CONTENTS

CONTENTS

PREFACE

PUBLIC LIBRARY CORE COLLECTION: NONFICTION is a curated list of collection development recommendations created by librarians for librarians for any kind of library serving general adult populations. It is derived from the NONFICTION CORE COLLECTION database from EBSCO*host*, updated weekly.

What's new in this edition?

The 17th edition of PUBLIC LIBRARY CORE COLLECTION: NONFICTION provides over 14,000 reference and nonfiction titles. A star (★) at the start of an entry indicates that a book is a "most highly recommended" title. These titles constitute a shortlist of the essential books in a given category or on a given subject. There are often a number of recommended titles on a single subject, and the star designation helps a user who wants only one or two. This edition includes 2,200 titles at the Most Highly Recommended level and over 12,000 at the Core Collection level.

Each new edition of PUBLIC LIBRARY CORE COLLECTION: NONFICTION is a mixture of the old and the new. Older titles, some in updated versions, are included if they remain the best titles in their field. Newer titles reflect new topics of interest and new interpretations of traditional knowledge.

History

The first of several installments of the "Standard Catalog" for the general library was published in 1918. It was called STANDARD CATALOG: SOCIOLOGY SECTION. Additional installments were issued over the next fourteen years, covering Biography; Fiction; Fine Arts; History and Travel; Science and Useful Arts; Literature and Philology; and Philosophy, Religion and General Works. Finally, a fully integrated first edition of the STANDARD CATALOG FOR PUBLIC LIBRARIES was assembled and published in 1934. The contents were displayed in classified order, according to the Dewey Decimal Classification. The name was changed to PUBLIC LIBRARY CATALOG with the publication of the fifth edition in 1969, and then to PUBLIC LIBRARY CORE COLLECTION: NONFICTION with the thirteenth edition in 2008. The collection subsequently evolved, along with the other Core Collections, into an online resource called WilsonWeb. EBSCO Information Services acquired H.W. Wilson in July 2011, and the collections became EBSCO*host* databases in January 2012. Despite many changes over the last 100 years, the 17th edition of PUBLIC LIBRARY CORE COLLECTION: NONFICTION remains a premier collection development tool for adult nonfiction recommendations.

Although a Fiction Section was issued in 1923, followed by supplements in 1928 and 1931, fiction was omitted from the first edition of the complete Catalog in 1934. A new expanded edition of the Fiction Section was published as FICTION CATALOG in 1942. In its preface that Catalog was referred to as "a companion volume to the Standard Catalog for Public Libraries." This complementary relationship has continued to the present. PUBLIC LIBRARY CORE COLLECTION: NONFICTION has always listed works of literary criticism and literary history and books about literary technique.

Scope and Purpose

This volume lists nonfiction books published in the United States or published in other countries and distributed in the United States. It excludes non-print materials; periodicals; non-English items (with the exception of dictionaries); and works of an ephemeral nature. Original paperback editions are included. Entries for hardcover editions provide information about the availability of paperback reprints where possible. This volume comprises over 14,000 book titles with multiple subject access.

The Core Collection is intended to serve the needs of public and undergraduate libraries and stand as a basic or "opening day" collection. The newer titles help in identifying areas in a collection that can be updated or strengthened. Retention of useful material from the previous edition enables the librarian to make informed decisions about weeding a collection. With its classified arrangement, complete bibliographical data, and descriptive and critical annotations, the Core Collection provides useful information for the acquisitions librarian, the reference librarian, and the cataloger. Entries provide information about the availability of electronic versions of books listed.

The Database

In 2017 EBSCO renamed PUBLIC LIBRARY CORE COLLECTION: NONFICTION with the broader term NONFICTION CORE COLLECTION, which brings it in line with the other database names, make it less cumbersome, and signifies suitability for a variety of library types. Although the title of this edition is different from the database from which it is excerpted, this volume is a derivation—the top two recommendation levels—of the NONFICTION CORE COLLECTION from EBSCO*host*, not a separate and distinct set of book recommendations. For more information or for a free trial, contact your EBSCO sales rep or visit https://www.ebscohost.com/public/core-collections

Preparation

Books included in this edition were selected by experienced librarians representing public library systems and academic libraries across the United States who also act as a committee of advisors on library policy and trends. The names of participating librarians and their affiliations are listed in the Acknowledgments. EBSCO invites feedback from Core Collections customers at corecollections@ebsco.com.

Organization

The Core Collection is organized into two parts: the Classified Collection; and an Author, Title, and Subject Index.

Part 1. Classified Collection. This is arranged according to the Dewey Decimal Classification. Within classes, arrangement is by main entry, with complete bibliographical and cataloging information given for each book. The classified arrangement, along with the descriptive and critical annotations, provides a useful guide to book selection. Entries include such information as price and ISBN to facilitate acquisitions.

Part 2. Author, Title, and Subject Index. This is a comprehensive key to the Classified List with entries for authors, titles, and subjects.

ACKNOWLEDGMENTS

H. W. Wilson and EBSCO Information Services express special gratitude to the following librarians who both advised the company in editorial matters and assisted in the selection and weeding of titles for this Core Collection:

Advisory Board

James Bobick
Science Librarian (Retired)
Pittsburgh, Pennsylvania

Julie Corsaro
Library Consultant & Adjunct
Professor of English,
Children's Literature
College of William & Mary
Williamsburg, Virginia

Gail de Vos
Adjunct Associate Professor
University of Alberta
Edmonton, Alberta

Francisca Goldsmith
Consulting Librarian
Worcester, Massachusetts

Mary Griffin
Librarian (Retired)
Omaha, Nebraska

Steven Jablonski
Collection Development
Librarian
Skokie Public Library
Skokie, Illinois

Joquetta Johnson
Library Media Specialist
Randallstown High School
Randallstown, Maryland

John Meier
Science Librarian
Penn State University
University Park, Pennsylvania

Liza Oldham
Research and Instructional
Design Librarian
Phillips Academy
Andover, Massachusetts

Rebecca Vargha
Head of Information and
Library Science Library
University of North Carolina
Chapel Hill, NC

Neal Wyatt
Columnist and Contributing
Editor, Library Journal
Richmond, Va

The editors would also like to thank NoveList librarians Krista Biggs, Kaitlin Conner, Halle Eisenman, and Ashley Lyons for their help in weeding this collection.

DIRECTIONS FOR USE OF THE
CORE COLLECTION

USES OF THE COLLECTION

PUBLIC LIBRARY CORE COLLECTION: NONFICTION is designed to serve a number of purposes:

As an aid in purchasing. The Core Collection is designed to assist in the selection and ordering of titles. Annotations are provided for each title along with information concerning the publisher, ISBN, price, and availability. Since Part 1, Classified Collection, is arranged according to the Dewey Decimal Classification, the Core Collection may be used to identify parts of the library collection that should be updated or strengthened. In evaluating the suitability of a work each library will want to consider the special character of the community it serves.

As an aid to the reader's advisor. The work of the reader's advisor is furthered by the information about sequels and companion volumes and the descriptive and critical annotations in the Classified Collection, and by the subject access in the Index.

As an aid in verification of information. For this purpose full bibliographical data are provided in the Classified Collection. Entries also include recommended subject headings based on *Sears List of Subject Headings* and a suggested classification derived from the *Abridged Dewey Decimal Classification and Relative Index*. Notes describe editions available, awards, publication history, and other titles in the series.

As an aid in collection maintenance. Information about titles available on a subject facilitates decisions to rebind, replace, or discard items. If a book has been deleted from the Core Collection in this edition because it is no longer in print, that deletion is not intended as a sign that the book is no longer valuable or that it should necessarily be weeded from the collection.

As an instructional aid. The Core Collection is useful in courses that deal with literature and book selection for public libraries.

ORGANIZATION

The Core Collection consists of two parts: a Classified Collection, and an Author, Title, and Subject Index.

Part 1. Classified Collection

The Classified Collection is arranged with nonfiction books first, classified according to the Dewey Decimal Classification in numerical order from 000 to 999. Individual biographies are classed at 92 and precede the 920s (collective biography). The information supplied for each book includes bibliographic description, suggested subject headings, an annotation, and frequently, an evaluation from a notable source.

An Outline of Classification, which serves as a table of contents for the Classified Collection, is reproduced following this section. It should be noted that many topics can be classified in more than one discipline. If a particular title is not found where it might be expected, the Index should be consulted to determine if it is classified elsewhere.

Within classes, works are arranged alphabetically under main entry, usually the author. Works of individual biography are arranged alphabetically under the biography's subject.

Each listing consists of a full bibliographical description. Prices, which are always subject to change, have been obtained from the publisher, when available, and are as current as possible. Entries include recommended subject headings derived from the *Sears List of Subject Headings*, a suggested classification number from the *Abridged Dewey Decimal Classification and Relative Index*, a brief description of the contents, and, whenever possible, an evaluation from a quoted source. The following is an example of a typical entry and a description of its components:

Roach, Mary, 1959-
★ **Stiff**; the curious lives of human cadavers. Norton 2003 303 p il $23.95; pa $13.95   **611**
    1. Dead 2. Dissection 3. Human experimentation in medicine
    ISBN 0-393-05093-9; 0-393-32482-6 pa
                  LC 2002-152908
    The author "explains how surgeons and doctors use cadavers donated for research purposes to help the living, and also examines potential new variations on how we bury the dead." Libr J
    "For those who are interested in the fields of medicine or forensics and are aware of some of the procedures, this book makes excellent reading." SLJ
    Includes bibliographical references

The star at the beginning of the entry indicates that this is a "most highly recommended" title.

The name of the author, Mary Roach, is given in conformity with *Anglo-American Cataloguing Rules*, 2nd edition, 2002 revision. The title of the book is *Stiff: the curious lives of human cadavers*. The book was published by Norton in 2003.

The book has 303 pages and contains illustrations. It is published in hardcover and paperback, and sells for $23.95 and $13.95, respectively. (Prices given were current when the Collection went to press.)

At the end of the last line of type in the body entry is 611 in boldface type. This is the classification number or category derived from the fifteenth edition of the *Abridged Dewey Decimal Classification*.

The numbered terms "1. Dead 2. Dissection 3. Human experimentation in medicine" are recommended subject headings for this book based on *Sears List of Subject Headings*.

The ISBN (International Standard Book Number) is included to facilitate ordering. The Library of Congress control number is provided when available.

Following are three notes supplying additional information about the book. The first is a description of the book's content, in this case, an excerpt from *Library Journal*. The second is a critical note from *School Library Journal*. Such annotations are useful in evaluating books for selection and in determining which of several books on the same subject is best suited for the individual reader. The final note describes special features, such as a bibliography, if applicable. Notes are also made to describe sequels and companion volumes, editions available, awards, and publication history.

Part 2. Author, Title, and Subject Index

The Index is a single alphabetical list of all the books entered in the Core Collection. Each book is entered under author; title (if distinctive); and subject. The classification number, displayed in boldface type, is the key to the location of the main entry for the book in the Classified Collection.

Appropriate added entries are made for joint authors and editors. "See" references are made from forms of names or subjects that are not used as headings. "See also" references are made to related or more specific headings.

The following are examples of Index entries for the book cited above:

	Roach, Mary, 1959-	
Author	Stiff	**611**
	Stiff. Roach, M.	**611**
Title		
	DEAD	
Subject	Roach, M. Stiff.	**611**

Standards Used

Anglo-American Cataloguing Rules, 2nd ed., 2002 revision, 2005 update. Chicago: American Library Association, 2005.

Bristow, Barbara A. and Christi Showman Farrar, eds. *Sears List of Subject Headings*. 21st ed. Ipswich, MA: The H. W. Wilson Company, 2014.

Dewey, Melvil. *Abridged Dewey Decimal Classification and Relative Index*. 15th ed. Edited by Joan S. Mitchell, et al. Dublin, Ohio: OCLC, 2012.

PUBLIC LIBRARY
CORE COLLECTION:
NONFICTION

A Selection Guide to Reference Books
and
Adult Nonfiction

SEVENTEENTH EDITION

Former title:

Public Library Catalog

EDITED BY

NEAL WYATT

KENDAL SPIRES

H. W. Wilson
A Division of EBSCO Information Services
Ipswich, Massachusetts
2019
GREY HOUSE PUBLISHING

R011 P

ISBN 978-1-68217-661-0

Abridged Dewey Decimal Classification and Relative Index, Edition 15 is © 2015 OCLC Online Computer Library Center, Inc. Used with Permission. DDC, Dewey, Dewey Decimal Classification, and WebDewey are registered trademarks of OCLC.

Public Library Core Collection, 2019, published by Grey House Publishing, Inc., Amenia, NY, under exclusive license from EBSCO Information Services, Inc.

A catalog record for this title is available from the Library of Congress.

PRINTED IN CANADA

PUBLIC LIBRARY CORE COLLECTION: NONFICTION
SEVENTEENTH EDITION
CLASSIFIED COLLECTION

000 COMPUTER SCIENCE, KNOWLEDGE & SYSTEMS

001.1 Intellectual life

Levine, Lawrence W.

The **opening** of the American mind; canons, culture, and history. Beacon Press 1996 xxiv, 212p hardcover o.p. pa $18   **001.1**

   1. Higher education 2. Multiculturalism 3. United States -- Intellectual life

ISBN 0-8070-3119-4 pa

LC 96-33866

"Levine's presentation is eloquent, eminently reasonable, and gratifyingly optimistic." Booklist

Includes bibliographical references

001.2 Scholarship and learning

Lima, Manuel

The **book** of trees; visualizing branches of knowledge. Manuel Lima. Princeton Architectural Press 2014 208 p. illustrations (chiefly color) (alkaline paper) $29.95   **001.2**

   1. Charts, diagrams, etc. 2. Statistics -- Graphic methods 3. Graphic methods -- History 4. Knowledge, Theory of -- History 5. Visual communication -- History 6. Learning and scholarship -- History 7. Trees -- Symbolic aspects -- History 8. Communication in learning and scholarship -- History

ISBN 1616892188; 9781616892180

LC 2013026128

In this book, "Manuel Lima examines the . . . history of the tree diagram, from its roots in the illuminated manuscripts of medieval monasteries to its current resurgence as an elegant means of visualization. Lima presents two hundred intricately detailed tree diagram illustrations on a remarkable variety of subjects--from some of the earliest known examples from ancient Mesopotamia to the manuscripts of medieval monasteries to contributions by leading contemporary designers." (Publisher's note)

"Sure to appeal to a diverse group of readers, the book beautifully combines art and science, as well as ancient and contemporary worldviews." Pub Wkly

Includes bibliographical references and index

001.4 Research; statistical methods

Feldman, Burton

The **Nobel** Prize; a history of genius, controversy, and prestige. Arcade Pub. 2000 489p il $29.95; pa $15.95   **001.4**

   1. Nobel Prizes

ISBN 1-55970-537-X; 1-55970-592-2 pa

LC 00-42002

The author provides a "history of the prizes awarded in the sciences, literature, social sciences, and humankind's . . . peace efforts. This is the first comprehensive critical history of the prizes to appear, and it's very good." Libr J

Includes bibliographical references

MacLeod, Don

How to find out anything; from extreme Google searches to scouring government documents, a guide to uncovering anything about everyone and everything. Don MacLeod. 1st ed. Prentice Hall Press 2012 x, 256 p.p (pbk.) $20   **001.4**

   1. Research 2. Internet searching 3. Information resources 4. Research -- Methodology 5. Electronic information resources 6. Electronic information resource searching

ISBN 0735204675; 9780735204676

LC 2012010974

In this book, "researcher Don MacLeod explains how to find what you're looking for quickly, efficiently, and accurately--and how to avoid the most common mistakes of the Google Age. . . . [The author] shows you how to unveil nearly anything about anyone. From top CEO's salaries to police records, . . . researching for a term paper or digging up dirt on an ex, the advice in this book arms you with the sleuthing skills to tackle any mystery." (Publisher's note)

Tufte, Edward R., 1942-

The **visual** display of quantitative information; 2nd ed; Graphics Press 2001 197p il $40   **001.4**

   1. Statistics -- Graphic methods

ISBN 0-9613921-4-2

LC 2001-271866

First published 1983

This book focuses "on statistical graphics, charts, tables. Theory and practice in the design of data graphics, 250 illustrations of the best (and a few of the worst) statistical graphics, with . . . analysis of how to display data for precise, effective, quick analysis." Publisher's note

001.42 Research methods

Williams, Joseph M.

The **craft** of research; Wayne C. Booth, Gregory G. Colomb, Joseph M. Williams, Joseph Bizup, William T. FitzGerald. Fourth edition University of Chicago Press 2016 xvi, 316 p.p illustrations (Chicago guides to writing, editing, and publishing) (pbk.: alk. paper) $18   **001.42**

   1. Technical writing 2. Research -- Methodology

ISBN 022623973X; 9780226239569; 9780226239736

1

LC 2016000143

This book by Wayne C. Booth, Gregory G. Colomb, Joseph M. Williams, Joseph Bizup, and William T. FitzGerald "explains how to find and evaluate sources, anticipate and respond to reader reservations, and integrate these pieces into an argument that stands up to reader critique. Its chapters on finding and engaging sources now incorporate recent developments in library and Internet research, emphasizing new techniques made possible by online databases and search engines." (Publisher's note)

"This thorough but inexpensive book is foundational for understanding the research process from beginning to end . . . ." Choice

Includes bibliographical references and index

001.9   Controversial knowledge

Shermer, Michael

Why people believe weird things; pseudoscience, superstition, and other confusions of our time. foreword by Stephen Jay Gould. rev and expanded; Freeman, W.H. 2002 xxvi, 349p il pa $16   **001.9**

1. Science 2. Parapsychology 3. Belief and doubt

ISBN 0-8050-7089-3

LC 2002-68784

First published 1997

The author "explores the very human reasons people find otherworldly phenomena, conspiracy theories, and cults so appealing. In . . . [the] chapter, 'Why Smart People Believe in Weird Things' he takes on science luminaries like physicist Frank Tippler and others, who hide their spiritual beliefs behind the trappings of science." Publisher's note

Includes bibliographical references

001.94   Mysteries

Krulos, Tea

Monster hunters; on the trail with ghost hunters, bigfooters, ufologists, and other paranormal investigators. by Tea Krulos. Chicago Review Press, Inc. 2015 320 p. illustrations (some color) (paperback) $16.95   **001.94**

1. Monsters 2. Supernatural -- Miscellanea 3. Parapsychology -- Miscellanea

ISBN 1613749813; 9781613749814

LC 2015002299

In this book, journalist Tea Krulos "spent over a year traveling nationwide to meet individuals who have made it their life's passion to hunt down evidence of entities that they believe exist, but that others might shrug off as nothing more than myths, fairytales, or overactive imaginations." (Publisher's note)

"This work is bound to be fascinating to those already interested in these fields and even to readers who are seeking an easy way to learn about people who work in these specialized areas. Recommended for public libraries." LJ

Includes bibliographical references and index

Prothero, Donald R., 1954-

UFOs, chemtrails, and aliens; what science says. Donald R. Prothero and Timothy D. Callahan; foreword by Michael Shermer. Indiana University Press 2017 xviii, 459 p.p illustrations (cloth: alk. paper) $28   **001.94**

1. Curiosities and wonders 2. Extraterrestrial beings 3. Unidentified flying objects 4. Occultism 5. Pseudoscience 6. Parapsychology

7. Human-alien encounters

ISBN 9780253034168; 9780253027061; 9780253026927

LC 2017006388

This book, by Donald R. Prothero and Timothy D. Callahan with foreword by Michael Shermer, "explore[s] why . . . false beliefs thrive despite decades of education and scientific debunking. Employing the ground rules of science and the standards of scientific evidence, Prothero and Callahan discuss a wide range of topics including . . . psychological research into why people want to believe in aliens and UFOs, and the role conspiratorial thinking plays in UFO culture." (Publisher's note)

"With their book's brisk pace and energetic writing, Prothero and Callahan offer entertainment as well as wisdom for everyone who's ever wondered what's behind so many conspiracy theories and paranormal phenomena." Pub Wkly

Includes bibliographical references (pages 433-447) and index.

001.942   Unidentified flying objects (UFOs)

Mezrich, Ben

The 37th parallel; The Secret Truth Behind America's UFO Highway. Ben Mezrich. Atria Books 2016 272 p. illustrations, maps (ebook) $19.99; (hardback) $26   **001.942**

1. Conspiracies 2. Parapsychology 3. Unidentified flying objects 4. Parapsychology -- Southwestern States 5. Unidentified flying objects -- Southwestern States

ISBN 9781501135545; 9781501135521

LC 2016021639

This book, by Ben Mezrich, "tells the true story of a computer programmer who tracks paranormal events along a 3,000-mile stretch through the heart of America and is drawn deeper and deeper into a vast conspiracy. . . . So begins an extraordinary and fascinating journey from El Paso and Rush, Colorado, to a mysterious space studies company and MUFON, from Roswell and Area 51 to the Pentagon and beyond." (Publisher's note)

"Mezrich probably won't sway the skeptical, but fans of Art Bell and company will find all the affirmation they need." Kirkus

001.944   Monsters and related phenomena

Kaplan, Matt

Medusa's gaze and vampire's bite; the science of monsters. Matt Kaplan. Scribner 2012 244 p. (hardcover: alk. paper) $26   **001.944**

1. Zombies 2. Monsters 3. Vampires 4. Anthropology 5. Cyclopes (Greek mythology) 6. Monsters -- History 7. Animals, Mythical -- History 8. Dangerous animals -- Folklore -- History

ISBN 1451667981; 9781451667981; 9781451667998; 9781451668001

LC 2012016553

In this book, journalist "[Matt] Kaplan sheds light on why people fear monsters, from the Calydonian Boar depicted on ancient Greek friezes to the creatures of films like Alien and Jurassic Park. He uses science and anthropology to make educated guesses about how figures like cyclopes, zombies, vampires, and dragons worked their way into humanity's collective imagination." (Library Journal)

Prothero, Donald R., 1954-

Abominable science! origins of the Yeti, Nessie, and other famous cryptids. Daniel Loxton and Donald R. Prothero. Columbia University Press 2013 432 p. (cloth: alk. paper)

$29.95 **001.944**

1. Cryptozoology 2. Pseudoscience 3. Mythical animals 4. Animals, Mythical

ISBN 0231153201; 9780231153201

LC 2013008424

In this book, "after examining the nature of science and pseudoscience and their relation to cryptozoology, [Daniel] Loxton and [Donald R.] Prothero take on Bigfoot; the Yeti . . .; the Loch Ness monster . . . [and] the Congo dinosaur. They conclude with an analysis of the psychology behind the persistent belief in paranormal phenomena . . . and consider . . . the challenge it poses to clear and critical thinking in our increasingly complex world." (Publisher's note)

Includes bibliographical references and index

002 The book

Basbanes, Nicholas A.

Patience & fortitude; a roving chronicle of book people, book places, and book culture. HarperCollins Pubs. 2001 636p il hardcover o.p. pa $19.95 **002**

1. Libraries 2. Book collecting 3. Books and reading

ISBN 0-06-019695-5; 0-06-051446-9 pa

LC 2001-16935

"Basbanes's fund of stories will delight readers who value books for more than just a good story, have a yen for second-hand books plucked from dusty shops or look to book catalogs for suspense and excitement." Publ Wkly

Includes bibliographical references

Buzbee, Lewis

The **yellow**-lighted bookshop; a memoir, a history. Graywolf Press 2006 216p $17 **002**

1. Booksellers and bookselling

ISBN 1-55597-450-3

LC 2005-938151

This "is a tribute to those who crave the cozy confines of a bookshop." Booklist

Darnton, Robert

The **case** for books; past, present, and future. PublicAffairs 2009 218p il $23.95 **002**

1. Books and reading -- History

ISBN 978-1-58648-826-0

"These essays bring balance and a refreshing perspective to the nervous predictions over the future of print." Libr J

Includes bibliographical references

002.03 The book -- Dictionaries

Berger, Sidney E.

The **dictionary** of the book; a glossary for book collectors, booksellers, librarians, and others. Sidney E. Berger. Rowman & Littlefield 2016 xiv, 319 p.p illustrations (cloth: alk. paper) $125 **002.03**

1. Bibliography 2. Book collecting 3. Encyclopedias and dictionaries 4. Bibliography -- Dictionaries 5. Book collecting -- Dictionaries 6. Library science -- Dictionaries 7. Book industries and trade -- Dictionaries

ISBN 9781442263390; 9781442263406

LC 2016013533

Written by Sidney E. Berger, "here is the definitive glossary of the book, offering readers all the terms they will need for thorough understanding of how books are made, the materials they are made of, and how they are described in the bookselling, book collecting, and library worlds. Every key term--over 1,300 different words--that could be used in booksellers' catalogs, library records, and collectors' descriptions of their holdings is represented in this dictionary." (Publisher's note)

"A former museum library director and curator of manuscripts at different institutions, Berger is highly qualified to compile this informative and important work." Booklist

Includes bibliographical references (pages 303-317)

002.07 Education, research, related topics

Lansky, Aaron

Outwitting history; the amazing adventures of a man who rescued a million Yiddish books. Algonquin Books of Chapel Hill 2004 316p **002.07**

1. Book collecting 2. Yiddish language 3. National Yiddish Book Center

ISBN 1-56512-429-4

LC 2004-51587

"The book is a testimony to [Lansky's] love of Judaism and literature and his desire to make a difference in the world." Publ Wkly

Includes bibliographical references

002.075 Book collecting

Occhipinti, Lisa

Novel living; collecting, decorating, and crafting with books. Lisa Occhipinti. STC Craft/A Melanie Falick Book 2014 143 p. illustrations (some color) $24.95 **002.075**

1. Books 2. Interior design

ISBN 1617690872; 9781617690877

LC 2014930834

In this book, "artist Lisa Occhipinti celebrates her love for physical books by presenting us with her unique ideas for collecting and displaying them, for conserving and preserving them, and for crafting with them. Guided by Occhipinti's artful eye, you'll be inspired to build and display collections based on your personal passions and to use books for crafting, either by deconstructing or by copying favorite elements." (Publisher's note)

"An elegant layout and excellent instructions pay appropriate homage to many of our best friends." Booklist

002.09 The book -- History

Houston, Keith

The **Book**; A Cover-to-Cover Exploration of the Most Powerful Object of Our Time. by Keith Houston. W W Norton & Co Inc 2016 448 p. illustrations (some color) $29.95 **002.09**

1. Books and reading -- History

ISBN 0393244792; 9780393244793

In this book, author "Keith Houston reveals that the paper, ink, thread, glue, and board from which a book is made tell as rich a story as the words on its pages—of civilizations, empires, human ingenuity, and madness. In an invitingly tactile history of this 2,000-year-old medium, Houston follows the development of writing, printing, the art of illustrations, and binding to show how we have moved from cuneiform tablets and papyrus scrolls to the hardcovers and paperbacks of today." (Publisher's note)

"Pulling together aspects of archaeology, history, literature, and biography, the author reveals the facts, conjecture, and educated guesses experts have made about how and when the first modern tome came to be, which is surprisingly difficult to pin down." LJ

Includes bibliographical references (pages 339-401) and index.

003   Systems

Domingos, Pedro

The **master** algorithm; how the quest for the ultimate learning machine will remake our world. Pedro Domingos. Basic Books, a member of the Perseus Books Group   2015   352 p. illustrations (hardcover) $29.99   **003**

1. Algorithms 2. Mathematics 3. Artificial intelligence 4. Cognitive science -- Mathematics 5. Artificial intelligence -- Philosophy 6. Artificial intelligence -- Social aspects 7. Knowledge representation (Information theory)
ISBN 0465065708; 9780465065707

LC 2015007615

In this book, author Pedro Domingos "lifts the veil for the first time to give us a peek inside the learning machines that power Google, Amazon, and your smartphone. He charts a course through machine learning's five major schools of thought, showing how they turn ideas from neuroscience, evolution, psychology, physics, and statistics into algorithms ready to serve you. Step by step, he assembles a blueprint for the future universal learner¿the Master Algorithm." (Publisher's note)

"Skeptics may dismiss Domingos' vision as hopelessly utopian, and libertarians may brand it as dangerously intrusive. But no one will find it boring. An exhilarating venture into groundbreaking computer science." Booklist

Taleb, Nassim Nicholas

The **black** swan; the impact of the highly improbable. [by] Nassim Nicholas Taleb. 2nd ed; Random House Trade Paperbacks 2010 xxxiii, 444p il pa $17   **003**

1. Forecasting
ISBN 0-8129-7381-X; 978-0-8129-7381-5

LC 2010-292618

First published 2007

Examines the role of the unexpected, discussing why improbable events are not anticipated or understood properly, and how humans rationalize the black swan phenomenon to make it appear less random.

The author "is really a philosopher in a businessman's clothing and his irreverent writing style, with its frequent first-person asides and tangential musings that go on for pages, actually helps make heavy intellectual discussions more accessible." Risk Management

Includes bibliographical references

004   Computer science; computer programming, programs, data; special computer methods

Dyson, George

Turing's cathedral; the origins of the digital universe. George Dyson. Pantheon Books 2012 xxii, 401 p.p (hardback) $29.95   **004**

1. Symbolic logic 2. Computers -- History 3. Mathematics -- History 4. Computer science -- History 5. Turing, Alan Mathison, 1912-1954 6. Turing machines 7. Computable functions 8.

Random access memory
ISBN 9780375422775

LC 2011030265

In this book, "science historian George Dyson shines light on the critical period when computers came into being. He begins with British mathematician Alan Turing's . . . 1936 description of a machine designed to resolve a problem in mathematical logic. . . . Dyson focuses on US efforts, when . . . a group of engineers, scientists and mathematicians, gathered together by Hungarian-American polymath John von Neumann . . . bent their minds to the making of the IAS machine." (New Scientist)

Includes bibliographical references and index

Isaacson, Walter

★ The **innovators**; how a group of inventors, hackers, geniuses, and geeks created the digital revolution. Walter Isaacson. Simon & Schuster 2014 560 p. illustrations (hardback) $35   **004**

1. Computer scientists 2. Internet -- History 3. Computers -- History 4. Computer science -- History
ISBN 147670869X; 9781476708690; 9781476708706

LC 2014021391

Los Angeles Times Book Prize Finalist: History (2014)
National Books Award: Nonfiction Longlist (2014)

This book, by Walter Isaacson, is the "story of the people who created the computer and the Internet. . . . [He] begins with Ada Lovelace, Lord Byron's daughter, who pioneered computer programming in the 1840s. He explores the fascinating personalities that created our current digital revolution, such as Vannevar Bush, Alan Turing, John von Neumann, J.C.R. Licklider, Doug Engelbart, Robert Noyce, Bill Gates, Steve Wozniak, Steve Jobs, Tim Berners-Lee, and Larry Page." (Publisher's note)

"Although full biographies of the individuals profiled here have been written in spades, Isaacson manages to bring together the entire universe of computing, from the first digitized loom to the web, presented in a very accessible manner that often reads like a thriller." Booklist

Markoff, John

What the dormouse said-- how the sixties counterculture shaped the personal computer industry. Viking Penguin 2005 xxiii, 310p il $25.95; pa $16   **004**

1. Counterculture 2. Computers and civilization 3. Counter culture 4. Computers -- History
ISBN 0-670-03382-0; 0-14-303676-9 pa

LC 2004-61181

"This book is a rare treat and a must-read for everyone who has had the pleasure of using the mysterious friend called the PC." Choice

Includes bibliographical references

Pogue, David

Pogue's basics; essential tips and shortcuts (that no one bothers to tell you) for simplifying the technology in your life. David Pogue. Flatiron Books 2014 368 p. illustrations (some color) (paperback) $19.99   **004**

1. Internet -- Miscellana 2. Electronic apparatus and appliances -- Miscellanea 3. Technology -- Miscellanea 4. Computer science -- Miscellanea 5. Online social networks -- Miscellanea
ISBN 125005348X; 9781250053480

LC 2014032515

This book, by David Pogue, presents tips for working with technology. "When it comes to technology, . . . somehow, you're just supposed to know how to use your phone, tablet, computer, camera, Web browser, e-mail, and social networks. . . . Tech expert David Pogue comes to the rescue with . . . a book that . . . collects every essential technique for making your gadgets seem easier, faster, and less of a hassle." (Publisher's note)

Syropoulos, Apostolos

Demystifying computation; a hands-on introduction. Apostolos Syropoulos. World Scientific 2017 xvii, 195 p.p illustrations (pbk: alk. paper) $48   **004**

    1. Data processing 2. Computer programming 3. Coding theory
    ISBN 1786342669; 9781786342652; 9781786342669
                 LC 2016045892

This book, by Apostolos Syropoulos, "introduces the theory of computation from its inception to current form of complexity; from explanations of how the field of computer science was formed using classical ideas in mathematics by Gödel, to conceptualization of the Turing Machine, to its more recent innovations in quantum computation, hypercomputation, vague computing and natural computing." (Publisher's note)

"The work will be an admirable reference book for courses in computing and also an excellent source for general readers in public libraries." Choice

    Includes bibliographical references and indexes

Vamosi, Robert

When gadgets betray us; the dark side of our infatuation with new technologies. Basic Books 2011 222p   **004**

    1. Computer crimes 2. Computer security 3. Electronic apparatus and appliances 4. Software failures 5. Computers -- Health aspects 6. Computers -- Social aspects
    ISBN 978-0-465-01958-8
                 LC 2010-43829

"The book is about hardware hacking and new kinds of identity fraud." (Publisher's note) Index.

"Read this, and you'll never again ignore the default security settings on accounts or your devices again. Gadget geeks and lay readers would benefit from Vamosi's information." Libr J

    Includes bibliographical references

White, Ron, 1944-

How Computers Work; the evolution of technology. by Ron White; illustrated by Tim Downs. 10th ed Que 2014 432 p. color illustrations pbk $39.99   **004**

    1. Personal computers
    ISBN 9780789749840; 078974984X

First published 1993 by Ziff-Davis Press. Frequently revised

An "illustrated guide to the world of PCs and technology. In this . . . edition, you'll find detailed information not just about every last component of hardware found inside your PC, but also . . . explanations about home networking, the Internet, PC security, and even how cell phone networks operate." (Publisher's note)

004.1   General works on specific types of computers

Johnson, George

A **shortcut** through time; the path to a quantum computer. Knopf 2003 204p il hardcover o.p. pa $13   **004.1**

    1. Computers 2. Quantum theory
    ISBN 0-375-41193-3; 0-375-72618-7 pa
                 LC 2002-73013

"Johnson has presented the fascinating science of quantum computing and its future development in a down-to-earth style." Libr J

Includes bibliographical references

004.16   Personal computers

Mueller, Scott

Upgrading and repairing PCs; Scott M. Mueller. 22nd edition Que 2015 1162 p. illustrations hbk $59.99   **004.16**

    1. Personal computers
    ISBN 9780789756107; 0789756102

"Scott Mueller delivers practical answers about PC processors, mother-boards, buses, BIOSes, memory, SSD and HDD storage, video, audio, networks, Internet connectivity, power, and much more. You'll find the industry's best coverage of diagnostics, testing, and repair--plus cutting-edge discussions of improving PC performance via overclocking and other techniques." (Publisher's note)

004.67   Wide-area networks

Arora, Pankaj

To the cloud; cloud powering an enterprise. Pankaj Arora, Raj Biyani, Salil Dave. McGraw Hill 2012 xx, 119 p.p ill. $30   **004.67**

    1. Cloud computing 2. Business planning 3. Web services 4. Information technology -- Management 5. Business enterprises -- Data processing
    ISBN 007179221X; 9780071792219
                 LC 2011277377

This book looks at cloud computing. This guide "lays out a four-step framework, leveraging the experience and best practices of Microsoft's own IT group. The book delivers end-to-end business and technology guidance, describing how to analyze application portfolios to identify good cloud candidates, choose the right cloud models, consider architecture and security, and understand how shifting operations to the cloud affects budgeting and staffing." (Publisher's note)

    Includes bibliographical references and index

Boyd, Danah

It's complicated; the social lives of networked teens. Danah Boyd. Yale University Press 2014 296 p. (clothbound: alk. paper) $25   **004.67**

    1. Teenagers 2. Internet and teenagers 3. Online social networks 4. Information technology -- Social aspects 5. Teenagers -- Social life and customs -- 21st century
    ISBN 0300166311; 9780300166316
                 LC 2013031950

Author Danah Boyd "uncovers some of the major myths regarding teens' use of social media. She explores tropes about identity, privacy, safety, danger, and bullying. Ultimately, Boyd argues that society fails young people when paternalism and protectionism hinder teenagers' ability to become informed, thoughtful, and engaged citizens through their online interactions. Yet despite an environment of rampant fear-mongering, Boyd finds that teens often find ways to engage and to develop a sense of identity." (Publisher's note)

"This groundbreaking survey of the online social habits and realities of American teens, based on extensive fieldwork, also serves as an important corrective to numerous persistent, widely held notions about young people, public life, and the Internet." (Library Journal)

    Includes bibliographical references and index

Dunckley, Victoria L.

Reset your child's brain; a four-week plan to end meltdowns, raise grades, and boost social skills by reversing the effects of electronic screen-time. Victoria L. Dunckley. New World Library 2015 384 p. illustrations (paperback) $18.95   **004.67**
    1. Parenting 2. Child psychology 3. Children -- Conduct of life 4. Internet and children 5. Electronics -- Social aspects 6. Problem children -- Behavior modification 7. Video games and children -- Health aspects 8. Behavior disorders in children -- Prevention
    ISBN 1608682846; 9781608682843

LC 2014046885

In this book "based on emerging scientific research and extensive clinical experience, integrative child psychiatrist Dr. Victoria Dunckley has pioneered a four-week program to treat the frequent underlying cause, Electronic Screen Syndrome (ESS). Dunckley provides hope for parents who feel that their child has been misdiagnosed or inappropriately medicated, by presenting an alternative explanation for their child's difficulties and a concrete plan for treating them." (Publisher's note)

"Decreasing childhood use of electronics often results in better behavior, but whether that's because parent and child find new ways of communicating and spending time together or because the electronics are creating long-term damage is still up for debate." LJ

Includes bibliographical references and index

Lessig, Lawrence

The **future** of ideas; the fate of the commons in a connected world. Random House 2001 352p hardcover o.p. pa $15   **004.67**
    1. Internet 2. Copyright 3. Information society
    ISBN 0-375-72644-6 pa

LC 2001-31968

"Some of Lessig's sweeping proposals are sure to spark a lively debate, but his well-reasoned, clearly written argument is powerful." Publ Wkly

McCullough, Brian

How the Internet happened; from Netscape to the iPhone. Brian McCullough. Liveright Publishing Corporation 2018 400 p. hardcover $28.95   **004.67**
    1. Internet -- History 2. Information networks 3. Technological innovations
    ISBN 9781631493072

LC 2018022765

In this book, author Brian McCullough, "chronicles the whole fascinating . . . [history of the Internet] for the first time, beginning in a dusty Illinois basement in 1993, when a group of college kids set off a once-in-an-epoch revolution with what would become the first 'dotcom.' . . . McCullough also reveals surprising quirks and unknown tales as he tracks both the technology and the culture around the internet's rise." (Publisher's note)

"Most of the individual components of McCullough's story, which closes with the arrival of the 'completely, conceptually perfect' iPhone in 2007, are well-documented, but few other histories of modern technology connect them so fluently." Kirkus

Includes bibliographical references and index

Moreno, Megan

Sex, drugs 'n Facebook; a parents' toolkit for promoting healthy Internet use. by Megan A. Moreno. Hunter House Inc. 2013 268 p. (trade paper) $17.95   **004.67**
    1. Social media 2. Internet and teenagers 3. Parenting 4. Online etiquette

ISBN 0897936590; 9780897936590; 9780897936606

LC 2012048533

In this book, author Megan Moreno presents "a guide to help [parents] teach your kids about balance and boundaries in their internet and media use and the skills they need to thrive online. This guide provides a clear toolkit for teaching our young people how to avoid the dangers of the internet while taking advantage of its full potential." (Publisher's note)

Includes bibliographical references and index

Naughton, John

From Gutenberg to Zuckerberg; Disruptive Innovation in the Age of the Internet. John Naughton. Quercus 2014 352 p. illustrations (hardcover) $24.95   **004.67**
    1. Internet 2. Technological innovations
    ISBN 1623650623; 9781623650629; 9781623650636

LC 2013937747

This book, by John Naughton, "is a . . . history of one of the most central, and yet most taken-for-granted, features of modern life: the internet. Once a technological novelty and now the very plumbing of the Information Age, the internet is something we have learned to take largely for granted. So, how exactly has our society become so dependent upon a utility it barely understands? And what does it say about us that this is so?" (Publisher's note)

"This is a solid overview of Internet technology for those who use it but who don't feel that they comprehend it. Experts might not find much new information here, but the author's observations and analysis will give any reader a better grasp of the web's big picture." LJ

Obee, Jennifer

Social networking; the ultimate teen guide. Jenna Obee. Scarecrow Press 2012 258 p.   **004.67**
    1. Social networking 2. Internet and teenagers 3. Online social networks
    ISBN 0810881209; 9780810881204; 9780810881211

LC 2011049875

This book by Jennifer Obee "helps young adults make the most of their online experience, giving them a complete understanding of social networking while also addressing online safety. . . . Author Jennifer Obee helps teens navigate through the challenging intricacies of social networks, covering such topics as: Facebook . . . Youtube . . . [and] Twitter." The book includes "quotes from teenagers about their favorite sites and personal stories." (Publisher's note)

Includes bibliographical references and index

Peters, Justin

The **Idealist**; Aaron Swartz and the Rise of Free Culture on the Internet. Justin Peters. Simon & Schuster 2016 352 p. $28   **004.67**
    1. Internet 2. Open access publishing
    ISBN 1476767726; 9781476767727

LC 2015044638

This book, by Justin Peters, presents a "history of the Internet free culture movement and its larger effects on society--and the life and shocking suicide of Aaron Swartz, a founding developer of Reddit and Creative Commons. [It] situates Swartz in the context of other 'data moralists' past and present, from lexicographer Noah Webster to ebook pioneer Michael Hart to NSA whistleblower Edward Snowden. In the process, the book explores the history of copyright statutes and the public domain." (Publisher's note)

"Swartz's writings and Peters' historically grounded and deeply involving biography illuminate the roots of today's thorny quandaries." Booklist

Includes bibliographical references (pages 309-317) and index.

Sales, Nancy Jo

★ **American** girls; social media and the secret lives of teenagers. Nancy Jo Sales. Alfred A. Knopf 2016 416 p. (hardcover) $26.95 **004.67**

    1. Social media 2. Teenage girls 3. Internet and teenagers
    ISBN 9780385353922; 9780385353939

LC 2016931806

For this book author Nancy Jo Sales "crisscrossed the country, speaking to more than two hundred girls, ages thirteen to nineteen, and documenting a massive change in the way girls are growing up. 'American Girls' provides a disturbing portrait of the end of childhood as we know it and of the inexorable and ubiquitous experience of a new kind of adolescence—one dominated by new social and sexual norms." (Publisher's note)

"Sales takes a broader view than simply being the scold of technology; she spoke with teens who point out the empowerment possibilities of a smartphone: being able to document injustices as they happen and broadcast them to the world. For parents with young daughters, this book is an ice-cold, important wake-up call." Kirkus

Stryker, Cole

Hacking the Future; Privacy, Identity, and Anonymity on the Web. Cole Stryker. Penguin Group USA 2012 255 p. (hardcover) $25.95 **004.67**

    1. Right of privacy 2. Internet -- Social aspects
    ISBN 1590209745; 9781590209745

This book, by Cole Stryker, offers "a broad look at how anonymity influences politics, activism, religion, and art. Stryker presents a strong defense of anonymity and explores some of the tools and organizations relating to this issue, especially as it has evolved with the ubiquity of the Internet." (Publisher's note)

"A multilayered and well-reasoned retort against all those who would seek to erase anonymity from the Web... The author explores the rich history of anonymity in politics, literature and culture, while also debunking the notion that only troublemakers fear revealing their identities to the world... One of the most well-informed examinations of the Internet available today." Kirkus

005   Computer programming, programs, data

Campbell-Kelly, Martin

From airline reservations to Sonic the Hedgehog; a history of the software industry. MIT Press 2003 372p il (History of computing) $42.50; pa $16.95 **005**

    1. Computer software industry
    ISBN 0-262-03303-8; 0-262-53262-X pa

LC 2002-75351

The author presents a "history of the software industry from the 1950s to 1995. Dividing the business into three sectors (software contracting, corporate software precuts, and mass-market software products), he examines the key products and players in each. . . . The result is a well-rounded look at the software industry from a business perspective." Libr J

Includes bibliographical references

Davis, Mark

Digital assassination; protecting your reputation, brand, or business against online attacks. by Richard Torrenzano and Mark Davis. 1st ed. St. Martin's Press 2011 viii, 289 p.p

(hardcover) $25.99 **005**

    1. Reputation 2. Public opinion 3. Internet security 4. Internet -- Security measures
    ISBN 0312617917; 9780312617912

LC 2011025849

In this book, authors [Richard] Torrenzano . . . and [Mark] Davis . . . discuss how various Internet tools are being used by digital maligners to harm reputations and perform character assassinations. The authors explain how anyone can tap into social media . . . to mount an electronic onslaught, severely altering the digital reputation of a person or a company. They argue that the dark side of human behavior, not technology, is the driving factor behind this phenomenon." (Library Journal)

Includes bibliographical references and index.

005.7   Data in computer systems

Mulgan, Geoff

Big mind; how collective intelligence can change our world. Geoff Mulgan. Princeton University Press 2017 280 p. (hardcover) $29.95 **005.7**

    1. Consciousness 2. Thought and thinking 3. Human-computer interaction
    ISBN 0691170797; 9780691170794

LC 2017954117

This book, by Geoff Mulgan, "explores how collective intelligence has to be consciously organized and orchestrated in order to harness its powers. He looks at recent experiments mobilizing millions of people to solve problems, and at groundbreaking technology like Google Maps and Dove satellites. He also considers why organizations full of smart people and machines can make foolish mistakes . . . and shows how to avoid them." (Publisher's note)

"In this brilliant, somewhat heady, but generally accessible book, Mulgan (The Locust and the Bee: Predators and Creators in Capitalism's Future, 2015, etc.), chief executive of Nesta, Britain's National Endowment for Science, Technology and the Arts, shows how the answers can be found in the emerging field of collective intelligence, which links people and machines to foster 'dramatic jumps' in group intelligence." (Kirkus)

O'Neil, Cathy

★ **Weapons** of math destruction; How Big Data Increases Inequality and Threatens Democracy. Cathy O'Neil. Crown Publishers 2016 272 p. (hardcover) $26 **005.7**

    1. Big data 2. Democracy -- United States 3. United States -- Social conditions 4. Big data -- Social aspects -- United States 5. Big data -- Political aspects -- United States 6. United States -- Social conditions -- 21st century 7. Social indicators -- Mathematical models -- Moral and ethical aspects
    ISBN 9780553418811; 9780553418835

LC 2016003900

National Book Award Longlist: Nonfiction (2016)

In this book, author Cathy O'Neil "sounds an alarm on the mathematical models that pervade modern life--and threaten to rip apart our social fabric. . . . Tracing the arc of a person's life, O'Neil exposes the black box models that shape our future, both as individuals and as a society. These 'weapons of math destruction' score teachers and students, sort résumés, grant (or deny) loans, evaluate workers, target voters, set parole, and monitor our health." (Publisher's note)

Includes bibliographical references (pages 219-252) and index

005.8   Data security

Mitnick, Kevin D. (Kevin David), 1963-

The **art** of invisibility; the world's most famous hacker teaches you how to be safe in the age of Big Brother and big data. Kevin Mitnick with Robert Vamosi. Little, Brown & Co. 2017 320 p. illustrations (ebook) $84; $28   **005.8**
1. Right of privacy 2. Computer security 3. Internet security 4. Data protection 5. Privacy, Right of 6. Internet -- Security measures
ISBN 9780316380515; 9780316380508

LC 2016024302

This book, by Kevin Mitnick with Robert Vamosi, "uses true-life stories to show exactly what is happening without your knowledge, teaching you 'the art of invisibility'--online and real-world tactics to protect you and your family, using easy step-by-step instructions. Reading this book, you will learn everything from password protection and smart Wi-Fi usage to advanced techniques designed to maximize your anonymity." (Publisher's note)

"You don't have to be a paranoiac to have enemies, and you don't need to be an outlaw to want to keep your personal information personal. Though with more than a whiff of conspiracy theory to it, Mitnick's book is a much-needed operating manual for the cyberage." Kirkus

Includes bibliographical references and index

Olson, Parmy

We are Anonymous; inside the hacker world of Lulzsec, Anonymous, and the global cyber insurgency. Parmy Olson. Little, Brown and Co. 2012 xi, 498 p.p $26.99   **005.8**
1. Hacktivism 2. Lulzsec (Group) 3. Computer hackers 4. Anonymous (Group)
ISBN 0316213543; 9780316213547

LC 2012936919

This book by Parmy Olson presents an "account of the hacker collective Anonymous and its splinter group, LulzSec. . . . A nebulous group of hackers and Internet activists . . . . [Anonymous] not only took down the Scientology website, but went on to attack other targets, including the anti-gay Westboro Baptist Church and the Tunisian government. . . . . [LulzSec] attacked companies just for the sake of publicly embarrassing them for laughs." (Kirkus Reviews)

Includes bibliographical references and index.

006.3   Artificial intelligence

Baker, Stephen

Final Jeopardy; man vs. machine and the quest to know everything. Houghton Mifflin Harcourt 2011 268p $24 **006.3**
1. Database management 2. Artificial intelligence 3. Watson (Computer) 4. Jeopardy (Television program) 5. Natural language processing (Computer science)
ISBN 9780547519432; 9780547483160; 0547483163

LC 2010051653

"In February 2011, the world watched as a computer named Watson handily beat the two greatest Jeopardy champions of all time. The contest was reminiscent of when IBM's Deep Blue defeated chess grandmaster Garry Kasparov, but Jeopardy was a much more difficult game for a computer to master. Although Baker . . . reviews the match in his last chapter, his primary focus here is on the compelling story of Watson's creation and education. . . . This is a thought-provoking view of one of IBM's major contributions to the computing field." Libr J

Includes bibliographical references

Bostrom, Nick, 1973-

Superintelligence; paths, dangers, strategies. Nick Bostrom. Oxford University Press 2014 352 p. (hardback) $29.95   **006.3**
1. Theory of knowledge 2. Artificial intelligence 3. Cognitive science 4. Artificial intelligence -- Philosophy
ISBN 0199678111; 9780199678112

LC 2013955152

This book, by Nick Bostrom, asks "[w]hat happens when machines surpass humans in general intelligence? Will artificial agents save or destroy us? . . . The human brain has some capabilities that the brains of other animals lack. . . . If machine brains surpassed human brains in general intelligence, then this new superintelligence could become extremely powerful - possibly beyond our control. . . . But we have one advantage: we get to make the first move." (Publisher's note)

Bostrom "delivers a comprehensive outline of the philosophical foundations of the nature of intelligence and the difficulty not only in agreeing on a suitable definition of that concept but in living with the possibly dire consequences of that concept." Choice

Includes bibliographical references and index

Dormehl, Luke

Thinking machines; the quest for artificial intelligence--and where it's taking us next. Luke Dormehl. TarcherPerigee 2017 xi, 275 p.p (paperback) $16   **006.309**
1. Artificial intelligence 2. Artificial intelligence -- Social aspects
ISBN 9780143130581; 9781524704414

LC 2016044018

This book, by Luke Dormehl, "takes you through the history of AI and how it makes up the foundations of the machines that think for us today. Furthermore, Dormehl speculates on the incredible--and possibly terrifying--future that's much closer than many would imagine. This remarkable book will invite you to marvel at what now seems commonplace and to dream about a future in which the scope of humanity may need to broaden itself to include intelligent machines." (Publisher's note)

"With interesting real-life characters . . . and stories about headline-news smart devices, Thinking Machines is an easy introduction for readers wanting insight into how technology fits into their lives." Booklist

Includes bibliographical references and index.

Favro, Terri

Generation robot; a century of science fiction, fact, and speculation. Terri Favro. Skyhorse Publishing 2018 256 p. $24.99   **006.3**
1. Robots 2. Artificial intelligence
ISBN 1510723102; 9781510723108

This book, by Terri Favro, "covers a century of science fiction, fact and, speculation--from the 1950 publication of Isaac Asimov's seminal robot masterpiece, I, Robot, to the 2050 Singularity when artificial and human intelligence are predicted to merge. . . . Favro offers a unique perspective on how our relationship with robotics and futuristic technologies has shifted over time." (Publisher's note)

"In every chapter, Favro shows how different actual robots are from many of their counterparts in science fiction. Her book's greatest achievement may be to get readers looking at their cell phones, computers, prosthetics, and other gadgets as robots in the real world." Pub Wkly

Kasparov, G. K. (Garri Kimovich), 1963-

Deep thinking; where machine intelligence ends and human creativity begins. Garry Kasparov; with Mig Greengard. PublicAffairs 2017 vii, 287 p.p portrait (hardcover) $28   **006.3**
1. Creative ability 2. Artificial intelligence 3. Chess 4. Deep

Blue (Computer)
ISBN 9781610397865; 9781610398916; 161039786X

LC 2017304768

In this book author Garry Kasparov "uses his unrivaled experience to look into the future of intelligent machines and sees it bright with possibility. As many critics decry artificial intelligence as a menace, particularly to human jobs, Kasparov shows how humanity can rise to new heights with the help of our most extraordinary creations, rather than fear them." (Publisher's note)

"Thoughtful reading for anyone interested in human and machine cognition and a must for chess fans." Kirkus

Includes bibliographical references and index.

Tegmark, Max

Life 3.0; being human in the age of artificial intelligence. Max Tegmark. Alfred A. Knopf 2017 xii, 364 p.p illustrations (hardback) $28 **006.3**
1. Artificial intelligence 2. Automation -- Social aspects 3. Technological forecasting 4. Artificial intelligence -- Philosophy 5. Automation -- Moral and ethical aspects 6. Artificial intelligence -- Social aspects 7. Artificial intelligence -- Moral and ethical aspects
ISBN 9781101946596; 9781101946602

LC 2017006248

This book, by Max Tegmark, addresses questions such as "how will artificial intelligence affect crime, war, justice, jobs, society and our very sense of being human? . . . How can we grow our prosperity through automation without leaving people lacking income or purpose? What career advice should we give today's kids? How can we make future AI systems more robust, so that they do what we want without crashing, malfunctioning or getting hacked?" (Publisher's note)

"Stretching the superhuman AI idea to intergalactic proportions by envisioning its colonization of the universe, Tegmark enthusiastically lays out concepts of AI, to the delight or disturbance of readers." Booklist

Includes bibliographical references (pages 337-347) and index

Zarkadakis, George

In Our Own Image; Savior or Destroyer? the History and Future of Artificial Intelligence. George Zarkadakis. W W Norton & Co Inc 2016 384 p. $27.95 **006.3**
1. Artificial intelligence 2. Human-computer interaction
ISBN 1605989649; 9781605989648

In this book, author George Zarkadakis "explores the history and future, as well as the societal and ethical implications, of Artificial Intelligence as we approach the cusp of a fourth industrial revolution. . . . He traces AI's origins in ancient myth, through literary classics like Frankenstein, to today's sci-fi blockbusters, arguing that a fascination with AI is hardwired into the human psyche." (Publisher's note)

"A delightfully lucid combination of the history, philosophy, and science behind thinking machines." Kirkus

Includes bibliographical references (pages [322]-347) and index.

006.7   Multimedia systems

Bilton, Nick

Hatching Twitter; a true story of money, power, friendship, and betrayal. Nick Bilton. Portfolio 2013 304 p. illustrations (hardback) $28.95 **006.7**
1. Twitter (Website) 2. Twitter 3. Twitter (Firm) 4. Internet industry -- United States 5. Online social networks -- United States 6. Businesspeople -- United States -- Biography

ISBN 1591846013; 9781591846017

LC 2013037924

This book examines "Twitter's contentious origins in the techie subculture of San Francisco." Author Nick Bilton "reconstructed this history from interviews and the digital trails . . . of his four principals: blogger, founder and chief investor Evan 'Ev' Williams and his friends and employees Noah Glass, Christopher 'Biz' Stone and Jack Dorsey. Each contributed an important share in the invention of the platform that . . . would revolutionize the way the world communicates and interrelates." (Kirkus Reviews)

Blakiston, Rebecca

Usability testing; a practical guide for librarians. Rebecca Blakiston. Rowman & Littlefield 2015 xiv, 133 p.p (Practical guides for librarians) (pbk.: alk. paper) $65 **006.7**
1. Libraries 2. Internet resources 3. Websites -- Design 4. Web site development 5. Library Web sites -- Design 6. User-centered system design 7. Library Web sites -- Testing
ISBN 9781442228993; 9781442229006

LC 2014024454

This book, in the Practical Guides for Librarians series, by Rebecca Blakiston, "will teach you how to: make the case for usability testing, define your audience and their goals, conduct an effective in-house usability test, . . . [and] create and implement a plan for ongoing, systematic usability testing. . . . [These] techniques are appropriate for libraries of all types, including academic, public, and special libraries." (Publisher's note)

Includes bibliographical references and index

Krug, Steve

★ **Don't** make me think, revisited; a common sense approach to Web usability. Steve Krug. New Riders 2014 xi, 200 p.p ill (some col) (pbk.) $45 **006.7**
1. Websites -- Design 2. Web sites -- Design 3. Web site development
ISBN 9780321965516; 0321965515

LC 2014397947

Previous ed.: 2006

This revised book on web design, by Steve Krug, is a "guide to help . . . understand the principles of intuitive navigation and information design . . . with updated examples and a new chapter on mobile usability." (Publisher's note)

Includes bibliographical references and index

Solomon, Laura

The **librarian's** nitty-gritty guide to social media; Laura Solomon. ALA Editions, an imprint of the American Library Association 2013 224 p. $52 **006.7**
1. Librarians 2. Social media 3. Online social networks -- Library applications
ISBN 0838911609; 9780838911600

LC 2012027302

Here, Laura Solomon offers a guide for the use of social media by libraries. The book "provides case studies of libraries that have excelled with their marketing efforts." She offers an "analysis of what success is and how to measure it to gain support from stakeholders." Also provided are "detailed sample postings that not only give suggestions for libraries to model but also examine unsuccessful posts and explain what makes them less than desirable." (Library Journal)

Includes bibliographical references and index

Stone, Biz

Things a little bird told me; confessions of the creative mind. Biz Stone. Grand Central Publishing 2014 240 p. illustrations (hardback) $26   **006.7**
1. Businesspeople 2. Internet industry 3. Twitter (Website) 4. Success in business 5. Twitter 6. Online social networks -- United States 7. Entrepreneurship -- United States -- Anecdotes
ISBN 1455528714; 9781455528714

LC 2013047280

In this book, Biz Stone "discusses the power of creativity and how to harness it, through stories from his remarkable life and career. . . . Biz tells fascinating, pivotal, and personal stories from his early life and his careers at Google and Twitter, sharing his knowledge about the nature and importance of ingenuity today. . . . Biz also addresses failure, the value of vulnerability, ambition, and corporate culture." (Publisher's note)

"Readers will enjoy the tales of the ups and downs of Silicon Valley among major players, from Google to Apple to Facebook, as well as the insightful advice that can be applied to any career or enterprise." Booklist

Wellman, Barry

Networked; the new social operating system. Lee Rainie and Barry Wellman. MIT Press 2012 xiii, 358 p.p ill.   **006.7**
1. Online social networks 2. Interpersonal relations 3. Internet -- Social aspects 4. Social networks
ISBN 0262017199; 9780262017190

LC 2011038146

This book "outline[s] the 'triple revolution'" in human communication: "the rise of social networking, the capacity of the Internet to empower individuals, and the always-on connectivity of mobile devices." The authors "examine how the move to networked individualism has expanded personal relationships . . . transformed work into less hierarchical, more team-driven enterprises; encouraged individuals to create and share content; and changed the way people obtain information." (Publisher's note)

Includes bibliographical references and index.

006.754   Online social networks

Van Susteren, Greta, 1954-

Everything you need to know about social media; (without having to call a kid) Greta Van Susteren. Simon & Schuster 2017 305 p. color illustrations (paperback) $19.99   **006.754**
1. Privacy 2. Social media 3. Computer crimes
ISBN 9781501132445; 9781501132452

LC 2017014973

This book, by Greta Van Susteren, presents "the most practical, thorough, and reader-friendly guide around to living well on social media. From answering basic questions like 'What's the best site for you?' to 'How to Tweet' and 'What does it mean to 'Tag' someone?' to addressing important moral and behavioral issues like how to protect your privacy, . . . this is the essential handbook for anyone who wants to stay up to date with today's changing technology." (Publisher's note)

"Readers who are curious about (but are still hesitant to use) social media will likely find Van Susteren's advice helpful." Pub Wkly

011   Bibliographies and catalogs

American reference books annual; edited by Juneal M. Chenoweth. Libraries Unlimited   **011**
1. Reference books -- Bibliography 2. Libraries -- Collection development
Cumulative indexes available 1990-1994; 2000-2004; 2005-2009
Annual. First published 1970

"Each issue covers the reference book output (including reprints) of the previous year (i.e., the 1970 volume covers 1969 publications). Offers descriptive and evaluative notes (many of them signed by contributors), with references to selected reviews. Limited to titles in English. Classed arrangement; author-subject-title index." Guide to Ref Books. 11th edition

Ellington, Elisabeth

A **year** of reading; a month-by-month guide to classics and crowd-pleasers for you and your book group. by H. Elisabeth Ellington and Jane Freimiller. Sourcebooks 2002 314p pa $14.95   **011**
1. Best books 2. Books and reading
ISBN 1-57071-935-7

LC 2002-6926

"Five titles designated as crowd pleasers, classics, challenges, memoirs, or potluck options are provided for each month. . . . There are brief descriptions of each book, thought-provoking discussion questions, information about the authors, video and Internet resources, and lists of related readings. Literary discussion groups will welcome this invaluable resource." Booklist

Guide to reference; essential general reference and library science sources. Jo Bell Whitlatch and Susan E. Searing, Editors. ALA Editions, An imprint of the American Library Association 2014 xiv, 230 p.p (paperback: alk. paper) $65   **011**
1. Reference services (Libraries) 2. Reference books -- Bibliography 3. Reference sources -- Bibliography
ISBN 083891232X; 9780838912324

LC 2014013098

This book, edited by Jo Bell Whitlatch and Susan E. Searing, "collects . . . sources of general reference and library science information. Encompassing internet resources, digital image collections, and print resources, it includes the full section on LIS Resources from the Guide to Reference database. . . . Organized by topic and thoroughly indexed, this guide makes it a snap to find the right sources." (Publisher's note)

Includes bibliographical references and indexes

Pearl, Nancy

Book lust; recommended reading for every mood, moment, and reason. Sasquatch Books 2003 287p pa $16.95   **011**
1. Best books 2. Books and reading
ISBN 1-57061-381-8

LC 2003-45796

Pearl's "recommendations are arranged under an alphabetical, subjective, but certainly comprehensive system of categories, which range from 'Academic Mysteries' to 'World War II Nonfiction' and from 'First Novels' to 'Three-Hanky Readers.' Within each category, Pearl's commentaries are concise and sound. A book difficult to put down and easy to be guided by." Booklist

★ **Recommended** reference books for small and medium-sized libraries and media centers, Vol. 34; volume 34 Shannon

Graff Hysell, associate editor. Libraries Unlimited 2014
301 p. $75 **011**
1. Reference books 2. Reference books -- Reviews 3. Reference
books -- Bibliography
ISBN 9781610695510
Annual. First published 1981
"This volume presents the top 550 reviews from the latest edition of
American Reference Books Annual (ARBA) to give collection development librarians working in small to medium-sized libraries the best
information for choosing new titles for their libraries. Overviewing the
breadth of reference products (both print and online) that became available in 2013, all of the titles . . . have price points that will appeal to
libraries on a budget." (Publisher's note)
Includes "books, e-books, free websites, and pay sites. These are
broken down into major subject headings and minor ones within the
major." VOYA

Reference Sources for Small and Medium-Sized Libraries;
Jack O'Gorman, editor. Amer Library Assn 2014 289 p.
$129 **011**
1. Book selection 2. Reference books -- Bibliography 3. Reference
books
ISBN 0838912125; 9780838912126
LC 200740026
"Focusing on new reference sources published since 2008 and reference titles that have retained their relevance, this new edition brings
[author Jack] O'Gorman's complete and authoritative guide to the best
reference sources for small and medium-sized academic and public libraries fully up to date. About 40 percent of the content is new to this
edition." (Publisher's note)

Saricks, Joyce G.
Read on--audiobooks; reading lists for every taste. Librar-
ies Unlimited 2011 145p (Read on series) pa $30 **011**
1. Audiobooks -- Catalogs 2. Libraries -- Special collections --
Audiobooks
ISBN 978-1-59158-804-7 pa; 978-1-59158-807-8 ebook
LC 2010051372
"More than 300 selections, fiction and nonfiction, are grouped into
five chapters according to their primary appeal: language (including
voice), mood, story, characters, or setting. Within each category, titles
are listed by shared themes, such as full-cast readings or armchair travel.
. . . All libraries that circulate audiobooks should shelve this guide along-
side." Booklist
Includes bibliographical references

**011.6   General bibliographies and catalogs of works for
young people and people with disabilities; for specific types
of libraries**

Rosow, La Vergne
★ **Accessing** the classics; great reads for adults, teens, and
English language learners. Libraries Unlimited 2006 301p pa
$40 **011.6**
1. Best books 2. Reading -- Remedial teaching
ISBN 1-56308-891-6; 978-1-56308-891-9
LC 2005-30838
"The intended audience is wide-ranging and includes anyone who
wishes to foster language and literacy skills. Essential reading." Booklist
Includes bibliographical references

Safford, Barbara Ripp
Guide to reference materials for school library media cen-
ters; 6th ed; Libraries Unlimited 2010 236p $60 **011.6**
1. Instructional materials centers 2. School libraries -- Catalogs 3.
Reference books -- Bibliography
ISBN 978-1-59158-277-9; 1-59158-277-6
LC 2009-51190
First edition by Christine Gehrt Wynar published 1973 with title:
Guide to reference books for school media centers
"This volume has been updated to include web-based reference offerings as well as listings of older sources, provided that their content
is still valid. . . . This title profiles resources recommended for use by
school librarians for collection management, readers' advisory, teaching,
general reference materials, the social sciences and humanities, and science and technology. This volume is an excellent starting point for new
school librarians, as well as for those who are building a library from
scratch." SLJ
Includes bibliographical references

011.62   Works for young people

Martin, William Patrick
Wonderfully wordless; the 500 most recommended graphic
novels and picture books. William Patrick Martin. Rowman &
Littlefield 2015 334 p. (hardcover: alk. paper) $38 **011.62**
1. Graphic novels -- Bibliography 2. Best books 3. Picture books
-- Bibliography 4. Picture books for children -- Bibliography
ISBN 9781442254770
LC 2015019482
Written by William Patrick Martin, "'Wonderfully Wordless: The
500 Most Recommended Graphic Novels and Picture Books' is the
first comprehensive best book guide to wordless picture books. . . . It
is an indispensable resource for parents and teachers who love graphic
storytelling or who recognize the value of these exceptional books in
working with different types of students, particularly preschool, English
as a Second Language (ESL), and special needs, and creative writers."
(Publisher's note)
"No dark corner is left unexplored, illuminating a far greater array of
choices than any reader might have guessed." Booklist
Includes bibliographical references

**016   Bibliographies and catalogs of works on specific
subjects**

Adamson, Lynda G.
Notable women in American history; a guide to recommended biographies and autobiographies. Greenwood Press
1999 450p $52.95 **016**
1. Reference books 2. Women -- Biography -- Dictionaries
ISBN 0-313-29584-0
LC 98-55350
Companion volume to Notable women in world history
This volume "concentrates on women who made contributions to
U.S. history from the colonial period through 1998. The 500 women
covered were born in America or became naturalized citizens; had a
full-length biography or autobiography published since 1970; and, in
the case of twentieth-century actors, authors, and poets, have been recognized by their peers." Booklist

All music guide to classical music; the definitive guide to classical music. edited by Chris Woodstra, Gerald Brennan, Allen Schrott. Backbeat Books 2005 1607p $34.95   **016**
1. Music -- Discography
ISBN 0-87930-865-6

LC 2005-23988

"The 1500 A-to-Z entries include established composers, performers, and ensembles of every style and era. . . . The final 25 pages are devoted to one-page discussions of form in classical music, historical periods (ten divisions), and genres such as ballet, film music, and opera. . . . This is an excellent resource for both classical novices and aficionados. There is simply no other single volume on the market as inclusive." Libr J

Alpert, Abby, 1961-
Read on-- graphic novels; reading lists for every taste. Abby Alpert. Libraries Unlimited 2012 xxi, 177 p.p (acid-free paper) $40   **016**
1. Best books 2. Graphic novels -- Bibliography 3. Readers' advisory services -- United States 4. Public libraries -- United States -- Book lists 5. Libraries -- Special collections -- Graphic novels
ISBN 1591588251; 1610691555; 9781591588252; 9781610691550

LC 2011039792

This book on graphic novels by Abby Alpert, part of the Read On series, offers "more than 500 original annotations organized within 70 thematic lists. The broad selection of titles is further categorized by key appeal elements, including story, character, setting, language, and mood, providing unique access points that allow discovery of interests to transcend subject headings in catalogs." (Publisher's note)

"This accessible guide is equally effective for collection building, readers' advisory, or individual perusal, and most public collections will find it perceptive and helpful. Recommended." Booklist

American foreign relations since 1600; a guide to the literature. Robert L. Beisner, editor. 2nd ed; ABC-CLIO 2003 2v set $255   **016**
1. Reference books 2. United States -- Foreign relations -- Bibliography
ISBN 1-57607-080-8

LC 2003-8684

First published 1983 under the editorship of Richard Dean Burns with title: Guide to American foreign relations since 1700

"The arrangement is essentially chronological, with the first of 32 chapters covering reference works and bibliographies and the second chapter, overviews and synthesis. Individual chapter editors . . . include journal articles, essays in collections, and dissertations. . . . Each chapter begins with a brief statement of the editor's selection criteria. Works in related specialties are listed for their influence on foreign relations, including Native American relations, gender and ethnic issues, and religious groups. . . . This is an excellent book; imaginative users will find ways to apply these listings to a wide variety of projects." Libr J
Includes bibliographical references

Barsanti, Chris
The **science** fiction movie guide; the universe of film from Alien to Zardoz. by Chris Barsanti. Visible Ink Press 2014 500 p. illustrations (pbk.: alk. paper) $19.95   **016**
1. Science fiction films -- Catalogs
ISBN 1578595037; 9781578595037

LC 2014017822

This book, by Chris Barsanti, "covers the broad and widening range

of science-fiction movies. From the trashy to the epic, from the classics to today's blockbusters, this cinefile's guidebook reviews nearly 1,000 of the biggest, baddest, and brightest from every age and genre of cinematic and TV science fiction." (Publisher's note)

"A great book for science fiction cinephiles and novices alike, this is a must for those interested in updating their film guidebook collections." Choice
Includes bibliographical referencfes

The **basic** business library; core resources and services. edited by Eric Forte and Michael R. Oppenheim. Libraries Unlimited 2012 xi, 227 p.p $50   **016**
1. Business libraries 2. Business -- Bibliography 3. Business -- Information services 4. Business libraries -- United States 5. Business -- Computer network resources 6. Business -- Reference books -- Bibliography 7. Business information services -- United States
ISBN 1598846116; 1598846124; 9781598846119; 9781598846126

LC 2011037666

This book, edited by Eric Forte and Michael R. Oppenheim, "is a modern sourcebook of core resources for the business library and the business information consumers and researchers it serves. This up-to-date guide also discusses strategies for acquiring and building the business collection in a Web 2.0/3.0 world and recommended approaches to providing reference service for business research." (Publisher's note)

"This is a valuable resource for small and medium-sized public libraries and an essential purchase for libraries that do not have an experienced business librarian or material selector on staff." Booklist
Includes bibliographical references and index

A **basic** music library; essential scores and sound recordings. compiled by the Music Library Association; Daniel F. Boomhower, editor; Edward Komara, Amanda Maple, and Liza Vick, associate editors. American Library Association 2013 752 p. (alk. paper) $258   **016**
1. Music libraries 2. Music -- Bibliography 3. Libraries -- Collection development 4. Music libraries -- Collection development
ISBN 0838910394; 9780838910399

LC 2013020223

This book, edited by Daniel F. Boomhower, Edward Komara, Amanda Maple, and Liza Vick on behalf of the Music Library Association, "constitutes the most authoritative music collection resource available. Completely revised and reorganized, this . . . reference is divided into" the three classical, popular, and world music genres. (Publisher's note)
Includes bibliographical references and index

Bleiler, Richard
★ **Reference** and research guide to mystery and detective fiction; [by] Richard J. Bleiler. 2nd ed; Libraries Unlimited 2003 828p (Reference sources in the humanities series) $78   **016**
1. Reference books 2. Mystery fiction -- Bibliography
ISBN 1-56308-924-6

LC 2003-58905

First published 1999 with title: Reference guide to mystery and detective fiction

"Separate chapters cover sources as diverse as maps and atlases, writers' associations and awards, character indexes, calendars, and quotations in addition to guides, encyclopedias, and dictionaries." Choice
Includes bibliographical references

Bosman, Ellen

Gay, lesbian, bisexual, and transgendered literature; a genre guide. [by] Ellen Bosman and John P. Bradford; edited by Robert B. Marks Ridinger. Libraries Unlimited 2008 422p (Genreflecting advisory series) $60 **016**

1. Homosexuality in literature
ISBN 978-1-59158-194-9; 1-59158-194-X

LC 2007-49022

"This addition to the Genreflecting Advisory Series fills a gap, focusing on popular literature with gay, lesbian, bisexual, and transgendered characters, themes, or authors. The first three chapters provide an excellent introduction and history of GLBT literature along with a discussion of collection develop-ment and readers'-advisory issues . . . An excellent tool for readers' advisory, as well as an outstanding reference on an important type of literature, this guide is highly recommended for public and academic libraries with GLBT collections." Booklist

Includes bibliographical references

Bouricius, Ann

The **romance** readers' advisory; the librarian's guide to love in the stacks. American Lib. Assn. 2000 107p pa $56 **016**

1. Reference books 2. Love stories -- Bibliography 3. Love stories -- History and criticism
ISBN 0-8389-0779-2

LC 99-57295

The author provides "information about the highly popular romance genre and its diverse subgenres; addresses key issues regarding the establishment of a romance collection; and, in a series of reading lists, recommends outstanding romances of all flavors for avid fans and new converts." Booklist

Burgess, Michael

Reference guide to science fiction, fantasy, and horror; [by] Michael Burgess, Lisa R. Bartle. 2nd ed; Libraries Unlimited 2002 605p (Reference sources in the humanities series) $75 **016**

1. Reference books 2. Science fiction -- Bibliography
ISBN 1-56308-548-8

LC 2002-151707

First published 1992

A guide to "amateur and professional reference materials in the related fields of science fiction, fantasy, and horror. . . . The book is divided into 32 sections . . . including 'Encyclopedias and Dictionaries,' 'Magazine and Anthology Indexes,' 'Subject Bibliographies,' 'Character Dictionaries and Author Cyclopedias,' and 'Film and Television Catalogs.'. . . . Complete bibliographic citations are followed by literature and readable annotations that vary from a brief note to three or four lengthy paragraphs. The annotations consist of description and succinct analysis of the strengths and weaknesses of each item. . . . 'Major On-Line Resources,' is a particularly valuable examination of 20 Web sites." Booklist

Includes bibliographical references

Burt, Daniel S.

The **biography** book; a reader's guide to nonfiction, fictional, and film biographies of the 500 most fascinating individuals of all time. Oryx Press 2001 629p $83.95 **016**

1. Reference books 2. Biography -- Bibliography
ISBN 1-57356-256-4

LC 00-10116

This "book provides annotated bibliographies of works on international historical figures. Entries are arranged alphabetically by person and begin with a paragraph on the individual's life and significance. Each entry contains a birth and death date, and recommended autobiographical and biographical studies. Primary sources include letters, memoirs, diaries, interviews, etc. Biographical novels, fictional portraits, films, documentaries, and theatrical performances are also identified. . . . A wonderful resource for students, biography lovers, and librarians." SLJ

Includes bibliographical references

Clark, Craig A.

Read on...sports; reading lists for every taste. Craig Clark, Richard T. Fox. Libraries Unlimited 2014 xv, 165 p.p (Read on series) (pbk.) $40 **016**

1. Books and reading 2. Sports -- Bibliography
ISBN 1610693574; 9781610693578

LC 2013034587

This library reference book, by Craig Clark and Richard T. Fox, "features reading lists of sports-oriented titles written by talented authors that are cataloged by character, story, setting, mood, and language. The lists are perfect for advising readers, creating thematic reading lists for library websites, and as plans for those who enjoy reading about athletic pursuits." (Publisher's note)

"This book would be useful for readers' advisory in libraries and will appeal to sports fans, so consider a copy in your circulating collection as well." Booklist

De Richemond, Jeanette

The **Medical** Library Association guide to finding out about heart disease; the best print and electronic resources. Jeanette de Richemond, Terry Paula Hoffman. Neal-Schuman, an imprint of the American Library Association 2013 468 p. (alk. paper) $88 **016**

1. Heart diseases 2. Reference books 3. Diet in disease -- Bibliography 4. Heart -- Diseases -- Bibliography 5. Diet in disease -- Computer network resources 6. Heart -- Diseases -- Computer network resources 7. Cardiovascular system -- Diseases -- Bibliography 8. Cardiovascular system -- Diseases -- Computer network resources
ISBN 1555707505; 9781555707507

LC 2013011592

"'The Medical Library Association Guide to Finding Out About Heart Disease' does the organizing for you and offers evaluated print and online resources to help you develop a collection or research your personal medical options. This . . . reference incorporates important data and key concepts about risk factors and symptoms of heart disease." (Publisher's note)

Includes bibliographical references and index

Dilevko, Juris

Contemporary world fiction; a guide to literature in translation. Juris Dilevko, Keren Dali, and Glenda Garbutt. Libraries Unlimited 2011 xxvi, 526 p.p $85 **016**

1. Translating and interpreting 2. Fiction -- 21st century
ISBN 1591583535; 9781591583530

LC 2010052517

In this book, by Juris Dilevko, Keren Dali, and Glenda Garbutt, "provides an overview of the tremendous range and scope of translated world fiction available in English. . . . Within the guide, approximately 1,000 contemporary non-English-language fiction titles are fully annotated and thousands of others are listed. Organization is primarily by language, . . . but also by country and culture." (Publisher's note)

"Highly recommended for the casual reader wishing to discover international contemporary fiction and for students of literature." LJ

Includes bibliographical references and indexes

Flora illustrata; great works on botany, horticulture, and garden design in the Luesther T. M. library. [edited by] Susan M. Fraser, Vanessa Bezemer Sellers. Yale University Press 2014 320 p. illustrations, maps, portraits (alk. paper) $50 **016**
1. Botanical illustration 2. Plants -- Collection and preservation
ISBN 0300196628; 9780300196627

LC 2014931108

This book, edited by Susan M. Fraser and Vanessa Bezemer Sellers, examines "exceedingly rare books, stunning botanical artworks, handwritten manuscripts, Renaissance herbals, nursery catalogs, explorers' notebooks, and more" from the LuEsther T. Mertz Library of The New York Botanical Garden. (Publisher's note)

"A wonderful title for the botanist and layperson—anyone who appreciates the aesthetic beauty of books, plants, and gardens." LJ

Fonseca, Anthony J.

Hooked on horror III; a guide to reading interests. [by] Anthony J. Fonseca and June Michele Pulliam. Libraries Unlimited 2009 xxiii, 515p (Genreflecting advisory series) $62 **016**
1. Horror films 2. Reference books 3. Horror fiction -- Bibliography
ISBN 978-1-59158-540-4

LC 2008-45518

First published 1999 with title: Hooked on horror
This book "provides annotations of horror books published between 2003 and 2008, including collections, anthologies, and series." Voice Youth Advocates
Includes bibliographical references

Frolund, Tina

Genrefied classics; a guide to reading interests in classical literature. Libraries Unlimited 2007 xxiv, 365p (Genreflecting advisory series) $45 **016**
1. Reference books 2. Fiction -- Bibliography
ISBN 1-59158-172-9; 978-1-59158-172-7

LC 2006-33740

"By identifying the genre characteristics of more than 400 classic fiction works, and organizing titles according to these features, this guide helps readers find the type of books they enjoy." Publisher's note
Includes bibliographical references

Read on...history; reading lists for every taste. Tina Frolund. Libraries Unlimited 2013 xiv, 195 p.p (Read on series) (pbk.) $30 **016**
1. Best books 2. History -- Bibliography 3. United States -- History -- Bibliography 4. Readers' advisory services -- United States 5. Public libraries -- United States -- Book lists
ISBN 1610690346; 9781610690348

LC 2013029492

"This invaluable resource offers reading lists of contemporary and classic non-fiction history books and historical fiction, covering all time periods throughout the world, and including practically all manner of human endeavors. . . . Organized by appeal characteristics, this book will help readers zero in on the history books they will like best." (Publisher's note)

Guide to Reference in Business and Economics; Steven W. Sowards, Elisabeth Leonard, editors. Amer Library Assn 2014 375 p. $65 **016**
1. Business -- Bibliography 2. Economics -- Bibliography 3. Reference books -- Bibliography
ISBN 0838912346; 9780838912348

This book, edited by Steven W. Sowards and Elisabeth Leonard, "focusing on print and electronic sources that are key to business and economics reference, . . . is a must-have [bibliography] for every reference desk. . . . This book will help connect librarians and researchers to the most relevant sources of information on business and economics." (Publisher's note)

★ **Genreflecting**; a guide to popular reading interests. edited by Cynthia Orr and Diana Tixier Herald, editors. Libraries Unlimited 2013 622 p. (Genreflecting advisory series) (Hardcopy: acid-free paper) $75 **016**
1. Reference books 2. Books and reading 3. Reading interests 4. Fiction -- Bibliography 5. Fiction genres -- Bibliography 6. English fiction -- Stories, plots, etc 7. American fiction -- Stories, plots, etc 8. Popular literature -- Stories, plots, etc
ISBN 9781598848403; 1598848402

LC 2012051480

First published 1982 under the authorship of Betty Rosenberg
This book for librarians on popular reading interests features "chapters devoted to each major genre with an overview of the genre's characteristics and appeal elements followed by definitions of popular subgenres, lists of benchmark titles, reader favorites, book-group selections, and resources for further investigation. Parts I and 2 focus on readers'-advisory services in the public library for the novice. . . . The chapters on the genres, found in part 3, are the series' stock-in-trade." (Booklist)
Includes bibliographical references

Herald, Diana Tixier

Fluent in fantasy; the next generation. [by] Diana Tixier Herald and Bonnie Kunzel. Libraries Unlimited 2008 312p (Genreflecting advisory series) $52 **016**
1. Reference books 2. Fantasy fiction -- Bibliography
ISBN 978-1-59158-198-7; 1-59158-198-2

LC 2007-28840

First published 1999
"More than 2,000 titles are arranged by author in 14 thematic chapters, including 'Epic Fantasy,' 'Arthurian Legend,' and 'Time Travel Romance.' . . . An essential collection development and readers'-advisory tool." Booklist
Includes bibliographical references

★ **Strictly** science fiction; a guide to reading interests. [by] Diana Tixier Herald, Bonnie Kunzel. Libraries Unlimited 2002 xxii, 297p (Genreflecting advisory series) $55 **016**
1. Reference books 2. Science fiction -- Bibliography 3. Science fiction -- History and criticism
ISBN 1-56308-893-2

LC 2002-3186

"Good indexing, by author, title, subject, and character name, along with chapters devoted to books written for children and young adults and genre-blended books (such as science fiction/ romance or science fiction/mystery), sets this reference apart." Libr J
Includes bibliographical references

Hollands, Neil

Read on . . . fantasy fiction; reading lists for every taste. Libraries Unlimited 2007 210p (Read on series) pa $30 **016**
1. Reference books 2. Fantasy fiction -- Bibliography
ISBN 978-1-59158-330-1; 1-59158-330-6

LC 2007-7841

"Librarians who do readers advisory for teens or adults will wonder how they ever got along without this funny, opinionated, wide-angle guide." SLJ

Honig, Megan

Urban grit; a guide to street lit. Megan Honig. Libraries Unlimited 2010 xxiv, 251 p.p $55 **016**
1. Fiction in libraries 2. Urban fiction, American -- Bibliography 3. Readers' advisory services -- United States 4. Urban fiction, American -- Stories, plots, etc
ISBN 159158857X; 9781591588573

LC 2010041099

In this book, by Megan Honig, "more than 400 entries appear in eleven chapters, each focusing on a different subgenre of street lit. The author has organized titles by popular subgenres and themes, such as prison life and urban erotica, to help librarians more easily identify read-alikes." (Publisher's note)

"Recommended for professional reading shelves as well as for researchers who will find value in Honig's defining the genre. This should be the definitive choice on the subject, with Andrew Ratner's practical teaching and classroom guide Street Lit: Teaching and Reading Fiction in Urban Schools as a good complement." LJ

Includes bibliographical references and index

Hooper, Brad

Read on....historical fiction; reading lists for every taste. by Brad Hooper. Libraries Unlimited 2006 xii, 152 p.p $40 **016**
1. Best books 2. Historical fiction -- Bibliography 3. Historical fiction
ISBN 1591582393; 9781591582397

LC 2006003711

In this book by Brad Hooper, part of the Read On series, "Hundreds of popular historical fiction titles are described and categorized according to their underlying appeal features, and under topics and themes you'll never find in the library catalog--women with true grit, greatest war stories, royalty rules, quick reads, humor, and many others." (Publisher's note)

This is definitely an unusual, thoughtful book that will be a useful addition to most professional and reference collections. Recommended." Library Media Connection

Includes bibliographical references and index

Husband, Janet

Sequels; an annotated guide to novels in series. [by] Janet G. Husband & Jonathan F. Husband. 4th ed; American Library Association 2009 782p pa $95 **016**
1. Reference books 2. Fiction -- Bibliography
ISBN 978-0-8389-0967-6

LC 2009-16426

First published 1982

"A selective, annotated list of the best, most enduring, and most popular novels in series. Short stories and children's books are excluded; classics, mysteries, and science fiction are included. Each work is listed in the best current edition, in the preferred order for reading. Arranged by author, with a title and subject index." Ref Sources for Small & Medium-sized Libr. 5th edition

Includes bibliographical references

Johnson, Sarah L.

Historical fiction II; a guide to the genre. Libraries Unlimited 2009 738p (Genreflecting advisory series) $65 **016**
1. Reference books 2. Historical fiction -- Bibliography
ISBN 978-1-59158-624-1

LC 2008-45537

"Johnson has updated her outstanding Historical Fiction: A Guide to

the Genre (2005) by covering historical fiction from 2004 through mid-2008 and adding such new features as ISBNs for each book and keyword descriptors after each annotation. . . . This volume continues rather than replaces the earlier work, adding more than 2,700 new titles." Booklist

Includes bibliographical references

Kallio, Jamie

Read on ... speculative fiction for teens; reading lists for every taste. Jamie Kallio. Libraries Unlimited 2012 126 p. (Read on series) (pbk.) $40 **016**
1. Fantasy fiction 2. Science fiction 3. Dystopian fiction 4. Apocalyptic fiction 5. Fiction in libraries -- United States 6. Young adults' libraries -- Book lists 7. Fantasy fiction, English -- Bibliography 8. Fantasy fiction, American -- Bibliography 9. Readers' advisory services -- United States 10. Speculative fiction, English -- Bibliography 11. Young adult fiction, English -- Bibliography 12. Speculative fiction, American -- Bibliography 13. Young adult fiction, American -- Bibliography 14. Teenagers -- Books and reading -- United States
ISBN 1598846531; 9781598846539

LC 2012014172

This book on speculative fiction for teens, by Jamie Kallio, "features popular, contemporary themes ranging from vampire love and ghost stories to epic fantasy and out-of-this-world science fiction. Each of the five chapters caters to a specific area of interest-- story, character, setting, mood, and language-- and within the chapter, numerous lists of novels are organized by topic, with the best titles highlighted." (Publisher's note)

"The summaries are well written, and the selection of books is very broad. The one missing feature that would be helpful is an indicator of which books are for older teens and which are for the junior high crowd. Nevertheless, this is a terrific book to have by the stacks or at the front desk of any school library, or in classrooms where the students are asking what to read next." VOYA

Includes bibliographical references and index

Ladd, Dana L.

The Medical Library Association guide to finding out about diabetes; the best print and electronic resources. Dana L. Ladd and Alyssa Altshuler. Neal-Schuman, an imprint of the American Library Association 2012 336 p. (alk. paper) $80 **016**
1. Diabetes 2. Diabetes -- Bibliography 3. Diabetes -- Computer network resources -- Directories
ISBN 1555708900; 9781555708900

LC 2012028333

This book, by Dana L. Ladd and Alyssa Altshuler, "provides . . . background on key diabetes concepts, encompassing reliable print and electronic resources, including hard-to-find periodicals and audiovisual sources. Each chapter in this guide presents an overview and description as well as an annotated list of multi-format resources on topics including Types 1 and 2 and gestational diabetes, diet, clinical trials, and support sources, and legal and insurance issues." (Publisher's note)

"This basic, plainly written bibliography is a must for any collection expected to provide current resources on diabetes to health-care students, medical professionals, or patients and their families." LJ

Includes bibliographical references and index

Martinez, Sara E.

Latino literature; A guide to reading interests. edited by Sara E. Martinez; foreword by Connie Van Fleet. Libraries Unlimited 2009 xxii, 364 p.p $60 **016**
1. American literature (Spanish) 2. American literature -- Latino

authors 3. Reference books 4. Hispanic American literature (Spanish) 5. American literature -- Hispanic American authors 6. American literature -- Hispanic American authors -- Bibliography
ISBN 159158292X; 9781591582922

LC 2009026355

"Focusing on popular works by Latino authors, i.e. U.S. authors of Latino heritage; and authors from Latin American countries or Spain," this book, edited by Sara E. Martinez, "organizes and describes approximately 750 titles by genre, subgenre and theme. . . . Complete bibliographic information is provided for each title, along with a concise plot summary, a subject list, award information, a brief quote from the book, and a list of similar reads." (Publisher's note)

"This well-written book is an essential resource for public and high-school libraries, especially if they serve Latino populations." Booklist
Includes bibliographical references and indexes

Montgomery, Denise L.
Ottemiller's index to plays in collections; an author and title index to plays appearing in collections published since 1900. Scarecrow Press, Inc. 2011 xlix, 781 p.p   **016**
1. Drama -- Indexes
ISBN 9780810877207; 9780810877214

LC 2010053010

"Returning after some 20 years, this volume (7th ed., 1988) remains the classic index to plays in collections and anthologies... Plays are indexed by title, author, and anthology title. Montgomery adds more than 2,300 new authors and 3,593 new plays, expanding the work's focus to include works from 103 countries and making works by women and LGBT authors more discoverable." Choice

Morris, Vanessa Irvin
The **readers'** advisory guide to street literature; Vanessa Irvin Morris; foreword by Teri Woods. American Library Association 2012 xxiii, 138 p.p ill. (alk. paper) $48.00   **016**
1. Readers' advisory services 2. Urban fiction -- Bibliography 3. Urban fiction -- History and criticism 4. Fiction in libraries 5. Street life -- Fiction -- Bibliography 6. Urban fiction, American -- Bibliography 7. Readers' advisory services -- United States 8. Young adult fiction, American -- Bibliography 9. Urban fiction, American -- History and criticism
ISBN 0838911102; 9780838911105

LC 2011029685

In this book, author Vanessa Irvin "Morris presents a[n] . . . overview of the genre [of street literature]. From exploring the genre's roots . . . to articulating the appeal of the books, this . . . volume covers unique . . . material. For example, there is an entire chapter on teen-friendly street lit as well as material on collection development. Appendixes include a list of publishers and unannotated book lists." (Booklist)
Includes bibliographical references (p. 113-130) and index

Moss, Rita W.
★ **Strauss's** handbook of business information; a guide for librarians, students, and researchers. Rita W. Moss and David G. Ernsthausen. 2nd ed; Libraries Unlimited 2012 xix, 399 p.p il (acid-free paper) $100   **016**
1. Business 2. Reference books 3. Business -- Databases -- Handbooks, manuals, etc 4. Government publications -- United States -- Handbooks, manuals, etc 5. Business -- Reference books -- Bibliography -- Handbooks, manuals, etc 6. Business -- Electronic information resources -- Handbooks, manuals, etc 7. Business information services -- United States -- Handbooks, manuals, etc
ISBN 1598848070; 1610692365; 9781598848076;

9781610692366

LC 2011041547

First edition by Diane Wheeler Strauss published 1988 with title: Handbook of business information

This business information handbook by Diane Wheeler Straus "is divided into two main parts. The first seven chapters cover business information according to the formats in which it is made available. The second part of the book covers specific topics within the area of business. Included are chapters on marketing; money, credit, and banking; and the many aspects of investment ranging from stocks through bonds, mutual funds, and futures and options." (Publisher's note)

This edition "first covers 'formats': directories, periodicals, loose-leaf services, government information services, and electronic sources. References are then organized by 'fields': banking, marketing, accounting, stocks and bonds, etc. Graphics include screen shots of e-sources." Libr J
Includes bibliographical references and indexes.

Niebuhr, Gary Warren
Caught up in crime; a reader's guide to crime fiction and nonfiction. [compiled by] Gary Warren Niebuhr. Libraries Unlimited 2009 xviii, 304 p.p $60   **016**
1. Crime 2. Organized crime 3. White collar crimes 4. Crime writing 5. Criminal investigation
ISBN 1591584280; 9781591584285

LC 2009008733

In this book, "librarian Gary Warren Niebuhr organizes and describes more than 600 crime titles according to popular reading tastes. . . . Books are arranged in three broad categories' professional criminals,' 'caught up in crime,' and 'criminal detectives.' Within these chapters, titles are organized in sections on the mob, serial killers, white-collar crime, criminals on the run, victims, cops-gone-bad, rogues, and more." (Publisher's note)

"The only challenge that readers or readers' advisors face when confronted with so many excellent choices is deciding where to begin reading. Whether you're after capers, serial-killer tales, white-collar crime, mobsters, dirty cops or lawyers, criminals on the lam, amateur criminals, or any other kind of crime tale, this work is recommended as a thoughtful starting point." Booklist

Make mine a mystery II; a reader's guide to mystery and detective fiction. Gary Warren Niebuhr. Libraries Unlimited 2011 xiv, 292 p.p (acid-free paper) $60   **016**
1. Mystery fiction 2. Detective and mystery stories -- Bibliography 3. Detective and mystery stories -- Stories, plots, etc
ISBN 1598845896; 9781598845891

LC 2011017226

This book, by Gary Warren Niebuhr, "examines works by prominent established authors and includes books from new writers not in the previous edition. Organizing some 700 titles in popular mystery series, the books within are divided into the broader types-- amateur, public, and private detective. Each of the selections within these groups is further categorized by the type of protagonist: classic, eccentric, lone wolf, police, lawyer, and so on." (Publisher's note)

"The authors included give a good representation of popular writers today. The bibliographies have also been updated. This is an excellent companion to the original volume and an essential readers' advisory tool." Booklist
Includes bibliographical references and indexes

Pearl, Nancy
Now read this II; a guide to mainstream fiction, 1990-2001. Libraries Unlimited 2002 300p il $55   **016**

1. Best books 2. Reference books 3. Fiction -- Bibliography
ISBN 1-56308-867-3

LC 2002-274079

This is an annotated list of 500 books categorized by setting, story, characterization, or language. "New features include a YA designation for selected titles, a section on fiction trends, and two appendixes, one on genre bridges (books that share elements with genre fiction) and one on book groups. Like others in the Genreflecting series, this work is a truly useful tool." Booklist

★ **Now** read this III; a guide to mainstream fiction. [by] Nancy Pearl and Sarah Statz Cords. Libraries Unlimited 2010 xxiii, 405p $60 **016**
1. Best books 2. Reference books 3. Fiction -- Bibliography
ISBN 978-1-59158-570-1

LC 2009-49898

An annotated list of over 500 books categorized by setting, story, characterization, or language. "This volume covers books published since 2002, with heavy emphasis on the last three years. Appendixes provide bridges to other genres, book award information, further resources, and advice for book groups, and everything is thoroughly indexed by author, title, and subject." Booklist
Includes bibliographical references

Perrault, Anna H.

Information resources in the humanities and the arts; by Anna H. Perrault, Elizabeth S. Aversa, Sonia Ramirez Wohlmuth, Cynthia Miller. Libraries Unlimited, an imprint of ABC-CLIO, LLC 2013 xvii, 461 p.p (Libraries Unlimited library and information science text series) (paperback) $65 **016**
1. Humanities 2. Reference books 3. Arts -- Bibliography 4. Humanities -- Bibliography 5. Arts -- Reference books -- Bibliography 6. Arts -- Electronic information resources 7. Arts -- Information services -- Directories 8. Humanities -- Reference books -- Bibliography 9. Humanities -- Electronic information resources 10. Humanities -- Information services -- Directories
ISBN 159884833X; 9781598848328; 9781598848335

LC 2012028606

This book "introduces new librarians to the breadth of humanities collections, experienced librarians to nature of humanities scholarship, and the scholars themselves to a wealth of information they might otherwise have missed. This new version . . . has been refreshed to account for the myriad of digital resources that have rewritten the rules of the reference and research world, and been expanded to include significantly increased coverage of world literature and languages." (Publisher's note)
Includes bibliographical references and indexes

Quillen, C. L.

Read on... romance; reading lists for every taste. C.L. Quillen and Ilene N. Lefkowitz. Libraries Unlimited 2014 xii, 136 p.p (paperback) $40 **016**
1. Best books 2. Romance fiction -- Bibliography 3. Books and reading 4. Reading interests 5. Love stories -- Bibliography 6. Love stories -- History and criticism
ISBN 1610694007; 9781610694001

LC 2014005515

Written by C. L. Quillen and Ilene N. Lefkowitz, "This book helps adult and teen readers quickly find the books they love to read, identifies other titles with shared qualities for more reading suggestions, and provides librarians with carefully reviewed read-alike lists that they can use with confidence. Featuring romance novels published from 2000 to the present day, this . . . guide offers you hundreds of reading suggestions."

(Publisher's note)

"Keep this slimmer, solid resource on the shelf next to Kristen Ramsdell's Romance Fiction: A Guide to the Genre (2012)." Booklist
Includes bibliographical references and index

Ramsdell, Kristin

Romance fiction; a guide to the genre. Kristin Ramsdell. Libraries Unlimited 2012 xxii, 719 p.p (hardcopy: acid-free paper) $55 **016**
1. Romances 2. Book selection 3. Romance language literature 4. Love stories -- Bibliography 5. Love stories -- History and criticism
ISBN 159158177X; 9781591581772; 9781610692359

LC 2011045879

Author Kristin Ramsdell explains in the preface that "this volume is actually the second edition of her 'Happily Ever After: A Guide to Reading Interests in Romance Fiction', published . . . in 1987. . . . [The book discusses] the definition and appeal of romance and contain[s] general information about advising readers and building collections, [while also looking at] subgenres of romance, from contemporary to ethnic/multicultural." (Booklist)
Includes bibliographical references and indexes.

Reisner, Rosalind

Read on-- life stories; reading lists for every taste. Rosalind Reisner. Libraries Unlimited 2009 xv, 175 p.p $40 **016**
1. Biography 2. Autobiographies
ISBN 1591587662; 9781591587668

LC 2009023222

This book, by Rosalind Reisner, "offers brief descriptions of nearly 450 published memoirs, from classics. . . to recent bestsellers. . . . Titles are grouped together by their appeal to readers, and there is something for everyone: humorous memoirs, thrilling adventure stories, chatty celebrity reminiscences, cathartic dramas of family dysfunction, fascinating career retrospectives, and insightful stories of family and personal lives in many eras and places." (Publisher's note)
"With both a detailed table of contents and an excellent index, this is a must-have tool for public libraries." Booklist
Includes bibliographical references and index.

Riechel, Rosemarie

Easy information sources for ESL, adult learners, & new readers. Neal-Schuman Publishers 2009 285p pa $65 **016**
1. Libraries -- Special collections 2. English as a second language -- Bibliography 3. High interest-low vocabulary books -- Bibliography
ISBN 978-1-55570-650-0; 1-55570-650-9

LC 2008-40028

"This work is aimed at educators and librarians working with adults whose English is poor. Advice on ways to use children's nonfiction for adults; reference interview strategies; book selection, placement, and utilization; collection development; and readers' advisory enables this work to not only suggest sources but also offer new ways of serving this growing and diverse population." Booklist
Includes bibliographical references

Roche, Rick

Read on-- biography; reading lists for every taste. Rick Roche. Libraries Unlimited 2012 xvi, 163 p.p (hardcover) $30 **016**
1. Autobiography 2. Book selection 3. Biography -- Bibliography 4. Autobiography -- Bibliography
ISBN 1610691792; 9781610691796; 1598847015; 9781598847017

LC 2011046293

In this book, author Rick Roche "focuses on life stories written in the third person, with subjects ranging from individuals who lived in ancient times to the present-day, hailed from myriad nations, and gained fame in diverse fields. The contents are organized in order to facilitate identification of read-alikes and easy selection of titles according to appeal features such as character, story, language, setting, and mood.

Includes bibliographical references and indexes.

Scales, Pat R.

★ **Books** under fire; a hit list of banned and challenged children's books. Pat Scales. ALA Editions, an imprint of the American Library Association 2015 xvi, 208 p.p illustrations (pbk.) $47   **016**
1. Books -- Censorship 2. Children -- Books and reading -- United States 3. School libraries -- Censorship -- United States 4. Challenged books -- United States -- Bibliography 5. Prohibited books -- United States -- Bibliography 6. Children's literature -- Censorship -- United States
ISBN 0838911099; 9780838911099

LC 2014023945

This book on banned and challenged books, by Pat R. Scales, "covers both children's and young adult books. The main section profiles 34 books (and series such as 'Harry Potter' and 'Captain Underpants') that have recently been challenged for library or curriculum suitability in the US. . . . Each entry includes a . . . synopsis, quotations from some reviews, details of known challenges, awards/accolades, and a 'Further Reading' section." (Choice)

Includes bibliographical references and index

Torres-Roman, Steven A.

Read on-- science fiction; reading lists for every taste. Steven A. Torres-Roman. Libraries Unlimited 2010 xxi, 252 p.p (pbk: acid-free paper) $40   **016**
1. Science fiction -- Bibliography 2. Fiction in libraries -- United States 3. Science fiction, English -- Bibliography 4. Science fiction, American -- Bibliography 5. Readers' advisory services -- United States 6. Public libraries -- United States -- Book lists
ISBN 1591587697; 9781591587699

LC 2010024075

This book, by Steven A. Torres-Roman, "is for new science fiction readers looking for a place to start exploring the genre, as well as for long-time fans who want to delve in deeper. The guide covers a broad spectrum of science fiction titles, organizing books into lists designed to appeal to a variety of reading tastes. . . . The book spans the genre's time stream, including classics . . . as well as the latest bestsellers." (Publisher's note)

Includes bibliographical references and index

Trott, Barry

Read on . . . crime fiction; reading lists for every taste. Libraries Unlimited 2008 146p (Read on series) pa $30   **016**
1. Reference books 2. Mystery fiction -- Bibliography
ISBN 978-1-59158-373-8

LC 2007-33858

The author organizes recommended crime fiction titles by "five 'appeal characteristics' commonly employed by RA professionals: story, character, setting, mood, and language. Under these broad categories, he offers an assortment of creatively titled reading lists ('Serf and Turf: Medieval Mysteries') that illustrate aspects of one of the appeal factors. Arrows designate one title per list selected as a good starting point for that category. . . . Both readers' advisors and crime-fiction fans will find all sorts of inventive ways to use this book, including, of course,

compiling their own lists of titles or categories that should have been represented." Booklist

Vnuk, Rebecca

Read on-- women's fiction; reading lists for every taste. Rebecca Vnuk. Libraries Unlimited 2009 126 p. $40   **016**
1. Women -- Fiction 2. American fiction -- Women authors
ISBN 1591586348; 9781591586340

LC 2009012315

This book, by Rebecca Vnuk, "offers new reading paths for women's fiction lovers. the organization and approach are based on various appeal factors of the genre, rather than on the formal genres and subgenres adhered to by other guides. Use these lists to advise readers; to create thematic reading lists for library websites, flyers, and newsletters; and as checklists or reading plans for those who enjoy women's fiction." (Publisher's note)

"The work also includes a combined index of titles and authors. Like others in the Read On . . . series, this book complements more formal genre guides and is intended to be used by readers as well as readers' advisors." Booklist

Includes bibliographical references and index

Women's fiction; a guide to popular reading interests. Rebecca Vnuk and Nanette Donohue. Libraries Unlimited, an imprint of ABC-CLIO, LLC 2013 xv, 233 p.p (Genreflecting advisory series) (hardback: acid-free paper) $55   **016**
1. Women -- Fiction 2. American fiction -- Women authors 3. Women -- Fiction -- Bibliography 4. Fiction in libraries -- United States 5. Readers' advisory services -- United States 6. Women -- Books and reading -- United States 7. Public libraries -- United States -- Book lists 8. American fiction -- 20th century -- Bibliography 9. American fiction -- 21st century -- Bibliography 10. American fiction -- Women authors -- Bibliography
ISBN 1598849204; 9781598849202

LC 2013023685

This book on women's fiction is part of the Libraries Unlimited Genreflecting Advisory series. "Nine chapters gather titles under such categories as 'Grande Dames of Women's Fiction,' 'Gentle Reads,' 'Chick Lit and Beyond,' and 'Multicultural Women's Fiction.' Each chapter begins with a brief explanation of the subgenre or classificadon; for each title presented within each chapter, a two-to- three-sentence annotation highlights plot, theme, and characters." (Booklist)

Includes bibliographical references and indexes

016.6   Bibliographies of technology (Applied sciences)

Covert, Jack

★ The **100** best business books of all time; what they say, why they matter, and how they can help you. [by] Jack Covert and Todd Sattersten. Portfolio 2009 335p il $25.95   **016.6**
1. Best books 2. Business -- Bibliography
ISBN 978-1-59184-240-8

LC 2008-36664

"Covert and Sattersten operate 800-CEO-READ, a specialty business-book retailer. Out of the countless business books they have read every year for a quarter century, they have culled 100 of the best and presented them in review format. . . . This list and the fine reviews are proof positive that business books can offer a rich treasure of stories and inspiration." Booklist

Includes bibliographical references

Introduction to reference sources in the health sciences; edited by Jeffrey T. Huber and Susan Swogger. ALA Neal-Schuman 2014 468 p. (Medical Library Association Guides) $118 **016.6**
1. Medicine -- Bibliography 2. Medicine -- Information services 3. Medicine -- Reference books -- Bibliography
ISBN 0838911846; 9780838911846

LC 2014004660

This book for medical librarians "lists classic and up-to-the-minute print and electronic resources in the health sciences, helping librarians find the answers that library users seek. Included are electronic versions of traditionally print reference sources, trustworthy electronic-only resources, and resources that library users can access from home or on the go through freely available websites or via library licenses." (Publisher's note)

"As with any reference work, particularly one that relies heavily on online materials, some of the resources mentioned likely will become outdated over time. Nevertheless, the larger context in which these resources are often presented should slow the inevitable decline in relevance." Choice

Includes bibliographical references and index

Stoeger, Melissa Brackney
Food lit; a reader's guide to epicurean nonfiction. Melissa Brackney Stoeger. Libraries Unlimited 2013 xx, 350 p.p (Real stories) (hardback) $60 **016.6**
1. Food in literature 2. Food -- Bibliography
ISBN 1598847066; 9781598847062

LC 2012038052

This book, by Melissa Brackney Stoeger, "provides a much-needed resource for librarians assisting adult readers interested in the topic of food. . . . Containing annotations of hundreds of nonfiction titles about food that are arranged into genre and subject interest categories for easy reference, the book addresses a diversity of reading experiences by covering everything from foodie memoirs and histories of food to extreme cuisine and food exposés." (Publisher's note)

"The hundreds of annotations alone make any librarian's job much, much easier, but Stoeger's inclusion of appendix materials from famous cooks and their books, food blogs, feature films and documentaries, fiction featuring food, and food-writing awards makes this an outstanding reference tool for any public library collection." Booklist

Includes bibliographical references and indexes

016.78 Music bibliographies

Friedwald, Will
The **great** jazz and pop vocal albums; Will Friedwald. Pantheon 2017 xxv, 402 p.p color illustrations (hardcover) $40 **016.78**
1. Singers 2. Jazz vocals 3. Popular music 4. Music -- Reviews 5. Singers -- Discography 6. Jazz vocals -- Discography 7. Sound recordings -- Reviews 8. Popular music -- Discography
ISBN 9781101871751; 9780307379078

LC 2016027178

This book, by Will Friedwald, features "great [jazz and pop] singers and their greatest work in an innovative and revelatory way. . . . It is through their albums that Ella Fitzgerald, Frank Sinatra, Peggy Lee, . . . Nat King Cole, Judy Garland, and the rest of the glorious honor roll of jazz and pop singers have been most tellingly and lastingly appreciated. . . . Each of the fifty-seven albums discussed here captures the artist at a high point . . . of her or his career." (Publisher's note)

"This absolutely indispensable compendium of essential jazz and pop vocal albums is a testament to the ongoing vibrancy of jazz music and the Great American Songbook . . . ." Booklist

020 Library and information sciences

ALA glossary of library and information science; edited by Michael Levine-Clark and Toni M. Carter. ALA Editions 2013 viii, 280 p.p (pbk.: alk. paper) $55 **020**
1. Library science -- Dictionaries 2. Information science -- Dictionaries
ISBN 0838911110; 9780838911112

LC 2012010060

This book, edited by Michael Levine-Clark and Toni M. Carter, "presents a thorough yet concise guide to the specific words that describe the materials, processes and systems relevant to the field of librarianship. Written by a panel of experts from across the LIS world, . . . [this edition is] updated to include the latest technology- and internet-related terms." (Publisher's note)

Includes bibliographical references (pages 277-280)

★ **Core** technology competencies for librarians and library staff; a LITA guide. Susan M. Thompson, editor. Neal-Schuman Publishers 2009 248p il pa $65 **020**
1. Library education 2. Information technology 3. Technological innovations 4. Librarians -- In-service training
ISBN 978-1-55570-660-9

LC 2008-46174

In this book, "a coterie of experts identify competencies for technology specialists and describe several competency implementation programs. Useful for everyone from the systems librarian to the 'lone information technology librarian.'" Am Libr

Includes bibliographical references

Defending professionalism; a resource for librarians, information specialists, knowledge managers, and archivists. Bill Crowley, editor. Libraries Unlimited, an imprint of ABC-CLIO, LLC 2012 235 p. (paperback) $50.00 **020**
1. Librarians 2. Professional ethics 3. Information scientists 4. Library education 5. Libraries and society 6. Archivists -- Training of 7. Knowledge workers -- Training of 8. Archivists -- Professional ethics 9. Librarians -- Professional ethics 10. Information scientists -- Training of 11. Knowledge workers -- Professional ethics 12. Information scientists -- Professional ethics
ISBN 1598848690; 9781598848694

LC 2012006410

This book, edited by Bill Crowley, offers "arguments and approaches for combating library and information deprofessionalization. . . . Composed of 14 chapters written by contemporary practitioners," the book "provides managers, funding authorities, educators, and practitioners with practical, political, and theoretical reasons why it is in their self-interest to employ professionally educated personnel." (Publisher's note)

Includes bibliographical references and index

Gleick, James
The **information**. Pantheon Books 2011 526p il $29.95 **020**
1. Information science
ISBN 978-0-375-42372-7; 0-375-42372-9

LC 2010-23221

"As he traces the evolution of intertwined ideas, [Gleick] provides

vivid portraits of [Claude] Shannon and other pioneers of our Information Age, including Charles Babbage, whose unbuilt 19th-century 'Analytical Engine' anticipated modern computers, and Alan Turing, whose machines helped the Allies crack German codes during World War II."
Wall Street J

Includes bibliographical references

Johnson, Marilyn

★ **This** book is overdue! how librarians and cybrarians can save us all. Harper 2010 272p $24.99   **020**
  1. Librarians 2. Library science
  ISBN 978-0-06-143160-9; 0-06-143160-5

LC 2010-07860

"In an information age full of Google-powered searches, free-by-Bittorrent media downloads and Wiki-powered knowledge databases, the librarian may seem like an antiquated concept. . . . [The author] is here to reverse that notion with a topical, witty study of the vital ways modern librarians uphold their traditional roles as educators, archivists, and curators of a community legacy. . . . Johnson's wry report is a must-read for anyone who's used a library in the past quarter century."
Publ Wkly

Includes bibliographical references

Lankes, R. David

The **atlas** of new librarianship. MIT Press; Association of College & Research Libraries 2011 408p il $55   **020**
  1. Library science 2. Libraries and community 3. Librarianship
  ISBN 978-0-262-01509-7

LC 2010-22788

The author initiates a "conversation about librarianship and its future. He builds this conversation using an atlas, or topical mapping, to engage librarians in exploring their profession, their mission, and their future. . . . Grounding the atlas in the why of librarianship, Lankes argues that libraries serve not only as repositories providing access to information but as fertile ground for actively using collections, resources, and information to create knowledge and foster learning via ongoing conversations with our communities. He invites librarians to expand librarianship beyond the support of information seeking, access, and literacy and toward participation in and co-ownership of a community's knowledge-creation processes. . . . Essential for all librarians." Libr J

Includes bibliographical references.

Library mashups; exploring new ways to deliver library data. edited by Nicole C. Engard. Information Today, Inc. 2009 334p il map pa $39.50   **020**
  1. Internet resources 2. Web sites -- Design
  ISBN 978-1-57387-372-7

LC 2009-25999

"Editor Engard assembles 21 articles from 25 international contributors to focus on mashups within the library environment. Readers with little knowledge of mashups will find chapters such as 'What Is a Mashup?' and 'Behind the Scenes: Some Technical Details on Mashups' especially helpful. Other portions of this book cover topics such as mashups in library Web sites, mashups of catalog data, and mashups and media (e.g., photos)." Booklist

Includes bibliographical references

What Do I Read Next? A Reader's Guide to Current Genre Fiction. Gale Cengage Learning. Gale / Cengage Learning 2012 738 p. (hardcover) $254   **020**
  1. Book selection 2. Books and reading
  ISBN 1414461372; 9781414461373

This volume is a book selection guide. It uses similarities in various books to help "readers to independently choose titles of interest published in the last year. Each entry describes a separate book, listing everything readers need to know to make selections. Arranged by author within six genre sections, detailed entries provide" information about the title, publisher, series, and temporal and geographical setting. (Publisher's note)

Palfrey, John G.

BiblioTech; why libraries matter more than ever in the age of Google. John Palfrey. Basic Books 2015 288 p. (hardback) $26.99   **020.285**
  1. Internet 2. Libraries 3. Libraries and electronic publishing 4. Digital preservation 5. Libraries -- Forecasting 6. Libraries and the Internet 7. Library information networks 8. Libraries -- Social aspects -- United States 9. Librarians -- Effect of technological innovations on 10. Library users -- Effect of technological innovations on
  ISBN 0465042996; 9780465042999

LC 2014041874

This book, by John Palfrey, "argues that anyone seeking to participate in the 21st century needs to understand how to find and use the vast stores of information available online. And libraries, which play a crucial role in making these skills and information available, are at risk. In order to survive our rapidly modernizing world and dwindling government funding, libraries must make the transition to a digital future as soon as possible." (Publisher's note)

Includes bibliographical references and index

Woodward, Jeannette

The **transformed** library; e-books, expertise, and evolution. Jeannette Woodward. ALA Editions, an imprint of the American Library Association 2013 131 p. $55   **020**
  1. Libraries 2. Technological innovations 3. Libraries and society 4. Libraries -- Forecasting 5. Libraries and the Internet 6. Library science -- Philosophy 7. Libraries -- Aims and objectives 8. Libraries -- Information technology 9. Libraries and electronic publishing 10. Librarians -- Effect of technological innovations on
  ISBN 0838911641; 9780838911648

LC 2012023767

In this book, Jeannette Woodward considers: are "librarians and libraries facing oblivion as some prognosticators claim? Woodward outlines the technological forces that have coalesced to 'threaten' the future of libraries including financial constraints, digital books, ebook-publisher approaches to libraries, outsourcing, downsizing library space, and librarians' reaction to perceived threats." (Library Journal)

Includes bibliographical references and index

020.1   Library and information sciences – Philosophy and theory

Lankes, R. David

The **new** librarianship field guide; R. David Lankes. The MIT Press 2016 240 p.   **020.1**
  1. Libraries and society 2. Librarians -- Attitudes 3. Libraries and community 4. Library science -- Philosophy
  ISBN 9780262529082

LC 2015039943

"The author argues that in order to become change agents and remain relevant, librarians can no longer be content to wait for their constituents to come to them. Instead, librarians must seek ways to engage community members through participatory systems which can include various avenues such as developing a web presence, literacy classes, or solid collections. In fact, the emphasis on participation with community members is so important that Lankes uses the term member, where others might use patron or customer. This field guide would make an excellent introductory text for library science students. Each chapter clearly presents its core concept, provides concrete examples, and offers stimulating discussion points." (Library Journal)

Includes bibliographical references and index

020.9   History, geographic treatment, biography

Wright, Alex

Cataloging the world; Paul Otlet and the birth of the information age. Alex Wright. Oxford University Press 2014 360 p. (acid-free paper) $27.95   **020.9**
1. Bibliographers -- Biography 2. Bibliographic control -- History 3. Documentation 4. Mundaneum -- History 5. Universal bibliography 6. Classification -- Books 7. World Wide Web -- History 8. Information organization -- History 9. Bibliographers -- Belgium -- Biography
ISBN 0199931410; 9780199931415
LC 2013035233
"In 'Cataloging the World,' Alex Wright introduces us to a figure who stands out in the long line of thinkers and idealists who devoted themselves to the task. Beginning in the late nineteenth century, Paul Otlet, a librarian by training, worked at expanding the potential of the catalog card, the world's first information chip." (Publisher's note)

"Wright ends his illuminating story in the present, where Otlet's thoughts about the connection of information to knowledge, and knowledge to insight, are still urgent." Kirkus

Includes bibliographical references and index

021.2   Relationships with the community

The **artist's** library; a field guide. edited by Laura C. Damon-Moore and Erinn P. Batykefer. Coffee House Press 2014 220 p. illustrations (Books in action) $23.95   **021.2**
1. Libraries and community 2. Creation (Literary, artistic, etc.) 3. Arts -- Library resources 4. Libraries -- Social aspects 5. Library users -- Case studies 6. Libraries -- Cultural programs 7. Libraries -- Problems, exercises, etc 8. Creation (Literary, artistic, etc.) -- Case studies
ISBN 1566893534; 9781566893534
LC 2013035168
This book, edited by Laura C. Damon-Moore and Erinn P. Batykefer, "offers the idea that an artist is any person who uses creative tools to make new things, and the guidance and resources to make libraries of all sizes and shapes come alive as spaces for art-making and cultural engagement. Case studies included in the book range from the crafty . . . to the community-minded . . . to documentary . . . to the technically complex." (Publisher's note)

"Librarians who wish to make their library the connecting point between artists and the community should purchase. Perfect for brainstorming planning guides, this book is a permission slip to have fun at the library." LJ

Brookover, Sophie

Pop goes the library; using pop culture to connect with your whole community. [by] Sophie Brookover and Elizabeth Burns. Information Today, Inc. 2008 298p il pa $39.50   **021.2**

1. Libraries and community 2. Libraries -- Special collections -- Popular culture
ISBN 978-1-57387-336-9
LC 2008-19509
"This work defines how popular culture can contribute to any library. . . . The authors explore what popular culture is and, more importantly, what it is not. Also examined are what it means to create a popular-culture collection and how to use popular culture to generate staff and public support. . . . This book is required reading." Booklist

Includes bibliographical references

Librarians as community partners; an outreach handbook. edited by Carol Smallwood. American Library Association 2010 204p pa $55   **021.2**
1. Cultural programs 2. Libraries and community 3. Libraries -- Public relations
ISBN 978-0-8389-1006-1
LC 2009-20359
"Thirty-seven public, school, and academic librarians here share 'how we did outreach good' and produce a joyful collection. . . . Beyond a bounty of ideas are practical suggestions and examples that can be used for the library to approach organizations, groups, and governmental entities for grant applications. While the creative is foremost, the financial and efficient are also addressed with the essential details of who did what, how it was funded, and the nature of follow-up. . . . Even the smallest library with a handful of staff could benefit from this book." Libr J

Includes bibliographical references

021.7   Promotion of libraries, archives, information centers

Imhoff, Kathleen R.

Library contests; a how-to-do-it manual. [by] Kathleen R.T. Imhoff, Ruthie Maslin. Neal-Schuman Publishers 2007 182p il pa $55   **021.7**
1. Contests 2. Libraries and community 3. Advertising -- Libraries 4. Libraries -- Public relations
ISBN 1-55570-559-6 pa; 978-1-55570-559-6 pa
LC 2006-33177
"This comprehensive book covers planning, implementing, and evaluating contests of all kinds, for all kinds of libraries. It addresses setting budgets and schedules, choosing prizes and judges, establishing rules, promoting the contest, and evaluating it once it is over. The final chapter details four tried-and-true programs various libraries have held." (School Library Journal)

Marketing your library; tips and tools that work. edited by Carol Smallwood, Vera Gubnitskaia and Kerol Harrod; foreword by Michael Germano. McFarland & Company, Inc., Publishers 2012 ix, 221 p.p ill. (softcover: acid-free paper) $55.00   **021.7**
1. Libraries -- Marketing 2. Libraries -- Public relations
ISBN 0786465433; 9780786465439
LC 2012004460
This book, edited by Carol Smallwood, Vera Gubnitskaia, and Kerol Harrod, presents "how-to case studies from practicing public, school, academic, and special librarians" intended to help librarians "improve brand management, campaign organization, community outreach, media interaction, social media, and event planning and implementation." (Publisher's note)

Includes bibliographical references and index

Phillips, Susan P.

Great displays for your library step by step. McFarland &
Co. 2008 234p il pa $45   **021.7**
1. Libraries -- Exhibitions
ISBN 978-0-7864-3164-9; 0-7864-3164-4

LC 2007-47450

This book "offers practical advice on utilizing everyday materials to
create lively but economical presentations on all sorts of topics including authors, world cultures, traditions, natural habitats and book genres.
Each of 46 featured displays includes a brief introduction to the subject;
an explanation of the genesis of the idea; specifics regarding the information included and its source; step-by-step instructions for assembly;
and ideas on how to customize the display to any available space." (Publisher's note)

Schall, Lucy

Teen talkback with interactive booktalks! Lucy Schall. Libraries Unlimited, an imprint of ABC-CLIO, LLC 2013 xviii,
305 p.p (hardcopy) $45   **021.7**
1. Reading 2. Book talks 3. Young adult literature 4. Library
services to young adults 5. Fiction genres -- Bibliography 6.
Reading promotion -- United States 7. Teenagers -- Books and
reading -- United States
ISBN 1610692896; 9781610692892

LC 2013000241

This book, by Lucy Schall, "is . . . a resource, supplying ready-to-
use, interactive booktalks and curriculum connections for more than 100
recently published young adult books. This . . . book is . . . [a] tool
for motivating teens to read. It shows how to make booktalks interactive and get teens participating in the presentation, rather than passively
listening. Book selections include titles published from 2008 to 2012
organized in seven categories." (Publisher's note)

"Although mostly fiction, there are some nonfiction choices included
and the balance of newer titles is respectable. Due to the plethora of topics, detail in descriptions, and variety of related works listed, librarians
will be able to locate books for the pickiest of readers." Lib Med Con

Includes bibliographical references and index

Thenell, Jan

The **library's** crisis communications planner; a PR guide
for handling every emergency. American Library Association
2004 77p il pa $25   **021.7**
1. Libraries -- Public relations
ISBN 0-8389-0870-5

LC 2004-10891

Offering "advice, firsthand experience, scenarios, and guidelines for
communicating effectively before, during, and after a crisis or crisis-
producing events, ... [the author's] guide is a ready-made workshop
on how to establish and maintain relationships with the media, including
how to write a press release, how to keep all staff informed and aware
of what to do when an emergency occurs, and how to make sure library
board members and other community stakeholders are notified and/or
involved. Whether or not you have a public relations office or officer,
this slim volume is a must for your professional shelf." Libr J

Includes bibliographical references

022   Administration of physical plant

Petroski, Henry

The **book** on the bookshelf. Knopf 1999 290p $26   **022**
1. Books 2. Libraries 3. Bookbinding
ISBN 0-375-40649-2

LC 99-14336

The author discusses the formatting and housing of books
throughout history

"The charm of this book lies in the way that it helps us take a fresh
look at an old, long-familiar object. . . . This survey of the subject is
probably definitive." Christ Sci Monit

Includes bibliographical references

023   Personnel management (Human resource management)

Giesecke, Joan

★ **Fundamentals** of library supervision; [by] Joan Giesecke and Beth McNeil. 2nd ed.; American Library Association
2010 189p il (ALA fundamentals series) pa $55   **023**
1. Personnel management 2. Libraries -- Administration
ISBN 978-0-8389-1016-0

LC 2009-28890

First published 2005

"The authors give advice on how to build relationships with bosses,
peers, and reports; establish good communication skills; create a healthy
work climate; motivate others; and build a team. . . . Each chapter includes a succinct bibliography, allowing the new manager to continue
his or her education—especially useful for more complex topics like
project management." Libr J

Includes bibliographical references

Stanley, Mary J.

Managing library employees; a how-to-do-it manual. Neal-Schuman Publishers 2008 247p il (How-to-do-it manuals
for libraries) pa $59.95   **023**
1. Personnel management 2. Libraries -- Handbooks, manuals, etc.
ISBN 978-1-55570-628-9; 1-55570-628-2

LC 2007-51961

"Oriented to librarians who do not have a human resources department in the library, Managing Library Employees is for the nonexpert
trying to come to terms with managing a library's largest expenditure
and asset—its employees. The chapters are divided into subtopics posed
as questions. . . . The chapters also provide information on writing an
effective job description, designing a disciplinary procedure, and identifying potential issues that might lead to a lawsuit. . . . This useful guide
for everyday situations should be on any library director or manager's
professional reference shelf." Booklist

Includes bibliographical references

Tucker, Dennis C.

Crash course in library supervision; meeting the key players. [by] Dennis C. Tucker and Shelley Elizabeth Mosley.
Libraries Unlimited 2008 139p il (Crash course series) pa
$30   **023**
1. Libraries -- Administration
ISBN 978-1-59158-564-0; 1-59158-564-3

LC 2007-30131

This book "covers the basics for new public library administrators,
with an emphasis on interpersonal relations. . . . The book should prove

valuable to all new library administrators." Booklist

Includes bibliographical references

025 Operations of libraries, archives, information centers

Bolan, Kimberly

Technology made simple; an improvement guide for small and medium libraries. [by] Kimberly Bolan and Robert Cullin. American Library Association 2007 213p il $40 **025**

1. Information technology 2. Libraries -- Automation

ISBN 0-8389-0920-5; 978-0-8389-0920-1

LC 2006-13191

The authors present an "overview of basic public library technologies. . . . Using examples from a plethora of small- and medium-sized libraries to illustrate how such specific issues as self-check, hiring for attitude, tech policies, staff and public training, and formal planning can be approached as doable and nonthreatening to the non-specialist, this guide is an excellent demonstration of how order can make big issues approachable. . . . Libraries should purchase it for their staff collections but also make reading and implementing various suggestions part of their work plans." Voice Youth Advocates

Includes bibliographical references

Burke, John (John J.)

Neal-Schuman library technology companion; a basic guide for library staff. [by] John J. Burke. 3rd ed.; Neal-Schuman Publishers 2009 279p il **025**

1. Information technology 2. Technological innovations 3. Libraries -- Automation

ISBN 978-1-55570-676-0

LC 2009-23646

First published 2001

"Separated into five parts, the work begins with a discussion of the basics, followed by descriptions of the tools, such as computers and networks. Next addressed are how to put technology to work and how to build and maintain the technology environment. The final chapter talks about future trends. . . . [This is] a valuable reference manual for practicing librarians and textbook for a library-school course. The work addresses all aspects of librarianship and technology—teaching, security, databases, social networking, and more." Booklist

Includes bibliographical references

Cohn, John M.

The **complete** library technology planner; a guidebook with sample technology plans and RFPs on CD-ROM. [by] John M. Cohn and Ann L. Kelsey; with a foreword by Keith Michael Fiels. Neal-Schuman Publishers 2010 xxiv, 163p il pa $99.95 **025**

1. Information technology 2. Planning, Library 3. Libraries -- Automation 4. Automation of library processes -- Handbooks, manuals, etc.

ISBN 978-1-55570-681-4; 1-55570-681-9

LC 2009-41008

"This book provides a comprehensive wealth of information for libraries in need of creating or updating a technology plan. Whether your goal is to introduce an integrated library system (ILS) or transfer from an existing system to a new one, Cohn and Kelsey make clear the strategic planning process involved and provide the tools needed to create a plan, including how to meet funding requirements, implement the plan, and evaluate its success. The accompanying CD-ROM contains 38 sample technology plans and requests for proposals (RFPs) that have been col-

lected from 32 different libraries." Libr J

Includes bibliographical references

Kovacs, Diane K.

The **Kovacs** guide to electronic library collection development; essential core subject collections, selection criteria, and guidelines. 2nd ed; Neal-Schuman Publishers 2009 xxiii, 303p il pa $150 **025**

1. Digital libraries

ISBN 978-1-55570-664-7; 1-55570-664-9

LC 2009-27772

First published 2004; written by Diane K. Kovacs and Kara L. Robinson

"Chapters cover general collection guidelines and licensing basics; especially useful are individual sections citing specific Web sites for e-collection sources in ready reference, business, medicine, biology, engineering, physical and earth sciences, and the social sciences and humanities. Kovacs . . . is a very diligent researcher, and her latest title again offers librarians much useful information. " Booklist

Includes bibliographical references

More technology for the rest of us; a second primer on computing for the non-IT librarian. Nancy Courtney, editor. Libraries Unlimited 2010 172p il pa $50 **025**

1. Digital libraries. 2. Digital preservation. 3. Libraries and the Internet. 4. Libraries -- Information technology. 5. Libraries -- Technological innovations.

ISBN 978-1-59158-939-6 pa; 1-59158-939-8 pa; 978-1-59158-941-9 ebook; 1-59158-941-X ebook

LC 2009051166

Continuation of Technology for the rest of us (2005)

"11 chapters provide readings on technology topics of interest to today's librarian. Each chapter, authored by a different practicing librarian, describes how the specific technology works and addresses its current and potential use in the library. . . . This book is a one-stop resource for gaining a basic overview of topics such as Web services, digital data preservation and curation, cloud computing, learning management systems, content management systems, metadata repurposing using XSLT, and more." Booklist

Includes bibliographical references

Pearl, Nancy

More book lust; recommended reading for every mood, moment, and reason. Sasquatch Books 2005 286p pa $16.95 **025**

1. Best books 2. Books and reading

ISBN 1-57061-435-0

LC 2004-66292

Sequel to: Book lust (2003)

The author presents a list of "books she or someone else really enjoyed reading, presented in more than 100 lists covering a delightful range of topics, from the biographical or geographical (Winston Churchill, Africa) to favorite writers categorized as 'too good to miss'. . . . If you're clueless about what to read next, you'll find something to pique your interest here." Publ Wkly

Includes bibliographical references

Pulliam, June Michele

Read on . . . horror fiction; [by] June Michele Pulliam and Anthony J. Fonseca. Libraries Unlimited 2006 xvii, 182 p (Read on series) **025**

1. Reference books 2. Horror tales -- Bibliography. 3. Fiction in libraries -- United States. 4. Horror tales, American -- Bibliography.

5. Readers' advisory services -- United States. 6. Public libraries -- United States -- Book lists.
ISBN 1-59158-176-1; 978-1-59158-176-5 (pbk.: alk. paper)
LC 2006012719

"Pulliam and Fonseca have taken 350 popular horror titles from the last decade and divided them by their appeal factors. The authors point out that some readers may prefer books that are plot driven, while others want books that emphasize characters, while still others are interested in the mood of the book, and these factors are not found in the library catalog. Five chapters analyze the appeal factors of story, mood, setting, character, and language, with each chapter further subdivided into various themes--complex plots, plot twists, intense endings, gross stories, home-alone frights, wilderness horror, and psychic detectives, to name just a few." (Publisher's note)

Includes bibliographical references and index..

025.04   Information storage and retrieval systems

Bell, Suzanne S.

Librarian's guide to online searching; cultivating database skills for research and instruction. Suzanne S. Bell. 4th edition Libraries Unlimitied 2015 xvii, 320 p.p illustrations $55   **025.04**
1. Internet searching 2. Librarians -- Training of
ISBN 161069998X; 9781610699983
LC 2014038457

"In its fourth edition, this work still serves as the best how-to on online searching for library degree students and those new to the profession. Bell . . . provides an updated version that includes a more thorough discussion on Google Scholar, and offers fresh discussions on discovery services and video tutorials. . . . Bell discusses the gamut of database basics, starting with database construction, moving to specialized databases by broad subject area and search strategies, and ending with advice on effectively working to engage the audience during instruction." LJ

Includes bibliographical references (pages 299-309) and index

Dornfest, Rael

Google hacks; [by] Rael Dornfest, Paul Bausch, and Tara Calishain. 3rd ed.; O'Reilly 2006 xxxii, 510p il $24.99 **025.04**
1. Google (Website) 2. Internet searching 3. Google (Web site)
ISBN 0-596-52706-3; 978-0-596-52706-8
LC 2006-285771

First published 2003 under the authorship of Tara Calishain and Rael Dornfest

This guide to the search engine Google gives instructions on how to use such tools as Google Earth, Google Maps, Google Blog Search, Video Search, and Music Search, as well as different ways of using Google products, such as using Google to keep track of new blog posts and building customized Google maps.

Includes bibliographical references

Gale directory of databases. Gale Res. 2008 2v in 4 parts set $585   **025.04**
1. Reference books 2. Information systems -- Directories
ISBN 978-0-7876-9755-6; 0-7876-9755-9

Annual. First published 1993. Formed by the merger of Directory of online databases, Directory of portable databases, and Computer-readable databases

"Descriptive entries include such details as producer name and contact information, summary of content, database language, geographic coverage, year first available, time span, updating, availability, rates, and more." Publisher's note

McClure, Charles R.

★ **Public** libraries and internet service roles; measuring and maximizing Internet services. [by] Charles R. McClure and Paul T. Jaeger. American Library Association 2009 112p il map $65   **025.04**
1. Internet 2. Public libraries 3. Libraries and the Internet 4. Internet -- Public libraries 5. Librarianship -- Social aspects 6. Public libraries -- Social aspects 7. Public libraries -- Aims and objectives
ISBN 978-0-8389-3576-7; 0-8389-3576-1
LC 2008-26622

The authors "summarize the existing research on the meanings of social roles and expectations of public libraries and the results of studies detailing those roles and expectations in relation to the Internet. . . . Their book raises our awareness of some very critical issues and is required reading for anyone who cares about public libraries." Booklist

Includes bibliographical references

Pariser, Eli

The **filter** bubble; what the Internet is hiding from you. Penguin Press 2011 294p $25.95   **025.04**
1. Internet 2. World Wide Web 3. Information systems 4. Semantic Web 5. Invisible Web 6. Internet -- Censorship 7. Information organization
ISBN 978-1-59420-300-8; 1-59420-300-8
LC 2011010403

The author examines "the personalization of search-engine results. . . . He is most concerned with its political and social implications, and particularly with what he believes to be its high toll on serendipitous discovery." (N Y Times Book Rev) Index.

"The distinction between citizen and consumer forms the core of [this book] . . . . Are we consumers whose role in society is primarily to purchase and use products, or are we citizens who make informed decisions in an attempt to make life better for ourselves and the world? The Internet, as Eli Pariser convincingly argues in the book, is hurtling toward a consumer model, existing primarily to sell people stuff at the expense of everything else. Pariser is focused on the 'personalization' model, as well as the 'filter bubble' that the gives the book its name. The biggest companies on the Internet, specifically Google and Facebook, are changing the Internet to match users' specific interests, habits, and purchasing preferences, often without us even knowing we're getting personalized content. Pariser isn't simply a disgruntled anticapitalist, though—he lays out the societal and cognitive reasons this particular form of personalization is threatening, using anecdotes, data, philosophy, and social as well as cognitive psychology." A V Club

Includes bibliographical references

Seife, Charles

Virtual unreality; just because the Internet told you, how do you know it's true? Charles Seife. Viking 2014 256 p. $26.95   **025.04**
1. Internet 2. Information literacy 3. Information resources 4. Internet literacy 5. Internet -- Safety measures 6. Internet fraud -- Prevention 7. Computer network resources -- Evaluation 8. Electronic information resource literacy
ISBN 0670026085; 9780670026081
LC 2013047849

This book, by Charles Seife, "explains how to separate fact from fantasy in the digital world. . . . Digital information is a powerful tool that spreads unbelievably rapidly . . ., even when that information is actually a lie. . . . Charles Seife uses the skepticism, wit, and sharp facility for analysis . . . to take us deep into the Internet information jungle and cut a path through the trickery, fakery, and cyber skullduggery that the online world enables." (Publisher's note)

"Intense and incisive, Seife's exposé of potent tricks on the mesmerizing, overpowering Internet makes us very wary about anything that cannot be verified with our own eyes." Pub Wkly

Includes bibliographical references and index

025.042   Search and retrieval

Devine, Jane

Going beyond Google again; strategies for using and teaching the Invisible Web. Jane Devine and Francine Egger-Sider. Amer Library Assn"||"Neal-Schuman, an imprint of the American Library Assn 2013 160 p. illustrations (paperback) $72   **025.042**

1. Internet in education 2. Internet searching -- Study and teaching 3. Invisible Web 4. Database searching 5. Internet searching 6. Invisible Web -- Study and teaching
ISBN 1555708986; 9781555708986

LC 2013010867

This book is a follow-up volume to book "Going Beyond Google" by Jane Devine and Francine Egger-Sider, "which placed teaching the Invisible Web into information literacy programs. [This volume] expands on the teaching foundation laid in the first book and continues to document the Invisible Web's existence and evolution, and suggests ways of teaching students to use it." (Publisher's note)

"Chapter summaries and extensive citations make this an attractive choice for students. It should also be of interest to librarians and anyone interested in optimizing their research resources and strategies." LJ

Includes bibliographical references and index

Hock, Randolph

The **Extreme** Searcher's Internet Handbook; A Guide for the Serious Searcher. by Randolph Hock. 3rd ed.; Information Today, Inc. 2013 xxi, 315 p.p ill.; (paperback) $24.95 **025.042**

1. Internet research 2. Internet searching 3. Web search engines
ISBN 1937290026; 9781937290023

LC 2012039960

This book by Randolph Hock presents a "guide for anyone who conducts research on the internet—including librarians, teachers, students, business professionals, and writers. This fully revised handbook details what users must know to take full advantage of internet search tools and resources. From the latest online tools to the new and enhanced services offered by standbys such as Google, the major search engines and their myriad of possibilities are thoroughly discussed." (Publisher's note)

025.06   Information storage and retrieval systems devoted to specific subjects

Guide to reference in medicine and health; Christa Modschiedler and Denise Bennett, editors. ALA Editions, an imprint of the American Library Association 2014 xviii, 468 p.p (print: alk. paper) $75   **025.06**

1. Medicine -- Bibliography 2. Reference books -- Bibliography 3. Medicine -- Information services 4. Medicine -- Reference books -- Bibliography 5. Reference Books, Medical -- Resource Guides
ISBN 0838912214; 9780838912218

LC 2014005002

This book, edited by Christa Modschiedler and Denise Bennett, "provides an annotated list of print and electronic biomedical and health-related reference sources, including internet resources and digital image collections. . . . Entries are selected and annotated by an editorial team of top reference librarians and are used internationally as a go-to source for identifying information as well as training reference professionals." (Publisher's note)

Includes bibliographical references and indexes
Reference in medicine and health

025.1   Administration

The **frugal** librarian; thriving in tough economic times. edited by Carol Smallwood. American Library Association 2011 277p il   **025.1**

1. Library finance 2. Libraries and community 3. Libraries -- United States
ISBN 0-8389-1075-0; 978-0-8389-1075-7

LC 2010034317

"More than 30 chapters in nine sections cover various aspects of running any library, from grant writing and programming to staffing. Also found here is advice on professional survival and career development for the librarian. The chapters are written by librarians from academic, public, and school libraries." (Booklist)

Includes bibliographical references

Johnson, Doug

★ The **indispensable** librarian; surviving and thriving in school libraries in the information age. Doug Johnson; illustrations by Brady Johnson. Linworth, an imprint of ABC-CLIO, LLC 2013 xix, 207 p.p illustrations (pbk.) $40   **025.1**

1. Librarians 2. School libraries 3. School librarians -- United States 4. School libraries -- United States -- Administration
ISBN 161069239X; 9781610692397

LC 2012051394

This book, by Doug A. Johnson, "defines and clarifies the role of the school library media specialist in a technologically enhanced school, providing relevant examples and useful advice on a variety of topics; and underscores the importance of strong management skills, especially regarding collaborative planning and communications. The book is written especially for K-12 school librarians, both new and experienced, and is also suitable for pre-service librarians as a textbook." (Publisher's note)

"Johnson offers both theory and practical suggestions on ways to embed [librarians] and [their] jobs into the fabric of a school's culture and curriculum." Lib Med Con

Includes bibliographical references and index

Landau, Herbert B.

The **small** public library survival guide; thriving on less. American Library Association 2008 159p pa $42   **025.1**

1. Library finance 2. Public libraries 3. Libraries and community
ISBN 978-0-8389-3575-0; 0-8389-3575-3

LC 2008-7425

This "volume covers many topics of interest to staff in small public libraries. Written in a conversational, accessible style, information is presented in short chapters with relevant examples and sample documents. . . . Covering topics from low-budget programming to building 'noncash support from the community,' this text has something for almost everyone involved in the operations of a small public library. . . . Easy and enjoyable to read." Voice Youth Advocates

Includes bibliographical references

Larson, Jeanette C.

★ The **public** library policy writer; a guidebook with model policies on CD-ROM. [by] Jeanette C. Larson and Herman L. Totten. Neal-Schuman Publishers 2008 xxi, 280p $75 **025.1**

1. Public libraries 2. Libraries -- Administration

ISBN 978-1-55570-603-6; 1-55570-603-7

LC 2008-17622

"This guidebook is written mainly for small to medium-sized library directors who need to analyze current policies, revise or update those still in use, and develop new ones. The book is organized by administrative and service areas such as employment practices, staff and patron conduct, use of materials, collection development, and access to facilities. . . . This practical tool should be useful to administrators, staff, and library boards." Booklist

Includes bibliographical references

Laughlin, Sara

The **quality** library; a guide to staff-driven improvement, better efficiency, and happier customers. [by] Sara Laughlin and Ray W. Wilson. American Library Association 2008 144p il pa $55 **025.1**

1. Customer services 2. Management 3. Planning, Library 4. Library administration 5. Libraries -- Management 6. Total quality management 7. Libraries -- Administration

ISBN 0-8389-0952-3; 978-0-8389-0952-2

LC 2007-30710

"Building on an earlier publication, The Library's Continuous Improvement Fieldbook: 29 Ready-to-Use Tools . . . Laughlin and Wilson have created a manual for administrators and employees who want to improve their libraries by improving their processes. . . . This can be a useful guide for libraries whose governing bodies are looking for businesslike solutions and for managers who want to heed input from those who do the job." Booklist

Includes bibliographical references

MacKellar, Pamela H.

Writing successful technology grant proposals; a LITA guide. Pamela H. MacKellar. Neal-Schuman Publishers, Inc. 2012 xviii, 227 p.p (alk. paper) $70.00 **025.1**

1. Information technology 2. Libraries -- Administration 3. Proposal writing for grants 4. Proposal writing for grants -- United States 5. Libraries -- Automation -- United States -- Finance 6. Proposal writing in library science -- United States 7. Libraries -- Information technology -- United States -- Finance

ISBN 1555707637; 9781555707637

LC 2011046318

This book, by Pamela H. MacKellar, offers instruction on grant writing. "[H]ow can you write a successful grant proposal? . . . This comprehensive book on grants for libraries focuses on technology, . . . specific sources and resources for technology grants, . . . and technology project success stories so you get real life examples of how others like you made their libraries stronger through technology grants." (Publisher's note)

Includes bibliographical references and index

Managing Electronic Resources; a LITA Guide. Edited by Ryan O. Weir. ALA TechSource, an imprint of the American Library Assoc. 2012 xii, 179 p.p (pbk.) $65 **025.1**

1. Digital libraries 2. Libraries -- Collection development 3. Electronic reference services (Libraries) 4. Electronic information resources -- Management 5. Libraries -- Special collections -- Electronic information resources

ISBN 155570767X; 9781555707675

LC 2012015102

In this book, Ryan O. Weir presents a "guide to developing and maintaining electronic library collections. Topics include evaluation, selection, and cataloging of electronic resources; strategies for contract negotiation; how to gather and interpret data about electronic resource use; . . . and staffing for electronic collections, as well as projections about how electronic resources will continue to evolve and impact libraries in the future." (Voice of Youth Advocates)

Includes bibliographical references and index

Matthews, Joseph R.

★ **Adding** value to libraries, archives, and museums; harnessing the force that drives your organization's future. Joseph R. Matthews. Libraries Unlimited, an imprint of ABC-CLIO, LLC 2016 xv, 271 p.p illustrations (paperback: acid-free paper) $70 **025.1**

1. Library science 2. Value added 3. Library planning 4. Library administration 5. Libraries and community 6. Libraries -- Technological innovations

ISBN 9781440842894; 9781440842887

LC 2015037584

This library management book, by Joseph R. Matthews, "explains the concept of adding value and shows staff at libraries and other organizations why they need to take steps now to ensure they are adding new value to their communities—whether it be a local town or neighborhood, a faculty and student body, or a school." (Publisher's note)

"This is a user-friendly, accessible guide that clearly outlines how institutions can enter the digital, global arena to reconnect with their clients and reclaim their positions as innovative, meaningful institutes of knowledge, culture, and community." VOYA

Includes bibliographical references (pages 255-256) and indexes

Mosley, Pixey Anne

The **challenge** of library management; leading with emotional engagement. by Wyoma vanDuinkerken and Pixey Anne Mosley. American Library Association 2011 169 p. $52 **025.1**

1. Personnel management 2. Libraries -- Administration 3. Leadership 4. Library administration 5. Organizational change -- Management 6. Library administration -- Problems, exercises, etc

ISBN 0838911021; 9780838911020

LC 2011011349

This book, by Wyoma vanDuinkerken and Pixey Anne Moseley, is designed to show library managers how to "engage library staff in the process and encourage their active participation, navigate successfully through common types of change, such as space planning, departmental reorganization, and changes in work responsibilities, [and] draw on concepts from psychology, communication, empowerment, planning, and evaluation to minimize friction." (Publisher's note)

"The information they provide mostly concerns dealing with employees in order to ensure an effective and successful change initiative in a library setting...While the authors tailor the advice to librarians by using example specific to libraries, the advice could be applied to any organizational setting. All in all, the suggestions contained here are helpful when planning change in a library. Each chapter concludes with a list of key ideas to keep in mind and questions for reflection.—" (VOYA)

Includes bibliographical references (p. 155-163) and index

Our new public, a changing clientele; bewildering issues or new challenges for managing libraries? edited by James R. Kennedy, Lisa Vardaman, and Gerard B. McCabe. Libraries

Unlimited 2008 305p (Libraries Unlimited library management collection) $45 **025.1**
1. Libraries and students 2. Libraries -- Administration
ISBN 978-1-59158-407-0

LC 2007-35907

"Several chapters in this . . . title discuss the milennials—children of the baby boomers—and digital natives and how they have already had an impact on library service. . . . Each chapter offers practical advice based on experiences, and each includes a list of references. Library managers and those aspiring to be managers will find help in providing services for a younger demographic." Booklist

Includes bibliographical references

Smith, G. Stevenson

Cost control for nonprofits in crisis; G. Stevenson Smith. American Library Association 2011 viii, 133 p.p ill. (pbk.: alk. paper) $75.00 **025.1**
1. Finance 2. Financial crises 3. Nonprofit organizations 4. Libraries -- Cost control 5. Libraries -- Cost effectiveness 6. Library finance -- United States 7. Nonprofit organizations -- Cost control 8. Library administration -- Decision making 9. Nonprofit organizations -- Cost effectiveness 10. Nonprofit organizations -- United States -- Finance 11. Nonprofit organizations -- Management -- Decision making
ISBN 083891098X; 9780838910986

LC 2011025285

Author G. Stevenson Smith's book provides financial advice and tips. "Libraries, like many other cultural institutions such as museums, art councils, and theater groups, are looking for answers to the pressing problem of financial stability, and ultimately survival . . . [Smith's book] helps managers and directors tackle the harsh realities before them . . . [He] offers [t]echniques for determining the most cost-effective methods of providing services to clients and patrons of nonprofit cultural institutions." (Publisher's note)

Includes bibliographical references and index

025.17 Administration of collections of special materials

★ **No** shelf required; e-books in libraries. edited by Sue Polanka. American Library Association 2011 182p pa $65 **025.17**
1. Electronic books
ISBN 978-0-83891-054-2

LC 2010-14045

"Following a chapter on e-book history are chapters discussing e-books and students' learning; e-books in school, public, and academic libraries; and e-book acquisitions and management. . . . An essential guide to a topic of high importance." Booklist

Includes bibliographical references

025.2 Acquisitions and collection development

Alabaster, Carol

Developing an outstanding core collection; a guide for libraries. 2nd ed; American Library Association 2010 191p il pa $60 **025.2**
1. Best books 2. Reference books 3. Libraries -- Collection development 4. Public libraries -- Collection development
ISBN 978-0-8389-1040-5

LC 2009-40342

First published 2002

The author suggests "that the general public needs materials beyond current best-sellers and ready-reference works; that those materials should be high-quality, enduring pieces; and that librarians are the best persons to decide what constitutes appropriate core collections for their communities. . . . [She also] addresses the technological changes that drastically affect reading habits and our ability to satisfy the needs of 'the people's university.'. . . [This book is] required reading for all those charged with the task of adult collection development." Booklist

Includes bibliographical references

Baker, Nicholson

Double fold; libraries and the assault on paper. Random House 2001 370p il hardcover o.p. pa $14 **025.2**
1. Paper 2. Libraries -- Special collections 3. Library resources -- Conservation and restoration
ISBN 0-375-72621-7 pa

LC 00-59171

Baker criticizes libraries for discarding books, magazines and newspapers and disputes the arguments for doing so "that libraries are running out of space, and that paper, because of its acid content, is rapidly turning to dust. . . . What the Library of Congress spends in a year on microfilming would, (according to Baker), buy a storage facility 'the size of a Home Depot, which would hold a century of newsprint.' . . . Librarians, he says, 'have lied to us shamelessly about the extent of paper's fragility, and they continue to lie about it.'" N Y Times Book Rev

Includes bibliographical references

Bartlett, Wendy K.

Floating collections; a collection development model for long-term success. Wendy K. Bartlett. Libraries Unlimited, an imprint of ABC-CLIO, LLC 2014 xix, 128 p.p (pbk.: acid-free paper) $55 **025.2**
1. Libraries -- Collection development 2. Public libraries -- Collection development -- United States 3. Cooperative collection development (Libraries) -- United States
ISBN 1598847430; 9781598847437

LC 2013033820

This book, by Wendy K. Bartlett, is "about floating and floating collections. . . . Not only does this book help librarians to decide rationally if, how, and when to float, it also outlines a how-to process for maximum success based on the real-world experience of many systems and identifies ways to maximize the advantages of a floating collection. In addition, the author addresses common collection concerns and outlines workable solutions for problematic issues that can arise." (Publisher's note)

"Chapters include tips on how to approach the practice with staff, how to ready facilities and collections, and, most importantly, how to manage new collections. Also offered are practical evaluations, FAQs, and a list of larger systems in the United States that offer floating collections." SLJ

Includes bibliographical references and index

Brenner, Robin E.

★ Understanding manga and anime. Libraries Unlimited 2007 335p il pa $40 **025.2**
1. Anime 2. Manga -- Study and teaching 3. Libraries -- Collection development 4. Libraries -- Special collections -- Graphic novels
ISBN 978-1-59158-332-5; 1-59158-332-2

LC 2007-9773

The author "provides thorough explanations of manga and anime vocabulary, potential censorship issues because of cultural disparities, and typical Manga conventions. . . . No professional collection could possibly be complete without this all-inclusive and exceptional work." Voice Youth Advocates

Building and managing e-book collections; a how-to-do-it manual for librarians. edited by Richard Kaplan. Neal-Schuman 2012 xv, 197 p.p (pbk.: alk. paper) $75   **025.2**
1. Libraries -- Collection development 2. Libraries and electronic publishing 3. Libraries -- Special Collections -- Electronic books 4. Electronic books 5. Libraries -- Special collections -- Electronic books
ISBN 1555707769; 9781555707767

LC 2012018143

This book on library collections of e-books, edited by Richard B. Kaplan, focuses on "collection development issues, including the selection process and development policies, the use of approval plans, patron-driven acquisition, and practical solutions for creating your e-book collection policies. Chapters on budgeting and licensing cover ownership versus leasing models . . . on digital rights management, and strategies for success in retention, access, and budgeting." (Publisher's note)

"This title features a wealth of useful information . . . the concepts and issues covered are applicable to all libraries. This book provides a solid snapshot of the current best practices in the world of e-book collecting." CHOICE

Includes bibliographical references and index

Charles, John A.

The **mystery** readers' advisory; the librarian's clues to murder and mayhem. [by] John Charles, Joanna Morrison, [and] Candace Clark. American Library Association 2002 227p (ALA readers' advisory series) pa $45   **025.2**
1. Reference books 2. Reference services (Libraries) 3. Mystery fiction -- Bibliography
ISBN 0-8389-0811-X; 978-0-8389-0811-2

LC 01-45083

"Covering everything a librarian would need to know to successfully build and promote a mystery collection, the authors include chapters on weeding and marketing the collection, with a great section on how to do a readers' advisory interview. . . . The text is peppered with authors and titles to know and plenty of plot teasers to fill your reading list. There are thorough discussions of the different subgenres, from police procedural to romantic suspense and other genre blends. . . . The lists of mystery periodicals, reference sources, and Web sites are well-rounded and up-to-date." Voice Youth Advocates

Includes bibliographical references

Disher, Wayne

Crash Course in Collection Development; Wayne Disher. Libraries Unlimited 2014 139 p. (paperback) $45   **025.2**
1. Libraries -- Collection development 2. Collection development -- Handbooks, manuals, etc.
ISBN 1610698134; 9781610698139

LC 2014018813

This book, by Wayne Disher, is a handbook on collection development "covering everything from community analysis through developing collection policies. Librarians will learn how to use reviews to acquire materials as well as to help weed the collection, how to market the collection to patrons, and how to handle censorship issues when collections are challenged." (Publisher's note)

"Disher, a seasoned practitioner and part-time instructor in San Jose State University's School of Library and Information Science, speaks primarily to public library staff with little, if any, experience in collection development. Short on theory but long on practicality, the book provides the reader with basic definitions and step-by-step outlines...

Recommended for all public library collections." Booklist

Evans, G. Edward

Collection management basics; G. Edward Evans and Margaret Zarnosky Saponaro. Libraries Unlimited 2012 xvi, 343 p.p (Library and information science text series) (paperback: acid-free paper) $48   **025.2**
1. Libraries -- Special collections 2. Libraries -- Collection development 3. Collection development (Libraries) 4. Libraries -- Special collections -- Electronic information resources
ISBN 159884864X; 9781598848632; 9781598848649

LC 2012008872

This book, by G. Edward Evans and Margaret Zarnosky Saponaro, "cover[s] all aspects of collection development and management, including subjects such as needs assessment, policies, selection process theory and practice, protection, legal issues, censorship, and intellectual freedom. The book represents a total restructuring of the previous work, and reflects changes brought on by new technology and the up-and-down economy." (Publisher's note)

Includes bibliographical references and index

Foerstel, Herbert N.

★ **Banned** in the U.S.A; a reference guide to book censorship in schools and public libraries. rev and expanded ed; Greenwood Press 2002 xxvii, 296p $54.95   **025.2**
1. Censorship 2. Books -- Censorship 3. Libraries -- Censorship 4. Censorship -- United States 5. Book selection -- United States 6. Textbooks -- Censorship -- United States 7. Public schools -- Censorship -- United States 8. Public libraries -- Censorship -- United States 9. Public libraries -- Book selection -- United States
ISBN 0-313-31166-8

LC 2001-55620

First published 1994

"Librarians and teachers need this book, but patrons who want to better understand the threats to their First Amendment rights should be led to it as well." SLJ

Includes bibliographical references

Gallaway, Beth

★ **Game** on! gaming at the library. Neal-Schuman Publishers 2009 306p il pa $55   **025.2**
1. Video games 2. Video games and children 3. Video games and teenagers 4. Multimedia library services 5. Electronic games -- Collections 6. Libraries -- Special collections
ISBN 1-55570-595-2; 978-1-55570-595-4

LC 2009-14110

"An essential guide for any librarian who plans on embracing the video-game phenomenon, or at the very least, understanding it. . . . [The chapters] are well organized and contain an abundance of practical information. The sections on selection, collection, and circulation of video games include relevant advice on policy, cataloging, marketing, storage, and displays. . . . The annotated list of video games for a core collection is wonderful for selection purposes." SLJ

Includes bibliographical references

Goldsmith, Francisca

The **readers'** advisory guide to graphic novels; Francisca Goldsmith. Second edition ALA Editions, an imprint of the American Library Association 2017 xvi, 215 p.p (paperback) $54   **025.2**
1. Readers' advisory services 2. Graphic novels -- Bibliography 3. Readers' advisory services -- United States 4. Libraries -- Special

collections -- Graphic novels
ISBN 0838915094; 9780838915097

LC 2016042034

Goldsmith "presents a readers' advisory guide to graphic novels. She discusses the key qualities of graphic novels and the characteristics of its readers; basic readers' advisory methods, with reference to the graphic novel format; tips for working with adults and teens experienced or not experienced with the format; working with teens who are becoming self-aware; reading development, interests, and advisory methods for children; materials by interest, topic, and age group; multimedia aspects; and professional tools." (Publisher's note)

"This is a book to spend time with, not flip through, although a strong index and table of contents make it easily consultable for patron interactions as well." VOYA

Includes bibliographical references and index

Graphic novels beyond the basics; insights and issues for libraries. Martha Cornog and Timothy Perper, editors. Libraries Unlimited 2009 xxx, 281p il pa $45   **025.2**
1. Graphic novels -- History and criticism 2. Comic books, strips, etc. -- History and criticism 3. Libraries -- Special collections -- Graphic novels
ISBN 978-1-59158-478-0; 1-59158-478-7

LC 2009-16189

Editors Cornog and Perper have collected essays by experts Robin Brenner, Francisca Goldsmith, Trina Robbins, Michael R. Lavin, Gilles Poitras, Lorena O'English, Michael Niederhausen, Erin Byrne, and Cornog herself, all about graphic novels in libraries. Topics covered range from the appeal of superheroes to manga, the appeal of comics to women and girls, anime, independent comics, dealing with challenges to the material, and more. Appendices provide resource information on African American-interest graphic novels, Latino-Interest graphic novels, LGBT-interest graphic novels, religious-themed graphic novels, a bibliography of books about graphic novels in libraries, and online resources.

"Whether you are serious about the genre, interested in the history, or looking for ammunition, this book should be on your shelf. The wealth of knowledge and research that went into these essays is impressive, and reading this book will put you on the road to becoming an expert." Libr Media Connect

Includes bibliographical references

★ **Intellectual** Freedom Manual; compiled by the Office for Intellectual Freedom of the American Library Association; Trina Magi, editor; Martin Garnar, assistant editor. 9th ed. ALA Editions, An imprint of the American Library Association 2015 434 p. $70   **025.2**
1. Censorship 2. Library science 3. Intellectual freedom 4. Freedom of information -- United States -- Handbooks, manuals, etc. 5. Libraries -- Censorship -- United States -- Handbooks, manuals, etc.
ISBN 0838912923; 9780838912928

LC 2014037437

First published 1974

This newest edition "is more than just an invaluable compendium of guiding principles and policies. It's also an indispensable resource for day-to-day guidance on maintaining free and equal access to information for all people. Fortifying and emboldening professionals and students from across the library spectrum, this manual includes . . . 34 ALA policy statements and documents [and] explanations of legal points." (Publisher's note)

"All libraries should have a copy of this book to use when writing or revising policies; indispensable." Libr J

Includes bibliographical references and index

Johnson, Peggy
Developing and managing electronic collections; the essentials. Peggy Johnson. ALA Editions, an imprint of the American Library Association 2013 ix, 186 p.p illustrations (paper) $65   **025.2**
1. Libraries -- Collection development 2. Libraries and electronic publishing 3. Electronic reference services (Libraries) 4. Libraries -- Special Collections -- Electronic books 5. Electronic information resources -- Management 6. Libraries and electronic publishing -- United States 7. Libraries -- Special collections -- Electronic information resources
ISBN 0838911900; 9780838911907

LC 2013005038

This book, by Peggy Johnson, discusses the "complex issues associated with developing and managing electronic collections [in libraries]." The book discusses "the evolving world of acquisition options, licenses, and contracts [as well as] budgeting and financial considerations, with guidance on how to collaborate across library organizational lines to acquire and manage e-content more efficiently." (Publisher's note)

"This short volume is a must-read for librarians who are just starting to explore how electronic collections will affect their libraries, and it would be a solid choice for most librarians currently working with electronic collections." Booklist

Includes bibliographical references and index

Fundamentals of Collection Development and Management; Peggy Johnson. Amer Library Assn 2014 554 p. $77   **025.2**
1. Libraries -- Administration 2. Libraries -- Collection development 3. Collection development (Libraries) 4. Collection development -- Administration
ISBN 0838911919; 9780838911914

LC 2008019989

This book, by Peggy Johnson, "addresses the art in controlling and updating your library's collection. Each chapter offers complete coverage of one aspect of collection development, including suggestions for further reading and a narrative case study exploring the issue. Johnson also integrates electronic resources throughout the book." (Publisher's note)

Laguardia, Cheryl
Marketing your library's electronic resources; a how-to-do-it manual. Marie R. Kennedy, Cheryl LaGuardia. Neal-Schuman, an imprint of the American Library Association 2013 177 p. (How-to-do-it manuals) $60   **025.2**
1. Library resources 2. Libraries -- Collection development 3. Libraries -- Special Collections -- Electronic books 4. Libraries -- Marketing 5. Electronic information resources -- Marketing 6. Libraries -- United States -- Marketing -- Case studies 7. Libraries -- Special collections -- Electronic information resources
ISBN 1555708897; 9781555708894

LC 2012028267

This book, by Marie R. Kennedy and Cheryl LaGuardia, "guides readers through every step of developing, implementing, and evaluating plans to market [a library's] e-resources in an approachable and user-friendly way. . . . Their book includes four complete programs from both public and academic libraries [and] a step-by-step organization guide, with a variety of feedback and assessment forms which can be used as models." (Publisher's note)

"Every library needs to know how to educate its patrons about these resources, and this book provides a well-organized, uncomplicated plan for doing so." VOYA

Includes bibliographical references and index

Lewis, Linda K.

The **complete** guide to acquisitions management; Frances C. Wilkinson, Linda K. Lewis, and Rebecca L. Lubas. Libraries Unlimited, An Imprint of ABC-CLIO, LLC 2015 xiv, 200 p.p (pbk: alk. paper) $60 **025.2**

1. Library education 2. Libraries -- Acquisitions 3. Acquisitions (Libraries) -- United States

ISBN 1610697138; 9781610697132

LC 2015007852

This book, by Frances C. Wilkinson, Linda K. Lewis, and Rebecca L. Lubas, part of the publisher's "Library and Information Science Text" series, "provides both library students and practitioners with a thorough understanding of procedural and philosophical approaches in acquisitions management. [It] incorporates thoroughly updated information that reflects today's fast-changing world of acquisitions management and addresses the changing landscape of publishing overall." (Publisher's note)

"This is an excellent introductory text for novice acquisitions librarians and students as well as a helpful reference for the more experienced." LJ

Includes bibliographical references and index

Pinnell-Stephens, June

★ **Protecting** intellectual freedom in your public library; scenarios from the front lines. June Pinnell-Stephens for the Office for Intellectual Freedom. American Library Association 2012 xi, 148 p.p (pbk.: alk. paper) $50.00 **025.2**

1. Censorship 2. Library science 3. Public libraries 4. Intellectual freedom 5. Intellectual freedom -- United States 6. Public libraries -- Censorship -- United States 7. Public libraries -- Censorship -- United States -- Case studies

ISBN 0838935834; 9780838935835

LC 2011029691

This book, by June Pinnell-Stephens, offers a guide to intellectual freedom concerns and rights as relating to public library administration. "When confronted with challenges like censorship and policy disputes, public librarians and paraprofessionals need reliable how-to guidance. . . . [T]his book provides . . . analysis of how IF plays out in the world of public libraries . . . and advice on how to effectively handle intellectual freedom challenges." (Publisher's note)

Includes bibliographical references and index.

Rethinking collection development and management; Becky Albitz, Christine Avery, and Diane Zabel, editors. Libraries Unlimited 2014 xiv, 394 p.p (pbk.: acid-free paper) $60 **025.2**

1. Libraries -- Acquisitions 2. Libraries -- Collection development 3. Acquisitions (Libraries) 4. Collection management (Libraries) 5. Collection development (Libraries) 6. Library materials -- Conservation and restoration

ISBN 1610693051; 9781610693059

LC 2013038447

"This collection of thought-provoking essays . . . covers theory, research, and best practices in collection development, examining how it has evolved, identifying how some librarians are creatively responding to these changes, and predicting what is coming next." (Publisher's note)

Includes bibliographical references and index

Serchay, David S.

The **librarian's** guide to graphic novels for adults. Neal-Schuman Publishers 2010 320p il $65 **025.2**

1. Graphic novels -- Collections 2. Graphic novels -- Administration 3. Libraries -- Special collections -- Graphic novels

ISBN 978-1-55570-662-3

LC 2009-41011

"This book will inspire librarians—and others—with little knowledge of graphic novels (GNs) for adults to pick one up and see what all the buzz is about. Serchay puts forth a complete guide that will enable any librarian, whether a GN novice or seasoned fan, to establish a brand-new collection, fully understanding what GNs are, where to purchase them, how to catalog them, and how to review, promote, and maintain the new collection." Libr J

Includes bibliographical references

Singer, Carol A.

Fundamentals of Managing Reference Collections; Carol A. Singer. American Library Association 2012 xii, 167 p.p (pbk.) $60 **025.2**

1. Reference books 2. Libraries -- Special collections 3. Electronic reference services (Libraries) 4. Reference books -- United States 5. Electronic reference sources -- United States 6. Libraries -- Special collections -- Reference sources 7. Collection management (Libraries) -- United States -- Case studies

ISBN 0838911536; 9780838911532

LC 2011044446

Author Carol A. "Singer's book offers information and insight on best practices for reference collection management, no matter the size, and shows why managing without a plan is a recipe for clutter and confusion." Singer discusses "the importance of collection development policies, and how to effectively involve others in the decision-making process," in addition to "new insights into selecting reference materials" and "strategies for collection maintenance." (Publisher's note)

Includes bibliographical references and index

Vnuk, Rebecca

The **weeding** handbook; a shelf-by-shelf guide. Rebecca Vnuk. ALA Editions, an imprint of the American Library Association 2015 196 p. (pbk.: alk. paper) $45 **025.2**

1. Libraries -- Collection development 2. Public libraries -- Collection development -- United States 3. Discarding of books, periodicals, etc. -- Handbooks, manuals, etc 4. Collection development (Libraries) -- United States -- Policy statements

ISBN 9780838913277

LC 2015008707

This guidebook, by Rebecca Vnuk, focuses on "weeding" libraries. "A library is an ever-changing organism; when done the right way, weeding helps a library thrive by focusing its resources on those parts of the collection that are the most useful to its users. Her handbook takes the guesswork out of this delicate but necessary process, giving public and school library staff the knowledge and the confidence to effectively weed any collection, of any size." (Publisher's note)

"Vnuk's clear writing and motivating tone will give confidence to reluctant weeders, resulting in a worthy purchase for all public libraries." LJ

Includes bibliographical references and index

White, Andrew C.

★ **E-metrics** for library and information professionals; how to use data for managing and evaluating electronic resource collections. Neal-Schuman Publishers 2006 249p il pa $75 **025.2**

1. Digital libraries

ISBN 1-55570-514-6

LC 2004-54678

"Designed to introduce readers to e-metrics ('the measurements of the use and activity of networked information'), this book is made up of 10 chapters that are divided among three major sections. Part 1 supplies a definition of e-metrics, explores their use in libraries, and discusses vendor-supplied electronic data reports. Part 2 explains why libraries need e-metrics, focusing on how they can be used for public relations, collection management, and library administration. Part 3 offers ways that libraries can build local e-metrics. Chapters cover the capturing and processing of statistics, infrastructure and technical requirements, and staffing needs. With its coherent structure, well-articulated language, and illustrative material (tables, figures, and examples), this book has much to recommend it." Booklist

Includes bibliographical references

025.3 Bibliographic analysis and control

The **card** catalog; books, cards, and literary treasures. the Library of Congress; foreword by Carla Hayden. Chronicle Books 2017 224 p. illustrations (chiefly color) (hardcover) $35   **025.3**
  1. Cataloging 2. Library catalogs 3. Card catalogs -- United States 4. Cataloging -- History 5. Library catalogs -- History 6. Library of Congress -- History 7. Classification -- Books -- History 8. Card catalogs -- United States -- History 9. Catalog cards -- United States -- History 10. Library of Congress -- Catalogs -- History
ISBN 9781452158587; 9781452145402

LC 2016017476

In this book, with foreword by Carla Hayden, "the Library of Congress brings booklovers an enriching tribute to the power of the written word. . . . Featuring more than 200 full-color images of original catalog cards, . . . and photographs from the library's magnificent archives, this collection is a visual celebration of the rarely seen treasures in one of the world's most famous libraries and the brilliant catalog system that has kept it organized for hundreds of years." (Publisher's note)

"An irresistible treasury for book and library lovers." Booklist

Includes bibliographical references and index.

Maxwell, Robert L.

FRBR; a guide for the perplexed. American Library Association 2008 151p il pa $50   **025.3**
  1. FRBR (Conceptual model)
ISBN 978-0-8389-0950-8; 0-8389-0950-7

LC 2007-27845

This book explains "Functional Requirements for Bibliographic Records (FRBR), an evolving conceptual model developed to assist users in navigating library catalogs to find the information they want and need. Maxwell . . . explains and illustrates the FRBR model, details why the document and model are important for the future of information organization, and explains what a catalog based on FRBR principles might look like. He also briefly illustrates the use of Functional Requirements for Authority Data (FRAD)." Booklist

Includes bibliographic references

Maxwell's handbook for RDA, resource description & access; explaining and illustrating RDA: resource description and access using MARC21. Robert L. Maxwell. ALA Editions, an imprint of the American Library Association 2013 x, 900 p.p (pbk.: alk. paper) $98   **025.3**
  1. Cataloging 2. Resource description and access -- Handbooks, manuals, etc. 3. Resource description & access -- Handbooks, manuals, etc 4. Descriptive cataloging -- Standards -- Handbooks,

manuals, etc
ISBN 0838911722; 9780838911723

LC 2013035124

In this book, "cataloging expert Robert Maxwell brings his trademark practical commentary to bear on the new, unified cataloging standard. Designed to interpret and explain RDA: Resource Description and Access, this handbook illustrates and applies the new cataloging rules in the MARC21 environment for every type of information format." (Publisher's note)

"Through full and numerous cataloging examples, the author covers FRBR (functional requirements for bibliographic records) basics and how to record the attributes for entities such as manifestations, items, persons, corporate bodies, places, expressions, and works. The examples are not limited to just the print format but also include electronic materials, music, series, and maps." LJ

Includes bibliographical references and index

Mitchell, Anne M.

★ **Cataloging** and organizing digital resources; a how-to-do-it manual for librarians. Neal-Schuman Publishers 2005 219p il (How-to-do-it manuals for librarians) pa $75   **025.3**
  1. Cataloging 2. Reference books 3. Digital libraries 4. Information systems
ISBN 1-55570-521-9

LC 2005-903

This "volume addresses the ways a library can manage electronic collections. The goal is to provide an overview of management concerns and issues regarding bibliographic control in an online environment and to suggest tools that are available. The 10 chapters address such topics as development of digital libraries, organization of work flow, alternatives to cataloging, cataloging rules and records, online monographs and serials, integration of resources, and trends. Each chapter offers an introduction; guidelines, instructions, or strategies; and a summary and references. The writing is clear, with plentiful examples that include figures and titles." Booklist

025.4 Subject analysis and control

★ **Sears** List of Subject Headings; Barbara A. Bristow, editor; Christi Showman Farrar, associate editor. 21st edition Grey House Publishing/H.W. Wilson 2014 946 pp. (hardcover) $165.00   **025.4**
  1. Cataloging 2. Library science 3. Subject headings
ISBN 9781619251908

LC 2013498263

This book, edited by Barbara A. Bristow and Christi Showman Farrar, presents the frameworks for the Sears List of Subject Headings cataloging system. "This resource lists subject headings used by small and medium-sized libraries, with patterns, examples, and notes on usage. The subject headings are listed alphabetically and aligned with the Dewey Decimal Classification system and include a list of canceled and replacement headings, as well as a discussion of the theoretical foundations of the list and the general principles of subject cataloging." (Book News)

025.5 Services for users

Berard, G. Lynn

Science and technology resources; a guide for information professionals and researchers. James E. Bobick and G.

Lynn Berard. Libraries Unlimited 2011 xiii, 285 p.p illustrations (Library and information science text series) (paperback) $60   **025.5**

1. Technology 2. Science -- Bibliography 3. Science -- Bibliography -- Methodology 4. Technology -- Bibliography -- Methodology 5. Technical literature -- Bibliography -- Methodology 6. Scientific literature -- Bibliography -- Methodology 7. Science and technology libraries -- Reference services

ISBN 159158793X; 1591587948; 1591588014; 9781591587934; 9781591587941; 9781591588016

LC 2011000461

This science and technology resource, by James E. Bobick and G. Lynn Berard, "begins with an overview of the nature of sci-tech literature, the information-seeking behavior of scientists and engineers, and an examination of the research cycle. . . . This practical guide will be invaluable to librarians, information specialists, engineering and science professionals, and students interested in acquiring a practical knowledge of science and technology resources." (Publisher's note)

"Database descriptions contain annotations, but the listings for websites, dictionaries, handbooks, and other materials do not. A timely resource to add to reference collections and to the library science curriculum." Booklist

Includes bibliographical references and index

Buker, Derek M.

The **science**-fiction and fantasy readers' advisory; the librarian's guide to cyborgs, aliens, and sorcerers. American Lib. Assn. 2002 230p (ALA readers' advisory series) pa $50 **025.5**

1. Reference books 2. Reference services (Libraries) 3. Fantasy fiction -- Bibliography 4. Science fiction -- Bibliography

ISBN 0-8389-0831-4; 978-0-8389-0831-0

LC 2002-1494

A "well-organized, humorous guide to providing readers' advisory to customers wanting science fiction or fantasy recommendations. . . . The book is divided into two parts, one dealing with science fiction and one with fantasy, and further divides these genres into their many subgenres, providing short annotated lists of recommended titles as well as longer lists without annotations. . . . What this guide does best is demonstrate the wide scope of science fiction and fantasy literature; it gives many suggestions and recommendations across this broad range." SLJ

Includes bibliographical references

Cords, Sarah Statz

The **real** story; a guide to nonfiction reading interests. edited by Robert Burgin. Libraries Unlimited 2006 xxxii, 460p (Genreflecting advisory series) $55   **025.5**

1. Books and reading 2. Reference services (Libraries)

ISBN 1-59158-283-0

LC 2006-3712

The author "describes more than 555 popular nonfiction titles published over the last 15 years, along with classic titles such as Truman Capote's In Cold Blood. . . . Cords has identified 11 broad categories based on subjects, genres, and appeal factors. Among the categories are 'Biography,' 'Travel,' 'True Adventure,' and 'True Crime.' . . . A must-read for any librarian who recommends popular reading titles, it belongs at the reference and readers'-advisory desks of most libraries." Booklist

Includes bibliographical references

Evans, G. Edward

Introduction to library public services; [by] G. Edward Evans and Thomas L. Carter. 7th ed; Libraries Unlimited 2009 401p il (Library and information science text series) $65; pa $50   **025.5**

1. Library services 2. Library circulation 3. Reference services (Libraries)

ISBN 978-1-59158-596-1; 978-1-59158-595-4 pa

LC 2008-37445

First published 1972 under the authorship of Marty Bloomberg with title: Introduction to public services for library technicians

"Each chapter covers the role, purpose, and philosophy related to major functional areas of public service, including points to ponder, forms and flowcharts, review questions and suggested readings." Publisher's note

Ford, Charlotte

Crash course in reference. Libraries Unlimited 2008 143p il (Crash course)   **025.5**

1. Reference books 2. Reference services (Libraries) 3. Reference services -- Handbooks, manuals, etc.

ISBN 978-1-59158-463-6

LC 2007-52948

"A basic explanation of reference services for those with little formal LIS training working in small rural libraries or others who have been working in other areas and wish to brush up on their skills, this author provides an introduction to reference services including search strategies." Publisher's note

Includes bibliographical references

Hernon, Peter

Assessing service quality; satisfying the expectations of library customers. [by] Peter Hernon + Ellen Altman. 2nd ed; American Library Association 2010 206p il pa $65   **025.5**

1. Library services 2. Libraries -- Public relations

ISBN 978-0-8389-1021-4; 0-8389-1021-1

LC 2009-40332

First published 1998

The authors "concentrate on how to assess service quality and customer satisfaction. Here they suggest . . . ways to think about library services, clarify the distinction between service quality and customer satisfaction, present strategies for developing a customer service plan, identify procedures to measure service quality and satisfaction, and . . . challenge conventional thinking about these powerful principles. . . . Kudos to these authors for providing an essential resource for librarians who understand that folks who walk into their libraries are not patrons but customers." Libr J

Includes bibliographical references

Jerrard, Jane

★ **Crisis** in employment; a librarian's guide to helping job seekers. foreword by Denise Davis. American Library Association 2009 66p il pa $40   **025.5**

1. Unemployment 2. Libraries and community 3. Reference services (Libraries) 4. Vocational guidance -- Information services

ISBN 978-0-8389-1013-9

LC 2009-16684

This "special report provides suggestions for providing low-cost assistance to job-seeking unemployed library users. With examples from various public libraries, the report offers advice for planning, how to get the most out of resources at hand, dealing with the need for additional computers, suggestions for community partnerships, and how to best assist users who need to become computer literate for a successful job search." Libr J

Includes bibliographical references

Kern, M. Kathleen

★ **Virtual** reference best practices; tailoring services to your library. American Library Association 2009 148p il pa $50   **025.5**
1. Reference services (Libraries)
ISBN 978-0-8389-0975-1

LC 2008-15379

The author "offers advice and assistance for libraries considering VR. . . . Kern's guidebook includes useful forms and exercises for every aspect of the VR process from a market assessment of the library's community served to an evaluation of the service. . . . Even those [libraries] which already offer virtual reference will find assistance and suggestions to improve their services." Voice Youth Advocates

Includes bibliographical references

Kroski, Ellyssa

The **makerspace** librarian's sourcebook; edited by Ellyssa Kroski. ALA Editions, an imprint of the American Library Association 2017 400 p. (pbk.: alk. paper) $85   **025.5**
1. Libraries 2. Information science 3. Information services 4. Maker movement 5. Makerspaces in libraries 6. Makerspaces -- Equipment and supplies
ISBN 9780838915042

LC 2016037887

This hands-on sourcebook, edited by Ellyssa Kroski, "includes everything libraries need to know about the major topics, tools, and technologies relevant to makerspaces today. . . . This collection leads librarians through how to start their own makerspace from the ground up, . . . discusses the transformative teaching and learning opportunities that makerspaces offer, . . . [and] delves into 11 of the most essential technologies and tools most commonly found in makerspaces." (Publisher's note)

"For librarians considering a Maker space or for those who already have one, this helpful selection covers all aspects of planning and implementation." Library Journal

Includes bibliographical references and index

Moyer, Jessica E.

The **readers'** advisory handbook; edited by Jessica E. Moyer and Kaite Mediatore Stover. American Library Association 2010 220p (ALA readers' advisory series) pa $55 **025.5**
1. Best books 2. Reference services (Libraries)
ISBN 978-0-8389-1042-9

LC 2009-45793

"This great generalist title offers guidelines not only on readers' advisory (RA) but on related matters of collection development and marketing books to different reading audiences. . . . [The authors] gather information and instruction from 15 contributing public and school librarians on self-education, managing and improving groups of selectors, making quick but thorough evaluations of different types of materials, writing reviews, and working with book groups as well as other kinds of programming." Libr J

Includes bibliographical references

Research-based readers' advisory; with contributions by Amanda Blau and others. American Library Association 2008 278p (ALA readers' advisory series) pa $50   **025.5**
1. Reference services (Libraries)
ISBN 978-0-8389-0959-1; 0-8389-0959-0

LC 2007-49421

"Following a survey of the current state of RA, 11 chapters cover topics such as 'Nonfiction Readers and Nonfiction Advisory,' 'Romance and Genre Readers,' and 'Tools for Readers' Advisory.' Each chapter begins with a 'Research View,' in which Moyer summarizes the latest literature. Following the 'Research View' is a 'Librarian's View,' in which an impressive array of contributors talk about practical applications." Booklist

Includes bibliographical references

Mulac, Carolyn M.

Fundamentals of reference; Carolyn M. Mulac. American Library Association 2012 xii., 131 p.p (pbk.: alk. paper) $52   **025.5**
1. Reference services (Libraries) 2. Reference books -- Bibliography 3. Electronic reference services (Libraries) 4. Reference sources -- Bibliography 5. Internet in library reference services 6. Reference services (Libraries) -- United States
ISBN 0838910874; 9780838910870

LC 2012010058

Author Carolyn M. Mulac's book offers an "introduction to reference sources and services for a variety of readers, from library staff members who are asked to work in the reference department to managers and others who wish to familiarize themselves with this important area of librarianship." Mulac "presents an overview of the basic tools and techniques of reference work, including" reference services and reference sources. (Publisher's note)

Includes bibliographical references and index

Nilsen, Kirsti

Conducting the reference interview; a how-to-do-it manual for librarians. [by] Catherine Sheldrick Ross, Kirsti Nilsen, and Marie L. Radford. 2nd ed; Neal-Schuman Publishers Inc. 2009 290p il (How-to-do-it manuals for librarians) pa $75   **025.5**
1. Reference services (Libraries) 2. Reference interview 3. Reference services -- Automation 4. Electronic reference services (Libraries)
ISBN 978-1-55570-655-5

LC 2009-17660

First published 2002

This book aims to teach librarians how "to understand the needs of public, academic and special library users across any virtual setting—email, text messaging, social networking websites—as well as in traditional and face-to-face models of communication." Publisher's note

Includes bibliographical references

Orr, Cynthia

★ **Crash** course in readers' advisory; Cynthia Orr. Libraries Unlimited 2015 125 p. (paperback) $45   **025.5**
1. Library services 2. Readers' advisory services
ISBN 1610698258; 9781610698252

LC 2014027064

This book on library services, by Cynthia Orr, "is built around understanding books, reading, and readers and will quickly show you how to identify reading preferences and advise patrons effectively. You'll learn about multiple RA approaches, such as genre, appeal features, and reading interests and about essential tools that can help with RA. Plus, you'll discover tips to help you keep up with this ever-changing field." (Publisher's note)

Includes bibliographical references and index

Reference reborn; breathing new life into public services librarianship. Diane Zabel, editor; preface by Linda C.

Smith. Libraries Unlimited 2010 xx, 401 p.p illustrations $65　　　　**025.5**
1. Library science 2. Library education 3. Reference services (Libraries) 4. Internet in library reference services 5. Electronic reference services (Libraries) 6. Public services (Libraries) -- United States 7. Reference services (Libraries) -- United States
ISBN 1591588286; 9781591588283

LC 2010041105

This book, edited by Diane Zabel, "is a collection of over two dozen essays on developments and trends in reference and public services librarianship, highlighting some of the best thinking on reference services, outreach initiatives, the migration from print to e-reference collections, staffing 21st century libraries, library school curriculum, and more." (Publisher's note)

"Essential for public service librarians—academic and public, both veterans and new to the profession—and for students or potential students in information science. Highly recommended." LJ

Includes bibliographical references and index

Saricks, Joyce G.

★ The **readers'** advisory guide to genre fiction; 2nd ed; American Library Association 2009 352p (ALA readers' advisory series) pa $65　　　　**025.5**
1. Reference services (Libraries) 2. Fiction -- Bibliography
ISBN 978-0-8389-0989-8

LC 2008-51029

First published 2001

"Each section includes three or four specific genres . . . and features a definition and introduction to the genre, the characteristics of the genre's appeal, suggested authors and titles, and other practical information. Well-crafted back matter add to the ease of navigation. This very readable text employs a playful tone that reflects Saricks's love of her work and will inspire readers to use RA techniques in a variety of ways. [This is] a useful tool for both new library employees and established practitioners." Voice Youth Advocates

Includes bibliographical references

★ **Readers'** advisory service in the public library; 3rd ed; American Library Association 2005 211p il pa $38　　**025.5**
1. Public libraries 2. Reference services (Libraries)
ISBN 0-8389-0897-7

LC 2004-29271

First published 1989

In this guide to readers' advisory, "online tools for identifying and evaluating titles to suggest to today's new adult leisure readers are described, in addition to . . . tried-and-true print sources. The value of personal reading suggestions from staff and patrons is addressed. Topics for discussion and techniques for marketing good reading material are offered. . . . A priority for all libraries involved in readers' advisory." Booklist

Includes bibliographical references

Spratford, Becky Siegel

The **horror** readers' advisory; the librarian's guide to vampires, killer tomatoes, and haunted houses. [by] Becky Siegel Spratford [and] Tammy Hennigh Clausen. American Library Association 2004 161p il (ALA readers' advisory series) pa $36　　　　**025.5**
1. Reference services (Libraries) 2. Horror fiction -- History and criticism
ISBN 0-8389-0871-3

LC 2003-25530

This is a "guide to horror fiction, explaining its appeal and advising on how librarians unfamiliar with the genre can broaden their own knowledge and build a viable collection. The text briefly outlines the characteristics of the main categories, or subgenres, including the usual monsters and occult creatures; extreme suspense of all types; hauntings and possession; and a section on classic works of horror, along with tips for interviewing readers of each subgenre. . . . [This] small, helpful book will be a boon to readers' advisors needing fresh meat for horror fans." Libr J

Includes bibliographical references

Virtual reference service; from competencies to assessment. edited by R. David Lankes . . . [et al.] Neal-Schuman Publishers 2008 206p il (Virtual reference desk series) $75　　　　**025.5**
1. Reference services (Libraries)
ISBN 978-1-55570-528-2

LC 2007-24104

"Featuring essays from the 2005 7th Annual Virtual Reference Desk Conference, this book focuses on the evolving aspects of virtual reference theory, research, and practice. . . . The topics explored include the implementation and expansion of virtual reference programs, and the training and assessment that is necessary to ensure the success of these services. . . . This is a valuable resource for library practitioners involved with reference services." Am Ref Books Annu, 2008

Includes bibliographical references

Wichman, Emily T.

Librarian's guide to passive programming; easy and affordable activities for all ages. Emily T. Wichman. Libraries Unlimited Inc. 2012 xvii, 152 p.p ill. (pbk.: acid-free paper) $40　　　　**025.5**
1. Librarians 2. Library finance 3. Library services 4. Libraries -- Activity programs -- United States
ISBN 159884895X; 9781598848953; 9781598848960

LC 2011045419

In her book, author Emily T. Wichman discusses library budget cuts, and how "librarians are seeking new ways to stretch their programming dollars and maximize staff resources. Passive programming allows libraries to inexpensively showcase their services while inviting visitors of all ages to enjoy the value that libraries bring to the community." (Publisher's note)

Includes bibliographical references and index.

Wyatt, Neal

The **readers'** advisory guide to nonfiction. American Library Association 2007 318p (ALA reader's advisory series) pa $48　　　　**025.5**
1. Public libraries 2. Reference services (Libraries)
ISBN 978-0-8389-0936-2; 0-8389-0936-1

LC 2006-102318

Wyatt "focuses on eight popular categories: history, true crime, true adventure, science, memoir, food/cooking, travel, and sports. Within each, she explains the scope, popularity, style, major authors and works, and the subject's position in readers' advisory interviews. Wyatt addresses who is reading nonfiction and why, while providing RAs with the tools and language to incorporate nonfiction into discussions that point readers to what to read next. . . . [This] guide includes nonfiction bibliography, key authors, benchmark books with annotations, and core collections." Publisher's note

Includes bibliographical references

025.52 Reference and information services

Goldsmith, Francisca

Crash course in contemporary reference; Francisca Goldsmith. Libraries Unlimited 2017 183 p. (Crash course) (acid-free paper) $45 **025.52**
    1. Reference services (Libraries) 2. Reference services (Libraries) -- United States
    ISBN 144084481X; 9781440844812

LC 2016030068
This book, by Francisca Goldsmith, is a "fresh, detailed, and thoughtful examination of reference services in the context of evolving community information needs and habits, a changing technological landscape, and new search strategies." (Publisher's note)
    Includes bibliographical references and index

025.7 Physical preparation for storage and use

Lavender, Kenneth

★ **Book** repair; a how-to-do-it manual. Kenneth Lavender. 2nd ed; Neal-Schuman Publishers Inc. 2011 xiv, 265 p.p il (How-to-do-it manuals for libraries) (alk. paper) $80 **025.7**
    1. Librarians 2. Paperback books 3. Bookbinding -- Repairing -- Handbooks, manuals, etc 4. Books -- Conservation and restoration -- Handbooks, manuals, etc
    ISBN 1555707475; 1555707483; 9781555707477; 9781555707484

LC 2011022636
First published 1992
Author Kenneth Lavender provides a "step-by-step manual . . . on basic book repair techniques and sound preservation practices . . . [which] offers illustrated sections on cleaning, mending, hinge and spine repair, strengthening paperbacks, and more. . . . A full discussion of when and how to make repairs is provided, as is a discussion of alternative conservation practices that will enable each librarian to develop procedures appropriate to his or her library." (Publisher's note)
"Covering both basic book repair techniques and . . . conservation practices, this . . . manual offers illustrated sections on cleaning, mending, hinge and spine repair, strengthening paperbacks, [etc.]. . . . Chapters cover: wet and water-damaged books; mold and mildew; repair of book linings and pamphlet bindings; using acid-free materials to repair damaged books; lining paper objects; affordable repair tools and supplies. . . . A full discussion of when and how to make repairs, and alternative conservation practices that enable each librarian to develop procedures appropriate to his or her library are also provided." Publisher's note
    Includes bibliographical references and index.

Schechter, Abraham A.

Basic book repair methods; illustrated by the author. Libraries Unlimited 1999 102p il pa $37 **025.7**
    1. Books -- Conservation and restoration
    ISBN 1-56308-700-6

LC 98-50950
Photographs accompany step-by-step instructions for common preservation techniques, from the cleaning of pages and their readhesion, to case reattachment and rebacking.
    Includes bibliographical references

025.8 Maintenance and preservation of collections

Halsted, Deborah D.

★ **Disaster** planning; a how-to-do-it manual for librarians with planning templates on CD-ROM. Neal-Schuman Publishers 2005 xx, 247p il (How-to-do-it manuals for librarians) pa $85 **025.8**
    1. Disaster relief 2. Accidents -- Prevention 3. Library resources -- Conservation and restoration
    ISBN 1-55570-486-7

LC 2003-65152
"Step-by-step instructions discuss creating a working disaster team, establishing a communications strategy, identifying relief and recovery agencies, developing response plans, and examining issues of cutting-edge library security. . . . This valuable resource is an important addition to most professional collections." Booklist
    Includes bibliographical references

Hammer, Joshua

★ The **bad**-ass librarians of Timbuktu; and their race to save the world's most precious manuscripts. Joshua Hammer. Simon & Schuster 2016 288 p. (hardcover) $26 **025.8**
    1. Librarians 2. Islamic literature 3. Cultural property -- Protection 4. Librarians -- Mali -- Tombouctou 5. Cultural property -- Protection -- Mali 6. Manuscripts, Arabic -- Mali -- Tombouctou 7. Centre de documentation et de recherches 'Ahmed Baba.' 8. Islamic learning and scholarship -- Mali -- Tombouctou 9. Libraries -- Destruction and pillage -- Mali -- Tombouctou 10. Mali -- History -- Tuareg Rebellion, 2012- -- Destruction and pillage
    ISBN 9781476777405; 9781476777412; 9781476777436

LC 2015030396
In this book, by Joshua Hammer, "To save precious centuries-old Arabic texts from Al Qaeda, a band of librarians in Timbuktu pulls off a brazen heist. . . . In the 1980s, a young adventurer and collector for a government library, Abdel Kader Haidara, . . . track[ed] down and salvag[ed] tens of thousands of ancient Islamic and secular manuscripts. . . . [This book] tells the incredible story of how Haidara . . . later became one of the world's greatest and most brazen smugglers." (Publisher's note)
"Hammer's clearly written and engaging chronicle of the achievements of Timbuktu, the risks presented to this area, and the portraits of several brave and dedicated individuals brings to light an important and unfamiliar story." LJ
    Includes bibliographical references and index.

Kahn, Miriam B.

Disaster response and planning for libraries; Miriam B. Kahn. 2nd ed; American Library Association 2012 158 p. bibl il (paperback) $60.00 **025.8**
    1. Libraries -- Safety measures 2. Disaster response and recovery 3. Library resources -- Conservation and restoration 4. Libraries -- Safety measures -- Planning 5. Library materials -- Conservation and restoration 6. Library materials -- Conservation and restoration -- Planning
    ISBN 083891151X; 9780838911518

LC 2011043703
This book by Miriam B. Kahn presents a "step-by-step, how-to guide for preparing and responding to all types of library disasters." It includes "guidance for creating protocols and response plans tailored to your own institution . . . pointers for handling . . . library materials when damaged . . . information on preparing for technology recovery . . . [and] reproducible checklists and forms." (Publisher's note)

Includes bibliographical references (pages 143-154) and index

026 Specific kinds of institutions

Baker, Jennifer S., 1953-

The **readers'** advisory guide to historical fiction; Jennifer S. Baker. ALA Editions, an imprint of the American Library Association 2015 176 p. (print: alk. paper) $48   **026**
1. Best books 2. Historical fiction 3. Historical fiction -- Bibliography 4. Fiction in libraries -- United States 5. Readers' advisory services -- United States 6. Libraries -- United States -- Special collections -- Historical fiction
ISBN 083891165X; 9780838911655

LC 2014018024

Written by Jennifer S. Baker, "this guide provides an overview of historical fiction's roots, highlighting foundational classics, as well as covering the latest and most popular authors and titles; explores the genre in terms of its scope, style, and appeal; [and] includes lists of recommendations, with a compendium of print and web-based resources." (Publisher's note)

"Although not as hefty as Sarah L. Johnson's Historical Fiction II, this volume strikes the perfect balance of thoroughness and accessibility. RA enthusiasts will be thrilled to add this book to their arsenal." LJ

Includes bibliographical references and indexes

★ **Directory** of special libraries and information centers; a guide to more than 35,000 special libraries, research libraries, information centers, archives, and data centers maintained by government agencies . . . Matthew Miskelly, content project editor. Thompson/Gale 3v   **026**
1. Reference books 2. Special libraries -- Directories

Annual. First published 1963. Volume one is kept up to date by mid-year supplementary volume (v3)

"Volume 1, in three parts, provides . . . contact and descriptive information on more than 35,800 subject-specific resource collections maintained by various government agencies, businesses, publishers, educational and nonprofit organizations, and associations around the world. . . . Volume 2, Geographic and Personnel Indexes, provides access to profiled libraries by geographic region, as well as by the professional staff that are cited in each listing." Publisher's note

027 General libraries, archives, information centers

Gunnels, Claire B.

Joint libraries; models that work. Claire B. Gunnels, Susan E. Green, and Patricia M. Butler. American Library Association 2012 220 p. $60.00   **027**
1. Public libraries 2. Academic libraries 3. Library cooperation 4. Joint-use libraries -- United States
ISBN 0838911382; 9780838911389

LC 2011044057

This book provides a "look at joint library models, including the determining factors that lead to increased success and issues that may lead to project failures. This title includes a brief discussion of the history behind school library joint partnerships; however, the authors primarily focus on joint academic/public libraries, giving concrete examples from their own experiences as well as information from examples of multi-use libraries across the country." (Voice of Youth Advocates)

Includes bibliographical references and index.

Johnson, Alex

Improbable libraries; a visual journey to the world's most unusual libraries. Alex Johnson. University of Chicago Press 2015 240 p. color illustrations (cloth: alk. paper) $27.50 **027**
1. Library architecture 2. Libraries -- Pictorial works 3. Curiosities and wonders 4. Libraries -- Miscellanea 5. Library architecture -- Miscellanea 6. Library architecture -- Pictorial works
ISBN 022626369X; 9780226263694

LC 2014035714

This book, by Alex Johnson, "showcases a wide range of unforgettable, never-before-seen images and interviews with librarians who are overcoming geographic, economic, and political difficulties to bring the written word to an eager audience. Alex Johnson charts the changing face of library architecture, as temporary pop-ups rub shoulders with monumental brick-and-mortar structures, and many libraries expand their mission to function as true community centers." (Publisher's note)

"This delightful book will give bibliophiles everywhere ideas for how to exhibit their collection as well as add some destinations to their bucket list. A great option for the children's room, too." LJ

Includes bibliographical references

Ryback, Timothy W.

Hitler's private library; the books that shaped his life. Alfred A. Knopf 2008 xx, 278p il map $25.95   **027**
1. Heads of state 2. Nazi leaders 3. Germany -- History -- 1933-1945
ISBN 978-1-4000-4204-3; 1-4000-4204-6

LC 2008-22010

"Thanks to [Ryback's] imaginative research—and his willingness to investigate a very creepy subject—we come closer to one of the most elusive men ever to shape world history." New Repub

Includes bibliographical references

027.009 History and biography

Kells, Stuart

The **library**; a catalogue of wonders. Stuart Kells. Counterpoint 2018 224 p. $26   **027.009**
1. Libraries 2. Library science
ISBN 1640090207; 9781640090200

"In this free-roaming history of libraries, [Stuart] Kells, well read, well traveled, ebullient, and erudite, relishes tales of innovation, obsession, and criminality . . . Kells' revelatory romp through the centuries cues us to the fact that, as has so often been the case, libraries need our passionate attention and support, our advocacy, gratitude, and . . . love." (Booklist)

"Kells' revelatory romp through the centuries cues us to the fact that, as has so often been the case, libraries need our passionate attention and support, our advocacy, gratitude, and (given Kells' tales of book-kissing, including Coleridge pressing his lips to his copy of Spinoza) love." Booklist

027.4 Public libraries

Matthews, Joseph R.

Scorecards for results; a guide for developing a library balanced scorecard. Libraries Unlimited 2008 112p pa $45 **027.4**
1. Public libraries 2. Libraries -- Administration
ISBN 978-1-59158-698-2

LC 2008-3689

"A balanced scorecard (BSC) is 'a process and culture for choosing, using, and revising measures' to help libraries focus on the success of their mission. . . . [The author] has developed a BSC workbook for public libraries. . . . Individual chapters here detail the six steps in developing and using a balanced scorecard, with sample vision statements, strategic themes, and performance measures." Libr J

Includes bibliographical references

McCook, Kathleen de la Peña

★ **Introduction** to public librarianship. Neal-Schuman Publishers 2004 406p il   **027.4**
1. Public libraries 2. Public librarianship 3. Public libraries -- United States
ISBN 1-55570-475-1

LC 2004-46012

"The book is a necessary addition to all professional collections, not to collect dust, but to become respectfully dog-eared and coffee-stained through repeated use." Florida Libraries

Includes bibliographical references

027.479 Public libraries – United States

★ The **library** book; by Susan Orlean. Simon and Schuster 2018 336 p. (hardcover) $28   **027.479**
1. Fires -- California -- Los Angeles 2. Public libraries -- California -- Los Angeles -- History 3. Los Angeles Public Library. Central Library -- History 4. Los Angeles Public Library. Central Library -- Fire, 1986
ISBN 1476740186; 9781476740188; 9781476740195

LC 2018022454

"On the morning of April 29, 1986, a fire alarm sounded in the Los Angeles Public Library. . . . The fire was disastrous: it reached 2000 degrees and burned for more than seven hours. . . . Investigators descended on the scene, but more than thirty years later, the mystery remains: Did someone purposefully set fire to the library[?]. . . . [Susan] Orlean chronicles the LAPL fire and its aftermath to showcase the larger, crucial role that libraries play in our lives." (Publisher's note)

"Bibliophiles will love this fact-filled, bookish journey." (Kirkus Reviews)

Includes bibliographical references

027.5 Government libraries

Conaway, James

America's library; the story of the Library of Congress, 1800-2000. foreword by James Billington; introduction by Edmund Morris. Yale Univ. Press 2000 226p il $48   **027.5**
1. Library of Congress
ISBN 978-0-300-08308-8; 0-300-08308-4

LC 99-58751

This history of the Library of Congress is organized "around that tiny, hardy band of men and women who have used both political acumen and intellectual vision to build the library's collections and establish those services that make the LC library to both Congress and nation. Richly supplemented with photographs, this history reaches out to touch all who love libraries." Booklist

Includes bibliographical references

027.6 Libraries for special groups and organizations

Moller, Sharon Chickering

Library service to Spanish speaking patrons; a practical guide. Libraries Unlimited 2001 207p pa $30   **027.6**
1. Public libraries 2. Libraries and Hispanic Americans
ISBN 1-56308-719-7

LC 00-45090

"Intended to stimulate discussion among library service planners and to offer counsel to service providers, this book should become required reading in any jurisdiction with an underserved Latino population." Voice Youth Advocates

Includes bibliographical references

Woodruff, John

Creating inclusive library environments; a planning guide for serving patrons with disabilities. Michelle Kowalsky, John Woodruff. ALA Editions, an imprint of the American Library Association 2017 x, 218 p.p (pbk.: alk. paper) $62   **027.6**
1. Libraries and people with disabilities 2. Libraries and people with disabilities -- United States
ISBN 9780838914854

LC 2016026241

In this book, by Michelle Kowalsky and John Woodruff, "librarians are continually faced with challenges of how to best meet the needs of patrons with disabilities, whether those patrons have physical or intellectual disabilities, differing learning styles, or even temporary problems which impact their access and may change over time. And because planning considerations range from policies and organizational culture to facilities, technologies, and beyond, librarians need a guide that covers everything." (Publisher's note)

"Demonstrated through their experiences and research, their expertise on the subject makes this work a valuable and credible resource." LJ

Includes bibliographical references and index

027.62 Libraries for specific age groups

Braafladt, Keith

Technology and literacy; 21st century library programming for children and teens. by Jennifer Nelson and Keith Braafladt. American Library Association 2012 129 p. (alk. paper) $50.00   **027.62**
1. Library services 2. Literacy programs 3. Literature and technology 4. Children's libraries -- Activity programs 5. Scratch (Computer program language) 6. Computer literacy -- Study and teaching 7. Technological literacy -- Study and teaching 8. Young adults' libraries -- Activity programs
ISBN 0838911080; 9780838911082

LC 2011035104

This book by Jennifer Nelson presents a "guide for creating and implementing technology-based programming in public libraries. . . . Beginning chapters explain and present a plan for offering such programs, providing steps on how to execute them. . . . The author explains the value of this type of programming and the process involved with adoption, and covers planning, gathering support from both administration and staff, marketing . . . managing time, etc." (School Library Journal)

Includes bibliographical references and index.

Brown, Amy

Let's start the music; programming for primary grades. Amy Brown. ALA Editions, an imprint of the American Library

Association 2014 xiii, 165 p.p (paperback) $48   **027.62**
1. Music -- Study and teaching 2. School libraries -- Activity programs 3. Children's libraries -- Activity programs 4. Music -- Instruction and study -- United States 5. School libraries -- Activity programs -- United States 6. Children's libraries -- Activity programs -- United States
ISBN 9780838911662; 9780838996928; 0838911668
LC 2013010871
In this book, author Amy Brown "explores several benefits of integrating music into story and literacy programs, then outlines simple strategies for all children's staff to feature more music and instruments in their events. Brown shares 13 themed programs, ranging from sing-alongs and animals to fairy tales and food, and each theme includes an extensive list of books, songs, an activity, and an instrument craft." (School Library Journal)
"Brown, an experienced programmer in public library settings, makes a solid case for weaving multiple intelligences into primary grade programs." SLJ
Includes bibliographical references and index

Del Negro, Janice M.
Folktales aloud; practical advice for playful storytelling. Janice M. Del Negro. American Library Association 2014 212 p. (alk. paper) $47   **027.62**
1. Fairy tales 2. Storytelling 3. Children's libraries -- Activity programs 4. Elementary school libraries -- Activity programs
ISBN 0838911358; 9780838911358
LC 2013028036
This book, by Janice M. Del Negro, "aims to show that storytelling is still vital in librarianship and throughout the greater community. . . . The text provides useful information for novice and seasoned storytellers alike while engaging the reader with its conversational tone. The chapters are broken down by audience age . . . and include information about audience needs and wants, stories, and resource information." (Booklist)
"Folktales are an integral part of children's literature and are the basis for many classic books librarians use daily in their work. These much loved tales are also the backbone of the art of storytelling...Del Negro leads novice tellers through the nuances of successful storytelling...Advice is offered in a very practical way on how to approach this group and suggestions are made as to how to grab and hold their interest with pacing, movement and suspense. If you have even a passing interest in the art of storytelling, this guide is not to be missed.—" SLJ
Includes bibliographical references and index

Eagle, MK
★ **Answering** teens' tough questions; a YALSA guide. mk Eagle. Neal-Schuman, an imprint of the American Library Association 2012 x, 125 p.p $49.95   **027.62**
1. Librarians 2. Library services 3. Teenagers -- Attitudes 4. Teenagers -- United States -- Attitudes 5. Libraries and teenagers -- United States 6. Young adults' libraries -- United States 7. Teenagers -- Services for -- United States 8. Teenagers -- United States -- Social conditions 9. Young adult services librarians -- United States -- Attitudes
ISBN 1555707947; 9781555707941
LC 2012015104
Author mk Eagle presents a book that "offers any librarian a quick primer on talking with young adults about the tough and often controversial topics of sex, drugs, alcohol, and violence." It provides "quick overviews on the issues themselves as well as tips for navigating these waters with teens. . . . . Chapters include sex, sexuality, homelessness, tattoos and piercings, dating violence, abuse, drugs and alcohol, emotional and

mental health, and the juvenile justice system." (Publisher's note)
Includes bibliographical references and index

Flowers, Sarah
Evaluating teen services and programs; Sarah Flowers. Neal-Schuman, an imprint of the American Library Association 2012 xv, 119 p.p (pbk.) $49.95   **027.62**
1. Library services 2. Libraries -- United States 3. Library services to young adults 4. Libraries and teenagers -- United States 5. Young adults' libraries -- Evaluation -- United States
ISBN 1555707939; 9781555707934
LC 2012015105
Author Sarah Flowers presents "a guide that provides basic information to help teen/youth services librarians, library directors, library school students studying teen services, and middle/high school librarians examine all aspects of their teen programs and services to determine where improvement is needed. Find out what you need to develop goals and objectives for evaluation, and learn how to collect the data that will give you a realistic picture of your library's strengths and weaknesses." (Publisher's note)
Includes bibliographical references and index

Ghoting, Saroj Nadkarni
STEP into storytime; using storytime effective practice to strengthen the development of newborns to five-year-olds. Saroj Nadkarni Ghoting and Kathy Fling Klatt. ALA Editions, an imprint of the American Library Association 2014 368 p. illustrations $59   **027.62**
1. Storytelling 2. Early childhood education 3. Children's libraries -- Activity programs 4. Storytelling -- United States 5. Libraries and preschool children -- United States 6. Children's libraries -- Activity programs -- United States
ISBN 0838912222; 9780838912225
LC 2014004162
This book, by Saroj Nadkarni Ghoting and Kathy Fling Klatt, focuses on "Story Time Effective Practice (STEP). . . . [It] is an approach that articulates the link between child development theory and storytimes. This important resource shows how presenters can use STEP to craft a storytime that is effective for mixed-age groups and adheres to best practices for emotional, social, physical, and cognitive support." (Publisher's note)
"It is a rare volume that could serve as both pleasure reading or as a textbook, but STEP into Storytime walks that fine line...The majority of children's librarians have studied childhood development and early literacy best practices; consider this book required reading to keep this knowledge fresh while reminding us of the importance—and delightful fun—of our work." Booklist
Includes bibliographical references and index

Pattee, Amy S.
Developing library collections for today's young adults; Amy S. Pattee. The Scarecrow Press, Inc. 2013 267 p. (cloth) $55   **027.62**
1. Multimedia 2. Library services 3. Libraries -- Special collections 4. Library services to young adults 5. Young adults' libraries 6. Libraries and teenagers -- United States 7. Multimedia library services -- United States
ISBN 0810887347; 9780810887343
LC 2013018596
This book, by Amy S. Pattee, "features policies that deal expressly with materials that respect the intellectual freedom of young library patrons. It emphasizes the importance of everything from needs assess-

ment to collection development, encouraging librarians to consider informational, recreational, and curricular needs and interests as the library staff select material on behalf of young adults." (Publisher's note)

"The book's greatest asset is that it manages to be extremely specific and thorough without becoming overwhelming." VOYA

Includes bibliographical references and index

Sweeney, Jennifer

Literacy; a way out for at-risk youth. Jennifer Sweeney. Libraries Unlimited 2012 xx, 133 pagesp (pbk.: acid-free paper) $40.00   **027.62**

1. Literacy 2. Prison librarians 3. Juvenile delinquents -- Books and reading 4. Prison libraries -- United States 5. Literacy programs -- United States 6. Juvenile corrections -- United States 7. Libraries and prisons -- United States 8. Literacy -- Social aspects -- United States 9. Juvenile delinquents -- Education -- United States 10. Libraries and juvenile delinquents -- United States 11. Problem youth -- Books and reading -- United States 12. Juvenile delinquents -- Rehabilitation -- United States 13. Juvenile delinquents -- Books and reading -- United States

ISBN 9781598846744; 9781598846751; 1598846744

LC 2011042804

This looks at corrections librarianship, focusing on juvenile institutions. The book "provides librarians in juvenile detention facilities with tools to face their unique challenges, such as collaborating with corrections staff and encouraging youth to maintain their connection to the library after release." (Barnes and Noble)

Includes bibliographical references and index.

Vaillancourt, Renee J.

Bare bones young adult services; tips for public library generalists. American Lib. Assn. 2000 142p il pa $33   **027.62**

1. Public libraries 2. Library services to young adults 3. Libraries and students 4. Young adults' libraries

ISBN 0-8389-3497-8

LC 99-35643

The author "provides guidelines for forming Teen Advisory Boards and focus groups, dealing with unruly adolescent patrons, providing homework support, as well as some basic programming ideas. She also discusses collection development and suggests resources that specialize in reviewing teen-level materials." SLJ

Includes bibliographical references

027.625   Libraries for children

Knoll, Debra J.

Engaging babies in the library; putting theory into practice. Debra J. Knoll. ALA Editions, an imprint of the American Library Association 2016 144 p. (print: alk. paper) $48 **027.625**

1. Libraries and families 2. Library services to children 3. Children's libraries 4. Libraries and infants 5. Libraries and toddlers 6. Children's libraries -- United States 7. Libraries and infants -- United States 8. Libraries and families -- United States 9. Libraries and toddlers -- United States

ISBN 9780838914342

LC 2015049312

"Focusing squarely on the how of providing quality library service to babies and families, [Debra] Knoll's new book provides sensible, sensitive advice on meeting their physical, emotional, intellectual, and social needs. Geared towards helping public libraries foster healthy growth and development for their littlest patrons, this book explores multiple

aspects in the developing life of a baby." (Publisher's note)

"This is a meaningful resource for libraries that are looking to increase meaningful service to infants and toddlers." Booklist

Includes bibliographical references and index

028   Reading and use of other information media

Basbanes, Nicholas A.

★ **Every** book its reader; the power of the printed word to stir the world. HarperCollins 2005 360p il $29.95; pa $15.95   **028**

1. Best books 2. Books and reading

ISBN 0-06-059323-7; 978-0-06-059323-0; 0-06-059324-5 pa; 978-0-06-059324-7 pa

LC 2005-46164

The author "focuses on peoples' reading habits and on the books they have read, both obscure and renowned, as well as on the importance of particular books in specific contexts. Basbanes begins by interviewing some of the best-read people alive, among them David McCullough, Harold Bloom, Helen Vendler, and Elaine Pagels; he also mentions a wide variety of contemporary and historical personages. The loosely related stories are often inspirational, making this an engrossing read." Libr J

Includes bibliographical references

The **books** that changed my life; reflections by 100 authors, actors, musicians, and other remarkable people. edited by Bethanne Patrick. Regan Arts 2016 304 p. (hardcover) $24.95   **028**

1. Books and reading 2. Celebrities -- Books and reading

ISBN 9781941393659; 9781942872290; 1941393659

LC 2015946442

In this book, edited by Bethanne Patrick, "leading authors, politicians, CEOs, actors, and other notables share the books that changed their life, why they love them, and their passion with readers everywhere. . . . Contributors include Al Roker, Carl Hiaasen, Dave Eggers, Emma Straub, Eric Idle, Fay Weldon, Fran Lebowitz, Gillian Flynn, Gregory Maguire, Jeff Kinney, Jim Shepard, Laura Lippmann, Lev Grossman, Liev Schreiber, . . . and Tommy Hilfiger, among others." (Publisher's note)

Dirda, Michael

Book by book; notes on reading and life. Henry Holt 2006 170p $17   **028**

1. Best books 2. Books and reading

ISBN 978-0-8050-7877-0; 0-8050-7877-0

LC 2005-55451

The author "writes a guide to reading and its life lessons ranging widely and pithily through the universal themes of learning, school, work, love, childhood and spiritual guidance. Dirda's message is simple: if reading is to be life enhancing, we need to focus our attention on books that are rewarding. . . . For those who enjoy books about reading, and for all those seeking to encourage others to read, Dirda's brief yet suggestive book will inspire." Publ Wkly

Browsings; A Year of Reading, Collecting, and Living With Books. by Michael Dirda. W W Norton & Co Inc. 2015 336 p. (hardcover) $24.95   **028**

1. Authors 2. Authorship 3. Books and reading

ISBN 9781605988443; 1605988448

This book, by Michael Dirda, "collects fifty of his witty and wide-ranging reflections on literary journalism, book collecting, and the writers he loves. Reaching from the classics to the post-moderns, his allusions dance from Samuel Johnson, Ralph Waldo Emerson and M. F. K. Fisher to Marilynne Robinson, Hunter S. Thompson, and David Foster Wallace." (Publisher's note)

"This joy-filled, reflective collection makes perfect bedside reading... Literate but never snobby, this collection of essays surely will entertain and enlighten book lovers of all stripes." Booklist

Hooper, Brad

The **short** story readers' advisory; a guide for librarians. American Lib. Assn. 2000 135p pa $32   **028**
    1. Short stories -- History and criticism
    ISBN 0-8389-0782-2

                                   LC 99-85751
This work contains over 200 critical essays covering short story authors past and present. A step-by-step guide on how to interview readers in order to match their tastes with appropriate stories is included.
Includes bibliographical references

Maatta, Stephanie L.

A **few** good books; using contemporary readers' advisory strategies to connect readers with books. Neal-Schuman Publishers 2010 xix, 387p pa $69.95   **028**
    1. Reference services (Libraries) 2. Books and reading -- History
    ISBN 978-1-55570-669-2; 1-55570-669-X

                                     LC 2009-40999
"This comprehensive and up-to-date guide is a treasure trove of practical advice and resources that will help make the RA experience even more effective and enjoyable." Libr J
Includes bibliographical references

Mendelsund, Peter

What we see when we read; a phenomenology, with illustrations. Peter Mendelsund. Vintage Contemporaries 2014 448 p. illustrations (Vintage original) (paperback) $16.95   **028**
    1. Phenomenology 2. Visual literacy 3. Books and reading 4. Visual perception in literature
    ISBN 0804171637; 9780804171632

                                     LC 2014007896
This book, by Peter Mendelsund, is an "exploration into the phenomenology of reading-- how we visualize images from reading works of literature. . . . The collection of fragmented images on a page-- a graceful ear there, a stray curl, a hat positioned just so-- and other clues and signifiers helps us to create an image of a character. But in fact our sense that we know a character intimately has little to do with our ability to concretely picture our beloved-- or reviled-- literary figures." (Publisher's note)

"This work was written for those who enjoy fully the creative experience of reading, and who read about reading." LJ

Mustich, James

★ **1,000** books to read before you die; a life-changing list. James Mustich; with Margot Greenbaum Mustich, Thomas Meagher, and Karen Templer. Workman Publishing 2018 960 p. (alk. paper) $35   **028**
    1. Best books 2. Books and reading 3. Books and reading -- United States
    ISBN 9781523504459

                                     LC 2018036090
"Covering fiction, poetry, science and science fiction, memoir, travel writing, biography, children's books, history, and more, . . . [this book,

by James Mustich] ranges across cultures and through time to offer an eclectic collection of works that each deserve to come with the recommendation, You have to read this. But it's not a proscriptive list of the 'great works'--rather, it's a celebration of the glorious mosaic that is our literary heritage." (Publisher's note)

"It might be wise to invest in several copies of this wonderful meditation on life lived with and enhanced by the written word."

Ross, Catherine Sheldrick

★ The **pleasures** of reading; a booklover's alphabet. Catherine Sheldrick Ross. Libraries Unlimited, An imprint of ABC-CLIO, LLC 2014 270 p. (paperback) $45   **028**
    1. Books and reading 2. Libraries and community 3. Reading interests 4. Reading -- Social aspects
    ISBN 159158695X; 9781591586951

                                     LC 2014008161
In this book, author Catherine Sheldrick Ross "takes a new look at pleasure reading through 30 thought-provoking essays based on themes arranged from A to Z. . . . Drawing on her own research as well as other published sources, Ross comments on the significance of each theme, provides examples of the phenomenon, and develops the topic chronologically, through further examples, or through reversals." (Publisher's note)

"Librarians who work with RA will not find much new information but will have their experiences validated. Those new to RA will receive a thorough introduction." LJ
Includes bibliographical references and index

★ **Reading** matters; what the research reveals about reading, libraries, and community. by Catherine Sheldrick Ross, Lynne E.F. McKechnie, and Paulette M. Rothbauer. Libraries Unlimited 2006 p. cm.   **028**
    1. Books and reading. 2. Reading interests. 3. Reading promotion. 4. Popular literature. 5. Libraries and community. 6. Reading -- Social aspects. 7. Public services (Libraries)
    ISBN 1-59158-066-8 (pbk.: alk. paper)

                                     LC 2005030839
Includes bibliographical references and index..

Young, Damon

The **art** of reading; Damon Young. Scribe US 2018 176 p. $14.95   **028**
    1. Reading 2. Books and reading
    ISBN 1947534025; 9781947534025
In this book author Damon Young, "reads passionately, selectively, surprisingly -- from superhero noir to speculative realism, from Heidegger to Heinlein -- and shows his reader how cultivating their inner critic can expand their own lives as well as the lives of those on the pages of the books they love." (Publisher's note)

"This literary study is serious but also witty and fun—a tough balance to strike, but Young nails it." Pub Wkly

028.1   Reviews

Naidoo, Jamie Campbell

★ **Rainbow** family collections; selecting and using children's books with lesbian, gay, bisexual, transgender, and queer content. Jamie Campbell Naidoo. Libraries Unlimited, an imprint of ABC-CLIO, LLC 2012 xvii, 260 p.p ill. (hardback) $50   **028.1**
    1. Libraries and sexual minorities 2. Sexual minorities in literature

3. Libraries and sexual minorities -- United States 4. Libraries -- Special collections -- Sexual minorities 5. Sexual minorities -- Juvenile literature -- Bibliography 6. Children's libraries -- Collection development -- United States 7. Children's libraries -- Services to minorities -- United States 8. Children of sexual minority parents -- Books and reading -- United States

ISBN 1598849603; 9781598849608

LC 2012008362

This book by Jamie Campbell Naidoo "highlight[s] titles for children from infancy to age 11" featuring lesbian, gay, bisexual, transgender, and queer content. It "supplies a synopsis of the title's content, lists awards it has received, cites professional reviews, and provides suggestions for librarians considering acquisition. The book also provides a brief historical overview of LGBTQ children's literature along with the major book awards for this genre." (Publisher's note)

Includes bibliographical references and index

Szymborska, Wislawa

Nonrequired reading; prose pieces. translated from the Polish by Clare Cavanagh. Harcourt 2002 233p $24   **028.1**
1. Books and reading
ISBN 0-15-100660-1

LC 2002-2440

"The skillful simplicity and lyric quality of these essays make them distinctive. With her poet's gift for compression, Szymborska captures large concepts and brilliantly reduces them to pithy, two-page essays." Libr J

Includes bibliographical references

028.5   Reading and use of other information media by young people

Allyn, Pam

What to read when; the books and stories to read with your child, and all the best times to read them. Avery 2009 318p pa $16.95   **028.5**
1. Children -- Books and reading
ISBN 978-1-58333-334-1

LC 2008-54501

The author "provides many ways to promote a love of reading to children and offers top-ten lists of reasons to read to kids that incorporate practical, easy-to-use tips to encourage literacy from a young age. . . . This is an indispensable guide to choosing age-appropriate books for children. Allyn provides a list of more than 300 titles on 50 themes including such issues as adoption, feelings about school, sharing, and coping with illness. This valuable resource for children's librarians, educators, and parents is highly recommended." Libr J

The **Cambridge** guide to children's books in English; [edited by] Victor Watson; advisory editors, Elizabeth L. Keyser, Juliet Partridge, Morag Styles. Cambridge Univ. Press 2001 814p il $75   **028.5**
1. Reference books 2. Children's literature -- Encyclopedias
ISBN 0-521-55064-5

LC 00-65163

This reference provides an "overview of historic and contemporary children's books published in English. The entries include authors, illustrators, and significant works primarily from Britain, the US, Canada, Australia, New Zealand, India, and Africa. . . . Major themes, such as fairy tales, fantasy, folktales, legends, mythology, and young adult fiction, are covered as well as less-expected entries on topics such as bias,

the bush, disability, ecology, and nudity in children's books. Nonbook media are also covered by entries on animated cartoons, comics, superheroes, and television for children." Choice

Includes bibliographical references

Helbig, Alethea

Dictionary of American young adult fiction, 1997-2001; books of recognized merit. {by} Alethea K. Helbig and Agnes Regan Perkins. Greenwood Press 2004 xxii, 558p $75   **028.5**
1. Best books 2. Reference books 3. Youth -- Books and reading 4. Young adult literature -- Dictionaries 5. Young adult literature -- Bio-bibliography
ISBN 0-313-32430-1

LC 2003-56804

"The 290 books included {in this volume} have been recognized by one or more of the following: Alex Award, ALA Best Books for Young Adults, Booklist, NYPL, and the Michael L. Printz Award. Approximately 60 of the listed books are adult books considered appropriate for young adults by the award committees. The 741 entries, which include books, their authors, major characters, and settings, are listed alphabetically and range in length from a couple of paragraphs to a bit more than a page. Book entries describe plot, themes, and characters, as well as relevant literary awards, while author entries consist of a brief biography and bibliography. . . . {The information is collected} usefully for selectors of young adult fiction, reader's advisers, teachers, and libraries supporting young adult fiction teaching." Libr J

Includes bibliographical references

Keane, Nancy J.

101 great, ready-to-use book lists for teens; Nancy J. Keane. Libraries Unlimited, an imprint of ABC-CLIO, LLC 2012 xiv, 263 p.p (paperback) $40; (ebook) $40   **028.5**
1. Book selection 2. Books and reading 3. Young adult literature -- Bibliography 4. High school libraries -- Book lists 5. Young adults' libraries -- Book lists 6. Teenagers -- Books and reading -- United States
ISBN 1610691342; 9781610691345; 9781610691352

LC 2011051428

This book offers a "compilation of YA [Young Adult] materials . . . published prior to August 2011. The book is divided . . . into themed lists such as 'Genres,' 'Readalikes,' and 'Teaching Literary Elements.' The themes . . . include . . . topics such as 'Romance,' 'Autism & Asperger's Syndrome,' 'Different Belief Systems,' and 'Crossing the Border.' Each entry includes the title, author, publisher, publication date, page numbers, an annotation, Lexile level when available, and interest level by grade or age range." (School Library Journal)

"This is a useful resource for new librarians and may also be helpful to seasoned librarians. The emphasis is on books published within the last ten years, but some older titles are included." Lib Med Con

Includes bibliographical references and index

028.7   Use of books and other information media as sources of information

Dorr, Christina

★ **LGBTQAI** + books for children and teens; providing a window for all. Christina Dorr and Liz Deskins, foreword by Jamie Campbell Naidoo. ALA Editions, an imprint of the American Library Association 2018 xxix, 132 p.p (softcover: acid-free paper) $45   **028.7**
1. Lesbians -- Bibliography 2. Bisexuals -- Bibliography

3. Intersex people -- Bibliography 4. Transgender people -- Bibliography 5. Sexual minorities -- Bibliography 6. Children's literature -- Study and teaching 7. Young adult literature -- Study and teaching 8. Children -- Books and reading -- United States 9. Sexual minorities in literature -- Bibliography 10. Teenagers -- Books and reading -- United States 11. Libraries -- Special collections -- Sexual minorities 12. Sexual minorities -- Juvenile literature -- Bibliography 13. Sexual minority youth -- Books and reading -- United States
ISBN 9780838916490

LC 2017052430

This resource book, by Christina Dorr and Liz Deskins, "for librarians who work with children and teens not only surveys the best in LGBTQAI+ lit but, just as importantly, offers guidance on how to share it in ways that encourage understanding and acceptance among parents, school administrators, and the wider community. . . . This guide discusses the path to marriage equality, how LGBTQAI+ terms have changed, and reasons to share LGBTQAI+ literature with all children." (Publisher's note)

"In addition to a survey of LGBTQAI+ literature for youth of all ages, this slim volume, intended for library staff who work with children and teens, contains practical advice for sharing each book, developmentally appropriate program ideas, and helpful talking points to discuss how diversity should factor into your collection." Booklist

Includes bibliographical references and indexes

LGBTQAI plus books for children and teens

028.9   Reading interests and habits

Prose, Francine

What to read and why; Francine Prose. HarperCollins 2018 336 p. $23.99   **028.9**
1. Best books 2. American essays
ISBN 0062397869; 9780062397867

In this book, author Francine Prose "passionately pushes great books and good writing in a wide-ranging assemblage of previously published and new essays Prose's stimulating collection of essays will move readers to pick up, for the first or the 15th time, the books she so enthusiastically recommends." (Publishers Weekly)

Schwalbe, Will

Books for Living; Will Schwalbe. Random House Inc 2016 288 p. $25.95   **028.9**
1. Books and reading
ISBN 0385353545; 9780385353540

LC 2016026088

In this book, author Will Schwalbe invites readers "on his quest for books that speak to the specific challenges of living in our modern world, with all its noise and distractions. In each chapter, he discusses a particular book—what brought him to it (or vice versa), the people in his life he associates with it, and how it became a part of his understanding of himself in the world." (Publisher's note)

"In an age when the number of readers is declining, a delightful book like this might just snare a few new recruits." Kirkus

Spence, Annie

Dear Fahrenheit 451; love and heartbreak in the stacks: a librarian's love letters and breakup notes to the books in her life. Annie Spence. Flatiron Books 2017 x, 244 p.p (hardcover) $19.99   **028.9**
1. Love letters 2. Books and reading 3. Librarians -- Books and reading 4. Books and reading -- United States 5. Authors -- Books and reading -- United States
ISBN 9781250113887; 9781250106490; 1250106494

LC 2017027324

In this book, author Annie Spence "has crafted love letters and breakup notes to the iconic and eclectic books she has encountered over the years. From breaking up with The Giving Tree . . . , to her love letter to The Time Traveler's Wife . . . , Spence will make you think of old favorites in a new way. Filled with suggested reading lists, Spence's take on classic and contemporary books is very much like the best of literature." (Publisher's note)

"A librarian delivers a charming epistolary volume that begs to be read with pencil in hand." Kirkus

Includes bibliographical references (pages 243-244).

Walter, Virginia A.

Transforming summer programs at your library; outreach and outcomes in action. Natalie Cole and Virginia A. Walter. ALA editions, an imprint of the American Library Association 2018 176 p. (print: alk. paper) $49   **028.9**
1. Children's libraries -- Activity programs 2. Reading promotion -- United States 3. Summer reading programs -- United States 4. Library outreach programs -- United States
ISBN 0838916287; 9780838916285

LC 2017052415

In this book, by Natalie Cole and Virginia A. Walter, "changes in public libraries, the communities they serve, children's lives, and educational research all demonstrate that traditional summer reading programs need to be reimagined. Working groups of librarians, in partnership with the California Library Association and the California State Library, have done just that, creating and implementing outcomes- and outreach-based summer reading programs." (Publisher's note)

"For well-cited research about summer reading, or readers who are looking to revamp their programs, this is a comprehensive place to begin." Booklist

Includes bibliographical references and index

030   General encyclopedic works

★ The **World** Almanac and Book of Facts. World Almanac Education   **030**
1. Almanacs 2. Geography 3. Popular culture
Originally published in 1868

"The World Almanac® and Book of Facts is America's top-selling reference book of all time, with more than 82 million copies sold. Since 1868, this compendium of information has been the authoritative source for all your entertainment, reference, and learning needs." (Publisher's note)

031   General encyclopedic works in specific languages and language families

Jacobs, A. J.

The **know-it-all**; one man's humble quest to become the smartest person in the world. Simon & Schuster 2004 386p $25   **031**
1. Encyclopaedia Britannica
ISBN 0-7432-5060-5

LC 2004-48233

This "book stems from the author's herculean effort to read every volume of the majestic Encyclopaedia Britannica. . . . Jacobs turns his quest for intellectual enlightenment into alphabetically ordered, humorous ruminations on all persons and events of his life. . . . Plenty of good fun pours out of this prose." Booklist

Includes bibliographical references

Lih, Andrew

The **Wikipedia** revolution; how a bunch of nobodies created the world's greatest encyclopedia. Hyperion 2009 246p il map $24.99   **031**

1. User generated content 2. Electronic encyclopedias
ISBN 978-1-4013-0371-6; 1-4013-0371-4

LC 2008-51137

"Wikipedia is a revolutionary phenomenon, changing fundamentally the landscape of networked collaboration, e-learning, and, as librarians know all too well, mediated information provision. Depicted here is a Wikipedia insider's narrative of the development of Wikipedia. . . . [Lih] characterizes this revolution as only partly technological. The real revolution is social—an apt point when one considers the philosophical underpinnings of this resource, the articles' neutral point of view, while remaining a free resource anyone can use and distribute." Libr J

Includes bibliographical references

The **World** Book Encyclopedia. World Book, Inc 22 v col ill, col maps   **031**

1. Reference books 2. Encyclopedias and dictionaries
New editions published yearly; revised frequently

"A 22-volume, highly illustrated, A-Z general encyclopedia for all ages, featuring sections on how to use World Book, other research aids, pronunciation key, a student guide to better writing, speaking, and research skills, and comprehensive index." (Publisher's note)

031.02   Books of miscellaneous facts

Famous first facts, international edition; a record of first happenings, discoveries, and inventions in world history. {edited by} Steven Anzovin & Janet Podell. Wilson, H.W. 2000 837p $140   **031.02**

1. Reference books 2. Encyclopedias and dictionaries
ISBN 0-8242-0958-3

LC 99-86869

This work "contains more than 5000 firsts from hundreds of countries and ranging in time from 3.5 billion years ago (the age of the oldest continental land discovered) to 2001 (the scheduled date of completion of the first building over 1500 feet tall). . . . {It} groups related entries under broad subject categories (arranged alphabetically) and subcategories. Within each category or sub-category, entries are arranged chronologically." Publisher's note

Henderson, Caspar

A **new** map of wonders; a journey in search of modern marvels. Caspar Henderson. University of Chicago Press 2017 371 p. illustrations, maps (cloth: alk. paper) $29   **031.02**

1. Curiosities and wonders 2. Technological innovations 3. Marvelous, The 4. Philosophy of nature
ISBN 022629191X; 9780226291918

LC 2017013309

This book, by Caspar Henderson, "borrows from the form of one of the oldest and most widely known sources of wonder: maps. Large, detailed mappae mundi invited people in medieval Europe to vividly imagine places and possibilities they had never seen before: manticores

with the head of a man, the body of a lion, and the stinging tail of a scorpion; tribes of one-eyed men who fought griffins for diamonds; and fearsome Scythian warriors who drank the blood of their enemies from their skulls." (Publisher's note)

"Part celebration and part meditation, an elegant study of things that should awe and amaze us—and why we are capable of awe and amazement in the first place." Kirkus

Includes bibliographical references and index

The **New** York Public Library desk reference; 4th ed; Hyperion 2002 999p il maps $34.95   **031.02**

1. Reference books 2. Encyclopedias and dictionaries
ISBN 0-7868-6846-5

LC 2002-27480

First published 1989 by Webster's New World

Divided into chapters, this reference features charts, tables, lists, and illustrations providing information in such categories as signs and symbols, mathematics and science basics, the arts, grammar and punctuation, etiquette, personal finance, first aid, and household tips.

Includes bibliographical references

032   General encyclopedic works in English

Guinness world records 2018; Guinness world records. Guinness World Records, Ltd. 2017 255 p. illustrations (hardcover) $28.95   **032**

1. World records 2. World records -- Periodicals 3. Curiosities and wonders -- Periodicals
ISBN 191056172X; 9781910561720

"The record-breaking records annual is back and packed with more incredible accomplishments, stunts, cutting-edge science and amazing sporting achievements than ever before. With more than 3,000 new and updated records and 1,000 eye-popping photos, it has thousands of new stats and facts and dazzling new features." (Publisher's note)

051   General serial publications in specific languages and language families

Highbrow, Lowbrow, Brilliant, Despicable; 50 Years of New York. by the editors of New York magazine; writer & historian, Christopher Bonanos. Simon & Schuster 2017 419 p. color illustrations (hardcover) $65   **051**

1. Periodicals 2. New York (N.Y.) 3. New York magazine 4. New York (N.Y.) -- Periodicals
ISBN 9781501166846; 9781501166853; 1501166840

"Since its founding in 1968, New York Magazine has told the story of that city's constant morphing, week after week. Covering culture high and low, the drama and scandal of politics and finance, through jubilant moments and immense tragedies, the magazine has hit readers where they live, with a sensibility as fast and funny and urbane as New York itself." (Publisher's note)

"A great magazine is commemorated with an equally top-flight anthology. . . . History, local and global, unfolds in this fine gathering that represents a half-century and more than 2,300 issues." Kirkus

Meyerowitz, Rick

Drunk stoned brilliant dead; the writers and artists who made the National Lampoon insanely great. Abrams 2010 319p il $40   **051**

1. Satire 2. American wit and humor 3. National lampoon

(Periodical)

ISBN 978-0-8109-8848-4; 0-8109-8848-8

This is the "first Lampoon book that celebrates the wild, eye-intoxicating diversity of its illustrations, photography, cartoons, comic strips, graphics—parodies of everything from matchbooks to Marvel Comics to modern art. In toto this volume is a testament to the dazzling design expertise of its formative art directors, Michael Gross and David Kaestle. Rick Meyerowitz, a charter member of the Lampoon crew . . ., has in effect edited a magnificent 320-page issue of the magazine that reprints much of its finest work. And in brief, funny, and for once malice-free memoirs from its principals, the collection evokes the sparkling camaraderie that drove it. If you grew up with the Lampoon, this book is a trip down memory lane like no other; if not, it will demonstrate that the much-maligned 70s could produce humor that has never been surpassed." Vanity Fair

060.4 Special topics of general organizations

American Institute of Parliamentarians standard code of parliamentary procedure; [by American Institute of Parliamentarians] McGraw-Hill 2012 x, 326 p.p (alk. paper) $19 **060.4**
1. Parliamentary practice
ISBN 0071778640; 9780071778640

LC 2011048926

This book, by American Institute of Parliamentarians, "for more than 60 years, . . . has been helping meeting organizers and participants ensure fairness and justice on a consistent basis. This updated edition provides important new motions and protocols pertaining to electronic meetings, discipline, and finance and audit committees." (Publisher's note)

Includes bibliographical references and index

Encyclopedia of Associations; An Associations Unlimited Reference. 53 edition Gale / Cengage Learning 2014 3700 p. 3v $1084 **060.4**
1. Associations 2. Encyclopedias and dictionaries
ISBN 1414477988; 9781414477985
Annual

This book, edited by Tara E. Atterberry, offers a "comprehensive source for detailed information on nonprofit American membership organizations of national scope. Every entry offers a wealth of valuable data, typically including the organization's complete name, address and phone number together with the primary official's name and title; . . . founding date, purpose, activities and dues; . . . and more." (Publisher's note)

Robert, Henry M.

Robert's rules of order newly revised; Henry M. Robert III, Daniel H. Honemann, and Thomas J. Balch; with the assistance of Daniel E. Seabold and Shmuel Gerber. 11th ed Da Capo Press 2011 lii, 716 p.p $18.95 **060.4**
1. Parliamentary practice 2. Life skills -- Handbooks, manuals, etc.
ISBN 030682020X; 9780306820205; 9780306820212

LC 2011932260

"'Robert's Rules of Order' is the book on parliamentary procedure for parliamentarians and anyone involved in an organization, association, club, or group. . . . . The eleventh edition has been thoroughly revised to address common inquiries and incorporate new rules, interpretations, and procedures made necessary by the evolution of parliamentary procedure, including new material relating to electronic communication and 'electronic meetings.'" (Publisher's note)

Robert's rules of order, newly revised, in brief; updated in accord with the eleventh edition of the complete manual. Henry M. Robert III ... [et al.] Da Capo Press 2011 vii, 197 p.p (alk. paper) $7.50 **060.4**
1. Parliamentary practice 2. Life skills -- Handbooks, manuals, etc.
ISBN 0306820196; 9780306820199

LC 2011932261

"'Robert's Rules of Order, Newly Revised, In Brief' was first published in 2005 to meet the need for a simple and short book on parliamentary procedure. This second edition of 'In Brief' is now updated and revised to match the new full edition of 'Robert's Rules of Order, Newly Revised,' also published this year. . . . This concise, user-friendly edition takes readers through the rules most often needed at meetings." (Publisher's note)

Webster's New World Robert's rules of order; simplified and applied. by Robert McConnell Productions. 3rd ed Houghton Mifflin Harcourt 2014 xxii, 388p $11.95 **060.4**
1. Parliamentary practice
ISBN 0764563998; 9780544236035

This book, by Robert McConnell Productions, is the "revised and updated edition of the clearest, most useful guide to parliamentary procedure. . . . Among its helpful features are sample scripts to help figure out what to say while conducting meetings, hands-on examples to show how the rules are applied, and timesaving tips to help make meetings more efficient." (Publisher's note)

"Organized so users can find what they need quickly and easily, this revised edition includes an entire new chapter on proper procedure for conducting homeowners' associations." Publisher's note

061 General organizations

The **Foundation** directory; compiled by The Foundation Center. Foundation Center 2730p **061**
1. Reference books 2. Endowments -- Directories
Annual. First published 1960 by Russell Sage. Replaces American foundations and their fields

"Provides detailed information concerning independent, corporate, community, and private foundations with assets of at least $2 million or annual giving of at least $200,000. Geographical arrangement. Entries give date founded; names of officers, contact, and donors; foundation type; financial data; fields of interest; types of support; limitations; application information; and number of staff. Six indexes: Donors, officers, and trustees; Geographic; Types of support; Subject; Foundations new to edition; Foundations name index." Guide to Ref Books. 11th edition

069 Museology (Museum science)

Conniff, Richard

House of Lost Worlds; Dinosaurs, Dynasties, and the Story of Life on Earth. Richard Conniff. Yale University Press 2016 352 p. illustrations (some color) (hardcover) $35 **069**
1. Natural history 2. Museums -- History
ISBN 9780300211634; 0300211635

This book, by Richard Conniff, "tells the story of how one museum changed ideas about dinosaurs, dynasties, and even the story of life on earth. . . . Delving into the [Yale Peabody Museum of Natural History's] storied and colorful past, award-winning author Richard Conniff introduces a cast of bold explorers, roughneck bone hunters, and visionary scientists." (Publisher's note)

"Colored, boxed sections highlighting people and events and over 100 illustrations and photos provide a pleasant coffee table-book feel, and 23 pages of footnotes attest to Conniff's exhaustive research." Kirkus

Includes bibliographical references (pages 293-316) and index.

Museums of the World; by De Gruyter Saur. De Gruyter Saur 2014 1553 p. $694.38 **069**
1. Museums
ISBN 3110337940; 9783110337945
First published 1973. Periodically revised.

This book "covers in its 18th edition about 55,000 museums in 202 countries, listed hierarchically by country and place, and within places, alphabetically by name. . . . A typical entry contains the following details: name of the museum, address, telephone number, fax, eMail address and URL, museum type, year of foundation, name of the director and museum staff, special collections and equipment, number of the entry." (Publisher's note)

070   Documentary media, educational media, news media; journalism; publishing

Avedon, Richard

Nothing Personal; James Baldwin, photographs by Richard Avedon. Taschen America Llc 2017 120 p. $70 **070**
1. Photojournalism 2. Artistic photography 3. Portrait photography
ISBN 3836569531; 9783836569538

"This meticulous reprint of Richard Avedon and James Baldwin's 'Nothing Personal' explores the complexities and contradictions still at the center of the American experience especially timely in the age of Donald Trump. Deploying both image and text, Avedon and Baldwin examine the formation of identity, and the bonds that both underlie and undermine human connection. An accompanying 72-page booklet features a fresh essay by Pulitzer Prize-winning critic Hilton Als." (Publisher's note)

Brokaw, Tom

A **long** way from home; growing up in the American heartland. Random House 2002 272p $24.95; pa $12.95 **070**
1. Journalists 2. Television news anchors
ISBN 0-375-50763-9; 0-375-75935-2 pa

LC 2002-31865

"Peppered with photographs . . . this tribute to an idyllic childhood should please Brokaw's loyal fans." Publ Wkly

Cronkite, Walter, 1916-2009

A **reporter's** life. Knopf 1997 384p il $26.95; pa $15 **070**
1. Radio reporters 2. Television news anchors
ISBN 0-394-57879-1; 0-345-41103-X pa

LC 96-21053

Cronkite's "memoir is a short course on the flow of events in the second half of this century—events the world knows more about because of Walter Cronkite's work, and some of which might not have happened without it." N Y Times Book Rev

Knight, Robert M., 1948-

Journalistic writing; building the skills, honing the craft. Robert M. Knight. Marion Street Press 2010 315 p. $29.95 **070**
1. Authorship 2. Journalism 3. Journalism -- Authorship
ISBN 1933338385; 1936863626; 9781933338385;

9781936863624

LC 2010012080

This book, by Robert M. Knight, "is the definitive handbook for aspiring journalists. Offering budding writers suggestions on how to improve their skills--even when faced with a tight deadline--this guide also reviews many elements essential to the occupation such as utilizing strong nouns and verbs, paring down adjectives and adverbs, describing with concrete detail, and avoiding clichés and the passive voice." (Publisher's note)

Includes bibliographical references (p. 301-305) and index

Kovach, Bill

Blur; how to know what's true in the age of information overload. [by] Bill Kovach and Tom Rosenstiel. Bloomsbury 2010 227p $26 **070**
1. Journalism -- Objectivity
ISBN 978-1-59691-565-7

LC 2010-19766

"Kovach and Rosenstiel combine journalism and civics in this valuable and insightful resource to help Americans adapt to an era that demands that readers become their own editors and news aggregators." Booklist

Includes bibliographical references

★ **Reporting** Iraq; an oral history of the war by the journalists who covered it. edited by Mike Hoyt, John Palattella, and the staff of the Columbia Journalism Review. Melville House 2007 191p il pa $21.95 **070**
1. Reporters and reporting 2. Iraq War, 2003-2011 -- Personal narratives
ISBN 978-1-93363-334-3; 1-93363-334-4

"44 reporters casually and directly discuss all angles of the War in Iraq, including their own shock, fear and incomprehension, in this compilation of interviews conducted by The Columbia Journalism Review. . . . This vital, breathtaking collection may be the closest contemporary reporting gets to cutting through the fog of war." Publ Wkly

Schorr, Daniel

Staying tuned; a life in journalism. Pocket Bks. 2001 354p il hardcover o.p. pa $14 **070**
1. Television reporters 2. Political commentators
ISBN 0-671-02088-9 pa

LC 2001-21014

Schorr tells of his life as a reporter for CBS, CNN and National Public Radio.

"Schorr's memoir is as much an inside look at the famous world figures of the latter half of the twentieth century as it is the story of one man's life and career." Booklist

Thompson, Hunter S.

★ **Fear** and loathing in America; the brutal odyssey of an outlaw journalist, 1968-1976. foreword by David Halberstam; edited by Douglas Brinkley. Simon & Schuster 2000 xxv, 756p il $30; pa $15 **070**
1. Authors 2. Novelists 3. Journalists 4. Satirists 5. Columnists 6. Nonfiction writers
ISBN 0-684-87315-X; 0-684-87316-8 pa

LC 00-47012

"During the period covered in this collection, Thompson was a vital, deliriously erratic force in journalism, covering the turbulent 1968 Democratic National Convention in Chicago, the 1968 election of Richard M. Nixon, the 1972 campaign, Watergate, the falls of Nixon and

Saigon." N Y Times Book Rev

070.1 Documentary media, educational media, news media

Weller, Sheila

The **News** Sorority; Diane Sawyer, Katie Couric, Christiane Amanpour and the (Ongoing, Imperfect, Complicated) Triumph of Women in TV News. by Sheila Weller. Penguin Group USA 2014 448 p. illustrations $29.95 **070.1**

    1. Women journalists

    ISBN 1594204276; 9781594204272

                         LC 2014009725

This book, by Sheila Weller, tells the story of how "Diane Sawyer, Katie Couric, and Christiane Amanpour . . . broke into the newsroom's once impenetrable 'boys' club.' . . . . Drawing on exclusive interviews with their colleagues and intimates from childhood on, . . . [it] crafts a lively and exhilarating narrative that reveals the hard struggles and inner strengths that shaped these women and powered their success." (Publisher's note)

"News junkies and fans will love all of the insider details on the media and the lives of these women." LJ

Wenger, Debora Halpern

Advancing the story; broadcast journalism in a multimedia world. [by] Debora Halpern Wenger and Deborah Potter. 2nd ed.; CQ Press 2011 xxxi, 380p il pa $36.95 **070.1**

    1. Broadcast journalism

    ISBN 978-1-60871-714-9

                         LC 2010049469

First published 2008

"While stressing basics of good journalism with emphasis on attention to detail, [the] authors explain how technology has changed the approach to content preparation among those invested in the Internet and integrated technology." Journalism and Mass Communication Educator [review of 2008 edition]

Includes bibliographical references

070.4 Journalism

Buell, Hal

Moments; Pulitzer Prize-winning photographs: a visual chronicle of our time. text by Hal Buell; introduction by David Halberstam. Hachette Books 2015 336 p. illustrations (some color) $24.99 **070.4**

    1. Photojournalism 2. Pulitzer Prizes 3. Pulitzer prizes 4. Photojournalism -- United States -- Awards

    ISBN 1631910086; 9781631910081

This book presents a "complete collection of more than 600 Pulitzer Prize-winning photographs, from the first awards in 1942 through the 2015 honors. Organized by year, the photographs . . . create a poignant visual chronicle of our times. The images here, many of which are seared into our collective consciousness, include raising the flag at Iwo Jima, a young Vietnamese girl fleeing her village, her body burned by napalm, and the collapse of the World Trade towers." (Publisher's note)

Includes index

Cronkite, Walter, 1916-2009

Cronkite's war; his World War II letters home. Walter

Cronkite IV and Maurice Isserman. National Geographic Society 2013 xxxiv, 318 p.p ill., map (hardcover) $28 **070.4**

    1. Letters 2. World War, 1939-1945 -- Journalists 3. Love-letters -- United States 4. United Press International -- Biography 5. World War, 1939-1945 -- Campaigns -- Europe 6. World War, 1939-1945 -- Personal narratives 7. World War, 1939-1945 -- Aerial operations, American 8. War correspondents -- United States -- Correspondence 9. World War, 1939-1945 -- Journalists -- Correspondence 10. World War, 1939-1945 -- England -- London -- Anecdotes

    ISBN 1426210191; 9781426210198

                         LC 2012045334

This book presents a selection of letters that journalist Walter Cronkite sent to his wife Betsy in Kansas City while he was in London, England reporting on World War II. These letters, "which barely mention any dangers the journalist faced, are mostly from England in the period 1943-45. They detail the daily routines of a journalist in wartime: arranging meetings, writing stories under deadline, dealing with military censors, struggling to travel anywhere, shortages and rationing of everything." (Library Journal)

Includes bibliographical references (pages 313-314) and index.

Friedlander, Edward Jay

Feature writing for newspapers and magazines; the pursuit of excellence. [by] Edward Jay Friedlander, John Lee. 6th ed.; Pearson/A&B 2008 334p pa $86.80 **070.4**

    1. Journalism

    ISBN 0-205-48466-2; 978-0-205-48466-9

                         LC 2007-20885

First published 1988

Through suggestions and examples this guide for the novice writer provides tips from Pulitzer Prize-winning journalists and other magazine and newspaper feature writers.

Fuller, Jack, 1946-2016

What is happening to news; the information explosion and the crisis in journalism. The University of Chicago Press 2010 214p $25 **070.4**

    1. Journalism 2. Information society 3. Journalistic ethics 4. Journalism -- United States

    ISBN 0-226-26898-5; 978-0-226-26898-9; 978-0-226-26899-6 ebook

                         LC 2009039090

"This worthy addition to the journalism bookshelf will stand the test of time." Choice

Includes bibliographical references

Hargreaves, Ian

Journalism; a very short introduction. Ian Hargreaves. 2nd edition Oxford University Press 2014 153 p. illustrations, map pbk $11.95 **070.4**

    1. Journalism 2. Mass media

    ISBN 0199686874; 9780199686872

                         LC 2014937968

First published as Journalism: truth or dare, 2003

Includes bibliographical references (p. 147-148) and index

In this book, author Ian Hargreaves "examines the world of contemporary journalism. He considers how technology has impacted the way major international events are reported, examines the development of online entertainment journalism, and chronicles the impact of the international financial crisis on the industry. . . . [M]ajor issues related to reportage, warfare, celebrity culture, privacy, and technology worldwide are closely examined." (Publisher's note)

Ross, Lillian, 1918-2017

Reporting always; writing for The New Yorker. Lillian Ross; foreword by David Remnick. Scribner 2015 320 p. illustrations (hardback) $27 **070.4**

    1. Journalism 2. Women journalists

    ISBN 1501116002; 9781501116001; 9781501116018

LC 2015013297

This book "collects a wide range of [author] Lillian Ross's New Yorker articles and 'Talk of the Town' pieces spanning sixty years, bringing readers into Robin Williams's living room; Harry Winston's office; the afterschool hangouts of Manhattan private-school children; the hotel rooms of Ernest Hemingway, John Huston, and Charlie Chaplin; onto the tennis court with John McEnroe; and into the lives of many other famous and not-so-famous characters." (Publisher's note)

"Readable and rewarding and, though more than a touch old-fashioned, full of exemplary reporting." Kirkus

Schieffer, Bob, 1937-

Overload; finding the truth in today's deluge of news. Bob Schieffer with H. Andrew Schwartz. Rowman & Littlefield 2017 xii, 204 p.p (cloth: alk. paper) $24.95 **070.4**

    1. Journalism 2. Mass media 3. Press and politics -- United States 4. Journalism -- Political aspects -- United States -- History -- 21st century 5. Mass media -- Political aspects -- United States -- History -- 21st century

    ISBN 9781538107225; 9781538107218

LC 2017021959

"From the explosion of fake news to the challenges of the 24 hour news cycle, legendary journalist Bob Schieffer examines political journalism today and those who practice it. Based on interviews with over 40 media leaders, Schieffer provides an inside look at the changing role of media and asks whether today's citizens are more informed or just overwhelmed." (Publisher's note)

"Succinct, savvy, and shrewd, this read-in-one-seating treatise on the Fourth Estate provides a crucial tool for critical analysis." Booklist

Spillman, Rob

All Tomorrow's Parties; Rob Spillman. Grove Press 2016 400 p. $25 **070.4**

    1. Arts 2. Berlin (Germany)

    ISBN 0802124836; 9780802124838

In this memoir, author Rob Spillman tells how "after an unsettled youth moving between divorced parents in disparate cities, Spillman would eventually find his way into the literary world of New York City, only to abandon it to return to Berlin just months after the Wall came down. Twenty-five and newly married, Spillman and his wife . . . moved to the anarchic streets of East Berlin in search of the bohemian lifestyle of their idols. But Spillman soon discovered he was chasing . . . a place, or person, to call home." (Publisher's note)

"Musically and culturally astute, this well-structured book is a delightful coming-of-age story couched within a travel narrative that deftly evokes one of the major historical moments of the 20th century. A richly detailed and always engaging memoir on artistic discovery." Kirkus

Tobin, James

Reporting America at war; an oral history. compiled by Michelle Ferrari with commentary by James Tobin. Hyperion 2003 241p il $23.95 **070.4**

    1. War 2. Reporters and reporting

    ISBN 1-401-30072-3

LC 2003-49966

"Beginning with Edward R. Morrow's live reports during the Lon-don blitz and ending with an epilogue on the second war in Iraq, this oral history contains transcripts of interviews with 11 top correspondents. Murrow is one of three deceased reporters included (the others are Martha Gellhorn and Homer Bigart), along with Walter Cronkite, Andy Rooney, Frank Gibney, Malcolm Browne, David Halberstam, Morley Safer, Ward Just, Gloria Emerson, Chris Hedges and Christiane Amanpour. . . . Tobin's introductions and transitional and informational interpolations within the transcripts hold this informative volume together." Publ Wkly

Includes bibliographical references

070.444 Miscellaneous information, advice, amusement

Havrilesky, Heather

How to be a person in the world; ask Polly's guide through the paradoxes of modern life. Heather Havrilesky. Doubleday 2016 272 p. illustrations (hardcover) $24.95 **070.444**

    1. Self-realization 2. Self-actualization (Psychology)

    ISBN 9780385540391

LC 2015023592

This book, by Heather Havrilesky, offers "a collection of brand new, impassioned, and inspiring letters by the author of the popular advice column Ask Polly, featured weekly on 'New York Magazine''s The Cut. Should you quit your day job to follow your dreams? How do you rein in an overbearing mother? Will you ever stop dating wishy-washy, noncommittal guys? Should you put off having a baby for your career?" (Publisher's note)

"Funny, frank advice for people searching for solutions to a myriad of relationship issues." Kirkus

070.449 Journalism --Specific subjects

Lascher, Bill

Eve of a Hundred Midnights; The Star-crossed Love Story of Two Wwii Correspondents and Their Epic Escape Across the Pacific. by Bill Lascher. HarperCollins 2016 288 p. illustrations $26.99 **070.449**

    1. Journalists 2. Married people 3. World War, 1939-1945 -- Journalists

    ISBN 0062375202; 9780062375209

LC 2015046489

This book, by Bill Lascher, is the "true story of two married journalists on an island-hopping run for their lives across the Pacific after the Fall of Manila during World War II. . . . The couple had worked in China as members of a tight community of foreign correspondents with close ties to Chinese leaders; if captured by invading Japanese troops, they were certain to be executed." (Publisher's note)

"From interviews and archival documents, Lascher creates a seamless narrative of daring and dedication." Kirkus

Includes bibliographical references (pages 382-398) and index.

Ryan, Bob

Scribe; my life in sports. Bob Ryan. Bloomsbury Press 2014 336 p. 16 plates; color illustrations (alk. paper) $27 **070.449**

    1. Sports journalism 2. Reporters and reporting 3. Sportswriters -- United States -- Biography

    ISBN 1620405067; 9781620405062

LC 2014012348

In this memoir, author Bob Ryan discusses his career in sports journalism. "As a young man, he became sports editor of his high school paper-and at age twenty-three, a year into his Boston Globe experience, he was handed the Boston Celtics beat. 'Scribe' reveals the people behind the stories, as only Bob Ryan can, from the NBA to eleven Olympics to his surprising favorite sport to cover-golf-and much more." (Publisher's note)

"This thoroughly engaging book is recommended to all sports enthusiasts, especially readers interested in Boston-area teams." LJ

070.49   Pictorial journalism

Ritchin, Fred

Magnum Photobook; The Catalogue Raisonne. Carole Naggar; Fred Ritchin. Phaidon Inc Ltd 2016 272 p. illustrations (some color) $79.95   **070.49**
 1. Artistic photography 2. Documentary photography
 ISBN 0714872113; 9780714872117
This book, by Carole Naggar and Fred Ritchin, "brings Magnum's history alive through the genre of the photobook, an essential vehicle for photographers to share their work. Its pages include unpublished behind-the-scenes material, together with ephemera from the photographers' archives about the making of their books. . . . This book explores the evolution of the photobook, as well as the important role that Magnum has played in the history of documentary photography." (Publisher's note)

"A valuable reference that will inform and delight those interested in photojournalism, as well as book and graphic design." LJ
Includes bibliographical references and index.

070.5   Publishing

★ **American** book trade directory. Information Today various pagings   **070.5**
 1. Book industry 2. Book collecting 3. Reference books 4. Publishers and publishing -- Directories
Annual. First published 1915 by Bowker with title: American book trade manual

"Includes lists of booksellers, wholesalers, and publishers in the United States, with related information on the book trade in Canada, the United Kingdom, and Ireland. Bookstores are arranged under state and city with speciality of each noted. Separate lists include exporters, importers, and dealers in foreign books. Index of retailers and wholesalers in the United States and Canada." Ref Sources for Small & Medium-sized LIbr. 6th edition

Germano, William P.

Getting it published; a guide for scholars and anyone else serious about serious books. William Germano. 3rd edition University of Chicago Press 2016 253 p. pbk $20   **070.5**
 1. Authors and publishers 2. Publishers and publishing
 ISBN 022628140X; 9780226281407
                                              LC 2015038629
"Today there are more ways to publish than ever, more challenges to traditional publishing, and more room for confusion among authors trying to understand their options. This extensively revised third edition brings Germano's classic up to date, charting a path across today's publishing landscape while showing why book publication rightly remains the highest aspiration for authors with big ideas and consequential arguments." (Publisher's note)
Includes bibliographical references and index

Guide to literary agents. Writer's Digest Bks.   **070.5**
 1. Authors and publishers -- Directories
Annual. Supersedes in part Guide to literary agents & art/photo reps
"An invaluable tool for writers in search of an agent, this guide is indexed by agency, agent, format, subject, and geographic location. Submission procedures, fees, contracts and what to ask a prospective agent are covered." Libr J

Herman, Jeff

Jeff Herman's guide to book publishers, editors, & literary agents. Writer Bks.   **070.5**
 1. Authors and publishers 2. Publishers and publishing
Annual. First published 1992 by Prima Pub. with title: Insider's guide to book editors, publishers, and literary agents. Variant title: Writer's guide to book editors, publishers, and literary agents

Herman provides "portraits of more than 100 agents plus tips on writing query letters and nonfiction book proposals, dealing with rejections, ghostwriting, and self-publishing. With an excellent glossary and sample author-agent and collaboration agreements." Libr J

Literary market place. Bowker 2v $399   **070.5**
 1. Reference books 2. Publishers and publishing -- Directories
Annual. First published 1940. In 1972 absorbed Names & numbers. Subtitle varies

"Directory of U.S. and Canadian book publishers and related businesses such as book clubs, literary agents, translators, and manufacturers. Gives names of executives and addresses, telephone numbers, and fields of specialization for each publishing company." N Y Public Libr Book of How & Where to Look It Up

No shelf required 2; use and management of electronic books. edited by Sue Polanka. American Library Association 2012 xiv, 254 p.p ill. (alk. paper) $65   **070.5**
 1. Electronic books 2. Library resources 3. Electronic publishing 4. Libraries and electronic publishing 5. Libraries -- Special collections -- Electronic books
 ISBN 0838911455; 9780838911457
                                              LC 2011040497
This book "brings together a variety of professionals to share their expertise about e-books with librarians and publishers. Providing forward-thinking ideas while remaining grounded in practical information that can be implemented in all kinds of libraries, the topics explored include an introduction to e-books . . . and an overview of their history and development . . . e-book technology . . . why e-books are good for learning, and how librarians can market them." (Publisher's note)
Includes bibliographical references and index

Pettegree, Andrew

The **book** in the Renaissance. Yale University Press 2010 421p il $40   **070.5**
 1. Printing 2. Renaissance 3. Book industry 4. Reformation -- Europe 5. Europe -- History -- 1492-1789 6. Books -- Europe -- History -- 1400-1600 7. Printing -- Europe -- History -- 16th century 8. Book industries and trade -- Europe -- History -- 16th century
 ISBN 978-0-300-11009-8; 0-300-11009-X
                                              LC 2009-26513
The author's "treatment is both thorough and engaging, ably situating the social, economic, and historical within the stories of individuals involved." Libr J
Includes bibliographical references

Publishers, distributors & wholesalers of the United States. Bowker 2v **070.5**
1. Reference books 2. Publishers and publishing -- Directories
Annual. First published 1979 with title: Publishers and distributors of the United States

This directory provides information on "more than 150,000 U.S. publishers, wholesalers, distributors, software firms, audiocassette producers, museum and association imprints, and trade organizations that publish." Publisher's note

Seaver, Richard

The **tender** hour of twilight; Paris in the '50s, New York in the '60s: a memoir of publishing's golden age. Richard Seaver; edited by Jeannette Seaver. Farrar, Straus and Giroux 2012 xxi, 457 p.p (alk. paper) $35 **070.5**
1. Translators -- United States -- Biography 2. Book editors -- United States -- Biography 3. Publishers and publishing -- United States -- Biography
ISBN 0374273782; 9780374273781

LC 2011024951

"[T]he first part of . . . [Richard Seaver's] memoir is about Paris in the Fifties and the adventure of publishing [Samuel] Beckett among others, [while] the second part is about Grove Press in New York, where he became one of the early editors of an enterprise financed and led by Barney Rosset. It's a story of Grove's long battles with censorship, with which Seaver was closely involved. . . . [One] censorship problem was encountered with Henry Miller's 'Tropic of Cancer,' about which Rosset had written an essay and which was banned in almost every country in the world. . . . [In addition,] Seaver's memoir testifies to Beckett's patience in dealing with collaborators, even if he held them to the highest standards." (New York Review of Books)

Shepard, Stephen B.

Deadlines and disruption; the turbulent road from print to digital. by Stephen Shepard. McGraw-Hill 2012 304 p. (hardback) $28 **070.5**
1. Journalism 2. Online journalism 3. Journalism -- Technological innovations 4. Newspaper publishing -- Technological innovations
ISBN 0071802649; 9780071802642

LC 2012016577

This book is "[Stephen B.] Shepard's story of his life in print journalism, and a . . . look at the way journalism is evolving due to electronic media, social networking, and the ability of anyone with a computer and an opinion to make him- or herself heard. Is journalism dying? Not according to Shepard. It's changing, yes, but in some respects it's also improving." (Booklist)

Suber, Peter

Open access; Peter Suber. MIT Press 2012 xii, 242 p.p (paperback) $12.95 **070.5**
1. Open access publishing
ISBN 0262517639; 9780262517638

LC 2011038297

This book, by Peter Suber, is part of the "MIT Press Essential Knowledge" series. "The Internet lets us share perfect copies of our work with a worldwide audience at virtually no cost. . . . In this concise introduction, . . . Suber tells us what open access is and isn't, how it benefits authors and readers of research, how we pay for it, how it avoids copyright problems, how it has moved from the periphery to the mainstream, and what its future may hold." Publisher's note

Includes bibliographical references (p. [177]-221) and index

070.92   Biography regardless of area, region, place

Bunnell, David Hugh

Good Friday on the Rez; a Pine Ridge odyssey. David Hugh Bunnell. St. Martin's Press 2017 288 p. $26.99 **070.92**
1. Travel writing 2. Autobiographies 3. Native Americans
ISBN 1250112532; 9781250112538

LC 2016052536

This book "introduces readers to places and people that author, writer, and entrepreneur David Bunnell encounters during his one day, 280-mile road trip from his boyhood Nebraska hometown to the Pine Ridge Indian Reservation to visit his longtime friend, Vernell White Thunder, a full-blooded Oglala Lakota, descendant of a long line of prominent chiefs and medicine men." (Publisher's note)

"This informative account should be placed alongside all books on Native American history and culture. It deserves to be read by all, particularly in light of the recent Dakota Access Pipeline protests." LJ

Kalb, Marvin

★ The **year** I was Peter the Great; 1956- Kruschev, Stalin's ghost, and a young American in Russia. Marvin Kalb. Brookings Institution Press 2017 xiv, 290 p.p $24.99 **070.92**
1. Russia -- History -- 1953-1991 2. Soviet Union -- History -- 1953-1985
ISBN 0815731612; 9780815731610

This book, by Marvin Kalb, is "a chronicle of the year that changed Soviet Russia. . . . 1956 was an extraordinary year in modern Russian history. It was called 'the year of the thaw'—a time when Stalin's dark legacy of dictatorship died in February only to be reborn later that December. This historic arc from rising hope to crushing despair opened with a speech by Nikita Khrushchev, then the unpredictable leader of the Soviet Union." (Publisher's note)

Rusbridger, Alan

Breaking news; the remaking of journalism and why it matters now. Alan Rusbridger. Farrar, Straus & Giroux 2018 384 p. $28 **070.92**
1. Journalism 2. Online journalism
ISBN 0374279624; 9780374279622

This book, by Alan Rusbridger, presents "an urgent account of the [Internet journalism] revolution that has upended the news business. . . . Rusbridger demonstrates how these decisive shifts have occurred, and what they mean for the future of democracy. In the twenty years he spent editing 'The Guardian,' Rusbridger managed the transformation of the progressive British daily into the most visited serious English-language newspaper site in the world." (Publisher's note)

"With social media and myriad blogs, 'vertical' reporting (from newspaper to reader) is being eclipsed by 'horizontal' communications that allow unverified and often wild stories to be accepted and shared in seconds. Rusbridger eloquently describes the dangers of this era." Booklist

071   Geographic treatment of journalism and newspapers

Baker, Nicholson

The **World** on Sunday; graphic art in Joseph Pulitzer's newspaper (1898-1911) [by] Nicholson Baker and Margaret Brentano. Bulfinch Press 2005 131p il $50 **071**
1. New York world (Newspaper)
ISBN 0-8212-6193-2

LC 2005-00224

This book collects 85 examples of graphic art from the Sunday edition of the New York World

This volume "offers a kaleidoscopic tour through, an ebullient moment in American history when the country was emerging from the shadowy gaslight age and bursting into the glare of the modern. It is a big, lush, coffee-table-size book suffused with gaiety and the optimism of an age blissfully unaware of darknesses soon to come. . . . The World on Sunday is the result of a heroic piece of cultural preservation." N Y Rev Books

Boynton, Robert S.

The **New** new journalism; conversations with America's best nonfiction writers on their craft. [edited and with an introduction by] Robert S. Boynton. Vintage Books 2005 xxxiv, 456p pa $13.95 **071**

1. Journalism

ISBN 1-400-03356-X; 9781435292185; 9780307429049

LC 2004-57161

The author "offers interviews with 19 writers who detail how and why they produce their work. . . . A fascinating book that makes the reader want to go out and get every book the writers have written as well as those mentioned as sources of inspiration." Booklist

Includes bibliographical references

Burns, Eric

Infamous scribblers; the founding fathers and the rowdy beginnings of American journalism. Public Affairs 2006 467p hardcover o.p. pa $15.95 **071**

1. Journalism 2. Newspapers -- United States

ISBN 978-1-58648-334-0; 1-58648-334-X; 978-1-58648-428-6 pa; 1-58648-428-1 pa

LC 2005-53542

"From the sniping feuds among Boston's first papers to sex scandals involving Alexander Hamilton and Thomas Jefferson, the snappy patter gives clear indication of how much Burns . . . relishes telling his story." Publ Wkly

Includes bibliographical references

Campbell, W. Joseph

Getting it wrong; ten of the greatest misreported stories in American journalism. University of California Press 2010 269p il $60; pa $24.95 **071**

1. Journalistic ethics 2. Journalism -- Objectivity

ISBN 0-520-25566-6; 0-520-26209-3 pa; 978-0-520-25566-1; 978-0-520-26209-6 pa

LC 2009047705

This "provocative book provides a wealth of case studies in the complexity of journalism and history. It reinforces the truism that journalists, authors and book reviewers alike should all be more skeptical—and definitely more humble." Am Journalism Rev

Includes bibliographical references

Carpini, Michael X. Delli

After broadcast news; media regimes, democracy, and the new information environment. Bruce A. Williams, Michael X. Delli Carpini. Cambridge University Press 2011 xii, 361 p.p (paperback) $32.99 **071**

1. Mass media 2. Online journalism 3. Broadcast journalism 4. Democracy -- United States 5. Press and politics -- United States 6. Mass media -- Political aspects -- United States 7. Popular culture -- Political aspects -- United States 8. Broadcast journalism -- Political aspects -- United States

ISBN 0521279836; 9780521279833; 9781107010314

LC 2011009191

This book posits that the "new media environment has challenged the role of professional journalists as the primary source of politically relevant information" and "puts this challenge into historical context, arguing that it is the latest of several critical moments, driven by economic, political, cultural, and technological changes, in which the relationship among citizens, political elites, and the media has been contested." (Publisher's note)

Includes bibliographical references and index.

Cullen, Art

Storm Lake; a chronicle of change, resilience, and hope from a heartland newspaper. Art Cullen. Viking 2018 336 p. $28 **071.77**

1. Newspapers -- United States -- History 2. Journalism -- Iowa -- Storm Lake -- History 3. Storm Lake times -- History 4. American newspapers -- Iowa -- Storm Lake -- History

ISBN 9780525558873

LC 2018025006

In this book, author Art Cullen "describes how the rural prairies have changed dramatically over his career, as seen from the vantage point of a farming and meatpacking town of 15,000 in Northwest Iowa. Politics, agriculture, the environment, and immigration are all themes in 'Storm Lake,' a chronicle of a resilient newspaper, as much a survivor as its town." (Publisher's note)

Kovach, Bill

The **elements** of journalism; Bill Kovach and Tom Rosenstiel. Three Rivers Press 2014 332 p. (pbk.) $15 **071**

1. Journalistic ethics 2. Journalism -- United States

ISBN 0804136785; 9780804136785

LC 2013049716

This book on journalism, by Bill Kovach and Tom Rosenstiel, is "[r]evised and updated with a new preface and material on the rise of social media, the challenges facing printed news, and how journalism can fulfill its purpose in the digital age." (Publisher's note)

"Kovach and Rosenstiel have issued a clarion call to their colleagues, and they hope that all journalists, editors and owners of news organizations will incorporate the principles of the profession as they've outlined them into their everyday work. However, the authors offer no specific suggestions as to how to enact these principles in a wide-reaching or systematic manner." Pub Wkly

Includes bibiographical references and index

Michaeli, Ethan

★ The **defender**; how the legendary black newspaper changed America: from the age of the Pullman porters to the age of Obama. Ethan Michaeli. Houghton Mifflin Harcourt 2016 656 p. (hardback) $32 **071**

1. Chicago (Ill.) -- History 2. African American newspapers 3. Newspapers -- United States 4. African Americans -- Chicago (Ill.) 5. Chicago defender -- History 6. African Americans -- Illinois -- Chicago -- Newspapers 7. African American press -- Illinois -- Chicago -- History 8. African American newspapers -- Illinois -- Chicago -- History

ISBN 0547560699; 9780547560694

LC 2015017437

This book, by Ethan Michaeli, presents the history of the newspaper the "Chicago Defender." "Drawing on dozens of interviews and extensive archival research, . . . Michaeli constructs a revelatory narrative of race in America and brings to life the reporters who braved lynch mobs and policemen's clubs to do their jobs, from the age of Teddy Roosevelt to the age of Barack Obama." (Publisher's note)

"Engagingly written and copiously sourced, Michaeli's stimulating read treating central personalities and an iconic institution offers general readers and scholars alike a focused look back at 20th-century battles against America's pervasive racism." LJ

Ostertag, Bob

   People's movements, people's press; the journalism of social justice movements. Beacon Press 2006 232p il $23.95 **071**
   1. Social movements 2. Alternative press
   ISBN 0-8070-6164-6; 978-0-8070-6164-0

LC 2005-31735

"Readers interested in the intersection of the media and social movements will appreciate this insightful book." Booklist

   Includes bibliographical references

   Written into history; Pulitzer Prize reporting of the twentieth century from the New York times. edited and with an introduction by Anthony Lewis. Times Bks. 2001 xxv, 355p hardcover o.p. pa $17 **071**
   1. Journalism 2. Pulitzer Prizes
   ISBN 0-8050-6849-X; 0-8050-7178-4 pa

LC 2001-35555

"For anyone interested in recent history or journalism at its best, this book will prove worthwhile." Publ Wkly

079.675 Journalism and newspapers -- Democratic Republic of the Congo, Rwanda, Burundi

Sundaram, Anjan

   Bad news; last journalists in a dictatorship. by Anjan Sundaram. Doubleday 2015 208 p. illustrations (ebook) $50.85; (hardcover) $25.95 **079.675**
   1. Journalists -- Rwanda 2. Rwanda -- Politics and government 3. Journalism -- Study and teaching -- Rwanda
   ISBN 9780385539579; 9780385539562; 9781101872154

LC 2015005625

This book, by Anjan Sundaram, is the story of "Sundaram's time running a journalist's training program out of Kigali, the capital city of . . . Rwanda. President Kagame's regime . . . is often held up as a beacon for progress and modernity in Central Africa. . . . Lurking underneath this shining vision of a modern, orderly state, however, is the powerful climate of fear springing from the government's brutal treatment of any voice of dissent." (Publisher's note)

"A chilling account of reporters in danger that heightens awareness of the importance of a free press." Kirkus

080 General collections

Adler, Mortimer J.

   How to think about the great ideas; from the great books of Western civilization. {by} Mortimer J. Adler; edited by Max Weismann. Open Court 2000 xxiv, 530p pa $24.95 **080**
   1. Great books of the Western world
   ISBN 0-8126-9412-0

LC 99-45251

This volume contains the transcripts of 52 half-hour segments of Adler's 1953-1954 television program The great ideas

"The book showcases Adler's ideas about all the big categories— truth, beauty, freedom, love, sex, art, justice, rationality, humankind's

nature, Darwinism, government." Publ Wkly

McPhee, John, 1931-

   ★ The **patch**; John McPhee. Farrar, Straus & Giroux 2018 256 p. (hardcover) $26 **080**
   1. American essays
   ISBN 9780374229481

LC 2018007631

This collection of essays, by John McPhee, "is divided into two parts. Part 1 . . . consists of pieces on fishing, football, golf, and lacrosse--from fly casting for chain pickerel in fall in New Hampshire to walking the linksland of St. Andrews at an Open Championship. Part 2 . . . is a montage of fragments of varying length from pieces done across the years that have never appeared in book form--occasional pieces, . . . reminiscences, and short items in various magazines." (Publisher's note)

"McPhee delights in cracking open subjects, both ordinary and esoteric, and making them accessible to the layperson in works that testify to his virtuosity as one of the greatest living American essayists." Publishers' Weekly

081 General collections in specific languages and language families

Pauling, Linus C.

   Linus Pauling in his own words; selections from his writings, speeches, and interviews. edited by Barbara Marinacci; introduction by Linus Pauling. Simon & Schuster 1995 320p hardcover o.p. pa $20 **081**
   1. Chemists 2. College teachers 3. Writers on science 4. Nobel laureates for peace 5. Nobel laureates for chemistry
   ISBN 0-6848-1387-4 ps

LC 95-31123

This book "attempts to follow the life and career of Dr. Pauling through his own writings, interspersed with narrative by the editor. The book succeeds wonderfully. Linus Pauling is unique among modern scientists, both for winning two Nobel Prizes and for his political and social views. Through his writings, the breadth and depth of his work become clear to the reader." Sci Books Films

   Includes bibliographical references

082 General collections in English

   Oxford dictionary of quotations; edited by Elizabeth Knowles. Oxford University Press 2014 xxvii, 1126 p.p $50 **082**
   1. Quotations 2. Quotations, English -- Dictionaries 3. Quotations -- Translations into English
   ISBN 0199668701; 9780199668700

LC 2014930368

This book, edited by Elizabeth Knowles, offers a dictionary of quotations. "Drawing on Oxford's unrivalled dictionary research program and unique language monitoring, over 700 new quotations have been added to this eighth edition from authors ranging from St Joan of Arc and Coco Chanel to Albrecht Durer and Thomas Jefferson." (Publisher's note)

   Dictionary of quotations

   ★ The **Yale** book of quotations; edited by Fred R. Shapiro; foreword by Joseph Epstein. Yale University Press 2006 1104p $50 **082**
   1. Quotations
   ISBN 978-0-300-10798-2; 0-300-10798-6

LC 2006-12317

The more than 12,000 "range over literature, history, popular culture, sports, computers, science, politics, law, and the social sciences, and although American quotations are emphasized, the book's scope is global. The authors represented are as diverse as William Shakespeare, John Lennon, Jack Dempsey, both Presidents Bush, J.K. Rowling, Rita Mae Brown, Confucius, Warren Buffet, and Deng Xiaoping. The entries are arranged by author, then chronologically and alphabetically by source title within the same year. A significant effort was made to trace the first published occurrence of a quotation, and whenever possible the wording is taken from the original source. . . . Electronic products such as the Times Digital Archive, JSTOR, Proquest Historical Newspapers and American Periodical Series, LexisNexis, Newspaperarchive.com, Questia, Eighteenth Century Collections Online, and Literature Online were all used." Libr J

091   Manuscripts

De Hamel, Christopher
★ **Meetings** with remarkable manuscripts; twelve journeys into the medieval world. Christopher de Hamel. Penguin Press 2017 vii, 632 p.p illustrations (some color) (hardcover) $45   **091**
1. Manuscripts 2. Illumination of books and manuscripts 3. Manuscripts, European 4. Manuscripts, Medieval 5. Illumination of books and manuscripts, Medieval
ISBN 1594206112; 9781594206115; 9780698163386

LC 2017031392

This book, by Christopher de Hamel, examines the "twelve illuminated manuscripts from the medieval period. . . . De Hamel . . . traces the . . . journeys which these . . . artifacts have made through time, shows us how they have been copied, who has owned them or lusted after them . . . , how they have been embroiled in politics, how they have been regarded as objects of supreme beauty and as symbols of national identity." (Publisher's note)
"A rare, erudite, and delightfully entertaining history." Kirkus
Includes bibliographical references and index.

098   Prohibited works, forgeries, hoaxes

Bosmajian, Haig A.
★ **Burning** books; [by] Haig Bosmajian. McFarland 2006 233p $39.95   **098**
1. Book burning
ISBN 0-7864-2208-4; 978-0-7864-2208-1

LC 2005-35201

"This work provides a detailed account of book burning worldwide over the past 2000 years. The book burners are identified, along with the works they deliberately set aflame." Publisher's note
Includes bibliographical references

100   PHILOSOPHY

100   Philosophy, parapsychology and occultism, psychology

Blackburn, Simon, 1944-
Think: a compelling introduction to philosophy. Oxford

Univ. Press 1999 312p $25   **100**
1. Philosophy
ISBN 0-19-210024-6

LC 00-265266

The author explores such areas as knowledge, mind, free will, identity, God, goodness and justice. "His method is to introduce what other philosophers—primarily Plato, Descartes, Locke, Berkeley, Leibniz, Hume, and Kant—have had to say about these themes. . . . Readers new to the subject could very well be captivated." Libr J
Includes bibliographical references

Ferry, Luc
A **brief** history of thought; Luc Ferry; translated by Theo Cuffe. HarperPerennial 2012 304p.   **100**
1. Philosophy 2. Christianity 3. Postmodernism 4. Existentialism
ISBN 9780062074249

This book "offers a thematic introduction to continental philosophy constructed around the biggest questions: how can we lead a meaningful life knowing that we will die but without the consolation of religion? . . . The author's episodic treatment starts with the Stoic concept of man as a fragment of a harmonious cosmos, moves on to Descartes, Rousseau, and Kant and their establishment of philosophy based on reason and individual freedom, climaxes with Nietzsche's demolition of modernist certitudes-a stance he finds both thrilling and unsatisfying--and ponders the abiding need to embrace a world we must ultimately lose." (Publishers Weekly)

Gutting, Gary
What philosophy can do; Gary Gutting. W W Norton & Co Inc 2015 320 p. (hardcover) $27.95   **100**
1. Philosophy 2. Social conditions
ISBN 0393242277; 9780393242270

LC 2015013783

In this book, author Gary Gutting presents his "approach to some of the most divisive [philosophical] issues on the table today. He scrutinizes our relationship to work and freedom in capitalism; our modern understanding of happiness and the good life; the value of liberal arts education and the humanities; the role of science and politics in shaping public policy today; and the value of art and popular culture." (Publisher's note)
"While Gutting applies complex philosophical and logical principles in his essays, he does so in an accessible way. The range of essays makes this work appealing to anyone with an interest in philosophy." LJ
Includes bibliographical references and index

Russell, Bertrand
★ The **problems** of philosophy. Hackett Pub. Co 1990 167p (Hackett classics) $27.95; pa $8.95   **100**
1. Philosophy
ISBN 978-0-87220-099-9; 0-87220-099-X; 978-0-87220-098-2 pa; 0-87220-098-1 pa

LC 90-81389

First published 1912 by Holt
The author discusses: appearance and reality, matter, idealism, theories of knowledge, universals, intuition, and truth
"The work is concise, free from technical terms and perfectly clear to the general reader with no prior knowledge of the subject." Booklist
Includes bibliographical references

103 Dictionaries, encyclopedias, concordances of philosophy

Blackburn, Simon, 1944-

The **Oxford** dictionary of philosophy; 2nd ed.; Oxford University Press 2005 407p il $45   **103**
1. Reference books 2. Philosophy -- Dictionaries
ISBN 0-19-861014-9; 978-0-19-861014-4

LC 2006-271895
First published 1994
This dictionary "contains over 2,500 entries, including biographies of nearly 500 influential philosophers. The dictionary provides . . . coverage of not only Western philosophical traditions, but also themes from Chinese, Indian, Islamic, and Jewish philosophy." Publisher's note
Includes bibliographical references

★ The **Cambridge** dictionary of philosophy; General editor Robert Audi. 3rd edition Cambridge University Press 2015 1161 p hardcover $102.95   **103**
1. Reference books 2. Philosophy -- Dictionaries
ISBN 9781107643796; 9781107015050

LC 2014021783
"The third edition of this authoritative volume . . . captures the dynamic nature of the field by substantially expanding coverage. The scope now includes some 500 new entries in addition to increased coverage of some of the more rapidly growing fields. Entries on ethics, cognitive science, and the philosophy of mind, for example, are substantially longer and reflect contemporary developments." (Choice Reviews)

★ The **Oxford** companion to philosophy; edited by Ted Honderich. 2nd ed., new ed; Oxford University Press 2005 1056p il $60   **103**
1. Reference books 2. Philosophy -- Encyclopedias
ISBN 0-19-926479-1

LC 2005-275452
First published 1995
"Including more than 2200 alphabetically arranged entries from nearly 300 contributors, . . . [this book] provides an encyclopedic view of philosophy's past and present, its ideas, disputes (the editor himself contributes an article on unlikely philosophical propositions), and key figures, living and dead. . . . This title makes an excellent companion for standard multivolume subject encyclopedias." SLJ
Includes bibliographical references

109 History and collected biography

Durant, William James

★ The **story** of philosophy; the lives and opinions of the great philosophers. by Will Durant. [2nd ed]; Simon & Schuster 1933 412p hardcover o.p. pa $15   **109**
1. Poets 2. Authors 3. Educators 4. Novelists 5. Dramatists 6. Historians 7. Philosophers 8. Psychologists 9. Mathematicians 10. Essayists 11. Logicians 12. Literary critics 13. Nonfiction writers 14. Writers on science 15. Writers on religion 16. Philosophy -- History 17. Nobel laureates for literature
ISBN 0-671-69500-2; 0-671-20159-X pa
First published 1926
A selective account of western thinkers from Socrates and Kant to Schopenhauer and Dewey.
Includes bibliographical references

Russell, Bertrand

A **history** of Western philosophy; and its connection with political and social circumstances from the earliest times to the present day. Simon & Schuster 1945 xxiii, 895p hardcover o.p. pa $25   **109**
1. Saints 2. Stoics 3. Authors 4. Bishops 5. Novelists 6. Statesmen 7. Historians 8. Franciscans 9. Theologians 10. Philosophers 11. Mathematicians 12. Catholic Church 13. Essayists 14. Memoirists 15. Writers on law 16. Science -- History 17. Writers on science 18. Writers on politics 19. Writers on religion 20. Rome -- Civilization 21. Philosophy -- History 22. Sparta (Extinct city) 23. Greece -- Civilization 24. Nobel laureates for literature 25. Political and social philosophers
ISBN 0-671-31400-9; 0-671-20158-1 pa
Originally designed and partly delivered as lectures at the Barnes Foundation in Pennsylvania
"My purpose is to exhibit philosophy as an integral part of social and political life; not as the isolated speculations of remarkable individuals." Preface

World philosophers and their works; editor, John K. Roth; managing editor, Christina J. Moose; project editor, Rowena Wildin. Salem Press 2000 3v il set $331   **109**
1. Philosophers
ISBN 0-89356-878-3

LC 99-55143
The editor "presents substantial entries that for 226 philosophers give brief biographies, justify the inclusion of each thinker, list their most important works, analyze their lifework, and locate them within the context of philosophy." Choice
Includes bibliographical references

111 Ontology

Barrow, John D.

The **book** of nothing; vacuums, voids, and the latest ideas about the origins of the universe. Pantheon Bks. 2001 361p il hardcover o.p. pa $15   **111**
1. Zero (The number) 2. Science -- History
ISBN 0-375-72609-8 pa

LC 00-58894
This volume traces the concept of nothing "from a Babylonian place holder, a Mayan decoration in the empty space where no number fell and an Indian dot signifying all the current aspects of zero, to one of the most essential elements in mathematics, physics and cosmology." Publ Wkly

The **infinite** book; a short guide to the boundless, timeless, and endless. Pantheon Books 2005 328p il $26   **111**
1. Infinite
ISBN 0-375-42227-7

LC 2004-60206
First published 2004 in the United Kingdom
The author "approaches the subject [of infinity] from the viewpoints of mathematics, physics, and scientific cosmology and also delves into philosophers' and theologians' reflections concerning infinity. . . . Well suited to a general audience, this book requires no specialized knowledge of mathematics or science." Libr J
Includes bibliographical references

Eco, Umberto

History of beauty; translated by Alastair McEwen. Rizzoli

Int. Pubs. 2004 438p il $40   **111**
1. Aesthetics 2. Arts -- Philosophy
ISBN 0-8478-2646-5
Published in the United Kingdom with title: On beauty: a history of a western idea

The editor "traces the protean subject of beauty in art, literature, philosophy, the mass media, and other humanities from ancient times to the present, setting forth various Western cultural aesthetic ideals ranging from ancient Greek to modern American. . . . This is not a quick, one-time coffee-table read but a nearly flawless presentation of the history of a fascinating and elusive idea that will delight and enlighten general readers as well as scholars." Libr J
Includes bibliographical references

Heidegger, Martin
   ★ **Being** and time; translated by John Macquarrie & Edward Robinson. Harper & Row 1962 589p hardcover o.p. pa $19.99   **111**
1. Ontology 2. Phenomenology
ISBN 0-06-063850-8; 0-06-157559-3 pa
Original German edition, 1927
"All of Heidegger's work revolves around the essential inquiry: what is the nature of being? In his most important book, . . . he distinguishes between two types of being: human existence (Dasein) and nonhuman presence (Vorhandensein)." Reader's Ency. 4th edition
Includes bibliographical references

On ugliness; edited byUmberto Eco; translated by Alastair McEwen. Rizzoli 2007 455p il $45   **111**
1. Aesthetics 2. Arts -- Philosophy
ISBN 978-0-8478-2986-6; 0-8478-2986-3
                   LC 2007-930249
In this "collection of images and written excerpts from ancient times to the present, all woven together with a provocative commentary and translated by Alastair McEwen, . . . [the editor] asks: Is repulsiveness, too, in the eye of the beholder? And what do we learn about that beholder when we delve into his aversions? Selecting stark visual images of gore, deformity, moral turpitude and malice, and quotations from sources ranging from Plato to radical feminists, Eco unfurls a taxonomy of ugliness. As gross-out contests go, it's both absorbing and highbrow." N Y Times Book Rev
Includes bibliographical references

111.85   Beauty

Whitefield-Madrano, Autumn
   Face value; the hidden ways that beauty shapes women's lives. Autumn Whitefield-Madrano. Simon & Schuster 2016 288 p. (hardcover) $25   **111.85**
1. Aesthetics 2. Body image 3. Self-perception 4. Personal appearance 5. Women -- Psychology 6. Body image in women 7. Appearance (Philosophy) 8. Self-perception in women 9. Aesthetics -- Social aspects 10. Beauty, Personal -- Social aspects 11. Feminine beauty (Aesthetics) -- Social aspects
ISBN 9781476754000; 9781476754048
                   LC 2015038730
In this book, "journalist Autumn Whitefield-Madrano thoughtfully examines the relationship between appearance and science, social media, sex, friendship, language, and advertising to show how beauty actually affects us day to day. Through meticulous research and interviews with dozens of women across all walks of life, she reveals surprising

findings." (Publisher's note)
"This is a valuable addition to contemporary feminist writing, providing much-needed perspective to a pervasive issue that young women and staunch feminists will glean much from, whether they agree with the author's findings or not." LJ
Includes bibliographical references (pages 233-266) and index.

113   Cosmology (Philosophy of nature)

Holt, Jim
   Why does the world exist? an existential detective story. Jim Holt. 1st ed. Liveright Pub. Corp. 2012 vi, 309 p.p ill. (hardcover) $27.95   **113**
1. Cosmology
ISBN 0871404095; 9780871404091; 9780871403599
                   LC 2012015177
It was the author's intent to answer the question "'why is there something rather than nothing?'" Author Jim Holt explores "the claims of evolutionary biology, neuropsychology, theoretical physics, natural religion theology, contemporary mysticism, and militant atheism. . . . He interviews several philosophers and scientists currently engaged in answering the question." (Library Journal)
Includes bibliographical references and index.

Teilhard de Chardin, Pierre
   ★ The **phenomenon** of man; with an introduction by Julian Huxley. Harper & Row 1959 318p hardcover o.p. pa $14.95   **113**
1. Universe 2. Evolution 3. Human beings
ISBN 0-06-090495-X pa
Original French edition, 1955; this translation by Bernard Wall
The author integrates scientific findings with the tenets of Christian faith in this study of human evolution and destiny

Wilson, Edward O.
   ★ **In** search of nature. Island Press 1996 214p il $22; pa $15   **113**
1. Human beings 2. Sociobiology 3. Human ecology 4. Philosophy of nature 5. Biological diversity
ISBN 1-55963-215-1; 1-55963-216-X pa
                   LC 96-11226
"Concerned people of all ages should enjoy the reasoning provided by the dedicated scientific writing presented in this attractive book." Sci Books Films
Includes bibliographical references

121   Epistemology (Theory of knowledge)

Blackburn, Simon, 1944-
   On truth; Simon Blackburn. Profile Books 2019 144 p. (pbk.) $12.95   **121**
1. Truth 2. Philosophy
ISBN 9780190867218; 9780190874407
                   LC 2017051643
"In this concise book Simon Blackburn provides an accessible explanation of what truth is and how we might think about it. The first half of the book details several main approaches to how we should think about, and decide, what is true. These are philosophical theories of truth such as the correspondence theory, the coherence theory, deflationism, and others." (Publisher's note)

"Blackburn (Distinguished Research Professor, Univ. of North Carolina at Chapel Hill; Think: A Compelling Introduction to Philosophy) offers an excellent, concise, and relatively accessible introduction to philosophical theories of truth." LJ

Includes bibliographical references and index

Blackburn, Simon, 1944-

★ **Truth**; a guide. Simon Blackburn. Oxford University Press 2005 xxi, 238p $25 **121**
1. Truth
ISBN 0-19-516824-0

LC 2004-19800

This book "traverses a broad terrain, exploring many points of the map of human knowledge and thinkers of all stripes." N Y Times Book Rev

Includes bibliographical references

Dennett, Daniel Clement, 1942-

Intuition Pumps and Other Tools for Thinking; Daniel C. Dennett. W W Norton & Co Inc 2013 512 p. $28.95 **121**
1. Thought experiments 2. Thought and thinking 3. Philosophy -- Miscellanea 4. Thought and thinking -- Miscellanea
ISBN 0393082067; 9780393082067

LC 2013000930

In this book, "opening with . . . [a] tutorial on argumentative strategies from reductio ad absurdum to Occam's Razor to rhetorical questions, [Daniel C.] Dennett expounds his ideas through a series of 'intuition pumps,' his term for the hypothetical scenarios philosophers contrive to explore difficult concepts." These include "conceiving of the body as a robotic survival vehicle for the genes, or the brain as a clueless man trapped in a sealed chamber." (Publishers Weekly)

Includes bibliographical references and index

Hecht, Jennifer Michael

Doubt: a history; the great doubters and their legacy of innovation, from Socrates and Jesus to Thomas Jefferson and Emily Dickinson. HarperSanFrancisco 2003 xxi, 551p il $27.95; pa $16.95 **121**
1. Belief and doubt
ISBN 0-06-009772-8; 0-06-009795-7 pa

LC 2004-266061

The author's "brief but splendid study of the great Renaissance skeptic Montaigne is alone worth the price of the book. Hecht's warm prose, lucid insights, and impeccable research combine for a lively, thoughtful, and first-rate study of a neglected idea." Libr J

Locke, John

An **essay** concerning human understanding; edited by Roger Woolhouse. Penguin Books 1997 xxvii, 784p pa $17 **121**
1. Theory of knowledge 2. Thought and thinking
ISBN 0-14-043482-8

LC 98-175907

This essay first published 1690, deals "with the nature and scope of human knowledge. Its basic premise is the empirical origin of ideas, which can be described as the raw material with which the mind works. Locke's essay contributed greatly to the growth of 18th-century empiricism." Reader's Ency. 4th edition

Includes bibliographical references

MacDonald, Hector

Truth; how the many sides to every story shape our reality. Hector Macdonald. Little, Brown and Co. 2018 346 p. (hardcover) $28 **121**
1. Truth 2. Critical thinking 3. Theory of knowledge 4. Knowledge, Theory of
ISBN 9780316412360; 9780316510820

LC 2017963338

In this book, "Hector Macdonald explores how truth is used and abused in politics, business, the media and everyday life. He shows how a clearer understanding of truth's many faces renders us better able to navigate our world and more influential within it. . . . [The book] is a sobering and engaging read about how profoundly our mindsets and actions are influenced by the truths that those around us choose to tell." (Publisher's note)

"Truth is a fascinating look at how such an abstract concept can be shaped to many purposes, the ethics of bending the truth, and what consumers can do to analyze the innumerable truths presented to us." Booklist

Includes bibliographical references (pages 307-332) and index.

Sartre, Jean Paul

★ **Truth** and existence; original text established and annotated by Arlette Elkaïm-Sartre; translated by Adrian van den Hoven; edited and with an introduction by Ronald Aronson. University of Chicago Press 1992 xlix, 94p hardcover o.p. pa $11 **121**
1. Theory of knowledge
ISBN 0-226-73523-0 pa

LC 92-5889

Written in 1948; original French edition, 1989

This book "presents Sartre's ontology of truth in terms of his characteristic key moral questions of freedom, action, and bad faith. Here is Sartre the existentialist at his most original and most provocative." Univ Press Books for Public and Second Sch Libr

Includes bibliographical references

Wilson, Edward O.

Consilience; the unity of knowledge. Knopf 1998 332p $27.50; pa $15 **121**
1. Philosophy 2. Theory of knowledge 3. Science -- Philosophy
ISBN 0-679-45077-7; 0-679-76867-X pa

LC 97-2816

The author's "extraordinarily clear, evocative imagery and elegant sentences make us see how a consilient world of knowledge might look. . . . Wilson's book of faith in the dream of reason and objective knowledge is a tour de force." Publ Wkly

Includes bibliographical references

128 Humankind

Becker, Ernest

★ The **denial** of death; Ernest Becker. Free Press Paperbacks 1997 xxii, 314 p.p **128**
1. Death -- Psychological aspects 2. Heroes and heroines -- Psychology 3. Mythology -- Psychological aspects
ISBN 0684832402; 9780684832401; 9781416590347

This book, by Ernest Becker, winner of the Pulitzer Prize, is a "brilliant and impassioned answer to the 'why' of human existence. In bold contrast to the predominant Freudian school of thought, Becker tackles the problem of the vital lie--man's refusal to acknowledge his own mortality. In doing so, he sheds new light on the nature of humanity and issues a call to life and its living that still resonates more than twenty years after its writing." (Publisher's note)

Includes bibliographical references and index.

Cannadine, David, 1950-

The **undivided** past; humanity beyond our differences. by David Cannadine. 1st ed. Alfred A. Knopf 2013 352 p. (hardcover) $26.95 **128**

1. Sociology 2. Human behavior 3. World history
ISBN 0307269078; 9780307269072

LC 2012029278

This book is David Cannadine's "examination of the fundamental ways in which humanity divides itself. While these all stem from an innate 'us vs. them' mentality, Cannadine takes the investigation a step further, looking at how we think of ourselves in terms of religion, class, nation, race, gender, and civilization. . . . He points out that . . . a wide variety of factors can create numerous factions and differences within any grouping." (Publishers Weekly)

Includes bibliographical references and index

Chittister, Joan

Between the Dark and the Daylight; Embracing the Contradictions of Life. Joan Chittister. Random House Inc 2015 176 p. (hardcover) $20 **128**

1. Quality of life 2. Self-realization
ISBN 9780804140942; 0804140944

This book, by Joan Chittister, "explores the concerns of modern life, of the overworked mind and hurting heart. These are the paradoxical-and often frustrating--moments when our lives feel at odds with everything around us. Only by embracing the contradictions, Chittister contends, may we live well amid stress, withstand emotional storms, and satisfy our yearnings for something transcendent and real." (Publisher's note)

"Chittister's beautifully crafted short reflections are salve for the soul and an antidote to the apathy, depression, and obsession with material goods that beset so many." Pub Wkly

Christian, Brian

The **most** human human; what talking with computers teaches us about what it means to be alive. Doubleday 2011 303p $27.95; ebook $13.99 **128**

1. Human beings 2. Artificial intelligence
ISBN 978-0-385-53306-5; 978-0-385-53307-2 ebook

LC 2010-48572

"In a fast-paced, witty, and thoroughly winning style, Christian documents his experience in the 2009 Turing Test, a competition in which judges engage in five-minute instant-message conversations with unidentified partners, and must then decide whether each interlocutor was a human or a machine. . . . This fabulous book demonstrates that we are capable of experiencing and sharing far deeper thoughts than even the best computers—and that too often we fail to achieve the highest level of humanness." Publ Wkly

Frayn, Michael

The **human** touch; our part in the creation of a universe. Metropolitan Books 2007 505p $32.50 **128**

1. Cosmology 2. Science -- Philosophy
ISBN 978-0-8050-8148-0; 0-8050-8148-8

LC 2006-48204

First published 2006 in the United Kingdom

"Beginning with a description of the continual 'traffic' between humans and the universe, Frayn shapes a cohesive introduction to philosophy that includes elements of science, determinism, physics, mathematics, psychology, linguistics, and epistemology." Libr J

Includes bibliographical references

Heath, Chip

★ The **power** of moments; why certain experiences have extraordinary impact. Chip Heath and Dan Heath. Simon & Schuster 2017 307 p. $29 **128**

1. Memories 2. Experience 3. Success (Concept)
ISBN 1501147765; 9781501147760

This book, by Christopher de Hamel, examines the "twelve illuminated manuscripts from the medieval period. . . . De Hamel . . . traces the . . . journeys which these . . . artifacts have made through time, shows us how they have been copied, who has owned them or lusted after them, . . . how they have been embroiled in politics, how they have been regarded as objects of supreme beauty and as symbols of national identity." (Publisher's note)

Includes bibliographical references (pages 279-295) and index.

Irvine, William Braxton

On desire; why we want what we want. [by] William B. Irvine. Oxford University Press 2005 322p $24 **128**

1. Desire
ISBN 0-19-518862-4

LC 2005-05938

The author "explains how desire–really a multitude of desires, uninvited and unannounced–manifests itself, how it can be identified and parsed, and how it can be mastered in a way that offers the best chance at self-fulfillment. He uses modern psychology to delineate desire but then shows how the world's great religions–here mainly Christianity and Buddhism, but also Hinduism, Islam, and Judaism–address this phenomenon. He advocates no particular approach, admitting instead that different tacks probably work for different people. And he never lets the reader think that mastering desire will be easy. This is that rare book that should appeal to a wide range of readers without necessarily trying to do so." Booklist

Louv, Richard, 1949-

The **nature** principle; human restoration and the end of nature-deficit disorder. Algonquin Books of Chapel Hill 2011 317p $24.95 **128**

1. Nature 2. Environmental influence on humans 3. Nature -- Psychological aspects
ISBN 9781565125810; 1565125819

LC 2011-3626

This book argues for the importance of fulfilling the "need to be outdoors" for adults. Author Richard Louv "believes that seven nature-based precepts can reshape our lives, including balancing technology with nature; achieving a mind/body/nature connection; incorporating biophilic design in our homes, communities and workplaces; and giving natural history more importance. . . . He affirms and expands on how nature is essential for our mental and physical health--and our very souls." (Christian Century)

An "exploration of nature's significance in our lives and what role it will play in the future. . . . [Louv discusses] seven precepts of natural power, introducing such concepts as the 'purposeful place,' where natural history is as highly valued as human history. While the author comes across as a bit self-obsessed and the book is written to suburban and urban audiences, his writing style is clear and raises many valid points. . . . Louv heartily exhorts readers to become more engaged in the world around them, as citizen naturalists out to discover their own bioregions. Taking time to find and create an everyday Eden is not only beneficial to the individual, but to the community as a whole." Kirkus

Includes bibliographical references and index.

★ The **Oxford** companion to the mind; edited by Richard L. Gregory. 2nd ed; Oxford University Press 2005 1004p il $75 **128**

1. Reference books 2. Psychology -- Dictionaries
ISBN 0-19-866224-6

LC 2004-275127

First published 1987

This book "contains over 1000 alphabetically arranged entries on all aspects of the mind, including topics in neurophysiology, communication, psychology, and philosophy, as well as people relevant to the field." Libr J

Terkel, Studs, 1912-2008

Will the circle be unbroken? reflections on death, rebirth, and a hunger for faith. New Press (NY) 2001 xxiv, 407p $25.95 **128**

1. Death 2. Faith
ISBN 1-56584-692-3

"Terkel talks to 60 people about their encounters with death. His subjects range from emergency room doctors and paramedics to public figures such as author Kurt Vonnegut and guitarist Doc Watson. A stirring celebration of life and exploration of death." Booklist

Trachtenberg, Peter

The **book** of calamities; five questions about suffering and its meaning. Little, Brown 2008 450p $23.99 **128**

1. Suffering
ISBN 978-0-316-15879-4; 0-316-15879-8

LC 2008-13351

This book "succeeds because it asks the right questions, calls on the experience of articulate witnesses and—through skillful narrative and trenchant observation—beguiles the reader into facing heartbreaking reality." Publ Wkly

Includes bibliographical references

Wilson, Edward O., 1929-

The **Meaning** of Human Existence; by Edward O. Wilson. W.W. Norton & Co Inc. 2014 207 p. $23.95 **128**

1. Human beings 2. Meaning (Philosophy)
ISBN 0871401002; 9780871401007

LC 2014016707

National Book Award Finalist: Nonfiction (2014)

In this book, author Edward O. Wilson, "bridges science and philosophy to create a twenty-first-century treatise on human existence. Once criticized for his over-reliance on genetics, Wilson unfurls here his most expansive and advanced theories on human behavior, recognizing that, even though the human and the spider evolved similarly, the poet's sonnet is wholly different from the spider's web." (Publisher's note)

"Wilson's suggested solutions to our paradoxical predicaments are firmly rooted in science and finely crafted with tonic common sense, unusual directness, and no small measure of valor." Booklist

130 Parapsychology and occultism

Dolnick, Barrie

Luck; understanding luck and improving the odds. [by] Barrie Dolnick and Anthony H. Davidson. Harmony Books 2007 236p $19.95 **130**

1. Chance 2. Superstition
ISBN 978-0-307-34750-3; 0-307-34750-8

LC 2007-13235

This "mini reference examines the concept of luck throughout history as observed by a variety of religious sects and practiced in many cultures. The authors help readers develop a personal-luck profile and detail how to apply astrology, numerology, and even herbology toward increasing the odds in one's favor. A practical section on gambling advises readers how to play cards, dice, or the roulette wheel with caution." Libr J

Includes bibliographical references

131 Parapsychological and occult methods for achieving well-being, happiness, success

Dale, Cyndi

Llewellyn's complete book of chakras; your definitive source of energy center knowledge for health, happiness, and spiritual evolution. Cyndi Dale. Llewellyn Worldwide, Ltd 2015 1056 p. (paperback) $39.99 **131**

1. Chakras
ISBN 9780738739625

LC 2015026134

This book, by Cyndi Dale, part of the "Llewellyn's Complete Book Series," presents a comprehensive overview of the Indian system of Chakras. "This definitive encyclopedia explores the science, history, practices, and structures of subtle energy systems, with chakras as the center point. . . . It features full-color illustrations, plus a wealth of exercises that you can use to immediately experience chakra healing and clearing." (Publisher's note)

"This is not a beginner's book (though Dale includes a "pocket guide" to orient new students), but it truly lives up to its "complete book" moniker; if it's related to chakras, it's in here." Pub Wkly

Includes bibliographical references and index

Mildon, Emma

The **soul** searcher's handbook; a modern girl's guide to the new-age world. Emma Mildon. Beyond Words 2015 272 p. illustrations $18.99 **131**

1. Women 2. Occultism 3. Spiritual life
ISBN 9781582705248

LC 2015018843

This book, by Emma Mildon, "offers easy tips, tricks, and how-tos for incorporating everything from dreamology and astrology to mysticism and alternative healing into your everyday life. . . . Your destiny, gifted to you at birth, is waiting. So plug into the universe, dig your toes into the soil of Mother Earth, and open your soul to your full potential." (Publisher's note)

"One of the best New Age texts without being preachy." LJ

Includes bibliographical references

133.1 Apparitions

Aykroyd, Peter

A **history** of ghosts; the true story of seances, mediums, ghosts, and ghostbusters. by Peter H. Aykroyd; with Angela Narth; foreword by Dan Aykroyd. Rodale 2009 237p il $25.99 **133.1**

1. Ghosts 2. Spiritualism
ISBN 978-1-60529-875-7; 1-60529-875-1

LC 2009-18360

The author's "grandfather was a spiritualist: he believed the human personality survives after bodily death, and practiced regular communication with ghosts—much of which he documented in journals. Aykroyd broadens the discussion with historical figures like Sir Arthur Conan Doyle, creator of Sherlock Holmes, who joined the Society of Psychical Research three weeks after his father's death. . . . This is a smart consideration of the paranormal and a curious artifact of the Aykroyd legacy." Publ Wkly

Includes bibliographical references

Dickey, Colin

Ghostland; An American History in Haunted Places. Colin Dickey. Penguin Group USA 2016 336 p. (ebook) $65; (hardcover) $27   **133.1**
1. Ghosts 2. Supernatural 3. Haunted houses -- United States
ISBN 1101980192; 9781101980217; 9781524703660; 9781101980194

LC 2016044006

This book, by Colin Dickey, takes readers "on a journey across the continental United States to decode and unpack the American history repressed in our most famous haunted places. Some have established reputations as 'the most haunted mansion in America,' or 'the most haunted prison'; others, like the haunted Indian burial grounds in West Virginia, evoke memories from the past our collective nation tries to forget." (Publisher's note)

"His book is a fascinating, measured assessment of phenomena more often exploited for sensationalism." Pub Wkly

Includes bibliographical references (pages 289-308) and index.

Guiley, Rosemary Ellen

★ The **encyclopedia** of ghosts and spirits; foreword by Troy Taylor. 3rd ed; Facts on File 2007 564p il $75   **133.1**
1. Reference books 2. Ghosts -- Encyclopedias
ISBN 978-0-8160-6737-4; 0-8160-6737-6

LC 2006-103302

First published 1992

This work examines famous hauntings, historical personages and happenings, and various legends and myths about ghosts and spirits throughout the world. Recent events, new findings about old myths and updated information on major figures in the field are covered.

"Believers and skeptics alike seeking information on various phenomena will find this book useful." Booklist

Includes bibliographical references

Ramsland, Katherine M., 1953-

Ghost; investigating the other side. {by} Katherine Ramsland. St. Martin's Press 2001 322p il $25.95; pa $6.99 **133.1**
1. Ghosts
ISBN 0-312-26164-0; 0-312-98373-5 pa

LC 2001-41725

"Although prepared to dismiss many so-called paranormal occurrences in favor of natural explanations, {the author} nevertheless encounters, experiences, and investigates a variety of inexplicable visual, photographic, and verbal manifestations. Both skeptics and believers will be intrigued by this first-person exploration of ghostly visitations." Booklist

Includes bibliographical references

133.122 Specific types of haunted places

Whitmer, Jamie Davis

America's most haunted hotels; Checking In with Uninvited Guests. by Jamie Davis Whitmer. Llewellyn Publications, a Division of Llewellyn Worldwide Ltd. 2016 264 p. illustrations $16.99; (ebook) $16.99   **133.122**
1. Ghosts -- United States 2. Haunted hotels -- United States
ISBN 9780738748009; 9780738750101

LC 2016024296

This book, by Jamie Davis Whitmer, explores "some of the most haunted hotels across the United States. From the Jerome Grand Hotel in Arizona to the Palmer House in Minnesota, each hotel is discussed in great detail, covering everything from the building's history and legends to first-hand accounts of spooky sounds and smells, ghost sightings, EVP sessions, and more. You'll also find . . . [everything] you need to plan your own visit to these iconic hotels." (Publisher's note)

"Though readers must decide just how much to believe in Whitmer's accounts of ghostly contact, everyone can enjoy the more straightforward travelogue aspects of the book, which provide handy contact information for the hotels and potential itineraries as part of its overview. Perhaps it'll help you plan your next trip." Pub Wkly

Includes bibliographical references

133.3 Divinatory arts

Crispin, Jessa

★ The **creative** tarot; a modern guide to an inspired life. Jessa Crispin. Touchstone 2016 352 p. illustrations (some color) $22   **133.3**
1. Tarot 2. Creative ability 3. Creative ability -- Miscellanea
ISBN 9781501120237

LC 2015038927

This book, by Jessa Crispin, "is a unique guidebook that reimagines tarot cards and the ways they can boost the creative process. . . . Thought to be esoteric and mystical, tarot cards are approachable and endlessly helpful to overcoming creative blocks. Crispin offers spiritual readings of the cards, practical information for the uninspired artist, and a wealth of fascinating anecdotes about famous artists including Virginia Woolf, Rembrandt, and David Bowie, and how they found inspiration." (Publisher's note)

"Even readers with no previous interest in the tarot will be intrigued and delighted by Crispin's ardently researched, spirited, creative, and inspiring elucidation." Booklist

133.4 Demonology and witchcraft

Adler, Margot

Drawing down the moon; witches, Druids, goddess-worshippers, and other pagans in America. [Rev and updated ed]; Penguin Books 2006 646p il pa $18   **133.4**
1. Paganism 2. Witchcraft
ISBN 0-14-303819-2; 978-0-14-303819-1

LC 2006-43786

First published 1979 by Viking

A survey of goddess worship and witchcraft movements discussing their basic philosophies and practices

"Despite its clear anti-Judaic and anti-Christian bias, this book is recommended for general and college audiences interested in religion, the occult, and modern social phenomena." Choice {review of 1979 edition}

Includes bibliographical references

Carlson, Laurie M.

A **fever** in Salem; a new interpretation of the New Eng-

land witch trials. Dee, I.R. 1999 197p hardcover o.p. pa $14.95 **133.4**
    1. Witchcraft 2. Salem (Mass.) -- History
    ISBN 1-56663-253-6; 1-56663-309-5 pa

LC 99-27520

"Carlson's compelling narrative begs for assessment by medical experts. A valuable purchase for libraries seeking more than a basic summary of the witch trials." Libr J
    Includes bibliographical references

Copenhaver, Brian

The **Book** of Magic; from antiquity to the enlightenment. edited, compiled and translated by Brian Copenhaver. Penguin Group USA 2016 672 p. illustrations $35 **133.4**
    1. Magic 2. Mythology 3. Occultism 4. Blacks -- Folklore
    ISBN 0241198569; 9780241198568

LC 2016009049

This book, in the A Penguin Classics Hardcover series, edited, compiled and translated by Brian Copenhaver, is "filled with incantations, charms, curses, summonings, cures, and descriptions of extraordinary, shadowy, only half-understood happenings from long ago. It features writers as various as Thomas Aquinas, John Milton, John Dee, Ptolemy, and Paracelsus along with anonymous ancient and medieval works that were, in some cases, viewed as simply too dangerous even to open." (Publisher's note)
    Includes bibliographical references.

Dell, Christopher

The **occult,** witchcraft and magic; an illustrated history. Christopher Dell. Thames & Hudson 2016 400 p. color ill., music, portraits (hardcover) $39.95 **133.4**
    1. Occultism 2. Witchcraft 3. Illustrated books
    ISBN 9780500518885

LC 2015959510

This book, by Christopher Dell, is an "invaluable source book on the history and practice of magic and occultism, filled with mystical symbols and perplexing charts. Whether the reader attempts to practice magic upon finishing this book is not as important to Dell as tracing the origins and roots of magic throughout the centuries. Layered throughout is a visually satisfying collection of eclectic and sometimes jarring photographs that will fascinate and stir curiosity." (Publishers Weekly)
    "A stunning treasury for anyone interested in the history of magic." Booklist
    Includes bibliographical references and index.

Durand, Sarah

Sister of darkness; the chronicles of a modern exorcist. R. H. Stavis and Sarah Durand. HarperCollins 2018 288 p. $26.99 **133.4**
    1. Exorcism 2. Demoniac possession
    ISBN 0062656147; 9780062656148

This book, by R. H. Stavis and Sarah Durand, "recounts [Stavis's] journey to becoming an exorcist and chronicles some of her most extreme cleansings cases. . . . [Stavis] teaches us that there are a diverse range of 'entities' surrounding us--some of these are playful or misguided, while some are dangerous and harmful. She introduces each of them and explains their power, helping us understand what is attacking and hurting us, and what we can do to protect ourselves." (Publisher's note)

Guiley, Rosemary Ellen

The **encyclopedia** of demons and demonology; foreword by John Zaffis. Facts On File 2009 302p il $82.50; pa $24.95 **133.4**
    1. Reference books 2. Demonology -- Encyclopedias
    ISBN 978-0-8160-7314-6; 0-8160-7314-7; 978-0-8160-7315-3 pa; 0-8160-7315-5 pa

LC 2008-52488

"This encyclopedia delineates beliefs about demons and demonology. The text emerges from an exploration of the darker aspects of folklore, myths, culture, and religion, covering major issues, people, and events in a historical and phenomenological perspective. Its over 400 A-to-Z entries cover topics such as demons in different cultures and religious traditions, possession, exorcism, and demon types. . . . Clear, concise, and balanced, this will attract a range of nonscholarly audiences, especially those interested in the occult, paranormal, folklore, myths, and religion. A solid addition to public libraries." Libr J
    Includes bibliographical references

The **encyclopedia** of witches, witchcraft, and Wicca; 3rd ed; Facts On File 2008 436p il $85; pa $24.95 **133.4**
    1. Reference books 2. Witchcraft -- Encyclopedias
    ISBN 978-0-8160-7103-6; 0-8160-7103-9; 978-0-8160-7104-3 pa; 0-8160-7104-7 pa

LC 2008-8917

First published 1989 with title: The encyclopedia of witches and witchcraft
    "Spanning centuries and continents, the book defines 480 of witchcraft's and wizardry's major historical events, figures, tools, sites, symbols, and abstract terms. The highly engaging, alphabetically organized entries run several paragraphs in length and deftly clarify a term's etymology as well as its spiritual, historical, or spell-making significance." Libr J
    Includes bibliographical references

Jones, Marie D.

Demons, the devil, and fallen angels; Marie D. Jones and Larry Flaxman. Visible Ink 2017 xv, 368 p.p (pbk.: alk. paper) $19.95 **133.4**
    1. Occultism 2. Demonology
    ISBN 9781578596133

LC 2017022073

This book, by Marie D. Jones and Larry Flaxman, "is a comprehensive resource of the many faces of the devil, his minions, ominous deities, and the darker side of nature and ourselves. From ancient demon worship to modern Satanism, the bloody era of the Inquisitions and later witch burnings to the Satanic Panic of the late-twentieth century, and secret occult societies to Hitler's involvement with demonology, this book covers it all." (Publisher's note)
    "An image-packed compendium on embodiments of evil, this overview incorporates significant historical events and modern phenomena. By salting pages with a portrait of mystic Antoinette Bourignon, photos of Santeria practitioners, and the title page of Malleus Maleficarum, the authors add weight to their entries on the impact of witch hunts in previous eras as well as current strands of the occult, including haunted dolls and the alleged satanic influence on rock and roll." Booklist

Karlsen, Carol F.

    ★ The **devil** in the shape of a woman; witchcraft in colonial New England. Norton 1987 360p hardcover o.p. pa $16.95 **133.4**
    1. Witchcraft 2. New England -- History -- 1600-1775, Colonial period
    ISBN 0-393-02478-4; 0-393-31759-5 pa

LC 87-16615

The author presents a "social history of witchcraft in Puritan New

England (1620-1725). She unearths detailed evidence which demonstrates that prosecuted and accused witches generally were older, married women who had violated the religious and/or economic Puritan social hierarchy. . . . A well-written, provocative addition to the . . . scholarship on New England witchcraft." Libr J

Includes bibliographical references

Levack, Brian P.

The **Devil** within; possession and exorcism in the Christian West. by Brian Levack. Yale University Press 2013 360 p. (cl: alk. paper) $35   **133.4**

1. Exorcism 2. Europe -- Religion 3. Demoniac possession 4. Exorcism -- Europe -- History 5. Demoniac possession -- Europe -- History

ISBN 0300114729; 9780300114720

LC 2012042933

This book "focuses on possession and exorcism in the Reformation period, but also reaches back to the fifteenth century and forward to our own times. . . . Challenging the commonly held belief that possession signals physical or mental illness, the author argues that demoniacs and exorcists--consciously or not--are following their various religious cultures, and their performances can only be understood in those contexts." (Publisher's note)

"In this riveting, readable study, Levack . . . offers readers a comprehensive view of reports of demon possession and efforts to rid victims of it." Pub Wkly

Ocker, J. W.

A **season** with the witch; The Magic and Mayhem of Halloween in Salem, Massachusetts. J.W. Ocker. Countryman Press 2016 352 p. illustrations (pbk.) $18.95; (ebook) $50   **133.4**

1. Witches -- Massachusetts -- Salem 2. Halloween -- Massachusetts -- Salem 3. Salem (Mass.) -- History -- Miscellanea 4. Haunted places -- Massachusetts -- Salem 5. Wiccans -- Massachusetts -- Salem

ISBN 9781581573398; 9781581575545

LC 2016023647

"For the fall of 2015, occult enthusiast and . . . writer J.W. Ocker moved his family of four to downtown Salem to experience firsthand a season with the witch, visiting all of its historical sites and macabre attractions. In between, he interviews its leaders and citizens, its entrepreneurs and visitors, its street performers and Wiccans, its psychics and critics, creating a picture of this unique place and the people who revel in, or merely weather, its witchiness." (Publisher's note)

"The result is a fresh, fun glimpse of a town that has come to grips with its sordid history and prospered. Armchair travelers will enjoy the trip." Booklist

The **Penguin** Book of Witches; edited by Katherine Howe. Penguin Group USA 2014 320 p. $17   **133.4**

1. Witchcraft 2. History -- Sources

ISBN 014310618X; 9780143106180

This book, edited by Katherine Howe, explores the history of witchcraft. "From a manual for witch hunters written by King James himself in 1597, to court documents from the Salem witch trials of 1692, to newspaper coverage of a woman stoned to death on the streets of Philadelphia while the Continental Congress met, . . . [this book] is a treasury of historical accounts of accused witches that sheds light on the reality behind the legends." (Publisher's note)

"Recent titles such as Lois Martin's The History of Witchcraft (2010) provide an accessible, albeit brief, overview of a well-covered phenomenon. The antiquated writing style of some of the original documents in Howe's collection is challenging, however, this superbly edited and annotated work provides in-depth material for those interested in the origins of witchcraft persecution in America." LJ

Robisheaux, Thomas

The **last** witch of Langenburg; murder in a German village. [by] Thomas Robisheaux. W. W. Norton & Co. 2009 427p il map   **133.4**

1. Homicide 2. Witchcraft 3. Murder -- Germany -- History 4. Germany -- History -- 1517-1740 5. Witchcraft -- Germany -- History

ISBN 0-393-06551-0; 9780393065510

LC 2008-43052

This "account of one of Europe's last witch panics draws on court documents, eyewitness testimonies, and an early autopsy report to chronicle the 1672 trial of Anna Schmeig and her family, who were accused of sorcery when a neighbor girl died after eating one of Anna's butter cakes." (Publisher's note) Bibliography. Index.

The author "gives us the story of one of the last witch hunts in Europe. In 1672, in a German village, a young woman who had just given birth to her second child died after eating a Shrovetide cake made by her neighbor. Stories of witches poisoning innocents were common in the Franconia region. The neighbor was arrested, and the entire family charged with witchcraft. You can't beat a witch hunt for drama. Every childhood nightmare is called to mind—the dark forest on the edge of town, the inaccessibility of God and, worse, our own friends and family. Forget memoir; this is nonfiction." Seattle Times

Includes bibliographical references

Roth, Harold

The **witching** herbs; 13 essential plants and herbs for your magical garden. Harold Roth. Weiser Books 2017 xviii, 263 p.p illustrations (6 x 9 tp: alk. paper) $18.95   **133.4**

1. Herbs 2. Witchcraft 3. Herbs -- Miscellanea

ISBN 9781578635993; 9781633410343

LC 2016044244

This book, by Harold Roth, "is an in-depth exploration of 13 essential plants and herbs most closely associated with witchcraft--13 because it's the witching number and reflects the 13 months of the lunar calendar. The plants are poppy, clary sage, yarrow, rue, hyssop, vervain, mugwort, wormwood, datura, wild tobacco, henbane, belladonna, and mandrake." (Publisher's note)

Includes bibliographical references (pages 247-263)

Saxena, Jaya

Basic witches; how to summon success, banish drama, and raise hell with your coven. Jaya Saxena and Jess Zimmerman; illustrated by Camille Chew. Quirk Books 2017 206 p. color illustrations (hardcover) $15.99   **133.4**

1. Witches 2. Witchcraft 3. Self-acceptance in women

ISBN 9781594749780; 9781594749773

LC 2016961079

This book, by Jaya Saxena and Jess Zimmerman, serves as "a magical lifestyle guide for everything from powering up a stylish crystal to banishing terrible Tinder dates. . . . DIY projects, rituals, and spells--along with fun historical sidebars--summon the best trends of the modern witchy lifestyle and the . . . traditions of the hell-raising women of the past. . . . [The authors] dispense witchy wisdom for the curious, the cynical, and anyone who could use a magical boost." (Publisher's note)

"This is a handy guide to boosting self-confidence and reaching positive outcomes." Pub Wkly

133.44 Spells, curses, charms

Abrev, Ileana

The **Little** Big Book of White Spells; Ileana Abrev. Llewellyn Worldwide Ltd 2017 408 p. (ebook) $9.99; $14.99 **133.44**

1. Magic 2. Incantations
ISBN 9780738755144; 0738751693; 9780738751696

LC 2017003810

This book, by Ileana Abrev, contains "the spells that you need. Find love, remove a curse, and bring the passion back into a relationship. Banish depression, protect yourself from negative energy, or make a business more profitable. With more than 200 spells, this book opens a whole universe of potential for making positive changes for yourself, your loved ones, and your community." (Publisher's note)

"For readers wishing to experiment with white magic, this book of mini recipes is a great starting point." Pub Wkly

133.5 Astrology

Lewis, James R.

★ The **astrology** book; the encyclopedia of heavenly influences. 2nd ed; Visible Ink Press 2003 928p il pa $24.95 **133.5**

1. Reference books 2. Astrology -- Encyclopedias
ISBN 1-57859-144-9

First published 1994 by Gale Res. with title: The astrology encyclopedia

"Although aimed at the believer, Lewis' work may be confidently consulted by the skeptic seeking basic information about astrology." Booklist

Miller, Susan

Planets and possibilities; explore the worlds beyond your sun sign. Warner Bks. 2001 418p il $30; pa $15.95 **133.5**

1. Astrology
ISBN 0-446-52434-4; 0-446-67806-6 pa

The author provides "character analysis of each sign. The cosmic gifts, relationship trends, financial tendencies, and career tendencies associated with each sign are all described in detail. The mythology of each sign is included as well, nicely rounding out the book." Libr J

133.8 Psychic phenomena

Bader, Christopher D.

Paranormal America; ghost encounters, UFO sightings, Bigfoot hunts, and other curiosities in religion and culture. [by] Christopher D. Bader, F. Carson Mencken, and Joseph O. Baker. New York University Press 2010 264p il $70; pa $20 **133.8**

1. Parapsychology 2. Curiosities and wonders
ISBN 978-0-8147-9134-9; 978-0-8147-9135-6 pa; 978-0-8147-8642-0 ebook

LC 2010-16525

Authors "Christopher D. Bader, F. Carson Mencken, and Joseph O. Baker take their readers on a . . . journey into 'the world of people who devote themselves to the "quest"' for contact with angels, aliens, and other unusual beings. . . . To flesh out the findings of the 2005 Baylor Religion Survey, a national random sample of American religious beliefs (two of the authors were principle investigators), and to understand who is attracted to paranormal beliefs, Bader, Mencken, and Baker accompany bigfoot hunters into the woods and listen to stories about alien abductions and ghostly apparitions. . . . By drawing on both the Baylor survey and qualitative research, these three sociologists conclude that 'the paranormal is normal' and challenge the stereotype that those drawn to the paranormal come from the margins of society." (Journal of American History)

The authors "examine America's belief in paranormal phenomena inside and outside of mainstream religion—from UFOs and Bigfoot to speaking in tongues and guardian angels. They look at how belief affects lives, examining common stereotypes faced by believers and considering whether belief in a mainstream religion makes one likely to ascribe to more otherworldly occurrences. . . . While this academic work showcases an astounding amount of research, the quick pacing and engaging language keep it from being a dry report of BRS findings. It is accessible to any reader with an interest in the convergence of paranormal beliefs and religion." Libr J

Includes bibliographical references

Clegg, Brian

Extra Sensory; The Science and Pseudoscience of Telepathy and Other Powers of the Mind. Brian Clegg. St. Martin's Press 2013 320 p. (hardcover) $25.99 **133.8**

1. Parapsychology 2. Extrasensory perception
ISBN 1250019060; 9781250019066

LC 2013004038

This book, by Brian Clegg, "look[s] at the untapped abilities of human beings, from ESP to Telekenesis and other real life sciences that are currently being studied today. . . . Is there any solid evidence to back up these talents, or are they nothing more than fantasy? . . . By looking at possible physical mechanisms for ESP and taking in the best scientific evidence, the reader can discover if this is all wishful thinking and deception, or a fascinating reality." (Publisher's note)

Sheldrake, Rupert

The **sense** of being stared at; and other aspects of the extended mind. Crown 2003 369p il hardcover o.p. pa $13.95 **133.8**

1. Extrasensory perception
ISBN 1-4000-5129-0 pa

LC 2002-9943

"A most unusual book—fascinating, scientifically sound, and fun to read—it posits that ESP and 'other aspects of the extended mind' are not paranormal but natural functions. Every library should make room on its shelves for this one." Libr J

Includes bibliographical references

133.9 Spiritualism

Blum, Deborah

Ghost hunters; William James and the search for scientific proof of life after death. Penguin Press 2006 370p $25.95; pa $15 **133.9**

1. Philosophers 2. Spiritualism 3. Psychologists 4. Parapsychology 5. Writers on science
ISBN 1-59420-090-4; 978-1-59420-090-8; 0-14-303895-8 pa; 978-0-14-303895-5 pa

LC 2006-44948

In this book, the author examines the Victorian era conflict between science and religion "by reviewing the history of the British Society for Psychical Research and its U.S. counterpart, the American Society for Psychical Research, both of which aimed to find scientific proof of the existence of the supernatural. . . . Her clearly written presentation of the history, frauds, and personalities involved in this unique slice of Victorian life is recommended for all history of science collections." Libr J

Includes bibliographical references

Moody, Raymond A.

★ **Life** after life; the investigation of a phenomenon--survival of bodily death. [by] Raymond A. Moody, Jr.; with a new preface by Melvin Morse and a foreword by Elizabeth Kübler-Ross. HarperSanFrancisco 2001 xxviii, 175p pa $14   **133.9**

1. Death 2. Future life 3. Near-death experiences

ISBN 0-06-251739-2

LC 00-46156

First published 1975 by MBB Inc.

The author "investigates more than one hundred case studies of people who experienced 'clinical death' and were subsequently revived." Publisher's note

Roach, Mary, 1959-

★ **Spook**; science tackles the afterlife. Norton 2005 311p il   **133.9**

1. Future life 2. Religion and science 3. Soul 4. Death

ISBN 0393059626

LC 2005-14450

The author investigates a range of theories and beliefs about the soul's migration after death.

"Roach perfectly balances her skepticism and her boundless curiosity with a sincere desire to know. . . . She is an original who can enliven any subject with wit, keen reporting and a sly intelligence." Publ Wkly

Includes bibliographical references

141   Idealism and related systems and doctrines

★ The **essential** transcendentalists; edited and introduced by Richard G. Geldard. J.P. Tarcher/Penguin 2005 265p pa $15.95   **141**

1. Transcendentalism

ISBN 1-58542-434-X

LC 2005-44016

This study "is divided into three main sections. . . . The first is 'Primary Texts,' with selections from the writings of Sampson Reed, James Marsh, Amos Alcott (father of Louisa May), and Ralph Waldo Emerson. The second, 'Individual Voices,' introduces selections from Frederic Hedge, Margaret Fuller, and Henry David Thoreau. The last is 'The Transcendental Heritage,' which features the works of Walt Whitman, Emily Dickinson, Wallace Stevens, Loren Eiseley, and Annie Dillard. This is a highly informed, elegantly written, fascinating story told through commentary, historical overview, and selections from classic works. It belongs in all libraries." Libr J

Includes bibliographical references

142   Critical philosophy

Bakewell, Sarah

★ **At** the Existentialist Cafe; Freedom, Being, and Apricot Cocktails With Jean-paul Sartre, Simone De Beauvoir, Albert Camus, Martin Heidegger, Maurice Merleau-ponty and Others. by Sarah Bakewell. Other Press 2016 439 p. illustrations (hbk.) $25   **142**

1. Paris (France) -- Intellectual life 2. Existentialism 3.

Philosophers -- France -- Biography 4. Philosophy, Modern -- 20th century"||Philosophy -- France -- History -- 20th century

ISBN 9781590514887; 1590514882

Kirkus Prize Finalist: Nonfiction (2016)

This book, by Sarah Bakewell, is an "account of one of the twentieth century's major intellectual movements and the revolutionary thinkers who came to shape it. . . . They are the young Jean-Paul Sartre, Simone de Beauvoir, and longtime friend Raymond Aron, a fellow philosopher who raves to them about a new conceptual framework from Berlin called Phenomenology." (Publisher's note)

"A fresh, invigorating look into complex minds and a unique time and place." Kirkus

Includes bibliographical references (pages 403-420) and index

Barrett, William

★ **Irrational** man; a study in existential philosophy. Doubleday 1958 278p hardcover o.p. pa $12.95   **142**

1. Existentialism

ISBN 0-385-03138-6 pa

This discussion of existentialism traces its origins and analyzes the contributions of chief exponents of existentialist thought—Nietzsche, Kierkegaard, Heidegger and Sartre

Existentialism from Dostoevsky to Sartre; rev and expanded; New Am. Lib. 1975 384p pa $15.95   **142**

1. Poets 2. Authors 3. Novelists 4. Dramatists 5. Theologians 6. Philosophers 7. Existentialism 8. Essayists 9. Biographers 10. Nonfiction writers 11. Short story writers 12. Writers on religion 13. Nobel laureates for literature

ISBN 0-452-00930-8

First published 1956 by World Pub.

This book contains selections from the basic writings of Dostoevsky, Kierkegaard, Nietzsche, Rilke, Ortega y Gasset, Jaspers, Heidegger, Sartre and Camus.

Sartre, Jean Paul

★ **Being** and nothingness; an essay on phenomenological ontology. translated and with an introduction by Hazel E. Barnes. Philosophical Lib. 1956 638p   **142**

1. Existentialism

Original French edition, 1943

This is "Sartre's major attempt to systematize his theoretical analysis of the human condition and human consciousness which underlies 'Existentialism.'" Reader's Ency. 4th edition

Existentialism and human emotions. Philosophical Library: Distributed to the Book trade by Citadel Press 1957 96p pa $9.95   **142**

1. Existentialism

ISBN 0-8065-0902-3 pa

"Sartre refutes the idea that existentialism drains meaning from human life, by claiming that the philosophy instead gives man total freedom to achieve his own significance." (Publisher's note)

146   Naturalism and related systems and doctrines

Dennett, Daniel Clement

Darwin's dangerous idea; evolution and the meanings of life. {by} Daniel C. Dennett. Simon & Schuster 1995 586p il hardcover o.p. pa $16   **146**

1. Authors 2. Evolution 3. Geologists 4. Mathematicians 5.

Natural selection 6. Paleontologists 7. College teachers 8. Writers on science

ISBN 0-684-82471-X pa

LC 94-49158

"Current controversies associated with the origin of life, sociobiology, punctuated equilibrium, the evolution of culture and language, and evolutionary ethics are investigated rigorously within the context of Darwinian science and philosophy. Dennett challenges the ideas of several imminent scientists, including Roger Penrose and Stephen Jay Gould, who, Dennett asserts, tend to limit the power or implications of Darwin's dangerous ideas." Libr J

Includes bibliographical references

150 Psychology

Colman, Andrew M.

★ A **dictionary** of psychology; 2nd ed; Oxford University Press 2006 861p il $45; pa $17.95 **150**

1. Reference books 2. Psychology -- Dictionaries

ISBN 978-0-19-280632-1; 0-19-280632-7; 978-0-19-861035-9 pa; 0-19-861035-1 pa

LC 2005-31810

First published 2001

"This work defines the most common as well as the most important issues facing psychology today. . . . [The book features] over 11,000 cross-referenced entries, covering everything from anxiety and cognitive impairment to hypolexia (another name for dyslexia) and postpartum depression. . . . For professionals and students of psychology, this is a good place to start their research." SLJ

Includes bibliographical references

Cordon, Luis A.

★ **Popular** psychology; an encyclopedia. Greenwood Press 2005 274p il $75 **150**

1. Reference books 2. Psychology -- Encyclopedias

ISBN 0-313-32457-3

LC 2004-17426

This book "provides a concise guide for anyone seeking to understand the true scientific nature of psychology." Libr Media Connect

Includes bibliographical references

Kubler-Ross, Elisabeth

The **wheel** of life; a memoir of living and dying. Scribner 1997 286p il hardcover o.p. pa $13 **150**

1. Psychiatrists 2. College teachers 3. Writers on medicine

ISBN 0-684-84631-4 pa

LC 97-6435

In this autobiography "Kübler-Ross describes her growing-up years in Switzerland as one of a set of triplet sisters, her fight to become a doctor, and later, the even stronger opposition she met when she began her research on death and dying. Despite the weightiness inherent in working with and writing about mortality, the book has a light, almost airy feel to it, which goes along with the author's central theme that death is merely a transformation." Booklist

150.19 Systems, schools, viewpoints

Bettelheim, Bruno

Freud and man's soul. Knopf 1983 111p hardcover o.p. pa $9 **150.19**

1. Psychoanalysis 2. Psychoanalysts 3. Writers on medicine

ISBN 0-394-71036-3 pa

LC 82-47809

The author argues that Freud was a great humanist and that mistranslation of his work has lead American psychoanalysis astray

Brill, A. A.

★ The **basic** writings of Sigmund Freud; translated and edited by A.A. Brill. Modern Lib. 1995 973p $24.95 **150.19**

1. Dreams 2. Psychoanalysis

ISBN 0-679-60166-X

LC 95-13411

A reissue of the 1938 edition

Includes Psychopathology of Everyday Life, The Interpretation of Dreams, Three Contributions to the Theory of Sex, Wit and Its Relation to the Unconscious, Totem and Taboo, and The History of the Psychoanalytic Movement.

Freud, Sigmund, 1856-1939

★ **Civilization** and its discontents; Sigmund Freud; introduction by Christopher Hitchens; translated and edited by James Strachey; biographical afterword by Peter Gay. W W Norton & Co. 2010 186 p. (pbk.) $14.95 **150.19**

1. Civilization 2. Psychoanalysis

ISBN 0393304515; 9780393304510

LC 2010011485

This book, written by Sigmund Freud, "may be his most famous and most brilliant work. It has been praised, dissected, lambasted, interpreted, and reinterpreted. Originally published in 1930, it seeks to answer several questions fundamental to human society and its organization: What influences led to the creation of civilization? Why and how did it come to be? What determines civilization's trajectory?" (Publisher's note)

Includes bibliographical references and index

★ The **Freud** reader; edited by Peter Gay. Norton 1989 832p hardcover o.p. pa $21.95 **150.19**

1. Psychoanalysis

ISBN 0-393-31403-0 pa

LC 89-2949

This "work includes some 50 of Freud's texts, organized chronologically with headnotes. The selections range from case studies and theoretical discussions about dreams, anxiety and anal eroticism to essays on lay analysis and religion as humankind's obsessional neurosis." Libr J

Includes bibliographical references

Fromm, Erich

On being human; foreword by Rainer Funk. Continuum 1994 180p hardcover o.p. pa $29.95 **150.19**

1. Humanism 2. Psychoanalysis 3. Social psychology

ISBN 0-8264-0576-2; 0-8264-1005-7 pa

LC 93-9243

This volume includes the author's writings on humanism, social psychology, and psychoanalysis from the 1960s, based on Fromm's lectures, works written for specific occasions, and manuscripts intended as books.

Includes bibliographical references

Gay, Peter

A **Godless** Jew; Freud, atheism, and the making of psychoanalysis. Yale Univ. Press 1987 182p hardcover o.p. pa $17 **150.19**

1. Atheism 2. Psychoanalysis 3. Psychoanalysts 4. Writers on medicine
ISBN 0-300-04008-3; 0-300-04608-1 pa

LC 87-8267

The author "reviews the various claims for the Jewishness of psychoanalysis and finds them to be wholly without merit. Paradoxically, he argues that Freud's position as an outsider—an atheist and Jew—enabled him to pierce the taboo topics of sexuality and the unconscious which led to his momentous discoveries." Publ Wkly

Includes bibliographical references

Hayman, Ronald

A **life** of Jung. Norton 2001 xxi, 522p il hardcover o.p. pa $18.95   **150.19**

1. Psychiatrists 2. Psychologists 3. Writers on medicine
ISBN 0-393-32322-6 pa

LC 00-54802

First published 1999 in the United Kingdom

"One of the many strengths of this candid and discerning biography is that Hayman enlists . . . provocative, alarming material to build a careful, nuanced portrait of his subject that neither excuses nor excoriates his actions and words." Publ Wkly

Includes bibliographical references

Judith, Anodea

Eastern body, Western mind; psychology and the chakra system as a path to the self. Anodea Judith. Celestial Arts 2004 xii, 488 p.p illustrations $18.99   **150.19**

1. Self 2. Psychology 3. Chakras -- Miscellanea
ISBN 1587612259; 9781587612251

LC 2004010256

Author "Anodea Judith brought a fresh approach to the yoga-based Eastern chakra system, adapting it to the Western framework of Jungian psychology, somatic therapy, childhood developmental theory, and metaphysics. This groundbreaking work in transpersonal psychology has been revised and redesigned for a more accessible presentation. Arranged schematically, the book uses the inherent structure of the chakra system as a map upon which to chart our Western understanding of individual development." (Publisher's note)

Includes bibliographical references (p. 465-474) and index

Jung, C. G.

★ The **basic** writings of C. G. Jung; edited with an introduction by Violet Staub de Laszlo. Modern Lib. 1993 xxxiii, 691p $21.95   **150.19**

1. Psychoanalysis
ISBN 0-679-60071-X

LC 93-17801

This is a reissue of the 1959 edition

This volume contains excerpts from Symbols of transformation, On the nature of the psyche, Relations between the ego and the unconscious, Psychological types, Psychology of the transference, and Psychology and religion. It also includes Archetypes of the collective unconscious, Psychological aspects of the mother archetype, On the nature of dreams, On the psychogenesis of schizophrenia, Introduction to the religious and psychological problems of alchemy, and Marriage as a psychological relationship.

Includes bibliographical references

★ **Man** and his symbols; {by} Carl G. Jung {et al.} Doubleday 1964 320p il $30; pa $7.99   **150.19**

1. Self 2. Dreams 3. Symbolism 4. Psychology 5. Art --

Psychology
ISBN 0-385-05221-9; 0-440-35183-9 pa

"The basic ideas of Jungian psychology are presented in popular language in six essays by Dr. Jung and {four} of his pupils; these are correlated to dreams and symbols and are shown in their archetypal relationships to ancient myths, present-day thought and art." Libr J

Includes bibliographical references

May, Rollo

★ The **discovery** of being; writings in existential psychology. Norton 1983 192p hardcover o.p.   **150.19**

1. Psychotherapy 2. Existentialism

LC 83-4282

The author "provides the reader with principles of his existential psychotherapy; delineates his view of the cultural-historical context that gave rise to both psychoanalysis and existentialism; and sets forth what he considers to be the contributions to therapy of an existential approach." Choice

Includes bibliographical references

Rogers, Carl R.

A **way** of being. Houghton Mifflin 1980 395p hardcover o.p. pa $15   **150.19**

1. Humanism 2. Psychology
ISBN 0-395-75530-1 pa

LC 80-20275

"This is a book rich in theoretical insights and experiential sharing, and full of invigorating optimism." Libr J

Includes bibliographical references

Skinner, B. F.

★ **About** behaviorism. Knopf 1974 256p hardcover o.p. pa $12   **150.19**

1. Behaviorism
ISBN 0-394-71618-3 pa

The author defines, analyzes and defends the science of behaviorism with chapters exploring the causes of behavior, operant behavior, verbal behavior, thinking, causes and reasons, knowledge, emotion and self

Includes bibliographical references

152.1   Sensory perception

Herz, Rachel S.

The **scent** of desire; discovering our enigmatic sense of smell. [by] Rachel Herz. William Morrow 2007 xxi, 266p $24.95; pa $13.95   **152.1**

1. Smell
ISBN 978-0-06-082537-9; 0-06-082537-5; 978-0-06-082538-6 pa; 0-06-082538-3 pa

LC 2007-33563

"This is one of those all-too-rare books that is involving, well written, and solidly grounded in research." Libr J

Includes bibliographical references

152.109   Sensory perception – History, geographic treatment, biography

Purnell, Carolyn

The **sensational** past; how the Enlightenment changed

the way we use our senses. Carolyn Purnell. W W Norton & Co Inc 2017 304 p. illustrations (ebook) $50; (hardcover) $26.95 **152.109**
1. Enlightenment -- Influence 2. Senses and sensation -- History -- 18th century
ISBN 9780393249361; 9780393249378
LC 2016031574

This book, by Carolyn Purnell, "focuses on the ways in which small, peculiar, and seemingly unimportant facts open up new ways of thinking about the past. You will explore the sensory worlds of the Enlightenment, learning how people in the past used their senses, understood their bodies, and experienced the rapidly shifting world around them." (Publisher's note)

"With a solid, well-researched core of intriguing facts and hints of academia, Purnell's fascinating first book appeals to history-philes, armchair trivia enthusiasts, and students of the senses alike." Booklist

Includes bibliographical references and index

152.14   Visual perception

Herman, Amy E.
Visual intelligence; sharpen your perception, change your life. Amy E. Herman. Houghton Mifflin Harcourt 2016 336 p. illustrations (chiefly color) (hardcover) $28 **152.14**
1. Visual literacy 2. Visual perception
ISBN 9780544381056
LC 2015037245

This book, by Amy E. Herman, is a "guide to seeing – and communicating – more clearly. . . . By showing people how to look closely at images, she helps them hone their 'visual intelligence,' a set of skills we all possess but few of us know how to use properly." (Publisher's note)

"Sharp and original, this book should alter how readers look at the world." Kirkus

Includes bibliographical references and index

152.3   Movements and motor functions

Provine, Robert R.
Curious behavior; yawning, laughing, hiccupping, and beyond. Robert R. Provine. Harvard University Press 2012 288 p. (alk. paper) $24.95 **152.3**
1. Hiccups 2. Sneezing 3. Human body 4. Human behavior 5. Human biology 6. Neuropsychology 7. Evolutionary psychology
ISBN 0674048512; 9780674048515
LC 2012007754

This book by author Robert R. Provine is "about many instinctive behaviors. . . which science has overlooked. Provine 'redresses historic debts' by focusing on such bodily behaviors as 'Farting and Belching.' Tickling, for example, may tap into a neural mechanism for distinguishing ourselves from others. . . . Contagious yawns--affecting 55% of those watching yawn videos--may reflect how our brains replicate observed behavior to create empathy." (Publishers Weekly)

Includes bibliographical references.

152.4   Emotions

Barrett, Lisa Feldman
★ **How** emotions are made; the secret life of the brain.

Lisa Feldman Barrett. Houghton Mifflin Harcourt 2017 448 p. $29; (ebook) $29 **152.4**
1. Brain 2. Emotions 3. Neuropsychology
ISBN 0544133315; 9780544133310; 9780544129962
LC 2016038354

In this book, author Lisa Feldman Barrett describes "her research [that] overturns the widely held belief that emotions are housed in different parts of the brain and are universally expressed and recognized. Instead, she has shown that emotion is constructed in the moment, by core systems that interact across the whole brain, aided by a lifetime of learning. This new theory means that you play a much greater role in your emotional life than you ever thought." (Publisher's note)

"The book is a challenging read and will offer the most rewards to researchers already familiar with the longstanding and apparently still unresolved arguments about what emotions are." Pub Wkly

Includes bibliographical references and index.

Beam, Cris
I feel you; the surprising power of extreme empathy. Cris Beam. Houghton Mifflin Harcourt 2018 272 p. (hardback) $26 **152.4**
1. Empathy 2. Compassion 3. Interpersonal relations 4. Emotions
ISBN 9780544558168
LC 2017045815

This book, by Cris Beam, presents "[an] exploration of how we perform empathy, how it is learned, what it can do. . . . She takes us to the labs where the neural networks of compassion are being mapped, and the classrooms where children are being trained to see others' views. Beam visits courtrooms and prisons, asking how empathy might transform our justice system. . . . And finally, she turns to how we, as individuals, can foster compassion for ourselves." (Publisher's note)

Includes bibliographical references and index

Bloom, Paul
How pleasure works; the new science of why we like what we like. W. W. Norton 2010 280p il $26.95 **152.4**
1. Pleasure
ISBN 0-393-06632-0; 978-0-393-06632-6
LC 2010-05803

Refuting the "explanation of pleasure as a simple sensory response, Bloom . . . [argues] that pleasure is grounded in our beliefs about the deeper nature or essence of a given thing." (Publisher's note) Index.

Bloom "presents essentialism as a weighty determinant of our pleasures. . . . [He] probes the history of sentimental objects, the contact and context that give them meaning; how we hope that qualities of the things we eat will pervade us; the ways in which we are attracted to the process of making art and storytelling; and the strange case of giving and receiving pain. A heartening, well-developed argument." Kirkus

Includes bibliographical references

Clark, Taylor
Nerve; poise under pressure, serenity under stress, and the brave new science of fear and cool. Little, Brown and Company 2011 310p $25.99; ebook $12.99 **152.4**
1. Fear 2. Anxiety
ISBN 978-0-316-04289-5; 978-0-316-12686-1 ebook
LC 2010-38835

"A compassionate psychological page-turner." Kirkus
Includes bibliographical references

Damasio, Antonio R.
Looking for Spinoza; joy, sorrow, and the feeling rain. {by}

Antonio Damasio. Harcourt 2003 355p il $28; pa $15 **152.4**
1. Authors 2. Emotions 3. Philosophers 4. Essayists 5. Writers on religion
ISBN 0-15-100557-5; 0-15-602871-9 pa

LC 2002-11347

This is a "discussion of the difference between emotions (of the body) and feelings (of the mind), various sites in the brain that trigger these states, and the . . . synthesis of the homeostatic process, memory, sensory input, imagination, and foresight that links the unconscious to consciousness and feelings to reasoning." Booklist

Includes bibliographical references

Fromm, Erich

★ The **art** of loving; Centennial ed; Continuum 2000 130p $18.95   **152.4**
1. Love
ISBN 0-8264-1260-2

LC 00-21030

A reissue of the title first published 1956

"An astonishingly simple presentation of an abstract subject." Booklist

Gardner, Daniel

The **science** of fear; why we fear the things we shouldn't-- and put ourselves in greater danger. Dutton 2008 339p $24.95   **152.4**
1. Fear
ISBN 978-0-525-95062-2; 0-525-95062-1

LC 2008-03024

Gardner "analyses everything from the media's predilection for irrational scare stories to the cynical use of fear by politicians pushing a particular agenda. . . . [He] never falls into the trap of becoming frustrated and embittered by the waste and needless worry that he is documenting. A personal anecdote about an unwise foray into a Nigerian slum in search of a stolen wallet disposes of the idea that the author is immune to the foibles he describes. What could easily have been a catalogue of misgovernance and stupidity instead becomes a cheery corrective to modern paranoia." Economist

Includes bibliographical references

Gilligan, Carol

★ The **birth** of pleasure. Knopf 2002 253p $24; pa $13   **152.4**
1. Love 2. Interpersonal relations
ISBN 0-679-44037-2; 0-679-75943-3 pa

LC 2001-50329

Gilligan's "mastery of literary sources and her intelligent but non-academic writing style make this an enjoyable, challenging work." Publ Wkly

Includes bibliographical references

Goleman, Daniel, 1946-

★ **Emotional** intelligence; 10th anniversary ed.; Bantam Books 2006 xxiv, 358p il $29; pa $18   **152.4**
1. Emotions 2. Marriage 3. Medicine 4. Intellect 5. Parenting 6. Temperament 7. Industrial relations 8. Emotionally disturbed children 9. Education -- Curricula
ISBN 978-0-553-80491-1; 0-553-80491-X; 978-0-553-38371-3 pa; 0-553-38371-X pa

LC 2006-283929

First published 1995

The author explains "how to develop our emotional intelligence in

ways that can improve our relationships, our parenting, our classrooms, and our workplaces. Goleman assures us that our temperaments may be determined by neurochemistry, but they can be altered." Booklist

Includes bibliographical references

Havrilesky, Heather

What if this were enough? essays. by Heather Havrilesky. Doubleday 2018 240 p. (hardcover) $25.95   **152.4**
1. Essays 2. Happiness 3. Conduct of life 4. Women -- Biography
ISBN 9780385542883

LC 2018001398

This essay collection, by Heather Havrilesky, "is a mantra and a clarion call. In its chapters--many of them original to the book . . . --Havrilesky takes on those cultural forces that shape us. . . . From the allure of materialism to our misunderstandings of romance and success, Havrilesky deconstructs some of the most poisonous and misleading messages we ingest today, all the while suggesting new ways to navigate our increasingly bewildering world." (Publisher's note)

Jamison, Kay R.

Exuberance; the passion for life. by Kay Redfield Jamison. Knopf 2004 405p il $24.95   **152.4**
1. Happiness
ISBN 0-375-40144-X

LC 2004-46561

The author "examines the contagious nature of exuberance, which she defines as 'a psychological state characterized by high mood and high energy,' offering diverse examples that range from John Muir and FDR to Mary Poppins and Peter Pan. Having in mind the simply put idea that 'those who are exuberant act,' the author details the energetic efforts of scientists, naturalists, politicians and even her meteorologist father." Publ Wkly

Includes bibliographical references

Jeffers, Susan J.

Feel the fear--and do it anyway; [by] Susan Jeffers. Ballantine Books 2007 214p il pa $13.95   **152.4**
1. Fear
ISBN 978-0-345-48742-1

LC 2007-271292

First published 1987 by Harcourt Brace Jovanovich

"By mixing positive thinking with situational exercises that examine basic fear responses, psychologist Jeffers shows that fear is what you make of it and that in most cases it is unfounded." Libr J

Includes bibliographical references

Lenoir, Frédéric

Happiness; a philosopher's guide. Frédéric Lenoir; translated by Andrew Brown. Melville House 2015 208 p. black and white illustrations (hardcover) $23.95   **152.4**
1. Happiness 2. Philosophy
ISBN 1612194397; 9781612194394

LC 2014040205

This book, edited by Frédéric Lenoir, translated by Andrew Brown, "examines how history's greatest philosophers and religious figures have answered life's most fundamental question: What is happiness and how do I achieve it? From the ancient Greeks . . . to the Buddha, Jesus, and Muhammad; from Voltaire . . . and Schopenhauer to Kant, Freud, and even modern neuroscientists--Lenoir considers the idea that true and lasting happiness is indeed possible." (Publisher's note)

"Throughout the book, Lenoir writes economically, devoting only enough words to particular thoughts and approaches as are necessary to stir questions in the minds of readers. A brief though well-considered guide to a wide range of the many schools of thought regarding contentment, joy and happiness." Kirkus

Includes bibliographical references

Lerner, Harriet Goldhor

★ The **dance** of anger; a woman's guide to changing the patterns of intimate relationships. [by] Harriet Lerner. Perennial Currents 2005 239p il pa $13.95   **152.4**

1. Anger 2. Women -- Psychology
ISBN 0-06-074104-X

LC 2004-60074

First published 1985

The author examines the ways women express anger, as well as how women's anger is viewed by society and throughout history.

Includes bibliographical references

Lewis, Thomas

★ A **general** theory of love; [by] Thomas Lewis, Fari Amini, Richard Lannon. Random House 2000 274p il hardcover o.p. pa $13   **152.4**

1. Love
ISBN 0-375-70922-3 pa

LC 99-49930

The authors "aim to help physicians treat patients by showing how the many and varied aspects of love, including the lack and the warping of it, affect patients' problems and strengths and by discussing what must, therefore, be involved in treating patients." Booklist

Includes bibliographical references

Marsh, Abigail

The **fear** factor; how one emotion connects altruists, psychopaths, and everyone in-between. Abigail Marsh. Basic Books 2017 320 p. (hardback) $28   **152.4**

1. Fear 2. Psychopaths -- Psychology -- Case studies 3. Philanthropists -- Psychology -- Case studies
ISBN 9781541697195

LC 2017014787

This book, by Abigail Marsh, focuses on "how the brains of psychopaths and heroes show that humans are wired to be good. . . . What is responsible for the . . . generosity and cruelty humans are capable of? By putting psychopathic children and extreme altruists in an fMRI, ... Marsh found that the answer lies in how our brain responds to others' fear. While the brain's amygdala makes most of us hardwired for good, its variations can explain heroic and psychopathic behavior." (Publisher's note)

"Recommend this fascinating text to readers of pop psychology and true crime fans who wish to better understand the minds of potential criminals." (Booklist)

Includes bibliographical references and index

Nettle, Daniel

Happiness; the science behind your smile. Oxford University Press 2005 216p il $21; pa $13.95   **152.4**

1. Happiness
ISBN 0-19-280558-4; 978-0-19-280558-4; 0-19-280559-2 pa; 978-0-19-280559-1 pa

LC 2004-30585

"With absolute clarity and admirable brevity, Nettle explores the pursuit of happiness and, happily, makes good sense of it all." Publ Wkly

Includes bibliographical references

Orloff, Judith

Emotional freedom; liberate yourself from negative emotions and transform your life. Harmony Books 2009 401p $24.95   **152.4**

1. Emotions 2. Self-realization
ISBN 978-0-307-33818-1

LC 2008-21482

"In Part 1, Orloff presents four components of emotion—biology, energy, spirituality, and psychology—and provides a 20-question assessment to highlight individuals' strengths and weaknesses. . . . Orloff divides Part 2 into seven chapters, each devoted to a difficult negative emotion. Throughout, Orloff details how one can use the four components of emotion to transform negative emotions into positive ones and become a more centered and emotionally healthy person. . . . This well-written book is full of good advice for anyone who wants to take more control of his or her emotional life." Libr J

Ronson, Jon

So you've been publicly shamed; a journey through the world of public humiliation. Jon Ronson. Riverhead Hardcover 2015 304 p. illustrations (hardback) $27.95   **152.4**

1. Shame 2. Interpersonal relations 3. Social control
ISBN 9781594487132; 1594487138

LC 2014038382

This book reports on how "for the past three years, [author] Jon Ronson has been immersing himself in the world of modern-day public shaming--meeting famous shamees, shamers, and bystanders who have been impacted." This book is "a radically empathetic book about public shaming, and about shaming as a form of social control." (Publisher's note)

"With confidence, verve, and empathy, Ronson skillfully informs and engages the reader without excusing those caught up in the shame game. As he stresses, we are the ones wielding this incredible power over others' lives, often with no regard for the lasting consequences of our actions." Booklist

Rosenblatt, Roger

The **book** of love; improvisations on a crazy little thing. by Roger Rosenblatt. HarperCollins 2015 177 p. $22.99   **152.4**

1. Love 2. Marriage 3. Interpersonal relations
ISBN 0062349422; 9780062349422

In this book, "Roger Rosenblatt looks at love in all its themes and variations--romantic love, courtship, marriage, battle, heartbreak, fury, confusion, melancholy, beauty, delirium, ecstasy; love of lovers, family, friends, of country, of work, writing, solitude, of art; love of nature; love of life itself. . . . Rosenblatt intersperses thoughts about love with fictional vignettes." (Publisher's note)

"True to its subtitle, this is a collection of "improvisations," meandering in a way that allows readers to pick it up and begin from any page in this tiny, precious book." LJ

Saviuc, Luminita D.

15 things you should give up to be happy; an inspiring guide to discovering effortless joy. Luminita D. Saviuc; foreword by Vishen Lakhiani. Perigee Books 2016 208 p. (paperback) $16   **152.4**

1. Happiness 2. Conduct of life 3. Self-help techniques
ISBN 9780399172823

LC 2015032168

This book, by Luminita D. Saviuc, offers "a simple and counterintuitive approach to finding true joy. . . . When . . . Luminita Saviuc posted a list of things to let go in order to be happy, she had no idea that it would go viral. . . . Based on that inspiring post, this heartfelt book gives readers permission to give up--that is, to let go of the bad habits that are holding them back from achieving authentic happiness and living their best lives." (Publisher's note)

"Therapeutic, compassionate prodding for those who feel like they're unable to move forward." Library Journal

Fifteen things you should give up to be happy

Tallis, Frank

The **incurable** romantic; and other tales of madness and desire. Frank Tallis. Basic Books 2018 304 p. (hardcover: alk. paper) $27   **152.4**
1. Sex 2. Love 3. Compulsive behavior 4. Psychotherapy 5. Behavior, Addictive
ISBN 9781541617551

LC 2017056452

In this book, author and psychologist "Frank Tallis recounts the extraordinary stories of patients who are, quite literally, madly in love: a woman becomes utterly convinced that her dentist is secretly infatuated with her and drives him to leave the country; a man destroys his massive fortune through trysts with over three thousand prostitutes--because his ego requires that they fall in love with him; a beautiful woman's pathological jealousy destroys the men who love her." (Publisher's note)

Includes bibliographical references and index

Waal, F. B. M. de (Frans B. M.), 1948-

The **age** of empathy; nature's lessons for a kinder society. with drawings by the author. Harmony Books 2009 291p il   **152.4**
1. Empathy 2. Animal behavior
ISBN 0-307-40776-4; 978-0-307-40776-4

The author "examines what he calls the behavioral 'glue' of primate societies: empathy, sympathy, a sense of fair play, and trust. In tracing the origins and evolution of empathy, de Waal points out that our ability to take another's perspective is an automatic impulse with a long evolutionary history in the mammalian line. . . . This insightful work . . . will appeal to a wide variety of general readers interested in the links between human evolution and animal behavior." Libr J

Includes bibliographical references

152.42 Happiness

King, Vanessa

10 keys to happier living; a practical handbook for happiness. Vanessa King. Headline Publishing Group 2017 336 p. illustrations (paperback) $19.99   **152.42**
1. Happiness 2. Conduct of life 3. Self-help techniques 4. Well-being 5. Mental health
ISBN 9781472233424; 1472233425

In this book, author Vanessa King describes "10 key evidence-based actions that have been shown to increase happiness and wellbeing . . . [She] has drawn on the latest scientific studies to create a set of evidence-based practical actions. They will help you connect with people, nurture your relationships and find purpose." (Publisher's note)

"Instructions for learning new things, connecting with people, and living mindfully will resonate with many readers, and their follow through will undoubtedly result in more fulfillment." LJ

Includes bibliographical references and index.

Leanse, Ellen Petry

The **happiness** hack; how to take charge of your brain

and program more happiness into your life. Ellen Petry Leanse. Simple Truths 2017 xvii, 109 p.p illustrations (some color) (hardcover: alk. paper) $14.99   **152.42**
1. Happiness 2. Self-realization 3. Self-help techniques 4. Self-actualization (Psychology)
ISBN 9781492670162; 9781492656913

LC 2017047527

This book, by Ellen Petry Leanse, describes "proven methods to hack your mind in order to: stop living your life on auto pilot, reclaim focus for the things that matter, have more time to do things you love, create real connections to the world around you, and most importantly, reduce stress. By the end of 'The Happiness Hack,' you'll be back in control of your mind and living the life you wish to live." (Publisher's note)

Includes bibliographical references

Lustig, Robert H.

The **hacking** of the American mind; the science behind the corporate takeover of our bodies and brains. Robert H. Lustig. Avery 2017 344 p. illustrations (hardcover: alk. paper) $27   **152.42**
1. Pleasure 2. Neuropsychology 3. Happiness 4. Contentment 5. Satisfaction
ISBN 9781101982587; 9781101982594

LC 2017031139

This book, by Robert H. Lustig, "reveals the corporate scheme to sell pleasure, driving the international epidemic of addiction, depression, and chronic disease. While researching the toxic and addictive properties of sugar for his New York Times bestseller Fat Chance, . . . [the author] made an alarming discovery--our pursuit of happiness is being subverted by a culture of addiction and depression from which we may never recover." (Publisher's note)

"This persuasive and eye-opening book reveals the downward spiral of our health and happiness . . . Well-researched and witty, Lustig's important inquiry will appeal to diverse readers." Booklist

Includes bibliographical references and index.

152.47 Anger

Lieberman, David J.

★ **Never** get angry again; the foolproof way to stay calm and in control in any conversation or situation. David J. Lieberman, Ph.D. St. Martin's Press 2018 vii, 225 p.p (hardcover) $25.99   **152.47**
1. Anger 2. Emotions 3. Adjustment (Psychology) 4. Calmness
ISBN 9781250154408; 1250154391; 9781250154392

LC 2017037537

In this book, author David J. Lieberman, "reveals how to see anger through a comprehensive, holistic lens, illuminates the underlying emotional, spiritual, and physical components of anger, and gives the readers simple, practical tools to snuff out anger before it even occurs. Take a deep breath and count to ten. Meditate. Visualize your happy place." (Publisher's note)

Includes bibliographical references

153 Conscious mental processes and intelligence

Eagleman, David

Incognito; the brains behind the mind. Pantheon 2011 290p il $26.95   **153**
1. Brain 2. Subconsciousness

ISBN 978-0-307-37733-3

LC 2010053184

"Eagleman's main theme is that what one calls 'me,' the conscious mind, is only the tip of the iceberg, and that most of the interesting and important things the brain does are inaccessible to the brain's 'owner.' . . . What Eagleman does is explain the idea to the neophyte through discussion of dozens of fascinating, engaging examples. . . . Eagleman's prose is vivid and, more important, accessible." Choice

Includes bibliographical references

Edelman, Shimon

★ The **happiness** of pursuit; what neuroscience can teach us about the good life. Shimon Edelman. Basic Books 2012 x, 237 p.p **153**

1. Happiness 2. Perception 3. Psychology 4. Thought and thinking 5. Ego 6. Self 7. Thinking 8. Cognition 9. Mind-Body Relations, Metaphysical

ISBN 0465022243; 9780465022243

LC 2011039326

This book by psychologist Shimon Edelman "offers a fundamental understanding of pleasure and joy via the brain. Using the concept of the mind as a computing device, he unpacks how the human brain is highly active, involved in patterned networks, and constantly learning from experience. As our brains predict the future through pursuit of experience, we are rewarded both in real time and in the long run. Essentially, as Edelman discovers, it's the journey, rather than the destination, that matters." (Publisher's note)

Includes bibliographical references and index.

Hallinan, Joseph T.

Why we make mistakes; how we look without seeing, forget things in seconds, and are all pretty sure we are way above average. Broadway Books 2009 283p $24.95 **153**

1. Errors 2. Failure (Psychology)

ISBN 978-0-7679-2805-2; 0-7679-2805-9

LC 2008-30818

"Hallinan examines 13 pitfalls that make us vulnerable to mistakes: 'we look but don't always see,' 'we like things tidy' and 'we don't constrain ourselves' among them. Each chapter takes on a different drawback, packing in an impressive range of intriguing and practical real-world examples. . . . He also looks at the serious consequences of multitasking and data overload on what is at best a two or three-track mind." Publ Wkly

Includes bibliographical references

Hofstadter, Douglas R.

I am a strange loop. Basic Books 2007 412p il 26.95 **153**

1. Self 2. Consciousness

ISBN 978-0-465-03078-1; 0-465-03078-5

The author's model of self is neither "spiritual—he's not a religious man—nor is it locked into the cold neurological materialism of cellular mechanics. . . . [The book] scales some lofty conceptual heights, but it remains very personal, and it's deeply colored by the facts of Hofstadter's later life." Time

Includes bibliographical references

Kandel, Eric R.

★ **In** search of memory; the emergence of a new science of mind. W. W. Norton & Company 2006 510p il $29.95 **153**

1. Memory 2. Nervous system 3. Neuroscientists 4. College teachers 5. Nobel laureates for physiology or medicine

ISBN 0-393-05863-8; 978-0-393-05863-5

LC 2005-28565

The author "recounts his own revolutionary research in establishing the molecular chemistry of short-term memory and the cellular dynamics of long-term memory, highlighting particularly the potential of his findings for the treatment of Alzheimer's and other mental disorders. But even as he outlines the biomechanics of memory, Kandel shares his personal reminiscences of the years during which he unraveled those mysteries. . . . An autobiography of exceptional substance." Booklist

Includes bibliographical references

Lewis, Michael

★ The **undoing** project; a friendship that changed our minds. by Michael Lewis. W.W. Norton & Company 2016 320 p. (hardcover) $28.95 **153**

1. Cognitive therapy 2. Cognitive psychology

ISBN 9780393254594; 0393254593

LC 2016046888

This book, by Michael Lewis, tells "how a Nobel Prize–winning theory of the mind altered our perception of reality. . . . Israeli psychologists Daniel Kahneman and Amos Tversky wrote a series of . . . studies undoing our assumptions about the decision-making process. . . . Their work created the field of behavioral economics, revolutionized Big Data studies, advanced evidence-based medicine, [and] led to a new approach to government regulation." (Publisher's note)

Markman, Art

Brain Briefs; Answers to the Most (and Least) Pressing Questions about Your Mind. Art Markman, Bob Duke PhD. Sterling Pub Co Inc 2016 288 p. $19.95 **153**

1. Brain 2. Brain -- Popular works 3. Psychology -- Popular works

ISBN 1454919078; 9781454919070

This book, by Art Markman and Bob Duke PhD., "answer all your questions about how the brain works and why we behave the way we do. Featuring the latest empirical findings, this is science served up in fun and revelatory bite-size bits, along with a complete set of references for further study." (Publisher's note)

"Markman... and Duke... cover a wide range of topics without taking themselves too seriously." Kirkus

Includes bibliographical references (pages 260-271) and index.

Medina, John, 1956-

Brain rules; 12 principles for surviving and thriving at work, home, and school. John Medina. 2nd ed. Pear Press 2014 288 p. illustrations pbk $15.95 **153**

1. Brain 2. Perception 3. Senses and sensation 4. Human information processing

ISBN 9780983263371

"Dr. John Medina, a molecular biologist, shares his lifelong interest in how the brain sciences might influence the way we teach our children and the way we work. In each chapter, he describes a brain rule--what scientists know for sure about how our brains work--and then offers transformative ideas for our daily lives." Publisher's note

Pinker, Steven, 1954-

How the mind works. Norton 1997 660p il hardcover o.p. pa $18.95 **153**

1. Brain 2. Emotions 3. Evolution 4. Intellect 5. Reasoning 6. Psychology 7. Natural selection

ISBN 978-0-393-33477-7 pa

LC 97-1855

Pinker "has a gift for making enormously complicated mechanisms—and human foibles—accessible." Publ Wkly

Includes bibliographical references

Rosenbaum, David A., 1952-

It's a jungle in there; how competition and cooperation in the brain shape the mind. David A. Rosenbaum. Oxford University Press 2014 272 p. ill. $29.95   **153**

1. Cognitive psychology 2. Competition (Psychology) 3. Brain 4. Neuropsychology

ISBN 0199829772; 9780199829774

LC 2013028959

In this book, author David A. Rosenbaum "argues that the overarching theory of biology, Darwin's theory, should be the overarching theory of cognitive psychology, the science of mental functioning. He explores this new and intriguing idea by showing how neural elements compete and cooperate in a kind of inner jungle, where only the fittest survive. Competition within your brain does as much to shape who you are as the physical and figurative competition you face externally." (Publisher's note)

"Tying the vicissitudes of psychology to any one principle, even loosely, is bold, but Rosenbaum's careful prose will ignite thoughtful debate." Pub Wkly

Includes bibliographical references and index

Sagan, Carl

The **dragons** of Eden; speculations on the evolution of human intelligence. Random House 1977 263p il hardcover o.p. pa $7.50   **153**

1. Brain 2. Genetics 3. Intellect

ISBN 0-345-34629-7 pa

LC 76-53472

In this study of human intellect "Sagan is principally preoccupied with the neocortex, with its left hemisphere, responsible for language and logic, a right hemisphere in charge of intuition and spatial dimension, and a corpus callosum that mediates and synthesizes the two." Atl Mon

Includes bibliographical references

Schulz, Kathryn

Being wrong; adventures in the margin of error. Ecco 2010 405p il $26.99; pa $20.99   **153**

1. Errors 2. Decision making 3. Error 4. Expertise 5. Fallibility 6. Errors -- Psychological aspects

ISBN 0-06-117604-4; 0-06-199793-5 pa; 978-0-06-117604-3; 978-0-06-199793-8 pa

Schulz explores "why we find it so gratifying to be right and so maddening to be mistaken, and how this attitude toward error corrodes relationships—whether between family members, colleagues, neighbors, or nations. Along the way, she takes us on a . . . tour of human fallibility, from wrongful convictions to no-fault divorce; medical mistakes to misadventures at sea; failed prophecies to false memories; 'I told you so!' to 'Mistakes were made.' Drawing on thinkers such as Augustine, Darwin, Freud, Gertrude Stein, Alan Greenspan, and Groucho Marx, she proposes a new way of looking at wrongness. In this view, error is both a given and a gift—one that can transform our worldviews, our relationships, and ourselves." (Publisher's note) Index.

The author discusses "how we make mistakes, how we behave when we find we have been wrong, and how our errors change us. . . . Schulz writes with such lucidity and wit that her philosophical enquiry becomes a page-turner." Publ Wkly

Includes bibliographical references

153.1   Memory and learning

Carey, Benedict

How we learn; the surprising truth about when, where, and why it happens. Benedict Carey. Random House 2014 338 p. illustrations $27   **153.1**

1. Psychology of learning 2. Learning 3. Learning, Psychology of

ISBN 0812993888; 9780812993882

LC 2013049850

In this book, "science reporter Benedict Carey sifts through decades of education research and landmark studies to uncover the truth about how our brains absorb and retain information. What he discovers is that, from the moment we are born, we are all learning quickly, efficiently, and automatically; but in our zeal to systematize the process we have ignored valuable, naturally enjoyable learning tools like forgetting, sleeping, and daydreaming." (Publisher's note)

"A totally fascinating look at learning, with helpful insights for students and any reader interested in learning everything from a new language to flying to playing chess." Booklist

Foer, Joshua

Moonwalking with Einstein; the art and science of remembering everything. Penguin Press 2011 307p $26.95   **153.1**

1. Memory 2. Memory disorders -- Treatment

ISBN 978-1-59420-229-2

LC 2010-30265

"Mr. Foer writes in these pages with fresh enthusiasm. His narrative is smart and funny and . . . it's informed by a humanism that enables its author to place the mysteries of the brain within a larger philosophical and cultural context." N Y Times (Late N Y Ed)

Includes bibliographical references

Fogler, Janet

Improving your memory; how to remember what you're starting to forget. Janet Fogler and Lynn Stern. Johns Hopkins University Press 2014 168 p. (pbk.: alk. paper) $18.95 **153.1**

1. Memory 2. Mnemonics 3. Memory in old age 4. Memory -- Age factors

ISBN 1421415704; 9781421415703

LC 2014008681

This book, by Janet Fogler and Lynn Stern, "have completely updated their friendly and usable guide to memory improvement techniques. Recognizing that people worry something is wrong with them when they forget things, Fogler and Stern suggest that the antidote to worry is taking positive actions to help us remember what we want to remember." (Publisher's note)

Goldman, Bob

Brain fitness; anti-aging strategies for achieving super mind power. {by} Robert M. Goldman with Ronald Klatz and Lisa Berger. Doubleday 1999 333p il hardcover o.p. pa $14.95   **153.1**

1. Aging 2. Sleep 3. Memory 4. Stress (Physiology)

ISBN 0-385-48869-6 pa

LC 98-18785

This is an "exploration of techniques—mental workouts, memory training, physical exercises, and nutrition and dietary supplements—that readers can use to maximize their concentration, memory, imagination, energy, intelligence, and creativity while decreasing fatigue and stress and preventing Alzheimer's disease and other brain diseases." Libr J

Includes bibliographical references

Malone, Michael S.

The **guardian** of all things; the epic story of human memory. Michael S. Malone. St. Martin's Press 2012 xii, 290 p.p (hardcover) $25.99 **153.1**

1. Memory 2. Civilization 3. Technology and civilization 4. Civilization -- History
ISBN 0312620314; 9780312620318; 9781250014924
LC 2012010246

This book by Michael S. Malone is an "exploration of the history of memory and human civilization. . . . [The book] is a sweeping scientific history that takes us on a 10,000-year-old journey replete with incredible ideas, inventions, and transformations. From cave drawings to oral histories to libraries to the internet, 'The Guardian of All Things' is the history of how humans have relentlessly pursued new ways to preserve and manage memory, both within the human brain and as a series of inventions external to it." (Publisher's note)

Includes bibliographical references and index.

Pink, Daniel H.

Drive; the surprising truth about what motivates us. Daniel H. Pink. Riverhead Books, a member of Penguin Group (USA) 2009 xii, 242 p.p illustrations $26.95 **153.1**

1. Psychology 2. Motivation (Psychology)
ISBN 1594488843; 9781594488849
LC 2009040651

Author Daniel H. Pink "exposes the mismatch between what science knows and what business does--and how that affects every aspect of our lives. He demonstrates that while the old-fashioned carrot-and-stick approach worked successfully in the 20th century, it's precisely the wrong way to motivate people for today's challenges." (Publisher's note)

"The author presents an integral addition to a growing body of literature that argues for a radical shift in how businesses operate in a world dominated by technology, and soon to be led by a generation that doesn't necessarily equate money with happiness.Important reading for frustrated but open-minded business leaders struggling to connect with stressed-out workers." Kirkus

Includes bibliographical references (p. [221]-229) and index

Schacter, Daniel L.

The **seven** sins of memory; how the mind forgets and remembers. Houghton Mifflin 2001 272p il hardcover o.p. **153.1**

1. Memory 2. Memory disorders 3. Recollection (Psychology)
ISBN 0-618-04019-6; 0-618-21919-6 pa
LC 00-53885

Schacter discusses "the 'different ways in which memory can get us into trouble.' . . . We forget things over time (transience). We often forget where we put our house keys because we were preoccupied with something else (absent-mindedness). We can't remember someone's name (blocking). We mistake an idealized version of our past for a real recollection (misattribution) or claim an 'implanted' memory as our own when it has been suggested by someone else (suggestibility). Our memories are often . . . influenced by our current beliefs (bias). In some cases, we obsessively remember traumatic or painful events that we'd much rather forget (persistence)." (N Y Times Book Rev) Index.

The author discusses "the curious processes of memory by classifying its malfunctions into seven categories: transience, absent-mindedness, blocking, misattribution, suggestibility, bias, and persistence. Schacter illustrates each of these 'sins' with examples of routine misfortunes common to all." Libr J

Includes bibliographical references

153.15 Learning

Boser, Ulrich

Learn better; mastering the skills for success in life, business, school, or, how to become an expert in just about anything. Ulrich Boser. Rodale Press 2017 xxvi, 277 p.p $24.99 **153.15**

1. Cognitive psychology 2. Psychology of learning 3. Learning 4. Learning, Psychology of
ISBN 1623365260; 9781623365264
LC 2017004366

This book, by Ulrich Boser, "maps out the new science of learning, showing how simple techniques like comprehension check-ins and making material personally relatable can help people gain expertise in dramatically better ways. He covers six key steps to help readers 'learn how to learn,' all illuminated with fascinating stories like how Jackson Pollock developed his unique painting style and why an ancient Japanese counting device allows kids to do math at superhuman speeds." (Publisher's note)

"This work infuses a sense of fresh excitement and accessibility into a topic sometimes considered stodgy or overly cerebral. Readers will be left craving something new to learn." Pub Wkly.

Includes bibliographical references and index.

153.3 Imagination, imagery, creativity

Bloomston, Carrie

The **little** spark; 30 ways to ignite your creativity. Carrie Bloomston. Stash Books 2014 128 p. illustrations (soft cover) $19.95 **153.3**

1. Creative ability 2. Creation (Literary, artistic, etc.) 3. Inspiration
ISBN 1607059606; 9781607059608
LC 2014009342

This book, by Carrie Bloomston, explores and seeks to foster creativity. "Do you look at yourself now and wonder if the spark has gone out? Ignite that inner fire with the 30 engaging exercises, fun activities, inspirational images, and motivating ideas in this book. Learn what your Little Spark of creative passion looks like, how to capture it, and how to make room for it in your life." (Publisher's note)

"Bloomston also offers her own personal anecdotes, as well as stories and tips from numerous others; the extensive list of contributors includes designers, artists and business owners.A sparkling blueprint for stimulating creativity." Kirkus

Csikszentmihalyi, Mihaly

Creativity; flow and the psychology of discovery and invention. HarperCollins Pubs. 1996 456p hardcover o.p. pa $15 **153.3**

1. Creative ability 2. Creative thinking
ISBN 0-06-092820-4 pa
LC 96-4116

"Utilizing the interviews garnered from 91 respondents (ranging from philosopher Mortimer Adler to biologist Edward O. Wilson to politician Eugene McCarthy), the author . . . demonstrates the processes that these acknowledged creative thinkers and doers go through and the characteristics that make them stand out. . . . Csikszentmihalyi also deals with creativity and aging and ways to enhance one's own personal creativity." Libr J

Includes bibliographical references

Gawain, Shakti

★ **Creative** visualization; use the power of your imagi-

nation to create what you want in your life. 30th anniversary ed.; Nataraj Pub./New World Library 2008 175p $25; pa $12.95   **153.3**
1. Imagination 2. Self-realization
ISBN 978-1-577-31636-7; 1-577-31636-3; 978-1-577-31229-1 pa; 1-577-31229-5 pa
LC 2008-14400
First published 1978 by Whatever Pub.
"The author asserts that people can achieve an ideal existence simply through mental visualization." Libr J
Includes bibliographical references

Gilbert, Elizabeth, 1969-

★ **Big** magic; creative living beyond fear. Elizabeth Gilbert. Riverhead Books 2015 288 p. (hardback) $24.95 **153.3**
1. Conduct of life 2. Creation (Literary, artistic, etc.) 3. Courage 4. Confidence 5. Inspiration 6. Creative ability 7. Magical thinking
ISBN 9781594634710
LC 2015010717
In this book, by Elizabeth Gilbert, "digs deep into her own generative process to share her wisdom and unique perspective about creativity. With profound empathy and radiant generosity, she offers potent insights into the mysterious nature of inspiration. She asks us to embrace our curiosity and let go of needless suffering." (Publisher's note)
"Gilbert serves as an enthusiastic coach for readers who want more out of life. Highly recommended." Library Journal

Grant, Adam, 1981-

Originals; how non-conformists move the world. Grant Adam; foreword by Sheryl Sandberg. Penguin Group USA 2016 336 p. illustrations (hardback) $27   **153.3**
1. Entrepreneurship 2. Creative thinking 3. Organizational change
ISBN 9780525429562; 0525429565
LC 2015041287
This book, by Grant Adam, "addresses the challenge of improving the world, but now from the perspective of becoming original: choosing to champion novel ideas and values that go against the grain, battle conformity, and buck outdated traditions. How can we originate new ideas, policies, and practices without risking it all?" (Publisher's note)
"No matter whether the reader is an original or a wannabe, this book is enjoyable and full of useful information." LJ

Livio, Mario

Why? what makes us curious. Mario Livio. Simon & Schuster 2017 xiii, 252 p.p illustrations (hardcover) $26 **153.3**
1. Curiosity 2. Human behavior 3. Curiosity -- History
ISBN 9781476792125; 9781476792095; 1476792097
LC 2016040604
In this book author Mario Livio "interviewed scientists in several fields to explore the nature of curiosity. He examined the lives of two of history's most curious geniuses, Leonardo da Vinci and Richard Feynman. He also talked to people with boundless curiosity: a superstar rock guitarist who is also an astrophysicist; an astronaut with degrees in computer science, biology, literature, and medicine. What drives these people to be curious about so many subjects?" (Publisher's note)
"The information presented is accessible to all readers and the tone is engaging, sometimes even playful." LJ
Includes bibliographical references (pages 197-237) and index

May, Rollo

The **courage** to create. Norton 1975 143p hardcover o.p. pa $11.95   **153.3**

1. Courage 2. Consciousness 3. Creative ability
ISBN 0-393-31106-6 pa
The author argues that creativity is an act of encounter and draws on examples from literature, art, and psychoanalysis
Includes bibliographical references

Zomorodi, Manoush

Bored and brilliant; how spacing out can unlock your most productive and creative self. Manoush Zomorodi. St. Martin's Press 2017 192 p. (hardback) $26.99   **153.3**
1. Time management 2. Creative ability 3. Human-computer interaction
ISBN 9781250124951; 9781250126658
LC 2017017719
This book, by Manoush Zomorodi, focuses on how the author, host of the "podcast and radio show 'Note to Self,' led . . . listeners through an experiment to help them unplug from their devices, get bored, [and] jump-start their creativity. . . . Manoush explains the connection between boredom and original thinking, exploring how we can harness boredom's hidden benefits to become our most productive and creative selves without totally abandoning our gadgets in the process." (Publisher's note)
"In this age of information, Zomorodi's book seems revolutionary, almost subversive. Sprinkled liberally with research and insights from some of the leading minds in technology and futurism, Bored and Brilliant is an important reminder that we are not beholden to our devices." BookPage.

153.35   Adaptability and adjustment

Brandt, Anthony

The **runaway** species; how human creativity remakes the world. Anthony Brandt and David Eagleman. Catapult 2017 304 p. $28   **153.35**
1. Imagination 2. Human behavior 3. Creative ability
ISBN 9781936787524; 9781936787678
LC 2016959435
This book, by Anthony Brandt and David Eagleman, "is a deep-dive into the creative mind, a celebration of the human spirit, and a vision of how we can improve our future by understanding and embracing our ability to innovate. . . . Brandt and . . . Eagleman seek to answer the question: what lies at the heart of humanity's ability--and drive--to create?" (Publisher's note)
"Packed with vivid images, countless examples, and fun facts that will leave readers eager to discuss it with friends, this is a refreshing and thought-provoking book that captures both the wonder of science and the beauty of the human spirit." Booklist

Harford, Tim

Messy; The Power of Disorder to Transform Our Lives. Tim Harford. Penguin Group USA 2016 304 p. (hardcover) $28; (ebook) $65   **153.35**
1. Chaos (Science) 2. Creative ability
ISBN 9781594634796; 9780698408906; 1594634793
LC 2016026363
This book by Tim Harford "celebrates the benefits that messiness has in our lives: why it's important, why we resist it, and why we should embrace it instead. Using research from neuroscience, psychology, social science, as well as captivating examples of real people doing extraordinary things, Harford explains that the human qualities we value – creativity, responsiveness, resilience – are integral to the disorder, confu-

sion, and disarray that produce them." (Publisher's note)

"Weaving together lessons from history, art, technology, and social and scientific research, Harford's theories have many potential benefits for individuals and businesses seeking to remain on the creative cutting edge, as well as profound implications for society." Pub Wkly

Includes bibliographical references and index.

Sonenshein, Scott

Stretch; unlock the power of less--and achieve more than you ever imagined. Scott Sonenshein. HarperBusiness 2017 304 p. (ebook) $27.99; (hardcover) $28.99 **153.35**

1. Success 2. Creative ability 3. Adjustment (Psychology) 4. Adaptability (Psychology) 5. Resourcefulness -- Psychological aspects
ISBN 9780062457233; 9780062457226

LC 2016028800

This book, by Scott Sonenshein, "examines why some people and organizations succeed with so little, while others fail with so much. . . . 'Stretch' shows why everyone--from executives to entrepreneurs, professionals to parents, athletes to artists--performs better with constraints; why seeking too many resources undermines our work and well-being; and why even those with a lot benefit from making the most out of a little." (Publisher's note)

"A convincing argument within a compelling narrative—recommended for business managers and resourceful individuals alike." Kirkus

Includes bibliographical references and index.

Wilson, Edward O., 1929-

The **origins** of creativity; Edward O. Wilson. Liveright Publishing Corporation 2017 243 p. (hardcover) $24.95 **153.35**

1. Creative ability 2. Science and the humanities
ISBN 1631493183; 9781631493195; 9781631493188

LC 2017017326

This book, by Edward O. Wilson, "offers a sweeping examination of the relationship between the humanities and the sciences. . . . Both endeavours, . . . Wilson reveals, have their roots in human creativity--the defining trait of our species. Reflecting on the deepest origins of language, storytelling, and art, Wilson demonstrates how creativity began not ten thousand years ago, as we have long assumed, but over one hundred thousand years ago in the Paleolithic age." (Publisher's note)

"Wilson (Half-Earth) makes a case for blending an understanding of the sciences into the humanities in his latest work, raising provocative questions in the process." Pub Wkly

Includes bibliographical references (pages [199]-213) and index.

153.4 Thought, thinking, reasoning, intuition, value, judgment

Berdik, Chris

Mind over mind; the surprising power of placebos, expectations, and assumptions. Chris Berdik. Current Hardcover 2012 272 p. (hardback) $26.95 **153.4**

1. Perception 2. Mind and body 3. Expectation (Psychology) 4. Cognitive psychology 5. Thought and thinking
ISBN 1591845092; 9781591845096

LC 2012019144

This book, by Chris Berdik, "offers a . . . look at the frontiers of expectations research, revealing how our brains work in the future tense and how our assumptions . . . bend reality. We learn how placebo calories can fill us up, . . . how fake surgery can sometimes work better than

real surgery, and how imaginary power can be corrupting. . . . Their influence seems based on illusion, even trickery, but they can create their own reality, for good or for ill." (Publisher's note)

Includes bibliographical references and index

Brotherton, Rob

Suspicious Minds; Why We Believe Conspiracy Theories. by Rob Brotherton. St. Martin's Press 2015 304 p. illustrations $27 **153.4**

1. Psychology 2. Conspiracies
ISBN 1472915615; 9781472915610

This book, by Rob Brotherton, focuses on "the psychology of believing in conspiracy theories. . . . We instinctively see events in the world in terms of human motives and intentions, leading us to discount the role of chance and unintended consequences, and we look for some hidden hand behind catastrophic events. These psychological quirks can lead us to suspect a conspiracy where none exists." (Publisher's note)

"Clearly written and with liberal use of humor and numerous examples from scholarly research, this title provides a valuable look at why conspiracy theories abound and why we should continually assess our thinking." Library Journal

Christian, Brian

Algorithms to live by; The computer science of human decisions. Brian Christian and Tom Griffiths. Henry Holt & Co. 2016 368 p. **153.4**

1. Computer simulation 2. Comptuter algorithms 3. Problem solving -- Mathematics 4. Human behavior -- Mathematical models
ISBN 9781627790369

LC 2015032177

This book "offers an intriguing, valuable approach to the examination of how computer-created algorithms assist with solving a number of important human decision-making problems. The work attempts to demonstrate how understanding these algorithms has wider relevance—one can apply algorithmic solutions to the human decision-making process. Overall, the book succeeds in this endeavor by illustrating and offering examples of how computer algorithms can be applied in typical situations arising in daily human life." (Choice Reviews)

Includes bibliographical references and index

Dobelli, Rolf

The **art** of thinking clearly; Rolf Dobelli; translated by Nicky Griffin. HarperBusiness 2013 384 p. (hardcover) $25.99 **153.4**

1. Decision making 2. Thought and thinking 3. Cognition 4. Reasoning (Psychology) 5. Errors -- Psychological aspects
ISBN 0062219707; 9780062219688

LC 2013003934

This book, by Rolf Dobelli, is a "look at human psychology and reasoning--essential reading for anyone who wants to avoid 'cognitive errors' and make better choices in all aspects of their lives. . . . [It offers] examples of cognitive biases, simple errors we all make in our day-to-day thinking. But by knowing what they are and how to spot them, we can avoid them and make better decisions." (Publisher's note)

Gladwell, Malcolm

Blink: the power of thinking without thinking. Little, Brown and Co 2005 277p il $25.95 **153.4**

1. Intuition 2. Decision making
ISBN 0-316-17232-4

LC 2004-13916

Gladwell "has a dazzling ability to find commonality in disparate fields of study. . . . Each case study is satisfying, and Gladwell imparts his own evident pleasure in delving into a wide range of fields and seeking an underlying truth." Publ Wkly

Includes bibliographical references

Herbert, Wray

On second thought; outsmarting your mind's hard-wired habits. Crown Publishers 2010 289p $25   **153.4**
1. Thought and thinking
ISBN 0-307-46163-7; 978-0-307-46163-6

LC 2010-03073

"The brain is like a dual processor, [Herbert] argues—one part is logical, deliberate, and cautious, while the other is much older and primitive. The latter is the heuristic brain—fast, impressionistic, and sometimes irrational. After years of evolution, the brain has become hardwired with mental shortcuts that help us quickly navigate our daily lives. However, they can also distort our thinking and lead to poor decision making. . . . Heuristics are neither good nor bad—the trick, Herbert says, is in recognizing when to question an instant response." Libr J

Jacob, Alan

How to think; a survival guide for a world at odds. Alan Jacobs. Currency 2017 157 p. (hardcover) $23   **153.4**
1. Reasoning 2. Thought and thinking
ISBN 9780451499615; 0451499603; 9780451499608

LC 2016052795

This book, by Alan Jacobs, "is a contrarian treatise on why we're not as good at thinking as we assume—but how recovering this lost art can rescue our inner lives from the chaos of modern life. . . . Drawing on sources as far-flung as novelist Marilynne Robinson, basketball legend Wilt Chamberlain, British philosopher John Stuart Mill, and Christian theologian C.S. Lewis, Jacobs digs into the nuts and bolts of the cognitive process." (Publisher's note)

"Witty, engaging, and ultimately hopeful, Jacobs's guide is sorely needed in a society where partisanship too often trumps the pursuit of knowledge." Pub Wkly

Includes bibliographical references.

Kahneman, Daniel, 1934-

Thinking, fast and slow; Daniel Kahneman. Farrar, Straus and Giroux 2011 499p. ill.   **153.4**
1. Intuition 2. Reasoning 3. Decision making 4. Thought and thinking
ISBN 0374275637; 9780374275631

LC 2011027143

In this book, author Daniel Kahneman examines "the mind and explains the two systems that drive the way we think. System 1 is fast, intuitive, and emotional; System 2 is slower, more deliberative, and more logical. Kahneman exposes the . . . capabilities--and also the faults and biases--of fast thinking, and reveals the pervasive influence of intuitive impressions on our thoughts and behavior." (Publisher's note)

Includes bibliographical references (p. 447-481) and index.

Konnikova, Maria, 1987-

Mastermind; how to think like Sherlock Holmes. Maria Konnikova. Viking Adult 2013 273 p. (hardback) $26.95 **153.4**
1. Perception 2. Logic 3. Reasoning
ISBN 0670026573; 9780670026579

LC 2012035455

In this book, psychologist Maria Konnikova "examines [fictional character Sherlock] Holmes's powers of perception and problem solving through the lens of her discipline. The book is part literary analysis and part self-help guide, teaching readers how to sharpen the ways they

observe the world, store and retrieve memories, and make decisions." (Scientific American)

Levitin, Daniel J.

★ A **field** guide to lies; critical thinking in the information age. Daniel J. Levitin. Dutton 2016 304 p. (hardcover) $28   **153.4**
1. Critical thinking 2. Information science 3. Truthfulness and falsehood 4. Reasoning 5. Fallacies (Logic)
ISBN 9780525955221; 0525955224

LC 2016007356

This book, by Daniel J. Levitin, asks "how do we distinguish misinformation, pseudo-facts, distortions, and outright lies from reliable information? Levitin groups his field guide into two categories--statistical information and faulty arguments--ultimately showing how science is the bedrock of critical thinking." (Publisher's note)

"Levitin (The Organized Mind) equips readers with tools to combat misinformation—bad data, false facts, distortions, and their ilk—in this useful primer on the importance of critical thinking in daily life. . . . In all three sections Levitin explores material that has often been written about elsewhere, but the book still serves its purpose as a valuable primer on critical thinking that convincingly illustrates the prevalence of misinformation in everyday life." PW

Includes bibliographical references and index

Manage your day-to-day; build your routine, find your focus, and sharpen your creative mind. by Jocelyn K. Glei. Amazon Pub 2013 253 p. $14.95   **153.4**
1. Work ethic 2. Work-life balance
ISBN 1477800670; 9781477800676

This book, by Jocelyn K. Glei, "will give you a toolkit for tackling the new challenges of a 24/7, always-on workplace. Featuring contributions from: Dan Ariely, Leo Babauta, Scott Belsky, Lori Deschene, Aaron Dignan, Erin Rooney Doland, Seth Godin, Todd Henry, Christian Jarrett, Scott McDowell, Mark McGuinness, Cal Newport, Steven Pressfield, Gretchen Rubin, Stefan Sagmeister, Elizabeth G. Saunders, Tony Schwartz, Tiffany Shlain, Linda Stone, and James Victore." (Publisher's note)

Mudd, Philip

The **Head** Game; A Spy's Guide to High-stakes Risk Management and Decision Making. by Philip Mudd. W W Norton & Co Inc 2015 288 p. $26.95   **153.4**
1. Management 2. Decision making
ISBN 0871407884; 9780871407887

LC 2015006002

This book, by Philip Mudd, "gives us the definitive guidebook for how to approach complex decisions today. Filled with logical yet counterintuitive answers to ordinary and extraordinary problems . . . Mudd's 'HEAD' (High Efficiency Analytic Decision-making) methodology provides readers with a battle-tested set of guiding principles that promise to bring order to even the most chaotic problems, all in five practical steps." (Publisher's note)

"How do you make decisions when the stakes are really, really high? The former deputy director of the CIA's Counterterrorist Center and the FBI's National Security Branch, currently director of enterprise risk at SouthernSun asset management, should know." LJ

Nisbett, Richard E.

Mindware; tools for smart thinking. Richard E. Nisbett. Farrar, Straus & Giroux 2015 336 p. illustrations (hardcover) $27   **153.4**

1. Problem solving 2. Critical thinking 3. Thought and thinking 4. Reasoning
ISBN 0374112673; 9780374112677

LC 2015005007

In this book, author Richard E. Nisbett explores how "scientific and philosophical concepts can change the way we solve problems by helping us to think more effectively about our behavior and our world. . . . Nisbett has made a . . . career of studying and teaching . . . the law of large numbers, statistical regression, cost-benefit analysis, sunk costs and opportunity costs, and causation and correlation, probing the best methods for teaching others how to use them effectively in their daily lives." (Publisher's note)

"Nisbett's goal is to help us look at problems and choices in new ways, to attack them from new analytic angles, to find clarity out of chaos. No psychological self-help book succeeds completely, but this one comes close." Booklist

Includes bibliographical references and index

Nye, Bill, 1955-
Everything all at once; how to unleash your inner nerd, tap into radical curiosity and solve any problem. by Bill Nye; edited by Corey S. Powell. Rodale Books 2017 ix, 374 p.p illustrations (hardback) $26.99   **153.4**
1. Biography 2. Problem solving 3. Critical thinking 4. Science television programs -- Anecdotes 5. Television personalities -- United States -- Biography 6. Bill Nye, the science guy (Television program) -- History
ISBN 9781623367923; 9781623367916

LC 2017022105

This biography, by Bill Nye, edited by Corey S. Powell, "is the story of how Bill Nye became Bill Nye and how he became a champion of change and an advocate of science. It's how he became The Science Guy. Bill teaches us that we have the power to make real change. Join him in dare we say it changing the world." (Publisher's note)

"Bow-tied nerd superhero Nye (Unstoppable: Harnessing Science to Change the World, 2015, etc.) serves up a tasty combination of memoir and manifesto." Kirkus

Shermer, Michael
The **believing** brain; from ghosts and gods to politics and conspiracies--how we construct beliefs and reinforce them as truths. Times Books 2011 385p il $28   **153.4**
1. Belief and doubt 2. Theory of knowledge 3. Knowledge, Theory of 4. Cognitive neuroscience
ISBN 9780805091250; 0805091254

LC 2010-30706

This book discusses the science of the human brain in relation to belief formation. "[T]he book is clearly less about the examples than about the theory Shermer uses to explain them all. . . . Shermer's theory looks like this: The human mind is inherently a 'belief engine'; we perceive endless bits of information, and we must posit beliefs as ways of organizing and making sense of them. . . . Having found a possible explanation, we then seek confirming evidence and deepenings of the patterns and agents we believe we have discerned. The result, Shermer claims, is that we live much of the time in 'belief-dependent realism,' which is to say that our beliefs are shaping what we see in the world, rather than the world shaping our beliefs. . . . Shermer also believes in a dividing line between benign or helpful beliefs and malignant ones (like religion)." (Commonweal)

"A timely, reasoned reflection on the nature of belief, offering a levelheaded corrective to the divisiveness of extreme partisanship." Kirkus

Includes bibliographical references and index.

Trivers, Robert
The **folly** of fools; the logic of deceit and self-deception in human life. Robert Trivers. Basic Books 2011 xvi, 397 p.p $28   **153.4**
1. Deception 2. Evolution 3. Psychology 4. Self-deception 5. Deception -- Social aspects 6. Deception -- Psychological aspects
ISBN 0465027555; 9780465027552; 9780465028054

LC 2011028453

The author "argues that self-deception evolved in the service of deceit--the better to fool others. We do it for biological reasons--in order to help us survive and procreate. From viruses mimicking host behavior to humans misremembering (sometimes intentionally) the details of a quarrel, science has proven that the deceptive one can always outwit the masses. But we undertake this deception at our own peril." (Publisher's note)

Includes bibliographical references (p. 355-383) and index

Watts, Duncan J.
Everything is obvious; once you know the answer. Crown Business 2011 335p il $26   **153.4**
1. Reasoning 2. Thought and thinking 3. Common sense
ISBN 978-0-385-53168-9; 0-385-53168-0

LC 2010031550

The author posits "that common sense is a shockingly unreliable guide to truth and yet we rely on it virtually to the exclusion of other methods of reasoning. Mr. Watts, a former sociology professor and physicist who is now a researcher for Yahoo, has written a fascinating book that ranges through psychology, economics, marketing and the science of social networks. He is especially interested in the mistakes we make when we reason about how people influence one another—such as our tendency to think of groups in terms of representative or important members rather than as whole entities. . . . The enterprise of prediction-making is another casualty of the limits of common sense. Mr. Watts suggests that the entire field of business strategy suffers from a delusion that the future can be forecast with enough numerical precision to enable accurate planning. One solution he endorses is a systematic process of imagining detailed alternative narratives of the future." Wall Street J

Includes bibliographical references

153.42   Thought and thinking

Sloman, Steven
The **knowledge** illusion; why we never think alone. Steven Sloman and Philip Fernbach. Riverhead Books 2017 304 p. $28   **153.42**
1. Theory of knowledge 2. Thought and thinking
ISBN 9780399184352

LC 2016036297

This book, by Steven Sloman and Philip Fernbach, argues "that we survive and thrive despite our mental shortcomings because we live in a rich community of knowledge. The key to our intelligence lies in the people and things around us. We're constantly drawing on information and expertise stored outside our heads: in our bodies, our environment, our possessions, and the community with which we interact—and usually we don't even realize we're doing it." (Publisher's note)

"In an increasingly polarized culture where certainty reigns supreme, a book advocating intellectual humility and recognition of the limits of understanding feels both revolutionary and necessary. The fact that it's a fun and engaging page-turner is a bonus benefit for the reader." Pub Wkly

Includes bibliographical references and index

153.6   Communication

Alda, Alan, 1936-

If I understood you, would I have this look on my face? my adventures in the art and science of relating and communicating. Alan Alda. Random House 2017 xviii, 213 p.p illustrations   **153.6**
1. Communication 2. Interpersonal relations 3. Interpersonal communication
ISBN 9780812989168; 9780812989144; 9781524781927
     LC 2016045922
This memoir, by Alan Alda, describes how the author "has been on a decades-long journey to discover new ways to help people communicate and relate to one another more effectively.... [This book] is the warm, witty, and informative chronicle of how Alda found inspiration in everything from cutting-edge science to classic acting methods." (Publisher's note)
"A sharp and informative guide to communication." Kirkus

Headlee, Celeste

We need to talk; how to have conversations that matter. Celeste Headlee. Harper Wave 2017 xix, 244 p.p (hardback) $26.99   **153.6**
1. Conversation 2. Communication 3. Interpersonal communication
ISBN 9780062669018; 9780062669025; 9780062669001
     LC 2017013596
This book, by Celeste Headlee, "shows us how to bridge what divides us--by having real conversations.... Studies show that Americans feel less connected and more divided than ever before.... The only way forward, says Headlee, is to start talking to each other. In [this book], she outlines the strategies that have made her a better conversationalist--and offers simple tools that can improve anyone's communication." (Publisher's note)
"Based on a popular TED talk, this unassuming but powerful debut offers 10 strategies for improving conversational skills." Pub Wkly
Includes bibliographical references (pages [237]-244).

McMillan, Ron

Crucial conversations; tools for talking when stakes are high. Kerry Patterson, Joseph Grenny, Ron McMillan, and Al Switzler. McGraw-Hill 2011 244 p. $32   **153.6**
1. Communication 2. Interpersonal relations 3. Interpersonal communication
ISBN 0071775307; 9780071775304
     LC 20021129
2nd edition.
This book, by Kerry Patterson, Joseph Grenny, Ron McMillan, and Al Switzler, "exploded onto the scene ten years ago and revolutionized the way people communicate when stakes are high, opinions vary, and emotions run strong.... Now, the authors have revised their bestselling classic to provide even more ways to help you take the lead in any tough conversation." (Publisher's note)
"Being an efficient advocate for the self and others depends on the ability to participate effectively in difficult and critical discussions. Readers will appreciate how Patterson's techniques apply both to interpersonal relationships and when acting in the interests of another." LJ
Includes bibliographical references and index

Pease, Allan

The **definitive** book of body language; [by] Allan & Barbara Pease. Bantam Books 2006 386p il $23   **153.6**
1. Nonverbal communication

ISBN 0-553-80472-3; 978-0-553-80472-0
     LC 2006-42657
"The book is amply and wittily illustrated with celebrity photographs.... This is a fascinating book." N Y Times Book Rev
Includes bibliographical references

153.7   Perceptual processes

Beilock, Sian

How the body knows its mind; the unseen influence of your physical environment on your thoughts and feelings. Sian Beilock. Atria Books 2015 288 p. (hardback) $26   **153.7**
1. Mind and body 2. Thought and thinking
ISBN 1451626681; 9781451626681; 9781451626698
     LC 2014007653
Author Sian Beilock offers a "new understanding of the mind-body connection and its profound impact on everything from advertising to romance. From the tricks used by advertisers to the ways body language can improve your memory, Beilock explains a wealth of fascinating interconnections between mind and body and how mastering them can make us happier, safer, and more successful." (Publisher's note)
"A must-read for those who want to understand and embrace a greater connection between body and brain." LJ
Includes bibliographical references and index

Chabris, Christopher

The **invisible** gorilla; and other ways our intuitions deceive us. [by] Christopher Chabris and Daniel Simons. Crown 2010 306p $27; pa $14   **153.7**
1. Memory 2. Perception 3. Thought and thinking
ISBN 978-0-307-45965-7; 0-307-45965-9; 978-0-307-45966-4 pa; 0-307-45966-7 pa
     LC 2009-45325
The authors "won a 2004 Ig Nobel Prize for their widely reported 'gorilla experiment,' which showed that when people focus on one thing, it's easy to overlook other things—even a woman in a gorilla suit. ... [In this book,] they explore this habit of 'inattentional blindness' and other common ways in which we distort our perception of reality. Their readable book offers surprising insights into just how clueless we are about how our minds work and how we experience the world." Kirkus
Includes bibliographical references

Ellard, Colin

★ **You** are here; why we can find our way to the moon but get lost in the mall. Doubleday 2009 328p il map $25 **153.7**
1. Direction sense 2. Space perception
ISBN 978-0-385-52806-1; 0-385-52806-X
     LC 2009-07822
Ellard argues that in the modern age the human sense of navigation and direction has diminished greatly.
"If you're looking for an eye-opening, if somewhat embarrassing, book to help understand why you keep getting lost when you know you shouldn't and what you can do about it well, here you are." Booklist
Includes bibliographical references

Goleman, Daniel, 1946-

Focus; the hidden driver of excellence. Daniel Goleman. Harper 2013 320 p. $28.99   **153.7**
1. Attention 2. Self-control 3. Thought and thinking
ISBN 0062114867; 9780062114860
     LC 2013007290

Author Daniel Goleman's book "delves into the science of attention in all its varieties, presenting a long overdue discussion of this little-noticed and under-rated mental asset. In an era of unstoppable distractions, Goleman persuasively argues that now more than ever we must learn to sharpen focus if we are to survive in a complex world." (Publisher's note)

Greenspan, Stanley I.

The **first** idea; how symbols, language, and intelligence evolved from our early primate ancestors to modern humans. [by] Stanley I. Greenspan, Stuart G. Shanker. 1st Da Capo Press ed; Da Capo Press 2004 504p $25   **153.7**
  1. Evolution 2. Theory of knowledge
  ISBN 0-7382-0680-6
           LC 2004-10658
"This book should appeal most to readers working in psychology and child development, but its revolutionary ideas no doubt will lead to lively and well-publicized debates." Publ Wkly
Includes bibliographical references

Parr, Ben

Captivology; the science of capturing people's attention. Ben Parr. HarperOne 2015 256 p. (hardback) $27.99   **153.7**
  1. Attention 2. Marketing
  ISBN 0062324195; 9780062324191
           LC 2014035615
This book, by Ben Parr, "presents a new understanding of attention-how it works, why it matters, and how we leverage psychological triggers to draw and retain attention for our passions, projects, and ideas. Parr combines the latest research on attention with interviews with more than fifty scientists and visionaries . . . who have successfully brought their ideas, projects, companies, and products to the forefront of cultural consciousness." (Publisher's note)

Zimbardo, Philip G.

The **time** paradox; the new psychology of time that will change your life. [by] Philip Zimbardo and John Boyd. Free Press 2008 358p il $27   **153.7**
  1. Time perception
  ISBN 978-1-4165-4198-1; 1-4165-4198-5
           LC 2008-2149
This is an "investigation of how attitudes toward time affect every aspect of human life. The authors help readers determine their personal time zone before revealing how to 'reclaim yesterday, enjoy today, and master tomorrow.' Balance never seemed so attainable." Libr J
Includes bibliographical references

153.753   Time and rhythm perception

Pink, Daniel H.

When; the scientific secrets of perfect timing. Daniel H. Pink. Riverhead Books 2018 258 p. (hardcover) $28 **153.753**
  1. Time perception 2. Time -- Psychological aspects
  ISBN 9780735210646; 9780735210622
           LC 2017033061
In this book, author Daniel H. Pink "shows that timing is really a science. Drawing on a rich trove of research from psychology, biology, and economics, Pink reveals how best to live, work, and succeed. How can we use the hidden patterns of the day to build the ideal schedule? Why do certain breaks dramatically improve student test scores? How can we turn a stumbling beginning into a fresh start? Why should we avoid going to the hospital in the afternoon?" (Publisher's note)

"Both those seeking this as a business resource and general readers interested in social psychology, time management, personal development, and decision making will find helpful, inspiring, and thoughtful advice from Pink." Booklist
Includes bibliographical references (pages 219-250) and index.

153.8   Will (Volition)

Akst, Daniel

We have met the enemy; self-control in an age of excess. Penguin Press 2011 303p $26.95   **153.8**
  1. Self-control 2. Supply and demand
  ISBN 978-1-59420-281-0
           LC 2010-28525
"Akst combines the disciplines of history, philosophy, psychology, economics, and literature in examining this phenomenon and inspires readers to view self-control in a positive light. Essential for all people concerned with their own overindulgences and with the future of society in general." Libr J
Includes bibliographical references

Cialdini, Robert B.

★ **Influence**: the psychology of persuasion; Rev. ed.; 1st Collins business essentials ed; Collins 2007 320p il pa $17.95   **153.8**
  1. Persuasion (Psychology)
  ISBN 0-06-124189-X; 978-0-06-124189-5
  First published 1984
The author "explains the psychology of why people say 'yes'—and how to apply these understandings." Publisher's note
Includes bibliographical references

Dennett, Daniel Clement

Freedom evolves; {by} Daniel C. Dennett. Viking 2003 347p il $24.95; pa $17   **153.8**
  1. Decision making 2. Free will and determinism
  ISBN 0-670-03186-0; 0-14-200384-0 pa
           LC 2002-28085
"Drawing on evolutionary biology, neuroscience, economic game theory, philosophy and Richard Dawkins's meme, the author argues that there is indeed such a thing as free will, but it 'is not a preexisting feature of our existence, like the law of gravity.' . . . This book comprises a kind of toolbox of intellectual exercises favoring cultural evolution, the idea that culture, morality and freedom are as much a result of evolution by natural selection as our physical and genetic attributes. Yet genetic determinism, he argues, does not imply inevitability, as his critics may claim, nor does it cancel out the soul. . . . Dennett clearly relishes pushing other scientists' buttons. Though natural selection itself is still a subject of controversy, the author . . . most certainly is in the vanguard of the philosophy of science." Publ Wkly
Includes bibliographical references

Dutton, Kevin

Split-second persuasion; the ancient art and new science of changing minds. Houghton Mifflin Harcourt 2011 296p il $26   **153.8**
  1. Persuasion (Psychology)
  ISBN 978-0-15-101279-4
           LC 2010-5739
First published 2010 in the United Kingdom

"This is a well-researched, wide-ranging treatise on the psychology of persuasion. The first section reviews research from an impressive variety of disciplines, from neuroscience to the biological and social sciences. The second section focuses on the author's main theme—split-second persuasion—a powerful 'superstrain' of persuasion that occurs quickly. Written for a less-experienced audience, the book is clear and nontechnical." Choice

Includes bibliographical references

Iyengar, Sheena

The **art** of choosing. Twelve 2010 329p il $25.99 **153.8**
1. Decision making 2. Choice (Psychology)
ISBN 978-0-446-50410-2; 0-446-50410-6

                                       LC 2009-37664

"In 'The Art of Choosing,' a broad and fascinating survey of current research on the subject, Iyengar stitches together personal anecdotes, examples from popular culture, and scientific evidence to explain the complex calculus that goes into our everyday choices, from picking our favorite soda to choosing our medical insurance. She also writes about the ways in which her blindness — Iyengar lost her sight as a teenager — has given her a unique perspective on the subject." Salon

Johnson, Steven, 1968-

Farsighted; how we make the decisions that matter the most. Steven Johnson. Riverhead Books 2018 256 p. (hardcover) $28   **153.8**
1. Decision making 2. Problem solving 3. Choice (Psychology)
ISBN 9781594488214

                                       LC 2017060305

In this book, author Steven Johnson, "uncovers powerful tools for honing the important skill of complex decision-making. . . . Johnson explains how we can most effectively approach the choices that can chart the course of a life, an organization, or a civilization. 'Farsighted' will help you imagine your possible futures and appreciate the subtle intelligence of the choices that shaped our broader social history." (Publisher's note)

"Science writer Johnson (Wonderland: How Play Made the Modern World) looks at decision-making, on both the individual and collective level, persuasively arguing that it should be approached not intuitively, but deliberately, rationally, and even scientifically." Pub Wkly

Includes bibliographical references and index

Lehrer, Jonah

How we decide. Houghton Mifflin Harcourt 2009 302p $25   **153.8**
1. Decision making
ISBN 978-0-618-62011-1; 0-618-62011-7

                                       LC 2008036769

"Lehrer is a delight to read, and this is a fascinating book . . . that will help everyone better understand themselves and their decision making." Publ Wkly

Includes bibliographical references

Levine, Robert

The **power** of persuasion; how we're bought and sold. Wiley 2003 278p hardcover o.p. pa $14.95   **153.8**
1. Interpersonal relations 2. Persuasion (Psychology)
ISBN 0-471-26634-5; 0-471-76317-9 pa

                                       LC 2002-9952

The author "opens by demonstrating that all of us . . . can be persuaded under the right circumstances. He goes on to study financial manipulation and the use of the sense of obligation . . . and then proceeds to a nuts-and-bolts analysis of salesmanship by describing what he learned and did (and had done to him) as an automobile salesman. . . . Inevitably, he moves to cults, the Moonies and the ultimate persuasion horror story, Jonestown." Publ Wkly

Includes bibliographical references

McKeown, Greg

Essentialism; the disciplined pursuit of less. Greg McKeown. Crown Business 2014 272 p. illustrations hbk $23 **153.8**
1. Decision making 2. Choice (Psychology) 3. Essentialism (Philosophy)
ISBN 0804137382; 9780804137386

                                       LC 2013038729

"Punctuated with zippy, thoughtful one-liners, this guide to doing 'less but better' offers strategies for determining what is truly necessary, and shedding what is not. Too many people fall for the having-it-all myth, and would benefit from shifting from a non-essentialist mindset (unable to distinguish and parse out the truly important) to an essentialist one (capable of identifying the goal), contends McKeown. Instead of attempting to achieve everything, readers need to figure out how to do the 'right thing the right way at the right time.'" (Pub Wkly)

Includes bibliographical references and index

Partnoy, Frank

Wait; the art and science of delay. Frank Partnoy. PublicAffairs 2012 xii, 290 p.p   **153.8**
1. Patience 2. Decision making 3. Thought and thinking 4. Procrastination
ISBN 1610390040; 9781610390040; 9781610390057

                                       LC 2012010970

In this book, Frank Partnoy "weaves together findings from hundreds of scientific studies and interviews with wide-ranging experts to craft a picture of effective decision-making that runs counter to our . . . fast-paced world. Even as technology exerts new pressures to speed up our lives, it turns out that the choices we make . . . benefit profoundly from delay. As this . . . book reveals, taking control of time and slowing down our responses yields better results in almost every arena of life." (Publisher's note)

Includes bibliographical references and index.

Vanderbilt, Tom

You may also like; taste in an age of endless choice. by Tom Vanderbilt. Alfred A. Knopf 2016 320 p. (hardcover) $26.95   **153.8**
1. Consumers 2. Aesthetics 3. Choice (Psychology) 4. Consumers' preferences 5. Aesthetics -- Psychological aspects
ISBN 9780307948595; 9780307958242

                                       LC 2015026997

This book, by Tom Vanderbilt, is "an enlightening and illuminating look at why we like the things we like, why we hate the things we hate, and what our preferences reveal about us. . . . Vanderbilt stalks the elusive beast of taste, probing research in psychology, marketing, and neuroscience to answer myriad complex and fascinating questions." (Publisher's note)

"Essential for readers who are interested in getting a glimpse of the decision-making process at influential online media companies, as well as those who are interested in the processes that govern individual preferences and taste making." LJ

Includes bibliographical references

153.9   Intelligence and aptitudes

Beilock, Sian L

Choke; what the secrets of the brain reveal about getting it right when you have to. Free Press 2010 294p il $26; ebook $12.99   **153.9**

1. Success 2. Failure (Psychology)

ISBN 978-1-4165-9617-2; 978-1-4391-0962-5 ebook

LC 2010-10595

"A star golfer misses a critical putt; a brilliant student fails to ace a test; a savvy salesperson blows a key presentation. Each of these people has suffered the same bump in mental processing: They have just choked under pressure. . . . By studying how the brain works when we are doing our best — and when we choke — Beilock has formulated practical ideas about how to overcome performance lapses at critical moments." Science Daily

Bloom, Harold

Genius; a mosaic of one hundred exemplary creative minds. Warner Bks. 2002 814p il $35.95; pa $19.95   **153.9**

1. Genius 2. Authors 3. Literature -- History and criticism

ISBN 0-446-52717-3; 0-446-69129-1 pa

LC 2002-16808

"Although the book is a delight to read, its real value lies in the author's ability to provoke the reader into thinking about literature, genius, and related topics. No similar work discusses literary genius in this way or covers this many writers." Libr J

Includes bibliographical references

Brogaard, Berit

The superhuman mind; free the genius in your brain. Berit Brogaard, PhD, and Kristian Marlow, MA. Hudson Street Press 2015 288 p. illustrations $25.95   **153.9**

1. Intellect 2. Psychology 3. Self-perception 4. Self-actualization (Psychology)

ISBN 1594633681; 9781594633683

LC 2014041967

This book by Berit Brogaard and Kristian Marlow "takes us inside the lives and brains of geniuses, savants, virtuosos, and a wide variety of ordinary people who have acquired truly extraordinary talents, one way or another. Delving into the neurological underpinnings of these abilities, the authors even reveal how we can acquire some of them ourselves--from perfect pitch and lightning fast math skills to supercharged creativity." (Publisher's note)

"An enjoyable book, but don't expect to make a major contribution to world civilization as a direct result of reading it." LJ

Includes bibliographical references and index

Ericsson, Anders

Peak; secrets from the new science of expertise. Anders Ericsson and Robert Pool. Houghton Mifflin Harcourt 2016 336 p. (hardcover) $28   **153.9**

1. Ability 2. Psychology of learning 3. Expertise 4. Performance -- Psychological aspects

ISBN 9780544456235; 9780544809703

LC 2015042796

This book, by Anders Ericsson and Robert Pool, offers "a powerful new approach to mastering almost any skill. . . . Expert performance guru Anders Ericsson has made a career studying chess champions, violin virtuosos, star athletes, and memory mavens. . . . [It] condenses three decades of original research to introduce an incredibly powerful approach to learning that is fundamentally different from the way people traditionally think about acquiring a skill." (Publisher's note)

"Throughout, the authors encourage dreaming big, even when conventional wisdom might dictate otherwise. This is an empowering, encouraging work that will challenge readers to reach for excellence." Pub Wkly

Includes bibliographical references and index

Gardner, Howard, 1943-

★ Frames of mind; the theory of multiple intelligences. Howard Gardner. Basic Books 2011 lii, 467 p.p (paperback) $19.99   **153.9**

1. Educational psychology 2. Multiple intelligences

ISBN 0465024335; 9780465024339

LC 2011294394

"First published in 1983 and now available with a new introduction by the author, Gardner's trailblazing book revolutionized the worlds of education and psychology by positing that rather than a single type of intelligence, we have several--most of which are neglected by standard testing and educational methods." (Publisher's note)

Includes bibliographical references (p. 413-451) and indexes

Gould, Stephen Jay

The mismeasure of man; rev & expanded ed; Norton 1996 444p il hardcover o.p. pa $15.95   **153.9**

1. Intelligence tests 2. Ability -- Testing

ISBN 0-393-31425-1 pa

LC 95-44442

First published 1981

The author examines the history of various scientific methods used to measure intelligence. He demonstrates how the research was used to perpetuate the myth of the intellectual superiority of the white male

Includes bibliographical references

Kurzweil, Ray, 1948-

★ The singularity is near; when humans transcend biology. [by] Ray Kurzweil. Viking 2005 652p il $29.95; pa $18   **153.9**

1. Robots 2. Genetics 3. Evolution 4. Nanotechnology

ISBN 0-670-03384-7; 0-14-303788-9 pa

LC 2004-61231

The book provides an "argument that a sudden acceleration in the growth of knowledge is about to make immortality technologically feasible. . . . A part of the argument concerns the transformation the human body will undergo as a result of the explosive increase of knowledge he believes is imminent. Nanotechnology will enable the design of nanobots . . . that will 'have myriad roles within the human body, including reversing human aging (to the extent that this task will not already have been completed through biotechnology, such as genetic engineering).' . . . But this will still not be immortality, and perfecting the human body is a phase in a much larger transformation. . . . 'Ultimately, the entire universe will become saturated with our intelligence.'" (New York Review of Books)

"Anyone can grasp Mr. Kurzweil's main idea: that mankind's technological knowledge has been snowballing, with dizzying prospects for the future. The basics are clearly expressed. But for those more knowledgeable and inquisitive, the author argues his case in fascinating detail." N Y Times (Late N Y Ed)

Includes bibliographical references

Murdoch, Stephen

IQ; a smart history of a failed idea. J. Wiley and Sons 2007 269p $24.95   **153.9**

1. Intelligence tests
ISBN 978-0-471-69977-4; 0-471-69977-2

LC 2006-32488

The author "traces now ubiquitous but still controversial attempts to measure intelligence to its origins in the late 19th and early 20th centuries. . . . This is a thoughtful overview and a welcome reminder of the dangers of relying on such standardized tests." Publ Wkly

Includes bibliographical references

154.2 The subconscious

Bargh, John

Before you know it; the unconscious reasons we do what we do. John Bargh, PhD. Touchstone 2017 vii, 343 p.p (hardcover) $26   **154.2**
1. Human behavior 2. Subconsciousness 3. Motivation (Psychology) 4. Cognition
ISBN 9781501101236; 9781501101212; 9781501101229

LC 2017008149

This book, by John Bargh, "gives us an entirely new understanding of the hidden mental processes that secretly govern every aspect of our behavior. . . . Telling personal anecdotes with infectious enthusiasm and disclosing startling and delightful discoveries, Dr. Bargh . . . and his colleagues have discovered how the unconscious guides our behavior, goals, and motivations in areas like race relations, parenting, business, consumer behavior, and addiction." (Publisher's note)

"In this impressive debut, Bargh, a professor of social psychology at Yale University, dives deep into human behavior and social psychology to unlock the enigmatic human unconscious." Pub Wkly

Includes bibliographical references and index.

Kandel, Eric R., 1929-

The **age** of insight; the quest to understand the unconscious in art, mind, and brain: from Vienna 1900 to the present. Eric R. Kandel. Random House 2011 636 p.   **154.2**
1. Intellect 2. Perception 3. Subconsciousness 4. Art -- Psychological aspects 5. Subconsciousness in art
ISBN 9781400068715; 9781588369307

LC 2011025274

This book examines "the interplay among art, psychology and brain science." It focuses on "Austrian artists Gustav Klimt, Oskar Kokoschka and Egon Schiele, each of whom was profoundly influenced by Sigmund Freud and by the emerging scientific approach to medicine in their day. Kandel describes the psychological and biological insights reflected in their paintings, as well as the neuroscience behind how the beholder perceives the paintings." (Scientific American)

Mlodinow, Leonard

Subliminal; how your unconscious mind rules your behavior. Leonard Mlodinow. Pantheon Books 2012 viii, 260 p.p ill. (hardcover) $25.95   **154.2**
1. Human behavior 2. Decision making 3. Subconsciousness 4. Applied psychology
ISBN 9780307378217; 0307378217

LC 2011048098

In this book about the unconscious, physicist Leonard "Mlodinow runs through study after study and some . . . real-life examples to reveal how subliminal processing controls our sensory systems, creates and distorts memories and guides our intuitions about people. . . . He is pragmatic about how completely it leads us astray and the near-impossibility of overriding it, but he . . . acknowledg[es] how lost he would be without

it." (New Scientist)
Includes bibliographical references and index

Tallis, Frank

Hidden minds; a history of the unconscious. Arcade Pub. 2002 194p $25.95   **154.2**
1. Subconsciousness
ISBN 1-55970-643-0

LC 2002-74566

"Highly readable and possessing a surprising degree of depth, this book manages to be both entertaining and informative." Libr J

Includes bibliographical references

Vedantam, Shankar

The **hidden** brain; how our unconscious minds elect presidents, control markets, wage wars, and save our lives. Spiegel & Grau 2009 270p $26; pa $16   **154.2**
1. Perception 2. Subconsciousness 3. Motivation (Psychology)
ISBN 978-0-385-52521-3; 0-385-52521-4; 978-0-385-52522-0 pa; 0-385-52522-2 pa

LC 2009-19717

"A tour into dark realms of the psyche by a personable guide." Kirkus

Includes bibliographical references

154.6 Sleep phenomena

Freud, Sigmund, 1856-1939

★ **Interpretation** of dreams; translated by Joyce Crick; edited with an introduction by Ritchie Robinson. Oxford University Press 2008 514p il (Oxford world's classics) pa $14.95   **154.6**
1. Dreams 2. Psychoanalysis
ISBN 978-0-19-953758-7; 0-19-953758-5
Original German edition, 1900; first English translation published 1913
Groundbreaking analysis of dreams as manifestations of suppressed unconscious desires

Lewis, James R.

★ The **dream** encyclopedia; [by] James R. Lewis and Evelyn Dorothy Oliver. 2nd ed.; Visible Ink Press 2009 xxi, 410p il pa $24.95   **154.6**
1. Reference books 2. Dreams -- Encyclopedias
ISBN 978-1-57859-216-6

LC 2009-5132

First published 1995 by Gale Res.

This "reference examines more than 250 dream-related topics, from art to history to science, including how factors such as self-healing, ESP, literature, religion, sex, cognition and memory, and medical conditions can all have an effect on dreams. Dream symbolism and interpretation is examined in historical, cultural, and psychological detail." Publisher's note

Includes bibliographical references

155 Differential and developmental psychology

Bailey, Rebecca Anne

Easy to love, difficult to discipline; the 7 basic skills for

turning conflict into cooperation. {by} Becky A. Bailey. Morrow 2000 285p hardcover o.p. pa $12.95 **155**
1. Parenting 2. Child rearing
ISBN 0-06-000775-3 pa

LC 99-44313

"Bailey contends that the difficult but rewarding task of guiding children's behavior starts only when parents are able to discipline themselves and become models of self-control. . . . Bailey's underlying message is positive and hopeful, supported with humorous anecdotes and helpful solutions." Publ Wkly

Includes bibliographical references

Kagan, Jerome

The **human** spark; the science of human development. Jerome Kagan. Basic Books 2013 352 p. (hardcover) $28.99 **155**
1. Psychology 2. Child development 3. Child psychology
ISBN 0465029825; 9780465029822

LC 2012047558

In this book, developmental psychologist Jerome Kagan points out that "a great deal of what we 'know' about human development isn't firmly anchored in empirical science. He aims to correct that by encouraging readers to question received knowledge . . . and he does so by presenting [a] . . . discussion of the epistemology of psychology, alongside . . . critiques of the methodologies used in psychological research and the social applications of misinterpreted findings." (Publishers Weekly)

Includes bibliographical references and index

Levine, Josh

Why don't you want my stuff? by Josh Levine. BookBaby 2018 132 p. (pbk.) $16.99 **155**
1. Aging 2. Parenting 3. Baby boom generation
ISBN 154392199X; 9781543921991

This book, by Josh Levine, is 'a Boomer's guide to downsizing, their Millennial kid's psyche and just things that are so An easy to understand (maybe even fun) guide through the secondary market of online retailing, auctions and estate sales. . . . From any perspective you will finish with an understanding of the disconnect between the generations as well as with actionable knowledge for your inevitable quest to liquidate seemingly unwanted stuff." (Publisher's note)

"Levine's insights into antiques economics along with his terrific needle-in-a-haystack anecdotes about discovering treasure among clutter will inspire readers to not only dig through their attic, but maybe visit some estate and tag sales." Publishers' Weekly

155.2 Individual psychology

Bluestein, Jane

The **perfection** deception; why striving to be perfect is sabotaging your relationships, making you sick, and holding your happiness hostage. Jane Bluestein. HCI 2015 312 p. charts (paperback) $15.95 **155.2**
1. Psychology 2. Self-help techniques 3. Perfectionism (Personality trait)
ISBN 0757318258; 9780757318252

LC 2015027944

In this book, Dr. Jane Bluestein "exposes the truth: perfectionism is actually a mask for a fear of making mistakes, a desperate need to avoid negative judgments and rejection. . . . Through personal interviews and the latest research, she explores how our culture fuels the dysfunction, how perfectionism develops, and how it can hurt our physical, mental, and social well-being. Further, she provides practical strategies for mov-

ing toward authenticity and wholeness.." (Publisher's note)

"An excellent and full description of the problems of perfectionism that helps readers alter their self-conceptions." LJ

Includes bibliographical references and index

Cain, Susan

Quiet; the power of introverts in a world that can't stop talking. Susan Cain. Crown Publishers 2012 x, 333 p.p **155.2**
1. Interpersonal relations 2. Introversion and extroversion 3. Introverts 4. Extraversion 5. Introversion
ISBN 9780307352149; 9780307452207

LC 2010053204

It was the author's intent to discuss "the one-third to one-half of the population who are introverts. She defines the term broadly, including 'solitude-seeking' and 'contemplative,' but also 'sensitive,' 'humble,' and 'risk-averse.' Such individuals, she claims . . . are "'disproportionately represented among the ranks of the spectacularly creative.' Yet the American school and workplace make it difficult for those who draw strength from solitary musing by overemphasizing teamwork. . . . She notes [that] introverts can negotiate as well as, or better than, alpha males and females because they can take a firm stand 'without inflaming [their] counterpart's ego.' Cain provides tips to parents and teachers of children who are introverted or seem socially awkward and isolated. She suggests, for instance, exposing them gradually to new experiences that are otherwise overstimulating." (Publishers Weekly)

Includes bibliographical references (p. [277]-323) and index

Crawford, Matthew B.

The **World** Beyond Your Head; On Becoming an Individual in an Age of Distraction. Farrar Straus & Giroux 2015 320 p. $26 **155.2**
1. Psychology 2. Thought and thinking
ISBN 0374292981; 9780374292980

LC 2015933043

Author Matthew B. Crawford "investigates the challenge of mastering one's own mind. [He] makes sense of an astonishing array of common experience, from the frustrations of airport security to the rise of the hipster. With implications for the way we raise our children, the design of public spaces, and democracy itself, this is a book of urgent relevance to contemporary life." (Publisher's note)

"This illuminating work will appeal to students of philosophy and sociology, as well as fans of good cultural analysis." LJ

Csikszentmihalyi, Mihaly

★ **Flow**: the psychology of optimal experience. Harper Perennial 2008 303p pa $14.95 **155.2**
1. Attention 2. Happiness 3. Applied psychology
ISBN 978-0-06-133920-2; 0-06-133920-2
First published 1990

This book offers a discussion of "'flow,' a field of behavioral science examining connections between satisfaction and daily activities. [According to the author], a flow state ensues when one is engaged in self-controlled, goal-related, meaningful actions. . . . This thoroughly researched study is an intriguing look at the age-old problem of the pursuit of happiness and how, through conscious effort, we may more easily attain it." Libr J

Ehrenreich, Barbara

★ **Bright**-sided; how the relentless promotion of positive thinking has undermined America. Metropolitan Books/Henry Holt and Co. 2009 235p $23 **155.2**
1. Success 2. Optimism 3. Happiness 4. Self-confidence

ISBN 978-0-8050-8749-9; 0-8050-8749-4

LC 2009-23588

"The author's tough-minded and convincing broadside raises troubling questions about many aspects of contemporary American life. . . . Bright, incisive, provocative thinking." Kirkus

Includes bibliographical references

Emre, Merve

The **personality** brokers; the strange history of Myers-Briggs and the birth of personality testing. by Merve Emre. Doubleday, a division of Penguin Random House LLC 2018 336 p. (hardcover) $27.95   **155.2**

1. Personality tests 2. Typology (Psychology) 3. Myers-Briggs Type Indicator 4. Personality tests -- History 5. Self-consciousness (Awareness)

ISBN 9780385541909; 9781101974148

LC 2018011977

Written by Merve Emre, "this combined dual biography and social history seeks explanations for why an admittedly flawed, unscientifically proven personality test--created in the 1920s by a mother-daughter team of two untrained pseudointellectuals--continues to be the most revered personality indicator in existence...[T]his eye-opening account gives readers insight into how one evaluation method morphed into a neat, satisfying packaging system for our complicated psyches." (Booklist)

Includes bibliographical references

Fanning, Patrick

★ **Self**-esteem; a proven program of cognitive techniques for assessing, improving, & maintaining your self-esteem. Matthew McKay, PhD, Patrick Fanning. Fourth edition New Harbinger Publications 2016 vii, 358 p.p illustrations (paperback) $17.95   **155.2**

1. Self-esteem

ISBN 9781626253933; 1626253935; 9781626253957

LC 2016461087

This book, by Matthew McKay and Patrick Fanning, "uses proven-effective methods of CBT and relevant components of ACT to help you raise low self-esteem by working on the way you interpret your life. You'll learn how to differentiate between healthy and unhealthy self-esteem, how to uncover and analyze negative self-statements, and how to create new, more objective and positive self-statements to support your self-esteem rather than undermine it." (Publisher's note)

Includes bibliographical references (pages 357-358).

Gladwell, Malcolm, 1963-

David and Goliath; underdogs, misfits, and the art of battling giants. Malcolm Gladwell. Little, Brown & Co. 2013 304 p. illustrations (hardcover) $29   **155.2**

1. Success 2. Self-help techniques 3. Opportunity 4. Motivation (Psychology) 5. Struggle -- Psychological aspects

ISBN 9780316204361; 0316204366; 9780316239851

LC 2013941807

In this book, author Malcolm Gladwell "examines and challenges our concepts of 'advantage' and 'disadvantage' in a way that may seem intuitive to some and surprising to others. Beginning with the classic tale of David and Goliath and moving through history with figures such as Lawrence of Arabia and Martin Luther King Jr., Gladwell shows how, time and again, players labeled 'underdog' use that status to their advantage and prevail through the elements of cunning and surprise." (Booklist)

"Gladwell rewards readers with moving stories, surprising insights and consistently provocative ideas." Kirkus

Includes bibliographical references and index

Goldsmith, Marshall

Triggers; creating behavior that lasts-- becoming the person you want to be. by Marshall Goldsmith and Mark Reiter. Random House Inc 2015 244 p. illustrations $27   **155.2**

1. Human behavior 2. Behavior modification

ISBN 0804141231; 9780804141239

In this book, authors Marshall Goldsmith and Mark Reiter examine "the environmental and psychological triggers that can derail us at work and in life. . . . These triggers are constant and relentless and omnipresent. . . . So often the environment seems to be outside our control. Even if that is true, as Goldsmith points out, we have a choice in how we respond." (Publisher's note)

Greitens, Eric, 1974-

Resilience; hard-won wisdom for living a better life. Eric Greitens. Houghton Mifflin Harcourt 2015 320 p. (hardback) $26   **155.2**

1. Life skills 2. Self-help techniques 3. Resilience (Personality trait)

ISBN 054432398X; 9780544323988

LC 2014035279

In this book, Navy SEAL Eric Greitens "offer[s] a masterpiece of warrior wisdom that will change your life. . . . There is a path through pain to wisdom, through suffering to strength, and through fear to courage if we have the virtue of resilience. . . . [Greitens] explains how we can build purpose, confront pain, practice compassion, develop a vocation, find a mentor, create happiness, and much more." (Publisher's note)

"Based on the practices he suggests to build compassion, confront pain and create happiness, readers can move beyond their fears and create creative, energized lives rich in wisdom and filled with friendships and mentorships. Robust, heart-to-heart lessons for moving beyond obstacles to create a better life." Kirkus

Harris, Judith Rich

No two alike; human nature and human individuality. W.W. Norton & Co. 2006 322p il $26.95   **155.2**

1. Personality 2. Individuality

ISBN 0-393-05948-0

LC 2005-25837

"Harris makes behavioral genetics and evolutionary psychology enjoyable and accessible to general readers as well as scholars." Libr J

Includes bibliographical references

Helgoe, Laurie A.

Introvert power; why your inner life is your hidden strength. [by] Laurie Helgoe. Sourcebooks 2008 xxiv, 256p il pa $15.95   **155.2**

1. Introversion and extroversion

ISBN 978-1-4022-1117-1; 1-4022-1117-1

LC 2008-4967

Shows readers how to use introversion not as a weakness but as a source of power.

"The author's voice is vivid and engaging, and she skillfully draws real-life examples of awkward scenarios introverts find themselves in when forced to play a role in society or the workplace. Readers will find much insight, as well as a comforting sense of being understood and validated." Publ Wkly

Includes bibliographical references

Hood, Bruce

The **self** illusion; how the social brain creates identity. Bruce Hood. Oxford University Press 2012 xvii, 349 p.p ill. (trade: alk. paper) $29.95   **155.2**
1. Self 2. Brain 3. Theory of knowledge 4. Cognition
ISBN 019989759X; 9780199897599

LC 2011047151

This book presents an "account of . . . developments in psychology and neuroscience that are helping to substantiate theories of selfhood positing that there is no concrete identity at the core of our being, and that our sense of self is an illusion spun from narratives we construct about our lives." It "explor[es] subjects such as free will, the unconscious, [and] the role of (false) memories in building identity." (New Scientist)
Includes bibliographical references (p. 297-341) and index.

Keltner, Dacher

Born to be good; the science of a meaningful life. W. W. Norton & Co. 2009 336p il $25.95   **155.2**
1. Altruism 2. Cooperation 3. Helping behavior 4. Interpersonal relations
ISBN 978-0-393-06512-1

LC 2008-42492

"A landmark book in the science of emotion and its implications for ethics and human universals, this is essential for all libraries." Libr J
Includes bibliographical references

Mischel, Walter, 1930-2018

The **marshmallow** test; mastering self-control. Walter Mischel. Little, Brown & Co. 2014 336 p. illustrations (paperback) $16.99   **155.2**
1. Self-control 2. Applied psychology
ISBN 0316230863; 9780316230865; 9780316230872; 9780316336192

LC 2014018058

In this book, by Walter Mischel, the "designer of the famous Marshmallow Test, explains what self-control is and how to master it. . . . [The author] explains how self-control can be mastered and applied to challenges in everyday life--from weight control to quitting smoking, overcoming heartbreak, making major decisions, and planning for retirement . . . , with profound implications for the choices we make in parenting, education, public policy and self-care." (Publisher's note)
Includes bibliographical references (pages 283-316) and index

Moran, Joe

Shrinking violets; the secret life of shyness. Joe Moran. Yale University Press 2017 272 p. (hardcover) $26   **155.2**
1. Shyness 2. Bashfulness 3. Bashfulness -- Social aspects
ISBN 0300222823; 9780300222821; 9780300234596

LC 2016948565

This book, by Joe Moran, is a "cultural history of shyness. . . . Shyness is a pervasive human trait: even most extroverts know what it is like to stand tongue-tied at the fringe of an unfamiliar group or flush with embarrassment at being the unwelcome center of attention. And yet the cultural history of shyness has remained largely unwritten—until now." (Publisher's note)
"This lovely book is like a stroll through the park on a lazy afternoon with an immensely erudite friend who knows everything there is to know about shyness, is self-confessedly shy himself, and knows how to weave his erudition into a deeply engrossing story." Choice
Includes bibliographical references (pages 237-254) and index

Myers, Isabel Briggs

Gifts differing; understanding personality type. [by] Isabel Briggs Myers with Peter B. Myers. Davies-Black Pub 1995 228p il pa $16.95   **155.2**
1. Personality
ISBN 0-89106-074-X

LC 95-4184

First published 1980 by Consulting Psychologists Press
This is a guide to the 16 personality types distinguished in the Myers-Briggs Type Indicator.
Includes bibliographical references

Northrup, Christiane

Dodging energy vampires; an empath's guide to evading relationships that drain you and restoring your health and power. Christiane Northrup, M.D. Hay House, Inc. 2018 xii, 230 p.p (hardcover: alk. paper) $24.99   **155.2**
1. Empathy 2. Well-being 3. Mental health 4. Sensitivity (Personality trait)
ISBN 1401954774; 9781401954772

LC 2017048779

This book, by Christiane Northrup, "draws on the latest research . . . [on empathy], along with stories from her global community and her own life, to explore the phenomenon of energy vampires and show us how we can spot them, dodge their tactics, and take back our own energy. You'll delve into the dynamics of vampire-empath relationships and discover how vampires use others' energy to fuel their own dysfunctional lives." (Publisher's note)
Includes bibliographical references and index

Pinker, Steven, 1954-

The **blank** slate; the denial of human nature in modern intellectual life. Viking 2002 509p $27.95; pa $16   **155.2**
1. Nature and nurture
ISBN 0-670-03151-8; 0-14-2003344 pa

LC 2002-22719

The author "attacks the notion that an infant's mind is a blank slate, arguing instead that human beings have an inherited universal structure shaped by the demands made upon the species for survival, albeit with plenty of room for cultural and individual variation." Publ Wkly
Includes bibliographical references

Rudder, Christian

Dataclysm; our life in numbers. Christian Rudder. Crown Publishers 2014 368 p. illustrations, maps (hardback) $28   **155.2**
1. Social media 2. Human behavior 3. Big data 4. Behavioral assessment
ISBN 0385347375; 9780385347372; 9780385347396

LC 2014007364

Los Angeles Times Book Prizes Finalist: Science and Technology (2014)

In this book, author Christian Rudder "explains how Facebook 'likes' can predict, with surprising accuracy, a person's sexual orientation and even intelligence; how attractive women receive exponentially more interview requests; and why you must have haters to be hot. He charts the rise and fall of America's most reviled word through Google Search and examines the new dynamics of collaborative rage on Twitter. He shows how people express themselves, both privately and publicly." (Publisher's note)
"Demographers, entrepreneurs, students of history and sociology, and ordinary citizens alike will find plenty of provocations and, yes,

much data in Rudder's well-argued, revealing pages." Kirkus
Includes bibliographical references (pages 249-281) and index

Seligman, Martin E. P.

★ **Learned** optimism; how to change your mind and your life. Vintage Books 2006 319p pa $14.95   **155.2**
1. Self-perception 2. Adjustment (Psychology)
ISBN 1-4000-7839-3; 978-1-4000-7839-4

LC 2006-277713
First published 1991
Seligman "has written a lively, very accessible book. . . . Presented for lay readers, this book can be highly recommended to professionals as well for its lucid and informative introduction to cognitive therapy and its approach to issues of mood and depression." Libr J
Includes bibliographical references

Shenk, David

The **genius** in all of us; why everything you've been told about genetics, talent, and IQ is wrong. Doubleday 2010 302p il $26.95   **155.2**
1. Ability 2. Heredity 3. Intellect
ISBN 978-0-385-52365-3; 0-385-52365-3

LC 2009-18376
Shenk "tells engaging stories, lucidly explains complex research and offers fresh insights into the nature of exceptional performance. . . . [This is] deeply interesting and important book." N Y Times Book Rev
Includes bibliographical references

Storr, Will

Selfie; how we became so self-obsessed and what it's doing to us. Will Storr. The Overlook Press 2018 416 p. $29.95 **155.2**
1. Self-perception 2. Identity (Psychology)
ISBN 1468315897; 9781468315899
This book, by Will Storr, "explores the mysterious power of the self and reveals the danger of our modern obsession with it. . . . Every day, we're bombarded with depictions of the beautiful, successful, slim, socially conscious, and extroverted individual that our culture has decided is the perfect self. . . . Journalist and novelist Will Storr began to wonder about this perfect self that torments so many of us: Where does this ideal come from? Why is it so powerful?" (Publisher's note)

Triandis, Harry C.

Fooling ourselves; self-deception in politics, religion, and terrorism. Harry C. Triandis. Praeger Publishers 2009 xxvi, 246p (alk. paper) $49.95   **155.2**
1. Deception 2. Psychology 3. Social psychology 4. Psychology of religion
ISBN 9780313364389; 0313364389

LC 2008033679
In this book, author Harry C. "Triandis shows how and why self-deception takes place, and its subtle and profound effects on our everyday lives. Self-deception occurs because we often see the world the way we would like it to be, rather than the way it is. Our brains so long for things the way we want them, we might not even be aware we are fooling ourselves. . . . Across cultures and around the world, self-deception is a phenomenon that has subtle and profound effects on everyday life, explains Triandis, . . . former president of the International Association of Cross-Cultural Psychology. In this work, he not only explains how and why self-deceptions occur in three areas - politics, religion, and terrorism - but also how to recognize and reduce the frequency of fooling ourselves." (Publisher's note)
Includes bibliographical references (p. [209]-235) and indexes.

Weber, Robert J.

The **created** self; reinventing body, persona, spirit. Norton 2000 350p il hardcover o.p. pa $14.95   **155.2**
1. Self 2. Psychology
ISBN 0-393-32121-5 pa

LC 99-37480
The author contends that "having a self enables the individual to pursue creative endeavors, which though often adaptive from an evolutionary standpoint, actually extend beyond what can be explained in terms of biological, reproductive aims. Using the model of the self developed by William James . . . Weber attempts to show that the self is a constantly developing, 'unitary system', consisting of bodily awareness, persona and spirit, over which the individual has control." Publ Wkly
Includes bibliographical references

Young-Eisendrath, Polly

The **self**-esteem trap; raising confident and compassionate kids in an age of self-importance. Little, Brown 2008 248p $25.99   **155.2**
1. Self-esteem 2. Child psychology
ISBN 978-0-316-01311-6; 0-316-01311-0

LC 2008-2224
The author argues that "those born between 1970 and 2000 (Gen Me-ers) . . . are a vastly discontented group who find their lives unsatisfying and feel entitled to success owing to an overestimation of what the world will bring. She views this as a cultural problem begun in the 1980s when the collapse of the traditional parental hierarchy coincided with a hyperfocus on self-esteem. . . . This is well written, accessible, soundly researched, and beautifully insightful." Libr J
Includes bibliographical references

155.24 Adaptability and adjustment

Abbott, Christmas

The **badass** life; 30 amazing days to a lifetime of great habits--body, mind, and spirit. Christmas Abbott. William Morrow & Co 2017 xiii, 290 p.p illustrations (chiefly color) (hardcover) $28.99   **155.24**
1. Lifestyles 2. Self-improvement 3. Habit 4. Health 5. Wellbeing 6. Conduct of life
ISBN 9780062645197; 9780062645210; 0062645196
This book by Christmas Abbott is "a day-by-day guide designed to encourage habit change through fun, dynamic daily tasks challenging your mind, body, and spirit. 'The Badass Life' is her month-long-program based on building positive daily habits, to help you achieve a higher quality of life and a heightened sense of self-worth." (Publisher's note)
"Readers seeking ways to jump-start their lives will find Abbot a companionable guide." Pub Wkly
Includes bibliographical references (pages 283-284) and index.

Wicks, Robert J.

Night call; embracing compassion and hope in a troubled world. by Robert J. Wicks. Oxford University Press 2018 xxviii, 248 p.p (hardcover) $24.95   **155.24**
1. Compassion 2. Counseling 3. Social work 4. Human services 5. Resilience (Personality trait) 6. Social service
ISBN 9780190669638; 9780190669645; 0190669632

LC 2017000502
This book, by Robert J. Wicks, "offers the stories and principles gleaned over many years of writing and mentoring for those in the help-

ing and healing professions. The stories are offered in ways that foster compassionate caring while encouraging initiative in those who seek to personally deepen and share their lives with others -- especially in times of significant need." (Publisher's note)

Includes bibliographical references and index

155.3 Sex psychology; psychology of people by gender or sex, by sexual orientation

Chemaly, Soraya

Rage becomes her; the power of women's anger. Soraya L. Chemaly. Atria Books 2018 416 p. (hardcover) $27 **155.3**
1. Anger 2. Women -- Psychology 3. Women -- Social conditions
ISBN 9781501189555; 9781501189562

LC 2018010867

This book, by Soraya Chemaly, "makes the case that anger is not what gets in our way, it is our way, sparking a new understanding of one of our core emotions that will give women a liberating sense of why their anger matters and connect them to an entire universe of women no longer interested in making nice at all costs." (Publishe's note)

Eldredge, Niles

★ **Why** we do it; rethinking sex and the selfish gene. Norton 2004 269p il $24.95 **155.3**
1. Evolution 2. Sociobiology 3. Sex (Biology)
ISBN 0-393-05082-3

LC 2003-27564

"This book, while written for the lay reader, is appropriate for a scientific audience as well. It could be used as supplementary reading in college courses in animal behavior." Sci Books & Films

Fine, Cordelia

Testosterone rex; myths of sex, science, and society. Cordelia Fine. W W Norton & Co Inc 2017 272 p. (ebook) $50; (hardcover) $26.95 **155.3**
1. Sex 2. Gender role 3. Sex differences (Psychology) 4. Sex (Biology) 5. Sex (Psychology)
ISBN 9780393253887; 9780393082081

LC 2016031608

In this book, psychologist Cordelia Fine "explains why past and present sex roles are only serving suggestions for the future, revealing a much more dynamic situation through an entertaining and well-documented exploration of the latest research that draws on evolutionary science, psychology, neuroscience, endocrinology, and philosophy. She uses stories from daily life, scientific research, and common sense to break through the din of cultural assumptions."

"A fascinating, greatly contemplative discussion of sex and gender and the embedded societal expectations of both." Kirkus

Includes bibliographical references and index

Gottman, John

The **man's** guide to women; scientifically proven secrets from the "love lab" about what women really want. John Gottman, PhD, Julie Schwartz Gottman, PhD, Douglas Abrams, Rachel Carlton Abrams, MD, with Lara Love Hardin. Rodale 2015 224 p. illustrations (trade hardcover) $22.99 **155.3**
1. Women -- Psychology 2. Man-woman relationship 3. Sex -- Psychological aspects 4. Sex (Psychology) 5. Sexual attraction 6. Man-woman relationships -- Psychological aspects
ISBN 9781623361846

LC 2015041297

This book, by John Gottman, Julie Schwartz Gottman, Douglas Abrams, and Rachel Carlton Abrams, is a "definitive guide for men, providing answers on everything from how to approach a woman and build a connection with her to how to truly satisfy her in bed and know when the relationship is on the right track. [It] is a must-have playbook for how to play—and win—the game of love." (Publisher's note)

"This should be required reading for men who are both baffled by and interested in women." Pub Wkly

Includes bibliographical references and index

Pincott, J.

Do gentlemen really prefer blondes? bodies, behavior and brains: the science behind sex, love, and attraction. [by] Jena Pincott. Delacorte Press 2008 351p il $20 **155.3**
1. Dating (Social customs) 2. Sexual behavior
ISBN 978-0-385-34215-5; 0-385-34215-2

LC 2008-23933

The author "argues that desire is strongly rooted in evolutionary biases and consults a variety of studies . . . to reveal the extent to which hormones dictate human behavior." Publ Wkly

Includes bibliographical references

155.333 Pschology -- Women

Huston, Therese

How women decide; what's true, what's not, and what strategies spark the best choices. Therese Huston. Houghton Mifflin Harcourt 2016 384 p. (hardcover) $28 **155.333**
1. Businesswomen 2. Decision making 3. Women -- Psychology 4. Decision making -- Sex differences 5. Decision making -- Psychological aspects
ISBN 9780544416093

LC 2015037243

In this book, by Therese Huston, "from confidence gaps to power poses, leaning in to calling bias out, bossypants to girl bosses, women have been hearing a lot of advice lately. Most of this aims at greater success, but very little focuses on a key set of skills that ensures such success—making the wisest, strongest decisions." (Publisher's note)

"Useful, practical strategies based on informed analysis." Kirkus
Includes bibliographical references

155.4 Psychology of specific ages

Brazelton, T. Berry

The **irreducible** needs of children; what every child must have to grow, learn, and flourish. {by} T. Berry Brazelton, Stanley I. Greenspan. Perseus Bks. 2000 xx, 228p hardcover o.p. pa $14 **155.4**
1. Child rearing 2. Child psychology 3. Child development
ISBN 0-7382-0516-8 pa

LC 2001-2290

This is "a practical, well-organized volume, of value to parents, physicians, teachers, sociologists, and others who wish to improve children's lives locally and globally." Booklist

Includes bibliographical references

★ **To** listen to a child; understanding the normal problems of growing up. photographs by B.A. King. Addison-Wesley 1984 184p il hardcover o.p. **155.4**

1. Sleep 2. Asthma 3. Child psychology 4. Child development 5. Parent-child relationship 6. Emotionally disturbed children 7. Children -- Health and hygiene

LC 84-6174

"Brazelton's sensible, authoritative, clear approach provides parents with the kinds of information they need to relax over the long pull, and to understand and cope with day-to-day difficulties." Publ Wkly

Elkind, David

★ The **power** of play; how spontaneous, imaginative activities lead to happier, healthier children. Da Capo Lifelong 2007 240p $24   **155.4**

1. Play

ISBN 0-7382-1053-6; 978-0-7382-1053-7

LC 2006-35592

"Prescribing the trinity of play, love, and work, . . . [the author] shows how the integration of these elements at various stages of development, from infancy to adolescence, leads to happier, well-adjusted individuals with a greater potential for academic success. Elkind will connect with parents when he reveals that 'Toys R Not Us' and argues that less is more; that children should use toys for inspiration, not distraction." Libr J

Includes bibliographical references

Gopnik, Alison

The **gardener** and the carpenter; What the New Science of Child Development Tells Us About the Relationship Between Parents and Children. Alison Gopnik. Farrar, Straus & Giroux 2016 320 p. illustrations (hardback) $26   **155.4**

1. Parenting 2. Child psychology 3. Child development 4. Developmental psychology

ISBN 9780374229702

LC 2015048667

In this book, "developmental psychologist and philosopher Alison Gopnik argues that the familiar twenty-first-century picture of parents and children is profoundly wrong. . . . Drawing on the study of human evolution and her own cutting-edge scientific research into how children learn, Gopnik shows that although caring for children is profoundly important, it is not a matter of shaping them to turn out a particular way." (Publisher's note)

"A highly thoughtful and entertaining treatment of a subject that merits serious consideration." Kirkus

Includes bibliographical references and index

The **scientist** in the crib; minds, brains, and how children learn. [by] Alison Gopnik, Andrew N. Meltzoff, Patricia K. Kuhl. Morrow 1999 279p hardcover o.p. pa $14   **155.4**

1. Child development 2. Psychology of learning

ISBN 0-688-17788-3 pa

LC 99-24247

The authors examine "how children learn to understand and use language, control their emotions and arouse the emotions of others, and establish relationships. . . . Prospective and actual parents stand to learn much that may be helpful to them and their children from this lively book." Booklist

Includes bibliographical references

Johnson, Ned

The **self**-driven child; the science and sense of giving your kids more control over their lives. William Stixrud, PhD, and Ned Johnson. Viking 2018 viii, 367 p.p (hardcover) $28 **155.4**

1. Parenting 2. Child psychology 3. Education -- Parent

participation 4. Child rearing 5. Self-reliance in children 6. Stress management for children 7. Achievement motivation in children

ISBN 9780735222533; 9780735222519; 0735222517

LC 2017301146

This book, by William Stixrud and Ned Johnson, "offers a combination of cutting-edge brain science, the latest discoveries in behavioral therapy, and case studies drawn from the thousands of kids and teens Bill and Ned have helped over the years to teach you how to set your child on the real road to success. As parents, we can only drive our kids so far. At some point, they will have to take the wheel and map out their own path." (Publisher's note)

"Neuropsychiatrist Stixrud and Johnson, founder of a test-prep service, provide a nuanced and enormously insightful look into the struggles facing so many children and teens." Booklist

Includes bibliographical references (pages 327-351) and index.

Linn, Susan

The **case** for make believe; saving play in a commercialized world. New Press 2008 258p $24.95   **155.4**

1. Play 2. Imagination 3. Advertising and children

ISBN 978-1-56584-970-9; 1-56584-970-1

LC 2007-42435

"Puppeteer and therapist Linn draws on years of work at Boston Children's Hospital to make a thoughtful case for creative play. She distinguishes between children who are familiar with concepts of imagination and make-believe versus those who know only how to play with manufactured toys linked to media campaigns or within the constructs of rule-driven environments. . . . None of this will be news to most parents, but Linn seeks to discover what it means for children to no longer spend time pretending to be someone or somewhere else. Her research is comprehensive, her firsthand knowledge is impressive, and her examples are damning in their conclusions." Booklist

Includes bibliographical references

Louv, Richard

Last child in the woods; saving our children from nature-deficit disorder. Algonquin Books of Chapel Hill 2005 323p $24.95   **155.4**

1. Child psychology 2. Environmental influence on humans

ISBN 1-56512-391-3

LC 2004-66034

"Louv's book is a call to action, full of warnings—but also full of ideas for change." Publ Wkly

Includes bibliographical references

Piaget, Jean

★ The **moral** judgment of the child; {translated by Marjorie Gabain} Free Press 1948 418p hardcover o.p. pa $15   **155.4**

1. Ethics 2. Human behavior 3. Child psychology

ISBN 0-684-83330-1 pa

Original French edition, 1932

Piaget studies, not the moral behavior of children, but their ideas about right and wrong, the rules of a game, adult authority, and cooperation and justice

Siegel, Daniel J.

The **yes** brain; how to cultivate courage, curiosity, and resilience in your child. Daniel J. Siegel, M.D. and Tina Payne Bryson, Ph.D. Bantam 2018 xii, 184 p.p illustrations (hardcover) $27   **155.4**

1. Parenting 2. Child rearing 3. Resilience (Personality trait) 4.

Resilience (Personality trait) in children
ISBN 9780399594670; 9780399594663; 0399594663

LC 2017037802

This book, by Daniel J. Siegel and Tina Payne Bryson, "is an essential tool for nurturing positive potential and keeping your child's inner spark glowing and growing strong--and gifting your children with a life of rich relational connections, meaningful interactions with the world, and emotional equanimity." (Publisher's note)

"Siegel and Bryson have taken a high-level concept and broken it down into an approach that is easy to understand and implement. Parents, grandparents, teachers, clinicians, and other caregivers will find something in the plan that they can use to help the children in their care to excel." Pub Wkly

Tuck, Shonna

Getting from me to we; how to help young children fit in and make friends. Shonna L. Tuck, M.A., SLP. Woodbine House Inc. 2015 220 p. (pbk.: alk. paper) $24.95 **155.4**
1. Friendship 2. Child development 3. Adjustment (Psychology) 4. Adjustment (Psychology) in children
ISBN 9781606132692

LC 2015023676

This book, by Shonna L. Tuck, "helps parents understand the roots of [children's social] problems, which take hold at a very young age, and give their kids the foundational skills necessary to form connections and friendships. The book explains how parents can teach their children social observing skills at an early stage in their development." (Publisher's note)

"This book joins Ross W. Greene's The Explosive Child as a helpful tool to aid those who love and work with children with social issues." LJ

Includes bibliographical references and index

White, Burton L.

The **new** first three years of life; 20th anniversary ed; Fireside Bks. 1995 384p il pa $14 **155.4**
1. Child psychology 2. Infants -- Development
ISBN 0-684-80419-0

LC 95-18297

First published 1975 with title: The first three years of life

"White describes the seven developmental phases of the first three years of life. He provides parents with a comprehensive treasury of techniques for enhancing development and establishing discipline that are refreshingly straight-forward and based on real-world experience." Publ Wkly

155.433   Girls

Tassler, Nina

What I Told My Daughter; Lessons from Leaders on Raising the Next Generation of Empowered Women. by Nina Tassler. Pocket Books 2016 320 p. $25 **155.433**
1. Mother-daughter relationship
ISBN 1476734674; 9781476734675

In this book, "entertainment executive Nina Tassler has brought together a powerful, diverse group of women—from Madeleine Albright to Ruth Bader Ginsburg, from Dr. Susan Love to Whoopi Goldberg—to reflect on the best advice and counsel they have given their daughters either by example, throughout their lives, or in character-building, teachable moments between parent and child." (Publisher's note)

155.44   Children by status and relationships

Wright, Lawrence

Twins; and what they tell us about who we are. Wiley 1997 202p $22.95; pa $14.95 **155.44**
1. Twins
ISBN 0-471-25220-4; 0-471-29644-9 pa

LC 97-38827

"Wright does an admirable job of sorting through the differing research in a well-reasoned, clearheaded manner." Publ Wkly

Includes bibliographical references

155.45   Exceptional children; children by social and economic levels, by ethnic or national group

Stephens, Kimberly

The **Prodigy's** Cousin; The Family Link Between Autism and Extraordinary Talent. by Joanne Ruthsatz and Kimberly Stephens. Penguin Group USA 2016 288 p. $28 **155.45**
1. Autism 2. Genius 3. Child psychology 4. Autistic children
ISBN 1617230189; 9781617230189

LC 2015048520

In this book, authors Joanne Ruthsatz and Kimberly Stephens "propose a startling possibility: What if the abilities of child prodigies stem from a genetic link with autism? And could prodigies— children who have many of the strengths of autism but few of the challenges—be the key to a long-awaited autism breakthrough? . . . Ruthsatz and Stephens narrate the poignant stories of the children they have studied." (Publisher's note)

"People with an interest in autism or prodigies will be intrigued by the interesting hypothesis posed by this psychologist-journalist duo, who provide a lovely epilogue about what their young prodigies are doing today." Booklist

Includes bibliographical references and index.

155.5   Psychology of young people twelve to twenty

Shatkin, Jess P.

Born to be wild; why teens take risks, and how we can help keep them safe. Jess P. Shatkin, MD, MPH. TarcherPerigee 2017 xv, 299 p.p (hardcover) $26 **155.5**
1. Adolescence 2. Adolescent psychology 3. Risk-taking (Psychology) 4. Risk-taking (Psychology) in adolescence
ISBN 9780143129790; 9781101993422

LC 2017016376

This book, by Jess P. Shatkin, "sheds new light on why young people make dangerous choices--and offers solutions that work. . . . Shatkin explains: Why 'scared straight,' adult logic, and draconian punishment don't work. Why the teen brain is 'born to be wild.' . . . The . . . role of brain development, hormones, peer pressure, screen time, and other key factors. What parents and teachers can do . . . to work with teens' need for risk, rewards and social acceptance." (Publisher's note)

"An accessible and compelling look at a frequently misunderstood developmental stage that will provoke talk around the family dinner table." Booklist

Includes bibliographical references and index

Siegel, Daniel J.

Brainstorm; the power and purpose of the teenage brain. Daniel J. Siegel, M.D. Jeremy P. Tarcher/Penguin 2013 336 p.

ill $27.95   **155.5**
1. Adolescent psychology 2. Brain 3. Cognition in adolescence
ISBN 158542935X; 9781585429356

LC 2013029724

This book, by Daniel J. Siegel, "illuminates how brain development impacts teenagers' behavior and relationships. Drawing on important new research in the field of interpersonal neurobiology, he explores exciting ways in which understanding how the teenage brain functions can help parents make what is in fact an incredibly positive period of growth, change, and experimentation in their children's lives less lonely and distressing on both sides of the generational divide." (Publisher's note)

"Smart advice . . . on providing the most supportive and brain-healthy environment during the tumultuous years of adolescence." Kirkus

Simmons, Rachel

★ **Enough** as she is; how to help girls move beyond impossible standards of success to live healthy, happy, and fulfilling lives. Rachel Simmons. HarperCollins 2018 304 p. $27.99   **155.5**
1. Self-confidence 2. Adolescent psychology 3. Teenage girls -- Conduct of life
ISBN 0062438395; 9780062438393

This book, by Rachel Simmons, "gives adults the tools to help girls in high school and college reject 'supergirl' pressure, overcome a toxic stress culture, and become resilient adults with healthy, happy, and fulfilling lives. . . . [It] . . . provides practical parenting advice--including teaching girls self-compassion as an alternative to self-criticism [and] how to manage overthinking." (Publisher's note)

"A fascinating read that provides ideas for combatting the 'not enough' ideals that are devastating young girls." LJ

155.6   Psychology of adults

Engel, Beverly

The **nice** girl syndrome; stop being manipulated and abused--and start standing up for yourself. John Wiley & Sons 2008 245p $24.95   **155.6**
1. Self-esteem 2. Conduct of life 3. Self-confidence 4. Women -- Psychology
ISBN 978-0-470-17938-3; 0-470-17938-4

LC 2008-8382

The author argues "that while society superficially rewards nice girls, they suffer deeply in their intimate and work relationships by losing personal power and parading inauthentic selves. . . . Most useful for its thorough treatment for how 'nice girls' are socialized and for Engel's concise antidote (the four 'Power C's': confidence, competence, conviction and courage) this book will challenge, entertain and empower its readers." Publ Wkly

Includes bibliographical references

Friday, Nancy

My mother/my self; the daughter's search for identity. Delta Trade Paperbacks 1997 425p pa $17   **155.6**
1. Mothers 2. Mother-daughter relationship 3. Women -- Psychology
ISBN 0-385-32015-9; 978-0-385-32015-3

LC 98-115632

First published 1977 by Delacorte Press

The author explores the psychological aspects of the mother-daughter relationship.

Includes bibliographical references

Rauch, Jonathan

The **happiness** curve; why life gets better after 50. Jonathan Rauch. Dunne Books 2018 256 p. (hardcover: alk. paper) $26.99   **155.6**
1. Happiness 2. Middle age 3. Interpersonal relations
ISBN 1250078806; 9781250078803

LC 2018005155

In this book, author Jonathan Rauch, "shows that from our 20s into our 40s, happiness follows a U-shaped trajectory, a 'happiness curve,' declining from the optimism of youth into what's often a long, low slump in middle age, before starting to rise again in our 50s. . . . Rauch reveals that this slump is instead a natural stage of life--and an essential one." (Publisher's note)

155.67   People in late adulthood

Cameron, Julia B., 1948-

It's never too late to begin again; discovering creativity and meaning at midlife and beyond. Julia Cameron, Emma Lively. TarcherPerigee 2016 304 p. (paperback) $17   **155.67**
1. Middle age 2. Creative ability 3. Aging
ISBN 9780399174216

LC 2015050216

In this book, by Julia Cameron and Emma Lively, the authors "turns [their] eye to a segment of the population that, ironically, while they have more time to be creative, are often reluctant or intimidated by the creative process. Cameron shows readers that retirement can, in fact, be the most rich, fulfilling, and creative time of their lives." (Publisher's note)

"Organized into a 12-week program designed to help individuals define and re-create their lives in middle age and beyond, Cameron's guide offers useful assigned tasks (warning: these include fill-in writing exercises), making this a must-read for all hoping to enhance their creativity in all aspects of life." Booklist

Includes bibliographical references and index

Hagerty, Barbara Bradley

Life Reimagined; The Science, Art, and Opportunity of Midlife. by Barbara Bradley Hagerty. Penguin Group USA 2016 464 p. (ebook) $48; $28   **155.67**
1. Middle age
ISBN 9781101622971; 1594631700; 9781594631702

LC 2016006516

In this book, author Barbara Bradley Hagerty "explains that midlife is about renewal. . . . Drawing from emerging information in neurology, psychology, biology, genetics, and sociology--as well as her own story of midlife transformation--Hagerty redraws the map for people in midlife and plots a new course forward in understanding our health, our relationships, even our futures." (Publisher's note)

"This work is a joyous reminder that the middle years can be satisfying, resilient, and significant." LJ

Moore, Thomas, 1940-

Ageless soul; the lifelong journey toward meaning and joy. Thomas Moore. St. Martin's Press 2017 304 p. $26.99 **155.67**
1. Conduct of life 2. Aging -- Psychological aspects
ISBN 1250135818; 9781250135810

In this book, author Thomas "Moore reveals a fresh, uplifting, and inspiring path toward aging, one that need not be feared, but rather embraced and cherished. In Moore's view, aging is the process by which one becomes a more distinctive, complex, fulfilled, loving, and connected person. . . . 'The book] teaches readers how to embrace the richness of experience and how to take life on, accept invitations to new vitality, and feel fulfilled as they get older." (Publisher's note)

"This gentle book, filled with specific suggestions and thought-provoking examples, will be inspiring to older readers and a comfort to their caregivers." (Booklist)

155.7 Evolutionary psychology

Clark, William R.

Are we hardwired? the role of genes in human behavior. by William R. Clark & Michael Grunstein. Oxford Univ. Press 2000 322p il hardcover o.p. pa $24.95   **155.7**
1. Behavior genetics
ISBN 0-19-513826-0; 978-0-19-517800-5 pa; 0-19-517800-9 pa
LC 99-54699
The authors offer an "overview of the current evidence supporting genetic causes for general behavioral tendencies, such as aggression, consumption, sexual preferences, and, most controversial, intelligence. Case studies of identical twins separated as infants provide some of the most compelling proofs." Libr J
Includes bibliographical references

Dunbar, Robin

Human evolution; Our Brains and Behavior. Robin Dunbar. Oxford University Press 2016 432 p. (hardback) $29.95 **155.7**
1. Evolutionary psychology
ISBN 9780190616786
LC 2016009401
In this book, author "Robin Dunbar appeals to the human aspects of every reader, as subjects of mating, friendship, and community are discussed from an evolutionary psychology perspective. With a table of contents ranging from prehistoric times to modern days, [it] focuses on an aspect of evolution that has typically been overshadowed by the archaeological record: the biological, neurological, and genetic changes that occurred with each 'transition' in the evolutionary narrative." (Publisher's note)

"Readers who pay attention and do not skim the many graphs, tables, and statistics will discover a rich trove of discoveries on how primitive primates became modern humans." Kirkus
Includes bibliographical references and index

Maestripieri, Dario

Games primates play; an undercover investigation of the evolution and economics of human relationships. Dario Maestripieri. Basic Books 2012 xviii, 302 p.p (hardcover: alk. paper): $27.99   **155.7**
1. Evolution 2. Interpersonal relations 3. Behavior evolution 4. Control (Psychology) 5. Primates -- Behavior 6. Dominance (Psychology)
ISBN 046502078X; 9780465020782
LC 2011045523
In this book, "[Dario] Maestripieri argues that human behaviour, like our anatomy, can be explained by looking at our biology. Natural selection strongly shaped our social behaviour, and the same pressures faced by our ancestors would also have influenced our closest living relatives--other primates. . . . In economic terms, he argues that we choose mates who enhance our material interests--but only so long as the benefits outweigh the costs." (New Scientist)
Includes bibliographical references (p. 277-295) and index

Miller, Kenneth R.

The **human** instinct; how we evolved to have reason, consciousness, and free will. Kenneth R. Miller. Simon & Schuster 2018 304 p. (hardcover: alk. paper) $26   **155.7**
1. Reason 2. Human behavior 3. Free will and determinism 4. Consciousness 5. Human evolution 6. Natural selection 7. Behavior evolution 8. Evolutionary psychology
ISBN 9781476790268
LC 2017006770
In this book, author Kenneth R. Miller "rejects the idea that our biological heritage means that human thought, action, and imagination are pre-determined, describing instead the trajectory that ultimately gave us reason, consciousness and free will. A proper understanding of evolution, he says, reveals humankind in its glorious uniqueness." (Publisher's note)

"Miller's latest work seamlessly crosses between science and philosophy, appealing to readers of both subjects. Those interested in the human condition or wishing to delve into an introspective text on the self and mind will appreciate the depth and thought." Booklist
Includes bibliographical references and index

Ridley, Matt

The **agile** gene; how nature turns on nurture. Perennial 2004 326p pa $13.99   **155.7**
1. Genetics 2. Nature and nurture
ISBN 978-0-06-000679-2; 0-06-000679-X
First published 2003 with title: Nature via nurture
"In February 2001 it was announced that the human genome contains not 100,000 genes, as originally postulated, but only 30,000. This . . . revision led some scientists to conclude that there are simply not enough human genes to account for all the different ways people behave: we must be made by nurture, not nature. . . . [Ridley argues that] nurture depends on genes, too, and genes need nurture. Genes not only predetermine the broad structure of the brain, they also absorb formative experiences, react to social cues, and even run memory. They are consequences as well as causes of the will." Publisher's note
Includes bibliographical references

155.8 Ethnopsychology and national psychology

Levi-Strauss, Claude

★ The **savage** mind. University of Chicago Press 1966 290p il (Nature of human society series) hardcover o.p. pa $18   **155.8**
1. Anthropology 2. Ethnopsychology
ISBN 0-226-47484-4 pa
Original French edition, 1962
"An anthropological study of the nature of thought, concepts and systems as they occur in various cultures." Chicago Public Libr
Includes bibliographical references

155.9 Environmental psychology

Aiken, Mary

The **cyber** effect; A Pioneering Cyberpsychologist Explains How Human Behavior Changes Online. Mary Aiken. Spiegel & Grau 2016 400 p. (ebook) $65; (hardback) $28   **155.9**
1. Internet 2. Human behavior 3. Social psychology 4. Interpersonal relations 5. Internet users -- Psychology 6. Interpersonal relations -- Psychological aspects

ISBN 9780812997866; 9780812997859

LC 2016007455

This book, by Mary Aiken, is an "exploration of how cyberspace is changing the way we think, feel, and behave. . . . Aiken covers a wide range of subjects from the impact of screens on the developing child to the explosion of teen sexting, and the acceleration of compulsive and addictive behaviors online (gaming, shopping, pornography). She examines the escalation of cyberchondria (anxiety produced by self-diagnosing online), cyberstalking, and organized cybercrime in the Deep Web." (Publisher's note)

"Aiken provides a thoughtful approach to the attractions, distractions, and pitfalls of our digital culture." Kirkus

Includes bibliographical references (pages 337-370) and index.

Benson, Herbert

★ The **relaxation** response; by Herbert Benson, with Miriam Z. Klipper. Updated & expanded [ed.]; Quill 2001 liv, 179p il pa $13.99 **155.9**
1. Rest 2. Stress (Physiology) 3. Stress (Psychology)
ISBN 0-380-81595-8

LC 2003-269877

First published 1975 by Morrow

This guide to relieving stress is "recommended for patients suffering from heart conditions, hypertension, chronic pain, and other ailments. A classic." Libr J

Includes bibliographical references

Bettencourt, Megan Feldman

Triumph of the heart; forgiveness in an unforgiving world. Megan Feldman Bettencourt. Avery 2015 288 p. (hardback) $25.95 **155.9**
1. Forgiveness
ISBN 1594632634; 9781594632631

LC 2014048570

This book, by Megan Feldman Bettencourt, explores the concept of forgiveness "from both a scientific perspective and a human one. She draws on cutting-edge research showing that forgiveness can provide a range of health benefits, from relieving depression to decreasing high blood pressure. She examines situations as mundane as road rage, as painful as cheating spouses, and as unthinkable as war crimes." (Publisher's note)

"This compelling investigation into an important subject may well inspire readers to give the concept of forgiveness a bigger place in their lives." Pub Wkly

Includes bibliographical references and index

★ **Breaking** sad; what to say after loss, what not to say, and when to just show up. edited by Shelly Fisher and Jennifer Jones. She Writes Press 2017 xi, 235 p.p $16.95 **155.9**
1. Grief 2. Loss (Psychology)
ISBN 1631522426; 9781631522420

This book, by Shelly Fisher and Jennifer Jones, presents "real stories and real feedback on what should be said, what should be kept to yourself, and what can be done when trying to support someone you care about as they navigate loss." (Publisher's note)

Doka, Kenneth J.

Grief is a journey; finding your path through loss. Dr. Kenneth J. Doka. Atria Books 2016 304 p. (hardback) $26 **155.9**
1. Grief 2. Bereavement 3. Loss (Psychology) 4. Death
ISBN 9781476771489; 1476771480

LC 2015014071

This book, by Kenneth J. Doka, "explores a new, compassionate way to grieve, explaining that grief is not an illness to get over but an individual and ongoing journey. . . . In doing so, he helps us realize that our experiences following a death are far more individual and much less predictable than the conventional 'five stages' model would have us believe." (Publisher's note)

"Well supported by footnotes, this is a useful and reassuring resource." Pub Wkly

Includes bibliographical references and index

Dresser, Norine

Saying goodbye to someone you love; your journey through end-of-life and grief. [by] Norine Dresser, Fredda Wasserman. DemosHealth Pub. 2010 210p pa $16.95 **155.9**
1. Death 2. Bereavement
ISBN 978-1-932603-85-9

LC 2010-2096

The authors "draw from their experience as hospice workers to illustrate how people have brought up the subject of death with the dying, made end-of-life decisions, and planned (or not held) a funeral service. Dresser and Wasserman not only offer comfort and companionship but provide practical suggestions for conversation starters, ideas for memorials, and a whole section on handling the grief of children. Essential for anyone experiencing end-of-life issues." Libr J

Includes bibliographical references

Edelman, Hope

Motherless daughters; the legacy of loss. 2nd ed; Da Capo Press 2006 pa $15.95 **155.9**
1. Bereavement 2. Loss (Psychology) 3. Mother-daughter relationship
ISBN 978-0-7382-1026-1

LC 2005-33840

First published 1994 by Addison-Wesley

"Writing of her own experiences of losing her mother when she was 17, and the grief of hundreds of women she interviewed who lost their mothers through death, abandonment or another form of separation . . . Edelman marshals a wealth of anecdotal evidence, supplemented with psychological research about bereavement, that indicates that one's longing for a mother never disappears." Publ Wkly

Includes bibliographical references

Motherless mothers; how mother loss shapes the parents we become. HarperCollins 2006 xxxiii, 410p hardcover o.p. pa $14.95 **155.9**
1. Parenting 2. Bereavement 3. Loss (Psychology) 4. Mother-daughter relationship
ISBN 0-06-053246-7 pa; 978-0-06-053246-8 pa

LC 2005-52812

Edelman "presents emotionally charged concepts in clear, memorable terms (e.g., reaching the 'neon number' of a mother's age of death) to encourage frank, cathartic discussion." Publ Wkly

Includes bibliographical references

Emswiler, Mary Ann

Guiding your child through grief; {by} Mary Ann Emswiler and James P. Emswiler. Bantam Bks. 2000 286p il pa $13.95 **155.9**
1. Death 2. Bereavement 3. Child rearing
ISBN 0-553-38025-7

LC 00-23645

"Thoroughly researched and bolstered with the wisdom of bereavement experts nationwide, this fine guide does those working through the loss of loved ones an enormous service. It should rank amongst the first line of defense and support for those facing a death in the family." Publ Wkly

Includes bibliographical references

Enayati, Amanda

Seeking serenity; the 10 new rules for health and happiness in the age of anxiety. Amanda Enayati. NAL Hardcover 2015 272 p. illustrations (hardback) $25.95   **155.9**

1. Health 2. Anxiety 3. Happiness 4. Well-being 5. Inner peace 6. Mental health 7. Stress management 8. Stress (Psychology)

ISBN 0451471512; 9780451471512

LC 2014029563

In this book, author "Amanda Enayati challenges our long-held assumptions about stress, painting a groundbreaking picture that separates myth from reality when it comes to what is commonly referred to as the plague of modern life. Weaving together stories, research from science, history, philosophy and diverse faiths, and everyday exercises, she crafts a fascinating tale that begins with the behind-the-scenes machinations of corporate villains and ends in the power of our stories to shape our realities." (Publisher's note)

"Enayati's work, while not earth-shattering, provides a positive, inexpensive avenue to inner peace." LJ

Gilbert, Sandra M.

★ **Death's** door; modern dying and the ways we grieve. Norton 2006 580p il $29.95; pa $17.95   **155.9**

1. Death 2. Bereavement

ISBN 0-393-05131-5; 978-0-393-05131-5; 0-393-32969-0 pa; 978-0-393-32969-8 pa

LC 2004-65430

"Those who have experienced the death of a loved one will recognize themselves in this meticulously researched, comprehensively organized, and exceptionally caring examination of society's attitudes about mortality and mourning." Booklist

Includes bibliographical references

Gonzales, Laurence, 1947-

Surviving survival; the art and science of resilience. Laurence Gonzales. W.W. Norton 2012 272 p. (hardcover) $26.95   **155.9**

1. Psychology 2. Brain -- Physiology 3. Adjustment (Psychology) 4. Resourcefulness 5. Resilience (Personality trait) 6. Disasters -- Psychological aspects

ISBN 0393083187; 9780393083187

LC 2012015592

This book examines "the mental processes that enable us to cope with the trauma that often sets in during and after a challenge to our survival. . . . [Laurence] Gonzales narrates . . . tales, not all of them elective; his survivors are those who have suffered war and terrorism as well as falls off mountains and into choppy surf." The book includes "explanations of the science behind . . . how the amygdala works. . . . One characteristic of success, writes Gonzales, is the ability to step outside oneself to help others." (Kirkus Reviews)

Includes bibliographical references and index

Gosling, Sam

Snoop; what your stuff says about you. Basic Books 2008 263p il map $25   **155.9**

1. Materialism 2. Social psychology

ISBN 978-0-465-02781-1; 0-465-02781-4

LC 2007-52071

"Unlike many current books on behaviour, Snoop does not contain a single brain scan or discussion of neural activity. Instead, it adopts a shamelessly social approach, focusing on how people behave in the real world rather than in a brain scanner, and presents explanations at the level of individual personalities and social interactions. It works, not least because it has the huge advantage of being exclusively concerned with the one topic that most people find endlessly fascinating: themselves." New Sci

Includes bibliographical references

Greenfield, Susan, 1950-

Mind change; how digital technologies are leaving their mark on our brains. Susan Greenfield. Random House Inc 2015 368 p. illustration (hardback) $28   **155.9**

1. Information technology 2. Technology -- Psychological aspects 3. Cognition 4. Information technology -- Social aspects 5. Information technology -- Psychological aspects

ISBN 0812993829; 9780812993820

LC 2014020059

In this book, author Susan Greenfield "explores whether incessant exposure to social media sites, search engines, and videogames is capable of rewiring our brains, and whether the minds of people born before and after the advent of the Internet differ. Stressing the impact on Digital Natives--those who've never known a world without the Internet--Greenfield exposes how neuronal networking may be affected by unprecedented bombardments of audiovisual stimuli." (Publisher's note)

"While Greenfield is cautious about making definitive statements, she is determined to persuade readers to think about how all our texting, e-mailing, and social networking may be affecting our very brains. Although densely written at times, Mind Change is exceedingly well organized and hits the right balance between academic and provocative. There is no question about the need for us to think more deeply about this topic." Booklist

Harding, Thomas

Kadian Journal; A Father's Memoir. Thomas Harding. St. Martin's Press 2017 256 p. $16.00; (ebook) $60   **155.9**

1. Grief 2. Father-son relationship

ISBN 1250065097; 9781250065094; 9781250065100

LC 2016039171

"In July 2012, Thomas Harding's fourteen-year-old son Kadian was killed in a bicycle accident. Shortly afterwards Thomas began to write. . . . Beginning on the day of Kadian's death, and continuing to the one-year anniversary, and beyond, . . . [this book] is a record of grief in its rawest form, and of a mind in shock and questioning a strange new reality." (Publisher's note)

"Both eloquent and heart-rending, Harding's book is not only a grieving father's testament of love to his dead son. It is also a reminder of the fragility of life and human relationships. An emotionally raw and uncompromising memoir." Kirkus

Karr-Morse, Robin

Scared sick; Robin Karr-Morse with Meredith S. Wiley. Basic Books 2012 xvii, 301p   **155.9**

1. Mothers 2. Diseases 3. Parenting 4. Child psychology 5. Child development 6. Psychic trauma

ISBN 9780465013548; 9780465028122

LC 2011029405

This book presents an "investigation of the importance of attachment between baby and caretaker—usually the mother—in setting the path to physical and mental health. . . . [The authors] write that without that bond, there is danger that a baby will be stressed, triggering the hypothalamus-pituitary-adrenal axis and flooding the baby's developing nervous system with flight-or-fight hormones. The baby, unable to flee or fight, may succumb to trauma, defined as being frozen in fear. Such trauma is the root of being 'scared sick': suffering ills that may not appear until later in life. Among many others, these can include autism, Alzheimer's, addiction, ADHD, schizophrenia, PTSD, suicide, chronic pain, obesity, heart disease, diabetes and cancer." (Kirkus)

Includes bibliographical references and index.

Kingma, Daphne Rose

The **ten** things to do when your life falls apart; an emotional and spiritual handbook. New World Library 2010 xxiv, 214p pa $14.95   **155.9**
1. Suffering 2. Adjustment (Psychology)
ISBN 978-1-57731-698-5

                 LC 2010-1049

The author "writes for readers whose lives are being wrenched apart by sudden job loss, the death of a loved one, financial ruin, or a dire medical diagnosis. When any of these things happens, either separately or simultaneously, Kingma offers a list of ten ways whereby readers can eventually learn that their difficulties have meaning and purpose. . . . For those lost in the turbulence of life, Kingma offers a genuine hand through." Libr J

Kubler-Ross, Elisabeth

★ **On** children and death. Macmillan 1983 279p hardcover o.p. pa $12   **155.9**
1. Death 2. Child psychology
ISBN 0-684-83939-3 pa

                 LC 83-11252

A look at how one copes with a child's death by disease, accident or murder

Includes bibliographical references

★ **On** death and dying. Scribner Classics 1997 286p il $23; pa $13   **155.9**
1. Death 2. Terminal care
ISBN 0-684-84223-8; 0-684-83938-5 pa

                 LC 97-177294

A reissue of the title first published 1969 by Macmillan

A look at the psychological, sociological and theological issues faced by the terminally ill and their caregivers

Includes bibliographical references

Lifton, Robert Jay, 1926-

The **climate** swerve; reflections on mind, hope, and survival. Robert Jay Lifton. The New Press 2017 xii, 178 p.p (hbk: alk. paper) $22.95   **155.9**
1. Climate change 2. Nuclear warfare -- Psychological aspects 3. Climatic changes -- Psychological aspects
ISBN 1620973472; 9781620973479; 9781620973486

                 LC 2017018185

In this book, author Robert Jay Lifton "shifts to climate change. . . . Lifton draws a message of hope from the Paris climate meeting of 2015 where representatives of virtually all nations joined in the recognition that we are a single species in deep trouble." (Publisher's note)

"In short chapters, this slim title engages readers on everything from the long-term damage to the Marshall Islands from nuclear testing to the ethics of fossil-fuel extraction in our enlightened age. Thoughtful, intelligent, and deeply human, Lifton will not disappoint his fans and will hopefully draw new readers with this deeply informative work." (Booklist)

Includes bibliographical references (pages 158-169) and index

Louv, Richard, 1949-

Vitamin N; the essential guide to a nature-rich life. Richard Louv. Algonquin Books of Chapel Hill 2016 304 p. illustrations (paperback) $15.95   **155.9**
1. Nature 2. Outdoor recreation 3. Nature study 4. Family recreation 5. Nature -- Psychological aspects
ISBN 9781616205782; 1616205784

                 LC 2015031470

This book, by Richard Louv, "is a complete prescription for connecting with the power and joy of the natural world right now, with 500 activities for children and adults, dozens of inspiring and thought-provoking essays, scores of informational websites, [and] down-to-earth advice." (Publisher's note)

"Louv has become a national leader in advocating for kids to connect with nature. His macrovision of ecological health speaks beyond the benefits of youngsters getting dirty." LJ

Includes bibliographical references (pages 243-251) and index.

Padgett, Jason

Struck by genius; how a brain injury made me a mathematical marvel. Jason Padgett, Maureen Ann Seaberg. Houghton Mifflin Harcourt 2014 256 p. colored illustrations (hardback) $27   **155.9**
1. Autobiographies 2. Savants (Savant syndrome) 3. Brain -- Wounds and injuries 4. Psychic trauma
ISBN 0544045602; 9780544045606

                 LC 2013041065

"In September 2002, author Padgett was brutally mugged as he exited a Tacoma karaoke bar. The hospital medical exam revealed a profound brain concussion, and Padgett was treated and released. The next day, the author began to experience a keen ability to understand high levels of math and physics, as well as grasp developed skills for drawing complex geometric shapes that he started to see in everything. Padgett's diagnosis was acquired savant syndrome, a condition that had formerly been diagnosed in only 30 other individuals.." (Library Journal)

A "beautiful, inspiring and intimate account of Padgett's struggles and breakthroughs. An exquisite insider's look into the mysteries of consciousness." Kirkus

Includes bibliographical references and index

Ripley, Amanda

The **unthinkable**; who survives when disaster strikes and why. Crown Publishers 2008 xx, 266p il $24.95   **155.9**
1. Disasters 2. Disaster relief 3. Survival skills
ISBN 978-0-307-35289-7

                 LC 2007-40315

Ripley "offers an elementary discussion of disaster and survival, drawing on both survivors' personal accounts and scientific studies that reveal how the human brain functions under duress. She shows how individuals and groups react when such disasters as shipwrecks, fires, terrorist attacks, and tsunamis occur, detailing the traits survivors demonstrate that help them respond effectively. . . . Offering tips on how we can boost our odds, her self-help approach to survival will attract readers." Libr J

Includes bibliographical references

Rosling, Hans, 1948-2017

Factfulness; ten reasons we're wrong about the world-and why things are better than you think. Hans Rosling, with Ola Rosling and Anna Rosling Ronnlund. Flatiron Books 2018 352

p. (hardcover) $27.99   **155.9**
1. Prejudices 2. Critical thinking 3. Information literacy 4. Reality 5. Stress management
ISBN 9781250107817

LC 2018000167

This book, by Hans Rosling, with Ola Rosling and Anna Rosling Ronnlund, presents "ten instincts that distort our perspective--from our tendency to divide the world into two camps . . . to the way we consume media . . . to how we perceive progress (believing that most things are getting worse). 'Factfulness' is an urgent and essential book that will change the way you see the world and empower you to respond to the crises and opportunities of the future." (Publisher's notes)

Includes bibliographical references and index

Sife, Wallace

The **loss** of a pet; 3rd ed; Howell Book House 2005 260p il pa $14.99   **155.9**
1. Pets 2. Death 3. Bereavement
ISBN 0-7645-7930-4

LC 2005-12603

First published 1993

The author "addresses the pet owner whose grief at a pet's death is largely misunderstood or even ridiculed by friends, associates and society in general. . . . Sife is to be commended for offering information that is not only compassionate but concise, wide-ranging and, above all, practical." Publ Wkly {review of 1993 edition}

Wickersham, Joan

The **suicide** index; putting my father's death in order. Harcourt 2008 316p $25; pa $14.95   **155.9**
1. Suicide 2. Father-daughter relationship
ISBN 978-0-1510-1490-3; 0-1510-1490-6; 978-0-1560-3380-0 pa; 0-1560-3380-1 pa

LC 2007-29299

National Book Award Finalist: Nonfiction (2008)

"Wickersham's memoir unravels the twisted branches of family ties in the aftermath of her father's suicide as she attempts to answer the question, Why did he do it? . . . Wickersham's effort is worth the read. . . . This book is beautifully written and haunts the reader long after it's closed. Recommended." Libr J

Williams, Florence

The **nature** fix; why nature makes us happier, healthier, and more creative. Florence Williams. W W Norton & Co Inc 2017 288 p. (hardcover) $26.95   **155.9**
1. Nature 2. Creative ability 3. Environmental psychology 4. Nature -- Psychological aspects
ISBN 9780393242713

LC 2016040709

In this book, by Florence Williams, the author "set out to uncover the science behind nature's positive effects on the brain. . . . demonstrates that our connection to nature is much more important to our cognition than we think and that even small amounts of exposure to the living world can improve our creativity and enhance our mood. . . . Williams show[s] how time in nature is not a luxury but is in fact essential to our humanity." (Publisher's note)

"This powerful environmental call to arms proposes that for optimal well-being, regular doses of nature are not only recommended but required." Pub Wkly

Includes bibliographical references

Winch, Guy

★ **How** to fix a broken heart; Guy Winch. Simon & Schuster 2018 128 p. $16.99   **155.9**
1. Loss (Psychology) 2. Adjustment (Psychology) 3. Separation (Psychology)
ISBN 1501120123; 9781501120121

This book, byGuy Winch, "reveals how and why heartbreak impacts our brain and our behavior in dramatic and unexpected ways, regardless of our age. Emotional pain lowers our ability to reason, to think creatively, to problem solve, and to function at our best. In 'How to Fix a Broken Heart' he focuses on two types of emotional pain--romantic heartbreak and the heartbreak that results from the loss of a cherished pet." (Publisher's note)

"Most importantly, he preaches self-compassion. This tender book reminds readers to be kind to others and themselves." Pub Wkly

Zimbardo, Philip

The **Lucifer** effect; understanding how good people turn evil. [by] Philip Zimbardo. Random House 2007 xx, 551p il $27.95   **155.9**
1. Good and evil 2. Social psychology 3. Good and evil -- Psychological aspects
ISBN 1-4000-6411-2; 978-1-4000-6411-3

LC 2006-50388

The author "masterminded the famous Stanford Prison Experiment, in which college students randomly assigned to be guards or inmates found themselves enacting sadistic abuse or abject submissiveness. In this penetrating investigation, he revisits . . . the SPE study and applies it to historical examples of injustice and atrocity, especially the Abu Ghraib outrages by the U.S. military. . . . Combining a dense but readable and often engrossing exposition of social psychology research with an impassioned moral seriousness, Zimbardo challenges readers to look beyond glib denunciations of evil-doers and ponder our collective responsibility for the world's ills." Publ Wkly

Includes bibliographical references

155.937   Death and dying

Cacciatore, Joanne

Bearing the unbearable; love, loss, and the heartbreaking path of grief. Joanne Cacciatore; foreword by Jeffrey B. Rubin, PhD. Wisdom Publications 2017 222 p. (pbk.: alk. paper) $15.95   **155.937**
1. Grief 2. Loss (Psychology) 3. Adjustment (Psychology) 4. Love
ISBN 9781614293170; 1614292965; 9781614292968

LC 2016044492

This book, by Joanne Cacciatore, with foreword by Jeffrey B. Rubin, "is a companion for life's most difficult times, revealing how grief can open our hearts to connection, compassion, and the very essence of our shared humanity. . . . Cacciatore . . . accompanies us along the heartbreaking path of love, loss, and grief." (Publisher's note)

"Cacciatore . . . has taken a unique, straightforward approach that will enlighten those who have not made this journey, offer guidance to those who are navigating loss, and provide validation for those who failed to meet society's expectations of how they should respond to their lives being forever changed." Choice

Grant, Adam, 1981-

Option B; facing adversity, building resilience, and finding joy. Sheryl Sandberg, Adam Grant. Alfred A. Knopf 2017 226 p. illustrations (hardcover) $25.95   **155.937**
1. Loss (Psychology) 2. Resilience (Personality trait) 3. Grief 4.

Bereavement
ISBN 9781524732691; 9781524732684

LC 2016057738

This book, by Sheryl Sandberg and Adam Grant, "illuminates how to help others in crisis, develop compassion for ourselves, raise strong children, and create resilient families, communities, and workplaces. Many of these lessons can be applied to everyday struggles, allowing us to brave whatever lies ahead." (Publisher's note)

"Option B is not simply a self-help book for those who are suffering; rather, it is a richly informed, engaging read that will broaden readers' understanding of empathy and reveal the strength of the human spirit." Booklist

Includes bibliographical references (pages [185]-216) and index.

Hone, Lucy

Resilient grieving; finding strength and embracing life after a loss that changes everything. Lucy Hone, PhD; foreword by Karen Reivich, PhD. The Experiment 2017 xii, 240 p.p illustrations (pbk.) $15.95　　**155.937**

1. Grief 2. Emotions 3. Future life 4. Death -- Psychological aspects 5. Resilience (Personality trait)
ISBN 9781615193752; 9781615193769

LC 2016056561

"Author and resilience/well-being expert Lucy Hone, a pioneer in fusing positive psychology and bereavement research, was faced with her own inescapable sorrow when, in 2014, her 12-year-old daughter was killed in a car accident. By following the strategies of resilient grieving, she found a proactive way to move through her grief, and, over time, embrace life again." (Publisher's note)

Includes bibliographical references.

James, John W.

★ The **grief** recovery handbook; the action program for moving beyond death, divorce, and other losses including health career, and faith. John W. James and Russell Friedman. 20th anniversary edition Collins Living 2009 208 p. illustrations pbk $16.99　　**155.93**

1. Grief 2. Bereavement 3. Loss (Psychology)
ISBN 0061686077; 9780061686078

LC 2010455458

Originally published 1988

"Incomplete recovery from grief can have a lifelong negative effect on the capacity for happiness. Drawing from their own histories as well as from others', the authors illustrate how it is possible to recover from grief and regain energy and spontaneity." (Publisher's note)

"A practical guide to coping with the grief of death or divorce, complemented by excellent exercises for finding peace and regaining energy." LJ

Samuel, Julia

Grief works; stories of life, death, and surviving. Julia Samuel. Scribner 2018 xx, 261 p.p (hardcover) $26 **155.937**

1. Grief 2. Bereavement 3. Loss (Psychology)
ISBN 9781501181535; 150118153X

LC 2017050279

This book, by Julia Samuel, "is a profoundly optimistic and compassionate handbook for anyone suffering a loss--from the expected death of a parent to the sudden death of a child or spouse--as well as a guide for those who want to help their grieving loved ones. . . . 'Grief Works' addresses the fear that surrounds death and grief and replaces it with confidence." (Publisher's note)

"As a guide for the newly grieving, the book succeeds on many

levels, and the author's compassionate storytelling skills provide even broader appeal. Though often touching on profoundly sad situations, Samuel's stories and reflections consistently hit an authentically inspiring note." Kirkus

Includes bibliographical references (pages 237-257).

155.94　Influence of community and housing

Warnick, Melody

This Is Where You Belong; The Art and Science of Loving the Place You Live. by Melody Warnick. Penguin Group USA 2016 320 p. (hardcover) $26　　**155.94**

1. Moving 2. Social integration 3. United States -- Social life and customs
ISBN 9780525429128; 0525429123

LC 2016017846

In this book, journalist Melody Warnick "embarks on a project to discover what it takes to love where you live. . . . She dives into the body of research around place attachment—the deep sense of connection that binds some of us to our cities and increases our physical and emotional well-being—then travels to towns across America to see it in action. Inspired by a growing movement of placemaking, she examines what its practitioners are doing to create likeable locales." (Publisher's note)

"Warnick shifts between sharing her stories and the results of her extensive research, crafting an enjoyable book for anyone who cherishes their hometown as well as for those who don't and would like to do so." LJ

Includes bibliographical references (pages 261-298) and index.

156　Comparative psychology

Miller, Peter

The **smart** swarm; how understanding flocks, schools, and colonies can make us better at communicating, decision making, and getting things done. Avery 2010 xx, 283p $26　　**156**

1. Human behavior 2. Animal behavior 3. Decision making
ISBN 978-1-58333-390-7

LC 2009-48619

The author "examines hives, mounds, colonies, and swarms, whose complex systems of engagement and collective decision making have catalyzed innovations in engineering and can suggest solutions to such problems as climate change. . . . Miller informs, engages, entertains, and even surprises in this thought-provoking study of problem making and problem solving, and through the comparison of human and insect scenarios, shows how social cues and signals can either bring about social cooperation or destruction." Publ Wkly

Includes bibliographical references

Peterson, Dale

The **moral** lives of animals. Bloomsbury Press 2010 342p　　**156**

1. Ethics 2. Animal behavior 3. Animal intelligence 4. Moral motivation 5. Animal psychology
ISBN 978-1-59691-424-7

LC 2010024662

Peterson "examines the moral behavior observed in animals and argues that human beings are not the only species to live by the principles of cooperation, kindness, and empathy." (Publisher's note) Bibliography. Index.

The author "develops his thoughts on how morality evolved in mammals, including humans. He initially concentrates on where morality comes from, covering basic concepts, linguistic bias, definitions of morality, and a theory of morality's structure. Rules of morality follow with topics such as authority, violence, sex, possession, and communication. . . . Although written for a general audience, this book challenges readers to absorb new information in an area unfamiliar to most. It is definitely worth the effort and is highly recommended for high school-age readers and up." Libr J

Includes bibliographical references

Suddendorf, Thomas

The **gap**; the science of what separates us from other animals. Thomas Suddendorf. Basic Books 2013 368 p. (hardcover) $29.99 **156**

1. Human beings 2. Comparative psychology 3. Psychology 4. Psychology, Comparative

ISBN 0465030149; 9780465030149

LC 2013017538

Author Thomas Suddendorf "provides a definitive account of the mental qualities that separate humans from other animals. Drawing on . . . research on apes, children, and human evolution, he surveys the abilities most often cited as uniquely human--language, intelligence, morality, culture, theory of mind--and finds that two traits account for most of the ways in which our minds appear so distinct: [the] ability to imagine . . .and our insatiable drive to link our minds together." (Publisher's note)

"A reader-friendly examination of the great gap that exists between human beings and the rest of the animal world and an explanation of how our minds came to be unique." Kirkus

Includes bibliographical references and index

Waal, Frans de

Our inner ape; a leading primatologist explains why we are who we are. photographs by the author. Riverhead Books 2005 274p il $24.95 **156**

1. Human behavior 2. Comparative psychology 3. Primates -- Behavior

ISBN 1-57322-312-3

LC 2005-42768

"Readers might be surprised at how much these apes and their stories resonate with their own lives, and may well be left with an urge to spend a few hours watching primates themselves at the local zoo." Publ Wkly

Includes bibliographical references

158 Applied psychology

Achor, Shawn

Before happiness; the 5 hidden keys to achieving success, spreading happiness, and sustaining positive change. by Shawn Achor. Crown Business 2013 256 p. (hc: alk. paper) $26 **158**

1. Happiness 2. Change (Psychology) 3. Success 4. Positive psychology

ISBN 0770436730; 9780770436735

LC 2013022564

In this book, "a happiness researcher investigates why some people can embrace positivity while others are mired in pessimism. Expanding on the theories he presented in 'The Happiness Advantage' . . . [Shawn] Achor now turns his attention to the question of how people learn to accept the possibility of happiness. . . . Happiness . . . is not the same as blind optimism but rather the ability to focus on the positive aspects of a situation while not becoming overwhelmed by the challenges." (Kirkus Reviews)

Includes bibliographical references and index

Bernstein, Gabrielle

Judgment detox; release the beliefs that hold you back from living a better life. Gabrielle Bernstein. North Star Way 2018 229 p. (hardback) $25.99 **158**

1. Happiness 2. Self-realization 3. Judgment 4. Self-actualization (Psychology)

ISBN 9781501168994; 1501168967; 9781501168963

LC 2017021778

This book, by Gabrielle Bernstein, "is an interactive six-step process that calls on spiritual principles from the text 'A Course in Miracles,' Kundalini yoga, the Emotional Freedom Technique (aka Tapping), meditation, prayer and metaphysical teachings. . . . Each lesson builds upon the next to support true healing." (Publisher's note)

"Readers concerned about the downsides of judgement—for both the judge and the accused—will find relief in Bernstein's comforting words and concrete plans for action." Pub Wkly

Bloomfield, Harold H.

Making peace with your past; the six essential steps to enjoying a great future. {by} Harold H. Bloomfield with Philip Goldberg. HarperCollins Pubs. 2000 269p hardcover o.p. pa $13 **158**

1. Self-realization 2. Applied psychology

ISBN 0-06-093314-3 pa

LC 99-89719

The author "addresses the syndrome Freud called 'repetition compulsion'—humans' tendency to re-create what they have not worked through. . . . With revealing exercises, Bloomfield shows readers how to rediscover 'the passion to live {their} highest destiny.'" Libr J

Includes bibliographical references

Brown, Brene

The **gifts** of imperfection; let go of who you think you're supposed to be and embrace who you are. by Brené Brown. Hazelden 2010 xvii, 137 p.p (paperback) $14.95 **158**

1. Self-esteem 2. Self-acceptance

ISBN 159285849X; 9781592859894; 9781592858491

LC 2010016989

In this book, "Brené Brown, a leading expert on shame, authenticity, and belonging, shares ten guideposts on the power of Wholehearted living—a way of engaging with the world from a place of worthiness. . . . In her ten guideposts, Brown engages our minds, hearts, and spirits as she explores how we can cultivate the courage, compassion, and connection." (Publisher's note)

"Brown offers exercises for readers to plumb their own emotions and begin to develop the kind of resilience needed to stand up to unrealistic expectations of others and ourselves." Booklist

Includes bibliographical references (p. 131-135)

Rising strong; Brené Brown. Spiegel & Grau 2015 336 p. (hardback) $27 **158**

1. Courage 2. Resilience (Personality trait) 3. Self-actualization (Psychology)

ISBN 0812995821; 9780812995824

LC 2015010832

In this book author Brene Brown "has listened as a range of people--from leaders in Fortune 500 companies and the military to artists, couples in long-term relationships, teachers, and parents--shared their stories of being brave, falling, and getting back up. They recognize the power of emotion and they're not afraid to lean in to discomfort." (Publisher's note)

"An innovative one-two-three-punch approach to self-help and healing from an author who has helped count less readers change their lives." Kirkus

Canfield, Jack

The **success** principles; how to get from where you are to where you want to be. by Jack Canfield with Janet Switzer. HarperCollins Publishers 2005 xxxiii, 473p il $24.95   **158**
  1. Success
  ISBN 0-06-059488-8

LC 2004-54259

A self-improvement guide for business professionals, teachers, students, parents, or anyone interested in promoting themselves within today's success-oriented culture shares sixty-four principles on how to reach desired goals

The author "has an easy style and talks directly to readers, responding to potential 'what ifs' and 'buts' with encouragement and sound advice. The book's layout is superb—small paragraphs are punctuated by italicized quotes, questions for self-study, and several appropriate cartoons." Libr J

Includes bibliographical references

Carnegie, Dale

★ **How** to win friends and influence people; editorial consultant, Dorothy Carnegie, editorial assistance, Arthur R. Pell. Pocket Books 1982 276p pa $6.99   **158**
  1. Success 2. Applied psychology
  ISBN 0-671-72365-0; 978-0-671-72365-1

LC 94-176452

First published 1936 by Simon & Schuster

An examination of the psychology of business and social success.

"This grandfather of all people-skills books was first published in 1937. It was an overnight hit, eventually selling 15 million copies. . . . [It] emphasizes fundamental techniques for handling people without making them feel manipulated. . . . Carnegie illustrates his points with anecdotes of historical figures, leaders of the business world, and everyday folks." Joan Price [This text refers to an out of print or unavailable edition of this title.]

Includes bibliographical references

Covey, Stephen R.

★ The **7** habits of highly effective people; restoring the character ethic. [Rev. ed.]; Free Press 2004 372p il $26; pa $15.95   **158**
  1. Success 2. Conduct of life
  ISBN 0-7432-7245-5; 0-7432-6951-9 pa

LC 2004-57494

First published 1989

The author describes seven habits designed to help people solve personal and professional problems.

The **8th** habit; from effectiveness to greatness. Free Press 2004 408p il $26   **158**
  1. Success 2. Self-realization
  ISBN 0-684-84665-9

LC 2004-56371

"Though conceived for individuals, Covey's book will be of tremendous importance to organizations and businesses." Libr J

Includes bibliographical references

Duhigg, Charles

Smarter faster better; the secrets of productivity in life and business. Charles Duhigg. Random House Inc 2016 400 p. illustrations $28   **158**
  1. Performance 2. Decision making 3. Self-help techniques 4. Motivation (Psychology) 5. Organizational behavior 6. Success 7. Mental efficiency
  ISBN 9780812993394

LC 2015034214

This book, by journalist Charles Duhigg, is "a ground-breaking exploration of the science of productivity, one that can help anyone learn to succeed with less stress and struggle, and to get more done without sacrificing what we care about most—to become smarter, faster, and better at everything we do." (Publisher's note)

"Duhigg shows an uncanny ability to find just the right exciting example of productivity-boosting methods, leaving readers to nod in recognition that they might act in the same way to improve their lives and work." Kirkus

Includes bibliographical references and index

Dyer, Wayne W.

★ The **power** of intention; learning to co-create your world your way. Hay House 2004 259p $24.95; pa $14.95   **158**
  1. Intentionalism
  ISBN 1-401-90215-4; 1-401-90216-2 pa

LC 2003-14622

The author argues that "there are seven faces, or energy fields, of intention: creativity, kindness, love, beauty, expansion, abundance and receptivity. Drawing on a variety of spiritual traditions and gurus, Dyer . . . describes how to surmount the barriers that may get in the way of connecting to this power, such as negative thinking, relying on the opinion of others or retaining a controlling ego." Publ Wkly

Foster, Rick

How we choose to be happy; the 9 choices of extremely happy people--their secrets, their stories. Rev; Berkley Publishing Group 2004 xxi, 228p pa $14.95   **158**
  1. Happiness
  ISBN 978-0-399-52990-0; 0-399-52990-X

First published 1999

The authors "interviewed happy people from all walks of life, from the United States to Eastern Europe. The resulting personal stories, writing exercises, and quotes together inform and instruct the reader in the nine principles discovered by the authors in their travels." Libr J

Gilbert, Daniel

★ **Stumbling** on happiness; [by] Daniel Gilbert. Alfred A. Knopf 2006 277p il   **158**
  1. Happiness
  ISBN 1-4000-4266-6; 1-4000-7742-7 pa; 978-1-4000-4266-1; 978-1-4000-7742-7 pa

LC 2005044459

This book argues that "events that we anticipate will give us joy make us less happy than we think; things that fill us with dread will make us less unhappy, for less long, than we anticipate." (N Y Times Book Rev) Index.

"The book is a sly, irresistible romp down, or through, memory lane—past, present, and future. It is not only wildly entertaining but also hilarious . . . and yet full of startling insight, imaginative conclusions, and even bits of wisdom." Booklist

Includes bibliographical references

Goleman, Daniel

★ **Social** intelligence; the new science of human relationships. Bantam Books 2006 403p il $28; pa $14 **158**

1. Emotions 2. Intellect

ISBN 0-553-80352-2; 978-0-553-80352-5; 0-553-38449-X pa; 978-0-553-38449-9 pa

LC 2006-45971

The author "argues for a new social model of intelligence drawn from the emerging field of social neuroscience. . . . Goleman illuminates new theories about attachment, bonding, and the making and remaking of memory as he examines how our brains are wired for altruism, compassion, concern and rapport." Publ Wkly

Includes bibliographical references

Hardy, Benjamin

Willpower doesn't work; discover the hidden keys to success. Benjamin Hardy. Hachette Books 2018 xviii, 235 p.p (hardcover) $26 **158**

1. Success 2. Self-help techniques 3. Identity (Psychology) 4. Proximity spaces 5. Becoming (Philosophy) 6. Self -- Social aspects

ISBN 9780316441353; 0316441325; 9780316441322

LC 2017042668

In this book, author Benjamin Hardy "explains that willpower is nothing more than a dangerous fad-one that is bound to lead to failure. Instead of 'white-knuckling' your way to change, you need to instead alter your surroundings to support your goals. . . . Hardy will show you that nurture is far more powerful than your nature, and teach you how to create and control your environment so your environment will not create and control you." (Publisher's note)

Hay, Louise L.

You can heal your life. Hay House 1987 226p pa $14.95 **158**

1. Mind and body 2. Health self-care 3. Self-realization 4. Holistic medicine

ISBN 0-937611-01-8

LC 88-200391

First published 1984

The author's "key message in this . . . work is: 'If we are willing to do the mental work, almost anything can be healed.' Louise explains how limiting beliefs and ideas are often the cause of illness." Publisher's note

Includes bibliographical references

Klauser, Henriette Anne

Write it down, make it happen; knowing what you want-- and getting it! Scribner 2000 250p hardcover o.p. pa $12 **158**

1. Applied psychology

ISBN 0-684-85002-8 pa

LC 99-43551

The author "instructs her readers to write down their most extravagant wishes and, merely by the act of recording them, make them come true. . . . Her technique is intended to clarify goals, increase self-confidence, and dispel self-doubt, and she describes how it has dramatically improved her life and the lives of her friends and acquaintances." Libr J

Includes bibliographical references

Langshur, Eric

Start here; master the lifelong habit of wellbeing. by Eric Langshur and Nate Klemp. North Star Way 2016 320 p. illustrations (hardback) $26 **158**

1. Well-being 2. Stress management 3. Self-help techniques 4.

Happiness 5. Satisfaction 6. Mental health

ISBN 1501129082; 9781501129087

LC 2015043325

This book, by Eric Langshur and Nate Klemp, "is the manual for anyone seeking to achieve emotional fitness. Combining ancient wisdom with modern neuroscience from the world's leading experts, LIFE XT is a groundbreaking training program to master the art of wellbeing. The program teaches practices proven to rewire the brain for increased focus, engagement, and resilience to stress." (Publisher's note)

"Personal anecdotes add interest to the nuts-and-bolts format. Other books have touched on these same principles, but this book does an especially good job, walking readers step-by-step through the practices, presenting achievable goals, and encouraging readers to take charge of their emotional lives." Booklist

Includes bibliographical references and index

May, Rollo

★ **Freedom** and destiny. Norton 1981 275p hardcover o.p. pa $14 **158**

1. Fate and fatalism 2. Applied psychology 3. Free will and determinism

ISBN 0-393-31842-7 pa

LC 81-4009

This book examines "the continuing tension in our lives between the possibilities freedom offers and the various limitations imposed upon us by our particular fate or destiny." America

Includes bibliographical references

McGraw, Phillip C.

Life strategies; doing what works, doing what matters. Hyperion 1999 282p il $21.95; pa $13.95 **158**

1. Success

ISBN 0-7868-6548-2; 0-7868-8459-2 pa

LC 98-46748

"McGraw claims that people in dire situations have serious problems, including denial and choosing initial assumptions without testing them for accuracy. To create a life strategy that works, McGraw lays out his ten 'Life Laws' along with checklists and 18 assignments." Libr J

Michels, Barry, 1954-

The **tools**; transform your problems into courage, confidence, and creativity. Phil Stutz and Barry Michels. 1st ed. Spiegel & Grau 2012 271 p. ill. (alk. paper) $25 **158**

1. Applied psychology 2. Change (Psychology) 3. Self-help techniques 4. Self-actualization (Psychology)

ISBN 067964444X; 9780679644446; 9780679644453

LC 2011044717

In this book, "psychiatrist [Phil] Stutz and psychotherapist [Barry] Michels promote a rapid and streamlined method of self-improvement. Michels . . . teaches readers to end procrastination and negativity by tapping into higher forces. . . . [T]he authors' techniques are designed to access intense intrapersonal areas. The 'Inner Authority' tool, for example, involves imagining the Jungian Shadow to reach greater self-expression." (Publishers Weekly)

Miller, Caroline Adams

★ **Creating** your best life; the ultimate life list guide. [by] Caroline Adams Miller and Dr. Michael B. Frisch. Sterling Pub. 2009 276p il $19.95; pa $14.95 **158**

1. Success 2. Happiness

ISBN 978-1-4027-6259-8; 1-4027-6259-3; 978-1-4027-7998-5 pa; 1-4027-7998-4 pa

LC 2010-275766

"Instead of making New Year's resolutions, it may be more beneficial to assemble a goal-setting list. So believe positive psychologist/life coach Miller and clinical psychologist Frisch . . . who have put together dozens of interactive exercises and assessments to guide readers in self-discovery and life-list creation. Whether or not readers follow through with every assignment, they will undoubtedly be inspired to think about goals and live more consciously and productively." Libr J

Includes bibliographical references

Peck, M. Scott

★ The **road** less traveled; a new psychology of love, traditional values, and spiritual growth. 25th anniversary ed; Simon & Schuster 2002 315p $22.95   **158**
1. Love 2. Applied psychology
ISBN 0-7432-3825-7

LC 2002-75858

A reissue of the title first published 1978

This book attempts to bring together "psychology and religion. It is divided into four areas—discipline, love, religion and growth, and grace—and within each Peck tackles the . . . struggle between stagnation and progress which goes on in all of us throughout our lives." Libr J

Robbins, Tony

Unlimited power; the new science of personal achievement. [by] Anthony Robbins. 1st Fireside ed.; Simon & Schuster 1997 425p il pa $15   **158**
1. Success 2. Applied psychology
ISBN 0-684-84577-6

LC 97-35403

First published 1986

The author offers advice and techniques for achieving personal and professional success using neurolinguistic programming (NLP).

Rowling, J. K., 1965-

Very good lives; the fringe benefits of failure and the importance of imagination. J.K. Rowling. Little, Brown & Co. 2015 80 p. illustrations $15   **158**
1. Imagination 2. Commencements 3. Failure (Psychology)
ISBN 0316369152; 9780316369152

LC 2014959607

In this book, which reproduces her 2008 commencement speech at Harvard University, author J.K. Rowling "asks the profound and provocative questions: How can we embrace failure? And how can we use our imagination to better both ourselves and others? Drawing from stories of her own post-graduate years, the world famous author addresses some of life's most important questions." (Publisher's note)

"Rowling makes neat connections between the challenges of modern life and the tutelary examples of Seneca, Plutarch, and the other ancients. While she discounts the ennobling aspects of poverty and misery, it's also clear that her education provided her with some steel to face those hardships." Kirkus

Salzberg, Sharon

Real happiness; learn the power of meditation: a 28-day program. Workman Publishing 2011 208p pa $14.99   **158**
1. Meditation
ISBN 978-0-7611-5925-4

LC 2010-52087

The author "provides a 28-day program for incorporating meditation into one's life. Written for beginners, the book explains breathing and sitting techniques, the science behind the practice, and 12 guided

meditations. Interspersed throughout are FAQs from Salzberg's students regarding their difficulties with the practice. The accompanying CD includes nine meditations to guide readers through breathing, walking, emotional, and loving-kindness exercises. This is one of the best guides for anyone interested in exploring meditation or mindfulness." Libr J

Includes bibliographical references

Schwartz, David Joseph

★ The **magic** of thinking big; 1st Fireside ed.; Simon & Schuster 1987 192p pa $14.95   **158**
1. Success
ISBN 0-671-64678-8

LC 87-8516

First published 1959 by Prentice-Hall

In this motivational book, the author presents a "program for getting the most out of your job, your marriage and family life, and your community." Publisher's note

Sugar, Lisa

Power your happy; Work Hard, Play Nice & Build Your Dream Life. Lisa Sugar. Dutton, a member of Penguin Random House LLC 2016 256 p. illustrations (hardcover) $25   **158**
1. Success 2. Happiness 3. Self-realization 4. Success in business
ISBN 9781101985069

LC 2016020264

In this book author Lisa Sugar, founder of POPSUGAR, "shares her personal and business story. [Sugar] knows that creating your dream job requires hard work, patience, and experience. She'll give advice, in big and small ways, about exactly how to do that, from starting a company to ditching a relationship that isn't working to becoming a fabulous boss." (Publisher's note)

"While the advice is often lighthearted ("eating ice cream" is frequently prescribed as a quick fix), readers will discover substantial guidance that is easy to implement on everything from networking to interviewing to parenting." LJ

Tolle, Eckhart

A **new** earth; awakening to your life's purpose. Dutton/Penguin Group 2005 315p $24.95   **158**
1. Spiritual life 2. Self-realization
ISBN 978-0-525-94802-5; 0-525-94802-3

LC 2005-23358

"According to Tolle, . . . humans are on the verge of creating a new world by a personal transformation that shifts our attention away from our ever-expanding egos." Publ Wkly

Includes bibliographical references

The **power** of now; a guide to spiritual enlightenment. New World Library 1999 193p $22.95; pa $14   **158**
1. Spiritual life 2. Self-realization
ISBN 978-1-57731-152-2; 1-57731-152-3; 978-1-57731-480-6 pa; 1-57731-480-8 pa

LC 99-42366

First published 1997 in Canada

"The author describes his transition from despair to self-realization soon after his 29th birthday. Tolle took another ten years to understand this transformation, during which time he evolved a philosophy that has parallels in Buddhism, relaxation techniques, and meditation theory. . . In The Power of Now he shows readers how to recognize themselves as the creators of their own pain, and how to have a pain-free existence by living fully in the present." Publisher's note

Yate, Martin

Knock 'em dead 2015; the ultimate job search guide. by Martin Yate. Adams Media Corp 2014 384 p. $16.99   **158**
1. Job hunting 2. Job interviews 3. Resumes (Employment)
ISBN 1440579059; 9781440579059

LC 2001242089

In this book on job searching, author Martin Yate "shares his proven, unique, and ever-evolving tactics for professional success. You'll learn how to create resumes that get results, maximize social networks to quadruple your interviews, turn those job interviews into job offers, [and] negotiate the best salary and benefits package." (Publisher's note)

158.1   Personal improvement and analysis

André, Christophe

Looking at Mindfulness; 25 Ways to Live in the Moment Through Art. by Christophe Andre. Penguin Group USA 2015 304 p. color illustrations $27.95   **158.1**
1. Mind and body 2. Art appreciation
ISBN 0399175636; 9780399175633

In this book, author Christophe Andre "guides readers through the art of mindfulness beginning with art itself. Beautifully illustrated in color throughout, André curates a collection of classic and esoteric works, from Rembrandt to Hopper to Magritte, providing a lucid commentary on the inner workings of each painting-- as he describes the dynamic on the canvas, he turns to the reader's own reactions, exploring the connection between what we see and what we feel." (Publisher's note)

"A fascinating book, suitable for those who are interested in art or the discipline of mindfulness." LJ

Benincasa, Sara

Real artists have day jobs; (and other awesome things they don't teach you in school) Sara Benincasa. William Morrow, an imprint of HarperCollins Publishers 2016 ix, 259 p.p (paperback) $14.99   **158.1**
1. Success 2. Self-realization 3. Adulthood
ISBN 9780062369819; 9780062369826; 0062369814

LC 2017394680

This book, by Sara Benincasa, offers "52 witty, provocative essays on how to live like a real adult--especially for those who have chosen a slightly more offbeat path to get there. Chock full of information and advice, Sara's warm, smart, empathetic, and quirky voice is relatable to everyone from twenty-somethings and recent college grads to anyone a bit older who's still trying to figure things out." (Publisher's note)

"Outspoken and matter of fact, Benincasa points self-deprecatingly to her own failures to emphasize just how important they are to living a full, happy, and meaningful life. It's hard to imagine an actual self-help book could be more inspirational." LJ

Cardillo, Joseph

Body intelligence; harness your body's energies for your best life. Joseph Cardillo. Atria Books 2015 272 p. (hardback) $24   **158.1**
1. Self-improvement 2. Self-realization 3. Mind and body 4. Self-actualization (Psychology)
ISBN 1582705186; 9781582705187

LC 2015015373

Author Joseph Cardillo "combines Western science, technology, psychology, and holistic medicine to show that we must first balance the body's energies before we can enhance the mind. Based on cutting-edge ideas, this perennial guide teaches us to tap into our energetic "sweet spot" and identify specific steps we must take to remove energy blocks. Packed with exercises, self-tests, and step-by-step instructions, [it] provides all the interactive tools for beginners and experienced energy-balancing practitioners alike." (Publisher's note)

"Although Cardillo's reasoning can be complex, his practical suggestions will be useful for all those wanting to tap into surrounding energy forces to correct their emotional and physical balance and fine-tune their minds." Booklist

Cuddy, Amy

Presence; bringing your boldest self to your biggest challenges. Amy Cuddy. Little, Brown & Co. 2015 352 p. illustrations (hardcover) $28   **158.1**
1. Self-perception 2. Self-realization
ISBN 0316256579; 9780316256575; 9780316305624; 9780316387804

LC 2015952382

In this book author Amy Cuddy suggests "we don't need to embark on a grand spiritual quest or complete an inner transformation to harness the power of presence. Instead, we need to nudge ourselves, moment by moment, by tweaking our body language, behavior, and mind-set in our day-to-day lives. 'Presence' is filled with stories of individuals who learned how to flourish during the stressful moments that once terrified them." (Publisher's note)

"Given the popularity of Cuddy's TED Talk, one would expect that this book will be in demand, and readers will not be disappointed." LJ

Duckworth, Angela

Grit; the power of passion and perseverance. Angela Duckworth. Scribner 2016 352 p. illustrations (hardback) $28   **158.1**
1. Perseverance 2. Success in business 3. Academic achievement 4. Success 5. Diligence 6. Perseverance (Ethics) 7. Expectation (Psychology)
ISBN 9781501111105; 9781501111112

LC 2015042880

In this book, author Angela Duckworth "shows anyone striving to succeed—be it parents, students, educators, athletes, or business people—that the secret to outstanding achievement is not talent but a special blend of passion and persistence she calls 'grit.' . . . She takes readers into the field to visit cadets struggling through their first days at West Point, teachers working in some of the toughest schools, and young finalists in the National Spelling Bee." (Publisher's note)

"Not your grandpa's self-help book, but Duckworth's text is oddly encouraging, exhorting us to do better by trying harder, and a pleasure to read." Kirkus

Includes bibliographical references and index

Duhigg, Charles

★ The **power** of habit; by Charles Duhigg. Random House 2012 xx, 371 p.p   **158.1**
1. Habit 2. Business planning 3. Change (Psychology) 4. Habit -- Social aspects
ISBN 9780679603856; 9781400069286

LC 2011029545

In this book, "science writer Charles Duhigg explores the reasons why we find it so hard to change ingrained behaviour. . . . [H]abits usually start with a simple sensory cue . . . which sets up a craving in the brain's reward centres. This yearning overrides the regions involved in self-control. . . . From nail-biting to alcoholism, Duhigg offers . . . insights into the triggers that set people on a downward spiral, and proven ways to fight those urges. . . . Habitual behaviours can propagate through an organisation or society, he argues, offering convincing anecdotes that cover everything from the success of Starbucks to the civil rights movement. . . . [Duhigg examines the] way advertising hijacks your brain's reward centres to set off a new, irresistible habit." (New Scientist)

Includes bibliographical references and index

Dunne, Linnea

Lagom; the Swedish art of balanced living. Linnea Dunne. Running Press 2017 160 p. color illustrations (hardcover) $16　　　　　**158.1**
1. Well-being 2. Self-realization 3. Work-life balance 4. Self-actualization (Psychology)
ISBN 9780762463756; 9780762464456

LC 2017942833

This book, by Linnea Dunne, edited by Jennifer Kasius, "provides simple solutions to juggle everyday priorities, reduce stress, eat well, and save money, with lessons on the importance of downtime, being outdoors, and Sweden's coffee break culture. Tips on removing clutter and creating a capsule wardrobe help readers achieve Sweden's famously clean and functional design aesthetic, while advice on going green and growing food gets their hands dirty." (Publisher's note)

"She covers everything from eating and styling lagom to feeling and socializing lagom in a clear upbeat tone, which encourages readers to participate." LJ

Ferriss, Tim

Tools of titans; the tactics, routines, and habits of billionaires, icons, and world-class performers. Tim Ferriss; foreword by Arnold Schwarzenegger; illustrations by Remie Geoffroi. Houghton Mifflin Harcourt 2016 xxvii, 673 p.p illustrations (hardcover) $28　　　　　**158.1**
1. Success 2. Interviews 3. Wealth 4. Wisdom 5. Conduct of life 6. Physical fitness 7. Self-realization 8. Change (Psychology) 9. Self-actualization (Psychology) 10. Successful people -- Interviews
ISBN 1328683788; 9781328683786

LC 2016304630

This book, by Tim Ferriss, presents edited transcripts from the author's podcast interviewing successful people and discussing their habits and practices. "The guests range from super celebs (Jamie Foxx, Arnold Schwarzenegger, etc.) and athletes (icons of powerlifting, gymnastics, surfing, etc.) to legendary Special Operations commanders and black-market biochemists." (Publisher's note)

Includes bibliographical references.

Harris, Dan

★ **10%** happier; how I tamed the voice in my head, reduced stress without losing my edge, and found self-help that actually works--a true story. Dan Harris. It Books 2014 256 p. (hardback) $25.99　　　　　**158.1**
1. Buddhism 2. Meditation 3. Mind and body 4. Stress management
ISBN 0062265423; 9780062265425; 9780062265432

LC 2013043037

News anchor Dan Harris "embarks on an . . . odyssey through the strange worlds of spirituality and self-help, and discovers a way to get happier. . . . After having a nationally televised panic attack on Good Morning America, . . . Harris knew he had to make some changes. . . . After learning about research that suggests meditation can do everything from lower your blood pressure to essentially rewire your brain, Harris . . . us[ed] it for increased calm, focus, and happiness." (Publisher's note)

Heller, Rick

Secular meditation; 32 practices for cultivating inner peace,

compassion, and joy: a guide from the humanist community at Harvard. Rick Heller. New World Library 2015 287 p. (paperback) $15.95　　　　　**158.1**
1. Happiness 2. Meditation 3. Relaxation 4. Secularism -- 21st century 5. Meditation -- Psychological aspects
ISBN 1608683699; 9781608683697

LC 2015027201

In this book, by Rick Heller, "step-by-step instructions, personal stories, and provocative questions teach empathy for others, stress reduction, and the kind of in-the-moment living that fosters appreciation for life and resilience in the face of adversity. Heller simplifies what is often found mysterious, describing and providing detailed instructions for 32 different practices, ensuring that anyone can find the right one." (Publisher's note)

"This book is an ideal guide for those who want to study meditation and mindfulness but are put off by the focus on Buddhism or religion in general." LJ

Includes bibliographical references and index

Knight, Sarah

The **life**-changing magic of not giving a f*ck; how to stop spending time you don't have with people you don't like doing things you don't want to do. Sarah Knight. Little, Brown & Co. 2015 xi, 208 p.p (hardcover) $17.99　　　　　**158.1**
1. Parodies 2. Self-realization 3. Self-help techniques
ISBN 9780316270724; 9780316271332

LC 2015952380

This book, by Sarah Knight, is a "brilliant, hilarious, and practical parody of Marie Kondo's bestseller 'The Life-Changing Magic of Tidying Up.' [It] explains how to rid yourself of unwanted obligations, shame, and guilt--and give your f*cks instead to people and things that make you happy." (Publisher's note)

"She offers suggestions on how to handle things based on beginner, intermediate, and expert level, and much of her advice is truly practical." Booklist

Magness, Steve

Peak performance; elevate your game, avoid burnout, and thrive with the new science of success. Brad Stulberg; Steve Magness. Rodale Books 2017 ix, 230 p.p illustrations (hardcover) $24.99　　　　　**158.1**
1. Self-realization 2. Self-help techniques 3. Psychology, Applied 4. Self-actualization (Psychology)
ISBN 162336793X; 9781623367947; 9781623367930

LC 2017021865

This book, by Brad Stulberg and Steve Magness, "combines the inspiring stories of top performers across a range of capabilities--from athletic, to intellectual, to artistic--with the latest scientific insights into the cognitive and neurochemical factors that drive performance in all domains. . . . Readers [will] learn how to enhance their performance via myriad ways including: optimally alternating between periods of intense work and rest." (Publisher's note)

"The accessible science and easy-to-grasp instructions on healthy ways of developing a sense of purpose are encouraging and inspiring, and readers looking to realize their potential without harming themselves would do well to take this advice." Pub Wkly

Includes bibliographical references (pages 203-216) and index.

Manson, Mark

The **subtle** art of not giving a fu*k; a counterintuitive approach to living a good life. Mark Manson. HarperOne 2016 224 p. (hardback) $24.99; (ebook) $23.99　　　　　**158.1**

1. Conduct of life 2. Self-realization 3. Self-help techniques
ISBN 0062457713; 9780062457714; 9780062457738

LC 2016011724

This book, by Mark Manson, is a "generation-defining self-help guide. . . . Manson makes the argument, backed both by academic research and well-timed poop jokes, that improving our lives hinges not on our ability to turn lemons into lemonade, but on learning to stomach lemons better." (Publisher's note)

"This book, full of counterintuitive suggestions that often make great sense, is a pleasure to read and worthy of rereading. A good yardstick by which self-improvement books should be measured." Kirkus

Rosenfeld, Edward

The **book** of highs; 255 ways to alter your consciousness without drugs. Edward Rosenfeld. Workman Publishing Company, Inc. 2018 320 p. (alk. paper) $17.95 **158.1**
    1. Meditation 2. Consciousness 3. Alternative medicine 4. Mind and body 5. Mindfulness (Psychology) 6. Self-actualization (Psychology)
ISBN 9780761193876

LC 2018014124

This book, by Edward Rosenfeld, catalogs "ways humans can alter consciousness, minus drugs and alcohol. Drawn from cultures around the world, here are positive techniques--Self-Hypnosis, Alterations of Breathing. . . . And here are 'negative' techniques--Self-Flagellation, Sleep Deprivation. . . . Methods derived from religious and mystic traditions. . . . [And] methods that use devices, from the domestic Metronome Watching, to the state-of-the-art Brain-Wave Biofeedback." (Publisher's note)

Roth, Bernard

The **Achievement** Habit; Stop Wishing, Start Doing, and Take Command of Your Life. Bernard Roth. HarperCollins 2015 288 p. illustrations $27.99 **158.1**
    1. Self-confidence 2. Self-realization 3. Thought and thinking
ISBN 0062356100; 9780062356109

LC 2015303295

This book by Bernard Roth presents a "primer to the basic elements of design theory, based on the premise that 'achievement can be learned.' Tenets include 'making the familiar unfamiliar,' individual responsibility, and reframing questions in order to find solutions. To illustrate the last principle's importance, Roth describes some D.school success stories, including presenting MRI testing to child patients as an 'adventure.'" (Publishers Weekly)

"Roth's excellent advice on how to overcome obstacles and triumph should be of interest to readers college age and up." LJ

Roth, Bob

Strength in stillness; the power of transcendental meditation. Bob Roth. Simon & Schuster 2018 224 p. (hardcover) $24 **158.1**
    1. Meditation 2. Stress management 3. Transcendental meditation 4. Transcendental Meditation
ISBN 9781501161216; 9781501161223

LC 2017035499

In this book, author Bob Roth "breaks down the science behind Transcendental Meditation in a new, accessible way. He highlights the three distinct types of meditation--Focused Attention, Open Monitoring, and Self-Transcending--and showcases the evidence that the third, Self-Transcending, or Transcendental Meditation, is a uniquely accessible, effective, and efficient way to reduce stress, access inner power, and build resilience." (Publisher's note)

" A thorough explanation of what transcendental meditation is and is not that will appeal to readers of mindfulness and seekers of stress reduction and mental composure." LJ

Includes bibliographical references

Roth, Geneen

This messy magnificent life; a field guide. by Geneen Roth, foreword by Anne Lamott. Simon & Schuster 2018 224 p. $26 **158.1**
    1. Self-acceptance 2. Self-realization 3. Women -- Psychology
ISBN 1501182463; 9781501182464

This book, by Geneen Roth, foreword by Anne Lamott, "explores the personal beliefs, hidden traumas, and social pressures that shape not just women's feelings about their bodies, but also their confidence, choices, and relationships. This . . . sometimes laugh-out-loud look at the imperfect path women take to step into their own power, presence, and ownership is based on the author's personal journey and her decades of work with thousands of women around the country." (Publisher's note)

" Though hardly groundbreaking, these chapters of simple advice are easily digestible, and reading one per day is a good way to start this practice. Empowering words for women—especially those struggling with body issues—to regain control of their lives." Kirkus

Rubin, Gretchen

Better than before; Mastering the Habits of Our Everyday Lives. Gretchen Rubin. Crown 2015 320 p. illustrations (hardback) $26 **158.1**
    1. Habit 2. Change (Psychology)
ISBN 0385348614; 9780385348614; 9780385348638

LC 2014031703

In this book, author Gretchen Rubin explains that "[h]abits are the invisible architecture of everyday life. It takes work to make a habit, but once that habit is set, we can harness the energy of habits to build happier, stronger, more productive lives. . . . Rubin uses herself as guinea pig, tests her theories on family and friends, and answers readers' most pressing questions." (Publisher's note)

Shankle, Melanie

★ **Church** of the small things; the million little pieces that make up a life. Melanie Shankle. Zondervan 2017 222 p. (hardcover: alk. paper) $22.99 **158.108**
    1. Anecdotes 2. Women -- Psychology 3. Women -- Conduct of life 4. Christian life 5. Christian women -- Religious life 6. Christian women -- Conduct of life
ISBN 9780310348870

LC 2017003557

In this book, author Melanie Shankle "speaks directly to the heart of women of all ages who are longing to find significance and meaning in the normal, . . . mundane world of . . . cooking meals for their family, or taking care of a sick loved one. . . . Through humorous stories[,] . . . Melanie helps women embrace what it means to live a simple, yet incredibly meaningful life and how to find all the beauty and laughter that lies right beneath the surface of every moment." (Publisher's note)

Shankle's winsome book will be well-received by Christian readers looking to be more conscientious in everyday life. --Publishers Weekly (August 2017)

Shriver, Maria, 1955-

I've been thinking; reflections, prayers, and meditations for a meaningful life. Maria Shriver. Penguin Group USA 2018 240 p. $20 **158.1**
    1. Prayer 2. Meditations 3. Christianity -- Spiritual life
ISBN 0525522603; 9780525522607

In this book, author Maria Shrive, "shares inspiring quotes, prayers, and reflections designed to get readers thinking, get them feeling, get them laughing, and help them in their journey to what she calls The Open Field--a place of acceptance, purpose, and passion--a place of joy. . . . Like talking with a close friend, it's the perfect daily companion--an exceptional gift for someone looking to move forward in life with hope and grace," (Publisher's note)

"Among the topics she covers are kindness, mental health, peace, time to reflect, grief, and power—of the mind, of women, of the pause, of empathy. The honesty of this uplifting book will please Shriver's established readership as well as new readers looking for inspiration." Pub Wkly

Siegel, Daniel J.

Aware; the science and practice of presence: the groundbreaking meditation practice. Dr. Daniel Siegel, M.D. TarcherPerigee 2018 400 p. (hardback) $28   **158.1**
1. Meditation 2. Mindfulness (Psychology) 3. Self-actualization (Psychology)
ISBN 1101993049; 9781101993040
                 LC 2018016987

This book, by Daniel Siegel, "provides practical instruction for mastering the Wheel of Awareness, a life-changing tool for cultivating more focus, presence, and peace in one's day-to-day life. . . . Siegel reveals how developing a Wheel of Awareness practice to focus attention, open awareness, and cultivate kind intention can literally help you grow a healthier brain and reduce fear, anxiety, and stress in your life." (Publisher's note)

Includes bibliographical references and index

Sincero, Jen

You Are a Badass; how to stop doubting your greatness and start living an awesome life. Jen Sincero. Running Press 2017 269 p. (hardcover) $25   **158.1**
1. Self-realization 2. Self-help techniques 3. Self-actualization (Psychology)
ISBN 9780762490622; 9780762490547; 0762490543
                 LC 2013932303

This book, by Jen Sincero, "has inspired even the snarkiest of skeptics--encouraging them to embrace their awesomeness, give fear the heave-ho, and start kicking some serious ass. Now it's dressed up in a deluxe hardcover edition, with a new foreword by the author. But it's the same 'classic' book that helps you create a life you love via hilariously inspiring stories, sage advice, easy exercises, and the occasional swear word." (Publisher's note)

"Sincero writes with candor about her own struggles, heightening the message's accessibility, particularly among a younger set." Pub Wkly

Includes bibliographical references (pages 257-267).

Tilcsik, Andras

Meltdown; why our systems fail and what we can do about it. Chris Clearfield and András Tilcsik. Penguin Group USA 2018 304 p. $28   **158.1**
1. Social systems 2. Organizational behavior 3. System theory -- Social aspects
ISBN 0735222630; 9780735222632

In this book, authors "Chris Clearfield and András Tilcsik explain how the increasing complexity of our systems creates conditions ripe for failure and why our brains and teams can't keep up. They highlight the paradox of progress: Though modern systems have given us new capabilities, they've become vulnerable to surprising meltdowns--and even to corruption and misconduct." (Publisher's note)

"Though the underlying argument isn't new—the authors draw

heavily on the work of social scientist Charles Perrow, particularly his 1984 book Normal Accidents—the authors' body of examples is relatively fresh, if sometimes not so well remembered today—e.g., the journalistic crimes of Jayson Blair, made possible by a complex accounting system that just begged to be gamed. Programmers, social engineers, and management consultants are among the many audiences for this useful, thought-provoking book." Kirkus

Tippett, Krista

★ **Becoming** Wise; An Inquiry into the Mystery and Art of Living. Krista Tippett. Penguin Group USA 2016 304 p. $28   **158.1**
1. Life 2. Meaning (Philosophy)
ISBN 1594206805; 9781594206801

This book, by Krista Tippett, " offers a grounded and fiercely hopeful vision of humanity for this century – of personal growth but also renewed public life and human spiritual evolution. It insists on the possibility of a common life for this century marked by resilience and redemption, with beauty as a core moral value and civility and love as muscular practice. The book is a master class in living, curated by Tippett and accompanied by a delightfully ecumenical dream team of teaching faculty." (Publisher's note)

"A hopeful consideration of the human potential for enlightenment." Kirkus

Vincent, Isabel

Dinner with Edward; the story of a remarkable friendship. Isabel Vincent. Algonquin Books of Chapel Hill 2016 224 p. $23.95   **158.1**
1. Widowers 2. Friendship 3. New York (N.Y.) -- Biography 4. Self-actualization (Psychology) 5. Friendship -- Psychological aspects 6. Dinners and dining -- New York (State) -- New York 7. Women authors, American -- New York (State) -- New York -- Biography
ISBN 9781616204228; 1616204222
                 LC 2015034310

Author Isabel Vincent presents this memoir "about sorrow and joy, love and nourishment. As Edward and Isabel meet weekly for . . . dinners that Edward prepares, he shares so much more than his recipes. Edward is teaching Isabel the luxury of slowing down and taking the time to think through everything she does, to deconstruct her own life, cutting it back to the bone and examining the guts, no matter how messy that proves to be." (Publisher's note)

"Delightfully combining the warmheartedness of Tuesdays with Morrie with the sensual splendor of Julie and Julia, this is a memoir to treasure." Booklist

Viorst, Judith

Imperfect control; our lifelong struggles with power and surrender. Simon & Schuster 1998 446p hardcover o.p. pa $14   **158.1**
1. Psychology
ISBN 0-684-84814-7 pa
                 LC 97-37302

"Referring to the works of social scientists, psychologists, and philosophers as well as literary examples and personal experiences, Viorst shows how issues of power and surrender confront and affect us throughout our lives. . . . Her book is very readable, with traces of the author's special brand of humor woven throughout." Libr J

Includes bibliographical references

Wade, Cleo

Heart talk; poetic wisdom for a better life. Cleo Wade. Atria / 37 INK 2018 224 p. (paperback) $17.99 **158.1**

    1. Conduct of life 2. Self-realization 3. Self-help techniques 4. Conduct of life -- Poetry 5. Self-realization -- Poetry

    ISBN 9781501177347; 9781501191138

        LC 2017057816

In this book, poet Cleo Wade "offers creative inspiration and life lessons through poetry, mantras, and affirmations. . . . Featuring over one hundred and twenty of Cleo's original poems, mantras, and affirmations, including fan favorites and never before seen ones, this book is a daily pep talk to keep you feeling empowered and motivated." (Publisher's note)

    Includes bibliographical references and index

Wax, Ruby

Sane new world; a user's guide to the normal-crazy mind. Ruby Wax. Perigee Trade 2014 247 p. illustrations (paperback) $16 **158.1**

    1. Mental health 2. Cognitive therapy 3. Mind and body 4. Mindfulness-based cognitive therapy

    ISBN 039917060X; 9780399170607

        LC 2014016530

In this book, Ruby Wax, "comedian, writer and mental health advocate--shows us just how our minds can send us mad as our internal critics play on a permanent loop tape. . . . Ruby knows those voices well. She has been on a tough but ultimately enlightening journey that has taken her from battling depression to achieving a Masters Degree from Oxford University in Mindfulness-based Cognitive Therapy." (Publisher's note)

    "Wax's unconventional approach may inspire others to seek help in coping with mental illness." LJ

Wiking, Meik

The **little** book of hygge; Danish secrets to happy living. by Meik Wiking. HarperCollins 2017 221 p. color illustrations $19.99; (ebook) $18.99 **158.1**

    1. Happiness 2. Meditation

    ISBN 0062658808; 9780062658807; 9780062658814

        LC 2016052564

In this book, by Meik Wiking, "Hygge is the sensation you get when you're cuddled up on a sofa, in cozy socks under a soft throw, during a storm. It's that feeling when you're sharing comfort food and easy conversation with loved ones at a candlelit table. It is the warmth of morning light shining just right on a crisp blue-sky day. [It] introduces you to this cornerstone of Danish life, and offers advice and ideas on incorporating it into your own life." (Publisher's note)

    "An exciting and intriguing guide, full of ideas for making everyday life more cozy." LJ

The **little** book of lykke; secrets of the world's happiest people. Meik Wiking. William Morrow, an imprint of HarperCollins Publishers 2017 285 p. color illustrations (hardcover) $19.99 **158.1**

    1. Happiness 2. Quality of life 3. Self-help techniques 4. Contentment

    ISBN 9780062820334; 9780062820341; 0062820338

In this book, author Meik Wiking "identifies the six factors that explain the majority of differences in happiness across the world--togetherness, money, health, freedom, trust, and kindness--and explores what actions we can take to become happier. As he reveals, we can deepen our blissfulness and contentment with little adjustments in our behavior, whether it's eating like the French . . . or dancing the tango like Argen-

tineans in Buenos Aires." (Publisher's note)

    "Wiking provides common-sense, real-life applications for his advice in a light-hearted, easy-to-read presentation laced with statistics and personal anecdotes in support of his findings. Whether it's used as a how-to or as inspirational reading, this little book is sure to bring a dose of happiness to all its readers." Booklist

158.12　Personal improvement and analysis through meditation

Adams, Louise

Mindful Moments; 30 Day Plan for Supercharged Results. Louise Adams. Wilkinson Press 2016 128 p. illustrations $14.95 **158.12**

    1. Mind and body 2. Self-perception 3. Mindfulness (Psychology)

    ISBN 1925265528; 9781925265521

This book, by Louise Adams, discusses ideas for bringing mindfulness into your life. "Awareness of the present moment is a tremendously important first step in developing mindfulness skills. . . . Once people have achieved mindful awareness, then what? . . . Adams discusses how compassion can transform your life and help build a better relationship with your mind and body." (Publisher's note)

    "Highly recommended for its presentation, simplicity, and concentration on self-care." LJ

Federle, Tim

★ **Life** is like a musical; how to live, love, and lead like a star. Tim Federle. Running Press 2017 179 p. $18 **158.12**

    1. Success 2. Self-realization 3. Theater -- Vocational guidance

    ISBN 9780762462643

        LC 2017943744

This book, by Tim Federle, "features 50 wry, witty tips on getting ahead in life and love--all learned in the showbiz trenches. . . . [It] features 50 tips learned backstage, onstage, and in between gigs, with chapters such as 'Dance Like Everyone's Watching' and 'Save the Drama for the Stage.' This charming and clever guide will appeal to all ages and inspire readers to step into the lead role of their own life, even if they're not a recovering theater major." (Publisher's note)

Warren, Jeff

Meditation for fidgety skeptics; a 10% happier how-to book. by Dan Harris and Jeff Warren, with Carlye Adler. Spiegel & Grau 2017 xi, 286 p.p (hardcover) $26 **158.12**

    1. Happiness 2. Meditation 3. Self-help techniques 4. Meditation -- Psychological aspects

    ISBN 9780399588945; 9780399588952

        LC 2017037570

This book, by Dan Harris and Jeff Warren, with Carlye Adler, is intended to get people started on meditation. "Harris and his friend Jeff Warren, a masterful teacher and 'Meditation MacGyver,' embark on a cross-country quest to tackle the myths, misconceptions, and self-deceptions that stop people from meditating. . . . They create a taxonomy of the most common issues . . . and offer up science-based life hacks to help people overcome them." (Publisher's note)

    "Making meditation's benefits clear, sharing countless ways to fit it into already-packed days, and, above all, stressing the evolving work-in-progress that is any meditation practice, this is highly useful for fidgety skeptics and true believers alike." Booklist

    Includes bibliographical references (pages 274-276).

Wellings, Nigel

Why can't I meditate? how to get your mindfulness practice on track. Nigel Wellings. TarcherPerigee 2016 384 p. (paperback) $16   **158.12**

1. Meditation 2. Mindfulness (Psychology)
ISBN 9781101983270

LC 2016007917

This book, by Nigel Wellings, is a "guide . . . on how to get the most out of meditation--and make the practice a permanent part of your daily life. . . . Full of practical ways to help our mindfulness practice flourish, it also features guidance from a wide spectrum of secular and Buddhist mindfulness teachers, and personal accounts by new meditators on what they find difficult and what helps them overcome those blocks." (Publisher's note)

"The instructions are clear, easy to follow, and kind, offering readers a path forward while leaving plenty of room for them to decide what works best. New students of mediation would be hard-pressed to find a more patient teacher." Booklist

Includes bibliographical references and index

Willink, Jocko

★ **Discipline** equals freedom; field manual. Jocko Willink. St. Martin's Press 2017 199 p. (hardcover) $24.99   **158.12**

1. Success 2. Motivation (Psychology)
ISBN 1250156947; 9781250156945; 9781250156952; 9781250184719

LC 2017953364

In this book, "Jocko Willink's methods for success were born in the SEAL Teams, where he spent most of his adult life. . . . [It] includ[es] strategies and tactics for conquering weakness, procrastination, and fear, and specific physical training presented in workouts for beginner, intermediate, and advanced athletes, and even the best sleep habits and food intake recommended to optimize performance." (Publisher's note)

158.2   Interpersonal relations

Bright, Deb

The **truth** doesn't have to hurt; how to use criticism to strengthen relationships, improve performance, and promote change. Deb Bright. American Management Association 2015 256 p. illustrations (pbk.) $17.95   **158.2**

1. Change (Psychology) 2. Feedback (Psychology) 3. Interpersonal relations 4. Performance 5. Criticism, Personal
ISBN 0814434819; 9780814434819

LC 2014020765

This book, by Deborah Bright, offers advice on utilizing criticism positively. "Executives, managers, team leaders--anyone who needs to temper praise with a dose of reality--will learn to: deliver the truth and have it taken as helpful; create an atmosphere of acceptance; avoid mistakes that sabotage an exchange; and control how they receive criticism so they benefit--even if it's badly presented." (Publisher's note)

"A useful book for almost anyone, giving helpful insight into ways to deliver (and receive) criticism so that it can do good, not harm." LJ

Dahl, Melissa

Cringeworthy; a theory of awkwardness. Melissa Dahl. Portfolio 2018 304 p. (hardback) $27   **158.2**

1. Emotions 2. Self-consciousness 3. Interpersonal relations
ISBN 9780735211636

LC 2017052219

In this book, editor Melissa Dahl, "explains the compelling psychology of awkwardness, and asks: what if the moments that make us feel most awkward are actually valuable? . . . Dahl explores the oddest, cringiest corners of our world. She chats with strangers on the busy New York City subway, goes on awkward friend dates using a 'Tinder-for-friendship' app, takes improv comedy lessons, and even reads aloud from her . . . middle school diary to a crowd of strangers." (Publisher's note)

Includes bibliographical references

Fontes, Lisa Aronson

Invisible chains; overcoming coercive control in your intimate relationship. Lisa Aronson Fontes. The Guilford Press 2015 220 p. (paperback) $14.95   **158.2**

1. Domestic violence 2. Interpersonal relations 3. Intimidation 4. Control (Psychology) 5. Dominance (Psychology) 6. Intimate partner violence
ISBN 1462520243; 9781462520244; 9781462520350

LC 2014048835

This book, by Lisa Aronson Fontes, asks "what happens when [male] attentiveness becomes domination? In some relationships, the desire to control leads to jealousy, threats, micromanaging--even physical violence. If you or someone you care about are trapped in a web of coercive control, this book provides answers, hope, and a way out." (Publisher's note)

"Excellent for people who are under someone's coercive control or know someone who might be. The book is also recommended for those who have the opportunity to help victims in their work such as therapists, lawyers, and police officers." LJ

Includes bibliographical references and index

Goodman, Ellen

I know just what you mean; the power of friendship in women's lives. {by} Ellen Goodman, Patricia O'Brien. Simon & Schuster 2000 300p il $25; pa $14   **158.2**

1. Friendship 2. Women -- Psychology
ISBN 0-684-84287-4; 0-7432-0171-X pa

LC 00-24859

"Heavy on insight and light on psychological jargon, this book is an intelligent, observant read." Publ Wkly

Grant, Adam, 1981-

Give and take; a revolutionary approach to success. Adam M. Grant. Viking 2013 320 p. $27.95   **158.2**

1. Success 2. Social networking 3. Success in business 4. Interpersonal relations
ISBN 0670026557; 9780670026555

LC 2012039995

This book, by Adam M. Grant, focuses on the topic of success. Grant "shows how one of America's best networkers developed his connections, why the creative genius behind one of the most popular shows in television history toiled for years in anonymity, how a basketball executive responsible for multiple draft busts transformed his franchise into a winner, and how we could have anticipated Enron's demise four years before the company collapsed." (Publisher's note)

Includes bibliographical references and index

Karlins, Marvin

The **like** switch; an ex-FBI agent's guide to influencing, attracting, and winning people over. Jack Schafer, Marvin Karlins. Simon & Schuster 2015 288 p. illustrations (A Touchstone book) (pbk.) $19.99   **158.2**

1. Personality 2. Influence (Psychology) 3. Friendship 4.

Interpersonal relations 5. Interpersonal attraction
ISBN 1476754489; 9781476754482

LC 2014009121

This book by Jack Schafer, with Marvin Karlins, presents "proven strategies on how to instantly read people and influence how they perceive you, so you can easily turn on the like switch. He presents these techniques for how you can influence, attract, and win people over. Learn how to think and react like your favorite TV investigators from Criminal Minds or CSI as Dr. Schafer shows you how to improve your LQ (Likeability Quotient)." (Publisher's note)

"The author's approach to observing human nature should prove practical and useful in a variety of situations, from romantic meetings to interviewing criminals. A unique and pragmatic tome." Pub Wkly

Miller, Donald

Scary close; dropping the act and finding true intimacy. Donald Miller. Thomas Nelson 2015 256 p. $19.99 **158.2**
1. Intimacy (Psychology) 2. Interpersonal relations
ISBN 078521318X; 9780785213185

LC 2014945329

This book, by Donald Miller, is "about the risk involved in choosing to impress fewer people and connect with more, about the freedom that comes when we stop acting and start loving. It is a story about knocking down old walls to create a healthy mind, a strong family, and a satisfying career. And it all feels like a conversation with the best kind of friend: smart, funny, true, important." (Publisher's note)

"Older, married readers might chuckle at the author's description of Betsy as near perfect, but younger readers will relate to the frankly expressed concerns about pressure to fit in, difficulties in the dating scene, and hard lessons learned, some with the help of counseling." Pub Wkly

Rollag, Keith

What to do when you're new; how to be confident, comfortable, and successful in new situations. Keith Rollag. AMACOM--American Management Association 2015 240 p. (pbk.) $17.95 **158.2**
1. Success 2. Self-confidence 3. Interpersonal relations
ISBN 9780814434895

LC 2015011043

This book, by Keith Rollag, "opens your eyes to the necessary skills and teaches you how to: Overcome fears, make great first impressions, talk to strangers with ease, get up to speed quickly, connect with people wherever you go. Blending stories and insights with simple techniques and exercises, this one-of-a-kind guide will get you out of your comfort zone and trying new things in no time." (Publisher's note)

"Key points are highlighted in this well-organized, comprehensive book." LJ

Includes bibliographical references and index

Waxman, Jamye

How to break up with anyone; letting go of friends, family, and everyone in-between. Jamye Waxman. Seal Press 2015 240 p. (paperback) $16 **158.2**
1. Conflict management 2. Breaking up (Interpersonal relations) 3. Friendship 4. Self-actualization (Psychology)
ISBN 9781580055970

LC 2015019613

In this book, by Jamye Waxman, a "relationship expert . . . has written a much-needed guide to every step of a non-romantic breakup. Drawing from her own experiences, Jamye provides strategies for disengaging from a friend, family member, community, or even former version of oneself, addressing both practical and emotional concerns." (Publisher's note)

"Sound guidance for those involved in toxic relationships and looking for a way out." LJ

158.4   Leadership

Fabritius, Friederike

The **leading** brain; Powerful Science-Based Strategies for Achieving Peak Performance. Friederike Fabritius, MS, and Hans W. Hagemann, PhD. TarcherPerigee 2017 352 p. (ebook) $65; (hardcover) $26 **158.4**
1. Leadership 2. Performance 3. Leadership -- Psychological aspects 4. Performance -- Psychological aspects
ISBN 9781101993200; 9780143129356

LC 2016038838

This book, by Friederike Fabritius and Hans W. Hagemann, is "a cutting-edge guide to applying the latest research in brain science to leadership - to sharpen performance, encourage innovation, and enhance job satisfaction. . . . Based on the authors' popular leadership programs, which have been delivered to tens of thousands of leaders all over the world, this clear, insightful, and engaging book will help both individuals and teams perform at their maximum potential, delivering extraordinary results." (Publisher's note)

"Concrete, energetic, and accessible, this is a must-read for anyone who takes a science-backed approach to business." Pub Wkly

Includes bibliographical references and index

158.5   Negotiation

Fisher, Roger, 1922-2012

★ **Getting** to yes; negotiating agreement without giving in. by Roger Fisher and William Ury; with Bruce Patton, editor. 3rd edition Penguin Books 2011 204 p. pbk $17 **158.5**
1. Negotiation
ISBN 0143118757; 9780143118756

LC 2011006319

Originally published 1981

"One of the primary business texts of the modern era, [Getting to Yes] is based on the work of the Harvard Negotiation Project, a group that deals with all levels of negotiation and conflict resolution. Getting to Yes offers a proven, step-by-step strategy for coming to mutually acceptable agreements in every sort of conflict. Thoroughly updated and revised, it offers readers a straight- forward, universally applicable method for negotiating personal and professional disputes without getting angry-or getting taken." (Publisher's note)

Includes bibliographical references

160   Philosophical logic

Copi, Irving M.

★ **Introduction** to logic; [by] Irving M. Copi, Carl Cohen. 13th ed; Pearson/Prentice-Hall 2008 670p il $104 **160**
1. Logic
ISBN 978-0-13-614139-6; 0-13-614139-0

LC 2007-41752

First published 1953. Periodically revised

This introduction to logic covers language, fallacies, definitions, categories, arguments, deduction, probability and other areas of logical inquiry such as thought and reasoning

Includes bibliographical references

169   Analogy

Hofstadter, Douglas

Surfaces and essences; Analogy As the Fuel and Fire of Thinking. Douglas Hofstadter, Emmanuel Sander. Basic Books 2013 608 p. (hardcover) $35   **169**
    1. Analogy 2. Thought and thinking
    ISBN 0465018475; 9780465018475

            LC 2013932688

This book, by Douglas Hofstadter and Emmanuel Sander, "put[s] forth a highly novel perspective on cognition. We are constantly faced with a swirling and intermingling multitude of ill-defined situations. Our brain's job is to try to make sense of this unpredictable, swarming chaos of stimuli. How does it do so? The ceaseless hail of input triggers analogies galore, helping us to pinpoint the essence of what is going on." (Publisher's note)

170   Ethics (Moral philosophy)

Aristotle

★ **Nicomachean** ethics; translation (with historical introduction) by Christopher Rowe; philosophical introduction and commentary by Sarah Broadie. Oxford University Press 2002 468p pa $29.95   **170**
    1. Ethics
    ISBN 978-0-19-875271-4; 0-19-875271-7

            LC 2002-283430

According to Aristotle's ethical treatises, "happiness is the goal of life. Pleasure, fame, and wealth, however, will not bring one the highest happiness, which is achieved only through the contemplation of philosophic truth, because it exercises man's peculiar virtue, the rational principle." Reader's Ency. 3d edition
    Includes bibliographical references

Brooks, David Benjamin, 1961-

The **Road** to Character; The Humble Journey to an Excellent Life. David Brooks. Random House Inc 2015 320 p. $28   **170**
    1. Character 2. Personality
    ISBN 081299325X; 9780812993257

            LC 2015001791

In this book author David Brooks "focuses on the deeper values that should inform our lives. Responding to what he calls the culture of the Big Me, which emphasizes external success, Brooks challenges us, and himself, to rebalance the scales between our 'résumé virtues'--achieving wealth, fame, and status--and our 'eulogy virtues,' those that exist at the core of our being: kindness, bravery, honesty, or faithfulness, focusing on what kind of relationships we have formed." (Publisher's note)

"Although Brooks goes after the selfie generation, he does so in a fairly nuanced way, noting that it was really the World War II Greatest Generation who started the ball rolling. He is careful to emphasize that no one—even those he profiles—is anywhere near flawless. The author's sincere sermon—at times analytical, at times hortatory—remains a hopeful one." Kirkus

Coles, Robert

★ **Lives** of moral leadership. Random House 2000 247p hardcover o.p. pa $13.95   **170**
    1. Ethics 2. Leadership 3. Conduct of life
    ISBN 0-375-75835-6 pa

            LC 00-27858

Drawing on interviews he conducted over the past four decades with public and private figures, Coles reflects on the meaning of moral leadership in the United States

Comte-Sponville, Andre

A **small** treatise on the great virtues; the uses of philosophy in everyday life. translated by Catherine Temerson. Metropolitan Bks. 2001 352p $27.50; pa $16   **170**
    1. Ethics
    ISBN 0-8050-4555-4; 0-8050-4556-2 pa

            LC 2001-30299

Original French edition, 1995

"His subject demands a sober seriousness, but Comte-Sponville still manages to avoid taking himself too seriously: humility makes it into his litany of virtues, as does humor. A laudable renewal of the ancient quest for ethical wisdom." Booklist
    Includes bibliographical references

Edelman, Marian Wright

The **measure** of our success; a letter to my children and yours. HarperPerennial 1993 97p pa $10   **170**
    1. Ethics 2. Child rearing 3. Human behavior 4. United States -- Moral conditions
    ISBN 0-06-097546-6; 978-0-06-097546-3

            LC 92-54846

First published 1992 by Beacon Press

The author presents her "beliefs on child rearing and moral values. . . She includes a personal letter to her three sons, who were born into a family with a shared African American and Jewish heritage, and offers 25 lessons, or 'road maps', for life." Libr J

★ **Ethics**; edited by John K. Roth. Rev. ed.; Salem Press 2005 3v set $331   **170**
    1. Reference books 2. Ethics -- Encyclopedias
    ISBN 1-58765-170-X

            LC 2004-21797

First published 1994

For a fuller review, see: Booklist, June 1 & 15, 2005

The aim of this set is "to provide accessible entry points for those grappling with ethical issues and concerns. The 1000-plus articles cover people, events, organizations, trends, and issues. . . . This well-organized, highly useful work will be popular with researchers and general readers." SLJ
    Includes bibliographical references

Gottlieb, Daniel

Learning from the heart; lessons on living, loving, and listening. Sterling Pub. 2008 170p $17.95   **170**
    1. Conduct of life
    ISBN 978-1-4027-4999-5; 1-4027-4999-6

            LC 2007-35100

"Having rebuilt his life after an accident that left him a quadriplegic in his thirties, . . . [the author] here shares his observations on what makes us human. . . . An uplifting book abounding with encouragement for daily living; recommended for public libraries." Libr J

Graham, Lauren, 1967-

In conclusion, don't worry about it; Lauren Graham. Ballantine Books 2018 64 p. (hardcover: alk. paper) $15   **170**
    1. Success 2. Conduct of life 3. Self-actualization (Psychology) 4. Success -- Psychological aspects
    ISBN 9781524799595

LC 2017061314

In this book, author Lauren Graham offers "advice for graduates and reflections on staying true to yourself. . . . In this expansion of the 2017 commencement speech she gave at her hometown Langley High, . . . Graham . . . reflects on growing up, pursuing your dreams, and living in the here and now. . . . [She] reminds us to be curious and compassionate, no matter where life takes us or what we've yet to achieve." (Publisher's note)

Greene, Joshua

Moral tribes; emotion, reason, and the gap between us and them. by Joshua D. Greene. Penguin Press 2013 432 p. $29.95 **170**
1. Ethics 2. Emotions 3. Social psychology 4. Civilization
ISBN 1594202605; 9781594202605

LC 2013007775

In this book, "[Joshua] Greene, a philosopher and scientist, draws on research in psychology and neuroscience to explore the roots of morality, particularly the tragedy of commonsense morality, when people of different races, religions, ethnic groups, and nationalities share the same sense of morality but apply it from different perspectives in whose differences lie the roots of conflict. Us-versus-them conflicts date back to tribal life." (Booklist)
Includes bibliographical references (pages 388-403) and index

Haidt, Jonathan

The **happiness** hypothesis; finding modern truth in ancient wisdom. Basic Books 2005 297p il $26; pa $15.95 **170**
1. Happiness
ISBN 978-0-465-02801-6; 0-465-02801-2; 978-0-465-02802-3 pa; 0-465-02802-0 pa

LC 2005-21163

"Using the wisdom culled from the world's greatest civilizations as a foundation, social psychologist Haidt comes to terms with 10 Great Ideas, viewing them through a contemporary filter to learn which of their lessons may still apply to modern lives. . . . Fascinating stuff, accessibly expressed." Booklist
Includes bibliographical references

Kubler-Ross, Elisabeth

★ **Life** lessons; two experts on death and dying teach us about the mysteries of life and living. [by] Elisabeth Kübler-Ross and David Kessler. Scribner 2000 224p $24; pa $13 **170**
1. Death 2. Conduct of life
ISBN 0-684-87074-6; 0-684-87075-4 pa

LC 00-57387

"As in each of their previous individual works, the authors provide useful and accessible information." Libr J

Lamott, Anne

Almost everything; notes on hope. Anne Lamott. Riverhead Books 2018 208 p. (hardcover) $20 **170**
1. Hope 2. Spirituality 3. Spiritual life 4. Hope -- Religious aspects 5. Life -- Religious aspects
ISBN 9780525537441

LC 2018013899

In this book, author Anne Lamott "calls for each of us to rediscover the nuggets of hope and wisdom that are buried within us that can make life sweeter than we ever imagined. Divided into short chapters that explore life's essential truths, . . . [the book] pinpoints these moments of insight as it shines an encouraging light forward." (Publisher's note)

McCullough, David, Jr.

You Are Not Special; And Other Encouragements. David G. McCullough. HarperCollins 2014 352 p. illustrations $21.99 **170**
1. Commencements 2. High school students
ISBN 006225734X; 9780062257345

"In 'You Are (Not) Special,' [author David] McCullough elaborates on his now-famous speech exploring how, for what purpose, and for whose sake, we're raising our kids. With wry, affectionate humor, McCullough takes on hovering parents, ineffectual schools, professional college prep, electronic distractions, club sports, and generally the manifestations, and the applications and consequences of privilege." (Publisher's note)
"The author tackles big issues, such as gender and race, with searching sincerity, open-heartedness, and a deft, light touch." Kirkus

Modern ethics in 77 arguments; a Stone reader. edited by Peter Catapano and Simon Critchley. Liveright Publishing Corp. 2017 xi, 435 p.p (hardcover) $28.95 **170**
1. Ethics 2. Modern philosophy 3. Newspapers -- Sections, columns, etc. 4. Ethics, Modern -- 21st century 5. Newspapers -- Sections, columns, etc. -- Ethics
ISBN 9781631492983; 9781631492990

LC 2017018086

This book, edited by Peter Catapano and Simon Critchley, presents a collection of ethics essays drawn from "The Stone" column from 'The New York Times.' It "explores long-standing ethical and moral issues in light of our most urgent dilemmas. Divided into twelve sections, the book opens with a series of broad arguments on existence, human nature and morality." (Publisher's note)
"An accessible volume of thoughtful, concise contributions." Kirkus

Reader's Digest Association

Everyday greatness; inspiration for a meaningful life. insights and commentary by Steven R. Covey; compiled by David K. Hatch. Rutledge Hill Press 2006 445p $24.99 **170**
1. Conduct of life
ISBN 978-1-4016-0241-3; 1-4016-0241-X

LC 2006-19786

"The stories, which the authors have gleaned from Reader's Digest, illustrate 21 principles such as integrity, gratitude, respect, and perseverance. Covey provides commentary, reflections, and further insights on how readers can apply each principle to their own lives in today's world. Truly inspiring." Libr J
Includes bibliographical references

This I believe; the personal philosophies of remarkable men and women. edited by Jay Allison and Dan Gediman, with John Gregory and Viki Merrick; photographs by Nubar Alexanian. H. Holt 2006 xxi, 281p il $23 **170**
1. Conduct of life 2. Belief and doubt
ISBN 0-8050-8087-2; 978-0-8050-8087-2

LC 2006-43522

This collection of essays from a popular radio series "draws transcripts from both the original series and its newer version, including some remarkable statements from the likes of dancer/choreographer Martha Graham, autistic academic Temple Grandin, writer and physicist Alan Lightman, novelist and social critic Thomas Mann, economic historian Arnold Toynbee, and feminist writer Rebecca West. Astonishing to hear and astonishing to read and reread, this work is a wonderful addition to any library." Libr J

This I believe II; more personal philosophies of remarkable men and women. edited by Jay Allison and Dan Gediman; with John Gregory and Viki Merrick; additional editing by Emily Botein . . . [et al.] Henry Holt 2008 268p $23 **170**

1. Conduct of life 2. Belief and doubt
ISBN 978-0-8050-8768-0; 0-8050-8768-0

LC 2008-10110

"Many [of these essays] will leave you breathless. And those that don't astonish may simply humble you." Christ Sci Monit

Tutu, Desmond, 1931-

Made for goodness; and why this makes all the difference. [by] Desmond M. Tutu and Mpho A. Tutu; edited by Douglas C. Abrams. HarperOne 2010 206p $25.99 **170**

1. Good and evil 2. Religious life 3. Conduct of life 4. Christian life
ISBN 978-0-06-170659-2

LC 2010-3774

In this book, the South African archbishop and his daughter, an Anglican priest, present their spiritual vision of hope for humanity.

"The book is founded on the broad notion that we are created with the freedom to choose good or evil but also incline fundamentally to the good. . . . A crucially important book from the Nobel Peace Prize winner; a witness to our tumultuous times." Libr J

Wolfe, Alan

Moral freedom; the impossible idea that defines the way we live now. Norton 2001 256p hardcover o.p. pa $14.95 **170**

1. Ethics 2. Values 3. Public opinion 4. United States -- Moral conditions
ISBN 0-393-04843-8; 0-393-32302-1 pa

LC 00-51969

"Wolfe here discusses the results of a national public opinion poll he helped design on American beliefs about values, which he supplemented with detailed interviews of people from eight different U.S. communities. These ranged widely, from the Castro district of San Francisco to San Antonio." Libr J

Includes bibliographical references

170.44   Normative ethics

Egan, Kerry

On living; Kerry Egan. Riverhead Books 2016 224 p. (hardback) $24 **170.44**

1. Life 2. Death 3. Spiritual life 4. Terminally ill 5. Conduct of life 6. Church work with the terminally ill
ISBN 9781594634819

LC 2016026365

This book, by Kerry Egan, is "a book about living. . . . An emergency procedure during the birth of her first child left her physically whole but emotionally and spiritually adrift. Her work as a hospice chaplain healed her. . . . Each of her patients taught her something—how to find courage in the face of fear or the strength to make amends; how to be profoundly compassionate and fiercely empathetic; how to see the world in grays instead of black and white." (Publisher's note)

"As the title suggests, this is not just a book about dying. It's one that will inspire readers to make the most of every day." Pub Wkly

Viljoen, Edward

Ordinary goodness; The Surprisingly Effortless Path to Creating a Life of Meaning and Beauty. Edward Viljoen.

TarcherPerigee 2017 240 p. illustrations (pbk.) $16; (ebook) $48 **170.44**

1. Good and evil 2. Spiritual life 3. Conduct of life
ISBN 9780399183911; 9780399183928

LC 2016029449

"People often struggle to find a life filled with passion, happiness—and just plain goodness. . . . [Author] Edward Viljoen argues that the struggle need not be an arduous or painful one—that through everyday acts of kindness, faith, and compassion we can create peaceful and contented lives. Using personal stories, practical tips, and exercises, this book shows us that regardless of our circumstances, we can create meaning and beauty in our lives and in the world." (Publisher's note)

"The student following this path will be neither social activist nor cloistered religious, but an everyday person making daily conscious small choices to live from goodness." Pub Wkly

Includes bibliographical references.

171   Ethical systems

Rand, Ayn

★ The **virtue** of selfishness; a new concept of egoism. with additional articles by Nathaniel Branden. Centennial ed; Signet/New American Library 2005 173p pa $7.99 **171**

1. Egoism 2. Objectivism (Philosophy)
ISBN 0-451-16393-1

First published 1964

The author "sets forth the moral principles of Objectivism, the philosophy that holds man's life—the life proper to a rational being—as the standard of moral values and regards altruism as incompatible with man's nature, with the creative requirements of his survival, and with a free society." Publisher's note

172   Applied ethics

Sandel, Michael J., 1953-

Justice; what's the right thing to do? Farrar, Straus & Giroux 2009 308p $25; pa $15 **172**

1. Ethics 2. Values 3. Justice
ISBN 0-374-18065-2; 0-374-53250-8 pa; 978-0-374-18065-2; 978-0-374-53250-5 pa

LC 2009-25438

This book is based on a course the author teaches at Harvard University. It is a companion to a series on public television. Sandel examines various philosophical approaches to justice and seeks to show how they relate to contemporary political debates on such issues as same-sex marriage, reparations for slavery, surrogate motherhood and immigration reform. Index.

"The author has a talent for making the difficult—Kant's 'categorical imperative' or Rawls's 'difference principle'—readily comprehensible, and his relentless, though never oppressive, reason shines throughout the narrative. Sparkling commentary from the professor we all wish we had." Kirkus

Includes bibliographical references

174   Occupational ethics

Callahan, David

The **cheating** culture; why more Americans are doing wrong to get ahead. Harcourt 2004 353p $26; pa $14 **174**

1. Social ethics 2. Business ethics
ISBN 0-15-101018-8; 0-15-603005-5 pa

LC 2003-15529

"If all business school students could be required to read one book, this should be it." Choice
Includes bibliographical references

Conway, Erik M.

Merchants of doubt; how a handful of scientists obscured the truth on issues from tobacco smoke to global warming. [by] Naomi Oreskes and Erik M. Conway. Bloomsbury Press 2010 355p $27 **174**
1. Science -- Ethical aspects
ISBN 978-1-59691-610-4; 1-59691-610-9

LC 2009-43183

"A well-documented, pulls-no-punches account of how science works and how political motives can hijack the process by which scientific information is disseminated to the public." Kirkus
Includes bibliographical references

Covey, Stephen M. R.

★ **Smart** trust; creating prosperity, energy and joy in a low-trust world. Stephen M.R. Covey and Greg Link; with Rebecca R. Merrill. Free Press 2012 xxiii, 296 p.p $27 **174**
1. Trust 2. Ethics 3. Business ethics 4. Organizational behavior 5. Leadership -- Moral and ethical aspects
ISBN 1451651457; 9781451651454; 9781451651478

LC 2011039458

It was the authors' intent to demonstrate that "the biggest impediment to global economic health is not the economics of the financial crisis but the loss of trust the crisis caused. . . . The authors make the case for the importance of trust and then teach readers how to trust in an untrustworthy world: by coupling the universal innate propensity to trust with a high level of critical analysis." (Library Journal)
Includes bibliographical references and index.

Gentile, Mary C.

Giving voice to values; how to speak your mind when you know what's right. Yale University Press 2010 xliv, 273p $26 **174**
1. Values 2. Leadership 3. Business ethics
ISBN 978-0-300-16118-2

LC 2010011905

Gentile "offers a powerful action-oriented manifesto for living with integrity, fighting for one's convictions, and building a more ethical workplace." Publ Wkly
Includes bibliographical references

Greenhouse, Linda

★ **Just** a journalist; on the press, life, and the spaces between. Linda Greenhouse. Harvard University Press 2017 xiii, 169 p.p $22.95 **174**
1. Journalistic ethics 2. Reporters and reporting 3. Journalism -- United States 4. Journalistic ethics -- United States -- 21st century 5. Reporters and reporting -- United States -- 21st century
ISBN 9780674980334

LC 2017013621

In this book in The William E. Massey Sr. Lectures in American Studies series, author Linda Greenhouse "trains an autobiographical lens on a moment of remarkable transition in American journalism. . . . Clearly, something has changed as the old rules of 'balance' and 'two sides to every story' have lost their grip. Is the change for the better? Will it last?.

. . . [The author] tackles these questions from the perspective of her own experience." (Publisher's note)
Includes bibliographical references and index.

Mackey, John, 1954-

Conscious capitalism; liberating the heroic spirit of business. John Mackey & Raj Sisodia. Harvard Business Review Press 2013 344 p. (hardcover) $27 **174**
1. Capitalism -- Ethical aspects 2. Social responsibility of business 3. Social values 4. Business ethics 5. Capitalism -- Moral and ethical aspects 6. Corporations -- Moral and ethical aspects
ISBN 1422144208; 9781422144206

LC 2012025305

"In this book, Whole Foods Market cofounder John Mackey and professor and Conscious Capitalism, Inc. cofounder Raj Sisodia argue for the inherent good of both business and capitalism. Featuring some of today's best-known companies, they illustrate how these two forces can--and do--work most powerfully to create value for all stakeholders: including customers, employees, suppliers, investors, society, and the environment." (Publisher's note)
Includes bibliographical references

174.2 Medical and health professions

Dreger, Alice

Galileo's middle finger; heretics, activists, and the search for justice in science. Alice Dreger. Penguin Press 2015 352 p. (hardback) $27.95 **174.2**
1. Heresy 2. Science and civilization 3. Science -- Ethical aspects 4. Heresy in science 5. Science -- Political aspects 6. Scientists -- Professional ethics 7. Science -- Moral and ethical aspects
ISBN 1594206082; 9781594206085

LC 2014036659

This book "begins with [author Alice] Dreger's own research into the treatment of people born intersex (once called hermaphrodites). Realization of the shocking surgical and ethical abuses conducted in the name of 'normalizing' intersex childre's gender identities moved Dreger to become an internationally recognized patient rights activist." (Publisher's note)
"A crusader in the mold of muckrackers from a century ago, Dreger doesn't try to hide her politics or her agenda. Instead she advocates for change intelligently and passionately. Highly recommended for those interested in academic freedom, controversial issues in academia, and intersex and gender issues." LJ
Includes bibliographical references and index

Elliott, Carl

White coat, black hat; adventures on the dark side of medicine. Beacon Press 2010 224p $24.95 **174.2**
1. Drug industry 2. Medical ethics 3. Medicine -- United States 4. Medical ethics -- United States 5. Drugs -- Effectiveness -- Evaluation 6. Conflict of interests -- United States 7. Pharmaceutical industry -- United States
ISBN 978-0-8070-6142-8

LC 201006119

The author argues that "over the past twenty-five years, the practice of medicine has been subverted by the business of medicine, sacrificing old-style doctoring to fit the values of consumer capitalism. In this . . . narrative, physician and moral philosopher Carl Elliott traces the evolutionary path of this new direction in health care." (Publisher's note)
Index.

Elliott "examines the part played by the pharmaceutical industry in constructing 'a medical system in which deception is often not just tolerated but rewarded.' While some abuses—including the use of subjects to test drugs without informed consent—are not new, these practices continue despite the existence of regulatory institutional-review boards set up by Congress, because these too have now become profit centers. Elliott writes that pharmaceutical companies hire PR specialists who not only supply educational materials to promote products, they also train medical professionals to be 'opinion leaders' and even write papers in their name." Kirkus

Includes bibliographical references

Tucker, Todd

★ The **great** starvation experiment; the heroic men who starved so that millions could live. Free Press 2006 270p il $26   **174.2**

1. Starvation 2. Human experimentation in medicine 3. Centenarians 4. Physiologists 5. College teachers

ISBN 0-7432-7030-4; 978-0-7432-7030-4

LC 2006-278255

"As WWII neared an end, 36 idealistic conscientious objectors, members of the Civilian Public Service, volunteered to be systematically starved. The project, headed by Dr. Ancel Keys, was designed to develop an understanding of the physiology and psychology of starvation and to provide strategies to manage the mass starvation that might follow the war's end in Europe. Tucker . . . provides a fascinating and moving history of the experiment, centering on the lives and experiences of the volunteers and the formidable obstacles they overcame." Publ Wkly

Includes bibliographical references and index

Washington, Harriet A.

★ **Medical** apartheid; the dark history of medical experimentation on Black Americans from colonial times to the present. Doubleday 2006 501p il hardcover o.p. pa $17   **174.2**

1. Human experimentation in medicine 2. African Americans -- Health and hygiene

ISBN 0-385-50993-6; 978-0-385-50993-0; 0-7679-1547-X pa; 978-0-7679-1547-2 pa

LC 2005-51873

The author offers a "history of medical experimentation on and mistreatment of black Americans in this stunning work, which is both broad in scope and well documented." Booklist

Includes bibliographical references

176   Ethics of sex and reproduction

Freitas, Donna

The **end** of sex; how hookup culture is leaving a generation unhappy, sexually unfulfilled, and confused about intimacy. Donna Freitas. Basic Books 2013 240 p. (pbk.: alk. paper) $25.99   **176**

1. Sex -- Psychological aspects 2. College students -- Sexual behavior 3. Sexual ethics 4. Intimacy (Psychology) 5. Dating (Social customs) 6. Youth -- Sexual behavior

ISBN 0465002153; 9780465002153

LC 2012042226

This book is an "attack on the casual-sex culture at American universities, which is marked not by free love, but by pressure to have as much sex with as little emotional connection as possible (and often while drunk). Through interviews and demographic surveys, [Donna] Freitas

constructs an anthropological survey on what hooking up and dating (or its absence) look like on campuses today. She lays out convincing arguments against this harmful kind of sexual culture." (Publishers Weekly)

Includes bibliographical references

Stock, Gregory

Redesigning humans; our inevitable genetic future. Houghton Mifflin 2002 277p $24; pa $14   **176**

1. Genetics 2. Genetic engineering 3. Reproductive technology

ISBN 0-618-06026-X; 0-618-34083-1 pa

LC 2001-51890

The author gives an "overview of the new biotechnology that will allow scientists to delay aging and to insert genes that enhance physical and cognitive performance, combat disease or improve looks into embryos. Stock thoughtfully weighs the ethical dilemmas such advances present, arguing that the real threat is not frivolous abuse of technology but the fact that we don't know the long-term effects of these genetic changes." Publ Wkly

Includes bibliographical references

Wilmut, Ian

★ **After** Dolly; the uses and misuses of human cloning. Norton 2006 335p il $24.95; pa $15.95   **176**

1. Cloning 2. Reproductive technology

ISBN 0-393-06066-7; 978-0-393-06066-9; 0-393-33026-5 pa; 978-0-393-33026-7 pa

LC 2006-2030

In this "account of the program that eventuated in Dolly, . . . [Wilmut] covers a variety of the social, medical, and scientific implications of cloning. . . . Wilmut, aided by science writer Highfield, well explains potentially confusing issues, in the end making a strong enough case to convince us that Dolly neither lived nor died in vain." Booklist

Includes bibliographical references

177   Ethics of social relations

Ariely, Dan

The **honest** truth about dishonesty; how we lie to everyone---especially ourselves. Dan Ariely. 1st ed. Harper 2012 xiii, 285 p.p (hardback) $26.99   **177**

1. Honesty 2. Deception 3. Truthfulness and falsehood 4. HISTORY -- Social History 5. BUSINESS & ECONOMICS -- General

ISBN 0062183591; 9780062183590; 9780062183613

LC 2012015990

This book "explains the psychological and economic factors that drive people to lie and cheat." Author Dan Ariely "explores the rational cost-benefit forces that propel dishonesty, such as the amount of money to be gained, the probability of being caught, and conflicts of interest. To illustrate his argument, Ariely cites examples ranging from the Enron scandal to Ponzi schemes to owning fake designer bags." (Library Journal)

Includes bibliographical references (pages 267-273) and index.

Armstrong, Karen, 1944-

Twelve steps to a compassionate life. Alfred A. Knopf 2010 222p $22.95; ebook $11.99   **177**

1. Compassion 2. Twelve-step programs 3. Ethics 4. Sympathy 5. Conduct of life

ISBN 978-0-307-59559-1; 978-0-307-59563-8 ebook

LC 2010-36870

The author of A History of God, Islam, and Buddha sets out a program that is intended to lead readers "toward a more compassionate life. The twelve steps Armstrong suggests begin with 'Imagine a World of Compassion' and close with 'Love Your Enemies.' In between, she takes up self-love, mindfulness, suffering, sympathetic joy, the limits of our knowledge of others, and 'concern for everybody.' She suggests concrete ways of putting compassion into action in our everyday lives." (Publisher's note)

"Armstrong weaves together the teachings of diverse religions in a graceful, approachable manner. A commendable effort well-executed." Kirkus

Includes bibliographical references

Campbell, Jeremy

The **liar's** tale; a history of falsehood. Norton 2001 363p $26.95; pa $15.95　　　　　　　　　　　　**177**
　　1. Truthfulness and falsehood
　　ISBN 0-393-02559-4; 0-393-32361-7 pa
　　　　　　　　　　　　　　　　　　LC 2001-30286
"This challenging romp through the underbelly of intellectual history . . . is fascinating and troublesome." NY Times Book Rev

Includes bibliographical references and index

★ **Count** on me; tales of sisterhoods and fierce friendships. by Las Comadres para las Americas. Atria Books 2012 272 p. $16.00　　　　　　　　　　　　　　　　**177**
　　1. Essays 2. Hispanic American women 3. Female friendship -- Fiction 4. Social networks -- America 5. Female friendship -- America 6. Las Comadres para las Americas 7. Social networks -- United States 8. Female friendship -- United States 9. Hispanic American women -- Biography 10. Hispanic American women -- Social conditions 11. Hispanic American women -- Social life and customs
　　ISBN 1451642016; 9781451642018
　　　　　　　　　　　　　　　　　　LC 2012015552
This book is "[a]n anthology celebrating sisterhood and the special bonds that connect Latinas from diverse backgrounds. . . . The stories in this collection [nearly] all deal with the topic of female friendship . . . . Several of the pieces deal with the relationship between a Latina author and a cherished teacher who became a lifelong 'comadre,' a Spanish word to describe complex relationships between women." (Kirkus)

Kortes-Miller, Kathy

Talking about death won't kill you; the essential guide to end-of-life conversations. Kathy Kortes-Miller. ECW Press 2018 216 p.　　　　　　　　　　　　　　**177**
　　1. Palliative treatment 2. Terminally ill -- Psychology 3. Death -- Psychological aspects
　　ISBN 1770414061; 9781770414068
This handbook, by Kathy Kortes-Miller, will "help Canadians navigate personal and medical decisions for the best quality of life for the end of our lives. Noted palliative-care educator and researcher . . . Miller shows readers how to identify and reframe limiting beliefs about dying with humor and compassion." (Publisher's note)

Sakyong Mipham, Rinpoche, 1962-

★ The **lost** art of good conversation; a mindful way to connect with others and enrich everyday life. Sakyong Mipham. Harmony Books 2017 ix, 226 p.p (hc) $19.99　　　**177**
　　1. Etiquette 2. Conversation 3. Conversation -- Religious aspects -- Buddhism 4. Oral communication -- Religious aspects -- Buddhism
　　ISBN 9780451499431

　　　　　　　　　　　　　　　　　　LC 2017014009
This book, by Sakyong Mipham, "offers simple and practical advice to help us increase our attentions spans, become better listeners, and strive to appreciate the people around us. In a world of iPhones and connectivity to social media and email, we are all in constant connection with one another. Then why are so many people feeling burned out, distant from colleagues, and abandoned by family and friends?" (Publisher's note)

Young, Kevin

Bunk; the true story of hoaxes, hucksters, humbug, plagiarists, forgeries, and phonies. Kevin Young. Graywolf Press 2017 560 p. (hardback) $30　　　　　　　　　**177**
　　1. Impostors and imposture
　　ISBN 9781555977917
　　　　　　　　　　　　　　　　　　LC 2017930117
Longlisted for the National Book Award for Nonfiction, 2017.

Longlisted for the Andrew Carnegie Medal for Excellence in Non-Fiction, 2018.

This book, by Kevin Young, "traces the history of the hoax as a peculiarly American phenomenon, examining what motivates hucksters and makes the rest of us so gullible. Disturbingly, Young finds that fakery is woven from stereotype and suspicion, race being the most insidious American hoax of all. He chronicles how Barnum came to fame by displaying figures like Joice Heth, a black woman whom he pretended was the 161-year-old nursemaid to George Washington." (Publisher's note)

"Young presents a rogue's gallery, including Grey Owl, Bernie Madoff, and Lance Armstrong, paying particular attention to the especially heinous frauds of journalists, including Stephen Glass and Jayson Blair. Young closes with an examination of today's constant bombardment of intertwined facts and factoids and the need for each of us to try to suss out the truth. Compelling and eye-opening." Booklist.

177.1　Courtesy, hospitality, politeness

Bernard, Jeremy

Treating people well; the extraordinary power of civility at work and in life. Lea Berman and Jeremy Bernard; foreword by Laura Bush. Scribner 2018 xxiv, 226 p.p color illustrations (hardcover) $27　　　　　　　　　　　　**177.1**
　　1. Courtesy 2. Etiquette 3. Conduct of life 4. Respect for persons
　　ISBN 9781501158001; 9781501157981; 1501157981
　　　　　　　　　　　　　　　　　　LC 2017061756
In this book, authors Lea Berman and Jeremy Bernard present a "practical guide to personal and professional success in modern life. Their daily experiences at 1600 Pennsylvania Avenue taught them valuable lessons about how to work productively with people from different walks of life and points of view. . . . [They] share what they've learned through first person examples of their own glamorous . . . moments with celebrities, foreign leaders and . . . American politician[s]." (Publisher's note)

"Berman and Bernard winningly call on their experiences as White House social secretaries under, respectively, George W. Bush and Barack Obama to make a case that manners and civility can be the basis for success in work and life." Pub Wkly

Includes bibliographical references (pages 223-226).

177.7   Love

Cousineau, Tara

The **kindness** cure; how the science of compassion can heal your heart & your world. Tara Cousineau, PhD. New Harbinger Publications, Inc. 2018 ix, 225 p.p illustrations (pbk.: alk. paper) $16.95   **177.7**

1. Caring 2. Kindness 3. Compassion
ISBN 9781626259713; 9781626259706; 1626259690; 9781626259690

LC 2017058866

This book, by Tara Cousineau, "draws on the latest social and scientific research to reveal how the seemingly 'soft skills' of kindness, cooperation, and generosity are fundamental to our survival as a species. In fact, it's our prosocial abilities that put us at the head of the line. Blended with moving case studies and clinical anecdotes, Cousineau offers practical ways to rekindle kindness from the inside out." (Publisher's note)

Includes bibliographical references

Velásquez, Lizzie

Dare to Be Kind; How Extraordinary Compassion Can Transform Our World. Lizzie Velasquez; with Catherine Avril Morris. Hachette Books 2017 192 p. $22   **177.7**

1. Kindness 2. Bullying
ISBN 0316272434; 9780316272438

LC 2017002974

This book, by Lizzie Velasquez, "reveals the hidden forces that give rise to self-doubt, shame, and cruelty, and empowers us to redirect them to unlock empathy and kindness for ourselves and others. She pulls from examples in her own life-such as battles with anxiety and coping with disappointment-to share uplifting insight on how we can overcome obstacles in our path and move forward with greater positivity and the right mental attitude." (Publisher's note)

"This is a wonderful and fast read, full of vitality that captures the luminous spirit of kindness that Velasquez so beautifully embodies." Booklist.

179   Other ethical norms

Baur, Gene

Farm Sanctuary; changing hearts and minds about animals and food. Simon & Schuster 2008 286p il $25   **179**

1. Animal welfare 2. Livestock industry
ISBN 978-0-7432-9158-3; 0-7432-9158-1

LC 2008-297873

A founder of an organization dedicated to promoting the compassionate treatment of animals and combating factory farming addresses the ethics of breeding animals for food, exposing inhumane practices utilized by typical food-production companies.

"Baur's report is not for the faint of heart, but it is critical reading for anyone willing to ask about the origin of their food, and readers are rewarded with tales of animals who have been saved, and the surprising things that have been learned about farm animals from close observation of their habits. A life-altering read." Booklist

Includes bibliographical references

Beers, Diane L.

★ **For** the prevention of cruelty; the history and legacy of animal rights activism in the United States. Swallow Press/Ohio University Press 2006 312p il $34.95; $19.95   **179**

1. Animal rights movement

ISBN 0-8040-1086-2; 978-0-8040-1086-3; 0-8040-1087-0 pa; 978-0-8040-1087-0 pa

LC 2006-4294

This "study of the animal advocacy movement in the U.S. since the ASPCA's founding in 1866 fills a glaring historical gap with exceptional style, accuracy and insight." Publ Wkly

Includes bibliographical references

Coetzee, J. M.

The **lives** of animals; {by} J.M. Coetzee; {reflections by} Marjorie Garber {et al.}; edited and introduced by Amy Gutmann. Princeton Univ. Press 1999 127p (University Center for Human Values series) $29.95; pa $13.95   **179**

1. Animal rights 2. Animal welfare
ISBN 0-691-00443-9; 0-691-07089-X pa

LC 98-39591

"This hybrid collection of fiction and essays is a provocative version of Socratic philosophy. It begins with a story about a Doris Lessing-like author who visits her conflicted son and his antagonistic wife while lecturing at the university where they teach. The mother's hobbyhorse, that Animals R Us, embarrasses the academic couple, and her suggestion that they are like Nazis because they eat meat infuriates them. Other distinguished academics carry on this dialogue in playful fiction and sober commentary, in which the most eloquent part may be the descriptions of communication with animals." New Yorker

Includes bibliographical references

Greek, C. Ray

Sacred cows and golden geese; the human cost of experiments on animals. {by} C. Ray Greek and Jean Swingle Greek; foreword by Jane Goodall. Continuum 2000 256p $24.95; pa $18.95   **179**

1. Animal experimentation
ISBN 0-8264-1226-2; 0-8264-1402-8 pa

LC 99-57157

This "covers the history of animal experimentation, legislation that promulgates it, the real cost to humans, and alternatives. It is a well-written, if disturbing, book." Libr J

Includes bibliographical references (p. {227}-251) and index

Hall, Stephen S.

Wisdom; from philosophy to neuroscience. Alfred A. Knopf 2010 333p $27.95   **179**

1. Decision making 2. Neuropsychology
ISBN 978-0-307-26910-2; 0-307-26910-2

LC 2009-27438

"Those searching for easy tips on achieving wisdom will not find them here, but diligent readers will be rewarded. A steady stream of insights into the psychology and neurological mechanisms of wise decision-makingand the researchers uncovering them." Kirkus

Magill, R. Jay

Sincerity; how a moral ideal born five hundred years ago inspired religious wars, modern art, hipster chic, and the curious notion that we all have something to say (no matter how dull) R. Jay Magill, Jr. W. W. Norton & Co. Inc. 2012 272 p. (hardcover) $25.95   **179**

1. Catholic Church 2. Christian heresies 3. Doctrinal theology 4. Sincerity
ISBN 0393080986; 9780393080988

LC 2012010360

Author R. Jay Magill "examines sincerity from a variety of perspectives--religious, philosophical, political, sociological, artistic--as Western culture has alternately feared sincerity, embraced it, or denied the very possibility of it. . . . Sincerity and irony, rather than polar opposites, are complementary correctives, with the latter exposing the hypocrisies within professions of the former. The author . . . traces the early equation of sincerity with heresy as a challenge to the dogmatic authority of the Catholic Church." (Kirkus Reviews)

Includes bibliographical references and index.

McCain, John S.

Why courage matters; the way to a braver life. [by] John McCain with Mark Salter. Random House 2004 209p il $16.95 **179**
1. Courage
ISBN 1-400-06030-3

LC 2003-58626

Senator McCain tells his favorite stories of courage. "In offering anecdotes of individuals whose actions embody the rarity of true courage, his well-drawn examples range from Navajo leaders to Colorado River explorers to Jewish freedom fighter Hannah Senesh and Burmese dissident and Nobel Peace Prize-recipient Aung San Suu Kyi. He reflects on the wellsprings of courage, defining it as conscious self-sacrifice 'for the sake of others or to uphold a virtue,' encompassing actions that may be spurred by honor, outrage, a sense of duty, one's conscience, or moral obligation." SLJ

Santi, Jenny

The **giving** way to happiness; stories and science behind the transformative power of giving. Jenny Santi; foreword by Deepak Chopra. Tarcher 2015 352 p. (hardback) $25.95 **179**
1. Happiness 2. Generosity 3. Self-realization 4. Self-actualization (Psychology)
ISBN 9780399175497

LC 2015027341

In this book, author Jenny Santi "overturns conventional thinking about what it takes to be happy by revealing how giving to others—whether in the form of money, expertise, time, or love—has helped people from all walks of life find purpose and joy. Drawing on the wisdom of great thinkers past and present, as well as cutting-edge scientific research, Santi makes an eloquent and passionate case that oftentimes the answers to the problems that haunt us." (Publisher's note)

"Both of these inspiring books will prompt readers to consider and act on making the world a better place." LJ

Includes bibliographical references and index

Shevelow, Kathryn

For the love of animals; the rise of the animal protection movement. Henry Holt and Co. 2008 352p il $27.50 **179**
1. Animal rights movement
ISBN 978-0-8050-8090-2; 0-8050-8090-2

LC 2007-47353

The author "documents the history of animal cruelty and the slow, controversial and much maligned rise of the animal protection movement in 17th and 18th-century England. . . . This is a fascinating, often disturbing and frequently funny book, a must read for anyone concerned with the treatment of animals and a call to action for the next generation of animal rights activists." Publ Wkly

Includes bibliographical references

Singer, Peter, 1946-

★ **Animal** liberation; the definitive classic of the animal movement. Peter Singer. Harper Perennial 2009 xiii, 311, 32

p.p illustrations (pbk.) $14.99 **179**
1. Animal rights 2. Vegetarianism 3. Animal welfare
ISBN 9781497645592; 0061711306; 9780061711305

LC 2011292483

This book, by Peter Singer, "exposes the chilling realities of today's 'factory farms' and product-testing procedures—destroying the spurious justifications behind them, and offering alternatives to what has become a profound environmental and social as well as moral issue. An important and persuasive appeal to conscience, fairness, decency, and justice, it is essential reading for the supporter and the skeptic alike." (Publisher's note)

Includes bibliographical references and index.

Tillich, Paul

★ The **courage** to be; with an introduction by Peter J. Gomes. 2nd ed; Yale Univ. Press 2000 197p (Yale Nota bene) pa $12.95 **179**
1. Anxiety 2. Courage 3. Ontology 4. Existentialism
ISBN 0-300-08471-4

LC 00-102364

First published 1952

The author offers advice on how to conquer the anxiety caused by the loss of meaning in one's life

Tutu, Desmond, 1931-

The **book** of forgiving; the fourfold path for healing ourselves and our world. Desmond Tutu and Mpho A. Tutu; edited by Douglas C. Abrams. HarperOne 2014 240 p. ill $25.99 **179**
1. Forgiveness 2. Reconciliation
ISBN 0062203568; 9780062203564; 9780062203571

LC 2013033890

In this book, Desmond Tutu and his daughter Mpho "lay out the simple but profound truths about the significance of forgiveness, how it works, why everyone needs to know how to grant it and receive it, and why granting forgiveness is the greatest gift we can give to ourselves when we have been wronged." (Publisher's note)

"The book is almost entirely practical in focus, geared toward helping people come to grips with issues of anger, grief and loss. It includes meditations, rituals and journal exercises after each chapter." Kirkus

Includes bibliographical references

Wise, Steven M.

★ **Drawing** the line; science and the case for animal rights. Perseus Bks. 2002 322p $26; pa $18 **179**
1. Animal rights
ISBN 0-7382-0340-8; 0-7382-0810-8 pa

Wise "sets out to determine whether animals ranging from dolphins to his family dog . . . have mental abilities meriting {legal} protection. . . . The key to granting any of them rights, Wise argues, is whether they possess 'practical autonomy'—desires and the ability to act to satisfy them." Christ Sci Monit

Includes bibliographical references

179.7 Respect and disrespect for human life

Durkheim, Emile

★ **Suicide,** a study in sociology; translated by John A. Spaulding and George Simpson; edited with an introduction by George Simpson. Free Press 1951 405p maps hardcover o.p. pa $18.95 **179.7**
1. Suicide

ISBN 0-684-83632-7 pa

Original French edition, 1897

Durkheim's "Suicide is a major sociological classic, one that is still read today, not so much for its data, which are limited and out-of-date, but for the brilliance of his analysis of suicide rates and other data that had been initially obtained for administrative rather than scientific purposes." Reader's Adviser

Includes bibliographical references

Humphry, Derek

★ **Final** exit; the practicalities of self-deliverance and assisted sucide for the dying. 3rd ed; Delta Trade Paperbacks 2002 xxviii, 220p pa $13.95   **179.7**

1. Suicide 2. Right to die

ISBN 0-385-33653-5

LC 2002-19403

First published 1991 by Hemlock Society

This offers information about how to commit suicide for the terminally ill and about the legality and ethics of assisted suicide and euthanasia

Includes bibliographical references

Kiernan, Stephen P.

★ **Last** rights; rescuing the end of life from the medical system. St. Martin's Press 2006 301p $25.95   **179.7**

1. Death 2. Terminal care

ISBN 978-0-312-34224-1; 0-312-34224-1

LC 2006-47449

"Anyone who has stood helplessly by as physicians insisted that a battery of tests and interventions could prolong the life of a loved one, only to see those expensive efforts fail, is certain to be moved by Kiernan's presentation." Booklist

Includes bibliographical references

Wanzer, Sidney H.

★ **To** die well; your right to comfort, calm, and choice in the last days of life. Da Capo 2007 209p $24; pa $15 **179.7**

1. Euthanasia 2. Right to die 3. Terminal care -- Ethical aspects

ISBN 0-7382-1083-8; 978-0-7382-1083-4; 0-7382-1163-X pa; 978-0-7382-1163-3 pa

The authors present "what individuals can do to achieve a peaceful death for themselves and their loved ones. Using a combination of patient stories and their own expert discussions, the authors describe the legal rights of terminally ill patients to end their medical care. They also address the controversial issue of hastening the death of terminally ill patients. . . . More useful than the many other recent books on death and dying, this influential volume should be on the shelves of every public and university library." Libr J

Warraich, Haider

Modern death; How Medicine Changed the End of Life. Haider Warraich. St. Martin's Press 2017 336 p. (ebook) $60; (hardback) $26.99   **179.7**

1. Right to die 2. Terminal care 3. Terminal care -- Decision making

ISBN 9781250104595; 9781250104588

LC 2016038746

This book, by Haider Warraich, "takes a broader look at how we die today, from the cellular level up to the very definition of death itself. The most basic aspects of dying—the whys, wheres, whens, and hows—are almost nothing like what they were mere decades ago. . . . [This] book will explore the rituals and language of dying that have developed in the last century, and how modern technology has not only

changed the hows, whens, and wheres of death, but the what of death." (Publisher's note)

"An important contribution to a serious discussion of profound life-and-death issues." Kirkus

Includes bibliographical references (pages 279-312) and index.

Watson, Katie

Scarlet A; the ethics, law & politics of ordinary abortion. Katie Watson. Oxford University Press 2018 296 p. (cloth: alk. paper) $29.95   **179.7**

1. Abortion -- Ethical aspects 2. Birth control -- Ethical aspects 3. Abortion -- Social aspects -- United States 4. Abortion -- Moral and ethical aspects -- United States

ISBN 9780190624859

LC 2017018856

This book, by Katie Watson, "explains the law of abortion, challenges the toxic politics that make it a public football and private secret, offers tools for more productive private exchanges, and leads the way to a more robust public discussion of abortion ethics. . . . [It] combines storytelling and statistics to bring the story of ordinary abortion out of the shadows, painting a rich, rarely seen picture of how patients and doctors currently think and act." (Publisher's note)

Includes bibliographical references and index

Wiesenthal, Simon

★ The **sunflower**; on the possibilities and limits of forgiveness. [by] Simon Wiesenthal; with a symposium edited by Harry James Cargas and Bonny V. Fetterman. rev and expanded ed, 2nd pa. ed; Schocken Books 1998 289p pa $14   **179.7**

1. Forgiveness 2. Holocaust, 1933-1945 -- Personal narratives

ISBN 0-8052-1060-1

LC 99-198049

Original French edition, 1969

"The responses to the author's question are as varied as their authors. The mystery of evil and atonement remain, and the reader is left challenged on these most basic issues of meaning in human life." Publ Wkly

Yount, Lisa

★ **Right** to die and euthanasia; rev ed; Facts on File 2007 312p il (Library in a book) $45   **179.7**

1. Euthanasia 2. Right to die

ISBN 978-0-8160-6275-1

LC 2006-33424

First published 2000 with title: Physician-assisted suicide and euthanasia

This reference source contains an overview of the subjects, a chronology of significant events (including the Terri Schiavo case), biographical information on important figures, a glossary of terms, and an annotated bibliography.

Includes glossary and bibliographical references

180   History, geographic treatment, biography

Gottlieb, Anthony

The **dream** of reason; a history of Western philosophy from the Greeks to the Renaissance. Norton 2000 468p $27.95; pa $17.95   **180**

1. Philosophy -- History

ISBN 0-393-04951-5; 0-393-32365-X pa

LC 00-49012

"This eloquent book offers a lively chronicle of the evolution of

Western philosophy." Publ Wkly
Includes bibliographical references

181   Eastern philosophy

Buber, Martin
★ **I** and thou; translated by Ronald Gregor Smith. Scribner 2000 126p $22; pa $11   **181**
1. God 2. Ontology 3. Jewish philosophy
ISBN 0-7432-0133-7; 0-7432-0133-7 pa
Original German edition, 1923; first published in English 1958
In this book, the author "conceived the individual as in permanent relationship with all forms of life, finding his fulfillment in the reciprocity of the relationship—the 'Thou' being God." Reader's Adviser

Confucius
★ The **Analects**; [by] Confucius; translated by Arthur Waley; with an introduction by Sarah Allan. Knopf 2000 xxxi, 257p $19   **181**
1. Chinese ethics 2. Chinese philosophy
ISBN 0-375-41204-2
LC 00-53460
This translation first published 1938 in the United Kingdom
"One of the Chinese 'Four Books.' A brief, unsystematic collection of fragmentary writings attributed to Confucius and his school. . . . It is one of the most influential works in the history of Chinese thought." Reader's Ency
Includes bibliographical references

Pacheco, Rebecca
Do your om thing; bending yoga tradition to fit your modern life. Rebecca Pacheco. HarperWave 2015 288 p. $26.99 **181**
1. Yoga 2. Health 3. Well-being 4. Spirituality 5. Spiritual life
ISBN 006227337X; 9780062273376
LC 2014044390
This book by Rebecca Pacheco "explores the traditional practice of yoga, from the eight limbs of the ancient path to the five koshas and the seven chakras of the yoga body. Pacheco translates these ancient texts for modern readers and puts them into the context of our everyday lives. Complete with a practical overview of the many different styles of yoga, simple poses, and sequences for daily balance." (Publisher's note)
"She taps into the lessons of ancient sages, discusses ethics as well as principles, and offers practical suggestions on how to apply these teachings in 'How You Can Do It' and 'Doing Your Om Thing' sections found at the end of each chapter. Her gift is her ability to weave traditional yoga wisdom into everyday life and to make the principles so accessible and nonthreatening that even beginning students can be enlightened without feeling overwhelmed." Booklist
Includes bibliographical references

183   Sophistic, Socratic, related Greek philosophies

Kreeft, Peter
★ **Philosophy** 101 by Socrates; an introduction to philosophy via Plato's apology: forty things philosophy is according to history's first and wisest philosopher. by Peter Kreeft. St. Augustines Press 2012 149 p. $12   **183**
1. Teaching 2. Philosophers 3. History -- Philosophy 4. Philosophy -- Introductions
ISBN 0898709253; 158731830X; 9781587318306

LC
2001098029 Author Peter "Kreeft uses the dialogues of Socrates in this book to help the reader grow in that love of wisdom. He says that no master of the art of philosophizing has ever been more simple, clear, and accessible to beginners as Socrates. He focuses on Plato's dialogues, the Apology of Socrates, as a model partner for the reader to dialogue with. Kreeft calls it 'the Magna Carta of philosophy,' a timeless classic that is 'a portable classroom.'" (Publisher's note)

Stone, I. F. (Isidor Feinstein), 1907-1989
The **trial** of Socrates. Anchor Bks. 1989 282p pa $14.95   **183**
1. Philosophers
ISBN 0-385-26032-6; 978-0-385-26032-9
First published 1988 by Little, Brown
The author attempts "to show that Athens was totally committed to free speech and did not normally place any check on it, and, therefore, that the trial of Socrates was a singular aberration which might be explicable, if finally not justifiable." Commentary
Includes bibliographical references

Waterfield, Robin
Why Socrates died; dispelling the myths. W. W. Norton & Co. 2009 253p il map $27.95   **183**
1. Trials 2. Hellenism 3. Philosophers 4. Philosophy, Ancient
ISBN 978-0-393-06527-5
LC 2009-4317
This "account of the trial and execution of the philosopher draws on Greek sources to separate truth from myth, . . . [arguing for] Socrates' character as a deeply moral thinker whose convictions strongly contrasted those of his former student, Alcibaides." (Publishers note)
The author "sets out to explain why Socrates died: he discusses his trial, but also offers an informed and well-written account of classical Athenian history." Times Higher Ed
Includes bibliographical references

184   Platonic philosophy

Hare, R. M.
Plato. Oxford Univ. Press 1982 82p (Past masters series) hardcover o.p. pa $9.95   **184**
1. Authors 2. Philosophers 3. Essayists
ISBN 0-19-287585-X pa
LC 83-159441
The author examines the chief Platonic concepts in their political and intellectual contexts
Includes bibliographical references

185   Aristotelian philosophy

Shields, Christopher John
Aristotle; Christopher Shields. Routledge, Taylor & Francis Group 2014 xviii, 505 pagesp (Routledge philosophers) (hardback: alk. paper) $160; (pbk.: alk. paper) $32.95   **185**
1. Values 2. Virtue 3. Philosophers 4. Ancient philosophy
ISBN 9780415622486; 9780415622493
LC 2013021013
This book, by Christopher John Shields, "introduces the whole of Aristotle's philosophy, showing . . . much of his thinking on the nature of the soul and the mind, ethics, politics, and the arts. Beginning with a

brief biography, Shields carefully explains the fundamental elements of Aristotle's thought. . . . Subsequently he discusses Aristotle's metaphysics, the theory of categories, logical theory, and his conception of the human being as a composite of soul and body." (Publisher's note)

Includes bibliographical references and index

187   Epicurean philosophy

Lucretius Carus, Titus

On the nature of things: De rerum natura; [by] Lucretius; edited and translated by Anthony M. Esolen. Johns Hopkins Univ. Press 1995 296p pa $25   **187**

   1. Poetry -- By individual authors

   ISBN 978-0-8018-5055-4; 0-8018-5055-X

                  LC 94-25165

"Writing in the waning days of the Roman Republic—as Rome's politics grew individualistic and treacherous, its high-life wanton, its piety introspective and morbid—Lucretius sets forth a rational and materialistic view of the world which offers a retreat into a quiet community of wisdom and friendship." Publisher's note

188   Stoic philosophy

Marcus Aurelius

  ★ **Meditations**; a new translation, with an introduction, by Gregory Hays. Modern Lib. 2002 lvii, 191p $19.95   **188**

   1. Ethics 2. Stoics

   ISBN 0-679-64260-9

                 LC 2001-57947

"An emperor and Stoic philosopher records his thoughts as he struggles for composure and order in the face of national disaster." Good Read

189   Medieval western philosophy

Rubenstein, Richard E.

Aristotle's children; how Christians, Muslims, and Jews rediscovered ancient wisdom and illuminated the Dark Ages. Harcourt 2003 368p $27   **189**

   1. Philosophers 2. Medieval philosophy 3. Writers on science

   ISBN 0-15-100720-9

                 LC 2003-6582

"Although the book purports to trace Aristotle's influence on Christianity, Islam and Judaism, it devotes more attention to Christianity. Even so, Rubenstein's lively prose, his lucid insights and his crystal-clear historical analyses make this a first-rate study in the history of ideas." Publ Wkly

Includes bibliographical references and index

Thomas, Aquinas, Saint, 1225?-1274

Selected writings; edited and translated with an introduction and notes by Ralph McInerny. Penguin Bks. 1998 xxxviii, 841p pa $14.95   **189**

   ISBN 0-14-043632-4

Arranged chronologically, this collection of theological and philosophical writings brings together sermons, commentaries, responses to criticism and lengthy extracts from the Summa theologia.

Includes bibliographical references

190   Modern western and other noneastern philosophy

★ The **Columbia** history of Western philosophy; edited by Richard H. Popkin. Columbia Univ. Press 1999 xxvi, 836p $64.50   **190**

   1. Philosophy -- History

   ISBN 0-231-10128-7

                 LC 98-15219

"This survey's coverage of medieval Islamic, Jewish, and Christian philosophy is particularly strong." Choice

Includes bibliographical references

Gay, Peter

The **rise** of modern paganism. Norton 1995 xviii, 555, xvp (The Enlightenment: an interpretation) pa $19.95   **190**

   1. Enlightenment 2. Modern philosophy 3. Europe -- Intellectual life

   ISBN 0-393-31302-6

   First published 1966 by Knopf

Voume one of a two volume series examining the ideas, experiences and impact of leading Enlightenment figures in 18th century Europe and America.

Includes bibliographical references

The **science** of freedom. Norton 1996 xx, 705, xviiip (The Enlightenment: an interpretation) pa $19.95   **190**

   1. Enlightenment 2. Modern philosophy 3. Europe -- Intellectual life

   ISBN 0-393-31366-2

   First published 1969

Volume two of a two-volume series examining the ideas, experiences and impact of leading Enlightenment figures in 18th century Europe and America.

Gottlieb, Anthony

  ★ The **dream** of enlightenment; the rise of modern philosophy. Anthony Gottlieb. Liveright Publishing Corporation, a division of W. W. Norton & Co. Inc. 2016 384 p. (hardcover) $27.95   **190**

   1. Modern philosophy

   ISBN 9780871404435

                 LC 2016015063

In this book, author Anthony Gottlieb "navigates a . . . great explosion of thought, taking us to northern Europe in the wake of its wars of religion and the rise of Galilean science. In a relatively short period—from the early 1640s to the eve of the French Revolution—Descartes, Hobbes, Spinoza, Locke, Leibniz, and Hume all made their mark. [This book] tells their story and that of the birth of modern philosophy." (Publisher's note)

"A former executive editor of the Economist who has held visiting fellowships at Harvard University and All Souls College, Oxford, Gottlieb won raves for The Dream of Reason, a history of philosophy from the Greeks to the Renaissance. Finally, after 16 years, we have the sequel, which focuses on the key philosophers Descartes, Hobbes, Spinoza, Locke, Leibniz, Hume, and Rousseau, who rethought thinking itself as Galilean science challenged previously held assumptions and religious beliefs. Accessibly written philosophical studies can be surprisingly popular as evidenced by the current success of Sarah Bakewell's At the Existentialist Café. Don't miss." LJ

Includes bibliographical references and index

Himmelfarb, Gertrude

The **moral** imagination; from Edmund Burke to Lionel Trilling. Ivan R. Dee 2006 259p $26   **190**
1. Modern philosophy 2. Political science
ISBN 1-56663-624-8

LC 2005-19838

The author "specializes in Victorian Britain and profiles some of its leading writers and statesmen, along with philosophical forerunners and descendants, to probe the complexities of two centuries of conservative thought. . . . Himmelfarb's stylish blend of literary criticism and intellectual history yields a stimulating reappraisal of a multifaceted and influential worldview." Publ Wkly
Includes bibliographical references

The **roads** to modernity; the British, French, and American enlightenments. Knopf 2004 284p $25   **190**
1. Enlightenment 2. Europe -- Intellectual life 3. United States -- Intellectual life
ISBN 1-400-04236-4

LC 2003-60576

"This is a book with important ideological implications that deserves to be read and debated across the political spectrum." Publ Wkly
Includes bibliographical references

Miller, Jim

Examined lives; [by] James Miller. Farrar, Straus and Giroux 2011 422p ill. $28   **190**
1. Biography 2. Philosophers 3. Conduct of life 4. Biography, Collective 5. Philosophers -- Biography 6. Philosophy -- Psychological aspects
ISBN 978-0-374-15085-3

LC 201014385

This book, a "New York Times" Notable Book for 2011, looks at the lives of "12 philosophers: Socrates, Plato, Diogenes the Cynic, . . . Aristotle, Seneca, Augustine, Montaigne, Descartes, Rousseau, Kant, Emerson and Nietzsche. In each case, he explores the life selectively, looking for 'crux' points and investigating how ideas of the philosophical life have changed. Few readers will be astounded to learn that philosophers make as much of a mess of their lives as anyone else. But [James] Miller . . . shows us philosophers becoming ever more inclined to reflect on these failings, and suggests that this makes their lives more rather than less studying." (N Y Times)
Includes bibliographical references

Nadler, Steven M.

The **best** of all possible worlds; a story of philosophers, God, and evil. [by] Steven Nadler. Farrar, Straus and Giroux 2008 300p $25   **190**
1. God 2. Theologians 3. Philosophers 4. Good and evil 5. Mathematicians 6. Modern philosophy 7. Essayists
ISBN 978-0-374-22998-6; 0-374-22998-8

LC 2008-29143

This book "is written simply and clearly, without condescension, flashiness or oversimplification. But it's a demanding book nonetheless, and you need to pay attention. You'll be amply rewarded if you do." Washington Post Book World
Includes bibliographical references

The **Oxford** history of Western philosophy; edited by Anthony Kenny. Oxford Univ. Press 1994 407p il maps hardcover o.p. pa $15   **190**
1. Philosophy -- History

ISBN 0-19-824278-6; 0-19-289329-7 pa

LC 94-9858

"The illustrations have been wisely chosen to show the constant play between art and idea. Some familiarity with analytic philosophy would be useful to gain the most from the text, but this is a significant addition to the literature." Libr J
Includes bibliographical references

Sedgwick, Peter

★ **Descartes** to Derrida; an introduction to European philosophy. Blackwell 2001 310p $76.95; pa $33.95   **190**
1. Modern philosophy
ISBN 0-631-20142-4; 0-631-20143-2 pa

LC 00-57917

"This book should take a place as one of the key texts in humanities programs throughout the English-speaking world." Choice
Includes bibliographical references

191   Philosophy of United States and Canada

Kaag, John

American philosophy; a love story. John Kaag. FSG 2016 272 p. (cloth) $26   **191**
1. Pragmatism 2. Rare books 3. Philosophers 4. American philosophy 5. Philosophy, American -- Miscellanea
ISBN 9780374154486

LC 2016001908

In this book, "John Kaag--a disillusioned philosopher at sea in his marriage and career--stumbles upon a treasure trove of rare books on an old estate in the hinterlands of New Hampshire that once belonged to the Harvard philosopher William Ernest Hocking. . . . As he begins to catalog and preserve these priceless books, Kaag rediscovers the very tenets of American philosophy--self-reliance, pragmatism, the transcendent--and sees them in a twenty-first-century context." (Publisher's note)

" Kaag's lively prose, acute self-examination, unfolding romance, and instructive history of philosophy as a discipline make for a surprisingly absorbing book." Kirkus
Includes bibliographical references and index

Rand, Ayn

The **voice** of reason; essays in objectivist thought; edited and with an introduction by Leonard Peikoff; and with additional essays by Leonard Peikoff and Peter Schwartz. New Am. Lib. 1989 353p hardcover o.p. pa $18   **191**
1. American philosophy 2. Objectivism (Philosophy)
ISBN 0-45-300634-5; 0-45-201046-2 pa

LC 88-18192

The late author opposed liberalism and championed "capitalism, self-interest, and objective reality against collectivism, altruism, and mysticism. . . . These lectures, newspaper columns, and magazine articles are entirely characteristic of her—surprisingly emotional and dogmatic for a professed rationalist. Additional essays by editor Peikoff and disciple Peter Schwartz are of a piece." Booklist
Includes bibliographical references

Romano, Carlin

America the philosophical; Carlin Romano. Knopf 2012 672 p.   **191**
1. American philosophy 2. Philosophy -- Social aspects 3. Popular culture -- United States 4. United States -- Intellectual life 5. Philosophy -- United States

ISBN 0679434704; 9780679434702

LC 2011034753

This book offers a "diagnosis of the condition of philosophical thinking in America today. . . . [Carlin Romano] realizes that philosophy has traditionally been the ballpark for white men to play in, so he . . . add[s] to the team some prominent women, African Americans, Native Americans, gays and others. But he begins with the famous white men (William James, George Santayana, John Dewey et al.) and looks at key figures later on--John Rawls and Richard Rorty among them." (Kirkus)

Includes bibliographical references (p. [611]-639) and index

192   Philosophy of British Isles

Edmonds, David

Wittgenstein's poker; the story of a ten-minute argument between two great philosophers. {by} David Edmonds and John Eidinow. Ecco Press 2001 340p il $24; pa $13.95 **192**
1. Philosophers 2. Logicians 3. Nonfiction writers
ISBN 0-06-621244-8; 0-06-093664-9 pa

LC 2002-276301

"On the Cambridge University campus in 1946, two of the twentieth-century's most notable philosophers, Ludwig Wittgenstein and Karl Popper, squared off in an intense 10-minute clash rumored to have culminated with Wittgenstein brandishing a red-hot poker. The authors explain what the fight was about and how it reflects the development of philosophy. Ivory-tower drama at its crackling best." Booklist

Includes bibliographical references

193   Philosophy of Germany and Austria

Hegel, Georg Wilhelm Friedrich

★ The **philosophy** of Hegel; edited with an introduction by Carl J. Friedrich. Modern Lib. 1954 552p pa $10.75 **193**
1. Philosophy
ISBN 0-07-553655-2 pa

Contents: The philosophy of history; The history of philosophy; The science of logic; Philosophy of right and law, or natural law and political science outlines; Lectures on aesthetics; The phenomenology of the spirit (1807); Political essays; Bibliography

Kaag, John

Hiking with Nietzsche; on becoming who you are. John Kaag. Farrar, Straus & Giroux 2018 272 p. (hardcover) $26 **193**
1. Biography 2. Spirituality 3. Mountaineering 4. Spiritual biography 5. Mountaineering -- Alps -- Miscellanea
ISBN 9780374170011

LC 2017057604

This book, by John Kaag, "is a tale of two philosophical journeys--one made by . . . Kaag as an introspective young man of nineteen, the other seventeen years later, in radically different circumstances: he is now a husband and father, and his wife and small child are in tow. Kaag sets off for the Swiss peaks above Sils Maria where Nietzsche wrote his landmark work 'Thus Spoke Zarathustra.'" (Publisher's note)

"A wonderful introduction to Nietzsche set against the unique backdrop of the landscape and cities he experienced. The tone and writing style make it accessible to general readers, while the content will reward those familiar with Nietzsche as well." LJ

Includes bibliographical references and index

Kant, Immanuel

★ **Basic** writings of Kant; edited and with an introduction by Allen W. Wood. Modern Lib. 2001 xxv, 478p pa $15.95 **193**
1. Philosophy
ISBN 0-375-75733-3

LC 2001-18303

First Modern Library edition published 1949 with title: The philosophy of Kant

This volume presents the essential works of the philosopher including "selected excerpts from his most frequently taught essays and book-length publications, including 'Critique of Pure Reason, Critique of Judgment,' and 'Eternal Peace.'" Publisher's note

★ **Critique** of pure reason; translated by Marcus Weigelt. Rev ed; Penguin 2003 lxxvi, 708p (Penguin classics) pa $20 **193**
1. Reason 2. Theory of knowledge
ISBN 978-0-14-044747-7; 0-14-044747-4
Original German edition, 1781

In this philosophical work Kant "attempted to define the possibility and limits of our knowledge. He denied that we can ever know how the world 'really' is. However, he tried to show that science nevertheless has a sort of universal validity, insofar as it consists of sense experience, which comes from the world, coupled with the mind, which orders this sense experience according to the 'categories of the understanding' and the intuitions of space and time." Reader's Ency. 4th edition

Nietzsche, Friedrich Wilhelm

★ **Basic** writings of Nietzsche; introduction by Peter Gay; translated and edited, with commentaries, by Walter Kaufmann. Modern Lib. 2000 xxiv, 862p pa $14.95 **193**
1. Philosophy
ISBN 0-679-78339-3

LC 00-64578

First Modern Library edition published 1968

"Gathers the complete texts of five of Nietzsche's most important works, from his first book to his last: The Birth of Tragedy, Beyond Good and Evil; On the Genealogy of Morals; The Case of Wagner; and Ecce Homo. . . . Included also are seventy-five aphorisms, selections from Nietzsche's correspondence, and variants from drafts for Ecce Homo." Publisher's note

The **portable** Nietzsche; selected and translated, with an introduction, prefaces, and notes, by Walter Kaufmann. Viking 1954 687p hardcover o.p. pa $17 **193**
1. Philosophy
ISBN 0-14-015062-5 pa

Includes the complete texts of Thus spake Zarathustra, Twilight of the idols, The antichrist, and Nietzsche contra Wagner. Selections from other works, notes and letters complete the volume

★ **Thus** spoke Zarathustra; a book for everyone and nobody. [by] Friedrich Nietzsche; translated with an introduction and notes by Graham Parkes. Oxford University Press 2005 xliii, 335p (Oxford world's classics) pa $14.95 **193**
1. Philosophy
ISBN 0-19-280583-5

LC 2005-19431

Written between 1883-1892

A philosophical narrative in which Nietzsche "transforms the ancient Persian philosopher Zarathustra . . . into a mouthpiece for his own views. Nietzsche develops his doctrine of the 'Ubermensch' in a prophetic, quasi-biblical style. Nietzsche's Zarathustra announces the death of God, and preaches a new 'faithfulness to the earth,' which includes a new respect for the body . . . and attentiveness to this world rather than the next. He also attacks pity and virtue as weapons of weakness." Reader's Ency. 4th edition

Includes bibliographical references

The **will** to power; a new translation by Walter Kaufmann and R. J. Hollingdale; edited with commentary by Walter Kaufmann; with facsimiles of the original manuscript. Random House 1967 xxxii, 576p hardcover o.p. pa $16 **193**
  1. Values 2. Nihilism
  ISBN 0-394-70437-1 pa
"Represents a selection from Nietzsche's notebooks to find out what he wrote on nihilism, art, morality, religion, and the theory of knowledge, among others." (Publisher's note)

Safranski, Rudiger
  Nietzsche; a philosophical biography. translated by Shelley Frisch. Norton 2001 409p $29.95; pa $18.95 **193**
  1. Authors 2. Philosophers 3. Essayists
  ISBN 0-393-05008-4; 0-393-32380-3 pa
                LC 2001-52130
"With brilliant insights and impressive scholarship, Safranski . . . here makes a major contribution to understanding and appreciating the lasting significance of Friedrich Nietzsche." Libr J
  Includes bibliographical references

Sherratt, Yvonne
  Hitler's philosophers; Yvonne Sherratt. Yale University Press 2012 328 p. (hardcover) $35 **193**
  1. Political philosophy 2. Philosophers -- Germany 3. Philosophy, German -- 20th century 4. Philosophers -- Germany -- History -- 20th century
  ISBN 0300151934; 9780300151930
                LC 2012026930
This book, by Yvonne Sherratt, explores the philosophical policy of Adolf Hitler. The author presents "evidence back to the 1920s of Hitler's vulgarization of noble thinkers of the past. . . . She reveals how philosophers of the 1930s eagerly collaborated to lend the Nazi regime a cloak of respectability. . . . And while these eminent men sanctioned slaughter, Semitic thinkers like Walter Benjamin and opponents like Kurt Huber were hunted down or murdered." (Publisher's note)

Solomon, Robert C.
  What Nietzsche really said; {by} Robert C. Solomon and Kathleen M. Higgins. Schocken Bks. 2000 263p hardcover o.p. pa $13 **193**
  1. Authors 2. Philosophers 3. Essayists
  ISBN 0-8052-1094-6 pa
                LC 99-33796
The authors offer an "overview of Friedrich Nietzsche's life, thought, and influence. . . . Particularly helpful are their brief annotations of Nietzsche's 14 books and short analyses of the thinkers who influenced him." Libr J
  Includes bibliographical references

196 Philosophy of Spain and Portugal

Ortega y Gasset, Jose
  What is philosophy? translated from the Spanish by Mildred Adams. Norton 1961 252p hardcover o.p. pa $10.95 **196**
  1. Philosophy
  ISBN 0-393-00126-1 pa
This volume by the influential Spanish philosopher, essayist and critic "consists of a series of lectures begun in 1929 at the University of Madrid. Interrupted when the University was closed as a result of political troubles, they were resumed in a Madrid theatre. Part of the lectures had been given earlier in Buenos Aires." N Y Times Book Rev

198 Philosophy of Scandinavia and Finland

Kierkegaard, Søren, 1813-1855
  Fear and trembling; Kierkegaard; dialectical lyric by Johannes de silentio (Kierkegaard); translated with and introduction by Alastair Hannay. Penguin Books"||"Viking Penguin 1985 158 p. (Penguin classics) (pbk) ($3.95 U.S.); $7.99 **198**
  1. Christian philosophy 2. Christianity -- Philosophy
  ISBN 0140444491 £2.50; 9780140444490; 9781101007143
                LC 86113797
This book, by Soren Kierkegaard, is "the infamous and controversial work that made a lasting impression on both modern Protestant theology and existentialist philosophers such as Sartre and Camus. . . . Alastair Hannay's introduction evaluates Kierkegaard's philosophy and the ways in which it conflicted with more accepted contemporary views." (Publisher's note)
  Bibliography: p. [149]-158

200 RELIGION

200 Religion

Ahlstrom, Sydney E.
  A **religious** history of the American people; Sydney E. Ahlstrom. Yale University Press 2004 xxiv, 1192 p.p $45 **200**
  1. United States -- Religion 2. United States -- Church history
  ISBN 0300100124; 9780300100129
                LC 2003116918
This book, by Sydney E. Ahlstrom, "winner of the 1973 National Book Award in Philosophy and Religion and Christian Century's choice as the Religious Book of the Decade (1979), is now issued with a new chapter by noted religious historian David Hall, who carries the story of American religious history forward to the present day." (Publisher's note)
  Includes bibliographical references (p. 1119-1162) and index

Armstrong, Karen
  A **history** of God; the 4000 year quest of Judaism, Christianity, and Islam. Knopf 1993 xxiii, 460p maps hardcover o.p. pa $15.95 **200**
  1. God 2. Islam 3. Judaism 4. Christianity
  ISBN 0-345-38456-3 pa
                LC 92-38318
This is a study of ideas and experiences of God in Judaism, Christi-

anity and Islam from Abraham to the twentieth century

"Public librarians should be aware that conservative readers may be offended by this book, and even religious scholars may find Armstrong's rather one-sided 'death of God' optimism about humanity a bit passé. Otherwise, this is an excellent and informative book." Libr J

Bowker, John

World religions; contributing consultants: David Bowker [et al.] DK Pub. 1997 200p il maps $35; pa $16.95 **200**
1. Religion 2. Religions
ISBN 0-7894-1439-2; 0-7566-1772-3 pa

LC 96-38277

Each chapter begins with an "introduction and is followed by one-or-two page sections that explain the basic tenets of the faith, symbols, events, people, buildings, works of art, and the differences and similarities to other religions. Hinduism, Buddhism, Judaism, Christianity, and Islam are included as are Jainism, Sikhism, Chinese and Japanese religions, and Native religions." SLJ

Chittister, Joan

The **gift** of years; growing older gracefully. BlueBridge 2008 222p $19.95 **200**
1. Older people 2. Elderly 3. Aging -- Religious aspects
ISBN 978-1-933346-10-6; 1-933346-10-8

LC 2008-00332

"This collection of inspirational reflections, 'not meant to be read in one sitting, or even in order, but one topic at a time,' abounds in gentle insights and arresting aphorisms." Publ Wkly
Includes bibliographical references

Dawkins, Richard

★ The **God** delusion. Houghton Mifflin Co. 2006 406p $27; pa $15.95 **200**
1. God 2. Atheism 3. Religion
ISBN 978-0-618-68000-9; 0-618-68000-4; 978-0-618-91824-9 pa; 0-618-91824-8 pa

LC 2006-15506

"Both fans of Dawkins and his many opponents will want to read this book." Libr J
Includes bibliographical references

De Botton, Alain, 1969-

Religion for atheists; Alain de Botton. Pantheon Books 2012 320p. ill. **200**
1. Atheism 2. Religious life 3. Conduct of life 4. Religion -- Philosophy 5. Atheists
ISBN 9780307379108

LC 2011021286

It was the author's intent to demonstrate "that the supernatural claims of religion are entirely false--but that it still has some very important things to teach the secular world." The author "suggests . . . that we look to religion for insights into how to, among other concerns, build a sense of community, make our relationships last, overcome feelings of envy and inadequacy, inspire travel and reconnect with the natural world." (Publisher's note)

The **encyclopedia** of cults, sects, and new religions; {edited by} James R. Lewis. 2nd ed; Prometheus Bks. 2002 951p il $180 **200**
1. Cults 2. Reference books 3. Sects -- Encyclopedias 4. United States -- Religion -- Encyclopedias
ISBN 1-57392-888-7

LC 2002-19180

First published 1998

This reference contains "information on approximately 1,000 religious groups, ranging from small churches with less than a hundred members (Chishti Order of America) to organizations such as the Assemblies of God that number in the millions. Most entries are relatively short. The more controversial religions, as well as religious groups that have had a high profile lately, receive more lengthy treatments. Also included are entries on broader religious movements such as the New Age and the Charismatic Movement. . . . Each article outlines the history of the group, its founders and leaders, its main teachings, and an approximate number of followers or congregations. The explanations are clearly written, interesting and understandable, without too much scholarly jargon." Booklist
Includes bibliographical references

★ **Encyclopedia** of religion; Lindsay Jones, editor in chief. 2nd ed; Macmillan Reference USA 2005 15v il set $1295 **200**
1. Reference books 2. Religions -- Encyclopedias
ISBN 0-02-865733-0

LC 2004-17052

First published 1987 in 16 volumes

"Treats theoretical (e.g., doctrines, myths, theologies, ethics), practical (e.g., cults, sacraments, meditations), and sociological (e.g., religious groups, ecclesiastical forms) aspects of religion; includes extensive coverage of non-Western religions. Signed articles by some 1,400 contributors worldwide end with bibliographies. Many composite entries treat two or more related topics. . . . Has quickly become the standard work." Guide to Ref Books. 11th edition [review of 1993 edition]
Includes bibliographical references

★ **Encyclopedia** of religious rites, rituals, and festivals; Frank A. Salamone, editor. Routledge 2004 487p il (Routledge encyclopedias of religion and society) $150 **200**
1. Reference books 2. Rites and ceremonies 3. Religions -- Encyclopedias
ISBN 0-415-94180-6

LC 2003-20389

"The entries can be understood by readers unfamiliar with the topics covered, but the work is suitable for all levels of scholars." Choice
Includes bibliographical references

Hexham, Irving

Understanding world religions. Zondervan 2011 512p il map $39.99; ebook $30.99 **200**
1. Religions
ISBN 978-0-310-25944-2; 0-310-25944-4; 978-0-310-31448-6 ebook; 0-310-31448-8 ebook

LC 2010013103

This "world religions text explores various religions under the broad categories of African Religions, the Yogic Traditions (including Buddhism), and the Abrahamic traditions." Publisher's note
Includes bibliographical references

Hitchens, Christopher

God is not great; how religion poisons everything. Twelve 2007 307p $24.99 **200**
1. Atheism 2. Religion
ISBN 978-0-44657-980-3; 0-44657-980-7

LC 2006-23039

National Book Award Finalist: Nonfiction (2007)
In this work Hitchens catalogs "the major arguments against reli-

gion, which he deems a pernicious force. First, he writes, faith misrepresents the origin of the cosmos as well as that of humanity; second, it fosters servility, solipsism, and sexual repression; and, third, it is based on wishful thinking. Hitchens spares no targets in this manifesto, criticizing both Western and Eastern faiths." Libr J

Includes bibliographical references

Minois, Georges

The **atheist's** Bible; the most dangerous book that never existed. Georges Minois; translated by Lys Ann Weiss. The University of Chicago Press 2012 249 p. map (cloth: alk. paper) $30 **200**

1. Atheism -- History 2. De tribus impostoribus 3. Rationalism -- History
ISBN 0226530299; 9780226530291

LC 2012011212

This book by Georges Minois, translated by Lys Ann Weiss, explains that "in 1239, Pope Gregory IX accused Frederick II, the Holy Roman Emperor, of . . . [writing] a supremely blasphemous book--'De tribus impostoribus,' or the 'Treatise of the Three Impostors'--in which Frederick denounced Moses, Jesus, and Muhammad as impostors. . . . Minois tracks the course of the book from its origins in 1239 to its most salient episodes in the seventeenth and eighteenth centuries." (Publisher's note)

Includes bibliographical references and index

National Geographic concise history of world religions; an illustrated time line. edited by Tim Cooke. National Geographic 2011 352 p. col. ill. (hardcover) $40.00 **200**

1. Ethics 2. World history 3. Religious institutions 4. Religions -- Encyclopedias 5. Religion -- History -- Chronology 6. Religions 7. Religion and ethics 8. Religions -- History
ISBN 1426206984; 9781426206986

LC 2011276808

This book "continues the 'Concise History' series with [a] . . . take on major religions and lesser-known faiths of all times and nations." It offers a "global perspective on the history of faith in the Americas, Europe, Asia and Oceania, and Africa and the Middle East. . . . 50 feature essays explore in detail the origins, development and influence of faith." (Publisher's Note)

Includes bibliographical references (p. 343-344) and index

Prothero, Stephen R.

God is not one; the eight rival religions that run the world-- and why their differences matter. [by] Stephen Prothero. HarperOne 2010 388p $26.99; ebook $9.99 **200**

1. Religions
ISBN 978-0-06-157127-5; 0-06-157127-X; 978-0-06-199120-2 ebook; 0-06-199120-1 ebook

LC 2009053372

Prothero argues that each of the major world religions have different worldviews and approaches to spiritual questions. The book contains chapters on Islam (the way of submission); Christianity (the way of salvation); Confucianism (the way of propriety); Hinduism (the way of devotion); Buddhism (the way of awakening); Yoruba religion (the way of connection); Judaism (the way of exile and return); Daoism (the way of flourishing); Atheism (the way of reason).

"Provocative, thoughtful, fiercely intelligent and, for both believing and nonbelieving, formal and informal students of religion, a must-read." Booklist

Includes bibliographical references

Religious literacy; what every American needs to know--

and doesn't. [by] Stephen Prothero. HarperSanFrancisco 2007 296p $24.95 **200**

1. Religions
ISBN 978-0-06-084670-1; 0-06-084670-4

LC 2006-41310

"In this book, the author combines a lively history of the rise and fall of American religious literacy with a set of proposed remedies based on his hope that 'the Fall into religious ignorance is reversible.' He also includes a useful multicultural glossary of religious definitions and allusions, in which religious illiterates can find the prodigal son, the promised land, the Quakers and the Koran." Washington Post Book World

Includes bibliographical references

Williams, Juan

This far by faith; stories from the African-American religious experience. [by] Juan Williams and Quinton Dixie. Morrow 2003 326p il hardcover o.p. pa $15.95 **200**

1. African Americans -- History 2. African Americans -- Religion
ISBN 0-06-018863-4; 0-06-093424-7 pa

LC 2002-71884

"Brief topical articles and captioned illustrations supplement the main text, creating a balanced, readable, and nuanced introduction to the power of faith to sustain the African American community." Libr J

200.1   Systems, scientific principles, psychology of religion

Barrett, Justin L.

Born believers; the science of children's religious belief. Justin L. Barrett. Free Press 2012 x, 302 p.p **200.1**

1. Belief and doubt 2. Child psychology 3. Faith -- Psychology 4. Children -- Religious life 5. God 6. Psychology, Religious
ISBN 1439196540; 9781439196540

LC 2011039581

In this book, "the author looks at cross-cultural studies of children conducted by experts in the 'cognitive science of religion.' The studies indicate that, from an early age, humans know the difference between inanimate objects and 'agents'--people or forces that can move or make things move. As they develop, children are prone to see agents as powerful forces unlike humans. By four or five, kids see a purpose, not only in objects, but also in creatures, rocks, rivers and mountains. . . . In the second part of the book, the author indicts atheism by arguing that if one accepts natural selection then one cannot reject the natural religion of childhood--it must have survival value." (Kirkus)

Includes bibliographical references and index

200.8   Groups of people

Circling faith; Southern women on spirituality. edited by Wendy Reed and Jennifer Horne. University of Alabama Press 2012 xiv, 230 p.p (trade cloth) $29.95 **200.8**

1. Women -- Religious life -- Southern states 2. Spirituality 3. Women authors -- Religious life 4. Southern women -- Religious life
ISBN 0817317678; 0817357017; 0817386084; 9780817317676; 9780817357016; 9780817386085

LC 2011034803

This book, edited by Wendy Reed and Jennifer Horne, "is a collection of essays by southern women that encompasses spirituality and the experience of winding through the religiously charged environment of the American South. . . . These essays showcase the large spectrum of spirituality that abides in the South, as well as the equally large spectrum of individual women who hold these faiths." (Publisher's note)

200.9   History, geographic treatment, biography

Almond, Gabriel Abraham

★ **Strong** religion; the rise of fundamentalisms around the world. {by} Gabriel A. Almond, R. Scott Appleby, and Emmanuel Sivan. University of Chicago Press 2003 281p il $49; pa $19   **200.9**

1. Religious fundamentalism

ISBN 0-226-01497-5; 0-226-01498-3 pa

LC 2002-13665

This "may be the single most cogent sociohistorical analysis of the modern religious phenomenon called fundamentalism. . . . This foundational work is essential for academic and major public libraries." Libr J

Includes bibliographical references

Armstrong, Karen

★ The **battle** for God; fundamentalism in Judaism, Christianity, and Islam. Knopf 2000 442p $29.95; pa $15.95 **200.9**

1. Judaism 2. Islamic fundamentalism 3. Christian fundamentalism 4. Religious fundamentalism 5. Israel -- History

ISBN 0-679-43597-2; 0-345-39169-1 pa

LC 99-34022

This is a "study of fundamentalism among Jews (in Israel), Christians (American Protestants), and Muslims (Sunni Egyptians and Shiite Iranians). Armstrong argues that all strains of fundamentalism, despite their differences, are fearful defenses against modernity. . . . The author is sympathetic to the human need for spiritual meaning, but she points out that the intellectual flaws of fundamentalist beliefs are customarily accompanied by paranoia, anger, and aggression—which, in turn, frequently betray the message of the faith." New Yorker

Includes bibliographical references

★ The **great** transformation; the beginning of our religious traditions. Knopf 2006 469p il map $30   **200.9**

1. Religion -- History

ISBN 0-375-41317-0

LC 2005-47536

"This could very possibly be one of the greatest intellectual histories ever written." Libr J

Includes bibliographical references

Believer, beware; first person dispatches from the margins of faith. selected by Jeff Sharlet, Peter Manseau, and the editors of Killing the Buddha. Beacon Press 2009 263p pa $16   **200.9**

1. Faith 2. United States -- Religion

ISBN 978-0-8070-7739-9; 0-8070-7739-9

LC 2008-47403

"The editors are among the smart, candid, and insightful authors whose personal narratives form the book's 35 brief chapters. The selections represent a wide range of experiences from cheating on bar mitzvah prep to discovering hunger as spiritual food in a Ramadan fast, from sabotaging Bible camp to stumbling upon barbershop theology. Contributions reflect the scope of religious diversity, including orthodox Judaism, Roman Catholicism, Islam, Zen Buddhism and even a meditation on agnosticism. Some are funny, others heartbreaking, and some are simply revelatory." Publ Wkly

Includes bibliographical references

★ The **Cambridge** illustrated history of religions; edited by John Bowker. Cambridge Univ. Press 2002 336p il (Cambridge illustrated history) $40   **200.9**

1. Religions

ISBN 0-521-81037-X

LC 2001-37866

"The major religions get thoroughgoing treatment, with short introductions also given to the Zoroastrianism; the religions of Greece, Rome, Egypt, and Mesopotamia; aboriginal religions; and new religious movements. . . . Christianity receives a separate chapter as well as substantial treatment in chapters on Chinese, Korean, and Japanese religions. . . . This volume presents a large amount of information in an engaging way, offering much scholarly insight for the lay reader." Libr J

Includes bibliographical references

Controversial New Religions; edited by James R. Lewis and Jesper Aa. Petersen. 2nd Edition Oxford University Press 2014 480 p. pa. $35   **200.9**

ISBN 9780199315314

LC 2013049363

"This volume collects papers on those specific New Religious Movements (NRMS) that have generated the most scholarly attention. With few exceptions, these organizations are also the controversial groups that have attracted the attention of the mass media, often because they have been involved in, or accused of, violent or anti-social activities. Among the movements . . . profiled are such groups as the Branch Davidians, Heaven's Gate, Aum Shinrikyo, Solar Temple, Scientology, and Falun Gong." (Publisher's note)

★ **Eastern** religions; origins, beliefs, practices, holy texts, sacred places. general editor, Michael D. Coogan; [contributors] Vasudha Narayanan . . . [et al.] Oxford University Press 2005 552p il $35; pa $19.95   **200.9**

1. Shinto 2. Taoism 3. Buddhism 4. Hinduism 5. Confucianism 6. East Asia -- Religion 7. South Asia -- Religion

ISBN 0-19-522190-7; 978-0-19-522190-9; 0-19-522191-5 pa; 978-0-19-522191-6 pa

LC 2004-30376

This is an introduction "to major South Asian and East Asian religious traditions. Four expert authors introduce Hinduism, Buddhism, Taoism, Confucianism, and Shinto. To aid comparison, each article has parallel sections on origins and historical development, aspects of the divine, sacred texts, sacred persons, ethical principles, sacred space, sacred time, death and the afterlife, and society and religion. The clear, crisp prose avoids academic jargon without losing the complexity and richness of the traditions being examined." Libr J

Includes bibliographical references

Leon, Luis D.

Religion and American cultures; an encyclopedia of traditions, diversity, and popular expressions. Gary Laderman and Luis León, editors; foreword by Amanda Porterfield. ABC-CLIO 2003 3v set $285   **200.9**

1. Reference books 2. United States -- Religion -- Encyclopedias

ISBN 1-57607-238-X

LC 2003-8644

"This resource explores the various ways Americans approach religion. Its first volume features chapters on ethnic groups and sectarian beliefs, the second comprises essay entries on distinct practices, and the third collects primary documents. Cotton Mather, Shirley MacLaine, and Elijah Muhammad are represented, along with such pivotal documents as The Maryland TolerationAct and the American Indian Reli-

gious Freedom Act." Libr J
   Includes bibliographical references

Melton, J. Gordon

   ★ **Melton's** encyclopedia of American religions; [by] J. Gordon Melton; James Beverley, associate editor; Constance Jones, assistant editor; Pamela S. Nadell, assistant editor; foreword by Rodney Stark. 8th ed.; Gale, Cengage Learning 2009 xxvi, 1386p il map $380   **200.9**
   1. Reference books 2. Sects -- Encyclopedias 3. United States -- Religion -- Encyclopedias
   ISBN 978-0-7876-9696-2

                                             LC 2008-37465
   First published 1978 by McGrath Publishing Company with title: Encyclopedia of American religions
   This encyclopedia features "coverage on more than 2,300 North American religious groups in the U.S. and Canada—from Adventists to Zen Buddhists. Information on these groups is presented in two . . . sections. These sections contain essays and directory listings that describe the historical development of religious families and give . . . information about each group within those families, including, when available, rubrics for membership figures, educational facilities and periodicals." Publisher's note
   Includes bibliographical references

Stark, Rodney

   For the glory of God; how monotheism led to reformations, science, witch-hunts, and the end of slavery. Princeton Univ. Press 2003 488p il $45; pa $18.95   **200.9**
   1. Slavery 2. Monotheism 3. Witchcraft 4. Reformation 5. Religion and science
   ISBN 0-691-11436-6; 0-691-11950-3 pa
                                             LC 2002-31746
   A "provocative volume—lucid and tightly reasoned." Booklist
   Includes bibliographical references

200.951   Religion – China

Johnson, Ian

   The **souls** of China; the return of religion after Mao. Ian Johnson. Pantheon Books 2017 x, 455 p.p (hardcover: alk. paper) $30   **200.951**
   1. Spiritual life 2. China -- Religion 3. China -- Religion -- 20th century 4. China -- Religion -- 21st century
   ISBN 9781101870051; 9781101870068
                                             LC 2016036412
   This book, by Ian Johnson, presents "a revelatory portrait of religion in China today--its history, the spiritual traditions of its Eastern and Western faiths, and the ways in which it is influencing China's future. . . . Following a century of violent anti-religious campaigns, China is now filled with new temples, churches, and mosques--as well as cults, sects, and politicians trying to harness religion for their own ends." (Publisher's note)
   "Johnson provides a fascinating account of how traditional activities recovered after enduring severe repression during China's Cultural Revolution (1966–76)." LJ
   Includes bibliographical references and index

200.973   Religion – United States

Ozment, Katherine

   Grace without God; The Search for Meaning, Purpose, and Belonging in a Secular Age. Katherine Ozment, Harper Wave. HarperCollins Publishers 2016 320 p. (hardcover) $25.99   **200.973**
   1. Spiritual life 2. United States -- Religion 3. Religion 4. Spirituality 5. Spiritual biography
   ISBN 9780062305114
                                             LC 2016004086
   This book, by Katherine Ozment, is an "exploration of secular America. . . . Ozment takes readers on a quest to understand the trends and ramifications of a nation in flight from organized religion. . . . Most Americans are raised in a religious tradition, but in recent decades many have begun to leave religion. . . . So how do the nonreligious fill the need for ritual, story, community, . . . purpose and meaning without . . . religion?"
   "Ozment successfully writes an informative and relatable discussion on the changing landscape of religion, society, and identity." LJ
   Includes bibliographical references and index

Schmidt, Leigh Eric

   The **religious** history of America; The Heart of the American Story from Colonial Times to Today. by Edwin S. Gaustad and Leigh E. Schmidt. Rev ed; HarperSanFrancisco 2002 x, 454 p.p illustrations $18.99   **200.973**
   1. United States -- Religion 2. United States -- Church history
   ISBN 0060630566; 9780060630560
                                             LC 2002190208
   This book on American religious history, by Edwin S. Gaustad and Leigh E. Schmidt, is a "fully revised, updated, and expanded version. . . . [It] expands its scope, increasing the emphasis on pluralism, religious practices, and spiritual seeking, as well as the direct connection of religion to social and political struggle. . . . [It also has] a new emphasis on African-American and Native American religious life, Eastern religions, and the recent boom in spirituality." (Publisher's note)
   "The overall result is a well-balanced enhancement of an excellent work." LJ
   Includes bibliographical references (p. 433-435) and index

201   Specific aspects of religion

Armstrong, Karen, 1944-

   ★ **Fields** of Blood; Religion and the History of Violence. by Karen Armstrong. Random House Inc 2014 496 p. $30 **201**
   1. Violence -- Religious aspects
   ISBN 0307957047; 9780307957047
   This book, by Karen Armstrong, is an "exploration of religion and the history of human violence. . . . While many historians have looked at violence in connection with particular religious manifestations (jihad in Islam or Christianity's Crusades), Armstrong looks at each faith--not only Christianity and Islam, but also Buddhism, Hinduism, Confucianism, Daoism, and Judaism--in its totality over time." (Publisher's note)
   Includes bibliographic references, notes, and index

Campbell, Joseph

   Creative mythology. Arkana 1991 730p (The masks of God) pa $18   **201**
   1. Mythology in literature
   ISBN 978-0-14-019440-1; 0-14-019440-1

First published 1968 by Viking

"This volume explores the whole inner story of modern culture since the Dark Ages, treating modern man's unique position as the creator of his own mythology." Publisher's note

Includes bibliographical references

Occidental mythology. Arkana 1991 564p (The masks of God) pa $18 **201**
1. Mythology
ISBN 978-0-14-019441-8; 0-14-019441-X
First published 1964 by Viking

"A systematic . . . comparison of the themes that underlie the art, worship, and literature of the Western world." Publisher's note

Includes bibliographical references

Oriental mythology. Arkana 1991 561p (The masks of God) pa $18 **201**
1. Oriental mythology
ISBN 978-0-14-019442-5; 0-14-019442-8
First published 1962 by Viking

"An exploration of Eastern mythology as it developed into the distinctive religions of Egypt, India, China, and Japan." Publisher's note

Includes bibliographical references

★ The **power** of myth; [by] Joseph Campbell, with Bill Moyers; Betty Sue Flowers, editor. Doubleday 1988 231p il hardcover o.p. pa $29.95 **201**
1. Mythology 2. Religious art 3. Spiritual life
ISBN 0-385-24773-7; 0-385-24774-5

LC 88-4218

This companion to a public television series records conversations between Campbell and Bill Moyers. Campbell reflects on themes and symbols from world religions and mythologies and explores their relevance for his own spiritual journey.

"Campbell is the hero on his own voyage of discovery. This well-bound book on lovely paper with helpful illustrations from art is highly recommended for all libraries." Choice

Primitive mythology. Arkana 1991 504p (The masks of God) pa $18 **201**
1. Mythology
ISBN 978-0-14-019443-2; 0-14-019443-6
First published 1959 by Viking

The author "discusses the primitive roots of mythology, examining them in light of . . . discoveries in archaeology, anthropology, and psychology." Publisher's note

Includes bibliographical references

Frank, Adam

The **constant** fire; beyond the science vs. religion debate. University of California Press 2009 288p $24.95 **201**
1. Religion and science
ISBN 978-0-520-25412-1; 0-520-25412-0

LC 2008-25402

"An elegant reimagining of the relationship between science and spirituality. . . . Challenges the assumption that science and religion are implacable foes." Chron Higher Educ

Includes bibliographical references (p. 269-281) and index

Haidt, Jonathan

The **righteous** mind; why good people are divided by politics and religion. Jonathan Haidt. Pantheon Books 2012 419

p. $28.95 **201**
1. Social values 2. Social psychology 3. Political psychology 4. Psychology of religion 5. Ethics -- Psychological aspects 6. Ethics 7. Psychology, Religious
ISBN 9780307377906

LC 2011032036

"The core of the book [by Jonathan Haidt] is an attempt at a Darwinian explanation of morality, contending that moral behavior emerges from a natural process of competition among human groups. . . . A part of 'The Righteous Mind' is a . . . critique of . . . [a] primitive type of rationalism. . . . Much of his book is an attempt to apply the findings of evolutionary psychology to the political gridlock that . . . exists in the United States." (New Republic)

Includes bibliographical references and index.

Harman, Oren

Evolutions; fifteen myths that explain our world. Oren Harman. Farrar, Straus & Giroux 2018 256 p. (hardcover) $26 **201**
1. Evolution 2. Mythology 3. Life sciences 4. Myth 5. Science 6. Evolution (Biology)
ISBN 9780374150709

LC 2017047954

This book, by Oren Harman, "brings to life the latest scientific thinking on the birth of the universe and the solar system, the journey from a single cell all the way to our human minds. . . . Harman uses modern science to create new and original mythologies. Here are the earth and the moon presenting a cosmological view of motherhood, . . . and the birth of language in evolution summoning humankind's struggle with truth." (Publisher's note)

The **History** of science and religion in the western tradition; an encyclopedia. Gary B. Ferngren, general editor; Edward J. Larson, Darrel W. Amundsen, co-editors; Anne-Marie E. Nakhla, assistant editor. Garland 2000 xxi, 586p (Garland reference library of the humanities) $195 **201**
1. Religion and science
ISBN 0-8153-1656-9

LC 00-25153

This is a collection of articles "grouped under ten headings covering everything from the relationship of science and religion to the approaches taken by specific religious traditions, from alchemy to chemistry to materialism to spiritualism. Ferngren . . . and his coeditors take the stand that the historical relationship between science and religion follows a complex model rather than the popularly understood model of unalterable conflict. The result is a work, well worth reading through or browsing, that is filled with respect for the roles and methodologies of both religion and science." Libr J

Includes bibliographical references and index

Jordan, Michael

Dictionary of gods and goddesses; 2nd ed; Facts on File 2004 402p il (Facts on File library of religion and mythology) $45 **201**
1. Reference books 2. Gods and goddesses -- Dictionaries
ISBN 0-8160-5923-3

LC 2004-13028

First published 1993

The author's "alphabetical list includes gods and goddesses from a variety of religions. Each entry provides a brief description with cross-references where appropriate; some supply translations of the names. Longer entries include origin, dates of observance, synonyms, geographic location of the cult center, art references by type (e.g., stone carvings), and literary sources. . . . This [is] a usable, well-written resource for short descriptions of cross-cultural deities." Choice

Includes bibliographical references

Karabell, Zachary

Peace be upon you; the story of Muslim, Christian, and Jewish coexistence. Random House 2007 343p map $26.95 **201**
1. Interfaith relations 2. Christianity and other religions 3. Islam -- Relations 4. Judaism -- Relations
ISBN 978-1-4000-4368-2; 1-4000-4368-9

LC 2006-31501

"This outstanding book . . . combines in a single volume centuries of interaction among the three great monotheistic religions." Choice

Includes bibliographical references (p. 317-326)

Kimball, Charles

When religion becomes lethal; the explosive mix of politics and religion in Judaism, Christianity, and Islam. Jossey-Bass 2011 254p $27.95; ebook $14.99 **201**
1. Islam and politics 2. Religion and politics 3. Religious fundamentalism 4. Christianity and politics 5. Judaism and politics
ISBN 978-0-470-58190-2; 0-470-58190-5; 978-1-1180-3056-1 ebook

LC 2010052515

The author "begins with a careful overview of how, in sacred text and history, religion and politics interact in Judaism, Christianity, and Islam. He then examines the constructive and destructive ways adherents of the faiths have interpreted and acted on their traditions in the public square, focusing specifically on Israel, the U.S., Iraq, and Iran." Sojourners

Includes bibliographical references (p. 229-232)

Leeming, David Adams

★ The **Oxford** companion to world mythology. Oxford University Press 2006 xxxvii, 469p $65 **201**
1. Reference books 2. Mythology -- Dictionaries
ISBN 0-19-515669-2

LC 2005-14216

"This volume presents approximately 2,000 concise entries in dictionary format. Leeming, . . . in an attempt to be 'inclusive and reasonably comprehensive,' ranges far outside the Western tradition to cover figures and folklore from Africa, Asia, and the Americas, as well as from the sacred narratives of religions. . . . Approximately 100 black-and-white illustrations, along with a few color plates, provide examples of artistic renderings of various myths. . . . This work should find a place in any general reference collection." Choice

Includes bibliographical references

Lombard, Jay

The **mind** of God; neuroscience, faith, and a search for the soul. Dr. Jay Lombard; foreword by Patrick J. Kennedy. Random House Inc 2017 xxi, 1977 pagesp $25 **201**
1. God 2. Neurosciences 3. Religion and science
ISBN 055341867X; 9780553418675

LC 2017285198

In this book, author Jay Lombard, "employs case studies from his own behavioral neurology practice to explore the spiritual conundrums that we all ask ourselves: What is the nature of God? Does my life have purpose? What's the meaning of our existence? Are we free? What happens to us when we die? For Lombard, these metaphysical questions are a jumping-off point for exploring the brain in search of the seat of the soul." (Publisher's note)

"Along the path carrying him from early years as an aimless druggie to professional maturity as an esteemed neurologist, Lombard has learned a great deal about the science of the brain. Surprisingly, he has also learned much about faith, especially as it manifests itself as a formative mental force." Booklist

Includes bibliographical references (pages 181-194).

Niebuhr, Gustav

Beyond tolerance; searching for interfaith understanding in America. Viking 2008 xxxviii, 218p $25.95 **201**
1. Religious tolerance 2. Interfaith relations
ISBN 978-0-670-01956-4; 0-670-01956-9

LC 2007-40479

"Niebuhr brings his reporter's eye for detail to this work, which he populates with people and organizations who strive to find religious meaning in our diverse lives. This is no dry, academic exposition. Written for a general audience, it is also valuable for scholars wishing to see an America many might have thought was calcifying into an insular continent, worshipping hard gods or God." Libr J

Includes bibliographical references (p. 208-212)

Nussbaum, Martha Craven, 1947-

★ The **new** religious intolerance; overcoming the politics of fear in an anxious age. Martha C. Nussbaum. Belknap Press of Harvard University Press 2012 xiii, 285 p.p (hbk.: alk. paper) $26.95 **201**
1. Freedom of religion 2. Religious tolerance 3. Islamophobia -- United States 4. Religious discrimination 5. Fear -- Religious aspects
ISBN 0674065905; 9780674065901

LC 2011051712

In this book Martha C. Nussbaum "enters the debate on anti-Muslim discrimination. . . . She invites us to examine disputes about women's use of the burka and the construction of an Islamic-initiated 'multifaith community center' near New York's Ground Zero. The author's argument for tolerant accommodation falls within the 'Socratic and Christian/Kantian' commitment to live an examined life in relations with religious minorities." (Library Journal)

Includes bibliographical references (p. 247-267) and index

201.5 Interreligious relations

Hutchison, William R.

Religious pluralism in America; the contentious history of a founding ideal. Yale University Press 2003 262p $32.50; pa $18 **201.5**
1. United States -- Religion
ISBN 0-300-09813-8; 0-300-10516-9 pa

LC 2002-151893

The author "illuminates the cultural transformations that enabled twentieth-century Americans to embrace belatedly the religious diversity that emerged in the nineteenth-century influx of Catholic and Jewish immigrants and in the rise of new American-born faiths such as Mormonism and Transcendentalism. . . . Though he acknowledges the concerns of critics worried about the moral balkanization of a society lacking shared religious premises, Hutchison hails America's new religious pluralism as a great achievement. A balanced and informative narrative." Booklist

Includes bibliographical references

201.65   Religion and science

Sacks, Jonathan, 1948-
★ The **great** partnership; science, religion, and the search for meaning. Jonathan Sacks. Schocken Books 2011 x, 370 p.p $28.95   **201.65**
  1. Faith 2. Religion and science
  ISBN 0805243011; 9780805243017

LC 2012006601

In this book Jonathan Sacks "argues not only that science and religion are compatible, but that they complement each other--and that the world needs both. . . . [According to Sacks,] Science teaches us where we come from. Religion explains to us why we are here. Science is the search for explanation. Religion is the search for meaning. We need scientific explanation to understand nature. We need meaning to understand human behavior." (Publisher's note)

Includes bibliographical references

202   Doctrines

Anderson, Herbert
The **divine** art of dying; How to Live Well While Dying. Karen Speerstra + Herbert Anderson; foreword by Ira Byock, MD. Divine Arts. 2014 268 p. $18.95   **202**
  1. Death 2. Death -- Religious aspects
  ISBN 1611250234; 9781611250237

LC 2013047709

This book, by Karen Speerstra and Herbert Anderson, "explores the unique moment when seriously ill people choose to turn toward death. Combining personal stories with solid research on palliative and hospice care, it provides a well-integrated look at the spiritual dimensions of living fully when death is near." (Publisher's note)

"A valuable resource; this books brims with wisdom and grace." Pub Wkly

202.3   Eschatology

Holloway, Richard
Waiting for the Last Bus; reflections on life and death. Richard Holloway. Canongate Books 2018 165 p. (hardcover) $24   **202.3**
  1. Life 2. Death 3. Future life
  ISBN 9781786890214; 9781786890238; 1786890216

In this book, Richard Holloway, "presents a positive, meditative and profound exploration of the many important lessons we can learn from death: facing up to the limitations of our bodies as they falter, reflecting on our failings, and forgiving ourselves and others. . . . [The book] is an invitation to reconsider life's greatest mystery by one of the most important and beloved religious leaders of our time." (Publisher's note)

"This powerful volume abounds with thoughtful guidance for soothing the dying, comforting the grieving, and preparing for one's own death." Pub Wkly

Includes bibliographical references (pages 161-165).

203   Public worship and other practices

★ **How** to be a perfect stranger; the essential religious etiquette handbook. edited by Stuart M. Matlins & Arthur J.

Magida. 5th ed.; SkyLight Paths Pub. 2011 402p (¿Perfect stranger¿ series) pa $19.99   **203**
  1. Etiquette 2. Rites and ceremonies
  ISBN 978-1-59473-294-2

LC 2010-31668

First published 1996-1997 in two volumes by Jewish Lights Pub.

This guide "provides brief overviews of many religions: services, life-cycle events, home celebrations. It explains rituals so that those unfamiliar with them will know what to expect, how to dress, whether to bring a gift, and so on. It also has a glossary, explains various religious calendars, and lists religious festivals." Booklist

204   Religious experience, life, practice

Nepo, Mark
★ **Things** that join the sea and the sky; field notes on living. Mark Nepo. Sounds True 2017 xvii, 236 p.p (pbk.) $18.95   **204**
  1. Spiritualism 2. Mind and body 3. Spiritual life 4. Life -- Miscellanea
  ISBN 9781622038992

LC 2017011750

In this book, author "Mark Nepo brings us a compelling treasury of short prose reflections to turn to when struggling to keep our heads above water, and to breathe into all of our sorrows and joys. Inspired by his own journal writing across 15 years, this book shares with us some of Mark's most personal work." (Publisher's note)

Includes bibliographical references.

Wathey, John C.
The **illusion** of God's presence; the biological origins of spiritual longing. John C. Wathey. Prometheus Books 2016 445 p. (hardcover) $28   **204**
  1. God 2. Faith 3. Religion and science 4. Experience (Religion)
  5. Biology -- Religious aspects -- Christianity
  ISBN 1633880745; 9781633880740

LC 2015030319

In this book, "starting with a vivid narrative account of the life-threatening hike that triggered his own mystical experience, biologist John Wathey takes the reader on a scientific journey to find the sources of religious feeling and the illusion of God's presence. His book delves into the biological origins of this compelling feeling, attributing it to innate neural circuitry that evolved to promote the mother-child bond." (Publisher's note)

Includes bibliographical references and index

Winfrey, Oprah, 1954-
The **wisdom** of Sundays; life-changing insights from Super Soul conversations. Oprah Winfrey. St. Martin's Press 2017 240 p. $27.99   **204**
  1. Spiritual life 2. Self-improvement 3. Spiritual healing
  ISBN 125013806X; 9781250138064

LC 2017022445

This book, by Oprah Winfrey, "features selections from the most meaningful conversations between Oprah and some of today's most-admired thought-leaders. Visionaries like Tony Robbins, Arianna Huffington, and Shonda Rhimes share their lessons in finding purpose through mindfulness and intention . . . , and award-winning and bestselling writers like Cheryl Strayed, Elizabeth Gilbert, and Elizabeth Lesser explore the beauty of forgiveness and spirituality." (Publisher's note)

208 Sources

Three Testaments; Torah, Gospel, and Quran. edited by Brian Arthur Brown, foreword by Amir Hussain. Rowman & Littlefield Pub Inc 2014 (paperback) $29.95 **208**
1. Islam -- Relations 2. Judaism -- Relations 3. Christianity and other religions
ISBN 1442214937; 9781442214927; 9781442214934; 9781442214941
This book "brings together for the first time the text of the Torah, the New Testament, and the Quran, along with commentaries from notable religion scholars, to help readers explore the connections, as well as the points of departure, of the three Abrahamic traditions." (Publisher's note)

209 Sects and reform movements

Pearson, Joanne
★ **Belief** beyond boundaries; Wicca, Celtic spirituality and the new age. edited by Joanne Pearson. Ashgate 2002 339p il maps (Religion today) $94.95; pa $29.95 **209**
1. Wicca 2. Paganism 3. New Age movement
ISBN 0-7546-0744-5; 0-7546-0820-4 pa
LC 2001-53654
"Though somewhat academic in tone, this is a solid overview of several New Age spiritual movements." Libr J
Includes bibliographical references

210 Philosophy and theory of religion

Gutting, Gary
Talking God; Philosophers on Belief. by Gary Gutting. W W Norton & Co Inc 2016 240 p. (ebook) $50; (pbk.) $16.95 **210**
1. Religion -- Philosophy 2. Philosophy and religion 3. Religions
ISBN 9780393352825; 9780393352818
LC 2016023255
This book, by Gary Gutting, "offers new perspectives on religion, including the challenge to believers from evolution, cutting-edge physics and cosmology; arguments both for and against atheism; and meditations on the value of secular humanism and faith in the modern world. Experts offer insights on Islam, Buddhism, and Hinduism, as well as Judaism and Christianity." (Publisher's note)
"An exceptional introduction to the philosophical questions surrounding God and atheism." Kirkus

Huxley, Aldous
★ The **perennial** philosophy. Harper & Row 1945 312p hardcover o.p. pa $14 **210**
1. Philosophy and religion 2. Religion -- Philosophy
ISBN 0-06-057058-X pa
An anthology and commentary on Chinese, Latin, Greek, Catholic and Protestant mysticism
Includes bibliographical references

James, William
★ The **varieties** of religious experience; a study in human nature. introduction by Reinhold Niebuhr. Simon & Schuster 2004 398p pa $15 **210**
1. Mysticism 2. Conversion 3. Psychology 4. New Thought 5. Religious life 6. Spiritual healing 7. Religion -- Philosophy
ISBN 978-0-7432-5787-9; 0-7432-5787-1
LC 2004-42870
First published 1902 by Longman
"Based on material James had collected on the psychology and philosophy of religion for lectures at the University of Edinburgh in 1901 and 1902. The varieties of religious experience contains numerous descriptions of religious states of consciousness, which James presented from a pragmatic point of view." HarperCollins Reader's Ency of Am Lit. 2nd edition
Includes bibliographical references

211 Concepts of God

Armstrong, Karen
The **case** for God. Knopf 2009 406p $27.95 **211**
1. God 2. Apologetics 3. Christian life 4. Religious life
ISBN 978-0-307-26918-8
LC 2009-14044
"'Magisterial' is the adjective of choice to describe Armstrong's work; her usual confident sweep across times and cultures rises above the 'answer-the-atheists' tired angle to make a passionate footnoted argument for the human need for a God." Publ Wkly
Includes bibliographical references

Aslan, Reza, 1972-
God; a human history. Reza Aslan. Random House 2017 320 p. $28 **211**
1. God 2. Agnosticism 3. Christianity and other religions
ISBN 9780553394726
LC 2017034711
Author Reza Aslan "explores humanity's quest to make sense of the divine in this concise and fascinating history of our understanding of God. . . . This book is an attempt to get to the root of this humanizing impulse in order to develop a more universal spirituality. Whether you believe in one God, many gods, or no god at all, 'God: A Human History,' will challenge the way you think about the divine and its role in our everyday lives." (Publisher's note)
Includes bibliographical references and index

Berlinerblau, Jacques
How to be secular; a call to arms for religious freedom. Jacques Berlinerblau. Houghton Mifflin Harcourt 2012 xxix, 306 p.p $26.00 **211**
1. Humanism 2. Freedom of religion 3. Christianity -- United States 4. United States -- Religion 5. Secularism -- United States 6. Church and state -- United States 7. Freedom of religion -- United States
ISBN 0547473346; 9780547473345
LC 2012014226
Author Jacques Berlinerblau looks at secularism. "Arguing that the revival of religion in the United States since the 1970s has led to the ascent of the Christian Right and the crackup of secularism, the author cites examples of ways in which traditional boundaries have been breached, including the creation of the White House Office of Faith-based and Neighborhood Partnerships and frequent threats by elected officials to establish Christianity as the national religion." (Kirkus)
Includes bibliographical references (p. [212]-290) and index

Hazleton, Lesley, 1945-

Agnostic; a spirited manifesto. Lesley Hazleton. Riverhead 2016 224 p. (print) $26   **211**
1. Religion 2. Agnosticism
ISBN 1594634130; 9781594634130

LC 2016006449

Author Lesley Hazleton "gives voice to the case for agnosticism, breaks it free of its stereotypes as watered-down atheism or amorphous 'seeking,' and celebrates it as a reasoned, revealing, and sustaining stance toward life. Stepping over the lines imposed by rigid conviction, she draws on philosophy, theology, psychology, science, and more to explore, with curiosity and passion, the vital role of mystery in a deceptively information-rich world." (Publisher's note)

"This engaging and highly accessible read will satisfy those who puzzle over the idea of infinity, question theological "truth" or what death means for the mind and body, and who wish to delve deeper into our belief system." Library Journal

Kramnick, Isaac

Godless citizens in a godly republic; atheists in American public life. R. Laurence Moore and Isaac Kramnick. W W Norton & Co Inc 2018 236 p. (hardcover) $26.95   **211**
1. Church and state -- United States 2. Religion and politics -- United States 3. Atheists -- Political activity -- United States 4. Religion and state -- United States
ISBN 0393254968; 9780393254969

LC 2018001550

"As R. Laurence Moore and Isaac Kramnick demonstrate in their sharp and convincing work, avowed atheists were derided since the founding of the nation. . . . [They] lay out this fascinating history and the legal cases that have questioned religious supremacy. . . . The authors discuss these cases and more current ones, such as Burwell v. Hobby Lobby Stores, Inc., which address whether personal religious beliefs supersede secular ones." (Publisher's note)

"This work provides important historical insights into a contentious contemporary issue. Highly recommended for readers interested in history, law, and political science, as well as those seeking positive approaches to expanding religious liberty." LJ

Includes bibliographical references and index

Niose, David

Nonbeliever nation; the rise of secular Americans. David Niose. Palgrave Macmillan 2012 262 p. (hardcover) $27 **211**
1. Secularism -- United States 2. Religion and politics -- United States 3. Culture conflict -- United States
ISBN 023033895X; 9780230338951

LC 2011049323

This book, by David Niose, explores trends in non-religious observance in the United States. "Nearly one in five Americans are nonbelievers . . . and they are flexing their muscles like never before. . . . From gay marriage to education policy to contentious church-state battles . . . [the author] shows how . . . secular Americans . . . are mobilizing and forming groups all over the country . . . to challenge the exaltation of religion in American politics and public life." (Publisher's note)

Zuckerman, Phil

Living the Secular Life; New Answers to Old Questions. Phil Zuckerman. Penguin Group USA"‖"Penguin Press 2014 288 p. $25.95   **211**
1. Secularism 2. United States -- Religion 3. Secularism -- United States 4. United States -- United States
ISBN 1594205086; 9781594205088

LC 2014009785

This book by Phil Zuckerman, "reveals that, despite opinions to the contrary, nonreligious Americans possess a unique moral code that allows them to effectively navigate the complexities of modern life. Spiritual self-reliance, clear-eyed pragmatism, and an abiding faith in the Golden Rule to adjudicate moral decisions: these common principles are shared across secular society." (Publisher's note)

"Highly recommended for all readers, both religious and nonreligious, seeking a more accurate understanding of this ever-growing segment of the American population." LJ

Includes bibliographical references and index

212   Existence of God, ways of knowing God, attributes of God

Overman, Dean L.

A **case** for the existence of God. Rowman & Littlefield 2008 xxxii, 229p $24.95   **212**
1. God 2. Religion and science
ISBN 978-0-7425-6312-4; 0-7425-6312-X

LC 2008-21731

"Drawing on modern cosmology and information theory, Overman exposes fallacies that have infested skeptics' thinking since Hume and Kant. Clearer reasoning establishes an astonishing harmony between quantum physics and religious orthodoxy, so providing a credible defense for free will and moral judgment. Still, readers looking for certainty will not find it here: Overman acknowledges that the believer must make a leap of faith. . . . The intensely personal character of spiritual conversion emerges in the lives of the nine remarkable believers—including St. Augustine and Pascal, Dostoyevsky and Weil—whose testimonies resonate with passionate conviction. A book for readers willing to wrestle with the largest questions." Booklist

Includes bibliographical references

215   Science and religion

Barr, Stephen M.

★ **Modern** physics and ancient faith. University of Notre Dame Press 2003 312p il hardcover o.p. pa $18   **215**
1. Physics 2. Religion and science
ISBN 0-268-03471-0; 978-0-268-02198-6 pa; 0-268-02198-8 pa

LC 2002-151565

The author "argues that the great discoveries of modern physics are more compatible with the central teachings of Christianity and Judaism about God, the cosmos, and the human soul than with the atheistic viewpoint of scientific materialism." Publ Wkly

Includes bibliographical references

Ecklund, Elaine Howard

Science vs. religion; what scientists really think. Oxford University Press 2010 228p $27.95   **215**
1. Religion and science 2. Scientists -- Attitudes 3. Universities and colleges -- United States -- Faculty
ISBN 978-0-19-539298-2; 0-19-539298-1

LC 2009-34731

Ecklund's "outstanding research, articulately presented, and judicious recommendations make this a valuable work for all who care about the subject of science and religion." Libr J

Includes bibliographical references

220.3 Encyclopedias and topical dictionaries

Eerdmans dictionary of the Bible; David Noel Freedman, editor-in-chief; Allen C. Myers, associate editor; Astrid B. Beck, managing editor. Eerdmans 2000 xxxiii, 1425p il maps $45 **220.3**
1. Reference books 2. Bible (as subject) -- Dictionaries
ISBN 0-8028-2400-5
LC 00-56124
"Up-to-date, comprehensive, and well written, the EDB is highly recommended." Libr J
Includes bibliographical references

The **HarperCollins** Bible dictionary; Mark Allan Powell, general editior; with the Society of Bible Literature. 3rd edition HarperCollins 2011 xxiii, 1142 p.p illustrations, maps hbk $47.99 **220.3**
1. Bible -- Dictionaries
ISBN 0061469068; 9780061469060
LC 2010007897
First published 1985 with title: Harper's Bible Dictionary
"This volume usefully aids readers in understanding the Bible, while avoiding polemics and personal theories. It incorporates contributions from a wide spectrum of confessional and ideological positions. Updates include entries for all the deuterocanonical books, and their citation where relevant; entries on all the fauna/flora in the Bible; entries on important theological terms and words used in the Bible in a significant way; and entries treating the phenomena of everyday life in the biblical world." (Choice Reviews)
Includes bibliographical references and index

Oxford University Press

The **Oxford** companion to the Bible; edited by Bruce M. Metzger, Michael D. Coogan. Oxford Univ. Press 1993 xxi, 874p il map $70 **220.3**
1. Reference books 2. Bible (as subject) -- Dictionaries
ISBN 0-19-504645-5
LC 93-19315
"The many contributors read as a veritable who's who among biblical scholars. Although this companion is not meant to be an exhaustive reference, it is a highly reliable guide." Booklist

Zondervan illustrated Bible dictionary; [edited by] J.D. Douglas and Merrill C. Tenney; revised by Moises Silva. Zondervan 2011 1571 p. col. ill., maps $29.99 **220.3**
1. Bible -- Dictionaries
ISBN 9780310229834
LC 2010034210
This reference book "provides a visual . . . journey for anyone interested in learning more about the world of the Bible. Through the articles, sidebars, charts, maps, and full-color images included in this volume, the text of the Old and New Testaments [is enhanced]. . . . As a condensation of the Zondervan Pictorial Encyclopedia of the Bible, the information contained within this reference work is . . . biblically sound. The material is based completely on the NIV [New International Version] and cross-referenced to the King James Version, and it contains over 7,200 entries, 500 full-color photographs, charts, and illustrations, 75 full-color maps, and a Scripture index." (Publisher's note)
Includes bibliographical references.

220.5 Modern versions and translations

★ The **Bible**: Authorized King James Version; with an introduction and notes by Robert Carroll and Stephen Prickett. Oxford University Press 2008 lxxiv, 1039, 248, 445p il map (Oxford world's classics) pa $18.95 **220.5**
ISBN 978-0-19-953594-1
LC 2008-273825
This Oxford World's Classics version first published 1997
The authorized or King James Version originally published 1611.
Includes bibliographical references

Cruden, Alexander

★ **Cruden's** Complete concordance; with index to proper names and their meanings. edited by A.D. Adams, C.H. Irwin, S.A. Waters. Zondervan Pub. House 1968 803p (Zondervan classic reference series) $24.99; pa $8.99 **220.5**
1. Bible -- Concordances
ISBN 0-310-22920-0; 0-310-48971-7 pa
First edition 1737. Frequently revised
"The special value of this title is that Cruden provides an index to the Apocrypha. Note that some reprints of the work omit the Apocrypha in the concordance." Ref Sources for Small & Medium-sized Libr. 5th edition

Ferrell, Lori Anne

The **Bible** and the people. Yale University Press 2008 273p il map $32.50 **220.5**
1. Bible -- History
ISBN 978-0-300-11424-9
LC 2008-26769
"The Christian Bible is not only a physical object but also a delivery system for spiritual and secular ideas, according to cultural historian Ferrell. . . . Examining the English Bible collection at the Huntington Library, Ferrell discusses these Bibles' historical, political, and social impact on Christian belief and practice in Great Britain and America from the Middle Ages to the present. . . . Written for a general audience, this is an engaging and accessible overview of the history of the English Bible." Libr J
Includes bibliographical references

★ The **New** American Bible; translated from the original languages with critical use of all the ancient sources including the revised Psalms and the revised New Testament. authorized by the Board of Trustees of the Confraternity of Christian Doctrine and approved by the Administrative Committee Board of the National Conference of Catholic Bishops and the United States Catholic Conference. Oxford University Press 2006 xxiii, 1514p $39.99 **220.5**
ISBN 978-0-19-528904-6; 0-19-528904-8
First published 1970 by Kenedy
"Roman Catholic version based on modern English translations; replaces the Douay edition." N Y Public Libr Book of How & Where to Look It Up

★ The **new** Jerusalem Bible; [general editor: Henry Wansbrough] Doubleday 1985 2108p map $45; pa $29.95 **220.5**
ISBN 0-385-14264-1; 978-0-385-14264-9; 0-385-24833-4 pa; 978-0-385-24833-4 pa
LC 85-16070
First published in this format 1966 with title: The Jerusalem Bible

"Derives from the French version edited at the Dominican Ecole Biblique de Jerusalem and known as 'La Bible de Jerusalem.' The introductions and notes are 'a direct translation from the French, though revised and brought up to date in some places' but translation of the Biblical text goes back to the original languages." Guide to Ref Books. 11th edition

Poets of the Bible; from Solomon's Song of Songs to John's Revelation. edited and translated from the Hebrew and Greek by Willis Barnstone. W W Norton & Co Inc 2017 xix, 522 p.p (hardcover) $35   **220.5**
1. Bible. New Testament 2. Bible. Old Testament 3. Bible -- History of Biblical events -- Poetry
ISBN 0393243893; 9780393243901; 9780393243895
LC 2017016681

In this book author Willis Barnstone "restores the lyricism and power of the poets' voices in both the New and Old Testaments. In the Hebrew Bible we hear Solomon rhapsodize in Song of Songs, David chant in Psalms, God and Job debate in grand rhetoric, and prophet poet Isaiah plead for peace. Jesus speaks in wisdom verse in the Gospel, Paul is a philosopher of love, and John of Patmos roars majestically in Revelation, the Bible's epic poem." (Publisher's note)

"Thoughtful selections, a visually arresting presentation, and intriguing translations make these collected poems a valuable addition to biblical literature." Pub Wkly

Includes bibliographical references and index.

Ruden, Sarah
The **face** of water; a translator on beauty and meaning in the Bible. Sarah Ruden. Pantheon Books 2017 xxxviii, 232 p.p (hard cover: alk. paper) $26.95   **220.5**
1. Bible -- Translating 2. Bible -- Criticism, interpretation, etc 3. Bible. English -- Versions -- Authorized
ISBN 9780307908575; 9780307908568
LC 2016014872

In this book, author Sarah Ruden "brilliantly and elegantly explains and celebrates the Bible's writings. Singling out the most famous passages, such as the Genesis creation story, the Ten Commandments, the Lord's Prayer, and the Beatitudes, Ruden reexamines and retranslates from the Hebrew and Greek what has been obscured and misunderstood over time." (Publisher's note)

"This combination of casual ease and serious scholarship allows Ruden to bring fresh insights into even the most familiar stories and will make the book a true pleasure for anyone with an interest in translation or the Bible." Pub Wkly

Includes bibliographical references (pages [215]-218) and index.

Strong, James
The **strongest** Strong's exhaustive concordance of the Bible; 21st century ed, fully rev and corrected by John R. Kohlenberger III and James A. Swanson; Zondervan 2001 1742p maps $34.99   **220.5**
1. Bible -- Concordances
ISBN 0-310-23343-7
LC 2001-26577

A version of Strong's exhaustive concordance of the Bible originally published 1894

"Kohlenberger has teamed with James A. Swanson to produce a volume that cross-indexes a . . . database with exhaustive Hebrew and Greek dictionaries and adds Nave's Topical Bible Reference System (essentially a Bible dictionary with subjects, persons, places, and biblical books in alphabetic order). . . . Charts plot the chronology of events in

the Old and New Testament, miracles and parables of Jesus, and messianic prophecies. There is a harmony (parallels) of gospel stories, lists of biblical kings, weights and measures, Old Testament feasts, sacred days, sacrifices, and the major social concerns of the Mosaic Covenant. There is also a chart of the Hebrew Calendar. The work is based on the King James Version of the Bible and is generally conservative." Am Ref Books Annu, 2003

Suggs, M. Jack
The **Oxford** study Bible; Revised English Bible with the Apocrypha. edited by M. Jack Suggs, Katharine Doob Sakenfeld, James R. Mueller. Oxford University Press 1992 xxviii, 199, 1597p map hardcover o.p. pa $34.99   **220.5**
ISBN 0-19-529001-1; 0-19-529000-3 pa
LC 92-137886

A revised edition of The new English Bible, published 1970

An annotated version of the Revised English Bible. "This volume combines a cultural guide to the biblical world and an annotated Bible. Its notes feature the reflections of Protestant, Roman Catholic, and Jewish scholars." Publisher's note

220.6   Interpretation and criticism (Exegesis)

Loveday, Simon
The **Bible** for grown-ups; a new look at the good book. Simon Loveday. Icon Books 2017 xv, 285 p.p illustrations, maps (hardcover) $16.95   **220.6**
1. Bible -- Criticism, interpretation, etc.
ISBN 1785781316; 9781785781315

This book, by Simon Loveday, "neither requires, nor rejects, belief. It sets out to help intelligent adults make sense of the Bible--a book that is too large to swallow whole, yet too important in our history and culture to spit out. Why do the creation stories in Genesis contradict each other? Did the Exodus really happen? Was King David a historical figure? Why is Matthew's account of the birth of Jesus so different from Luke's? Why was St Paul so rude about St Peter?" (Publisher's note)

"After first setting aside belief, the late Loveday intelligently and successfully assesses the Bible in ways that are accessible and useful for those with open, inquiring minds." Pub Wkly

Includes bibliographical references (pages 267-275) and index.

Manser, Martin H.
Critical companion to the Bible; a literary reference. [by] Martin H. Manser; associate editors, David Barratt, Pieter J. Lalleman, Julius Steinberg. Facts On File, Inc. 2009 488p il (Facts on File library of world literature) $75   **220.6**
1. Bible as literature 2. Bible -- Criticism
ISBN 978-0-8160-7065-7
LC 2008-29257

"This reference provides an excellent introduction to not only just the literary but also the theological studies of the Bible through the ages." Booklist

Includes bibliographical references

Wray, T. J.
What the Bible really tells us; the essential guide to biblical literacy. Rowman & Littlefield Publishers 2011 249p $24.95; ebook $23.99   **220.6**
1. Bible -- Criticism
ISBN 978-0-7425-6253-0; 978-1-4422-1293-0 ebook
LC 2011011778

"Wray devotes a couple of introductory chapters to the biblical world and the tools and methods scholars use in their exegetical work. But her intention is to get people reading the Bible, not to offer an academic, verse-by-verse commentary. Subsequent chapters, therefore, explore what the Bible says about such issues as wealth, heaven, hell, sex, and the environment, dispelling many commonly held assumptions and pointing out where disagreements in interpretation lie along the way. Wray succeeds in sharing the wisdom of the Bible by making it accessible, interesting, and fun." Booklist

Includes bibliographical references

220.9 Geography, history, chronology, persons of Bible lands in Bible times

Currie, Robin

The **letter** and the scroll; what archaeology tells us about the Bible. [by] Robin Currie and Stephen Hyslop. National Geographic 2009 335p il map $40   **220.9**
   1. Bible (as subject) -- Antiquities
   ISBN 978-1-4262-0514-9

LC 2009-8572

"This gorgeous book . . . covering the people and events of the Bible, placed into their archaeological context, will delight and inform those who are interested in the Bible from a religious, cultural, or historical perspective. . . . [The book] investigates a variety of topics—such as cities, languages, luxury goods, wars, taxes, writings, and ancient art—through artifacts and archaeological evidence to provide an extensive background for the reader." Libr J

Includes bibliographical references

Curtis, Adrian

Oxford Bible atlas; edited by Adrian Curtis. 4th ed.; Oxford University Press 2007 229p il map $35   **220.9**
   1. Reference books 2. Bible -- Geography
   ISBN 0-19-100158-9; 978-0-19-100158-1
   First published 1962

This atlas includes "81 full-color illustrations as well as 27 maps—e.g., of Jerusalem and the Holy Land, the Middle East and the eastern Mediterranean lands—all with terrain modeling. The text is divided into four main sections: 'The Setting,' 'The Hebrew Bible,' 'The New Testament,' and 'Archaeology in Bible Lands.' . . . [This is] a handsome background resource for Bible study." Libr J

Includes bibliographical references

Kee, Howard Clark

The **Cambridge** companion to the Bible; Bruce Chilton, general editor; Howard Clark Kee . . . [et al.] 2nd ed; Cambridge University Press 2008 724p il $100; pa $34.99 **220.9**
   1. Bible -- History of Biblical events
   ISBN 978-0-521-86997-3; 978-0-521-69140-6 pa

LC 2008-270190

First published 1997

"This is an excellent, single-volume resource for serious students of the Bible. . . . The text is generally accessible; extensive maps and illustrations add to its popular appeal." Booklist [review of 1997 edition]

Includes bibliographical references

The **Oxford** history of the biblical world; edited by Michael D. Coogan. Oxford Univ. Press 1998 643p il maps $60; pa $19.95   **220.9**
   1. Ancient civilization 2. Bible -- History of biblical events

ISBN 0-19-508707-0; 0-19-513937-2 pa

LC 98-16042

"Organized chronologically, the essays explore the many cultures of ancient Canaan, Israel, Judea, and Palestine from 10,000 B.C.E. to the rise of Islam in the seventh century C.E. Illustrations, maps, charts, chronologies, and bibliographies enhance the uniformly well-written essays. But the strengths of the work are its currency and breadth of coverage and perspective." Libr J

Includes bibliographical references

Tischler, Nancy M.

Men and women of the Bible; a readers guide. Greenwood Press 2002 267p il $59.95   **220.9**
   1. Bible -- Biography
   ISBN 0-313-31714-3

LC 2002-75347

This resource provides "information on 100 biblical characters and their cultural significance in Western civilization. . . . Entries are arranged alphabetically from Aaron to Zephaniah, concisely written, and adhere to a uniform pattern. Subjects are listed by name with the addition of etymological information. A synopsis of the relevant biblical story follows, utilizing the King James version of the Bible. . . . The author also includes information on each person as a character in later works, including Western literature, legend, and painting." Booklist

Includes bibliographical references

221 Old Testament (Tanakh)

The **Jewish** Bible. The Jewish Publication Society 2008 291p il map (JPS guide) pa $22   **221**
   1. Bible -- O.T. -- Introductions
   ISBN 978-0-8276-0851-1; 0-8276-0851-9

LC 2008-10794

"One in a series of concise reference books on different aspects of Judaism, this includes a history of the Jewish scriptures, translations through the centuries, how to read the Bible, summaries of each book, and an extensive glossary." Univ Press Books for Public and Second Sch Libr, 2009

Includes bibliographical references

Kugel, James L.

How to read the Bible; a guide to scripture, then and now. Free Press 2007 819p il map $35   **221**
   1. Bible -- O.T. -- Criticism
   ISBN 978-0-7432-3586-0; 0-7432-3586-X

LC 2007-23466

"Kugel has written a wonderful book, one that lays bare the worlds both of modern biblical scholarship and of ancient biblical interpretation with wit and erudition." Commentary

Includes bibliographical references

221.92 Old Testament – Persons

Zornberg, Avivah Gottlieb, 1944-

Moses; A Human Life. Avivah Gottlieb Zornberg. Yale University Press 2016 240 p. (hardback: alk. paper) $25 **221.92**
   1. Bible. Old Testament
   ISBN 9780300209624

LC 2016941501

This book in the Jewish Lives series, by Avivah Gottlieb Zornberg, "offers a vivid and original portrait of the biblical Moses. Moses's vexing personality, his uncertain origins, and his turbulent relations with his own people are acutely explored by Zornberg, who sees this story, told and retold, as crucial not only to the biblical past but also to the future of Jewish history." (Publisher's note)

"A meaty, worthwhile biography by a great interpreter of Jewish texts." Kirkus

Includes bibliographical references (pages 195-210) and indexes.

222   Historical books of Old Testament

The **contemporary** Torah; a gender-sensitive adaptation of the JPS translation. revising editor, David E.S. Stein; consulting editors, Adele Berlin, Ellen Frankel, and Carol L. Meyers. Jewish Publication Society 2006 xlii, 412p $28   **222**
ISBN 0-8276-0796-2; 978-0-8276-0796-5

LC 2006-40608

A modern adaptation of the Jewish Publication Society's translation of the Torah. "In places where the ancient audience probably would not have construed gender as pertinent to the text's plain sense, the editors changed words into gender-neutral terms; where gender was probably understood to be at stake, they left the text as originally translated, or even introduced gendered language where none existed before. They made these changes regardless of whether words referred to God, angels, or human beings." Publisher's note

Feiler, Bruce

The **first** love story; Adam, Eve, and us. Bruce Feiler. Penguin Press 2017 306 p. illustrations (hardcover) $28 **222**
1. Love -- Biblical teaching
ISBN 9780698409958; 9781594206818

LC 2016043490

This book, by Bruce Feiler, is a "revelatory journey across four continents and 4,000 years exploring how Adam and Eve introduced the idea of love into the world, and how they continue to shape our deepest feelings about relationships, family, and togetherness. . . . [It] reminds us that even our most familiar stories still have the ability to surprise, inspire, and guide us today." (Publisher's note)

"Part travelogue, part historical survey, the book presents an impressive array of perspectives and a broad archive." Booklist

Includes bibliographical references (pages 275-296) and index.

★   The **five** books of Moses; a translation with commentary. {by} Robert Alter. Norton 2004 xlviii, 1064p map $39.95   **222**
ISBN 0-393-01955-1

LC 2004-14067

In "this new translation of the first five books of the Bible {Alter} . . . seeks to reproduce as faithfully as possible in standard English the nuances, literary devices, and metaphors of the original Hebrew text. In doing so, he aims to show where many modern translations (including the King James Bible) have failed to represent the original Hebrew's varied nuances. In his commentary, found in the introductions to each book and on many individual verses, Alter expounds the theological meaning of the text's narrative in its larger biblical context." Libr J

Includes bibliographical references

Kass, Leon

The **beginning** of wisdom; reading Genesis. {by} Leon R. Kass. Free Press 2003 576p $35   **222**
1. Bible -- O.T. -- Genesis -- Criticism

ISBN 0-7432-4299-8

LC 2002-45593

The author "sees Genesis as a text that offers wisdom about the nature of man and how we ought to live, while it also calls for interpretation, reflection, and judgment. . . . Kass presents many enlightening insights, the result of his attempts to understand the text on its own terms and relating it to contemporary concerns, especially tradition and parenthood. While not everyone will agree with his interpretations, which tend to the conservative, Kass offers much to be pondered by thoughtful readers, both academics and, especially, educated laypeople." Libr J

Includes bibliographical references

Moyers, Bill

Genesis: a living conversation. Doubleday 1996 361p il hardcover o.p. pa $22.95   **222**
1. Bible -- O.T. -- Genesis -- Criticism
ISBN 0-385-49043-7 pa

LC 96-15318

Companion volume to the PBS series led by Bill Moyers in which writers and religious thinkers discussed episodes from the first book of the Bible. Among the participants are Burton Visotzky, a rabbi who initiated the conversations which gave rise to the series, "Elaine Pagels, Karen Armstrong, . . . John Barth, and Oscar Hijuelos. The book is divided by biblical tale (Adam and Eve, Cain and Abel, the blinding of Isaac) with five or six of the participants discussing the moral, literary, and personal meanings of the stories." Booklist

★   The **Torah**: the five books of Moses; a new translation of the Holy Scriptures according to the Masoretic text; first section. Jewish Publication Society 1963 393p $20; pa $15   **222**
ISBN 0-8276-0015-1; 0-8276-0680-X pa

This "translation of Genesis, Exodus, Leviticus, Numbers, and Deuteronomy was prepared . . . to present a version of the Bible that takes into account modern insights and knowledge of ancient times. . . . Of chief value to persons of the Jewish religion but of interest to Bible scholars of any religion." Booklist

223   Poetic books of Old Testament

Kushner, Harold S., 1935-

The **book** of Job; when bad things happened to a good person. Harold S. Kushner. Nextbook: Schocken 2012 201 p. $24   **223**
1. God 2. Suffering -- Religious aspects 3. Bible. O.T. Job -- Commentaries 4. Suffering -- Religious aspects -- Judaism
ISBN 0805242929; 9780805242928

LC 2011051531

This book by Harold S. Kushner presents a "guide to that most fascinating of biblical texts, the book of Job, and what it can teach us about living in a troubled world. Kushner examines the questions raised by Job's experience, questions that have challenged wisdom seekers and worshippers for centuries. What kind of God permits such bad things to happen to good people? Why does God test loyal followers? Can a truly good God be all-powerful?" (Publisher's note)

225   New Testament

Borg, Marcus J., 1942-2015

Evolution of the Word; reading the New Testament in the order it was written. Marcus J. Borg. 1st ed. HarperOne 2012

viii, 608 p.p $29.99 **225**

1. Bible. New Testament 2. Bible. N.T. -- Chronology 3. Bible. N.T. -- Criticism, interpretation, etc

ISBN 9780062082121; 0062082108; 9780062082107

LC 2012001947

This New Testament with commentary, edited by Marcus J. Borg, changes "the order of the New Testament, . . . putting the books in . . . the order in which they were written. By doing so, [he] allows us to read these documents in their historical context. . . . Borg offers . . . introductions for each book so that as we read through these biblical documents . . . we see afresh what concerns and pressures shaped this movement as it evolved into a new religion." (Publisher's note)

Includes bibliographical references.

Brown, Raymond Edward

An **introduction** to the New Testament; by Raymond E. Brown. Yale University Press 1997 xxxviii, 878p map (Anchor Bible reference library) $55 **225**

1. Bible -- N.T. -- Criticism

ISBN 978-0-300-14016-3; 0-300-14016-9

A reissue of the title first published 1997 by Doubleday

Brown's book "culminates his life's work and synthesizes the best of his generation's historical-critical scholarship clearly and cogently for beginners and advanced students alike." N Y Times Book Rev

225.9 Geography, history, chronology, persons of New Testament lands in New Testament times

Ruden, Sarah

Paul among the people; the Apostle reinterpreted and reimagined in his own time. Pantheon Books 2010 214p $25; ebook $25 **225.9**

1. Saints 2. Apostles 3. Writers on religion 4. Bible -- N.T. -- Epistles of Paul -- Criticism

ISBN 978-0-375-42501-1; 978-0-307-37902-3 ebook

LC 2009-20969

"In 'reimagining' Paul with the aid of her intimate knowledge of classical literature, Ruden hasn't only helped us to better understand him and his message in the context of his time (as indispensable as that service is). She has also brought Paul to us, to our time. . . . In an uncanny way, her book is animated by the apostle's style: his urgency, his argumentative agility, his bluntness, his exasperation, his vision of great felicity." Natl Rev

Includes bibliographical references

225.92

Wright, N. T. (Nicholas Thomas), 1948-

Paul; a biography. N.T. Wright. HarperOne 2018 xiii, 464 p.p maps (hardcover) $29.99 **225.92**

1. Christian saints -- Biography 2. Christianity

ISBN 9780062198273; 9780061730580

LC 2017027846

In this biography, "author N. T. Wright offers a radical look at the apostle Paul, illuminating the humanity and remarkable achievements of this intellectual who invented Christian theology--transforming a faith and changing the world. . . . 'Paul' is a compelling modern biography that reveals the apostle's greater role in Christian history . . . and celebrates his stature as one of the most effective and influential intellectuals in human history." (Publisher's note)

"A very human Paul, brought to life by an experienced teacher and pastor—an excellent introduction for general readers." Kirkus

Includes bibliographical references (pages 435-446) and indexes.

226 Gospels and Acts

Kloppenborg, John S.

Q, the earliest Gospel; an introduction to the original stories and sayings of Jesus. Westminster John Knox Press 2008 170p il pa $19.95 **226**

1. Q hypothesis (Synoptics criticism)

ISBN 978-0-664-23222-1; 0-664-23222-1

LC 2008-8394

The author is an "authority on the Q Gospel, a 'sayings gospel' that is thought to be a source (from the German Quelle for source) for the Gospels of Matthew and Luke. No copy of Q has been found, but scholars have recreated it through analysis of the three synoptic Gospels, looking for common elements and focusing on the sayings of Jesus. This book is a succinct introduction to Q, addressing questions about its composition and importance. . . . A complete reconstruction of Q is included as well as notes and a bibliography." Libr J

226.2 Specific Gospels

Spong, John Shelby

Biblical literalism; a gentile heresy: a journey into a new Christianity through the doorway of Matthew's gospel. John Shelby Spong. HarperOne 2016 416 p. (hardcover) $26.99 **226.2**

1. Bible 2. Judaism 3. Bible. Matthew -- Criticism, interpretation, etc

ISBN 9780062362308; 9780062362315; 0062362313

LC 2015018099

This book, by John Shelby Spong, "explores the Bible's literary and liturgical roots—its grounding in Jewish culture, symbols, icons, and storytelling tradition—to explain how the events of Jesus' life, including the virgin birth, the miracles, the details of the passion story, and the resurrection and ascension, would have been understood by both the Jewish authors of the various gospels and by the Jewish audiences for which they were originally written." (Publisher's note)

"A worthwhile read for the progressive layperson concerned with living out one's faith and applying the Bible as a touchstone." Library Journal

226.3 Mark

Bible/N.T./Gospels

The **three** Gospels; {by} Reynolds Price. Scribner 1996 288p $23; pa $13 **226.3**

ISBN 0-684-80336-4; 0-684-83281-X pa

LC 95-39948

"Although there is so much to appreciate in these commentaries and in the translated texts, the best part of the book . . . is left to last: Price's own joyously written account of Jesus' life." Booklist

227   Epistles

Borg, Marcus J.

The **first** Paul; reclaiming the radical visionary behind the Church's conservative icon. [by] Marcus J. Borg, John Dominic Crossan. HarperOne 2009 230p $24.99; pa $13.99   **227**
1. Saints 2. Apostles 3. Writers on religion 4. Bible -- N.T. -- Epistles of Paul -- Criticism
ISBN 978-0-06-143072-5; 0-06-143072-2; 978-0-06-143073-2 pa; 0-06-143073-0 pa
                     LC 2009-004881

"The great epistolary apostle is revealed as neither anti-Semitic, anti-sex, nor misogynist, but a preacher of social and political equality." Booklist

Includes bibliographical references

229   Apocrypha, pseudepigrapha, intertestamental works

★ The **Apocrypha**; new revised standard version. Cambridge University Press 1993 262p pa $14.99   **229**
ISBN 978-0-521-50776-9; 0-521-50776-6

"These books form part of the sacred literature of the Alexandrian Jews. . . . Some of them form an historical link between the Old and New Testament, others have a linguistic value in connexion with the Hellenistic phraseology of the latter. The narratives of Apocrypha are partly historical records, and partly allegorical." Oxford Univ. Press

Pagels, Elaine H.

★ **Beyond** belief; the secret Gospel of Thomas. {by} Elaine Pagels. Random House 2003 241p $26.95   **229**
1. Christianity 2. Gospel of Thomas 3. Bible -- N.T. -- John -- Criticism
ISBN 0-375-50156-8
                     LC 2002-36840

"Even those who possess only a nodding acquaintance with Gnostic writings will find themselves stimulated by the author's arguments and perhaps transformed by her conclusions. A fresh and exciting work of theology and spirituality." Booklist

Includes bibliographical references

230   Christianity

Christian reconstruction; R.J. Rushdoony and American religious conservatism. Michael J. McVicar. University of North Carolina Press 2015 326 p.   **230**
1. Dominion theology 2. United States -- Church history 3. Christian conservatism -- United States 4. Conservatism -- Religious aspects -- Christianity
ISBN 9781469622743
                     LC 2014035500

Includes bibliographical references and index

Dark, David

Life's too short to pretend you're not religious; David Dark. InterVarsity Press 2016 192 p. (hardcover: alk. paper) $20 **230**
1. Apologetics 2. Philosophical theology
ISBN 9780830844463
                     LC 2015036062

In this book, author David Dark "persuasively argues that the fact of religion is the fact of relationship. It's the shape our love takes, the lived witness of everything we're up to for better or worse, because witness knows no division. Looking hard at our weird religious background (Dark maintains we all have one) can bring the actual content of our everyday existence—the good, the bad and the glaringly inconsistent—to fuller consciousness." (Publisher's note)

"Dark's argument couched in a memoir is a persuasive, well-grounded case for religion's place in modern society." Pub Wkly

Includes bibliographical references

Edman, Elizabeth M., 1962-

Queer virtue; what LGBTQ people know about life and love and how it can revitalize Christianity. The Reverend Elizabeth M. Edman. Beacon Press 2016 216 p. (hardcover: alk. paper) $25.95   **230**
1. Christianity 2. Queer theory 3. Queer theology 4. Sex -- Religious aspects -- Christianity
ISBN 0807061344; 9780807061343
                     LC 2015027701

In this book, by Elizabeth M. Edman, the author, "an openly lesbian Episcopal priest and professional advocate for LGBTQ justice, . . . posits that Christianity, at its scriptural core, incessantly challenges its adherents to rupture false binaries, to 'queer' lines that pit people against one another. . . . Edman proposes that queer experience be celebrated as inherently valuable, ethically virtuous, and illuminating the sacred." (Publisher's note)

"An intellectual and provocative perspective challenging Christians and others to reconsider the confines of spiritual interconnection, harmony, and progressive inclusion in modern religion." Kirkus

Includes bibliographical references

Harrington, Joel F.

Dangerous mystic; Meister Eckhart's path to the God within. Joel F. Harrington. Penguin Group USA 2018 384 p. $30   **230**
1. Mysticism 2. Theologians -- Biography
ISBN 1101981563; 9781101981566

This book, by Joel F. Harrington, recounts the "life and times of the 14th century German spiritual leader Meister Eckhart, whose theory of a personal path to the divine inspired thinkers from Jean Paul Sartre to Thomas Merton, and most recently, Eckhart Tolle. Meister Eckhart was a medieval Christian mystic whose wisdom powerfully appeals to seekers seven centuries after his death." (Publisher's note)

Holifield, E. Brooks

★ **Theology** in America; Christian thought from the age of the Puritans to the Civil War. Yale University Press 2003 617p hardcover o.p. pa $23   **230**
1. Doctrinal theology
ISBN 0-300-09574-0; 978-0-300-10765-4 pa; 0-300-10765-X pa
                     LC 2003-42289

"In this majestic achievement, Holifield . . . provides a first-rate, richly evocative and unrivaled history of theology in America. . . . This masterfully narrated, splendid book will become the definitive study of the development of American theology." Publ Wkly

Includes bibliographical references

Kung, Hans

Great Christian thinkers. Continuum 1994 235p hardcover o.p. pa $19.95   **230**
1. Saints 2. Bishops 3. Apostles 4. Theology 5. Theologians 6. Philosophers 7. Social reformers 8. Religious leaders 9. Writers on religion

ISBN 0-8264-0848-6 pa

LC 94-883

The author "attempts a new approach to the introduction-to-theology genre by critically tracing the developing thought of key, usually 'paradigm-shifting,' theologians (Paul, Origen, Augustine, Aquinas, Luther, Schleiermacher, and Karl Barth) in relation to their social, intellectual, and religious environment. He explores the significance of their life and work for the Christian world in an interesting, quite understandable manner." Libr J

Includes bibliographical references

Lewis, C. S (Clive Staples), 1898-1963

★ **Mere** Christianity; a revised and amplified edition, with a new introduction, of the three books, Broadcast talks, Christian behaviour, and Beyond personality. HarperSanFrancisco 2001 xx, 227p $19.95; pa $10 **230**
    1. Christian philosophy
    ISBN 0-06-065288-8; 0-06-065292-6 pa

LC 00-49862

First published 1952

This omnibus edition includes most of C. S. Lewis' writings on Christian theology and moral philosophy
    Includes bibliographical references

Moore, Russell

Onward; engaging the culture without losing the gospel. Russell D. Moore. B & H Books 2015 224 p. $24.99 **230**
    1. Culture 2. Christianity
    ISBN 1433686171; 9781433686177

Author Russell D. Moore suggests "as the culture changes all around us, it is no longer possible to pretend that we are a Moral Majority. That may be bad news for America, but it can be good news for the church. What's needed now, in shifting times, is neither a doubling-down on the status quo nor a pullback into isolation. Instead, we need a church that speaks to social and political issues with a bigger vision in mind: that of the gospel of Jesus Christ." (Publisher's note)

"Mainline Christian readers will wonder whether this is old wine in new bottles, but Moore may be pointing the way for a new guard, as the Christian Right ages and loses key cultural battles. This important book is sure to provoke interesting discussions among many different kinds of Christians." Pub Wkly

Oxford companion to Christian thought; edited by Adrian Hastings {et al.} Oxford Univ. Press 2000 xxviii, 777p $75 **230**
    1. Reference books 2. Theology -- Dictionaries
    ISBN 0-19-860024-0

LC 2001-267818

This volume focuses "on the movement of ideas among Christians. The articles (more than 500) by 268 scholars (mostly British) range in length from half a column . . . to seven pages. . . . They broadly cover the themes . . . persons . . . places . . . and historical periods . . . that characterize Christian thought." Choice
    Includes bibliographical references

231 Christian doctrinal theology

Bass, Diana Butler

Grounded; finding God in the world--a spiritual revolution. Diana Butler Bass. HarperOne 2015 336 p. (hardcover) $26.99 **231**

    1. God -- Christianity 2. Christianity -- Spiritual life 3. God (Christianity) 4. Christianity -- 21st century 5. Spirituality -- Christianity
    ISBN 0062328549; 9780062328540; 9780062328564

LC 2015018071

This book, by Diana Butler Bass, argues "that what appears to be a decline [in religion] actually signals a major transformation in how people understand and experience God. The distant God of conventional religion has given way to a more intimate sense of the sacred that is with us in the world. This shift . . . is at the heart of a spiritual revolution that surrounds us – and that is challenging not only religious institutions but political and social ones as well." (Publisher's note)

"It's a deeply theological book, but also a practical one; a book that causes one to ponder the spiritual implications of farmers' markets in altogether new ways." Booklist

Cairns, Scott

The **end** of suffering; finding purpose in pain. Paraclete Press 2009 126p pa $15.99 **231**
    1. Suffering
    ISBN 978-1-55725-563-1; 1-55725-563-6

LC 2009-18728

The author "offers a profoundly touching and deeply considered treatment of the notion of suffering, especially grief, in a Christian's life. For Cairns, suffering is not about the presence of evil; instead, it provides occasions where God can be known more intimately. . . . Eloquent in its simplicity, Cairns's brief book is a superb treatment of the thorny issues of suffering and grief." Libr J

Includes bibliographical references

231.7 Relation to the world

Lewis, C. S (Clive Staples), 1898-1963

Miracles; a preliminary study. HarperSanFrancisco 2001 294p pa $13.95 **231.7**
    1. Miracles
    ISBN 0-06-065301-9; 978-0-06-065301-9

LC 00-49863

First published 1947 by Macmillan

"Mr. Lewis casts his net fairly wide and, under the guise of a book on miracles, offers a rational justification both of theism and of doctrinal Christianity." Times Lit Suppl

McKnight, Scot

Kingdom conspiracy; returning to the radical mission of the local church. Scot McKnight. Brazos Press 2014 304 p. (pbk.) $21.99 **231.7**
    1. Church 2. Church work 3. Pastoral theology 4. Kingdom of God 5. Mission of the church
    ISBN 1587433605; 9781587433603

LC 2014015580

This book, by Scot McKnight, "defines the biblical concept of kingdom, offering a thorough corrective and vision for the contemporary church. The most important articulation of kingdom was that of Jesus, who contended that the kingdom was in some sense present and in some sense in the future. . . . McKnight explains that kingdom mission is local church mission and that the present-day fetish with influencing society, culture, and politics distracts us from the mission of God." (Publisher's note)

"This is a must-read for church leaders today." Pub Wkly
    Includes bibliographical references and index

Panagore, Peter Baldwin

Heaven Is Beautiful; How Dying Taught Me That Death Is Just the Beginning. Peter Baldwin Panagore. Red Wheel/Weiser 2015 256 p. illustrations $16.95   **231.7**

1. Spiritual life 2. Near-death experiences

ISBN 1571747346; 9781571747341

In this book, author Peter Baldwin Panagore "combines the thrills of a wilderness adventure with the awe inspiring elements of a paranormal novel.In March of 1980, . . . Panagore went ice climbing on the world-famous Lower Weeping Wall . . . Alberta, Canada. He died on the side of that mountain. He experienced hell, forgiveness, and unconditional love. Heaven was beautiful.Panagores near death experience (NDE) changed his life and resulted in an intense spiritual journey." (Publisher's note)

"Readers who have a fascination with near-death experiences and mysticism will be drawn into Panagore's remembrances of dying on the side of that mountain and the unexplainable feelings he encountered, and may find comfort in his assurance that death is not to be feared." Pub Wkly

Winner, Lauren F.

Wearing God; clothing, laughter, fire, and other overlooked ways of meeting God. Lauren F. Winner. HarperOne 2015 304 p. (hardcover) $24.99   **231.7**

1. Christian life 2. Spiritual life 3. Image of God 4. Spirituality -- Christianity 5. Spiritual life -- Christianity 6. Christian women -- Religious life

ISBN 006176812X; 9780061768125; 9780061768132

LC 2015001455

In this book, author Lauren F. Winner presents "this exploration of little known--and, so, little used--biblical metaphors for God, metaphors which can open new doorways for our lives and spiritualities. . . . Lauren Winner gathers a number of lesser-known tropes, reflecting on how they work biblically and culturally, and reveals how they can deepen our spiritual lives." (Publisher's note)

"Winner's honest, charming reflections stir the imagination and invite the reader to explore not just the metaphors she has chosen, but the treasure trove the Bible provides. Prayers and quotations promote further contemplation." Pub Wkly

Includes bibliographical references and index

Wintz, Jack

Will I see my dog in heaven? God's saving love for the whole family of creation. Paraclete Press 2009 153p pa $14.99   **231.7**

1. Future life 2. Animals -- Religious aspects

ISBN 978-1-55725-568-6

LC 2009-259

The author, a Franciscan friar, argues that "God's promise of a new creation at the end of time extends to the animal companions we have known and loved in this life. . . . Strongly recommended." Libr J

Includes bibliographical references

Woodward, Kenneth L.

The **book** of miracles; the meaning of the miracle stories in Christianity, Judaism, Buddhism, Hinduism, Islam. Simon & Schuster 2000 429p hardcover o.p. pa $16   **231.7**

1. Miracles

ISBN 0-7432-0029-2 pa

LC 99-88083

"A great resource for studies in comparative religions and interfaith dialog." Libr J

Includes bibliographical references

232   Jesus Christ and his family

Blum, Edward J.

★ The **color** of Christ; the Son of God and the saga of race in America. Edward J. Blum and Paul Harvey. University of North Carolina Press 2012 340 p. ill. $32.5   **232**

1. Racism 2. African Americans -- Religion 3. United States -- Church history 4. Racism -- United States 5. Indians of North America -- Religion 6. Racism -- Religious aspects -- Christianity

ISBN 0807835722; 9780807835722

LC 2012004088

This book, by Edward J. Blum and Paul Harvey, discusses Christianity and racism in the U.S., discussing "how, in a country founded by Puritans who destroyed depictions of Jesus, Americans came to believe in the whiteness of Christ. Some envisioned a white Christ who would sanctify the exploitation of Native Americans and African Americans and bless imperial expansion. Many others gazed at a messiah, not necessarily white, who was willing and able to confront white supremacy." (Publisher's note)

Includes bibliographical references (p. [283]-325) and index

Gordon, Mary

Reading Jesus; a writer's encounter with the Gospels. Pantheon Books 2009 205p $24.95   **232**

1. Bible -- N.T. -- Gospels -- Criticism

ISBN 978-0-375-42457-1

LC 2009-04975

Gordon "examines her faith by closely reading, in a kind of literary lectio divina (sacred reading), the four Christian gospels that recount the life of Christ. The accounts by evangelists Matthew, Mark, Luke and John of the life of Jesus have a common subject and amazingly different treatments. Gordon tackles the power and puzzle of the Christian gospels with measure and imagination, providing welcome relief for those left cold by scholarly or fundamentalist parsing." Publ Wkly

232.9   Family and life of Jesus

Benedict XVI, Pope, 1927-

Jesus of Nazareth. part two; Holy week, from the entrance into Jerusalem to the Resurrection. by Joseph Ratzinger, Pope Benedict XVI. Ignatius Press 2011 362p $24.95   **232.9**

1. Holy Week 2. Biography, Individual 3. Bible -- N.T. -- Gospels -- Criticism 4. Bible -- N.T. -- Gospels -- Criticism, interpretation, etc.

ISBN 978-1-58617-500-9; 1-58617-500-9

This is "the second volume in [the author's] 'Jesus of Nazareth' series. . . . [This book] is a worthy contribution to the field not only because it was written by a pope, but also because it combines solid scholarship with deep spirituality. As such it joins the Jesus of history to the Christ of faith in an accessible narrative. This volume explores the drama of Holy Week. . . . The focus is on the meaning of the events, with a strong reiteration of recent church teaching against imputing guilt for Jesus' death to the Jews of that time or now." Publ Wkly

Fredriksen, Paula

Jesus of Nazareth, King of the Jews; a Jewish life and the emergence of Christianity. Knopf 1999 327p hardcover o.p. pa $14   **232.9**

ISBN 0-679-76746-0 pa

LC 99-31054

"To Fredriksen, Jesus was an observant Jew immersed in a context bounded by Galilee and Jerusalem. He was crucified as an imperial Roman deterrent to unruly inhabitants of a region prone to rebellion, and the emergence of Christianity is a work of creative theological reinterpretation as much as of historical memory." Booklist

Includes bibliographical references

Girzone, Joseph F.

A **portrait** of Jesus. Doubleday 1998 179p il hardcover o.p. pa $11.95 **232.9**
1. Christian life
ISBN 0-385-48477-1 pa

LC 98-15618

"This is popular liberal Catholic theology, more filled with forgiveness and fellowship than shaming and hierarchy. Many a non-Catholic and even non-Christian may embrace it, too." Booklist

Meier, John P.

A **marginal** Jew; rethinking the historical Jesus. Doubleday 1991 3v maps (Anchor Bible reference library) v1 $45; v2 $42.50; v3 $45 **232.9**
ISBN 0-385-26425-9 v1; 0-385-46992-6 v2; 0-385-46993-4 v3
LC 91-10538

The first three volumes in a projected series of four devoted to an examination of the historical Jesus and his Jewish environment

The author "summarizes the first two volumes of A Marginal Jew and forecasts the next while meticulously documenting his understanding of the relations between the historical Jesus, his historical companions, and his historical competitors—Pharisees, Sadduccees, Essenes, and others. . . . The only thing common about Meier's project is fascination with the character of Jesus. Those who share that will find this dense, academic work worth their effort." Booklist {review of volume 3}

Includes bibliographical references

Pelikan, Jaroslav Jan

The **illustrated** Jesus through the centuries. Yale Univ. Press 1997 254p il $25 **232.9**
ISBN 0-300-07268-6

LC 97-7360

Companion volume to Mary through the centuries

In this revision of Jesus through the centuries (1985) the author "has abridged the text and turns to illustrations to convey his interpretations. . . . Very beautiful and very appealing for the general reader, this edition by no means replaces the scholarship and documentation of the first; those notations and references are missing in the illustrated edition. However, the illustrations enhance this interesting and insightful text." Libr J

Wilson, A. N.

Jesus. Norton 1992 269p $22.95 **232.9**
ISBN 0-393-03087-3

LC 92-37046

The author attempts to understand Jesus as a historical figure and ethical teacher within the context of first-century Judaism

Includes bibliographical references

232.91 Mary, mother of Jesus

Pelikan, Jaroslav Jan

Mary through the centuries; her place in the history of culture. Yale Univ. Press 1996 267p il $40; pa $14.95 **232.91**
1. Saints

ISBN 0-300-06951-0; 0-300-07661-4 pa

LC 96-24726

Companion volume to The illustrated Jesus through the centuries

"Although volumes have been written about the Virgin Mary from a wide variety of perspectives, it is rare to find a scholarly work that is easily accessible to the general, educated reader." Choice

Includes bibliographical references

232.96 Passion and death of Jesus

Wright, N. T. (Nicholas Thomas), 1948-

The **day** the revolution began; Reconsidering the Meaning of Jesus's Crucifixion. N.T. Wright. HarperOne 2016 440 p. (ebook) $27.99; (hardcover) $28.99 **232.96**
1. Salvation 2. Theology of the cross 3. Salvation -- Christianity
ISBN 9780062334404; 9780062334381

LC 2016028318

In this book, author N.T. Wright "contemplates the central event at the heart of the Christian faith—Jesus' crucifixion—arguing that the Protestant Reformation did not go far enough in transforming our understanding of its meaning. . . . Wright argues that Jesus' death on the cross was not only to absolve us of our sins; it was actually the beginning of a revolution commissioning the Christian faithful to a new vocation—a royal priesthood responsible for restoring and reconciling all of God's creation." (Publisher's note)

"Although demanding reading, Wright's bracing and thought-provoking exegesis should inform and encourage everyone concerned with Christianity's continuing vitality." Booklist

233 Humankind

Jacobs, Alan

Original sin; a cultural history. HarperOne 2008 286p $24.95; pa $14.99 **233**
1. Sin
ISBN 978-0-06-078340-2; 0-06-078340-0; 978-0-06-087257-1 pa; 0-06-087257-8 pa

LC 2008-06582

This is "a playful, wide-ranging, erudite meditation on the nagging question of whether human beings enter the world predisposed to evil and sinfulness. . . . Original Sin has a great deal to offer both the general reader and those already well versed in this most controversial of theological arenas." America

Includes bibliographical references

Kierkegaard, Søren, 1813-1855

The **concept** of anxiety; a simple psychologically oriented deliberation in view of the dogmatic problem of hereditary sin. Soren Kierkegaard; edited and translated with introduction and notes by Alastair Hannay. Liveright Publishing Corporation 2014 288 p. (hardcover) $27.95 **233**
1. Sin 2. Anxiety 3. Psychology of religion 4. Psychology, Religious 5. Anxiety -- Religious aspects -- Christianity
ISBN 0871407191; 9780871407191

LC 2013037399

In this book, author Soren Kierkegaard "describes the nature and forms of anxiety, placing the domain of anxiety within the mental-emotional states of human existence that precede the qualitative leap of faith to the spiritual state of Christianity. It is through anxiety that the self becomes aware of its dialectical relation between the finite and the infinite, the temporal and the eternal." (Publisher's note)

"Almost as valuable as the translation is Hannay's introduction in which he provides the background necessary to grapple with Kierkegaard and a heartfelt argument for the value of studying this fountainhead of existentialism in general and Anxiety in particular." LJ

Includes bibliographical references

233.14   Original sin and fall

Greenblatt, Stephen, 1943-

★ The **rise** and fall of Adam and Eve; Stephen Greenblatt. W W Norton & Co Inc 2017 419 p. illustrations (hardcover) $27.95   **233.14**
1. Eden 2. Fall of man 3. Anthropology
ISBN 9780393634587; 9780393240801; 0393240800
LC 2017014743

This book, by Stephen Greenblatt, "explores the enduring story of humanity's first parents. Comprising only a few ancient verses, the story of Adam and Eve has served as a mirror in which we seem to glimpse the whole, long history of our fears and desires, as both a hymn to human responsibility and a dark fable about human wretchedness." (Publisher's note)

"Greenblatt has shaped an enjoyable and well-paced narrative that effectively draws from many disciplines." LJ

Includes bibliographical references (pages [325]-391) and index.

234   Salvation and grace

Carter, Jimmy, 1924-

Faith; a journey for all. Jimmy Carter. Simon & Schuster 2018 192 p. (hardcover: alk. paper) $25.99   **234**
1. Faith 2. Christianity 3. Christianity and culture 4. History -- Religious aspects -- Christianity
ISBN 9781501184413; 9781501184437
LC 2018003986

In this book, former U.S. President Jimmy Carter contemplates how faith has sustained him in happiness and disappointment. He considers how we may find it in our own lives. . . . As President Carter examines faith's many meanings, he describes how to accept it, live it, how to doubt and find faith again. A serious and moving reflection from one of America's most admired and respected citizens." (Publisher's note)

Eldredge, John

All things new; heaven, earth, and the restoration of everything you love. John Eldredge. Thomas Nelson 2017 xii, 224 p.p $24.99   **234**
1. Heaven 2. Paradise 3. Salvation 4. Redemption 5. Heaven -- Christianity
ISBN 0718037995; 9780718037994
LC 2017011696

Includes bibliographical references

Strobel, Lee

The **Case** for Grace; A Journalist Explores the Evidence of Transformed Lives. Lee Stroble. Harpercollins Christian Pub 2015 240 p. $22.99   **234**
1. God 2. Grace (Theology)
ISBN 0310259177; 9780310259176

Author Lee Strobel "draws upon his own journey from atheism to Christianity to explore the depth and breadth of God's redeeming love

for spiritually wayward people. He travels thousands of miles to capture the inspiring stories of everyday people whose values have been radically changed and who have discovered the 'how' and 'why' behind God's amazing grace." (Publisher's note)

"This eloquent and honest book should appeal to those who have found grace, as well as those seeking it." Pub Wkly

234.5   Repentance and forgiveness

Teresa, Mother, Saint, 1910-1997.

A **call** to mercy; Mother Teresa; edited and with a preface and introduction by Brian Kolodiejchuk, MC. Image 2016 xx, 364 p.p (ebook) $65; (hardcover) $25   **234.5**
1. Corporal works of mercy 2. Spiritual works of mercy 3. Catholic Church -- Doctrines 4. Mercy
ISBN 0451498208; 9780451498212; 9780451498205
LC 2016288106

This book "offers Mother Teresa's profound yet accessible wisdom on how we can show mercy and compassion in our day-to-day lives. . . . Compiled and edited by Brian Kolodiejckuk, M.C., the postulator of Mother Teresa's cause for sainthood, [the book] . . . discusses such topics as: the need for us to visit the sick and the imprisoned, the importance of honoring the dead and informing the ignorant, [and] the necessity to . . . forgive willingly, [among others]." (Publisher's note)

"These reflections, stories, and testimonials will challenge and inspire readers to bear witness to a venerable spiritual legacy." Pub Wkly

Includes bibliographical references (pages 333-364)

235   Spiritual beings

McCarthy, David Matzko

Sharing God's Good Company; A Theology of the Communion of Saints. David Matzko McCarthy. W.B. Eerdmans Pub. Co. 2012 viii, 174 p.p (pbk.: alk. paper) $28   **235**
1. Christian saints 2. Christian saints -- Biography -- History and criticism
ISBN 080286709X; 9780802867094
LC 2011049265

This book by David Matzko McCarthy "explores the role and significance of the saints in Christians' lives today. While examining the lives of specific saints like Martin de Porres, Thérèse de Lisieux, and Mother Teresa, McCarthy especially focuses on such topics as the veneration of martyrs, realism and hagiography, science and miracles, images and pilgrimage, and why the saints continue to captivate Christians and inspire devotion." (Publisher's note)

Includes bibliographical references and index.

Wray, T. J.

The **birth** of Satan; tracing the devil's biblical roots. [by] T.J. Wray, Gregory Mobley. Palgrave Macmillan 2005 211p $24.95   **235**
1. Devil
ISBN 1-4039-6933-7
LC 2005-43046

The authors find Satan's "origins in a biblical character and in early Jewish and Christian writings outside of the scriptures. They try to understand why we as a species strive to feel fearful, why being frightened—vicariously, at least—is so appealing. . . . A thoughtful, informative examination." Booklist

Includes bibliographical references

236   Eschatology

Brown, Samuel Morris

In heaven as it is on earth; Samuel Morris Brown. Oxford University Press 2012 xii, 392 p illustrations **236**
1. Death 2. Church of Jesus Christ of Latter-day Saints -- History
ISBN 9780199793570

LC 2011002848

'This book examines Mormonism "through the lens of founder Joseph Smith's profound preoccupation with the specter of death. Revisiting historical documents and scripture from this . . . perspective, Brown offers . . . insight into the origin and meaning of some of Mormonism's earliest beliefs and practices. The world of early Mormonism was besieged by death--infant mortality, violence, and disease were rampant. A prolonged battle with typhoid fever, punctuated by painful surgeries including a threatened leg amputation, and the sudden loss of his beloved brother Alvin cast a long shadow over Smith's own life. Smith embraced and was deeply influenced by the culture of 'holy dying'--with its emphasis on deathbed salvation, melodramatic bereavement, and belief in the Providential nature of untimely death--that sought to cope with the widespread mortality of the period." (Publisher's note)
Includes bibliographical references and index

Eire, Carlos M. N.

A very brief history of eternity; [by] Carlos Eire. Princeton University Press 2010 268p il $24.95; ebook $24.95 **236**
1. Eternity 2. Western civilization
ISBN 978-0-691-13357-7; 978-1-4008-3187-6 ebook

LC 2009-22951

The author's "skill at engaging readers conceals the rigorous, thoughtful research and methodology that went into this volume. . . . This thought-provoking book is sure to be a classic." Choice
Includes bibliographical references

Miller, Lisa

Heaven; our enduring fascination with the afterlife. Harper 2010 331p $25.99 **236**
1. Heaven 2. United States -- Religion
ISBN 978-0-06-055475-0; 0-06-055475-4

LC 2009-26063

In this "sweeping historical and literary geography of heaven . . . [Miller] talks to priests, a Dominican monk, Muslim clerics, rabbis, and professors (and even visits a psychic, who channels a balding Ed Asner look-alike — no one she knows, though she racks her brain). She doesn't ignore pop culture, either, touching on everything from The Lovely Bones to the hugely popular Left Behind series. . . . But once she has finished reporting and researching, Miller's book loses its hard journalistic edge and becomes something else: a memoir. Her own qualms about faith have danced around the edges of the story, but finally they come front and center. What Miller ultimately concludes may surprise you. It certainly surprised her." Entertainment Wkly

Spong, John Shelby

Eternal life; a new vision: beyond religion, beyond theism, beyond heaven and hell. Harper One 2009 xx, 268p $24.99 **236**
1. Death 2. Eternity 3. Future life
ISBN 978-0-06-076206-3

LC 2008-51443

This book "offers new insights into religion's big questions about life and death, making an invaluable contribution to both religious scholarship and faithful exploration." Publ Wkly

Includes bibliographical references

Wright, N. T.

Surprised by hope; rethinking heaven, the resurrection, and the mission of the church. HarperOne 2008 332p $24.95 **236**
1. Hope 2. Eschatology 3. Future life
ISBN 978-0-06-155182-6; 0-06-155182-1

"Readers will need a Bible handy to appreciate this work fully, as Wright prefers to cite rather than print Scripture. His prose, deep but not murky, is lightened by glints of humor. For any library serving patrons who are willing to think a bit about religion." Libr J
Includes bibliographical references

239   Apologetics and polemics

Augustine

Concerning the city of God against the pagans; [by] St. Augustine; translated by Henry Bettenson; with a new introduction by G.R. Evans. Penguin Books 2003 lxxi, 1097p (Penguin classics) pa $16 **239**
1. Apologetics
ISBN 978-0-14-044894-8; 0-14-044894-2

LC 2004-269353

This translation first published 1972

"Written as an eloquent defence of the faith at a time when the Roman Empire was on the brink of collapse, it examines the ancient pagan religions of Rome, the arguments of the Greek philosophers and the revelations of the Bible. Pointing the way forward to a citizenship that transcends worldly politics and will last for eternity, City of God represents a dramatic turning point in the unfolding of Christian doctrine. The new introduction by Gill Evans examines the text in the light of contemporary Greek and Roman thought and political change." Publisher's note
Includes bibliographical references

Keller, Timothy J.

The reason for God; belief in an age of skepticism. Dutton 2008 293p $24.95 **239**
1. Faith 2. Skepticism 3. Apologetics
ISBN 978-0-525-95049-3; 0-525-95049-4

LC 2007-43745

"Using literature, philosophy, and pop culture, the author gives . . . reasons for a strong belief in God. . . . [The author] presents a religious view without being overly critical of the secular side presented in other books. . . . This book presents a valid, well-written, and well-researched argument." Libr J

241   Christian ethics

Bass, Diana Butler

Grateful; the transformative power of giving thanks. Diana Butler Bass. HarperOne 2018 256 p. (hardcover) $26.99 **241**
1. Gratitude 2. Christianity -- Spiritual life
ISBN 9780062659477

LC 2017047233

In this book, author Diana Butler Bass, "explores why gratitude is missing as a modern spiritual practice, offers practical suggestions for reclaiming it, and illuminates how the shared practice of gratitude can lead to greater connection with God, our world, and our own souls. . . . Bass challenges readers to think about the impact gratitude has in our spiritual lives.'" (Publisher's note)

Becker, Josh, 1958-

The **more** of less; finding the life you want under everything you own. Joshua Becker. WaterBrook Press 2016 230 p. (hardback) $17.99   **241**

1. Consumers 2. Simplicity 3. Quality of life 4. Simplicity -- Religious aspects -- Christianity 5. Consumption (Economics) -- Religious aspects -- Christianity
ISBN 1601427964; 9781601427960

LC 2015042586

This book, by Joshua Becker, focuses on non-consumption and minimalism. The book seeks to help "recognize the life-giving benefits of owning less, realize how all the stuff you own is keeping you from pursuing your dreams, craft a personal, practical approach to decluttering your home and life, experience the joys of generosity, [and] learn why the best part of minimalism isn't a clean house, it's a full life." (Publisher's note)

"With action plans, lists, and appeals to the reader's quiet nature, Becker successfully presents a well-rounded argument that a journey toward minimalism is possible and even enjoyable." Pub Wkly

Includes bibliographical references (pages 223-230).

Chapman, Gary D.

Love as a way of life; seven keys to transforming every aspect of your life. [by] Gary Chapman. Doubleday 2008 239p $19.95; pa $13.95   **241**

1. Love -- Religious aspects 2. Interpersonal relations -- Religious aspects
ISBN 978-0-385-51858-1; 0-385-51858-7; 978-1-4000-7259-0 pa; 1-4000-7259-X pa

LC 2007-50546

"All self-help books run the risk of cliché, but Chapman manages to make tried-and-true material feel fresh through carefully chosen examples from his pastoral counseling practice and his own life. . . . Although Christian faith provides the scaffolding for his program and a concluding chapter makes the need for God's help explicit, Chapman's judicious counsel can be implemented by people of many religious traditions." Publ Wkly

Includes bibliographical references

Davis, Will

Enough; finding more by living with less. Will Davis, Jr. Revell 2012 232 p. (pbk.) $13.99   **241**

1. Simplicity 2. Christian life 3. Conduct of life 4. Simplicity -- Religious aspects -- Christianity 5. Contentment -- Religious aspects -- Christianity
ISBN 0800720024; 9780800720025

LC 2012003547

This Christian book, by Will Davis Jr., "challenges readers to discover the peace that comes through contentment with what we have and compassion for those in need. Through . . . statistics, scriptural insight, and real-life stories, Davis gently leads readers to consider living with less in order to do more for the kingdom." (Publisher's note)

Includes bibliographical references (p. 231-232)

Price, Reynolds

A **serious** way of wondering; the ethics of Jesus imagined. Scribner 2003 146p hardcover o.p. pa $14.95   **241**

1. Christian ethics
ISBN 0-7432-3008-6; 0-7432-3009-4 pa

LC 2003-41506

"In three . . . . apocryphal gospel stories, Price's Jesus engages in conversations about homosexuality, suicide and the plight of women

in male-dominated societies. . . . Elegant and passionate, Price's provocative parables provide no simple answers to the saccharine question 'What would Jesus do?' Rather, they compel us to imagine creatively our engagements with Jesus' teachings and the impact of those teachings on our lives." Publ Wkly

Includes bibliographical references

241.4   Virtues

Lamott, Anne

★ **Hallelujah** anyway; rediscovering mercy. Anne Lamott. Riverhead Books 2017 192 p. $20   **241.4**

1. Mercy
ISBN 9780735213586

LC 2016036301

In this book, author Anne Lamott "ventures to explore where to find meaning in life. We should begin, she suggests, by 'facing a great big mess, especially the great big mess of ourselves.' It's up to each of us to recognize the presence and importance of mercy everywhere--'within us and outside us, all around us'--and to use it to forge a deeper understanding of ourselves and more honest connections with each other." (Publisher's note)

"As in previous works, Lamott's courageous honesty and humility, laced with wit and compassion, offer wisdom and hope for difficult times." Pub Wkly

242   Devotional literature

Augustine

Confessions; translated with an introduction and notes by Henry Chadwick. Oxford University Press 1998 xxviii, 311p (Oxford world's classics) pa $7.95   **242**

ISBN 978-0-19-283372-3; 0-19-283372-3

"These confessions were written at the end of the fourth century by the most distinguished of the Latin fathers as a revelation of his spiritual experience. They have been a source of religious inspiration through the centuries." Pratt Alcove

Includes bibliographical references

Confessions; Augustine; a new translation by Sarah Ruden. The Modern Library 2017 xli, 484 p.p (hardcover) $28 **242**

1. Catholic Church 2. Christian saints 3. Hippo (Extinct city) -- Biography 4. Christian saints -- Algeria -- Hippo (Extinct city) -- Biography 5. Catholic Church -- Algeria -- Hippo (Extinct city) -- Bishops -- Biography
ISBN 0812996569; 9780812996562

LC 2016033647

In this book, translated by Sarah Ruden, author "Augustine tells the story of his sinful youth and his conversion to Christianity. He describes his ascent from a humble farm in North Africa to a prestigious post in the Roman Imperial capital of Milan, his struggle against his own overpowering sexuality, his renunciation of secular ambition and marriage, and the recovery of the faith his mother had taught him during his earliest years." (Publisher's note)

"In this lively translation filled with vivid, personal prose, Ruden introduces readers to a saint whom many will realize they only thought they knew." Pub Wkly

Includes bibliographical references

King, Martin Luther, Jr., 1929-1968

Thou, dear God; Martin Luther King, Jr.; foreword by the Julius R. Scruggs; edited and introduced by Lewis V. Baldwin. Beacon Press 2012 245 p.   **242**

1. Prayers

ISBN 9780807086032

LC 2011031431

This book "is the first and only collection of sixty-eight prayers by Martin Luther King, Jr. Arranged thematically in six parts--with prayers for spiritual guidance, special occasions, times of adversity, times of trial, uncertain times, and social justice--Baptist minister and King scholar Lewis Baldwin introduces the book and each section with short essays. Included are both personal and public prayers King recited as a seminarian, graduate student, preacher, pastor, and, finally, civil rights leader, along with a special section that reveals the biblical sources that most inspired King. Collectively they illustrate how King turned to private prayer for his own spiritual fulfillment and to public prayer as a way to move, inspire, and reaffirm a quest for peace and social justice." (Publisher's note)

Includes bibliographical references (p. 239-245).

Lewis, C. S. (Clive Staples), 1898-1963

★ A **grief** observed; C.S. Lewis. HarperSanFrancisco 2001 xxxi, 76 p.p (pbk.: alk. paper) $13.99   **242**

1. Death 2. Grief 3. Bereavement 4. Consolation 5. Bereavement -- Religious aspects -- Christianity

ISBN 0060652381; 9780060652388

LC 00063227

This book, "written after his wife's tragic death, . . . is C.S. Lewis's honest reflection on the fundamental issues of life, death, and faith in the midst of loss. . . . This is a beautiful and unflinchingly honest record of how even a stalwart believer can lose all sense of meaning in the universe, and how he can gradually regain his bearings." (Publisher's note)

Thomas, à Kempis, 1380-1471

The **imitation** of Christ; {by} Thomas à Kempis. Vintage Books 1998 xliii, 242p pa $12.95   **242**

ISBN 978-0-375-70018-7; 0-375-70018-8

This devotional classic originally written in Latin in the 15th century "traces in four books the gradual progress of the soul to Christian perfection, its detachment from the world, and its union with God." Oxford Companion to Engl Lit. Concise edition

Ugolino di Monte Santa Maria

The **little** flowers of St. Francis of Assisi; written by Ugolino di Monte Santa Maria; edited by and adapted from a translation by W. Heywood; with a new preface by Madeleine L'Engle. Vintage Books 1998 xxxviii, 120p (Vintage spiritual classics) pa $13   **242**

1. Saints 2. Writers on religion

ISBN 978-0-375-70020-0; 0-375-70020-X

LC 97-48815

This translation first published 1906 in the United Kingdom

These "simple anecdotes exemplify St. Francis' love of nature, man and of God." Bookman's Manual

Includes bibliographical references

248   Christian experience, practice, life

Brizendine, Judy

Stunned by grief; remapping your life when loss chang-

es everything. BennettKnepp Publishing 2011 274p il pa $18.95   **248**

1. Bereavement 2. Loss (Psychology) 3. Spiritual healing 4. Adjustment (Psychology)

ISBN 978-0-9831688-1-2

"A former market analyst and interior designer, . . . [the author] found her world turned upside down when her husband died. She uses her own experience combined with the advice of psychologists, grief counselors, the Bible, and fellow mourners to provide a sort of roadmap for the unwelcome journey of grief. In bite-size pieces, she covers the progression of grief, the intrinsic anger and guilt felt in the process, and the possibility of dealing with and planning a new future. . . . This book will comfort and support anyone new to grief and will serve as a companion in times of loneliness. Realistic, practical, and highly recommended." Libr J

Includes bibliographical references

Evans, Rachel Held

Searching for Sunday; loving, leaving, and finding the church. Rachel Held Evans. Thomas Nelson 2015 288 p. $16.99   **248**

1. Christian life

ISBN 0718022122; 9780718022129

LC 2014956181

This book, by Rachel Held Evans, is an "ode to the past and hopeful gaze into the future of what it means to be a part of the Church. . . . Centered around seven sacraments, Evans' quest takes readers through a liturgical year with stories about baptism, communion, confirmation, confession, marriage, vocation, and death that are funny, heartbreaking, and sharply honest." (Publisher's note)

"Elegantly structured and thoughtfully written, Evans's approach to church through the metaphors of the sacraments should please many reading groups and individual seekers." LJ

Lamott, Anne

Small victories; spotting improbable moments of grace. Anne Lamott. Riverhead Books, a member of Penguin Group (USA) 2014 304 p. (hardback) $22.95   **248**

1. Hope 2. Christianity -- Spiritual life 3. Joy 4. Grace 5. Spiritual life 6. Christian biography -- United States 7. Life -- Religious aspects -- Christianity 8. Novelists, American -- 20th century -- Biography

ISBN 1594486298; 9781594486296

LC 2014026967

This book, by Anne Lamott, is a "collection of new and selected essays on hope, joy, and grace. . . . Our victories over hardship and pain may seem small, . . . but they change us-- our perceptions, our perspectives, and our lives. Lamott writes of forgiveness, restoration, and transformation, how we can turn toward love even in the most hopeless situations, how we find the joy in getting lost and our amazement in finally being found." (Publisher's note)

"Lamott confronts each situation with humor and rectitude and shows readers how she found something redeeming in each one. Sage advice on finding beauty and happiness in life despite bad circumstances." Kirkus

Spotting improbable moments of grace

Lewis, C. S (Clive Staples), 1898-1963

★ The **Screwtape** letters; with, Screwtape proposes a toast. HarperSanFrancisco 2001 209p $22.95; pa $11.95 **248**

1. Satire 2. Christian life

ISBN 0-06-065289-6; 0-06-065293-4 pa

LC 00-49860

The Screwtape letters first published 1943 by Macmillan; this combined edition first published 1961 by Macmillan

"A popular work on Christian moral and theological problems. . . . It is in the form of a series of letters in which a devil, Screwtape, advises his nephew, Wormwood, on how to deal with his human 'patients.'" Reader's Ency. 4th edition

Lucado, Max

Fearless; imagine your life without fear. Thomas Nelson 2009 221p $24.99 **248**

1. Fear -- Religious aspects

ISBN 978-0-8499-2139-1

LC 2009-707

The author offers a faith-based primer on how to live without fear.

"Skillful as a surgeon, . . . [Lucado] discerns and identifies the cancer of fear that touches every human being, and with like precision speaks healing words that cut right the heart. While there exists no fast fix or simple cure for the fear-bound individual, Lucado's tempered counsel and faith-driven remedies will offer day-by-day spiritual medicine of the most potent kind." Publ Wkly

Includes bibliographical references

Peale, Norman Vincent

★ The **power** of positive living. Fawcett Columbine 1996 224p pa $13.95 **248**

1. Success 2. Applied psychology 3. Pastoral psychology

ISBN 0-449-91166-7; 978-0-449-91166-2

LC 96096721

First published 1952 by Prentice-Hall

In this volume "Peale strings together dozens of personal success stories ('success' is always materialistic) that make readers feel good. Believing (in yourself, others, values, God) is all-important, and the stories of wealthy business executives who made it on their own grab center stage." Libr J

Zondervan dictionary of Christian spirituality; Glen G. Scorgie, general editor; consulting editors: Simon Chan, Gordon T. Smith, James D. Smith III. Zondervan 2011 852p $39.99 **248**

1. Reference books 2. Christianity -- Dictionaries

ISBN 978-0-310-29066-7

LC 2010037314

"The first section presents six to seven-page entries on topics such as spiritual theology, human personhood, education and spiritual formation, and liturgical spirituality. Also included are articles describing the history of Christian spirituality from 100 C.E. to the present. Each article is followed by a bibliography and a further-reading list. The second section is a dictionary with entries on a broad variety of subjects: biblical figures, popes, mystics, saints, philosophers, spiritual leaders, and educators, as well as concepts and areas of concern including poverty, humanism, suffering, vows, the Kingdom of God, and peace." Libr J

Includes bibliographical references

248.2 Religious experience

Armstrong, Karen

Visions of God; four medieval mystics and their writings. Bantam Bks. 1994 228p pa $19 **248.2**

1. Authors 2. Hermits 3. Mysticism 4. Mystics 5. Writers on religion

ISBN 0-553-35199-0

LC 94-20217

"The collection is eminently readable and should serve to make these important sources more accessible to a general audience. The selections are arranged chronologically, but Armstrong's reflections also place them in a 'developmental sequence.'" Booklist

Includes bibliographical references

Downing, David C.

Into the region of awe; mysticism in C. S. Lewis. InterVarsity Press 2005 207p $17 **248.2**

1. Authors 2. Mysticism 3. Novelists 4. Theologians 5. Essayists 6. Satirists 7. Literary critics 8. Children's authors

ISBN 0-8308-3284-X; 978-0-8308-3284-2

LC 2004-29844

This is a "book on the writer/thinker's complex attitudes toward mysticism and mystical experience. Downing is keenly responsible in his approach to Lewis's biography and background and candid about Lewis's reservations about mysticism in his own theology; the author's affection for his subject ably informs this sensitive reading of Lewis's life and writings." Libr J

Includes bibliographical references

248.3 Worship

Lucado, Max

Before amen; the power of a simple prayer. Max Lucado. Thomas Nelson 2014 192 p. $19.99 **248.3**

1. Prayer 2. Christian life 3. Devotional literature 4. Prayer -- Christianity

ISBN 0849948487; 9780849948480

LC 2014007855

In this Christian devotional book, by Max Lucado, "joins readers on a journey to the very heart of biblical prayer, offering hope for doubts and confidence even for prayer wimps. Distilling prayers in the Bible down to one pocket-sized prayer, Max reminds readers that prayer is not a privilege for the pious nor the art of a chosen few. Prayer is simply a heartfelt conversation between God and his child." (Publisher's note)

"The concept that there is power in a simple prayer normally wouldn't take a whole book to convey, but Lucado (You'll Get Through This), a prolific author with 92 million books in print, succeeds in getting readers to approach communication with God in a whole new way." Pub Wkly

Includes bibliographical references

248.4 Christian life and practice

Carter, Jimmy

Sources of strength; meditations on scripture for a living faith. Times Bks. 1997 252p hardcover o.p. pa $14.99 **248.4**

1. Christian life 2. Bible -- Meditations

ISBN 0-8129-3236-6 pa

LC 97-27501

Companion volume to Living faith

This "is a collection of 52 brief Bible lessons—one for each week of the year—written by former president Jimmy Carter. All were used in adult Sunday school classes he taught himself. Carter's lessons are open-minded and socially progressive while remaining unapologetically conservative and Christian theologically. . . . The lessons are grouped in nine categories, such as 'What We Believe' and 'Christians in the

World,' but each lesson stands well on its own." Libr J

Chittister, Joan

Following the path; the search for a life of passion, purpose, and joy. Image 2012 188 p. $18.00   **248.4**

    1. Self-help techniques

    ISBN 030795398X; 9780307953988

This book considers "the questions 'What am I supposed to do with my life?' and 'How do I know when I've found my purpose?' [which] can seem endless and overwhelming. . . . [Author] Sister Joan [Chittister] brings the insights of her years of teaching and contemplation to bear on this issue." She examin[es] . . . spiritual calling and gifts, change and discernment." (Publisher's note) This book "is meant to give someone in the process of making a life decision at any age—in early adulthood, at the point of middle-age change and later, when we find ourselves at the crossroads without a name—some ideas against which to pit their own minds, their own circumstances." (Author's note)

Francis, Pope, 1936-

Happiness in this life; a passionate meditation on earthly existence. Pope Francis; translated from the Italian by Oonagh Stransky. Random House 2017 viii, 259 p.p (hardcover) $27   **248.4**

    1. Christian life 2. Spiritual life 3. Happiness -- Religious aspects 4. Christian life -- Catholic authors 5. Joy -- Religious aspects -- Catholic Church 6. Happiness -- Religious aspects -- Catholic Church

    ISBN 9780525510970; 9780525510987

    LC 2017045759

This book, by Pope Francis, translated by Oonagh Stransky, is "[a] collection of homilies, speeches, and 'messages of the day' that brings together [the] Pope['s] . . . wisdom on finding happiness. . . . For Pope Francis, the appreciation of our everyday lives is a spiritual undertaking. . . . Along the way, Pope Francis discusses the sanctity of women's rights . . . and explains why fighting discrimination is the essence of loving thy neighbor." (Publisher's note)

"A book as loving and encouraging as the man himself seems to be." Booklist

Heim, Tami

@stickyjesus; how to live out your faith online. Toni Birdsong, Tami Heim. Abingdon Press 2012 224 p.   **248.4**

    1. Christian life 2. Computer literacy 3. Online social networks 4. Internet -- Social aspects 5. Christian life -- Meditations

    ISBN 1426741898; 9781426741890

    LC 2011044377

This book instructs Christian readers in incorporating technology, computers, and the Internet into their faith. The book "is a fusion of discipleship, faith sharing, marketing, and a Get Started 101 on Twitter, Facebook and blogging. '@stickyJesus' . . . challenges Christ followers to regain [their] God-given dominion on earth, which includes the Internet. With knowledge, skills, and Holy Spirit guidance, [the authors] encourage believers to dig in and learn how to navigate this online world. . . . The book also includes personal testimonies. . . . These are real people and ministries (about a dozen) making a difference because they walk, talk and connect differently online." (Publisher's Note)

Includes bibliographical references.

Jakes, T. D., 1957-

Destiny; step into your purpose. T.D. Jakes. Faith Words 2015 272 p. (hardcover) $25   **248.4**

    1. Self-realization 2. Fate and fatalism 3. Vocation -- Christianity

4. Fate and fatalism -- Religious aspects -- Christianity 5. Self-actualization (Psychology) -- Religious aspects -- Christianity

    ISBN 1455553972; 9781455553976; 9781455589630

    LC 2015017111

This inspirational self-help book, by T. D. Jakes, encourages readers to embrace their self-confidence and sense of having a destiny. "Life offers more when destiny is our focus! Our divine purpose maneuvers us past challenges, pains, and shortcuts and even what appears on the surface to be failure. On deeper reflection, we understand them as catalysts that shift us toward authentic self-identity, greater exposure, and bold life adventures." (Publisher's note)

"Readers will specifically learn how to prioritize wisely; decide what works best for their unique gifts and talents; protect the undervalued commodity of time; push past failure; and find the courage to actively pursue their destinies. Jakes's passion for life and colloquial style translate effortlessly from screen to page. This book of hard-nosed spiritual advice is an uplifting rally cry for self-determination." Pub Wkly

Instinct; the power to unleash your inborn drive. T.D. Jakes. Faith Words 2014 271 p. (hardcover) $25   **248.4**

    1. Spiritual life 2. Self-help techniques 3. Instinct 4. Christian life

    ISBN 1455554049; 9781455554041

    LC 2014007406

In this book, author T. D. Jakes "outlines how to re-discover your natural aptitudes and re-claim the wisdom of your past experiences." He claims that "Knowing when to close a deal, when to take a risk, and when to listen to your heart will become possible when you're in touch with the instincts that God gave you." (Publisher's note)

"This positive book encourages readers to get in touch with their instincts, trust them, and rely on them." Pub Wkly

Lentz, Carl

Own the moment; Carl Lentz. Simon & Schuster 2017 352 p. (hardcover) $24.99   **248.4**

    1. Clergy 2. Christian life

    ISBN 9781501177002; 9781501191954

    LC 2017049418

In this book, author and pastor Carl Lentz "shares the unlikely and inspiring story of how he went from being an average teenager who couldn't care less about church to leading one of the country's fastest-growing congregations--how one day he is trying to convince a Virginia Beach 7-Eleven clerk to attend his service, and just a few years later he is baptizing a global music icon in an NBA player's Manhattan bathtub." (Publisher's note)

Lucado, Max

Unshakable hope; building our lives on the promises of God. Max Lucado. Thomas Nelson 2018 xiv, 216 p.p $22.99 **248.4**

    1. Christian life 2. God (Christianity) -- Promises 3. Despair -- Religious aspects -- Christianity 4. Trust in God 5. Hope -- Religious aspects -- Christianity

    ISBN 0718096142; 9780718096144

    LC 2018936435

"In 'Unshakable Hope,' Max Lucado unpacks 12 of the Bible's most significant promises, equipping you to overcome difficult circumstances by keeping your focus on the hope found in the promises of Scripture rather than dwelling on the problems in front of you. For every problem in life, God has given you a promise." (Publisher's note)

Includes bibliographical references

Martin, James

The **Jesuit** guide to almost everything; a spirituality for real life. HarperOne 2010 420p il $26.99; ebook $11.99 **248.4**

1. Saints 2. Priests 3. Spiritual life 4. Catholic Church 5. Religious leaders 6. Writers on religion
ISBN 978-0-06-143268-2; 978-0-06-198140-1 ebook

LC 2009030505

"In this digestible account of all things Jesuit, James Martin, S.J., encapsulates the uniquely Ignatian concept of spirituality. Translating the essence of the Jesuit philosophy into layman's terms, he uses both traditional stories and personal anecdotes to vividly illustrate the Jesuit approach to God, friendship, social justice, decision-making, prayer, simplicity, obedience, and self-actualization. Martin's engaging, intimate tone will appeal to anyone interested in understanding the history, the efficacy, and the universality of the Jesuit mission and way of life." Booklist

Includes bibliographical references

Meyer, Joyce

Seize the day; living on purpose and making every day count. Joyce Meyer. Faith Words 2016 234 p. (hardcover) $24   **248.4**
1. Christian life 2. Older persons -- Religious life
ISBN 145555989X; 9781455559893; 9781455559923

LC 2016015536

This book, by Joyce Meyer, "shares a purposeful approach to everyday living, helping readers claim the good things God has in store for them each day. Today is no ordinary day. You may perform simple routines, feel uninspired, or lack the excitement of hope. But today could be the most important one of your life--depending on how you choose to spend it." (Publisher's note)

"Meyer advocates seizing control of one's schedule to focus on life's purpose, but also recommends being flexible, finding a system that fits one's style, and taking time to laugh." Pub Wkly

Nouwen, Henri

Discernment; reading the signs of daily life. Henri J. M. Nouwen, with Michael J. Christensen and Rebecca J. Laird. HarperOne 2013 xxix, 223 p.p (hc) $25.99   **248.4**
1. Theology 2. Christian life 3. Christian ethics 4. Discernment (Christian theology)
ISBN 9780061686153; 0061686158; 9780061686160

LC 2013004593

This book "features the wisdom that spiritual leader and counselor Henri J. M. Nouwen brought to the essential question asked by every Christian and seeker: What should I do with my life? Nouwen emphasizes listening to the Word of God--in our hearts, in the Bible, in the community of faith, and in the voice of the poor as a way to discern God's plan." (Publisher's note)

Includes bibliographical references

Osteen, Joel, 1963-

The **power** of I am; two words that will change your life today. Joel Osteen. Faith Words 2015 269 p. (hardcover) $26   **248.4**
1. Self-realization 2. Motivation (Psychology) 3. Affirmations 4. Self-talk -- Religious aspects -- Christianity 5. Self-confidence -- Religious aspects -- Christianity
ISBN 0892969962; 9780892969968; 9781455536207

LC 2015025973

Author Joel Osteen attempts to "help you discover your unique abilities and advantages to lead a more productive and happier life. His insights and encouragement are illustrated with many amazing stories of people who turned their lives around by focusing on the positive power of this principle. You can choose to rise to a new level and invite God's goodness by focusing on these two words: I AM!" (Publisher's note)

"Directing believers to look beyond their own needs and wants, Osteen advances his message to a higher plane, advocating a life of reaching out and sharing your blessings." Publisher's Weekly

Think better, live better; A Victorious Life Begins in Your Mind. Joel Osteen. FaithWords 2016 224 p. (ebook) $72; (hardcover) $24.00   **248.4**
1. Christian life 2. Thought and thinking 3. Attitude (Psychology) 4. Thought and thinking -- Religious aspects -- Christianity 5. Attitude (Psychology) -- Religious aspects -- Christianity
ISBN 9780892968671; 9780892969678; 9781455541706

LC 2016022264

This book, by Joel Osteen, "offers a simple yet life-changing strategy for erasing the thoughts that keep you down and reprogramming your mind with positive thinking to reach a new level of victory. As a child of the Most High God, you are equipped to handle anything that comes your way. To claim your destiny, start thinking about yourself the way God does and delete the thoughts that tear down your confidence." (Publisher's note)

"Osteen writes in this uplifting call to action that, one way or another, you are going to become what you think." Pub Wkly

Riess, Jana

Flunking sainthood; a year of breaking the Sabbath, forgetting to pray, and still loving my neighbor. Paraclete Press 2011 179p pa $16.99   **248.4**
1. Success 2. Christian life 3. Spiritual life 4. Failure (Psychology)
ISBN 978-1-55725-660-7

LC 2011022595

The author "intended to devote an entire year ('a year-long experiment') to mastering 12 different spiritual challenges, including praying at fixed times during the day, exhibiting gratitude, observing the Sabbath, practicing hospitality according to the rules set by St. Benedict, abstaining from eating meat, and amply demonstrating her generosity. But nothing turned out as planned. . . . Although her spiritual quest falls far short, she can still proffer spiritual lessons. Anyone who has failed to live up to expectations, which means most everyone, will love this book." Booklist

Includes bibliographical references

Smith, Myquillyn

The **nesting** place; your home doesn't have to be perfect to be beautiful. Myquillyn Smith. Zondervan 2014 199 p. color illustrations (hardcover) $19.99   **248.4**
1. Apartments 2. Interior design 3. Home economics 4. Rental housing 5. Home -- Religious aspects -- Christianity
ISBN 0310337909; 9780310337904

LC 2013034145

"Popular blogger and self-taught decorator Myquillyn Smith (The Nester) is all about

embracing reality--especially when it comes to decorating a home bursting with boys, pets, and all the unpredictable messes of life. In 'The Nesting Place,' Myquillyn shares the secrets of decorating for real people--and it has nothing to do with creating a flawless look to wow your guests. It has everything to do with embracing the natural imperfection and chaos of daily living." (Publisher's note)

248.8   Guides to Christian life for specific groups of people

Billings, J. Todd

Rejoicing in lament; wrestling with incurable cancer and life in Christ. J. Todd Billings. Brazos Press 2015 224 p. (pbk.) $18.99 **248.8**

1. Christianity -- Doctrines 2. Suffering -- Religious aspects 3. Cancer patients -- Religious life 4. Cancer -- Patients -- Religious life 5. Cancer -- Religious aspects -- Christianity 6. Suffering -- Religious aspects -- Christianity
ISBN 1587433583; 9781587433580

LC 2014040099

This book, by J. Todd Billings, "shares . . . [the author's] journey, struggle, and reflections on providence, lament, and life in Christ in light of his illness, moving beyond pat answers toward hope in God's promises. Theologically robust yet eminently practical, it engages the open questions, areas of mystery, and times of disorientation in the Christian life." (Publisher's note)

"His poignant insight into the role of lament in faithful Christian living makes this a work of both astute scholarship and powerful testimony." Pub Wkly

Includes bibliographical references and index

DiFelice, Bekah

Almost There; Searching for Home in a Life on the Move. Bekah DiFelice. NavPress 2017 172 p. (paperback) $14.99 **248.8**

1. Spiritual life 2. Self-improvement 3. Christian life
ISBN 9781631464720; 9781631464713; 163146471X

This book, by Bekah DiFelice, "is for those on the move and those who feel restless right where they are. It's for those who struggle with not belonging, with feeling unsettled, with believing that home is out of their reach, at least for the moment. And Almost There is for those who find themselves in a transient lifestyle they didn't expect—say, moving across the country for a new job or the military or an opportunity to begin again." (Publisher's note)

"This book will appeal broadly to those who have lived a wandering existence, and Christian readers in particular will appreciate DiFelice's tangents on the lives of biblical characters . . ." Pub Wkly

Hatmaker, Jen

Of mess and moxie; wrangling delight out of this wild and glorious life. Jen Hatmaker. Thomas Nelson 2017 xxi, 266 p.p (hardcover) $22.99 **248.8**

1. Christian life 2. Women -- Religious life 3. Women -- Religious life -- Christianity
ISBN 9780718031862; 9780718031848

LC 2017933589

In this book, author Jen Hatmaker "parlays her own triumphs and tragedies into a sigh of relief for all normal, fierce women everywhere. Whether it's the time she drove to the wrong city for a fourth-grade field trip . . . or the way she learned to forgive . . . , she offers a reminder to those of us who sometimes hide in the car eating crackers that we do have the moxie to get back up and get back out." (Publisher's note)

"Hatmaker shares the importance of reaching beyond comfort zones and extending welcomes. She owns the moxie she's writing about." Booklist

Includes bibliographical references (pages 262-265).

Hendey, Lisa M.

A **book** of saints for Catholic moms; 52 companions for your heart, mind, body, and soul. Lisa M. Hendey. Ave Maria Press 2011 xiv, 334 p.p ill. **248.8**

1. Prayers 2. Catholics 3. Motherhood 4. Christian saints 5. Devotional exercises 6. Mothers -- Prayers and devotions 7. Catholic Church -- Prayers and devotions 8. Christian saints -- Prayers and devotions
ISBN 1594712735; 9781594712739

LC 2011025284

In this book, Lisa M. Hende "familiarizes readers with saints — one for each week of the year — who are relevant to nearly every aspect of a Catholic mother's life, divided into categories of heart, mind, body and soul. She offers related Scripture verses for the week as well as practical suggestions and activities. . . . [The book covers] topics such as 'overflowing mounds of dirty laundry' or serious issues such as mental illness and single parenthood. . . . Hendey . . . details the saints' trials and triumphs that . . . people struggle with the same intrinsic issues today. Although many of the individual saints are patrons to various groups or issues . . . Hendey . . . relat[es] each saint's legacy to common dilemmas faced by mothers." (Our Sunday Visitor)

Jaynes, Sharon

When you feel you're not enough; silencing the lies that steal your confidence. Sharon Jaynes. Harvest House Publishers 2018 272 p. (pbk.) $15.99 **248.8**

1. Self-perception 2. Self-esteem in women 3. Women -- Religious aspects -- Christianity 4. Christian women -- Religious life 5. Self-esteem -- Religious aspects -- Christianity 6. Self-perception -- Religious aspects -- Christianity
ISBN 0736973540; 9780736973540

LC 2017039262

In this book, author "Sharon Jaynes exposes the lies that keep you bogged down in shame, insecurity, and feelings of inadequacy. By recognizing the lies and replacing them with truth, you'll be able to silence the voice inside that whispers you're just not good enough, accept God's grace and move past failures that have defined and confined you, [and] preload your heart with truth to fight your deepest insecurities." (Publisher's note)

Includes bibliographical references

Yoder, Brenda L.

Fledge; launching your kids without losing your mind. Brenda L. Yoder. Herald Press 2018 239 p. (pbk.: alk. paper) $15.99 **248.8**

1. Parenting 2. Motherhood 3. Child rearing -- Religious aspects -- Christianity 4. Parenting -- Religious aspects -- Christianity
ISBN 9781513802367; 9781513802534

LC 2017038550

In this book, author "Brenda L. Yoder helps Christian parents navigate the many transitions of the launching years. How do you parent tweens at home and young adults away from home at the same time? What's a good balance between boundaries and freedom? How can you pray for your fledgling youth? And what do you do with all that mom grief? Your job as a parent isn't over; it's just changing." (Publisher's note)

248.843 Women

Brownback, Lydia

Finding God in my loneliness; Lydia Brownback. Crossway 2017 174 p. (trade paperback) $12.99 **248.843**

1. Loneliness 2. Encouragement 3. Christian life 4. Christian women -- Prayers and devotions 5. Loneliness -- Biblical teaching -- Meditations 6. Loneliness -- Religious aspects -- Christianity 7. Encouragement -- Biblical teaching -- Meditations 8. Encouragement -- Religious aspects -- Christianity
ISBN 1433553937; 9781433553936

LC 2016031222

This book, by Lydia Brownback, "reminds us of God's power to redeem our loneliness and use it in our lives to draw us to himself. Ultimately, she helps us see that even when we feel misunderstood, forsaken, or abandoned, we're never really alone. God is always with us, and only he can meet all of our needs in Christ Jesus." (Publisher's note)

"Brownback's encouraging book is a sharp, thoroughly readable entreaty to readers looking for grace in loneliness." Pub Wkly Annex.

Includes bibliographical references and index.

248.844   Married people

Evans, Jimmy

Strengths based marriage; build a stronger relationship by understanding each other's gifts. Jimmy Evans and Allan Kelsey. Thomas Nelson 2016 208 p. (ebook) $14.99; $16.99   **248.844**

1. Marriage -- Religious aspects 2. Marriage -- Religious aspects -- Christianity

ISBN 9780718083632; 0718083628; 9780718083625

LC 2016017800

This book, by Jimmy Evans and Allan Kelsey, "show readers how to have a happier, stronger marriage by applying the concepts from the popular StrengthsFinder assessment to their relationship. . . . Applying the revelatory concepts from the popular Clifton StrengthsFinder assessment to marriage (assessment itself not included in purchase price), Evans and Kelsey break new ground in helping readers understand themselves and others." (Publisher's note)

"A superb tool for those wanting to understand and be understood by others." LJ

Includes bibliographical references

248.86   People experiencing illness, trouble, bereavement

Lucado, Max

Anxious for nothing; finding calm in a chaotic world. Max Lucado. Thomas Nelson 2017 xii, 222 p.p (hardcover) $22.99   **248.86**

1. Anxiety -- Treatment 2. Self-help techniques 3. Anxiety -- Religious aspects -- Christianity

ISBN 9780718096120; 9780718096441

LC 2017933165

This book, by Max Lucado, "provides a roadmap for battling with and healing from anxiety. . . . Max writes, 'The news about our anxiety is enough to make us anxious.' [The book] invites readers to delve into Philippians 4:6-7. . . . Max guides readers through this Scripture passage and explains the key concepts of celebration, asking for help, leaving our concerns, and meditating." (Publisher's note)

"A compulsively readable book focused on an aspect of Christian living that many find challenging: overcoming guilt to find peace in life." Pub Wkly

Includes bibliographical references (pages 219-222).

252   Texts of sermons

American sermons; the pilgrims to Martin Luther King, Jr. Library of Am. 1999 939p $40   **252**

1. Sermons

ISBN 1-88301-165-5

LC 98-34295

"To peruse this work is to become reacquainted with the literary eloquence of our distant and recent past and to observe what has happened to rhetoric itself over the centuries." N Y Times Book Rev

Includes bibliographical references

King, Martin Luther, Jr., 1929-1968

★ **Strength** to love; foreword by Coretta Scott King. Fortress 2010 168p il pa $20   **252**

1. Sermons

ISBN 978-0-8006-9740-2

First published 1963 by Harper & Row

A collection of sermons addressing social injustice and racism.

Includes bibliographical references

253   Pastoral office and work (Pastoral theology)

McKibben, Bill

Eaarth; making a life on a tough new planet. Times Books 2010 253p $24   **253**

1. Environmental degradation 2. Human influence on nature 3. Greenhouse effect 4. Climate -- Environmental aspects

ISBN 978-0-8050-9056-7; 0-8050-9056-8

LC 2009-30040

The author "demonstrates how global warming has already occurred and is irreversible. He describes a new 'Eaarth,' where the cumulative effects of the release of carbon dioxide in the atmosphere have already changed the planet. . . . McKibben envisions a future in which humanity transitions from unfettered growth and a dependence on external markets for sustenance and fossil-fuel-driven energy, to smaller, self-contained communities, growing food locally and generating sustainable distributed electricity. An absolute must-read." Kirkus

Includes bibliographical references

Pattison, John

Slow church; cultivating community in the patient way of Jesus. C. Christopher Smith, John Pattison. InterVarsity Press 2014 247 p. (pbk.: alk. paper) $16   **253**

1. Church 2. Religion and sociology 3. Communities -- Religious aspects -- Christianity

ISBN 0830841148; 9780830841141

LC 2014011067

In this book, authors C.Christopher Smith and John Pattison suggests we "leave franchise faith behind and enter into the ecology, economy and ethics of the kingdom of God, where people know each other well and love one another as Christ loved the church." (Publisher's note)

"Though primarily focused upon church communities, the ideas presented here may appeal to other types of religious or intentional communities. Individuals who are attempting to bring their own lives into line with their ethics and values will also find help." Pub Wkly

Includes bibliographical references

261.2   Christianity and other systems of belief

Kertzer, David I.

The **Popes** against the Jews; the Vatican's role in the rise of modern anti-semitism. Knopf 2001 355p $27.95; pa $15   **261.2**

1. Antisemitism 2. Catholic Church -- Relations -- Judaism

ISBN 0-375-40623-9; 0-375-70605-4 pa

LC 2001-33728

"This is a devastating indictment, and fair-minded critics will find flaws in Kertzer's methodology and sweeping conclusions. Nevertheless, he has opened a window that should be opened." Booklist

Includes bibliographical references (p.) and index

261.27   Christianity and Islam

Dardess, George

Meeting Islam; a guide for Christians. by George Dardess. Paraclete Press 2005 xiv, 242 p.p (Many mansions) (paperback) $18.95 **261.27**

1. Christianity and other religions 2. Islam -- Relations -- Christianity 3. Islam -- Doctrines 4. Christianity and other religions -- Islam

ISBN 9781557254337; 1557254338

LC 2005013504

This book, by George Dardess, "invites readers to explore some of Islam's key facts, chief concepts, and practices. . . . He shares his own experiences as a deacon in the Catholic Church in Rochester, New York, seeking to build bridges with the local Muslim community, and how his own faith has been expanded and enhanced by the relationships and understandings that have resulted." (Publisher's note)

"This brief book provides some introductory information about Islam and is excellent reading for Christians who are curious about one of the world's fastest-growing religions." Pub Wkly

Includes bibliographical references (p. 242).

261.5   Christianity and secular disciplines

Barbour, Ian G.

When science meets religion; enemies, strangers, or partners? HarperSanFrancisco 2000 205p pa $16.95 **261.5**

1. Religion and science

ISBN 0-06-060381-X

LC 99-55579

The author "guides readers through a four-fold typology of the science/religion relationship—Conflict, Independence, Dialogue and Integration. . . . Barbour's own sympathies are markedly on the side of dialogue and integration, but he makes an unusually sucessful effort to represent other perspectives in a fair light." Publ Wkly

Includes bibliographical references

Grant, Edward

★ **Science** and religion, 400 B.C. to A.D. 1550; from Aristotle to Copernicus. Greenwood Press 2004 xxvi, 307p il (Greenwood guides to science and religion) $67.95 **261.5**

1. Religion and science

ISBN 0-313-32858-7

LC 2004-17429

"With this new book, grounded in five decades of active scholarship, Edward Grant provides a synthetic account of the relationship between science and religion from Greek antiquity to the beginnings of the Scientific Revolution. Intended as an introduction for the general reader, the book successfully argues its central point–namely, that contrary to popular belief today, the medieval Church promoted scientific thought, which in turn profoundly influenced theological understanding. . . . Grant's book, along with the eight primary documents it provides, is an introduction students and teachers will welcome." Journal of the History of Science in Society

Includes bibliographical references

Olson, Richard

★ **Science** and religion, 1550-1900; from Copernicus to Darwin. [by] Richard G. Olson. Greenwood Press 2004 292p il (Greenwood guides to science and religion) $65 **261.5**

1. Religion and science

ISBN 0-313-32694-0

LC 2004-47501

The issues discussed "should be especially helpful to those who are interested in the historical background to current science-religion issues being debated in the United States." Sci Books Films

Includes bibliographical references

261.7   Christianity and political affairs

Volf, Miroslav

Public faith in action; how to think carefully, engage wisely, and vote with integrity. Miroslav Volf and Ryan McAnnally-Linz. Brazos Press 2016 xiii, 240 p.p (ebook) $21.99; (cloth) $21.99 **261.7**

1. Christianity and politics 2. Church and social problems 3. Christians -- Political activity

ISBN 9781493404667; 9781587433849

LC 2016003425

This book, by Miroslav Volf and Ryan McAnnally-Linz, "offers Christians practical guidance for thinking through complicated public issues and faithfully following Jesus as citizens of their countries. The book focuses on enduring Christian commitments that should guide readers in their judgments and encourages legitimate debate among Christians over how to live out core values." (Publisher's note)

"The authors draw conclusions without pushing an agenda and suggest that moral issues don't always have to trump the law." Pub Wkly

Includes bibliographical references and index.

261.8   Christianity and socioeconomic problems

Chu, Jeff, 1977-

Does Jesus Really Love Me? A Gay Christian's Pilgrimage in Search of God in America. by Jeff Chu. HarperCollins 2013 368 p. $26.99 **261.8**

1. Gay men 2. Christianity 3. Homosexuality -- United States 4. Christian gays -- United States 5. Homosexuality -- Religious aspects -- Christianity

ISBN 0062049739; 9780062049735

LC 2013464818

Lambda Literary Awards Finalist (2014)

This book, by Jeff Chu, "is part memoir and part investigative analysis that explores the explosive and confusing intersection of faith, politics, and sexuality in Christian America. . . . From Brooklyn to Nashville to California, from Westboro Baptist Church and their 'God Hates Fags' protest signs, to the pioneering Episcopalian bishop Mary Glasspool--who proclaims a message of liberation and divine love, Chu captures spiritual snapshots of Christian America." (Publisher's note)

"[T]he book brings complexity and humanity to a discourse often lacking in both." Pub Wkly

D'Antonio, Michael

★ **Mortal** Sins; Sex, Crime, and the Era of Catholic Scandal. Michael D'Antonio. St. Martin's Press 2013 416 p. $26.99 **261.8**

1. Child sexual abuse by clergy 2. Catholic Church -- Clergy --
Sexual behavior 3. Catholic Church -- Discipline 4. Catholic
Church -- United States
ISBN 0312594895; 9780312594893

LC 2013003725

This book presents a "history of the Catholic Church's 'most severe
crisis since the Reformation': the revelations of endemic sexual abuse
of minors by priests in the United States and Europe. . . . In 1984,
American priest Thomas Doyle learned of a lawsuit brought by parents
of a victim, and was deeply troubled. . . . Along with plaintiffs' attorney
Jeffrey Anderson, Doyle and a few others worked tirelessly to get the
church, the media, and the public to pay attention." (Publishers Weekly)

Gilliard, Dominique DuBois

Rethinking incarceration; advocating for justice that restores. Dominique DuBois Gilliard. IVP Books 2018 240 p.
$17   **261.8**
1. Prisons -- United States 2. Discrimination in criminal justice
administration -- United States
ISBN 0830845291; 9780830845293

This book, by Dominique DuBois Gilliard, "explores the history and
foundation of mass incarceration, examining Christianity's role in its
evolution and expansion. He assesses our nation's ethic of meritocratic
justice in light of Scripture and exposes the theologies that embolden
mass incarceration. Gilliard then shows how Christians can pursue justice that restores and reconciles, offering creative solutions and highlighting innovative interventions." (Publisher's note)

"In his debut, Gilliard, an Evangelical Covenant Church pastor,
builds on the work of Michelle Alexander (The New Jim Crow), Bryan
Stevenson (Just Mercy), and Christopher D. Marshall (Compassionate
Justice) to create a readable narrative history of racialized incarceration
in the U.S." Pub Wkly

Lehmann, Chris

The **money** cult; Capitalism, Christianity, and the Unmaking of the American Dream. Chris Lehmann. Melville House
2016 403 p. (hardback) $28.95   **261.8**
1. Capitalism 2. Christianity and economics 3. Wealth -- Religious
aspects -- Christianity 4. Capitalism -- United States -- History 5.
Christianity -- United States -- History 6. Capitalism -- Religious
aspects -- Christianity 7. Christianity -- Economic aspects -- United
States -- History
ISBN 9781612195087

LC 2016001439

In this book, author Chris Lehmann "reveals how America's religious leaders became less worried about sin and the afterlife and more
concerned with the material world, until the social gospel was overtaken
by the gospel of wealth. Showing how American Christianity came to
accommodate—and eventually embrace—the pursuit of profit, as well
as the inescapability of economic inequality, [it is a wide-ranging . . .
book." (Publisher's note)

"This book is unlikely to embarrass believers into a social conscience or different political allegiance, but Lehmann does reveal the
modern evangelical right as deeply faithful to an American economic
model—one focused on industrial production—that no longer exists."
Pub Wkly

Includes bibliographical references and index.

261.835   Sexual relations, marriage, family

Griffith, R. Marie

Moral combat; how sex divided American Christians and

fractured American politics. R. Marie Griffith. Basic Books
2017 xx, 395 p.p illustrations (hardback) $32   **261.835**
1. Catholic Church -- Relations 2. Christians -- Political activity 3.
Christianity and politics -- United States 4. United States -- Church
history 5. Sex -- Religious aspects -- Christianity 6. Sex -- Political
aspects -- United States 7. Christians -- Political activity -- United
States 8. Catholic Church -- Relations -- Protestant churches 9.
Protestant churches -- Relations -- Catholic Church
ISBN 9781541698062; 9780465094752

LC 2017037768

In this book, author R. Marie Griffith "offers a carefully reasoned
examination of the century-long political and religious controversies
over sexuality that color our national character. Given the passions engendered by these controversies on both sides--conservative and liberal-
-she demonstrates that comity and compromise are perennially elusive,
while consensus seems to be a word in an incomprehensible language."
(Booklist)

"Griffith's remarkably comprehensive book will be of interest to
scholars and lay readers alike." Pub Wkly

Includes bibliographical references (pages 327-374) and index.

263.042   Holy places

Mullins, Edwin

The **four** roads to heaven; France and the Santiago pilgrimage. Edwin Mullins. Interlink Pub Group Inc 2018 224 p.
$20   **263.042**
1. Religious literature 2. Christian pilgrims and pilgrimages
ISBN 1623719917; 9781623719913

In this book, author "Edwin Mullins follows the same four roads
[used during the great pilgrimage of the Middle Ages] to as they exist
today in the footsteps of those medieval travelers. He explores the magnificent churches, abbeys, and works of art which are the proud legacy
of the pilgrimage, as well as reconstructing a turbulent period of history
that encompassed wars, crusades, and the re-conquest of Spain." (Publisher's note)

264   Public worship

Episcopal Church

★ The **Book** of common prayer and administration of the
sacraments and other rites and ceremonies of the church; together with the Psalter or Psalms of David according to the use
of the Episcopal Church. Church Hymnal Corp, Seabury Press
1979 1001p pew ed., black $19   **264**
ISBN 0-89869-081-1

LC 81-204603

The official liturgy of the Episcopal Church.

Lucatero, Heliodoro

★ The **living** Mass; changes to the Roman missal and how
we worship. Liguori 2011 64p il pa $4.99   **264**
1. Catholic Church -- Liturgy
ISBN 978-0-7648-2007-6
This book seeks to answer questions about the changes made to the
Roman Missal "as well as to give some insight into the history of the
development of the Roman Missal from early Church times, through
the Middle Ages, through the different Church councils, and up to the
present day. A comparison of each change features old and new text
side-by-side with the changes highlighted in bold type." Publisher's note

Includes bibliographical references

269 Spiritual renewal

Martin, William

A **prophet** with honor; the Billy Graham story. William Martin. Zonderkidz 2010 832 p. $29.99   **269**
1. Biography 2. Clergy -- Biography 3. Evangelists -- United States -- Biography -- Juvenile literature
ISBN 0310353300; 9780310353300; 9780310719359
LC 2009054208

This book, by William Martin, presents "the biography preacher Billy Graham. . . . Carefully documented, eminently fair, and gracefully written, it raises and answers key questions about Graham's character, contributions, and influence on the world religious scene. In this engaging and comprehensive book, . . . Martin gives readers a better understanding of the most successful evangelist in modern history, and the movement he led for over fifty years." (Publisher's note)

270 History, geographic treatment, biography of Christianity; Church history; Christian denominations and sects

The **Bloomsbury** Guide to Christian Spirituality. Bloomsbury Academic 2012 356 p. $49.95   **270**
1. Spiritual life 2. Christianity -- Encyclopedias
ISBN 1441184848; 9781441184849

This book is a "single-volume orientation to Christian spirituality. . . . Topics are . . . inclusive (sources, traditions, practices, dialogue with other faiths, contemporary issues). Three indexes (biblical citations, names, subjects) enable rapid searches through the text. The 30-plus contributors include world-class scholars Bernard McGinn, Richard Rohr, Benedicta Ward, and coeditor [Richard] Woods." (Choice)

Jenkins, Philip

The **new** faces of Christianity; believing the Bible in the global south. Oxford University Press 2006 252p $26   **270**
1. Forecasting 2. Christianity
ISBN 978-0-19-530065-9; 0-19-530065-3
LC 2006-15490

Jenkins explores the growth of Christianity in Africa, Asia and Latin America.
"Those interested in religious trends across the globe, the Muslim-Christian friction, and world politics will benefit from this resource." Libr J
Includes bibliographical references

MacCulloch, Diarmaid

★ **Christianity**; the first three thousand years. Viking 2010 1161p il map $45   **270**
1. Church history
ISBN 978-0-670-02126-0; 0-670-02126-1
LC 2009-40184

First published 2009 in the United Kingdom
"It is difficult to imagine a more comprehensive and surprisingly accessible volume on the subject than MacCulloch's. . . . Want a refresher on the rise of the papacy? It is here. On Charlemagne and Carolingians? That is here, too. On the Fourth Crusade and its aftermath? Look no farther." N Y Times Book Rev
Includes bibliographical references

Tickle, Phyllis, 1934-2015

The **great** emergence; how Christianity is changing and why. Baker Books 2008 172p il $17.99   **270**
1. Christianity
ISBN 0-8010-1313-5; 978-0-8010-1313-3
LC 2008-21706

"This is a must-read for anyone seeking to understand the face and future of Christianity." Publ Wkly
Includes bibliographical references

270.092 Christians – Biography

Marsh, Karen Wright

★ **Vintage** saints and sinners; 25 Christians who transformed my faith. Karen Wright Marsh; foreword by Lauren Winner. IVP Books, an imprint of InterVarsity Press 2017 215 p. (hardcover: alk. paper) $20   **270.092**
1. Christian biography 2. Christian saints -- Biography
ISBN 0830845135; 9780830845132
LC 2017033889

This book, by Karen Wright Marsh, "introduces us afresh to twenty-five brothers and sisters who challenge and inspire us with their honest faith. Join Karen on her journey with the likes of Augustine, Brother Lawrence, and Saint Francis, as well as Amanda Berry Smith, Søren Kierkegaard, Dorothy Day, Howard Thurman, Flannery O'Conner, and many more. Let their lives and their wisdom be an invitation to authentic life in Christ." (Publisher's note)
Includes bibliographical references.

270.1 Historical periods

Ehrman, Bart D.

The **triumph** of Christianity; how a forbidden religion swept the world. Bart D. Ehrman. Simon & Schuster 2018 xiv, 335 p.p (hardcover) $28   **270.1**
1. Christianity 2. Church history -- 30-600, Early church 3. Christian civilization -- History 4. Church history -- Primitive and early church, ca. 30-600
ISBN 9781501136702; 9781501136726
LC 2016056895

This book, by Bart D. Ehrman, "shows how [Christianity,] a religion whose first believers were twenty or so illiterate day laborers in a remote part of the empire, became the official religion of Rome, converting some thirty million people in just four centuries. . . . [It] combines deep knowledge and meticulous research in an eye-opening, immensely readable narrative that upends the way we think about the single most important cultural transformation our world has ever seen." (Publisher's note)
"The author maps out the early growth of Christianity against a detailed background of Roman society and history . . . He not only brings a clear presentation of his own views but also gives alternative interpretations a fair hearing." LJ
Includes bibliographical references (pages 295-322) and index.

Riley, Gregory J.

The **river** of God; a new history of Christian origins. HarperSanFrancisco 2001 252p hardcover o.p. pa $14.95   **270.1**
1. Church history -- 30-600, Early church
ISBN 0-06-066979-9; 0-06-066980-2 pa
LC 2001-16888

"This volume will become one of the most important books on the

subject." Libr J
Includes bibliographical references

Voices of early Christianity; documents from the origins of Christianity. Kevin W. Kaatz, editor. Greenwood 2013 xxii, 277 p.p (Voices of an era) (hardcopy: alk. paper) $100   **270.1**
1. Christianity 2. Religion -- History 3. Women in Christianity 4. Church history -- Primitive and early church, ca. 30-600 -- Sources
ISBN 1598849522; 9781598849523

LC 2012041162

The "editor's intention with this book is to teach about early Christianity using primary-source documents, with the title also offering a treatise on how to evaluate and think critically about primary sources." Topics include "'Early Christian Life,' 'The Church,' 'Early Christian Women,' 'Conflicts of the Early Church,' 'Persecution,' and 'Church and Politics.'" (Library Journal)
Includes bibliographical references (pages 255-264) and index

270.2   Period of ecumenical councils, 325-787

Brown, Peter
Through the eye of a needle; wealth, the fall of Rome, and the making of Christianity in the West, 350-550 AD. Peter Brown. Princeton University Press 2012 759 p.   **270.2**
1. Rome -- History 2. Church history -- 30-600, Early church 3. Wealth -- Religious aspects -- Christianity 4. Rome -- History -- Empire, 284-476 5. Wealth -- Religious aspects -- Christianity -- History 6. Church history -- Primitive and early church, ca. 30-600
ISBN 069115290X; 9780691152905

LC 2011045697

This book, by Peter Brown, is a history "of the vexing problem of wealth in Christianity in the waning days of the Roman Empire. . . . Peter Brown examines the rise of the church through the lens of money and the challenges it posed to an institution that espoused the virtue of poverty and called avarice the root of all evil, . . . challeng[ing] the widely held notion that Christianity's growing wealth sapped Rome of its ability to resist the barbarian invasions." (Publisher's note)
Includes bibliographical references and index

Wills, Garry
Saint Augustine. Viking 1999 xx, 152p (Penguin lives series) $19.95   **270.2**
1. Saints 2. Bishops 3. Theologians 4. Philosophers 5. Writers on religion
ISBN 0-670-88610-6

LC 98-50317

Wills begins "by addressing centuries of misconceptions. Though his admiration for the saint is occasionally tainted by defensiveness, his account of Augustine's search for a faith and a philosophy engages our sympathy. He also conveys the turbulence of the era, when the Roman Empire was beleaguered by barbarians and the Catholic Church by heretics, and shows how Augustine's responses to the troubles of his time have shaped Christianity down to our own." New Yorker
Includes bibliographical references

270.6   Period of Reformation and Counter-Reformation, 1517-1648

MacCulloch, Diarmaid
The **Reformation**; a house divided. Viking 2004 xxiv, 792p il map $34.95; pa $18   **270.6**
1. Reformation
ISBN 0-670-03296-4; 0-14-303538-X pa

LC 2003-61607

First published 2003 in the United Kingdom
The author "has produced the definitive survey for this generation. . . . This well-written book is a joy to read, with new facts and interpretations on nearly every page." Libr J
Includes bibliographical references

Massing, Michael
Fatal discord; Erasmus, Luther, and the fight for the western mind. Michael Massing. HarperCollins 2018 976 p. $45   **270.609**
1. Religion -- History 2. Intellectual life -- History
ISBN 0060517603; 9780060517601

In this book, author "Michael Massing seeks to restore [Desiderius] Erasmus to his proper place in the Western tradition. The conflict between him and [Martin] Luther, he argues, forms a fault line in Western thinking--the moment when two enduring schools of thought, Christian humanism and evangelical Christianity, took shape. . . . Massing concludes that Europe has adopted a form of Erasmian humanism while America has been shaped by Luther-inspired individualism." (Publisher's note)
"As we commemorate the 500th anniversary of the Protestant Reformation, this engaging tale of the contentious relationship between two precursors of the modern world—one who remained a Catholic, the other whose teaching spawned the various Protestant denominations—provides much-needed historical background and reflection on a major period in church and world history." LJ

270.82   History of Christianity – 1900-1999

Stanley, Brian
★ **Christianity** in the twentieth century; a world history. Brian Stanley. Princeton University Press 2018 xxi, 477 p.p maps (Princeton history of Christianity) (hardcover: alk. paper) $35   **270.82**
1. Religion -- History 2. Church history -- 20th century
ISBN 9780691157108

LC 2017039619

This book in The Princeton History of Christianity series, by Brian Stanley "charts the transformation of one of the world's great religions during an age marked by world wars, genocide, nationalism, decolonization, and powerful ideological currents, many of them hostile to Christianity. . . . The book traces how Christianity evolved from a religion defined by the culture and politics of Europe to the expanding polycentric and multicultural faith it is today." (Publisher's note)
"A finely crafted exploration of Christianity in the 20th century." Kirkus
Includes bibliographical references (pages 429-469) and index.

271 Religious congregations and orders in church history

Butcher, Carmen Acevedo

Man of blessing; a life of St. Benedict. Paraclete Press 2006 180p map $21.95 **271**
1. Monks 2. Saints 3. Writers on religion
ISBN 1-55725-485-0; 978-1-55725-485-6

LC 2005-35827

This is the "story of the life of St. Benedict of Nursia, who founded Western monasticism in the sixth century and later became the patron saint of Europe. . . . The book's readability will make it easy for patrons to escape into late Roman culture and find peace in a monastic simplicity." Libr J
Includes bibliographical references

Haag, Michael

The **Tragedy** of the Templars; The Rise and Fall of the Crusader States. Michael Haag. HarperCollins 2013 384 p. $16.99 **271**
1. Crusades 2. Templars -- History
ISBN 0062059750; 9780062059758

In this book, Michael Haag provides an "account of the Crusades, including the history of the Crusader states--known as Outremer--established by the Franks after the First Crusade. He . . . examines the Crusades from both the Christian and Muslim perspectives, drawing from contemporary chronicles, church records, and correspondence by Templars. Haag covers the motivations for the Crusades, why both Muslims and Christians wanted control of the Holy Land, and how the Templars were established." (Library Journal)

Jones, Dan

The **Templars**; the rise and spectacular fall of God's holy warriors. Dan Jones. Viking 2017 xvi, 428 p.p color illustrations, maps (hardcover) $30 **271**
1. Templars -- History 2. Religious literature 3. Military religious orders -- History
ISBN 9780525428305; 9780698186439; 0525428305

LC 2017025385

This book, by Dan Jones, "tells the true story of the Templars . . ., drawing on extensive original sources to build a gripping account of these Christian holy warriors. . . . They fought the forces of Islam in hand-to-hand combat . . ., finding their nemesis in Saladin, who vowed to drive all Christians from the lands of Islam. . . . They established the medieval world's first global bank and waged private wars against anyone who threatened their interests." (Publisher's note)

"This is an engrossing examination of a period whose conflicts are still reverberating today." Pub Wkly
Includes bibliographical references and index.

Spink, Kathryn

Mother Teresa; a complete authorized biography. Harper-SanFrancisco 1997 306p il hardcover o.p. pa $15.95 **271**
1. Nuns 2. Missionaries 3. Missions -- India 4. Missionaries of Charity 5. Nobel laureates for peace
ISBN 0-06-251553-5 pa

LC 97-41349

"Spink's biography benefits from her own 18-year involvement with the work of the Missionaries of Charity Order as well as from the intimate relationship she developed over the years with Mother Teresa. . . . A final chapter in the book provides glimpses of Mother Teresa's affection for Princess Diana, a brief description of Mother Teresa's funeral and a short account of the election of Sister Nirmal as her successor."

Publ Wkly

What I am living for; lessons from the life and writings of Thomas Merton. edited by Jon M. Sweeney. Ave Maria Press 2018 224 p. (pbk.: alk. paper) $16.95 **271**
1. Spiritual life
ISBN 9781594717413

LC 2017044813

This book, edited by Jon M. Sweeney, "offers readers new to [Thomas] Merton, as well as longtime enthusiasts, an opportunity to see how the influential twentieth-century monk and writer continues to encourage the awakening of faith in the twenty-first century. . . . Each contributor . . . focuses on an aspect of the spiritual life that is of vital importance today and on which Merton made a profound impact." (Publisher's note)

"Many of the writers list Merton's 1948 autobiography The Seven Storey Mountain as an influence when deciding to write about their spiritual inner life and discuss topics such as spiritual identity, sexual relationships, interfaith dialogue, and expansive (as opposed to constrictive) theology. A time line of Merton's life and world events that happened during his life (1915–1968) is also helpfully included in Sweeney's well-rounded collection." Pub Wkly
Includes bibliographical references and index

272 Persecutions in general church history

Perez, Joseph

★ The **Spanish** Inquisition; a history. trans. by Janet Lloyd. Yale University Press 2005 248p $26; pa $17 **272**
1. Inquisition 2. Spain -- History
ISBN 0-300-10790-0; 0-300-11982-8 pa

LC 2004-114614

The author "tells the history of the Spanish Inquisition from its medieval beginnings to its nineteenth-century ending. . . . He explores the inner workings of its councils, and shows how its officers, inquisitors, and leaders lived and worked." Univ Press Books for Public and Second Sch Libr, 2006
Includes bibliographical references

272.6 Persecutions of Anglican reformers by Mary I

Rounding, Virginia

The **burning** time; Henry VIII, Bloody Mary, and the Protestant martyrs of London. Virginia Rounding. St. Martin's Press 2017 xvi, 459 p.p color illustrations (hardcover) $29.99 **272.6**
1. Martyrs 2. Church history 3. England -- Church history -- 16th century 4. Great Britain -- History -- Mary I, 1553-1558 5. Great Britain -- History -- Edward VI, 1547-1553 6. Great Britain -- History -- Henry VIII, 1509-1547 7. Persecution -- England -- History -- 16th century 8. Martyrdom -- Christianity -- History -- 16th century 9. Smithfield (London, England) -- History -- 16th century 10. Christian martyrs -- England -- London -- History -- 16th century 11. Christian heretics -- England -- London -- History -- 16th century
ISBN 9781466836242; 9781250040640

LC 2017023617

This book, by Virginia Rounding, "is a vivid insight into an era in which what was orthodoxy one year might be dangerous heresy the next. The first martyrs were Catholics, who cleaved to Rome in defiance of Henry VIII's break with the papacy. But with the accession of Henry's daughter Mary - soon to be nicknamed 'Bloody Mary' - the charge of heresy was leveled against devout Protestants, who chose to burn rather than recant." (Publisher's note)

"An excellent account of 16th-century religious persecution and martyrdom." Pub Wkly

Includes bibliographical references and index

274 Christianity by specific continents, countries, localities in modern world

Gregory, Brad S.

★ **Rebel** in the ranks; Martin Luther, the Reformation, and the conflicts that continue to shape our world. Brad S. Gregory. HarperOne 2017 304 p. (hardcover) $27.99 **274**

1. Reformation 2. Protestantism 3. Reformation -- Influence
ISBN 9780062471178

LC 2017027346

This book, by Brad S. Gregory, explores "How [Martin] Luther inadvertently fractured the Catholic Church and reconfigured Western civilization. . . . While recasting the portrait of Luther as a deliberate revolutionary, Gregory describes the cultural, political, and intellectual trends that informed him and helped give rise to the Reformation, which led to conflicting interpretations of the Bible, as well as the rise of competing churches . . . across Europe." (Publisher's note)

Includes bibliographical references

275 Christianity in Asia

Liao Yiwu

God is red; the secret story of how Christianity survived and flourished in Communist China. Liao Yiwu; translated by Wen Huang. HarperOne 2011 231 p. $25.99 **275**

1. Persecution 2. Communism -- China 3. Christianity -- China 4. China -- Church history -- 21st century 5. China -- Church history-- 20th century 6. Communism and Christianity -- China -- History -- 20th century 7. Communism and Christianity -- China -- History -- 21st century
ISBN 0062078461; 9780062078469; 9780062078483

LC 2010051154

"The author examines Christianity, which survived under China's Cultural Revolution despite attempts to eradicate it as a 'lackey of the imperialists.' . . . In an attempt to understand why a foreign religion gained such popularity, Liao interviews a wide range of Chinese Christians, from an elderly nun who witnessed both the closing and eventual reopening of her church by the Communist regime, to a missionary doctor treating impoverished villagers in lieu of working in a government-run hospital, to a dying tailor who finds meaning in his recent conversion to the faith. . . . Will appeal to both Christian and secular readers interested in the cultural realities of China's Great Leap Forward." Kirkus

276 Christianity in Africa

Majors, Katie Davis

★ **Daring** to hope; finding God's goodness in the broken and the beautiful. Katie Davis Majors. Multnomah 2017 xiv, 214 p.p (hardcover) $25.99 **276**

1. Orphans 2. Orphanages 3. Orphanages -- Uganda 4. Orphans -- Services for -- Uganda 5. Church work with orphans -- Uganda 6. Orphans -- Uganda -- Social conditions
ISBN 9780735290518

LC 2017017869

This book, by Katie Davis Majors, "is an invitation to cling to the God of the impossible--the God who whispers His love to us in the quiet, in the mundane, when our prayers are not answered the way we want or the miracle doesn't come. It's about a mother discovering the extraordinary strength it takes to be ordinary. It's about choosing faith no matter the circumstance and about encountering God's goodness in the least expected places." (Publisher's note)

Includes bibliographical references.

277 Christianity in North America

Boyle, Gregory

Tattoos on the heart; the power of boundless compassion. [by] Gregory Boyle. Free Press 2010 217p $25; pa $14; ebook $11.99 **277**

1. Church work 2. Christian life 3. Priests 4. Youth workers 5. Homeboy Industries 6. Church work with juvenile delinquents -- California -- East Los Angeles
ISBN 1-4391-5302-7; 1-4391-5315-9 pa; 1-4391-7177-7 ebook; 978-1-4391-5302-4; 978-1-4391-5315-4 pa; 978-1-4391-7177-6 ebook

LC 2009-32970

"'Nothing stops a bullet like a job' is the motto of Homeboy Industries, [a] . . . gang intervention program. . . . Founded in 1986 by Gregory Boyle, a Jesuit priest, Homeboy offers job training, tattoo removal and employment to Los Angeles gang members who are seeking to leave gang life behind. . . . Boyle—a k a Father Greg, G-Dog, or simply G—has written a new book about his experiences. . . . The book is less about Boyle, though, than about his 'homies,' the young men and women who come to Homeboy in search of a better life." (America)

"Jesuit priest Boyle recounts his two decades of working with 'homies' in Los Angeles County, which contains 1,100 gangs with nearly 86,000 members. Boyle's Homeboy Industries is the largest gang intervention program in the country, offering job training, tattoo removal, and employment to members of enemy gangs." Publ Wkly

Dochuk, Darren

From Bible belt to sunbelt; plain-folk religion, grassroots politics, and the rise of evangelical conservatism. W.W. Norton 2011 520p il **277**

1. Conservatism 2. Evangelicalism 3. California 4. Evangelicalism -- Southern California 5. Christianity and politics -- Evangelicalism 6. California -- Church history -- 20th century 7. Conservatism -- Religious aspects -- Christianity -- History -- 20th century
ISBN 0393066827; 9780393066821

LC 2010032740

"A five-decade history of the evangelical movement in southern California [argues that] . . . the influx of migrants from the Bible Belt during the Great Depression ultimately led to the rise of the New Right and modern conservatism in the late twentieth century." (Publisher's note) Bibliography. Index.

"Well-written and documented, a supremely helpful guide in sorting out how we arrived at that odd state of affairs." Kirkus

Includes bibliographical references and index

Marty, Martin E.

Pilgrims in their own land; 500 years of religion in America. Penguin Books 1985 500p il pa $18 **277**

1. United States -- Religion 2. United States -- Church history
ISBN 0-14-008268-9; 978-0-14-008268-5

LC 85-3596

First published 1984 by Little, Brown

This book examines "the force of religion in the United States since colonial times. Marty considers not only the religious beliefs and rituals brought to America by the various European settlers, but also those of native Americans. The clashes between Protestant, Catholic, Judaic, and other religious groups are perceived in light of their influence upon the development of this nation up to the present." Booklist

Includes bibliographical references

Miller, Donald, 1971-

Blue like jazz; nonreligious thoughts on Christian spirituality. Donald Miller. Thomas Nelson 2008 ix, 243 p.p illustrations $16.99   **277**

1. Christian life 2. Spiritual life 3. Christian biography -- United States

ISBN 0785263705; 1400204585; 9781400204588

LC 2003002223

This spiritual memoir, by Donald Miller, describes how "when [the author] came to know Jesus Christ, he pursued the Christian life with great zeal. Within a few years he had a successful ministry that ultimately left him feeling empty, burned out, and, once again, far away from God. In this intimate, soul-searching account, Miller describes his remarkable journey back to a culturally relevant, infinitely loving God." (Publisher's note)

Sutton, Matthew Avery

American apocalypse; a history of modern evangelicalism. Matthew Avery Sutton. Belknap Press 2014 480 p. illustrations (alk. paper) $35   **277.3**

1. United States -- Religion 2. Evangelicalism -- United States 3. Evangelicalism -- History 4. United States -- Church history -- 20th century

ISBN 0674048369; 9780674048362

LC 2014014034

Author "Matthew Avery Sutton draws on extensive archival research to document the ways an initially obscure network of charismatic preachers and their followers reshaped American religion, at home and abroad, for over a century. [He] shows how a group of radical Protestants, anticipating the end of the world, paradoxically transformed it." (Publisher's note)

"The result is so seamless a history that readers may wonder whether he engages in overstatement at times. Factual errors, such as stating the U.S. pummeled Iraq with Scud missiles during the first Gulf War (Scuds were never part of the U.S. arsenal), or that Reverend Billy Graham is dead (as of this writing, he is not), don't help. Despite these caveats, this remains an important story, and it is exceedingly well told." Booklist

Includes bibliographical references and index

277.307   Great Awakening

Manseau, Peter

Objects of devotion; religion in early America. Peter Manseau. Smithsonian Books 2017 vii, 251 p.p illustrations (chiefly color) (hardcover) $29.95   **277.307**

1. Material culture 2. United States -- Church history 3. Material culture -- United States 4. United States -- Religion -- History 5. Material culture -- Religious aspects 6. Material culture -- Religious aspects -- Christianity

ISBN 9781588345929

LC 2016038040

This book, by Peter Manseau, "tells the story of religion in the United States through the material culture of diverse spiritual pursuits in the nation's colonial period and the early republic. The beautiful, full-color companion volume to a Smithsonian National Museum of American History exhibition, the book explores the wide range of religious traditions vying for adherents, acceptance, and a prominent place in the public square from the 1630s to the 1840s." (Publisher's note)

"This landmark study of the role of religion in the early history of the U.S.—from the mid-17th century to the mid-19th century—demonstrates how deeply religion influenced America's founders and their descendants." Pub Wkly

Includes bibliographical references and index

277.308   Christianity – United States

Fitzgerald, Frances, 1940-

★ The **Evangelicals**; The Struggle to Shape America. Frances FitzGerald. Simon & Schuster 2017 752 p. (hardcover: alk. paper) $35   **277.308**

1. Evangelicalism 2. United States -- Church history 3. Christianity and politics -- United States 4. Evangelicalism -- United States -- History 5. Fundamentalism -- United States -- History 6. Christianity and politics -- United States -- History

ISBN 9781439131336; 9781439131343

LC 2016025851

National Book Critics Circle Award: Nonfiction (2017)

National Book Award Finalist: Nonfiction (2017)

This book, by Frances FitzGerald, "is the first to tell the powerful, dramatic story of the Evangelical movement in America—from the Puritan era to the 2016 presidential election. The evangelical movement began in the revivals of the eighteenth and nineteenth centuries, known in America as the Great Awakenings. . . . Evangelicals now constitute twenty-five percent of the American population, but they are no longer monolithic in their politics." (Publisher's note)

"This is a timely and accessible contribution to the rapidly growing body of literature on Christianity in modern America." Pub Wkly

Includes bibliographical references and index

Hartke, Austen

Transforming; the Bible and the lives of transgender Christians. Austen Hartke. Westminster John Knox Press 2018 225 p. (pbk.: alk. paper) $16   **277.308**

1. Spiritual life 2. Transsexualism 3. Transgender people 4. Christian transgender people -- Religious life 5. Gender nonconformity -- Religious aspects -- Christianity

ISBN 9780664263102

LC 2017050167

This book, by Austen Hartke, "provides access into an underrepresented and misunderstood community and will change the way readers think about transgender people, faith, and the future of Christianity. By introducing transgender issues and language and providing stories of both biblical characters and real-life narratives from transgender Christians living today, Hartke helps readers visualize a more inclusive Christianity." (Publisher's note)

"It's an informative and illuminating quest, supplemented by an extensive appended list of further reading and resources. This is an important book that fills an urgent need. " Booklist

Includes bibliographical references

280   Denominations and sects of Christian church

Atwood, Craig D.
  ★ **Handbook** of denominations in the United States; [by] Craig D. Atwood, Frank S. Mead, Samuel S. Hill. 13th ed.; Abingdon Press 2010 416p il $24   **280**
    1. Sects 2. United States -- Religion
    ISBN 978-1-4267-0048-4; 1-4267-0048-2
                      LC 2010-07092
  First published 1951. Periodically revised
  "History and present structure of Christian religious bodies in the United States. Reports on doctrines of different churches. Includes bibliography and index." NY Public Libr Book of How & Where to Look It Up
  Includes bibliographical references

281.9   Orthodox churches

Mathewes-Green, Frederica
  Welcome to the Orthodox Church; an introduction to Eastern Christianity. Frederica Mathewes-Green. Paraclete Press 2015 xviii, 361 p.p (paperback) $19.99   **281.9**
    1. Christian life 2. Orthodox Eastern Church
    ISBN 1557259216; 9781557259219
                      LC 2014041905
  This book, by Frederica Mathewes-Green, "provides a comprehensive introduction to [Eastern] Orthodoxy, but with a twist: readers learn by making a series of visits to a fictitious church, and get to know the faith as new Christians did for most of history, by immersion. Mathewes-Green provides commentary and explanations on everything from how to 'venerate' an icon, the Orthodox understanding of the atonement, to the Lenten significance of tofu." (Publisher's note)
  Includes bibliographical references and index

282   Roman Catholic Church

Allen, John L., 1965-
  The **Catholic** church; what everyone needs to know. by John L. Allen. Oxford University Press 2013 298 p. (What Everyone Needs to Know) $16.95   **282**
    1. Catholic Church -- History 2. Catholic Church -- Doctrines 3. Theology, Doctrinal -- Popular works
    ISBN 0199975108; 9780199975105; 9780199975112
                      LC 2012038594
  In this book, author John L. Allen, Jr, "one of the world's leading authorities on the Vatican, offers an authoritative and accessible guide to the past, present, and future of the Church. The Catholic Church remains by far the largest branch of the worldwide Christian family, and is growing at a remarkable clip. Yet the Church has also been rocked by a series of scandals related to the sexual abuse of minors by clergy, and, even more devastating, the cover-up by the Church hierarchy." (Publisher's note)

Betrayal; the crisis in the Catholic Church. by the Investigative Staff of the Boston Globe. Little, Brown & Co. 2015 304 p. illustrations $16.99   **282**
    1. Catholic Church 2. Child sexual abuse 3. Child sexual abuse by clergy
    ISBN 0316271535; 9780316271530
                      LC 2015951503

  This book, by the Investigative Staff of the Boston Globe, presents "the devastating revelations that triggered a crisis within the Catholic Church. Here is the truth about the scores of abusive priests who preyed upon innocent children and the cabal of senior Church officials who covered up their crimes." (Publisher's note)
  Includes bibliographical references (p. 251-263) and index

Buckley, William F.
  Nearer, my God; an autobiography of faith. Harcourt Brace & Co. 1998 xx, 313p il pa $14   **282**
    1. Authors 2. Novelists 3. Columnists 4. Magazine editors
    ISBN 0-15-600618-9
                      LC 98-16194
  First published 1997 by Doubleday
  "As we might expect, Nearer My God is rich in anecdote, witty, and animated by what Buckley refers to as his 'polemical inclinations.'. . . But what gives it unity as a book, and not just a loose collection of pieces bound in cloth, is the warmth and the depth of Buckley's faith, at once complex and many-sided." Christ Today

Duffy, Eamon
  Saints & sinners; a history of the popes. 3rd ed.; Yale Nota Bene/Yale University Press 2006 474p il pa $22   **282**
    1. Papacy 2. Catholic Church -- History
    ISBN 978-0-300-11597-0
  First published 1997
  This illustrated volume is a companion piece to a six-part television series of the same name. The book offers an overview of the 2,000-year history of the papacy.
  Includes bibliographical references

Francis, Pope, 1936-
  ★ The **church** of mercy; a vision for the Church. Pope Francis. Loyola Press 2014 200 p. (hardcover) $22.95   **282**
    1. Popes 2. Catholic Church
    ISBN 9780829441680; 9780829441697; 9780829441703
                      LC 2014934036
  This book, "[c]ollected from Pope Francis's speeches, homilies, and papers presented during the first year of his papacy, . . . is the first Vatican-authorized book detailing his vision for the Catholic Church. From how to be citizens of the world to answering God's call for evangelization, Pope Francis's deep wisdom reminds us that the Church must move beyond its own walls and joyfully bring God's mercy wherever suffering, division, or injustice exists." (Publisher's note)
  "Refreshingly humane, focusing on people rather than institutions. Admirers of Francis and students of church history alike will find this a useful introduction to the pontiff's thought." Kirkus
  Includes bibliographical references

  Walking with Jesus; a way forward for the church. Pope Francis. Loyola Press 2015 160 p. (hardcover) $22.95   **282**
    1. Christianity
    ISBN 0829442480; 9780829442489; 9780829442496; 9780829442540
                      LC 2015930346
  In this book, Pope Francis "urges us to make Jesus central in our individual lives and in the collective life of the Church--to walk toward him, and ultimately to walk with him at all times and in all places. Each chapter of this Vatican-authorized book helps us put one foot in front of the other as we move ever closer to God and to our neighbors through the sacraments, prayer, evangelization, the gifts of the Spirit, and service to others." (Publisher's note)
  "Perhaps no one has as much potential to buoy the human spirit

through his words as Francis, whose life and public speeches are closely watched by so many. The book's foreword is by Archbishop Blase J. Cupich of Chicago, the pope's first major U.S. appointment." Pub Wkly

Guiley, Rosemary Ellen

The **encyclopedia** of saints. Facts on File 2001 419p il $82.50; pa $24.95 **282**

1. Reference books 2. Christian saints -- Dictionaries

ISBN 0-8160-4133-4; 0-8160-4134-2 pa

LC 00-69176

This volume offers "accounts of the lives and experiences of more than 400 principal saints, from early martyrs such as Lucy of Syracuse to recently canonized saints such as Katherine Drexel. Entries provide a biographical overview, a record of the saint's religious journeys and mystical experiences, a discussion of personal philosophies and important theological influences, as well as his or her patronage, feast days and popular role within the Church." Publisher's note

★ **New** Catholic encyclopedia; prepared by an editorial staff at the Catholic University of America. 2nd ed; Gale Group 2003 15v il maps set $1,981 **282**

1. Reference books 2. Catholic Church -- Encyclopedias

ISBN 978-0-7876-4004-0; 0-7876-4004-2

LC 2002-924

First published 1967 as an update to the Catholic encyclopedia. Kept up-to-date-by yearly supplements

This encyclopedia "covers the history of the eastern churches, the churches of the Protestant Reformation, and other ecclesial communities as well as the Christian roots based in ancient Israel and Judaism. No comprehensive resource on Catholicism can be complete without touching on other world religions as well, including Islam, Buddhism, and Hinduism. This resource provides entries not only on the doctrine, organization, and history of the church, but also on the people, institutions, and social changes that have affected the church over the years. Arranged alphabetically, the entries run in length from half a page to several pages in length. All entries provide the name of the contributor and a bibliography. Cross-references to related articles are located throughout the work. Adding to the usefulness of the set are more than 3,000 black-and-white photographs, maps, and charts that complement the scholarly articles." Am Ref Books Annu, 2003

Our Sunday Visitor Catholic almanac. Our Sunday Visitor **282**

1. Almanacs 2. Catholic Church -- Directories

Annual. First published 1904. Title varies

"Includes much miscellaneous information, e.g., annual survey of news, ecclesiastical calendar, glossary of terms in Catholic use, the Catholic church in various countries of the world, statistics, directory of information, etc." Guide to Ref Books. 11th edition

Politi, Marco

Pope Francis among the wolves; the inside story of a revolution. Marco Politi; translated by William McCuaig. Columbia University Press 2015 288 p. (cloth: alk. paper) $27.95 **282**

1. Catholic Church 2. Catholic Church -- History -- 21st century

ISBN 9780231174145

LC 2014046193

This book, by Marco Politi, translated by William McCuaig, "takes us deep inside the power struggle roiling the Roman Curia and the Catholic Church worldwide, beginning with Benedict XVI . . . and intensifying with the contested and unexpected election of . . . Francis. Politi's account balances the perspectives of Pope Francis's supporters, Benedict's sympathizers, and those disappointed members of the Catholic laity who feel alienated by the institution." (Publisher's note)

"This book is well translated and accessible to a wide audience of Francis's admirers and opponents, both inside and outside of the Catholic Church." LJ

Includes bibliographical references and index

Wills, Garry, 1934-

The **Future** of the Catholic Church With Pope Francis; Garry Wills. Penguin Group USA 2015 320 p. 24 cm $27.95 **282**

1. Catholic Church

ISBN 0525426965; 9780525426967

LC 2014038534

This book, by Garry Wills, "argues that changes have been the evidence of life in the Catholic Church. It has often changed, sometimes with bad consequences, more often with good. . . . In this . . . study, . . . [the author] gives seven examples of deep and serious changes that have taken place (or are taking place) within the last century. None of them was effected by the pope all by himself." (Publisher's note)

"Highly recommended for all interested in a fact-based study of the church's evolution." LJ

282.092　Roman Catholics -- Biography

Nouwen, Henri J. M.

Love, Henri; letters on love, hope, faith, and vocation. Henri J.M. Nouwen; edited with a preface by Gabrielle Earnshaw; foreword by Brené Brown. Convergent 2016 384 p. (ebook) $65; (alk. paper) $24 **282.092**

1. Authors -- Correspondence

ISBN 9781101906361; 1101906359; 9781101906354

LC 2016034448

This book, by Henri J.M. Nouwen, edited by Gabrielle Earnshaw, is a "collection of over 100 unpublished letters. . . . Over the course of his life, Henri Nouwen wrote thousands of letters to friends, acquaintances, parishioners, students, and readers of his work all around the world. He corresponded in English, Dutch, German, French, and Spanish, and took great care to store and archive the letters decade after decade." (Publisher's note)

"The courage and kindness with which Nouwen shares his vulnerabilities and honest feelings, combined with his willingness to provide direction, advice, companionship, and affection, ensure that Nouwen's legacy as inspired spiritual guide will continue, enhanced by this testimony to his sincere desire to live with gratitude, faith, and love." Pub Wkly

Includes bibliographical references and index

Weigel, George, 1951-

★ **Lessons** in hope; my unexpected life with St. John Paul ll. George Weigel. Basic Books, an imprint of Perseus Books, a subsidiary of Hachette Book Group 2017 x, 357 p.p (hardcover) $32 **282.092**

1. Popes 2. Friendship 3. Autobiographies

ISBN 9780465094295

LC 2017948323

In this book, author "George Weigel tells the story of his unique friendship with St. John Paul II. As Weigel learns the pope 'from inside,' he also offers a firsthand account of the tumult of post-Vatican II Catholicism and the Cold War's endgame, introducing readers to the heroes who brought down European communism. Later, he shows us the aging pope grappling with the post-9/11 world order and teaching new lessons in dignity through his own suffering." (Publisher's note)

284   Protestant denominations of Continental origin and related bodies

Ryrie, Alec

    Protestants; the faith that made the modern world. Alec Ryrie. Viking 2017 528 p. (ebook) $65; (hardcover) $35 **284**

    1. Protestants 2. Protestantism

    ISBN 9780735222816; 0670026166; 9780670026166

LC 2016056692

    This book, by Alec Ryrie, "makes the case that Protestants made the modern world. . . . If you look at any of the great confrontations of the last five centuries, you will find Protestants defining the debate on both sides: for and against colonialism, slavery, fascism, communism, women's rights, and more. Protestants have also fought among themselves. What unites them all is a passion for God and a vital belief in the principle of self-determination." (Publisher's note)

    "Rarely has an author of such deep faith offered such a tolerant, engaging history of any religion." Kirkus

    Includes bibliographical references and index

284.1   Lutheran churches

Bolz-Weber, Nadia

    Accidental saints; finding God in all the wrong people. Nadia Bolz-Weber. Convergent Books 2015 224 p. $23   **284.1**

    1. Christianity 2. Christian biography 3. House for All Sinners and Saints (Denver, Colo.) -- Biography

    ISBN 1601427557; 9781601427557

LC 2015012506

    This memoir, by Nadia Bolz-Weber, "invites readers into a surprising encounter with what she calls 'a religious but not-so-spiritual life.' Tattooed, angry and profane, this former standup comic turned pastor stubbornly, sometimes hilariously, resists the God she feels called to serve. But God keeps showing up in the least likely of people--a church-loving agnostic, a drag queen, a felonious Bishop and a gun-toting member of the NRA." (Publisher's note)

    "Recommended for readers who enjoyed Bolz-Weber's previous books or authors such as Anne Lamott and Brian McClaren. An entertaining, reality-based alternative to the polished "professional Christian" memoir." LJ

287   Methodist churches; churches related to Methodism

Tomkins, Stephen

    ★ **John** Wesley; a biography. Eerdmans 2003 208p pa $20   **287**

    1. Theologians 2. Methodist Church 3. Evangelists 4. Writers on religion

    ISBN 0-8028-2499-4

LC 2003-54328

    In this biography of the founder of the Methodist religion "Tomkins presents a keenly engaging portrait of a great man full of contradictoriness. Wesley insisted he was loyal to the Church of England yet consented to his followers setting up establishments and engaging in practices that flouted Anglican authority. . . . He altered the face of Christianity in the West by inspiring modern evangelicalism and Pentecostalism. A fascinating figure, fascinatingly limned." Booklist

    Includes bibliographical references

289.3   Latter-Day Saints (Mormons)

Beam, Alex

    American crucifixion; the murder of Joseph Smith and the fate of the Mormon church. Alex Beam. PublicAffairs 2014 352 p. illustrations, maps (hardcover) $26.99   **289.3**

    1. Mormons 2. Church of Jesus Christ of Latter-day Saints 3. Mormon Church -- History 4. Church of Jesus Christ of Latter-day Saints -- History

    ISBN 1610393139; 9781610393133; 9781610393140

LC 2014004063

    This book, by Alex Beam, focuses on "founding prophet of Mormonism, Joseph Smith. . . . Beam tells how Smith went from charismatic leader to public enemy: How his most seismic revelation--the doctrine of polygamy--created a rift among his people; how that schism turned to violence; and how, ultimately, Smith could not escape the consequences of his ambition and pride . . . Smith's brutal assassination propelled the Mormons to colonize the American West." (Publisher's note)

    "Beam offers a captivating saga of Smith's rise and fall and of a colorful cast of characters who contributed to the internal politics and rivalries that led to Smith's death and drove the Mormons forward to their destiny." Booklist

    Includes bibliographical references and index

Book of Mormon

    ★ The **Book** of Mormon; another testament of Jesus Christ. [translated by Joseph Smith, Jr.] Doubleday 2004 586p $24.95   **289.3**

    1. Mormons 2. Church of Jesus Christ of Latter-day Saints

    ISBN 0-385-51316-X

LC 2004-51982

    First published 1830

    "Based on golden plates which Joseph Smith claimed were revealed to him, and which he unearthed from Cumorah Hill, New York, this book is roughly similar in structure to the Bible. . . . Emphasized are the doctrines of pre-existence, perfection, the afterlife, and Christ's second coming." Haydn. Thesaurus of Book Dig

Bushman, Richard L.

    Mormonism; a very short introduction. [by] Richard Lyman Bushman. Oxford University Press 2008 130p il (Very short introductions) pa $11.95   **289.3**

    1. Church of Jesus Christ of Latter-day Saints

    ISBN 978-0-19-531030-6

LC 2007-44444

    This is an "outstanding, reliable overview of Mormon history and beliefs." Libr J

    Includes bibliographical references (p. 121-123)

Givens, Terryl

    By the hand of Mormon; the American scripture that launched a new world religion. [by] Terryl L. Givens. Oxford Univ. Press 2002 230p il maps hardcover o.p. pa $16.95 **289.3**

    1. Book of Mormon

    ISBN 0-19-513818-X; 0-19-516888-7 pa

LC 2001-53118

    The author "investigates the history and theology of the Book of Mormon, which he calls 'perhaps the most religiously influential, hotly contested, and, in the secular press at least, intellectually under-investigated book in America.' Givens persuasively demonstrates how the Book of Mormon was trumpeted by early Latter-day Saints more for the fact of its existence . . . than for its content per se." Publ Wkly

Includes bibliographical references

Gutjahr, Paul C.

The **Book** of Mormon; a biography. Paul C. Gutjahr. Princeton University Press 2012 xix, 255 p.p   **289.3**
1. Mormons 2. Sacred books 3. Church of Jesus Christ of Latter-day Saints -- History 4. Book of Mormon -- History 5. Book of Mormon -- Criticism, interpretation, etc
ISBN 9780691144801

LC 2011044063

This book presents a history of the Book of Mormon. "[Paul C.] Gutjahr recounts the life of Joseph Smith, whose status as the prophet of the Church of Jesus Christ of Latter-Day Saints rests upon his claim that he translated the Book of Mormon from ancient gold plates delivered to him by an angel. . . . Undeterred by skeptics' allegations of fraud, a small army of missionaries have made the book a powerful proselytizing tool, attracting millions . . . to their faith." (Booklist)
Includes bibliographical references (pages 209-246) and index

Hardy, Grant

★ **Understanding** the Book of Mormon; a reader's guide. Oxford University Press 2010 336p $29.95   **289.3**
1. Book of Mormon -- Criticism
ISBN 978-0-19-973170-1

LC 2009-26675

In this analysis of the Book of Mormon's narrative structure, the author describes the work's "characters, events, and ideas, as he explores the story and its messages. He identifies the book's literary techniques, such as characterization, embedded documents, allusions, and parallel narratives." Publisher's note
Includes bibliographical references

Turner, John G.

★ **Brigham** Young, pioneer prophet; John G. Turner. The Belknap Press of Harvard University Press 2012 500 p. (alk. paper) $35.00   **289.3**
1. Biography 2. Religious life 3. Mormon Church -- Presidents -- Biography 4. Church of Jesus Christ of Latter-day Saints -- Presidents -- Biography
ISBN 0674049675; 9780674049673

LC 2012015555

Author John G. Turner tells the story of "Brigham Young, [who] was Joseph Smith's lieutenant in spreading the newly coined doctrine of Mormonism and his successor on Smith's murder." Turner chronicles "Young's rise in the early hierarchy. . . . The author looks at the various strains of Protestantism, 'ecstatic' and otherwise, that fed into early Mormonism, drawing particularly on Methodism in the British Isles, where Young worked as one of the church's first missionaries." (Kirkus Reviews)
Includes bibliographical references and index

289.5 Church of Christ, Scientist (Christian Science)

Eddy, Mary Baker

★ **Science** and health, with key to the Scriptures; Trustees under the will of Mary Baker G. Eddy. Christian Science Pub. Soc. 2000 pa $9.95   **289.5**
1. Christian Science
ISBN 978-0-87952-259-9; 0-87952-259-3
First published 1875
This work is the foundation of the Christian Science religion, setting

forth Mrs. Baker's interpretations of the Holy Scriptures and the method of healing. It has not been revised since her death in 1910.

Schoepflin, Rennie B.

Christian Science on trial; religious healing in America. Johns Hopkins Univ. Press 2002 301p il (Medicine, science, and religion in historical context) $39.95   **289.5**
1. Christian Science
ISBN 0-8018-7057-7

LC 2001-8512

"A historical examination of Christian Science's evolution during the late 19th and early 20th centuries and the faith's struggle for existence and respectability in the midst of organized American medicine's efforts to curtail its influence." Libr J
Includes bibliographical references

289.6 Society of Friends (Quakers)

Hamm, Thomas D.

★ The **Quakers** in America. Columbia Univ. Press 2003 293p il (Columbia contemporary American religion series) $48.50; pa $27   **289.6**
1. Society of Friends
ISBN 0-231-12362-0; 0-231-12363-9 pa

LC 2002-41422

The author provides an "introduction to Quaker origins abroad, their influences on American politics and culture, as well as their beliefs and traditions as they are played out on American soil. Though this is a serious history with a glossary, chronology, and 40 pages of notes, cartoons and anecdotes leaven the text. For both public and academic libraries." Libr J
Includes bibliographical references

289.7 Mennonite churches

Hostetler, John A.

Amish society; 4th ed; Johns Hopkins Univ. Press 1993 435p il maps hardcover o.p. pa $20   **289.7**
1. Amish
ISBN 0-8018-4441-X; 0-8018-4442-8

LC 92-19304

First published 1963
This book discusses the sectarian origins of the Amish, immigration history, family and community life, population trends, farming practices, technological innovations, education, medicine and the effects of government regulation.
Includes bibliographical references

Kraybill, Donald B.

Concise encyclopedia of Amish, Brethren, Hutterites, and Mennonites; Donald B. Kraybill. Johns Hopkins University Press 2010 302p ill., maps   **289.7**
1. Amish 2. Mennonites 3. Hutterian Brethren
ISBN 9780801896576; 0801896576

LC 2009046015

In this book author "[Donald B.] Kraybill [provides an] . . . overview of the beliefs and cultural practices of Amish, Brethren, Hutterites, and Mennonites in North America. Found throughout Canada, Central America, Mexico, and the United States, these religious communities include more than 200 different groups with 800,000 members in 17 countries. Through 340 short entries, Kraybill offers readers information on a wide range of topics related to religious views and social practices. With . . . consideration of how these diverse communities are related, this compact reference provides a . . . synopsis of these groups in the twenty-first century." (Publisher's note)

Includes bibliographical references (p. 259-285) and index.

★ **On** the backroad to heaven; Old Order Hutterites, Mennonites, Amish, and Brethren. {by} Donald B. Kraybill, Carl F. Bowman. Johns Hopkins Univ. Press 2001 330p il maps (Center books in Anabaptist studies) $57; pa $16.95 **289.7**
  1. Amish 2. Mennonites 3. Hutterian Brethren
  ISBN 0-8018-6565-4; 0-8018-7089-5 pa
                           LC 00-10406

"This look at the history, similarities and differences between four groups of Old Order faithful in North America—Hutterites, Mennonites, Amish and Brethren—is fascinating. . . . A book that, in one volume, tackles history, sociology and future trends—and does it well." Christ Century

Includes bibliographical references

The **riddle** of Amish culture; rev ed; Johns Hopkins Univ. Press 2001 397p il maps (Center books in Anabaptist studies) $65; pa $16.95 **289.7**
  1. Amish
  ISBN 0-8018-6771-1; 0-8018-6772-X pa
                           LC 00-13054

First published 1989

The author examines the history and culture of the Amish, discussing such topics as the social structure of Amish society, rites of redemption and purification, recreation and social gatherings, work, technology, public relations, and social change

Includes bibliographical references (p. {369}-390) and index

Mackall, Joe
  Plain secrets; an outsider among the Amish. Beacon Press 2007 xxxiv, 208p $24.95; pa $13 **289.7**
  1. Amish
  ISBN 0-80701-064-2; 978-0-80701-064-8; 0-80701-065-0 pa; 978-0-80701-065-5 pa
                     LC 2007-924329

"This is a loving portrait, warts and all, of an often-misunderstood people." Booklist

Includes bibliographical references

289.9   Denominations and sects not provided for elsewhere

Guinn, Jeff
  The **road** to Jonestown; Jim Jones and Peoples Temple. Jeff Guinn. Simon & Schuster 2017 ix, 531 p.p illustrations (hardcover) $28 **289.9**
  1. Homicide 2. Jonestown (Guyana) mass deaths, 1978 3. Peoples Temple 4. Jonestown Mass Suicide, Jonestown, Guyana, 1978
  ISBN 1476763828; 9781476763842; 9781476763828
                    LC 2016051471

This book, by Jeff Guinn, "examines [Jim] Jones's life, from his extramarital affairs, drug use, and fraudulent faith healing to the fraught decision to move almost a thousand of his followers to a settlement in the jungles of Guyana in South America. Guinn provides stunning new details of the events leading to the fatal day in November, 1978 when more than nine hundred people died . . . after being ordered to swallow a cyanide-laced drink." (Publisher's note)

"A vivid, fascinating revisitation of a time and series of episodes fast receding into history even as their forgotten survivors still walk among us." Kirkus

Includes bibliographical references (pages 473-508) and index.

292   Classical religion (Greek and Roman religion)

Graves, Robert
  ★ The **Greek** myths; Combined ed; Penguin Books 1992 782p pa $19.95 **292**
  1. Classical mythology
  ISBN 0-14-017199-1
  First published 1955
  A collection of the author's interpretations of Greek myths based on anthropological and archaeological findings

★ The **Oxford** dictionary of classical myth and religion; edited by Simon Price and Emily Kearns. Oxford University Press 2003 599p maps $39.95; pa $17.95 **292**
  1. Reference books 2. Classical mythology -- Dictionaries
  ISBN 0-19-280288-7; 0-19-280289-5 pa
                    LC 2004-298013

"Instead of separating mythology and Judeo-Christian religion into separate references, this work covers all religious life in the ancient Greco-Roman world. The result is a generally accessible and academically current compendium of information on gods and holy beings, religious practices, festivals, sacred sites, myths, authors, and texts of the period. The reader will find not only Athena and Zeus but also Jesus Christ and St. Augustine, Mani and Zoroaster." Libr J

292.1   Specific elements

Hamilton, Edith L.
  Mythology; timeless tales of gods and heroes, 75th anniversary illustrated edition. Edith Hamilton, Jim Tierny. 75th anniversary illustrated Black Dog & Leventhal 2017 371 p. illustrated (hardcover) $29.99 **292.1**
  1. Greek mythology 2. Norse mythology 3. Roman mythology
  ISBN 0316438529; 9780316438520; 9780316438537
                    LC 2017936387

This book, by Edith Hamilton, with artwork by Jim Tierny, "will be beloved by fans of Greek, Roman, and Norse mythology of all ages. . . . This exciting new deluxe, large-format hardcover edition, published in celebration of the book's 75th anniversary, will be beautifully packages and fully-illustrated throughout with all-new, specially commissioned four-color art, making it a true collector's item." (Publisher's note)

293   Germanic religion

Larrington, Carolyne
  Norse myths; a guide to the gods and heroes. Carolyne Larrington. Thames & Hudson 2017 208 p. illustrations, maps (hardcover) $24.95 **293**
  1. Norse mythology 2. Gods and goddesses 3. Mythology, Norse
  ISBN 9780500251966; 9780500773789
                    LC 2016941839

This book, by Carolyne Larrington, "presents the infamous Viking gods, from ... Asyr, led by Ódinn, and ... Vanir, to Thor and the mythological cosmos they inhabit. Passages translated from Old Norse bring this legendary world to life, from the myths of creation to ragnarök, the prophesied end of the world at the hands of Loki's army of monsters and giants, and everything that comes in between." (Publisher's note)

"Larrington ... presents readers with a succinct survey of Norse gods, heroes, and their myths." LJ

Includes bibliographical references (page 203) and index.

294   Religions of Indic origin

Dalrymple, William
    Nine lives; in search of the sacred in modern India. A.A. Knopf 2010 275p il map $26.95   **294**
        1. India -- Religion
    ISBN 978-0-307-27282-9; 0-307-27282-6
                                    LC 2010-06362
    First published 2009 in the United Kingdom
    "Throughout the book, Dalrymple showcases his knowledge of the breadth of India and his fearless willingness to penetrate its sometimes unsavory nooks and crannies, rendering this a truly heartfelt work for readers craving a deeper connection to India and its rich spiritual heritage. A remarkable feat of journalism." Kirkus
    Includes bibliographical references

Iyengar, B. K. S.
    Light on life; the yoga journey to wholeness, inner peace, and ultimate freedom. [by] B.K.S. Iyengar, with John J. Evans and Douglas Abrams. Rodale 2005 xxii, 282p il $24.95; pa $15.95   **294**
        1. Yoga
    ISBN 1-59486-248-6; 978-1-59486-248-9; 1-59486-524-8 pa
                                    LC 2005-15700
    The author "expounds the philosophy of yoga—its metaphysics, of which yoga poses, or asanas, represent the physical component. ... Not the book with which to begin the yoga journey, it is highly recommended for those advanced on the path and interested in learning from a master of flexibility and wisdom." Publ Wkly

294.3   Buddhism

Armstrong, Karen
    Buddha. Viking 2001 xxix, 205p map (Penguin lives series) hardcover o.p. pa $13   **294.3**
        1. Philosophers 2. Buddhist leaders
    ISBN 0-670-89193-2; 0-14-303436-7 pa
                                    LC 00-43808
    "Armstrong interprets the mythologized story of the Buddha's abandonment of his life of comfort and privilege; commitment to practicing advanced forms of yoga and nearly fatal asceticism; enlightenment beneath a bodhi tree; and 45 years of wandering and teaching until his death in 483. And as she does so, she lucidly explains his revelations and influence." Booklist
    Includes bibliographical references

Chödrön, Pema
    How to meditate; a practical guide to making friends with your mind. Pema Chodron. Sounds True 2013 viii, 175 p.p $19.95   **294.3**
        1. Buddhism 2. Meditation

ISBN 1604079339; 9781604079333
                                    LC 2012046126
    In this book, by Pema Chödrön, the author, an "American-born Tibetan Buddhist nun ..., explores in-depth what she considers the essentials for an evolving practice [of meditation] that helps you live in a wholehearted way.... Meditation, Pema explains, gives us a golden key to address this yearning. This comprehensive guide shows readers how to honestly meet and openly relate with the mind to embrace the fullness of our experience." (Publisher's note)
    "At all times Chodron is careful not to overwhelm readers or make meditation feel like an Everest expedition, and she features her own practice as an example of challenges and successes." LJ

Dalai Lama, XIV, 1935-
    Approaching the Buddhist path; Bhikṣu Tenzin Gyatso, the Fourteenth Dalai Lama and Bhikṣuṇi Thubten Chodron. Wisdom Publications 2017 xxviii, 323 p.p (The library of wisdom and compassion) (hardcover.: alk. paper) $29.95   **294.3**
        1. Enlightenment 2. Buddhism -- Doctrines
    ISBN 1614294410; 9781614294412; 9781614294573
                                    LC 2016053409
    This book in The Library of Wisdom and Compassion series, features Dalai Lama's "presentations of every step of the path to enlightenment, compiled and coauthored by one of his chief Western disciples, the American nun Thubten Chodron.... [The book] provides a wealth of reflections on Buddhist history and fundamentals, contemporary issues, and the Dalai Lama's own personal experiences." (Publisher's note)
    "An excellent and intellectually stimulating introduction to the Buddhist way of life." Pub Wkly
    Includes bibliographical references and index

    The **book** of joy; lasting happiness in a changing world. His Holiness the Dalai Lama and Archbishop Desmond Tutu, with Douglas Abrams. Avery 2016 x, 354 p.p (hardcover) $26   **294.3**
        1. Joy and sorrow 2. Happiness -- Religious aspects 3. Joy -- Religious aspects
    ISBN 9780399185045; 9780399185069
                                    LC 2016026669
    In this book, the Dalai Lama and Desmond Tutu "explore the Nature of True Joy and confront each of the Obstacles of Joy - from fear, stress, and anger to grief, illness, and death. They then offer us the Eight Pillars of Joy, which provide the foundation for lasting happiness. Throughout, they include stories, wisdom, and science. Finally, they share their daily Joy Practices that anchor their own emotional and spiritual lives." (Publisher's note)
    "This narrative recounts a multiday meeting of two highly regarded spiritual leaders and dear friends—the Dalai Lama and Archbishop Desmond Tutu—during which they discussed living a life filled with joy." LJ

    ★ **How** to be compassionate; a handbook for creating inner peace and a happier world. [by] His Holiness the Dalai Lama; translated from oral teachings and edited by Jeffrey Hopkins. Atria Books 2011 xi, 147 p.p $14   **294.3**
        1. Buddhism 2. Compassion 3. Religious life
    ISBN 1451623917; 9781451623901; 9781451623925
                                    LC 2011281813
    In this book, the Tibetan Buddhist spiritual leader the Dalai Lama demonstrates that "the surest path to true happiness lies in being intimately concerned with the welfare of others," or "in compassion." (Publisher's note) The author "works ... from the Buddhist places (aware-

ness, nonattachment) to speak to general readers about habits that make for unhappiness (anger, for one) and the attitudes that increase contentment." (Library Journal)

"Light on politics and even lighter on the more abstruse points of Tibetan Buddhism, this is a fine and accessible book for the everyday reader." Libr J

Includes bibliographical references (p. [145]-147)

Violence and compassion; {by} the Dalai Lama and Jean-Claude Carrière. Doubleday 1996 248p hardcover o.p. pa $11.50 **294.3**

1. Buddhism
ISBN 0-385-50144-7 pa

LC 95-30694

"This is a rich and invigorating volume, full of ponderable wisdom." Booklist

Emet, Joseph

Finding the blue sky; A Mindful Approach to Choosing Happiness Here and Now. Joseph Emet. TarcherPerigee, an imprint of Penguin Random House, LLC 2016 208 p. (ebook) $48; $16 **294.3**

1. Buddhism 2. Happiness 3. Spiritual life 4. Spiritual life -- Buddhism 5. Happiness -- Religious aspects -- Buddhism
ISBN 9781101992364; 9780143109631

LC 2016022074

This book, by Joseph Emet, "explores the intersection between Positive Psychology--the study of what makes people happy--and the ancient wisdom of Buddhism. . . . As Joseph explains in this work, the blue sky of happiness is found just beyond the grey clouds of sadness, everyday concerns, stress, or anxiety." (Publisher's note)

"While Emet's teaching of mindfulness is fairly basic for those already familiar with the subject, his approach through positive psychology is fresh and welcome; the newcomer will find a fount of compassionate wisdom to begin the work of personal growth." Pub Wkly

Includes bibliographical references

Epstein, Mark

Advice not given; a guide to getting over yourself. Mark Epstein, M.D. Penguin Press 2018 204 p. (hardcover) $26 **294.3**

1. Egoism 2. Psychotherapy 3. Buddhism -- Doctrines 4. Buddhism -- Psychology 5. Psychotherapy -- Religious aspects 6. Egoism -- Religious aspects -- Buddhism
ISBN 9780399564338; 9780399564321

LC 2017025261

In this book, author "Mark Epstein reveals how Buddhism and Western psychotherapy, two traditions that developed in entirely different times and places and, until recently, had nothing to do with each other, both identify the ego as the limiting factor in our well-being, and both come to the same conclusion: When we give the ego free reign, we suffer; but when it learns to let go, we are free." (Publisher's note)

"Epstein's book of practical suggestions will leave readers educated, inspired, and equipped with new tools for psychological health." Pub Wkly

Includes bibliographical references (pages 195-198) and index.

Greenblat, Musho Rodney Alan

Dharma Delight; a visionary post pop comic guide to Buddhism and Zen. Rodney Allan Greenblat. Tuttle Pub 2016 128 p. color illustrations (paperback) $16.95 **294.3**

1. Buddhism 2. Zen Buddhism
ISBN 0804845263; 9780804845267

This book, by Rodney Allan Greenblat, "illustrates how seeking the path of compassion and acceptance can be as zany and exuberant as it is profound. It is a happy exploration of Buddhist Enlightenment--what it is, where to seek it--and how to recognize the perfection in ourselves." (Publisher's note)

"The relatively brief text invites rereading, and those readers who truly want to learn more will do so. Thoughtful older teens and adults seeking a spiritual outlet may find much to enjoy here. Though the format is graphic-novel-like, this would be just as at home in the religion section." Booklist

Includes bibliographical references.

Johnson, Tim

Tragedy in crimson; how the Dalai Lama conquered the world but lost the battle with China. Nation Books 2011 333p map pa $26.99 **294.3**

1. Buddhist leaders 2. Political leaders 3. Nobel laureates for peace 4. China -- Politics and government 5. Tibet (China) -- Description and travel
ISBN 978-1-56858-601-4

LC 2010-37497

"A current, objective, basic primer on the Free Tibet movement and the Dalai Lama was sorely needed, and . . . [the author] has provided exactly that." Natl Rev

Includes bibliographical references

Keown, Damien

★ A **dictionary** of Buddhism; contributors, Stephen Hodge, Charles Jones, Paoli Tinti. Oxford Univ. Press 2003 357p il maps hardcover o.p. pa $15.95 **294.3**

1. Buddhism
ISBN 0-19-860560-9; 978-0-19-280062-6 pa; 0-19-280062-0 pa

LC 2003-276701

"The entries are short . . . but such accessibility is the very reason why this should be on the bookshelf of every student of Buddhism." Publ Wkly

Nichtern, Ethan

The **road** home; a contemporary exploration of the Buddhist path. Ethan Nichtern; foreword by Sharon Salzberg. North Point Press 2015 288 p. (hardback) $25 **294.3**

1. Buddhism 2. Meditation 3. Meditation -- Buddhism
ISBN 0374251932; 9780374251932

LC 2014030912

In this book, by Ethan Nichtern, the author "drawing from contemporary research on meditation and mindfulness and his experience as a Buddhist teacher and practitioner, . . . describes in fresh and deeply resonant terms the basic existential experience that gives rise to spiritual seeking--and also to its potentially dangerous counterpart, spiritual materialism." (Publisher's note)

"Valuable for readers looking for an introduction to Buddhist teachings as they relate to meditation practice or for those searching for ways to live their lives in the here and now." LJ

Olson, Carl

Historical dictionary of Buddhism. Scarecrow Press 2009 xxix, 327p il map (Historical dictionaries of religions, philosophies, and movements) $105; ebook $105 **294.3**

1. Reference books 2. Buddhism -- Dictionaries
ISBN 978-0-8108-5771-1; 0-8108-5771-5; 978-0-8108-6317-0 ebook; 0-8108-6317-0 ebook

LC 2009-7383

First published 1993 under the authorship of Charles S. Prebish

This dictionary covers "Buddhist concepts, significant figures, movements, schools, places, activities, and periods. . . . [It also features] a chronology, an introductory essay, a bibliography, and over 700 cross-referenced dictionary entries." Publisher's note

Includes bibliographical references

Rinzler, Lodro

The **Buddha** walks into a bar; a guide to life for a new generation. Lodro Rinzler. Shambhala 2012 211 p. pbk.: alk. paper $14.95 **294.3**

1. Buddhism 2. Spiritual life 3. Spiritual life -- Buddhism

ISBN 1590309375; 9781590309377

LC 2011014498

This book, by Lodro Rinzler, offers an "introduction to Buddhism for anyone who wants to ride the waves of life with mindfulness and compassion. You'll learn how to use meditation techniques to work with your own mind, how to manage the pervasive 'Incredible Hulk Syndrome,' how to relax into your life despite external pressures, and ultimately how you can start to bring light to a dark world." (Publisher's note)

"A fine beginning resource for younger adults ready to try the approaches of Buddhism; this is Eastern spirituality for the Harry Potter generation." LJ

Includes bibliographical references (p. 210-211)

Love hurts; Buddhist advice for the heartbroken. Lodro Rinzler. Shambhala 2016 170 p. (ebook) $11.99; (pbk.: alk. paper) $12.95 **294.3**

1. Buddhism 2. Consolation 3. Interpersonal relations 4. Suffering -- Religious aspects 5. Suffering -- Religious aspects -- Buddhism

ISBN 9780834840515; 1611803543; 9781611803549

LC 2016013202

This book, by Lodro Rinzler, presents "Buddhist-inspired advice for working through romantic breakups and other painful emotional periods. . . . The wisdom he presents applies to any kind of emotional suffering. It's a great, practical offering of consolation for someone you know who's going through a tough time, and for yourself when you're looking for the light at the end of the tunnel in your own situation." (Publisher's note)

"Rinzler melds his Shambhala training with sharp humor, an eye for detail, and deep empathy in this superb book for any heartbroken reader." Pub Wkly

Includes bibliographical references

Siff, Jason

Thoughts are not the enemy; an innovative approach to meditation practice. Jason Siff. Shambhala 2014 224 p. (paperback) $16.95 **294.3**

1. Meditation 2. Meditation -- Buddhism

ISBN 1611800439; 9781611800432

LC 2013046153

In this book, author Jason Siff offers a "new approach to meditation. . . . In most forms of meditation, the meditator is instructed to let go of thoughts as they arise. . . . [Siff argues,] if we allow thoughts to arise and become mindful of the thoughts themselves, we gain tranquillity and insight just as in other methods without having to reject our natural mental processes." (Publisher's note)

"Though Siff emphasizes open and unstructured exploration, some instructions veer toward technical, which may leave inexperienced meditators behind. Meditation scenarios, in which he presents fictionalized accounts of practitioners using different methods, often serve as awkward detours in this otherwise excellent work. Unafraid to go against the grain, Siff teaches readers how to adequately approach conceptual thought, the everyday state of existence, in all of its messiness." Pub Wkly

Includes bibliographical references and index

Sogyal

The **Tibetan** book of living and dying; edited by Patrick Gaffney and Andrew Harvey. rev and updated ed; HarperSanFrancisco 2002 441p il $28.95; pa $17.95 **294.3**

1. Death 2. Buddhism

ISBN 0-06-250793-1; 0-06-250834-2 pa

LC 2002-523084

First published 1992

The author "is well qualified to pass on his tradition. He does this beautifully, in limpid prose free of the scholastic list making that deadens many Tibetan Buddhist primers." N Y Times Book Rev {review of 1992 edition}

Includes bibliographical references

Sutin, Lawrence

★ **All** is change; the two-thousand year journey of Buddhism to the West. Little, Brown 2006 403p il $25.99 **294.3**

1. Buddhism

ISBN 978-0-316-74156-9; 0-316-74156-6

LC 2006-40824

"Greeks and Buddhists in India found common metaphysical ground 2,000 years ago, and Sutin also documents parallels between Buddist and Gnostic teachings in this vital study of a remarkable spiritual migration." Booklist

Includes bibliographical references

Suzuki, Daisetz Teitaro

★ **Manual** of Zen Buddhism. Grove Press 1960 192p il pa $13 **294.3**

1. Buddhist art 2. Zen Buddhism

ISBN 0-8021-3065-8

Fisrt published 1950 in the United Kingdom

In this volume, D. T. Suzuki has brought together some of Zen Buddhism's original sources. Included are the sutras or sermons of the Buddha: the gathas or hymns; the philosophical puzzles known as koan; and the dharanis or invocations to expel evil spirits. In addition to the written selections there are reproductions of Buddhist drawings and paintings, including religious statues found in Zen temples

Thich Nhat Hanh, 1926-

The **art** of living; peace and freedom in the here and now. Thich Nhat Hanh. HarperOne 2017 ix, 206 p.p (hardcover) $25.99 **294.3**

1. Buddhism 2. Religious life 3. Religious life -- Buddhism 4. Life -- Religious aspects -- Buddhism

ISBN 9780062434722; 9780062434661; 9780062434678

LC 2017013611

This book, by Thich Nhat Hanh, "presents, for the first time, seven transformative meditations that open up new perspectives on our lives, our relationships and our interconnectedness with the world around us. Based on the last full talks before his sudden hospitalization, and drawing on intimate examples from his own life, Thich Nhat Hanh shows us how these seven meditations can free us to live a happy, peaceful and active life, and face aging and dying with curiosity and joy and without fear." (Publisher's note)

Thurman, Robert A. F.

Why the Dalai Lama matters; his act of truth as the solution for China, Tibet, and the world. [by] Robert Thurman. Beyond Words Pub. 2008 xxiv, 231p il map $23   **294.3**
1. Buddhism 2. Tibet (China) 3. Buddhist leaders 4. Political leaders 5. Nobel laureates for peace
ISBN 978-1-58270-220-9; 1-58270-220-9

LC 2008-8529

The author presents an "introduction to Buddhism and the Tibetan concept of the Dalai Lama before focusing on the current 'living embodiment of the Buddha'—a man born as Tenzin Gyatso—the 14th Dalai Lama. Thurman sympathetically renders his lifelong friend as a 'simple Buddhist monk,' a teacher, philosopher, scientist and the political representative of the Tibetan people. . . . The book concludes with a five-step plan to broker peace between Tibet and China—an agenda simultaneously pragmatic and idealistic, demonstrating truly the talent and power of faith." Publ Wkly

Includes bibliographical references

Van Buren, Mark

A **fool's** guide to actual happiness; Mark Van Buren. Wisdom Publications 2018 264 p. (pbk.: alk. paper) $16.99 **294.3**
1. Buddhism 2. Meditation 3. Happiness -- Religious aspects 4. Buddhism -- Psychology 5. Happiness -- Religious aspects -- Buddhism
ISBN 9781614294481

LC 2017048415

This book, by Mark Van Buren, "offers a realistic roadmap for working towards inner peace without needing to be someone you're not. With humor and refreshing simplicity, Van Buren shows how everything life throws at you, good or bad, can be used as a means to cultivate compassion, wisdom, and loving-kindness. This book allows you to explore who you are—warts and all—and gives you tools to love and accept what you find." (Publisher's note)

"Van Buren (Your Life Is Meditation) lays out a concise but informative crash course on finding happiness through Buddhist concepts and practices in this powerful book." Pub Wkly

Includes bibliographical references and index

Watts, Alan

The **way** of Zen. Vintage Books 1999 236p il pa $13.95   **294.3**
1. Zen Buddhism
ISBN 0-375-70510-4
First published 1957 by Pantheon Bks.

This is an historical and cultural survey of Zen, tracing its origins in Indian and Chinese thought. The author describes the Zen way of living and its techniques for overcoming the mind's conflict between symbolic thought and actual experience.

Includes bibliographical references

Wright, Robert, 1957-

Why Buddhism is true; the science and philosophy of meditation and enlightenment. Robert Wright. Simon & Schuster 2017 xii, 321 p.p (hardcover) $27   **294.3**
1. Buddhism 2. Meditation 3. Buddhism -- Apologetic works
ISBN 9781439195451; 9781439195475

LC 2016041766

In this book, author Robert Wright "leads readers on a journey through psychology, philosophy, and a great many silent retreats to show how and why meditation can serve as the foundation for a spiritual life in a secular age. At once excitingly ambitious and wittily accessible, this

is the first book to combine evolutionary psychology with cutting-edge neuroscience to defend the radical claims at the heart of Buddhist philosophy." (Publisher's note)

"Wright's joyful and insightful book is both entertaining and informative, equally accessible to general audiences and more experienced practitioners." Pub Wkly

Includes bibliographical references and index

294.337   Social theology -- Buddhism

Chödrön, Pema

Practicing peace; Pema Chodron. Random House Inc 2018 104 p. $12.95   **294.337**
1. Religious life 2. Peace -- Religious aspects -- Buddhism
ISBN 1611806135; 9781611806137

"Can there be hope for a peaceful future in times like these? How can we overcome our sense of helplessness when problems seem so big and tensions so strong? Pema Chödrön here shows us how to look deeply at the underlying causes of these tensions and how we really can create a more peaceful world--by starting right where we are and learning to see the seeds of hostility in our hearts." (Publisher's note)

"Chodron teaches readers how to pause and let experiences pierce the heart so that the sparks of aggression may burn themselves out, leaving a positive sense of groundlessness and insecurity. These are familiar teachings to those acquainted with her work, but her approach remains invaluable for guidance on working with hatred and anger." Publishers' Weekly

294.342   Doctrines

Thubten Zopa Rinpoche

The **four** noble truths; a guide for everyday life. Lama Zopa Rinpoche, edited by Yeo Puay Huei. Wisdom Publications 2018 312 p. (pbk.: alk. paper) $17.95   **294.342**
1. Buddhism 2. Religion 3. Four Noble Truths
ISBN 9781614293941

LC 2017048508

In this book, by Lama Zopa Rinpoche, edited by Yeo Puay Huei, "Buddha's profound teachings on the four noble truths are illuminated by a Tibetan master simply and directly, so that readers gain an immediate and personal understanding of the causes and conditions that give rise to suffering as well as the spiritual life as the path to liberation." (Publisher's note)

"Though treatments of some complex topics—such as Vajrayana and the path of tantra—are hard to follow, this useful book clearly explains the Buddhist belief that the mind creates suffering through the mistaken notion of the self's inherent existence." Publishers' Weekly

Includes bibliographical references and index

294.35   Buddhist ethics

Dalai Lama, XIV, 1935-

An **appeal** to the world; the way to peace in a time of division. His Holiness the Dalai Lama with Franz Alt. William Morrow, an imprint of HarperCollins Publishers 2017 vii, 112 p.p illustrations (hardcover) $14.99   **294.35**
1. Peace 2. Ethics 3. Buddhism 4. Religion and ethics
ISBN 9780062835550; 9780062835536; 006283553X

In this book, "His Holiness the Dalai Lama of Tibet reveals that we all hold the seeds of world peace within us. . . . [He] outlines both the inward and outward paths to peace, addressing a wide range of contemporary topics--from the rise of nationalism, Trump presidency, refugee crisis, climate catastrophes, and materialism to meditation, universal ethics, and even neuroscience." (Publisher's note)

"Always inspiring and accessible, this lovely book is, itself, readers will discover, worth meditation and contemplation." Booklist

294.392   Mahayana Buddhism (Northern Buddhism)

Connelly, Ben

Inside Vasubandhu's Yogacara; A Practitioner's Guide. Ben Connelly; with a new translation from Sanskrit by Ben Connelly and Weijen Teng; foreword by Norman Fischer. Wisdom Publications 2016 248 p. (paperback: alk. paper) $16.95; (ebook) $16.99   **294.392**
  1. Buddhism 2. Yogācāra (Buddhism)
  ISBN 1614292841; 9781614292845; 9781614293088
                                                      LC 2016008752
"In this down-to-earth book, Ben Connelly sure-handedly guides us through the intricacies of Yogacara and the richness of the 'Thirty Verses.' Dedicating a chapter of the book to each line of the poem, he lets us thoroughly lose ourselves in its depths. His warm and wise voice unpacks and contextualizes its wisdom, showing us how we can apply its ancient insights to our own modern lives, to create a life of engaged peace, harmony, compassion, and joy." (Publisher's note)

"Newcomers and adherents to this lesser-known Buddhist school alike are lucky to have Connelly as an exceptional guide to the central themes of Yogacara." Pub Wkly

  Includes bibliographical references and index

294.5   Hinduism

Calasso, Roberto

Ardor; Roberto Calasso; translated from the Italian by Richard Dixon. Farrar Straus & Giroux 2014 432 p. illustrations (some color) (hardback) $35   **294.5**
  1. Vedas 2. Hinduism 3. Vedas -- Criticism, interpretation, etc
  ISBN 0374182310; 9780374182311
                                                      LC 2013044345
This book by Roberto Calasso "explores the ancient texts known as the Vedas. Often at odds with modern thought, these texts illuminate the nature of consciousness more than anybody else has managed up to now. Following the 'hundred paths of the Śatapatha Brāhmaṇa, an impressive exegesis of Vedic ritual, 'Ardor' indicates that it may be possible to reach what is closest to us by passing through that which is most remote." (Publisher's note)

"Richard Dixon's supple and elegant translation brings Calasso's poetic meditations to life. Readers will return again and again for wisdom and insight." Pub Wkly

Davis, Richard H.

The **Bhagavad** Gita; a biography. Richard H. Davis. Princeton University Press 2014 256 p. illustrations (Lives of great religious books) (hardback) $24.95   **294.5**
  1. Hinduism 2. Sacred books 3. Bhagavadgītā -- History 4. Bhagavadgītā -- Criticism, interpretation, etc
  ISBN 0691139962; 9780691139968
                                                      LC 2014023890
This book, by Richard H. Davis, part of the "Lives of great religious books" series, "tells the story of [the Bhagavad Gita,] . . . from its origins in ancient India to its reception today as a spiritual classic that has been translated into more than seventy-five languages. . . . [The author] highlights the place of this legendary dialogue in classical Indian culture, and then examines how it has lived on in diverse settings and contexts." (Publisher's note)

"Davis neatly organizes a great deal of material, and he presents it in utterly accessible prose." Choice

  Includes bibliographical references and index

Doniger, Wendy

On Hinduism; Wendy Doniger. Oxford University Press, USA 2014 680 p. (hardback: alk. paper) $39.95   **294.5**
  1. Hinduism
  ISBN 0199360073; 9780199360079
                                                      LC 2013038952
  Includes bibliographical references (pages 627-648) and index
This book of essays, by Wendy Doniger, is about Hinduism. "The essays contemplate the nature of Hinduism; Hindu concepts of divinity; attitudes concerning gender, control, and desire; the question of reality and illusion; and the impermanent and the eternal in the two great Sanskrit epics, the 'Ramayana' and the 'Mahabharata.' . . . Doniger concludes with . . . autobiographical essays in which she reflects on . . . the influence of Hinduism on her own philosophy of life." (Publisher's note)

"This book assumes some basic knowledge of the subject, but [Doniger's] writing is clear and direct and will be intelligible to readers unacquainted with the technicalities of Hindu doctrine and literature." LJ

Goldberg, Philip

American Veda; from Emerson and the Beatles to yoga and meditation: how Indian spirituality changed the West. Doubleday Religion 2010 398p il ebook $26; $26   **294.5**
  1. Yoga 2. Vedanta 3. Hinduism 4. United States -- Religion
  ISBN 978-0-307-71961-4 ebook; 978-0-385-52134-5
                                                      LC 2010-11040
"From meditating movie stars, scandalous gurus, and psychedelic drugs to genuine spiritual breakthroughs and devotion to helping others, Goldberg's history of 'American Veda' takes measure of a powerful, if underappreciated, force." Booklist

  Includes bibliographical references

Mahabharata/Bhagavadgita

★ **Bhagavad** Gita; a new translation. [translated by] Stephen Mitchell. Harmony Bks. 2000 223p hardcover o.p. pa $13.95   **294.5**
  ISBN 0-609-60550-X; 0-609-81034-0 pa
                                                      LC 00-28286
"An eighteen-part discussion between the god Krishna, an avatar of Vishnu appearing as a charioteer, and Arjuna, a warrior about to enter battle, on the nature and meaning of life. Sometimes called the New Testament of Hinduism, it is an interpolation in the great Hindu epic the Mahabharata." Reader's Ency. 4th edition

Majmudar, Amit

★ **Godsong**; a verse translation of the Bhagavad Gita, with commentary. by Amit Majmudar. Alfred A. Knopf 2018 256 p. (hardback) $25   **294.5**
  1. Hinduism 2. Religious poetry
  ISBN 9781524733476
                                                      LC 2017025404
This book, by Amit Majmudar presents poems about the relationship of the soul and god. "His verse translation captures the many tones and

strategies Krishna uses with Arjuna--strict and berating, detached and philosophical, tender and personable. 'Listening guides' to each section follow the main text, and expand in accessible terms on the text and what is happening between the lines." (Publisher's note)

"This is a well-crafted and exceptional translation of a spiritual and cultural masterpiece." Library Journal

Sengupta, Hindol

Being Hindu; understanding a peaceful path in a violent world. Hindol Sengupta. Rowman & Littlefield 2017 ix, 189 p.p (hardback: alk. paper) $35   **294.5**
  1. Hindus 2. Hinduism 3. Religious literature
  ISBN 9781442267466; 9781442267459

  LC 2017023126

This book, by Hindol Sengupta, "is a practitioner's guide that takes the reader on a journey to very simply understand what the Hindu message is, where it stands in the clash of civilizations between Islam and Christianity, and why the Hindu way could yet be the path for plurality and progress in the twenty-first century." (Publisher's note)

"Sengupta's enlightening elucidation is invaluable for understanding Hinduism, India, and the growing Hindu community in the U.S." Booklist

Includes bibliographical references and index

294.592   Sacred books and scriptures

The **illustrated** Mahabharata; the definitive guide to India's greatest epic. DK; [foreword by Bibek Debroy] DK Publishing 2017 509 p. illustrations (chiefly color) (hardcover) $50   **294.592**
  1. Indian epic poetry 2. Epic literature -- History and criticism 3. Mahābhārata -- Illustrations 4. Mahābhārata -- Criticism, interpretation, etc
  ISBN 9781465462916; 1465462910

  LC 2017285524

"The Illustrated Mahabharata brings the world's longest epic to life. With more than 500 stunning images showcasing India's varied art forms, the book encapsulates the complete stories in a uniquely accessible way. Providing details of the principal cities and kingdoms from the epic, . . .The Illustrated Mahabharata also includes detailed family trees to help unfamiliar readers understand the relationships of the Mahabharata's various characters." (Publisher's note)

"The content is detailed, covering people, mythology and folklore, history and culture, key concepts, and art. The layout is dazzling, with quotes, pull-out boxes of analysis, and more than 500 full-color illustrations." LJ

Mahabharata

294.6   Sikhism

Singh, Patwant

The **Sikhs**. Knopf 2000 276p il hardcover o.p. pa $14   **294.6**
  1. Sikhs
  ISBN 0-375-40728-6; 0-385-50206-0 pa

  LC 99-31807

The author "traces Sikh history from its origins in the 15th century through Indira Gandhi's 1984 storming of the Golden Temple. . . . Sikhs, he argues, have for centuries been an embattled people because their culture and religion defy the predominant religions in the region, as well

as the Indian caste system with its ruling elite." Publ Wkly

Includes bibliographical references

296   Judaism

Bronfman, Edgar M., 1929-2013

Why be Jewish? a testament. Edgar M. Bronfman. Twelve 2016 256 p. (hardback) $26   **296**
  1. Judaism 2. Jews -- Identity 3. Jewish way of life 4. Judaism -- Essence, genius, nature
  ISBN 9781455562886; 9781455562893; 9781478961024

  LC 2015039135

In this book, author Edgar M. Bronfman "walks readers through the major tenets and ideas in Jewish life. . . . Bronfman shares . . . insights gleaned from his own personal journey and makes a compelling case for the meaning and transcendence of a secular Judaism that is still steeped in deep moral values, authentic Jewish texts, and a focus on deed over creed or dogma." (Publisher's note)

"Excellent for nontheistic and unaffiliated readers, Jewish or not, who want to better understand this religion." LJ

Includes bibliographical references and index

The **Cambridge** history of Judaism; v2 edited by W.D. Davies [and] Louis Finkelstein; assistant editor, John Sturdy. Cambridge Univ. Press 1990 738p v2 il maps $205   **296**
  1. Judaism -- History
  ISBN 0-521-21929-9

This "second volume in the four-volume Cambridge History of Judaism deals with Judaism's encounter with Hellenism under Alexander the Great and his successors, the efforts of Jews led by the Maccabees to counter this influence and to establish their own state and the resulting Jewish ideologies and literary activities. The 18 chapters treat the archaeology of Hellenistic Palestine, languages, the interpenetration of Judaism and Hellenism in the pre-Maccabean period, the Hasmonean revolt and dynasty, the matrix of apocalyptic and the Samaritans, as well as various writings and historical movements." America

Includes bibliographical references

Encyclopaedia Judaica; Fred Skolnik, editor-in-chief; Michael Berenbaum, executive editor. 2nd ed; Macmillan Reference USA in association with the Keter Pub. House 2007 22v il map   **296**
  1. Jews 2. Judaism 3. Reference books 4. Judaism -- Encyclopedias
  ISBN 0-02-865928-7; 978-0-02-865928-2

  LC 2006020426

First published 1972 in 16 volumes

ALA RUSA Dartmouth Medal (2007)

This "is a welcome addition to reference collections. By documenting the modern Jewish experience while retaining links with its rich past, it provides users with information about all aspects of Jewish religion and culture." Booklist

Includes bibliographical references

Freedman, Samuel G.

Jew vs. Jew; the struggle for the soul of American Jewry. Simon & Schuster 2000 397p $26; pa $14   **296**
  1. Judaism 2. Jews -- United States
  ISBN 0-684-85944-0; 0-684-85945-9 pa

  LC 00-33907

The author "describes the paradoxical situation faced by today's American Jews, living in a country where religious freedom has yielded unreconcilable devisiveness. . . . This is a helpful guide for anyone seeking an understanding of intra-Jewish conflicts in contemporary America." Libr J

Includes bibliographical references

★ The **New** encyclopedia of Judaism; editor-in-chief, Geoffrey Wigoder; coeditors, Fred Skolnik & Shmuel Himelstein. New York Univ. Press 2002 856p il $79.95 **296**

1. Reference books 2. Judaism -- Dictionaries
ISBN 0-8147-9388-6

LC 2002-16614

First published 1989 with title: The Encyclopedia of Judaism

This reference "seeks to present a balanced picture, offering current thinking among scholars in Reform, Conservative, and Orthodox movements and a roster of contributors hailing from Israel, England, and the United States. While the scholarship is solid, the material is readily accessible to a popular audience, and the work is magnificently illustrated." Libr J

Includes bibliographical references

★ The **Oxford** dictionary of the Jewish religion; editor in chief, Adele Berlin. 2nd ed. Oxford University Press 2011 xxiv, 934 p.p (hardcover) $195 **296**

1. Judaism -- Dictionaries 2. Judaism -- Encyclopedias
ISBN 0199730040; 9780199730049; 9780199759279

LC 2010035774

This book, by Maxine Grossman, edited by Adele Berlin, presents an updated, second edition of its original 1997 publication. It "focuses on recent and changing rituals in the Jewish community. . . . Nearly 200 internationally renowned scholars have created a new edition that incorporates updated bibliographies, biographies of 20th-century individuals who have shaped the recent thought and history of Judaism, and an index with alternate spellings of Hebrew terms." (Publisher's note)

Includes bibliographical references and index.

Reader's guide to Judaism; editor, Michael Terry. Fitzroy Dearborn Pubs. 2000 718p (Reader's guide) $135 **296**

1. Reference books 2. Judaism -- Encyclopedias
ISBN 1-57958-139-0

LC 2001-274119

This "work covers over 400 topics, including interfaith relations, historical periods, philosophical and mystical movements, important figures, and more. Preceding each essay is a bibliography of five to ten English-language titles. . . . Written by librarians and scholars . . . these 1000 to 2000-word essays include a descriptive and often analytical overview of each book. . . . This is an excellent tool for building Judaica collections in public and academic libraries." Libr J

Includes bibliographical references

Robinson, George

Essential Judaism; a complete guide to beliefs, customs and rituals. George Robinson. 2nd edition Atria Books 2016 680 p. illustrations pbk $24 **296**

1. Judaism
ISBN 1501117750; 9781501117756

"Robinson has updated this valuable introductory text with information on topics including denominational shifts, same-sex marriage, the intermarriage debate, transgender Jews, the growth of anti-Semitism, and the changing role of women in worship, along with many other hotly debated topics in the contemporary Jewish world and beyond." (Publisher's note)

Sarna, Jonathan D.

★ **American** Judaism; a history. Yale University Press 2004 xx, 490p il $35 **296**

1. Judaism 2. Jews -- United States
ISBN 0-300-10197-X

LC 2003-14464

"This comprehensive and insightful study of the American Jewish experience is much more than just a record of events. It is an account of how people shaped events: establishing and maintaining communities, responding to challenges, and working for change. It is compelling reading for Jews and non-Jews alike." Booklist

Includes bibliographical references

Weisman, Steven R.

The **chosen** wars; how Judaism became an American religion. Steven R. Weisman. Simon & Schuster 2018 368 p. illustrations (hardcover: alk. paper) $30 **296**

1. Judaism -- United States -- History 2. Judaism -- United States -- History -- 18th century 3. Judaism -- United States -- History -- 19th century
ISBN 9781416573265; 9781416573272

LC 2017058478

In this book author Steven R. Weisman, "tells the dramatic history of how Judaism redefined itself in America in the eighteenth and nineteenth centuries. . . . [This book] tells the stories of the colorful rabbis and activists, including women, who defined American Judaism and whose disputes divided it into the Reform, Conservative, and Orthodox branches that remain today." (Publisher's note)

Includes bibliographical references and index

296.09   History, geographic treatment, biography

The **Cambridge** history of Judaism; v3 edited by William Horbury, John Sturdy and W.D. Davies. Cambridge Univ. Press 1999 1254p v3 il maps $190 **296.09**

1. Judaism -- History
ISBN 0-521-24377-7

This third volume of a four-volume history "contains thirty-two essays on aspects of Judaism in the early Roman period, primarily the period between Pompey and Vespasian but often ranging into the rabbinic period." J Relig

Includes bibliographical references

Cole, Peter

★ **Sacred** trash; [by] Adina Hoffman & Peter Cole. Nextbook: Schocken 2011 283p. ill., ports. **296.09**

1. Manuscripts 2. Jews -- History 3. Cultural property 4. Cairo Genizah 5. Judaism -- History -- Sources
ISBN 978-0-8052-4258-4; 0-8052-4258-9

LC 201016751

Sophie Brody Award (2012)

This is an account of the discovery, about 120 years ago, of a cache of documents in the storeroom of a synagogue in Cairo. The cache, referred to as a geniza, includes "letters, wills, bills of lading, prayers, marriage contracts and writs of divorce, Bibles, money orders, court depositions, business inventories, leases, magic charms and receipts." (N Y Times Book Rev)

Includes bibliographical references.

Goodman, Martin

★ A **history** of Judaism; Martin Goodman. Princeton

University Press 2018 656 p. (cloth) $39.95 **296.09**
1. Judaism -- History 2. Religion -- History
ISBN 9780691181271

LC 2017957814

This book, by Martin Goodman, "provides the first truly comprehensive look in one volume at how . . . [Judaism] came to be, how it has evolved from one age to the next, and how its various strains, sects, and traditions have related to each other. . . . Goodman takes readers from Judaism's origins in the polytheistic world of the second and first millennia BCE to the temple cult at the time of Jesus." (Publisher's note)

"While dense and detailed, this volume is ideal for anyone looking for a comprehensive history of Judaism. Even experts will find something new to consider." (LJ)

296.1 Sources

Abegg, Martin G.

The **Dead** Sea scrolls; a new translation. [by] Michael O. Wise, Martin G. Abegg Jr., and Edward M. Cook. Rev ed; HarperSanFrancisco 2005 662p pa $24.95 **296.1**
ISBN 0-06-076662-X

LC 2005-46285
First published 1996

"An engaging necessity for updating Dead Sea Scrolls collections." Booklist

Includes bibliographical references

The **Encyclopedia** of the Dead Sea scrolls; {edited by} Lawrence H. Schiffman and James C. VanderKam. Oxford Univ. Press 2000 2v set $295 **296.1**
1. Dead Sea scrolls
ISBN 0-19-508450-0

LC 99-55300
"In addition to individual texts, coverage extends to the archeological sites themselves; important historical figures (Moses) and groups (Essenes, Pharisees) as they are represented in the scrolls; scholars important to Dead Sea scroll research . . . and methods employed both to date and to preserve these ancient documents." Booklist

Freedman, Harry

The **Talmud**; A Biography - Banned, Censored and Burned. the Book They Couldn't Suppress. St. Martin's Press 2014 256 p. $26 **296.1**
1. Jewish diaspora 2. Talmud -- Biography
ISBN 1472905946; 9781472905949

LC 2015376128
In this book, "Jewish scholar Harry Freedman tells the . . . story of an ancient classic, the legal and mystical pillar of Judaism and recounts the story of a book which, in many ways, parallels the history of the Jewish people. . . . Freedman traces the spiraling paths of the Jewish diaspora and explores the story of the Talmud's early origins in Babylon, its role during the Enlightenment and its influence over traditional Judaism." (Publisher's note)

"Freedman (independent scholar) makes clear that this is no academic volume; his goal is to make the Talmud's story interesting and perhaps even inspiring to the unacquainted reader." Choice

Schiffman, Lawrence H.

Reclaiming the Dead Sea scrolls; the history of Judaism, the background of Christianity, the lost library of Qumran. with a foreword by Chaim Potok. Jewish Publ. Soc. 1994 xxvii,

529p il maps **296.1**
1. Dead Sea scrolls 2. Judaism -- History

LC 94-26489
Schiffman provides a "description and evaluation of the scrolls, the archeology of Qumran (the site near the Dead Sea from which the scrolls originated), the history and nature of the Jewish community that lived at Qumran and the setting of the scrolls in Jewish history and thought from the second century B.C. through the first century A.D." N Y Times Book Rev

Includes bibliographical references

296.3 Theology, ethics, views of social issues

Epstein, Lawrence J.

The **basic** beliefs of Judaism; a twenty-first-century guide to a timeless tradition. Lawrence J. Epstein. Jason Aronson 2013 203 p. (cloth: alk. paper) $35 **296.3**
1. Judaism 2. Jews -- Social life and customs 3. Jewish way of life
ISBN 0765709694; 9780765709691; 9780765709707

LC 2013015985

In this book, Lawrence J. Epstein "culls from nearly 3,000 years of Jewish moral, ethical, and philosophical thought to present an overview of fundamentals for an educated, 21st-century audience. In ten chapters, he discusses themes such as the mystery of God, the suffering of the innocent, and ethical foundations for a good life, from a broad array of Jewish perspectives." (Choice: Current Reviews for Academic Libraries)

Includes bibliographical references and index

Kushner, Harold S.

★ **When** bad things happen to good people; with a new preface by the author. 20th anniversary ed; Schocken Bks. 2001 202p $21 **296.3**
1. Suffering 2. Providence and government of God
ISBN 0-8052-4193-0

LC 2001-531062

A reissue of the title first published 1981

"A bright and happy infant, Rabbi Kushner's first-born son gradually succumbed to progeria, 'rapid aging': he never grew beyond three feet tall, looked like a hairless, wizened old man, and died in his teens. This book is his father's attempt to make sense out of his son's fate, his own pain, and the pain of others enduring undeserved misfortunes." Libr J

296.311 God

Kugel, James L.

The **great** shift; encountering God in biblical times. James L Kugel. Houghton Mifflin Harcourt 2017 xvi, 476 p.p maps (hardcover) $30 **296.311**
1. God 2. Bible. Old Testament 3. God (Judaism) 4. Spirituality -- Judaism 5. Bible. Old Testament -- Criticism, interpretation, etc
ISBN 9780544520578; 9780544520554

LC 2017019809

This book, by James L Kugel, "fuses revelatory close readings of ancient texts with modern scholarship from a range of fields, including neuroscience, anthropology, psychology, and archaeology, to explain the origins of belief, worship, and the sense of self, and the changing nature of God through history." (Publisher's note)

"Biblical exegesis at its best: a brilliant and sensitive reading of ancient texts, all with an eye to making them meaningful to our time by making sense of what they meant in their own." Kirkus

Includes bibliographical references (pages [413]-441) and index.

296.4 Traditions, rites, public services

Ashton, Dianne

Hanukkah in America; a history. by Dianne Ashton. New York University Press 2013 368 p. illustrations (The Goldstein-Goren series in American Jewish history) (cl: alk. paper) $29.95 **296.4**
  1. Hanukkah 2. Jews -- United States 3. Hanukkah -- United States 4. Judaism -- United States -- History -- 21st century
  ISBN 0814707394; 9780814707395

LC 2013014009

In this history of Hanukkah in the U.S. author Diane Ashton argues that the holiday "has been a vehicle for asserting solidarity among a never-large American minority and establishing that minority's credentials as faithful Americans as well as faithful Jews. Further, Ashton asserts, Hanukkah has always played a role in response to the successive challenges American Jews have faced over the course of the last century and a half." (Booklist)
Includes bibliographical references and index

Axelrod, Matt

Your guide to the Jewish holidays; from shofar to Seder. cantor Matt Axelrod. Jason Aronson 2013 214 p. (cloth: alk. paper) $30 **296.4**
  1. Jewish holidays 2. Fasts and feasts -- Judaism
  ISBN 0765709899; 9780765709899; 9780765709905

LC 2013033886

This book, by cantor Matt Axelrod, "takes a . . . look at the 11 most important Jewish holidays. Instead of simply explaining that Jews are obligated to observe in a certain way because of a biblical text, Axelrod shows where each holiday, along with its rituals, came from in a historical context. He provides a humorous retelling of the biblical passages relating to the holiday, explorations of rituals associated with each holiday, and descriptions of traditional foods." (Publisher's note)

Bolsta, Hyla Shifra

The **illuminated** Kaddish; interpretations of the Mourner's Prayer. paintings, calligraphy, and interpretations by Hyla Shifra Bolsta. KTAV Pub. House, Inc. 2012 108 p. col. ill. $27.50 **296.4**
  1. Prayer 2. Judaism -- Customs and practices 3. Illumination of books and manuscripts 4. Kaddish 5. Judaism -- Liturgy -- Texts 6. Jewish illumination of books and manuscripts
  ISBN 1602801916; 9781602801912

LC 2011033483

This book from author and illustrator Hyla Bolsta is an illuminated version of the Kaddish, "a prayer recited as part of the funeral rites of a Jewish believer." Here, "she connects the words throughout by a motif of leaves and branches from the tree of life." The prayer "is a kind of perennial puzzle . . . . Why praise God, in the words of Ezekiel, rather than mourn the death? Bolsta's scholarship, insights, and art suggest some answers." (Library Journal)
Includes bibliographical references

Diamant, Anita

The **Jewish** wedding now; Anita Diamant. Third edition Scribner 2017 xxi, 224 p.p illustrations (paperback) $18 **296.4**
  1. Weddings 2. Marriage customs and rites 3. Judaism -- Customs and practices 4. Weddings -- Planning 5. Jewish marriage customs

and rites
  ISBN 1501153943; 9781501153945; 9781416576549

This book, by Anita Diamant, "explains everything you need to know to plan your own Jewish wedding in today's ever-changing world. . . . [Diamant] provides choices for every stage of a wedding. . . . She explains the Jewish tradition of love and marriage with references drawn from Biblical, Talmudic, and mystical texts and stories. She guides you step by step through planning the ceremony and the party that follows." (Publisher's note)
"This provides a very helpful framework for couples who want to honor tradition with contemporary values." Booklist
Includes bibliographical references (pages 193-197) and index.

Eisenberg, Ronald L.

★ The **JPS** guide to Jewish traditions; [by] Ron Eisenberg. The Jewish Publication Society 2004 xxiii, 806p $40 **296.4**
  1. Reference books 2. Judaism -- Encyclopedias
  ISBN 0-8276-0760-1

LC 2004-6399

This "work covers the major elements of Jewish life, including life-cycle events (birth, bar and bat mitzvah, marriage, divorce, parenting, and death), the Sabbath and holidays, the synagogue, prayer, and the Bible and Jewish literature. . . . The author has done a masterful job in distilling the major beliefs and practices of a 3,000-year-old religion into lively and informative prose and in creating an accessible, essential reference work." Booklist
Includes bibliographical references

Goldman, Ari L.

Being Jewish; the spiritual and cultural practice of Judaism today. Simon & Schuster 2000 286p $25 **296.4**
  1. Jewish holidays 2. Judaism -- Customs and practices
  ISBN 0-684-82389-6

LC 00-44047

"An excellent resource." Booklist
Includes bibliographical references

★ **New** American Haggadah; edited by Jonathan Safran Foer; with a new translation by Nathan Englander; designed by Oded Ezer; commentaries by Nathaniel Deutsch ("House of Study") . . . [et al.]; timeline created by Mia Sara Bruch. Little, Brown & Co. 2012 149 p. ill. $29.99 **296.4**
  1. Seder 2. Prayers 3. Jews -- History 4. Rites and ceremonies 5. Haggadah 6. Haggadot -- Texts 7. Seder -- Liturgy -- Texts 8. Judaism -- Liturgy -- Texts
  ISBN 0316069868; 9780316069861

LC 2011040637

Author Jonathan Foer retells a major story in Jewish history. "Read each year around the seder table, the Haggadah recounts through prayer, song, and ritual the extraordinary story of Exodus, when Moses led the Israelites out of slavery in Egypt to wander the desert for forty years before reaching the Promised Land. . . . [This prayer book includes] commentary by major Jewish writers and thinkers [including] Jeffrey Goldberg, Lemony Snicket, Rebecca Newberger Goldstein, and Nathaniel Deutsch." (Publisher's note)

Shulevitz, Judith

The **Sabbath** world; glimpses of a different order of time. Random House 2010 246p $26 **296.4**
  1. Sabbath 2. Rest -- Religious aspects 3. Time -- Religious aspects
  ISBN 978-1-4000-6200-3; 1-4000-6200-4

LC 2009-26417

"In personal terms, and without sanctimony, [the author] explores the history of the Sabbath, its philosophical foundations, its consolations, its purposes, and, in doing so, writes a swift, penetrating book intent on shattering the habits of mindless workaholism and the inability to recognize the blessings of rest, reflection, spirit, and family." New Yorker

Wagner, Jordan Lee

The **synagogue** survival kit; A Guide to Understanding Jewish Religious Services. Jordan Lee Wagner. Jason Aronson 1997 xvi, 347 p.p illustrations $35   **296.4**
    1. Judaism 2. Synagogues 3. Siddur 4. Prayer -- Judaism 5. Judaism -- Liturgy 6. Synagogue etiquette 7. Judaism -- Customs and practices
    ISBN 0765709686; 1568219679; 9780765709684; 9781568219677
LC 96039695

This book, by Jordan Lee Wagner, "offers introductions and instructions for all aspects of the synagogue experience. No matter what kind of synagogue you attend, the roadmap is the same. Some synagogues may read certain prayers in English translation rather than the original Hebrew or replace some traditional prayers with newer versions, but the service will still touch on the same topics in the same order for the same reasons." (Publisher's note)

"Extensive notes follow each chapter, and a cross-reference to selections in the most commonly used prayer books fleshes out this carefully crafted primer, which is perfect for Jews rediscovering their own traditions, Jews by choice and others who wish to participate in Jewish events." Pub Wkly

Includes bibliographical references and index

296.43   Festivals, holy days, fasts

Pogrebin, Abigail

My Jewish year; 18 holidays, one wondering Jew. Abigail Pogrebin; foreword by A. J. Jacobs. Fig Tree Books LLC 2017 336 p. $22.95   **296.43**
    1. Judaism 2. Jewish holidays 3. Fasts and feasts -- Judaism
    ISBN 1941493203; 9781941493205

This book, by Abigail Pogrebin, with foreword by A. J. Jacobs, "travels through this calendar's signposts with candor, humor, and a trove of information, capturing the arc of Jewish observance through the eyes of a relatable, wandering--and wondering--Jew. The chapters are interspersed with brief reflections from prominent rabbis and Jewish thinkers." (Publisher's note)

"A sentimental journey through Judaic practice and thought." Kirkus
Includes bibliographical references.

296.7   Religious experience, life, practice

Davidson, Sara

The **December** Project; an extraordinary Rabbi and a skeptical seeker confront life's greatest mystery. Sara Davidson. HarperOne 2014 224 p.   **296.7**
    1. Death 2. Rabbis 3. Skepticism 4. Self-actualization (Psychology) -- Religious aspects -- Judaism
    ISBN 9780062281746; 9780062281753; 0062281755
LC 2013020725

National Jewish Book Award Finalist: Contemporary Jewish Life and Practice (2014)

"Author Sara Davidson met every Friday with 89-year-old Rabbi

Zalman Shachter-Shalomi, the iconic founder of the Jewish Renewal movement. This is Davidson's memoir of what they learned and how they changed. Interspersed with their talks are sketches from Reb Zalman's extraordinary life. Together they created strategies to deal with pain and memory loss, and found tools to cultivate simplicity, fearlessness, and joy." (Publisher's note)

"Both a kind of biography of Zalman and a moving manual on dying, this book should reach far beyond a Jewish or aging readership." LJ

Diamant, Anita

Pitching my tent; on marriage, motherhood, friendship, and other leaps of faith. Scribner 2003 223p hardcover o.p. pa $15   **296.7**
    1. Jewish women
    ISBN 0-7432-4616-0; 0-7432-4617-9 pa
LC 2003-45440

"This collection of short essays, culled primarily from the Boston Globe Sunday Magazine and then reworked, . . . [are] organized around such themes as love and marriage, child rearing, friendship and living a religious life. . . . The book's strength lies in its woman-to-woman conversational tone, especially in the opening section about married life and its dark side. . . . These morsels will make a tasty snack for Diamant's admirers." Publ Wkly

Isaacs, Ronald H.

★ **Kosher** living; it's more than just the food. [by] Ron Isaacs. Jossey-Bass 2005 xlvii, 286p $22.95   **296.7**
    1. Judaism -- Customs and practices
    ISBN 0-7879-7642-3
LC 2004-26727

"The book not only covers the expected Jewish topics— circumcision, marriage, prayer, Shabbat, synagogue behavior and more—but also . . . [items] such as employer-employee relations, shopping and even war. . . . This resource offers timeless wisdom through a contemporary lens." Publ Wkly

Includes bibliographical references

Kushner, Harold S.

Who needs God; [by] Harold Kushner. Fireside 2002 212p pa $14   **296.7**
    1. God -- Judaism
    ISBN 0-7432-3477-4
    First published 1989 by Summit Bks.

The author "believes that 'human life has meaning . . . but only in religious terms.' According to this crucial realization, it is religion that connects us to God and community." Libr J

Reuben, Steven Carr

★ **Becoming** Jewish; the challenges, rewards, and paths to conversion. [by] Steven Carr Reuben and Jennifer S. Hanin; [foreword by Bab Saget] Rowman & Littlefield Publishers 2011 256p $22.95; ebook $22.95   **296.7**
    1. Conversion 2. Converts to Judaism
    ISBN 978-1-4422-0848-3; 978-1-4422-0849-0 ebook
LC 2011014083

"The authors explain such details as finding the right denomination, choosing a rabbi, selecting a Hebrew name, and the need to learn Hebrew. They also discuss Jewish culture and beliefs, holidays, and traditions. Chapters on telling family and friends about the decision to convert, raising Jewish children, kabbalah, anti-Semitism, and Israel help those converting understand important issues. . . . Written in a casual, friendly style with good humor and warmth, this accessible guide will help anyone considering conversion to Judaism." Booklist

297 Islam, Babism, Bahai Faith

Abou El Fadl, Khaled

The **great** theft; wrestling Islam from the extremists. Khaled Abou El Fadl. HarperSanFrancisco 2005 308 p. $21.95 **297**

1. Islam 2. Islamic fundamentalism
ISBN 9780060563394; 0060563397

LC 2005283877

This "book is a fulfilling read for moderate Muslims concerned about conservative leadership and any non-Muslims who want to inform themselves about the extremists' misuse of Islam." Publ Wkly

Includes bibliographical references

Armstrong, Karen

★ **Islam**; a short history. Modern Lib. 2000 xxxiv, 222p maps $19.95; pa $11.95 **297**

1. Islam
ISBN 0-679-64040-1; 0-8129-6618-X pa

LC 00-25285

This history of the Islamic faith focuses on the religion's attitude toward politics

The author "does an admirable job of presenting Islamic history from an objective, unbiased point of view." Libr J

Includes bibliographical references

Muhammad; a prophet for our time. Atlas Books/HarperCollins Publishers 2006 249p map (Eminent lives) $21.95; pa $14.95 **297**

1. Islam 2. Prophets 3. Islamic leaders 4. Writers on religion
ISBN 0-06-059897-2; 978-0-06-059897-6; 0-06-115577-2 pa; 978-0-06-115577-2 pa

LC 2006-45864

First published 1991 in the United Kingdom with subtitle: A Western attempt to understand Islam; Original American edition published 1992 with subtitle: A biography of the prophet

This is a biography of the founder of Islam.

"Readers of these pages cannot escape the genius of Muhammad and his aim for peace and compassion among nations and among Muslims themselves. . . . Recommended for all libraries." Libr J

Includes bibliographical references

Aslan, Reza

★ **No** god but God; the origins, evolution, and future of Islam. Random House 2005 xxiv, 310p $25.95; pa $14.95 **297**

1. Islam
ISBN 1-4000-6213-6; 0-8129-7189-2 pa

LC 2004-54053

"Beginning with an exploration of the religious climate in the years before the Prophet's Revelation, Aslan traces the story of Islam from the Prophet's life and the so-called golden age of the first four caliphs all the way through European colonization and subsequent independence. . . . This is an excellent overview that doubles as an impassioned call to reform." Booklist

Includes bibliographical references

Bawer, Bruce

Surrender; appeasing Islam, sacrificing freedom. Doubleday 2009 321p $24.95 **297**

1. Freedom of speech 2. Islam -- Relations
ISBN 978-0-385-52398-1; 0-385-52398-X

LC 2008-35743

"Bawer files a hefty brief of case reports on Muslim campaigns against free speech, primarily in western Europe but also in Canada and the U.S. Official infatuation with political correctness (PC), the determination that no one ever be offended, and multiculturalism, the dogma that all cultural perspectives are equally and universally valid, undergird what Bawer believes amounts to a surrender of Western liberal traditions. What may seal the fate of free speech, he argues, are the apparent inabilities of Western ruling elites to be offended by Muslims rioting, threatening by fatwa, and murdering non-Muslims . . . and to assert the priority of Western liberal values in the West. . . . Sublimely literate and rational, Bawer is no crank, however angry he gets." Booklist

Includes bibliographical references

Ben Jelloun, Tahar

Islam explained. New Press (NY) 2002 120p hardcover o.p. pa $13.95 **297**

1. Islam
ISBN 1-56584-781-4; 1-56584-897-7 pa

LC 2002-30500

"Cast in the form of an extended conversation between Ben Jelloun and his young daughter. . . . Father and child discuss the history of Islam, what it means to be a Muslim today, the challenges facing the Islamic world, and terrorism. . . . Its openness and emotional honesty, particularly when discussing the tragedy of 9/11, make it a valuable addition to a growing public discourse. As an introduction to the religion, it is spotty, but as a liberal Muslim voice of reconciliation, heartbreak, and compassion, it is priceless." Booklist

Campo, Juan Eduardo

Encyclopedia of Islam; [by] Juan E. Campo. Facts On File 2008 750p il map (Encyclopedia of world religions) $85 **297**

1. Reference books 2. Islam -- Encyclopedias
ISBN 978-0-8160-5454-1; 0-8160-5454-1

LC 2008-5621

"In about 600 A-to-Z entries, this encyclopedic guide explores the terms, concepts, personalities, historical events, and institutions that helped shape the history of this religion and the way it is practiced today." Publisher's note

Includes bibliographical references

Ernst, Carl W.

Following Muhammad; rethinking Islam in the contemporary world. University of North Carolina Press 2003 244p il (Islamic civilization & Muslim networks) $24.95; pa $16.95 **297**

1. Islam
ISBN 0-8078-2837-8; 0-8078-5577-4 pa

LC 2003-11162

The author "informs readers of the roles played by colonialism, Christian missionary efforts, and Western conceptions of just what 'religion' is, all in relation to American conceptions of Islam." Libr J

Includes bibliographical references

Esposito, John L.

What everyone needs to know about Islam. Oxford Univ. Press 2002 204p $18.95 **297**

1. Islam
ISBN 0-19-515713-3

LC 2002-8387

In question-and-answer format the author presents information on a variety of aspects of Islam. The "format allows readers to skip ahead to areas that interest them, including hot-button issues such as 'Why are Muslims so violent?' or 'Why do Muslim women wear veils and long garments?' In his answers, which are anywhere from a paragraph to several pages long, Esposito elegantly educates the reader through what the Qur'an says, how Muslims are influenced by their local cultures, and how the unique politics of Islamic countries affects Muslims' views." Publ Wkly

Includes bibliographical references

Esposito, John L., 1940-

Islam; the straight path. Rev. 3rd ed., updated with new epilogue; Oxford University Press 2005 304p map pa $39.95 **297**
1. Islam
ISBN 0-19-518266-9

                                               LC 2004-61688

First published 1988

This "survey text introduces the faith, belief, and practice of Islam from its earliest origins up to its contemporary resurgence." Publisher's note

Includes bibliographical references

Fuller, Graham E., 1937-

A **world** without Islam. Little, Brown and Co. 2010 328p $25.99 **297**
1. East and West 2. Islamic civilization 3. Islam -- History 4. Islam -- Relations
ISBN 978-0-316-04119-5; 978-0-316-07201-4 ebook

                                               LC 2009-54078

"A cogent argument demonstrating that a knowledgeable awareness of the rich dynamics that drive societies will better help diffuse tensions." Kirkus

Includes bibliographical references

Gardell, Mattias

In the name of Elijah Muhammad; Louis Farrakhan and the Nation of Islam. Duke Univ. Press 1996 482p (C. Eric Lincoln series on the black experience) $59.95; pa $23.95   **297**
1. Black Muslims 2. Black Muslim leaders 3. Civil rights activists
ISBN 0-8223-1852-0; 0-8223-1845-8 pa

                                               LC 96-22666

"Some will appreciate the author's brief critical airing of claims of pre-Columbian Africans in America and accounts of Muslims and the slave trade, but he is at his best when focusing on the leaders and on the changing theology of the Nation of Islam (NOI) and similar African American groups in the 20th-century US. The book is balanced and well researched." Choice

Includes bibliographical references

Glassé, Cyril

The **new** encyclopedia of Islam; Cyril Glassé. Rowman & Littlefield Pub Inc 2013 736 p. ill., maps $95   **297**
1. Islam 2. Muslims
ISBN 1442223480; 9781442223486

This book, by Cyril Glassé, "revised, updated, and re-designed in a fresh larger-format, with more than 1,500 entries . . . [is] a single-volume work that encompasses the beliefs, practices, history, and culture of the Islamic world. . . . In this expanded new edition, with an extensive chronology, Cyril Glasse provides a . . . study of one of the world's great religions." (Publisher's note)

"This beautifully illustrated and clearly written book provides a myriad of facts and insights about Islam that many readers--novices

and scholars alike--will find informative, interesting, and enlightening." Choice

Gordon, Matthew

Understanding Islam; origins, beliefs, practices, holy texts, sacred places. [by] Matthew S. Gordon. Sterling Pub. Co. 2010 112p pa $9.95   **297**
1. Islam
ISBN 978-1-90748-616-6

                                               LC 2010-2376

First published 2001 by Facts on File

This "exploration of Islam's history, beliefs, and practices . . . [addresses] issues such as political Islam, Islam and Israel, and Islamic fundamentalism." Publisher's note

Includes bibliographical references

Grieve, Paul

★ A **brief** guide to Islam; history, faith and politics: the complete introduction. Carroll & Graf 2006 433p il map pa $13.95   **297**
1. Islam
ISBN 0-7867-1804-8; 978-0-7867-1804-7

                                               LC 2006-282191

"If you read only one book about Islam this year, this should be it." Publ Wkly

Griswold, Eliza

The **tenth** parallel; dispatches from the fault line between Christianity and Islam. Farrar, Straus and Giroux 2010 317p il map $27; ebook $12.99   **297**
1. Christianity and other religions 2. Islam -- Relations -- Christianity
ISBN 978-0-374-27318-7; 0-374-27318-9; 978-1-4299-7966-5 ebook; 1-4299-7966-6 ebook

                                               LC 2010-1480

This "is a beautifully written book, full of arresting stories woven around a provocative issue—whether fundamentalism leads to violence—which Griswold investigates through individual lives rather than caricatures or abstractions." N Y Times Book Rev

Includes bibliographical references

Hazleton, Lesley, 1945-

After the prophet; the epic story of the Shia-Sunni split in Islam. Doubleday 2009 239p map $26.95   **297**
1. Shi'ah 2. Sunnis 3. Prophets 4. Imams 5. Caliphs 6. Islamic leaders 7. Islam -- History 8. Writers on religion 9. Spouses of prominent persons
ISBN 978-0-385-52393-6

                                               LC 2009-6498

"In June 632, the founder of Islam died without having clearly designated a successor. It seemed obvious to some that Muhammad's first cousin, Ali, who occupied the place of a son in the prophet's circle, would assume leadership. But Aisha, Muhammad's favorite, youngest, and most forceful wife, favored her father, and others backed Muhammad's greatest warrior. Ali would succeed, but not until 25 years later. Thus began the turmoil that eventuated in the bisection of Muslims into Sunni and Shia and that Hazleton describes in a new masterpiece of a kind of history seldom seen these days, in which the telling of a complicated, eventful story takes precedence over constant quotation of documents and squabbling with other historians." Booklist

Includes bibliographical references

Husain, Ed

The **house** of Islam; a global history. Ed Husain. St. Martin's Press 2018 336 p. $30 **297**
1. Islamic sects 2. Islam -- History
ISBN 1632866390; 9781632866394

This book, by Ed Husain, "explores the events and issues that have come from and contributed to the broadening gulf between Islam and the West, from the United States' overthrow of Iran's first democratically elected leader to the emergence of ISIS, from the declaration of a fatwa on Salman Rushdie to the attack on the offices of 'Charlie Hebdo.' . . . Husain leads us clearly and carefully through the nuances of Islam and its people." (Publisher's note)

"By explaining the contours of global Islam, Husain ends up making a strong case against Koranic textual literalism that readers of all backgrounds will appreciate." Publishers' Weekly

★ **Islam** in the world today; a handbook of politics, religion, culture, and society. edited by Werner Ende and Udo Steinbach. Cornell University Press 2010 1114p il $85 **297**
1. Islamic civilization 2. Islam -- History
ISBN 978-0-8014-4571-2
LC 2009-39910

First published 1989 in Germany

This is "one of the most authoritative works on Islam in the modern world. . . . The volume is divided into three parts; the first is a historical overview of the Islamic world from its beginnings in the seventh century to the present, including a description of the different sects and movements of Islam and their influence in the world today. The second, and most extensive, section discusses the political role of Islam in the modern world, Islamic economics, social systems, and law. . . . The final section describes Islamic culture and civilization, including art, literature, and architecture, and their intersection with the West." Libr J

Includes bibliographical references

Johnson, Ian

A **mosque** in Munich; Nazis, the CIA, and the Muslim brotherhood in the West. Houghton Mifflin Harcourt 2010 318p $27 **297**
1. Mosques 2. Cold war 3. Islam and politics 4. Islamic fundamentalism 5. Munich (Germany) 6. Mosques -- Germany 7. Islamic Brotherhood 8. Islamic fundamentalism -- Germany 9. United States -- Central Intelligence Agency
ISBN 978-0-15-101418-7; 0-15-101418-3
LC 2009-35285

"Mr. Johnson brings to life a previously overlooked episode in the Muslim Brotherhood's story and thus in the story of Islamism as a whole: How a radical European beachhead came to be established in Munich. It should be said that the story takes some confusing turns; even alert readers may find themselves flipping to the list of characters at the back of the book, or to the index, to help them follow the narrative. But many of the details are astonishing and the larger implications for our own time disturbing." Wall Street J

Includes bibliographical references

Karsh, Efraim

Islamic imperialism; a history. Yale University Press 2006 276p map $30 **297**
1. Jihad 2. Imperialism 3. Islam and politics
ISBN 0-300-10603-3
LC 2005-34836

The author "surveys for a general audience the region's Islamic political past. Parallel to his narrative, Karsh frequently contrasts the universalistic proclamations of Islam with cycles of imperial consolidation

and fragmentation. After recounting the Prophet Muhammad's religio-political establishment of Islam, and the discord about his legacy that continues today, Karsh narrates the battles over Muhammad's caliphate that eventuated in the Umayyad and Abbasid Empires. Karsh's commentary often looks forward to contemporary ideologues of Islam who ransack history to justify grievances. . . . An informative foundation for further exploration of Islamic history." Libr J

Kepel, Gilles

Jihad; the trail of political Islam. translated by Anthony F. Roberts. Harvard Univ. Press 2002 454p $33.95; pa $15.95 **297**
1. Islam and politics
ISBN 0-674-00877-4; 0-674-01090-6 pa
LC 2002-17181

Original French edition, 2000

"Kepel argues that the terrorism seen today throughout the world results from the failure of Islamic fundamentalism and not its success. . . . Fascinating despite its copious detail." Booklist

Kugle, Scott Siraj al-Haqq

Living out Islam; voices of gay, lesbian, and transgender Muslims. Scott Siraj al-Haqq Kugle. NYU Press 2014 x, 265 p.p (hardback) $85 **297**
1. Homosexuality 2. Islam -- Customs and practices 3. Homosexuality -- Religious aspects -- Islam
ISBN 0814744486; 9780814744482; 9781479894673
LC 2013023734

Stonewall Book Award: Nonfiction (2015)

This book "documents the rarely-heard voices of Muslims who live in secular democratic countries and who are gay, lesbian, and transgender. It weaves original interviews with Muslim activists into a compelling composite picture which showcases the importance of the solidarity of support groups in the effort to change social relationships and achieve justice." (Publisher's note)

Includes bibliographical references and index

Lewis, Bernard

★ The **crisis** of Islam; holy war and unholy terror. Modern Library 2003 xxxii, 184p map hardcover o.p. pa $13.95 **297**
1. Islam and politics 2. Islamic fundamentalism 3. Terrorism -- Religious aspects
ISBN 0-679-64281-1; 0-8129-6785-2 pa
LC 2002-45219

"Written in an easily accessible style, this analysis provides a digestible overview for Westerners still asking why." Booklist

Includes bibliographical references

The **Many** faces of Islam; perspectives on a resurgent civilization. Nissim Rejwan {editor} University Press of Fla. 2000 282p $55 **297**
1. Islam 2. Islamic countries -- Politics and government
ISBN 0-8130-1807-2
LC 00-32587

The editor offers "perspectives on modern Islamic culture and religious practice. Seeking to dispel the perception that Islamic fundamentalism and extremism represent Islam in its entirety, Rejwan surveys the issues and provides numerous excerpts from modern writers and scholars, Muslim and non-Muslim, summarizing the many problems and dilemmas facing contemporary Muslims." Univ. Press Books for Public and Second Sch Libr, 2001

Nasr, Seyyed Hossein

Islam: religion, history, and civilization. HarperSanFrancisco 2002 xx, 198p pa $12.95 **297**
1. Islam 2. Islamic civilization
ISBN 0-06-050714-4

LC 2002-32810

This introduction to the world of Islam explores the following topics: What is Islam?; The doctrines and beliefs of Islam; Islamic practices and institutions; The history of Islam; Schools of Islamic thought; Islam in the contemporary world; Islam and other religions; The spiritual and religious significance of Islam

"Provides compelling analysis of contemporary Islam and its conflicts without overwhelming the reader with information." Booklist

Includes bibliographical references

Nasr, Vali

★ The **Shia** revival; how conflicts within Islam will shape the future. Norton 2006 287p map $25.95 **297**
1. Shi'ah 2. Islam and politics
ISBN 0-393-06211-2; 978-0-393-06211-3

LC 2006-12361

"So enlightening and perspective altering that no one concerned about the Middle East should miss reading it." Booklist

Includes bibliographical references

★ The **Oxford** dictionary of Islam; John L. Esposito, editor in chief. Oxford Univ. Press 2003 359p hardcover o.p. pa $18.95 **297**
1. Reference books 2. Islam -- Dictionaries
ISBN 0-19-512558-4; 0-19-512559-2 pa

LC 2002-30261

"This is an excellent resource for ready-reference collections in any library." Libr J

Includes bibliographical references

The **Oxford** history of Islam; {edited by} John Esposito. Oxford Univ. Press 1999 749p il map $49.95 **297**
1. Islam
ISBN 0-19-510799-3

LC 99-13219

"Contributors treat, among other things, Muslim history, law, and society; art and architecture; and regional differences. Chapters on the 'Globalization of Islam' and 'Contemporary Islam' are particularly relevant to current events.... An ideal one-volume source." Libr J

Includes bibliographical references

Power, Carla

If the oceans were ink; an unlikely friendship and a journey to the heart of the Quran. Carla Power. Henry Holt & Co. 2015 352 p. (hardcover) $19 **297**
1. Islam 2. Friendship 3. Interfaith relations 4. Islam -- Appreciation 5. Islamophobia -- Europe 6. Islam -- Public opinion 7. Muslim converts -- Biography 8. Islam -- Essence, genius, nature
ISBN 0805098194; 9780805098198; 9780805098242

LC 2014017543

Pulitzer Prize Finalist: General Nonfiction (2016)

National Book Award Finalist: Nonfiction (2015)

This book, by Carla Power, offers the author's story of how she "and her longtime friend Sheikh Mohammad Akram Nadwi found a way to confront ugly stereotypes and persistent misperceptions that were cleaving their communities.... Both knew that a close look at the Quran would reveal a faith that preached peace and not mass murder; respect for women and not oppression. And so they embarked on a yearlong journey through the controversial text." (Publisher's note)

"Power's narrative offers an accessible and enlightening route into a topic fraught with misunderstanding." Pub Wkly

Includes bibliographical references and index

Ramadan, Tariq

Introduction to Islam; Tariq Ramadan; translated by Fred A. Reed. Oxford University Press 2017 xxii, 250 p.p map (paperback) $18.95 **297**
1. Islam 2. Religious literature 3. Islam -- Doctrines 4. Islam -- Customs and practices
ISBN 9780190467494; 9780190467487; 9780190467500

LC 2017004515

In this book, author Tariq Ramadan "walks readers through Islam and its principles, rituals, diversity, and evolution. Ramadan, known for his efforts to reform and change the understanding of Islam in the West, avoids ideology and idealism, instead attempting to depict the true meaning of Islam for readers who have no previous experience with the religion. The book is therefore focused on defining the basic principles of Islam and offering an overview of the faith's history." (Publisher's note)

"For non-Muslims, it is an invitation to understand the basics of Islam as well as to dive a bit deeper into its history, theology, and various manifestations over time and across the globe." Pub Wkly

Includes bibliographical references (pages [227]-231) and index.

Renard, John

The **handy** Islam answer book; John Renard. Visible Ink Press 2015 435 p. illustrations, maps (paperback) $21.95 **297**
1. Islam
ISBN 157859510X; 9781578595105

LC 2014033780

This book, by John Renard, "provides detailed descriptions of the history, beliefs, symbols, rituals, observations, customs, leaders, and organization of the world's second largest religion. [The author] . . . explains the significance of the Five Pillars, Muhammad, various sects, the Qur'an, Islamic law, and much more." (Publisher's note)

"This very well-written and captivating resource explains Islam using an accessible and balanced approach and rectifies the more egregious misconceptions about the religion that are often popularly cited. A strong choice for anyone of high school age and above who wishes to know about Islam and for those who provide ready reference." LJ

Zafar, Harris, 1979-

Demystifying Islam; tackling the tough questions. Harris Zafar. Rowman & Littlefied 2014 218 p. map (cloth: alk. paper) $35 **297**
1. Islamophobia 2. Islam -- Relations 3. Islam 4. Islam -- Doctrines
ISBN 1442223278; 9781442223271; 9781442223288

LC 2014004827

This book, by Harris Zafar, asks questions such as "What really is Shariah law? How is a Muslim to understand Jihad? Does Islam oppose Western values such as free speech or freedom of religion? What place do women have according to Islam? . . . Author Harris Zafar . . . is forthright about issues where Muslims disagree, and he digs into history through vast research and scholarship to track the origins of differing beliefs." (Publisher's note)

"This book is less of a spiritual introduction than it is a cultural one, and an excellent starting point for people navigating interfaith relationships or working to improve understanding and representation in organizations and public discussion." Pub Wkly

Includes bibliographical referencees and index

297.082   Muslim women

Living Islam out loud; American Muslim women speak. edited by Saleemah Abdul-Ghafur. Beacon Press 2005 209 p. (pbk.) $18   **297.082**
1. Muslim women 2. Women in Islam 3. Women in Islam -- United States 4. Muslim women -- United States -- Biography 5. Muslim women -- Religious life -- United States
ISBN 9780807096925; 0807083836; 9780807083833
                              LC 2004028161
This book, edited by Saleemah Abdul-Ghafur, "presents the first generation of American Muslim women who have always identified as both American and Muslim. These pioneers have forged new identities for themselves and for future generations, and they speak out about the hijab, relationships, sex and sexuality, activism, spirituality, and much more." (Publisher's note)
"Muslim activist Abdul-Ghafur edits this book of essays and poems, all related to the experience of growing up Muslim and female in the United States." Pub Wkly

297.09   History, geographic treatment, biography

Abdul Rauf, Feisal, 1948-
Moving the mountain; beyond ground zero to a new vision of Islam in America. Feisal Abdul Rauf. Free Press 2012 xiv, 225 p.p (hardcover) $24   **297.09**
1. Islamic law 2. Religious tolerance 3. Muslims -- United States 4. Islam -- United States
ISBN 1451656009; 9781451656008
                              LC 2011050797
Author Feisal Abdul Rauf "offers a . . . comparative study of the 'People of the Book,' focusing partly on the similarities between the three Abrahamic faiths. . . . Rauf delves into the 'bogeyman' of Shariah law, comparing it to the U.S. Constitution." He also discusses "Islam since 9/11" and his time as "imam of the al-Farah Mosque in New York City." (Kirkus Reviews)
Includes bibliographical references

Ghobash, Omar Saif
Letters to a Young Muslim; Omar Saif Ghobash. St. Martin's Press 2017 256 p. (ebook) $60; $22   **297.09**
1. Muslim youth 2. Islam -- 21st century
ISBN 9781250119834; 1250119847; 9781250119841
                              LC 2016039168
"In a series of personal letters to his son, Omar Saif Ghobash offers a short and highly readable manifesto that tackles our current global crisis with the training of an experienced diplomat and the personal responsibility of a father. . . . The burning question, Ghobash argues, is how moderate Muslims can unite to find a voice that is true to Islam while actively and productively engaging in the modern world. What does it mean to be a good Muslim?" (Publisher's note)
"He urges them to pursue a middle path that is simultaneously true to Islam and yet effectively and energetically engaged in the modern world. This is a fantastic book for Muslims and non-Muslims alike." Pub Wkly

Nasr, Amir Ahmad
My Isl@m; how fundamentalism stole my mind--and doubt freed my soul. Amir Ahmad Nasr. St. Martin's Press 2013 304 p.   **297.09**
1. Belief and doubt 2. Internet and religion 3. Islamic fundamentalism 4. Muslims -- Malaysia -- Biography
ISBN 9781250016485; 9781250016799
                              LC 2013004044
The author, "a Sudanese blogger . . . blends memoir with political thought and activism in his book, a distillation of his last few years blogging about Islam and the Muslim world. [Amir Ahmad] Nasr, who grew up in Qatar and Malaysia, recounts his early religious education. . . . The book . . . follows his journey out of a simplistic understanding of Islam, through rationalism and semi-atheism, towards a conversion to Sufism, the mystical school of Islam." (Publishers Weekly)

297.092   Biography

All-American; 45 American men on being Muslim. edited by Wajahat Ali & Zahra T. Suratwala; foreword by Congressman Keith Ellison. White Cloud Press 2012 xiv, 256 p.p ill. (pbk.) $16.95   **297.092**
1. Muslims -- United States 2. Muslim men -- United States 3. Muslim men -- United States -- Biography
ISBN 1935952595; 9781935952596
                              LC 2012014744
"In this second book in the 'I Speak For Myself' series," edited by Wajahat Ali, "American Muslim men speak out on their lives and how their Muslim beliefs play out in private and on the public stage. Contributors include high profile figures in the American Muslim community, representing a new generation that is making a profound impact inside and outside the Muslim world." (Publisher's note)

297.1   Islam

Cook, Michael
The **Koran**; a very short introduction. Michael Cook. Oxford University Press 2000 162 p. illustrations (Very Short Introductions) (paperback) $11.95   **297.1**
1. Qur'an 2. Qur'an -- Criticism, interpretation, etc
ISBN 9780192853448; 0192853449
                              LC 99057686
This book, by Michael Cook, "provides a lucid and direct account of the significance of the Koran both in the modern world and in that of traditional Islam. He gives vivid accounts of its role in Muslim civilization, illustrates the diversity of interpretations championed by traditional and modern commentators, discusses the processes by which the book took shape, and compares it to other scriptures and classics of the historic cultures of Eurasia." (Publisher's note)
Includes bibliographical references (p. 149-151) and indexes

Mattson, Ingrid
★ The **story** of the Qur'an; its history and place in Muslim life. Ingrid Mattson. Second Edition Wiley-Blackwell 2013 xiii, 298 p.p illustrations, maps (pbk.) $32.95   **297.1**
1. Qur'an 2. Islam -- History 3. Qur'an -- History 4. Qur'an -- Theology 5. Qur'an -- Criticism, interpretation, etc
ISBN 9780470673492; 9781118257067; 9781118257074; 9781118257104
                              LC 2012042779
This book, by Ingrid Mattson, is a "popular introduction by a well-known Islamic scholar . . . , offering a balanced portrayal of the Qur'an

and its place in historic and contemporary Muslim society. [It] features new sections on the Qur'an and its relationship to democracy, science, human rights, and the role of women. [It also] contains expanded sections on the Qur'an in the life cycle of Muslims, and in Islamic ethics and law." (Publisher's note)

"An excellent companion resource for study and understanding of the Qur'an." LJ

Includes bibliographical references (p. [271]-286) and index.

★ The **meaning** of the glorious Koran; an explanatory translation by Marmaduke Pickthall; with an introduction by William Montgomery Watt. A.A. Knopf 1992 xxiv, 693p il $22   **297.1**
1. Qur'an
ISBN 0-679-41736-2; 978-0-679-41736-1
                     LC 92-52928
This translation first published 1930

"The sacred scripture of Islam, regarded by Muslims as the Word of God, and except in sura I.—which is a prayer to God—and some few passages in which Muhammad or the angels speak in the first person, the speaker throughout is God." Ency Britannica

The **Qur'an**; English translation and parallel Arabic text. translated, with an introduction and notes, by M.A.S. Abdel Haleem. Oxford University Press 2010 xxxix, 624 p.p maps (hardcover) $45   **297.1**
1. Qur'an
ISBN 019957071X; 9780199570713
                LC 2010281328
This book, by M. A. S. Abdel Haleem, offers an English translation of the Qur'an with Arab text presented in parallel. "This translation is written in contemporary language . . . , set page-for-page against the most widespread traditional calligraphic Arabic text. . . . Furthermore, Haleem includes notes that explain geographical, historical, and personal allusions as well as an index in which Qur'anic material is arranged into topics for easy reference." (Publisher's note)

"Because the Koran stresses its Arabic nature, devout Muslims believe that only an Arabic version is the actual Koran and insist that its translation cannot be more than an approximate interpretation. . . Yet anyone wishing to understand Islamic civilization and global affairs may find this Koran very useful. . . . Highly recommended." LJ

Includes bibliographical references and index

The **Qur'an**: an encyclopedia; edited by Oliver Leaman. Taylor & Francis Group 2006 xxvii, 771p $280; pa $45 **297.1**
1. Reference books 2. Koran -- Encyclopedias
ISBN 0-415-32639-7; 978-0-415-32639-1; 0-415-77529-9 pa; 978-0-415-32639-1 pa

"The objective of this encyclopedia is to fill a gap between general introductions and more technical works and provide the non-specialist with a resource covering all aspects of the text and its reception." Booklist

Includes bibliographical references

Wagner, Walter H.
Opening the Qur'an; introducing Islam's holy book. University of Notre Dame Press 2008 547p $45   **297.1**
1. Koran -- Criticism
ISBN 978-0-268-04415-2; 0-268-04415-5
                LC 2008-27221
This "work makes an important contribution to the contemporary Muslim-Christian conversation." Catholic Hist Rev

Includes bibliographical references

Wills, Garry, 1934-
What the Qur'an meant and why it matters; Garry Wills. Viking 2017 x, 226 p.p (hardcover) $25   **297.1**
1. Qur'an 2. Islam -- Doctrines 3. Qur'an -- Criticism, interpretation, etc
ISBN 9781101981030; 9781101981023
              LC 2017025389
In this book, "[Gary] Wills, as a non-Muslim with an open mind, reads the Qur'an with sympathy but with rigor, trying to discover why other non-Muslims—such as Pope Francis—find it an inspiring book, worthy to guide people down through the centuries. There are many traditions that add to and distort and blunt the actual words of the text. What Wills does resembles the work of art restorers who clean away accumulated layers of dust to find the original meaning." (Publisher's note)

Includes bibliographical references and index.

297.2   Islamic doctrinal theology ('Aqa'id and Kalam); Islam and secular disciplines; Islam and other systems of belief

Akyol, Mustafa
The **Islamic** Jesus; how the King of the Jews became a prophet of the Muslims. Mustafa Akyol. St. Martin's Press 2017 288 p. (hardcover) $26.99; (ebook) $60   **297.2**
1. Islam -- Relations -- Judaism 2. Islam -- Relations -- Christianity 3. Islam -- History 4. Judaism -- Relations -- Islam 5. Christianity and other religions -- Islam
ISBN 9781250088697; 9781250088703
             LC 2016038747
This book, by Mustafa Akyol, "not only tells the story of Jesus, and his mother Mary, as narrated in the Qur'an. It also explores how this Islamic picture of the Nazarene resonates with pre-existing Christian sources, especially Apocrypha. In particular, it unveils the fascinating similarity between Islam and 'Jewish Christianity,' a strain in the early church that got branded as a heresy." (Publisher's note)

"A fascinating bridge text between Islam and Christianity." Kirkus

Includes bibliographical references and index

Harris, Sam, 1967-
Islam and the future of tolerance; a dialogue. Sam Harris, Maajid Nawaz. Harvard University Press 2015 138 p. (alk. paper) $17.95   **297.2**
1. Islam 2. Religious tolerance 3. Dialogue -- Religious aspects 4. Toleration -- Religious aspects -- Islam
ISBN 9780674088702; 0674088700
            LC 2015009535
In this book, authors "Sam Harris and Maajid Nawaz invite [readers] to join an urgently needed conversation: Is Islam a religion of peace or war? Is it amenable to reform? Why do so many Muslims seem drawn to extremism? What do words like Islamism, jihadism, and fundamentalism mean in today's world? Harris and Nawaz demonstrate how two people with very different views can find common ground." (Publisher's note)

"Those interested in a deferential and detailed dialogue about human rights, Islam, jihadism, and pluralism will find this book both enlightening and engaging." Pub Wkly

Includes bibliographical references

Hirsi Ali, Ayaan, 1969-
Heretic; why Islam needs a reformation now. Ayaan Hirsi Ali. Harper 2015 x, 272 p.p (hardcover) $27.99   **297.2**

1. Religious awakening 2. Islam -- 21st century 3. Islam and secularism 4. Islam and world politics 5. Islamic countries -- Politics and government -- 21st century
ISBN 9780062333957; 9780062333940; 9780062333933; 0062333933

LC 2015385062

A book written by activist Ayaan Hirsi Ali, "Interweaving her own experiences, historical analogies and powerful examples from contemporary Muslim societies and cultures, 'Heretic' is not a call to arms, but a passionate plea for peaceful change and a new era of global toleration." (Publisher's note)

"This an urgent, complicated, risky subject, and Hirsi Ali, valiant, indomitable, and controversial, offers a potent indictment, idealistic blueprint, and galvanizing appeal to both conscience and reason." Booklist
Includes bibliographical references (pages 251-272)

Miles, Jack

God in the Qur'an; Jack Miles. Alfred A. Knopf 2019 272 p. (hardcover) $26.95   **297.2**
1. Islam 2. Qur'an 3. Women in Islam 4. God (Islam) 5. Qur'an -- Criticism, interpretation, etc
ISBN 9780307269577

LC 2018005105

This book in the God in Three Classic Scriptures series, by Jack Miles, presents "an erudite, hugely informative portrait of the God of Islam, the world's second largest, fastest-growing, and perhaps most tragically misunderstood religion. . . . Setting passages from the Hebrew Bible, the New Testament, and the Qur'an side by side, Miles illuminates what is unique about Allah, His teachings and His temperament." (Publisher's note)

"Readers will discover that writings in the Qur'an have less literary complexity but consistently show God (Allah) as full of forgiveness and compassion. Miles concludes by urging Christians to rethink their ideas about Islam and to respond with charity and tolerance." LJ
Includes bibliographical references and index

297.3   Islamic worship

Islamic images and ideas; essays on sacred symbolism. edited by John Andrew Morrow. McFarland & Company, Inc., Publishers 2014 x, 277 p.p (softcover: alk. paper) $45   **297.3**
1. Islam 2. Symbolism 3. Religious art 4. Islamic art and symbolism
ISBN 9780786458486; 9781476612881

LC 2013037134

This book, edited by John Andrew Morrow, contains "24 studies on specific symbols, images and icons from the Muslim tradition. . . . Divided into four sections, the Divine, the Spiritual, the Physical, and the Societal, they examine theological issues, such as divine unity, creation, wrath, and justice, as well as spiritual subjects, such as the straight path, servitude, perfection, the jinn, intoxication, and the status of Fatimah, the daughter of the Prophet Muhammad." (Publisher's note)
Includes bibliographical references and index

297.6   Islamic leaders and organization

Hazleton, Lesley, 1945-

The **First** Muslim; The Story of Muhammad. Lesley Hazleton. Riverhead Hardcover 2013 320 p. map (hardcover)

$27.95   **297.6**
1. Islam -- History
ISBN 1594487286; 9781594487286

LC 2012038501

This book, by Lesley Hazleton, offers a biography of the Prophet Muhammad. "Muhammad's was a life of almost unparalleled historical importance; yet for all the iconic power of his name, the intensely dramatic story of the prophet of Islam is not well known. . . . Hazleton's account follows the arc of Muhammad's rise from powerlessness to power, from anonymity to renown, from insignificance to lasting significance." (Publisher's note)
Includes bibliographical references (p. [299]-310) and index.

297.8   Islamic sects and reform movements

Evanzz, Karl

The **messenger**: the rise and fall of Elijah Muhammad. Pantheon Bks. 1999 667p hardcover o.p. pa $18   **297.8**
1. Black Muslim leaders 2. Civil rights activists
ISBN 0-679-77406-8 pa

LC 99-11826

A "critical biography of one of America's leading black nationalists of the 20th century. One of the founders of the Nation of Islam (NOI), Muhammad helped convert thousands of African Americans to the religion popularly known as the Black Muslims. Evanzz concludes that Muhammad was essentially a con man who used his considerable powers of persuasion to get rich and seduce women. Especially fascinating is Evanzz's extensive use of FBI files to make his case." Libr J
Includes bibliographical references

Levinsohn, Florence Hamlish

Looking for Farrakhan. Dee, I.R. 1997 305p $25   **297.8**
1. Black Muslims 2. Black Muslim leaders
ISBN 1-56663-157-2

LC 97-11335

Levinsohn's "biography, which reflects on the black experience and how it changed young Eugene Walcott into Louis Farrakhan, leader of the Nation of Islam, attempts to make sense of this prominent figure in American politics." Libr J

299   Religions not provided for elsewhere

Callow, John

Embracing the darkness; a cultural history of witchcraft. John Callow. I B Tauris & Co Ltd 2018 264 p. $39.95   **299**
1. Magic 2. Wicca 3. Witchcraft
ISBN 1845114698; 9781845114695

This book, by John Callow, "is an enthralling account of . . . [witchcraft in the western world]. A belief in the supernatural, and in black magic, has been central to western cultural life for 3000 years. From the Salem witch trials . . . to the seductive sorceresses of Warner Brother's 'Charmed,' . . . witchcraft has profoundly shaped the western imagination. In this . . . [book,] Callow brings the twilight world of the witch, mage and necromancer vividly to life." (Publisher's note)

★ The **Gnostic** Bible; edited by Willis Barnstone and Marvin Meyer. Rev. ed.; Shambhala 2009 881p pa $29.95   **299**
1. Gnosticism
ISBN 978-1-59030-631-4; 1-59030-631-7

LC 2008-36431

First published 2003

"The book provides Gnostic texts from their Jewish origins, into early Christianities, on into the medieval world. Though it concentrates on the early Jewish-Christian matrix of early Gnosticism, the collection . . . manifests the breadth and depth of Gnostic variations in neo-Platonist, Manichean, Mandean, Islam, and Cathar movements." Choice

Includes bibliographical references

Mar, Alex

Witches of America; Alex Mar. Sarah Crichton Books 2015 288 p. (hardcover) $26   **299**
1. Paganism 2. Occultism 3. Wicca -- United States 4. Neopaganism -- United States
ISBN 0374291373; 9780374291372

LC 2015010897

This book follows author Alex Mar "on her immersive five-year trip into the occult, charting modern Paganism from its roots in 1950s England to its current American mecca in the San Francisco Bay Area; from a gathering of more than a thousand witches in the Illinois woods to the New Orleans branch of one of the world's most influential magical societies. Along the way she takes part in dozens of rituals and becomes involved with a wild array of characters." (Publisher's note)

A top-notch read for pagans and open-minded seekers curious about the fascinating beginnings of American witchcraft and some of the various directions its form is taking." Library Journal

Reitman, Janet

★ **Inside** Scientology. Houghton Mifflin Harcourt 2011 xx, 444p $28   **299**
1. Scientology 2. United States -- Religion
ISBN 978-0-618-88302-8; 0-618-88302-9

LC 2010-49837

An expose "culled from hundreds of interviews with active Scientologists and defectors alike. Reitman brings an almost clinical detachment to the religion's story, from its birth in the sci-fi imagination of founder L. Ron Hubbard to its current Hollywood heyday. Her revelations—including abuse allegations against church leader David Miscavige and details about the organization's aggressive courtship of Tom Cruise—come with impressive backup." Entertainment Wkly

Includes bibliographical references

Wilkinson, Richard H.

★ The **complete** gods and goddesses of ancient Egypt. Thames & Hudson 2003 256p il $39.95   **299**
1. Egyptian mythology 2. Gods and goddesses 3. Egypt -- Religion
ISBN 0-500-05120-8

LC 2002-110321

"Wilkinson's gorgeously illustrated book adds new dimension to popular literature on ancient Egypt. . . . And once readers open the book to look at the pictures, they well may stay to read the well-organized, comprehensive, clearly written text." Booklist

Includes bibliographical references

Wright, Lawrence, 1947-

★ **Going** Clear; Scientology, Hollywood, and the Prison of Belief. Lawrence Wright. Random House Inc 2013 xiii, 430 p.p ill. $28.95   **299**
1. Cults 2. Scientology 3. Scientology. 4. Scientology --Doctrines.
ISBN 0307700666; 9780307700667

LC 2012532009

National Book Critics Circle Award Finalist: Nonfiction (2013); National Book Award Finalist (2013)

National Book Award Finalist: Nonfiction (2013)

This book from Pulitzer Prize winner Lawrence Wright looks at the Church of Scientology. It begins "with the life of L. Ron Hubbard, a manic-depressive, wannabe naval hero, sci-fi writer and self-styled shaman" whose book "Dianetics" "laid the groundwork for a 'religion' where 'thetans' (souls) are stymied by 'engrams,' self-destructive suggestive impulses lodged in the brain." The Church's connections to the U.S. entertainment industry and its behavior toward outsiders are examined. (Kirkus Reviews)

Includes bibliographical references (p. [373]-418) and index.

299.31   Ancient Egyptian religion

Wilkinson, Richard H.

Complete gods and goddesses of ancient Egypt; Richard H. Wilkinson. Thames & Hudson 2017 256 p. (pbk.) $26.95   **299.31**
1. Theocracy 2. Egypt -- Religion 3. Gods and goddesses 4. Gods, Egyptian 5. Goddesses, Egyptian 6. Mythology, Egyptian
ISBN 0500284245; 9780500284247

LC 2016943970

This book by Richard H. Wilkinson "examines the evolution, worship, and eventual decline of the numerous gods and goddesses--from minor household figures such as Bes and Tawaret to the all-powerful deities Amun and Re--that made Egypt the most theocratic society of the ancient world." (Publisher's note)

"This elegant and comprehensive resource thoroughly illustrates and catalogs the Egyptian deities, from early pharaonic times to the Roman period." LJ

299.5   Religions of East and Southeast Asian origin

Lao-tzu

★ **Tao** te ching; the new translation from Tao te ching: the definitive edition. translation by Jonathan Star. Jeremy P. Tarcher/Penguin 2008 103p pa $10   **299.5**
ISBN 978-1-58542-618-8

LC 2007-44948

This translation first published 2001 with title: Tao te ching: the definitive edition

"Chinese Taoist text attributed to Lao Tzu, supposedly an elder contemporary of Confucius (551?-479 BC). . . . A brief work in eighty-one-paragraphs in both verse and prose, it probably dates from the 4th or 3rd century BC, although some believe it may be as early as the 6th century BC. Because of its concise, poetic language, its meaning is subject to many interpretations. It is generally agreed that it is both a mystical book about union with the absolute, and a political handbook on how to rule and survive in chaotic times." Reader's Ency. 4th edition

Yang Lihui

★ **Handbook** of Chinese mythology; [by] Lihui Yang and Deming An, with Jessica Anderson Turner. ABC-CLIO 2005 293p il (Handbooks of world mythology) $75   **299.5**
1. Asian mythology
ISBN 1-57607-806-X

LC 2005-13851

"This volume provides useful information to the reader. The authors' credibility and in-depth scholarship offer a rare opportunity to experience Chinese mythology through Chinese eyes." Booklist

Includes bibliographical references

299.561   Shinto

Hardacre, Helen

Shinto; a history. Helen Hardacre. Oxford University Press 2016 xiii, 698 p.p illustrations (cloth: alk. paper) $39.95   **299.561**
1. Shinto 2. Shinto -- History
ISBN 9780190621728; 9780190621711

LC 2016021265

This book, by Helen Hardacre, "offers the first comprehensive history of Shinto, the ancient and vibrant tradition whose colorful rituals are still practiced today. Under the ideal of Shinto, a divinely descended emperor governs through rituals offered to deities called Kami. These rituals are practiced in innumerable shrines across the realm, so that local rites mirror the monarch's ceremonies." (Publisher's note)

"Hardacre, a professor of Japanese religions and society at Harvard, surveys the history of Shinto from ancient Japan to the present in this even-handed and detailed treatment of the topic." Pub Wkly

Includes bibliographical references (pages 659-680) and index.

299.6   Religions originating among Black Africans and people of Black African descent

★ The **Encyclopedia** of African and African-American religions; Stephen D. Glazier, editor. Routledge 2000 xx, 452p il maps $150   **299.6**
1. Reference books 2. Blacks -- Religion 3. African Americans -- Religion -- Encyclopedias
ISBN 0-415-92245-3

LC 00-59136

"This encyclopedia is a good starting point for understanding the complex interrelationships among African, African American, and European religious beliefs, practices, and traditions in a global context." Libr J

299.7   Religions of North America native origin

Emrys, Barbara

The **Toltec** art of life and death; a story of discovery. Don Miguel Ruiz and Barbara Emrys. HarperElixir 2015 416 p. (hardback) $25.99   **299.7**
1. Near-death experiences 2. Spiritual biography
ISBN 0062390929; 9780062390929; 9780062390936; 9780062423559

LC 2015009856

This book, by Don Miguel Ruiz and Barbara Emrys, responds to how, "in 2002, Don Miguel Ruiz suffered a near fatal heart attack that left him in a nine-weeks-long coma. The spiritual journey he undertook while suspended between this world and the next forms the heart of . . . [the book.] As his body lies unconscious, Ruiz's spirit encounters the people, ideas, and events that have shaped him, illuminating the eternal struggle between life . . . and death." (Publisher's note)

"Readers might find it difficult to follow Ruiz's winding road to the truth, but will come away from this book with a deeper understanding of life's complexities." Publisher's Weekly

Nabokov, Peter

Where the lightning strikes; the lives of American Indian sacred places. Viking 2005 350p hardcover o.p. pa $17 **299.7**
1. Sacred space 2. Native Americans -- Religion

ISBN 0-670-03432-0; 0-14-303881-8 pa

LC 2005-42227

The author presents "16 'biographies of place,' each of a habitat illustrating the bond between North American Indian cultures and their environment perpetuated by myths, legends, and rituals. . . . The author's careful documentation of unbroken reverence for these sacred places powerfully illuminates Native American attachment to the earth itself." Booklist

Includes bibliographical references

299.93   New Age religions

Williamson, Marianne

Tears to triumph; The Spiritual Journey from Suffering to Enlightenment. Marianne Williamson. HarperOne 2016 240 p. (hardcover) $25.99   **299.93**
1. Suffering -- Religious aspects
ISBN 9780062205445; 9780062441591

LC 2016011730

In this book, author Marianne Williamson "argues that our desire to avoid pain is actually detrimental to our lives, disconnecting us from our deepest emotions and preventing true healing and spiritual transcendence. . . . In refusing to acknowledge our suffering, we actually prolong it and deny ourselves the opportunity for profound wisdom—ultimately limiting our personal growth and opportunity for enlightenment." (Publisher's note)

"Those who are searching for a spiritual, not religious answer to the aspects of hurt and hardship will find it here." LJ

299.94   Modern paganism, neopaganism, wicca

Crosson, Monica

The **magickal** family; pagan living in harmony with nature. Monica Crosson. Llewellyn Worldwide, Ltd. 2017 xv, 300 p.p illustrations (paperback) $19.99   **299.94**
1. Magic 2. Paganism 3. Nature -- Religious aspects 4. Neopaganism -- Rites and ceremonies 5. Environmentalism -- Religious aspects
ISBN 9780738750934; 9780738753225

LC 2017025403

This book, by Monica Crosson, "is a real-life guide for those who want to practice magick and simplicity but need a little nudge to take a break from the workaday world. Filled with tips, ideas, stories, and projects to bring you and your family closer to nature and to celebrate the God and the Goddess, this book shows how to be true to your magickal self while raising little Witchlings—or helping others with theirs." (Publisher's note)

"In this delightful mix of memoir and Wiccan ritual advice guide, Crosson (Summer Sage) relates anecdotes of her children's spiritual awakening and celebrations of the pagan lifestyle." Pub Wkly

Includes bibliographical references (pages 281-285) and index.

300 SOCIAL SCIENCES, SOCIOLOGY & ANTHROPOLOGY

300 Social sciences

Calhoun, Craig J.

★ **Dictionary** of the social sciences; edited by Craig Calhoun. Oxford Univ. Press 2002 563p $75   **300**
1. Reference books 2. Social sciences -- Dictionaries
ISBN 0-19-512371-9

                      LC 00-68151

This dictionary provides "definitions of key terms, offering entries that also discuss the intellectual issues behind the terms' usage. The entries cover all the social sciences except for law, education, and public administration.... Some 275 biographies are included." Libr J
Includes bibliographical references

★ **ProQuest** Statistical Abstract of the United States; The National Data Book. ProQuest. Rowman & Littlefield $199   **300**
1. United States -- Statistics

"The Statistical Abstract of the United States has provided a statistical portrait of social, political, demographic and economic conditions of America since 1878. This 2017 edition continues the heritage begun so long ago by the U.S. government, with the U.S. Census Bureau being the last agency to produce the compendium at government expense. Now in our fifth annual edition, Bernan and ProQuest carry on the proud tradition and responsibility of creating the statistical portrait of America." (Publisher's note)

Rosenblatt, Roger

★ **Kayak** morning; Roger Rosenblatt. Ecco 2012 160p.   **300**
1. Grief 2. Autobiographies 3. Kayaks and kayaking
ISBN 9780062084033

In this memoir, the author questions "why [he] cannot come to terms with his grief [over the death of his 38-year-old daughter] two and a half years later. As [Roger] Rosenblatt, a writer and professor of English and writing at Stony Brook University, takes up kayaking near his home in Quogue on Long Island, he begins to contemplate his connection to nature and his place in it by observing the sea. The kayak becomes a metaphorical conveyance as he floats from one topic to the next . . . everything from life versus death to personal memories and classical literature. . . . The piece . . . combines short vignettes, poetic verses, snippets of conversations and meaningful quotations." (Publishers Weekly)

301 Sociology and anthropology

Lefebvre, Henri, 1901-1991

Critique of everyday life; Henri Lefebvre, translated by John Moore and Gregory Elliott. Random House Inc. 2014 912 p. (paperback) $44.95   **301**
1. Marxism 2. Modern philosophy
ISBN 9781781683170; 9781781683187; 1781683174

This book, by Henri Lefebvre, translated by John Moore and Gregory Elliott, "written at the birth of post-war consumerism, . . . was a philosophical inspiration for the 1968 student revolution in France and is considered to be the founding text of all that we know as cultural studies, as well as a major influence on the fields of contemporary philoso-

phy, geography, sociology, architecture, political theory and urbanism." (Publisher's note)

Morris, Aldon D.

The **scholar** denied; W.E.B. Du Bois and the birth of modern sociology. Aldon D. Morris. University of California Press 2015 320 p. 8 plates; illustrations (cloth: alk. paper) $29.95   **301**
1. Sociology -- History 2. Sociologists -- United States 3. Sociology -- United States -- History
ISBN 0520276353; 0520286766; 9780520276352; 9780520286764

                      LC 2014042410

This book, by Aldon D. Morris, seeks "to help rewrite the history of sociology and to acknowledge the primacy of W. E. B. Du Bois's work in the founding of the discipline. Calling into question the prevailing narrative of how sociology developed, Morris, a major scholar of social movements, probes the way in which the history of the discipline has traditionally given credit." (Publisher's note)

"Morris's provocative exposé of how economic and political power elevates the ideas, images, and intellectuals America publicly embraces. A must-read for anyone interested in American sociology and/or the U.S. marketplace of ideas." Library Journal
Includes bibliographical references and index

World of sociology; Joseph M. Palmisano, editor. Gale Group 2001 2v il set $160   **301**
1. Reference books 2. Sociology -- Encyclopedias
ISBN 0-7876-4965-1

                      LC 00-48399

This is a "subject-specific guide to concepts, theories, discoveries, pioneers, issues and ethical questions associated with sociology. It includes approximately 1,000-1,500 alphabetically arranged topical essays, definitions and biographies." Publisher's note
Includes bibliographical references

302 Specific topics in sociology and anthropology

Gladwell, Malcolm, 1963-

Outliers; the story of success. Little, Brown and Co. 2008 309p $27.99   **302**
1. Success
ISBN 978-0-316-01792-3; 0-316-01792-2

                      LC 2008-32824

Gladwell's "subject is success — an 'outlier' is a superachiever, like Bill Gates or the four Beatles, and Gladwell wants to know what sets these titans apart. It's not mere talent, he insists, offering up instead one thrilling, exquisitely unfurled counterargument after another. . . . There are both brilliant yarns and life lessons here: Outliers is riveting science, self-help, and entertainment, all in one book." Entertainment Wkly
Includes bibliographical references

The **tipping** point; how little things can make a big difference. Malcolm Gladwell. Little, Brown 2000 viii, 279 p $27.99   **302**
1. Causation 2. Social psychology 3. Contagion (Social psychology)
ISBN 0316316962; 9780316316965

                      LC 99047576

It was the author's intent to demonstrate "that ideas, products, messages and behaviors 'spread just like viruses do.' . . . [Malcolm Gladwell] follows the growth of 'word-of-mouth epidemics' triggered with the help of three pivotal types. These are Connectors, sociable personalities who bring people together; Mavens, who like to pass along knowledge; and Salesmen, adept at persuading the unenlightened. (Paul Revere, for example, was a Maven and a Connector). . . . [The book] offers a smorgasbord of . . . snippets summarizing research on topics such as conversational patterns, infants' crib talk, judging other people's character, cheating habits in schoolchildren, memory sharing among families or couples, and the dehumanizing effects of prisons." (Publishers Weekly)

Includes bibliographical references and index.

Lieberman, Matthew D., 1970-

Social; why our brains are wired to connect. Matthew D. Lieberman. Crown Publishers 2013 384 p. $26 **302**
1. Neurosciences 2. Social networking 3. Social psychology 4. Cognitive psychology 5. Social networks 6. Social interaction 7. Cognitive neuroscience
ISBN 0307889092; 9780307889096; 9780307889119

LC 2013006226

LA Times Book Prize Finalist: Science & Technology (2013)

This book, by Matthew D. Lieberman, "shows readers how their brains may be wired . . . to harmonize and connect with others, rather than simply to act in their own interests. With the help of new functional MRI technology, Lieberman . . . investigat[es] how our perceptions of others affect our cognition and, even more elementally, how social interaction and its absence can produce the same mental responses as physical pain and pleasure." (Publishers Weekly)

"A fascinating explanation of why 'a broken heart can feel as painful as a broken leg' and social recognition is frequently prized above money." Kirkus

Stryker, Kitty

Ask; building consent culture. Kitty Stryker; afterword by Carol Queen; foreword by Laurie Penny. Thorntree Press 2017 212 p. (paperback) $14.95 **302**
1. Feminism 2. Self-acceptance 3. Interpersonal relations 4. Feminist theory 5. Mentally ill -- Psychology 6. Offenses against the person -- Prevention
ISBN 1944934251; 9781944934255

LC 2017022470

"A vibrant treatise from the very first page, this radical collection provides a multifaceted view of consent as an essential concept in not only the bedroom but in the realms of politics, technology, education, and society overall." (LJ)

Wright, Jennifer

It Ended Badly; Thirteen of the Worst Breakups in History. Jennifer Wright. Henry Holt & Co. 2015 256 p. illustrations $21 **302**
1. Marriage 2. Interpersonal relations 3. Breaking up (Interpersonal relations)
ISBN 1627792864; 9781627792868

LC 2015004347

In this book author Jennifer Wright "digs deep into the archives to bring these thirteen terrible breakups to life. [She] guides [readers] through the worst of the worst in historically bad breakups. In the throes of heartbreak, Emperor Nero had just about everyone he ever loved . . . put to death. Oscar Wilde's lover . . . abandoned him when faced with being cut off financially. And poor volatile Caroline Lamb sent Lord Byron one hell of a torch letter." (Publisher's note)

"Wright's ability to blend historical facts with humor will make this book attractive to readers looking for a delightful page-turner, as well as those who enjoy the dynamic people who have been peppered throughout history." LJ

302.1　General topics of social interaction

Kaufman, Sarah L.

The **art** of grace; on moving well through life. Sarah L. Kaufman. W W Norton & Co Inc 2015 336 p. illustrations (hardcover) $24.95; (ebook) $40 **302.1**
1. Aesthetics 2. Manners and customs 3. Grace (Aesthetics)
ISBN 9780393243956; 9780393243963

LC 2015028036

In this book, author "Sarah L. Kaufman sifts the graceful from the graceless, celebrating heart-catching moments of physical elegance in sports, movies, dance, fashion, and music; rare sightings of celebrity grace; the secrets of gracious hosts; and grace found unexpectedly, in the kitchen of a high-end restaurant and among strippers in a basement bar." (Publisher's note)

"Kaufman reminds us that even in a world where most eyes are locked on smart phones, there are still people who really listen, think before they speak, and move gracefully. It's up to us to notice and emulate their techniques." Booklist

Includes bibliographical references and index

302.12　Social understanding

Abramsky, Sasha

Jumping at shadows; the triumph of fear and the end of the American dream. Sasha Abramsky. Nation Books 2017 ix, 324 p.p (hardcover) $28 **302.12**
1. Social change 2. Social perception -- United States 3. Risk -- United States -- Sociological aspects
ISBN 9781568585192; 9781568587646; 1568585195

LC 2017012751

This book, by Sasha Abramsky, is a searing account of America's most dangerous epidemic: irrational fear. Taking readers on a dramatic journey through a divided nation, where everything from immigration to disease, gun control to health care has become fodder for fearmongers and conspiracists, he delivers an eye-popping analysis of our misconceptions about risk and threats." (Publisher's note)

"In this fascinating examination of fear, journalist Abramsky (The American Way of Poverty) reveals how it has infected the collective American psyche, influencing everything from child rearing to government." LJ

Includes bibliographical references (pages 285-307) and index.

302.13　Social choice

Berger, Jonah

Invisible Influence; The Hidden Forces That Shape Behavior. by Jonah Berger. Simon & Schuster 2016 288 p. illustrations (hardcover) $26.99 **302.13**
1. Decision making 2. Social sciences 3. Influence (Psychology)
ISBN 9781476759692; 1476759693

This book, by Jonah Berger, "explores the subtle, secret influences that affect the decisions we make—from what we buy, to the careers we choose, to what we eat. . . . Berger integrates research and thinking from business, psychology, and social science to focus on the subtle, invisible influences behind our choices as individuals. By understanding how social influence works, we can decide when to resist and when to embrace it." (Publisher's note)

"Berger's unique knowledge will appeal to readers from many backgrounds, especially individuals interested in making better decisions."

LJ

Includes bibliographical references and index.

302.2   Communication

Biedermann, Hans

★ **Dictionary** of symbolism; cultural icons and the meanings behind them. translated by James Hulbert. Meridan Book 1994 465p il pa $25   **302.2**
1. Reference books 2. Signs and symbols
ISBN 0-452-01118-3

LC 93-30616

Original German edition, 1989

This dictionary "incorporates symbols that originated in Asia, Africa, Europe and the 'New World'. There are almost 600 entries from mythology, fairy tale, psychology, religion, and sociology, plus historical and legendary figures. With 2000 black-and-white illustrations, the book is highly attractive. The symbols are accompanied by thorough interpretations based on various sources." SLJ

Includes bibliographical references

Colier, Nancy

The **power** of off; The Mindful Way to Stay Sane in a Virtual World. Nancy Colier. Sounds True 2017 256 p. (ebook) $16.95; (pbk.) $16.95   **302.2**
1. Attention 2. Self-control 3. Mindfulness (Psychology) 4. Information technology -- Social aspects 5. Information technology -- Psychological aspects
ISBN 9781622037964; 9781622037957

LC 2016022006

This book, by Nancy Colier, explores technology and how it "will make our lives easier; yet to realize that promise, we cannot be passive users--we must bring awareness and mindfulness to our relationships with our devices. . . . [it] offers us a path for making use of the virtual world while still feeling good, having healthy relationships, and staying connected with what is genuinely meaningful in life." (Publisher's Note)

"Readers fascinated by how digital technology has changed the world, particularly everyday human interaction, will appreciate the author's thought-provoking viewpoint." Pub Wkly

Includes bibliographical references (pages 224-228).

Tannen, Deborah

You just don't understand; women and men in conversation. Quill 2001 342p pa $13.95   **302.2**
1. Conversation 2. Sex differences (Psychology)
ISBN 978-0-06-095962-3; 0-06-095962-2

First published 1990 by Morrow

"Aside from the vivid examples and lively prose, what makes this book particularly engaging is that the author makes linguistics . . . interesting and usable." N Y Times Book Rev

Includes bibliographical references

302.222   Nonverbal communication

Von Petzinger, Genevieve

The **first** signs; unlocking the mysteries of the world's oldest symbols. by Genevieve von Petzinger. Atria Books, an imprint of Simon & Schuster, Inc. 2016 320 p. illustrations (ebook) $18.99; (hardcover: alkaline paper) $27   **302.222**
1. Stone Age 2. Symbolism in art 3. Signs and symbols 4. Europe

-- Antiquities 5. Glacial epoch -- Europe 6. Rock paintings -- Europe 7. Art, Prehistoric -- Europe 8. Geometry in art -- History 9. Symbolism in art -- History 10. Paleolithic period -- Europe 11. Social archaeology -- Europe 12. Signs and symbols -- Europe -- History

ISBN 9781476785516; 9781476785493; 9781476785509

LC 2015051281

This book, by Genevieve von Petzinger, "is the first-ever exploration of the little-known geometric images that accompany most cave art around the world—the first indications of symbolic meaning, intelligence, and language. . . . Part travel journal, part popular science, part personal narrative, von Petzinger's groundbreaking book starts to crack the code on the first form of graphic communication." (Publisher's note)

"An exceptional read that should capture the imagination of anyone fascinated by time, humanity, and prehistory." LJ

Includes bibliographical references and index

302.23   Media (Means of communication)

Bartlett, Jamie

The **Dark** Net; Jamie Bartlett. William Heinemann 2014 320 p. $27.95   **302.23**
1. Internet 2. Internet industry
ISBN 0434023159; 1612194893; 9780434023158; 9781612194899

LC 2015013287

This book by Jamie Bartlett, presents an "examination of the internet today, and of its most innovative and dangerous subcultures: trolls and pornographers, drug dealers and hackers, political extremists and computer scientists, Bitcoin programmers and self-harmers, libertarians and vigilantes." (Publisher's note)

"A provocative excursion to the darker side of human nature set free by the anonymous and unregulated boundaries of cyberspace." Kirkus

Clark, Lynn Schofield

The **parent** app; understanding families in the digital age. Lynn Schofield Clark. Oxford University Press 2013 xx, 299 p.p (alk. paper) $29.95   **302.23**
1. Digital media and families 2. Parent and child 3. Internet and families 4. Internet -- Social aspects
ISBN 0199899614; 9780199899616

LC 2012006687

This book by Lynn Schofield Clark provides families with "strategies for coping with the dilemmas of digital and mobile media in modern life. . . . Clark set about interviewing scores of mothers and fathers, identifying not only their various approaches, but how they differ according to family income. Clark tackles a host of issues, such as family communication, online predators, cyber bullying, sexting, gamer drop-outs, helicopter parenting, . . . and much more." (Publisher's note)

Includes bibliographical references (p. 275-291) and index

Durham, M. Gigi

The **Lolita** effect; the media sexualization of young girls and what we can do about it. [by] M. Gigi Durham, Ph.D. Overlook Press 2008 320p $24.95; pa $14.95   **302.23**
1. Body image 2. Mass media 3. Girls -- Sexual behavior 4. United States -- Social conditions
ISBN 978-1-5902-00636; 1-5902-0063-2; 978-1-5902-0215-9 pa; 1-5902-0215-5 pa

In this "exploration of the media's exploitation of girls, Durham exposes the links between destructive teenage self-images and the popular, highly sexed, and negative representations of girls in magazines, television programs, and movies. . . . [Her] provocative and erudite study of the demeaning way society views girls serves to both alarm and educate; consider it required reading for parents and their daughters." Booklist

Includes bibliographical references

Gladstone, Brooke

The **influencing** machine; Brooke Gladstone on the media. illustrated by Josh Neufeld; with additional penciling by Randy Jones and Susann Ferris-Jones. W. W. Norton 2011 xxii, 170p ill. (chiefly col.) (hbk.) $23.95; (hbk.) $16.95   **302.23**
1. Journalism 2. Mass media 3. Broadcast journalism 4. Comic books, strips, etc. 5. Graphic novels 6. Journalism -- Graphic novels 7. Broadcast journalism -- Graphic novels
ISBN 0393077799; 9780393077797
LC 2011009820

This work of graphic nonfiction explores the "history of media's influence. . . . [F]rom the 'Acta Diurna' posted in ancient Rome to the outcries over President Adams's Alien and Sedition Acts and McCarthy's Red Scare, [Brooke] Gladstone traces not only the birth of the press, but also its various muzzles. The press will not always stay silent, as she illustrates with Daniel Ellsberg and the Pentagon Papers. . . . Yet government opacity still abounds, and Gladstone pointedly wonders if secrecy really makes us safer. . . . Gladstone points to seven key biases that cognizant media consumers should worry about: commercial, bad news, status quo, access, visual, narrative, and fairness. These dovetail . . . into a . . . discussion of war journalism." (Publishers Weekly)

"Gladstone's is an indispensible guide to our ever-evolving media landscape that's brought vividly to life." Publ Wkly

Includes bibliographical references (p. 163-170).

Gonzalez, Juan, 1969-

News for all the people; Juan Gonzalez and Joseph Torres. Verso 2011 432p $29.95   **302.23**
1. Mass media 2. United States -- Race relations
ISBN 978-1-84467-687-3

This book "provide[s] a history of the development of 'the American system of news,' with emphasis on the government's role . . . and . . . construct[s] an account of the struggle across the 'fundamental faultline' of race and ethnicity that shaped both mainstream and dissident media. . . . The stories of Hispanic, Native-American, African-American, and Asian-American journalists risking lives and wellbeing to raise their voices, constitute the true heart of this book. Some of the pioneers' names are reasonably familiar, . . . [b]ut there are dozens of others rescued from obscurity, ranging from Joaquín de Lisa and Joseph Antonio Boniquet, founders in 1809 of 'El Mensajero' of New Orleans, to Ruben Salazar of Los Angeles, assassinated while covering a riot in 1970." (Columbia Journalism Review)

Includes bibliographical references

Harris, Michael

The **End** of absence; reclaiming what we've lost in a world of constant connection. Michael Harris. Current 2014 256 p. (hardback) $26.95   **302.23**
1. Information society 2. Information technology -- Social aspects 3. Internet -- Social aspects 4. Technology -- Social aspects
ISBN 1591846935; 9781591846932
LC 2014009772

In this book, author "Michael Harris argues that amid all the changes we're experiencing, the most interesting is the one that future generations will find hardest to grasp. That is the end of absence--the loss of lack. The daydreaming silences in our lives are filled; the burning solitudes are extinguished. There's no true 'free time' when you carry a smartphone. Today's rarest commodity is the chance to be alone with your own thoughts." (Publisher's note)

"Harris' core argument regarding the values of technological disengagement feels valid, and his prose is graceful, but as a social narrative, the book becomes repetitive and less focused as it proceeds.A thoughtful addition to the bookshelf addressing the unintended consequences of a wired world." Kirkus

Includes bibliographical references and index

Iyer, Pico

The **Art** of Stillness; Adventures in Going Nowhere. by Pico Iyer. Simon & Schuster 2014 96 p. color illustrations $14.99   **302.23**
1. Spiritual life 2. Conduct of life
ISBN 1476784728; 9781476784724
LC 2014498836

This book, by Pico Iyer, "considers the unexpected adventure of staying put and reveals a counterintuitive truth: The more ways we have to connect, the more we seem desperate to unplug. . . . Iyer investigate[s] the lives of people who have made a life seeking stillness: from Matthieu Ricard, a Frenchman with a PhD in molecular biology who left a promising scientific career to become a Tibetan monk, to revered singer-songwriter Leonard Cohen." (Publisher's note)

"Rather than reading it quickly and filing it, readers will likely slow down to meet its pace and might continue carrying it around as a reminder." Kirkus

Keen, Andrew

The **Internet** Is Not the Answer; Andrew Keen. Atlantic Monthly Press 2015 256 p. $25   **302.23**
1. Internet 2. Internet industry 3. Technological innovations
ISBN 0802123139; 9780802123138

In this book, author Andrew Keen "traces the technological and economic history of the internet from its founding in the 1960s through the rise of the big data companies to the increasing attempts to monetize almost every human activity, and investigates how the internet is reconfiguring our world--often at great cost." (Library Journal)

"A must-read for technophiles and business leaders, or those curious about technology's societal effects." LJ

McChesney, Robert Waterman, 1952-

Digital disconnect; how capitalism is turning the Internet against democracy. Robert W. McChesney. The New Press 2013 320 p. (hardcover) $27.95   **302.23**
1. Democracy 2. Capitalism 3. Internet -- Political aspects
ISBN 1595588671; 9781595588678
LC 2012035748

This book, by Robert W. McChesney, "address[es] the relationship between economic power and the digital world. . . . McChesney . . . argues that the sharp decline in the enforcement of antitrust violations, the increase in patents on digital technology . . . and other policies have made the internet a place of numbing commercialism. . . . Robert McChesney . . . urg[es] us to reclaim the democratizing potential of the digital revolution while we still can." (Publisher's note)

Includes bibliographical references and index

McLuhan, Marshall, 1911-1980

Understanding media; the extensions of man. by Marshall McLuhan; edited by W. Terrence Gordon. Critical ed.; Gingko Press 2003 611p ill.;   **302.23**
1. Mass media 2. Mass media -- United States -- History
ISBN 1584230738

LC 2003012174

"Terms and phrases such as "the global village" and "the medium is the message" are ow part of the lexicon, and McLuhan's theories continue to challenge our sensibilities and our assumptions about how and what we communicate." (Publisher's Note)

Includes bibliographical references (p. 569-574) and index..

Palfrey, John

Born digital; understanding the first generation of digital natives. [by] John Palfrey and Urs Gasser. Basic Books 2008 375p $25.95   **302.23**

1. Information society 2. Internet and children 3. Information technology 4. Internet and teenagers 5. Internet -- Social aspects
ISBN 9780465005154

LC 2008-21538

The authors "document the myriad ways downloading, text-messaging, Massively Multiplayer Online Games-playing, YouTube-watching youth are transforming society. Energetic, expert, and forward-looking, the authors serve as envoys between the generations, addressing issues that worry parents and educators, from privacy and safety concerns to the quality of digital information, the psychological and physical effects of information overload and excessive online time, and legal and ethical issues, all the while stressing the need for digital literacy and critical thinking." Booklist

Includes bibliographical references

Singer, P. W.

Likewar; the weaponization of social media. P.W. Singer and Emerson T. Brooking. Eamon Dolan/Houghton Mifflin Harcourt 2018 416 p. (hardback) $28   **302.23**

1. Cyberterrorism 2. Internet -- Political aspects 3. Social media -- Political aspects 4. Mass media and propaganda 5. Hacking -- Political aspects
ISBN 9781328695741

LC 2018017519

In this book, authors "P. W. Singer and Emerson Brooking tackle the mind-bending questions that arise when war goes online and the online world goes to war. They explore how ISIS copies the Instagram tactics of Taylor Swift, . . . internet trolls shape elections, and China uses a smartphone app to police the thoughts of 1.4 billion citizens. What can be kept secret in a world of networks? . . . . And what role do ordinary people now play in international conflicts?" (Publisher's note)

Includes bibliographical references and index

Standage, Tom

Writing on the wall; Social Media - the First 2,000 Years. Tom Standage. St. Martin's Press 2013 288 p. illustrations $26   **302.23**

1. Social media -- History 2. Social networking -- History
ISBN 1620402831; 9781620402832

In this book, author Tom Standage "draws comparisons between modern social media and the forms of communication and information dissemination used over 2,000 years to show how, in fact, 'History retweets itself.' Examples include ancient Roman graffiti that bears a strong resemblance to a Facebook status update . . . and Martin Luther's 95 theses, perhaps the first document to go viral." (Publishers Weekly)

"Standage offers historical perspective on such concerns about evolving social media as faddishness, coarsening of discourse, distraction from serious work, and erosion of social skills." Booklist

Includes bibliographical references and index

Thompson, David C.

The **reputation** economy; how to optimize your digital footprint in a world where your reputation is your most valuable asset. Michael Fertik, David C. Thompson. Crown Business 2015 256 p. (hardback) $25   **302.23**

1. Reputation 2. Technology 3. Public relations 4. Success in business 5. Internet in publicity 6. Online social networks 7. Online identities -- Social aspects
ISBN 0385347596; 9780385347594; 9780804139236

LC 2014038611

In this book, authors Michael Fertik and David C. Thompson "will draw on the insider tools, insights, research, and secrets that has make Reputation.com the leading reputation management firm, to show how to capitalize on the trends the Reputation Economy will trigger to improve your professional, financial, and even social prospects." (Publisher's note)

Turkle, Sherry

Reclaiming Conversation; The Power of Talk in a Digital Age. by Sherry Turkle. Penguin Group USA 2015 448 p. (ebook) $32.50; $27.95   **302.23**

1. Conversation
ISBN 9781101617397; 1594205558; 9781594205552

This book, by Sherry Turkle, "investigates how a flight from conversation undermines our relationships, creativity, and productivity—and why reclaiming face-to-face conversation can help us regain lost ground. . . . Based on five years of research and interviews in homes, schools, and the workplace, Turkle argues that we have come to a better understanding of where our technology can and cannot take us and that the time is right to reclaim conversation." (Publisher's note)

"A timely wake-up call urging us to cherish the intimacy of direct, unscripted communication." Kirkus

Includes bibliographical references (pages 367-416) and index.

Zuckerman, Ethan

Rewire; digital cosmopolitans in the age of connection. Ethan Zuckerman. W W Norton & Co Inc 2013 288 p. (hardcover) $26.95   **302.23**

1. Internet 2. Cosmopolitanism 3. Internet -- Social aspects 4. Social media
ISBN 0393082830; 9780393082838

LC 2013007124

This book is a reflection "on what it means to be a citizen of the world in the Internet age," where Ethan Zuckerman "declares that, far from aspiring to full engagement with others around the world, we seek to connect with people who share our values, nationality, gender, and race. . . . He argues that we all possess the capacity to build networks that 'rewire' our world with a better sense of interdependence." (Publishers Weekly)

Includes bibliographical references and index

302.231   Digital media

Alter, Adam

Irresistible; the rise of addictive technology and the business of keeping us hooked. Adam Alter. Penguin Press 2017 354 p. illustrations $27   **302.231**

1. Applied psychology 2. Digital media -- Psychological aspects
ISBN 1594206643; 9781594206641

LC 2016043481

In this book, "Adam Alter, a professor of psychology and marketing at NYU, tracks the rise of behavioral addiction, and explains why so many of today's products are irresistible. Though these miraculous products melt the miles that separate people across the globe, their extraordinary and sometimes damaging magnetism is no accident. The companies that design these products tweak them over time until they become almost impossible to resist." (Publisher's note)

"An excellent offering for those interested in technology, especially those grappling with the topic themselves." LJ.

Includes bibliographical references (pages 323-344) and index.

Harrison, Guy P.

Think before you like; social media's effect on the brain and the tools you need to navigate your newsfeed. by Guy P. Harrison. Prometheus Books 2017 380 p. (pbk.) $18 **302.231**
  1. Social media 2. Critical thinking 3. Social networking 4. Brain -- Psychology 5. Online social networks 6. Social media -- Psychological aspects
  ISBN 9781633883529; 9781633883512

  LC 2017022168

In this book, author Guy P. Harrison "demonstrates how critical thinking can enhance the benefits of social media while giving users the skills to guard against its dangers. . . . [He] will teach you how to resist the psychological and behavioral manipulation of social media and avoid the mistakes that millions have already made and now regret." (Publisher's note)

"In this skillfully written and researched survey, journalist Harrison (Good Thinking) makes an argument for appreciating social media's good points while exercising prudence to avoid its downside." Pub Wkly

Includes bibliographical references (pages 321-360) and index.

McLaughlin, Rhett

Rhett & Link's book of mythicality; a field guide to curiosity, creativity, & tomfoolery. by Rhett McLaughlin & Link Neal with Jake Greene. Crown Archetype 2017 269 p. illustrations (chiefly color) (hardback) $21 **302.231**
  1. Wit and humor 2. American wit and humor 3. Good mythical morning (YouTube) 4. Internet personalities -- United States -- Biography
  ISBN 9780451496317; 0451496299; 9780451496294

  LC 2017032473

In this book, authors Rhett McLaughlin & Link Neal with Jake Greene, present their "ultimate guide to living a 'Mythical' life, featuring stories and photos from their lifelong friendship, as well as awesomely illustrated guides, charts, and activities aimed at laughing more, learning more, and never taking yourself too seriously. . . . Within its pages, you'll discover twenty ways to fill your life with curiosity, creativity, and tomfoolery." (Publisher's note)

Includes bibliographical references (pages 266-267) and index.

302.3   Social interaction within groups

Ferguson, Niall, 1964-

The **square** and the tower; networks and power, from the Freemasons to Facebook. Niall Ferguson. Penguin Press, an imprint of Penguin Random House LLC 2018 xxvii, 563 p.p illustrations (some color) (hardcover) $30 **302.3**
  1. Secret societies 2. Social networking 3. Social networks -- History
  ISBN 9780735222915; 9780735222922; 0735222916

  LC 2017301143

In this book, author "Niall Ferguson argues that [social] networks

have always been with us, from the structure of the brain to the food chain, from the family tree to freemasonry. . . . [He] tells the story of the rise, fall and rise of networks, and shows how network theory--concepts such as clustering, degrees of separation, weak ties, contagions and phase transitions--can transform our understanding of both the past and the present." (Publisher's note)

"Making profitable use of information science, Ferguson offers a novel way of examining data that will be highly intriguing to students of history and current affairs." Kirkus

Includes bibliographical references (pages 436-536) and index

Fisher, Helen, ca. 1947-

Anatomy of Love; A Natural History of Mating, Marriage, and Why We Stray. by Helen Fisher. W W Norton & Co Inc 2016 400 p. illustrations, charts $26.95 **302.3**
  1. Sex 2. Marriage 3. Natural history 4. Man-woman relationship
  ISBN 0393285227; 9780393285222

  LC 2015037510

In this book, anthropologist Helen Fisher presents a " four-million-year history of the human species. She demystifies much about romance and pairing that we tend to believe is willfull or just plain careless. She offers new explanations for why men and women fall in love, marry, and divorce, and discusses the future of sex in a way that will surprise you." (Publisher's note)

"This work remains a solid introduction to the nature of sex and relationships, albeit cursory in depth of coverage. Highly recommended to readers interested in human sexuality." LJ

Junger, Sebastian, 1962-

Tribe; On Homecoming and Belonging. by Sebastian Junger. Grand Central Pub 2016 160 p. $22 **302.3**
  1. Tribes
  ISBN 1455566381; 9781455566389

  LC 2016013022

This book, by Sebastian Junger, "explores what we can learn from tribal societies about loyalty, belonging, and the eternal human quest for meaning. It explains the irony that-for many veterans as well as civilians-war feels better than peace, adversity can turn out to be a blessing, and disasters are sometimes remembered more fondly than weddings or tropical vacations." (Publisher's note)

"Junger uses every word in this slim volume to make a passionate, compelling case for a more egalitarian society." Booklist

Includes bibliographical references (pages 139-168).

O'Connor, Rory

Friends, followers, and the future; how social media are changing politics, threatening big brands, and killing traditional media. Rory O'Connor. City Lights Books 2012 285 p. (pbk.) $15.95 **302.3**
  1. Mass media 2. Communication 3. Social networking 4. Social media 5. Social media -- Economic aspects 6. Social media -- Political aspects
  ISBN 0872865568; 9780872865563

  LC 2012005506

This book, by Rory O'Connor, offers "a look at how social media are transforming our world. . . . O'Connor explains the trends and explores what tech visionaries, media makers, political advisers, and business-people are saying about the meteoric rise of the various social networks of friends and followers, and what they bode for our future." (Publisher's note)

O'Hagan, Andrew, 1968-

The **secret** life; three true stories of the digital age. Andrew O'Hagan. Farrar, Straus & Giroux 2017 xvi, 218 p.p (hardcover) $26 **302.3**

1. Internet 2. Identity (Psychology) 3. Bitcoin 4. Secrecy 5. Online identities 6. WikiLeaks (Organization) 7. Internet -- Moral and ethical aspects
ISBN 9780374277918; 9780374717094

LC 2017001315

In this book, author Andrew O'Hagan "issues three bulletins from the porous border between cyberspace and IRL. 'Ghosting' introduces us to the beguiling and divisive Wikileaks founder Julian Assange. . . . 'The Invention of Ronnie Pinn' finds the author using the actual identity of a deceased young man to construct an entirely new one. . . . And 'The Satoshi Affair' chronicles the strange case of Craig Wright, . . . who may or may not be the mysterious inventor of Bitcoin." (Publisher's note)

"Taken as a whole, this is an unmissable collection of up-to-the-moment insights about life in our digital era." Pub Wkly

Sciolino, Elaine

La seduction; how the French play the game of life. Times Books/Henry Holt 2011 338p il **302.3**

1. Seduction 2. Sex customs -- France -- History 3. France -- Social life and customs
ISBN 0-8050-9115-7; 9780805091151

LC 2010049572

According to the author, "seduction plays a crucial role in how the French relate to one another—not just in romantic relationships but also in how they conduct business, enjoy food and drink, define style, engage in intellectual debate, elect politicians, and project power around the world. While sexual repartee and conquest remain at the heart of seduction, for the French seduction has become a philosophy of life, even an ideology, that can confuse outsiders. In [this book, Sciolino looks at] . . . how seduction works in all areas, analyzing its limits as well as its power." (Publisher's note)

The author "deals with the subtle and cultural ways seduction shapes all aspects of French life. She takes a broad approach and writes less about the sexual associations of the word and more about the pleasure game the French play in order to 'attract or influence, to win over, even if just for fun.' Ms. Sciolino's pedigree as a commentator on things French is first class. She was a student in France in 1969 and returned to live and work there as a correspondent for Newsweek, then later as the Bureau Chief of The New York Times in Paris, and now as a correspondent for the paper. She finds French life permeated with the seduction factor, and in a journalistic fashion looks at it in an array of fields, including politics, foreign affairs, literature, history, film, advertising, beauty, scent, fashion, entertaining, food and wine, and sex, and makes her mostly French victims unveil some rules and secrets." Daily Beast

Includes bibliographical references

302.34 Social interaction in primary groups

Bazelon, Emily, 1971-

★ **Sticks** and stones; defeating the culture of bullying and rediscovering the power of character and empathy. by Emily Bazelon. Random House 2013 viii, 386 p.p ill. (hardcover) $27 **302.34**

1. Bullies 2. Adolescence 3. Social media 4. Bullying 5. Bullying in schools 6. Bullying -- Prevention 7. Bullying in schools -- Prevention
ISBN 0812992806; 9780679644002; 9780812992809

LC 2012022773

This book, by Emily Bazelon, discusses teen culture in the U.S., focusing on bullying. "Being a teenager has never been easy, but in recent years, with the rise of the Internet and social media, it has become exponentially more challenging. . . . Bazelon defines what bullying is and, just as important, what it is not. She explores when intervention is essential and when kids should be given the freedom to fend for themselves. She also dispels persistent myths." (Publisher's note)

"While less prescriptive than other books on the topic, very useful FAQs are included, as are resource lists for readers. Masterfully written, Bazelon's book will increase understanding, awareness, and action." Pub Wkly

Includes bibliographical references and index

Hitchcock, J. A.

Cyberbullying and the wild, wild web; what everyone needs to know. J. A. Hitchcock. Rowman & Littlefield 2016 140 p. illustrations (cloth) $30 **302.34**

1. Cyberbullying 2. Computer crimes 3. Cyberbullying -- Prevention
ISBN 9781442251175

LC 2016042062

This book, by J.A. Hitchcock, "explains how someone can become victim to cyberbullying and how they can stay safer online. Offering victims, and parents, the chance to be able to relate to and truly understand the unfortunate reality of cyberbullying through real-life examples of what happened to someone who had been through a similar situation." (Publisher's note)

"This book will be a useful resource for anyone who wants to know how to deal with cyberbullying." Booklist

Includes bibliographical references and index

Kowalski, Robin M.

Cyberbullying; bullying in the digital age. Robin M. Kowalski, Susan P. Limber, and Patricia W. Agatston. Wiley-Blackwell 2012 xi, 282 p.p (pbk.) $24.95 **302.34**

1. Social media 2. Cyberbullying 3. School children 4. Computers and children 5. Bullying
ISBN 1444334816; 9781444334814; 9781444334807

LC 2011046026

In this book, "psychologists explore the reality of cyberbullies. . . . Advances in social media, email, instant messaging, and cell phones . . . have moved bullying from a schoolyard fear to a constant threat. The second edition of "Cyberbullying' offers the most current information on this constantly-evolving issue and outlines the unique concerns and challenges it raises for children, parents, and educators." (Publisher's note)

Includes bibliographical references and index

Schaefer, Kayleen

Text me when you get home; the evolution and triumph of modern female friendship. Kayleen Schaefer. Penguin Group USA 2018 288 p. $24 **302.340**

1. Autobiographies 2. Female friendship 3. Friendship -- Fiction
ISBN 1101986123; 9781101986127

In this book author Kayleen Schaefer "relays her journey of modern female friendship: from being a competitive teenager to trying to be one of the guys in the workplace to ultimately awakening to the power of female friendship and the soulmates, girl squads, and chosen families that come with it. Schaefer has put together a completely new sociological perspective on the way we see our friends today, one that includes interviews with dozens of other women across the country." (Publisher's note)

"Schaefer provides an engaging, deeply researched sociological perspective into the evolution of female friendships. Consider purchasing where women's studies topics circulate well." LJ

Scheff, Sue

Shame nation; the global epidemic of online hate. Sue Scheff, with Melissa Schorr. Sourcebooks Inc 2017 352 p. (hardcover: alk. paper) $25.99   **302.34**

1. Hate speech 2. Cyberbullying 3. Shame -- Social aspects 4. Humiliation 5. Online hate speech 6. Internet -- Moral and ethical aspects

ISBN 9781492648994

LC 2017013493

This book, by Sue Scheff with Melissa Schorr, "presents an eye-opening examination around the rise in online shaming, and offers practical advice and tips including: preventing digital disasters; defending your online reputation; building digital resilience; [and] reclaiming online civility. Armed with the right knowledge and skills, everyone can play a positive part in the prevention and protection against online cruelty." (Publisher's note)

"Parents will find the book's advice useful in protecting their children from danger as they explore online, as will anyone who has made a hasty comment or tweet and lived to regret it. Shame Nation is a strong addition to any collection." (Booklist)

Includes bibliographical references and index

Strauss, Susan L.

★ **Sexual** harassment and bullying; a guide to keeping kids safe and holding schools accountable. Susan L. Strauss. Rowman & Littlefield Publishers 2012 290 p. (cloth: alk. paper) $34.95   **302.34**

1. Bullies 2. Social media 3. Sexual harassment 4. Bullying 5. Bullying -- Prevention 6. Sexual harassment in education 7. Sexual harassment -- Prevention

ISBN 1442201622; 9781442201620

LC 2011031731

In this book, "[Susan L.] Strauss draws on her experiences as consultant, former high-school teacher, and parent of a child who was sexually harassed to advise parents, teachers, and other adults on how to protect children" from bullying and harassment. She gives definitions of bullying and harassment, "offers a particular focus on the kind of harassment of gay, bisexual, and transgendered students," and examines "how social media . . . have ramped up bullying and harassment." (Booklist)

Includes bibliographical references and index.

Tannen, Deborah

You're the only one I can tell; inside the language of women's friendships. Deborah Tannen. Ballantine Books 2017 xviii, 276 p.p (hardcover) $27   **302.34**

1. Conversation 2. Female friendship 3. Conversation analysis 4. Interpersonal communication

ISBN 9781101885802; 9781101885819; 1101885807

LC 2017288647

In this book, author Deborah Tannen "deconstructs the ways women friends talk and how those ways can bring friends closer or pull them apart. From casual chatting to intimate confiding, from talking about problems to telling what you had for dinner, Tannen uncovers the patterns of communication and miscommunication that affect friendships at different points in our lives." (Publisher's note)

"Tannen sets out to help women make friendships stronger, accomplishing this in a highly accessible manner with both scientific research and a warm heart." LJ

Includes bibliographical references (pages 257-263) and index.

Whitson, Signe

8 keys to end bullying; strategies for parents & schools. Signe Whitson; foreword by Babette Rothschild. W.W. Norton & Co Inc. 2014 240 p. (8 keys to mental health series) (pbk.) $19.95   **302.34**

1. Bullies 2. Classroom management 3. Bullying -- Prevention 4. Aggressiveness in children 5. Bullying in schools -- Prevention

ISBN 0393709280; 9780393709285

LC 2014001241

This book by Signe Whitson discusses how "social media bullying . . . has given the widespread problem a new dimension. While no magic cure-all exists, adults can learn . . . techniques that can make a huge difference in the lives of kids. In 8 core strategies, this book lays them out, from establishing meaningful connections with kids to creating a positive school climate, addressing cyberbullying, building social emotional competence, . . . and much more." (Publisher's note)

"Complete with example scenarios, exercises for readers, and sample responses, the author does a convincing job of helping adults feel empowered to address this important issue." LJ

Includes bibliographical references and index

302.35 Social interaction in complex groups

Davis, Todd

Get better; 15 proven practices to build effective relationships at work. by Todd Davis. Simon & Schuster 2017 230 p. $28   **302.35**

1. Work environment 2. Success in business

ISBN 1501158309; 9781501158308

LC 2017301150

This book, by Todd Davis, "explains that an organization's greatest asset isn't its people; rather, it's the relationships between its people that is the greatest predictor of personal effectiveness. In the end, employees' ability to build and sustain great relationships is an organization's ultimate competitive advantage." (Publisher's note)

"Making the office a safe place to speak the truth, trusting oneself as well as others, and reflecting on the intentions that drive one's actions are all sage practices, but the foundation of Davis's fundamental points is observing and listening to business partners, colleagues, and supervisors." Library Journal

302.5 Relation of individual to society

Appiah, Anthony, 1954-

The **lies** that bind; rethinking identity. Kwame Anthony Appiah. W W Norton & Co Inc 2018 256 p. $27.95   **302.5**

1. Philosophy 2. Group identity 3. Identity (Psychology)

ISBN 1631493833; 9781631493836

This book, by Kwame Anthony Appiah, "is an incandescent exploration of the nature and history of the identities that define us. It challenges our assumptions about how identities work. We all know there are conflicts between identities, but Appiah shows how identities are created by conflict. Religion, he demonstrates, gains power because it isn't primarily about belief. . . . This book will transform the way we think about who--and what--'we' are." (Publisher's note)

"Written in a clear, nontechnical style, this book by an outstanding contemporary philosopher presents critical thinking about public issues at its best and should appeal widely to anyone interested in serious thought." Library Journal

Olds, Jacqueline

The **lonely** American; drifting apart in the twenty-first century. [by] Jacqueline Olds and Richard S. Schwartz. Beacon Press 2008 228p $24.95   **302.5**

1. Loneliness 2. Loneliness -- United States 3. Social isolation -- United States

ISBN 978-0-8070-0034-2; 0-8070-0034-5

LC 2008-19339

The authors "paint a tragic picture of a nation of individual units—families, couples and, increasingly, single people—that have all but ceased to function as a society. While the authors focus largely on the psychological impact of all this isolation, they also explain its physical toll on Americans and their world. Not only is social isolation an indicator for substance abuse, violent crime and early death, it is also linked to greater consumption of consumer goods. . . . In keeping with their profession as psychoanalysts, Olds and Schwartz maintain a kind and caring tone throughout The Lonely American, neither scolding nor scoffing at the nation of individuals Americans have become" PopMatters

Includes bibliographical references and index.

303.3   Coordination and control

Huxley, Aldous

★ **Brave** new world revisited. Harper & Row 1958 147p hardcover o.p. pa $11.95   **303.3**

1. Culture 2. Propaganda 3. Brainwashing 4. Totalitarianism

ISBN 0-06-089852-6 pa

In response to his 1932 novel Brave new world "Huxley reconsiders his prophecies and fears that some of these may be coming true much sooner than he thought." Oxford Companion to Engl Lit. 5th edition

Nader, Ralph

Told you so; the big book of weekly columns. by Ralph Nader. Seven Stories Press 2013 xv, 520 p.p (pbk.) $29.95 **303.3**

1. Social problems 2. United States -- Social conditions 3. Social justice -- United States 4. Corporate power -- United States 5. United States -- Social policy -- 21st century 6. United States -- Economic policy -- 21st century 7. United States -- Social conditions -- 21st century 8. United States -- Politics and government -- 21st century

ISBN 1609804740; 9781609804749

LC 2013001625

Author Ralph Nader "presents a panoramic portrait of the problems confronting our society and provides examples of the many actions an organized citizenry could and should take to create a more just and environmentally sustainable world. Drawing on decades of experience, Nader's columns document the consequences of concentrated corporate power; threats to our food, water and air; the corrosive effect of commercialism on our children; the dismantling of worker rights; and the attacks on our civil rights." (Publisher's note)

Includes index

Surowiecki, James

The **wisdom** of crowds; why the many are smarter than the few and how collective wisdom shapes business, economies, societies and nations. Doubleday 2004 xxi, 296p $24.95; pa $14   **303.3**

1. Crowds 2. Social psychology 3. Intellect 4. Consensus (Social sciences)

ISBN 0-385-50386-5; 0-385-72170-6 pa

LC 2003-70095

The author argues that "large groups of people are smarter than an elite few, no matter how brilliant: better at solving problems, fostering innovation, coming to wise decisions, even predicting the future." (Publisher's note)

The author "analyzes the concept of collective wisdom and applies it to various areas of the social sciences, including economics and politics. . . . This work is an intriguing study of collective intelligence and how it works in contemporary society." Libr J

Includes bibliographical references

Taibbi, Matt, 1970-

The **divide**; American injustice in the age of the wealth gap. Matt Taibbi; illustrations by Molly Crabapple. Spiegel & Grau 2014 448 p. illustrations (hardback) $27   **303.3**

1. Equality 2. Social policy -- United States 3. Administration of criminal justice -- United States 4. Poor -- United States 5. Rich people -- United States 6. Social justice -- United States 7. Income distribution -- United States

ISBN 081299342X; 9780812993424

LC 2013024907

Taibbi "takes readers on a galvanizing journey through both sides of our new system of justice--the fun-house-mirror worlds of the untouchably wealthy and the criminalized poor. . . . Through . . . accounts of the high-stakes capers of the wealthy and nightmare stories of regular people caught in the Divide's punishing logic, Taibbi lays bare one of the greatest challenges we face in contemporary American life." (Publisher's note)

"Taibbi's chapters are high-definition photographs contrasting the ways we pursue small-time corruption and essentially reward high-level versions of the same thing. [He mixes] case studies, interviews and anecdotes with comprehensive research on his topics." Kirkus

Includes bibliographical references and index

Wills, Garry

Certain trumpets; the call of leaders. Simon & Schuster 1994 336p il hardcover o.p. pa $16   **303.3**

1. Leadership 2. Power (Social sciences) 3. Leadership -- Case studies. 4. Social participation -- Case studies. 5. Power (Social sciences) -- Case studies.

ISBN 0-671-65702-X; 978-0-684-80138-4 pa; 0-684-80138-8 pa

LC 94-6526

The author "has chosen 16 figures who exemplify a distinctive leadership type—for example, military (Napoleon), charismatic (King David), saintly (Catholic worker activist Dorothy Day). Each leader is contrasted with an 'anti-type' who, in Wills's judgment, failed to capitalize on strengths similar to those of his or her successful counterpart. . . . Wills pairs Martha Graham with Madonna, Socrates with Ludwig Wittgenstein, Eleanor Roosevelt with Nancy Reagan in a wise, witty, entertaining look at the psychology of leaders and their followers." Publ Wkly

Includes bibliographical references

303.34   Leadership

Koehn, Nancy

Forged in crisis; the power of courageous leadership in turbulent times. Nancy Koehn. Scribner 2017 ix, 517 p.p illustrations (hardcover) $35   **303.34**

1. Historical literature 2. Leadership -- History

ISBN 1501174444; 9781501174445; 9781501174469

LC 2017297073

This book, by Nancy Koehn, "spotlights five masters of crisis: polar explorer Ernest Shackleton; President Abraham Lincoln; legendary abolitionist Frederick Douglass; Nazi-resisting clergyman Dietrich Bonhoeffer; and environmental crusader Rachel Carson. What do such disparate figures have in common? . . . Koehn offers a remarkable template by which to judge those in our own time to whom the public has given its trust." (Publisher's note)

"Wise, thoughtful, and valuable, this book will foster a new appreciation for effective leadership and prompt many readers to lament the lack of it in the world today." Kirkus

Includes bibliographical references (pages 459-496) and index.

Viroli, Maurizio

How to choose a leader; Machiavelli's Advice to Citizens. Maurizio Viroli. Princeton University Press 2016 144 p. (hardback: acid-free paper) $16.95   **303.34**
1. Political leadership -- Philosophy 2. Political participation -- Philosophy
ISBN 9780691170145

LC 2015043592

"One of the greatest political advisers of all time, Niccolò Machiavelli thought long and hard about how citizens could identify great leaders--ones capable of defending and enhancing the liberty, honor, and prosperity of their countries. Drawing on the full range of the Florentine's writings, acclaimed Machiavelli biographer Maurizio Viroli gathers and interprets Machiavelli's timeless wisdom about choosing leaders." (Publisher's note)

Includes bibliographical references

303.38   Public opinion

Salvanto, Anthony

Where did you get this number? a pollster's guide to making sense of the world. Anthony Salvanto. Simon & Schuster 2018 256 p. (hardcover) $26   **303.38**
1. Public opinion polls 2. United States. Congress 3. United States -- Politics and government -- Public opinion 4. Public opinion -- United States 5. Voter research -- United States 6. Public opinion polls -- United States 7. United States. Congress -- Public opinion 8. Presidents -- United States -- Public opinion
ISBN 9781501174834; 9781501174858

LC 2018013690

In this book "CBS News' Elections and Surveys Director Anthony Salvanto takes you behind the scenes of polling to show you how to think about who we are and where we're headed as a nation. . . . Salvanto demystifies jargon with plain language and answers readers' biggest questions about polling and pollsters. . . . [He] offers data-driven perspective on how Americans see the biggest issues of our time." (Publisher's note)

"General interest readers and news junkies alike will come away with a greater appreciation of how polls and surveys are conducted, as well as a much clearer sense of what they mean." Publishers' Weekly

303.4   Social change

Carr, Nicholas G., 1959-

The **big** switch; rewiring the world, from Edison to Google. W. W. Norton & Company 2008 278p $25.95; pa $16.95 **303.4**

1. Internet 2. Information technology 3. Technological innovations 4. Computers and civilization
ISBN 0-393-06228-7; 0-393-33394-9 pa; 978-0-393-06228-1; 978-0-393-33394-7 pa

LC 2007-38084

The author "examines the future of the Internet, which he says may one day completely replace the desktop PC as all computing services are delivered over the Net as a utility, the Internet morphing into one giant 'World Wide Computer.'" Booklist

Includes bibliographical references

Diamond, Jared M.

★ **Guns,** germs, and steel; the fates of human societies. [by] Jared Diamond. Norton 2005 518p il map $24.95 **303.4**
1. Ethnology 2. Food supply 3. Social change 4. Technology and civilization 5. Environmental influence on humans
ISBN 0-393-06131-0; 978-0-393-06131-4

LC 2005-284261

First published 1997

"This book poses a simple but profound question about the distribution of wealth and power in the modern world: 'Why weren't Native Americans, Africans, and Aboriginal Australians the ones who decimated, subjugated, or exterminated Europeans and Asians?'. . . To explore the discrepancies in technological and cultural development he looks not at peoples but at places, and at the natural resources available to different indigenous populations since 11,000 B.C. The scope and the explanatory power of this book are astounding." New Yorker [review of 1997 edition]

Includes bibliographical references

Gore, Albert, 1948-

The **future**; six drivers of global change. Al Gore. Random House 2013 xxxi, 558 p.p (hardback) $30   **303.4**
1. Forecasting 2. Climate change 3. World history -- 21st century 4. Globalization 5. Social change 6. Technological innovations 7. Global environmental change 8. Economic history -- 21st century
ISBN 0812992946; 9780812992946

LC 2012039890

This book, by Al Gore, offers an "assessment of six critical drivers of global change in the decades to come. . . . Al Gore surveys . . . ever-increasing economic globalization . . . , worldwide digital communications, . . . the balance of global political, economic, and military power . . ., unsustainable growth in consumption, pollution flows, and depletion of the planet's strategic resources . . . , [and] genomic, biotechnology, neuroscience, and life sciences revolutions." (Publisher's note)

"Gore's strengths lie in his passion for the subject and in his ability to take the long view by putting current events and trends in historical context." PubWkly

Includes bibliographical references (pages 379-387) and index

Heath, Chip

Switch; how to change things when change is hard. [by] Chip Heath and Dan Heath. Broadway Books 2010 305p $26; pa $15.95; ebook $11.99   **303.4**
1. Change (Psychology)
ISBN 978-0-385-52875-7; 978-0-307-74235-3 pa; 978-0-307-59016-9 ebook

LC 2009-27814

This book "offers many insights about human behavior and psychology that marketing professionals, communications experts, and public-policy makers might all appreciate." Futurist

Includes bibliographical references

Hessler, Peter

Country driving; a journey through China from farm to factory. Harper 2010 438p map $27.99   **303.4**

1. Highway transportation 2. Journalists 3. China -- Description and travel 4. Transportation, Automotive -- China

ISBN 0-06-180409-6; 978-0-06-180409-0

LC 2009-27502

In 2001, Peter Hessler, the Beijing correspondent for The New Yorker, acquired his Chinese driver's license. For the next seven years, he traveled the country, tracking how the automobile and improved roads were transforming China. . . . Country Driving begins with Hessler's 7,000-mile trip across northern China, following the Great Wall, from the East China Sea to the Tibetan plateau. He investigates a historically important rural region being abandoned, as young people migrate to jobs in the southeast. Next Hessler spends six years in Sancha, a small farming village in the mountains north of Beijing, which changes dramatically after the local road is paved and the capital's auto boom brings new tourism. Finally, he turns his attention to urban China, researching development . . . in Lishui, a small southeastern city where officials hope that a new government-built expressway will transform a farm region into a major industrial center. (Publisher's note)

"Full of exotic detail, solid reporting, and ironic observation, Country Driving offers a personal snapshot of the world's second superpower hurtling through the 21st century." Boston Globe

Includes bibliographical references

Ladd, Brian

Autophobia; love and hate in the automotive age. University of Chicago Press 2008 227p il $22.50   **303.4**

1. Automobiles 2. Environmental degradation 3. Automobiles -- Social aspects 4. Transportation, Automotive -- United States

ISBN 0-226-46741-4; 978-0-226-46741-2

LC 2008-14520

This is "a look at the car and its critics." (N Y Times Book Rev) Index.

Ladd "documents a century of expanding U.S. reliance on vehicles powered by oil, most of which has to be imported. He frames his analysis in familiar concepts: the automotive industry as employer, urban migration from cities by families relying on automobiles for transportation, traffic/congestion/roadways, and damage to the environment from burning fossil fuels. . . . [The author shows] how the car is completely woven into the fabric of our cultural and economic history. As such, he writes, we have accepted the dark side of the automobile—pollution, congestion, high energy costs, and accidental loss of life—in exchange for personal mobility." Libr J

Includes bibliographical references

Lanier, Jaron

★ **You** are not a gadget; a manifesto. Alfred A. Knopf 2010 209p $24.95   **303.4**

1. Information technology 2. Technological innovations 3. Technology and civilization 4. Web sites -- Design 5. Digital media -- Social aspects 6. Information technology -- Social aspects 7. Technological innovations -- Social aspects

ISBN 0-307-26964-7; 978-0-307-26964-5

LC 2009-20298

"In the nineteen-eighties, Lanier belonged to what he calls a 'merry band' of Internet pioneers who believed that the digital revolution would mean a groundswell of creativity. But, he argues in this manifesto, around the turn of this century the dream was hijacked by 'digital Maoists,' who value the crowd above the individual. Their influence, he writes, has led to an online culture of mashups, 'pervasive anonymity' (which encourages bullying and moblike behavior), open access (so

that individual ownership is devalued or lost), and social-networking sites that reduce 'the deep meaning of personhood.' He fears that these characteristics are perilously close to 'lock-in': becoming permanent features of the Web. Lanier's detractors have accused him of Ludditism, but his argument will make intuitive sense to anyone concerned with questions of propriety, responsibility, and authenticity." New Yorker

Linden, Eugene

The **ragged** edge of the world; encounters at the frontier where modernity, wildlands, and indigenous peoples meet. Viking 2011 260p $26.95   **303.4**

1. Ethnology

ISBN 978-0-670-02251-9

LC 2010043578

"Traveling to the rain forests of Borneo and to the Amazon, the Antarctic, and Africa, Linden provides firsthand accounts of cargo cults in New Guinea, practices of Pygmy tribes in Africa, and conservation efforts in Cuba—some of which show positive responses to deforestation and loss of habitat for wildlife, while others reveal the downward spiral to extinction for rain forests and many animal species. He highlights cultural extinction as much as environmental devastation to habitats. . . . . Linden provides an original look at globalization and its impact on various cultures and species throughout the world. Anyone interested in global environmental issues will find this book informative." Libr J

Mortimer, Ian

Millennium; From Religion to Revolution: How Civilization Has Changed Over a Thousand Years. by Ian Mortimer. W W Norton & Co Inc 2016 416 p. illustrations (ebook) $50; $28.95   **303.4**

1. World history

ISBN 9781681772868; 1681772434; 9781681772431

LC 2016042500

This book, by Ian Mortimer, "takes the reader on a whirlwind tour of the last ten centuries of Western history. It is a journey into a past vividly brought to life and bursting with ideas, that pits one century against another in his quest to measure which century saw the greatest change." (Publisher's note)

"A quirky but always delightful social history that w ill convince most readers that social revolutions have been happening for a long time." Kirkus

Includes bibliographical references (pages 355-377) and index.

Otto, Shawn

Fool me twice; fighting the assault on science in America. [by] Shawn Lawrence Otto. Rodale 2011 376p $25.99 **303.4**

1. Learning and scholarship 2. Science -- United States 3. Science -- Study and teaching 4. United States -- Intellectual life

ISBN 978-1-60529-217-5; 1-60529-217-6

LC 2011033902

The author "explores the devaluation of science in America. His exhaustively researched text explains the three-pronged attack on science: how right-wing Christian fervor discredits evolution; how postmodernism and cultural sensitivity makes people believe that objective truth doesn't exist; and how corporations discredit scientists in order to further economic agendas. . . . The accessible book will inform scientists about what has happened to their field, provide an overview for laypeople, and allow educators to equip themselves to address these issues for the next generation and reverse this troubling trend." Publ Wkly

Includes bibliographical references

Pagel, Mark

Wired for culture; origins of the human social mind. Mark Pagel. W. W. Norton & Company 2012 416 p. **303.4**

1. Culture 2. Evolution 3. Social change 4. Social sciences 5. Language and languages 6. Human evolution 7. Social evolution 8. Evolution (Biology) 9. Evolutionary genetics

ISBN 0393065871; 9780393065879

LC 2011044465

This book "frames cultural development in the language of Richard Dawkins's selfish gene theory. . . . Dawkins . . . coined the term 'meme' as the cultural analogue of a gene. [Mark] Pagel . . . [argues that m]emes . . . have built vehicles around themselves made up of groups of people. . . . [He] explores the implications of the emerging consensus across . . . religion, the arts and economics, . . . consciousness, deception, conflict and thevery idea of truth." (New Scientist)

Includes bibliographical references and index

Pipher, Mary

The **green** boat; reviving ourselves in our capsized culture. Mary Pipher. Riverhead Books 2013 240 p. $16 **303.4**

1. Environmental movement 2. Culture shock 3. Adjustment (Psychology) 4. Social change -- Psychological aspects 5. Social problems -- Psychological aspects

ISBN 1594485852; 9781594485855

LC 2012043406

Here, Mary Pipher offers an "approach to acknowledging the global environmental crisis." She "explains, the overwhelming amount of information about the desperate state of our planet leads to stress, avoiding discussion, willful ignorance, and outright denial. . . . Piper distinguishes between 'distractionable intelligence,' which makes us feel helpless, and 'actionable intelligence,' which combines information with suggestions for addressing problems." (Publishers Weekly)

The **Radical** reader; a documentary history of the American radical tradition. edited by Timothy Patrick McCarthy and John McMillian; foreword by Eric Foner. New Press 2003 688p $65; lib bdg $21.95 **303.4**

1. Radicalism

ISBN 1-56584-827-6; 1-56584-682-6 lib bdg

LC 2002-41051

"By bringing many hard-to-find documents under one cover, this anthology will excite readers in discussing why radicals from all walks of life have made progressive ideals meaningful to Americans. Recommended for college, high school, and public libraries." Libr J

Includes bibliographical references

Solnit, Rebecca

A **paradise** built in hell; the extraordinary communities that arise in disasters. Viking 2009 353p $27.95 **303.4**

1. Disasters

ISBN 978-0-670-02107-9; 0-670-02107-5

LC 2009-04101

"An engaging book, full of fascinating detail, 'Paradise' especially deserves a close reading by political leaders at every level, as well as the news media who cover disasters." Christ Sci Monit

Includes bibliographical references

Solomon, Andrew

★ **Far** and away; reporting from the brink of change: seven continents, twenty-five years. Andrew Solomon. Scribner 2016 592 p. illustrations (ebook) $16.99; (hbk) $30 **303.4**

1. Essays 2. Travel 3. Social change 4. Social movements

ISBN 1476795045; 9781476795065; 9781476795041

LC 2016304584

This book, "collects [journalist] Andrew Solomon's writings about places undergoing seismic shifts--political, cultural, and spiritual. Chronicling his stint on the barricades in Moscow in 1991, . . . resisting the coup whose failure ended the Soviet Union, his 2002 account of the rebirth of culture in Afghanistan following the fall of the Taliban, his insightful appraisal of a Myanmar seeped in contradictions . . . , and many other stories of profound upheaval." (Publisher's note)

"Agile, informative, even revelatory pieces that, together, show us both the great variety of humanity and the interior of a gifted writer's heart." Kirkus

Includes bibliographical references (pages 533-554) and index.

Toffler, Alvin

★ **Future** shock. Bantam Books 1990 561p pa $7.99 **303.4**

1. Family 2. Children 3. Democracy 4. Education 5. Social change 6. Adaptation (Biology) 7. Interpersonal relations 8. Technology and civilization 9. Modern civilization -- 1950-

ISBN 978-0-553-27737-1; 0-553-27737-5

First published 1970 by Random House

According to the author, "future shock is 'the dizzying disorientation brought on by the premature arrival of the future.' . . . Toffler outlines some interesting strategies for survival, writing in a clear popular style." Publ Wkly

Includes bibliographical references

Turkle, Sherry

Alone together; why we expect more from technology and less from each other. Sherry Turkle. 3rd edition Basic Books 2017 361 p paperback $17.99 **303.4**

1. Interpersonal relations 2. Human-computer interaction 3. Information technology -- Social aspects 4. Online social networks -- Social aspects 5. Communication & technology -- Social aspects 6. Online social networks -- Psychological aspects

ISBN 9780465093656

This book "is the third in a trilogy, part of a project [author Sherry Turkle] . . . has been working on since she joined MIT in 1976 and noticed that the people there were using the language of psychology to talk about their machines. . . . Turkle picks out the contradictions of the networked life that everyone has now come to take for granted, but adolescents especially: the desire for attention and the desire to hide, constantly online but dreading the exposure of a phone call. . . . Turkle argues that people risk impairing the quality of their thought and communication by so often resorting to media designed only for short, simplified messages." (London Review of Books)

"Turkle argues that people are increasingly functioning without face-to-face contact. For all the talk of convenience and connection derived from texting, e-mailing, and social networking, Turkle reaffirms that what humans still instinctively need is each other, and she encounters dissatisfaction and alienation among users. . . . Turkle's prescient book makes a strong case that what was meant to be a way to facilitate communications has pushed people closer to their machines and further away from each other." Publ Wkly

Includes bibliographical references

303.409 Social change -- History

Giridharadas, Anand

Winners take all; the elite charade of changing the world. by Anand Giridharadas. Alfred A. Knopf 2018 304 p. $26.95 **303.409**

1. Elite (Social sciences) 2. Social change -- United States 3. United States -- Social conditions 4. Elite (Social sciences) -- United States 5. United States -- Social conditions -- 1980-
ISBN 9780451493248

LC 2017045477

In this book, author "Anand Giridharadas takes us into the inner sanctums of a new gilded age, where the rich and powerful fight for equality and justice any way they can--except ways that threaten the social order and their position atop it. We see how they rebrand themselves as saviors of the poor; how they lavishly reward 'thought leaders' who redefine 'change' in winner-friendly ways; and how they constantly seek to do more good, but never less harm." (Publisher's note)

Includes bibliographical references and index

303.44 Growth and development

Pinker, Steven, 1954-
★ **Enlightenment** now; the case for reason, science, humanism, and progress. Steven Pinker. Viking 2018 xix, 556 p.p illustrations, charts (hardcover) $35   **303.44**
1. Reason 2. Humanism 3. Critical thinking
ISBN 9780525427575; 9780698177888; 0525427570

LC 2017301147

In this book, Steven Pinker "proposes that human progress is the gift of a coherent value system that many of us embrace without even knowing it. The values of the Enlightenment underlie all our modern institutions and deserve credit for the stupendous progress we have made. The progress we have enjoyed is not, of course, an excuse for complacency: Some of the challenges we face today are unprecedented in their complexity and scope." (Publisher's note)

"Pinker's sober, lucid, and meticulously researched vision of human progress is heartening and important." Pub Wkly

Includes bibliographical references (pages 455-524) and index.

303.48 Causes of change

Bingham, Clara
Witness to the revolution; radicals, resisters, vets, hippies, and the year America lost its mind and found its soul. Clara Bingham. Random House 2016 656 p. illustrations (ebook) $65; (hardback) $30   **303.48**
1. Vietnam War, 1961-1975 -- Protest movements 2. Radicalism -- United States -- History -- 20th century 3. Social movements -- United States -- History -- 20th century 4. Nineteen seventy, A.D. -- Interviews 5. Nineteen sixty-nine, A.D. -- Interviews 6. United States -- Social conditions -- 1960-1980 -- Interviews 7. Radicalism -- United States -- History -- 20th century -- Interviews 8. Social movements -- United States -- History -- 20th century -- Interviews 9. Vietnam War, 1961-1975 -- Protest movements -- United States -- Interviews 10. Student movements -- United States -- History -- 20th century -- Interviews
ISBN 9780679644743; 9780812993189

LC 2015046134

"From August 1969 to August 1970, the nation witnessed nine thousand protests and eighty-four acts of arson or bombings at schools across the country. It was the year of the My Lai massacre investigation, the Cambodia invasion, Woodstock, and the Moratorium to End the War. . . . [Author] Clara Bingham's . . . [book] unveils anew that moment when America careened to the brink of a civil war at home, as it fought a long, futile war abroad." (Publisher's note)

"While Bingham's is one of many retrospective looks at that period, it is one of the most immediate and personal." Booklist

Brooks, Mike
Tech generation; raising balanced kids in a hyper-connected world. Mike Brooks and Jon Lasser. Oxford University Press 2018 328 p. (hardcover) $24.95   **303.48**
1. Child rearing 2. Internet and children 3. Internet and families 4. Computers and families 5. Technology and children
ISBN 9780190665296

LC 2017047898

This book, by Mike Brooks and Jon Lasser, "guides parents in teaching their children how to reap the benefits of living in a digital world while also preventing its negative effects. . . . [The authors] combine cutting-edge research and expertise to create an engaging and helpful guide that emphasizes the importance of the parent-child relationship." (Publisher's note)

Brynjolfsson, Erik
Machine, platform, crowd; harnessing our digital future. Andrew McAfee & Erik Brynjolfsson. W W Norton & Co Inc 2017 402 p. illustrations (hardcover) $28.95   **303.48**
1. Forecasting 2. Information technology -- Social aspects 3. Information technology -- Economic aspects 4. Economic development -- Technological innovations
ISBN 9780393254303; 9780393254297

LC 2017016682

This book, by Andrew McAfee and Erik Brynjolfsson, describes "what it takes to master this digital-powered shift: we must rethink the integration of minds and machines, of products and platforms, and of the core and the crowd. In all three cases, the balance now favors the second element of the pair, with massive implications for how we run our companies and live our lives." (Publisher's note)

"Provocative reading for futurists, investors, and inventors." Kirkus
Includes bibliographical references and index

Burrough, Bryan
Days of Rage; America's Radical Underground, the FBI, and the First Age of Terror. Bryan Burrough. Penguin Group USA 2015 464 p. 16 plates; illustrations $29.95   **303.48**
1. Revolutionaries 2. United States -- Civilization -- 1970- 3. United States. Federal Bureau of Investigation
ISBN 1594204292; 9781594204296

LC 2014036663

This book by Bryan Burrough presents an "account of the decade-long battle between the FBI and the homegrown revolutionary movements of the 1970s. [It] is filled with revelations and fresh details about the major revolutionaries and their connections and about the FBI and its desperate efforts to make the bombings stop. The result is a mesmerizing book that takes us into the hearts and minds of homegrown terrorists and federal agents." (Publisher's note)

"The author's history is thoroughgoing and fascinating, though with a couple of curious notes—e.g., the likening of the Weathermen et al. to the Nazi Werewolf guerrillas 'who briefly attempted to resist Allied forces after the end of World War II.' A superb chronicle, long—but no longer than needed—and detailed, that sheds light on how the war on terror is being waged today." Kirkus

Dear, Brian
The **friendly** orange glow; the story of the PLATO system and the dawn of cyberculture. Brian Dear. Pantheon Books 2017 xv, 613 p.p illustrations (some color) (hardcover: alk.

paper) $40 **303.48**

1. Cyberspace 2. Computer operating systems 3. Cyberspace -- History 4. PLATO (Electronic computer system) -- History
ISBN 9781101871553; 9781101871560

LC 2017013007

This book, by Brian Dear, "is the first history to recount in fascinating detail the remarkable accomplishments and inspiring personal stories of the PLATO community. The addictive nature of PLATO both ruined many a college career and launched pathbreaking multimillion-dollar software products. Its development, impact, and eventual disappearance provides an instructive case study of technological innovation and disruption, project management, and missed opportunities." (Publisher's note)

"An exploration of the computer system that was too far ahead of its time to succeed but whose legacy quietly endures." Kirkus

Includes bibliographical references (pages [543]-555) and index.

Encyclopedia of mathematics and society; Sarah J. Greenwald , Jill E. Thomley, [editors] Salem Press 2012 3 v. (xxxi, 1191 p.)p **303.48**

1. Mathematics -- History 2. Mathematics -- Encyclopedias 3. Mathematics -- Social aspects
ISBN 1587658445; 1587658453; 1587658461; 158765847X; 9781587658440; 9781587658457; 9781587658464; 9781587658471

LC 2011021856

This encyclopedia of mathematics "focus[es] on how the basic concepts of figures relate to everyday life. As the editors phrase it, the purpose of these compact volumes is to 'weave multilayered connections between society, history, people, applications, and mathematics.' . . . [T]opics covered include 'Cooking,' 'Earthquakes,' 'Mathematics and Religion,' and 'Skydiving.' While some purely mathematical principles are discussed, they are always placed in relation to the larger context of human affairs, such as in the essay 'Algebra in Society.' Pieces open with boldface headword(s), a classification of the subject matter, and a one-line summary of the material to follow. A short bibliography and cross-references follow." (Libr J)

Includes bibliographical references and index

Freeberg, Ernest

The **Age** of Edison; Electric Light and the Invention of Modern America. Ernest Freeberg. Penguin Group USA 2013 368 p. ill. (hardcover) $27.95 **303.48**

1. Electric lighting 2. Technological innovations -- History 3. Electric lighting -- United States -- History 4. Technological innovations -- United States -- History 5. Technological innovations -- Social aspects -- United States -- History
ISBN 1594204268; 9781594204265

LC 2012039513

This book, by Ernest Freeberg, discusses the social impact of the invention of electricity, as part of the "Penguin History of American Life" series. It "places the story of Edison's invention in the context of a technological revolution that transformed America and Europe. . . . Edison and his fellow inventors emerged from a culture shaped by . . . a lively popular press that took an interest in science and technology, and an American patent system that encouraged innovation." (Publisher's note)

Includes bibliographical references (pages 317-341) and index

Hedges, Chris

Wages of rebellion; by Chris Hedges. Nation Books 2015 304 p. (hardback) $26.99 **303.48**

1. Revolutions 2. Social movements 3. Protest movements 4. Revolutions -- Social aspects

ISBN 1568589662; 9781568589664

LC 2014044940

In this book, author Chris Hedges "investigates what social and psychological factors cause revolution, rebellion, and resistance. Drawing on an ambitious overview of prominent philosophers, historians, and literary figures he shows not only the harbingers of a coming crisis but also the nascent seeds of rebellion. Hedges' message is clear: popular uprisings in the United States and around the world are inevitable in the face of environmental destruction and wealth polarization." (Publisher's note)

"People tend to either love or hate Hedges, but librarians in public, academic, and relevant special libraries will want this book because, even if the revolution isn't about to happen, Hedges's voice is an important one." LJ

Includes bibliographical references and index

Heffernan, Virginia

Magic and Loss; The Internet as Art. by Virginia Heffernan. Simon & Schuster 2016 272 p. $26 **303.48**

1. Internet
ISBN 1439191700; 9781439191705

In this book, author Virginia Heffernan "reveals the logic and aesthetics behind the Internet. Since its inception, the Internet has morphed from merely an extension of traditional media into its own full-fledged civilization. It is among mankind's great masterpieces—a massive work of art. . . . Heffernan presents an original and far-reaching analysis of what the Internet is and does." (Publisher's note)

"A thoroughly engrossing examination of the Internet's past, present, and future." Kirkus

Kotler, Steven, 1967-

Abundance; the future is better than you think. Peter H. Diamandis and Steven Kotler. Simon & Schuster 2012 p. cm. **303.48**

1. Population 2. Food supply 3. Natural resources 4. Technological forecasting 5. Technology -- Social aspects 6. Technological innovations -- Forecasting
ISBN 1451614217; 9781451614213

LC 2011039926

"Diamandis, a tech-entrepreneur turned philanthropist, and journalist Kolter . . . contend that widespread pessimism about the future is due in part to our cognitive biases and the effects of mass media. Bad news sells newspapers, while good news escapes our attention or remains hidden in statistics. This engaging book is a needed corrective, a whirlwind tour of the latest developments in health care, agriculture, energy, and other fields as well as an introduction to thinkers and innovators such as Daniel Kahneman, Ray Kurzweil, and Craig Venter." (Choice)

Kunstler, James Howard

Too much magic; wishful thinking, technology, and the fate of the nation. James Howard Kunstler. Atlantic Monthly Press 2012 245 p. (hardcover) $25.00 **303.48**

1. Technological innovations 2. Technology and civilization 3. United States -- Economic conditions
ISBN 080212030X; 9780802120304

In this book, James Howard Kunstler "recount[s] the evidence supporting his predictions about our radically altered future. . . . The dangerously stressed systems that underpin the society we've known since World War II -- 'agriculture, commerce, manufacturing, transport, finance, the oil-gas-coal industry, the electric grid' -- are too large, too complex and too expensive to sustain any longer." (Kirkus Reviews)

Otto, Shawn

The **war** on science; who's waging it, why it matters, what we can do about it. Shawn Otto. Milkweed Editions 2016 x, 514 p.p (pbk.: alk. paper) $20   **303.48**

1. Science -- Social aspects 2. Science -- Political aspects 3. Science -- Social aspects -- History 4. Science -- Political aspects -- History

ISBN 1571313532; 9781571313539; 9781571319524

LC 2016002797

"Shawn Lawrence Otto's provocative new book investigates the historical, social, philosophical, political, and emotional reasons for why and how evidence-based politics are in decline and authoritarian politics are once again on the rise, and offers a vision, an argument, and some compelling solutions to bring us to our collective senses, before it's too late." (Publisher's note)

Includes bibliographical references (pages 429-488) and index

Razsa, Maple

Bastards of Utopia; Living Radical Politics After Socialism. by Maple Razsa. Indiana University Press 2015 296 p. $30   **303.48**

1. Protest movements 2. Yugoslavia -- History

ISBN 0253015839; 0253015863; 9780253015839; 9780253015860

LC 2014044169

This book, by Maple Razsa, "the companion to a feature documentary film of the same name, explores the experiences and political imagination of young radical activists in the former Yugoslavia, participants in what they call alterglobalization or 'globalization from below.' . . . Razsa follows individual activists from the transnational protests against globalization of the early 2000s through the Occupy encampments." (Publisher's note)

Ridley, Matt

The **evolution** of everything; how new ideas emerge. Matt Ridley. Harper, an imprint of HarperCollinsPublishers 2015 360 p. (hardcover) $28.99   **303.48**

1. Evolution 2. Thought and thinking 3. Civilization, Modern 4. Diffusion of innovations 5. Technology and civilization

ISBN 9780062296009; 9780062296016

LC 2015026886

This book by Matt Ridley "is about bottom-up order and its enemy, the top-down twitch--the endless fascination human beings have for design rather than evolution, for direction rather than emergence. Drawing on anecdotes from science, economics, history, politics and philosophy, Matt Ridley's wide-ranging, highly opinionated opus demolishes conventional assumptions that major scientific and social imperatives are dictated by those on high, whether in government, business, academia, or morality." (Publisher's note)

"All along, Ridley shows how hard it has been for even the most definite evolutionists to fully abandon the notion of a guiding intelligence, whether divine or human. Yet that is what the hard evidence to the effect that good things come by undirected means that Ridley adduces in every chapter compels us all to do." Booklist

Includes bibliographical references (pages 323-341) and index

Rushkoff, Douglas

Present Shock; When Everything Happens Now. Douglas Rushkoff. Penguin Group USA 2013 vii, 296 p.p (hardcover) $26.95   **303.48**

1. Conduct of life 2. Mass media -- Social aspects 3. Information technology -- Social aspects 4. Technology -- Philosophy 5.

Technology -- Social aspects

ISBN 1591844762; 9781591844761

LC 2012039915

This book, by Douglas Rushkoff, explains how 21st-century society has "created technologies that would help connect us faster, gather news, map the planet, compile knowledge, and connect with anyone, at anytime. . . . And the dissonance between our digital selves and our analog bodies has thrown us into a new state of anxiety: present shock." (Publisher's note)

Includes bibliographical references and index

Steiner-Adair, Catherine

The **Big** Disconnect; Protecting Childhood and Family Relationships in the Digital Age. HarperCollins 2013 384 p. $26.99   **303.48**

1. Parenting 2. Parent-child relationship 3. Internet -- Social aspects

ISBN 0062082426; 9780062082428

"Parents text relentlessly or worship the computer screen, while children learn more from social media than from school. The result? Distorted family dynamics and children unable to develop sustaining relationships. Advice from a clinical psychologist." (Library Journal)

Taplin, Jonathan

Move fast and break things; how Facebook, Google, and Amazon cornered culture and undermined democracy. Jonathan Taplin. Little, Brown & Co. 2017 x, 308 p.p illustrations (hardcover) $29   **303.48**

1. Social media 2. Mass media -- Social aspects 3. Internet -- Political aspects 4. Google (Firm) 5. Facebook (Firm) 6. Amazon. com (Firm) 7. Electronic commerce 8. Information society 9. Art and the Internet 10. Music and the Internet 11. Internet -- Social aspects 12. Literature and the Internet

ISBN 9780316275774; 9780316508513

LC 2016959692

This book, by Jonathan Taplin, "is the riveting account of a small group of libertarian entrepreneurs who in the 1990s began to hijack the original decentralized vision of the Internet, in the process creating three monopoly firms--Facebook, Amazon, and Google--that now determine the future of the music, film, television, publishing and news industries." (Publisher's note)

"In this insightful analysis of the intersection of technology and culture, Taplin . . . explains how the rise of modern Internet monopolies has changed the face of information and entertainment." Pub Wkly

Includes bibliographical references (pages 287-297) and index.

Tenner, Edward

Our own devices; How Technology Remakes Humanity. Alfred A. Knopf 2004 336p hardcover o.p. pa $14.95; pa $18   **303.48**

1. Technological innovations 2. Technology and civilization

ISBN 0-375-70707-7 pa; 9780375707070

LC 2002-40694

"For a work that covers such a broad topic, this book is a page-turner, largely due to its clear prose and the author's approach to the material. While not lavishly illustrated, there seems to be a picture every time one is needed to illustrate the technology being discussed." SLJ

Includes bibliographical references

Thompson, Clive

Smarter Than You Think; How Technology Is Changing Our Minds for the Better. Clive Thompson. Penguin Group

USA 2013 352 p. $27.95 **303.48**

1. Internet -- Social aspects 2. Technological innovations -- Social aspects 3. Social media 4. Thought and thinking 5. Internet -- Psychological aspects 6. Information technology -- Social aspects 7. Information technology -- Psychological aspects

ISBN 1594204454; 9781594204456

LC 2013017155

In this book "about the advent of technology and its influence on humans, journalist [Clive] Thompson . . . admits that we often allow ourselves to be used by facets of new technologies and that we must exercise caution to avoid this; yet, he demonstrates, digital tools can have a huge positive impact on us, for they provide us with infinite memory, the ability to discover connections . . . previously unknown to us, and new and abundant avenues for communication and publishing." (Publishers Weekly)

Includes bibliographical references and index

Venter, J. Craig, 1946-

Life at the Speed of Light; From the Double Helix to the Dawn of Digital Life. by J. Craig Venter. Penguin Group USA 2013 240 p. $26.95 **303.48**

1. Biology 2. Genomes 3. Genomics 4. Artificial life 5. Biology -- Philosophy 6. Science -- Social aspects

ISBN 0670025402; 9780670025404

LC 2013017049

In this book author J. Craig Venter "presents a fascinating and authoritative study of [synthetic genomics]—detailing its origins, current challenges and controversies, and projected effects on our lives. This scientific frontier provides an opportunity to ponder anew the age-old question 'What is life?' and examine what we really mean by 'playing God.'" (Publisher's note)

Includes bibliographical references and index

Weinberger, David

Too big to know; rethinking knowledge now that the facts aren't the facts, experts are everywhere, and the smartest person in the room is the room. David Weinberger. Basic Books 2011 xiv, 231 p.p (alk. paper) $25.99 **303.48**

1. Internet 2. Theory of knowledge 3. Information technology 4. Knowledge, Sociology of 5. Internet -- Social aspects 6. Information technology -- Social aspects

ISBN 0465021425; 9780465021420; 9780465028139

LC 2011034727

It was the author's intent to demonstrate "that the collaborative, hyperlinked, instant nature of the Internet has fundamentally altered the way humans relate with knowledge. . . . The democratizing of knowledge is not without its dangers. Bad information has equal access to the common well with good information, and is just as viral. But crowdsourced and refereed resources like Wikipedia give [David] Weinberger hope." (Kirkus Reviews)

Includes bibliographical references (p. 199-218) and index.

Young, Ralph

Dissent; the history of an American idea. Ralph Young. New York University Press 2015 640 p. illustrations (cl: alk. paper) $39.95 **303.48**

1. United States -- History 2. Dissenters -- United States 3. Dissenters -- United States -- History 4. United States -- Politics and government 5. Social reformers -- United States -- History 6. Protest movements -- United States -- History 7. United States -- Social conditions -- Sources

ISBN 147980665X; 9781479806652

LC 2014040999

This book, by Ralph Young, "examines the key role dissent has played in shaping the United States. It focuses on those who, from colonial days to the present, dissented against the ruling paradigm of their time: from the Puritan Anne Hutchinson and Native American chief Powhatan in the seventeenth century, to the Occupy and Tea Party movements in the twenty-first century." (Publisher's note)

Includes bibliographical references and index

303.482 Contact between cultures

Foer, Franklin

How soccer explains the world; an unlikely theory of globalization. by Franklin Foer. HarperCollins 2004 261p (ebook) $13.99 **303.482**

ISBN 0-06-621234-0; 9780061864704; 9780061978050

This book, by Franklin Foer, "is a unique and . . . illuminating look at soccer, the world's most popular sport, as a lens through which to view the pressing issues of our age, from the clash of civilizations to the global economy." (Publisher's note)

"Though the globalism thread sometimes disappears, the author is unfailingly interesting. Lively and provocative-even for those who just don't get what FIFA is all about." Kirkus

Includes bibliographical references and index.

303.483 Development of science and technology

Botsman, Rachel

Who can you trust? how technology brought us together and why it might drive us apart. Rachel Botsman. PublicAffairs 2017 322 p. illustrations (hardcover) $27 **303.483**

1. Trust 2. Technology and civilization 3. Technology -- Social aspects 4. Public administration -- Public opinion 5. Associations, institutions, etc. -- Public opinion 6. Representative government and representation -- Public opinion

ISBN 9781541773677; 9781541773684

LC 2017949042

In this book, author "Rachel Botsman reveals that we are at the tipping point of one of the biggest social transformations in human history--with fundamental consequences for everyone. . . . If we are to benefit from this radical shift, we must understand the mechanics of how trust is built . . . and repaired in the digital age. In the first book to explain this new world, Botsman provides a detailed map of this uncharted landscape--and explores what's next for humanity." (Publisher's note)

"A sharp, thoughtful, sometimes-surprising account of how we build trust with strangers now." Kirkus

Includes bibliographical references (pages 263-308) and index.

Carr, Nicholas G., 1959-

Utopia is creepy; And Other Provocations. Nicholas Carr. W W Norton & Co Inc 2016 384 p. (hardcover) $26.95 **303.483**

1. Social sciences 2. Technology and civilization

ISBN 9780393254549

LC 2016018920

This book, by Nicholas Carr, "offers an alternative history of the digital age, chronicling its roller-coaster crazes and crashes, its blind triumphs and its unintended consequences. . . . Carr offers searching assessments of the future of work, the fate of reading, and the rise of artificial intelligence, challenging us to see our world anew." (Publisher's note)

"A collection that reminds us that critical thinking is the best way to view the mixed blessings of rampant technology." Kirkus

Colvile, Robert

The **Great** Acceleration; How the World is Getting Faster, Faster. by Robert Colvile. St. Martin's Press 2016 400 p. $28   **303.483**

1. Speed 2. Social change 3. Quality of life
ISBN 163286455X; 9781632864550

In this book, author Robert Colvile "inspects the various ways in which the pace of life in our society is increasing and examines the evolutionary science behind our rapidly accelerating need for change, as well as why it's unlikely we'll be able to slow down . . . or even want to. Exploring theories surrounding the effect of this speed on our minds and bodies, Colvile reveals how . . . living in a faster age might be beneficial for us, both physically and mentally." (Publisher's note)

"Anyone worried about our increasingly frenetic lives will find food for thought" Booklist

Includes bibliographical references (pages 329-374) and an index.

Friedman, Thomas L., 1953-

★ **Thank** you for being late; an optimist's guide to thriving in the age of accelerations. Thomas L. Friedman. Farrar, Straus and Giroux 2016 496 p. illustrations (hardcover) $28 **303.483**

1. Geopolitics 2. Globalization 3. Political participation 4. Technological innovations 5. Technology and civilization 6. Climatic changes -- Social aspects 7. Civilization, Modern -- 21st century 8. Technological innovations -- Social aspects
ISBN 9780374715144; 9780241300978; 9780374273538

LC 2016034910

In this book, author "Thomas L. Friedman exposes the tectonic movements that are reshaping the world today and explains how to get the most out of them and cushion their worst impacts. . . . How you understand the news, the work you do, the education your kids need, the investments your employer has to make, and the moral and geopolitical choices our country has to navigate will all be refashioned by Friedman's original analysis." (Publisher's note)

"Required reading for a generation that's 'going to be asked to dance in a hurricane.'" Kirkus

Ito, Joi

Whiplash; how to survive our faster future. Joi Ito and Jeff Howe. Grand Central Publishing 2016 320 p. (ebook) $84; (hardcover) $28   **303.483**

1. Technological innovations 2. Technology and civilization 3. Massachusetts Institute of Technology. -- Media Laboratory 4. Technological innovations -- Social aspects 5. Technological innovations -- Economic aspects 6. Digital communications -- Research -- United States 7. Massachusetts Institute of Technology. Media Laboratory
ISBN 9781455552689; 9781455544592

LC 2016032313

In this book about surviving in an unpredictable future world, authors Joi Ito and Jeff Howe present "nine organizing principles for navigating and surviving this tumultuous period. From strategically embracing risks rather than mitigating them (or preferring 'risk over safety') to drawing inspiration and innovative ideas from your existing networks (or supporting 'pull over push'), this dynamic blueprint can help you rethink your approach to all facets of your organization." (Publisher's note)

"A standout among titles on technology and innovation, it will repay reading—and rereading—by leaders in all fields." Kirkus

Includes bibliographical references

Kelly, Kevin, 1952-

The **Inevitable**; Understanding the 12 Technological Forces That Will Shape Our Future. Kevin Kelly. Penguin Group USA 2016 336 p. (ebook) $65; $28   **303.483**

1. Industrial research 2. Technological innovations 3. Technology -- Social aspects
ISBN 9780698183650; 0525428089; 9780525428084

LC 2016287123

This book, by Kevin Kelly, "provides an optimistic road map for the future, showing how the coming changes in our lives--from virtual reality in the home to an on-demand economy to artificial intelligence embedded in everything we manufacture--can be understood as the result of a few long-term, accelerating forces." (Publisher's note)

"Kelly's arguments ring true, and his enthusiasm is contagious." Kirkus

Includes bibliographical references and index.

Rid, Thomas

Rise of the machines; A Cybernetic History. Thomas Rid. W. W. Norton & Company, Inc. 2016 432 p. illustrations (ebook) $50; (hardcover) $27.95   **303.483**

1. Automation 2. Cybernetics 3. Technology -- Social aspects 4. Machinery -- History 5. Cybernetics -- History 6. Automation -- Social aspects 7. Information warfare -- History
ISBN 9780393286014; 9780393286007

LC 2016007022

This book, by Thomas Rid, "delivers a thought-provoking portrait of our technology-enraptured era. Springing from the febrile mind of mathematician Norbert Wiener . . . , the cybernetic vision underpinned a host of seductive myths about the future of machines. . . . From the Cold War's monumental SAGE bomber defense system to enhanced humans, Wiener's scheme turned computers from machines of assured destruction into engines of brilliant utopias." (Publisher's note)

"Not a history of computers but an ingenious look at how brilliant and not-so-brilliant thinkers see—usually wrongly but with occasional prescience—the increasingly intimate melding of machines and humans." Kirkus

Includes bibliographical references and index

Sumpter, David

Outnumbered; from Facebook and Google to fake news and filter-bubbles - the algorithms that control our lives. David Sumpter. Bloomsbury Sigma 2018 272 p. $27 **303.483**

1. Big data 2. Mathematical models 3. Big data -- Social aspects 4. Algorithms -- Social aspects 5. Human behavior -- Mathematical models 6. Mathematical models -- Social aspects 7. Social indicators -- Mathematical models
ISBN 147294741X; 1472947436; 9781472947413; 9781472947437

LC 2017473502

In this book, David Sumpter "takes an algorithm-strewn journey to the dark side of mathematics. He investigates the equations that analyze us, influence us and will (maybe) become like us, answering questions like: Who are Cambridge Analytica, and what are they doing with our data? How does Facebook build a 100-dimensional picture of your personality? Are Google algorithms racist and sexist? . . . What does the future hold as we relinquish our decision-making to machines?" (Publisher's note)

"In his clear account of how algorithms work, Sumpter provides comfort to those who fear them as an insidious form of mind control, concluding that the real work is to address human biases." Publishers' Weekly

Includes bibliographical references and index

Wachter-Boettcher, Sara

Technically wrong; sexist apps, biased algorithms, and other threats of toxic tech. Sara Wachter-Boettcher. W W Norton & Co Inc 2017 232 p. (hardcover) $24.95 **303.483**
1. New products 2. Business failures 3. Technology -- Social aspects 4. System failures (Engineering) 5. New products -- Moral and ethical aspects
ISBN 9780393634648; 9780393634631

LC 2017031829

This book, by Sara Wachter-Boettcher, "look[s] at how tech industry bias and blind spots get baked into digital products--and harm us all. . . . 'Technically Wrong' demystifies the tech industry, leaving those of us on the other side of the screen better prepared to make informed choices about the services we use--and demand more from the companies behind them." (Publisher's note)

"In straightforward prose, Wachter-Boettcher lays out a convincing and damning argument about the small daily failures and large systemic issues that stem from Silicon Valley's diversity problem." SLJ

Includes bibliographical references and index

303.49 Social forecasts

Kaku, Michio

Physics of the future; how science will shape human destiny and our daily lives by the year 2100. Doubleday 2011 389p il $28.95; ebook $12.99 **303.49**
1. Science 2. Forecasting 3. Science -- Social aspects 4. Science -- History -- 21st century
ISBN 978-0-385-53080-4; 978-0-385-53081-1 ebook

LC 2010-26569

"The book's lively, user-friendly style should appeal equally to fans of science fiction and popular science." Booklist

Includes bibliographical references

303.6 Conflict and conflict resolution

Camus, Albert

The rebel; an essay on man in revolt. with a foreword by Sir Herbert Read; a revised and complete translation of L'homme révolté by Anthony Bower. Vintage Bks. 1991 306p pa $12 **303.6**
1. Authors 2. Nihilism 3. Novelists 4. Revolutions 5. Philosophers 6. Essayists 7. Memoirists 8. Revolutionaries 9. Short story writers 10. Writers on politics 11. Political and social philosophers
ISBN 0-679-73384-1

LC 91-50022

Original French edition, 1951; this translation first published 1956 by Knopf

The author describes how the theories of philosophers have been used with disastrous effect by political leaders from the French Revolution through the nihilist revolutions of Russia and the governments of Lenin, Hitler and Stalin. The conclusion calls for a return to a political philosophy having as its aim the happiness and development of living human beings

Carr, Caleb

The lessons of terror; a history of warfare against civilians: why it has always failed and why it will fail again. Random House 2002 272p hardcover o.p. pa $12.95 **303.6**
1. Terrorism
ISBN 0-375-76074-1 pa

LC 2002-280604

The author argues "that terrorism must be viewed in terms of 'military history, rather than political science or sociology,' and that the refusal to label terrorists as soldiers, rather than criminals, is a mistake. . . . This often fascinating, accessible tome skillfully contends that the terrorizing of civilians has a long and controversial history but, as an inferior method, is prone to failure." Publ Wkly

Includes bibliographical references

Grossman, Dave

Assassination Generation; Video Games, Aggression, and the Psychology of Killing. Lt. Col. Dave Grossman, and Kristine Paulsen, with Katie Miserany. Little, Brown & Co. 2016 224 p. $26; (ebook) $78 **303.6**
1. Children and violence 2. Violence in video games 3. Video games -- Social aspects
ISBN 0316265934; 9780316265935; 9780316269360

LC 2016938567

This book, by Dave Grossman and Kristine Paulsen, with Katie Miserany, focuses "on the threat posed to our society by violent video games. Drawing on crime statistics, cutting-edge social research, and scientific studies of the teenage brain, Col. Grossman shows how video games that depict antisocial, misanthropic, casually savage behavior can warp the mind - with potentially deadly results." (Publisher's note)

Includes bibliographical references (pages 233-251) and index.

Morris, Ian

War! What is it good for? conflict and the progress of civilization from primates to robots. Ian Morris. Farrar Straus & Giroux 2014 512 p. illustrations, maps (hardback) $30 **303.6**
1. War 2. Military history 3. War and civilization 4. War and society
ISBN 0374286000; 9780374286002

LC 2013038722

This book, by Ian Morris, "tells the gruesome . . . story of fifteen thousand years of war, going beyond the battles and brutality to reveal what war has really done to and for the world. . . . War, and war alone, has created bigger, more complex societies, ruled by governments that have stamped out internal violence. Strangely enough, killing has made the world safer, and the safety it has produced has allowed people to make the world richer too." (Publisher's note)

"A profoundly uncomfortable but provocative argument that 'productive war' promotes greater safety, a decrease in violence and economic growth." Kirkus

Includes bibliographical references and index

Pinker, Steven, 1954-

The better angels of our nature; why violence has declined. Steven Pinker. Penguin Books 2012 xxviii, 802 p.p illustrations (paperback) $20 **303.6**
1. Violence 2. Nonviolence 3. Violence -- Social aspects 4. Violence -- Psychological aspects 5. Nonviolence -- Psychological aspects
ISBN 0143122010; 9781101544648; 9780143122012

LC 2011015201

This book, by Steven Pinker "shows that despite the ceaseless news about war, crime, and terrorism, violence has actually been in decline over long stretches of history. Exploding myths about humankind's inherent violence and the curse of modernity, this ambitious book continues Pinker's exploration of the essence of human nature, mixing psychology and history to provide a remarkable picture of an increasingly enlightened world." Publisher's note)

"This long, well-researched, comprehensive tour-de-force provides a helpful look at the human condition." Booklist

Includes bibliographical references (pages 739-771) and index.

Sontag, Susan

Regarding the pain of others. Farrar, Straus & Giroux 2003 131p hardcover o.p. pa $12   **303.6**
1. Violence 2. Atrocities 3. Photojournalism 4. War photography 5. Documentary photography
ISBN 978-0-312-42219-6

LC 2002-192527

Companion volume to On photography (1977)

"All libraries, regardless of type, size, or demographics, should own this book." Libr J

Younge, Gary

Another day in the death of America; A Chronicle of Ten Short Lives. Gary Younge. Nation Books 2016 304 p. (hardback) $25.99   **303.6**
1. Violence -- United States -- Case studies 2. Violent crimes -- United States -- Case studies 3. Youth and violence -- United States -- Case studies 4. United States -- Social conditions -- 1980- 5. Firearms and crime -- United States -- Case studies 6. Firearms ownership -- United States -- Case studies
ISBN 9781568589756

LC 2016014076

Carnegie Medal Longlist: Nonfiction (2017)

"On an average day in America, seven children and teens will be shot dead. In . . . [this book,] award-winning journalist Gary Younge tells the stories of the lives lost during one such day. It could have been any day, but he chose November 23, 2013. Black, white, and Latino, aged nine to nineteen, they fell." (Publisher's note)

"Younge provides nuance and context to a polarizing issue. The personal touches, however, are most affecting, as Younge pieces together each story from news reports and interviews with friends and family, weaving a tragic narrative of wasted potential. " Pub Wkly

Includes bibliographical references

304   Factors affecting social behavior

Davies, William

The **happiness** industry; how the government and big business sold us well-being. William Davies. Verso 2015 320 p. (hardcover: U.K.: alkaline paper) $26.95   **304**
1. Happiness 2. Capitalism 3. Social psychology 4. Happiness -- Social aspects 5. Marketing -- Social aspects 6. Capitalism -- Social aspects 7. Well-being -- Social aspects 8. Well-being -- Economic aspects 9. Neoliberalism -- Social aspects 10. Well-being -- Political aspects 11. Economics -- Psychological aspects 12. Well-being -- Social aspects -- Great Britain
ISBN 1781688451; 9781781688458

LC 2014041594

This book by William Davies is a "guide to the marketization of modern life. Davies shows that the science of happiness is less a science than an extension of hyper-capitalism. Davies shows how this philosophy, first pronounced by Jeremy Bentham in the 1780s, has dominated the political debates that have delivered neoliberalism." (Publisher's note)

Includes bibliographical references and index

304.2   Human ecology

Ackerman, Diane, 1948-

The **Human** Age; The World Shaped by Us. by Diane Ackerman. W.W. Norton & Co Inc. 2014 352 p. $27.95 **304.2**
1. Human ecology
ISBN 0393240746; 9780393240740

LC 2014027691

This book, by Diane Ackerman, "confronts the unprecedented reality that one prodigiously intelligent and meddlesome creature, Homo sapiens, is now the dominant force shaping the future of planet Earth." According to Ackerman, "we tinker with nature at every opportunity; we garden the planet with our preferred species of plants and animals, many of them invasive; and we have even altered the climate, threatening our own extinction." (Publisher's note)

Barnosky, Anthony D.

Tipping point for planet earth; how close are we to the edge? Anthony D. Barnosky and Elizabeth A. Hadly. Thomas Dunne Books 2016 272 p. (hardback) $25.99   **304.2**
1. Environmental degradation 2. Human influence on nature 3. Conservation of natural resources 4. Human security 5. Population ecology 6. Global environmental change 7. Nature -- Effect of human beings on 8. Climatic changes -- Effect of human beings on
ISBN 9781250051158; 9781466852013

LC 2015045236

In this book scientists Anthony D. Barnosky and Elizabeth A. Hadly explains "the growing threats to humanity as the planet edges toward resource wars for remaining space, food, oil, and water. And as they show, these wars are not the nightmares of a dystopian future, but are already happening today. Finally, they ask: at what point will inaction lead to the break-up of the intricate workings of the global society?" (Publisher's note)

"Frequently unsettling, often surprising, yet not without a modicum of hope, the authors' cogent and articulate analysis of our past and present offers an urgent view of the steps required to ensure a livable future." Booklist

Biello, David

The **unnatural** world; the race to remake civilization in Earth's newest age. David Biello. Scribner, an Imprint of Simon & Schuster, Inc. 2016 304 p. $26.00   **304.2**
1. Human ecology 2. Climate change 3. Human influence on nature 4. Nature and civilization 5. Global environmental change 6. Nature -- Effect of human beings on 7. Civilization, Modern -- 21st century
ISBN 9781476743905; 9781476743929

LC 2016018491

This book, by David Biello, "argues that we must innovate and adapt to save planet Earth. . . . [It] chronicles a disparate band of unlikely heroes: an effervescent mad scientist who would fertilize the seas; a pigeon obsessive bent on bringing back the extinct; a low-level government functionary in China doing his best to clean up his city, and more." (Publisher's note)

"In this well-written, significant book, Biello insists that humans, the world's most successful invasive species, have the ability to engage in planetary protection and human survival, but it will require wisdom, innovation, and restraint." Kirkus

Diamond, Jared M.

★ **Collapse**: how societies choose to fail or succeed. Viking 2005 575p il $29.95; pa $17   **304.2**

1. Social change 2. Environmental policy
ISBN 0-670-03337-5; 0-14-303655-6 pa

LC 2004-57152

The author "examines storied examples of human economic and social collapse, and even extinction, including Easter Island, classical Mayan civilization and the Greenland Norse. He explores patterns of population growth, overfarming, overgrazing and overhunting, often abetted by drought, cold, rigid social mores and warfare, that lead inexorably to vicious circles of deforestation, erosion and starvation prompted by the disappearance of plant and animal food sources. . . . Readers will find his book an enthralling, and disturbing, reminder of the indissoluble links that bind humans to nature." Publ Wkly

Includes bibliographical references

Hertsgaard, Mark

Hot; living through the next fifty years on earth. Houghton Mifflin Harcourt 2011 339p $25   **304.2**

1. Greenhouse effect 2. Climate -- Environmental aspects
ISBN 978-0-618-82612-4; 0-618-82612-2

LC 2010-12416

"The author notes that we have entered the 'second era of global warming.' Even if greenhouse-gas emissions ceased today, the consequences would continue for hundreds of years. Consequently, the author persuasively argues that we need to begin adapting to those changes, which does not mean that mitigating global warming is no longer important; in fact, it grows more urgent every day. . . . Starkly clear and of utmost importance. " Kirkus

Includes bibliographical references

Jensen, Derrick

What we leave behind; [by] Derrick Jensen and Aric McBay. Seven Stories Press 2009 453p pa $24.95   **304.2**

1. Pollution 2. Refuse and refuse disposal
ISBN 978-1-58322-867-8

LC 2008-47287

Jensen and McBay argue that "the global industrial system . . . produces massive amounts of unsustainable and toxic wastes. . . . The authors focus on some of these harmful products, discuss reasons why our culture produces so much waste, and explain why individual action is insufficient to solve our enormous problems. . . . This compelling book has a refreshing style, at once very personal and very passionate. It is also thorough, with historical, scientific, statistical, and anecdotal evidence filtered through a lot of anger and some quirky humor." Libr J

Includes bibliographical references

Owen, David, 1955-

Green metropolis; why living smaller, living closer, and driving less are the keys to sustainability. Riverhead Books 2009 357p $25.95   **304.2**

1. Human ecology 2. Urban ecology 3. Sustainable architecture 4. Green technology 5. Urban ecology -- Social aspects
ISBN 1-59448-882-7; 978-1-59448-882-5

LC 2009-17116

Owen argues "that Manhattan, Hong Kong and large, old European cities are inherently greener than less densely populated places because a higher percentage of their inhabitants walk, bike and use mass transit than drive; they share infrastructure and civic services more efficiently; they live in smaller spaces and use less energy to heat their homes." (N Y Times Book Rev) Index.

This is "a compelling analysis of the world's environmental predicament that upends orthodox opinion and points the way to practical solutions." Publ Wkly

Includes bibliographical references

Raygorodetsky, Gleb

The **archipelago** of hope; wisdom and resilience from the edge of climate change. Gleb Raygorodetsky. W W Norton & Co Inc 2017 336 p. $28.95   **304.2**

1. Climate change 2. Indigenous peoples
ISBN 1681775328; 9781681775326

This book, by Gleb Raygorodetsky, "reveals the . . . links between Indigenous cultures and their lands--and how it can form the foundation for climate change resilience around the world. . . . Raygorodetsky shows how these communities are actually islands of biological and cultural diversity in the ever-rising sea of development and urbanization." (Publisher's note)

" Filled with admiration for those at the center of his study, Raygorodetsky delivers a valuable addition for all environmental collections and readers interested in cultural studies and international relations." (LJ)

Smith, Laurence C.

The **world** in 2050; four forces shaping civilization's northern future. Dutton 2010 322p il map $26.95   **304.2**

1. Forecasting 2. Climate -- Environmental aspects
ISBN 978-0-525-95181-0

LC 2010-29553

"Smith demonstrates the breadth of geography and emerges as a champion of the discipline. His engaging style and understandable prose will appeal to a wide range of readers interested in social and environmental sciences." Libr J

Includes bibliographical references

Weintraub, Robert

No better friend; one man, one dog, and their extraordinary story of courage and survival in wwii. by Robert Weintraub. Little, Brown & Co. 2015 400 p. 8 plates; illustrations, maps $28   **304.2**

1. Human-animal relationship 2. World War, 1939-1945 -- Prisoners and prisons
ISBN 0316337064; 9780316337069

LC 2015932606

This book, by Robert Weintraub, is a "tale of survival and friendship between a man and a dog in war. Flight technician Frank Williams and Judy, a purebred pointer, met in the most unlikely of places: a World War II internment camp in the Pacific. Judy was a fiercely loyal dog, with a keen sense for who was friend and who was foe, and the pair's relationship deepened throughout their captivity." (Publisher's note)

"By mutual trust and aid, dog and man survived several brutal Japanese camps together, braving hunger, sadistic guards, snakes, and tigers. Weintraub's research on the prisoners' experiences in the camps is remarkable as he narrates Judy and Frank's heroic tale." Kirkus

Weisman, Alan

Countdown; Our Last, Best Hope for a Future on Earth? Alan Weisman. Little, Brown and Co. 2013 528 p. $28 **304.2**

1. Population 2. Sustainability 3. Overpopulation 4. Population ecology 5. Nature -- Effect of human beings on
ISBN 0316097756; 9780316097758

LC 2013017113

LA Times Book Prize Winner: Science & Technology (2013)

In this book, author Alan Weisman "visits an extraordinary range of the world's cultures, religions, nationalities, tribes, and political systems to learn what in their beliefs, histories, liturgies, or current circumstances might suggest that sometimes it's in their own best interest to limit their growth. [He] reveals what may be the fastest, most acceptable, practical, and affordable way of returning our planet and our presence on it to balance." (Publisher's note)

"Provocative and sobering, this vividly reported book raises profound concerns about our future." Pub Wkly

Includes bibliographical references (pages 442-496) and index

The **world** without us. Thomas Dunne Books/St. Martin's Press 2007 324p il pbk $18; hbk $24.95   **304.2**

1. Human influence on nature 2. Material culture 3. Human-plant relationships 4. Human-animal relationships 5. Nature -- Effect of human beings on

ISBN 978-0-312-34729-1; 0312427905; 0-312-34729-4

LC 2007-11565

Weisman speculates on what would become of the Earth if the human population disappeared.

"Weisman is a thoroughly engaging and clarion writer fueled by curiosity and determined to cast light rather than spread despair. His superbly well researched and skillfully crafted stop-you-in-your-tracks report stresses the underappreciated fact that humankind's actions create a ripple effect across the web of life." Booklist.

Includes bibliographical references

Wohlforth, Charles

The **fate** of nature; rediscovering our ability to rescue the earth. Thomas Dunne Books/St. Martin's Press 2010 434p map $27.99   **304.2**

1. Human ecology 2. Environmental protection 3. Conservation of natural resources 4. Human ecology -- Alaska 5. Natural history -- Alaska 6. Alaska -- Environmental conditions 7. Conservation of natural resources -- Alaska

ISBN 0-312-37737-1; 978-0-312-37737-3

LC 2009-45779

The author "examines humanity's emotional and spiritual relationship with the physical world." (Sci Books Films) Index.

The author "considers the consequences of Captain John Cook's hasty visit to the gulf in 1778, the Russian conquest of coastal Alaska, . . . the crash of the herring fisheries, and the cruel fates of the region's indigenous peoples. But Wohlforth believes that our 'consuming nature' is balanced by the impulse to understand and cherish the living world, which is borne out in his compelling profiles of whale biologist Eva Saulitis; Geerat Vermeij, a blind evolutionary scientist who discovered an arms race among crustaceans; and various environmental heroes.... By analyzing competition and evolution, culture and economics, habits of living and of mind, science and suffering, Wohlforth brings a truly ecological perspective to the global debate over how to protect the biosphere." Booklist

Includes bibliographical references

Worster, Donald

Shrinking the Earth; The Rise and Decline of American Abundance. by Donald Worster (Author) Oxford University Press 2016 280 p. ill. (some color), color maps $27.95 **304.2**

1. Human ecology 2. Human influence on nature 3. United States -- History -- 20th century

ISBN 019984495X; 9780199844951

LC 2016301463

In this book, environmental historian Donald Worster "takes a global view in his examination of the ways in which complex issues of worldwide abundance and scarcity have shaped American society and behavior over three centuries. Looking at the limits nature imposes on human ambitions, he questions whether America today is in the midst of a shift from a culture of abundance to a culture of limits and whether American consumption has become reliant on the global South." (Publisher's note)

"A bracing, intelligent survey of wealth become immiseration, es-

sential for students of environmental history." Kirkus

Includes bibliographical references (pages 227-252) and index.

304.5   Genetic factors

Taylor, Shelley E.

The **tending** instinct; how nurturing is essential for who we are and how we live. Times Bks. 2002 290p $25; pa $16   **304.5**

1. Sociobiology 2. Stress (Psychology) 3. Sex differences (Psychology)

ISBN 0-8050-6837-6; 0-8050-7289-6 pa

LC 2002-19879

The author "launched a series of innovative experiments that led her to believe that humans are biologically wired to nurture. She thus devised no less than a whole new psychology of women, presented in this accessible and well-grounded work." Libr J

Includes bibliographical references

304.6   Population

Encyclopedia of the U.S. Census; from the constitution to the American community survey. editors, Margo J. Anderson, Constance F. Citro, and Joseph J. Salvo. 2nd ed. CQ Press 2013 456 p. Hardcover $195   **304.6**

1. United States -- Census -- Encyclopedias

ISBN 9781608710256

LC 2011036339

"The Encyclopedia of the U.S. Census, Second Edition" updates and expands a critically-acclaimed resource for the history, politics, content, procedures and uses of the decennial census of the American population. The new edition highlights changes in the Census Bureau's data collection and dissemination practices for the 2010 enumeration, including the use of a short-form questionnaire for the actual population count, and the release in late 2010 of the American Community Survey (ACS) 5-year data set based on rolling samples of the U.S. population and gathered using the long-form questionnaire. The second edition also comprehensively covers the fallout from the 2000 census and recent issues affecting the administration of the 2010 count." (Publisher's Note)

The alphabetically arranged articles "explain the history, methodology, and results of U.S. censuses since 1790...Maps, tables, and charts show how the composition of the population has changed, where the center of population has moved over time, and how the address lists and census tracts are developed." Booklist

Includes bibliographical references and index

Encyclopedia of the United States census

Hitchens, Christopher, 1949-2011

★ **Mortality**; Christopher Hitchens. 1st ed. Twelve 2012 160 p. (hardcover) $22.99; (paperback) $14.99; (ebook) $21.80   **304.6**

1. Terminally ill 2. Cancer patients 3. Cancer -- Chemotherapy 4. Death 5. Mortality 6. Authors, American -- Biography 7. Terminally ill -- United States -- Biography 8. Cancer -- Patients -- United States -- Biography

ISBN 1455502758; 9781455502752; 9781455523474; 9781742695198

LC 2012014024

This memoir chronicles the decline of cultural critic Christopher Hitchens during the later stages of esophageal cancer. Here, he "shares his thoughts about his suffering, the etiquette of illness and wellness, and religion." He talks about the battle metaphors doctors and friends use to describe his illness and his feelings about the loss of his voice from the treatment. (Publishers Weekly)

Peake, Riley

Mapping Census 2010; the geography of American change. Riley Peake. Esri Press 2012 1 atlas (xiv, 90 p.)p col. maps (pbk.) $18.95 **304.6**
    1. Minorities 2. United States -- Census 3. United States -- Population 4. United States -- Census, 23rd, 2010 -- Maps 5. United States -- Population -- Statistics -- Maps 6. Minorities -- United States -- Population -- Statistics -- Maps
ISBN 1589483197; 9781589483194
LC 2012288678

Author Riley Peake's book "is an atlas of the American people--who we are, and where we are. Using the latest census data and geographic information system (GIS) technology, this atlas examines how our unique population is moving and changing. These large, full-color maps illustrate population density, age, and racial and ethnic composition with clarity." (Publisher's note)
    Includes bibliographical references

304.64 Deaths (Mortality)

Mannix, Kathryn

With the end in mind; death, dying, and wisdom in an age of denial. Kathryn Mannix. Little, Brown & Co. 2018 viii, 341 p.p illustrations (hardcover) $27 **304.64**
    1. Death 2. Terminal care
ISBN 9780316510691; 9780316504485
LC 2017951362

In this book, author Kathryn Mannix, "shares beautifully crafted stories from a lifetime of caring for the dying. . . . With insightful meditations on life, death, and the space between them, . . . [the book] describes the possibility of meeting death gently, with forethought and preparation, and shows the unexpected beauty, dignity, and profound humanity of life coming to an end." (Publisher's note)
    "Using case histories, Mannix provides poignant insight into the way people live when they know they are dying, and what those around them may be thinking and wishing to say." LJ
    Includes bibliographical references.

305 Groups of people

Azam Zanganeh, Lila

My sister, guard your veil; my brother guard, your eyes; uncensored Iranian voices. Lila Azam Zanganeh, editor. Beacon Press 2006 132p il pa $12 **305**
    1. Women -- Iran 2. Iran -- Social conditions
ISBN 0-8070-0463-4; 978-0-8070-0463-0
LC 2005-27496

This "volume features frank interviews with an array of reputable Iranians intellectuals, artists, and writers, some of whom live in exile. Their compelling personal experiences, views, and opinions answer some persistent questions about the lives of ordinary people in Iran and challenge established myths and stereotypes. . . . This volume opens a window on the irrepressible talents, aspirations, and energy of Iranians both at home and abroad, despite their adverse conditions" MultiCult Rev

Baldwin, Neil

★ **Henry** Ford and the Jews; the mass production of hate. PublicAffairs 2001 416p il $27.50; pa $16 **305**
    1. Antisemitism 2. Philanthropists 3. Automobile industry 4. Automobile executives 5. Jews -- United States
ISBN 1-891620-52-5; 1-58648-163-0 pa
LC 2001-41679

"The strength of this biography lies in context: by emphasizing Ford's background, influences and the world around the auto manufacturer, Baldwin . . . brings a fresh approach to what has long been known about one of America's most famous anti-Semites." Publ Wkly
    Includes bibliographical references

Bergner, Daniel

★ **What** Do Women Want? Adventures in the Science of Female Desire. Daniel Burgner. HarperCollins 2013 224 p. (hardcover) $25.99 **305**
    1. Women -- Sexual behavior 2. Sex -- Psychological aspects
ISBN 0061906085; 9780061906084

This book, by Daniel Bergner, "disseminates the latest scientific research and paints an unprecedented portrait of female lust: the triggers, the fantasies, the mind-body connection (and disconnection), the reasons behind the loss of libido, and, most revelatory, that this loss is not inevitable. . . . While debunking the myths popularized by evolutionary psychology, Bergner also looks at the future of female sexuality." (Publisher's note)
    "Stylishly written and cogently organized, making it easy and rewarding for lay readers to understand and appreciate some fairly complex science." Kirkus

Gates, Henry Louis

The **African**-American century; how Black Americans have shaped our country. {by} Henry Louis Gates, Jr. and Cornel West. Free Press 2000 414p il hardcover o.p. pa $16 **305**
    1. African Americans -- Biography 2. African Americans -- Intellectual life
ISBN 0-684-86414-2; 0-684-86415-0 pa
LC 00-63596

"Gates and West have listed and written biographies of their choices of the 100 most important and influential [African Americans] of the . . . twentieth century. In their opinion the subjects that they have selected have made significant impacts and contributions to American society. . . . The entries are arranged by decade and by the person's period of prominence in society, 1900-1909 through 1990-1999. Profiles include Madame C.J. Walker, Langston Hughes, Carter G. Woodson, Paul Robeson, Thurgood Marshall, and Colin Powell." MultiCult Rev
    Includes bibliographical references

Morrison, Toni, 1931-

★ The **origin** of others; Toni Morrison; foreword by Ta-Nehisi Coates. Harvard University Press 2017 xvii, 114 p.p (The Charles Eliot Norton lectures) (hardcover) $22.95 **305**
    1. Speeches 2. Race relations 3. Race in literature 4. Racism in literature 5. Identity (Psychology) 6. Belonging (Social psychology) 7. African Americans in literature 8. United States -- Race relations -- History 9. Literature, Modern -- History and criticism
ISBN 9780674983120; 9780674976450
LC 2017019077

This book in the Charles Eliot Norton Lectures series, by Toni Morrison, "reflects on the themes that preoccupy . . . [Morrison's] work and increasingly dominate national and world politics: race, fear, borders, the mass movement of peoples, the desire for belonging. What is race and why does it matter? What motivates the human tendency to construct Others? Why does the presence of Others make us so afraid?" (Publisher's note)

"Nobel laureate Morrison, long known for her penetrating exploration of race in the U.S., continues that examination with essays derived from a lecture series at Harvard." Booklist

Reef, Catherine

Working in America. Facts On File 2007 xxviii, 484p il map (American experience) $80   **305**
1. Labor -- United States
ISBN 978-0-8160-6239-3; 0-8160-6239-0

          LC 2006-31191

First published 2000

"Each chapter begins with a . . . narrative that chronicles the experience of workers in the United States—from factory workers, cowboys, seamstresses, and newsboys to truck drivers, migrant farm workers, computer programmers, and genetic engineers. Chronologies of important events follow, along with eyewitness testimonies on the experience of working in a wide range of professions and trades—from Thomas Jefferson, Malcolm X, Samuel Gompers, Charlotte Perkins Gilman, Jesse Jackson, Cesar Chavez, and Jane Addams, as well as a wide range of American workers." Publisher's note

Includes bibliographical references

Shraya, Vivek

I'm afraid of men; Vivek Shraya. Penguin Group USA 2018 96 p. $16   **305**
1. LGBT people -- Biography 2. Transgender people -- Biography
ISBN 0735235937; 9780735235939

In this memoir, transgender artist Vivek Shraya "explores how masculinity was imposed on her as a boy and continues to haunt her as a girl--and how we might reimagine gender for the twenty-first century. . . . Shraya delivers an important record of the cumulative damage caused by misogyny, homophobia, and transphobia, releasing trauma from a body that has always refused to assimilate." (Publisher's note)

305.23   Young people

Canada, Geoffrey

Fist, stick, knife, gun; a personal history of violence in America. Beacon Press 1995 179p pa $13   **305.23**
1. Children 2. Violence 3. New York (N.Y.) -- Social conditions
ISBN 0-8070-0422-7; 978-0-8070-0423-4 pa; 0-8070-0423-5 pa

          LC 94-41357

"This is a graphic adaptation of famous activist and educator Canada's work of the same name. It explores his Bronx, NY, childhood and foray into increasingly violent activity. The use of violence as self-protection in a rough neighborhood and the introduction of guns into the mix make for a profound reflection on inner-city violence." (Library Journal)

"A more powerful depiction of the tragic life of urban children and a more compelling plea to end 'America's war against itself' cannot be imagined." Publ Wkly

Clinton, Hillary Rodham, 1947-

It takes a village; and other lessons children teach us. Hillary Rodham Clinton. Simon & Schuster 2006 xviii, 331 p.p illustrations (ebook) $13.99; $26   **305.23**
1. Parenting 2. Child welfare 3. Child development 4. Family -- United States 5. Presidents' spouses -- United States 6.

Parenting -- United States 7. Child welfare -- United States 8. Child development -- United States 9. Presidents' spouses -- Family relationships -- United States -- Case studies
ISBN 9781416574644; 1416540644; 9781416540649

          LC 2007297957

This book, by Hillary Rodham Clinton, "reflects on how our village has changed over the last decade—from the impact of the Internet to new research in early child development and education. She discusses issues of increasing concern—security, the environment, the national debt—and looks at where we have made progress and where there is still work to be done." (Publisher's note)

Coles, Robert

Children of crisis; selections from the Pulitzer Prize-winning five-volume Children of crisis series; with a new introduction by the author. Little, Brown 2003 714p il pa $22.95   **305.23**
1. Children with social disabilities 2. Children -- United States
ISBN 9780316151023

          LC 2003-47522

These are selections of Coles' social study of "African American children caught in the throes of the South's racial integration; the young children of impoverished sharecroppers, migrant workers, and mountaineers in Appalachia; children whose families were transformed by the migration from South to North, from rural to urban communities; Latino, Native American, and Eskimo children in the poorest communities of the American West; the children of America's wealthiest families, wrestling with the burden of their own privilege." Publisher's note

Kozol, Jonathan

Ordinary resurrections; children in the years of hope. Harper Perennial 2001 388p pa $14   **305.23**
1. Children 2. Bronx (New York, N.Y.) -- Social conditions
ISBN 978-0-06-095645-5; 0-06-095645-3

First published 2000 by Crown

"Kozol tells of his continued visits with the children who attend the afterschool program at St. Ann's Episcopal Church in the racially segregated, impoverished South Bronx." SLJ

Includes bibliographical references

Luiselli, Valeria, 1983-

★ **Tell** me how it ends; an essay in forty questions. Valeria Luiselli. Coffee House Press 2017 119 p. (softcover) $12.95   **305.23**
1. Essays 2. Children of immigrants 3. Unauthorized immigrants 4. Immigrant children -- United States -- Social conditions 5. Illegal alien children -- United States -- Social conditions 6. Immigrant children -- Legal status, laws, etc. -- United States 7. United States -- Emigration and immigration -- Government policy 8. Illegal alien children -- Legal status, laws, etc. -- United States
ISBN 1566894956; 9781566894951

          LC 2017000414

National Book Critics Circle Award Finalist: Criticism (2017)
Kirkus Prize Finalist: Nonfiction (2017)

Introduction -- Border -- Court -- Home -- Community -- Coda (Eight brief postscripta)

This essay documents how "from 2014 to 2015, . . . [the author] Valeria Luiselli . . . volunteered as an interpreter with an immigration court in New York, where she administered a 40-question survey to unaccompanied and undocumented minors who fled Central America for the United States. . . . [She] explores the plights these children are fleeing . . . as well as their harrowing journeys, many riding atop Mexican freight trains (known as la Bestia, the Beast) to the border."

(Publishers Weekly)
Includes bibliographical references

Mintz, Steven

★ **Huck's** raft; a history of American childhood. Belknap Press of Harvard University Press 2004 445p il $29.95 **305.23**
1. Children -- United States
ISBN 0-674-01508-8

LC 2004-42220

The author "revisits the treatment of children from the Puritan era up to the edge of the millennium, . . . showing that we have alternately vilified our offspring . . . and glorified them. . . . In addition, the roles children have assumed in the workforce have fluctuated with the needs of the era—economic expansion led to harsh child labor, while its aftermath, prosperity, led to an interest in child welfare. . . . Mintz's thorough yet accessibly written study delves into the external forces that have shaped the lives of our young while also probing the internal developments in their collective consciousness." Libr J
Includes bibliographical references

Orenstein, Peggy

Cinderella ate my daughter; dispatches from the frontlines of the new girlie-girl culture. HarperCollins 2011 244p $25.99 **305.23**
1. Mother-daughter relationship 2. Femininity 3. Girls -- Psychology 4. Mothers and daughters
ISBN 0061711527; 9780061711527

LC 2010-28724

Orenstein examines aspects and manifestations of sexualized girlhood such as child beauty pageants and Disney Princess dolls. Bibliography. Index.

The author "finds today's pink and princess-obsessed girl culture grating when it threatens to lure her own young daughter, Daisy. In her quest to determine whether princess mania is merely a passing phase or a more sinister marketing plot with long-term negative impact, Orenstein travels to Disneyland, American Girl Place, the American International Toy Fair; visits a children's beauty pageant; attends a Miley Cyrus concert; tools around the Internet; and interviews parents, historians, psychologists, marketers, and others. . . . With insight and biting humor, the author explores her own conflicting feelings as a mother as she protects her offspring and probes the roots and tendrils of the girlie-girl movement." Publ Wkly
Includes bibliographical references

Shachtman, Tom

★ **Rumspringa**; to be or not to be Amish. North Point Press 2006 286p hardcover o.p. pa $16 **305.23**
1. Amish 2. Teenagers -- Religious life
ISBN 0-86547-687-X; 978-0-86547-687-5; 0-86547-742-6 pa; 978-0-86547-742-1 pa

LC 2006-4329

"Rumspringa is Tom Shachtman's celebrated look at a little-known Amish coming-of-age ritual, the rumspringa--the period of "running around" that begins for their youth at age sixteen. During this time, Amish youth are allowed to live outside the bounds of their faith, experimenting with alcohol, premarital sex, revealing clothes, telephones, drugs, and wild parties. By allowing such broad freedoms, their parents hope they will learn enough to help them make the most important decision of their lives--whether to be baptized as Christians, join the church, and forever give up worldly ways, or to remain in the world." (Publisher's note)

"Shachtman is like a maestro, masterfully conducting an orchestra of history, anthropology, psychology, sociology, and journalism together in a harmonious and evocative symphony of all things Amish." Christ Sci Monit
Includes bibliographical references

Simmons, Rachel

★ **Odd** girl out; the hidden culture of aggression in girls. Revised and updated Harcourt 2011 296p pa $15 **305.23**
1. Girls 2. Aggressiveness (Psychology) 3. Girls -- Psychology 4. Aggressiveness in children
ISBN 9780547520193

LC 2001-6864

"In this updated edition, educator and bullying expert Rachel Simmons gives girls, parents, and educators proven and innovative strategies for navigating social dynamics in person and online, as well as brand new classroom initiatives and step-by-step parental suggestions for dealing with conventional bullying. With up-to-the-minute research and real-life stories, Odd Girl Out continues to be the definitive resource on the most pressing social issues facing girls today." (Publisher's note)

"Why are girls inclined to relational rather than physical aggression? Simmons contends that girls are socialized into a psychological double bind. They are told that they must be good, nice and quiet and that they should value close and intimate relationships. . . . According to Simmons, girls fear that an expression of conflict will damage their relationships. . . . Trapped in a constraining, stereotypical gender role, some girls craft ways of expressing their anger covertly. . . . Odd Girl Out explores this grim side of girlhood with {stories} . . . about girls hurting other girls." (Women's Rev Books) Index.
Includes bibliographical references

Tanenbaum, Leora

I Am Not a Slut; Slut-shaming in the Age of the Internet. Leora Tanenbaum. HarperCollins 2015 416 p. $15.99 **305.23**
1. Shame 2. Internet -- Social aspects 3. Stereotype (Social psychology)
ISBN 006228259X; 9780062282590

In this book by Leora Tanenbaum, "as the Internet's omnipresence continues to realign attitudes regarding what constitutes appropriate behavioral standards, the author revisits former arguments on issues of female empowerment and verbal sexual harassment, refreshing her research with new interviews with girls on the frontlines of name-calling and bullying. She updates readers on what has changed on the name-calling landscape, noting that the term 'slut' has 'metastasized' outward throughout our culture". (Kirkus Reviews)

"This brilliant, thoughtful, and compelling investigation of young womanhood commands the reader's attention from beginning to end." Booklist

305.232 Infants

Collings, Sally

7 secrets of the newborn; secrets and (happy) surprises of the first year. Robert C. Hamilton, M.D. with Sally Collings. St. Martin's Press 2018 336 p. (hardcover) $27.99 **305.232**
1. Child rearing 2. Infants -- Care 3. Infants -- Health and hygiene
ISBN 9781250114426

LC 2018022132

In this book, physician Robert C. Hamilton, with Sally Colling, "shares his clear, sensible, warm advice--as well as all the latest scientific data and research--on how to: Offer comfort to a crying newborn using the 'Hold,' gently teach your baby how to sleep . . . , establish healthy patterns, breastfeed, formula-feed, or bottle-feed using either, play, manage screen time in your home and more to help you navigate the unforgettable first year of your child's life." (Publisher's note)

305.233　Children three to five

Santomero, Angela C.

Preschool clues; raising smart, inspired, and engaged kids in a screen-filled world. Angela C. Santomero, Deborah Reber, foreword by Daniel R. Anderson. Simon & Schuster 2018 320 p. $16.99 **305.233**

1. Children 2. Child rearing 3. Children's television programs
ISBN 1501174339; 9781501174339

In this book, author Angela Santomero "shares the secret sauce behind her shows' powerful, transformative results in the form of eleven research-based, foundational 'clues' to ensure that preschoolers flourish academically, socially, and emotionally during this critical time. . . . She breaks down the philosophy behind her shows . . . into concrete strategies that parents and educators can incorporate into their family and classroom to set their preschoolers up for success." (Publisher's note)

"Fans of Blue's Clues and Santomero's other popular children's shows will enjoy her practical advice and conversational tone. Educators and parents will likely find a takeaway or two in this breezy, informative read." LJ

305.235　Young people twelve to twenty

Connolly, Daniel

The **Book** of Isaias; A Child of Hispanic Immigrants Seeks His Own America. by Daniel Connolly. St. Martin's Press 2016 272 p. $26.99 **305.235**

1. Children of immigrants -- Education
ISBN 1250083060; 9781250083067

In this book, by Daniel Connolly, "a bright 18-year-old Hispanic student named Isaias Ramos sets out on the journey to college. Isaias, who passed a prestigious national calculus test as a junior and leads the quiz bowl team, is the hope of Kingsbury High in Memphis. . . . Isaias also doubts the value of college and says he might go to work in his family's painting business after high school, despite his academic potential. Is Isaias making a rational choice?" (Publisher's note)

"Connolly unearths the human element behind one of today's most debated issues, asking expert and everyday readers alike to consider how the immigrant experience is affecting one of the fastest-growing youth populations in the nation." Pub Wkly

Damour, Lisa

Untangled; guiding teenage girls through the seven transitions into adulthood. Lisa Damour. Ballantine Books 2016 352 p. hbk $27 **305.235**

1. Adolescence 2. Teenage girls 3. Adulthood 4. Adolescent psychology 5. Teenage girls -- Psychology
ISBN 9780553393057; 0553393057

LC 2015040046

"Damour offers a hopeful, helpful new way for parents to talk about--and with--teenage girls. Raising a teenage girl doesn't have to be the proverbial roller-coaster ride or feel like a 'tangled mess,' she asserts. There is a predictable pattern to teenage development, and parents can learn how to understand and support their daughters. Damour identifies seven distinct, sequential 'strands,' one per chapter, from middle school through high school: parting with childhood; joining a new tribe; harnessing emotions; contending with adult authority; planning for the future; entering the romantic world; and caring for herself."

(Publishers Weekly)
Includes bibliographical references and index

Hine, Thomas

The **rise** and fall of the American teenager. Bard 1999 322p $24; pa $14; prebind $23.99 **305.235**

1. Teenagers 2. Adolescence
ISBN 0-380-97358-8; 0-380-72853-2 pa; 9781439573587

LC 99-24381

In this social history Hine "writes about ways the culture has affected what teenage has meant for youth and how youth have been perceived, as in World War II when teenagers readily took on roles supporting the war effort. Interesting, enjoyable, and multifaceted, Hine's work defies pigeonholing by covering anthropology, psychology, communications, and sociology." Libr J

Includes bibliographical references

Sengupta, Somini

The **end** of karma; hope and fury among India's young. Somini Sengupta. W W Norton & Co Inc 2016 256 p. illustrations, map (hardcover) $26.95; (ebook) $50 **305.235**

1. Women -- India 2. Youth -- India 3. India -- Social life and customs 4. Women and democracy -- India 5. Youth -- India -- History -- 21st century
ISBN 9780393071009; 9780393292879

LC 2015041519

This book, by Somini Sengupta, is an exploration of modern India "through the lens of young people from different worlds: a woman who becomes a Maoist rebel; a brother charged for the murder of his sister, who had married the 'wrong' man; a woman who . . . hopes to become a police officer. Driven by aspiration—and thwarted at every step by state and society—they are making new demands on India's democracy for equality of opportunity, dignity for girls, and civil liberties." (Publisher's note)

"A compelling portrait of what will soon be the world's most populous nation, one on the verge of great change—for better or worse." Kirkus

Includes bibliographical references

305.24　Adults

Sasse, Ben, 1972-

The **vanishing** American adult; our coming-of-age crisis--and how to rebuild a culture of self-reliance. Ben Sasse. St. Martin's Press 2017 306 p. (hardcover) $27.99 **305.24**

1. Adulthood 2. Self-reliance 3. Adulthood -- United States 4. Young adults -- United States 5. Self-reliance -- United States
ISBN 9781250114419; 9781250114402

LC 2017005552

This book, by Ben Sasse, "diagnoses the causes of a generation that can't grow up and offers a path for raising children to become active and engaged citizens. He identifies core formative experiences that all young people should pursue: hard work to appreciate the benefits of labor, travel to understand deprivation and want, the power of reading, the importance of nurturing your body--and explains how parents can encourage them." (Publisher's note)

"Deeply thoughtful, delightfully personal, and bravely ecumenical in scope, Sasse's guide for stemming the tide of delayed responsibility showcases what is both practical and possible." Booklist

Includes bibliographical references and index

305.242   People in early adulthood

Burge, Kimberly

The **born** frees; writing with the girls of Gugulethu. Kimberly Burge. W.W. Norton & Co. Inc. 2015 384 p. (hardcover) $26.95   **305.242**

1. Creative writing 2. Women -- South Africa 3. Youth -- South Africa 4. South Africa -- Social life and customs 5. Post-apartheid era -- South Africa 6. Young women -- South Africa -- Social conditions 7. Creative writing (Study and teaching) -- South Africa
ISBN 0393239160; 9780393239164

LC 2015010037

In this book, by Kimberly Burge, a "creative writing group unites and inspires girls of the first South African generation 'born free.' Born into post-apartheid South Africa, the young women of the townships around Cape Town still face daunting challenges. . . . Yet, as . . . Burge discovered when she set up a writing group in the township of Gugulethu, the spirit of these girls outshines their circumstances." (Publisher's note)

"Incredible and inspiring, this account belongs in every library and on every bookshelf." LJ

Includes bibliographical references

Our black sons matter; mothers talk about fears, sorrows, and hopes. edited by George Yancy, Maria del Guadalupe Davidson, and Susan Hadley. Rowman & Littlefield 2016 xii, 227 p.p (cloth: alk. paper) $34   **305.242**

1. African American boys 2. Mother-son relationship -- United States 3. African Americans -- Family relationships 4. African American young men 5. Black lives matter movement 6. Mothers and sons -- United States
ISBN 9781442269125; 9781442269118

LC 2016023174

This book, edited by George Yancy, Maria del Guadalupe Davidson, and Susan Hadley, is a "collection of original essays, letters, and poems that addresses both the deep joys and the very real challenges of raising black boys today. From Trayvon Martin to Tamir Rice, the list of young black men who have suffered racial violence continues to grow. Young black people also deal with profound stereotypes and structural barriers." (Publisher's note)

"This collection offers powerful and thoughtful reflections on the impact of racism on black males and the women who witness and offer as much love and protection as they can." Booklist

Includes bibliographical references and index
Mothers talk about fears, sorrows, and hopes

Smith, Mychal Denzel

Invisible man, got the whole world watching; A Young Black Man's Education. Mychal Denzel Smith. Nation Books 2016 240 p. (hardcover) $24   **305.242**

1. African Americans -- Education 2. United States -- Race relations 3. African American young men -- Education 4. African American young men -- Race identity 5. African American young men -- Social conditions -- 21st century
ISBN 9781568585284; 9781568585291

LC 2016006482

In this book, "Mychal Denzel Smith chronicles his own personal and political education during these tumultuous years, describing his efforts to come into his own in a world that denied his humanity. Smith unapologetically upends reigning assumptions about black masculinity, rewriting the script for black manhood so that depression and anxiety aren't considered taboo, and feminism and LGBTQ rights become part of the fight." (Publisher's note)

"This is a commanding read that deserves a place in all libraries. It will make a great book group discussion, especially when paired with Coates's memoir." SLJ

305.244   People in middle adulthood

Corrigan, Kelly

Tell me more; and 11 other important things I'm learning to say. Kelly Corrigan. Random House Inc 2018 240 p. $26   **305.244**

1. Adulthood 2. Conduct of life 3. Middle aged women
ISBN 039958837X; 9780399588372

This essay collection, by Kelly Corrigan, is "a deeply personal, unfailingly honest, and often hilarious examination of the essential phrases that turn the wheel of life. In 'I Don't Know,' Corrigan wrestles to make peace with uncertainty. . . . In 'No,' she admires her mother's ability to set boundaries and her liberating willingness to be unpopular. In 'Tell Me More,' a facialist named Tish teaches her something important about listening." (Publisher's note)

"Moving and deeply personal, Corrigan's portraits of love and loss urge readers to speak more carefully and hold on tighter to the people they love." (Kirkus)

305.26   People in late adulthood

Carter, Jimmy

The **virtues** of aging. Ballantine Pub. Group 1998 140p (Library of contemporary thought) hardcover o.p. pa $11.95   **305.26**

1. Aging
ISBN 0-345-42826-9; 0-345-42592-8 pa

LC 98-25298

"At age 56, Jimmy Carter 'involuntarily retired' when he was defeated for a second term as president by Ronald Reagan in 1980. . . . Carter sketches how he and Rosalynn created new careers and new lives for themselves—as authors, educators, and senior family members and as a couple growing old together. He adds statistics about the aging population, makes suggestions for healthy living, and defines successful aging." Libr J

Jacoby, Susan

Never say die; the myth and marketing of the new old age. Pantheon Books 2011 332p $27.95   **305.26**

1. Aging 2. Old age 3. Older people 4. Elderly 5. Aged -- United States
ISBN 978-0-307-37794-4; 0-307-37794-6

LC 2010-17123

In this book, author "Susan Jacoby turns an . . . eye on the marketers of longevity--pharmaceutical companies, lifestyle gurus, and scientific businessmen who suggest that there will soon be a 'cure' for the 'disease' of aging. She separates wishful hype from realistic hope. . . . Finally, Jacoby raises the fundamental question of whether living longer is a desirable thing unless it means living better, and she considers the profound moral and ethical concerns raised by increasing longevity." (Publisher's note)

The author "offers an important reality check for Americans enamored of the images of healthy, active seniors featured in advertisements." Booklist

Includes bibliographical references

Jenkins, Jo Ann

Disrupt aging; a bold new path to living your best life at every age. Jo Ann Jenkins, CEO, AARP with Boe Workman. PublicAffairs 2016 265 p. (ebook) $14.99; (hardback) $26.99   **305.26**
   1. Aging 2. Old age 3. Older people 4. Older people -- Societies and clubs 5. Self-actualization (Psychology) in old age
   ISBN 9781610396776; 9781610396769
                   LC 2016002025

This book, by Jo Ann Jenkins with Boe Workman, "focuses on three core areas—health, wealth, and self—to show us how to embrace opportunities and change the way we look at getting older. Here, she chronicles her own journey and that of others who are making their mark as disruptors to show readers how we can be active, healthy, and happy as we get older. . . . She touches on all the important issues . . . , from caregiving and mindful living to . . . making our money last." (Publisher's note)

"With a positive outlook and many creative suggestions, this straightforward book will be an inspiration to boomers and millennials." Booklist

Lawrence-Lightfoot, Sara

The **third** chapter; passion, risk, and adventure in the 25 years after 50. Farrar, Straus and Giroux 2009 260p $25 **305.26**
   1. Aging 2. Old age 3. Elderly -- United States
   ISBN 978-0-374-27549-5; 0-374-27549-1
                   LC 2008-29147

"New opportunities for creativity and self-fulfillment await men and women between the ages of 50 and 75. . . . [The author] coins the term 'Third Chapter' to describe the rich possibilities as illustrated in her extended interviews with 40 well-educated, affluent Americans. Founding her thesis on classic formulations of life-stage development, particularly that of Erik Erikson, the author offers a wide range of models for people who feel burned out, restless or dissatisfied with their lives, describing how each of her subjects became 'a different person.' . . . Readers feeling that something is missing from their lives, that there is something more they can contribute, will find this book a helpful guide." Publ Wkly

Includes bibliographical references

Leland, John, 1959-

Happiness is a choice you make; lessons from a year among the oldest old. John Leland. Farrar, Straus & Giroux 2018 242 p. illustrations (hardcover) $26   **305.26**
   1. Happiness 2. Older people 3. Conduct of life 4. Wisdom 5. Happiness in old age
   ISBN 9780374717056; 9780374168186
                   LC 2017028940

In this book, author John Leland details his quest "to meet some of . . . [New York] city's oldest inhabitants for a series on America's fastest-growing age group: those over eighty-five. . . . [It presents] a rare, intimate glimpse into the end of life, and the insight that can enhance the years preceding. What he finds is deeply heartening: Even as our faculties decline, we still wield extraordinary influence over the quality of our lives. Happiness is a choice." (Publisher's note)

"Leland entertains and intrigues readers as six unique personalities emerge, sharing their reminiscences about love, heartache, aches and pains, and joy. This is a sympathetic and honest look at growing old." Booklist

Includes bibliographical references (pages 235-240).

Pillemer, Karl A.

30 lessons for living; tried and true advice from the wisest Americans. [by] Karl Pillemer. Hudson Street Press 2011 271p $25.95   **305.26**
   1. Aging 2. Old age 3. Happiness 4. Conduct of life 5. Elderly -- United States
   ISBN 978-1-59463-084-2
                   LC 2011017113

"Who better to teach lessons on living . . . than the thousands of Americans over the age of 65 who have successfully navigated the territories of marriage, career, money, and aging? By conducting innumerable interviews, Pillemer found that their advice upends contemporary wisdom: they suggest marrying a person like oneself, choosing a career for intrinsic rewards, and spending more time with one's children. The author skillfully weaves a prevailing theme (e.g., parenting, aging fearlessly) with self-disclosing statements from interviewees to create a compelling, inspirational book. One of the best of its kind. " Libr J

Includes bibliographical references

305.3   People by gender or sex

Browning, Frank

The **Fate** of Gender; nature, nurture, and the human future. Frank Browning. St. Martin's Press 2016 320 p. (ebook) $66; $28   **305.3**
   1. Gender role 2. Gender identity 3. Sex differences (Psychology)
   ISBN 9781620406212; 1620406195; 9781620406199
                   LC 2015050790

In this book, author Frank Browning "takes us into human gender geographies around the world, from gender-neutral kindergartens in Chicago . . . to women's masturbation classes in Shanghai, from conservative Catholics in Paris . . . to transsexual Mormon parents in Utah. . . . Browning goes on to show equally that no one is born a man but learns how to perform as a man, and that there is no fixed way of being masculine or feminine." (Publisher's note)

"Although the author sacrifices depth for range, this account provides a solid overview of the shifting landscape of gender issues today." LJ

Includes bibliographical references (pages 299-302) and index

Lipman, Joanne

That's what she said; what men need to know (and women need to tell them) about working together. Joanne Lipman. William Morrow, an imprint of HarperCollins Publishers 2018 xxi, 297 p.p illustrations (hardcover) $28.99   **305.3**
   1. Leadership 2. Gender role 3. Businesswomen 4. Sex discrimination 5. Sex discrimination against women -- United States 6. Sex discrimination in employment -- United States 7. Sex role in the work environment -- United States
   ISBN 9780062437235; 9780062437211; 0062437216

This book, by Joanne Lipman, is "filled with illuminating anecdotes, data from the most recent studies, and stories from . . . Lipman's own journey to the top of a male-dominated industry, it shows how we can win by reaching across the gender divide. . . . How does brain chemistry help explain men's fear of women's emotions at work? . . . What can we learn from Iceland's campaign to 'feminize' an entire nation?" (Publisher's note)

"A solid start to an essential, gender-inclusive conversation." Kirkus
   Includes bibliographical references (pages 248-297).

305.31 Men

Bly, Robert

★ **Iron** John; a book about men. Robert Bly. 25th anniversary edition Da Capo Press 2015 292 p paperback $16.99 **305.31**

1. Men -- Psychology
ISBN 9780306824265

LC 2015024336

First published 1990 by Addison-Wesley

"Drawing vitally upon such diverse sources as ancient mythology, classic literature (including his own poetry), anthropology, psychology, and even the responses of the real-life men who have participated in his seminars ('gatherings'), Bly staunchly redefines male identity, emphasizing the importance of what he calls 'warrior energy' and all its positive implications." Booklist

305.4 Women

Beauvoir, Simone de

★ The **second** sex; translated and edited by H. M. Parshley; with an introduction by Margaret Crosland. Knopf 1993 lv, 786p $23; pa $17 **305.4**

1. Women
ISBN 0-679-42016-9; 0-679-72451-6 pa

LC 92-54303

Original French edition, 1949; this translation first published 1953

This "thorough analysis of women's secondary status in society, became a classic of feminist literature." Reader's Ency. 3d edition

Collins, Gail

When everything changed; the amazing journey of American women from 1960 to the present. Little, Brown and Co. 2009 471p il $27.99 **305.4**

1. Women -- United States -- History
ISBN 978-0-316-05954-1; 0-316-05954-4

LC 2008-54933

"Collins can be deadly serious and great fun to read at the same time. A revelatory book for readers of both sexes, and sure to become required reading for any American women's-studies course." Kirkus

Includes bibliographical references

Doyle, Sady

Trainwreck; the women we love to hate, mock, and fear... and why. Sady Doyle. Melville House 2016 320 p. (ebook) $25.95; (hardcover) $25.99 **305.4**

1. Feminism 2. Women -- Conduct of life 3. Celebrities -- Conduct of life 4. Feminist theory 5. Women in mass media 6. Women -- Conduct of life -- Press coverage 7. Women -- Conduct of life -- Public opinion 8. Celebrities -- Conduct of life -- Press coverage 9. Celebrities -- Conduct of life -- Public opinion
ISBN 9781612195643; 9781612195636

LC 2016015117

This book, by Sady Doyle, "dissects a centuries-old phenomenon [of the fallen woman in popular culture] and asks what it means now, in a time when we have unprecedented access to celebrities and civilians alike, and when women are pushing harder than ever against the boundaries of what it means to 'behave.' Where did these women come from? What are their crimes? And what does it mean for the rest of us?" (Publisher's note)

"With compassion for its subjects and a vibrantly satirical tone,

Doyle's debut book places her on the A-list of contemporary feminist writers." Pub Wkly

Includes bibliographical references and index

The **essential** feminist reader; edited and with an introduction by Estelle B. Freedman. Modern Library 2007 472p pa $17.95 **305.4**

1. Feminism
ISBN 0-8129-7460-3; 978-0-8129-7460-7

This collection of writings by feminist authors "features primary source material from around the globe, including short works of fiction and drama, political manifestos, and the work of less well-known writers." Publisher's note

Includes bibliographical references

Friedan, Betty

★ The **feminine** mystique; with a new introduction. Norton 1997 xlviii, 452p hardcover o.p. pa $15.95 **305.4**

1. Feminism 2. Women -- United States
ISBN 0-393-32257-2 pa

LC 97-8877

A reissue of the title first published 1963

An "analysis of the dilemma facing the educated American woman; the post-war emphasis on the feminine image of the role as wife and mother has caused the American woman to lose her identity, says the author." Cincinnati Public Libr

Includes bibliographical references

Grunwald, Lisa

★ **Women's** letters; America from the Revolutionary War to the present. edited by Lisa Grunwald & Stephen J. Adler. Dial Press 2005 824p il hardcover o.p. pa $18; pa $18 **305.4**

1. Women -- United States -- History -- Sources
ISBN 9780385335560; 0-385-33553-9; 0-385-33556-3 pa

LC 2005-41446

"Historical events of the last three centuries come alive through these women's singular correspondences—often their only form of public expression. In 1775, Rachel Revere tries to send financial aid to her husband, Paul, in a note that is confiscated by the British; First Lady Dolley Madison tells her sister about rescuing George Washington's portrait during the War of 1812; one week after JFK's assassination, Jacqueline Kennedy pens a heartfelt letter to Nikita Khrushchev; and on September 12, 2001, a schoolgirl writes a note of thanks to a New York City firefighter, asking him, "Were you afraid?" (Publisher's note)

"This collection of more than 400 entries begins with a letter written by Abigail Grant, accusing her husband of cowardice in battle, and ends with an e-mail by Wall Street Journal correspondent Farnaz Fassihi on the stark state of affairs in war-torn Iraq. In between, a wide variety of compelling subjects is covered. . . . The letters are accompanied by information about the topics included, biographical details about the author and the recipient, and other interesting facts." SLJ

Includes bibliographical references

Petersen, Anne Helen

Too fat, too slutty, too loud; the rise and reign of the unruly woman. Anne Helen Petersen. Plume 2017 xxii, 266 p.p (hardcover) $25 **305.4**

1. Women -- Identity 2. Women celebrities -- United States 3. American literature -- 21st century 4. Women -- United States 5. Celebrities -- United States
ISBN 9780399576867; 9780399576850

LC 2016058237

This book, by Anne Helen Petersen, presents "an accessible, analytical look at how female celebrities are pushing boundaries of what it means to be an 'acceptable' woman. . . . [The author] uses the lens of 'unruliness' to explore the ascension of pop culture powerhouses like Lena Dunham, Nicki Minaj, and Kim Kardashian, exploring why the public loves to love (and hate) these controversial figures." (Publisher's note)

"Media studies scholar Petersen (BuzzFeed News) offers a trenchant and intersectional analysis of the celebrity narratives we create around famous women who, in some way, defy the cultural scripts of classed and raced femininity." LJ

Includes bibliographical references (pages 237-266).

Rodriguez, Deborah

Kabul Beauty School; an American woman goes behind the veil. Random House 2007 275p $24.95; pa $14.95   **305.4**
1. Beauty shops 2. Women -- Afghanistan 3. Kabul Beauty School (Afghanistan)
ISBN 978-1-4000-6559-2; 1-4000-6559-3; 978-0-8129-7673-1 pa; 0-8129-7673-8 pa

LC 2006-50384

"Rodriguez's experiences will delight readers as she recounts such tales as two friends acting as 'parents' and negotiating a dowry for her marriage to an Afghan man or her students puzzling over a donation of a carton of thongs. Most of all, they will share her admiration for Afghan women's survival and triumph in chaotic times." SLJ

Saini, Angela

Inferior; how science got women wrong - and the new research that's rewriting the story. Angela Saini. Beacon Press 2017 213 p. (hardback) $25.95   **305.4**
1. Women's studies 2. Women -- Physiology 3. Women -- Psychology
ISBN 9780807071717; 9780807010037; 9780807071700

LC 2016048808

In this book, author "Angela Saini weaves together a fascinating--and sorely necessary--new science of women. As Saini takes readers on a journey to uncover science's failure to understand women, she finds that we're still living with the legacy of an establishment that's just beginning to recover from centuries of entrenched exclusion and prejudice." (Publisher's note)

"In admirably subtle prose, Saini questions, considers, and refuses to accept traditional generalizations. A brilliant approach to a long overlooked topic, Inferior is impossible to ignore and invaluable." Booklist

Includes bibliographical references and index

Schnall, Marianne

What will it take to make a woman president? conversations about women, leadership, and power. by Marianne Schnall. Seal Press 2013 384 p. $17   **305.4**
1. Women politicians 2. Gender and politics 3. Presidential candidates -- United States 4. Women -- United States -- Interviews 5. Politicians -- United States -- Attitudes 6. Women political activists -- United States 7. Women presidential candidates -- United States
ISBN 158005496X; 9781580054966

LC 2013031218

Amelia Bloomer Project (2014)

This book, by Marianne Schnall, "features interviews with politicians, public officials, thought leaders, writers, artists, and activists in an attempt to discover the obstacles that have held women back and what needs to change in order to elect a woman into the White House. With insights and personal anecdotes . . . , this book addresses timely, provoc-

ative issues involving women, politics, and power." (Publisher's note)

"Through far-ranging conversations, Schnall gained insight into factors contributing to the country's failure to elect a woman to its highest office and sought advice as to how we can not only better prepare for the next presidential election but create a world in which today's young women feel empowered to break out of stereotypical roles. The good news is that there is universal agreement among those profiled that the country will, indeed, elect a woman president. The more disconcerting message is that there is still much work to do in order to achieve true gender parity." (Booklist)

Sebba, Anne

Les Parisiennes; how the women of Paris lived, loved and died under Nazi occupation. Anne Sebba. St. Martin's Press 2016 480 p. illustrations (some color) (ebook) $60; (hardcover) $27.99   **305.4**
1. Paris (France) -- History 2. World War, 1939-1945 -- France 3. Paris (France) -- Biography 4. World War, 1939-1945 -- Influence 5. Women -- France -- Paris -- Biography 6. Paris (France) -- History -- 1940-1944 7. France -- History -- German occupation, 1940-1945 8. Paris (France) -- Social conditions -- 20th century 9. Women -- France -- Paris -- History -- 20th century 10. Paris (France) -- Politics and government -- 20th century 11. World War, 1939-1945 -- Social aspects -- France -- Paris
ISBN 9781466849563; 9781250048592

LC 2016020685

In this book "author Anne Sebba explores a devastating period in Paris's history and tells the stories of how women survived—or didn't—during the Nazi occupation. Sebba focuses on the role of women, many of whom faced life and death decisions every day. After the war ended, there would be a fierce settling of accounts between those who made peace with or, worse, helped the occupiers and those who fought the Nazis in any way they could." (Publisher's note)

"Paris history buffs will enjoy a new look at the city during World War II." LJ

Includes bibliographical references and index

Spruill, Marjorie J.

Divided We Stand; the battle over women's rights and family values that polarized American politics. Marjorie J. Spruill. St. Martin's Press 2017 448 p. illustrations (ebook) $66; $33   **305.4**
1. Women's rights 2. Feminism -- United States -- History 3. Women -- Political activity -- United States
ISBN 9781632863157; 1632863146; 9781632863140

LC 2017007810

This book, by Marjorie J. Spruill, "reveals how the battle between feminists and their conservative challengers divided the nation as Democrats continued to support women's rights and Republicans cast themselves as the party of family values. The women's rights . . . [and] conservative women's [movements] have irrevocably affected the course of modern American history. We cannot fully understand the present without appreciating the events leading up to Houston and thereafter." (Publisher's note)

"There are countless kernels of amazing achievement and courage throughout this jam-packed, engaging history." Kirkus

Includes bibliographical references (pages 351-425) and index.

Ulrich, Laurel

Well-behaved women seldom make history; [by] Laurel Thatcher Ulrich. Alfred A. Knopf 2007 xxxiv, 284p il $24   **305.4**

1. Poets 2. Authors 3. Feminism 4. Novelists 5. Suffragists 6. Women in literature 7. Essayists 8. Biographers 9. Women -- History 10. Short story writers
ISBN 978-1-4000-4159-6; 1-4000-4159-6

LC 2006-100581

This book "is by no means jargon-ridden or academic in tone. Ulrich's style is plain and direct, agreeable but without frills, and she moves efficiently right along. The book is a pleasure to read." Washington Post Book World

Includes bibliographical references

Wolf, Naomi

The **beauty** myth; how images of beauty are used against women. Perennial 2002 348p pa $14.95   **305.4**
1. Women 2. Gender role 3. Personal appearance 4. Sex role
ISBN 0-06-051218-0

LC 2002-72516

First published 1991 by Morrow

The author "presents a provocative and persuasive account of the pervasiveness of the beauty ideal in all facets of Western culture." Libr J

Includes bibliographical references

Xinran

Message from an unknown Chinese mother; stories of loss and love. translated from Chinese by Nicky Harman. Scribner 2011 xxvii, 239p $25; ebook $11.99   **305.4**
1. Mothers 2. Children -- China 3. China -- Social conditions
ISBN 978-1-4516-1089-5; 978-1-4516-1095-6 ebook

First published 2010 in the United Kingdom

The author "collects the heartbreaking stories of Chinese women forced to give up their baby girls because of the one-child-only policy or feudal traditions that prefer boys, in an oral history written for those abandoned daughters. . . . This is a brutally honest book written for those relinquished children, so that they will know how much their birth mothers loved them and how—in the words of one mother who gave up her daughter—'they paid for that love with an endless stream of bitter tears.'" Publ Wkly

305.409   History, geographic treatment, biography

Beard, Mary, 1955-

★ **Women** & power; a manifesto. Mary Beard. Liveright Publishing Corporation 2018 128 p. (hardcover) $15.95   **305.409**
1. Women -- History 2. Leadership in women 3. Women -- Political activity
ISBN 9781631494758

LC 2017054169

In this book, author "Mary Beard addresses . . . the misogynists and trolls who mercilessly attack and demean women the world over, including, very often, Mary herself. . . . She traces the origins of this misogyny to its ancient roots, examining the pitfalls of gender and the ways that history has mistreated strong women since time immemorial. . . . Beard draws illuminating parallels between our cultural assumptions about women's relationship to power." (Publisher's note)

"This slim and timely volume leaves readers to contemplate how women can reconfigure society's current perceptions of power." Pub Wkly

Includes bibliographical references and index

Women and power

Jewell, Hannah

She caused a riot; 100 unknown women who built cities, sparked revolutions, and massively crushed it. Hannah Jewell. Sourcebooks, Inc. 2018 320 p. (pbk.: alk. paper) $22.99   **305.409**
1. Women -- History 2. Women -- Biography
ISBN 9781492662921

LC 2017046004

This book, by Hannah Jewell, is "an empowering, no-holds-barred look into the epic adventures and dangerous exploits of 100 inspiring women who were too brave, too brilliant, too unconventional, too political, too poor, not ladylike enough and not white enough to be recognized by their . . . contemporaries." (Publisher's note)

Includes bibliographical references and index

305.42   Social role and status of women

Adichie, Chimamanda Ngozi, 1977-

Dear Ijeawele, or a feminist manifesto in fifteen suggestions; Chimamanda Ngozi Adichie. Alfred A. Knopf 2017 63 p. (hardcover: alk. paper) $15   **305.42**
1. Feminism 2. Women -- Social conditions 3. Mothers and daughters 4. Child rearing -- Social aspects
ISBN 9781524733148; 9781524733131

LC 2017930564

This memoir tells how author "Chimamanda Ngozi Adichie received a letter from a dear friend . . . asking her how to raise her baby girl as a feminist. 'Dear Ijeawele' is Adichie's letter of response. Here are fifteen invaluable suggestions--compelling, direct, wryly funny, and perceptive--for how to empower a daughter to become a strong, independent woman. 'Dear Ijeawele' goes right to the heart of sexual politics in the twenty-first century." (Publisher's note)

"This excellent series of essays is award-winning author Adichie's (Americanah) response to a friend's question on how to raise her daughter as a feminist." LJ

★ **We** should all be feminists; Chimamanda Ngozi Adichie. Random House Inc 2015 64 p. $7.95   **305.42**
1. Women 2. Feminism 3. Women's rights
ISBN 110191176X; 9781101911761

In this book, author Chimamanda Ngozi Adichie "offers readers a unique definition of feminism for the twenty-first century, one rooted in inclusion and awareness. Drawing extensively on her own experiences and her deep understanding of the often masked realities of sexual politics, here is one remarkable author's exploration of what it means to be a woman now--and an of-the-moment rallying cry for why we should all be feminists." (Publisher's note)

"An eloquent, stirring must-read for budding and reluctant feminists." SLJ

Anderson, Gillian, 1968-

We; a manifesto for women everywhere. Gillian Anderson and Jennifer Nadel. Atria Books 2017 xxiii, 360 p.p (hardcover) $25   **305.42**
1. Self-improvement 2. Women -- Psychology 3. Women -- Mental health 4. Women -- Conduct of life 5. Self-realization
ISBN 150112627X; 9781501126277; 9781501126291

LC 2016052691

This book, by Gillian Anderson and Jennifer Nadel, is an "inspirational, and intensely practical manual for change, providing nine universal principles that offer a path for dealing with life's inevitable emotional and spiritual challenges. It's for anyone who wants to see her own life and the world around her change for the better.... [This book] is a rallying cry for women to join together and create lasting change in our own lives, our communities, and across the world." (Publisher's note)

Includes bibliographical references and index.

Armstrong, Jennifer Keishin

Sexy feminism; a girl's guide to love, success, and style. Jennifer Keishin Armstrong and Heather Wood Rudúlph. Mariner Books 2013 xxii, 228 p.p (paperback) $15.95   **305.42**
1. Feminism 2. Self-realization 3. Women -- Social conditions 4. Success 5. Self-realization in women
ISBN 0547738307; 9780547738307

LC 2012040351

This book, by Jennifer Keishin Armstrong and Heather Wood Rudulph, discusses feminism in the 21st century. "For many young women the radicalism of the Second Wave is unappealing, and the . . . Third Wave feels out of date.... [This book offers] an inclusive, approachable kind of feminism--miniskirts, lip gloss, and waxing permitted. Covering a range of topics from body issues and workplace gender politics to fashion, dating, and sex." (Publisher's note)

Includes bibliographical references (p. [217]-228).

The **bitch** is back; edited by Cathi Hanauer. HarperCollins 2016 368 p. (ebook) $25.99; $26.99   **305.42**
1. Women authors 2. American essays 3. Man-woman relationship 4. Middle aged women -- Fiction
ISBN 9780062389534; 0062389513; 9780062389510

LC 2016041569

In this book, "Cathi Hanauer, Kate Christensen, Sarah Crichton, Debora Spar, Ann Hood, Veronica Chambers, and nineteen other women offer unique views on womanhood and feminism today. Some of the 'original bitches' (OBs) revisit their earlier essays to reflect on their previous selves. All reveal how their lives have changed in the intervening years-whether they stayed coupled, left marriages, or had affairs, . . . or experienced other meaningful life transitions." (Publisher's note)

"Like an all-night gab session with one's best friend, these essays shed sincere and searing light on subjects that are often hard for women to face. In doing so, Hanauer and company give voice to topics all too frequently hidden under a damaging cone of silence." Booklist

Chocano, Carina

You play the girl; on Playboy bunnies, Stepford wives, trainwrecks, & other mixed messages. Carina Chocano. Houghton Mifflin Harcourt 2017 xxvi, 275 p.p (paperback) $16.95   **305.42**
1. Women -- Psychology 2. Identity (Psychology) 3. Women -- Social conditions 4. Sexism 5. Women -- Identity 6. Women in mass media 7. Women in popular culture
ISBN 9780544648944; 9780544648968; 0544648943

LC 2017289231

National Book Critics Circle Award: Criticism (2017)

In this book, pop culture critic Carina Chocano "merges memoir and commentary to explore how our culture shapes ideas about who women are, what they are meant to be, and where they belong.... She explains how growing up in the shadow of 'the girl' taught her to think about herself and the world and what it means to raise a daughter in the face of these contorted reflections." (Publisher's note)

"A sharply perceptive look at the myths that constrain women." Kirkus

Includes bibliographical references (pages 264-275)

Coontz, Stephanie

A **strange** stirring; the Feminine mystique and American women at the dawn of the 1960s. Stephanie Coontz. Basic Books 2011 xxiii, 222 p.p (hc: alk. paper) $25.95   **305.42**
1. Authors 2. Feminism 3. Feminism -- United States -- History -- 20th century 4. Women -- United States -- Social conditions -- 20th century
ISBN 0465002005; 9780465002009

LC 2010022163

The book "documents the circumstances of middle-class American women in the early 1960s and the impact of Betty Friedan's The Feminine Mystique (1963). Stephanie Coontz makes it clear that although Friedan, and many observers since, have exaggerated the book's role in launching the second wave of the feminist movement, thousands of women were profoundly affected by it. . . . [Stephanie] Coontz begins with a stark look at the circumstances facing women in the early 1960s, including legal discrimination and widely held cultural beliefs about women's nature and proper role.... The book ends with a chapter on the circumstances of women today. Despite the gains of the feminist movement, gender expectations still limit women's possibilities." (Journal of American History)

Includes bibliographical references (p. 191-208) and index

Double bind; women on ambition. edited by Robin Romm. Liveright Publishing Corporation 2017 viii, 303 p.p (hardcover) $27.95   **305.42**
1. Women authors 2. Feminism 3. Women in the professions
ISBN 9781631491214; 1631491210

LC 2016054987

In this collection of essays, "editor Robin Romm has marshaled a stunning constellation of thinkers to examine their relationships with ambition with candor, intimacy, and wit. Roxane Gay discusses how race informs and feeds her ambition. Theresa Rebeck takes on Hollywood and confronts her own unquenchable thirst to overcome its sexism. Francine Prose considers the origins of the stigma; Nadia Manzoor discusses its cultural weight." (Publisher's note)

"Romm's collection, which also includes contributions from Roxane Gay, Francine Prose, and others, is a welcome addition to the discourse on a topic that rarely receives the kind of honest and wide-ranging consideration these essays offer." Kirkus.

Includes bibliographical references.

Filipovic, Jill

The **H**-spot; the feminist pursuit of happiness. Jill Filipovic. Nation Books 2017 320 p. (hardcover) $27   **305.42**
1. Happiness 2. Women -- Psychology 3. Feminism -- History
ISBN 9781568585482; 9781568585475

LC 2016050782

In this book, author Jill Filipovic "argues that the main obstacle standing in-between women and happiness is a rigged system.... [She contends] that it is more important than ever to prioritize women's happiness--and that doing so will make men's lives better, too. Here, she provides an outline for a feminist movement we all need and a blueprint for how policy, laws, and society can deliver on the promise of the pursuit of happiness for all." (Publisher's note)

"A timely, enlightening exploration of what American women truly want and need to live purposeful, fulfilling, happy lives." Kirkus

Includes bibliographical references (pages 285-306) and index.

Gray, Emma

A **girl's** guide to joining the resistance; a feminist handbook on fighting for good. Emma Gray. HarperCollins 2018

144 p. $16.99   **305.42**

1. Feminism 2. Women political activists

ISBN 0062748084; 9780062748089

"Interweaving the interviews with her own experiences covering resistance events and being a member of the media in a time when the media has been under assault, Emma has created a down and dirty guide for women of all ages to roll up their sleeves and resist the forces that are a threat to our rights. . . . Whether you're new to the front or an activism vet, there has never been a better time to jump into the fray." (Publisher's note)

Nasty women; feminism, resistance, and revolution in Trump's America. edited by Samhita Mukhopadhyay and Kate Harding. Picador 2017 vi, 248 p.p (trade pbk.) $16   **305.42**

1. Feminism -- United States 2. Advocacy (Political science) 3. United States -- Politics and government -- 21st century 4. Women -- Political activity -- United States 5. United States -- Politics and government -- 2017- 6. Women -- United States -- Social conditions -- 21st century

ISBN 9781250155511; 9781250155504

LC 2017027142

This book, edited by Samhita Mukhopadhyay and Kate Harding, presents "inspiring essays from a diverse group of talented women writers who seek to provide a broad look at how we got here and what we need to do to move forward. . . . [It includes] essays by Rebecca Solnit on Trump and his 'misogyny army,' Cheryl Strayed on grappling with the aftermath of Hillary Clinton's loss, [and] Sarah Hepola on resisting the urge to drink after the election." (Publisher's note)

"The writers are emotionally generous as they meditate on this pivotal moment in American history. . . . This book invites readers to converse, comfort, and hold one another accountable in the hope of igniting radical, intersectional change." Booklist

Morris, Bonnie J.

★ The **feminist** revolution; the struggle for women's liberation. Bonnie J. Morris, D-M Withers; foreword by Roxane Gay. Smithsonian Books 2018 224 p. (hardback) $34.95   **305.420**

1. Women's rights 2. Women's studies 3. Feminism -- History

ISBN 9781588346124

LC 2017039814

This book, by Bonnie J. Morris and D-M Withers, with foreword by Roxane Gay, "offers an overview of women's struggle for equal rights in the late twentieth century. Beginning with the auspicious founding of the National Organization for Women in 1966 . . . , the book traces a path through political campaigns, protests, the formation of women's publishing houses and groundbreaking magazines, and other events that shaped women's history." (Publisher's note)

"Much like a museum exhibition, this collection uses accessible text and rich visual materials that invite readers to explore in a nonlinear fashion. It will appeal to both those deeply familiar with the topic as well as beginners of this influential moment in feminist history." LJ

Includes bibliographical references and index

Nordberg, Jenny

★ The **underground** girls of Kabul; in search of a hidden resistance in Afghanistan. Jenny Nordberg. Crown Publishers 2014 288 p. hbk $25   **305.42**

1. Gender role 2. Women -- Afghanistan 3. Afghanistan -- Social conditions 4. Girls -- Afghanistan 5. Gender Identity -- Afghanistan 6. Male impersonators -- Afghanistan

ISBN 0307952495; 9780307952493

LC 2014000295

Author Jenny Nordberg presents this book on the Afghan custom of "bacha posh . . . a third kind of child--a girl temporarily raised as a boy and presented as such to the outside world. Nordberg, the reporter who broke the story of this phenomenon for the New York Times, constructs a powerful and moving account of those secretly living on the other side of a deeply segregated society where women have almost no rights and little freedom. " (Publisher's note)

"Nordberg's subtle, sympathetic reportage makes this one of the most convincing portraits of Afghan culture in print; through a small breach in the wall of gender apartheid, she reveals the harsh ironies of a system that so devalues women that it forces them to become men." Pub Wkly

Includes bibliographical references and index

Orenstein, Peggy

Don't call me princess; essays on girls, women, sex, and life. Peggy Orenstein. HarperCollins 2018 xii, 378 p.p (paperback) $16.99   **305.42**

1. Girls 2. Feminism 3. Women -- Social conditions

ISBN 0062688901; 9780062688903; 9780062688910

In this essay collection, author Peggy Orenstein "delivers her first ever collection of essays--funny, poignant, deeply personal and sharply observed pieces, drawn from three decades of writing, which trace girls' and women's progress (or lack thereof) in what Orenstein once called a 'half-changed world.'" (Publisher's note)

"Compelling and intelligent, Orenstein's book offers a powerful vision of the challenges of modern womanhood and of what it means to be female in 21st-century America. A sharp, timely collection of essays." Kirkus

Outrageous acts and everyday rebellions; Gloria Steinem; with a new foreword by Emma Watson and new material by the author. 3rd edition Picador USA 2019 432 p paperback $20   **305.42**

1. Feminism

ISBN 9781250204868

"Outrageous Acts and Everyday Rebellions has sold over half a million copies since its original publication in 1983, acclaimed for its witty, warm, and life-changing view of the world, 'as if women mattered.' Steinem's truly personal writing is here, from the now-famous exposé, 'I Was a Playboy Bunny,' to the moving tribute to her mother 'Ruth's Song (Because She Could Not Sing It).'" (Publisher's note)

Paglia, Camille, 1947-

Free Women, Free Men; Sex, Gender, Feminism. by Camille Paglia. Pantheon Books 2017 xxvi, 315 p.p illustrations $26.95   **305.42**

1. Essays 2. Gender role 3. Gender identity 4. Feminism 5. Sex role

ISBN 0375424776; 9780375424779

LC 2016034574

This book, by Camille Paglia, is an "essay collection that both celebrates modern feminism and challenges us to build an alliance of strong women and strong men. . . . At once illuminating, witty, and inspiring, these essays are essential reading that affirm the power of men and women and what we can accomplish together." (Publisher's note)

"Intriguing and thought provoking for readers interested in different perspectives of feminism." LJ.

Includes bibliographical references and index.

Rosin, Hanna

The **end** of men; and the rise of women. Hanna Rosin. Riverhead Books 2012 310 p. (hbk.) $27.95   **305.42**

1. Women -- History 2. Man-woman relationship 3. Feminism 4. Women -- Social conditions -- 21st century 5. Women -- Economic conditions -- 21st century
ISBN 1594488045; 9781594488047

LC 2012018005

This book by Hanna Rosin is a "portrait of women, men, and power in a transformed world. Men have been the dominant sex since, well, the dawn of mankind. . . . [But] this unprecedented moment, by almost every measure, women are no longer gaining on men: They have pulled decisively ahead. Rosin reveals how this new state of affairs is radically shifting the power dynamics between men and women at every level of society, with profound implications for marriage, sex, children, work, and more." (Publisher's note)

Includes bibliographical references and index.

Scutts, Joanna

The **extra** woman; how Marjorie Hillis led a generation of women to live alone and like it. Joanna Scutts. Liveright Publishing Corporation 2017 335 p. illustrations (hardcover) $27.95 **305.42**

1. Feminism -- United States 2. Single women -- United States -- History 3. Women authors -- Biography 4. Feminism -- United States -- History 5. Living alone -- United States -- History
ISBN 9781631492747; 9781631492730; 163149273X

LC 2017027416

This book, by Joanna Scutts, presents "a cultural history of single women in the city through the reclaimed life of glamorous guru Marjorie Hillis. . . . [It] is both a brilliant exposé of women who forged their independent paths before the domestic backlash of the 1950s trapped them behind picket fences, and an illuminating excursion into the joys of fashion, mixology, decorating, and other manifestations of shameless self-love." (Publisher's note)

"A sparklingly intelligent and well-researched cultural history." Kirkus

Includes bibliographical references (pages 293-316) and index.

Solnit, Rebecca

The **mother** of all questions; further reports from the feminist revolutions. Rebecca Solnit; images by Paz de la Calzada. Haymarket Books 2017 176 p. illustrations (paperback) $14.95 **305.42**

1. Feminism 2. Violence against women 3. Sex differences (Psychology) 4. Women -- Violence against
ISBN 1608467406; 9781608467204; 9781608467402

This collection of essays, by Rebecca Solnit, illustrated by Paz de la Calzada, "offers indispensable commentary on women who refuse to be silenced, misogynistic violence, the fragile masculinity of the literary canon, the gender binary, the recent history of rape jokes, and much more. In characteristic style, Solnit mixes humor, keen analysis, and powerful insight in these essays." (Publisher's note)

"Solnit's voice is calm, clear, and unapologetic; each essay balances a warm wit with confident, thoughtful analysis, resulting in a collection that is as enjoyable and accessible as it is incisive." Booklist

Spar, Debora L.

Wonder Women; Sex, Power, and the Quest for Perfection. Sarah Crichton Books 2013 320 p. $27 **305.42**

1. Feminism 2. Women -- Social conditions
ISBN 0374298750; 9780374298753

This book "addresses the state of feminism and suggests that, despite historic gains in education, the workforce, and equal rights, American women suffer under 'an excruciating set of mutually exclusive expec-

tations' resulting, paradoxically, from the proliferation of options that feminism made possible." Debora L. Spar "traces how the movement's 'expansive and revolutionary' political goals have evolved into a set of 'vast and towering expectations' that trouble women at every stage of their lives." (Publishers Weekly)

Suh, Krista

★ **DIY** rules for a WTF world; how to speak up, get creative, and change the world. Krista Suh. Grand Central Publishing 2018 248 p. $25 **305.42**

1. Feminism 2. Women -- Conduct of life 3. Self-actualization (Psychology) in women 4. Pussyhat Project 5. Self-realization in women
ISBN 1538712334; 9781538712337

LC 2017951263

In this book, "Krista Suh shares the tools, tips, experiences, 'rules,' and knitting patterns she uses to get creative, get bold, and change the world. . . . [The book] not only inspires you to demolish the patriarchy, but also enables you to create your own rules for living, and even a movement of your own, all with gusto, purpose, and joy.' (Publisher's note)

Includes bibliographical references (pages 247-248)

Together we rise; the Women's March: behind the scenes at the protest heard around the world. The Women's March Organizers and Conde Nast. HarperCollins 2018 319 p. $30 **305.42**

1. Protest movements 2. Women in politics 3. Women's rights -- History
ISBN 0062843435; 9780062843432

"In celebration of the one-year anniversary of Women's March, this . . . book, [by The Women's March Organizers and Conde Nast] offers an unprecedented, front-row seat to one of the most galvanizing movements in American history, with exclusive interviews with Women's March organizers, never-before-seen photographs, and essays by feminist activists.

"Interspersed between the organizers' narratives are accounts of the day from women all over the world, explaining how that show of dissent impacted their lives, and notes from celebrities like America Ferrera, Roxane Gay, and Jill Solloway detailing their own views of the march. Large and plentiful photos show many shades of hope and inclusion in this energizing and emotional trip through the movement." Booklist

The **unfinished** revolution; voices from the global fight for women's rights. edited by Minky Worden. Seven Stories Press 2012 xviii, 361 p.p col. ill. (paperback) $25.95 **305.42**

1. Human rights 2. Women's rights
ISBN 1609803876; 9781609803872

LC 2011052738

This book edited by Minky Worden is a collection of "essays assessing the progress of worldwide rights for women and girls since the UN's human rights conferences in the 1990s. The ongoing global struggle consists of three distinct spheres: economic issues (human trafficking, property rights); violence against women and their health rights (including genital mutilation); and harmful traditions (religious clothing restraints, so-called honor crimes)." (Booklist)

Includes bibliographical references and index

Valenti, Jessica, 1978-

Full Frontal Feminism; A Young Woman's Guide to Why Feminism Matters. Jessica Valenti. Pgw 2014 279 p. illustrations $17 **305.42**

1. Feminism 2. Women's movement 3. Women -- Social conditions
ISBN 1580055613; 9781580055611

LC 200638573

This book, by Jessica Valenti, is an updated "guide to the issues that matter to today's young women. . . . With new openers from Valenti in every chapter, the book covers a range of topics, including pop culture, health, reproductive rights, violence, education, relationships, and more." (Publisher's note)

"These are lessons we already know; little in this book will prove useful to most women. Most public libraries will want the Siegel book; a few may want Valenti's." LJ

Wolf, Naomi

Vagina; A New Biography. Naomi Wolf. HarperCollins 2012 xii, 381 p., [8] p. of platesp ill. $27.99   **305.42**
1. Vagina 2. Femininity 3. Nervous system 4. Reproductive system 5. Women -- Sexual behavior
ISBN 0061989169; 9780061989162

LC 2012454997

This book by Naomi Wolf "explores the effect of new neurobiological discoveries on our understanding of female sexuality. When the author began noticing . . . diminished sexual response at age 46, she visited a gynecologist, who diagnosed her with an impacted pelvic nerve. . . . Wolf set out to document the mind-body link with the goal of informing women of the crucial role that neurology plays not only in their sex lives, but also in . . . their creativity and sense of well-being." (Kirkus Reviews)

Includes bibliographical references (p. [335]-365) and index.

Zoepf, Katherine

Excellent Daughters; The Secret Lives of Young Women Who Are Transforming the Arab World. Katherine Zoepf. Penguin Group USA 2016 272 p. illustrations (ebook) $51; (hardcover) $28   **305.42**
1. Feminism -- Arab countries 2. Young women -- Arab countries -- Social conditions 3. Young women -- Political activity -- Arab countries
ISBN 9780698411470; 1594203881; 9781594203886

LC 2015043395

This book by Katherine Zoepf describes how "today, young Arab women outnumber men in universities, and a few are beginning to face down religious and social tradition in order to live independently, to delay marriage, and to pursue professional goals. Hundreds of thousands of devout girls and women are attending Qur'anic schools." (Publisher's note)

"In her absorbing, window-opening book, Zoepf reveals the variety of women's lives and interests away from political headlines and conventional stereotypes, and their power, often by small steps, to transform their world." Pub Wkly

Includes bibliographical references (pages [247]-248) and index.

305.48   Specific groups of women

Black girls rock! owning our magic. rocking our truth. edited by Beverly Bond. Simon & Schuster 2018 256 p. $30   **305.488**
1. Black women 2. African American women
ISBN 1501157922; 9781501157929

This book, edited by Beverly Bond, "pays tribute to the achievements and contributions of black women around the world. Fueled by the insights of women of diverse backgrounds, including Michelle

Obama, Angela Davis, Shonda Rhimes, Misty Copeland Yara Shahidi, and Mary J. Blige, this book is a celebration of black women's voices and experiences that will become a collector's items for generations to come." (Publisher's note)

Carruthers, Charlene A.

Unapologetic; a black, queer, and feminist mandate for radical movements. Charlene A. Carruthers. Beacon Press 2018 182 p. (pbk.: alk. paper) $22.95   **305.488**
1. Black power 2. Feminism -- United States 3. African American women -- Political activity 4. Black power -- United States 5. African Americans -- Civil rights 6. Feminism -- United States -- 21st century 7. Black lives matter movement -- United States 8. African American women -- Political activity -- United States -- 21st century 9. African American lesbians -- Political activity -- United States -- 21st century
ISBN 9780807019412

LC 2017058987

This book, by Charlene Carruthers, "challenges all of us engaged in the social justice struggle to make the movement for Black liberation more radical, more queer, and more feminist. This book provides a vision for how social justice movements can become sharper and more effective through principled struggle, healing justice, and leadership development." (Publisher's note)

"Incantatory without being incendiary, strong but not strident, Carruthers argues for "a world in which everyone is able to live with dignity and in right relationship with the land we inhabit." This handbook for the revolution is a rousing call for collective liberation." Publishers' Weekly

Includes bibliographical references and index

Cooper, Brittney

Eloquent rage; a black feminist discovers her superpower. Brittney Cooper. St. Martin's Press 2018 279 p. (hardcover) $25.99   **305.48**
1. Feminism -- United States 2. Feminists -- United States -- Biography 3. African American feminists -- Biography
ISBN 9781250112897; 9781250112576

LC 2017036275

This book, by Brittney Cooper, "reminds us that anger is a powerful source of energy that can give us the strength to keep on fighting. . . . This book argues that ultimately feminism, friendship, and faith in one's own superpowers are all we really need to turn things right side up again." (Publisher's note)

"Deftly blending the conversational tone of a memoir with pointed critique, Cooper offers a comprehensive and accessible analysis of topics from the Bible to pop music to U.S. politics past and present." LJ

De Courcy, Anne

The **husband** hunters; American heiresses who married into the British aristocracy. Anne de Courcy. St. Martin's Press 2018 320 p. (hardcover) $27.99   **305.48**
1. Heiresses 2. Aristocracy -- Great Britain 3. Americans -- Great Britain -- Biography 4. Heiresses -- Great Britain -- Biography 5. Americans -- Great Britain -- History -- 19th century 6. Heiresses -- Great Britain -- History -- 19th century 7. Aristocracy (Social class) -- Great Britain -- History 8. Great Britain -- Social life and customs -- 19th century
ISBN 9781250164599

LC 2018013474

This book, by Anne de Courcy, presents a "group biography of the young, rich, American heiresses who married into the impoverished British aristocracy at the turn of the twentieth century. . . . From 1874 - the year that Jennie Jerome, the first known 'Dollar Princess', married

Randolph Churchill - to 1905, dozens of young American heiresses married into the British peerage, bringing with them all the fabulous wealth, glamour and sophistication of the Gilded Age." (Publisher's note)

Includes bibliographical references and index

Scroggins, Deborah

Wanted women; faith, lies, and the war on terror: the lives of Ayaan Hirsi Ali and Aafia Siddiqui. by Deborah Scroggins. Harper 2011 p. cm.   **305.48**

1. Feminism 2. Terrorism 3. Muslim women 4. Women political activists 5. Muslim women -- Social conditions 6. Muslim women -- Political activity

ISBN 9780060898977

LC 2011022153

This book explores the topics of "militant Islam, Muslim women's rights, and the war on terror--brought into focus through two lives on opposite sides: activist Ayaan Hirsi Ali and religious extremist Aafia Siddiqui. . . . Ayaan Hirsi Ali, a Somali-born former member of the Dutch Parliament and the author of the international bestseller 'Infidel,' was raised as a Muslim fundamentalist in Kenya. A feminist, political analyst, writer, and fierce critic of her former religion, she champions the West in what she insists must be a war against Islam. . . . Aafia Siddiqui, a native of Pakistan, moved to the United States to pursue a doctorate in neuroscience. A decade later, she returned to Pakistan, where her involvement with al-Qaeda, including her marriage to one of the 9/11 plotters, led the CIA to regard her as one of the most dangerous terrorists in the world." (Publisher's note)

305.5   People by social and economic levels

Bageant, Joe

Deer hunting with Jesus; dispatches from America's class war. Crown Publishers 2007 273.   **305.5**

1. Social classes -- United States. 2. United States -- Social conditions -- 1980-

ISBN 978-0-307-33936-2

LC 2007-01343

"Returning after 30 years to the 'dirt-poor' neighborhoods of his native Winchester, VA, Bageant examines the lives of the working poor using the stories of his friends and neighbors. Through these bleak tales, he paints a picture of a permanent underclass exploited by the Right and forgotten or even disdained, by the Left." (Library Journal)

Boo, Katherine

★ **Behind** the beautiful forevers; Katherine Boo. Random House 2012 xxii, 256 p.p   **305.5**

1. Poverty 2. Bombay (India) 3. Political corruption 4. Creative nonfiction 5. Urban poor -- India -- Bombay 6. Urban poor -- India -- Mumbai

ISBN 1400067553; 9780679645504; 9781400067558

LC 2011019555

National Book Award Finalist: Nonfiction (2012)

This book examines "the stark lives of the inhabitants of Annawadi, a slum across from Mumbai's Sahar Airport, to reveal the . . . inequality and urban poverty still endemic in India's democracy. Using recorded and videotaped conversations, interviews, documents, and the assistance of interlocutors, [Katherine] Boo profiles the lives of some of the slum dwellers from November 2007 to March 2011. . . . [Boo] claims she witnessed most of the events described in the book." (Library Journal)

Brooks, David

The **social** animal; the hidden sources of love, character, and achievement. Random House 2011 424p $27; ebook $13.99   **305.5**

1. Character 2. Social status 3. Elite (Social sciences)

ISBN 978-1-4000-6760-2; 1-4000-6760-X; 978-0-679-60393-1 ebook; 0-679-60393-X ebook

LC 2010045785

"Brooks offers fictional characters Harold and Erica to illustrate how humans communicate, are educated, and succeed—or don't. Synthesizing research on human unconsciousness, Brooks meshes sociology, psychology, and economics to show how character is formed and how we strive for happiness and success. . . . [The author] offers a new look at the assumptions we make about life and a close, deep examination of the failure of social and economic policies that do not take into account the complexities of human behavior, treating us as if we were totally rational and guided by our thoughts rather than some combination of intellect and emotion." Booklist

Includes bibliographical references

Ehrenreich, Barbara

★ **Nickel** and dimed; on (not) getting by in America. Metropolitan Bks. 2001 221p hardcover o.p. pa $15   **305.5**

1. Poverty 2. Minimum wage 3. Labor -- United States

ISBN 0-8050-6388-9; 0-8050-8838-5 pa

LC 00-52514

"No real answers to the problem but a compelling sketch of its reality and pervasiveness." Libr J

Epstein, Joseph, 1937-

Snobbery; The American Version. Houghton Mifflin 2002 274p $25; pa $14   **305.5**

1. Snobs and snobbishness 2. Social status -- United States 3. Snobs and snobbishness -- United States

ISBN 0-395-94417-1; 0-618-34073-4 pa

LC 2001-51623

Epstein tracks the evolution of intellectual and cultural snobbery in the United States. He suggests that the traditional snobbery associated with the class system has given way in recent decades to a more complex phenomenon based on taste. Index.

"Every bracing page is a mirror in which readers can't help but recognize themselves, and each offers a quotable quip . . . and much to think about." Booklist

Includes bibliographical references

Freeland, Chrystia, 1968-

Plutocrats; the rise of the new global super-rich and the fall of everyone else. Chrystia Freeland. Penguin Press 2012 p. cm.   **305.5**

1. Poor 2. Rich people -- Conduct of life

ISBN 9781594204098

LC 2012015119

This book, by Chrystia Freeland, offers an "examination of wealth disparity, income inequality, and the new global elite. . . . In the last few decades what it means to be rich has changed dramatically. . . . The wealthiest 0.1 percent . . . are outpacing the rest of us at break-neck speed. . . . [The book] demonstrates how social upheavals generated by the first Gilded Age may pale in comparison to what is in store for us." (Publisher's note)

Hayes, Christopher

Twilight of the elites; America after meritocracy. Christo-

pher Hayes. Crown Publishers 2012 292 p. **305.5**
1. Equality 2. Leadership 3. Elite (Social sciences) 4. United States -- Politics and government -- 21st century 5. Power (Social sciences) 6. Corporate power -- United States 7. Business and politics -- United States 8. Elite (Social sciences) -- United States 9. United States -- Social conditions -- 21st century 10. United States -- Economic conditions -- 21st century
ISBN 9780307720450; 9780307720474

LC 2012002435

This book looks at the meritocracy and income inequality in the U.S. since the 1960s. Combining "political analysis, . . . social commentary, . . . and . . . historical understanding, 'Twilight of Elites' describes how the society we have come to inhabit -- utterly forgiving at the top and relentlessly punitive at the bottom -- produces leaders who are out of touch with the people they have been trusted to govern." (Publisher's note)

Includes bibliographical references and index.

Hedges, Chris
Days of destruction, days of revolt; Chris Hedges and Joe Sacco. Nation Books 2012 xv, 302 p.p ill. (hardback) $28 **305.5**
1. Camden (N.J.) 2. Social conflict 3. Poor -- United States 4. Pine Ridge Indian Reservation (S.D.) 5. Mines and mineral resources -- United States 6. Crime -- United States 7. Social classes -- United States 8. United States -- Social conditions -- 20th century
ISBN 1568586434; 9781568586434; 9781568587103

LC 2012004701

This book by Chris Hedges and Joe Sacco examines the impact of capitalism in America's society through a "tour of some of the worst places in America: the Pine Ridge reservation in South Dakota, which paces the nation in drug abuse, alcoholism, and teen suicide rates; Camden, NJ, one of the country's poorest and most dangerous cities; Welch, WV, where coal companies have relentlessly mined both human and natural resources; and Immokalee, FL, where migrant farm workers toil in virtual slavery." (Columbia Journalism Review)

Includes bibliographical references (p. 287-291) and index

Isenberg, Nancy, 1958-
★ **White** Trash; the 400-year untold history of class in America. Nancy Isenberg. Viking 2016 xvii, 460 p.p illustrations (ebook) $51; (hbk) $28 **305.5**
1. Poor -- United States -- History 2. Working class -- United States -- History 3. Social classes -- United States -- History 4. Poor whites -- United States -- Social conditions -- History 5. Working class whites -- United States -- Social conditions -- History
ISBN 9781101608487; 0670785970; 9780670785971

LC 2016302095

Carnegie Medal Longlist: Nonfiction (2017)

In this book, "surveying political rhetoric and policy, popular literature and scientific theories over four hundred years, [author Nancy] Isenberg upends assumptions about America's supposedly class-free society--where liberty and hard work were meant to ensure real social mobility." (Publisher's note)

"A riveting thesis supported by staggering research." Kirkus

Includes bibliographical references and index

Jadhav, Narendra
★ **Untouchables**; my family's triumphant journey out of the caste system in modern India. Scribner 2005 307p $26 **305.5**
1. Caste 2. India -- Social conditions
ISBN 0-7432-7079-7

LC 2005-44166

Original Indian edition, 1993; first published in English 2003 by Vi-

king with title: Outcaste, a memoir

"This moving story of perseverance from a sector of India rarely represented to American readers will be a standard text on Indian and Dalit themes for years to come." Libr J

Laskas, Jeanne Marie, 1958-
★ **Hidden** America; from coal miners to cowboys, an extraordinary exploration of the unseen people who make this country work. Jeanne Marie Laskas. Penguin Group USA 2012 318 p. **305.5**
1. Cheerleading 2. Migrant labor 3. Coal mines and mining 4. Subculture -- United States 5. United States -- Description and travel 6. United States -- Social conditions -- 1980- 7. Working class -- United States -- Biography 8. Manual work -- Social aspects -- United States 9. United States -- Social life and customs -- 1971- 10. Working class -- United States -- Social conditions 11. Working class -- United States -- Social life and customs
ISBN 0399159002; 9780399159008

LC 2012025457

Author Jeanne Marie Laskas presents a book "about the people who make our lives run every day--and yet we barely think of them. Laskas spent weeks in an Ohio coal mine and on an Alaskan oil rig; in a Maine migrant labor camp, a Texas beef ranch, the air traffic control tower at New York's LaGuardia Airport, a California landfill, an Arizona gun shop, the cab of a long-haul truck in Iowa, and the stadium of the Cincinnati Ben-Gals cheerleaders." (Publisher's note)

LeBlanc, Adrian Nicole
Random family; love, drugs, trouble, and coming of age in the Bronx. Scribner 2003 408p $25 **305.5**
1. Poor -- New York (N.Y.) 2. Youth -- New York (N.Y.) 3. Bronx (New York, N.Y.) -- Social conditions
ISBN 0-684-86387-1

LC 2002-26673

"A painstaking feat of reporting and empathy that resulted from 10 years of hanging out with a hard-pressed, loosely defined family in the Bronx." N Y Times Book Rev

Painter, Nell Irvin, 1942-
★ **Sojourner** Truth; a life, a symbol. Norton 1996 370p il hardcover o.p. pa $15.95 **305.5**
1. Feminism 2. Abolitionists 3. Memoirists 4. Biography, Individual 5. African American women -- Biography
ISBN 0-393-02739-2; 0-393-31708-0 pa

LC 95-47595

This is a biography of the public "speaker and advocate of abolitionism and women's rights. . . . The first section deals with {Truth's} early life as Isabella, who was born a slave in New York State, and with the beginning of her lifelong religious searching and preaching. Part 2 describes her self-transformation in the mid-1840s to Sojourner Truth and her strength and perseverance in pursuing her causes. A final section addresses the symbolic impact of her life down to the present day." (Libr J) Index.

"Painter persuasively offers us the real woman behind the myth." Publ Wkly

Includes bibliographical references

Quart, Alissa
Squeezed; why our families can't afford America. Alissa Quart. Ecco 2018 320 p. (hardback) $27.99 **305.5**
1. Social problems 2. Middle class -- United States 3. Middle class -- United States -- Economic conditions

ISBN 9780062412256; 9780062412263; 9780062847904; 9780062847911

LC 2017056972

In this book, author Alissa Quart "examines the lives of many middle-class Americans who can now barely afford to raise children. Through gripping firsthand storytelling, Quart shows how our country has failed its families. Her subjects--from professors to lawyers to caregivers to nurses--have been wrung out by a system that doesn't support them, and enriches only a tiny elite." (Publisher's note)

"Quart details sound policy-related solutions—an adjunct rights movement; free preschool; welfare-type assistance for elder care and childcare; an end to federal funding for sketchy, for-profit schools; and universal basic income. Her ambitious, top-tier reportage tells a powerful story of America today." Pub Wkly

Includes bibliographical references (pages 271-295) and index

Smith, Douglas

Former people; the final days of the Russian aristocracy. Douglas Smith. 1st ed. Farrar, Straus and Giroux 2012 xvii, 464 pages, 32 unnumbered pages of platesp illustrations, maps (hardcover: alk. paper) $30.00   **305.5**
1. Communism 2. Russia -- History 3. Nobility -- Russia 4. Aristocracy (Social class) -- Soviet Union 5. Aristocracy (Social class) -- Russia -- History -- 20th century
ISBN 0374157618; 9780374157616

LC 2012003819

This book "examines the . . . 'fate of the nobility in the decades following the Russian Revolution,' when they were sometimes given the Orwellian title 'former people.' The author of several books on Russia . . . , [Douglas] Smith focuses on three generations of two families: the Sheremetsevs of St. Petersburg and the Golitsyns of Moscow." (Publishers Weekly)

Includes bibliographical references (pages 416-435) and index.

Stiglitz, Joseph E., 1943-

★ The **price** of inequality; how today's divided society endangers our future. Joseph E. Stiglitz. W.W. Norton & Co. 2012 xxxi, 414 p.p (hbk.) $27.95   **305.5**
1. Wealth 2. Finance -- United States 3. Equality -- United States 4. Global Financial Crisis, 2008-2009 5. United States -- Social conditions -- 21st century 6. United States -- Economic conditions -- 21st century 7. Income distribution -- Social aspects -- United States
ISBN 0393088693; 9780393088694

LC 2012014811

In this book, author Joseph E. Stiglitz "insists that increasing inequality in the United States stems from a breakdown of the country's political and economic systems." Stiglitz suggests that "inequality is a by-product of the ability to exploit consumers through monopoly power. . . . He shows that the consequences include a monopolistic redistribution powerful enough to have caused massive distortions in the U.S. financial system." (Kirkus Reviews)

Includes bibliographical references and index.

Veblen, Thorstein

★ The **theory** of the leisure class; edited with an introduction and notes by Martha Banta. Oxford University Press 2007 (Oxford world's classics) pa $15.95   **305.5**
1. Social classes
ISBN 978-0-19-280684-0; 0-19-280684-X

LC 2007-8544

First published 1899 by Macmillan

In this economic treatise, "Veblen held that the feudal subdivision of classes had continued into modern times, the lords employing themselves uselessly . . . while the lower classes labored at industrial pursuits to support the whole of society. The leisure class, Veblen said, justifies itself solely by practicing 'conspicuous leisure and conspicuous consumption'; he defined waste as any activity not contributing to material productivity." Benet Reader's Ency. 4th edition

Warren, Elizabeth, 1949-

This fight is our fight; the battle to save America's middle class. Elizabeth Warren. Metropolitan Books/Henry Holt and Company 2017 337 p. illustrations (hardcover) $28   **305.5**
1. Middle class -- United States 2. Economic policy -- United States 3. United States -- Social conditions 4. United States -- Economic policy -- 2009- 5. United States -- Social conditions -- 1980- 6. United States -- Economic conditions -- 2009- 7. United States -- Politics and government -- 2009-2017
ISBN 9781250120618; 9781250120625

LC 2017007458

This book, by U.S. Senator Elizabeth Warren, is "a passionate, inspiring book about why our middle class is under siege and how we can win the fight to save it. . . . [It offers] an illuminating account of how we built the strongest middle class in history,. . . and a rousing call to action. . . . [The book] tells eye-opening stories about . . . [Warren's] battles in the Senate and vividly describes the experiences of hard-working Americans. . . ." (Publisher's note)

"Warren's education in maneuvering through the powers that be is eye-opening, and she shares her experiences with grim frankness." Kirkus

Includes bibliographical references (pages 271-315) and index.

305.513   Social mobility

Cowen, Tyler

The **Complacent** Class; the self-defeating quest for the American dream. Tyler Cowen. St. Martin's Press 2017 256 p. (ebook) $60; $28.99   **305.513**
1. Economic conditions 2. Social classes -- United States 3. United States -- Social conditions
ISBN 9781250108708; 1250108691; 9781250108692

LC 2016049031

This book, by Tyler Cowen, examines the trend how Americans "are postponing change, due to . . . extreme desire for comfort. . . . The forces unleashed by the Great Stagnation will eventually lead to a major fiscal and budgetary crisis: impossibly expensive rentals, . . . worsening of residential segregation, and a decline in our work ethic. The only way to avoid this difficult future is for Americans to . . . embrace their restless tradition again." (Publisher's note)

"A book that will undoubtedly stir discussion—as many of Cowen's books do—with readers divided about how they stand based on where they currently sit." Kirkus

Includes bibliographical references (pages 205-231) and index.

305.55   Middle class

Reeves, Richard V.

Dream hoarders; how the American upper middle class is leaving everyone else in the dust, why that is a problem, and what to do about it. Richard V. Reeves. Brookings Institution Press 2017 196 p. (hardback) $24   **305.55**

1. Equality 2. Middle class -- United States 3. Income distribution -- United States
ISBN 9780815729129; 9780815729136

LC 2017010289

In this book author Richards V. Reeves "argues that society can take effective action to reduce opportunity hoarding and thus promote broader opportunity. This fascinating book shows how American society has become the very class-defined society that earlier Americans rebelled against--and what can be done to restore a more equitable society." (Publisher's note)

Includes bibliographical references and index.

305.8   Ethnic and national groups

★ The **African** American almanac; Christopher A. Brooks, editor; foreword by Benjamin Jealous. 11th ed; Gale Cengage Learning 2011 1601p il map $297   **305.8**
1. Reference books 2. African Americans
ISBN 978-1-4144-4547-2

First edition under the editorship of Harry A. Ploski published 1967 by Bellwether with title: The Negro almanac. Periodically revised. Editors vary

"Reference covering the cultural and political history of Black Americans. Includes generous amount of statistical information and biographies of Black Americans, both historical and contemporary." N Y Public Libr. Book of How & Where to Look It Up

Anderson, Carol (Carol Elaine), 1959-
White Rage; The Unspoken Truth of Our Racial Divide. by Carol Anderson. St. Martin's Press 2016 272 p. $26   **305.8**
1. Racism -- History 2. United States -- Race relations -- History
ISBN 1632864126; 9781632864123

LC 2015049398

National Book Critics Circle Award: Criticism (2017)

In this book, by Carol Anderson, "since 1865 and the passage of the Thirteenth Amendment, every time African Americans have made advances towards full participation in our democracy, white reaction has fueled a deliberate and relentless rollback of their gains. . . . Anderson pulls back the veil that has long covered actions made in the name of protecting democracy, fiscal responsibility, or protection against fraud, rendering visible the long lineage of white rage." (Publisher's note)

Includes bibliographical references (pages 167-229) and index.

Asch, Chris Myers
★ **Chocolate** City; a history of race and democracy in the nation's capital. Chris Myers Asch and George Derek Musgrove. University of North Carolina Press 2017 xii, 609 p.p (cloth: alk. paper) $39.95   **305.8**
1. Democracy -- United States 2. Washington (D.C.) -- History 3. United States -- Race relations 4. Washington (D.C.) -- Race relations 5. African Americans -- Washington (D.C.) -- History
ISBN 1469635860; 9781469635866

LC 2017026934

This book, by Chris Myers Asch and George Derek Musgrove, "tells the tumultuous, four-century story of race and democracy in our nation's capital. Emblematic of the ongoing tensions between America's expansive democratic promises and its enduring racial realities, Washington often has served as a national battleground for contentious issues, including slavery, segregation, civil rights, the drug war, and gentrification." (Publisher's note)

An ambitious, kaleidoscopic history of race and politics in Washington, D.C. . . Essential American history, deeply researched and written with verve and passion.

Includes bibliographical references and index.

Bayoumi, Moustafa
How does it feel to be a problem? being young and Arab in America. Penguin Press 2008 290p pa $15; $24.95   **305.8**
1. Arab American youth 2. Young men -- Psychology 3. Young men -- United States 4. Race awareness -- United States 5. United States -- Race relations 6. Arab Americans -- Ethnic identity 7. Arab Americans -- Social conditions 8. Brooklyn (New York, N.Y.) -- Ethnic relations
ISBN 978-0-14-311541-0 pa; 978-1-59420-176-9

LC 2007-49272

This book is based on interviews with seven young Arab Americans who live in Brooklyn. It "evaluates their daily encounters with such factors as prejudice, the Christian faith, and their relationships with friends and family members in the Middle East." (Publisher's note)

The author "wondered how younger generations of Arab Americans were faring in a post-9/11 U.S. against the backdrop of fear and suspicion. By focusing on the lives of seven young people living in Brooklyn, Bayoumi offers a revealing portrait of life for people who are often scrutinized but seldom heard from." Booklist

Includes bibliographical references

Berlin, Ira, 1941-2018
The **making** of African America; the four great migrations. Viking 2010 304p $27.95   **305.8**
1. Slave trade 2. Internal migration 3. African Americans -- History 4. Slave trade -- United States 5. African Americans -- Migrations -- History 6. United States -- Immigration and emigration 7. Migration, Internal -- United States -- History 8. United States -- Emigration and immigration -- History
ISBN 978-0-670-02137-6; 0-670-02137-7

LC 2009-28366

"This . . . book proposes a new framework for African American history. Breaking with what he calls the 'master narrative' that frames the subject as an ongoing struggle for freedom and equality, Ira Berlin argues that the experience of relocation and the formation of new communities in new contexts have been pivotal in the making and remaking of African American society. . . . Based on secondary sources, this . . . book briskly narrates four hundred years of history, highlighting the 'four great migrations.' . . . 'The Making of African America' aims to show how migrations reorganized culture and social life. Each of his four major relocations yields a new African America." (Journal of American History)

"Berlin's neat synthesis offers the sharp insights and provocative commentary of one of the foremost historians of black America. Essential for library collections, general readers, and scholars of African American history." Libr J

Includes bibliographical references

Bishop, Bill
The **big** sort; why the clustering of like-minded America is tearing us apart. with Robert G. Cushing. Houghton Mifflin 2008 370p il map $25   **305.8**
1. Minorities 2. Minorities -- United States 3. Regionalism -- United States 4. Segregation -- United States 5. Regionalism -- Political aspects 6. Social conflict -- United States 7. Political culture -- United States 8. United States -- Social conditions 9. Group identity -- Political aspects 10. United States -- Social conditions -- 1980- 11. United States -- Politics and government -- 1989-

ISBN 0-618-68935-4; 978-0-618-68935-4

LC 2007-43907

This volume originated in a series of articles written by journalist Bill Bishop and sociologist Robert Cushing, contending that "Americans have been sorting themselves over the past three decades into . . . homogeneous communities, not by region or by red state or blue state, but by city and even neighborhood." (Publisher's note) Index.

"Bishop's argument is meticulously researched—surveys and polls proliferate—and his reach is broad. . . . [The] portrait of our 'post materialistic' society will . . . generate chatter [and] the idea is catchy." Publ Wkly

Includes bibliographical references

Biss, Eula

Notes from no man's land; American essays. Graywolf Press 2009 230p **305.8**

1. Poets 2. Authors 3. Essayists 4. Group identity -- United States 5. United States -- Race relations 6. United States -- Description and travel

ISBN 1-55597-518-6; 978-1-55597-518-0

LC 20080935599

"In a book that begins with a series of lynchings and ends with a series of apologies, Eula Biss explores race in America. Her response to the topic is informed by the experiences chronicled in these essays--teaching in a Harlem school on the morning of 9/11, reporting for an African American newspaper in San Diego, watching the aftermath of Katrina from a college town in Iowa, and settling in Chicago's most diverse neighborhood." (Publisher's note)

"These essays are about many things, but the theme of race runs through them all. They are not 'about' race, however, not in the way essays are usually 'about' something. Instead of presenting her opening gambits and using the body of the essay to support her initial points, Biss finds her jumping-off point and examines her observations and experiences. Although her juxtapositions are occasionally forced, it is impossible to remain unmoved by Biss's work." Libr J

Blackmon, Douglas A.

Slavery by another name; the re-enslavement of Black people in America from the Civil War to World War II. Doubleday 2008 466p il $29.95; pa $16.95 **305.8**

1. Slavery -- United States 2. United States -- Race relations 3. African Americans -- Civil rights

ISBN 978-0-385-50625-0; 0-385-50625-2; 978-0-385-72270-4 pa; 0-385-72270-2 pa

LC 2007-34500

The author "gives a groundbreaking and disturbing account of a sordid chapter in American history—the lease (essentially the sale) of convicts to commercial interests between the end of the 19th century and well into the 20th. . . . [The] book reveals in devastating detail the legal and commercial forces that created this neoslavery along with deeply moving and totally appalling personal testimonies of survivors." Publ Wkly

Includes bibliographical references (p. 444-459)

Brown, Brene

Braving the wilderness; the quest for true belonging and the courage to stand alone. Brene Brown. Random House 2017 194 p. (hardback) $28 **305.8**

1. Spiritual life 2. Interpersonal relations 3. Individuality 4. Group identity

ISBN 9780812995848

LC 2017030221

In this book, Brene "Brown redefines what it means to truly belong in an age of increased polarization. With her trademark mix of research, storytelling, and honesty, Brown will again change the cultural conversation while mapping a clear path to true belonging. Brown argues that we're experiencing a spiritual crisis of disconnection, and introduces four practices of true belonging that challenge everything we believe about ourselves and each other." (Publisher's note)

"Grounded by moving interviews, case studies, her experience spearheading four educational companies, and a winning combination of perceptiveness and humor, Brown's enthusiastic narrative urges readers to discover their own 'wilderness' by culling the strength and determination (and risk) necessary to truly live 'from our wild heart rather than our weary hurt.' Nothing truly groundbreaking, but an enthusiastic, practical guide to achieving a healthy sense of interconnectedness within one's culture and community." Kirkus.

Chang, Jeff

We gon' be alright; notes on race and resegregation. Jeff Chang. Picador 2016 208 p. (ebook) $60; (trade pbk.) $16 **305.8**

1. Racism -- United States 2. Segregation -- United States 3. Multiculturalism -- United States 4. Equality -- United States 5. Minorities -- United States 6. Social change -- United States 7. United States -- Race relations 8. Cultural pluralism -- United States

ISBN 9781250114792; 9780312429485

LC 2016038855

In this book of essays, author Jeff Chang "explores the rise and fall of the idea of 'diversity,' the roots of student protest, changing ideas about Asian Americanness, and the impact of a century of racial separation in housing. He argues that resegregation is the unexamined condition of our time, the undoing of which is key to moving the nation forward to racial justice and cultural equity." (Publisher's note)

"A compelling and intellectually thought-provoking exploration of the quagmire of race relations." Kirkus

Includes bibliographical references

Chesler, Phyllis

The **new** anti-semitism; the current crisis and what we must do about it. Jossey-Bass 2003 307p $24.95; pa $15.95 **305.8**

1. Antisemitism 2. Israel-Arab conflicts

ISBN 0-7879-6851-X; 0-7879-7803-5 pa

LC 2003-6448

The author "addresses what she sees as a re-emergence of virulent anti-Jewish hatred cloaked in 'political correctness,' closely linked to anti-American attitudes, sustained by many liberal feminists, intellectuals and Jewish leftists, acted upon by Islamic terrorists and jihadists, and fueled by a 'demonization of Jews' in the media. One of the main thrusts of Chesler's argument is that in our contemporary world anti-Zionism is nearly inseparable from anti-Semitism, and that while there are valid criticisms to be made of Israeli policies—for instance, she sees the West Bank settlements as an impediment to peace—many of these critiques are, she contends, rooted in a profound and socially accepted anti-Semitism." Publ Wkly

Includes bibliographical references

Coates, Ta-Nehisi, 1975-

★ **Between** the World and Me; Ta-Nehisi Coates. Random House Inc. 2015 176 p. illustrations (hardback) $24.00 **305.8**

1. United States -- Race relations 2. African Americans -- Social conditions

ISBN 0812993543; 9780812993547

LC 2015008120

Alex Award (2016)

National Book Critics Circle Award Finalist: Criticism (2015)

NAACP Image Award: Outstanding Literary Work- Biography/Autobiography (2016)

National Book Award: Nonfiction (2015)

Pulitzer Prize Finalist: General Nonfiction (2016)

Kirkus Prize: Nonfiction (2015)

This book, by Ta-Nehisi Coates, argues "Americans have built an empire on the idea of 'race,' a falsehood that damages us all but falls most heavily on the bodies of black women and men--bodies exploited through slavery and segregation and, today, threatened, locked up, and murdered out of all proportion. What is it like to inhabit a black body and find a way to live within it? And how can we all honestly reckon with this fraught history and free ourselves from its burden?" (Publisher's note)

"In this brief book, which takes the form of a letter to the author's teenage son, Coates . . . comes to grips with what it means to be black in America today. . . . There is awesome beauty in the power of his prose and vital truth on every page." Booklist

Curtis, Edward E., 1970-

Muslims in America; a short history. Oxford University Press 2009 144p il (Religion in American life) pa $12.95 **305.8**

1. Muslims 2. Ethnic relations 3. Islam 4. Muslims -- United States 5. Islam -- United States -- History 6. Muslims -- United States -- History 7. United States -- Religious life and customs

ISBN 978-0-19-536756-0

LC 2008-47566

The author "has authored a fine and succinct history that spans centuries. . . . Although geared toward non-Muslims, American Muslims would also learn a great deal from reading about their own history. . . . [Readers] will undoubtedly be intrigued by Curtis's compelling little read." Publ Wkly

Includes bibliographical references

DiAngelo, Robin

White fragility; why it's so hard for white people to talk about racism. Robin DiAngelo, with foreword by Michael Eric Dyson. Beacon Press 2018 192 p. (pbk.: alk. paper) $16 **305.8**

1. Racism 2. Whites 3. Race relations

ISBN 9780807047415

LC 2018003562

This book, by Robin DiAngelo, with foreword by Michael Eric Dyson, explores "the counterproductive reactions white people have when their assumptions about race are challenged, and how these reactions maintain racial inequality. . . . [DiAngelo and Dyson] deftly illuminates the phenomenon of white fragility and allows us to understand racism as a practice not restricted to 'bad people.'" (Publisher's note)

"While especially helpful for those new to the critical analysis of whiteness, this work also offers a useful refresher to anyone committed to the ongoing process of self-assessment and antioppression work." Library Journal

Includes bibliographical references

Du Bois, W. E. B.

The **souls** of Black folk; edited with an introduction and notes by Brent Hayes Edwards. Oxford University Press 2007 xxxvi, 223p il (Oxford world's classics) pa $12.95 **305.8**

1. African Americans

ISBN 978-0-19-280678-9; 0-19-280678-5

LC 2006-35193

First published 1903 by McClurg

"A collection of fifteen essays and sketches by W.E.B. Du Bois. In it he describes the lives of African American farmers, sketches the role of music in their churches, details the history of the Freedman's Bureau, discusses the career of Booker T. Washington, and advocates a commitment to higher education for the most talented African American youth." Benet's Reader's Ency of Am Lit

Includes bibliographical references

Dyson, Michael Eric

★ The **Black** presidency; Barack Obama and the politics of race in America. Michael Eric Dyson. Houghton Mifflin Harcourt 2016 346 p. (hardcover) $27 **305.8**

1. Racism 2. United States -- Race relations 3. African Americans -- Politics and government 4. United States -- Politics and government -- 2009- 5. Race -- Political aspects -- United States 6. Racism -- Political aspects -- United States 7. United States -- Race relations -- Political aspects 8. African Americans -- Politics and government -- 21st century

ISBN 9780544387669; 9780544811805

LC 2015037026

Kirkus Prize Finalist: Nonfiction (2016)

This book, by Michael Eric Dyson, "explores the powerful, surprising way the politics of race have shaped Barack Obama's identity and groundbreaking presidency. How has President Obama dealt publicly with race—as the national traumas of Tamir Rice, Trayvon Martin, Michael Brown, Eric Garner, Freddie Gray, and Walter Scott have played out during his tenure? What can we learn from Obama's major race speeches about his approach to racial conflict and the black criticism it provokes?" (Publisher's note)

"Dyson succeeds admirably in creating a base line for future interpretations of this historic presidency. His well-written book thoroughly illuminates the challenges facing a black man elected to govern a society that is far from post-racial." Kirkus

Includes bibliographical references (pages 282-333) and index.

Tears We Cannot Stop; A Sermon to White America. by Michael Eric Dyson. St. Martin's Press 2017 208 p. $24.99; (ebook) $60 **305.8**

1. United States -- Race relations 2. Racism -- United States -- History -- 21st century

ISBN 1250135990; 9781250135995; 9781250136008

LC 2016498068

This book, by Michael Eric Dyson, "is the book that all Americans who care about the current and long-burning crisis in race relations will want to read. . . . Dyson argues that if we are to make real racial progress we must face difficult truths, including being honest about how black grievance has been ignored, dismissed, or discounted." (Publisher's note)

"With a reading list to encourage further learning, Dyson offers an intellectual framework for everyone to adopt in order to understand and embrace each other's struggles to be united." Booklist

What truth sounds like; Robert F. Kennedy, James Baldwin, and our unfinished conversation about race in America. Michael Eric Dyson. St. Martin's Press 2018 304 p. (hardcover) $24.99 **305.8**

1. Social policy -- United States 2. United States -- Race relations 3. African American civil rights workers -- History -- 20th century 4. African Americans -- Intellectual life 5. Civil rights movements -- United States 6. Cocktail parties -- New York (State) -- New York City 7. Intercultural communication -- United States -- Case studies

ISBN 9781250199416

LC 2018017174

In this book, author Michael Eric Dyson describes how, "in 1963 Attorney General Robert Kennedy sought out James Baldwin to explain the rage that threatened to engulf black America. Baldwin brought along some friends, including . . . activist Jerome Smith. . . . Kennedy walked away from the nearly three-hour meeting angry--that the black folk assembled didn't understand politics. . . . Every big argument about race that persists to this day got a hearing in that room." (Publisher's note)

"Dyson's much-recommended work puts forth the artists and activists who continue to celebrate blackness, offering a welcome reminder of the power of art to maintain dialog with and within America." Library Journal

Includes bibliographical references

Else, Jon

True South; Henry Hampton and Eyes on the prize, the landmark television series that reframed the civil rights movement. Jon Else. Penguin Group USA 2017 416 p. illustrations $30; (ebook) $65   **305.8**

1. African Americans on television 2. Television programs -- Social aspects

ISBN 1101980931; 9781101980934; 9781101980958

LC 2016044049

This book, by Jon Else, "focuses on the tumultuous eighteen months in 1985 and 1986 when 'Eyes on the Prize' was finally created. It's a point where many wires cross: the new telling of African American history, the complex mechanics of documentary making, the rise of social justice film, and the politics of television. . . . [Else's] book braids together battle tales from . . . [the] experiences . . . [of] civil rights workers in the south in the 1960s." (Publisher's note)

"An illuminating look at racial strife and TV history." Kirkus
Includes bibliographical references and index.

Encyclopedia of diversity and social justice; Sherwood Thompson. Rowman & Littlefield 2015 791 p. illustrations (ebook) $295; (cloth: set: alk. paper) $236   **305.8**

1. Social justice 2. Pluralism (Social sciences) 3. Social justice -- Encyclopedias 4. Cultural pluralism -- Encyclopedias

ISBN 9781442216068; 9781442216044

LC 2014028212

This book by Sherwood Thompson "contains over 300 entries alphabetically arranged for straightforward and convenient use by scholars and general readers alike. This reference is a comprehensive and systematic collection of designated entries that describe, in detail, important diversity and social justice themes." (Publisher's note)

"The clarity and depth of the entries make the set suitable for general readers as well as specialists looking to broaden their knowledge." Booklist

Includes bibliographical references and index

Everett, Daniel Leonard

Don't sleep, there are snakes; life and language in the Amazonian jungle. [by] Daniel L. Everett. Pantheon Books 2008 283p il $26.95   **305.8**

1. Pirahã Indians 2. Amazon River valley -- Languages

ISBN 978-0-375-42502-8; 0-375-42502-0

LC 2008-16306

The author "has crafted a fascinating account of his 30 years of linguistics work among the Pirahã (pronounced pee-da-HAN) Indians, a tribal group living along the Maici and Marmelos Rivers in a remote area of western Brazil. . . . With a clear, detail-rich writing style, Everett provides evocative ethnographic descriptions of Pirahã life and culture as well as perceptive linguistic analysis." Libr J

Includes bibliographical references

Franklin, John Hope

★ **From** slavery to freedom; a history of African Americans. [by] John Hope Franklin, Evelyn Higginbotham. 9th ed.; McGraw-Hill 2010 xxv, 710p il map $100.63   **305.8**

1. Slavery -- United States 2. African Americans -- History

ISBN 978-0-07-296378-6; 0-07-296378-6

LC 2009-42935

First published 1947

A survey of African-Americans history from slavery to the present. Includes bibliographical references

★ **Freedom** on my mind; the Columbia documentary history of the African American experience. Manning Marable, general editor; Nishani Frazier and John McMillian, assistant editors. Columbia University Press 2003 734p $80 **305.8**

1. African Americans -- History -- Sources

ISBN 0-231-10890-7

LC 2003-51605

This "anthology features the works of noteworthy figures of African American history and culture . . . and provides a tapestry of personal correspondence, excerpts from slave narratives and autobiographies, leaflets, speeches, oral histories and interviews, political manifestos, song lyrics, and important statements of black institutions and organizations. . . . A necessary text of readings for both introductory and advanced African American studies courses." Choice

Includes bibliographical references

Gates, Henry Louis

In search of our roots; how 19 extraordinary African Americans reclaimed their past. Crown Publishers 2008 438p il map $27.50   **305.8**

1. Genealogy 2. African Americans

ISBN 978-0-307-38240-5

LC 2008-11860

"Bright, inquisitive take on the multifarious murky stories and relationships that make up the history of a dispossessed people." Kirkus

Includes bibliographical references

Life upon these shores; looking at African American history, 1513-2008. Knopf 2011 487p il $50   **305.8**

1. African Americans -- History 2. United States -- Civilization

ISBN 978-0-307-59342-9

LC 2011014277

"With nearly 900 illustrations (formal portraits, news photos, historic lithographs, broadsides, flyers, posters, newspaper clippings, advertisements) complemented by a succinct but informing text, Harvard professor Gates (Black in Latin America) provides a visual sojourn through African-American history, a generally upbeat march from Juan Garrido, accompanying Cortés in 1519, to Barack Obama taking the presidential oath in 2008. Gathered in this chronologically arranged compendium, with its focus on the accomplishments and moments of achievement in the African-American community, is a wealth of materials about the historical, political, social, literary, and scientific events influencing American social and political culture." Publ Wkly

Includes bibliographical references

Griffin, John Howard

★ **Black** like me; 2nd ed; Houghton Mifflin 1977 208p   **305.8**

1. Prejudices 2. African Americans -- Southern States

LC 76-47690

First published 1961

The author, "who is white, a Catholic, and a Texan, conceived and carried out the unusual notion of blackening his skin with a newly developed pigment drug and traveling through the Deep South as a Negro. This book, part of which appeared in the Negro magazine Sepia, is a journal account of that experience." New Yorker

Hahn, Steven

A **nation** under our feet; Black political struggles in the rural South, from slavery to the great migration. Steven Hahn. Belknap Press of Harvard University Press 2003 610p il $35; pa $18.95 **305.8**
1. Southern States -- Race relations 2. African Americans -- Political activity
ISBN 0-674-01169-4; 0-674-01765-X pa

LC 2003-45326

This book "is one of the most important works in American social history to appear in recent years." Nation
Includes bibliographical references

Hargrave, Courtney

Burden; a preacher, a klansman, and a true story of redemption in the modern South. Courtney Hargrave. Convergent Books 2018 xii, 227 p.p $26 **305.8**
1. Ku Klux Klan 2. Race relations 3. White supremacy movements 4. Ku Klux Klan (1915-) 5. Laurens (S.C.) -- Race relations 6. White supremacy movements -- South Carolina -- Laurens
ISBN 1984823337; 9781524762704; 9781984823335

LC 2018013781

This book, by Courtney Hargrave, "explores the choices that led to [Reverend David] Kennedy and [white supremacist Michael] Burden's friendship, the social factors that drive young men to join hate groups, the intersection of poverty and racism in the divided South, and the difference one person can make in confronting America's oldest sin." (Publisher's note)
Includes bibliographical references

Hill, Anita, 1956-

Reimagining equality; stories of gender, race, and finding home. Beacon Press 2011 xxiv, 195p $25.95 **305.8**
1. African American women 2. African Americans -- Housing 3. Houses -- Buying and selling 4. African Americans -- Social conditions
ISBN 978-0-8070-1437-0

LC 2011020232

The author "addresses the prime mortgage debacle, specifically how 'owning a home, and thus acquiring this piece of the American Dream has become increasingly difficult for people of color and single women,' and presents an indictment of subprime and predatory lending." Publ Wkly
Includes bibliographical references

Johnson, Walter

River of dark dreams; slavery and empire in the cotton kingdom. Walter Johnson. The Belknap Press of Harvard University Press 2013 560 p. (hardcover) $35 **305.8**
1. Cotton manufacture 2. Slavery -- United States 3. Mississippi River Valley -- History 4. Slavery -- Mississippi River Valley -- History -- 19th century 5. Mississippi River Valley -- Commerce -- History -- 19th century 6. Cotton growing -- Mississippi River Valley -- History -- 19th century 7. Mississippi River Valley -- Race relations -- History -- 19th century
ISBN 0674045556; 9780674045552

LC 2012030065

This book, by Walter Johnson, explores how "when Jefferson acquired the Louisiana Territory, he envisioned an 'empire for liberty' populated by self-sufficient white farmers . . . , [but] was transformed instead into a booming capitalist economy . . . dependent on the coerced labor of slaves. [The book] places the Cotton Kingdom at the center of worldwide webs of exchange and exploitation that extended across oceans and drove an insatiable hunger for new lands." (Publisher's note)
Includes bibliographical references and index

Kaleka, Pardeep

The **gift** of our wounds; a Sikh and a former white supremacist find forgiveness after hate. Arno Michaelis and Pardeep Singh Kaleka. St. Martin's Press 2018 288 p. $26.99 **305.8**
1. Hate crimes 2. Human rights 3. Social action
ISBN 1250107547; 9781250107541

In this book, Arno Michaelis and Pardeep Singh Kaleka, tell how they establish an organization called Serve 2 Unite [after the Oak Creek tragedy], which works with students to create inclusive, compassionate and nonviolent climates in their schools and communities. Their story is one of triumph of love over hate, and of two men who breached a great divide to find compassion and forgiveness." (Publisher's note)

Kendi, Ibram X.

★ **Stamped** from the beginning; the definitive history of racist ideas in America. Ibram X. Kendi. Nation Books 2016 592 p. (hardcover) $32.99 **305.8**
1. Racism -- History 2. United States -- Race relations 3. Racism -- United States -- History
ISBN 1568584636; 9781568584638

LC 2015033671

National Book Award: Nonfiction (2016)
In this book, author Ibram X. Kendi chronicles "the entire story of anti-Black racist ideas. . . . [He] uses the life stories of five major American intellectuals to offer a window into the contentious debates between assimilationists and segregationists and between racists and antiracists. From Puritan minister Cotton Mather to Thomas Jefferson, from fiery abolitionist William Lloyd Garrison to brilliant scholar W.E.B. Du Bois to legendary anti-prison activist Angela Davis." (Publisher's note)
"Kendi's provocative egalitarian argument combines prodigious reading and research with keen insights into the manipulative power of racist ideologies that suppress the recognition of diversity." LJ
Includes bibliographical references and index

Landrieu, Mitch

In the shadow of statues; a white southerner confronts history. Mitch Landrieu. Viking 2018 240 p. (hardcover) $25 **305.8**
1. Monuments 2. Racism -- United States 3. Monuments -- United States 4. Racism -- Louisiana -- New Orleans 5. Statues -- Louisiana -- New Orleans 6. New Orleans (La.) -- Politics and government 7. Soldiers' monuments -- Louisiana -- New Orleans
ISBN 9780525559443

LC 2018006748

In this book, Mayor Mitch Landrieu, "discusses his personal journey on race as well as the path he took to making the decision to remove . . . [Confederate] monuments, tackles the broader history of slavery, race and institutional inequities that still bedevil America, and traces his personal relationship to this history. His father, as state legislator and mayor, was a huge force in the integration of New Orleans in the 1960s and 19070s." (Publisher's note)

Lehr, Dick

★ The **Birth** of a Nation; how a legendary director and a crusading editor reignited America's Civil War. Dick Lehr. PublicAffairs 2014 368 p. illustrations (hardcover: alk. paper) $26.99   **305.8**

1. United States -- Race relations 2. Motion pictures -- United States 3. Birth of a nation (Motion picture) 4. United States -- History -- Civil War, 1861-1865
ISBN 1586489879; 9781586489878

LC 2014029679

This book, by Dick Lehr, focuses on the 1915 film "The Birth of a Nation," by D. W. Griffith and the efforts to censor it. The film "dramatized the Civil War and Reconstruction in a post-Confederate South. . . . [It] included actors in blackface, heroic portraits of Knights of the Ku Klux Klan, and . . . [f]reed slaves were portrayed as villainous. . . . Monroe Trotter's titanic crusade to have the film censored became a blueprint for dissent during the 1950s and 1960s." (Publisher's note)

"The book culminates, as expected, with the highly publicized battle in Boston over the censorship of Griffith's film. However, the larger story for the reader is Lehr's fascinating portrait of simmering American racial tensions moving into the early 20th century, and his spotlight on men and women who, intentionally or not, helped galvanize painful and necessary conversations about civil rights, race relations, and the power of mass media for decades to come." LJ

Includes bibliographical references and index

Lukas, J. Anthony

Common ground; a turbulent decade in the lives of three American families. Knopf 1985 659p il maps hardcover o.p. pa $18   **305.8**

1. School integration 2. Busing (School integration) 3. Boston (Mass.) -- Race relations
ISBN 0-394-74616-3 pa

LC 85-127

"By focusing on three families—one of them welfare black, one upper-middle-class white and one working-class Irish—a veteran journalist recreates the school-busing struggles of Boston in the 1970s, and delineates . . . the moral complexities of caste and class in America." Newsday

McWhorter, John H.

Losing the race; self-sabotage in Black America. [with a new afterword by the author] Perennial 2001 299p pa $13.95   **305.8**

1. African Americans -- Education 2. African Americans -- Social conditions
ISBN 978-0-06-093593-1; 0-06-093593-6

LC 2001-24092

First published 2000 by Free Press

McWhorter discusses what he sees as "a cult of anti-intellectualism 'that has infected black America. . . . He concluded [black students] were held back by three defeatist thought patterns': the Cult of Victimology, which leads blacks to blame their problems on racism; the Cult of Separatism, which makes blacks think that whatever whites do, they should do the opposite; and the Cult of Anti-Intellectualism, which holds that scholastic excellence is a white thing." Time

Includes bibliographical references

Monterrey, Manuel

Americanos; Latino life in the United States. [by] Edward James Olmos, Lea Ybarra, Manuel Monterrey; preface by Edward James Olmos; introduction by Carlos Fuentes. Little,

Brown 1999 176p il $39; pa $25   **305.8**

1. Latinos (U.S.) 2. Hispanic Americans
ISBN 0-316-64914-7; 0-316-64909-0 pa

LC 98-51930

This work includes essays, poetry, and commentary in English and Spanish by such authors as Carlos Fuentes and Maya Angelou and over 200 photographs of Latin Americans from many parts of the United States.

"This is a beautiful, vibrant . . . book; it may also be one of the more socially important books to appear in some time." Booklist

Murray, Charles, 1943-

Coming apart; Charles Murray. Crown Forum 2012 407 p.   **305.8**

1. Equality 2. Upper class 3. Working class 4. Social conflict 5. Social classes -- United States 6. Social mobility -- United States 7. United States -- Social conditions -- 1980- 8. Whites -- United States -- Social conditions 9. United States -- Economic conditions -- 1945- 10. Whites -- United States -- Economic conditions 11. United States -- Social conditions -- 1960-1980
ISBN 0307453421; 9780307453426; 9780307453440

LC 2011501987

This book argues "that a new upper class and a new lower class have diverged so far in core behaviors and values that they barely recognize their underlying American kinship." It argues that "[t]he top and bottom of white America increasingly live in different cultures, . . . with the powerful upper class living in enclaves surrounded by their own kind, ignorant about life in mainstream America, and the lower class suffering from erosions of family and community life." (Publisher's note)

"Though it provides much to argue with, the book is a timely investigation into a worsening class divide no one can afford to ignore." (Publishers Weekly)

Includes bibliographical references and index

Nelson, Jimmy

Before they pass away; Jimmy Nelson; text, Mark Blaisse. teNeues Verlag 2013 423 p. chiefly color illustrations (hardcover: alk. paper) $150   **305.8**

1. Indigenous peoples 2. Indigenous peoples -- Portraits 3. Indigenous peoples -- Pictorial works
ISBN 3832797599; 9783832797591

LC 2013940504

This book, by Jimmy Nelson, "showcases tribal cultures around the world. With globalization, these societies are to be prized for their distinctive lifestyles, art and traditions. They live in close harmony with nature, now a rarity in our modern era. . . . Nelson not only presents us with . . . images of customs and artifacts, but also offers insightful portraits of people who are the guardians of a culture that they--and we--hope will be passed on to future generations in all its glory." (Publisher's note)

Oluo, Ijeoma

★ **So** you want to talk about race; Ijeoma Oluo. Seal Press 2018 v, 248 p.p (hardback) $27   **305.8**

1. Race awareness 2. United States -- Race relations 3. Race discrimination -- United States 4. Racism -- United States 5. Intercultural communication
ISBN 9781580057561; 9781580056779

LC 2017041919

In this book, author "Ijeoma Oluo offers a contemporary, accessible take on the racial landscape in America, addressing head-on such issues as privilege, police brutality, intersectionality, micro-aggressions, the Black Lives Matter movement, and the 'N' word. . . . Oluo answers the questions readers don't dare ask, and explains the concepts that continue to elude everyday Americans." (Publisher's note)

"A clear and candid contribution to an essential conversation." Kirkus

Includes bibliographical references.

Ortiz, Paul

An **African** American and Latinx history of the United States; Paul Ortiz. Beacon Press 2018 xi, 276 p.p (ReVisioning American history) (hardcover: alk. paper) $27.95 **305.8**

1. African Americans -- History 2. Hispanic Americans -- History 3. Working class -- United States -- History 4. United States -- Race relations 5. United States -- Ethnic relations 6. Anti-imperialist movements -- United States 7. Latin America -- Relations -- United States 8. United States -- Relations -- Latin America 9. Internationalists -- United States -- History 10. Blacks -- Caribbean Area -- Politics and government

ISBN 9780807013908; 9780807013106

LC 2017020565

In this book, author Paul "Ortiz traces . . . the rise and violent fall of a powerful tradition of Mexican labor organizing in the twentieth century, to May 1, 2006, International Workers' Day, when migrant laborers--Chicana/os, Afro-Cubanos, and immigrants from nearly every continent on earth--united in resistance on the first 'Day Without Immigrants.'" (Publisher's note)

"A sleek, vital history that effectively shows how, 'from the outset, inequality was enforced with the whip, the gun, and the United States Constitution.'" Kirkus

Includes bibliographical references (pages 196-259) and index.

Painter, Nell Irvin

The **history** of White people. W.W. Norton 2010 496p il map $27.95 **305.8**

1. Whites 2. United States -- Race relations

ISBN 978-0-393-04934-3; 0-393-04934-5

LC 2009-34515

The author "examines the history of 'whiteness' as a racial category and rhetorical weapon: who is considered to be 'white,' who is not, what such distinctions mean, and how notions of whiteness have morphed over time in response to shifting demographics, aesthetic tastes, and political exigencies. . . . Painter's narrative succeeds as an engaging and sophisticated intellectual history, as well as an eloquent reminder of the fluidity (and perhaps futility) of racial categories." Booklist

Includes bibliographical references

Phillips, Patrick

★ **Blood** at the root; A Racial Cleansing in America. Patrick Phillips. W W Norton & Co Inc 2016 320 p. illustrations (hardcover) $26.95 **305.8**

1. Racism -- Georgia 2. Race discrimination 3. United States -- Race relations -- History 4. Forsyth County (Ga.) -- Race relations -- History

ISBN 0393293017; 9780393293012

LC 2016018237

Carnegie Medal Finalist: Nonfiction (2017)

This book by Patrick Phillips tells "Forsyth's tragic story in vivid detail and traces its long history of racial violence all the way back to antebellum Georgia. Recalling his own childhood in the 1970s and '80s, Phillips sheds light on the communal crimes of his hometown and the violent means by which locals kept Forsyth 'all white' well into the 1990s." (Publisher's note)

"This is a gripping, timely, and important examination of American racism, and Phillips tells it with rare clarity and power." Pub Wkly

Includes bibliographical references and index

Roberts, Dorothy

Fatal invention; how science, politics, and big business recreate race in the twenty-first century. New Press 2011 388p $29.95 **305.8**

1. Race 2. Physical anthropology 3. Genomics 4. Human population genetics

ISBN 9781595584953; 1595584951

LC 2011012830

In this book, "legal scholar and social critic Dorothy Roberts argues that America is once again at the brink of a virulent outbreak of classifying population by race. By searching for differences at the molecular level, a new race-based science is obscuring racism in our society and legitimizing state brutality against communities of color at a time when America claims to be post-racial." (Publisher's note)

The author "examines the development and contemporary consequences of 'race as a political system,' bringing science, law, commerce, and race ideologies, virtual thickets of controversy, under one canopy. . . . Roberts is consistently lucid. Her book is alarming but not alarmist, controversial but evidential, impassioned but rational." Publ Wkly

Includes bibliographical references and index.

Robinson, Eugene

Disintegration; the splintering of Black America. Doubleday 2010 254p $24.95 **305.8**

1. United States -- Race relations 2. African Americans -- Race identity 3. United States -- Social conditions 4. African Americans -- Social conditions 5. African Americans -- Economic conditions

ISBN 978-0-385-52654-8; 0-385-52654-7

LC 2010-20405

"This book will have great appeal to African Americans and others concerned about issues of race and equality." Libr J

Includes bibliographical references

Rothstein, Richard

The **color** of law; a forgotten history of how our government segregated America. Richard Rothstein. Liveright Publishing Corporation 2017 xvii, 345 p.p illustrations, maps (hardcover) $27.95 **305.8**

1. Segregation -- History 2. African Americans -- Segregation 3. Discrimination in housing -- Government policy 4. Urban Planning -- Social aspects 5. Urban Planning -- United States 6. United States -- Politics & government 7. Segregation -- United States -- History -- 20th century 8. United States -- Race relations -- History -- 20th century 9. African Americans -- Segregation -- History -- 20th century 10. Discrimination in housing -- Government policy -- United States -- History -- 20th century

ISBN 1631492853; 9781631492860; 9781631492853

LC 2017004962

This book, by Richard Rothstein, "explores the myth that America's cities came to be racially divided through de facto segregation—that is, through individual prejudices, income differences, or the actions of private institutions like banks and real estate agencies. . . . [It chronicles] nothing less than an untold story that begins in the 1920s, showing how this process of de jure segregation began with explicit racial zoning." (Publisher's note)

"This is essential reading for anyone interested in social justice, poverty, American history, and race relations, and its narrative nonfiction style will also draw general readers." Booklist

Includes bibliographical references and index.

Sabar, Ariel

My father's paradise; a son's search for his Jewish past in

Kurdish Iraq. Algonquin Books of Chapel Hill 2008 332p il map $25.95   **305.8**

1. Sephardim 2. Linguists 3. Jews -- Iraq 4. College teachers
ISBN 978-1-56512-490-5; 1-56512-490-1

LC 2008-24811

Sabar writes about his father's early life as a Sephardic Jew in Iraq and his father's authorship of a dictionary of Neo-Aramaic.

This "is an engaging account of a wonderful, enlightening journey, a voyage with the power to move readers deeply even as it stretches across differences of culture, family, and memory." Christ Sci Monit

Includes bibliographical references

Sokol, Jason

There goes my everything; white Southerners in the age of civil rights, 1945-1975. Knopf 2006 433p il $27.95   **305.8**

1. African Americans -- Civil rights 2. Southern States -- Race relations
ISBN 0-307-26356-8; 978-0-307-26356-8

LC 2005-44488

"This chronicle of the destruction of the white Southern hierarchy belongs in all libraries, public and academic." Libr J

Includes bibliographical references

Thompson, Tracy

★ The **new** mind of the South; an unconventional portrait for the twenty-first century. Tracy Thompson. 1st Simon & Schuster hc. ed. Simon & Schuster 2013 263 p. (hardcover) $26   **305.8**

1. Group identity 2. Southern States -- Civilization 3. Group identity -- Southern States 4. Southern States -- Race relations 5. Southern States -- Civilization -- 21st century
ISBN 1439158037; 9781439158036; 9781439160138

LC 2012021581

This book, by Tracy Thompson, explores the culture of the American South. "Thompson spent years traveling through the region and discovered a South both amazingly similar and radically different from the land she knew as a child. . . . Drawing on mountains of data, interviews, and a whole new set of historic archives, Thompson upends stereotypes and fallacies to reveal the true heart of the South today--a region still misunderstood by outsiders and even by its own people." (Publisher's note)

Includes bibliographical references and index

Thorpe, Helen

Just like us; the true story of four Mexican girls coming of age in America. Scribner 2009 387p $27.99   **305.8**

1. Mexican Americans 2. Hispanic American women 3. Unauthorized immigrants 4. Illegal aliens
ISBN 978-1-4165-3893-6

LC 2009-22722

"Thorpe does a masterful job of exploring issues of class, race, and culture in the American amalgam through the lives of four young Mexican women." Booklist

Those who forget the past; the question of anti-Semitism. edited and with an introduction by Ron Rosenbaum; afterword by Cynthia Ozick. Random House Trade Paperbacks 2004 lxix, 649p pa $16.95   **305.8**

1. Antisemitism
ISBN 0-8129-7203-1

LC 2003-65542

"This is an important and vital contribution to efforts to comprehend what is new and what is the same in this ancient virus of ignorance and hatred." Booklist

Includes bibliographical references

Trillin, Calvin, 1935-

Jackson, 1964; and other dispatches from fifty years of reporting on race in America. Calvin Trillin. Random House 2016 304 p. (hardcover) $27; (ebook) $65   **305.8**

1. Minorities -- United States 2. United States -- Race relations 3. African Americans -- Social conditions 4. Racism -- United States -- History -- 20th century 5. African Americans -- Social conditions -- 20th century 6. United States -- Race relations -- History -- 20th century 7. Minorities -- United States -- Social conditions -- 20th century
ISBN 9780399588242; 9780399588259

LC 2015045274

This book, by Calvin Trillin, offers a "career-spanning collection of articles on race and racism, from the 1960s to the present. In the early sixties, Calvin Trillin got his start as a journalist covering the Civil Rights Movement in the South. Over the next five decades of reporting, he often returned to scenes of racial tension. Now, for the first time, the best of Trillin's pieces on race in America have been collected in one volume." (Publisher's note)

"Haunting pieces that show how our window on the past is often a mirror." Kirkus

★ **We** wear the mask; 15 true stories of passing in America. edited by Brando Skyhorse and Lisa Page. Beacon Press 2017 xii, 204 p.p (pbk.: alk. paper) $18   **305.8**

1. Ethnicity 2. Identity (Psychology) 3. Ethnicity -- United States 4. Passing (Identity) -- United States
ISBN 9780807078983

LC 2016058349

This book, edited by Brando Skyhorse and Lisa Page, "is an illuminating and timely anthology that examines the complex reality of passing in America. Skyhorse, a Mexican American, writes about how his mother passed him as an American Indian before he learned who he really is. Page shares how her white mother didn't tell friends about her black ex-husband or that her children were, in fact, biracial." (Publisher's note)

Includes bibliographical references.

305.868   Spanish Americans

Grande, Reyna

A **dream** called home; a memoir. Reyna Grande. Atria Books 2018 336 p. (hardcover) $26   **305.868**

1. Biography 2. Women authors -- Biography 3. Mexican Americans -- Biography 4. Mexican American women authors -- Biography 5. Mexican Americans -- California -- Biography 6. Iguala de la Independencia (Mexico) -- Biography 7. Teachers -- California -- Los Angeles -- Biography 8. Mexico -- Emigration and immigration -- Social aspects 9. United States -- Emigration and immigration -- Social aspects 10. University of California, Santa Cruz -- Students -- Biography 11. Mexican Americans -- California -- Social conditions -- 20th century 12. University of California, Santa Cruz -- Student life -- 20th century
ISBN 9781501171420

LC 2017053844

In this memoir, author Reyna Grande recounts the emotional and practical challenges she encountered as a young immigrant in the U.S. "When Reyna . . . was nine-years-old, she walked across the US-Mexico border in search of a home, desperate to be reunited with the parents who had left her behind years before for a better life in the City of Angels. What she found instead was an indifferent mother, an abusive, alcoholic father, and a school system that belittled her heritage." (Publisher's note)

Markham, Lauren

★ The **far** away brothers; two young migrants and the making of an American life. Lauren Markham. Crown Publishers 2017 xvi, 298 p.p (hardcover) $27   **305.868**
1. Brothers 2. Unauthorized immigrants 3. United States -- Immigration and emigration 4. Twin brothers -- Biography 5. El Salvador -- Emigration and immigration 6. United States -- Emigration and immigration 7. Salvadorans -- California -- Oakland -- Biography 8. Unaccompanied immigrant children -- United States 9. Refugees -- California -- Oakland -- Social conditions 10. Salvadoran Americans -- California -- San Francisco Bay Area -- Social conditions
ISBN 9781101906187; 9781101906200; 9781101906194
LC 2017000952

This book, by Lauren Markham, "follows the seventeen-year-old Flores twins as they . . . [illegally emigrate to the U.S. from El Salvador.] Soon these unaccompanied minors are navigating a new school in a new language, working to pay down their mounting coyote debt, and facing their day in immigration court, while also encountering the triumphs and pitfalls of life as American teenagers—girls, grades, Facebook—with only each other for support." (Publisher's note)

"This is a timely and thought-provoking exploration of a international quagmire. Markham provides a sensitive and eye-opening take on what's at stake for young immigrants with nowhere else to go." Pub Wkly

Includes bibliographical references and index

305.892   Semites

Goldhagen, Daniel Jonah

The **Devil** That Never Dies; The Rise and Threat of Global Antisemitism. Daniel Jonah Goldhagen. Little, Brown and Co. 2013 432 p. $30   **305.892**
1. Antisemitism 2. Globalization -- Social aspects 3. Antisemitism -- History -- 20th century 4. Antisemitism -- History -- 21st century
ISBN 031609787X; 9780316097871
LC 2013941806

In this book, by Daniel Jonah Goldhagen, "reveals the unprecedented, global form of [antisemitism]; its strategic use by states; its powerful appeal to individuals and groups; and how technology has fueled the flames that had been smoldering prior to the millennium." (Publisher's note)

"Goldhagen . . . comes out swinging in this frontal assault on anti-Semitism and its practitioners . . . . A frightening photograph of a mutable demon so many fail to recognize and continue to embrace." Kirkus

Includes bibliographical references (pages 460-472) and index

Keinan, Tal

God is in the crowd; Twenty-first-century Judaism. Tal Keinan. Spiegel & Grau 2018 352 p. $28   **305.892**
1. Judaism 2. Jews -- Identity 3. Jewish civilization 4. Jews -- Civilization 5. Judaism -- 21st century 6. Judaism and state -- Israel
ISBN 9780525511168; 9780525511175
LC 2018000337

This book, by Tal Keinan, "is an original and provocative blueprint for Judaism in the twenty-first century. Presented through the lens of . . .

Keinan's unusual personal story, it is a sobering analysis of the threat to Jewish continuity. As the Jewish people has become concentrated in just two hubs--America and Israel--it has lost the subtle code of governance that endowed Judaism with dynamism and relevance in the age of Diaspora." (Publisher's note)

"A thoughtful and relevant assessment of the current state of Judaism." Kirkus

Includes bibliographical references and index

Thornhill, Teresa

Hara Hotel; a tale of Syrian refugees in Greece. Teresa Thornhill. Random House Inc 2018 352 p. $26.95   **305.892**
1. Greece 2. Refugees -- Syria 3. Immigration and emigration
ISBN 1786635194; 9781786635198

This book, by Teresa Thornhill, "chronicles everyday life in a makeshift refugee camp on the forecourt of a petrol station in northern Greece. In the first two months of 2016, more than 100,000 refugees arrived in Greece. Half of them were fleeing war-torn Syria, seeking a safe haven in Europe. As the numbers seeking refuge soared, many were stranded in temporary camps, staffed by volunteers." (Publisher's note)

Vincent, Leah

Cut me loose; sin and salvation after my ultra-Orthodox girlhood. by Leah Vincent. Nan A. Talese/Doubleday 2014 viii, 228 p.p (alk. paper) $25.95   **305.892**
1. Jewish women 2. Jewish women -- New York (State) -- New York -- Biography 3. Ultra-Orthodox Jews -- New York (State) -- New York -- Biography
ISBN 038553809X; 9780385538091
LC 2013016764

This book, by Leah Vincent, is a "memoir about a young woman's self-destructive spiral after being cast out by her ultra-Orthodox Jewish family. . . . Sent to live on her own in New York City, adrift and unprepared for the freedoms of secular life, Leah's desperate loneliness coupled with her stubborn loyalty to the dogma of her past pulled her into a vicious cycle of promiscuity and self-harm." (Publisher's note)

Wasserstein, Bernard

On the eve; the Jews of Europe before the Second World War. Bernard Wasserstein. Simon & Schuster 2012 xxi, 552 p.p   **305.892**
1. Antisemitism 2. Jews -- Europe 3. Jews -- History 4. Jews -- Social conditions 5. World War, 1939-1945 -- Causes 6. Jews -- Europe -- History -- 20th century 7. Jews -- Persecutions -- Europe -- History -- 20th century
ISBN 1416594272; 9781416594277; 9781416594284; 9781439101698
LC 2011020529

This book by Bernard Wasserstein "presents a[n] . . . interpretation of the collapse of European Jewish civilization even before the Nazi onslaught." Wasserstein "focuses not on the anti-Semites but on the Jews . . . refut[ing] the common misconception that they were unaware of the gathering forces of their enemies. . . . It explores their hopes, anxieties, and ambitions, their family ties, social relations, and intellectual creativity." (Publisher's note)

Includes bibliographical references and index.

Weisman, Jonathan

(((Semitism))) being Jewish in America in the age of Trump. Jonathan Weisman. St. Martin's Press 2017 240 p. (hardcover) $25.99   **305.892**
1. Antisemitism 2. Jews -- United States -- History 3. United

States -- Politics and government -- 21st century 4. Religious right -- United States 5. Jews -- United States -- Public opinion 6. Jews -- United States -- Ethnic relations 7. Jews -- United States -- History -- 21st century 8. Antisemitism -- United States -- History -- 21st century

ISBN 9781250169938; 9781250169945

LC 2017043692

This book, by Jonathan Weisman, is "a short, literary, powerful contemplation on how Jews are viewed in America since the election of Donald J. Trump, and how we can move forward to fight anti-Semitism. . . . Weisman explores the disconnect between his own sense of Jewish identity and the expectations of his detractors and supporters. He delves into the rise of the Alt Right, their roots in older anti-Semitic organizations . . . and their aims." (Publisher's note)

" An urgent and compelling report on the clear and present danger of proto-fascism in the U.S." Kirkus

305.893   Non-Semitic Afro-Asiatic peoples

Iftin, Abdi Nor

Call me American; a memoir. Abdi Nor Iftin. Alfred A. Knopf 2018 320 p. (hardcover) $26.95   **305.893**
1. Muslims -- Biography 2. Somali Americans -- Biography 3. Immigrants -- United States -- Biography 4. Muslims -- Maine -- Biography 5. Immigrants -- Maine -- Biography 6. Somali Americans -- Maine -- Biography

ISBN 9780525433026; 9781524732196

LC 2017043213

In this memoir, Abdi Nor Iftin describes his experiences as "a boy living in war-torn Somalia who escapes to America. . . . Sporting American clothes and dance moves, he became known around Mogadishu as Abdi American. . . . As life in Somalia grew more dangerous, Abdi was left with no choice but to flee to Kenya as a refugee. In an amazing stroke of luck, Abdi won entrance to the U.S. in the annual visa lottery, though his route to America . . . did not come easily." (Publisher's note)

305.896   Africans and people of African descent

Badkhen, Anna, 1976-

Walking With Abel; Journeys With the Nomads of the African Savannah. by Anna Badkhen. Penguin Group USA 2015 320 p. illustrations $27.95   **305.896**
1. Africa 2. Nomads

ISBN 1594632480; 9781594632488

LC 2015004476

In this book, journalist Anna Badkhen "embeds herself with a family of Fulani cowboys-- nomadic herders in Mali's Sahel grasslands-- as they embark on their annual migration across the savanna. It[s a cycle that connects the Fulani to their past even as their present is increasingly under threat-- from Islamic militants, climate change, and the ever-encroaching urbanization that lures away their young." (Publisher's note)

"Readers with hectic lives may find the pace a bit slow, but the poetry in Badkhen's prose demands that readers slow down and savor her gentle, elegant story." Kirkus

Brown, Austin Channing

I'm still here; Black dignity in a world made for whiteness. Austin Channing Brown. Random House Inc 2018 192 p. $25   **305.896**
1. United States -- Race relations 2. African American women --

Biography 3. Women political activists -- Biography

ISBN 1524760854; 9781524760854

LC 2017301173

This memoir of Austin Channing Brown, "is a powerful account of how and why our actions so often fall short of our words. Austin writes in breathtaking detail about her journey to self-worth and the pitfalls that kill our attempts at racial justice, in stories that bear witness to the complexity of America's social fabric--from Black Cleveland neighborhoods to private schools in the middle-class suburbs, from prison walls to the boardrooms at majority-white organizations." (Publisher's note)

"An eloquent argument for meaningful reconciliation focused on racial injustice rather than white feelings." Booklist

Du Bois, W. E. B.

The **Oxford** W. E. B. Du Bois reader; edited by Eric J. Sundquist. Oxford Univ. Press 1996 680p pa $34.95 **305.896**
1. African Americans 2. United States -- Race relations

ISBN 0-19-509178-7

LC 95-21307

This reader covers Du Bois's "writing career, from the 1890s through the early 1960s. The volume selects key essays and longer works that portray the range of Du Bois's thought on such subjects as African American culture, the politics and sociology of American race relations, art and music, black leadership, gender and women's rights, Pan-Africanism and anti-colonialism, and Communism in the U.S. and abroad." Publisher's note

Includes bibliographical references

★ The **Fire** This Time; A New Generation Speaks About Race. edited by Jesmyn Ward. Simon & Schuster 2016 288 p. $26   **305.896**
1. Racism 2. African Americans 3. United States -- Race relations

ISBN 1501126342; 9781501126345

LC 2016005371

This book, by Jesmyn Ward, is a "collection of essays and poems about race. . . . In light of recent tragedies and widespread protests across the nation, The Progressive magazine republished one of its most famous pieces: James Baldwin's 1962 'Letter to My Nephew.' . . . Ward knows that Baldwin's words ring as true as ever today. In response, she has gathered short essays, memoir, and a few essential poems to engage the question of race in the United States." (Publisher's note)

"Ward's remarkable achievement is the gift of freshly minted perspectives on a tale that may seem old and twice-told. Readers in search of conversations about race in America should start here." Pub Wkly

Gates, Henry Louis

The **future** of the race; by Henry Louis Gates, Jr. and Cornel West. Knopf 1996 196p hardcover o.p. pa $12.95 **305.896**
1. Authors 2. Novelists 3. Historians 4. Editors 5. Essayists 6. Sociologists 7. Nonfiction writers 8. Civil rights activists 9. United States -- Race relations 10. African Americans -- Intellectual life 11. African Americans -- Social conditions

ISBN 0-679-44405-X; 0-679-76378-3 pa

LC 96-14450

"Gates and West explore the challenge of W.E.B. DuBois's famous essay 'The Talented Tenth' and consider the future of African American society in light of it. . . . The authors examine the responsibility of the successful and talented black middle and upper classes to uplift the impoverished. . . . The text includes DuBois's 'The Talented Tenth' and, reprinted for the first time, his 1948 critique of it." Libr J

Includes bibliographical references

Jerkins, Morgan

This will be my undoing; living at the intersection of black, female, and feminist in (white) America. Morgan Jerkins. Harper Perennial 2018 258 p. (paperback) $15.99 **305.896**
1. African American women 2. Women -- Social conditions 3. Women -- Economic conditions 4. African Americans -- Social conditions 5. African Americans -- Economic conditions 6. African American women -- Social conditions 7. African American women -- Economic conditions
ISBN 9780062666161; 9780062666154; 0062666150

In this essay collection, author Morgan Jenkins takes on "one of the most provocative contemporary topics: What does it mean to 'be'--to live as, to exist as--a black woman today? This is a book about black women, but it's necessary reading for all Americans. . . . [She] becomes both narrator and subject to expose the social, cultural, and historical story of black female oppression that influences the black community as well as the white, male-dominated world at large." (Publisher's note)

"Jerkins has penned a complex look at what it means to be an African American woman who subscribes to the tenets of feminism but finds herself marginalized by and chained to a narrative crafted for her, not by her." SLJ
Includes bibliographical references.

Johnson, Yvette

The **song** and the silence; a story about family, race, and what was revealed in a small town in the Mississippi Delta while searching for Booker Wright. Yvette Johnson. Atria Books 2017 xx, 315 p.p (hardcover) $26 **305.896**
1. Racism 2. Victims of crimes 3. African Americans -- Southern States 4. Murder victims -- Mississippi -- Greenwood -- Biography 5. African Americans -- Mississippi -- Greenwood -- Biography 6. Racism -- Mississippi -- Greenwood -- History -- 20th century 7. Greenwood (Miss.) -- Race relations -- History -- 20th century
ISBN 1476754942; 9781476754949; 9781476754963
LC 2016055229

In this book, the author "travels to Greenwood, Mississippi, a beautiful Delta town steeped in secrets and a scarred past, to interview family members and townsfolk about the real Booker Wright. As she uncovers her grandfather's compelling story and gets closer to the truth behind his murder, she also confronts her own conflicted feelings surrounding race, family, and forgiveness." (Publisher's note)

"Johnson brilliantly constructs a complex and empathetic look at racism in the South." Pub Wkly
Includes bibliographical references.

Kelly, Joseph

America's longest siege; Charleston, slavery, and the slow march toward Civil War. by Joseph Kelly. Overlook Duckworth 2013 384 p. ill., maps (hardcover) $28.95 **305.896**
1. Slavery -- United States 2. Charleston (S.C.) -- History -- Siege, 1863 3. Charleston (S.C.) -- History -- 1775-1865 4. Charleston (S.C.) -- Race relations -- History 5. Slaves -- South Carolina -- Charleston -- History 6. Slavery -- South Carolina -- Charleston -- History 7. African Americans -- South Carolina -- Charleston -- Social conditions
ISBN 159020719X; 9781590207192
LC 2013015841

In this book, Joseph Kelly "examines the great ideological dispute [around slavery] that underpinned the Civil War by focusing on [Charleston, South Carolina's] long-running internal conflict regarding its moral distaste for and economic addiction to slave labor (Charleston was a major port for incoming slaves)." Kelly "traces the development

of the town's views on slavery while simultaneously relating attempts to break down or bulwark the institution." (Publishers Weekly)
Includes bibliographical references and index.

King, Gilbert, 1962-

★ **Devil** in the grove; Thurgood Marshall, the Groveland Boys, and the dawn of a new America. Gilbert King. Harper 2012 x, 434 p.p ill. **305.896**
1. Civil rights 2. Florida -- Race relations 3. United States -- History -- 1945-1953 4. Rape -- Florida -- Groveland 5. African Americans -- Civil rights 6. Groveland (Fla.) -- Race relations 7. National Association for the Advancement of Colored People 8. Discrimination in criminal justice administration -- Florida -- Groveland
ISBN 9780061792267; 9780061792281; 9780062097712
LC 2011033757

Pulitzer Prize: General Nonfiction (2013)

This book presents an "account of Thurgood Marshall's role as a prominent civil rights attorney in challenging racist 'justice' in the South. . . . Principally . . . the 1949 arrest and unjust prosecution of four young black men, designated 'the Groveland Boys.' In this case, Marshall and the NAACP pursued every legal remedy to save the lives of these young men falsely accused of rape by a white woman, whose preposterous story went unquestioned by authorities. At great personal risk, Marshall tenaciously challenged the hegemony of McCall, eventually bringing to an end the racist reign of terror in Lake County and drawing it and its underlying mentality to national attention." (Libr J)
Includes bibliographical references (p. [413]-416) and index.

Lebron, Christopher J.

The **making** of Black lives matter; a brief history of an idea. Christopher J. Lebron. Oxford University Press 2017 xxii, 187 p.p (hardcover: alk. paper) $27.95 **305.896**
1. United States -- Race relations 2. African Americans -- Social conditions -- 21st century 3. Racism -- United States 4. Equality -- United States 5. Black lives matter movement 6. African Americans -- Politics and government -- 21st century
ISBN 9780190601348
LC 2016042413

This book, by Christopher J. Lebron, "presents a condensed and accessible intellectual history that traces the genesis of the ideas that have built into the #BlackLivesMatter movement. Drawing on the work of revolutionary black public intellectuals, including Frederick Douglass, Ida B. Wells, . . . and Martin Luther King Jr., Lebron clarifies what it means to assert that 'Black Lives Matter' when faced with contemporary instances of anti-black law enforcement." (Publisher's note)

"Throughout five brief essays, an introduction, and an afterword, black scholars consider the persistent failure of the U.S. justice system to redress or remedy the white terrorism responsible for harming black lives." LJ
Includes bibliographical references and index

Lowery, Wesley, 1990-

They can't kill us all; Ferguson, Baltimore & a new era in America's racial justice movement. Wesley Lowery. Little, Brown & Co. 2016 256 p. (ebook) $81; $27 **305.896**
1. African Americans -- Civil rights 2. Racial profiling in law enforcement 3. Race discrimination -- United States
ISBN 9780316502160; 9780316312479
LC 2016948558

This book, by Wesley Lowery, explores the Black Lives Matter movement. It "examines the cumulative effect of decades of racially biased policing in segregated neighborhoods with failing schools, crumbling infrastructure and too few jobs. . . . [The author] offers a historically informed look at the standoff between the police and those they are sworn to protect, showing that civil unrest is just one tool of resistance in the broader struggle for justice." (Publisher's note)

"A timely, significant book." Kirkus

Includes bibliographical references (pages 237-240) and index.

Raboteau, Emily

Searching for Zion; The Quest for Home in the African Diaspora. by Emily Raboteau. Atlantic Monthly Press 2013 320 p. $25 **305.896**
1. Home 2. Blacks
ISBN 0802120032; 9780802120038

This book by Emily Raboteau focuses on "black communities that left home in search of a Promised Land. . . . On her ten-year journey back in time and around the globe, through the Bush years and into the age of Obama, Raboteau wanders to Jamaica, Ethiopia, Ghana, and the American South to explore the complex and contradictory perspectives of Black Zionists." (Publisher's note)

Remembering Jim Crow; African Americans tell about life in the segregated South. edited by William H. Chafe [et al.] New Press (NY) 2001 xxxv, 346p il $55; pa $16.95 **305.896**
1. African Americans -- Segregation 2. Southern States -- Race relations 3. African Americans -- Southern States
ISBN 1-56584-697-4; 1-56584-778-4 pa

LC 2001-31224

Companion volume to Remembering slavery

This work offers "views into the thoughts, activities, and anxieties of black Americans. . . . Included are two one-hour CDs of the radio documentary produced by American Radio Works, a transcript of the audio program, 50 rare segregation-era photographs, biographical information, and suggestions for further reading. This [is a] superb primary source." Libr J

Includes bibliographical references

Starks, Glenn L.

African Americans at Risk; Issues in Education, Health, Community, and Justice. Glenn L. Starks. Greenwood, An Imprint of ABC-CLIO, LLC 2015 832 p. (print: alk. paper) $189 **305.896**
1. African Americans -- Education -- 21st century 2. African Americans -- Social conditions -- 21st century 3. African Americans -- Health and hygiene -- 21st century
ISBN 9781440800764; 9781440800757

LC 2014045530

This book by Glenn L. Starks, examines the issues and policies that put African Americans at risk in our culture today. "Examines up-to-date statistical data on the primary issues negatively impacting African Americans. . . . Provides extensive literary and data analysis of the issues addressed. . . . Supplies concise background and investigates the implications of each key issue . . . [and] includes an extensive bibliographic list of references for all issues discussed." (Publisher's note)

"This is an excellent resource for high-school, public, and academic libraries because it offers comprehensive coverage of important issues facing all communities." Booklist

Includes bibliographical references and index

Whitaker, Mark

Smoketown; the untold story of the other great Black Renaissance. by Mark Whitaker. Simon & Schuster 2018 xxi,

404 p.p illustrations, map (hardcover: alk. paper) $30 **305.896**
1. African Americans -- History 2. African Americans -- Intellectual life 3. African Americans -- Social conditions 4. Pittsburgh (Pa.) -- Civilization 5. Jazz musicians -- Pennsylvania -- Pittsburgh 6. Pittsburgh (Pa.) -- Intellectual life -- 20th century 7. African Americans -- Intellectual life -- 20th century 8. African American athletes -- Pennsylvania -- Pittsburgh 9. African Americans -- Pennsylvania -- Pittsburgh -- History 10. African Americans -- Pennsylvania -- Pittsburgh -- Intellectual life 11. African Americans -- Pennsylvania -- Pittsburgh -- Social conditions -- 20th century
ISBN 9781501122392; 9781501122422; 9781501122439

LC 2017019428

This book, by Mark Whitaker, "is a captivating portrait of [the Black Pittsburgh] community and a vital addition to the story of black America. It depicts how ambitious Southern migrants were drawn to a steel-making city on a strategic river junction; how they were shaped by its schools and a spirit of commerce with roots in the Gilded Age; and how their world was eventually destroyed by industrial decline and urban renewal." (Publisher's note)

"An expansive, prodigiously researched, and masterfully told history." Kirkus

Includes bibliographical references (pages [345]-384) and index.

Young, R. J.

Let it bang; a young black man's reluctant odyssey into guns. R. J. Young. Houghton Mifflin Harcourt 2018 192 p. (hardcover) $25 **305.896**
1. Guns -- Social aspects 2. African Americans -- Social life and customs 3. African Americans -- Race relations 4. African American journalists -- Biography 5. Firearms -- Social aspects -- United States
ISBN 9781328826336

LC 2018012248

In this book, author R. J. Young, tells "the compelling story of [his] unexpected obsession [with guns]--he eventually becomes an NRA-certified pistol instructor--and of his deep dive into the heart of America's gun culture. . . . Through indelible profiles, Young brings us up to the current rocketing rise in gun ownership among black Americans, most notably women. . . . [This is] the story of a young black man's hard-won nonviolent path to self-protection." (Publisher's note)

Includes bibliographical references and index

305.897 North American native peoples

Burns, Mike

The **only** one living to tell; the autobiography of a Yavapai Indian. Mike Burns; edited by Gregory McNamee. University of Arizona Press 2012 179 p. (pbk.: alk. paper) $17.95 **305.897**
1. Yavapai Indians -- History 2. Yavapai Indians -- Biography
ISBN 0816501203; 9780816501205

LC 2011046513

This book is an autobiography of Mike Burns edited by Gregory McNamee. "Mike Burns--born Hoomothya--was around eight years old in 1872 when the US military murdered his family and as many as seventy-six other Yavapai men, women, and children in the Skeleton Cave Massacre in Arizona. One of only a few young survivors, he was adopted by an army captain and ended up serving as a scout in the US army and adventuring in the West." (Publisher's note)

Includes bibliographical references.

Fenn, Elizabeth A. (Elizabeth Anne), 1959-

Encounters at the heart of the world; a history of the mandan people. Elizabeth A. Fenn. Hill and Wang, a division of Farrar, Straus and Giroux 2014 480 p. illustrations, maps (hardback) $35 **305.897**

1. Mandan Indians 2. Native Americans -- History
ISBN 0809042398; 9780809042395

LC 2013032994

Pulitzer Prize: History (2015)

This book, by Elizabeth A. Fenn, tells the "history of the tribe that once thrived on the upper Missouri River in present-day North Dakota. . . . Peaking at a population of 12,000 by 1500, and still a vital presence when Lewis and Clark visited in 1804, the Mandans were besieged by a 'daunting succession of challenges,' including Norway rats that decimated their corn stores, two waves of smallpox, whooping cough, and cholera, reducing their numbers to 300 by 1838." (Booklist)

"A nonpolemical, engaging study of a once-thriving Indian nation of the American heartland whose origins and demise tell us much about ourselves." Kirkus

Includes bibliographical references and index

Talaga, Tanya

Seven fallen feathers; racism, death, and hard truths in a northern city. Tanya Talaga. House of Anansi Press 2017 361 p. maps (paperback) $18.95 **305.897**

1. Indigenous peoples 2. Native peoples -- Canada 3. Native Americans -- Social conditions 4. Canada -- Race relations 5. Thunder Bay (Ont.) -- Race relations 6. Indigenous peoples -- Civil rights -- Canada 7. Indians of North America -- Education -- Ontario, Northern 8. Indigenous peoples -- Ontario, Northern -- Social conditions 9. Indigenous peoples -- Ontario, Northern -- Government relations 10. Indigenous peoples -- Violence against -- Ontario -- Thunder Bay 11. Indigenous peoples -- Ontario -- Thunder Bay -- Social conditions
ISBN 9781487002275; 9781487002268

LC 2016958341

In this book, by Tanya Talaga, "in 1966, twelve-year-old Chanie Wenjack froze to death on the railway tracks after running away from residential school. . . . More than a quarter of a century later, from 2000 to 2011, seven indigenous high school students died in Thunder Bay, Ontario. . . . Talaga delves into the history of this small northern city that has come to manifest Canada's long struggle with human rights violations against indigenous communities." (Publisher's note)

"Talaga's incisive research and breathtaking storytelling could bring this community one step closer to the healing it deserves." Booklist

Includes bibliographical references and index.

305.9 People by occupation and miscellaneous social statuses; people with disabilities and illnesses, gifted people

The **displaced**; refugee writers on refugee lives. Viet Thanh Nguyen. Abrams 2018 240 p. $25 **305.9**

1. Essays 2. Refugees
ISBN 9781419729485

LC 2017949746

In this book, editor and refugee Viet Nguyen "brings together writers originally from Mexico, Bosnia, Iran, Afghanistan, Soviet Ukraine, Hungary, Chile, Ethiopia, and others to make their stories heard. . . . [Their] essays reveal moments of uncertainty, resilience in the face of trauma, and a reimagining of identity, forming a compelling look at what it means to be forced to leave home and find a place of refuge." (Publisher's note)

Martinez, Ruben

★ The **new** Americans; photographs by Joseph Rodríguez. New Press 2004 251p il $25 **305.9**

1. United States -- Immigration and emigration
ISBN 1-565-84792-X

LC 2003-70621

"Masterfully evoking such diverse settings as a Palestinian wedding in Chicago, a raucous ball game in Guatemala City and a torpid migrant trailer camp in California, Martínez's writing is clear-eyed and incisive—and sometimes heartbreaking and hilarious." Publ Wkly

Includes bibliographical references

McDonald-Gibson, Charlotte

Cast away; true stories of survival from Europe's refugee crisis. Charlotte McDonald-Gibson. New Press 2016 xiv, 336 p.p map (ebook) $25.99; (hardcover: alk. paper) $25.95 **305.9**

1. Refugees -- Europe 2. Europe -- Immigration and emigration 3. Mediterranean Region -- Emigration and immigration 4. Refugees -- Mediterranean Region 5. Refugees -- Legal status, laws, etc. -- Europe 6. Europe -- Emigration and immigration -- History -- 21st century 7. Mediterranean Region -- Emigration and immigration -- History -- 21st century
ISBN 9781620972649; 9781620972632

LC 2016019359

Carnegie Medal Longlist: Nonfiction (2017)

This book on Europe's refugee crisis, by Charlotte McDonald-Gibson, "describes the agonizing stories and the impossible decisions that migrants have to make as they head toward what they believe is a better life: a pregnant Eritrean woman, four days overdue, chooses to board an obviously unsafe smuggler's ship to Greece; a father, swimming from a sinking ship, has to decide whether to hold on to one child or let him go to save another." (Publisher's note)

"A powerfully written, well-documented account of a humanitarian crisis of epic proportions." Kirkus

Includes bibliographical references

Nugent, Benjamin

American nerd; the story of my people. Scribner 2008 224p $20 **305.9**

1. Gifted children 2. Creative ability 3. Popular culture -- United States
ISBN 978-0-7432-8801-9; 0-7432-8801-7

A study of the nerd in American popular culture and throughout history discussed in such contexts as the rise of online gaming, the science fiction club, ethnicity, Asperger's syndrome, autism, and high school and college debating.

"In a lighthearted, often laugh-out-loud manner, Nugent challenges us to reexamine our long-held belief of what it means to be a nerd and to reposition the nerd as, if not an American hero, at least an American antihero. Great fun and remarkably insightful between the laughs." Booklist

Pipher, Mary Bray

The **middle** of everywhere; the world's refugees come to our town. {by} Mary Pipher. Harcourt 2002 xxv, 390p $25; pa $14; $23.95 **305.9**

1. Refugees
ISBN 0-15-100600-8; 0-15-602737-2 pa; 9781439560235

LC 2001-5863

"In cities all over the country, refugees arrive daily. Lost Boys from Sudan, survivors from Kosovo, families fleeing Afghanistan and Vietnam: they come with nothing but the desire to experience the American dream. Their endurance in the face of tragedy and their ability to hold on to the virtues of family, love, and joy are a lesson for Americans. Their stories will make you laugh and weep--and give you a deeper understanding of the wider world in which we live. The Middle of Everywhere moves beyond the headlines into the homes of refugees from around the world. Working as a cultural broker, teacher, and therapist, Mary Pipher has once again opened our eyes--and our hearts--to those with whom we share the future." (Publisher's Note)

The author "writes in rich, empathetic language and with a keen, observant eye for detail and nuance." Publ Wkly

Includes bibliographical references

Shannon, Lisa

A **thousand** sisters; my journey into the worst place on earth to be a woman. [by] Lisa J. Shannon; foreword by Zainab Salbi. Seal Press 2010 335p il $24.95   **305.9**
   1. Women -- Congo (Republic)
   ISBN 978-1-58005-296-2

LC 2009-25391

"Shannon presents images of the uncensored horror stories that, to many Congolese, have become regrettably routine: Congo's vile colonial history and the Rwandan genocide spillover that has caused the murders of more than five million Congolese people; children forced to kill and rape in their own communities; daily child deaths from easily curable illnesses; grisly murders of men and children in front of their wives and mothers; families burned alive inside their homes; women who must choose between rape and watching their children starve. . . . Juxtaposing brutality with beauty, Shannon's direct prose is a stirring reminder that these horrors are real and ongoing. An alarming and inspiring message that will hopefully spur much-needed action." Kirkus

Includes bibliographical references

Stephenson, Michael

The **last** full measure; how soldiers die in battle. Michael Stephenson. Crown Publishers 2012 xvi, 464 p.p $28.00; $28.00   **305.9**
   1. Ordnance 2. Soldiers 3. Weapons -- History 4. Military art and science -- History 5. Military history 6. Battle casualties -- History
   ISBN 0307395847; 0307952770; 9780307395849; 9780307952776

LC 2011005874

In this book, "[Michael] Stephenson . . . provides . . . descriptions of the ways in which soldiers have died in battle throughout history. Arranged chronologically, the book begins with analyses of ancient weapons and armor, and the deaths and destruction they caused, and then proceeds through history to discuss modern warfare. The physical and psychological effects of weapons are constant themes." (Library Journal)

Includes bibliographical references (p. [441]-452) and index

305.906 People by miscellaneous social statuses

McDonell, Nick

The **bodies** in person; an account of civilian casualties in American wars. Nick McDonell. Penguin Group USA 2018 304 p. $28   **305.906**
   1. War casualties 2. Iraq War, 2003-2011
   ISBN 0735211574; 9780735211575

In this book, journalist Nick McDonell "introduces us to some of the civilians who died [as a result of America's recent wars,] along with the rescue workers who tried to save them, U.S. soldiers grappling with

their deaths, and everyone in between. He shows us how decent Americans, inside and outside the government and military, looked away from the mounting death toll, even as they claimed to do everything in their power to prevent civilian casualties." (Publisher's note)

306   Culture and institutions

Abby, Laura Leigh

2brides 2be; A Same-sex Guide for the Modern Bride. by Laura Leigh Abby. Archer 2017 224 p. $15.95   **306**
   1. Lesbians 2. Weddings 3. Same-sex marriage
   ISBN 1941729177; 9781941729175

This book, by Laura Leigh Abby, "is a wedding guide for the bride who exudes youth and style no matter what her age, who is inspired by innovation, and who wants to marry the woman of her dreams and do it her way. She is a visionary who is up to the task of blending tradition and rebellion, but she is looking for some practical wedding planning advice. . . . Abby shares her own experiences navigating the world of lesbian wedding planning with a sense of humor and a dose of sass." (Publisher's note)

"An accomplished book about the meaning of marriage for same-sex couples and how to represent that in the wedding." LJ

Brill, Steven, 1950-

★ **Tailspin**; the people and forces behind America's fifty-year fall--and those fighting to reverse it. Steven Brill. Alfred A. Knopf 2018 441 p. illustrations (hardback) $28.95   **306**
   1. Democracy -- United States 2. Social change -- United States 3. United States -- Politics and government 4. Equality -- United States 5. Political culture -- United States 6. United States -- Social conditions -- 1980- 7. United States -- Social conditions -- 1960-1980 8. United States -- Politics and government -- 1989- 9. United States -- Politics and government -- 1945-1989
   ISBN 9781524731649; 9781524731632

LC 2017051857

"In this revelatory narrative covering the years 1967 to 2017, [journalist] Steven Brill gives us a stunningly cogent picture of the broken system at the heart of our society. He shows us how, over the last half-century, America's core values--meritocracy, innovation, due process, free speech, and even democracy itself--have somehow managed to power its decline into dysfunction." (Publisher's note)

"He brings both detailed reporting and wide-ranging perspective to this insightful account of how America reached its current state." Pub Wkly

Includes bibliographical references and index.

Calcaterra, Regina

Girl Unbroken; a sister's harrowing story of survival from the streets of Long Island to the farms of Idaho. Regina Calcaterra. HarperCollins 2016 416 p. (paperback) $15.99   **306**
   1. Adult child abuse victims
   ISBN 9780062412584; 0062412582

In this book, by Regina Calcaterra, the author "pairs with her youngest sister Rosie to tell Rosie's harrowing, yet ultimately triumphant, story of childhood abuse and survival. They were five kids with five different fathers and an alcoholic mother who left them to fend for themselves for weeks at a time. Yet through it all they had each other." (Publisher's note)

"As engrossing as Etched in Sand, this book is a testament to Maloney's remarkable resilience and a moving tribute to the unbreakable bond of love she shared with her siblings. Courageous and emotionally intense." Kirkus

Partanen, Anu

The **Nordic** Theory of Everything; in search of a better life. Anu Partanen. HarperCollins 2016 432 p. $27.99   **306**
1. Scandinavia -- Civilization 2. Social policy -- Scandinavia 3. Scandinavia -- Social conditions
ISBN 0062316540; 9780062316547

LC 2016016859

In this book, author Anu Partanen "compares and contrasts life in the United States with life in the Nordic region, focusing on four key relationships—parents and children, men and women, employees and employers, and government and citizens. She debunks criticism that Nordic countries are socialist 'nanny states,' revealing instead that it is we Americans who are far more enmeshed in unhealthy dependencies than we realize." (Publisher's note)

"An earnest, well-written work worth heeding, especially in our current toxic political climate." Kirkus

Includes bibliographical references (pages 339-397) and index.

Pomerantsev, Peter

Nothing is true and everything is possible; the surreal heart of the new Russia. Peter Pomerantsev. PublicAffairs 2014 256 p. (hardcover) $25.99   **306**
1. Russia 2. Social problems 3. Political corruption 4. Corruption -- Russia (Federation) 5. Interviews -- Russia (Federation) 6. Social change -- Russia (Federation) 7. Social problems -- Russia (Federation) 8. Power (Social sciences) -- Russia (Federation) 9. Russia (Federation) -- Social conditions -- 1991- 10. Russia (Federation) -- Economic conditions -- 1991- 11. Russia (Federation) -- History -- 1991- Biography 12. Authoritarianism -- Social aspects -- Russia (Federation)
ISBN 1610394550; 9781610394550

LC 2014018638

In this book "when British producer Peter Pomerantsev plunges into the booming Russian TV industry, he gains access to every nook and corrupt cranny of the country. As the Putin regime becomes more aggressive, Pomerantsev finds himself drawn further into the system. [He recounts his] voyage into a country spinning from decadence into madness." (Publisher's note)

Shadid, Anthony

House of stone; a memoir of home, family, and a lost Middle East. Anthony Shadid. Houghton Mifflin Harcourt 2012 xviii, 311 p.p (hardback) $26   **306**
1. Family life 2. Arab Americans 3. Houses -- Remodeling 4. Families -- Lebanon 5. Home -- Lebanon -- History 6. Middle East -- Social conditions 7. Lebanon -- Emigration and immigration -- Social aspects
ISBN 0547134665; 9780547134666

LC 2011036906

National Book Awards Finalist (2012)

This memoir offers the following: "an Arab-American story of immigrant roots; an evocation of Lebanon and its anguished history; a lament for a vanishing Middle East; an exploration of the meaning of home. . . . The story of [the] . . . effort [of rebuilding a house in Marjayoun, Lebanon,] forms the frame of the book, with each stage of building intercut by tales of [Anthony] Shadid's globe-straddling family across four generations." (New York Review of Books)

Solnit, Rebecca

★ **Call** them by their true names; American crises (and essays) Rebecca Solnit. Haymarket Books 2018 166 p. $15.95   **306**
1. Social action 2. Social justice -- United States 3. Political culture -- United States
ISBN 1608469468; 9781608469468
Kirkus Prize: Nonfiction (2018)

In this essay collection, author Rebecca Solnit "turns her attention to battles over meaning, place, language, and belonging at the heart of the defining crises of our time. She explores the way emotions shape political life, electoral politics, police shootings and gentrification, the life of an extraordinary man on death row, the pipeline protest at Standing Rock, and the existential threat posed by climate change." (Publisher's note)

"Solnit is careful with her words (she always is) but never so much that she mutes the infuriated spirit that drives these essays." Kirkus

Talbot, David

Season of the witch; enchantment, terror, and deliverance in the City of Love. David Talbot. Free Press 2012 xvii, 452 p.p   **306**
1. Social problems 2. San Francisco (Calif.) -- History 3. Political culture -- San Francisco (Calif.) 4. Social change 5. Counterculture 6. Culture conflict 7. Political culture 8. City and town life 9. San Francisco (Calif.) -- History -- 20th century 10. San Francisco (Calif.) -- Social conditions -- 20th century 11. San Francisco (Calif.) -- Social life and customs -- 20th century
ISBN 1439108218; 9781439108215

LC 2011032082

In this book, author David Talbot "recounts the . . . story of San Francisco in the turbulent years between 1967 and 1982. . . . The cool gray city of love was the epicenter of the 1960s cultural revolution. But by the early 1970s, San Francisco's ecstatic experiment came crashing down from its starry heights. The city was rocked by savage murder sprees, mysterious terror campaigns, political assassinations, street riots, and finally a terrifying sexual epidemic. . . . David Talbot takes us deep into the riveting story of his city's ascent, decline, and heroic recovery. He draws intimate portraits of San Francisco's legendary demons and saviors. . . . He reveals how the city emerged from the trials of this period with a new brand of 'San Francisco values.'" (Publisher's note)

Includes bibliographical references, discography, filmographies, and index.

Underhill, Paco

The **call** of the mall; a walking tour through the crossroads of our shopping culture. Simon & Schuster 2004 227p hardcover o.p. pa $14   **306**
1. Consumers 2. Consumption (Economics) 3. Shopping centers and malls
ISBN 0-7432-3591-6; 0-7432-3592-4 pa

LC 2003-64960

The author takes readers on a "tour of a typical Saturday at a large, regional mall. He examines the routes there, the shopping center itself, the stores, food, entertainment, ambience. and the customers. He shows why the mall is the way it is and how it could be improved. He provides insight into how the stores are arranged, how they display merchandise. and the different ways that men and women respond to this environment." SLJ

Wann, David

The **new** normal; an agenda for responsible living. St. Martin's Griffin 2011 274p il pa $14.99   **306**
1. Lifestyles 2. Social values 3. Conduct of life 4. Quality of life

ISBN 978-0-312-57543-4

LC 2010-37913

"Wann pulls from the disciplines of biology, anthropology, history, and psychology to make his case that the current paradigm of bigger and more is not working. He proposes the 'Era of Emerging Restoration,' in which healthy families, communities, and ecosystems are the best measures of wealth. . . . This is one of the best approaches to promoting a sustainable world." Libr J

Includes bibliographical references

Wilkinson, Richard

The **spirit** level; why greater equality makes societies stronger. Richard Wilkinson and Kate Pickett. Bloomsbury Press 2010 xv, 330 p.p il (hardcover: alk. paper) $28   **306**
1. Equality 2. Social policy 3. Social classes 4. Quality of life 5. Social mobility
ISBN 1608193411; 9781608193417; 9781608190362; 1608190366

LC 2009030428

First published in Great Britain by Allen Lane, 2009

It was the authors' intent to "rank the quality of life in twenty-three countries, mainly European, but with Singapore, Israel, and the United States also on the list. To evaluate the well-being of each society, Richard Wilkinson and Kate Pickett use indices ranging from obesity and incarceration rates to teenage births and the feelings people have about their fellow countrymen. They then relate these variables to how income is distributed in each society. . . . Linking social indicators to economic disparities, the authors conclude that 'reducing inequality is the best way of improving the quality of the social environment.'" (New York Review of Books)

The authors "make an eloquent case that the income gap between a nation's richest and poorest is the most powerful indicator of a functioning and healthy society. . . . Felicitous prose and fascinating findings make this essential reading." Publ Wkly

Includes bibliographical references (p. 27-1297) and index.

306.09   Social history

Easterbrook, Gregg

It's better than it looks; reasons for optimism in an age of fear. Gregg Easterbrook. PublicAffairs 2018 352 p. (hardcover) $28   **306.09**
1. Progress 2. Quality of life 3. Social conditions 4. Social history 5. Economic history 6. Civilization, Modern -- 21st century
ISBN 9781610397414

LC 2017048518

In this book, author Gregg "Easterbrook offers specific policy reforms to address climate change, inequality, and other problems, and reminds us that there is real hope in conquering such challenges. In an age of discord and fear-mongering, . . . [this book] will profoundly change your perspective on who we are, where we're headed, and what we're capable of." (Publisher's note)

Includes bibliographical references and index

Hill, Marc Lamont

Nobody; casualties of America's war on the vulnerable, from Ferguson to Flint and beyond. Marc Lamont Hill. Atria Books 2016 272 p. (ebook) $13.99; (hardback) $26 **306.09**
1. United States -- Race relations 2. United States -- Social conditions 3. Discrimination -- United States 4. Social classes -- United States 5. Social conflict -- United States 6. Police shootings

-- United States 7. African Americans -- Violence against 8. United States -- Social conditions -- 1980- 9. United States -- Race relations -- 21st century
ISBN 9781501124976; 9781501124945; 9781501124969

LC 2016023107

This book, by Marc Lamont Hill, "presents a powerful and thought-provoking analysis of race and class by examining a growing crisis in America: the existence of a group of citizens who are made vulnerable, exploitable and disposable through the machinery of unregulated capitalism, public policy, and social practice. These are the people considered 'Nobody' in contemporary America." (Publisher's note)

"A thought-provoking and important analysis of oppression, recommended for those seeking clarity on current events." LJ

Includes bibliographical references and index

Whippman, Ruth

America the anxious; how our pursuit of happiness is creating a nation of nervous wrecks. Ruth Whippman. St. Martin's Press 2016 272 p. (ebook) $60; (hardcover) $25.99 **306.09**
1. Happiness 2. American national characteristics 3. United States -- Social conditions
ISBN 9781466882669; 9781250071521

LC 2016016272

This book, by Ruth Whippman, reveals "a paradox: despite the fact that Americans spend more time and money in search of happiness than any other nation on earth, research shows that the United States is one of the least contented, most anxious countries in the developed world. Stoked by a multi-billion dollar 'happiness industrial complex' intent on selling the promise of bliss, America appeared to be driving itself crazy in pursuit of contentment." (Publisher's note)

"After putting the book down, readers may well agree with the author that if we want to be happy, what we really need to do is stop chasing after happiness and focus on living fuller lives. A delightfully witty, enjoyable read." Kirkus

Includes bibliographical references and index

306.097   North America – Culture

Fallows, James

★ **Our** towns; a 100,000-mile journey into the heart of America. James Fallows and Deborah Fallows. Pantheon Books 2018 432 p. (hardback) $28.95   **306.097**
1. Social surveys -- United States 2. United States -- Social conditions -- Public opinion 3. United States -- Politics and government -- Public opinion 4. Public opinion -- United States 5. United State -- Social conditions -- Public opinon
ISBN 9781101871843; 9781101871850

LC 2017052007

"For the last five years, James and Deborah Fallows have been traveling across America in a single-engine prop airplane. Visiting dozens of towns, they have met hundreds of civic leaders, workers, immigrants, educators, environmentalists, artists, public servants, librarians, business people, city planners, students, and entrepreneurs to take the pulse and understand the prospects of places that usually draw notice only after a disaster or during a political campaign." (Publisher's note)

"With a commitment to observation and a sincere desire to understand each place on their journey, they offer a fascinating review of the many economic, environmental, educational, and cultural efforts taking place all over America. Far from the national narrative of crisis and decay, the authors suggest that a more hopeful renewal may be under way." Booklist

Haynes, Douglas

★ **Every** day we live is the future; surviving in a city of disasters. Douglas Haynes. University of Texas Press 2017 283 p. (cloth: alk. paper) $27 **306.097**

1. Poor -- Nicaragua 2. Internal migration 3. Women -- Nicaragua 4. Poor -- Nicaragua -- Managua 5. Women -- Nicaragua -- Managua 6. Urbanization -- Nicaragua -- Managua 7. Environmental justice -- Nicaragua -- Managua 8. Rural-urban migration -- Nicaragua -- Managua 9. Managua (Nicaragua) -- Social conditions -- 21st century 10. Managua (Nicaragua) -- Economic conditions -- 21st century

ISBN 9781477313121

LC 2016058954

In this book, by Douglas Haynes, "Dayani Baldelomar. . . . was among tens of thousands of rural migrants to Managua in the 1980s and 1990s. After years of homelessness, Dayani landed in a shantytown called The Widows. . . Her neighbor, Yadira Castellón, also migrated from the mountains. Driven by hope for a better future for their children, Dayani, Yadira, and their husbands invent jobs in . . . spreading markets . . . , joining the planet's burgeoning informal economy." (Publisher's note)

Includes bibliographical references

LeDuff, Charlie

Sh*tshow! the country's collapsing...and the ratings are great. Charlie LeDuff. Penguin Press 2018 288 p. (hardcover) $27 **306.097**

1. United States -- Politics and government -- 2009- 2. United States -- Social conditions -- 21st century 3. United States -- Race relations -- History -- 21st century

ISBN 9780525522027

LC 2018006192

This book, by Charlie LeDuff, is "a daring, firsthand, and utterly-unscripted account of crisis in America, from Ferguson to Flint to Cliven Bundy's ranch to Donald Trump's unstoppable campaign for President. . . . A soul-baring, irreverent, and iconoclastic writer, LeDuff speaks the language of everyday Americans, and is unafraid of getting his hands dirty. He scrambles the tired-old political, social, and racial categories, taking no sides--or prisoners." (Publisher's note)

"This timely portrait of America is a superb example of contemporary gonzo journalism." Pub Wkly

306.2   Cultural institutions

Frank, Thomas

Rendezvous with oblivion; reports from a sinking society. Thomas Frank. Metropolitan Books, Henry Holt & Co. 2018 240 p. (hardcover) $24 **306.209**

1. Political science 2. Political parties -- United States 3. Political culture -- United States 4. Polarization (Social sciences) -- Political aspects -- United States

ISBN 9781250293664

LC 2017060877

This book, by Thomas Frank, "is a collection of interlocking essays examining how inequality has manifested itself in our cities, in our jobs, in the way we travel--and of course in our politics, where in 2016, millions of anxious ordinary people rallied to the presidential campaign of a billionaire who meant them no good. . . . [The essays] capture a society where every status signifier is hollow, where the allure of mobility is just another con game." (Publisher's note)

Freeman, Joanne B.

Affairs of honor; national politics in the new republic. Yale Univ. Press 2001 xxiv, 376p $29.95; pa $16.95 **306.2**

1. United States -- Politics and government -- 1783-1865

ISBN 0-300-08877-9; 0-300-09755-7 pa

LC 2001-915

"Freeman's prose is lively, and she balances entertaining narrative with sharp analysis." Publ Wkly

Includes bibliographical references and index

Goldwag, Arthur

The **new** hate; a history of fear and loathing on the populist right. Arthur Goldwag. Pantheon Books 2012 368 p. $27.95 **306.2**

1. Conspiracies 2. Radicalism -- United States 3. Conservatism -- United States -- History 4. United States -- Politics and government 5. United States -- Ethnic relations -- History 6. Politics and culture -- United States 7. Right-wing extremists -- United States 8. Hate groups -- Political aspects -- United States 9. Conspiracy theories -- Political aspects -- United States

ISBN 0307379698; 9780307379696

LC 2011028589

The author "[Arthur] Goldwag . . . delivers an . . . history of organized hate groups and their role in U.S. politics. Less about prejudice than America's 'relentless quest for scapegoats,' he traces the American conspiratorial tradition from colonial times--where the Puritans feared Jesuit conspiracies as much as Indian ambushes--to the present, covering the movements and vitriolic commentary against the Masons, Catholics, Jews, Communists, and Muslims. . . . Goldwag combines his research with contemporary analysis to explain what conspiracy theories all have in common and to show how the new hate is the same as the old, though it's now 'hiding in plain sight.'" (Publishers Wkly)

Includes bibliographical references and index

Kakutani, Michiko

The **death** of truth; notes on falsehood in the age of Trump. Michiko Kakutani. Tim Duggan Books 2018 208 p. (hardcover) $22 **306.2**

1. Political culture -- United States 2. United States -- Politics and government -- 2017- 3. Truth -- Political aspects -- United States

ISBN 9780525574828

LC 2018010263

In this book, former New York Times critic Michiko Kakutani looks at "how did truth become an endangered species in contemporary America? . . . . Kakutani takes a penetrating look at the cultural forces that contributed to this gathering storm. In social media and literature, television, academia, and politics, Kakutani identifies the trends--originating on both the right and the left--that have combined to elevate subjectivity over factuality, science, and common values." (Publisher's note)

Includes bibliographical references and index

Maddow, Rachel, 1973-

Drift; the unmooring of American military power. Rachel Maddow. Crown 2012 275 p. **306.2**

1. Military policy -- United States 2. United States -- Military history 3. National security -- United States 4. United States -- Foreign relations 5. United States -- Politics and government -- 2001- 6. Militarism -- United States 7. United States -- Military policy 8. Political culture -- United States 9. United States -- Foreign relations -- 1989- 10. United States -- Politics and government -- 1989- 11. United States -- Armed Forces -- Appropriations and expenditures

ISBN 9780307460981; 9780307461001

LC 2012000998

The author "examines how the country has lost control of its national-security policy. The author holds Dick Cheney . . . responsible, . . . associating . . . [him] with the presidential prerogative of war-making powers. . . . American forces are now accompanied by . . . private contractors who perform functions that used to be reserved to the military, without either accountability or military control. . . . She grounds her argument in the Founding Fathers' debates about going to war." (Kirkus Reviews)

Includes bibliographical references and index

Nussbaum, Martha Craven, 1947-

The **monarchy** of fear; a philosopher looks at our political crisis. Martha C. Nussbaum. Simon & Schuster 2018 272 p. (hardcover: alk. paper) $25.99   **306.209**

1. Political psychology -- United States 2. United States -- Politics and government -- 21st century
ISBN 9781501172496; 9781501172519

LC 2017049444

In this book, author Martha C. Nussbaum "turns her attention to the current political crisis that has polarized American since the 2016 election. . . . Nussbaum focuses on what so many pollsters and pundits have overlooked. She sees a simple truth at the heart of the problem: the political is always emotional. Globalization has produced feelings of powerlessness in millions of people in the West. That sense of powerlessness bubbles into resentment and blame." (Publisher's note)

"Nussbaum's erudite but very readable investigation engages figures from Aristotle to Donald Trump in lucid and engaging prose, though some readers may feel she psychologizes politics without grappling sufficiently with positions' substance. Still, Nussbaum offers fresh, worthwhile insights into the animosities that roil contemporary public life." Publishers' Weekly

Includes bibliographical references and index

Sehat, David

The **Jefferson** rule; why we think the founding fathers have all the answers. David Sehat. Simon & Schuster 2015 320 p. (hardcover: alk. paper) $27   **306.2**

1. Political philosophy 2. Founding Fathers of the United States 3. United States -- Politics and government 4. Persuasion (Rhetoric) 5. Political culture -- United States 6. Collective memory -- Political aspects -- United States
ISBN 1476779775; 9781476779775; 9781476779782

LC 2014034708

This book, by David Sehat, "describes how liberals, conservatives, secessionists, unionists, civil rights leaders, radicals, and libertarians have sought out the Founding Fathers to defend their policies. [The author begins] . . . with the debate between Thomas Jefferson and Alexander Hamilton over the future of the nation, and continuing through the Civil War, the New Deal, the Reagan Revolution, and Obama and the Tea Party." (Publisher's note)

Includes bibliographical references and index

Weiler, Jonathan

Prius or pickup? how the answers to four simple questions explain America's great divide. Marc Hetherington and Jonathan Weiler. Houghton Mifflin Harcourt 2018 288 p. (hardback) $28   **306.209**

1. Political science 2. Political psychology -- United States 3. Political culture -- United States 4. Polarization (Social sciences) -- United States
ISBN 9781328866783

LC 2018012316

In this book, "political scholars Marc Hetherington and Jonathan Weiler explains [that] even our smallest choices speak volumes about us--especially when it comes to our personalities and our politics. . . . If we're to overcome our seemingly intractable differences, Hetherington and Weiler show, we must first learn to master the psychological impulses that give rise to them, and to understand how politicians manipulate our mindsets for their own benefit." (Publisher's note)

Includes bibliographical references and index

Wilentz, Sean

The **Politicians** and the Egalitarians; The Hidden History of American Politics. by Sean Wilentz. W W Norton & Co Inc 2016 400 p. $28.95   **306.2**

1. Political parties 2. United States -- Politics and government
ISBN 0393285022; 9780393285024

LC 2016009662

This book, by Sean Wilentz, "reminds us of the commanding role party politics has played in America's enduring struggle against economic inequality. . . . First, America is built on an egalitarian tradition. . . . Second, partisanship is a permanent fixture in America. . . . With these two insights . . . Wilentz offers a crystal-clear portrait of American history, told through politicians and egalitarians including Thomas Paine, Abraham Lincoln, and W. E. B. Du Bois." (Publisher's note)

"In other hands, this would seem silly and lacking force; in Wilentz's, it's authoritative and telling. The result is wonderfully readable and the best kind of serious, sharp argumentation from one of the leading historians of the United States." Pub Wkly

Includes bibliographical references and index.

306.3   Economic institutions

Baptist, Edward E.

★ The **half** has never been told; slavery and the making of American capitalism. Edward E. Baptist. Basic Books 2014 528 p. illustrations, maps (hardcover) $35   **306.3**

1. Capitalism 2. Slavery -- United States 3. Slavery -- Economic aspects 4. African Americans -- Social conditions
ISBN 046500296X; 9780465044702; 9780465002962

LC 2014012546

"As historian Edward Baptist reveals in 'The Half Has Never Been Told,' the expansion of slavery in the first eight decades after American independence drove the evolution and modernization of the United States. . . . Until the Civil War, Baptist explains, the most important American economic innovations were ways to make slavery ever more profitable. Through forced migration and torture, slave owners extracted continual increases in efficiency from enslaved African Americans." (Publisher's note)

"Through an incredible amount of detail and the use of an array of primary sources, the author argues that the South's use of slave labor in cotton production was the primary factor in the United States becoming a leading modern industrial nation." LJ

Includes bibliographical references and index

Davis, David Brion, 1927-

★ The **problem** of slavery in the age of emancipation; by David Brion Davis. Knopf 2014 448 p. (hardback) $30 **306.3**

1. Slavery -- History 2. Slaves -- Emancipation 3. Antislavery movements 4. Free African Americans 5. American Colonization Society
ISBN 0307269094; 9780307269096

LC 2013032893

National Book Critics Circle Award: General Nonfiction (2014)

Author David Brion Davis "offers . . . insights into what slavery and emancipation meant to Americans. He explores how the Haitian Revolution respectively terrified and inspired white and black Americans, hovering over the antislavery debates like a bloodstained ghost, and he offers a surprising analysis of the complex and misunderstood significance of colonization. Davis presents the age of emancipation as a model for reform." (Publisher's note)

"This is a well-researched and broad historical and global analysis of the complex motives and actions on all fronts, highlighting the transcontinental tension between efforts by white society to dehumanize and the fight by freedmen and slaves for freedom, full humanity, and citizenship." Booklist

Includes bibliographical references and index

Dewitt, David

Precious Cargo; How Foods from the Americas Changed the World. by David DeWitt. Counterpoint 2014 256 p. illustrations (chiefly color) $28 **306.3**

1. Food -- History
ISBN 1619023091; 9781619023093

IACP Cookbook Award Winner: Culinary History (2015)

This book, by David DeWitt, "tells the fascinating story of how western hemisphere foods conquered the globe and saved it from not only mass starvation, but culinary as well. Focusing heavily American foods—specifically the lowly crops that became commodities, plus one gobbling protein source, the turkey—Dewitt describes how these foreign and often suspect temptations were transported around the world, transforming cuisines and the very fabric of life on the planet." (Publisher's note)

"Both public and academic libraries will find this a welcome addition to sociological, anthropological, and culinary collections." LJ

DeWolf, Thomas Norman

Gather at the table; the healing journey of a daughter of slavery and a son of the slave trade. Thomas Norman DeWolf and Sharon Leslie Morgan; foreword by Joy Angela DeGruy. Beacon Press 2012 xvii, 212 p.p (hbk.: alk. paper) $25.95 **306.3**

1. Slavery -- United States 2. United States -- Race relations 3. Slavery -- United States -- History
ISBN 0807014419; 9780807014417

LC 2012009318

In this book by Thomas Norman DeWolf and Sharon Morgan "two people--a black woman and a white man--confront the legacy of slavery and racism head-on. . . . [DeWolf and Morgan] visit[ed] ancestral towns, courthouses, cemeteries, plantations, antebellum mansions, and historic sites. They spent time with one another's families and friends and engaged in deep conversations about how the lingering trauma of slavery shaped their lives." (Publisher's note)

Includes bibliographical references (p. 210-212)

Dunbar, Erica Armstrong

Never Caught; The Washingtons' Relentless Pursuit of Their Runaway Slave, Ona Judge. Erica Armstrong Dunbar. Simon & Schuster 2017 304 p. $26 **306.3**

1. Fugitive slaves
ISBN 1501126393; 9781501126390

LC 2016056908

National Book Award Finalist: Nonfiction (2017)

This book, by Erica Armstrong Dunbar, presents "the powerful narrative of Ona Judge, George and Martha Washington's runaway slave who risked it all to escape the nation's capital and reach freedom. . .

. At just twenty-two-years-old, Ona became the subject of an intense manhunt led by George Washington, who used his political and personal contacts to recapture his property." (Publisher's note)

"A startling, well-researched slave narrative that seriously questions the intentions of our first president." Kirkus

Grandin, Greg

The **empire** of necessity; freedom, slavery, and deception in the New World. Greg Grandin. Metropolitan Books/Henry Holt and Company 2013 320 p. illustrations, maps (hardcover) $30 **306.3**

1. Slave revolts 2. Slavery -- History 3. Slavery in literature 4. Slavery -- South America -- History -- 19th century 5. Slave trade -- South America -- History -- 19th century 6. Slave insurrections -- South America -- History -- 19th century
ISBN 0805094539; 9780805094534

LC 2013014309

"Drawing on research on four continents, 'The Empire of Necessity' explores the multiple forces that culminated in [an] extraordinary event--an event that already inspired Herman Melville's masterpiece Benito Cereno. Now historian Greg Grandin . . . uses the dramatic happenings of that day to map a new transnational history of slavery in the Americas, capturing the clash of peoples, economies, and faiths that was the New World in the early 1800s." (Publisher's note)

Hurston, Zora Neale, 1891-1960

★ **Barracoon**; The Story of the Last Black Cargo. by Zora Neale Hurston, with foreword by Alice Walker and introduction by Deborah G. Plant. HarperCollins 2018 208 p. $24.99 **306.3**

1. African Americans -- History 2. Slavery -- United States -- History
ISBN 0062748203; 9780062748201

In this book, "author Zora Neale Hurston, brilliantly illuminates the horror and injustices of slavery as it tells the true story of one of the last-known survivors of the Atlantic slave trade--abducted from Africa on the last 'Black Cargo' ship to arrive in the United States. . . . 'Barracoon' masterfully illustrates the tragedy of slavery and of one life forever defined by it." (Publisher's note)

"This is a fascinating look at the journey of one man, reflective of the African American experience. It also attests to Hurston's development as an author and ethnographer, and stands as a work of profound relevance, its illumination of slavery, freedom, and race as timely as ever." Booklist

Levs, Josh

All in; how our work-first culture fails Dads, families, and businesses--and how we can fix it together. Josh Levs. HarperOne 2015 272 p. (hardcover) $25.99 **306.3**

1. Work and family 2. Father-child relationship 3. Families -- United States 4. Parental leave -- United States 5. Work and family -- United States 6. Father and child -- United States
ISBN 0062349619; 9780062349613; 9780062349620

LC 2014042031

This book, by Josh Levs, "explores the changing face of fatherhood and what it means for our individual lives, families, workplaces, and society. . . . Stay-at-home dads are increasingly common, and growing numbers of men are working part-time or flextime schedules to spend more time with their children. . . . Dads today are . . . 'all in' and--like mothers--they are struggling with work-life balance and doing it all." (Publisher's note)

"Lev's thoughtful plea for men and women to work together is more persuasive, providing a useful guide for those looking to effect change in their own workplaces and communities." PW

Includes bibliographical references

Nathans, Sydney

To free a family; Sydney Nathans. Harvard University Press 2012 330 p. [20] p of plates, ill, maps **306.3**

1. Family 2. Fugitive slaves 3. United States -- History -- 1783-1865 4. Cambridge (Mass.) -- Biography 5. Orange County (N.C.) -- Biography 6. Fugitive slaves -- Northeastern States -- Biography 7. Women slaves -- North Carolina -- Orange County -- Biography 8. African American women -- Massachusetts -- Cambridge -- Biography 9. Family reunions -- Massachusetts -- Cambridge -- History -- 19th century

ISBN 9780674062122

LC 2011023122

This book "tells the . . . story of Mary Walker, who in August 1848 fled her owner for refuge in the North and spent the next seventeen years trying to recover her family. . . . This story is anchored in two . . . collections of letters and diaries, that of her former North Carolina slaveholders and that of the northern family--Susan and Peter Lesley--who protected and employed her." (Publisher's note)

Includes bibliographical references and index

Postma, Johannes

The **Atlantic** slave trade. Greenwood Press 2003 xxii, 177p map (Greenwood guides to historic events, 1500-1900) $45 **306.3**

1. Slave trade

ISBN 0-313-31862-X

LC 2002-35338

The author "covers the entire Atlantic slave trade era, from the 1400s to the final abolition of chattel slavery in the New World in 1888. The focus is on Africa and the entire New World. While he describes the many horrors of the Middle Passage, he also examines how the slave trade contributed to the development of the modern international economy. The last chapters discuss the efforts to abolish the slave trade and its legacy." SLJ

Includes bibliographical references

Rae, Noel

★ The **great** stain; witnessing American slavery. Noel Rae. Overlook Press 2018 592 p. $40 **306.3**

1. Slavery -- United States -- History 2. Slaves -- Emancipation -- United States

ISBN 1468315137; 9781468315134

In this book, author "Noel Rae integrates firsthand accounts into a narrative history that brings the reader face to face with slavery's everyday reality, expertly weaving together narratives that span hundreds of years. . . . Most significant are the texts from and interviews with former slaves themselves. . . . Meticulously researched, this is a work of history that is profoundly relevant to our world today." (Publisher's note)

"Highly recommended for U.S. colonial, middle period, and Civil War scholars, and general readers." LJ

Reséndez, Andrés

★ The **other** slavery; the uncovered story of Indian enslavement in America. Andrés Reséndez. Houghton Mifflin Harcourt 2016 448 p. (hardcover) $30 **306.3**

1. Slave trade 2. Native Americans 3. Slavery -- History 4. Native Americans -- United States 5. Slavery -- North America -- History 6. Slavery -- United States -- History 7. Slave trade -- North America -- History 8. Slave trade -- United States -- History

ISBN 9780547640983

LC 2015037557

National Book Award Finalist: Nonfiction (2016)

This book, by Andrés Reséndez, presents "the sweeping story of the enslavement of tens of thousands of Indians across America, from the time of the conquistadors up to the early 20th century. . . . New evidence, including testimonies of courageous priests, rapacious merchants, Indian captives, and Anglo colonists, sheds light too on Indian enslavement of other Indians." (Publisher's note)

"This eye-opening exposure of the abuse of the indigenous peoples of America is staggering; that the mistreatment continued into the 20th century is beyond disturbing." Kirkus

Includes bibliographical references and index

Sax, David

The **revenge** of analog; real things and why they matter. David Sax. PublicAffairs 2016 304 p. (ebook) $17.99; (hardback) $25.99 **306.3**

1. Marketing 2. Entrepreneurship -- History 3. Electronic commerce -- History

ISBN 9781610395724; 9781610395717

LC 2016012413

Carnegie Medal Longlist: Nonfiction (2017)

In this book, author "David Sax has uncovered story after story of entrepreneurs, small business owners, and even big corporations who've found a market selling not apps or virtual solutions but real, tangible things. . . . [His] work reveals a deep truth about how humans shop, interact, and even think. Blending psychology and observant wit with first-rate reportage, Sax shows the limited appeal of the purely digital life-and the robust future of the real world outside it." (Publisher's note)

"This book has a calming effect, telling readers, one analog page at a time, that tangible goods, in all their reassuring solidity, are back and are not going anywhere." Pub Wkly

Includes bibliographical references and index

Thompson, Derek

Hit makers; the science of popularity in an age of distraction. Derek Thompson. Penguin Press 2017 344 p. illustrations (ebook) $65; (hardcover) $28 **306.3**

1. Consumers 2. Marketing 3. Popularity 4. Product management 5. Marketing -- Social aspects 6. Popularity -- Social aspects

ISBN 9781101980347; 110198032X; 9781101980323

LC 2016043453

In this book, author Derek Thompson "uncovers the hidden psychology of why we like what we like and reveals the economics of cultural markets that invisibly shape our lives. Shattering the sentimental myths of hit-making that dominate pop culture and business, Thompson shows quality is insufficient for success, nobody has 'good taste,' and some of the most popular products in history were one bad break away from utter failure." (Publisher's note)

"Good reading for anyone who aspires to understand the machinery of pop culture—and perhaps even craft a hit of his or her own." Kirkus

Includes bibliographical references (pages 311-334) and index.

Williams, Heather Andrea

Help me to find my people; the African American search for family lost in slavery. by Heather Andrea Williams. University of North Carolina Press 2012 251 p. ill. (cloth: alk. paper) $30 **306.3**

1. Archives 2. Family reunions 3. Slave narratives 4. African American families -- History 5. Slavery -- Social aspects -- United States -- History 6. Slaves -- Family relationships -- United States

-- History
ISBN 0807835544; 9780807835548

LC 2011050216

Author "Heather Andrea Williams uses slave narratives, letters, interviews, public records, and diaries to guide readers back to devastating moments of family separation during slavery when people were sold away from parents, siblings, spouses, and children. . . . [She tells the] stories of separation and the long, usually unsuccessful journeys toward reunification. . . . Williams follows those who were separated, chronicles their searches, and documents the rare experience of reunion." (Publisher's note)

Includes bibliographical references (p. [225]-233) and index

306.36   Systems of labor

Brody, Lauren Smith

The **fifth** trimester; The Working Mom's Guide to Style, Sanity, and Big Success After Baby. by Lauren Smith Brody. Doubleday 2016 352 p. (ebook) $65; (hardcover) $25.95   **306.36**
1. Work and family 2. Working mothers 3. Work-life balance
ISBN 9780385541428; 9780385541411

LC 2016019667

This book, by Lauren Smith Brody, "is your one-stop shop for the honest, funny, and comforting tips, to-do lists, and take-charge strategies you'll need to embrace your new identity as a working parent and set yourself up for success. Based on interviews with 700+ candidly speaking moms in wildly varied fields and incredible expert advice, [it] tackles every personal and professional detail with the wit, warmth, and inspiration you need to win when you head back to work." (Publisher's note)

"Working moms will find a wealth of ideas to help navigate the challenging transition period in this friendly and practical guide." Pub Wkly

Includes bibliographical references and index

Downey, Allyson

Here's the plan; Your Practical, Tactical Guide to Advancing Your Career During Pregnancy and Parenthood. Allyson Downey. Seal Press 2015 272 p. $16; (ebook) $10.99 **306.36**
1. Working mothers 2. Work-life balance 3. Work and family 4. Career development 5. Vocational guidance for women
ISBN 9781580056182; 9781580056199

LC 2015040214

This book, by Allyson Downey, "offers an inventive and inspiring roadmap for working mothers steering their careers through the parenting years. . . . Downey—founder of weeSpring, the 'Yelp for baby products,' and mother of two young children—advises readers on all practical aspects of ladder-climbing while parenting, such as negotiating leave, flex time, and promotions." (Publisher's note)

"A highly useful guide for anyone considering starting a family and working." Booklist

Stromberg, Lisen

Work pause thrive; how to pause for parenthood without killing your career. Lisen Stromberg. BenBella Books, Inc. 2017 288 p. illustrations (trade cloth: alk. paper) $24.95; (ebook) $24.99   **306.36**
1. Work and family 2. Working mothers 3. Work-life balance 4. Career development 5. Women -- Vocational guidance
ISBN 9781942952732; 9781942952749

LC 2016034628

This book, by Lisen Stromberg, focuses on work-life balance. "After

the birth of her second child, she did something she never imagined she would do: she opted out to focus on her family. But her career didn't end there. Lisen paused then pivoted to become first a social entrepreneur and then an award-winning journalist writing about women, work, and life in Silicon Valley. Along the way, she learned she wasn't alone." (Publisher's note)

"Stuffed with realistic but inspiring stories and concrete advice, this is a healthy reminder that those who pause to place the personal before the professional are not failures." Pub Wkly

Includes bibliographical references and index

306.362   Slavery

Bales, Kevin

Blood and earth; modern slavery, ecocide, and the secret to saving the world. Kevin Bales. Spiegel & Grau 2016 304 p. illustrations (ebook) $65; (hardback) $27   **306.362**
1. Slavery -- Environmental aspects 2. Environmental degradation -- Developing countries 3. Slave labor -- Environmental aspects -- Developing countries 4. Consumption (Economics) -- Environmental aspects 5. Slavery -- Environmental aspects -- Developing countries -- History -- 21st century
ISBN 9780812995770; 9780812995763

LC 2015008438

This book, by Kevin Bales, is "the product of seven years of travel and research, . . . [and] brings us dramatic stories from the world's most beautiful and tragic places, the environmental and human-rights hotspots where this crisis is concentrated. But it also tells the stories of some of the most common products we all consume--from computers to shrimp to jewelry--whose origins are found in these same places." (Publisher's note)

"Readers will be deeply disturbed to learn how the links connecting slavery, environmental issues, and modern convenience are forged." Pub Wkly

Includes bibliographical references and index

Marques, Leonardo

The **United** States and the slave trade to the Americas, 1776-1867; Leonardo Marques. Yale University Press 2016 xi, 313 p.p illustrations (hardcover: alk. paper) $40 **306.362**
1. Historical literature 2. Slave trade -- History 3. Slavery -- United States 4. Slave trade -- Cuba -- History 5. Slave trade -- Brazil -- History 6. Slave trade -- America -- History 7. Slave trade -- United States -- History 8. Slave traders -- United States -- History
ISBN 9780300212419

LC 2016942711

This book, by Leonardo Marques, presents "an investigation of US participation in the transatlantic slave trade to the Americas, from the American Revolution to the Civil War. . . . Marques outlines the multiple forms of U.S. involvement in this traffic amid various legislation and shifting international relations, exploring the global processes that shaped the history of this participation." (Publisher's note)

"Marques's ambitious and well-researched study delivers on its promise to shed new light on the economic and ideological forces that led to the Civil War." Pub Wkly

Includes bibliographical references and index.

Warren, Wendy

★ **New** England Bound; slavery and colonization in early America. Wendy Warren. Liveright Publishing Corporation

2016 352 p. illustrations, map (hardcover) $29.95 **306.362**
1. Slavery -- History 2. United States -- History
ISBN 9780871406729; 0871406721

LC 2016007276

Pulitzer Prize Finalist: History (2017)

This book, by Wendy Warren, "links the growth of the northern colonies to the Atlantic slave trade, demonstrating how New England's economy derived its vitality from the profusion of slave-trading ships coursing through its ports. Warren documents how Indians were systematically sold into slavery in the West Indies and reveals how colonial families like the Winthrops were motivated not only by religious freedom but also by their slave-trading investments." (Publisher's note)

"For students of early American history, this is an eye-opening book about Puritans and Anglicans who disapproved of slavery but accepted it as a normal part of life and reaped its profits." Kirkus

Includes bibliographical references and index.

306.4 Specific aspects of culture

Ekirch, A. Roger, 1950-
At day's close; night in times past. Norton 2005 447p il $25.95 **306.4**
1. Night 2. Social history 3. Night -- Social aspects
ISBN 0-393-05089-0

LC 2005-2784

This is a social history of night before the industrial age. Index.

"This history finds Ekirch reminding us of how preindustrial Westerners lived during the nocturnal hours, when most were plunged into almost total darkness. . . . A rich weave of citation and archival evidence, Ekirch's narrative is rooted in the material realities of the past, evoking a bygone world of extreme physicality and preindustrial survival stratagems." Publ Wkly

Includes bibliographical references

Fadiman, Anne
★ The **spirit** catches you and you fall down; a Hmong child, her American doctors, and the collision of two cultures. Anne Fadiman. Farrar, Straus & Giroux 1997 xi, 339p $25; (pbk.) $15 **306.4**
1. Epilepsy 2. Medical care 3. Culture conflict 4. Hmong (Asian people) 5. Epilepsy in children 6. Hmong Americans -- Medicine 7. Intercultural communication 8. Hmong American children -- Medical care -- California 9. Transcultural medical care -- California -- Case studies
ISBN 0374267812; 9780374533403

LC 97005175

Los Angeles Times Book Prizes: Current Interest (1997), National Book Critics Circle Award: General Nonfiction (1997)

This book presents an "anthropological exploration of the Hmong population in Merced County, California. Following the case of Lia (a Hmong child with a progressive and unpredictable form of epilepsy), Fadiman maps out the controversies raised by the collision between Western medicine and holistic healing traditions of Hmong immigrants. Unable to enter the Laotian forest to find herbs for Lia that will 'fix her spirit,' her family becomes resigned to the Merced County emergency system, which has little understanding of Hmong animist traditions. [Anne] Fadiman reveals the rigidity and weaknesses of these two ethnographically separated cultures." (Library Journal)

Includes bibliographical references (p. [311]-324) and index.

Francis, Gavin
Shapeshifters; a journey through the changing human body. Gavin Francis. Basic Books 2018 304 p. (hardcover) $27 **306.4**
1. Physiology 2. Life sciences 3. Life cycle, Human
ISBN 9781541697515; 9781541697522

LC 2018938201

In this book author Gavin Francis "considers the inevitable changes all of our bodies undergo--such as birth, puberty, and death, but also laughter, sleeping, and healing-and those that only some of our bodies will: like getting a tattoo, experiencing psychosis, . . . or undergoing a gender transition. In Francis's hands, each event becomes an opportunity to explore the meaning of identity and the natures-biological, psychological, and philosophical-of our selves." (Publisher's note)

Kugel, Seth
Rediscovering travel; a guide for the globally curious. Seth Kugel. Liveright Publishing Corporation 2018 320 p. (hardcover) $26.95 **360.4**
1. Travel 2. Tourism
ISBN 9780871408501

LC 2018028589

This book, by Seth Kugel, is "an indispensable companion for rookie and veteran travelers alike that promises to revolutionize both how and why we vacation. . . . [It] explains . . . how to make the most of new digital technologies without being shackled to them. For the tight-belted tourist and the first-class flyer, the eager student and the comfort-seeking retiree, Kugel shows how we too can rediscover the joy of discovery." Publisher's note)

Includes bibliographical references

Leonard, Annie
The **story** of stuff; how our obsession with stuff is trashing the planet, our communities, and our health--and a vision for change. [by] Annie Leonard with Ariane Conrad. Free Press 2010 xxxiv, 317p il $26 **306.4**
1. Material culture 2. Consumption (Economics)
ISBN 978-1-4391-2566-3

LC 2009-42207

"Leonard explains that our consumer goods undergo extraction, production, distribution, consumption, and disposal processes that are trashing the planet, diminishing our resources, exploiting workers, and contributing to high levels of disease and death. She advocates an international cooperative effort to develop domestic and international policies and laws that will reverse our planet's ecological decline and leave a sustainable world for future generations. . . . An important work for consumers of all ages." Libr J

McGonigal, Jane
Reality is broken; why games make us better and how they can change the world. Jane McGonigal. Penguin Press 2011 388 p. $16.00 **306.4**
1. Video games 2. Computer games 3. Simulation games 4. Educational games 5. Computers and civilization 6. Computer games -- Social aspects
ISBN 0143120611; 1594202850; 9780143120612; 9781594202858

LC 2010029619

In this book, author Jane McGonigal offers a vision of "how we can harness the power of games to boost global happiness. . . . [Why] should games be used for escapist entertainment alone? . . . [The author] shows how we can leverage the power of games to fix what is wrong with the real world--from social problems . . . to global issues-- . . . and introduces us to cutting-edge games that are already changing the business, education, and nonprofit worlds." (Publisher's note)

Includes bibliographical references.

Pollan, Michael, 1955-

The **botany** of desire; Michael Pollan. Random House 2001 xxv, 271 p.p $24.95; pa $13.95   **306.4**

1. Apples 2. Tulips 3. Potatoes 4. Marijuana 5. Economic botany 6. Human-plant relationships

ISBN 0-375-50129-0; 0-375-76039-3 pa; 9780375760396; 9780375501296

LC 00066479

In this book, author "Michael Pollan . . . demonstrates how people and domesticated plants have formed a similarly reciprocal relationship. He . . . links four fundamental human desires--sweetness, beauty, intoxication, and control--with the plants that satisfy them: the apple, the tulip, marijuana, and the potato. In telling the stories of four familiar species, Pollan illustrates how the plants have evolved to satisfy humankind's most basic yearnings. And just as we've benefited from these plants, we have also done well by them. So who is really domesticating whom?" (Publisher's note)

"Pollan intertwines history, anecdote, and revelation as he investigates the connection between four plants that have thrived under human care—apples, tulips, marijuana, and potatoes—and the four human desires they satisfy in return: sweetness, beauty, intoxication, and control. . . . Pollan's dynamic, intelligent, and intrepid parsing of the wondrous dialogue between plants and humans is positively paradigm-altering." Booklist

Includes bibliographical references and index.

Robinson, Jo

Eating on the wild side; the missing link to optimum health. Jo Robinson; illustrations by Andie Styner. Little Brown & Co 2013 416 p. ill. $16   **306.4**

1. Nutrition 2. Natural foods

ISBN 0316227935; 9780316227933; 9780316227940

LC 2013934815

IACP Cookbook Award (2014)

This book, by Jo Robinson. discusses how "ever since farmers first planted seeds . . . , humans have been destroying the nutritional value of their fruits and vegetables. Unwittingly, we've been selecting plants that are high in starch and sugar and low in vitamins, minerals, fiber, and antioxidants." Robinson "reveals the solution--choosing modern varieties that approach the nutritional content of wild plants but that also please the modern palate." (Publisher's note)

Rose, Frank

The **art** of immersion; how the digital generation is remaking Hollywood, Madison Avenue, and the way we tell stories. W.W. Norton & Co. 2011 354p $26.95   **306.4**

1. Internet marketing 2. Internet entertainment 3. Internet -- Social aspects

ISBN 978-0-393-07601-1

LC 2010-38676

The author "theorizes that we are encountering a profound shift in the way we play, consume, and communicate. He explains that our experiences with television, movies, games, and advertisements are becoming increasingly more immersive and consumer-driven. . . . This engrossing study of how new media is reshaping the entertainment, advertising, and communication industries is an essential read for professionals in the fields of digital communications, marketing, and advertising, as well as for fans of gaming and pop culture." Libr J

Includes bibliographical references

Trumble, Angus

The **finger**; a handbook. Farrar, Straus and Giroux 2010 300p il $28   **306.4**

1. Fingers

ISBN 978-0-374-15498-1; 0-374-15498-8

LC 2009-42220

On the whole, The Finger is a deft, enjoyable and often provocative investigation into some overlooked and interrelated aspects of human experience. Washington Post

Includes bibliographical references

306.44   Language

Dorren, Gaston

Lingo; Around Europe in Sixty Languages. Gaston Dorren. Atlantic Monthly Press 2015 303 p. illustrations, maps $25   **306.44**

1. Europe 2. Language and languages

ISBN 0802124070; 9780802124074

This book, by Gaston Dorren, brings the "reader on a whirlwind tour of sixty European languages and dialects, sharing quirky moments from their histories and exploring their commonalities and differences. Most European languages are descended from a single ancestor, a language not unlike Sanskrit known as Proto-Indo-European (or PIE for short), but the continent's ever-changing borders and cultures have given rise to a linguistic and cultural diversity." (Publisher's note)

"This intriguing, thoughtful book will delight those who love words; it is also a round, solid education in the vastness of the world's citizens' ability and desire to express themselves, intended, Dorren states, 'as an amuse-bouche.' Amusing, too!" Booklist

Includes bibliographical references and index.

Lepore, Jill

A is for American; letters and other characters in the newly United States. Knopf 2002 241p il $25; pa $13   **306.44**

1. Slaves 2. Artists 3. Painters 4. Inventors 5. Architects 6. Americanisms 7. Sociolinguistics 8. Artisans 9. Essayists 10. Metalworkers 11. Indian leaders 12. Lexicographers 13. Writers on law 14. Teachers of the deaf 15. Telecommunications executives 16. English language -- Social aspects

ISBN 0-375-40449-X; 0-375-70408-6 pa

LC 2001-38057

"Each man's story delivers a wealth of irony along with valuable history. . . . Some familiar accounts, some not well known, but all told with a fresh eye to their national significance." Booklist

Includes bibliographical references

306.46   Culture and institutions -- technology

Langlands, Alex

Cræft; an inquiry into the origins and true meaning of traditional crafts. Alexander Langlands. W W Norton & Co Inc 2018 344 p. illustrations (hardcover) $26.95   **306.46**

1. Material culture 2. Antiquities -- Europe 3. Artisans -- Europe -- History 4. Antiquities, Prehistoric -- Europe 5. Material culture -- Europe -- History 6. Handicraft industries -- Europe -- History

ISBN 9780393635911; 9780393635904

LC 2017047723

This book, by Alexander Langlands "takes us into the ancient world of traditional crafts to uncover their deep, original histories. . . . [The author] argues that our modern understanding of craft only skims the surface. His journeys from his home in Wales have taken him along the Atlantic seaboard of Europe, from Spain through France and England to Scotland and Iceland in search of the lost meaning of craft." (Publisher's note)

"Langlands offers a fascinating history of what's setting trends today." Booklist

306.461 Medicine and health

O'Connell, Mark

To be a machine; Adventures among cyborgs, utopians, hackers, and the futurists solving the modest problem of death. Mark O'Connell. Doubleday 2017 256 p. (hardback) $26.95; (ebook) $65 **306.461**

1. Humanism 2. Medical technology 3. Technological innovations 4. Prosthesis -- Social aspects 5. Medical technology -- Social aspects 6. Technological innovations -- Social aspects
ISBN 9780385540414; 9780385540421

LC 2016021725

This book, by Mark O'Connell, "explores the staggering possibilities and moral quandaries that present themselves when you of think of your body as a device. He visits the world's foremost cryonics facility to witness how some have chosen to forestall death. He discovers an underground collective of biohackers, implanting electronics under their skin to enhance their senses. He meets a team of scientists urgently investigating how to protect mankind from artificial superintelligence." (Publisher's note)

"An unsettling but informative and sometimes-optimistic view of mostly legitimate efforts at life extension." Kirkus

Includes bibliographical references (pages [239]-241).

306.7 Sexual relations

Bader, Michael J.

Arousal, the secret logic of sexual fantasies. Thomas Dunne Bks./St. Martin's Press 2002 293p $23.95; pa $14.95 **306.7**

1. Sexual behavior
ISBN 0-312-26933-1; 0-312-30242-8 pa

LC 2001-51290

"Bader covers how arousal works, how fantasies assist in arousal, the role of fantasies in therapy, and the social meaning of fantasies. Throughout, he gives numerous case studies, examples, and sensible and compassionate conjectures about particular fantasies and the fantasizing process. Bader is a clear, graceful writer, and he makes his points with rare facility in a way useful to both lay people and therapeutic professionals." Libr J

Includes bibliographical references

Barash, David P.

The myth of monogamy; fidelity and infidelity in animals and people. [by] David P. Barash, Judith Eve Lipton. Freeman, W.H. 2001 227p $24.95; pa $15 **306.7**

1. Adultery 2. Marriage 3. Sexual behavior
ISBN 0-7167-4004-4; 0-8050-7136-9 pa

This is "guaranteed to entertain and may even pique thoughtful readers' interests." Sci Books Films

Includes bibliographical references

Berkowitz, Eric

The boundaries of desire; bad laws, good sex, and changing identities. Eric Berkowitz. Counterpoint 2015 468 p. (hardback) $28 **306.7**

1. Sex 2. Sex -- Social aspects 3. Sex customs -- History
ISBN 9781619025295

LC 2015005123

This book, by Eric Berkowitz, "traces the fast-moving bloodsport of sex law over the past century, and challenges our most cherished notions about family, power, gender, and identity. Starting when courts censored birth control information as pornography and let men rape their wives, and continuing through the 'sexual revolution' and into the present day, . . . Berkowitz shows how the law has remained out of synch with the convulsive changes in sexual morality." (Publisher's note)

"A bracing look at the often-strange relationship between sexuality and the legal system over six tumultuous decades." Booklist

Includes bibliographical references (pages 343-458) and index.

Coles, Joanna, 1962-

Love rules; how to find a real relationship in a digital world. Joanna Coles. HarperCollins 2018 256 p. $25.99 **306.7**

1. Online dating 2. Man-woman relationship 3. Women -- Conduct of life
ISBN 0062652583; 9780062652584

"A diet book for romantic relationships, Love Rules[, by Joanna Coles,] first asks women to re-assess the way they think about their relationships, and then helps them use that newfound awareness to navigate their love lives more successfully in this very modern, fast-paced--and often lonely--digital age. . . . Coles provides a series of simple guidelines for finding worthwhile love: fifteen rules--love 'hacks.'" (Publisher's note)

Coviello, Peter

Long players; a love story in eighteen songs. Peter Coviello. Penguin Books 2018 272 p. (pbk.) $16 **306.7**

1. Men -- Biography 2. Man-woman relationship 3. Interpersonal relations 4. Men -- United States -- Biography 5. Man-woman relationships -- United States 6. Popular music fans -- United States -- Biography
ISBN 9780143132332

LC 2017037330

This book, by Peter Coviello, is "a story of heartbreak, (ex)stepparenthood, and the limitless grace of pop songs. . . . We follow . . . Coviello through his happy marriage, his blindsiding divorce, and his fumbling post marital forays into sex and romance. Above all we travel with him as he calibrates, mix by mix and song by song, his place in the lives of two little girls, his suddenly ex-stepdaughters." (Publisher's note)

Love story in eighteen songs

Keenan, Jillian

Sex With Shakespeare; here's much to do with pain, but more with love. Jillian Keenan. HarperCollins 2016 400 p. (ebook) $14.99; $25.99 **306.7**

1. Sex in literature
ISBN 9780062378736; 0062378716; 9780062378712

LC 2016017608

"Four hundred years after [William] Shakespeare's death, [author Jillian] Keenan's smart and passionate memoir brings new life to his work. With fourteen of his plays as a springboard, she explores the many facets of love and sexuality--from desire and communication to fetish and fantasy." (Publisher's note)

"A raunchy memoir revealing a visceral connection to the Bard."

Kirkus

Includes bibliographic references (pages 317-322) and index.

Koenig, Emma

Moan; essays on female orgasm. collected by Emma Koenig; foreword by Rachel Bloom. Grand Central Publishing 2018 240 p. (trade pbk.) $15.99   **306.7**

1. Sex 2. Women -- Sexual behavior 3. Female orgasm 4. Sexual excitement 5. Sexual intercourse

ISBN 9781455540556

LC 2017025281

In this book author Emma Koenig "tackles the ideas surrounding the sometimes elusive orgasm head on. Here is a look into the spectrum of desire. Of frustration. Of experiences that have left an impact. From the hilarious to the tragic, . . . these essays will leave you feeling inspired and excited to embark on your own journey of sexual exploration and empower women to do what most of the time is hardest for us: asking for what we want and don't in the bedroom and beyond." (Publisher's note)

McConnachie, James

The **book** of love; the story of the Kamasutra. Metropolitan Books 2008 267p il $27.50; pa $17   **306.7**

1. Kamasutra 2. Sexual behavior

ISBN 978-0-8050-8818-2; 0-8050-8818-0; 978-0-8050-9019-2 pa; 0-8050-9019-3 pa

LC 2007-47172

"In an impressively researched, charming volume, McConnachie traces the Kamasutra's history from its creation by the third-century sage Vatsyayana as a guide to the good life for urbane dandies. . . . Since not a single posture is described, consider it G-rated." Booklist

Includes bibliographical references

McLaughlin, August

Girl boner; the good girl's guide to sexual empowerment. by August McLaughlin. Amberjack Publishing 2018 320 p. (hardcover: alk. paper) $24.99   **306.708**

1. Women -- Sexual behavior 2. Sex -- Physiological aspects

ISBN 9781944995713

LC 2018002591

In this book, author "August McLaughlin offers an unfiltered blend of personal narrative and practical tips on relationships, solo play, journaling, gender issues, and more. From the perks of 'Jilling off' to the 7 types of 'gasms, 'Girl Boner' will 'empower you to own your sexual self and enjoy your whole life a great deal more.'" (Publisher's note)

"McLaughlin carefully homes in on the myriad ways that mental and physical health connect with sexuality in this uplifting and refreshingly inclusive guide to women's sexual health based on a podcast of the same name." Pub Wkly

Orenstein, Peggy

★ **Girls** and Sex; Navigating the Complicated New Landscape. by Peggy Orenstein. HarperCollins 2016 320 p. $26.99   **306.7**

1. Young women 2. Teenage girls 3. Sex -- Psychological aspects 4. Teenagers -- Sexual behavior

ISBN 0062209728; 9780062209726

In this book, by Peggy Orenstein, "A generation gap has emerged between parents and their girls. Even in this age . . . the mothers and fathers of tomorrow's women have little idea what their daughters are up to sexually. . . . Drawing on in-depth interviews with over seventy young women and a wide range of psychologists, academics, and experts, . . . Orenstein goes where most others fear to tread." (Publisher's note)

"Ample, valuable information on the way young women in America perceive and react to their sexual environment." Kirkus

Includes bibliographical references (pages 239-290) and index.

Shlain, Leonard

Sex, time, and power; how women's sexuality shaped human evolution. Viking 2003 xx, 420p il $25.95; pa $16 **306.7**

1. Evolution 2. Women -- Sexual behavior

ISBN 0-670-03233-6; 0-14-200467-7 pa

LC 2002-41186

The author "takes an evolutionary approach to solving the conundrums of misogyny and patriarchy, guiding his . . . readers through . . . speculations about the purpose of such seemingly impractical, even dangerous traits as bipedalism, menstruation, the perils of childbirth, and the helplessness of infants. . . . Lucid and compelling, Shlain asks startling and crucial questions about human nature and presents truly imaginative and mind-stretching answers." Booklist

Includes bibliographical references

Spiegel, Amy Rose

Action; a book about sex. Amy Rose Spiegel. Grand Central Pub. 2016 240 p. illustrations (ebook) $48; (paperback) $15.99   **306.7**

1. Sex 2. Sex education 3. Sex instruction 4. Sexual excitement 5. Sexual intercourse

ISBN 9781455534524; 9781455534494

LC 2015050562

This book, by Amy Rose Spiegel, "is a book about sex that people won't feel embarrassed about owning. . . . Spiegel exhorts you to trust yourself and be respectful of others--and to have the best possible time doing the things you search for on the Internet, except in reality. The book covers consent, safety, group sex, gender, and the best breakfast to make for a one-night stand." (Publisher's note)

"This should be required reading for anyone even considering having sex for the first time." Pub Wkly

Includes bibliographical references and index.

Wade, Lisa

American Hookup; the new culture of sex on campus. W W Norton & Co Inc 2017 288 p. $26.95; (ebook) $50 **306.7**

1. Sex 2. United States -- Social conditions 3. College students -- Sexual behavior

ISBN 039328509X; 9780393285093; 9780393285109

LC 2016035704

In this book about hookups, author "Lisa Wade offers the definitive account of this new sexual culture and demonstrates that the truth is both more heartening and more harrowing than we thought. Offering invaluable insights for parents, educators, and students, Wade situates hookup culture within the history of sexuality, the evolution of higher education, and the unfinished feminist revolution." (Publisher's note)

"An eye-opening, conversation-starting examination of sex on the American college campus." Kirkus

Includes bibliographical references (pages [265]-284) and index.

Yes means yes! visions of female sexual power & a world without rape. [by] Jaclyn Friedman & Jessica Valenti [editors]; foreword by Margaret Cho. Seal Press 2008 361p pa $16.95   **306.7**

1. Rape 2. Sexism 3. Gender role 4. Sex role 5. Women -- Sexual behavior

ISBN 978-1-58005-257-3; 1-58005-257-6

LC 2008-20989

The editors "present an extraordinary, eye-opening essay collection that focuses on the importance of sexual identity and ownership in the struggle against rape in the U.S., as well as a number of related issues, including sexual pleasure, self-esteem and the mixed societal messages that turn 'nice guys' bad." Publ Wkly

Includes bibliographical references

306.73   General institutions

Perel, Esther

The **state** of affairs; rethinking infidelity. Esther Perel. Harper 2017 xvi, 319 p.p (hardcover) $26.99   **306.73**
1. Adultery 2. Marriage 3. Married people 4. Man-woman relationships
ISBN 0062322583; 9780062322609; 9780062322586; 9780062322593

This book, by Esther Perel, offers a "provocative look at relationships through the lens of infidelity. Affairs, she argues, have a lot to teach us about the human heart. . . . They offer a unique window into our personal and cultural attitudes about love, lust, and commitment. Through examining illicit love from multiple angles, Perel invites readers into an honest, enlightened, and entertaining exploration of modern marriage in its many variations." (Publisher's note)

"This is a thought-provoking take on relationships and essential reading for couples dealing with infidelity." Pub Wkly

Includes bibliographical references (pages 303-310) and index.

Weigel, Moira

Labor of love; The Invention of Dating. Moira Weigel. Farrar, Straus & Giroux 2016 304 p. (hardback) $26; (ebook) $60   **306.73**
1. Dating (Social customs) 2. Interpersonal relations
ISBN 9780374182533; 9780374713133

LC 2015041606

This book, by Moira Weigel, "offers a fresh feminist perspective on how we came to date the ways we do. This isn't a guide to 'getting the guy.' There are no ridiculous 'rules' to follow. Instead, Weigel helps us understand how looking for love shapes who we are—and hopefully leads us closer to the happy ending that dating promises." (Publisher's note)

"Timely and provocative, this work is a solid choice for readers interested in contemporary social behaviors and their antecedents." LJ

Includes bibliographical references (pages [269]-273) and index.

306.74   Prostitution

Moran, Rachel

Paid for; my journey through prostitution. Rachel Moran. Gill & Macmillan 2013 295 p. $15.95   **306.74**
1. Homelessness 2. Women -- Ireland 3. Juvenile prostitution 4. Sex -- Psychological aspects 5. Prostitution -- Ireland 6. Prostitutes -- Ireland -- Dublin -- Biography
ISBN 9780393351972; 0717156028; 9780717156023

LC 2013412048

In this memoir, author Rachel Moran was "Born into a troubled family [and left] home at the age of fourteen. Being homeless, she was driven into prostitution to survive. . . . She describes the exploitation she and others endured on the streets and in the brothels. Moran also speaks to the psychological damage inherent to prostitution and the inevitable estrangement from one's body. At twenty-two, Moran escaped the sex

trade." (Publisher's note)

"Moran's thoughtful, highly readable, and provocative treatise shines a necessary light on a dark and underdiscussed topic." Kirkus

Includes bibliographical references.

306.76   Sexual orientation, transgenderism, intersexuality

Arceneaux, Michael

I can't date Jesus; love, sex, family, race, and other reasons I've put my faith in Beyoncé. Michael Arceneaux. Pocket Books 2018 256 p. $17   **306.76**
1. Essay 2. African American gay men 3. Coming out (Sexual orientation)
ISBN 1501178857; 9781501178856

This book "is Michael Arceneaux's impassioned, forthright, and refreshing look at minority life in today's America. Leaving no bigoted or ignorant stone unturned, he describes his journey in learning to embrace his identity when the world told him to do the opposite. He eloquently writes about coming out to his mother . . . and the persistent challenges of young people who feel marginalized and denied the chance to pursue their dreams." (Publisher's note)

Beachy, Robert

Gay Berlin; birthplace of a modern identity. by Robert Beachy. Alfred A. Knopf 2014 336 p. (hardback) $27.95 **306.76**
1. Gay men 2. Homosexuality 3. Germany -- History 4. Gay culture -- Germany -- Berlin 5. Homosexuality -- Germany -- Berlin 6. Gender identity -- Germany -- Berlin 7. Gay men -- Germany -- Berlin -- Identity
ISBN 0307272109; 9780307272102

LC 2014004986

Stonewall Honor Book: Nonfiction (2015)

"Berlin, before the turn of the twentieth century, became a place where scholars, activists, and medical professionals could explore and begin to educate both themselves and Europe about new and emerging sexual identities. . . . Chapter by chapter [author Robert] Beachy's scholarship illuminates forgotten firsts, including the life and work of Dr. Magnus Hirschfeld, first to claim (in 1896) that same-sex desire is an immutable, biologically determined characteristic." (Publisher's note)

Bianchi, Anna

Becoming an ally to the gender-expansive child; a guide for parents and carers. by Anna Bianchi. Jessica Kingsley Pub 2017 247 p. illustrations (paperback) $19.95   **306.76**
1. Parenting 2. Transgender people 3. Transgender children 4. Gender identity disorders in children 5. Transgender children -- Family relationships
ISBN 9781785920516; 9781784503055; 1785920510

LC 2017448702

This book, by Anna Bianchi, "draws deeply on four areas: her own experience, current research, interviews with children and their families, and a discussion of power, both in society and between children and adults. She shows how the inner journey of the adult inevitably impacts on the outer journey of the child and, given the significance of this, offers a step-by-step guide to becoming an ally to the gender-expansive child." (Publisher's note)

"Bianchi walks a graceful path, seamlessly exploring her own experience, that of her grandchild, the politics of society, and the human conditions of fear and love." LJ

Includes bibliographical references and index.

Blank, Hanne

Straight; the surprisingly short history of heterosexuality. Hanne Blank. Beacon Press 2012 xxvii, 228 p.p (hardcover: acid-free paper) $26.95   **306.76**

1. Homosexuality -- History 2. Heterosexuality -- History
ISBN 0807044431; 9780807044438

LC 2011031432

In this book, Hanne Blank "sets out to explore the changing views of marriage, heterosexuality, and conceptions of biological sex itself over the past 150 years, systematically exploring the history from scientific, philosophical, and sociological perspectives. . . . She argues that although sexual contact between men and women has existed since time immemorial, the word and idea of heterosexuality as an identity is a relatively recent invention." (Library Journal)

Includes bibliographical references and index

Bronski, Michael

★ A **queer** history of the United States. Beacon Press 2011 xx, 287p $27.95   **306.76**

1. Homosexuality -- United States -- History
ISBN 978-0-8070-4439-1

LC 2010-50225

"This enthralling history spans 500 years of evolving perspectives on sexuality in America—from the European setters' violent responses to the more fluid gender roles of Native Americans to how the birth control pill, which separated sex from reproduction, contributed to the cause of LGBT liberation. . . . A savvy political, legal, literary (and even fashion) history, Bronski's narrative is as intellectually rigorous as it is entertaining." Publ Wkly

Carter, David

Stonewall; David Carter. 2nd edition Griffin 2010 336 p. ill., maps $17.99   **306.76**

1. Gay men 2. Lesbians 3. Gay rights 4. Gay liberation movement 5. Greenwich Village (New York, N.Y.) -- History 6. Stonewall Riots, New York, N.Y., 1969
ISBN 9780312671938

Originally published 2004

"In 1969, a series of riots over police action against The Stonewall Inn, a gay bar in New York City's Greenwich Village, changed the longtime landscape of the homosexual in society literally overnight. Since then the event itself has become the stuff of legend, with relatively little hard information available on the riots themselves. Now, based on hundreds of interviews, an exhaustive search of public and previously sealed files, and over a decade of intensive research into the history and the topic, Stonewall: The Riots That Sparked the Gay Revolution brings this singular event to vivid life." (Publisher's note)

"The author depicts the Stonewall riots as a unique convergence of time, place, and circumstance and performs some gentle revisionism on the received version of events, emphasizing the contributions of lesbians and street youth while downplaying, but not discounting, the role of drag queens." LJ

Coyote, Ivan E., 1969-

Tomboy survival guide; Ivan Coyote. Arsenal Pulp Press 2016 239 p. illustrations (ebook) $17.99; $17.95   **306.76**

1. Canadians 2. Transgender people 3. Tomboys -- Canada -- Biography 4. Transgender people -- Identity
ISBN 9781551526577; 1551526565; 9781551526560

LC 2016497455

Stonewall Honor Book in Nonfiction

This book, by Ivan Coyote, "is a funny and moving memoir told in stories, in which Ivan recounts the pleasures and difficulties of growing up a tomboy in Canada's Yukon, and how they learned to embrace their tomboy past while carving out a space for those of us who don't fit neatly into boxes or identities or labels." (Publisher's note)

"Stylishly illustrated with sketches of tools and enriched with poems and stories others have shared with Coyote, this book is highly recommended for transgender readers as well as those exploring their own gender identities or wanting to better understand non-binary experiences of a gendered world." Pub Wkly

Davis, Heath Fogg

★ **Beyond** trans; does gender matter? Heath Fogg Davis. New York University Press 2017 vii, 184 p.p illustrations (hardcover) $25   **306.76**

1. Gender studies 2. Gender identity 3. Sexism -- United States 4. Sex role -- United States 5. Gender identity -- United States 6. Transgender people -- United States
ISBN 9781479855407

LC 2017003478

This book, by Heath Fogg Davis, "offers an impassioned call to rethink the usefulness of dividing the world into not just Male and Female categories but even additional categories of Transgender and gender fluid. . . . explores the underlying gender-enforcing policies and customs in American life . . . arguing that it is necessary for our society to take real steps to challenge the assumption that gender matters." (Publisher's note)

"This book is a rare example of a text that speaks fluently to experts and novices alike. Indispensable for all libraries and readership levels." Choice

Includes bibliographical references and index

Downs, Jim

★ **Stand** by me; the forgotten history of gay liberation. Jim Downs. Basic Books 2016 vii, 261 p.p (hardcover) $27.99   **306.76**

1. Gay liberation movement 2. Gay rights -- United States 3. Gays -- United States -- History -- 20th century 4. Gay liberation movement -- United States -- History 5. Gay rights -- United States -- History -- 20th century 6. Gays -- Political activity -- United States -- History -- 20th century
ISBN 9780465032709

LC 2015040030

In this book, author "Jim Downs rewrites the history of gay life in the 1970s, arguing that the decade was about much more than sex and marching in the streets. Drawing on a vast trove of untapped records at LGBT community centers in Los Angeles, New York, and Philadelphia, Downs tells moving, revelatory stories of gay people who stood together . . . to create a sense of community among people who felt alienated from mainstream American life." (Publisher's note)

Includes bibliographical references and index.

Duberman, Martin B., 1930-

★ **Has** the gay movement failed? Martin Duberman. University of California Press 2018 272 p. (cloth: alk. paper) $27.95   **306.76**

1. Gay liberation movement 2. Gay rights -- United States 3. Gay Liberation Front (New York, N.Y.) 4. Gay rights -- United States -- History 5. Gay liberation movement -- United States -- History
ISBN 9780520298866

LC 2017056078

In this book, social-justice activist Martin Duberman "reviews the half century since Stonewall with an immediacy and rigor that informs and energizes. He revisits the early gay movement and its progressive vision for society and puts the left on notice as failing time and again to embrace the queer potential for social transformation." (Publisher's note)

"Duberman challenges gay readers and their allies to become active within a complex caucus he feels has become unfocused and misled. A relevant, fiery, and dizzying treatise certain to provoke debate and discussion." Kirkus

Includes bibliographical references and index

The **Martin** Duberman reader; the essential historical, biographical, and autobiographical writings. Martin Duberman. The New Press 2013 384 p. (paperback) $21.95   **306.76**
1. LGBT people 2. United States -- Social conditions 3. United States -- History 4. Gays -- United States -- History 5. Gay rights -- United States -- History 6. United States -- Politics and government
ISBN 1595586792; 9781595586797

LC 2012041856

This book, by Martin Duberman, offers a reader featuring essays and autobiographical writings of the LGBT scholar. "For the past fifty years, prize-winning historian Martin Duberman's groundbreaking writings have established him as one of our preeminent public intellectuals. Founder of the first graduate program in LGBT studies in the country, . . . Duberman is also an equally gifted playwright and essayist." (Publisher's note)

Eisner, Shiri

Bi; notes for a bisexual revolution. Shiri Eisner. Seal Press 2013 345 p. $16   **306.76**
1. Sex 2. Bisexuality
ISBN 1580054749; 9781580054744

LC 2012047200

Lambda Literary Award Finalist (2014)

This book, by Shiri Eisner, offers a "comprehensive look at bisexual politics—from the issues surrounding biphobia/monosexism, feminism, and transgenderism to the practice of labeling those who identify as bi as either 'too bisexual' . . . or 'not bisexual enough'. . . . In this . . . book, feminist bisexual and genderqueer activist Shiri Eisner takes readers on a journey through the many aspects of the meanings and politics of bisexuality." (Publisher's note)

Erickson-Schroth, Laura

★ **You're** in the wrong bathroom! and 20 other myths and misconceptions about transgender and gender-nonconforming people. Laura Erickson-Schroth, MD; Laura A. Jacobs, LCSW-R. Beacon Press 2017 182 p. (pbk.: alk. paper) $16   **306.76**
1. Gender identity 2. Transgender people 3. Sexual minorities 4. Gender nonconformity
ISBN 9780807033883; 9780807033890

LC 2016055090

This book, by Laura Erickson-Schroth and Laura A. Jacobs, brings "together the medical, social, psychological, and political aspects of being trans in the United States today, . . . [and] unpacks the twenty-one most common myths and misconceptions about transgender and gender-nonconforming people." (Publisher's note)

"A timely and worthwhile purchase for libraries as well as middle- and high-school counseling offices, community centers, and places of worship." Booklist

Includes bibliographical references

Faderman, Lillian, 1940-

The **gay** revolution; the story of the struggle. Lillian Faderman. Simon & Schuster 2015 512 p. 16 plates; illustrations (hardcover: alk. paper) $35   **306.76**
1. Gay men 2. Lesbians 3. Same-sex marriage 4. Gay rights -- United States 5. LGBT people in the military 6. Gays -- United States -- History 7. Gay rights -- United States -- History 8. Gay liberation movement -- United States -- History
ISBN 1451694113; 9781451694116; 9781451694123

LC 2015007285

Stonewall Honor Book: Nonfiction (2016)

This book, by Lillian Faderman, presents the "story of the modern struggle for gay, lesbian, and trans rights--from the 1950s to the present--based on . . . interviews with politicians, military figures, legal activists, and members of the entire LGBT community who face these challenges every day." (Publisher's note)

"Throughout this engaging and extremely well-documented book, Faderman clearly shows that for the LGBT community, equality is not a completed goal. Yet the ideal of fully integrated citizenship is closer to becoming reality than ever before. Inspiring and necessary reading for all Americans interested in social justice." Kirkus

Includes bibliographical references and index

Hirshman, Linda

Victory; the triumphant gay revolution. Linda Hirshman. Harper 2012 464 p. $27.99   **306.76**
1. Civil rights 2. LGBT people -- Legal status, laws, etc. 3. Gays -- Legal status, laws, etc. -- United States 4. United States -- Social conditions -- 21st century 5. Gay liberation movement -- United States -- History
ISBN 0061965502; 9780061965500

LC 2012406399

This book by Linda Hirshman discusses the "triumph of the gay-rights movement. Drawing on previous histories and more than 100 interviews, the author shows how the movement has been successful over the years in countering bigoted notions. . . . Hirshman . . . [presents] discussions of court cases and their attendant legal issues, and on occasion she offers perceptive comparisons between the gay-rights movement and other, concurrent movements for equality." (Kirkus Reviews)

Includes bibliographical references (p. [357]-423) and index

Jacques, Juliet

Trans; A Memoir. Juliet Jacques. Random House Inc 2015 320 p. (hbk.) $26.95; (pbk.) $24.95   **306.76**
1. Sex 2. Transgender people
ISBN 1784781649; 9781784781675; 9781784781644; 1784781673

This memoir by Juliet Jacques is an "exploration of debates that comprise trans politics, issues which promise to redefine our understanding of what it means to be alive. In July 2012, aged thirty, Juliet Jacques underwent sex reassignment surgery—a process she chronicled with unflinching honesty in a serialised national newspaper column. Trans tells of her life to the present moment." (Publisher's note)

Langford, Jo

★ The **pride** guide; a guide to sexual and social health for LGBTQ youth. Jo Langford. Rowman & Littlefield 2018 382 p. (cloth: alk. paper) $36   **306.76**
1. LGBT youth 2. Sex education 3. Gender identity -- Social aspects 4. Sexual minority youth -- Psychology -- United States 5. Sexual minority youth -- Social aspects -- United States 6. Sexual minority youth -- Violence against -- United States
ISBN 9781538110768; 9781538110775

LC 2018005997

"Longtime therapist and sex educator [Jo] Langford has written an indispensable guide to a universe of things sexual and social for LG-

BTQ+ youth and their parents or caregivers. Written in an accessible and always empathetic style, the book is never dreary or didactic. . . . The content is near encyclopedic, ranging from biology to coming out, from dating to 'the religion thing,' and from casual sex to personal safety." (Booklist)

"Aside from its intended audience, this excellent book will be useful for therapists and teachers. It belongs in every library." Booklist

Includes bibliographical references and index

Lester, C. N.

Trans like me; conversations for all of us. C.N. Lester. Seal Press 2018 240 p. (pbk.) $16.99   **306.76**

1. Sex 2. LGBT people 3. Transgender people 4. Transgender people -- Identity 5. Transgender people -- Biography 6. Transgender people -- Conduct of life

ISBN 1580057853; 9781580057844; 9781580057851

LC 2017051262

In this book, author C. N. Lester "takes readers on a measured, thoughtful, intelligent yet approachable tour through the most important and high-profile narratives around the trans community, turning them inside out and examining where we really are in terms of progress. From the impact of the media's wording in covering trans people and issues, to the way parenting gender variant children is portrayed, Lester brings their charged personal narrative to every topic." (Publisher's note)

Mock, Janet

Redefining Realness; My Path to Womanhood, Identity, Love & So Much More. by Janet Mock. Atria Books 2014 288 p. (hardback) $24.99   **306.76**

1. Self-realization 2. Transgender people 3. Identity (Psychology) 4. Racially mixed people 5. Self-actualization (Psychology) -- Case studies 6. Gender identity -- United States -- Case studies 7. Transgender people -- United States -- Biography 8. Racially mixed people -- United States -- Biography

ISBN 1476709122; 9781476709123

LC 2013047625

Stonewall Honor Book: Nonfiction (2015)

This memoir follows author Janet Mock's "quest for identity, from an early, unwavering conviction about her gender to a turbulent adolescence in Honolulu that saw her transitioning during the tender years of high school, self-medicating with hormones at fifteen, and flying across the world alone for sex reassignment surgery at just eighteen. . . . Mock uses her own experience to impart vital insight about the unique challenges and vulnerabilities of trans youth." (Publisher's note)

Nealy, Elijah C.

★ **Transgender** children and youth; cultivating pride and joy with families in transition. Elijah C. Nealy. W W Norton & Co Inc 2017 xxii, 423 p.p (hardcover) $27.95   **306.76**

1. Mental health 2. LGBT literature 3. Transgender people 4. Gender nonconformity 5. Transgender people -- Identity 6. Transgender people -- Services for 7. Transgender youth -- Mental health 8. Transgender children -- Mental health 9. Transgender people -- Family relationships

ISBN 9780393711400; 9780393711394

LC 2016036762

Written by Elijah C. Nealy, this book is his "first-ever comprehensive guide to understanding, supporting, and welcoming trans[gender] kids. Covering everything from family life to school and mental health issues, as well as the physical, social, and emotional aspects of transition, this book is full of best practices to support trans kids." (Publisher's note)

"A must-read for anyone who wants to help trans youth." Booklist
Includes bibliographical references and index

Nutt, Amy Ellis

Becoming Nicole; the transformation of an American family. Amy Ellis Nutt. Random House Inc 2015 304 p. (hardback) $27   **306.76**

1. Family 2. Transgender people 3. Transgender teenagers 4. Families -- United States 5. Transgender youth -- United States 6. Transgender people -- United States

ISBN 0812995414; 9780812995411

LC 2015031162

Stonewall Honor Book in Non-Fiction (2016)

"The inspiring true story of a transgender girl, her identical twin brother, and an ordinary American family's extraordinary journey to understand, nurture, and celebrate the right to be different--from the Pulitzer Prize-winning science reporter for The Washington Post." (Publisher's note)

"This poignant account of a transgender girl's transition offers a heartfelt snapshot of a family whose only objective is to protect their daughter. Tackling the subject from a biological, social, and psychological viewpoint, Pulitzer-winning reporter Nutt . . . weaves complex elements of what being transgender means into a compelling narrative about a young woman who has identified as female since early childhood. . . . Writing in a very journalistic tone, Nutt succeeds in placing Nicole's individual story within the more general narrative of transgender rights in the United States and humanizes the issues currently at play." Pub Wkly

Includes bibliographical references

Parkinson, R. B.

A **little** gay history; desire and diversity across the world. Richard Parkinson; with contributions by Kate Smith and Max Carocci. Columbia University Press 2013 128 p. col. ill., map (pbk.: alk. paper) $19.95   **306.76**

1. Art 2. Homosexuality -- History

ISBN 023116663X; 9780231166638

LC 2013001699

Stonewall Book Awards: Nonfiction Honor Book (2014)

Author R.B. Parkinson presents answers to questions such as "When was the first chat line between men established? Who was the first 'lesbian'? Were ancient Greek men who had sex with each other necessarily 'gay' and what did Shakespeare think about crossdressing? . . . through close readings of art objects from the British Museum's far-ranging collection." (Publisher's note)

"This little gay history is a little terrific book. . . . Parkinson . . . explore[s] the subject of homosexual desire throughout history; he discusses artistic movements, ordinary material culture, facades of conventional life, warrior traditions, legal persecutions, and definitions of the sacred." (Library Journal)

Includes bibliographical references

Robb, Graham

Strangers: homosexual love in the nineteenth century. W.W. Norton 2004 341p il $26.95; pa $15.95   **306.76**

1. Homosexuality

ISBN 0-393-02038-X; 0-393-32649-7 pa

LC 2003-66239

The author "has produced a brilliant work of social archaeology. . . . In excavating the long-buried lives of our gay great-great-granduncles and lesbian great-great-grandaunts, Robb has done more than make a major historical contribution. He has, as it were, provided their distant nieces and nephews, gay and straight, with a family tree that we have never had before." N Y Times Book Rev

Savage, Dan, 1964-

American Savage; insights, slights, and fights on faith, sex, love, and politics. by Dan Savage. Dutton 2013 320 p. (hardcover) $26.95   **306.76**

1. Sex 2. LGBT people 3. Gays -- United States 4. Gay men -- United States -- Biography
ISBN 0525954104; 9780525954101

LC 2013001374

This book by sex columnist and gay rights advocate Dan Savage presents a "collection of 17 new essays. . . . Savage introduces readers to his son's coming out as straight . . . . Sexual mores such as debates over monogamy and the closeted are grappled with. He also takes on conservative opponents . . . his Roman Catholic upbringing and his mother." (Library Journal)

Schwartz, John

Oddly normal; one family's struggle to help their teenage son come to terms with his sexuality. John Schwartz. 1st ed. Gotham Books 2012 xiv, 290 p.p ill. (hardcover) $26 **306.76**

1. Gay teenagers 2. Parents of gays 3. Families 4. Parent and teenager
ISBN 1592407285; 9781592407286

LC 2012014369

This book by John Schwartz is a "memoir by the father of a gay teen. . . . After mustering the courage to come out to his classmates, [Shwartz's] thirteen-year-old son, Joe, was in the hospital following a failed suicide attempt. . . . 'Oddly Normal' is Schwartz's . . . attempt to address his family's own struggles within a culture that is changing fast, but not fast enough to help gay kids like Joe." (Publisher's note)

Includes bibliographical references (p. 279-290)

Singer, Bennett

LGBTQ stats; Lesbian, Gay, Bisexual, Transgender, and Queer People by the Numbers. David Deschamps and Bennett Singer. New Press 2016 352 p. illustrations, map (ebook) $14.99; (pb: alk. paper) $17.95   **306.766**

1. Gays -- United States -- Statistics 2. Sexual minorities -- United States -- Statistics
ISBN 9781620972458; 9781620972441

LC 2016032471

This book, by David Deschamps and Bennett Singer, "chronicles the ongoing LGBTQ revolution, providing the critical statistics, and draws upon and synthesizes newly collected data. Deschamps and Singer . . . provide chapters on family and marriage, workplace discrimination, education, youth, criminal justice, and immigration, as well as evolving policies and laws affecting LGBTQ communities." (Publisher's note)

"An important and indispensable research tool for every library collection." Booklist

Includes bibliographical references and index

Smith, Rachelle Lee

Speaking Out; Queer Youth in Focus. Rachelle Lee Smith. Independent Pub Group 2014 128 p. 7 plates; color photographs (paperback) $14.95   **306.76**

1. LGBT youth 2. Documentary photography
ISBN 1629630411; 9781629630410

This book by Rachelle Lee Smith, is "a photographic essay that explores a wide spectrum of experiences told from the perspective of a diverse group of young people, ages 14-24, identifying as queer (lesbian, gay, bisexual, transgender, or questioning). . . . [It] presents portraits without judgment or stereotype by eliminating environmental influence with a stark white backdrop." (Publisher's note)

"A salutary addition to the growing body of LGBTQ literature." Booklist

Trans bodies, trans selves; a resource for the transgender community. edited by Laura Erickson-Schroth. Oxford University Press, USA 2014 672 p. illustrations (paperback) $41.95   **306.76**

1. Transgender people 2. Gender identity
ISBN 9780199325351

LC 2014007921

This book, edited by Laura Erickson-Schroth, is "a comprehensive, reader-friendly guide for transgender people, with each chapter written by transgender or genderqueer authors. . . . Each chapter takes the reader through an important transgender issue, such as race, religion, employment, medical and surgical transition, mental health topics, relationships, sexuality, parenthood, arts and culture, and many more." (Publisher's note)

"A glossary and biographical information for each contributor round out this much-needed and well-done workbook, suitable for all types of libraries." Booklist

Viloria, Hida

Born both; An Intersex Life. Hida Viloria. Hachette Books 2017 352 p. (hardback) $27   **306.76**

1. Intersexuality 2. Intersex people -- United States -- Biography 3. Intersex people -- Identity
ISBN 9780316347846

LC 2016030284

This book, by intersex activist Hida Viloria, is the story of the author's "life-long journey toward finding love and embracing . . . [his/her] authentic identity in a world that insists on categorizing people into either/or, and of . . . [his/her] decades-long fight for human rights and equality for intersex people everywhere." (Publisher's note)

"This brave and empowering book deserves a wide audience." LJ
Includes bibliographical references

306.768   Transgender identity and intersexuality

Stein, Arlene

Unbound; transgender men and the remaking of identity. Arlene Stein. Pantheon Books 2018 336 p. (hard cover: alk. paper) $27.95   **306.768**

1. Gender identity 2. Transgender people 3. Gender nonconformity 4. Female-to-male transsexuals 5. Transgender people -- Identity
ISBN 9781524747459

LC 2017046998

In this book, "sociologist Arlene Stein takes us into the lives of four strangers who find themselves together in a sun-drenched surgeon's office, having traveled to Florida from across the United States in order to masculinize their chests. . . . Following them over the course of a year, Stein shows how members of this young transgender generation, along with other gender dissidents, are refashioning their identities and challenging others' conceptions of who they are." (Publisher's note)

"Stein posits that trans identity as it exists right now in younger people is less an act of survival and more an act of self-reinvention. Though Stein finds no tidy conclusions, her book succeeds in documenting what it means to be trans today." Publishers' Weekly

Includes bibliographical references and index

To my trans sisters; edited by Charlie Craggs. Jessica Kingsley Publishers 2017 344 p. (paperback) $18.95   **306.768**
   1. Transsexualism 2. Transgender people
   ISBN 9781784506681; 9781785923432

   LC 2017026096

This book, edited by Charlie Craggs, presents "letters written by successful trans women . . . [who share] the lessons they learnt on their journeys to womanhood, celebrating their achievements and empowering the next generation to become who they truly are. . . . These letters capture the diversity of the trans experience and offer advice from make-up and dating through to fighting dysphoria and transphobia." (Publisher's note)

"This invigorating anthology, written by trans women for trans women, is a welcome departure from the established genre of texts about trans individuals that seek to explain their lives and experiences for a presumed audience of primarily cisgendered individuals." Pub Wkly

306.8   Marriage and family

Because I said so; 33 mothers write about children, sex, men, aging, faith, race, and themselves. from the editors of Mothers who think Camille, Peri, & Kate Moses. HarperCollins 2005 xxi, 372p $24.95; pa $13.95   **306.8**
   1. Mothers
   ISBN 0-06-059878-6; 0-06-059879-4 pa

   LC 2004-62007

"Women will appreciate the humor and candor, and men will gain insight into the stunning challenges of motherhood." Booklist
   Includes bibliographical references

Ray, Barbara E.

Not quite adults; why 20-somethings are choosing a slower path to adulthood, and why it's good for everyone. [by] Rick Settersten and Barbara E. Ray. 1st ed. Delacorte Press 2010 xxiii, 239 p.p (paperback) $15.00   **306.8**
   1. Adulthood 2. Youth -- Education 3. Youth -- Employment 4. Youth -- United States
   ISBN 0553807404; 9780440339793; 9780553807400

   LC 2010027109

This authors of this book "document the many ways that touch points of adulthood . . . are happening years later for people currently in their twenties and thirties than for their parents and grandparents" as well as "the vast disparity of resources and opportunities . . . between 'swimmers,' as the authors term college-educated youth with strong family support and wide social networks, and 'treaders,' a larger group of young people suffering chronic, generational resource deficits." (Library Journal)

"Drawing on eight years of data and more than 500 interviews with young people between 18 and 34, Richard Settersten and Barbara Ray dismantle the common belief that this generation has been coddled into laziness. Rather, these young adults have come of age at a particularly merciless moment. . . . 'Not Quite Adults' offers a valuable portrait of the diverging destinies of young people today." Economist
   Includes bibliographical references

Warner, Judith

Perfect madness; motherhood in the age of anxiety. Riverhead Books 2005 327p $23.95; pa $15   **306.8**
   1. Mothers 2. Dual-career families
   ISBN 1-573-22304-2; 1-594-48170-9 pa

   LC 2004-56615

"Writing from the perspective of her first few years of motherhood spent in France and her subsequent return to the U.S., Warner ponders the cultural factors driving the madness of pursuing perfect motherhood and the toll it is taking on American women." Booklist
   Includes bibliographical references

306.81   Marriage and marital status

Calhoun, Ada

Wedding toasts I'll never give; Ada Calhoun. W W Norton & Co Inc 2017 192 p. (hardcover) $24.95   **306.81**
   1. Marriage 2. Autobiographies 3. Man-woman relationship 4. Love -- United States 5. Spouses -- United States 6. Marriage -- United States
   ISBN 0393254798; 9780393254808; 9780393254792

   LC 2017005487

In this memoir, author Ada Calhoun "presents an unflinching but also loving portrait of her own marriage, opening a long-overdue conversation about the institution as it truly is: not the happy ending of a love story or a relic doomed by high divorce rates, but the beginning of a challenging new chapter of which 'the first twenty years are the hardest.'" (Publisher's note)

"This realistic, empathetic book of advice is worthy of a spot on any newlyweds' bookshelf." Pub Wkly
   Includes bibliographical references.

Carroll, Jim

Marriage boot camp; defeat the top 10 marriage killers and build a rock-solid relationship. Elizabeth and James Carroll. New American Library 2015 288 p. (ebook) $45; (paperback) $15   **306.81**
   1. Marriage 2. Married people 3. Interpersonal relations 4. Marital quality 5. Interpersonal conflict 6. Married people -- Psychology
   ISBN 9780698406599; 9780451476777

   LC 2015011862

In this book "relationship experts Elizabeth and Jim Carroll have created a program proven to mend marriages, revive relationships, and make the happily-ever-afters come true. After twenty years of resuscitating thousands of marriages, the Carrolls bring their wisdom directly to readers through this do-it-yourself relationship bible. Filled with advice, exercises, quizzes, and games, Marriage Boot Camp will teach couples to fight the Top Ten Marriage Killers." (Publisher's note)

"The authors make it clear that they've faced their own rocky times, which will endear them to couples trying to find their own happy endings." Pub Wkly

Flock, Elizabeth

The **heart** is a shifting sea; love and marriage in Mumbai. Elizabeth Flock. HarperCollins 2018 xxii, 358 p.p illustrations (hardcover) $27.99   **306.81**
   1. Marriage -- India -- Mumbai 2. Married people -- India -- Mumbai 3. Marriage -- India -- Mumbai -- Case studies
   ISBN 9780062456502; 9780062456489; 0062456482

This book, by Elizabeth Flock, "introduces three couples whose relationships illuminate . . . cultural shifts in dramatic ways. . . . Though these three middle-class couples are at different stages in their lives and come from diverse religious backgrounds, their stories build on one another to present a layered, nuanced, and fascinating mosaic of the universal challenges, possibilities, and promise of matrimony in its present state." (Publisher's note)

"Flock writes about these sensitive topics with generosity and empathy in this beautifully rendered, intricate, and human exploration of love and marriage in Mumbai." LJ

Klinenberg, Eric

Going solo; the extraordinary rise and surprising appeal of living alone. Eric Klinenberg. Penguin Press 2012 273 p.   **306.81**

1. Housing 2. Social psychology 3. Youth -- United States 4. Single people -- United States 5. Living alone -- United States 6. Single people -- United States -- Psychology

ISBN 9781594203220

LC 2011031522

This book explores why more than 50 percent of American adults are single--and why the usually prefer to live that way. . . . The author examines both ends of the age spectrum in an attempt to understand the social implication of this trend. He finds that among relatively affluent young adults in the 25-to-34 age bracket, living solo is seen as a rite of passage into adulthood--a period allowing more sexual freedom, a chance to explore relationships without commitment and a major focus on career building. A similar increase in solitary living is becoming the norm among the elderly. . . . [Eric] Klinenberg suggests that public support is needed to provide affordable, urban assisted-living facilities in which the elderly can maintain their independence for as long as possible. (Kirkus)

Includes bibliographical references and index

Traister, Rebecca, 1975-

★ **All** the single ladies; unmarried women and the rise of an independent nation. Rebecca Traister. Simon & Schuster 2016 352 p. (ebook) $18.99; (hardback) $27   **306.81**

1. Feminism -- United States -- History 2. Single women -- United States -- History 3. Women -- United States -- Social conditions 4. United States -- History 5. United States -- Civilization 6. United States -- Social conditions

ISBN 9781476716589; 9781476716565; 9781476716572

LC 2015045131

"Over the course of her vast research and more than a hundred interviews with academics and social scientists and prominent single women, [author Rebecca] Traister discovered a startling truth: the phenomenon of the single woman in America is not a new one. And historically, when women were given options beyond early heterosexual marriage, the results were massive social change--temperance, abolition, secondary education, and more." (Publisher's note)

"Traister is funny and fair in how she deals with the prevalent stereotypes and remaining stigmas attached to being an unmarried woman in society. She sticks to her central argument that the world is changing and policies need to catch up to the social reality. The result is an invigorating study of single women in America with refreshing insight into the real life of the so-called spinster." Pub Wkly

306.82   Patterns in mate selection

Catron, Mandy Len

How to fall in love with anyone; Mandy Len Catron. Simon & Schuster 2017 ix, 238 p.p (hardcover) $26   **306.82**

1. Love 2. Courtship 3. Mate selection

ISBN 9781501137457; 9781501137464; 1501137441; 9781501137440

LC 2017000307

This essay collection and memoir, by Mandy Len Catron, "explores the romantic myths we create and explains how they limit our ability to

achieve and sustain intimacy. . . . In a series of candid, vulnerable, and wise essays that takes a closer look at what it means to love someone, be loved, and how we present our love to the world, Catron deconstructs her own personal canon of love stories." (Publisher's note)

"Personal musings and reminiscences paired with solid research provide an interesting stroll through an abstract topic." Kirkus

Includes bibliographical references (pages 231-238).

306.84   Types of marriage and relationships

Cleves, Rachel Hope

Charity and Sylvia; a same-sex marriage in early America. Rachel Hope Cleves. Oxford University Press 2014 296 p. $29.95   **306.84**

1. Same-sex marriage 2. Same-sex marriage -- United States -- To 1865

ISBN 0199335427; 9780199335428

LC 2013050416

Stonewall Honor Book: Nonfiction (2015)

"Born in 1777, Charity Bryant was raised in Massachusetts. A brilliant and strong-willed woman with a clear attraction for her own sex, Charity found herself banished from her family home at age twenty. . . . At age twenty-nine, still defiantly single, Charity visited friends in Weybridge, Vermont. There she met a pious and studious young woman named Sylvia Drake. . . . In 1809, they moved into their own home together, and over the years, came to be recognized, essentially, as a married couple. Revered by their community, Charity and Sylvia operated a tailor shop employing many local women, served as guiding lights within their church, and participated in raising their many nieces and nephews." (Publisher's note)

"This volume provides an exhaustive and valuable look into a relatively unknown lesbian relationship in Colonial America, proving that Puritans could be accepting in their own way of 'marriages' between women." LJ

Includes bibliographical references and index

Johnson, Sophie Lucido

Many love; a memoir of polyamory and finding love(s) Sophie Lucido Johnson. Touchstone 2018 272 p. (paperback) $16   **306.84**

1. Sex 2. Love 3. Man-woman relationship 4. Sex customs 5. Non-monogamous relationships

ISBN 9781501189784

LC 2017059117

In this memoir, author Sophie Lucido Johnson "explores her sexuality, her values, and the versions of love our society accepts and practices. Along the way, she shares what it's like to play on Tinder side-by-side with your boyfriend, encounter--and surmount--many types of jealousy, learn the power of female friendship, and other amazing things that happened when she stopped looking for 'the one.'" (Publisher's note)

Sheff, Elisabeth

Stories from the Polycule; Real Life in Polyamorous Families. by Dr. Elisabeth Sheff; illustrated by Tikva Wolf. Itasca Books 2015 288 p. illustrations (ebook) $7.99; $17.99 **306.84**

1. Polygamy

ISBN 9780991399789; 0991399773; 9780991399772

This book, by Dr. Elisabeth Sheff, with illustrations by Tikva Wolf, is "an anthology of work from people living in polyamorous families of all configurations." (Publisher's note)

"Readers engaged in or curious about polyamorous families will find plenty to ponder in this eclectic and enlightening collection." Pub Wkly

306.85   Family

Carbone, June

Marriage markets; how inequality is remaking the American family. June Carbone and Naomi Cahn. Oxford University Press, USA 2014 272 p. illustrations (hardback) $29.95 **306.85**

1. Marriage 2. Family -- Economic aspects 3. United States -- Economic conditions 4. Equality -- United States 5. Social classes -- United States 6. Domestic relations -- United States 7. Families -- Economic aspects -- United States 8. Marriage -- Economic aspects -- United States 9. Working class -- Economic aspects -- United States

ISBN 0199916586; 9780199916580

LC 2013045704

In this book, authors "June Carbone and Naomi Cahn examine how macroeconomic forces are transforming our most intimate and important spheres, and how working class and lower income families have paid the highest price. Why is this so? The book provides the answer: greater economic inequality has profoundly changed marriage markets, the way men and women match up when they search for a life partner." (Publisher's note)

"This book is a methodical and skillful discussion of how the American family has changed and what needs to happen to rescue it. Social scientists, family advocates, and policymakers will find it thought provoking." LJ

Gerson, Stéphane

Disaster Falls; A Family Story. Stéphane Gerson. Random House Inc. 2017 272 p. $26; (ebook) $65 **306.85**

1. Family crises 2. Drowning -- Utah -- Green River

ISBN 1101906693; 9781101906699; 9781101906705

LC 2016016306

"On a rafting trip down Utah's Green River, Stéphane Gerson's eight-year-old son, Owen, drowned in a spot known as Disaster Falls. That night, as darkness fell, Stéphane huddled in a tent with his wife, Alison, and their older son, Julian, trying to understand what seemed inconceivable.... [This book] chronicles the aftermath of that day and ... [offers] an unflinching portrait of a marriage tested." (Publisher's note)

"While asserting that one can never recover from the death of a child, Gerson evocatively describes the process of a struggle that allows him to continue living." Pub Wkly

Includes bibliographical references.

Janning, Michelle

The **stuff** of family life; how our homes reflect our lives. Michelle Janning. Rowman & Littlefield 2017 xii, 225 p.p (hardcover) $34 **306.85**

1. Family life 2. House furnishings 3. Families 4. Domestic space 5. House furnishings -- Psychological aspects 6. Personal belongings -- Psychological aspects

ISBN 9781442254800; 9781442254794

LC 2016058386

This book, by Michelle Janning, "takes readers inside the changing world of families through a unique examination of their stuff. From digital family photo albums to the growing popularity of 'man caves.' . . . The book takes readers through various phases of family life, including dating, marriage, parenting, divorce, and aging, while paying attention to how our choices about our spaces and objects impact our lives." (Publisher's note)

"Whether familiar with sociological methods or not, readers will be fascinated by Janning's ideas and the connections she draws between household items and family life." Booklist

Includes bibliographical references and index

306.87   Intrafamily relationships

Duron, Lori

Raising my rainbow; adventures in raising a slightly effeminate, possibly gay, totally fabulous son. Lori Duron. Crown Trade 2013 224 p. $15 **306.87**

1. LGBT youth 2. Gender role 3. Parent-child relationship 4. Child rearing 5. Child psychology

ISBN 0770437729; 9780770437725

LC 2012042444

Stonewall Book Award: Israel Fishman Non-Fiction Award (2014)

This book, by Lori Duron, is the author's "account of her and her family's adventures of distress and happiness raising a gender-creative son. . . . C.J. is gender variant or gender nonconforming, . . . whatever the term, Lori has a boy who likes girl stuff. . . . He floats on the gender-variation spectrum from super-macho-masculine on the left all the way to super-girly-feminine on the right." (Publisher's note)

"In Duron's story, parents will find support for a 'love them, not change them' style of parenting, optimism about the outcomes for their gender-creative children, sympathy for the difficulties of parenting, and an affirmation of the appropriateness and necessity for fierce advocacy." Pub Wkly

Schuitemaker, Lisette

The **Eldest** Daughter Effect; how firstborn women--like Oprah Winfrey, Sheryl Sandberg, JK Rowling and Beyoncé-harness their strengths. Lisette Schuitemaker & Wies Enthoven; translation by Lisette Schuitemaker. Findhorn Press 2016 192 p. $15.99 **306.87**

1. Siblings 2. Daughters 3. Birth order

ISBN 1844097072; 9781844097074

LC 2017002540

In this book, by Lisette Schuitemaker and Wies Enthoven, translated by Lisette Schuitemaker, the authors "set out to discover the big five qualities that characterize all eldest daughters to some degree. Eldest daughters are responsible, dutiful, thoughtful, expeditious and caring. Firstborns are more intelligent than their siblings, more proficient verbally and more motivated to perform. Yet at the same time they seriously doubt that they are good enough." (Publisher's note)

"Eldest daughters and those who love them will find this book fascinating." LJ

Includes bibliographical references.

Tannen, Deborah

I only say this because I love you; how the way we talk can make or break family relationships throughout our lives. Random House 2001 xxvii, 336p hardcover o.p. pa $15.95 **306.87**

1. Family 2. Communication

ISBN 0-345-40752-0 pa

LC 00-68851

"With lively prose and genuine concern for people, Tannen brings linguistic concepts—metamessage, re-framing, indirect request—to bear on dozens of situations to help lay readers strenghten family ties." Libr J

Includes bibliographical references

306.872   Spousal relationship

Yalom, Marilyn

A **history** of the wife. HarperCollins Pubs. 2001 441p il
hardcover o.p. pa $14.95   **306.872**
   1. Marriage 2. Women -- History
   ISBN 0-06-093156-6 pa

                      LC 00-58153

Yalom "has apparently written the first truly comprehensive history
of the Western female spousal experience; indeed, there are precious
few long views of either marriage or the family to which this book can
be compared." Libr J

306.874   Parent-child relationship

Babul, Denna D.

The **fatherless** daughter project; understanding our losses
and reclaiming our lives. Denna D. Babul, RN, and Karin Luise, PhD. Avery 2015 304 p. (alk. paper) $26; (ebook)
$65   **306.874**
   1. Loss (Psychology) 2. Children of single parents 3. Father-
daughter relationship 4. Fathers and daughters 5. Parent and adult
child
   ISBN 9781594633690; 9780698194410

                      LC 2015025161

In this book, by Denna D. Babul and Karin Luise, "the authors have
found that fatherless daughters tend to push their emotions underground.
These issues in turn become distinct patterns in their relationships as
adult women and they often can't figure out why. Delivered with compassion and expertise, this book allows readers support and understanding they never had when they first needed it, and it encourages the conversation to continue." (Publisher's note)

"With interesting personal stories woven throughout, fatherless
daughters will find this to be a supportive and encouraging guidebook to
reclaiming their lives and healing their wounds." Pub Wkly

Includes bibliographical references and index

Bradley, Michael J.

Crazy-stressed; saving today's overwhelmed teens with
love, laughter, and the science of resilience. Michael J. Bradley.
AMACOM 2017 xxiv, 256 p.p (pbk.) $17.95   **306.874**
   1. Parenting 2. Advice literature 3. Adolescent psychology 4.
Teenagers 5. Parent and teenager
   ISBN 9780814438053; 9780814438046

                      LC 2016044192

This book, by Michael J. Bradley, "sheds light on the teen brain and
offers a wealth of resiliency-boosting strategies. In it, Dr. Bradley reveals: what kids these days are really going through; ways to strengthen
the seven skills every teen needs to survive and thrive; what-to-do-when
suggestions for common behavior, school, and social issues; tactics for
coping with conflict, teaching consequences, improving communication, staying connected, and more." (Publisher's note)

"Bradley's book is aimed at teaching parents to help teens develop
resilience. It is also a useful and important book for those who work
with teens." VOYA

Includes bibliographical references (pages 245-248) and index

Brooks, Kim

Small animals; parenthood in the age of fear. Kim Brooks.
Flatiron Books 2018 256 p. (hardcover) $26.99   **306.874**
   1. Motherhood 2. Child welfare 3. Parenthood -- United States 4.

Child welfare -- United States 5. Fear -- United States 6. Mother
and child -- United States
   ISBN 9781250089557

                      LC 2017061165

This book, by Kim Brooks, "is a riveting examination of the ways
our culture of competitive, anxious, and judgmental parenting has profoundly altered the experiences of parents and children. . . . Brooks offers a provocative, compelling portrait of parenthood in America and
calls us to examine what we most value in our relationships with our
children and one another." (Publisher's note)

"Compassionate and empathetic, appalled and angry, this fierce, intimate blend of memoir, reportage, and critique is essential reading for
parents, policymakers, and all others concerned about our children and
their future." LJ

Includes bibliographical references

Chabon, Michael, 1963-

   ★ **Pops**; fatherhood in pieces. Michael Chabon. Harper-
Collins 2018 144 p. $19.99   **306.874**
   1. Fathers 2. Fatherhood 3. Father-son relationship
   ISBN 0062834622; 9780062834621

                      LC 2018045348

In this book, author Michael Chabon "delivers a collection of essays-
-heartfelt, humorous, . . . wise--on the meaning of fatherhood. For the
September 2016 issue of 'GQ,' . . . [he] wrote a piece about accompanying his son Abraham Chabon, then thirteen, to Paris Men's Fashion Week. . . . With the 'GQ' story as its centerpiece, and featuring six
additional essays plus an introduction, 'Pops' illuminates the meaning,
magic, and mysteries of fatherhood as only Michael . . . can." (Publisher's note)

"The author combines perfect pitch of tone with an acute eye for
detail, whether reporting on his 13-year-old son's unlikely emergence as
a fashion savant...or trying to navigate his way through reading Huckleberry Finn aloud to his children without repeating a word that makes
him recoil. Even when he's driving at cruising speed, Chabon takes his
readers for an enjoyable ride." Kirkus

Chua, Amy

Battle hymn of the tiger mother. Penguin Press 2011 237p
il   **306.874**
   1. Lawyers 2. Mothers 3. Parenting 4. Child rearing 5. Memoirists
6. Law teachers 7. College teachers 8. Biography, Individual 9.
Mothers and daughters 10. Chinese American families
   ISBN 9781594202841; 1594202842; 9780143120582

                      LC 2010029623

It was the author's "stated intent . . . to present the differences between Western and Chinese parenting styles by sharing experiences with
her own children. . . . As the daughter of Chinese immigrants, she is
poised to contrast the two disparate styles, even as she points out that
being a 'Chinese Mother' . . . is more a state of mind than a genetic trait.
. . . She insists that Western children are no happier than Chinese ones."
(Booklist)

Includes bibliographical references

Cusk, Rachel

A **life's** work; on becoming a mother. Picador 2002 213p
$22; pa $13   **306.874**
   1. Mothers 2. Parenting 3. Motherhood
   ISBN 0-312-26987-0; 0-312-31130-3 pa

                      LC 2001-54894

First published 2001 in the United Kingdom
The author discusses childbirth and motherhood.
"This is not a happy guide; instead, it is a penetrating, sometimes

joyful and amusing, sometimes frightening and disturbing look at pregnancy and motherhood." Booklist

DeGarmo, John

The **foster** parenting manual; a practical guide to creating a loving, safe and stable home. John DeGarmo; foreword by Mary Perdue. Jessica Kingsley Publishers 2013 160 p. $17.95   **306.874**
1. Parenting 2. Foster children 3. Foster home care 4. Foster parents
ISBN 184905956X; 9781849059565

LC 2013012292

This book, by John Degarmo, "is a comprehensive guide offering proven, friendly advice for novice and experienced parents alike.... He describes what to expect from the process, how to access help and how to ensure the best care for your child. He tackles thorny issues such as children's use of the Internet and social media, managing contact with birth parents and how to support your child at school." (Publisher's note)

"DeGarmo includes both big-picture ideas about child development and nuts-and-bolts considerations for fostering, such as how often a caseworker must visit a home, what foster families are reimbursed for, and what training is required." LJ

Includes bibliographical references (page 142-154) and index

Dell'Antonia, K. J.

How to be a happier parent; raising a family, having a life, and loving (almost) every minute. K. J. Dell'Antonia. Avery, an imprint of Penguin Random House 2018 311 p. (hbk) $27   **306.874**
1. Parenthood 2. Stress management 3. Parent-child relationship 4. Parent and child
ISBN 0735210470; 9780735210479

LC 2017301186

This book, by K. J. Dell'Antonia, presents "an encouraging guide to helping parents find more happiness in their day-to-day family life. ... KJ discovers that it's possible to do more by doing less, and make our family life a refuge and pleasure, rather than another stress point in a hectic day. She focuses on nine common problem spots that cause parents the most grief, ... and offers small, doable, sometimes surprising steps you can take to make them better." (Publisher's note)

Includes bibliographical references (pages 299-311)

Gallagher, Shaun

Experimenting with babies; 50 amazing science projects you can perform on your kid. by Shaun Gallagher. Perigee Book 2013 224 p. (pbk.) $16   **306.874**
1. Infants 2. Science -- Experiments 3. Parent and child
ISBN 0399162461; 9780399162466

LC 2013021018

This book, by Shaun Gallagher, "shows you how to re-create landmark scientific studies on cognitive, motor, language, and behavioral development—using your [infant] as the research subject. Simple [and] engaging, ... each project sheds light on how your baby is acquiring new skills--everything from recognizing faces, voices, and shapes to understanding new words, learning to walk, and even distinguishing between right and wrong." (Publisher's note)

"This is a unique work that presents an enjoyable and intelligent look at child development." LJ

Includes bibliographical references

Giffels, David

★ **Furnishing** eternity; a father, a son, a coffin, and a mea-

sure of life. David Giffels. Scribner 2018 243 p. $24 **306.874**
1. Death 2. Father-son relationship 3. Fathers and sons
ISBN 1501105949; 9781501105944

This book, by David Giffels, is "a vibrant, heartfelt memoir about confronting mortality, surviving loss, finding resilience in one's Midwest roots and seeking a father's wisdom through an unusual woodworking project—constructing his own coffin." (Publisher's note)

Greene, Ross W.

Raising human beings; Creating a Collaborative Partnership with Your Child. Ross W. Greene, Ph.D. Scribner 2016 304 p. (hardcover: alk. paper) $26   **306.874**
1. Parenting 2. Child rearing 3. Parent-child relationship 4. Parent and child
ISBN 9781476723747; 9781476723761

LC 2016021664

This book by Ross W. Greene "explains how to cultivate a better parent-child relationship while also nurturing empathy, honesty, resilience, and independence.... Parents have an important task: figure out who their child is--his or her skills ... beliefs, values, ... goals and direction. ... Greene offers ... guide for raising kids in a way that enhances relationships, improves communication, and helps kids learn how to resolve disagreements without conflict." (Publisher's note)

"This book is a game-changer for parents, teachers, and other caregivers of children. Its advice is reasonable and empathetic, and readers will feel ready to start creating a better relationship with the children in their lives." Pub Wkly

Holroyd, Michael

A **book** of secrets; Michael Holroyd. Farrar, Straus and Giroux 2011 xiv, 258p.p ill.   **306.874**
1. Essays 2. Biography 3. Illegitimacy 4. Gifted women 5. Women -- Biography 6. Biography, Collective
ISBN 0-374-11558-3; 978-0-374-11558-6 0-374-11558-3

LC 2011003839

In this book, "Holroyd brings a company of unknown women into the light. From Alice Keppel, the mistress of both the second Lord Grimthorpe and the Prince of Wales; to Eve Fairfax, a muse of Auguste Rodin; to the novelist Violet Trefusis, the lover of Vita Sackville-West--these women are always on the periphery of the respectable world. Also on the margins is the ... biographer, who on occasion turns an ... eye upon himself as part of his investigations in the maze of biography." (Publisher's note)

Includes bibliographical references and index.

Hurley, Katie

No more mean girls; the secret to raising strong, confident, and compassionate girls. Katie Hurley, LCSW. TarcherPerigee 2018 xxvi, 303 p.p (pbk) $17   **306.874**
1. Daughters 2. Parenting 3. Girls -- Psychology 4. Compassion 5. Self-confidence
ISBN 9781524704674; 9780143130864

LC 2017031973

This book, by Katie Hurley, "is a guide for parents to help their young daughters navigate tricky territories such as friendship building, creating an authentic self, standing up for themselves and others, and expressing themselves in a healthy way.... This book offers actionable steps to help parents empower young girls to be kind, confident leaders who work together and build each other up." (Publisher's note)

"Hurley's user-friendly layout and compassionate advice ensure that her book will be a useful workbook not just for parents, but also for youth counselors, teachers, and other caregivers." Pub Wkly

Includes bibliographical references and index.

Isay, Jane

Unconditional love; a guide to navigating the joys and challenges of being a grandparent today. Jane Isay. HarperCollins 2018 x, 226 p.p (hardcover) $27.99   **306.874**
1. Grandparents 2. Grandparenting 3. Grandparent-grandchild relationship 4. Grandparent and child
ISBN 9780062427175; 9780062427168; 0062427164

This book, by Jane Isay, is "a beautiful meditation on the joys of being a grandparent and a practical guide to help you and your adult children make the most of your relationship with a grandchild. . . . [Isay] explores the realities of today's multigenerational families, identifying problems and offering solutions to enhance love, trust, and understanding between grandparents, parents, and grandchildren." (Publisher's note)

"Isay . . . shares what it is to be a grandparent and how to keep family conflicts to a minimum and joy at the maximum in this lovely treatment of a widely shared experience." Pub Wkly

Includes bibliographical references (pages 211-213) and index.

Johnson, Plum

They left us everything; a memoir. Plum Johnson. G.P. Putnam's Sons 2014 279 p. illustrations (ebook) $65; (hardcover) $26   **306.874**
1. Caregivers 2. Aging parents 3. Parent-child relationship 4. Houses -- Buying and selling 5. Parent and adult child 6. Aging parents -- Care -- Canada 7. Caregivers -- Canada -- Biography 8. Families -- Psychological aspects 9. House selling -- Psychological aspects 10. House furnishings -- Psychological aspects 11. Personal belongings -- Psychological aspects 12. Adult children of aging parents -- Family relationships -- Canada
ISBN 9780399184116; 0399184090; 9780399184093
LC 2016023486

This book is a "memoir of family, loss, and a house jam-packed with decades of goods and memories. After almost twenty years of caring for elderly parents—first for their senile father, and then for their cantankerous ninety-three-year old mother—author Plum Johnson and her three younger brothers have finally fallen to their middle-aged knees with conflicted feelings of grief and relief. Now they must empty and sell the beloved family home, twenty-three rooms bulging with history, antiques, and oxygen tanks." (Publisher's note)

"It is an uplifting affirmation of human relationships and the cycle of life itself. A warmly candid memoir of navigating family, aging, and death." Kirkus

Leap, Jorja

Project Fatherhood; a story of courage and healing in one of America's toughest communities. Jorja Leap. Beacon Press 2015 256 p. (hardback) $24.95   **306.874**
1. Fathers 2. Parenting 3. Parenting -- California -- Los Angeles 4. Fatherhood -- California -- Los Angeles 5. Father and child -- California -- Los Angeles
ISBN 0807014524; 9780807014523
LC 2014043792

This book by Jorja Leap "follows the lives of the men as they struggle with the pain of their own losses, the chronic pressures of poverty and unemployment, and the unquenchable desire to do better and provide more for the next generation. Although the group begins as a forum for them to discuss issues relating to their roles as parents, it slowly grows to mean much more: it becomes a place where they can share jokes and traumatic experiences, joys and sorrows." (Publisher's note)

"Leap observes and captures, in the members' own words, the group's development and its members' four years of progress toward healing their families and, perhaps, their community." Pub Wkly

Lythcott-Haims, Julie

How to raise an adult; break free of the overparenting trap and prepare your kid for success. Julie Lythcott-Haims. Henry Holt & Co. 2015 368 p. illustrations (hardback) $27 **306.874**
1. Parenting 2. Parent-child relationship
ISBN 1627791779; 9781627791779
LC 2014044394

This book by Julie Lythcott-Haims "draws on research . . . and on her own insights as a mother and as a student dean to highlight the ways in which overparenting harms children, their stressed-out parents, and society at large. While empathizing with the parental hopes and, especially, fears that lead to overhelping, Lythcott-Haims offers practical alternative strategies that underline the importance of allowing children to make their own mistakes." (Publisher's note)

"Well-presented, solid facts that address the many detriments of helicopter parenting." Kirkus

Includes bibliographical references

McConville, Brigid

On Becoming a Mother; Welcoming Your New Baby and Your New Life With Wisdom from Around the World. Brigid McConville. Pgw 2014 304 p. illustrations $16.99 **306.874**
1. Infants 2. Mother-child relationship
ISBN 1780743890; 9781780743899
Includes index

This book by Brigid McConville discusses mothering practices around the world, "From the Mexican rebozo used to rock the belly and ease back pain during pregnancy to the Bengali practice of taking off a woman's bangles to help her visualize a speedy labor, . . . from the proverbs printed on the kangas used to carry East African newborns to the Japanese ritual where Sumo wrestlers are asked to make infants cry." (Publisher's note)

"The American baby shower, Islamic naming ceremonies, and first birthdays in Korea sit comfortably next to each other in this global celebration of motherhood." Pub Wkly

McGlynn, David

One day you'll thank me; lessons from an unexpected fatherhood. David McGlynn. Counterpoint Press 2018 272 p. (alk. paper) $25 **306.874**
1. Fatherhood 2. Father-child relationship 3. African American authors -- Biography 4. Fatherhood -- Humor 5. Fatherhood -- Anecdotes 6. Father and child -- Humor 7. Father and child -- Anecdotes 8. Authors, American -- Biography
ISBN 9781640090392
LC 2017052590

In this book, David McGlynn, "translates the small, often hilarious moments common among parents of young children, especially dads, into 'life lessons' about fatherhood. Comprised of interconnected chapters--many of which have appeared in . . . publications as 'The New York Times,' 'Men's Health,' 'Parents,' 'Real Simple,' and 'O, The Oprah Magazine'--the stories invoke a sense of humor and honesty that expand our understanding of what it means to be an American dad." (Publisher's note)

Morris, Virginia

How to Care for Aging Parents; A One-Stop Resource for All Your Medical, Financial, Housing, and Emotional Issues. Virginia Morris. Workman Pub Co 2014 688 p. **306.874**
1. Aging parents
ISBN 0761166769; 9780761166764

"Morris's authoritative guide on caring for aging parents, now in its third edition, is a must-read for anyone who wants to prepare for emotionally strenuous challenge head on. She thoroughly addresses the subject, covering most topics imaginable from standards such as exercise and healthy diet to uncomfortable ones such as STDs, Alzheimer's, and delusions and hallucinations. The vast amounts of information are succinctly communicated often using visual aids as inset boxes, checklists, at-a-glance comparison charts, and blocked quotes from a variety players involved in the process with reassuring personal testimonies." (Publishers Weekly)

Newman, Katherine S., 1953-

The **accordion** family; boomerang kids, anxious parents, and the private toll of global competition. Katherine S. Newman. Beacon Press 2012 xxiii, 261 p.p charts $25.95 **306.874**
   1. Parent-child relationship 2. Globalization -- Economic aspects 3. Adult children living with parents 4. Parent and adult child 5. Competition, International 6. Adult children -- Family relationships
   ISBN 0807007439; 9780807007433
                      LC 2011027846

This book "examines the proliferation of 'accordion families,' in which children continue to live with their parents late into their 20s and 30s. . . . [Katherine] Newman's inquiry takes her around the world to examine how family structures are responding to societal changes. She examines how high unemployment rates, the rise of short-term employment, staggered birth rates, longer life expectancies, and the high cost of living have affected the younger generation's transition to adulthood." (Publishers Weekly)

Includes bibliographical references and index

Rosswood, Eric

Journey to Same-sex Parenthood; Firsthand Advice, Tips and Stories from Lesbian and Gay Couples. Eric Rosswood: foreword by Melissa Gilbert; introduction by Charlie Condou; epilogue by Gabriel Blau. New Horizon Press 2016 240 p. (paperback) $15.95 **306.874**
   1. Adoption 2. Parenthood 3. Gay couples
   ISBN 9780882825144; 0882825143
                      LC 2015913633

This book, by Eric Rosswood, "guides and helps prospective LGBT parents to explore . . . five popular options [of parenting]: Adoption, Foster Care, Assisted Reproduction, Surrogacy and Co-Parenting. Each section includes a description of the specific family-building approach, followed by personal stories from same-sex couples and individuals who have chosen and gone through that particular journey." (Publisher's note)

"This supportive and helpful volume is full of warmth, encouragement, and advice, and it's a good place for prospective parents to start." Pub Wkly

Sandahl, Iben Dissing

The **Danish** way of parenting; Jessica Joelle Alexander and Iben Sandahl. TarcherPerigee 2016 208 p. (ebook) $48; $16 **306.874**
   1. Parenting -- Denmark 2. Parent-child relationship 3. Parenting -- Cross-cultural studies
   ISBN 9781101992975; 9780143111719
                      LC 2016006963

This book on parenting in Denmark, by Jessica Joelle Alexander and Iben Sandahl, "presents six essential principles, which spell out P-A-R-E-N-T: Play is essential for development and well-being. Authenticity fosters trust. . . . Reframing helps kids cope with setbacks and look on the bright side. Empathy allows us to act with kindness toward others.

No ultimatums means no power struggles, . . . [and] Togetherness is a way to celebrate family time." (Publisher's note)

"This pithy, practical little volume is the ideal guide for parents seeking to change their child-rearing habits." Pub Wkly

Includes bibliographical references and index

Sandler, Lauren

One and only; the freedom of having an only child, and the joy of being one. Lauren Sandler. Simon & Schuster 2013 224 p. $24.99 **306.874**
   1. Parenting 2. Only child 3. Families 4. Family size
   ISBN 1451626959; 9781451626957
                      LC 2013000707

Author Lauren Sandier, an only child, considers only children. "Though she says this is not a memoir, her personal story is woven throughout, beginning with her mother's decision to have one child and ending with the author's apparent decision not to have a second child . . . The focus of the book, however, is on dissecting the research surrounding the myth of the lonely, selfish, maladjusted only child." (Publishers Weekly)

Includes bibliographical references

Senior, Jennifer

All Joy and No Fun; The Paradox of Modern Parenthood. by Jennifer Senior. HarperCollins 2014 320 p. hbk $26.99 **306.874**
   1. Happiness 2. Parenting 3. Gender role 4. Home economics
   ISBN 0062072226; 9780062072221
                      LC 2013498720

In this book, author Jennifer Senior "argues that changes in the last half century have radically altered the roles of today's mothers and fathers. . . . Recruiting from a wide variety of sources--in history, sociology, economics, psychology, philosophy, and anthropology--she dissects both the timeless strains of parenting and the ones that are brand new, and then brings her research to life in the homes of ordinary parents around the country." (Publisher's note)

"Full of fascinating ideas and information about the family structure and its history, this work is sure to be of strong interest to parents, in particular, as they look for meaning beyond the day to day." LJ

Includes bibliographical references and index

Thiagarajan, Maya

Beyond the tiger mom; East-West parenting for the global age. by Maya Thiagarajan. Tuttle Publishing 2016 224 p. illustrations (hardcover) $18.95; (ebook) $17.99 **306.874**
   1. Parenting 2. East and West 3. Parent-child relationship 4. Parent and child -- Asia
   ISBN 9780804846028; 9781462918416
                      LC 2015027385

This book on parenting, by Maya Thiagarajan, "examines the stereotypes and goes beneath the surface to explore what really happens in Asian households. How do Asian parents think about childhood, family and education—and what can Western parents learn from them? Through interviews with hundreds of Asian parents and kids, Thiagarajan offers a detailed look at their values, hopes, fears and parenting styles." (Publisher's note)

"This is an excellent resource for both parents and teachers." Booklist

Includes bibliographical references

Tsabary, Shefali

   ★ The **awakened** family; a revolution in parenting. Shefali

Tsabary, Ph.D. Viking 2016 368 p. (hardcover) $27 **306.874**
1. Parenting 2. Parent-child relationship 3. Families 4. Parent and child
ISBN 9780399563966

LC 2016003716

This book, by Shefali Tsabary, "will take you on a journey to transcending your fears and illusions around parenting and help you become the parent you always wanted to be: fully present and conscious. It will arm you with practical, hands-on strategies and real-life examples from [the author's] experience as a parent and clinical psychologist that show the extraordinary power of being a conscious parent." (Publisher's note)

"Readers of Tsabary's first book will find this follow-up useful and encouraging, and those starting here will find everything they need without having to refer back." Pub Wkly

Uhls, Yalda T.

Media moms & digital dads; a fact-not-fear approach to parenting in the digital age. Yalda Uhls. Bibliomotion 2015 xxiv, 238 p.p (paperback) $18.95   **306.874**
1. Parenting 2. Social media 3. Child rearing 4. Parenting -- Social aspects
ISBN 1629560847; 9781629560847

LC 2015021252

This book, by Yalda T. Uhls, "breaks down complex issues in a friendly, accessible fashion, making it a highly useful and, ultimately, reassuring read for anyone worries about the impact that media might be having on young minds. Dr. Uhls ends each chapter with summaries of the science, bottom lines for quick takeaways, and tips and guidance for parents. Each chapter delves into a different issue, so parents can easily turn to their own particular needs and skip what doesn't concern them." (Publisher's note)

"Research-based information, common sense, and opinion drive the discussion as questions are raised concerning when, where, and how the use of digital media is appropriate." ForeWord

Includes bibliographical references (pages 191-222) and index

Waichler, Iris

Role reversal; how to take care of yourself and your aging parents. Iris Waichler, MSW, LCSW. She Writes Press 2016 xvii, 283 p.p illustrations (paperback) $16.95   **306.874**
1. Caregivers -- Handbooks, manuals, etc. 2. Aging parents -- Care 3. Caregivers -- Family relationships 4. Parent and adult child -- Psychological aspects 5. Adult children of aging parents -- United States 6. Aging parents -- Family relationships -- United States
ISBN 9781631520921; 9781631520914; 1631520911

LC 2016935741

This book, by Iris Waichler, is "designed to help caregivers understand how to cope with and overcome the overwhelming challenges that arise while caregiving for a loved one--especially an aging parent. . . . [The book] is a comprehensive guide to navigating the enormous daily challenges faced by caregivers. In these pages, Waichler blends her personal experience caring for her beloved father with her forty years of expertise as a patient advocate and clinical social worker." (Publisher's note)

"By offering so much advice about managing the difficult and even heartbreaking situations the author experienced, the book offers the reader a sense of speaking to a well-informed and personally invested friend rather than an impersonal medical professional." Pub Wkly

Includes bibliographical references.

Waters, Lea

The **strength** switch; how the new science of strength-based parenting can help your child and your teen to flourish.

Lea Waters. Avery 2017 340 p. illustrations (hardcover) $27   **306.874**
1. Parenting 2. Advice literature 3. Parent-child relationship 4. Parent and child
ISBN 9781101983669; 9781101983645

LC 2016054068

This book, by Lea Waters, reveals "the extraordinary results of focusing on our children's strengths rather than always trying to correct their weaknesses. . . . [It also shows] how we can not only help our children build resilience, optimism, and achievement but . . . also help inoculate them against today's pandemic of depression and anxiety. . . . Waters demonstrates how to . . . deal with problem behaviors and talk about difficult situations and emotions." (Publisher's note)

"Waters's clearly presented, easily implemented ideas will make sense to parents looking to escape the corrective mind-set . . ." Pub Wkly

Includes bibliographical references (pages 301-306) and index.

When I first held you; 22 critically acclaimed writers talk about the triumphs, challenges, and transformative experience of fatherhood. edited by Brian Gresko; introduction by Darin Strauss. Berkley Books 2014 304 p. $15   **306.874**
1. Fatherhood 2. Authors -- Family life 3. Fathers
ISBN 0425269248; 9780425269244

LC 2013050514

In this book, edited by Brian Gresko, "22 of today's masterful writers get straight to the heart of modern fatherhood. . . . From making that ultimate decision to have a kid to making it through the birth to tangling with a toddler mid-tantrum, and eventually letting a teen loose in the world, these fathers explore every facet of fatherhood and show how being a father changed the way they saw the world--and themselves." (Publisher's note)

"This impressive collection deeply probes both the exterior and interior changes that come with fatherhood." Pub Wkly

306.88   Alteration of family arrangements

Aikman, Becky

Saturday night widows; the adventures of six friends remaking their lives. Becky Aikman. Crown 2013 337 p. $26   **306.88**
1. Widows 2. Self-help groups 3. Widowhood
ISBN 0307590437; 9780307590435

LC 2012021057

This book, by Becky Aikman, profiles "six marriages, six heartbreaks, [and] one shared beginning. . . . In this . . . memoir, she explores surprising new discoveries about how people experience grief and transcend loss and, following her own remarriage, forms a group with five other young widows to test these unconventional ideas. Together, these friends summon the humor, resilience, and striving spirit essential for anyone overcoming adversity." (Publisher's note)

306.89   Separation and divorce

Emery, Robert E.

Two homes, one childhood; a parenting plan to last a lifetime. Robert E. Emery Ph.D. Avery 2016 336 p. (ebook) $65; (hardback) $26   **306.89**
1. Parenting 2. Part-time parenting 3. Children of divorced parents 4. Parent and child
ISBN 9780698404243; 9781594634154

LC 2016010866

This book, by Robert Emery, "details a new approach to sharing custody with children in two homes. Huge numbers of children are affected by separation, divorce, cohabitation breakups, and childbearing outside of marriage. These children have two homes. But their parents have only one chance to protect their childhood. . . . Emery explains that a parenting plan that lasts a lifetime is one that grows and changes along with children's—and families'—developing needs." (Publisher's note)

"Research and common sense back solid strategies that allow children to navigate the ups and downs of divorce with minimal damage." Kirkus

Includes bibliographical references (pages [313]-317) and index.

Moffett, Kay

Not your mother's divorce; a practical, girlfriend-to-girlfriend guide to surviving the end of an early marriage. [by] Kay Moffett and Sarah Touborg. Broadway Bks. 2003 259p pa $12.95 **306.89**

1. Divorce
ISBN 0-7679-1350-7

LC 2003-58531

The authors "help young divorcées tackle both legal and emotional problems. . . . Overwhelming issues like mutual photographs, wedding rings, and family, as well as legal console, mediators, and even Internet divorce, are discussed with authority and sensitivity. The authors realize that each person is different and comes out her relationship with a different set of circumstances, so they also provide many personal stories—including their own." Libr J

Sexton, James J.

If you're in my office, it's already too late; a divorce lawyer's guide to staying together. James J. Sexton, Esq. Henry Holt & Co. 2018 288 p. (hardcover) $26 **306.89**

1. Divorce 2. Marriage 3. Interpersonal relations 4. Spouses 5. Interpersonal conflict
ISBN 9781250130778

LC 2017042566

In this book, "hard-hitting divorce lawyer James Sexton shares his insights and wisdom from the front lines of divorce to keep you out of his office and improve your relationship. . . . Sexton tells the unvarnished truth about relationships, diving straight into the most common marital problems. These usually derive from dishonest . . . communication. . . . Symptom and root cause get confused all the time." (Publisher's note)

Wallerstein, Judith S.

The **unexpected** legacy of divorce; a 25 year landmark study. by Judith Wallerstein, Julia Lewis and Sandy Blakeslee. Hyperion 2000 xxxv, 347p o.p.; pbk $16.99 **306.89**

1. Divorce 2. Children of divorced parents
ISBN 0-7868-6394-3; 9780786886166

LC 00-35071

The author follows her two studies "on the effects of divorce on children (Surviving the Breakup, 1980; Second Chances, 1989) with this third study of 93 adults whom she first interviewed as children 25 years ago. Her findings are presented through five very readable case studies interwoven with other data." Libr J

Includes bibliographical references

306.893   Separation and divorce – Women

Riss, Suzanne

The **optimist's** guide to divorce; how to get through your breakup and create a new life you love. Suzanne Riss & Jill Sockwell. Workman Publishing 2016 288 p. illustrations (ebook) $14.95; (alk. paper) $14.95 **306.893**

1. Divorce 2. Divorced women -- Life skills guides 3. Divorce -- Psychological aspects
ISBN 9780761189763; 9780761187424

LC 2016053408

This book, by Suzanne Riss and Jill Sockwell, "captures the experience of sisterhood through the voices of its authors and their community of women in the Maplewood Divorce Club. . . . This book prepares you for each phase of divorce, from having 'the talk,' to breaking the news to family and friends, to figuring out where to live, to co-parenting with an ex, to rebounding and rebooting your life." (Publisher's note)

"From varying backgrounds and portrayed with their identifying details obscured, they've left passionless, abusive, or faithless unions, or been left themselves. The overall effect is a chorus of relatable, emotional, and true-feeling stories about the many facets of divorce that will have newly single advice-seekers feeling less alone and more sure they'll get through it, too." Booklist

306.9   Institutions pertaining to death

Ehrenreich, Barbara, 1941-

★ **Natural** causes; an epidemic of wellness, the certainty of dying, and killing ourselves to live longer. Barbara Ehrenreich. Twelve 2018 xv, 234 p.p (hardcover) $27 **306.9**

1. Aging 2. Death 3. Longevity 4. Death -- Sociological aspects
ISBN 9781455535910; 9781478971085; 1455535915

In this book, author Barbara Ehrenreich "takes on the task of investigating America's peculiar approach to aging, health, and wellness. She comes down hard on what she describes as 'medicalized life': the unending series of doctor's visits, fads in wellness, and preventative-care screenings that can dominate the life of an aging person. Ehrenreich's core philosophy holds that aging people have the right to determine their quality of life." (Publishers Weekly)

"In assessing our quest for a longer, healthier life, Ehrenreich provides a contemplative vision of an active, engaged health care that goes far beyond the physical restraints of the body and into the realm of metaphysical possibilities." Booklist

Includes bibliographical references (pages 213-234).

Lovejoy, Bess

Rest in pieces; the curious fates of famous corpses. Bess Lovejoy. Simon & Schuster 2013 xviii, 329 p.p ill. (hardcover) $22 **306.9**

1. Dead -- Miscellanea 2. Celebrities -- Biography 3. Celebrities -- Death -- Miscellanea 4. Celebrities -- Biography -- Miscellanea
ISBN 1451654987; 9781451654981

LC 2012034706

This book, by Bess Lovejoy, discusses how "the famous deceased have been stolen, burned, sold, pickled, frozen, stuffed, impersonated, and even filed away in a lawyer's office. . . . From Mozart to Hitler, [the book] . . . connects the lives of the famous dead to the hilarious and horrifying adventures of their corpses, and traces the evolution of cultural attitudes toward death." (Publisher's note)

Includes bibliographical references and index

O'Mahony, Seamus

The **way** we die now; Seamus O'Mahoney. Thomas Dunne Books 2017 xii, 292 p.p (hardcover) $26.99 **306.9**
1. Death 2. Terminal care 3. Self-help techniques 4. Terminally ill -- Care 5. Death -- Social aspects 6. Death -- Sociological aspects
ISBN 9781250112804; 9781250112798
LC 2017009494

This book, by Seamus O'Mahony, deals with "the western way of death. Dying has never been more exposed, with public figures writing memoirs of their illness, but in private we have done our best to banish all thought of death. . . . 'The Way We Die Now' asks us to consider how we have gotten to this age of spiritual poverty and argues that giving up our fantasies of control over death can help restore its significance." (Publisher's note)

"O'Mahony's clear-eyed analysis is important, poignant, and immensely humane." Pub Wkly

Includes bibliographical references

Sacks, Oliver, 1933-2015

Gratitude; Oliver Sacks. Alfred A. Knopf 2015 64 p. illustrations, portraits (hadcover: alk. paper) $20 **306.9**
1. Neurologists -- Biography 2. Death -- Psychological aspects
ISBN 9780451492937; 9780451492968
LC 2015952928

This book, by Oliver Sacks, "chronicles the famous author's thoughts, wishes, regrets, and, above all, feelings of love, happiness, and gratitude even as he faced the cancer that ended his life last year at 82 . the material offers incisive, poignant observations. . . . [This is] a title that belongs in science and biography collections." (Library Journal)

"A perfect gift for thoughtful readers, and a title that belongs in science and biography collections." LJ

Schechter, Harold

The **whole** death catalog; a lively guide to the bitter end. Ballantine Books 2009 304p il pa $18 **306.9**
1. Death
ISBN 978-0-345-49964-6
LC 2009-13779

The author "offers readers a scholarly yet wildly hilarious romp through the cultural history of death and dying. It is not only rollicking entertainment but also provides a wealth of practical and historical information about death." Libr J

Includes bibliographical references

307 Communities

Wilkerson, Isabel

★ The **warmth** of other suns; the epic story of America's great migration. Random House 2010 622p $30; ebook $30 **307**
1. Internal migration 2. African Americans -- History 3. African Americans -- Migrations -- History -- 20th century 4. Migration, Internal -- United States -- History -- 20th century 5. Rural-urban migration -- United States -- History -- 20th century
ISBN 978-0-679-44432-9; 0-679-44432-7; 978-0-679-60407-5 ebook; 0-679-60407-3 ebook
LC 2009-49753

This book focuses on "the Great Migration (1910-1970)--the six-million-strong African American flights from the U.S. South." Author Isabel Wilkerson "seeks to tell the 'larger emotional truths' of the Migration in such ways that spotlight 'people's interior lives and motivations.'

. . . Wilkerson contends that this movement was more than a demographic shift, but an action of then-unparalleled collective black agency: [I]t was the first big step the nation's servant class ever took without asking.'" (Contemporary Sociology)

An "account of the Great Migration, the 55-year stretch (1915–70) during which 6 million black Americans fled the Jim Crow South. Wilkerson, a Pulitzer Prize-winning journalist, uses the journeys of three of them — a Mississippi sharecropper, a Louisiana doctor, and a Florida laborer — to etch an indelible and compulsively readable portrait of race, class, and politics in 20th-century America. History is rarely distilled so finely." Entertainment Wkly

Includes bibliographical references

307.1 Planning and development

Cornett, Mick

The **next** American city; the big promise of our midsize metros. Mick Cornett with Jayson White. G.P. Putnam's Sons 2018 272 p. (hardback) $27 **307.1**
1. Cities and towns -- Growth 2. City planning -- United States 3. Urban sociology -- United States 4. Sociology, Urban -- United States
ISBN 9780399575099
LC 2018022150

In this book, by four-term Oklahoma City Mayor Mick Cornett with Jayson White, "Cornett translates his city's success--and the success of cities like his--into a vision for the future of our country. 'The Next American City' is a story of civic engagement, inventive public policy, and smart urban design. It is a study of the changes re-shaping American urban life-and a blueprint for those to come." (Publisher's note)

307.3 Structure

Duneier, Mitchell

★ **Ghetto**; the invention of a place, the history of an idea. Mitchell Duneier. Farrar, Straus & Giroux 2015 304 p. illustrations, portraits (hardcover) $28 **307.3**
1. Inner cities 2. Jewish ghettos 3. Segregation -- History 4. Jewish ghettos -- History 5. Inner cities -- United States -- History
ISBN 9780374161804; 9781429942751
LC 2015036373

This book, by Mitchell Duneier, "traces the idea of the ghetto from its beginnings in the sixteenth century and its revival by the Nazis to the present. As Duneier shows, we cannot comprehend the entanglements of race, poverty, and place in America today without recalling the ghettos of Europe, as well as earlier efforts to understand the problems of the American city." (Publisher's note)

"Americans did not create the ghetto, but in this well-documented study, we see clearly how those urban areas have come to embody so many of our shortcomings when it comes to matters of race." Kirkus

Includes bibliographical references and index

Philp, Drew

A **$500** house in Detroit; rebuilding an abandoned home and an American city. Drew Philp. Scribner 2017 xi, 290 p.p illustrations (hardcover) $26.00 **307.3**
1. House construction 2. Detroit (Mich.) -- Economic conditions 3. Generation Y -- Biography 4. Detroit (Mich.) -- Biography 5. Detroit (Mich.) -- Race relations 6. Subculture -- Michigan -- Detroit 7. Community development -- Michigan -- Detroit 8.

Dwellings -- Remodeling -- Michigan -- Detroit 9. Working class whites -- Michigan -- Detroit -- Biography 10. Urban renewal -- Michigan -- Detroit -- Citizen participation 11. African Americans -- Michigan -- Detroit -- Social conditions -- 21st century
ISBN 9781476797984; 1476797994; 9781476798011; 9781476797991

LC 2016046283

In this book, author Drew Philip recounts how he "[bought] a ramshackle house for five hundred dollars in the east side neighborhood [of Detroit] known as Poletown. [The book] is Philp's raw and earnest account of rebuilding everything but the frame of his house, nail by nail and room by room. As he assimilates into the community of Detroiters around him, Philp guides readers through the city's vibrant history and engages in urgent conversations about gentrification, racial tensions, and class warfare." (Publisher's note)

"Philp ably outlines the broad issues of race and class in the city, but it is the warmth and liveliness of his storytelling that will win many readers." Kirkus

307.7 Specific kinds of communities

Grandin, Greg

Fordlandia; the rise and fall of Henry Ford's forgotten jungle city. Metropolitan Books 2009 416p il map **307.7**
1. Plantations 2. Philanthropists 3. Ford Motor Co. 4. Automobile executives 5. Planned communities -- Brazil 6. Fordlandia Plantation (Brazil)
ISBN 0-8050-8236-0; 978-0-8050-8236-4

LC 2008049642

National Book Award Finalist: Nonfiction (2009)

This is an account of Henry Ford's attempt to recreate small-town America in the . . . Amazon. In 1927, Ford . . . bought a tract of land twice the size of Delaware in the Brazilian Amazon. . . . Ford's early success in imposing time clocks and square dances on the jungle soon collapsed, as indigenous workers . . . turned the place into a . . . tropical boomtown. (Publisher's note) Index.

Grandin's account is an epic tale of a clash between cultures, values, man, and nature. Booklist

Includes bibliographical references

Green, Hardy

The **company** town; the industrial Edens and Satanic mills that shaped the American economy. Basic Books 2010 248p il $26.95 **307.7**
1. Cities and towns 2. Industrial relations 3. Industries -- United States 4. Industries -- United States -- History 5. Company towns -- United States -- History 6. Industrial relations -- United States -- History
ISBN 978-0-465-01826-0

LC 2010-13434

"The book provides a valuable perspective on a well-worn history, detailing the heinous, lofty, and occasionally absurd ways companies have tried to shape their workers' lives beyond factory walls." Publ Wkly
Includes bibliographical references

Wilson, David Sloan

The **neighborhood** project; using evolution to improve my city, one block at a time. Little, Brown and Company 2011 432p $25.99; ebook $12.99 **307.7**
1. Cities and towns -- Growth 2. Cities and towns -- Civic improvement

ISBN 978-0-316-03767-9; 978-0-316-17525-8 ebook

LC 2011002752

"Although the book meanders—Wilson gives a vivid, in-depth description of several scientific studies, and offers a biography for each scientist he cites—the tangents are mostly pleasurable and provide more evidence for how lives, like ideas, intersect in fascinating ways." Publ Wkly
Includes bibliographical references

307.76 Urban communities

Duany, Andrés, 1949-

Suburban nation; the rise of sprawl and the decline of the American dream. [by] Andres Duany, Elizabeth Plater-Zyberk and Jeff Speck. 10th anniversary ed. North Point Press 2010 xxiv, 294 p.p ill., maps $20 **307.76**
1. Suburbs 2. Urbanization 3. City planning 4. Urban renewal 5. Suburbs -- United States 6. Urban policy -- United States 7. Urbanization -- United States 8. Urban renewal -- United States 9. Community development, Urban -- United States
ISBN 0865477507; 9780865477506

LC 2011292714

Originally published 2000

"In this culmination of a 20-year crusade against suburban sprawl, the husband-and-wife architectural firm of Duany and Plater-Zyberk (DPZ) presents its manifesto for city planning. Armed with studies and statistics, the authors fault unchecked suburban growth for sapping vitality from urban centers, depleting natural resources, and breeding an alienated, enslaved automobile citizenry. Their solution is to reconsider pre-World War II methods of mixed-use planning and pedestrian-centered, environmentally sensitive design." (Library Journal)

Includes bibliographical references (p. 273-280) and index

Klinenberg, Eric

Palaces for the people; how social infrastructure can help fight inequality, polarization, and the decline of civic life. Eric Klinenberg. Crown 2018 288 p. (hardback) $28 **307.76**
1. Equality -- United States 2. City planning -- United States 3. Quality of life -- United States 4. Infrastructure (Economics) -- United States
ISBN 9781524761165; 9781524761172

LC 2018002837

In this book, author Eric Klinenberg "believes that the future of democratic societies rests not simply on shared values but on shared spaces: the libraries, childcare centers, bookstores, churches, synagogues, and parks where crucial, sometimes life-saving connections, are formed. Klinenberg calls this the 'social infrastructure,' . . . [and] urges us to acknowledge the crucial role these spaces play in civic life." (Publisher's note)

Smith, P. D.

City; a guidebook for the urban age. P.D. Smith. Bloomsbury 2012 383 p. **307.76**
1. Civilization 2. Urban sociology 3. Cities and towns -- HIstory 4. City and town life -- History 5. City life -- History 6. Cities and towns -- History 7. Sociology, Urban -- History
ISBN 1608196763; 9781608196760

LC 2011051430

This book is an "illustrated guide to 7,000 years of urban life for an age when more than half of the world's population lives in cities. From the earliest Sumerian city of Eridu to the wired eco-cities of the future,

[P.D.] Smith embarks on a multicentury tour highlighting urban history, customs, infrastructure, architecture, language, markets, crime, parks, cemeteries, transportation, food, and leisure activities across cultures. He . . . provid[es] panoramic yet focused views of a particular subject, such as . . . the development of language from cuneiform script to 16th-century street speech and its effect on cockney, to the new London dialect of the 21st century, Jafaican." (Publishers Weekly)

Includes bibliographical references and index

Winkless, Laurie

Science and the City; The Mechanics Behind the Metropolis. Laurie Winkless. St. Martin's Press 2016 304 p. illustrations (ebook) $66; (hardcover) $27   **307.76**

1. Cities and towns 2. Technological innovations 3. Technology and civilization

ISBN 9781472913227; 1472913213; 9781472913210

This book by physicist Laurie Winkless guides readers "through the technology of everyday city life: how new approaches to building materials help to construct the tallest skyscrapers in Dubai, how New Yorkers use light to treat their drinking water, how Tokyo commuters' footsteps power gates in train stations. . . . [It uncovers] the science and engineering that shapes our cities, . . . [and] how technology will help us meet the challenges of a soaring world population." (Publisher's note)

"Where necessary, Winkless includes diagrams of scientific processes, but this is mainly a packed-with-detail, textual work that will be a hit with both young adult and adult patrons curious about what makes cities tick." Booklist

Includes bibliographical references (pages 271-280) and index.

307.762   Small urban communities

Badkhen, Anna, 1976-

Fisherman's blues; a West African community at sea. Anna Badkhen. Riverhead Books 2018 287 p. illustrations, maps (hardback) $27   **307.762**

1. Fishers 2. Fishing 3. Senegal -- Social conditions 4. Fishers -- Senegal -- Joal-Fadiout 5. Ecological disturbances -- Atlantic Ocean 6. Fishing villages -- Senegal -- Joal-Fadiout 7. Joal-Fadiout (Senegal) -- Social conditions 8. Joal-Fadiout (Senegal) -- Economic conditions 9. Climatic changes -- Economic aspects -- Senegal 10. Joal-Fadiout (Senegal) -- Social life and customs

ISBN 9780698410848; 9781594634864

LC 2017030225

This book, by Anna Badkhen, presents "an intimate account of life in a West African fishing village, tugged by currents ancient and modern, and dependent on an ocean that is being radically transformed. . . . For centuries, fishermen have launched their pirogues from the Senegalese port of Joal, where the fish used to be so plentiful. . . . But in an Atlantic decimated by overfishing and climate change, the fish are harder and harder to find." (Publisher's note)

"Badkhen is a spellbinding writer, her observations at once hypnotic and elegiac, witnessing a fragile community just barely getting by." Booklist

Dawson, Ashley

★ **Extreme** cities; the peril and promise of urban life in the age of climate change. Ashley Dawson. Verso 2017 v, 378 p.p $29.95   **307.762**

1. Environmental literature 2. Cities and towns -- Growth 3. City planning -- Environmental aspects

ISBN 1784780367; 9781784780364

In this book, author Ashley Dawson "argues that cities are ground zero for climate change, contributing the lion's share of carbon to the atmosphere, while also lying on the frontlines of rising sea levels. Today, the majority of the world's megacities are located in coastal zones, yet few of them are adequately prepared for the floods that will increasingly menace their shores." (Publisher's note)

Includes bibliographical references (pages 311-359) and index.

307.77   Self-contained communities

Wayland-Smith, Ellen

Oneida; From Free Love Utopia to the Well-Set Table. Ellen Wayland-Smith. Picador 2016 320 p. illustrations (ebook) $60; (hardback) $27   **307.77**

1. Free love 2. Collective settlements 3. Oneida, ltd. -- History 4. Oneida Community -- History 5. Social reformers -- United States -- Biography 6. Collective settlements -- New York (State) -- History 7. Tableware -- United States -- History -- 20th century 8. Free love -- New York (State) -- History -- 19th century 9. Silver flatware -- United States -- History -- 19th century

ISBN 9781250043108; 9781250043085

LC 2015044336

In this book, by Ellen Wayland-Smith, "in the early nineteenth century, many Americans were looking for an alternative to the Puritanism that had been the foundation of the new country. Amid the fervor of the religious revival known as the Second Great Awakening, John Humphrey Noyes, a spirited but socially awkward young man, attracted a group of devoted followers with his fiery sermons about creating Jesus' millennial kingdom here on Earth." (Publisher's note)

"This book is a fascinating look into the strange history of Oneida silverware and how its origins reflect an exhilarating period of American history." Pub Wkly

Includes bibliographical references (pages 271-294) and index.

307.951   Communities – China

Chu, Lenora

Little soldiers; an American boy, a Chinese school, and the global race to achieve. Leonora Chu. Harper 2017 x, 347 p.p map (hardcover) $27.99   **307.951**

1. Education -- China 2. Cross-cultural studies 3. Education -- Aims and objectives 4. Education and state -- China 5. Education -- Cross-cultural studies

ISBN 9780062367877; 9780062367853; 0062367854

This book, by Lenora Chu, explores "China's widely acclaimed yet insular education system . . . that raises important questions for the future of American parenting and education. . . . Chu and her husband decided to enroll three-year-old Rainer in China's state-run public school system. . . . What she discovered is a military-like education system driven by high-stakes testing, . . . using bribes to reward students who comply, and shaming to isolate those who do not." (Publisher's note)

"Little Soldiers offers fascinating peeks inside the world's largest educational system and at the future intellectual 'soldiers' American kids will be facing." Booklist

Includes bibliographical references (pages 329-347).

310 Collections of general statistics

★ The **Europa** world year book. Europa Publications 2v **310**
1. Statistics 2. Reference books 3. Political science
Annual. First published 1959 with title: The Europa year book
"The best annual directory of the nations of the world. For each country it includes demographic and economic statistics, and facts about constitution and government, political parties, press, trade and industry, publishers, etc. Also incorporates a substantive section with listings and information about international organizations." Ref Sources for Small & Medium-sized Libr. 6th edition

"The best annual directory of the nations of the world. For each country it includes demographic and economic statistics, and facts about constitution and government, political parties, press, trade and industry, publishers, etc. Also incorporates a substantive section with listings and information about international organizations." Ref Sources for Small & Medium-sized Libr. 6th edition

★ The **statesman's** yearbook; the politics, cultures, and economies of the world. Palgrave Macmillan illustrations, maps **310**
1. Political science
Annual. First published 1864
"Descriptive and statistical information about international organizations and countries of the world-brief history, area, political status, economy, etc." N Y Public Libr. Ref Books for Child Collect. 2nd edition
Includes bibliographical references

Vital Statistics of the United States 2018; Births, Life Expectancy, Deaths, and Selected Health Data. edited by Shana Hertz Hattis. 8th edition Bernan Press 2018 390 p $137 **310**
1. Vital statistics
ISBN 9781598889925
Updated biennially
Vital Statistics of The United States: Births, Life Expectancy, Deaths, and Selected Health Data brings together a comprehensive collection of birth, mortality, and health data into a single volume. It provides a wealth of information compiled by the National Center for Health Statistics and other government agencies.

317.3 Statistics - United States

The **who**, what, and where of America; understanding the American Community Survey. edited by Deirdre A. Gaquin and Mary Meghan Ryan. 6th edition Bernan 2018 458 p. illustrations $135 **317.3**
1. United States -- Census 2. Cities and towns -- United States 3. Cities and towns -- United States -- Statistics
ISBN 9781641432863
Updated biennially
The Who, What, and Where of America: Understanding the American Community Survey pulls details from the American Community Survey (ACS) which provides a portrait of America at a certain point in time. This book covers each U.S. state, county, metropolitan area, and city with a population of 20,000 or more.
"This would be a useful resource for libraries that find themselves in need of population information." Booklist

320 Political science (Politics and government)

Aristotle
Politics. Oxford University Press 1998 480p (Oxford world's classics) pa $12.95 **320**
1. Political science
ISBN 978-0-19-283393-8
"Discussion of public affairs by the most eminent of the Greek philosophers in terms applicable to many of the problems of modern political science." Pratt Alcove

Bawer, Bruce
The **victims'** revolution; the rise of identity studies and the closing of the liberal mind. Bruce Bawer. Broadside Books 2012 378 p. **320**
1. Humanities 2. Group identity 3. Learning and scholarship 4. United States -- Intellectual life 5. Identity politics -- United States 6. Group identity -- Political aspects -- United States
ISBN 0061807370; 9780061807374
LC 2012032311
This book, by Bruce Bawer, offers a "critique of the identity-based revolution that has transformed American campuses." In "the 1960s and '70s, . . . a new generation of scholar-activists rejected traditional humanism in favor of a radical ideology that denied esthetic merit and objective truth. . . . Bawer concludes that . . . these programs ha[ve] impoverished our thought [and] confused our politics . . . with politically correct mush." (Publisher's note)
Includes bibliographical references and index

Brookhiser, Richard
What would the Founders do? our questions, their answers. Basic Books 2006 261p $26 **320**
1. Statesmen -- United States 2. Presidents -- United States 3. United States -- Politics and government -- 2001-
ISBN 0-465-00819-4; 978-0-465-00819-3
The author "uses the Founders' written and oral statements to imagine their thoughts concerning contemporary issues ranging from stem cells and terrorism to censorship and gay marriage. The short answers he gives for each question can be serious or witty and are often infused with interesting historical facts." Libr J
Includes bibliographical references

Edwards, Mickey
The **parties** versus the people; how to turn Republicans and Democrats into Americans. Mickey Edwards. Yale University Press 2012 xxiii, 208 p.p (hardcover) $25 **320**
1. Democratic Party (U.S.) 2. Republican Party (U.S.) 3. United States -- Politics and government 4. Democracy -- United States 5. Political parties -- United States 6. Two-party systems -- United States 7. Divided government -- United States 8. Polarization (Social sciences) -- United States
ISBN 0300184565; 9780300184563
LC 2012013008
This book, by Mickey Edwards, "identifies exactly how [the American] . . . political and governing systems reward intransigence, discourage compromise, and undermine our democracy. He then describes exactly what must be done to banish the negative effects of partisan warfare from our political system. . . . He offers graphic examples of how this problem has intensified and reveals how political battles have become nothing more than conflicts between party machines." (Publisher's note)
Includes bibliographical references (p. 187-192) and index.

Fukuyama, Francis

The **origins** of political order; from prehuman times to the French Revolution. Farrar, Straus and Giroux 2011 585p $35   **320**

1. Democracy 2. State, The 3. Comparative government

ISBN 978-0-374-22734-0; 0-374-22734-9

LC 2010-38534

"Political theorist Fukuyama presents nothing less than a unified theory of state formation, a comparative study of how tribally organized societies in various parts of the world and various moments in history have transformed into societies with political systems and institutions and, in some cases, political accountability. Drawing upon a diverse range of sources--sociobiology and anthropology as well as macroeconomics and legal history--and paying particular attention to political development in Asia, Fukuyama describes a somewhat evolutionary mechanism wherein political systems develop in response to certain societal conditions and become institutionalized because of, among other things, their ability to adapt." (Booklist)

Includes bibliographical references

Judt, Tony, 1948-2010

Thinking the twentieth century; Tony Judt, with Timothy Snyder. Penguin 2012 414 p. $36   **320**

1. Historians 2. Jews -- History 3. Political science 4. Philosophy -- History 5. United States -- Politics and government -- 20th century 6. College teachers 7. Nonfiction writers 8. History -- Philosophy

ISBN 9781594203237; 1594203237

LC 2011031473

"The book is a history of twentieth-century thought. It begins with . . . [author Tony Judt's] reflections on Jewish idealism and Jewish suffering in Europe and ends with a devastating account of the failure of American politics in the post-cold war world. It is also an intellectual autobiography. . . . [Topics include] the argument . . . for a one-state solution in Israel . . . [and] Friedrich Hayek's ideas about economics and state planning." (New York Review of Books)

Includes bibliographical references

Kaplan, Robert D.

Warrior politics; why leadership demands a pagan ethos. Random House 2002 xxii, 198p $22.95; pa $12   **320**

1. Leadership 2. Political ethics 3. International relations

ISBN 0-375-50563-6; 0-375-72627-6 pa

LC 2001-31862

"This is a provocative, smart and polemical work that will stimulate lively discussion." Publ Wkly

Includes bibliographical references

Paine, Thomas

★ **Rights** of man; and, Common sense. Knopf 1994 lii, 306p $19   **320**

1. Political science 2. France -- History -- 1789-1799, Revolution 3. United States -- Politics and government -- 1775-1783, Revolution

ISBN 0-679-43314-7

LC 94-5989

This volume combines Rights of man with Common sense which was "published anonymously at Philadelphia (Jan. 10, 1776). . . . Over 100,000 copies were sold by the end of March, and it is generally considered the most important literary influence on the movement for independence." Oxford Companion to Am Lit. 5th edition

Includes bibliographical references

Washington Information Directory. Congressional Quarterly   **320**

1. Washington (D.C.) -- Directories

Annual. First published 1975-76

"Lists names, telephone numbers, addresses, and responsibilities of 5,000 key personnel and agencies, both private and governmental, in the Washington, DC area; includes detailed indexes." N Y Public Libr Book of How & Where to Look It Up

"This substantial and user-friendly guide . . . [is] a vital resource for navigating Washington's intricate bureaucratic web." Libr J

320.01 Philosophy and theory

Fukuyama, Francis, 1952-

Identity; the demand for dignity and the politics of resentment. Francis Fukuyama. Farrar, Straus & Giroux 2018 240 p. (hardcover) $26   **320.01**

1. Political participation 2. Polarization (Social sciences) 3. Group identity -- Political aspects 4. Dignity 5. Resentment 6. Identity politics 7. World politics -- 21st century 8. Political participation -- Social aspects 9. Polarization (Social sciences) -- Political aspects

ISBN 9780374129293

LC 2018004954

In this book, author Francis Fukuyama "offers a provocative examination of modern identity politics. . . . In 2014, . . . Fukuyama wrote that American institutions were in decay, as the state was progressively captured by powerful interest groups. Two years later, his predictions were borne out by the rise to power of a series of political outsiders whose economic nationalism and authoritarian tendencies threatened to destabilize the entire international order." (Publisher's note)

Includes bibliographical references and index

The **politics** book; Big ideas simply explained. edited by Rebecca Warren and Kate Johnsen; illustrated by James Graham. 1st American ed. DK Pub. 2013 352 p. ill. (some col.) (Big ideas simply explained) (hardcover) $25.00   **320.01**

1. Political philosophy

ISBN 1465402144; 9781465402141

LC 2012533724

This book, part of the Big Ideas Simply Explained series, looks at political philosophy. "More than 100 political philosophers, among them Confucius, Plato, Machiavelli, Mary Wollstonecraft, Karl Marx, Ito Hirobumi, Emiliano Zapata, Jomo Kenyatta, and Mao Zedong, are covered in seven chronological sections ranging from 'Ancient Political Thought' to 'Postwar Politics.'" (Library Journal)

Ryan, Alan

On politics; a history of political thought from Herodotus to the present. Alan Ryan. W. W. Norton & Co. 2012 1114 p. (hardcover) $75   **320.01**

1. Political science 2. Political philosophy 3. Political scientists -- History 4. Political science -- Philosophy -- History

ISBN 1846147794; 9780871404657; 9781846147791

LC 2012012351

This is a two-volume work that looks at the "history of political theory." The first volume covers writings "from Herodotus through Aristotle, the ancient Roman theorists of law, St. Augustine and the medievals, right up to Machiavelli." The second volume "covers the turn of the 17th century to the present. Starting with Thomas Hobbes, whom Ryan regards as the father of our modern conceptions of politics, the book ranges through Locke, Rousseau, Hegel, and Marx." (Publishers Weekly)

Includes bibliographical references and index

320.082   Women in politics

Fitzpatrick, Ellen

The **highest** glass ceiling; women's quest for the American presidency. Ellen Fitzpatrick. Harvard University Press 2016 318 p. (alk. paper) $25.95   **320.082**

1. Presidential candidates -- United States -- Biography 2. Women -- Political activity -- United States -- History 3. Women presidential candidates -- United States -- Biography
ISBN 9780674496071; 9780674088931

LC 2015045620

In this book, historian Ellen Fitzpatrick "tells the story of three remarkable women who set their sights on the American presidency. Victoria Woodhull (1872), Margaret Chase Smith (1964), and Shirley Chisholm (1972) each challenged persistent barriers confronted by women presidential candidates. Their quest illuminates today's political landscape, showing that Hillary Clinton's 2016 campaign belongs to a much longer, arduous, and dramatic journey." (Publisher's note)

"The book illuminates the continuity of discrimination female candidates face and should work well in classes dedicated to political and women's history." Choice

Includes bibliographical references (pages 259-302) and index

Unger, Craig

When women win; EMILY's list and the rise of women in American politics. Ellen R. Malcolm with Craig Unger. Houghton Mifflin Harcourt 2016 384 p. (ebook) $15.99; (hardcover) $28   **320.082**

1. Women politicians -- United States 2. Women -- Political activity -- United States 3. United States -- Politics and government -- 1989-
ISBN 9780544443389; 9780544443310

LC 2015037242

This book on the rise of women in elected office, by Ellen R. Malcolm with Craig Unger, "delivers stories of some of the toughest political contests of the past three decades, including the historic victory of Barbara Mikulski as the first Democratic woman elected to the Senate in her own right; the defeat of Todd Akin . . . by Claire McCaskill; and Elizabeth Warren's dramatic win over incumbent Massachusetts senator Scott Brown." (Publisher's note)

"An inspiring portrait of a gutsy activist who produced a transformation in the political landscape." Kirkus

Includes bibliographical references and index

320.092   Biography

Love, Reggie

Power forward; my presidential education. Reggie Love. Simon & Schuster 2015 224 p. 16 plates; illustrations (hardback) $26   **320.092**

1. Presidents -- United States -- Staff 2. Presidents -- United States -- Staff -- Biography 3. United States -- Politics and government -- 2009- 4. United States -- Politics and government -- 2001-2009
ISBN 1476763348; 9781476763347; 9781476763354

LC 2014040838

NAACP Image Award Nominee: Outstanding Literary Work- Biography/Autobiography (2016)

In this memoir, author Reggie Love describes his time "as 'body man' to [Barack] Obama during his first presidential campaign, . . . [and]

as President Obama's personal aide during that momentous first term. Keeping the President company at every major turning point of his historic first campaign and administration, . . . Love learned how persistence and passion can lead not only to success, but to a broader concept of adulthood." (Publisher's note)

"Though Love admits to his share of mistakes, both he and the president he served emerge from this memoir as admirable and likable." Kirkus

320.1   The state

Cicero, Marcus Tullius

The **republic;** and, The laws; [by] Cicero; translated by Niall Rudd; with an introduction and notes by Jonathan Powell and Niall Rudd. Oxford University Press 1998 xliii, 242p (Oxford world's classics) pa $12.95   **320.1**

1. State, The 2. Political science 3. Rome -- History
ISBN 978-0-19-283236-8; 0-19-283236-0

LC 97-23394

"Cicero's The Republic is an impassioned plea for responsible government written just before the civil war that ended the Roman Republic in a dialogue following Plato. Drawing on Greek political theory, the work embodies the mature reflections of a Roman ex-consul on the nature of political organization, on justice in society, and on the qualities needed in a statesman. Its sequel, The Laws , expounds the influential doctrine of Natural Law, which applies to all mankind, and sets out an ideal code for a reformed Roman Republic, already half in the realm of utopia." Publisher's note

Includes bibliographical references

Fukuyama, Francis, 1952-

★ **Political** Order and Political Decay; From the Industrial Revolution to the Globalization of Democracy. Francis Fukuyama. Farrar Straus & Giroux 2014 752 p. illustrations hbk $35   **320.1**

1. Democracy 2. Comparative government 3. Globalization 4. Order -- History 5. State, The -- History
ISBN 0374227357; 9780374227357

LC 2014016973

"The distinction between strong and accountable government is seen as a driver of history in this second volume of . . . [Francis Fukuyama's] study of politics and the state. Following up 'The Origins of Political Order,' Stanford scholar Fukuyama surveys political developments of the past 250 years, from the French Revolution to the Arab Spring, focusing on the often clashing imperatives of democratic accountability, rule of law, and effective governmental administration." (Publishers Weekly)

A "compelling historical overview of a useful template for the retooling of institutions in the modern state. . . . Systematic, thorough and even hopeful fodder for reform-minded political observers." Kirkus

Includes bibliographical references and index

Hobbes, Thomas

★ **Leviathan**; edited with an introduction and notes by J.C.A. Gaskin. Oxford University Press 2008 lv, 508p (Oxford world's classics) pa $9.95   **320.1**

1. State, The 2. Political science
ISBN 978-0-19-953728-0

First published 1651

"A treatise on the origin and ends of government. . . . This work, a defense of secular monarchy, written while the Puritan Commonwealth ruled England, contains Hobbes's famous theory of the sovereign state."

Benet's Reader's Ency. 4th edition

Machiavelli, Niccolo

★ The **prince**. Knopf 1992 xxxi, 190p (Everyman's library) $16 **320.1**

1. Political ethics 2. Political science

ISBN 0-679-41044-9

LC 91-53225

Written in 1513

"A handbook of advice on the acquisition, use, and maintenance of political power, dedicated to Lorenzo de Medici." Haydn. Thesaurus of Book Dig

Rousseau, Jean-Jacques

★ The **social** contract; translated by Maurice Cranston. Penguin Books 2006 167p pa $10 **320.1**

1. Political science

ISBN 978-0-14-303749-1; 0-14-303749-8

LC 2006-43772

First published 1762

"A treatise on the origins and organization of government and the rights of citizens. Rousseau's thesis states that, since no man has any natural authority over another, the social contract, freely entered into, creates natural reciprocal obligations between citizens." Benet's Reader's Ency. 4th edition

Includes bibliographical references

320.4 Structure and functions of government

Han, Lori Cox

Handbook to American democracy; Lori Cox Han and Tomislav Han. Facts On File 2011 224 p. **320.4**

1. United States -- History 2. Democracy -- United States -- History 3. United States -- Politics and government 4. United States -- Politics and government -- Handbooks, manuals, etc

ISBN 0816078548; 9780816078547

LC 2011005185

The authors "address the foundations of American democracy and the three branches of American government. The books introduce offices, history, and issues in eight chapters each (e.g., 'The Founding Fathers and the American Revolution,' 'How Congress Is Organized,' and 'Vice Presidents, Presidential Advisers, and America's First Ladies'). The material is complemented by black-and-white photos and sidebars on legal cases, laws and legislation, statistics, maps, biographies of major figures such as Henry VIII, and other primary materials, and chapters close with a summary. . . . [The volumes] each include an individual glossary, index, selected bibliography, and table of contents." (Libr J)

Includes bibliographical references and index

320.473 Structure and functions of government – United States

Moss, David A.

Democracy; a case study. David A. Moss. The Belknap Press of Harvard University Press 2017 784 p. $35; (ebook) $43.95 **320.473**

1. Democracy -- United States -- History -- Case studies 2. United States -- Politics and government -- Case studies 3. Social conflict -- Political aspects -- United States -- Case studies

ISBN 9780674971455; 9780674974098

LC 2016020796

In this book, author David Moss "adapts the case study method made famous by Harvard Business School to revitalize our conversations about governance and democracy and show how the United States has often thrived on political conflict. . . . These vibrant cases ask readers to weigh choices and consequences, wrestle with momentous decisions, and come to their own conclusions." (Publisher's note)

"It's hard to imagine a timelier book, given America's tumultuous 2016 elections, than this eminently readable survey of political disputes by Moss (Preventing Regulatory Capture), a Harvard professor of business administration." Pub Wkly

Includes bibliographical references and index

320.5 Political ideologies

Allitt, Patrick

★ The **conservatives**; ideas and personalities throughout American history. Yale University Press 2009 325p $35 **320.5**

1. Conservatism 2. United States -- Politics and government

ISBN 978-0-300-11894-0; 0-300-11894-5

LC 2008-42559

"From present-day questions of taxation and big government, Allitt traces conservative principles to the earliest days of the republic. . . . Cutting across the stereotypes of present-day conservatism, this nuanced, thoughtful history should educate the unaffiliated and help the disillusioned recover." Publ Wkly

Includes bibliographical references

Brown, Archie

★ The **rise** and fall of communism. Ecco 2009 720p il map $35.99 **320.5**

1. Communism

ISBN 0-06-113879-7; 978-0-06-113879-9

Brown has crafted a readable and judicious account of Communist history, from its theoretical beginnings in 19th-century Europe to its practical collapse at the end of the 1980s, that is both controversial and commonsensical. . . . Given the immense sweep of time, ideology and geography he strives to cover in 600-odd pagesas Brown observes, almost every one of his chapters could be a book on its ownThe Rise and Fall of Communism is a work of considerable delicacy and nuance. Salon

Includes bibliographical references

Jones, Van, 1968-

Beyond the messy truth; how we came apart, how we come together. Van Jones. Ballantine Books 2017 xvi, 233 p.p (hardback) $27 **320.5**

1. Political parties -- United States 2. United States -- Politics and government -- 2001- 3. Right and left (Political science) -- United States 4. Presidents -- United States -- Election -- 2016 5. United States -- Politics and government -- 21st century 6. Political parties -- United States -- History -- 21st century

ISBN 9780399180026; 9780399180033

LC 2017036063

In this book, Van "Jones offers a blueprint for transforming our collective anxiety into meaningful change. Tough on Donald Trump but showing respect and empathy for his supporters, Jones takes aim at the failures of both parties before and after Trump's victory. He urges both sides to abandon the politics of accusation and focus on real solutions. . . . [H]e shows us how to get down to the vital business of solving, together, some of our toughest problems." (Publisher's note)

"Speaking with heartfelt conviction and clarity of purpose, Jones proffers an achievable pathway to harmony for ideologues of both conservative and liberal persuasions." Booklist

Potter, Will

Green is the new red. City Lights Books 2011 301 p. **320.5**
1. Ecoterrorism 2. Political activists 3. Environmental movement
ISBN 9780872865389

LC 2010053209

It was the author's intent to demonstrate that "the U.S. government is using post-9/11 anti-terrorism resources to target environmentalists and animal rights activists. . . . Tracing funds from animal-exploiting corporations to Congress and the passing of the big business-friendly Animal Enterprise Terrorism Act, Potter reports on an increased usage of the terrorism enhancement in court cases. . . . [Will] Potter warns of the crumbling of the 'legal wall separating "terrorist" from "dissident" or "undesirable" and concludes his account with a call to action and a decry of the injustice that results in the "terrorist" label being put on those who threaten American corporate interests." (Publishers weekly)

Includes bibliographical references and index.

320.51   Liberalism

Brennan, Jason

Libertarianism; what everyone needs to know. by Jason Brennan. Oxford University Press 2012 xvi, 213 p.p (hardback) $74; (pbk.) $16.95 **320.51**
1. Libertarianism 2. Republican Party (U.S.) 3. Libertarianism -- United States 4. United States -- Politics and government
ISBN 0199933898; 019993391X; 9780199933891; 9780199933914

LC 2012020049

Author Jason Brennan "offers a nuanced portrait of libertarianism, proceeding through a series of questions to illuminate the essential elements of libertarianism and the problems the philosophy addresses, including such topics as the Value of Liberty, Human Nature and Ethics, Economic Liberty, Civil Rights, Social Justice and the Poor, Government and Democracy, and Contemporary Politics." (Publisher's note)

Includes bibliographical references (p. [191]-198) and index

Carville, James

★ It's the middle class, stupid! James Carville and Stan Greenberg. Blue Rider Press 2012 321 p. $26.95 **320.51**
1. Middle class 2. Equality -- United States 3. United States -- Social conditions 4. Politics, Practical -- United States 5. United States -- Politics and government -- 2009- 6. United States -- Politics and government -- 2001-2009
ISBN 0399160396; 9780399160394

LC 2012018191

In this book, "[James] Carville . . . and [Stan] Greenberg offer a plea to save America's floundering middle class. . . . The authors outline a grim cycle of 'institutionalize inequality,' declining wages, reduced benefits, and skyrocketing higher education prices, all of which that are blocking middle class children from top educations and, later on, career benefits." (Publishers Weekly)

Includes bibliographical references.

320.52   Conservatism

Dionne, E. J., 1952-

Why the right went wrong; Conservatism--From Goldwater to the Tea Party and Beyond. E.J. Dionne, Jr. Simon & Schuster 2016 560 p. (hardcover) $30 **320.52**
1. Conservatism -- United States -- History
ISBN 9781476763798; 9781476763804

LC 2015027336

This book, by E. J. Dionne, "offers a historical view of the right since the 1960s. Its core contention is that American conservatism and the Republican Party took a wrong turn when they adopted Barry Goldwater's worldview during and after the 1964 campaign." (Publisher's note)

Includes bibliographical references and index

Flake, Jeff, 1962-

Conscience of a conservative; a rejection of destructive politics and a return to principle. Jeff Flake. Random House 2017 xi, 140 p.p (hardcover) $27 **320.52**
1. Political science literature 2. Conservatism -- United States 3. United States -- Politics and government -- 2009- 4. Conservatism 5. United States -- Politics and government -- 2017-
ISBN 9780399592911; 9780399592928; 0399592911

LC 2017302576

In this book, author Jeff Flake, a Republican Senator in the U.S., shows how he "takes his party to task for embracing nationalism, populism, xenophobia, and the anomalous [Donald] Trump presidency. The book is an urgent call for a return to bedrock conservative principle and a cry to once again put country before party." (Publisher's note)

"The junior senator from Arizona offers a critical (in both senses of the word) look at the Republican Party." Booklist

Includes bibliographical references (pages 139-140)

Gibson, Chris

★ Rally point; five tasks to unite the country and revitalize the American dream. Chris Gibson. Twelve 2017 246 p. $26 **320.52**
1. Conservatism -- United States 2. Political culture -- United States 3. United States -- Politics and government -- 2009-
ISBN 1538760584; 9781538760581

In this book, author Chris Gibson "provides incisive and frank analysis of the current political environment, including President Trump, and provides a roadmap based on time-tested Founding principles to help unite our country and revitalize the American Dream. 'RALLY POINT' is a thoughtful, compelling, enjoyable read - a must for serious-minded Americans looking for answers in this challenging political environment." (Publisher's note)

Includes bibliographical references (pages 233-242).

Hochschild, Arlie Russell

★ Strangers in their own land; Anger and Mourning on the American Right. Arlie Russell Hochschild. New Press, The 2016 288 p. illustrations (ebook) $27.99; (hardback) $27.95 **320.52**
1. Political psychology 2. Liberalism -- United States 3. Conservatism -- United States 4. Liberalism -- United States -- History -- 21st century 5. Conservatism -- United States -- History -- 21st century
ISBN 9781620972267; 9781620972250

LC 2016017892

National Book Award Finalist: Nonfiction (2016)

In this book author Arlie Russell Hochschild "embarks on a . . . journey from her liberal hometown of Berkeley, California, deep into Louisiana bayou country--a stronghold of the conservative right. As she gets to know people who strongly oppose many of the ideas she . . . champions, Hochschild . . . warms to the people she meets. . . . people whose concerns are actually ones that all Americans share: the desire for community, the embrace of family, and hopes for their children." (Publisher's note)

"A well-told chronicle of an ambitious sociological project of significant current importance." Kirkus

Includes bibliographical references (pages 317-338) and index.

Mayer, Jane

★ **Dark** money; the hidden history of the billionaires behind the rise of the radical right. Jane Mayer. Doubleday 2016 464 p. chart (hardcover) $29.95	**320.52**

    1. Journalists 2. Rich -- United States 3. United States -- Politics and government

ISBN 9780385535595; 9780385535601

LC 2015957180

Author "Jane Mayer spent five years conducting hundreds of interviews--including with several sources within the network--and scoured public records, private papers, and court proceedings in reporting this book. . . . She traces the byzantine trail of the billions of dollars spent by the network and provides vivid portraits of the colorful figures behind the new American oligarchy." (Publisher's note)

Includes bibliographical references (pages 381-425) and index.

Roth, Zachary

The **great** suppression; voting rights, corporate cash, and the conservative assault on democracy. Zachary Roth. Crown 2016 256 p. (hardback) $26; (ebook) $65	**320.52**

    1. Republican Party (U.S.) 2. Democracy -- United States 3. United States -- Politics and government -- 2001- 4. Voting -- United States 5. Conservatism -- United States 6. Campaign funds -- United States 7. Political culture -- United States 8. Right-wing extremists -- United States

ISBN 9781101905760; 9781101905777; 9781101905784

LC 2016003489

In this book, author Zachary Roth "unearths the deep historical roots of [the] anti-egalitarian worldview, and introduces us to its modern-day proponents: The GOP officials pushing to make it harder to cast a ballot; the lawyers looking to scrap all limits on money in politics; the libertarian scholars reclaiming judicial activism to roll back the New Deal; and the corporate lobbyists working to ban local action on everything from the minimum wage to the environment." (Publisher's note)

"Roth explains that once-per-decade redistricting will allow the GOP to dominate American electoral politics for years to come. His book should be required reading for understanding the ultimate goals of American conservatism." Pub Wkly

Includes bibliographical references (pages 183-235) and index.

Sykes, Charles J.

How the right lost its mind; Charles J. Sykes. St. Martin's Press 2017 xix, 267 p.p (hardcover) $27.99	**320.52**

    1. Conservatism -- United States 2. United States -- Politics and government 3. Right and left (Political science) -- United States 4. Political culture -- United States

ISBN 9781250147172; 9781250147219

LC 2017018870

In this book, author Charles J. Sykes "presents an impassioned, regretful, and deeply thoughtful account of how the American conservative movement came to lose its values. How did a movement that was defined by its belief in limited government, individual liberty, free markets, traditional values, and civility find itself embracing bigotry, political intransigence, demagoguery, and outright falsehood?" (Publisher's note)

"Exceedingly readable, Syke's voice comes across as clearly as if

over the airwaves." LJ

Includes bibliographical references and index

320.53   Collectivism and fascism

Albright, Madeleine Korbel, 1937-

Fascism; a warning. Madeleine Albright. HarperCollins 2018 256 p. $27.99	**320.53**

    1. Fascism 2. World politics 3. National socialism

ISBN 0062802186; 9780062802187

This book, by Madeleine Albright, is "a personal and urgent examination of Fascism in the twentieth century and how its legacy shapes today's world. . . . Fascism, as she shows, not only endured through the twentieth century but now presents a more virulent threat to peace and justice than at any time since the end of World War II." (Publisher's note)

MacLean, Nancy

★ **Democracy** in chains; the deep history of the radical right's stealth plan for America. Nancy MacLean. Viking 2017 368 p. (hardback) $28	**320.53**

    1. Radicalism -- United States 2. Right and left (Political science) 3. Democracy -- United States -- History 4. Right-wing extremists -- United States 5. Economics -- Political aspects -- United States

ISBN 1101980966; 9781101980965

LC 2017009048

LA Times Book Prize: Current Interest (2017)

National Book Award Finalist: Nonfiction (2017)

This book, by Nancy MacLean, examines how "the capitalist radical right has been working . . . to fundamentally alter the rules of democratic governance. But billionaires did not launch this movement; a white intellectual in the embattled Jim Crow South did. . . . [MacLean] names its true architect--the Nobel Prize-winning political economist James McGill Buchanan--and dissects the operation he and his colleagues designed over six decades to alter every branch of government." (Publisher's note)

"MacLean's intense and extensive examination of the right-wing's rise to power is perhaps the best explanation to date of the roots of the political divide that threatens to irrevocably alter American government." Booklist

Includes bibliographical references (pages 241-321) and index

Snyder, Timothy D., 1969-

The **road** to unfreedom; Russia, Europe, America. Timothy Snyder. Random House Inc 2018 368 p. $27	**320.53**

    1. Totalitarianism 2. Democracy -- History 3. World politics -- 21st century

ISBN 0525574468; 9780525574460

Kirkus Prize Finalist: Nonfiction (2018)

This book, by Timothy Snyder, is a "chronicle of the rise of authoritarianism from Russia to Europe and America. . . . Authoritarianism returned to Russia, as Putin found fascist ideas that could be used to justify rule by the wealthy. In the 2010s, it has spread from east to west, aided by Russian warfare in Ukraine and cyberwar in Europe and the United States." (Publisher's note)

320.533   Fascism

Riemen, Rob

To fight against this age; on fascism and humanism. Rob Riemen. W W Norton & Co Inc 2018 171 p. (hardcover)

$19.95   **320.533**

1. Fascism 2. Humanism 3. Political ethics 4. World politics -- 21st century

ISBN 9780393635874; 0393635864; 9780393635867

LC 2017043652

This book, by Rob Riemen, "consists of two beautifully written, cogent, and urgent essays about the rise of fascism and the ways in which we can combat it. In 'The Eternal Return of Fascism,' Rob Riemen explores the theoretical weakness of fascism. . . . Riemen's own response to what he sees as the spiritual crisis of our age is articulated in 'The Return of Europa.'" (Publisher's note)

"His erudite essays add an enriching element to the ongoing conversation of a contentious political moment." Pub Wkly

320.54   Nationalism, regionalism, internationalism

Avineri, Shlomo

Herzl's vision; Theodor Herzl and the foundation of the Jewish state. Shlomo Avineri. BlueBridge / United Tribes Media Inc. 2014 304 p. illustrations $22.95   **320.54**

1. Zionism

ISBN 1933346981; 9781933346984

LC 2014948524

National Jewish Book Award Finalist: History (2014)

This book, by Shlomo Avineri, is a biography of the Swiss Zionist Theodor Herzl. The author portrays "Herzl's intellectual and spiritual odyssey from a private and marginal individual into a Jewish political leader and shows how it was the political crisis of the Austro-Hungarian Habsburg Empire, torn apart by contending national movements, which convinced Herzl of the need for a Jewish polity." (Publisher's note)

320.557   Islamic ideologies

Hamid, Shadi

Islamic exceptionalism; how the struggle over Islam is reshaping the World. Shadi Hamid. St. Martin's Press 2016 304 p. (hardback) $26.99   **320.557**

1. Islam and politics 2. Middle East -- Politics and government 3. Middle East -- Politics and government -- 20th century 4. Middle East -- Politics and government -- 21st century 5. Arab countries -- Politics and government -- 20th century 6. Arab countries -- Politics and government -- 21st century

ISBN 9781250061010; 9781466866720

LC 2015049286

This book, by Shadi Hamid, "offers a novel and provocative argument on how Islam is, in fact, 'exceptional in how it relates to politics, with profound implications for how we understand the future of the Middle East. Divides among citizens aren't just about power but are products of fundamental disagreements over the very nature and purpose of the modern nation state—and the vexing problem of religion's role in public life." (Publisher's note)

Includes bibliographical references and index.

320.6   Policy making

Collins, Gail

As Texas goes; how the Lone Star State hijacked the American agenda. Gail Collins. Liveright Pub. Corporation 2012 267 p.   **320.6**

1. Texas -- History 2. Social policy -- Texas 3. Economic policy -- Texas 4. Texas -- Politics and government 5. Texas -- Social policy 6. Texas -- Economic policy 7. Texas -- Politics and government -- 1951-

ISBN 0871404079; 9780871404077

LC 2012007794

This book is a "study of Texas's government and its discontents. New York Times columnist [Gail] Collins . . . argues . . . [that Texas] is a disastrous model of public policy that inspired the Republican Party's national platform: a rickety economic boom based on insecure, poverty-level jobs and massive state incentives to corporations; financial deregulation that led to banking meltdowns; a raft of ill-advised education nostrums." (Publishers Weekly)

Includes bibliographical references and index

Rabin-Havt, Ari

Lies, Incorporated; The World of Post-truth Politics. by Ari Rabin-Havt. Random House Inc 2016 256 p. $15; (ebook) $45   **320.6**

1. Deception 2. Truthfulness and falsehood 3. United States -- Politics and government

ISBN 0307279596; 9780307279590; 9781101972274

LC 2016012087

This book is a "stunning investigation of the history of organized misinformation in politics. . . . Ari Rabin-Havt and Media Matters for America present a revelatory history of this industry—which they've dubbed Lies, Incorporated—and show how it has crippled legislative progress on issues including tobacco regulation, public health care, climate change, gun control, immigration, abortion, and same-sex marriage." (Publisher's note)

"Powerfully crafted accusations sounding the alarm on an insidious trend in political manipulation." Kirkus

Includes bibliographical references and index.

320.9   Political situation and conditions

Perry, Alex

The Rift; A New Africa Breaks Free. Alex Perry. Little, Brown & Co. 2015 448 p. 16 plates; illustrations; maps $30   **320.9**

1. Africa -- Social conditions 2. Africa -- Description and travel

ISBN 0316333778; 9780316333771

LC 2015946918

This book by Alex Perry takes a "look at how the world gets Africa wrong, and how a resurgent Africa is forcing it to think again. Perry traveled the continent for most of a decade, meeting with entrepreneurs and warlords, professors and cocaine smugglers, presidents and jihadis. Beginning with a devastating investigation into a largely unreported war crime-in 2011, when the US and the major aid agencies helped cause a famine in which 250,000 Somalis died-he finds Africa at a moment of furious self-assertion." (Publisher's note)

"This in-depth, investigative report will intrigue readers concerned with U.S. policy and its impact on African nations." Library Journal

320.956   Politics – Middle East

Bergman, Ronen

Rise and kill first; the secret history of Israel's targeted assassinations. Ronen Bergman; translated by Ronnie Hope. Random House Inc 2018 753 p. (hardcover) $35   **320.956**

1. Assassination 2. World politics 3. Israel -- History 4. Israel -- Politics and government
ISBN 1400069718; 9781400069712

LC 2017301148

In this book, author Ronen Bergman "offers a riveting inside account of . . . [Israel Defense Forces'] targeted killing programs: their successes, their failures, and the moral and political price exacted on the men and women who approved and carried out the missions. . . . Bergman traces . . . the gripping events and thorny ethical questions underlying Israel's targeted killing campaign, which has shaped the Israeli nation, the Middle East, and the entire world." (Publisher's note)

"The senior political and military analyst for Israel's largest daily newspaper, Yedioth Ahronoth, Bergman interviewed dozens of current and former government officials in Israel to tell the story of its state-sponsored assassination programs. Billed as news-breaking." LJ

Includes bibliographical references (pages 637-725) and index.

320.973   Politics – United States

Goldfield, David

The **gifted** generation; when government was good. David Goldfield. Bloomsbury USA 2017 544 p. (hardcover: alk. paper) $35   **320.973**

1. United States -- History -- 1945- 2. United States -- Social conditions -- 1945- 3. Social change -- United States -- History -- 20th century 4. Public opinion -- United States 5. Baby boom generation -- Attitudes 6. United States -- Politics and government -- 1989- 7. Federal government -- United States -- Public opinion 8. Public investments -- United States -- Public opinion 9. United States -- Politics and government -- 1945-1989
ISBN 9781620400883

LC 2017020004

This book, by David Goldfield, "examines the generation immediately after World War II and argues that the federal government was instrumental in the great economic, social, and environmental progress of the era. . . . Goldfield brings this unprecedented surge in American legislative and cultural history to life as he explores the presidencies of Harry S. Truman, Dwight D. Eisenhower, and Lyndon Baines Johnson." (Publisher's note)

" Drawing on two excellent accounts of presidential civil rights policies: Michael Gardner's Harry Truman and Civil Rights, and David Nichol's A Matter of Justice, Goldfield acknowledges that this is primarily a history of public policy, which includes exhaustive detail. A valuable resource for historians and informed readers." (LJ)

Includes bibliographical references

When government was good

King, Josh

Off script; an advance man's guide to White House stagecraft, campaign spectacle, and political suicide. Josh King. St. Martin's Press 2016 384 p. illustrations (hardback) $27.99   **320.973**

1. Presidents -- United States -- Press relations 2. Communication in politics -- United States 3. Presidents -- Press coverage -- United States 4. Mass media -- Political aspects -- United States 5. United States -- Politics and government -- 1989- 6. Political campaigns -- United States -- Press coverage 7. Presidents -- United States -- Election -- Press coverage
ISBN 9781137280060; 9781466878921

LC 2015045855

In this book, by Josh King, "Donald Trump won election as the 45th President of the United States by studying American political stagecraft

and learning what helped previous candidates succeed and doomed others to failure. A figure on the periphery of campaigns for decades, he glided down the Trump Tower escalator on June 16, 2015, declared his candidacy and took his place, permanently, as an actor in the country's greatest spectacle." (Publisher's note)

"King presents one of the liveliest and funniest political books of recent years; it will keep political junkies and campaign professionals guffawing and learning." LJ

Includes bibliographical references (p. [328]-351) and index.

Pfeiffer, Dan

Yes we (still) can; politics in the age of Obama, Twitter, and Trump. Dan Pfeiffer. Twelve, an imprint of Grand Central Publishing 2018 284 p.   **320.973**

1. Presidents -- United States -- Staff -- Biography 2. United States -- Politics and government -- 2017- 3. United States -- Politics and government -- 2009-2017
ISBN 9781478992462; 9781538711712; 9781538711729

LC 2018932320

This book by Dan Pfeiffer is "a colorful account of how politics, the media, and the Internet changed during the Obama presidency and how Democrats can fight back in the Trump era. . . . [It] examines how Obama succeeded despite Twitter trolls, Fox News . . . , and a Republican Party that lost its collective mind. . . . [It] is a must-read for everyone who is disturbed by Trump, misses Obama, and is marching, calling, and hoping for a better future for the country." (Publisher's note)

"Those who share Pfeiffer's admiration of Obama and his hopes for a Democratic resurgence--and, of course, fans of his podcast--will love both the chatty insider anecdotes and the advice." Pub Wkly

Includes bibliographical references

320.977   Politics – North central United States

Kaufman, Dan

The **fall** of Wisconsin; The Conservative Conquest of a Progressive Bastion and the Future of American Politics. Dan Kaufman. W W Norton & Co Inc 2018 336 p. $26.95 **320.977**

1. Conservatism -- Wisconsin -- History 2. Progressivism (United States politics) -- History
ISBN 0393635201; 9780393635201

This book, by Dan Kaufman, "is a deeply reported, searing account of how the . . . [Wisconsin's] progressive tradition was undone and turned into a model for national conservatives bent on remaking the country. . . . [It] traces the history of progressivism that made Wisconsin so widely admired. . . . Kaufman also chronicles the remarkable efforts of citizens who are fighting to reclaim Wisconsin's progressive legacy against tremendous odds." (Publisher's note)

"Still, the author's vivid reportage and trenchant insights illuminate America's changing political landscape." Publishers' Weekly

321.8   Democratic government

Achen, Christopher H.

Democracy for realists; why elections do not produce responsive government. Christopher H. Achen, Larry M. Bartels. Princeton University Press 2016 408 p. illustrations (cloth) $29.95   **321.8**

1. Democracy -- United States 2. Elections -- United States 3. Political participation -- United States
ISBN 9780691169446

LC 2016930927

In this book, authors Christopher Achen and Larry Bartels "deploy a wealth of social-scientific evidence . . . to show that the familiar ideal of thoughtful citizens steering the ship of state from the voting booth is fundamentally misguided. They demonstrate that voters . . . mostly choose parties and candidates on the basis of social identities and partisan loyalties, not political issues. . . . Voters do not control the course of public policy, even indirectly." (Publisher's note)

"A comprehensive analysis that lays the foundation for a discussion of necessary reforms and how they can be achieved." Kirkus

Includes bibliographical references (p. 335-369) and index

Cartledge, Paul

Democracy; a life. Paul Cartledge. Oxford University Press 2016 416 p. illustrations (hardback) $29.95 **321.8**
1. Political science 2. Democracy -- History 3. Greece -- Politics and government 4. Democracy -- Greece -- History -- To 1500 5. Greece -- Politics and government -- To 146 B.C
ISBN 9780190494322; 9780199837458; 9780199837465

LC 2015034058

This book, by Paul Cartledge, "surveys the emergence and development of Greek politics, the invention of political theory, and-intimately connected to the latter- the birth of democracy, first at Athens in c. 500 bce and then at its greatest flourishing in the Greek world 150 years later. Cartledge then traces the decline of genuinely democratic Greek institutions at the hands of the Macedonians and-subsequently and decisively-the Romans." (Publisher's note)

"No library should be without this wonderful book, in which Cartledge has abundantly shared his love and knowledge of ancient Greece with us." Kirkus

Includes bibliographical references and index

Dobson, William J.

The **dictator's** learning curve; inside the global battle for democracy. by William J. Dobson. Doubleday 2012 341p. $28.95 **321.8**
1. Democracy 2. Dictators 3. Dictatorship 4. Democratization
ISBN 0385533357; 9780385533355

LC 2011050286

This book presents a "study of how heavy-handed repression by authoritarian regimes has given way to more subtle forms of control. Despite some reassuring advances in democracy over the last 40 years. . . . [William J.] Dobson sees a pernicious, no-less-repressive shift in the tactics of autocrats still hanging on. . . . Dobson travels around the globe, from Malaysia to Venezuela, chronicling his encounters with both camps." (Kirkus Reviews)

Includes bibliographical references and index

Levitsky, Steven

★ **How** democracies die; Steven Levitsky and Daniel Ziblatt. Crown Publishing 2018 320 p. (hbk.) $26 **321.8**
1. Democracy 2. Political culture 3. Democracy -- United States 4. Political culture -- United States 5. United States -- Politics and government -- 2017-
ISBN 0525574530; 9780241317983; 978-0525574538; 0241317983; 1524762938; 9781524762933

LC 2017045872

"Drawing on decades of research and a wide range of historical and global examples, from 1930s Europe to contemporary Hungary, Turkey, and Venezuela, to the American South during Jim Crow, [Steven] Levitsky and [Danie] Ziblatt show how democracies die--and how ours can be saved." (Publisher's note)

"A provocative analysis of the parallels between Donald Trump's ascent and the fall of other democracies." Kirkus

Includes bibliographical references

Miller, James

Can democracy work? a short history of a radical idea from ancient Athens to our world. James Miller. Farrar, Straus & Giroux 2018 320 p. (hardcover) $27 **321.8**
1. Ideology 2. Political science 3. Democracy -- History 4. Democracy -- Philosophy
ISBN 9780374137649

LC 2018002536

In this book, author James Miller, "offers a lively, surprising, and urgent history of the democratic idea from its first stirrings to the present. As he shows, democracy has always been rife with inner tensions. . . . Ranging from the theaters of Athens to the tents of Occupy Wall Street, 'Can Democracy Work?' is an entertaining and insightful guide to our most cherished--and vexed--ideal." (Publisher's note)

Includes bibliographical references and index

Rice, Condoleezza, 1954-

Democracy; Stories from the Long Road to Freedom. Condoleezza Rice. Twelve 2017 viii, 486 p.p illustrations, maps (hardcover) $35 **321.8**
1. Democracy -- History 2. United States -- Foreign relations 3. World politics -- 1989- 4. Cabinet officers -- United States -- Biography 5. United States -- Foreign relations -- 2001-2009 6. Democratization -- Government policy -- United States
ISBN 9781455540181; 9781538760383; 1455540188

LC 2016056710

This book, by Condoleezza Rice, presents "a sweeping look at the global struggle for democracy and why America must continue to support the cause of human freedom. . . . Using America's long struggle as a template, Rice draws lessons for democracy around the world -- from Russia, Poland, and Ukraine, to Kenya, Colombia, and the Middle East. She finds that no transitions to democracy are the same because every country starts in a different place." (Publisher's note)

"George W. Bush's secretary of state returns to her academic roots with this accessibly written study of that imperfect but ideal form of government." Kirkus

Includes bibliographical references (pages 449-466) and index.

321.9 Authoritarian government

Kalder, Daniel

★ The **infernal** library; on dictators, their books, and other catastrophes of literacy. Daniel Kalder. Henry Holt & Co. 2018 400 p. (hardcover) $32 **321.9**
1. Dictators 2. Literature and politics 3. Dictatorships -- History 4. Dictators as authors -- History 5. Revolutionary literature -- Authorship
ISBN 9781627793421

LC 2017009633

This book, by Daniel Kalder, offers "a harrowing tour of 'dictator literature' in the twentieth-century, featuring the soul-killing prose and poetry of Hitler, Mao, and many more, which shows how books have sometimes shaped the world for the worse. . . . The titans of the genre . . . produced theoretical works, spiritual manifestos, poetry, memoirs, and even the occasional romance novel and established a literary tradition of boundless tedium that continues to this day." (Publisher's note)

"The author renders his highly compelling narrative in a cheeky yet erudite tone that will keep readers smirking despite the monstrousness

of the book's protagonists. Dictators have never looked so educated."
Kirkus

Paxton, Robert O.

★ The **anatomy** of fascism; [by] Robert Paxton. Knopf
2004 321p $26; pa $15   **321.9**

1. Fascism
ISBN 1-4000-4094-9; 1-4000-3391-8 pa

LC 2004-100489

"While there are countless studies on fascism, readers will be hard
pressed to find anything more in-depth from a scholar with Paxton's
credentials." Libr J

Includes bibliographical references

Snyder, Timothy D., 1969-

On tyranny; twenty lessons from the twentieth century.
Timothy Snyder. Tim Duggan Books 2017 126 p. (trade pbk.)
$7.99   **321.9**

1. Despotism 2. World history -- 20th century 3. Political culture
-- United States 4. Political ethics 5. Democracy -- United States
6. History, Modern -- 20th century
ISBN 0804190119; 9780804190114; 9780804190121

LC 2017000492

In this book, author Timothy Snyder claims that "our [American] political order faces new threats, not unlike the totalitarianism of the twentieth century. We are no wiser than the Europeans who saw democracy
yield to fascism, Nazism, or communism. Our one advantage is that we
might learn from their experience." (Publisher's note)

Stanley, Jason

How fascism works; the politics of US and them. Jason
Stanley. Random House Inc 2018 256 p. $26   **321.9**

1. Fascism 2. Polarization (Social sciences)
ISBN 9780525511830

LC 2018013266

In this book, author Jason Stanley "identifies the ten pillars of fascist
politics, and charts their horrifying rise and deep history. . . . Alarmed by
the pervasive rise of fascist tactics both at home and around the globe,
Stanley focuses here on the structures that unite them, laying out and
analyzing the ten pillars of fascist politics--the language and beliefs that
separate people into an 'us' and a 'them.'" (Publisher's note)

322   Relation of the state to organized groups and their members

Kertzer, David I., 1948-

The **Pope** and Mussolini; the secret history of Pius XI and
the rise of Fascism in Europe. David I. Kertzer. Random House
2014 576 p. illustrations, maps hbk $32   **322**

1. Church and state -- Italy -- History 2. Fascism and the Catholic
Church -- Italy
ISBN 0812993462; 9780812993462

LC 2013019402

Pulitzer Prize: Biography or Autobiography (2015)

"'The Pope and Mussolini' tells the story of two men who came to
power in 1922, and together changed the course of twentieth-century
history. . . . Pius XI and 'Il Duce' had many things in common. They
shared a distrust of democracy and a visceral hatred of Communism. .
. . In a challenge to the conventional history of this period . . . [author
David I.] Kertzer shows how Pius XI played a crucial role in making
Mussolini's dictatorship possible and keeping him in power." (Publish-

er's note)

"Kertzer unravels the relationship between two of 20th-century Europe's most important political figures and does so in an accessible style
that makes for a fast-paced must-read." Pub Wkly

Includes bibliographical references and index

Kruse, Kevin M.

One nation under God; how corporate America invented
Christian America. Kevin M. Kruse. Basic Books 2015 448 p.
(hardback: alkaline paper) $29.99   **322**

1. New Deal, 1933-1939 2. Church and state -- United States 3.
Christianity and politics -- United States 4. New Deal, 1933-1939
-- Public opinion 5. United States -- Religion -- 20th century 6.
United States -- Politics and government -- 1933-1945 7. United
States -- Politics and government -- 1945-1989 8. Conservatism --
United States -- History -- 20th century 9. Social conflict -- United
States -- History -- 20th century 10. Church and state -- United
States -- History -- 20th century 11. Political culture -- United
States -- History -- 20th century 12. Christianity and politics --
United States -- History -- 20th century 13. Corporations -- Political
activity -- United States -- History -- 20th century
ISBN 0465049494; 9780465049493

LC 2014035883

In this book, "historian Kevin M. Kruse reveals that the idea of
'Christian America' is an invention--and a relatively recent one at that.
As Kruse argues, the belief that America is fundamentally and formally a
Christian nation originated in the 1930s when businessmen enlisted reli-
gious activists in their fight against FDR's New Deal." (Publisher's note)

"In a book for readers from both parties, Kruse ably demonstrates
how the simple ornamental mottoes 'under God' and 'In God We Trust,'
as well as the fight to define America as Christian, were parts of a clever
business plan."

Includes bibliographical references and index

Preston, Andrew

Sword of the spirit, shield of faith; religion in American war
and diplomacy. by Andrew Preston. Alfred A. Knopf 2012 815
p.   **322**

1. Protestantism 2. Military policy -- United States 3. United
States -- Foreign relations 4. Religion and politics -- United States
5. International relations -- Religious aspects 6. United States --
Military policy -- Religious aspects 7. United States -- Foreign
relations -- Religious aspects 8. United States -- History, Military
-- Religious aspects 9. Religion and international relations -- United
States -- History
ISBN 9781400043231

LC 2011035138

It was the author's intention to provide an "examination of the consistent application of the founding religious principles to American foreign policy, from the colonists' sense of a Protestant exceptionalism to
President Obama's 'Good Niebuhr Policy.' . . . [Author Andrew] Preston
explores this fascinating paradox of a nation founded on freedom of religion yet exhibiting, in its relations with the wider world, a profound belief in a Judeo-Christian sense of 'exceptional virtue.'" (Kirkus Reviews)

Includes bibliographical references and index

Rothkopf, David

Power, Inc. the epic rivalry between big business and gov-
ernment-- and the reckoning that lies ahead. David Rothkopf.
Farrar, Straus and Giroux 2011 436 p. $30   **322**

1. Capitalism 2. Industrial policy 3. Economics -- History 4.
Business and politics 5. Big business 6. Capitalism -- Political
aspects

ISBN 9780374151287; 0374151288

LC 2011036672

In this book, "[David] Rothkopf . . . uses . . . examples . . . to show the massive influence big business wields in our world and claims that our current economic struggles are not new but, rather, have their roots in history. The rivalry between public and private power has existed for centuries, and, Rothkopf argues, must be managed to achieve a balance that will work for the future. He examines the watershed years of 1288, 1648, 1776, and 1848 to illustrate the common threads of this struggle through history. Whether it is the Treaty of Westphalia, the Industrial Revolution, or the fall of communism, Rothkopf puts an economic spin on historic events and times of change. (Libr J)

Includes bibliographical references and index

Tobin, Jacqueline

★ **From** Midnight to Dawn; the last tracks of the underground railroad. [by] Jacqueline Tobin with Hettie Jones. Doubleday 2006 272p il hardcover o.p. pa $14   **322**

1. Abolitionists 2. Underground railroad 3. Slavery -- United States

ISBN 978-0-385-51431-6; 0-385-51431-X; 978-1-4000-7936-0 pa; 1-4000-7936-5 pa

LC 2006-46304

"There's an enlightening portrait of Josiah Henson (the model for Stowe's Uncle Tom) as a political activist, a fascinating look at the pioneering journalist and early feminist Mary Ann Shadd and an intriguing section on the deep 'Canadian connection to Harpers Ferry,' as John Brown meets with the fugitives in Chatham. Accessible and fluidly written, the book will appeal to general readers." Publ Wkly

Includes bibliographical references

322.4 Political action groups

Chalmers, David Mark

Hooded Americanism: the history of the Ku Klux Klan; 3rd ed; Duke Univ. Press 1987 477p il hardcover o.p. pa $24.95   **322.4**

1. Ku Klux Klan

ISBN 0-8223-0772-3 pa

LC 86-29133

First published 1965 by Doubleday; this is a reissue of the 1981 edition published by Watts

This book recounts the history of the Klan. It describes the sociological and psychological forces behind the Klan, and sets forth its dogmas

"The book is written in a breezy, journalistic style. . . . Especially instructive and sobering is Chalmers' account of the role of the Klan in politics." J Am Hist

Includes bibliographical references

Conner, Claire

Wrapped in the flag; a personal history of America's radical right. Claire Conner. Beacon Press 2013 264 p. (alk. paper) $25.95   **322.4**

1. Conservatism 2. John Birch Society 3. United States -- Politics and government -- 1945-1989 4. Right-wing extremists -- United States -- History -- 20th century 5. Right and left (Political science) -- United States -- History -- 20th century

ISBN 080707750X; 9780807077504

LC 2012049353

This book provides an insider's view of the John Birch Society (JBS), "the most radical right-wing organization of the Cold War era." It

"describes the seeming paranoia and questionable logic of the most devoted JBS members. [Claire] Conner provides . . . descriptions of many of the eccentric JBS leaders, including founder Robert Welch. . . . She describes her evolution from a fervently pro-life organizer to a somewhat disillusioned woman who is more" pro-choice. (Library Journal)

Includes bibliographical references and index

Esposito, John L.

Unholy war; terror in the name of Islam. Oxford Univ. Press 2002 196p hardcover o.p. pa $15.95   **322.4**

1. Islam and politics 2. Terrorism -- Religious aspects 3. United States -- Foreign opinion

ISBN 0-19-515435-5; 0-19-516886-0 pa

LC 2001-58009

The author "explains the teachings of Islam—the Quran, the example of the Prophet, Islamic law—about jihad or holy war, the use of violence, and terrorism. He chronicles the rise of extremist groups and examines their frightening worldview and tactics." Publisher's note

Includes bibliographical references

Gandhi, Mahatma

★ **Gandhi** on non-violence; selected texts from Mohandas K. Gandhi's Non-violence in peace and war. edited with an introduction by Thomas Merton; preface by Mark Kurlansky. New Directions 2007 101p pa $13.95   **322.4**

1. Passive resistance 2. India -- Politics and government

ISBN 978-0-8112-1686-9

LC 2007-32262

First published 1965

In an introductory essay Merton "considers Gandhi's ideas, not in relation to their Indian context, but in terms of their applicability to all men's lives. Brief quotations from Gandhi's writings make up most of the book." Asia: a Guide to Paperbacks

Includes bibliographical references

McCarter, Jeremy

Young radicals; in the war for American ideals. Jeremy McCarter. Random House 2017 xvii, 368 p.p (hardback: acid-free paper) $30   **322.4**

1. Political activists -- United States -- Biography 2. Radicals -- United States -- Biography 3. Idealism, American -- History -- 20th century 4. United States -- Politics and government -- 1901-1953 5. World War, 1914-1918 -- Social aspects -- United States

ISBN 9780679644545; 9780812993059

LC 2016055051

This book, by Jeremy McCarter, "tells the story of five activists, intellectuals and troublemakers who agitated for freedom and equality in the hopeful years before the war, then fought to defend those values in a country pitching into violence and chaos. . . . [It] brings to life the exploits of Randolph Bourne, the bold social critic . . .; Max Eastman, the charismatic poet-propagandist of Greenwich Village; . . . [and] Alice Paul, a suffragist leader." (Publisher's note)

"A brisk pace and sympathetic portraits make for an entertaining, well-researched history of a decade marked by ebullience, hope, and pain." Kirkus

Includes bibliographical references and index

Ronson, Jon

Them: adventures with extremists. Simon & Schuster 2002 330p $24; pa $13   **322.4**

1. Radicalism 2. Conspiracies

ISBN 0-7432-2707-7; 0-7432-3321-2 pa

LC 2001-47411

First published 2001 in the United Kingdom

This book "is at times funny, other times unsettling, but always astonishing. So difficult to accept are Ronson's narratives that any conclusions must be left up to the reader." Booklist

Toobin, Jeffrey, 1960-

★ **American** Heiress; The Wild Saga of the Kidnapping, Crimes and Trial of Patty Hearst. Jeffrey Toobin. Random House Inc 2016 368 p. illustrations, portratis $28.95   **322.4**

1. Kidnapping

ISBN 0385536712; 9780385536714

LC 2016016625

In this book, author Jeffrey Toobin shows how "the saga of Patty Hearst highlighted a decade in which America seemed to be suffering a collective nervous breakdown. Based on more than a hundred interviews and thousands of previously secret documents, [it[thrillingly recounts the craziness of the times. Toobin portrays the lunacy of the half-baked radicals of the SLA and the toxic mix of sex, politics, and violence that swept up Patty Hearst and re-creates her melodramatic trial." (Publisher's note)

"His thorough research, careful parsing of all the evidence, and superior prose make the book read like a summertime thriller." Pub Wkly

Includes bibliographical references (pages [345]-351) and index.

322.42   Revolutionary and subversive groups

The **Black** Panthers; portraits from an unfinished revolution. Bryan Shih and Yohuru Williams. Nation Books 2016 288 p. illustrations (ebook) $16.99; (pbk.) $24.99   **322.42**

1. Black Panther Party 2. African Americans -- Political activity 3. Black Panther Party -- History 4. Black Panther Party -- Interviews 5. Black Panther Party -- Pictorial works 6. African American radicals -- Interviews 7. Black Panther Party -- History -- Sources 8. African American social reformers -- Interviews 9. African American political activists -- Interviews 10. Black power -- United States -- History -- 20th century -- Sources 11. African Americans -- Politics and government -- 20th century -- Sources

ISBN 9781568585567; 9781568585550

LC 2016012694

In this book, "photojournalist Bryan Shih and historian Yohuru Williams offer a reappraisal of the party's history and legacy. Through stunning portraits and interviews with surviving Panthers, as well as illuminating essays by leading scholars, 'The Black Panthers' reveals party members' grit and battle scars-and the undying love for the people that kept them going." (Publisher's note)

"Readers interested in the current Black Lives Matter movement will find resonance in the Panthers' stories." LJ

Includes bibliographical references and index

Gordon, Linda

The **second** coming of the KKK; the Ku Klux Klan of the 1920s and the American political tradition. Linda Gordon. Liveright Publishing Corporation 2017 xiv, 272 p.p illustrations (hardcover) $27.95   **322.42**

1. Ku Klux Klan 2. Racism -- United States 3. Ku Klux Klan (1915-) -- History -- 20th century 4. Racism -- United States -- History -- 20th century 5. Hate groups -- United States -- History -- 20th century 6. United States -- Race relations -- History -- 20th century 7. Political culture -- United States -- History -- 20th century

ISBN 9781631493690; 9781631493706; 1631493698

LC 2017037229

This book, by Linda Gordon, looks at the emergence of the Ku Klux Klan in the early 1920s. [The] "Klan recruited openly, through newspaper ads, in churches, and through extravagant mass 'Americanism' pageants, often held on Independence Day. As Gordon shows, the themes of 1920s Klan ideology were not aberrant, but an indelible part of American history." (Publisher's note)

" A revealing, well-researched—and, unfortunately, contemporarily relevant—investigation of the KKK's wide support in the 1920s." Kirkus

Includes bibliographical references and index.

323   Civil and political rights

Arsenault, Raymond

★ **Freedom** riders; 1961 and the struggle for racial justice. Oxford University Press 2006 690p il map (Pivotal moments in American history) $32.50   **323**

1. Congress of Racial Equality 2. Segregation in transportation 3. African Americans -- Segregation 4. African Americans -- Civil rights 5. Southern States -- Race relations 6. Civil rights -- Constitutional history 7. Civil rights movements -- Southern States 8. Civil rights workers -- Southern states -- History 9. African Americans -- Segregation -- Southern States 10. Civil rights activists -- Southern States -- History 11. Segregation in transportation -- Southern States -- History 12. Civil rights workers -- United States -- History -- 20th century 13. African Americans -- Civil rights -- Southern States -- History -- 20th century

ISBN 0-19-513674-8; 978-0-19-513674-6

LC 2005-18108

This is a history of the "six months [in 1961] in which black and white volunteers descended on the South to challenge segregated travel." N Y Times (Late N Y Ed)

Includes bibliographical references

Cleaver, Eldridge

Target zero; a life in writing. edited by Kathleen Cleaver; foreword by Henry Louis Gates, Jr.; afterword by Cecil Brown. Palgrave Macmillan 2005 xxvi, 336p $27.95; pa $16.95 **323**

1. Dissenters 2. Memoirists 3. Civil rights activists

ISBN 978-1-4039-6237-9; 1-4039-6237-5; 978-1-4039-7657-4 pa; 1-4039-7657-0 pa

LC 2005-51252

"The book's four parts chart Cleaver's life trhough his essays, short stories, letters, interviews, and poems, many previously unpublished. . . . This well-crafted reader . . . is a rich experience." Choice

Includes bibliographical references

Dershowitz, Alan M.

★ **Rights** from wrongs; a secular theory of the origins of rights. Basic Books 2004 261p $24   **323**

1. Civil rights 2. Human rights

ISBN 0-465-01713-4

LC 2004-20006

The author "asserts that human rights derive from the world's experience with 'wrongs,' i.e., injustice. Only after seeing genocide, for example, did the notion develop that this was a violation of human rights. Dershowitz . . . has a rare ability to develop complex ideas in readable prose. . . . Whether conservative or liberal, absolutist or relativist, readers will find areas of disagreement, but most will concur that a talented and creative legal mind is at work." Publ Wkly

Includes bibliographical references

Dyson, Michael Eric

I may not get there with you: the true Martin Luther King, Jr. Free Press 2000 404p $25; pa $15   **323**
1. Clergy 2. Nonfiction writers 3. Civil rights activists 4. Nobel laureates for peace 5. African Americans -- Biography 6. African Americans -- Civil rights
ISBN 0-684-86776-1; 0-684-83037-X pa

LC 99-40478

Dyson "believes that the ministry fostered King's rhetorical gifts but also encouraged his authoritarian personality. We learn much about his flaws, and about conflict, dissent, and generational differences within the black community, as Dyson insists that King, properly understood, remains a controversial figure." New Yorker

Includes bibliographical references

Hartman, Saidiya V.

★ Lose your mother; a journey along the Atlantic slave route. [by] Saidiya Hartman. Farrar, Straus and Giroux 2007 270p il $25; pa $14   **323**
1. Slave trade 2. Ghana -- Description and travel
ISBN 978-0-374-27082-7; 0-374-27082-1; 978-0-374-53115-7 pa; 0-374-53115-3 pa

LC 2006-29407

This "is a groundbreaking book for its ability to combine autobiography, history, and politics in an unprecedented style. . . . Hartman's book is not just to be read by historians of slavery or the Atlantic World, but by all of those who desire to write of the past." Rev Am Hist

Includes bibliographical references

Honey, Michael K.

To the promised land; Martin Luther King and the fight for economic justice. Michael K. Honey. W.W. Norton & Company 2018 241 p. illustrations (hardcover) $25.95   **323**
1. African Americans -- Biography 2. Civil rights workers -- Biography 3. Poor People's Campaign 4. Civil rights workers -- United States -- Biography 5. African Americans -- Economic conditions -- 20th century 6. Right to labor -- United States -- History -- 20th century 7. African Americans -- Civil rights -- History -- 20th century 8. Civil rights movements -- United States -- History -- 20th century 9. Discrimination in employment -- United States -- History -- 20th century 10. Equality -- Economic aspects -- United States -- History -- 20th century
ISBN 9780393651270; 9780393651263

LC 2017060268

This book, by Michael K. Honey, "goes beyond the iconic view of Martin Luther King Jr. as an advocate of racial harmony to explore his profound commitment to the poor and working class and his call for 'nonviolent resistance' to all forms of oppression, including the economic injustice that 'takes necessities from the masses to give luxuries to the classes.' Phase one of King's agenda led to the Civil Rights and Voting Rights Acts." (Publisher's note)

"Honey encourages the many who revere his memory to continue his work toward this goal. His book contains both insight and inspiration to activists of many stripes." Pub Wkly

Includes bibliographical references (pages 199-224) and index.

King, Martin Luther Jr, 1929-1968

The **autobiography** of Martin Luther King, Jr; edited by Clayborne Carson. Warner Bks. 1998 400p il $25; pa $15.95   **323**

1. Clergy 2. Nonfiction writers 3. Civil rights activists 4. Nobel laureates for peace 5. African Americans -- Biography 6. African Americans -- Civil rights
ISBN 0-446-52412-3; 0-446-67650-0 pa

LC 98-35704

"Carson, director of Martin Luther King Jr. Papers Project, brings together selections from King's writings, speeches, and recordings to create this fascinating 'autobiography' of the famed civil rights leader and Nobel Peace Prize winner. The writings trace King's struggles with religion, philosophy, and the racial politics of the U.S." Booklist

Includes bibliographical references

The **radical** King; Martin Luther King, Jr.; edited and introduced by Cornel West. Beacon Press 2014 320 p. illustrations $26.95   **323**
ISBN 9780807012826

LC 2014022515

Featuring works by Martin Luther King, Jr., "Arranged thematically in four parts, 'The Radical King' includes twenty-three selections, curated and introduced by Dr. Cornel West, that illustrate King's revolutionary vision, underscoring his identification with the poor, his unapologetic opposition to the Vietnam War, and his crusade against global imperialism." (Publisher's note)

"This volume features a popularly referenced spiritual giant too seldom recognized in his true dimensions. Readers looking to discover the 'real' Martin Luther King Jr., revolutionary Christianity, social justice, or the state of contemporary America will enjoy West's provocative and pithy work as it calls on King to speak again about America, the world, and 'where we go from here.'" LJ

Includes bibliographical references and index

Kotz, Nick

★ Judgment days; Lyndon Baines Johnson, Martin Luther King, Jr., and the laws that changed America. Houghton Mifflin 2005 522p $26   **323**
1. Clergy 2. Presidents 3. Vice-presidents 4. Senators 5. Nonfiction writers 6. Members of Congress 7. Civil rights activists 8. Civil Rights Act of 1964 9. Nobel laureates for peace 10. Voting Rights Act of 1965 11. United States -- Race relations 12. United States -- Politics and government -- 1961-1974
ISBN 0-618-08825-3

LC 2004-59852

This is a "narrative of how President Johnson and King temporarily overcame their mutual suspicion to battle successfully for the Civil Rights Acts of 1964 and 1968 and the 1965 Voting Rights Act. . . . This book is an informed political investigation of these two civil rights warriors and the cause for which they fought and, in King's case, died." Libr J

Schulz, William F.

In our own best interest; how defending human rights benefits us all. foreword by Mary Robinson. Beacon Press 2001 235p $25; pa $15   **323**
1. Human rights
ISBN 0-8070-0226-7; 0-8070-0227-5 pa

LC 2001-392

According to the author, "defending human rights pays off not only in terms of justice, but also in ways that can include greater economic growth, a more protected environment, better public health, and a generally less violent world." America

Includes bibliographical references

Shipler, David K.

The **rights** of the people; how our search for safety invades our liberties. Alfred A. Knopf 2011 366p $27.95; ebook $13.99   **323**

1. Civil rights 2. Law enforcement 3. Rule of law -- United States 4. Civil rights -- United States

ISBN 978-1-4000-4362-0; 978-0-307-59550-8 ebook

LC 2010-34255

The book "offers provocative real-life accounts of how privacy has been sacrificed in the modern era. The outlines of some of the stories he tells are familiar, such as the arrest of Brandon Mayfield, a Muslim lawyer in Portland, Oregon, whose fingerprint the FBI erroneously 'matched' to fingerprints from the Madrid train bombing in 2004. . . . [David K.] Shipler's goal is not to reformulate legal doctrine but to show us, through the experience of Americans subject to intrusive police tactics, where existing doctrine has left us; we live in a world where a federal judge can resignedly say, as Shipler quotes US District Judge Paul Friedman, 'I don't think that there's much left of the Fourth Amendment in criminal law.' As Shipler . . . illustrates, the dual wars on drugs and terror have brought us to this point. Time and again, constitutional law has bent to the imperatives of the state in conflict." (New York Review of Books)

"Identifying five periods in American history when the Bill of Rights has been under particular assault, Shipler . . . argues that we are in the middle of a sixth, a post-9/11 era in which our liberties are once again endangered. . . . A timely call for vigilance, for insisting on the protections the Framers provided against an always overreaching government." Kirkus

Includes bibliographical references

Sugrue, Thomas J.

Sweet land of liberty; the forgotten struggle for civil rights in the North. Random House 2008 xxviii, 688p il $35   **323**

1. United States -- Race relations 2. African Americans -- Civil rights 3. African American civil rights workers 4. Northeastern States -- Race relations 5. Civil rights movements -- Northeastern States 6. United States -- Race relations -- History -- 20th century 7. African Americans -- Civil rights -- History -- 20th century 8. Civil rights workers -- United States -- History -- 20th century 9. Civil rights movements -- United States -- History -- 20th century

ISBN 0-679-64303-6; 978-0-679-64303-6

LC 2008-2081

This is a an account of the civil rights movement in the North from the 1920s to the present. Index.

The author "shows that black exclusion, poverty, and racial violence permeated America on both sides of the Mason-Dixon Line. . . . This splendid read brims with insights broadening and deepening understanding of the black-white mold of modern America. Highly recommended and essential for collections on U.S. history, social movements, race relations, or civil rights." Libr J

Includes bibliographical references

323.092   Civil rights leaders

Hancock, Larry

Killing King; racial terrorists, James Earl Ray, and the plot to assassinate Martin Luther King Jr. Stuart Wexler and Larry Hancock. Counterpoint Press 2018 304 p. $26   **323.092**

1. Conspiracies 2. Racism -- United States 3. Conspiracies -- United States -- History -- 20th century

ISBN 9781619029194

LC 2017054596

This book, by Stuart Wexler and Larry Hancock, "uncovers previously unknown FBI files and sources, as well as new forensics to convincingly make the case that [Martin Luther] King [Jr.] was assassinated by a long-simmering conspiracy orchestrated by the racial terrorists who were responsible for the Mississippi Burning murders. . . . [T]he book reveals a network of racist militants led by Sam Bowers, . . . who were dedicated to the cause of killing King." (Publisher's note)

Includes bibliographical references and index

Sokol, Jason

The **heavens** might crack; the death and legacy of Martin Luther King, Jr. Jason Sokol. Basic Books 2018 352 p. (hardback) $32   **323.092**

1. African Americans -- Social conditions 2. United States -- Race relations -- History 3. Public opinion -- United States

ISBN 9780465055913; 9781541697393

LC 2017042658

This book on the aftermath of Martin Luther King Jr.'s assassination, by Jason Sokol, "places King in a balanced perspective both at home and abroad. This even-handed account helps explain the irony that King, in his day, was largely unpopular outside of African American communities yet now has become a symbol of American democracy. A highly readable volume that will appeal to a spectrum of scholars, students, and the general public interested in African American politics." (Library Journal)

Includes bibliographical references and index

323.1   Civil and political rights of nondominant groups

Black Power 50; edited by Sylviane A. Diouf and Komozi Woodward. The New Press 2016 160 p. illustrations (some color) (paperback) $24.95   **323.1**

1. Black power 2. Schomburg Center for Research in Black Culture 3. African Americans -- History -- 1964- -- Exhibitions 4. Black power -- United States -- History -- Exhibitions 5. Schomburg Center for Research in Black Culture -- Exhibitions 6. United States -- Civilization -- African American influences -- Exhibitions

ISBN 9781620971482

LC 2015022627

This book, edited by Sylviane A. Diouf and Komozi Woodward, "includes original interviews with key figures from the [Black Arts] movement, essays from today's leading Black Power scholars, and over one hundred stunning images, offering a beautiful and compelling introduction to this pivotal movement." (Publisher's note)

"The text and visuals combine for an educational, eye-opening experience." Kirkus

Includes bibliographical references and index

Black Power fifty

Boyd, Herb

★ **We** shall overcome; a living history of the civil rights struggle told in words, pictures and the voices of the participants. Sourcebooks 2004 272p il $45   **323.1**

1. African Americans -- Civil rights

ISBN 1-402-20213-X

LC 2004-12509

"Through text, images, and actual recordings (found on 2 CDs), Boyd . . . presents some of the major events in the Civil Rights Movement, including the murder of Emmett Till, the march on Washington, and the life and death of Martin Luther King Jr." Libr J

Includes bibliographical references

Euchner, Charles

Nobody turn me around; a people's history of the 1963 march on Washington. Beacon Press 2010 226p $26.95 **323.1**
1. Civil rights demonstrations 2. Washington (D.C.) 3. African Americans -- Civil rights
ISBN 978-0-8070-0059-5

LC 2009-46943

Draws on the oral histories of more than one hundred participants to provide a behind-the-scenes look at the historic 1963 March on Washington that culminated in Martin Luther King Jr.'s "I Have a Dream" speech.

"A sweeping, comprehensive look at a pivotal march in American history." Booklist

Includes bibliographical references

The **Eyes** on the prize civil rights reader; documents, speeches, and firsthand accounts from the black freedom struggle, 1954-1990. general editors, Clayborne Carson {et al.} Penguin Bks. 1991 764p pa $18 **323.1**
1. United States -- Race relations 2. African Americans -- Civil rights
ISBN 0-14-015403-5

LC 91-9507

First published 1987 with title: Eyes on the prize: America's civil rights years, a reader and guide

"An anthology of primary material important in the historiography of this country's civil rights movement. . . . Not simply for reference use, this compilation makes provocative cover-to-cover reading and is extremely worthy of consideration by every library." Booklist

Includes bibliographical references

Greenhaw, Wayne

Fighting the devil in Dixie; how civil rights activists took on the Ku Klux Klan in Alabama. Lawrence Hill Books 2011 316p il $26.95 **323.1**
1. Ku Klux Klan (1915-) 2. Alabama -- Race relations 3. African Americans -- Civil rights
ISBN 978-1-56976-345-2

LC 2010-30114

"The author skillfully weaves a rich historical tapestry from his deeply engaged, firsthand observations. Impressively captures stark, stunning history in the making." Kirkus

Includes bibliographical references

Halberstam, David

★ The **children**. Fawcett Books 1999 783p il pa $18.95 **323.1**
1. Clergy 2. Mayors 3. Educators 4. Physicians 5. Psychiatrists 6. Songwriters 7. College teachers 8. Social activists 9. Members of Congress 10. School administrators 11. Civil rights activists 12. Local government officials 13. United States -- Race relations 14. African Americans -- Civil rights
ISBN 978-0-449-00439-5; 0-449-00439-2
First published 1998 by Random House

This is a "recreation of the early days of the civil rights movement. . . . The author focuses on a small group of young African Americans who attended the Reverend James Lawson's workshop for nonviolent demonstrators in Nashville in 1959, then went on to play active roles in the movement. . . . A masterful achievement in reporting, research and understanding." Publ Wkly

Includes bibliographical references

Hoxie, Frederick E.

This Indian country; American Indian political activists and the place they made. Frederick E. Hoxie. Penguin Press 2012 467 p. $32.95 **323.1**
1. Native Americans -- History 2. Native American political activists 3. Native Americans -- Politics and government 4. United States -- Race relations 5. United States -- Politics and government 6. Political activists -- United States -- History
ISBN 1594203652; 9781594203657

LC 2012009287

This book by Frederick E. Hoxie "profiles eight Native American lawyers, lobbyists, writers, and politicians who 'chose to oppose the oppressions of the United States with words and ideas rather than violence.'" These include 'mid-19th-century leader William Potter Ross . . . who negotiated with the Union Pacific Railroad over its claims to tribal lands . . . and writer Vine Deloria Jr., who . . . argued that U.S. policies should forward Indian self-governance." (Publishers Weekly)

Includes bibliographical references and index.

Joseph, Peniel E.

★ **Waiting** 'til the midnight hour; a narrative history of Black power in America. Henry Holt and Co. 2006 399p il hardcover o.p. pa $17 **323.1**
1. Black power 2. African Americans -- Civil rights
ISBN 978-0-8050-7539-7; 0-8050-7539-9; 978-0-8050-8335-4 pa; 0-8050-8335-9 pa

LC 2005-46765

"Rather than simply detailing the history of radical organizations, Joseph . . . also profiles several famous leaders and uses their stories to spearhead a discussion of the intellectual and practical history of Black Power as a political movement. . . . Enthusiastically recommended for public and academic libraries." Libr J

Includes bibliographical references

Kantrowitz, Stephen

More than freedom; fighting for black citizenship in a white republic, 1829-1889. Stephen Kantrowitz. Penguin Press 2012 514 p. **323.1**
1. Abolitionists 2. Slaves -- Emancipation 3. Reconstruction (1865-1876) 4. African Americans -- Civil rights 5. United States -- History -- 1861-1865, Civil War 6. Boston Region (Mass.) -- Race relations -- History -- 19th century 7. African Americans -- Civil rights -- Massachusetts -- Boston Region -- History -- 19th century
ISBN 1594203423; 9781594203428

LC 2011044724

This book by Stephen Kantrowitz provides a "narrative account of the long struggle of Northern activists-both black and white, famous and obscure-to establish African Americans as free citizens, from abolitionism through the Civil War, Reconstruction, and its demise. . . . [Kantrowitz] chronicles this epic struggle through the lived experiences of black and white activists in and around Boston. . . . [T]heir goals and achievements went far beyond emancipation." (Publisher's note)

Includes bibliographical references (p. [442]-499) and index

Katznelson, Ira

★ **When** affirmative action was white; an untold history of racial inequality in twentieth-century America. W.W. Norton 2005 238p $25.95; pa $16.95 **323.1**
1. Race discrimination 2. Affirmative action programs 3. United

States -- Race relations　4.　African Americans -- Economic conditions 5. African Americans -- Civil rights -- History -- 20th century 6. Race discrimination -- United States -- History -- 20th century

ISBN 0-393-05213-3; 9780393328516

LC 2004-24359

"Katznelson principal focus is on the . . . social programs of Franklin Roosevelt's New Deal and Harry Truman's Fair Deal in the 1930's and 1940's. He contends that those programs not only discriminated against blacks, but actually contributed to widening the gap between white and black Americans—judged in terms of educational achievement, quality of jobs and housing, and attainment of higher income." (N Y Times Book Rev) Index.

"Katznelson offers a penetrating . . . analysis, supported by vivid examples and statistics." N Y Times Book Rev

Includes bibliographical references

Kelley, Kitty

Let Freedom Ring; Stanley Tretick's Iconic Images of the March on Washington. Kitty Kelly. St. Martin's Press　2013　176 p.　$24.99　　　　**323.1**

1.　Civil rights demonstrations -- United States -- Pictorial works 2. March on Washington for Jobs and Freedom (1963: Washington, D.C.)　3.　Documentary photography　4.　Photographers -- United States　5.　African Americans -- Civil rights -- History -- 20th century -- Pictorial works　6.　March on Washington for Jobs and Freedom (1963: Washington, D.C.) -- Pictorial works　7.　Civil rights demonstrations -- Washington (D.C.) -- History -- 20th century -- Pictorial works

ISBN 1250021464; 9781250021465

LC 2013009956

This book presents photographs of the 1963 "March on Washington to urge passage of the civil rights bill." It includes "never-before-published photographs of the historic march as well as the events that led up to it. [Photographer Stanley] Tretick . . . documents the rising hopes and tensions as blacks and whites pressed for equity and obstructionists fought their efforts. . . . [Kitty] Kelley provides narrative background and context." (Booklist)

Includes bibliographical references and index

King, Martin Luther, 1929-1968

★ **A testament** of hope; the essential writings of Martin Luther King, Jr. edited by James Melvin Washington. Harper & Row　1986　xxvi, 676p　hardcover o.p.　pa $23.95　　**323.1**

1.　United States -- Race relations　2.　African Americans -- Civil rights

ISBN 0-06-250931-4; 0-06-064691-8 pa

LC 85-45370

"King's most important writings are gathered together in one source. The arrangement is topical: philosophy, sermons and public addresses, essays, interviews and excerpts of his books. The material within each of these categories is arranged chronologically. Included are Dr. King's writings on nonviolence, integration and politics." SLJ

Includes bibliographical references

Where do we go from here; chaos or community? [by] Martin Luther King, Jr.; [foreword by Coretta Scott King; introduction by Vincent Harding] Beacon Press　2010　xxiv, 223p (King legacy series)　$24.95; pa $14　　　　**323.1**

1.　Racism 2. United States -- Race relations　3. African Americans -- Civil rights

ISBN 978-0-8070-0076-2; 978-0-8070-0067-0 pa

LC 2009035950

First published 1967 by Harper & Row

The author reaffirms his belief in the power of nonviolence to achieve full citizenship for black people in America and defines his attitude toward the Black Power movement and the white backlash.

Includes bibliographical references

Why we can't wait; [by] Martin Luther King, Jr.　Harper & Row　1964　178p il　hardcover o.p.　pa $6.95　　　　**323.1**

1.　African Americans -- Civil rights　2.　Birmingham (Ala.) -- Race relations

ISBN 0-06-012395-8; 0-451-52753-4 pa

The author first reviews the background of the 1963 civil rights demands. He then describes the strategy of the Birmingham campaign and outlines future action

Lewis, Andrew B.

The shadows of youth; the remarkable journey of the civil rights generation. Hill and Wang　2009　356p　$28　　**323.1**

1.　Political activists　2.　African Americans -- Biography　3.　United States -- Race relations　4.　African Americans -- Civil rights　5.　Student Nonviolent Coordinating Committee

ISBN 978-0-8090-8598-9; 0-8090-8598-4

LC 2009-9980

The author "offers an engaging look at some of the major figures in the budding civil rights movement: John Lewis, son of a poor tenant cotton farmer; Marion Barry, ambitious son of poor southern parents; Diane Nash, from a middle-class Chicago family; Stokely Carmichael, who learned black culture from his Caribbean roots and politics from a leftist friend; and Julian Bond, born of black privilege. Lewis chronicles the coming together of these young people, and others, in the formation of the Student Nonviolent Coordinating Committee." Booklist

Includes bibliographical references (p. 329-335)

McGuire, Danielle L.

At the dark end of the street; Black women, rape, and resistance: a new history of the civil rights movement, from Rosa Parks to the rise of Black Power. Alfred A. Knopf　2010　324p il $27.95; e-book $27.95　　　　**323.1**

1.　Rape　2.　African American women　3.　African Americans -- Civil rights　4.　Southern States -- Race relations　5.　African American women -- Violence against　6.　Rape -- Political aspects -- Southern States　7.　Southern States -- Race relations -- History -- 20th century 8. African American women -- Civil rights -- History -- 20th century 9.　Civil rights movements -- Southern States -- History -- 20th century

ISBN 978-0-307-26906-5; 978-0-307-59447-1 e-book

LC 2010-12072

"McGuire restores to memory the courageous black women who dared seek legal remedy, when black women and their families faced particular hazards for doing so. McGuire brings the reader through a dark time via a painful but somehow gratifying passage in this compelling, carefully documented work." Publ Wkly

Includes bibliographical references and index

Peck, Raoul

I am not your negro; a major motion picture directed by Raoul Peck. from texts by James Baldwin; compiled and edited by Raoul Peck. Vintage Books　2017　xxiii, 118 p.p　(pbk.) $15.00　　　　**323.1**

1.　Racism　2.　African Americans -- Civil rights　3.　Racism -- United States　4.　United States -- Race relations　5.　African Americans -- Civil rights -- History -- 20th century　6.　Civil rights movements

-- United States -- History -- 20th century
ISBN 9780525434719; 0525434690; 9780525434696

LC 2016053419

"To compose his stunning documentary film I Am Not Your Negro, acclaimed filmmaker Raoul Peck mined James Baldwin's published and unpublished oeuvre, selecting passages from his books, essays, letters, notes, and interviews that are every bit as incisive and pertinent now as they have ever been." (Publisher's note)

Includes bibliographical references

★ **Reporting** civil rights. Library of Am. 2003 2v ea $40 **323.1**
1. Journalism 2. United States -- Race relations 3. African Americans -- Civil rights
ISBN 1-931082-28-6 v1; 1-931082-29-4 v2

LC 2002-27459

"From A. Philip Randolph's defiant call in 1941 for African Americans to march on Washington to Alice Walker in 1973, Reporting Civil Rights presents firsthand accounts of the revolutionary events that overthrew segregation in the United States. This two-volume anthology brings together for the first time nearly 200 newspaper and magazine reports and book excerpts, and features 151 writers, including James Baldwin, Robert Penn Warren, David Halberstam, Lillian Smith, Gordon Parks, Murray Kempton, Ted Poston, Claude Sitton, and Anne Moody. A newly researched chronology of the movement, a 32-page insert of rare journalist photographs, and original biographical profiles are included in each volume." (Publisher's note)

"An important anthology for readers interested in the history of the civil rights movement." Booklist

Rieder, Jonathan

Gospel of freedom; Martin Luther King, Jr.'s letter from Birmingham Jail and the struggle that changed a nation. Jonathan Rieder. St. Martin's Press 2013 240 p. illustrations $25 **323.1**
1. Nonviolence 2. African Americans -- Civil rights 3. Birmingham (Ala.) -- Race relations 4. African Americans -- Civil rights -- Alabama -- Birmingham 5. Civil disobedience -- Alabama -- Birmingham -- History -- 20th century 6. Civil rights movements -- Alabama -- Birmingham -- History -- 20th century
ISBN 1620400588; 9781620400586

LC 2012044387

This book, by Jonathan Rieder, focuses on "[t]he letter that Martin Luther King Jr. penned from a Birmingham, Alabama, jail 50 years ago. . . . The letter was King's impassioned response to eight white Birmingham clergymen who had appealed to him for moderation. Here Rieder first discusses the events that led to King's arrest, then addresses the letter's importance during the civil rights struggle." (Library Journal)

"Rieder's trenchant comments approach the letter on historical and literary grounds but also as a way to better understand the often elusive King. Several chapters offer a close analysis of the letter, while later chapters trace the impact it had on subsequent events." Booklist

Includes bibliographical references and index

Sokol, Jason

All eyes are upon us; race and politics from Boston to Brooklyn. Jason Sokol. Basic Books 2014 416 p. illustrations (hardback) $32 **323.1**
1. Race relations 2. African Americans -- Civil rights 3. Progressivism (United States politics) 4. Northeastern States -- Politics and government 5. Racism -- Political aspects -- Northeastern States -- History 6. African Americans -- Segregation -- Northeastern States -- History 7. Northeastern States -- Race relations -- Political aspects -- History 8. African Americans -- Civil rights -- Northeastern States -- History -- 20th century 9. African Americans -- Civil rights -- Northeastern States -- History -- 21st century
ISBN 046502226X; 9780465022267

LC 2014023616

This book by Jason Sokol "exposes the troubled truth about the North's racial integration. The Northern states could point to the Southern states' ongoing practices of Jim Crow legislation, white supremacist violence and suppression of voting rights with righteous disgust, but the author shows how, in unsubtle and pernicious ways, the North, too, was 'at war with itself.'" (Kirkus Reviews)

"Sokol provides some of the participants' previously unavailable recollections, based on interviews conducted for this history. Ultimately, the book provides a much-needed reminder of the difficult battles discrimination's enemies faced, even in the heart of what was supposed to be an already color-blind society." Choice

Includes bibliographical references and index

Sullivan, Patricia

Lift every voice; the NAACP and the making of the Civil Rights Movement. New Press 2009 514p il $26.95 **323.1**
1. United States -- Race relations 2. African Americans -- Civil rights 3. Civil rights -- United States -- History -- 20th century 4. National Association for the Advancement of Colored People 5. United States -- Race relations -- History -- 20th century 6. African Americans -- Civil rights -- History -- 20th century 7. National Association for the Advancement of Colored People -- History
ISBN 978-1-59558-446-5

LC 2009-9473

This is an "examination of the NAACP's growth and influence, from its inception in 1909 to the present." Index.

The author "delivers a solidly researched examination of the organization's growth and influence, leaving us with a vital account of 100 years of foundational civil rights activism." Publ Wkly

Includes bibliographical references

Theoharis, Jeanne

A **more** beautiful and terrible history; the uses and misuses of civil rights history. Jeanne Theoharis. Beacon Press 2018 xxv, 253 p.p (hardcover: alk. paper) $26.95 **323.1**
1. Historical literature 2. United States -- Race relations -- History 3. African Americans -- Civil rights -- History 4. United States -- Race relations -- Historiography 5. African Americans -- Civil rights -- Historiography 6. Civil rights movements -- United States -- Historiography 7. United States -- Race relations -- History -- 20th century 8. African Americans -- Civil rights -- History -- 20th century 9. Civil rights movements -- United States -- History -- 20th century
ISBN 9780807075883; 9780807075876

LC 2017030979

This book, by Jeanne Theoharis, features several civil rights activists in the U.S. in different light. "We see Rosa Parks not simply as a bus lady but a lifelong criminal justice activist and radical; Martin Luther King, Jr. as not only challenging Southern sheriffs but Northern liberals, too; and Coretta Scott King not only as a 'helpmate' but a lifelong economic justice and peace activist who pushed her husband's activism in these directions." (Publisher's note)

"Chronicling the efforts of many activists, the author underscores her message that reform requires courage and hard work. An impassioned call for continued efforts for change." Kirkus

Includes bibliographical references and index

Voices in our blood; America's best on the civil rights movement. edited by Jon Meacham. Random House 2001 561p hardcover o.p. pa $16.95   **323.1**

1. United States -- Race relations 2. African Americans -- Civil rights

ISBN 0-375-75881-X pa

LC 00-41474

A "collection of acclaimed 'voices' narrating the environment, origin, and progress of the Civil Rights movement, as told by reporters, artists, novelists, historians, and authors such as Maya Angelou, Eudora Welty, James Baldwin, Richard Wright, Willie Morris, Robert Penn Warren, Alice Walker, Murray Kempton, E. B. White, William Faulkner, Ralph Ellison, and Rebecca West." Libr J

Watson, Bruce

Freedom summer; the savage season that made Mississippi burn and made America a democracy. Viking 2010 369p il $27.95   **323.1**

1. African Americans -- Suffrage 2. Mississippi -- Race relations 3. African Americans -- Civil rights 4. Student Nonviolent Coordinating Committee

ISBN 978-0-670-02170-3

LC 2009-47211

This book "combines a political overview of the Mississippi civil rights struggle in the summer of 1964 with more than 50 personal accounts from those who were there, both the famous (including Sidney Poitier, Pete Seeger, John Lewis, Stokely Carmichael) and the lesser known, including the more than 200 volunteer students from the North who lived and worked with local residents and taught in the Freedom Schools in converted shacks and church basements. . . . The personal interviews, some from people telling their stories for the first time, make gripping drama, as they recount the standoffs, the struggle for voter registration, the reign of terror that encompassed church burnings and murders." Booklist

Includes bibliographical references

Williams, Juan

Eyes on the prize: America's civil rights years, 1954-1965; [by] Juan Williams with the Eyes on the prize production team; introduction by Julian Bond. Viking 1987 300p il hardcover o.p. pa $20   **323.1**

1. United States -- Race relations 2. African Americans -- Civil rights

ISBN 0-670-81412-1; 0-14-009653-1 pa

LC 86-40271

"Highly recommended both as a socio-historical document and as a heartfelt, poignant remembrance of a movement and its activists." Booklist

Includes bibliographical references

323.11   Civil rights – Ethnic and national groups

Calloway, Colin G.

The **Indian** world of George Washington; the first President, the first Americans, and the birth of the nation. Colin G. Calloway. Oxford University Press 2018 640 p. (hardback: alk. paper) $34.95   **323.11**

1. Native Americans -- History 2. United States -- History -- 1775-1783, Revolution 3. Indians of North America -- Wars -- 1750-1815 4. Indians of North America -- Government relations 5. United States -- History -- Revolution, 1775-1783 6. Indians of North

America -- History -- 18th century 7. United States -- History -- French and Indian War, 1754-1763

ISBN 9780190652166

LC 2017028686

National Book Award Finalist: Nonfiction (2018)

"In this sweeping new biography, Colin Calloway uses the prism of George Washington's life to bring focus to the great Native leaders of his time--Shingas, Tanaghrisson, Bloody Fellow, Joseph Brant, Red Jacket, Little Turtle--and the tribes they represented: the Iroquois Confederacy, Lenape, Miami, Creek, Delaware; in the process, he returns them to their rightful place in the story of America's founding." (Publisher's note)

Includes bibliographical references and index

Haney Lopez, Ian

★ **Dog** whistle politics; how coded racial appeals have reinvented racism and wrecked the middle class. Ian Haney-López. Oxford University Press 2014 xiv, 277 p.p (hardback: alk. paper) $24.95   **323.11**

1. United States -- Politics and government 2. United States -- Race relations -- History 3. Racism -- United States -- History -- 21st century 4. United States -- Politics and gov 5. Post-racialism -- United States -- History 6. United States -- Politics and government -- 1945-1989 7. Communication in politics -- United States -- History -- 20th century 8. Communication in politics -- United States -- History -- 21st century 9. Racism -- Political aspects -- United States -- History -- 20th century 10. Racism -- Political aspects -- United States -- History -- 21st century 11. United States -- Race relations -- Political aspects -- History 21st century 12. United States -- Race relations -- Political aspects -- History -- 20th century

ISBN 9780199964277

LC 2013015913

In this book, author "Ian Haney López offers a sweeping account of how politicians and plutocrats deploy veiled racial appeals to persuade white voters to support policies that favor the extremely rich yet threaten their own interests. Dog whistle appeals generate middle-class enthusiasm for political candidates who promise to crack down on crime, curb undocumented immigration, and protect the heartland against Islamic infiltration." (Publisher's note)

Includes bibliographical references and index.

323.4   Specific civil rights; limitation and suspension of civil rights

Conroy, John

Unspeakable acts, ordinary people; the dynamics of torture. University of California Press 2001 304p pa $19.95   **323.4**

1. Torture 2. Persecution 3. Police brutality 4. Israel 5. Northern Ireland

ISBN 0-520-23039-6

LC 2001-33218

First published 2000 by Knopf

The author "interviews torturers, torture victims, and government officials from such diverse locations as Israel, Northern Ireland, and a Chicago police interrogation room, focusing on how torture is performed and why." Booklist

Includes bibliographical references

McCoy, Alfred W.

★ A **question** of torture; CIA interrogation from the Cold War to the War on Terror. Metropolitan Books 2006 290p il

(The American empire project) $25; pa $15 **323.4**
1. Torture 2. Intelligence service -- United States 3. United States
-- Central Intelligence Agency
ISBN 978-0-8050-8041-4; 0-8050-8041-4; 978-0-8050-8248-7
pa; 0-8050-8248-4 pa

LC 2005-51124

The author "shows how, since 1950, the CIA and various nations
have augmented traditional physical torture with psychological abuse
techniques of 'sensory disorientation' and 'self-inflicted pain,' which he
documents with some gruesome first-person accounts by victims and
with stories of doctors who conducted horrific experiments." Libr J

Includes bibliographical references

323.44   Freedom of action (Liberty)

Angwin, Julia

Dragnet nation; a quest for privacy, security, and freedom
in a world of relentless surveillance. Julia Angwin. Times
Books, Henry Holt & Co. 2014 304 p. (hardcover) $28 **323.44**
1. Right of privacy 2. Electronic surveillance 3. Civil rights 4.
Privacy, Right of 5. National security -- Moral and ethical aspects
6. Information technology -- Moral and ethical aspects
ISBN 0805098070; 9780805098075

LC 2013042041

In this book "Julia Angwin reports from the front lines of America's
surveillance economy, offering a revelatory and unsettling look at how
the government, private companies, and even criminals use technology
to indiscriminately sweep up vast amounts of our personal data." (Publisher's note)

"A solid work for both privacy freaks and anyone seeking tips on
such matters as how to strengthen passwords (make them longer and
avoid simple dictionary words)." Kirkus

Includes bibliographical references and index

Fischer, David Hackett

Liberty and freedom. Oxford University Press 2004 851p
il (America, a cultural history) $50 **323.44**
1. Freedom 2. American national characteristics 3. Liberty --
History 4. United States -- History 5. National characteristics,
American
ISBN 0-19-516253-6

LC 2004-5197

"This book studies American ideas of liberty and freedom as visions
of an open society, through the symbols they have inspired from the
Revolutionary era through 9/11." (Publisher's note) Index.

This "beautifully illustrated book shifts subtly from a rich graphic
survey, incorporating painting, flags and sculpture, to a broader chronicle of the many ways Americans have articulated their most cherished
ideals." Publ Wkly

Includes bibliographical references

Shipler, David K.

Freedom of speech; mightier than the sword. David K. Shipler. Alfred A. Knopf 2015 352 p. (hardback) $28.95 **323.44**
1. Freedom of speech -- United States 2. Constitutional law --
United States 3. United States. Constitution. 1st Amendment
ISBN 0307957322; 9780307947611; 9780307957320;
9781101874691

LC 2014032127

This book presents author David K. Shipler's "investigations of the
cultural limits on both expression and the willingness to listen build to

expose troubling instabilities in the very foundations of our democracy.
Focusing on recent free speech controversies across the nation, Shipler
maps a rapidly shifting topography of political and cultural norms."
(Publisher's note)

"This book addresses a timely subject and is written by someone
with a deep interest in the controversies and difficulties surrounding
freedom of speech." LJ

Includes bibliographical references and index

Stone, Geoffrey R.

★ **Perilous** times; free speech in wartime from the Sedition
Act of 1798 to the war on terrorism. Norton 2004 xx, 730p il
$35 **323.44**
1. Freedom of speech
ISBN 0-393-05880-8

LC 2004-17871

The author "delivers rich material in an engaging, character-based
narrative. Stone offers deep insight into rhetorical history and the men
and women who made it—resisters like Clement Vallandingham, Emma
Goldman, Fred Korematsu and Daniel Ellsberg; presidents faced with
wartime dilemmas; and the prosecutors, defenders and Supreme Court
justices who shaped our understanding of the First Amendment today."
Publ Wkly

Includes bibliographical references

323.6   Citizenship and related topics

Duina, Francesco

★ **Broke** and patriotic; why poor Americans love their
country. Francesco Duina. Stanford University Press 2017 227
p. (cloth: alk. paper) $26.95 **323.6**
1. Patriotism 2. Poor -- United States 3. Patriotism -- United States
4. Poor -- United States -- Attitudes
ISBN 0804799695; 9780804799690

LC 2017005639

This book, by Francesco Duina, "speak[s] directly to America's
most impoverished. Spending time in bus stations, laundromats, senior
citizen centers, homeless shelters, public libraries, and fast food restaurants, Duina conducted over 60 revealing interviews in which the people
he met explain how they view themselves and their country. He masterfully weaves their words into three narratives." (Publisher's note)

Includes bibliographical references and index

323.65   Duties and obligations of citizens

Rather, Dan, 1931-

What unites us; reflections on patriotism. Dan Rather &
Elliot Kirschner. Algonquin Books of Chapel Hill 2017 274 p.
(hardcover: alk. paper) $22.95 **323.65**
1. Patriotism 2. American national characteristics 3. Patriotism
-- United States 4. Social values -- United States 5. National
characteristics, American
ISBN 9781616207847; 9781616207823

LC 2017028401

In this book, by Dan Rather and Elliot Kirschner, a venerated television journalist "celebrates our shared values and what matters most
in our great country, and shows us what patriotism looks like. Writing
about the institutions that sustain us, . . . the values that have transformed
us, . . . and the drive toward science and innovation that has made the
United States great, Rather will bring to bear his decades of experience

on the frontlines of the world's biggest stories." (Publisher's note)

"Rather has issued a stirring call for overcoming today's strident partisanship." Pub Wkly

324   The political process

Larson, Edward J.

A **magnificent** catastrophe; the tumultuous election of 1800, America's first presidential campaign. Free Press 2007 335p il $27   **324**

1. Statesmen 2. Architects 3. Presidents 4. Vice-presidents 5. Essayists 6. Secretaries of the treasury 7. Presidents -- United States -- Election -- 1800 8. United States -- Politics and government -- 1783-1809

ISBN 978-0-7432-9316-7; 0-7432-9316-9

LC 2007-16017

The author "recreates the dramatic presidential race of 1800, which, Larson says, stamped American democracy with its distinctive partisan character as Republicans and Federalists battled for the presidency. . . . [This is] an invaluable study of a crucial chapter in the lives of the founding fathers—and of the nation." Publ Wkly

Includes bibliographical references

Schoen, Douglas E.

The **power** of the vote; electing presidents, overthrowing dictators, and promoting democracy around the world. William Morrow 2007 396p pa $25.95   **324**

1. Democratic Party (U.S.) 2. Political consultants 3. United States -- Politics and government

ISBN 978-0-06-123188-9; 0-06-123188-6

LC 2006-52877

The author presents an account of his work as a politcal strategist.

Includes bibliographical references

Traister, Rebecca

Big girls don't cry; the election that changed everything for American women. Free Press 2010 336p $26   **324**

1. Mayors 2. Lawyers 3. Feminism 4. Governors 5. Senators 6. Secretaries of state 7. Spouses of presidents 8. Hospital administrators 9. Presidential candidates 10. Women -- Political activity 11. Women in politics -- United States 12. Presidents -- United States -- Election -- 2008

ISBN 978-1-4391-5028-3; 1-4391-5028-1

LC 2010-09631

This is "a passionate, visionary and very personal account of the cultural ferment that accompanied the election of '08." N Y Times Book Rev

Includes bibliographical references

324.1   International party organizations, auxiliaries, activities

Lichtblau, Eric

The **Nazis** next door; how America became a safe haven for Hitler's men. Eric Lichtblau. Houghton Mifflin Harcourt 2014 288 p. 8 plates; illustrations (hardback) $28   **324.1**

1. Cold war 2. American espionage 3. National socialists 4. Cold War 5. Espionage, American -- History -- 20th century 6. United States -- Foreign relations -- 1945-1989 7. Nazis -- United States -- History -- 20th century 8. Refugees -- United States -- History

-- 20th century 9. United States -- Politics and government -- 1945-1989 10. War criminals -- United States -- History -- 20th century 11. Anti-communist movements -- United States -- History -- 20th century 12. United States. Central Intelligence Agency -- History -- 20th century 13. United States. Federal Bureau of Investigation -- History -- 20th century

ISBN 0547669194; 9780547669199

LC 2014023543

Written by Eric Lichtblau, this book describes how "thousands of Nazis--from concentration camp guards to high-level officers in the Third Reich--came to the United States after World War II and quietly settled into new lives. They had little trouble getting in. . . . The CIA, the FBI, and the military all put Hitler's minions to work as spies, intelligence assets, and leading scientists and engineers, whitewashing their histories." (Publisher's note)

"An essential read for all those interested in World War II, the Cold War, and 20th-century history." LJ

Includes bibliographical references and index

324.2   Political parties

McGerr, Michael E.

A **fierce** discontent; the rise and fall of the Progressive movement in America, 1870-1920. [by] Michael McGerr. Oxford University Press 2005 395p pa $19.95   **324.2**

1. Progressivism (United States politics)

ISBN 978-0-19-518365-8; 0-19-518365-7

LC 2004-30592

First published 2003 by the Free Press

The author "examines the social, cultural and political currents of a movement that, through its early successes and ultimate failure, has defined today's 'disappointing' political climate. . . . In three parts, McGerr illuminates the origins of Progressive thought, the movement's meteoric ascent in American life and its descent into 'the Red scare, race riots, strikes and inflation,' positing that the Progressive vision of remaking America in its own middle-class image eventually sparked a backlash that persists to this day. . . . Simply put, this is history at its best." Publ Wkly

Includes bibliographical references

McGregor, Richard

The **Party**; the secret world of China's communist rulers. Harper 2010 302p il map   **324.2**

1. Communism -- China 2. Communist Party (China) 3. Economic policy -- China 4. China -- Politics and government

ISBN 9780061708770; 9780061998089

McGregor "examines China's Communist Party, with a focus on the large role it has played in the nation's competition with the United States." (Publisher's note) Index.

"An astute, well-crafted work that should be enormously useful in understanding China's role in the world." Kirkus

Includes bibliographical references

324.209   Political parties -- History

Lewis, David Levering

The **improbable** Wendell Willkie; the businessman who saved the Republican Party and his country, and conceived a new world order. David Levering Lewis. W W Norton & Co Inc 2018 352 p. $28.95   **324.209**

1. Politicians -- United States -- Biography 2. Presidential candidates -- United States -- Biography
ISBN 0871404575; 9780871404572

In this biography of Wendell Lewis Willkie, author David Levering Lewis "demonstrates that the corporate chairman–turned–presidential candidate must be regarded as one of the most exciting, intellectually able, and authentically transformational figures to stride the twentieth-century American political landscape. . . . Successful at outwitting the isolationist wing of his own party, Willkie took on Roosevelt during one of the nation's darkest periods." (Publisher's note)

324.273   Parties of United States

Golway, Terry

Frank and Al; FDR, Al Smith, and the unlikely alliance that created the modern Democratic Party. Terry Golway. St Martin's Press 2018 336 p. $29.99   **324.273**
1. Democratic Party (U.S.)
ISBN 1250089646; 9781250089649

This book, by Terry Golway, focuses on the "relationship between [Al] Smith and [Franklin] Roosevelt, . . . [which] is one of the most dramatic untold stories of early 20th Century American politics. It was Roosevelt who said once that everything he sought to do in the New Deal had been done in New York under Al Smith when he was governor in the 1920s. It was Smith who persuaded a reluctant Roosevelt to run for governor in 1928." (Publisher's note)

Gould, Lewis L.

★ **Grand** Old Party; a history of the Republicans. Random House 2003 597p il $35   **324.273**
1. Republican Party (U.S.)
ISBN 0-375-50741-8

LC 2003-46604

This is an "account of the Grand Old Party that spans its earliest days under Abraham Lincoln to its conservative bent today. Much of the book documents the shifts of its platform. . . . Gould also discusses the leadership qualities, farsighted policies, conservative federal spending, and willingness to provide social programs at the cost of future generations of four Republican presidents—Lincoln, Theodore Roosevelt, Eisenhower, and Reagan." Libr J

Includes bibliographical references

Lofgren, Mike

The **party** is over; how Republicans went crazy, Democrats became useless, and the middle class got shafted. Mike Lofgren. Viking 2012 p. cm.   **324.273**
1. Democratic Party (U.S.) 2. Republican Party (U.S.) 3. United States -- Politics and government 4. Democratic Party (U.S.) -- History -- 20th century 5. Democratic Party (U.S.) -- History -- 21st century 6. Republican Party (U.S.: 1854-) -- History -- 20th century 7. Republican Party (U.S.: 1854-) -- History -- 21st century 8. Political parties -- United States -- History -- 20th century 9. Political parties -- United States -- History -- 21st century
ISBN 9780670026265

LC 2012014990

This New York Times bestselling book, by Mike Lofgren, criticizes 21st-century American politics. "There was a time, not so very long ago, when perfectly rational people ran the Republican Party. So how did the party of Lincoln become the party of lunatics? That is what this book aims to answer. Fear not, the [Democrats] come in for their share of tough talk--they are zombies, a party of the living dead." (Publish-

er's note)
Includes bibliographical references and index

324.6   Election systems and procedures; suffrage

Anderson, Carol (Carol Elaine), 1959-

One person, no vote; how voter suppression is destroying our democracy. Carol Anderson; foreword by Senator Dick Durbin. Bloomsbury Publishing 2018 256 p. (hardcover) $27   **324.6**
1. African Americans -- Suffrage 2. Race discrimination -- United States 3. Minorities -- Suffrage -- United States 4. Suffrage -- United States 5. Race discrimination -- Political aspects -- United States
ISBN 9781635571370

LC 2018015633

"In her New York Times bestseller 'White Rage,' Carol Anderson laid bare an insidious history of policies that have systematically impeded black progress in America, from 1865 to our combustible present. With 'One Person, No Vote,' she chronicles . . . the rollbacks to African American participation in the vote since the 2013 Supreme Court decision that eviscerated the Voting Rights Act of 1965." (Publisher's note)

"This a whiplash-inducing chronicle of how a nation that just a few short years ago elected its first black president now finds itself in the throes of a deceitful and craven effort to rip this most essential of American rights from millions of its citizens." (Booklist)

Includes bibliographical references

Berman, Ari

★ **Give** us the ballot; the modern struggle for voting rights in America. Ari Berman. Farrar, Straus & Giroux 2015 384 p. (hardback) $27   **324.6**
1. Suffrage 2. Minorities -- Suffrage -- United States 3. United States. Voting Rights Act of 1965 4. Suffrage -- United States -- History -- 20th century 5. Suffrage -- United States -- History -- 21st century
ISBN 0374158274; 9780374158279; 9780374711498

LC 2015004989

National Book Critics Circle Award Finalist: Nonfiction (2015)

This book, by Ari Berman, focuses on "the Voting Rights Act (VRA) [of] 1965. . . . The act enfranchised millions of Americans and is widely regarded as the crowning achievement of the civil rights movement. And yet, fifty years later, we are still fighting heated battles over race, representation, and political power, with lawmakers devising new strategies to keep minorities out of the voting booth and with the Supreme Court declaring a key part of the Voting Rights Act unconstitutional." (Publisher's note)

"General readers will appreciate the panoramic survey of the cases in which the VRA has been challenged and defended in federal and state courts and legislatures, and the fair inclusion of voices from both sides of the arguments. A timely and needed addition to the voting rights debate." LJ

Includes bibliographical references (pages 315-351) and index

Congressional Quarterly, Inc.

★ **Presidential** elections 1789-2008. CQ Press 2010 295p il map pa $65   **324.6**
1. Presidents -- United States -- Election
ISBN 978-1-60426-541-5

LC 2009-40267

First published 1995 with title: Presidential elections, 1789¿1992

This book offers information about the electoral college, electoral votes and popular votes in each presidential election, voter turnout, primary returns, and Democratic and Republican Party conventions.

Includes bibliographical references

Dudden, Faye E.

Fighting chance; the struggle over woman suffrage and Black suffrage in Reconstruction America. Oxford University Press 2011 287p il $34.95   **324.6**

1. Reconstruction (1865-1876) 2. Women -- Suffrage 3. African Americans -- Suffrage

ISBN 978-0-19-977263-6; 0-19-977263-0

LC 2010053188

"Likely to be a classic study, it is recommended for all readers in American studies and Reconstruction history." Libr J

Includes bibliographical references

Lichtman, Allan J.

The **embattled** vote in America; from the founding to the present. Allan J. Lichtman. Harvard University Press 2018 336 p. $27.95   **324.6**

1. Suffrage -- United States 2. Elections -- United States 3. Suffrage -- United States -- History

ISBN 9780674972360

LC 2018006882

In this book, author Allan J. Lichtman "gives us the deep history behind today's headlines and shows that calls of voter fraud, political gerrymandering and outrageous attempts at voter suppression are nothing new. The players and the tactics have changed--we don't outright ban people from voting anymore--but the battle and the stakes remain just as high." (Publisher's note)

Includes bibliographical references and index

Waldman, Michael

★ The **Fight** to Vote; by Michael Waldman. Simon & Schuster 2016 288 p. $28   **324.6**

1. Suffrage 2. United States -- Politics and government

ISBN 1501116487; 9781501116483

LC 2015030899

In this book, author Michael Waldman "takes a succinct and comprehensive look at a crucial American struggle: the drive to define and defend government based on 'the consent of the governed.' From the beginning, and at every step along the way, as Americans sought to right to vote, others have fought to stop them. This is the first book to trace the full story from the founders' debates to today's challenges." (Publisher's note)

"Waldman urges citizens to find a way to celebrate democracy and reinvigorate political engagement for all. A timely contribution to the discussion of a crucial issue." Kirkus

Includes bibliographical references (pages 285-353) and index.

324.623   Women's suffrage

Weiss, Elaine

★ The **woman's** hour; the great fight to win the vote. Elaine Weiss. Viking 2018 404 p. illustrations (hardcover) $28   **324.623**

1. Women's rights 2. Women -- Suffrage -- United States 3. Women -- Political activity -- United States 4. Suffragists -- United States -- History 5. United States. Constitution. 19th Amendment -- History 6. Women -- Suffrage -- United States -- History -- 20th

century 7. Women -- Political activity -- United States -- History -- 20th century

ISBN 9780525429722; 9780698407831; 0525429727

LC 2018006746

This book, by Elaine Weiss, narrates the "climax of one of the greatest political battles in American history: the ratification of the constitutional amendment that granted women the right to vote. . . . [It] is an inspiring story of activists winning their own freedom in one of the last campaigns forged in the shadow of the Civil War, and the beginning of the great 20th-century battles for civil rights." (Publisher's note)

"Weiss brings to life the fascinating characters at the heart of one of the most pivotal events in U.S. history with striking similarity to the social and political tensions of today." Booklist

Includes bibliographical references (pages 345-391) and index.

324.7   Conduct of election campaigns

Litman, Amanda

Run for something; a real-talk guide to fixing the system yourself. Amanda Litman. Atria Paperback 2017 240 p. (pbk.) $16.99   **324.709**

1. Local elections 2. Local government 3. Political participation -- United States 4. Local elections -- United States 5. Local government -- United States -- Citizen participation

ISBN 9781501180446

LC 2017027814

This book, by Amanda Litman, is "an essential and inspiring guide that encourages and educates young progressives to run for local office, complete with contributions from elected officials and political operatives. . . . Run for local office and become the change you want to see in the world. Forget about Congress. Forget about the Senate. Focus on the offices that get the real sh*t done: state legislatures, city councils, school boards, and mayors." (Publisher's note)

Includes bibliographical references

Roberts, Robert North

Campaigning for president in America, 1788-2016; Scott John Hammond, Robert North Roberts, and Valerie A. Sulfaro. Greenwood 2016 xxxv, 954 p.p (hardback) $68   **324.7**

1. Presidents -- United States -- Election -- History 2. Presidential candidates -- United States -- History 3. Political campaigns -- United States -- History

ISBN 1440848904; 9781440848889; 9781440848902; 9781440850790

LC 2015046107

This book by Scott John Hammond, Robert North Roberts, and Valerie A. Sulfaro offers "readers insight into the major issues and events surrounding American presidential elections across more than two centuries, from the earliest years of the Republic through the campaigns of the 21st century. . . . [It] presents a chronological account of presidential campaigns that showcases the key personalities, issues, and campaign themes as they emerged in American political history." (Publisher's note)

"Both the topical and historical sections of this consistently objective and analytical encyclopedia-cum-history will reward readers who want to understand recurring and one-off phenomena in electoral history." Booklist

Includes bibliographical references (pages 881-898) and index

Vogel, Kenneth P.

Big money; 2.5 billion dollars, one suspicious vehicle, and a pimp-on the trail of the ultra-rich hijacking American politics. Kenneth P. Vogel. PublicAffairs 2014 304 p. (hardback) $27.99 **324.7**

1. Economic policy -- United States 2. United States -- Politics and government 3. Campaign funds -- United States 4. Citizens United -- Trials, litigation, etc 5. United States. Congress -- Elections -- Finance 6. Presidents -- United States -- Election -- Finance 7. Campaign funds -- Law and legislation -- United States
ISBN 1610393384; 9781610393386

LC 2014004954

This book by Kenneth P. Vogel is a "tour of a new political world dramatically reordered by ever-larger flows of cash. From the casino magnate Sheldon Adelson to the bubbling nouveau cowboy Foster Friess; from the Texas trial lawyer couple, Amber and Steve Mostyn, to the micromanaging Hollywood executive Jeffrey Katzenberg--the multimillionaires and billionaires are swaggering up to the tables for the hottest new game in politics." (Publisher's note)

Includes bibliographical references and index

324.9   History and geographic treatment of elections

Halperin, Mark

★ **Double** Down; Game Change 2012. Mark Halperin, John Heilemann. Penguin Group USA 2013 499 p. ill. (hardback) $29.95 **324.9**

1. Presidents -- United States -- Election -- 2012 2. Presidential candidates -- United States 3. United States -- Politics and government -- 2009- 4. Political campaigns -- United States -- History -- 21st century
ISBN 1594204403; 9781594204401

LC 2013431166

This book by Mark Halperin and John Heileman chronicles the 2012 U.S. Presidential election. "Their focus is always on the candidates with the most buzz among not just voters, but the Washington, D.C., cognoscenti." Candidates profiled include Barack Obama, Mitt Romney, Jon Huntsman, Newt Gingrich, and Chris Christie. (Kirkus Reviews)

"The well-connected authors have worked their sources thoroughly to give readers a warts-and-all look at what went on behind the scenes." Booklist

Karabell, Zachary

The **last** campaign; how Harry Truman won the 1948 election. Knopf 2000 308p hardcover o.p. pa $14 **324.9**

1. Governors 2. Presidents 3. Vice-presidents 4. Senators 5. District attorneys 6. Presidential candidates 7. Presidents -- United States -- Election -- 1948
ISBN 0-375-70077-3 pa

LC 99-28567

This is an account of the presidential campaign which pitted Truman against Dewey.

"The author is strongest discussing the impact of the press, polls, and radio and describing the importance of the convention, which was then 'a mix of high politics, low politics and entertainment.'" Libr J

Includes bibliographical references

Morris, Roy

Fraud of the century; Rutherford B. Hayes, Samuel Tilden, and the stolen election of 1876. {by} Roy Morris, Jr. Simon & Schuster 2003 311p il hardcover o.p. pa $14 **324.9**

1. Lawyers 2. Generals 3. Governors 4. Presidents 5. Political corruption 6. Political leaders 7. Presidential candidates 8. Presidents -- United States -- Election

ISBN 0-7432-2386-1; 978-0-7432-5552-3; 0-7432-5552-6 pa

LC 2002-36507

"Morris has an eye for detail and a lively writing style that make this highly detailed, first-rate work of history read more like a whodunnit than a historical examination." Libr J

Includes bibliographical references

Popkin, Samuel L.

The **candidate**; what it takes to win, and hold the White House. Samuel L. Popkin. Oxford University Press 2012 viii, 350 p.p (hardcover) $27.95 **324.9**

1. Presidents -- United States -- Election 2. Presidential candidates -- United States 3. Presidents -- United States -- Election -- History 4. Presidential candidates -- United States -- History 5. Presidential candidates -- United States -- Case studies
ISBN 9780199922079

LC 2012006845

In this book, Samuel L. Popkin "analyzes what it takes to win [a political] campaign. . . . Based on detailed analyses of the winners--and losers--of the last 60 years of presidential campaigns, Popkin explains how challengers get to the White House, how incumbents stay there for a second term, and how successors hold power for their party." (Publisher's note)

Includes bibliographical references and index

324.973   Elections -- United States

Allen, Jonathan

★ **Shattered**; inside Hillary Clinton's doomed campaign. Jonathan Allen and Amie Parnes. Crown 2017 xii, 464 p.p (hardcover: alkaline paper) $28 **324.973**

1. Presidents -- United States -- Election -- 2016 2. United States -- Politics and government -- 2009- 3. Presidential candidates -- United States -- Biography 4. Women presidential candidates -- United States -- Biography 5. Political campaigns -- United States -- History -- 21st century
ISBN 9780553447088; 9780553447118; 9780553447095

LC 2017010338

This book, by Jonathan Allen and Amie Parnes, explores "how Hillary Clinton lost the 2016 election to Donald Trump. . . . Through deep access to insiders from the top to the bottom of the campaign, political writers Jonathan Allen and Amie Parnes have reconstructed the key decisions and unseized opportunities, the well-intentioned misfires and the hidden thorns that turned a winnable contest into a devastating loss." (Publisher's note)

"A top-notch campaign examination." Kirkus

Includes bibliographical references and index

Bordo, Susan

The **destruction** of Hillary Clinton; untangling the political forces, media culture, and assault on fact that decided the 2016 election. Susan Bordo. Melville House 2017 244 p. (hardback) $24.99 **324.973**

1. Presidents -- United States -- Election 2. Presidential candidates -- United States 3. Presidents -- United States -- Election -- 2016 4. United States -- Politics and government -- 2009- 5. Public opinion -- United States -- History -- 21st century 6. Presidential candidates -- United States -- History -- 21st century 7. Sexism in political culture -- United States -- History -- 21st century 8. Women -- Political activity -- United States -- History -- 21st century 9. Women presidential candidates -- United States -- History --

21st century 10. Mass media -- Political aspects -- United States -- History -- 21st century 11. Right and left (Political science) -- United States -- History -- 21st century

ISBN 9781612196640; 1612196632; 9781612196633

LC 2017006567

Author Susan Bordo offers "an answer to the question many have been asking: How did an extraordinarily well-qualified, experienced, and admired candidate--whose victory would have been as historic as Barack Obama's--come to be seen as a tool of the establishment, a chronic liar, and a talentless politician? Bordo unpacks the Rights' assault on [Hillary] Clinton and her reputation [and] the way the left provoked suspicion and indifference among the youth vote." (Publisher's note)

"This perceptive, thoroughly readable book will strike a chord with her supporters and prove enlightening to many others hoping to make sense of a contentious election." Booklist

Includes bibliographical references (pages 193-233) and index

Clinton, Hillary Rodham, 1947-

★ **What** happened; Hillary Rodham Clinton. Simon & Schuster 2017 xiv, 494 p.p (hardcover) $30   **324.973**

1. Elections -- United States 2. Women presidential candidates -- United States 3. Legislators -- United States -- Biography 4. Presidents -- United States -- Election -- 2016 5. Women legislators -- United States -- Biography 6. Presidential candidates -- United States -- Biography 7. Women presidential candidates -- United States -- Biography

ISBN 9781501175572; 9781501175565; 1501175564

In this memoir, Hillary Rodham Clinton "reveals what she was thinking and feeling during one of the most controversial and unpredictable presidential elections in history. . . . Hillary takes you inside the intense personal experience of becoming the first woman nominated for president by a major party in an election marked by rage, sexism, exhilarating highs and infuriating lows, stranger-than-fiction twists, Russian interference, and an opponent who broke all the rules." (Publisher's note)

"Writing in her smart, sometimes self-deprecating voice, Clinton brings much-needed perspective to the election, especially for her millions of supporters, who also want to know what happened and why." Booklist

Davis, Lanny J.

The **unmaking** of the president 2016; how FBI Director James Comey cost Hillary Clinton the presidency. Lanny J. Davis. Simon & Schuster 2017 224 p. $25   **324.973**

1. Presidents -- United States -- Election -- 2016

ISBN 1501177729; 9781501177729

"During the week of October 24, 2016, Hillary Clinton was decisively ahead of Donald Trump in many polls. . . . Then FBI Director James Comey sent his infamous letter to Congress . . . , saying the bureau was investigating additional emails . . . [related] to the Hillary Clinton email case. In . . . [this book], attorney Lanny J. Davis shows how Comey's misguided announcement . . . swung a significant number of voters away from Clinton, winning Trump . . . the presidency." (Publisher's note)

"Lapsed Trump supporters might well open their minds to this attorney's scholarly, entirely convincing proof of the damage done." Kirkus

Dickerson, John, 1968-

Whistlestop; my favorite stories from presidential campaign history. John Dickerson. Twelve 2016 439 p. illustrations (hardcover) $30   **324.973**

1. United States -- Politics and government -- Anecdotes 2. Presidents -- United States -- Election -- History -- Anecdotes 3. Presidential candidates -- United States -- History -- Anecdotes 4. Campaign management -- United States -- History -- Anecdotes 5.

Political campaigns -- United States -- History -- Anecdotes

ISBN 9781455540464; 9781455540488; 9781478912866

LC 2016941542

This book, by John Dickerson, presents "the stories behind the stories of the most memorable moments in American presidential campaign history. . . . [It] tells the human story of nervous gambits hatched in first-floor hotel rooms, failures of will before the microphone, and the cross-country crack-ups of long-planned stratagems. At the bar at the end of a campaign day, these are the stories reporters rehash for themselves and embellish for newcomers." (Publisher's note)

"A politically astute, timely book that will also have great historical value for future campaigns." Kirkus

Includes bibliographical references (pages 393-423) and index.

Fountain, Ben

★ **Beautiful** country burn again; democracy, rebellion, and revolution. Ben Fountain. HarperCollins 2018 448 p. hardcover $27.99   **324.973**

1. Political science literature 2. United States -- Politics and government 3. Presidents -- United States -- Election -- 2016

ISBN 9780062688842; 0062688847

LC 2018022055

This book, by Ben Fountain, "narrates a shocking year in American politics, moving from the early days of the Iowa Caucus to the crystalizing moments of the Democratic and Republican national conventions, and culminating in the aftershocks of the weeks following election night. Along the way, Fountain probes deeply into history. . . . Fountain has fused history and the present day to paint a startling portrait of the state of our nation." (Publisher's note)

"Month by month, Fountain recaps campaign absurdities and national and international tragedies. Interspersed are essays pinpointing relevant historic events that have influenced the current political climate. Marry the two, and the result is a chronicle of past existential threats to our democracy and a warning-cum-prediction of what most probably lies ahead." Booklist

Green, Joshua

Devil's bargain; Steve Bannon, Donald Trump, and the storming of the presidency. Joshua Green. Penguin Press 2017 xiii, 272 p.p (hardcover) $27   **324.973**

1. Political science literature 2. Presidents -- United States -- Election 3. United States -- Politics and government -- 2009- 4. Campaign management -- United States 5. Presidents -- United States -- Election -- 2016 6. United States -- Politics and government -- 2009-2017

ISBN 9780735225039; 9780735225022; 0735225028

LC 2017304376

This book, by Joshua Green, "is a tour-de-force telling of the remarkable confluence of circumstances that decided the [2016 U.S. presidential] election, many of them orchestrated by [Steve] Bannon and his allies, who really did plot a vast, right-wing conspiracy to stop [Hillary] Clinton. To understand [Donald] Trump's extraordinary rise and Clinton's fall, you have to weave Trump's story together with Bannon's, or else it doesn't make sense." (Publisher's note)

"Behind the scenes and ripped from the headlines, Green's saga exuberantly traces Trump's wild ride to the presidency." Kirkus

Includes bibliographical references and index.

Greene, John Robert, 1955-

I like Ike; the presidential election of 1952. John Robert Greene. University Press of Kansas 2017 xvi, 254 p.p illustrations (American presidential elections) (hardback) $45 **324.973**

1. Presidents -- United States -- Election 2. Presidents -- United

States -- Election -- 1952 3. United States -- Politics & government -- 1945-1953

ISBN 9780700624041; 9780700624058; 9780700624065

LC 2016047603

This book on the 1952 U.S. presidential election, by John Robert Greene, "looks in detail at how Stevenson and Eisenhower faced demands that they run for an office neither originally wanted. He examines the campaigns of their opponents—Harry Truman and Robert Taft, but also Estes Kefauver, Richard B. Russell, Averell Harriman and Earl Warren." (Publisher's note)

"Using primary and secondary sources with aplomb, Greene has produced an excellent work, one that should stand the test of time for its accuracy and interpretation of this important postwar election." LJ

Includes bibliographical references and index

Harding, Luke

Collusion; secret meetings, dirty money, and how Russia helped Donald Trump win. Luke Harding. Vintage Books, a division of Penguin Random House LLC 2017 354 p. illustrations (trade paperback) $16.95   **324.973**

1. Political corruption 2. Presidents -- United States -- Election -- 2016 3. Political corruption -- United States 4. Political campaigns -- Corrupt practices -- United States 5. Russia (Federation) -- Foreign relations -- United States

ISBN 9780525520931; 0525562516; 9780525562511

LC 2017470511

This book, by Luke Harding, presents "an explosive exposé that lays out the story behind the Steele Dossier, including Russia's decades-in-the-making political game to upend American democracy and the Trump administration's ties to Moscow. . . . Harding takes the reader through every bizarre and disquieting detail of the 'Trump-Russia' story--an event so huge it involves international espionage, off-shore banks, . . . and the most shocking election in American history." (Publisher's note)

"One point not in dispute is Harding's ability to bring together diverse strands of a complicated story to make a book that is informative, accessible, and hard to put down." Pub Wkly Annex

Includes bibliographical references (pages 337-338) and index

Ingraham, Laura, 1963-

Billionaire at the barricades; the populists vs. the establishment from Reagan to Trump. Laura Ingraham. St. Martin's Press 2017 307 p. (hardcover) $27.99   **324.973**

1. Right and left (Political science) 2. Presidents -- United States -- Election -- 2016 3. Populism -- United States -- History 4. United States -- Politics and government -- 1989- 5. Right and left (Political science) -- United States

ISBN 1250150647; 9781250150646

LC 2017036170

This book, by Laura Ingraham, "gives readers a front row seat to the populist revolution as she witnessed it. She reveals the origins of this movement and its connection to the Trump presidency. She unmasks the opposition, forecasts the future of the Make America Great Again agenda and offers her own prescriptions for bringing real change to the swamp of Washington." (Publisher's note)

Includes bibliographical references and index

Kasich, John, 1952-

Two paths; America divided or united. John Kasich with Daniel Paisner. Thomas Dunne Books 2017 308 p. illustrations (chiefly color) (hardcover) $27.99   **324.973**

1. Presidents -- United States -- Election 2. United States -- Politics and government -- 21st century 3. Presidents -- United States

-- Election -- 2016 4. Presidential candidates -- United States -- Biography 5. United States -- Politics and government -- 2009-2017

ISBN 9781250138477; 9781250138460; 1250138469

In this book Ohio governor John Kasich reflects "on the tumultuous 2016 [presidential] campaign, sharing his concerns for America and his hopes for our future, and sounding a clarion call to reason and purpose, humility and dignity, righteousness and calm. . . . As Governor Kasich reminds us in these pages, America is great because America is good--and because Americans have stayed true to who we are: one nation, under God, indivisible." (Publisher's note)

O'Donnell, Lawrence

Playing with fire; the 1968 election and the transformation of American politics. Lawrence O'Donnell. Penguin Press 2017 484 p. illustrations (hardcover) $28   **324.973**

1. Elections -- United States 2. United States -- Politics and government -- 1961-1974 3. Presidents -- United States -- Election -- 1968 4. United States -- Politics and government -- 1963-1969

ISBN 9780399563157; 9780399563140

LC 2017031414

This book, by Lawrence O'Donnell, is an account of the 1968 presidential election. "[Lyndon B. Johnson] was confident he'd dispatch with [Richard] Nixon, the GOP frontrunner; Johnson's greatest fear and real nemesis was [Robert F. Kennedy]. But Kennedy and his team . . . weren't prepared to challenge their own party's incumbent. Then, out of nowhere, Eugene McCarthy shocked everyone with his disloyalty and threw his hat in the ring to run against the president." (Publisher's note)

"A careful, circumstantial study that compares favorably to Theodore H. White's presidents series and that politics junkies will find irresistible." Kirkus

Includes bibliographical references and index

O'Rourke, P. J., 1947-

How the hell did this happen? the election of 2016. P. J. O'Rourke. Atlantic Monthly Press 2017 xiv, 216 p.p (hardcover) $25   **324.973**

1. Wit and humor 2. Presidents -- United States -- Election 3. Presidential candidates -- United States -- Humor 4. Presidents -- United States -- Election -- 2016 -- Humor

ISBN 9780802189387; 9780802127655; 9780802126191; 0802126197

LC 2016058368

This book, by comedian P. J. O'Rourke, discusses the U.S. election of 2016, and "offers a brief history of how our insane process for picking who will run for president evolved. . . . He takes us through the debates and key primaries and analyzes everything from the campaign platforms (or lack thereof) to presidential style. And he rises from the depths of despair to come up with a better way to choose a president." (Publisher's note)

"For those interested in one more look at the unusual road leading to the unlikely outcome of the unforgettable 2016 U.S. presidential election, humorist O'Rourke delivers a wry, dry, and occasionally laugh-out-loud take." Pub Wkly

Rove, Karl, 1950-

★ The **triumph** of William McKinley; why the election of 1896 still matters. Karl Rove. Simon & Schuster 2015 viii, 482 p.p (hardcover) $32.50   **324.973**

1. United States -- Politics and government 2. Presidents -- United States -- Election -- 1896 3. United States -- Politics and government -- 1893-1897

ISBN 9781476752952; 9781476752969

LC 2015032290

This book by Karl Rove describes how "President William McKinley, whose 1896 campaign ended a bitter period of political gridlock and reformed and modernized his party, thereby creating a governing majority that dominated American politics for the next thirty-six years. . . . McKinley found ways to address these challenges and win, which is why his campaign is so relevant to our politics now." (Publisher's note)

Sexton, Jared Yates

The **people** are going to rise like the waters upon your shore; a story of American rage. Jared Yates Sexton. Counterpoint 2017 xi, 302 p.p (hardcover) $26   **324.973**
1. Presidents -- United States -- Election -- 2016 2. United States -- Politics and government -- 21st century 3. Public opinion -- United States 4. Political culture -- United States 5. Political campaigns -- United States 6. Political psychology -- United States 7. Polarization (Social sciences) -- United States
ISBN 9781619029637; 9781619029569; 1619029561

LC 2017015327

This book, by Jared Yates Sexton, presents "a firsthand account of the events that shaped the 2016 presidential election and the cultural forces that divided both parties and powered Donald Trump into the White House. . . . Sexton's book is not just the story of the most unexpected and divisive election in modern political history. It is also a sobering chronicle of our democracy's political polarization." (Publisher's note)

"Sexton's is a critical and important voice in helping readers understand the cultural and political sea change the election created." Booklist
Includes bibliographical references (pages 291-302).

Tur, Katy

Unbelievable; my front-row seat to the craziest campaign in American history. Katy Tur. Dey St., an imprint of William Morrow 2017 xii, 291 p.p maps (hardcover) $26.99 **324.973**
1. Elections -- United States 2. Presidential candidates -- United States 3. Presidents -- United States -- Election -- 2016 4. United States -- Politics and government -- 2009-2017
ISBN 9780062684943; 9780062684929; 0062684922

In this memoir, "Katy Tur lived out of a suitcase for a year and a half, following Trump around the country. . . . She visited forty states with the candidate. . . . From day 1 to day 500, Tur documented Trump's inconsistencies, fact-checked his falsities, and called him out on his lies. In return, Trump repeatedly singled Tur out. He tried to charm her, intimidate her, and shame her. . . . None of it worked." (Publisher's note)

"A thoughtful account of covering what the author rightly calls 'the most unlikely, exciting, ugly, trying, and all-around bizarre campaign in American history.'" Kirkus

325   International migration and colonization

Cannato, Vincent J.

American passage; the history of Ellis Island. [by] Vincent J. Cannato. Harper 2009 487p il $27.99   **325**
1. Immigrants -- United States 2. Ellis Island (N.J. and N.Y.) 3. Ellis Island Immigration Station 4. Immigrants -- United States -- History 5. United States -- Immigration and emigration 6. United States -- Emigration and immigration -- History
ISBN 978-0-06-074273-7; 0-06-074273-9

LC 2008-52245

"The author reaches back to the island's beginnings in the early 19th century, when, then named Gibbet Island, it served as a venue for hanging convicted pirates. Cannato then chronicles the many different people—immigrants, immigration officials, politicians and others—who made Ellis Island what it was in the early 20th century. . . . Ambitious in scope and rooted in solid storytelling." Kirkus
Includes bibliographical references

Handlin, Oscar

The **uprooted**; 2nd ed; Little, Brown 1973 333p hardcover o.p. pa $18.99   **325**
1. Acculturation 2. United States -- Immigration and emigration
ISBN 0-316-34313-7 pa
First published 1951

This account of the American immigrant experience and the acculturation process describes employment, religion, ghetto life, benevolent societies, boss politics, family life, and social alienation

Truax, Eileen

Dreamers; an immigrant generation's fight for their American dream. Eileen Truax. Beacon Press 2015 224 p. (paperback) $15   **325**
1. Unauthorized immigrants 2. Immigrants -- United States 3. Illegal aliens -- Education (Higher) -- United States 4. Illegal alien children -- Government policy -- United States 5. United States -- Emigration and immigration -- Social aspects 6. Children of illegal aliens -- Education -- Law and legislation -- United States
ISBN 9780807030332; 0807030333

LC 2014031771

This book by Eileen Truax describes how, "in the face of congressional inertia and furious opposition from some, the DREAM Act has yet to be passed. But recently, this young generation has begun organizing, and with their rallying cry 'Undocumented, Unapologetic, and Unafraid' they are the newest face of the human rights movement." (Publisher's note)

"Immigration buffs and ethnic studies aficionados will not be disappointed. Truax's informative, engaging read provides a new perspective on this country's ongoing immigration debate." LJ
Includes bibliographical references

Urrea, Luis Alberto

★ The **devil's** highway; a true story. Luis Alberto Urrea. Little, Brown 2004 xii, 239p (pbk.) $13.99   **325**
1. Unauthorized immigrants 2. Mexico -- Immigration and emigration 3. United States -- Immigration and emigration 4. Illegal aliens -- Crimes against -- Mexican-American Border Region
ISBN 9780316746717; 9780316010801

LC 2003058930

"In May 2001, 26 Mexican men scrambled across the border and into an area of the Arizona desert known as the Devil's Highway. Only 12 made it safely across. . . . In artful yet uncomplicated prose, Urrea captivatingly tells how a dozen men squeezed by to safety, and how 14 others whom the media labeled the Yuma 14 did not. But while many point to the group's smugglers (known as coyotes) as the prime villains of the tragedy, Urrea unloads on, in the words of one Mexican consul, 'the politics of stupidity that rules both sides of the border.'" (Publishers Weekly)

325.73   International migration – United States

Ramos, Jorge

Stranger; the challenge of a Latino immigrant in the Trump era. Jorge Ramos. Vintage 2018 224 p. $15   **325.73**
1. Latinos (U.S.) 2. Immigrants -- United States 3. United States -- Immigration and emigration -- Government policy

ISBN 0525563792; 9780525563792

In this book, author Jorge Ramos "sets out to examine what it means to be a Latino immigrant, or just an immigrant, in present-day America. Using current research and statistics, with a journalist's nose for a story, and interweaving his own personal experience, Ramos shows us the changing face of America while also trying to find an explanation for why he, and millions of others, still feel like strangers in this country." (Publisher's note)

" An insightful read about prejudice against Latinx individuals in America. Readers of politics and culture will find Ramos's book enlightening." LJ

326 Slavery and emancipation

Berlin, Ira

Generations of captivity; a history of African-American slaves. Belknap Press 2003 374p maps $29.95; pa $16.95 **326**
1. Slavery -- United States
ISBN 0-674-01061-2; 0-674-01624-6 pa

LC 2002-28142

"Berlin has given us a moving, insightful account of slavery in the United States. Readers will not soon forget the story he has told, nor should they." N Y Times Book Rev

Includes bibliographical references

Blight, David W.

A **slave** no more; two men who escaped to freedom: including their own narratives of emancipation. Harcourt 2007 307p il map **326**
1. Slaves 2. Diarists 3. Slavery -- United States 4. African Americans -- Biography
ISBN 978-0-15-101232-9; 0-15-101232-6

LC 2007-14467

"Required reading for scholars or even casual students, this signal [sic] contribution is essential for any collection on slavery, emancipation, or African American or U.S. history and literature." Libr J

Includes bibliographical references

Douglass, Frederick, 1818-1895

★ **Frederick** Douglass: selected speeches and writings; edited by Philip S. Foner; abridged and adapted by Yuval Taylor. Hill Bks. 1999 789p hardcover o.p. pa $32.95 **326**
1. Speeches, addresses, etc., American 2. African Americans -- Civil rights -- History -- 19th century 3. Slaves -- United States -- Social conditions -- 19th century 4. Antislavery movements -- United States -- History -- 19th century
ISBN 1-55652-352-1 pa

LC 99-23180

Based on Foner's five-volume The life and writings of Frederick Douglass (1950-1975), this volume "covers Douglass' speeches and writings over a 54-year period. The breadth and depth of his focus and concerns reflected in more than 2,000 speeches, editorials, articles, and letters provide a wellspring of knowledge about the man and his intellect." Booklist

Includes bibliographical references

Hochschild, Adam

★ **Bury** the chains; prophets, slaves, and rebels in the first human rights crusade. Houghton Mifflin 2005 468p il $26.95 **326**
1. Slavery

ISBN 0-618-10469-0

LC 2004-54091

National Book Award Finalist: Nonfiction (2005)

The author "brings drama and incredible research to this thrilling look at the little-celebrated abolition movement in Britain and its reverberations throughout modern democracies." Booklist

Includes bibliographical references

Horton, James Oliver

★ **Slavery** and the making of America; [by] James Oliver Horton [and] Lois E. Horton. Oxford University Press 2004 254p il maps $35; pa $18.95 **326**
1. Slavery -- United States 2. African Americans -- History
ISBN 0-19-517903-X; 0-19-530451-9 pa

LC 2004-13617

"The oft-told tale is made fresh through up-to-date slavery scholarship, the extensive use of slave narratives and archival photos and, especially, a focus on individual experience." Publ Wkly

Jordan, Don

White cargo; the forgotten history of Britain's white slaves in America. [by] Don Jordan and Michael Walsh. New York University Press 2008 320p il map hardcover o.p. pa $20 **326**
1. Contract labor 2. Slavery -- History 3. Great Britain -- Social conditions 4. United States -- History -- 1600-1775, Colonial period
ISBN 978-0-8147-4272-3; 0-8147-4296-3; 978-0-8147-4296-9 pa; 0-8147-4296-3 pa

LC 2007-37976

First published 2007 in the United Kingdom

This "is a colorful series of portraits of villains and victims, exploiters and exploited, rendered with bemused outrage." Choice

Includes bibliographical references

Rediker, Marcus

★ The **Amistad** rebellion; an Atlantic odyssey of slavery and freedom. Marcus Rediker. Viking 2012 288 p. $27.95 **326**
1. Slave trade 2. Slave revolts 3. Slavery -- United States 4. Amistad (Schooner) 5. Slave trade -- America -- History 6. Slave insurrections -- United States 7. Antislavery movements -- United States 8. Sierra Leoneans -- United States -- History -- 19th century
ISBN 0670025046; 9780670025046

LC 2012014810

In this book, Marcus Rediker "reframes the story [of the Spanish slave schooner Armistad] to show how a small group of courageous men fought and won an epic battle against Spanish and American slaveholders and their governments. He reaches back to Africa to find the rebels' roots, narrates their cataclysmic transatlantic journey, and unfolds a prison story . . . featuring . . . portraits of the Africans, their captors, and their abolitionist allies." (Publisher's note)

Includes bibliographical references and index

White, Shane

★ The **sounds** of slavery; discovering African American history through songs, sermons, and speech. [by] Shane White and Graham White. Beacon Press 2005 xxii, 241p hardcover o.p. pa $17 **326**
1. Plantation life 2. Slavery -- United States 3. African Americans -- History
ISBN 0-8070-5026-1; 0-8070-5027-X pa

LC 2004-21447

"Drawing on WPA interviews with former slaves, slave narratives, and other historical documents from the 1700s through the 1850s, the authors provide the context for the field calls, work songs, sermons, and other sounds and utterances of slaves on American plantations. The authors also focus on recollections of the wails of slaves being whipped, the barking of hounds hunting down runaways, and the keening of women losing their children to the slave block. The combination of the CD and the book brings vibrancy and texture to a complex history that has been long neglected." Booklist

Includes discography and bibliographical references

Wills, Garry

'Negro president' Jefferson and the slave power. Houghton Mifflin 2003 274p il $25; pa $14   **326**
1. Architects 2. Presidents 3. Vice-presidents 4. Essayists 5. Slavery -- United States 6. United States -- Politics and government -- 1783-1865
ISBN 0-618-34398-9; 0-618-48537-6 pa
LC 2003-56710
"Wills makes a valuable contribution to our understanding of Jefferson and the new American nation." Choice
Includes bibliographical references

326.8 Emancipation

Berlin, Ira, 1941-2018

The **long** emancipation; the demise of slavery in the United States. Ira Berlin. Harvard University Press 2015 240 p. (The Nathan I. Huggins lectures) (alk. paper) $22.95; (ebook) $28.95   **326.8**
1. Slaves -- Emancipation -- United States 2. African American abolitionists -- History 3. Antislavery movements -- United States -- History
ISBN 9780674286085; 9780674495487
LC 2015005604
In this book, author Ira Berlin "draws upon decades of study to offer a framework for understanding slavery's demise in the United States. Freedom was not achieved in a moment, and emancipation was not an occasion but a near-century-long process—a shifting but persistent struggle that involved thousands of men and women." (Publisher's note)
Includes bibliographical references and index

327 International relations

Burk, Kathleen

Old world, new world; Great Britain and America from the beginning. Atlantic Monthly Press 2008 830p il map $35 **327**
1. Great Britain -- Foreign relations -- United States 2. United States -- Foreign relations -- Great Britain
ISBN 978-0-87113-971-9
First published 2007 in the United Kingdom
This is "the most reliable, lucidly narrated and generous history of the mutual entanglement of Britain and America we are likely to have for some time." Times Lit Suppl
Includes bibliographical references

Crist, David

★ The **twilight** war; the secret history of America's thirty-year conflict with Iran. David Crist. Penguin Press 2012 638 p., [16] p. of platesp ill., maps $36.00   **327**
1. Iran -- History -- 1979- 2. Iran -- Politics and government 3. United States -- Foreign relations -- Iran 4. United States --

Politics and government -- 1945- 5. Espionage, Iranian -- History 6. Espionage, American -- History 7. Iran -- Foreign relations -- United States 8. United States. Central Intelligence Agency 9. Iran -- Military relations -- United States 10. United States -- Foreign relations -- 1989- 11. United States -- Military relations -- Iran 12. United States -- Foreign relations -- 1981-1989
ISBN 1594203415; 9781594203411
LC 2011050573
This book by David Crist presents an "account of American-Iranian hostilities since the 1979 revolution. . . . Crist makes the case that the United States is already enmeshed in a hidden war with Iran that has raged unacknowledged for decades. This shadow war is characterized by espionage, assassination plots, and frequent eruptions of open hostilities, and exacerbated by egregious missteps and blunders by both sides." (Publishers Weekly)
Includes bibliographical references (p. [576]-623) and index

Feingold, Russ, 1953-

While America sleeps; Russ Feingold. Crown Publishers 2011 viii, 304 p col. ill., maps   **327**
1. International relations 2. United States -- Foreign relations 3. September 11 terrorist attacks, 2001 4. United States -- Politics and government 5. September 11 Terrorist Attacks, 2001 -- Influence 6. Political culture -- United States -- History -- 21st century 7. Progressivism (United States politics) -- History -- 21st century 8. Terrorism -- Government policy -- United States -- History -- 21st century
ISBN 9780307952523; 9780307952547
LC 2011051735
In this book, former U.S. Senator Russ "Feingold revisits the U.S. reaction in the wake of the [September 2001 terrorist] attacks, which set off an 'unfortunate trend' in soured international relations that is only presently being arrested under President Obama. While Feingold graciously allows former President Bush accolades for his initial words of resolve and restraint after 9/11, he grew increasingly alarmed by the hysterical fear gripping Washington, and cast the lone vote against the Patriot Act. . . . In the post-9/11 Risk game, as he calls it, Feingold urged the government not to lose sight of other important strategic spots like Yemen, Indonesia and Somalia. . . . [H]e first urged the troop withdrawal from Iraq in 2005. . . . He has been a vocal proponent for 'restoring the rule of law' to the presidency and of Obama's health-care legislation." (Kirkus)
Includes bibliographical references and index

Gates, Robert Michael, 1943-

From the shadows; the ultimate insider's story of five presidents and how they won the Cold War. Simon & Schuster 1996 604p il hardcover o.p. pa $16   **327**
1. Cold war 2. Cold War 3. Soviet Union -- Foreign relations -- United States 4. United States -- Foreign relations -- Soviet Union
ISBN 0-684-83497-9 pa
LC 95-51704
This book on U.S. politics during the Cold War details author Robert Gates' "career in the Central Intelligence Agency, where he rose from his entry-level job as a Soviet analyst in 1969 to become director in 1991 lays out his insider's view of the agency's role in the collapse of the Soviet Union. He defends himself against charges that his CIA overestimated Soviet military power and the threat it posed." (Commonwealth)
This is an "often entertaining, frequently self-serving but always thoughtful account of the United States' long effort to contain the Soviet Union." N Y Times Book Rev
Includes bibliographical references

Herring, George C., 1936-

From colony to superpower; U.S. foreign relations since 1776. Oxford University Press 2008 1035p il map (Oxford history of the United States) $35; pa. $24.95   **327**

1. United States -- Foreign relations
ISBN 978-0-19-507822-0; 0-19-507822-5; 9780199765539
LC 2008-07996

The author "recaptures a quarter-millennium of American foreign policy with fluidity and felicity." N Y Times Book Rev

Includes bibliographical references (p. 965-995)

Jacques, Martin

When China rules the world; the end of the western world and the birth of a new global order. Penguin Press 2009 xxv, 550p il map $29.95   **327**

1. Globalization 2. Forecasting 3. China -- History 4. China -- Foreign relations 5. China -- Economic conditions 6. China -- Foreign economic relations
ISBN 1-59420-185-4; 978-1-59420-185-1
LC 2009-27298

The author contends "that we are moving into an era of contested modernity. The central player in this new world will be China. . . . Although clearly influenced by the west, its extraordinary size and history mean that it will remain highly distinct, and as it exercises its rapidly growing power it will change much more than the world's geopolitics. The nation-state as we understand it will no longer be globally dominant, and the Westphalian state-system will be transformed; ideas of race will be redrawn." (Publisher's note)

This "comprehensive and richly detailed analysis will be an indispensable resource for anyone who wants to understand contemporary China." New Statesman

Includes bibliographical references

Kaplan, Robert D., 1952-

Monsoon; the Indian Ocean and the future of American power. Random House 2010 366p map $28   **327**

1. National security -- United States 2. Indian Ocean region -- Strategic aspects 3. National security -- Indian Ocean region 4. Indian Ocean region -- Foreign relations -- United States 5. United States -- Foreign relations -- Indian Ocean region
ISBN 1-4000-6746-4; 978-1-4000-6746-6
LC 2009-49752

This is an "examination of the Indian Ocean region and the countries known as 'Monsoon Asia.'" (Publisher's note) Glossary. Index.

"The book's political and economic focus and forecasts are smart and brim with apercus on the intersection of power, politics, and resource consumption (especially water), and give full weight to the impact of colonialism. An ambitious and prescient study equally at ease analyzing the work of the Indian poet Rabindranath Tagore, the finer points of the Indian state of Gujarat's flirtation with fascism, and the economic impact of the Asian tsunami on Indonesia." Publ Wkly

Includes bibliographical references

Kinzer, Stephen

All the Shah's men; an American coup and the roots of Middle East terror. John Wiley & Sons 2003 258p il map hardcover o.p. pa $14.95   **327**

1. Prime ministers 2. Iran -- Politics and government 3. United States -- Foreign relations -- Iran
ISBN 0-471-26517-9; 0-471-67878-3 pa
LC 2003-9968

"This comprehensive . . . account of the nationalization of the Anglo-Iranian Oil Company under the leadership of Mohammad Mossadegh in 1951 . . . is a valuable and informative work." Choice

Includes bibliographical references

Kissinger, Henry, 1923-

World Order; Henry Kissinger. Penguin Press 2014 384 p. maps $36   **327**

1. World politics 2. International relations 3. Geopolitics 4. Security, International 5. World politics -- 21st century
ISBN 1594206147; 9781594206146
LC 2014028152

Author Henry Kissinger offers "a deep meditation on the roots of international harmony and global disorder. Drawing on his experience as one of the foremost statesmen of the modern era . . . Kissinger now reveals his analysis of the ultimate challenge for the twenty-first century: how to build a shared international order in a world of divergent historical perspectives, violent conflict, proliferating technology, and ideological extremism." (Publisher's note)

"Critics are unlikely to find much interest in this volume as it largely summarizes Kissinger's thinking, but students and historians of political science may appreciate his suggestion that both realism and idealism are necessary in modern times." LJ

Includes bibliographical references (pages 379-403) and index

Klimburg, Alexander

The **darkening** web; the war for cyberspace. Alexander Klimburg. Penguin Press 2017 xii, 420 p.p (hardcover) $30   **327**

1. Cyberspace 2. International security 3. Power (Social sciences) 4. Internet -- Political aspects 5. Security, International 6. Computer crimes -- Prevention 7. Cyberspace -- Government policy 8. Internet and international relations 9. Information warfare -- Risk assessment 10. Information society -- Political aspects
ISBN 9780698402768; 9781594206665
LC 2017008579

This book, by Alexander Klimburg, "explains why we underestimate the consequences of states' ambitions to project power in cyberspace at our peril: Not only have hacking and cyber operations fundamentally changed the nature of political conflict, . . . but the rise of covert influencing and information warfare has enabled these same global powers to create and disseminate their own distorted versions of reality in which anything is possible." (Publisher's note)

"The dark side of cyberspace is a daunting subject, but Klimburg's narrative is very accessible, and frankly, this is all far too important to ignore." Booklist

Includes bibliographical references and index

Moynihan, Daniel Patrick

On the law of nations. Harvard Univ. Press 1990 211p $37; pa $10.95   **327**

1. International law 2. United States -- Foreign relations
ISBN 0-674-63575-2; 0-674-63576-0 pa
LC 90-33227

"In the seven essays in this volume, Moynihan traces U.S. attitudes toward international law from the American Revolution to the current administration, and he makes a powerful argument for a return to the conventions of international behavior set out by Woodrow Wilson and the United Nations." Libr J

O'Sullivan, Meghan L.

★ **Windfall**; how the new energy abundance upends global politics and strengthens America's power. Meghan L.

O'Sullivan. Simon & Schuster 2017 xii, 479 p.p (hardcover: alk. paper) $29   **327**
1. Energy development 2. World politics -- 21st century 3. Power resources
ISBN 9781501107931; 9781501107948

LC 2016057135

This book, by Meghan L. O'Sullivan, "describes how new energy realities have profoundly affected the world of international relations and security. New technologies led to oversupplied oil markets and an emerging natural gas glut. This did more than drive down prices. It changed the structure of markets and altered the way many countries wield power and influence." (Publisher's note)

Includes bibliographical references and index

Toumani, Meline

There was and there was not; a journey through hate and possibility in Turkey, Armenia, and beyond. Meline Toumani. Metropolitan Books/Henry Holt and Company 2014 304 p. map (hardback) $28   **327**
1. Ethnicity 2. Social change 3. Armenian Americans 4. Turkey -- Foreign relations 5. Armenian massacres, 1915-1923 6. Social change -- Turkey 7. Armenia -- Relations -- Turkey 8. Turkey -- Relations -- Armenia 9. Turkey -- Social conditions -- 1960- 10. Armenian Americans -- Ethnic identity 11. Armenian massacres, 1915-1923 -- Influence 12. Genocide -- Armenia -- Psychological aspects
ISBN 0805097627; 9780805097627

LC 2014018362

National Book Critics Circle Award Finalist: Autobiography (2014)

In this memoir, "young Armenian-American . . . Meline Toumani grew up in a close-knit Armenian community in New Jersey where Turkish restaurants were shunned and products made in Turkey were boycotted. The source of this enmity was the Armenian genocide of 1915 at the hands of the Ottoman Turkish government, and Turkey's refusal to acknowledge it. . . . Frustrated by her community's all-consuming campaigns for genocide recognition, Toumani . . . moves to Istanbul." (Publisher's note)

"This remarkable memoir serves as a moving examination of the complex forces of ethnicity, nationality and history that shape one's sense of self and foster, threaten or fray the fragile tapestry of community." Kirkus

Tuchman, Barbara Wertheim

★ **Stilwell** and the American experience in China, 1911-45; [by] Barbara W. Tuchman. Grove Press 2001 621p map pa $20   **327**
1. Generals 2. Presidents 3. Sino-Japanese Conflict, 1937-1945 4. World War, 1939-1945 -- China 5. China -- Foreign relations -- United States 6. United States -- Foreign relations -- China
ISBN 0-8021-3852-7; 978-0-8021-3852-1

LC 2001-40154

First published 1970 by Macmillian

Using the career of General "Vinegar Joe" Stilwell as a vehicle, this is a history of America's relations with China from the end of the Manchu Empire to the rise of Mao Tse-tung.

Includes bibliographical references

Westad, Odd Arne

Restless empire; China and the world since 1750. Odd Arne Westad. Basic Books 2012 ix, 515 p.p maps   **327**
1. China -- Foreign relations -- History 2. China -- Foreign relations -- 1949- 3. China -- Foreign relations -- 1644-1912 4. China --

Foreign relations -- 1912-1949
ISBN 0465019331; 9780465019335; 9780465029365

LC 2012021635

This book by Odd Arne Westad "traces China's complex foreign affairs over the past 250 years, identifying the forces that will determine the country's path in the decades to come. . . . Since the height of the Qing Empire in the eighteenth century, China's interactions--and confrontations--with foreign powers have caused its worldview to fluctuate wildly between extremes of dominance and subjugation, emulation and defiance." (Publisher's note)

Includes bibliographical references (p. 479-499) and index

327.1 Foreign policy and specific topics in international relations

Brzezinski, Zbigniew, 1928-2017

Strategic vision; America and the crisis of global power. Zbigniew Brzezinski. Basic Books 2012 viii, 208 p.p (hbk.) $26   **327.1**
1. Economic development 2. World politics -- 1991- 3. Balance of power -- Forecasting 4. World politics -- 21st century -- Forecasting 5. Geopolitics -- History -- 21st century -- Forecasting 6. International relations -- History -- 21st century -- Forecasting 7. United States -- Foreign relations -- 21st century -- Forecasting
ISBN 046502954X; 0465029558; 9780465029549; 9780465029556

LC 2011033312

This book, by Zbigniew Brzezinski, "argues that without an America that is economically vital, socially appealing, responsibly powerful, and capable of sustaining an intelligent foreign engagement, the geopolitical prospects for the West could become increasingly grave. The ongoing changes in the distribution of global power and mounting global strife make it all the more essential that America does not retreat into an ignorant garrison-state mentality or wallow in cultural hedonism." (Publisher's note)

"Jimmy Carter's national security advisor offers an astute, elegant appraisal of the waning of America's "global appeal" and the severe consequences of the shifting of power from West to East." Kirkus

Includes bibliographical references (p. 195-196) and index

Schlesinger, Arthur M. (Arthur Meier), 1917-2007

★ **War** and the American presidency; [by] Arthur M. Schlesinger, Jr. W. W. Norton 2004 160p   **327.1**
1. Iraq War, 2003-2011 2. Governors 3. Presidents 4. Baseball executives 5. Children of presidents 6. Democracy -- United States 7. Energy industry executives 8. United States -- Foreign relations 9. War and emergency powers -- United States
ISBN 0393060020; 0393327698

LC 200409872

This book by Arthur M. Schlesinger Jr. "offers a 21st-century . . . examination of the revolution in foreign policy that defines the US response to the terrorist attacks of 2001. Schlesinger places the Bush Doctrine and the war against Iraq in historical context, tracing the evolution of presidential power and US national security doctrine from the early presidencies to the Bush presidency." (Choice: Current Reviews for Academic Libraries)

This book "explores the war in Iraq, the presidency, and the future of democracy." Publisher's note

Zak, Dan

Almighty; Dan Zak. Blue Rider Press, an imprint of Penguin Random House 2016 416 p. illustrations (ebook) $65; (print: alkaline paper) $27 **327.1**

1. Antinuclear movement 2. Nuclear weapons -- Government policy 3. Y-12 National Security Complex (U.S.) 4. Courage -- United States 5. United States -- Military policy 6. Government, Resistance to -- United States 7. Nuclear weapons -- United States -- History 8. Pacifists -- Tennessee -- Oak Ridge -- Biography 9. Nuclear weapons -- Social aspects -- United States 10. Nuclear weapons industry -- United States -- History 11. Nuclear weapons -- Moral and ethical aspects -- United States 12. Antinuclear movement -- United States -- History -- 21st century
ISBN 9780698189232; 9780399173752

LC 2016011566

This book, by Dan Zak, focuses on how "a trio of peace activists infiltrated the Y-12 National Security Complex in Oak Ridge, Tennessee . . . [and] reexamines America's love-hate relationship to the bomb, from the race to achieve atomic power before the Nazis did to the solemn 70th anniversary of Hiroshima. At a time of concern about proliferation in such nations as Iran and North Korea, the U.S. arsenal is plagued by its own security problems." (Publisher's note)

"Zak gracefully synthesizes the stories of the politicians and bureaucrats controlling stockpiles of weapons and those of the activists working to disarm them." Pub Wkly

Includes bibliographical references and index

327.12   Espionage and subversion

Andrew, Christopher

Defend the realm; the authorized history of MI5. [by] Christopher Andrew. Alfred A. Knopf 2009 xxii, 1032p il $40 **327.12**

1. Great Britain -- MI5 2. Intelligence service -- Great Britain
ISBN 978-0-307-26363-6; 0-307-26363-0

LC 2009-25463

"This unique publication is definitive and fascinating. Definitive because, after decades of ill-informed or partial accounts this book fully defines and describes its subject; no future writer can ignore it. Fascinating because the fluent clarity of Andrew's narrative, his eye for colourful individual detail and the sheer interest of his subjects. . . . This book is essential reading for anyone with even the slightest interest in intelligence in the modern period." Spectator

Includes bibliographical references

The **secret** world; a history of intelligence. Christopher Andrew. Yale University Press 2018 960 p. (alk. paper) $40 **327.12**

1. Espionage -- History 2. Intelligence service -- History
ISBN 9780300238440

LC 2018947154

This book, by Christopher Andrew, presents a "comprehensive history of intelligence, from Moses and Sun Tzu to the present day. . . . Those who do not understand past mistakes are likely to repeat them. Intelligence is a prime example. At the outbreak of World War I, the grasp of intelligence shown by U.S. President Woodrow Wilson and British Prime Minister Herbert Asquith was not in the same class as that of George Washington during the Revolutionary War." (Publisher's note)

Bamford, James

The **shadow** factory; the ultra-secret NSA from 9/11 to the eavesdropping on America. Doubleday 2008 395p $27.95 **327.12**

1. Intelligence service 2. Electronic surveillance 3. United States -- National Security Agency 4. United States -- Politics and government -- 2001-
ISBN 978-0-385-52132-1; 0-385-52132-4

LC 2008-26448

The book is "full of technical details and insider politics for those who follow such things, but Bamford's overarching theme is the grand scale of the threat to privacy." San Francisco Chron

Includes bibliographical references

Blum, Howard

In the enemy's house; the secret saga of the FBI agent and the code breaker who caught the Russian spies. Howard Blum. HarperCollins 2018 336 p. $29.99 **327.124**

1. United States. Federal Bureau of Investigation 2. United States -- Foreign relations -- Soviet Union 3. Intelligence officers -- United States -- Biography
ISBN 0062458248; 9780062458247

In this book, author Howard Blum, "illuminates the lives of . . . [linguist and codebreaker Meredith Gardner and FBI supervisor Bob Lamphere] who played a significant role in America's history. . . . [Gardner and Lamphere] worked together on Venona, a top-secret mission to uncover the Soviet agents and protect the Holy Grail of Cold War espionage--the atomic bomb." (Publisher's note)

"There's a lot of excitement throughout, as Blum shows how a piece of paper left on a desk, an overheard conversation, and a New York Times article (read by a Russian spy) contributed to hair-raising outcomes. Blum is a standout in the field of espionage history." Booklist

Corera, Gordon

Cyberspies; the secret history of surveillance, hacking, and digital espionage. Gordon Corera. W W Norton & Co Inc 2016 448 p. (ebook) $50; $29.95 **327.12**

1. Computer security 2. Internet in espionage 3. Computer crimes -- Prevention
ISBN 9781681771946; 1681771543; 9781681771540

LC 2016498084

This book, by Gordon Corera, offers a "compelling narrative [that] takes us from the Second World War through the Cold War and the birth of the internet to the present era of hackers and surveillance. The book is rich with historical detail and characters, as well as astonishing revelations about espionage carried out in recent times by the UK, US, and China." (Publisher's note)

"A convincing argument that the most secure way to communicate is via snail mail." Kirkus

Includes bibliographical references (pages 393-420) and index.

Dillon, Eva

Spies in the family; an American spymaster, his Russian crown jewel, and the friendship that helped end the Cold War. Eva Dillon. HarperCollins 2017 xvi, 327 p.p illustrations (hardcover) $28.99 **327.12**

1. Cold war 2. Spies -- Biography 3. Cold War -- Biography 4. Friendship -- Political aspects 5. Spies -- Soviet Union -- Biography 6. Spies -- United States -- Biography 7. Children of spies -- United States -- Biography 8. Soviet Union -- Foreign relations -- United States 9. United States -- Foreign relations -- Soviet Union
ISBN 9780062385918; 9780062385888; 9780062385901

LC 2017010000

This book, by Eva Dillon, "is a[n] account of two families on opposite sides of the lethal espionage campaigns of the Cold War, and two men whose devoted friendship lasted a lifetime. . . . Dillon goes beyond the fog of secrecy to craft an unforgettable story of friendship and betrayal, double agents and clandestine lives, that challenges our notions of patriotism, exposing the commonality between peoples of opposing political economic systems." (Publisher's note)

"Reads like a fine spy novel whose ending we know but whose story transports us nonetheless." Kirkus

Includes bibliographical references (pages 307-310) and index.

Dorril, Stephen

MI6; inside the covert world of Her Majesty's secret intelligence service. Free Press 2000 907p $40; pa $22   **327.12**
1. Great Britain -- MI6 2. Intelligence service -- Great Britain
ISBN 0-7432-0379-8; 0-7432-1778-0 pa

LC 00-29385

This study of the British secret intelligence service "focuses on the years since World War II, when MI6 was dedicated to winning the cold war. . . . The book is invaluable for readers who want to separate spy fact from spy fiction." Booklist

Epstein, Edward Jay

How America lost its secrets; Edward Snowden, the Man and the Theft. by Edward Jay Epstein. Alfred A. Knopf 2017 368 p. illustrations (ebook) $65; (hardcover) $27.95 **327.12**
1. Whistle blowing 2. Electronic surveillance 3. Leaks (Disclosure of information) 4. National security -- United States 5. Whistle blowing -- United States 6. Electronic surveillance -- United States 7. Leaks (Disclosure of information) -- United States 8. United States. National Security Agency--Central Security Service
ISBN 9780451494573; 9780451494566

LC 2016026940

This book, by Edward Jay Epstein, is a "groundbreaking exposé that convincingly challenges the popular image of Edward Snowden as hacker turned avenging angel, while revealing how vulnerable our national security systems have become--as exciting as any political thriller, and far more important." (Publisher's note)

"A wild and harrowing detective story and impressively evenhanded portrait of a very sticky case." Kirkus

Includes bibliographical references and index

Garton-Ash, Timothy

The **file**; a personal history. Random House 1997 262p hardcover o.p. pa $14   **327.12**
1. Authors 2. Essayists 3. Historians 4. Nonfiction writers 5. Secret service -- Germany (East) 6. Intelligence service -- Germany (East) 7. Germany (East) -- Ministerium für Staatssicherheit
ISBN 0-679-77785-7 pa

"For much of 1980, while working on a doctorate in history, Garton Ash lived in East Berlin. . . . He became an object of interest to East Germany's . . . secret police known by the acronym Stasi. In The File, Garton Ash, now 42, tries to reconstruct that year . . . by comparing his private notes from the period with what he found in Stasi's newly opened records. Going further, he located and interviewed some of the informers and bureaucrats who had spied on him." (Time)

"The author went to Berlin to study in 1978 and soon came under the scrutiny of the Stasi, the notorious East German secret police. In 1993, Garton Ash had the opportunity to examine the secret file kept on him. Comparing the file reports with his private diary of the time, he finds distortions, fabrications, and surprising omissions in the file. . . . This work makes an important contribution to the literature of the new Europe." Libr J

Greenwald, Glenn, 1967-

★ **No** place to hide; Edward Snowden, the NSA, and the

U.S. surveillance state. Glenn Greenwald. Henry Holt & Co. 2014 320 p. illustrations (hardcover) $27   **327.12**
1. Whistle blowing 2. Intelligence service -- United States
ISBN 162779073X; 9781627790734; 9781627790741

LC 2014932888

This book tells how "In May 2013, [author] Glenn Greenwald set out for Hong Kong to meet an anonymous source who claimed to have astonishing evidence of pervasive government spying. . . . That source turned out to be the 29-year-old NSA contractor Edward Snowden, and his revelations about the agency's widespread, systemic overreach proved to be some of the most explosive and consequential news in recent history." (Publisher's note)

"In his analysis, the author breaks down the dense NSA subject matter and uses excerpts and slides from the documents to illustrate his points, making this work readable for even those unfamiliar with the technical concepts." LJ

Includes bibliographical references and index

Gup, Ted

Book of honor; covert lives and classified deaths at the CIA. Doubleday 2000 390p il hardcover o.p. pa $15   **327.12**
1. Spies 2. United States -- Central Intelligence Agency
ISBN 0-385-49541-2 pa

LC 99-89017

This exposé "reveals the names—and personal stories—of some three dozen CIA agents who died in the line of duty and whose identities have been kept secret—sometimes for decades. . . . Gup's sleuthing is a remarkable coup, full of high-level intrigue, cover-ups and drama." Publ Wkly

Hanson, Jason

Survive like a spy; real CIA operatives reveal how they stay safe in a dangerous world and how you can too. Jason Hanson. Penguin Group USA 2018 256 p. $26   **327.12**
1. Tactics 2. Espionage 3. Lifesaving
ISBN 0143131591; 9780143131595

In this book author Jason Hanson, "takes the reader deep inside the world of espionage, . . . [with] accounts of spy missions in Eastern Europe, the Middle East, Asia, and elsewhere, the book reveals how to: Achieve mental sharpness to be ready for anything, escape if taken hostage, . . . [and] master the 'Weapons of Mass Influence' to recruit others, build rapport, and make allies when you need them most." (Publisher's note)

"The macho tone will repel some, but the book is chock-full of amusing and colorful tips that readers can hope they never actually have to use." Pub Wkly

Harden, Blaine

King of spies; the dark reign of America's spymaster in Korea. Blaine Harden. Viking 2017 viii, 260 p.p illustrations (hardcover) $27   **327.12**
1. Biography 2. Spies -- United States -- Biography 3. Korean War, 1950-1953 -- Secret service 4. Korean War, 1950-1953 -- Atrocities 5. Korean War, 1950-1953 -- Secret service -- United States
ISBN 9780525429937; 9780698410152; 052542993X

LC 2017025386

In this book, author Blaine Harden "traces [Donald] Nichols's unlikely rise and tragic ruin, from his birth in an operatically dysfunctional family in New Jersey to his sordid postwar decline, which began when the U.S. military sacked him in Korea, sent him to an air force psych ward in Florida, and subjected him--against his will--to months of electroshock therapy." (Publisher's note)

"The author ably connects his ominous central figure to the larger mysterious, unresolved narrative of the Korean conflict. An engrossing hidden history of wartime espionage, with elements of derring-do and moral barbarity." Kirkus

Includes bibliographical references and index.

Harding, Luke

A **very** expensive poison; the assassination of Alexander Litvinenko and Putin's war with the West. by Luke Harding. Random House Inc 2017 454 p. illustrations $16　**327.12**

1. Journalists 2. Poisons and poisoning 3. Russia -- Politics and government

ISBN 1101973994; 9781101973998

LC 2017301006

This book, by Luke Harding, is "a true story of murder and conspiracy that points directly to Vladimir Putin. . . . On November 1, 2006, journalist and Russian dissident Alexander Litvinenko was poisoned in London. He died twenty-two days later. The cause of death? Polonium—a rare, lethal, and highly radioactive substance. Here . . . Harding unspools a real-life political assassination story—complete with KGB, CIA, MI6, and Russian mobsters." (Publisher's note)

"Hard-hitting and timely given Russia's continued sway in international politics as well as its documented influence over an incoming American administration that is also hostile to the press" Kirkus

Hayes, Paddy

Queen of Spies; Daphne Park, Britain's Cold War Spy Master. by Paddy Hayes. Overlook Press 2016 336 p. illustrations, portraits (ebook) $50; $29.95　**327.12**

1. Intelligence service -- Great Britain

ISBN 9781468313253; 1468312685; 9781468312683

LC 2015039895

This book, by Paddy Hayes, "recounts the . . . story of the evolution of the British Secret Intelligence Service (SIS) from World War II to the Cold War through the eyes of Daphne Park, one of its outstanding and most unusual operatives. He provides the reader with one of the most intimate narratives yet of how the modern SIS actually went about its business, . . . and shows how Park was able to rise through the ranks of a field that had been comprised almost entirely of men." (Publisher's note)

"She was forthright and obdurate, and she had an infectious sense of humor. Most importantly, she personified the qualities required: loyalty, respect, tradition, and absolute secrecy. As exciting as any good spy thriller—but it's all true." Kirkus

Includes bibliographical references and index.

Haynes, John Earl

Spies; the rise and fall of the KGB in America. [by] John Earl Haynes, Harvey Klehr, and Alexander Vassiliev; with translations by Philip Redko and Steven Shabad. Yale University Press 2009 liii, 650p il $35; pa $24　**327.12**

1. Spies 2. Russian espionage 3. KGB

ISBN 978-0-300-12390-6; 0-300-12390-6; 978-0-300-16438-1 pa; 0-300-16438-6 pa

LC 2008-45628

This history of Soviet espionage in the United States "offers a remarkable portrait of the KGB's efforts—drawn largely from the KGB's own files. This achievement is possible only because Alexander Vassiliev, a former KGB agent, was allowed extensive access to the raw espionage files for two years in the mid-1990s. . . . Spies is chockablock with poignant individual tales." Newsweek

Includes bibliographical references

Hemming, Henry

Agent M; the lives and spies of MI5's Maxwell Knight. Henry Hemming. PublicAffairs 2017 xi, 354 p.p illustrations (hardcover) $28　**327.12**

1. British espionage 2. Intelligence officers -- Great Britain -- Biography 3. Intelligence service -- Great Britain -- History -- 20th century

ISBN 9781610396844; 9781610398855

LC 2016047678

This book by Henry Hemming "reveals not only the story of one of the world's greatest intelligence operators, but the sacrifices and courage required to confront fascism during a nation's darkest time. Maxwell Knight was perhaps the greatest spymaster in history, rumored to be the real-life inspiration for the James Bond character 'M.' Knight's work revolutionized British intelligence, pioneering the use of female agents, among other accomplishments." (Publisher's note)

"Many spy stories are page-turners, but the author proves that the story of one man can be equally thrilling." Kirkus

Includes bibliographical references (pages 335-339) and index.

The **ingenious** Mr. Pyke; inventor, fugitive, spy. Henry Hemming. PublicAffairs 2015 512 p. illustrations (hardcover) $26.99　**327.12**

1. Inventors

ISBN 1610395778; 9781610395779; 9781610395786

LC 2014952648

This book presents a biography of Geoffrey Pyke, who "audaciously planned to enter Germany in 1914 to get the scoop as a war correspondent for the British newspaper Daily Chronicle. He successfully sneaked in, was imprisoned, escaped with a spy, and had a heart attack, but made it back to England . . . While Pyke did not graduate from college, this never hindered his copious writing and inventing; his creations caught the imagination of Winston Churchill and the British military." (Library Journal)

"Those fond of biographies and 20th-century European war tales told in a modern vein will enjoy this book." LJ

Herrington, Stuart A.

Traitors among us; inside the spy catcher's world. Harcourt 2000 409p il pa $14　**327.12**

1. Spies 2. Soldiers 3. Russian espionage 4. Berlin (Germany) 5. Intelligence service -- United States

ISBN 0-15-601117-4

LC 00-38893

First published 1999 by Presidio Press

"Herrington, former head of the U.S. Army Counterintelligence Unit . . . offers a fascinating view of life as a spy catcher in West Berlin during the height of the Cold War. His description of the search for and capture of Clyde Conrad and James Hall . . . (who for 13 years handed over America's secret war plans to the Soviets) surpasses any spy fiction." Libr J

Hoffman, David E., 1953-

The **Billion** Dollar Spy; A True Story of Cold War Espionage and Betrayal. by David E. Hoffman. Random House Inc 2015 352 p. illustrations, map $28.95　**327.12**

1. Cold war 2. Espionage 3. Intelligence service 4. Russia -- History -- 1917-1991, Soviet Union

ISBN 0385537603; 9780385537605

LC 2015003370

In this book, by David E. Hoffman, "it was the height of the Cold War, and a dangerous time to be stationed in the Soviet Union. One evening, while the chief of the CIA's Moscow station was filling his gas tank, a stranger approached and dropped a note into the car. The chief, suspicious of a KGB trap, ignored the overture. But the man had made up his mind. . . . In the years that followed, that man, Adolf Tolkachev, became one of the most valuable spies ever for the U.S." (Publisher's note)

"Hoffman ably navigates the many strands of this complex espionage story. An intricate, mesmerizing portrayal of the KGB-CIA spy culture." Kirkus

Includes bibliographical references (pages 267-297) and index.

Laird, Thomas

Into Tibet; the CIA's first atomic spy and his secret expedition to Lhasa. Grove Press 2002 364p il $26; pa $15 **327.12**
1. American espionage 2. Tibet (China) 3. China -- Foreign relations -- United States 4. United States -- Foreign relations -- China
ISBN 0-8021-1714-7; 0-8021-3999-X pa
LC 2001-58459

The author "traces the story of two CIA agents, Douglas Mackiernan and Frank Bessac, sent on an intelligence expedition to Tibet in 1949-1950. . . . Focusing on the heart-stopping details of the expedition itself, Laird gives the now familiar story of callous CIA manipulation an absorbing twist." Publ Wkly

Includes bibliographical references

Macintyre, Ben, 1963-

A **Spy** Among Friends; Kim Philby and the Great Betrayal. Ben Macintyre. Crown Publishers 2014 384 p. illustrations, portraits $27 **327.12**
1. Spies 2. Betrayal 3. Spies -- Great Britain -- Biography 4. Espionage, Soviet -- Great Britain -- History
ISBN 0804136637; 9780804136631
LC 2014003296

This book by Ben MacIntyre describes how "even as the web of suspicion closed around him, and [spy Kim] Philby was driven to greater lies to protect his cover, his two friends never abandoned him--until it was too late. The stunning truth of his betrayal would have devastating consequences on the two men who thought they knew him best, and on the intelligence services he left crippled in his wake." (Publisher's note)

"A tale of espionage, alcoholism, bad manners and the chivalrous code of spies--the real world of James Bond, that is, as played out by clerks and not superheroes." Kirkus

Includes bibliographical references (pages 309-359) and index

Moran, Christopher

Company confessions; secrets, memoirs, and the CIA. Christopher R. Moran; foreword by Tony Mendez. Thomas Dunne Books/St. Martin's Press 2016 368 p. illustrations (ebook) $60; (hardback) $27.99 **327.12**
1. Intelligence officers -- United States -- Biography 2. United States. Central Intelligence Agency -- Officials and employees -- Biography 3. United States. Central Intelligence Agency. Publications Review Board
ISBN 9781466847491; 9781250047137
LC 2016003324

In this book, author Christopher R. Moran "digs deep into . . . [the] tumultuous relationship between the CIA and former agents who try to go public about their careers. . . . [This book] examines why America's spies are so willing to share their stories, the damage inflicted when they leak the nation's secrets, and the fine line between censorship on the grounds of security and censorship for the sake of reputation." (Publisher's note)

"Moran's book is s cholarly in intent but proves a surprisingly cracking read. An informative historical summation of CIA memoirs with enough skulduggery to entertain casual readers." Kirkus

Includes bibliographical references and index.

Navarro, Joe

Three minutes to doomsday; an agent, a traitor, and the worst espionage breach in U.S. history. Joe Navarro. Scribner 2017 xiv, 349 p.p illustrations (hardcover) $26 **327.12**
1. American espionage 2. Military intelligence -- United States -- History -- 20th century 3. Espionage -- Soviet Union -- History -- 20th century 4. Espionage -- United States -- History -- 20th century 5. United States. Federal Bureau of Investigation -- Officials and employees -- Biography
ISBN 1501128272; 9781501128271; 9781501128295
LC 2017288630

This book, by Joe Navarro, offers an "insider's story [that] shows how a massive giveaway of secret war plans and nuclear secrets threatened America with annihilation. . . . The dueling antagonists: an FBI agent who couldn't overtly tip to his target that he suspected him of wrongdoing lest he clam up, and a traitor whose weakness was the enjoyment he derived from sparring with his inquisitor." (Publisher's note)

"A fascinating account of counterintelligence in the pre-cyber era . . . ." Kirkus

Plokhy, Serhii

The **man** with the poison gun; a Cold War spy story. Serhii Plokhy. Basic Books 2016 384 p. maps (hardcover) $28.99; (ebook) $18.99 **327.12**
1. Russian espionage 2. Spies -- Biography 3. Spies -- Soviet Union -- Biography 4. Ukrainians -- Germany -- Biography 5. Espionage, Soviet -- Germany -- History 6. Poisoning -- Germany -- History -- 20th century 7. Ukraine -- Politics and government -- 1945-1991 8. Political refugees -- Germany (West) -- Biography 9. Political crimes and offenses -- Germany -- History -- 20th century
ISBN 9780465035908; 9780465096602
LC 2016019612

This book, by Serhii Plokhy, presents the story of KGB assassin Bogdan Stashinsky, who defected to West Germany in 1961. "The publicity stirred up by the Stashinsky case forced the KGB to change its modus operandi abroad and helped end the career of Aleksandr Shelepin, one of the most ambitious and dangerous Soviet leaders. Stashinsky's testimony, implicating the Kremlin rulers in political assassinations carried out abroad, shook the world of international politics." (Publisher's note)

"A thrilling, well-researched tale of espionage that has all the spycraft hallmarks of a blockbuster movie." Kirkus

Includes bibliographical references and index

Priess, David

The **president's** book of secrets; the untold story of intelligence briefings to America's presidents from Kennedy to Obama. David Priess; foreword by George H. W. Bush. PublicAffairs 2016 400 p. illustrations (ebook) $16.99; (hardback) $29.99 **327.127**
1. Intelligence service -- United States 2. Presidents -- United States -- History 3. United States. Central Intelligence Agency 4. National security -- United States 5. United States -- Foreign relations 6. Intelligence service -- United States -- History 7. United States. Central Intelligence Agency -- History
ISBN 9781610395960; 9781610395953
LC 2015041833

"David Priess, a former intelligence officer and daily briefer, has interviewed every living president and vice president as well as more than one hundred others intimately involved with the production and delivery of the president's book of secrets. [In this book,] he offers an unprecedented window into the decision making of every president from Kennedy to Obama, with many character–rich stories revealed here for the first time." (Publisher's note)

"Recommended for those interested in a different perspective on the U.S. presidency, political scientists, and historians." LJ

Includes bibliographical references and index

Reel, Monte

A **brotherhood** of spies; the U-2 and the CIA's secret war. Monte Reel. Doubleday 2018 352 p. (hardcover: alk. paper) $28.95   **327.127**
    1. U-2 Incident, 1960 2. Intelligence service -- United States 3. United States. Central Intelligence Agency -- History -- 20th century 4. U-2 (Reconnaissance aircraft) 5. Intelligence service -- United States -- History -- 20th century
ISBN 9780385540209
                   LC 2017053819

In this book, "Monte Reel reveals how the U-2 spy program, principally devised by four men working in secret, upended the Cold War and carved a new mission for the CIA. This secret fraternity, made up of Edwin Land, best known as the inventor of instant photography and the head of Polaroid Corporation; Kelly Johnson, a hard-charging taskmaster from Lockheed; Richard Bissell, the secretive and ambitious spymaster; and ace Air Force flyer Powers." (Publisher's note)

"A richly detailed, well-researched, and engagingly written book that takes us behind the scenes of one of the twentieth-century's most nail-bitingly tense episodes." Booklist

Includes bibliographical references and index

Richelson, Jeffrey

The **wizards** of Langley; inside the CIA's Directorate of Science and Technology. {by} Jeffrey T. Richelson. Westview Press 2001 386p il hardcover o.p. pa $17   **327.12**
    1. United States -- Central Intelligence Agency -- Directorate of Science and Technology
ISBN 0-8133-4059-4 pa

The author "provides a richly detailed account of the agency's work." Libr J

Solomon, Jay

The **Iran** wars; spy games, bank battles, and the secret deals that reshaped the Middle East. Jay Solomon. Random House Inc 2016 352 p. illustrations $28; (ebook) $65 **327.12**
    1. Nuclear weapons -- Iran 2. Iran -- Foreign relations -- United States 3. United States -- Foreign relations -- Iran 4. Nuclear arms control -- Iran 5. Economic sanctions, American -- Iran
ISBN 9780812993646; 9780812993653
                   LC 2016016783

This book, by Jay Solomon, explores how "through a combination of economic sanctions, global diplomacy, and intelligence work, successive U.S. administrations have struggled to contain Iran's aspirations to become a nuclear power and dominate the region--what many view as the most serious threat to peace in the Middle East. Meanwhile, Iran has used regional instability to its advantage to undermine America's interests." (Publisher's Note)

"In addition to in-depth research, Solomon enlists his own countless interviews and extensive on-site reporting to provide a sound, timely, authoritative exposé." Kirkus

Includes bibliographical references (pages 307-320) and index.

Weiner, Tim

★ **Legacy** of ashes; the history of the CIA. Tim Weiner. Doubleday 2007 702p ill. (pbk.) $17.95; o.p.; o.p. **327.12**
    1. United States -- History -- 1945- 2. Intelligence service -- United States 3. United States. Central Intelligence Agency 4. United States -- Central Intelligence Agency 5. United States. Central Intelligence Agency -- History
ISBN 9780307389008; 9780385514453; 038551445X
                   LC 2007004077

Los Angeles Times Book Prizes: History (2007); National Book Awards: Nonfiction (2007)

This book is a "chronicle of the [U.S.] Central Intelligence Agency . . . [and] C.I.A. incompetence. . . . The author has . . . studied the archival record, teased out newly declassified primary documents and done numerous interviews to glean as much as can be publicly known about the agency's history. Some of the most damning criticism of the C.I.A.'s past performance in this book comes . . . from ex-officials and long-secret authorized accounts by C.I.A. historians. . . . [Author Tim] Weiner argues that a bad C.I.A. track record has encouraged many of . . . [the U.S.'s] gravest contemporary problems: Iran, Iraq, Afghanistan, terrorism." (New York Times)

This book "takes the CIA from its creation after World War II, through its battles in the cold war and the war on terror, to its . . . [circumstances] after 9/11." Publisher's note

Includes bibliographical references and index.

Wise, David

Spy: the inside story of how the FBI's Robert Hanssen betrayed America. Random House 2002 309p $24.95; pa $13.95   **327.12**
    1. Spies 2. Espionage 3. FBI agents 4. United States -- Federal Bureau of Investigation
ISBN 0-375-50745-0; 0-375-75894-1 pa
                   LC 2002-31867

"A relentless reporter and true expert on the world of spying, Wise recounts Hanssen's story and the hunt to catch him in precise, if sometimes overwhelming detail." N Y Times Book Rev

327.2   Diplomacy

Grandin, Greg

Kissinger's Shadow; The Long Reach of America's Most Controversial Statesman. by Greg Grandin (Author) Henry Holt & Co. 2015 288 p. $28   **327.2**
    1. Military policy -- United States 2. United States -- Foreign relations
ISBN 1627794492; 9781627794497
                   LC 2015003553

This book, written by Greg Grandin, "reveals how Richard Nixon's top foreign policy advisor . . . was helping to revive a militarized version of American exceptionalism centered on an imperial presidency. Believing that reality could be bent to his will . . . and vowing that past mistakes should never hinder future bold action, [Henry] Kissinger anticipated, even enabled, the ascendance of the neoconservative idealists who took America into crippling wars in Afghanistan and Iraq." (Publisher's note)

"Grandin will win no friends among Kissinger supporters, yet this book will find its audience among political scientists, historians, and informed readers attempting to assess the statesman's complex legacy." LJ

Includes bibliographical references (pages 231-259) and index.

Kissinger, Henry, 1923-

Diplomacy. Simon & Schuster 1994 912p il maps hardcover o.p. pa $22   **327.2**

1. Actors 2. Princes 3. Cold war 4. Emperors 5. Generals 6. Diplomacy 7. Governors 8. Statesmen 9. Historians 10. Presidents 11. Heads of state 12. Prime ministers 13. Vice-presidents 14. World War, 1914-1918 15. Vietnam War, 1961-1975 16. People with disabilities 17. Senators 18. Memoirists 19. Nazi leaders 20. Philatelists 21. Cabinet members 22. Communist leaders 23. Political leaders 24. College presidents 25. Nonfiction writers 26. Members of Congress 27. Members of Parliament 28. Nobel laureates for peace 29. Nobel laureates for literature 30. World War, 1939-1945 -- Children 31. United States -- Foreign relations

ISBN 0-671-51099-1 pa

LC 93-44001

"This is an important contribution to the theoretical literature on foreign affairs and will also serve quite ably as a one-volume synthesis of modern diplomatic history. All libraries should have this impressive book." Libr J

Includes bibliographical references

327.42   International relations – England

Brotton, Jerry

The **sultan** and the queen; the untold story of Elizabeth and Islam. Jerry Brotton. Viking 2016 352 p. color ill., map, portraits (ebook) $65; (hardcover) $30   **327.42**

1. Great Britain -- Foreign relations -- Turkey 2. Turkey -- History -- Ottoman Empire, 1288-1918 3. Great Britain -- History -- 1558-1603, Elizabeth 4. Turkey -- History -- Murad III, 1574-1595 5. Turkey -- Foreign relations -- Great Britain 6. Great Britain -- History -- Elizabeth, 1558-1603

ISBN 9780698191631; 9780525428824

LC 2016029495

This book, by Jerry Brotton, tells the "story of Queen Elizabeth's secret alliance with the Ottoman sultan and outreach to the Muslim world. . . . Brotton reveals that Elizabethan England's relationship with the Muslim world was far more amicable—and far more extensive—than we have ever appreciated as he tells the riveting story of the traders and adventurers who first went East to seek their fortunes." (Publisher's note)

"An erudite work that presents a fresh facet to Elizabeth's reign." Kirkus

Includes bibliographical references and index

327.51   International relations – China

French, Howard W.

Everything under the heavens; How the past helps shape China's push for global power. Howard W. French. Alfred A. Knopf 2017 352 p. illustrations, map (hardcover) $27.95; (ebook) $65   **327.51**

1. Geopolitics -- Asia 2. Strategic culture -- China 3. Asia -- Foreign relations -- China 4. China -- Foreign relations -- Asia 5. China -- Foreign relations -- 21st century

ISBN 9780385353328; 9780385353335

LC 2016021957

This book, by Howard W. French, presents "an incisive investigation of China's ideological development as it becomes an ever more aggressive player in regional and global diplomacy. . . . After its reform and opening in 1978, China maintained an attitude of false modesty about its ambitions. . . . Underlying this attitude is a strain of thinking that casts China's present-day actions in decidedly historical terms, as the path to restoring the dynastic glory of the past." (Publisher's note)

"This will be a useful, and necessary, starting point for informed discussion." Pub Wkly

Includes bibliographical references and index

327.73   Foreign relations -- United States

Allison, Graham

Destined for war; can America and China escape Thucydides's trap? Graham Allison. Houghton Mifflin Harcourt 2017 xx, 364 p.p   **327.73**

1. War 2. China -- Foreign relations -- United States 3. War -- Causes 4. United States -- Foreign relations -- China

ISBN 9780544935273; 0544935276; 9780544935334

LC 2017005351

In this book author "Graham Allison explains why Thucydides's Trap is the best lens for understanding U.S.-China relations in the twenty-first century. Through uncanny historical parallels and war scenarios, he shows how close we are to the unthinkable. Yet, stressing that war is not inevitable, Allison also reveals how clashing powers have kept the peace in the past — and what painful steps the United States and China must take to avoid disaster today." (Publisher's note)

"A timely, reasoned treatise by a keen observer and historian." Kirkus

Bass, Gary Jonathan, 1969-

The **Blood** telegram; Nixon, Kissinger, and a forgotten genocide. by Gary J. Bass. Alfred A. Knopf 2013 528 p. $30   **327.73**

1. Bangladesh 2. Nixon, Richard M. (Richard Milhous), 1913-1994 3. Genocide -- Bangladesh 4. United States -- Foreign relations -- 1969-1974 5. South Asia -- Foreign relations -- United States 6. United States -- Foreign relations -- South Asia 7. Bangladesh -- History -- Revolution, 1971 -- Atrocities

ISBN 0307700208; 9780307700209

LC 2013014788

Pulitzer Prize Finalist: History (2014)

This book by Gary J. Bass examines the "humanitarian crisis that propelled the creation of Bangladesh." Particular focus is given to how "[Richard] Nixon's deep distrust of India--which he viewed as an ungovernable cauldron of Soviet-leaning liberals, lefties and hippies--and his longtime support of the military in Pakistan disastrously steered his and [Henry] Kissinger's resolve not to stay the hand of Gen. Agha Mohammad Yahya Khan against a dissenting East Pakistan in March 1971." (Kirkus Reviews)

Includes bibliographical references and index

Bernstein, Richard, 1944-

China 1945; Mao's revolution and America's fateful choice. Richard Bernstein. Alfred A. Knopf 2014 464 p. illustrations, maps (hardcover) $30   **327.73**

1. China -- History -- 1912-1949 2. China -- Foreign relations -- United States 3. Taiwan -- History -- 1945- 4. China -- History -- Republic, 1912-1949 5. United States -- Foreign relations -- China

ISBN 0307595889; 9780307595881; 9780307743213

LC 2014003598

This book by Richard Bernstein "examines the first episode in which

American power and good intentions came face-to-face with a powerful Asian revolutionary movement, and challenges familiar assumptions about the origins of modern Sino-American relations." (Publisher's note)

"This thoroughly researched and well-argued work is highly recommended for those interested in Sino-American relations during the World War II and Cold War periods. The inclusion of stories from individuals impacted by these events adds to the book's value. Readers interested in China's World War II experience should also consider Rana Mitter's Forgotten Ally." LJ

Includes bibliographical references and index

Bordewich, Fergus M.

The **First** Congress; How James Madison, George Washington, and a Group of Extraordinary Men Invented the Government. by Fergus M. Bordewich. Simon & Schuster 2016 448 p. 8 plates; illustrations $30   **327.73**

1. United States -- Politics and government -- 1783-1809
ISBN 1451691939; 9781451691931

LC 2015017286

This book, by Fergus M. Bordewich, is about "the most productive Congress in US history, the First Federal Congress of 1789–1791. . . . The Constitution was a broad set of principles. It was left to the members of the First Congress and President George Washington to create the machinery that would make the government work. Fortunately, James Madison, John Adams, Alexander Hamilton, and others less well known today, rose to the occasion." (Publisher's note)

"This engaging and accessible book sheds new light on the meaning of constitutionality." LJ

Budiansky, Stephen

Code warriors; NSA's codebreakers and the secret intelligence war against the Soviet Union. by Stephen Budiansky. Alfred A. Knopf 2016 416 p. illustrations (ebook) $65; $30   **327.73**

1. Cryptography -- United States -- History 2. United States -- Foreign relations -- Soviet Union 3. United States. National Security Agency -- History 4. Soviet Union -- Foreign relations -- United States
ISBN 9780385352673; 9780385352666

LC 2015045330

In this book, author Stephen Budiansky tells "how NSA came to be, from its roots in World War II through the fall of the Berlin Wall. Along the way, he guides us through the . . . challenges faced by cryptanalysts, and how they broke some of the most complicated codes of the [20th] century. With access to new documents, Budiansky shows where the agency succeeded and failed during the Cold War, but his account also offers crucial perspective for assessing NSA today." (Publisher's note)

"Budiansky leavens the history and technology with colorful profiles of cryptographers and spies; the result is a lively account of how today's information controversies emerged." Pub Wkly

Includes bibliographical references and index

Chomsky, Noam, 1928-

Who rules the world? Noam Chomsky. Metropolitan Books 2016 320 p. (hardback) $28   **327.73**

1. Power (Social sciences) 2. World politics -- 21st century 3. United States -- Foreign relations -- 21st century
ISBN 9781627793810; 9781627793827

LC 2016010018

In this book, author Noam Chomsky "argues that the United States, through its military-first policies and its . . . devotion to maintaining a world-spanning empire, is both risking catastrophe and wrecking the global commons. Drawing on a wide range of examples, from the . . . drone assassination program to the . . . flashpoints of Iraq, Iran, Afghanistan, and Israel/Palestine, he offers . . . insights into the workings of imperial power on our increasingly chaotic planet." (Publisher's note)

"Chomsky, fierce and unapologetic, has a strong fan base and continues to be an important voice." Booklist

Includes bibliographical references (pages 259-293) and index.

Farrow, Ronan, 1987-

War on peace; the end of diplomacy and the decline of American influence. Ronan Farrow. W W Norton & Co Inc 2018 432 p. (hardcover) $27.95   **327.73**

1. Diplomacy 2. World politics -- 21st century 3. United States -- Foreign relations -- 21st century 4. United States. Department of State 5. United States -- Foreign relations administration
ISBN 9780393652109

LC 2018006827

This book, by Ronan Farrow, presents "a harrowing exploration of the collapse of American diplomacy and the abdication of global leadership. . . . Farrow illuminates one of the most consequential and poorly understood changes in American history. . . . Diplomacy, Farrow argues, has declined after decades of political cowardice, shortsightedness, and outright malice--but it may just offer America a way out of a world at war." (Publisher's note)

"Excellent, wide-ranging reporting and sharp-edged analysis make this a book that's sure to be talked about inside the Beltway—and that deserves a wide audience beyond." Kirkus Reviews

Includes bibliographical references and index

Ferreiro, Larrie D.

★ **Brothers** at arms; American independence and the men of France & Spain who saved it. Larrie D. Ferreiro. Alfred A. Knopf 2016 464 p. illustrations, maps (ebook) $65; (hardback) $30   **327.73**

1. United States -- Foreign relations -- 1775-1783 2. United States -- History -- 1775-1783, Revolution -- French participation 3. United States -- History -- 1775-1783, Revolution -- Spanish participation 4. Great Britain -- Foreign relations -- Spain 5. Spain -- Foreign relations -- Great Britain 6. France -- Foreign relations -- Great Britain 7. Great Britain -- Foreign relations -- France 8. Great Britain -- Foreign relations -- 1760-1789 9. United States -- History -- Revolution, 1775-1783 -- Participation, French 10. United States -- History -- Revolution, 1775-1783 -- Participation, Spanish
ISBN 9781101875254; 9781101875247

LC 2016007136

Pulitzer Prize Finalist: History (2017)

This book, by Larrie Ferreiro, presents the "untold story of how the American Revolution's success depended on substantial military assistance provided by France and Spain, and places the Revolution in the context of the global strategic interests of those nations in their fight against England. . . . Ferreiro adds to the historical records the names of French and Spanish diplomats, merchants, soldiers, and sailors whose contribution is at last given recognition." (Publisher's note)

"A largely untold, engrossing history of our nation's fraught, and unlikely, path to liberty." Kirkus

Includes bibliographical references (pages [339]-412) and index.

Haass, Richard N., 1951-

Foreign policy begins at home; the case for putting America's house in order. by Richard Haass. Basic Books 2013 viii, 195 p.p (hardcover) $25.99   **327.73**

1. Economic policy -- United States 2. United States -- Foreign

relations 3. World politics 4. International relations 5. Security, International 6. United States -- Politics and government
ISBN 0465057985; 9780465057986

LC 2012049203

Here, Richard N. Haass focuses on "domestic economic policy as the foundation of U.S. power. He notes the current national budget debates, which, he says, result from systemic changes in the U.S. economy and in international geoeconomic realities that impact our national security." He explores the post-Cold War world, the effects of 9/11 and the 2008 global financial crisis, and discusses a "more discriminating and pragmatic foreign policy that is supported by a more disciplined domestic policy." (Library Journal)

Includes bibliographical references (pages 169-183) and index.

Hersh, Seymour, 1937-

The **killing** of Osama Bin Laden; Seymour M. Hersh. Verso Books 2016 144 p. (hardback: alk. paper) $19.95   **327.73**
  1. United States -- Foreign relations 2. United States -- Military policy 3. United States -- Foreign relations -- 2009-
ISBN 9781784784362

LC 2016002833

This book, by Seymour M. Hersh, is an "investigation of White House lies about the assassination of Osama bin Laden. . . . At the same time, the full story of the United States' involvement in the Syrian civil war has been kept behind a diplomatic curtain, concealed by double-speak. It is a policy of obfuscation that has compelled the White House to turn a blind eye to Turkey's involvement in supporting ISIS and its predecessors in Syria." (Publisher's note)

"The Pulitzer Prize winner builds on his reputation as an iconic investigative journalist, skewering the conventional wisdom about the death of Osama bin Laden." Kirkus

Kagan, Robert, 1958-

The **jungle** grows back; America and our imperiled world. by Robert Kagan. Alfred A. Knopf 2018 192 p. (hardback) $22.95   **327.73**
  1. World politics 2. International security 3. United States -- Foreign relations 4. Security, International 5. World politics -- 1989- 6. World politics -- 1945-1989 7. United States -- Foreign relations -- 1989- 8. United States -- Foreign relations -- 1945-1989
ISBN 9780525521655

LC 2018011882

This book, by Robert Kagan, presents "a brilliant and visionary argument for America's role as an enforcer of peace and order throughout the world--and what is likely to happen if we withdraw and focus our attention inward. . . . Like a jungle that keeps growing back after being cut down, the world has always been full of dangerous actors who, left unchecked, possess the desire and ability to make things worse." (Publisher's note)

Kaplan, Robert D., 1952-

The **return** of Marco Polo's world; war, strategy, and American interests in the twenty-first century. Robert D. Kaplan. Random House 2018 xiv, 280 p.p (hardcover) $28   **327.73**
  1. Democracy -- United States 2. Military policy -- United States 3. United States -- Foreign relations -- 21st century 4. World politics -- 21st century 5. United States -- Military policy 6. Democracy -- Government policy -- United States
ISBN 9780812996791; 9780812996807; 0812996798

LC 2018005845

"Drawing on decades of firsthand experience as a foreign correspondent and military embed for The Atlantic, . . . [Robert D.] Kaplan outlines the timeless principles that should shape America's role in a turbulent world: a respect for the limits of Western-style democracy; a delineation between American interests and American values; an awareness of the psychological toll of warfare; a projection of power via a strong navy; and more." (Publisher's note)

"An astute, powerfully stated, and bracing presentation." Booklist
Includes bibliographical references and index.

Kinzer, Stephen

★ The **true** flag; Theodore Roosevelt, Mark Twain, and the Birth of American Empire. Stephen Kinzer. Henry Holt and Company 2016 320 p. illustrations, portraits (hardcover) $28; (ebook) $60   **327.730**
  1. Imperialism -- History 2. United States -- Territorial expansion 3. United States -- Foreign relations -- History 4. Imperialism -- History -- 19th century 5. Imperialism -- History -- 20th century 6. Spanish-American War, 1898 -- Influence 7. United States -- Foreign relations -- 1897-1901 8. United States -- Foreign relations -- 1901-1909 9. United States -- Politics and government -- 1897-1901 10. United States -- Politics and government -- 1901-1909
ISBN 9781627792165; 9781627792172

LC 2016019840

This book, by Stephen Kinzer, "brings to life the forgotten political debate that set America's interventionist course in the world for the twentieth century and beyond. . . . The country's best-known political and intellectual leaders took sides. Theodore Roosevelt, Henry Cabot Lodge, and William Randolph Hearst pushed for imperial expansion; Mark Twain, Booker T. Washington, and Andrew Carnegie preached restraint." (Publisher's note)

"A tremendously elucidating book that should be required reading for civics courses." Kirkus

Includes bibliographical references and index

Leverett, Flynt

Going to Tehran; why the United States must come to terms with the Islamic Republic of Iran. Flynt Leverett and Hillary Mann Leverett. Henry Holt & Co 2013 496 p. (hardback) $32   **327.73**
  1. Nuclear weapons 2. Iran -- Foreign relations -- United States 3. United States -- Foreign relations -- Iran 4. United States -- Foreign relations -- 2001-
ISBN 0805094199; 9780805094190

LC 2012036700

This book offers an "analysis of the Islamic Republic's policies, intentions, and capabilities," focusing particularly on Iran's developing nuclear capabilities. The authors "call for a reset in relations and substantial engagement rather than saber-rattling and sanctions" and "accuse the American government of 'shameless duplicity.'" (Publishers Weekly)

McFaul, Michael Anthony, 1963-

From Cold War to hot peace; an American ambassador in Putin's Russia. Michael McFaul. Houghton Mifflin Harcourt 2018 528 p. (hardcover) $30   **327.73**
  1. Ambassadors 2. Russia -- Foreign relations -- United States 3. United States -- Foreign relations -- Russia 4. United States -- Foreign relations -- 1989- 5. Ambassadors -- Russia (Federation) -- Biography 6. United States -- Foreign relations -- 2009-2017 7. Russia (Federation) -- Foreign relations -- United States 8. United States -- Foreign relations -- Russia (Federation)
ISBN 9780544716247

LC 2017045603

This book, by Michael McFaul, is "a revelatory, inside account of U.S.-Russia relations from 1989 to the present. . . . This riveting inside account combines history and memoir to tell the full story of U.S.-Russia relations from the fall of the Soviet Union to the new rise of the hostile, paranoid Russian president. From the first days of McFaul's ambassadorship, the Kremlin actively sought to discredit and undermine him." (Publisher's note)

Includes bibliographical references and index

Morris, Seymour

Supreme Commander; MacArthur's Triumph in Japan. by Seymour Morris Jr. HarperCollins 2014 368 p. illustrations $26.99   **327.73**

1. World War, 1939-1945 -- Peace 2. Japan -- History -- 1945-1952, Allied occupation
ISBN 0062287931; 9780062287939

LC 2013498721

Includes bibliographical references and index

In this book, author Seymour Morris Jr. "combines political history, military biography, and business management to tell the story of General Douglas MacArthur's tremendous success in rebuilding Japan after World War II. . . . As the uniquely titled Supreme Commander for the Allied Powers, he was charged with transforming a defeated, militarist empire into a beacon of peace and democracy." (Publisher's note)

"A well-crafted history of an underappreciated aspect of MacArthur's career." LJ

Nasr, Vali

The **dispensable** nation; American foreign policy in retreat. Vali Nasr. Doubleday 2013 336 p. $28.95   **327.73**

1. Political science 2. United States -- Foreign relations 3. Middle East -- Foreign relations -- United States 4. United States -- Foreign relations -- Middle East 5. Islamic countries -- Foreign relations -- United States 6. United States -- Foreign relations -- Islamic countries
ISBN 038553647X; 9780385536479

LC 2012043100

In this book, author Vali Nasr "questions America's . . . choice to engage less and matter less in the world. Nasr makes a compelling case that behind specific flawed decisions lurked a desire by the White House to pivot away from the complex problems of the Muslim world. Drawing on his . . . expertise in Middle East affairs and firsthand experience in diplomacy, Nasr demonstrates why turning our backs is dangerous and, what's more, sells short American power." (Publisher's note)

Includes bibliographical references (pages 259-283) and index

Pomfret, John

The **beautiful** country and the Middle Kingdom; America and China, 1776 to the present. John Pomfret. Henry Holt & Co. 2016 704 p. ill. (some color), maps (ebook) $60; (hardback) $40   **327.73**

1. China -- Foreign relations -- United States 2. United States -- Foreign relations -- China
ISBN 9781429944120; 9780805092509

LC 2016009016

This book, by John Pomfret, presents a "history of the two-centuries-old relationship between the United States and China, from the Revolutionary War to the present day. . . . Drawing on personal letters, diaries, memoirs, government documents, and contemporary news reports, . . . Pomfret reconstructs the surprising, tragic, and marvelous ways Americans and Chinese have engaged with one another through the centuries." (Publisher's note)

"An occasionally too-dense but impressively wide-ranging history demonstrating that the U.S.–China relationship began decades before Richard Nixon arrived on the scene." Kirkus

Includes bibliographical references and index

Rice, Condoleezza, 1954-

No higher honor; A Memoir of My Years in Washington. Condoleezza Rice. Random House Inc. 2011 xviii, 766 p.p illustrations, maps $35   **327.73**

1. Israel-Arab conflicts 2. September 11 terrorist attacks, 2001 3. United States -- Politics and government 4. War on Terrorism, 2001-2009 5. Stateswomen -- United States -- Biography 6. United States. Dept. of State -- Biography 7. National Security Council (U.S.) -- Biography 8. Cabinet officers -- United States -- Biography 9. United States -- Foreign relations -- 2001-2009 10. Women cabinet officers -- United States -- Biography
ISBN 030758786X; 9780307587862; 9780307952479

LC 2011534059

Author Condoleezza Rice "takes the reader into secret negotiating rooms where the fates of Israel, the Palestinian Authority, and Lebanon often hung in the balance, and it draws back the curtain on how frighteningly close all-out war loomed . . . [in response to] the September 11, 2001, terrorist attacks . . . [and] in clashes involving Pakistan-India and Russia-Georgia, and in East Africa." (Publisher's note)

Ross, Dennis, B., 1948-

Doomed to succeed; the U.S.-Israel relationship from Truman to Obama. Dennis Ross. Farrar, Straus & Giroux 2015 496 p. (hardcover) $30   **327.73**

1. Presidents -- United States 2. United States -- Foreign relations -- Israel 3. United States -- Politics and government -- 1945- 4. United States -- Foreign relations -- 1989- 5. Israel -- Foreign relations -- United States 6. United States -- Foreign relations -- 1945-1989
ISBN 0374141460; 9780374141462

LC 2015010959

This book, by Dennis Ross, discusses the Israeli-U.S. diplomatic relationship since World War II. The author "takes us through every administration from [Harry] Truman to [Barack] Obama, throwing into dramatic relief each president's attitudes toward Israel and the region, the often tumultuous debates between key advisers, and the events that drove the policies and at times led to a shift in approach." (Publisher's note)

"Ross provides a learned, wise template for understanding the long-term relationship between two countries tethered to one another out of shared self-inter e st and geopolitical necessity and yet with sometimes-conflicting senses of the way forward." Kirkus

Includes index

Walt, Stephen M., 1955-

The **hell** of good intentions; America's foreign policy elite and the decline of U.S. primacy. Stephen M. Walt. Farrar, Straus & Giroux 2018 400 p. (hardcover) $28   **327.73**

1. Political consultants 2. World politics -- 1991- 3. United States -- Foreign relations 4. Political consultants -- United States 5. United States -- Foreign relations -- 1989-
ISBN 9780374280031

LC 2018007639

This book, by Stephen M. Walt, "dissects the faults and foibles of recent American foreign policy--explaining why it has been plagued by disasters like the 'forever wars' in Iraq and Afghanistan and outlining what can be done to fix it. In 1992, the United States stood at the pinnacle of world power and Americans were confident that a new era of peace and prosperity was at hand. Twenty-five years later, those hopes have been dashed." (Publisher's note)

Includes bibliographical references and index

The **WikiLeaks** files; the world according to US empire. by WikiLeaks, with an introduction by Julian Assange. Verso 2015 624 p. (ebook) $29.95 **327.73**
1. Government information 2. WikiLeaks (Organization) 3. Leaks (Disclosure of information) 4. United States -- Foreign relations 5. Official secrets -- United States 6. Government information -- United States 7. United States -- Foreign relations -- 2009- 8. United States -- Foreign relations -- 2001-2009 9. Leaks (Disclosure of information) -- United States
ISBN 9781781688755; 9781781689448; 9781784782719; 9781781689448
LC 2015017220
This book by WikiLeaks "exposes the machinations of the United States as it imposes a new form of imperialism on the world, one founded on tactics from torture to military action, to trade deals and 'soft power,' in the perpetual pursuit of expanding influence. The book also includes an introduction by Julian Assange examining the ongoing debates about freedom of information, international surveillance, and justice." (Publisher's note)
"The insights from researchers provide an excellent resource and solid foundation for further research by scholars or lay readers." Pub Wkly
Includes bibliographical references (pages 546-588) and index.

328 The legislative process

Cohen, Richard E.
The **almanac** of American politics 2018; Richard E. Cohen with James A. Barnes. Columbia Books 2017 2181 p. paperback $89 **328**
1. Almanacs 2. United States -- Politics and government -- 2001-
ISBN 9781938939563
The 2018 edition includes: In-depth profile of every governor, Senator, and House member. Updated demographic information for every state and district, including information from the Census Bureau's American Community Survey, with new categories of economic, occupational, social and geographic data.

Congressional Quarterly, Inc.
★ **Congress** A to Z; 5th ed.; CQ Press 2008 xxxiv, 704p il map (CQ's American government A to Z series) $85 **328**
1. Reference books 2. United States -- Congress
ISBN 978-0-87289-558-4
LC 2008-11284
First published 1988
This work provides information on the structure and work of Congress in some 340 alphabetical entries.
Includes bibliographical references

Kaiser, Robert Greeley
So damn much money; the triumph of lobbying and the corrosion of American government. [by] Robert G. Kaiser. Knopf 2009 398p il $27.95 **328**
1. Lobbying 2. Political corruption 3. Lobbyists 4. United States -- Congress
ISBN 978-0-307-26654-5; 0-307-26654-0
LC 2008-33862
"Lobbying, Kaiser writes, is a business of 'huge numbers and vague standards,' forever reorienting itself in an effort to skate just inside the limits of legality. Kaiser follows the career of Gerald S. J. Cassidy, a kid from a poor family who became a lawyer for migrant workers, an aide to George McGovern, and, latterly, a lobbyist for universities, cranber-

ries, defense contractors, and Taiwan. Cassidy pioneered the use of earmarks, fought to save the Seawolf submarine, and took congressmen to N.C.A.A. Final Four games. . . . Kaiser's account dwells less on blatant corruption than on what is perfectly, depressingly legal." New Yorker
Includes bibliographical references

Robert C. Byrd Center for Legislative Studies
Congress investigates; a critical and documentary history. edited by Roger A. Bruns, David L. Hostetter, Raymond W. Smock; Robert C. Byrd Center for Legislative Studies. Rev. ed; Facts on File 2011 2v il (Facts on File library of American history) set $195 **328**
1. Reference books 2. Governmental investigations -- United States
ISBN 978-0-8160-7679-6; 978-1-4381-3545-8 ebook
LC 2010020268
First published 1975
The editors "have gathered here information on congressional investigations from the Colonial period to the 21st century. The entries, written by U.S. historians and archivists, each offer an overview, chronology, documents, excerpts from congressional committee reports and testimony, and a bibliography; many also include black-and-white illustrations, photographs, or political cartoons. They cover well-known events such as the Teapot Dome scandal, the burning of Washington in 1814, the Hurricane Katrina inquiry of 2005–06, and several lesser-known happenings—General St. Clair's defeat of 1792–93 and the Pujo Committee on the 'Money Trust,' for example. . . . This well-researched and richly detailed resource provides an excellent overview of major congressional investigations and will be a quality addition to a high school, public, or undergraduate academic library." Libr J
Includes bibliographical references

328.73 Legislative process -- United States

Abrams, Stacey, 1973-
Minority leader; how to lead from the outside and make real change. Stacey Abrams. Henry Holt & Co. 2018 272 p. $28 **328.73**
1. Political participation 2. Political leadership -- United States 3. African American women politicians -- Georgia -- Biography
ISBN 1250191297; 9781250191298
In this book, author "Stacey Abrams argues that knowing your own passion is the key to success, regardless of the scale or target. From launching a company . . . to running a successful political campaign, finding what you want to fight for is as critical as knowing how to turn thought into action. Stacey uses her experience . . . to break down how ambition . . . and failure function in leadership, while offering personal stories that illuminate practical strategies." (Publisher's note)

Bai, Matt
All the truth is out; the week politics went tabloid. Matt Bai. Alfred A. Knopf 2014 288 p. illustrations (hardback) $26.95 **328.73**
1. Scandals 2. Public opinion 3. Presidential candidates -- United States 4. Legislators -- United States -- Biography 5. United States. Congress. Senate -- Biography 6. Scandals -- United States -- History -- 20th century 7. Public opinion -- United States -- History -- 20th century 8. Press and politics -- United States -- History -- 20th century 9. Tabloid newspapers -- United States -- History -- 20th century 10. Character -- Political aspects -- United States -- History -- 20th century 11. Mass media -- Political aspects -- United States -- History -- 20th century 12. Presidential candidates -- Press

coverage -- United States -- History -- 20th century

ISBN 0307273385; 9780307273383; 9780307474681

LC 2014001033

In this book, political correspondent Matt Bai "offers a poignant, highly original, and news-making reappraisal of [Gary] Hart's fall from grace (and overlooked political legacy) as he makes the compelling case that this was the moment when the paradigm shifted-private lives became public, news became entertainment, and politics became the stuff of Page Six." (Publisher's note)

"The author takes inspiration from Richard Ben Cramer, whose What It Takes (1992) is often considered the best book about any presidential campaign. Here Bai shows he is Cramer's worthy successor—his important cautionary tale will resonate with journalists and members of the media as well as with political players and readers of current history." LJ

Baker, Richard A.

The **American** Senate; an insider's history. Neil MacNeil and Richard A. Baker. Oxford University Press, Inc. 2013 472 p. (hardcover) $29.95 **328.73**

1. United States. Congress. Senate -- History

ISBN 0195367618; 9780195367614

LC 2012046807

This book by Richard A. Baker and Neil MacNeil "explore[s] the [U.S.] Senate's historical evolution with one eye on persistent structural pressures and the other on recent transformations. Here, for example, are the Senate's struggles with the presidency--from George Washington's first, disastrous visit . . . through now-forgotten conflicts with Presidents Garfield and Cleveland, to current war powers disputes. The authors also explore the Senate's potent investigative power." (Publisher's note)

Includes bibliographical references and index.

Brazile, Donna

Brazile, Donna. **For** colored girls who have considered politics; Donna Brazile, Yolanda Caraway, Leah Daughtry, and Minyon Moore with Veronica Chambers. St. Martin's Press 2018 336 p. $28.99 **328.73**

1. African American women -- Biography 2. United States -- Politics and government -- 20th century 3. African American women -- Political activity -- History -- 20th century 4. African American women politicians -- Biography 5. African American women -- Political activity -- History 6. United States -- Politics and government -- 21st century

ISBN 9781250137715

LC 2018017175

This book presents the sweeping view of American history from the vantage points of four women who have lived and worked behind the scenes in politics for over thirty years--Donna Brazile, Yolanda Caraway, Leah Daughtry, and Minyon Moore--a group of women who call themselves The Colored Girls. . . . Over the years, they've filled many roles: in the corporate world, on campaigns, in unions, in churches, in their own businesses and in the White House." (Publisher's note)

Lawrence, John A.

The **class** of '74; Congress after Watergate and the roots of partisanship. John A. Lawrence. Johns Hopkins University Press 2018 416 p. illustrations (hardcover: alk. paper) $29.95 **328.73**

1. Political parties -- United States 2. United States -- Politics and government 3. United States -- Politics and government -- History 4. United States. Congress (94th: 1977-1979) 5. United States -- Politics and government -- 1977-1981

ISBN 142142469X; 9781421424699

LC 2017022924

In this book, author "John A. Lawrence examines how . . . elected representatives [after the Watergate scandal] bucked the status quo in Washington, helping to effectuate unprecedented reforms. Lawrence's long-standing work in Congress afforded him unique access to former members, staff, House officers, journalists, and others, enabling him to challenge the time-honored reputation of the Class as idealistic, narcissistic, and naïve 'Watergate Babies.'" (Publisher's note)

Includes bibliographical references and index

Spieler, Matthew

The **U.S.** House of Representatives; the fundamentals of American government. Matthew Spieler. Thomas Dunne Books/ St. Martin's Press 2015 192 p. (hardback) $22.99 **328.73**

1. United States. Congress. House

ISBN 9781250040367; 9781466835641

LC 2015028828

This book, by Matthew Spieler, part of the Fundamentals of American Government civics series, "carefully examines and explains exactly how the House of Representatives operates. From its voting procedure to historic beginnings and modern day issues, there is no area of this governmental body left un-revealed." (Publisher's note)

"A concise civics handbook that focuses a spotlight on the House's design and where its leadership does not measure up." Kirkus

Includes bibliographical references and index.

330 Economics

Acemoglu, Daron

Why nations fail; the origins of power, prosperity and poverty. Daron Acemoglu and James A. Robinson. Crown Publishers 2012 529 p. ill., map $30 **330**

1. Nations 2. Economic conditions 3. Poverty -- Developing countries 4. Economics -- Political aspects 5. Revolutions -- Economic aspects 6. Developing countries -- Social policy 7. Economic history -- Political aspects 8. Developing countries -- Economic policy 9. Economic development -- Developing countries

ISBN 0307719219; 9780307719218

LC 2011023538

This book attempts to answer the question "'Why Nations Fail.' . . . [The authors] favour . . . an approach rooted solely in institutional economics, which studies the impact of political environments on economic outcomes. . . . They offer [the following] . . . diagnosis: some governments get it wrong on purpose. . . . Inclusive institutions protect individual rights and encourage investment and effort. Where inclusive governments emerge, great wealth follows." (Economist)

"The authors make what could be a weighty topic both engaging and accessible. It will appeal not only to students of economics and political science but also to anyone looking to gain insight into the current state of our global economy, its origins, and the kind of transformations that might level the playing field." LJ

Includes bibliographical references (p. [465]-509) and index

Adler, Moshe

Economics for the rest of us; debunking the science that makes life dismal. New Press 2009 217p il $24.95; ebook $24.95 **330**

1. Income 2. Economics 3. Salaries, wages, etc.

ISBN 978-1-59558-101-3; 978-1-59558-527-1 ebook

LC 2009-24968

"Only occasionally relying on graphs or tables, Adler provides an accessible summary of quite complex debates in economic theory." Choice

Includes bibliographical references

Bregman, Rutger

Utopia for realists; How we can build the ideal world. Rutger Bregman, Translated from the dutch by Elizabeth Manton. Little, Brown & Co. 2017 336 p. illustrations (ebook) $81; (hbk.) $27   **330**

1. Utopias

ISBN 9780316559263; 0316471895; 9780316471893

LC 2016962005

This book, by Rutger Bregman, "is one of those rare books that takes you by surprise and challenges what you think can happen. From a Canadian city that once completely eradicated poverty, to Richard Nixon's near implementation of a basic income for millions of Americans, Bregman takes us on a journey through history, and beyond the traditional left-right divides, as he champions ideas whose time have come." (Publisher's note)

"A provocative pleasure to contemplate." Kirkus

Includes bibliographical references (pages 265-305) and index.

Chang, Ha-Joon

Economics; The User's Guide. Ha-Joon Chang. St. Martin's Press 2014 384 p. illustration $30   **330**

1. Finance 2. Economics

ISBN 1620408120; 9781620408124

LC 2014498623

In this book author Ha-Joon Chang "explains how the global economy actually works--in real-world terms. Writing with irreverent wit, a deep knowledge of history, and a disregard for conventional economic pieties, Chang offers insights that will never be found in the textbooks." (Publisher's note)

"A solid choice for those who want to learn more about economics without feeling like they are back in the classroom." LJ

Dubner, Stephen J., 1963-

★ **Freakonomics**; a rogue economist explores the hidden side of everything. [by] Steven D. Levitt and Stephen J. Dubner. William Morrow 2005 242p hardcover o.p. pa $15.99   **330**

1. Economics 2. Economics -- Sociological aspects 3. Economics -- Psychological aspects

ISBN 0-06-073132-X; 0-06-073133-8 pa

LC 2004-65478

The authors "evaluate intriguing questions such as 'What do Schoolteachers and Sumo Wrestlers Have in Common?' 'How is the Ku Klux Klan Like a Group of Real Estate Agents?' 'Where Have All the Criminals Gone?' and 'What Makes a Perfect Parent?' . . . This excellent, readable book will enlighten many library patrons." Booklist

Includes bibliographical references

The **economics** book; [Niall Kishtainy, consultant editor; George Abbot ... [et al.], contributors] DK Pub. 2012 352 p. col. ill. $25   **330**

1. Economics 2. Economic conditions 3. Economists 4. Economic history

ISBN 0756698278; 9780756698270

LC 2011279835

This book "takes a unique approach to elucidating" economics. "Arranged by both subtopic and time frame, the history of economic theory, notable world events, and biographies of key players are presented in six chapters, titled 'Let the Trading Begin (400 BCE-1770 CE),' 'The

Age of Reason (1770-1820),' 'Industrial and Economic Revolutions (1820-1929),' 'War and Depressions (1929-1945),' 'Post-War Economics (1945-1970),' and 'Contemporary Economics (1970-present).' (Booklist)

Encyclopedia of Business Information Sources; edited by Virgil L. Burton. Gale / Cengage Learning 2013 1210 p. (paperback) $657   **330**

1. Businesspeople 2. Business -- Encyclopedias

ISBN 1414478119; 9781414478111

The 23rd edition of this book, edited by Virgil L. Burton, offers "a bibliographic guide to citations covering over 1,100 subjects of interest to business personnel." It "includes abstracts and indexes, almanacs and yearbooks, bibliographies, online databases, research centers and institutes and much more." (Publisher's note)

Ferguson, Niall

★ The **ascent** of money; a financial history of the world. Penguin Press 2008 441p $29.95   **330**

1. Money 2. International finance 3. Economics -- History

ISBN 978-1-59420-192-9; 1-59420-192-7

The author "presents the history of money within these contexts: the rise of money and the history of credit, and the histories of the bond market, the stock market, insurance, the real-estate market, and international finance. There is an ease to his prose that leaves this complicated subject interesting to and approachable by any general reader." Booklist

Includes bibliographical references

Kwak, James

Economism; bad economics and the rise of inequality. James Kwak; foreword by Simon Johnson. Pantheon Books 2016 256 p. illustrations (hard cover: alk. paper) $25.95 **330**

1. Economics 2. Economic policy -- United States 3. Economic policy 4. Economics -- United States 5. United States -- Economic policy 6. Economics -- Sociological aspects

ISBN 9781101871195; 9781101871201

LC 2016024099

In this book about economism, author James Kwak "first offers a primer on supply and demand, market equilibrium, and social welfare: the underpinnings of most popular economic arguments. Then he provides a historical account of how economism became a prevalent mode of thought in the United States—focusing on the people who packaged Econ 101 into sound bites that were then repeated until they took on the aura of truth." (Publisher's note)

"It should be companion reading to every introductory economics text." Pub Wkly

Includes bibliographical references and index

Levitt, Steven D.

Superfreakonomics; global cooling, patriotic prostitutes, and why suicide bombers should buy life insurance. [by] Steven D. Levitt & Stephen J. Dubner. William Morrow 2009 270p $29.99; pa $15.99; ebook $9.99   **330**

1. Economics

ISBN 978-0-06-088957-9; 0-06-088957-8; 978-0-06-088958-6 pa; 0-06-088958-6 pa; 978-0-06-195993-6 ebook; 0-06-195993-6 ebook

LC 2009035852

Sequel to Freakonomics (2005)

The authors "assert that the unifying principle in the various topics they address is people responding to incentives in ways that are not necessarily predictable or manifest. Major themes are explored using a wide range of examples, e.g., life and death issues, terrorism, altruism, medical care, crime, and the environment. . . . Levitt and Dubner succeed in applying economic analysis to timely topics with stimulation, wit, and humor. Best of all, their book will appeal to a broad segment of the population." Choice

Includes bibliographical references

Mezrich, Ben

Once Upon a Time in Russia; The Rise of the Oligarchs. by Ben Mezrich. Pocket Books 2015 288 p. $28   **330**

1. Businessmen 2. Russia -- History -- 1991- 3. Russia -- History -- 1953-1991
ISBN 1476771898; 9781476771892

    LC 2015295889

This book, by Ben Mezrich, "is the untold true story of the larger-than-life billionaire oligarchs who surfed the waves of privatization to reap riches after the fall of the Soviet regime: 'Godfather of the Kremlin' Boris Berezovsky, a former mathematician whose first entrepreneurial venture was running an automobile reselling business, and Roman Abramovich, his dashing young protégé who built a multi-billion-dollar empire of oil and aluminum." (Publisher's note)

"Mezrich's ability to tell a true (and well-documented) story, in a way that makes it look and feel like the most involving of narratives, is nearly unparalleled. He is one of the few writers whose name on a piece of nonfiction guarantees not only quality but also interest, no matter the subject, and this fine book is one more example of just how talented a storyteller he is." Booklist

Oxford University Press

The **Oxford** encyclopedia of economic history; Joel Mokyr, editor in chief. Oxford University Press 2003 5v set $695 **330**

1. Reference books 2. Economic history -- Encyclopedias
ISBN 0-19-510507-9

    LC 2003-8992

This encyclopedia includes "over 900 contributions from 800 scholars to explore key concepts of economics, firms and individuals, institutions, countries, and cities. Although scholarly in tone, this volume is an excellent starting point for those wishing to trace ideas and industries across chronological boundaries." Libr J

Includes bibliographical references and index

Sowell, Thomas

Basic economics; a common sense guide to the economy. 4th ed.; Basic Books 2011 689p $39.95   **330**

1. Economics
ISBN 978-0-465-02252-6
First published 2000

Thomas Sowell explains the principles of economics in plain jargon for the general public, answering questions like: Why are homeless people sleeping on the sidewalks of New York in the winter, when the abandoned apartment buildings have four times as many dwelling units as there are homeless people in the city? Why did Russians have to import food to feed people in Moscow, when Russia itself had vast amounts of some of the richest farmland in Europe?

"Sowell's volume does a fantastic job in cultivating the reader's 'economic imagination.'" Choice

Taylor, Timothy

The **instant** economist; Timothy Taylor. Plume 2012 x, 260p.p ill. pa $16   **330**

1. Economics
ISBN 978-0-452-29752-4

    LC 2011033416

This book provides an introduction to "[e]conomics [which] isn't just about numbers: It's about politics, psychology, history, and so much more. We are all economists-when we work, save for the future, invest, pay taxes, and buy our groceries. Yet many of us feel lost when the subject arises. . . . Timothy Taylor tackles all the key questions and hot topics of both microeconomics and macroeconomics, including: Why do budget deficits matter? What exactly does the Federal Reserve do? Does globalization take jobs away from American workers? Why is health insurance so costly?" (Publisher's note)

Includes bibliographical references

Yunus, Muhammad, 1940-

A **world** of three zeros; the new economics of zero poverty, zero unemployment, and zero carbon emissions. Muhammad Yunus with Karl Weber. PublicAffairs 2017 vii, 288 p.p (hardcover) $28   **330**

1. Equality 2. Economics 3. Capitalism 4. Economic development 5. Sustainable development 6. Capitalism -- Social aspects 7. Equality -- Economic aspects 8. Social responsibility of business 9. Economic development -- Social aspects
ISBN 1610397576; 9781610397575

    LC 2017017988

"Yunus, winner of the Nobel Peace Prize and originator of microcredit, calls for capitalism to be more inclusive. He outlines a new economic system incorporating human selflessness, entrepreneurship, and opportunities for the poor. He espouses creating businesses that prioritize social outcomes over investor profits. In a social business, explains the author, the entrepreneur repays any invested capital within a period of time and then reinvests future profits to operate and expand the business. Yunus sets as goals eliminating poverty, unemployment, and environmental degradation. He demonstrates the possibilities of his vision with myriad examples including beekeeping in Kenya, industrial waste recycling in Japan, and solar energy in Bangladesh." (Library Journal)

Includes bibliographical references and index

330.01   Philosophy and theory

Roth, Alvin E., 1951-

Who gets what--and why; the new economics of matchmaking and market design. Alvin E. Roth. Eamon Dolan/Houghton Mifflin Harcourt 2015 272 p. (ebook) $15.95; (hardback) $28   **330.01**

1. Markets 2. Economics 3. Game theory 4. Matching theory
ISBN 9780544288393; 9780544291133

    LC 2015010771

This book, by Alvin E. Roth, "guides us through the jungles of modern life, pointing to the many markets that are hidden in plain view all around us. . . . Most of the study of economics deals with commodity markets, where the price of a good connects sellers and buyers. But what about other kinds of 'goods' like a spot in the Yale freshman class or a position at Google?" (Publisher's note)

"An exciting practical approach to economics that enables both individuals and institutions to achieve their goals without running afoul of the profit motive." Kirkus

Includes bibliographical references (pages 233-246) and index.

Thaler, Richard H., 1945-

Misbehaving; the making of behavioral economics. Richard H. Thaler. W W Norton & Co Inc 2015 432 p. illustrations (hardcover: alk. paper) $27.95   **330.01**

1. Human behavior 2. Economics -- Psychological aspects

ISBN 0393080943; 9780393080940

LC 2015004600

Author Richard Thaler won the Nobel Prize in Economics in 2017.

In this book, by Richard H. Thaler, "coupling recent discoveries in human psychology with a practical understanding of incentives and market behavior, . . . [the author] enlightens readers about how to make smarter decisions in an increasingly mystifying world. He reveals how behavioral economic analysis opens up new ways to look at everything from household finance to assigning faculty offices in a new building, to TV game shows, the NFL draft, and businesses like Uber." (Publisher's note)

"Misbehaving chronicles Thaler's participation in the development of behavioral economics, describes how it happened, and details some of what he and his colleagues learned along the way. This challenging book is written in an understandable manner and contains valuable insight for those interested in economics, psychology, other social sciences, public policy, and business." Booklist

Includes bibliographical references and index

330.1 Systems, schools, theories

Appleby, Joyce, 1929-2016

The **relentless** revolution; a history of capitalism. [by] Joyce Appleby. W.W. Norton 2010 494p $29.95   **330.1**

1. Capitalism 2. Economic conditions 3. Economic history 4. Capitalism -- History

ISBN 978-0-393-06894-8; 0-393-06894-3

LC 2009-35676

"Whether masterfully discussing the significance of agricultural progress that made capitalism possible, or touching lightly on the impact of Amazon and e-mail, Appleby offers consistently illuminating commentary. A useful introduction to a vast, complex topic." Kirkus

Includes bibliographical references

Heilbroner, Robert L.

★ The **worldly** philosophers; the lives, times, and ideas of the great economic thinkers. Rev. 7th ed.; Simon & Schuster 1999 365p pa $16   **330.1**

1. Authors 2. Utopias 3. Economics 4. Capitalism 5. Economists 6. Depressions 7. Imperialism 8. Journalists 9. Social critics 10. Nonfiction writers 11. Patrons of the arts 12. Writers on politics 13. Political and social philosophers

ISBN 0-684-86214-X

LC 99-14050

First published 1953

The author traces the story of economics and the great economists from Adam Smith, Malthus, Ricardo, the Utopians, Marx, Veblen and Keynes to those working with the problems of our contemporary world

Includes bibliographical references

Keynes, John Maynard

★ The **general** theory of employment, interest and money. Harcourt Brace & Co. 1936 403p hardcover o.p. pa $15 **330.1**

1. Money 2. Economics 3. Interest (Economics)

ISBN 0-15-634711-3 pa

This work "revolutionized economic theory by showing how unemployment could occur 'involuntarily'. For 30 years after the Second World War governments of western nations pursued 'Keynesian' full-employment policies." Oxford Companion to Engl Lit. 5th edition

Lanchester, John

How to Speak Money; What the Money People Say--and What It Really Means. John Lanchester. W W Norton & Co Inc 2014 288 p. illustrations $26.95   **330.1**

1. Economics 2. Personal finance 3. Economics -- Terminology

ISBN 0393243370; 9780393243376

LC 2014028529

In this book, John Lanchester "reveals how the world of finance really works: from the terms and conditions of your personal checking account to the evasions of bankers appearing in front of Congress. As Lanchester writes, we need to understand what the money people are talking about so that those who speak the language don't just write the rules for themselves." (Publisher's note)

"This entertaining, informative, useful reference, written in a lively style, is suitable for both practitioners and newcomers to the subject of economics." Choice

Includes bibliographical references and index

Marx, Karl

★ **Capital**: an abridged edition; edited with an introduction and notes by David McLellan. Oxford University Press 2008 xxxii, 499p (Oxford world's classics) pa $16.95   **330.1**

1. Capital 2. Economics

ISBN 978-0-19-953570-5

LC 2008-274361

Abridged edition first published 1995

This abridged edition of Marx's three-volume "denunciation of mid-Victorian capitalist society . . . offers virtually all of Volume 1, which Marx himself published in 1867; excerpts from a . . . translation of 'The Result of the Immediate Process Production'; and a selection of key chapters from Volume 3, which Engels published in 1895." Publisher's note

Patel, Raj

The **value** of nothing; how to reshape market society and redefine democracy. Picador 2010 250p pa $14   **330.1**

1. Democracy 2. Economic policy 3. Free enterprise

ISBN 978-0-312-42924-9

LC 2009-41546

The author "lays bare the social, political, and environmental damage caused by free markets and the commoditization of every facet of any market society. . . . Patel debunks the myth that markets are the perfect form of social organization, effectively arguing that the tyranny they exert can and must be replaced by strategies benefiting all humanity and ensuring our very survival. This work is written calmly and sensibly enough that it could change some readers' minds, although it will leave free-market apologists spluttering. Highly recommended." Libr J

Includes bibliographical references

Sandel, Michael J., 1953-

What money can't buy; the moral limits of markets. Michael J. Sandel. Farrar Straus & Giroux 2012 244 p.   **330.1**

1. Capitalism 2. Business ethics 3. Free enterprise 4. Economics -- Philosophy

ISBN 0374203032; 9780374203030

LC 2011052182

In this book author Michael J. Sandel "takes on . . . the . . . ethical questions . . . Is there something wrong with a world in which everything is for sale? If so, how can we prevent market values from reaching into spheres of life where they don't belong? What are the moral limits of markets? In recent decades, market values have crowded out nonmarket norms in almost every aspect of life, medicine, education, government, law, art, sports, even family life and personal relations. Without quite re-alizing it, Sandel argues, we have drifted from having a market economy to being a market society. . . . What is the proper role of markets in a democratic society, and how can we protect the moral and civic goods that markets don't honor and that money can't buy?"(Publisher's note)

Includes bibliographical references and index

Smith, Adam, 1723-1790

★ The **wealth** of nations; introduction by Robert Reich; edited, with notes, marginal summary, and enlarged index by Edwin Cannan. Modern Library 2000 xxvi, 1154p pa $15.95 **330.1**

  1. Economics

  ISBN 0-679-78336-9; 978-0-679-78336-7

                       LC 00-64573

  First published 1776

This treatise "is the first comprehensive treatment of the whole sub-ject of political economy, and is remarkable for its breadth of view. . . . In it, the author presents an attack on the mercantile system, and an advocacy of freedom of commerce and industry." Oxford Companion to Engl Lit. 6th edition

  Includes bibliographical references

330.12 Systems

King, Mervyn A., 1948-

The **End** of Alchemy; Money, Banking, and the Future of the Global Economy. by Mervyn King. W W Norton & Co Inc 2016 368 p. $28.95 **330.12**

  1. Money 2. Economics 3. Banks and banking

  ISBN 0393247023; 9780393247022

                      LC 2015048306

In this book, author Mervyn King "offers us an essential work about the history and future of money and banking, the keys to modern fi-nance. . . . Common paper became as precious as gold, and risky long-term loans were transformed into safe short-term bank deposits. As King argues, this is financial alchemy—the creation of extraordinary financial powers that defy reality and common sense." (Publisher's note)

King "provides a terrific analysis of what went wrong in the global financial system and with economics in general." LJ

  Includes bibliographical references and index.

McMillan, John

Reinventing the bazaar; a natural history of markets. Nor-ton 2002 278p $25.95; pa $15.95 **330.12**

  1. Capitalism

  ISBN 0-393-05021-1; 0-393-32371-4 pa

                      LC 2002-521

The author "examines how markets in ancient times evolved and shows how countries experimented with markets, some successfully and some not. . . . He takes a refreshingly commonsense approach to his subject, doesn't talk down to his readers, and refrains from excessive economic jargon." Libr J

  Includes bibliographical references

Soto, Hernando de

The **mystery** of capital; why captitalism triumphs in the West and fails everywhere else. Basic Bks. 2000 276p il $27.50; pa $17 **330.12**

  1. Capitalism

  ISBN 0-465-01614-6; 0-465-01615-4 pa

                      LC 00-34301

The author contends that "the poor do not really 'own' the property they work, because they are not registered as owning it, and because of this, they cannot turn it into capital. . . . The market is restricted and the growth of wealth retarded. His solution is simple: give the poor title to the property they own de facto, and their countries will become capital rich." N Y Times Book Rev

330.9 Economic situation and conditions

Bartiromo, Maria

The **weekend** that changed Wall Street; an eyewitness ac-count. [by] Maria Bartiromo, with Catherine Whitney. Portfo-lio Penguin 2010 232p $26.95 **330.9**

  1. Bank failures 2. Global Financial Crisis, 2008-2009

  ISBN 978-1-59184-351-1

                      LC 2010026892

"Bartiromo lays out the facts of the Lehman Brothers downfall using both her own account and those of the most powerful people on Wall Street. . . . The most fascinating aspects of . . . [this book] were not so much the details of the collapse . . . but the book's early focus on the lavish lives of those involved in the Wall Street game; Bartiromo details the parties they threw, the apartments they owned that resembled art galleries and the confidence they exuded, which came across not only in their business conversations, but also in the casual talks between the author and her trusting subjects. " Risk Management

  Includes bibliographical references

De Graaf, John

What's the economy for, anyway? why it's time to stop chasing growth and start pursuing happiness. [by] John de Graaf and David K. Batker; foreword by James Gustave Speth. Bloomsbury Press 2011 292p il $25 **330.9**

  1. Happiness 2. Economic development 3. United States -- Economic conditions

  ISBN 978-1-60819-510-7; 1-60819-510-4

                      LC 2011017438

De Graaf and Batker "examine new ways to think about economic processes, specifically as they relate to human happiness and well-being. The authors show that the indicators of performance developed during World War II—the 'Gross National Product'—have become both ob-scurantist and counterproductive. They argue that human purposes and needs ought to provide the basis for much more broadly based measures of performance, which would consider what is the greatest good and benefit for the greatest number of people over the longest period of time. . . . An entertaining presentation of important ideas and information about how lives could be improved." Kirkus

  Includes bibliographical references

Epping, Randy Charles

The **21st** century economy; a beginner's guide: with 101 easy-to-learn tools for surviving and thriving in the new global marketplace. Vintage Books 2009 316p pa $14.95 **330.9**

  1. Globalization 2. Economic conditions 3. International trade 4. International finance

  ISBN 978-0-307-38790-5

                      LC 2008-41554

This is an "explanation of the workings of our modern economy and hundreds of terms, such as subprime debt, CDO, IMF, money supply, and discount rate. . . . [The author] is able to explain the global economy in language that most readers will find both understandable and interesting." Libr J

Hickel, Jason

The **divide**; global inequality from conquest to free markets. Jason Hickel. W W Norton & Co Inc 2018 344 p. illustrations (hardcover) $26.95   **330.9**

1. Poverty 2. Equality 3. Globalization 4. Economic history
ISBN 9780393651362; 0393651363; 9780393651379

LC 2017052787

In this book, author Jason Hickel, "argues that . . . global poverty--and the growing inequality between the rich countries of Europe and North America and the poor ones of Africa, Asia, and South America--has come about because the global economy has been designed over the course of five hundred years of conquest, colonialism, regime change, and globalization to favor the interests of the richest and most powerful nations." (Publisher's note)

"A sharply argued analysis of the traditional explanations for wealth and poverty in the world, offering a program for easing misery while addressing structural inequalities." Kirkus

Includes bibliographical references (pages 287-328) and index.

Huffington, Arianna

Third World America; how our politicians are abandoning the middle class and betraying the American dream. Crown Publishers 2010 276p $23.99; ebook $9.99   **330.9**

1. Social policy -- United States 2. Economic policy -- United States 3. United States -- Politics and government -- 2001-
ISBN 978-0-307-71982-9; 978-0-307-71997-3 ebook

LC 2010-26871

The author "argues that overspending on war at the expense of domestic issues and the alarming decline of the middle class are troubling signals that the U.S. is losing its economic, political, and social stability—a stability that has always been maintained by the middle class. . . . An engaging analysis of troubling economic and political trends." Booklist

Krugman, Paul R., 1953-

★ **End** this depression now! Paul Krugman. W.W. Norton & Co. 2012 xii, 259 p.p ill. $24.95   **330.9**

1. Recessions 2. Unemployment 3. Economic policy -- United States 4. United States -- Economic conditions 5. United States -- Economic policy -- 21st century 6. Recessions -- United States -- History -- 21st century 7. Unemployment -- United States -- History -- 21st century 8. Financial crises -- United States -- History -- 21st century
ISBN 0393088774; 9780393088779

LC 2012009067

This book, by Nobel Prize-winning economist Paul Krugman, discusses the U.S. Great Recession of 2008 and following. It asks why "'nations rich in resources, talent, and knowledge--all the ingredients for prosperity and a decent standard of living for all--remain in a state of intense pain.' . . . How did we get stuck in what now can only be called a depression? And above all, how do we free ourselves?" (Publisher's note)

"Krugman's forceful jargon-free criticisms and solutions directed at a general audience are a thoughtful contribution to both economic and political discourse in this election year. Highly recommended for a broad readership." LJ

Lanchester, John

★ **I.O.U.** why everyone owes everyone and no one can pay. Simon & Schuster 2010 260p $25   **330.9**

1. Economic conditions 2. International finance 3. Global Financial Crisis, 2008-2009
ISBN 978-1-4391-6984-1; 1-4391-6984-5

LC 2009-36465

This book is "equal parts history, economic primer, and social commentary—that manages to be, by turns, acidic, frightening, and sharply funny." Entertainment Wkly

Includes bibliographical references

Lewis, Michael

The **big** short; inside the doomsday machine. W.W. Norton 2010 266p   **330.9**

1. Financial crises 2. Global Financial Crisis, 2008-2009 3. Financial crises -- United States 4. United States -- Economic conditions 5. United States -- Economic conditions -- 2001-2009
ISBN 0-393-07223-1; 0-393-33882-7 pa; 978-0-393-07223-5; 978-0-393-33882-9 pa

LC 201004804

This is a study of the financial crisis that began in 2008. Michael Lewis, the author of Liar's Poker (1989) contends that "the roots of the meltdown of 2008 can be found in the 1980s, . . . when complex financial products like mortgage derivatives were developed." (N Y Times (Late N Y Ed))

"'The Big Short' manages to give us the truest picture yet of what went wrong on Wall Street—and why. At times, it reads like a morality play, at other times like a modern-day farce. But as with any good play, its value lies in the way it reveals character and motive and explores the cultural context in which the plot unfolds." Washington Post

Liveris, Andrew

Make it in America; the case for re-inventing the economy. Wiley 2011 xxi, 208p il $24.95; ebook $16.99   **330.9**

1. Manufactures 2. Economic forecasting 3. Industrial policy -- United States 4. United States -- Economic conditions
ISBN 978-0-470-93022-9; 0-470-93022-5; 9781118019405 ebook

LC 2010045654

The author "calls for a national strategy to revive manufacturing. We need manufacturing jobs, he says, if we are to keep a growing population busy and start paying off our debts to the rest of the world." Wall Street J

Includes bibliographical references

Madrick, Jeffrey G.

Age of greed; the triumph of finance and the decline of America, 1970 to the present. [by] Jeff Madrick. Alfred A. Knopf 2011 464p il $30; ebook $14.99   **330.9**

1. Wealth 2. Financial crises 3. Capitalists and financiers 4. Wealth -- Moral and ethical aspects 5. Financial crises -- United States -- History 6. United States -- Economic policy -- 2001-2009 7. United States -- Economic policy -- 20th century 8. United States -- Politics and government -- 20th century 9. United States -- Politics and government -- 21st century
ISBN 978-1-4000-4171-8; 978-0-307-59671-0 ebook

LC 2011003399

This book "is a fascinating and deeply disturbing tale of hypocrisy, corruption, and insatiable greed. But more than that, it's a much-needed reminder of just how we got into the mess we're in—a reminder that is greatly needed when we are still being told that greed is good." New York Rev Books

Includes bibliographical references

Martínez, Rubén

Desert America; boom and bust in the new Old West.

Rubén Martínez. Metropolitan Books/ Henry Holt and Company 2012 333 p. $28.00 **330.9**
1. Poverty 2. West (U.S.) 3. Drugs and crime 4. Immigrants -- United States 5. New Mexico -- Race relations 6. New Mexico -- Social conditions -- 21st century 7. New Mexico -- Economic conditions -- 21st century
ISBN 0805079777; 9780805079777

LC 2011040587

"In this first-person report . . . [Rubén] Martínez . . . sojourns in the more remote regions of the Southwest . . . and finds the front line of a battle over the American past and future. . . . Martínez does his best to immerse himself in a largely Latino community that is extremely aware of outsiders, weighing the stark realities of his neighbors' lives while musing on disparities and dislocations teaching back hundreds of years." (Publishers Weekly)

McLean, Bethany
All the devils are here; the hidden history of the financial crisis. [by] Bethany McLean and Joe Nocera. Portfolio/Penguin 2010 380p il $32.95 **330.9**
1. Mortgages 2. International finance 3. Global Financial Crisis, 2008-2009 4. Mortgage-backed securities 5. Financial crises -- United States
ISBN 978-1-59184-363-4; 1-59184-363-4

LC 2010-32893

This is an "account of the late financial meltdown, when, in the words of one analyst, 'we went from a collective belief in soundness to a collective belief in insolvency.' . . . Hard-hitting reporting and fluent writing bring the utter devastation of the Great Recession to life." Kirkus
Includes bibliographical references

Paulson, Henry M.
★ **On** the brink; inside the race to stop the collapse of the global financial system. Business Plus 2010 478p il $28.99 **330.9**
1. Global Financial Crisis, 2008-2009 2. Economic policy -- United States
ISBN 978-0-446-56193-8; 0-446-56193-2

LC 2009-939043

"This is the ultimate insider's account of the crisis, and, owing to its evenhanded tone and penetrating insights into government actions, it will also remain an important contribution to the historical record of the crisis, essential reading for everyone interested in knowing what happened." Libr J

Perino, Michael A.
The **hellhound** of Wall Street; how Ferdinand Pecora's investigation of the Great Crash forever changed American finance. [by] Michael Perino. Penguin Press 2010 341p il $27.95 **330.9**
1. Judges 2. Lawyers 3. Stock exchanges 4. Financial crises 5. Stock market crash, 1929 6. Regulatory agency officials
ISBN 978-1-59420-272-8

LC 2010-19157

The author "recounts the 1933 investigation into Wall Street abuses by the Senate Committee on Banking and Currency, focusing on the 10-day interrogation by chief counsel Ferdinand Pecora of executives of National City Bank (precursor to Citigroup). . . . Perino's book is a trenchant, entertaining study of the New Deal's heroic beginnings, one with obvious relevance to latter-day efforts to rein in Wall Street's excesses." Publ Wkly
Includes bibliographical references

Phillips-Fein, Kim
★ **Fear** city; New York's fiscal crisis and the rise of austerity politics. Kimberly Phillips-Fein. Metropolitan Books 2017 xii, 401 p.p (hardback) $32 **330.9**
1. Financial crises 2. New York (N.Y.) -- History 3. Fiscal policy -- United States -- History 4. New York (N.Y.) -- Politics and government 5. New York (State) -- New York -- Economic conditions -- 20th century 6. Fiscal policy -- New York (State) -- New York -- History -- 20th century 7. Financial crises -- New York (State) -- New York -- History -- 20th century
ISBN 9780805095258

LC 2016033559

Pulitzer Prize Finalist: History (2018)

This book, by Kimberly Phillips-Fein, presents a "history of New York City on the edge of disaster--and an anatomy of the austerity politics that continue to shape the world today. When the news broke in 1975 that New York City was on the brink of fiscal collapse, few believed it was possible. How could the country's largest metropolis fail? How could the capital of the financial world go bankrupt?" (Publisher's note)

"Paced like a thriller and extremely well written, the book chronicles the slow descent of the city into a fiscal abyss and its unlikely rescue by a group of hardened bureaucrats, altruistic investment bankers, and political power players . . . ." Pub Wkly Annex
Includes bibliographical references and index

Piscione, Deborah Perry
Secrets of Silicon Valley; what everyone else can learn from the innovation capital of the world. Deborah Perry Piscione. Palgrave Macmillan 2013 256 p. (hardcover) $27 **330.9**
1. High technology industry 2. Santa Clara Valley (Santa Clara County, Calif.) -- Economic conditions 3. Technological innovations -- California -- Santa Clara County 4. High technology industries -- California -- Santa Clara County
ISBN 0230342116; 9780230342118

LC 2012038481

This book, by Deborah Perry Piscione, explores the economics of Silicon Valley. "While the global economy languishes, one place just keeps growing . . .: Silicon Valley. . . . Piscione takes us inside this vibrant ecosystem where meritocracy rules the day. She explores Silicon Valley's exceptionally risk-tolerant culture, and why it thrives despite the many laws that make California one of the worst states in the union for business." (Publisher's note)

Reich, Robert B.
Aftershock; the next economy and America's future. Alfred A. Knopf 2010 174p il $25; ebook $11.99 **330.9**
1. United States -- Economic policy 2. United States -- Social conditions 3. United States -- Economic conditions 4. United States -- Social conditions -- Forecasting
ISBN 978-0-307-59281-1; 0-307-59281-2; 978-0-307-59452-5 ebook

LC 2010-04134

Reich "argues that America will not have a sustained economic recovery until the middle class has more buying power. In this call for reform, the author writes that the increasing concentration of wealth among a small percentage of Americans was the main culprit in the destabilization of the U.S. economy in 2008. . . . Lucid and cogent." Kirkus
Includes bibliographical references

Sachs, Jeffrey, 1954-
The **price** of civilization; reawakening American virtue and prosperity. Random House 2011 324p il $27; ebook

$12.99   **330.9**

1. Economic policy -- United States 2. United States -- Economic policy -- 2009- 3. Environmental responsibility -- United States 4. United States -- Economic conditions -- 2009- 5. Social responsibility of business -- United States 6. United States -- Economic conditions -- 21st century 7. United States -- Politics and government -- 21st century

ISBN 9781400068418; 140006841X; 9780679605027 ebook; 0679605029 ebook

LC 2011014631

The author "explores the economic, political, social, and psychological roots of the U.S.'s 30-year journey 'from decades of consensus and high achievement to an era of deep division and growing crisis.' He indicts America's elites for abandoning social responsibility, politicians for giving up on solving problems, the media for distraction and hyper-commercialization, and citizens for surrendering to that distraction. He urges mindfulness, clear goals for political reform, and significant tax changes, and he suggests that the millennial generation will lead the way to a restoration of the nation's highest aspirations" Booklist

Includes bibliographical references (p. [277]-307) and index.

Sharma, Ruchir

The **rise** and fall of nations; forces of change in the post-crisis world. Ruchir Sharma. W W Norton & Co Inc 2016 480 p. maps (ebook) $50; (hardcover) $27.95   **330.9**

1. Economic conditions 2. Economic forecasting 3. Global Financial Crisis, 2008-2009 4. State, The 5. Economic history -- 21st century

ISBN 9780393248906; 9780393248890

LC 2016012023

This book, by Ruchir Sharma, "rethinks the 'dismal science' of economics as a practical art. Narrowing the thousands of factors that can shape a country's fortunes to ten clear rules, Sharma explains how to spot political, economic, and social changes in real time. He shows how to read political headlines, black markets, the price of onions, and billionaire rankings as signals of booms, busts, and protests." (Publisher's note)

"Evenhanded, measured, sage advice on the global economy." Kirkus

Includes bibliographical references and index

Sorkin, Andrew Ross

★ **Too** big to fail; the inside story of how Wall Street and Washington fought to save the financial system from crisis--and themselves. Viking 2009 xx, 600p il pa $18; $32.95 **330.9**

1. Financial crises 2. Global Financial Crisis, 2008-2009 3. Financial crises -- United States 4. United States -- Economic policy -- 2001-2009

ISBN 0-14-311824-2 pa; 0-670-02125-3; 978-0-14-311824-4 pa; 978-0-670-02125-3

LC 2009-36494

This is an account of the recent financial crisis.

"Sorkin boasts of the hours spent interviewing, emailing, inspecting telephone call logs, billing time sheets and even expense reports [for this book], and his reward is the fullest and most convincing account of the Lehman debacle. Conversations are reconstructed, and an air of authenticity created by the accumulation of thousands of small facts." Times Lit Suppl

Includes bibliographical references

330.91   Areas, regions, places in general

Sharma, Ruchir

★ **Breakout** nations; in pursuit of the next economic miracles. Ruchir Sharma. W.W. Norton & Co. 2012 x, 292 p.p $26.95   **330.91**

1. Economic development 2. Economic forecasting 3. Developing countries -- Economic conditions 4. Economic history -- 21st century

ISBN 0393080269; 9780393080261

LC 2012005810

This book, by Ruchir Sharma, examines how "[a]fter a decade of rapid growth, the world's most celebrated emerging markets are poised to slow down. . . . To identify the economic stars of the future we should abandon the habit of extrapolating from the recent past and lumping wildly diverse countries together. . . . What emerges is a clear picture of the shifting balance of global economic power and how it plays out for emerging nations and for the West." (Publisher's note)

Includes bibliographical references and index.

330.941   Economics – British Isles

Satia, Priya

Empire of guns; the violent making of the Industrial Revolution. Priya Satia. Penguin Group USA 2018 544 p. $35   **330.941**

1. Firearms industry 2. Historical literature 3. Industrial revolution

ISBN 0735221863; 9780735221864

This book, by Priya Satia, "[places] war and Britain's prosperous gun trade at the heart of the Industrial Revolution and the state's imperial expansion. Satia brings to life this bustling industrial society with the story of a scandal: Samuel Galton of Birmingham, one of Britain's most prominent gunmakers, has been condemned by his fellow Quakers, who argue that his profession violates the society's pacifist principles." (Publisher's note)

330.973   Economics – United States

Alexander, Brian

Glass House; The 1% Economy and the Shattering of the All-American Town. by Brian Alexander. St. Martin's Press 2017 336 p. $26.99; (ebook) $60   **330.973**

1. United States -- Economic conditions 2. Economic policy -- United States -- History

ISBN 1250085802; 9781250085801; 9781250085818

LC 2016044045

In this book, "journalist Brian Alexander uses the story of one town to show how seeds sown 35 years ago have sprouted to give us Trumpism, inequality, and an eroding national cohesion. The Anchor Hocking Glass Company, once the world's largest maker of glass tableware, was the base on which Lancaster's society was built. . . . With access to the company and its leaders, and Lancaster's citizens, Alexander shows how financial engineering took hold in the 1980s, accelerated in the 21st Century, and wrecked the company." (Publisher's note)

"This is a particularly timely read for our tumultuous and divisive era." Pub Wkly

Includes bibliographical references (pages 301-312) and index.

Barlett, Donald L.

The **betrayal** of the American dream; Donald L. Barlett

and James B. Steele. 1st ed. PublicAffairs 2012 xxi, 289 p.p ill. (hardcover) $26.99; (ebook) $26.99 **330.973**
1. Middle class -- United States 2. Economic policy -- United States 3. United States -- Economic conditions 4. United States -- Economic policy -- 2009- 5. United States -- Economic conditions -- 2009- 6. Middle class -- United States -- Economic conditions -- 21st century 7. Working class -- United States -- Economic conditions -- 21st century
ISBN 1586489690; 9781586489694; 9781586489700
LC 2012012879
In this book, authors Donald L. Barlett and James B. Steele "maintain that the deficit is less the result of government programs than plummeting tax revenue from the rich. . . . The authors' solutions include: Revise the tax code so corporations and the rich pay more than the middle class instead of less, discard the clueless ideology of free trade . . . re-regulate disastrously unregulated areas, and enforce current laws equally instead of giving the influential a free pass." (Kirkus Reviews)
Includes bibliographical references and index.

Blinder, Alan S.
After the music stopped; the financial crisis, the response, and the work ahead. Alan S. Blinder. Penguin Press 2013 xix, 476 p.p ill. (hardcover) $29.95 **330.973**
1. Global Financial Crisis, 2008-2009 2. United States -- Economic conditions 3. Finance -- United States 4. Financial crises -- United States 5. United States -- Economic policy -- 2009- 6. United States -- Economic conditions -- 2009-
ISBN 1594205302; 9781594205309
LC 2012031025
In this book, "[Alan S.] Blinder, a corporate executive and former vice chairman of the Federal Reserve, sets out to tell the American people what happened during the financial crisis of 2007-09. He explains the events that are still reverberating in the U.S. and globally and will challenge public policy for years." (Booklist)
Includes bibliographical references (p. [455]-462) and index.

Dayen, David
Chain of title; how three ordinary Americans uncovered Wall Street's great foreclosure fraud. David Dayen. The New Press 2016 320 p. (hardback) $27.95; (ebook) $17.99 **330.973**
1. Global Financial Crisis, 2008-2009 2. Foreclosure -- United States -- Corrupt practices 3. Global Financial Crisis, 2008-2009 -- Popular works 4. Foreclosure -- United States -- Corrupt practices -- Popular works
ISBN 9781620971581; 9781620971598
LC 2016005544
This book, by David Dayen, describes how "in the depths of the Great Recession, a cancer nurse, a car dealership worker, and an insurance fraud specialist helped uncover the largest consumer crime in American history. . . . While struggling with their shame and isolation they committed a revolutionary act: closely reading their mortgage documents, discovering the deceit behind them, and building a movement to expose it." (Publisher's note)
"Dayen relates how prosecutors, judges, and the Department of Justice have caved to powerful mortgage industry donors while illegal foreclosures continue. An inspiring, well-rendered, deeply reported, and often infuriating account." Kirkus
Includes bibliographical references and index

Ferguson, Charles
Predator nation; corporate criminals, political corruption, and the hijacking of America. Charles Ferguson. Crown Business 2012 vii, 369 p.p ill. $27.00 **330.973**
1. Securities fraud 2. Elite (Social sciences) 3. Wall Street (New York, N.Y.) 4. Manufacturing industries -- United States 5. Equality -- United States 6. United States -- Economic policy 7. Financial crises -- United States 8. Banks and banking -- United States 9. Global Financial Crisis, 2008-2009 10. United States -- Politics and government 11. United States -- Economic conditions -- 2009-
ISBN 030795255X; 9780307952554
LC 2011052366
In this book, "author Charles H. Ferguson . . . explains how a predator elite took over the country, step by step, and he exposes the networks of academic, financial, and political influence, in all recent administrations, that prepared the predators' path to conquest." Topics include the decline of the manufacturing industry, fraud in the finance industry, and income inequality in the U.S. (Publisher's note)
Includes bibliographical references (p. 333-349) and index

Greenspan, Alan, 1926-
Capitalism in America; a history. Alan Greenspan, Adrian Wooldridge. Penguin Press 2018 496 p. (hardback) $35 **330.973**
1. Capitalism 2. United States -- Economic conditions 3. Economic policy -- United States -- History 4. Economic history 5. United States -- Economic policy 6. Capitalism -- United States -- History
ISBN 9780735222441
LC 2018020397
This book, by Alan Greenspan and Adrian Wooldridge, presents "the full, epic story of America's evolution from a small patchwork of threadbare colonies to the most powerful engine of wealth and innovation the world has ever seen. . . . [T]he authors argue [that] America's genius has been its unique tolerance for the effects of creative destruction, the ceaseless churn of the old giving way to the new, driven by new people and new ideas." (Publisher's note)

Lind, Michael, 1962-
Land of promise; an economic history of the United States. by Michael Lind. Broadside Books 2012 586 p. (hardback) $29.99 **330.973**
1. United States -- History 2. Technological innovations -- History 3. United States -- Economic conditions
ISBN 0061834807; 9780061834806; 9780061834813
LC 2011047794
Author Michael Lind presents an "account of how a weak collection of former British colonies became an industrial, financial, and military colossus. From the eighteenth to the twenty-first centuries, the American economy has been transformed by wave after wave of emerging technology: the steam engine, electricity, the internal combustion engine, computer technology." Lind "demonstrates that Americans, since the earliest days of the republic, have reinvented the American economy--and have the power to do so again." (Publisher's note)

McCraw, Thomas K., 1940-2012
★ The **founders** and finance; how Hamilton, Gallatin, and other immigrants forged a new economy. Thomas K. McCraw. Belknap Press of Harvard University Press 2012 485 p. (hardcover) $35 **330.973**
1. Fiscal policy -- United States -- History 2. United States -- Economic policy 3. United States -- History -- 1783-1865 4. Finance, Public -- United States -- History 5. Monetary policy -- United States -- History 6. United States. Dept. of the Treasury -- History 7. United States -- History -- Revolution, 1775-1783 8. United States -- Politics and government -- 1783-1865

ISBN 0674066928; 9780674066922

LC 2012014006

This book, by Thomas K. McCraw, shows how "analyzes the skills and worldliness of Alexander Hamilton . . . , Albert Gallatin . . . , and other immigrant founders who guided the [United States] to prosperity. . . . Innovations designed by Hamilton, Gallatin, and other immigrants enabled the United States to control its debts, to pay for the Louisiana Purchase of 1803, and . . . preserve[] the nation's hard-won independence from Britain." (Publisher's note)

"McCraw is a talented storyteller. His highly readable and fascinating work portrays the brilliance of Hamilton and Gallatin against the difficulty of their time and is strongly recommended to all readers interested in American and financial history." LJ

Includes bibliographical references and index

Nations, Scott

A **history** of the United States in five crashes; stock market meltdowns that defined a nation. Scott Nations. William Morrow, an imprint of HarperCollinsPublishers 2017 xiv, 336 p.p (hardcover) $28.99   **330.973**

1. Stock exchanges 2. Financial crises 3. Stock exchanges -- United States -- History -- 20th century 4. Stock exchanges -- United States -- History -- 21st century 5. Financial crises -- United States -- History -- 20th century 6. Financial crises -- United States -- History -- 21st century

ISBN 9780062467270; 9780062467294; 0062467271

In this book author "Scott Nations, a longtime trader, financial engineer, and CNBC contributor, takes [readers] on a journey through the five significant stock market crashes in the past century to reveal how they defined the United States today. Taken together they tell the larger story of a nation reaching enormous heights of financial power while experiencing precipitous dips that alter and reset a market where millions of Americans invest their savings, and on which they depend for their futures." (Publisher's note)

"An eye-opening examination of the many ways money can be made—and disappear." Kirkus

Includes bibliographical references (pages 303-320) and index.

Reich, Robert B.

Saving capitalism; for the many, not the few. Robert B. Reich. Alfred A. Knopf 2015 304 p. illustrations (hardcover: alk. paper) $26.95   **330.973**

1. Capitalism 2. Economic policy -- United States 3. Business and politics -- United States 4. Capitalism -- United States 5. Income distribution -- United States 6. Democracy -- Economic aspects -- United States

ISBN 9780345806222; 9780385350570

LC 2015001873

In this book, author Robert B. Reich exposes "one of the most pernicious obstructions to progress today: the enduring myth of the 'free market' when, behind the curtain, it is the powerful alliances between Washington and Wall Street that control the invisible hand. . . . Reich shows that the truly critical choice ahead is between a market organized for broad-based prosperity and one designed to deliver ever more gains to the top." (Publisher's note)

"Reich's overriding message is that we don't have to put up with things as they are. It's a useful and necessary one, if not likely to sway the powers that be to become more generous of their own volition." Kirkus

Includes bibliographical references and index

Stone, James M.

Five easy theses; common-sense solutions to America's greatest economic challenges. James M. Stone. Houghton Mifflin Harcourt 2016 288 p. (hardcover) $26   **330.973**

1. Social policy -- United States 2. Economic policy -- United States 3. United States -- Social conditions 4. United States -- Economic conditions -- 2009- 5. United States -- Social policy -- 1993- 6. United States -- Economic policy -- 2009- 7. United States -- Social conditions -- 1980-

ISBN 9780544749009

LC 2015037880

In this book, author James M. Stone "presents specific, common-sense solutions to a handful of our most pressing challenges, showing how simple it would be to shore up Social Security, rein in an out-of-control financial sector, reduce inequality, and make healthcare and education better and more affordable." (Publisher's note)

"In a presidential election year, Stone does a wonderful job summarizing these critical topics clearly for a wide readership" LJ

Includes bibliographical references and index.

331   Economics of labor, finance, land, energy

Crawford, Matthew B.

Shop class as soulcraft; an inquiry into the value of work. Penguin Press 2009 246p il $25.95   **331**

1. Work

ISBN 978-1-59420-223-0

LC 2009-1789

The author "extols the value of making and fixing things in this masterful paean to what he calls 'manual competence,' the ability to work with one's hands. . . . With wit and humor, the author deftly mixes the details of his own experience as a tradesman and then proprietor of a motorcycle repair shop with more philosophical considerations." Publ Wkly

Includes bibliographical references

De Botton, Alain, 1969-

The **pleasures** and sorrows of work. Pantheon Books 2009 326p il $26   **331**

1. Work 2. Labor 3. Work -- Social aspects

ISBN 978-0-375-42444-1

LC 2008-46060

In this study of the workplace, the author visits "the under-charted worlds of the office, the factory, the fishing fleet and the logistics centre. . . . [He discusses such questions about work as]: Why do we do it? What makes it pleasurable? What is its meaning? And why do we daily exhaust not only ourselves but also the planet?" (Publisher's note)

"De Botton's sprightly mix of reportage and rumination expands beyond the workplace to investigate the broader meaning of life." Publ Wkly

Murolo, Priscilla

From the folks who brought you the weekend; a short, illustrated history of labor in the United States. {by} Priscilla Murolo and A.B. Chitty; illustrations by Joe Sacco. New Press (NY) 2001 xx, 364p hardcover o.p. pa $17.95   **331**

1. Working class 2. Labor movement 3. Labor -- United States

ISBN 1-56584-776-8 pa

LC 2001-30978

"Brandishing little-known facts, the authors reshape common views of social history." Publ Wkly

Includes bibliographical references

Murray, R. Emmett

★ The **lexicon** of labor; more than 500 key terms, biographical sketches, and historical insights concerning labor in America. Rev. and updated ed.; New Press 2010 235p pa $16.95 **331**

1. Reference books 2. Labor -- United States -- Dictionaries
ISBN 978-1-59558-226-3

LC 2010-8276

First published 1998

This is an "encyclopedia of 500 entries for terms, concepts, people, legislation, places, and events in U.S. labor history." Booklist

Includes bibliographical references

331.1 Labor force and market

Johnson, Jean

Where did the jobs go-- and how do we get them back? your guided tour to America's employment crisis. Scott Bittle and Jean Johnson. WilliamMorrow 2012 xix, 342 p.p (paperback) $16.99 **331.1**

1. Employment 2. Unemployment 3. United States -- Economic conditions 4. Employment (Economic theory) 5. Unemployment -- United States 6. Unemployment -- Government policy -- United States
ISBN 0061715662; 9780061715662

LC 2012371737

This book by Scott Bittle and Jean Johnson presents a "discussion and study guide on unemployment. . . . The authors provide a[n] . . . analysis of the many problems caused by the unemployment crisis, as well as possible solutions. . . . The authors . . . provide a[n] . . . historical discussion of the 1930s Depression and FDR's WPA program, as well as estimates of the financial costs of possible solutions and the ramifications for other sectors of American society." (Kirkus Reviews)

Includes bibliographical references (p. [302]-342)

Taylor, Nick

★ **American**-made; the enduring legacy of the WPA: when FDR put the nation to work. Bantam Books 2008 630p il $27 **331.1**

1. New Deal, 1933-1939 2. United States -- Works Progress Administration
ISBN 978-0-553-80235-1; 0-553-80235-6

LC 2007-34563

"Lavishly illustrated, the book also has a list of New Deal organizations, a partial list of construction projects, a New Deal chronology, and endnotes. It will be a boon to all 20th-century history collections." Libr J

Includes bibliographical references

Woodward, Bob, 1943-

Maestro: Greenspan's Fed and the American boom. Simon & Schuster 2000 270p il $25; pa $14 **331.1**

1. Economists 2. Bankers 3. Government officials 4. Presidential advisers 5. Regulatory agency officials 6. Monetary policy -- United States 7. Board of Governors of the Federal Reserve System 8. Federal Reserve System (U.S.) -- Board of Governors 9. Monetary policy -- United States -- History -- 20th century
ISBN 0-7432-0412-3; 0-7432-0562-6 pa

LC 00-52627

Woodward discusses the influence exerted over the American economy by the chairman of the Federal Reserve Board, Alan Greenspan. Index.

"In a surprisingly short book, Woodward lucidly explains the axes of intellectual and political disagreement over monetary policy, productivity growth, irrational exuberance and more, shedding new light on major conflicts of the Greenspan era and demystifying this most political of ostensibly technical institutions." N Y Times Book Rev

Includes bibliographical references

331.13 Discrimination in employment, labor shortages, unemployment

Ford, Martin

Rise of the robots; technology and the threat of a jobless future. Martin Ford. Basic Books 2015 352 p. illustrations (hardback) $28.99 **331.13**

1. Labor supply 2. Industrial robots 3. Technological innovations 4. Employment forecasting 5. Labor supply -- Effect of automation on 6. Technological innovations -- Economic aspects 7. Labor supply -- Effect of technological innovations on
ISBN 0465059996; 9780465059997

LC 2014041327

"As technology continues to accelerate and machines begin taking care of themselves, fewer people will be necessary. Ford details what machine intelligence and robotics can accomplish, and implores employers, scholars, and policy makers alike to face the implications." (Publisher's note)

Includes bibliographical references and index

331.2 Conditions of employment

Clifford, Steven

The **CEO** pay machine; how it trashes America and how to stop it. Steven Clifford. Blue Rider Press 2017 277 p. illustrations (hardcover) $23 **331.2**

1. Corporate governance 2. Salaries, wages, etc. 3. Executives -- Salaries, etc. 4. Executives -- Salaries, etc. -- United States
ISBN 0735212392; 9780735212404; 9780735212398

LC 2016052097

This book, by Steven Clifford, "examines the scandalous and corrupt reasons behind obscene pay packages for corporate executives--and explains how this hurts all of us--and how we can stop it. . . . 'The CEO Pay Machine' is Clifford's thorough and shocking explanation of the 'machine'--how it works, how its parts interact, and how every step pushes CEO pay to higher levels." (Publisher's note)

"Clifford . . . takes an enlightening and refreshingly candid look at the contentious topic of chief executive compensation." Pub Wkly

Includes bibliographical references (pages [239]-263) and index.

Jayaraman, Saru

Forked; a new standard for American dining. Saru Jayaraman. Oxford University Press 2016 240 p. illustrations (hardcover) $24.95 **331.2**

1. Restaurants 2. Salaries, wages, etc.
ISBN 9780199380473; 0199380473

LC 2015033657

This book, by Saru Jayaraman, "is an enlightening examination of what we don't talk about when we talk about restaurants. . . . [The author] offers an insider's view of the highest--and lowest--scoring restaurants for worker pay and benefits in each sector of the restaurant industry, and with it, a new way of thinking about how and where we eat." (Publisher's note)

"A revealing exposé of the realities of restaurant work that makes a strong case for reform." Kirkus

Includes bibliographical references and index.

Schultz, Ellen

Retirement heist; how companies plunder and profit from the nest eggs of American workers. [by] Ellen E. Schultz. Portfolio/Penguin 2011 245p $26.95   **331.2**

1. Pensions 2. Corporations 3. Life insurance
ISBN 978-1-59184-333-7; 1-59184-333-2

LC 2011015064

"Readers are no stranger to the grumblings of their corporate overlords: Pensions are untenable; health-care costs too high; retiree benefits hurt competitiveness. But according to . . . Schultz, employee pensions actually make money for corporations, and the funds diverted from them help feather the beds of multimillionaire executives. She exposes all this and more in a rapid-fire narrative. Individual stories of retired men and women (some with more than 40 years of service) robbed of their nest eggs put a human face on the proceedings. . . . Essential reading for anyone who works for a living." Kirkus

Includes bibliographical references

Terkel, Studs, 1912-2008

Working; people talk about what they do all day and how they feel about what they do. The New Press 1997 589p pa $16.95   **331.2**

1. Work 2. Labor -- United States 3. United States -- Social conditions
ISBN 978-1-56584-342-4; 1-56584-342-8

First published 1974 by Pantheon Bks.

Based on interviews, this study describes the working lives and feelings of people engaged in occupations ranging from interstate truck driver to stockbroker to bookbinder to corporation president.

This "is not a dry, academic treatise but a sensitive portrayal of the experience of working, with all its pain, tension, frustrations, and occasional satisfactions." Best Sellers

331.25   Other conditions of employment

Chertavian, Gerald.

A **Year** Up; how a pioneering program that teaches young adults real skills for real jobs- - with real success. Gerald Chertavian. Viking 2012 viii, 358 p.p   **331.25**

1. Mentoring 2. Youth -- Employment 3. Year Up (Organization) 4. Internship programs -- United States 5. Occupational training -- United States 6. Internship programs -- New York (State) 7. Young adults -- Employment -- United States 8. Poor youth -- Employment -- New York (State) 9. Poor youth -- Education, Higher -- New York (State) 10. Young adults -- Vocational education -- United States 11. Poor youth -- Vocational education -- New York (State)
ISBN 9780670023776

LC 2012000606

This book is an "account of the origins and growth of Year Up, a groundbreaking employment program. Year Up founder and [chief executive officer] [Gerald] Chertavian debuts with this memoir about his nationwide program, which is aimed at 'closing the ever-widening Opportunity Divide in this country.'" (Kirkus)

331.3   Labor force by personal attributes

Fideler, Elizabeth F.

Men still at work; professionals over sixty and on the job. Elizabeth F. Fideler. Rowman & Littlefield Pub Inc. 2014 232 p. (cloth: alk. paper) $36   **331.3**

1. Age and employment 2. Older men -- Employment 3. Retirement age -- United States 4. Age and employment -- United States 5. Professional employees -- United States 6. Older men -- Employment -- United States
ISBN 1442222751; 9781442222755

LC 2013040402

This book, by Elizabeth F. Fideler, "explores the reasons why many men are continuing to work well beyond the traditional retirement age. In today's challenging economy, they are the second-fastest growing group of workers (just behind older women). Filled with profiles of older working men, . . . [it] explores thorny issues such as masculinity and the 'need to provide,' as well as economic issues, job satisfaction, and more." (Publisher's note)

"Overall, an engaging, accessible overview of what the future holds for many younger men who will undoubtedly work into their 60s ... and beyond." Choice

Includes bibliographical references and index

331.398   Older workers

Bruder, Jessica

★ **Nomadland**; surviving America in the twenty-first century. Jessica Bruder. W W Norton & Co Inc 2017 xiv, 273 p.p illustrations (hardcover) $26.95   **331.398**

1. Older people -- Employment 2. United States -- Social conditions 3. Van life -- United States 4. Casual labor -- United States 5. Working poor -- United States 6. Migrant labor -- United States 7. Retirees -- Employment -- United States 8. Older people -- Employment -- United States 9. Recreational vehicle living -- United States 10. Retirement -- Economic aspects -- United States
ISBN 9780393249316; 9780393249323; 039324931X

LC 2017018056

This book, by Jessica Bruder, is "about low-income Americans eking out a living while driving from locale to locale for seasonal employment. . . . [Bruder] makes it clear that the nomads--many of them senior citizens--refuse to think of themselves as 'homeless.' Rather, they refer to themselves as 'houseless,' as in no longer burdened by mortgage payments, repairs, and other drawbacks, and they discuss 'wheel estate' instead of real estate." (Kirkus Reviews)

"Engaging, highly relevant immersion journalism." Kirkus
Includes bibliographical references (pages [257]-273).

331.4   Women workers

Berebitsky, Julie

Sex and the office; a history of gender, power, and desire. Julie Berebitsky. Yale University Press 2012 x, 359 p.p (cloth: alk. paper) $38   **331.4**

1. Sexual harassment 2. Sex in the workplace 3. Women employees -- United States -- History 4. Sex role -- United States -- History -- 20th century 5. Women -- Employment -- United States -- History -- 20th century
ISBN 0300118996; 9780300118995

LC 2011026337

This book by Julie Berebitsky "explores how Americans' attitudes toward sexuality and gender in the office have changed since the 1860s. . . . Berebitsky recounts the actual experiences of female and male office workers; draws on archival sources . . . and explores how popular sources--including cartoons, advertisements, advice guides, and a wide array of fictional accounts--have represented wanted and unwelcome romantic and sexual advances." (Publisher's note)

Includes bibliographical references and index

Bohnet, Iris
What works; gender equality by design. Iris Bohnet. The Belknap Press of Harvard University Press 2016 400 p. illustrations (alk. paper) $26.95 **331.4**
1. Gender role 2. Organizational behavior 3. Sex discrimination in employment 4. Gender mainstreaming
ISBN 9780674089037

LC 2015039199

In this book, by Iris Bohnet, "Gender equality is a moral and a business imperative. But unconscious bias holds us back, and de-biasing people's minds has proven to be difficult and expensive. Diversity training programs have had limited success, and individual effort alone often invites backlash. Behavioral design offers a new solution. By de-biasing organizations instead of individuals, we can make smart changes that have big impacts." (Publisher's note)

Includes bibliographical references and index

Carlson, Gretchen, 1966-
Be fierce; stop harassment and take your power back. by Gretchen Carlson. Center Street 2017 244 p. (hardcover) $27 **331.41**
1. Work environment 2. Sexual harassment 3. Women in the workplace 4. Sexual harassment of women 5. Women television journalists -- United States -- Biography
ISBN 9781478992172; 9781546083184; 1478992174

LC 2017289389

In this book, author Gretchen Carlson "shares her views on what women can do to empower and protect themselves in the workplace or on a college campus, what to say when someone makes suggestive remarks, how an employer's Human Resources department may not always be your friend, and how forced arbitration clauses in work contracts often serve to protect companies rather than employees. Her . . . message encourages women to stand up and speak up in every aspect of their lives." (Publisher's note)

Includes bibliographical references (pages 209-229) and index.

Chang, Emily
Brotopia; breaking up the boys' club of Silicon Valley. Emily Chang. Portfolio 2018 320 p. (hardback) $28 **331.4**
1. Women -- Employment 2. Industrial relations
ISBN 9780735213531

LC 2017052180

In this book, "TV journalist Emily Chang reveals how Silicon Valley got so sexist despite its utopian ideals, why bro culture endures despite decades of companies claiming the moral high ground . . . --and how women are finally starting to speak out and fight back. . . . Chang shows how women such as former Uber engineer Susan Fowler, entrepreneur Niniane Wang, and game developer Brianna Wu, have risked their careers and sometimes their lives to pave a way for other women." (Publisher's note)

Includes bibliographical references

Chang, Leslie T.
Factory girls; from village to city in a changing China.

Spiegel & Grau 2008 420p map $26; pa $16 **331.4**
1. Migrant labor 2. Manufacturing industries 3. Women -- China
ISBN 978-0-385-52017-1; 0-385-52017-4; 978-0-385-52018-8 pa; 0-385-52018-2 pa

LC 2008-12880

This "is an exceptionally vivid and compassionate depiction of the day-to-day dramas, and the fears and aspirations, of the real people who are powering China's economic boom." N Y Times Book Rev

Includes bibliographical references

Featherstone, Liza
Selling women short; the landmark battle for workers' rights at Wal-Mart. Basic Bks. 2004 282p $25 **331.4**
1. Sex discrimination 2. Wal-Mart Stores, Inc.
ISBN 0-465-02315-0

LC 2004-10298

Using an "investigation of the class action suit Dukes v. Wal-Mart Stores, Inc. and . . . interviews with female workers, Featherstone indicts Wal-Mart for low wages, discriminatory policies and sexist practices. . . . This is a clearly written and compelling book." Publ Wkly

Includes bibliographical references

Fideler, Elizabeth F.
Women still at work; professionals over sixty and on the job. Elizabeth S. Fideler. Rowman & Littlefield Publishers 2012 vii, 209 p.p (cloth: alk. paper) $37.50; (ebook) $36.99 **331.4**
1. Age and employment 2. Older women -- Employment 3. Age and employment -- United States 4. Older women -- Employment -- United States
ISBN 144221550X; 9781442215504; 9781442215528

LC 2012017802

In this book on older women in the workforce, Elizabeth F. Fideler "tells the everyday stories of hard-working women and the reasons they're still on the job, with a focus on women in the professional workforce. . . . Their stories showcase some of the key themes women choose to stay at work -- including job satisfaction, diminishing retirement savings, the need to support children or parents longer in life, exercising the hard-won right to work, and more." (Publisher's note)

Includes bibliographical references.

Kessler-Harris, Alice
★ **Out** to work; a history of wage-earning women in the United States. 20th anniversary ed; Oxford Univ. Press 2003 414p il pa $19.95 **331.4**
1. Women -- Employment -- History
ISBN 0-19-515709-5

LC 2003-267644

First published 1982

"This work remains a landmark in the field of analyzing the history of women's work in the United States from Colonial times to the Reagan era." Libr J

Includes bibliographical references

Pao, Ellen, 1969-
Reset; my fight for inclusion and lasting change. Ellen K. Pao. Spiegel & Grau 2017 274 p. (hardcover) $28 **331.4**
1. Women executives 2. Success in business 3. Computer industry -- United States 4. Industrial relations -- United States 5. Businesswomen -- United States -- Biography 6. Internet industry -- California -- Santa Clara Valley (Santa Clara County) 7. Discrimination in employment -- California -- Santa Clara

Valley (Santa Clara County) 8. Sex discrimination against women -- California -- Santa Clara Valley (Santa Clara County) 9. Sex discrimination in employment -- California -- Santa Clara Valley (Santa Clara County)

ISBN 9780399591013; 9780399591037; 039959101X

LC 2017301132

In this book, author Ellen Pao describes how she "sued a powerhouse Silicon Valley venture capital firm, [Kleiner Perkins,] calling out workplace discrimination and retaliation against women and other underrepresented groups. . . . She and seven other women [technology] leaders formed Project Include, an award-winning nonprofit for accelerating diversity and inclusion in [the industry]. In her book, Pao shines a light on troubling issues that plague today's workplace." (Publisher's note)

Includes bibliographical references (pages 271-274).

Povich, Lynn

★ The **good** girls revolt; how the women of Newsweek sued their bosses and changed the workplace. Lynn Povich. PublicAffairs 2012 xx, 249 p.p (hardcover) $25.99   **331.4**

1. Sexism 2. Women journalists 3. Sex discrimination in employment 4. Sex discrimination -- Law and legislation 5. Newsweek 6. Women journalists -- United States 7. Sex discrimination in employment -- United States 8. Sex role in the work environment -- United States

ISBN 161039173X; 9781610391733; 9781610391740

LC 2012006936

Amelia Bloomer Project (2014)

This book by Lynn Povich explains how, in 1970, "forty-six 'Newsweek' women charged the magazine with discrimination in hiring and promotion. It was the first female class action lawsuit--the first by women journalists--and it inspired other women in the media to quickly follow suit. . . . 'The Good Girls Revolt' also explores why changes in the law didn't solve everything. Through the lives of young female journalists at Newsweek today, Lynn Povich shows what has--and hasn't--changed in the workplace." (Publisher's note)

Includes bibliographical references and index.

Ryckman, Pamela

Stiletto network; inside the women's power circles that are changing the face of business. Pamela Ryckman. American Management Association 2013 256 p. (hardcover) $22.95   **331.4**

1. Women executives 2. Women -- Social conditions 3. Businesswomen 4. Business networks 5. Strategic alliances 6. Women in the professions

ISBN 0814432530; 9780814432532

LC 2012051563

This book by Pamela Ryckman looks at the "female heads of industry [who] are the forerunners of a radical shift in power. It's about what happens when bright, extraordinary women, from captains of industry to aspiring entrepreneurs, come together to celebrate and unwind, debate and compare notes. It's about how they mine their collective intelligence to realize their dreams or champion a cause, . . . how they join forces to ensure each woman gets what she needs." (Publisher's note)

Zahidi, Saadia

Fifty million rising; the new generation of working women transforming the Muslim world. Saadia Zahidi. Nation Books 2018 288 p. (hardcover) $28   **331.409**

1. Women in Islam 2. Women -- Employment 3. Muslim women -- Social conditions 4. Muslim women -- Employment 5. Feminism -- Islamic countries 6. Muslim women -- Economic conditions

7. Women -- Employment -- Islamic countries 8. Economic development -- Islamic countries

ISBN 9781568585901

LC 2017029076

In this book, economist Saadia Zahidi illuminates . . . [the increase of] women [workers in Islamic countries] through the stories of the remarkable women who are at the forefront of this shift--a McDonald's worker in Pakistan who has climbed the ranks to manager; the founder of an online modest fashion startup in Indonesia; . . . and an executive in a Saudi corporation who is altering the culture of her workplace; among many others." (Publisher's note)

"In this fascinating look at a monumental shift, Zahidi elevates the voices of women across the world who speak about their motivations, successes, and challenges in forging new paths." Booklist

Includes bibliographical references and index

331.44   Working mothers

Lacy, Sarah

A **uterus** is a feature, not a bug; the working woman's guide to overthrowing the partriarchy. by Sarah Lacy. Harper Business 2017 x, 306 p.p (hardcover) $26.99   **331.44**

1. Working mothers 2. Women -- Employment 3. Work and family 4. Career development 5. Women -- Vocational guidance

ISBN 9780062641823; 9780062641816; 0062641816

LC 2017277180

In this book, by Sarah Lacy, "working mothers aren't a liability. They are assets you—and every manager and executive—want in your company, in your investment portfolio, and in your corner. There is copious academic research showing the benefits of working mothers on families and the benefits to companies who give women longer and more flexible parental leave. There are even findings that demonstrate women with multiple children actually perform better at work than those with none or one." (Publisher's note)

"A fierce and persuasive call to action that demands women, especially millennials, rethink the relationship b e tween maternity and career ambitions." Kirkus

Includes bibliographical references (pages 287-291) and index.

331.5   Workers by personal attributes other than age

Browne, John

The **Glass** Closet; Why Coming Out Is Good Business. John Browne. HarperCollins Publishers 2014 240 p. $27.99   **331.5**

1. LGBT people 2. Businesspeople 3. Autobiographies

ISBN 0062316974; 9780062316974

1st U.S. edition

"Part memoir and part social criticism, 'The Glass Closet' addresses the issue of homophobia that still pervades corporations around the world and underscores the immense challenges faced by LGBT employees. . . . In 'The Glass Closet,' Lord John Browne . . . seeks to unsettle business leaders by exposing the culture of homophobia that remains rampant in corporations around the world, and which prevents employees from showing their authentic selves." (Publisher's note)

"Brown's rhetoric is businesslike and a little dry but also to the point, supported by research, and culturally significant. He has taken pains to provide strikingly honest personal narratives and uses them to put a face on the problems at hand.—" Booklist

Includes bibliographical references (p. 203-234) and index

331.6 Workers by ethnic and national origin

Bacon, David

Illegal people; how globalization creates migration and criminalizes immigrants. Beacon Press 2008 261p $25.95; pa $18 **331.6**

1. Labor policy 2. Globalization 3. Migrant labor 4. Unauthorized immigrants 5. Illegal aliens

ISBN 978-0-8070-4226-7; 978-0-8070-4230-4 pa

LC 2008-15394

The author "follows the lives of undocumented workers at the Westin Suite Hotel in California and a Smithfield meatpacking plant in North Carolina, who travel back and forth from Mexico to the U.S. He examines the economic and social forces in both countries that lure workers to a market where they can earn higher wages but are vulnerable to exploitation. . . . A fascinating look at trade and immigration policies and the people directly affected by them." Booklist

Includes bibliographical references

Breslin, Jimmy

The **short** sweet dream of Eduardo Gutierrez. Crown 2002 213p hardcover o.p. pa $12 **331.6**

1. Construction workers

ISBN 1-400-04682-3 pa

LC 2001-47283

"A true-life account of an illegal Mexican immigrant who died on a New York construction site, and of the dreary lives and modest ambitions common to Mexicans in this country." N Y Times Book Rev

331.7 Labor by industry and occupation

Bureau of Labor Statistics

Occupational outlook handbook. U.S. Dept. of Labor Bureau of Labor Statistics il **331.7**

1. Occupations 2. Reference books 3. Vocational guidance

Biennial. First published 1949.

"Gives information on employment trends and outlook in more than 800 occupations. Indicates nature of work, qualifications, earnings and working conditions, how to enter, where to go for more information, etc." Guide to Ref Books. 11th edition

Fisher, James Terence

On the Irish waterfront; the crusader, the movie, and the soul of the port of New York. [by] James T. Fisher. Cornell University Press 2009 370p il map (Cushwa Center studies of Catholicism in Twentieth-century America) $29.95 **331.7**

1. Stevedores 2. Irish Americans 3. Catholic Church -- Missions 4. New York Harbor (N.Y. and N.J.) 5. On the waterfront (Motion picture)

ISBN 978-0-8014-4804-1; 0-8014-4804-2

LC 2009-13058

The author presents a "history of the New York-New Jersey waterfront depicted in Elia Kazan's Oscar-winning 1954 film, On the Waterfront. Fischer's impeccable research delves into the real-life stories behind the characters, particularly Pete Corridan, the crusading Catholic priest who tried to reform the longshoremen's union and the recently deceased Bud Schulberg, who adapted Malcolm Johnson's 1949 Pulitzer Prize-winning 'Crime on the Waterfront' newspaper series for the screen. . . . This engaging narrative is essential reading for both labor historians and cinema buffs, plus anyone studying the waterfront, working-class and immigrant history, anticommunism, blacklisting, and the

House Un-American Activities Committee." Libr J

Includes bibliographical references

J.G. Ferguson Publishing Company

★ **Encyclopedia** of careers and vocational guidance; 15th ed.; Ferguson 2010 5v il set $249.95 **331.7**

1. Reference books 2. Occupations -- Encyclopedias 3. Vocational guidance -- Encyclopedias

ISBN 978-0-8160-8313-8; 0-8160-8313-4

LC 2010-17724

First published 1967

"These five volumes contain more than 700 . . . [articles] on careers in nearly 100 industries. Each three to five-page entry provides a concise and engaging profile of fields like accounting, animal care, computers, the environment, publishing, sales, and the visual arts. Included in each job entry are an overview, a history, a description, requirements, employers, advancement, earnings, work environment, outlook, and more." Libr J [review of 2008 edition]

Includes bibliographical references

Nagle, Robin

Picking up; on the streets and behind the trucks with the sanitation workers of New York City. Robin Nagle. Farrar, Straus & Giroux 2013 x, 280 p., [8] p. of platesp ill., map (hardcover) $28 **331.7**

1. Municipal officials and employees 2. Refuse and refuse disposal -- New York (N.Y.) 3. Sanitation workers -- New York (State) -- New York

ISBN 0689825528; 9780374299293

LC 2012028941

In this book, "Robin Nagle introduces us to the men and women of New York City's Department of Sanitation and makes clear why this small army of uniformed workers is the most important labor force on the streets. Seeking to understand every aspect of the Department's mission, Nagle accompanied crews on their routes, questioned supervisors and commissioners, and listened to story after story about blizzards, hazardous wastes, and the insults of everyday New Yorkers." (Publisher's note)

Includes bibliographical references and index

Wartzman, Rick

The **end** of loyalty; the rise and fall of good jobs in America. Rick Wartzman. PublicAffairs 2017 vii, 418 p.p illustrations (hardcover) $30 **331.7**

1. Corporations -- United States 2. Social responsibility of business 3. Industrial relations -- United States -- History 4. Labor -- United States -- History 5. Corporations -- United States -- History 6. Labor policy -- United States -- History 7. Industrial policy -- United States -- History 8. United States -- Economic conditions -- 1945-

ISBN 9781610399708; 9781586489144

LC 2017006668

In this book, author Rick Wartzman "chronicles the erosion of the relationship between American companies and their workers. Through the stories of four major employers--General Motors, General Electric, Kodak, and Coca-Cola--he shows how big businesses once took responsibility for providing their workers and retirees with an array of social benefits. . . . But the corporate social contract didn't last." (Publisher's note)

"A sharp-edged examination of why large American employers shifted from loyalty to their workers to loyalty focused primarily on stockholders." Kirkus

Includes bibliographical references (pages 369-392) and index

331.702   Choice of vocation

Anders, George

You can do anything; the suprising power of a "useless" liberal arts education. George Anders. Little, Brown & Co. 2017 342 p. (hardcover) $27   **331.702**
1. Advice literature 2. Vocational guidance 3. Liberal arts education 4. Vocational guidance -- United States 5. Education, Humanistic -- United States 6. Bachelor of arts degree -- United States 7. College graduates -- Employment -- United States
ISBN 9780316548809; 9780316548816

LC 2017932050

This book, by George Anders, "explains the remarkable power of a liberal arts education--and the ways it can open the door to thousands of cutting-edge jobs every week. . . . In this book, you will learn why resume-writing is fading in importance and why 'telling your story' is taking its place. You will learn how to . . . translate your campus achievements into a new style of expression that will make employers' eyes light up. . . . You will be ready for anything." (Publisher's note)

"An argument for the usefulness of a major in liberal arts. . . . Useful guidance for newly minted job hunters." Kirkus

Includes bibliographical references (pages 297-330) and index.

McKenna, Amy

Nontraditional careers for women and men; more than 30 great jobs for women and men with apprenticeships through phds. by Andrew Morkes and Amy McKenna. College & Career Press 2012 280 p. $19.95   **331.702**
1. Occupations 2. Professions 3. Vocational guidance 4. Men -- Employment -- United States -- Juvenile literature 5. Vocational guidance -- United States -- Juvenile literature 6. Women -- Employment -- United States -- Juvenile literature
ISBN 0974525197; 9780974525198

LC 2011046915

This book about nontraditional employment with an emphasis on gender "is chock-full of career articles encompassing a wide variety of fields. Each career article includes salary information, skills needed, minimum education level, employment outlook, information about the career, certification and licensing information, tips for getting a job in this career, and industry resources." (Voice of Youth Advocates)

331.8   Labor unions, labor-management bargaining and disputes

Dray, Philip

There is power in a union; the epic story of labor in America. Doubleday 2010 772p il $35; ebook $35   **331.8**
1. Labor movement 2. Industrialization 3. Labor unions -- United States 4. United States -- Social conditions 5. Labor unions -- United States -- History 6. Labor movement -- United States -- History 7. Industrialization -- United States -- History
ISBN 978-0-385-52629-6; 0-385-52629-6; 978-0-385-53360-7 ebook

LC 201002357

This is a "narrative history of American labor. . . . From the textile mills of Lowell, Massachusetts . . . to the triumph of unions in the twentieth century and their waning influence today, the contest between labor and capital for their share of American bounty has shaped our national experience. Philip Dray's ambition is to show us the vital accomplishments of organized labor in that time and illuminate its central role in our social, political, economic, and cultural evolution." (Publisher's note)

Bibliography. Index.

The author "follows organized labor from the struggles of early 19th-century female textile workers to the present-day retreat of organized labor following the failed 1981 air traffic controllers' strike. . . . Packed with vivid characters and dramatic scenes, Dray's fine recap of a neglected but vital tradition has much to say about labor's current straits." Publ Wkly

Includes bibliographical references

Dubofsky, Melvyn

★ **Labor** in America; a history. Melvyn Dubofsky, Joseph A. McCartin. 9th edition Blackwell 2017 il   **331.8**
1. Labor unions 2. Working class 3. Labor -- United States
ISBN 9781118976852

LC 2003-13265

First published 1949 by Crowell under the authorship of Foster Rhea Dulles. Periodically revised

A study of the social and political impact of the American labor movement since colonial times

Includes bibliographical references

★ **Historical** encyclopedia of American labor; edited by Robert Weir and James P. Hanlan. Greenwood Press 2003 2v set $175   **331.8**
1. Reference books 2. Labor movement -- Encyclopedias 3. Labor -- United States -- Encyclopedias
ISBN 0-313-31840-9

LC 2003-52847

This "encyclopedia includes approximately 400 entries designed for the general researcher, students, and lay readers interested in learning more about such topics as unions, union leaders, union history, important laws and court cases, and labor terminology. An appendix contains excerpts from over 50 primary documents." Libr J

Includes bibliographical references

Shaw, Randy

Beyond the fields; Cesar Chavez, the UFW, and the struggle for justice in the 21st century. University of California Press 2008 347p il   **331.8**
1. Social action 2. Agricultural laborers 3. Labor leaders 4. United Farm Workers of America 5. Social justice -- United States 6. Social action -- United States -- History -- 20th century
ISBN 0520251075; 0520268040; 9780520251076; 9780520268043

LC 2008-31252

This book explores the impact of César Chávez and the United Farm Workers "on 21st-century social justice movements. Beyond the Fields [aims to show] . . . how Chávez and the UFW's imprint can be found in the modern reshaping of the American labor movement, the building of Latino political power, the transformation of Los Angeles and California politics, the fight for environmental justice, and the . . . movement for immigrant rights. [According to the author], many of the ideas, tactics, and strategies that Chávez and the UFW initiated or revived—including the boycott, the fast, clergy-labor partnerships and door-to-door voter outreach—are now so commonplace that their roots in the farmworkers' movement [are] forgotten. . . . UFW volunteers and staff were dedicated to furthering economic justice, and many devoted their post-UFW lives to working for social change." (Publisher's note) Index.

"Shaw's book is the product of extensive research, and it's invaluable for anyone interested in the evolution of unionization over the past forty years." Washington Monthly

Includes bibliographical references and index

★ **St.** James encyclopedia of labor history worldwide; major events in labor history and their impact. with introductions by Willie Thompson and Daniel Nelson; Neil Schlager, editor; produced by Schlager Groups. St. James Press 2003 2v set $260 **331.8**
1. Reference books 2. Labor movement -- Encyclopedias
ISBN 1-558-62542-9

LC 2003-294

"This reference promises to fill an important niche for larger public and academic libraries." Libr J

Stepan-Norris, Judith
Left out; Reds and America's industrial unions. [by] Judith Stepan-Norris, Maurice Zeitlin. Cambridge Univ. Press 2002 375p $75; pa $27 **331.8**
1. Labor -- United States 2. Labor unions -- United States
ISBN 0-521-79212-6; 0-521-79840-X pa

LC 2001-37655

"In 1947, ten 'Communist-dominated unions' were expelled from the CIO. The mythology that developed is that these unions sacrificed the interests of the American worker to the foreign policy dictates of the Statlin-era Soviet Union. The authors, both sociologists, use statistical analysis of contracts to argue that these unions actually had the most democracy, the most pro-labor contracts, and the best track record in fighting for gender and racial equality in the labor movement." Libr J
Includes bibliographical references

Zieger, Robert H.
American workers, American unions; the twentieth century. {by} Robert H. Zieger & Gilbert J. Gall. 3rd ed; Johns Hopkins Univ. Press 2002 292p (The American moment) pa $17.95 **331.8**
1. Labor unions 2. Labor -- United States
ISBN 0-8018-7078-X

LC 2002-3250

First published 1986
"This standard work of American labor history from the Gilded Age onward has been updated to almost the present, with the last paragraph discussing September 11. Zieger's strength lies in his striving for a balanced survey." Libr J
Includes bibliographical references

331.88 Labor unions (Trade unions)

Labor rising; the past and future of working people in America. edited by Richard A. Greenwald, Daniel Katz. New Press, The 2012 318 p. (paperback) $20.95 **331.88**
1. Working class 2. Labor economics 3. Labor movement -- History 4. Working class -- United States -- History 5. Labor movement -- United States -- History
ISBN 1595585184; 9781595585189

LC 2012001464

Editors Daniel Katz and Richard A. Greenwald present a "volume [that] provides readers with an understanding of the history that is directly relevant to the economic and political crises working people face today, and points the way to a revitalized twenty-first-century labor movement. With original contributions from leading labor historians, social critics, and activists," the book "makes crucial connections between the past and present, and then looks forward, asking how we might imagine a different future for all Americans." (Publisher's note)

331.892 Strikes

Loomis, Erik
A **history** of America in ten strikes; Erik Loomis. The New Press 2018 288 p. (hc: alk. paper) $27.99 **331.892**
1. Strikes 2. Labor disputes 3. Industrial relations -- United States -- History 4. Labor disputes -- United States -- History 5. Strikes and lockouts -- United States -- History
ISBN 9781620971611

LC 2018017580

In this book, "labor historian Erik Loomis recounts ten critical workers' strikes in American labor history that everyone needs to know about (and then provides an annotated list of the 150 most important moments in American labor history in the appendix). From the Lowell Mill Girls strike in the 1830s to Justice for Janitors in 1990, these labor uprisings do not just reflect the times in which they occurred, but speak directly to the present moment." (Publisher's note)
"This concise history, seen through the lens of 10 labor strikes from the nineteenth century on, uses those encounters between capitalists and workers to tell a broader and very sad story." Booklist
Includes bibliographical references and index

332 Financial economics

Gasparino, Charles
The **sellout**; how three decades of Wall Street greed and government mismanagement destroyed the global financial system. Harper Business 2009 553p $27.99 **332**
1. Wall Street (New York, N.Y.) 2. Global Financial Crisis, 2008-2009
ISBN 978-0-06-169716-6; 0-06-169716-8

LC 2009-28097

"Of all the books documenting the financial crisis . . . The Sellout tells it better than most. Filled with very little of the boring, complex financial jargon that comprises many books of the genre, this tome makes for a surprisingly entertaining and easy read." Risk Management
Includes bibliographical references

Mayer, Robert
Quick cash; the story of the loan shark. Northern Illinois University Press 2010 293p $35 **332**
1. Loans 2. Usury
ISBN 978-0-8758-0430-9; 0-8758-0430-6

LC 2010014718

This book "traces high-interest lending from the late 19th century through the latest financial crisis. While the book focuses on Chicago, it does reference lending practices throughout the South and New York City. Chapters delve into the social issues of the early 20th century that created a market for these high-interest loans, the various government policies that tried to regulate the lenders, and the legal and economic changes that gave rise to the current methods of payday lending since the 1980s. . . . [The author] has created an original and multidisciplinary look at subprime lending in the United States that is accessible to a wide variety of readers, including students and professionals." Libr J
Includes bibliographical references

O'Rourke, P. J., 1947-
None of my business; P.J. explains money, banking, debt, equity, assets, liabilities, and why he's not rich and neither are you. P. J. O'Rourke. Atlantic Monthly Press 2018 304 p. (hardcover: alk. paper) $27 **332**

1. Money -- Humor 2. Investments -- Humor 3. Banks and banking -- Humor
ISBN 9780802128485

LC 2018026530

"After decades covering war and disaster, bestselling author and acclaimed satirist P. J. O'Rourke takes on his scariest subjects yet--business, investment, finance, and the political chicanery behind them. P.J.'s approach to business, investment, and finance is different. . . . He offers a brief history of economic transitions before exploring the world of high tech innovation with a chapter on 'Unnovations.'" (Publisher's note)

Includes bibliographical references and index

Palmer, Kimberly

Smart mom, rich mom; How to Build Wealth While Raising a Family. Kimberly Palmer. American Management Association 2016 256 p. (pbk.) $14.95; (ebook) $12.95   **332**
1. Work and family 2. Working mothers 3. Women -- Personal finance 4. Family -- Economic aspects 5. Career development 6. Women -- Finance, Personal 7. Families -- Economic aspects 8. Working mothers -- Finance, Personal
ISBN 9780814436806; 9780814436813

LC 2015050487

This book, by Kimberly Palmer, "explores how women today are navigating the financially challenging career/parenting years. Written by a national money columnist and mom of two, the book chronicles people who have stayed in the game--full-time, freelance, self-employed, and more--and emerged more prosperous and empowered." (Publisher's note)

Includes bibliographical references and index

Piketty, Thomas, 1971-

★ **Capital** in the twenty-first century; Thomas Piketty; translated by Arthur Goldhammer. The Belknap Press of Harvard University Press 2014 696 p. illustrations (alk. paper) $39.95   **332**
1. Equality 2. Economic forecasting 3. Economic development -- History 4. Wealth 5. Capital 6. Labor economics 7. Income distribution
ISBN 067443000X; 9780674430006

LC 2013036024

Kirkus Prize Finalist: Nonfiction (2014); National Book Critics Circle Finalist: Nonfiction (2014)

"In 'Capital in the Twenty-First Century,' Thomas Piketty analyzes a unique collection of data from twenty countries, ranging as far back as the eighteenth century, to uncover key economic and social patterns. . . . Piketty shows that modern economic growth and the diffusion of knowledge have allowed us to avoid inequalities on the apocalyptic scale predicted by Karl Marx. . . . Political action has curbed dangerous inequalities in the past, Piketty says, and may do so again." (Publisher's note)

Shows "that plain language can be put to work explaining the most complex of ideas, foremost among them the fact that economic inequality is at an all-time high--and is only bound to grow worse." Kirkus

Includes bibliographical references and index

332.024   Personal finance

Ariely, Dan

★ **Dollars** and sense; how we misthink money and how to spend smarter. Dan Ariely and Jeff Kreisler; with illustrations by Matt Trower. HarperCollins 2017 xii, 275 p.p illustrations (hardcover) $27.99   **332.024**

1. Personal finance 2. Consumption (Economics) 3. Finance, Personal -- Psychological aspects
ISBN 9780062651228; 9780062651204; 006265120X

This book, by Dan Ariely and Jeff Kreisler, "challenge[s] many of our most basic assumptions about the precarious relationship between our brains and our money. . . . [The authors] demonstrate how our misplaced confidence in our spending habits frequently leads us astray, costing us more than we realize. . . . [The book] provides the practical tools we need to understand and improve our financial choices, save and spend smarter, and ultimately live better." (Publisher's note)

"A user-friendly and often entertaining treatise on how to be a more discerning, vastly more aware handler of money." Kirkus

Includes bibliographical references (pages 261-268) and index.

Choudhri, Nihara K.

Preparing for baby; all the legal, financial, tax, and insurance information new and expectant parents need. Nihara K. Choudri. American Bar Association 2015 xii, 320 p.p illustrations (ebook) $19.99; (pbk.) $19.95   **332.024**
1. Parenting 2. Child care -- United States 3. Domestic relations -- United States 4. Parent and child (Law) -- United States 5. Children -- Legal status, laws, etc. -- United States 6. Pregnant women -- Legal status, laws, etc. -- United States
ISBN 9781634251884; 9781634251877

LC 2015034391

This book, by Nihara K. Choudri, "provides plain-English information about the basic legal and financial issues most new parents' face, broken down into an easy to digest and reference Q&A format for parents busy with the day-to-day aspects of caring for their babies. This guide gives readers the information they need to make smart legal decisions in the months before and after baby arrives." (Publisher's note)

"Preparing for Baby is essential for public libraries, where it should be promoted to expectant parents or parents with minors." Booklist

Includes bibliographical references and index.

D'Agnese, Joseph

The **money** book for freelancers, part-time, and the self-employed; the only personal finance system for people with not-so-regular jobs. [by] Joseph D'Agnese & Denise Kiernan. Three Rivers Press 2010 306p il pa $15   **332.024**
1. Self-employed 2. Personal finance
ISBN 978-0-307-45366-2; 0-307-45366-9

LC 2009-31596

"The authors describe how one can maximize financial security without compromising success by addressing debts, taxes, emergency funds, and retirement savings using their 'Freelance Finance System.' They preach commonsense ideas such as accountability and restraint but also describe plenty of clever ways to make one's money go further. . . . Developed from the personal experiences of the authors, this book is fun and relevant. . . . Recommended for anyone who is self-employed now or is facing a new work-life situation." Libr J

Economides, Annette, 1961-

The **moneysmart** family system; teaching financial independence to children of every age. Steve Economides, Annette Economides. Thomas Nelson 2012 272 p. $16.99   **332.024**
1. Child rearing 2. Personal finance 3. Household budgets 4. Finance, Personal 5. Families -- Economic aspects 6. Children -- Finance, Personal
ISBN 1400202841; 9781400202843

LC 2012941594

This book, by Steve and Annette Economides, teaches how to "raise financially responsible kids of any age in a society filled with consumer-ism." The "Economides raised their five kids while spending 77 percent less than the USDA predicted. And the money they did spend was also used to train their children to become financially independent." Their "system will show you how to teach your children to manage money and have a good attitude while they're learning." (Publisher''s note)

Fagan, Chelsea
The **financial** diet; a total beginner's guide to getting good with money. by Chelsea Fagan; designed by Lauren Ver Hage. Henry Holt & Co. 2018 196 p. (pbk.) $19   **332.024**
1. Personal finance 2. Self-improvement 3. Finance, Personal 4. Women -- Finance, Personal
ISBN 9781250176172; 9781250176165
LC 2017027973
Written by Chelsea Fagan and designed by Lauren Ver Hage, "'The Financial Diet' is the personal finance book for people who don't care about personal finance. Whether you're in need of an overspending de-tox, buried under student debt, or just trying to figure out how to live on an entry-level salary, [this book] gives you tools to make a budget, understand investments, and deal with your credit." (Publisher's note)
"The breezy lifestyle-magazine-like writing style and easy-to-digest layout make this guide a useful and readable resource." Pub Wkly

Hirshman, Susan L.
Does this make my assets look fat? a woman's guide to finding financial empowerment and success. St. Martin's Press 2010 302p il $24.99; ebook $11.99   **332.024**
1. Investments 2. Personal finance 3. Women -- United States
ISBN 978-0-312-38553-8; 0-312-38553-6; 978-1-4299-5006-0 ebook; 1-4299-5006-4 ebook
LC 2010-21668
"Comparing getting one's financial house in order to dieting, Hirsh-man . . . presents chapters on assessing personal finance fitness and gives comprehensive definitions and explanations of, as well as practical sug-gestions on, various investment strategies." Libr J

Kiyosaki, Robert T., 1947-
Why "A" Students Work for "C" Students and Why "B" Students Work for the Government; Rich Dad's Guide to Finan-cial Education for Parents. Robert T. Kiyosaki. Perseus Distri-bution Services 2013 453 p. (paperback) $16.95   **332.024**
1. Creative ability 2. Education -- Aims and objectives
ISBN 1612680763; 9781612680767
In this book, Robert T. Kiyosaki "expands on his belief that the school system was created to churn out . . . 'A Students' who read well, memorize well and test well . . . and not the creative thinkers . . . who grow up to be the innovators and creators of new ideas, businesses, ap-plications and products. The book urges parents . . . to . . . focus, instead, on concepts, ideas, and helping their child find their true genius, their special gift." (Publisher's note)

Kobliner, Beth
Make your kid a money genius (even if you're not) a par-ents' guide for kids 3 to 23. Beth Kobliner. Simon & Schuster 2017 256 p. illustrations (hardcover) $19.99   **332.024**
1. Parenting 2. Personal finance 3. Finance, Personal 4. Children -- Finance, Personal
ISBN 9781476766812; 9781476766829
LC 2016021573
This book, by Beth Kobliner "is a jargon-free, step-by-step guide to help parents of all income levels teach their kids—from ages three to

twenty-three—about money. It turns out the key to raising a money ge-nius is . . . about instilling values that have been proven to make people successful—not just financially, but in life: delaying gratification, work-ing hard, living within your means, getting a good education, and acting generously toward others." (Publisher's note)
"Best-selling financial author Kobliner (Get a Financial Life) here provides a step-by-step look at developing financial literacy skills throughout childhood." LJ
Includes bibliographical references (pages 223-242) and index.

Lieber, Ron
The **Opposite** of Spoiled; Raising Kids Who Are Ground-ed, Generous, and Smart About Money. Ron Lieber. Harper-Collins 2015 256 p. $26.99   **332.024**
1. Parenting 2. Personal finance
ISBN 0062247018; 9780062247018
LC 2014035600
This book, by Ron Lieber, "delivers a . . . manifesto that explains how talking openly to children about money can help parents raise mod-est, patient, grounded young adults who are financially wise beyond their years. . . . It identifies a set of traits and virtues that embody the opposite of spoiled, and shares how to embrace the topic of money to help parents raise kids who are more generous and less materialistic." (Publisher's note)
"Humble stories of kids raising money for Down syndrome research or creating kit bags to give to people living on the street offer inspiration for those who do have money to spend it wisely in the world and to teach their children to do the same. Sound advice on managing family finances but only if you have sufficient finances to manage." Kirkus

Mecham, Jesse
You need a budget; the proven system for breaking the paycheck-to-paycheck cycle, getting out of debt, and living the life you want. Jesse Mecham. HarperBusiness 2017 207 p. illustrations (hardcover) $23.99   **332.024**
1. Personal finance 2. Self-help techniques 3. Budgets, Personal 4. Finance, Personal
ISBN 9780062567581; 9780062567604; 0062567586
In this book, author Jesse Mecham describes "his proven method--four, simple rules--[that] will transform money management from a paralyzing burden to a powerful tool . . . This tried-and-true system has changed the lives of hundreds of thousands of people by teaching them how to take charge, adjust money habits, eliminate stress, and build the life they want to live." (Publisher's note)
"Mecham's book is a handy guide for readers looking to increase their financial literacy and manage their money carefully and success-fully." Booklist

Miller, Mark
The **hard** times guide to retirement security; practical strat-egies for money, work, and living. Wiley 2010 223p il pa $16.95; ebook $11.99   **332.024**
1. Retirement income
ISBN 978-1-57660-362-8 pa; 978-0-470-90834-1 ebook
LC 2010-14478
This guide to retirement after the financial crisis touches upon "is-sues such as insuring against the risk of outliving your assets, recali-brating damaged retirement portfolios, managing the risk of health-care expenses in retirement, and career strategies for workers who are 50 years old and up." Publisher's note

Morduch, Jonathan

The **financial** diaries; how American families cope in a world of uncertainty. Jonathan Morduch & Rachel Schneider. Princeton University Press 2017 xii, 233 p.p illustrations (alk. paper) $27.95 **332.024**

1. Personal finance 2. Poor -- United States 3. United States -- Economic conditions 4. Poor families -- United States 5. Finance, Personal -- United States 6. Financial security -- United States 7. Middle class families -- United States 8. United States -- Economic conditions -- 21st century
ISBN 9780691172989

LC 2016955128

In this book, authors Jonathan Morduch and Rachel Schneider "draw on the groundbreaking U.S. Financial Diaries, which follow the lives of 235 low- and middle-income families as they navigate through a year. Through the Diaries, Morduch and Schneider challenge popular assumptions about how Americans earn, spend, borrow, and save--and they identify the true causes of distress and inequality for many working Americans." (Publisher's note)

"This is a must-read for anyone interested in causes of—and potential solutions to—American poverty." Pub Wkly

Includes bibliographical references (pages 179-223) and index.

Orman, Suze

The **money** class; learn to create your new American dream. Spiegel & Grau 2011 281p $26; ebook $13.99 **332.024**

1. Wealth 2. Personal finance
ISBN 978-1-4000-6973-6; 978-0-679-60470-9 ebook

LC 2011-1394

"Organized into nine 'classes,' with each class/chapter further divided into related lessons, . . . [this book is] upbeat and no-nonsense, offering lessons on family matters, homeownership, saving for college, emergencies, retirement, and more. Orman firmly guides readers when dealing with parenting issues or underwater mortgages. . . . After finishing Orman's book, and completing her exercises, readers will have a very clear sense of how they can achieve what she has rechristened the 'New American Dream.'" Publ Wkly

Pepper, Carol

The **seven** pearls of financial wisdom; a woman's guide to enjoying wealth and power. Carol Pepper and Camilla Webster. 1st ed. St. Martin's Press 2012 viii, 338 p.p (hardcover) $25.99; (paperback) $19.99 **332.024**

1. Businesswomen 2. Life cycle, Human 3. Women -- Personal finance 4. New business enterprises 5. Women -- Finance, Personal 6. Investments -- Psychological aspects
ISBN 0312641664; 1250008328; 9780312641665; 9781250008329; 9781250035486

LC 2012010250

"The goal of wealth-management adviser [Carol] Pepper and financial journalist [Camilla] Webster is to assist with common issues that arise in women's financial lives and to turn those issues into assets. . . . They discuss romance, children, crises ranging from health problems to natural disasters, leadership, wealth accrual, leaving a legacy, and mapping out a path to financial security. . . . Women are encouraged to start their own businesses, invest wisely . . . and live well." (Library Journal)

Includes bibliographical references and index.

Quinn, Jane Bryant

Making the most of your money now; the classic bestseller. Completely rev. for the new economy; Simon & Schuster hardcover ed.; Simon & Schuster 2010 1242p $35 **332.024**

1. Investments 2. Personal finance
ISBN 978-0-7432-6996-4; 0-7432-6996-9

LC 2009-32610

First published 1991 with title: Making the most of your money

This guide includes information about investing, buying a home, life and health insurance, retirement planning, checklists for life changes, finding a financial advisor, and financing college.

"This is an excellent primer, especially for those new to managing their money." Libr J

Tobias, Andrew P.

★ The **only** investment guide you'll ever need; Andrew Tobias. Second Mariner Books edition Mariner Books 2016 296 p **332.024**

1. Investments 2. Personal finance
ISBN 9780544781931

This book offers advice on such topics as personal investments, tax strategies, life insurance, stock market trading, college funds, real estate, and inheritance.

Walsh, Peter

Lighten up; love what you have, have what you need, be happier with less. Free Press 2011 288p $26; pa $15; ebook $12.99 **332.024**

1. Happiness 2. Conduct of life 3. Personal finance
ISBN 978-1-4391-5514-1; 978-1-4391-5515-8 pa; 978-1-4391-6008-4 ebook

LC 2010030244

The author "coaches readers in dealing with psychological clutter tied to money and finances so they can live thrifty lives that are also liberating, pleasurable, and rewarding. . . . At the crux of this book are three audits designed to instigate life changes: a financial audit combined with assessments of the physical junk filling our homes and the emotional junk causing tension in our lives. Throughout, Walsh challenges readers to face not just the physical clutter overwhelming their homes but also the psychological underpinnings to their habits and attitudes, to confront family members, and to establish tough boundaries within the limits of their family's means. . . . Motivated readers will find plenty of helpful tips to jump-start their self-transformations." Publ Wkly

Yeager, Jeff

The **cheapskate** next door; the surprising secrets of Americans living happily below their means. Broadway Books 2010 231p pa $12.99; ebook $12.99 **332.024**

1. Personal finance
ISBN 978-0-7679-3132-8 pa; 978-0-307-59247-7 ebook

LC 2009-42287

"The amazing fact about this book is that in addition to his instructions making perfect sense, like no other book of its kind, this one can be read simply for the humor of the author's prose." Booklist

332.042 International finance

Perkins, John, 1945-

The **new** confessions of an economic hit man; John Perkins. Berrett-Koehler Publishers, Inc. 2015 384 p. (paperback: acid-free paper) $17.95 **332.042**

1. Corporations -- Corrupt practices 2. United States. National Security Agency -- Biography 3. Chas. T. Main, Inc 4. World Bank -- Developing countries 5. Imperialism -- History -- 20th century 6. Imperialism -- History -- 21st century 7. Economists -- United

States -- Biography 8. Corporations, American -- Corrupt practices 9. Energy consultants -- United States -- Biography 10. Intelligence officers -- United States -- Biography
ISBN 9781626566743

LC 2015036436

In this book, "former economic hit man John Perkins shares new details about the ways he and others cheated countries around the globe out of trillions of dollars. Then he reveals how the deadly EHM cancer he helped create has spread far more widely and deeply than ever in the US and everywhere else—to become the dominant system of business, government, and society today. Finally, he gives an insider view of what we each can do to change it." (Publisher's note)

"An intriguing, vivid account of Perkins's 'living on the edge' experiences, this fascinating read is of the truth-is-stranger-than-fiction variety." LJ

Includes bibliographical references and index

332.1   Banks

Ahamed, Liaquat

Lords of finance; the bankers who broke the world. Penguin Press 2009 564p il $32.95   **332.1**
    1. Capitalists and financiers
    ISBN 978-1-59420-182-0

LC 2008-44512

"A grand, sweeping narrative of immense scope and power." N Y Times Book Rev

Includes bibliographical references

Farrell, Greg

Crash of the titans; greed, hubris, the fall of Merrill Lynch, and the near-collapse of Bank of America. Crown Business 2010 471p $27; pa $17; ebook $12.99   **332.1**
    1. Bank failures 2. Corporate mergers and acquisitions 3. Bank of America NA 4. Merrill Lynch & Co., Inc.
    ISBN 978-0-307-71786-3; 978-0-307-71787-0 pa; 978-0-307-71788-7 ebook

LC 2010485623

This is an account of the decline of Merrill Lynch & Co. and Bank of America Corp. The author claims that "at the moment they should have been minding their balance sheets, . . . many of the financial industry's masters of the universe were preoccupied with their bonuses, expense accounts, and office renovations." Businessweek

Includes bibliographical references

Johnson, Simon

13 bankers; the Wall Street takeover and the next financial meltdown. [by] Simon Johnson and James Kwak. Pantheon Books 2010 304p il $26.95; pa $15.95; ebook $11.99 **332.1**
    1. Bank failures 2. Financial crises 3. Finance -- United States 4. Financial crises -- United States 5. Banks and banking -- United States
    ISBN 0-307-37905-1; 0-307-47660-X pa; 978-0-307-37905-4; 978-0-307-37922-1 ebook; 978-0-307-47660-9 pa

LC 2010-00168

This book argues that financial markets are not self-correcting and that government regulation is necessary to prevent destructive panics and recessions. Index.

"The book is a thoughtful, stimulating read on a topic of much ongoing debate and concern." Choice

Includes bibliographical references

Lefevre, John

Straight to Hell; true tales of deviance, debauchery, and billion-dollar deals. John LeFevre. Atlantic Monthly Press 2015 288 p. (hardback) $26   **332.1**
    1. Banks and banking -- Corrupt practices
    ISBN 0802123309; 9780802123305; 9781611855548

LC 2015460485

This book, by John LeFevre, is "an unapologetic . . . account of a career as a globe-conquering investment banker spanning New York, London, and Hong Kong. . . . [The author] pulls back the curtain on a world that is both hated and envied, taking readers from the trading floors and roadshows to private planes and after-hours overindulgence." (Publisher's note)

"This will appeal readily to heterosexual males with an inflated sense of entitlement and a mental age below 30, particularly those working in large corporations." LJ

Lowenstein, Roger

America's Bank; The Epic Struggle to Create the Federal Reserve. by Roger Lowenstein. Penguin Group USA 2015 368 p. illustrations $29.95   **332.1**
    1. Federal Reserve banks 2. Banks and banking -- United States
    ISBN 1594205493; 9781594205491

This book, by Roger Lowenstein, "illuminates the tumultuous era and remarkable personalities that spurred the unlikely birth of America's modern central bank, the Federal Reserve. Today, the Fed is the bedrock of the financial landscape, yet the fight to create it was so protracted and divisive that it seems a small miracle that it was ever established." (Publisher's note)

"Readers seeking a comprehensive history of the Federal Reserve from its conception to modern times will find this work especially appealing." LJ

Meltzer, Allan H.

★ A **history** of the Federal Reserve; v1 with a foreword by Alan Greenspan. University of Chicago Press 2002 800p v1 $75; pa $25   **332.1**
    1. Federal Reserve banks 2. Federal Reserve System (U.S.) -- Board of Governors
    ISBN 0-226-51999-6; 0-226-52000-5 pa

LC 2002-72007

The author "provides a definitive history of the U.S. Federal Reserve from its founding in 1913 to its establishment as a separate, independent entity in 1951. Using meeting minutes, correspondence, and internal Federal Reserve documents, he traces the reasons behind Federal Reserve policy decisions, highlights the impact that individuals and events had on the Fed, and examines the Fed's influence on international affairs. . . . This well-written and thoroughgoing account is recommended for academic, business, and public libraries." Libr J

Includes bibliographical references

Overtveldt, Johan van

Bernanke's test; Ben Bernanke, Alan Greenspan, and the drama of the central banker. Agate 2009 287p il $26   **332.1**
    1. Economists 2. Bankers 3. Government officials 4. Presidential advisers 5. Regulatory agency officials 6. Economic policy -- United States 7. Monetary policy -- United States 8. Banks and banking -- United States 9. Federal Reserve System (U.S.) -- Board of Governors
    ISBN 978-1-932841-37-4; 1-932841-37-7

LC 2008-45741

"Anyone who wants to understand the role of the Fed in the current crisis will find this an accessible primer." Publ Wkly

Includes bibliographical references

Parks, Tim

Medici money; banking, metaphysics, and art in fifteenth-century Florence. W. W. Norton & Co. 2005 273p il map (Enterprise) $22.95   **332.1**

1. Banks and banking 2. Bankers 3. Political leaders 4. Florence (Italy) -- History

ISBN 0-393-05827-1

LC 2004-30516

"The general reader will learn from this book a great deal about the era, and those who bestrode it, without getting bogged down in excessive scholarly detail." Natl Rev

Includes bibliographical references

Prins, Nomi

Collusion; how central bankers rigged the world. Nomi Prins. Nation Books 2018 384 p. $28   **332.1**

1. Monetary policy 2. Financial crises 3. Banks and banking

ISBN 1568585624; 9781568585628

In this book, author "Nomi Prins shows how the 2007-2008 financial crisis turbo-boosted the influence of central bankers and triggered a massive shift in the world order. . . . Prins reveals how five regions and their central banks reshaped economics and geopolitics. She discloses how Mexico navigated its relationship with the US while striving for independence and how Brazil led the BRICS countries to challenge the US dollar's hegemony." (Publisher's note)

Rockefeller, David

Memoirs. Random House 2002 517p $35; pa $17.95 **332.1**

1. Philanthropists 2. Bankers 3. Chase Manhattan Bank, N.A.

ISBN 0-679-40588-7; 0-8129-6973-1 pa

LC 2002-24800

"Rockefeller's style is restrained and self-deprecating; the account of his attempts to modernize and globalize Chase makes for excellent business history, and his sketch of his complicated relationship with his brother is especially convincing." New Yorker

Servon, Lisa

The **Unbanking** of America; How the New Middle Class Survives. Lisa Servon. Houghton Mifflin Harcourt 2017 272 p. $27; (ebook) $27   **332.1**

1. Financial services industry 2. Middle class -- United States 3. Banks and banking -- United States

ISBN 0544602315; 9780544602311; 9780544611184

LC 2016498797

In this book, author Lisa Servon "delivers a stunning indictment of America's banks, together with eye-opening dispatches from inside a range of banking alternatives. . . . She works as a teller at RiteCheck, a check-cashing business in the South Bronx, and as a payday lender in Oakland. She looks closely at the workings of a tanda, an informal lending club. And she delivers fascinating . . . portraits of the entrepreneurs reacting to the unbanking of America." (Publisher's note)

"This well-written book offers a fascinating read." LJ

Includes bibliographical references (pages 227-240) and index.

Wessel, David

★ In Fed we trust; Ben Bernanke's war on the great panic. Crown Business 2009 323 p. (hbk.) $26.99   **332.1**

1. Economists 2. Banks and banking 3. Global Financial Crisis, 2008-2009 4. Government officials 5. Regulatory agency officials

6. Federal Reserve System (U.S.) 7. Monetary policy -- United States 8. Financial crises -- United States 9. Federal Reserve System (U.S.) -- Board of Governors

ISBN 9780307459688; 0307459683

LC 2009-289789

This book reviews events of 2008 as the U. S. government attempted to stave off financial panic. Under the leadership of Ben Bernanke, the Federal Reserve "spearheaded the biggest government intervention in more than half a century. . . . [Wessel discusses questions such as]: What did Bernanke and his team at the Fed know—and what took them by surprise? Which of their actions stretched—or even ripped through—the Fed's legal authority? . . . What were they thinking at pivotal moments during the race to sell Bear Stearns, the unsuccessful quest to save Lehman Brothers, and the virtual nationalization of AIG, Fannie Mae, and Freddie Mac? . . . How well did Bernanke, former treasury secretary Hank Paulson, and then New York Fed president Tim Geithner perform under intense pressure?" (Publisher's note)

The author "has written a gripping blow-by-blow account of how the top brass at the Federal Reserve and Treasury flailed against financial collapse. . . . [The story] is a thrilling one, deftly told by a veteran journalist with access to those involved. Mr Wessel has an eye for enlivening detail, . . . and he has a knack for making finance accessible to the layman without boring the specialist." Economist

Includes bibliographical references

332.3   Credit and loan institutions

Grind, Kirsten

The **lost** bank; the story of Washington Mutual--the biggest bank failure in American history. Kirsten Grind. Simon & Schuster 2012 389 p.   **332.3**

1. Bank failures 2. Financial crises 3. Washington Mutual, Inc. 4. Savings and loan associations 5. Banks and banking -- United States 6. Washington Mutual, Inc 7. Bank failures -- United States -- History 8. Banks and banking -- Washington (State) -- Seattle -- History 9. Savings and loan association failures -- United States -- History 10. Savings and loan associations -- Washington (State) -- Seattle -- History

ISBN 1451617925; 9781451617924; 9781451617931; 9781451617948

LC 2011048587

In this book, "reporter [Kirsten] Grind chronicles the rise of Washington Mutual from a sleepy Seattle-based thrift to America's biggest savings and loan bank, its reckless plunge into the can't-lose subprime mortgage market, and its 2008 failure. . . . [The book includes] personalities like Kerry Killinger, WaMu's . . . CEO, and Jamie Dimon, the . . . JPMorgan leader who swallowed WaMu, . . . [as well as the] WaMu salespeople. . . . Grind pens a . . . guide to the delusions and frauds powering the debacle, from Fed chief Alan Greenspan's . . . economic forecasts down to the falsified documents that put people with no income, assets, or perhaps even pulses into mortgages they could never repay." (Publishers Weekly)

Includes bibliographical references.

332.4   Money

Ledbetter, James

One nation under gold; how one precious metal has dominated the American imagination for four centuries. James Ledbetter. Liveright Publishing Corp. 2017 xvii, 380 p.p illustrations (hardcover) $28.95   **332.4**

1. Gold 2. Gold -- United States -- History 3. Gold standard --
United States -- History

ISBN 9781631493966; 9780871406835

LC 2017005139

This book, by James Ledbetter, "examines the countervailing forces
that have long since divided America--whether gold should be a repository of hope, or a damaging delusion. . . . [The book] begins with the
nation's founding in the 1770s. . . . [S]ome Founding Fathers believed
that a national currency would not only unify the fledgling nation but
provide a perfect solution for a country that was believed to be lacking
in natural silver and gold resources." (Publisher's note)

"A vibrant and fascinating account of monetary gold's volatile fortunes in the U.S." Booklist

Includes bibliographical references (pages 341-369) and index.

Popper, Nathaniel

Digital gold; bitcoin and the inside story of the misfits and
millionaires trying to reinvent money. Nathaniel Popper. Harper 2015 416 p. (hardback) $27.99   **332.4**

1. Money 2. Internet industry 3. Internet -- Economic aspects 4.
Credit 5. Electronic commerce 6. Electronic funds transfers

ISBN 0062362496; 9780062362490

LC 2015002576

In this book author Nathaniel Popper presents a "history of Bitcoin,
the landmark digital money and financial technology that has spawned
a global social movement. [He] charts the rise of the Bitcoin technology through the eyes of the movement's colorful central characters, including an Argentinian millionaire, a Chinese entrepreneur, Tyler and
Cameron Winklevoss, and Bitcoin's elusive creator, Satoshi Nakamoto."
(Publisher's note)

Rickards, James

Currency wars; the making of the next global crisis. Port-
folio/Penguin 2011 288p $26.95   **332.4**

1. Monetary policy 2. Financial crises 3. Foreign exchange

ISBN 978-1-59184-449-5

LC 2011026906

The author "tells us we are in a new currency war that could destroy
faith in the U.S. dollar; he examines that war through the lens of economic policy, national security, and historical precedent. As a national
security issue, he tells a fascinating story of his involvement with the
Pentagon and other agencies in designing and participating in a war
game using currencies and capital markets, instead of ships and planes,
to gain early warning of attacks on the U.S. dollar. . . . He presents a
compelling case for his views and offers thought-provoking information
for library patrons. This is a must-read book." Booklist

Includes bibliographical references

332.401   Philosophy and theory

Hammond, Claudia

Mind over Money; The Psychology of Money and How to
Use It Better. by Claudia Hammond. HarperCollins 2016 384
p. $15.99; (ebook) $14.99   **332.401**

1. Money 2. Economics

ISBN 0062317008; 9780062317001; 9780062317018

In this book, author Claudia Hammond "tackles the very latest research in the fields of neuroscience, psychology, and biology to provide
a fresh, fascinating, and thought-provoking look at our relationship with
money. . . . She also reveals some simple and effective tricks that will

help you use and save money better—from how being grumpy can stop
you getting ripped off to why you should opt for the more expensive pain
relief." (Publisher's note)

"Part history, part anecdotes, part research, part tips, Hammond's
deep look into our conflicted, world-shaping involvement with money provides striking insights, sage advice, humor, and much food for
thought." Booklist

Includes bibliographical references (page [363]) and index.

332.6   Investment

Bernstein, William

The **four** pillars of investing; lessons for building a winning portfolio. [by] William J. Bernstein. McGraw Hill 2010
331p il $30   **332.6**

1. Investments

ISBN 978-0-07-174705-9

First published 2002

The author discusses "the four pillars—the theory of investing, the
history of investing, the psychology of investing, and the business of
investing. . . . Using humor, Bernstein advises readers to employ sound
tenets of investing to manage risk while building a foundation of assests
for the long term." Libr J

Includes bibliographical references

The **investor's** manifesto; preparing for prosperity, Armageddon, and everything in between. [by] William J. Bernstein.
Wiley 2010 xxii, 201p il $24.95; ebook $24.95   **332.6**

1. Stocks 2. Securities 3. Investments

ISBN 978-0-470-50514-4; 978-0-470-55807-2 ebook

LC 2009-20116

"Touching on lessons from the dot.com and 2008 market sell-offs, . .
. [the author] discusses market and investor psychology, asset allocation,
the unpredictability of returns, how to keep costs low, and, ultimately,
how to avoid dying poor." Libr J

Includes bibliographical references

Bogle, John C., 1929-

The **clash** of the cultures; investment vs. speculation. John
C. Bogle. John Wiley & Sons 2012 xxv, 353 p.p ill. (hardcover) $29.95; (ebook) $29.95; (ebook) $40.00   **332.6**

1. Investments 2. Speculation 3. Mutual funds 4. Capital gains

ISBN 9781118122778; 9781118224748 pdf; 9781118414378

LC 2012026770

This book, by John C. Bogle, explores how "speculation has come
to dominate investment. . . . Over the course of his sixty-year career in
the mutual fund industry, Vanguard Group founder John C. Bogle has
witnessed . . . the prudent, value-adding culture of long-term investment
. . . crowded out by an aggressive, value-destroying culture of short-term
speculation. . . . [This book] urges a return to the common sense principles of long-term investing." (Publisher's note)

Includes bibliographical references and index.

Buffett, Mary

Warren Buffett and the art of stock arbitrage; proven strategies for arbitrage and other special investment situations. [by]
Mary Buffett & David Clark. Scribner 2010 153p $25; ebook
$11.99   **332.6**

1. Investments 2. Financiers

ISBN 978-1-4391-9882-7; 978-1-4516-0645-4 ebook

LC 2011280299

Analyzes Buffett's techniques for arbitrage and special situations investing and offers step-by-step instructions on how to take advantage of such events as spin-offs, liquidations, recapitalizations, and tender offers.

"The writing is concise and straightforward, the examples are current and clear, and there are simple formulas on how to determine risk in both arbitrage and valuing liquidations." Libr J

Includes glossary

Cohan, William D.

Money and power; how Goldman Sachs came to rule the world. Doubleday 2011 658p $30.50; ebook $14.99   **332.6**
1. Securities 2. Investments 3. Banks and banking 4. Goldman Sachs & Co. 5. Goldman Sachs Group, Inc.
ISBN 978-0-385-52384-4; 978-0-385-53497-0 ebook

This is a history of the New York-based banking and investment firm from its founding in 1869 to the present.

"The book offers the best analysis yet of Goldman's increasingly tangled web of conflicts. . . . The writing is crisp and the research meticulous, drawing on reams of documents made publicly available by congressional committees and the Financial Crisis Inquiry Commission." Economist

Includes bibliographical references

Cortese, Amy

Locavesting; the revolution in local investing and how to profit from it. John Wiley 2011 252p $22.95; ebook $10.99   **332.6**
1. Investments 2. Small business 3. Community development
ISBN 978-0-470-91138-9; 978-1-1180-8578-3 ebook

LC 2011005647

"With the recent crash of the financial markets, many investors are looking for new places to put their money. At the same time, many small businesses are finding it ever more difficult to get credit. Cortese . . . covers this current confluence, providing examples of how investing in local small businesses can be beneficial to all parties. . . . Various types of funding methods are discussed, including cooperatives, credit unions, local stock exchanges, community development funds, public venture capital, and raising money through social networking. . . . Timely and easy to read, this is a nice introduction to something many of us have never considered. A good choice for public libraries and fruitful reading for small businesses and investors." Libr J

Includes bibliographical references

Fox, Justin

★ The **myth** of the rational market; a history of risk, reward, and delusion on Wall Street. Harper Business 2009 382p $27.99; pa $16.99   **332.6**
1. Economics 2. Wall Street (New York, N.Y.) 3. Economics -- History 4. Economics -- Psychological aspects 5. Rational expectations (Economic theory)
ISBN 0-06-059899-9; 0-06-059903-0 pa; 978-0-06-059899-0; 978-0-06-059903-4 pa

LC 2008-52718

This book chronicles "the rise and fall of the efficient market theory. . . . The theory holds that the market is always right, and that the decisions of millions of rational investors, all acting on information to outsmart one another, always provide the best judge of a stock's value." (Publisher's note) Index.

"A must-read for anyone interested in the markets, our economy or government, this dense but spellbinding work brings modern finance and economics to life." Publ Wkly

Includes bibliographical references

Hagstrom, Robert G., 1956-

The **Warren** Buffett Way; Robert G. Hagstrom. 3rd edition Wiley 2013 281 p. hbk $29.95   **332.6**
1. Investments 2. Capitalists and financiers
ISBN 1118503252; 9781118503256

LC 2013023887

First published 1994

"Warren Buffett is the most famous investor of all time and one of today's most admired business leaders. He became a billionaire and investment sage by looking at companies as businesses rather than prices on a stock screen. . . . The new edition updates readers on the latest investments by Buffett. And, more importantly, it draws on the new field of behavioral finance to explain how investors can overcome the common obstacles that prevent them from investing like Buffett." (Publisher's note)

Hudson, Michael

The **monster**; how a gang of predatory lenders and Wall Street bankers fleeced America--and spawned a global crisis. [by] Michael W. Hudson. Times Books 2010 365p $26; ebook $12.99   **332.6**
1. Mortgages 2. Global Financial Crisis, 2008-2009 3. Banks and banking -- Corrupt practices
ISBN 978-0-8050-9046-8; 978-1-4299-4004-7 ebook

LC 2010-3223

The author "exposes the source of the so-called toxic subprime mortgages that led to the 2008 financial crisis. He picks his way through a warren of mortgage brokers and lending companies that sat just outside banking regulations in the years following the savings and loan crisis. The book concentrates on the practices of mortgage lenders FAMCO and Ameriquest Mortgage, at one point the largest U.S. subprime lender. . . . This is essential reading for anyone concerned with the mortgage crisis." Libr J

Includes bibliographical references

Kelly, Kate

Street fighters; the last 72 hours of Bear Stearns, the toughest firm on Wall Street. Portfolio 2009 247p hardcover o.p. pa $16   **332.6**
1. Investments 2. Wall Street (New York, N.Y.) 3. Bear, Stearns & Co. Inc.
ISBN 978-1-5918-4273-6; 1-5918-4273-5; 978-1-5918-4318-4 pa; 1-5918-4318-9 pa

LC 2009-07694

This is an account of the collapse of the Bear Stearns investment bank in March 2008.

"Enlivened by graphic descriptions of executive disarray and cameo profiles of scrambling financiers as they come to appreciate the magnitude of the disaster they unleashed . . . this riveting account puts the ensuing worldwide financial crises in stark perspective." Publ Wkly

Includes bibliographical references

Lewis, Michael

Flash boys; a Wall Street revolt. Michael Lewis. W.W. Norton & Co Inc. 2014 288 p. (hardcover: alk. paper) $27.95   **332.6**
1. Financial services industry 2. Wall Street (New York, N.Y.) 3. Business -- Corrupt practices 4. Stockbrokers -- United States 5. Finance -- United States -- History -- 21st century
ISBN 0393244660; 9780393244663

LC 2014003208

Written by Michael Lewis, "'Flash Boys' is about a small group of

Wall Street guys who figure out that the U.S. stock market has been rigged for the benefit of insiders and that, post-financial crisis, the markets have become not more free but less, and more controlled by the big Wall Street banks. Working at different firms, they come to this realization separately; but after they discover one another, the flash boys band together and set out to reform the financial markets." (Publisher's note)

An "engrossing true-life morality play that unmasks the devil in the details of high finance." Pub Wkly

Includes bibliographical references and index

Lowenstein, Roger

The **end** of Wall Street. Penguin Press 2010 xxv, 339p $27.95 **332.6**

    1. Wall Street (New York, N.Y.) 2. Global Financial Crisis, 2008-2009

ISBN 978-1-59420-239-1; 1-59420-239-7

            LC 2009-50864

Lowenstein "examines the past three years of economic collapse, chronicling actions and inactions from dozens of villains and a few heroes. . . . [He] identifies more than 100 key players, almost all of them middle-aged white males from Wall Street, private mortgage companies, law firms, federal government agencies and the U.S. Congress. The narrative consistently demonstrates how almost all of those who could have halted the coming recession by employing common sense instead decided that the housing market would never collapse." Kirkus

Includes bibliographical references

Lutnick, Howard

On top of the world; Cantor Fitzgerald and 9/11: a story of loss and renewal. {by} Howard Lutnick and Tom Barbash. HarperCollins Pubs. 2002 282p il $25.95; pa $14.95 **332.6**

    1. September 11 terrorist attacks, 2001 2. Cantor Fitzgerald LP 3. World Trade Center (New York, N.Y.)

ISBN 0-06-051029-3; 0-06-051030-7 pa

            LC 2002-27550

The bond-trading firm Cantor Fitzgerald lost 658 employees on September 11, 2001. "'On Top of the World' sets out to tell the story of Cantor Fitzgerald's tragedy, and its survival, largely from its chairman's point of view; the book is interspersed with . . . passages in {Howard} Lutnick's own voice." N Y Times Book Rev

Mahar, Maggie

★ **Bull!**: a history of the boom, 1982-1999; what drove the breakneck market--and what every investor needs to know about financial cycles. HarperBusiness 2003 xxii, 486p il $27.95; pa $16.95 **332.6**

    1. Business cycles 2. Wall Street (New York, N.Y.)

ISBN 0-06-056413-X; 0-06-056414-8 pa

            LC 2003-51131

This is a "history of the 1982-99 bull market in U.S. stocks. {The author} explains that this bull market got its initial impetus from both the undervaluation of equities during the 1970s and the end of the Cold War. . . . Mahar concludes by summarizing how investors who haven't seen a bear market for 17 years might plan their investing strategies. Mahar takes complicated topics and explains them clearly for the average reader. Her exceptional book is most highly recommended to even the smallest public or academic library." Libr J

Includes bibliographical references

Malkiel, Burton Gordon, 1932-

★ A **random** walk down Wall Street; the time-tested strategy for successful investing. [by] Burton G. Malkiel. Rev. ed.;

W.W. Norton & Co. 2011 445p il $29.95 **332.6**

    1. Stocks 2. Investments

ISBN 978-0-393-08143-5

            LC 2010-41866

  First published 1973

The author argues "that it is extremely rare for an individual investor to consistently beat the stock-market averages. Investors are better off buying and holding an index fund than attempting to buy and sell individual securities or actively managed mutual funds. . . . This readable investment guide for individuals offers information on the full range of new investment products available, the results of current research by academics and other marketplace professionals, and a section on investment strategies for retired investors or those anticipating retirement. This excellent book offers important information for individual investors and is a valuable resource for library patrons." Booklist

McGee, Suzanne

Chasing Goldman Sachs; how the masters of the universe melted Wall Street down--and why they'll take us to the brink again. Crown Publishers 2010 398p $27; ebook $13.99 **332.6**

    1. Banks and banking 2. Global Financial Crisis, 2008-2009 3. Goldman Sachs & Co.

ISBN 978-0-307-46011-0; 0-307-46011-8; 978-0-307-46012-7 ebook

            LC 2009-53440

This " is an exceptionally lucid, well-written account of how and why the financial system broke down." Washington Post

Includes bibliographical references

Tengler, Nancy

The **women's** guide to successful investing; achieving financial security and realizing your goals. Nancy Tengler. Palgrave Macmillan 2014 210 p. illustrations (hardback) $28 **332.6**

    1. Investments 2. Women -- Personal finance 3. Stocks -- Prices 4. Women -- Finance, Personal

ISBN 1137403349; 9781137403346

            LC 2014005402

In this book, wealth advisor Nancy Tengler "delivers advice about building a rational, reliable investment portfolio. Investing, she writes, is not gambling. And it's not rocket science. In fact, the value-based approaches employed by the most successful investors will resonate with women who manage their own finances and households. Filled with fascinating case studies and engaging, personal stories of financial management, Tengler entertains as she educates." (Publisher's note)

Tett, Gillian

Fool's gold; how the bold dream of a small tribe at J.P. Morgan was corrupted by Wall Street greed and unleashed a catastrophe. Free Press 2009 293p $26; pa $16 **332.6**

    1. Investments 2. Wall Street (New York, N.Y.)

ISBN 978-1-4165-9857-2; 1-4165-9857-X; 978-1-4391-0013-4 pa; 1-4391-0013-6 pa

            LC 2009-5127

Traces the relationship between a team of JP Morgan banking gurus and the current financial crisis, documenting their invention of a bold variety of allegedly risk-free investments that sparked a frenzy in the banking world and may have directly contributed to the market crash.

Tett "deploys a remarkable sense of pacing, generating real suspense over rapidly inflating debt on bank balance sheets; by the time Lehman Brothers fails, the book has become a bonafide page-turner. . . . Tett's explosive, illuminating narrative is the one to read for anyone confused

by the present financial mess." Publ Wkly
Includes bibliographical references

Town, Phil

Invested; how Warren Buffett and Charlie Munger taught me to master my mind, my emotions, and my money (with a little help from my dad) Danielle Town and Phil Town. Harper-Collins 2018 336 p. $24.99   **332.6**
1. Investments 2. Personal finance
ISBN 0062672657; 9780062672650

In this book, author Danielle Town "shares her yearlong journey learning to invest, as taught to her by her father, investor and bestselling author Phil Town. . . . Danielle shows you how to . . . take command of your own life and finances by choosing companies with missions that match your values, using the same gold standard strategies that have catapulted Warren Buffet and Charlie Munger to the top of the Forbes 400." (Publisher's note)

332.601   Philosophy and theory

Dreman, David

Contrarian investment strategies; the psychological edge. David Dreman. Free Press 2012 viii, 481 p.p $30   **332.601**
1. Profit 2. Stocks 3. Stock exchanges 4. Investment analysis 5. Investments -- Psychological aspects
ISBN 0743297962; 9780743297967

LC 2011023716

Author David Dreman discusses "new findings in psychology that explain why the stock market is inescapably given to bubbles, panics, and periods of high volatility. He also shows how we can use these findings to reliably profit from market errors, crash-proof our portfolios, and earn market-beating long-term returns. . . . [The book] shows why the 'best' stocks are consistently overvalued while the so-called worst, contrarian stocks are undervalued, and [Dreman] lays out his proven and simple rules for avoiding the pitfalls and spotting the bargains." (Publisher's note)

Includes bibliographical references and index.

332.63   Specific forms of investment

Shiller, Robert J., 1946-

Irrational exuberance; Robert J. Shiller. Princeton University Press 2015 392 p. illustrations (hardcover: alk. paper) $29.95   **332.63**
1. Economics 2. Financial crises 3. Capitalists and financiers 4. Risk 5. Stocks -- United States 6. Dow Jones industrial average 7. Stock exchanges -- United States 8. Stocks -- Prices -- United States 9. Real property -- Prices -- United States
ISBN 0691166269; 9780691166261

LC 2014036705

This book by "Robert Shiller, who warned of both the tech and housing bubbles, now cautions that signs of irrational exuberance among investors have only increased since the 2008–9 financial crisis. It shows how investor euphoria can drive asset prices up to dizzying and unsustainable heights, and how, at other times, investor discouragement can push prices down to very low levels." (Publisher's note)

Includes bibliographical references and index

Siegel, Jeremy J.

Stocks for the long run; the definitive guide to financial market returns & long-term investment strategies. Jeremy J. Siegel. Fifth edition McGraw-Hill Education 2014 422 p illustrations $40   **332.63**
1. Stocks 2. Rate of return
ISBN 9780071800518; 0071800514

LC 2013037218

First published 1994 by Irwin

This book, by Jeremy J. Siegel, "answers all the important questions of today: How did the crisis alter the financial markets and the future of stock returns? What are the sources of long-term economic growth? How does the Fed really impact investing decisions? Should you hedge against currency instability?" (Publisher's note)

"New material encompasses the causes and consequences of the 2008-09 financial crises. . . . The writing is so lucid that lay investors can readily comprehend the concepts." Choice

Includes bibliographical references and index

Weatherall, James Owen

The **physics** of Wall Street; a brief history of predicting the unpredictable. James Owen Weatherall. Houghton Mifflin Harcourt 2013 304 p. $27   **332.63**
1. Finance 2. Physics 3. Securities -- United States 4. Wall Street (New York, N.Y.)
ISBN 0547317271; 9780547317274

LC 2012017323

In this book, professor "[James Owen] Weatherall looks at the role played by physicists and their ideas in financial markets, and argues . . . that their contributions should be more widely used and recognized. Himself a physicist, philosopher, and mathematician, Weatherall suggests that the profession's essential contribution to finance is to develop models of how financial markets operate using insights from science." (Publishers Weekly)

Includes bibliographical references and index

332.64   Exchange of securities and commodities; speculation

Henriques, Diana B.

A **first**-class catastrophe; the road to Black Monday, the worst day in Wall Street history. Diana B. Henriques. Henry Holt & Co. 2017 xviii, 393 p.p (hardcover) $32   **332.64**
1. Stock exchanges 2. Financial crises 3. Stock Market Crash, 1987 4. Finance -- United States -- History -- 20th century 5. Stock exchanges -- United States -- History -- 20th century 6. Financial crises -- United States -- History -- 20th century
ISBN 9781627791649; 1627791647; 9781627791656

LC 2017002890

In this book, author Diana B. Henriques presents an "account of the [stock market] crash of 1987, a cautionary tale of how the U.S. financial system nearly collapsed. . . . Black Monday was more than seven years in the making and threatened nearly every U.S. financial institution. Drawing on superlative archival research and dozens of original interviews[,] . . . Henriques weaves a tale of missed opportunities, market delusions, and destructive actions." (Publisher's note)

"It's a must-read for anyone who wants to understand why financial markets lurch from crisis to crisis and are still so frighteningly susceptible to crashes today." Pub Wkly

Includes bibliographical references and index

332.67 Investments in specific industries, in specific kinds of enterprise, by specific kinds of investors; international investment; investment guides

Nolan, Peter
Is China buying the world? Peter Nolan. Polity 2012 147 p. $19.95 **332.67**
1. International competition 2. China -- Economic conditions -- 1970-
ISBN 0745660789; 9780745660783
This book by Peter Nolan "probes behind the media rhetoric and shows that the idea that China is buying the world is a myth. . . . Giant firms from high income countries with leading technologies and brands have greatly increased their investments in developing countries, with China at the forefront. . . . By contrast, Chinese firms have a negligible presence in the high-income countries." (Publisher's note)

332.7 Credit

Acharya, Viral V.
Guaranteed to fail; Fannie Mae, Freddie Mac, and the debacle of mortgage finance. [by] Viral V. Acharya [et al.] Princeton University Press 2011 232p il $24.95; ebook $24.95 **332.7**
1. Housing 2. Mortgages 3. Financial crises 4. Business failures 5. Fannie Mae 6. Federal Home Loan Mortgage Corporation
ISBN 978-0-691-15078-9; 978-1-4008-3809-7 ebook
LC 2011000247
"The authors of Guaranteed to Fail are specialists in applied financial and housing economics. They believe in the necessity of choosing among three options: should Fannie Mae and Freddie Mac exist? Should there be a private-public partnership of mortgage guarantees? Should government end housing subsidies? . . . The authors argue that overextension in housing came from the private sector, Congress, and government-sponsored enterprises." Choice
Includes bibliographical references

Atwood, Margaret, 1939-
Payback; debt and the shadow side of wealth. House of Anansi Press 2008 230p (CBC Massey lectures) **332.7**
1. Debt 2. Wealth 3. Debt in literature 4. Debt -- Social aspects 5. Debt -- Moral and ethical aspects
ISBN 978-0-88784-800-1
This volume collects novelist Margaret Atwood's Massey Lectures, originally broadcast on the CBC. She investigates the "subject of debt, exploring debt as an ancient and central motif in religion, literature, and the structure of human societies." (Publisher's note) Bibliography. Index.
"Delivered with . . . [Atwood's] trademark wit and imagination, this is a meditation that challenges conventional thinking on one of the most morally pressing issues we face." Booklist
Includes bibliographical references

Davenport, Anthony
Your Score; An Insider's Secrets to Understanding, Controlling, and Protecting Your Credit Score. Anthony Davenport with Matthew Rudy. Houghton Mifflin Harcourt 2018 xvi, 202 p.p (hardcover) $22 **332.7**
1. Consumer credit 2. Personal finance 3. Consumer credit -- United States 4. Finance, Personal -- United States
ISBN 9781328695277; 9781328694652; 1328695271
LC 2017044246
This book, by Anthony Davenport, is a "comprehensive insider's look at what every consumer needs to know about their credit score. . . . Like it or not, a healthy credit score is essential if you want to participate in today's financial world. But very few people actually understand how their credit score is determined. Worse yet, most don't know how their score is used by all kinds of companies and banks to dictate financial terms that will strongly affect their daily lives." (Publisher's note)
"All readers who seek to better their knowledge of financial literacy, personal finance, and banking will find this a valuable resource." Booklist
Includes bibliographical references and index.

Halpern, Jake
Bad paper; chasing debt from wall Street to the underworld. Jake Halpern. Farrar Straus & Giroux 2014 256 p. (hardback) $25 **332.7**
1. Consumer credit 2. Collecting of accounts 3. Finance, Personal 4. Collection agencies
ISBN 0374108234; 9780374108236
LC 2014013576
This book, by Jake Halpern, explores why "the Federal Trade Commission receives more complaints about rogue debt collecting than about any activity besides identity theft. . . . It tells the story of Aaron Siegel, a former banking executive, and Brandon Wilson, a former armed robber, who become partners and go in quest of 'paper'-- the uncollected debts that are sold off by banks for pennies on the dollar." (Publisher's note)
"Colorful and chilling, this work is an important peek into the dark corner of consumer finance and recommended for all consumers and true crime aficionados." LJ

Howard, Timothy
The **mortgage** wars; inside Fannie Mae, big-money politics, and the collapse of the American dream. Timothy Howard. McGraw-Hill 2013 304 p. (hardback) $30 **332.7**
1. Mortgages 2. Housing -- United States -- History 3. Federal National Mortgage Association 4. Mortgage loans -- United States 5. Subprime mortgage loans -- United States 6. Mortgage banks -- United States -- History
ISBN 0071821090; 9780071821094
LC 2013033450
In this book "former Fannie Mae CFO [Timothy] Howard lays bare . . . how the agency was undermined, and its executive leadership framed, by a confederation of political opponents. . . . His . . . account traces behind-the-scenes activity beginning around 1998. He describes a bipartisan league of free market ideologues, political hatchet men operating as financial regulators, and major business and corporate interests eager to privatize Fannie Mae's mortgage business for their own benefits." (Kirkus Reviews)

Leonard, Robin
★ **Credit** repair; make a plan, improve your credit, avoid scams. Robin Leonard, J.D.; updated by Attorney Amy Loftsgordon. 12th edition Nolo 2015 394 p. pbk $24.99 **332.7**
1. Consumer credit
ISBN 9781413321548; 1413321542
LC 2014043496
First published 1996. Periodically revised
Includes bibliographical references
This book offers advice on assessing your debt situation, avoiding overspending, handling existing debts, cleaning your credit file, how credit reports are used, and building and maintaining good credit.

Morgenson, Gretchen

Reckless endangerment; how outsized ambition, greed, and corruption led to economic armageddon. [by] Gretchen Morgenson, Joshua Rosner. Times Books 2011 331p il $30; ebook $12.99   **332.7**

1. Mortgages 2. Financial crises 3. Global Financial Crisis, 2008-2009 4. Fannie Mae 5. Subprime mortgage loans 6. Financial crises -- United States -- 21st century

ISBN 978-0-8050-9120-5; 978-1-4299-6577-4 ebook

LC 2010047594

"A sobering account of some sordid recent history that's so clear and detailed that pros and novices will find its account rich and informative, and deeply depressing." Publ Wkly

333   Economics of land and energy

Clover, Charles

The **end** of the line; how overfishing is changing the world and what we eat. New Press 2006 386p $26.95   **333**

1. Commercial fishing

ISBN 978-1-59558-109-9; 1-59558-109-X

LC 2006-12058

First published 2004 in the United Kingdom

"Clover's hard-hitting approach will probably anger some, but his argument that we will soon run out of fish unless we take drastic measures . . . is persuasive." Publ Wkly

Includes bibliographical references

Renewable energy; sustainable concepts for the energy change. edited by Roland Wengenmayr and Thomas Bührke, translated by William D. Brewer. Wiley-VCH 2013 vi, 164 p.p $44.95   **333**

1. Energy policy 2. Energy development 3. Renewable energy resources 4. Renewable energy sources

ISBN 3527411879; 9783527411870

LC 2012540474

This book, edited by Roland Wengenmayr and Thomas Bührke, examines "changes in terms of energy sources.The increasing number of wind power plants, solar collectors and photovoltaic installations demonstrates perceptibly that many innovations for tapping renewable energy sources have matured: very few other technologies have developed so dynamically in the past years. Nearly all the chapters were written by professionals in the respective fields." (Publisher's note)

Includes bibliographical references and index

Turner, Brandon

The **book** on rental property investing; how to create wealth and passive Income through smart buy & hold real estate investing. by Brandon Turner. BiggerPockets 2015 347 p. (paperback) $24.99   **333**

1. Real estate business 2. Real estate investment 3. Lease and rental services

ISBN 099071179X; 9780990711797

This book, by Brandon Turner, is intended "to give you every strategy, tool, tip, and technique needed to become a millionaire rental property investor--while helping you avoid the junk that pulls down so many wannabes! . . . [Here] you'll find practical, up-to-date, exciting strategies that investors across the world are using to build wealth and significant cash flow through rental properties." (Publisher's note)

"A thorough and accessible introduction to the complex world of real estate investments." Kirkus

333.3   Private ownership of land

Linklater, Andro

Owning the earth; the transforming history of land ownership. by Andro Linklater. Bloomsbury USA 2013 496 p. illustrations, maps (alk. paper) $30   **333.3**

1. Feudalism 2. Land tenure 3. Landlord and tenant 4. Land tenure -- History

ISBN 1620402890; 9781620402894

LC 2013011970

In this book, author Andro Linklater "focuses on the history of land ownership as driving human activity from the earliest ages and being the key to the creation of democracy. . . . Evolving from the collision of crown and chief barons that resulted in the Magna Carta, the impetus for owning land gained steam in the 1500s in England with the land revolution, which displaced subsistence farming via the feudal system in favor of a few rich owners profiting from the buying of land and increasing yields." (Kirkus Reviews)

"Many aspire to land ownership, taking the concept--that individuals may obtain a sliver of our planet as their own--for granted. Linklater's global study looks at land ownership--feudal, private, communal--through the lens of history and politics, rather than as merely a matter for economic study. The results are enlightening for our understanding not only of the past but of our future." (Library Journal)

Includes bibliographical references and index

333.33   Transfer of possession and of right to use

Ilgunas, Ken

This land is our land; how we lost the right to roam and how to take it back. Ken Ilgunas. Plume, an imprint of Penguin Random House, LLC 2018 288 p. (hardcover) $14   **333.33**

1. Land use 2. Land tenure 3. Right of property 4. Land use -- United States 5. Land tenure -- United States 6. Public lands -- United States 7. Right of way -- United States 8. Recreation areas -- United States 9. Right of property -- United States 10. Land use -- Government policy -- United States

ISBN 9780735217843

LC 2017036689

In this book, author Ken Ilgunas, "calls into question our entrenched understanding of private property and provocatively proposes something unheard of: opening up American private property for public recreation. He imagines a future in which folks everywhere will have the right to walk safely, explore freely, and roam boldly--from California to the New York island, from the Redwood Forest to the Gulf Stream waters." (Publisher's note)

Includes bibliographical references and index

333.7   Natural resources and energy

Duncan, Dayton

The **national** parks; America's best idea: an illustrated history. with a preface by Ken Burns; picture research by Susanna Steisel and Aileen Silverstone. Alfred A. Knopf 2009 403p il map $50   **333.7**

1. Nature conservation 2. United States -- Local history 3. National parks and reserves -- United States 4. United States -- National Park Service -- History

ISBN 978-0-307-26896-9

LC 2009-20880

The author delves "into the history of the park idea, from the first sighting by white men in 1851 of the valley that would become Yosemite and the creation of the world's first national park at Yellowstone in 1872, through the most recent additions to a system that now encompasses nearly four hundred sites and 84 million acres." Publisher's note

Includes bibliographical references

Encyclopedia of global resources; editor, Craig W. Allin. Salem Press 2010 4v il map set $395   **333.7**
   1. Reference books 2. Natural resources -- Encyclopedias
ISBN 978-1-58765-644-6; 1-58765-644-2

                      LC 2010-1984

First published 1998 with title: Natural resources

"This four-volume set provides a wide variety of perspectives about Earth's natural resources and explains the interrelationships among resource exploitation, environmentalism, geology, and biology. Allin . . . presents 576 articles on resources such as oil and tar sands, nations from Argentina to Zimbabwe, government laws and conventions, and historical events. . . . [This encyclopedia] offers real value and sheds important light on where we derive our mineral and biological resources, how they are processed, what they are used for, and how they fit into the global economy." Libr J

Includes bibliographical references

Goleman, Daniel
   Ecological intelligence; how knowing the hidden impacts of what we buy can change everything. Doubleday 2009 276p $26   **333.7**
   1. Consumers 2. Industries 3. Environmental protection
ISBN 0-385-52782-9; 978-0-385-52782-8

                      LC 2008-41811

"Brimming with intriguing, useful, and galvanizing information, this is an exceptionally sharp, innovative, and realistic approach to raising the demand for environmentally safe merchandise." Booklist

Miller, Char
   Gifford Pinchot and the making of modern environmentalism. Island Press (Washington, D.C.) 2001 458p il $28 **333.7**
   1. Governors 2. Conservationists 3. Foresters
ISBN 1-55963-822-2

                      LC 2001-5665

"Charismatic, progressive, and controversial, Gifford Pinchot (1865-1946) established and directed the Forest Service under Theodore Roosevelt, lobbied hard for responsible logging practices, expressed prescient warnings about pollution, and called for sustainable energy. Miller's animated biography portrays Pinchot in all his fervor, and environmentalism in all its complexity." Booklist

Includes bibliographical references

Park, Chris
   A **dictionary** of environment and conservation; by Chris Park. 2nd ed. Oxford University Press 2013 484 p. (Oxford paperback reference) (paperback) $21.95   **333.7**
   1. Environment 2. Conservation of natural resources 3. Environmental sciences -- Dictionaries 4. Conservation of natural resources -- Dictionaries
ISBN 0199641668; 9780199641666

                      LC 2008006450

This book by Michael Allaby and Chris Park "provides over 9,000 alphabetically arranged entries on scientific and social aspects of the environment, including concise and authoritative information on key thinkers, treaties, movements, organizations, concepts, and theories. For the second edition, Allaby has added over 700 new entries, including

'aerial plankton,' 'cyclone collector,' 'oasis,' and 'supertramp.'" (Publisher's note)

333.72   Conservation and protection

★   **American** earth; environmental writing since Thoreau. edited by Bill McKibben; foreword by Al Gore. Literary Classics of the United States 2008 1047p il (Library of America) $40   **333.72**
   1. Nature conservation 2. Environmental movement 3. Environmental protection 4. Literature -- Collections
ISBN 978-1-59853-020-9; 1-59853-020-8

                      LC 2007-940683

This book "can be read as a survey of the literature of American environmentalism, but above all, it should be enjoyed for the sheer beauty of the writing." Publ Wkly

Includes bibliographical references

Brinkley, Douglas
   The **quiet** world; saving Alaska's wilderness kingdom, 1879-1960. Harper 2011 576p il map $29.99; ebook $23.99   **333.72**
   1. Nature conservation 2. Environmental protection 3. Natural history -- Alaska
ISBN 978-0-06-200596-0; 978-0-06-203533-2 ebook

This book "brims over with information and insight, passion and insistence and some carelessness. In fact, it's a bit like Alaska itself: large, formidable, raw and ultimately unforgettable." Washington Post

Includes bibliographical references

Freeman, Scott
   Saving Tarboo Creek; one family's quest to heal the land. by Scott Freeman; illustrations by Susan Leopold Freeman. Timber Press 2018 224 p. (hardcover) $25.95   **333.72**
   1. Human ecology 2. Nature conservation 3. Tarboo Creek (Wash.) 4. Human ecology -- Washington (State) -- Olympic Peninsula 5. Nature conservation -- Washington (State) -- Olympic Peninsula
ISBN 9781604698381; 9781604697940

                      LC 2016055648

This book, by Scott Freeman, illustrated by Susan Leopold Freeman, tells the story of how "the Freeman family decided to restore a damaged creek in Washington's Olympic Peninsula. . . . Scott . . . artfully blends his family's story with powerful universal lessons about how we can all live more constructive, fulfilling, and natural lives by engaging with the land rather than exploiting it." (Publisher's note)

"Thought-provoking and unsettling, this highly readable book is made lovely by homey drawings sprinkled throughout." Booklist

Includes bibliographical references and index

Horn, Miriam
   Rancher, farmer, fisherman; Conservation Heroes of the American Heartland. Miriam Horn. W W Norton & Co Inc 2016 384 p. illustrations, map (hardcover) $27.95; (ebook) $50   **333.72**
   1. Conservationists 2. Conservation of natural resources
ISBN 9780393247343; 9780393247350

                      LC 2016018263

This book, by Miriam Horn, " tells the stories of five representatives of this stewardship movement: a Montana rancher, a Kansas farmer, a Mississippi riverman, a Louisiana shrimper, and a Gulf fisherman. In exploring their work and family histories and the essential geographies they protect, [it] challenges pervasive and powerful myths about American and environmental values." (Publisher's note)

"Horn's intimate profiles reveal undervalued environmental change makers while countering popular notions of what it means to be a conservationist." Pub Wkly

Includes bibliographical references and index

McDaniel, Carl N.

Wisdom for a livable planet; the visionary work of Terri Swearingen, Dave Foreman, Wes Jackson, Helena Norberg-Hodge, Werner Fornos, Herman Daly, Stephen Schneider, and David Orr. Trinity University Press 2005 277p hardcover o.p. pa $17.95   **333.72**
1. Environmental sciences
ISBN 1-595-34008-4; 1-595-34009-2 pa
        LC 2004-19081

The author personalizes "critical environmental issues via profiles of eight 'visionaries' agitating for a more livable planet. . . . His subjects are prominent in the areas of hazardous waste incineration, biodiversity, sustainable agriculture, appropriate technology, population control, rational economic planning, climate concerns and environmental education. . . . The stories of these eight ecological warriors are profoundly appealing in that they show the diverse ways that people can commit to a common cause." Publ Wkly

Includes bibliographical references

McKibben, Bill

★ The **Bill** McKibben reader; pieces from an active life. Henry Holt 2008 442p pa $18   **333.72**
1. Environmental protection
ISBN 978-0-8050-7627-1 pa; 0-8050-7627-1 pa
        LC 2007-39609

This is a "collection of essays gleaned from books and periodicals published between 1982 and 2007. Most of the 44 essays come from a diverse array of magazines, including The New Yorker, Mother Jones, Outside, Gourmet, and Christian Century. . . . Essays are loosely divided into categories that include consumerism, activism, the changing planet, the meaning of community, and the sufficiency of nature. . . . Readers new to McKibben will be entertained, informed, and perhaps even inspired to make the positive changes that McKibben desires for the world." Libr J

333.73   Land

Biggers, Jeff

Reckoning at Eagle Creek; the secret legacy of coal in the heartland. Nation Books 2010 300p il $26.95   **333.73**
1. Coal mines and mining 2. Shawnee National Forest region (Ill.)
ISBN 978-1-56858-421-8; 1-56858-421-0
        LC 2009-32686

Biggers "takes a look at coal and its role in the history of southern Illinois as well as its human and environmental costs. Biggers also tells a personal story as he chronicles the saga of his family's strip-mined homestead in an area that one day would be a part of the Shawnee National Forest. . . . A lot of history is presented here in a personal style by a cultural historian with a keen eye. A valuable read for followers of environmental history." Libr J

Includes bibliographical references

333.75   Forest lands

Quammen, David, 1948-

Yellowstone; a journey through America's wild heart. David Quammen. National Geographic Partners 2016 222 p. ill. (some color), color map (harcback) $28   **333.75**
1. Yellowstone National Park 2. National parks and reserves -- United States 3. National parks and reserves -- Idaho 4. National parks and reserves -- Montana 5. National parks and reserves -- Wyoming 6. Public spaces -- Social aspects -- Yellowstone National Park 7. Outdoor recreation -- Social aspects -- Yellowstone National Park 8. Nature conservation -- Social aspects -- Yellowstone National Park
ISBN 9781426217548
        LC 2016014893

"Author David Quammen takes readers on a breathtaking journey through America's most inspiring and imperiled ecosystem--Yellowstone National Park--in this monumental book on America's first national park. Yellowstone's storied past, rich ecosystem, and dynamic landscape are brilliantly portrayed in a captivating mosaic of photographs and eloquently written text that blend history, science, and research from the field." (Publisher's note)

Includes bibliographical references (pages 216-219)

333.78   Recreational and wilderness areas

A **thinking** person's guide to America's national parks; 23 essays on America's national parks. edited by Robert Manning, Rolf Diamant, Nora Mitchell and David Harmon; foreword by Denis Galvin. George Braziller Publishers 2016 300 p. color illustrations (ebook) $50; $24.95   **333.78**
1. Nature conservation -- United States 2. Landscape protection -- United States 3. National parks and reserves -- United States 4. National parks and reserves -- United States -- History 5. National parks and reserves -- Study and teaching -- United States 6. National parks and reserves -- Conservation and restoration -- United States
ISBN 9780807600238; 9780807600191
        LC 2015038434

This book, edited by Robert Manning, Rolf Diamant, Nora Mitchell and David Harmon, with foreword by Denis Galvin, "delves into issues affecting an array of parks: the iconic western national parks like Yellowstone; the urban parks such as Golden Gate National Recreation Area; historic sites including the Statue of Liberty National Monument and Gettysburg National Military Park; and cultural areas like Mesa Verde National Park that are among America's over 400 national parks." (Publisher's note)

"A worthwhile title for prospective visitors who want more than a straightforward travel guide." LJ

Includes bibliographical references and index

Williams, Terry Tempest, 1955-

★ The **hour** of land; a personal topography of America's national parks. Terry Tempest Williams. Sarah Crichton Books/Farrar, Straus & Giroux 2016 416 p. illustrations (hardback) $27; (ebook) $60   **333.78**
1. Natural history -- United States 2. United States -- Environmental conditions 3. National parks and reserves -- United States 4. Human ecology -- United States -- Philosophy 5. Landscapes -- Social aspects -- United States 6. National parks and reserves -- Social aspects -- United States 7. National parks and reserves -- United States -- Pictorial works

ISBN 9780374280093; 9780374712266

LC 2015042477

Carnegie Medal Longlist: Nonfiction (2017)

This book, by Terry Tempest Williams, offers "a literary celebration of our national parks, an exploration of what they mean to us and what we mean to them. From the Grand Tetons in Wyoming to Acadia in Maine to Big Bend in Texas and more, Williams creates a series of lyrical portraits that illuminate the unique grandeur of each place while delving into what it means to shape a landscape with its own evolutionary history into something of our own making." (Publisher's note)

"An important, well-informed, and moving read for anyone interested in learning more about America's national parks." Kirkus

Includes bibliographical references (pages 375-382).

333.79   Energy

Barnham, Keith

The **Burning** Answer; The Solar Revolution: a Quest for Sustainable Power. by Keith Barnham. W.W. Norton & Co. Inc. 2015 400 p. illustrations $27.95   **333.79**

1. Solar energy

ISBN 160598776X; 9781605987767

In this book, author Keith Barnham "uncovers the connections between physics and politics that have resulted in our dependence on a high-carbon lifestyle, which only a solar revolution can now overcome. . . . While everyone is aware of solar energy, people are still not paying enough attention, and so as well as explaining the science behind it, Barnham takes his subject forward to advise on what we should be doing to utilize this amazing energy source." (Publisher's note)

"The author makes some big claims about the viability (and necessity) of solar energy, and while he seems oblivious to the strength of NIMBYism (Not In My Backyard), many readers will be inclined to agree with him. He persuades not with charts and graphs but with the power of his storytelling and his passion for science." LJ

Ferguson, Charles D.

Nuclear energy; what everyone needs to know. Charles D. Ferguson. Oxford University Press 2011 xvii, 222 p.p (What everyone needs to know) (hardback) $74   **333.79**

1. Nuclear energy 2. Nuclear power plants

ISBN 0199759456; 9780199759453; 9780199759460

LC 2010044449

In this book, "Charles D. Ferguson provides an authoritative account of the key facts about nuclear energy. What is the origin of nuclear energy? What countries use commercial nuclear power, and how much electricity do they obtain from it? How can future nuclear power plants be made safer? What can countries do to protect their nuclear facilities from military attacks? How hazardous is radioactive waste? Is nuclear energy a renewable energy source?" (Publisher's note)

"This compelling assembly of historical and scientific information deftly steps through the essential discoveries, definitions, and theory that led to the development of nuclear reactors and nuclear bombs. . . . [F]ollowing chapters . . . cover safety, climate change, nuclear proliferation concerns, security, and the politically charged options for disposal of radioactive waste." Choice

Includes bibliographical references and index

Helm, Dieter

The **carbon** crunch; how we're getting climate change wrong--and how to fix it. Dieter Helm. Yale University Press 2012 xiii, 273 p.p (hardcover) $35   **333.79**

1. Energy policy 2. Climate change 3. Renewable energy resources 4. Energy conservation 5. Renewable energy sources 6. Greenhouse gas mitigation 7. Climatic changes -- Prevention

ISBN 0300186592; 9780300186598

LC 2012017386

In this book Dieter Helm examines the economics of climate change regulation policies, finding fault in "their basic design. They have caused people to focus on the most expensive ways of mitigating climate change, rather than the cheapest, imposing high cost for little gain. . . .The heart of Mr Helm's book is an examination of the economics of renewable energy" and wind energy in particular. (Economist)

Includes bibliographical references and index

Koerth-Baker, Maggie

Before the lights go out; conquering the energy crisis before it conquers us. Maggie Koerth-Baker. John Wiley & Sons 2012 xii, 290 p.p $27.95   **333.79**

1. Solar energy 2. Biomass energy 3. Climate change 4. Energy policy -- United States 5. Energy consumption -- United States 6. Energy development -- United States 7. Energy conservation -- United States 8. Renewable energy sources -- United States

ISBN 0470876255; 9780470876251

LC 2011043334

Author Maggie KoerthBaker tells "how our energy systems really work today, and what we'll have to do to keep them working in the years to come. . . . [She discusses] climate change, [solar farms,] and conversion efficiency. . . . [KoerthBaker provides information on the future of] economics and social incentives [and how they] will be the things that build our new world." (maggiekb.com)

Includes bibliographical references and index.

Levi, Michael

Power surge; energy, opportunity, and the battle for America's future. by Michael Levi. Oxford University Press 2013 260 p. (hardback: alk. paper) $27.95   **333.79**

1. Energy resources 2. Energy policy -- United States 3. Renewable energy -- United States 4. Energy industries -- United States

ISBN 0199986169; 9780199986163

LC 2012043264

In this book, author Michael Levi "takes on the big claims made by both sides in the fight over American energy, showing what the changes underway mean for the United States and the world. Both unfolding revolutions in American energy offer big opportunities for the country to strengthen its economy, bolster its security, and protect the environment. Levi shows how to seize those with a new strategy that blends the best of old and new energy while avoiding the real dangers." (Publisher's note)

"Readers seeking to understand America's energy policies and prospects will welcome this even-handed, smart, and accessible book on a topic of incomparable economic importance." Pub Wkly

Includes bibliographical references and index

McGraw, Seamus

The **end** of country. Random House 2011 245p $26; ebook $13.99   **333.79**

1. Energy policy 2. Energy resources 3. Pennsylvania

ISBN 978-1-4000-6853-1; 978-0-679-60431-0 ebook

LC 2010035972

"In 2006, in a hardscrabble part of Pennsylvania that had long lost its allure as a farming and industrial area, geologists began investigating the Marcellus Shale. It turned out to be the richest deposit of natural gas ever discovered anywhere. When his widowed mother was approached about permitting natural-gas exploration on their farm, journalist McGraw had to weigh their need for money against the future prospects of the farmland. Chronicling the impact of the find on his mother and her neighbors, McGraw's research led to this impressively detailed, highly engaging look at issues of energy policy, economics, and sociology that arose when a bucolic town was suddenly faced with the 'traveling circus' of energy exploration. . . . A completely engaging look at how energy policy affected a quiet, rural town." Booklist

Muller, Richard A., 1944-

Energy for future presidents; the science behind the headlines. Richard A. Muller. W. W. Norton 2012 xvii, 350 p.p ill., maps (hardcover) $26.95   **333.79**
1. Energy resources 2. Energy development 3. Energy policy -- United States 4. Technology and state 5. Energy policy -- Social aspects 6. Power resources -- Social aspects
ISBN 0393081613; 9780393081619

LC 2012015586

This book, by Richard A. Muller, discusses U.S. energy policy. "The near-meltdown of Fukushima, the upheavals in the Middle East, the BP oil rig explosion, and the looming reality of global warming have reminded . . . all U.S. citizens that nothing has more impact on our lives than the supply of and demand for energy. Its procurement dominates our economy and foreign policy. . . . But the 'energy question' is more confusing, contentious, and complicated than ever before." (Publisher's note)

Includes bibliographical references and index

Newton, David E.

World energy crisis; a reference handbook. David E. Newton. ABC-CLIO 2013 xviii, 334 p.p ill. (Contemporary world issues. Science, technology, and medicine) (hardcover) $58   **333.79**
1. Energy policy 2. Energy consumption 3. Energy conservation 4. Energy security 5. Energy industries 6. Energy development
ISBN 1610691474; 9781610691475; 9781610691482

LC 2012016975

This book, by David E. Newton, is part of the "Contemporary World Issues" reference series. It "provides a thorough investigation of . . . our current global energy situation, and what actions should be taken to prevent a crippling fuel-supply catastrophe in the future. The book presents a historical background for current energy problems that discusses the supply and consumption of various forms of energy at different periods of history." (Publisher's note)

Includes bibliographical references (p. 269-305) and index

Rhodes, Richard

★ **Energy**; a human history. Richard Rhodes. Simon & Schuster 2018 xiv, 464 p.p illustrations, maps (hardcover) $30   **333.79**
1. Coal 2. Electricity 3. Energy development 4. Power resources -- History 5. Energy development -- History 6. Power resources -- Social aspects 7. Energy development -- Social aspects
ISBN 9781501105371; 9781501105357; 1501105353

In this book, author "Richard Rhodes explains how wood gave way to coal and coal made room for oil, as we now turn to natural gas, nuclear power, and renewable energy. . . . He addresses how we learned from such challenges, mastered their transitions, and capitalized on their opportunities. Rhodes also looks at the current energy landscape, with a focus on how wind energy is competing for dominance with cast supplies of coal and natural gas." (Publisher's note)

"Pulitzer Prize-winning historian and author Rhodes . . . takes on entangled issues around the use of science and technology and makes complicated matters more approachable." LJ

Includes bibliographical references (pages 347-397) and index.

Vollmann, William T., 1959-

No immediate danger; William T. Vollmann. Viking 2018 624 p. (hbk.) $40   **333.79**
1. Climate change 2. Global warming 3. Fukushima Nuclear Accident, Fukushima, Japan, 2011
ISBN 0399563490; 9780399563492

This book, the first volume of Carbon Ideologies, by William T. Vollmann, "[begins] by examining and quantifying the many causes of climate change. . . . Turning to nuclear power first, Vollmann then recounts multiple visits that he made . . . to the contaminated no-go zones and sad ghost towns of Fukushima, Japan, beginning shortly after the tsunami and reactor meltdowns of 2011. . . . [The book] builds up a powerful, sobering picture of the ongoing nightmare of Fukushima." (Publisher's note)

Yergin, Daniel

The **quest**; energy, security and the remaking of the modern world. Penguin Press 2011 804p il map $37.95   **333.79**
1. Energy policy 2. Globalization 3. Energy resources 4. Money -- Political aspects 5. Power resources -- Political aspects
ISBN 978-1-59420-283-4; 1-59420-283-4

LC 2011013100

This book "combines four books. The first . . . provides global history of oil, natural gas, and nuclear power from 1991 to 2011. . . . The second part of 'The Quest' traces a path from the discovery of climate change as an esoteric interest of a few scientists in the nineteenth century to the introduction of 'new climate change policies . . . intended to make a profound transformation of the energy foundations that support the world economy.' . . . 'The Quest''s third part looks at nuclear and renewable alternatives to fossil fuels. . . . When Yergin looks to the future in his fourth book, he asks how the economic benefits from an average megawatt of power can be increased while at the same time reducing its negative effects on the environment and health." (New York Review of Books)

This book "is a masterly piece of work and, as a comprehensive guide to the world's great energy needs and dilemmas, it will be hard to beat." Economist

Includes bibliographical references

333.792   Primary forms of energy

Mahaffey, James

Atomic adventures; secret islands, forgotten N-rays, and isotopic murder: a journey into the wild world of nuclear science. James Mahaffey. Pegasus Books 2017 xxxiii, 363 p.p illustrations (some color) (hardcover) $29.95   **333.792**
1. Nuclear physics 2. Nuclear engineering 3. Nuclear facilities -- History 4. Nuclear energy -- Government policy -- History
ISBN 9781681774800; 9781681774213; 1681774216

In this book, author James Mahaffey "unearths lost reactors on far flung Pacific islands and trees that were exposed to active fission that changed gender or bloomed in the dead of winter. He explains why we have nuclear submarines but not nuclear aircraft and why cold fusion doesn't exist." (Publisher's note)

"His expertise and astonishing stories are matched by his writing skills, creating a sometimes humorous book that offers a valuable history of a deadly modern force and uncommonly clear, enjoyable explanations of related physics." Booklist

Includes bibliographical references (pages 335-345) and index.

333.793 Secondary forms of energy

Bakke, Gretchen

The **grid**; the fraying wires between Americans and our energy future. Gretchen Bakke. Bloomsbury USA 2016 384 p. (hardback) $27; (ebook) $63   **333.793**

1. Electric power systems 2. Electric power distribution 3. Energy policy -- Social aspects -- United States 4. Clean energy -- United States 5. Electric power failures -- United States 6. Electric power distribution -- United States -- History 7. Electric power systems -- Technological innovations -- United States

ISBN 9781608196104; 9781620401248

LC 2016001376

In this book, author Gretchen Bakke "unveils the many facets of America's energy infrastructure, its most dynamic moments and its most stable ones, and its essential role in personal and national life. The grid, she argues, is an essentially American artifact, one which developed with us: a product of bold expansion, the occasional foolhardy vision, some genius technologies, and constant improvisation. Most of all, her focus is on how Americans are changing the grid [now]." (Publisher's note)

"A lively analysis of the challenges renewables present to the production and distribution of electricity." Kirkus

Includes bibliographical references and index.

Couch, Julianne

Traveling the power line; from the Mojave Desert to the Bay of Fundy. Julianne Couch. University of Nebraska Press 2013 xx, 214 p.p (Our sustainable future) (paperback) $19.95   **333.793**

1. Electric power 2. Power resources -- United States 3. Electric power plants -- United States

ISBN 0803245068; 9780803245068

LC 2012035997

In this book, journalist Julianne Couch "chronicles her visits to nine electrical power stations across the country, examining the pros and cons of the fuel sources used at each site." She looks at sources including "wind, water, geothermal, solar and nuclear power. Between 2008 and 2010, Couch traveled . . . to talk to 'scientists, engineers, policy advocates, environmental activists, industry experts and the folks who work in or live around various sites of energy production.'" (Kirkus)

Includes bibliographical references (pages 213-216).

333.794 Renewable energy sources

Pernick, Ron

Clean Tech Nation; How the U.S. Can Lead in the New Global Economy. Ron Pernick. HarperCollins 2012 320 p. $29.99   **333.794**

1. Economic development 2. Sustainable development 3. Technological innovations 4. Economic policy -- United States

ISBN 0062088440; 9780062088444

This book, by Ron Pernick and Clint Wilder, discusses how "the United States risks losing out on the most critical opportunity for job creation and global economic leadership in the 21st century. . . . If the U.S. is to remain dominant, as it has in the earlier high-tech and Internet revolutions, it needs to supercharge efforts at every level--in federal, state, and city governments, and in schools, small businesses, and large companies." (Publisher's note)

333.8 Subsurface resources

Goodstein, David L.

Out of gas; the end of the age of oil. {by} David Goodstein. Norton 2004 140p il $21.95; pa $13.95   **333.8**

1. Petroleum

ISBN 0-393-05857-3; 0-393-32647-0 pa

LC 2003-10376

"Goodstein's predictions are based on a sophisticated understanding of physics and thermodynamics, and on a simple observation about natural resources." N Y Times Book Rev

Includes bibliographical references

Wilber, Tom

Under the surface; fracking, fortunes and the fate of the Marcellus Shale. Tom Wilber. Cornell University Press 2012 272 p. (cloth: alk. paper) $27.95   **333.8**

1. Natural gas 2. Shale gas industry 3. Hydraulic fracturing 4. Marcellus Shale 5. Shale gas industry -- Pennsylvania 6. Hydraulic fracturing -- Pennsylvania 7. Shale gas industry -- New York (State) 8. Hydraulic fracturing -- New York (State)

ISBN 0801450160; 9780801450167

LC 2011047166

This book by Tom Wilber is a "journalistic overview of shale gas development and the controversies surrounding it. . . . [Wilber] gives a voice to all constituencies, including farmers and landowners tempted by the prospects of wealth but wary of the consequences, policymakers struggling with divisive issues, and activists coordinating campaigns based on their visions of economic salvation and environmental ruin." (Publisher's note)

Includes bibliographical references and index.

333.91 Water and lands adjoining bodies of water

Dean, Cornelia

Against the tide; the battle for America's beaches. Columbia Univ. Press 1999 279p il $60; pa $18.95   **333.91**

1. Coasts 2. Beaches 3. Seashore ecology

ISBN 0-231-08418-8; 0-231-08419-6 pa

LC 98-50755

Dean discusses the ecology of American beaches and contends that they are threatened by coastal development and erosion

"This thoroughly researched and thoughtful book is destined to become a classic of environmental science writing." Libr J

Includes bibliographical references

Doyle, Martin

The **source**; how rivers made America and America remade its rivers. Martin Doyle. W W Norton & Co Inc 2018 349 p. (hardcover) $26.95   **333.91**

1. Water resources development 2. Rivers -- United States -- History 3. Water conservation -- United States 4. Water conservation -- United States -- History 5. Floodplain management -- United States -- History 6. Water resources development -- United States -- History

ISBN 9780393242362; 9780393242355; 0393242358

LC 2017051192

In this book, author "Martin Doyle tells the epic story of America and its rivers, from the U.S. Constitution's roots in interstate river navigation . . . to the failure of the levees in Hurricane Katrina and the water wars in the west. Along the way, he explores how rivers have often been the source of arguments at the heart of the American experiment--over federalism, sovereignty and property rights, taxation, regulation, conservation, and development." (Publisher's note)

"Doyle tackles the shifts in how America has viewed and used its extensive waterways, producing a comprehensive and enjoyable account." Pub Wkly

Includes bibliographical references and index.

Fishman, Charles

The **big** thirst; Charles Fishman. Free Press 2011 388p. ebook $12.99; $26.99   **333.91**
1. Water supply 2. Infrastructure (Economics) 3. Water resources development
ISBN 978-1-4391-2493-2 ebook; 978-1-4391-0207-7
LC 2010033989

This is a "lively and invaluable assessment of the current politics, economics, and culture of water. Lyrical in his descriptions of the beauty and wonder of water, Fishman is rigorous when explaining that the water we have now is all the water we will ever have and that our 'golden age' of 'abundant, safe, and cheap' water may soon end, thanks to deteriorating infrastructure (7 billion gallons leak out of our water systems every day), rising urban populations, and climate change." Booklist

Includes bibliographical references and index.

Rothfeder, Jeffrey

Every drop for sale; our desperate battle over water in a world about to run out. Tarcher/Putnam 2001 205p hardcover o.p. pa $14.95   **333.91**
1. Water supply
ISBN 1-58542-114-6; 978-1-58542-367-5 pa; 1-58542-367-X pa
LC 2001-27903

"Like the drip of water on stone, Rothfeder's steady exposition of horrors will wear down any reader's doubts that water is the next flashpoint of global politics, human rights and health issues." Publ Wkly

Includes bibliographical references

333.95   Biological resources

Alexander, Jane, 1939-

Wild things, wild places; adventurous tales of wildlife and conservation on planet Earth. by Jane Alexander. Alfred A. Knopf 2016 336 p. illustrations (some color) (hardcover: alk. paper) $28.95   **333.95**
1. Wildlife conservation
ISBN 9780385354363
LC 2016007803

In this book, author Jane Alexander "writes of her steady and fervent immersion into the worlds of wildlife conservation, of her coming to know the scientists throughout the world--to her, the prophets in the wilderness--who are steeped in this work, of her travels with them--and on her own--to the most remote and forbidding areas of the world as they try to save many species, including ourselves." (Publisher's note)

"Highly recommended for all interested in travel, natural history, and environmental issues." LJ

Includes bibliographical references and index

Barrow, Mark V.

Nature's ghosts; confronting extinction from the age of Jefferson to the age of ecology. [by] Mark V. Barrow, Jr. University of Chicago Press 2009 497p il $35   **333.95**
1. Biologists 2. Extinct animals 3. Endangered species 4. Wildlife

conservation 5. Extinction (Biology) 6. Endangered species -- Law and legislation 7. Wildlife conservation -- United States -- History
ISBN 978-0-226-03814-8; 0-226-03814-9
LC 2008-49085

The author "retraces the history of the earliest European and North American naturalists, from those who refused to believe that species comprising a perfect, stable world could go extinct, to the acceptance of extinction at the hands of humans and the legal mechanisms created to halt it. . . . Professionals in ecology, conservation biology, and wildlife management and readers interested in natural history will find this book hard to put down." Choice

Includes bibliographical references

Cousteau, Jacques Yves

The **human,** the orchid, and the octopus; exploring and conserving our natural world. [by] Jacques Cousteau and Susan Schiefelbein. Bloomsbury 2007 305p hardcover o.p. pa $16   **333.95**
1. Oceanography 2. Nature conservation 3. Human influence on nature
ISBN 978-1-59691-417-9; 1-59691-417-3; 978-1-59691-418-6 pa; 1-59691-418-1 pa
LC 2007-18824

Original French edition, 1997

"Cousteau's reverence for life's miracles . . . shines through in this eloquent testimony on the importance of pursuing higher ideals, particularly the preservation of the oceans and the natural world for future generations." Publ Wkly

Includes bibliographical references

Ellis, Richard

Tuna; a love story. Alfred A. Knopf 2008 334p il $27.95; pa $16   **333.95**
1. Tuna 2. Commercial fishing 3. Endangered species
ISBN 978-0-307-26715-3; 0-307-26715-6; 978-0-307-38710-3 pa; 0-307-38710-0 pa
LC 2007-52253

"Ellis loves this fish. His rapt description of the physiology that makes tunas one of the fastest things in the ocean . . . lends emotional urgency to his account of the collapsing tuna fishery." Orion

Includes bibliographical references

Fraser, Caroline

Rewilding the world; dispatches from the conservation revolution. Metropolitan Books 2009 400p map $28.50 **333.95**
1. Ecology 2. Endangered species 3. Wildlife conservation
ISBN 978-0-8050-7826-8; 0-8050-7826-6
LC 2009-32989

"Heavily researched with endnotes for those looking for more information, this truly is an essential read for conservationists, biologists, and anyone interested in the natural world." Libr J

Includes bibliographical references

Goldfarb, Ben

Eager; the surprising, secret life of beavers and why they matter. Ben Goldfarb. Chelsea Green Publishing 2018 304 p. (hc) $24.95   **333.95**
1. Mammals 2. Wildlife conservation 3. Beavers -- Habitations 4. Beavers -- Ecology -- North America 5. Wildlife conservation -- North America 6. Colonization (Ecology) -- North America 7. Beavers -- Habitations -- North America -- History
ISBN 9781603587396; 9781603587402; 9781603588386

LC 2018004621

In this book, "environmental journalist Ben Goldfarb reveals that our modern idea of what a healthy landscape looks like and how it functions is wrong, distorted by the fur trade that once trapped out millions of beavers from North America's lakes and rivers. The consequences of losing beavers were profound: streams eroded, wetlands dried up, and species from salmon to swans lost vital habitat. Today, a growing coalition of 'Beaver Believers.'"(Publisher's note)

"Goldfarb traveled the country to observe researchers, beaver damage mitigators, county engineers, hydrologists, and wildlife biologists, all working with beavers and studying their positive effects on ecosystems from the western deserts to the replenishing forests of the east. Beavers are kind of magical, Goldfarb tells us: they can make wetlands appear." Booklist

Includes bibliographical references and index

Goodall, Jane

★ The **ten** trusts; what we must do to care for the animals we love. {by} Jane Goodall and Marc Bekoff. HarperSanFrancisco 2002 xx, 200p hardcover o.p. pa $14.95   **333.95**
1. Animal rights 2. Animal welfare 3. Wildlife conservation 4. Human influence on nature
ISBN 0-06-251757-0; 0-06-055611-0 pa

LC 2002-68717

"An accessible, compelling, and important exposé." Booklist
Includes bibliographical references

Greenberg, Paul

American catch; the fight for our local seafood. Paul Greenberg. The Penguin Press 2014 320 p. $26.95   **333.95**
1. Seafood industry -- United States 2. Commercial fishing -- United States 3. Fish trade 4. Local foods -- United States 5. Fishes -- Conservation -- United States
ISBN 1594204489; 9781594204487

LC 2014005395

In this book, author Paul Greenberg tells "the surprising story of why Americans stopped eating from their own waters. In 2005, the United States imported five billion pounds of seafood, nearly double what we imported twenty years earlier. . . . During that same period, our seafood exports quadrupled. 'American Catch' examines New York oysters, Gulf shrimp, and Alaskan salmon to reveal how it came to be that 91 percent of the seafood Americans eat is foreign." (Publisher's note)

Includes bibliographical references and index

Four fish; the future of the last wild food. Penguin Press 2010 284p $25.95   **333.95**
1. Tuna 2. Salmon 3. Codfish 4. Bass (Fish) 5. Fish culture 6. Commercial fishing
ISBN 978-1-59420-256-8

LC 2010-1276

"The narrative is grounded in common sense and anchored by first-rate, on-scene reporting from the Yukon and Mekong Rivers, Lake Bardawil in the Sinai Peninsula and the waters off the coasts of Long Island, Greece, Hawaii and the Shetland Islands. Hugely informative, sincere and infectiously curious and enthusiastic." Kirkus

Includes bibliographical references

Hanes, Stephanie

White man's game; saving animals, rebuilding Eden, and other myths of conservation in Africa. Stephanie Hanes. Metropolitan Books, Henry Holt & Co. 2017 287 p. maps (hardcover) $28   **335.954**

1. Environmental literature 2. Wildlife conservation -- Africa 3. National parks and reserves -- Mozambique 4. Environmental ethics 5. Wildlife conservation -- Mozambique 6. Parque Nacional da Gorongosa (Mozambique) 7. Wildlife conservation -- Africa, Southern 8. Wildlife conservation -- Social aspects -- Mozambique 9. Wildlife conservation -- Social aspects -- Africa, Southern
ISBN 9780805097177; 9780805097160

LC 2016034296

This book, by Stephanie Hanes, offers "a probing examination of Western conservation efforts in Africa, where our feel-good stories belie a troubling reality. The . . . Gorongosa National Park, once the crown jewel of Mozambique. . . . looked . . . perfect . . . for Western philanthropy: revive the park and tourists would return. . . . So why did. . . . efforts to bring back wildlife become far more difficult than expected?" (Publisher's note)

"In straightforward and fervent prose, Hanes gives readers 'a new way of thinking about nature, conservation, and the pitfalls of best intentions.'" Pub Wkly

Includes bibliographical references (pages [263]-271) and index.

Hoekstra, Jonathan M.

The **atlas** of global conservation; changes, challenges and opportunities to make a difference. [by] Jonathan Hoekstra ... [et al.]; edited by Jennifer L. Molnar. University of California Press 2010 234p il map $49.95   **333.95**
1. Atlases 2. Globalization 3. Reference books 4. Environmental protection 5. Conservation of natural resources
ISBN 978-0-520-26256-0

LC 2009-23617

"Focusing primarily on biomes and ecosystems, this valuable atlas promotes a deeper understanding of the challenges involved in preserving and maintaining these habitats and resources. Basically an analysis of the current state of the globe, the book highlights conservation challenges through chapters on habitats, species distributions, deforestation, global warming, coastal development, and pollution. . . . The book is unique and well done." Voice Youth Advocates

Includes bibliographical references

Horwitz, Joshua

War of the Whales; A True Story. by Joshua Horwitz. Simon & Schuster 2014 448 p. ill. (some col.), col. map $28   **333.95**
1. Whales 2. Military research 3. United States. Navy
ISBN 1451645015; 9781451645019

This book, by Joshua Horwitz, "is the gripping tale of a crusading attorney who stumbles on one of the US Navy's best-kept secrets: a submarine detection system that floods entire ocean basins with high-intensity sound--and drives whales onto beaches. As Joel Reynolds launches a legal fight to expose and challenge the Navy program, marine biologist Ken Balcomb witnesses a mysterious mass stranding of whales near his research station in the Bahamas." (Publisher's note)

"Based on years of interviews and research, Horwitz delivers a powerful, engrossing narrative that raises serious questions about the unchecked use of secrecy by the military to advance its institutional power." Kirkus

Kurlansky, Mark

Cod; a biography of the fish that changed the world. Penguin Bks. 1998 294p il pa $14   **333.95**
1. Codfish 2. Commercial fishing 3. Cooking -- Fish
ISBN 0-14-027501-0

LC 97-12165

First published 1997 by Walker & Co.

Kurlansky discusses the history of commercial cod fishing and the plight of the Atlantic fish and fisheries today as the cod faces extinction.

This book offers "maximum readability, plenty of handsome illustrations, and a 40-page appendix of superlatively annotated recipes." Booklist

Includes bibliographical references

Lebbin, Daniel J.

The **American** Bird Conservancy guide to bird conservation; [by] Daniel J. Lebbin, Michael J. Parr, and George H. Fenwick; with a foreword by Jonathan Franzen. University of Chicago Press 2010 446p il map $45; ebook $27   **333.95**
  1. Wildlife conservation 2. Birds -- United States
  ISBN 978-0-226-64727-2; 0-226-64727-7; 978-0-226-6472-6 ebook

LC 2010007646

The authors survey "the comprehensive status of bird conservation in the Americas, primarily focusing on North America. . . . 'WatchList Birds' provides accounts for 212 US birds—priority species for conservation—with a color plate, map, and text sections on distribution, threats, conservation, and action. 'Habitats' gives an overview of 12 major North American habitats (tundra, wetlands, grasslands, etc.) and includes several prime site descriptions within each, accompanied by the same features as the 'WatchList' accounts. The third major section, 'Threats,' includes sections such as 'Habitat Loss,' 'Pollution and Toxics,' and 'Climate Change,' and describes problems, solutions, and actions. . . . A beautiful production visually, the book is inviting as well as an unprecedented, rewarding conservation reference source." Choice

Includes glossary and bibliographical references

Magdalena, Carlos

The **plant** messiah; adventures in search of the world's rarest species. by Carlos Magdalena. Doubleday 2018 272 p. (hardcover) $26.95   **333.95**
  1. Rare plants 2. Plant conservation 3. Horticulturists -- Biography 4. Personal narratives
  ISBN 9780385543613; 9780525436669; 0385543611

LC 2017027303

In this book, author Carlos Magdalena "takes readers from the Amazon to the jungles of Mauritius to deep within the Australian Outback in search of the rare and the vulnerable. Back in the lab, we watch as he develops groundbreaking, left-field techniques for rescuing species from extinction, encouraging them to propagate and thrive once again. Along the way, he offers moving, heartfelt stories about the secrets contained within these incredible organisms." (Publisher's note)

"Magdalena's paean to flora is bound to enthrall readers and get them thinking more fully about plants." Pub Wkly

Includes bibliographical references

Mooallem, Jon

Wild ones; a sometimes dismaying, weirdly reassuring story about looking at people looking at animals in America. Jon Mooallem. The Penguin Press 2013 339 p. (hardcover) $27.95   **333.95**
  1. Ecology 2. Human-animal relationship 3. Endangered species -- United States 4. Wildlife conservation -- United States 5. Endangered species -- United States -- Psychological aspects
  ISBN 159420442X; 9781594204425

LC 2012047006

In this book, the "plights of polar bears, Lange's metalmark butterflies and whooping cranes frame [a] discussion of humankind's relations with the animal kingdom, the environment and itself." Author

Jon Mooallem "contrasts the perilous circumstances threatening some species with the conflicts that arise among sentiment, commerce and environmental science." (Kirkus Reviews)

Includes bibliographical references and index

Orenstein, Ronald

Ivory, horn and blood; behind the elephant and rhinoceros poaching crisis. Ronald Orenstein. Firefly Books 2013 216 p. color illustrations $29.95   **333.95**
  1. Ivory 2. Poaching 3. Elephants 4. Rhinoceros 5. Ivory industry -- Corrupt practices 6. Rhinoceroses -- Effect of poaching on 7. African elephant -- Effect of poaching on 8. Asiatic elephant -- Effect of poaching on 9. Rhinoceros horn industry -- Corrupt practices
  ISBN 1770852271; 9781770852273

LC 2013427986

This book, by Ronald Orenstein, describes how "today a new ivory crisis has arisen, fuelled by internal wars in Africa and a growing market in the Far East. . . . Bands of militia have crossed from one side of Africa to the other, slaughtering elephants with automatic weapons. A market surge in Vietnam and elsewhere has led to a growing criminal onslaught against the world's rhinoceroses. The situation, for both elephants and rhinos, is dire." (Publisher's note)

"Orenstein brings his considerable expertise to bear on this complex catastrophe, presenting all sides of some of the most polarizing issues." LJ

Includes bibliographical references (pages [194]-211) and index

Owens, Delia

The **eye** of the elephant; an epic adventure in the African wilderness. [by] Delia and Mark Owens. Houghton Mifflin 1992 305p il hardcover o.p. pa $16   **333.95**
  1. Elephants 2. Wildlife conservation 3. Endangered species 4. North Luangwa National Park (Zambia)
  ISBN 0-395-42381-3; 0-395-68090-5 pa

LC 92-17691

This is an account of the authors' experiences attempting to stop elephant poaching in North Luangwa National Park in Zambia. Index.

This "is a provocative, disturbing, and eminently readable work." Nat Hist

Includes bibliographic references

Followed by Secrets of the savanna

★ **Sustaining** life; how human health depends on biodiversity. edited by Eric Chivian and Aaron Bernstein; Center for Health and the Global Environment Harvard Medical School; foreword by Edward O. Wilson; prologue by Kofi Annan. Oxford University Press 2008 542p il map $34.95   **333.95**
  1. Environmental health 2. Biological diversity
  ISBN 978-0-19-517509-7; 0-19-517509-3

LC 2007-20609

"A collaborative survey of biodiversity issues written and/or reviewed for accuracy by more than 100 scientists, this volume is motivated by its UN sponsors' sense of the world populace's indifference to the consequences of environmental degradation. Conceiving that implicating human health with the health of other species may enlist its concern, the authors collectively warn that present extinction rates are abnormally high. Seven categories of endangered species stand in as portents of the dire effects to ecosystems when extinction occurs. . . . Abundantly illustrated, this is a valuable, urgent resource suited to any general-interest library." Booklist

Includes bibliographical references (p. 445-514)

Wilson, Edward O., 1929-

The **future** of life. Knopf 2002 xxiv, 229p il $22; pa $13   **333.95**
1. Endangered species 2. Nature conservation
ISBN 0-679-45078-5; 0-679-76811-4 pa
LC 2001-38316
Wilson "proposes that there is yet time to avoid a grand planetary environmental crash provided we get serious, acknowledge a duty of stewardship and recognize an emotional affiliation . . . with other kinds of life." NY Times Book Rev

Half-earth; Our Planet's Fight for Life. W W Norton & Co Inc 2016 256 p. illustrations (ebook) $50; $25.95   **333.95**
1. Science 2. Extinction (Biology)
ISBN 9781631490835; 1631490826; 9781631490828
LC 2015041784
Written by Edward O. Wilson, "'Half-Earth' proposes an achievable plan to save our imperiled biosphere: devote half the surface of the Earth to nature. . . . 'Half-Earth' argues that the situation facing us is too large to be solved piecemeal and proposes a solution commensurate with the magnitude of the problem: dedicate fully half the surface of the Earth to nature." (Publisher's note)
"This startling, courageous, many will say wildly quixotic vision of a truly global preservation effort is guaranteed to stoke the fires of environmental debate." Booklist
Includes bibliographical references (pages 213-226) and index.

A **window** on eternity; A Biologist's Walk Through Gorongosa National Park. Edward O. Wilson; photographs by Piotr Naskrecki. Simon & Schuster 2014 228 p. col illustrations, color maps (hardback) $30   **333.95**
1. Ecology 2. Mozambique 3. Biodiversity 4. Nature conservation 5. Biodiversity -- Mozambique -- Parque Nacional da Gorongosa 6. Parque Nacional da Gorongosa (Mozambique) -- Pictorial works 7. Natural history -- Mozambique -- Parque Nacional da Gorongosa 8. Nature conservation -- Mozambique -- Parque Nacional da Gorongosa 9. Restoration ecology -- Mozambique -- Parque Nacional da Gorongosa 10. Parque Nacional da Gorongosa (Mozambique) -- Description and travel 11. Parque Nacional da Gorongosa (Mozambique) -- Environmental conditions
ISBN 1476747415; 9781476747415
LC 2013032607
In this book, author Edward O. Wilson presents a book of "prose and . . . photography about . . . Gorongosa National Park in Mozambique. . . . Wilson takes readers to the summit of Mount Gorongosa, sacred to the local people and the park's vital watershed. From the forests of the mountain he brings us to the deep gorges on the edge of the Rift Valley, previously unexplored by biologists, to search for new species and assess their ancient origins." (Publisher's note)
"Wilson . . . presents a lyrical ode to biodiversity within the framework of a memoir of his work in Mozambique's Gorongosa National Park, helping to rebuild it from the loss of nearly all of its megafauna as it was neglected, repurposed as a battleground, and destroyed by poachers during the 16-year civil war." Pub Wkly

335 Socialism and related systems

Avrich, Karen

Sasha and Emma; the anarchist odyssey of Alexander Berkman and Emma Goldman. Paul Avrich and Karen Avrich.

Belknap Press of Harvard University Press 2012 x, 490 p.p (hbk.: alk. paper) $35   **335**
1. Anarchism and anarchists 2. Anarchism -- United States -- History 3. Anarchists -- United States -- Biography
ISBN 0674065980; 9780674065987
LC 2012008659
This book, by Paul and Karen Avrich, is a biography of the anarchists, terrorists and political extremists Emma Goldman and Alexander Berkman. "Berkman shocked the country in 1892 with . . . the failed assassination of the industrialist Henry Clay Frick. . . . Through an attempted prison breakout, multiple bombing plots, and a dramatic deportation from America, these two unrelenting activists insisted on the improbable ideal of a socially just, self-governing utopia." (Publisher's note)
Includes bibliographical references and index.

Butterworth, Alex

The **world** that never was; a true story of dreamers, schemers, anarchists and secret agents. Pantheon Books 2010 482p il ebook $30.00; $30.00   **335**
1. Anarchism and anarchists 2. Anarchism -- History
ISBN 9780307379030; 9780375425110
LC 2009-48115
Butterworth "presents a history of anarchism from the 1871 Paris Commune to the 1905 Russian Revolution through stories of violent revolutionaries, the secret police who tracked them, and famous figures who played lesser-known roles." (Publisher's note) Index.
"A narrative taut with intrigue and freighted with contemporary significance." Booklist
Includes bibliographical references

335.4   Marxian systems

Marx, Karl

★ The **Communist** manifesto; [by] Karl Marx and Friedrich Engels; with an introduction and notes by Gareth Stedman Jones. Penguin Books 2002 287p pa $7   **335.4**
1. Communism
ISBN 0-14-044757-1
First published 1848
This document "analyzes history in terms of class conflict, predicts the imminent overthrow of the ruling bourgeoisie by the oppressed proletariat, and envisions a resulting classless society in which personal property would be abolished. The 'Manifesto' calls upon the proletariat of the world to unite and strengthen itself for this final revolution." Benet's Reader's Ency 4th edition
Includes bibliographical references

Pipes, Richard

★ **Communism**: a history. Modern Lib. 2001 175p hardcover o.p. pa $10.95   **335.4**
1. Communism
ISBN 0-679-64050-9; 0-8129-6864-6 pa
LC 2001-275458
"As a brief, polemical diatribe . . . this short account of communism should provoke and instruct." Libr J
Includes bibliographical references

Priestland, David

The **red** flag; a history of communism. Grove Press 2009 xxvii, 675p il $30   **335.4**

1. Communism

ISBN 978-0-8021-1924-7

"Starting with the origins of communist ideology in the French Revolution, . . . [this book] presents an interesting analysis of Marx's thinking as being shaped as much by Romanticism as by the Enlightenment. Priestland also examines communist governments and movements in Africa, Asia, Europe and Latin America as well as the Soviet Union, and discusses the Nazi-Soviet pact as well as Stalin's ban on anti-fascist activity in Europe, concluding with a level-headed account of the communist collapse." New Statesman

Includes bibliographical references

Wheen, Francis

Karl Marx; a life. Norton 2000 431p il $27.95; pa $14.95 **335.4**

1. Communism 2. Writers on politics 3. Political and social philosophers

ISBN 0-393-04923-X; 0-393-32157-6 pa

LC 99-87466

First published 1999 in the United Kingdom

"Following Marx from his childhood in Trier, Germany, through his exile in London, Wheen . . . takes readers from hovel to grand house, from the International Working Man's Association to Capital, from obscurity to notoriety and back again." Publ Wkly

Includes bibliographical references

335.43 Communism (Marxism-Leninism)

McAdams, A. James

★ **Vanguard** of the revolution; the global idea of the Communist Party. A. James McAdams. Princeton University Press 2017 xvii, 564 p.p (alk. paper) $35 **335.43**

1. Communism 2. Revolutions

ISBN 9780691168944

LC 2017941546

This book, by A. James McAdams, "argues that the rise and fall of communism can be understood only by taking into account the origins and evolution of this compelling idea. He shows how the leaders of parties in countries as diverse as the Soviet Union, China, Germany, Yugoslavia, Cuba, and North Korea adapted the original ideas of revolutionaries like Karl Marx and Vladimir Lenin to profoundly different social and cultural settings." (Publisher's note)

Includes bibliographical references (pages 503-541) and index.

336.2 Taxes

★ **J.K.** Lasser's your income tax; prepared by the J.K. Lasser Tax Institute. Wiley il **336.2**

1. Income tax

Annual. First published by Simon & Schuster. Began publication with 1936 issue. Title varies. Early issues prepared by J.K. Lasser

This "guide offers line-by-line instructions on filling out tax forms and what to do to prepare throught the year." Libr J

Reid, T. R.

A **Fine** Mess; A Global Quest for a Simpler, Fairer, and More Efficient Tax System. by T. R. Reid. Penguin Press 2017 278 p. illustrations $27 **336.2**

1. Taxation 2. Economics 3. Taxation -- United States 4. Income tax -- United States

ISBN 1594205515; 9781594205514

LC 2017301115

In this book, "T. R. Reid crisscrosses the globe in search of the exact solutions to these urgent problems. With an uncanny knack for making a complex subject not just accessible but gripping, he investigates what makes good taxation (no, that's not an oxymoron) and brings that knowledge home where it is needed most. Never talking down or reflexively siding with either wing of politics, T. R. Reid presses the case for sensible root-and-branch reforms with a companionable ebullience." (Publisher's note)

"Washington Post correspondent Reid...examines taxation in countries around the world to find alternatives to the American system in this highly readable and informative book." Pub Wkly

Includes bibliographical references (pages 263-269) and index.

Slemrod, Joel

Taxes in America; what everyone needs to know. Leonard E. Burman, Joel Slemrod. Oxford University Press 2013 280 p. (pbk.: alk. paper) $16.95 **336.2**

1. Taxation -- United States

ISBN 0199890269; 9780199890262; 9780199890279

LC 2012026106

In this book, Leonard E. Burman and Joel Slemrod provide an "explanation of how . . . [the U.S.] tax system works, how it affects people and businesses, and how it might be improved. They address such questions as how to recognize Fool's Gold tax reform plans. How much more tax could the IRS collect with better enforcement? How do tax burdens vary around the world? Why do corporations pay so little tax, even though they earn trillions of dollars every year?" (Publisher's note)

Includes bibliographical references and index

336.3 Public debt and expenditures

Johnson, Simon

White House burning; the founding fathers, our national debt, and why it matters to you. Simon Johnson, James Kwak. 1st ed. Pantheon Books 2012 352 p. ill. $26.95 **336.3**

1. Public debts -- United States 2. Deficit financing -- United States 3. United States -- Appropriations and expenditures 4. Debts, Public -- United States 5. Budget deficit -- United States 6. Government spending policy -- United States

ISBN 0307906965; 9780307906960

LC 2012000435

In this book, "[Simon] Johnson (Entrepreneurship and Management/ MIT) and [James] Kwak (Univ. of Connecticut School of Law) . . . explain how the [U.S.] national debt began to grow, why it is willfully misrepresented by politicians and misunderstood by much of the citizenry and whether it is ever likely to cripple the richest nation in the world. . . . The authors . . . [also offer a] demonstration of the fallacy of likening government debt to the debt of an individual family." (Kirkus Reviews)

Includes bibliographical references (p. [241]-324) and index.

Kleinbard, Edward D.

We are better than this; how government should spend our money. Edward D. Kleinbard. Oxford University Press 2015 544 p. illustrations (hardback) $29.95 **336.3**

1. Public finance 2. United States -- Appropriations and expenditures 3. Fiscal policy -- United States 4. Finance, Public -- United States 5. Government spending policy -- United States

ISBN 019933224X; 9780199332243

LC 2014024466

This book "fundamentally reframes budget debates in the United States. Author Edward D. Kleinbard explains how the public's preoccupation with tax policy alone has obscured any understanding of government's ability to complement the private sector through investment and insurance programs that enhance the general welfare and prosperity of our society at large." (Publisher's note)

Includes bibliographical references and index

Lane, Carl

A **Nation** Wholly Free; The Elimination of the National Debt in the Age of Jackson. by Carl Lane. Westholme Pub Llc 2014 256 p. 6 plates; illustrations $28   **336.3**

1. South Carolina -- History 2. Public debts -- United States 3. Banks and banking -- United States
ISBN 1594162093; 9781594162091

This book, by Carl Lane, "shows that the great and disparate issues that confronted [U.S. President Andrew] Jackson, such as internal improvements, the 'war' against the Second Bank of the United States, and the crisis surrounding South Carolina's refusal to pay federal tariffs, become unified when debt freedom is understood as a core element of Jacksonian Democracy." (Publisher's note)

"Lane brings life to the dry topics of debt, tariffs, taxes, and banks, and he's not above calling participants to account when he thinks criticism is warranted. His only error is holding figures of the past to today's standards. Otherwise, this is first-rate history rendered with unusual clarity and verve." Pub Wkly

337   International economics

Friedman, Thomas L.

The **Lexus** and the olive tree; Updated and expanded ed; Farrar, Straus, Giroux 2000 xxi, 469p $30   **337**

1. Free trade 2. Business and politics 3. International economic relations 4. United States -- Foreign economic relations
ISBN 978-0-374-18552-7; 0-374-18552-2

LC 00-29411

First published 1999

Friedman "explains, with anecdotes as well as analyses, what the instant electronic global economy is and what it may take to live there." N Y Times Book Rev

Stiglitz, Joseph E.

Globalization and its discontents. Norton 2002 xxii, 282p $24.95; pa $15.95   **337**

1. Globalization 2. International finance 3. International economic relations 4. International Monetary Fund 5. Developing countries -- Economic conditions
ISBN 0-393-05124-2; 0-393-32439-7 pa

LC 2002-23148

"This smart, provocative study contributes significantly to the ongoing globalization debate." Publ Wkly

Includes bibliographical references

338   Production

Clark, Taylor

Starbucked; a double tall tale of caffeine, commerce, and culture. Little, Brown 2007 297p $25.99   **338**

1. Coffeehouses 2. Coffee industry 3. Starbucks Corporation
ISBN 978-0-316-01348-2; 0-316-01348-X

LC 2007-13074

This "is a breezily written business yarn with plenty of big-picture punch." Christ Sci Monit

Includes bibliographical references

Dauch, Richard E., 1942-2013

American drive; how manufacturing will save our country. Richard E. Dauch with Hank H. Cox. St. Martin's Press 2012 xii, 334 p.p ill. (chiefly col.)   **338**

1. Banks and banking 2. Automobile industry 3. United States -- Economic conditions 4. Job creation -- United States 5. Industrial management -- United States
ISBN 9781250010827; 9781250010834

LC 2012028235

Author Richard E. "Dauch narrates the story of AAM [American Axle and Manufacturing] against the backdrop of his nearly fifty years in the auto industry, from . . . foreign competition, government bailouts, battles with unions, and the recent Great Recession . . . [He provides] lessons on leadership, advanced product technology, communication, negotiation, and making profits in the most difficult times . . . [The book] transcends the auto industry and draws a blueprint for job creation, manufacturing competitiveness, economic growth, and excellence in America." (Amazon)

★ **Encyclopedia** of American business; general editor, W. Davis Folsom; associate editor, Stacia N. VanDyne. Rev. ed.; Facts On File 2011 2v (Facts on File library of American history) set $150   **338**

1. Reference books 2. Business -- Encyclopedias
ISBN 978-0-8160-8112-7

LC 2010-28372

First published 2004

"Five general areas of business are covered: accounting, banking, finance, marketing, and management. This encyclopedia focuses on the terms, concepts, and associations that one is most likely to encounter in business." Publisher's note

Includes bibliographical references

O'Reilly, Tim

★ **WTF?** what's the future and why it's up to us. by Tim O'Reilly. HarperCollins 2017 xxvi, 419 p.p $32.99   **338**

1. Management 2. Business ethics 3. Economic development
ISBN 0062565710; 9780062565716

In this book, author Tim O'Reilly "shares the techniques he's used at O'Reilly Media to make sense of and predict past innovation waves and applies those same techniques to provide a framework for thinking about how today's world-spanning platforms and networks, on-demand services, and artificial intelligence are changing the nature of business, education, government, financial markets, and the economy as a whole." (Publisher's note)

Includes bibliographical references (pages 377-406) and index.

Schwantes, Carlos A.

The **West** the railroads made; [by] Carlos A. Schwantes, James P. Ronda. University of Washington Press in association with Washington State Historical Society and the John 2008 xx, 229p il map $39.95   **338**

1. West (U.S.) -- History 2. Railroads -- United States
ISBN 978-0-295-98769-9

LC 2007-29363

"Sprinkled throughout with marvelous reproductions of photos, maps, artwork and railroad memorabilia, this book highlights a fascinating era in our history. . . . A stunning work using well chosen archival resources to tell the story." Univ Press Books for Public and Second Sch Libr, 2009

Includes bibliographical references

338.04   Entrepreneurship

Stone, Brad

The **upstarts**; how Uber, Airbnb and the killer companies of the new Silicon Valley are changing the world. Brad Stone. Little, Brown & Co. 2017 x, 372 p.p color illustrations (hardcover) $30   **338.04**

1. Airbnb (Firm) 2. Entrepreneurship 3. New business enterprises 4. Electronic commerce -- United States 5. Ridesharing -- United States -- 21st century 6. Entrepreneurship -- United States -- Case studies 7. New business enterprises -- United States -- Case studies 8. Bed and breakfast accommodations -- United States -- 21st century

ISBN 0316388394; 9780316388399; 9780316388405

               LC 2016958932

This book, by Brad Stone, shows how "Uber and Airbnb . . . [are] redefining neighborhoods, challenging the way governments regulate business, and changing the way we travel. . . . Another generation of entrepreneurs is using technology to upend convention and disrupt entire industries. . . . They are rewriting the rules of business and often sidestepping serious ethical and legal obstacles in the process." (Publisher's note)

"Stone's account is illuminating reading for the business-minded." Kirkus

Includes bibliographical references (pages 337-358) and an index.

338.09   History, geographic treatment, biography

Waterhouse, Benjamin C.

The **land** of enterprise; a business history of the United States. Benjamin C. Waterhouse. Simon & Schuster 2017 vii, 280 p.p (hardcover) $28   **338.09**

1. Entrepreneurship 2. Business enterprises -- United States 3. Entrepreneurship -- United States -- History 4. Business enterprises -- United States -- History 5. Industrial management -- United States -- History

ISBN 1476766649; 9781476766676; 9781476766645

               LC 2017288586

This book, by Benjamin C. Waterhouse, "charts the development of American business from the colonial period to the present. It explores the nation's evolving economic, social, and political landscape by examining how different types of enterprising activities rose and fell, how new labor and production technologies supplanted old ones . . . and how Americans of all stripes responded to the tumultuous world of business." (Publisher's note)

"A historian makes his case that the story of private enterprise has been undervalued as a window into the history of the United States." Kirkus

Includes bibliographical references (pages 245-260) and index.

338.092   Biography

Bonney, Grace

★ In the company of women; Inspiration and Advice from over 100 Makers, Artists, and Entrepreneurs. by Grace Bonney; principal photography by Sasha Israel. Artisan 2016 360 p. color ill., color portraits (ebook) $35; (hardback, paper over board) $35   **338.092**

1. Businesswomen 2. Women executives 3. Businesswomen -- United States -- Biography 4. Women executives -- United States -- Biography 5. Minority businesswomen -- United States -- Biography 6. Women in the professions -- United States -- Biography 7. Minority women executives -- United States -- Biography 8. Minority women in the professions -- United States -- Biography

ISBN 9781579657260; 9781579655976

               LC 2016013010

This book, by Grace Bonney, "profiles over 100 . . . influential and creative women. . . . These interviews detail the keys to success (for example, going with your gut; maintaining meaningful and lasting relationships), highlight the importance of everyday rituals (meditating; creating a daily to-do list), and dispense advice for the next generation of women entrepreneurs and makers (stay true to what you believe in; have patience)." (Publisher's note)

"An excellent source of inspiration for women (and men) of all ages." LJ

338.1   Specific kinds of industries

Ackerman-Leist, Philip

Rebuilding the foodshed; how to create local, sustainable, and secure food systems. Philip Ackerman-Leist. Post Carbon Institute""||"Chelsea Green Pub. 2013 360 p. (A community resilience guide) (paperback) $19.95   **338.1**

1. Local foods 2. Agriculture -- Government policy 3. Food supply 4. Food security

ISBN 1603584234; 9781603584234; 9781603584241

               LC 2012043955

This book is about food policy. Farmer and professor Philip Ackerman-Leist "ruminates his way through the conundrums and possibilities of local food, demonstrating how words and their definitions can shed light on and transform our understanding of the rapidly evolving, often confusing, emotion-fraught questions of what people eat, where the food comes from, who has access to what, and how the answers to these questions affect the lives of eaters and growers." (Publishers Weekly)

Includes bibliographical references and index

Astyk, Sharon

A **nation** of farmers; defeating the food crisis on American soil. [by] Sharon Astyk & Aaron Newton. New Society Publishers 2009 392p il pa $19.95   **338.1**

1. Food relief 2. Food supply

ISBN 978-0-86571-623-0

               LC 2009-483077

The authors "argue that it is both possible and necessary to stop the harm caused by industrial agriculture. They show how the food crisis is tied to the energy crisis, global warming, and resource depletion and conclude that worldwide food shortages are imminent. . . . This outstanding and well-written compendium of insights and recommendations, of fervent idealism and practical solutions, is highly recommended." Libr J

Includes bibliographical references

Berry, Wendell, 1934-

The **art** of loading brush; new agrarian writings. Wendell Berry. Counterpoint 2017 270 p. (hardcover) $26   **338.1**

1. Nature writing 2. Agriculture -- United States 3. Agriculture -- Government policy 4. Agriculture -- Social aspects -- United States
ISBN 9781619020603; 9781619020382; 1619020386

LC 2017034645

This book, by Wendell Berry, "is an energetic mix of essays and stories, including 'The Thought of Limits in a Prodigal Age,' which explores Agrarian ideals as they present themselves historically and as they might apply to our work today. 'The Presence of Nature in the Natural World' is added here as the bookend of this developing New Agrarianism. Four stories from an as-yet-unfinished novel, better described as 'an essay in imagination,' extend the Port William story." (Publisher's note)

"About everything he loves and everything he regrets, he has never written better." Booklist

Includes bibliographical references (pages 172-175).

Bittman, Mark, 1950-

A **bone** to pick; the good and bad news about food, along with wisdom, insights, and advice on diets, food safety, GMOs policy, farming, and more. Mark Bittman. Clarkson Potter 2015 272 p. (hardback) $26 **338.1**
1. Diet 2. Food industry -- United States 3. Diet -- United States 4. Nutrition policy -- Untied States 5. Agriculture and state -- United States 6. Food industry and trade -- United States
ISBN 0804186545; 9780804186544

LC 2014044874

This book, by Mark Bittman, collects the author's "most memorable and thought-provoking columns . . . into a single volume. . . . As abundant and safe as the American food supply appears to be, the state of our health reveals the presence of staggering deficiencies in both the system that produces food and the forces that regulate it. Bittman leaves no issue unexamined: agricultural practices, government legislation, fad diets, and corporate greed." (Publisher's note)

"The author's keen analysis of the weakness of the Food and Drug Administration and its failures regarding food safety proves especially informative and enraging. Bittman successfully links a sound food system not just to the tastes of foodies (a word the author dislikes), but also to larger public health issues. An intelligent rallying cry for anyone seeking a safe and healthy food supply, and all that entails." Kirkus

Faruqi, Sonia

Project Animal Farm; An Accidental Journey into the Secret World of Farming and the Truth About Our Food. Sonia Faruqi. W.W. Norton & Co. Inc. 2015 336 p. illustrations $27.95; (ebook) $59.95 **338.1**
1. Food industry 2. Animal welfare 3. Livestock industry
ISBN 1605987980; 9781605987989; 9781504609326

LC 2015490657

This book by Sonia Faruqi offers a "look at what truly happens behind farm doors. . . . Over the course of living with farmers, hitchhiking with strangers, and risking her life, she developed surprising insights and solutions—both about the food industry and herself. . . . Sonia takes readers on an unforgettable adventure from top-secret egg warehouses in Canada to dairy feedlots in the United States, from farm offices in Mexico to lush pastures in Belize." (Publisher's note)

"Not for the fainthearted, but a good wake-up call for those concerned with decent treatment of animals and healthy food on the table." Kirkus

Includes bibliographical references (pages 357-390).

Hamilton, Lisa M.

Deeply rooted; unconventional farmers in the age of agribusiness. Counterpoint 2009 313p $25 **338.1**

1. Farmers
ISBN 978-1-5937-6180-6; 1-5937-6180-5

LC 2008-50526

Hamilton "profiles farmers and ranchers who believe that 'agriculture is not an industry' but, rather, 'a fundamental act that determines whether we as a society will live or die.'. . . Hamilton's in-depth portraits of independent farmers offer invaluable perspectives on American agriculture, past and present, while offering hope for a life-sustaining future." Booklist

Includes bibliographical references

Hesterman, Oran B.

Fair food; growing a healthy, sustainable food system for all. PublicAffairs 2011 302p il $24.99; ebook $9.99 **338.1**
1. Food supply 2. Food industry 3. Sustainable agriculture
ISBN 978-1-61039-006-4; 978-1-61039-007-1 ebook

LC 2010-53129

Hesterman "writes that our food system is broken and will not be able to continue supporting the world population for much longer. The author's deft explanation of our current cultivation and consumption of food should have families moving away from their supermarket aisles and into farmers' markets and community-supported agriculture programs. Hesterman urges much-needed change on the federal level, as well. . . . Guides and resources are included to help the average consumer source food locally, and the author also includes a breakdown of federal legislation and how it should be amended. A thorough, inspiring guide on how to restructure the food system for a long and healthy future, for consumers and legislators alike." Kirkus

Includes bibliographical references

Hewitt, Ben

The **town** that food saved; how one community found vitality in local food. Rodale 2009 234p $24.99 **338.1**
1. Food supply 2. Food industry 3. Entrepreneurship 4. Sustainable agriculture
ISBN 978-1-60529-686-9; 1-60529-686-4

LC 2009-34294

"Adroitly balancing professional neutrality with personal commitment, Hewitt engagingly examines this paradigm shift in the way a community feeds its citizens." Booklist

Koehler, Jeff

★ **Where** the wild coffee grows; the untold story of coffee from the cloud forests of Ethiopia to your cup. Jeff Koehler. Bloomsbury USA 2017 xvii, 268 p.p (hardcover) $28 **338.1**
1. Coffee 2. Coffee industry 3. Coffee -- History
ISBN 9781632865090

LC 2017000709

This book, by Jeff Koehler, tells "the story of . . . [coffee's] origins, its history, and the threat to its future. . . . Located between the Great Rift Valley and the Nile, the cloud forests in southwestern Ethiopia are the original home of Arabica, the most prevalent and superior of the two main species of coffee being cultivated today. . . . Koehler takes readers from these forest beginnings along the spectacular journey of its spread around the globe." (Publisher's note)

Includes bibliographical references and index

Logsdon, Gene

Letter to a young farmer; how to live richly without wealth on the new garden farm. Gene Logsdon; foreword by Wendell Berry. Chelsea Green Publishing 2017 xiv, 210 p.p (hardcover) $22.50 **338.1**

1. Farm life -- United States 2. Agriculture -- United States 3. Farm life -- United States -- Anecdotes 4. Agriculture -- United States -- Anecdotes
ISBN 9781603587259

LC 2016050357

In this book of essays, author Gene Logsdon "addresses the next generation--young people who are moving back to the land to enjoy a better way of life as small-scale 'garden farmers.' It's a lifestyle that isn't defined by accumulating wealth or by the 'get big or get out' agribusiness mindset. Instead, it's one that recognizes the beauty of nature, cherishes the land, respects our fellow creatures, and values rural traditions." (Publisher's note)

"This work serves as a guiding light and lodestar for farmers facing the modern challenges of any farming operation, large or small." Pub Wkly Annex.

Rebanks, James

★ The **shepherd's** view; modern photographs from an ancient landscape. James Rebanks. Flatiron Books 2016 176 p. color illustrations (ebook) $60; (hardcover) $24.99 **338.1**
1. Sheep -- England -- Lake District 2. Sheep farming -- England -- Lake District 3. Lake District (England) -- Pictorial works 4. Shepherds -- England -- Lake District -- Anecdotes 5. Sheep -- England -- Lake District -- Pictorial works 6. Sheep farming -- England -- Lake District -- Pictorial works
ISBN 9781250103376; 9781250103369

LC 2016033305

This book, by James Rebanks, "chronicles an ancient way of living that deeply resonates in our modern world. With over eighty full color photographs The English Lake District comes into full focus: the sheep competitions of the spring, the sweeping pastures of the summer, beloved sheep dogs in the fall and the harsh snows of winter." (Publisher's note)

"Rebanks' prose and the photographs make the landscape come alive, and woolly sheep pictured against beautiful craggy meadows will entice readers to dream of shepherding. A true gem." Booklist

Stuart, Andrea

Sugar in the Blood; A Family's Story of Slavery and Empire. Andrea Stuart. Knopf 2013 xix, 353 p.p ill., maps, geneal. tables $27.95 **338.1**
1. Stuart family 2. Slavery -- History 3. Barbados -- History 4. Slavery -- Barbados -- History 5. Sugar trade -- Barbados -- History 6. Sugarcane industry -- Barbados -- History
ISBN 0307272834; 9780307272836

LC 2012034259

This book, by Andrea Stuart, is a family history and overview of slavery and the sugar industry. "In the late 1630s, . . . George Ashby . . . fell into the life of a sugar plantation owner by mere chance, but by the time he harvested his first crop, a revolution was fully under way. . . . Stuart uses her own family story--from the seventeenth century through the present--as the pivot for this . . . tale of migration, settlement, survival, slavery and the making of the Americas." (Publisher's note)

Includes bibliographical references (p. [335]-341) and index

338.2   Extraction of minerals

Burgis, Tom

The **looting** machine; warlords, oligarchs, corporations, smugglers, and the theft of Africa's wealth. Tom Burgis. PublicAffairs 2015 352 p. illustrations, map (hardcover)

$27.99   **338.2**
1. Natural resources 2. International relations 3. Africa -- Social conditions 4. Africa -- Politics and government
ISBN 1610394399; 9781610394390; 9781610394406

LC 2015930296

In this book, "Tom Burgis exposes the truth about the African development miracle. . . . As global demand for Africa's resources rises, a handful of Africans are becoming legitimately rich but the vast majority, like the continent as a whole, is being fleeced. Outsiders tend to think of Africa as a great drain of philanthropy. But look more closely at the resource industry and the relationship between Africa and the rest of the world looks rather different." (Publisher's note)

"Essential for understanding the colonial Africa of the past and, even more so, the diverse Africa of today." LJ

Burrough, Bryan

The **big** rich; the rise and fall of the greatest Texas oil fortunes. Penguin Press 2009 466p il $29.95; pa $16   **338.2**
1. Petroleum industry
ISBN 978-1-59420-199-8; 1-59420-199-4; 978-0-14-311682-0 pa; 0-14-311682-7 pa

LC 2008-27043

"Full of schadenfreude and speculation—and solid, timely history too." Kirkus

Includes bibliographical references

House, Silas

Something's rising; Appalachians fighting mountaintop removal. [by] Silas House and Jason Howard; foreword by Lee Smith. University Press of Kentucky 2009 xiv, 306 p.p $27.95   **338.2**
1. Landscape protection 2. Coal mines and mining 3. Appalachian region 4. Mountaintop mining 5. Environmentalism -- Appalachian Region, Southern 6. Appalachian Region, Southern -- Environmental conditions 7. Celebrities -- Appalachian Region, Southern -- Interviews 8. Landscape protection -- Appalachian Region, Southern -- Citizen participation 9. Mountaintop removal mining -- Environmental aspects -- Appalachian Region, Southern
ISBN 978-0-8131-2546-6; 0813125464; 9780813125466

LC 2008049846

The authors focus on "the long-growing mining crisis in Central Appalachia. Twelve Appalachians—among them a college student, former union organizers, community activists and the octogenarian 'mother of folk,' Jean Ritchey—provide firsthand accounts of a disappearing way of life, a vital ecology in rapid decline, an industry that refuses to take responsibility for the devastation it causes (blowing the tops off mountains is only the latest, most destructive technique), and a nation too hooked on cheap energy to help. . . . This important collection illuminates the ongoing betrayal of the American mining town." Publ Wkly

Includes bibliographical references (p. [287]-290) and index

LeCain, Timothy J.

Mass destruction; the men and giant mines that wired America and scarred the planet. Rutgers University Press 2009 273p il map $26.95   **338.2**
1. Mining engineering 2. Copper mines and mining 3. Mining engineers 4. Copper industry and trade -- History 5. Copper mines and mining -- Western States 6. Copper mines and mining -- Environmental aspects
ISBN 978-0-8135-4529-5; 0-8135-4529-3

LC 2008-35434

The author writes "about the history, the engineering challenges, the successes of production and resulting consumption, and the environmental consequences of open-pit copper mining, mainly in the first half of the 20th century.... This book provokes serious second thoughts about the future of the exploitation of nature's bounty, and it should appeal to a wide audience." Choice

Includes bibliographical references and index

Maass, Peter

Crude world; the violent twilight of oil. Alfred A. Knopf 2009 276p il $27　　**338.2**

1. Petroleum industry

ISBN 978-1-4000-4169-5

LC 2009-12303

"An absorbing, relentlessly discouraging account of the disastrous effect of oil wealth on nearly everyone." Kirkus

Includes bibliographical references (p. 233-62)

Margonelli, Lisa

Oil on the brain; adventures from the pump to the pipeline. Doubleday 2007 324p hardcover o.p. pa $14.95　　**338.2**

1. Petroleum industry

ISBN 0-385-51145-0; 978-0-385-51145-2; 0-7679-1697-2 pa; 978-0-7679-1697-4 pa

LC 2006-20789

Margonelli examines how oil travels from petroleum fields to neighborhood gas stations.

The author "adds something fresh to the discussion by eschewing the popular (but dreary) doomsday angle in favor of an 'adventures in . . .' approach. . . . By giving voice to the people who are the links in the global oil chain, Margonelli invites us to leapfrog all the rhetoric, dry statistics, and dire pronouncements about oil in order to truly understand it." Fast Company

Includes bibliographical references

Rao, Maya

Great American outpost; dreamers, mavericks, and the making of an oil frontier. Maya Rao. PublicAffairs 2018 336 p. $27　　**338.2**

1. North Dakota 2. Petroleum industry -- United States

ISBN 1610396464; 9781610396462

In this book, author Maya Rao describes how, "as North Dakota became the nation's second-largest oil producer, [she] set out in steel-toe boots to join a wave of drifters, dreamers, entrepreneurs, and criminals. . . . Rao fearlessly immersed herself in their world to chronicle this modern-day gold rush, from its heady beginnings to OPEC's price war against the US oil industry." (Publisher's note)

Yergin, Daniel

★ The **prize**; the epic quest for oil, money & power. Free Press 2008 908p il map pa $22　　**338.2**

1. World politics 2. Petroleum industry

ISBN 978-1-4391-1012-6; 1-4391-1012-3

LC 2009-291302

First published 1991

This is a "history of the oil industry, from the first oil well ever drilled (near Titusville, Pennsylvania, in 1859) to the Iraqi invasion of Kuwait. It recalls advances in technology, innovations in salesmanship, and wars and truces among corporations and nations." New Yorker

Includes bibliographical references

Zuckerman, Gregory

The **frackers**; the outrageous inside story of the new billionaire wildcatters. Gregory Zuckerman. Portfolio Penguin 2013 416 p. (hardback) $29.95　　**338.2**

1. Energy resources 2. Shale gas industry 3. Hydraulic fracturing 4. Businesspeople -- United States -- Biography 5. Energy industries -- United States -- Biography 6. Petroleum industry and trade -- United States -- Biography

ISBN 1591846455; 9781591846451

LC 2013037926

This book explores "one of America's biggest economic and scientific revolutions of recent decades: the tapping of abundant oil and natural gas reserves within our own borders using a technique called fracking. . . . Focusing on a half dozen 'wildcatters,' the ones who seek out potential drilling sites, Zuckerman takes us through their decades long drought while they refined the techniques of horizontal hydraulic drilling." (Publishers Weekly)

"[S]hows us the beneficial side of fracking and the potentially environmentally disastrous side, and lets us find our own ground to stand on. A lively, exciting, and definitely thought-provoking book." Booklist

Includes bibliographical references

338.3　Other extractive industries

Fagan, Brian

Fishing; how the sea fed civilization. Brian Fagan. Yale University Press 2017 xvi, 346 p.p $30　　**338.3**

1. Fishing 2. Aquaculture 3. Civilization -- History 4. Fishers -- History 5. Fishing -- History 6. Fish trade -- History 7. Fishing -- Anthropological aspects

ISBN 0300215347; 9780300215342

LC 2017934016

In this book, author Brian Fagan "argues that fishing was an indispensable and often overlooked element in the growth of civilization. It sustainably provided enough food to allow cities, nations, and empires to grow. . . . This history of the long interaction of humans and seafood tours archaeological sites worldwide to show readers how fishing fed human settlement, rising social complexity, the development of cities, and ultimately the modern world." (Publisher's note)

"A much-needed volume for serious students of world history. Highly recommended for readers interested in archaeology, anthropology, ecology, and environmental science." LJ

Includes bibliographical references (pages 311-331) and index

Hilborn, Ray

Overfishing; what everyone needs to know. Ray Hilborn with Ulrike Hilborn. Oxford University Press 2012 xviii, 150 p.p (pbk.: alk. paper) $16.95　　**338.3**

1. Overfishing 2. Commercial fishing 3. Sustainable fisheries 4. Fisheries -- Environmental aspects

ISBN 0199798141; 9780199798131; 9780199798148

LC 2011031308

This book by Ray and Ulrike Hilborn provides an "explanation of the broad issues associated with overfishing. Guiding readers through the scientific, political, economic, and ethical issues associated with harvesting fish from the ocean, it will provide answers to questions about which fisheries are sustainably managed and which are not. Overall, the authors present a hopeful view of the future of fisheries." (Publisher's note)

Includes bibliographical references (p. [131]-139) and index

338.4 Secondary industries and services

Almond, Steve

★ **Candyfreak**: a journey through the chocolate underbelly of America. Algonquin Books of Chapel Hill 2004 266p $21.95   **338.4**
1. Candy 2. Authors 3. Chocolate 4. Humorists 5. Journalists 6. Short story writers
ISBN 1-56512-421-9

LC 2003-70801

The author tells how candy "shaped his childhood and continues to define his life in ways large and small. . . . Once hundreds of American confectioners delivered regional favorites to consumers, but now the big three of candy—Hershey, Mars, and Nestlé—control the market. To find out what happened to those candies of yesteryear, Almond talks to candy collectors and historians and visits a few of the remaining independent candy companies. . . . Flavored with the author's amusingly tart sense of humor, Candyfreak is an intriguing chronicle of the passions that candy inspires and the pleasures it offers." Libr J

Includes bibliographical references

Becker, Elizabeth

Overbooked; the exploding business of travel and tourism. Elizabeth Becker. Simon & Schuster 2013 464 p. (hardback) $28   **338.4**
1. Travel 2. Cultural tourism 3. Tourism 4. TRAVEL -- General 5. Tourism -- Political aspects 6. Tourism -- Cross cultural studies 7. Tourism -- Moral and ethical aspects
ISBN 1439160996; 9781439160992; 9781439161005

LC 2012032848

In this book, Elizabeth Becker explores the growing global tourism industry. She "travels widely, experiencing and analyzing 'the stealth industry of the twenty-first century,' which is proliferating across regions, cultures, and ecosystems, and developing in specialized niches like 'sex tourism,' 'dark tourism,' and 'heritage tourism.'" (Publishers Weekly)

Beckert, Sven

Empire of cotton; a global history. Sven Beckert. Alfred A. Knopf 2014 704 p. illustrations, maps (hardback) $35 **338.4**
1. Textile industry 2. Cotton manufacture 3. Slaves 4. Textile workers 5. Labor -- History 6. Capitalism -- History 7. Cotton trade -- History 8. Slavery -- Economic aspects 9. Cotton textile industry -- History 10. Cotton plantation workers -- History
ISBN 0375414142; 9780375414145

LC 2014009320

Pulitzer Prize Finalist: History (2015)

This book by Sven Beckert "tells the story of how, in a remarkably brief period, European entrepreneurs and powerful statesmen recast the world's most significant manufacturing industry, combining imperial expansion and slave labor with new machines and wage workers to change the world. . . . The empire of cotton was, from the beginning, a fulcrum of constant global struggle between slaves and planters, merchants and statesmen, workers and factory owners." (Publisher's note)

"Both chronologically and geographically, this is a wide-ranging saga that examines the role of nation-states, politicians, entrepreneurs, and laborers on every continent. This is not a pretty story, since Beckert shows that this empire often depended upon coercion and violence for its growth and maintenance. This is a highly detailed, provocative work that combines history, economics, and sociology in an effort to show how cotton shaped the modern world." Booklist

Burhans, Dirk E.

Crunch! a history of the great American potato chip. [by] Dirk Burhans. University of Wisconsin Press 2008 203p il $26.95   **338.4**
1. Potato chips
ISBN 978-0-299-22770-8

LC 2008-11962

"A wonderfully readable history that spans popular culture, local history, agriculture, economics, business and biography. Pass the chips please!" Univ Press Books for Public and Second Sch Libr, 2009

Includes bibliographical references

Burningham, Lucy

My beer year; Adventures with Hop Farmers, Craft Brewers, Chefs, Beer Sommeliers, and Fanatical Drinkers as a Beer Master in Training. Lucy Burningham. Roost Books, an imprint of Shambhala Publications, Inc. 2016 288 p. (pbk.: acid-free paper) $16.95; (ebook) $15.99   **338.4**
1. Beer 2. Brewing 3. Brewers -- Biography 4. Beer industry -- Biography
ISBN 9781611802719; 9780834840539

LC 2016010941

In this book, "Lucy Burningham made it her career to write about craft beer, traveling to hop farms, attending rare beer tasting parties, and visiting as many taprooms, breweries, and festivals as possible. With this as her introduction, Lucy decided to take her relationship with beer to the next level: to become a certified beer expert." (Publisher's note)

"As Burningham shares the successes, failures, and stresses of her journey, readers will be drawn more and more into the bubbly, exciting, deliciously intoxicating world of beer." Booklist

Includes bibliographical references (page 270) and index.

Diaz, Tom

The **last** gun; how changes in the gun industry are killing Americans and what it will take to stop it. Tom Diaz. The New Press 2013 319 p. (hardcover) $26.95   **338.4**
1. Gun control 2. Firearms industry -- United States 3. Firearms ownership -- United States 4. Gun control -- United States 5. Firearms industry and trade -- United States 6. Firearms -- Law and legislation -- United States
ISBN 1595588302; 9781595588302

LC 2012047230

This book, by Tom Diaz, explores gun control in the U.S. "By any account, gun violence in the United States has reached epidemic proportions. . . . Tom Diaz presents a chilling, up-to-date survey of the changed landscape of gun manufacturing and marketing. [The book] explores how the gun industry and the nature of gun violence have changed . . . [and arguing] that now is the time for a renewed political effort to attack gun violence at its source--the guns themselves." (Publisher's note)

Includes bibliographical references (pages 255-319).

Fine, Doug

Too high to fail; cannabis and the new green economic revolution. Doug Fine. Gotham Books 2012 xlv, 314 p.p (hardcover) $28.00; (paperback) $16.00   **338.4**
1. Marijuana industry 2. Marijuana -- Economic aspects
ISBN 1592407099; 9781592407095; 9781592407613

LC 2012014437

It was author "[Doug] Fine's intention . . . to track one cloned female cannabis plant, later named Lucille, from the farmer who tended her to the first patient who inhaled her smoke. Along the way, the author explores the intertwined history of humans and cannabis, as well as potential future benefits of cannabis, including biofuel, textiles, foodstuffs, farming and substantial economic boosts for cash-strapped communities." (Kirkus Reviews)

Futterman, Matthew

Players; the story of sports and money--and the visionaries who fought to create a revolution. by Matthew Futterman. Simon & Schuster 2016 336 p. (ebook) $18.99; (Hardcover) $26.95 **338.4**

1. Sports -- Economic aspects 2. Athletes -- Salaries, etc. -- United States
ISBN 9781476716978; 9781476716954; 9781476716961
LC 2015025635

This book, by Matthew Futterman, "is the first book to tell the astonishing narrative behind the creation of the modern sports business—a true revolution that moved athletes from the bottom of the financial pyramid to the top. It started in 1960, when a young Cleveland lawyer named Mark McCormack convinced a young golfer named Arnold Palmer to sign with him. McCormack simply believed that the best athletes had more commercial value than they realized—and he was right." (Publisher's note)

"This lively take on the money game in contemporary sports should be read widely." LJ

Includes bibliographical references and index

García Martínez, Antonio

★ **Chaos** Monkeys; Obscene Fortune and Random Failure in Silicon Valley. by Antonio Garcia Martinez. HarperCollins 2016 528 p. $29.99 **338.4**

1. Privacy 2. Internet 3. Marketing 4. Social media
ISBN 0062458191; 9780062458193

This book, by Antonio Garcia Martinez, "unravels the chaotic evolution of social media and online marketing and reveals how it is invading our lives and shaping our future. Weighing in on everything from start-ups and credit derivatives to Big Brother and data tracking, social media monetization and digital 'privacy,' García Martínez shares his scathing observations and outrageous antics, taking us on a humorous, subversive tour of the fascinatingly insular tech industry." (Publisher's note)

Goldstone, Lawrence

Drive! Henry Ford, George Selden, and the Race to Invent the Auto Age. Lawrence Goldstone. Ballantine Books 2016 384 p. $28 **338.4**

1. Automobile industry 2. Automobiles -- Design and construction
ISBN 0553394185; 9780553394184
LC 2016002581

Author Lawrence Goldstone "tells the fascinating story of how the internal combustion engine, a 'theory looking for an application,' evolved into an innovation that would change history. Debunking many long-held myths along the way, Drive! shows that the creation of the automobile was not the work of one man, but very much a global effort. Long before anyone had heard of Henry Ford, men with names like Benz, Peugeot, Renault, and Daimler were building and marketing the world's first cars." (Publisher's note)

"A splendid dissection of the Selden/Ford patent face-off and its place in automotive historiography." LJ

Includes bibliographical references and index.

Haag, Pamela

★ The **gunning** of America; Business and the Making of American Gun Culture. Pamela Haag. Basic Books, a member of the Perseus Books Group 2016 528 p. illustrations (hard-

cover) $29.99; (ebook) $20.99 **338.4**

1. Guns -- Social aspects 2. Winchester Repeating Arms Company 3. Firearms industry -- United States 4. United States -- Social conditions 5. United States -- Economic conditions 6. Capitalism -- United States -- History 7. Firearms -- Social aspects -- United States -- History 8. Firearms industry and trade -- United States -- History
ISBN 9780465048953; 9780465098569
LC 2015036679

In this book, historian Pamela Haag argues that "American gun culture . . . developed not because the gun was exceptional, but precisely because it was not: guns proliferated in America because throughout most of the nation's history, they were perceived as an unexceptional commodity. . . . Focusing on the history of the Winchester Repeating Arms Company, . . . Haag challenges many basic assumptions of how and when America became a gun culture." (Publisher's note)

"A refreshingly unusual approach by an author admirably transparent about why she wrote the book and why she chose to avoid more traditional approaches." Kirkus

Includes bibliographical references and index

Lalli, Frank

★ **Your** best health care now; get better health insurance, score doctor discounts, find . . . affordable prescriptions. Frank Lalli. Simon & Schuster 2016 352 p. (ebook) $15.99; (hardback) $19.99 **338.4**

1. Health education 2. Medical economics 3. Medical care -- Costs 4. Medical care, Cost of 5. Health education -- Research
ISBN 9781501132902; 9781501132865
LC 2016011242

In this book author Frank Lalli "details how he mastered the ins and outs of health care-and how you, too, can get the best care for your money. . . . Based on three years of research and more than 300 first-hand interviews, . . . [this book] is your easy-to-follow, real-world guide to making today's health system work for you. You'll learn all the smart moves and timely tips to get better care and save hundreds . . . of dollars--no matter what your concerns may be." (Publisher's note)

"With facts and advisories from patients' rights organizations and think tanks, plus the author's personal experience and clear directions, this handbook is a must-have for everyone needing health care." Pub Wkly

Includes bibliographical references and index.

McMillan, Tracie

★ The **American** way of eating; undercover at Walmart, Applebee's, farm fields, and the dinner table. Tracie McMillan. Scribner 2012 x, 319 p.p $25 **338.4**

1. Poverty 2. American cooking 3. Agriculture -- United States 4. Food industry -- United States 5. Cooking, American 6. Food supply -- United States 7. Food industry and trade -- United States 8. Food habits -- Economic aspects -- United States
ISBN 1439171955; 9781439171950; 9781439171974
LC 2012372266

This book by journalist Tracie McMillan discusses the economics of the food industry of the United States. "[S]he watched the debate about America's meals unfold, one that urges us to pay food's true cost—which is to say, pay more. So in 2009 McMillan embarked on a[n] . . . undercover journey to see what it takes to eat well in America. For nearly a year, she worked, ate, and lived alongside the working poor to examine how Americans eat when price matters." (Publisher's note)

"Full of personal stories of the daily struggle to put food of any kind on the table in today's economy, McMillan's book will force readers to question their own methods of purchasing and preparing food." Kirkus

Includes bibliographical references (p. 255-318)

McNish, Jacquie

Losing the signal; the untold story behind the extraordinary rise and spectacular fall of Blackberry. Jacquie McNish, Sean Silcoff. Flatiron Books 2015 279 p. (hardback) $27.99 **338.4**

1. Smartphones 2. BlackBerry Limited 3. BlackBerry (Smartphone)
ISBN 1250060176; 9781250060174

LC 2015012152

This book, by Jacquie McNish and Sean Silcoff, "is a riveting story of a company that toppled global giants before succumbing to the ruthlessly competitive forces of Silicon Valley. This is not a conventional tale of modern business failure by fraud and greed. The rise and fall of BlackBerry reveals the dangerous speed at which innovators race along the information superhighway." (Publisher's note)

Includes bibliographical references and index

Mitford, Jessica

★ The **American** way of death revisited. Knopf 1998 296p hardcover o.p. pa $14 **338.4**

1. Cremation 2. Undertakers and undertaking 3. Funeral rites and ceremonies
ISBN 0-679-77186-7 pa

LC 97-49349

First published 1963 by Simon & Schuster with title: The American way of death

"Very interesting, informative, and easy to read, this book is written with wit, solid information, and refreshing bluntness." Libr J

Noonan, Meg Lukens

The **coat** route; craft, luxury, and obsession on the trail of a $50,000 coat. Meg Lukens Noonan. Spiegel & Grau 2013 272 p. (alk. paper) $27 **338.4**

1. Luxuries 2. Men's clothing 3. Luxury 4. Custom-made clothing
ISBN 1400069939; 9781400069934

LC 2012042994

In this book, Meg Lukens Noonan follows the making of a $50,000 overcoat. The "journey begins in the Peruvian mountains with the elusive . . . vicuna (the animal that provides the fleece for the coat), and is followed by stops in Florence, to meet the creator of the coat's silk lining—enigmatic menswear designer Stefano Ricci; Yorkshire, where a textile mill spins vicuna fleece into yarn that Gary Eastwood's Pennine Weavers turns into cloth; and Birmingham, for hand-carved buffalo horn buttons." (Publishers Weekly)

Includes bibliographical references and index

Pein, Corey

Live work work work die; a journey into the savage heart of Silicon Valley. Corey Pein. Metropolitan Books 2017 320 p. (hardcover) $28 **338.4**

1. Internet industry 2. High technology industry 3. Technological innovations 4. Entrepreneurship -- California 5. Internet industry -- California 6. New business enterprises -- California 7. Technological innovations -- California 8. High-technology industries -- California
ISBN 9781627794855

LC 2017040258

This book, by Corey Pein, is "a scathing, sardonic exploration of Silicon Valley tech culture, laying bare the greed, hubris, and retrograde politics of an industry that aspires to radically transform society for its own benefit. . . . In showing us this frantic world, Pein challenges the positive, feel-good self-image that the tech tycoons have crafted-- . . .

revealing their self-justifying views and their insidious visions for the future." (Publisher's note)

Includes bibliographical references and index

Petersen, Melody

Our daily meds; how the pharmaceutical companies transformed themselves into slick marketing machines and hooked the nation on prescription drugs. Farrar, Straus and Giroux 2008 432p $26 **338.4**

1. Drug industry
ISBN 978-0-374-22827-9; 0-374-22827-2

LC 2008-2097

The author shows how corporate salesmanship has triumphed over science inside the biggest pharmaceutical companies and, in turn, how this promotion driven industry has taken over the practice of medicine and is changing American life.

"Petersen takes readers beyond glossy advertising and celebrity endorsements to glimpse the alarming dark side of the American pharmaceutical industry." Libr J

Includes bibliographical references (p. 409-412)

Quigley, Fran

Prescription for the people; an activist's guide to making medicine affordable for all. Fran Quigley. ILR Press, an imprint of Cornell University Press 2017 xiii, 243 p.p (Culture and politics of health care work) (pbk.: alk. paper) $19.95 **338.4**

1. Drugs 2. Popular medicine 3. Drugs -- Prices -- United States 4. Drug accessibility -- United States 5. Health care reform -- United States 6. Prescription pricing -- United States 7. Pharmaceutical policy -- United States 8. Pharmaceutical industry -- United States
ISBN 9781501713927; 1501713752; 9781501713750

LC 2017020499

In this book, "Fran Quigley diagnoses our inability to get medicines to the people who need them and then prescribes the cure. He delivers a clear and convincing argument for a complete shift in the global and U.S. approach to developing and providing essential medicines—and a primer on how to make that change happen." (Publisher's note)

"Quigley (law, Indiana Univ.) offers a focused analysis of the problem and advice for those who wish to help change the system." LJ

Includes bibliographical references and index

Rudacille, Deborah

Roots of steel; the boom and bust of an American mill town. Pantheon Books 2010 290p $27 **338.4**

1. Steel industry 2. Maryland -- History 3. United States -- Economic conditions
ISBN 9780375423680; 978-0-375-42368-0

LC 2009020962

"Rudacille has delivered a book that would do Studs Terkel proud, partaking of his oral-historical approach to the past at turns, imbued with his pro-labor spirit throughout. Required reading for activists and for those wondering where things went wrong for America's working people." Kirkus

Includes bibliographical references

Suisman, David

Selling sounds; the commercial revolution in American music. Harvard University Press 2009 356p il $29.95 **338.4**

1. Music industry 2. Music -- United States 3. Music trade -- United States 4. Music -- United States -- History and criticism
ISBN 0-674-03337-X; 978-0-674-03337-5

LC 2008-55620

"Suisman investigates the early decades of the popular music industry, from 1880 to 1930." (Nation) Index.

"A fascinating, well-written, richly detailed story of how music became a commodity in America. . . . [Suisman's] scholarship is amazingly wide-ranging." Washington Times

Includes bibliographical references

Vlasic, Bill

Once upon a car; the fall and resurrection of America's big three auto makers--GM, Ford, and Chrysler. William Morrow 2011 394p **338.4**

1. Automobile industry 2. Chrysler Corp. 3. Ford Motor Co. 4. General Motors Corp.

ISBN 978-0-06-184562-8; 978-0-06-204222-4 ebook

LC 2011020572

The author "examines the perfect storm of overseas competition, economic downturn, rising gas prices, union pressures, legacy costs, and lumbering bureaucracy that brought the U.S. auto industry to its knees. He takes us into the boardrooms and inside the heads of such people as Rick Wagoner, former GM CEO, who was ousted by Steve Rattner; Obama's 'car czar,' Bill Ford Jr., great-grandson of Henry Ford and chairman of Ford Motor Company; and billionaire financier Kirk Kerkorian, who at different times held 10-percent stakes in both GM and Ford. This is an engrossing look at big business in crisis, forever changed but never willing to give up." Booklist

Includes bibliographical references

Washington, Harriet A.

Deadly monopolies; the shocking corporate takeover of life itself, and the consequences for your health and our medical future. Doubleday 2011 433p il $28.95; ebook $14.99 **338.4**

1. Drug industry 2. Medical ethics 3. Drugs -- Marketing

ISBN 978-0-385-52892-4; 978-0-385-53405-5 ebook

LC 2011013033

"Extensively documented with minimal scientific jargon, this book is recommended for any reader interested in the future of our health system." Libr J

Includes bibliographical references

338.476 Technology industry

Berlin, Leslie

Troublemakers; Silicon Valley's coming of age. Leslie Berlin. Simon & Schuster 2017 xvi, 494 p.p illustrations (chiefly color) (hardcover) $30 **338.476**

1. San Francisco (Calif.) 2. High technology industry 3. Computer industry -- United States -- History 4. Santa Clara Valley (Santa Clara County, Calif.) -- History 5. Entrepreneurship -- California -- Santa Clara Valley (Santa Clara County) 6. Technological innovations -- California -- Santa Clara Valley (Santa Clara County) 7. High technology industries -- California -- Santa Clara Valley (Santa Clara County) 8. Santa Clara Valley (Santa Clara County, Calif.) -- Social life and customs -- 21st century

ISBN 9781451651522; 9781451651508; 1451651503

In this book, "historian Leslie Berlin introduces the people and stories behind the birth of the Internet and the microprocessor, as well as Apple, Atari, Genentech, Xerox PARC, ROLM, ASK, and the iconic venture capital firms Sequoia Capital and Kleiner Perkins Caufield & Byers. In the space of only seven years and thirty-five miles, five major industries . . . were born." (Publisher's note)

"A sturdy, skillfully constructed work of business and technological

history." Kirkus

Includes bibliographical references (pages 381-387) and index.

338.5 General production economics

Cox, Eli P. III

★ **Seeking** Adam Smith; finding the shadow curriculum of business. Eli P Cox III, University of Texas at Austin, USA. World Scientific 2017 xvii, 261 p.p (pbk.: alk. paper) $30 **338.5**

1. Capitalism 2. Microeconomics

ISBN 9789813206724; 9789813206731

LC 2016049469

This book, by Eli P. Cox III, "demonstrates that greed is highly destructive motive for conducting business and the notion that greed is good is nowhere to be found in the 'Wealth of Nations' despite claims by some of the world's leading economists. Cox offers alternative economic perspectives that are more realistic and less prone to misuse than those permeating the current business curricula." (Publisher's note)

Includes bibliographical references (pages 231-252) and index.

Galbraith, John Kenneth

★ The **great** crash, 1929; with a new introduction by the author; foreword by James K. Galbraith. Houghton Mifflin Co. 2009 206p pa $14.95 **338.5**

1. Great Depression, 1929-1939 2. United States -- Economic conditions -- 1919-1933

ISBN 978-0-547-24816-5

First published 1955

Beginning with the bull market of Coolidge and Hoover and continuing through the stock market crash, the author analyzes its causes and speculates about the chances of another crash.

Includes bibliographical references

Panic; the story of modern financial insanity. [edited by] Michael Lewis. W. W. Norton & Company 2009 391p il $27.95; pa $18.95 **338.5**

1. Financial crises

ISBN 978-0-393-06514-5; 978-0-393-33798-3 pa

LC 2008-39523

The editor "has compiled an anthology of articles related to five major financial crises in recent decades: the 1987 stock market crash, the Russian default, the Asian currency crisis, the Internet bubble and . . . the subprime mortgage collapse (the final article included is from January 2008). For each crisis, Lewis offers articles from journals, books, transcripts, and newspapers, all written immediately before, during, or after the event. . . . Timely and highly readable, this work includes in one accessible source two decades' worth of some of the best writing on the various crises and panics." Libr J

Reinhart, Carmen M., 1955-

This time is different; eight centuries of financial folly. [by] Carmen M. Reinhart, Kenneth S. Rogoff. Princeton University Press 2009 xlv, 463p il $35 **338.5**

1. Fiscal policy 2. Business cycles 3. Financial crises 4. International finance

ISBN 978-0-691-14216-6; 0-691-14216-5

LC 2009-22616

The authors "have compiled an impressive database, which covers eight centuries of government debt defaults from around the world. They have also collected statistics on inflation rates from every country where information is available and on banking crises and international capital flows over the past couple of centuries. This lengthy historical study gives what they call a 'panoramic view' of the unending cycle of boom and bust, showing how claims that 'this time is different' are invariably proven wrong. . . . [This] is an important addition to the literature of financial history." Wall Street J

Includes bibliographical references (p. 400-433)

Shafir, Eldar
Scarcity; why having too little means so much. Sendhil Mullainathan and Eldar Shafir. Times Books, Henry Holt and Company 2013 304 p. $28   **338.5**
  1. Scarcity 2. Decision making 3. Supply and demand
  ISBN 0805092641; 9780805092646

LC 2013004167

In this book, authors Sendhil Mullainathan and Eldar Shafir "discuss how scarcity affects our daily lives, recounting anecdotes of their own foibles and making . . . connections that bring this research alive. Their book provides a new way of understanding why the poor stay poor and the busy stay busy, and it reveals not only how scarcity leads us astray but also how individuals and organizations can better manage scarcity for greater satisfaction and success." (Publisher's note)

Includes bibliographical references and index

The **value** of a dollar; prices and incomes in the United States, 1860-2009. [edited] by Scott Derks. 4th ed; Grey House Pub. 2009 690p il $155   **338.5**
  1. Prices 2. Reference books 3. Salaries, wages, etc. 4. Cost and standard of living
  ISBN 978-1-59237-403-8
  First published 1994

"Both great-grandparents and serious students in historical research will benefit from this book. It will be an especially valuable study to students of American history, economics, and even mathematics." Libr J

Includes bibliographical references

The **value** of a dollar: colonial era to the Civil War, 1600-1865; [edited by] Scott Derks and Tony Smith. Grey House Pub. 2005 436p il $155   **338.5**
  1. Prices 2. Reference books 3. Salaries, wages, etc. 4. Cost and standard of living
  ISBN 1-59237-094-2; 978-1-59237-094-8

LC 2006-275331

"This source is an engaging statistical summary that looks at the history of the American people through the eyes of everyday workers and consumers. The 265 years it covers are presented in six chronological chapters: '1600-1749: The Development of the Colonies,' '1750-1774: The Run up to the War of American Independence,' and so on, ending with the close of the Civil War in 1865. . . . [This book] will find a happy audience among students, researchers, and general browsers. It offers a fascinating and detailed look at early American history from the viewpoint of everyday people trying to make ends meet." Booklist

Includes bibliographical references

338.6   Organization of production

Freeman, Joshua B., 1949-
  ★ **Behemoth**; a history of the factory and the making of the modern world. Joshua B. Freeman. W W Norton & Co Inc 2018 448 p. $27.95   **338.6**
  1. Factories 2. Industrial relations 3. Manufacturing industries

ISBN 0393246310; 9780393246315

In this book, "historian Joshua B. Freeman tells the story of the factory and examines how it has reflected both our dreams and our nightmares of industrialization and social change. . . . He chronicles protests against standard industry practices from unions and workers' rights groups that led to shortened workdays, child labor laws, protection for organized labor, and much more." (Publisher's note)

" Freeman has provided an ambitious, sweeping, and well-researched history of factories, which remains accessible and relevant to general readers." LJ

338.7   Business enterprises

Auletta, Ken
  Googled; the end of the world as we know it. Penguin Press 2009 384p $27.95   **338.7**
  1. Internet industry 2. Internet searching 3. Web search engines 4. Computer scientists 5. Social responsibility of business 6. Google, Inc. 7. Internet executives 8. Information technology executives
  ISBN 978-1-594-20235-3

LC 2009-24770

The author's "thorough reporting and declarative writing provide a crisp, informative read. . . . Auletta displays the skill of a responsible journalist in both researching and crafting this snapshot of today's technological landscape. " Christ Sci Monit

Includes bibliographical references

Bissonnette, Zac
  The **great** Beanie Baby bubble; mass delusion and the dark side of cute. Zac Bissonnette. Portfolio 2015 272 p. illustrations (some color) (hardback) $26.95   **338.7**
  1. Fads 2. Teddy bears 3. Ty, Inc. -- History 4. Toy industry -- United States -- History 5. Beanie Babies (Trademark) -- Collectors and collecting -- History
  ISBN 9781591846024; 1591846021

LC 2014038639

This book, by Zac Bissonnette, "delivers the never-before-told story of the plush animal craze that became the tulip mania of the 1990s. . . . Beanie Babies were ten percent of eBay's sales in its early days, with an average selling price of $30--six times the retail price. . . . The end of the craze was swift and devastating, with 'rare' Beanie Babies deemed worthless as quickly as they'd once been deemed priceless." (Publisher's note)

Includes bibliographical references and index

Breen, Bill
  Brick by brick; by David C. Robertson and Bill Breen. 1st ed. Crown Business 2013 xii, 305 p.p (hardcover) $26.00   **338.7**
  1. LEGO toys 2. Toy industry 3. LEGO toys -- History 4. LEGO koncernen (Denmark) 5. Toy industry -- Denmark -- Management
  ISBN 030795160X; 9780307951601

LC 2013004798

This book, written by David Robertson and Bill Breen, examines toy manufacturer LEGO. "it spotlights the company's disciplined approach to harnessing creativity and recounts one of the most remarkable business transformations in recent memory." It "reveals how LEGO failed to keep pace with the revolutionary changes in kids' lives and began sliding into irrelevance. It took a new LEGO management team – faced with the growing rage for electronic toys, few barriers to entry, and ultra-demanding consumers – to . . . transform LEGO." (Publisher's note)

Brenner, Joel Glenn

The **emperors** of chocolate; inside the secret world of Hershey and Mars. Random House 1999 366p il hardcover o.p. pa $14.95 **338.7**

1. Chocolate 2. Mars, Inc. 3. Hershey Foods Corp. 4. Food industry executives

ISBN 0-7679-0457-5 pa

LC 98-21610

"Brenner examines the candy industry, focusing on the rivalry between Hershey and Mars. Milton Hersey was and Forrest Mars is highly secretive and eccentric, and they both amassed huge fortunes. A wonderful inside look at successful businessmen." Booklist

Includes bibliographical references

Brinkley, Douglas

★ **Wheels** for the world; Henry Ford, his company, and a century of progress, 1903-2003. Viking 2003 xxii, 858p il $34.95; pa $18 **338.7**

1. Philanthropists 2. Automobile industry 3. Ford Motor Co. 4. Automobile executives

ISBN 0-670-03181-X; 0-14-200439-1 pa

LC 2003-33066

"Car lovers will appreciate this amazing account of the birth of the automobile industry, including funny anecdotes about the trusty Model T, the evolution of the V-8 engine, the artistic design of the Thunderbird, sophistication of the Lincoln Continental, and popularity of the Mustang." Booklist

Includes bibliographical references

Bruck, Connie

When Hollywood had a king; the reign of Lew Wasserman, who leveraged talent into power and influence. Random House 2003 512p il hardcover o.p. pa $16.95 **338.7**

1. MCA Inc. 2. Talent agents 3. Motion picture executives

ISBN 0-375-50168-1; 978-0-8129-7217-7 pa; 0-8129-7217-1 pa

LC 2003-41418

"Those who are interested in comprehensive details about the inner workings of the entertainment industry—its history, business, customs, people, and gossip—will find this a fascinating read and a solid resource." Libr J

Includes bibliographical references

Burrows, Peter

Backfire: Carly Fiorina's high-stakes battle for the soul of Hewlett-Packard. Wiley 2003 296p il $27.95 **338.7**

1. Computer industry 2. Hewlett-Packard Co. 3. Compaq Computer Corporation 4. Computer industry executives 5. Telecommunications executives

ISBN 0-471-26765-1

LC 2002-156443

This is an account "of the bitter boardroom fight that erupted after Hewlett-Packard announced plans to merge with Compaq in the late summer of 2001 . . . [with a focus on] the charismatic Carleton S. Fiorina, who became one of the highest-ranking women in American business in 1999 when she was tapped as the first outside chief executive of the Hewlett-Packard company. . . . [This] is a riveting, colorful, fastpaced account of the Compaq battle." N Y Times Book Rev

Includes bibliographical references

Cabot, Heather

Geek girl rising; inside the sisterhood shaking up tech. Heather Cabot and Samantha Walravens. St. Martin's Press

2017 xii, 258 p.p (hardcover) $26.99 **338.7**

1. Women engineers 2. Entrepreneurship 3. Computer industry 4. Computer industry -- United States 5. Women in technology -- United States 6. Women computer engineers -- United States 7. Women in computer science -- United States

ISBN 9781250112262; 9781250112279

LC 2017001937

In this book, "veteran journalists Heather Cabot and Samantha Walravens introduce readers to the fearless female entrepreneurs and technologists fighting at the grassroots level for an ownership stake in the revolution that's changing the way we live, work and connect to each other. . . . At a time when women hold 26% of computing jobs in the U.S. and make up a tiny fraction of the entrepreneurs launching new tech companies, their stories shine a light on new role models." (Publisher's note)

"This enlightening read reveals many problems embedded in startup culture, but, more importantly, it is an invigorating call to action and testament to the wide-ranging successes of women in this field." Booklist

Includes bibliographical references and index

Carreyrou, John, ca. 1973-

★ **Bad** blood; secrets and lies in a Silicon Valley startup. John Carreyrou. Knopf 2018 352 p. (hardback) $27.95 **338.7**

1. Fraud 2. White collar crimes 3. Fraud -- United States 4. Theranos (Firm) -- History 5. Hematologic equipment industry -- United States

ISBN 9781524731656

LC 2018000263

This book, by John Carreyrou, is "the full inside story of the breathtaking rise and shocking collapse of Theranos, the multibillion-dollar biotech startup. . . . In 2014, Theranos founder and CEO Elizabeth Holmes was widely seen as the female Steve Jobs. . . . Theranos sold shares in a fundraising round that valued the company at more than $9 billion, putting Holmes's worth at an estimated $4.7 billion. There was just one problem: The technology didn't work." (Publisher's note)

"Crime thriller authors have nothing on Carreyrou's exquisite sense of suspenseful pacing and multifaceted character development in this riveting, read-in-one-sitting tour de force. Investigative journalists are perhaps the country's last true protectors of truth and justice, and Carreyrou's commitment to unraveling Holmes' crimes has been literally of life-saving value." Booklist

Cohen, Rich

The **fish** that ate the whale; the life and times of America's banana king. Rich Cohen. Farrar, Straus and Giroux 2012 xiii, 270 p.p **338.7**

1. Biography 2. Businessmen 3. Business and politics 4. United Fruit Company -- Biography 5. Banana trade -- Louisiana -- New Orleans -- History 6. Jewish businesspeople -- Louisiana -- New Orleans -- Biography

ISBN 0374299277; 9780374299279

LC 2011041207

This biography describes the life of the 20th-century American fruit businessman Samuel Zemurray. "He worked as . . . a banana hauler, a dockside hustler, and a plantation owner. He battled and conquered the United Fruit Company, becoming a symbol of the best and worst of the United States. . . . Starting with nothing but a cart of freckled bananas, he built a sprawling empire . . . connected to the birth of modern American diplomacy, public relations, business, and war." (Publisher's note)

Includes bibliographical references.

Coll, Steve, 1958-

★ **Private** empire; ExxonMobil and American power. Steve Coll. Penguin Press 2012 685 p. $36.00   **338.7**

1. Global warming 2. Petroleum industry 3. Iraq War, 2003-2011 4. Corporate mergers and acquisitions 5. Exxon Corporation 6. Exxon Mobil Corporation 7. Big business -- United States 8. Corporate power -- United States 9. Petroleum industry and trade -- Political aspects -- United States

ISBN 1594203350; 9781594203350

LC 2011044722

In this book "two-time Pulitzer winner [Steve] Coll . . . demonstrates how the merger of Exxon and Mobil has allowed the company to wield more power and wealth than even the American government, in the manner of John D. Rockefeller. . . . The Exxon-Mobil merger in 1999 created a global behemoth and also provoked small wars at drilling spots where the poor and disenfranchised deeply resented the foreign workers on native soil and disrupted the extraction by violence and insurgency." (Kirkus Reviews)

Includes bibliographical references (p. [659]-664) and index

Denton, Sally

The **Profiteers**; Bechtel and the Men Who Built the World. by Sally Denton. Simon & Schuster 2016 448 p. illustrations (some color) $30   **338.7**

1. Corporations 2. Hoover Dam (Ariz. and Nev.) 3. Family-owned business enterprises

ISBN 1476706468; 9781476706467

LC 2015510596

In this book, by Sally Denton, "The tale of the Bechtel family dynasty is a classic American business story. It begins with Warren A. 'Dad' Bechtel, who led a consortium that constructed the Hoover Dam. From that auspicious start, the family and its eponymous company would go on to 'build the world,' from the construction of airports in Hong Kong and Doha, to pipelines and tunnels in Alaska and Europe, to mining and energy operations around the globe." (Publisher's note)

"However readers view the company, Denton's extensively researched work informs readers about the firm's maintenance as a privately held concern during its growth into a huge, multinational enterprise." Booklist

Includes bibliographical references (pages 317-408) and index.

Doran, Peter B.

Breaking Rockefeller; the incredible story of the ambitious rivals who toppled an oil empire. Peter B. Doran. Penguin Group USA 2016 352 p. illustrations $28; (ebook) $65 **338.7**

ISBN 0525427392; 9780525427391; 9780698170773

LC 2016429238

This book, by Peter B. Doran, "traces [Marcus] Samuel's rise from outsider to the heights of the British aristocracy, [Henri] Deterding's conquest of America, and the collapse of [John D.] Rockefeller's monopoly. The beginning of the twentieth century is a time when vast fortunes were made and lost. . . . Doran offers a richly detailed, fresh perspective on how Samuel and Deterding beat the world's richest man at his own game." (Publisher's note)

"A readable popular history told largely through the actions of swashbuckling tycoons." Kirkus

Includes bibliographical references (pages 291-322) and index.

Elmore, Bartow J.

Citizen Coke; the making of Coca-Cola capitalism. Bartow J. Elmore. W W Norton & Co Inc 2015 304 p. 9 plates; illustrations (hardcover) $27.95   **338.7**

1. Coca-Cola Company 2. Soft drink industry 3. Sustainable development 4. Social responsibility of business 5. Soft drink industry -- United States

ISBN 0393241122; 9780393241129

LC 2014022329

This book, by Bartow J. Elmore, is a "history of how Coke's insatiable thirst for natural resources shaped the company and reshaped the globe. How did Coca-Cola build a global empire by selling a low-price concoction of mostly sugar, water, and caffeine? The easy answer is advertising, but the real formula to Coke's success was its strategy, from the start, to offload costs and risks onto suppliers, franchisees, and the government." (Publisher's note)

"Without a doubt, Coke has been a good public citizen that stimulates economies and improves lives, writes the author, but the costs to taxpayers—for recycling systems, public pipes and subsidized farms—and the environment call into question how such unsustainable practices can continue in an age of scarcity. A superb, quietly devastating environmental and business history." Kirkus

Includes bibliographical references and index

Ewing, Jack

Faster, Higher, Farther; The Volkswagen Scandal. by Jack Ewing. W.W . Norton & Company 2017 x, 337 p.p illustrations (some color) (hardcover) $27.95   **338.7**

1. Automobile industry 2. Volkswagenwerk -- History 3. Corporations -- Corrupt practices -- United States 4. Automobile industry and trade -- Germany -- History 5. Volkswagen automobiles -- Motors (Diesel) -- Exhaust gas

ISBN 9780393254525; 9780393254501; 039325450X

LC 2017012672

This book, by Jack Ewing, is an "exposé of Volkswagen's fraud. . . . He describes VW's rise from 'the people's car' during the Nazi era to one of Germany's most prestigious and important global brands, touted for being 'green.' He paints vivid portraits of Volkswagen chairman Ferdinand Piëch and chief executive Martin Winterkorn, arguing that the corporate culture they fostered drove employees, working feverishly in pursuit of impossible sales targets, to illegal methods." (Publisher's note)

"Capturing the public fascination with craven financial scandals, and with a movie in the works, Ewing's sordid saga is the latest addition to the history of corporate fraud." Booklist

Includes bibliographical references and index.

Galloway, Scott

The **four**; the hidden DNA of Amazon, Apple, Facebook, and Google. Scott Galloway. Penguin Group USA 2017 310 p. $28   **338.7**

1. Entrepreneurship 2. Internet industry 3. Strategic planning

ISBN 0735213658; 9780735213654

This book, by Scott Galloway, focuses on "Amazon, Apple, Facebook, and Google[,] . . . the four most influential companies on the planet. . . . [The author] shows how they manipulate the fundamental emotional needs that have driven us since our ancestors lived in caves, at a speed and scope others can't match. And he reveals how you can apply the lessons of their ascent to your own business or career." (Publisher's note)

"Readers interested in innovation and strategies in technology and business management will find this book to be a provocative and insightful look at four powerful forces that dominate our social, psychological, and economic states today." (Booklist)

Genoways, Ted

The **chain**; farm factory. Ted Genoways. Harper 2014 320 p. illustrations $26.99   **338.7**

1. Food industry 2. Meat industry 3. Occupational health and safety 4. Factory farms 5. Industrial safety 6. Hormel Foods Corporation 7. Food processing plants -- United States 8. Meat industry and trade -- United States
ISBN 006228875X; 9780062288752

LC 2014019018

James Beard Foundation Award Nominee: Writing and Literature (2015)

This book, by Ted Genoways, is a "work of investigative journalism that explores the runaway growth of the American meatpacking industry and its dangerous consequences. . . . Genoways uses the story of Hormel Foods and soaring recession-era demand for its most famous product, Spam, to probe the state of the meatpacking industry, including the expansion of agribusiness and the effects of immigrant labor on Middle America." (Publisher's note)

"Readers curious about meatpacking and agriculture as well as the social, economic, and environmental impacts of the food industry will find Genoways's nonfiction debut a valuable and stimulating read." LJ

Includes bibliographical references

Harris, Blake J.

Console wars; Sega, Nintendo, and the battle that defined a generation. Blake J. Harris. It Books 2014 576 p. (hardback) $22.99 **338.7**
1. Video games 2. Video games -- History 3. Video games industry -- History 4. Electronic games industry -- History
ISBN 0062276719; 9780062276698; 9780062276704

LC 2013050668

This book, by Blake J. Harris, is a "behind-the-scenes business thriller that chronicles how Sega . . . took on the juggernaut Nintendo and revolutionized the video game industry. In 1990, Nintendo had a virtual monopoly on the video game industry. Sega, on the other hand, was just a faltering arcade company with big aspirations and even bigger personalities. But that would all change with the arrival of Tom Kalinske." (Publisher's note)

"Harris defines the players immediately, honing in on their most notable characteristics, and puts the reader in the thick of the meetings and deal-making with a confidence stemming from hundreds of interviews." Booklist

Kealing, Bob

Tupperware, unsealed; Brownie Wise, Earl Tupper, and the home party pioneers. University Press of Florida 2008 250p il $28 **338.7**
1. Containers 2. Sales personnel 3. Tupperware Corp. 4. Household products industry executives
ISBN 0-8130-3227-X; 978-0-8130-3227-6

LC 2007-47539

The author "explores the origins of the Tupperware industry as seen through the insightful genius of Brownie Wise, the impetus behind the home party craze that catapulted Tupperware revenues into the millions. . . . This work proves to be a valuable contribution to the growing body of literature that focuses on the individual contributions of women to US business and industry." Choice

Includes bibliographical references

Kirkpatrick, David

The **Facebook** effect; the inside story of the company that is connecting the world. Simon & Schuster 2010 372p il $26 **338.7**
1. Internet industry 2. Social networking 3. Online social networks 4. Facebook Inc. 5. Internet executives 6. Internet -- Social aspects
ISBN 978-1-4391-0211-4; 1-4391-0211-2

LC 2009-51983

The author was encouraged by Mark Zuckerberg, the founder and chief executive of Facebook.com, to write this book and was granted extensive access to him and his associates. Their cooperation has resulted in a mostly sympathetic at times, gushingly laudatory account of the company, though Mr. Kirkpatrick does not shy away from dissecting its missteps and successive disputes over privacy. He gives the reader a detailed understanding of how the company grew from a 2004 Harvard dorm-room project into the world's second-most-visited site after Google. N Y Times (Late NY Ed)

Includes bibliographical references

Knoedelseder, William

Bitter brew; the rise and fall of Anheuser-Busch and America's kings of beer. William Knoedelseder. HarperBusiness 2012 396 p. $27.99 **338.7**
1. Anheuser-Busch, inc. -- History 2. Beer industry -- United States -- History 3. Brewing industry -- United States -- History
ISBN 0062009265; 9780062009265

LC 2012026942

This book by William Knoedelseder is a history of the Anheuser-Busch beer company. It is a "saga of one of the wealthiest, longest-lasting, and most colorful family dynasties in the history of American commerce--a cautionary tale about prosperity, profligacy, hubris, and the blessings and dark consequences of success. . . . [The] narrative captures the Busch saga through five generations. At the same time, it weaves a broader story of American progress and decline over the past 150 years." (Publisher's note)

Krass, Peter

Carnegie. Wiley 2002 612p il $35; pa $19.95 **338.7**
1. Philanthropists 2. Metal industry executives
ISBN 0-471-38630-8; 0-471-46883-5 pa

LC 2002-10162

"From bobbin boy in a cotton mill to one of American history's most famous characters, Carnegie's life was one of contradictions. In his lifetime, Carnegie gave away a staggering $350 million, setting a standard for social conscience. Krass used original sources such as letters, diaries, and other writings by primary and peripheral characters in Carnegie's life to penetrate the public persona and show the man who crusaded for universal literacy and world peace." Booklist

Includes bibliographical references

Kurlansky, Mark, 1948-

Birdseye; the adventures of a curious man. Mark Kurlansky. Doubleday 2012 251 p. **338.7**
1. Businessmen 2. Frozen foods 3. Inventors -- Biography 4. Food industry -- United States 5. Inventors -- United States -- Biography 6. Businessmen -- United States -- Biography 7. Frozen foods industry -- United States -- History
ISBN 0385527055; 9780385527057; 9780385535885

LC 2011044891

This book explains that "[t]here was far more to American inventor Clarence Birdseye (1886-1956) than met the eye; he was slight and cheerful but restlessly curious. He was drawn into a life of travel to remote parts of the continent in search of adventure and new experiences. He invented tools and processes, notably that which enabled quick freezing of foodstuffs and revolutionized culinary habits. Birdseye launched not just the frozen-vegetable company that bears his now-famous name but an entire industry. [Mark] Kurlansky, whose past works include the popular histories 'Salt' and 'Cod,' paints a complete picture of Birdseye's unusual career and accomplishments." (Libr J)

Includes bibliographical references and index

Lashinsky, Adam

Inside Apple; how America's most admired-and secretive-company really works. Adam Lashinsky. Business Plus 2012 223 p. $26.99   **338.7**
1. Business planning 2. Apple Computer, Inc 3. Corporate culture -- United States 4. Success in business -- United States 5. Computer industry -- United States -- Management
ISBN 145551215X; 9781455512157

LC 2011044773

In this book, "[Adam] Lashinsky . . . investigates the core of Apple before, during, and after the reign of the late Steve Jobs, not only to discover how the company works and if its success can be replicated, but also to speculate about Apple's future." He "outlines salient factors that concurrently contribute to Apple's success and deviate from standard business practice." (Publishers Weekly)

Levy, Steven

In the plex; how Google thinks, works, and shapes our lives. Simon & Schuster 2011 424p $26; ebook $12.99 **338.7**
1. Google (Website) 2. Google, Inc. 3. Google (Web site)
ISBN 978-1-4165-9658-5; 1-4165-9658-5; 978-1-4165-9671-4 ebook; 1-4165-9671-2 ebook

LC 2010049964

The author presents a behind-the-scenes story of the Internet search engine company Google.

This is "the most comprehensive, intelligent and readable analysis of Google to date. Levy is particularly good on how those behind Google think and work. . . . [This work] teems with original insight into Google's most controversial affairs." New Sci

Includes bibliographical references

Lutz, Bob, 1932-

Car guys vs. bean counters; the battle for the soul of American business. [by] Bob Lutz. Portfolio/Penguin 2011 241p il $26.95   **338.7**
1. Automobile industry 2. Automobile executives 3. Corporate turnarounds 4. General Motors Corp. -- Bankruptcy 5. Automobile industry and trade -- United States -- Finance
ISBN 978-1-59184-400-6; 1-59184-400-2

LC 2011010720

The author "describes how he was pulled out of retirement to turn around a bankrupt General Motors in 2008, recounting how he transitioned the company away from office politics and penny pinching." Publisher's note

Macy, Beth

★ **Factory** man; how one furniture maker battled offshoring, stayed local - and helped save an american town. Beth Macy. Little, Brown and Co. 2014 464 p. illustrations (hardcover) $28   **338.7**
1. Outsourcing 2. Furniture making 3. American furniture
ISBN 0316231436; 9780316231411; 9780316231435; 9780316231565

LC 2014937343

"With over $500 million a year in sales, the Bassett Furniture Company was once the world's biggest wood furniture manufacturer. . . . But beginning in the 1980s, the Bassett company suffered from an influx of cheap Asian furniture as the first wave of imports struck, and ultimately moved nearly all its production to Asia. Only one man fought back: John Bassett III, a shrewd and determined third-generation factory man who used grit, tenacity, and will to compete against China and ultimately save his family's company." (Publisher's note)

"Macy's down-to-earth writing style and abundance of personal stories from manufacturing's beleaguered front lines make her work a stirring critique of globalization." Booklist

Includes bibliographical references (pages [415]-442) and index

Magner, Mike

Poisoned legacy; the human cost of BP's rise to power. Mike Magner. St. Martin's Press 2011 432 p. $18   **338.7**
1. Oil wells -- Blowouts 2. Oil spills -- Environmental aspects 3. Petroleum industry -- Ethical aspects 4. Offshore oil well drilling -- Safety measures 5. British Petroleum Company 6. Petroleum refineries -- Accidents -- United States 7. Petroleum workers -- Health and hygiene -- United States 8. Petroleum industry and trade -- Moral and ethical aspects
ISBN 9780312554941

LC 2010054461

In this book, an 'exposé of the British oil giant,' BP, "gives a comprehensive rundown of the [2010] Gulf oil well explosion and leak, and of the rushed scheduling, substandard engineering, skipped tests, and faulty equipment that precipitated that disaster. That's just the capstone of [Mike Magner's] detailed account of BP's misadventures in North America, which include a 2005 explosion at the company's Texas refinery that killed 15 people, a 200,000-gallon leak from a corroded Alaskan oil pipeline, a steady drip of workplace accidents, fatalities, and pollution violations and a drumbeat of callow apologies, lawsuits, fines, and criminal probes." (Publishers Wkly)

Includes bibliographical references (p. [381]-398) and index

Maxfield, Katherine

Starting up Silicon Valley; how ROLM became a cultural icon and Fortune 500 company. Katherine Maxfield. Greenleaf Book Group 2014 368 p. color illustrations $21.95   **338.7**
1. Technology 2. New business enterprises 3. ROLM Corporation -- History 4. Corporate culture -- California -- Santa Clara County 5. Success in business -- California -- Santa Clara County 6. Santa Clara Valley (Santa Clara County, Calif.) -- History 7. Computer industry -- California -- Santa Clara County -- History 8. Technological innovations -- California -- Santa Clara County -- History
ISBN 1937110621; 9781937110628

LC 2013955281

Author Katherine Maxfield "draws from materials collected by the Silicon Valley Historical Association, newspaper and magazine articles, and interviews with the founders and former employees of ROLM to write a corporate history unusual in its candor. Readers don't need to know the difference between a PBX and a CBX--although they'll know after reading this book--to appreciate the intense emotions and exuberant personalities Maxfield portrays." (Publisher's note)

"Few authors have Maxfield's knack for describing both the forest and the trees, which makes her history of ROLM a worthy model for other histories of Silicon Valley companies.Corporate history with enough drama for a movie." Kirkus

Includes bibliographical references and index

Mazzeo, Tilar J.

The **secret** of Chanel No. 5; the intimate history of the world's most famous perfume. Harper 2010 281p il $25.99   **338.7**
1. Perfumes 2. Fashion designers 3. Perfumers 4. Chanel (Firm) 5. Cosmetics industry executives
ISBN 978-0-06-179101-7; 0-06-179101-6

LC 2010-15284

This "'unauthorized biography of a scent' unearths the roots of the creation and fame of Coco Chanel's famous perfume. . . . Mazzeo's lush prose covers relevant aspects of Coco Chanel's life, from the stark beauty of the orphanage where she was raised to the glamour and luxury of her adulthood, to the scents that wove through her life and shaped the development of her signature perfume. However, the book never bogs down in the details—despite the extensive research showcased in the bibliography—and a smooth pacing keeps it moving along at a fast clip." Libr J

Includes bibliographical references

Micklethwait, John

The **company**; a short history of a revolutionary idea. [by] John Micklethwait and Adrian Wooldridge. Modern Library 2003 xxiii, 227p (Modern Library chronicles) hardcover o.p. pa $14.95   **338.7**

1. Corporations 2. Business enterprises
ISBN 0-679-64249-8; 0-8129-7287-2 pa

LC 2002-26429

In this history of the joint-stock company, Micklethwait and Wooldridge "trace its progress from Assyrian partnership agreements through the 16th- and 17th-century European 'charter companies' that opened trade with distant parts of the world, to today's multinationals. The authors' breadth of knowledge is impressive. They infuse their engaging prose with a wide range of cultural, historical and literary references, with quotes from poets to presidents. . . . Moreover, the authors argue that for all the change companies have engendered over time, their force has been for an aggregate good." Publ Wkly

Includes bibliographical references

Nalebuff, Barry, 1958-

Mission in a bottle; the honest guide to doing business differently--and succeeding. by Seth Goldman and Barry J. Naelbuff and illustrated by Sungyoon Choi. Crown Business 2013 288 p. $23   **338.7**

1. Entrepreneurship 2. Business enterprises 3. Graphic novels 4. Iced tea -- United States -- Comic books, strips, etc 5. Tea trade -- United States -- Comic books, strips, etc 6. Honest Tea (Firm) -- History -- Comic books, strips, etc 7. Soft drink industry -- United States -- Comic books, strips, etc
ISBN 0770437494; 9780770437497

LC 2013004799

Authors Seth Goldman and Barry Nalebuff, "cofounders of Honest Tea tell the engaging story of how they created and built a mission-driven business, offering a wealth of insights and advice to entrepreneurs, would-be entrepreneurs, and millions of Honest Tea drinkers about the challenges and hurdles of creating a successful business--and the importance of perseverance and creative problem-solving." (Publisher's note)

"[T]his candid portrait of leveraging resources to build a business from the ground up is a useful and cleverly conceptualized read." Pub Wkly

Orbanes, Philip

The **game** makers; the story of Parker Brothers from Tiddledy Winks to Trivial Pursuit. {by} Philip E. Orbanes. Harvard Business School Press 2003 272p il $29.95   **338.7**

1. Parker Brothers (Firm)
ISBN 1-591-39269-1

LC 2003-10768

This is a study of the Parker Brothers, who developed such games as Monopoly, Clue and Risk. The author contends that the games "reflect the American world view of the 20th century. Life is a ruthless struggle in which there are many losers, but it takes place within a framework of unbendable and fairminded rules." Economist

Includes bibliographical references

Shaw, Greg

★ **Hit** refresh; the quest to rediscover Microsoft's soul and imagine a better future for everyone. by Satya Nadella, with Greg Shaw and Jill Tracie Nichols. HarperBusiness 2017 272 p. $29.99   **338.7**

1. Artificial intelligence 2. Technology and civilization
ISBN 0062652508; 9780062652508

This book, by Satya Nadella, with Greg Shaw and Jill Tracie Nichols, "is about individual change, about the transformation happening inside of Microsoft and the technology that will soon impact all of our lives—the arrival of the most exciting and disruptive wave of technology humankind has experienced: artificial intelligence, mixed reality, and quantum computing." (Publisher's note)

Includes bibliographical references (pages 247-255) and index.

Vaidhyanathan, Siva

The **Googlization** of everything; (and why we should worry) University of California Press 2011 265p $26.95; ebook $22   **338.7**

1. Google (Website) 2. Internet industry 3. Google, Inc. 4. Google (Web site) 5. Internet -- Social aspects
ISBN 978-0-520-25882-2; 978-0-520-94869-3 ebook

LC 2010-27772

The author "shows how Google's methods of capturing, storing and filtering information are often elitist and increasingly invasive. . . . Citing some of the company's most controversial headlines, from the toddler who was captured naked in his grandmother's garden with Google Street View to the settlement between Google and the Author's Guild over copyrights, the author unmasks the monster behind the friendly interface with the suspense of a horror novel. An urgent reminder to look more closely at dangers that lurk in plain sight. " Kirkus

Includes bibliographical references

338.76   Business enterprises by industry

Lashinsky, Adam

Wild ride; inside Uber's quest for world domination. Adam Lashinsky. Portfolio 2017 228 p. illustrations (hardback) $28   **338.76**

1. Success in business 2. Historical literature 3. Corporations -- Growth 4. Ridesharing 5. Uber (Firm) 6. Transportation -- Forecasting
ISBN 9780735211407; 9780735211391

LC 2017006832

This book, by Adam Lashinsky, presents the "story of Uber's meteoric rise, and the massive ambitions of its larger-than-life founder and CEO. Before Travis Kalanick became famous as the public face of Uber, he was a scrappy, rough-edged, loose-lipped entrepreneur. . . . [Lashinsky] traces the origins of Kalanick's massive ambitions in his humble roots, and he explores Uber's murky beginnings and the wild ride of its rapid growth and expansion into different industries." (Publisher's note)

338.8   Combinations

Bown, Stephen R.

Merchant kings; when companies ruled the world, 1600-1900. [by] Stephen Bown. Thomas Dunne Books 2010 314p il map $26.99   **338.8**

1. Merchants 2. Multinational corporations 3. Europe -- Commerce
ISBN 978-0-312-61611-3

LC 2010-34783

The author "has produced a magnificent description of the six great companies, and their leaders, that dominated the 'Heroic Age of Commerce.' Bown demonstrates how the corporations served as stalking horses for kings and parliaments while enriching shareholders and the powerful managers themselves. . . . Bown presents a fascinating look at the men who exploited resources and native peoples while laying the foundations of empires." Publ Wkly

Includes bibliographical references

MacIntosh, Julie

Dethroning the king; the hostile takeover of Anheuser-Busch, an American icon. Wiley 2010 408p il $27.95 **338.8**

1. Corporate mergers and acquisitions 2. Anheuser-Busch, Inc. 3. Beverage industry executives
ISBN 978-0-470-59270-0

LC 2010-32279

"In a narrative that reads as fast as any fiction thriller, . . . MacIntosh details the 2008 takeover of the iconic Anheuser-Busch brewing company by Belgian corporation InBev, focusing particularly on the company's importance to the St. Louis region; its management, or lack thereof, by the Busch family (particularly the August Busches III and IV); and the broader unsettled economic climate of 2008." Libr J

Includes bibliographical references

338.9   Economic development and growth

Byrd, Rosaly

Sustainability made simple; small changes for big impact. Rosaly Byrd and Laurèn DeMates. Rowman & Littlefield 2017 x, 203 p.p (cloth: alk. paper) $36   **338.9**

1. Sustainability 2. Sustainable development 3. Sustainable living
ISBN 9781442269101; 9781442269095

LC 2016032731

This book, by Rosaly Byrd and Laurèn DeMates, offers "an optimistic yet realistic perspective on our impact on the environment, giving much needed guidance to those who are interested in finding new and relatively easy ways to incorporate sustainability into daily life. . . . [It] shows that adopting a sustainable lifestyle doesn't require 'going off the grid' or making drastic life changes that take time and cost money." (Publisher's note)

"An essential guidebook for anyone who wants to make a difference." Booklist

Includes bibliographical references (pages 159-199) and index.

Sachs, Jeffrey, 1954-

The **age** of sustainable development; Jeffrey D. Sachs. Columbia University Press 2015 544 p. illustrations, maps, portraits (pbk.: alk. paper) $34.95   **338.9**

1. Sustainable development 2. Economic development -- Environmental aspects
ISBN 0231173156; 9780231173148; 9780231173155

LC 2014034070

In this book, Jeffrey D. Sachs "argues that it's time for humankind to reconcile its needs with those of the planet, in this sprawling manifesto. He surveys the great dilemma facing civilization: how to ensure broadly inclusive economic growth, especially in the poorest countries, without destroying the natural environment and deranging the climate on which

survival depends." (Publishers Weekly)

"Overall, Sachs's book provides a basic but ambitious argument: to reverse current unsustainable trends, global warming must be mitigated, extreme poverty must end, gender imbalance must be corrected, and access to basic health care and education must be granted to all." Choice

Includes bibliographical references and index

Speth, James Gustave, 1942-

★ **America** the possible; manifesto for a new economy. James Gustave Speth. Yale University Press 2012 249 p. (hardback) $30.00   **338.9**

1. Economics 2. Democracy -- United States 3. United States -- Politics and government 4. Social justice -- United States 5. United States -- Economic policy 6. Environmental policy -- United States 7. Progressivism (United States politics)
ISBN 0300180764; 9780300180763

LC 2012012170

The book, by author James Gustave Speth, "spells out the specific changes that are needed to move toward a new political economy--one in which the true priority is to sustain people and planet. Supported by a . . . "theory of change" that explains how system change can come to America, the book also presents a vision of political, social, and economic life in a renewed America. . . . In short, this is a book about the American future and the strong possibility that we . . . have it in ourselves to use our freedom and our democracy in powerful ways to create . . . a reborn America." (Publisher's note)

Includes bibliographical references and index

338.91   International development and growth

Steil, Benn

★ The **Marshall** Plan; dawn of the cold war. Benn Steil. Simon & Schuster 2018 624 p. $35   **338.91**

1. American foreign aid 2. Reconstruction (1939-1951) 3. Europe -- Foreign relations -- United States
ISBN 1501102370; 9781501102370

This book, by Benn Steil, "reveals the gripping history behind the Marshall Plan. . . . Steil's thrilling account brings to life the seminal episodes marking the collapse of postwar US-Soviet relations--the Prague coup, the Berlin blockade, and the division of Germany. In each case, we see and understand like never before Stalin's determination to crush the Marshall Plan and undermine American power in Europe." (Publisher's note)

"Political history is often a tough slog, but Steil writes a vivid, opinionated narrative full of colorful characters, dramatic scenarios, villains, and genuine heroes, and the good guys won. It will be the definitive account for years to come." Kirkus

339.2   Distribution of income and wealth

Garson, Barbara

Down the up escalator; how the 99 percent live in the Great Recession. Barbara Garson. Doubleday 2013 288 p. (hardcover) $26.95; (electronic) $80.85   **339.2**

1. Employment 2. Global Financial Crisis, 2008-2009 3. United States -- Economic conditions 4. Equality -- United States -- History -- 21st century 5. Income distribution -- United States -- History -- 21st century
ISBN 0385532741; 9780385532747; 9780385532754

LC 2012020359

This book, by Barbara Garson, explores how "the Great Recession has thrown huge economic challenges at almost all Americans save the super-affluent few. . . . Garson has interviewed an economically and geographically wide variety of Americans to show the painful waste in all this loss and insecurity, and describe how individuals are coping." (Publisher's note)

Milanovi¿, Branko

The **haves** and the have-nots; a short and idiosyncratic history of global inequality. Basic Books 2010 258p il map $27.95   **339.2**
  1. Wealth 2. Poverty 3. Wealth -- History 4. Poverty -- History 5. Income distribution
  ISBN 0-465-01974-9; 978-0-465-01974-8

LC 2010-29295

The first essay in this book discusses "how economists think about income inequality within a country—in particular, how it is measured, and how it is related to a country's overall economic health. . . . In his second and third essays, Milanovic switches to . . . inequality around the world." (N Y Times Book Rev) Index.

"Students, practitioners, and anyone interested in economics and the issue of inequality would enjoy this." Libr J

Includes bibliographical references

Noah, Timothy

The **great** divergence; America's growing inequality crisis and what we can do about it. Timothy Noah. Bloomsbury 2012 264 p.   **339.2**
  1. Wealth 2. Poverty 3. Equality 4. Economic policy -- United States 5. United States -- Economic conditions 6. Wealth -- United States 7. Poverty -- United States 8. Equality -- United States 9. United States -- Economic policy 10. Income distribution -- United States
  ISBN 9781608196333

LC 2011048447

This book examines the "political dimensions of the outrageous disparity in incomes that has developed since 1979. . . . [Timothy] Noah discusses the rise and fall of the trade-union movement and demonstrates that turning points in that movement were also turning points in the growth of income inequality. . . . Noah also calls out financial deregulation as a major offender, and he lists measures that he believes can help the situation." (Kirkus Reviews)

Piketty, Thomas, 1971-

The **economics** of inequality; Thomas Piketty; translated by Arthur Goldhammer. Belknap Press of Harvard University Press 2015 160 p. illustrations (alk. paper) $22.95   **339.2**
  1. Income 2. Equality 3. Economics 4. Income distribution 5. Equality -- Economic aspects
  ISBN 0674504801; 9780674504806

LC 2015008813

This book, by Thomas Piketty, is "an introduction to the conceptual and factual background necessary for interpreting changes in economic inequality over time. . . . Piketty begins by explaining how inequality evolves and how economists measure it. In subsequent chapters, he explores variances in income and ownership of capital and the variety of policies used to reduce these gaps." (Publisher's note)

"Most readers will be better served by Capital in the Twenty-First Century, leaving students and economists as the likeliest audience for this title." LJ

Includes bibliographical references and index

Ridley, Matt

The **rational** optimist; how prosperity evolves. Fourth Estate, Harper 2010 438p il $26.99   **339.2**
  1. Reason 2. Wealth 3. Optimism
  ISBN 978-0-06-145205-5

LC 2010-4907

The author posits that as long as civilization engages in exchange and specialization, we will be able to reinvent ourselves and responsibly use earthly resources ad infinitum. . . . Ridley puts current perceptions about violence, wealth, and the environment into historical perspective, reaching back thousands of years to advocate global free trade, smaller government, and the use of fossil fuels. He confidently takes on the experts, from modern sociologists who fret over the current level of violence in the world to environmentalists who disdain genetically modified crops. An ambitious and sunny paean to human ingenuity, this is an argument for why ambitious optimism is morally mandatory. Publ Wkly

Includes bibliographical references

339.4   Factors affecting income and wealth

Banerjee, Abhijit V.

Poor economics; a radical rethinking of the way to fight global poverty. [by] Abhijit V. Banerjee and Esther Duflo. PublicAffairs 2011 303p $26.99   **339.4**
  1. Poverty 2. Foreign aid 3. Poverty -- Prevention 4. Economic assistance -- Developing countries
  ISBN 9781586487980; 1586487981

LC 2010-50938

This book "draws on a variety of evidence, not limiting itself to the results of randomised trials, as if they are the only route to truth. And the authors' interest is not confined to 'what works', but also to how and why it works. Indeed, Ms Duflo and Mr Banerjee, perhaps more than some of their disciples, are able theorists as well as thoroughgoing empiricists." Economist

Includes bibliographical references

Cohen, Lizabeth

A **consumer's** republic; the politics of mass consumption in postwar America. Knopf 2003 567p il $35; pa $16.95 **339.4**
  1. Consumers 2. Consumption (Economics) 3. United States -- Social conditions
  ISBN 0-375-40750-2; 0-375-70737-9 pa

LC 2002-141599

"Without question, this is a difficult, demanding, and dense book—but it is also a greatly significant contribution to business literature. . . . Cohen submits a copiously researched, brilliantly conceived, and ultimately quite instructive study of American economics since the Depression." Booklist

Includes bibliographical references

Desmond, Matthew, ca. 1970-

★ **Evicted**; poverty and profit in the American city. Matthew Desmond. Crown 2016 432 p. (ebook) $20; (hardback) $28   **339.4**
  1. Profit -- United States 2. Poverty -- United States 3. Eviction -- United States 4. Cities and towns -- United States 5. Low-income housing -- United States
  ISBN 9780553447446; 9780553447439; 9780553447453

LC 2015027374

Pulitzer Prize: General Nonfiction (2017)
Carnegie Medal: Nonfiction (2017)

Kirkus Prize Finalist: Nonfiction (2016)

National Book Critics Circle Award: Nonfiction (2017)

This book by Matthew Desmond describes "Sherrena Tarver, a former schoolteacher turned inner-city entrepreneur, and Tobin Charney, who runs one of the worst trailer parks in Milwaukee. They loathe some of their tenants and are fond of others, but as Sherrena puts it, 'Love don't pay the bills.' She moves to evict Arleen and her boys a few days before Christmas." (Publisher's note)

"This stunning, remarkable book--a scholar's 21st-century How the Other Half Lives--demands a wide audience." Kirkus

Includes bibliographical references (pages 343-405) and index.

Gerth, Karl

As China goes, so goes the world; how Chinese consumers are transforming everything. Hill and Wang 2010 258p il $26; ebook $12.99 **339.4**

1. Consumers 2. Consumption (Economics) 3. China -- Economic conditions

ISBN 978-0-8090-3429-1; 978-1-4299-6246-9 ebook

LC 2010-12647

"Nuanced, balanced and accessible—essential reading for anyone trying to make sense of China today." Kirkus

Includes bibliographical references

Gordon, Robert J.

★ The **rise** and fall of American growth; the U.S. standard of living since the Civil War. Robert J. Gordon. Princeton University Press 2016 768 p. illustrations (ebook) $74.95; (hardcover: alk. paper) $39.95 **339.4**

1. United States -- Economic conditions 2. United States -- Economic conditions -- 1945- 3. United States -- Economic conditions -- 1865-1918 4. United States -- Economic conditions -- 1918-1945 5. Cost and standard of living -- United States -- History

ISBN 9781400873302; 0691147728; 9780691147727

LC 2015027560

This book, by Robert J. Gordon, "challenges the view that economic growth will continue unabated, and demonstrates that the life-altering scale of innovations between 1870 and 1970 cannot be repeated. Gordon contends that the nation's productivity growth will be further held back by the headwinds of rising inequality, stagnating education, an aging population, and the rising debt of college students and the federal government, and that we must find new solutions." (Publisher's note)

"A masterful study to be read and reread by anyone interested in today's political economy." Kirkus

Includes bibliographical references and index

Miller, Geoffrey F.

Spent; sex, evolution, and consumer behavior. [by] Geoffrey Miller. Viking 2009 374p $26.95 **339.4**

1. Consumers 2. Consumption (Economics)

ISBN 978-0-670-02062-1; 0-670-02062-1

LC 2008-51554

"Since evolutionary psychology seeks to examine how natural selection acts on psychological and mental traits, Miller applies this knowledge to help us understand what actually motivates us to buy. He pokes fun at popular culture and at the things we buy and flaunt to inflate our self-esteem and try to make ourselves more attractive. Personality research can inform the study of consumer behavior, and Miller shows us how having a better understanding of our own personalities will help us avoid the pitfalls of runaway consumerism." Libr J

Includes bibliographical references

Novogratz, Jacqueline

The **blue** sweater; bridging the gap between rich and poor in an interconnected world. Jacqueline Novogratz. Rodale"||"Distrib. to the trade by Macmillan 2009 x, 262 p.p $15.99 **339.4**

1. Globalization 2. Poverty -- Developing countries 3. Philanthropists -- Personal narratives 4. Domestic economic assistance -- Developing countries 5. Poverty 6. Charities 7. Microfinance 8. Economic assistance

ISBN 1594869154 (hardcover); 9781594869150 (hardcover)

LC 2008043621

This book, "[p]art coming-of-age story, part blueprint for effecting real change, . . . explores what it means to create meaningful solutions to global poverty and release human potential in an interconnected world. For [author] Jacqueline Novogratz it all started back home in Alexandria, Virginia, with the blue sweater . . . she outgrew . . . and gave . . . to Goodwill. Eleven years later in Africa, she spotted a young boy wearing that very sweater, with her name still on the tag inside. . . . Novogratz relates her experiences over two decades, first in Africa and later in India and Pakistan. She began as a banker and philanthropist, and now works as a venture capitalist, trying to effect real change in countries where the average citizen lives on less than $4 a day." (Publisher's note)

Rivlin, Gary

Broke, USA; from pawnshops to Poverty, Inc.: how the working poor became big business. Harper 2010 358p $26.99 **339.4**

1. Poor -- United States 2. United States -- Economic conditions

ISBN 978-0-06-173321-5

LC 2010-2874

"A timely, important, and deeply disturbing look at the cycle of debt of the nation's most vulnerable." Publ Wkly

Includes bibliographical references

Roberts, James A.

Shiny objects; why we spend money we don't have in search of happiness we can't buy. James A. Roberts. HarperOne 2011 368 p. $25.99 **339.4**

1. Consumers 2. American dream 3. Consumption (Economics) -- United States 4. American Dream 5. Materialism -- United States

ISBN 0062093606; 9780062093608

LC 2010005086

In this book James A. Roberts "studies why Americans believe and behave as if possessions will induce, increase, and enhance happiness -- when, as studies show, materialism 'negatively correlate[s]' with well-being. He examines the psychological underpinnings of our desire to purchase -- even beyond our means. . . . Roberts offers a history of American consumerism, drawing parallels between different eras." (Publishers Weekly)

Includes bibliographical references.

Shaefer, H. Luke

$2.00 a Day; Living on Almost Nothing in America. Kathryn J. Edin; H. Luke Shaefer. Houghton Mifflin Harcourt 2015 240 p. (hardback) $28 **339.4**

1. Poverty -- United States 2. Income gap -- United States 3. United States -- Social conditions

ISBN 0544303180; 9780544303188

LC 2015004337

This book by Kathryn J. Edin and H. Luke Shaefer describes how "American families in urban and rural areas, across all races and family structures, are living on wages so low they can barely sustain themselves. Focusing on families in the inner cities of Chicago and Cleveland; the small Appalachian town of Johnson City, Tennessee; and the small rural towns of Jefferson and Percy, Mississippi, the authors highlight the day-to-day struggle of families living well below the poverty line." (Booklist)

"An eye-opening account of the lives ensnared in the new poverty cycle." Kirkus

Includes bibliographical references (pages 179-199) and index.

339.5 Macroeconomic policy

Conway, Ed

The **Summit**; Bretton Woods, 1944: J. M. Keynes and the Reshaping of the Global Economy. Ed Conway. W W Norton & Co Inc 2015 480 p. 16 plates; illustrations $28.95 **339.5**

1. Monetary policy 2. International finance
ISBN 160598681X; 9781605986814

This book, by Ed Conway, discusses the history of the 1944 Bretton Woods meeting, the "most colorful and important economic summit in history-- held during the height of World War II. . . . Countries from around the world . . . agreed to overhaul the structure of the international monetary system. Against all odds, they were successful. The system they set up presided over the longest, strongest and most stable period of growth the world economy has ever seen." (Publisher's note)

"This is a gripping story for both general readers and scholars interested in World War II, the Cold War, and domestic and international political economy. The author knows how to write for those who are less informed about economics while telling the history of the turbulent conference through its leading characters and updating its legacy today. An essential purchase on this topic." LJ

Steil, Benn

The **battle** of Bretton Woods; John Maynard Keynes, Harry Dexter White, and the making of a new world order. Benn Steil. Princeton University Press 2013 472 p. (hardcover) $29.95 **339.5**

1. Economic conditions 2. World War, 1939-1945 3. Monetary policy -- History -- 20th century 4. International finance -- History -- 20th century
ISBN 0691149097; 9780691149097

LC 2012035709

Author Benn Steil, the director of international economics at the Council on Foreign Relations, "revisits the 1944 conference that created 'the new global monetary architecture' for the postwar world. As the American Army entered Rome and the Russians drove the Nazis out of Minsk, delegates from 44 Allied nations gathered in Bretton Woods, N.H., to hammer out the ground rules for international economic equilibrium following the defeat of the Axis powers." (Kirkus Reviews)

Includes bibliographical references and index

340 Law

Black's law dictionary; Bryan A. Garner, editor in chief. 10th edition Thomson Reuters 2014 2016 p. deluxe $140; hbk $81.95 **340**

1. Law -- United States -- Dictionaries
ISBN 9780314621306; 031462130X; 9780314613004; 0314613005

LC 2015372206

First published 1891 with title: A dictionary of law. (7th edition

1999) Periodically revised to bring terms up to date

"Contains more than 50,000 terms, earliest usage dates for nearly all terms, pronunciation guidance, Latin maxims, and more." (Publisher's note)

Feinman, Jay M.

★ **Law** 101; 3rd ed.; Oxford University Press 2010 363p $27.95 **340**

1. Law -- United States
ISBN 978-0-19-539513-6

LC 2010-487303

First published 2000

This book "covers the main subjects taught in the first year of law school. Readers are introduced to every aspect of the legal system, from constitutional law and the litigation process to tort law, contract law, property law, and criminal law." Publisher's note

Legal systems of the world; a political, social, and cultural encyclopedia. edited by Herbert M. Kritzer. ABC-CLIO 2002 4v il maps set $385 **340**

1. Reference books 2. Law -- Encyclopedias
ISBN 1-57607-231-2

LC 2002-2659

"Written by an international team of more than 350 legal scholars, the more than 400 signed entries cover legal systems of countries from around the world, Australia, and the provinces of Canada; transnational systems (International Court of Justice); general systems (Islamlic law, indigenous, and folk legal systems); and key concepts. Each country profile includes a map with an inset of its location on the globe, general information about the country, its history, diagrams of its court structure, the evolution of its legal framework, its current structure, staffing or how judges are appointed, any specialized judicial bodies (i.e. military court), and the impact that the legal system has had on the country. Articles conclude with references and a bibliography. Academic and public libraries will find this source invaluable for comparative studies in legal and judicial systems."—"The Best of the Best Reference Sources." Am Libr

Includes bibliographical references

Nolo (Firm)

★ **Nolo's** encyclopedia of everyday law; answers to your most frequently asked legal questions. by Shae Irving & Nolo editors. 8th ed.; Nolo 2011 494p pa $34.99 **340**

1. Law -- United States
ISBN 978-1-4133-1321-5 pa; 1-4133-1321-3 pa; 978-1-4133-1347-5 ebook; 1-4133-1347-7 ebook

LC 2010-31328

First published as a replacement of Nolo's everyday law book. Frequently revised

This offers answers to frequently asked legal questions about such topics as credit and debt, workplace rights, wills, divorce, bankruptcy, social security, tenant's rights, child custody and visitation, patents and trademarks, travel, partnerships, healthcare directives and powers of attorney.

Includes bibliographical references

Tamanaha, Brian Z.

Failing law schools; Brian Z. Tamanaha. The University of Chicago Press 2012 xvi, 235 p.p (cloth) $25.00 **340**

1. Debt 2. Law schools 3. Lawyers -- United States 4. American Bar Association 5. Law schools -- United States -- Finance 6. Law -- Study and teaching -- United States
ISBN 0226923614; 0226923622; 9780226923611; 9780226923628

LC 2012006829

In this book, Brian Z. Tamanaha "argues that ABA [American Bar Association] accreditation was established to keep out poor and immigrant students, 'U.S. News' doesn't verify schools' self-reported numbers, most professors have little or no experience practicing law, and schools artificially inflate the employment numbers of their graduates. The result is that too many schools produce impossibly indebted graduates who can't find work and, when they do, make legal services unaffordable." (Library Journal)

Tucker, Virginia

Finding the answers to legal questions; Virginia M. Tucker, Marc Lampson. ALA Neal-Schuman 2018 xxiv, 232 p.p $75   **340**

1. Library science 2. Information science 3. Law -- United States 4. Legal research -- United States 5. Law -- United States -- Popular works

ISBN 9780838915691; 0838915698

LC 2017056093

This book, by Virginia M. Tucker and Marc Lampson, "is a comprehensive guide to help librarians confidently assist users in finding the legal information they need. Newly revised and updated, this timely, clearly organized, and easy-to-use resource is packed with guidance to help librarians answer questions that span the gamut of the law. . . . [The] book will help librarians connect users to the most accurate, up-to-date legal information." (Publisher's note)

"Libraries of all types lacking both a legal reference collection and staff with sufficient expertise in the area are often called upon to provide assistance and direction to those seeking legal information. This book will help libraries serve that need." Booklist

Includes bibliographical references and index

340.09   History, geographic treatment, biography of law

Roffer, Michael H.

The **Law** Book; from Hammurabi to the International Criminal Court: 250 milestones in the history of law. Michael H. Roffer. Sterling Pub Co Inc 2015 528 p. color illustrations $29.95   **340.09**

1. Law -- History

ISBN 1454901683; 9781454901686

This book in the Sterling Milestones series, by Michael H. Roffer, "presents a comprehensive look at the rules by which we live our lives. It covers such diverse topics as the Code of Hammurabi, the Ten Commandments, the Trial of Socrates, the Bill of Rights, women's suffrage, the insanity defense, and more. . . . [It tackles] everything from civil rights, . . . assisted suicide, to the 2000 U.S. presidential election, Google Books, and the fight for marriage equality." (Publisher's note)

"This high quality and engaging book is recommended for most public libraries, where it will be appreciated more in a browsing collection than on a reference shelf." Booklist

Includes bibliographical references (pages 511-524) and index.

340.59   Islamic law

Kamali, Mohammad Hashim

Shariah Law; Questions and Answers. Mohammad Hashim Kamali. Oneworld 2017 viii, 278 p.p (paperback) $19.99   **340.59**

1. Islamic law 2. Human rights 3. Women (Islamic law) 4.

Muslims -- United States 5. Islam -- Customs and practices 6. Equality before the law -- Islamic countries 7. Women's rights -- Religious aspects -- Islam

ISBN 1786071509; 9781786071514; 9781786071507

This book on Shariah Law, by Mohammad Hashim Kamali, "connects the theoretical aspects of the law with how it is applied in the world today. At once scholarly and accessible, it is sure to be a vital resource for students, teachers and general readers, addressing as it does a range of contemporary concerns, including jihad, democracy, the environment, genetic engineering, human cloning, euthanasia and abortion." (Publisher's note)

"Using a question-and-answer format, Islamic jurisprudence and legal scholar Kamali . . . endeavors to make the Islamic legal field both accessible and understandable, especially for the nonspecialist." LJ

Includes bibliographical references (pages 251-262) and index.

341.23   United Nations

Annan, Kofi A. (Kofi Atta), 1938-2018

Interventions; a life in war and peace. Kofi Annan with Nader Mousavizadeh. Penguin Press 2012 xiv, 383 p.p $36   **341.23**

1. Diplomats 2. World politics -- 1989- 3. United Nations -- Biography 4. Statesmen -- Ghana -- Biography

ISBN 1594204209; 9781594204203

LC 2012008173

In this memoir, "with the assistance of . . . [Nader] Mousavizadeh . . ., former United Nations Secretary-General [Kofi] Annan discusses the major benchmarks of his life and career. The author, born in 1934, passes briefly over his education and early career at the World Health Organization and U.N., where he worked until his retirement in 2006, and moves rapidly into his main topic: the transformation of U.N. Peacekeeping Operations since the late 1980s and early '90s." (Kirkus Reviews)

Fasulo, Linda M.

★ An **insider's** guide to the UN; Linda Fasulo. 3rd edition Yale University Press 2015 302 p paperback $20   **341.23**

1. United Nations

ISBN 9780300203653

First published 2003

"In this third edition, prominent news correspondent Linda Fasulo updates and revises her lively, comprehensive, and authoritative guide to the United Nations, including candid insights from US and UN diplomats and officials as well as experts. Fasulo's popular book carefully describes the UN system while covering issues as diverse as terrorism, peacekeeping, climate change, R2P (responsibility to protect), and sustainable development." (Publisher's note)

Includes bibliographical references

Mires, Charlene

Capital of the world; the race to host the United Nations. Charlene Mires. New York University Press 2013 320 p. (hardcover) $29.95   **341.23**

1. United Nations 2. United States -- History 3. United Nations -- Headquarters 4. New York (N.Y.) -- Buildings, structures, etc

ISBN 0814707947; 9780814707944

LC 2012035350

In this book, Pulitzer Prize winner Charlene Mires "investigates a largely unexamined aspect of the birth of the United Nations: the attempt by many U.S. cities during the closing days of World War II to persuade it to base its headquarters in their respective communities.

Mires has tracked down . . . archival sources and forgotten newspaper accounts, uncovering a . . . chronicle involving countless American politicians, foreign diplomats, and community promoters who participated." (Library Journal)

Includes bibliographical references and index

Moore, John Allphin

★ **Encyclopedia** of the United Nations; [by] John Allphin Moore, Jr., Jerry Pubantz. 2nd ed.; Facts On File 2008 2v il (Facts on File library of world history) set $125   **341.23**

1. United Nations 2. Reference books 3. International relations -- Encyclopedias

ISBN 978-0-8160-6913-2

LC 2007-29559

First published 2002

This set features entries on "the United Nations's institutions, procedures, policies, specialized agencies, historic personalities, initiatives, and involvement in world affairs. . . . The appendixes contain important UN documents, such as the Charter of the United Nations, the Universal Declaration of Human Rights, the Statute of the International Court of Justice, and the recent Security Council Resolution." Publisher's note

Includes bibliographical references

341.4   Jurisdiction over physical space; human rights

Fabey, Michael

★ **Crashback**; the power clash between the U.S. and China in the pacific. Michael Fabey. Scribner 2017 xiii, 305 p.p $27   **341.4**

1. Maritime law 2. China -- Foreign relations -- United States 3. United States -- Foreign relations -- China

ISBN 150111204X; 9781501112041

This book, by Michael Fabey, look[s] at the 'warm war' [between the U.S. and China] over control of the South China Sea--one that is threatening to flare into full-scale conflict. . . . The Chinese regard the Pacific, and especially the South China Sea, as their ocean, and they're ready to defend it. Each day the heat between the two countries increases as the Chinese try to claim the South China Sea. . . , and the United States insists on asserting freedom of navigation." (Publisher's note)

Includes bibliographical references (pages 257-281) and index.

341.44   Bodies of water

Engdal, Eskil

Catching thunder; the true story of the world's longest sea chase. by Eskil Engdal and Kjetil Sæter, translated by Diane Oatley. University of Chicago Press 2018 400 p. $21.95 **341.44**

1. Boats and boating 2. Environmental protection

ISBN 1786990873; 9781786990877

In this book, by Eskil Engdal and Kjetil Sæter, translated by Diane Oatley, "wanted by Interpol, the Thunder has for years evaded justice: accumulating millions in profits, hunting endangered species and ruthlessly destroying ocean habitats. The authors follow this incredible expedition from the beginning . . [which] leads them to trail of criminal kingpins, rampant corruption, modern slavery, and an international community content to turn a blind eye." (Publisher's note)

341.5   Disputes and conflicts between states

Bass, Gary Jonathan, 1969-

Freedom's battle; the origins of humanitarian intervention. Alfred A. Knopf 2008 509p $35   **341.5**

1. Humanitarian intervention

ISBN 978-0-307-26648-4; 0-307-26648-6

LC 2007-52252

This "history of nineteenth-century campaigns to stop atrocities in Greece, Syria, and Bulgaria is a corrective to the idea that humanitarian interventions are a product of the 'dreamy interlude' between 1989 and 9/11. The compelling narrative, rich with accounts of parliamentary debate and battlefield confrontation, presents a world of familiar political and military concerns, from the pressure of nonstop media coverage to the importance of a clear exit strategy. Bass's thesis that humanitarianism long preceded the crises of Bosnia and Rwanda is persuasive." New Yorker

Includes bibliographical references

341.69   War crimes

Rashke, Richard

★ **Useful** Enemies; John Demanjuk and America's Open-Door Policy for Nazi War Criminals. Delphinium 2013 621 p. $29.95   **341.69**

1. War criminals 2. United States -- Immigration and emigration

ISBN 1883285518; 9781883285517

This book looks at John Demjanjuk, convicted of Nazi war crimes in 2011. Richard Rashke "uses Demjanjuk's story to explore the troubling implications of U.S. immigration patterns after WWII; the author contends that the United States knowingly accepted Nazis while simultaneously denying entry to Holocaust survivors, a trend motivated by a political agenda concerned with monitoring Europe in the postwar period and during the cold war." (Publishers Weekly)

342   Branches of law; laws, regulations, cases; law of specific jurisdictions, areas, socioeconomic regions

Amar, Akhil Reed

★ **America's** constitution; a biography. Random House 2005 657p il $29.95; pa $16.95   **342**

1. Constitutional history -- United States

ISBN 1-400-06262-4; 0-8129-7272-4 pa

LC 2004-61464

"Only rarely do you find a book that embodies scholarship at its most solid and invigorating; this is such a book." Publ Wkly

Includes bibliographical references

The **annotated** U.S. Constitution and Declaration of Independence; edited by Jack N. Rakove. Belknap Press 2009 354p il $24.95   **342**

1. United States -- Constitution 2. Constitutional law -- United States 3. Constitutional history -- United States 4. United States -- Declaration of Independence 5. United States -- Constitution -- 1st-10th amendments

ISBN 0-674-03606-9; 978-0-674-03606-2

LC 2009-22907

This is an explication of the Declaration of Independence, the Bill of Rights, and the Constitution. Bibliography.

The author "presents both the Declaration and the Constitution with carefully laid out annotation that's accessible to general readers as well as high school and college students. His extended introduction provides a readable and instructive analysis of how the writing of the Constitution progressed, especially on matters concerning representation, executive power, and creation of the amendments. His annotations often rely upon contemporary usage and meaning from the time of the Declaration of Independence and Constitution . . . and he compares such usage to other documents of the time." Libr J

Includes bibliographical references

Beeman, Richard

★ **Plain,** honest men; the making of the American Constitution. [by] Richard Beeman. Random House 2009 514p il $30   **342**

1. Constitutional history -- United States 2. United States -- Constitutional Convention (1787)

ISBN 978-1-4000-6570-7; 1-4000-6570-4

LC 2008-28841

"Masterfully told American history for the scholar and general reader alike." Kirkus

Includes bibliographical references

Berkin, Carol

A **brilliant** solution; inventing the American Constitution. Harcourt 2002 310p $26; pa $14   **342**

1. Constitutional history -- United States 2. United States -- Constitutional Convention (1787) 3. United States -- Politics and government -- 1783-1809

ISBN 0-15-100948-1; 0-15-602872-7 pa

LC 2002-5648

This history of the 1787 Constitutional Convention "emphasizes the importance of the delegates' anxieties, showing how they insinuated themselves into some of the compromises, such as the equality of the states in the Senate. Shrewd at integrating biographical detail on the delegates into their debates, Berkin fares well in comparison with previous historians on the topic." Booklist

Bray, Ilona M.

★ **U.S.** Immigration Made Easy; Ilona Bray, J.D.; updated by Attorney Richard Link. 18th edition Nolo 2017 688 p. $44.99   **342**

1. Immigration law -- United States 2. United States -- Immigration and emigration

ISBN 1413323677; 9781413323672

First published 1989 by Sheridan Chandler Co. under the authorship of Martha S. Siegel and Laurence A. Canter. Periodically revised

This guide "discusses immigration paperwork, green cards, and other types of temporary visas and when to involve a lawyer." Libr J

"Thoroughly updated and revised, this edition covers the latest changes in immigration law, including expansion of the new 'provisional waiver of unlawful presence' to family members of lawful permanent residents living in the U.S.), the latest average processing times, and much more." (Publisher's note)

Breyer, Stephen G.

Active liberty; interpreting our democratic Constitution. [by] Stephen Breyer. Knopf 2005 161p $21   **342**

1. United States -- Supreme Court 2. Constitutional law -- United States

ISBN 0-307-26313-4

LC 2005-44242

The Supreme Court Justice presents his view on the Constitution of the United States.

"This will be essential reading at a possibly watershed moment for the Supreme Court." Publ Wkly

Includes bibliographical references

★ The **Constitution** of the United States of America; analysis and interpretation: analysis of cases decided by the Supreme Court of the United States to June 28, 2012. prepared by the Congressional Research Service, Library of Congress; Kenneth R. Thomas, editor-in-chief; Larry M. Eig, managing editor; Henry Cohen, George Costello, contributing editors. Centennial edition U.S. Government Printing Office 2013 2789 p. hbk $290   **342**

1. Constitutional law -- United States

ISBN 0160917352; 9780160917356

"Sometimes known by its short title, the Constitution Annotated provides commentary on every article, section, and clause of the basic instrument, as well as the amendments, with citations to selected United States Supreme Court decisions construing these provisions." Introd to U.S. Govt Info Sources. 5th edition

Davis, Thomas J.

Plessy v. Ferguson; Thomas J. Davis. Greenwood 2012 xx, 238 p.p (Landmarks of the American mosaic) (hardcover) $58   **342**

1. Segregation 2. United States -- Race relations -- History 3. Segregation -- Law and legislation -- United States -- History 4. Segregation in transportation -- Law and legislation -- Louisiana -- History

ISBN 0313391874; 9780313391873

LC 2012011735

This book, by Thomas J. Davis, discusses the U.S. Supreme Court case Plessy v. Ferguson as part of the "Landmarks of the American Mosaic" series. "Contrary to popular misconceptions, Plessy v. Ferguson was not a simple case of black vs. white separation, but rather a challenging and complex protest for U.S. law to fully accept mixed ancestry and multiculturalism." (Publisher's note)

Includes bibliographical references (p. 219-222) and index.

The **Debate** on the Constitution; Federalist and Antifederalist speeches, articles, and letters during the struggle over ratification. Library of Am. 1993 2v ea $35   **342**

1. Constitutional history -- United States 2. United States -- Politics and government -- 1783-1809

ISBN 0-940450-42-9; 0-940450-64-X

LC 92-25449

In addition to the documents themselves, these volumes contain "brief biographical notes on the various speakers and writers, a chronology of key events in American independence and the establishment of the new governmental system, notes on contemporary state constitutions, and notes explicating the text of the reprinted documents." Christ Sci Monit

★ **Encyclopedia** of the First Amendment; edited by John R. Vile, David L. Hudson Jr., David Schultz. CQ Press 2009 2v il set $275   **342**

1. Reference books 2. United States -- Constitution -- 1st-10th amendments -- Encyclopedias

ISBN 978-0-87289-311-5; 0-87289-311-1

LC 2008-36077

This "is an excellent resource for anyone who wants to learn more about broadcast regulation, the establishment of religion clause, students' rights, or a myriad of other topics involving the First Amendment and its political, cultural, and legal significance." Booklist

Includes bibliographical references

★ The **Federalist**; edited, with introduction and notes, by Jacob E. Cooke. Wesleyan Univ. Press 1982 xxx, 672p pa $27.95   **342**

1. United States -- Constitution

ISBN 0-8195-6077-4

LC 82-2815

A reissue of the 1961 edition

"From 27 Oct. 1787 to 2 April 1788, 77 essays were published in the semi-weekly 'Independent Journal' of New York, entitled 'The Federalist,' and signed first 'A Citizen of Nwe York' then 'Publius.' Eight more were added when they were collected in book form {in 1789}. . . . They were so acute and massively learned in their exposition of the true intent of the Constitution, that even the courts have accepted them as authoritative comments in doubtful cases; and they are held by all the civilized world as among the noblest storehouses of political philosophy in existence. A classic textbook of political science." Ency Americana

Ford, Richard T.

Rights gone wrong; Richard Thompson Ford. Farrar, Straus and Giroux 2011 272p.   **342**

1. Racism 2. Civil rights 3. Discrimination 4. United States -- Social conditions

ISBN 9780374250355

LC 2011010705

It was the author's intent to demonstrate "that both the progressive left and the colorblind right are guilty of the same error: defining discrimination too abstractly and condemning it too categorically, with similarly perverse results. According to Ford, the urge to condemn discrimination in all its forms . . . has led people on the left and the right to reject 'reasonable, prudent and innocent distinctions.' It has also led activists, judges and government officials to concentrate on eliminating even trivial forms of discrimination at the expense of more effective means to social justice, like expanding economic opportunities for the poor." (N Y Times)

Includes bibliographical references and index.

Hennessey, Jonathan

The **United** States Constitution; a graphic adaptation. written by Jonathan Hennessey; art by Aaron McConnell. Hill and Wang 2008 149p il $35; pa $16.95   **342**

1. Graphic novels 2. United States -- Constitution -- Graphic novels 3. Constitutional history -- United States -- Graphic novels

ISBN 978-0-8090-9487-5; 0-8090-9487-8; 978-0-8090-9470-7 pa; 0-8090-9470-3 pa

LC 2008-17927

The author and illustrator go "through the entire U. S. Constitution, article by article, amendment by amendment, explaining their meaning and implications—in comics format. Avoiding the didactic, the book succeeds in being both consistently entertaining and illuminating." Publ Wkly

Includes bibliographical references

Lewis, Loida Nicolas

How to Get a Green Card; Ilona Bray, J.D. & Loida Nicolas Lewis, J.D.; updated by Attorney Kristina Gasson. 12 edition Nolo 2016 402 p. pbk $39.99   **342**

1. Noncitizens -- United States 2. United States -- Immigration and emigration

ISBN 1413322557; 9781413322552

First published 1993. Periodically revised

This guide covers different ways to get a green card, alternatives to a green card, fiancé and fiancée visas, visa lotteries, applying for refugee status and political asylum, and immigration applications.

Maddex, Robert L.

The **U.S.** Constitution A to Z; 2nd ed.; CQ Press 2008 xxix, 736p il map (CQ's American government A to Z series) $85   **342**

1. Reference books 2. Constitutional law -- United States -- Encyclopedias 3. Constitutional history -- United States -- Encyclopedias

ISBN 978-0-87289-764-9

LC 2008-21902

First published 2002

"Maddex offers over 200 articles about issues (abortion, gun control), legal concepts (due process, privacy), landmark cases (Roe v. Wade, Brown v. Board of Education) and people (John Adams, Thurgood Marshall) related to the Constitution. . . . The unique feature of this work is its collection of source materials. . . . It is an excellent, concise reference." Choice [review of 2002 edition]

Includes bibliographical references

Madison, James

★ The **Constitutional** Convention; a narrative history from the notes of James Madison. [edited by] Edward J. Larson and Michael P. Winship. Modern Library 2005 229p pa $13.95   **342**

1. Constitutional history -- United States 2. United States -- Constitutional Convention (1787) 3. United States -- Politics and government -- Sources

ISBN 0-8129-7517-0

LC 2005-41649

"This book tells the convention's turbulent story in Madison's own words, drawn from the notes he took at the scene and giving us a daily blow-by-blow. . . . [The editors] steer readers through the fierce debates with helpful explanations and editorial asides, as well as a cogent epilogue, making this primary source far more than a tidy civics lesson." Publ Wkly

Includes bibliographical references

Maier, Pauline, 1938-2013

Ratification; the people debate the Constitution, 1787-1788. Simon & Schuster 2010 589p il map $30   **342**

1. Constitutional history -- United States

ISBN 978-0-684-86854-7; 0-684-86854-7

LC 2010-27709

In this book on the ratification of the U.S. Constitution, Pauline Maier explores "dynamics within the individual state ratification conventions" with a focus on "how the structure of debate within the individual state conventions affected the final votes in each state. Rather than demonstrate the inevitability of the Constitution's triumph, Maier . . . shows how remarkable the Federalist victory was." (Reviews in American History)

"On Sept. 17, 1787, the convention that had been sitting in Philadelphia for four months to design a new form of government for the United States adjourned, offering its handiwork to the nation. Almost a year later, on Sept. 13, 1788, Congress declared that the Constitution had been duly ratified, and prescribed the rules for the first presidential election the following year. . . . [This] book shows how America got from the first date to the second—and ultimately to today, since we still live with the same document, however modified." N Y Times Book Rev

Includes bibliographical references

Meyerson, Michael

   Liberty's blueprint; how Madison and Hamilton wrote the Federalist Papers, defined the constitution, and made democracy safe for the world. [by] Michael I. Myerson. Basic Books 2008 309p $26.95   **342**
   1. Constitutional law -- United States 2. Constitutional history -- United States
   ISBN 978-0-465-00264-1; 0-465-00264-1

                                 LC 2007-35376

   "This fine book is the fullest and most insightful account we have of the collaboration between Alexander Hamilton and James Madison." J Am Hist
   Includes bibliographical references

Nussbaum, Martha Craven

   Liberty of conscience; in defense of America's tradition of religious equality. [by] Martha Nussbaum. Basic Books 2008 406p $28.95   **342**
   1. Freedom of religion
   ISBN 978-0-465-05164-9; 0-465-05164-2

                                   LC 2007-38176

   This "is a historical and conceptual study of the American tradition of religious freedom." (Publisher's note) Index.
   The author "plumbs the historical, political, philosophical, and legal debates surrounding religious freedom." Booklist

   The **Oxford** guide to United States Supreme Court decisions; edited by Kermit L. Hall, James W. Ely, Jr. 2nd ed.; Oxford University Press 2009 499p $35   **342**
   1. Reference books 2. United States -- Supreme Court 3. Constitutional law -- United States
   ISBN 978-0-19-537939-6

                                   LC 2008-23763

   First published 1999
   The editors "assemble the scholarship of 161 field specialists, who summarize the Supreme Court's 440 most significant cases. Scholar-signed, multiparagraph entries are alphabetized by case name, include argued and decided dates, and detail vote divisions. The book closes with a glossary, an appendix containing the complete Constitution, a chronology of justices since 1789, and a list of presidential appointments. An outstanding single-volume reference." Libr J
   Includes bibliographical references

Rehnquist, William H.

   All the laws but one; civil liberties in wartime. Knopf 1998 254p il $27.50; pa $14   **342**
   1. Civil rights 2. World War, 1914-1918 3. World War, 1939-1945 4. National security -- United States 5. United States -- History -- 1861-1865, Civil War 6. Japanese Americans -- Evacuation and relocation, 1942-1945
   ISBN 0-679-44661-3; 0-679-76732-0 pa

                                   LC 98-12641

   This is "Supreme Court Chief Justice Rehnquist's narrative of the conflict between civil liberties and military necessity. . . . Fully two-thirds of the book covers Civil War issues. . . . One chapter discusses World War I espionage and draft resistance cases; three, the World War II internment of Japanese Americans and the imposition of martial law in Hawaii. . . . Far from a complete survey of wartime civil liberties—reviewing only cases that reached the Supreme Court before 1950—this is nonetheless both enlightening and entertaining." Booklist

Includes bibliographical references

Schultz, David A.

   Encyclopedia of the United States Constitution; [by] David Schultz. Facts On File 2009 2v il (Facts on File library of American history) set $150   **342**
   1. Reference books 2. Constitutional law -- United States -- Encyclopedias
   ISBN 978-0-8160-6763-3; 0-8160-6763-5

                                   LC 2008-23349

   "This reference source can help high-school students, the general public, and other interested parties comprehend the fundamental concepts, evolutionary character, and historic people and events that have shaped the [Constitution.] . . . The alphabetically arranged entries cover terms, events, people, landmark cases, and issues that help explain the Constitution's history. The appendix provides the Declaration of Independence, the Articles of Confederation, the Constitution, and the Bill of Rights as well as 'Other Amendments to the Constitution,' a 'U.S. Constitution Time Line,' and instructions on locating court cases." Booklist
   Includes bibliographical references

Simon, James F.

   What kind of nation; Thomas Jefferson, John Marshall, and the epic struggle to create a United States. Simon & Schuster 2002 348p $27.50; pa $14   **342**
   1. Architects 2. Presidents 3. Executive power 4. Vice-presidents 5. Essayists 6. Biographers 7. Writers on law 8. Secretaries of state 9. Supreme Court justices 10. United States -- Supreme Court 11. Constitutional history -- United States 12. United States -- Politics and government -- 1783-1809
   ISBN 0-684-84870-8; 0-684-84871-6 pa

                                   LC 2001-55027

   "Simon's enlivening account proves that writing about constitutional law needn't be the dry preserve of academics." Booklist
   Includes bibliographical references

Strebeigh, Fred

   Equal; women reshape American law. W.W. Norton 2009 582p $35   **342**
   1. Trials 2. Women's rights 3. Women -- Law and legislation
   ISBN 978-0-393-06555-8; 0-393-06555-3

                                     LC 2008-44463

   "This book generates a genuine appreciation for the legal entrepreneurs who fought long and hard to make possible the careers of many a professional woman." Wilson Quarterly
   Includes bibliographical references

Vile, John R.

   Encyclopedia of constitutional amendments, proposed amendments, and amending issues, 1789-2010; 3rd ed.; ABC-CLIO 2010 2v set $165   **342**
   1. Reference books 2. Constitutional law -- United States -- Encyclopedias 3. Constitutional history -- United States -- Encyclopedias
   ISBN 978-1-59884-316-3; 1-59884-316-8; 978-1-59884-317-0 ebook; 1-59884-317-6 ebook

                                   LC 2010-2113

   First published 1996, covering 1789-1995
   The author "discusses the Constitution, its 27 ratified amendments, and the approximately 11,700 amendments proposed within the titular time frame to present 'a unique window into American history and politics.' The alphabetical format and detailed index make information

access a breeze, and the six appendixes provide a reprint of the Constitution along with charts of the number of proposals by decade, key events, and names of individuals submitting the proposals." Libr J

Includes bibliographical references

Waldman, Steven

Founding faith; providence, politics, and the birth of religious freedom in America. Random House 2008 277p $26 **342**

    1. Freedom of religion 2. United States -- Religion 3. Freedom of religion -- United States 4. United States -- Religion -- History 5. Founding Fathers of the United States -- Religious life

    ISBN 1400064376; 9781400064373

                LC 2007-21710

Walman examines the religious attitude of various founding fathers, focusing particularly on Benjamin Franklin, John Adams, George Wshington, Thomas Jefferson, and James Madison. He argues that "our nation's Founders forged a new approach to religious liberty, a revolutionary formula that promoted faith by leaving it alone. . . . [Waldman contends that] neither side in the culture war has accurately depicted the true origins of the First Amendment." (Publisher's note) Index.

This "is an excellent book about an important subject: the inescapable—but manageable—intersection of religious belief and public life. With a grasp of history and an understanding of the exigencies of the moment, Waldman finds a middle ground between those who think of the Founders as apostles in powdered wigs and those who assert, equally inaccurately, that the Founders believed religion had no place in politics." Newsweek

Includes bibliographical references

Weiner, Mark Stuart

Black trials; citizenship from the beginnings of slavery to the end of caste. [by] Mark S. Weiner. Alfred A. Knopf 2004 421p $26.95; pa $16.95 **342**

    1. Trials 2. African Americans -- Civil rights

    ISBN 0-375-40981-5; 0-375-70884-7 pa

                LC 2004-40860

The author "examines how court proceedings involving black people—and whites trying to assist them—have served as windows onto race relations and the power of whites over blacks in the U.S. from its earliest days. . . . This book is the best of its kind—a serious, deeply felt reflection on the weight of history on contemporary affairs." Publ Wkly

Includes bibliographical references

Wexler, Jay

Holy hullabaloos; a road trip to the battlegrounds of the church/state wars. Beacon Press 2009 251p pa $20 **342**

    1. Freedom of religion 2. Church and state 3. Religious minorities 4. Church and state -- United States

    ISBN 0-8070-0044-2; 978-0-8070-0044-1

                LC 2008-47405

"This is a rare treat, a combination of thoughtful analysis and quirky humor that illuminates an issue that rarely elicits a laugh—and that is central to the American body politic." Publ Wkly

Includes bibliographical references

Wise, Steven M.

Though the heavens may fall; the landmark trial that led to the end of human slavery. Da Capo Press 2005 282p il $25; pa $17.95 **342**

    1. Slaves 2. Trials 3. Slavery

    ISBN 0-7382-0695-4; 0-306-81450-1 pa

                LC 2004-25346

The author "has an eye for evocative detail and an interest in the trappings and procedures of an 18th-century courtroom that do as much to engage the reader as the drama of the trials themselves." N Y Times Book Rev

Includes bibliographical references

342.08　Jurisdiction over persons

Strossen, Nadine

Hate; why we should resist it with free speech, not censorship. Nadine Strossen. Oxford University Press 2018 232 p. (hardback) $24.95 **342.08**

    1. Freedom of speech -- United States 2. Hate speech -- Law and legislation -- United States

    ISBN 9780190859121; 9780190859138; 9780190859145

                LC 2017054213

This book, by Nadine Strossen, "dispels misunderstandings plaguing our perennial debates about 'hate speech vs. free speech,' showing that the First Amendment approach promotes free speech and democracy, equality, and societal harmony. . . . Citing evidence from many countries, this book shows that 'hate speech' laws are at best ineffective and at worst counterproductive." (Publisher's note)

"Strossen succeeds in lucidly explaining the relevant legal issues in a way that benefits both professional and lay readers." LJ

Includes bibliographical references and index

342.73　Constitutional law -- United States

Barron, David J.

Waging war; David J. Barron. Simon & Schuster 2016 576 p. illustrations, portraits (ebook) $20.99; (hardback) $30.00 **342.73**

    1. War 2. United States. Congress 3. Presidents -- United States 4. IS (Organization) 5. United States. Congress -- History 6. Presidents -- United States -- History 7. Constitutional history -- United States 8. Executive power -- United States -- History 9. Legislative power -- United States -- History 10. War, Declaration of -- United States -- History 11. War and emergency powers -- United States -- History

    ISBN 9781451681994; 9781451681970; 9781451681987

                LC 2016025789

In this book, author David J. Barron presents an "account of a raging debate: The history of the ongoing struggle between the presidents and Congress over who has the power to declare and wage war. [It] opens with an account of George Washington and the Continental Congress over Washington's plan to burn New York City before the British invasion. Barron takes us through all the wars that followed." (Publisher's note)

Includes bibliographical references and index

Brettschneider, Cory

The **oath** and the office; a guide to the Constitution for future presidents. Corey Brettschneider. W W Norton & Co. Inc. 2018 224 p. (hardcover) $22.95 **342.73**

    1. Executive power -- United States 2. Constitutional law -- United States 3. Presidents -- Legal status, laws, etc. -- United States

    ISBN 9780393652123

                LC 2018016664

In this book "Constitutional law scholar and political science professor Corey Brettschneider guides us through the Constitution and explains the powers--and limits--that it places on the presidency. . . . [This book] empowers all readers, voters, and future presidents with the knowledge and confidence to read and understand one of our nation's most important founding documents." (Publisher's note)

"The author offers a clear explanation of many complex issues, such as the provisions of the 14th Amendment, which guarantees equal protection under the law; and the process involved in impeachment, including the question of whether obstruction of justice is an impeachable offense. A cleareyed, accessible, and informative primer: vital reading for all Americans." Kirkus Reviews

Includes bibliographical references and index

Carpenter, Dale

Flagrant conduct; the story of Lawrence v. Texas: how a bedroom arrest decriminalized gay Americans. Dale Carpenter. W. W. Norton & Company 2012 xv, 345 p.p   **342.73**
1. Gay rights -- United States 2. United States. Supreme Court 3. Right of privacy -- United States 4. Gay men -- Legal status, laws, etc. 5. Homosexuality -- Law and legislation -- Texas 6. Trials (Sodomy) -- Texas 7. Texas -- Trials, litigation, etc. 8. Gays -- Legal status, laws, etc. -- United States 9. Homosexuality -- Law and legislation -- Texas -- Criminal provisions
ISBN 0393062082; 9780393062083

LC 2011047245

"The 2003 landmark Lawrence v. Texas Supreme Court case established the right of homosexuals to engage in private sexual conduct. After setting the sociopolitical and legal scene, [Dale] Carpenter . . . describes the 1998 arrest of John Lawrence and Tyron Garner and the ensuing events as gay rights groups in Houston grasped the potential of the case as a national test. Chapters introduce participants, describe the so-called crime, compare differing accounts of the arrest, follow court events, and explain the stakes. Carpenter . . . discuss[es] legal strategies and Supreme Court arguments, and the elite lawyers and strategists of the defense team . . . in stark contrast to the ill-prepared Harris County district attorney." (Libr J)

Includes bibliographical references and index

Conley, Richard S.

Historical dictionary of U.S. Constitution; Richard S. Conley. Rowman & Littlefield 2016 474 p. (hardcover: alk. paper) $105; (ebook) $131   **342.73**
1. United States. Constitution 2. Constitutional law -- United States 3. Constitutional history -- United States 4. United States. Constitution -- Dictionaries 5. Constitutional law -- United States -- Dictionaries 6. Constitutional history -- United States -- Dictionaries 7. United States -- Politics and government -- Dictionaries 8. Constitutional history -- United States -- Dictionaries -- Sources
ISBN 9781442271883; 9781442271876

LC 2016011954

This book in the Historical Dictionaries of U.S. Politics and Political Eras series, by Richard S. Conley, "covers the Founding of the American Republic and the Framers, the drafting of the Constitution, constitutional debates over ratification, and traces key events, Supreme Court chief justices, amendments, and Supreme Court cases regarding the interpretation of the Constitution from 1789-2016." (Publisher's note)

"This reference will be well received by both academic and armchair historians." Booklist

Includes bibliographical references

Davis, Lennard J.

Enabling acts; the hidden story of how the Americans with Disabilities Act gave the largest US minority its rights. Lennard Davis. Beacon Press 2015 296 p. illustrations (hardback)

$26.95   **342.73**
1. Legislation -- United States 2. People with disabilities -- Legal status, laws, etc. 3. United States. Americans with Disabilities Act of 1990 4. People with disabilities -- Services for -- United States 5. People with disabilities -- United States -- Social conditions 6. People with disabilities -- Legal status, laws, etc. -- United States 7. Discrimination against people with disabilities -- Law and legislation -- United States
ISBN 9780807071564

LC 2014046510

This book on the Americans with Disabilities Act (ADA) by Lennard J. Davis delivers a behind-the-scenes narrative "of how a band of leftist Berkeley hippies managed to make an alliance with upper-crust, conservative Republicans to bring about a truly bipartisan bill. . . . From inside the offices of newly formed disability groups to secret breakfast meetings . . . , here we meet countless unsung characters, including political heavyweights and disability advocates." (Publisher's note)

"A lively and well-researched legal saga suited to general readers interested in current events and disability issues." LJ

Includes bibliographical references and index

Healy, Thomas

The **great** dissent; how Oliver Wendell Holmes changed his mind and changed the history of free speech in America. by Thomas Healy. Henry Holt and Company 2013 336 p. $28   **342.73**
1. Freedom of speech 2. United States. Constitution. 1st-10th amendments 3. Freedom of speech -- United States 4. Trials (Anarchy) -- New York (State) -- New York -- History -- 20th century
ISBN 0805094563; 9780805094565

LC 2012047539

Author Thomas Healy examines U.S. Supreme Court Justice Oliver Wendell Holmes' "1919 the court opinion that solidified free speech rights in American political doctrine. Holmes' change of heart has long been pondered by legal scholars and historians. Drawing on newly uncovered letters and memos, legal scholar Healy recounts Holmes' long, slow process of advocating for free speech at a time of great national turmoil." (Booklist)

Includes bibliographical references and index

Klarman, Michael J.

The **framers'** coup; the making of the United States constitution. Michael J. Klarman. Oxford University Press 2016 880 p. illustrations (hardcover: alk. paper) $39.95   **342.73**
1. United States. Constitution 2. Constitutions -- United States 3. Constitutional history -- United States 4. United States Constitution
ISBN 9780199942039

LC 2016009496

This book, by Michael J. Klarman, "narrates how the Framers' clashing interests shaped the Constitution--and American history itself. The Philadelphia convention could easily have been a failure, and the risk of collapse was always present. Had the convention dissolved, any number of adverse outcomes could have resulted, including civil war or a reversion to monarchy." (Publisher's note)

"A monumental project carried off to a high degree of excellence." Kirkus

Includes bibliographical references (pages 815-824) and index.

Paulsen, Michael Stokes

The **Constitution**; an introduction. Michael Stokes Paulsen and Luke Paulsen. Basic Books, a member of the Perseus Books Group 2015 368 p. portraits (hardback) $29.99   **342.73**

1. Constitutional history 2. United States. Constitution 3. Constitutional law -- United States 4. Constitutional history -- United States

ISBN 0465053726; 9780465053711; 9780465053728

LC 2014041943

"Beginning with the Constitution's birth in 1787, [author Michael Stokes] Paulsen and [Luke] Paulsen offer a grand tour of its provisions, principles, and interpretation, introducing readers to the characters and controversies that have shaped the Constitution in the 200-plus years since its creation. Along the way, the authors provide correctives to the shallow myths and partial truths that pervade so much popular treatment of the Constitution." (Publisher's note)

"This is a highly accessible and scholarly but lively look at the nation's guiding document." Booklist

Includes bibliographical references and index

Purdum, Todd S., 1959-

An **idea** whose time has come; two presidents, two parties, and the battle for the Civil Rights Act of 1964. Todd S. Purdum. Henry Holt & Co 2014 416 p. 8 plates; illustrations (hardback) $30   **342.73**

1. Civil Rights Act of 1964 2. Civil rights -- United States 3. United States -- Politics and government -- 1961-1974 4. United States. Civil Rights Act of 1964 5. United States -- Politics and government -- 1961-1963 6. United States -- Politics and government -- 1963-1969 7. Civil rights -- United States -- History -- 20th century

ISBN 0805096728; 9780805096729

LC 2013038545

In this book, "Todd S. Purdum tells the story of the Civil Rights Act of 1964, recreating the legislative maneuvering and the larger-than-life characters who made its passage possible. . . . Purdum shows how these all-too-human figures managed, in just over a year, to create a bill that prompted the longest filibuster in the history of the U.S. Senate yet was ultimately adopted with overwhelming bipartisan support." (Publisher's note)

"Those battling the neo-Confederates and nullificationists of today will want this book to see how it's done. Readers with an interest in American history and the American promise will find it a must-read as well." Kirkus

Includes bibliographical references and index

Raphael, Ray

Constitutional myths; what we get wrong and how to get it right. by Ray Raphael. The New Press 2013 xiii, 316 p.p (hardcover) $26.95   **342.73**

1. United States. Constitution 2. Founding Fathers of the United States 3. Constitutional history -- United States 4. United States -- History -- 1783-1815 5. Constitutional history -- United States -- 18th century

ISBN 1595588329; 9781595588326

LC 2012041849

This book on the U.S. Constitution is "more concerned with contextualizing the Founder Fathers than in interpreting them. One by one, [Ray] Raphael . . . addresses some of the more pervasive interpretations of the Constitution and the men who crafted it. . . .Through careful analysis of the 1787 Constitutional Convention, Raphael demonstrates that nothing about the Constitution is as simple as contemporary discourse makes it seem." (Publishers Weekly)

Includes bibliographical references and index.

Richards, Leonard L.

Who freed the slaves? the fight over the Thirteenth Amend-ment. Leonard L. Richards. University of Chicago Press 2015 320 p. illustrations, portraits (cloth: alk. paper) $30   **342.73**

1. Slavery -- United States 2. Slaves -- Emancipation -- United States 3. United States. Constitution. 13th Amendment -- History 4. Slaves -- Emancipation -- United States -- History -- 19th century 5. United States. President (1861-1865: Lincoln). Emancipation Proclamation 6. Slavery -- Law and legislation -- United States -- History -- 19th century

ISBN 022617820X; 9780226178202

LC 2014023200

In this book, historian Leonard L. Richards "tells the little-known story of the battle over the Thirteenth Amendment, and of James Ashley, the unsung Ohio congressman who proposed the amendment and steered it to passage. Taking readers to the floor of Congress and the back rooms where deals were made, Richards brings to life the messy process of legislation—a process made all the more complicated by the bloody war and the deep-rooted fear of black emancipation." (Publisher's note)

"It... provides a perceptive explanation as to how and why the promise of the 13th Amendment as an instrument for civil rights never came to fruition. In doing so, it reminds us that freedom is not a given; principled, pragmatic, and persistent advocates must work to realize and secure it." LJ

Includes bibliographical references and index

Risen, Clay

The **bill** of the century; the epic battle for the Civil Rights Act. Clay Risen. Bloomsbury Press 2014 320 p. illustrations (hardback) $28   **342.73**

1. United States. Civil Rights Act of 1964 2. Civil rights -- United States -- History

ISBN 1608198243; 9781608198245

LC 2014004662

"Clay Risen shows [that] the battle for the Civil Rights Act was a . . . broad, epic struggle, a sweeping tale of unceasing grassroots activism, ringing speeches, backroom deal-making and finally, hand-to-hand legislative combat. The larger-than-life cast of characters ranges from Senate lions like Mike Mansfield and Strom Thurmond to NAACP lobbyist Charles Mitchell, called 'the 101st senator' for his Capitol Hill clout, and industrialist J. Irwin Miller, who helped mobilize a powerful religious coalition for the bill." (Publisher's note)

"A work of high academic quality written with a journalist's flair for telling a tale." Choice

Includes bibliographical references and index

Sunstein, Cass R. (Cass Robert), 1954-

Impeachment; a citizen's guide. Cass R. Sunstein. Harvard University Press 2017 199 p. (paperback) $7.95 342.73

1. Impeachments -- United States 2. Presidents -- United States -- Impeachment 3. Presidents -- Legal status, laws, etc. -- United States

ISBN 9780674984196; 9780674983793

LC 2017034532

This book, by Cass R. Sunstein, "illuminates the constitutional design behind impeachment and emphasizes the people's role in holding presidents accountable. . . . Sunstein identifies and corrects a number of misconceptions. For example, he shows that the Constitution, not the House of Representatives, establishes grounds for impeachment, and that the president can be impeached for abuses of power that do not violate the law." (Publisher's note)

"The resulting book is an essential guide to understanding impeachment's function within the 'constitutional system as a whole' and a persuasive argument that the impeachment clause places 'the fate of the republic' in the hands of its citizenry." Pub Wkly

Includes bibliographical references and index

Tribe, Laurence H., 1941-

Uncertain justice; the Roberts court and the constitution. Laurence Tribe, Joshua Matz. Henry Holt & Co. 2014 416 p. (hardback) $32   **342.73**

1. Roberts, John G., 1955- 2. United States. Supreme Court 3. Constitutional law -- United States 4. Constitutional law -- Social aspects -- United States

ISBN 0805099093; 9780805099096

LC 2014002845

This book, by Laurence Tribe and Joshua Matz, argues that "the Roberts Court is shaking the foundation of our nation's laws. . . . Tribe . . . and Matz dig deeply into the court's recent rulings, stepping beyond tired debates over judicial 'activism' to draw out hidden meanings and silent battles. The undercurrents they reveal suggest a strikingly different vision for the future of our country, one that is sure to be hotly debated." (Publisher's note)

"A well-researched, unsettling investigation of recent trends in the nation's highest court." Kirkus

Includes bibliographical references and index

Urofsky, Melvin I.

Dissent and the Supreme Court; Its Role in the Court's History and the Nation's Constitutional Dialogue. Melvin I. Urofsky. Pantheon Books 2015 544 p. illustrations (hard cover: alk. paper) $35   **342.73**

1. United States. Constitution 2. United States. Supreme Court 3. Judicial opinion -- United States 4. Constitutional law -- United States 5. Dissenting opinions -- United States 6. Government, Resistance to -- United States 7. Dissenters -- Legal status, laws, etc. -- United States

ISBN 9780307379405; 9781101870631

LC 2014048245

This book, by Melvin I. Urofsky, "looks at the role of dissent in the Supreme Court and the meaning of the Constitution through the greatest and longest lasting public-policy debate in the country's history, among members of the Supreme Court, between the Court and the other branches of government, and between the Court and the people of the United States." (Publisher's note)

"This is an insightful look at dissents as dialogues between the justices that reflect broader dialogues among citizens on the controversial issues of our time." Kirkus

Includes bibliographical references (pages 429-488) and index.

343   Military, defense, public property, public finance, tax, commerce (trade), industrial law

Benedict, Jeff

Little pink house; a true story of defiance and courage. Grand Central Publishing 2009 397p il $26.99   **343**

1. Nurses 2. Eminent domain

ISBN 978-0-446-50862-9; 0-446-50862-4

LC 2008-17650

"Benedict has pieced together a fascinating narrative, using e-mail messages, planning documents, interviews and personal diaries to produce a sordid account of ruthless local politicians working hand-in-medical-glove with big business to drive hardworking Americans from their homes." N Y Times Book Rev

Fishman, Stephen

Working for yourself; law & taxes for independent contractors, freelancers & consultants. Stephen Fishman, J.D. 11th edition Nolo 2018 360p pa $39.99   **343**

1. Self-employed

ISBN 9781413325812

First published 1997 with title: Wage slave no more. Frequently revised

"There's a good chance having a side business will mean being an independent contractor, a freelancer, or a consultant. This thorough and well-organized volume will guide individuals through the legal and tax issues that come with the territory. From deciding on legal structures to drafting contracts to collecting payment from deadbeat clients, this is excellent information." Libr J

Includes bibliographical references

Witt, John Fabian

Lincoln's code; the laws of war in American history. John Fabian Witt. Free Press 2012 viii, 498 p., [16] p.p ill. (hbk.) $32   **343**

1. Law 2. War 3. United States -- History -- 1861-1865, Civil War 4. War -- United States -- History 5. War (International law) -- History 6. Military law -- United States -- History 7. United States -- History -- Civil War, 1861-1865 8. War and emergency legislation -- United States -- History

ISBN 1416569839; 9781416569831

LC 2012006187

This book by author John Fabian Witt "reviews the background of U.S. laws of war. Witt . . . examines the laws of war in the 18th and 19th centuries from the French and Indian Wars to the Spanish American War. The focus is on the Civil War, where an entirely new rulebook on the laws of war was drafted by Franz Lieber and approved by President Lincoln." (Library Journal)

Includes bibliographical references (p. 401-470) and index

343.73   Military, defense, public property, public finance, tax, commerce (trade), industrial law – United States

Bray, Chris

Court- martial; how military justice has shaped America from the revolution to 9/11 and beyond. Chris Bray. W W Norton & Co Inc 2016 416 p. (hardcover) $28.95; (ebook) $50   **343.73**

1. Military law 2. Military offenses 3. Courts martial and courts of inquiry 4. Courts-martial and courts of inquiry -- United States -- History

ISBN 9780393243406; 9780393243413

LC 2016002824

This book, by Chris Bray, "tells the sweeping story of military justice from the earliest days of the republic to contemporary arguments over using military courts to try foreign terrorists or soldiers accused of sexual assault. . . . [It] recounts the stories of famous American court-martials, . . . [the] encounters of freed slaves with the military justice system during the Civil War, and . . . how the Uniform Code of Military Justice came about after World War II." (Publisher's note)

"A thoroughly impressive debut." Kirkus

Includes bibliographical references and index

Chertoff, Michael, 1953-

Exploding data; reclaiming our cybersecurity in the digital age. Michael Chertoff. Atlantic Monthly Press 2018 288 p.

(hardcover) $26 **343.73**

1. Computer security 2. Internet security 3. Right of privacy -- United States 4. Privacy, Right of -- United States 5. Information warfare (International law) 6. Internet -- Law and legislation -- United States 7. Conflict of laws -- Data protection -- United States 8. Data protection -- Government policy -- United States 9. Computer security -- Government policy -- United States 10. Data protection -- Law and legislation -- United States 11. Computer security -- Law and legislation -- United States
ISBN 9780802127938

LC 2018012763

In this book, author "Michael Chertoff makes clear that our laws and policies surrounding the protection of personal information, written for an earlier time, need to be completely overhauled in the Internet era. . . . Chertoff explains the complex legalities surrounding issues of data collection and dissemination today, and charts a path that balances the needs of government, business, and individuals alike." (Publisher's note)

"A tremendous resource for any reader about ever-shifting threats embedded in data collection and control." LJ

Includes bibliographical references

344 Labor, social service, education, cultural law

Ball, Howard, 1937-

At liberty to die; the battle for death with dignity in America. Howard Ball. New York University Press 2012 ix, 229 p.p (alk. paper) $30.00 **344**

1. Euthanasia 2. Brain death 3. Right to die -- Law and legislation 4. Euthanasia -- Law and legislation -- United States 5. Right to die -- Law and legislation -- United States 6. Assisted suicide -- Law and legislation -- United States
ISBN 081474527X; 0814769756; 0814791042; 9780814745274; 9780814769751; 9780814791042

LC 2011052258

In this book, political scientist Howard Ball offers a "legal history of the right to die in America. He starts with the case of Nancy Cruzan, who was left in a persistent vegetative state after a car accident, and the Supreme Court's ruling that the state had the right to require 'clear and convincing evidence' of Cruzan's intentions before removing her from life support. He then traces battles to legalize physician-assisted death (PAD) in Oregon, Washington State, Montana, Vermont, and Hawaii." (Library Journal)

Includes bibliographical references and index.

Barrett, Paul M.

Law of the jungle; the $19 billion brawl over oil, indians, and the fate of the rainforest. by Paul M. Barrett. Crown Publishers 2014 viii, 290 p.p map (hbk.) $26 **344**

1. Trials 2. Petroleum industry 3. Chevron Corporation -- Trials, litigation, etc 4. Liability for oil pollution damages -- Ecuador 5. Environmental lawyers -- United States -- Biography
ISBN 9780770436360; 0770436366; 9780770436346; 077043634X

LC 2013038226

This book by Paul M. Barrett describes how "Steven Donziger, a self-styled social activist and Harvard educated lawyer, signed on to a budding class action lawsuit against multinational Texaco (which later merged with Chevron to become the third-largest corporation in America). The suit sought reparations for the Ecuadorian peasants and tribes people whose lives were affected by decades of oil production near their villages and fields." (Publisher's note)

"Although legal jargon appears often here, Barrett's prose is far from

tedious in telling a story that is almost Shakespearean in scope, featuring a flawed protagonist with good intentions but tragically overreaching ambitions." Booklist

Includes bibliographical references (pages 277-280) and index.

Cohen, Adam

★ **Imbeciles**; The Supreme Court, American Eugenics, and the Sterilization of Carrie Buck. Adam Cohen. Penguin Group USA 2016 416 p. $28 **344**

1. United States. Supreme Court 2. Sterilization (Birth control)
ISBN 1594204187; 9781594204180

LC 2015044207

National Book Award Longlist: Nonfiction (2016)

This book by Adam Cohen tells of "one of the darkest moments in the American legal tradition: the Supreme Court's decision to champion eugenic sterilization for the greater good of the country. In 1927, when the nation was caught up in eugenic fervor, the justices allowed Virginia to sterilize Carrie Buck, a perfectly normal young woman, for being an 'imbecile.'" (Publisher's note)

"A shocking tale about science and law gone horribly wrong, an almost forgotten case that deserves to be ranked with Dred Scott, Plessy, and Korematsu as among the Supreme Court's worst decisions." Kirkus

Green, Lisa

On Your Case; A Comprehensive, Compassionate (And Only Slightly Bossy) Legal Guide for Every Stage of a Woman's Life. Lisa Green. HarperCollins 2015 320 p. $26.99 **344**

1. Law 2. Women -- Law and legislation
ISBN 0062307991; 9780062307996

LC 2015372846

This book, by Lisa Green, "offers . . . a witty, direct and empowering legal guide for women, filled with accessible information they can employ to understand and respond to common legal issues throughout their lives, from dating, marriage, and kids to jobs, retirement, aging parents, and wills." (Publisher's note)

"Green's confident voice resonates like a smart, funny girlfriend giving solid counsel over a glass of wine. It's personal, practical, and backed up with plenty of legal reality. This book will appeal to women with legal troubles and to those hoping to avoid them." LJ

Hull, N. E. H.

★ **Roe** v. Wade; the abortion rights controversy in American history. [by] N.E.H. Hull and Peter Charles Hoffer. 2nd ed., rev. & expanded.; University Press of Kansas 2010 370p (Landmark law cases & American society) $39.95; pa $19.95 **344**

1. Roe v. Wade 2. District attorneys 3. Pro-choice activists 4. Abortion -- Law and legislation
ISBN 978-0-7006-1753-1; 0-7006-1753-1; 978-0-7006-1754-8 pa; 0-7006-1754-X pa

LC 2010-21294

First published 2001

Thsi book "highlights the abortion issue's historical background; highlights Roe v. Wade's core issues, essential personalities, and key precedents; tracks the case's path through the courts; clarifies the jurisprudence behind the court's ruling in Roe; and gauges its impact on American society and subsequent challenges to it in Webster v. Reproductive Services (1989) and Casey v. Planned Parenthood (1992). . . . [It includes] chapters covering abortion politics and legal battles in the post-9/11 era." Publisher's note

Includes bibliographical references

James, Vaughn E.

The **Alzheimer's** advisor; a caregiver's guide to dealing with the tough legal and practical issues. AMACOM - American Management Association 2009 300p pa $19.95   **344**

1. Caregivers 2. Alzheimer's disease 3. Medicine -- Law and legislation
ISBN 978-0-8144-0924-4; 0-8144-0924-5

LC 2008-20258

The author "deals with the often overlooked but difficult legal and financial responsibilities associated with caring for elders with memory loss and/or dementia." Libr J

Includes bibliographical references

Lombardo, Paul A.

Three generations, no imbeciles; eugenics, the Supreme Court, and Buck v. Bell. Johns Hopkins University Press 2008 365p il   **344**

1. Eugenics 2. Sterilization (Birth control) 3. People with mental disabilities 4. Buck v. Bell 5. Forced sterilization 6. Constitutional history 7. Sterilization, Eugenic 8. Constitutional law -- United States 9. United States -- Supreme Court -- History 10. Insanity -- Jurisprudence -- United States 11. Eugenics -- United States -- History -- 20th century
ISBN 0-8018-9010-1; 978-0-8018-9010-9

LC 2008-6546

This book examines the case of Buck v. Bell, covering the events of the trial and the 1927 Supreme Court decision that upheld Virginia's 1924 Eugenical Sterilization Act, which called for compulsory sterilization of the "feeble-minded." Index.

The author "traces a seminal 1927 Supreme Court case arising from the attempt by authorities in Virginia to force the sterilization of a woman believed to be mentally and socially 'insufficient.'" Libr J

Includes bibliographical references

Matthews, Joseph L.

★ **Social** security, Medicare & government pensions; get the most out of your retirement & medical benefits. Joseph Matthews. Nolo   **344**

1. Medicare 2. Pensions 3. Social security

First published 1983 with title: Sourcebook for older Americans. Revised annually.

This guide discusses such topics as how to claim social security benefits, social security disability, civil service and veterans benefits, and Medicare procedures.

Nourse, Victoria F.

In reckless hands; Skinner v. Oklahoma and the near-triumph of American eugenics. W.W. Norton & Company 2008 240p il map $24.95   **344**

1. Thieves 2. Eugenics 3. Prisoners 4. Sterilization (Birth control) 5. Sterilization, Eugenic 6. Constitutional law -- United States 7. Eugenics -- United States -- History -- 20th century
ISBN 978-0-393-06529-9; 0-393-06529-4

LC 2008-13140

The author "provides a legal history of the Supreme Court case that served to increase the recognition of individual rights, although it fell short of ending the practice and debate of eugenics in the US. . . . This book deserves attention from those interested in the history and politics of the legal system." Choice

Includes bibliographical references

Sack, Steven Mitchell

The **employee** rights handbook; effective legal strategies to protect your job from interview to pink slip. 3rd ed., rev. & enlarged ed.; Legal Strategies Publications 2010 620p $39.95   **344**

1. Employee rights 2. Labor -- Law and legislation
ISBN 978-0-9636306-7-4

LC 2010-926886

First published 1990 by Facts on File

The author "advises readers on topics from avoiding prehiring abuses and protecting on-the-job rights through postemployment litigation and finding and hiring a lawyer. . . . Readers looking for an all-in-one employee legal primer or layperson's quick reference should find this a useful tool." Libr J

Steingold, Fred S.

The **employer's** legal handbook; manage your employees & workplace effectively. Fred S. Steingold. 13th edition Nolo 2017 496 p. pbk $49.99   **344**

1. Labor -- Law and legislation
ISBN 9781413323993; 1413323995

"This guide for employers discusses "how to comply with the most recent workplace laws and regulations, run a safe and fair workplace and avoid lawsuits." Publisher's note

344.73   Labor, social service, education, cultural law – United States

Driver, Justin

The **schoolhouse** gate; public education, the Supreme Court, and the battle for the American mind. Justin Driver. Pantheon 2018 576 p. (hardback) $35   **344.73**

1. Students -- Civil rights 2. Education -- Government policy 3. Educational law and legislation 4. Students -- Civil rights -- United States 5. Educational law and legislation -- United States 6. Constitutional law -- Social aspect -- United States
ISBN 9781101871652

LC 2017058167

This book, by Justin Driver, "aims to vindicate the rights of public school students, which have so often been undermined by the Supreme Court in recent decades. . . . From racial segregation to unauthorized immigration, from antiwar protests to compulsory flag salutes, from economic inequality to teacher-led prayer--these are but a few of the cultural anxieties dividing American society that the Supreme Court has addressed in elementary and secondary schools." (Publisher's note)

"Readers with the ability to grapple with complex constitutional issues will find much to learn from Driver's independent thinking and unique insights." Publishers' Weekly

Friedman, Barry

Unwarranted; policing without permission. Barry Friedman. Farrar, Straus & Giroux 2017 448 p. (hardback) $28   **344.73**

1. Right of privacy -- United States 2. Intelligence service -- United States 3. Electronic surveillance -- United States 4. Espionage -- United States 5. Civil rights -- United States 6. Law enforcement -- United States 7. Privacy, Right of -- United States 8. Electronic surveillance -- Law and legislation -- United States
ISBN 9780374280451; 9780374710903

LC 2016033246

In this book, law professor Barry Friedman "examines what he identifies as the crisis in 21st-century U.S. policing. Drawing on landmark court cases, extensive history, and incisive analysis, Friedman takes a hard look at current problems and proposes astute and well-researched solutions in favor of more 'democratic and constitutional' policing." (Publisher's Weekly)

"This book is the definitive guide to contemporary policing and its necessary reforms." Pub Wkly

Includes bibliographical references and index.

Thomas, Gillian

Because of sex; one law, ten cases, and fifty years that changed American women's lives at work. Gillian Thomas. St. Martin's Press 2016 304 p. (ebook) $40; (hardback) $26.99 **344.73**

1. Women's rights 2. Sex discrimination in employment 3. Sex discrimination -- Law and legislation 4. Women's rights -- United States -- Cases 5. Sex discrimination against women -- Law and legislation -- United States -- Cases 6. Sex discrimination in employment -- Law and legislation -- United States -- Cases

ISBN 9781466878976; 9781137280053

LC 2015033086

This book, by Gillian Thomas, narrates how "the 1964 Civil Rights Act also revolutionized the lives of America's working women. Title VII of the law made it illegal to discriminate 'because of sex.' But that simple phrase didn't mean much until ordinary women began using the law to get justice on the job—and some took their fights all the way to the Supreme Court." (Publisher's note)

"The author merges the personal stories with the legal intricacies of the litigation, and crafts a moving and informative account of a struggle for equality that remains incomplete." Pub Wkly

Includes bibliographical references (pages [247]-280) and index.

345 Criminal law

Bogira, Steve

Courtroom 302; a year behind the scenes in an American criminal courthouse. Knopf 2005 404p hardcover o.p. pa $16 **345**

1. Courts 2. Administration of criminal justice

ISBN 0-679-43252-3; 0-679-75206-4 pa

LC 2004-57636

Bogira provides "a balanced view of the realities of the day-to-day, assembly-line grind that marks so much of the process from arrest to final disposition.... The brilliance of Bogira's insights will lead many to hope that he will follow this debut with proposals to cure the many ills he has diagnosed." Publ Wkly

Includes bibliographical references

Boyle, Kevin

Arc of justice; a saga of race, rights, and murder in the Jazz Age. Holt & Co. 2004 415p il $26; pa $15 **345**

1. Physicians 2. Trials (Homicide) 3. Lawyers 4. Memoirists 5. Writers on law 6. Trials (Murder) 7. State legislators 8. African Americans -- Civil rights 9. Detroit (Mich.) -- Race relations 10. African Americans -- Michigan -- Detroit 11. African Americans -- Civil rights -- History -- 20th century

ISBN 0-8050-7145-8; 0-8050-7933-5 pa

LC 2004-47352

National Book Award: Nonfiction (2004)

In 1925, Dr. Ossian Sweet, an African American, moved into an all-white neighborhood in Detroit with his wife, Gladys. Mobs attacked his home. He and his friends fired on the attackers in self-defense and a white man was killed. "The Sweets and the nine other men there that night were charged with first-degree murder. The case was a significant moment in the early civil rights movement.... {This is an} account of the incident and trial.... {Clarence Darrow} joined the defense team three months after the end of the Scopes trial." (N Y Times (Late N Y Ed)) Bibliography. Index.

Boyle "has brilliantly rescued from obscurity a fascinating chapter in American history that had profound implications for the rise of the Civil Rights movement." Publ Wkly

Includes bibliographical references

Colmez, Coralie

Math on trial; how numbers get used and abused in the courtroom. Leila Schneps and Coralie Colmez. Basic Books 2013 xi, 256 p.p ill., ports. (hardcover) $26.99 **345**

1. Mathematics 2. Judicial error 3. Forensic sciences 4. Forensic statistics

ISBN 0465032923; 9780465032921

LC 2012040624

In this book, "Leila Schneps and Coralie Colmez describe ten trials spanning from the nineteenth century to today, in which mathematical arguments were used--and disastrously misused--as evidence.... Offering a fresh angle on cases from the nineteenth-century Dreyfus affair to the murder trial of Dutch nurse Lucia de Berk, Schneps and Colmez show how the improper application of mathematical concepts can mean the difference between walking free and life in prison." (Publisher's note)

Includes bibliographical references and index.

Feige, David

Indefensible; one lawyer's journey into the inferno of American justice. Little, Brown and Co. 2006 276p $24.95 **345**

1. Lawyers 2. Administration of criminal justice 3. Writers on law

ISBN 978-0-316-15623-3; 0-316-15623-X

LC 2006-1283

The author "takes us through a typically harrowing day as a public defender, dealing with arbitrary judges and clients who are often victims of the judicial system.... Feige skillfully shares his wisdom and his humanity and sheds light on a justice system that too often works irrationally." Publ Wkly

Hoffer, Peter Charles

The **Salem** witchcraft trials; a legal history. University Press of Kan. 1997 165p (Landmark law cases & American society) hardcover o.p. pa $12.95 **345**

1. Trials 2. Salem (Mass.) -- History

ISBN 0-7006-0858-3; 0-7006-0859-1 pa

LC 97-19986

"Hoffer discusses the legal nature of the charges of witchcraft, the evidential and procedural characteristics of the trials of the accused, and the roles and attitudes of the ministers and magistrates who controlled the proceedings.... Hoffer offers little that is new in terms of interpretation, but he presents it well and in a manner easily grasped by the general reader." Choice

Includes bibliographical references

Kadri, Sadakat

The **trial**; a history, from Socrates to O. J. Simpson. Random House 2005 459p il $29.95 **345**

1. Trials

ISBN 0-375-50550-4

LC 2005-42925

This "history of the trial from ancient times to the present provides . . . [a] history of the various forms and purposes of trials throughout Western civilization. . . . The result is a magnificent book suitable for all sorts of people, from inquisitive high school students to blue-chip lawyers." Choice

Includes bibliographical references

Lipstadt, Deborah E.

The **Eichmann** trial. Nextbook/Schocken 2011 237p (Jewish encounters) $24.95 **345**

1. War criminals 2. War crime trials 3. Nazi leaders 4. Holocaust, 1933-1945 5. Holocaust, Jewish (1939-1945)
ISBN 978-0-8052-4260-7; 0-8052-4260-0

LC 2010-28620

"Lipstadt has done a great service by untethering the trial from [Hannah] Arendt's polarizing presence, recovering the event as a gripping legal drama, as well as a hinge moment in Israel's history and in the world's delayed awakening to the magnitude of the Holocaust." N Y Times Book Rev

Includes bibliographical references

Malcolm, Janet

Iphigenia in Forest Hills; anatomy of a murder trial. Yale University Press 2011 155p $25 **345**

1. Dentists 2. Trials (Homicide) 3. Murderers 4. Internists 5. Murder victims 6. Trials (Murder) -- Queens (New York, N.Y.)
ISBN 978-0-300-16746-7; 0-300-16746-6

LC 2010-35851

"Malcolm's book chronicles the fate of Mazoltuv Borukhova, a 35-year-old doctor and a member of the Bukharan Jewish sect who stands accused of hiring an assassin to kill her ex-husband, Daniel Malakov. On the morning of Oct. 28, 2007, Malakov was shot to death in a park in Queens, N.Y., in front of his and Borukhova's 4-year-old daughter. . . . Malcolm shows us what happens when the abstract ideals of the law are applied, as they always are, by human beings. We meet one judge who, acting out of incompetence or malice, makes an inexplicable and terrible child-custody decision. Another proves less interested in serving justice than in wrapping up proceedings in time for his Caribbean vacation. A lawyer who, on the stand, appears to be 'intelligent and well-spoken' turns out to be both negligent and delusional. . . . All told, it's such a damning portrait of American jurisprudence that Malcolm scarcely need editorialize. As lawyers would say, res ipsa loquitur: the thing speaks for itself." Boston Globe

Newton, Michael A.

Enemy of the state; the trial and execution of Saddam Hussein. [by] Michael A. Newton & Michael P. Scharf. St. Martin's Press 2008 305p il $26.95 **345**

1. Trials 2. Presidents
ISBN 978-0-312-38556-9; 0-312-38556-0

LC 2008-21087

The authors "provided judicial assistance to the trial of Saddam Hussein and other Ba'athists, including training of judicial personnel, writing rules for the Iraqi Tribunal, and observing the nine-month trial proceedings. Here, they write of their experiences and provide perspective on the trial, which began in October 2005, including gavel-to-gavel coverage of the proceedings. . . . Their insiders' account is directed toward general adult audiences and will effectively aid them in understanding this crucial phase as Iraq struggles toward its future." Libr J

Includes bibliographical references

Rabinowitz, Dorothy

No crueler tyrannies; accusation, false witness, and other terrors of our times. Simon & Schuster 2003 239p (A Wall Street Journal book) $25; pa $13 **345**

1. Trials 2. Child sexual abuse
ISBN 0-7432-2834-0; 0-7432-2840-5 pa

LC 2002-44670

This book "reexamines high-profile cases of the 1980s and 1990s involving mass sexual abuse. Demonstrating that overzealous prosecutors and indifferent courts led to the prosecution of many innocents, Rabinowitz provides . . . analyses of the major cases, especially those that involved child-care workers. . . . This gripping, well-written book about social injustice and public hysteria is recommended for social science and law collections." Libr J

Sands, Philippe

East West Street; on the origins of genocide and crimes against humanity. Philippe Sands. Alfred A. Knopf 2016 448 p. illustrations, maps (hardcover) $32.50 **345**

1. Lawyers 2. Genocide 3. War crimes
ISBN 9780385350716; 9780385350723; 0385350716

LC 2016933268

This book, by Philippe Sands, "looks at the personal and intellectual evolution of [Rafael Lemkin and Hersch Lauterpacht,] the two men who simultaneously originated the ideas of 'genocide' and 'crimes against humanity.' And the author writes of a third man, Hans Frank, Hitler's personal lawyer. Sands . . . writes of how all three men came together, in October 1945 in Nuremberg." (Publisher's note)

"Readers interested in history, political science, and/or religion shouldn't miss this compelling work with unforgettable characters." LJ

Includes bibliographical references (pages 381-409) and index.

Schiff, Stacy, 1961-

★ The **Witches**; Salem, 1692. Stacy Schiff. Little, Brown & Co. 2015 512 p. 16 plates; color illustrations (hardcover) $32 **345**

1. Salem witch trials 2. Salem (Mass.) -- History
ISBN 9780316200608; 0316200603

LC 2015939026

This book, by Stacy Schiff, "unpacks the mystery of the Salem Witch Trials. It began in 1692, over an exceptionally raw Massachusetts winter, when a minister's daughter began to scream and convulse. It ended less than a year later, but not before 19 men and women had been hanged and an elderly man crushed to death. . . . In curious ways, the trials would shape the future republic." (Publisher's note)

"This fully documented narrative, if a bit exhausting and disorganized, will find a welcome audience among readers of witchcraft or colonial histories as well as Schiff's legion of fans." LJ

Stone, Geoffrey R.

★ **Sex** and the constitution; sex, religion, and law from America's origins to the twenty-first century. Geoffrey R. Stone. Liveright Publishing Corporation 2017 xxxii, 668 p.p illustrations (hardcover) $35 **345**

1. Sex -- Religious aspects 2. Sexual rights -- United States 3. Sex -- Law and legislation -- United States
ISBN 9781631493652; 0871404699; 9780871404695

LC 2016047264

In this book about sex-related legislation in America, author Geoffrey R. Stone "demonstrates how the Founding Fathers, deeply influenced by their philosophical forebears, saw traditional Christianity as an impediment to the pursuit of happiness and to the quest for human progress.

Acutely aware of the need to separate politics from the divisive forces of religion, the Founding Fathers crafted a constitution that expressed the fundamental values of the Enlightenment." (Publisher's note)

"This title is a commanding synthesis of scholarship on over two centuries of American legal debate and practice regarding these issues, and would work well as the core text for a course of the subject." Pub Wkly

Includes bibliographical references and index.

Strang, Dean A.

Worse than the devil; anarchists, Clarence Darrow, and justice in a time of terror. Dean A. Strang. The University of Wisconsin Press 2013 xviii, 268 p.p ill., map (paperback) $26.95 **345**
1. Trials 2. Judicial error 3. Anarchism and anarchists 4. Milwaukee (Wis.) -- History -- 20th century 5. Bay View (Milwaukee, Wis.) -- History -- 20th century 6. Anarchists -- Wisconsin -- Milwaukee -- History -- 20th century 7. Trials (Riots) -- Wisconsin -- Milwaukee -- History -- 20th century 8. Italian Americans -- Wisconsin -- Milwaukee -- History -- 20th century 9. Judicial corruption -- Wisconsin -- Milwaukee -- History -- 20th century
ISBN 0299293947; 9780299293932; 9780299293949
LC 2012032689

This book, by Dean A. Strang, profiles how "in 1917 a bomb exploded in . . . Milwaukee. . . . Those responsible never were apprehended, but . . . all assumed that the perpetrators were Italian. Days later, eleven alleged Italian anarchists went to trial on unrelated charges involving a fracas that had occurred two months before. Against the backdrop of World War I . . . and . . . a prevailing hatred and fear of radical immigrants, the Italians had an unfair trial." (Publisher's note)

Includes bibliographical references and index

Temkin, Moshik, 1971-

The **Sacco**-Vanzetti Affair; America on trial. Yale University Press 2009 316p il $35 **345**
1. Trials (Homicide) 2. Sacco-Vanzetti case 3. Sacco-Vanzetti Trial, Dedham, Mass., 1921 4. Sacco-Vanzetti trial, Dedham (Mass.), 1921 5. Trials (Murder) -- Massachusetts -- Dedham 6. United States -- Foreign public opinion, European -- History
ISBN 978-0-300-12484-2; 0-300-12484-8
LC 2008-45606

This "study of the trial and appeals of these two condemned murderers and of the life and times of the country, which feared foreign contamination, surpasses all prior analyses of this subject in terms of scope, erudition, and objectivity. . . . This book discusses many fascinating elements of controversy, not least the long-term views held by Sacco and Vanzetti's defenders and accusers and how their participation in the search for justice was perceived by their peers." Libr J

Includes bibliographical references

Turow, Scott

★ **Ultimate** punishment; a lawyer's reflections on dealing with the death penalty. Farrar, Straus and Giroux 2003 164p $18 **345**
1. Capital punishment
ISBN 0-374-12873-1
LC 2003-7873

"In 2000 Governor George Ryan of Illinois declared a moratorium on executions. . . . Ryan established a commission to study the state's capital punishment system and propose reforms. In 2002 the commission issued its report. . . . Among the people Ryan appointed to the commission was Scott Turow, a . . . novelist and practicing attorney, with experience in death penalty cases. He was, at the time of his appointment,

a self-described 'agnostic' on capital punishment. Ultimate Punishment is Turow's account of his struggle to resolve for himself the question, Should we retain the death penalty?" Christ Century

Includes bibliographical references

Walsh, John Evangelist

Moonlight; Abraham Lincoln and the Almanac trial. St. Martin's Press 2000 166p il $22.95 **345**
1. Trials 2. Lawyers 3. Presidents 4. State legislators 5. Members of Congress
ISBN 0-312-22922-4
LC 99-59606

This is "the story of how Abraham Lincoln secured the acquittal of murder suspect William 'Duff' Armstrong, the son of an old New Salem friend, by making use of an almanac to discredit a witness's description of the position of the moon on the night in question." Libr J

Includes bibliographical references

Watson, Bruce

★ **Sacco** and Vanzetti; the men, the murders and the judgment of mankind. Viking 2007 433p il $25.95; pa $16 **345**
1. Trials (Homicide) 2. Sacco-Vanzetti case 3. Anarchists
ISBN 978-0-670-06353-6; 0-670-06353-3; 978-0-14-3114284 pa; 0-14-311428-X pa
LC 2006-103092

The author "has written a well-researched page-turner. Highly recommended." Libr J

Includes bibliographical references

345.02   Criminal offenses

George, Cherian

Hate spin; the manufacture of religious offense and its threat to democracy. Cherian George. MIT Press 2016 xviii, 308 p.p (hardcover: alk. paper) $29.95; (ebook) $44.95 **345.02**
1. Hate speech 2. Freedom of speech 3. Religion and politics 4. Political persecution 5. Hate speech -- Law and legislation 6. Offenses against religion -- Political aspects 7. Offenses against religion -- Law and legislation
ISBN 0262035308; 9780262035309; 9780262336086
LC 2016014335

In this book, by Cherian George, "outbreaks of religious intolerance are usually assumed to be visceral and spontaneous. . . . George shows that they often involve sophisticated campaigns manufactured by political opportunists to mobilize supporters and marginalize opponents. Right-wing networks orchestrate the giving of offense and the taking of offense as instruments of identity politics, exploiting democratic space to promote agendas that undermine democratic values." (Publisher's note)

"This timely work provides an essential warning against the misuse of perceived religious-based bias and an unmasking of the real motives of those who incite manufactured offense." Pub Wkly

Includes bibliographical references (pages 267-292) and index

345.73   Criminal justice -- law -- United States

Beloof, Douglas E.

Victims' rights; a documentary and reference guide. Douglas E. Beloof. Greenwood 2012 xi, 313 p.p (hbk.: alk. paper) $100.00 **345.73**
1. Victims of crimes 2. Victims of crimes -- Legal status, laws,

etc. 3. Victims of crimes -- Legal status, laws, etc. -- United States
ISBN 0313393451; 9780313393457; 9780313393464

LC 2011043292

This book by Douglas E. Beloof "traces the origins, evolution, and results of the victims' rights movement. It puts victims' rights in a legal, historical, and contemporary context, and . . . collects important victims' rights documents in a single volume." It "bring[s] together dozens of varied documents such as presidential task force reports and recommendations, Supreme Court cases, state constitutions, human rights reports, critical articles, and political documents." (Publisher's note)

Includes bibliographical references and index.

Duane, James

You Have the Right to Remain Innocent. Amazon Pub 2016 152 p. $9.99   **345.73**
1. United States. Constitution 2. United States. Supreme Court
ISBN 1503933393; 9781503933392

In this book Professor James Duane "demonstrates the critical importance of a constitutional right not well or widely understood by the average American. Reflecting the most recent attitudes of the Supreme Court, Professor Duane argues that it is now even easier for police to use your own words against you. This lively and informative guide explains what everyone needs to know to protect themselves and those they love." (Publisher's note)

"Well-informed, scary, sobering, and sure to tick off police officers and prosecutors even as it contributes to keeping innocent people out of jail." Kirkus

Includes bibliographical references.

Garrett, Brandon L.

Too big to jail; how prosecutors compromise with corporations. Brandon L. Garrett. Belknap Press 2014 384 p. illustrations (hardcover: alk. paper) $29.95   **345.73**
1. Corporation law 2. Administration of criminal justice -- United States 3. Prosecution -- United States 4. Tort liability of corporations -- United States 5. Corporations -- Corrupt practices -- United States 6. Corporation law -- United States -- Criminal provisions 7. Criminal liability of juristic persons -- United States 8. Corporate governance -- Law and legislation -- United States
ISBN 0674368312; 9780674368316

LC 2014013351

Author Brandon L. Garrett "takes readers into a complex, compromised world of backroom deals, for an unprecedented look at what happens when criminal charges are brought against a major company in the United States. Presenting detailed data from more than a decade of federal cases, . . . Garrett reveals a pattern of negotiation and settlement in which prosecutors demand admissions of wrongdoing, impose penalties, and require structural reforms." (Publisher's note)

"A well-written, detailed exposé for all audiences." LJ

Includes bibliographical references and index

Houppert, Karen

Chasing Gideon; the elusive quest for poor people's justice. Karen Houppert. The New Press 2013 288 p. (hardcover) $26.95   **345.73**
1. Legal aid 2. Right to counsel 3. Right to counsel -- United States 4. Legal assistance to the poor -- United States
ISBN 1595588698; 9781595588692

LC 2012047464

This book, by Karen Houppert, profiles public defense in U.S. law. "On March 18, 1963, . . . the U.S. Supreme Court unanimously ruled in Gideon v. Wainright that all defendants facing significant jail time have the constitutional right to a free attorney if they cannot afford their own. . . . [The] book . . . chronicles the stories of people in all parts of the country who have relied on Gideon's promise." (Publisher's note)

Includes bibliographical references.

Mandery, Evan J.

A wild justice; the death and resurrection of capital punishment in America. Evan J. Mandery. W W Norton & Co Inc 2013 496 p. (hardcover) $29.95   **345.73**
1. Capital punishment -- United States 2. Constitutional law -- United States 3. Capital punishment -- United States. -- History -- 20th century
ISBN 0393239586; 9780393239584

LC 2013010126

In this book, Evan J. Mandery "traces the building momentum within the country and the court to question the legality of a punishment the Founding Fathers took for granted", the death penalty. He starts with "when the Supreme Court declined to accept the appeal of a 1963 rape case, [and] Justice Arthur Goldberg published an unusual dissent questioning the constitutionality of the death penalty." (Kirkus Reviews)

Includes bibliographical references and index

Smith, Clive Stafford

The **injustice** system; a murder in Miami and a trial gone wrong. Clive Stafford Smith. Viking 2012 xi, 352 p.p $27.95   **345.73**
1. Trials (Homicide) 2. Capital punishment -- United States 3. Administration of criminal justice -- United States 4. Trials (Murder) -- Florida 5. Criminal justice, Administration of -- United States
ISBN 0670023701; 9780670023707

LC 2012019068

This book presents an "account of a questionable 1989 death penalty case by the lawyer who tried to get it overturned. By the time [Clive Stafford] Smith . . . became involved in the case of Kris Maharaj . . . [he] had been convicted and sentenced to death in Miami for the murder of a former business partner and his son. . . . In the author's view, the case is a glaring, but by no means unique, example of massive flaws in the American criminal justice system." (Kirkus Reviews)

Includes bibliographical references and index

Toobin, Jeffrey, 1960-

The **run** of his life; the people v. O.J. Simpson. {by} Jeffrey Toobin. Random House 2015 466p $16   **345.73**
1. Football players 2. Trials (Homicide) 3. Sportscasters
ISBN 9780812988543; 081298854X

LC 96-210907

Originally published 1996

"The definitive account of the O. J. Simpson trial, The Run of His Life is a prodigious feat of reporting that could have been written only by the foremost legal journalist of our time. First published less than a year after the infamous verdict, Jeffrey Toobin's nonfiction masterpiece tells the whole story, from the murders of Nicole Brown Simpson and Ronald Goldman to the ruthless gamesmanship behind the scenes of 'the trial of the century.' Rich in character, as propulsive as a legal thriller, this enduring narrative continues to shock and fascinate with its candid depiction of the human drama that upended American life." (Publisher's note)

Trainum, James L.

How the police generate false confessions; an inside look at the interrogation room. James L. Trainum. Rowman & Littlefield 2016 328 p. (ebook) $45; (hardcover) $36   **345.73**

1. Interrogation 2. Administration of criminal justice -- United States

ISBN 144224464X; 9781442244658; 9781442244641

This book, by James L. Trainum, "expos[es] the tactics that law enforcement uses to make confessions happen. James L. Trainum reveals how innocent people can become suspects and then confessed criminals even when they have not committed a crime. Using real stories, he looks at the inherent coerciveness of the interrogation process and why so many false confessions contain so many of the details that only the true perpetrator would know." (Publisher's note)

"Using numerous examples and backed by persuasive academic research, Trainum proposes a better way that is already at work in countries with similar criminal justice systems. His book will hit a nerve with a public newly concerned with abuses of police power, and hopefully will influence those tasked with law enforcement and public policy as well." Pub Wkly

Includes bibliographical references (pages 293-299) and index.

345.747   Criminal law – New York

Davis, Kevin

The **brain** defense; murder in Manhattan and the dawn of neuroscience in America's courtrooms. Kevin Davis. Penguin Press 2017 336 p. (ebook) $65; (hardback) $28   **345.747**

1. Trials (Homicide) 2. Criminal law -- United States 3. Insanity (Law) -- New York (State) 4. Forensic neurology -- New York (State) 5. Trials (Murder) -- New York (State) -- New York 6. Brain -- Diseases -- Law and legislation -- New York (State)

ISBN 9780698183353; 9781594206337

LC 2016043485

This book, by Kevin Davis, "combines true crime, brain science, and courtroom drama. . . . Davis uses the perplexing story of the Weinstein murder to present a riveting, deeply researched exploration of the intersection of neuroscience and criminal justice. . . . It was the first case in the United States in which a judge allowed a scan showing a defendant's brain activity to be admitted as evidence to support a claim of innocence." (Publisher's note)

"A thoroughly researched, clearly presented book that suggests that imprecise brain science will become increasingly more common as evidence in criminal cases." Kirkus

Includes bibliographical references (pages 297-313) and index.

345.761   Criminal law – Alabama

Morrison, Melanie S.

Murder on Shades Mountain; the legal lynching of Willie Peterson and the struggle for justice in Jim Crow Birmingham. Melanie S. Morrison. Duke University Press 2018 288 p. (hardcover: alk. paper) $26.95   **345.761**

1. African Americans -- Crimes against 2. Birmingham (Ala.) -- Race relations 3. Trials (Rape) -- Alabama -- Birmingham 4. African Americans -- Crimes against -- Alabama -- Birmingham 5. Birmingham (Ala.) -- Race relations -- History -- 20th century

ISBN 9780822371175

LC 2017039036

In this book, by Melanie S. Morrison, "in 1931, . . . three young white women were brutally attacked. The sole survivor, Nell Williams, . . . said a black man . . . [shot] them and . . . [disappeared] into the woods. . . . Weeks later, Nell identified Willie Peterson as the attacker. . . . With the exception of being black, Peterson bore little resemblance to the description Nell gave the police. An all-white jury convicted Peterson of murder and sentenced him to death." (Publisher's note)

Includes bibliographical references and index

345.764   Criminal law – Texas

Graves, Anthony

Infinite hope; how wrongful conviction, solitary confinement and 12 years on death row failed to kill my soul. Anthony Graves. Beacon Press 2018 xvi, 197 p.p (hardback) $25.95   **345.764**

1. Judicial error 2. Prisoners -- Biography 3. Judicial error -- Texas 4. Trials (Murder) -- Texas 5. Death row inmates -- Texas -- Biography

ISBN 9780807062548; 9780807062524

LC 2017035843

In this book, author Anthony Graves recounts his wrongful conviction, the 16 years he spent in solitary confinement and 12 years on death row. "Through years of suffering the whims of rogue prosecutors, vote-hungry district attorneys, and Texas State Rangers who played by their own rules, Graves was frequently exposed to the dire realities of being poor and black in the criminal justice system." (Publisher's note)

"A well-written, matter-of-fact, inspirational account of how a man prevailed against a criminal justice system that is deeply flawed." Kirkus

346   Private law

American Bar Association

★ The **American** Bar Association legal guide for small business; everything you need to know about small business, from start-up to employment to financing and selling. 2nd ed.; Random House Reference 2010 472p pa $16.99   **346**

1. Small business

ISBN 978-0-375-72303-2; 0-375-72303-X

LC 2009-49394

First published 2000

Topics covered "include legal forms of operating businesses, buying an existing business or a franchise, hiring and firing employees, managing temps and independent contractors, dealing with contracts and scams, taxes of all types, and, finally, closing, selling, or bequeathing the business." Libr J [review of 2000 edition]

Baldwin, Peter

The **copyright** wars; three centuries of trans-Atlantic battle. Peter Baldwin. Princeton University Press 2014 552 p. (alk. paper) $35   **346**

1. Copyright 2. Right of property 3. Intellectual property 4. Copyright -- Europe -- History 5. Copyright -- United States -- History

ISBN 0691161828; 9780691161822

LC 2013049603

In this book, author "Peter Baldwin explains why the copyright wars have always been driven by a fundamental tension. Should copyright assure authors and rights holders lasting claims, much like conventional property rights, as in Continental Europe? Or should copyright be primarily concerned with giving consumers cheap and easy access to a shared culture, as in Britain and America? 'The Copyright Wars' describes how the Continental approach triumphed." (Publisher's note)

"This book will be of interest to readers in comparative law and history as it includes discussions of both policy and national history."

Choice
Includes bibliographical references and index

Butler, Rebecca P.

★ **Copyright** for teachers & librarians in the 21st century.
Neal-Schuman Publishers 2011 274p il pa $70   **346**
1. Copyright 2. Fair use (Copyright)
ISBN 978-1-55570-738-5

LC 2011012600

First published 2004 with title: Copyright for teachers and librarians
"Library educator Rebecca Butler explains fair use, public domain,
documentation and licenses, permissions, violations and penalties, policies and ethics codes, citations, creation and ownership, how to register
copyrights, and gives tips for staying out of trouble." Publisher's note
Includes bibliographical references

Dickey, Lisa

Then comes marriage; United States v. Windsor and the
defeat of DOMA. Roberta Kaplan with Lisa Dickey; Foreword
by Edie Windsor. W W Norton & Co Inc 2015 336 p. 8 plates;
illustrations (hardcover) $27.95   **346**
1. Same-sex marriage -- United States 2. Marriage law -- United
States 3. United States. Defense of Marriage Act 4. Gay couples
-- Legal status, laws, etc. -- United States 5. Same-sex marriage
-- Law and legislation -- United States
ISBN 0393248674; 9780393248678

LC 2015023636

This book, by Roberta Kaplan with Lisa Dickey, presents the author's "story of her defeat of the Defense of Marriage Act (DOMA)
before the Supreme Court. . . . In this . . . account . . . , Kaplan describes meeting Windsor and their journey together to defeat DOMA.
She shares the behind-the-scenes highs and lows, the excitement and
the worries, and provides intriguing insights into her historic argument
before the Supreme Court." (Publisher's note)
"Readers with an interest in constitutional law and Supreme Court
politics, as well as the road to marriage equality, will find this account
deliciously gripping." Library Journal

Elias, Stephen

Chapter 13 bankruptcy; keep your property & repay debts
over time. Cara O'Neill. 14th edition Nolo 2018 394 p il
paperback $39.99   **346**
1. Bankruptcy
ISBN 9781413325157
First published 1995. Periodically revised
Answers questions about bankruptcy that range from how to face the
reality of being in debt and possible alternatives to filing procedures and
strategies for rebuilding credit after the process is complete.

The **foreclosure** survival guide; keep your house or walk
away with money in your pocket. attorneys Stephen Elias and
Amy Loftsgordon; with bankruptcy updates by attorney Leon
Bayer. 5th edition Nolo 2015 346 p. pbk $24.99   **346**
1. Foreclosure
ISBN 1413321844; 9781413321845

LC 2015009962

First published 2008. Frequently revised
"Elias explains how foreclosure works, what options there may be
for keeping a home when in default, and what to do when that is not
possible. He includes instruction on negotiating a workout with a lender
as well as chapters on how to use bankruptcy to avoid foreclosure. . . .
Straightforward and timely." Libr J

Includes bibliographical references and index

Encyclopedia of crime and punishment; edited by David
Levinson. Sage Publs. 2002 4v set $600   **346**
1. Reference books 2. Administration of criminal justice 3. Crime
-- Encyclopedias
ISBN 0-7619-2258-X

LC 2002-1220

"The 439 signed entries cover 13 major themes: crimes and related
behaviors, law and justice, policing, forensics, corrections, victimology,
punishment, social and cultural context, international aspects, concepts
and theories, research methods and information, organizations and institutions, and special populations. . . . {This is} easy to understand and
useful for beginning research in the field of criminal justice." Booklist
Includes bibliographical references

Fishman, Stephen

The **public** domain; find and use free content for your website, book, app, music, video, art, and more. Stephen Fishman.
8th edition Nolo 2017 433p il map pa $39.99   **346**
1. Copyright
ISBN 9781413324013
First published 2001. Frequently revised
This book offers "information about finding copyright-free writings,
music, art, photography, software, maps, databases, videos, and more."
Publisher's note

Leonard, Robin

★ **Solve** your money troubles; Strategies to get out of debt
and stay that way. Robin Leonard; updated by Amy Loftsgordon. 15th edition Nolo 2015 375 p. pbk $24.99   **346**
1. Credit 2. Debtor and creditor
ISBN 1413321704; 9781413321708
First published 1991 with title: Money troubles. Frequently revised
This guide offers advice on how to manage debts, including how to
create a budget, negotiate with creditors, and rebuild your credit.
Includes bibliographical references

Lessig, Lawrence

Remix; making art and commerce thrive in the hybrid economy. Penguin Press 2008 xxii, 327p $25.95   **346**
1. Copyright
ISBN 978-1-59420-172-1

LC 2008-32392

As Lessig "sees it, if intellectual-property law is left as it is an entire
generation will be criminalized. He argues that the ways in which young
people break copyright laws help them to become the sort of people
we want them to be—creative and collaborative. Kids today are simply
not going to give up downloading music and using copyrighted material
in YouTube videos: they belong to a culture for which 'remix' is 'the
essential art.' Lessig's proposals for revising copyright are compelling,
because they rethink intellectual-property rights without abandoning
them." New Yorker
Includes bibliographical references

McGinty, Brian

Lincoln's Greatest Case; The River, the Bridge, and the
Making of America. Brian McGinty. W W Norton & Co Inc
2015 320 p. illustrations, maps $26.95   **346**
1. Trials 2. Bridges
ISBN 0871407841; 9780871407849

LC 2014036938

This book, by Brian McGinty, examines the 1850s "case . . . Hurd et al. v. The Railroad Bridge Company. In the early hours of May 6, 1856, the steamboat Effie Afton barreled into a pillar of the Rock Island Bridge--the first railroad bridge ever to span the Mississippi River. McGinty . . . animates this legal cauldron of the late 1850s, which turned out to be the most consequential trial in [Abraham] Lincoln's nearly quarter century as a lawyer." (Publisher's note)

"McGinty's book gives us the best accounting of Lincoln, the lawyer, to date. Highly recommended." LJ

Pakroo, Peri

★ The **small** business start-up kit; by Peri H. Pakroo; edited by Marcia Stewart. 10th edition Nolo 2018 352p pa $29.99   **346**

1. Commercial law 2. Small business 3. Business enterprises
ISBN 9781413324747

First published 2000. Frequently revised

"In addition to covering essential legal basics, . . . [the author] advises on picking a business name and the best location, drafting and using contracts, managing business finances using technology, choosing the right business structure, and reaching customers using social media. . . . The CD-ROM includes contact information for state agencies that deal with businesses and taxes." Libr J

Pascoe, Peggy

What comes naturally; miscegenation law and the making of race in America. Oxford University Press 2009 404p il map   **346**

1. Interracial marriage 2. Racially mixed people 3. United States -- Race relations 4. Miscegenation -- United States -- History 5. Interracial marriage -- United States -- History 6. Racially mixed people -- Legal status, laws, etc. -- United States
ISBN 0-19-509463-8; 978-0-19-509463-3

LC 2008-18035

"Peggy Pascoe's book, 'What Comes Naturally,' has won five major book awards--two from the American Historical Association, two from the Organization of American Historians, and one from the Law and Society Association; it was also a finalist for another from the American Studies Association. . . . It . . . [examines] laws banning interracial marriage in the United States, . . . informed by sociological, anthropological, and feminist theories of race-making, the state, law, and the intersections of race, class, and gender." (Contemporary Sociology)

"This compelling history of the United States miscegenation law demonstrates its centrality to maintaining white supremacy in the century following the Civil War. Pascoe, broadening her focus beyond black-white relations, considers Western states' prohibition of marriage between whites and American Indians, Chinese, Japanese, and Filipinos, as well as blacks. She weaves a fascinating story out of significant court cases." New Yorker

Includes bibliographical references and index

Pressman, David

Patent it yourself; your step-by-step guide to filing at the U.S. Patent Office. David Pressman and David E. Blau. 19th edition Nolo 2018 656 p il paperback $49.99   **346**

1. Patents 2. Inventions
ISBN 9781413325393

First published 1979. Periodically revised

This guide for the amateur inventor covers patent searching, filing and infringement.

Includes bibliographical references

346.01   Persons and domestic relations

American Civil Liberties Union

★ The **rights** of women; the authoritative ACLU guide to women's rights. [by] Lenora M. Lapidus, Emily J. Martin, and Namita Luthra. 4th ed.; New York University 2009 412p (American Civil Liberties Union handbook) $75; pa $19   **346.01**

1. Women's rights 2. Women -- Law and legislation
ISBN 978-0-8147-5230-2; 0-8147-5230-6; 978-0-8147-5229-6 pa; 0-8147-5229-2 pa

LC 2008-47033

First published 1973 by Sunrise Books/Dutton

Topics covered include "employment, education, housing, and public accommodations. This handbook also examines the specific issues of trafficking, violence against women, welfare reform, and reproductive freedom." Publisher's note

Includes bibliographical references

Doskow, Emily

★ **Nolo's** essential guide to divorce; Emily Doskow. 7th edition Nolo 2018 496p il paperback $24.99   **346.01**

1. Divorce -- Law and legislation
ISBN 9781413325317

First published 2006

The author "covers the before, during, and after of divorce, counseling readers on the types of divorces, how to make decisions about living arrangements and the division of property, and how custody decisions are made. She advocates minimizing conflict but includes sections on domestic violence and kidnapping if the worst happens. Appendixes contain state-to-state grounds for divorce and financial inventory forms." Libr J

Hertz, Frederick

A **legal** guide for lesbian and gay couples; Frederick Hertz and Emily Doskow. 18th edition Nolo 2016 pbk $34.99 **346.01**

1. Gay couples -- Legal status, laws, etc.
ISBN 9781413322798; 1413322794

LC 2016019762

First published 1980 by Addison-Wesley under the authorship of Hayden Curry and Denis Clifford

This handbook addresses "legal issues with which gay and lesbian couples are certain to contend . . . [including] advice for GLBT parents and prospective parents. Moreover, it addresses other legal considerations such as finanical arrangements. Indispensable for gay and lesbian readers, as well as for attorneys who may lack familiarity in this area." Libr J

Includes bibliographical references

346.04   Property

Crews, Kenneth D.

Copyright law for librarians and educators; creative strategies and practical solutions. with contributions from Dwayne K. Buttler . . . [et al.] 2nd ed; American Library Association 2012 xii, 192 p.p ill. (alk. paper) $57   **346.04**

1. Copyright 2. Sound recordings 3. Fair use (Copyright) 4. Copyright -- United States 5. Fair use (Copyright) -- United States 6. Teachers -- United States -- Handbooks, manuals, etc 7. Librarians -- United States -- Handbooks, manuals, etc
ISBN 0838910920; 9780838910924

LC 2011027604

First published 2000 with title: Copyright essentials for librarians and educators

Author Kenneth D. Crews' book "allows readers to get up to speed on current interpretations of the Digital Millennium Copyright Act from a librarian-educator viewpoint." It also "draws on cutting-edge case law in 18 discrete areas of copyright, including specialized and controversial music and sound recording issues. [This guide offers] information professionals . . . the tools they need to take control of their rights and responsibilities as copyright owners and users." (Publisher's note)

The author "addresses 18 areas of copyright in 5 parts. He begins with the scope of protectable works as well as works without copyright protection. Next, he discusses the rights of ownership, including duration and exceptions. He then explains fair use and its related guidelines. Part 4 focuses on the TEACH Act, Section 108, and responsibilities and liabilities. Lastly, Crews examines special issues such as the Digital Millennium Copyright Act." Booklist

Includes bibliographical references and index.

Fishman, Stephen

★ The **copyright** handbook; what every writer needs to know. Stephen Fishman. 12th edition Nolo 2014 458 p. pbk $49.99   **346.04**

1. Copyright
ISBN 9781413320480; 1413320481

First published 1991. Frequently revised

"Designed as a practical handbook for writers and publishers. Includes a list of legal aid groups and sample forms." Guide to Ref Books. 11th edition

Includes bibliographical references

Hyde, Lewis, 1945-

Common as air; revolution, art, and ownership. Farrar, Straus and Giroux 2010 306p $26   **346.04**

1. Arts 2. Culture 3. Patents 4. Copyright 5. Intellectual property 6. Information commons
ISBN 0-374-22313-0; 978-0-374-22313-7

LC 2010-02388

Hyde argues against "efforts to close off sectors of knowledge so as to exploit them for private profit." (N Y Times Book Rev) Index.

This is "an eloquent and erudite plea for protecting our cultural patrimony from appropriation by commercial interests." N Y Times Book Rev

Includes bibliographical references

Hylton, Keith N.

Laws of creation; property rights in the world of ideas. by Ronald A. Cass and Keith N. Hylton. Harvard University Press 2013 275 p. $55   **346.04**

1. Copyright 2. Intellectual property
ISBN 9780674066458; 0674066456

LC 2012011488

In this book authors Ronald A. Cass and Keith N. Hylton "look closely at the [intellectual property] doctrines that have been developed over many years in patent, copyright, trademark, and trade secret law. Over time, the authors show, a set of rules has emerged that supports wealth-creating innovation while generally avoiding overly expansive, growth-retarding licensing regimes." (Publisher's note)

Includes bibliographical references and index

Jameson, Marni

Downsizing the family home; what to save, what to let go.

Marni Jameson. Sterling Pub Co Inc 2016 237 p. illustrations $16.95   **346.04**

1. Moving 2. Personal belongings
ISBN 1454916338; 9781454916338

LC 2015510856

This book, by Marni Jameson, focuses on the "emotional journey of downsizing your or your aging parents' home. Jameson sensitively guides readers through the process, from opening that first closet, to sorting through a lifetime's worth of possessions, to selling the homestead itself. Using her own personal journey as a basis, she helps you figure out a strategy and create a mindset to accomplish the task quickly, respectfully, rewardingly--and, in the best of situations, even memorably." (Publisher's note)

"The common-sense advice and practical information here will be of interest to persons facing downsizing or needing to get rid of stuff they no longer use." LJ

Includes bibliographical references (pages 228-229) and index.

Portman, Janet

★ **Every** tenant's legal guide; by Janet Portman and Marcia Stewart. 14th edition Nolo 2018 489p il pa $44.99   **346.04**

1. Landlord and tenant
ISBN 9781413325171

First published 1997. Frequently revised

This guide explains how to find and inspect a home, negotiate clauses in a lease or rental agreement, understand rules on rent increases and late rent, get repairs and maintenance, protect privacy rights, fight discrimination, deal with environmental hazards, security deposits, evictions and legal procedures.

Stewart, Marcia

★ **Every** landlord's legal guide; Marcia Stewart & Attorney Janet Portman. 14th edition Nolo 2018 462p   **346.04**

1. Landlord and tenant
ISBN 9781413325171

First published 1996. Frequently revised

This guide covers how to "screen and choosing tenants; prepare leases and rental agreements; collect and returning deposits; avoid discrimination charges; keep up with repairs and maintenance; hire the right property manager; minimize your liability; [and] deal with problem tenants." Publisher's note

346.05   Inheritance, succession, fiduciary trusts, trustees

Clifford, Denis

★ **Plan** your estate; Denis Clifford. 14th edition Nolo 2018 539p paperback $44.99   **346.05**

1. Estate planning
ISBN 9781413325119

First published 1989. Periodically revised

This guide covers basic estate planning, probate avoidance, living wills, federal estate and gift taxes, trusts, durable powers of attorney, and more.

346.07   Commercial law

Elias, Stephen

★ **How** to file for Chapter 7 bankruptcy; Attorney Cara O'Neill & Albin Renauer, J.D. 20th edition Nolo 2017 452 p il pa $39.99   **346.07**

1. Bankruptcy
ISBN 9781413324327

First published 1989. Periodically revised. Variant title: How to file for bankruptcy

This guide offers advice on such topics as personal debt, property liability, asset protection, rebuilding credit, and filling out and filing forms.

Includes bibliographical references

346.73   Private law – United States

Becker, Jo

★ **Forcing** the spring; inside the fight for marriage equality. Jo Becker. The Penguin Press 2014 480 p. illustrations (hardback) $29.95   **346.73**

1. United States. Supreme Court 2. Same-sex marriage -- United States 3. California. Proposition 8 (2008) 4. Locus standi -- United States -- Cases 5. United States. Defense of Marriage Act 6. Same-sex marriage -- Law and legislation -- United States -- Cases
ISBN 1594204446; 9781594204449

LC 2014005342

Written by Jo Becker, this book offers an "account of five remarkable years in American civil rights history: when the United States experienced a tectonic shift on the issue of marriage equality. Beginning with the historical legal challenge of California's ban on same-sex marriage, Becker expands the scope to encompass all aspects of this momentous struggle, offering a . . . behind-the-scenes narrative." (Publisher's note)

"Becker's chronicle of a legal battle reveals deeper changes in the cultural and political landscape of a nation grappling with old prejudices and changing public opinion that continue to resonate." Booklist

Includes bibliographical references and index

Cenziper, Debbie

★ **Love** wins; The Lovers and Lawyers Who Fought the Landmark Case for Marriage Equality. Debbie Cenziper and Jim Obergefell. William Morrow, an imprint of HarperCollinsPublishers 2016 304 p. color illustrations (ebook) $18.89; (hardback) $27.99   **346.73**

1. Lawyers -- United States 2. Gay rights -- United States 3. Same-sex marriage -- United States 4. Gay couples -- Legal status, laws, etc. 5. Gays -- United States -- Biography 6. Lawyers -- United States -- Biography 7. Same-sex marriage -- Law and legislation -- United States -- Cases
ISBN 9780062456090; 0062456083; 9780062456083; 9780062456106

LC 2016014548

This book, by Debbie Cenziper and Jim Obergefell, is the "story of the lovers, lawyers, judges and activists behind the groundbreaking Supreme Court case that led to one of the most important, national civil rights victories in decades—the legalization of same-sex marriage." (Publisher's note)

"Uplifting, well-written story of personal courage and political empowerment." Kirkus

Decherney, Peter

Hollywood's copyright wars; from Edison to the internet. Peter Decherney. Columbia University Press 2012 287 p. (cloth: alk. paper) $34.50   **346.73**

1. Copyright 2. Motion picture industry 3. Television supplies industry 4. Copyright -- Motion pictures -- United States -- History 5. Copyright -- Broadcasting rights -- United States -- History
ISBN 0231159463; 9780231159463

LC 2011041745

This book by Peter Decherney "follows the struggle of the film, television, and digital media industries to influence and adapt to copyright law . . . beginning with Thomas Edison's aggressive patent and copyright disputes and concluding with recent lawsuits against YouTube and Universal. Decherney shows that the history of intellectual property in Hollywood has not always mirrored the evolution of the law. Many landmark decisions have barely changed the industry's behavior." (Publisher's note)

Includes bibliographical references and index

Gasaway, Laura N., 1945-

Copyright questions and answers for information professionals; from the columns of Against the Grain. by Laura N. Gasaway. Purdue University Press 2013 xiii, 284 p.p (paperback) $24.95; (ebook) $11.99; (ebook) $11.99   **346.73**

1. Copyright 2. Fair use (Copyright) 3. Intellectual property 4. Copyright -- United States 5. Fair use (Copyright) -- United States 6. Photocopying -- Fair use(Copyright) -- United States
ISBN 1557536392; 9781557536396; 9781612492537 pdf; 9781612492544

LC 2012032276

Laura N. Gasaway's "book begins with a basic primer on copyright. Then each topical chapter (e.g., Licensing, Performance and Displays, Digitization, etc.) presents a short introduction to the issues involved, followed by related questions and answers. The author includes reference to the applicable section of the copyright law as well as to other laws dealing with the subject. All in all, there are answers to well over 300 questions concerning copyright, fair use, and related issues." (Library Journal)

Kaiser, Robert G.

Act of Congress; how America's essential institution works, and how it doesn't. Robert G. Kaiser. 1st ed. Alfred A. Knopf 2013 xxvi, 417 p.p (hardcover) $27.95   **346.73**

1. United States. Congress 2. United States. Dodd-Frank Wall Street Reform and Consumer Protection Act 3. Global Financial Crisis, 2008-2009 4. Financial services industry -- Law and legislation -- United States
ISBN 030770016X; 9780307700162

LC 2012038245

In this book, journalist Robert G. Kaiser "chronicles the journey of the Dodd-Frank act, a complex package of banking and market regulations passed in 2011 that few voters paid attention to. . . . While the bill was moving through Congress, Kaiser had access to lawmakers of both parties and their staffs, executive-branch officials, and lobbyists; he finds the drama in arcane parliamentary procedure and paints . . . fly-on-the-wall scenes of legislative sausage making." (Publishers Weekly)

Includes bibliographical references (pages 391-400) and index.

Leamer, Laurence

The **price** of justice; a true story of two lawyers' epic battle against corruption and greed in coal country. Laurence Leamer. Times Books 2013 xii, 432 p.p (hardcover) $30.00   **346.73**

1. Fair trial -- United States 2. Judges -- Recusal -- United States 3. Massey Energy (Firm) -- Trials, litigation, etc 4. Coal trade -- Corrupt practices -- West Virginia
ISBN 9780805094718

LC 2012041537

"Not content to dominate the coal-mining industry through Massey Energy and the West Virginia judicial system that indirectly supported it, CEO Don Blankenship ferociously punished anyone who dared to challenge that dominance. So, in 1998, when attorneys Bruce Stanley and Dave Fawcett went after Massey on behalf of their client, a small mining company, they set off a 14-year-long struggle that eventually took them to the U.S. Supreme Court to argue against corporate corruption of the judicial system." (Booklist)

Includes bibliographical references and index.

★ **Legal** rights; the guide for deaf and hard of hearing people. National Association of the Deaf. Gallaudet University Press 2015 304 p. (pbk.: alk. paper) $34.95   **346.73**

1. Deaf -- Legal status, laws, etc. -- United States 2. Hearing impaired -- Legal status, laws, etc. -- United States
ISBN 9781563686443; 9781563686450

LC 2015005783

This book by the National Association of the Deaf "describes those statutes that prohibit discrimination against deaf and hard of hearing people, and any others with physical challenges. . . . The new edition describes the core legislation and laws and their critical importance since their inception: The Rehabilitation Act of 1973, the Individuals with Disabilities Education Act (IDEA), and the Americans with Disabilities Act (ADA)." (Publisher's note)

"Highly recommended for those with hearing impairments and their loved ones, along with students and practitioners of law, education, medicine, and politics. A necessity for all public library collections." LJ
Includes bibliographical references and index.

Lindner, Dan

★ A **guide** to federal contracting; principles and practices. Dan Lindner. Bernan Press 2017 632 p. (pbk.: alk. paper) $95   **346.73**

1. Contracts 2. Purchasing 3. Government purchasing 4. Public contracts -- United States 5. Letting of contracts -- United States 6. Government purchasing -- Law and legislation -- United States
ISBN 1598889656; 9781598889659

LC 2017046917

This book, by Dan Lindner, demystifies "the volumes of regulations and policies, and provide . . . a succinct yet thorough treatment of Federal contracting requirements and regulations. Bringing together concepts of business law, politics, public and social policy, pricing, and procedures for contract placement and administration, the author draws on . . . [his] Federal Government experience to cover . . . this . . . process which impacts our daily Government operations." (Publisher's note)

"There are other, less-expensive guides, but none are as complete or authoritative. This is an essential resource for large public and academic libraries where federal contracts play an important role." Booklist
Includes bibliographical references and index

Lobel, Orly

You don't own me; how Mattel v. MGA Entertainment exposed Barbie's dark side. Orly Lobel. W W Norton & Co Inc 2017 xxi, 282 p.p (hardcover) $27.95   **346.73**

1. Toy industry 2. Bratz dolls 3. Barbie dolls 4. Labor contract -- United States -- Cases 5. Mattel, Inc. -- Trials, litigation, etc. 6. MGA Entertainment (Firm) -- Trials, litigation, etc. 7. Dolls -- Law and legislation -- United States -- Cases 8. Intellectual property infringement -- Law and legislation -- United States -- Cases
ISBN 0393254070; 9780393254082; 9780393254075

LC 2017027183

In this book, by Orly Lobel, "when Carter Bryant began designing what would become the billion-dollar line of Bratz dolls, he was taking time off from his job at Mattel, where he designed outfits for Barbie. Later, back at Mattel, he sold his concept for Bratz to rival company MGA. Law professor Orly Lobel reveals the colorful story behind the

ensuing decade-long court battle." (Publisher's note)

"The end result is a thoroughly researched book that explains the legalese of patent, property, and copyright law in layman's terms while providing an entertaining narrative." Pub Wkly
Includes bibliographical references and index.

Love unites us; edited by Kevin M. Cathcart, Leslie J. Gabel-Brett; foreword by Eric Holder. New Press, The 2016 352 p. illustrations (ebook) $27.99; (hardback) $27.95 **346.73**

1. Gay rights -- United States 2. Same-sex marriage -- United States 3. Gay couples -- Legal status, laws, etc. 4. Gay rights -- United States -- History 5. Gay couples -- Legal status, laws, etc. -- United States 6. Same-sex marriage -- Law and legislation -- United States -- History
ISBN 9781620971772; 9781595585509

LC 2016006203

This book, edited by Kevin M. Cathcart, Leslie J. Gabel-Brett, is an "anthology documenting the road to marriage equality in the United States. . . . Beginning with an account of the earliest marriage cases (1970–74) and ending with a survey of religious freedom challenges to LGBT rights protections, the book situates the recent Supreme Court victories in United States v. Windsor and Obergefell v. Hodges within the context of . . . shifts in public opinion." (Library Journal)

"As a core text about one of our society's most significant developments, this volume belongs in every library." Booklist
Includes bibliographical references and index.

Winkler, Adam

We the corporations; how American businesses won their civil rights. Adam Winkler. Liveright Publishing Corp., a Division of W W Norton & Co. 2018 xxiv, 471 p.p illustrations (hardcover) $28.95   **346.73**

1. Commercial law 2. Corporations -- United States 3. Civil rights of corporations -- United States
ISBN 9780871403841; 9780871407122

LC 2017051893

National Book Award Finalist: Nonfiction (2018)

This book, by Adam Winkler, "reveals how American businesses won equal rights and transformed the Constitution to serve the ends of capital. . . . Uncovering the deep historical roots of Citizens United, Adam Winkler shows how that controversial 2010 Supreme Court decision was the capstone of a two-hundred-year battle over corporate personhood and constitutional protections for business." (Publisher's note)

"Winkler employs an evocative, fast-paced storytelling style, making for an entertaining and enlightening book that will likely complicate the views of partisans on both sides of the issue." Pub Wkly
Includes bibliographical references and index

Yoshino, Kenji

Speak now; marriage equality on trial. Kenji Yoshino. Crown 2015 336 p.   **346.73**

1. Same-sex marriage 2. Gay couples -- Legal status, laws, etc. 3. California. Proposition 8 (2008) 4. United States. Defense of Marriage Act 5. Gay couples -- Legal status, laws, etc. -- United States -- Cases 6. Same-sex marriage -- Law and legislation -- United States -- Cases
ISBN 9780385348805; 9780385348812; 9780385348829

LC 2014042967

Stonewall Book Awards: Israel Fishman Non-Fiction Award (2016)

"'Speak Now' tells the story of a watershed trial that unfolded over twelve tense days in California in 2010. . . . In telling the story of Hollingsworth v. Perry, the groundbreaking federal lawsuit against Proposition 8, Kenji Yoshino has also written a paean to the vanishing civil trial--an oasis of rationality in what is often a decidedly uncivil debate." (Publisher's note)

"This is the well-told story of one of the most important civil trials in recent American history, Hollingsworth v. Perry, the 12-day trial challenging the constitutionality of California's Proposition 8. Because this case was tried in federal court, most of America was aware that it might end up being argued before the US Supreme Court. Yoshino (New York Univ. School of Law) takes the reader behind the scenes of both sides of this civil trial. . . . Well beyond its outcome, however, this case is all about why trials can be crucial to the American system of justice." Choice

347 Procedure and courts

Breyer, Stephen G., 1938-

Making our democracy work; a judge's view. [by] Stephen Breyer. Alfred A. Knopf 2010 270p il $26.95   **347**
1. United States -- Supreme Court 2. Judicial review -- United States 3. Separation of powers -- United States 4. United States -- Politics and government 5. Judicial review -- United States -- History 6. Political questions and judicial power -- United States
ISBN 0-307-26991-4; 978-0-307-26991-1

LC 2010-16839

"Why does the public accept the Court's decisions as legitimate and follow them, even when those decisions are highly unpopular? What must the Court do to maintain the public's faith? How can the Court help make . . . democracy work? These are the questions that Justice Stephen Breyer [examines]." (Publisher's note) Index.

"A sitting Justice explains how the Supreme Court won the public trust and what it must do to keep it. Employing a succession of cases from Marbury v. Madison to Bush v. Gore, Breyer . . . offers a short, highly accessible course on the evolution of judicial review, the doctrine permitting the Court to invalidate laws conflicting with the Constitution. . . . Speaking out without talking down, Breyer renders a signal service to his fellow citizens." Kirkus
Includes bibliographical references

Faigman, David L.

Laboratory of justice; the Supreme Court's 200-year struggle to integrate science and the law. Times Books, Henry Holt 2004 417p $27.50; pa $17   **347**
1. Science -- Governmental policy 2. United States -- Supreme Court 3. Constitutional law -- United States
ISBN 0-8050-7274-8; 0-8050-7845-2 pa

LC 2003-57049

"This insightful and accessible study throws light on how new ways of understanding the world produce new readings of our Constitution." Publ Wkly
Includes bibliographical references

Finkelman, Paul

★ **Landmark** decisions of the United States Supreme Court; [by] Paul Finkelman, Melvin I. Urofsky. 2nd ed.; CQ Press 2008 791p il $250   **347**
1. United States -- Supreme Court 2. Constitutional law -- United States
ISBN 978-0-87289-409-9

LC 2007-42588

First published 2003

This "provides the historical context and constitutional perspective of more than 1,000 of the most important Supreme Court cases." Pub-

lisher's note
Includes bibliographical references

Friedman, Barry

The **will** of the people; how public opinion has influenced the Supreme Court and shaped the meaning of the Constitution. Farrar, Straus and Giroux 2009 614p   **347**
1. Public opinion 2. United States -- Supreme Court 3. Public opinion -- United States 4. United States -- Supreme Court -- Public opinion 5. Judicial process -- United States -- Public opinion
ISBN 0374220344; 0374532370 pa; 9780374220341; 9780374532376 pa

LC 2008054247

This is an account of the relationship between popular opinion and the Supreme Court from the Declaration of Independence to the end of the Rehnquist court in 2005. (Publisher's note) Index.

This book is a thought-provoking and authoritative history of the Supreme Court's relationship to popular opinion. . . . Friedman's contribution to [the] discussion is the breadth and detail of his historical canvas, and it's a significant one. N Y Times Book Rev
Includes bibliographical references

★ **Great** American trials; Edward W. Knappman, editor; Stephen G. Christianson and Lisa Paddock, consulting legal editors. 2nd ed; Gale Group 2002 2v il set $170   **347**
1. Trials
ISBN 0-7876-4901-5
First published 1994
Featuring approximately 360 trials from the 1800s to the present, entries "cover the principals involved, the crime charged, the verdict and sentence, and the significance and impact of each trial." Publisher's note
Includes bibliographical references

Leiter, Richard A.

Landmark Supreme Court cases; the most influential decisions of the Supreme Court of the United States. [by] Gary Hartman, Roy M. Mersky, [and] Cindy Tate Slavinski. Facts on File 2004 594p (Facts on File library of American history) $70; pa $21.95   **347**
1. Law -- United States 2. United States -- Supreme Court
ISBN 0-8160-2452-9; 0-8160-6923-9 pa

LC 2003-57776

This is "an excellent source for beginning researchers. . . . The discussion of the case's significance and its implications will be useful for students." SLJ
Includes bibliographical references

Marshall, Thurgood

Thurgood Marshall; his speeches, writings, arguments, opinions, and reminiscences. edited by Mark Tushnet; foreword by Randall Kennedy. Hill Bks. 2001 xxvi, 548p (Library of Black America) $40; pa $24.95   **347**
1. Lawyers 2. Solicitors general 3. Civil rights activists 4. Supreme Court justices 5. African Americans -- Biography 6. United States -- Supreme Court 7. African Americans -- Civil rights
ISBN 1-55652-385-8; 1-55652-386-6 pa

LC 2001-16793

"In a career ranging from his trial and appellate work for the NAACP to his tenure as an associate justice of the Court, Marshall wrought revolutionary changes in U.S. law and politics, and this collection of his legal briefs, writings, speeches, and judicial opinions, plus a never-before-published oral interview, gives us a superior analysis of the advocate, the democrat, the dissenter, and the unflagging fighter for equality." Libr J

Includes bibliographical references

O'Brien, David M.

   Storm center; the Supreme Court in American politics. David M. O'Brien. 11th edition Norton 2017 456 p il   **347**

   1. United States -- Supreme Court

   ISBN 9780393603538

   First published 1986. Periodically revised

   The author discusses "the day-to-day workings of the Court justices and their law clerks, how cases are accepted for hearing, what negotiations and compromises go on, how case opinions get written—and what happens to American society when two conservative presidents, Reagan and Bush, appoint the majority of justices." Publisher's note

   Includes bibliographical references

★ The **Oxford** companion to the Supreme Court of the United States; editor in chief, Kermit L. Hall; editors, James W. Ely, Jr., Joel B. Grossman. 2nd ed.; Oxford University Press 2005 xxv, 1239p il $65   **347**

   1. Reference books 2. United States -- Supreme Court

   ISBN 0-19-517661-8

   LC 2004-29463

   First published 1992

   This encyclopedia includes over 1200 articles "on all aspects of the court's history, justices, operations, and cases. Over 300 experts contributed the entries, which vary in length; some have bibliographic references. The organization . . . [includes] alphabetical entries, portraits of the justices, cross-references, and indexes by both case name and topic." Choice

Shesol, Jeff

   ★ **Supreme** power; Franklin Roosevelt vs. the Supreme Court. W. W. Norton & Co. 2010 644p il $27.95   **347**

   1. Governors 2. Presidents 3. People with disabilities 4. Philatelists 5. United States -- Supreme Court 6. United States -- Politics and government -- 20th century 7. Political questions and judicial power -- United States -- History

   ISBN 978-0-393-06474-2; 0-393-06474-3

   LC 2009-46365

   The book examines the interaction between U.S. President Franklin Delano Roosevelt and the Supreme Court. "FDR took up the idea of expanding the number of justices on the Court. This was the famous 'court-packing plan.' The story of the plan and the . . . political battle over it . . . [is] told . . . by Jeff Shesol in his . . . [book] 'Supreme Power.' Shesol looks at the battle through the eyes of all the major players--FDR and his advisers, the congressional leadership that was handed the unappealing job of putting the plan into effect, the congressional opposition, the many politicians and interest groups that organized over the plan, and the justices themselves." (New York Review of Books)

   This "is an impressive and engaging book—an excellent work of narrative history. It is deeply researched and beautifully written. Even readers who already know the outcome will find it hard not to feel the suspense that surrounded the battle, so successfully does Shesol recreate the atmosphere of this great controversy." N Y Times Book Rev

   Includes bibliographical references

Toobin, Jeffrey R.

   ★ The **nine**; inside the secret world of the Supreme Court. [by] Jeffrey Toobin. Doubleday 2007 369p il $27.95   **347**

   1. United States -- Supreme Court

   ISBN 978-0-385-51640-2

   LC 2007-20287

"Beautifully written, this is an essential purchase for all libraries interested in the contemporary Supreme Court." Libr J

   Includes bibliographical references

Warner, Ralph E.

   ★ **Everybody's** guide to small claims court; Cara O'Neill. 17th edition Nolo 2018 480p paperback $29.99   **347**

   1. Small claims court

   ISBN 9781413324907

   First published 1980 by Addison-Wesley. Periodically revised

   Presents resources and step-by-step instructions for defending one's case in small claims court, and discusses specific kinds of cases, such as motor vehicle repair and purchase, vehicle accident, and landlord-tenant cases.

347.73   Civil procedure and courts of the United States

Coyle, Marcia

   ★ The **Roberts** court; the struggle for the constitution. Marcia Coyle. Simon & Schuster 2013 352 p. (hardcover) $28   **347.73**

   1. Roberts, John G., 1955- 2. United States. Constitution 3. United States. Supreme Court 4. United States. Supreme Court -- History -- 21st century 5. Political questions and judicial power -- United States -- History -- 21st century

   ISBN 1451627513; 9781451627510; 9781451627527; 9781451627534

   LC 2012051637

   In this book, author Marcia Coycle "reveals the fault lines in the conservative-dominated [U.S. Supreme] Court led by Chief Justice John Roberts Jr." It "captures four landmark decisions--concerning health care, money in elections, guns at home, and race in schools. Her analysis shows how dedicated conservative lawyers and groups are strategizing to find cases and crafting them to bring up the judicial road to the Supreme Court with an eye on a receptive conservative majority." (Publisher's note)

   Includes bibliographical references and index

Gibson, Larry S.

   Young Thurgood; the making of a Supreme Court Justice. by Larry S. Gibson. Prometheus Books 2012 413 p. (cloth: alk. paper) $28   **347.73**

   1. Judges -- United States -- Biography 2. United States. Supreme Court -- History 3. United States. Supreme Court -- Officials and employees

   ISBN 1616145714; 9781616145712

   LC 2012027517

   This book by Larry S. Gibson is a biography of U.S. Supreme Court Justice Thurgood Marshall. "He transformed the nation's legal landscape by challenging the racial segregation that had relegated millions to second-class citizenship. . . . Marshall's personality, attitudes, priorities, and work habits had crystallized during earlier years in Maryland. . . . [This book] is the first close examination of the formative period in Marshall's life." (Publisher's note)

   Includes bibliographical references and index.

Graetz, Michael J.

   The **Burger** Court and the Rise of the Judicial Right; Michael J. Graetz and Linda Greenhouse. Simon & Schuster 2016 480 p. illustrations (ebook) $20.99; (hbk.) $30   **347.73**

   1. United States. Supreme Court 2. United States. Supreme Court

-- History -- 20th century 3. Political questions and judicial power
-- History -- 20th century
ISBN 9781476732527; 1476732507; 9781476732503

LC 2015031713

In this book Supreme Court reporter Michael J. Graetz and Linda Greenhouse "have written a detailed, accessible revisionist history of Warren Burger's tenure as chief justice from 1969 to 1986. . . . They convincingly argue that the Supreme Court decisions rendered during that era paved the way for more recent conservative landmark decisions such as the highly controversial 2010 Citizens United ruling on campaign finance." (Publishers Weekly)

"Two powerhouse law historians/journalists deliver a major contribution to the history of the Supreme Court." Kirkus

Includes bibliographical references and index

Haygood, Wil

★ **Showdown**; Thurgood Marshall and the Supreme Court nomination that changed America. by Wil Haygood. Alfred A. Knopf 2015 416 p. illustrations, portraits (hardcover) $32.50 **347.73**
1. Judges 2. United States. Supreme Court 3. Judges -- Selection and appointment -- United States -- History -- 20th century 4. United States. Supreme Court -- Officials and employees -- Selection and appointment -- History -- 20th century
ISBN 0307957195; 9780307957191

LC 2014044440

NAACP Image Award Nominee: Outstanding Literary Work- Nonfiction (2016)

Haygood "examines the confirmation battle over the first African-American nominated to the Supreme Court. During the summer of 1967, Thurgood Marshall (1908-1993) appeared for an unprecedented fifth day before the Senate Judiciary Committee. This confrontation between arguably the most consequential appellate attorney ever and the 'Old Bulls' who dominated the interrogating panel is both the spine of Haygood's narrative and the occasion for a number of ancillary stories that lend blood and guts to the superficial civilities of a Senate hearing." (Kirkus Reviews)

"The behind-the-scenes look at the hard-fought battle that Lyndon Johnson and his supporters waged on Marshall's behalf creates suspense, even though readers will already know of their ultimate success." Pub Wkly

Includes bibliographical references and index

Hirshman, Linda

Sisters in law; how Sandra Day O'Connor and Ruth Bader Ginsburg went to the Supreme Court and changed the world. Linda Hirshman. HarperCollins 2015 416 p. illustrations $28.99; (ebook) $15.99 **347.73**
1. Women judges 2. United States. Supreme Court 3. Judges -- United States -- Biography 4. Women judges -- United States -- Biography
ISBN 9780062238467; 9780062238481

LC 2015002577

This book, by Linda Hirshman, "tells the fascinating story of the intertwined lives of Sandra Day O'Connor and Ruth Bader Ginsburg, the first and second women to serve as Supreme Court justices. The relationship between Sandra Day O'Connor and Ruth Bader Ginsburg— Republican and Democrat, Christian and Jew, western rancher's daughter and Brooklyn girl—transcends party, religion, region, and culture." (Publisher's note)

"Hirshman's conversational style and deep analysis of several precedent-setting constitutional cases should appeal to both casual and professional readers." Pub Wkly

Includes bibliographical references and index

Jost, Kenneth

★ The **Supreme** Court A to Z; Kenneth Jost. 5th ed. CQ Press 2012 xvii, 668 p.p ill. (hardcover: alk. paper) $125.00 **347.73**
1. United States. Supreme Court -- Biography 2. United States. Supreme Court -- Encyclopedias
ISBN 1608717445; 9781608717446

LC 2012000642

This book by Kenneth Jost "offers . . . information about the Supreme Court, including its history, traditions, organization, dynamics, and personalities. The entries in The Supreme Court A to Z are arranged alphabetically and are . . . cross-referenced to related information. This volume also has a detailed index, reference materials on Supreme Court nominations, a seat chart of the justices, the U.S. Constitution, online sources of decisions, and a bibliography." (Publisher's note)

Includes bibliographical references (p. 617-630) and index.

Justices of the United States Supreme Court; their lives and major opinions. edited by Leon Friedman & Fred L. Israel. Facts On File 2013 1600 p. (hbk. alk. paper) $375 **347.73**
1. Judges -- Biography 2. Judges -- United States -- Biography 3. United States. Supreme Court -- Biography
ISBN 0816070156; 9780816070152

LC 2009021252

This book by Leon Friedman and Fred L. Israel "examines the biographical facts of each Supreme Court justice's life, including his or her background in the law, the paths that led each one to the Supreme Court, and each justice's major decisions, as well as how these decisions reveal an underlying legal philosophy. All entries and their corresponding bibliographies have been thoroughly updated in this revised four-volume set." (Publisher's note)

Includes bibliographical references and index

Mersky, Roy M.

Landmark Supreme Court cases; the most influential decisions of the Supreme Court of the United States. Richard A. Leiter, Roy M. Mersky. 2nd ed. Facts on File 2012 3 v., xx, 1224 p.p (hardbound: alk. paper) $250.00 **347.73**
1. Civil rights 2. Freedom of speech 3. Freedom of the press 4. United States. Supreme Court 5. Law -- United States -- Cases 6. United States -- Supreme Court
ISBN 9780816069576; 0816069573

LC 2010048195

Authors Richard A. Leiter and Roy M. Mersky's book discusses landmark U.S. Supreme Court "cases on such issues as freedom of speech, freedom of the press, civil rights, labor unions, abortion, antitrust and competition, due process, search and seizure, executive privilege, and more. Organized chronologically by issue, each entry includes the case title and legal citation, year of decision, key issue, historical background, legal arguments, decision (majority and dissenting opinions), aftermath and significance, related cases, and recommended reading." (Publisher's note)

"The authors describe some 350 influential US Supreme Court decisions. Arranged by subjects such as abortion and taxation, the . . . entries include an abstract of the decision, . . . the case's history, summary of the arguments, the salient issues involved, its significance, related cases, and recommended readings including law journal articles." Choice

Includes bibliographical references and index.

O'Connor, Sandra Day, 1930-

★ **Out** of order; stories from the history of the Supreme Court. Sandra Day O'Connor. 1st ed. Random House Inc. 2013 xviii, 233 p.p ill. (hardcover) $26; (ebook) $78.00   **347.73**
1. Courts -- History 2. United States. Supreme Court 3. Law -- United States -- History 4. United States. Supreme Court -- History 5. United States. Supreme Court -- Anecdotes 6. Courts of last resort -- United States -- History 7. Courts of last resort -- United States -- Anecdotes
ISBN 0812993926; 9780812993929; 9780812993936

LC 2012025708

This book, by Sandra Day O'Connor, "the first woman to sit on the United States Supreme Court, . . . [discusses] the history and evolution of the highest court in the land. . . . [This book] sheds light on the centuries of change and upheaval that transformed the Supreme Court from its uncertain beginnings into the . . . institution that thrives and endures today." (Publisher's note)

Includes bibliographical references and index

Scalia, Antonin, 1936-2016

Scalia speaks; reflections on law, faith, and life well lived. Antonin Scalia, edited by Christopher J. Scalia and Edward Whelan; foreword by Ruth Bader Ginsburg. Crown Forum 2017 xi, 420 p.p (hardback) $30   **347.73**
1. American speeches 2. Judges -- United States 3. Judicial opinions -- United States 4. Speeches, addresses, etc., American 5. United States. Supreme Court -- Officials and employees
ISBN 9780525573333; 9780525573326

LC 2017034660

This book, presents the "finest speeches [by U.S. Supreme Court Justice Antonin Scalia, which] covers topics as varied as the law, faith, virtue, pastimes, and his heroes and friends. . . . 'Scalia Speaks' will give readers the opportunity to encounter the legendary man more fully, helping them better understand the jurisprudence that made him one of the most important justices in the Court's history and introducing them to his broader insights on faith and life." (Publisher's note)

"This fine representative assemblage of Supreme Court Justice Scalia's speeches pays tribute to his ready wit and facility with language." LJ

Includes bibliographical references and indexes.

The **Supreme** Court justices; illustrated biographies, 1789-2012. edited by Clare Cushman, the Supreme Court Historical Society; foreword by Chief Justice John G. Roberts, Jr. 3rd ed. CQ Press, an imprint of SAGE Publications 2013 xx, 562 p.p ill., ports. (hardcover) $135   **347.73**
1. Judges -- Biography 2. Judges -- United States -- Biography 3. United States. Supreme Court -- History 4. United States. Supreme Court -- Officials and employees -- Biography
ISBN 1608718328; 9781608718320

LC 2012031502

This book, edited by Clare Cushman, is "a single-volume reference profiling every Supreme Court justice from John Jay through Elena Kagan. An original essay on each justice paints a . . . picture of his or her individuality as shaped by family, education, pre-Court career, and the times in which he or she lived. Each biographical essay also presents the major issues on which the justice presided. Essays are arranged in the order of the justices' appointments." (Publisher's note)

"Written by leading constitutional scholars, the well-researched essays are arranged in chronological order of the justices' appointment to the Court. The volume includes a revised bibliography organized by individual justices, and a thorough index. . . . Recommended." Choice

Includes bibliographical references (pages 516-538) and index.

Toobin, Jeffrey, 1960-

The **oath**; the Obama White House and the Supreme Court. Jeffrey Toobin. Doubleday 2012 viii, 325 p.p $28.95 **347.73**
1. Roberts, John G., 1955- 2. United States. Supreme Court 3. United States -- Politics and government -- 2009- 4. Constitutional history -- United States 5. United States. Supreme Court -- History -- 21st century 6. Political questions and judicial power -- United States -- History -- 21st century
ISBN 0385527209; 9780385527200

LC 2012029205

This book by Jeffrey Toobin offers an "account of the current struggle over constitutional interpretation." It "interweaves three topics: the leading cases that illustrate the ambition of the [John] Roberts Court; the four appointments since 2006 ([John] Roberts, Samuel Alito, Sonia Sotomayor, and Elena Kagan) that have turned the court into an institution . . . divided between five committed Republicans and four committed Democrats; and . . . sketches of all the justices, including the three recent retirees (Sandra Day O'Connor, David Souter, and John Paul Stevens)." (Bookforum)

Includes bibliographical references and index.

Tushnet, Mark

In the balance; law and politics on the Roberts Court. Mark Tushnet. W W Norton & Co Inc 2013 352 p. (hardcover) $28.95   **347.73**
1. Judicial power 2. Roberts, John G., 1955- 3. United States. Supreme Court 4. Judges -- United States 5. Law -- Political aspects -- United States 6. Political questions and judicial power -- United States
ISBN 0393073440; 9780393073447

LC 2013012744

In this book, "constitutional law expert Mark Tushnet clarifies the lines of conflict and what is at stake on the Supreme Court as it hangs 'in the balance' between its conservatives and its liberals." He "cover[s] the legal philosophies that have informed decisions on major cases such as the Affordable Care Act, the political structures behind Court appointments, and the face-off between John Roberts and Elena Kagan for intellectual dominance of the Court." (Publisher's note)

Includes bibliographical references and index

Zirin, James D.

Supremely partisan; How Raw Politics Tips the Scales in the United States Supreme Court. James D. Zirin. Rowman & Littlefield 2016 312 p. (cloth: alk. paper) $28; (ebook) $35   **347.73**
1. Judicial power 2. United States. Supreme Court 3. Judicial review -- United States 4. Political questions and judicial power -- United States
ISBN 9781442266360; 9781442266377

LC 2016016520

This book, by James D. Zirin, "argues that the [Supreme] Court has become increasingly partisan, rapidly making policy choices right and left on bases that have nothing to do with law or the Constitution. Zirin explains how we arrived at the present situation and looks at the current divide through its leading partisans, Justices Ruth Bader Ginsburg and Sonia Sotomayor on the left and Antonin Scalia and Clarence Thomas on the right. He also examines four of the Court's most controversial recent decisions." (Publisher's note)

"A top-notch book about the Supreme Court. Zirin has his finger on its pulse, and he shows the rest of us how it works and how it doesn't." Kirkus

Includes bibliographical references and index

347.732   Federal courts

Chemerinsky, Erwin

Closing the courthouse door; how your constitutional rights became unenforceable. Erwin Chemerinsky. Yale University Press 2017 280 p. (hardcover: alk. paper) $32.50   **347.732**
1. Due process of law 2. United States. Supreme Court 3. Constitutional law -- United States
ISBN 9780300211580

LC 2016941955

This book, by Erwin Chemerinsky, "explores how the constitutional right to seek justice has been restricted by the Supreme Court. . . . Using many stories of people whose rights have been trampled yet who had no legal recourse, Chemerinsky argues that enforcing the Constitution should be the federal courts' primary purpose, and they should not be barred from considering any constitutional question." (Publisher's note)

"A dramatic challenge to understand the shakiness of the foundations we take for granted and where energies committed to redress should be directed." Kirkus

Includes bibliographical references (pages 211-242) and index.

348.73   Federal laws, regulations, cases of the United States

Stathis, Stephen W.

Landmark legislation 1774-2012; Major U.S. acts and treaties. Stephen W. Stathis. 2nd edition CQ Press 2014 hardcover $190   **348.73**
1. Legislation -- United States
ISBN 9781452292304

"In just a single volume, Landmark Legislation effectively covers hundreds of the most significant pieces of legislation and treaties in US history, beginning with the Continental Congress in 1774 and concluding with the first Obama Administration in 2012. Some of the legislation has had a far-reaching impact, such as the 14th Amendment; other legislation was significantly more important at the time of passage, such as the Greek-Turkish Aid Act of 1947. Stathis (formerly, Congressional Research Service) includes 113 chronological entries, each one devoted to the period that a particular body of Congress met." (Choice Reviews)

349   Law of specific jurisdictions, areas, socioeconomic regions, regional intergovernmental organizations

Friedman, Lawrence Meir

American law in the 20th century; {by} Lawrence M. Friedman. Yale Univ. Press 2002 722p $38   **349**
1. Law -- United States
ISBN 0-300-09137-0

LC 2001-3332

The author "examines the American legal system as an integral part of the larger society, both reflecting and causing changes therein. By adopting such a focus, the author makes his book accessible to readers who are not legal scholars." Booklist

Includes bibliographical references

★ **Gale** encyclopedia of American law; 3rd ed.; Gale/Cengage Learning 2011 14v il map set $1604   **349**
1. Reference books 2. Law -- United States -- Encyclopedias
ISBN 978-1-4144-3684-5; 1-4144-3684-X; 978-1-4144-4302-7 ebook; 1-4144-4302-1 ebook

LC 2010-45527

First published 1983-1985 with title: The Guide to American law. Previous edition published with title: West's encyclopedia of American law

Explains legal terms and concepts in everyday language, covering a wide variety of persons, entities, and events that have shaped the U.S. legal system and influenced public perceptions of it.

Includes bibliographical references

★ **Gale** encyclopedia of everyday law; Jeffrey Wilson, editor. 2nd ed.; Thomson Gale 2006 2v set $325   **349**
1. Law -- United States
ISBN 1-4144-0353-4

LC 2006-10071

First published 2003

This encyclopedia includes "descriptions of each issue's historical background, covering important statutes and cases; profiles of various U.S. laws and regulations; details of how laws and regulations vary from state to state, and; . . . bibliographies, including print and Web resources and lists of relevant organizations." Publisher's note

Includes bibliographical references

351   Public administration

Kettl, Donald F.

The **next** government of the United States; why our institutions fail us and how to fix them. W. W. Norton & Co. 2009 288p il $25.95   **351**
1. Administrative agencies 2. United States -- Politics and government -- 2001-
ISBN 978-0-393-05112-4; 0-393-05112-9

LC 2008-38584

"Kettl's cogent and unbiased analysis of the failure of government institutions posits that current challenges, whether in health care or disaster response, have outgrown the capacity of monolithic government agencies, even while the size of government continues to swell. . . . He presents a balanced and unpartisan analysis of the Hurricane Katrina debacle, examining human error and generations of poor decision making as well as the intricacies of federalism and the organizational complexity of government institutions." Publ Wkly

Includes bibliographical references

352.13   Administration of subordinate jurisdictions

★ The **book** of the states; [compiled by] the Council of State Governments. 2010 ed; Council of State Governments 2010 627p il map $125   **352.13**
1. State governments
ISBN 978-0-87292-7667

Biennial, 1935-2001, Annual from 2002. Began publication 1935

"In addition to general articles on various aspects of state government, this source provides many statistical and directory data, the principal state officials, and such information as the nickname, motto, flower, bird, song, and tree of each state." Ref Sources for Small & Medium-sized Libr. 6th edition

352.23   Chief executives

Brower, Kate Andersen

First in line; presidents, vice presidents, and the pursuit of power. Kate Andersen Brower. HarperCollins 2018 352 p. $28.99   **352.23**

1. Biography 2. Vice-presidents -- United States 3. Vice-Presidents -- United States 4. United States -- Politics and government -- 20th century 5. United States -- Politics and government -- 21st century
ISBN 0062668943; 9780062668943

LC 2018056073

In this book, Kate Andersen Brower, "pulls back the curtain and reveals the sometimes cold, sometimes close, and always complicated relationship between our modern presidents and their vice presidents. Brower took us inside the lives of the White House staff and gave us an intimate look at the modern First Ladies; now, in her signature style, she introduces us to the second most powerful men in the world, exploring the lives and roles of thirteen modern vice presidents." (Publisher's note)

"Notwithstanding the famous assessment that the vice presidency is not worth a bucket of warm spit, 14 of the 47 U.S. vice presidents have gone on to the presidency. CNN contributor Brower interviewed 200 people, including VPs and their families, to find out what the job is really like." LJ

Includes bibliography and index.

Encyclopedia of the U.S. presidency; a historical reference. edited by Nancy Beck Young. Facts On File 2013 6 v., 2500 p.p ill., maps (hardcover) $550   **352.23**

1. Presidents -- United States -- Encyclopedias 2. Presidents -- United States -- Encyclopedias, Juvenile 3. Presidents -- United States -- History -- Encyclopedias, Juvenile 4. United States -- Politics and government -- Encyclopedias, Juvenile
ISBN 0816067449; 9780816067442

LC 2010020746

This six-volume set looks at the American presidency. The "opening volume includes 19 thematic essays dealing with various topics surrounding the history of the presidency including 'Origins of the Presidency,' 'Presidency and the Politics of Race,' and 'The Presidency and Popular Culture.' The ensuing volumes follow a chronological arrangement of individually signed entries covering from Washington to Obama." (Library Journal)

Includes bibliographical references and index

Fellow citizens; the Penguin book of U.S. presidential inaugural addresses. edited with an introduction and commentaries by Robert V. Remini and Terry Golway. Penguin Books 2008 476p $16   **352.23**

1. American speeches 2. Presidents -- United States -- Inaugural addresses
ISBN 978-0-14-311453-6; 0-14-311453-0

LC 2008-19970

"Two distinguished historians round up every presidential inaugural address and preface it with commentary on the rhetoric and historical context of the discourse. . . . Reflecting the major events of American history, as well as a rhetorical evolution from prolixity to brevity, this . . . is a great resource." Booklist

Includes bibliographical references

Guide to the presidency and the executive branch; Michael Nelson, editor. 5th ed. CQ Press 2013 2 v. (xix, 2141 p.)p ill. (cloth: alk. paper) $425   **352.23**

1. Political science 2. Presidents -- United States

ISBN 9781608719068

LC 2012023291

This two-volume guide is a source "for researchers seeking an understanding of those who have occupied the White House and on the institution of the U.S. presidency." Its chapters "explain the structure, powers, and operations of the office and the president's relationship with Congress and the Supreme Court." In this fifth edition, there is "coverage of the George W. Bush presidency, the 2008 election, and the first 3 years of the presidency of Barack Obama." (Publisher's note)

Includes bibliographical references and index

My fellow citizens; the inaugural addresses of the presidents of the United States, 1789-2009. with an introduction by Arthur M. Schlesinger, Jr. and commentary by Fred L. Israel. Facts On File 2010 428p (Facts on File library of American history) $45   **352.23**

1. Presidents -- United States -- Inaugural addresses
ISBN 978-0-8160-8253-7; 0-8160-8253-7

LC 2009-32184

First published 2007

"Features the original text of all 56 inaugural speeches, each with an explanatory essay." Publisher's note

Owen, Roger

The **rise** and fall of Arab presidents for life; Roger Owen. Harvard University Press 2012 xi, 248 p.p (alk. paper) $24.95   **352.23**

1. Dictators 2. Presidents -- Middle East 3. Middle East -- Politics and government 4. Monarchy -- Middle East 5. Monarchy -- Arab countries 6. Authoritarianism -- Middle East 7. Middle East -- Kings and rulers 8. Arab countries -- Kings and rulers 9. Authoritarianism -- Arab countries 10. Presidents -- Middle East -- History 11. Presidents -- Arab countries -- History 12. Middle East -- Politics and government -- 1945- 13. Arab countries -- Politics and government -- 1945-
ISBN 0674065832; 9780674065833

LC 2011045764

This book, by Roger Owen, examines the political history of Arab political regimes in the 20th century. "Monarchical presidential regimes in the Arab world looked as though they would last indefinitely--until events in Tunisia and Egypt made clear their time was up. This . . . book [seeks] to lay bare the dynamics of a governmental system that largely defined the Arab Middle East in the twentieth century, and the popular opposition they engendered." (Publisher's note)

Includes bibliographical references (p. 217-226) and index

Raphael, Ray

Mr. president; how and why the founders created a chief executive. by Ray Raphael. Alfred A. Knopf 2012 324 p. **352.23**

1. Executive power -- United States 2. Founding Fathers of the United States 3. Presidents -- United States -- Biography 4. Constitutional conventions -- United States 5. United States -- Politics and government -- 1783-1809 6. Presidents -- United States -- History -- 18th century
ISBN 9780307595270

LC 2011033471

This book presents a "biography of the Constitutional Convention and the herculean task faced by the representatives. The author paints a picture of heroes--Edmund Randolph, George Mason, James Wilson and James Madison, among others--noting that the founders developed a government presupposing that George Washington would be the first chief executive. . . . In order to show how their views evolved as they toiled, Raphael explores the founders' writings in chronological order."

(Kirkus Reviews)

Includes bibliographical references (p. [289]-309) and index

State of the union; presidential rhetoric from Woodrow Wilson to George W. Bush. CQ Press 2007 1185p il $140 **352.23**

1. American speeches 2. Presidents -- United States -- Messages 3. Presidents -- United States -- Inaugural addresses 4. United States -- Politics and government -- Sources

ISBN 978-0-87289-433-4; 0-87289-433-9

LC 2006-35973

"This volume includes over 100 full-text addresses delivered by Presidents from 1913 to 2006 and comes complete with prefatory notes for context." Libr J

Includes bibliographical references

Witcover, Jules

America's vice presidents; from irrelevance to power. Jules Witcover. Smithsonian Institution Press 2014 592 p. illustrations $34.95 **352.23**

1. Vice-presidents -- United States 2. United States -- Politics and government 3. Vice-Presidents -- United States -- History 4. Vice-Presidents -- United States -- Biography

ISBN 1588344711; 9781588344717

LC 2014004242

This book by Jules Witcover is an "examination of the vice presidency throughout American history. Witcover chronicles each of the 47 vice presidents, including their personal biographies and their achievements--or lack thereof--during their vice presidential tenures." (Publisher's note)

"The essays included here are well-rounded, concise perspectives of the vice president's time in office, and in many cases, his pursuits after leaving that position. Adults and motivated high school students could pick and choose from among the entries or read straight through for an inside view of an oft-overlooked position." Library Jorunal

Includes bibliographical references

352.3   Executive management

Moynihan, Daniel Patrick

Secrecy; the American experience. {by} Daniel Patrick Moynihan; introduction by Richard Gid Powers. Yale Univ. Press 1998 262p il $38; pa $16 **352.3**

1. Executive power 2. National security -- United States

ISBN 0-300-07756-4; 0-300-08079-4 pa

LC 98-8144

"Using his background as chairman of the bipartisan Commission on Protecting and Reducing Government Secrecy, Moynihan provides a fascinating account of the development of secrecy as a mode of regulation for the U.S. government since World War I: how it was born, how world events shaped it, how it has adversely affected momentous political decisions—dropping the bomb on Hiroshima, the Bay of Pigs fiasco, the Iran-contra affair—and how it has eluded efforts to curtail or end it." America

Includes bibliographical references

352.4   Financial administration and budgets

Kramer, Mattea

★ A **people's** guide to the federal budget; National Priorities Project; written by Mattea Kramer ... [et al.]; foreword by Barbara Ehrenreich; afterword by Josh Silver. Interlink Books 2012 219 p. (pbk.) $15.00 **352.4**

1. Budget -- United States 2. United States. Congress 3. United States -- Appropriations and expenditures 4. Fiscal policy -- United States 5. Budget deficits -- United States 6. Government spending policy -- United States

ISBN 1566568870; 9781566568876

LC 2012007930

This book focuses on U.S. fiscal policy, government spending, and the federal budget. It "addresses such issues as discretionary and mandatory spending; how the federal government creates a budget; where the money comes from and goes; and the federal debt. . . . Other important priorities include construction of roads and highways, law enforcement, and veterans' assistance." (Booklist)

Includes bibliographical references.

353.4   Public administration of justice

Stevenson, Bryan

★ **Just** Mercy; a story of justice and redemption. Bryan Stevenson. First edition Random House Inc 2014 336 p. $28 **353.4**

1. Lawyers 2. Administration of criminal justice 3. Social reformers

ISBN 0812994523; 9780812994520

LC 2014430900

Carnegie Medal: Nonfiction (2015)

Los Angeles Times Book Prize Finalist: Current Interest (2014)

Kirkus Prize Finalist: Nonfiction (2014)

"Bryan Stevenson was a young lawyer when he founded the Equal Justice Initiative, a legal practice dedicated to defending those most desperate and in need: the poor, the wrongly condemned, and women and children trapped in the farthest reaches of our criminal justice system. One of his first cases was that of Walter McMillian, a young man who was sentenced to die for a notorious murder he insisted he didn't commit." (Publisher's note)

"Stevenson details changes in victims' rights, incarceration of juveniles, death penalty reforms, inflexible sentencing laws, and the continued practices of injustice that see too many juveniles, minorities, and mentally ill people imprisoned in a frenzy of mass incarceration in the U.S. A passionate account of the ways our nation thwarts justice and inhumanely punishes the poor and disadvantaged." Booklist

Includes bibliographical references

353.9   Public administration of safety, sanitation, waste control

Hilts, Philip J.

★ **Protecting** America's health; the FDA, business, and one hundred years of regulation. University of North Carolina Press 2004 394p pa $19.95 **353.9**

1. Drug industry 2. Food adulteration and inspection 3. Food -- Law and legislation 4. United States -- Food and Drug Administration

ISBN 978-0-8078-5582-9; 0-8078-5582-0

First published 2003 by Knopf

"This fascinating look at the inside story reveals how disastrous unfettered capitalism would be without reasonable regulation." Booklist

Includes bibliographical references

355   Military science

★ **Amazons** to fighter pilots; a biographical dictionary of military women. Reina Pennington, editor; foreword by Gerhard Weinberg. Greenwood Press 2003 2v il set $175   **355**
1. Reference books 2. Women soldiers -- Biography -- Dictionaries
ISBN 0-313-29197-7
LC 2002-44777
"This peerless work, situated at the nexus of military history and women's studies, is an essential companion to more male-biased biographical resources." Choice
Includes bibliographical references

Arnold, James R.
Jungle of snakes; a century of counterinsurgency warfare from the Philippines to Iraq. Bloomsbury Press 2009 291p map $28   **355**
1. Military history 2. Counterinsurgency
ISBN 978-1-59691-503-9; 1-59691-503-X
LC 2008-54018
The author "studies past insurgency responses to help clarify the U.S. efforts in Iraq. The author investigates four counterinsurgencies that either proved successful in putting down rebellion—the United States in the Philippines following war with Spain in 1898; the British response to the Malayan Emergency in 1948—or disastrous—the French invasion of Algeria in 1830; the U.S. quagmire in Vietnam—and offers lessons to be drawn from them. . . . A reasonably argued work that delivers needed insight and historical precedent to the current war debate." Kirkus
Includes bibliographical references

Axelrod, Alan
★ The **encyclopedia** of the American armed forces. Facts on File 2005 2v il (Facts on File library of American history) set $175   **355**
1. Reference books 2. United States -- Armed forces -- Encyclopedias
ISBN 0-8160-4700-6
LC 2004-20549
"The four sections each document a major branch of the United States military: Army, Navy, Marine Corps, and Air Force. Each branch has an initial list of entries, a list of branch-specific abbreviations and acronyms, and a short bibliography." Choice
Includes bibliographical references

Bacevich, Andrew J., 1947-
Washington rules; America's path to permanent war. [by] Andrew J. Bacevich. Metropolitan Books 2010 286p $25 **355**
1. Military policy -- United States 2. United States -- Foreign relations 3. United States -- Military policy -- Decision making 4. United States -- Foreign relations -- Decision making
ISBN 978-0-8050-9141-0; 0-8050-9141-6
LC 2010-06302
"From Harry S. Truman's presidency to today, Bacevich argues, Americans have trumpeted the credo that they alone must 'lead, save, liberate and ultimately transform the world.'" (N Y Times Book Rev) Index.
"The U.S. spends more on the military than the entire rest of the world combined and maintains 300,000 troops abroad in an 'empire of bases,' all part of a credo of global leadership and a consensus that the U.S. must maintain a state of semiwar. . . . [The author offers an] analysis of the assumptions behind the credo of global leadership and eternal military vigilance that has become increasingly expensive and unsustainable." Booklist
Includes bibliographical references

Belfiore, Michael
★ The **department** of mad scientists; how DARPA is remaking our world, from the Internet to artificial limbs. Smithsonian Books/Harper 2009 xxiii, 295p $26.99; ebook $12.99   **355**
1. Science -- Governmental policy 2. United States -- Advanced Research Projects Agency
ISBN 978-0-06-157793-2; 0-06-157793-6; 978-0-06-195937-0 ebook; 0-06-195937-5 ebook
LC 2009-18015
"Founded by Eisenhower in response to Sputnik and the Soviet space program, DARPA [Defense Advanced Research Projects Agency] mixes military officers with sneaker-wearing scientists, seeking paradigm-shifting ideas in varied fields—from energy, robotics, and rockets to peopleless operating rooms, driverless cars, and planes that can fly halfway around the world in just hours. DARPA gave birth to the Internet, GPS, and mind-controlled robotic arms. . . . Michael Belfiore was given unprecedented access to write this first-ever popular account of DARPA." Bookmarks
Includes bibliographical references

Boot, Max
★ **War** made new; technology, warfare, and the course of history, 1500 to today. Gotham Books 2006 624p il map $24.95   **355**
1. Military history 2. Military art and science
ISBN 978-1-592-40222-9; 1-592-40222-4
LC 2006-15518
"Throughout, Boot provides a vivid and engaging mix of historical narrative and analysis, showing the bloody real-world results of abstract decisionmaking about the nature and degree of a country's military preparedness. His twelve case studies, stretching from the defeat of the Spanish Armada to the current situation in Iraq, point to a variety of disparate lessons but some themes that are surprisingly constant over time and space." Commentary

Brooks, Rosa
★ **How** everything became war and the military became everything; Tales from the Pentagon. Rosa Brooks. Simon & Schuster 2016 448 p. (ebook) $20.99; (hardcover) $29.95 **355**
1. War 2. United States -- Armed forces 3. Military policy -- United States 4. National security -- United States 5. Just war doctrine 6. Militarism -- United States 7. United States -- Military policy 8. Strategic culture -- United States 9. War (International law) -- Philosophy 10. Armed Forces -- Operations other than war 11. Terrorism -- Prevention -- Government policy -- United States 12. United States -- History, Military -- 20th century -- Anecdotes 13. United States -- History, Military -- 21st century -- Anecdotes
ISBN 9781476777887; 9781476777863; 9781476777870
LC 2016005348
This book by Rosa Brooks traces the shift "in how America wages war from an unconventional perspective—that of a former top Pentagon official who is the daughter of two anti-war protesters and a human rights activist married to an Army Green Beret. Her experiences lead her to an urgent warning: When the boundaries around war disappear, we risk destroying America's founding values and the laws and institutions we've built." (Publisher's note)
Includes bibliographical references and index

Buckley, Gail Lumet

★ **American** patriots; the story of Blacks in the military from the Revolution to Desert Storm. [by] Gail Buckley. Random House 2001 xxiv, 534p il hardcover o.p. pa $15.95 **355**
    1. African American soldiers 2. United States -- Race relations 3. United States -- Military history
    ISBN 0-375-50279-3; 0-375-76009-1 pa

                    LC 00-51825
    This is an account "of blacks in the U.S. military, both at home and abroad, from the 1770s to the 1990s. . . . This readable, spirited story deserves a place in every U.S. history collection, as well as in the black or military collections." Libr J
    Includes bibliographical references

Carroll, James

House of war; the Pentagon and the disastrous rise of American power. Houghton Mifflin Co. 2006 657p il $30 **355**
    1. Military policy -- United States 2. United States -- Dept. of Defense 3. Pentagon (Arlington, Va.: Building)
    ISBN 0-618-18780-4; 978-0-618-18780-5

                  LC 2005-24014
    "Chronicling the ascent of America's military establishment from 1943 to the aftermath of 9/11, Carroll uses the Pentagon as a metaphor for a U.S. political culture that values military power over human rights and seeks to project U.S. influence and values abroad by force, if necessary, whether invited by other countries or not. . . . Certain to be a widely read and discussed book, this is worthy of space on the shelves of all libraries." Libr J
    Includes bibliographical references

Clausewitz, Carl von

★ **On** war; {by} Carl von Clausewitz; edited and translated by Michael Howard and Peter Paret; introductory essays by Peter Paret, Michael Howard and Bernard Brodie; with commentary by Bernard Brodie. Princeton Univ. Press 1976 717p $95; pa $26.95 **355**
    1. War 2. Military art and science
    ISBN 0-691-05657-9; 0-691-01854-5 pa
    Original German edition, 1833
    "Drawing on the experiences of Frederick the Great and Napoleon, Clausewitz tried to analyze the workings of military genius by isolating the factors that decide success in war. His conclusions have remained generally applicable, and since his work contains a minimum of technical discussion, it has retained a wide appeal." Ency Britannica

Cohen, Eliot A.

Conquered into liberty. Free Press 2011 405p il map $30; ebook $14.99 **355**
    1. New York (State) -- History 2. United States -- Military history 3. United States -- History -- 1755-1763, French and Indian War
    ISBN 978-0-7432-4990-4; 978-1-4516-2733-6 ebook

                  LC 2011023717
    It was the author's intent to demonstrate "that there is more to the American military heritage than the U.S.'s conventional war-fighting and its European antecedents. We should expand the concept of 'American' to include pre-revolutionary times, and so include nearly 200 years of frontier fighting . . . . In . . . [an] examination of 18th-century warfare along the northeastern seaboard . . . Cohen sees two less-appreciated sources for the way Americans currently fight. First was the birth of a unique strain of raiding, ambushing, subversion, living off the land, ad hoc alliance-building with indigenous peoples, long-range reconnaissance, and patrolling behind enemy lines. Second, writes Cohen, was the

very fact that these non-traditional tactics were rooted in the distinctiveness of colonial society. . . . Cohen believes that this legacy endures". (National Review)
    This is "an engaging account of the wars fought on the 'Great Warpath.' These were the trails, especially around Lakes George and Champlain, which marked a kind of western border for early settlers. The author recounts the eight major battles in those successive campaigns. He includes two naval battles: Plattsburgh, during the War of 1812, and Valcour Island in 1776, both of which he presents as decisive but underrated contributions to securing the young republic from foreign threat. . . . A delightful-to-read piece of American history." Kirkus
    Includes bibliographical references

Daalder, Ivo H.

In the shadow of the Oval Office; profiles of the national security advisers and the presidents they served: from JFK to George W. Bush. [by] Ivo H. Daalder and I.M. Destler. Simon & Schuster 2009 386p $27 **355**
    1. National security -- United States 2. Presidents -- United States -- Staff 3. United States -- Special Assistant to the President for National Security Affairs
    ISBN 978-1-416-55319-9; 1-416-55319-3

                  LC 2008-40699
    "A revealing, unsettling look at how our presidents receive advice on foreign policy." Kirkus
    Includes bibliographical references

Dower, John W., 1938-

Cultures of war; Pearl Harbor, Hiroshima, 9-11, Iraq. New Press 2010 596p il $29.95 **355**
    1. Iraq War, 2003-2011 2. War and civilization 3. World War, 1939-1945 4. September 11 terrorist attacks, 2001 5. Military policy -- United States 6. United States -- Military policy 7. War and society -- United States 8. United States -- History, Military -- 20th century 9. United States -- History, Military -- 21st century
    ISBN 978-0-393-06150-5; 0-393-06150-7

                  LC 2010-20395
    National Book Award Finalist: Nonfiction (2010)
    The author "draws astute ironies between Pearl Harbor and 9/11 in terms of the overweening arrogance of military superpowers. The author moves back and forth between these two definitive eras in history, providing a brilliant examination of the willful self-delusion and selective reasoning involved in the highest levels of decision making—from Japan's spectacularly ill-advised bombing of Pearl Harbor to the Bush Administration's bundling of 'weapons of mass destruction' and Osama bin Laden as justification for invasion of Iraq. . . . An unrelenting, incisive, masterly comparative study." Kirkus
    Includes bibliographical references and index.

★ **Encyclopedia** of American military history; Spencer C. Tucker, general editor; associate editors David Coffey, John C. Fredriksen, Justin D. Murphy. Facts on File 2003 3v il maps set $225 **355**
    1. Reference books 2. United States -- Military history -- Encyclopedias
    ISBN 0-8160-4355-8

                  LC 2002-29658
    "More than 1,200 entries cover military leaders, wars, campaigns, battles, events, famous soldiers, military branches, key technological developments, overviews of weapons systems, and more. It covers the period from the colonial wars to the present, and gives special attention to the minorities and women who have contributed significantly to American military success." Publisher's note

Includes bibliographical references

France, John

Perilous glory; the rise of western military power. John France. Yale University Press 2011 ix, 448 p.p ill., maps $35   **355**
1. War -- History 2. War and civilization 3. Military art and science -- History 4. Military history
ISBN 0300120745; 9780300120745

LC 2011006437

In this book, "[John] France acknowledges the significance of democracy . . . and technology in the nineteenth-century transformation of warfare . . . [but] argues . . . that the resulting rise of the 'Western' style of warfare to international significance was largely fortuitous, coinciding with the decline and stagnation of the Ottomans and the Mughals, inheritors of the previously dominant form of steppe warfare that had emerged from Eurasia in antiquity." (Times Literary Supplement)

Gordin, Michael D.

Red cloud at dawn; Truman, Stalin, and the end of the atomic monopoly. Farrar, Straus and Giroux 2009 402p il map $27   **355**
1. Arms race 2. Presidents 3. Heads of state 4. Nuclear weapons 5. Vice-presidents 6. Senators 7. Communist leaders 8. Political leaders 9. Nuclear weapons -- History 10. World politics -- 1945-1955 11. Arms race -- History -- 20th century 12. Soviet Union -- Foreign relations -- 1945-1991 13. United States -- Foreign relations -- 1945-1953 14. Soviet Union -- Foreign relations -- United States 15. United States -- Foreign relations -- Soviet Union
ISBN 0-374-25682-9; 978-0-374-25682-1

LC 2009-01424

Gordin examines the years from 1945 to 1949 "in which only the United States possessed atomic weapons." (N Y Times Book Rev) Index.

The author "brings considerable scholarship to the subject of how the Soviets succeeded in building an atomic bomb. He weaves an impressively wide range of sources, including new material from ex-Soviet and western archives, into a brilliant narrative about the intelligence war." Hist Today

Includes bibliographical references

Hagedorn, Ann

The **invisible** soldiers; how America outsourced our security. Ann Hagedorn. Simon & Schuster 2014 352 p. $28 **355**
1. Private military companies 2. National security -- United States 3. United States -- Military policy 4. United States -- Politics and government
ISBN 1416598804; 9781416598800

LC 2014015007

This book, by Ann Hagedorn, is "about the privatization of America's national security. . . . [P]rivate military and security companies (PMSCs) . . . are a bona-fide industry, an indispensable part of American foreign and military policy. PMSCs assist US forces in combat operations and replace them after the military withdraws from combat zones; they guard our embassies; they play key roles in US counterterrorism strategies; and Homeland Security depends on them." (Publisher's note)

"A brisk, disturbing account that adds to the sense that liberties taken in the war on terror have created long-term liabilities for American society." Kirkus

Includes bibliographical references and index

Hanson, Victor Davis

The **father** of us all; war and history, ancient and modern.

Bloomsbury 2010 259p $25   **355**
1. War 2. Military history
ISBN 978-1-60819-165-9; 1-60819-165-6

LC 2009-41714

"This anthology brings together 13 of Hanson's essays and reviews, revised and re-edited. They have appeared over the past decade in periodicals from the American Spectator to the New York Times. Hanson's introductory generalization that war is a human enterprise that seems inseparable from the human condition structures such subjects as an eloquent answer to the question 'Why Study War?', a defense of the historicity of the film 300, about the Persian Wars, in a masterpiece of envelope pushing, and a comprehensive and dazzling analysis of why America fights as she does. . . . The pieces are well written, sometimes elegantly so, and closely reasoned." Publ Wkly

Includes bibliographical references

The **soul** of battle; from ancient times to the present day, how three great liberators vanquished tyranny. Anchor Books 2001 480p pa $16.95   **355**
1. Generals 2. Military history 3. Memoirists 4. Army officers 5. Secretaries of war
ISBN 0-385-72059-9; 978-0-385-72059-5

LC 00-63979

First published 1999 by Free Press

"Hanson narrates the success of three military campaigns-Epaminondas defeat of the Spartans in the fourth century B.C., Sherman's march through Georgia and the Carolinas during the Civil War, and Patton's race into Germany at the head of the Third Army in 1944-45. . . . In Hanson's view, the individual traits of spontaneity and creativity that are nourished in a free society are assets, not hindrances, in warfare." Booklist

Includes bibliographical references

Hastings, Max

Warriors; portraits from the battlefield. Knopf 2006 xxiii, 354p il maps $27.50   **355**
1. Soldiers 2. Military history
ISBN 1-4000-4441-3; 978-1-4000-4441-2

LC 2005-44302

The author "selects memoirs and biographies about 15 combatants (one of them a woman) and distills accounts of their lives and trenchant observations about their personalities. . . . Filled with poignant psychological insight, Hastings' remarkable sketches will provoke greater-than-average demand from the military affairs readership." Booklist

Includes bibliographical references

Jacobsen, Annie

The **Pentagon's** Brain; An Uncensored History of DARPA, America's Top-secret Military Research Agency. by Annie Jacobsen. Little, Brown & Co. 2015 560 p. 16 plates; illustrations $30   **355**
1. United States. Dept. of Defense 2. United States -- Politics and government
ISBN 0316371769; 9780316371766

LC 2015304581

Pulitzer Prize Finalist: History (2016)

This book, by Annie Jacobsen, is the "definitive history of DARPA, the Defense Advanced Research Project Agency. . . . Jacobsen draws on inside sources, exclusive interviews, private documents, and declassified memos to paint a picture of DARPA, or 'the Pentagon's brain,' from its Cold War inception in 1958 to the present." (Publisher's note)

"This engrossing, conversation-starting read is highly recommended for policymakers, historians, scientists, and others who study technology's implications. It will complement Jonathon Moreno's Mind Wars and Sarah Bridger's Scientists at War." LJ

Karpin, Michael I.

The **bomb** in the basement; how Israel went nuclear and what that means for the world. [by] Michael Karpin. Simon & Schuster 2006 404p il map $26; pa $15   **355**

   1. Nuclear weapons 2. Israel -- Military history

   ISBN 0-7432-6594-7; 978-0-7432-6594-2; 0-7432-6595-5 pa; 978-0-7432-6595-9 pa

                                  LC 2005-51689

"For all those interested in understanding how Israel's idealistic origins dovetail with its hawkish position in the game of nuclear deterrence and fraught relationship with other countries in the Middle East, this well-researched study is a must-read." Publ Wkly

   Includes bibliographical references

Kindsvatter, Peter S.

American soldiers; ground combat in the World Wars, Korea, and Vietnam. foreword by Russell F. Weigley. University Press of Kan. 2003 432p il (Modern war studies) $34.95 **355**

   1. Soldiers -- United States 2. United States -- Marine Corps 3. United States -- Army -- Infantry 4. United States -- Military history

   ISBN 0-7006-1229-7

                                  LC 2002-12957

"Mining twentieth-century foot soldiers' memoirs and novels, Kindsvatter integrates this literature of personal experience into a generalized assessment of what combat was like and how men reacted to it. . . . Kindsvatter's illuminating work is about coping with . . . fear at the foxhole level, and it . . . powerfully conveys the psychology and military sociology of combat in the draft-era armies." Booklist

   Includes bibliographical references

Langewiesche, William

The **atomic** bazaar; the rise of the nuclear poor. Farrar, Straus and Giroux 2007 179p map $22   **355**

   1. Arms control 2. Nuclear weapons

   ISBN 978-0-374-10678-2; 0-374-10678-9

                                  LC 2006-102539

"Langewiesche's bracing expose of nuclear criminality blasts away the ubiquitous misinformation usually attendant on this alarming subject." Booklist

Lipsky, David

Absolutely American; four years at West Point. Houghton Mifflin 2003 317p il $25   **355**

   1. United States Military Academy

   ISBN 0-618-09542-X

                                  LC 2002-191339

"The book must have been extremely hard to organize. And yet it reads with a novelistic flow. . . . It turns out that how teenagers get turned into leaders is not a simple story, but it is wonderfully told in this book." N Y Times Book Rev

Nicholson, Alexander

Fighting to serve; behind the scenes in the war to repeal "don't ask, don't tell" Alexander Nicholson. Chicago Review Press 2012 288 p. $26.95   **355**

   1. Military policy -- United States 2. Don't ask, don't tell (Military policy) 3. LGBT people -- Legal status, laws, etc. 4. Nicholson, Alexander 5. Servicemembers United (United States) 6. United States. Army -- Gays -- Biography 7. Gay military personnel -- United States -- Biography 8. Gay rights -- United States -- History -- 21st century 9. Gay military personnel -- Government policy -- United States 10. Homosexuality -- Political aspects -- United States -- History -- 21st century

   ISBN 1613743726; 9781613743720

                                  LC 2012021821

This book "provides an . . . account of the road to repeal the 'Don't Ask, Don't Tell' (DADT) law prohibiting the open service of" LGBT "military members." Author Alexander Nicholson "offer[s] commentary on a range of incidents: being personally forced out of the army by the DADT policy; meeting and persuading former chairman of the Joint Chiefs of Staff, Gen. John Shalikashvili, of the cause's benefits . . .; leading and speaking at rallies; and coordinating directly with the White House." (Publishers Weekly)

Rhodes, Richard

Arsenals of folly; the making of the nuclear arms race. Alfred A. Knopf 2007 386p il $28.95   **355**

   1. Arms race 2. Nuclear weapons

   ISBN 978-0-375-41413-8; 0-375-41413-4

                                  LC 2007-17613

"This historical record, drawing upon many firsthand accounts and interviews, details pivotal events in world history and should be necessary reading for anyone interested in 20th-century history." Libr J

   Includes bibliographical references

Rose, Gideon

How wars end; why we always fight the last battle: a history of American intervention from World War I to Afghanistan. Simon & Schuster 2010 413p $27   **355**

   1. War 2. War -- Termination 3. Disengagement (Military science) 4. Military policy -- United States 5. United States -- Military policy 6. United States -- Military history 7. Military planning -- United States 8. United States -- History, Military -- 20th century 9. United States -- History, Military -- 21st century

   ISBN 978-1-4165-9053-8; 1-4165-9053-6

                                  LC 2010-34817

"Surveying the settlements of America's wars since WWI, Rose analyzes reasons for the manner and substance of their conclusions. . . . Public spirited and accessible, Rose's presentation should impress anyone hoping for better management of war and peace by Washington." Booklist

   Includes bibliographical references

Singer, P. W.

Wired for war; the robotics revolution and conflict in the twenty-first century. Penguin Press 2009 499p il $29.95 **355**

   1. Robots 2. Military weapons 3. Military art and science

   ISBN 978-1-59420-198-1; 1-59420-198-6

This is "a vivid picture of the current controversies and dazzling possibilities of war in the digital age." Kirkus

   Includes bibliographical references

Sites, Kevin

The **things** they cannot say; stories soldiers won't tell you about what they've seen, done or failed to do in war. Kevin Sites. HarperCollins 2013 336 p. $15.99   **355**

   1. Soldiers -- Psychology 2. Afghan War, 2001- -- Personal narratives 3. Iraq War, 2003-2011 -- Personal narratives

   ISBN 0061990523; 9780061990526

In this book author Kevin Sites asks soldiers, "many of whom Sites first met while in Afghanistan and Iraq, . . . difficult questions. . . . One struggles to recover from a head injury he believes has stolen his ability to love; another attempts to make amends for the killing of an innocent man; yet another finds respect for the enemy fighter who tried to kill him. Sites also shares the unsettling narrative of his own failures during war--including his complicity in a murder." (Publisher' note)

Sun-tzu

★ The **illustrated** art of war; [by] Sun Tzu; the definitive English translation by Samuel B. Griffith. Oxford University Press 2005 272p il map $29.95   **355**
1. Military art and science
ISBN 0-19-518999-X; 978-0-19-518999-5

LC 2005-10651

An illustrated version of The art of war, a military treatise written in China during the 6th century BC discussing different military tactics and strategies.
Includes bibliographical references

Sutherland, Jonathan

★ **African** Americans at war; an encyclopedia. [by] Jonathan D. Sutherland. ABC-CLIO 2004 2v set $185   **355**
1. Reference books 2. African American soldiers 3. United States -- Armed forces -- Encyclopedias 4. African Americans -- Biography -- Encyclopedias
ISBN 1-57607-746-2

LC 2003-21501

"There are more than 250 [alphabetically arranged] entries conveying biographical, thematic, and conceptual information. Well-known leaders (Colin Powell), groups (Buffalo Soldiers), specific units [and battles] . . . have their own entries. . . . This is a superb resource for any . . . library looking to enrich its history, military or African American studies collections." Booklist

Tucker, Spencer C.

The **encyclopedia** of Middle East wars; the United States in the Persian Gulf, Afghanistan, and Iraq conflicts. Spencer C. Tucker, editor; Priscilla Mary Roberts, editor, documents volume; foreword by Anthony C. Zinni. ABC-CLIO 2010 1887p 5v il map set $495   **355**
1. Reference books 2. Afghan War, 2001- -- Encyclopedias 3. Iraq War, 2003-2011 -- Encyclopedias 4. Persian Gulf War, 1991 -- Encyclopedias 5. Middle East -- Military history -- Encyclopedias
ISBN 978-1-85109-947-4; 978-1-85109-948-1 ebook

LC 2010-33812

"An essential resource for anyone seeking detailed information and in-depth reading on U.S. actions and involvement in the Middle East region during the last 15 years." Libr J
Includes bibliographical references

★ **Voices** of war; stories of service from the home front and the front lines. edited by Tom Wiener. National Geographic Society 2004 336p il $30; pa $6.95   **355**
1. Veterans 2. United States -- Military history 3. United States -- Armed forces -- Military life
ISBN 0-7922-7838-0; 0-7922-4204-1 pa

LC 2004-49986

This book showcases "the oral histories collected by the Veteran's History Project, the Library of Congress's nationwide effort to collect and preserve the stories not only of war veterans, but also of those who served in support of the frontline troops. . . . The personal accounts cover the major conflicts of the 20th century, from World War I to the Persian Gulf War, and include letters, diaries, and journals. The chapters are nicely arranged to show the commonalities of military experience, e.g., basic training, daily life, combat, the home front, and returning home." Libr J

★ **War**: from ancient Egypt to Iraq; editorial consultant, Saul David. DK 2009 512p il $50   **355**
1. Reference books 2. War -- Encyclopedias 3. Military history -- Encyclopedias
ISBN 978-0-7566-5572-3

LC 2010-278612

"From the Punic wars to the Crusades to the wars of the league of Cognac and modern conflicts like those in the former Yugoslavia, War is an outstanding catalog of conflict. Each of the seven chapters . . . opens with a time line and is peppered with sidebars of military superlatives such as youngest commanders, famous female warriors, and even landmark war movies. . . . An essential reference title for all libraries." Libr J

Watts, Clint

Messing with the enemy; surviving in a social media world of hackers, terrorists, Russians, and fake news. Clint Watts. HarperCollins 2018 289 p. $27.99   **355**
1. Social networking 2. Information warfare 3. Online social networks
ISBN 0062795988; 9780062795984

This book, by Clint Watts, "offers a devastating and essential look at the misinformation campaigns, fake news, and electronic espionage operations that have become the cutting edge of modern warfare--and how we can protect ourselves and our country against them. . . . Watts examines a range of social media platforms . . . and nefarious actors . . . to illuminate exactly how they use Western social media for their nefarious purposes." (Publisher's note)

355.001   Philosophy and theory

Tyson, Neil deGrasse, 1958-

★ **Accessory** to war; the unspoken alliance between astrophysics and the military. by Neil deGrasse Tyson and Avis Lang. W W Norton & Co Inc 2018 448 p. $30   **355.001**
1. Astrophysics 2. Astronautics -- United States 3. Military research -- United States
ISBN 0393064441; 9780393064445

In this book, "acclaimed astrophysicist Neil deGrasse Tyson and writer-researcher Avis Lang examine how the methods and tools of astrophysics have been enlisted in the service of war. . . . Spanning early celestial navigation to satellite-enabled warfare, 'Accessory to War' is a richly researched and provocative examination of the intersection of science, technology, industry, and power." (Publisher's note)

" Tracing the military's influence on fact-finding as far back as the Greeks and the Egyptians, when stargazers helped guide warships into battle, the authors demonstrate how the invention of devices such as chronometers, astrolabes, and telescopes were motivated as much by a given country's drive to dominate another as by the search for knowledge."

355.007   Education and related topics

Dobson, Michael Singer

How to get into a military service academy; a step-by-step guide to getting qualified, nominated, and appointed. Michael Singer Dobson. Rowman & Littlefield 2015 214 p. (cloth: alk.

paper) $34; (ebook) $41.99 **355.007**
1. Military education 2. United States Naval Academy -- Admission 3. United States Military Academy -- Admission 4. United States Air Force Academy -- Admission
ISBN 9781442243149; 9781442243156

LC 2015019469

This book, by Michael Singer Dobson, offers "practical advice on how to decide if a [military] service academy is the right fit for them. The author covers high school coursework and extracurricular activities, including leadership and community service. Students and parents will appreciate the step-by-step discussion of the application process. The explanation of how to secure a nomination to an academy will be of special interest to those unfamiliar with the system." (Publisher's note)

"Attending a U.S. military academy isn't for everyone, but Dobson's guide is a must-read for anyone considering this career path. Highly recommended for high school, public, and college libraries." LJ

Includes bibliographical references and index

355.008   Groups of people

Buckley, Gail Lumet, 1937-
Fighting for Freedom; Photographs from the National Museum of African American History and Culture. National Museum of African American History and Culture; Earl W. and Amanda Stafford Center for African American Media Arts. D. Giles Limited 2017 80 p. ills. (some color), portraits (Double exposure) (paperback) $16.95 **355.008**
1. African American soldiers 2. African American soldiers -- Portraits 3. African American soldiers -- History -- Pictorial works
ISBN 1911282018; 9781911282013

This book "presents fifty images of African Americans in uniform, from the Civil War to the War in Iraq. The selection of photographs, which exemplify stories of patriotism, courage, and dignity, are enriched by the unique perspective of Frank Bolden, Jr., 12th Administrator of NASA and Gail Lumet Buckley, author of American Patriots." (Publisher's note)

"The fifth volume in the Double Exposure series . . . is a short yet powerful pictorial history of black men and women who served in the United States Armed Forces, from the Civil War to today." Pub Wkly

Includes bibliographical references (page 80) and index.

355.009   History, geographic treatment, biography

Beschloss, Michael R., 1955-
★ **Presidents** of war; Michael Beschloss. Random House Inc 2018 752 p. $35 **355.009**
1. United States -- Military history 2. Presidents -- United States -- History 3. Political leadership -- United States -- History
ISBN 0307409600; 9780307409607

This book, by Michael Beschloss, offers a "look at a procession of American leaders as they took the nation into conflict and mobilized their country for victory. It brings us into the room as they make the most difficult decisions that face any President, at times sending hundreds of thousands of American men and women to their deaths. . . . We come to understand how these Presidents were able to withstand the pressures of war . . . or were broken by them." (Publisher's note)

"The author's highly readable style and ability to pinpoint the most relevant facts make this a perfect book for any student of American history and its presidents."

Brands, H. W.
★ The **man** who saved the union; Ulysses Grant in war and peace. H. W. Brands. Doubleday 2012 736 p. $35.00 **355.009**
1. Civil rights 2. Presidents -- United States 3. Generals -- United States -- Biography 4. Presidents -- United States -- Biography
ISBN 0385532415; 9780385532419

LC 2011043795

This book offers a biography of U.S. President Ulysses S. Grant. Here, "Pulitzer [prize] finalist [H. W.] Brands . . . treats Grant's entire life, showing its full arc. He breaks with earlier interpretations . . . , concluding that Grant did the best he could in trying circumstances, particularly in the area of civil and minority rights." (Library Journal)

Danner, Mark
Spiral; trapped in the forever war. Mark Danner. Simon & Schuster 2016 288 p. (ebook) $19.99; (hardback) $26 **355.009**
1. World politics 2. Terrorism -- Prevention 3. United States -- Military history 4. World politics -- 21st century 5. Military history, Modern -- 21st century 6. United States -- Military policy -- 21st century 7. Terrorism -- Prevention -- History -- 21st century 8. United States -- Foreign relations -- 21st century 9. United States -- History, Military -- 21st century 10. War on Terrorism, 2001-2009 -- Political aspects -- United States
ISBN 9781476747781; 9781476747767; 9781476747774

LC 2016000732

This book, by Mark Danner, "describes a nation that has been altered in fundamental ways. President Bush declared a war of choice and without an exit plan, and President Obama has proven unable to take the country off what he has called its 'permanent war footing.' . . . Bush's promise that we have 'taken the gloves off' and Obama's inability to define an end game have had a profound effect on us even though the actual combat is fought by a tiny percentage of our citizens." (Publisher's note)

"A chilling cautionary tale of Orwellian repercussions." Kirkus
Includes bibliographical references and index.

Keegan, John
Fields of battle; the wars for North America. Knopf 1996 348p il maps hardcover o.p. pa $15 **355.009**
1. North America -- Military history
ISBN 0-679-42413-X; 0-679-74664-1 pa

LC 96-154385

First published 1995 in the United Kingdom with title: Warpaths: travels of a military historian in North America

The author "demonstrates how North America's geography has influenced its history: how its mountain chains and river systems have determined where people fought, and fought repeatedly. For example, the defenses that Cornwallis built at Yorktown to deter American forces were improved and reused by the Confederates almost a century later. Keegan's tour of the continent skips the Mexican War, and his book is atypically discursive. For Americans, the charm is the familiarity of its sites—Brooklyn, Pittsburgh, Laramie, and other home towns." New Yorker

Jaffe, Steven H.
★ **New York** at war; Steven H. Jaffe. Basic Books 2012 p. cm. **355.009**
1. War 2. New York (N.Y.) -- History, Military
ISBN 9780465029709; 9780465036424

LC 2012000454

In this book "historian Steven H. Jaffe offers a . . . history of New York City" from a local, military perspective. "Beginning with an Indian attack on one of Henry Hudson's crewmen (who in 1609 became the first recorded fatality of an act of war in the region's history), Jaffe describes, in turn, each of the city's encounters with war over the past four centuries. . . . [including] how New York became hugely powerful . . . during the Civil War . . . during the build-up to World War I . . . during World War II, and in the atomic era." The book's scope discusses the impact of military and ethnic conflicts in the city "stretching from the colonial era to 9/11 and beyond." (Publisher's note)

Includes bibliographical references

Ricks, Thomas E.

★ The **generals**; American military command from World War II to today. Thomas E. Ricks. Penguin Press 2012 576 p.   **355.009**

1. Generals 2. Command of troops 3. United States -- Military history 4. Generals -- United States -- History -- 20th century 5. Command of troops -- History -- 20th century -- Case studies 6. United States -- History, Military -- 20th century -- Case studies

ISBN 1594204047; 9781594204043

LC 2012015110

This book, by Thomas E. Ricks, presents an overview of U.S. military leadership since 1945. "History has been kind to the American generals of World War II--Marshall, Eisenhower, Patton, and Bradley--and less kind to the generals of the wars that followed. . . . Thomas E. Ricks sets out to explain why that is. . . . [W]e meet great leaders and suspect ones, generals who rose to the occasion and those who failed themselves and their soldiers." (Publisher's note)

Includes bibliographical references and index

Wheelan, Joseph

★ **Terrible** swift sword; the life of General Philip H. Sheridan. Joseph Wheelan. Da Capo Press 2012 387 p. (hardcover: alk. paper) $26   **355.009**

1. Native Americans -- History 2. United States -- History -- 1861-1865, Civil War -- Campaigns 3. Native Americans -- Wars 4. United States. Army -- Biography 5. Generals -- United States -- Biography 6. United States -- History -- Civil War, 1861-1865 -- Campaigns

ISBN 0306820277; 9780306820274; 9780306821097

LC 2012018587

This book, by Joseph Wheelan, is a biography of the Civil War general Philip H. Sheridan. "Sheridan is the least known of the triumvirate of generals most responsible for winning the Civil War. . . . It was General Sheridan who introduced scorched-earth warfare to the South. . . . After the war, Sheridan ruthlessly suppressed the raiding Plains Indians much as he had the Confederates, . . . but he also defended reservation Indians from corrupt agents and contractors." (Publisher's note)

Includes bibliographical references and index

355.02 War and warfare

Armitage, David, 1965-

Civil wars; A History in Ideas. David Armitage. Alfred A. Knopf 2017 368 p. (ebook) $65; (hardback) $27.95 **355.02**

1. Military history 2. Civil war -- Philosophy

ISBN 9780385353090; 9780307271136; 9780307456175

LC 2016023404

This book, by David Armitage, presents a "highly original history, tracing the least understood and most intractable form of organized human aggression from Ancient Rome through the centuries to the present day. We think we know civil war when we see it. Yet ideas of what it is, and what it isn't, have a long and contested history, from its fraught origins in republican Rome to debates in early modern Europe to our present day." (Publisher's note)

"A profound contribution to political philosophy." Booklist
Includes bibliographical references and index

Ellsberg, Daniel, 1931-

The **doomsday** machine; confessions of a nuclear war planner. Daniel Ellsberg. St. Martin's Press 2017 384 p. $30   **355.02**

1. Autobiographies 2. Nuclear warfare -- Government policy -- United States -- History -- 20th century 3. Nuclear weapons -- Government policy -- United States -- History -- 20th century

ISBN 1608196704; 9781608196708

Carnegie Medal Finalist: Nonfiction (2018)

In this book, author "Daniel Ellsberg reveals his shocking firsthand account of America's nuclear program in the 1960s. From the remotest air bases in the Pacific Command, where he discovered that the authority to initiate use of nuclear weapons was widely delegated, to the secret plans for general nuclear war under [Dwight] Eisenhower, . . . Ellsberg shows that the legacy of this most dangerous arms buildup in the history of civilization . . . threatens our very survival." (Publisher's note)

"Ellsberg's book is essential for facilitating a national discussion about a vital topic." (LJ)

Gentile, Gian P.

Wrong turn; America's deadly embrace of counterinsurgency. Colonel Gian Gentile. The New Press 2013 208 p. (hardback) $24.95   **355.02**

1. Counterinsurgency 2. Iraq War, 2003-2011 3. Counterinsurgency -- Case studies 4. Counterinsurgency -- Iraq -- History -- 21st century 5. Counterinsurgency -- Malaya -- History -- 20th century 6. Counterinsurgency -- Government policy -- United States 7. Counterinsurgency -- Vietnam -- History -- 20th century 8. Counterinsurgency -- Afghanistan -- History -- 21st century

ISBN 1595588744; 9781595588746

LC 2012049114

In this book about the U.S. Iraq war, Gian Gentile "argues that the U.S. military's appropriation of COIN [counterinsurgency], a strategy with a long and fraught history, as the author explains, was a dangerously misguided attempt 'to refight the Vietnam War—but this time in Iraq.' COIN, in Gentile's estimation, is little more than 'a recipe for perpetual war.'" (Publishers Weekly)

Includes bibliographical references and index

Hedges, Chris

War is a force that gives us meaning. PublicAffairs 2002 211p $23   **355.02**

1. War

ISBN 1-58648-049-9

LC 2002-68136

"This should be required reading in this post-9/11 world." Libr J
Includes bibliographical references

Latiff, Robert H.

Future war; preparing for the new global battlefield. by Robert H. Latiff. Alfred A. Knopf 2017 192 p. (hardcover) $25   **355.02**

1. War -- Forecasting 2. War -- Ethical aspects 3. Military art and science -- History 4. War -- Moral and ethical aspects 5. Military art and science -- Moral and ethical aspects 6. Military art and science -- United States -- History -- 21st century

ISBN 9781101947609; 9781101947616

LC 2017002411

In this book, author Robert H. Latiff "maps out the changing ways of war and the weapons technologies we will use to fight them, seeking to describe the ramifications of those changes and what it will mean in the future to be a soldier. He also recognizes that the fortunes of a nation are inextricably linked with its national defense, and how its citizens understand the importance of when, how, and according to what rules we fight." (Publisher's note)

"This is a quick and stimulating read, and its focus on ethics makes it an important part of the growing literature related to managing the continuing acceleration of technological development." Pub Wkly

Includes bibliographical references and index

Ruane, Kevin

Churchill and the bomb in war and Cold War; Kevin Ruane. Bloomsbury Academic, an imprint of Bloomsbury Publishing Plc 2016 xxi, 402 p.p illustrations (hardback) $34 **355.02**
1. Cold war 2. Atomic bomb 3. Nuclear warfare -- History -- 20th century 4. Great Britain -- Politics and government -- 1936-1945 5. Great Britain -- Politics and government -- 1945-1964 6. Nuclear weapons -- Great Britain -- History -- 20th century
ISBN 9781472523389; 9781472530806

LC 2016000484

This book "explores a still neglected aspect of Winston Churchill's career--his relationship with and thinking on nuclear weapons. [Author] Kevin Ruane shows how Churchill went from regarding the bomb as a weapon of war in the struggle with Nazi Germany to viewing it as a weapon of communist containment (and even punishment) in the early Cold War before, in the 1950s, advocating and arguably pioneering what would become known as 'mutually assured destruction' as the key to preventing the Cold War flaring into a calamitous nuclear war." (Publisher's note)

"An important story very well told." Choice

Includes bibliographical references (pages 373-388) and index

Scahill, Jeremy, 1974-

Dirty wars; the world is a battlefield. Jeremy Scahill. Nation Books 2013 680 p. (hbk.) $29.99 **355.02**
1. Military intelligence 2. Terrorism -- Prevention 3. Military art and science 4. United States -- History, Military -- 21st century 5. United States -- Military policy -- History -- 21st century 6. Targeted killing -- United States -- History -- 21st century 7. United States -- Military policy -- Moral and ethical aspects 8. Intelligence service -- United States -- History -- 21st century 9. Special operations (Military science) -- United States -- History -- 21st century 10. Terrorism -- Prevention -- United States -- Government policy -- History -- 21st century
ISBN 156858671X; 9781568586717

LC 2012051769

In this book, author Jeremy Scahill "questions the legality and command methods of the ongoing war against al-Qaida. Focusing on the career of Anwar al Awlaki, an American citizen and reported al-Qaida leader killed by a drone in Yemen, and the evolution of special forces-led global strikes, the author seeks to establish his case that Barack Obama's military policies are best seen as a continuation of the policies of George W. Bush." (Kirkus Reviews)

Includes bibliographical references (pages 531-613) and index

★ **Sleepwalking** to armageddon; the threat of nuclear annihilation. edited by Helen Caldicott. The New Press 2017 xviii, 232 p.p (hardcover: alk. paper) $25.95 **355.02**
1. Arms control 2. Nuclear warfare 3. Nuclear weapons 4. Nuclear disarmament 5. Nuclear warfare -- Prevention 6. World politics -- 21st century
ISBN 9781620972465

LC 2017004869

In this book, editor and activist Helen Caldicott "assembles the world's leading nuclear scientists and thought leaders to assess the political and scientific dimensions of the threat of nuclear war today. Chapters address the size and distribution of the current global nuclear arsenal, the history and politics of nuclear weapons, the culture of modern-day weapons labs, the militarization of space, and the dangers of combining artificial intelligence with nuclear weaponry." (Publisher's note)

Includes bibliographical references (pages 209-226).

Wilson, Ward

Five myths about nuclear weapons; Ward Wilson. Houghton Mifflin Harcourt 2013 208 p. $22 **355.02**
1. Arms control 2. Nuclear warfare 3. Nuclear weapons 4. Strategy 5. Nuclear weapons -- Psychological aspects
ISBN 054785787X; 9780547857879

LC 2012017322

This book, by Ward Wilson, offers a "rethinking of the power and purpose of nuclear weapons--and a call for radical action. Nuclear weapons have always been a serious but seemingly insoluble problem: while they're obviously dangerous, they are also, apparently, necessary. This . . . study shows why five central arguments promoting nuclear weapons are, in essence, myths." (Publisher's note)

"This slim, persuasively argued, tightly written book provides much food for thought." Booklist

355.07 Military research and development

Roach, Mary, 1959-

★ **Grunt**; The Curious Science of Humans at War. Mary Roach. W W Norton & Co Inc 2016 256 p. illustrations $26.95 **355.07**
1. War 2. Soldiers -- Psychology
ISBN 0393245446; 9780393245448

LC 2016008754

Carnegie Medal Longlist: Nonfiction (2017)

This book, by Mary Roach, examines "the science behind some of a soldier's most challenging adversaries--panic, exhaustion, heat, noise--and introduces us to the scientists who seek to conquer them. Roach samples caffeinated meat, sniffs an archival sample of a World War II stink bomb, and stays up all night with the crew tending the missiles on the nuclear submarine USS Tennessee." (Publisher's note)

"Roach's book is not for the squeamish or those who envision war as a glorious enterprise; it is a captivating look at the lengths scientists go to in order to reduce the horrors of war." Pub Wkly

Includes bibliographical references (pages [277]-285).

355.009 Military science – History, geographic treatment, biography

Matloff, Judith

No friends but the mountains; dispatches from the world's violent highlands. Judith Matloff. Basic Books 2017 viii, 253 p.p maps (hardback) $27 **355.009**
1. Violence -- History 2. Mountain life -- Political aspects -- History 3. Civil war -- History 4. Ethnic conflict -- History 5. Social conflict -- History 6. Uplands -- Political aspects -- History 7. Military history, Modern -- 20th century 8. Military history,

Modern -- 21st century 9. Mountains -- Political aspects -- History
ISBN 9780465097883; 9781541698079

LC 2016043569

In this book about remote mountain communities, author Judith Matloff "introduces us to Albanian teenagers involved in ancient blood feuds; Mexican peasants hunting down violent poppy growers; and Jihadists who have resisted the Russian military for decades. At every stop, Matloff reminds us that the drugs, terrorism, and instability cascading down the mountainside affect us all." (Publisher's note)

"A tightly focused study of mountain societies that hints at future conflicts." Kirkus

Includes bibliographical references (pages 227-238) and index.

355.1   Military life and customs

Farley, Janet I.

Military life 101; basic training for new military families. Janet I. Farley. Rowan & Littlefield 2016 228 p. illustrations (ebook) $44.99; (cloth: alk. paper) $36.00   **355.1**
1. Military spouses 2. United States -- Armed forces -- Military life 3. Military spouses -- United States -- Handbooks, manuals, etc 4. United States -- Armed Forces -- Military life -- Handbooks, manuals, etc 5. Families of military personnel -- United States -- Handbooks, manuals, etc
ISBN 9781442256026; 144225601X; 9781442256019

LC 2015050849

In this book, author Janet I. Farley "addresses what to expect from life on the home front in the military and how this career path not only affects the service members but their families. This useful, concise guide effectively introduces new service members and their families to the culturally relevant and need-to- know information required to survive and thrive in the ever-evolving military lifestyle." (Publisher's note)

"Farley... has created an accessible and important guide, suitable for most public libraries—essential for base libraries and libraries in military-service areas." Booklist

Includes bibliographical references and index

Basic training for new military families

Hickman, Joseph

Murder at Camp Delta; a staff sergeant's pursuit of the truth about Guantanamo Bay. Joseph Hickman. Simon & Schuster 2014 240 p. (hardcover: alk. paper) $28   **355.1**
1. Civil rights 2. Prisoners of war 3. Guantanamo Bay Detention Camp 4. War on Terrorism, 2001-2009 5. Guantánamo Bay Detention Camp 6. United States. Marine Corps -- Officers 7. Reporters and reporting -- United States 8. Prisoners -- Civil rights -- United States 9. Political prisoners -- Cuba -- Guantánamo Bay Naval Base 10. Detention of unlawful combatants -- Cuba -- Guantánamo Bay Naval Base
ISBN 9781451650792; 9781451650808

LC 2014012099

This book by Joseph Hickman presents an "account of abuse and secrecy at the Guantánamo Bay military prison. . . . Although Hickman suspected that many detainees were potentially dangerous jihadi, he was disturbed by the unprovoked harassment and abuse handed out by the guards. His unease climaxed in June 2006, when, on his supervisory watch, three inmates died mysteriously." The book recounts Hickman's participation in "a six-year investigation" of the deaths. (Kirkus Reviews)

"Some readers will see this book as a traitorous attack on patriots protecting the United States from fanatics by any means, while others will view it as confirmation from a veteran that an out-of-control government and individuals went way beyond the law—and gained nothing but trouble from it." LJ

Scott, Jeff

Raising children in the military; Cheryl Lawhorne-Scott, Don Philpott, and Jeff Scott. Rowman & Littlefield 2014 224 p. (Military life) (cloth: alk. paper) $36   **355.1**
1. Children of military personnel 2. Military personnel -- United States 3. Child rearing -- United States -- Handbooks, manuals, etc 4. United States -- Armed Forces -- Military life -- Handbooks, manuals, etc 5. Children of military personnel -- United States -- Handbooks, manuals, etc 6. Families of military personnel -- United States -- Handbooks, manuals, etc
ISBN 1442227486; 9781442227484

LC 2013046688

This book by Cheryl Lawhorne-Scott, Don Philpott, and Jeff Scott, part of the Military Life series, describes how "[m]ilitary life places unique demands on military families with children including frequent moves, disruptions in schooling, family separation, health care issues, loss of friends. . . . It also covers other critical issues such as wellness, family solidarity, benefits, insurance and problems such as addiction and domestic violence." (Publisher's note)

"This is a helpful guide aimed at the special challenges of military families." Booklist

355.3   Organization and personnel of military forces

Geraghty, Tony

Soldiers of fortune; a history of the mercenary in modern warfare. Pegasus Books 2009 392p il $27.95   **355.3**
1. Mercenary soldiers
ISBN 978-1-60598-048-5; 1-60598-048-X

"Covering the 1960s to the present, with revealing interviews, Geraghty looks at the virtues and failings of the world's second-oldest profession. . . . This serious study should find its way to most readers of military history." Libr J

Includes bibliographical references

Harris, Shane

@WAR; the rise of the military-Internet complex. Shane Harris. Houghton Mifflin Harcourt 2014 304 p. (hardcover) $27   **355.3**
1. War 2. Technology 3. Military art and science 4. Information warfare -- United States 5. United States. National Security Agency 6. Cyberterrorism -- Prevention -- Government policy 7. Computer crimes -- Prevention -- Government policy 8. Cyberspace -- Security measures -- Government policy 9. United States. Strategic Command (2002-). Cyber Command
ISBN 0544251792; 9780544251793

LC 2014016741

Author "Shane Harris delves into the frontlines of America's new cyber war. As recent revelations have shown, government agencies are joining with tech giants like Google and Facebook to collect vast amounts of information. The military has also formed a new alliance with tech and finance companies to patrol cyberspace, and Harris offers a deeper glimpse into this partnership than we have ever seen before." (Publisher's note)

Includes bibliographical references and index

Jacobsen, Annie

Phenomena; the secret history of the U.S. government's

investigations into extrasensory perception and psychokinesis. Annie Jacobsen. Little, Brown & Co. 2017 viii, 527 p.p illustrations (some color) (hardcover) $28   **355.3**

1. Military research -- United States 2. Parapsychology -- Military aspects -- United States 3. Psychokinesis 4. Extrasensory perception 5. Military research -- United States -- History
ISBN 9780316349369; 9780316349345

LC 2016959021

This book, by Annie Jacobsen, reveals how, "for more than forty years, the U.S. government has researched extrasensory perception, using it in attempts to locate hostages, fugitives, secret bases, and downed fighter jets, to divine other nations' secrets, and even to predict future threats to national security. The intelligence agencies and military services involved include CIA, DIA, NSA, DEA, the Navy, Air Force, and Army-and even the Joint Chiefs of Staff." (Publisher's note)

"Jacobsen artfully deals card after dutifully researched card in her enthralling reportage on one of America's most curious defense endeavors." Pub Wkly

Includes bibliographical references (pages 493-507) and index.

Lawhorne-Scott, Cheryl

★ **Military** mental health care; a guide for service members, veterans, families, and community. Cheryl Lawhorne and Don Philpott. Rowman & Littlefield Publishers, Inc. 2012 240 p. (Military life) (cloth: alk. paper) $34.95   **355.3**

1. Mental health services 2. Military personnel -- Health and hygiene 3. Psychology, Military -- Handbooks, manuals, etc 4. Veterans' families -- United States -- Handbooks, manuals, etc 5. Soldiers -- Mental health -- United States -- Handbooks, manuals, etc 6. Veterans -- Mental health -- United States -- Handbooks, manuals, etc
ISBN 1442220937; 9781442220935; 9781442220942

LC 2012034879

This book is a "reference guide on mental health for returning veterans. Chapters cover problems (e.g., PTSD, head injuries), symptoms (e.g., stress, anger, depression), social issues (e.g., suicide, homelessness, family relationships), resilience, and wellness. Self-help sections include bulleted lists, suggested websites, and resources from the Veterans Administration and other service agencies." (Library Journal)

Includes bibliographical references and index

Paglen, Trevor, 1974-

Blank spots on the map; the dark geography of the Pentagon's secret world. Dutton/Penguin Group 2009 324p il map   **355.3**

1. Military bases 2. Intelligence service -- United States
ISBN 9780525951018

LC 2008042862

The author "explores the clandestine activities of the U.S. military and the CIA, giving readers a thorough and provocative tour of places that officially do not exist. Paglen has a brisk reporting style and is an engaging storyteller. His journey into what he calls the 'black world' of classified locations—from research facilities to secret prisons—this time takes him across the country and around the world." Libr J

Includes bibliographical references

355.4   Military operations

Gaddis, John Lewis, 1941-

On grand strategy; John Lewis Gaddis. Penguin Group USA 2018 384 p. $26   **355.4**

1. Strategy -- History 2. Military art and science
ISBN 1594203512; 9781594203510

"John Lewis Gaddis, the distinguished historian of the Cold War, has for almost two decades co-taught grand strategy at Yale University. . . . Now, in On Grand Strategy, Gaddis reflects on what he has learned. In chapters extending from the ancient world through World War II, Gaddis assesses grand strategic theory and practice in Herodotus, Thucydides, Sun Tzu, . . . and Isaiah Berlin." (Publisher's note)

Kilcullen, David

The **accidental** guerrilla; fighting small wars in the midst of a big one. Oxford University Press 2009 xxviii, 346p il map $27.95   **355.4**

1. Guerrilla warfare 2. War on terrorism
ISBN 978-0-19-536834-5

LC 2008-54870

This "excellent book has an anthropologist's sense of social dynamics and a reporter's eye for telling detail. . . . [The author's] account of how the Americans use soft and hard power to pacify parts of eastern Afghanistan . . . should be compulsory reading in military academies on both sides of the Atlantic." Economist

Includes bibliographical references

355.409   Military operations – History

Nolan, Cathal J., 1956-

The **allure** of battle; a history of how wars have been won and lost. Cathal J. Nolan. Oxford University Press 2017 viii, 709 p.p illustrations, maps (hardcover: alk. paper) $34.95   **355.409**

1. War 2. Battles 3. Military history
ISBN 9780195383782

LC 2016016391

This book, by Cathal J. Nolan, "examines the great battles, tracing what he calls 'short-war thinking,' the hope that victory might be swift and wars brief. As he proves persuasively, however, such has almost never been the case. . . . Massive conflicts, . . . beginning with Napoleon and continuing until 1945, have consisted of and been determined by prolonged stalemate and attrition, industrial wars in which the determining factor has been not military but matériel." (Publisher's note)

"Nonetheless, this is one of the most valuable military histories in years. A must - read for students of military history." Kirkus

Includes bibliographical references (pages 583-652) and index.

355.5   Military training

Ambinder, Marc

The **brink**; president Reagan and the nuclear war scare of 1983. Marc Ambinder. Simon & Schuster 2018 384 p. $27   **355.5**

1. Nuclear warfare -- United States 2. Nuclear weapons -- Government policy -- United States -- History -- 20th century
ISBN 1476760373; 9781476760377

This book, by Marc Ambinder, offers the "story of the 1983 war game that triggered a tense, brittle period of nuclear brinkmanship between the United States and the former Soviet Union. . . . Ambinder explains the anxious period between the United States and the Soviet Union from 1982 to 1984, with the 'Able Archer '83' war game as the fulcrum of the tension." (Publisher's note)

Man, John

Ninja; 1,000 years of the shadow warrior. John Man. William Morrow 2013 304 p. (hardcover) $25.99   **355.5**
1. Ninja 2. Ninjutsu 3. Ninja -- History 4. Ninjutsu -- History
ISBN 0062222023; 9780062222022

LC 2012031912

This book, by John Man, offers a popular history "of the Japanese stealth assassins.... [The book] is a ... blend of mythology, anthropology, travelogue, and history of the legendary shadow warriors. Spies, assassins, saboteurs, and secret agents, Ninja have become the subject of countless legends that continue to enthrall us in modern movies, video games, and comics--and their arts are still practiced in our time by dedicated acolytes who study the ancient techniques." (Publisher's note)

Includes bibliographical references and index

355.6 Military administration

Vogel, Steve

The **Pentagon**; a history: the untold story of the wartime race to build the Pentagon--and to restore it sixty years later. Random House 2007 xxv, 626p il map $32.95   **355.6**
1. Public buildings -- United States 2. United States -- Dept. of Defense 3. Pentagon (Arlington, Va.: Building)
ISBN 978-1-4000-6303-1; 1-4000-6303-5

LC 2006-50873

Vogel's "work recounts the construction of one of the world's most iconic buildings—the Pentagon. But more compelling by far, he relates the human stories underlying this huge construction effort.... All this would of itself be enough to warrant a book but Vogel plunges on to an appropriate second story: the terrorist assault of 9/11 and the Pentagon's subsequent resurrection. This section of the book, due perhaps to the proximity of the event, is all the more compelling." New York Post

Includes bibliographical references

355.8 Military equipment and supplies (Mat??riel)

Baggott, Jim

The **first** war of physics; the secret history of the atom bomb, 1939-1949. [by] Jim Baggott. Pegasus Books 2010 576p il $35   **355.8**
1. Atomic bomb
ISBN 978-1-60598-084-3; 1-60598-084-6

First published 2009 in the United Kingdom with title: Atomic

"Baggott contributes a novel perspective to the story, looking at the Anglo-American, German, and Soviet atomic programs, and as such provides a broad thematic history." Libr J

Includes bibliographical references

Levy, Joel

Fifty Weapons That Changed the Course of History; Joel Levy. Firefly Books Ltd 2014 224 p. illustrations (some color) $29.95   **355.8**
1. Weapons 2. Military history
ISBN 1770854266; 9781770854260

Author Joel Levy presents this "guide to the arms and armaments that have had the greatest impact on the development of human civilization. Like the other titles in this series, the book organizes the weapons into brief illustrated chapters. The stories span human history, from our hunter-gatherer ancestors who devised the spear and the wheel, which brought about the war chariot, to gunpowder, which democratized warfare and has been the basis for almost every weapon used in war from that point on." (Publisher's note)

"The format, layout, and liveliness of the text enhance its readability. A list of further reading, useful websites, and an accurate index further the volume's usefulness. With its modest price, this book is recommended for a wide range of public, school, and academic libraries." Booklist

Light, Michael

100 suns, 1945-1962. Knopf 2003 208p il $49.95   **355.8**
1. Nuclear weapons -- Pictorial works
ISBN 1-4000-4113-9

LC 2003-106275

"The 'suns' Light presents to readers in this ... photography collection are manmade: aboveground atomic detonations captured on film both in the Nevada desert and at sea, terrifyingly beautiful images that remind readers of the apocalyptic might of nuclear weapons." Booklist

Includes bibliographical references

Pollack, Kenneth M.

Unthinkable; Iran, the Bomb, and American Strategy. Kenneth M. Pollack. Simon & Schuster 2013 560 p. illustration, maps $30   **355.8**
1. Nuclear weapons 2. Iran -- Foreign relations -- United States 3. United States -- Foreign relations -- Iran 4. Nuclear weapons -- Iran 5. Nuclear nonproliferation -- Iran 6. Iran -- Politics and government -- 21st century 7. Nuclear arms control -- Government policy -- United States
ISBN 1476733929; 9781476733920

LC 2013431171

In this book on U.S. relations with Iran, author Kenneth Pollack "clearly states his preference for containment but not before thoroughly exploring the pros and cons of a military attack (including one by Israel) and not without conceding the dangers of the policy he recommends. As the Cold War demonstrated, the path of nuclear deterrence and containment is a difficult slog, but this choice ... is likely less bad than the alternative." (Kirkus Reviews)

Includes bibliographical references (pages 429-512) and index

Preston, Diana

Before the fallout; from Marie Curie to Hiroshima. Walker 2005 438p il $27   **355.8**
1. Atomic bomb
ISBN 0-8027-1445-5

LC 2004-61953

"Avidly researched and gracefully constructed, Preston's revelatory history is rich in telling moments, powerful personalities, intense confrontations, and indelible images of the devastation delivered by nuclear weapons, our Damoclean sword." Booklist

Includes bibliographical references

356 Specific kinds of military forces and warfare

Carney, John T.

No room for error; the covert operations of America's special tactics units from Iran to Afghanistan. {by} John T. Carney Jr. and Benjamin F. Schemmer. Ballantine Books 2003 334p il map $25.95   **356**
1. Military art and science 2. United States -- Army -- Special Forces
ISBN 0-345-45333-6

LC 2002-28158

The author's "dramatic tales place special operations history in perspective, particularly as the war in Afghanistan has been led by special forces units." Publ Wkly

Includes bibliographical references

Couch, Dick

Sua sponte; the forging of a modern American Ranger. Dick Couch. Berkley Books 2012 364 p.   **356**

1. Commando troops 2. United States. Army 3. Special forces (Military science) -- United States 4. United States. Army. Ranger Regiment, 75th 5. United States. Army -- Commando troops -- Training of 6. United States. Army. Ranger Regiment, 75th -- Recruiting, enlistment, etc

ISBN 0425247589; 9780425247587

LC 2011038693

This book, by Dick Couch, profiles the U.S. Army Rangers. "They stand alone, even among our other Special Operations forces, as the most active brigade-sized force in the current Global War on Terrorism. . . . Granted . . . access to the training of this highly-restricted component of America's Special Operations Forces in a time of war, . . . Couch tells the personal story of the young men who begin this difficult and dangerous journey to become a Ranger." (Publisher's note)

Halevi, Yossi Klein

Like dreamers; the story of the Israeli paratroopers who reunited Jerusalem and divided a nation. Yossi Klein Halevi. HarperCollins Publishers 2013 608 p. (hardcover: alk. paper) $35   **356**

1. Israel -- History 2. Israel-Arab War, 1967 3. Arab-Israeli conflict -- 1967-1973 4. Arab-Israeli conflict -- 1973-1993 5. Israel -- Parachute troops -- Biography 6. Israel. Tseva haganah le-Yiśra'el -- Parachute troops -- History -- 20th century 7. Israel. Tseva haganah le-Yiśra'el. Ḥel-ha-tsanḥanim -- History -- 20th century

ISBN 0060545763; 9780060545765; 9780060545772; 9780062274823

LC 2013018850

National Jewish Book Awards: Jewish Book of the Year (2013)

In this book, author Yossi Klein Halevi, "interweaves the stories of a group of 1967 paratroopers who reunited Jerusalem, tracing the history of Israel and the divergent ideologies shaping it from the Six-Day War to the present. Following the lives of seven young members from the 55th Paratroopers Reserve Brigade . . . Halevi reveals how this band of brothers played pivotal roles in shaping Israel's destiny long after their historic victory." (Publisher's note)

Includes bibliographical references

Haney, Eric L.

★ **Inside** Delta Force; the story of America's elite counter-terrorist unit. Delacorte Press 2002 324p il hardcover o.p. pa $14   **356**

1. United States -- Army -- Delta Force

ISBN 0-385-33603-9; 0-385-33936-4 pa

LC 2001-58408

The author relates his "experiences during the formation and early operations of 1st Special Forces Operational Detachment-Delta. . . . He served three times in Beirut guarding the American ambassador, participated in the invasion of Grenada, served in several Central American countries and narrowly escaped death during the abortive rescue attempt of the American hostages in Iran. . . . Readers of other special forces memoirs will find this one distinctive for Haney's attention to interservice rivalries . . . that he believes compromised several missions, as well as for Haney's nuanced, often disgusted descriptions of the human cost of war." Publ Wkly

Mazzetti, Mark

The **way** of the knife; the CIA, a secret army, and a war at the ends of the Earth. Mark Mazzetti. The Penguin Press 2013 400 p. $29.95   **356**

1. Terrorism 2. Military policy -- United States 3. United States. Dept. of Defense 4. Interagency coordination -- United States 5. United States. Central Intelligence Agency 6. United States -- Military policy -- Decision making 7. National security -- United States -- Decision making

ISBN 1594204802; 9781594204807

LC 2013006820

Washington Post Notable Nonfiction (2013)

In this book, "Pulitzer Prize-winning New York Times national security correspondent [Mark] Mazzetti demonstrates in . . . detail how the new-style warfare approved by both George W. Bush and Barack Obama has led to controversial assassinations by the U.S. government and blowback yielding new terrorists determined to harm American citizens." (Kirkus Reviews)

Includes bibliographical references and index

357   Mounted forces and warfare

Cotterell, Arthur

Chariot; from chariot to tank, the astounding rise and fall of the world's first war machine. Overlook Press 2005 344p il map $29.95   **357**

1. Military art and science

ISBN 1-58567-667-5

LC 2004-65980

"This work is a welcome addition to a collection specializing in military history or ancient history but will appeal to general readers as well because the writing is accessible despite the plethora of detail." Libr J

Includes bibliographical references

358   Air and other specialized forces and warfare; engineering and related services

Engelberg, Stephen

Germs; America's secret war against biological weapons. Judith Miller, Stephen Engelberg, William Broad. Simon & Schuster 2001 382p $27; pa $14   **358**

1. Biological warfare

ISBN 0-684-87158-0; 0-684-87159-9 pa

LC 2001-42690

Three reporters survey the history of biological weapons and recount incidents of their use by terrorist groups. They explain why advances in biology and the spread of germ weapons poses grave risks as countries such as Iran, Iraq and North Korea continually engage in research

Includes bibliographical references

Guillemin, Jeanne

★ **Biological** weapons; from the invention of state-sponsored programs to contemporary bioterrorism. Columbia University Press 2005 258p $75; pa $22.95   **358**

1. Biological warfare

ISBN 0-231-12942-4; 0-231-12943-2 pa

LC 2004-51911

This is a "history of biological weaponry, beginning with the British, American and Japanese programs that predate WWII. . . . Admirably free of finger-pointing, shrillness and Luddite tendencies, the book ranks high as a historical introduction to the subject and a handbook on contemporary remedies." Publ Wkly

Includes bibliographical references

Lockwood, Jeffrey A.

Six-legged soldiers; using insects as weapons of war. Oxford University Press 2009 xx, 377p il $27.95   **358**

1. Biological warfare 2. Insects as carriers of disease

ISBN 978-0-19-533305-3; 0-19-533305-5

LC 2008-6935

"Both science and military history buffs will learn much from Lockwood." Publ Wkly

Includes bibliographical references (p. 315-322)

Tucker, Jonathan B.

★ **War** of nerves; chemical warfare from World War I to al-Qaeda. Pantheon Books 2006 479p il $30; pa $17.95 **358**

1. Chemical warfare

ISBN 0-375-42229-3; 978-0-375-42229-4; 1-4000-3233-4 pa; 978-1-4000-3233-4 pa

LC 2005-50053

This "book makes a sobering case for a less poisonous world." N Y Times Book Rev

Includes bibliographical references

358.34   Chemical warfare

Emery, Theo

Hellfire boys; the birth of the U.S. Chemical Warfare Service and the race for the world's deadliest weapons. Theo Emery. Little, Brown & Co. 2017 xxi, 535 p.p illustrations (hardcover) $29   **358.34**

1. Chemical warfare 2. World War, 1914-1918 3. World War, 1914-1918 -- United States 4. World War, 1914-1918 -- Chemical warfare 5. United States. Army. Chemical Warfare Service -- History 6. Chemical warfare -- United States -- History -- 20th century 7. Chemical warfare -- Research -- United States -- History -- 20th century

ISBN 9780316264105; 9780316264099

LC 2017942376

In this book, author Theo Emery "shows how World War I quickly spiraled into a chemists' war, one led by the companies of young American engineers-turned-soldiers who would soon become known as the 'Hellfire Boys.' As gas attacks began to mark the heaviest and most devastating battles, these brave and brilliant men were on the front lines, racing against the clock-and the Germans-to protect, develop, and unleash the latest weapons of mass destruction." (Publisher's note)

"This is a timely and often unsettling examination of a previously well-hidden government program." Booklist

Includes bibliographical references (pages 443-519) and index.

358.4   Air forces and warfare

Jacobsen, Annie

Area 51; an uncensored history of America's top secret military base. Annie Jacobsen. Little, Brown 2011 523p il map $27.99   **358.4**

1. Area 51 (Nev.)

ISBN 0-316-13294-2; 978-0-316-13294-7

Written by Annie Jacobsen, "this the first book based on interviews with eye witnesses to Area 51 history, which makes it the seminal work on the subject. Filled with formerly classified information that has never been accurately decoded for the public, [it] weaves the mysterious activities of the top-secret base into a gripping narrative, showing that facts are often more fantastic than fiction, especially when the distinction is almost impossible to make." (Publisher's note)

"Seventy-five miles north of Las Vegas sits a land parcel in the middle of the desert. Called Area 51, the parcel is just outside of the abandoned Nevada Test and Training Range, where more than 100 atmospheric bomb tests were conducted in the 1950s. Officially, the U.S. government has never acknowledged the existence of Area 51. Unofficially, it has become a place associated with conspiracy theories, alien landings and tiny spaceships. Journalist Annie Jacobsen . . . [reveals] that the site has remained classified for many years — not because of aliens or spaceships, but because the government once used the site for top-secret nuclear testing and weapons development. . . Jacobsen details how several agencies — including the Atomic Energy Commission, the Department of Defense and the CIA — once used the site to conduct controversial and secretive research on aircraft and pilot-related projects." NPR

Includes bibliographical references

Scahill, Jeremy, 1974-

The **assassination** complex; inside the government's secret drone warfare program. by Jeremy Scahill and the staff of The Intercept. Simon & Schuster 2016 256 p. illustrations (ebook) $20.99; $30   **358.4**

1. National security -- United States 2. Terrorism -- Prevention -- United States 3. Drone aircraft -- Government policy -- United States 4. Military intelligence -- United States -- Evaluation 5. Terrorism -- Prevention -- United States -- Decision making 6. Drone aircraft -- Moral and ethical aspects -- United States 7. Targeted killing -- United States -- History -- 21st century 8. United States -- Military policy -- Moral and ethical aspects 9. Targeted killing -- Moral and ethical aspects -- United States 10. Military intelligence -- Technological innovation -- Moral and ethical aspects

ISBN 9781501144158; 1501144138; 9781501144134

LC 2016001115

This book, by Jeremy Scahill and the staff of The Intercept, "expose stunning new details about America's secret assassination policy, . . . [allowing] us to understand at last the circumstances under which the US government grants itself the right to sentence individuals to death without the established checks and balances of arrest, trial, and appeal." (Publisher's note)

"There's nothing revelatory here—the drone assassinations and their problems are well-known—but this pointillistic portrait provides illuminating new detail and insight." Pub Wkly

Includes bibliographical references (pages 191-212) and index.

Wildsmith, Snow

Joining the United States Air Force; a handbook. Snow Wildsmith. McFarland & Co. 2012 x, 229 p.p (Joining the military) (pbk.: alk. paper) $25   **358.4**

1. Employment 2. United States -- Armed forces 3. Military personnel -- United States 4. United States. Air Force -- Vocational guidance

ISBN 0786447583; 9780786447589

LC 2012010677

Author Snow Wildsmith presents a book on the U.S. Air Force. "This book is for the teenager or young adult who is interested in enlisting in the United States Air Force. It will walk him or her through the enlistment and recruit training process: making the decision to join the military, talking to recruiters, getting qualified, preparing for and learning what to expect at basic recruit training." (Publisher's note)

Includes bibliographical references and index

359   Sea forces and warfare

Crowley, Roger

Empires of the sea; the siege of Malta, the battle of Lepanto, and the contest for the center of the world. Random House 2008 336p il map $30; pa $16   **359**

1. Naval battles 2. Christianity and other religions 3. Europe -- Naval history 4. Islam -- Relations -- Christianity

ISBN 978-1-4000-6624-7; 1-4000-6624-7; 978-0-8129-7764-6 pa; 0-8129-7764-5 pa

LC 2007-33794

This book "is well-crafted narrative history in the best sense of the word, lucid, colorful, and beautifully written. . . . Crowley draws on a wealth of sources reflecting a multiplicity of viewpoints and the results are convincing." Journal of Military History

Includes bibliographical references

Grant, R. G.

Battle at sea; 3,000 years of naval warfare. written by R.G. Grant. DK Pub. 2008 360p il map $40   **359**

1. Naval history 2. Naval art and science

ISBN 978-0-7566-3973-0

LC 2008-10019

"This oversized book . . . is perhaps the most comprehensive one-volume history of war at sea, covering engagements large and small, from 1200 B.C.E. to the present day. . . . Highly recommended." Libr J

★ **Naval** warfare; an international encyclopedia. edited by Spencer C. Tucker; associate editors, John Fredriksen {et al.}; introduction by James C. Bradford. ABC-CLIO 2002 3v il maps set $295   **359**

1. Reference books 2. Naval art and science -- Encyclopedias

ISBN 1-57607-219-3

LC 2002-4401

This set "explores the history of combat at sea, from ancient Greek galleys to the sophisticated ships of the U.S. Sixth Fleet. More than 1500 signed entries . . . describe the three key eras: Age of Galley Warfare, Age of Sail, and Age of Steam or Modern Era. . . . Each new development is examined in painstaking detail." Libr J

Includes bibliographical references

Stavridis, James

Sea power; the history and geopolitics of the world's oceans. Admiral James Stavridis, USN (Ret.) Penguin Press 2017 363 p. (hardcover) $28   **359**

1. Sea power 2. United States -- Naval history 3. Naval history 4. Sea-power -- History 5. Geopolitics -- History

ISBN 9780735220591; 9780735220607; 073522059X

LC 2016056758

In this book, author James Stavridis "takes us with him on a tour of the world's oceans from the admiral's chair, showing us how the geography of the oceans has shaped the destiny of nations, and how naval power has in a real sense made the world we live in today, and will shape the world we live in tomorrow. . . . [The book] is marvelous naval history, giving us fresh insight into great naval engagements." (Publisher's note)

"A highly readable, instructive look at the role of the oceans in our civilization, past and present." Kirkus

Includes bibliographical references (pages [347]-351) and index.

Toll, Ian W.

★ **Six** frigates; the epic history of the founding of the U.S. Navy. Norton 2006 560p il map $27.95   **359**

1. United States -- Navy

ISBN 978-0-393-05847-5; 0-393-05847-6

LC 2006-20769

This is "a must-read for fans of naval history and the early American Republic." Publ Wkly

Includes bibliographical references

359.9   Specialized combat forces; engineering and related services

Couch, Dick

The **warrior** elite; the forging of Seal Class 228. photographs by Cliff Hollenbeck. Crown 2001 319p il hardcover o.p. pa $14.95   **359.9**

1. United States -- Navy -- Sea Air Land Team

ISBN 1-4000-4695-5 pa

LC 2001-28368

This is an account of the Basic Underwater Demolition course, (BUD) training for the U.S. Navy Sea Air Land Team (SEALs)

This book "is unique. Couch, a Vietnam-era SEAL and retired naval reserve captain was given the most complete access possible. . . . On view is much serious thought by serious thinkers on the making of warriors at the dawn of the twenty-first century." Booklist

Parrish, Thomas

★ The **submarine**; a history. Viking 2004 576p il $29.95; pa $16   **359.9**

1. Submarines

ISBN 0-670-03313-8; 0-14-303519-3 pa

LC 2003-70515

"This brilliant, dramatic account of submarines and the men who sailed in them is a required acquisition for every military history collection." Choice

Includes bibliographical references

359.93   Submarine forces

Dean, Josh

The **taking** of K-129; how the CIA used Howard Hughes to steal a Russian sub in the most daring covert operation in history. Josh Dean. Dutton, an imprint of Penguin Random House LLC 2017 431 p. (hardcover) $28   **359.93**

1. Submarine warfare 2. Nuclear submarines 3. Historical literature 4. Jennifer Project 5. K-129 (Submarine) 6. Glomar Explorer (Ship) 7. Submarine disasters -- Soviet Union 8. United States. Central Intelligence Agency -- History 9. Soviet Union. Voenno-Morskoĭ Flot -- Submarine forces -- History

ISBN 9781101984437; 9781101984444

LC 2017011991

This book, by Josh Dean, is "an incredible true tale of espionage and engineering set at the height of the Cold War . . . about how the CIA, the U.S. Navy, and America's most eccentric mogul spent six years and nearly a billion dollars to steal the nuclear-armed Soviet submarine K-129 after it had sunk to the bottom of the Pacific Ocean; all while the Russians were watching." (Publisher's note)

"Dean delivers an engaging rendition of the high-profile espionage effort." Booklist

Includes bibliographical references (pages 415-420) and index.

359.984 Special warfare services

Henican, Ellis

Worth dying for; a Navy Seal's call to a nation. Rorke Denver and Ellis Henican. Howard Books, an imprint of Simon & Schuster, Inc. 2016 230 p. (hardcover) $24   **359.984**

1. Heroes and heroines 2. Military policy -- United States 3. Military personnel -- United States 4. Terrorism -- Prevention 5. United States. Navy. SEALs 6. War on Terrorism, 2001-2009 7. United States. Navy -- Commando troops

ISBN 1501124110; 9781501124112; 9781501125683

LC 2015034024

In this book, by Rorke Denver and Ellis Henican, "tackles the questions that have emerged about America's past decade at war—from what makes a hero to why we fight and what it does to us. Heroes are not always the guys who jump on grenades. Sometimes, they are the snipers who decide to hold their fire, the wounded operators who find fresh ways to contribute, or the wives who keep the families together back home." (Publisher's note)

361.7 Private action

Addams, Jane

Twenty years at Hull-House.   **361.7**

1. Authors 2. Philanthropists 3. Hull House (Chicago, Ill.) 4. Essayists 5. Pacifists 6. Social welfare leaders 7. Nobel laureates for peace 8. Chicago (Ill.) -- Social conditions

ISBN 9780486457499

"This classic of the reform era is actually an autobiography of the woman who practically founded social service work in this country. . . . It tells her life story, but the greater part of it is devoted to the setting up of Chicago's Hull House, the first settlement house in the United States." Guide to Read in Am Hist

Callahan, David

The **givers**; wealth, power, and philanthropy in a new gilded age. David Callahan. Alfred A. Knopf 2017 343 p. (hardcover) $28.95   **361.7**

1. Rich -- United States 2. Lobbying -- United States 3. Philanthropists -- United States 4. Rich people -- United States 5. Pressure groups -- United States 6. Liberalism -- United States -- History -- 21st century 7. Conservatism -- United States -- History -- 21st century

ISBN 9781101947050; 9781101947067; 9781101971048

LC 2016963048

In this book, author David Callahan charts the rise of new philanthropists "and the ways they are converting the fortunes of a second Gilded Age into influence. He shows how this elite works behind the scenes on education, the environment, science, LGBT rights, and many other issues--with deep impact on government policy. Above all, he shows that the influence of the Givers is only just beginning, as new waves of billionaires like Mark Zuckerberg turn to philanthropy." (Publisher's note)

"An eye-opening view of a vast sector of the economy that lies in the shadows but has undue influence, for ill or good." Kirkus

Includes bibliographical references and index.

Simon, Morgan

Real impact; the new economics of social change. Morgan Simon. Nation Books 2017 viii, 246 p.p (hardback) $26 **361.7**

1. Charities 2. Social change 3. Foreign investments 4. Economic development 5. Social responsibility of business 6. Investments, Foreign -- Moral and ethical aspects

ISBN 9781568588216; 9781568589800

LC 2017005419

In this book, investment professional Morgan Simon "teaches us how to get it right, leveraging the world's resources to truly transform the economy. Over the past seventeen years, Simon has influenced over $150 billion from endowments, families, and foundations. . . . [She] shares her experience as both investor and activist to offer clear strategies for investors, community leaders, and entrepreneurs alike." (Publisher's note)

"A cleareyed case for socially conscious investment, of much interest to those who want their dollars to do good." Kirkus

Includes bibliographical references (pages 227-234) and index.

362 Specific social problems and services

Manguso, Sarah

The **two** kinds of decay. Farrar, Straus and Giroux 2008 184p $22; pa $14   **362**

1. Poets 2. Authors 3. Editors 4. Guillain-Barré syndrome

ISBN 978-0-374-28012-3; 0-374-28012-6; 978-0-312-42844-0 pa; 0-312-42844-8 pa

LC 2008-1766

"What makes this lightning-quick book extraordinary is not just Manguso's deadpan delivery of often unthinkable details, nor her poet's struggle with the damaging metaphors of disease, but the compassion she acquires as she comes to understand her pain in relation to the pain of others." Publ Wkly

362.1 People with illnesses and disabilities

Blumenthal, David

The **heart** of power; health and politics in the Oval Office. [by] David Blumenthal and James A. Morone. University of California Press 2009 484p il $26.95   **362.1**

1. Medical care -- Government policy 2. Presidents -- United States -- Health

ISBN 978-0-520-26030-6; 0-520-26030-9

LC 2008-54361

"More than an excellent primer on American health policy, the book offers a thorough, incisive look at the presidency as an institution and the men who have occupied the office." Publ Wkly

Includes bibliographical references

Encyclopedia of public health; edited by Lester Breslow. Macmillan Ref. USA 2001 4v set $475   **362.1**

1. Reference books 2. Public health -- Encyclopedias

ISBN 0-02-865354-8

LC 2001-31501

"Information on more than 900 programs, services, organizations, health behaviors, and the prevalence, epidemiology, and costs of communicable diseases. Although the work focuses on the United States, there are also references to worldwide problems." Libr J

France, David

★ **How** to survive a plague; The Inside Story of How Citizens and Science Tamed AIDS. by David France. Alfred A. Knopf 2016 640 p. (hardback) $30 **362.1**

1. AIDS (Disease) 2. Gay liberation movement 3. Activism -- United States -- History 4. AIDS activists -- New York (State) -- New York 5. HIV-positive persons -- New York (State) -- New York 6. AIDS (Disease) -- Research -- New York (State) -- New York 7. AIDS (Disease) -- Treatment -- New York (State) -- New York

ISBN 9780307700636

LC 2016010685

Stonewall Book Award, Nonfiction (2017)
Carnegie Medal Longlist: Nonfiction (2017)

"Intimately reported, this is the story of the men and women who, watching their friends and lovers fall, ignored by public officials, religious leaders, and the nation at large, and confronted with shame and hatred, chose to fight for their right to live. We witness the founding of ACT UP and TAG (Treatment Action Group), the rise of an underground drug market in opposition to the prohibitively expensive (and sometimes toxic) AZT, and the gradual movement toward a lifesaving medical breakthrough. . . Expansive yet richly detailed, this is an insider's account of a pivotal moment in the history of American civil rights." (Publisher's note)

"Prepare to have your heart buoyed and broken in this riveting account of the response to the AIDS epidemic that's as educational as it is difficult to put down. Based on thorough research and the author's own experience as a gay man and a reporter in New York when the disease emerged, this book presents the fear, hope, and civil rights struggles of the 1980s and 1990s. . . This highly engaging account is a must-read for anyone interested in epidemiology, civil rights, gay rights, public health, and American history." LJ

Includes bibliographical references and index

Garrett, Laurie

Betrayal of trust; the collapse of global public health. Hyperion 2000 754p il $30; pa $16.95 **362.1**

1. Medical care 2. Public health

ISBN 0-7868-6522-9; 0-7868-8440-1 pa

LC 00-33425

This book examines contemporary "health systems in the former Soviet Union, India, central Africa, and the United States." N Y Times Book Rev

Hurley, Dan

Diabetes rising; how a rare disease became a modern pandemic, and what to do about it. foreword by Zachary T. Bloomgarden. Kaplan Pub. 2010 xxiii, 312p $26.95 **362.1**

1. Diabetes

ISBN 978-1-60714-458-8

LC 2009-29382

The author, "diagnosed at age 18 with type 1 diabetes, recounts the 3500-year history of the disease, its possible causes, and the latest promising treatments and cures with a professional writer's skills and a patient's passion. . . . [This is] a compelling layperson's overview of diabetes research, enlivened by multiple interviews with scientists in the field. Diabetics and those who love them will find this a fascinating and hope-filled read." Libr J

Includes bibliographical references

Kaufman, Sharon R.

--And a time to die; how American hospitals shape the end of life. Scribner 2005 400p $28 **362.1**

1. Death 2. Terminal care -- Ethical aspects

ISBN 0-7432-6476-2

LC 2004-52530

The author "reveals the dilemmas of hospital death in America today: the shift to patients' control of decision making despite the doctors' greater knowledge; the ethics and practical effects of resuscitation versus pain relief; the complexities of assessing 'quality of life' while guessing at the desires of an unconscious patient. . . . This deeply probing study lays bare the cultural and institutional assumptions and rhetoric that frame our search for 'a good death.'" Publ Wkly

Includes bibliographical references

Keene, Nancy

Your Child in the Hospital; A Practical Guide for Parents. Nancy Keene & Rachel Prentice. Childhood Cancer Guides 2015 176 p. $14.95 **362.1**

1. Children -- Medical care 2. Parent-child relationship 3. Parent and child 4. Children -- Hospital care 5. Sick children -- Psychology

ISBN 1941089992; 9781941089996

LC 99019134

Author Nancy Keene offers "tips and home-grown wisdom that will make any visit to the hospital easier. It explains how cope with procedures, plan for surgery, communicate with doctors and nurses, and deal with insurance companies. Woven throughout the text are dozens of practical and encouraging stories from parents who have been through the experience of having a child in the hospital." (Publisher's note)

"The brevity of information, while somewhat dry in presentation, may be just what the doctor ordered for the concerned or uninitiated parent." LJ

Includes bibliographical references (p. 155-157)

Khan, Ali S.

The **next** pandemic; On the Front Lines Against Humankind's Gravest Dangers. Ali S. Khan with William Patrick. PublicAffairs 2016 288 p. illustrations (hardcover) $26.99 **362.1**

1. Disasters 2. Epidemics 3. Disease management 4. Internationality 5. Disease Outbreaks

ISBN 9781610395915

LC 2016001718

This book, by Ali S. Khan with William Patrick, offers an "account of the fight to contain the world's deadliest diseases—and the panic and corruption that make them worse. Throughout history, humankind's biggest killers have been infectious diseases: the Black Death, the Spanish Flu, and AIDS alone account for over one hundred million deaths. We ignore this reality most of the time, but when a new threat . . . seems imminent, we send our best . . . doctors to contain it." (Publisher's note)

"The details are sometimes disturbing, but Khan writes with verve, clarity, and a touch of humor." Kirkus

Includes bibliographical references and index

Offit, Paul A.

Bad advice; or why celebrities, politicians, and activists aren't your best source of health information. Paul A. Offit, M.D. Columbia University Press 2018 272 p. (cloth: alk. paper) $24.95 **362.101**

1. Medicine 2. Virology 3. Public health 4. Health in mass media 5. Communication in medicine 6. Communication in public health

ISBN 9780231186988

LC 2017056425

In this book, author "Paul A. Offit shares hard-earned wisdom on the dos and don'ts of battling misinformation. For the past twenty years, Offit has been on the front lines in the fight for sound science and public health. . . . 'Bad Advice' discusses science and its adversaries: not just the manias stoked by slick charlatans and their miracle cures but also corrosive, dangerous ideologies such as Holocaust and climate-change denial." (Publisher's note)

Includes bibliographical references and index

Pearson, Rachel

No apparent distress; a doctor's coming-of-age on the front lines of American medicine. Rachel Pearson. W W Norton & Co Inc 2017 260 p. (hardcover) $26.95   **362.1**
1. Medical care 2. Socioeconomics 3. Sociobiology 4. Medical students 5. Medical education 6. Health care rationing
ISBN 9780393249255; 9780393249248

LC 2016055803

This book, by Rachel Pearson, is a "memoir about doctors and patients in a health care system that puts the poor at risk. . . . Pearson confronted these harsh realities when she started medical school in Galveston, Texas. Pearson, herself from a working-class background, remains haunted by the suicide of a close friend, experiences firsthand the heartbreak of her own errors in a patient's care, and witnesses the ruinous effects of a hurricane on a Texas town's medical system." (Publisher's note)

"On the whole, Pearson's well-balanced book provides a smooth combination of personal history and patient care cases. Educative and thoughtful—important reading for patients and fellow medical professionals alike." Kirkus

Reid, T. R.

The **healing** of America; a global quest for better, cheaper, and fairer health care. Penguin Press 2009 277p il $25.95 **362.1**
1. Insurance, Health 2. Medical care -- Europe 3. Medical policy -- United States 4. Medical care -- Government policy 5. Health care reform -- United States
ISBN 9781594202346

LC 2009-9555

Reid "discusses successful health-care systems worldwide, challenging American myths of 'socialized medicine' to find possible paths toward reform." (Publisher's note) Index.

"Reid's concise—and surprisingly humorous—study is recommended to anyone following the ongoing debate over health-care reform." Libr J

Includes bibliographical references

Rosenthal, Elisabeth

An **American** sickness; how healthcare became big business and how you can take it back. Elisabeth Rosenthal. Penguin Press 2017 416 p. (hardcover) $28   **362.1**
1. Health care reform 2. Right to health care 3. Medical care -- United States 4. Health care -- United States 5. Medical policy -- United States
ISBN 1594206759; 9781594206757

LC 2016042934

In this book, "Dr. Elisabeth Rosenthal reveals the dangerous, expensive, and dysfunctional American healthcare system, and tells us exactly what we can do to solve its myriad of problems. . . . Breaking down the monolithic business into its individual industries—the hospitals, doctors, insurance companies, drug manufacturers—that together constitute our healthcare system, Rosenthal tells the story of the history of American medicine as never before." (Publisher's note)

"After laying out the problem, Rosenthal presents solutions both personal and societal in this commanding and necessary call to arms." Booklist

Shah, Sonia

The **body** hunters; testing new drugs on the world's poorest patients. New Press 2006 242p $24.95   **362.1**
1. Drug industry 2. Medical ethics 3. Developing countries
ISBN 1-56584-912-4; 978-1-56584-912-9

LC 2005-58394

The author "uncovers a series of recent unethical drug trials conducted on impoverished and sick people in the developing world. . . . Meticulously researched and packed with documentary evidence, Shah's tautly argued study will provoke much needed public debate about this disturbing facet of globalization." Publ Wkly

Includes bibliographical references

Pandemic; tracking contagions, from cholera to ebola and beyond. Sonia Shah. Sarah Crichton Books/Farrar, Straus & Giroux 2016 288 p. illustrations (chiefly color) (hardback) $26; (ebook) $40   **362.1**
1. Epidemics 2. Communicable diseases 3. Public health surveillance 4. Communicable diseases -- Epidemiology -- History
ISBN 9780374122881; 9780374708740

LC 2015010246

In this book, "prizewinning journalist Sonia Shah . . . interweaves history, original reportage, and personal narrative to explore the origins of contagions, drawing parallels between cholera, one of history's most deadly and disruptive pandemic-causing pathogens, and the new diseases that stalk humankind today. To reveal how a new pandemic might develop, Sonia Shah tracks each stage of cholera's dramatic journey." (Publisher's note)

"Shah's warning is certainly troubling, and this important medical and social history is worthy of attention—and action." Pub Wkly

Includes bibliographical references (pages [221]-253) and index.

Shilts, Randy

★ **And** the band played on; politics, people, and the AIDS epidemic. 20th anniversary ed.; St Martin's Griffin 2007 630p pa $17.95   **362.1**
1. AIDS (Disease)
ISBN 978-0-312-37463-1
First published 1987

The author traces the history of the AIDS epidemic in the United States.

"Shilts successfully weaves comprehensive investigative reporting and commercial page-turner pacing, political intrigue and personal tragedy into a landmark work." Publ Wkly

Includes bibliographical references

Smith, Tom

A **balanced** life; 9 strategies for coping with the mental health problems of a loved one. Hazelden 2008 147p pa $14.95   **362.1**
1. Mentally ill
ISBN 978-1-59285-662-6

LC 2008-18794

"Through extensive research and his own experience with his daughter's mental illness and subsequent suicide, . . . [the author] suggests nine strategies for coping, including helping loved ones find and continue to take their medication, urging them to maintain a supportive relationship with a therapist, and recognizing the warning signs. . . . Smith provides empathetic information that has the potential to buoy people up." Libr J

Includes bibliographical references

Starr, Paul

Remedy and reaction; the peculiar American struggle over health care reform. Yale University Press 2011 324p $28.50 **362.1**

1. Health insurance 2. Medical care -- Government policy
ISBN 978-0-300-17109-9

LC 2011019577

The author "recounts the long and largely unsuccessful fight to provide all Americans with health care. . . . Starr shows how the window of opportunity for health-care reform has opened several times in the last 100 years and how each time it has been slammed shut by powerful interests including the American Medical Association, big insurance companies, and the conservative politicians they support. . . . This is a must-read in order to understand why health-care reform has been and continues to be so difficult to achieve in America." Libr J

Includes bibliographical references

Torrey, E. Fuller (Edwin Fuller), 1937-

The **insanity** offense; how America's failure to treat the seriously mentally ill endangers its citizens. W.W. Norton 2008 265p il **362.1**

1. Mentally ill -- Institutional care
ISBN 0-393-06658-4; 978-0-393-06658-6

LC 2008-2697

"Released en masse from institutions beginning in the 1960s, the most severely ill are most likely to become homeless, incarcerated, victimized, and/or violent. Torrey details how civil liberties suits have prevented such people from being involuntarily institutionalized, leaving them a danger both to themselves and to others. . . . Chilling and well documented, this text has many no-nonsense solutions to protect the mentally ill themselves as well as society as a whole." Publ Wkly

Includes bibliographical references

362.108 Groups of people

Glezerman, Marek

Gender medicine; the groundbreaking new science of gender- and sex-related diagnosis and treatment. Marek Glezerman; foreword by Amos Oz. Overlook Press 2016 288 p. illustrations $29.95; (ebook) $50 **362.108**

1. Social medicine 2. Health -- Sex differences 3. Medical care -- Sex differences
ISBN 1468313185; 9781468313185; 9781468313499

LC 2016028905

This book, by Marek Glezerman, with foreword by Amos Oz, calls "for reform, challenging the dangerous assumption that male and female patients can be effectively treated in the same way. Over millions of years, male and female bodies developed crucial physiological differences to improve the chances for human survival. These differences . . . [are] very real, and they go well beyond the obvious sexual and reproductive variances." (Publisher's note)

"This fascinating work will teach readers a great deal about sex, gender, and the human body." LJ

Includes bibliographical references (pages 251-277) and index.

362.109 History, geographic treatment, biography

Brawley, Otis Webb

How we do harm; Otis Webb Brawley with Paul Goldberg.

St. Martin's Press 2012 256p. **362.109**

1. Medical care 2. Access to health care 3. Medical policy -- United States 4. Medical care -- United States 5. Health care reform -- United States
ISBN 9780312672973

LC 2011035843

'In this book, Dr. Otis Webb Brawley, M.D., explores "how medicine is really practiced in America. Brawley tells of doctors who select treatment based on payment they will receive, rather than on demonstrated scientific results; hospitals and pharmaceutical companies that seek out patients to treat even if they are not actually ill (but as long as their insurance will pay); a public primed to swallow the latest pill, no matter the cost; and rising healthcare costs for unnecessary—and often unproven—treatments that we all pay for. Brawley calls for rational healthcare, healthcare drawn from results-based, scientifically justifiable treatments, and not just the peddling of hot new drugs." (Publisher's note)

362.11 Services of specific kinds of institutions

Cosgrove, Toby

The **Cleveland** Clinic way; lessons in excellence from one of the world's leading health care organizations. by Toby Cosgrove, MD., President and CEO of Cleveland Clinic. McGraw-Hill Education 2014 xvi, 222 p.p (alk. paper) $30 **362.11**

1. Medical care 2. Health facilities 3. Integrative medicine 4. Cleveland Clinic Foundation 5. Integrative medicine -- United States -- Ohio 6. Health facilities -- Standards -- United States -- Ohio
ISBN 0071827242; 9780071827249

LC 2013038181

This book, by Dr. Toby Cosgrove, "is a blueprint for fixing what's wrong with healthcare. . . . It's all happening at Cleveland Clinic, one of the most innovative, forward-looking medical institutions in the nation. . . . Cosgrove . . . reveals how the Clinic works so well and argues persuasively for why it should be the model for the nation. He details how Cleveland Clinic focuses on the eight key trends that are shaping the future of medicine." (Publisher's note)

Includes bibliographical references and index

Fink, Sheri

★ **Five** days at Memorial; life and death in a storm-ravaged hospital. Sheri Fink. Crown Publishers 2013 432 p. $27 **362.11**

1. Hospitals 2. Disaster relief 3. Hurricane Katrina, 2005 4. Memorial Medical Center (New Orleans, La.) 5. Disaster medicine -- Louisiana -- New Orleans -- Case studies 6. Disaster hospitals -- Louisiana -- New Orleans -- Case studies 7. Forensic pathology -- Louisiana -- New Orleans -- Case studies 8. Health facilities -- Louisiana -- Administration -- Case studies
ISBN 0307718964; 9780307718969

LC 2013019693

Andrew Carnegie Medal for Excellence in Nonfiction Shortlist (2014)

LA Times Book Prize Winner: Current Interest (2013)

National Book Critics Circle Award Winner: Nonfiction (2013)

"Fink reconstructs 5 days at Memorial Medical Center and draws the reader into the lives of those who struggled mightily to survive and to maintain life amid chaos. After Katrina struck and the floodwaters rose, the power failed, and the heat climbed, exhausted caregivers chose to designate certain patients last for rescue. Months later, several health professionals faced criminal allegations that they deliberately injected numerous patients with drugs to hasten their deaths." (Publisher's note)

"Fink draws those few days in the hospital's life with a fine, lively pen, providing stunningly framed vignettes of activities in the hospital and sharp pocket profiles of many of the characters. She gives measured consideration to such explosive issues as class and race discrimination in medicine, end-of-life care, medical rationing and euthanasia, and she presents the injection of some patients with a cocktail of drugs to reduce their breathing in such a manner that readers will be able to fully fashion their own opinions." Kirkus

Includes bibliographical references and index

Manheimer, Eric

Twelve patients; life and death at Bellevue Hospital. Eric Manheimer. Grand Central Pub. 2012 vii, 355 p.p (regular) $26.99   **362.11**

1. Patients 2. Hospitals 3. Cancer patients 4. Physicians -- Biography 5. Bellevue Hospital 6. Hospital care -- New York (State) -- New York -- Case studies 7. Hospital patients -- New York (State) -- New York -- Case studies

ISBN 1455503886; 9781455503889

LC 2012005513

This book presents "a memoir from the Medical Director of Bellevue Hospital that uses the plights of twelve very different patients -- from dignitaries at the nearby UN . . . to illegal immigrants, and Wall Street tycoons -- to illustrate larger societal issues. . . . As the book unfolds, the narrator is diagnosed with cancer, and he is forced to wrestle with the end of his own life even as he struggles to save the lives of others." (Publisher's note)

Oshinsky, David M., 1944-

Bellevue; three centuries of medicine and mayhem at America's most storied hospital. David Oshinsky. Doubleday 2016 384 p. illustrations (some color) (hardcover: alk. paper) $30.00; (ebook) $65   **362.11**

1. Bellevue Hospital 2. Hospitals -- New York (State) -- New York -- History 3. New York City 4. History, Modern 1601- 5. Hospitals, Urban -- History

ISBN 9780385523363; 9780385540858

LC 2016027568

This book, by David Oshinsky, presents the "history of New York's iconic public hospital that charts the turbulent rise of American medicine. Bellevue Hospital, on New York City's East Side, . . . a den of mangled crime victims, vicious psychopaths, assorted derelicts, lunatics, and exotic-disease sufferers. In its two and a half centuries of service, there was hardly an epidemic or social catastrophe--or groundbreaking scientific advance—that did not touch Bellevue." (Publisher's note)

"This readable, smoothly flowing, and well-documented account should fascinate readers with interests touching on all aspects of the history of medicine and the American health-care system." LJ

Includes bibliographical references and index

362.17 Specific services

Gawande, Atul

★ **Being** mortal; medicine and what matters in the end. Atul Gawande. Henry Holt & Co. 2014 288 p. illustrations (hardcover) $26   **362.17**

1. Hospices 2. Terminal care 3. Older people -- Medical care 4. Prognosis 5. Quality of life 6. Attitude to death 7. Aging -- Physiology

ISBN 0805095152; 9780805095159

LC 2014017442

Los Angeles Times Book Prize Finalist: Current Interest (2014)

"In 'Being Mortal,' . . . author Atul Gawande . . . addresses his profession's ultimate limitation, arguing that quality of life is the desired goal for patients and families. Gawande offers examples of freer, more socially fulfilling models for assisting the infirm and dependent elderly, and he explores the varieties of hospice care to demonstrate that a person's last weeks or months may be rich and dignified." (Publisher's note)

"A sensitive, intelligent and heartfelt examination of the processes of aging and dying." Kirkus

Includes bibliographical references

Robbins, Alexandra

The **nurses**; a year of secrets, drama, and miracles with the heroes of the hospital. Alexandra Robbins. Workman Publishing 2015 368 p. (alk. paper) $24.95   **362.17**

1. Nurses 2. Nursing 3. Emergency medicine 4. Nursing Care -- United States -- Popular Works 5. Nursing Care -- United States -- Personal Narratives 6. Nurse-Patient Relations -- United States -- Popular Works 7. Nursing Staff, Hospital -- United States -- Popular Works 8. Nursing Service, Hospital -- United States -- Popular Works 9. Physician-Nurse Relations -- United States -- Popular Works 10. Nurse-Patient Relations -- United States -- Personal Narratives 11. Nursing Staff, Hospital -- United States -- Personal Narratives 12. Nursing Service, Hospital -- United States -- Personal Narratives 13. Physician-Nurse Relations -- United States -- Personal Narratives

ISBN 0761171711; 9780761171713

LC 2015011380

In this book, Alexandra Robbins "trains her sights on the adrenaline-infused world of emergency nursing, offering a disturbing snapshot of the barriers imposed on healthcare providers by colleagues, myopic bosses, and a changing healthcare system. She follows four ER nurses at four hospitals where patients range from the wealthy and privileged to the down and out, aiming to represent the varied perspectives of America's 3.5 million nurses." (Publishers Weekly)

"Robbins works in lots of fascinating facts as she argues for improved working conditions for nurses, citing research that shows how much that benefits patients. An educational, sometimes alarming read for anyone interested in learning behind-the-scenes details about hospital life." Booklist

Includes bibliographical references and index

362.19 Services to patients with specific conditions

Taylor, Jill Bolte

My stroke of insight; a brain scientist's personal journey. Jill Bolte Taylor. Plume 2009 206 p. illustrations $16 **362.19**

1. Stroke patients 2. Neuroanatomy 3. Biography, Individual 4. Brain -- Hemorrhage -- Patients

ISBN 0452295548; 9780452295544

LC 2008271243

This book, by Jill Bolte Taylor, "chronicles how a brain scientist's own stroke led to enlightenment. . . . On December 10, 1996, Jill Bolte Taylor, a thirty-seven- year-old Harvard-trained brain scientist experienced a massive stroke in the left hemisphere of her brain. . . . For Taylor, her stroke . . . taught her that by 'stepping to the right' of our left brains, we can uncover feelings of well-being that are often sidelined by 'brain chatter.'" (Publisher's note)

362.196   Specific conditions

Brzezinski, Mika, 1967-

Obsessed; America's Food Addiction -- And My Own. Perseus Books Group 2013 256 p. $26   **362.196**
1. Eating habits 2. Eating disorders
ISBN 1602861765; 9781602861763

This book by Mika Brzezinski looks at eating habits in the U.S. As a television host for "Morning Joe," she "admonish[es] viewers about the importance of proper diet and exercise. Few would suspect that her vehemence stems from a personal addiction to junk food and binge eating that has plagued her all her life and that her ironclad willpower actually border on an unhealthy obsession to stay thin at any cost." (Booklist)

Cody, Joshua

[Sic] W.W. Norton 2011 266 p.   **362.196**
1. Autobiographies 2. Cancer patients
ISBN 9780393081060

LC 2011026035

In this book "Joshua Cody, a . . . young composer, was about to receive his PhD when he was diagnosed with an aggressive cancer. Facing a bone-marrow transplant and full radiation, he charts his struggle: the fury, the tendency to self-destruction, and the ruthless grasping for life and sensation; the encounter with a strange woman on Canal Street that leads to sex at his apartment; the detailed morphine fantasy complete with a bride called Valentina while, in reality, hospital staff are pinning him to his bed." (Publisher's note)

Includes bibliographical references.

Forrest, Emma

Your voice in my head; a memoir. Other Press 2011 215 p.   **362.196**
1. Authors 2. Bulimia 3. Novelists 4. Journalists 5. Self-mutilation 6. Screenwriters 7. Biography, Individual
ISBN 1590514467; 9781590514467; 978-1-59051-446-7; 1-59051-446-7

LC 201030930

This book presents a memoir by writer Emma Forrest which details a period in her life in which, despite "the support of her parents . . . as well as a precocious career in journalism and a first novel . . . already on the way, she became a bulimic and an obsessive cutter, and soon began walking 'hand in hand with the thought of suicide.' She also had a knack for acquiring terrible boyfriends whose bad behavior inspired her to hurt herself more, and who sometimes aided and abetted the abuse." Particular focus is given to "the therapist who ultimately changed her life, a man she refers to as Dr. R. . . . [and his] unexpected death." Also included are "letters from Dr. R.'s other patients . . . [and] a sermon by her rabbi." (N Y Times)

Geiger, Chris

The **Cancer** Survivors' Club; A Collection of Inspirational and Uplifting Stories. Chris Geiger. Oneworld Publication 2015 272 p. $15.99   **362.196**
1. Cancer patients 2. Cancer -- Chemotherapy
ISBN 1780747268; 9781780747262

This book by author Chris Geiger " brings together firsthand accounts of ordinary people who have beaten cancer. They are old and young, their diagnoses common and rare, their courses of treatment long and short, but all are survivors. In these honest, unflinching and deeply personal stories, they write about the most difficult times in their lives, telling us how they found a strength and determination that they never knew they possessed." (Publisher's note)

"An inspiring compilation for anyone struggling with cancer. Read-ers will find comfort and even a few laughs in the pages. A note: this book is from the UK; the survivors refer to the nation's National Health Service, and the list of cancer-related websites and blogs is mostly from the UK." LJ

Hatch, Steven

Inferno; A Doctor's Ebola Story. by Steven Hatch. St. Martin's Press 2017 320 p. (ebook) $60; $27.99   **362.196**
1. Ebola virus
ISBN 9781250085146; 1250085136; 9781250085139

LC 2016052533

In this book, "Dr. Steven Hatch first came to Liberia in November 2013, to work at a hospital in Monrovia. Six months later, several of the physicians Dr. Hatch had mentored and served with were dead or barely clinging to life, and Ebola had become a world health emergency. Hundreds of victims perished each week; whole families were destroyed in a matter of days; so many died so quickly that the culturally taboo practice of cremation had to be instituted to dispose of the bodies." (Publisher's note)

"Hatch's analysis is intelligent, nuanced, and tempered, a necessary departure from the panicked response of most American media outlets." Kirkus

Includes bibliographical references (pages [289]-294) and index.

Leavitt, Sarah

Tangles; A Story About Alzheimer's, My Mother, and Me. Sarah Leavitt. Skyhorse Pub. 2012 127 p. ill., port. (paperback) $14.95   **362.196**
1. Family life 2. Autobiographies 3. Alzheimer's disease
ISBN 1616086394; 9781616086398

"In this . . . graphic memoir, Sarah Leavitt reveals how Alzheimer's disease transformed her mother Midge -- and her family -- forever. . . . Sarah shares her family's journey . . . managing to find moments of happiness. Midge, a Harvard-educated intellectual, struggles to comprehend the simplest words; Sarah's father Rob slowly adapts to his new role as full-time caretaker . . . Sarah and her sister Hannah argue, laugh, and grieve together." (Publisher's note)

Stratton, Stephen E.

The **encyclopedia** of HIV and AIDS; Stephen E. Stratton, Evelyn J. Fisher; foreword by Edward A. Morales. 3rd ed. Facts On File 2012 414 p. (hardcover) $75   **362.196**
1. AIDS (Disease) 2. HIV infections 3. Reference books 4. AIDS (Disease) -- Dictionaries
ISBN 0816077231; 9780816077236

LC 2011017597

First published 1998 with title: The AIDS dictionary

This book is the third edition of an encyclopedia of HIV and AIDS. "Coverage includes definitions of AIDS and HIV; information on medications used to treat the conditions--including side effects, dosage, and drug interactions; and related medical conditions. Further research is supported by the inclusion of a bibliography for each essay. The appendixes include frequently used abbreviations, lists of online resources, and U.S. and global HIV and AIDS statistics." (Library Journal)

This volume includes "entries covering the basic biological, medical, financial, legal, political, and social issues and terms associated with HIV and AIDS. Entries explain symptoms and treatments, opportunistic infections, prevention strategies, and much more. Appendixes include HIV/AIDS associations, education centers, clinical trials, hotlines, publications, and additional material." Publisher's note

Includes bibliographical references and index.

Weldon, Michele

Escape Points; A Memoir. by Michele Weldon. Chicago Review Press 2015 272 p. (ebook) $21.99; $26.95 **362.196**

1. Mothers 2. Single parents 3. Divorced people 4. Women journalists

ISBN 9781613733554; 1613733526; 9781613733523

LC 2015008965

In this memoir, "journalist Michele Weldon provides a potent antidote to the harried single mom stereotype. . . . Untethered from a seemingly idyllic life with a handsome but abusive attorney husband, Weldon relates the challenges and triumphs of the years that followed her divorce as she maneuvers through a complicated life of long daily commutes, radiation treatments, [and] supporting [her three] boys." (Publisher's note)

"Weldon pins life to the mat in this valiant, passionate, purposeful memoir." Kirkus

Zimmer, Carl

A **planet** of viruses; Carl Zimmer. University of Chicago Press 2011 x, 109p.p col. ill. **362.196**

1. Viruses

ISBN 9780226983356 pa; 0226983358 pa; 9780226983363; 9780226983332

LC 2010036742

"This . . . book explores the hidden world of viruses. . . . Here Carl Zimmer, popular science writer and author of Discover magazine's award-winning blog The Loom, presents the latest research on how viruses hold sway over our lives and our biosphere, how viruses helped give rise to the first life-forms, how viruses are producing new diseases, how we can harness viruses for our own ends, and how viruses will continue to control our fate for years to come. In this . . . tour of the frontiers of biology, . . . we learn that some treatments for the common cold do more harm than good; that the world's oceans are home to an astonishing number of viruses; and that the evolution of HIV is now in overdrive, spawning more mutated strains than we care to imagine." (Publisher's note)

Includes bibliographical references (p. 97-101) and index.

362.198   Gynecology and pediatrics

Oberman, Michelle

Her body, our laws; on the front lines of the abortion war, from El Salvador to Oklahoma. Michelle Oberman. Beacon Press 2018 ix, 174 p.p (hardcover) $27.95 **362.198**

1. Reproduction 2. Women's rights 3. Abortion -- Law and legislation 4. Abortion -- Case studies 5. Women drug addicts -- Case studies 6. Reproductive rights -- Case studies 7. Abortion -- Law and legislation -- Case studies

ISBN 9780807045534; 9780807045527

LC 2017041184

In this book, author Michelle Oberman "explores what happens when abortion is a crime. Oberman reveals the practical challenges raised by a thriving black market in abortion drugs, as well as the legal challenges to law enforcement. She describes a system in which doctors and lawyers collaborate in order to identify and prosecute those suspected of abortion-related crimes, and the troubling results of such collaboration." (Publisher's note)

"Oberman . . . uses her extensive knowledge of the legal system and the ethics of issues such as pregnancy and motherhood to disrupt easy narratives based on artificial binary oppositions." LJ

Includes bibliographical references and index

Peters, Rebecca Todd

Trust women; a progressive Christian argument for reproductive justice. Rebecca Todd Peters. Beacon Press 2018 248 p. (hardback: alk. paper) $27.95 **362.198**

1. Motherhood 2. Birth control 3. Abortion -- Religious aspects 4. Abortion -- United States 5. Motherhood -- United States 6. Abortion -- Religious aspects -- Christianity

ISBN 9780807069981

LC 2017042045

This book, by Rebecca Todd Peters, "offers a compelling case for radically revising the way we think and speak about women's reproductive experience. . . . While written specifically for Christians, this will be a valuable read for anyone who questions the pronatalism and misogyny that constrains reproductive decision-making in the United States and seeks to shift our public debate in a more just direction." (Library Journal)

Includes bibliographical references and index

362.2   People with mental illness and disabilities

Bering, Jesse

★ **Suicidal**; why we kill ourselves. Jesse Bering. University of Chicago Press 2018 272 p. (cloth: alk. paper) $27.50 **362.2**

1. Suicide

ISBN 9780226463322

LC 2018021904

In this book author Jesse Bering, takes us "through the science and psychology of suicide, revealing its cognitive secrets and the subtle tricks our minds play on us when we're easy emotional prey. Scientific studies, personal stories, and remarkable cross-species comparisons come together to help readers critically analyze their own doomsday thoughts while gaining broad insight into a problem that, tragically, will most likely touch all of us at some point in our lives." (Publisher's note)

"The author lays bare the possible root causes and outward complications when someone with periodic depression or a fleetingly sporadic compulsion ends their life. For such a fiercely complex subject with varying nuances, viewpoints, and interpretations, Bering imparts accessible information through an affable, conversational tone."

Includes bibliographical references and index

Horn, Stacy

Damnation island; poor, sick, mad & criminal in 19th-century New York. by Stacy Horn. Algonquin Books of Chapel Hill 2018 304 p. (hardcover: alk. paper) $27.95 **362.2**

1. Mental illness -- Treatment 2. Psychiatric hospitals -- History -- United States 3. Roosevelt Island (New York, N.Y.) -- 19th century -- History 4. Psychiatric hospitals -- New York (State) -- New York -- 19th century -- History 5. Mental illness -- Treatment -- New York (State) -- New York -- 19th century -- History

ISBN 9781616205768

LC 2017052414

"In the first contemporary investigative account of Blackwell's, Stacy Horn tells this chilling narrative through the gripping voices of the island's inhabitants, as well as the period's officials, reformers, and journalists, including the celebrated Nellie Bly. . . . Horn brings this forgotten history alive: there was terrible overcrowding; prisoners were enlisted to care for the insane; punishment was harsh and unfair; and treatment was nonexistent. (Publisher's note)

Includes bibliographical references

Schüll, Natasha Dow

Addiction by design; machine gambling in Las Vegas. Natasha Dow Schüll. Princeton University Press 2012 xi, 442 p.p (hardcover) $35
362.2

1. Las Vegas (Nev.) 2. Compulsive gambling 3. Casinos -- Nevada -- Las Vegas 4. Gambling -- Nevada -- Las Vegas 5. Compulsive gambling -- Nevada -- Las Vegas 6. Gambling -- Equipment and supplies -- Nevada -- Las Vegas

ISBN 0691127557; 9780691127552

LC 2012004339

In this book, Natasha Dow Schüll looks at problem gambling. "She begins by tracing the spectacular growth of machine gambling over the last several decades to where it now stands as the dominant gambling form in the US. Applying an anthropological perspective, the author focuses especially on the Las Vegas gambling industry." (Choice)

Includes bibliographical references (p. 385-423) and index

362.26 Psychoses

Powers, Ron

No One Cares About Crazy People; The Chaos and Heartbreak of Mental Health in America. Ron Powers. Hachette Books 2017 342 p. $28
362.26

1. Mentally ill 2. Schizophrenia -- History 3. Mental health services -- History

ISBN 0316341177; 9780316341172

LC 2016046019

This book, by Ron Powers, "offers a searching, richly researched narrative of the social history of mental illness in America paired with the deeply personal story of his two sons' battles with schizophrenia. . . . [It covers] the centuries of torture of 'lunatiks' at Bedlam Asylum to the infamous eugenics era to the follies of the anti-psychiatry movement to the current landscape in which too many families struggle alone to manage afflicted love ones." (Publisher's note)

"Readers will surely be moved by this double portrait of one family's days of happiness and sorrow, and the world's halting and flawed attempts to care for troubled people." Pub Wkly

362.28 Suicide

Bateson, John

The **last** and greatest battle; finding the will, commitment, and strategy to end military suicides. John Bateson. Oxford University Press 2015 xviii, 360 p.p (hardback) $29.95 **362.28**

1. Veterans -- Mental health 2. Soldiers -- Suicidal behavior -- United States -- History 3. Veterans -- Suicidal behavior -- United States -- History 4. Military psychology 5. Combat -- Psychological aspects 6. Suicide -- United States -- Prevention 7. Soldiers -- Mental health -- United States 8. Veterans -- Mental health -- United States

ISBN 9780199392322

LC 2014017942

In this book, John Bateson, "former executive director of a nationally certified suicide prevention center, surveys the history of suicide in the United States military from the Civil War to the present day and outlines a plan to save lives-and ultimately end the tragedy of military suicides. . . . Transitioning from the front lines to the home front is difficult for many service members, and many need help both during and after their deployments." (Publisher's note)

"Poetry lovers will want Levine's last word." LJ

Includes bibliographical references (pages 311-343) and index

362.29 Substance abuse

Clegg, Bill

Ninety days; a memoir of recovery. Bill Clegg. Little, Brown and Co. 2012 194 p. $24.99
362.29

1. New York (N.Y.) 2. Drug addicts -- Rehabilitation 3. Literary agents -- Personal narratives 4. Recovering addicts -- Personal narratives 5. Drug addicts -- United States -- Biography 6. Literary agents -- United States -- Biography

ISBN 9780316122528; 0316122521

LC 2011032542

"In this . . . memoir, a follow-up to Portrait of an Addict as a Young Man, literary agent and author [Bill] Clegg describes his struggle to stay clean. Returning to New York City after a stint in rehab, Clegg faces the ruin he's made of his life: his literary agency has closed, his lover has moved on, and he faces mounting debts with no income to speak of. Making matters worse, in spite of the many meetings Clegg attends, he's helplessly drawn to vice. Many organizations dealing with substance abuse emphasize 90 days sober as a real signpost toward recovery. Clegg discovers that reaching that signpost is going to take him a lot longer than three months." (Publishers Weekly)

Dahl, Linda

Loving Our Addicted Daughters Back to Life; A Guidebook for Parents. Linda Dahl. Central Recovery Press 2015 200 p. $16.95
362.29

1. Parenting 2. Drug addicts 3. Drug abuse counseling

ISBN 1937612856; 9781937612856

This book, by Linda Dahl, offers "the latest information on gender-specific treatment of addiction and recovery . . . for parents seeking direction to help their daughters. Step-by-step guidelines present tools for recognizing substance abuse in young women; communicating with them and their care providers; dealing with relapse and long-term recovery; and managing parental shame, guilt, fear, anger, and loving detachment." (Publisher's note)

"This book's down-to-earth style is for parents or any reader seeking facts and guidance. The female focus is atypical and makes this an essential addition to the literature." LJ

Feiling, Tom

Cocaine nation; how the white trade took over the world. Pegasus Books 2010 350p $27.95
362.29

1. Cocaine 2. Drug traffic

ISBN 978-1-60598-101-7; 1-60598-101-X

First published 2009 in the United Kingdom with title: The candy machine

"Studying the cultivation, distribution, and use of cocaine, . . . [the author] probes the drug's meteoric rise in sales and traces traffic from Colombian coca fields to Miami, Kingston, Tijuana, London, and New York. He follows consumers, traders, producers, police officers, doctors, and custom officials. . . . Packed with facts and figures, this is a well-researched survey of the subject." Publ Wkly

Includes bibliographical references

Fletcher, Anne M.

Inside rehab; the surprising truth about addiction treatment: and how to get help that works. Anne M. Fletcher. Penguin Group USA 2013 448 p. $27.95
362.29

1. Substance abuse 2. Drug abuse -- Treatment 3. Drug addicts

-- Rehabilitation 4. Addicts -- Rehabilitation 5. Substance abuse
-- Treatment
ISBN 0670025224; 9780670025220

LC 2012037030

This book is an "overview of modern treatment methods for substance abuse." Anne M. Fletcher "conducted interviews with patients and the administrators and staff of addiction programs, visiting more than a dozen such programs (both residential and outpatient). The author challenges the notion that an addict is powerless to overcome an addiction on his or her own or with minimal professional counseling." (Kirkus)

Includes bibliographical references and index

Hampton, Ryan

American fix; inside the opioid addiction crisis - and how to end it. Ryan Hampton, with Claire Rudy Foster. All Points Books 2018 304 p. (hardcover: alk. paper) $27.99　　**362.29**
1. Social problems 2. Drug abuse -- United States 3. Substance abuse -- United States 4. Drug abuse -- United States -- History 5. Opioid abuse -- United States -- History 6. Drug abuse -- Political aspects -- United States -- History
ISBN 1250196264; 9781250196262

LC 2018025770

In this book, Ryan Hampton, with Claire Rudy Foster, "describes his personal struggle with addiction, outlines the challenges that the [Facing Addiction] recovery movement currently faces, and offers a concrete, comprehensive plan of action towards making America's addiction crisis a thing of the past." (Publisher's note)

"This sobering story by a recovering heroin addict makes a strong case for why tackling the opioid crisis must be a top priority for the country." Booklist

Includes bibliographical references and index

Hart, Carl

High Price; A Neuroscientist's Journey of Self-discovery That Challenges Everything You Know About Drugs and Society. Carl Hart. HarperCollins 2013 352 p. $26.99　　**362.29**
1. Scientists 2. Drug education
ISBN 0062015885; 9780062015884

In this book, "combining memoir, popular science, and public policy" author Carl Hart "lambasts current drug laws as draconian and repressive, arguing that they're based more on assumptions about race and class than on a real understanding of the physiological and societal effects of drugs. . . . Central to his work is the idea that addiction is actually a combination of physiological and social factors, and the use of drugs does not itself lead to violence and crime." (Publishers Weekly)

"An eye-opening, absorbing, complex story of scientific achievement in the face of overwhelming odds." Kirkus

Larsen, Laura

Drug abuse sourcebook; basic consumer health information about the abuse of cocaine, club drugs, marijuana, inhalants, heroin, hallucinogens, and other illicit substances . . . edited by Laura Larsen. Omnigraphics, Inc. 2014 xx, 636 p.p (hardcover: acid-free paper) $95　　**362.29**
1. Drug abuse 2. Drug abuse -- Treatment -- Handbooks, manuals, etc 3. Drug abuse -- Prevention -- Handbooks, manuals, etc 4. Drug addiction -- Treatment -- Handbooks, manuals, etc
ISBN 9780780813076; 0780813073

LC 2013037324

This book, edited by Laura Larsen, "provides basic consumer health information about the abuse of illegal drugs and misuse of prescription and over-the-counter medications, along with facts about prevention, treatment, and recovery. Includes index, glossary of related terms and directory of resources." (Publisher's note)

Includes bibliographical references and index

Macy, Beth

★ **Dopesick**; dealers, doctors, and the drug company that addicted America. Beth Macy. Little, Brown & Co. 2018 384 p. (hc) $28　　**362.29**
1. Drug abuse 2. Substance abuse
ISBN 9780316551243

LC 2017961068

Kirkus Prize Finalist: Nonfiction (2018)

In this book, author "Beth Macy takes us into the epicenter of America's twenty-plus year struggle with opioid addiction. . . . [She] endeavors to answer a grieving mother's question--why her only son died--and comes away with a harrowing story of greed and need. From the introduction of OxyContin in 1996, Macy parses how America embraced a medical culture where overtreatment with painkillers became the norm." (Publisher's note)

"Award-winning Virginia-based journalist Macy, author of bestsellers Factory Man (2014) and Truevine (2016), carefully constructs the through line from the midnineties introduction of the prescription painkiller OxyContin to the current U.S. opioid crisis: 300,000 deaths over the last 15 years, with that number predicted to double in the next 5." Booklist

Mohammad, Akikur

The **anatomy** of addiction; what science and research tell us about the true causes, best preventive techniques, and most successful treatments. Akikur Mohammad, MD. Periger 2016 272 p. (ebook) $65; (hardback) $27　　**362.29**
1. Substance abuse 2. Compulsive behavior 3. Substance abuse -- Etiology 4. Substance abuse -- Treatment 5. Compulsive behavior -- Etiology
ISBN 9781101983034; 9781101981832

LC 2015041635

In this book on addiction, by Akikur Mohammad, "readers will discover information and advice on: normal vs. problem drinking; new medications that are now available; medical and psychiatric complications of different addictions; the importance of treating a dual diagnosis (such as addiction and borderline personality disorder or depression); maintenance therapy; [and] when and how to seek treatment, and the roles family members should play." (Publisher's note)

"A useful and educative primer introducing but not elaborating on a new clinical perspective on addiction." Kirkus

Includes bibliographical references and index

Ohler, Norman

Blitzed; drugs in the Third Reich. Norman Ohler; translated by Shaun Whiteside. Houghton Mifflin Harcourt 2017 292 p. (hardcover) $28　　**362.29**
1. Drugs -- History 2. National socialists 3. World War, 1939-1945 -- Germany 4. Nazis -- Drug use 5. Drugs -- Germany -- History -- 20th century 6. Soldiers -- Drug use -- Germany -- History -- 20th century 7. Pharmaceutical industry -- Germany -- History -- 20th century
ISBN 9781328663795; 9781328664099

LC 2016056346

This book, by Norman Ohler, translated by Shaun Whiteside, is a "narrative that discovers a surprising perspective on World War II: Nazi Germany's all-consuming reliance on drugs. . . . Drugs seeped all the way up to the Nazi high command and, especially, to Hitler himself. Over the course of the war, Hitler became increasingly dependent on injections of a cocktail of drugs—including a form of heroin—administered by his personal doctor." (Publisher's note)

"Although Morell is not unknown to Nazi history, descriptions of his medicating the Führer here are new and fascinating. Stories of drug use among German soldiers are culled from old letters, anecdotes, and interviews with veterans." LJ

Includes bibliographical references and index

Proctor, Robert N.

Golden holocaust; origins of the cigarette catastrophe and the case for abolition. Robert N. Proctor. University of California Press 2011 x, 737 p.p ill. (cloth: alk. paper) $49.95 **362.29**
1. Cigarettes 2. Tobacco habit 3. Smoking cessation programs 4. Tobacco use -- Health aspects 5. Smoking -- Psychological aspects 6. History, 20th Century -- United States 7. Smoking -- psychology -- United States 8. Persuasive Communication -- United States 9. Smoking -- adverse effects -- United States 10. Tobacco Industry -- history -- United States 11. Tobacco industry -- United States -- History 12. Tobacco Industry -- economics -- United States 13. Government Regulation -- history -- United States
ISBN 0520270169; 9780520270169
LC 2011003825
Author Robert N. Proctor discusses the cigarette, "the deadliest artifact in the history of human civilization . . . [and] how the cigarette came to be the most widely-used drug on the planet, with six trillion sticks sold per year . . . [He looks at] tobacco manufacturers conspiring to block the recognition of tobacco-cancer hazards, even as they ensnare legions of scientists and politicians in a web of denial." (Publisher's note)

Includes bibliographical references and index

Quinones, Sam

Dreamland; the true tale of America's opiate epidemic. by Sam Quinones. Bloomsbury Press 2014 384 p. maps (alk. paper) $28 **362.29**
1. Narcotics 2. Drug abuse 3. Heroin abuse 4. American dream 5. Drug traffic -- Mexico 6. American Dream 7. Narcotics -- United States 8. Oxycodone -- United States 9. Heroin abuse -- United States 10. Drug addiction -- United States
ISBN 1620402505; 9781620402504
LC 2014025398
National Book Critics Circle Award Finalist: Nonfiction (2015)
This book, by Sam Quinones, "delves into the heart of America's obsession with opiates like heroin, morphine, and OxyContin. He looks at how aggressive marketing and irresponsible business tactics led to the widespread use of addictive prescription painkillers (especially OxyContin) and how Mexican drug cartels introduced black tar heroin into small towns and vulnerable areas around the U.S." (Publishers Weekly)

"Journalist Quinones weaves an extraordinary story, including the personal journeys of the addicted, the drug traffickers, law enforcement, and scores of families affected by the scourge, as he details the social, economic, and political forces that eventually destroyed communities in the American heartland and continues to have a resounding impact." Booklist

Includes bibliographical references and index

Reding, Nick

Methland; the death and life of an American small town. Bloomsbury 2009 255p $25 **362.29**
1. Methamphetamine 2. Iowa 3. Methamphetamine abuse
ISBN 1-59691-650-8; 978-1-59691-650-0
LC 2008-45398

This is an account of the effect of crystal methamphetamine on "the community of Oelwein, Iowa (pop. 6,159), a once-thriving farming and railroad community." (Publisher's note)

The author traces "rise of meth use across the Midwest, focusing on Oelwein, an Iowa railroad town (pop. 6,772) that by 2005 had been 'destroyed' by the drug. . . . An important report on an extremely dangerous drug and the consequences of addiction." Kirkus

Includes bibliographical references

Ruta, Domenica

With or without you; a memoir. Domenica Ruta. Spiegel & Grau 2013 224 p. $25 **362.29**
1. Substance abuse 2. Children of drug addicts 3. Drug addicts -- Massachusetts -- Biography 4. Children of drug addicts -- Massachusetts -- Biography
ISBN 0812993241; 9780679645023; 9780812993240
LC 2012017991
This book is Domenica Ruta's memoir of her relationship with "her drug-dealer, addict mother. . . . Ruta holds nothing back as she . . . portrays her childhood in Massachusetts, whether she's writing about school events at her Catholic school, her mother's ascent as a millionaire and subsequent loss of money due to drug use, or the sexual abuse at the hands of . . . one of her mother's friends." (Kirkus Reviews)

Sederer, Lloyd I.

The **addiction** solution; treating our dependence on opioids and other drugs. Lloyd I. Sederer. Scribner 2018 224 p. (hc) $26 **362.29**
1. Drug abuse 2. Substance abuse 3. Drug abuse -- Treatment -- Popular works 4. Opioid abuse -- Treatment -- Popular works 5. Substance abuse -- Treatment -- Popular works
ISBN 9781501179440; 9781501179457
LC 2017061754
"The Addiction Solution is a practical guide through the world of drug use and abuse and addiction treatment. Here, Lloyd I. Sederer, MD, Chief Mental Health Officer of the NYS Office of Mental Health, brings together scientific and clinical knowledge, policy suggestions, and case studies, to describe our current drug crisis and establish a clear path forward to recovery and health." (Publisher's note)

"Enriched with patient case studies that illustrate the complex nature of this disease, Sederer's balanced and compassionate approach makes this a valuable addition to the conversation on this timely topic." LJ

Includes bibliographical references and index

Streatfeild, Dominic

Cocaine; an unauthorized biography. Thomas Dunne Bks./ St. Martin's Press 2002 510p il $27.95; pa $15 **362.29**
1. Cocaine 2. Drug abuse 3. Drug traffic
ISBN 0-312-28624-4; 0-312-42226-1 pa
First published 2001 in the United Kingdom
"Thorough, engrossing, balanced, and entertaining, it is important social history in palatable form." Booklist

Includes bibliographical references

362.292   Alcohol

Bowman, Dana

Bottled; A Mom's Guide to Early Recovery. Dana Bowman. Central Recovery Press 2015 264 p. $16.95 **362.292**
1. Alcoholism 2. Motherhood
ISBN 193761297X; 9781937612979

This memoir by Dana Bowman "explains the perils moms face with drinking and chronicles the author's path to recovery, from hitting bottom to the months of early sobriety--a blur of pain and chaos--to her now (in)frequent moments of peace. [It] offers practical suggestions on how to be a sober, present-in-the-moment mom, one day at a time, and provides much needed levity on an issue too often treated with deadly seriousness." (Publisher's note)

Glaser, Gabrielle

Her best-kept secret; why women drink -- and how they can regain control. Gabrielle Glaser. Simon & Schuster 2013 256 p. $24   **362.292**
1. Alcoholism 2. Women -- Alcohol use 3. Women -- Alcohol use -- United States 4. Women alcoholics -- Rehabilitation -- United States
ISBN 1439184380; 9781439184387
                                            LC 2013001088
This book by Gabrielle Glaser looks at U.S. women's alcohol consumption. She "traces the increasingly besotted history of women's relationship with alcohol (focusing mostly on middle-class women), but . . . argues against the efficacy of Alcoholics Anonymous (AA) for women. Rather than guiding women down a healing path of humility and acceptance, AA and its Twelve Steps, Glaser argues, have failed to protect women from predatory men, thereby consigning many" women to failure. (Publishers Weekly)
Includes bibliographical references

Johnston, Ann Dowsett

Drink; the intimate relationship between women and alcohol. by Ann Dowsett Johnston. HarperWave 2013 320 p. (hardback) $27.99   **362.292**
1. Alcoholism 2. Women -- Alcohol use 3. Women alcoholics
ISBN 0062241796; 9780062241795
                                            LC 2013026103
In this book, author "Anne Dowsett Johnston combines in-depth research with her own personal story of recovery, and delivers a[n] . . . examination of a shocking yet little recognized epidemic threatening society today: the precipitous rise in risky drinking among women and girls." (Publisher's note)
Includes bibliographical references

362.295   Cannabis

Dufton, Emily

Grass roots; the rise and fall and rise of marijuana in America. Emiliy Dufton. Basic Books, an imprint of Perseus Books, a subsidiary of Hachette Book Group 2017 320 p. (hardcover) $28   **362.295**
1. Advocacy (Political science) 2. Marijuana -- United States -- History
ISBN 9780465096169
                                            LC 2017956164
In this book, by Emily Dufton, is "a comprehensive history of marijuana legalization in America. . . . Dufton puts years of dedicated research, interviews, and social scrutiny to impressive use. . . . The author's astute, well-rounded report spotlights the virtual tug of war of the movement and pays close attention to each side's setbacks and advancements. She presents an engrossing, evenhanded timeline of the marijuana legalization revolution and its backlash." (Kirkus Reviews)
"Dufton's balanced and thoroughly researched book traces the long and still unwinding history of marijuana policy and activism in the U.S."

Booklist

362.384   People with mental disabilities

Barry, Dan

The **Boys** in the Bunkhouse; Servitude and Salvation in the Heartland. Dan Barry. HarperCollins 2016 352 p. illustrations (ebook) $25.99; $26.99   **362.384**
1. Peonage 2. Atalissa (Iowa) -- History 3. People with mental disabilities
ISBN 9780062372154; 0062372130; 9780062372130
                                            LC 2016013131
In this book, by Dan Barry, "in the tiny Iowa farm town of Atalissa, dozens of men, all with intellectual disability and all from Texas, lived in an old schoolhouse. Before dawn each morning, they were bussed to a nearby processing plant, where they eviscerated turkeys in return for food, lodging, and $65 a month. They lived in near servitude for more than thirty years, enduring increasing neglect, exploitation, and physical and emotional abuse." (Publisher's note)
"Gently, empathetically, and indelibly, Barry conveys a tale of unthinkable brutality." Kirkus
Includes bibliographical references (pages [337]-340).

362.4   People with physical disabilities

Nielsen, Kim E.

A **disability** history of the United States; Kim E. Nielsen. Beacon Press 2012 272 p. (alk. paper) $26.95   **362.4**
1. Autonomy (Psychology) 2. United States -- History 3. People with disabilities -- Legal status, laws, etc. 4. Sociology of disability -- United States -- History 5. People with disabilities -- United States -- History 6. People with disabilities -- Legal status, laws, etc. -- United States -- History
ISBN 0807022020; 9780807022023
                                            LC 2012014236
This book "seeks to define the pivotal role of people with disabilities in [the U.S.'s] past and their contribution to our laws, policy, economics, popular culture, and our collective identity. Disability, with its presumed need for dependency, challenges the American ideal of independence and autonomy. [Kim E.] Nielsen uses various concepts of disability and dependency that go to 'the heart of both human and American experience.'" (Publisher's Weekly)
Includes bibliographical references and index.

Sacks, Oliver W.

Seeing voices; a journey into the world of the deaf. [by] Oliver Sacks. Vintage Books 2000 222p il pa $13.95 **362.4**
1. Deaf 2. Sign language 3. Gallaudet University
ISBN 0-375-70407-8
                                            LC 00-42340
First published 1989 by University of California Press
"With his philosopher's penchant for profound discovery and his neurologist's knowledge of biology and the brain, Sacks offers provocative connections and acute observations about the nature of language and culture." Booklist
Includes bibliographical references

Solomon, Andrew

★ **Far** from the tree; parents, children and the search for identity. Andrew Solomon. Scribner 2012 962 p. (hbk.: alk.

paper) $37.50   **362.4**

1. Parenting 2. Family life 3. Exceptional children 4. Slow learning children 5. Identity (Psychology) -- United States 6. Parents of exceptional children -- United States 7. Exceptional children -- United States -- Psychology 8. Parents of children with disabilities -- United States 9. Children with disabilities -- United States -- Psychology 10. Parent and child -- United States -- Psychological aspects

ISBN 0743236718; 9780743236713; 9780743236720; 9781439183106; 9781442356108; 9781442357433

LC 2012020878

In this book, Andrew Solomon "writes about families coping with deafness, dwarfism, Down syndrome, autism, schizophrenia, multiple severe disabilities, with children who are prodigies, who are conceived in rape, who become criminals, who are transgender. . . . All parenting turns on a crucial question: to what extent parents should accept their children for who they are, and to what extent they should help them become their best selves." (Publisher's note)

Includes bibliographical references (p. 831-906) and index.

Witter, Bret

Until Tuesday; a wounded warrior and the golden retriever who saved him. [by] Luis Carlos Montalvan with Bret Witter. Hyperion 2011 272p illustrations hardcover $23   **362.4**

1. Veterans 2. Army officers

ISBN 9781401324292

LC 2010051147

"A highly decorated captain in the U.S. Army, Luis Montalvan never backed down from a challenge during his two tours of duty in Iraq. After returning home from combat, however, the pressures of his physical wounds, traumatic brain injury, and crippling post-traumatic stress disorder began to take their toll. . . . Then Luis met Tuesday, a beautiful and sensitive golden retriever trained to assist the disabled. Tuesday had lived amongst prisoners and at a home for troubled boys, blessing many lives; he could turn on lights, open doors, and sense the onset of anxiety and flashbacks. But because of a unique training situation and sensitive nature, he found it difficult to trust in or connect with a human being--until Luis." (Publisher's note)

"Montalvan's mixture of memoir, military history, and pet story results in an urgently important tale." Booklist

362.43   People with mobility impairments

Crosby, Christina

A **body,** undone; living on after great pain. Christina Crosby. New York University Press 2016 213 p. (cl: alk. paper) $22.95   **362.43**

1. Lesbians -- United States -- Biography 2. Quadriplegics -- United States -- Biography 3. Feminists -- United States -- Biography 4. Authors, American -- 21st century -- Biography 5. Women college teachers -- United States -- Biography

ISBN 9781479833535

LC 2015034127

In this book in the Sexual Cultures series, author Christina Crosby "puts into words a broken body that seems beyond the reach of language and understanding. She writes about a body shot through with neurological pain, disoriented in time and space, incapacitated by paralysis and deadened sensation. To address this foreign body, she calls upon the readerly pleasures of narrative, critical feminist and queer thinking, and the concentrated language of lyric poetry." (Publisher's note)

"A potent memoir that rips open a most human heart." Kirkus

Includes bibliographical references and index

362.5   Poor people

Edelman, Peter

★ **Not** a crime to be poor; the criminalization of poverty in America. Peter Edelman. The New Press 2017 xix, 293 p.p $26.95   **362.5**

1. Poor -- Government policy -- United States 2. Poverty -- Government policy -- United States 3. Administration of criminal justice -- United States

ISBN 1620971631; 9781620971635

LC 2017025523

This book, by Peter Edelman, explains that "Ferguson is everywhere in America today. Through money bail systems, fees and fines, strictly enforced laws and regulations against behavior including trespassing and public urination that largely affect the homeless, and the substitution of prisons and jails for the mental hospitals that have traditionally served the impoverished, in one of the richest countries on Earth we have effectively made it a crime to be poor." (Publisher's note)

Includes bibliographical references (pages 253-276) and index.

Kozol, Jonathan

Rachel and her children; homeless families in America. Three Rivers Press 2006 303p pa $13.95   **362.5**

1. Homeless persons

ISBN 0-307-34589-0

LC 2007-281899

A reissue of the title first published 1988

"While the individual stories that Kozol tells so affectingly point out the vivid realities of urban poverty, the book also supplies statistics that detail the more abstract-and-inhuman-attitudes that contemporary society assumes when attempting to deal with its victims." Booklist

Includes bibliographical references

Tirado, Linda

Hand to mouth; living in bootstrap America. Linda Tirado. G.P. Putnam's Sons, a member of Penguin Group (USA) 2014 224 p. (hardback) $25.95   **362.5**

1. Poor -- United States 2. Poverty -- United States 3. Social classes -- United States

ISBN 9780399171987

LC 2014023347

This book, by Linda Tirado, "articulates not only what it is to be working poor in America (yes, you can be poor and live in a house and have a job, even two), but what poverty is truly like—on all levels. Frankly and boldly, Tirado discusses openly how she went from lower-middle class, to sometimes middle class, to poor and everything in between, and in doing so reveals why 'poor people don't always behave the way middle-class America thinks they should.'" (Publisher's note)

"Outspoken and vindictive, Tirado embodies the cyclical vortex of today's struggle to survive." Kirkus

Vollmann, William T.

★ **Poor** people. Ecco 2007 314p il $29.95; pa $16.95   **362.5**

1. Poor 2. Poverty

ISBN 0-06-087882-7; 978-0-06-087882-5; 0-06-087884-3 pa; 978-0-06-087884-9 pa

LC 2006-48547

The author "brings to bear his keen powers of observation on the world around him and, not incidentally, on himself; he is unabashed about allowing his emotional reactions to inform his thoughts about what it means to be poor. This remarkable book is sui generis and should be in all collections." Libr J

362.6   People in late adulthood

Delehanty, Hugh

Caring for your parents; the complete AARP guide. [by] Hugh Delehanty & Elinor Ginzler; foreword by Mary Pipher. Rev. and expanded ed.; Sterling Pub. 2008 xvii, 238p il pa $12.95   **362.6**

1. Aging parents 2. Elderly -- Care
ISBN 1-4027-5857-X; 978-1-4027-5857-7

LC 2008-277441

First published 2005

The authors "provide information on everything from the first difficult conversations with parents about their changing situation to coping with terminal illness and death. The book has a wealth of data on long-distance caregiving, financial matters, community-based and professional case management, Medicare, and age-related physical changes." Libr J

Includes bibliographical references

Hogan, Paul Ross

Stages of senior care; your step-by-step guide to making the best decisions. by Paul Hogan and Lori Hogan. McGraw-Hill 2009 292p il pa $18.95   **362.6**

1. Aging parents 2. Elderly -- Care
ISBN 978-0-07-162109-0

LC 2009-20572

This is "a helpful guide for families choosing among home caregiving and other assisted-living options for aging or ailing parents." Publ Wkly

Includes bibliographical references

362.7   Young people

Caughman, Susan

You can adopt; an Adoptive Families guide. [by] Susan Caughman and Isolde Motley; with the editors and readers of Adoptive Families magazine. Ballantine Books 2009 296p il pa $16   **362.7**

1. Adoption
ISBN 978-0-345-50401-2; 0-345-50401-1

LC 2009-20252

"This thorough and honest resource stands out among other books on the topic in both its comprehensiveness and the authors' candor in discussing potentially controversial adoption-related issues. Domestic or international adoption? An infant or an older child? A sibling group? What about adopting transracially? These questions and many more are addressed here via a straightforward text interspersed with firsthand, sometimes wrenching accounts by adoptive parents, birth parents, and adoptees themselves." Booklist

Includes bibliographical references

Gammage, Jeff

China ghosts; my daughter's journey to America, my passage to fatherhood. William Morrow 2007 255p il $25.95 **362.7**

1. Adoption
ISBN 978-0-06-124029-4; 0-06-124029-X

LC 2007-61204

"A father's account of going to China with his wife to adopt their first and second daughters. . . . Gammage, a staff writer for the Philadelphia Inquirer, had been happily married without children for many years, although he knew his wife really wanted children. By the time they discovered they couldn't have biological children, the best option was adopting from China. While there were tensions over their first daughter's medical problems (an infected scalp injury), both adoptions went reasonably smoothly. Back home, Gammage wrestled with his mixed feelings about the birth parents and his burden of good fortune, that guilty knowledge that his own happiness came from someone else's misfortune. Realizing that his own relationship to China was being shaped by the process of raising two Chinese girls, he ends this upbeat memoir by wondering about the impact of this new wave of immigrants on the future of Sino-American relations." Publ Wkly

Groza, Victor

Adopting older children; a practical guide to adopting and parenting children over age four. Stephanie Bosco-Ruggiero, Gloria Russo-Wassell, Victor Graza. New Horizon Press 2014 240 p. $15.95   **362.7**

1. Adoption 2. Parenting
ISBN 0882824821; 9780882824826

LC 2014938451

This book by Stephanie Bosco-Ruggiero, Gloria Russo Wassell, and Victor Groza "addresses the most significant challenges surrounding older-child adoption (both domestically and internationally), including mental health, behavioral, and educational concerns. This thorough guide enumerates the issues an older adopted child faces and provides a comprehensive overview of problems and how adopting parents can successfully deal with them, including critical information about developmental issues." (Publisher's note)

An appendix of online resources —websites, video interviews, documentaries, etc.—rounds out this helpful, if far from comprehensive, addition to the literature on adoption." Publisher's Weekly

Kozol, Jonathan

Amazing grace; the lives of children and the conscience of a nation. HarperPerennial 1996 284p pa $14.95   **362.7**

1. Inner cities 2. Children with social disabilities 3. Poor -- New York (N.Y.)
ISBN 0-06-097697-7; 978-0-06-097697-2

First published 1995 by Crown

Kozol's "powerfully understated report takes us inside rat-infested homes that are freezing in winter, overcrowded schools, dysfunctional clinics, soup kitchens. . . . While his narrative offers no specific solutions, it forcefully drives home his conviction: a civilized nation cannot allow this situation to continue." Publ Wkly

Includes bibliographical references

Kozol, Jonathan, 1936-

Fire in the ashes; twenty-five years among the poorest children in America. Jonathan Kozol. 1st ed. Crown Publishers 2012 x, 368 p.p $27   **362.7**

1. Poor -- United States 2. Poor children -- United States 3. Children -- United States -- Social conditions 4. Child welfare -- United States 5. Poor families -- United States
ISBN 1400052467; 9781400052462

LC 2012005183

In this book, author Jonathan Kozol profiles "a group of inner-city children he has known for many years, . . . as they grow into adulthood. . . . Jonathan tells the stories of young men and women who have come of age in one of the most destitute communities of the United States. Some of them never do recover from the battering they undergo in their early years, but many more battle back with fierce . . . determination to overcome the formidable obstacles they face." (Publisher's note)

Includes bibliographical references and index.

Tough, Paul

Whatever it takes; Geoffrey Canada's quest to change Harlem and America. Houghton Mifflin Co. 2008 296p il map **362.7**

1. Poverty 2. Poverty -- Prevention 3. Organization officials 4. Social welfare leaders 5. Poor -- Social conditions 6. Education -- United States 7. African American children -- Education 8. Harlem (New York, N.Y.) -- Economic conditions

ISBN 0-618-56989-8; 978-0-618-56989-2

LC 2008-13303

This is an account of Geoffrey Canada's creation of "the Harlem Children's Zone, a ninety-seven-block . . . [area] in central Harlem where he is testing new . . . ideas about poverty in America." (Publisher's note) Index.

"Tough profiles educational visionary Geoffrey Canada, whose Harlem Children's Zone—currently serving more than 7,000 children and encompassing 97 city blocks—represents an audacious effort to end poverty within underserved communities. . . . This book gives readers a solid look at the problems facing poor communities and their reformers, as well as good cause to be optimistic about the future." Publ Wkly

Includes bibliographical references

Wides-Muñoz, Laura

The **making** of a dream; how a group of young undocumented immigrants helped change what it means to be American. Laura Wides-Munoz. HarperCollins 2018 384 p. $27.99 **362.7**

1. Unauthorized immigrants 2. Immigration law -- United States 3. United States -- Immigration and emigration

ISBN 0062560123; 9780062560124

In this book, by Laura Wides-Muñoz, "a journalist chronicles the next chapter in civil rights--the story of a movement and a nation, witnessed through the poignant and inspiring experiences of five young undocumented activists who are transforming society's attitudes toward one of the most contentious political matters roiling America today: immigration." (Publisher's note)

"This inspiring, well-written, well-documented account is an important read for Americans on all sides of this lingering issue." LJ

362.71 Specific kinds of services to young people

Vanover, Sarah Taylor

Finding Quality Early Childcare; A Step-by-Step Guide for Parents about What Matters Most. Sarah Vanover. Rowman & Littlefield 2016 122 p. $24; (ebook) $30 **362.71**

1. Child rearing 2. School choice 3. Day care centers 4. Child development 5. Preschool education 6. Early childhood education

ISBN 1475827733; 9781475827736; 9781475827750

LC 2017006230

This book, by Sarah Vanover, "reviews foundational elements of childcare, such as health and safety features, while explaining educational strategies, including styles of teaching and daily classroom activities. . . . [It] also covers types of specialized childcare, such as infant care and childcare for children with special needs, reviews Transitional Kindergarten, and discusses when children are ready to transition from preschool to Kindergarten." (Publisher's note)

"The information is straightforward and clearly presented and gives parents a good understanding of both general theory and practical appli-

cation of early-childhood education, allowing them to make an informed choice for their children." Booklist

362.73 Institutional and related services

Beam, Cris

★ **To** the end of June; the intimate life of American foster care. Cris Beam. Houghton Mifflin Harcourt 2013 336 p. $26 **362.73**

1. Foster home care 2. United States -- Social conditions 3. Foster home care -- United States

ISBN 0151014124; 9780151014125

LC 2013001331

This book looks at the foster care system in the U.S. "Following the lives of foster children, meeting their natural and foster parents, and interviewing experts, [Cris] Beam developed a broad overview. Intended to be a temporary arrangement, foster care frequently fails to lead either to resolution of the biological parents' problems and restoration of the birth family or to the children's permanent adoption into a new home." (Kirkus Reviews)

Includes bibliographical references

Bernstein, Nina

The **lost** children of Wilder; the epic struggle to change foster care. Pantheon Bks. 2001 482p hardcover o.p. pa $15 **362.73**

1. Child welfare 2. Foster home care

ISBN 0-679-75834-8 pa

LC 00-57456

National Book Award Finalist: Nonfiction (2001)

"Bernstein explores the genesis and aftermath of the landmark 1973 legal case filed by young ACLU attorney Marcia Lowry against the New York State foster-care system. Known as Wilder for its 14-year-old African-American plaintiff, Shirley 'Pinky' Wilder, the suit claimed Jewish and Catholic child welfare services had a lock on foster care funding and placements. . . . This viscerally powerful history of institutionalized child abuse and the criminalization of poverty, of civil rights and social change, is compelling and essential reading." Publ Wkly

Includes bibliographical references

Moody, Anne, 1940-2015

The **children** money can buy; stories from the frontlines of foster care and adoption. Anne Moody. Rowman & Littlefield 2018 266 p. (cloth: alk. paper) $38 **362.73**

1. Adoption 2. Foster home care -- United States 3. Adoption -- United States

ISBN 9781538108024

LC 2017034191

This book, by Anne Moody, "illuminates the worlds of foster care and adoption through the personal stories . . . [the author] witnessed and experienced in her many years working in the foster care and adoption systems. These compelling stories about real people and situations illustrate larger life lessons about the way our society values--and fails to value--parents and children." (Publisher's note)

362.734 Adoption

Aronson, Jane

Carried in Our Hearts; The Gift of Adoption: Inspiring Stories of Families Created Across Continents. Penguin 2013 336

p. $25.95   **362.734**

ISBN 0399161058; 9780399161056

"There is a wealth of information--and hope--here for people looking at possibilities for international adoption, and there is certainly no better advocate on the long journey than the upbeat, passionate Aronson." Pub Wkly

Joyce, Kathryn

★ The **child** catchers; rescue, trafficking, and the new gospel of adoption. Kathryn Joyce. PublicAffairs 2013 352 p. (hardback) $26.99   **362.734**

1. Adoption 2. Evangelicalism -- United States 3. Abortion -- Religious aspects -- Christianity 4. Adoption -- Religious aspects -- Christianity

ISBN 1586489429; 9781586489427; 9781586489434

LC 2012044316

This book "examines the rise of adoption as a practice and cause among American evangelical communities . . . . The more than 150 million so-termed orphans and vulnerable children worldwide frequently have living family members . . . capable of raising them, circumstances . . . lost in the mix of aggressive agencies, inadequate regulation, vulnerable families lacking understanding of the concept of adoption as permanent, and adoptive families with emotional and financial resources invested." (Library Journal)

Includes bibliographical references and index

Sweeney, Julia

If it's not one thing, it's your mother; Julia Sweeney. Free Press 2013 256 p. (hardcover) $26   **362.734**

1. Working mothers 2. Adopted children 3. Parenting -- California 4. Motherhood -- California 5. Adopted children -- California

ISBN 145167404X; 9781451674040; 9781451674057

LC 2012049503

This book is comedian Julia Sweeney's "memoir on adopting and raising a family." She writes about "her childhood, finding a suitable nanny during her daughter's childhood, her failed relationships and life as a working mother . . . . Her thoughts swirled around the complexities of educating her daughter about human anatomy and sex." (Kirkus)

362.74   Specific kinds of young people

Phelps, Carissa

Runaway girl; escaping life on the streets, one helping hand at a time. Carissa Phelps with Larkin Warren. Viking 2012 311 p. $19.99   **362.74**

1. Runaway children 2. Juvenile prostitution 3. Prostitution -- California 4. Runaway children -- California -- Biography 5. Sexually abused children -- California -- Biography

ISBN 1561636150; 9780670023721

LC 2011038441

In this memoir, Carissa Phelps discusses "her loveless, troubled childhood." After running away from a state group home at age 12, "she meets crack-addicted Natara, a prostitute, and Icey, a pimp, a pair who promise to take care of her." Eventually, "she lands in the Youth Authority detention center. There, she meets her first mentor, counselor Ron Jenkins. Slowly and with setbacks, Phelps rebuilds her life and graduates from high school thanks to the perseverance of a teacher." (Publishers Weekly)

Includes bibliographical references.

362.785   Transgender young people and intersex young people

Whittington, Hillary

Raising Ryland; Our Story of Parenting a Transgender Child With No Strings Attached. HarperCollins 2016 304 p. illustrations (some color) (ebook) $7.34; $15.99   **362.785**

1. Deaf children 2. Transgender people

ISBN 9780062388896; 0062388886; 9780062388889

LC 2016440367

"From the earliest stages of deciphering Ryland through clothing choices to examining the difficult conversations that have marked every stage of Ryland's transition, [author] Hillary Whittington shares her experiences as a mother through it all, demonstrating both the resistance and support that their family has encountered as they try to erase the stigma surrounding the word 'transgender.'" (Publisher's note)

"An uplifting testimonial to the power of unconditional familial love and acceptance." Kirkus

362.786   Young people by sexual orientation

Berg, Ryan

No house to call my home; Love, Family, and Other Transgressions. Ryan Berg. Nation Books 2015 320 p. (hardback) $25.99; (ebook) $9.99   **362.786**

1. LGBT youth -- New York (State) -- New York 2. Gay teenagers -- Counseling of -- New York (State) -- New York 3. Residence counselors -- New York (State) -- New York 4. Group homes for youth -- New York (State) -- New York 5. Gay teenagers -- Services for -- New York (State) -- New York 6. Sexual minority youth -- Services for -- New York (State) -- New York 7. Sexual minority youth -- Counseling of -- New York (State) -- New York

ISBN 9781568585093; 9781568585109

LC 2015011424

This book by Ryan Berg focuses "on the lives and loves of eight unforgettable youth. . . [and] traces their efforts to break away from dangerous sex work and cycles of drug and alcohol abuse. . . . From Bella's fervent desire for stability to Christina's . . . dreams of stardom to Benny's . . . efforts to find someone to love him, Berg uncovers the real lives behind the harrowing statistics: over 4,000 youth are homeless in New York City—43 percent of them identify as LGBTQ." (Publisher's note)

"Through their compelling stories, Berg looks at inequalities suffered by LGBTQ youth in housing, public safety, health care, prison, immigration, employment, poverty, and homelessness." Booklist

Includes bibliographical references and index

362.82   Families

Dalpiaz, Christina M.

Breaking free, starting over; parenting in the aftermath of family violence. Praeger 2004 232p $39.95   **362.82**

1. Parenting 2. Domestic violence

ISBN 0-275-98167-3

LC 2003-62436

This guide provides "techniques for reparenting children who've been exposed to domestic violence. Lacking a safe haven, many of these children exhibit significant behavior, communication, and self-management problems." Libr J

Includes bibliographical references

Denham, Wes

Arrested; what to do when your loved one's in jail. Chicago Review Press 2010 263p il pa $16.95   **362.82**

1. Prisoners

ISBN 978-1-55652-834-7; 1-55652-834-5

LC 2009-42270

This book is an "extended checklist for those coping with the incarceration of a family member or significant friend, from the time the phone rings with news of the arrest onward. Denham shares the jargon, procedures, tricks, and traps in his coverage of jail visits, bail, public defenders, jail medical care, and legal and jail costs, and he outlines a decision-making process that considers the well-being of the entire family. . . .Hard-hitting, blunt, and practical, this book is packed with inside knowledge of the jail experience. It's a necessary purchase for criminal justice collections in public libraries." Libr J

Includes bibliographical references

Domestic violence sourcebook; edited by Joyce Brennfleck Shannon. 3rd ed.; Omnigraphics 2009 665p il (Health reference series) $84   **362.82**

1. Reference books 2. Domestic violence

ISBN 978-0-7808-1038-9; 0-7808-1038-4

LC 2009-4386

First published 2000 under the editorship of Helene Henderson with title: Domestic violence & child abuse sourcebook

"Provides basic consumer health information about the physical, mental, and social effects of violence against intimate partners, children, teens, parents, and the elderly, along with prevention and intervention strategies." Publisher's note

Includes bibliographical references

Fessler, Ann

The **girls** who went away; the hidden history of women who surrendered children for adoption in the decades before Roe v. Wade. Penguin Press 2006 354p hardcover o.p. pa $16   **362.82**

1. Adoption

ISBN 1-59420-094-7; 0-14-303897-4 pa

LC 2005-58179

"These knowing oral histories are an emotional boon for birth mothers and adoptees struggling to make sense of troubled pasts." Publ Wkly

Includes bibliographical references

Lambert, Carol A.

Women with controlling partners; taking back your life from a manipulative or abusive partner. Carol Lambert, MSW. New Harbinger Publications, Inc. 2016 226 p. (ebook) $13.95; (pbk.: alk. paper) $16.95   **362.82**

1. Self-esteem 2. Abused women 3. Domestic violence 4. Self-help techniques 5. Self-esteem in women 6. Family violence -- Prevention 7. Psychological abuse -- Prevention 8. Intimate partner violence -- Prevention

ISBN 9781626254725; 1626254710; 9781626254718

LC 2016041010

This book, by Carol Lambert, MSW, "will help you identify the coercive constraints that can be predictive of intimate partner abuse, recognize the harmful effects of psychological abuse on your mental and physical health, and gain the personal strength and power to break free. Using the author's three-stage recovery model, you'll be empowered to move out of denial, deconstruct what holds you psychologically captive, and take back your life." (Publisher's note)

"A poignant and necessary book for all women who live in fear in their own homes." LJ

Includes bibliographical references

Marshall, Samantha

Reunited; an investigative genealogist unlocks some of life's greatest family mysteries. Pamela Slaton; with Samantha Marshall. St. Martin's Griffin 2012 248 p. (trade pbk.) $14.99   **362.82**

1. Adoption 2. Genealogy 3. Adoptees -- United States -- Identification -- Case studies 4. Birthparents -- United States -- Identification -- Case studies

ISBN 0312617321; 9780312617325; 9781250012135

LC 2012004630

This book shares the experience of investigative genealogist Pamela Slaton. An "adopted child herself, the author's sleuthing career began 15 years ago when her husband hired an investigator to locate her birth mother. Although she was raised by a loving adoptive family, Slaton had always wondered about her roots. . . . The author tells about finding her own extended birth family and the touching stories of some of the clients she has helped." (Kirkus Reviews)

Sundberg, Kelly

Goodbye, sweet girl; a story of domestic violence and survival. Kelly Sundberg. HarperCollins 2018 272 p. $26.99   **362.829**

1. Biography 2. Domestic violence 3. Abused women -- United States -- Biography

ISBN 0062497677; 9780062497673

This memoir, by Kelly Sundberg, "chronicles how her marriage devolved from a love story into a shocking tale of abuse--examining the tenderness and violence entwined in the relationship, why she endured years of physical and emotional pain, and how she eventually broke free. . . . [Sundberg] offers an intimate record of the joys and terrors that accompanied her long, difficult awakening, and presents a . . . glimpse into why women remain too long in dangerous relationships." (Publisher's note)

Weiss, Elaine

Family & friends' guide to domestic violence; how to listen, talk, and take action, when someone you care about is being abused. Volcano Press 2003 143p pa $17.95   **362.82**

1. Domestic violence

ISBN 1-88424-422-X

LC 2003-4642

This is a "guide for family and friends, with practical tips for communicating with a likely victim of abuse, including how to broach the subject." Libr J

Includes bibliographical references

Surviving domestic violence; voices of women who broke free. Volcano Press 2004 214p pa $17.95   **362.82**

1. Domestic violence

ISBN 1-88424-427-0

LC 2003-27829

First published 2000 by Agreka Bks.

The author tells the "stories of 12 survivors, ranging in age and socioeconomic circumstances. She concludes each case study with a reflective commentary that emphasizes the strength and courage of these women." Libr J

Includes bibliographical references

362.83   Women

Kristof, Nicholas D., 1959-

★ **Half** the sky; turning oppression to opportunity for women worldwide. [by] Nicholas D. Kristof and Sheryl Wu-Dunn. Alfred A. Knopf 2009 xxii, 294p il $27.95; ebook $15.95; pa $15.95   **362.83**

1. Women's rights 2. Women -- Developing countries 3. Women's rights -- Developing countries 4. Women -- Crimes against -- Developing countries 5. Women -- Developing countries -- Social conditions

ISBN 9780307267146; 9780307273154; 9780307387097

LC 2009-12270

Kristof and WuDunn address what they consider to be "our era's most pervasive human rights violation: the oppression of women in the developing world. They show that a little help can transform the lives of women and girls abroad and that the key to economic progress lies in unleashing women's potential." (Publisher's note) Index.

This book "is a call to arms, a call for help, a call for contributions, but also a call for volunteers. It asks us to open our eyes to this enormous humanitarian issue. It does so with exquisitely crafted prose and sensationally interesting material." Washington Post Book World

Includes bibliographical references

362.84   Ethnic and national groups

Youngstedt, Scott M.

★ **Surviving** with dignity; Hausa communities of Niamey, Niger. by Scott M. Youngstedt. Lexington Books 2012 xv, 226 p.p ill., map (hbk.: alk. paper) $65   **362.84**

1. Niger 2. Internal migration 3. Rural-urban migration -- Niger 4. Hausa (African people) -- Niger -- Niamey -- Social conditions 5. Hausa (African people) -- Niger -- Niamey -- Economic conditions

ISBN 0739173502; 9780739173503; 9780739173510

LC 2012040502

This book, by Scott M. Youngstedt, "explores three key interconnected themes—structural violence, suffering, and surviving with dignity—through examining the lived experiences of first and second-generation migrant Hausa men in Niamey over the past two decades in the current neoliberal moment.The central goal of the book is to explain the material (migration and informal economy work) and symbolic (meaning-making) strategies that Hausa individuals and communities have deployed in their struggles . . . to survive with dignity." (Publisher's note)

Includes bibliographical references (p. [213]-223) and index

362.86   Veterans of military service

Bannerman, Stacy

Homefront 911; how families of veterans are wounded by our wars. Stacy Bannerman. Arcade Publishing 2015 304 p. (hardcover: alkaline paper) $24.99   **362.86**

1. Afghan War, 2001- 2. Iraq War, 2003-2011 3. Veterans -- United States 4. Civil-military relations -- United States 5. Veterans -- Services for -- United States 6. Veterans -- Mental health -- United States 7. Afghan War, 2001- -- Veterans -- United States 8. Families of military personnel -- United States 9. Iraq War, 2003-2011 -- Veterans -- United States 10. Veterans -- Family relationships -- United States 11. Families of military personnel -- Services for -- United States 12. Families of military personnel -- Mental health -- United States

ISBN 9781628725698

LC 2015019123

This book, by Stacy Bannerman, "provides an insider's view of how more than a decade of war has contributed to the emerging crisis we are experiencing in today's military and veteran families as they battle with overwhelmed VA offices, a public they feel doesn't understand their sacrifices, and a nation that still isn't fully prepared to help those who have given so much." (Publisher's note)

"An activist, Bannerman has set up programs for women, drafted legislation, and testified before congressional committees. Here, she takes her message to a broader public in a disturbing cry for help." Kirkus

Includes bibliographical references (pages 270-282).

Finkel, David

★ **Thank** You for Your Service; by David Finkel. Farrar, Straus and Giroux 2013 272 p. $27   **362.86**

1. Veterans -- Employment 2. Veterans -- United States 3. Iraq War, 2003-2011 -- Psychological aspects 4. Post-traumatic stress disorder -- United States 5. Iraq War, 2003-2011 -- Veterans -- United States

ISBN 0374180660; 9780374180669

LC 2013021990

National Book Critics Circle Award Finalist: Nonfiction (2013); LA Times Book Prize Finalist: Current Interest (2013)

In this book, author David Finkel "has embedded with some of the men of the 2-16 [Infantry Battalion]--but this time he has done it . . . after their deployments have ended. He is with them in their most intimate, painful, and hopeful moments as they try to recover, and in doing so, he creates a . . . portrait of what life after war is like." (Publisher's note)

"It is impossible not to be moved, outraged, and saddened by these stories, and Finkel's deeply personal brand of narrative journalism is both heartbreaking and gut-wrenching in its unflinching honesty." Booklist

Includes bibliographical references and index

362.88   Victims of crimes and war

Crompton, Vicki

Saving beauty from the beast; how to protect your daughter from an unhealthy relationship. by Vicki Crompton and Ellen Zelda Kessner. Little, Brown 2003 259p il $22.95; pa $13.95   **362.88**

1. Parenting 2. Abused women

ISBN 0-316-09058-1; 0-316-73552-3 pa

LC 2002-19153

This book "illuminates the problems of dangerous relationships by describing their characteristics, mapping out warning signs of abuse and offering sound advice for parents seeking to empower their daughters. The authors interviewed psychologists, counselors and girls who have had violent boyfriends; the girls' stories, as well as first-person accounts from parents and abusive boyfriends, are woven throughout the text. . . . This book serves as both fervent friend and practical coach to parents whose daughters may be facing abuse." Publ Wkly

Includes bibliographical references

Kushner, David

Alligator candy; a memoir. David Kushner. Simon & Schuster 2016 256 p. (hardcover) $26   **362.88**

1. Brothers 2. Homicide 3. Children of anthropologists -- Biography 4. Murder victims -- Florida -- Tampa -- Biography 5.

Murder victims' families -- Florida -- Tampa -- Biography
ISBN 9781451682533; 9781451682601; 9781451682632
LC 2015022792

This memoir, by David Kushner, "is the story of [his brother] Jon's murder at the hands of two sadistic drifters and everything that happened after. [It] isn't only the chronicle of Jon's death, it is also the story of how parenting in America changed, casting light on the transition between two generations of children—one raised on freedom, the other on fear. Jon's death was one of the first in what turned out to be a rash of child abductions and murders that dominated headlines for much of the 1970s and 80s." (Publisher's note)

"This emotional account invites readers to journey down a path that at first is in the shade but eventually wanders through strands of sunlight. You will hold those close to you tight after reading. For fans of true crime, books about getting past tragedy, and memoirs." Library Journal

Nelson, Maggie, 1973-

The **red** parts; Autobiography of a Trial. Maggie Nelson. Graywolf Press 2016 201 p. illustrations (alk. paper) $16   **362.88**
1. Evidence 2. Trials (Homicide) 3. Cold cases (Criminal investigation)
ISBN 9781555977368
LC 2015953598

In this memoir, "in 2004, Maggie Nelson was looking forward to the publication of her book Jane: A Murder, . . . about the life and death of her aunt, who had been murdered thirty-five years before. The case remained unsolved, but Jane was assumed to have been the victim of an infamous serial killer. . . . Then, one November afternoon, Nelson received a call from her mother, who announced that the case had been reopened; a new suspect would be arrested and tried." (Publisher's note)

Surviving sexual violence; a guide to recovery and empowerment. edited by Thema Bryant-Davis. Rowman & Littlefield Publishers 2011 ix, 372 p.p (cloth: alk. paper) $49.95; (electronic) $49.95   **362.88**
1. Rape 2. Sex crimes 3. Sexual harassment 4. Sexual abuse victims -- Psychology 5. Sexual abuse victims -- Rehabilitation
ISBN 144220639X; 9781442206397; 9781442206410
LC 2011013937

Author Thema Bryant-Davis's "book outlines and describes the impact of particular types of sexual violation . . . [including] childhood sexual abuse, sexual assault during adulthood, marital rape, sexual harassment, sex trafficking, or sexual violence within the military. . . . [Readers] are introduced to various pathways to surviving sexual violence and moving forward. . . . Survivors can make use of the particular approaches, which include mind-body practices, counseling, group therapies, self-defense training, and others." (Publisher's note)

Includes bibliographical references and index.

362.883   Rape

Elva, Thordis

South of forgiveness; a story of rape and responsibility. Thordis Elva and Tom Stranger. Skyhorse Publishing 2017 307 p. (hc: alk. paper) $24.99   **362.883**
1. Rape victims 2. Sex offenders 3. Rapists -- South Africa -- Biography 4. Rape victims -- South Africa -- Biography
ISBN 9781510730021; 9781510730014
LC 2017008561

This book, by Thordis Elva and Tom Stranger, "is an unprecedented

collaboration between a survivor and a perpetrator, each equally committed to exploring the darkest moment of their lives. It is a true story about being bent but not broken, facing fear with courage, and finding hope even in the most wounded of places. . . . [It presents a] look at a gendered violence, rape culture, personal responsibility, and the effect that patriarchal cultures have on both men and women." (Publisher's note)

Includes bibliographical references and index

Krakauer, Jon, 1954-

Missoula; by Jon Krakauer. Doubleday 2015 384 p. (hardcover: alk. paper) $28.95   **362.883**
1. Date rape 2. Trials (Rape) 3. Missoula (Mont.) 4. Rape -- Montana -- Missoula 5. Rape victims -- Montana -- Missoula 6. Trials (Rape) -- Montana -- Missoula
ISBN 0385538731; 9780385538732
LC 2015002686

This book "follows a rash of rapes at the University of Montana in Missoula from 2010 to 2012." Author Jon Krakauer "sticks with two cases in particular through agonizing courtroom dramas, spotlighting the two obstacles to justice. The first is haphazard investigation, made worse by . . . callousness and suspicion about the motives of women making rape allegations. . . . The second is the counterintuitive behavior of traumatized victims, which often undermines their claims." (Kirkus Reviews)

"Krakauer has done considerable research into acquaintance rape, and his recounting of trials, both legal and university proceedings, is riveting. His focus on quoting from testimony means that it is harder for readers to understand the motivations of someone like Kirsten Pabst, a former prosecutor who became a lawyer for an accused football player; an interview with her could have been useful. A raw and difficult but necessary read." Kirkus

Includes bibliographical references and index

Ream, Anne K.

Lived through this; listening to the stories of sexual-violence survivors. Anne K. Ream; with photographs by Patricia Evans. Beacon Press 2014 216 p. illustrations (hardcover: alk. paper) $24.95   **362.883**
1. Sex crimes 2. Rape victims 3. Sex crimes -- Case studies 4. Sexual abuse victims -- Case studies
ISBN 0807033367; 9780807033364
LC 2013045411

This book, by Anne K. Ream, is about "rape and sexual violence survivors. . . . In these pages we are introduced to . . . the women of Atenco, Mexico, victims of rape and political torture who are speaking out about gender-based violence in Latin America; Beth Adubato, a woman who was raped by a popular athlete; . . . and Jenny and Steve Bush, a rape survivor and her father who are working together to share Jenny's testimony of surviving rape at the hands of a veteran." (Publisher's note)

"Ream's prose is approachable, making the book a useful introductory primer for anyone studying sexual violence. The helpful inclusion of statistics at the end, which puts quantitative weight behind these individual stories, enhances the book's educational value." Pub Wkly

Includes bibliographical references

Sebold, Alice

Lucky. Back Bay Books 2002 246p pa $11.95   **362.883**
1. Rape
ISBN 0-316-09619-9
First published 1999 by Scribner

When the author "was a college freshman at Syracuse University, she was attacked and raped on the last night of school. . . . Sebold launches her memoir headlong into the rape itself, laying out its visceral physical as well as mental violence, and from there spins a narrative of her life before and after the incident, weaving memories of parental alcoholism together with her post-rape addiction to heroin. In the midst of each wrenching episode, from the initial attack to the ensuing courtroom drama, Sebold's wit is as powerful as her searing candor." Publ Wkly

Winslow, Emily

Jane Doe January; my twenty-year search for truth and justice. Emily Winslow. William Morrow 2016 288 p. (ebook) $25.99; (hardback) $26.99   **362.883**

1. Rape 2. Rape victims 3. Trials (Rape) -- United States 4. Rape victims -- United States -- Biography 5. Serial rape investigation -- United States 6. Authors, American -- 21st century -- Biography
ISBN 9780062434845; 9780062434807

LC 2015046675

This book, by Emily Winslow, is a "real-life crime mystery.... Winslow was a young drama student . . . in Pittsburgh when a man brutally attacked and raped her in January 1992. While the police's search for her rapist proved futile, Emily reclaimed her life. Over the course of the next two decades, she fell in love, married, had two children, and began writing mystery novels. . . . Then, in fall 2013, she received shocking news—the police had found her rapist." (Publisher's note)

"A potently rendered chronicle of rape and the clarity and closure achieved even when justice is only partially served." Kirkus

363.1 Public safety programs

Pringle, Peter

★ **Food,** inc; Mendel to Monsanto--the promises and perils of the biotech harvest. Simon & Schuster 2003 239p hardcover o.p. pa $13   **363.1**

1. Farm produce 2. Food -- Biotechnology
ISBN 0-7432-2611-9; 0-7432-6763-X pa

LC 2003-42823

"This is a book to satisfy curiosity and engender concern, and any of its chapters would provide an excellent subject for discussion groups." SLJ

Puleo, Stephen

Dark tide; the great Boston molasses flood of 1919. Beacon Press 2003 263p il $23   **363.1**

1. Industrial accidents 2. Boston (Mass.) -- History
ISBN 0-8070-5020-2

LC 2003-10433

"On January 15, 1919, a fifty-foot tall steel tank filled with 2.3 million gallons of molasses collapsed on Boston's waterfront, disgoring its contents as a fifteen-foot high wave of molasses that briefly traveled at thirty-five miles per hour. The Great Boston Molasses Flood claimed the lives of twenty-one people and scores of animals, injured 150, and caused widespread destruction. Tracing the era from the tank's construction in 1915 through the multiyear lawsuit that followed the tragedy, Dark Tide uses the drama of the flood to examine the sweeping changes brought about by World War I, Prohibition, the Anarchist movement, the Red Scare, Immigration, and the role of big business in society." Univ Press Books 2004

Includes bibliographical references

Wilson, Bee

Swindled; the dark history of food fraud, from poisoned candy to counterfeit coffee. Princeton University Press 2008

384p il map $26.95   **363.1**

1. Food industry 2. Food contamination
ISBN 978-0-691-13820-6

LC 2008-9688

"In this day and age of tainted milk, pet food and genetically altered food, Bee Wilson has given us an immensely readable history from the 1820's to the 21st century. Timely and purposeful, this book should bring many people to the whole foods world." Univ Press Books for Public and Second Sch Libr, 2009

Includes bibliographical references (351-361)

363.11 Occupational and industrial hazards

Galuszka, Peter A.

Thunder on the Mountain; Death at Massey and the Dirty Secrets Behind Big Coal. Peter A. Galuszka. St. Martin's Press 2012 xvii, 283 p., [8] p. of plates p ill. (hardcover) $25.99   **363.11**

1. Coal mines and mining 2. Massey Energy (Firm) 3. Coal trade -- Appalachian Region 4. Coal mines and mining -- Appalachian Region
ISBN 1250000211; 9781250000217

LC 2012028241

This book by journalist Peter A. Galuszka focuses on the U.S. coal industry. He examines a "central dichotomy: the geographical and cultural isolation of the Appalachian people, perpetuated by inaccurate and condescending popular conceptions, has fostered a big-profit environment for Big Coal even as the region remains impoverished." (Publishers Weekly)

Koppel, Ted, 1940-

Lights out; a cyberattack: a nation unprepared: surviving the aftermath. Ted Koppel. Crown Publishers 2015 272 p. (ebook) $48; (hardcover) $26   **363.11**

1. Cyberterrorism -- United States 2. Emergency management -- United States 3. Electric utilities -- Security measures -- United States 4. Preparedness -- United States 5. Self-reliant living -- United States
ISBN 9780553419979; 9780553419962; 9780553419986

LC 2015019999

This book, by Ted Koppel, reveals that a major cyberattack on America's power grid is not only possible but likely, that it would be devastating, and that the United States is shockingly unprepared. . . . Koppel makes clear, the federal government, while well prepared for natural disasters, has no plan for the aftermath of an attack on the power grid. . . . In the absence of a government plan, some individuals and communities have taken matters into their own hands." (Publisher's note)

"Easy to read and understand; recommended for all libraries." LJ

Includes bibliographical references and index

Raimi, Daniel

The **fracking** debate; the risks, benefits, and uncertainties of the shale revolution. Daniel Raimi. Columbia University Press 2017 280 p. (cloth: alk. paper) $30   **363.11**

1. Shale gas industry 2. Hydraulic fracturing 3. Hydraulic fracturing -- Social aspects 4. Hydraulic fracturing -- Environmental aspects -- Risk assessment
ISBN 9780231184861

LC 2017024122

This book, by Daniel Raimi, "directly addresses the most common questions and concerns associated with fracking: What is fracking? Does fracking pollute the water supply? . . . Does fracking cause earthquakes? How is fracking regulated? . . . Coupling a deep understanding of the scholarly research with lessons from his travels to every major U.S. oil- and gas-producing region, Raimi highlights stories of the people and communities affected by the shale revolution." (Publisher's note)

"A deft, fair analysis that clarifies the issues for both the general public and concerned policymakers." Kirkus

Includes bibliographical references and index

Tobar, Héctor

★ **Deep** down dark; the untold stories of 33 men buried in a Chilean mine, and the miracle that set them free. Hector Tobar. Fararr, Straus & Giroux 2014 320 p. illustrations (cloth) $26 **363.11**

1. Chile 2. Rescue work 3. Gold mines and mining 4. Copper mines and mining 5. San José Mine Accident, Chile, 2010
ISBN 0374280606; 9780374280604

LC 2014008385

National Book Critics Circle Finalist: Nonfiction (2014)

Los Angeles Times Book Prize Finalist: Current Interest (2014)

This book, by Hector Tobar, focuses on "the San José mine [collapse] outside of Copiapó, Chile, in August 2010, [which] trapped thirty-three miners beneath thousands of feet of rock for a record-breaking sixty-nine days. . . . Even while still buried, they all agreed that if by some miracle any of them escaped alive, they would share their story only collectively." (Publisher's note)

"Rich in local color, this is a sensitive, suspenseful rendering of a legendary story." Pub Wkly

363.12   Transportation hazards

Gonzales, Laurence, 1947-

Flight 232; A Story of Disaster and Survival. Laurence Gonzales. W.W. Norton & Co Inc. 2014 432 p. illustrations (some color) $27.95 **363.12**

1. Journalism 2. Aircraft accidents
ISBN 0393240029; 9780393240023

LC 2014005238

"United Airlines Flight 232 wallowed drunkenly over the bluffs northwest of Sioux City. The plane slammed onto the runway and burst into a vast fireball. . . . Drawing on interviews with hundreds of survivors, crew, and airport and rescue personnel, [author] Laurence Gonzales, a commercial pilot himself, captures, minute by minute, the harrowing journey of pilots flying a plane with no controls and flight attendants keeping their calm in the face of certain death." (Publisher's note)

"Gonzalez presents an absorbing account of the delicate machinery of flight-—and the titanic forces it must withstand-—-and of the investigation that traced the disaster to a tiny flaw therein." Pub Wkly

Includes bibliographical references and index

363.124   Air and space transportation

Leinbach, Michael D.

Bringing Columbia home; the untold story of a lost space shuttle and her crew. Michael D. Leinbach and Jonathan H. Ward; foreword by astronaut Robert Crippen; epilogue by astronaut Eileen Collins. Arcade Publishing 2018 xii, 356 p.p illustrations (chiefly color) (hardcover: alk. paper) $25.99 **363.124**

1. Columbia (Spacecraft) 2. Space vehicles -- Recovery 3. Space shuttles -- Accidents 4. Columbia (Spacecraft) -- Accidents 5.

Astronauts -- Accidents -- United States 6. Space vehicle accidents -- United States 7. Space shuttles -- Accidents -- United States
ISBN 9781628728521; 9781628728514

LC 2017046190

This book, by Michael D. Leinbach and Jonathan H. Ward, foreword by Robert Crippen, epilogue by Eileen Collins, presents "the definitive inside story of the Columbia [space shuttle] disaster and recovery and the inspiring message it ultimately holds. . . . [It] shares the deeply personal stories that emerged as NASA employees looked for lost colleagues and searchers overcame immense physical . . . and emotional challenges and worked together to accomplish the impossible." (Publisher's note)

"A gripping account of a fatal tragedy and the impressive and deeply emotional human response that ensued." Kirkus

Includes bibliographical references and index

363.14   Hazards in sports and recreation

Chowdhury, Bernie

The **last** dive; a father and son's fatal descent into the ocean's depths. Bernie Chowdhury. HarperCollins 2000 xi, 356 p.p illustrations (some color) (ebook) $14.99; $25 **363.14**

1. Shipwrecks 2. Scuba diving 3. Shipwrecks -- Atlantic Coast (U.S.) 4. Scuba diving -- Accidents -- Atlantic Coast (U.S.)
ISBN 9780062196828; 0060194626; 9780060194628

LC 00033426

In this book, author Bernie Chowdhury "recounts the (eventually) fatal adventures of the Rouses, a father-and-son pair of divers who met their match eight years ago in the wreck of a German U-boat that lies under 230 feet of water off the coast of New Jersey. The Rouses practiced a sport called technical diving, in which divers seek depths as great as 1,000 feet using elaborate equipment and multiple air tanks." (N Y Times Book Rev)

"A sorrowful education in diving history and technique, in the psychology of the adventurer, and in the dominion of death." Kirkus

363.17   Hazardous materials

Brown, Kate

Plutopia; nuclear families, atomic cities, and the great Soviet and American plutonium disasters. Kate Brown. Oxford University Press 2013 416 p. (acid-free paper) $27.95 **363.17**

1. Cold war 2. Arms race 3. Plutonium 4. Working class families -- Russia (Federation) -- Ozërsk (Cheliabinskaia oblast) -- History -- 20th century 5. Plutonium industry -- Accidents -- Russia (Federation) -- Ozërsk (Cheliabinskaia oblast) -- History -- 20th century 6. Plutonium industry -- Social aspects -- Russia (Federation) -- Ozërsk (Cheliabinskaia oblast) -- History -- 20th century 7. Richland (Wash.) -- History -- 20th century 8. Industrial safety -- Government policy -- Soviet Union -- Case studies 9. Industrial safety -- Government policy -- United States -- Case studies 10. Working class families -- Washington (State) -- Richland -- History -- 20th century 11. Plutonium industry -- Accidents -- Washington (State) -- Richland -- History -- 20th century 12. Plutonium industry -- Social aspects -- Washington (State) -- Richland -- History -- 20th century 13. Ozërsk (Cheliabinskaia oblast, Russia) -- History -- 20th century
ISBN 0199855765; 9780199855766

LC 2012041758

This book, written by Kate Brown, "draws on official records and dozens of interviews to tell the extraordinary stories of Richland, Washington and Ozersk, Russia-the first two cities in the world to produce plutonium. An untold . . . piece of Cold War history, Plutopia invites readers to consider the nuclear footprint left by the arms race and the enormous price of paying for it." (Publisher's note)

Includes bibliographical references and index

Iversen, Kristen

★ **Full** body burden; growing up in the nuclear shadow of Rocky Flats. Kristen Iversen. Crown Publishers 2012 400 p. ill. $25.00　　　　**363.17**

1. Nuclear weapons 2. Women journalists 3. Rocky Flats Plant (U.S.) 4. Rocky Flats Plant (U.S.) -- History 5. Plutonium -- Health aspects -- Colorado 6. Jefferson County (Colorado) -- Biography 7. Rocky Flats Plant (U.S.) -- Health aspects 8. Radioactive waste sites -- Cleanup -- Colorado 9. Rocky Flats Plant (U.S.) -- Environmental aspects 10. Nuclear weapons plants -- Health aspects -- Colorado 11. Radioactive pollution -- Colorado -- Jefferson County

ISBN 030795563X; 9780307955630

LC 2011045902

This book is about "[t]he Rocky Flats nuclear weapons plant near Denver [that] began production in 1953; within four years, the plutonium factory had its first major accident, the first of many. In fact, by the end of its forty-year run, the plant would gain notoriety as 'the most contaminated site in America.' Kristen [Iversen], the author . . . , grew up in the radioactive shadow of this secret facility and she witnessed at close quarters the disastrous effects of its activities." Here, "she combines . . . personal experiences and . . . investigative reporting to expose [the U.S.] government's betrayal of its responsibility to its citizens." (Barnes & Noble)

Includes bibliographical references and index

Lyman, Edwin

Fukushima; the story of a nuclear disaster. David Lochbaum, Edwin Lyman, Susan Q. Stranahan, and The Union of Concerned Scientists. The New Press 2014 320 p. illustrations, maps (hc.: alk. paper) $27.95　　　　**363.17**

1. Tsunamis 2. Nuclear reactors 3. Fukushima Nuclear Accident, Fukushima, Japan, 2011 4. Fukushima Nuclear Disaster, Japan, 2011 5. Nuclear power plants -- Accidents -- Japan -- Fukushima-ken

ISBN 1595589082; 9781595589088

LC 2013035284

Authors David Lochbaum, Edwin Lyman, and Susan Q. Stranahan present an "account of the Fukushima disaster. [It] combines a fast-paced . . . account of the tsunami and the nuclear emergency it created with an explanation of the science and technology behind the meltdown as it unfolded in real time." (Publisher's note)

Includes bibliographical references and index

Moore, Kate

The **radium** girls; the dark story of America's shining women. Kate Moore. Sourcebooks Inc 2017 xvi, 479 p.p illustrations (hardcover: alk. paper) $26.99　　　　**363.17**

1. Young women 2. Women -- Employment 3. Radium -- Toxicology 4. Radium paint -- Toxicology 5. Consumers' leagues -- United States -- History 6. World War, 1914-1918 -- Women -- United States 7. World War, 1914-1918 -- War work -- United States 8. Watch dial painters -- Diseases -- United States -- History 9. Industrial hygiene -- United States -- History -- 20th century

ISBN 9781492649359; 9781492649366

LC 2016040681

This book, by Kate Moore, shares the story of young women working at radium-dial factories during World War I who were exposed to radium. . . . "The . . . girls find themselves embroiled in one of the biggest scandals of America's early 20th century, and in a groundbreaking battle for workers' rights that will echo for centuries to come. . . . Their courage and tenacity led to life-changing regulations, research into nuclear bombing, and ultimately saved . . . [many] lives." (Publisher's note)

"Moore's well-researched narrative is written with clarity and a sympathetic voice that brings these figures and their struggles to life." LJ

Includes bibliographical references (pages [415]-467) and index. Includes reading group guide, pages [409]-410.

Schlosser, Eric, 1959-

★ **Command** and control; nuclear weapons, the Damascus Accident, and the illusion of safety. Eric Schlosser. The Penguin Press 2013 640 p. $36　　　　**363.17**

1. Nuclear weapons -- United States -- History 2. Nuclear weapons -- Accidents -- United States -- History 3. Titan (Missile) -- History 4. Nuclear weapons -- Accidents -- Arkansas -- History 5. Nuclear weapons -- United States -- Safety measures 6. Nuclear weapons -- Government policy -- United States 7. United States. Air Force. Strategic Air Command. Strategic Missile Wing, 308th

ISBN 1594202273; 9781594202278

LC 2013017151

Pulitzer Prize Finalist: History (2014)

This book "interweaves the minute-by-minute story of an accident at a nuclear missile silo in rural Arkansas with a historical narrative that spans more than fifty years. It depicts the urgent effort by American scientists, policymakers, and military officers to ensure that nuclear weapons can't be stolen, sabotaged, used without permission, or detonated inadvertently." (Publisher's note)

Includes bibliographical references and index

363.2　Police services

Bell, Suzanne

Encyclopedia of forensic science; foreword by Barry A.J. Fisher; preface by Robert C. Shaler. rev ed; Facts on File 2008 402p il (Facts on File science library) $85　　　　**363.2**

1. Reference books 2. Forensic sciences -- Encyclopedias

ISBN 978-0-8160-6799-2; 0-8160-6799-6

LC 2008-5862

First published 2003

"In addition to explaining the science of forensics, Bell . . . reviews various disciplines related to forensic science, among them entomology, odontology, and psychology. Other entries cover professional organizations, government agencies, famous names in the field of forensics, evidence, and legal issues. . . . With its clear language and brief entries [this] volume will provide readers with a nuts-and-bolts understanding of the real world of forensic science." Booklist [review of 2003 edition]

Includes bibliographical references

Campisi, Charles

Blue on blue; an insider's story of good cops catching bad cops. Charles Campisi with Gordon Dillow. Simon & Schuster 2017 368 p. illustrations (ebook) $18.99; $28　　　　**363.2**

1. Police corruption 2. Police -- New York (State) -- New York

ISBN 9781501127212; 1501127195; 9781501127199

LC 2016056300

This book, by Charles Campisi, "describes the fascinating inner workings of the world's largest police force and Chief . . . Campisi's unprecedented two decades putting bad cops behind bars. From 1996 through 2014 . . . [he] headed NYPD's Internal Affairs Bureau. . . . During Campisi's IAB tenure, the number of New Yorkers shot, wounded, or killed by cops every year declined by ninety percent, and the number of cops failing integrity tests shrank to an equally startling low." (Publisher's note)

"The breadth and depth of his experience makes this a must-read for those interested in how police misconduct has been handled." Pub Wkly

Chadwick, Bruce

Law & disorder; the chaotic birth of the NYPD. Bruce Chadwick. Thomas Dunne Books 2017 viii, 368 p.p illustrations (hardcover) $28.99 **363.2**

1. Police -- New York (N.Y.) 2. New York (N.Y.) -- History 3. New York (N.Y.). Police Department -- History -- 19th century 4. Police -- New York (State) -- New York -- History -- 19th century
ISBN 1250082587; 9781250082596; 9781250082589
LC 2016047035

Author "Bruce Chadwick examines how rampant violence led to the founding of the first professional police force in New York City. Chadwick brings readers into the bloody and violent city, where race relations and an influx of immigrants boiled over into riots, street gangs roved through town with abandon, and thousands of bars, prostitutes, and gambling emporiums clogged the streets." (Publisher's note)

Includes bibliographical references and index.

Englert, Rod

Blood secrets; a forensic expert reveals how blood spatter tells the crime scene's story. [by] Rod Englert, with Kathy Passero; foreword by Ann Rule. Thomas Dunne Books 2010 286p il $25.99; ebook $12.99 **363.2**

1. Blood 2. Forensic sciences 3. Criminal investigation
ISBN 978-0-312-56400-1; 0-312-56400-7; 978-1-4299-2921-9 ebook; 1-4299-2921-9 ebook
LC 2009-40294

"Englert deftly balances real-life examples and detailed scientific analysis, giving readers a richer understanding of this developing avenue of forensic science." Publ Wkly

Includes bibliographical references

Geary, Rick

J. Edgar Hoover; a graphic biography. Hill and Wang 2008 102p il $16.95 **363.2**

1. Graphic novels 2. Biographical graphic novels 3. FBI officials 4. United States -- Federal Bureau of Investigation -- Graphic novels
ISBN 978-0-8090-9503-2; 0-8090-9503-3
LC 2007-25193

Rick Geary has written a biography of J. Edgar Hoover, who served in the federal government for 55 years and under eight presidents, most notably as director of the Federal Bureau of Investigation. He was appointed to that position on May 10, 1924. Geary covers Hoover's sometimes controversial career, including his refusal to involve the FBI directly into investigations of crimes against civil rights workers and the 1963 bombing in Birmingham, Alabama, and the bureau's investigation of Martin Luther King, Jr. He tastefully discusses Hoover's undercover sexual life.

"As solid, thrilling and informative a guide to the life of the America's most powerful authoritarian as one could ask for." Kirkus

Neme, Laurel A.

Animal investigators; how the world's first wildlife forensics lab is solving crimes and saving endangered species. foreword by Richard Leakey. Scribner 2009 230p il $25 **363.2**

1. Poaching 2. Forensic sciences 3. Wild animal trade 4. Endangered species 5. Wildlife conservation 6. U.S. Fish and Wildlife Service -- Forensics Laboratory
ISBN 978-1-4165-5056-3; 1-4165-5056-9
LC 2008-56004

"Illegal wildlife trafficking is worth an estimated $20 billion a year. That makes it the third most lucrative criminal activity, coming in just behind drug and human trafficking and, incredibly, ahead of arms smuggling. . . . Animal Investigators documents this black market in unflinching and often depressing detail. But the book is more than just a journey into the criminal underworld, a litany of dismal statistics or a roll-call of cowardly, greedy intermediaries. Instead, Laurel A. Neme centres her book on a more inspiring place: the US Fish and Wildlife Service Forensics Lab in Ashland, Oregon, the world's only laboratory dedicated to solving crimes against wildlife." New Sci

Includes bibliographical references

Renner, James

True crime addict; how I lost myself in the mysterious disappearance of Maura Murray. James Renner. Thomas Dunne Books 2016 288 p. maps (ebook) $60; (hardback) $25.99 **363.2**

1. Missing persons -- United States -- Case studies 2. Criminal investigation -- United States -- Case studies 3. Journalists -- United States -- Psychology -- Case studies
ISBN 9781250089021; 9781250089014
LC 2015049511

This book, by James Renner, "is the story of his spellbinding investigation of the missing person's case of Maura Murray, which has taken on a life of its own for armchair sleuths across the web. . . . It is a fascinating look at a case that has eluded authorities and one man's obsessive quest for the answers." (Publisher's note)

"An entrancing, brilliant next step for fans of the podcast Serial, Netflix's Making a Murderer, and other true crime cases." LJ

Stamper, Norm

To protect and serve; how to fix America's police. Norm Stamper. Nation Books 2016 336 p. (ebook) $18.99; (hardback) $27.99 **363.2**

1. Police -- United States 2. Law enforcement -- United States 3. Police misconduct -- United States 4. Community policing -- United States
ISBN 9781568585413; 9781568585406
LC 2016000403

In this book author Norm Stamper "delivers a revolutionary new model for American law enforcement: the community-based police department. It calls for fundamental changes in the federal government's role in local policing as well as citizen participation in all aspects of police operations: policymaking, program development, crime fighting and service delivery, . . . education and training, oversight of police conduct, and . . . joint community-police crisis management." (Publisher's note)

"A vivid, well-written, vitally important book." Kirkus

Includes bibliographical references (pages 279-297) and index.

Taibbi, Matt, 1970-

★ **I** can't breathe; a killing on Bay Street. Matt Taibbi. Spiegel & Grau 2017 xii, 322 p.p (hardcover) $28 **363.2**

1. Police brutality -- United States 2. Racial profiling in law enforcement 3. Police brutality -- New York (State) -- New York 4. Discrimination in law enforcement -- New York (State) -- New York 5. Racial profiling in law enforcement -- New York (State) -- New York 6. Discrimination in criminal justice administration -- New York (State) -- New York

ISBN 9780812988840; 9780812988864; 0812988841

"On July 17, 2014, a forty-three-year-old black man named Eric Garner died on a Staten Island sidewalk after a police officer put him in what has been described as an illegal chokehold during an arrest for selling bootleg cigarettes. . . . [Author] Matt Taibbi's deeply reported retelling of these events liberates Eric Garner from the abstractions of newspaper accounts and lets us see the man in full--with all his flaws and contradictions intact." (Publisher's note)

"This is a necessary and riveting work." Booklist

Tucker, Holly

City of light, city of poison; murder, magic, and the first police chief of Paris. Holly Tucker. W W Norton & Co Inc 2017 336 p. illustrations (hardcover) $26.95   363.2

1. Crime -- History 2. Paris (France) -- History 3. Paris (France) -- History -- 17th century 4. Crime -- France -- Paris -- History -- 17th century 5. Murder -- France -- Paris -- History -- 19th century 6. Police -- France -- Paris -- History -- 17th century

ISBN 9780393239782

LC 2016046270

In this book, by Holly Tucker, "the first police chief of Paris faces an epidemic of murder in the late 1600s. Assigned by Louis XIV, Nicolas de La Reynie begins by clearing the streets of filth and installing lanterns throughout Paris, turning it into the City of Light. . . . He unearths a tightly knit cabal of poisoners, witches, and renegade priests. As he exposes their unholy work, he soon learns that no one is safe from black magic—not even the Sun King." (Publisher's note)

"Tucker...vividly brings to life a slice of Parisian history in this rigorously researched true-crime epic, set during the reign of Louis XIV." Pub Wkly.

Includes bibliographical references and index

Wagner, E. J.

The science of Sherlock Holmes; from Baskerville Hall to the Valley of Fear, the real forensics behind the great detective's greatest cases. Wiley 2006 244p il $24.95; pa $16.95 363.2

1. Forensic sciences 2. Criminal investigation 3. Holmes, Sherlock (Fictitious character)

ISBN 0-471-64879-5; 978-0-471-64879-6; 0-470-12823-2 pa; 978-0-470-12823-7 pa

LC 2005-22236

The author discusses forensic science in Arthur Conan Doyle's stories of the 'consulting detective' Sherlock Holmes. She compares Holmes's investigative techniques to those used in actual cases such as the killing of Lizzie Borden's parents in 1892, the 1902 murder of Joseph Browne Elwell, and the disappearance of Dr. George Parkman in 1849.

This book "will intrigue readers with incredible stories and amazing tales from the early days of forensic science." Christ Sci Monit

Includes bibliographical references

363.25 Detection of crime (Criminal investigation)

Comey, James B., 1960-

A higher loyalty; Truth, Lies, and Leadership. James Comey. St. Martin's Press 2018 304 p. $29.99   363.25

1. Biography 2. Political leadership -- United States 3. United States. Federal Bureau of Investigation

ISBN 1250192455; 9781250192455

In this book, "former FBI director James Comey shares his never-before-told experiences from some of the highest-stakes situations of his career in the past two decades of American government, exploring what good, ethical leadership looks like, and how it drives sound decisions. His journey provides an unprecedented entry into the corridors of power, and a remarkable lesson in what makes an effective leader." (Publisher's note)

Halber, Deborah

The skeleton crew; how amateur sleuths are solving America's coldest cases. Deborah Halber. Simon & Schuster 2014 304 p. (hardcover) $25   363.25

1. Private investigators 2. Cold cases (Criminal investigation) 3. Criminal investigation -- United States

ISBN 1451657587; 9781451657586; 9781451657593

LC 2013034949

This book, by Deborah Halber, "provides an entree into the gritty and tumultuous world of Sherlock Holmes-wannabes who race to beat out law enforcement--and one another--at matching missing persons with unidentified remains. In America today, upwards of forty thousand people are dead and unaccounted for. These murder, suicide, and accident victims, separated from their names, are being adopted by the bizarre online world of amateur sleuths." (Publisher's note)

"The author paints a colorful picture of armchair investigators pursuing their first 'solves' amid the conflicting motivations of their peers and of various law enforcement agencies—." LJ

Includes bibliographical references

Lance, Peter

Deal With the Devil; The FBI's Secret Thirty-Year Relationship with a Mafia Killer. by Peter Lance. William Morrow 2013 672 p. (hardcover) $29.99   363.25

1. Mafia 2. Criminal investigation -- United States

ISBN 0061455342; 9780061455346

In this book, author Peter Lance draws on three decades of once secret FBI files—and exclusive new interviews—to tell the . . . story of Gregory Scarpa Sr., aka "The Grim Reaper;" a Mafia capo, who "stopped counting" after 50 murders, while secretly betraying the Colombo crime family as a Top Echelon Criminal Informant for the Bureau. Lance draws on thousands of pages of court transcripts, interviews and declassified FBI files, to trace Scarpa's . . . relationship with the Bureau starting in 1960." (Publisher's note)

McCrery, Nigel

Silent witnesses; the often gruesome but always fascinating history of forensic science. by Nigel McCrery. Chicago Review Press, Inc. 2014 288 p. illustrations (some color) (paperback) $16.95   363.25

1. Forensic sciences 2. Criminal investigation 3. Forensic sciences -- History 4. Forensic sciences -- Case studies 5. Criminal investigation -- Case studies

ISBN 1613730020; 9781613730027

LC 2014006713

This book, by Nigel McCrery, "provides an account of all the major areas of forensic science from around the world over the past two centuries. The book weaves dramatic narrative and scientific principles together in a way that allows readers to figure out crimes along with the experts." (Publisher's note)

"Where McCrery really shines is in his storytelling, which is no surprise given his background as a successful crime novelist. While certain technical portions may be difficult for some readers, true-crime enthusiasts will find the payoff worth the effort." Kirkus

Weiner, Tim

Enemies; the history of the FBI at war. Tim Weiner. 1st ed. Random House 2011 537 p. (alk. paper) $30   **363.25**
    1. National security -- United States 2. Intelligence service -- United States 3. United States -- History -- 20th century 4. Espionage -- United States -- History -- 20th century 5. United States. Federal Bureau of Investigation -- History -- 20th century
    ISBN 9780679643890; 9781400067480
                          LC 2011005353

This book "delivers a . . . history of what has been, in effect, America's secret police.The history of the FBI is easily divided into two periods: the J. Edgar Hoover period and after. In 1924, before he was 30, Hoover took over a tiny, tawdry Bureau and built it into a fearsome empire he ruled as a personal fiefdom until his death in 1972. . . . Weiner focuses on the FBI's activities investigating and attempting to prevent subversion and terrorism." (Kirkus Reviews)

Includes bibliographical references and index

Wilber, Del Quentin

A **good** month for murder; the inside story of a homicide squad. Del Quentin Wilber. Henry Holt & Co. 2016 288 p. map (hardback) $30   **363.25**
    1. Homicide 2. Detectives 3. Washington (D.C.) 4. Criminal investigation -- United States 5. Homicides -- Washington Metropolitan Area 6. Criminal investigation -- Washington Metropolitan Area
    ISBN 9780805098815
                          LC 2015036515

This book, by Del Quentin Wilber, "tells the inside story of how a homicide squad---a dedicated, colorful team of detectives—does its almost impossible job. Twelve homicides, three police-involved shootings and the furious hunt for an especially brutal killer--February 2013 was a good month for murder in suburban Washington, D.C." (Publisher's note)

"A fascinating report written in a relentless, real-life noir tone." Booklist

363.28   Services of special kinds of security and law enforcement agencies

Hill, Clint

Five presidents; my extraordinary journey with Eisenhower, Kennedy, Johnson, Nixon, and Ford. Clint Hill with Lisa McCubbin. Gallery Books 2016 464 p. illustrations (some color) $28   **363.28**
    1. Secret service -- United States 2. Presidents -- United States -- Staff 3. Presidents -- Protection -- United States 4. United States. Secret Service -- Officials and employees -- Biography
    ISBN 9781476794136; 9781476794143
                          LC 2015050618

In this book, "Secret Service agent Clint Hill brings history . . . to life as he reflects on his seventeen years protecting . . . Presidents Dwight D. Eisenhower, John F. Kennedy, Lyndon B. Johnson, Richard M. Nixon, and Gerald R. Ford, seeing them through a long, tumultuous era—the Cold War; the Cuban Missile Crisis; the assassinations of John F. Kennedy, Martin Luther King, Jr., and Robert F. Kennedy; the Vietnam War; Watergate." (Publisher's note)

"An eloquently written travelog through midcentury America from the periphery of political power." LJ

Miller, Todd

Border patrol nation; dispatches from the front lines of homeland security. Todd Miller. City Lights Publishers 2014 256 p. ill., maps (City lights open media) (pbk.) $16.95 **363.28**
    1. Border patrols 2. Immigration law -- United States 3. United States. Immigration Border Patrol -- History 4. Mexican-American Border Region -- Economic conditions
    ISBN 0872866319; 9780872866317
                          LC 2013043754

In this book, author "Todd Miller sounds an alarm as he chronicles the changing landscape. Traveling the country--and beyond--to speak with the people most involved with and impacted by the Border Patrol, he combines these first-hand encounters with careful research to expose a vast and booming industry for high-end technology, weapons, surveillance, and prisons." (Publisher's note)

An "alarming story of U.S. Border Patrol and Homeland Security's ever-widening reach into the lives of American citizens and legal immigrants as well as the undocumented." Pub Wkly

Includes bibliographical references and index. (p. 326-343) and index

363.283   Secret police

Goodavage, Maria

Secret Service Dogs; The Heroes Who Protect the President of the United States. by Maria Goodavage. Penguin Group USA 2016 304 p. $28   **363.283**
    1. Service dogs 2. Secret service -- United States
    ISBN 1101984732; 9781101984734
                          LC 2016025219

This book, by Maria Goodavage, "immerses readers into the heart of this elite world of canine teams who protect first families, popes, and presidential candidates: the selection of dogs and handlers, their year-round training, their missions around the world, and, most important, the bond—the glue that holds the teams together and can mean the difference between finding bombs and terrorists or letting them slip by." (Publisher's note)

363.31   Censorship

Simon, Joel

The **new** censorship; inside the global battle for media freedom. Joel Simon. Columbia University Press 2014 248 p. (Columbia journalism review books) (cloth: alk. paper) $27.95   **363.31**
    1. Censorship 2. Journalism 3. Freedom of the press 4. Journalists -- Violence against 5. Censorship -- History -- 21st century 6. Press and politics -- History -- 21st century 7. Freedom of the press -- History -- 21st century 8. Journalism -- Political aspects -- History -- 21st century
    ISBN 023116064X; 9780231160643
                          LC 2014012961

This book, by Joel Simon, part of the "Columbia Journalism Review Books" series, "warns that we can no longer assume that our global information ecosystem is stable, protected, and robust. Journalists are increasingly vulnerable to attack by authoritarian governments, militants, criminals, and terrorists, who all seek to use technology, political pressure, and violence to set the global information agenda." (Publisher's note)

"Most moving are Simon's wrenching stories of the ordeals journalists have suffered, from kidnappings through imprisonment through death. Simon's assessment of what it means to be a journalist and his call to action at book's end are moving and practical. A must-read." Booklist

Includes bibliographical references and index

363.32   Social conflict

Allison, Graham T.

Nuclear terrorism; the ultimate preventable catastrophe. [by] Graham Allison. Times Books\Henry Holt 2004 263p il $24   **363.32**

1. Terrorism 2. Nuclear warfare

ISBN 0-8050-7651-4

LC 2004-47427

"Allison's comprehensive but accessible treatment of this vital subject is a major contribution to public understanding." N Y Times Book Rev

Includes bibliographical references

Bobbitt, Philip

Terror and consent; the wars for the twenty-first century. Alfred A. Knopf 2008 672p il $35   **363.32**

1. Terrorism 2. United States -- Foreign relations

ISBN 1-4000-4243-7; 978-1-4000-4243-2

LC 2007-34194

The author examines "the relationship between the emergent constitutional order and the emergence of modern 'market state terrorism,' which, mirroring the market state and availing itself of the same technological advances, may be lethal enough to pose an existential threat to the very possibility of government by consent of the governed." Booklist

Includes bibliographical references

Elshtain, Jean Bethke

Just war against terror; the burden of American power in a violent world. Basic Books 2003 240p $23; pa $14 **363.32**

1. Terrorism 2. War on terrorism

ISBN 0-465-01910-2; 0-465-01911-0 pa

LC 2002-154549

"While this volume is not a radical departure from the abundance of post-September 11 books, it presents well the moral case for U.S. military engagement in the world and gives credence to those who advocate the use of force as a response to terrorism." Publ Wkly

Includes bibliographical references

Encyclopedia of terrorism; Peter Chalk, editor. ABC-CLIO 2013 xviii, 871 p.p ill. (hardcopy) $205; (ebook) $205.00   **363.32**

1. Terrorism -- Encyclopedias

ISBN 0313308950; 9780313308956; 9780313385353

LC 2012016710

This book, edited by Peter Chalk, "provides comprehensive coverage of the events, individuals, groups, incidents, and trends in terrorism in the modern era. [It] . . . presents . . . information on developments since the watershed events of September 11, 2001, providing readers with an invaluable reference tool for understanding major developments that have occurred in domestic and international terrorism." (Publisher's note)

Includes bibliographical references and index

Gillon, Steven M.

Separate and unequal; the Kerner Commission and the unraveling of American liberalism. Steven M. Gillon. Basic Books 2018 400 p. (hardback) $32   **363.32**

1. Poor -- United States 2. Riots -- United States 3. United States -- Race relations 4. Liberalism -- United States -- 20th century 5. Riots -- Political aspects -- United States 6. United States -- Social policy -- 20th century 7. Urban poor -- Social conditions -- United States 8. United States -- Race relations -- Political aspects 9. United States -- Politics and government -- 1963-1969 10. African Americans -- Social conditions -- United States 11. United States. National Advisory Commission on Civil Disorders. Report 12. United States. National Advisory Commission on Civil Disorders -- History

ISBN 9780465096084

LC 2017035839

In this book, "historian Steven M. Gillon offers a revelatory new history of the National Advisory Commission on Civil Disorders--popularly known as the Kerner Commission. Convened by President Lyndon Johnson after riots in Newark and Detroit left dozens dead and thousands injured, the commission issued a report in 1968 that attributed the unrest to 'white racism' and called for aggressive new programs to end discrimination and poverty." (Publisher's note)

Includes bibliographical references and index

Harris, Shane

The **watchers**; the rise of America's surveillance state. Penguin Press 2010 418p il $27.95; pa $17   **363.32**

1. Terrorism 2. National security -- United States 3. Intelligence service -- United States

ISBN 978-1-59420-245-2; 978-0-14-311890-9 pa

LC 2009-37205

The author examines the development of domestic surveillance programs in the United States intended to prevent terrorist attacks.

"A sharply written, wise analysis of the complex mashup of electronic sleuthing, law, policy and culture." Kirkus

Includes bibliographical references

Herridge, Catherine

The **next** wave; on the hunt for al Qaeda's American recruits. Crown Forum 2011 258p il $25   **363.32**

1. Terrorists 2. Qaida (Organization) 3. Islamic fundamentalism 4. Muslims -- United States 5. Terrorism -- Religious aspects

ISBN 978-0-307-88525-8; 0-307-88525-9

LC 2010-53585

A "report on a new generation of terrorists and the American-born Islamic cleric Anwar al-Awlaki, who has inspired many of them to commit violent acts. Now believed to be in Yemen, al-Awlaki was targeted for killing by the U.S. government in 2010. He is linked to three of the 9/11 hijackers, the massacre at Foot Hood, the attempted Christmas Day 2009 bombing and the cargo printer plot in October 2010. Drawing on documents and interviews, the author shows how the charismatic al-Awlaki has become a leading al-Qaeda propagandist, using the Internet to recruit alienated American youths, many newly arrived in America, to join the terrorist cause. . . . A sobering view of why the 9/11 nightmare continues a decade later. " Kirkus

Includes bibliographical references

363.321   Aspects of social conflict

Okeowo, Alexis

★ A **moonless,** starless sky; ordinary women and men fighting extremism in Africa. Alexis Okeowo. Hachette Books

2017 xv, 240 p.p (hardcover) $26 **363.321**
1. Slavery 2. Political activists 3. Islamic fundamentalism 4. Abduction -- Uganda 5. Abduction -- Nigeria 6. Slavery -- Mauritania 7. Forced marriage -- Uganda 8. Political activists -- Africa 9. Human rights workers -- Africa 10. Extremists -- Africa, Sub-Saharan 11. Islamic fundamentalism -- Nigeria 12. Islamic fundamentalism -- Somalia
ISBN 9780316382915; 9780316382939; 9781478941200

LC 2017020071

In this book, author "Alexis Okeowo weaves together four narratives that form a powerful tapestry of modern Africa: a young couple, kidnap victims of Joseph Kony's LRA; a Mauritanian waging a lonely campaign against modern-day slavery; a women's basketball team flourishing amid war-torn Somalia; and a vigilante who takes up arms against the extremist group Boko Haram. This debut book . . . illuminates the inner lives of ordinary people doing the extraordinary." (Publisher's note)

"In this memorable debut, Okeowo's in-depth, perceptive reporting gives a voice to the extraordinarily courageous—and resilient—women and men fighting malevolent ideologies and organizations in their native countries." Pub Wkly

363.325 Terrorism

Bakos, Nada

The **targeter**; my life in the CIA, on the hunt of the godfather of Isis. Nada Bakos, Davin Coburn. Little, Brown & Co. 2017 368 p. (hc) $28.00 **363.325**
1. Women spies 2. United States. Central Intelligence Agency
ISBN 9780316269780; 9780316260473

LC 2016944050

This memoir, by Nada Bakos with Davin Coburn, tells "the story of a young woman from Montana who joined the CIA and worked her way up through the ranks to the frontline of the fight against Islamic extremists. . . . Bakos reveals the inner workings of the Agency and the largely hidden world of intelligence gathering post 9/11." (Publisher's note)

Bergen, Peter

United States of Jihad; investigating America's homegrown terrorists. by Peter Bergen. Crown 2016 416 p. color illustrations (hardcover) $28 **363.325**
1. Jihad 2. Terrorism -- United States 3. Terrorists -- United States 4. Terrorism -- Religious aspects -- Islam 5. Terrorists -- Recruiting -- United States
ISBN 9780804139540; 9780804139564

LC 2015034447

This book on Islamist terrorism, by Peter Bergen, tells the "stories of the key actors on the American front. Among the perpetrators are Anwar al-Awlaki, the New Mexico-born radical cleric who became the first American citizen killed by a CIA drone . . .; Samir Khan, whose Inspire webzine has rallied terrorists around the world, including the Tsarnaev brothers; and Omar Hammami, an Alabama native and hip hop fan who became a fixture in al Shabaab's propaganda videos." (Publisher's note)

"Both balanced and galvanizing, Bergen's meticulous portrait of violent extremism is required reading for anyone who truly wants to understand the nature of the evolving threats from within and without." Booklist

Includes bibliographical references and index

Bergen, Peter L.

Manhunt; the ten-year search for Bin Laden from 9/11 to Abbottabad. Peter L. Bergen. 1st ed. Crown Publishers 2012

xxi, 359 p.p col. ill., maps $26 **363.325**
1. Terrorists 2. Special forces (Military science) -- United States 3. Qaida (Organization) 4. Terrorists -- Saudi Arabia 5. War on Terrorism, 2001-2009 6. Fugitives from justice -- United States 7. Terrorism -- United States -- Prevention 8. Special operations (Military science) -- United States
ISBN 0307955575; 9780307955579

LC 2012004258

This book provides an "account of the . . . effort to track and kill the al-Qaeda leader. . . . Only in 2010 did the monitoring of a Kuwaiti courier's cellphone use suggest ties to bin Laden, and they followed his car to the compound in the quiet Pakistani town of Abbottabad, where he actually lived with bin Laden's extended family. . . . Bergen . . . delineates the U.S. government decision-making process in pursuing the Special Operations infiltration of the compound, despite the lack of certainty that bin Laden was actually there." (Kirkus Reviews)

Includes bibliographical references and index

Cannell, Michael

Incendiary; the psychiatrist, the mad bomber, and the invention of criminal profiling. Michael Cannell. Minotaur Books 2017 ix, 289 p.p illustrations (hardcover) $26.99 **363.325**
1. Serial Killers -- History 2. New York (N.Y.) -- History 3. Criminal psychology -- Case studies 4. Bombings -- New York (State) -- New York -- Case studies
ISBN 9781250048936; 9781250048943; 125004894X

LC 2017000713

In this book, by Michael Cannell, "a serial bomber stalked the streets of 1950s New York. . . . Grand Central, Penn Station, Radio City Music Hall—for almost two decades, no place was safe from the man who signed his anonymous letters 'FP' and left his lethal devices in phone booths, storage lockers, even tucked into the plush seats of movie theaters. His victims were left cruelly maimed." (Publisher's note)

"A fascinating study not just of a historical crime and its consequences, but also of its unintended effects." Kirkus

Includes bibliographical references (pages 261-279) and index.

Gerges, Fawaz A.

Isis; a history. Fawaz A. Gerges. Princeton University Press 2016 384 p. (cloth: alk. paper) $27.95 **363.325**
1. Jihad 2. Terrorism 3. Islamic fundamentalism 4. Middle East -- Politics and government 5. IS (Organization) 6. Terrorism -- Middle East 7. Terrorism -- Religious aspects -- Islam 8. Middle East -- Politics and government -- 21st century
ISBN 9780691170008

LC 2015956950

This book, by Fawaz A. Gerges, "explains the rise of ISIS, and what does it portend for the future of the Middle East? . . . This unique history shows how decades of dictatorship, poverty, and rising sectarianism in the Middle East, exacerbated by foreign intervention, led to the rise and growth of ISIS--and why addressing those problems is the only way to ensure its end." (Publisher's note)

"A specific, timely, well-rendered exegesis of the unfolding global threat." Kirkus

Includes bibliographical references (pages 295-351) and index.

Johnsen, Gregory D.

The **last** refuge; Yemen, al-Qaeda, and America's war in Arabia. Gregory D. Johnsen. W W Norton & Co Inc 2013 352 p. (hbk.) $27.95 **363.325**
1. Yemen 2. Qaida (Organization) 3. War on Terrorism, 2001-2009 4. Terrorism -- Yemen (Republic) 5. United States -- Military policy 6. Terrorism -- Persian Gulf Region -- Prevention

ISBN 9780393082425; 0393082423

LC 2012027875

In this book on Yemen, Gregory D. Johnson presents an "analysis of how a nation that had been a success story in the U.S. effort to defeat al-Qaeda and stabilize the region has been the site for resurgence instead. He examines the historical factors that have contributed to the buildup of al-Qaeda in Yemen as young men were recruited by the government, Yemeni tribes, and mosques in a concerted effort to turn the war in Afghanistan into a broader jihad." (Booklist)

Includes bibliographical references and index

Kaplan, Fred, 1937-

Dark territory; the secret history of cyber war. Fred Kaplan. Simon & Schuster 2016 352 p. (ebook) $20.99; (hardback) $28   **363.325**

1. Cyberterrorism -- Prevention -- United States -- History

ISBN 9781476763279; 9781476763255; 9781476763262

LC 2015027335

In this book, author Fred "Kaplan probes the inner corridors of the National Security Agency, the beyond-top-secret cyber units in the Pentagon, the 'information warfare' squads of the military services, and the national security debates in the White House, to tell this never-before-told story of the officers, policymakers, scientists, and spies who devised this new form of warfare and who have been planning . . . these wars for decades." (Publisher's note)

"An important, disturbing, and gripping history arguing convincingly that, as of 2015, no defense exists against a resourceful cyberattack." Kirkus

Includes bibliographical references and index

McDermott, Terry

The **hunt** for KSM; inside the pursuit and takedown of the real 9/11 mastermind, Khalid Sheikh Mohammed. Terry McDermott and Josh Meyer. Little, Brown and Co. 2012 350 p.   **363.325**

1. Terrorists 2. September 11 terrorist attacks, 2001 3. Terrorism -- Prevention -- United States 4. Qaida (Organization) 5. Terrorists -- Islamic countries 6. September 11 Terrorist Attacks, 2001 7. Terrorism -- United States -- Prevention

ISBN 9780316186599

LC 2011041533

This book follows "[t]he cat-and-mouse game between American investigators and Khalid Sheikh Mohammed, architect of the 9/11 attacks and other terrorist spectaculars. . . . Journalists [Terry] McDermott . . . and [Josh] Meyer (the L.A. Times's chief terrorism reporter) present a police procedural starring an FBI agent, Frank Pellegrino, Port Authority detective Matt Besheer, and the inter-agency anti-terrorism experts who tracked KSM and his confederates for a decade before his 2003 capture. . . . The authors" . . . profile of Khalid Sheikh Mohammed depicts a resourceful, charismatic man . . . and paints a . . . portrait of the workaday terrorist life of fund-raising, recruitment, bomb-rigging, and general plotting, all carried out while dodging a global manhunt." (Publishers Weekly)

Includes bibliographical references

Morell, Michael J.

The **great** war of our time; an insider's account of the CIA's fight against al Qa'ida. Michael Morell with Bill Harlow. Twelve 2015 384 p. illustrations (hardback) $28   **363.325**

1. Terrorism -- Prevention 2. United States. Central Intelligence Agency 3. Qaida (Organization) 4. War on Terrorism, 2001-2009 5. Terrorism -- United States -- Prevention 6. United States. Central

Intelligence Agency -- Officials and employees -- Biography

ISBN 1455585661; 9781455585663

LC 2014049799

In this book, author Michael Morrell "offer[s] an unblinking and insightful assessment of CIA's counterterrorism successes and failures of the past twenty years and, perhaps most important, shows readers that the threat of terrorism did not die with Bin Ladin in Abbottabad. Morell describes how efforts to throw off the shackles of oppression have too often resulted in broken nation states unable or unwilling to join the fight against terrorism." (Publisher's note)

"Recently retired as the CIA's deputy director, Morell was the only person with President Bush on 9/11 and President Obama when Osama Bin Laden was killed. No wonder 60 Minutes calls him 'the most important spook you have never heard of.' Here he goes inside the CIA to reveal its operations during the war on terror.' LJ

Russell, Jenna

Long mile home; Boston under attack, the city's courageous recovery, and the epic hunt for justice. Scott Helman and Jenna Russell, reporters for the Boston Globe. Penguin Group 2014 352 p. ill. (chiefly col.), col map (hardcover) $27.95 **363.325**

1. Bombings 2. Boston Marathon 3. Terrorism -- United States 4. Boston Marathon Bombing, Boston, Mass., 2013 5. Terrorism -- Massachusetts -- Boston -- Case studies

ISBN 0525954481; 9780525954484

LC 2014000091

This book, by Scott Helman and Jenna Russell, is about "the Boston Marathon bombing and subsequent manhunt for the Tsarnaev brothers. [It tells] the . . . story of the tragic, surreal, and ultimately inspiring week of April 15, 2013: the preparations of the bombers; the glory of the race; the . . . emergency response to the explosions; the massive deployment of city, state, and federal law enforcement personnel; and the . . . world's emotional and humanitarian response." (Publisher's note)

"Despite the multitude of sources drawn upon, the writing is seamless and riveting. . . . Sensitive in its treatment and thrilling in its pace and immediacy." LJ

Includes bibliographical references and index

Sanger, David E.

The **perfect** weapon; war, sabotage, and fear in the cyber age. David E. Sanger. Crown Publishers, an imprint of the Crown Publishing Group 2018 xxiii, 357 p.p $28   **363.325**

1. Cyberterrorism 2. Internet and international relations 3. Technology and international relations 4. Internet in espionage 5. Cyberterrorism -- Prevention 6. Hacking -- Political aspects 7. Cyberspace -- Political aspects

ISBN 0451497899; 9780451497895

LC 2018285788

This book, by David E. Sanger, "is the startling inside story of how the rise of cyberweapons transformed geopolitics like nothing since the invention of the atomic bomb. Cheap to acquire . . . and usable for a variety of malicious purposes--from crippling infrastructure to sowing discord and doubt--cyber is now the weapon of choice for democracies, dictators, and terrorists. . . . [Sanger] reveals a world coming face-to-face with the perils of technological revolution." (Publisher's note)

Includes bibliographical references (pages 315-342) and index

Seierstad, Åsne

One of Us; The Story of Anders Breivik and the Massacre in Norway. by Asne Seierstad, Sarah Death (translator) Farrar, Straus & Giroux 2015 544 p. $28   **363.325**

1. Domestic terrorism -- Norway

ISBN 0374277893; 9780374277895

LC 2015932749

This book, by Asne Seierstad, translated by Sarah Death, provides "a harrowing and thorough account of the [July 22, 2011 terrorism] massacre that upended Norway, and the trial that helped put the country back together. . . . [The book] is at once a psychological study of violent extremism, a dramatic true crime procedural, and a compassionate inquiry into how a privileged society copes with homegrown evil." (Publisher's note)

"A powerful read that sociologists, historians, and political science students alike will find very informative." LJ

Skarlatos, Alek, 1992-

The **15**:17 to Paris; the true story of a terrorist, a train, and three American heroes. Anthony Sadler, Alek Skarlatos, Spencer Stone, with Jeffrey E. Stern. PublicAffairs 2016 245 p. map (hardback) $25.99; (ebook) $15.99 **363.325**
1. Railroad travel 2. Terrorism -- Prevention 3. Americans -- Foreign countries 4. Heroes -- United States -- Biography 5. Soldiers -- United States -- Biography 6. Railroad trains -- Belgium -- History -- 21st century 7. Terrorism -- Prevention -- European Union countries -- History -- 21st century
ISBN 1610397339; 9781610397339; 9781610397346

LC 2016015296

In this book, by Anthony Sadler, Alek Skarlatos, and Spencer Stone, with Jeffrey E. Stern, "on August 21, 2015, Ayoub El-Khazzani boarded train #9364 in Brussels, bound for Paris. . . . Another major ISIS attack was about to begin. . . . [But] near tragedy [was] averted by three young men who found the heroic unity and strength inside themselves at the moment when they, and 500 other innocent travelers, needed it most." (Publisher's note)

Includes bibliographical references and index.

Soufan, Ali H.

★ **Anatomy** of terror; from the death of Bin Laden to the rise of the Islamic State. Ali Soufan. W W Norton & Co Inc 2017 xix, 359 p.p (hardcover) $27.95 **363.325**
1. Terrorism 2. Radicalism 3. Qaida (Organization) 4. IS (Organization) 5. Terrorism -- Religious aspects -- Islam 6. Radicalism -- Religious aspects -- Islam
ISBN 9780393241174

LC 2016055805

This book, by Ali Soufan, is an "account of how and why [Osama] bin Laden's ideology keeps rising from the dead. . . . This riveting account examines the new Islamic radicalism through the eyes of its flag-bearers, including a Jordanian former drug dealer whose cruelties shocked even his fellow militants, an Air Force colonel who once served Saddam Hussein, and a provincial bookworm who declared himself caliph of all Muslims." (Publisher's note)

"Former FBI agent Soufan . . . composes a concise, accessible, enormously readable account of the trajectory of al-Qaida, especially through the actions of its murderous main protagonists." Kirkus

Includes bibliographical references and index

Wright, Lawrence, 1947-

★ The **terror** years; from al-Qaeda to the Islamic State. Lawrence Wright. Knopf 2016 400 p. (hardback) $28.95 **363.325**
1. Terrorism 2. Terrorists 3. Qaida (Organization) 4. United States -- Foreign relations 5. Middle East -- Politics and government 6. IS (Organization) 7. Terrorism -- Middle East 8. Middle East -- History -- 1979- 9. Terrorism -- Religious aspects -- Islam 10.

Terrorism -- United States -- Prevention 11. Middle East -- Politics and government -- 1945-
ISBN 9780385352055

LC 2015046064

In this book, journalist Lawrence Wright "recalls the path that terror in the Middle East has taken, from the rise of al-Qaeda in the 1990s to the recent beheadings of reporters and aid workers by ISIS. . . . The American response is covered in profiles of two FBI agents and the head of the intelligence community. The book ends with a devastating piece about the capture and slaying by ISIS of four American journalists and aid workers, and our government's failed response." (Publisher's note)

"The research that Wright did for the 10 essays contained in his latest work, all of which first appeared in the magazine, also contributed to Wright's deeper insight into the jihadist mindset, including its latest embodiment in ISIS. In "The Man behind Bin Laden" Wright recounts his return to Egypt, where he taught English decades earlier, to investigate the background of Bin Laden's sidekick Ayman al-Zawahiri, describing a country embroiled in post-9/11 political turmoil. . . . Other pieces on Saudi Arabia, ISIS violence, and Israel round out a brilliant volume that is a must-read for anyone looking for greater illumination of the baffling world of religious extremism." Booklist

363.33 Control of firearms

Giffords, Gabrielle D. (Gabrielle Dee), 1970-

Enough; Our Fight to Keep America Safe from Gun Violence. Gabrielle Giffords and Mark Kelly; with Harry Jaffe. Simon & Schuster 2015 256 p. $25 **363.33**
1. Gun control 2. Firearms ownership -- United States 3. Violence -- United States 4. Gun control -- United States 5. Firearms -- Law and legislation 6. United States. Constitution. 2nd Amendment
ISBN 1476750076; 9781476750071

LC 2013497343

In this book, by Gabrielle Giffords and Mark Kelly, with Harry Jaffe, the authors "share their impassioned argument for responsible gun ownership. . . . As gun owners and strong supporters of the Second Amendment, Gabby and Mark offer a bold but sensible path forward, preserving the right to own guns for collection, recreation, and protection while taking common-sense actions to prevent the next Tucson, Aurora, or Newtown." (Publisher's note)

"Lay readers and political science students who want to understand the emotional debate surrounding gun ownership and current efforts to limit access to lethal weapons will appreciate the balanced discussion of the issues facing those who intend to change current firearms legislation." LJ

Guns in American society; an encyclopedia of history, politics, culture, and the law. Gregg Lee Carter, editor. ABC-CLIO 2012 3 v. lxx, 1096 p.p ill. **363.33**
1. Weapons 2. Law -- United States 3. Violence -- Encyclopedias 4. Gun control -- United States -- Encyclopedias 5. Violent crimes -- United States -- Encyclopedias 6. Social movements -- United States -- Encyclopedias 7. Firearms -- Social aspects -- United States -- Encyclopedias 8. Firearms -- Law and legislation -- United States -- Encyclopedias
ISBN 0313386706; 0313386714; 9780313386701; 9780313386718

LC 2011043435

In this book, editor Gregg Lee Carter focuses on the following questions: Is "the high rate of violence in the United States linked to the prevalence of guns--or to a lack of social homogeneity and economic inequality? Should there be support for stricter or more lenient gun control? Should people carry concealed weapons for personal protection? . . . The encyclopedia . . . [offers] the latest thinking and research in the fields of criminology, history, law, medicine, politics, and sociology, [while] providing objective information." (Publisher's note)

Includes bibliographical references and index

Hogg, David

#NeverAgain; a new generation draws the line. Random House Inc 2018 165 p. $10   **363.33**
1. Gun control 2. School shootings
ISBN 198480183X; 9781984801838

LC 2018108177

This book, by David Hogg and Lauren Hogg, presents "an in-depth look at the making of the #NeverAgain movement, [after the February 14, 2018 school shooting in Parkland, Florida. The] . . . book is a manifesto for the movement begun that day, one that has already changed America. . . . With moral force and clarity, a new generation has made it clear that problems previously deemed unsolvable due to powerful lobbies and political cowardice will be theirs to solve." (Publisher's note)

Overton, Iain

★ The **Way** of the Gun; A Bloody Journey into the World of Firearms. Iain Overton. HarperCollins 2016 368 p. illustrations (ebook) $14.99; $26.99   **363.33**
1. Gun control 2. Guns -- Social aspects
ISBN 9780062346087; 0062346067; 9780062346063

LC 2016498146

In this book, author Iain Overton attempts "to understand how . . . [guns] have become an integral part of twenty-first century life, beyond the economics of supply and demand. Overton travels through more than twenty-five countries around the world and meets with ER doctors dealing with gun trauma, SWAT team leaders, gang members, and weapons smugglers. . . . He unearths some hard truths about the terrible realities of war and gun crime, and what can be done to stop it." (Publisher's note)

"A passionate mix of rhetoric and travelogue, Overton's book takes the gun debate into impressive new territory." Kirkus

Includes bibliographical references (pages 311-354).

363.34   Disasters

Andrés, José, 1969-

We fed an island; the true story of rebuilding Puerto Rico, one meal at a time. José Andrés. Anthony Bourdain/Ecco 2018 288 p. $27.99   **363.34**
1. Hurricanes 2. Food relief 3. Disaster relief
ISBN 0062864483; 9780062864482

This book, by José Andrés , presents "the true story of how a group of chefs fed hundreds of thousands of hungry Americans after Hurricane Maria. . . . Chef . . . Andrés arrived in Puerto Rico . . . [and] addressed the humanitarian crisis the only way he knew how: by feeding people, one hot meal at a time. . . . Andrés and his team fed hundreds of thousands of people . . . [and a]t the same time . . . confronted a crisis with deep roots." (Publisher's note)

Cross, Kim

What Stands in a Storm; Three Days in the Worst Superstorm to Hit the South's Tornado Alley. Kim Cross. Pocket Books 2015 320 p. illustration $25   **363.34**
1. Storms 2. Tornadoes 3. Natural disasters -- United States
ISBN 1476763062; 9781476763064

LC 2014035817

In this book by Kim Cross "immersive reporting and dramatic storytelling set you right in the middle of the horrific superstorm of April 2011, a weather event that killed 348 people. Cross weaves together the heart-wrenching stories of several characters--including three college students, a celebrity weatherman, and a team of hard-hit rescuers--to create a nail-biting chronicle in the Tornado Alley of America." (Publisher's note)

"Though topographical media and photographs aren't included, Cross journalistically illustrates the storm's unrelenting fury, heartbreaking aftermath and organized recovery efforts through dramatic firsthand stories, putting a human face on a tragic chain of events that claimed a devastating 348 casualties in 72 hours. The author also includes an 'In Memoriam' section that lists the 'Alabamians who lost their lives and the people who face a world without them.' Armchair storm chase r s will find much to savor in this grippingly detailed, real-time chronicle of nature gone awry." Kirkus

Ehrlich, Gretel

Facing the wave; a journey in the wake of the tsunami. Gretel Ehrlich. Pantheon Books 2012 240 p. $25   **363.34**
1. Tsunamis 2. Sendai Earthquake, Japan, 2011 3. Fukushima Nuclear Accident, Fukushima, Japan, 2011 4. Tohoku Earthquake and Tsunami, Japan, 2011 5. Tsunami damage -- Japan -- Tōhoku Region 6. Tsunami relief -- Japan -- Tōhoku Region 7. Disaster victims -- Japan -- Tōhoku Region
ISBN 0307907317; 9780307907318

LC 2012020400

National Book Awards: Nonfiction Long List (2013)

In this book, Gretel Ehrlich, winner of PEN New England's Henry David Thoreau Prize, "explains how a fascination with Japanese art and poetry drove her to Japan's devastated Tohoku coast after last year's tsunami." (Library Journal) Ehrlich "made several visits to Japan in the months after the shattering earthquake and tsunami" and tried to make sense of the event by "recording accounts by traumatized survivors and [sharing] her own . . . on-the-ground observations." (Kirkus)

Includes bibliographical references

Halberstam, David

Firehouse. Hyperion 2002 201p $22.95; pa $14 **363.34**
1. Fire fighters 2. World Trade Center terrorist attack, 2001 3. New York (N.Y.) -- Fire Dept.
ISBN 1-4013-0005-7; 0-7868-8851-2 pa

"A journalist's homage to firefighters, their values, their culture and their courage during the martyrdom imposed on the New York Fire Department by the catastrophe of the attack on the World Trade Center." N Y Times Bk Rev

Jones, Lucy

The **big** ones; how natural disasters have shaped us (and what we can do about them) Lucy Jones. Doubleday 2018 256 p. (hardback) $26.95   **363.34**
1. Tsunamis 2. Earthquakes 3. Natural disasters -- History 4. Natural disasters -- Social aspects
ISBN 9780385542708

LC 2017036796

In this book "seismologist Dr. Lucy Jones offers a bracing look at some of the world's greatest natural disasters, whose reverberations we continue to feel today. . . . She examines the California floods of 1862 and the limits of human memory. And she probes more recent events--such as the Indian Ocean tsunami of 2004 and the American hurricanes of 2017--to illustrate the potential for globalization to humanize and heal." (Publisher's note)

"For all her impressive expertise, Jones delivers a very accessible book—without sacrificing the scientific content, the text is sprinkled with relatable analogies to help readers better understand some of the more technical geological processes." LJ

Includes bibliographical references

Katz, Jonathan M.

The **big** truck that went by; how the world came to save Haiti and left behind a disaster. Jonathan Katz. Palgrave Macmillan 2013 306 p. ill., maps hbk $26   **363.34**
  1. Humanitarian intervention 2. Haiti Earthquake, Haiti, 2010 3. Disaster response and recovery 4. Haiti 5. Disaster relief -- Haiti 6. Earthquake relief -- Haiti
  ISBN 023034187X; 9780230341876
                                                              LC 2012037217
This book by Jonathan M. Katz is "about the January 2010 earthquake and its aftermath. . . . Katz, a former AP correspondent, was the only full-time American reporter stationed in Haiti when the quake hit; he stayed for more than a year thereafter, reporting on the charitable aftershocks--as small donations were mishandled by NGOs, as big donations never materialized, and as the world gradually lost interest and left Haiti to fend for itself." (Columbia Journalism Review)

"The author reports how promised aid funds didn't arrive and NGO relief funds were misspent, while Haitians, presumed to be corrupt, were shut out of involvement in relief efforts. . . . An eye-opening, trailblazing exposé." Kirkus

Includes bibliographical references and index

Muir-Wood, Robert

The **cure** for catastrophe; How We Can Stop Manufacturing Natural Disasters. Robert Muir-Wood. Basic Books, a Member of the Perseus Books Group 2016 368 p. maps (ebook) $20.99; (hardcover) $29.99   **363.34**
  1. Natural disasters 2. Environmental risk assessment 3. Hazardous geographic environments 4. Hazard mitigation 5. Natural disasters -- Planning 6. Natural disasters -- Prevention
  ISBN 9780465096473; 9780465060948
                                                              LC 2016004281
In this book, author Robert Muir-Wood "argues that our natural disasters are in fact human ones: We build in the wrong places and in the wrong way, putting brick buildings in earthquake country, timber ones in fire zones, and coastal cities in the paths of hurricanes. We then blindly trust our flood walls and disaster preparations, and when they fail, catastrophes become even more deadly. No society is immune to the twin dangers of complacency and heedless development." (Publisher's note)

"Readers will find it hard to stop reading this excellent book and will share the author's perhaps futile yearning that elected officials have the courage to pass inconvenient laws and spend the electorate's money to prevent disasters." Kirkus

Includes bibliographical references and index

Olson, Steve

Eruption; the untold story of Mount St. Helens. Steve Olson. W W Norton & Co Inc 2016 320 p. ill., maps, portraits (hardcover) $27.95   **363.34**
  1. Volcanoes 2. Mount Saint Helens (Wash.) 3. Volcanoes -- Washington (State) 4. Volcanic eruptions -- Washington (State) 5. Saint Helens, Mount (Wash.) -- Eruption, 1980
  ISBN 9780393242799
                                                              LC 2015038842
This book, by Steve Olson, presents "scientific, natural, and social history. . . . For months in early 1980, scientists, journalists, sightseers, and nearby residents listened anxiously to rumblings in Mount St.

Helens. . . . Still, no one was prepared when an immense eruption took the top off of the mountain and laid waste to hundreds of square miles of verdant forests in southwestern Washington State." (Publisher's note)

Includes bibliographical references and index

Smith, Dennis

Report from ground zero; the story of the rescue efforts at the World Trade Center. Viking 2002 366p il maps $24.95; pa $14   **363.34**
  1. Fire fighters 2. World Trade Center terrorist attack, 2001 3. New York (N.Y.) -- Fire Dept.
  ISBN 0-670-03116-X; 0-452-28395-7 pa
                                                              LC 2002-19840
Based on his personal observations and interviews with other rescue workers, the author describes the efforts of the New York City Fire Department to rescue survivors of the September 11 attack on the World Trade Center

Tougias, Mike

Ten hours until dawn; the true story of heroism and tragedy aboard the Can Do. [by] Michael Tougias. St. Martins Press 2005 322p il map $24.95   **363.34**
  1. Blizzards 2. Shipwrecks 3. Rescue work
  ISBN 0-312-33435-4
The author "delivers a well-researched, vividly written tale of brave men overwhelmed by the awesome forces of nature." Publ Wkly

Welky, David

The **thousand**-year flood; the Ohio-Mississippi disaster of 1937. University of Chicago Press 2011 355p il $27.50 **363.34**
  1. Disaster relief 2. New Deal, 1933-1939 3. Floods -- Mississippi River 4. Floods -- Ohio River valley 5. United States -- Politics and government -- 1933-1945
  ISBN 978-0-226-88716-6; 0-226-88716-2; 978-0-226-88718-0 ebook
                                                              LC 2011014875
"Vividly written and carefully documented, . . . [this book] masterfully brings a turning point in American history back to life." Wilson Quarterly

Includes bibliographical references

Zeilinga de Boer, Jelle

Earthquakes in human history; the far-reaching effects of seismic disruptions. [by] Jelle Zeilinga de Boer and Donald Theodore Sanders. Princeton University Press 2005 278p il maps $24.95   **363.34**
  1. Earthquakes
  ISBN 0-691-05070-8
                                                              LC 2004-40122
The authors provide "facts and insights on geologic processes and the effects of . . . natural disasters on the course of human history. Narratives on especially impactful earthquakes include events in the Holy Land, Ancient Greece, England, Portugal, Missouri, San Francisco, Japan, Peru and Chile, and Nicaragua. The influence of the earthquakes on religion, politics, economy, wars, and literature is portrayed in fascinating prose, embellished with carefully selected photos, drawings, and maps." Choice

Includes bibliographical references

363.35　Civil defense

Graff, Garrett M.

Raven Rock; the story of the U.S. Government's secret plan to save itself--while the rest of us die. Garrett M. Graff. Simon & Schuster 2017 xxv, 529 p.p illustrations, map (hardcover) $28 **363.35**

1. Crisis management 2. Military readiness 3. Civil defense -- United States 4. Nuclear warfare -- United States 5. Cold War 6. Nuclear warfare 7. United States -- Defenses 8. Military planning -- United States 9. Civil defense -- United States -- History 10. Crisis management in government -- United States -- History 11. Emergency management -- Government policy -- United States -- History
ISBN 9781476735405; 9781476735429

LC 2017004895

This book, by Garrett M. Graff, tells "the eye-opening true story of the government's secret plans to survive and rebuild after a catastrophic attack on US soil--a narrative that spans from the dawn of the nuclear age to today. . . . Equal parts a presidential, military, and political history, Raven Rock tracks the evolution of the government's plans and the threats of global war from the dawn of the nuclear era through the present day." (Publisher's note)

"A chilling portrait of how the government planned to continue to function during and after a nuclear holocaust is brilliantly told in this new valuable addition to Cold War literature that goes beyond policy and delves into logistical plans." LJ

Includes bibliographical references and index

363.37　Fire hazards

Dickman, Kyle

On the burning edge; a fateful fire and the men who fought it. by Kyle Dickman. Random House Inc 2015 277 p. color illustrations, maps $26 **363.37**

1. Wildfires 2. Fire fighters
ISBN 0553392123; 9780553392128

This book, by Kyle Dickman, "is the definitive account of the Yarnell Hill Fire. On June 28, 2013, a single bolt of lightning sparked an inferno that devoured more than eight thousand acres in northern Arizona. Twenty elite firefighters—the Granite Mountain Hotshots—walked together into the blaze, tools in their hands and emergency fire shelters on their hips. Only one of them walked out." (Publisher's note)

Kodas, Michael

Megafire; the race to extinguish a deadly epidemic of flame. Michael Kodas. Houghton Mifflin Harcourt 2017 xvi, 365 p.p illustrations (hardcover) $28 **363.37**

1. Wildfires 2. Natural disasters 3. Wildfire fighters
ISBN 9780547792088; 9780547792125; 0547792085

LC 2017019810

In this book journalist and forest fire expert, Michael Kodas "travels to the most dangerous and remote wildernesses, as well as to the backyards of people faced with . . . [megafires,] to look at the heart of this phenomenon and witness firsthand the heroic efforts of the firefighters and scientists racing against time to stop it--or at least to tame these deadly flames." (Publisher's note)

"Journalist Kodas addresses the increasing destructiveness of forest fires, a topic gaining in significance as the climate warms. . . . This is a must-read for all as forest fires spread across the country." Booklist

Includes bibliographical references (pages [321]-349) and index

363.379　Fire hazards in specific situations

McDonough, Brendan

My Lost Brothers; The Untold Story by the Yarnell Hill Fire's Lone Survivor. by Brendan McDonough. Hachette Books 2016 288 p. illustrations (ebook) $81; $27 **363.379**

1. Wildfires 2. Fire fighters
ISBN 9780316308168; 0316308188; 9780316308182

LC 2016016931

In this book, "Brendan McDonough was on the verge of becoming a hopeless, inveterate heroin addict when he, for the sake of his young daughter, decided to turn his life around. He enlisted in the Granite Mountain Hotshots, a team of elite firefighters based in Prescott, Arizona. Their leader, Eric Marsh, was in a desperate crunch after four hotshots left the unit, and perhaps seeing a glimmer of promise in the skinny would-be recruit, he took a chance on the unlikely McDonough, and the chance paid off." (Publisher's note)

"With his insightful barbs aimed at our increasingly unrealistic ideal of life in the West and the many ways in which wildland firefighters are let down by those who fund and rely upon them, and brutally honest assessment of his struggles with PTSD, McDonough gives readers a unique and bracing literary experience." Booklist

363.4　Controversies related to public morals and customs

McGirr, Lisa

The **war** on alcohol; prohibition and the rise of the American state. Lisa McGirr. W W Norton & Co Inc 2015 352 p. 8 plates; illustrations (hardcover) $27.95 **363.4**

1. Prohibition 2. United States -- History -- 20th century 3. Prohibition -- United States
ISBN 0393066959; 9780393066951

LC 2015028038

This book, by Lisa McGirr, presents an alternative analysis of prohibition in U.S. history. "Prohibition was the seedbed for a pivotal expansion of the federal government, the genesis of our contemporary penal state. . . . [The author] uncovers patterns of enforcement still familiar today: the war on alcohol was waged disproportionately in African American, immigrant, and poor white communities." (Publisher's note)

"McGirr's new perspective on Prohibition is recommended for all readers interested in American history." LJ

Includes bibliographical references and index

Okrent, Daniel, 1948-

Last call; the rise and fall of Prohibition, 1920-1933. Scribner 2010 468p $30 **363.4**

1. Prohibition 2. Drinking of alcoholic beverages 3. United States -- History -- 20th century 4. Prohibition -- United States -- History -- 20th century 5. Drinking of alcoholic beverages -- United States -- History -- 20th century
ISBN 978-0-7432-7702-0; 0-7432-7702-3

LC 2009-51127

"Okrent's style is bracing and wry, his research is vast and impressive and his insight is penetrating. Intoxicating." Kirkus

Includes bibliographical references

Watman, Max

Chasing the white dog; an amateur outlaw's adventures in moonshine. Simon & Schuster 2010 292p $25 **363.4**

1. Liquors 2. Distillation
ISBN 978-1-4165-7178-0; 1-4165-7178-7

LC 2009-24657

"No matter where the chase takes him, from policing a lobster pot full of boiling molasses to getting schnockered at a conference for hobby distillers, Watman is a hands-on, no-holds-barred participant. He gamely learns to race cars to absorb the moonshine/NASCAR culture, and sits through the trial of a group of large-scale bootleggers in a multistate investigation. He profiles local color like Daytona 500 winner Junior Johnson, onetime moonshiner, famous for inventing the 'bootleg turn' to outrun the feds; and 'whitecollar' distillers like George Stranahan in Colorado." PopMatters

363.45   Drug traffic

Ainslie, Ricardo C.
The **fight** to save Juárez; life in the heart of Mexico's drug war. by Ricardo C. Ainslie. 1st ed. University of Texas Press 2013 xii, 282 p.p ill. (paperback) $25   **363.45**
1. Ciudad Juarez (Mexico) 2. Drug traffic -- Mexico 3. Law enforcement -- Mexico 4. Drug control -- Mexico -- Ciudad Juárez 5. Drug traffic -- Mexico -- Ciudad Juárez 6. Violent crime -- Mexico -- Ciudad Juárez
ISBN 9780292738904

LC 2012035822

This book, by Ricardo C. Ainslie, discusses the Mexican drug war. "The city of Juárez is ground zero for the drug war that is raging across Mexico and has claimed close to 60,000 lives since 2007. . . . [The book] takes us into the heart of Mexico's bloodiest city through the lives of four people who experienced the drug war from very different perspectives--Mayor José Reyes Ferriz, a mid-level cartel player's mistress, a human rights activist, and a photojournalist." (Publisher's note)

Includes bibliographical references and index.

Deutsch, Kevin
Pill city; How Two Honor Roll Students Foiled the Feds and Built a Drug Empire. Kevin Deutsch. St. Martin's Press 2016 288 p. illustrations (hardcover) $26.99; (ebook) $60 **363.45**
1. Drug dealers -- United States -- Case studies 2. Drug traffic -- United States -- Case studies 3. Medication abuse -- United States -- Case studies 4. Drug control -- United States -- Case studies
ISBN 9781250110039; 9781250110046

LC 2016036712

This book, by Kevin Deutsch, "chronicles the rise of . . . [two] gangland upstarts as they help steal $100 million worth of high-powered opiates, and build a national narcotics empire from scratch. . . . [It] takes readers into the heat of the action as Brick and Wax outwit the FBI and DEA, gang members like Damage and Lyric live and die by their own brutal code, the cops battle to stop the carnage, and a high-school coach risks a bullet to get addicts into rehab." (Publisher's note)

"The book shows communities both torn apart by and responding to an opioid epidemic. Deutsch's analysis looks at the two young men, a mob war, and the neighborhood caught in the middle... This story is not well known, but it should be." LJ

Includes bibliographical references

Schou, Nicholas
Orange sunshine; the Brotherhood of Eternal Love and its quest to spread peace, love, and acid to the world. Thomas Dunne Books 2010 306p il $24.99   **363.45**
1. Drug traffic 2. Dissenters 3. Narcotics dealers 4. Brotherhood of Eternal Love
ISBN 978-0-312-55183-4; 0-312-55183-5

LC 2009-40284

"Blue Cheer. Window Pane. Orange Sunshine. Maui Wowie. These were the brand names of the psychedelic counterculture of the 1960s and '70s, a culture led by the Brotherhood of Eternal Love. Chances are, if a brand of acid, pot or hashish was known to stoners, it first made its way into the underground market via the Brotherhood. Originally a marijuana-dealing motorcycle gang of toughs, the Brotherhood had a mass religious experience with LSD in 1965-they believed they'd found a lysergic shortcut to God. They resolved, under the charismatic leadership of John 'the Farmer' Griggs, whom Timothy Leary called 'the holiest man ever to live in this country,' to become apostles of acid with a mission to turn on the entire world. . . . A fascinating read for any audience and essential history for anyone interested in the roots of psychedelia." Kirkus

Includes bibliographical references

Wainwright, Tom
Narconomics; how to run a drug cartel. Tom Wainwright. PublicAffairs 2016 288 p. illustrations, map (ebook) $15.99; (hardcover) $26.99   **363.45**
1. Drug traffic 2. Organized crime 3. Drug dealers 4. Drug control -- Economic aspects 5. Drug traffick -- Economic aspects
ISBN 9781610395847; 9781610395830

LC 2015032727

This book, by Tom Wainwright, "provides a fresh, innovative look into the drug trade. . . . The cast of characters includes . . . [a] Bolivian coca guide . . . , [a] Salvadoran gang leader . . . , [and a] New Zealand pill maker. . . . Along with presidents, cops, and teenage hitmen, they explain such matters as the business purpose for head-to-toe tattoos, how gangs decide whether to compete or collude, and why cartels care . . . about corporate social responsibility." (Publisher's note)

"Readers interested in the intersection of crime, economics, entrepreneurship, and law enforcement will find this work fascinating." LJ

Includes bibliographical references and index

363.46   Abortion

Palmer, Louis J.
Encyclopedia of abortion in the United States; [by] Louis J. Palmer, Jr. and Xueyan Z. Palmer. 2nd ed.; McFarland & Co. 2009 624p il $150   **363.46**
1. Reference books 2. Abortion -- Encyclopedias
ISBN 978-0-7864-3838-9; 0-7864-3838-X

LC 2008-31047

First published 2002

"Ranging in length from a single paragraph to several pages, the A-to-Z entries define noteworthy events, significant figures, state and federal legislation, prochoice and prolife organizations, case specifics, abortion methods, and contraceptive devices. . . . This balanced, unblinking, and comprehensive subject reference makes complex legal details accessible to the lay reader." Libr J

Includes bibliographical references

Pollitt, Katha, 1949-
Pro; Reclaiming Abortion As Good for Society. Katha Pollitt. St. Martin's Press 2014 256 p. $25   **363.46**
1. Abortion 2. Pro-life movement
ISBN 0312620543; 9780312620547

LC 2014017553

"In this . . . book, Katha Pollitt reframes abortion as a common part of a woman's reproductive life, one that should be accepted as a moral right with positive social implications. In 'Pro,' Pollitt takes on the personhood argument, reaffirms the priority of a woman's life and health, and discusses why terminating a pregnancy can be a force for good for women, families, and society." (Publisher's note)

"Although the 'muddled middle' may not welcome the ascription, pro-choice advocates will find Pollitt's summation helpful in recruitment." LJ

Press, Eyal

Absolute convictions; my father, a city, and the conflict that divided America. Henry Holt and Co. 2006 292p il map hardcover o.p. pa $15   **363.46**
1. Abortion 2. Gynecologists 3. Pro-life movement 4. Abortion providers
ISBN 0-8050-7731-6; 978-0-312-42657-6 pa; 0-312-42657-7 pa
LC 2005-34064

The author "manages the extraordinary feat of bringing light to a political issue that for far too long has generated nothing but blistering heat." N Y Times Book Rev
Includes bibliographical references

Sanger, Carol

★ **About** abortion; terminating pregnancy in twenty-first-century America. Carol Sanger. The Belknap Press of Harvard University Press 2017 xv, 304 p.p illustrations (hardcover) $29.95   **363.46**
1. Abortion -- Ethical aspects 2. Abortion -- Law and legislation 3. Unwanted pregnancy -- United States 4. Abortion -- Political aspects -- United States 5. Abortion -- Law and legislation -- United States 6. Abortion -- United States -- Psychological aspects 7. Abortion -- Moral and ethical aspects -- United States
ISBN 9780674977303; 9780674737723
LC 2016041934

It this book, author Carol Sanger, "distinguishes . . . abortion privacy, a form of nondisclosure based on a woman's desire to control personal information, and abortion secrecy, a woman's defense against the many harms of disclosure. . . . Sanger takes these prejudicial views of women's abortion decisions into the twenty-first century by uncovering new connections between abortion law and American culture and politics." (Publisher's note)

"This is perhaps the best book ever written on the multiple facets surrounding abortion politics, law, and regulation. An excellent addition to collections on reproductive rights, gender politics, women and the law, and American politics." Choice
Includes bibliographical references and index

Underwood, Kassi

May cause love; an unexpected journey of enlightenment after abortion. Kassi Underwood. HarperOne 2017 352 p. (ebook) $25.99; (hardback) $26.99   **363.46**
1. Abortion 2. Spiritual life 3. Self-acceptance 4. Self-realization 5. Loss (Psychology) 6. Abortion -- Psychological aspects
ISBN 9780062458650; 0062458639; 9780062458636
LC 2016030271

In this memoir, "at age nineteen, Kassi Underwood discovered she was pregnant. Broke, unwed, struggling with alcohol, and living a thousand miles away from home, she checked into an abortion clinic. While her abortion sparked her 'feminist awakening,' she also felt lost and lawless. . . . Three years later, just when she had settled into a sober life at her dream job, the ex-boyfriend with whom she had become pregnant had a baby with someone else. She shattered." (Publisher's note)

"A poignant memoir about the years of healing that are often re-

quired after having an abortion." Kirkus
Includes bibliographical references (pages [323]-338).

363.5 Housing

Loewen, James W.

Sundown towns; a hidden dimension of American racism. New Press 2005 562p il $29.95   **363.5**
1. Discrimination in housing 2. United States -- Race relations 3. African Americans -- Segregation
ISBN 1-56584-887-X
LC 2005-43855

"This book is sure to become a landmark in several fields and a sure bet among Loewen's many fans." Publ Wkly
Includes bibliographical references

Satter, Beryl

Family properties; race, real estate, and the exploitation of Black urban America. Metropolitan Books 2009 495p il $30   **363.5**
1. Lawyers 2. Discrimination in housing 3. Social activists 4. African Americans -- Chicago (Ill.)
ISBN 978-0-8050-7676-9; 0-8050-7676-X
LC 2008-33005

The author "leaps from the particulars of one man's story to become a panoramic retelling of the Chicago real-estate wars during a period when, after the postwar migration of Southern blacks, that city was the most segregated in the North." N Y Times (Late N Y Ed)
Includes bibliographical references

363.6 Public utilities and related services

Farabee, Charles R.

National park ranger; an American icon. {by} Charles R. "Butch" Farabee Jr. Roberts Rinehart Publishers 2003 180p il pa $18.95   **363.6**
1. United States -- National Park Service 2. National parks and reserves -- United States
ISBN 1-570-98392-5
LC 2003-1022

"In this study of the vocation of park ranger since Maryland's park caretakers in 1696 to the present day, former ranger Farabee not only explores a ranger's role but also touches on the establishment of the National Park Service, the introduction of women rangers, and early resource management. Readers will enjoy the abundance of archival photographs, ranger profiles, and numerous other features." Libr J
Includes bibliographical references

Heacox, Kim

National Geographic the national parks; an illustrated history. Kim Heacox. National Geographic 2015 367 p. color illustrations (hardcover: alk. paper) $50   **363.6**
1. National parks and reserves -- United States -- History
ISBN 1426215592; 9781426215599
LC 2015014107

This book is a "celebration of the 100th anniversary of the National Park Service. [It] collects the very best of National Geographic's photographs, combined with an expertly told history: from the multi-hued layers of the Grand Canyon to the verdigris flame of the Statue of Liberty, this book presents a breathtaking panorama of the National Parks.

With the stories behind the first female park ranger, a decidedly amateur scuba expedition that unearthed a submerged Civil War treasure trove, and so much more, Heacox takes readers on a VIP tour of America's rich natural and cultural heritage." (Publisher's note)

"Gorgeous in every way, and essential for travel and history shelves." LJ

363.61 Water supply

Clark, Anna

The **poisoned** city; Flint's water and the American urban tragedy. Anna Clark. Henry Holt & Co. 2018 336 p. $30 **363.61**

1. Water supply 2. Flint (Mich.) 3. Drinking water -- Contamination
ISBN 1250125146; 9781250125149

This book, by Anna Clark, "recounts the gripping story of Flint's poisoned water through the people who caused it, suffered from it, and exposed it. It is a chronicle of one town, but could also be about any American city, all made precarious by the neglect of infrastructure and the erosion of democratic decision making." (Publisher's note)

"A compelling must-read about issues of environmental activism, urban issues, systemic racism, and the accountability of the government to the people whom it serves." Library Journal

363.7 Environmental problems

Berners-Lee, Mike

How bad are bananas? the carbon footprint of everything. Greystone Books 2011 232p il pa $16.95 **363.7**

1. Carbon 2. Greenhouse effect
ISBN 978-1-55365-831-3 pa; 978-1-55365-832-0 ebook
First published 2010 in the United Kingdom

Discusses the carbon footprint—the carbon emissions used to manufacture and transport—of everyday items, including paper bags and imported produce, and provides information to help build carbon considerations into everyday purchases.

"A book like this risks being preachy or overly serious, but Berners-Lee approaches his topics with humor and curiosity. He rarely advocates radical change. Rather, he gives readers information." Christ Sci Monit
Includes bibliographical references

Bloom, Jonathan

American wasteland; how America throws away nearly half of its food (and what we can do about it) Da Capo Press 2010 360p il $26 **363.7**

1. Salvage 2. Food supply 3. Food industry 4. Waste (Economics)
ISBN 978-0-7382-1364-4

LC 2010-15075

"An eye-opening account of what used to be considered a sin—the willful waste of perfectly edible food. . . . An urgent, necessary book." Kirkus
Includes bibliographical references

Bloomberg, Michael R., 1942-

Climate of hope; how cities, businesses, and citizens can save the planet. Michael Bloomberg and Carl Pope. St. Martin's Press 2017 264 p. color illustrations, maps (hardcover) $26.99 **363.7**

1. Climate change 2. Business enterprises -- Environmental aspects 3. Global warming -- Political aspects 4. Climatic changes --

Political aspects
ISBN 9781250142092; 1250142075; 9781250142078

LC 2016055992

Authors Michael Bloomberg and Carl Pope present this "manifesto on how the benefits of taking action on climate change are concrete, immediate, and immense. They explore climate change solutions that will make the world healthier and more prosperous, aiming to begin a new type of conversation on the issue that will spur bolder action by cities, businesses, and citizens—and even, someday, by Washington." (Publisher's note)

"Whether this is an exercise in thinking globally and acting locally or vice versa, a thoughtful, eminently reasonable set of proposals for saving New York—and therefore the world." Kirkus

Carson, Rachel, 1907-1964

★ **Silent** spring; introduction by Linda Lear; afterword by Edward O. Wilson. 40th anniversary ed; Houghton Mifflin 2002 378p il **363.7**

1. Pesticides and wildlife 2. Pesticides -- Environmental aspects
ISBN 0-618-24906-0 pa; 0-618-25305-X
First published 1962

In The silent spring, Carson "contended that the indiscriminate use of weed killers and insecticides constituted a hazard to wildlife and to human beings. Her provocative work inspired many subsequent environmental studies." Reader's Ency. 4th edition

Flannery, Tim F.

The **weather** makers; how man is changing the climate and what it means for life on Earth. [by] Tim Flannery. Atlantic Monthly Press 2006 357p il maps hardcover o.p. pa $15 **363.7**

1. Climate 2. Greenhouse effect
ISBN 0-8711-3935-9; 0-8021-4292-3 pa

LC 2005-52350

"This work is distinctive in its marriage of science to an act-now attitude and should energize environmentally minded readers." Booklist
Includes bibliographical references (p. 289-297)

Freudenburg, William R.

Blowout in the Gulf; the BP oil spill disaster and the future of energy in America. [by] William R. Freudenburg and Robert Gramling. MIT Press 2010 254p il $18.95 **363.7**

1. Oil spills 2. Drilling platforms 3. Offshore oil well drilling 4. British Petroleum Co. plc
ISBN 978-0-262-01583-7

LC 2010-937510

The authors "set the deadly BP blowout within a technologically precise history of oil in America, from the first primitively constructed well on land to the development of offshore rigs, explaining that the Deepwater Horizon was actually a technical marvel—if only its operation hadn't been compromised. . . . Science, commerce, and the politics of oil are all newly illuminated here, accompanied by invaluable explanations of the risks of offshore drilling and a pragmatic look at the energy conundrums we now face." Booklist
Includes bibliographical references

Friedman, Thomas L.

Hot, flat, and crowded; why we need a green revolution--and how it can renew America. Farrar, Straus & Giroux 2008 438p il $27.95 **363.7**

1. Energy resources 2. Environmental movement 3. Climate -- Environmental aspects 4. Environmental policy -- United States

ISBN 978-0-374-16685-4; 0-374-16685-4

LC 2008-930589

"Friedman's big, passionate, and solidly specific ecological primer, social manifesto, and realistic plan for a green revolution aimed at restoring America's greatness and securing a sustainable future should serve as a playbook for innovators and civic leaders." Booklist

Gates, Alexander E.

Encyclopedia of pollution; [by] Alexander E. Gates and Robert P. Blauvelt. Facts on File 2011 2v il map (Facts on File science library) set $170   **363.7**

1. Pollution 2. Reference books 3. Pollution -- Encyclopedias

ISBN 978-0-8160-7002-2

LC 2009048190

"Broad topics encompass all aspects of pollutants, including properties, production, uses, environmental release and fate, regulations, and adverse health effects in response to exposure. Summary entries on general subjects, such as water pollution, provide topical overviews. Case studies of pollution events supply instructive background information." Booklist

Includes bibliographical references

George, Rose

The **big** necessity; the unmentionable world of human waste and why it matters. Metropolitan Books 2008 288p il $26   **363.7**

1. Sanitation 2. Sewage disposal

ISBN 978-0-8050-8271-5; 0-8050-8271-9

LC 2008-29999

The author "breaks the embarrassed silence over the economic, political, social and environmental problems of human waste disposal. . . . From the depths of the world's oldest surviving urban sewers in to Japan's robo-toilet revolution, George leads an intrepid, erudite and entertaining journey through the public consequences of this most private behavior." Publ Wkly

Includes bibliographical references

Gessner, David

All the Wild That Remains; Edward Abbey, Wallace Stegner, and the American West. David Gessner. W W Norton & Co Inc 2015 320 p. illustrations $26.95   **363.7**

1. West (U.S.)

ISBN 0393089991; 9780393089998

LC 2014036995

In this book about writers Edward Abbey and Wallace Stegner, author " David Gessner follows the ghosts of these two remarkable writer-environmentalists from Stegner's birthplace in Saskatchewan to the site of Abbey's pilgrimages to Arches National Park in Utah, braiding their stories and asking how they speak to the lives of all those who care about the West." (Publisher's note)

"Highly recommended for everyone interested in literature, environmentalism, and the American West." LJ

Gore, Al

★ An **inconvenient** truth; the planetary emergency of global warming and what we can do about it. Rodale 2006 325p il map pa $23.95   **363.7**

1. Human ecology 2. Environmental protection 3. Greenhouse effect 4. Environmental policy -- United States

ISBN 978-1-59486-567-1; 1-59486-567-1

LC 2006-926537

"Gore has put together a coherent account of a complex topic that

Americans desperately need to understand. . . . By telling the story of climate change with striking clarity . . . Al Gore may have done for global warming what [Rachel Carson's] Silent Spring [1962] did for pesticides." N Y Rev Books

Our choice; a plan to solve the climate crisis. Rodale 2009 414p il map pa $26.99   **363.7**

1. Human ecology 2. Environmental policy 3. Environmental protection 4. Greenhouse effect

ISBN 978-1-59486-734-7; 1-59486-734-8

LC 2009-38291

The former vice president addresses key environmental issues while profiling and evaluating possible solutions.

This "is an inviting and momentous compendium of environmental discovery . . . that addresses one of the greatest threats our species has encountered with intelligence, knowledge, wisdom, and faith in human empowerment. This is a book that should be displayed and talked about everywhere." Booklist

Hansen, James E.

Storms of my grandchildren; the truth about the coming climate catastrophe and our last chance to save humanity. [by] James Hansen; illustrations by Makiko Sato. Bloomsbury USA 2009 304p il $25   **363.7**

1. Environmental influence on humans 2. Greenhouse effect 3. Climate -- Environmental aspects

ISBN 978-1-60819-200-7

LC 2009-44553

"Rich in invaluable insights into the geopolitics as well as the geophysics of climate change, Hansen's guaranteed-to-be-controversial manifesto is the most comprehensible, realistic, and courageous call to prevent climate change yet. It belongs in every library." Booklist

Includes bibliographical references

Keizer, Garret

The **unwanted** sound of everything we want; a book about noise. PublicAffairs 2010 385p $27.95   **363.7**

1. Noise 2. Sound 3. Noise -- Psychological aspects 4. Sound -- Psychological aspects

ISBN 1586485520; 9781586485528

LC 2010-05391

This book presents an "argument about the politics of sound. [Garret] Keizer acknowledges the subjective dimension of noise, which is sometimes defined as unwanted sound. What I deem noise may not be bothersome to someone else, and what bothers me in one context could be acceptable to me in another." Keizer offers an "analysis of power and inequality, noting the disproportionate effect of noise on people on the margins. . . . In response, he argues for a renewed human community of civility and sustainability." (Christian Century)

This "book explores the unforeseen (and sometimes unwanted) side effects of our inventive natures. We usually use the word noise as a pejorative, a term denoting unwanted sound: somebody's loud music, a blaring car alarm, the din from a nearby airport. But, as Keizer points out, noise is often—perhaps even usually—a product of human achievement, invention, or ambition. In broad terms, you can't have civilization without noise. . . . An enlightening look at an issue most of us ignore." Booklist

Includes bibliographical references

Kirby, David

Animal factory; the looming threat of industrial pig, dairy, and poultry farms to humans and the environment. St. Martin's

Press 2010 492p $26.99 **363.7**
1. Livestock industry 2. Agriculture -- Environmental aspects
ISBN 0-312-38058-5; 978-0-312-38058-8

"Thanks to Kirby's extraordinary journalism, we have the most re-latable, irrefutable, and unforgettable testimony yet to the hazards of industrial animal farming." Booklist

Kolbert, Elizabeth
★ **Field** notes from a catastrophe; man, nature, and climate change. Bloomsbury Pub. 2006 210p il map hardcover o.p. pa $14.95 **363.7**
1. Climate 2. Greenhouse effect
ISBN 1-59691-125-5; 978-1-59691-125-3; 1-59691-130-1 pa; 978-1-59691-130-7 pa

LC 2005-30972

"On the burgeoning shelf of cautionary but occasionally alarmist books warning about the consequences of dramatic climate change, Kolbert's calmly persuasive reporting stands out for its sobering clarity." Publ Wkly
Includes bibliographical references

Mann, Charles C.
★ The **wizard** and the prophet; two remarkable scientists and their dueling visions of tomorrow's world. Charles C. Mann. Alfred A. Knopf 2018 x, 616 p.p illustrations, maps (hardcover) $28.95 **363.7**
1. Environmental sciences 2. Food security 3. Water security 4. Energy security 5. Climatic changes 6. Environmentalists -- United States -- Biography 7. Environmental sciences -- History -- 20th century
ISBN 9780307961709; 9780307961693

LC 2017024776

This book, by Charles C. Mann, presents "an incisive portrait of the two little-known twentieth-century scientists, Norman Borlaug and William Vogt, whose diametrically opposed views shaped our ideas about the environment, laying the groundwork for how people in the twenty-first century will choose to live in tomorrow's world. In forty years, Earth's population will reach ten billion. Can our world support that? What kind of world will it be?" (Publisher's note)

"This unique, encompassing, clarifying, engrossing, inquisitive, and caring work of multifaceted research, synthesis, and analysis humanizes the challenges and contradictions of modern environmentalism and our struggle toward a viable future." Booklist
Includes bibliographical references (pages 481-584) and index.

McKibben, Bill, 1960-
Oil and Honey; The Education of an Unlikely Activist. Bill McKibben. Times Books 2013 272 p. $26 **363.7**
1. Beekeeping 2. Environmentalists 3. Environmental movement 4. Environmentalism -- United States 5. Beekeepers -- United States -- Biography 6. Climatic changes -- Environmental aspects 7. Environmentalists -- United States -- Biography 8. Petroleum industry and trade -- Environmental aspects 9. Petroleum industry and trade -- Political aspects -- United States
ISBN 0805092846; 9780805092844

LC 2013010995

This book is a memoir by environmental activist Bill McKibben. "McKibben intersperses his accounts of his intense and wide-ranging efforts as an environmental activist with his sometimes-humbling experiences as a novice beekeeper, learning from [farmer Kirk] Webster the art and science of raising bees and making honey." (Kirkus Reviews)

Mooney, Chris
Storm world; hurricanes, politics, and the battle over global warming. Harcourt 2007 392p il map $26 **363.7**
1. Hurricanes 2. Greenhouse effect
ISBN 978-0-15-101287-9; 0-15-101287-3

LC 2007-09742

"This is certainly one of the most thought-provoking and accessible accounts of climate change to appear since Katrina." Booklist
Includes bibliographical references

Moore, Charles
Plastic ocean; how a sea captain's chance discovery launched a determined quest to save the oceans. [by] Capt. Charles Moore with Cassandra Phillips. Avery 2011 358p il map $26 **363.7**
1. Plastics 2. Marine pollution
ISBN 978-1-58333-424-9; 1-58333-424-6

LC 2011034559

"The author is an impassioned, fiercely inquisitive writer, detailing the many unorthodox ways he's managed to get these issues into the news and in peer-reviewed science journals. . . . Fast-paced and electrifying, Moore's story is 'gonzo science' at its best." Kirkus
Includes bibliographical references

Pooley, Eric
The **climate** war; true believers, power brokers, and the fight to save the earth. Hyperion 2010 481p $27.99 **363.7**
1. Environmental policy 2. Climate -- Environmental aspects
ISBN 978-1-4013-2326-4

LC 2010-12422

This "is a fascinating, well-researched, behind-the-scenes account of the political twists and turns and efforts of corporate bosses and climate activists. Pooley . . . puts a human face on the topic and writes a gripping account—whether one reads it cover to cover or consults individual chapters in any order." Choice
Includes bibliographical references

Robinson, Mary
Climate justice; hope, resilience, and the fight for a sustainable future. Mary Robinson. Bloomsbury Publishing 2018 176 p. illustrations hardcover $26 **363.7**
1. Climate change 2. Environmental movement 3. Environmental protection 4. Environmental justice 5. Climatic changes -- Social aspects
ISBN 9781632869289

LC 2018027314

In this book, author Mary Robinson shows "that an irrepressible driving force in the battle for climate justice could be found at the grassroots level, mainly among women, many of them mothers and grandmothers like herself. From Sharon Hanshaw, . . . to Constance Okollet, . . . Robinson met with ordinary people whose resilience and ingenuity had already unlocked extraordinary change." (Publisher's note)

"This brief but cogent account reminds readers that climate change is not academic or abstract; it is real and it has consequences." Pub Wkly
Includes bibliographical references and index

Rogers, Heather
Gone tomorrow; the hidden life of garbage. New Press 2005 288p il $23.95 **363.7**
1. Refuse and refuse disposal
ISBN 1-56584-879-9

LC 2005-41562

The author "analyzes the contents of America's garbage and its disposal while also revealing the corporate strategies behind the disposable-goods explosion and assessing the ecological toll of our consumer habits." Booklist

Includes bibliographical references

Royte, Elizabeth

Garbage land; on the secret trail of trash. Little, Brown 2005 311p hardcover o.p. pa $14.99 **363.7**

1. Refuse and refuse disposal

ISBN 0-316-73826-3; 0-316-15461-X pa

LC 2004-24732

"There's little waste in Royte's winning words. . . . Seldom has garbage been handled with such care." Christ Sci Monit

Includes bibliographical references

Shulman, Seth

Cooler smarter; practical steps for low-carbon living: expert advice from the Union of Concerned Scientists. Seth Shulman ... [et al.] Island Press 2012 321 p. (pbk.) $21.95 **363.7**

1. Fuel 2. Environmental health 3. Transportation -- Environmental aspects 4. Sustainable living -- United States 5. Environmental protection -- United States -- Citizen participation

ISBN 161091192X; 9781610911924

LC 2012008656

In the book, the Union of Concerned Scientists discusses "proven strategies to cut carbon, with chapters on transportation, home energy use, diet, personal consumption, as well as how best to influence your workplace, your community, and elected officials. The book explains how to make the biggest impact and when not to sweat the small stuff. It also turns many eco-myths on their head, like the importance of locally produced food or the superiority of all hybrid cars." (Publisher's note)

Stager, Curt

Deep future; Curt Stager. Thomas Dunne Books 2011 284p ill. **363.7**

1. Global warming 2. Geological time 3. Historical geology 4. Climate -- Research

ISBN 9780312614621; 9780312614638

LC 2010040381

This book, a 'Kirkus Reviews' Best Nonfiction of 2011 title, presents an "exploration of the impact of climate change over geological time. [Curt] Stager takes the long view of global climate change . . . [and] examines both moderate and extreme scenarios. . . . A key point is that humanity has the ability to moderate the release of carbon, shaping the long-range impact on climate. While we are already past the point where significant global warming can be prevented, the author points out that cutting carbon now preserves some for a future era when its release could help prevent another ice age -- a global disaster every bit as threatening to the human race as warming." (Kirkus)

Includes bibliographical references (p. 243-270) and index.

Watts, Jonathan

When a billion Chinese jump; how China will save mankind--or destroy it. Scribner 2010 435p map pa $17; ebook $9.99 **363.7**

1. China -- Economic conditions 2. Environmental policy -- China 3. China -- Politics and government

ISBN 978-1-4165-8076-8 pa; 1-4165-8076-X pa; 978-1-4391-4193-9 ebook; 1-4391-4193-2 ebook

LC 2010-29901

"Watts' comprehensive, revealing study is eye-opening, not only for the way it illuminates how China's population growth and rapid modernization affect the environment, but also for its exposure of the way Western waste contributes to the problem." Booklist

Includes bibliographical references

363.72 Sanitation

Fagin, Dan

★ **Toms** River; a small town, a cancer cluster, and the epic quest to expose pollution's hidden consequences. Dan Fagin. Bantam Books 2013 560 p. $28 **363.72**

1. Rivers 2. Pollution 3. Industrial waste 4. Cancer -- Toms River Region 5. Water quality -- New Jersey -- Toms River Watershed 6. Toms River Watershed (N.J.) -- Environmental conditions 7. Groundwater -- Pollution -- Health aspects -- Toms River Region 8. Drinking water -- Contamination -- Health aspects -- Toms River Region

ISBN 055380653X; 9780345538611; 9780553806533

LC 2012017030

Pulitzer Prize: General Nonfiction (2014)

This book by Dan Fagin "recounts the sixty-year saga of rampant pollution and inadequate oversight that made Toms River [New Jersey] a cautionary example for fast-growing industrial towns from South Jersey to South China. He tells the stories of the pioneering scientists and physicians who first identified pollutants as a cause of cancer, and brings to life the everyday heroes in Toms River who struggled for justice." (Publisher's note)

Includes bibliographical references and index

363.73 Pollution

Blackwell, Andrew

★ **Visit** sunny Chernobyl; and other adventures in the world's most polluted places. Andrew Blackwell. Rodale 2012 xiii, 306 p.p maps (hardcover) $25.99 **363.73**

1. Pollution 2. Ecotourism 3. Environmental degradation 4. Tourism -- Environmental aspects

ISBN 1605294454; 9781605294452

LC 2011053229

"[I]n 'Visit Sunny Chernobyl,' Andrew Blackwell embraces a different kind of travel, taking a jaunt through the most gruesomely polluted places on Earth. . . . From the hidden bars and convenience stores of a radioactive wilderness to the sacred but reeking waters of India, 'Visit Sunny Chernobyl' fuses . . . first-person reporting with satire and analysis, making the case that it's time to start appreciating our planet as it is--not as we wish it would be." (Publisher's note)

Griswold, Eliza

Amity and prosperity; one family and the fracturing of America. Eliza Griswold. Farrar, Straus & Giroux 2018 336 p. (hardcover) $27 **363.73**

1. Pollution 2. Hydraulic fracturing 3. Energy policy -- United States 4. Prosperity (Pa.) -- Social conditions 5. Amity (Washington County, Pa.: Township) -- Social conditions 6. Gas wells -- Hydraulic fracturing -- Environmental aspects -- Pennsylvania -- Prosperity 7. Gas wells -- Hydraulic fracturing -- Environmental aspects -- Pennsylvania -- Amity (Washington County: Township)

ISBN 9780374103118

LC 2017057605

In this book, "Eliza Griswold tells the story of the energy boom's impact on . . . [Amity, Pennsylvania] and . . . [Stacey Haney's] transformation from a struggling single parent to an unlikely activist. . . . Haney joins with neighbors and a committed husband-and-wife legal team to investigate what's really in the water and air. . . . [They] doggedly pursue their case in court and begin to expose the damage that's being done to the land her family has lived on for centuries." (Publisher's note)

"Griswold's (The Tenth Parallel, 2010) empathetic yet analytical account of Haney's indefatigable role as advocate for justice is a thorough and thoroughly blood-pressure-raising account of the greed and fraud embedded in the environmentally ruinous natural-gas industry. As honest and unvarnished an account of the human cost of corporate corruption as one will find." Booklist

Includes bibliographical references

Jenkins, McKay

Poison spring; the secret history of pollution and the EPA. by E.G. Vallianatos with McKay Jenkins. Bloomsbury Press 2013 304 p. (alk. paper) $28   **363.73**
1. Political corruption 2. United States. Environmental Protection Agency 3. Corporate power -- United States 4. Pollution -- Research -- United States 5. Environmental responsibility -- United States
ISBN 1608199142; 9781608199143
LC 2013041923

"For twenty-five years [author] E.G. Vallianatos saw the EPA from the inside, with rising dismay over how pressure from politicians and threats from huge corporations were turning it from the public's watchdog into a 'polluter's protection agency.' Based on his own experience . . . and hundreds of documents Vallianatos collected inside the EPA, 'Poison Spring' [co-authored by McKay Jenkins] reveals how the agency has continually reinforced the chemical-industrial complex." (Publisher's note)

"The authors tout healthier living through small, nontoxic family farms while delivering an alarming, comprehensive account of a 'fatally compromised' EPA mission crippled by bad enforcement practices and numerous corrupting influences." Pub Wkly

Includes bibliographical references and index

363.738   Pollutants

Climate change; an encyclopedia of science and history. Brian C. Black, general editor; David M. Hassenzahl, Jennie C. Stephens, Gary Weisel, and Nancy Gift, associate editors. ABC-CLIO, LLC 2013 xx, 1774 p.p ill. (hardcover) $399   **363.738**
1. Climate change 2. Global warming 3. Climatic changes -- History -- Encyclopedias 4. Climatic changes -- Research -- Encyclopedias
ISBN 1598847619; 9781598847611
LC 2012034673

This book afford a "historical overview of the topic" of climate change. "The volume provides a foundational understanding of climate change for students, policymakers, and the general public. . . . More than 100 subject experts contributed more than 225 articles, typically several pages in length, to the compilation. The articles examine the potential effects of climate change on both human and natural systems; many contain climate change mitigation" strategies. (Booklist)

Includes bibliographical references (pages 1651-1693) and index.

Encyclopedia of global warming & climate change; general editor, S. George Philander. SAGE Publications, Inc. 2012 3 v.,1641 p. 3v il (cloth) $375   **363.738**
1. Climate change 2. Encyclopedias and dictionaries 3. Global warming -- Encyclopedias 4. Climatic changes -- Encyclopedias
ISBN 1412992613; 9781412992619
LC 2012002545

This encyclopedia has "40 new articles . . . and extensive revision" and "offers students and . . . 'laymen' close looks at recent developments. The set also examines broad historical, scientific, national, geographical, political, and thematic pictures of climate change's mechanisms, effects, and controversies." (School Library Journal)

"The set includes more than 750 articles addressing major topics related to global warming and climate change ranging geographically from the North Pole to the South Pole and thematically from social effects to scientific causes. Coverage encompasses the science and history of climate change, the polarizing controversies over climate-change theories, the role of societies, the industrial and economic factors, and the sociological aspects of climate change. . . . This valuable resource provides an excellent historical overview and framework of this topic and serves as a general resource for geography, oceanography, biology, climatology, history, and many other subjects." Libr J

Includes bibliographical references and index

The **global** warming reader; A Century of Writing About Climate Change. Penguin Books 2012 421 p. (paperback) $18.00   **363.738**
1. Climate change 2. Global warming 3. Environmental sciences 4. Human influence on nature
ISBN 0143121898; 9780143121893

This book, edited by Bill McKibben, "brings together the essential voices on global warming, from its 19th-century discovery to the present. . . . [The book] provides more than thirty-five answers . . . from more than one hundred years of engagement with the topic. Here is Elizabeth Kolbert's groundbreaking essay 'The Darkening Sea,' . . . NASA scientist James Hansen's testimony before the U.S. Congress, and clarion calls for action by Al Gore, Arundhati Roy, Naomi Klein, and many others." (Publisher's note)

Gore, Albert, 1948-

An **inconvenient** sequel; truth to power: your action handbook to learn the science, find your voice, and help solve the climate crisis. Al Gore. Rodale 2017 319 p. illustrations (paperback) $25.99   **363.738**
1. Global warming 2. Human ecology 3. Climatic changes 4. Environmental policy
ISBN 9781635651089; 9781635651096; 1635651085

This book, by Al Gore, "is a daring call to action. It exposes the reality of how humankind has aided in the destruction of our planet and delivers hope through groundbreaking information on what you can do now. . . . Gore . . . brings together cutting-edge research from top scientists around the world; approximately 200 photographs and illustrations to visually articulate the subject matter; and personal anecdotes and observations to document the fast pace and wide scope of global warming." (Publisher's note)

"This clarifying and inspiring call to stand with the facts and support the sustainable revolution belongs in every library." Booklist

Guzman, Andrew T.

Overheated; The Human Cost of Climate Change. Andrew T. Guzman. Oxford University Press 2013 280 p. (hardcover) $29.95   **363.738**

1. Human ecology 2. Climate change 3. Climatic changes -- Social aspects 4. Climatic changes -- Economic aspects 5. Climatic changes -- Effect of human beings on
ISBN 0199933871; 9780199933877

LC 2012047000

This book, by Andrew T. Guzman, discusses the political aspects surrounding climate change. "Guzman takes climate change out of the realm of scientific abstraction to explore its real-world consequences. . . . He takes as his starting point a fairly optimistic outcome in the range predicted by scientists. . . . Even this modest rise would lead to catastrophic . . . problems. . . . He shows in vivid detail how climate change is already playing out in the real world." (Publisher's note)

Includes bibliographical references and index

Hauter, Wenonah

Frackopoly; the battle for the future of energy and the environment. Wenonah Hauter. The New Press 2016 xii, 364 p.p illustrations (hardback) $27.95   **363.738**
1. Energy development 2. Hydraulic fracturing 3. Environmental policy -- United States 4. United States -- Environmental conditions 5. Energy industries -- Environmental aspects -- United States 6. Energy development -- Environmental aspects -- United States 7. Hydraulic fracturing -- Environmental aspects -- United States
ISBN 1620970074; 9781620970072

LC 2015050032

This book, by Wenonah Hauter, "argues that the rush to fracking is dangerous to the environment and treacherous to human health. [It] describes how the fracking industry began; the technologies that make it possible; and the destruction and poisoning of clean water sources and the release of harmful radiation from deep inside shale deposits, creating what the author calls "sacrifice zones" across the American landscape." (Publisher's note)

Includes bibliographical references and index

Klein, Naomi

This changes everything; capitalism vs. the climate. Naomi Klein. Simon & Schuster 2014 576 p. (hardback) $30 **363.738**
1. Capitalism 2. Climate change 3. Environmental policy 4. Environmental economics 5. Climatic changes -- Economic aspects 6. Environmental policy -- Economic aspects 7. Global environmental change -- Economic aspects
ISBN 1451697384; 9781451697384

LC 2014013864

Los Angeles Times Book Prize Finalist: Science and Technology (2014)

In this book, author "Naomi Klein argues that climate change isn't just another issue to be neatly filed between taxes and health care. It's an alarm that calls us to fix an economic system that is already failing us in many ways. Klein . . . builds the case for how massively reducing our greenhouse emissions is our best chance to simultaneously reduce gaping inequalities, re-imagine our broken democracies, and rebuild our gutted local economies." (Publisher's note)

"In part, Klein's narrative is a personal story about her own awakening to and increasing engagement with the climate issue. But this always-interesting polemic is built mostly on her interviews with experts, environmentalists and activists and her colorful on-site reporting from various international meetings and conferences." Kirkus

Includes bibliographical references and index

Terry, Beth

Plastic-free; how I kicked the plastic habit and you can too. Beth Terry. Skyhorse Pub. 2012 viii, 344 p.p (alk. paper) $19.95   **363.738**

1. Pollution 2. Recycling 3. Environmental health 4. Plastic scrap -- Environmental aspects 5. Plastic waste -- Environmental aspects
ISBN 1616086246; 9781616086244

LC 2012002817

In this book, author Beth "Terry provides personal anecdotes, stats about the environmental and health problems related to plastic, and personal solutions and tips on how to limit your plastic footprint. Terry includes . . . lists and charts for easy reference, ways to get involved in larger community actions, and profiles of individuals . . . who have gone beyond personal solutions to create a change on a larger scale." (Publisher's note)

Includes bibliographical references.

363.739   Pollution of specific environments

Kelly, William J.

The **People's** Republic of Chemicals; William J. Kelly and Chip Jacobs. Rare Bird Books 2014 280 p. map $24.95 **363.739**
1. Climate change 2. Environmental policy -- China
ISBN 1940207258; 9781940207254

In this book authors "William J. Kelly and Chip Jacobs follow up their acclaimed Smogtown with a provocative examination of China's ecological calamity already imperling a warming planet. Kelly and Jacobs describe China's ancient love affair with coal, Bill Clinton's blunders cutting free-trade deals, . . . Communist Party manipulation of eco-statistics, the horror of cancer villages, the deception of the 2008 Beijing Olympics, and spellbinding peasant revolts." (Publisher's note)

"A powerful warning that "a growing cloud of toxin s aloft [are] swirling in the winds around the world" and recirculating the pollution we hoped to shed." Kirkus

363.75   Disposal of the dead

Doughty, Caitlin

From here to eternity; traveling the world to find the good death. Caitlin Doughty; illustrations by Landis Blair. W W Norton & Co Inc 2017 xiii, 248 p.p illustrations (hardcover) $24.95   **363.75**
1. Autobiographies 2. Undertakers and undertaking 3. Funeral rites and ceremonies 4. Death -- Social aspects -- Cross-cultural studies 5. Funeral rites and ceremonies -- Cross-cultural studies
ISBN 0393249891; 9780393249897; 9780393249903

LC 2017025059

In this book, author Caitlin Doughty "set out to discover how other cultures care for the dead. . . . [The book] is an immersive global journey that introduces compelling, powerful rituals almost entirely unknown in America. . . . With boundless curiosity and gallows humor, Doughty vividly describes decomposed bodies and investigates the world's funerary history. She introduces deathcare innovators researching body composting and green burial." (Publisher's note)

"These observances demonstrate how to diminish the stigma associated with death, burial, and eternal remembrance. Death gets the last word in this affably written, meticulously researched study of funerary customs." Kirkus

Includes bibliographical references.

363.8　Food supply

Stuart, Tristram

Waste; uncovering the global food scandal. W.W. Norton & Co. 2009 xxii, 451p il $27.95　**363.8**

1. Recycling　2. Food industry　3. Waste minimization

ISBN 978-0-393-06836-8

The author "shows how we could have much more food overnight simply by not tossing away so much of it. This simple concept ingeniously unites many food scandals that often do not get the attention they deserve: the mould that destroys a third or more of Third World harvests; . . . [and] the millions of tonnes of edible food wasted by modern food processing and 'sell-by' dates. . . . Usefully, Stuart offers examples of what we could be doing better, from processing technologies to offal sausages." New Sci

Includes bibliographical references

363.9　Population problems

Bruinius, Harry

Better for all the world; the secret history of forced sterilization and America's quest for racial purity. Knopf 2006 401p il hardcover o.p. pa $16.95; ebook $16.95　**363.9**

1. Eugenics　2. Sterilization (Birth control)

ISBN 0-375-41371-5; 0-375-71305-0 pa; 978-0-307-42496-9 ebook

LC 2005-44150

"Bruinius' account of one of America's dirty little secrets is . . . a real page-turner." Booklist

Includes bibliographical references

May, Elaine Tyler, 1947-

America and the pill; a history of promise, peril, and liberation. Basic Books 2010 214p $25.95　**363.9**

1. Birth control　2. Oral contraceptives　3. Women -- Social conditions　4. Oral contraceptives -- Social aspects　5. Birth control -- United States -- History　6. Women -- United States -- Social conditions -- 20th century

ISBN 978-0-465-01152-0

LC 2009-46957

The author describes "the now extravagant-seeming hopes and fears the pill first elicited, how the pill became a symbol of the 1960s sexual revolution without demonstrably affecting it, how feminists used the pill to push for an analogue for men as part of their gender-egalitarian agenda, and how reaction to the pill's ill effects on many women contributed to the late-twentieth-century dissipation of respect for professional and institutional authority. . . . Understanding that the book is fundamentally, nonargumentatively pro-pill, one couldn't ask for a better short history of its subject." Booklist

Includes bibliographical references and index

Overdevelopment, Overpopulation, Overshoot; Edited by Tom Butler. Goff Books 2015 330 p. chiefly color illustrations $50　**363.9**

1. Overpopulation　2. Community development

ISBN 1939621232; 9781939621238

This book, edited by Tom Butler, presents a "series of photo essays illuminating the depth of the damage that human numbers and behavior have caused to the Earth¿and which threatens humanity's future. [It answers] why is the demographic explosion and its effects ignored by policymakers and the media? Why do important people within the global environmental movement itself avoid the great challenges of the population issue?" (Publisher's note)

"This accessible work ought to make readers uncomfortable: it tells us there are too many people now and that there are soon to be many more, and our collective activities, including industrial agriculture and feedlots, are degrading our only home." LJ

364　Criminology

Flynn, Kevin

The **New** York Times book of crime; more than 166 years of covering the beat. edited by Kevin Flynn; foreword by Richard Price. Sterling Pub Co Inc 2017 xv, 400 p.p illustrations, portraits (hardcover) $26.95　**364**

1. True crime stories　2. Crime -- United States　3. New York times　4. Crime and the press　5. United States -- History　6. United States -- Social conditions　7. Investigative reporting -- United States

ISBN 9781402793233; 1402793235

This book, edited by Kevin Flynn, with foreword by Richard Price, "captures the full sweep of the newspaper's coverage of the subject--from the assassinations of icons like Lincoln, John F. Kennedy, and Malcolm X to the deadly trails left behind by serial killers like H. H. Holmes (America's first recognized serial killer), the Son of Sam, and Jeffrey Dahmer. This comprehensive review examines issues like incarceration, organized crime, and vice." (Publisher's note)

"The great virtue of all these pieces is the immediacy of breaking news, now read with the hindsight of history. Wonderfully well executed." Booklist

Slater, Dan

Wolf boys; two American teenagers and Mexico's most dangerous drug cartel. Dan Slater. Simon & Schuster 2016 352 p. (hardcover) $26.95　**364**

1. Drug traffic -- Mexico　2. Organized crime -- Mexico　3. Zetas (Drug cartel)　4. Narco-terrorism -- Mexico　5. Drug traffic -- Texas -- Laredo

ISBN 1501126547; 9781501126543

This book, by Dan Slater, offers "the story of two American teens recruited as killers for a Mexican cartel, and their pursuit by a Mexican-American detective who realizes the War on Drugs is unwinnable. What's it like to be an employee of a global drug-trafficking organization? And how does a fifteen-year-old American boy go from star quarterback to trained assassin, surging up the cartel corporate ladder?" (Publisher's note)

"Engrossing and readable yet nightmarish vision of a hyperviolent and corporatized narcotics industry, seducing a new generation with minimal alternatives." Kirkus

Zuckoff, Mitchell

Ponzi's scheme; the true story of a financial legend. Random House 2005 390p il $25.95; pa $14.95　**364**

1. Swindlers

ISBN 1-400-06039-7; 0-8129-6836-0 pa

LC 2004-46770

The author "chronicles Ponzi's mercurial rise and fall as he conjured up one get-rich-quick scheme after another. . . . Zuckoff provides not only a definitive portrait of Ponzi's life but also insights into immigrant life and the social world of early 20th-century Boston." Publ Wkly

Includes bibliographical references

364.1   Criminal offenses

Anderson, Devery S.

Emmett Till; the murder that shocked the world and propelled the civil rights movement. by Devery S. Anderson; foreword by Julian Bond. University Press of Mississippi 2015 560 p. illustrations (cloth: alk. paper) $45   **364.1**

1. Lynching 2. Hate crimes 3. Racism -- History 4. Trials (Homicide) 5. African Americans -- History 6. Hate crimes -- Mississippi 7. Mississippi -- Race relations 8. Trials (Murder) -- Mississippi -- Sumner 9. Racism -- Mississippi -- History -- 20th century 10. African Americans -- Crimes against -- Mississippi 11. Lynching -- Mississippi -- History -- 20th century 12. United States -- Race relations -- History -- 20th century

ISBN 9781496802842

LC 2015005681

This book, by Devery S. Anderson, "offers the first truly comprehensive account of the 1955 murder and its aftermath. It tells the story of Emmett Till, the fourteen-year-old African American boy from Chicago brutally lynched for a harmless flirtation at a country store in the Mississippi Delta. His death and the acquittal of his killers by an all-white jury set off a firestorm of protests that reverberated all over the world and spurred on the civil rights movement." (Publisher's note)

"At times, Anderson's devotion to detail can bury the reader, but historians will welcome his commitment to the story. It will become the go-to reference for scholars and those who teach the Till case in classrooms." Choice

Includes bibliographical references and index

Atwood, Roger

Stealing history; tomb raiders, smugglers, and the looting of the ancient world. St. Martin's Press 2004 337p il map hardcover o.p. pa $15.95   **364.1**

1. Art thefts 2. Antiquities -- Collection and preservation

ISBN 0-312-32406-5; 0-312-32407-3 pa

LC 2004-50862

The author's "ability to bring a story dramatically to life and his keen interest in stemming the illegal antiquities trade makes this an important book for anyone interested in archeology, preservation or the potentially tangled provenance of works they love." Publ Wkly

Includes bibliographical references

Burns, Sarah

The **Central** Park Five. Alfred A. Knopf 2011 240p il map $25.95   **364.1**

1. Rape 2. False accusation 3. Victims of crimes 4. Administration of criminal justice 5. Rape victims 6. Investment bankers 7. Crime -- New York (N.Y.) 8. Criminal justice, Administration of -- New York (N.Y.)

ISBN 978-0-307-26614-9; 0-307-26614-1

LC 2010039661

This book recounts "the public frenzy surrounding the April 19, 1989, attack on Trisha Meili in Central Park. The 28-year-old investment banker was out for a run when she was . . . raped, beaten and left for dead. The assault, pinned on a group of black and Hispanic boys aged 13 to 16 who'd been misbehaving in the park that night, incited media diatribes about civic decay. . . . [C]ourt cases found five of the boys guilty in 1990. Then, in 2002, convicted rapist and murderer Matias Reyes confessed to the attack and the five convictions were overturned. [Sarah] Burns's deconstruction of how justice was hijacked is part police procedural, part courtroom drama, part cultural critique . . . Burns . . . reveals how 'winning the case trumped investigating the evidence.'" Particular focus is given to "media and public resistance to Reyes's confession: so

entrenched was the 'wilding' narrative that many refused to give it up. " (Maclean's)

"An important cultural document, and unquestionably worth reading. . . . Burns's gripping tale may serve as an allegory for some of the most pressing criminal justice issues of our time." N Y Times Book Rev

Includes bibliographical references

Campbell, Greg

Flawless; inside the largest diamond heist in history. by Scott Andrew Selby and Greg Campbell. Sterling Pub. Co. 2010 319p il map $24.95   **364.1**

1. Theft 2. Diamonds

ISBN 978-1-4027-6651-0

LC 2009-40766

The authors "provide an engrossing nonfiction thriller with a truly improbable story at its center, but they also provide a colorful look at the shadowy world of the diamond trade—how they're graded, sold, secured and stolen." Kirkus

Includes bibliographical references

Capote, Truman

★ **In** cold blood; a true account of a multiple murder and its consequences. Random House 2002 343p $22; pa $13 **364.1**

1. Homicide 2. Murderers

ISBN 0-375-50790-6; 0-679-74558-0 pa

LC 2002-282920

A reissue of the title first published 1966

"Truman Capote called his account of the 1959 murder of a Kansas farm family a nonfiction novel. Using information he collected through interviews with townspeople and the killers, Capote created a vivid portrait of the criminals and graphically described the crime, the criminals' escape to Mexico, capture, trial, appeals, and hanging." HarperCollins Reader's Ency of Am Lit. 2nd edition

Carney, Scott

The **red** market; on the trail of the world's organ brokers, bone thieves, blood farmers, and child traffickers. William Morrow 2011 254p il $25.99   **364.1**

1. Procurement of organs, tissues, etc.

ISBN 978-0-06-193646-3; 0-06-193646-4

LC 2010-47807

"The 'red market' of Scott Carney's lucid and alarming book refers to the various medical activities through which the human body can generate a profit: surrogate motherhood, organ transplantation, drug testing, baby selling and blood farming, to mention just a few items on Mr. Carney's disturbing list. The buyers of red-market goods are usually well-to-do Westerners, while the sellers tend to come from developing countries. A surprisingly large number of the sellers are women, and many appear to be forced into the business. Middlemen, beyond taking large profits, encourage the trade by assuring buyers that the transaction is conducted ethically. . . . [This] is not an abstract philosophical meditation or an ethnographic treatise, though it has elements of both. It is a work of investigative journalism, written by an experienced health reporter who lived in India for more than 10 years. Mr. Carney knows how to tell a story and digs deeply." Wall Street J

Includes bibliographical references

Chayes, Sarah

Thieves of state; why corruption threatens global security. Sarah Chayes. W W Norton & Co Inc 2015 272 p. illustrations (hardcover) $26.95   **364.1**

1. Political corruption 2. International security 3. Political

corruption -- Case studies 4. Security, International -- Case studies
ISBN 0393239462; 9780393239461

LC 2014031700

Los Angeles Times Book Prize: Current Interest (2015)

In this book on corruption, author Sarah Chayes "reveals that canonical political thinkers such as John Locke and [Niccolo] Machiavelli, as well as the great medieval Islamic statesman Nizam al-Mulk, all named corruption as a threat to the realm. In . . . [an] argument connecting the Protestant Reformation to the Arab Spring, [it] presents a powerful new way to understand global extremism." (Publisher's note)

"From ancient tales of avaricious rulers to modern headlines of greedy politicians, Chayes offers insightful analysis of how government corruption invites instability and insurgency and why we will never see peace in some of the world's hot spots until we address that corruption." Booklist

Includes bibliographical references and index

Cullen, Kevin

Whitey Bulger; America's most wanted gangster and the manhunt that brought him to justice. Kevin Cullen and Shelley Murphy. 1st ed. W W Norton & Co Inc 2013 viii, 478 p., 16 unnumbered pages of platesp (hardcover) $26.95   **364.1**
  1. Fugitives from justice 2. Organized crime -- United States 3. Gangsters -- Massachusetts -- Boston -- Biography 4. Fugitives from justice -- United States -- Biography 5. Organized crime -- Massachusetts -- Boston -- Case studies
ISBN 0393087727; 9780393087727

LC 2012050752

National Book Critics Circle Award Finalist: Nonfiction (2013)

This book, by Kevin Cullen and Shelley Murphy, "follows the astonishing career and epic manhunt for Whitey Bulger. . . . Raised in a South Boston housing project, James 'Whitey' Bulger became the most wanted fugitive of his generation. . . . Reporters Kevin Cullen and Shelley Murphy follow Whitey's extraordinary criminal career--from teenage thievery to bank robberies to the building of his underworld empire and a string of brutal murders." (Publisher's note)

Includes bibliographical references (pages 431-464) and index.

Dash, Mike

The **first** family; terror, extortion, revenge, murder, and the birth of the American mafia. Random House 2009 375p il map $27   **364.1**
  1. Mafia 2. Organized crime 3. Mobsters 4. Mafia -- History 5. Biography, Individual 6. Mafia -- United States -- History 7. Organized crime -- United States -- History
ISBN 978-1-4000-6722-0

LC 2009-5681

This "history of the birth of the Italian mafia in America traces the life of Giuseppe Morello, describing his rise from poverty in rural Sicily to one of the nation's most influential underworld crime heads, in a portrait that also evaluates the contributions of Morello's brothers, police officer Joseph Petrosino, and secret service agent William Flynn." (Publisher's note) Index.

"Essential for students of organized crime in America. Murder and mayhem buffs will enjoy it too." Kirkus

Includes bibliographical references (p. 350-357)

Del Bosque, Melissa

Bloodlines; the true story of a drug cartel, the FBI, and the battle for a horse-racing dynasty. Melissa del Bosque. Ecco 2017 394 p. (hardback) $27.99   **364.1**
  1. Drug traffic 2. Organized crime -- Mexico 3. Horse racing -- United States 4. Zetas (Drug cartel) 5. Drug traffic -- Mexico -- Case studies 6. Organized crime -- Mexico -- Case studies 7. Drug control -- United States -- Case studies 8. Horse racing -- United States -- Case studies 9. United States. Federal Bureau of Investigation 10. Money laundering -- United States -- Case studies
ISBN 9780062448484; 9780062448491

LC 2017014612

This book, by Melissa del Bosque, "follows [Scott] Lawson and [Alma] Perez's harrowing attempt to dismantle a cartel leader's American racing dynasty built on extortion and blood money. . . . 'Bloodlines' offers us an unprecedented look at the inner workings of the Zetas and US federal agencies, and opens a new vista onto the changing nature of the drug war and its global expansion." (Publisher's note)

"Del Bosque breaks up the complex tale into brief, fluidly narrated, suspenseful chapters. Fully portraying the many key players and following the intricacies of the Treviños' sophisticated plan, the FBI's race against other federal agencies and the press to crack it, the gut-dropping dynamics of cartel coercion and retribution, and the eventual, dramatic trial, del Bosque recounts a true story that reads like crime fiction." Booklist.

Douglas, John E.

The **cases** that haunt us; from Jack the Ripper to JonBenet Ramsey, the FBI's legendary mindhunter sheds light on the mysteries that won't go away. [by] John Douglas, Mark Olshaker. Pocket Books 2001 487p il pa $7.99   **364.1**
  1. Homicide 2. Criminal psychology
ISBN 978-0-671-01706-4; 0-671-01706-3

First published 2000 by Scribner

The authors discuss "eight controversial cases that include the Lindbergh baby kidnapping, the Boston Strangler, the Zodiac Killer, and the JonBenet Ramsey killing." Libr J

Dray, Philip

At the hands of persons unknown; the lynching of Black America. Random House 2002 528p il hardcover o.p. pa $14.95   **364.1**
  1. Lynching 2. Southern States -- Race relations 3. African Americans -- Southern States
ISBN 0-375-75445-8 pa

LC 2001-40366

"Dray balances moral indignation with a sound understanding of history and politics. The result is vital, hard-hitting cultural history." Publ Wkly

Includes bibliographical references

Fisher, Kenneth L.

How to smell a rat; the five signs of financial fraud. [by] Ken Fisher with Lara Hoffmans. Wiley 2009 209p (Fisher investments series) $24.95   **364.1**
  1. Fraud 2. Investments 3. Swindlers and swindling
ISBN 978-0-470-52653-8

LC 2009-21631

"With five straightforward rules that would have saved any investor from Bernie Madoff, . . . [Fisher] gives readers a secure plan for fraud-proof investing, worthwhile for novices and sophisticated financiers alike. . . . Much more than what to avoid, Fisher's concise guide should be highly illuminating and confidence-building for anyone with a bank account." Publ Wkly

Includes bibliographical references

Geary, Rick

The **Lindbergh** child; America's hero and the crime of the century. written and illustrated by Rick Geary. NBM/ComicsLit 2008 un il map (Treasury of XXth century murder) pa $15.95 **364.1**

1. Generals 2. Air pilots 3. Graphic novels 4. Mystery graphic novels 5. Memoirists 6. Air force officers 7. Homicide -- Graphic novels 8. Kidnapping -- Graphic novels
ISBN 978-1-56163-529-0

Charles Lindbergh was an American hero following his solo crossing of the Atlantic in an airplane. He married into a wealthy family, he and his wife had a baby, they were building their dream home. Then, one night, the baby was abducted from the house. Geary's account retraces all the highly publicized events, ransom notes (false and otherwise), as well as the string of colorful characters who all claimed they could help but instead snookered the Lindberghs. While Bruno Hauptmann was arrested, tried, convicted, and executed, there remain many questions about what really happened. Geary brings them up for readers to consider.

"A good example of the origins of modern forensics, crime-scene investigation, and celebrity hysteria, this work is an excellent choice for most collections." SLJ

Glenny, Misha

McMafia; a journey through the global criminal underworld. Alfred A. Knopf 2008 375p il map $27.95 **364.1**

1. Organized crime
ISBN 978-1-4000-4411-5; 1-4000-4411-1

LC 2007-30522

"Readers yearning for a deeper understanding of the real-life, international counterparts to The Sopranos need look no further than Glenny's engrossing study." Publ Wkly

Includes bibliographical references

Goldhagen, Daniel Jonah

Worse than war; genocide, eliminationism, and the ongoing assault on humanity. [by] Daniel Jonah Goldhagen. PublicAffairs 2009 658p il **364.1**

1. Racism 2. Genocide 3. Prejudices 4. Mass murder 5. Racism -- Psychological aspects 6. Genocide -- Psychological aspects
ISBN 1-58648-769-8; 978-1-58648-769-0

LC 2009-28035

This is an investigation into the phenomenon of genocide and mass killing—explaining why genocides begin, are sustained, and end; why societies support them and why they happen so frequently; and how the international community should and can successfully stop them.

The author "convincingly disparages bureaucratic 'banality of evil' explanations of genocide and spotlights the ideologies of leaders who exploit ordinary citizens' hate-filled beliefs to instigate mass murder. It's not easy reading, but Goldhagen's vehemence and the sheer weight of horrors that he recounts move one's conscience." Publ Wkly

Includes bibliographical references

Guinn, Jeff

Go down together; the true, untold story of Bonnie and Clyde. Simon & Schuster 2009 467p il $27 **364.1**

1. Criminals 2. Outlaws 3. Murderers 4. Biography, Individual
ISBN 1-4165-5706-7; 978-1-4165-5706-7

LC 2008-53342

In this true crime book by Jeff Guinn, "Clyde Barrow, a scrawny kid in poverty-stricken West Dallas in the late 1920s, stole chickens before moving on to cars, following in the footsteps of his older brother,

Buck. In 1930, he met 19-year-old Bonnie Parker, and during the next four years Clyde, Bonnie and the ever-revolving members of the Barrow Gang robbed banks and armories all over the South, murdering at least seven people." (Publishers Weekly)

"As Guinn relates, Bonnie and Clyde didn't commit many of the acts—particularly the murders—they were accused of. Their crime spree only lasted from spring 1932 to May 1934. But in the worst of the Depression, Americans ate up accounts of the Barrow exploits as a form of entertainment. The gang fed the newspapers terrific stuff, including the staged photo of Bonnie holding a gun and smoking a cigar. For folks living hardscrabble lives, the fact that the gang robbed the same bankers who were foreclosing on their farms made the exploits of Bonnie and Clyde even sweeter. Guinn succeeds marvelously in recreating the spirit of the times, the desperation of unemployment and financial ruin." PopMatters

Includes bibliographical references

Ifill, Sherrilyn A.

On the courthouse lawn; confronting the legacy of lynching in the twenty-first century. Beacon Press 2007 xx, 204p il $25.95; pa $16 **364.1**

1. Lynching 2. Reconciliation 3. United States -- Race relations 4. Lynching -- United States -- History
ISBN 978-0-8070-0987-1; 0-8070-0987-3; 978-0-8070-0988-8 pa; 0-8070-0988-1 pa

LC 2006-16618

The author explores the continued effects of lynching. Ifill contends that "the lynchings implicated average white citizens, some of whom actively participated in the violence while many others witnessed the lynchings but did nothing to stop them. Ifill observes that this history of complicity has become embedded in the social and cultural fabric of local communities, who either supported, condoned, or ignored the violence. She . . . [presents] ideas to help communities heal. . . . Ifill argues that reconciliation and reparation efforts must also be locally based in order to bring both black and white Americans together in an efficacious dialogue." (Publisher's note) Index.

"An intriguing, immodest proposal that itself warrants discussion—and action." Kirkus

Includes bibliographical references

James, Bill, 1949-

Popular crime; reflections on the celebration of violence. Scribner 2011 482p il **364.1**

1. Crime 2. Homicide 3. Crime -- United States -- History
ISBN 1416552731; 9781416552734

LC 2010-36180

This "book is primarily a history of the murders that have obsessed American newspaper readers since Dec. 22, 1799, when the body of a young Manhattan woman named Elma Sands was found floating in a well at what is now 89 Greene Street. Between . . . accounts of Lizzie Borden, the Boston Strangler and the Zodiac killer, Mr. James offers proposals for penal and judicial reform, theories about the cultural significance of crime stories and brief book reviews." (N Y Times (Late N Y Ed)) Index.

This is a "very entertaining book, and it will instigate arguments even as it scores many important points. . . . James's layman status is a big part of this book's bracing charm. And his real point is more universal. He loves crime books and wants you to love them, too, and not just because they're a good way to pass the time in a motel room or airport. He wants you to take them seriously, as he does, and consider the ways they reflect and reshape the culture, what they say about our justice system and our very concept of justice." Washington Post Book World

Javers, Eamon

Broker, trader, lawyer, spy; inside the secret world of corporate espionage. Harper 2010 306p $26.99; ebook $11.99   **364.1**

1. Espionage 2. Business intelligence
ISBN 978-0-06-169720-3; 978-0-06-196938-6 ebook
LC 2009031010

"Javers traces spying activity, which began in Washington, D.C., in 1790, when the city became the capital, through the Civil War, when Allan Pinkerton was chasing Confederate spies, to Allen Dulles and the CIA developing drugs to enhance interrogations and in 2002 capturing traitor Robert Hanssen. The author also offers a fascinating explanation of the role of spies in today's world economy with hundreds of firms globally in the corporate espionage business using as operatives alumni from the FBI, CIA, Secret Service, British M15 and Russian KGB, and military intelligence officers. . . . This is a must-read, excellent book." Booklist

Includes bibliographical references

Jimenez, Stephen

The **Book** of Matt; Hidden Truths About the Murder of Matthew Shepard. Stephen Jimenez. Steerforth Press 2013 viii, 360 p.p $26; $16   **364.1**

1. Homicide 2. Drug traffic 3. Mass media and gays -- United States 4. Gays -- Crimes against -- United States 5. Mass media -- United States -- Influence 6. Hate crimes -- United States -- Public opinion 7. Mass media and public opinion -- United States
ISBN 1586422146; 9781586422141; 9781586422264
LC 2013431178

Author Stephen Jiminez presents his story of "determination to ascertain why Matthew Shepard--a gay University of Wyoming student--was viciously killed in 1998. Jimenez makes a strong case that the unappreciated lesson of the Shepard murder is one about the dangers of methamphetamine. Shepard and his killer, Aaron McKinney, were not strangers after all. In fact Aaron McKinney was a bisexual, who had had sex with Shepard. And both were dealers of methamphetamine." (Amazon)

"In claiming that Shepard was killed because of drugs, and the 'gay panic' story was offered as a cover and heavily pushed by media and politicians as part of a larger agenda, Jimenez completely changes the meaning and impact of Shepard's death." Pub Wkly

Includes bibliographical references (pages 355-357)

Keefe, Patrick Radden

The **snakehead**; an epic tale of the Chinatown underworld and the American dream. Doubleday 2009 414p map   **364.1**

1. Smuggling 2. Unauthorized immigrants 3. Smugglers 4. Businesspeople 5. Illegal aliens 6. Illegal aliens -- United States 7. Human trafficking -- United States 8. China -- Emigration and immigration 9. United States -- Emigration and immigration 10. United States -- Immigration and emigration
ISBN 0-307-27927-8 pa; 0-385-52130-8; 978-0-307-27927-9 pa; 978-0-385-52130-7
LC 2008-50049

This book tells the story of human smuggling and trafficking among Fujianese immigrants to the United States. It focuses on Cheng Chui Ping, a Chinese immigrant who came to New York in the early 1980s. Her path to the American "dream began with an underground bank . . . run out of a noodle shop. . . . She became known as Sister Ping and built a global people-smuggling conglomerate that stretched from China's Fujian province to Africa, Europe, and South America, relying on one of Chinatown's . . . gangs to protect her power and profits. Sister Ping's empire came to light in 1993, when [the Golden Venture], a ship loaded with 300 near-starving immigrants ran aground off Queens. It took . . . nearly ten years to untangle the criminal network and home in on its mastermind." (Publisher's note) Index.

"This is one of the freshest accounts of modern-day migration I've read, one filled with moral ambiguity, one that doesn't pretend to have the answers, one that . . . feels like essential reading." Washington Post Book World

Includes bibliographical references

Lebsock, Suzanne

A **murder** in Virginia; Southern justice on trial. Norton 2003 442p il $26.95; pa $15.95   **364.1**

1. Trials (Homicide) 2. Virginia 3. Southern States -- Race relations
ISBN 0-393-04201-4; 0-393-32606-3 pa
LC 2002-15946

"On a warm afternoon in June 1895, a 56-year-old white woman was brutally murdered in Lunenburg County, VA. Despite the absence of any truly incriminating eyewitness testimony or physical evidence, four blacks—three women and one man—were arrested and tried for the murder. Lebsock . . . recreates the subsequent trials, introducing the defendants, their prosecutors, and the witnesses and placing the proceedings within the context of the black and white communities and deteriorating conditions for African Americans in the post-Reconstruction South. Here historical narrative is every bit as intriguing as fictional mystery but more edifying for the information it gives its readers concerning race relations and criminal justice in the latter part of the 19th century." Libr J

Includes bibliographical references

Lehr, Dick

The **fence**; a police cover-up along Boston's racial divide. Harper 2009 383p il map $25.99; pa $14.99   **364.1**

1. Police brutality 2. Police corruption 3. Boston (Mass.) -- Race relations
ISBN 978-0-06-078098-2; 0-06-078098-3; 978-0-06-078099-9 pa; 0-06-078099-1 pa

The author "details one of the most controversial cases in the annals of the Boston Police Department, involving a brutal assault on a black plainclothes officer by his fellow cops and the resulting 1998 civil rights trial against the police force. Not only does Lehr paint the racial and political turbulence of Boston at the time, but he explores the cultural backgrounds of the black officer, Michael Cox; his attacker and fellow officer, Kenny Conley; and Robert 'Smut' Brown, a drug dealer involved in the killing that started it all. . . . Jolting, nightmarish and potent, this true cop yarn bests any bogus reality show or overblown tabloid tale with its hardboiled spin." Publ Wkly

Includes bibliographical references

Longman, Jere

Among the heroes; United Flight 93 and the passengers and crew who fought back. HarperCollins Pubs. 2002 288p il $24.95; pa $13.95   **364.1**

1. Hijacking of airplanes 2. September 11 terrorist attacks, 2001
ISBN 0-06-009908-9; 0-06-009909-7 pa
LC 2002-68530

This is an account of the United Airlines flight which was hijacked on September 11, 2001 and crashed in Pennsylvania before reaching its intended target

This book "gives us an incredibly detailed and personal tale of that horrific episode." Booklist

Includes bibliographical references

Malkus, Chuck

Full circle; the remarkable true story of two all-American wrestling teammates pitted against each other in the war on drugs and then reunited as coaches. Chuck Malkus with Jerry Langton. Skyhorse Publishing 2018 244 p. $24.99   **364.1**

1. Wrestling 2. Friendship 3. Coaching (Athletics)

ISBN 1510724664; 9781510724662

This book, by Chuck Malkus with Jerry Langton, tells the story of Kevin Pedersen and Alex DeCubas, . . . best friends and star high school wrestling teammates. . . . When a series of tragedies derailed . . . [Alex's] dreams . . . he used his natural strength . . . to start robbing drug dealers. . . . [while] Kevin . . . became a wrestling champion. . . . Years later, . . . the pair reunited and teamed up to . . . [coach] high school wrestling together." (Publisher's note)

Mallon, Thomas

Mrs. Paine's garage and the murder of John F. Kennedy. Pantheon Bks. 2002 211p $22; pa $13   **364.1**

1. Homemakers 2. Presidents 3. Senators 4. Murderers 5. Members of Congress 6. Spouses of prominent persons

ISBN 0-375-42117-3; 0-15-602755-0 pa

LC 2001-36157

"A journalistic inquiry into Ruth Paine, the woman who welcomed Marina Oswald—and sometimes her husband, Lee—into her suburban Dallas home in 1963; it offers a new theory about the antecedents of the assassination." N Y Times Book Rev

Matthews, Joe

Bringing Adam home; the abduction that changed America. [by] Les Standiford with Detective Sergeant Joe Matthews. Ecco 2011 291p il map   **364.1**

1. Children 2. Homicide 3. Kidnapping 4. Kidnap victims 5. Murder victims

ISBN 0-06-198390-X; 978-0-06-198390-0

LC 2010-43572

"This is the ultimate cold case—tragic, high-profile, and, finally, successfully solved. Six-year-old Adam Walsh was abducted from a crowded Sears store in Hollywood, Florida, in 1981. Later, he was murdered and decapitated. Identifying Adam's killer took 25 years. His parents turned into tireless advocates for missing and abused children; Adam's father, John Walsh, moved from a sales job to being the executive producer and host of America's Most Wanted. This forceful account . . . gives readers the ultimate insider's account of the grueling search for Adam's killer and for the evidence to convict him. While many true-crime books claim to shine a light on society by examining one particular case, this account actually does." Booklist

Maurer, Kevin

American radical; inside the world of an undercover Muslim FBI agent. Tamer Elnoury with Kevin Maurer. Dutton 2017 368 p. (hardcover) $28   **364.1**

1. Terrorism -- United States 2. Spies -- United States -- Biography 3. United States. Federal Bureau of Investigation 4. United States. Federal Bureau of Investigation -- Officials and employees -- Biography

ISBN 9781101986172; 9781101986158

LC 2017029950

This memoir, by Tamer Elnoury with Kevin Maurer, narrates his life as "a Muslim American FBI agent fighting terror from the inside. . . . Elnoury joined an elite counterterrorism unit after September 11. Its express purpose is to gain the trust of terrorists whose goals are to take out as many Americans in as public and as devastating a way possible.

It's a furious race against the clock for Tamer and his unit to stop them before they can implement their plans." (Publisher's note)

"Elnoury heightens the suspense in vividly described scenes, such as when he nearly gets run over by a train while scouting locations for the attack with two suspected terrorists, and provides insight into the world-view and intentions of al-Qaeda affiliates. There is never a dull moment in this intimate story of an American Muslim going to great lengths to serve and protect his country." PW.

May, Elaine Tyler, 1947-

★ **Fortress** America; how we embraced fear and abandoned democracy. Elaine Tyler May. Basic Books 2017 vii, 247 p.p (hardcover) $30   **364.1**

1. Crime -- United States 2. United States -- Social conditions -- 21st century 3. United States -- Civilization -- 21st century 4. Crime -- United States -- History -- 21st century 5. Violence -- United States -- History -- 21st century 6. Public safety -- Social aspects -- United States -- History -- 21st century

ISBN 9780465055920

LC 2017023376

This book, by Elaine Tyler May, "demonstrates how our obsession with security has made citizens fear each other and distrust the government, making America less safe and less democratic. 'Fortress America' charts the rise of a muscular national culture, undercutting the common good. Instead of a thriving democracy of engaged citizens, we have become a paranoid, bunkered, militarized, and divided vigilante nation." (Publisher's note)

This is a must-read for anyone seeking to understand the anxieties that occupy American politics. --Publishers Weekly

Includes bibliographical references and index.

McGinniss, Joe

★ **Fatal** vision. New American Library 1989 684p il pa $7.99   **364.1**

1. Homicide 2. Surgeons 3. Murderers

ISBN 978-0-451-16566-4; 0-451-16566-7

First published 1983 by Putnam

"This is a wisely observant, well-written, and understated book." Harpers

Includes bibliographical references

Murakami, Haruki

Underground; translated from the Japanese by Alfred Birnbaum and Philip Gabriel. Vintage Bks. 2001 366p map pa $14   **364.1**

1. Terrorism 2. Aum Shinrikyō

ISBN 0-375-72580-6

LC 00-69310

"On March 20, 1995, followers of the religious cult Aum Shinrikyo unleashed lethal sarin gas into cars of the Tokyo subway system. Many died, many more were injured. This is {Murakami's} . . . account of this episode." Publ Wkly

Olsen, Jack

I: the creation of a serial killer. St. Martin's Press 2002 365p il $24.95; pa $6.99   **364.1**

1. Homicide 2. Murderers

ISBN 0-312-24198-4; 0-312-98384-0 pa

LC 2001-58892

"A truly horrifying account of a serial killer, told with shocking candor." Booklist

The author draws "on interviews and his subject's own diaries to . .

. reveal the life and inner workings of Keith Hunter Jesperson, currently serving life in prison for the murders of eight women in the 1990s." Publ Wkly

Pepper, William F.

An **act** of state; the execution of Martin Luther King. Norton 2003 334p il map $25   **364.1**

1. Clergy 2. Conspiracies 3. Nonfiction writers 4. Civil rights activists 5. Nobel laureates for peace

ISBN 1-85984-695-5

Companion volume to Orders to kill (1995)

This book continues the author's examination of the life and death of Martin Luther King Jr.

"Forget everything you think you know, Pepper insists. James Earl Ray did not pull the trigger. . . . Pepper gradually introduces the vast cast of characters in a dizzying murder conspiracy that winds from a Memphis bar through the shadows of organized crime to the far reaches of national government. He carefully maps each player's place and role in the tangled web and doggedly tries to stick to a straightforward narrative. . . . Pepper attempts nothing less than a rewrite of history, and a spurring of further investigation." Publ Wkly

Includes bibliographical references

Queen, William

Under and alone; the true story of the undercover agent who infiltrated America's most violent outlaw motorcycle gang. Random House 2005 270p il $24.95   **364.1**

1. Gangs

ISBN 1-400-06084-2

LC 2004-51176

"The strength and white-hot intensity of the writing make this read like a movie, and Hollywood is certain to take note." Publ Wkly

Raab, Selwyn

Five families; the rise, decline, and resurgence of America's most powerful Mafia empires. Thomas Dunne Books 2005 765p il $29.95   **364.1**

1. Mafia 2. Organized crime

ISBN 0-312-30094-8

LC 2005-48416

"With vivid characterizations of a cavalcade of thugs, Raab's account is the most lively and informative Mafia history in years." Booklist

Includes bibliographical references

Rule, Ann

--and never let her go; Thomas Capano, the deadly seducer. Pocket Star Books 2000 680p il pa $7.99   **364.1**

1. Lawyers 2. Homicide 3. Secretaries 4. Missing persons 5. Trials (Homicide) 6. Murderers 7. Murder victims 8. District attorneys 9. State government employees

ISBN 0-671-86871-3; 978-0-671-86871-0

First published 1999 by Simon & Schuster

"In June 1996, Anne Marie Fahey, a 30-year-old secretary to the governor of Delaware, disappeared and was reported missing by her family. In the weeks that followed, a charming, successful, and well-connected attorney, Tom Capano, was charged with her murder. Rule . . . tells the riveting story of the three-year secret affair between Fahey and Capano and a cruel obsession that led to murder." Booklist

Saviano, Roberto

Gomorrah; translated from the Italian by Virginia Jewiss. Farrar, Straus & Giroux 2007 301p map $25   **364.1**

1. Organized crime 2. Italy

ISBN 978-0-374-16527-7; 0-374-16527-0

LC 2007-31004

Original Italian edition, 2006

This "is an eyepopping, hair-raising, stomach-turning book. The mob has never looked so bad—or read so well." Christ Sci Monit

Sifakis, Carl

The **mafia** encyclopedia; 3rd ed; Facts on File 2005 510p il (Facts on File crime library) $65; pa $21.95   **364.1**

1. Reference books 2. Mafia -- Dictionaries

ISBN 0-8160-5694-3; 0-8160-5695-1 pa

LC 2004-58487

First published 1987

"Sifakis provides detailed, informed, and colorful information." Libr J

Smith, Jennie Erin

Stolen world; a tale of reptiles, smugglers and skulduggery. Crown 2011 322p il $25; ebook $25   **364.1**

1. Reptiles 2. Smuggling 3. Rare animals 4. Wild animal trade 5. Rare reptiles 6. Animal dealers 7. Wildlife smuggling 8. Wild animal trade -- Corrupt practices

ISBN 978-0-307-38147-7; 0-307-38147-1; 978-0-307-72026-9 ebook; 0-307-72026-8 ebook

LC 2010-9548

"Smith's affection for these unsavory people gives the book an intriguing moral ambiguity (which might make some environmentalists cringe), but the subculture's brazen shenanigans make for a convoluted, fascinating tale." Publ Wkly

Tinti, Peter

Migrant, Refugee, Smuggler, Savior; by Peter Tinti and Tuesday Reitano. Oxford University Press 2017 xv, 331 p.p (hardcover) $29.95   **364.1**

1. Refugees 2. Smuggling 3. Human smuggling 4. Refugees -- Europe

ISBN 0190668598; 9780190668594

LC 2016049649

"As millions of people seek passage to Europe in order to escape conflict, repression, poverty and natural catastrophe, their movements are enabled and encouraged by . . . criminal networks that earn billions of pounds from this insidious new trade. . . . This book is a measured attempt . . . to better understand how people-smuggling networks function, the ways in which they have evolved, and their long term impact on both migration and global organised crime." (Publisher's note)

"Advocacy journalism in the service of the refugees, most from Africa and the Middle East, who are now flooding Europe." Kirkus

Includes bibliographical references and index.

Tone, Joe

Bones; brothers, horses, cartels, and the borderland dream. Joe Tone. One World 2017 329 p. (hardcover) $28   **364.1**

1. Brothers 2. Drug traffic -- Mexico 3. Zetas (Drug cartel) 4. Drug traffic -- Mexico -- Case studies 5. Organized crime -- Mexico -- Case studies 6. Drug control -- United States -- Case studies 7. Horse racing -- United States -- Case studies 8. United States. Federal Bureau of Investigation 9. Money laundering -- United States -- Case studies

ISBN 9780812989625; 9780812989601; 0812989600

LC 2017008111

This book, by Joe Tone, is "the dramatic true story of two brothers living parallel lives on either side of the U.S.-Mexico border--and how their lives converged in a major criminal conspiracy. José and Miguel Treviño were bonded by blood and a shared vision of a better life. But they chose different paths that would end at the same violent crossroads--with considerable help from the FBI and an enigmatic, all-American snitch." (Publisher's note)

"A suspenseful story as well as a fascinating depiction of the mechanics of money laundering, the largely unfamiliar world of quarter horse racing, and the dynamics of an extended family, the book draws readers into the complexities of life at the border." Kirkus

Includes bibliographical references.

Venegas, Maria

★ **Bulletproof** vest; the ballad of an outlaw and his daughter. Maria Venegas. Farrar Straus & Giroux 2014 x, 305 p.p (hardcover) $26   **364.1**
1. Autobiography 2. Father-daughter relationship 3. Criminals -- Family relationships -- Mexico 4. Fathers and daughters -- Mexico 5. Children of criminals -- Family relationships -- Mexico
ISBN 9780374117313

         LC 2013038777

This autobiography presents "the haunting story of a daughter's struggle to confront her father's turbulent-and often violent-legacy.... Moving between Mexico and New York, between past and present, Venegas traces her own life and her father's as, over time, a new closeness and understanding develops between them." (Publisher's note)

Watkins, D.

The **Cook** Up; A Crack Rock Memoir. by D. Watkins. Grand Central Publishing 2016 272 p. $26   **364.1**
1. Drug traffic 2. Baltimore (Md.)
ISBN 1455588636; 9781455588633

This memoir, by D. Watkins, is a "look inside the Baltimore drug trade.... D. was certain he would escape the life of drugs, decadence, and violence that had surrounded him since birth. But when his brother Devin is shot-only days after D. receives notice that he's been accepted into Georgetown University-the plans for his life are exploded, and he takes up the mantle of his brother's crack empire." (Publisher's note)

"Watkins, whose essays often appear in Salon and the New York Times, is a powerful writer, and he uses short chapters to heighten the quick-strike effect of his words, which often land like a punch in the stomach. The treatment of women in the drug subculture, as it is described here, will disturb many readers, but there's no doubting that Watkins is the real deal." Booklist

Welch, Craig

Shell games; rogues, smugglers, and the hunt for nature's bounty. William Morrow 2010 274p il map $25.99   **364.1**
1. Poaching 2. Smuggling 3. Puget Sound region (Wash.)
ISBN 978-0-06-153713-4; 0-06-153713-6

         LC 2009-38980

"Welch covers the wildlife crime beat in Puget Sound, where shellfish poachers wreak havoc on the region's once bountiful, now imperiled marine ecosystem. Writing with the sizzle of a mystery novelist, Welch portrays a complex, driven, and irresistible cast of real-life characters, from fish cops Ed Volz and Kevin Harrington to Doug Tobin, a larger-than-life Native American fisherman. . . . Welch's utterly compelling true tale of black-market trade in endangered ocean wildlife is astounding and infuriating." Booklist

Includes bibliographical references

Wittman, Robert

Priceless; how I went undercover to rescue the world's stolen treasures. [by] Robert K. Wittman with John Shiffman.

Crown Publishers 2010 324p il $25; ebook $25   **364.1**
1. Art thefts 2. Criminal investigation
ISBN 978-0-307-46147-6; 978-0-307-46149-0 ebook

         LC 2009-49083

This "book has the excitement of an espionage novel. It's suspenseful, thought provoking, and funny." ARTnews

Wood, Cutter

Love and death in the Sunshine State; the story of a crime. Cutter Wood. Algonquin Books of Chapel Hill 2018 240 p. (hardcover: alk. paper) $26.95   **364.1**
1. True crime stories 2. Murder victims -- Florida 3. Murder -- Investigation -- Florida 4. Murder victims -- Florida -- Case studies 5. Murder -- Investigation -- Florida -- Case studies
ISBN 9781616207304

         LC 2017045041

In this book, by Cutter Wood, "when a stolen car is recovered on the Gulf Coast of Florida, it sets off a search for a missing woman, local motel owner Sabine Musil-Buehler. Three men are named persons of interest--her husband, her boyfriend, and the man who stole the car. . . . Then, with the days passing quickly, her motel is set on fire, her boyfriend flees the county, and detectives begin digging on the beach." (Publisher's note)

"Part true crime and part memoir, Wood's debut, at its heart, is a work of creative nonfiction that explores the conflicts that exist within every relationship." Booklist

364.106   Organized crime

Dickinson, Rachel

The **notorious** Reno Gang; the wild story of the West's first brotherhood of thieves, assassins, and train robbers. Rachel Dickinson. Lyons Press 2017 xii, 248 p.p (hardcover: alk. paper) $22.95   **364.106**
1. Thieves 2. Railroad trains 3. True crime stories 4. Middle West -- History -- 19th century 5. Outlaws -- Middle West -- History -- 19th century 6. Train robberies -- Middle West -- History -- 19th century 7. Brigands and robbers -- Middle West -- History -- 19th century
ISBN 9781493026401; 9781493026395

         LC 2016052560

This book, by Rachel Dickinson, is "the true story of the world's first robbery of a moving train, and the real origins of the Wild West. They were the first outlaws to rob a moving train. But from 1864 to 1868, the Reno brothers and their gang of counterfeiters, robbers, burglars, and safecrackers also held the town of Seymour, Indiana, hostage, making a large hotel near the train station their headquarters." (Publisher's note)

"Evocative prose and rich historical context add depth and broad appeal to this captivating account of the men behind the first-ever robbery of a moving train, their wave of crimes in the 1860s, and their deaths at the hands of vigilantes." Pub Wkly

Includes bibliographical references and index

English, T. J.

The **Corporation**; an epic story of the Cuban American underworld. T.J. English. William Morrow 2018 viii, 584 p.p illustrations (some color) (hardcover) $28.99   **364.106**
1. Mafia -- Cuba 2. Cubans -- United States 3. Organized crime -- United States
ISBN 9780062568977; 0062568965; 9780062568960

         LC 2017039510

"An epic story of gangsters, drugs . . . and murder rooted in the streets, The Corporation reveals how an entire generation of political exiles, . . . hitmen, and their wives and girlfriends became caught up in an American saga of desperation and empire building. T. J. English interweaves the voices of insiders speaking openly for the first time with a trove of investigative material he has gathered over many decades to tell the story of this successful criminal enterprise." (Publisher's note)

"English capably covers half a century of criminal enterprise, avoiding the clichés of the true-crime genre while stocking his narrative with familiar players: the capos and goons, the cops and informants, a mistress or two, and John F. Kennedy." Kirkus

Includes bibliographical references and index

Green, Jonathan

Sex money murder; a story of crack, blood, and betrayal. Jonathan Green. W W Norton & Co Inc 2018 432 p. (hardcover) $27.95 **364.106**

1. Crime -- New York (State) -- New York 2. Gangs -- New York (State) -- New York 3. Drug traffic -- New York (State) -- New York 4. Crime -- New York (State) -- New York -- Case studies 5. Gangs -- New York (State) -- New York -- Case studies 6. Murder -- New York (State) -- New York -- Case studies 7. Crack (Drug) -- New York (State) -- New York -- Case studies 8. Drug traffic -- New York (State) -- New York -- Case studies

ISBN 9780393244489

LC 2017061642

In this book, "reporter Jonathan Green creates a visceral and devastating portrait of a New York City borough, and the dedicated detectives and prosecutors struggling to stop the tide of violence. The setting is Soundview, one of the city's most dangerous projects, where we encounter the gangsters Suge and Pipe, and the charismatic leader of Sex Money Murder, Pistol Pete. We also meet the dedicated policemen . . . risking their lives to make a difference." (Publisher's note)

Includes bibliographical references and index

Grillo, Ioan

Gangster Warlords; Drug Dollars, Killing Fields, and the New Politics of Latin America. Ioan Grillo. St. Martin's Press 2016 384 p. color illustrations $28 **364.106**

1. Gangs 2. Drug traffic 3. Latin America -- Politics and government

ISBN 162040379X; 9781620403792

LC 2015021253

Author Ioan Grillo presents this "definitive account of the crime wars now wracking Central and South America and the Caribbean, regions largely abandoned by the U.S. after the Cold War. Moving between militia-controlled ghettos and the halls of top policy-makers, Grillo provides a disturbing new understanding of a war that has spiraled out of control." (Publisher's note)

"A striking exploration of the horrors of mass violence in the Western Hemisphere, with the author offering hope that radical policies could provide positive change." Kirkus

Includes bibliographical references and index.

Perry, Alex

The **good** mothers; the true story of the women who took on the world's most powerful mafia. Alex Perry. William Morrow 2018 352 p. (hardback) $27.99 **364.106**

1. Mafia -- Italy 2. Organized crime -- Italy 3. Women and the mafia -- Italy

ISBN 0062655604; 9780062655608

LC 2018000498

This book, by Alex Perry, presents "the riveting story of a high-stakes battle pitting a brilliant, driven woman fighting to save a nation against ruthless mafiosi fighting for their existence. Caught in the middle are three women fighting for their children and their lives. Not all will survive." (Publisher's note)

Reavill, Gil

Mafia summit; J. Edgar Hoover, the Kennedy Brothers, and the meeting that unmasked the mob. Gil Reavill. Thomas Dunne Books 2012 320 p. (hbk.) $26.99 **364.106**

1. Mafia 2. Mafia -- United States 3. Organized crime -- United States

ISBN 0312657757; 9780312657758; 9781250021106

LC 2012038009

Author Gil Reavill presents a book on the Mafia in the U.S. "For years, FBI director J. Edgar Hoover had adamantly denied the existence of the Mafia, but young Robert Kennedy immediately recognized the shattering importance of the Appalachian summit. As attorney general when his brother JFK became president, Bobby embarked on a campaign to break the spine of the mob, engaging in a furious turf battle with the powerful Hoover." Reavill details "mob killings, the early days of the heroin trade, and the crusade to loosen the hold of organized crime." (Publisher's note)

Includes bibliographical references

Seligman, Scott D.

Tong wars; the untold story of vice, money, and murder in New York's Chinatown. Scott D. Seligman. Penguin Group USA 2016 368 p. illustrations (hardcover) $29 **364.106**

1. Gangs 2. Chinese -- United States 3. Crime -- New York (N.Y.) 4. New York (N.Y.) -- History 5. Chinatown (New York, NY) -- History -- 20th century 6. Crime -- New York (State) -- New York -- History -- 20th century 7. Chinese American criminals -- New York (State) -- New York--History--20th century 8. Chinese American gangs -- New York (State) -- New York -- History -- 20th century

ISBN 9780399562273; 0399562273

LC 2016029498

This book, by Scott D. Seligman, is the "true story of money, murder, gambling, prostitution, and opium: the Chinese gang wars that engulfed New York's Chinatown from the 1890s through the 1930s. . . . The city government was already corrupt from top to bottom, so once one tong began taxing the gambling dens and paying off the authorities, a rival, jealously eyeing its lucrative franchise, co-opted a local reformist group to help eliminate it." (Publisher's note)

"The depth of this research is remarkable—the product of uncovering and analyzing accounts in old newspapers, census and court records, and material in the National Archives—and his results are delivered compellingly. A story about immigrants and their suffering that needed to be told." Booklist

Includes bibliographical references and index.

Talty, Stephan

The **Black** Hand; the epic war between a brilliant detective and the deadliest secret society in American history. Stephan Talty. Houghton Mifflin Harcourt 2017 xix, 298 p.p illustrations (hardcover) $28 **364.106**

1. Mafia 2. Organized crime -- United States 3. Italian Americans -- Crimes against 4. Mafia -- United States -- Case studies 5. Murder -- United States -- Case studies 6. Extortion -- United States -- Case studies 7. Organized crime -- United States -- Case studies 8. Italian Americans -- Crimes against -- Case studies 9. Italians -- Crimes against -- United States -- Case studies

ISBN 9780544633384; 9780544635357

LC 2016048168

This book, by Stephan Talty, presents "the story of what [detective Joseph Petrosino] did almost single-handedly, as well as the systems he devised to do so. . . . The persecution, low pay, abuse, and ignorance of the immigrants' rich culture strike a chord close to home these days. Talty is an excellent storyteller, and this particular story is highly relevant as America's next set of immigrants struggles for acceptance." (Kirkus Review)

Includes bibliographical references and index

364.131   Political offenses

Bhattacharjee, Yudhijit

The **spy** who couldn't spell; a dyslexic traitor, an unbreakable code, and the FBI's hunt for America's stolen secrets. Yudhijit Bhattacharjee. New American Library 2016 304 p. (ebook) $65; (hardback) $27   **364.131**

1. Spies -- United States -- Biography 2. United States. Federal Bureau of Investigation 3. Dyslexics -- United States -- Biography 4. United States. National Reconnaissance Office 5. Espionage, American -- History -- 21st century 6. Intelligence service -- United States -- History -- 21st century

ISBN 9780698404090; 9781592409006

LC 2016012584

This book, by Yudhijit Bhattacharjee, describes how "in December of 2000, FBI Special Agent Steven Carr of the bureau's Washington, D.C., office received a package from FBI New York: a series of coded letters from an anonymous sender to the Libyan consulate, offering to sell classified United States intelligence. . . . Leading a diligent team of investigators and code breakers, Carr spent years hunting down a dangerous spy and his cache of stolen secrets." (Publisher's note)

"Readers interested in spy thrillers, cybercryptology, and the history of U.S. espionage will find this book to be both entertaining and helpful in understanding today's complex landscape of leaked classified information." Booklist

364.134   Offenses against administration of justice

Brannan, Karen

The **Family** Tree; A Kinship Lynching in Jim Crow Georgia. Pocket Books 2016 320 p. ill., maps, genealogical table $26   **364.134**

1. Racism 2. Lynching 3. Family secrets

ISBN 1476717184; 9781476717180

LC 2015043375

"Harris County, Georgia, 1912. A white man, the beloved nephew of the county sheriff, is shot dead on the porch of a black woman. Days after the sheriff is sworn into office, he allows the lynching of a woman and three men, all African American. Now, in a personal account like no other, the great-granddaughter of that sheriff, Karen Branan, digs deep into the past to deliver a shattering historical memoir a century after that gruesome day." (Publisher's note)

"A ghastly, dizzying descent into the coldblooded clannishness of the Southern racist mindset."

Includes bibliographical references and index.

Leamer, Laurence

The **lynching**; the epic courtroom battle that brought down the Klan. Laurence Leamer. HarperCollins 2016 384 p. illustrations (hardback) $27.99   **364.134**

1. Lynching 2. Ku Klux Klan 3. United States -- Race relations 4. Wrongful death -- Alabama 5. Southern Poverty Law Center 6. Lynching -- Law and legislation -- Alabama 7. Liability for human rights violations -- Alabama 8. United Klans of America -- Trials, litigation, etc.

ISBN 0062458345; 9780062458346

LC 2016022037

This book, by Laurence Leamer, "chronicles the . . . true story of a brutal race-based killing in 1981 and subsequent trials that undid one of the most pernicious organizations in American history—the Ku Klux Klan. . . . In addition to telling a gripping and consequential story, . . . Leamer chronicles the KKK and its activities in the second half the twentieth century, and illuminates its lingering effect on race relations in America today." (Publisher's note)

"The writing is solid, the research (especially the interviews) imposing, the case important, and the book's unquestionable hero, Dees, emerges powerfully." Booklist

Includes bibliographical references (pages 355-358) and index.

Tyson, Timothy B.

The **blood** of Emmett Till; Timothy B. Tyson. Simon & Schuster 2017 304 p. (ebook) $18.99; (hardcover) $27   **364.134**

1. African Americans -- Crimes against 2. Lynching -- Mississippi -- History -- 20th century 3. Hate crimes -- Mississippi 4. Mississippi -- Race relations 5. Trials (Murder) -- Mississippi -- Sumner 6. Racism -- Mississippi -- History -- 20th century 7. African Americans -- Crimes against -- Mississippi 8. United States -- Race relations -- History -- 20th century

ISBN 9781476714868; 9781476714844; 9781476714851

LC 2016021595

This book, by Timothy Tyson, is "part detective story, part political history . . . [and] draws on a wealth of new evidence, including the only interview ever given by Carolyn Bryant, the white woman in whose name Till was killed. Tyson's gripping narrative upends what we thought we knew about the most notorious racial crime in American history." (Publisher's note)

"Cinematically engaging, harrowing, and poignant, Tyson's monumental work illuminates Emmett Till's murder and serves as a powerful reminder that certain stories in history merit frequent retelling." Pub Wkly

Includes bibliographical references and index

364.15   Offenses against the person

Blum, Ben

Ranger games; a story of soldiers, family, and an inexplicable crime. Ben Blum. Doubleday 2017 x, 412 p.p (hardcover) $28.95   **364.15**

1. Bank robberies 2. United States. Army 3. Criminals -- United States 4. Bank robberies -- United States 5. Soldiers -- United States -- Case studies 6. Criminals -- United States -- Case studies 7. United States. Army. Ranger Regiment, 75th 8. Bank robberies -- Washington (State) -- Case studies

ISBN 9780385538435; 9780804169691; 9780385538442

LC 2016058715

In this book, by Ben Blum, "before deployment to Iraq, Alex [Blum] was supposed to fly home to see his family and beloved girlfriend. Instead, he got into his car with two fellow soldiers and two strangers, drove to a local bank in Tacoma, and committed armed robbery. . . . In . . . the hopes of helping both Alex and his splintering family cope, . . . [the author], Alex's first cousin, delved into these mysteries, growing closer to Alex in the process." (Publisher's note)

"The result is a well-researched, spellbinding work of narrative non-fiction that opens up the psychology of Ranger training, as well as giving the reader a compassionate view of the interlocking forces that can feed into one spectacularly bad decision." Booklist

Boynton, Robert S.

The **invitation**-only zone; the true story of North Korea's abduction project. Robert S. Boynton. Farrar, Straus & Giroux 2016 xiii, 271 p.p illustrations, maps (hardback) $26 **364.15**
1. Kidnapping 2. Korea (North) 3. Kidnapping victims -- Japan 4. Kidnapping victims -- Korea (North) 5. Korea (North) -- Politics and government -- 1994-2011 6. Kidnapping -- Korea (North) -- History -- 20th century
ISBN 9780374536725; 9780374712662; 9780374175849
LC 2015010957

In this book, author Robert S. Boynton "untangles the bizarre logic behind the abductions. Drawing on extensive interviews with the ab-ductees, Boynton reconstructs the story of their lives inside North Korea and ponders the existential toll the episode has had on them, and on Japan itself. He speaks with nationalists, spies, defectors, diplomats, abductees, and even crab fishermen, exploring the cultural and racial tensions between Korea and Japan." (Publisher's note)

"More than anecdotal stories, his work zeroes in on the deeply un-easy makeup of the Korean-Japanese relationship. Engaging reading, surreal in some of the Orwellian detail." Kirkus

Includes bibliographical references (pages 251-255) and index.

Cohan, William D.

★ The **price** of silence; the Duke lacrosse scandal, the power of the elite, and the corruption of our great universities. Willam D. Cohan. Scribner 2014 672 p. (hardcover: alk. pa-per) $35 **364.15**
1. Rape 2. College sports 3. Duke University 4. Lacrosse players 5. Malicious accusation 6. Prosecution -- Corrupt practices
ISBN 1451681798; 9781451681796; 9781451681802
LC 2013043923

This book, by Willam D. Cohan, presents an account of the "Duke lacrosse team scandal that reveals the pressures faced by America's elite colleges and universities and pulls back the curtain . . . on the larger is-sues of sexual misconduct, underage drinking, and bad-boy behavior. . . . What transpired at Duke followed upon the university's . . . effort to compete directly with the Ivy League for the best students and with its Division I rivals for supremacy in selected sports." (Publisher's note)

"Cohan explores the usual disconnects that occur in high-profile crime cases between what is reported by the press, chronicled in official records, and perceived as public opinion and what really happened. A gripping account of a sensational case." Booklist

Includes bibliographical references and index.

Connors, Joanna

I Will Find You; A Reporter Investigates the Life of the Man Who Raped Her, a memoir. by Joanna Connors (Author) Atlantic Monthly Press 2016 272 p. $25 **364.15**
1. Rape victims 2. Women journalists 3. Women -- Biography 4. Crime -- United States 5. Violence against women
ISBN 0802122604; 9780802122605

This book is a memoir by newspaper reporter and rape victim Joanna Connors. "Once her assailant was caught and sentenced, Joanna never spoke of the trauma again, until 21 years later. . . . Connors embarked on a journey to find out who [her attacker] was. . . . What she discov-ers stretches beyond one violent man's story and back into her own,

interweaving a narrative about strength and survival with one about rape culture and violence in America." (Publisher's note)

"The author insightfully reflects on the idea that the greatest monster anyone, including victims of violent crime, must face is the monster within. A courageous and unsettlingly forthright memoir of overcoming trauma." Kirkus

Delisle, Guy, 1966-

Hostage; Guy Delisle; translated by Helge Dascher. Drawn & Quarterly 2017 436 p. chiefly col. ill., col. map $29.95 **364.15**
1. Hostages
ISBN 1770462791; 9781770462793

"In the middle of the night in 1997, Doctors Without Borders admin-istrator Christophe André was kidnapped by armed men and taken away to an unknown destination in the Caucasus region. For three months, André was kept handcuffed in solitary confinement, with little to survive on and almost no contact with the outside world." (Publisher's note)

"Delisle brings the reader so fully into André's world that a simple change in his routine becomes either harrowing or hopeful, and the mundane details of his daily existence, saving a piece of bread from his morning meal for a snack, enjoying some music drifting through the wall into his cell, become heroic acts of defiance." LJ

Garcia Marquez, Gabriel

News of a kidnapping; translated from the Spanish by Edith Grossman. Knopf 1997 291p $25 **364.15**
1. Hostages 2. Kidnapping 3. Drug traffic
ISBN 0-375-40051-6
LC 97-5445

The author discusses kidnappings in Colombia orchestrated by "Pablo Escobar, once head of the Medellín drug cartel. . . . The writer's respondents are mainly the survivors of a group of prominent residents of Bogotá whom the drug lord held hostage during 1990 and 1991." Time

Hatch, Thom

The **Last** Outlaws; The lives and legends of Butch Cassidy and the Sundance Kid. by Thom Hatch. New American Library 2013 xii, 350 p.p ill., maps (The last outlaws) (hardcover) $26.95 **364.15**
1. West (U.S.) -- Biography 2. Outlaws -- West (U.S.) -- Biography
ISBN 0451239199; 9780451239198
LC 2012031697

This book, by Thom Hatch, presents a biography of "Butch Cassidy and the Sundance Kid--as leaders of the Wild Bunch, they planned and executed the most daring bank and train robberies of the day. . . . For sev-eral years at the end of the 1890s, the two friends, along with a revolving cast who made up their band of thieves, eluded local law enforcement and bounty hunters, all while stealing from the rich bankers and eastern railroad corporations who exploited western land." (Publisher's note)

Holleeder, Astrid

Judas; how a sister's testimony brought down a criminal mastermind. Astrid Holleeder. Little, Brown & Co. 2018 416 p. $28 **364.15**
1. Serial killers 2. Criminals -- Netherlands 3. Kidnapping -- Netherlands
ISBN 9780316475303
LC 2018937003

This memoir, by Astrid Holleeder, "chronicles Astrid's terrifying experience working as a double agent, preserving her brother, [Willem

Holleeder's] trust just so that she could get enough information to put him away for life. . . . [This book] is the intimate account of Astrid's deeply personal betrayal, set against the backdrop of their haunting family history and the astonishing world of the criminal underground." (Publisher's note)

"In her compulsively readable memoir, a best-seller in the Netherlands, Holleeder tells the story of how she became a witness against her criminal brother." Booklist

King, Gilbert, 1962-

★ **Beneath** a ruthless sun; a true story of violence, race, and justice lost and found. Gilbert King. Riverhead Books 2018 432 p. (hardcover) $28   364.15
1. Race relations 2. Discrimination in criminal justice administration -- United States 3. Discrimination in criminal justice administration -- Florida
ISBN 9780399183386

LC 2017053110

This book, by Gilbert King, "exposes the corruption of racial bigotry and animus that shadows a community, a state and a nation. . . . [The book] tells a powerful, page-turning story rooted in the fears that rippled through the South as integration began to take hold, sparking a surge of virulent racism that savaged the vulnerable, debased the powerful, and roils our own times still." (Publisher's note)

"From the opening pages, King's narrative barrels forward, leaving readers wondering what it will take for justice to prevail. By turns sobering, frightening, and thrilling, this meticulous account of the power and tenacity of officially sanctioned racism recalls a dark era that America is still struggling to leave behind." Kirkus

Includes bibliographical references

Koerner, Brendan I.

The **skies** belong to us; love and terror in the golden age of hijacking. Brendan I. Koerner. Crown Publishers 2013 336 p. illustrations $26   364.15
1. Hijacking of airplanes 2. Hijacking of aircraft -- United States -- Case studies
ISBN 0307886107; 9780307886101

LC 2012043203

This book on the history of airplane hijacking "follows the strange and romantic exploits of Willie Roger Holder and Cathy Kerkow, lovers and radicals who became international celebrities when they hijacked Western Airlines Flight 701 in June 1972, demanding a ransom and the release of Angela Davis. Their escape to Algiers and their subsequent adoption by French radicals contributed to the cachet of hijacking." (Library Journal)

"A riveting, highly readable tale of terror in the skies." Kirkus

Includes bibliographical references and index

Larson, Erik

★ The **devil** in the white city; murder, magic, and madness at the fair that changed America. Erik Larson. Crown 2003 xi, 447p ill., maps $25.95   364.15
1. Homicide 2. Murderers 3. World's Columbian Exposition (1893: Chicago, Ill.)
ISBN 0609608444; 9780609608449

LC 20020154046

International Horror Guild Awards: Best Nonfiction (2003); Edgar Allan Poe Awards: Best Fact Crime (2004)

This nonfiction "tale of Chicago Worlds' Fair of 1893 focuses primarily on two men: Daniel H. Burnham, the architect who was the driving force behind the fair, and Henry H. Holmes, a sadistic serial killer working under the cover of the busy fair. . . Burnham and his partner,

John Root, the leading architects in Chicago, were tapped for the job, and they in turn called on Frederick Law Olmstead, Louis Sullivan, and Richard M. Hunt to help them build the world's greatest fair. . . . Unbeknownst to any of them, Holmes, a charismatic, handsome doctor, had arrived in the city and built a complex with apartments, a drugstore, and a vault, which he used to trap his victims until they suffocated." (Booklist)

This is an account of how "H.H. Holmes (born Herman Webster Mudgett) dispatched somewhere between 27 and 200 people, mostly single young women, in the churning new metropolis of Chicago; many of the murders occurred during (and exploited) the city's finest moment, the World's Fair of 1893. Larson's breathtaking new history is a novelistic yet wholly factual account of the fair and the mass murderer who lurked within it." Publ Wkly

Includes bibliographical references (p. [423]-429) and index.

McConnell, David

American honor killings; desire and rage among men. David McConnell. Akashic Books 2013 256 p. (trade pbk. original) $15.95   364.15
1. Homicide 2. Hate crimes 3. Crime -- United States 4. Murder -- United States -- Case studies 5. Murderers -- United States -- Case studies 6. Victims of crimes -- United States -- Case studies
ISBN 1617751324; 9781617751325; 9781617751530

LC 2012939273

Stonewall Book Award: Israel Fishman Non-Fiction Award

Author David McConnell presents a "look at the subculture of violent crime [and] shows how fluid terms like 'gay' and 'straight' can actually be. The author's case studies reflect an intensive investigation into the economic and cultural backgrounds of a wide variety of extremist cultures, research that involved interviews with law enforcement officials, families of victims and the convicted criminals themselves." (Kirkus)

"With no clear answers, but some very intriguing questions, these vignettes of masculine pride and rage will appeal to those interested in gender politics and gay studies as well as true crime fans." LJ

Schiller, Lawrence

Perfect murder, perfect town. HarperCollins Pubs. 1999 621p hardcover o.p. pa $7.99   364.15
1. Children 2. Homicide 3. Homemakers 4. Murder victims 5. Beauty contest winners 6. Computer industry executives 7. Parents of murdered children 8. Boulder (Colo.) -- Police Dept.
ISBN 0-06-109696-2 pa

LC 99-207248

Schiller investigates the JonBenet Ramsey murder case.

Schiller argues that the "Boulder Police Department bungled the investigation, in large part out of ego and inexperience." N Y Times Book Rev

Sexual violence and abuse; an encyclopedia of prevention, impacts, and recovery. edited by Judy L. Postmus. ABC-CLIO, LLC 2013 2 v. (xxxii, 841 p.)p (hardcover) $189; (ebook) $189.00   364.15
1. Sex crimes 2. Sexual harassment 3. Sex crimes -- Prevention
ISBN 1598847554; 9781598847550; 9781598847567 pdf

LC 2012018355

This book, by Judy L. Postmus, provides a "resource on sexual violence and abuse for students, practitioners, and general readers. . . . The two-volume work contains 264 fully cross-referenced entries in alphabetical order, starting with abortion and ending with yoga therapy. The bibliography [also] provides important books, articles, online resources, and videos on a wide range of topics." (Publisher's note)

Includes bibliographical references and index.

Stiles, T. J.

Jesse James; last rebel of the Civil War. Knopf 2002 510p
il maps $27.50; pa $16   **364.15**
1. Thieves 2. Outlaws
ISBN 0-375-40583-6; 0-375-70558-9 pa

LC 2002-25493

"This is a well-written and often surprising reinterpretation of the
life of a legendary and enigmatic figure." Booklist
Includes bibliographical references

The **Ultimate** Jack the Ripper companion; an illustrated encyclopedia. {compiled by} Stewart P. Evans & Keith Skinner.
Carroll & Graf Pubs. 2000 692p il $35; pa $16   **364.15**
1. Homicide 2. Murderers
ISBN 0-7867-0768-2; 0-7867-0926-X pa

LC 00-711560

Published in the United Kingdom with title: Ultimate Jack the
Ripper sourcebook
This is a collection of primary and secondary source material per-
taining to the Whitechapel murders
"This volume is undoubtedly the single largest resource on this case
ever published." Libr J
Includes bibliographical references

Van Dyk, Jere

★ The **trade**; my journey into the labyrinth of political
kidnapping. Jere van Dyk. PublicAffairs, an imprint of Perseus
Books, a subsidiary of Hachette Book Group 2017 xxvii, 418
p.p $28   **364.15**
1. Kidnapping 2. Political crimes and offenses 3. Taliban 4.
Political kidnapping -- Afghanistan 5. Political kidnapping --
Middle East 6. Prisoners -- Afghanistan -- Biography 7. Journalists
-- Afghanistan -- Biography
ISBN 9781610394314; 9781610394321

LC 2017017361

In this book experienced investigative reporter Jere Van Dyk "traveled to Afghanistan to try to discover the motives behind a kidnapping
that had occurred six years earlier--his own. . . . In pursuing his kidnappers, and the stories of the intermediaries and money men, Van Dyk
uncovered not just the story of his own abduction but the operation of
what he calls the Trade: the business of kidnapping." (Publisher's note)
Includes bibliographical references and index

364.152   Homicide

Appelman, J. Reuben

The **kill** jar; obsession, descent, and a hunt for Detroit's
most notorious serial killer. J. Reuben Appleman. Gallery
Books 2017 288 p. (hardcover) $24.99   **364.152**
1. Serial killers 2. Serial murders 3. Serial murders -- Michigan
-- Detroit -- Case studies 4. Serial murder investigation -- Michigan
-- Detroit -- Case studies
ISBN 9781507204023

LC 2017031080

In this book, author "J. Reuben Appelman cracks open one of America's most notorious murder sprees while simultaneously banging the
gavel on his own history with violence. . . . Four children were abducted
and murdered outside of Detroit during the winters of 1976 and 1977,
their bodies eventually dumped in snow banks around the city. . . . Ap-

pelman was six years old at the time the murders began and had evaded
an abduction attempt during that same period." (Publisher's note)

Appignanesi, Lisa

Trials of passion; crimes in the name of love and madness.
Lisa Appignanesi. W W Norton & Co Inc 2015 434 p. illustrations $28.95   **364.152**
1. Love 2. Crime 3. Emotions 4. Crimes of passion -- Case
studies
ISBN 1605988146; 9781605988146

LC 2014450096

Author Lisa Appignanesi "brings to life some sensational trials between 1870 and 1914, a period when the psychiatric professions were
consolidating their hold on our understanding of what is human. Appignanesi teases out the vagaries of passion and the clashes between
the law and the clinic as they stumble towards a (sometimes reviled)
collaboration." (Publisher's note)
"An endlessly fascinating account of the history of insanity pleas
that will find an audience with social history fans as well as enthusiasts
of true crime." LJ
Includes bibliographical references (pages 399-416) and index

Baatz, Simon

The **girl** on the velvet swing; sex, murder, and madness at
the dawn of the twentieth century. Simon Baatz. Mulholland
Books 2018 392 p. illustrations (hardcover) $29   **364.152**
1. Trials (Homicide) 2. Murder -- New York (State) -- New York 3.
Trials (Murder) -- New York (State) -- New York
ISBN 9780316396653; 9780316510677

LC 2017942372

This book, by Simon Baatz, is "the first comprehensive account of
the murder that shocked the world. In 1901 Evelyn Nesbit . . . dined
alone with the architect Stanford White. . . . That evening, after drinking
champagne, Nesbit lost consciousness and awoke to find herself naked
in bed with White[, who allegedly raped her]. . . . She . . . confided in
Harry Thaw, . . . who would later become her husband. Thaw, thirsting
for revenge, shot and killed White in 1906." (Publisher's note)
"An entertaining recital of a notorious scandal." Kirkus
Includes bibliographical references and index.

Blum, Howard

American lightning; terror, mystery, movie-making, and
the crime of the century. Crown Publishers 2008 339p il
$24.95   **364.152**
1. Bombings 2. Terrorism
ISBN 978-0-307-34694-0

LC 2008-2974

"Blum's prose is tight, his speculations unfailingly sound and his
research extensive—all adding up to an absorbing and masterful true
crime narrative." Publ Wkly
Includes bibliographical references

Bowden, Charles

Murder city; Ciudad Juarez and the global economy's new
killing fields. photographs by Julian Cardona. Nation Books
2010 320p il $27.50   **364.152**
1. Homicide 2. Drug traffic 3. Ciudad Juarez (Mexico)
ISBN 978-1-56858-449-2; 1-56858-449-0

LC 2010-01716

"Bowden uses his tremendous talents to tell a haunting, darkly poetic story of a city's horrifying descent into madness and anarchy. A potent
book that readers won't soon forget, and a warning of what can come of

an insatiable market that knows no borders." Kirkus

Braude, Joseph

The **honored** dead; Joseph Braude. 1st ed. Spiegel & Grau 2011 xvi, 318p.p   **364.152**

1. Arabs 2. Morocco 3. Homicide 4. Friendship 5. Journalism
ISBN 9780385527033; 0385527039; 9780679604327 ebook

LC 2010046496

This book recounts the author's experiences as a journalist with "'embed-style access' to a police precinct in Casablanca, [Morocco]. . . . The Judiciary Police, an FBI-like agency, were . . . proud of their low crime rate compared to the United States, although bedeviled by a pesky sect of Islamist militants. . . . The particular murder that fascinated the author during this period involved a 41-year-old homeless Berber man, Ibrahim Dey, who was beaten to death in a warehouse where he had been sleeping for five years—ostensibly for theft. Dey was well liked and considered a majdub, or someone who brings fortune to others, and his best friend, Muhammad Bari, whom Braude befriended, swore to vindicate the suspicious murder." (Kirkus)

Brown, Ethan

Shake the devil off; a true story of the murder that rocked New Orleans. Henry Holt and Co. 2009 286p il $25 **364.152**

1. Homicide 2. Soldiers 3. Murderers 4. Bartenders 5. New Orleans (La.)
ISBN 978-0-8050-8893-9; 0-8050-8893-8

LC 2009-06698

Drawing the parallel between Katrina's aftermath and Bowen's unraveling psyche, Brown creates a riveting portrait of a gruesome crime while detailing the heart of a city in distress. A grim murder-suicide story delivered with skill and verve. Kirkus

Includes bibliographical references

Bryan, Patricia L.

Midnight assassin; a murder in America's heartland. [by] Patricia L. Bryan & Thomas Wolf. Algonquin Books of Chapel Hill 2005 278p $23.95   **364.152**

1. Farmers 2. Homemakers 3. Trials (Homicide)
ISBN 1-565-12306-9

LC 2004-59782

Bryan and Wolf offer "not only an interesting trial drama but also a look into social attitudes of rural America at the beginning of the 20th century, especially toward women." Libr J

Includes bibliographical references

Buruma, Ian

Murder in Amsterdam; the death of Theo van Gogh and the limits of tolerance. Penguin Press 2006 278p $24.95 **364.152**

1. Ethnic relations 2. Netherlands 3. Television producers 4. Motion picture directors
ISBN 1-59420-108-0; 978-1-59420-108-0

LC 2006-43606

This is a "shrewd, subtly argued inquiry into the tensions and resentments underlying two of the most shocking events in the recent history of the Netherlands." N Y Times (Late N Y Ed)

Includes bibliographical references

Chaudry, Rabia

Adnan's Story; The Search for Truth and Justice After Serial. Rabia Chaudry. St. Martin's Press 2016 416 p. facsimilies $26.99   **364.152**

1. Homicide 2. Criminals 3. Criminal investigation -- United States
ISBN 1250087104; 9781250087102

LC 2016024062

This book by Rabia Chaudry focuses on the case of Adnan Syed, who "was convicted and sentenced to life plus thirty years for the murder of his ex-girlfriend Hae Min Lee. . . . In this . . . narrative, . . . Chaudry presents new key evidence that she maintains dismantles the State's case: a potential new suspect, forensics indicating Hae was killed and kept somewhere for almost half a day, and documentation withheld by the State." (Publisher's note)

"Any murder is a tragedy, but a young, potentially innocent suspect sentenced to life in prison after a cursory, slipshod investigation full of cultural bias—and defended by an inept attorney—only magnifies the travesty. For Serial and true-crime fans, this book is a page-turner perfect for a quiet weekend." Kirkus

Collins, Paul

Blood & ivy; the 1849 murder that scandalized Harvard. Paul Collins. W W Norton & Co Inc 2018 368 p. (hardcover) $26.95   **364.152**

1. Forensic sciences 2. Harvard University 3. Harvard University -- History -- 19th century 4. Murder -- Massachusetts -- Boston -- Case studies
ISBN 9780393245165

LC 2017057354

The book, by Paul Collins, presents "a delectable true-crime story of scandal and murder at America's most celebrated university. On November 23rd of 1849, in the heart of Boston, one of the city's richest men simply vanished. Dr. George Parkman, a Brahmin . . . , was last seen that afternoon visiting his alma mater, Harvard Medical School. . . . One Harvard janitor [suspected] . . . that . . . [Parkman] had never left the Medical School building alive." (Publisher's note)

"A vivid true-crime tale from a fascinating bygone era." Kirkus

Includes bibliographical references and index

Blood and ivy

Duel With the Devil; The True Story of How Alexander Hamilton and Aaron Burr Teamed Up to Take on America's First Sensational Murder Mystery. by Paul Collins. Random House Inc 2013 viii, 289 p.p map (hardcover) $26.00   **364.152**

1. Trials (Homicide)
ISBN 0307956458; 9780307956453

LC 2013371593

This book, written by Paul Collins, is the "true account of a . . . turn-of-the-19th century murder and the trial that ensued — a showdown in which iconic political rivals Alexander Hamilton and Aaron Burr joined forces to make sure justice was done. Still our nation's longest running 'cold case,' the mystery of Elma Sands finally comes to a close with this book, which delivers the first substantial break in the case in over 200 years." (Publisher's note)

The **murder** of the century; Paul Collins. Crown 2011 viii, 325p ill.   **364.152**

1. Homicide 2. Journalism 3. Newspapers -- United States
ISBN 9780307592200; 0307592200

LC 2011009390

This book discusses "a sensational 1897 murder case that fascinated the public as it played out across the front pages of the New York City's leading newspapers: Joseph Pulitzer's 'New York World' and William Randolph Hearst's 'New York Journal.' After a group of children discovered the ghastly severed trunk of William Guldensuppe, a Turkish bath-house attendant, the rival news organs spared no expense to ferret out the culprits, eventually tracking the purchase of an oilcloth used to wrap the torso to Mrs. Augusta Nack, a German immigrant midwife and rumored back-room abortionist. Guldensuppe had been Nack's lover before being replaced by Martin Thorn, a hotheaded barber. Things failed to progress smoothly." (Kirkus)

Includes bibliographical references and index.

Colquhoun, Kate

Did she kill him? a Victorian tale of deception, adultery, and arsenic. Kate Colquhoun. Overlook Press 2014 432 p. illustrations (hardback) $27.95   **364.152**
1. Trials (Homicide) 2. Murder -- England -- Case studies 3. Poisoning -- England -- Case studies
ISBN 146830934X; 9781468309348

LC 2014034054

This book, by Kate Colquhoun, explores how "in the summer of 1889, young Southern belle Florence Maybrick stood trial for the alleged arsenic poisoning of her much older husband, Liverpool cotton merchant James Maybrick. . . . The case cracked the varnish of Victorian respectability, shocking and exciting the public in equal measure as they clambered to read the latest revelations of Florence's past and glimpse her likeness in Madame Tussaud's." (Publisher's note)

Colquhoun "employs again her fine storytelling sense, eye for detail, and impeccable research to ensure that contemporary readers will snap up this tale of treachery, deceit, love gone awry, poison, and 'the slipperiness of truth.'" Booklist

Includes bibliographical references (pages 351-361) and index

Corbett, Ken

A **murder** over a girl; justice, gender, junior high. Ken Corbett. Henry Holt & Co. 2016 288 p. illustrations (hardback) $27; (ebook) $60   **364.152**
1. Murder -- California -- Oxnard -- Case studies 2. School shootings -- California -- Oxnard -- Case studies 3. Transgender teenagers -- California -- Oxnard -- Case studies 4. Transgender youth -- California -- Oxnard -- Case studies 5. Transsexual youth -- California -- Oxnard -- Case studies 6. High school students -- California -- Oxnard -- Case studies 7. Transsexual students -- California -- Oxnard -- Case studies
ISBN 9780805099201; 9780805099218

LC 2015023835

This book, by psychologist Ken Corbett, presents an "exploration of the brutal murder of a possibly transgender middle school student by an eighth grade classmate. On Feb. 12, 2008, at E. O. Green Junior High in Oxnard, CA, 14-year-old Brandon McInerney shot and killed his classmate, Larry King, who had recently begun to call himself 'Leticia' and wear makeup and jewelry to school." (Publisher's note)

"Profound and disturbing, this heartbreaking testimony of our culture's worst fissures suggests that understanding is the only way to heal." Pub Wkly

Cornwell, Patricia Daniels, 1956-

Ripper; the secret life of Walter Sickert. Patricia Cornwell. Amazon Pub 2017 570 p. ill. (some color), maps $29.99   **364.152**
1. Serial killers 2. Jack the Ripper murders, London, England, 1888
ISBN 1503936872; 9781503936874

LC 2017000501

This book, by Patricia Cornwell, presents "a comprehensive and intriguing exposé of one of the world's most chilling cases of serial murder--and the police force that failed to solve it. Vain and charismatic Walter Sickert made a name for himself as a painter in Victorian London. But the ghoulish nature of his art--as well as extensive evidence--points to another name, one that's left its bloody mark on the pages of

history: Jack the Ripper." (Publisher's note)

Includes bibliographical references (pages 511-528) and index.

Cullen, Dave

Columbine. Twelve 2009 417p $26.99   **364.152**
1. School shootings 2. Columbine High School (Littleton, Colo.)
ISBN 978-0-446-54693-5; 0-446-54693-3

LC 2008-31441

This is an account of the shootings at Columbine High School in 1999.

This book "is an excellent work of media criticism, showing how legends become truths through continual citation; a sensitive guide to the patterns of public grief . . . and, at the end of the day, a fine example of old-fashioned journalism." N Y Times Book Rev

Includes bibliographical references

Davis, Miriam C.

The **axeman** of New Orleans; the true story. Miriam C. Davis. Chicago Review Press 2017 xiii, 306 p.p illustrations (hardcover) $26.99   **364.152**
1. Serial killers 2. Serial murders -- Louisiana -- New Orleans 3. True crime stories
ISBN 161374868X; 9781613748688; 9781613748695

LC 2016047629

"From 1910 to 1919, New Orleans suffered at the hands of its very own Jack the Ripper–style killer. . . . The Axeman repeatedly broke into the homes of Italian grocers in the dead of night, leaving his victims in a pool of blood. . . . [Author] Miriam C. Davis here expertly tells the story of the search for the Axeman and of the eventual exoneration of the innocent Jordanos. She proves that the person mostly widely suspected of being the Axeman was not the killer." (Publisher's note)

"A riveting story of a serial-killer investigation in a time long before modern-day investigative techniques, even before the term 'serial killer' was invented." Booklist

Includes bibliographical references and index.

Dawson, Kate Winkler

Death in the air; the true story of a serial killer, the great London smog, and the strangling of a city. Kate Winkler Dawson. Hachette Books 2017 viii, 341 p.p illustrations, maps (hardcover) $27   **364.152**
1. London (England) -- History 2. Smog -- England -- London -- History -- 20th century 3. London (England) -- Social conditions -- 20th century 4. Serial murderers -- England -- London -- Case studies 5. London (England) -- Environmental conditions -- 20th century
ISBN 9780316506847; 0316506869; 9780316506861

LC 2017020079

This book, by Kate Winkler Dawson, is a "historical narrative of a serial killer, an environmental disaster, and an iconic city struggling to regain its footing. In winter 1952, London automobiles and thousands of coal-burning hearths belched particulate matter into the air. But the smog that descended on December 5th of 1952 was different; it was a type that held the city hostage for five long days. Mass transit ground to a halt, criminals roamed the streets, and 12,000 people died." (Publisher's note)

Includes bibliographical references and index

Epstein, Edward Jay

The **annals** of unsolved crime; by Edward Jay Epstein. Melville House 2013 347 p. (hardcover) $26   **364.152**
1. Cold cases (Criminal investigation) 2. Criminal investigation 3.

Assassination -- History 4. Assassination -- Investigation
ISBN 1612190480; 9781612190488

LC 2012049984

This book by Edward Jay Epstein presents "case studies of 35 controversial crimes. Several involve conspiracy theories, e.g., JFK's assassination and the Dominique Strauss-Kahn case. He includes well-known historical cases (e.g., Jack the Ripper, the Lindbergh baby kidnapping) . . . and media-sensation cases such as those of Amanda Knox, O.J. Simpson, and JonBenet Ramsey. . . . After describing each case, he outlines theories, and offers his opinion on the most likely solution." (Library Journal)

Includes bibliographical references (pages [335]-338) and index.

Fieseler, Robert W.

★ **Tinderbox**; the untold story of the Up Stairs Lounge fire and the rise of gay liberation. Robert W. Fieseler. Liveright Publishing Corp. 2018 320 p. (hardcover) $26.95   **364.152**
1. Gays 2. Arson 3. Gay liberation movement 4. Arson -- Louisiana -- New Orleans -- History -- 20th century 5. Gay bars -- Louisiana -- New Orleans -- History -- 20th century 6. Homophobia -- Louisiana -- New Orleans -- History -- 20th century 7. Mass murder -- Louisiana -- New Orleans -- History -- 20th century 8. Gay liberation movement -- Louisiana -- New Orleans -- History -- 20th century 9. Gays -- Violence against -- Louisiana -- New Orleans -- History -- 20th century
ISBN 9781631491641

LC 2018004765

This book, by Robert W. Fieseler, "reconstructs the 1973 fire that devastated New Orleans' subterranean gay community. . . . Fieseler chronicles the tragic event that claimed the lives of thirty-one men and one woman on June 24, 1973, at a New Orleans bar, the largest mass murder of gays until 2016. . . . [He] creates an indelible portrait of a closeted, blue-collar gay world that flourished before an arsonist ignited an inferno that destroyed an entire community." (Publisher's note)

"Though Fieseler's prose leans toward overreach—"Humidity, so thick with vapor that breathing air could feel like crying tears, would almost routinely reach 100 percent"—his attention to detail and intricate exploration of the material is spot-on. Fieseler shines a bright light on a dark and largely forgotten moment in the history of the gay rights movement." PW

Includes bibliographical references and index

Flanders, Judith

★ The **invention** of murder; how the Victorians revelled in death and detection and created modern crime. by Judith Flanders. Thomas Dunne Books 2013 576 p. il (hardcover) $26.99   **364.152**
1. Homicide 2. Detectives -- Fiction 3. Great Britain -- History -- Victoria, 1837-1901 4. Murder -- Great Britain -- History -- 19th century
ISBN 1250024870; 9781250024879

LC 2013010535

This book by Judith Flanders is an "exploration of murder in the nineteenth century, [which] examines some of the most gripping cases that captivated the Victorians and gave rise to the first detective fiction. Flanders retells the gruesome stories of many different types of murder, both famous and obscure. Through these stories of murder—from the brutal to the pathetic—Flanders builds a rich and multi-faceted portrait of Victorian society." (Publisher's note)

Fox, Margalit

Conan Doyle for the defense; the true story of a sensational British murder, a quest for justice, and the world's most famous

detective writer. Margalit Fox. Random House Inc 2018 384 p. $27   **364.152**
1. Forensic sciences 2. Criminal investigation
ISBN 0399589457; 9780399589454

In this book, author Margalit Fox describes how "Arthur Conan Doyle, creator of the most famous detective in the world, . . . becomes a real-life detective on an actual murder case. . . . Fox takes us step by step inside Conan Doyle's investigative process and illuminates a murder mystery that is also a morality play for our time--a story of ethnic, religious, and anti-immigrant bias." (Publisher's note)

Graeber, Charles

The **good** nurse; America's most prolific serial killer, the hospitals that allowed him to thrive, and the detectives who brought him to justice. Charles Graeber. 1st ed. Twelve 2013 320 p. (hardcover) $26.99   **364.152**
1. Serial killers 2. Nurses -- United States -- Biography 3. Serial murderers -- United States -- Biography
ISBN 0446505293; 9780446505291

LC 2012041982

This book, by Charles Graeber, profiles the serial murderer and registered nurse "Charlie Cullen. . . . Implicated in the deaths of as many as 300 patients, he was also perhaps the most prolific serial killer in American history. . . . Graeber's portrait of Cullen depicts a surprisingly intelligent and complicated young man whose promising career was overwhelmed by his compulsion to kill, and whose shy demeanor masked a twisted interior life hidden even to his family and friends." (Publisher's note)

Includes bibliographical references

Guinn, Jeff

★ **Manson**; the life and times of Charles Manson. Jeff Guinn. Simon & Schuster 2013 512 p. $27.50   **364.152**
1. Criminals -- United States -- Biography 2. Murderers -- United States -- Biography
ISBN 1451645163; 9781451645163

LC 2012050176

This book by Jeff Guinn "reexamines the life of Charles Manson, interviewing Manson's sister and cousin, who have not previously spoken out, and gleaning new information from childhood friends, cellmates, and Manson Family members. Guinn argues that while Manson spouted incoherent race-war rhetoric, the killings were in fact related to his failed ambitions to be a rock star." (Library Journal)

Includes bibliographical references and index

Hempel, Sandra

The **inheritor's** powder; a tale of arsenic, murder, and the new forensic science. by Sandra Hempel. W W Norton & Co Inc 2013 288 p. (hardcover) $25.95   **364.152**
1. Arsenic 2. Forensic sciences 3. Poisons and poisoning 4. Forensic toxicology 5. Murder -- Great Britain -- History -- 19th century 6. Poisoning -- Great Britain -- History -- 19th century 7. Toxicology -- Great Britain -- History -- 19th century 8. Arsenic -- Toxicology -- Great Britain -- History -- 19th century
ISBN 0393239713; 9780393239713

LC 2013024989

Author Sandra Hempel presents a "look at how the science of poison detection developed. Hempel focuses on a different dilemma for the Victorian medical profession: how to successfully determine when poison is the cause of death. In 1833 the strange death of farmer George Bodle and the investigation of his family members, with whom he lived, frames the history of scientists' struggles to develop foolproof tests for the presence, in the victims' digestive tracts, of arsenic." (Publishers Weekly)

"An unexpected verdict and its aftermath make this a satisfying murder mystery in the grand tradition." Kirkus

Includes bibliographical references and index

Hollandsworth, Skip

The **midnight** assassin; panic, scandal, and the hunt for America's first serial killer. Skip Hollandsworth. Henry Holt & Co. 2016 336 p. (ebook) $60; (hardback) $30   **364.152**
1. Serial killers 2. Serial murders -- Texas -- Austin 3. Austin (Tex.) -- History -- 19th century 4. Serial murders -- Texas -- Austin -- History -- 19th century 5. Serial murderers -- Texas -- Austin -- History -- 19th century
ISBN 9780805097689; 9780805097672

LC 2015024689

This book, by Skip Hollandsworth, presents a "narrative history of a terrifying serial killer--America's first--who stalked Austin, Texas in 1885. . . . Beginning in December 1884, Austin was terrorized by someone equally as vicious . . . [as] London's infamous Jack the Ripper. For almost exactly one year, the Midnight Assassin crisscrossed the entire city, striking on moonlit nights, using axes, knives, and long steel rods to rip apart women from every race and class." (Publisher's note)

"The lively social history of a town on the brink combines with a riveting true crime story that will make this a favorite in regional history collections as well as true crime collections." LJ

Includes bibliographical references and index

James, Bill, 1929-

The **man** from the train; the solving of a century-old serial killer mystery. Bill James and Rachel McCarthy James. Scribner 2017 xi, 464 p.p (hardback) $30   **364.152**
1. Crime 2. Serial Killers -- History 3. Mass murder -- Middle West -- History 4. Mass murder -- Iowa -- Villisca -- History 5. Serial murderers -- Middle West -- History 6. Serial murderers -- Iowa -- Villisca -- History 7. Mass murder investigation -- Middle West -- History 8. Mass murder investigation -- Iowa -- Villisca -- History
ISBN 9781476796277; 9781476796253; 9781476796260

LC 2017005190

This book, by Bill James and Rachel McCarthy James, "paints a vivid, psychologically perceptive portrait of America at the dawn of the twentieth century, when crime was regarded as a local problem, and opportunistic private detectives exploited a dysfunctional judicial system. James shows how these cultural factors enabled such an unspeakable series of crimes to occur, and his groundbreaking approach to true crime will . . . change the way we view criminal history." (Publisher's note)

"Pioneering baseball analyst Bill James . . . successfully transfers his detail-oriented mind-set to true crime in this suspenseful historical account, cowritten with his daughter, Rachel McCarthy James." Pub Wkly

Kirn, Walter

Blood will out; the true story of a murder, a mystery, and a masquerade. Walter Kirn. First edition Liveright Publishing Corporation 2014 272 p. (hardcover) $25.95   **364.152**
1. Murderers -- United States -- Case studies 2. Impostors and imposture -- United States -- Case studies
ISBN 0871404516; 9780871404510

LC 2013046327

This book, by Walter Kirn, is the true story of Clark Rockefeller, an "eccentric son of privilege who ultimately would be unmasked as a brazen serial impostor, child kidnapper, and brutal murderer. . . . As Kirn uncovers the truth about his friend, a psychopath masquerading as a gentleman, he also confronts hard truths about himself. Why, as a

writer of fiction, was he susceptible to the deception of a sinister fantasist whose crimes, Kirn learns, were based on books and movies?" (Publisher's note)

"Kirn's reflecting, musing, and personal dealings add a killer punch to this true-crime memoir." Booklist

Kolker, Robert

Lost Girls; An Unsolved American Mystery. by Robert Kolker. HarperCollins 2013 xiv, 399 p.p (hardcover) $25.99   **364.152**
1. Crime 2. Prostitution 3. Serial murders 4. Computer crimes
ISBN 006218363X; 9780062183637

LC 2013021815

This book from Robert Kolker looks at the murder of five prostitutes in Oak Beach, Long Island. He "probes the 21st-century innovations that facilitated these crimes, which launched a media blitz." A major focus of the book is the author's attention to "the girls' back stories and to the efforts of their families and friends to bring the killer to justice." (Kirkus Reviews)

Kraybill, Donald B.

Amish grace; how forgiveness transcended tragedy. [by] Donald B. Kraybill, Steven M. Nolt, [and] David L. Weaver-Zercher. Jossey-Bass 2007 237p $24.95   **364.152**
1. Amish 2. Forgiveness 3. Amish -- Doctrines 4. West Nickel Mines Amish School (Pa.) 5. Amish School Shooting, Nickel Mines, Pa., 2006 6. Forgiveness -- Religious aspects -- Christianity
ISBN 978-0-7879-9761-8; 0-7879-9761-7

This book explains "Amish reaction to the horrific Nickel Mines shootings. . . . This anguished and devastating account of a national tragedy and a hopeful, life-affirming lesson in how to live is itself a marvel of grace." Booklist

Includes bibliographical references

Larson, Erik

Thunderstruck. Crown Publishers 2006 463p il map $25.95   **364.152**
1. Radio 2. Homicide 3. Inventors 4. Murderers 5. Electrical engineers 6. Homeopathic physicians 7. Nobel laureates for physics
ISBN 1-4000-8066-5; 978-1-4000-8066-3

LC 2006-11908

This book "alternates the story of Marconi's quest for the first wireless transatlantic communication amid scientific jealousies and controversies with the tale of [Dr. Hawley Harvey Crippen,] a mild-mannered murderer caught as a result of the invention. . . . A thrilling read." SLJ

Includes bibliographical references

Leovy, Jill

★ **Ghettoside**; a true story of murder in America. Jill Leovy. 1st edition Spiegel & Grau 2015 336 p. hbk $28 **364.152**
1. Homicide 2. Detectives 3. Los Angeles (Calif.) 4. United States -- Social conditions 5. Murder -- United States
ISBN 0385529988; 9780385529983

LC 2013046367

NAACP Image Award Nominee: Outstanding Literary Work - Nonfiction (2016)

National Book Critics Circle Award Finalist: Nonfiction (2015)

In this book, author Jill Leovy "uses the senseless murder of a policeman's progeny as a jumping-off point to investigate broader issues. Leovy's big-picture thesis is . . . that the gang violence in [Los Angeles] is the result of the local police simply not doing their jobs. On a microcosmic level, the author follows the lives of two LAPD officers, John Skaggs and Wally Tennelle, the former investigating the murder of the latter's son." (Kirkus Reviews)

"Readers may come for Leovy's detective story; they will stay for her lucid social critique." Pub Wkly

Includes bibliographical references and index

Liebman, James S.

The **wrong** Carlos; anatomy of a wrongful execution. James S. Liebman, Shawn Crowley, Andrew Markquart, Lauren Rosenberg, Lauren Gallo White, and Daniel Zharkovsky. Columbia University Press 2014 464 p. illustrations (pbk.: alk. paper) $27.95   **364.152**

1. Judicial error 2. Trials (Homicide) 3. Capital punishment -- United States 4. Judicial error -- Texas 5. Trials (Murder) -- Texas 6. Capital punishment -- Texas
ISBN 0231167237; 9780231167222; 9780231167239; 9780231536684

LC 2013044147

This book focuses on the history of a wrongful execution. "In 1989, Texas executed Carlos DeLuna, a poor Hispanic man with childlike intelligence, for the murder of Wanda Lopez, a convenience store clerk. His execution passed unnoticed for years until a team of Columbia Law School faculty and students almost accidentally chose to investigate his case and found that DeLuna almost certainly was innocent." (Publisher's note)

"A masterpiece of its type and a disturbing true crime account." LJ

Includes bibliographical references and index

Mann, William J.

Tinseltown; Murder, Morphine, and Madness at the Dawn of Hollywood. by William J. Mann. Harper, an imprint of HarperCollins Publishers 2014 xi, 463 p.p illustrations $27.99   **364.152**

1. Motion picture industry -- History 2. Motion picture producers and directors -- United States 3. Murder -- Investigation -- California -- Los Angeles -- Case studies 4. Motion picture producers and directors -- Crimes against -- United States 5. Cold cases (Criminal investigation) -- California -- Los Angeles -- Case studies
ISBN 0062242164; 9780062242167

LC 2015410477

Edgar Award: Best Fact Crime (2015)

This book, by William J. Mann, is the "true tale of ambition, scandal, intrigue, murder, and the creation of the modern film industry. By 1920, the movies had suddenly become America's new favorite pastime. . . . Yet Hollywood's glittering ascendency was threatened by a string of headline-grabbing tragedies—including the murder of William Desmond Taylor, the popular president of the Motion Picture Directors Association, a legendary crime that has remained unsolved until now." (Publisher's note)

"Fans of historical true crime and those who enjoy Old Hollywood gossip will like this title, which could spur the curious to further research of the Taylor case." LJ

Includes bibliographical references (pages 429-463)

Marzano-Lesnevich, Alexandria

The **fact** of a body; a murder and a memoir. Alexandria Marzano-Lesnevich. Flatiron Books 2017 viii, 326 p.p (hardcover) $26.99   **364.152**

1. Murder -- Louisiana 2. Women lawyers -- United States -- Biography 3. Child abuse 4. True crime stories 5. Child molesters -- Louisiana

ISBN 9781250080561; 9781250080547; 1250080541

LC 2017003049

This book, by Alexandria Marzano-Lesnevich, is "not only about how the story of one crime was constructed--but about how we grapple with our own personal histories. Along the way it tackles questions about the nature of forgiveness, and if a single narrative can ever really contain something as definitive as the truth. This . . . [work] shows how the law is more personal than we would like to believe--and the truth more complicated, and powerful, than we could ever imagine." (Publisher's note)

"She poses a greater philosophical and legal question of one's past and how that determines cause in an exquisite and thought-provoking comparison study." LJ

Includes bibliographical references.

Millman, Lawrence

At the end of the world; a true story of murder in the Arctic. Lawrence Millman. Thomas Dunne Books 2017 208 p. illustrations, map (hardback) $24.99   **364.152**

1. Inuit 2. Homicide 3. Arctic regions 4. Murder -- Arctic regions 5. Violence -- Arctic regions
ISBN 9781250111401

LC 2016037251

This book, by Lawrence Millman, "is the remarkable story of a series of murders that occurred in an extremely remote corner of the Arctic in 1941. Those murders show that senseless violence in the name of religion is not only a contemporary phenomenon, and that a people as seemingly peaceful as the Inuit can become unpeaceful at the drop of a hat or, in this instance, a meteor shower." (Publisher's note)

"The result is a smart, emotional, and thought-provoking analysis of this sad occurrence's lingering trauma...Millman has created a quiet and stunning investigative masterpiece." Booklist.

Morris, Errol, 1948-

A **wilderness** of error; the trials of Jeffrey MacDonald. Errol Morris; illustrations by Niko Skourti. Penguin Press 2012 xviii, 524 p.p ill. $29.95   **364.152**

1. Administration of criminal justice 2. Murder -- North Carolina -- Case studies 3. Murderers -- United States -- Case studies
ISBN 1594203431; 9781594203435

LC 2012017906

This book by Errol Morris is about the murder trials of Jeffrey MacDonald "that led to the conviction and imprisonment for life of this man for butchering his wife and two young daughters. . . . It shows us that almost everything we have been told about the case is deeply unreliable, and crucial elements of the case against MacDonald simply are not true. . . . Along the way Morris poses bracing questions about the nature of proof, criminal justice, and the media." (Publisher's note)

Includes bibliographical references and index

Murphy, Paul Thomas

Pretty Jane and the Viper of Kidbrooke Lane; A True Story of Victorian Law and Disorder: the First Unsolved Murder of the Victorian Age. by Paul Thomas Murphy. W W Norton & Co Inc 2016 400 p. illustrations, map (ebook) $60; $28.95 **364.152**

1. Crime -- History 2. London (England) -- History
ISBN 9781681771205; 1605989827; 9781605989822

LC 2016014288

This book, by Paul Thomas Murphy, is "a vivid investigation into the unsolved murder case that shocked Victorian England. . . . On April 26th, 1871, a police constable walking one of London's remotest beats stumbled upon a brutalized young woman kneeling in the muddy road. . . . Five days later, she died. . . . On the day of her death, the police discovered the girl's identity: Jane Maria Clouson, a sixteen-year-old servant to the Pooks, a respectable Greenwich family." (Publisher's note)

"This fascinating account of a Victorian murder, complemented by the added strength of a rich description of the period's society and judicial system, should be a solid addition to academic and true crime collections." LJ

Includes bibliographic notes and index (p. 223-270)

Parry, Richard Lloyd

People who eat darkness; the true story of a young woman who vanished from the streets of Tokyo and the evil that swallowed her up. Richard Lloyd Parry. Farrar, Straus and Giroux 2012 454 p. **364.152**

    1. Homicide 2. Trials (Homicide) 3. Victims of crimes 4. Murder -- Investigation -- Japan -- Tokyo 5. Young women -- Crimes against -- Japan -- Tokyo

ISBN 9780224079174 Jonathan Cape; 0224079174 Jonathan Cape; 0374230595 Farrar, Straus and Giroux; 9780374230593 Farrar, Straus and Giroux

                                                LC 2011047019

This true crime book by Richard Lloyd Parry tells the story of how "Lucie Blackman--tall, blond, twenty-one years old--stepped out into the vastness of Tokyo in the summer of 2000, and disappeared forever. The following winter, her dismembered remains were found buried in a seaside cave. . . . [The author], an award-winning foreign correspondent, covered Lucie's disappearance and followed the massive search for her, the long investigation, and the even longer trial." (Publisher's note)

Includes bibliographical references.

Patterson, James, 1947-

Home sweet murder; true-crime thrillers. James Patterson. Grand Central Publishing 2018 297 p. $15.99 **364.152**

    1. Crime -- United States -- Case studies 2. Murder -- United States -- Case studies 3. Homicide 4. Law Enforcement -- Biography 5. Attempted murder -- United States -- Case studies

ISBN 1538744813; 1538746565; 9781538744819; 9781538746561

                                               LC 2017956662

This book in the James Patterson's Murder Is Forever series, by James Patterson, presents two true-crime thrillers as seen on Discovery's 'Murder is Forever' TV series-- premiering January 2018. [In] HOME SWEET MURDER . . . , Lawyer Leo Fisher and his wife Sue . . . [were] shot, stabbed, and tortured [inside their home]. . . . [In] MURDER ON THE RUN . . . , a middle-aged housekeeper [and a little boy were] found dead [in] Omaha, Nebraska." (Publisher's note)

Presley, James

The **Phantom** Killer; Unlocking the Mystery of the Texarkana Serial Murders: the Story of a Town in Terror. W.W. Norton & Co. Inc. 2014 400 p. 16 plates; illustrations $27.95 **364.152**

    1. Homicide 2. Texas -- History 3. Cold cases (Criminal investigation)

ISBN 1605986429; 9781605986425

                                               LC 2015452738

In this book, "the salacious and scandalous murders of a series of couples on Texarkana's 'lovers lanes' in seemingly idyllic post-WWII America created a media maelstrom and cast a pall of fear over an entire region. What is even more surprising is that the case has remained cold for decades. Combining archival research and investigative journalism, . . . James Presley reveals evidence that provides crucial keys to unlocking this decades-old puzzle." (Publisher's note)

"A thoroughgoing but occasionally plodding story that awaits a better writer. For now, though, this is the best available account of a crime

that, though a cold case, still has people talking." Kirkus

Preston, John

A **very** English scandal; sex, lies and a murder plot at the heart of the establishment. John Preston. Other Press 2016 352 p. illustrations (ebook) $15.99; (hardcover) $27.95 **364.152**

    1. Politicians -- Great Britain -- Biography 2. Great Britain. Parliament. House of Commons -- Biography 3. Trials (Conspiracy) -- England -- London 4. Scandals -- England -- History -- 20th century 5. Great Britain -- Politics and government -- 1964-1979

ISBN 9781590518151; 9781590518144

                                               LC 2016005086

This book, by John Preston, presents a "true crime account of the scandalous private life of Jeremy Thorpe, the British MP whose covert homosexual affair led to blackmail, cover ups, a hired hitman, and ended with the 'Trial of the Century.' . . . Thorpe's climactic case at the Old Bailey in London was the first time that a leading British politician had stood trial on a murder charge, and the first time that a murder plot had been hatched in the House of Commons." (Publisher's note)

"Though knee-deep in politics, scandal, and betrayal, the book also conveys the sobering, grim reality of lives destroyed by dirty politics and homophobic culture." Pub Wkly

Includes bibliographical references (page [324]) and index.

Rowe, Claudia

The **spider** and the fly; A Reporter, a Serial Killer, and the Meaning of Murder. Claudia Rowe. Dey Street 2017 288 p. (ebook) $24.99; (hardcover) $26.99 **364.152**

    1. Serial killers 2. Serial murderers -- New York (State) -- Case studies 3. Serial murders -- New York (State) -- Poughkeepsie -- Case studies

ISBN 9780062416148; 9780062416124; 9780062416131; 9780062497628; 9780062656599

                                               LC 2016036818

This book is a "combination of memoir and psychological suspense, . . . [as] journalist Claudia Rowe, chronicles her unusual connection with a convicted serial killer and her search to understand the darkness inside us. . . . Rowe had always been secretly fascinated by the darkness, and soon became obsessed with the story and with [Kendall] Francois. She was consumed with the desire to understand just how a man could abduct and strangle eight women." (Publisher's note)

"Rowe leaves readers wishing for a more satisfying solution to one puzzle while feeling relief in the resolution of the other." Kirkus

Rule, Ann

Too late to say goodbye; a true story of murder and betrayal. Free Press 2007 456p il $26 **364.152**

    1. Homicide 2. Homemakers 3. Murder victims

ISBN 978-0-7432-3852-6; 0-7432-3852-4

                                               LC 2007-9168

"Rule's meticulous 2½ years of research provides a cinematically satisfying look into how police in two jurisdictions worked together to prove Corbin was a serial murderer of women who tried to leave him." USA Today

Safran, John

God'll Cut You Down; The Tangled Tale of a White Supremacist, a Black Hustler, a Murder, and How I Lost a Year in Mississippi. Penguin Group USA 2014 368 p. $27.95 **364.152**

    1. Homicide 2. Southern States -- Race relations

ISBN 1594633355; 9781594633355

                                               LC 2014017207

Author John Safran presents a true "story about race, money, sex, and power in the modern American South from an outsider's point of view. White supremacist . . . Richard Barrett was brutally murdered in Mississippi in 2010 by a young black man named Vincent McGee. Maybe it was a dispute over money rather than race--or, maybe and intriguingly, over sex." (Publisher's note)

"Safran discovers that the truth behind the crime is driven as much by sex, money, and power as it is by race. Safran's account is at turns hilarious and often bizarre as he riffs on his perspective as an outsider mixing into a complex environment and failing to understand all manner of nuances." Booklist

Sanders, Eli

★ **While** the city slept; a love lost to violence and a young man's descent into madness. Eli Sanders. Viking 2016 336 p. map (ebook) $51; (hardback) $28   **364.152**
1. Murder -- Washington (State) -- Seattle -- Case studies 2. Mentally ill offenders -- Washington (State) -- Seattle -- Case studies 3. Rape -- Washington (State) -- Seattle -- Case studies 4. Lesbians -- Crimes against -- Washington (State) -- Seattle -- Case studies
ISBN 9781101634677; 9780670015719

LC 2015041289

This book, by Eli Sanders, "offers a deeply reported portrait in microcosm of the state of mental health care in this country—as well as an inspiring story of love and forgiveness. Culminating in [Isaiah] Kalebu's dangerous slide toward violence—observed by family members, police, mental health workers, lawyers, and judges, but stopped by no one—'While the City Slept' is the story of a crime of opportunity and of the string of missed opportunities that made it possible." (Publisher's note)

"Handled with delicacy and delivered with a powerful sense of both dismay and compassion, Sanders offers an unflinching portrait of the human casualties of one city's and, by extrapolation, our country's overburdened health-care and judicial systems." Booklist

Schechter, Harold

Psycho USA; famous american killers you never heard of. Harold Schechter. Ballantine Books 2012 xiii, 396 p.p **364.152**
1. Homicide 2. Serial Killers -- History 3. Murder -- United States -- Case studies 4. Murderers -- United States -- Biography
ISBN 0345524470; 9780345524478; 9780345524485

LC 2012004990

This book by Harold Schechter focuses on "a bevy of all-but-forgotten homicidal fiends studding the bloody margins of U.S. history. . . . Spurred by profit, passion, paranoia, or perverse pleasure, these killers -- the Witch of Staten Island, the Smutty Nose Butcher, the Bluebeard of Quiet Dell, and many others -- span three centuries and a host of harrowing murder methods." (Publisher's note)

Includes bibliographical references and index

Sides, Hampton

★ **Hellhound** on his trail; the stalking of Martin Luther King, Jr., and the international hunt for his assassin. Doubleday 2010 459p il $28.95   **364.152**
1. Clergy 2. Murderers 3. Nonfiction writers 4. Civil rights activists 5. Nobel laureates for peace
ISBN 978-0-385-52392-9; 0-385-52392-0

LC 2009-43659

"Sides begins with Ray's escape from a maximum security prison in Missouri the prior April. In short, crisp chapters, Sides then cuts back and forth between Ray's movements during the ensuing year and King's increasing challenges during the same period, as a fraying civil rights movement struggled to transform hard-won legal equality into economic justice. Along the way, we're treated to vignettes featuring J. Edgar

Hoover's vicious antiKing smear tactics; George Wallace's race-driven politics of hate during the 1968 presidential campaign; and an embittered Lyndon Johnson's estrangement from King over the ongoing war in Vietnam. None of this is new, but Sides ensures that it's still compulsively readable." Milwaukee Journal Sentinel

Includes bibliographical references

Siegel, Barry

Manifest injustice; the true story of a convicted murderer and the lawyers who want him freed. by Barry Siegel. 1st ed. Henry Holt and Co. 2012 xiv, 384 p.p (hardcover) $28 **364.152**
1. Miscarriage of justice 2. Macumber, William, 1935- -- Trials, litigation, etc. 3. Judicial error 4. Arizona Justice Project 5. Trials (Murder) -- Arizona -- Maricopa County
ISBN 0805094156; 9780805094152

LC 2012028986

LA Times Book Prize Finalist: Current Interest (2013)

In this book, Pulitzer Prize-winning journalist Barry Siegel "describes the efforts of the Arizona Justice Project to free Bill Macumber, who has spent 38 years in prison for a double murder he denies committing. In 1962, a young couple was shot on a lovers lane in Maricopa County, AZ. There were no credible leads at the time, but a decade later Carol Macumber, a clerk in the sherriff's office, claimed that her ex-husband [Bill] was the murderer." (Library Journal)

Includes bibliographical references (p. [365]-371) and index.

Singular, Stephen

The **Spiral** Notebook; The Aurora Theater Shooter and the Epidemic of Mass Violence Committed by American Youth. by Stephen Singular and Joyce Singular. Counterpoint 2015 304 p. $26   **364.152**
1. School shootings 2. Youth -- United States
ISBN 1619025345; 9781619025349

This book, by Stephen and Joyce Singular, "investigates why America keeps producing twenty-something mass killers. . . . While following the legal proceedings in the Aurora shooting, [it] is full of interviews with Generation Z, a group dogged by big pharma and anti-depressants and ADHD drugs, by a doomsday/apocalyptic mentality present since birth, and by an entertainment industry that has turned violence into parlor games." (Publisher's note)

"Tragic, gripping, and authentic, this book deserves a wide audience." Kirkus

Stanton, Tom

Terror in the city of champions; murder, baseball, and the secret society that shocked Depression-era Detroit. Tom Stanton. Lyons Press 2016 352 p. illustrations, portraits (ebook) $31.99; (hardcover: alk. paper) $26   **364.152**
1. Homicide 2. Baseball -- History 3. Detroit (Mich.) -- History 4. Black Legion 5. Detroit (Mich.) -- History -- 20th century 6. Murder -- Michigan -- Detroit -- History -- 20th century 7. Baseball -- Michigan -- Detroit -- History -- 20th century 8. Professional sports -- Michigan -- Detroit -- History -- 20th century
ISBN 9781493018185; 9781493015702

LC 2015043482

This book, by Tom Stanton, "opens with the arrival of Mickey Cochrane, a fiery baseball star who roused the Great Depression's hardest-hit city by leading the Tigers to the 1934 pennant. A year later he guided the team to its first championship. Within seven months the Lions and Red Wings follow in football and hockey—all while Joe Louis chased boxing's heavyweight crown." (Publisher's note)

"First-rate reporting and a seminar in how to employ context in investigative and historical journalism." Kirkus

Includes bibliographical references and index

Stapinski, Helene

Murder in Matera; A True Story of Passion, Family, and Forgiveness in Southern Italy. Helene Stapinski. Dey St., an imprint of William Morrow Publishers 2017 xv, 300 p.p (hardcover) $26.99 **364.152**

1. Italy 2. Grandmothers 3. Basilicata (Italy) 4. Murder -- Italy -- Basilicata 5. Family secrets -- Italy -- Basilicata 6. Women murderers -- Italy -- Basilicata

ISBN 006243845X; 9780062438447; 9780062438454

LC 2017448193

In this book, "since childhood, Helene Stapinski heard lurid tales about her great-great-grandmother, Vita. In Southern Italy, she was a loose woman who had murdered someone. Immigrating to America with three children, she lost one along the way. Helene's youthful obsession with Vita deepened as she grew up, eventually propelling the journalist to Italy, where, with her own children in tow, she pursued the story, determined to set the record straight." (Publisher's note)

Includes bibliographical references (pages 297-300)

Starr, Douglas

The **killer** of little shepherds; a true crime story and the birth of forensic science. A.A. Knopf 2010 300p il $26.95 **364.152**

1. Homicide 2. Physicians 3. Forensic sciences 4. Trials (Homicide) 5. Murderers 6. Criminologists 7. Law enforcement officials

ISBN 978-0-307-26619-4; 0-307-26619-2

LC 2010-14930

This book is "like an episode of CSI: 19th-Century France. As he prowled the countryside, Joseph Vacher preyed on young shepherds, ultimately slaughtering four times as many people as Jack the Ripper. How the bumbling French authorities finally pieced together the evidence — while learning to study bodies and crime scenes for clues and to compare details about the killings — represents, Starr says, nothing less than the birth of forensic science. In gripping, almost novelistic chapters, he alternates between Vacher and Alexandre Lacassagne, the criminologist who helped crack the case." Entertainment Wkly

Includes bibliographical references

Stashower, Daniel

The **beautiful** cigar girl; Mary Rogers, Edgar Allan Poe, and the invention of murder. Dutton 2006 326p il $25.95 **364.152**

1. Poets 2. Authors 3. Homicide 4. Essayists 5. Murder victims 6. Short story writers

ISBN 0-525-94981-X; 978-0-525-94981-7

LC 2006-19335

The author "tells the story of New York City cigar store clerk Mary Rogers, whose violent death in 1841 brought on a frenzy of sensational newspaper stories and prompted the interest of Edgar Allan Poe.... [He] details how the mystery surrounding Rogers's murder became the inspiration for Poe's story 'The Mystery of Marie Rogêt.'... Well researched and accessible, here is a gripping story that is hard to put down." Libr J

Includes bibliographical references

Summerscale, Kate

The **suspicions** of Mr. Whicher; a shocking murder and the undoing of a great Victorian detective. Walker & Company 2008 360p il map $24.95 **364.152**

1. Homicide 2. Detectives 3. London (England)

ISBN 978-0-8027-1535-7; 0-8027-1535-4

LC 2008-00247

This is the story of Inspector Jonathan Whicher of Scotland Yard, who investigated the 1860 murder of three-year-old Francis Saville Kent in the village of Road, Wiltshire.

The author's "clean writing makes . . . [this book] so dynamic that she can't be accused of 'freezing' the past—instead, she has done a masterly job of reviving it, with all its curiosities and contradictions. But, most strikingly, she has created an enthralling mystery by overlaying the fictional tools of misdirection and suspense onto a nonfiction narrative." Am Scholar

Includes bibliographical references

The **Wicked** Boy; the mystery of a Victorian child murderer. Kate Summerscale. Penguin Group USA 2016 400 p. ill., genealogical table, maps (ebook) $65; $28 **364.152**

1. Murder -- Investigation -- England -- London -- History -- 19th century

ISBN 9780698135000; 1594205787; 9781594205781

LC 2016498145

This book, by Kate Summerscale, presents the story of Victorian-era murderer Robert Coombes and his brother Nattie. In 1895, the boys "were arrested for matricide and sent for trial at the Old Bailey. Robert confessed to having stabbed his mother, but his lawyers argued that he was insane. Nattie struck a plea and gave evidence against his brother. . . . The judge sentenced the thirteen-year-old to detention in Broadmoor, the most infamous criminal lunatic asylum in the land." (Publisher's note)

"This well-written story is not so much a true-crime tale or murder mystery as an excellent sociological study of turn-of-the-20th-century England." Kirkus

Includes bibliographical references (pages 309-360) and index.

Swanson, James L.

Manhunt; the 12-day chase for Lincoln's killer. William Morrow 2006 448p il $26.95 **364.152**

1. Actors 2. Lawyers 3. Presidents 4. Murderers 5. State legislators 6. Members of Congress

ISBN 0-06-051849-9

LC 2005-44911

While this book "belongs in the history section . . . it's as gripping a page-turner as anything you'll find on the mystery shelf." Entertainment Weekly

Includes bibliographical references

Tillman, Laura

★ The **Long** Shadow of Small Ghosts; Murder and Memory in an American City. Laura Tillman. Simon & Schuster 2016 256 p. illustrations $26; (ebook) $11.99 **364.152**

1. Homicide 2. Poverty -- United States 3. Violence -- United States -- Case studies

ISBN 150110425X; 9781501104251; 9781501104305

LC 2015039963

This book, by Laura Tillman, presents an "investigation of the causes, effects, and communal toll of a deeply troubling crime—the brutal murder of three young children by their parents in the border city of Brownsville, Texas. . . . The apartment building in which the brutal crimes took place was already rundown, and in their aftermath a consensus developed in the community that it should be destroyed." (Publisher's note)

"Tillman's book exemplifies provocative long-form journalism that does not settle for easy answers." Pub Wkly

Trillin, Calvin, 1935-

Killings; by Calvin Trillin. [Expanded edition] Random House Inc 2017 xviii, 293 p.p (hardcover) $26   **364.152**

    1. Crime 2. Homicide 3. Murder -- United States -- Case studies

    ISBN 9780399591419; 9780399591402; 0399591400

This book, by Calvin Trillin, presents "true stories of sudden death. . . . These stories, which originally appeared in The New Yorker between 1969 and 2010, are vivid portraits of lives cut short." (Publisher's note)

    "Violent deaths illuminate complex lives and desperate circumstances in this expanded reissue of the classic collection of the author's true-crime reporting for the New Yorker." Pub Wkly

Urschel, Joe

The **Year** of Fear; Machine Gun Kelly and the Manhunt That Changed the Nation. by Joe Urschel. St. Martin's Press 2015 304 p. $26.99   **364.152**

    1. Organized crime 2. Great Depression, 1929-1939

    ISBN 1250020794; 9781250020796

                   LC 2015022093

In this book by Joe Urschel "it's 1933 and Prohibition has given rise to the American gangster. . . . Gangster George 'Machine Gun' Kelly and his wife, Kathryn, are some of the most celebrated criminals of the Great Depression. With gin-running operations facing extinction and bank vaults with dwindling stores of cash, Kelly sets his sights on the easy-money racket of kidnapping. His target: rich oilman, Charles Urschel." (Publisher's note)

    "Many true-crime books claim to shine a light on their chosen eras. This one is the real deal." Booklist

    Includes bibliographical references (pages [271]-274) and index.

Wideman, John Edgar, 1941-

Writing to save a life; the Louis Till file. John Edgar Wideman. Simon & Schuster 2016 224 p. (ebook) $18.99; (hardcover) $25.00   **364.152**

    1. African American soldiers 2. World War, 1939-1945 -- African Americans 3. African American soldiers -- Biography 4. World War, 1939-1945 -- African Americans -- Biography 5. African American men -- Social conditions -- 20th century

    ISBN 1501147285; 9781501147302; 9781501147289

                   LC 2016015604

    Carnegie Medal Longlist: Nonfiction (2017)

This book, by John Edgar Wideman, "traces the life of the father of iconic Civil Rights martyr Emmett Till--a man who was executed by the Army ten years before Emmett's murder. . . . Wideman's personal interaction with the story began when he learned of Emmett's murder in 1955; Wideman was also fourteen years old. After reading decades later about Louis's execution, he couldn't escape the twin tragedies of father and son, and tells their stories together for the first time." (Publisher's Note)

    "A book seething with the passion and sense of outrage behind the Black Lives Matter movement that also traces specific roots of the movement's genealogy." Kirkus

Wiehl, Lis

Hunting Charles Manson; the quest for justice in the days of helter skelter. Lis Wiehl with Caitlin Rother. Nelson Books, an imprint of Thomas Nelson 2018 xv, 319 p.p $26.99 **364.152**

    1. Murderers -- California -- Los Angeles -- Case studies 2. Mass murder investigation -- California -- Los Angeles -- Case studies 3. Murder -- California -- Los Angeles -- Case studies

    ISBN 9780718092085

                   LC 2017059418

    "Drawing upon deep archival research and exclusive personal interviews--including unique access to Manson Family parole hearings--former federal prosecutor and Fox News legal analyst Lis Wiehl has written a propulsive, page-turning historical thriller of the crimes and manhunt that mesmerized the nation. And in the process, she reveals how the social and political context that gave rise to [Charles] Manson is eerily similar to our own." (Publisher's note)

    "Mystery writer, lawyer, and legal analyst Wiehl presents an accessible reboot of prosecutor Vincent Bugliosi's classic Helter Skelter that for the most part doesn't add new information to the highly publicized case." LJ

364.153   Sex offenses

Armstrong, Ken

    ★ A **false** report; a true story of rape in America. T. Christian Miller and Ken Armstrong. Crown Publishers 2018 291 p. maps (hardcover) $28   **364.153**

    1. Rape 2. Rape victims 3. Rape -- United States -- Case studies 4. Rape victims -- United States -- Case studies 5. Police charges -- United States -- Case studies 6. Rape -- Investigation -- United States -- Case studies

    ISBN 9781524759957; 9781524759933

                   LC 2017037935

This book, by T. Christian Miller and Ken Armstrong, "tel[s]l the riveting true story of Marie, a teenager who was charged with lying about having been raped, and the detectives who followed a winding path to arrive at the truth. . . . 'A False Report' is a serpentine tale of doubt, lies, and a hunt for justice, unveiling the disturbing truth of how sexual assault is investigated today--and the long history of skepticism toward rape victims." (Publisher's note)

    "This timely, well-researched, highly readable account will appeal to readers interested in true crime and social justice issues." Booklist

    Includes bibliographical references (pages 261-280) and index.

364.154   Abduction, kidnapping, taking and holding of hostages

Moore, Michael Scott

The **desert** and the sea; 977 days captive on the Somali pirate coast. Michael Scott Moore. HarperCollins 2018 464 p. $27.99   **364.154**

    1. Journalists -- United States -- Biography

    ISBN 0062449176; 9780062449177

This book, by Michael Scott Moore, "falls at the intersection of reportage, memoir, and history. Caught between Muslim pirates, the looming threat of Al-Shabaab and the rise of ISIS, Moore observes the worlds that surrounded him--the economics and history of piracy; the effects of post-colonialism; the politics of hostage negotiation and ransom; while also conjuring the various faces of Islam--and places his ordeal in the context of the larger political and historical issues." (Publisher's note)

364.16   Offenses against property

Bilton, Nick

    American kingpin; the epic hunt for the criminal mastermind behind the Silk Road. Nick Bilton. Portfolio/Penguin 2017 xv, 329 p.p illustrations (hardcover) $27   **364.16**

    1. Drug traffic 2. Computer crimes 3. Criminals -- United States

-- Case studies 4. Black market -- United States -- Case studies 5. Drug traffic -- United States -- Case studies 6. Electronic commerce -- United States -- Case studies 7. Computer crimes -- Investigation -- United States -- Case studies

ISBN 1591848148; 9781591848141; 9780698405738

LC 2016050581

This book by Nick Bolton tells how "in 2011, a twenty-six-year-old libertarian programmer named Ross Ulbricht launched the ultimate free market: the Silk Road, a clandestine Web site hosted on the Dark Web where anyone could trade anything—drugs, hacking software, forged passports, counterfeit cash, poisons. As Ross made plans to disappear forever, the Feds raced against the clock to catch a man they weren't sure even existed, searching for a needle in the haystack of the global Internet." (Publisher's note)

"A fast-paced, readable true-crime tale that frames the likely future of the underground economy." Kirkus

Includes bibliographical references (page 329).

Goodman, Marc

Future crimes; everything is connected, everyone is vulnerable and what we can do about it. Marc Goodman. Doubleday 2015 464 p. (hbk.) $27.95   **364.16**

1. Computer crimes 2. Computer security 3. Technological innovations -- Social aspects 4. Data protection 5. Computer crimes -- Prevention 6. Technological innovations -- Moral and ethical aspects

ISBN 0385539002; 0593073665; 9780593073667; 9780385539005

LC 2014038053

In this book, author "Marc Goodman takes readers on a vivid journey through the darkest recesses of the Internet. Reading like science fiction, but based in science fact, 'Future Crimes' explores how bad actors are primed to hijack the technologies of tomorrow, including robotics, synthetic biology, nanotechnology, virtual reality, and artificial intelligence." (Publisher's note)

Includes bibliographical references

Hesse, Monica

American Fire; Love, Arson, and Life in a Vanishing Land. Monica Hesse. Liveright Publishing Corporation 2017 255 p. illustrations (hardcover) $26.95   **364.16**

1. Arson 2. Unmarried couples 3. Arson -- Virginia -- Accomack County 4. Accomack County (Va.) -- Social conditions 5. Accomack County (Va.) -- Economic conditions

ISBN 1631490516; 9781631490514; 9781631490521

LC 2017014161

This book by Monica Hesse tells how she "first drove down to [Accomack County, Virginia] to cover a hearing for Charlie Smith, a struggling mechanic who upon his capture had promptly pleaded guilty to sixty-seven counts of arson. But as Charlie's confession unspooled, it got deeper and weirder. He wasn't lighting fires alone; his crimes were galvanized by a surprising love story. Over a year of investigating, Hesse uncovered the motives of Charlie and his accomplice, girlfriend Tonya Bundick." (Publisher's note)

"A captivating narrative about arson, persistent law enforcers, an unlikely romantic relationship, and a courtroom drama." Kirkus

Kolhatkar, Sheelah

Black edge; inside information, dirty money, and the quest to bring down the most wanted man on Wall Street. Sheelah Kolhatkar. Random House Inc 2017 368 p. (hardback) $28   **364.16**

1. Hedge funds 2. Global Financial Crisis, 2008-2009 3. Global financial crisis, 2008-2009 4. Hedge funds -- United States -- History -- 21st century 5. Financial crises -- United States -- History -- 21st century

ISBN 9780812995800

LC 2016031776

This book, by Sheelah Kolhatkar, "shows how Steve Cohen became one of the richest and most influential figures in finance—and what happened when the Justice Department put him in its crosshairs. Cohen and his fellow pioneers of the hedge fund industry . . . made their billions through speculation, . . . and for this they have gained not only extreme personal wealth but formidable influence throughout society." (Publisher's note)

"Well-written, with pointed characterizations of the ambitious players and their motives, this book is highly recommended for readers interested in finance, crime, and politics." LJ

Includes bibliographical references (pages [305]-336) and index.

Krebs, Brian

Spam nation; the inside story of organized cybercrime -from global epidemic to your front door. Brian Krebs. Sourcebooks, Inc. 2014 256 p. $24.99   **364.16**

1. Fraud 2. Internet 3. Computer crimes 4. Phishing 5. Spam (Electronic mail) 6. Internet fraud -- United States 7. Computer crimes -- United States 8. Organized crime -- United States

ISBN 1402295618; 9781402295614

LC 2014023007

This book, by Brian Krebs, "unmasks the criminal masterminds driving some of the biggest spam and hacker operations targeting Americans and their bank accounts. Tracing the rise, fall, and alarming resurrection of the digital mafia behind the two largest spam pharmacies--and countless viruses, phishing, and spyware attacks--[the author] . . . delivers the first definitive narrative of the global spam problem and its threat to consumers everywhere." (Publisher's note)

"For lay readers, an effectively revealing closing chapter offers tips on how anyone can safeguard their personal online information from hacker infiltration. An eye-opening, immensely distressing exposé on the current state of organized cyberspammers." Kirkus

Manaugh, Geoff

A **burglar's** guide to the city; Geoff Manaugh. Farrar, Straus & Giroux 2016 304 p. (ebook) $60; (pbk.) $16 **364.16**

1. Theft 2. Crime prevention 3. Burglary protection 4. Thieves -- Psychology 5. Burglary 6. Burglary -- Planning 7. Burglars -- Psychology

ISBN 9780374710286; 9780374117269

LC 2015034638

This book, by Geoff Manaugh, "takes readers through walls, down elevator shafts, into panic rooms, up to the buried vaults of banks, and out across the rooftops of an unsuspecting city. With the help of FBI Special Agents, reformed bank robbers, private security consultants, the L.A.P.D. Air Support Division, and architects past and present, the book dissects the built environment from both sides of the law." (Publisher's note)

"This fascinating look at how burglars analyze every nook and cranny of buildings will make readers see their homes anew. For fans of true crime, architecture, and surveillance." LJ

Includes bibliographical references

Mitnick, Kevin D. (Kevin David), 1963-

Ghost in the wires; my adventures as the world's most wanted hacker. by Kevin Mitnick, with William L. Simon. Little, Brown and Company 2011 xiv, 413 p.p ill. $25.99 **364.16**

1. Thieves 2. Computer hackers 3. Computer crimes -- United States 4. Computer security -- United States 5. Computer hackers -- United States -- Biography 6. Information superhighway -- Security measures -- United States

ISBN 0316037702; 9780316037709

LC 2010043461

In this book, computer hacker Kevin Mitnick "recounts his epic illegal computer hacks of Sun Microsystems, Digital Equipment Corporation, and any number of cellphone makers; his exploits triggered a manhunt that made headlines. He insists he did it not for money but for the transgressive thrill of looking at big, secret computer programs." (Publishers Weekly)

Posner, Gerald

God's Bankers; A History of Money and Power at the Vatican. By Gerald Posner. Simon & Schuster 2015 728 p. 16 plates; illustrations $30   **364.16**

1. Vatican City 2. Church finance 3. Political corruption 4. Catholic Church -- Finance 5. Banks and banking -- Vatican City 6. Catholic Church -- Corrupt practices 7. Catholic Church -- History -- 20th century 8. Catholic Church -- History -- 21st century 9. Catholic Church -- Controversial literature 10. Istituto per le opere di religione -- Corrupt practices

ISBN 1416576576; 9781416576570

LC 2014021061

Author Gerald Posner offers an "exposé of the money and the cardinals-turned-financiers at the heart of the Vatican . . .marked by poisoned business titans, murdered prosecutors, mysterious deaths of private investigators, and questionable suicides; . . . and a set of moral and political circumstances that clarify not only the church's aims and ambitions, but reflect the larger dilemmas of the world's more recent history." (Publisher's note)

"The destruction of documents, stonewalling by prelates, and closed Vatican archives made Posner's work harder, necessitating conjectures. This sad tale is known in its outlines, but Posner provides much more detail." Choice

Potter, Maximillian

Shadows in the vineyard; the true story of a plot to poison the world's greatest wine. Maximillian Potter. Grand Central Publishing 2014 304 p. (hardback) $27   **364.16**

1. Crime 2. Wine and wine making -- France 3. Crime -- France -- Burgundy -- Case studies 4. Wineries -- France -- Burgundy -- Case studies 5. Viticulture -- France -- Burgundy -- Case studies 6. Grapes -- France -- Burgundy -- Herbicide injuries -- Case studies

ISBN 1455516104; 9781455516100

LC 2014015787

In this book, the author "uncovers a fascinating plot to destroy the vines of La Romanée-Conti, Burgundy's finest and most expensive wine. . . . [The author] takes us deep into a captivating world full of . . . small-town French politics . . . and a local culture defined by the twinned veins of excess and vitality and the deep reverent attention to the land that runs through it." (Publisher's note)

"Digressions on the wine market and various viticultural techniques, as well as profiles of the police officers and the criminal they pursued, give the story depth and context. Even the most devout teetotaler will have a hard time putting this one down." Pub Wkly

Wright, Tom

Billion dollar whale; the man who fooled Wall Street, Hollywood, and the world. Bradley Hope and Tom Wright. Hachette Books 2018 400 p. (hardcover) $28   **364.16**

1. Fraud 2. Wall Street (New York, N.Y.) 3. Fraud -- United States

4. Swindlers and swindling -- United States -- Biography

ISBN 9780316436502

LC 2018011725

This book, by Bradley Hope and Tom Wright, reveals how Jho Low, a Wharton graduate, "pulled off one of the biggest heists in history--right under the nose of the global financial industry. Federal agents who helped unravel Bernie Madoff's Ponzi scheme say the 1MDB affair will become the textbook case of financial fraud in the modern age--and its fallout is already being credited for taking down the prime minister of Malaysia." (Publisher's note)

" For fans of business books about financial misdealings, this is a must-read." Booklist

364.162   Theft

Johnson, Kirk Wallace

★ The **feather** thief; beauty, obsession, and the natural history heist of the century. Kirk Wallace Johnson. Viking 2018 x, 308 p.p illustrations (some color) (hardcover) $27 **364.162**

1. Museums 2. Thieves 3. True crime stories 4. Natural History Museum (London, England) 5. Fly tying -- Great Britain -- Case studies 6. Theft from museums -- Great Britain -- Case studies 7. Zoological specimens -- Great Britain -- Case studies

ISBN 9781101981627; 9780525559092; 9781101981610

LC 2018013162

This book, by Kirk Wallace Johnson, "documents the astonishing 2009 theft of an invaluable collection of ornithological displays from the British Museum of Natural History by a talented American musician, tracing the author's years-long investigation to track down the culprit and understand his motives, which were possibly linked to an obsession with the Victorian art of salmon fly-tying." (Publisher's note)

"This is a remarkably compelling story of obsession and history and a man who so loved his art that he would break the law for it." Booklist

Includes bibliographical references and index.

364.163   Fraud

Konnikova, Maria, 1987-

The **Confidence** Game; Why We Fall for It--Every Time. by Maria Konnikova. Penguin Group USA 2016 352 p. (ebook) $65; $28   **364.163**

1. Deception 2. Ponzi schemes 3. Swindlers and swindling

ISBN 9780698170995; 0525427414; 9780525427414

LC 2015041266

"From multimillion-dollar Ponzi schemes to small-time frauds, [author Maria] Konnikova pulls together a selection of fascinating stories to demonstrate what all cons share in common, drawing on scientific, dramatic, and psychological perspectives. . . . 'The Confidence Game' asks not only why we believe con artists, but also examines the very act of believing and how our sense of truth can be manipulated by those around us." (Publisher's note)

"With meticulous research and a facility for storytelling, Konnikova makes this intriguing topic absolutely riveting." Kirkus

Includes bibliographical references and index.

364.168   Business, financial, professional offenses

Eisinger, Jesse

The **chickenshit** club; why the Justice Department fails

to prosecute executives. by Jesse Eisinger. Simon & Schuster 2017 xxi, 377 p.p (hardcover) $28 **364.168**
1. Political corruption 2. United States. Dept. of Justice 3. Administration of justice -- United States 4. Commercial crimes 5. White collar crimes 6. Prosecution -- United States 7. Prosecution -- Decision making 8. United States. Department of Justice 9. White collar crimes -- United States 10. Corporations -- Corrupt practices -- United States 11. Criminal justice, Administration of -- Social aspects
ISBN 9781501121364; 9781501121388; 1501121367

LC 2017301124

In this book, author Jesse Eisinger explores "the evolution of the [U.S.] Justice Department's approach to pursuing corporate criminals through the early 2000s and into the Justice Department of today, including the prosecutorial fiascos, corporate lobbying, trial losses, and culture shifts that have stripped the government of the will and ability to prosecute top corporate executives." (Publisher's note)

"Pulitzer Prize–winning journalist Eisinger does a masterful job of assembling this riveting dossier of the legal scholars, jurists, and elected officials who played a role in turning the U.S. into a nation in which white-collar criminals are celebrated for their cunning instead of incarcerated for their offenses." Booklist

Includes bibliographical references and index.

Enrich, David

The **spider** network; the wild story of a math genius, a gang of backstabbing bankers, and one of the greatest scams in financial history. David Enrich. Custom House 2017 xiii, 509 p.p (hardback) $29.99 **364.168**
1. Derivative securities 2. Banks and banking -- Corrupt practices 3. Interest rates 4. Commercial crimes 5. International finance
ISBN 9780062452993; 9780062453006; 9780062452986

LC 2016048389

This book, by David Enrich, "unveils the bizarre and sinister story of how a math genius named Tom Hayes, a handful of outrageous confederates, and a deeply corrupt banking system ignited one of the greatest financial scandals in history. . . . Hayes, a brilliant but troubled mathematician, became the lynchpin of shadowy team that used hook and crook to take over the process and set rates that made them a fortune, no matter the cost to others." (Publisher's note)

"Written in a lively style reminiscent of Ben Mezrich's financial best-sellers, the book is full of colorful characters, high-flying wheeling and dealing, and intrigue." Booklist

Includes bibliographical references (pages 473-483) and index.

364.3 Offenders

Benforado, Adam

Unfair; the new science of criminal injustice. Adam Benforado. Crown Publishers 2015 400 p. (hardback) $26 **364.3**
1. Discrimination 2. Criminal psychology 3. Administration of criminal justice 4. Criminal justice, Administration of -- Psychological aspects 5. Discrimination in criminal justice administration -- Psychological aspects
ISBN 0770437761; 9780770437763; 9780770437787

LC 2014041693

This book, by Adam Benforado, argues "our system of justice is fundamentally broken. . . . Even if the system operated exactly as it was designed to, we would still end up with wrongful convictions, trampled rights, and unequal treatment. This is because the roots of injustice lie not inside the dark hearts of racist police officers or dishonest prosecutors, but within the minds of each and every one of us." (Publisher's note)

"A stimulating critique of today's criminal justice system with applications to recent cases in Ferguson, MO, and elsewhere, this authoritative and accessible book is suited to a general audience and students." LJ

Paradis, Cheryl

The **measure** of madness; inside the disturbed and disturbing criminal mind. Citadel Press 2010 272p pa $16.95 **364.3**
1. Forensic sciences 2. Criminal psychology
ISBN 978-0-8065-3105-2

LC 2010-924994

The author "has spent more than two decades evaluating mentally ill and violent individuals and giving expert testimony in court. Here she details criminal cases in which the prosecution or defense asked her to establish whether defendants were competent to stand trial, or to vet such psychiatric defenses as insanity and extreme emotional disturbance. The cases, all tried in New York City, are fascinating, unsettling and often horrifying. . . . The author also discusses the psycho-legal issues of cases involving juveniles and abused wives. . . . A welcome inside account." Kirkus

Includes bibliographical references

364.38 Offenders with mental illnesses and disabilities

Roth, Alisa

Insane; America's criminal treatment of mental illness. Alisa Roth. Basic Books, an imprint of Perseus Books, a subsidiary of Hachette Book Group 2018 320 p. (hardcover) $28 **364.38**
1. Prisoners 2. Mental health 3. Mentally ill -- United States
ISBN 9780465094196

LC 2018933315

In this book, author "Alisa Roth goes deep inside the criminal justice system to show how and why it has become a warehouse where [mentally ill] inmates are denied proper treatment, abused, and punished in ways that make them sicker. Through intimate stories of people in the system and those trying to fix it, Roth reveals the hidden forces behind this crisis and suggests how a fairer and more humane approach might look." (Publisher's note)

364.6 Penology

Beer, Daniel

The **house** of the dead; Siberian exile under the tsars. Daniel Beer. Alfred A. Knopf 2016 496 p. ill. (some color), maps (ebook) $65; (hardcover) $35 **364.6**
1. Exiles 2. Siberia (Russia) -- History 3. Political prisoners -- Russia 4. Exile (Punishment) -- Russia -- History 5. Russia -- Social conditions -- 1801-1917 6. Siberia (Russia) -- History -- 19th century 7. Siberia (Russia) -- History -- 20th century 8. Exiles -- Russia (Federation) -- Siberia -- History 9. Convict labor -- Russia (Federation) -- Siberia -- History 10. Penal colonies -- Russia (Federation) -- Siberia -- History 11. Revolutionaries -- Russia (Federation) -- Siberia -- History 12. Exile (Punishment) -- Russia (Federation) -- Siberia -- History 13. Political prisoners -- Russia (Federation) -- Siberia -- History
ISBN 9780307958914; 9780307958907

LC 2016009610

"From the beginning of the nineteenth century until the Russian Revolution, the tsars exiled more than one million prisoners and their families beyond the Ural Mountains to Siberia. [In this book,] Daniel Beer illuminates both the brutal realities of this inhuman system and the tragic and inspiring fates of those who endured it." (Publisher's note)

"An eye-opening, haunting work that delineates how a vast imperial penal system crumbled from its rotten core." Kirkus

Includes bibliographical references (pages [379]-440) and index.

Berman, Greg

Start here; a road map to reducing mass incarceration. Greg Berman, Julian Adler. The New Press 2018 224 p. (hc: alk. paper) $24.99   **364.6**

1. Law reform -- United States 2. Administration of criminal justice -- United States 3. Imprisonment -- United States 4. Correctional law -- United States 5. Prisons -- Law and legislation -- United States 6. Criminal justice, Administration of -- United States

ISBN 9781620972236

LC 2017043125

"In this forward-looking, next-generation criminal justice reform book, Greg Berman and Julian Adler of the Center for Court Innovation highlight the key lessons from these programs--engaging the public in preventing crime, treating all defendants with dignity and respect, and linking people to effective community-based interventions rather than locking them up." (Publisher's note)

Includes bibliographical references

364.66   Capital punishment

Echols, Damien, 1974-

★ **Life** after death; Damien Echols. Blue Rider Press 2012 399 p.   **364.66**

1. Prisons 2. False imprisonment -- United States 3. Prisoners -- United States -- Biography 4. Death row inmates -- United States -- Biography

ISBN 0399160205; 9780399160202

LC 2012026115

Author Damien Echols, "sentenced to death . . . for the murders of three eight-year-old boys in Arkansas, [and] known worldwide as a symbol of wrongful conviction and imprisonment, . . . shares his story in full -- from abuse by prison guards and wardens, to portraits of fellow inmates and deplorable living conditions, to the incredible reserves of patience, spirituality, and perseverance that kept him alive and sane while incarcerated for nearly two decades." (Publisher's note)

Heard, Alex

The **eyes** of Willie McGee; a tragedy of race, sex, and secrets in the Jim Crow South. Harper 2010 404p il $26.99   **364.66**

1. Trials 2. Veterans 3. Capital punishment 4. Alleged criminals 5. Mississippi -- Race relations

ISBN 978-0-06-128415-1; 0-06-128415-7

LC 2009-51769

"McGee was mourned in poems, novels and memoirs. But while he clearly did not get a fair trial, was he innocent? Was Willette Hawkins really the guilty party? 'The Eyes of Willie McGee' leaves us wondering, and wondering how many other ghosts remain in Jim Crow's closet." Los Angeles Times

Prejean, Helen

★ The **death** of innocents; an eyewitness account of wrongful executions. Random House 2005 310p $25.95   **364.66**

1. Capital punishment

ISBN 0-679-44056-9

LC 2004-54154

The author "reexamines the cases of two men she fervently believes were executed for crimes they did not commit. . . . In addition to providing a searing indictment of capital punishment, Prejean also exposes the fundamental inadequacies of the American court system. Expect demand for this extremely thought-provoking book." Booklist

Includes bibliographical references

364.973   Crime – United States

Anatomy of innocence; testimonies of the wrongfully convicted. edited by Laura Caldwell and Leslie S. Klinger, introduced by Scott Turow and Barry Scheck. W W Norton & Co Inc 2017 320 p. (ebook) $50; $26.95   **364.973**

1. Actual innocence 2. Administration of criminal justice -- United States

ISBN 9781631490897; 1631490885; 9781631490880

In this book, edited by Laura Caldwell and Leslie S. Klinger, "fourteen exonerated inmates narrate their stories to a roster of high-profile mystery and thriller writers--including Lee Child, Sara Paretsky, Laurie R. King, Jan Burke and S. J. Rozan--while another exoneree's case is explored in a previously unpublished essay by legendary playwright Arthur Miller. . . . [These stories] detail every aspect of the experience of wrongful conviction." (Publisher's note)

"A searing, unforgettable anthology, with valuable insights provided at the end of each chapter by the editors." Kirkus

Forman, James

★ **Locking** up our own; crime and punishment in Black America. James Forman, Jr. Farrar, Straus & Giroux 2017 306 p. illustrations (hardback) $27   **364.973**

1. Social justice -- United States 2. African Americans -- Social conditions 3. Administration of criminal justice -- United States 4. African American judges 5. African American police 6. Life and death, Power over 7. African American politicians 8. United States -- Race relations 9. Criminal justice, Administration of -- United States 10. Discrimination in criminal justice administration -- United States

ISBN 9780374189976

LC 2016041345

Pulitzer Prize: General Nonfiction (2018)

In this book, author James Forman points out that "the war on crime that began in the 1970s was supported by many African American leaders. . . . [He] shows us that the first substantial cohort of black mayors, judges, and police chiefs took office amid a surge in crime and drug addiction. . . . [This book] enriches our understanding of why our society became so punitive and offers important lessons to anyone concerned about the future of race and the criminal justice system." (Publisher's note)

"Possibly controversial, undoubtedly argumentative, Forman's survey offers a refreshing breath of fresh air on the crisis in American policing." Pub Wkly.

Includes bibliographical references and index.

Greenberg, Karen J.

Rogue justice; the making of the security state. Karen J. Greenberg. Crown Publishers 2016 320 p. (ebook) $65; (hardback) $28   **364.973**

1. Civil rights -- United States 2. Internal security -- United States 3. National security -- United States 4. War on Terrorism, 2001-2009 -- Influence 5. Detention of persons -- United States 6. United States -- Politics and government -- 2009- 7. Human rights -- Government policy -- United States 8. United States -- Politics

and government -- 2001-2009 9. Political questions and judicial power -- United States 10. National security -- Law and legislation -- United States 11. War on Terrorism, 2001-2009 -- Political aspects -- United States 12. Criminal justice, Administration of -- Political aspects -- United States

ISBN 9780804138222; 9780804138215; 9780804138239

LC 2015041144

This book, by Karen J. Greenberg, is "the definitive account of how America's War on Terror sparked a decade-long assault on the rule of law. . . . The day after September 11, President Bush tasked the attorney general with preventing another terrorist attack on the United States. From that day forward, the Bush administration turned to the Department of Justice to give its imprimatur to activities that had previously been unthinkable." (Publisher's note)

"A sophisticated study of executive tyranny in the never-ending war on terror." Kirkus

Includes bibliographical references and index

Hayes, Christopher, 1979-

A **Colony** in a Nation; by Chris Hayes. W W Norton & Co Inc 2017 256 p. $26.95   **364.973**

1. United States -- Politics and government 2. African Americans in criminal justice administration 3. Discrimination in criminal justice administration -- United States

ISBN 0393254224; 9780393254228

LC 2016053392

This book, by Chris Hayes, "contends our country has fractured in two: the Colony and the Nation. In the Nation, we venerate the law. In the Colony, we obsess over order, fear trumps civil rights, and aggressive policing resembles occupation. . . . [It] explains how a country founded on justice now looks like something uncomfortably close to a police state." (Publisher's note)

"A timely and impassioned argument for social justice." Kirkus.

Includes bibliographical references and index.

Sharkey, Patrick

Uneasy peace; the great crime decline, the renewal of city life, and the next war on violence. Patrick Sharkey. W W Norton & Co Inc 2018 xxii, 244 p.p illustrations (hardcover) $26.95   **364.973**

1. Crime prevention 2. Crime -- United States 3. Violence -- Prevention 4. Crime prevention -- United States 5. City and town life -- United States 6. Crime -- United States -- History -- 20th century 7. Crime -- United States -- History -- 21st century

ISBN 9780393609615; 039360960X; 9780393609608

LC 2017051652

In this book, author Patrick "Sharkey draws on original data and textured accounts of neighborhoods across the . . . [U.S.] to document the most successful proven strategies for combatting violent crime and to lay out innovative and necessary approaches to the problem of violence. At a time when crime is rising again and powerful political forces seek to disinvest in cities, the insights in this book are indispensable." (Publisher's note)

"This is a well-documented, thoughtful look at major American cities and their comeback from deserted ghost towns to thriving urban centers." Booklist

Includes bibliographical references and index

365   Penal and related institutions

Applebaum, Anne

★ **Gulag**; a history. Doubleday 2003 677p il maps

$35   **365**

1. Convict labor 2. Concentration camps 3. Soviet Union -- Politics and government

ISBN 0-7679-0056-1

LC 2002-41344

National Book Award Finalist: Nonfiction (2003)

This "describes how, largely under Stalin's watch, a regulated, centralized system of prison labor—unprecedented in scope—gradually arose out of the chaos of the Russian Revolution. . . . Applebaum details camp life, including strategies for survival; the experiences of women and children in the camps; sexual relationships and marriages between prisoners; and rebellions, strikes and escapes. . . . Applebaum's lucid prose and painstaking consideration of the competing theories about aspects of camp life and policy are always compelling." Publ Wkly

Includes bibliographical references

Bauer, Shane

American prison; a reporter's undercover journey into the business of punishment. Shane Bauer. Penguin Press 2018 368 p. (hardback) $28   **365**

1. Prisons 2. Prisons -- United States 3. Law enforcement -- United States 4. Imprisonment -- United States

ISBN 9780735223585

LC 2018018293

Kirkus Prize Finalist: Nonfiction (2018)

In this book, author Shane Bauer "weaves . . . his experiences together with a thoroughly researched history of for-profit prisons in America from their origins in the decades before the Civil War. . . . To his horror, Bauer finds himself becoming crueler and more aggressive the longer he works in the prison, and he is far from alone. . . . 'American Prison' is a necessary human document about the true face of justice in America." (Publisher's note)

"Bauer's amazing book examines one of slavery's toxic legacies, using convicted people to make profit, through a dual approach." Booklist

Includes bibliographical references and index

Bernstein, Nell

Burning down the house; the end of juvenile prison. Nell Bernstein. New Press, The 2014 384 p. (hardback) $26.95 **365**

1. Juvenile courts 2. Juvenile delinquency 3. Administration of justice -- United States 4. Juvenile justice, Administration of -- United States

ISBN 1595589562; 9781595589569

LC 2013043709

In this book journalist Nell Bernstein "turns her attention to the U.S. juvenile justice system in which more than 66,000 youths are confined. . . . Bernstein introduces adolescents in and out of detention centers, capturing their struggles to overcome traumatic histories. . . . Visiting 'therapeutic' prisons in Minnesota, California, and New York, she concludes that . . . these institutions remain embedded in a larger culture that seems impervious to reform." (Publishers Weekly)

"The combination of muckraking research and absolutism make the book passionate and convincing as advocacy." Kirkus

Includes bibliographical references

Buser, Mary E.

Lockdown on Rikers; shocking stories of abuse and injustice at New York's notorious jail. Mary E. Buser. Palgrave Macmillan 2015 288 p. (hardcover) $26.99; (ebook) $40 **365**

1. Prisons -- New York (State) -- Rikers Island 2. Prisoners -- New York (State) -- Rikers Island 3. Jails -- New York (State) -- Rikers Island 4. Prison administration -- Moral and ethical aspects -- New York (State) -- Rikers Island

ISBN 9781250077844; 9781466890169

LC 2015007502

"Mary Buser began her career at Rikers Island as a social work intern. . . . Following her promotion to assistant chief, she was transferred to different jails, working in the Mental Health Center, and finally, at Rikers's notorious 'jail within jail,' the dreaded solitary confinement unit, where she saw horrors she'd never imagined." (Publisher's note)

"A full-bore view of prison life, the appalling conditions in solitary confinement, and the need for reform." Booklist

Dreisinger, Baz

Incarceration nations; a journey to justice in prisons around the world. Baz Dreisinger. Other Press 2016 336 p. (hardcover) $27.95; (ebook) $21.99   **365**

1. Prisons 2. Corrections 3. Administration of criminal justice 4. Imprisonment 5. Criminal justice, Administration of 6. Discrimination in criminal justice administration
ISBN 9781590517277; 9781590517284

LC 2015018691

"Beginning in Africa and ending in Europe, 'Incarceration Nations' is a first-person odyssey through the prison systems of the world. Professor . . . and founder of the Prison-to-College-Pipeline, [Baz] Dreisinger looks into the human stories of incarcerated men and women and those who imprison them, creating a jarring, poignant view of a world to which most are denied access, and a rethinking of one of America's most far-reaching global exports: the modern prison complex." (Publisher's note)

"An eye-opening, damning indictment of the American prison system and the way its sins reverberate around the globe." Kirkus

Includes bibliographical references (pages 311-325).

Ferro, Jeffrey

Prisons; Rev. ed; Facts On File, Inc. 2011 312p (Library in a book) $45   **365**

1. Prisons -- United States
ISBN 978-0-8160-8236-0; 978-1-4381-3398-0 ebook

LC 2010-49855

First published 2006

This book "examines the state of U.S. prisons and related issues. It focuses on the development of prisons in the United States and how the competing goals of punishment and rehabilitation have shaped the evolution of criminal correction. An overview presents statistics on U.S. prisons and explores the issues behind those statistics, including racial disparity among prisoners and the causes of recidivism. The financial costs of running prisons and the mixed record of private prisons are examined, and laws and legislation relating to issues of incarceration are reviewed." Publisher's note

Includes bibliographical references

Figes, Orlando, 1959-

Just send me word; a true story of love and survival in the Gulag. Orlando Figes. Metropolitan Books/Henry Holt and Company 2012 333 p.   **365**

1. Romance fiction 2. Political prisoners -- Russia 3. Russia -- History -- 1917-1991, Soviet Union 4. Imprisonment -- Soviet Union 5. Fiancées -- Soviet Union 6. Fiancées -- Soviet Union -- Correspondence 7. Labor camps -- Russia (Federation) -- Pechora (Komi) 8. Political prisoners -- Russia (Federation) -- Pechora (Komi) 9. Political prisoners -- Russia (Federation) -- Pechora (Komi) -- Correspondence
ISBN 0805095225; 9780805095227

LC 2011048355

In this book, "[d]rawing on more than 1,200 letters between Lev and Svetlana 'Sveta' Mishchenko, and interviews with the couple, veteran historian Figes . . . tells their remarkable tale of love and devotion during the worst years of the USSR. Having fallen in love as physics students at Moscow University, they were separated for 13 years: first while Lev seized in WWII, and then after he was sentenced to a Siberian labor camp for the 'crime' of serving as a translator for a German officer while a POW. Lev's letters illustrate the extreme hardships of .the Stalinist camps. . . . Her letters express her extraordinary devotion and determination to visit Lev, which she managed to do four times, despite the long trek, subterfuges, necessary bribes, and dangers involved in the illegal journeys." (Publishers Weekly)

Includes bibliographical references and index

Gessen, Masha

Never remember; searching for Stalin's Gulags in Putin's Russia. by Masha Gessen, photographs by Misha Friedman. Columbia Global Reports 2018 176 p. $27.99   **365**

1. Political prisoners -- Russia 2. Concentration camps -- Russia -- History
ISBN 0997722967; 9780997722963

In this book, author "Masha Gessen and photographer Misha Friedman set out across Russia in search of the memory of the Gulag. They journey from Moscow to Sandarmokh, a forested site of mass executions during [Joseph] Stalin's Great Terror; to the only Gulag camp turned into a museum, outside of the city of Perm in the Urals; and to Kolyma, where prisoners worked in deadly mines in the remote reaches of the Far East." (Publisher's note)

" Friedman's moody, panoramic black-and-white photos of the memorial sites convey a narrative that's fragmented, blurry, and ultimately incomplete, perfectly underscoring Gessen's text. The combination is a powerful meditation on contemporary Russia as seen through its relationship to the past." Pub Wkly

Kizny, Tomasz

Gulag; life and death inside the Soviet concentration camps. Firefly Books 2004 495p il maps $69.95   **365**

1. Convict labor 2. Concentration camps 3. Soviet Union -- Politics and government
ISBN 1-55297-964-4

LC 2005-357207

This book "contains 550 black-and-white photographs of life in the Soviet Gulag. . . . The photos gathered here range from official archival snapshots, showing both inmates and their captors, to scenes of enormous construction projects and snowbound ruins. Kizny has added his own photographs of the abandoned camps or work projects and included a brief history of the camps and personal accounts of survivors. These rare and historically significant photographs can only hint at the appalling horrors committed within the camps, and the importance of the book cannot be overstated." Booklist

Liao Yiwu

For a song and one hundred songs; a poet's journey through a Chinese prison. Liao Yiwu; translated from the Chinese by Wen Huang. Houghton Mifflin Harcourt 2013 432 p. (hardcover) $26   **365**

1. Political prisoners -- China 2. Tiananmen Square Incident, Beijing (China), 1989 -- Poetry 3. Prisoners -- China -- Biography
ISBN 0547892632; 9780547892634

LC 2012019558

In this book, "exiled Chinese poet Liao [Yiwu] . . . recounts . . . his politicization and imprisonment in the wake of the 1989 government crackdown on the democracy movement centered in Beijing's Tiananmen Square." His poem, "Massacre," about the protest and a subsequent film project resulted in his 1990 arrest. The "bulk of the memoir concerns Liao's four-year imprisonment at a series of facilities in the harrowing Chongqing prison system." (Publishers Weekly)

Solzhenitsyn, Aleksandr Isaevich, 1918-2008

★ The **Gulag** Archipelago, 1918-1956 v1; an experiment in literary investigation. [by] Aleksandr I. Solzhenitsyn; translated from the Russian by Thomas P. Whitney; foreword by Anne Applebaum. Harper Perennial Modern Classics 2007 xx, 660p pa $21.95   **365**

    1. Political prisoners 2. Soviet Union -- Politics and government
ISBN 978-0-06-125371-3; 0-06-125371-5
First published 1974
The first volume of the author's three-volume "'literary investigation' of the network of Soviet prison camps as they existed between 1918 and 1956.... A mixture of autobiography, history, and analysis, the relentlessly grim picture of life inside the camps forms the basis for an attack not only on Stalinism and Leninism but also on the whole process of substituting Western rational and secular ideas for Russia's traditional mysticism." Benét's Reader's Ency. 4th edition

★ The **Gulag** Archipelago, 1918-1956 v2; an experiment in literary investigation. [by] Aleksandr I. Solzhenitsyn; translated from the Russian by Thomas P. Whitney; foreword by Anne Applebaum. Harper Perennial Modern Classics 2007 712p il map pa $21.95   **365**

    1. Political prisoners 2. Soviet Union -- Politics and government
ISBN 978-0-06-125372-0; 0-06-125372-3
First published 1975
This second volume of a two-volume series describes "the story of Solzhenitsyn's entrance into the Soviet prison camps, where he would remain for nearly a decade." Publisher's note

★ The **Gulag** Archipelago, 1918-1956 v3; an experiment in literary investigation. [by] Aleksandr I. Solzhenitsyn; translated from the Russian by Harry Willetts; foreword by Anne Applebaum. Harper Perennial Modern Classics 2007 558p il map pa $21.95   **365**

    1. Political prisoners 2. Soviet Union -- Politics and government
ISBN 978-0-06-125373-7; 0-06-125373-1
First published 1978
The final volume of a three-volume series, this book contains the author's "account of resistance within the Soviet labor camps and his own release after eight years." Publisher's note

Thompson, Heather Ann, 1963-

★ **Blood** in the water; the Attica prison uprising of 1971 and its legacy. Heather Ann Thompson. Pantheon 2016 724 p. illustrations (hardback) $35   **365**

    1. Attica Prison 2. Prisoners -- Civil rights 3. Law enforcement -- History 4. Prison riots -- New York (State)
ISBN 0375423222; 9780375423222

                         LC 2016000477
National Book Award Finalist: Nonfiction (2016)
Pulitzer Prize: History (2017)
This book by Heather Ann Thompson discusses the 1971 uprising by inmates at Attica Prison in New York "to protest years of mistreatment. Holding guards and civilian employees hostage, the prisoners negotiated with officials for improved conditions. . . . On September 13, the state abruptly sent hundreds of heavily armed troopers and correction officers to retake the prison by force. Their gunfire killed thirty-nine men . . . [and] wounded more than one hundred others." (Publisher's note)

"Thompson's superb and thorough study serves as a powerful tale of the search for justice in the face of the abuses of institutional power." Pub Wkly
Includes bibliographical references (pages 579-684) and index.

365.34   Institutions by purpose or type of program

Dum, Christopher P.

Exiled in America; life on the margins in a residential motel. Christopher P. Dum. Columbia University Press 2016 320 p. (cloth: alk. paper) $35   **365.34**

    1. Loneliness 2. Sex offenders -- Housing 3. Hotels and motels -- United States 4. Motels -- United States 5. Social isolation -- United States 6. Marginality, Social -- United States 7. Sex offenders -- Housing -- United States
ISBN 9780231176422

                         LC 2016009591
Carnegie Medal Longlist: Nonfiction (2017)
This book in the Studies in Transgression series, by Christopher P. Dum, "paints a portrait of a vibrant community whose members forged identities in response to overwhelming stigma and created meaningful lives despite crushing economic instability. In addition to chronicling daily life at the Boardwalk [motel], Dum follows local neighborhood efforts to shut the establishment down, leading to a wider analysis of legislative attempts to sanitize shared social space." (Publisher's note)
"The author places the painful experiences of these residents in the larger societal context: rising rates of incarceration, foreclosures, evictions, and homelessness have in recent years turned many nonchain motels into shelters for the marginalized." Kirkus
Includes bibliographical references and index

Reed, Austin

The **life** and the adventures of a haunted convict; by Austin Reed; edited by Caleb Smith; with a preface by David W. Blight and Robert B. Stepto. Random House 2016 384 p. (ebook) $54; (hardback) $30   **365.34**

    1. African Americans -- Biography 2. United States -- Social conditions -- 19th century 3. Prisons -- New York (State) -- History -- 19th century 4. United States -- Race relations -- History -- 19th century 5. African American prisoners -- New York (State) -- Biography 6. Reformatories -- New York (State) -- History -- 19th century
ISBN 9780812997101; 9780812997095

                         LC 2015017693
This book, edited by Caleb Smith, presents "the memoir of Austin Reed, a free black man born in the 1820s who spent most of his early life ricocheting between forced labor in prison and forced labor as an indentured servant. Lost for more than one hundred and fifty years, the handwritten document is the first known prison memoir written by an African American." (Publisher's note)
"A moving, significant narrative that affords both an elegantly produced glimpse of 19th-century prison life and a new chapter in African-American history through a convict's eyes." Kirkus
Includes bibliographical references.

365.45   Institutions for political prisoners and related
groups of people

Pitzer, Andrea

One long night; a global history of concentration camps.

Andrea Pitzer. Little, Brown & Co. 2017 x, 466 p.p illustrations, maps (hardcover) $30   **365.45**
1. Concentration camps -- History 2. Detention of persons -- History 3. Concentration camps -- History -- 20th century 4. Detention of persons -- History -- 20th century
ISBN 9780316303606; 9780316303590

LC 2017941135

This book, by Andrea Pitzer, discusses the "history of concentration camps. Beginning with 1890s Cuba, . . . from the Philippines and Southern Africa in the early twentieth century to the Soviet Gulag and detention camps in China and North Korea during the Cold War, camp systems have been used as tools for civilian relocation and political repression. . . . [These] camps have . . . served as brutal and dehumanizing sites that have claimed the lives of millions." (Publisher's note)

"An informative and unsettling survey of the abuses states can inflict on targeted groups." Booklist

Includes bibliographical references (pages 413-451) and index.

365.6   Inmates

Bozella, Dewey, 1959-
Stand Tall; Fighting for My Life, Inside and Outside the Ring. by Dewey Bozella. HarperCollins 2016 256 p. $27.99   **365.6**
1. Actual innocence
ISBN 0062208152; 9780062208156

In this memoir "Dewey Bozella recounts his life and the twenty-six years he spent behind bars for a murder he did not commit. . . . Bozella was wrongfully accused of murdering Emma Crapser, a ninety-two-year-old resident of Poughkeepsie, New York. Sentenced to twenty years to life in prison, Bozella fiercely maintained his innocence throughout his ordeal at Sing Sing, and even refused the prosecutor's offer of instant freedom in exchange for admission of guilt." (Publisher's note)

"His writing is concise, never self-congratulatory or self-pitying, and always graceful." Pub Wkly

365.66   Services to prisoners

Brottman, Mikita
The **Maximum** Security Book Club; Reading Literature in a Men's Prison. by Mikita Brottman. HarperCollins 2016 272 p. $26.99   **365.66**
1. Books and reading 2. Prisoners -- Education
ISBN 0062384333; 9780062384331

LC 2016013355

This book is an "account of the two years literary scholar Mikita Brottman spent reading literature with criminals in a maximum-security men's prison outside Baltimore, and what she learned from them. . . . The book club members struggle with their assigned reading through solitary confinement; on lockdown; in between factory shifts; in the hospital; and in the middle of the chaos of blasting televisions, incessant chatter, and the constant banging of metal doors." (Publisher's note)

"Will not appeal to hard-core law-and-order types, but others will find this a brave and empathetic story of how literature brings light into shadows." Kirkus

366   Secret associations and societies

Ridley, Jasper Godwin
The **Freemasons**; a history of the world's most powerful secret society. [by] Jasper Ridley. Arcade Pub. 2001 357p $25.95; pa $14.95   **366**
1. Freemasons
ISBN 1-55970-601-5; 1-55970-654-6 pa

LC 2001-45745

The author "traces the origins of freemasonry back to the craft guilds in medieval Europe, and then he chronicles their growth and evolution through the modern era. . . . This work of popular history sheds light on a frequently obscure subject." Booklist

Includes bibliographical references

368   Insurance

Boyd, Roddy
Fatal risk; a cautionary tale of AIG's corporate suicide. Wiley 2011 349p   **368**
1. Insurance 2. Financial crises 3. Insurance executives 4. American International Group, Inc.
ISBN 978-0-470-88980-0

LC 2011-01512

"A vivid portrait of the giant insurer at the center of the 2008 financial crisis." Wall Street J

An "inside account of how Maurice 'Hank' Greenberg, the storied combat veteran and driven entrepreneur, took a motley collection of insurance companies and built them into the world's most innovative and daring financial conglomerate—only to see it all crash and burn. Made rich and powerful through Greenberg's iron will and vision, AIG was unprepared for his dramatic ouster in 2005. As the company recovered from a bruising regulatory battle, its management did not understand what risks were being taken onto its once mighty balance sheet in the name of a quick buck. . . . Boyd argues that, contrary to conventional wisdom, Goldman Sachs, and the billions in collateral calls it made on AIG's Financial Products unit, was not the sole cause of the company's downfall. Drawing upon a host of sources—from Hank Greenberg to senior Goldman executives; current and former AIG leaders and board members; to legendary short-seller Jim Chanos and Federal Reserve officials—Boyd makes a . . . case that AIG's collapse was an inside job." Publisher's note

368.009   Insurance – Biography

Benmosche, Robert H., 1944-2015
Good for the money; my fight to pay back America. Bob Benmosche; with Peter Marks and Valerie Hendy. St. Martin's Press 2016 288 p. illustrations (hardback) $27.99   **368.009**
1. Financial crises 2. American International Group, Inc 3. Insurance companies -- United States -- Management 4. Chief executive officers -- United States -- Biography 5. Financial crises -- United States -- History -- 21st century
ISBN 9781250072184

LC 2015044720

This book, by Bob Benmosche, "is an unyielding leader's memoir of a career spent fixing companies through thoughtful, unconventional strategy. With his brash, no-holds-barred approach to the job, Benmosche restored AIG's employee morale and good name. His is a story of perseverance, told with refreshing irreverence in unpretentious terms."

(Publisher's note)

"This is a definite must-read for anyone who wants to learn about the financial crisis, turnarounds in business, or leadership." Pub Wkly

368.38   Health insurance, accident insurance, disability income insurance

Brill, Steven, 1950-

America's bitter pill; money, politics, backroom deals, and the fight to fix our broken healthcare system. Steven Brill. Random House 2015 528 p. (hardback) $28; (paperback) $18   **368.38**

1. Health insurance -- United States 2. Medical policy -- United States 3. Health care reform -- United States 4. United States -- Politics and government -- 2009- 5. United States. Patient Protection and Affordable Care Act

ISBN 9780812996951; 9780812996968; 9780812986686

LC 2014037908

"'America's Bitter Pill' is Steven Brill's much-anticipated, sweeping narrative of how the Affordable Care Act, or Obamacare, was written, how it is being implemented, and, most important, how it is changing--and failing to change--the rampant abuses in the healthcare industry.... It's a fly-on-the-wall account of the fight, amid an onslaught of lobbying, to pass a 961-page law aimed at fixing America's largest, most dysfunctional industry." (Publisher's note)

Brill "breaks down insider language, asks fundamental and surprising questions, and leaves the reader . . . full of more questions yet with a much clearer map of the lines of debate." NYT

Includes bibliographical references (pages and index

Tomes, Nancy

Remaking the American patient; how Madison Avenue and modern medicine turned patients into consumers. Nancy Tomes. University of North Carolina Press 2016 538 p. (cloth: alk. paper) $45   **368.38**

1. Medicine -- United States 2. Medical care -- United States -- History 3. History, 20th Century -- United States 4. Consumer Participation -- history -- United States 5. Delivery of Health Care -- history -- United States 6. Marketing of Health Services -- history -- United States

ISBN 9781469622774

LC 2015029217

In this book in the Studies in Social Medicine series, author Nancy Tomes "questions the popular--and largely unexamined--idea that in order to get good health care, people must learn to shop for it. 'Remaking the American Patient' explores the consequences of the consumer economy and American medicine having come of age at exactly the same time." (Publisher's note)

"This fascinating book with copious notes and an extensive bibliography will intrigue health care professionals and policymakers as well as interested lay readers." LJ

Includes bibliographical references and index

368.4   Government-sponsored insurance

Altman, Nancy J.

The **battle** for Social Security; from FDR's vision to Bush's gamble. Wiley 2005 362p $24.95   **368.4**

1. Social security

ISBN 978-0-471-77172-2; 0-471-77172-4

LC 2005-20700

The author "traces the history of Social Security from its introduction in 1935, and provides a thoughtful, well-researched case against the ... [Bush] administration's efforts to reduce Social Security protection." Booklist

Includes bibliographical references

Frank, Joshua

The **people's** pension; the struggle to defend social security since Reagan. Eric Laursen, Joshua Frank; [edited by] 674-A 23rd Street. AK Press 2012 818 p. ill. (alk. paper) $13.99   **368.4**

1. Privitization 2. Social security 3. United States -- Politics and government -- 2001-

ISBN 9781849351010

LC 2012933068

This book looks at the issue of Social Security in terms of the U.S. 2012 presidential election. In "the aftermath of the debt reduction deal between Barack Obama and congressional Republicans, the 2012 election promises to be a kind of referendum on the size and role of government—including economic support programs like Social Security. . . . Eric Laursen suggests that the only solution for Social Security is taking it out of the government's hands altogether." (Barnes and Noble)

Includes bibliographical references (p. [727]-783) and index.

Social security handbook; overview of social security programs, 2014. by Social Security Administration. Rowman & Littlefield Publishers, Inc. 2014 703 p. $69   **368.4**

1. Social security

ISBN 1598887068; 9781598887068

This book "provides information about Social Security programs and services, and identifies rights and obligations under the Social Security laws. The handbook also contains information about related programs administered by agencies other than the Social Security Administration." (Publisher's note)

Solman, Paul

Get what's yours; the secrets to maxing out your social security. Laurence J. Kotlikoff, Philip Moeller, Paul Solman. Simon & Schuster 2015 288 p. (hardback) $19.99   **368.4**

1. Social security 2. Personal finance 3. Retirement income 4. Social security -- United States 5. Retirement income -- United States

ISBN 1476772290; 9781476772295

LC 2014034384

This book by Laurence J. Kotlikoff, Philip Moeller, and Paul Solman explains "Social Security benefits in an easy to understand and user-friendly style. . . . It explains what to do if you're a retired parent of dependent children, disabled, or an eligible beneficiary who continues to work, and how to plan wisely before retirement. It addresses the tax consequences of your choices, as well as the financial implications for other investments." (Publisher's note)

"This book works as a thorough overview and as a reference for those with specific questions about Social Security. The authors present the information from the unwieldy system clearly but without dumbing it down." LJ

Includes bibliographical references and index

370   Education

Uncle Tom or new Negro; African Americans reflect on Booker T. Washington and Up from slavery one hundred years later. edited by Rebecca Carroll. Broadway Books/Harlem Moon 2006 320p pa $15.95   **370**
1. Slaves 2. Authors 3. Educators 4. African American educators 5. Memoirists 6. Nonfiction writers 7. Tuskegee Institute 8. Civil rights activists 9. African Americans -- Biography
ISBN 0-7679-1955-6; 978-0-7679-1955-5

LC 2005-50161

"This collection of 20 commentaries by contemporary writers offers new perspectives on Booker T. Washington's autobiography and his place in the struggle for racial equality. Among the commentators are Debra Dickerson, Julianne Malveaux, Bill Ethanson, Ronald Walkers, Earl Ofari Hutchinson, and John McWhorter. The book also includes the complete text of Up from Slavery." Booklist

Includes bibliographical references

370.1   Philosophy and theory, education for specific objectives, educational psychology

Dewey, John, 1859-1952
Democracy and education; an introduction to the philosophy of education. Free Press 1997 378p pa $17.95   **370.1**
1. Education -- Philosophy
ISBN 0-684-83631-9; 978-0-684-83631-7
First published 1916 by Macmillan

"The author's aim here is to detect and state the ideas implied in a democratic society and to apply those ideas to the problems of education." Boston Transcr

370.113   Vocational education

Newman, Katherine S., 1953-
Reskilling America; learning to labor in the twenty-first century. Katherine S. Newman, Hella Winston. Metropolitan Books 2016 272 p. (hardback) $28; (ebook) $60   **370.113**
1. Labor policy 2. Skilled labor 3. Vocational education 4. Occupational training 5. Skilled labor -- United States 6. Manpower policy -- United States 7. Vocational education -- United States 8. Occupational training -- United States
ISBN 9781627793285; 9781627793292

LC 2015048810

In this book, authors Katherine S. Newman and Hella Winston "call for a radical reevaluation of the idea of vocational training. . . . The United States can prepare a new, high-performance labor force if we revamp our school system to value industry apprenticeship and rigorous technical education. By doing so, we will not only be able to meet the growing demand for skilled employees in dozens of sectors, . . . we will make the American Dream accessible to all." (Publisher's note)

"A top-notch, highly accessible contribution to the business and popular economics literature." Kirkus

Includes bibliographical references (pages 217-240) and index.

370.15   Educational psychology

Levine, Melvin D.
A **mind** at a time; {by} Mel Levine. Simon & Schuster 2002 352p $26; pa $14   **370.15**
1. Child development 2. Learning disabilities 3. Educational psychology
ISBN 0-7432-0222-8; 0-7432-0223-6 pa

LC 2001-57670

The author discusses "eight areas of learning (the memory system, the language system, the spatial ordering system, the motor system, etc.). He provides chapters describing how each type of learning works and advises parents and teachers on how to help kids struggling in these areas. . . . This is a must-read for parents and educators who want to understand and improve the school lives of children." Publ Wkly

Includes bibliographical references

Schwartz, Daniel L.
The **ABCs** of how we learn; 26 scientifically proven approaches, how they work, and when to use them. Daniel L. Schwartz, Jessica M. Tsang, and Kristen P. Blair. W.W. Norton & Company, Inc. 2016 xvi, 367 p.p illustrations (ebook) $60; (pbk.) $24.95   **370.15**
1. Education 2. Educational psychology 3. Psychology of learning 4. Learning
ISBN 9780393709407; 9780393709261

LC 2015047247

In this book in the Norton Books in Education series, by Daniel L. Schwartz, Jessica M. Tsang, and Kristen P. Blair, "each chapter offers a concise and approachable breakdown of one way people learn, how it works, how we know it works, how and when to use it, and what mistakes to avoid. The book presents learning research in a way that educators can creatively translate into exceptional lessons and classroom practice." (Publisher's note)

Includes bibliographical references and index

370.71   Education

McKeown, Rosalyn
Into the classroom; a practical guide for starting student teaching. Rosalyn McKeown. University of Tennessee Press 2011 xv, 165 p.p (pbk.) $14.95   **370.71**
1. Teaching 2. Student teaching 3. Student teaching -- United States
ISBN 1572338164; 9781572338166

LC 2011011282

This book offers suggestions to those "just starting out in a secondary school classroom. . . . After exploring the pitfalls of inexperience and providing . . . guidance on maintaining order in the classroom, [Rosalyn] McKeown focuses on teaching skills. She advises readers on writing objectives and lesson plans, creating interesting ways to start and end class, introducing variety into the classroom, lecturing, asking meaningful questions, and using visual aids." (Amazon.com)

Includes bibliographical references and index.

370.9   History, geographic treatment, biography

Falk, Beverly
Teaching matters; stories from inside city schools. Bev-

erly Falk and Megan Blumenreich with Adesina Abani ... [et al.] New Press 2012 xii, 196 p.p ill. (paperback) $19.95 **370.9**
1. Teaching 2. Urban schools 3. Education -- Case studies 4. Teachers -- United States -- Case studies 5. Education, Urban -- United States -- Case studies 6. Children of minorities -- Education -- United States -- Case studies
ISBN 1595584900; 9781595584908

LC 2012004564

This book, by Beverly Falk and Megan Blumenreich, discusses inner city public schools. "As public schools become increasingly embattled . . . , the burden of these restrictions has drastically changed the way children are expected to learn. . . . Leading education experts Beverly Falk and Megan Blumenreich provide an enlightening account of what our students really need--and how teachers are stepping up to provide what state standards and political posturing cannot." (Publisher's note)

Includes bibliographical references (p. 189-196)

McCluskey, Audrey Thomas

A **forgotten** sisterhood; pioneering black women educators and activists in the Jim Crow South. Audrey Thomas McCluskey. Rowman & Littlefield 2014 192 p. (cloth: alk. paper) $42 **370.9**
1. African American educators 2. Southern States -- Race relations 3. African Americans -- Education -- History 4. Southern States -- Social conditions 5. Southern States -- Race relations -- History 6. African Americans -- Education -- Southern States 7. Civil rights movements -- Southern States -- History 8. African American women civil rights workers -- Biography 9. African Americans -- Southern States -- Social conditions 10. African American educators -- Southern States -- Biography 11. African Americans -- Segregation -- Southern States -- History 12. African Americans -- Civil rights -- Southern States -- History 13. African American women educators -- Southern States -- Biography
ISBN 9781442211384

LC 2014025293

This book by Audrey Thomas McCluskey reveals how "black activist women Lucy Craft Laney, Mary McLeod Bethune, Charlotte Hawkins Brown, and Nannie Helen Burroughs founded schools aimed at liberating African-American youth from disadvantaged futures in the segregated and decidedly unequal South. . . . These individuals fought discrimination as members of a larger movement . . . [to uplift] future generations through . . . education, social service, and cultural transformation." (Publisher's note)

"McCluskey's well-researched account articulates the importance of this particular movement in education, appropriately and skillfully, to memorialize the four pioneering women at the forefront." Pub Wkly

Includes bibliographical references and index.

Ripley, Amanda

The **smartest** kids in the world; and how they got that way. Amanda Ripley. Simon & Schuster 2013 320 p. $28 **370.9**
1. Foreign students 2. Education -- United States 3. Education -- Poland 4. Education -- Finland 5. Comparative education 6. Education -- Korea (South)
ISBN 1451654421; 9781451654424

LC 2013002021

This book looks at the educational disparities between the U.S. and other world nations. Journalist Amanda Ripley "recounts the experiences of three American teens studying abroad for a year in the education superpowers. Fifteen-year-old Kim raises $10,000 so she can go to high school in Finland; Eric, 18, trades a leafy suburb in Minnesota for a 'city stacked on top of a city' in South Korea; and Tom, 17, leaves Gettysburg, Pa., for Poland." (Publishers Weekly)

Includes bibliographical references and index

370.92 Educators – Biography

Walker, Vanessa Siddle

The **lost** education of Horace Tate; uncovering the hidden heroes who fought for justice in schools. Vanessa Siddle Walker. The New Press 2018 448 p. $32.99 **370.92**
1. Race relations 2. African American educators 3. Segregation in education -- United States
ISBN 1620971054; 9781620971055

This book, by Vanessa Siddle Walker, presents an "account of the devoted black educators who battled southern school segregation and inequality. . . . [It] offers fresh insight into the southern struggle for human rights, revealing little-known accounts of leaders such as W.E.B. Du Bois and James Weldon Johnson, as well as hidden provocateurs like Horace Tate." (Publisher's note)

"Walker's extensively documented work is a much-needed corrective contextualizing the landscape of school desegregation; required reading for those interested in the past, present, and future of education of African American children." Library Journal

371.01 Specific kinds of schools

Paley, Rebecca

The **Bridge** to Brilliance; how one principal in a tough community Is inspiring the world. Nadia Lopez and Rebecca Paley. Penguin Group USA 2016 288 p. (ebook) $65; $26 **371.01**
1. Educators 2. Poor children -- Education
ISBN 9781101980279; 1101980257; 9781101980255

LC 2016287199

In this book, by Nadia Lopez and Rebecca Paley, "in 2010, Nadia Lopez started her middle-grade public school, Mott Hall Bridges Academy, in one of America's poorest communities. . . . Everything was an uphill battle-to get the school approved, to recruit faculty and students, to solve a million new problems every day, from violent crime to vanishing supplies—but Lopez was determined to break the downward spiral that had trapped too many inner-city children." (Publisher's note)

"Filled with narratives about overcoming adversity and of seeing the good where others see only trouble, and success where others see failure, this feel-good story will resonate with just about any reader." LJ

Rhee, Michelle A., 1969-

Radical; fighting to put students first. Michelle Rhee. Harper 2013 304 p. (hardcover) $27.99 **371.01**
1. Education -- United States 2. Education -- Aims and objectives 3. Public schools -- United States 4. Educational change -- United States 5. School improvement programs -- United States 6. Education -- Aims and objectives -- United States
ISBN 0062203983; 9780062203984

LC 2012038474

This book, by education reformer Michelle Rhee, "draws on her own life story and delivers her plan for better American schools. . . . Informing her critique are her . . . experiences in education. . . . Rhee draws on dozens of compelling examples from schools she's worked in and studied, from students who've left behind unspeakable home lives and thrived in the classroom to teachers whose groundbreaking methods have produced unprecedented leaps in student achievement." (Publisher's note)

371.1   Schools and their activities

Kozol, Jonathan

Letters to a young teacher. Crown Publishers 2007 288p hardcover o.p. pa $14   **371.1**

1. Teaching

ISBN 978-0-307-39371-5; 0-307-39371-2; 978-0-307-39372-2 pa; 0-307-39372-0 pa

LC 2007-2689

"The book will delight and encourage first-year (or for that matter, 40th-year) teachers who need Kozol's reminders of the ways that their beautiful profession can bring joy and beauty, mystery and mischievous delight into the hearts of little people in their years of greatest curiosity." Publ Wkly

Includes bibliographical references

Parini, Jay

The **art** of teaching. Oxford University Press 2005 160p $17.95   **371.1**

1. Teaching 2. Vocational guidance

ISBN 0-19-516969-7

LC 2004-5443

The author offers "musings about teaching's demands and what it takes to not lose one's other, creative self while meeting those demands in this memoir-cum-advice book for novice instructors. . . . This warm guide should inform, entertain, and inspire young teachers as they seek to 'waken a student to his or her potential.'" Publ Wkly

371.102   Teaching

Espinoza, Roberta

Pivotal moments; how educators can put all students on the path to college. Roberta Espinoza. Harvard Education Press 2011 200 p. (pbk.) $26.95   **371.102**

1. Higher education

ISBN 1612501192; 9781612501192; 9781612501208

LC 2011937500

In this book, "sociologist Roberta Espinoza introduces the idea of pivotal moments[:] interventions that point the way toward college, particularly for students from working-class or ethnic minority backgrounds. These pivotal encounters and the relationships that spring from them can help students accumulate procedural knowledge about attending college (cultural capital) and interpersonal support (social capital)." (Amazon.com)

Includes bibliographical references and index.

371.14   Organization of teaching force

Baker, Nicholson, 1957-

Substitute. Penguin Group USA 2016 736 p. (ebook) $65; $30   **371.14**

1. Teachers 2. Teaching 3. Education -- United States

ISBN 9780399576379; 0399160981; 9780399160981

LC 2016030181

In this book, "Nicholson Baker became an on-call substitute teacher in a Maine public school district. He awoke to the dispatcher's five-forty a.m. phone call and headed to one of several nearby schools; when he got there, he did his best to follow lesson plans and help his students get something done. What emerges from Baker's experience is a complex, often touching deconstruction of public schooling in America." (Pub-

lisher's note) Also

"An affecting (long-exposure) snapshot revealing real-life concerns." Kirkus

Includes bibliographical references and index.

371.192   Parent-school relations

Bauer, Susan Wise

Rethinking school; how to take charge of your child's education. Susan Wise Bauer. W W Norton & Co Inc 2018 xiv, 264 p.p (hardcover) $25.95   **371.192**

1. Home schooling 2. Education -- Parent participation 3. Academic achievement

ISBN 9780393285963; 9780393285970; 0393285960

LC 2017051513

In this book, author Susan Wise Bauer, "teaches parents how to flex the K–12 system, rather than the child. She closely analyzes the traditional school structure, gives trenchant criticisms of its weaknesses, and offers a wealth of advice for parents of children whose difficulties may stem from struggling with learning differences, maturity differences, toxic classroom environments, and even from giftedness." (Publisher's note)

"Bauer's guide to the various options available to struggling kids, inside and outside the educational system, will be both comforting and instructive to their parents." Pub Wkly

Includes bibliographical references and index.

371.2   School administration; administration of student academic activities

Aronica, Lou

Creative schools; the grassroots revolution that's transforming education. Ken Robinson and Lou Aronica. Viking 2015 292 p. illustrations $27.95   **371.2**

1. Creative ability 2. Creative thinking 3. Educational change 4. Education -- United States 5. Educational change -- United States 6. School improvement programs -- United States 7. Creative ability -- Study and teaching -- United States 8. Creative thinking -- Study and teaching -- United States

ISBN 0670016713; 9780670016716

LC 2015001098

This book, by Ken Robinson and Lou Aronica, is a "reappraisal of how to educate our children and young people. . . . [Robinson] argues for an end to our outmoded industrial educational system and proposes a highly personalized, organic approach that draws on today¿s unprecedented technological and professional resources to engage all students, develop their love of learning, and enable them to face the real challenges of the twenty-first century." (Publisher's note)

"For readers who are ardent about changing education for the better, believing that they can be part of the forces that will revolutionize the future." LJ

Includes bibliographical references and index

Russakoff, Dale

The **prize**; who's in charge of America's schools? Dale Russakoff. Houghton Mifflin Harcourt 2015 246 p. (hardback) $27   **371.2**

1. Educational change 2. Education -- Government policy 3. Public schools -- United States 4. Education and state -- United States -- History 5. Education and state -- New Jersey 6. Public

schools -- New Jersey -- Newark 7. Educational change -- New Jersey -- Newark 8. Education -- Political aspects -- New Jersey -- Newark
ISBN 9780547840055

LC 2015017454

In this book, by Dale Russakoff, "Mark Zuckerberg pledged $100 million to transform Newark's public schools. . . . Then Newark mayor Cory Booker teamed with Governor Chris Christie to turn around one of the most troubled urban school districts in the nation, favoring the creation of charter schools. It would mean massive reform of the way teachers were paid, rewarded, or let go, with accountability tied to student test scores. . . . But along the way, the plan ran into massive resistance." (Booklist)

"An absorbing entry into the burgeoning genre about necessary education reforms." Kirkus

Includes bibliographical references and index

371.26   Examinations and tests; academic prognosis and placement

More Than a Score; The New Uprising Against High-stakes Testing. edited by Jess Hagopian. Haymarket Books 2014 302 p. illustrations $18   **371.26**
1. Educational change 2. Educational tests and measurements
ISBN 1608463923; 9781608463923

This book, edited by Jesse Hagopian, is a " collection of essays, poems, speeches, and interviews--accounts of personal courage and trenchant insights--from frontline fighters who are defying the corporate education reformers, often at great personal and professional risk, and fueling a national movement to reclaim and transform public education." (Publisher's note)

"An array of outraged, insightful, and inspiring selections, this necessary collection should be required reading for educators, parents, and students affected by unremitting corporate education strategies." Booklist

Reese, William J.
Testing wars in the public schools; a forgotten history. William J. Reese. Harvard University Press 2013 298 p. $45   **371.26**
1. Public schools -- United States 2. Educational tests and measurements 3. Public schools -- United States -- History -- 19th century 4. Educational tests and measurements -- United States -- History -- 19th century
ISBN 0674073045; 9780674073043

LC 2012033665

Author William J. Reese provides an "examination of the roots of the testing culture in American education and the ramifications for administrators, teachers, and students. Reese organizes the book into six chapters, including those that concentrate upon the origins of large-scale testing, the reform-minded reasons for using such instruments, the procedures by which testing was implemented, the effects of testing, how the content was selected, and how the culture of testing evolved." (Choice)

Includes bibliographical references and index

371.3   Methods of instruction and study

Jackson, Rebecca
The learning habit; a groundbreaking approach to homework and parenting that helps our children succeed in school and life. Stephanie Donaldson-Pressman, Rebecca Jackson, Robert Pressman. Perigee Trade 2014 320 p. illustrations (paperback) $17   **371.3**
1. Homework 2. Family life 3. Psychology of learning 4. Families 5. Parenting 6. Study skills
ISBN 0399167110; 9780399167119

LC 2014011124

Written by Stephanie Donaldson-Pressman, Rebecca Jackson, and Robert Pressman, this book "presents new solutions based on the largest study of family routines ever conducted. 'The Learning Habit' offers a blueprint for navigating the maze of homework, media use, and . . . everyday stress . . .; turning those 'stress times' into opportunities to develop . . . skills including concentration and focus, time management, decision-making, goal-setting, and self-reliance." (Publisher's note)

"The book lists eight essential skill sets that parents should help children cultivate, from time management to fostering self-reliance. An especially useful chapter focuses on ways to help children concentrate." Pub Wkly

Includes bibliographical references and index

371.33   Teaching aids, equipment, materials

Miles, Matt
★ **Screen** schooled; two veteran teachers expose how technology overuse is making our kids dumber. Joe Clement and Matt Miles. Chicago Review Press 2017 xi, 260 p.p (paperback) $18.99   **371.332**
1. Computers and children 2. Educational technology 3. Technology -- Social aspects 4. Education -- Effect of technological innovations on
ISBN 9781613739518

LC 2017027686

In this book, authors Joe Clement and Matt Miles "show how screen saturation at home and school has created a wide range of cognitive and social deficits in our young people. They lift the veil on what's really going on in schools: teachers who are often powerless to curb cell phone distractions; zoned-out kids who act helpless and are unfocused, unprepared, and unsocial; administrators who are influenced by questionable science sponsored by corporate technology purveyors." (Publisher's note)

Includes bibliographical references (pages 239-252) and index.

Vander Ark, Tom, 1959-
Getting smart; how digital learning is changing the world. Tom Vander Ark; foreword by Bob Wise. 1st ed. Jossey-Bass 2011 xxi, 213 p.p $26.95   **371.33**
1. Internet in education 2. Computer-assisted instruction 3. Education -- Experimental methods 4. Blended learning -- United States 5. Internet in education -- United States 6. Computer-assisted instruction -- United States
ISBN 1118007239; 9781118007235

LC 2011024028

This book, by Tom Vander Ark, "examines the various facets of educational innovation in the United States and abroad. Vander Ark . . . makes a . . . case for a new model of education that blends online and on-site learning. [He] explains that through the use of technology it is now possible to provide 24/7 access to learning and increase student engagement. . . . By customizing learning . . . each hour of learning can become more effective for all students at all levels." (Publisher's note)

Includes bibliographical references and index

371.4   Student guidance and counseling

Morgan, Genevieve

Undecided; navigating life and learning after high school. Genevieve Morgan. Zest Books 2014 256 p. $14.99   **371.4**

1. College choice 2. Vocational guidance 3. Life skills -- Handbooks, manuals, etc.

ISBN 1936976323; 9781936976324

LC 2013951198

"This comprehensive handbook outlines the different options available to teens after high school and provides suggestions on how to follow each path. . . . It covers everything from SAT preparation and personal statements to trade school pros and cons and advice on how to prepare for life in the military. Full of checklists, anecdotes, brainstorming activities, and journal exercises, 'Undecided' leaves no stone unturned and no option unconsidered." (Publisher's note)

"A helpful guide full of good, sensible advice to teens feeling overwhelmed by the prospect of major life transitions." Kirkus

Includes bibliographical references and index

371.5   School discipline and related activities

Bully; an action plan for teachers and parents to combat the bullying crisis. edited by Lee Hirsch and Cynthia Lowen; with Dina Santorelli. Perseus Books Group 2012 viii, 295 p.p ill. $15.99   **371.5**

1. Bullies 2. Bullying 3. Bullying -- Prevention 4. Cyberbullying -- Prevention 5. Bullying in schools -- Prevention

ISBN 1602861846; 1602861854; 9781602861848; 9781602861855

LC 2012289039

"This companion book to the documentary film Bully was edited by filmmaker [Lee]Hirsch and writer/producer [Cynthia] Lowen, with contributing chapters by a number of celebrities, authors, experts, government officials, and educators. Part homage to the film, part resource, the book interweaves the stories of children who have been bullied with practical information and advice for parents and other readers." (Publishers Weekly)

Includes bibliographical references (p. 281-289) and index

371.7   Student welfare

Fisher, Robin Gaby

Choosing hope; moving forward from life's darkest hours. Kaitlin Roig-DeBellis with Robin Gaby Fisher. G. P. Putnam's Sons, an imprint of Penguin Group (USA) 2015 272 p. $26.95   **371.7**

1. Hope 2. School shootings

ISBN 0399174451; 9780399174452

LC 2015015834

This book, by Kaitlin Roig-DeBellis with Robin Gaby Fisher, is the memoir of "the first-grade teacher at Sandy Hook Elementary School who saved her entire class of fifteen six- and-seven-year-olds from the tragic events that took place on December 14, 2012." In it the author describes the events of the tragedy along with the emotional struggles which followed it. (Publisher's note)

"Though it may strike some readers as Pollyannaish, the author's sunny optimism about the teaching profession is sincere. Her account of the shooting, her struggle to keep despair at bay in both herself and her students, and her ultimate triumph as a survivor seeking to make a differ-

ence help balance the book and redeem it from excessive sentimentality. A flawed but still courageous and inspiring book from a genuine hero." Kirkus

Grigoriadis, Vanessa

Blurred lines; rethinking sex, power, and consent on campus. Vanessa Grigoriadis. Houghton Mifflin Harcourt 2017 332 p. (hardback) $28   **371.7**

1. College students -- Sexual behavior

ISBN 9781328511935; 9780544702554

LC 2017297003

This book, by Vanessa Grigoriadis, "presents a host of new truths. She reveals which times and settings are most dangerous for women (for instance, beware the 'red zone'); she demystifies the welter of conflicting statistics about the prevalence of campus rape; she makes a strong case that not all 'sexual assault' is equivalent; and she offers convincing if controversial advice on how schools, students, and parents can make college a safer, richer experience." (Publisher's note)

"Grigoriadis adds context to the often-polarizing topics with numerous first-person accounts. Her view that 'we, as a society, are terrified to look at boys as boys rather than men and give them a break as such' seems to make excuses for criminal behavior. However, the breadth of her research, including her discussion of how university administrators deal with rape allegations and her exploration of toxic gender roles and stereotypes, are reason enough to pick up this book." PW.

Includes bibliographical references (pages 297-321) and index.

371.8   Students

Hechinger, John

★ **True** gentlemen; the broken pledge of America's fraternities. John Hechinger. PublicAffairs 2017 vii, 306 p.p (hardback) $28   **371.8**

1. Hazing 2. Fraternities and sororities 3. College students -- Alcohol use 4. Sigma Alpha Epsilon 5. Hazing -- United States 6. Misogyny -- United States 7. Greek letter societies -- United States 8. Racism in higher education -- United States 9. College students -- Alcohol use -- United States 10. Male college students -- United States -- Conduct of life

ISBN 9781610399401; 9781610396820

LC 2017008179

In this book, author John Hechinger "embarks on a deep investigation of [Sigma Alpha Epsilon] and fraternity culture generally, exposing the vast gulf between its founding ideals and the realities of its impact on colleges and the world at large. He shows how national fraternities are reacting to a slowly dawning new reality, and asks what the rest of us should do about it." (Publisher's note)

"A highly disquieting but important investigation of one of the most influential subcultures in American higher education." Kirkus

Includes bibliographical references (pages 259-286) and index.

371.82   Specific groups of students; schools for specific groups of students

Cahill, Sean

LGBT youth in America's schools; Jason Cianciotto and Sean Cahill. The University of Michigan Press 2012 236 p. (pbk.: alk. paper) $30   **371.82**

1. Bullies 2. Gay youth 3. LGBT people 4. Discrimination 5. Schools -- Administration 6. Gay students -- United States

7. Sexual minorities -- Education 8. Lesbian students -- United States 9. Bisexual students -- United States 10. Homosexuality and education -- United States 11. Transgender youth -- Education -- United States
ISBN 0472031406; 9780472028320; 9780472031405; 9780472118229

LC 2011045478

In this book, "[Jason] Cianciotto and [Sean] Cahill use statistics and real-life anecdotes to show the pervasiveness of gender- and sexual orientation-based harassment in American schools, and argue for institutional reform and policy changes. . . . [R]esearch shows that . . . more young people are coming out . . . while still technically a minor, and thus subject to the rules of their educational institutions, and increasingly the abuse of their peers, teachers, and school administrators." (Publishers Weekly)

Includes bibliographical references and index.

Kuo, Michelle

Reading with Patrick; a teacher, a student, and a life-changing friendship. Michelle Kuo. Random House 2017 xxi, 296 p.p (hardcover) $27   **371.826**
1. Race relations 2. Prisoners -- Education 3. Teacher-student relationship 4. Race discrimination -- United States 5. United States -- Race relations 6. Alternative schools -- United States 7. Prisoners -- Education -- United States 8. Prisoners -- Books and reading -- United States
ISBN 9780812997323; 9780812997316; 9780812987140

LC 2016036759

This book, by Michelle Kuo, is "a memoir of race, inequality, and the power of literature told through the life-changing friendship between an idealistic young teacher and her gifted student, jailed for murder in the Mississippi Delta. . . . Convinced she can make a difference in the lives of her teenaged students, Michelle Kuo puts her heart into her work. . . . Though Michelle loses some students to truancy and even gun violence, she is inspired by some such as Patrick." (Publisher's note)

"Honest, thoughtful, and humane, Kuo's book is not only a testament to a remarkable friendship, but a must-read for anyone interested in social justice and race in America. Thoughtfully provocative reading." Kirkus

Perez, William

We are Americans; undocumented students pursuing the American dream. foreword by Daniel Solorzano. Stylus 2009 xxxiv, 161p $70; pa $22.50   **371.82**
1. Unauthorized immigrants 2. Discrimination in education 3. Illegal aliens 4. United States -- Immigration and emigration
ISBN 978-1-57922-375-5; 978-1-57922-376-2 pa

LC 2009-26206

The author "plumbs the stories of students living with the constant threat of deportation for an answer to the question, 'What does it mean to be an American?' Raised in this country by parents who gained access illegally, the 16 high school, college and postgraduate students profiled here (standing in for 65,000 nationwide) have each embraced our language, culture and collective dream, but are denied pathways to success. . . . No matter what one's position is on legalizing immigrants, this collection of inspiring, heartbreaking stories puts a number of unforgettable faces to the issue, making it impossible to defend any one side in easy terms or generalities." Publ Wkly

Includes bibliographical references

371.9 Special education

Chura, David

I don't wish nobody to have a life like mine; tales of kids in adult lockup. Beacon Press 2010 xxiii, 216p $24.95; pa $14   **371.9**
1. Juvenile delinquency 2. Prisoners -- Education
ISBN 978-0-8070-0064-9; 978-0-8070-0123-3 pa

LC 2009027664

Shares the experiences of teenagers incarcerated in an adult prison in New York, as well as those of the men and women hired to teach and watch over them.

"Chura offers a compelling personal look at the failings of the juvenile justice system." Booklist

Flink, David

Thinking Differently; An Inspiring Guide for Parents of Children With Learning Disabilities. David Flink. HarperCollins 2014 320 p. illustrations $15.99   **371.9**
1. Learning disabilities 2. Students with disabilities
ISBN 0062225936; 9780062225931

This book by David Flink "enlarges our understanding of the learning process and offers powerful, innovative strategies for parenting, teaching, and supporting the 20 percent of students with learning disabilities. . . . Focusing on how to arm students who think and learn differently with essential skills, including meta-cognition and self-advocacy, Flink offers real, hard advice, providing the tools to address specific problems they face." (Publisher's note)

Includes bibliographical references and index

Kozol, Jonathan, 1936-

Savage inequalities; children in America's schools. HarperPerennial 1992 261p pa $14.95   **371.9**
1. Public schools 2. Segregation in education 3. Children with social disabilities
ISBN 0-06-097499-0; 978-0-06-097499-2

First published 1991 by Crown

"Jonathan Kozol has written an impassioned book, laced with anger and indignation, about how our public education system scorns so many of our children. 'Savage Inequalities' is also an important book, and warrants widespread attention" N Y Times Book Rev

Includes bibliographical references

Salzman, Mark

True notebooks. Alfred A. Knopf 2003 330p hardcover o.p. pa $13.95   **371.9**
1. Creative writing 2. Juvenile delinquency
ISBN 0-375-41308-1; 0-375-72761-2 pa

LC 2002-43435

"While teaching writing to 17-year-olds detained in Los Angeles Central Juvenile Hall, Salzman found himself surprised by the boys' talent. The teens' heartwarming, funny voices are included in his irresistible, provocative memoir." Booklist

Siegel, Lawrence M.

The **complete** IEP guide; how to advocate for your special ed child. 7th ed.; Nolo 2011 380p pa $34.99   **371.9**
1. Special education 2. Children with disabilities 3. Individualized instruction 4. Individuals with Disabilities Education Act
ISBN 978-1-4133-1313-0 pa; 1-4133-1313-2 pa; 978-1-4133-1336-9 ebook; 1-4133-1336-1 ebook

LC 2010-38386

First published 1999. Frequently revised

This legal guide offer strategies and advice for parents of children who need an individualized education program. Includes information on special education laws and eligibility rules, how to draw up a blueprint of a child's educational needs, and what to look for in a special education program.

371.91   Students with physical disabilities

Hauser, Peter C.

★ **How** deaf children learn; what parents and teachers need to know. Marc Marschark Peter C. Hauser. Oxford University Press 2012 156 p. $26.50   **371.91**
   1. Teaching 2. Deaf children 3. Elementary education 4. Deaf -- Education 5. Deaf -- Means of communication
   ISBN 0195389751; 9780195389753
                                                      LC 2011012553
This book is "about teaching deaf children. Written primarily for parents and teachers of deaf or hard-of-hearing children, this work covers general information about their education, gives insights into their cognitive development, and provides steps to their school success. The authors also discuss issues such as the value of cochlear implants and the debate over signing vs. speaking." (Library Journal)

Includes bibliographical references.

371.93   Delinquent and problem students

Shalaby, Carla

Troublemakers; lessons in freedom from young children at school. Carla Shalaby. The New Press 2017 xl, 196 p.p illustrations (hardcover) $25.95   **371.93**
   1. School discipline 2. Classroom management 3. Emotionally disturbed children 4. Behavior disorders in children 5. Inclusive education -- United States
   ISBN 1620972360; 9781620972373; 9781620972366
                                                      LC 2016048199
In this book, author Carla Shalaby, "a former elementary school teacher, explores the everyday lives of four young 'troublemakers,' challenging the ways we identify and understand so-called problem children. . . . Through delicately crafted portraits of these memorable children--Zora, Lucas, Sean, and Marcus--'Troublemakers' allows us to see school through the eyes of those who know firsthand what it means to be labeled a problem." (Publisher's note)

"Teachers and noneducators alike will appreciate Shalaby's sensitive reorientation of the idea of troublemakers." Booklist

Includes bibliographical references.

371.95   Gifted students

Hulbert, Ann

Off the charts; the hidden lives and lessons of American child prodigies. by Ann Hulbert. Alfred A. Knopf 2018 xviii, 372 p.p illustrations (hardcover) $27.95   **371.95**
   1. Gifted people 2. Gifted children 3. Gifted children -- United States
   ISBN 9781101947302; 9781101947296
                                                      LC 2017003438
This book, by by Ann Hulbert, "examines the lives of children whose rare accomplishments have raised hopes about untapped human potential and questions about how best to nurture it. She probes the changing role of parents and teachers, as well as of psychologists and a curious press. Above all, she delves into the feelings of the prodigies themselves." (Publisher's note)

"In this beautifully written, thoroughly reported look at young 'geniuses,' Hulbert . . . poses fascinating questions about the roles of both genetics and pushy parents." Booklist

Includes bibliographical references and index

372.1   Organization and activities in primary education

Tough, Paul

Helping Children Succeed; What Works and Why. by Paul Tough. Houghton Mifflin Harcourt 2016 144 p. $18.99 **372.1**
   1. Parenting 2. Child rearing 3. Child development
   ISBN 0544935284; 9780544935280
In this book, author Paul Tough "takes on . . . pressing questions: What does growing up in poverty do to children's mental and physical development? How does adversity at home affect their success in the classroom, from preschool to high school? And what practical steps can the adults who are responsible for them—from parents and teachers to policy makers and philanthropists—take to improve their chances for a positive future?" (Publisher's note)

"Tough's research demonstrates that all children have the capacity for self-control, grit, and success if given the right tools to work with from birth. Informative and effective methods to help children overcome issues and thrive at home and in school." Kirkus

372.133   Instructional materials -- Primary education

Lambert, Megan Dowd

Reading picture books with children; how to shake up storytime and get kids talking about what they see. Megan Dowd Lambert in association with the Eric Carle Museum of Picture Book Art. Charlesbridge 2015 176 p. color illustrations (reinforced for library use) $21.95; (ebook) $64.99   **372.133**
   1. Storytelling 2. Language arts 3. Picture books for children 4. School children -- Books and reading 5. Picture books for children -- Educational aspects
   ISBN 9781580896627; 9781607346951
                                                      LC 2014010501
This book, by Megan Dowd Lambert, is a "a practical guide for reshaping storytime and getting kids to think with their eyes. Traditional storytime often offers a passive experience for kids, but the Whole Book approach asks the youngest of readers to ponder all aspects of a picture book and to use their critical thinking skills." (Publisher's note)

"The author's storytime anecdotes are funny, touching, and ultimately illuminating, highlighting how this approach can open new avenues to explore with children." SLJ

372.21   Preschool education

Christakis, Erika

The **Importance** of Being Little; What Preschoolers Really Need from Grownups. by Erika Christakis. Penguin Group USA 2016 400 p. $28   **372.21**
   1. Children 2. Parenting 3. Preschool education
   ISBN 0525429077; 9780525429074
In this book, author Erika Christakis "explains what it's like to be

a young child in America today. . . . She offers real-life solutions to real-life issues, with nuance and direction that takes us far beyond the usual prescriptions for fewer tests, more play. She looks at children's use of language, their artistic expressions, the way their imaginations grow, and how they build deep emotional bonds to stretch the boundaries of their small worlds." (Publisher's note)

"A deep, provocative analysis of the current modes of teaching pre-school e rs and what should be changed to create a more effective learning environment for everyone." Kirkus

Includes bibliographical references (pages [305]-364) and index.

Tough, Paul

★ **How** children succeed; grit, curiosity, and the hidden power of character. Paul Tough. Houghton Mifflin Harcourt 2012 231 p. $27.00   **372.21**
    1. Rich 2. Equality 3. Social classes 4. Poor -- United States 5. Children -- United States 6. Early childhood education -- United States 7. Cognitive styles in children -- United States
ISBN 0547564651; 9780547564654

                   LC 2012019000

In this book Paul Tough "argues that non-cognitive skills (persistence, self-control, curiosity, conscientiousness, grit and self-confidence) are the most critical to success in school and life. . . . When policymakers favor the belief that disadvantaged kids have insufficient cognitive training, Tough finds that a new generation of researchers are questioning the cognitive hypothesis." (Kirkus Reviews)

"Well-written and bursting with ideas." Kirkus

Includes bibliographical references and index

372.4   Reading

Fertig, Beth

Why cant U teach me 2 read? three students and a mayor put our schools to the test. Farrar, Straus and Giroux 2009 354p $27   **372.4**
    1. Reading disability 2. Students with disabilities 3. Reading -- Remedial teaching 4. New York (N.Y.) -- Board of Education
ISBN 978-0-374-29905-7; 0-374-29905-6

                   LC 2009-11520

This is "an overall excellent, thoroughly grounding survey of the state of literacy and education." Publ Wkly

Includes bibliographical references

Grover, Sharon

Listening to learn; audiobooks supporting literacy. by Sharon Grover and Lizette D. Hannegan. American Library Association 2011 xi, 188 p.p (alk. paper) $45   **372.4**
    1. Literacy 2. Audiobooks 3. Educational technology 4. Reading -- United States 5. Children -- Books and reading 6. Libraries -- Special collections -- Audiobooks 7. Literacy -- Study and teaching -- United States 8. School librarian participation in curriculum planning
ISBN 0838911072; 9780838911075

                   LC 2011041814

Authors Sharon Grover and Lizette D. Hannegan "make the case that audiobooks not only present excellent opportunities to engage the attention of young people but also advance literacy. 'Listening to Learn' connects audiobooks with K-12 curricula and demonstrates how the format can support national learning standards and literacy skills." (Publisher's note)

"This informative resource establishes the literacy benefits of au-

diobooks as an alternate reading delivery method...Discussions of audiobook formats and recommended sources for building an audiobook collection are also included. The authors provide a collaborative resource that would benefit a classroom, library, or home setting." (Library Media Connection)

Includes bibliographical references (p. 175-178) and index

372.5   The arts

Art and social justice education; culture as commons. edited by Therese Quinn, John Ploof, and Lisa Hochtritt. Routledge 2012 xxiii, 201 p.p ill. (some col.)   **372.5**
    1. Culture 2. Educators 3. Education -- Curricula 4. Arts -- Study and teaching 5. Art in education -- Social aspects 6. Social justice -- Study and teaching 7. Teaching -- Social aspects -- United States 8. Education -- Social aspects -- United States
ISBN 0415879078; 9780203852477; 9780415879064; 9780415879071

                   LC 2011027006

Editor Therese Quinn "offers inspiration and tools for educators to craft critical, meaningful, and transformative arts education curriculum and arts integration projects. The images, descriptive texts, essays, and resources are grounded within a clear social justice framework and linked to ideas about culture . . . Proposing that art can contribute in a wide range of ways to the work of envisioning and making a more just world, this imaginative . . . sourcebook of contemporary artists' works and education resources advances the field of arts education." (Amazon)

Includes bibliographical references and index

372.6   Language arts (Communication skills)

Maguire, James

American bee; the National Spelling Bee and the culture of word nerds: the lives of five top spellers as they compete for glory and fame. Rodale 2006 371p $24.95   **372.6**
    1. Spelling bees 2. English language -- Spelling
ISBN 978-1-59486-214-4; 1-59486-214-1

                   LC 2005-37443

"From the nail-biting denouement of the 2004 Bee, Maguire . . . moves on to brief sketches of some past winners and then takes an informative and wryly humorous look at the English language itself and the evolution of the American spelling bee from Puritan pastime to major media event." Libr J

Includes bibliographical references

373   Secondary education

Klebold, Sue

A **mother's** reckoning; living in the aftermath of tragedy. Sue Klebold. Crown 2016 272 p. illustrations (hardcover) $28; (ebook) $65   **373**
    1. Columbine High School (Littleton, Colo.) 2. Columbine High School Massacre, Littleton, Colo., 1999 3. School shootings -- Colorado -- Littleton 4. Mothers -- Colorado -- Littleton -- Biography
ISBN 9781101902752; 9781101902769

                   LC 2015018513

This memoir by Sue Klebold, mother of mass murderer Dylan Klebold of the Columbine High School massacre, chronicles "her journey as a mother trying to come to terms with the incomprehensible. In the hope that the insights . . . she has gained may help other families recognize when a child is in distress, she tells her story in full, drawing upon her personal journals, the videos and writings that Dylan left behind, and on . . . interviews with mental health experts." (Publisher's note)

"Klebold's painful memoir unfolds with more sorrow than drama; readers will be left with the sense that even the 'best' mother cannot know what her child may be feeling or thinking." Booklist

Includes bibliographical references (pages 285-292) and index.

The official guide to the HiSET exam; Educational Testing Service. McGraw-Hill 2016 768 p. illustrations (paperback) $23   **373**
1. Examinations -- Study guides 2. High school equivalency examinations
ISBN 1259640795; 9781259640797

This resource in the Official Guide to the Hiset Exam series from Educational Testing Service "shows you exactly what the real exam is like. You'll learn how the test is structured, which topics are tested, and how to approach specific HiSET questions, so there will be no surprises on test day. You'll also get HiSET-style exercises, review material, scoring information, and proven test-taking strategies." (Publisher's note)

373.1   Organization and activities in secondary education

Keizer, Garret
Getting Schooled; The Reeducation of an American Teacher. Garret Keizer. Henry Holt & Co 2014 320 p. $27   **373.1**
1. Teachers 2. Teaching 3. High schools 4. Rural schools 5. Public schools -- Vermont -- Case studies 6. High school teaching -- Vermont -- Case studies 7. High school teachers -- Professional relationships -- Vermont -- Case studies
ISBN 0805096434; 9780805096439
                 LC 2013042594

In this book, "teacher and writer Garret Keizer takes us to school--literally--in this arresting account of his return to the same rural Vermont high school where he taught fourteen years ago. Much has changed since then--a former student is his principal, standardized testing is the reigning god, and smoking in the boys' room has been supplanted by texting in the boys' room." (Publisher's note)

"[A]t once a sympathetic portrait of a school, a searing indictment of a culture that uses working-class children as cannon fodder, and, unexpectedly, a page-turner." Pub Wkly

Thorpe, Helen
The **newcomers**; finding refuge, friendship, and hope in an American classroom. Helen Thorpe. Simon & Schuster 2017 416 p. $28   **373.182**
1. Americanization 2. Multicultural education 3. English as a second language 4. Immigrants -- Colorado -- Denver 5. English language -- Study and teaching
ISBN 1501159097; 9781501159091
                 LC 2018286419

This book, by Helen Thorpe, "follows the lives of 22 immigrant teenagers throughout the course of the 2015-2016 school year as they land at South High School in Denver, Colorado, in an English Language Acquisition class created specifically for them. Speaking no English, unfamiliar with American culture, their stories are poignant and remarkable as they face the enormous challenge of adapting. These newcomers . . . come from nations convulsed by drought or famine or war." (Publisher's note)

373.22   Private and public secondary schools

Brick, Michael
Saving the school; the true story of a principal, a teacher, a coach, a bunch of kids, and a year in the crosshairs of education reform. Michael Brick. Penguin Press 2012 288 p. (hardback) $25.95   **373.22**
1. High schools 2. Schools -- Administration 3. School superintendents and principals 4. John H. Reagan High School (Austin, Tex.) 5. School improvement programs -- Texas -- Austin
ISBN 159420344X; 9781594203442
                 LC 2011050569

This book presents an "account of a troubled Austin, Texas, school that endured a year of tough medicine while facing shutdown. . . . When Reagan was given one more chance to bring up test scores or face closure as part of the national get-tough approach to school reform headed by the new president, . . . [Michael] Brick immersed himself in the lives of the teachers and students. . . . He focuses especially on . . . the school's principal, Anabel Garza." (Kirkus Reviews)

373.236   Lower level

Haddad, Douglas
The **ultimate** guide to raising teens and tweens; Strategies for unlocking your child's full potential. Douglas Haddad. Rowman & Littlefield 2016 286 p. (cloth: alk. paper) $18.95; (ebook) $23.95   **373.236**
1. Parenting 2. Teenagers 3. Parent-child relationship 4. Home and school 5. Parent and child 6. Parent and teenager 7. Education -- Parent participation
ISBN 9781442256958; 9781442256965
                 LC 2016025359

This book, by Douglas Haddad, "offers a step-by-step plan for raising your adolescent through this tumultuous time. . . . Haddad provides specific, proven tools for you to help your child become a problem solver and grow to be smart, successful, and self-disciplined." (Publisher's note)

"This is a crucial, thoughtful guide that will aid any adults with responsibility for mentoring children between 10 and 19." Pub Wkly

Includes bibliographical references and index

374   Adult education

John, Lauren Z.
Running book discussion groups; a how-to-do-it manual. [by] Lauren Zina John. Neal-Schuman Publishers 2006 250p (How-to-do-it manual for librarians) pa $55   **374**
1. Books and reading 2. Discussion groups
ISBN 1-55570-542-1; 978-1-55570-542-8
                 LC 2006-704

This is a "step-by-step guide to the tasks and responsibilities librarians are likely to encounter as book-group leaders conducting booktalks both on-site and online. . . . This is essential reading for anyone who may be considering taking on the role of a book-discussion-group leader and a refresher for the more experienced among us." Booklist

Includes bibliographical references

Rose, Mike
Back to school; why everyone deserves a second chance at

education. Mike Rose. New Press, The 2012 224 p. (hardcover) $21.95 **374**

1. Adult education 2. College students 3. Higher education
ISBN 9781595587862

LC 2012021135

This book by Mike Rose "look[s] at the schools that serve a growing population of . . . [non-traditional students] exploring what higher education . . . can offer our rapidly changing society." (Publisher's note) "Rose explores the need for a reassessment of the post–K-12 educational system, noting that growing sectors of the labor market require a four- or even two-year degree." (Kirkus Reviews)

Includes bibliographical references

378 Higher education (Tertiary education)

Book of Majors; the only book that describes majors and lists the colleges that offer them. College Board **378**

1. Colleges and universities -- Curricula 2. Colleges and universities -- United States

Annual. First published 1977 with title: The college handbook index of majors. Variant titles: The College Board book of majors; The College Board index of majors and graduate degrees; Index of majors and graduate degrees

Provides information on over nine hundred college majors, including related fields, prior high school subjects, possible courses of study, and career options and trends for graduates.

Dreifus, Claudia

Higher education? how colleges are wasting our money and failing our kids--and what we can do about it. [by] Andrew Hacker and Claudia Dreifus. Times Books 2010 271p il $26 **378**

1. College costs 2. Higher education 3. College teachers -- United States 4. Colleges and universities -- Faculty 5. Education, Higher -- United States -- Finance
ISBN 978-0-8050-8734-5; 0-8050-8734-6

LC 2010-07219

Hacker and Dreifus "draw up a powerful, if rambling, indictment of academic careerism. The authors are not shy about making biting judgments along the way. . . . [They conclude] with capsule summaries of, as they put it, 'Schools We Like'—that is, schools that offer superior undergraduate educations at relatively low cost." Wall Street J

Includes bibliographical references

Fiske, Edward B.

Fiske guide to colleges. Sourcebooks **378**

1. College choice 2. Colleges and universities -- United States

Annual. First published 1982 with title: The New York Times selective guide to colleges

This guide to over 300 of the best colleges and universities nationwide includes information on admissions, costs, financial aid, housing, social life, and academic strengths and weaknesses.

Selingo, Jeffrey J.

College (un)bound; the future of higher education and what it means for students. Jeffrey J. Selingo. Houghton Mifflin Harcourt 2013 xviii, 238 p.p (hardcover) $26 **378**

1. Higher education 2. Colleges and universities -- Finance 3. College students -- United States 4. Educational planning -- United States 5. Universities and colleges -- United States 6. Education, Higher -- Aims and objectives -- United States

ISBN 0544027078; 9780544027077

LC 2013001941

This book offers an analysis of "middle-tier American colleges" and highlights "forward-thinking educational models. [Jeffrey J.] Selingo . . . describes a climate in which colleges compete for rankings by improving amenities, falling into an escalating cycle of tuition increases and larger financial aid packages that leave students with crushing debt, and a sense of students as consumers that leads to grade inflation and teaching compromises." (Publishers Weekly)

Includes bibliographical references and index.

Williams, Juan

I'll find a way or make one; a tribute to historically Black colleges and universities. by Juan Williams and Dwayne Ashley. Amistad/HarperCollins 2004 xxiv, 453p il $35 **378**

1. African American universities and colleges 2. African Americans -- Education
ISBN 0-06-009453-2

LC 2004-46450

The authors "explore America's 107 historically black colleges and universities, in existence for 172 years, showing how the schools were created and how black and white abolitionists united to educate newly freed slaves." Libr J

Includes bibliographical references

378.1 Organization and activities in higher education

Albom, Mitch, 1958-

Tuesdays with Morrie; an old man, a young man, and life's greatest lesson. Mitch Albom. Doubleday 1997 192 p. pa $13.99; $20.00 **378.1**

1. Amyotrophic lateral sclerosis 2. Sociologists 3. College teachers 4. Brandeis University -- Faculty -- Biography 5. Death -- Psychological aspects -- Case studies 6. Teacher-student relationships -- United States -- Case studies 7. Amyotrophic lateral sclerosis -- Patients -- United States -- Biography
ISBN 076790592X pa; 0385484518

LC 96052535

This book discusses the author's relationship with his former teacher and mentor, "sociologist Morrie Schwartz. Here [Mitch] Albom recounts how . . . as the old man was dying, he renewed his warm relationship with his revered mentor. This is the . . . record of the teacher's battle with muscle-wasting amyotrophic lateral sclerosis, or Lou Gehrig's disease. The dying man, largely because of his life-affirming attitude toward his death-dealing illness, became a sort of thanatopic guru, and was the subject of three Ted Koppel interviews on Nightline. That was how the author first learned of Morrie's condition. Albom . . . calls his weekly visits to his teacher his last class, and the present book a term paper. The subject: The Meaning of Life . . . Albom does not present a full transcript of the regular Tuesday talks. Rather, he expands a little on the professor's aphorisms." (Kirkus)

"As a student at Brandeis University in the late 1970s, Albom was especially drawn to his sociology professor, Morris Schwartz. On graduation he vowed to keep in touch with him, which he failed to do until 1994, when he saw a segment about Schwartz on the TV program Nightline, and learned that he had just been diagnosed with Lou Gehrig's disease. By then a sports columnist for the Detroit Free Press . . . Albom was idled by the newspaper strike in the Motor City and so had the opportunity to visit Schwartz in Boston every week until the older man died. Their dialogue is the subject of this moving book." Publ Wkly

Bain, Ken

What the best college students do; Ken Bain. The Belknap Press of Harvard University Press 2012 289 p. (alk. paper) $24.95   **378.1**

1. College students 2. Academic achievement 3. College students -- United States 4. Academic achievement -- United States

ISBN 0674066642; 9780674066649

LC 2012015548

In this book, author Ken Bain "identifies the key attitudes that distinguished the best college students from their peers. These individuals started out with the belief that intelligence and ability are expandable, not fixed. This led them to make connections across disciplines, to develop a 'meta-cognitive' understanding of their own ways of thinking, and to find ways to negotiate ill-structured problems rather than simply looking for right answers." (Publisher's note)

"A soundly encouraging guide for college students to think deeply and for as long as it takes." Kirkus

Includes bibliographical references and index

Bergman, Dave

The **enlightened** college applicant; A New Approach to the Search and Admissions Process. Andrew Belasco and Dave Bergman. Rowman & Littlefield 2016 240 p. (ebook) $38; (cloth: alk. paper) $30   **378.1**

1. College choice 2. College applications 3. Colleges and universities -- United States 4. College choice -- United States 5. Universities and colleges -- United States -- Admission

ISBN 9781475826920; 9781475826906

LC 2016032477

This book, by Andrew Belasco and Dave Bergman, "presents a nononsense account of how students should approach the college search and admissions process. Instead of providing recycled entrance statistics or anecdotal generalizations about campus life, authors Belasco and Bergman incorporate cutting-edge data and research to pull back the curtain on critical topics." (Publisher's note)

"Families seeking enlightenment about how to rationally and reasonably advise their teens in the higher-education arms race would do well to seek out this title." Booklist

Includes bibliographical references and index

Beyond the asterisk; understanding Native students in higher education. edited by Heather Shotton, Shelly Lowe, and Stephanie J. Waterman. Stylus 2013 xvi, 189 p.p (cloth: alk. paper) $85   **378.1**

1. Students -- United States 2. Native Americans -- Education

ISBN 157922623X; 9781579226237; 9781579226244

LC 2012040238

Editor Heather J. Shotton's book discusses Native American students in higher education. "The purpose of this book is to move beyond the asterisk in an effort to better understand Native students, challenge the status quo, and provide an informed base for leaders in student and academic affairs, and administrators concerned with the success of students on their campuses." (Publisher's note)

Includes bibliographical references and index

Crossman, Anne

Getting the best out of college; insider advice for success from a professor, a dean, and a recent grad. Peter Feaver, Sue Wasiolek, Anne Crossman. Rev. and updated, 2nd ed. Ten Speed Press 2012 xiv, 289 p.p (pbk.) $14.99   **378.1**

1. Counseling 2. College students 3. Colleges and universities -- United States 4. College student orientation -- United States

ISBN 160774144X; 9781607741442

LC 2011051246

This book, by authors Peter Feaver, Sue Wasiolek, and Anne Crossman, "reveals insider advice that makes the hefty price tag worth it: how to impress professors, live with a roommate, pick the best courses (and do well in them), design a meaningful transcript, earn remarkable internships, prepare for a successful career after graduation, and much more." (Publisher's note)

Fiske, Edward B.

Fiske Guide to Getting Into The Right College; Edward B. Fiske & Bruce G. Hammond. 6th edition Sourcebooks 2016 385 p. pbk $16.99   **378.1**

1. College choice 2. College applications 3. Colleges and universities -- United States

ISBN 9781492633303; 1492633305

This book by Edward Fiske and Bruce Hammond is designed to "help you generate a list of schools you love and walk you step-by-step through the process of applying to them. [It] will show you how to: Discover which schools are right for you based on academic programs, size, location, institutional culture, and more." (Publisher's note)

Jager-Hyman, Joie

B + grades, A+ college application; how to present your strongest self, write a stand-out admissions essay, and get into the perfect school for you. by Joie Jager-Hyman, EdD. Random House Inc 2013 ix, 246 p.p (paperback) $14.99   **378.1**

1. Student aid 2. College applications 3. Exposition (Rhetoric) 4. College applications -- United States 5. Universities and colleges -- United States -- Admission

ISBN 1607743418; 9781607743415

LC 2013004970

In this book, college admissions consultant Joie Jager-Hyman "guides students (and their parents) through the college-admissions process, offering a wealth of insider advice. . . . Jager-Hyman covers the usual steps: developing a list of target, reach, and safety schools; writing essays; prepping for the college interview; taking the SATs; and demystifying financial aid." (Publishers Weekly)

The **Latino** student's guide to college success; Leonard A. Valverde, editor. Greenwood 2012 xiv, 270 p.p (alk. paper) $58   **378.1**

1. Hispanic Americans -- Education (Higher) -- Handbooks, manuals, etc. 2. Universities and colleges -- United States -- Directories 3. Hispanic Americans -- Education (Higher) -- Handbooks, manuals, etc

ISBN 031339797X; 0313397988; 9780313397974; 9780313397981

LC 2012010827

This book, edited by Leonard A. Valverde, provides "advice directed specifically to Latinos contemplating, preparing for, or already in the university or community college setting. This volume contains the 8 Steps to College Success, numerous vignettes of notable Latinos in many fields who give their personal story of how they succeeded in college and their advice for today's students, and a directory of top Latino universities and community colleges." (Publisher's note)

Pekar, Harvey

Students for a Democratic Society; a graphic history. written by Harvey Pekar; art by Gary Dumm; edited by Paul Buhle. Hill & Wang 2008 214p il pa $16; $22   **378.1**

1. Graphic novels 2. College students -- Political activity -- Graphic

novels 3. Students for a Democratic Society -- Graphic novels -- History

ISBN 978-0-8090-8939-0 pa; 978-0-8090-9539-1

LC 2007-40641

Students for a Democratic Society formed as an organization in 1960, but had its roots as a New Left group in the League for Industrial Democracy, founded in 1905 with members such as Jack London and Upton Sinclair. The members in 1960 included Al Haber and Tom Hayden, and one of their most famous documents is the Port Huron Statement of 1962. By the late 1960s, with opposition to the Vietnam War in full swing, a radical subgroup called the Weathermen became more violent. Graphic novelist Pekar is joined by members of the SDS in telling the story of the organization, which dissolved soon after its 1969 convention. The book includes some harsh language and violence.

"The book acts like a sophisticated handbook on an often misunderstood organization. It's good comics and excellent history." Publ Wkly

Rosenfeld, Seth, 1956-

Subversives; the FBI's war on student radicals, and Reagan's rise to power. Seth Rosenfeld. Farrar, Straus and Giroux 2012 752 p. ill., map (alk. paper) $40.00   **378.1**

1. United States. Federal Bureau of Investigation 2. California -- Politics and government -- 1951- 3. Student movements -- California -- Berkeley -- History 4. University of California, Berkeley -- Students -- History 5. Subversive activities -- California -- Berkeley -- History 6. College students -- Political activity -- California -- Berkeley -- History

ISBN 0374257000; 9780374257002

LC 2011041204

This book "traces the FBI's secret involvement with three iconic figures at Berkeley during the 1960s: the ambitious neophyte politician Ronald Reagan, the fierce but fragile radical Mario Savio, and the liberal university president Clark Kerr. Through these converging narratives, the award-winning investigative reporter Seth Rosenfeld tells . . . of FBI surveillance, illegal break-ins, infiltration, planted news stories, poison-pen letters, and secret detention lists." (Publisher's note)

Includes bibliographical references

Shachtman, Tom

Airlift to America; how Barack Obama, Sr., John F. Kennedy, Tom Mboya, and 800 East African students changed their world and ours. St. Martin's Press 2009 273p il $24.99 **378.1**

1. College students 2. African-American Students Federation 3. East Africa -- Foreign relations -- United States 4. United States -- Foreign relations -- East Africa

ISBN 978-0-312-57075-0

LC 2009-13186

"In the late 1950s, before Kenya's independence from Britain, Kenyan leader Tom Mboya and American philanthropist William Scheinman joined to develop a cadre of educated young people to staff the government and schools. Between 1959 and 1963, nearly 800 African students were flown to the U.S. to be educated and to return to become the 'founding brothers and sisters' of their East African nations. Among them were Wangari Maathai, who went on to become an environmentalist and 2004 Nobel Peace Prize winner, and Barack Obama Sr., father of the future president of the U.S. Shachtman provides historical perspective of cold war politics in African nations, countervailing loyalties to European colonial powers, and the appeal of U.S. ideals of independence." Booklist

Includes bibliographical references

Steinberg, Jacques

The **gatekeepers**; inside the admissions process of a pre-mier college. Viking 2002 xxiii, 292p hardcover o.p. pa $15   **378.1**

1. College applications 2. Wesleyan University (Middletown, Conn.)

ISBN 0-670-03135-6; 0-14-200308-5 pa

LC 2002-16884

"This insightful and readable book should be purchased by all academic and large public libraries." Libr J

Includes bibliographical references

Ventrone, Jillian

From the Marine Corps to college; transitioning from the service to higher education. by Jillian Ventrone. Rowan & Littlefield 2014 224 p. (cloth: alk. paper) $35   **378.1**

1. Veterans -- Education 2. United States. Marine Corps 3. Marines -- Education -- United States 4. Veterans -- Education -- United States

ISBN 9781442237209

LC 2014013314

This book, by Jillian Ventrone, was designed "to help Marines navigate the world of higher education and their available state and federal benefits. . . . [It] will better prepare veterans for tackling their new mission: college. . . . [It] can be read as a book from cover-to-cover, or as a reference manual section-by-section. The easy to follow format will assist Marines in furthering their educational goals." (Publisher's note)

"Despite its limitations, this title will appeal to marines and do well in libraries serving this population; otherwise, it is a supplemental purchase." LJ

Includes bibliographical references and index

378.161   College admissions

Bruni, Frank

Where You Go Is Not Who You'll Be; An Antidote to the College Admissions Mania. by Frank Bruni. Grand Central Pub 2016 262 p. $14.99   **378.161**

1. College choice 2. College applications

ISBN 1455532681; 9781455532681

LC 2014049043

In this book, author Frank Bruni "shows that the Ivy League has no monopoly on corner offices, governors' mansions, or the most prestigious academic and scientific grants. Through statistics, surveys, and the stories of hugely successful people who didn't attend the most exclusive schools, he demonstrates that many kinds of colleges-large public universities, tiny hideaways in the hinterlands-serve as ideal springboards." (Publisher's note)

"Written in a lively style but carrying a wallop, this is a book that family and educators cannot afford to overlook as they try to navigate the treacherous waters of college admissions." Kirkus

Chatterjee, Pria

The **dirty** little secrets of getting into a top college; Pria Chatterjee. Regan Arts 2015 180 p. illustrations $22.95 **378.161**

1. College choice 2. College applications

ISBN 1941393020; 9781941393024

LC 2014955519

In this book, author Pria Chatterjee "simplifies the complicated process of college admissions, providing parents and students with the tools needed to secure a spot at one of America's most competitive colleges. . . . Through a series of real-world case studies and with a store of deep insider knowledge, Chatterjee will help you navigate the thicket of college admissions." (Publisher's note)

378.3 Student aid and related topics

Collinge, Alan

The **student** loan scam; the most oppressive debt in U.S. history, and how we can fight back. Beacon Press 2008 167p $22.95 **378.3**

1. Student loan funds

ISBN 978-0-8070-4229-8; 0-8070-4229-3

LC 2008-12230

"Comprehensive and stirring, this extraordinary book is whistle-blowing at its finest." Publ Wkly

Includes bibliographical references

Getting financial aid; scholarships, grants, loans, and jobs. College Board **378.3**

1. College costs 2. Student loan funds

Annual. First published with title: The college cost book. Variant titles: College Board guide to getting financial aid, The college costs & financial aid handbook

This guide covers over 3000 two- and four-year institutions. Provides information on what each college really costs, describes aid packages and includes tips on application procedures.

Peterson's how to get money for college 2015; Peterson's. Petersons 2014 944 p. $29.95 **378.3**

1. Student aid

ISBN 0768938686; 9780768938685

This book "is a great resource for anyone looking to supplement his or her federal financial aid package with aid from colleges and universities. This comprehensive directory points you to complete and accurate information on need-based and non-need gift aid, loans, work-study, athletic awards, and more. The unique and easy-to-use Colleges-at-a-Glance comparison chart lists the full costs that can be expected, aid packages, and more." (Publisher's note)

378.38 Cost of higher education

Goldrick-Rab, Sara, ca. 1977-

Paying the price; College Costs, Financial Aid, and the Betrayal of the American Dream. Sara Goldrick-Rab. University of Chicago Press 2016 368 p. (cloth: alk. paper) $27.50 **378.38**

1. Student aid 2. College costs 3. Federal aid to education 4. Student aid -- Wisconsin 5. College costs -- Wisconsin 6. Student aid -- Social aspects -- United States 7. College costs -- Social aspects -- United States 8. Federal aid to higher education -- United States 9. Education, Higher -- Economic aspects -- United States

ISBN 9780226404349

LC 2016007474

In this book, by Sara Goldrick-Rab, "college is far too expensive for many people today, and the confusing mix of federal, state, institutional, and private financial aid leaves countless students without the resources they need to pay for it. Drawing on an unprecedented study of 3,000 young adults who entered public colleges and universities in Wisconsin in 2008 with the support of federal aid and Pell Grants, Goldrick-Rab reveals the devastating effect of these shortfalls." (Publisher's note)

"This cogent and persuasive argument for a more humane and efficient program to make higher education accessible to all capable students draws upon thorough research and an array of personal portraits.

Highly recommended for parents and taxpayers." LJ

Includes bibliographical references and index

378.73 Colleges -- United States

Bok, Derek Curtis, 1930-

The **struggle** to reform our colleges; Derek Bok. Princeton University Press 2017 x, 228 p.p (hardcover) $29.95 **378.73**

1. Educational change -- United States 2. Academic achievement -- United States 3. Colleges and universities -- United States 4. Education, Higher -- Aims and objectives -- United States 5. Universities and colleges -- United States -- Administration

ISBN 9780691177472

LC 2017012202

In this book, author Derek Bok seeks to explain "why efforts to improve American higher educational attainment haven't worked, and where to go from here. . . . Bok identifies a number of initiatives that could improve the performance of colleges and universities. The final chapter examines the process of change itself and describes the strategy best calculated to quicken the pace of reform and enable colleges to meet the challenges that confront them." (Publisher's note)

Includes bibliographical references and index

Delbanco, Andrew

College; what it was, is, and should be. Andrew Delbanco. Princeton University Press 2012 xiv, 229 p.p (hardcover) $24.95 **378.73**

1. Higher education 2. Colleges and universities 3. Education, Higher -- Aims and objectives -- United States

ISBN 0691130736; 9780691130736

LC 2011039399

This book presents an "assessment of how American higher education has lost its way. [Andrew Delbanco] starts with the American ideal, dating back to the Puritans, of college as a place that trained the whole person. . . . In modern America, that focus has shifted: Now it's less about the eternal verities than chasing after dollars, more about filling seats than heads and more about science than the humanities." (Kirkus Reviews)

Includes bibliographical references and index

Mettler, Suzanne

Degrees of inequality; how the politics of higher education sabotaged the American dream. Suzanne Mettler. Basic Books, a member of the Perseus Books Group 2014 272 p. illustrations (hardback) $27.99 **378.73**

1. College costs 2. American dream 3. Higher education 4. Education -- United States 5. Educational change -- United States

ISBN 0465044964; 9780465044962

LC 2013043678

In this book, political scientist Suzanne Mettler "explains why the . . . American Dream is increasingly out of reach for so many. . . . She illuminates how political partisanship has overshadowed America's commitment to equal access to higher education. As politicians capitulate to corporate interests, owners of for-profit colleges benefit, but for far too many students, higher education leaves them with little besides crippling student loan debt." (Publisher's note)

"Though the book orbits the central theme of the for-profits and their outsized political influence, [Mettler] frames this with a history of higher education and its attendant laws, as well as an excellent introduction to political science that explains----in approachable language----the myriad impacts of law and the ways in which the intentions of legislators are often deformed." Pub Wkly

Includes bibliographical references and index

Peterson's four-year colleges; by Peterson's. Petersons illustrations **378.73**

1. College choice 2. Colleges and universities

Annual. First published 1966 as part of Peterson's annual guide to undergraduate study. Formerly titled Peterson's guide to four-year colleges.

This reference compiles profiles of over 2,500 accredited institutions in the United States with four year undergraduate degree programs.

LC 2002258012

This book "includes information on every accredited four-year undergraduate institution in the U.S. and Canada (and many international schools). . . . It also includes detailed two-page descriptions written by admissions personnel for over 300 colleges and universities. College-bound students and their parents can access details including campus setting, enrollment, academic programs, entrance difficulty, expenses, student-faculty ratio, application deadline, and contact information." (Publisher's note)

Peterson's two-year colleges; Petersons illustrations **378.73**

1. College choice 2. Junior colleges

LC 2002258012

Annual. First published 1966 as part of Peterson's annual guide to undergradute study. Formerly titled Peterson's guide to two-year colleges

This reference compiles profiles of over 1,500 accredited institutions in the United States with two year associate degree programs.

Profiles of American colleges 2015; by Barron's College Division Staff. Barrons Educational Series Inc **378.73**

1. College choice 2. Colleges and universities

Annual. First published 1964

This guidebook "gives college-bound students online information and guidance to help them match their academic plans and aptitudes with the admission requirements and academic programs of every accredited four-year college in the country." (Publisher's note)

379 Public policy issues in education

Duncan, Arne, 1964-

How schools work; an inside account of failure and success from one of the nation's longest-serving secretaries of education. Arne Duncan. Simon & Schuster 2018 352 p. $26.99 **379.097**

1. Public schools -- United States 2. Educational change -- United States 3. Education -- Aims and objectives -- United States

ISBN 1501173057; 9781501173059

LC 2018016716

"Drawing on nearly three decades in education--from his mother's after-school program on Chicago's South Side to his tenure as Secretary of Education . . . --'How Schools Work' follows Arne [Duncan] . . . as he takes on challenges at every turn. . . . [The book] exposes the lies that have caused American kids to fall behind their international peers, from early childhood all the way to college graduation rates. But it also identifies what really does make a school work." (Publisher's note)

"Duncan's experienced perspective will interest anyone invested in American public education." Pub Wkly

Greenawalt, Kent

Does God belong in public schools? Princeton University Press 2005 261p $29.95 **379**

1. Church and state 2. Religion in the public schools

ISBN 0691121117

LC 2004-45779

The author "considers issues ranging from the teaching of evolution to parents' rights that their children not be exposed to offensive curriculum. He grounds his analyses in a review of the history and purposes of schooling. . . . His legal and philosophical lines of scholarship come together to produce a nonpartisan consideration of the crucial issues facing US courts and the country." Choice

Includes bibliographical references

Kozol, Jonathan

★ The **shame** of the nation; the restoration of apartheid schooling in America. Crown Publishers 2005 404p $25; pa $14.95 **379**

1. Segregation in education

ISBN 1-4000-5244-0; 1-4000-5245-9 pa

LC 2005-8626

"Readers interested in public education will appreciate—and be challenged by—this compelling book." Booklist

Includes bibliographical references

Ravitch, Diane, 1938-

The **death** and life of the great American school system; how testing and choice are undermining education. Basic Books 2010 283p $26.95 **379**

1. School choice 2. Educational tests and measurements 3. Public schools -- United States 4. Educational accountability -- United States 5. Educational tests and measurements -- United States

ISBN 978-0-465-01491-0; 0-465-01491-7

LC 2009-50406

Ravitch critiques "ideas for restructuring schools, including privatization, standardized testing, punitive accountability, and the . . . multiplication of charter schools." (Publisher's note) Index.

The author "provides an important and highly readable examination of the educational system, how it fails to prepare students for life after graduation, and how we can put it back on track. . . . Anyone interested in education should definitely read this accessible, riveting book." Libr J

Includes bibliographical references

379.26 Equal educational opportunity

Green, Kristen

Something Must Be Done About Prince Edward County; A Family, a Virginia Town, a Civil Rights Battle. HarperCollins 2015 336 p. 8 plates; illustrations $25.99 **379.26**

1. Blacks -- Segregation 2. Segregation in education

ISBN 0062268678; 9780062268679

LC 2015295454

This book by Kristen Green "reveals a little-known chapter of American history: the period after the Brown v. Board of Education decision when one Virginia school system refused to integrate. In the wake of the Supreme Court's unanimous decision in the case of Brown v. Board of Education, Virginia's Prince Edward County refused to obey the law. Rather than desegregate, the county closed its public schools." (Publisher's note)

"Green's work brims with real-life detail from the journalist's eye and ear and joins the likes of Diane McWhorter's Carry Me Home in further developing the dimensions of the South's desegregation struggle—particularly from the perspective of white communities—for general readers and scholars of the late 20th-century civil rights movement." LJ

Wilder, Craig Steven

★ **Ebony** and Ivy; Race, Slavery, and the Troubled History of America's Universities. by Craig Wilder. Bloomsbury 2013 448 p. $30   **379.26**

    1. Higher education 2. Slavery -- United States -- History 3. Race discrimination -- United States 4. Slavery -- United States 5. United States -- Race relations 6. Racism in education -- United States 7. African Americans -- Education (Higher) History 8. Discrimination in higher education -- United States 9. Universities and colleges -- United States -- History 10. Minorities -- Education (Higher) -- United States -- History

ISBN 1596916818; 9781596916814

       LC 2013011971

In this book, author Craig Steven Wilder examines the relationship among "race, slavery, and the American academy. Wilder shows, our leading universities, dependent on human bondage, became breeding grounds for the racist ideas that sustained them . . . revealing a history of oppression behind the institutions usually considered the cradle of liberal politics." (Publisher's note)

Includes bibliographical references and index

381   Commerce (Trade)

Bond's Top 100 Franchises, 2015; edited by Robert E. Bond. Source Book Publications 2015 392 p. $24.95   **381**

    1. Franchises (Retail trade)

    ISBN 1887137939; 9781887137935

This book, edited by Robert E. Bond, "assesses a wide variety of variables to give readers the leading franchises out of more than 3,500 under consideration. The final selection is based on a number of factors, including historical performance, competitive advantage, franchisee satisfaction, and financial stability." (Publisher's note)

Cassidy, John

How markets fail; the logic of economic calamities. Farrar, Straus and Giroux 2009 390p il   **381**

    1. Monetary policy 2. Stock exchanges 3. Financial crises 4. Banks and banking

    ISBN 0374173206; 9780374173203

       LC 2009029529

"Cassidy describes the rising influence of what he calls utopian economics—thinking that is blind to how real people act and that denies the many ways an unregulated free market can produce disastrous unintended consequences." (Publisher's note) Index.

"The author focuses primarily on the rise and fall of free market ideology and the mostly unrealistic ideal of a self-correcting marketplace. An excellent comprehensive history of the economic thought that led to this kind of utopian economics provides a refresher course in Adam Smith, Friedrich August von Hayek, Kenneth Arrow and Hyman Minsky." Publ Wkly

Includes bibliographical references

Dolin, Eric Jay

Fur, fortune, and empire; the epic history of the fur trade in America. W.W. Norton & Co. 2010 442p il map $29.95 **381**

    1. Fur trade 2. Europe -- Colonies -- America 3. Fur trade -- North America -- History 4. Fur trade -- Western States -- History 5. Frontier and pioneer life -- North America

    ISBN 978-0-393-06710-1

       LC 2010016212

This is an "overview of the American fur trade from Colonial times

until the beginnings of the conservation movement of the late 19th century. . . . From the Iroquoian 'Beaver Wars' of the mid-1600s to the brutal Russian domination of Alaskan native hunters, Dolin successfully shows how America's natural history is a vital part of our collective national history." Libr J

Includes bibliographical references

Eltis, David

Atlas of the transatlantic slave trade; [by] David Eltis and David Richardson; foreword by David Brion Davis; afterword by David W. Blight. Yale University Press 2010 xxvi, 307p il map (The Lewis Walpole series in eighteenth-century culture and history) $50   **381**

    1. Atlases 2. Reference books 3. Slave trade -- Maps

    ISBN 978-0-300-12460-6

"For nearly 20 years, the Trans-Atlantic Slave Trade Database project has been diligently tabulating all the slave ship crossings of the Atlantic Ocean, from 1500 to 1900. . . . With 189 informative and handsome maps, Eltis and Richardson relay and interpret the information contained in this rich database, mixing in beautiful historical illustrations and key passages from relevant texts. An accessible narrative, meanwhile, expands on the information in the maps. . . . This marvelous book will change how people think of the slave trade." Foreign Affairs

Fili, Louise

★ The **cognoscenti's** guide to Florence; shop and eat like a Florentine. Louise Fili & Lise Apatoff. Princeton Architectural Press 2015 224 p. $15.95   **381**

    1. Florence (Italy) 2. Italy -- Description and travel 3. Florence (Italy) -- Guidebooks 4. Walking -- Italy -- Florence -- Guidebooks 5. Shopping -- Italy -- Florence -- Guidebooks 6. Restaurants -- Italy -- Florence -- Guidebooks

    ISBN 1616896361; 9781616893217; 9781616896362

       LC 2014028202

"Shop and eat like a Florentine with this pocket-sized guide to the best of the magnificent Tuscan city known for its art, culture, and cuisine. . . . Graphic designer . . . Louise Fili, with . . . Lisa Apatoff, takes you on eight walks through Florence, discussing more than seventy of the city's most alluring shops—some run by the same families for generations, others offering young entrepreneurs' fresh interpretations of traditional techniques." (Publisher's note)

"Fili designs food packaging and restaurant identities, while Apatoff is an official guide for the city, and their expertise is apparent. It is worth noting that the guide itself is beautifully designed with vibrant photographs that truly capture the lovely, varied boutiques presented within." (LJ)

Korschun, Daniel

We are Market Basket; the story of the unlikely grassroots movement that saved a beloved business. by Daniel Korschun and Grant Welker. American Management Association 2015 256 p. illustrations (hardcover) $24.95   **381**

    1. Supermarkets 2. Grocery trade 3. Grocery shopping 4. Corporate governance 5. Market Basket (Firm) 6. Supermarkets -- United States -- Management 7. Grocery trade -- United States -- Management 8. Corporate governance -- United States -- Case studies

    ISBN 081443665X; 9780814436653

       LC 2015006561

This book, by Daniel Korschun and Grant Welker, focuses on "Market Basket, a popular New England supermarket chain. After long-time, CEO Arthur T. Demoulas was ousted by his cousin Arthur S. Demoulas, the company's managers and rank-and-file workers struck back. Risking their own livelihoods to restore the job of their beloved boss they walked out. . . . All openly challenged the Market Basket board of directors to make things right. And, in the end, they prevailed." (Publisher's note)

Includes bibliographical references and index

Mitchell, Stacy

Big-box swindle; the true cost of mega-retailers and the fight for America's independent businesses. Beacon Press 2006 318p $24.95; pa $15   **381**

1. Chain stores 2. Retail trade 3. Small business
ISBN 978-0-8070-3500-9; 0-8070-3500-9; 978-0-8070-3501-6 pa; 0-8070-3501-7 pa

LC 2006-13818

Mitchell's "call to action reveals the hidden costs of those 'low prices' promoted by the big-box bullies and gives hope to local entrepreneurs and concerned citizens alike." Booklist

Includes bibliographical references

Sennett, Frank

Groupon's biggest deal ever; the inside story of how one insane gamble, tons of unbelievable hype, and millions of wild deals made billions for one ballsy joker. Frank Sennett. St. Martin's Press 2012 310 p. (hbk.) $25.99   **381**

1. Groupon (Firm) 2. Internet industry 3. Internet marketing 4. Coupons (Retail trade) 5. Internet advertising
ISBN 125000084X; 1250014948; 9781250000842; 9781250014948

LC 2012009440

This book looks at daily deal website Groupon. The firm's "CEO Andrew Mason takes center stage in this story about the company's founding, development, and explosive assent." Author Frank Sennett starts "from November 2006, when Mason first pitched the idea for Policy Tree (Groupon's precursor) to Eric Lefkofsky, the man who became Groupon's chairman, to early November 2011, when Groupon finally went public on the NASDAQ stock exchange." (Publishers Weekly)

Spector, Robert

The **mom** & pop store; how the unsung heroes of the American economy are surviving and thriving. Walker Pub. Co. 2009 293p $26   **381**

1. Small business 2. Business enterprises
ISBN 978-0-8027-1605-7

LC 2009-19198

"Lively lessons about business ethics and practices that Fortune 500 companies, the author suggests, would be wise to follow." Kirkus

Includes bibliographical references

Stanton, Maureen

Killer stuff and tons of money; seeking history and hidden gems in flea-market America. Penguin Press 2011 326p $26.95   **381**

1. Antiques 2. Flea markets
ISBN 978-1-59420-293-3; 1-59420-293-1

LC 2010-53099

Before Stanton "reconnected with her pseudonymous old college friend, 'Curt Avery,' who had become a professional antiques dealer, she was 'the self-anointed Queen of the Flea-Market Dollar Table.' Like many Americans, she was on the lookout for an appealing bargain and just as happy with an inexpensive reproduction as the real thing. When she and Avery met again in 2000, she agreed to fly across the country to attend an auction where some old bottles that he coveted were on offer.

He asked her to be his proxy bidder while he hid at the back and signaled his bids. This was her introduction to a fascinating subculture, which she calls 'the flea realm.' Over the years, she attended many fairs and flea markets with Avery as what she calls a 'participant observer,' getting up before dawn to help him set up displays, grabbing food on the run and camping out next to his truck at night. . . . A treasure-trove of a book, especially for would-be antiquers." Kirkus

Includes bibliographical references

Whitaker, Jan

Service and style; how the American department store fashioned the middle class. St. Martin's Press 2006 342p il $35   **381**

1. Middle class 2. Department stores
ISBN 978-0-312-32635-7; 0-312-32635-1

LC 2006-40542

"At their peak, department stores were the nation's largest booksellers and many major chains also sold groceries. But it was clothes that made the stores a prime destination for women of all social classes, and Whitaker discusses at significant length the subtle movements through which major chains from one end of the country to the other cultivated their reputations for being up-to-date with the latest Paris fashions, then tapped into additional markets for young adult and children's wear. More than 100 photographs and illustrations are integrated into the text, aptly demonstrating the lengths to which stores went in order to present themselves as elegant yet modern and convenient." Publ Wkly

Includes bibliographical references

Ziegler, Mel

Wild company; the untold story of Banana Republic. Mel and Patricia Ziegler. Simon & Schuster 2012 208 p.   **381**

1. Clothing industry 2. Banana Republic Travel and Safari Company 3. Clothing trade -- United States 4. Fashion merchandising -- United States
ISBN 1451683480; 9781451683486; 9781451683509; 9781451683516

LC 2012030040

This book, by Mel and Patricia Ziegler, describes how the authors "turned a wild idea into a company that would become the international retail colossus Banana Republic. Re-imagining military surplus as safari and expedition wear, the former journalist and artist created a world that captured the zeitgeist for a generation and spoke to the creativity, adventure, and independence in everyone." (Publisher's note)

381.1 Marketing channels

Holiday, Ryan

Perennial seller; the art of making and marketing work that lasts. Ryan Holiday. Portfolio/Penguin 2017 248 p. (hardcover) $26   **381.1**

1. Selling 2. Marketing 3. Creative ability 4. Creative ability in business 5. Branding (Marketing)
ISBN 9780143109013; 9781101992142; 0143109014

LC 2017288786

In this book author Ryan Holiday explores the mystery of perennial sellers "by drawing on his extensive experience working with businesses and creators such as Google, American Apparel, and the author John Grisham, as well as his interviews with the minds behind some of the greatest perennial sellers of our time. . . . Holiday reveals that the key to success for many perennial sellers is that their creators don't distinguish between the making and the marketing." (Publisher's note)

"Holiday . . . brings a contemporary sensibility to the subject of making and marketing creative work. In clean, inspiring prose he lays out a process of setting goals, being diligent, making the product sell, and building a career out of what you love." Pub Wkly

Includes bibliographical references (pages 232-242) and index.

382   International commerce (Foreign trade)

Dolin, Eric Jay

When America first met China; an exotic history of tea, drugs, and money in the Age of Sail. Eric Jay Dolin. Liveright Pub. Corp. 2012 394 p.   **382**
1. China -- History 2. United States -- History 3. China -- Commerce -- United States 4. China -- Foreign economic relations 5. United States -- Foreign economic relations 6. China -- Commerce -- United States -- History -- 18th century 7. China -- Commerce -- United States -- History -- 19th century 8. United States -- Commerce -- China -- History -- 18th century 9. United States -- Commerce -- China -- History -- 19th century
ISBN 0871404338; 9780871404336

LC 2012016598

In this book, Eric Jay Dolin profiles the early history of United States-China trade. The author "traces . . . [America's] fraught relationship with China back to its roots: . . . a brash, rising naval power . . . [and] a battered ancient empire. . . . [T]he furious trade in furs, opium, and beche-de-mer . . . might have catalyzed America's emerging economy, but it also sparked an ecological and human rights catastrophe . . . that . . . can still be felt today." (Publisher's note)

Includes bibliographical references and index

Goldstein, Natalie

Globalization and free trade; Natalie Goldstein; foreword by Joanna G. Moss. 2nd ed. Facts On File 2012 428 p. (ebook) $54.00; (hardcover) $45.00; (paperback) $18.95; (hardcover) $45.00   **382**
1. Free trade 2. Globalization 3. International economic relations 4. Free trade -- Case studies 5. Globalization -- Economic aspects -- Case studies 6. International economic integration -- Case studies
ISBN 9781438109008; 9780816068081; 9780816077397; 0816083657; 9780816083657

LC 2011004940

This encyclopedia, by Natalie Goldstein, examines international economic issues and "provides an overview of the history of globalization and how it has evolved into its present state." It gives "opinions by proponents and detractors of the issue, and case studies of the United States, East Asia, China, Cochabamba, and Iceland are presented to provide real-world context." (Publisher's note)

Includes bibliographical references and index.

Nabhan, Gary Paul, 1952-

Cumin, camels, and caravans; a spice odyssey. Gary Paul Nabhan. University of California Press 2014 332 p. illustrations some color (California studies in food and culture) (cloth: alk. paper) $29.95   **382**
1. Spices -- History 2. International trade 3. Spice trade 4. Spice trade -- History
ISBN 0520267206; 9780520267206; 9780520956957

LC 2013032714

IACP Cookbook Award Finalist: Culinary History (2015)

In this book author "Gary Paul Nabhan takes the reader on a vivid and far-ranging journey across time and space in this fascinating look at the relationship between the spice trade and culinary imperialism. Drawing on his own family's history as spice traders, as well as travel narratives, historical accounts, and his expertise as an ethnobotanist, Nabhan describes the critical roles that Semitic peoples and desert floras had in setting the stage for globalized spice trade." (Publisher's note)

Includes bibliographical references and index

Rose, Sarah

For all the tea in China; how England stole the world's favorite drink and changed history. Viking 2010 261p $25.95 **382**
1. Tea 2. Horticulturists 3. China -- Description and travel
ISBN 0-670-02152-0; 978-0-670-02152-9

LC 2009-41482

First published 2009 in the United Kingdom

In this book, author Sarah Rose "reconstructs what she posits as the 'greatest theft of trade secrets in the history of mankind.' Tea was grown in China. Great Britain wanted

tea. . . . So the East India Company sent hunter [Robert] Fortune, undercover . . . to penetrate the depths of China and surreptitiously gather -steal, in other words--seeds and young plants and send them to India, where they would flourish in soil that was part of the British Empire." (Booklist)

"With her probing inquiry and engaging prose, Sarah Rose paints a fresh and vivid account of life in rural 19th-century China and Fortune's fateful journey into it." Washington Post

Includes bibliographical references

Snyder, Rachel Louise

Fugitive denim; a moving story of people and pants in the borderless world of global trade. W.W. Norton & Company 2008 352p $26.95; pa $16.95   **382**
1. Jeans (Clothing) 2. Clothing industry 3. International trade
ISBN 978-0-393-06180-2; 0-393-06180-9; 978-0-393-33542-2 pa; 0-393-33542-9 pa

LC 2007-24335

"Snyder's investigation is an essential read for those curious about fashion or the globe-spanning business that produces their clothes." Publ Wkly

Includes bibliographical references

383   Communications and transportation

National five digit zip code and post office directory. U.S. Postal Service 2v maps pa $45   **383**
1. Zip code
ISBN 978-1-59804-282-5; 1-59804-282-3

Annual. Continuation of National zip code and post office directory

"Besides ZIP codes and post offices, this directory includes information on the organization of the Postal Service, addressing, parcel weights and sizes, delivery statistics, and other matters." Recomm Ref Books in Paperback. 2d edition

383.143   Overland mail

DeFelice, Jim

West like lightning; the brief, legendary ride of the Pony Express. Jim DeFelice. William Morrow, an imprint of HarperCollins Publishers 2018 viii, 357 p.p illustrations, maps (hardcover) $27.99   **383.143**
1. Pony express 2. Frontier and pioneer life -- United States 3.

Postal service -- United States -- History 4. West (U.S.) -- History 5. Pony express -- History 6. Pony express -- History -- Juvenile literature
ISBN 9780062496768; 9780062496799; 006249676X

This book, by Jim DeFelice "is the first major history of the Pony Express to put its birth, life, and legacy into the full context of the American story. The Central Overland California and Pikes Peak Express Company--or 'Pony Express,' as it came to be known--was part of a plan by [three businessmen] to create the next American Express. . . . The Pony used a relay system of courageous horseback riders to ferry mail halfway across a continent in just ten days." (Publisher's note)

"A lively history of the short-lived but much-evoked Pony Express." Kirkus

Includes bibliographical references and index (pages 271-357).

383.49   Postal systems – History

Gallagher, Winifred

How the Post Office created America; a history. Winifred Gallagher. Penguin Group USA 2016 336 p. (hardcover) $28   **383.49**
1. Postal service -- United States -- History 2. United States Postal Service -- History
ISBN 9781594205002; 1594205000
LC 2016288042

This book, by Winifred Gallagher, "examines the surprising role of the postal service in our nation's political, social, economic, and physical development. . . . This was no conventional mail network but the central nervous system of the new body politic, designed to bind . . . the United States by delivering news about public affairs to every citizen— a radical idea that appalled Europe's great powers." (Publisher's note)

"Gallagher compellingly argues that mail delivery played a vital role in creating American unity via interpersonal communication and points a way forward to a postal service that can remain relevant even in the Internet age." Booklist

384   Communications

Elberse, Anita

Blockbusters; hit-making, risk-taking, and the big business of entertainment. Anita Elberse. Henry Holt & Co. 2013 320 p. illustrations (ebook) $40; (hardcover) $30   **384**
1. Celebrities 2. Music trade 3. Motion picture industry 4. Mass media -- Economic aspects
ISBN 9781429945325; 0805094334; 9780805094336
LC 2013014320

This book by Anita Elberse presents "the story of the entertainment blockbuster model and why it isn't going anywhere." It was the author's intent to "identify the strategies entertainment companies employ to maximize profits in a uniquely competitive and unpredictable market. Her . . . conclusion is that there is no surer bet than focusing the lion's share of resources on 'blockbusters,' products intended to make the biggest initial splash with the largest possible audience." (Kirkus Reviews)

"This thought-provoking book will appeal to students of all ages, those in the classroom and well beyond." Booklist

Includes bibliographical references and index

Gertner, Jon

The **idea** factory; Bell Labs and the great age of American innovation. Jon Gertner. Penguin Press 2012 422 p. ill.

$29.95   **384**
1. Bell Telephone Laboratories 2. Telecommunication -- History 3. Technological innovations -- History 4. Inventors -- United States -- History -- 20th century 5. Bell Telephone Laboratories -- History -- 20th century 6. Creative ability -- United States -- History -- 20th century 7. Telecommunication -- United States -- History -- 20th century 8. Technological innovations -- United States -- History -- 20th century
ISBN 1594203288; 9781594203282
LC 2011040207

This book "traces the history of Bell Labs through more than five decades of brilliant thinking and innovation. From the transistor to lasers to satellites and cellular technology, Bell Labs and its scientists invented machines and techniques that . . . ultimately presaged all of modern communications. . . . Bell Labs became a haven for creative and technical minds due to a unique culture of encouraged interdisciplinary research." (Kirkus Reviews)

"The book is a celebration of basic exploratory research. . . . [T] he writing and the longitudinal biographical portraits are engaging." LJ

Includes bibliographical references (p. [409]-412) and index

Gordon, Robert

Respect yourself; Stax Records and the soul explosion. Robert Gordon. Bloomsbury 2013 480 p. (alk. paper) $30 **384**
1. Soul music 2. Record producers 3. Stax Records -- History 4. Memphis (Tenn.) -- History
ISBN 1596915773; 9781596915770
LC 2013014533

This book by Robert Gordon on the history of Stax Records "situat[es] the story of Stax within the cultural history of the 1960s in the South. . . . Gordon . . . narrates the stories of the many musicians who called Stax home, from . . . Otis Redding to Isaac Hayes, Sam and Dave, and the Staples Singers, as well as the creative marketing and promotional strategies. . . . By the early 1970s, bad business decisions and mangled personal relationships shuttered the doors of Stax." (Publishers Weekly)

"Although treading much of the same ground as Rob Bowman's Soulsville, U.S.A., Gordon's title brings the story up to the present and is both less dense and more objective. For anyone interested in independent record labels and their music in mid-20th-century America." LJ

Includes bibliographical references and index

Knopper, Steve

Appetite for self-destruction; the spectacular crash of the record industry in the digital age. Free Press 2009 301p $26   **384**
1. Music industry
ISBN 978-1-4165-5215-4; 1-4165-5215-4
LC 2008-38739

Knopper "provides a wide-angled, morally complicated view of the current state of the music business. He doesn't let those rippers and burners among us—that is, those who download digital songs without paying for them, and you know who you are—entirely off the hook. But he suggests that with even a little foresight, record companies could have adapted to the Internet's brutish and quizzical new realities and thrived." N Y Times Book Rev

Includes bibliographical references

Lapsley, Phil

Exploding the Phone; The Untold Story of the Teenagers and Outlaws Who Hacked Ma Bell. by Phil Lapsley; forward by Steve Wozniak. Grove Press 2013 xvi, 431 p.p (hardcover)

$26   **384**

1. AT&T (Firm) 2. Telecommunication -- History
ISBN 080212061X; 9780802120618

In this book, Phil Lapsley "uses more than 100 interviews and 400 Freedom of Information Act requests to present the virtually unknown battle between phone companies and overcurious young tech whizzes determined to explore Ma Bell's networks." He "pieces together a . . . re-creation of 1967, a highly significant period in telecommunications history." (Library Journal)

Wu, Tim, ca. 1973-

The **master** switch; the rise and fall of information empires. Alfred A. Knopf 2010 366p il $27.95   **384**

1. Telecommunication 2. Information technology 3. Mass media -- History 4. Telecommunication -- History 5. Information technology -- History
ISBN 978-0-307-26993-5; 0-307-26993-0

LC 2010-04137

"Policy quibbles aside, there's a sharp insight and a surprising fact on nearly every page of Wu's masterful survey. Above all, Wu shows that each new communications technology spawns the same old quest for power." Boston Globe

Includes bibliographical references

384.1   Telegraphy

Gordon, John Steele

A **thread** across the ocean; the heroic story of the transatlantic cable. Walker & Co. 2002 240p il $26   **384.1**

1. Telegraph 2. Submarine cables
ISBN 0-8027-1364-5

LC 2002-66385

The author "has written a lively, engaging account of the extraordinary efforts that brought about this remarkable scientific, technological, and business feat." Libr J

Includes bibliographical references

384.3   Computer communication

Blum, Andrew

Tubes; a journey to the center of the Internet. Andrew Blum. Ecco 2012 294 p.   **384.3**

1. Internet 2. Computer networks 3. Information networks 4. Information technology 5. Information highway 6. Internet -- History 7. Telecommunication systems 8. Internet -- Social aspects
ISBN 0061994936; 9780061994937

LC 2012009519

In this book, "journalist Andrew Blum goes inside the Internet's physical infrastructure. . . . From the room in Los Angeles where the Internet first flickered to life . . . [to] a ten-thousand-mile undersea cable just two thumbs wide [that] connects Europe and Africa, to the wilds of the Pacific Northwest, where Google, Microsoft, and Facebook have built monumental data centers--Blum chronicles the . . . Internet's development, explains how it all works, and takes . . . [a] look inside its hidden monuments." (Publisher's note)

Includes bibliographical references and index.

Dwyer, Jim

More awesome than money; four boys and their heroic quest to save your privacy from Facebook. Jim Dwyer. Viking

2014 384 p. (hardback) $27.95   **384.3**

1. Business failures 2. Social networking 3. New business enterprises 4. Diaspora (Project) 5. Business failures -- United States 6. Internet industry -- United States 7. Privacy, Right of -- United States 8. Online social networks -- United States 9. New business enterprises -- United States
ISBN 0670025607; 9780670025602

LC 2014004511

"Four NYU undergrads wanted to build a social network that would allow users to control their personal data, instead of surrendering it to big businesses like Facebook. They called it Diaspora. In days, they raised $200,000, and reporters, venture capitalists, and the digital community's most legendary figures were soon monitoring their progress. . . . author Jim Dwyer tells a . . . story of four ambitious and naïve young men who tried to rebottle the genie of personal privacy." (Publisher's note)

"A thoroughly compelling account recommended for those interested in general technology books and business narratives. This book is a welcome addition to the literature on start-ups, particularly for its focus on notions of privacy in the digital era and how entrepreneurs are working to address these critical needs." LJ

Includes bibliographical references and index

Mitchell, Charlie

Hacked; The inside story of America's struggle to secure cyberspace. Charlie Mitchell. Rowman & Littlefield 2016 xvi, 301 p.p (cloth: alk. paper) $27   **384.3**

1. Internet 2. Computer security 3. Cyber intelligence (Computer security) 4. Internet -- Government policy -- United States 5. Computer security -- Government policy -- United States
ISBN 9781442255210

LC 2016006180

In this book, "veteran cybersecurity journalist Charlie Mitchell reveals the innovative, occasionally brilliant, and too-often hapless government and industry responses to growing cybersecurity threats. He examines the internal power struggles in the federal government, the paralysis on Capitol Hill, and the industry's desperate effort to stay ahead of both the bad guys and the government." (Publisher's note)

"The author does a stellar job of remaining impartial and sticking with the facts, and the reviewer would be hard-pressed to identify the author's biases in this work." Choice.

Includes bibliographical references and index

384.38   Computer communications in multimedia systems

Gallagher, Billy

How to turn down a billion dollars; the Snapchat story. Billy Gallagher. St. Martin's Press 2018 304 p. (hardcover) $26.99   **384.38**

1. Entrepreneurship 2. Businesspeople -- United States 3. Internet industry -- United States 4. Snap Inc 5. Snapchat (Electronic resource) 6. Entrepreneurship -- United States
ISBN 9781250108616

LC 2017037545

In this book, tech journalist Billy Gallagher takes us inside the rise of one of Silicon Valley's hottest start-ups. Snapchat developed from a simple wish for disappearing pictures as Stanford junior Reggie Brown nursed regrets about photos he had sent. After an epic feud between best friends, Brown lost his stake in the company, while [Evan] Spiegel has gone on to make a name for himself as a visionary--if ruthless--CEO worth billions." (Publisher's note)

384.51 Satellite communication

Bloom, John

Eccentric Orbits; The Iridium Story. John Bloom. Atlantic Monthly Press 2016 496 p. illustrations (some color) (ebook) $27.50; $27.50   **384.51**
1. Iridium Communications Inc. 2. Telecommunication -- History 3. Artificial satellites in telecommunication
ISBN 9780802192820; 0802121683; 9780802121684
LC 2016020769

In this book, author John Bloom "masterfully traces the conception, development, and launching of Iridium and [Dan] Colussy's tireless efforts to stop it from being destroyed, from meetings with his motley investor group, to the Clinton White House, to the Pentagon, to the hunt for customers in special ops, shipping, aviation, mining, search and rescue—anyone who would need a durable phone at the end of the Earth." (Publisher's note)

"A tour de force history of a star-crossed technological leap." Kirkus

384.54 Radiobroadcasting

Heil, Alan L.

Voice of America; a history. Columbia University Press 2003 538p $75; pa $26.50   **384.54**
1. Radio broadcasting 2. Voice of America
ISBN 0-231-12674-3; 0-231-12675-1 pa
LC 2002-41019

This is a "history of America's largest publicly funded overseas broadcasting network. . . . From the crises in eastern Europe to the student uprising in Tiananmen Square, Mr Heil provides countless examples of people clinging to their shortwave radios to listen to VOA and other international broadcasters, in spite of intense jamming, to know what was really going on in their own countries. . . . Readers fascinated by the technical intricacies of radio and the arcana of Washington's broadcasting policies will no doubt be riveted." Economist

Includes bibliographical references

385 Railroad transportation

Ambrose, Stephen E.

Nothing like it in the world; the men who built the transcontinental railroad, 1863-1869. Simon & Schuster 2000 471p $28; pa $16   **385**
1. West (U.S.) -- History 2. Central Pacific Railroad 3. Railroads -- United States 4. Union Pacific Railroad Company
ISBN 0-684-84609-8; 0-7432-0317-8 pa
LC 00-41005

This is an account of the construction of the transcontinental railroad by the Central Pacific and Union Pacific companies.

"Ambrose's scholarship seems impeccable. . . . He writes a brisk, colloquial, straightforward prose that not only is easy to read but also bears the reader on shoulders of wonder and excitement." N Y Times Book Rev

Includes bibliographical references

Drabelle, Dennis

The **great** American railroad war; how Ambrose Bierce and Frank Norris took on the notorious Central Pacific Railroad. Dennis Drabelle. St. Martin's Press 2012 306 p. $26.99 **385**
1. Whistle blowing 2. Central Pacific Railroad Company --

History 3. Norris, Frank, 1870-1902 -- Criticism and interpretation 4. Bierce, Ambrose, 1842-1914? -- Criticism and interpretation 5. Railroads -- California -- History -- 19th century 6. Political corruption -- Press coverage -- California
ISBN 0312667590; 9780312667597; 9781250015051
LC 2012010247

Author Dennis Drabelle "examines the role of literature in battling the Central Pacific Railroad monopoly. He recounts the financing of the transcontinental railroad with U.S. government bonds and how the railroad's owners such as Leland Stanford and Collis Huntington enriched themselves in various quasi-legal ways. Though the railroad worked to make itself untouchable by buying influence, Drabelle chronicles how writers Ambrose Bierce and Frank Norris challenged that position." (Library Journal)

Includes bibliographical references

Hayes, Derek

Historical atlas of the North American railroad. University of California Press 2010 224p il map $39.95   **385**
1. Reference books 2. Historical atlases 3. Railroads -- Canada -- Maps 4. Railroads -- North America -- Maps 5. Railroads -- United States -- Maps 6. North America -- Historical geography 7. Railroads -- North America -- History
ISBN 978-0-520-26616-2
LC 2009-943592

"With 400-plus color maps ranging from 1821 to President Obama's report 'A Vision for High Speed Rail,' this historical atlas reveals the richly variegated visual culture of railroad mapping in the US and Canada. Always utilitarian, railroad maps are differentiated into four types: those required to survey the land for construction and attracting investments, timetable maps for passengers, maps in advertising, and engineering maps. . . . The wealth of visual information, comprehensive coverage, and optimistic stance for the future of railroads on the North American continent make this an important purchase for all reference collections." Choice

Includes bibliographical references

McCommons, James

Waiting on a train; the embattled future of passenger rail service. foreword by James Howard Kunstler. Chelsea Green Pub. Company 2009 285p map pa $17.95   **385**
1. Transportation 2. Railroads -- United States
ISBN 978-1-60358-064-9; 1-60358-064-6
LC 2009-30142

"McCommons spent almost all of 2008 riding Amtrak trains back and forth across the country, telling folks he met along the way that he was doing research for a book on the future of passenger rail. . . . [The resulting work] is part travel log, chronicling both the horrors and the pleasures of riding Amtrak, and part solid political and business reporting on the rail industry that hardly any other journalist is doing." Washington Monthly

White, Richard

Railroaded; the transcontinentals and the making of modern America. Norton 2011 xxxix, 660p il map $35   **385**
1. American national characteristics 2. Railroads -- United States 3. Land settlement -- United States 4. National characteristics, American 5. Railroads -- United States -- History -- 19th century
ISBN 978-0-393-06126-0; 0-393-06126-4
LC 2010-54054

In this book, author Richard White "takes on the task of explaining the achievements and failings of the few transcontinental railroads that spanned North America in the latter half of the 19th century. He concentrates on their financial, political, and social impact. . . . He describes the corruption that made the railroad's founders wealthy but hamstrung the companies . . . , the antipathy between management and workers . . . [and] the antimonopoly movements against railroad practices." (Library Journal)

"Focusing on the entrepreneurs who between the 1860s and 1890s built and operated the transcontinental railroads, White judges them and their companies as failures and malignant influences on the settlement of the West." Booklist

Includes bibliographical references

Wolmar, Christian

Blood, iron, & gold; how the railroads transformed the world. PublicAffairs 2009 376p il map $28.95   **385**
1. Railroads -- History
ISBN 978-1-58648-834-5

LC 2009-38340

First published 2009 in the United Kingdom

This is "a fascinating study not just of a transportation system, but of the Promethean spirit of the modern age." Publ Wkly

Includes bibliographical references

Zoellner, Tom

Train; riding the rails that created the modern world: from the Trans-Siberian to the Southwest Chief. Tom Zoellner. Viking Adult 2014 384 p. (hardback) $27.95   **385**
1. Railroads 2. Railroad engineering 3. Railroad travel -- History
ISBN 0670025283; 9780670025282

LC 2013036816

In this book, Tom Zoellner "examines both the mechanics of the rails and their engines and how they helped societies evolve. Not only do trains transport people and goods in an efficient manner, but they also reduce pollution and dependency upon oil. Zoellner also considers America's culture of ambivalence to mass transit, using the perpetually stalled line between Los Angeles and San Francisco as a case study in bureaucracy and public indifference." (Publisher's note)

"An absorbing and lively reflection on an enduring marvel of modern industrial technology." Booklist

Includes bibliographical references and index

386   Inland waterway and ferry transportation

Bernstein, Peter L.

Wedding of the waters; the Erie Canal and the making of a great nation. W.W. Norton 2005 448p il map $24.95; pa $15.95   **386**
1. Erie Canal (N.Y.)
ISBN 0-393-05233-8; 0-393-32795-7 pa

LC 2004-22792

The author discusses the building of the Erie Canal and how, in his opinion, it changed the course of American history.

This "is an important window into a vital and too often neglected period in the American past." Foreign Affairs

Includes bibliographical references

Karabell, Zachary

Parting the desert; the creation of the Suez Canal. Knopf 2003 310p il map $27.50   **386**
1. Diplomats 2. Suez Canal (Egypt)
ISBN 0-375-40883-5

LC 2002-34209

Karabell "has written a thorough and entertaining work. . . . The author is quite comfortable discussing any issue, period, or personality in the canal's history, and many of the references in his 150-title bibliography are from primary sources. This is simply an excellent book." Libr J

Kelly, Jack

Heaven's ditch; God, Gold, and Murder on the Erie Canal. by Jack Kelly. St. Martin's Press 2016 304 p. illustrations, map (hardback) $27.99   **386**
1. Erie Canal (N.Y.) 2. New York (State) -- History 3. United States -- History -- 1783-1865 4. Erie Canal (N.Y.) -- History 5. New York (State) -- History -- 1775-1865
ISBN 9781137280091

LC 2016003174

In this book by Jack Kelly, "the technological marvel of its age, the Erie Canal grew out of a sudden fit of inspiration. Proponents didn't just dream; they built a 360-mile waterway entirely by hand and largely through wilderness. . . . The Erie Canal made New York the financial capital of America. . . . Kelly illuminates the spiritual and political upheavals along this 'psychic highway' from its opening in 1825 through 1844." (Publisher's note)

"An intriguing account of often overlooked events that significantly impacted the lives and times of individuals living during one of the most tumultuous times in American history." LJ

Includes bibliographical references (pages 265-281) and index.

387.155   Navigational aids

Dolin, Eric Jay

Brilliant beacons; a history of the American lighthouse. Eric Jay Dolin. Liveright Publishing Corp., a division of W.W. Norton & Co. 2016 448 p. illustrations (ebook) $50; (hardcover) $29.95   **387.155**
1. United States. -- Lighthouse Service 2. United States. Bureau of Light-Houses 3. Lighthouses -- United States -- History 4. United States. Lighthouse Service -- History 5. United States. Bureau of Light-Houses -- History
ISBN 9781631491535; 9780871406682

LC 2015044089

This book, by Eric Jay Dolin, "traces the evolution of America's lighthouse system from its earliest days, highlighting the political, military, and technological battles fought to illuminate the nation's hardscrabble coastlines. Beginning with 'Boston Light,' America's first lighthouse, Dolin shows how the story of America, from colony to regional backwater, to fledging nation, and eventually to global industrial power, can be illustrated through its lighthouses." (Publisher's note)

"A delightful journey with excellent sketches, renderings, and resources for museums and organizations." Kirkus

Includes bibliographical references and index

387.2   Ships

Graham, Ian

Fifty ships that changed the course of history; a nautical history of the world. Ian Graham. Firefly Books Ltd. 2016 224 p. ills., maps, portraits (hardcover) $29.95   **387.2**
1. Ships 2. Maritime law 3. Ships -- History 4. Navigation -- History 5. Ships -- History -- Pictorial works 6. Navigation -- History -- Pictorial works
ISBN 9781770857193

LC 2016416044

This book, by Ian Graham, "is a beautiful guide to fifty water vessels that played a key role in world history and had a great impact on human civilization. The book presents the ships chronologically, beginning with Pharaoh Khufu's Solar Barge from about 2566 BCE.... The book closes with another sun-seeking ship four thousand years later. The epitome of an ocean cruise ship, the MS Allure of the Seas is the biggest passenger ship ever built." (Publisher's note)

"Well researched and illustrated, this 'reference-y' title will be a good addition to any collection covering seafaring and transport." Booklist

Includes bibliographical references (page 218) and index

387.5   Ocean transportation (Marine transportation)

Ujifusa, Steven

Barons of the sea; and their race to build the world's fastest clipper ship. Steven Ujifusa. Simon & Schuster 2018 448 p. (hardcover: alk. paper) $29.99   **387.5**

1. Clipper ships 2. Shipping -- United States 3. Merchant marine -- United States 4. Shipping -- United States -- History -- 19th century 5. Clipper ships -- United States -- History -- 19th century 6. Merchant marine -- United States -- History -- 19th century
ISBN 9781476745978

LC 2017037340

This book, by Steven Ujifusa, "tells the story of a handful of cut-throat competitors who raced to build the fastest, finest, most profitable clipper ships to carry their precious cargo to American shores.... [The book tells] a riveting tale of innovation and ingenuity that draws back the curtain on the making of some of the nation's greatest fortunes, and the rise and fall of an all-American industry as sordid as it was genteel." (Publisher's note)

"A vivid account of larger-than-life if not always attractive characters and a technological marvel that briefly captivated the Victorian world." Kirkus

Includes bibliographical references and index

387.7   Air transportation

Fallows, James

China airborne; James Fallows. Pantheon Books 2012 xiii, 268 p.p   **387.7**

1. China -- History -- 1976- 2. Aerospace industry -- China 3. China -- Economic conditions 4. Commercial aeronautics -- China 5. Aeronautics -- China 6. Aerospace industries -- China 7. Aeronautics, Commercial -- China 8. China -- Economic conditions -- 2000-
ISBN 0375422110; 9780375422119

LC 2011046805

This book by James Fallows "analyzes the problems and promises of China's economic development through an examination of the efforts to create a world-class aerospace industry. With its unprecedented manufacturing prowess, China has become a world economic power. But how real and sustainable is the development? The test, writes the author, is how well China succeeds in its current effort to build an aerospace industry." (Kirkus Reviews)

Includes bibliographical references (p. [237]-251) and index

Holmes, Richard, 1945-

★ **Falling** upwards; how we took to the air. Richard Holmes. Pantheon Books 2013 416 p. $35   **387.7**

1. Flight 2. Balloons 3. Ballooning -- History 4. Balloonists -- History
ISBN 0307379663; 9780307379665

LC 2013011128

This book by Richard Holmes looks at ballooning. He "mentions Daedalus and Icarus, some balloons in literature, films and popular culture, and then lifts off into another of his ... histories. He notes that the French were the first to use balloons for military purposes (reconnaissance), then tells us about some of the most notable balloon pioneers, including André-Jacques Garnerin, who also pioneered parachutes." (Kirkus Reviews)

Includes bibliographical references and index

McGee, William J.

Attention all passengers; the airlines' dangerous descent and how to reclaim our skies. William J. McGee. HarperCollins 2012 xii, 354 p.p $26.99   **387.7**

1. Airlines 2. Air travel 3. Aeronautics -- Safety measures 4. Airlines -- United States
ISBN 0062088378; 9780062088376

LC 2012026940

Author William J. McGee "derives most of the book from his interviews with, among others, flight attendants, congressmen, [and] an FAA whistleblower.... McGee explains how the shortcomings of airlines can and do cost consumers more than a comfortable flight; they result in unsafe conditions.... The author exposes the common practice of outsourcing repairs, which can result in crashes because the companies doing the repairs are not as competent or as tightly regulated." (Kirkus Reviews)

Mondor, Colleen Catherine

The **map** of my dead pilots; Colleen Mondor. Lyons Press 2012 256p   **387.7**

1. Alaska 2. Air pilots 3. Aircraft accidents
ISBN 9780762773619

LC 2011033005

This book explores the author's experiences "as operations manager for a commercial airline servicing Alaska's remote villages and hamlets.... [Colleen] Mondor has had a bird's-eye view of the rigors of flying cargo that often as not included carcasses as well as crates, sleds as well as the dogs that hauled them, and passengers who had no other means of traversing a state whose isolation was both allure and aggravation. The men who flew these missions are—and, all too sadly, were—a lethal combination of danger junkies and hotshots, dreamers and schemers, dedicated professionals and determined daredevils who reveled in the challenges that Alaska's climate and terrain threw their way." (Booklist)

388   Transportation

McPhee, John A.

Uncommon carriers; [by] John McPhee. Farrar, Straus & Giroux 2006 248p $24   **388**

1. Freight 2. Transportation
ISBN 0-374-28039-8; 978-0-374-28039-0

LC 2006-7953

"McPhee's eye for idiosyncratic detail keeps the stories ... lively and frequently moves them in interesting directions." Publ Wkly

388.09   Transportation – History, geographic treatment, biography

Humes, Edward

Door to door; the magnificent, maddening, mysterious world of transportation. Edward Humes. Harper 2016 384 p. (hardcover: alk. paper) $27.99; (ebook) $26.99   **388.09**

1. Transportation 2. Transportation -- History 3. Transportation -- Social aspects -- History

ISBN 9780062372079; 9780062372086; 9780062372093

LC 2015037315

This book, by Edward Humes, "explores the hidden and costly wonders of our buy-it-now, get-it-today world of transportation, revealing the surprising truths, mounting challenges, and logistical magic behind every trip we take and every click we make. . . . Humes breaks down the complex movements of humans, goods, and machines as never before, from increasingly car-less citizens to the distance UPS goes to deliver a leopard-printed phone case." (Publisher's note)

"This timely book will inspire many readers to change their habits and their views of the future." Booklist

Includes bibliographical references

388.1   Roads

Conover, Ted

The **routes** of man; how roads are changing the world, and the way we live today. Alfred A. Knopf 2010 333p il map $26.95   **388.1**

1. Roads

ISBN 978-1-4000-4244-9; 1-4000-4244-5

LC 2009-24007

"A readable, fact-filled, well-written exploration of how roads work, for good and ill, and what their future likely holds." Kirkus

Includes bibliographical references

388.3   Vehicular transportation

Burns, Lawrence D.

Autonomy; the quest to build the driverless car and how it will reshape our world. Lawrence D. Burns with Christopher Shulgan. HarperCollins 2018 368 p. $27.99   **388.3**

1. Autonomous vehicles 2. Automobiles -- Automatic control

ISBN 0062661124; 9780062661128

LC 2018108714

This book, by Lawrence D. Burns and Christopher Shulgan, "investigates the quest to develop and perfect the driverless car--an innovation that promises to be the most disruptive change to our way of life since the smartphone. . . . [The book] is a page-turner that represents a chronicle of the past, diagnosis of the present, and prediction of the future--the ultimate guide to understanding the driverless car and navigating the revolution it sparks." (Publisher's note)

"A provocative look at a rising industry that may soon change the nature of the world's too-busy roadways." Kirkus

Sperling, Daniel

Two billion cars; driving toward sustainability. [by] Daniel Sperling [and] Deborah Gordon. Oxford University Press 2009 304p il $24.95   **388.3**

1. Automobile industry 2. Alternative fuel vehicles 3. Automobiles

-- Fuel consumption

ISBN 978-0-19-537664-7; 0-19-537664-1

LC 2008-21647

"With statistical data, charts, graphs, and erudite analysis, Sperling and Gordon present the most thorough study of the automobile industry general readers could hope to find." Booklist

Includes bibliographical references and index

Walker, Peter

How cycling can save the world; Peter Walker. TarcherPerigee 2017 xv, 270 p.p (paperback) $16   **388.3**

1. Cycling 2. City planning 3. Bicycle lanes 4. Bicycle commuting 5. Cycling -- Health aspects 6. Cycling -- Social aspects 7. Pedestrian facilities design

ISBN 9781101993033; 9780143111771

LC 2016048499

This book, by Peter Walker, "takes readers on a tour of cities like Copenhagen and Utrecht, where everyday cycling has taken root, demonstrating cycling's proven effect on reducing smog and obesity, and improving quality of life and mental health. Interviews with public figures--such as Janette Sadik-Khan, who led the charge to create more pedestrian, . . . provides case studies on how it can be done, and prove that you can make a big change with just a . . . paradigm shift." (Publisher's note)

"Walker . . . offers a fascinating read that informs, educates, and inspires." LJ

Includes bibliographical references (pages [243]-270).

388.4   Local transportation

Lenzer, Jeanne

★ The **danger** within us; America's untested, unregulated medical device industry and one man's battle to survive it. Jeanne Lenzer. Little, Brown & Co. 2017 336 p. $28   **388.4**

1. Medical ethics 2. Biomedical engineering

ISBN 0316343765; 9780316343763

In this book, author Jeanne Lenzer, explores the dark side of the medical device industry. "What Lenzer exposes will shock readers: rampant corruption, elaborate cover-ups, shameless profiteering, and astonishing lack of oversight, all of which leads to dangerous devices (from artificial hips to pacemakers) going to market and into our bodies." (Publisher's note)

" An impassioned expose that uncovers a significant danger within the contemporary health care industry." Kirkus

390   Customs, etiquette, folklore

Jenkins, Jessica Kerwin

All the time in the world; a book of hours. Jessica Kerwin Jenkins. Nan A. Talese 2013 320 p. (hardback) $28.95   **390**

1. Culture 2. Hobbies 3. Manners and customs -- History 4. Manners and customs -- Miscellanea

ISBN 0385535414; 9780385535410

LC 2013000795

In this book, author Jessica Kerwin Jenkins "uses the template of the medieval book of hours, which provided readings and meditations for certain times of the day and seasons, to create an unusual look at 'how we pass the time.'" (Booklist) "Subjects covered include the daylong ceremony of laying a royal Elizabethan tablecloth; the radicalization of sartorial chic in 1890s Paris; [and] Nostradamus's belief in the aphrodisiac power of jam". (Publisher's note)

Includes bibliographical references

Narayan, Shoba

The **milk** lady of Bangalore; an unexpected adventure. by Shoba Narayan. Algonquin Books of Chapel Hill 2017 272 p. (hardcover) $24.95 **390**

1. Community life -- India 2. Cattle -- Social aspects 3. India -- Social life and customs 4. Cows -- Social aspects -- India 5. Milk -- Social aspects -- India 6. Community life -- India -- Bangalore

ISBN 9781616206154

LC 2017023398

This book, by Shoba Narayan, "immerses us in the culture, customs, myths, religion, sights, and sounds of a city in which the twenty-first century and the ancient past coexist like nowhere else in the world. It's a true story of bridging divides, of understanding other ways of looking at the world, and of human connections and animal connections, and it's an irresistible adventure of two strong women and the animals they love." (Publisher's note)

"An absolute joy to read. Through her close encounters with the bovine kind, Narayan shows how Indian traditions are incorporated into contemporary ways of life." LJ

Includes bibliographical references

391 Customs

Bowles, Hamish

Vogue and the Metropolitan Museum of Art Costume Institute; parties, exhibitions, people. Hamish Bowles; [edited by] Chloe Malle. Abrams 2014 272 p. illustrations (chiefly color) $50 **391**

1. Fashion

ISBN 9781419714245

LC 2014934398

This book, by Hamish Bowles and edited by Chloe Malle, profiles "the Metropolitan Museum of Art's annual Costume Institute exhibition. . . . Covering the Costume Institute's history and highlighting exhibitions of the 21st century curated by Harold Koda and Andrew Bolton, this book offers insider access of the first order." (Publisher's note)

Crowe, Lauren Goldstein

The **towering** world of Jimmy Choo; a glamorous story of power, profits and the pursuit of the perfect shoe. [by] Lauren Goldstein Crowe and Sagra Maceira de Rosen. Bloomsbury USA 2009 228p il $26; pa $15 **391**

1. Shoes 2. Fashion design 3. Jimmy Choo (Firm) 4. Clothing industry executives

ISBN 978-1-59691-391-2; 1-59691-391-6; 978-1-60819-040-9 pa; 1-60819-040-4 pa

LC 2008-44378

"A fascinating, well-written chronology that draws a chillingly accurate behind-the-scenes portrait of a contemporary fashion brand." Booklist

Includes bibliographical references

DeJean, Joan E.

The **essence** of style; how the French invented high fashion, fine food, chic cafes, style, sophistication, and glamour. Free Press 2005 303p il $25; pa $15 **391**

1. Kings 2. Fashion -- History 3. France -- Social life and customs

ISBN 0-7432-6413-4; 0-7432-6414-2 pa

LC 2005-40019

"An unusual and delightfully educational perspective on snob appeal." Booklist

Includes bibliographical references

391.009 History, geographic treatment, biography

Cox, Caroline

The **world** atlas of street fashion; Caroline Cox. Yale University Press 2017 400 p. (hardcover: alk. paper) $35 **391.009**

1. Street life 2. Fashion -- Social aspects 3. Clothing and dress -- History

ISBN 9780300224030

LC 2017938947

This book, by Caroline Cox, "examines street style in all its global diversity. The book shows how Punk's generic language of anarchy is redeployed in London, Berlin, Tokyo, or Jakarta and takes on the unique flavor of each. It also reveals how street style can be overtly political: the Sapeurs of Kinshasa use elegance to reframe themselves as gentlemen, and the cholo gangs of East Los Angeles took strength from the Chicano movement of the 1960s." (Publisher's note)

"A lavishly photographed work that will entice anyone who devours fashion and pop culture." LJ

Dirix, Emmanuelle

Dressing the Decades; Twentieth-Century Vintage Style. Emmanuelle Dirix. Yale University Press 2016 224 p. illustrations (some color) $30 **391.009**

1. Fashion designers 2. Fashion -- History

ISBN 0300215525; 9780300215526

Author Emmanuelle Dirix "examines in depth the origins of the most important luxury garments. Each . . . chapter features a detailed overview of a particular decade, including the historical events, politics, technology, and advertising that inspired its most celebrated designs. The book provides a new perspective on such iconic items and significant trends as the cocktail dress, the Chanel suit, the tunic dress, boho chic, Futuristic chic, and others." (Publisher's note)

"Her well-informed narrative is often laced with socioeconomic observations, including discussion of Hollywood's impact on designers and vice versa, the class divisions of haute couture vs. ready-to-wear, and how various social and political movements transformed how we dress and consume fashion. The accompanying photos and illustrations ... are stunning and often drool-worthy." LJ

Includes bibliographical references (pages 218) and index.

Stevenson, N. J.

Fashion; a visual history from regency & romance to retro & revolution: a complete illustrated chronology of fashion from the 1800s to the present day. NJ Stevenson. 1st US ed. St. Martin's Griffin 2012 288 p. ill. (chiefly col.) $29.99 **391.009**

1. Hats 2. Painting 3. Women's clothing 4. Clothing and dress 5. Fashion -- History 6. Fashion design -- History 7. Clothing and dress -- History 8. Fashion -- History -- 19th century 9. Fashion -- History -- 20th century 10. Fashion -- History -- 21st century

ISBN 031262445X; 9780312624453

LC 2011278257

Author N. J. Stevenson describes "when distinctive styles that began as extravagances of the very rich permeated through well-dressed society until a cut of cloth or choice of accessory defined fashion. . . . Each spread focuses on a definitive item--be it bowler hat or little black dress, stiletto or caftan--or identifies key shifts in fashion that reflect excess, liberation, austerity, nostalgia, and technology, displaying it in contemporary images ranging from paintings and illustrated fashion plates to cartoons and photographs." (Publisher's note)

Includes bibliographical references and index

391.2   Women's clothing

Edwards, Lydia

How to read a dress; a guide to changing fashion from the 16th to the 20th century. Lydia Edwards. Bloomsbury Academic 2017 211 p. color illustrations (pbk.) $33.95   **391.2**

1. Fashion -- History 2. Women's clothing -- History
ISBN 9781472533272; 9781472534521

LC 2016029748

This book, by Lydia Edwards, "is an authoritative visual guide to women's fashion across five centuries. Each entry includes annotated color images of historical garments, outlining important features and highlighting how styles have developed over time, whether in shape, fabric choice, trimming, or undergarments. Readers will learn how garments were constructed and where their inspiration stemmed from at key points in history." (Publisher's note)

"Although the intended audience is fashion students, anyone interested in history or women's fashion will enjoy this volume." Booklist

Includes bibliographical references and index

391.5   Hairstyles

Tarlo, Emma

Entanglement; The secret lives of hair. Emma Tarlo. Oneworld Publications 2016 416 p. illustrations (some color) (ebook) $14.99; $22.99   **391.5**

1. Hair 2. Beauty shops 3. Personal grooming 4. Personal appearance
ISBN 9781780749938; 1780749929; 9781780749921

LC 2016051771

In this book, author "Emma Tarlo travels the globe, tracking its movement across India, Myanmar, China, Africa, the United States, Britain and Europe, where she meets people whose livelihoods depend on hair. Viewed from inside Chinese wig factories, Hindu temples and the villages of Myanmar, or from Afro hair fairs, Jewish wig parlours, fashion salons and hair loss clinics in Britain and the United States, hair is oddly revealing of the lives of all it touches." (Publisher's note)

"From eccentric wig makers in China to hair hunters in India and customers in Europe, Tarlo takes us on an eye-opening journey that will make us wonder if our own hair doesn't have a secret life of its own." Booklist

Includes bibliographical references (pages 363-368, 376-393) and index.

391.6   Personal appearance

Eldridge, Lisa

Face paint; the story of makeup. Lisa Eldridge. Abrams Image 2015 240 p. colour illustrations $29.95   **391.6**

1. Fashion 2. Cosmetics
ISBN 1419717960; 9781419717963

LC 2014959338

This book by Lisa Eldridge "explores the practical and idiosyncratic reasons behind makeup's use, the actual materials employed over generations, and the glamorous icons that people emulate, it is also a social

history of women and the ways in which we can understand their lives through the prism and impact of makeup." (Publisher's note)

391.65   Tattooing and scarification

Aitken-Smith, Trent

The **tattoo** dictionary; an A-Z guide to the secret language of tattoos. by Trent Aitken-Smith and illustrated by Ashley Tyson. Octopus Pub Group 2017 256 p. $20   **391.65**

1. Tattooing -- Encyclopedias 2. Signs and symbols -- Encyclopedias
ISBN 1784721778; 9781784721770

LC 2017046237

In this book, by Trent Aitken Smith, "discover the true meanings behind over 200 popular tattoos. . . . From sailors' swallows and Mexican skulls to prisoners' barbed wire and intricate Maori patterns, tattoos have been used as a means of communication by cultures all over the world for thousands of years. . . . [This book] uncovers the history of the most popular symbols in tattoo history, revealing their hidden meanings and the long-forgotten stories behind them." (Publisher's note)

"... this small volume will prove useful to those wanting to know the stories behind more than 200 popular tattoos, such as the Ace of Spades, anchors, the charming little devil known as Hot Stuff, the nautical star, and the QR code." Booklist

Cao, K. L.

DIY temporary tattoo art; easy step-by-step instructions for watercolor, henna, flash tattoos, and more! K.L. Cao. Adams Media 2017 176 p. color illustrations (paperback) $16.99   **391.65**

1. Body art 2. Henna (Dye) 3. Temporary tattoos
ISBN 9781507202388; 1507202377; 9781507202371

LC 2017009996

This book, by K.L. Cao, is a "step-by-step temporary tattoo book to help you rock a variety of on-trend tattoo styles for any occasion. . . . Cao uses a variety of easy-to-find materials like tissue paper, pressed flowers, gold leaf, henna ink, and more to give you what you need to amp up your style." (Publisher's note)

Includes bibliographical references and index

392   Customs of life cycle and domestic life

Gollaher, David

Circumcision; a history of the world's most controversial surgery. [by] David L. Gollaher. Basic Bks. 2000 253p hardcover o.p. pa $18   **392**

1. Circumcision
ISBN 0-465-02653-2 pa

LC 99-40015

This history of circumcision discusses Jewish, Muslim, and tribal rituals, medical procedures and complications, reasons for the procedure, and its social significance in various cultures and eras

Jellison, Katherine

It's our day; America's love affair with the white wedding, 1945-2005. University Press of Kansas 2008 297p il (CultureAmerica) $29.95   **392**

1. Marriage customs and rites 2. United States -- Social life and customs
ISBN 978-0-7006-1559-9

LC 2007-35444

The author "takes an in-depth look at the history and popularity of the American 'white wedding' and in doing so provides a unique exploration of late 20th- and early 21st-century American culture. She starts right after World War II and progresses through celebrity, royal, and movie weddings to the 'reality weddings' of today and how the ritual of a white wedding has been adapted in many same-sex marriages. . . . An enlightening and fascinating read, her book is sure to be of interest in most libraries." Libr J

Includes bibliographical references

Mead, Rebecca

One perfect day; the selling of the American wedding. Penguin Press 2007 245p $25.95; pa $15   **392**
1. Weddings
ISBN 978-1-59420-088-5; 978-0-14-311384-3 pa

LC 2006-52461

"Part investigative journalism, part social commentary, Mead's wry, insightful work offers an illuminating glimpse at the ugly underbelly of our Bridezilla culture." Publ Wkly

392.5   Wedding and marriage customs

Style your perfect wedding. DK Publishing 2015 253 p. color illustrations (hardcover) $40   **392.5**
1. Weddings 2. Wedding decorations 3. Weddings -- Planning
ISBN 1465429824; 9781465429827

LC 2015301664

This book presents wedding planning and decoration advice, "from unique wedding ideas to creative wedding themes, from fun bridal shower ideas to handmade wedding crafts, from a beautiful bouquet to the best dresses for your bridal party. . . . It's filled with over 50 . . . projects, including: save-the-date cards, centerpieces, linens, ring cushions, and confetti. This book also has . . . ideas for getting your bridal party involved in designing and planning your wedding." (Publisher's note)

392.6   Customs of sexual relations

Forbes, Sarah

Sex in the museum; my unlikely career at New York's most provocative museum. Sarah Forbes. St. Martin's Press 2016 224 p. (hardcover) $24.99; (ebook) $60   **392.6**
1. Sex -- History 2. Museums -- New York (N.Y.) 3. Sexology 4. Sex -- History -- Museums 5. Museum of Sex (New York, N.Y.) 6. Sex customs -- History -- Exhibitions 7. Museum curators -- New York (State) -- New York
ISBN 9781250041678; 9781466838574

LC 2015038926

This book, by Sarah Forbes, "invites readers to travel from suburban garages where men and women build sex machines, to factories that make sex toys, to labyrinthine archives of erotica collectors. Escorting us in to the hidden world of sex, illuminating the never-talked-about communities and eccentricities of our sexual subcultures, and telling her own personal story of a decade at The Museum of Sex, Sarah asks readers to grapple with the same questions she did: when it comes to sex, what is good, bad, deviant, normal?" (Publisher's note)

"A provocative chronicle steeped in eyebrow-raising details and personal honesty." Kirkus

393   Death customs

Jokinen, Tom

Curtains; adventures of an undertaker-in-training. Da Capo Press 2010 279p pa $15.95   **393**
1. Undertakers and undertaking 2. Funeral rites and ceremonies
ISBN 978-0-306-81891-2; 0-306-81891-4

LC 2010-920629

"The narrative pinballs between the many roles Jokinen takes on within the industry—hearse driver, embalming assistant, theatrically solemn host who gestures at coat racks and restrooms. All the while, Jokinen dutifully remains the voice of the curious reader, channeling skepticism, the weirds and awe into laugh-out-loud observations grounded in just enough research to provide context without weighing down the plot." PopMatters

Kammen, Michael G.

Digging up the dead; a history of notable American reburials. [by] Michael Kammen. University of Chicago Press 2010 260p il $25   **393**
1. Burial 2. Exhumation 3. Funeral rites and ceremonies
ISBN 978-0-226-42329-6; 0-226-42329-8

LC 2009-23515

"Kammen has a good sense of the details that make historical stories memorable. His occasional flashes of humor add a winsome, professionally geeky element to the telling." Dallas Morning News

Includes bibliographical references

Pringle, Heather Anne

The **mummy** congress; science, obsession, and the everlasting dead. {by} Heather Pringle. Hyperion 2001 368p il hardcover o.p. pa $13.95   **393**
1. Mummies 2. Forensic anthropology
ISBN 0-7868-6551-2; 0-7868-8463-0 pa

LC 00-54487

"Besides outstanding members of the scientific association that gathers as the Mummy Congress, Pringle limns the many varieties of mummies, from the world's oldest, preserved by the high-altitude climate of the Andes, to modern Communist dictators, self-mummifying Buddhists, and the subjects of extreme cosmetic surgery. More astounding than all the fright flicks about shambling, gauze-wrapped menaces wound together." Booklist

Includes bibliographical references

394   General customs

Visser, Margaret

The **gift** of thanks; the roots and rituals of gratitude. Houghton Mifflin Harcourt 2009 458p $27   **394**
1. Gratitude
ISBN 978-0-15-101331-9

LC 2009-14018

First published 2008 in Canada

"A book to be thankful for—sympathetic to human foible, deeply learned and a pleasure to read." Kirkus

Includes bibliographical references

394.1   Eating, drinking; using drugs

Anthony, Jason C.

Hoosh; roast penguin, scurvy day, and other stories of Antarctic cuisine. Jason C. Anthony. University of Nebraska Press 2012 286 p. (pbk.: alk. paper) $26.95 **394.1**

1. Food 2. Scientific expeditions 3. Antarctica -- Exploration 4. Food habits -- Antarctica 5. Outdoor cooking -- Antarctica 6. Antarctica -- History -- Anecdotes 7. Antarctica -- Social life and customs

ISBN 0803226667; 9780803226661

LC 2012011994

This book is "[Jason C.] Anthony's debut . . . [and] traces hardships during Antarctic expeditions and the sometimes disconcerting fare borne of isolation. From blubber to penguin meat, and on infamous occasions, sled dogs and horses, supplemented by canned foods as well as pemmican (a concentrated mixture of fat and protein, the 'perfect endurance food used by Native Americans for millennia'), polar cuisine has always had a storied history." (Kirkus)

Includes bibliographical references.

Cheever, Susan

Drinking in America; Our Secret History. Susan Cheever. Grand Central Publishing 2015 272 p. (hardcover) $28 **394.1**

1. United States -- Civilization 2. Drinking of alcoholic beverages -- United States

ISBN 9781455513871; 1455513873

LC 2015025648

First edition

This book, by Susan Cheever, presents an overview and analysis of the U.S. "national love affair with liquor, taking a long, thoughtful look at the way alcohol has changed . . . [the] nation's history. This is the often-overlooked story of how alcohol has shaped American events and the American character from the seventeenth to the twentieth century." (Publisher's note)

"As implicated as she is in the history of drinking in America, Cheever does not condemn it. Instead, she offers a colorful portrait of a society that, like her own family, has been indelibly shaped by its drinking habits. An intelligently argued study of our country's 'passionate connection to drinking.'" Kirkus

Collingham, E. M. (Elizabeth M.)

Curry; a tale of cooks and conquerors. Oxford University Press 2006 315p il maps $28 **394.1**

1. Eating customs 2. India -- Civilization

ISBN 978-0-19-517241-6; 0-19-517241-8

LC 2005-16641

The author "with incredibly engrossing detail, unravels the tantalizing mystery of 'curry' in its innumerable forms, which have ravished the taste buds in far-flung kitchens and dining rooms." MultiCult Rev

Includes bibliographical references

Cowen, Tyler

An **economist** gets lunch; new rules for everyday foodies. Tyler Cowen. Dutton 2012 x, 293 p.p **394.1**

1. Restaurants 2. Food industry and trade 3. Eating habits -- Economic aspects 4. Food habits -- Economic aspects 5. Food preferences -- Economic aspects

ISBN 0525952667; 9780525952664

LC 2011035174

In this book, economist Tyler Cowen "steers his audience through the contemporary world of eating and drinking. Like many staunch foodies, he respects the local. . . . Cowen finds that, despite what logic may suggest, the most expensive food is not necessarily the best. And he reveals that the same principle holds true in urban America as well as in the Third World. He expands this insight with a survey of barbecue restaurants in the U.S." (Booklist)

Includes bibliographical references and index

Downie, David

A **taste** of Paris; a history of the Parisian love affair with food. David Downie. St. Martin's Press 2017 280 p. (hardcover) $26.99 **394.1**

1. Gastronomy -- France 2. Paris (France) -- Description and travel 3. Food -- France -- Paris -- History

ISBN 9781250082930

LC 2017018869

This book, by David Downie, "embarks on a quest to discover 'What is it about the history of Paris that has made it a food lover's paradise?'. . . Following the contours of history and the geography of the city, Downie sweeps readers on an insider's gourmet walking tour of Paris and its environs . . . revealing the locations of Roman butcher shops, classic Belle Epoque bistros serving diners today and Marie Antoinette's exquisite vegetable garden." (Publisher's note)

"Downie relishes in debunking myths about French culinary exceptionalism (Curnonsky, one of Paris's best-known gastronomists in the early 20th century, 'only got into the gastro-journalism racket after a taste-bud-stimulating voyage to China') while unabashedly proclaiming his adoration for French culture and history in and out of the kitchen. Readers don't have to be foodies to get the flavor of the French character in this delightful, thoroughly researched culinary history." PW

Fernandez-Armesto, Felipe

Near a thousand tables; a history of food. Free Press 2002 258p $25; pa $14 **394.1**

1. Food -- History

ISBN 0-7432-2644-5; 0-7432-2740-9 pa

LC 2002-23318

This is a "well-written, thought-provoking overview of food history." Libr J

Includes bibliographical references and index

The **food** of a younger land; a portrait of American food: before the national highway system, before chain restaurants . . . edited and illustrated by Mark Kurlansky. Riverhead Books 2009 397p il $27.95 **394.1**

1. Cooking 2. Eating customs

ISBN 978-1-59448-865-8

LC 2009-8100

"In the late 1930s the WPA farmed out a writing project with the ambition of other New Deal programs: an encyclopedia of American food and food traditions from coast-to-coast similar to the federal travel guides. After Pearl Harbor, the war effort halted the project for good; the book was never published, and the files were archived in the Library of Congress. . . . [The editor] brought the unassembled materials to light and created this version of the guide that never was. . . . This extraordinary collection—at once history, anthropology, cookbook, almanac and family album—provides a vivid and revitalizing sense of the rural and regional characteristics and distinctions that we've lost and can find again here." Publ Wkly

Includes bibliographical references

Goulding, Matt

Grape, olive, pig; Deep Travels Through Spain's Food Culture. Matt Goulding; edited by Nathan Thornburgh. HarperCollins Publishers 2016 368 p. color illustrations, maps (ebook) $32.99; (hardcover) $35 **394.1**

1. Eating customs 2. Spanish cooking 3. Spain -- Description and travel 4. Food habits -- Spain 5. Food -- Spain -- History

ISBN 9780062394149; 9780062394132

LC 2016018185

This book, by Matt Goulding, "is a deeply personal exploration of Spain. . . . Goulding introduces you to . . . his adoptive home, and offers an intimate portrait of this multifaceted country, its remarkable people, and its complex history. Fall in love with Barcelona's tiny tapas bars and modernist culinary temples. Explore the movable feast of small plates and late nights in Madrid. Join the three-thousand-year-old hunt for Bluefin tuna off the coast of Cadiz." (Publisher's note)

"Deeply satisfying for the armchair traveler, this can't-miss book should be required reading prior to visiting Spain." LJ

Mayle, Peter

French lessons; adventures with knife, fork, and corkscrew. Knopf 2001 227p il $24; pa $12.95 **394.1**

1. Eating customs 2. France -- Social life and customs

ISBN 0-375-40590-9; 0-375-70561-9 pa

Mayle "relives some of his most precious moments reveling in the cuisine of his adopted homeland. . . . {He tells} savory, sensual, positively transporting stories about his encounters with Gallic gustatory delights and about his growing appreciation of the central place food occupies in French life." Booklist

McWilliams, James E.

Just food; where locavores get it wrong and how we can truly eat responsibly. Little, Brown and Company 2009 258p $25.99 **394.1**

1. Food industry 2. Natural foods 3. Eating customs

ISBN 978-0-316-03374-9

LC 2009-15514

The author "argues for moderation and compromise in today's raging food fights. Until recently, the author was a locavore—one who eats locally produced food. Though he still believes that it is a dietary commitment with many virtues, he argues that it's also a feeble, ineffective way to feed the world's hungry billions. . . . McWilliams presents some appealing alternatives to the views of both the agrarian romantics on the left and the agribusiness capitalists on the right. . . . Rich in research, provocative in conception and nettlesome to both the right and the left." Kirkus

Includes bibliographical references

Pollan, Michael, 1955-

★ The **omnivore's** dilemma; a natural history of four meals. Penguin Press 2006 450p pa $16; $26.95 **394.1**

1. Eating customs 2. Agriculture -- United States 3. Food supply -- United States 4. Food consumption -- United States

ISBN 0-14-303858-3 pa; 1-59420-082-3

LC 2005-56557

"Pollan has divided The Omnivore's Dilemma into three parts, one for each of the food chains that sustain us: industrialized food, alternative or 'organic' food, and food people obtain by dint of their own hunting, gathering, or gardening. Pollan follows each food chain . . . from the ground up to the table, emphasizing our dynamic co-evolutionary relationship with the species we depend on. He concludes each section by sitting down to a meal—at McDonald's, at home with his family sharing a dinner from Whole Foods, and in a revolutionary 'beyond organic' farm in Virginia. For each meal he traces the provenance of everything

consumed, [aiming to] and explain how our taste for particular foods reflects our environmental and biological inheritance." (Publisher's note)

The author "defines the Omnivore's Dilemma as the confusing maze of choices facing Americans trying to eat healthfully in a society that he calls 'notably unhealthy.' He seeks answers to this dilemma by taking readers through the industrial, organic, and hunter-gatherer stages of the food chain. . . . This folksy narrative provides a wealth of information about agriculture, the natural world, and human desires." Libr J

Includes bibliographical references

Schlosser, Eric

★ **Fast** food nation; the dark side of the all-American meal. Houghton Mifflin 2001 356p il $25 **394.1**

1. Restaurants 2. Food industry 3. Convenience foods

ISBN 0-395-97789-4

LC 00-53886

"Schlosser documents the effects of fast food on America's economy, its youth culture, and allied industries. . . . Starting with a young woman who makes minimum wage working at a Colorado fast-food restaurant, Schlosser relates the oft-told story of Ray Kroc's founding of McDonald's. The author also tells about the development of the franchise method of business ownership and the health and nutrition implications of fast-food consumption." Booklist

Includes bibliographical references

Standage, Tom

An **edible** history of humanity. Walker & Company 2009 269p il map $26 **394.1**

1. Food 2. Agriculture 3. Eating customs

ISBN 0-8027-1588-5; 978-0-8027-1588-3

LC 2009-5610

"This meaty little volume [is] cogent, informative and insightful." Kirkus

Includes bibliographical references

A **history** of the world in 6 glasses. Walker & Co. 2005 311p il $25 **394.1**

1. Beverages 2. World history 3. Tea -- History 4. Coffee -- History 5. Beverages -- History 6. Drinking of alcoholic beverages -- History

ISBN 0-8027-1447-1

LC 2004-61209

Mr. Standage's "book divides world history into beer, wine, spirits, coffee, tea and Coca-Cola ages. . . . He begins with humanity's shift from hunting and gathering to agriculture. This transition led to the cultivation of grain, which led to storage and fermentation and, eventually, beer." (N Y Times (Late N Y Ed)) Index.

Standage "has the ability to connect the smallest detail to the big picture and a knack for summarizing vast concepts in a few sentences." Publ Wkly

Includes bibliographical references

394.12 Eating and drinking

Goulding, Matt

Rice, noodle, fish; Deep Travels Through Japan's Food Culture. Matt Goulding; edited by Nathan Thornburgh. HarperWave 2015 352 p. color illustrations (Hardcover) $35; (ebook) $32.99 **394.12**

1. Japanese cooking 2. Food tourism -- Japan 3. Food habits -- Japan

ISBN 9780062394033; 9780062394040

LC 2015005013

IACP Cookbook Award Nominee: Literary Food Writing (2016)

This book by Matt Goulding, edited by Nathan Thornburgh, "explores Japan's most intriguing culinary disciplines in seven key regions, from the kaiseki tradition of Kyoto and the sushi masters of Tokyo to the street food of Osaka and the ramen culture of Fukuoka. You . . . will find a brilliant narrative that interweaves immersive food journalism with intimate portraits of the cities and the people who shape Japan's food culture." (Publisher's note)

"Goulding's gift for phrasing and razor-sharp prose elevate what could have been yet another rote travelogue into something much better." Pub Wkly

Kauffman, Jonathan

Hippie food; how back-to-the-landers, longhairs, and revolutionaries changed the way we eat. Jonathan Kauffman. William Morrow, an imprint of HarperCollins Publishers 2018 344 p. (hardcover) $26.99   **394.12**

1. Natural foods 2. Eating customs 3. Natural foods -- United States -- History 4. Natural foods industry -- United States -- History 5. Food habits -- United States -- History -- 20th century

ISBN 9780062437303; 9780062437327; 0062437305

In this book, author "Jonathan Kauffman journeys back more than half a century . . . to tell the story of how a coterie of unusual men and women embraced an alternative lifestyle that would ultimately change how modern Americans eat. Impeccably researched, 'Hippie Food' chronicles how the longhairs, revolutionaries, and back-to-the-landers . . . turned to a more idealistic and wholesome communal way of life and food." (Publisher's note)

"An astute, highly informative food exposé that educates without bias, leaving the culinary decision-making to readers." Kirkus

Includes bibliographical reference (pages 293-332) and index.

394.26   Holidays

Baker, James W.

Thanksgiving; the biography of an American holiday. foreword by Peter J. Gomes. University of New Hampshire Press 2009 273p il (Revisiting New England) pa $26.95   **394.26**

1. Thanksgiving Day

ISBN 978-1-58465-801-6

LC 2009-12348

The author shows "how Thanksgiving is seen through each generation's reality, having morphed from a holiday for pilgrim hats and turkeys to a cause for Native American protests to a holy day to several ancient holidays combined and a full-scale orgy of food and football. . . . [This is] an enjoyable, fascinating read both for students and for anyone looking for a good story." Libr J

Includes bibliographical references

Forbes, Bruce David

Christmas; a candid history. University of California Press 2007 179p il $19.95; pa $12.95   **394.26**

1. Christmas

ISBN 978-0-520-25104-5; 978-0-520-25802-0 pa

LC 2007-00366

The author "presents a brief social history of Christmas from pre-Christian winter celebrations to the commercialization of the holiday in American popular culture. The growth of the holiday to include Christmas cards, music and movies are included in this easy to read overview."

Univ Press Books for Public and Second Sch Libr, 2008

Includes bibliographical references

Hillstrom, Laurie

The **Thanksgiving** book; [by] Laurie C. Hillstrom. Omnigraphics 2008 328p il $65   **394.26**

1. Thanksgiving Day

ISBN 978-0-7808-0403-6

LC 2007-25708

"This book is definitely a wonderful tribute to the holiday of Thanksgiving." Am Ref Books Annu, 2008

Includes bibliographical references

Holiday symbols and customs; 4th ed.; Omnigraphics 2009 1321p $94   **394.26**

1. Holidays 2. Festivals

ISBN 978-0-7808-0990-1

LC 2008-28403

First published 1998 with title: Holiday symbols

"Describes the origins of 323 holidays around the world. Explains where, when, and how each event is celebrated, with detailed information on the symbols and customs associated with the holiday. Includes contact information and web sites for related organizations." Publisher's note

Includes bibliographical references

Holidays, festivals, and celebrations of the world dictionary; detailing more than 3,000 observances from all 50 states and more than 100 nations: a compendious reference guide to popular, ethnic, religious, national, and ancient holidays. . . edited by Cherie D. Abbey. 4th ed.; Omnigraphics 2010 1323p $144   **394.26**

1. Reference books 2. Holidays -- Dictionaries 3. Festivals -- Dictionaries

ISBN 978-0-7808-0994-9

LC 2009-41138

First edition published 1994 compiled by Sue Ellen Thompson and Barbara W. Carlson

"A comprehensive dictionary that describes more than 3,000 holidays and festivals celebrated around the world. Features both secular and religious events from many different cultures, countries, and ethnic groups. Includes contact information for events; multiple appendices with background information on world holidays; extensive bibliography; multiple indexes." Publisher's note

Rajtar, Steve

United States holidays and observances; by date, jurisdiction, and subject, fully indexed. McFarland & Co. 2003 165p $45   **394.26**

1. Holidays 2. Festivals

ISBN 0-7864-1446-4

LC 2002-154293

This "concentrates on observances and holidays established by statute in the U.S. and American Samoa, District of Columbia, Guam, the Northern Mariana Islands, Puerto Rico, and the U.S. Virgin Islands. In addition, UN-designated holidays are included. . . . The text is arranged by month, and chapters for each month are divided into 'Observances with Variable Dates' and 'Observances with Fixed Dates.' Each entry identifies the observance as federal or specific to a state and offers a description that ranges in length from three or four lines to a quarter page. . . . [This] would be a good addition to ready-reference desks in public libraries and information centers in schools." Booklist

394.264   Halloween

Morton, Lisa

Trick or Treat; A History of Halloween. Lisa Morton. University of Chicago Press 2012 229 p. (hardcover) $29 **394.264**
1. Halloween
ISBN 1780230478; 9781780230474

This book, by Lisa Morton, offers a history of Halloween. "The popularity of Halloween has spread around the globe to places as diverse as Russia, China, and Japan, but its association with death and the supernatural and its inevitable commercialization has made it one of our most misunderstood holidays. How did it become what it is today? . . . Lisa Morton provides a thorough history of this spooky day." (Publisher's note)

394.266   Christmas

Flanders, Judith

Christmas; a biography. Judith Flanders. Thomas Dunne Books 2017 245 p. (hardback) $24.99   **394.266**
1. Christmas 2. Santa Claus 3. Christmas trees 4. Christmas -- History
ISBN 9781250118349; 9781250118356

LC 2017027330

This book, by Judith Flanders, "explores the Christmas holiday, from the original festival through present day traditions. . . . Flanders casts a sharp eye on myths, legends and history, deftly moving from the origins of the holiday in the Roman empire, through Christmas trees in central Europe, to what might be the first appearance of Santa Claus -- in Switzerland -- to draw a picture of the season as it has never been seen before." (Publisher's note)

"Christmas evokes both memories of the past and expectations for future celebrations, but Flanders (The Making of Home, 2015) posits that the holiday never was the quiet, thoughtful, religious observance we think it was. Separating fact from myth and traditional practice, Flanders provides a well-researched 'biography' of how Christmas came to be observed through the ages and in various cultures." Booklist

394.909   Cannibalism – History

Schutt, Bill

Cannibalism; A Perfectly Natural History. by Bill Schutt. Algonquin Books of Chapel Hill 2017 352 p. illustrations (ebook) $26.95; $26.95   **394.909**
1. Cannibalism 2. Cannibalism -- Cross-cultural studies
ISBN 9781616206550; 9781616204624

LC 2016023112

This book, by Bill Schutt, investigates "our new understanding of cannibalism's role in biology, anthropology, and history. . . . Schutt takes readers from Arizona's Chiricahua Mountains, where . . . tadpoles . . . [devour] their siblings, to the Sierra Nevadas, where he joins researchers who are shedding new light on . . . the most infamous episode of cannibalism in American history. He even meets with an expert on the preparation and consumption of human placenta." (Publisher's note)

"With plenty of examples of cannibalism in humans past and present, Schutt's well researched and suspenseful work is a must read for anyone who's interested in the topic—and can stomach the gore." Pub Wkly

395   Etiquette (Manners)

Baldrige, Letitia

Letitia Baldrige's new manners for new times; a complete guide to etiquette. illustrations by Denise Cavalieri Fike. Scribner 2003 xxvi, 709p il $35   **395**
1. Etiquette
ISBN 0-7432-1062-X

LC 2003-65666

First published 1990 with title: Letitia Baldrige's complete guide to the new manners for the 90's

"Combining correctness, consideration, and common sense in equal measure, Baldrige advises readers on proper ways to approach intricate situations. She addresses same-sex unions, pregnant brides, blended and extended families, and sexual harassment with aplomb." Libr J

Blyth, Catherine

The **art** of conversation; a guided tour of a neglected pleasure. Gotham Books 2009 289p $22.50   **395**
1. Conversation
ISBN 978-1-592-40419-3; 1-592-40419-7

LC 2008-24276

"Adopting a chatty, conversational manner to write about conversation, Blyth mixes personal anecdotes into a salmagundi of selected quotes from anthropology, history, literature, philosophy and pop culture to analyze and give advice on the dynamics of good conversation, not to mention the perfect riposte for every situation. She examines everything from small talk to pillow talk, from riotous raconteurs to crashing bores, from flattery to false smiles. . . . Witty, eloquent and insightful, Blyth's book is a delightful encouragement to rediscover conversation as the best communication technology." Publ Wkly

Dresser, Norine

Multicultural manners; essential rules of etiquette for the 21st century. Rev ed; John Wiley & Sons 2005 285p map pa $16.95   **395**
1. Etiquette 2. Manners and customs
ISBN 978-0-471-68428-2; 0-471-68428-7

LC 2004-27079

First published 1996

"From body language and table manners to classroom behavior and gift giving, this guide to etiquette provides fascinating information about relations in our multicultural society." Booklist
Includes bibliographical references

Forni, Pier Massimo

The **civility** solution; what to do when people are rude. [by] P.M. Forni. St. Martin's Press 2008 xxi, 166p $19.95 **395**
1. Courtesy 2. Etiquette
ISBN 978-0-312-36849-4; 0-312-36849-6

LC 2008-9448

"In Part 1 . . . [the author] describes some of the causes of rudeness (e.g., anger, fear, inflated self-worth) and the negative consequences of rude behavior in daily life. . . . In Part 2, Forni provides over 70 examples of situations in which rudeness arises and solutions for dealing with them. Readers who have been criticized in public or annoyed by a loud cell phone conversation get realistic help." Libr J
Includes bibliographical references

Martin, Judith

Miss Manners' guide to excruciatingly correct behavior; illustrated by Gloria Kamen. freshly updated; Norton 2005

858p il $35   **395**
1. Etiquette
ISBN 0-393-05874-3
     LC 2005-00264
First published 1982 by Atheneum Pubs.
"Miss Manners is always as entertaining as she is civilized." Booklist

Morrison, Terri

★ **Kiss,** bow, or shake hands; the bestselling guide to doing business in more than 60 countries. [by] Terri Morrison and Wayne A. Conaway. 2nd ed.; Adams Media 2006 593p il pa $24.95   **395**
1. Negotiation 2. Business etiquette 3. Business communication
ISBN 1-59337-368-6
     LC 2006-13587
First published 1994
"The definitive reference for doing business around the world." Libr J

Oliver, Vicky

301 smart answers to tough business etiquette questions. Skyhorse Pub. 2010 370p pa $12.95   **395**
1. Business etiquette
ISBN 978-1-61608-141-6; 1-61608-141-4
     LC 2010021474
This guide to business etiquette covers "making a good first impression (and how to fix a bad one!); how to behave in elevators, airplanes, and supply closets; surviving cabs, commutes, and coffee shops; why time is not necessarily money everywhere on the planet; pre-approved conversational topics from A to Z; dining rules and regulations for the twenty-first century; what to do when you are suddenly unemployed; [and] electronic communication." Publisher's note
Includes bibliographical references

Outcalt, Todd

Your beautiful wedding on any budget. Sourcebooks 2009 227p pa $12.99   **395**
1. Weddings
ISBN 978-1-4022-1788-3
     LC 2008-46864
"A terrific resource for couples trying to start their marriage on a financially sound footing. The Methodist pastor offers suggestions for building a wedding fund and creative cost-cutting measures based on his debt-free wedding seminars and blog." Libr J

Post, Peggy

Emily Post's etiquette; manners for a new world. by Peggy Post, Anna Post, Lizzie Post, and Daniel Post Senning; illustrations by Janice Richter. 18th ed. William Morrow 2011 xi, 723 p.p illustrations $39.99   **395**
1. Etiquette
ISBN 0061740233; 9780061740237
     LC 2010042228
This book on etiquette, by Peggy Post, Anna Post, Lizzie Post, and Daniel Post Senning, "tackle[s] the latest issues and demands of the twenty-first century—from texting and tweeting to iPhones, Facebook, and all forms of social media. The perfect guide for Millennials living on their own for the first time who wish to establish themselves properly in the workplace, . . . [it] remains the essential handbook to proper social behavior." (Publisher's note)

Includes bibliographical references and index

Emily Post's The etiquette advantage in business; personal skills for professional success. Peggy Post and Peter Post. Third edition HarperResource 2005 xvi, 366 p.p illustrations $30   **395**
1. Job hunting 2. Business etiquette 3. Success in business
ISBN 0060760028; 006227046X; 9780062270467
     LC 2005283037
This book, by Peggy Post and Peter Post, "provide[s] you with the all-important tools for building solid, productive relationships with your business associates. . . . In this completely revised and updated edition, which includes three new chapters on ethics, table manners, and electronic communication, the Posts show you how to handle both everyday and unusual situations that are essential to professional and personal success." (Publisher's note)

Vivaldo, Denise

Do it for le$$! weddings; how-to create your dream wedding without breaking the bank. Sellers Pub., Inc. 2008 272p il pa $19.95   **395**
1. Weddings
ISBN 978-1-4162-0519-7
     LC 2008-923779
The author "focuses on receptions—venues, logistics, and menus (including numerous recipes). Detailed information and instructive illustrations make this a solid choice for those catering their own affairs." Libr J
Includes bibliographical references

Weiss, Mindy

The **wedding** book; the big book for your big day. by Mindy Weiss with Lisbeth Levine. Workman Pub. Company, Inc. 2007 485p il $35; pa $19.95   **395**
1. Weddings
ISBN 978-0-7611-5094-7; 978-0-7611-3960-7 pa
     LC 2008-15510
This book offers wedding planning advice on topics such as announcing the wedding, setting up a budget, planning the ceremony, wedding parties, and designing the dress and tuxedo.
This "comprehensive, well-organized guide offers good details on contracts and setting priorities." Libr J

395.2   Etiquette for stages in life cycle

Post, Lizzie

Emily Post's wedding etiquette; Anna Post and Lizzie Post; with illustrations by Happy Menocal. Sixth edition William Morrow, an imprint of HarperCollins Publishers 2014 xx, 380 p.p illustrations (hardcover) $29.99   **395.2**
1. Weddings 2. Etiquette 3. Wedding etiquette
ISBN 0062326104; 9780062326102
     LC 2013498453
This book, by Anna Post and Lizzie Post, "is the classic indispensable, comprehensive guide to creating the wedding of your dream[s], now in its sixth edition. Today's weddings are more complicated than ever, with new traditions replacing old, and new relationships to consider as family life grows more complex. [It] has everything a bride will ever need to know to have the perfect wedding." (Publisher's note)

395.4 Social correspondence

Scott, Andy

One kiss or two? the art and science of saying hello. Andy Scott. Overlook Pr 2018 320 p. $25.95 **395.4**

1. Etiquette 2. Social interaction 3. Interpersonal relations
ISBN 146831601X; 9781468316018

In this book, author "Andy Scott--a well-traveled former diplomat . . . takes a closer look at what greetings are all about. In discovering how they have developed over human history, he uncovers a kaleidoscopic world of etiquette, body-language, evolution, neuroscience, anthropology, and history. . . . By the end of it, we are able to make more sense of what lies behind greetings--and what it means to be human in the modern, cross-cultural age." (Publisher's note)

"Emphasizing the virtue of human connection throughout, Scott's buoyant study is reminiscent of the work of A.J. Jacobs in its breezy mix of pop sociology, personal anecdote, and self-help." Pub Wkly

395.5 Etiquette by situations

Alexander, Liz

Access to Asia; your multicultural guide to building trust, inspiring respect, and creating long-lasting business relationships. Sharon Schweitzer, Liz Alexander. John Wiley & Sons, Inc. 2015 374 p. illustrations (cloth) $30 **395.5**

1. Corporate culture 2. Business etiquette 3. Business communication 4. Cross-cultural studies 5. Management -- Asia 6. Corporate culture -- Asia 7. Business etiquette -- Asia 8. Intercultural communication 9. Management -- Cross-cultural studies
ISBN 9781118919019

LC 2014039933

This book, by Sharon Schweitzer and Liz Alexander, "presents a deeply insightful framework for today's global business leaders and managers, whether traveling from Toronto to Taipei, Baltimore to Bangalore, or San Francisco to Shanghai. . . . Readers will find in-the-trenches advice and stories from 80 regional experts in 10 countries, including China, Hong Kong, India, Japan, and Korea." (Publisher's note)

"Beautifully constructed and expertly written in straightforward language; will make it far easier for anyone to navigate the cultural differences of doing business in Asia." Kirkus

Includes bibliographical references and index

395.54 Table manners

Tower, Jeremiah

Table manners; how to behave in the modern world and why bother. Jeremiah Tower; illustrations by Libby Vander-Ploeg. Farrar, Straus & Giroux 2016 160 p. illustrations (ebook) $60; (hardback) $20 **395.54**

1. Table etiquette
ISBN 9780374714826; 9780374272340

LC 2016007141

This book by Jeremiah Tower answers table etiquette questions such as, "What do you do when you're running late? What can you eat with your hands? Are you the guest who runs late and texts real-time updates? . . . Whether your manners are a disaster or you simply need some fine-tuning, here is an authoritative and witty guide to table manners for everyone and every occasion." (Publisher's note)

"Tower successfully narrates the dos and don'ts of entertaining for all partygoers and planners." LJ

Includes bibliographical references (pages 139-140) and index.

398 Folklore

Bane, Theresa

Encyclopedia of vampire mythology. McFarland & Company, Inc., Publishers 2010 199p $75 **398**

1. Reference books 2. Vampires -- Encyclopedias
ISBN 978-0-7864-4452-6

LC 2010-15576

The "introduction presents a survey of the vampire myth's historical roots and continued evolution. Subsequent entries, organized alphabetically by vampire name, include phonetic pronunciations and define the many tangible and intangible vampiric forms that hail from every continent around the globe. . . . A thorough resource for dark mythologists and vampire enthusiasts." Libr J

Includes bibliographical references

Encyclopedia of American folklife; Simon J. Bronner, editor. M.E. Sharpe 2006 4v il set $399 **398**

1. Reference books 2. Folklore -- United States -- Encyclopedias 3. United States -- Social life and customs -- Encyclopedias
ISBN 0-7656-8052-1; 978-0-7656-8052-5

LC 2005-32119

This encyclopedia "provides a survey of the cultural patterns and experiences of diverse communities throughout the United States and the territories of Guam, Samoa, and Puerto Rico as well as other countries and ethnic groups that have influenced American social practices. . . . The encyclopedia covers crafts, foods, architecture, remedies, customs, holidays, narratives, speech, and stereotypes, with an emphasis on contemporary practices." Libr J

Includes bibliographical references

Guiley, Rosemary Ellen

The **encyclopedia** of vampires & werewolves; foreword by Jeanne Keyes Youngson. 2nd ed; Facts On File 2011 430p il $85; pa $24.95 **398**

1. Reference books 2. Monsters -- Encyclopedias 3. Vampires -- Encyclopedias 4. Werewolves -- Encyclopedias
ISBN 978-0-8160-8179-0; 0-8160-8179-4; 978-0-8160-8180-6 pa; 0-8160-8180-8 pa; 978-1-4381-3632-5 ebook; 1-4381-3632-3 ebook

LC 2010034839

First published 2004 with title: The encyclopedia of vampires, werewolves, and other monsters

"Entries describe supposed true historical accounts, how vampires and werewolves come into existence, beliefs about vampires and werewolves, and real-life creatures and cases that may have inspired their legends. . . . Fictional vampires from a range of media are discussed, along with the people who helped create them." Publisher's note

Includes bibliographical references

Hurston, Zora Neale

Folklore, memoirs, and other writings. Library of Am. 1995 1001p il $35 **398**

ISBN 0-940450-84-4

LC 94-21384

Companion volume to Novels and stories (1995)

"This is the first time the unexpurgated version of Hurston's 1942 autobiography, Dust Tracks on the Road, is being published; sections deemed too provocative (dealing with politics, race, and sex) have been restored. Mules and Men (1935) is a collection of African American folklore she gleaned on travels in the South, while Tell My Horse (1938) tenders her personal findings on African-based religion in Jamaica and Haiti. Additionally, 22 magazine and book articles with anthropological themes . . . that have never been gathered into book form are corralled here." Booklist

Melton, J. Gordon

The **vampire** book; the encyclopedia of the undead. Completely revamped, fully rev. and expanded, 3rd ed.; Visible Ink Press 2010 909p il pa $29.95   **398**
1. Reference books 2. Vampires -- Encyclopedias
ISBN 978-1-57859-281-4

LC 2010-24263
First published 1994
"This vampire lore tome covers legends from around the world, both classical and current, presenting an overview of the historical, literary, mythological, biographical, and popular aspects of vampires. . . . This book is an excellent and comprehensive addition to any collection serving readers interested in learning more about the vampire in time, place, and society. Aficionados of vampires in popular culture will enjoy it." Libr J
Includes bibliographical references

Prahlad, Anand

The **Greenwood** encyclopedia of African American folklore; edited by Anand Prahlad. Greenwood Press 2005 xl, 1557p 3v il set $299.95   **398**
1. Reference books 2. African Americans -- Folklore -- Encyclopedias 3. African Americans -- Social life and customs -- Encyclopedias
ISBN 0-313-33035-2

LC 2005-19214
For a fuller review, see: Booklist, Feb. 1, 2006
"The three volume set gives special attention to music, art, folktales, spiritual beliefs, foodways, proverbs, and other topics central to African American folklore, and discusses the Caribbean and African roots of traditional African American culture." Libr Media Connect
Includes bibliographical references

World folklore for storytellers; tales of wonder, wisdom, fools, and heroes. Josepha Sherman, editor. Sharpe Reference 2010 368p il $95   **398**
1. Folklore 2. Storytelling
ISBN 978-0-7656-8174-4

LC 2009-10525
This is "a wonderfully wide-ranging collection of nearly 200 ethnically diverse folktales. Particularly vital is that the stories are organized thematically rather than geographically, allowing for broader symbolic and anthropological comparisons. Each narrative runs several pages, includes a brief explanatory introduction, and consistently concludes with at least two bibliographic references. Pockets of multipage color plates offer images from native folktale anthologies and other relevant artistic renderings." Libr J
Includes bibliographical references

398.2   Folk literature

Ackroyd, Peter

The **death** of King Arthur; Thomas Malory's Le morte d'Arthur. Sir Thomas Malory; a retelling by Peter Ackroyd. Viking 2011 316p $26.95   **398.2**
1. Authors 2. Kings 3. Britons -- Fiction. 4. Great Britain -- Kings and rulers -- Fiction. 5. Knights and knighthood -- Great Britain -- Fiction.
ISBN 978-0-670-02307-3; 0-670-02307-8

LC 2011-21800
First published 2010 in the United Kingdom
"Ackroyd takes the daunting Middle English verse and retells the ancient legends in modern English prose. He also omits most of Malory's medieval tales as perhaps too creaky for modern minds, or maybe simply to make his retelling a niftier little book. All the essential stories are here, among them: Arthur lifting the great sword Excalibur from the stone to become king; the adulterous quarter-century-long love affair of Queen Guinevere and Arthur's most powerful and trusted knight, Lancelot du Lake; the love of Tristram and Isolte; Sir Galahad and the search for the Holy Grail; the awesome power of the wizard Merlin, the exquisite evil of Morgan le Fay, Arthur's half-sister, and finally the doom of Camelot and the death of Arthur at the hand of Sir Mordred, his own son born from an incestuous union of Arthur and Morgan le Fay. . . . Ackroyd tells these stories in such simple, vivid language that they seem as new as they must have when first heard around the peat fires of cold and gloomy England perhaps 1,000 years ago. And they're still a lot of fun." Dallas Morning News

African American folklore; Anand Prahlad, editor. Greenwood, an Imprint of ABC-CLIO, LLC 2016 xviii, 413 p.p illustrations (alk. paper) $100   **398.2**
1. Encyclopedias and dictionaries 2. Folklore -- United States -- Encyclopedias 3. African Americans -- Social life and customs -- Encyclopedias 4. Tales -- United States -- Encyclopedias 5. African Americans -- Folklore -- Encyclopedias
ISBN 9781610699297; 9781610699303

LC 2016005233
Edited by Anand Prahlad, "This encyclopedia provides accessible entries on key elements of this long history, including folklore originally derived from African cultures that have survived here and those that originated in the United States." It "Offers the most comprehensive compilation of resources on African American folklore, in the forms of bibliographical citations, lists of websites, and lists of cultural centers." (Publisher's note)
"Prahlad sets out to have an encyclopedia that celebrates the spirit of African Americans without shying away from the history that shaped the culture. In this, he can be proud." Booklist
Includes bibliographical references and index

Armstrong, Karen

★ A **short** history of myth. Canongate 2005 159p hardcover o.p. pa $14   **398.2**
1. Mythology
ISBN 1-84195-716-X; 1-84195-800-X pa
This is an "overview of the ever-evolving partnership between myth and man from Paleolithic times to the present. Succinct and cleanly written, it is hugely readable and, in its journey across the epochs of human experience, often moving. . . . Armstrong's exposition is streamlined and uncluttered without being simplistic." N Y Times Book Rev
Includes bibliographical references

Asma, Stephen T.

On monsters; an unnatural history of our worst fears. Oxford University Press 2009 351p il $27.95   **398.2**
1. Monsters
ISBN 978-0-19-533616-0

LC 2009-7219

The author "is insightful and entertaining in his discussion of monsters of the deep, supernatural doppelgangers, zombies, and vampires, and intense in his discussion of Freud and the science of monstrous feelings. . . . Asma's far-reaching book of monsterology is original, captivating, and profoundly elucidating." Booklist

Includes bibliographical references

Bly, Robert, 1926-

More than true: the wisdom of fairy tales; Robert Bly. Henry Holt and Company 2018 192 p. (hardcover: alk. paper) $27 **398.2**

1. Wisdom in literature 2. Fairy tales -- History and criticism 3. Truth in literature 4. Conduct of life in literature 5. Tales -- History and criticism 6. Fairy tales -- Psychological aspects
ISBN 9781250158192

LC 2017024789

In this book, author "Robert Bly revisits a selection of fairy tales and examines how these enduring narratives capture the essence of human nature. Few forms of storytelling have greater power to captivate the human mind than fairy tales, but where do these tales originate from, and what do they mean? . . . Bly has been asking these questions throughout his career. Here Bly looks at six tales that have stood the test of time and have captivated the poet for decades." (Publisher's note)

Includes bibliographical references and index
Wisdom of fairy tales

Bulfinch, Thomas

★ **Bulfinch's** mythology; foreword by Alberto Manguel. Modern Library pbk. ed.; Modern Library 2004 862p pa $17.95 **398.2**

1. Chivalry 2. Emperors 3. Mythology 4. Mabinogion 5. Folklore -- Europe
ISBN 0-375-75147-5

LC 2005-271850

First combined edition published 1913 by Crowell. Originally published in three separate volumes 1855, 1858 and 1862 respectively

"The classic work on mythology, Bulfinch's gives brief summations of Greek, Roman, Norse, Arthurian, and other miscellaneous myths and includes notes on the 'Iliad,' the 'Odyssey,' and the 'Aeneid.'" N Y Public Libr Book of How & Where to Look It Up

Includes bibliographical references

Encyclopedia of Jewish folklore and traditions; Raphael Patai, founding editor; Haya Bar-Itzhak, editor. M.E. Sharpe 2012 44 p. (hardcover: alk. paper) $299 **398.2**

1. Jewish folk literature 2. Judaism -- Encyclopedias 3. Folklore -- Encyclopedias 4. Jews -- Folklore -- Encyclopedias 5. Jews -- Social life and customs -- Encyclopedias
ISBN 0765620251; 9780765620255

LC 2012042203

"This encyclopedia covers the long and multifarious history of Jewish folklore and customs from the Bible to bagels. . . . The eclectic content covers holidays (Purim), material artifacts (illuminated manuscripts), and mythical beliefs (Dybbuk) and offers country studies (Afghanistan, Iran) and biographies of notable Jewish ethnographers." (Library Journal)

Includes bibliographical references and index

Favorite folktales from around the world; edited by Jane Yolen. Pantheon Bks. 1986 498p hardcover o.p. pa $18 **398.2**

1. Folklore 2. Fairy tales
ISBN 0-394-75188-4 pa

LC 86-42644

"Selections include tales from the American Indians, the brothers Grimm, Italo Calvino's Italian folk-tales, as well as stories from Iceland, Afghanistan, Scotland, and many other countries. Yolen provides each section with a relevant introduction, often including historical and literary factors, thus alerting readers as to what to look for." SLJ

Grimm, Wilhelm, 1786-1859

The **Original** Folk and Fairy Tales of the Brothers Grimm; the complete first edition. [Jacob Grimm, Wilhelm Grimm; translated by] Jack Zipes; [illustrated by Andrea Dezsö] Princeton University Press 2014 xliii, 519 p.p illustrations (hardback: acid-free paper) $35 **398.2**

1. Fairy tales 2. Folklore -- Germany 3. Tales -- Germany 4. Fairy tales -- Germany
ISBN 9780691160597

LC 2014004127

"For the very first time, 'The Original Folk and Fairy Tales of the Brothers Grimm' makes available in English all 156 stories from the 1812 and 1815 editions. These narrative gems, newly translated and brought together in one. . . book, are accompanied by . . . new illustrations from . . . artist Andrea Dezsö." (Publisher's note)

Includes bibliographical references and index

Haase, Donald

The **Greenwood** encyclopedia of folktales and fairy tales; edited by Donald Haase. Greenwood Press 2008 3v il set $299.95 **398.2**

1. Reference books 2. Folklore -- Encyclopedias 3. Fairy tales -- Encyclopedias
ISBN 978-0-313-33441-2

LC 2007-31698

"Meticulously documented and firmly grounded in scholarly research, most articles feature straightforward language and sufficient background material to be accessible to lay readers and novice researchers." Booklist

Includes bibliographical references

Lavers, Chris

The **natural** history of unicorns. William Morrow 2009 258p il $26.99 **398.2**

1. Unicorns
ISBN 978-0-06-087414-8; 0-06-087414-7
First published 2008 in the United Kingdom

This "is an erudite, scholarly book which uses the unicorn to illuminate millennia of social and geographical change. Unicorns appear in many guises in many cultures. . . . Lavers's achievement is to show how each of these is a chimera based on startlingly accurate reports of real animals, carried over trade routes. . . . Lavers's book offers revelations not only about mythical creatures, but about the extent and effects of globalisation in ancient times. It's eminently readable, too." New Sci

Includes bibliographical references p. 245-248)

Malory, Thomas

Le morte Darthur, or, The hoole book of Kyng Arthur and of his noble knyghtes of the Rounde Table; authoritative text, sources and backgrounds, criticism. [by] Sir Thomas Malory; edited by Stephen H.A. Shepherd. Norton 2004 lii, 954p (A Norton critical edition) pa $16.95 **398.2**

1. Kings
ISBN 0-393-97464-2

LC 2002-26534

Originally published 1485

"The work is a skillful selection and blending of materials taken from the mass of Arthurian legends. The central story consists of two main elements: the reign of King Arthur ending in catastrophe and the dissolution of the Round Table; and the quest of the Holy Grail." Oxford Companion to Engl Lit

Includes bibliographical references

Orenstein, Catherine

Little Red Riding Hood uncloaked; sex, morality, and the evolution of a fairy tale. Basic Bks. 2002 289p il hardcover o.p. pa $14.95 **398.2**

1. Little Red Riding Hood

ISBN 0-465-04126-4 pa; 0-465-04125-6

LC 2002-4240

"Once upon a time, Red Riding Hood was a good little girl. When she foolishly strayed from the path in the forest and spoke to strangers, she fell prey to the wicked wolf, but fortunately, the heroic woodcutter rescued her just in time. . . . With wit and insight, Orenstein makes us look again at the old childhood story, how it has changed and what that says about us. From Perrault and the Brothers Grimm to Bruno Bettelheim and Andrea Dworkin, the lively informal narrative surveys the stories and the scholarship in terms of folklore, psychology, feminism, and pornography." Booklist

Includes bibliographical references

Pullman, Philip, 1946-

★ **Fairy** tales from the Brothers Grimm; a new English version. [edited by] Philip Pullman. Viking 2012 405 p. $27.95 **398.2**

1. Fairy tales 2. Fairy tales -- Germany 3. Pullman, Philip, 1946-

ISBN 067002497X; 9780670024971

LC 2012027181

In this book "[Philip] Pullman retells [fairy tales by Jacob and Wilhelm Grimm], . . . from much-loved stories like 'Cinderella' and 'Rumpelstiltskin,' 'Rapunzel' and 'Hansel and Gretel' to lesser-known treasures like 'The Three Snake Leaves,' 'Godfather Death' and 'The Girl with No Hands.' At the end of each tale he offers a brief personal commentary, opening a window on the sources of the tales, the various forms they've taken over the centuries and their everlasting appeal." (Publisher's note)

Includes bibliographical references

Sir Gawain and the Green Knight; a new verse translation. [translated by] Simon Armitage. W. W. Norton & Company 2007 198p $25.95; pa $14.95 **398.2**

1. Arthurian romances 2. Poetry -- By individual authors

ISBN 978-0-393-06048-5; 0-393-06048-9; 978-0-393-33415-9 pa; 0-393-33415-5 pa

LC 2007-28520

Armitage "clearly feels a special kinship with the Gawain poet. He captures his dialect and his landscape and takes great pains to render the tale's alliterative texture and drive. . . . His vernacular translation isn't literal—sometimes he alliterates different letters, sometimes he foreshortens the number of alliterations in a line, sometimes he changes lines altogether and so forth—but his imitation is rich and various and recreates the gnarled verbal texture of the Middle English original, which is presented in a parallel text." N Y Times Book Rev

Wroe, Ann

Orpheus; the song of life. Ann Wroe. Overlook 2012 262 p. $26.95 **398.2**

1. Greek mythology 2. Cross-cultural studies 3. Literature -- History and criticism 4. Orpheus (Greek mythology)

ISBN 9780224091367; 0224091360; 1590207785; 9781590207789

LC 2011508687

This book by Ann Wroe "traces the obscure origins and tangled relationships of the Orpheus myth from ancient times through today." (Library Journal). After tracing "his adventures with Jason and the Argonauts, his eternal love of Eurydice and interminable mourning for her and descent into Hades . . . the author recounts the influence of Orpheus on a veritable pantheon of writers and musicians, including Ovid, Virgil, Milton, Shelley, Keats, Cocteau and a host of others." (Kirkus Reviews)

398.209 History, geographic treatment, biography

Schönwerth, Franz Xaver von, 1809-1886

The **turnip** princess; and other newly discovered fairy tales. Franz Xaver von Schonwerth; edited by Erika Eichenseer; illustrated by Engelbert Suss; translated by Maria Tatar. Penguin Group USA 2015 288 p. illustrations (paperback) $17 **398.209**

1. Fairy tales 2. Princesses -- Fiction

ISBN 0143107429; 9780143107422

LC 2015302549

This book edited by Erika Eichenseer; illustrated by Engelbert Suss; translated by Maria Tatar, presents author Franz Xavier von Schonwerth's fairy tales in English. "Violent, dark, and full of action, and upending the relationship between damsels in distress and their dragon-slaying heroes, these more than seventy stories bring us closer than ever to the unadorned oral tradition in which fairy tales are rooted, revolutionizing our understanding of a hallowed genre." (Publisher's note)

"These eminently enjoyable tales offer a rich new take on the material of the Grimms and Andersen." LJ

Zipes, Jack

The **irresistible** fairy tale; the cultural and social history of a genre. Jack Zipes. Princeton University Press 2012 xvii, 235 p.p (hardcover; alk. paper) $29.95 **398.209**

1. Fairy tales 2. Fairy tales -- Social aspects 3. Fairy tales -- History and criticism

ISBN 0691153388; 9780691153384

LC 2011040188

This book, by Jack Zipes, presents "a provocative new theory about why fairy tales were created and retold--and why they became such an indelible and infinitely adaptable part of cultures around the world. . . . Zipes presents a nuanced argument about how fairy tales originated in ancient oral cultures, how they evolved through the rise of literary culture and print, and how, in our own time, they continue to change through their adaptation in an ever-growing variety of media." (Publisher's note)

Includes bibliographical references and index.

398.23 Tales and lore of places and times

Adams, Mark, 1967-

Meet Me in Atlantis; My Obsessive Quest to Find the Sunken City. Mark Adams. Penguin Group USA 2015 336 p. illustrations $27.95 **398.23**

1. Exploration 2. Atlantis (Legendary place)

ISBN 0525953701; 9780525953708

LC 2014025735

Author Mark Adams examines why "mateur explorers are still actively searching for [Atlantis] this sunken city all around the world, based entirely on the clues Plato left behind. He visits scientists who use cutting-edge technology to find legendary civilizations once thought to be fictional. He examines the numerical and musical codes hidden in Plato's writings, and . . . traces their roots back to Pythagoras, the sixth-century BC mathematician." (Publisher's note)

"Adams's excellent examination frames much of Atlantis research on an intimate level. In its own right, this work serves as an important contribution to the search for Atlantis. Readers of history, adventure, travel, scientific inquiry, or the history of science will find this book provocative and entertaining." LJ

398.8 Rhymes and rhyming games

The **Oxford** dictionary of nursery rhymes; edited by Iona and Peter Opie. 2nd ed; Oxford Univ. Press 1997 xxix, 559p il $55 **398.8**
   1. Reference books 2. Nursery rhymes -- Dictionaries
   ISBN 0-19-860088-7
LC 98-140995
First published 1951
"The novice as well as the professional will find it an enjoyable read, as well as a learning experience." Am Ref Books Annu, 1999

398.9 Proverbs

Manser, Martin H.
The **Facts** on File dictionary of proverbs; associate editors, Rosalind Fergusson, David Pickering. 2nd ed.; Facts On File 2006 499p (Facts on File library of language and literature) $55; pa $19.95 **398.9**
   1. Proverbs
   ISBN 0-8160-6673-6; 978-0-8160-6673-5; 0-8160-6674-4 pa; 978-0-8160-6674-2 pa
LC 2006-24535
Original edition published 1983 compiled by Rosalind Fergusson
This dictionary "includes more than 1,700 English-language proverbs . . . that are widely recognized today. Arranged alphabetically, entries provide the meaning of each proverb, the date it was first recorded, variant forms of the proverb, other proverbs that are similar and opposite to it in meaning, and examples of the proverb's use." Publisher's note
   Includes bibliographical references

400 LANGUAGE

400 Language

Crystal, David
  ★ The **Cambridge** encyclopedia of language; 3rd ed; Cambridge University Press 2010 516p il map $99; pa $45 **400**
   1. Reference books 2. Language and languages -- Encyclopedias
   ISBN 978-0-521-51698-3; 978-0-521-73650-3 pa
LC 2010-502889
First published 1987

"A valuable and concise . . . handbook for linguistic beginners, linguistic researchers looking for a quick overview and, most of all, the general reader interested in language." Linguist List
   Includes bibliographical references

Everett, Daniel L.
  Language; the cultural tool. Daniel L. Everett. Pantheon Books 2012 351 p. ill. $27.95 **400**
   1. Intellect 2. Communication 3. Sociolinguistics 4. Language and culture
   ISBN 0307378535; 9780307378538
LC 2011034829
This book looks at whether language is "a genetically programmed instinct or something we pick up from the culture around us . . . . Challenging Noam Chomsky, Steven Pinker, and other partisans of 'nativism,' which holds that certain kinds of knowledge are hard-wired into us . . . , linguist [Daniel L. Everett . . . argues that language is a practical tool for communicating and social bonding . . . that children learn through general intelligence." (Publishers Weekly)

"Everett unfolds a compelling analysis of how language informs all the activities we recognize as distinctively human. A linguistic study certain to attract many general readers." Booklist
   Includes bibliographical references (p. [334]-337) and index

Kenneally, Christine
  The **first** word; the search for the origins of language. Viking 2007 357p $26.95 **400**
   1. Evolution 2. Language and languages
   ISBN 978-0-670-03490-1; 0-670-03490-8
LC 2007-3182
The author "explains difficult ideas concisely and clearly, and she maintains a firm grip on the steering wheel, moving the overall argument along in a straight line. Above all, she is scrupulously fair-minded." N Y Times (Late N Y Ed)
   Includes bibliographical references

Pinker, Steven, 1954-
  The **language** instinct; how the mind creates language. Harper Perennial 2007 526p il pa $15.95 **400**
   1. Language and languages
   ISBN 978-0-06-133646-1; 0-06-133646-7
First published 1994 by Morrow
The author "argues that an 'innate grammatical machinery of the brain' exists, which allows children to 'reinvent' language on their own. Basing his ideas on Noam Chomsky's Universal Grammar theory, Pinker describes language as a 'discrete combinatorial system' that might easily have evolved via natural selection. Pinker steps on a few toes . . . but his work, while controversial, is well argued, challenging, often humorous, and always fascinating." Libr J
   Includes bibliographical references

Tammet, Daniel
  Every word is a bird we teach to sing; encounters with the mysteries and meanings of language. Daniel Tammet. Little, Brown & Co. 2017 262 p. (hardcover) $27 **400**
   1. Vocabulary 2. Historical literature 3. English language -- History 4. Linguistics 5. Communication 6. Language and languages
   ISBN 9780316353052; 9780316510141
LC 2017935940
In this book, author Daniel Tammet "goes back in time to London to explore the numeric language of his autistic childhood; in Iceland, he learns why the name Blær became a court case; in Canada, he meets one of the world's most accomplished lip readers. . . . [He] explores the way

communication shapes reality. From the art of translation to the lyricism of sign language, these essays display the stunning range of Tammet's literary and polyglot talents." (Publisher's note)

"A fascinating journey through language and some of its many varied forms and uses." Booklist

401   Philosophy and theory

Crystal, David

★ **How** language works; how babies babble, words change meaning, and languages live or die. Overlook Press 2006 500p $32.50   **401**

1. Linguistics 2. Language and languages
ISBN 1-58567-848-1
Crystal "offers an impeccably organized guide to language and communication that brings clarity to a scholarly subject, and is sure to become a standard reference." Publ Wkly

Includes bibliographical references

Everett, Daniel L.

How language began; the story of humanity's greatest invention. Daniel L. Everett. Liveright Publishing Corporation 2017 xviii, 330 p.p illustrations (hardcover) $28.95   **401**

1. Semiotics 2. Historical literature 3. Language and languages -- Origin 4. Communication 5. Psycholinguistics
ISBN 9780871407955; 9780871404770; 0871407957
                                LC 2017025673

This book, by Daniel L. Everett, "provides . . . a comprehensive examination of the evolutionary story of language, from the earliest speaking attempts by hominids to the more than seven thousand languages that exist today. . . . Challenging long-standing principles in the field, Everett now builds on the theory that language was not intrinsic to our species. In order to truly understand its origins, a more interdisciplinary approach is needed." (Publisher's note)

"In this provocative and ambitious book, linguist Everett . . . demonstrates the complex and expansive nature of human language and its many communicative forms." LJ

Includes bibliographical references and index.

Pinker, Steven, 1954-

The **stuff** of thought; language as a window into human nature. Viking 2007 499p il $29.95   **401**

1. Thought and thinking 2. Language and languages
ISBN 978-0-670-06327-7; 0-670-06327-4
                                LC 2007-26601

The author's "vivid prose and down-to-earth attitude will once again attract an enthusiastic audience outside academia." Publ Wkly

Includes bibliographical references

Words and rules; the ingredients of language. Perennial 2000 349p il pa $15   **401**

1. Grammar 2. Language and languages
ISBN 978-0-06-095840-4; 0-06-095840-5
First published 1999 by Basic Books
This book "with its crisp prose and neat analogies, makes required reading for anyone interested in cognition and language." Publ Wkly

Includes bibliographical references

Yang, Charles

★ The **infinite** gift; how children learn and unlearn the languages of the world. Scribner 2006 275p il $25   **401**

1. Language and languages
ISBN 978-0-7432-3756-7; 0-7432-3756-0
The author explains the "process by which children acquire language. He discusses everything from the sounds they hear in the womb to how they distinguish between different languages at three months to their mastery of their language by age five. Throughout this learning process, posits Yang, a child has tested the grammar and sounds that exist in many other languages (and would presumably have no trouble acquiring them) but ultimately settles on the relevant one, and soon after, can no longer distinguish between or articulate nonrelevant sounds. . . . Anyone with the slightest interest in the English language should read his book." Libr J

401.9   Psychological principles, language acquisition, speech perception

Wolfe, Tom, 1930-2018

The **Kingdom** of Speech; Tom Wolfe. Little, Brown & Co. 2016 160 p. (ebook) $78; $26   **401.9**

1. Evolution 2. Linguistics 3. Language and languages
ISBN 9780316269315; 0316404624; 9780316404624
                           LC 2016942707

This book, by Tom Wolfe, argues "that speech--not evolution--is responsible for humanity's complex societies and achievements. From Alfred Russel Wallace, the Englishman who beat Darwin to the theory of natural selection but later renounced it, and through the controversial work of modern-day anthropologist Daniel Everett, . . . Wolfe examines the solemn, long-faced, laugh-out-loud zig-zags of Darwinism, old and Neo, and finds it irrelevant here in the Kingdom of Speech." (Publisher's note)

"Wolfe is at his best when portraying the lives of the scientists and their respective eras, and his vibrant study manages to be clever, funny, serious, satirical, and instructive." Pub Wkly

Includes bibliographical references (pages 170-185).

410   Linguistics

Crystal, David

★ A **dictionary** of language; 2nd ed; University of Chicago Press 2001 390p il pa $17.50   **410**

1. Reference books 2. Language and languages -- Dictionaries
ISBN 0-226-12203-4
                            LC 00-69076

First published 1992 with title: An encyclopedic dictionary of language and languages; present edition first published in the United Kingdom with title: The Penguin dictionary of language

This dictionary "offers explanations of the most frequently used linguistic terms, particularly those that can occur in texts read by beginners and by interested laypersons. . . . There are also entries concerned with graphology, shorthand writing, and similar peripheral, but interesting, topics. The impression that this dictionary has been written mainly for the general public is enhanced by the humorous jocose caricatures interspersed throughout the text, but the information is still solid. The author has succeeded in creating a handy dictionary that will serve students and laypeople equally well, for both browsing and study." Am Ref Book Annu, 2002

Deutscher, Guy

Through the language glass; why the world looks different in other languages. Metropolitan Books / Henry Holt and Co.

2010 304p il $28; ebook $14.99 **410**
1. Linguistics 2. Language and languages
ISBN 978-0-8050-8195-4; 978-1-4299-7011-2 ebook

LC 2010-1042

Deutscher "combines erudition, wry humor, and serious interpretation in this elegant and charmingly accessible study of the relation among language, culture, and thought and of how we have engaged in and reflected upon language over the years." Libr J

Includes bibliographical references

410.92 Linguists

Chomsky, Noam, 1928-
Global Discontents; Conversations on the Rising Threats to Democracy. by Noam Chomsky and David Barsamian. Henry Holt & Co. 2017 240 p. $18 **410.92**
1. Democracy 2. International security 3. Anarchism and anarchists
ISBN 1250146186; 9781250146182

LC 2017276923

This book, by Noam Chomsky and David Barsamian, "examine[s] the latest developments around the globe: the rise of ISIS, the reach of state surveillance, growing anger over economic inequality, conflicts in the Middle East, and the presidency of Donald Trump. In personal reflections on his Philadelphia childhood, Chomsky also describes his own intellectual journey and the development of his uncompromising stance as America's premier dissident intellectual." (Publisher's note)

"Every page of this lively, probing, and sharp collection delivers a searing observation from linguist and political-thinker Chomsky." Pub Wkly

411 Writing systems of standard forms of languages

Houston, Keith
Shady characters; the secret life of punctuation, symbols, & other typographical marks. Keith Houston. W W Norton & Co Inc 2013 352 p. $25.95 **411**
1. Typography 2. Punctuation 3. Writing -- History 4. Punctuation -- History 5. Signs and symbols -- History 6. Type and typefounding -- History
ISBN 0393064425; 9780393064421

LC 2013017324

This book is a "bestiary of lesser-known punctuation marks. . . . Nearly every punctuation symbol in this book gained its start from the annotation marks of monks, scribes, or scholars. (The chapter on daggers and asterisks, of course, uses those symbols to mark the asides.) Some game-changers, like the sudden confines of the typing press or the yet-more-restrictive typewriter, extend their influence across numerous chapters." (Publishers Weekly)

Includes bibliographical references and index

413.028 Auxiliary techniques and procedures; apparatus, equipment, materials

Stamper, Kory
Word by word; The Secret Life of Dictionaries. Kory Stamper. Pantheon Books 2017 320 p. (ebook) $65; (hardback) $26.95 **413.028**
1. Lexicography 2. Encyclopedias and dictionaries 3. Lexicography

-- History 4. Lexicographers -- Biography 5. Encyclopedias and dictionaries -- History and criticism
ISBN 9781101870952; 9781101870945

LC 2016024253

This book, by Kory Stamper, "cracks open the complex, obsessive world of lexicography--from the agonizing decisions about what and how to define, to the knotty questions of usage in an ever-changing language. She explains why small words are the most difficult to define (have you ever tried to define 'is'?), how it can take nine months to define a single word, and how our biases about language and pronunciation can have tremendous social influence." (Publisher's note)

"Word by Word offers marvelous insight into the messy world behind the tidy definitions on the page." Booklist

Includes bibliographical references and index

417.22 Pidgins, creoles, mixed languages

Valdman, Albert
★ **English-**Haitian Creole bilingual dictionary; project director, Albert Valdman ; editors, Albert Valdman, Marvin D. Moody, Thomas E. Davies ; assistant editor, Michael A. Kunz ; editorial assistant, Karen S. Smith. IUniverse 2017 xxxvii, 1103 p.p (softcover; alk. paper) $39.95 **417.22**
1. Encyclopedias and dictionaries 2. Creole dialects, French -- Haiti -- Dictionaries -- English
ISBN 9781532015991; 9781532016004; 9781532016011

LC 2017903469

This bilingual dictionary, by Albert Valdman, " aims to assist anglophone users in constructing written and oral discourse in HC; it also will aid HC [Haitian Creole] speakers to translate from English to their language. As the most elaborate and extensive linguistic tool available, it contains about 30,000 individual entries, many of which have multiple senses and include subentries, multiword phrases or idioms." (Publisher's note)

Includes bibliographical references (pages xxxiii-xxxvii).

418 Standard usage (Prescriptive linguistics)

Deheane, Stanislas
Reading in the brain; the science and evolution of a cultural invention. Viking 2009 388p il $27.95 **418**
1. Reading
ISBN 978-0-670-02110-9; 0-670-02110-5

LC 2009-09389

"Dense with ideas and experiments, but richly rewarding for readers willing to put in the effort." Kirkus

Includes bibliographical references

Grossman, Edith
Why translation matters. Yale University Press 2010 135p (Why X matters) **418**
1. Translating and interpreting 2. Literature -- Translations
ISBN 0-300-12656-5; 978-0-300-12656-3

LC 2009-26510

Grossman "argues for the cultural importance of translation and a more encompassing and nuanced appreciation of the translator's role." (Publisher's note) Index.

"In the end, Grossman warmly (after all) and gratefully rehearses the twofold answer to the question of her title: translation matters because it is an expression and an extension of our humanity, the secret metaphor of all literary communication; and because the creation of any literary translation is (or at least must be) an original writing, not a pathetic shadow or tracing of the inaccessible 'original' but the creation, indeed, of a second — and as we have seen, a third and a ninth — but always a new work, in another language." N Y Times Book Rev

Includes bibliographical references

Wolf, Maryanne

Reader, come home; the reading brain in a digital world. Maryanne Wolf. HarperCollins 2018 272 p. $24.99   **418**

1. Reading comprehension 2. Books and reading -- Psychological aspects

ISBN 0062388789; 9780062388780

"This book comprises a series of letters [Maryanne] Wolf writes to us--her beloved readers--to describe her concerns and her hopes about what is happening to the reading brain as it unavoidably changes to adapt to digital mediums. . . . Wolf draws on neuroscience, . . . technology, and philosophy and blends historical . . . and scientific facts with down-to-earth examples . . . to illuminate complex ideas that culminate in a proposal for a biliterate reading brain." (Publisher's note)

"Overall, a hopeful look at the future of reading that will resonate with those who worry that we are losing our ability to think in the digital age." Library Journal

419   Sign languages

Costello, Elaine

Random House Webster's American Sign Language dictionary: unabridged. Random House Reference 2008 xxxii, 1200p $55   **419**

1. Reference books 2. Sign language -- Dictionaries

ISBN 978-0-375-42616-2; 0-375-42616-7

First published 1994 with title: Random House American Sign Language dictionary

This dictionary includes "over 5,600 signs for the novice and experienced user alike. It includes complete descriptions of each sign, plus full-torso illustrations. There is also a subject index for easy reference as well as alternate signs for the same meaning." Publisher's note

★ The **Gallaudet** dictionary of American Sign Language; Clayton Valli, editor in chief; illustrated by Peggy Swartzel Lott, Daniel Renner, and Rob Hills. Gallaudet University Press 2005 xli, 558p il $49.95   **419**

1. Reference books 2. Sign language -- Dictionaries

ISBN 1-56368-282-6; 978-1-56368-282-7

LC 2005-51129

"This is a very valuable language resource for parents, students, and teachers learning ASL as a first language and as a second language." Choice

Includes bibliographical references

Grayson, Gabriel

Talking with your hands, listening with your eyes; a complete photographic guide to American Sign Language. Square One Pubs. 2002 373p il pa $26.95   **419**

1. Sign language

ISBN 0-7570-0007-X

LC 2002-1125

"An outstanding, user-friendly resource for those interested in learning ASL." SLJ

Sternberg, Martin L. A.

American Sign Language; a comprehensive dictionary. illustrated by Herbert Rogoff. Unabridged; HarperCollins Pubs. 1998 xxi, 983p il $60; pa $24   **419**

1. Reference books 2. Sign language -- Dictionaries

ISBN 0-06-271608-5; 0-06-273634-5 pa

LC 98-26649

First published 1981

Arranged alphabetically, this dictionary features 7,000 sign entries, with cross-references and more than 12,000 illustrations

Includes bibliographical references

420   Specific languages

Bragg, Melvyn

The **adventure** of English; the biography of a language. Arcade Pub. 2004 322p il $27.95   **420**

1. English language -- History

ISBN 1-55970-710-0

LC 2003-19583

First published 2003 in the United Kingdom

The author offers a "biography of the English language, highlighting key individuals, places, and literature that advanced it, as well as the political and social trends that influenced it. . . . Bragg discusses its evolution in the English colonies, devoting four chapters to the United States and one each to India, the West Indies, and Australia. . . . Well researched yet more accessible to a wide audience than scholarly treatments by linguists or historians." Libr J

Bryson, Bill

Made in America; an informal history of the English language in the United States. Avon Books 1996 417p pa $14.95   **420**

1. Americanisms 2. English language -- History

ISBN 978-0-380-71381-3; 0-380-71381-0

First published 1994 by Morrow

"For Bryson's wonderfully sane and reasoned discussion of the issues surrounding 'politically correct' language alone, this book is a worthwhile read." Libr J

Includes bibliographical references

Crystal, David

★ The **Cambridge** encyclopedia of the English language; 2nd ed; Cambridge Univ. Press 2003 499p il hardcover o.p. pa $35   **420**

1. English language

ISBN 0-521-82348-X; 0-521-53033-4 pa

LC 2003-272259

First published 1995

This "volume is divided into six broad topics that cover the English language's history, vocabulary, grammar, writing and speech systems, usage, and acquisition. Within these major topics, the book is divided into logical subtopics and finally into the basic unit of the text—the two-page spread. . . . The clear and spirited text is stunning, enhanced with over 500 illustrations, making this a particularly rich reference work and a browser's dream." Libr J {review of 1995 edition}

★ **English** as a global language; David Crystal. 2nd edition Cambridge University Press 2012 212 p. illustrations pbk $16.99   **420**

1. English language -- Social aspects

ISBN 1107611806; 9781107611801

LC 2013498883

First published 1997

Crystal's "account of the rise of English as a global language explores the history, current status and potential of English as the international language of communication. {Includes} sections on the future of English as a world language, English on the Internet, and the possibility of an English 'family' of languages." (Publisher's note)

Hitchings, Henry

The **language** wars; a history of proper English. Farrar, Straus and Giroux 2011 408p $28 **420**

1. English language -- Usage 2. English language -- History

ISBN 978-0-374-18329-5; 0-374-18329-5

LC 2011-10701

"As the author points out, there is probably not a person alive who does not have some bee in his bonnet about the way other people speak and write. Maybe it is the errant apostrophe, the splitting of the poor old infinitive, or the use of 'like' as a comma. Or perhaps it is the exclamation mark, once known as the 'shriek mark'. Mr Hitchings's book is a corrective to some of these linguistic prejudices. It is bracing to learn, for example, that the prohibition on splitting the infinitive is fairly recent. Pre-Victorians did not object. Chaucer was a splitter, and even Shakespeare had a go. Same story with the apostrophe: in the 18th-century authors were sprinkling apostrophes over everything. . . . Mr Hitchings reviews such matters with cool erudition. He is resolutely relaxed about usage, understanding that correctitude and intelligibility are not the same." Economist

Includes bibliographical references

McCrum, Robert

★ The **story** of English; [by] Robert McCrum, Willam Cran [and] Robert MacNeil. 3rd rev ed; Penguin Bks. 2003 xxi, 468p pa $16 **420**

1. English language -- History

ISBN 0-14-200231-3

LC 2002-29818

First published 1986 by Viking

A "companion to the PBS television series of the same name. . . . The text covers the history of our language from its roots in Latin through its transplanting to other shores and its infusions from other cultures and languages. . . . Good for browsing, this book is a must for word and history buffs." SLJ [review of 1986 edition]

Includes bibliographical references

Metcalf, Allan A.

Predicting new words; the secrets of their success. {by} Allan Metcalf. Houghton Mifflin 2002 206p il $22 **420**

1. New words 2. English language -- Terms and phrases

ISBN 0-618-13006-3

LC 2002-68593

This book traces the origins of an "array of words and phrases: Marlboro Man, Frankenfood, blurb, skycap, quark, scofflaw. It also introduces us to a fascinating array of would-be words, coinages that never quite caught on. . . . The book is jam-packed with treats for word lovers." Booklist

421 Writing system, phonology, phonetics of standard English

★ **Acronyms**, initialisms, & abbreviations dictionary; 40th ed; Gale Res. 2008 4v set $1,190 **421**

1. Reference books 2. Acronyms -- Dictionaries

ISBN 978-1-4144-1902-2; 1-4144-1902-3

First published 1960 in one volume with title: Acronyms dictionary. Frequently revised

A guide to acronyms, initialisms, abbreviations, contractions, alphabetic symbols, and similar condensed apellations

Crystal, David

Spell It Out; The Curious, Enthralling and Extraordinary Story of English Spelling. David Crystal. St. Martin's Press 2013 336 p. $22.99 **421**

1. English language -- Spelling 2. English language -- Orthography and spelling 3. English language -- Orthography and spelling -- History

ISBN 1250003474; 9781250003478

LC 2013010521

In this book author David Crystal "takes readers on a history of English spelling, starting with the Roman missionaries' sixth century introduction of the Roman alphabet and ending with where the language might be going. He looks individually at each letter in the alphabet and its origins. He considers the question of vowels and how people developed a way to tell whether or not it was long or short. He looks at influences from other cultures." (Publisher's note)

Rosen, Michael, 1946-

Alphabetical; how every letter tells a story. Michael Rosen. Counterpoint Press 2015 448 p. illustrations (hardback) $25 **421**

1. Alphabet 2. Language and languages 3. Writing 4. Alphabet -- History 5. Alphabet in literature

ISBN 1619024837; 9781619024830

LC 2014035051

This book by Michael Rosen looks at the alphabet. "Each letter receives a brief description of its written evolution and the pronunciation of its name and its sounds, followed by a relevant topic beginning with that letter, such as 'D is for Disappeared Letters' and 'O is for OK.' . . .The diverse topics he covers also include printing fonts, diacritics ('U is for Umlauts'), and the ways that the alphabet can be manipulated to encrypt secrets." (Publishers Weekly)

"Rosen also is mellow about "correctness" in usage and punctuation ("Our personal histories and feelings are wrapped up in what the letters and their means of transmission mean to each of us") and shows little sorrow for the disappearance of handwriting in schools; in fact, he thinks our current emphasis on it doesn't make much sense. A delightfully informative book about letters, their meanings, and the words and meanings we derive from them." Kirkus

Includes bibliographical references and index

Truss, Lynne

Eats, shoots & leaves; the zero tolerance approach to punctuation. Gotham Books 2004 xxvii, 209p $19.95; pa $12 **421**

1. Punctuation

ISBN 1-59240-087-6; 1-59240-203-8 pa

LC 2004-40646

First published 2003 in the United Kingdom

The author "dissects common errors that grammar mavens have long deplored (often, as she readily points out, in isolation) and makes . . .

arguments for increased attention to punctuation correctness. . . . Truss serves up delightful, unabashedly strict and sometimes snobby little book, with cheery Britishisms ('Lawks-a-mussy!') dotting pages that express a more international righteous indignation." Publ Wkly

Includes bibliographical references

422   Etymology of standard English

Adonis to Zorro; Oxford dictionary of reference and allusion. edited by Andrew Delahunty and Sheila Dignen. 3rd ed.; Oxford University Press 2010 406p $34.95   **422**
   1. Allusions 2. Reference books
   ISBN 978-0-19-956745-4; 0-19-956745-X
                                                       LC 2010-549367
   First published 2001 with title: The Oxford dictionary of allusions
   "This guide to allusions and common references is a moderately priced volume well worth adding to a public, school, community college, or college shelf. Neat and user-friendly, the 1,900 entries, their provenance, definitions, models, and starred cross-references identify a range of familiar terms, from 'Terminator' to 'hobbit,' and from 'My Lai' to the 'sword of Damocles' and 'thirty pieces of silver.' The text makes clever use of fonts, dingbats, and point count to identify authors, sources, and dates." Choice

Crystal, David
   The **story** of English in 100 words; David Crystal. St. Martin's Press 2012 260 p.   **422**
   1. Vocabulary 2. English language -- History 3. English language -- Etymology 4. English language -- Foreign words and phrases 5. English language -- Foreign elements
   ISBN 9781250003461; 9781466805088
                                                       LC 2012003038
   This book presents "information about how English grows, changes, adopts and plays. . . . The author . . . teach[es] 100 lessons about English by picking out 100 words from our history, telling us their origin story and showing us how they've changed and spawned. Roughly chronological-beginning in the fifth century, ending in the 21st-[David] Crystal's text begins with what may be the first written word in our language, raihan, the word for roe-deer, and ends with something awfully recent, twittersphere. In between are not just the stories of individual words but the stories of how words become words. Why do we sometimes spell yogurt with an -h? Has there always been a difference between disinterested and uninterested? Why do only poets use certain words like swain?"(Kirkus)

Forsyth, Mark
   The **etymologicon**; a circular stroll through the hidden connections of the English language. Mark Forsyth. Berkley Books 2012 XVIII, 252 p.p $16   **422**
   1. English language -- Etymology
   ISBN 0425260798; 9780425260791; 9781848313071
                                                       LC 2011535421
   This book by Mark Forsyth presents a "guide to the strange underpinnings of the English language. It explains: how you get from 'gruntled' to 'disgruntled'; why you are absolutely right to believe that your meager salary barely covers 'money for salt'; how the biggest chain of coffee shops in the world (hint: Seattle) connects to whaling in Nantucket; and what precisely the Rolling Stones have to do with gardening." (Publisher's note)

★ **From** bonbon to cha-cha; Oxford dictionary of foreign words and phrases. edited by Andrew Delahunty. 2nd ed; Oxford University Press 2008 411p $24.95; pa $18.99 **422**
   1. Reference books 2. English language -- Foreign words and phrases -- Dictionaries
   ISBN 978-0-19-954369-4; 0-19-954369-0; 978-0-19-954368-7 pa; 0-19-954368-2 pa
                                                       LC 2008-482026
   First published 1997 with title: The Oxford dictionary of foreign words and phrases. Paperback has title: Oxford dictionary of foreign words and phrases
   This reference "offers coverage of more than 6,000 foreign words and phrases that are in regular use in English today." Publisher's note

Hendrickson, Robert
   ★ The **Facts** on File encyclopedia of word and phrase origins; 4th ed., [Updated and expanded ed.]; Facts On File 2008 948p (Facts on File library of language and literature) $95; pa $27.95   **422**
   1. Reference books 2. English language -- Terms and phrases 3. English language -- Etymology -- Dictionaries
   ISBN 978-0-8160-6966-8; 978-0-8160-6967-5 pa
                                                       LC 2007-48223
   First published 1987
   "Because the entries have both scholarly value and the capacity to entertain, the book is ideal for both linguists and lay readers." Libr J

Hitchings, Henry
   The **secret** life of words; how English became English. Farrar, Straus and Giroux 2008 440p $27   **422**
   1. English language -- Etymology
   ISBN 978-0-374-25410-0; 0-374-25410-9
                                                       LC 2008-26055
   "Hitchings here provides a colorful, thematic history of the English language. Treating borrowings and coinages as psychological windows to history, the author takes the reader on a tour of the lexicon from Anglo-Saxon to the present day and shows how new words answer linguistic needs. . . . Hitchings treats the reader to some 3,000 word histories. . . . With 90-plus pages of notes, sources, and useful indexes, this is a fine choice for libraries and a 'smorgasbord' for language aficionados." Choice
   Includes bibliographical references

Manser, Martin H.
   The **Facts** on File dictionary of allusions; David H. Pickering, associate editor. Facts on File 2008 532p (Facts on File library of language and literature) $75; pa $18.95   **422**
   1. Allusions 2. Reference books 3. Literature -- Dictionaries
   ISBN 978-0-8160-7105-0; 0-8160-7105-5; 978-0-8160-7907-0 pa; 0-8160-7907-2 pa
                                                       LC 2007-51375
   "In approximately 4,000 entries, this . . . resource explores well-known events, places, people, and phenomena whose names have acquired linguistic significance, conveying a particular message beyond a mere reference to the objects referred to. Entries are drawn from a . . . range of sources, including Shakespeare and the Bible; Greek, Roman, and Norse mythology; texts from literature through the ages; historical events; popular culture; and film and television. Individual entries contain pronunciation guides, definitions, examples, information on derived forms, and more." Publisher's note
   Includes bibliographical references

★ The **Facts** on File dictionary of foreign words and phrases; [by] Martin H. Manser; associate editors: Alice Grandison and David H. Pickering. 2nd ed., [New ed.]; Facts on File 2008 469p (Facts on File library of language and literature) $55; pa $19.95 **422**

1. Reference books 2. English language -- Foreign words and phrases -- Dictionaries

ISBN 978-0-8160-7035-0; 978-0-8160-7036-7 pa

LC 2007-29711

First published 2002

This dictionary includes more than 4,500 entries for terms that have entered the English lexicon from foreign languages in the fields of language and literature, religion, law, politics, economics, music, entertainment and cuisine. Examples or quotations are provided to illustrate usage.

"This is a captivating title to browse." SLJ

Includes bibliographical references

More word histories and mysteries; from aardvark to zombie. from the editors of the American Heritage dictionaries. Houghton Mifflin 2006 288p il pa $12.95 **422**

1. Reference books 2. English language -- Etymology

ISBN 978-0-618-71681-4; 0-618-71681-5

LC 2006020835

This "emphasizes the huge number of source languages from which English draws its vast vocabulary—from Sanskrit to French and beyond. The introductory pages give the reader a brief overview of the methods and aims of etymology and a potted history of the origins of English. . . . The editors then present an alphabetical listing of words and their etymology. Each of the 300-plus entries is about half a page to a page long and briefly outlines the origins of the word, its use, and the evolution of its meaning. . . . The book's informative yet informal writing style would appeal to the amateur enthusiast, and accessibility is further enhanced by a useful glossary of linguistic terms." Libr J

Quinion, Michael

★ **Ballyhoo,** buckeroo, and spuds; ingenious tales of words and their origins. Smithsonian Books 2004 288p $19.95 **422**

1. English language -- Etymology 2. English language -- Terms and phrases

ISBN 1-588-34219-0

LC 2004-52235

A look at common English "words and phrases most readers will probably have wondered about. We're all familiar with the phrase 'happy as a clam.' but why a clam? We know what a 10-gallon hat is, but how did it get its name? And what the heck is a ballyhoo, anyway? The book is simply organized—alphabetically, of course—and endlessly illuminating. Quinion's research and documentation are impeccable, and when he needs to make a leap of imagination, he does so gracefully. For word lovers, this book is indispensable." Booklist

Includes bibliographical references

Rosten, Leo

The **new** joys of Yiddish; revisions and commentary by Lawrence Bush; illustrations by R. O. Blechman. Rev ed; Crown 2001 xxxii, 458p il $35; pa $18 **422**

1. Yiddish language 2. English language -- Foreign words and phrases

ISBN 0-609-60785-5; 0-609-80692-0 pa

LC 2001-28366

First published 1968 with title: The joys of Yiddish

This "work explores the nuances and complexities of language, clarifying the interrelationship between Yiddish and English (Yinglish, according to Rosten). The lengthy alphabetical listing not only presents multiple spellings, pronunciation guides, definitions, and cross references but also illustrates usage with background information, anecdotes, and jokes, as well as breezy erudition in the form of tidbits of cultural history, Talmudic and biblical references, tips on pronunciation, and thoughtful commentary. . . . The revision incorporates additional material on modern Yiddish literature and culture and updates on changes in American Jewish life and faith. Also included as an appendix is an English-Yiddish dictionary." Libr J

Includes bibliographical references

Stevens, Christopher

Written in Stone; A Journey Through the Stone Age and the Origins of Modern Language. Christopher Stevens. W W Norton & Co Inc 2015 272 p. $27.95 **422**

1. Stone Age 2. Language and languages

ISBN 160598907X; 9781605989075

In this book author Christopher Stevens "combines detective work, mythology, ancient history, archaeology, the roots of society, technology and warfare, and the sheer fascination of words to explore that original mother tongue, sketching the connections woven throughout the immense vocabulary of English--with some surprising results." (Publisher's note)

"The history of English is fascinating and this is a delightful distraction from a more serious linguistic approach to the topic." LJ

Word histories and mysteries; from abracadabra to Zeus. from the editors of the American Heritage dictionaries. Houghton Mifflin Co. 2004 xvi, 348p il pa $12.95 **422**

1. Reference books 2. English language -- Etymology

ISBN 978-0-618-45450-1; 0-618-45450-0

LC 2004014798

"The 400 alphabetically arranged entries here illustrate the diversity from which the English language draws its vocabulary, particularly from the prehistoric base that linguists call Proto-Indo-European. As a result, the editors aim to demonstrate links between the ancient base and modern English. . . . An overall quality resource." Libr J

423 Dictionaries of standard English

Adelson-Goldstein, Jayme

The **Oxford** picture dictionary; [by] Jayme Adelson-Goldstein and Norma Shapiro. 2nd ed.; Oxford University Press 2008 285p il pa $16.95 **423**

1. Reference books 2. Picture dictionaries 3. English language -- Dictionaries

ISBN 978-0-19-436976-3; 0-19-436976-5

LC 2007-41017

First published 1998

This picture dictionary features "4,000 words and phrases illustrated with . . . artwork." Publisher's note

★ The **American** Heritage dictionary of the English language; revised 5th edition Houghton Mifflin Harcourt 2016 2084 p illustrations $60 **423**

1. Reference books 2. Encyclopedias and dictionaries 3. English language -- Dictionaries 4. English language -- Usage -- Dictionaries

ISBN 9780544454453

"This dictionary presents the most up-to-date research about the words in our language in an accessible and elegant design. The landmark

Fifth Edition, with 10,000 new words and senses, over 4,000 new full-color images, and comprehensive, up-to-date guidance on usage from the celebrated American Heritage® Usage Panel, is now updated for 2016 with more than 1,000 revisions, including nearly 100 new words and senses." (Publisher's note)

★ **Bartlett's** Roget's thesaurus. Little, Brown 1996 xxxii, 1415p $21.95; pa $16.95 **423**
1. Americanisms 2. Reference books 3. English language -- Synonyms and antonyms
ISBN 0-316-10138-9; 0-316-73587-6 pa
LC 96-18343

This thesaurus "reflects the current state of American English, including terminology from the worlds of composers and television, with such sub-categories as 'Living Things,' 'The Arts,' 'Feelings.' But what really makes the book a joy to use is the tremendously useful lists—everything from phobias to styles and periods of furniture." Am Libr

★ **Concise** Oxford American thesaurus. Oxford University Press 2006 996p $19.95 **423**
1. Reference books 2. English language -- Synonyms and antonyms
ISBN 0-19-530485-3; 978-0-19-530485-5
LC 2005-35868

First published 1997 in the United Kingdom with title: The concise Oxford thesaurus; Original American edition published 1999 with title: The Oxford American thesaurus of current English

This "thesaurus contains over 15,000 entries with more than 350,000 synonyms and is . . . arranged with the typical synonyms listed first. . . . This simple arrangement makes this thesaurus particularly user-friendly." Libr J

★ **Concise** Oxford English dictionary; edited by Angus Stevenson and Maurice Waite. 12th edition Oxford University Press 2011 1682 p $40 **423**
1. Reference books 2. English language -- Dictionaries
ISBN 9780199601080

First published 1911 under the editorship of H. W. Fowler and F. G. Fowler with title: The Concise dictionary of current English

Offers definitions for English words and phrases, along with observations about the evolution of the dictionary since its first edition and tables that contain information for such topics as countries and chemical elements.

Davidson, Mark
★ **Right,** wrong, and risky; a dictionary of today's American English usage. Norton 2006 570p $29.95 **423**
1. Americanisms 2. Reference books 3. English language -- Usage 4. English language -- Dictionaries
ISBN 0-393-06119-1
LC 2005-17628

The author "offers a dictionary that 'views the real world of today's American English, identifying usage questions that are debatable, citing conflicting answers, and offering risk-free solutions for each conflict.' . . . Browsers will enjoy the colorful, interesting backstories on the origins of terms such as ground zero, on the sudden warming to the phrase girl talk, and on the widely misunderstood use of the word Neanderthal." Booklist

Includes bibliographical references

★ **Dictionary** of confusable words; {edited by} Adrian Room. Fitzroy Dearborn Pubs. 2000 251p $35 **423**
1. English language -- Usage 2. English language -- Synonyms and antonyms

ISBN 1-57958-271-0

A "guide to potentially confusing words. . . . The brief entries give definitions of each of the terms. Each word is then used in at least one sample sentence, clarifying the differences between like terms. The definitions and examples are in simple language and are easy to understand." Libr J

Espy, Willard R.
Words to rhyme with; a rhyming dictionary. 3rd ed.; Facts On File 2006 683p (Facts on File library of language and literature) $75; pa $19.95 **423**
1. English language -- Rhyme
ISBN 0-8160-6303-6; 978-0-8160-6303-1; 0-8160-6304-4 pa; 978-0-8160-6304-8 pa
LC 2005-51122

First published 1986

"Including a primer of prosody, a list of more than 80,000 words that rhyme, a glossary defining 9,000 of the more eccentric rhyming words, and a variety of exemplary verses, one of which does not rhyme at all." Title page

Garner, Bryan A.
★ **Garner's** modern American usage; 3rd ed; Oxford University Press 2009 lx, 942p $45 **423**
1. Reference books 2. Americanisms -- Dictionaries 3. English language -- Usage -- Dictionaries
ISBN 978-0-19-538275-4
LC 2009-9539

First published 1998 with title: A dictionary of modern American usage

"One would be tempted to say that this is clearly one of the best works on the topic, but doing so would be using one of Garner's weasel words (intensives such as clearly that 'actually have the effect of weakening a statement'). Suffice it to say that it is highly recommended for most libraries." Booklist

Includes bibliographical references (p. 925-938)

Historical thesaurus of the Oxford English dictionary; with additional material from A Thesaurus of Old English. [edited by] Christian Kay [et al.] Oxford University Press 2009 3952p 2v set $395 **423**
1. Reference books 2. English language -- Synonyms and antonyms
ISBN 978-0-19-920899-9
LC 2009-935029

"The knowledge compiled in this 40-year project is stunning, and promises to revolutionize the study of the language by making wholly new kinds of questions possible." Choice

Includes bibliographical references

Houghton Mifflin Co.
★ The **American** Heritage guide to contemporary usage and style. Houghton Mifflin 2005 512p $19.95 **423**
1. English language -- Usage
ISBN 978-0-618-60499-9; 0-618-60499-5
LC 2005-16513

"Drawing on the authoritative knowledge of its lexicographers and the considered collective judgment of a panel of noted writers, the book offers guidance on the simple (the pronunciations of bouquet); the perplexingly redundant (free gift); the often imprecisely used (impeach); the no longer distinct (healthful/healthy); the needless but persistent (irregardless); the easily confused (stationary/stationery); the unfortunately conflated (lay/lie); and many more pitfalls. Articles embodying the precision and lucidity of dictionary definitions explain the history of a word's or expression's usage issue, how and why the issue exists, and the preferred usage." Booklist

Merriam-Webster Inc.

★ **Merriam**-Webster's collegiate dictionary; Eleventh ed; Merriam-Webster 2003 1623p il $23.95 **423**
1. Reference books 2. English language -- Dictionaries
ISBN 0-87779-808-7

LC 2003-3674

First published 1898
This edition includes over 165,000 entries, 10,000 new words and meanings, 38,000 etymologies, a handbook of style, an essay on the English language, a special section on signs and symbols, and a free one-year subscription to the Collegiate Web site.

★ **Merriam**-Webster's collegiate thesaurus; 2nd ed.; Merriam-Webster 2010 16a, 1162p $21.95 **423**
1. Reference books 2. English language -- Synonyms and antonyms
ISBN 978-0-8777-9269-7; 0-8777-9269-0

LC 2009-42161

First published 1976 with title: Webster's collegiate thesaurus
"Employs a conventional dictionary arrangement, and gives synonyms, related terms, idiomatic equivalents, antonyms, and contrasted words as applicable. Cross-references in small capitals." Guide to Ref Books. 11th edition

★ **Merriam**-Webster's visual dictionary. Merriam-Webster, Inc. 2012 1112 p. (hbk.) $39.95 **423**
1. English language -- Dictionaries
ISBN 0877791511; 9780877791515

This visual dictionary, edited by Jean-Claude Corbeil, has "more than 8,000 highly detailed, full-color illustrations, organized by subject in specialized fields from all aspects of life, . . . [and] nearly 25,000 . . . technical and everyday terms with clear, concise definitions. . . . Themes include a wide variety of fields: astronomy, the earth, human beings, the animal kingdom, plants and gardening, . . . food, arts and architecture, . . . sports and games" and more. (Publisher's note)

Mugglestone, Lynda

Lost for words; the hidden history of the Oxford English Dictionary. Yale University Press 2005 xxi, 273p il $30 **423**
1. Oxford English dictionary
ISBN 0-300-10699-8

LC 2004-29344

"Serious word lovers will appreciate . . . [this book's] fascinating revelations." Booklist
Includes bibliographical references

★ **New** Oxford American dictionary; 3rd ed.; Oxford University Press 2010 xxvi, 2018p il map $60 **423**
1. Reference books 2. Americanisms -- Dictionaries 3. English language -- Dictionaries
ISBN 978-0-19-539288-3

LC 2010-20033

First published 1980 with title: The Oxford American dictionary. Editors vary
"This dictionary arranges definitions by most current usage and provides additional guidance in usage notes. Although U.S. English is the focus here, regionalisms from other English-speaking areas are also included. More than 1000 illustrations (e.g., photos, drawings, diagrams) clarify definitions. . . . A labor of love and an unparalleled gift to writers and readers worldwide, the New Oxford American Dictionary should be on the reference shelves of every library." Libr J

★ **Oxford** American writer's thesaurus; compiled by Christine A. Lindberg. 3rd edition Oxford University Press 2012 1050 p hardcover $40 **423**
1. Reference books 2. English language -- Synonyms and antonyms
ISBN 9780199829927

"Much more than a word list, the Oxford American Writer's Thesaurus is a browsable source of inspiration as well as an authoritative guide to selecting and using vocabulary. This essential guide for writers provides real-life example sentences and a careful selection of the most relevant synonyms, as well as new usage notes, hints for choosing between similar words, a Word Finder section organized by subject, and a comprehensive language guide. The text is also peppered with thought-provoking reflections on favorite (and not-so-favorite) words by noted contemporary writers, including Joshua Ferris, Francine Prose, David Foster Wallace, Zadie Smith, and Simon Winchester, many newly commissioned for this edition." (Publisher's note)

★ **Oxford** dictionary of English idioms; 3rd ed., Oxford pbk ed.; Oxford University Press 2010 408p (Oxford paperback reference) pa $16.95 **423**
1. Reference books 2. English language -- Idioms
ISBN 978-0-19-954378-6

LC 2010-935315

First published 1999 with title: The Oxford dictionary of idioms
This book "contains entries for over 6,000 idioms. . . . These include a range of idioms such as 'the elephant in the corner,' 'go figure,' 'step up to the plate,' 'a walk in the park,' and 'win ugly.'" Publisher's note

The **Oxford** English dictionary; 2nd ed; Oxford Univ. Press 1989 20v apply to publisher for price **423**
1. Reference books 2. English language -- Dictionaries
ISBN 0-19-861186-2

LC 88-5330

First published 1888 with title: New English dictionary on historical principles
"This is an etymological or word-source dictionary. In addition to definitions, this work gives the history of 290,500 words, both current and archaic, in the English language. Slang entries are very limited. Word histories include early forms, variant forms and roots, and first or exemplary usages in English from ancient to modern times. Short explanatory notes are provided for more common words." N Y Public Libr Book of How & Where to Look It Up

★ **Random** House Webster's unabridged dictionary; 2nd ed.; Random House 2005 xxvi, 2230p il map $59.95 **423**
1. Reference books 2. English language -- Dictionaries
ISBN 0-375-42599-3

First published 1966 with title: The Random House dictionary of the English language
This dictionary contains over 315,000 entries. A new-words section and an essay on the growth of English are included. 2,400 spot maps and illustrations complement the text

★ **Roget's** 21st century thesaurus in dictionary form; the essential reference for home, school, or office. edited by the Princeton Language Institute; Barbara Ann Kipfer, head lexicographer. 3rd ed; Bantam Dell 2005 962p $15; pa $5.99 **423**
1. Reference books 2. English language -- Synonyms and antonyms
ISBN 0-385-33895-3; 0-440-24269-X pa

First published 1992

This thesaurus, cross referencing each word with the same concept, provides 500,000 synonyms and antonyms in a dictionary format and includes recently coined and common slang terms and commonly used foreign terms.

★ **Roget's** international thesaurus; edited by Barbara Ann Kipfer. 7th edition HarperReference 2011 1282 p paperback $19.99; hardcover $24.99   **423**
1. English language -- Synonyms and antonyms
ISBN 9780061715211; 0061715212; 9780061715228; 0061715239; 9780061715235
LC 2008055359

First copyright edition published 1911 with title: The standard thesaurus of English words and phrases classified and arranged so as to facilitate the expression of ideas and assist in literary composition

"The most comprehensive, user-friendly thesaurus available, Roget's features more than 325,000 words and phrases, including more than 2,000 all-new entries that reflect the very latest in culture and technology, from "alpha male" to"zero tolerance." The seventh edition has reduced archaic terminology and added 50 new word lists." (Publisher's note)

★ **Shorter** Oxford English dictionary on historical principles; [editor-in-chief, Lesley Brown] 6th ed.; Oxford University Press 2007 2v il map set $175   **423**
1. Reference books 2. English language -- Dictionaries
ISBN 978-0-19-923324-3; 0-19-923324-1
LC 2007-37226

First published 1933

This dictionary "has more than half a million definitions drawn from the Oxford English Corpus database of more than 1.5 billion words. . . . It includes 'all words in current English from 1700 to the present day, plus the vocabulary of Shakespeare, the Authorized Version of the Bible and other major works from before 1700.'" Booklist

Includes bibliographical references

Simpson, John

The **word** detective; searching for the meaning of it all at the Oxford English Dictionary. John Simpson. Basic Books 2016 384 p. (ebook) $18.99; (hardback) $27.99   **423**
1. Lexicographers 2. English language 3. Oxford English dictionary 4. English language -- Lexicography 5. Lexicographers -- Great Britain -- Biography
ISBN 9780465096527; 9780465060696
LC 2016025594

In this book, by John Simpson, "an intensely personal memoir and a joyful celebration of English, he weaves a story of how words come into being (and sometimes disappear), how culture shapes the language we use, and how technology has transformed not only the way we speak and write but also how words are made." (Publisher's note)

"Simpson's vibrant and inspiring memoir gives us a glimpse into life as detective in the realm of words." Pub Wkly

Upton, Clive

★ **Oxford** rhyming dictionary; {by} Clive Upton, Eben Upton. Oxford University Press 2004 659p $37.95   **423**
1. English language -- Rhyme
ISBN 0-19-280115-5
LC 2004-53133

In this dictionary "an index of words leads to numbered sections of phonic groupings of end, double, and triple syllable rhymes, with proximate groupings of near rhymes. But the index (95,000 words) . . . provides many word variations." Choice

Winchester, Simon

The **professor** and the madman; a tale of murder, insanity, and the making of the Oxford English dictionary. HarperCollins Pubs. 1998 242p il $22; pa $13   **423**
1. Surgeons 2. Mentally ill 3. Editors 4. Murderers 5. Lexicographers 6. Oxford English dictionary 7. New English dictionary on historical principles 8. English language -- Lexicography -- History -- 19th century 9. United States -- History -- Civil War, 1861-1865 -- Veterans -- Biography
ISBN 0-06-017596-6; 0-06-099486-X pa
LC 98-10204

Winchester examines the relationship between James Murray, editor of the Oxford English Dictionary, and "William C. Minor (1834-1920), . . . a Civil War surgeon whose war experience caused his personality to change. He became paranoid and was eventually diagnosed as schizophrenic. After three years in an asylum, he went to Europe in 1871. . . . {In London} he killed George Merritt. An English court found him not guilty on the ground of insanity, and Minor was sent to Broadmoor. Coming across a leaflet for volunteers to help compile a history of the English language, Minor offered his services. . . . After 17 years of correspondence, the editor of the Oxford English Dictionary came to meet Minor, who had submitted 10,000 definitions to the project." (Libr J)

The author relates the "story of the Oxford English Dictionary's first editor and the expatriate American murderer who contributed more than 10,000 quotations as examples. Best of all, among the entertaining tangents one learns a great deal about the making of that grandest of all reference works." Libr J

Includes bibliographical references

423.13   Dictionaries of idioms

Ammer, Christine.

The **American** Heritage dictionary of idioms. Christine Ammer. Houghton Mifflin 2013 506 p (pa) $15.95   **423.13**
1. English language -- United States -- Idioms -- Dictionaries
ISBN 0547676581 ; 9780547676586
LC 9780547676586

"This book surveys 10,000 American English expressions. Idioms predominate, but common figures of speech (e.g., blind as a bat), interjections, proverbs, colloquialisms (out in left field), emphatic redundancies whose word order cannot be reversed (far and wide), and slang phrases are also included. Entries and their variants are listed alphabetically in boldface. Where a phrase has more than one meaning, definitions are numbered and ordered by frequency of use. Keywords to phrases are listed alphabetically among the entries and note all the entries that contain that keyword. Entries are labeled to indicate the degree of formality or offensiveness: colloquial, slang, and vulgar slang." (Booklist)

"This book makes for fun browsing and could be very helpful to foreign speakers." Choice

Includes bibliographical references

425   Grammar of standard English

Huddleston, Rodney D.

★ The **Cambridge** grammar of the English language; {by} Rodney Huddleston, Geoffrey K. Pullum in collaboration with Laurie Bauer {et al.} Cambridge Univ. Press 2002 1842p il $160   **425**
1. English language -- Grammar
ISBN 0-521-43146-8

LC 2001-25630

This "comprehensive and detailed look at the principles of the English language . . . {is} an authoritative addition to the fields of both English grammar and linguistics." Libr J

Includes bibliographical references

425.55 English language – Pronouns

Bongiovanni, Archie

A **quick** and easy guide to they/them pronouns; Archie Bongiovanni, Tristan Jimerson ; [edited by] Ari Yarwood. Limerence Press 2018 64 p. illustrations $7.99 **425.55**
1. Gender identity 2. Pronouns (Grammar) 3. Interpersonal communication
ISBN 1620104997; 9781620104996

LC 2017959095

"Archie [Bongiovanni], a snarky genderqueer artist, is tired of people not understanding gender neutral pronouns. Tristan [Jimerson], a cisgender dude, is looking for an easy way to introduce gender neutral pronouns to his increasingly diverse workplace. The longtime best friends team up in this short and fun comic guide that explains what pronouns are, why they matter, and how to use them." (Publisher's note)

"In addition to supplying best practices for allies, situational examples illustrate what it's like to be misgendered and how that feels to someone who identifies as nonbinary." LJ

427 Historical and geographic variations, modern nongeographic variations of English

Axelrod, Alan

Whiskey tango foxtrot; the real language of the modern American military. Alan Axelrod. Skyhorse Publishing 2013 240 p. (pbk.; alk. paper) $12.95 **427**
1. English language -- Slang 2. United States -- Armed forces 3. Sailors -- United States -- Language -- Dictionaries 4. Soldiers -- United States -- Language -- Dictionaries 5. Military art and science -- United States -- Dictionaries 6. English language -- United States -- Slang -- Dictionaries
ISBN 1620876477; 9781620876473

LC 2013011431

In this book, Alan Axelrod "tours modern military slang via six topical chapters, including 'Cake Eaters and Chicken Guts.' As the author acknowledges, the sources for some of his entries are from 'official' authorities such as the Department of Defense Dictionary of Military Terms . . . , but Axelrod's main focus is 'unofficial' terms, such as soldiers' rework of the 'What the . . . ' curse as expressed in this book's title." (Library Journal)

Ayto, John

The **Oxford** dictionary of slang. Oxford University Press 2003 (Oxford paperback reference) pa $16.95 **427**
ISBN 0-19-860763-6

LC 427

A reissue of the title first published 1998

"The 10,000 slang terms defined here originated mainly in the United States, Britain, Australia, or New Zealand and include both old and new coinages. The dictionary's arrangement is topical in thesaurus fashion." Libr J

Bailey, Richard W.

Speaking American; a history of English in the United States. Richard W. Bailey. Oxford University Press 2012 xvi, 207 p.p (alk. paper) $27.95 **427**
1. Americanisms 2. English language -- History 3. English language -- Lexicography -- United States 4. English language -- United States -- Usage 5. English language -- United States -- Grammar 6. English language -- United States -- History 7. English language -- Variation -- United States
ISBN 019517934X; 9780195179347

LC 2011011042

In this book, Richard W. Bailey "identifies eight major centers of influence on American English and describes how each has helped shape the tongue of today. . . . In his introduction, he" refutes "the idea that language can somehow be perfected and standardized and celebrates the ability of English to change, adapt, adopt, steal and transform. Then he offers a series of . . . chapters, each focusing on a certain region whose influence on the language has been profound." (Kirkus Reviews)

Includes bibliographical references and index.

Crystal, David

By hook or by crook; a journey in search of English. Overlook Press 2008 314p il map $27.95 **427**
1. English language -- Dialects
ISBN 978-1-59020-061-2; 1-59020-061-6

First published 2007 in the United Kingdom

Combines personal reflections, historical allusions, and traveler's observations about the author's encounters with language and its users throughout the English-speaking world.

"In a conversational style that includes plenty of quirky facts, Crystal captures the exploratory, seductive, teasing, quirky, tantalizing nature of language study, and in doing so illuminates the fascinating world of words in which we live." Publ Wkly

Includes bibliographical references

The **stories** of English. Overlook Press 2004 584p il map $35 **427**
1. English language -- History
ISBN 1-585-67601-2

LC 2004-54727

The author "traces the diverse and unpredictable influences that have shaped English into an unruly family of dialects, creoles, and patois. . . . Crystal acknowledges the emergence during the fourteenth and fifteenth centuries of a prestigious standard version of English. Yet he shows in instance after instance that the tempests of linguistic change have often overwhelmed the custodians of the King's English, compelling them to accommodate forces they could not control. And though he never loses his focus on language, Crystal allows some of its more colorful users—including Chaucer, Shakespeare, Samuel Johnson, and Thomas Jefferson—to bring their personalities and voices into the chronicle." Booklist

Includes bibliographical references

Décharné, Max

Vulgar tongues; an alternative history of English slang. Max Décharné. Pegasus Books 2017 388 p. (hardcover) $26.95 **427**
1. Vocabulary 2. English language 3. English language -- Slang 4. English language -- Slang -- History
ISBN 9781681775005; 9781681774640; 168177464X

This book, by Max Décharné, "traces the many routes of slang, beginning with the thieves and prostitutes of Elizabethan London and ending with the present day, where the centuries-old terms rap and hip-hop still survive, though their meanings have changed. . . . [Readers] will meet Dr. Johnson, World War II flying aces, pickpockets, . . . hardboiled private eyes, carnival geeks and the many eccentric characters who have tried to record slang throughout its checkered past." (Publisher's note)

"Songwriter, musician, and author Décharné gives a breathtaking history and overview of English slang as an ever-evolving language of 'pop culture, street culture and secret society.'" LJ

Includes bibliographical references (pages 339-357) and index.

Holder, R. W.

★ **How** not to say what you mean; a dictionary of euphemisms. 4th ed.; Oxford University Press 2007 410p pa $18.95   **427**

1. Reference books 2. Euphemism -- Dictionaries
ISBN 978-0-19-920839-5; 0-19-920839-5

LC 2007-37558

First published 1987 by Bath University Press with title: A dictionary of American and British euphemisms

"Here are almost five thousand euphemistic expressions listed in alphabetical order, ranging from well-known favorites such as 'push up the daisies,' 'fly-by-night,' 'red light district,' 'take to the cleaners,' 'get lucky,' and 'five-fingered discount,' to less amusing expressions from the bureaucratic and military world such as 'restructuring,' 'collateral damage,' and 'extrajudicial killing.' For each word or expression, Holder includes examples from . . . authors, along with . . . explanations of the words' origins and meaning." Publisher's note

Includes bibliographical references

MacNeil, Robert

Do you speak American? [by] Robert MacNeil and William Cran. 1st Harvest ed.; Harcourt 2005 228p map pa $13 **427**

1. Americanisms 2. English language -- Dialects
ISBN 978-0-15-603288-9; 0-15-603288-0

LC 2005-23093

Sequel to The story of English (1986)

First published 2005 by Nan A. Talese/Doubleday

"Whether talking to crab fishermen in Maryland or country-and-western singers in Tennessee, the authors discover that regional dialects are thriving despite the uniformity of our national tastes in clothing, fast-food chains, and movies. . . . The authors show how mobility, immigration, and racial and ethnic mixing are rapidly and profoundly changing the language. . . . This is colorful, witty, and insightful commentary on American speech patterns." Booklist

Includes bibliographical references

McMahon, Sean

Brewer's dictionary of Irish phrase & fable; [by] Sean McMahon and Jo O'Donoghue. Brewer's 2009 867p $34.95 **427**

1. Allusions 2. Reference books 3. Folklore -- Ireland 4. Irish literature -- Dictionaries
ISBN 978-0-550-10565-3

First published 2004 by Weidenfeld & Nicholson

"Entries explore the island's history, literature, language, folklore and mythology . . . [with a] mix of people, places, historical events, facts and phrases. . . . 6,000 entries focus on the phrase and fable of Ireland, from ancient myth to modern politics." Publisher's note

★ The **new** Partridge dictionary of slang and unconventional English; Tom Dalzell (senior editor) and Terry Victor (editor) Routledge 2006 2v set $220 **427**

1. Reference books 2. English language -- Slang -- Dictionaries
ISBN 0-415-21258-8; 978-0-415-21258-8

First published 1937

This slang dictionary places "emphasis on post-Word War II slang and unconventional English." (Publisher's note)

"Entries list the term, identify its part of speech, explain its meaning, identify the country of origin, and cite sources or provide quotations showing how the term is used. . . . This dictionary informs, but it also entertains." Booklist

Includes bibliographical references

Nunberg, Geoffrey

The **ascent** of the A-word; assholism, the first sixty years. Geoffrey Nunberg. PublicAffairs 2012 251 p. (hardcover) $25.99   **427**

1. Popular culture 2. English language -- Slang 3. English language -- History 4. Words, Obscene 5. English language -- Obscene words
ISBN 1610391756; 9781610391757; 9781610391764

LC 2012017027

Author Geoffrey "Nunberg's study of the word 'asshole' . . . breaks down the important place the word 'asshole' occupies in our language and culture. Nunberg begins by charting the rise of 'asshole' from its origins as WWII barracks slang, to its popularization in post-war literature . . . to its eventual adoption as part of Standard English in the 1970s." (Publishers Weekly)

The **Routledge** dictionary of modern American slang and unconventional English; edited by Tom Dalzell. 2nd edition Routledge 2017 1200 p. hardcover $80; paperback $80   **427**

1. Americanisms 2. English language -- Slang
ISBN 9781138779655; 1138779652; 9781138722088

"The 25,000 entries are accompanied by citations that authenticate the words as well as offer examples of usage from popular literature, newspapers, magazines, movies, television shows, musical lyrics, and Internet user groups. Etymology, cultural context, country of origin and the date the word was first used are also provided. . . . This new edition includes over 500 new headwords collected with citations from the last five years." (Publisher's note)

Spears, Richard A.

★ **McGraw**-Hill's dictionary of American slang and colloquial expressions; 4th ed.; McGraw-Hill 2006 xxix, 546p pa $19.95   **427**

1. Americanisms 2. Reference books 3. English language -- Slang -- Dictionaries
ISBN 0-07-146107-8; 978-0-07-146107-8

LC 2005-52220

First published 1989 with title: NTC's dictionary of American slang and colloquial expressions

This book offers "definitions of more than 12,000 slang and informal expressions from various sources, ranging from golden oldies such as . . . golden oldie, to recent coinages like shizzle (gangsta), jonx (Wall Street), and ping (the Internet). Each entry is followed by examples illustrating how an expression is used in everyday conversation and, where necessary, International Phonetic Alphabet pronunciations are given, as well as cautionary notes for crude, inflammatory, or taboo expressions." Publisher's note

Includes bibliographical references

427.973   American English dialects

McWhorter, John

Talking back, talking Black; truths about America's lingua franca. John McWhorter. Bellevue Literary Press 2017 192 p. $19.99   **427.973**
1. Linguistics 2. Dialect literature 3. Black English -- United States
ISBN 1942658206; 9781942658207

This book, by John McWhorter, is "devoted solely to the form, structure, and development of Black English. . . . McWhorter clearly explains its fundamentals and rich history while carefully examining the cultural, educational, and political issues that have undermined recognition of this transformative, empowering dialect." (Publisher's note)

"This is an engaging look at the English language as spoken by many black Americans as well as the long history of stereotyping that has prevented an objective analysis of a rich language tradition." Booklist

Includes bibliographical references (pages 169-173) and index

428   Standard English usage (Prescriptive linguistics)

Adolescent literacy in the academic disciplines; general principles and practical strategies. edited by Tamara L. Jetton, Cynthia Shanahan. The Guilford Press 2012 xiv, 274 p.p ill. (paper) $30   **428**
1. Reading 2. Literacy 3. Teaching 4. Secondary education 5. Language arts (Secondary) 6. Language arts -- Correlation with content subjects
ISBN 1462502806; 9781462502806; 9781462502837
LC 2011035689

This book, edited by Tamara L. Jetton and Cynthia Shanahan, "addresses the particular challenges of literacy learning in each of the major academic disciplines. Chapters focus on how to help students successfully engage with texts and ideas in English/literature, science, math, history, and arts classrooms. The book shows that . . . students also need to learn processing strategies that are quite specific to each subject and its typical tasks or problems." (Publisher's note)

Includes bibliographical references and index

Dunn, Patricia A.

Grammar rants. Heinemann/Boynton/Cook Publishers 2011 xvi, 134 p   **428**
1. Grammar 2. Textbooks 3. English language -- Grammar
ISBN 0867096055; 9780867096057
LC 2011005689

This book presents an analysis of debates and complaints concerning the moral and social implications of grammar. "Each chapter includes actual rants along with . . . editorial commentary, instructional activities and classroom lessons" intended to facilitate student discussion on the social aspects of grammar and the assumptions people make when they encounter incorrect usage. According to the publisher, these "lessons will promote savvy writing by empowering students and teachers to see for themselves how best to raise the quality of their written and spoken language without resorting to ranting." (Publisher's note)

Includes bibliographical references and index.

Florey, Kitty Burns

Sister Bernadette's barking dog; the quirky history and lost art of diagramming sentences. Melville House 2006 154p $19.95   **428**
1. English language -- Grammar

ISBN 978-1-933633-10-7; 1-933633-10-7
LC 2006-24703

The author "writes with verve about the nuns who taught her to render the English language as a mess of slanted lines, explains how diagrams work, and traces the bizarre history of the men who invented this odd pedagogical tool. And unlike so many of today's microhistorians, who seek to demonstrate how zippers, azaleas, or hopscotch explain the world, Florey is refreshingly content to recount her tale without any suggestion that the diagramming of sentences somehow illuminates the American character. It's a great read." Slate

Fowler, H. W. (Henry Watson), 1858-1933

★ A **dictionary** of modern English usage; H.W. Fowler ; with an introduction and notes by David Crystal. Oxford University Press 2010 784 p.   **428**
1. English language -- Usage 2. English language -- Idioms 3. English language -- Etymology
ISBN 019958589X; 9780199585892
LC 2011389197

First published 1926

"Much loved for his firm opinions, passion, and dry humor, Fowler has stood the test of time and is still considered by many to be the best arbiter of good practice. Now Oxford is bringing back the original long-out-of-print first edition of this beloved work, enhanced with a new introduction by one of today's leading experts on the language, David Crystal. Drawing on a wealth of entertaining examples, Crystal offers an insightful reassessment Fowler's reputation and his place in the history of linguistic thought. Most important, Crystal examines nearly 300 of Fowler's entries in detail, offering a modern perspective on them, and showing how English has changed since the 1920s." (Publisher's note)

Hult, Christine A.

The **Handy** English grammar answer book; Christine A. Hult. Visible Ink Press 2015 419 p. illustrations (paperback) $21.95   **428**
1. English language -- Usage 2. English language -- Grammar 3. English language -- Grammar -- Handbooks, manuals, etc
ISBN 9781578595204; 1578595207
LC 2015015787

Author Christine A. Hult presnts this "guide to writing with clarity for all occasions. It offers fundamental principles, grammar rules, and punctuation advice, as well as insights on writing for different occasions and audiences. From a brief history of the English language to the deconstruction—and explanation—of the different parts of a sentence, and from showing how to punctuate correctly to how to organize a well-argued essay, this easy-to-use reference answers nearly 500 questions." (Publisher's note)

"This grammar guide distills a lot of technical grammar rules into a digestible format directed toward a wide audience and those new to the English language." Booklist

Includes bibliographical references and index.

Norris, Mary

Between you & me; confessions of a Comma Queen. Mary Norris. W W Norton & Co Inc 2015 240 p. (hardcover) $24.95   **428**
1. English language -- Grammar 2. English language -- Errors of usage 3. Comma 4. English language -- Punctuation 5. English language -- Errors in usage
ISBN 0393240185; 9780393240184
LC 2014043252

In this book, professional editor Mary Norris "brings her vast experience, good cheer, and finely sharpened pencils to help the rest of us in a boisterous language book as full of life as it is of practical advice. . . . [The book offers] descriptions of some of the most common and vexing problems in spelling, punctuation, and usage . . . and her clear explanations of how to handle them." (Publisher's note)

"In countless laugh-out-loud passages, Norris displays her admirable flexibility in bending rules when necessary. She even makes her serious quest to uncover the reason for the hyphen in the title of the classic novel Moby-Dick downright hilarious. A funny book for any serious reader." Kirkus

Includes bibliographical references and index

O'Conner, Patricia T.

★ **Woe** is I; the grammarphobe's guide to better English in plain English. Riverhead Bks. 2003 240p $19.95; pa $14 **428**
  1. English language -- Usage 2. English language -- Grammar
  ISBN 1-57322-252-6; 1-59448-006-0 pa
                                                    LC 2003-41416
First published 1996

This guide to good English offers advice on punctuation, usage, style and grammar as well as e-mail.

"The author doesn't take herself or the subject matter too seriously, offering a delightful romp through the intricacies of our language. . . . She knows her subject, can convey her message with wit and ease, and does it all in a compact, easy-to-read format. In short, this is an entertaining and useful grammar reference." Libr J

Includes bibliographical references

Peters, Pam

★ The **Cambridge** guide to English usage. Cambridge University Press 2004 608p il $35 **428**
  1. Reference books 2. English language -- Usage
  ISBN 0-521-62181-X
                                                    LC 2004-301888
"Considering the abundance of peculiarities and challenges in English usage, Cambridge will strengthen even a library well stocked with other guides. It is a serious book for those serious about language." Booklist

Strumpf, Michael

The **grammar** bible; everything you always wanted to know about grammar but didn't know whom to ask. [by] Michael Strumpf and Auriel Douglas. Holt 2004 489p pa $18 **428**
  1. English language -- Grammar
  ISBN 0-8050-7560-7
                                                    LC 2003-57129
The authors move "from the parts of speech to the parts of the sentence and then to spelling, vocabulary, and punctuation, even encompassing thorny issues (e.g., sexist language, split infinitives) and complex grammatical terms (e.g., objective complements, gerund phrases). The authors also include a useful list of collocations and intersperse informative and often amusing 'Hot Line' queries throughout. . . This book is thorough, combining practical information not easily found in trade books, and is lively without trying to be too witty, cute, or humorous." Libr J

Includes bibliographical references

428.2 English language grammar

Garner, Bryan A.

The **Chicago** guide to grammar, usage, and punctuation;

Bryan A. Garner. University of Chicago Press 2016 552 p. (cloth; alkaline paper) $45 **428.2**
  1. English language -- Grammar 2. English language -- Grammar -- Handbooks, manuals, etc 3. English language -- Grammar -- Study and teaching (Higher)
  ISBN 9780226188850
                                                    LC 2015047425
This book, by Bryan A. Garner, is the "definitive guide for writers who want their prose to be both memorable and correct. Throughout the book Garner describes standard literary English—the forms that mark writers and speakers as educated users of the language. He also offers historical context for understanding the development of these forms." (Publisher's note)

"Punctuation guidance separates out uses and misuses, drawing example uses from a diverse group of mostly 20th-century writers." Choice Reviews

Includes bibliographical references

433 Dictionaries of standard German

★ **Random** House Webster's German-English, English-German dictionary; Rev. ed; Random House Reference 2006 547p $12.95 **433**
  1. Reference books 2. German language -- Dictionaries
  ISBN 0-375-72194-0; 978-0-375-72194-6
First published 1997 with title: Random House German-English English-German dictionary

In addition to more than 60,000 entries this dictionary also includes notes on pronunciation, lists of abbreviations, tables of irregular verbs and lists of geographical names.

439 Other Germanic languages

Comprehensive Yiddish-English Dictionary; Hayem Bokhner, Sholem Beynfeld, shef-redaktorn ; Berish Goldshteyn, Yankl Salant, asotsyirte redaktorn = Solon Beinfeld, Harry Bochner, editors-in-chief ; Barry Goldstein, Yankl Salant, associate editors. Indiana University Press 2013 xxxix, 704 p.p (hardcover) $45 **439**
  1. Encyclopedias and dictionaries 2. Yiddish language -- Dictionaries 3. Yiddish language -- Dictionaries -- English
  ISBN 0253009839; 9780253009838
                                                    LC 2012491596
This book is a Yiddish-English dictionary. It contains "more than 37,000 words and a treasure horde of idiomatic phrases." It provides "readers with the most contemporary grammatical and semantic nuances. . . . Included is a . . . user's guide, an introduction and road map through the difficulties inherent in working with two distinct alphabets and language systems." (Choice)

440 French and related Romance languages

Nadeau, Jean-Benoit

★ The **story** of French; [by] Jean-Benoît Nadeau [and] Julie Barlow. St. Martin's Press 2006 483p map $25.95 **440**
  1. French language
  ISBN 9780312341831; 0312341830
                                                    LC 2006-49348

This book explores the origins and evolution of the French language.

This is "a well-told, highly accessible history of the French language that leads to a spirited discussion of the prospects for French in an increasingly English-dominated world." N Y Times (Late N Y Ed)

Includes bibliographical references

443 Dictionaries of standard French

Correard, Marie-Helene

★ The **Oxford**-Hachette French dictionary; French-English, English-French. edited by Marie-Hélène Corréard, Valerie Grundy. 4th ed.; Oxford University Press/Hachette Livre 2007 xxxviii, 1945p $55 **443**

1. Reference books 2. French language -- Dictionaries
ISBN 978-0-19-861422-7; 0-19-861422-5

LC 2007-14213

First published 1994

This work provides coverage of French and English vocabulary in general as well as scientific and technical areas with over 350,000 words and phrases and over 530,000 translations. Supplementary material includes information on French society and culture, including famous places, people and much practical information for those planning to reside in France.

460 Spanish, Portuguese, Galician

Barlow, Julie

The **story** of Spanish; Jean-Benoit Nadeau and Julie Barlow. St. Martin's Press 2013 496 p. (hardcover) $27.99 **460**

1. Linguistics 2. Spanish language -- History
ISBN 0312656025; 9780312656027

LC 2013002633

This book, by Jean-Benoit Nadeau and Julie Barlow, asks "just how did a dialect spoken by a handful of shepherds in Northern Spain become the world's second most spoken language, the official language of twenty-one countries on two continents, and the unofficial second language of the United States? . . . [The authors] look at the roots and spread of modern Spanish." (Publisher's note)

Includes bibliographical references and index.

463 Dictionaries of standard Spanish

Houghton Mifflin Co.

The **Concise** American Heritage Spanish dictionary; 2nd ed; Houghton Mifflin 2001 xxiv, 616p $14 **463**

1. Reference books 2. Spanish language -- Dictionaries
ISBN 0-618-11769-5

LC 00-66461

"This bilingual dictionary includes more than 70,000 words and phrases. The emphasis on American English and Latin American Spanish as well as the informative guides and tables will assist students of either language." Booklist

470 Latin and related Italic languages

Ostler, Nicholas

Ad infinitum; a biography of Latin. Walker & Company

2007 382p il map $27.95 **470**

1. Latin language
ISBN 978-0-8027-1515-9; 0-8027-1515-X

"In four parts, Ostler covers the origins and development of Latin in the Roman world, Latin's "taking over the church," its medieval continuation and fracturing into vernaculars, and a nuanced rebirth in the Renaissance and its legacy in the contemporary world. Incredibly well documented, with examples from antiquity to the modern era." Libr J

473 Dictionaries of classical Latin

★ **Oxford** Latin dictionary; edited by P. G. W. Glare. Oxford Univ. Press 1982 xxiii, 2126p **473**

1. Reference books 2. Latin language -- Dictionaries 3. Latin language -- Dictionaries -- English
ISBN 0198642245

LC 8208162

This dictionary looks at the meaning and development of more than 40,000 classical Latin words and phrases

"Authorized in 1931 and begun two years later, {this dictionary} appeared in eight fascicles published between 1968 and 1982. These have been combined in a single volume." Wilson Libr Bull

Stone, Jon R.

★ **Latin** for the illiterati; a modern phrase book for an ancient language. 2nd ed.; Routledge 2009 xxii, 338p pa $24.95 **473**

1. Reference books 2. Latin language -- Dictionaries
ISBN 978-0-415-77767-4; 0-415-77767-4

First published 1996

"Organized alphabetically within the categories of verba (common words and expressions), dicta (common phrases and familiar sayings), and abbreviations, this . . . [is a] compendium of more than 7,000 Latin words, expressions, phrases, and sayings taken from the world of art, music, law, philosophy, theology, medicine and the theatre, as well as . . . [remarks and] advice from ancient writers such as Virgil, Ovid, Cicero, and more." Publisher's note

Includes bibliographical references

487 Preclassical and postclassical Greek

Fox, Margalit

★ The **Riddle** of the Labyrinth. HarperCollins 2013 384 p. $27.99 **487**

1. Ciphers 2. Greece -- Antiquities
ISBN 0062228838; 9780062228833

This book looks at the deciphering of Linear B, a "script first found on clay tablets excavated on the island of Crete and later at Pylos on the Greek mainland and dating to the Mycenaean period, circa 1400 BCE." It was deciphered by Michael Ventris. This book focuses on the "work of American classical scholar Alice Kober (1906-50) whose syllabic grids made Ventris's breakthrough possible." (Library Journal)

492.4 Hebrew

Glinert, Lewis

The **story** of Hebrew; Lewis Glinert. Princeton University Press 2017 xii, 281 p.p illustrations (Library of Jewish ideas)

(hardcover; alk. paper) $27.95   **429.4**
1. Hebrew language 2. Hebrew language -- Usage 3. Hebrew language -- History 4. Hebrew language -- Revival
ISBN 9780691153292

LC 2016022084

This book in the Library of Jewish Ideas series, by Lewis Glinert, "explores the extraordinary hold that Hebrew has had on Jews and Christians, who have invested it with a symbolic power far beyond that of any other language in history. Preserved by the Jews across two millennia, Hebrew endured long after it ceased to be a mother tongue, resulting in one of the most intense textual cultures ever known." (Publisher's note)

"This is a must-read for students of language and Jewish history." Pub Wkly

Includes bibliographical references and index.

Zilkha, Avraham

★ **Modern** English-Hebrew dictionary. Yale Univ. Press 2002 457p (Yale language series) $55; pa $30   **492.4**
1. Reference books 2. Hebrew language -- Dictionaries
ISBN 0-300-09004-8; 0-300-09005-6 pa

LC 2001-26830

This dictionary includes 30,000 entries, with listings for translating words with multiple meanings, newly coined and slang words, common idioms, vocalization of Hebrew words, acronyms, and gender identification and plural forms of irregular nouns

493   Non-Semitic Afro-Asiatic languages

Robinson, Andrew, 1957-

Cracking the Egyptian code; the revolutionary life of Jean-François Champollion. Andrew Robinson. Oxford University Press 2012 272 p. (telework) $29.95   **493**
1. Hieroglyphics 2. Rosetta stone 3. Egyptologists -- France -- Biography 4. Egyptian language -- Writing, Hieroglyphic
ISBN 0199914990; 9780199914999

LC 2011046769

This book, by Andrew Robinson, "is the first biography in English of [Jean-François] Champollion, widely regarded as the founder of Egyptology. . . . Robinson . . . reconstructs how Champollion cracked the code of the hieroglyphic script, describing how Champollion . . . sailed the Nile for a year, studied the tombs in the Valley of the Kings . . . and carefully compared the three scripts on the Rosetta Stone to penetrate the mystery of the hieroglyphic text." (Publisher's note)

Includes bibliographical references and index.

495.1   Chinese

Cheng & Tsui English-Chinese lexicon of business terms with pinyin; compiled by Andrew C. Chang = [Jianqiao Ying Han shang yong ci hui pin ying ci dian / Zhang Jiezhou bian] Cheng & Tsui Co. 2001 442p (C & T Asian dictionary series) $36.95   **495.1**
1. Reference books 2. Business -- Dictionaries 3. Chinese language -- Dictionaries
ISBN 978-0-88727-394-0; 0-88727-394-7

LC 2001-94244

"A book to hand to your patrons who need to know the Chinese expressions for terms such as Chief Executive Officer, market penetration, and stockholder. More than 9,000 English-language words and phrases are listed with their Chinese simplified characters, with pinyin translit-

eration equivalents." Booklist

495.7   Korean

Berlitz Korean compact dictionary. Berlitz Publishing 2006 672p pa $12.95   **495.7**
1. Reference books 2. Korean language -- Dictionaries
ISBN 978-981-246-949-6; 981-246-949-4

This book has "45,000 entries that aim to capture the core words of the language. This dictionary features bold, blue headwords [for navigation]." Publisher's note

499   Non-Austronesian languages of Oceania, Austronesian languages, miscellaneous languages

Okrent, Arika

In the land of invented languages; Esperanto rock stars, Klingon poets, Loglan lovers, and the mad dreamers who tried to build a perfect language. Spiegel & Grau 2009 342p il $26   **499**
1. Artificial languages
ISBN 978-0-385-52788-0; 0-385-52788-8

LC 2008-38732

The author "explores some of the themes and shortcomings of 900 years worth of artificial languages. . . . [Her] prose is a model of clarity and grace; through it, she conveys fascinating insights into why natural language, with its corruptions, ambiguities and arbitrary conventions, trips so fluently off our tongues." Publ Wkly

Includes bibliographical references

499.992   Esperanto

Schor, Esther

Bridge of words; Esperanto and the Dream of a Universal Language. Esther Schor. Metropolitan Books 2016 384 p. illustrations (hardback) $32   **499.992**
1. Esperanto -- History 2. Language and languages
ISBN 9780805090796

LC 2015018907

In this history of a constructed language, "scholar Esther Schor traces the life of Esperanto. She follows the path from its invention by [Ludwig Lazarus] Zamenhof, through its . . . golden age as the great hope of embattled cosmopolites, to its suppression by nationalist regimes and its resurgence as a bridge across the Cold War. She plunges into the mechanics of creating a language . . . that would be easy to learn, politically neutral, and allow all to speak to all." (Publisher's note)

"Must reading for those fascinated by linguistics and utopian endeavors and an essential volume for every library's language collection." Booklist

Includes bibliographical references (pages 329-348) and index.

500 SCIENCE

500 Natural sciences and mathematics

Bais, Sander

In praise of science; curiosity, understanding, and progress. MIT Press 2010 192p il $24.95 **500**
1. Science
ISBN 978-0-262-01435-9; 0-262-01435-1
LC 2009-35675

"Over the course of four short chapters, Sander Bais illustrates in entertaining and often poetic ways not only how all of the sciences are connected to each other, but how they comprise a vital (if not the most vital) endeavor humans has ever undertaken. . . . Among others, the stories in In Praise of Science include the origin of Santa Claus, the history of quantum theory, the invention of the lightning rod, and religious attacks that distorted the theory of evolution and facts surrounding HIV and AIDS. The polemical nature of Bais' arguments might spark debate for some readers, but he never comes across as ranting. He employs many (at times lengthy) quotes from a variety of sources, and near the end of the book there's a tendency to let the quotes make the case for him. But for the vast majority of the book, Bais seems like the quirky professor everyone loves and/or wishes they had, one who inspires lifelong interests." PopMatters

Includes bibliographical references

Bloom, Howard

The God problem; how a godless cosmos creates. by Howard Bloom. Prometheus Books 2012 708 p. (hardcover) $28.00 **500**
1. Cosmology 2. Religion and science 3. Cosmology -- Miscellanea 4. Science -- Social aspects
ISBN 161614551X; 9781616145514
LC 2012013460

This book, by Howard Bloom, asks "how does an inanimate universe generate stunning new forms and unbelievable new powers without a creator? . . . [The book explains] . . . Howard Bloom's provocative new theory of the . . . universe--the Bloom toroidal model, also known as the big bagel theory--which explains two of the biggest mysteries in physics: dark energy and why, if antimatter and matter are created in equal amounts, there is so little antimatter in this universe." (Publisher's note)

Includes bibliographical references and index

Bryson, Bill, 1951-

★ A **short** history of nearly everything. Broadway Bks. 2003 544p $27.50; pa $15.95 **500**
1. Science 2. Science -- Popular works
ISBN 0-7679-0817-1; 0-7679-0818-X pa
LC 2003-46006

"Neither oversimplified nor overstuffed, this exceptionally skillful tour of the physical world covers the basic principles and still has room for profiles of some of the more engaging scientists." N Y Times Book Rev

Includes bibliographical references

Dawkins, Richard, 1941-

Science in the soul; selected writings of a passionate rationalist. Richard Dawkins ; edited by Gillian Somerscales. Random House 2017 438 p. (hardback) $28 **500**
1. Essays 2. Evolution 3. Science -- Philosophy
ISBN 9780399592256; 9780399592249
LC 2017025118

This book, by Richard Dawkins, "brings together forty-two essays, polemics, and paeans--all written with Dawkins's characteristic erudition, remorseless wit, and unjaded awe of the natural world. . . . In the essays themselves, newly annotated by the author, he investigates a number of issues, including the importance of empirical evidence, and decries bad science, religion in the schools, and climate-change deniers." (Publisher's note)

"These 41 short pieces suitably capture evolutionary biologist Dawkins's . . . reputation as a fierce proponent of rationalism, who possesses an exacting and questioning scientific mind and an acerbic wit." LJ

Includes bibliographical references (pages 419-427) and index.

Dean, Cornelia

Making sense of science; separating substance from spin. Cornelia Dean. The Belknap Press of Harvard University Press 2017 xi, 281 p.p $19.95 **500**
1. Research 2. Science -- Social aspects 3. Science news 4. Science in popular culture 5. Research -- Political aspects 6. Research -- Moral and ethical aspects
ISBN 9780674059696
LC 2016037738

In this book, author Cornelia Dean attempts "to expose the flawed reasoning and knowledge gaps that handicap readers with little background in science. Shortcomings in K–12 education are partly to blame, but so too is the public's indifference to the way science is done and communicated. Dean shows how venues such as courtrooms and talk shows become fonts of scientific misinformation. She also calls attention to the conflicts of interest that color scientific research." (Publisher's note)

"Dean's excellent primer will be welcomed by those who find themselves lost in the fog of rival claims about scientific issues that affect us all." Pub Wkly.

Includes bibliographical references and index

Du Sautoy, Marcus, 1965-

The great unknown; seven journeys to the frontiers of science. Marcus du Sautoy. Viking 2017 450 p. illustrations (hardcover) $30 **500**
1. Theory of knowledge 2. Discoveries in science 3. Knowledge, Theory of
ISBN 0735221804; 9780735221802; 9780735221819
LC 2016056835

This book, by Marcus du Sautoy, "takes us into the minds of science's greatest innovators and reminds us that major breakthroughs were often ridiculed at the time of their discovery. Then he carries us on a . . . tour of seven 'Edges' of knowledge--inviting us to consider the problems in quantum physics, cosmology . . . and neuroscience. . . . He [also explores] some of science's thorniest questions in simple concepts like the roll of dice . . . or how a clock measures time." (Publisher's note)

"his brilliant, well-written exploration of our universe's biggest mysteries will captivate the curious and leave them pondering 'natural phenomena that will never be tamed and known.'" Pub Wkly

Includes bibliographical references (pages 431-435) and index

Dyson, Freeman J., 1923-

Dreams of earth and sky; by Freeman Dyson. New York Review Books 2015 300 p. (alk. paper) $27.95 **500**
1. Science 2. Discoveries in science 3. Serendipity in science
ISBN 1590178548; 9781590178546
LC 2014038482

Author "Freeman Dyson's new collection of pieces from 'The New

York Review of Books' investigates and celebrates what he calls openness to unconventional ideas in science. His subjects range from the seventeenth-century scientific revolution, to the scientific inquiries of the Romantic generation, to important recent works by Daniel Kahneman and Malcolm Gladwell." (Publisher's note)

"Readers who enjoyed the first volume of reviews will be pleased with this follow-up, and new readers will be delighted by the fascinating insider's view of the scientific community and its intersection with the political establishment." Kirkus

Feynman, Richard Phillips

★ The **meaning** of it all; thoughts of a citizen scientist. Basic Books 2005 133p pa $13.95   **500**
1. Science 2. Religion
ISBN 0-465-02394-0
First published 1998 by Addison-Wesley
"Originally delivered as a three-part lecture series at the University of Washington in 1963, this collection touches on such far-ranging topics as the existence or nonexistence of God; the Constitution; and UFOs. . . . These memorable lectures confirm that Feynman's gift of insight extended from the subatomic world to the cosmic, and to the very human as well." Publ Wkly

The **pleasure** of finding things out; the best short works of Richard P. Feynman. by Richard P. Feynman; edited by Jeffrey Robbins; foreword by Freeman Dyson. Perseus Bks. 1999 270p hardcover o.p. pa $15.95   **500**
1. Science
ISBN 0-7382-0349-1 pa
LC 99-64775
These lectures and interviews are "expositions about [Feynman's] life, about technical topics in computing and physics, and about science's general place in society." Booklist

Gardner, Martin, 1914-2010

Did Adam and Eve have navels? discourses on reflexology, numerology, urine therapy and other dubious subjects. Norton 2000 333p il hardcover o.p. pa $15.95   **500**
1. Science
ISBN 0-393-32238-6 pa
LC 00-34870
This is a collection of the author's pieces culled from the Skeptical Inquirer. Gardner "gives succinct and amusing critiques of a number of the fallacies that abound in alternative medicine (including the very peculiar urine-therapy treatment) and many other 'dubious subjects.'" Libr J
Includes bibliographical references

Goldacre, Ben

Bad science; quacks, hacks, and big pharma flacks. Faber and Faber 2010 288p il pa $15   **500**
1. Errors 2. Medical misconceptions
ISBN 978-0-86547-918-0
LC 2010-14401
First published 2008 in the United Kingdom
The author "has written a very funny and biting book critiquing what he calls 'Bad Science.' Under this heading he includes homeopathy, cosmetics manufacturers whose claims about their products defy plausibility, proponents of miracle vitamins, and drug companies and physicians who design faulty studies and manipulate the results. . . . While it is a very entertaining book, it also provides important insight into the horrifying outcomes that can result when willful anti-intellectualism is al-

lowed equal footing with scientific methodology." Boston Globe
Includes bibliographical references

Gribbin, John R.

Almost everyone's guide to science; the universe, life and everything. [by] John Gribbin with Mary Gribbin. Yale Univ. Press 1999 232p $30; pa $11.95   **500**
1. Science
ISBN 0-300-08101-4; 0-300-08460-9 pa
LC 99-26755
First published 1998 in the United Kingdom
In this "general guide to science for the layperson . . . Gribbin combines biographies and history, on the one hand, with the major theories in science, on the other. . . . The text is clear, is based on solid research, and clearly reflects a lifetime love for science." Sci Books Films
Includes bibliographical references

The **handy** science answer book; compiled by the Carnegie Library of Pittsburgh; [edited by] Naomi E. Balaban and James E. Bobick. 4th ed.; Visible Ink Press 2011 679p il pa $21.95   **500**
1. Science 2. Technology
ISBN 978-1-57859-321-7
LC 2011-429
First published 1994
"The text is divided into various subject areas including physics and chemistry, space, earth, climate and weather, minerals and other materials, energy, technology, and environment, gathering answers to reference questions. . . . A comprehensive index . . . makes the material accessible and easy to find. Pages are full of fascinating tidbits, complemented by illustrations, photos, charts, graphs, and maps." Voice Youth Advocates
Includes bibliographical references

Henderson, Mark

100 most important science ideas; key concepts in genetics, physics and mathematics. [by] Mark Henderson, Joanne Baker, Tony Crilly. Firefly Books 2009 431p il $19.95   **500**
1. Physics 2. Genetics 3. Mathematics
ISBN 978-1-55407-527-0
This book aims to encourage the reader to explore "the 100 most important, groundbreaking ideas that have emerged from the scientific disciplines of genetics, physics, and mathematics. Divided into three sections, each written by one of the authors . . . this work presents complex scientific topics in a simple, understandable way. . . . Text boxes, entertaining quotations, frequent diagrams, and everyday examples hold the reader's attention and make this work engaging to anyone interested in the world of science." Libr J

Munroe, Randall, 1984-

Thing Explainer; Complicated Stuff in Simple Words. by Randall Munroe. Houghton Mifflin Harcourt 2015 64 p. illustrations $24.95   **500**
1. Technological innovations 2. Science -- Juvenile literature 3. Outer space -- Juvenile literature
ISBN 0544668251; 9780544668256
In this book, author Randall Munroe "uses line drawings and only the thousand (or, rather, 'ten hundred') most common words to provide simple explanations for some of the most interesting stuff there is. . . . Funny, interesting, and always understandable, this book is for anyone—age 5 to 105—who has ever wondered how things work, and why." (Publisher's note)

What if? serious scientific answers to absurd hypothetical questions. Randall Munroe. Houghton Mifflin Harcourt 2014 320 p. (hardback) $24 **500**
1. Wit and humor 2. Science -- Miscellanea
ISBN 0544272994; 9780544272996

LC 2014016311

This book, by Randall Munroe, offers "hilarious and informative answers to important questions you probably never thought to ask. . . . In pursuit of answers, Munroe runs computer simulations, pores over stacks of declassified military research memos, solves differential equations, and consults with nuclear reactor operators." (Publisher's note)

"Those who enjoyed the irreverent style of Allie Brosh's best-selling memoir, Hyperbole and a Half, will enjoy Munroe's serious and silly musings on everything from science to romance. One question submitted to his blog: 'If all digital data were stored on punch cards, how big would Google's data warehouse be?' was even answered by the search-engine behemoth. The response, 'No comment.'" LJ

Orzel, Chad

Eureka! discovering your inner scientist. Chad Orzel. Basic Books, a member of the Perseus Books Group 2014 368 p. illustrations (hardcover; alk. paper) $17.99 **500**
1. Discoveries in science 2. Science -- Popular works
ISBN 0465074960; 9780465044917; 9780465074969

LC 2014034615

In this book, author Chad Orzel "shows that science isn't something alien and inscrutable beyond the capabilities of ordinary people, it's central to the human experience. Every human can think like a scientist, and regularly does so in the course of everyday activities. The disconnect between this reality and most people's perception is mostly due to the common misconception that science is a body of (boring, abstract, often mathematical) facts." (Publisher's note)

Park, Robert L.

Voodoo science; the road from foolishness to fraud. Oxford Univ. Press 2000 230p hardcover o.p. pa $17.95 **500**
1. Fraud 2. Science
ISBN 0-19-513515-6; 978-0-19-514710-0 pa; 0-19-514710-3 pa

LC 99-40911

The author "aims to expose various beliefs and schemes put forth in the popular press and other places as scientifically real and factual. . . . {He} turns a critical eye on cold fusion, magnet therapy, homeopathy, perpetual motion, and other recent examples of fringe science. . . . Park's book should be required reading for all science writers, journalists, and politicians." Libr J

Randall, Lisa

Knocking on heaven's door; how physics and scientific thinking illuminate the universe and the modern world. Ecco 2011 xxi, 442p il $29.99; ebook $14.99 **500**
1. Physics 2. Science
ISBN 978-0-06-172372-8; 978-0-06-209689-0 ebook

LC 2011010521

"To explain how science works, Randall analyzes the way two researchers at Bell Labs turned the annoying static coming through their radio telescope into a cosmic breakthrough. For in this piquant episode—and others that Randall examines—science advances by testing theoretical ingenuity against technologically acquired data. . . . Randall offers an insider's perspective into this cutting-edge science. Yet she illuminates that science with lucid language, laced with references to popular culture, political controversy, and even comic-strip art. The general reader's indispensable passport to the frontiers of science." Booklist

Includes bibliographical references

Rees, Martin J., 1942-

From here to infinity; a vision for the future of science. Martin Rees. W.W. Norton 2012 144 p (hardcover) $23.95 **500**
1. Overpopulation 2. Nuclear warfare 3. Science and civilization 4. Science -- Philosophy
ISBN 0393063070; 9780393063073

LC 2012003421

This book on science by Martin Rees offers "four of the distinguished Reith lectures, delivered annually over BBC radio by renowned thinkers. . . . He reviews our planet's looming problems, from climate change to overpopulation to nuclear war, emphasizing that there are no solutions outside of science. . . . He also warns about the 'tendency for long-term strategies, however important, to be trumped by more immediate issues that can be resolved within an electoral cycle.'" (Kirkus Reviews)

Sagan, Carl

Billions and billions; thoughts on life and death at the brink of the millennium. Random House 1997 241p hardcover o.p. pa $14.95 **500**
1. Science
ISBN 0-345-37918-7 pa

LC 96-52730

This collection of essays covers such topics as: "the invention of chess, life on Mars, global warming, abortion, international affairs, the nature of government, and the meaning of morality. Writing with clarity and an understanding of human nature, Sagan offers hope for humanity's future." Libr J

Includes bibliographical references

★ **Broca's** brain; reflections on the romance of science. Random House 1979 347p hardcover o.p. pa $7.99 **500**
1. God 2. Science 3. Religion 4. Astronomy 5. Machinery 6. Philosophy 7. Physicians 8. Physicists 9. Psychologists 10. Writers on science 11. Nobel laureates for physics
ISBN 0-345-33689-5 pa

LC 78-21810

The author "is a lucid, logical writer with a gift for explaining science to the layman and infecting the reader with his own boundless enthusiasm and curiosity." Natl Rev

Includes bibliographical references

Scientific American's ask the experts; answers to the most puzzling and mindblowing science questions. by the editors of Scientific American. HarperCollins Pubs. 2003 267p il pa $14.95 **500**
1. Science
ISBN 0-06-052336-0

LC 2004-555579

This "is a book that answers questions big, little, and in between. . . . The book uses the familiar question-and-answer format, with a table of contents allowing the reader to flip to a specific question. The questions are answered by a variety of experts. . . . This is one of those books you put on your reference shelf, and pull out whenever the subject turns to matters of scientific interest. Great for trivia buffs, too." Booklist

This explains everything; deep, beautiful, and elegant theories of how the world works. edited by John Brockman. 1st ed. Harper Perennial 2013 xx, 411 p.p (paperback) $15.99 **500**
1. Physics 2. American essays 3. Pattern perception 4. Explanation 5. Science -- Miscellanea

ISBN 0062230174; 9780062230171

LC 2012032107

This book is a "collection of brief essays [that] started with a question posed to the readers of Edge.org, founded by [editor John] Brockman . . .; What is your favorite deep, elegant, or beautiful explanation? The result is 150 brief essays that present . . . explanations of the world around us. The authors include Richard Dawkins, Eric Kandel, Alan Alda, and Brian Eno." (Library Journal)

This idea is brilliant; lost, overlooked, and underappreciated scientific concepts everyone should know. edited by John Brockman. HarperCollins 2018 515 p. $18.99   **500**
1. Biology 2. Life sciences 3. Science -- Miscellanea
ISBN 0062698214; 9780062698216

This book, edited by John Brockman, "takes readers on a tour of the bold, exciting, and underappreciated scientific concepts that will enrich every mind. . . . [These include] the lost brilliance of common sense, . . . how to extend our grasp of reality beyond what we can see and touch . . . [and] Navier-Stokes equations, which govern everything from weather prediction to aircraft design and blood flow." (Publisher's note)

Wilkinson, Karen

The **Art** of tinkering; meet 150+ makers working at the intersection of art, science & technology. Karen Wilkinson, Mike Petrich. Weldon Owen Inc. 2013 223 p. illustrations (chiefly color) $32.50   **500**
1. Tinkers -- United States
ISBN 1616286091; 9781616286095

LC 2013948536

This book, by Karen Wilkinson and Mike Petrich, "is a collection of exhibits, artwork, and projects that celebrate a whole new way to learn, in which people create their own knowledge through making and doing, working with readily available materials, getting their hands dirty, collaborating with others, problem-solving in the most fun sense of the word, and, yes, oftentimes failing and bouncing back from getting stuck." (Publisher's note)

500.2   Physical sciences

Ball, Philip, 1962-

Patterns in nature; why the natural world looks the way it does. Philip Ball. University of Chicago Press 2016 288 p. illustrations (chiefly color) (cloth; alk. paper) $35   **500.2**
1. Nature 2. Ecology 3. Fractals 4. Physical sciences 5. Environmental science 6. Patterns (Mathematics) 7. Geometry in nature 8. Pattern formation (Biology) 9. Pattern formation (Physical sciences)
ISBN 9780226332420

LC 2015034568

In this book, by Philip Ball, "Though at first glance the natural world may appear overwhelming in its diversity and complexity, there are regularities running through it, from the hexagons of a honeycomb to the spirals of a seashell and the branching veins of a leaf. Revealing the order at the foundation of the seemingly chaotic natural world, [this book] explores not only the math and science but also the beauty and artistry of nature's awe-inspiring designs." (Publisher's note)

"This is formidable eye candy for the I-love-science crowd, sure to spark a sense of impressed wonder at the beauty of our universe and our ability to photograph it." Pub Wkly

Includes bibliographical references (page 283) and index.

Nature's patterns; a tapestry in three parts. Oxford University Press 2009 308p il $29.95   **500.2**
1. Shape 2. Chaos (Science) 3. Patterns (Mathematics)
ISBN 978-0-19-923796-8; 0-19-923796-4

LC 2009-280579

"From the curl of a ram's horn to patterns of spider webs and the development of an embryo, Mr Ball examines the possible causes of the shapes and forms we observe. His book contains a lot of fascinating detail about the different physical, chemical and evolutionary processes at work." Economist

Includes bibliographical references

501   Philosophy and theory

Arbesman, Samuel

★ The **half**-life of facts; why everything we know has an expiration date. Samuel Arbesman. Current 2012 viii, 242 p,p ill. (hardback) $25.95   **501**
1. Science 2. Probabilities 3. Theory of knowledge 4. Evolution 5. Science -- Philosophy
ISBN 159184472X; 9781591844723

LC 2012019142

This book by Samuel Arbesman presents a "treatise on the nature of facts: what they are, how and why they change and how they sometimes don't (despite being wrong). . . . [Arbesman argues that] what we know 'changes in understandable and systematic ways.' . . . He introduces 'scientometrics,' the science of science. With scientometrics, we can measure the exponential growth of facts, how long it will take, exponentially, for knowledge in any field to be disproved." (Kirkus Reviews)

Includes bibliographical references (pages 215-234) and index

Costa, Rebecca D.

The **watchman's** rattle; thinking our way out of extinction. with a foreword by E.O. Wilson. Vanguard Press 2010 347p $26.95   **501**
1. Civilization 2. Problem solving 3. Complexity (Philosophy)
ISBN 978-1-59315-605-3; 1-59315-605-7

LC 2010-927900

Explains why the human brain has such difficulty dealing with complex global problems and provides a method for surmounting these limitations in order to end the blights of worldwide recession, global warming, fast-spreading viruses, famine, and poverty.

This book "will give concerned readers new hope in human capability." Libr J

Includes bibliographical references

Dawkins, Richard, 1941-

The **magic** of reality; how we know what's really true. illustrated by Dave McKean. 1st Free Press hardcover ed; Free Press 2011 271p il map   **501**
1. Nature 2. Reality 3. Science -- Philosophy
ISBN 1439192812; 1451628927 ebook; 9781439192818; 9781451628920 ebook

LC 2011025607

"In this outstanding 'graphic science book,' evolutionary biologist Dawkins . . . teams up with illustrator Dave McKean . . . to examine questions in everyday science, such as: why seasons occur; what things are made of; and whether there's life on other planets. They explain the answers from mythological and cultural points of view before diving into the chemistry, biology, and physics—all in language that advanced middle school, or most high school, students can absorb." Publ Wkly

Deutsch, David

The **beginning** of infinity; explanations that transform the world. Viking Adult 2011 487p il $30 **501**

1. Infinite 2. Science -- Philosophy

ISBN 978-0-670-02275-5; 0-670-02275-6

LC 2011004120

The book discusses the interaction between humans and the universe they inhabit, challenging concepts such as "the Earth is a maternally inclined spacefaring vessel . . . [and] the utter insignificance of human beings in the cosmic scheme of things. . . . Our cosmic importance derives from our capacity to acquire knowledge, and use it to transform our lives and surroundings. . . . In the short term, this means that we should seek to understand and control the Earth's entire ecosystem. . . . In the medium term we should colonize the Moon, followed by the other planets in our solar system. In the longer term we should aim for the stars - and even beyond: Deutsch argues in some detail that extremely empty intergalactic space is easily capable of sustaining a high population of technologically advanced space-dwellers." (TLS)

"Anyone who loves to grapple with profound ideas should love reading this very ambitious and challenging look at the history and (possibly unlimited) future of human understanding." Sci Books Films

Includes bibliographical references

Firestein, Stuart

Ignorance; how it drives science. Stuart Firestein. Oxford University Press 2012 viii, 195 p.p **501**

1. Ignorance 2. Discoveries in science 3. Science -- Methodology 4. Science -- Philosophy 5. Ignorance (Theory of knowledge)

ISBN 0199828075; 9780199828074

LC 2011051395

This book argues that "[t]he fundamental attribute of successful scientists . . . is a form of ignorance characterised by knowing what you don't know, and being able to ask the right questions. . . . To demonstrate the crucial role of this type of informed ignorance, [Stuart] Firestein highlights two well-known examples. The first, Heisenberg's uncertainty principle, asserts that we cannot know the position and momentum of a particle simultaneously. . . . His second example is Godel's incompleteness theorems. . . . Firestein also includes more modern examples of productive ignorance." (New Scientist)

Includes bibliographical references and index

Henry, John

A **short** history of scientific thought; John Henry. Palgrave Macmillan 2012 xvii, 306 p.p ill. (hbk.) $90 **501**

1. Science -- History 2. Science -- Philosophy 3. Science and civilization 4. Natural history -- History 5. Civilization, Western -- History 6. Science -- Philosophy -- History 7. Science and civilization -- History

ISBN 0230019420; 0230019439; 9780230019423; 9780230019430

LC 2011049038

This book by John Henry offers a "historical survey of the major developments in scientific thought and the impact of science on Western culture, this book takes the reader from ancient times through to the twentieth century. Organized chronologically, the book explores the history of studies of the natural world, and man's role within that world, in a single volume." (Publisher's note)

Includes bibliographical references and index

Mitchell, Melanie

Complexity; a guided tour. Oxford University Press 2009 349p il map $29.95 **501**

1. Complexity (Philosophy) 2. Science -- Philosophy

ISBN 978-0-19-512441-5; 0-19-512441-3

LC 2008023794

The sciences of complexity "seek to explain how large-scale complex, organized, and adaptive behavior can emerge from simple interactions among myriad individuals. . . . Based on her work at the Santa Fe Institute and drawing on its interdisciplinary strategies, Mitchell [attempts to] bring clarity to the workings of complexity across a . . . range of biological, technological, and social phenomena, seeking out the general principles or laws that apply to all of them. She explores as well the relationship between complexity and evolution, artificial intelligence, computation, genetics, information processing, and [other fields]." (Publisher's note) Bibliography. Index.

The author offers a "snapshot of the growing field of complex-systems science. . . . Mitchell explores the historical roots of this area in the work of visionaries such as Henri Poincaré and Edward Lorenz in dynamical-systems theory, and of John von Neumann, Alan Turing and others in computation. . . . The book hits its stride in its latter half, with an insightful survey of recent developments in complex-network theory and scaling in biology." Nature

Includes bibliographical references (p. 326-336)

Nothing; surprising insights everywhere from zero to oblivion. edited by Jeremy Webb. Workman Publishing Company 2014 266 p. illustrations $14.95 **501**

1. Science 2. Cosmology 3. Nothing (Philosophy) 4. Science -- Philosophy

ISBN 1615192050; 9781615192052

LC 2014002254

"There's a lot about nothing in this fun assortment of pop science essays culled from the New Scientist. . . . The collection on a whole takes a fun and accessible tone with easily digestable insights and discoveries, like the history and differences between zero as a number and zero as a symbol (which surprisingly people didn't always use it or even have it to represent nothing) or the critical benefits of doing nothing for certain animals." (Publishers Weekly)

Includes bibliographical references and index

Olson, Randy

★ **Don't** be such a scientist; talking substance in an age of style. Island Press 2009 206p il pa $19.95 **501**

1. Science 2. Communication 3. College teachers 4. Marine biologists 5. Communication in science 6. Motion picture directors 7. Science in motion pictures 8. Science -- Study and teaching

ISBN 1-59726-563-2; 978-1-59726-563-8

LC 2009-7081

Olson discusses his evolution "from science professor to Hollywood filmmaker. In Don't Be Such a Scientist, he . . [discusses] talking substance in an age of style. The key, he argues, is to stay true to the facts while tapping into something more primordial, more irrational, and ultimately more human." (Publisher's note) Filmography of movies by Randy Olson. Index.

The author argues "that 'scientists need artists.' He delves into the principle of 'arouse and fulfill,' suggesting that while scientists are great with the fulfillment part, the power of art can help arouse the interest of the broader audience." Publisher's note

Includes bibliographical references

Shtulman, Andrew

Scienceblind; why our intuitive theories about the world are so often wrong. Andrew Shtulman. Basic Books 2017 viii, 311 p.p illustrations (hardcover) $30 **501**

1. Errors 2. Science -- Methodology 3. Intuition 4. Reasoning 5. Fallacies (Logic) 6. Errors, Scientific

ISBN 9781541698178; 9780465053940

LC 2016050643

This book, by Andrew Shtulman, "shows that the root of our misconceptions lies in the theories about the world we develop as children. They're not only wrong, they close our minds to ideas inconsistent with them, making us unable to learn science later in life. So how do we get the world right? We must dismantle our intuitive theories and rebuild our knowledge from its foundations." (Publisher's note)

"Although this book is thoroughly researched with a wealth of scholarly sources cited, Shtulman reaches a broad audience by investigating topics that everyone can understand." LJ

Includes bibliographical references (pages 273-298) and index.

Sigmund, Karl
★ **Exact** thinking in demented times; the Vienna Circle and the epic quest for the foundations of science. Karl Sigmund. Basic Books 2017 xviii, 449 p.p (hardcover) $32   **501**
1. Vienna circle 2. Logical positivism 3. Science -- Philosophy -- History -- 20th century
ISBN 9780465096954

LC 2017037770

Many readers will agree that we are currently living in "demented times," and Sigmund adeptly lays out a history that has great relevance for today. --Kirkus

Includes bibliographical references and index.

This will change everything; ideas that will shape the future. edited by John Brockman; [introduction by Daniel C. Dennett] HarperCollins 2010 xxiii, 390p pa $14.99   **501**
1. Science 2. Forecasting
ISBN 978-0-06-189967-6

"With contributions from Ian McEwan, Steven Pinker, Lee Smolin, Craig Venter, Richard Dawkins and 130 others of their ilk, the book is like an intellectual lucky dip." New Sci

502   Miscellany

Woodford, Chris
Atoms Under the Floorboards; The Surprising Science Hidden in Your Home. Chris Woodford. Excelsior Editions/State University of New York Press 2015 336 p. illustrations $27   **502**
1. Houses 2. Science -- Popular works
ISBN 1472912225; 9781472912220

This book, by Chris Woodford, "presents the fascinating and surprising scientific explanations behind a variety of common (and often entertainingly mundane) household phenomena, from gurgling drains and squeaky floorboards to rubbery custard and shiny shoes. . . . Each chapter focuses on the objects and processes familiar in everyday life and slowly unpicks the science behind them." (Publisher's note)

"The author's writing is clear and precise; he explains complex matters simply, using scientific terminology without getting bogged down by it." Booklist

503   Dictionaries, encyclopedias, concordances

★ **Van** Nostrand's scientific encyclopedia; 10th ed.; Wiley 2008 3v il map set $450   **503**
1. Reference books 2. Science -- Encyclopedias
ISBN 978-0-471-74338-5

LC 2007-46658

First published 1938

This encyclopedia contains articles contains over 10,000 entries on topics such as biology, chemistry, earth science, mathematics and engineering, anatomy and physiology, physics, botany, and space science.

Includes bibliographical references

506   Organizations and management

Seeing further; the story of science, discovery, and the genius of the Royal Society. edited & introduced by Bill Bryson; contributing editor, Jon Turney. William Morrow 2010 506p il $35; ebook $21.99   **506**
1. Science 2. Royal Society (Great Britain)
ISBN 978-0-06-199976-5; 978-0-06-203622-3 ebook

Bryson "presents a remarkable collection of essays celebrating the 350th anniversary of the founding of the Royal Society of London and its many contributions to science. Society members have included such illustrious names as Darwin, Newton, Leibniz, and Francis Bacon, to name a few. The volume's 23 contributors are both uniformly excellent and remarkable for their diversity." Publ Wkly

Includes bibliographical references (p. 486-489)

507.1   Science education

Tesoriero, Heather Won
The **class**; a life-changing teacher and his world-changing kids. Heather Won Tesoriero. Ballantine Books 2018 448 p. (hardback; alk. paper) $27   **507.1**
1. STEM education 2. Science -- Exhibitions 3. Science -- Study and teaching 4. Science fairs -- United States 5. Greenwich High School (Greenwich, Conn.) 6. Science teachers -- Connecticut -- Greenwich 7. High school students -- Connecticut -- Greenwich 8. Science projects -- Competitions -- United States 9. Science -- Study and teaching (Secondary) -- Connecticut -- Greenwich
ISBN 9780399181849

LC 2018014535

This book, by Heather Won Tesoriero, is an inspiring account of how Andy Bramante, a corporate scientist turned public school teacher, "mentors and motivates his prize-winning pupils . . . [at] Greenwich High School's science research class, where his students have been cleaning up awards on the science fair circuit for years." (Publishers Weekly)

Includes bibliographical references and index

507.8   Use of apparatus and equipment in study and teaching

Johnson, George
The **ten** most beautiful experiments. Alfred A. Knopf 2008 192p il $22.95   **507.8**
1. Science -- Experiments
ISBN 978-1-4000-4101-5; 1-4000-4101-5

LC 2007-27839

"Writing up Luigi Galvani's study of frog's legs, James Joule's of heat, Albert Michelson's of light's speed, and Robert Millikan's of the electron's charge, Johnson exerts classic appeal to science readers: presenting the lone genius making a great discovery. Good to go in any library." Booklist

Includes bibliographical references

508 Natural history

Alvarez, Walter

A **Most** Improbable Journey; A Big History of Our Planet and Ourselves. Walter Alvarez. W W Norton & Co Inc 2016 288 p. $26.95 **508**

1. Geology 2. Cosmology 3. Evolution 4. Earth sciences
ISBN 039329269X; 9780393292695

This book by geologist Walter Alvarez "expands our view of human history by revealing the cosmic, geologic, and evolutionary forces that have shaped us. . . . Almost fourteen billion years of cosmic history, over four billion years of Earth history, a couple million years of human history . . .--it's staggering to consider. Yet behind everything in our world, . . . lies a similarly grand procession of highly improbable events." (Publisher's note)

Carroll, Sean B.

Remarkable creatures; epic adventures in the search for the origins of species. Houghton Mifflin Harcourt 2009 331p il map $26; pa $14.95 **508**

1. Evolution 2. Naturalists
ISBN 978-0-15-101485-9; 0-15-101485-X; 978-0-547-24778-6 pa; 0-547-24778-8 pa

LC 2008-25438

National Book Award Finalist: Nonfiction (2009)

"A stirring introduction to the wonder of evolutionary biology." Kirkus

Includes bibliographical references

Darwin, Charles

★ The **voyage** of the Beagle; journal of researches into the natural history and geology of the countries visited during the voyage of H.M.S. Beagle round the world. introduction by Steve Jones. Modern Lib. 2001 468p il pa $12.95 **508**

1. Natural history 2. Beagle Expedition (1831-1836) 3. South America -- Description and travel
ISBN 0-375-75680-9

LC 00-46294

This journal records the author's five year voyage around the world as a naturalist aboard H.M.S. Beagle. The trip was influential in the formulation of Darwin's theories of evolution. During the journey he collected data on wildlife, geological formations, weather, and local customs.

De Villiers, Marq

Sahara ; a natural history; {by} Marq de Villiers and Sheila Hirtle. Walker & Co. 2002 326p il maps $28; pa $13 **508**

1. Sahara Desert 2. Natural history -- Africa
ISBN 0-8027-1372-6; 0-8027-7678-7 pa

LC 2002-71391

"Insightful and intelligent, this fascinating book will appeal to anyone with a curiosity about the world's largest desert and the people who inhabit it." Booklist

Includes bibliographical references

Flannery, Tim F.

The **eternal** frontier; an ecological history of North America and its peoples. {by} Tim Flannery. Atlantic Monthly Press 2001 404p il maps $27.50; pa $16 **508**

1. Natural history -- North America
ISBN 0-87113-789-5; 0-8021-3888-8 pa

LC 2001-18841

"This book weaves ecological, cultural, and social history together in a marvelous way." Sci Books Films

Fothergill, Alastair

Planet Earth; as you've never seen it before. [by] Alastair Fothergill [et al.]; foreword by David Attenborough. University of California Press 2007 309p il map $39.95 **508**

1. Habitat (Ecology) 2. Earth
ISBN 978-0-520-25054-3; 0-520-25054-0

LC 2006-50073

In this collection of over 400 photographs of natural landscapes and wildlife, the author "takes readers on a kaleidoscopic tour of the flora, fauna and natural history of the Earth's poles, forests, plains, deserts, mountains and oceans." Publ Wkly

Gould, Stephen Jay

★ The **richness** of life; the essential Stephen Jay Gould. edited by Paul McGarr and Steven Rose; with an introduction by Steven Rose and a foreword by Oliver Sacks. Norton 2007 654p il $35 **508**

1. Evolution 2. Natural history
ISBN 978-0-393-06498-8; 0-393-06498-0

LC 2006-29208

Frist published 2006 in the United Kingdom

"For collections that have room for only one volume of his writing, this is the essential one." SLJ

Includes bibliographical references

Heinrich, Bernd

A **naturalist** at large; the best essays of Bernd Heinrich. Bernd Heinrich. Houghton Mifflin Harcourt 2018 304 p. (hardcover; alk. paper) $26 **508**

1. Essays 2. Science 3. Natural history 4. Science -- Popular works 5. Natural history -- Popular works
ISBN 9780544986831

LC 2017046210

"From one of the finest scientist/writers of our time comes an engaging record of a life spent in close observation of the natural world. . . . In essays that span several decades, [Bernd] Heinrich finds himself at home in Maine, where he plays host to visitors from Europe (the cluster flies) and more welcome guests from Asia (ladybugs); and as far away as Botswana, where he unravels the far-reaching ecological consequences of elephants' bruising treatment of mopane trees." (Publisher's note)

Includes bibliographical references and index

Leach, Amy

Things that are; Amy Leach ; illustrations by Nate Christopherson. Milkweed Editions 2012 xiii, 185 p.p (acid-free paper) $18.00 **508**

1. Essays 2. Natural history 3. Natural history literature
ISBN 1571313346; 9781571313348

LC 2011040887

This book of essays by Amy Leach, winner of a Whiting Writers' Award and a Rona Jaffe Foundation Writers' Award, "explores fantastical and curious subjects pertaining to natural phenomena." It is "divided into two sections -- 'Things of Earth' and 'Things of Heaven' -- containing essays with names such as 'Goats, and Bygone Goats,' 'When Trees Dream of Being Trees' and 'Sail On, My Little Honeybee.' Each of the essays range from three to seven pages, and they are accompanied by . . . pen-and-ink drawings by [Nate] Christopherson." (Kirkus Reviews)

Leopold, Aldo, 1886-1948

A **Sand** County almanac & other writings on ecology & conservation; a sand county almanac & other writings on ecology and conservation. Aldo Leopold ; [edited by] Curt Meine. Literary Classics of the United States, Inc. 2013 832 p. illustrations, maps (Library of America)   **508**

1. Nature conservation 2. Environmental protection
ISBN 9781598532067

LC 2012948207

A reissue of the title first published 1949

By Aldo Leopold and edited by Curt Meine, "the collection opens with Leopold's classic A Sand County Almanac," which "is joined here by over fifty uncollected articles, essays, speeches, and other writings that chart the evolution of Leopold's ideas over the course of three decades. . . . The volume also presents a freshly prepared version of Leopold's extraordinary field journals." (Publisher's note)

"The volume also includes a chronology of Leopold's life; extensive notes; an index to plants/animals, with a mixture of common and scientific nomenclature; and a general index." Choice

Includes bibliographical references and indexes

Leslie, Clare Walker

The **Curious** Nature Guide; Explore the Natural Wonders All Around You. by Clare Walker Leslie. Storey Publishing 2015 144 p. illustrations (chiefly color) (pbk.; alk. paper) $14.95   **508**

1. Nature 2. Ecology 3. Natural history
ISBN 9781612125091

LC 2015010780

This book, by Clare Walker Leslie, "will inspire you to use all of your senses to notice the colors, sounds, smells, and textures of the trees, plants, animals, birds, insects, clouds, and other features that can be seen right outside your home, no matter where you live. Sketch or write about one exceptional nature image each day; learn to identify cloud types and the weather they bring; or create a record of what you see each day as you walk your dog." (Publisher's note)

"A remarkable book for solitary reading or sharing with children." LJ

Includes bibliographical references and index

Matthiessen, Peter

End of the earth; voyaging to Antarctica. National Geographic Soc. 2003 242p il maps $26   **508**

1. Animals -- Antarctica 2. Antarctica -- Exploration
ISBN 0-7922-5059-1

LC 2003-51254

This account of the author's voyage describes the wildlife he encountered in the region

"Vivid and empathic accounts of the high drama and petty rivalries of Antarctic exploration alternate with Matthiessen's own adventures as he shares his indelible impressions of this cold, white wonderland in the hope that they will inspire readers to appreciate the beauty and bounty of the earth's 'shimmering web of biodiversity' enough to defend and preserve it." Booklist

Includes bibliographical references

Natural history; the ultimate visual guide to everything on Earth. [senior project editor, Kathryn Hennessy] DK 2010 648p il map $50   **508**

1. Natural history 2. Reference books
ISBN 978-0-7566-6752-8; 0-7566-6752-6

LC 2010-283659

"This is an international encyclopedia of life-forms—e.g., fossils, fungi, plants, animals, mammals—that includes vital facts and two to three sentences about each as well as more than 5000 color illustrations in all. Each grouping is introduced by an essay that puts it in biological and evolutionary perspective." Libr J

Nicholls, Steve

Paradise found; nature in America at the time of discovery. University of Chicago Press 2009 524p $30   **508**

1. Human influence on nature 2. America -- Exploration 3. Natural history -- North America
ISBN 978-0-226-58340-2; 0-226-58340-6

LC 2008-36076

The author "turns to the writings of forgotten early naturalists to gain understanding both of the natural abundance of the New World when the first Europeans arrived and of how so much of this living bounty was destroyed so quickly. . . . Not only does Nicholls present arresting material, he also offers fresh interpretations and connections in this grandly spanning and affecting look to the past for guidance in facing a future of further diminishment." Booklist

Includes bibliographical references and index

Peck, Robert McCracken, 1952-

The **natural** history of Edward Lear (1812-1888) Robert McCracken Peck ; with a foreword by Sir David Attenborough. David R. Godine, Publisher 2016 224 p. color illustrations (alk. paper) $40.00   **508**

1. Natural history 2. Animals -- Pictorial works 3. Natural history illustration 4. Artists -- Great Britain -- Biography 5. Poets, English -- 19th century -- Biography 6. Natural history illustrators -- Great Britain -- Biography
ISBN 9781567925838

LC 2016016171

This book, by Robert McCracken Peck, presents work by the amateur naturalist Edward Lear, who produced "an impressive number of drawings for scientific publications, a large number of superb natural history paintings, and countless detailed and delicate drawings for public institutions and private patrons, not just of English species, but of birds and mammals from as far afield as Australia, New Zealand, and the Americas." (Publisher's note)

"Highly recommended for all academic libraries and larger public library systems. Readers of all levels will find this book useful." LJ

Includes bibliographical references

Rothman, Julia

Nature anatomy; the curious parts & pieces of the natural world. by Julia Rothman, with John Niekrasz. Storey Publishing 2015 224 p. color illustrations, color map (paper w/ flaps; alk. paper) $16.95   **508**

1. Earth sciences 2. Earth sciences -- Study and teaching (Middle school) -- Pictorial works
ISBN 1612122310; 9781612122311

LC 2014033664

This book, by Julia Rothman with John Niekrasz, "celebrates the diverse curiosities and beauty of the natural world. . . . With whimsically hip illustrations, every page is an extraordinary look at all kinds of subjects, from mineral formation and the inside of a volcano to what makes sunsets, monarch butterfly migration, the ecosystem of a rotting log, the parts of a bird, the anatomy of a jellyfish, and much, much more." (Publisher's note)

"With its wide range of topics, from landforms to leaf identification, bird beaks, and water bugs, Nature Anatomy is designed as the ultimate book for browsers with an insatiable curiosity about the great outdoors. Rothman has clearly found a structure and design in which she excels; this title is an informative charmer from start to finish. More, please." Booklist

Safina, Carl

The **view** from Lazy Point; a natural year in an unnatural world. with drawings by Trudy Nicholson; maps by Jon Luoma. Henry Holt and Co. 2011 401p il map $32; ebook **$16.99 508**
1. Human ecology 2. Marine ecology 3. Coastal ecology 4. Environmental degradation
ISBN 978-0-8050-9040-6; 0-8050-9040-1; 978-1-4299-5035-0 ebook; 1-4299-5035-8 ebook
LC 2009-40108

A conservationist explores various global regions to investigate examples of environmental degradation and renewal while identifying a link between environmental dangers and human rights issues.

"A superb work of environmental reportage and reflection." Kirkus Includes bibliographical references

Sampson, Scott D.

How to raise a wild child; the art and science of falling in love with nature. Scott D. Sampson. Houghton Mifflin Harcourt 2015 352 p. (hardback) $25 **508**
1. Parenting 2. Child rearing 3. Outdoor education 4. Nature study 5. Child development 6. Natural history -- Study and teaching
ISBN 0544279328; 9780544279322
LC 2014048565

This book, by Scott D. Sampson, offers "an easy-to-use guide for parents, teachers, and others looking to foster a strong connection between children and nature, complete with engaging activities, troubleshooting advice, and much more. . . . Distilling the latest research in multiple disciplines, Sampson reveals how adults can help kids fall in love with nature--enlisting technology as an ally, taking advantage of urban nature, and instilling a sense of place along the way." (Publisher's note)

"This timely, significant work carries a far-reaching message for families and the planet." Pub Wkly

Shetterly, Susan Hand

Settled in the wild; notes from the edge of town. Algonquin Books of Chapel Hill 2010 240p $21.95 **508**
1. Wildlife 2. Natural history -- Maine
ISBN 1565126181; 9781565126183
LC 2009-30802

Shetterly "notes the interplay of humanity and wilderness through fishing, forestry, conservation, preservation, hunting, trapping, development and wildlife rehabilitation, but also in quiet, personal appreciation. Shetterly is a less verbose Thoreau, allowing nature's wisdom to seep through her simple yet thorough observations." Kirkus

Spencer, Edgar W.

★ **Guide** to the geology & natural history of the Blue Ridge Mountains; Edgar W. Spencer. Edgar W. Spencer"||"Distributed by University of Virginia Press 2017 388 p. $29.95 **508**
1. Blue Ridge Mountains region 2. Natural history -- Blue Ridge Mountains 3. Blue Ridge Mountains -- Guidebooks 4. Geology -- Virginia -- Blue Ridge Region 5. Geology -- Blue Ridge Mountains -- Guidebooks 6. Natural history -- Blue Ridge Mountains -- Guidebooks
ISBN 0983747164; 9780983747161
LC 2017288751

"Full of rich detail and easy to use, this beautifully illustrated full-color guide to the [Blue Ridge Mountains] region was written [by Edgar W. Spencer] and designed for great accessibility, whether you're a first-time visitor looking to understand the Parkway's spectacular views or an experienced geology or nature enthusiast. . . . [It offers] an overview of the major geological and environmental processes that shape the Blue Ridge." (Publisher's note)
Includes bibliographical references and index
Guide to the geology and natural history of the Blue Ridge Mountains

Steelquist, Robert

The **Northwest** coastal explorer; your guide to the places, plants, and animals of the Pacific Coast. Robert Steelquist. Timber Press 2016 283 p. color illustrations (paperback) $24.95 **508**
1. Coastal ecology 2. Travel guidebooks 3. Northwest Coast of North America -- Guidebooks 4. Northwest, Pacific -- Guidebooks 5. Pacific Coast (North America) -- Guidebooks 6. Natural areas -- Northwest, Pacific -- Guidebooks 7. Coastal ecology -- Northwest, Pacific -- Guidebooks 8. Natural history -- Northwest, Pacific -- Guidebooks 9. Natural areas -- Pacific Coast (North America) -- Guidebooks 10. Coastal ecology -- Pacific Coast (North America) -- Guidebooks 11. Natural history -- Pacific Coast (North America) -- Guidebooks
ISBN 1604696311; 9781604696318; 9781604697711
LC 2015047572

This book, by Robert Steelquist, "is a fun, engaging, lushly-illustrated guide to the marine life of Oregon, Washington, and British Columbia. Profiles of the flora and fauna include tips on where and how to find them--like the ochre sea stars commonly discovered on exposed rocks and the olive snails found on sandy beaches--while the included getaway guide highlights the best weekend trips for each area." (Publisher's note)

"This book will be very helpful to those exploring these areas who want to learn more about the terrain, plants, and animals they are likely to encounter." Choice
Includes bibliographical references (pages 271-273) and index

Steinberg, Ted

★ **Gotham** unbound; an ecological history of greater New York, from Henry Hudson to Hurricane Sandy. Ted Steinberg. Simon & Schuster 2014 544 p. illustrations, maps (hardcover; alk. paper) $32 **508**
1. Natural history -- New York (State) -- New York
ISBN 1476741247; 9781476741246; 9781476741284; 9781476741307
LC 2013036197

This book, by Ted Steinberg, "is a powerful account of the relentless development that New Yorkers wrought as they plunged headfirst into the floodplain and transformed untold amounts of salt marsh and shellfish beds into a land jam-packed with people, asphalt and steel, and the reeds and gulls that thrive among them." (Publisher's note)

A "fascinating and cautionary unnatural history, a staggering epic of human will, might, and folly that affirms a crucial truth, 'the control of nature is an illusion.'" Booklist
Includes bibliographical references and index

Stroud, Patricia Tyson

A **glorious** enterprise; the Academy of Natural Sciences of Philadelphia and the making of American science. Robert McCracken Peck and Patricia Tyson Stroud ; photographs by Rosamond Purcell. University of Pennsylvania Press 2012 xvii, 437 p.p (alk. paper) $75 **508**

1. Natural history 2. Science -- History 3. Academy of Natural Sciences of Philadelphia -- History 4. Natural history -- Research -- Pennsylvania -- Philadelphia
ISBN 0812243803; 9780812243802

LC 2011034991

This book by Robert McCracken Peck and Patricia Tyson Stroud focuses on the history of the Academy of Natural Sciences of Philadelphia, which "stands today as the oldest natural history museum in the Western hemisphere. . . . What began as a small gathering of devoted amateurs has grown into a vibrant international center for scientific education and research." (Publisher's note)

Includes bibliographical references and index.

509 History, geographic treatment, biography

Al-Khalili, Jim

The **house** of wisdom; how Arabic science saved ancient knowledge and gave us the Renaissance. Penguin Press 2011 xxix, 302p il map $29.95   **509**
1. Medieval civilization 2. Science -- Philosophy 3. Science -- Arab countries 4. Arab countries -- Intellectual life
ISBN 1-59420-279-6; 978-1-59420-279-7

LC 2010-53136

This is a history of early "Islamic astronomy, mathematics, medicine and philosophy." (N Y Times Book Rev) Glossary. Chronology. Index.

"There is a commonly held view that during the Middle Ages, Arabic scientists focused mainly on translating into Arabic the scientific knowledge of ancient civilizations while contributing little to scientific advancement. Physicist al-Khalili . . . challenges this theory by documenting the remarkable contributions of Arabic astronomers, mathematicians, physicians, physicists, chemists, and philosophers, who were scholars at a scientific academy in Baghdad known as the House of Wisdom. . . . Al-Khalili brings to life a vibrant intellectual period of Islamic history when there was not only tolerance for other religions and cultures but a synergy between science and Islam. Anyone interested in the early history of science or the development of the scientific method before Galileo will find this an engaging study." Libr J

Includes bibliographical references

Bauer, Susan Wise

The **story** of Western science; From the writings of Aristotle to the big bang theory. Susan Wise Bauer. W.W. Norton & Co. Inc. 2015 336 p. illustrations (hardcover) $26.95   **509**
1. Science -- History 2. Astronomy -- History
ISBN 0393243265; 9780393243260

LC 2015000136

This book by Susan Wise Bauer "shows us the joy and importance of reading groundbreaking science writing for ourselves and guides us back to the masterpieces that have changed the way we think about our world, our cosmos, and ourselves. Each chapter recommends one or more classic books and provides entertaining accounts of crucial contributions to science, vivid sketches of the scientist-writers, and clear explanations of the mechanics underlying each concept." (Publisher's note)

"What is especially enriching in the text is the focus on the science writing of these inquiring pioneers, and each chapter contains names of websites and e-book versions and recommendations for books written by individual scientists. A remarkable resource for a wide audience." Choice

Includes bibliographical references and index

Concise history of science & invention; an illustrated time line. edited by Jolyon Goddard. National Geographic 2010 352p il map $40   **509**
1. Science -- History 2. Inventions -- History 3. Reference books 4. Science -- History -- Chronology 5. Inventions -- History -- Chronology
ISBN 978-1-4262-0544-6; 1-4262-0544-9

LC 2009-18460

This book presents "a panoramic perspective on humankind's restless quest for the laws, theories, and tools by which we can grasp and master our universe. . . . All human scientific endeavors and achievement are divided into four general fields of inquiry and arrayed into four basic geocultural regions . . . highlighted by 350 photographs, maps, illustrations, and diagrams that add graphic emphasis to key information." (Publisher's note)

"The topical essays and wonderful photos and illustrations make this source useful as a circulating book as well as a reference book." Booklist

Includes glossary and bibliographical references

Crease, Robert P.

The **great** equations; breakthroughs in science from Pythagoras to Heisenberg. W.W. Norton & Co. 2009 315p il $25.95   **509**
1. Equations 2. Science -- History 3. Science -- Philosophy
ISBN 978-0-393-06204-5; 0-393-06204-X

LC 2008-42494

The author "explores 10 rather beautiful equations. He begins with the beguiling simplicity of the equation that bears Pythagoras' name . . . and moves on to Newton's second law of motion and law of universal gravitation, the second law of thermodynamics, Maxwell's celebrated equations, discoveries by Einstein and Schrödinger and, finally, Heisenberg's famous uncertainty principle. . . . Any reader who aspires to be scientifically literate will find this a good starting place." Publ Wkly

Includes bibliographical references

Dolnick, Edward

The **clockwork** universe; Isaac Newton, the Royal Society, and the birth of the modern world. HarperCollins 2011 378p il $27.99; ebook $23.99   **509**
1. Science 2. Physicists 3. Mathematicians 4. Writers on science 5. Royal Society of London 6. Royal Society (Great Britain) 7. Scientists -- Great Britain -- History
ISBN 9780061719516; 9780062042262

LC 2010-24321

The subject is "how the scientific attempt to describe the underlying order of the cosmos played out in the life of Isaac Newton." (N Y Times Book Rev) Bibliography. Index.

"Colorful, entertainingly written and nicely paced—a fine introductory text on Newton and the scientific revolution." Kirkus

Includes bibliographical references

Fara, Patricia

★ **Science**; a four thousand year history. Oxford University Press 2009 408p il map pa $18.95; $34.95   **509**
1. Science and civilization 2. Science -- History
ISBN 019922689X; 0199580278 pa; 9780199226894; 9780199580279 pa; 978-0-19-922689-4; 978-0-19-958027-9 pa; 0-19-958027-8 pa; 0-19-922689-X

LC 2008-50975

This "book explores how science has become so powerful by describing the financial interests and imperial ambitions behind its success. . . . [Fara challenges] notions of European superiority by emphasising the importance of scientific projects based around the world. . . . [This] volume challenges scientific supremacy itself, arguing that science is successful not because it is always indubitably right, but because people have said that it is right. Science dominates modern life, but perhaps the globe will be better off by limiting science's powers and undoing some of its effects." (Publisher's note) Index.

"This survey of 4,000 years of scientific discovery from Babylon to the present confirms that historians of science often have quite different perspectives from those of the actual practitioners. . . . Readers learn about the contributions of famous scientists as though they were almost puppets responding to religious, social, and practical influences in both their choices of research topics and their methods of investigation—in contrast to their possessing an inherent desire to better understand the behavior of nature. In this highly readable book that tells a magnificent story, Fara . . . weaves together the bits and pieces in a unique way." Choice

Includes bibliographical references

Freely, John

The **flame** of Miletus; the birth of science in ancient Greece (and how it changed the world) John Freely. I.B. Tauris 2012 238 p. (hbk.) $29.95 **509**
1. Ancient philosophy 2. Greece -- Civilization 3. Science, Ancient 4. Science -- Greece -- History 5. Greece -- Intellectual life -- To 146 B.C
ISBN 1780760515; 9781780760513

LC 2012472537

This book looks at Ancient Greece and "the great scientific thinkers of that distant age. [John Freely] narrates . . . the story of how the ancient flame lit by Thales and others survived the centuries after the fall of Hellas and Rome, resurfaced in the Islamic world, and was transmitted to western Europe. There it rekindled the spirit of scientific inquiry that led to the germination of modern science." (Choice)

Includes bibliographical references (p. 226-235) and index

Gribbin, John R.

The **scientists**; a history of science told through the lives of its greatest inventors. [by] John Gribbin. Random House 2003 xxii, 646p il hardcover o.p. pa $16.95 **509**
1. Scientists 2. Science -- History
ISBN 1-4000-6013-3; 0-8129-6788-7 pa

LC 2003-46607

First published 2002 in the United Kingdom with title: Science: a history, 1543-2001

"Replete with scientific clarity, Gribbin's work is the epitome of what a general-interest history of science should be." Booklist

Includes bibliographical references

Hofstadter, Dan

The **Earth** moves; Galileo and the Roman Inquisition. W.W. Norton 2009 240p il **509**
1. Popes 2. Astronomy 3. Astronomers 4. Inquisition 5. Writers on science 6. Inquisition -- Italy 7. Science, Renaissance 8. Catholic Church -- Italy -- History 9. Astronomy -- Religious aspects -- Christianity 10. Catholic Church -- Doctrines -- History -- 17th century
ISBN 0-393-06650-9; 978-0-393-06650-0

LC 2009-4325

This book examines the Inquisition in relation to Galileo's arrest, trial, conviction, and the legal processes involved. Bibliography. Index.

This book "allows a clear understanding of one of the major events in the history of science." Sci Books Films

Includes bibliographical references

Holmes, Richard, 1945-

★ The **age** of wonder; how the romantic generation discovered the beauty and terror of science. Pantheon Books 2009 xxi, 552p il $40; pa $17.95 **509**
1. Science -- Great Britain -- History
ISBN 978-0-375-42222-5; 978-1-4000-3187-0 pa

LC 2008-49587

"In this big two-hearted river of a book, the twin energies of scientific curiosity and poetic invention pulsate on every page." N Y Times Book Rev

Includes bibliographical references

Ignotofsky, Rachel

Women in science; 50 Fearless Pioneers Who Changed the World. written and illustrated by Rachel Ignotofsky. Ten Speed Press 2016 127 p. color illustrations (hardcover; alk. paper) $16.99 **509**
1. Women scientists 2. Women scientists -- Biography -- Juvenile literature
ISBN 1607749769; 9781607749769

LC 2015050246

This book, by Rachel Ignotofsky, "highlights the contributions of fifty notable women to the fields of science, technology, engineering, and mathematics (STEM) from the ancient to the modern world. . . . The trailblazing women profiled include well-known figures like primatologist Jane Goodall, as well as lesser-known pioneers such as Katherine Johnson, the African-American physicist and mathematician who calculated the trajectory of the 1969 Apollo 11 mission to the moon." (Publisher's note)

Includes bibliographical references and index

Ings, Simon

Stalin and the Scientists; A History of Triumph and Tragedy, 1905-1953. Simon Ings. Atlantic Monthly Press 2017 528 p. illustrations (ebook) $28; $28 **509**
1. Communism 2. Science -- Government policy
ISBN 9780802189868; 0802125980; 9780802125989

LC 2017006682

This book, by Simon Ings, "tells the story of the many gifted scientists who worked in Russia from the years leading up to the Revolution through the death of the 'Great Scientist' himself, Joseph Stalin. It weaves together the stories of scientists, politicians, and ideologues into an intimate and sometimes horrifying portrait of a state determined to remake the world. They often wreaked great harm." (Publisher's note)

"A provocative and increasingly chilling work that shows how scientists in the nascent Soviet Union were sacrificed to the Soviet dream of building the ideal state." Kirkus

Includes bibliographical references (pages 437-495) and index.

Lightman, Alan P.

★ The **discoveries**; great breakthroughs in 20th century science. [by] Alan Lightman. Pantheon Books 2005 553p il $32.50; pa $16.95 **509**
1. Science -- History
ISBN 0-375-42168-8; 0-375-71345-X pa

LC 2005-40854

This book "chronicles 25 landmark findings in astronomy, physics, chemistry, and biology in the 20th century. Beginning with Max Planck's quantum theory and ending with Paul Berg's recombinant DNA, these breakthroughs are academically and playfully explored via the nature of the unknown, the circumstances and influences of discovery, and, most originally, the actual words of the scientists." Libr J

Includes bibliographical references

McCray, W. Patrick

The **visioneers**; how a group of elite scientists pursued space colonies, nanotechnologies, and a limitless future. W. Patrick McCray. Princeton University Press 2012 351 p. (hardback; acid-free paper) $29.95   **509**

1. Nanotechnology 2. Space colonies 3. Visionaries 4. Science -- History

ISBN 0691139830; 9780691139838

LC 2012017061

This book looks at visioneers, a term coined by author W. Patrick McCray "to describe an individual with an an inquiring mind that is not merely scientific or technical but posed imaginatively toward the future. . . . The two primary visioneers examined by McCray are Gerard O'Neil, a prominent Princeton physicist who saw space colonization as an answer to Earth's growing population, and Eric Drexler, who was fascinated by the new field of nanotechnology." (Library Journal)

Includes bibliographical references and index

Mlodinow, Leonard

The **upright** thinkers; the human journey from living in trees to understanding the cosmos. Leonard Mlodinow. Pantheon Books 2015 352 p. illustrations (hard cover; alk. paper) $27.95   **509**

1. Evolution 2. Science -- History

ISBN 0307908232; 9780307908230; 9780307908247

LC 2014040067

This book, by Leonard Mlodinow, offers a "tour through the exciting history of human progress and the key events in the development of science. . . . He presents a . . . new look at the unique characteristics of our species and our society that helped propel us from stone tools to written language and through the birth of chemistry, biology, and modern physics to today's technological world." (Publisher's note)

"Attending to the real people involved in the story he tells, and gifted with a knack for inserting a personal anecdote, a biographical tidbit, or a laugh line just when one is needed, Mlodinow never bores or exhausts. His structuring of the book is also exemplary. It's in three sections, the first ranging from H. habilis to Aristotle and the formalization of reason, the second from Renaissance cosmology to Darwin, and the third from Planck's and Einstein's invention of the quantum onward. Amateur science mavens couldn't ask for a better brief, introductory text." Booklist

Snyder, Laura J.

The **philosophical** breakfast club; four remarkable friends who transformed science and changed the world. Broadway Books 2011 439p il map $27; ebook $27   **509**

1. Clergy 2. Economists 3. Scientists 4. Astronomers 5. Philosophers 6. Photographers 7. Mathematicians 8. Writers on science 9. Science -- Philosophy 10. Great Britain -- Intellectual life 11. Scientists -- Great Britain -- History

ISBN 978-0-7679-3048-2; 978-0-7679-3048-2 ebook

LC 2010-25790

This book "gives a unique view of the background and times in which these men lived, and a peek at the implications that their work and philosophy had on today's modern science." Sci Books Films

Includes bibliographical references

Teresi, Dick

Lost discoveries; the ancient roots of modern science, from the Babylonians to the Maya. Simon & Schuster 2002 453p il $27; pa $15   **509**

1. Ancient civilization 2. Science -- History

ISBN 0-684-83718-8; 0-7432-4379-X pa

LC 2002-75457

"Teresi offers a great deal of fascinating material largely ignored by many histories of science." Publ Wkly

Includes bibliographical references

Watson, Peter, 1943-

Convergence; the idea at the heart of science. Peter Watson. Simon & Schuster 2017 576 p. (ebook) $23.99; (hardcover) $35   **509**

1. Science -- History 2. Interdisciplinary approach to knowledge

ISBN 9781476754369; 9781476754345; 9781476754352

LC 2016059213

In this book, by Peter Watson, "various scientific disciplines, despite their very different beginnings, have been coming together over the past 150 years, converging and coalescing. Intimate connections have been discovered between physics and chemistry, psychology and biology, genetics and linguistics. . . . Watson identifies one extraordinary master narrative, capturing how the sciences are slowly resolving into one overwhelming, interlocking story about the universe." (Publisher's note)

"Bringing in ideas from geology, mythology, psychology, economics, and more to investigate the origins of civilization, Watson persuasively presents a deep and challenging idea." Pub Wkly

Includes bibliographical references and index

Weinberg, Steven, 1933-

To explain the world; the discovery of modern science. Steven Weinberg. Harper 2015 432 p. illustrations (hardback) $28.99   **509**

1. Ancient history 2. Science -- History 3. Medieval civilization 4. Science -- Greece -- History 5. Science, Ancient 6. Science, Medieval 7. Science -- Methodology -- History

ISBN 0062346652; 9780062346650

LC 2014030253

This book, by Steven Weinberg, is a "commentary on the history of science from the Greeks to modern times. . . . He shows that the scientists of ancient and medieval times . . . did not understand what there is to understand, or how to understand it. Yet over the centuries, through the struggle to solve such mysteries as the curious backward movement of the planets and the rise and fall of the tides, the modern discipline of science eventually emerged." (Publisher's note)

"The author provides an almost 100-page appendix of "technical notes," mathematical explanations of many of the theories and ideas discussed in the book. Overall, the book is interesting because it shows a scientist's perspective on the history of science; however, it does not measure up to the strict requirements of historiography expected by professional historians. Summing Up: Optional. General readers." Choice

Includes bibliographical references

Wiggins, Arthur W.

The **human** side of science; Edison and Tesla, Watson and Crick, and other personal stories behind science's big ideas. by Arthur W. Wiggins and Charles M. Wynn Sr. ; with cartoon commentary by Sidney Harris. Prometheus Books 2016 364 p. illustrations, maps (hardcover) $25   **509**

1. Scientists 2. Science -- Anecdotes 3. Discoveries in science 4. Scientists -- Anecdotes 5. Discoveries in science -- Anecdotes

ISBN 9781633881570; 9781633881563

LC 2016007462

This book, by Arthur W. Wiggins and Charles M. Wynn Sr., with commentary by Sidney Harris, "focuses attention on the fact that science is a human enterprise. The reader learns about the foibles and quirks as well as the admirable ingenuity and impressive accomplishments of famous scientists who made some of the greatest discoveries of the past and present." (Publisher's note)

"A good addition to any popular-science collection." Booklist

Includes bibliographical references and index

Wilson, Derek K.

A **magical** world; superstition and science from the Renaissance to the Enlightenment. Derek K. Wilson. Pegasus Books 2018 x, 310 p.p (hardcover) $27.95   **509**

1. Superstition 2. Science -- History 3. Religion and science 4. Renaissance 5. Enlightenment 6. Science -- Europe -- History 7. Religion and science -- History 8. Superstition -- Europe -- History
ISBN 9781681776453; 9781681777061; 1681776456

This book, by Derek K. Wilson, "reveals a society filled with an ardent desire for knowledge and astounding discoveries---and the fantastic discoveries that flowered from it. There was the discovery of the movement of blood around the body; the movement of the earth around the sun; the velocity of falling objects. . . . [The book] is a reminder of humanity's paradoxical nature--our passionate pursuit of knowledge alongside deep-rooted fears, superstitions, and traditions." (Publisher's note)

"A dazzling chronicle, a bracing challenge to modernity's smug assumptions." Booklist

Includes bibliographical references (pages 291-297) and index

Wootton, David

The **Invention** of Science; A New History of the Scientific Revolution. by David Wootton. HarperCollins 2015 784 p. 16 plates; illustrations; maps $35   **509**

1. Science -- History
ISBN 006175952X; 9780061759529

This book, by David Wootton, is an "examination of the . . . the Scientific Revolution, and how it came to change the way we understand ourselves and our world. . . . From gunpowder technology, the discovery of the new world, movable type printing, perspective painting, and the telescope to the practice of conducting experiments, the laws of nature, and the concept of the fact, Wotton shows how these discoveries codified into a social construct and a system of knowledge." (Publisher's note)

"Although academics, who will catch the foreshadowing, will have no trouble following Wootton's argument, casual readers are likely to quit before they reach the payoff." LJ

510   Mathematics

Adam, John A.

★ A **mathematical** nature walk. Princeton University Press 2009 248p il $27.95   **510**

1. Mathematics 2. Mathematical analysis
ISBN 978-0-691-12895-5; 0-691-12895-2

LC 2008-44828

"The general reader will find here a remarkably lucid explanation of how mathematicians create a formulaic model that mimics the key features of some natural phenomenon. . . . Ordinary math becomes adventure." Booklist

Includes bibliographical references

Barrow, John D.

100 essential things you didn't know you didn't know; math explains your world. by John D. Barrow. W W Norton & Co Inc

2009 284 p. il $16.95   **510**

1. Mathematics
ISBN 0393338673; 9780393070071; 9780393338676

LC 200855910

First published 2008 in the United Kingdom

In this book, author John D. Barrow "takes the most baffling of everyday phenomena and—with simple math, lucid explanations, and illustrations—explains why they work the way they do. His witty, crystal-clear answers shed light on the dark and shadowy corners of the physical world we all think we understand so well." (Publisher's note)

"Barrow (Mathletics), a Cambridge University professor of mathematical sciences and the director of the Millennium Mathematics Project, delves into the many ways mathematics informs art, and more broadly, our daily lives. Barrow is well versed in mathematics and is fascinated by the topics, but he does not consistently provide accessible explanations. That said, even when he misses, Barrow successfully conveys the idea that mathematics provides a key to understanding both ordinary and extraordinary phenomena." Pub Wkly.

Includes bibliographical references

Benjamin, Arthur

The **Magic** of Math; Solving for X and Figuring Out Why. Basic Books 2015 336 p. illustrations $26.99   **510**

1. Mathematics 2. Sequences (Mathematics)
ISBN 0465054722; 9780465054725

LC 2015936185

This book on mathematics by Arthur Benjamin "empowers you to see the beauty, simplicity, and truly magical properties behind those formulas and equations that once left your head spinning. You'll learn the key ideas of classic areas of mathematics like arithmetic, algebra, geometry, trigonometry, and calculus, but you'll also have fun fooling around with Fibonacci numbers, investigating infinity, and marveling over mathematical magic tricks." (Publisher's note)

"Forget magic. Benjamin delivers a primer generously filled with insights and intuitions that make math approachable, interesting, and, yes, beautiful." Kirkus

Beveridge, Colin

The **math** behind... discover the mathematics of everyday events. Colin Beveridge. Firefly Books 2017 192 p. $24.95   **510**

1. Probabilities 2. Mathematics -- Popular works 3. Mathematics -- Miscellanea 4. Probabilities -- Miscellanea 5. Probabilities -- Popular works
ISBN 1770859985; 9781770859982

LC 2017302920

This book, by Colin Beveridge, "is a fascinating compilation of everyday events analyzed for their probability of occurring and how those odds are determined using mathematical equations and science. The book examines everything from how predictive text works to why buses come in threes and the likelihood that toast will land butter side down." (Publisher's note)

"Whether readers are math geeks looking for new ways of applying mathematics principles or just curious to see how math might actually be applicable in everyday life, this fun, enlightening book will not disappoint." Pub Wkly

Boyer, Carl B.

A **history** of mathematics; [by] Carl B. Boyer and Uta Merzbach. 3rd ed.; Wiley 2010 xx, 668p il (pbk.) $39.95 **510**

1. Mathematics 2. Mathematics -- History
ISBN 9780470525487

LC 2010-3424

First published 1969

This book explores the "history of humankind's relationship with numbers, shapes, and patterns. This revised edition features up-to-date coverage of topics such as Fermat's Last Theorem and the Poincaré Conjecture, in addition to recent advances in areas such as finite group theory and computer-aided proofs." (Publisher's note)

"This good general history of mathematics is understandable to the student as well as authoritative for the mathematician." Malinowsky. Best Sci & Technol Ref Books for Young People

Includes bibliographical references

Clegg, Brian

Are numbers real? the uncanny relationship of mathematics and the physical world. Brian Clegg. St. Martin's Press 2016 304 p. illustrations (hardcover) $28.99; (ebook) $60   **510**
1. Number theory 2. Mathematics -- Popular works
ISBN 9781250081049; 1250081041; 9781466892965

LC 2016027287

This book, by Brian Clegg, "explores the way that math has become more and more detached from reality, and yet despite this is driving the development of modern physics. From devising a new counting system based on goats, . . . to the debate over whether mathematics has too much influence on the direction of science, this . . . book opens the reader's eyes to the hidden reality of the strange yet familiar entities that are numbers." (Publisher's note)

"Clegg is an outstanding science writer, and this book lives up to his usual standard. Highly recommended for those interested in math or science." LJ

Includes bibliographical references (pages [263]-273) and index.

Darling, David J.

The **universal** book of mathematics; from Abracadabra to Zeno's paradoxes. [by] David Darling. Wiley 2004 383p il $40   **510**
1. Reference books 2. Mathematics -- Encyclopedias
ISBN 0-471-27047-4

LC 2003-24670

"The book's entries include numerous mathematical terms, brief biographies of mathematicians from ancient times to the present, and famous mathematical problems (both solved and unsolved), as well as problems and puzzles of a more recreational nature. It is a spirit of whimsy, the fanciful, and the outrageous that makes this book much more than a dry encyclopedia of mathematical terms, however. Darling's writing style and choice of entries make this an easy book to pick up and page through." Choice

Includes bibliographical references

Ellenberg, Jordan, 1971-

★ **How** not to be wrong; the power of mathematical thinking. Jordan Ellenberg. The Penguin Press 2014 480 p. illustrations (hardback) $27.95   **510**
1. Life skills 2. Mathematics 3. Mathematical analysis
ISBN 1594205221; 9781594205224

LC 2014005394

"The math we learn in school can seem like a dull set of rules, laid down by the ancients and not to be questioned. In 'How Not to Be Wrong,' Jordan Ellenberg shows us how terribly limiting this view is: Math isn't confined to abstract incidents that never occur in real life, but rather touches everything we do--the whole world is shot through with it. . . . Ellenberg chases mathematical threads through a vast range of time and space, from the everyday to the cosmic." (Publisher's note)

"Ellenberg finds the common-sense math at work in the everyday world, and his vivid examples and clear descriptions show how 'math is

woven into the way we reason.'" Pub Wkly

Includes bibliographical references and index

Huber, Michael R.

Mythematics; solving the twelve labors of Hercules. Princeton University Press 2009 183p il $24.95   **510**
1. Problem solving 2. Hercules (Legendary character)
ISBN 978-0-691-13575-5

LC 2009-8535

The author takes the ancient Greeks' "early interest in puzzles and the descriptions of Hercules' various labors and reinterpreted each of those labors in terms of several 'tasks,' after which he gives a 'solution' to the mathematical problem(s) implicit in each of the tasks. . . . Given that we tend to think of early Greek mathematics in terms of geometry or, possibly, number theory, the breadth of mathematics required for the various tasks may be surprising." Sci Books Films

Includes bibliographical references

Kanigel, Robert

The **man** who knew infinity; a life of the genius Ramanujan. Washington Sq. Press 1992 438p map il pa $15   **510**
1. Mathematicians
ISBN 0-671-75061-5; 978-0-671-75061-9

LC 91-37763

First published 1991 by Charles Scribner's Sons

"Kanigel deserves high praise for a work of arduous research and rare insight." Booklist

Includes bibliographical references

Mahajan, Sanjoy

Street-fighting mathematics; the art of educated guessing and opportunistic problem solving. MIT Press 2010 134p il pa $25   **510**
1. Problem solving 2. Approximate computation
ISBN 0-262-51429-X; 978-0-262-51429-3

LC 2009-28867

The author argues that the key to solving complex arithmetic questions "lies in having informal tools on hand that let us attack the problem. Though the result may not be perfectly precise, he believes, intuitive mathematical reasoning is often sufficient for our needs. . . . [The book] is not organized around traditional math topics, such as differential equations, but ways of thinking: reasoning by analogy, visualizing geometric problems, and more. Readers can then answer all manner of questions: Guessing the number of babies in the United States, calculating the bond angles in methane, or determining the drag that air exerts on a 747." Dr. Dobb's

Includes bibliographical references

The **New** York Times book of mathematics; edited by Gina Kolata ; forward by Paul Hoffman. Sterling 2013 xvi, 480 p.p (hardcover) $24.95   **510**
1. Mathematics
ISBN 1402793227; 9781402793226

LC 2012045019

This book about mathematics is "divided into thematic sections and is only occasionally chronological. Among topics covered are the National Security Agency's (NSA's) threats to mathematicians writing papers with code-breaking applications; the celebrated story of Andrew Wiles's proof of Fermat's Last Theorem; Grigori Perelman's confirmation of the Poincaré conjecture and his subsequent, Bobby Fischer-like, disappearance." (Library Journal)

Parker, Matt

★ **Things** to make and do in the fourth dimension; a mathematician's journey through narcissistic numbers, optimal dating algorithms, at least two kinds of infinity, and more. Matt Parker. Farrar, Straus & Giroux 2014 464 p. illustrations (hardcover) $28   **510**

1. Mathematics
ISBN 0374275653; 9780374275655

LC 2014950271

In this book, "mathematician and comedian Matt Parker . . . sets out to convince his readers to revisit the very math that put them off the subject as fourteen-year-olds. Starting with the foundations of math familiar from school (numbers, geometry, and algebra), he reveals how it is possible to climb all the way up to the topology and to four-dimensional shapes, and from there to infinity--and slightly beyond." (Publisher's note)

"Parker makes it sound easy, even when it is not, and some of the material can be pretty heavy going. However, most important, he reveals the social aspects of the field, describing his interactions with other mathematicians as they bounce problems around, challenging one another's imaginations." LJ

Pasles, Paul C.

Benjamin Franklin's numbers; an unsung mathematical odyssey. Princeton University Press 2008 254p il $26.95   **510**

1. Authors 2. Diplomats 3. Inventors 4. Statesmen 5. Scientists 6. Mathematics 7. Writers on science 8. Members of Congress
ISBN 978-0-691-12956-3; 0-691-12956-8

LC 2006-102508

The author "documents the famous scientist-statesman's lively interest in numerical enigmas, most particularly those known as Magic Squares. . . . An unexpected but welcome perspective on the genial genius of Philadelphia." Booklist
Includes bibliographical references

Pickover, Clifford A.

The **math** book; from Pythagoras to the 57th dimension, 250 milestones in the history of mathematics. Clifford A. Pickover. Sterling 2009 527 p. il pbk $19.95; $29.95   **510**

1. Mathematics -- History
ISBN 1402788290; 9781402788291; 9781402757969

LC 200843214

In this book, "beginning millions of years ago with ancient 'ant odometers' and moving through time to our modern-day quest for new dimensions, prolific polymath Clifford Pickover covers 250 milestones in mathematical history. Among the numerous concepts readers will encounter as they dip into this inviting anthology: cicada-generated prime numbers, magic squares, and the butterfly effect." (Publisher's note)

"Pickover's love of mathematics shines through the text and images, and it is likely that the reader will catch at least some of his enthusiasm." Choice
Includes bibliographical references

Posamentier, Alfred S.

Magnificent mistakes in mathematics; by Alfred S. Posamentier and Ingmar Lehmann. Prometheus Books 2013 300 p. (hardback) $24   **510**

1. Errors 2. Mathematics 3. Errors, Scientific 4. Discoveries in science 5. Mathematics -- Miscellanea
ISBN 1616147474; 9781616147471

LC 2013012126

Authors Alfred S. Posamentier and Ingmar Lehmann "demonstrate

how some mistakes had profound consequences for our understanding of mathematics' key concepts. The authors show that when we "prove" that every triangle is isosceles, we are violating a concept not even known to Euclid [and how] even using correct procedures can sometimes lead to absurd - but enlightening - results." (Publisher's note)
Includes bibliographical references and index

Rudman, Peter Strom

The **Babylonian** theorem; the mathematical journey to Pythagoras and Euclid. [by] Peter S. Rudman. Prometheus Books 2010 248p il $26   **510**

1. Philosophers 2. Mathematicians 3. Writers on science 4. Mathematics -- History
ISBN 978-1-59102-773-7; 1-59102-773-X

LC 2009-39196

Sequel to How mathematics happened (2007)

"Topics covered include Pythagorean triplets, . . . similar triangles, square-root calculations, and calculations of the volume of a pyramid. . . . This is a well-researched volume on what forms of mathematics existed when similar ideas developed again and again in different cultures. The book's numerous mathematical equations would delight any math student." Sci Books Films
Includes bibliographical references

Seife, Charles

★ **Proofiness**; the dark arts of mathematical deception. Viking 2010 295p il map $25.95   **510**

1. Mathematics
ISBN 978-0-670-02216-8

LC 2010-12127

The author "examines the many ways that people fudge with numbers, sometimes just to sell more moisturizer but also to ruin our economy, rig our elections, convict the innocent and undercount the needy. . . . [This book] reveals the truly corrosive effects on a society awash in numerical mendacity. This is more than a math book; it's an eye-opening civics lesson." N Y Times Book Rev
Includes bibliographical references

Sherlock Holmes in Babylon; and other tales of mathematical history. edited by Marlow Anderson, Victor Katz, Robin Wilson. Mathematical Association of America 2004 387p il maps (Spectrum series) $51.95   **510**

1. Mathematics -- History
ISBN 0-88385-546-1

LC 2003-113541

This "is a compilation of journal articles written by various mathematical historians and published by the Mathematical Association of America over the past 100 years. The stories deal with many important and fundamental topics from ancient up through 18th-century mathematics. The papers are all self-contained, so the reader with some degree of mathematical maturity can jump around in the book." Sci Books Films
Includes bibliographical references

Singh, Simon

The **Simpsons** and their mathematical secrets; Simon Singh. Bloomsbury USA 2013 272 p. (hardback) $26   **510**

1. Mathematics 2. Television programs 3. Simpsons (Television program)
ISBN 1620402777; 9781620402771

LC 2013020884

Author Simon Singh discusses the television series "The Simpsons," examining how "embedded in many plots are subtle references to mathematics, ranging from well-known equations to cutting-edge theorems and conjectures. That they exist, Simon Singh reveals, underscores the brilliance of the shows' writers, many of whom have advanced degrees in mathematics in addition to their unparalleled sense of humor." (Publisher's note)

"Perhaps Simpsons nerds have known this all along, but for the rest of us who think of the TV show as primarily a sharp piece of comic writing, it may come as a surprise to learn that it is riddled with sophisticated mathematics. . ." Kirkus

Includes bibliographical references and index

Stewart, Ian

Professor Stewart's casebook of mathematical mysteries; Ian Stewart. Basic Books, a member of the Perseus Books Group 2014 307 p. black and white illustrations (paperback) $16.99   **510**
    1. Mathematics -- Miscellanea
    ISBN 0465054978; 9780465054978
                   LC 2014940655

In this book, by Ian Stewart, "guided by stalwart detective Hemlock Soames and his sidekick, Dr. John Watsup, readers will delve into almost two hundred mathematical problems, puzzles, and facts. Tackling subjects from mathematical dates (such as Pi Day), what we don't know about primes, and why the Earth is round, this clever, mind-expanding book demonstrates the power and fun inherent in mathematics." (Publisher's note)

"Add a few jokes, a few serious applications, and plenty of references for further online exploration, and the result is another fine book from Stewart. Summing Up: Highly recommended. All levels/libraries." Choice

Casebook of mathematical mysteries

Visions of Infinity; The Great Mathematical Problems. Perseus Books Group 2013 352 p. $26.99   **510**
    1. Mathematics
    ISBN 0465022405; 9780465022403

This looks at mathematical problems. Mathematician Ian Stewart argues that "mathematics is as creative as physics." He discusses Goldbach's Conjecture "that every even number can be written as the sum of two prime numbers," Squaring the Circle, or "constructing a square with an area identical to a given circle," pi, and Newton's laws of motion. (Kirkus)

Strogatz, Steven, 1959-

★ The **joy** of X; a guided tour of math, from one to infinity. Steven Strogatz. Houghton Mifflin Harcourt 2012 336 p. (hardback) $27.00   **510**
    1. Mathematics
    ISBN 0547517653; 9780547517650
                   LC 2012017320

In this book on mathematics, author Steven Strogatz "begins with arithmetic, by way of Sesame Street, then explores algebra, geometry, and, finally, the wonders of calculus. . . . From addition and subtraction, with a glimpse into negative numbers and 'the black art of borrowing,' it's a quick step into the hardcore detective work of algebra's search for the unknown x, with algorithms like the quadratic equation." (Publishers Weekly)

Szpiro, George G.

Numbers rule; the vexing mathematics of democracy from Plato to the present. Princeton University Press 2010 226p **510**
    1. Mathematics 2. Voting 3. Democracy -- History

ISBN 978-0-691-13994-4
                   LC 2009-28615

Szpiro "traces the quest of philosophers, statesmen and mathematicians throughout history to create a more perfect democracy and adapt to the ever-changing demands of each new generation by analyzing the mathematical anomalies in voting results." (Publisher's note) Index,

The author "presents a refreshingly different presentation of the mathematics of voting and apportionment. Topics are organized chronologically, and historical contexts are presented in an engaging way. Unlike mathematics textbooks, the book reads like a collection of stories describing the origin of many mathematical ideas. The mathematical content is not trivial, and it is well written, very clear, and should be accessible to readers with an understanding of arithmetic and a willingness to play with numbers." Choice

Includes bibliographical references

Poincare's prize; the hundred-year quest to solve one of math's greatest puzzles. Dutton 2007 309p $24.95   **510**
    1. Mathematics 2. Mathematicians
    ISBN 978-0-525-95024-0; 0-525-95024-9
                   LC 2007-12792

The author "recounts the story of how a geometrical puzzle worthy of the most voracious sphinx finally yielded to an eccentric Russian genius who has since refused the honors and million-dollar prize proffered by an astonished world. The mathematical puzzle, readers learn, originated with the French polymath Henri Poincaré, whose revolutionary topology generated a tantalizing conjecture about how multidimensional bodies might all be transformed into spheres. . . . Never has mathematics provided more fascinating human drama!" Booklist

Includes bibliographical references

Tammet, Daniel

★ **Thinking** in numbers; on life, love, meaning, and math. Daniel Tammet. Little, Brown and Co. 2013 288 p. $26 **510**
    1. Numbers 2. Statistics 3. Mathematics
    ISBN 0316187372; 9780316187374
                   LC 2013935728

This is a book of essays by Daniel Tammet. "His topics include the concept of zero, the calendar, prime numbers, chess, time and statistics. . . . Several of his pieces have an autobiographical component. His essay on infinity shows him as a young boy discovering the infinity of fractions between two points on his walk home from school, and readers learn of his amazing memory in his account of reciting aloud the decimals of pi to 22,514 places at the University of Oxford's Pi Day." (Kirkus Reviews)

Tanton, James S.

Encyclopedia of mathematics; [by] James Tanton. Facts on File 2005 568p il (Facts on File science library) $75   **510**
    1. Reference books 2. Mathematics -- Encyclopedias
    ISBN 0-8160-5124-0
                   LC 2004-16785

This encyclopedia "offers more than 800 entries from abacus and compound interest to Bertrand Russell and vector along with essays on the history and evolution of equations and algebra, calculus, functions, geometry, probability and statistics, and trigonometry." SLJ

Includes bibliographical references

Tymony, Cy

Sneaky math; a graphic primer with projects; ace the basics of algebra, geometry, trigonometry, and calculus with everyday things. by Cy Tymony. Andrews McMeel Pub 2014 179 p.

illustrations $12.99 **510**

1. Mathematics

ISBN 1449445209; 9781449445201

In this book, author Cy Tymony "shows us how math is all around us through intriguing and easy projects, including 20 pass-along tools to complement math education programs. The book is divided into seven sections: 1. Fundamentals of Numbers and Arithmetic 2. Algebra Primer 3. Geometry Primer 4. Trigonometry Primer 5. Calculus Primer 6. Sneaky Math Challenges, Tricks, and Formulas [and] 7. Resources." (Publisher's note)

"Math lessons in school have a reputation for being rote and forgettable, but the content has a way of sneaking into everyday life, and by capitalizing on these real-world applications, Tymony helps conquer much of the fear and dread associated with traditional math lessons." Booklist

510.1   Philosophy and theory

Cheng, Eugenia

How to bake pi; an edible exploration of the mathematics of mathematics. Eugenia Cheng. Basic Books 2015 304 p. illustrations (hardcover) $27.50 **510.1**

1. Cooking 2. Mathematics -- Popular works

ISBN 0465051715; 9780465051694; 9780465051717

LC 2014957937

This book, by Eugenia Cheng, "provides an accessible introduction to the logic and beauty of mathematics, powered, unexpectedly, by insights from the kitchen: we learn, for example, how the béchamel in a lasagna can be a lot like the number 5, and why making a good custard proves that math is easy but life is hard." (Publisher's note)

"Despite her zeal for mathematical logic, Cheng recognizes that such logic begins in faith—irrational faith—and ultimately requires poetry and art to complement its findings. A singular humanization of the mathematical project." Booklist

510.92   Mathematicians

Shetterly, Margot Lee, 1969-

Hidden Figures; The Story of the African-American Women Who Helped Win the Space Race. Margot Lee Shetterly. HarperCollins 2016 384 p. $27.99 **510.92**

1. Women mathematicians 2. African American women 3. United States. National Aeronautics and Space Administration

ISBN 006236359X; 9780062363596

Carnegie Medal Longlist: Nonfiction (2017)

This book, by Margot Lee Shetterly, tells the "true story of the black female mathematicians at NASA whose calculations helped fuel some of America's greatest achievements in space. [It] follows the interwoven accounts of Dorothy Vaughan, Mary Jackson, Katherine Johnson and Christine Darden, four African American women who participated in some of NASA's greatest successes." (Publisher's note)

"Shetterly's highly recommended work offers up a crucial history that had previously and unforgivably been lost. We'd do well to put this book into the hands of young women who have long since been told that there's no room for them at the scientific table." LJ

Includes bibliographical references (pages 273-328) and index.

Stewart, Ian

★ **Significant** figures; the lives and work of great mathematicians. Ian Stewart. Basic Books 2017 352 p. (hardcover)

$28 **510.92**

1. Mathematics -- History 2. Mathematicians -- Biography

ISBN 9780465096121; 9780465096138

LC 2017947338

In this book, author Ian Stewart "introduces the visionaries of mathematics throughout history. . . . Stewart examines the roles they played in creating, inventing, and discovering the mathematics we use today. Through these short biographies, we get acquainted with the history of mathematics from Archimedes to Benoit Mandelbrot, and learn about those too often left out of the cannon, such as Muhammad ibn Musa al-Khwarizmi . . . and Augusta Ada King." (Publisher's note)

Includes bibliographical references (pages 283-290) and index.

511   General principles of mathematics

Alexander, Amir

Infinitesimal; how a dangerous mathematical theory shaped the modern world. Amir Alexander. Scientific American/Farrar, Straus and Giroux 2014 368 p. illustrations (hardback) $27 **511**

1. Calculus 2. Geometry 3. Mathematics

ISBN 0374176817; 9780374176815

LC 2013033923

Amir Alexander "look[s] at the history of a . . . mathematical concept. According to classic geometry, a line is made of a string of points, or 'indivisibles,' which cannot be broken down into anything smaller. . . . Churchmen and respected thinkers like Descartes railed against infinitesimals, while Galileo, Newton, and others insisted the concept defined the real world. . . . [B]eginning with the German Jesuit mathematician Christopher Clavius, Alexander explores this war of ideas." (Publishers Weekly)

"The author navigates even the most abstract mathematical concepts as deftly as he does the layered social history, and the result is a book about math that is actually fun to read. A fast-paced history of the singular idea that shaped a multitude of modern achievements." Kirkus

Includes bibliographical references and index

Michael, T. S.

How to guard an art gallery and other discrete mathematical adventures. Johns Hopkins University Press 2009 257p il $60; pa $25 **511**

1. Algorithms 2. Computer science 3. Mathematical analysis

ISBN 978-0-8018-9298-1; 0-8018-9298-8; 978-0-8018-9299-8 pa; 0-8018-9299-6 pa

LC 2009-00435

"The time-honored story problem, central to mathematics and an expression of its fascination or frustration (depending on the student's success), is the protagonist of this delightful work on discrete mathematics. Written for . . . [readers with a knowledge of] algebra and geometry, the text contains 7 chapters, each one devoted to a different story problem and its variations. Pick's formula, art gallery problems, quadratic residues of primes and squares, and stamps and coins and Sylvester's formula are some of the problems presented, with each chapter consisting of a group of problems of increasing difficulty." Sci Tech Book News

Includes bibliographical references

511.3   Mathematical logic (Symbolic logic)

Fortnow, Lance

The **golden** ticket; P, NP, and the search for the impossible.

Lance Fortnow. Princeton University Press 2013 188 p. (hardback) $26.95 **511.3**

1. Computer algorithms 2. NP-complete problems
ISBN 0691156492; 9780691156491

LC 2012039523

This book by Lance Fortnow "tackles one of the biggest open problems in mathematics. P vs. NP can be succinctly phrased as the issue of whether some of the hardest and most important questions in mathematics have easily computable solutions. The questions themselves can range from how best to match up organ donors and recipients to how one can use the smallest number of different colors when creating a map." (Library Journal)

Includes bibliographical references and index

Stillwell, John

Roads to infinity; the mathematics of truth and proof. A K Peters 2010 203p il $39 **511.3**

1. Infinite 2. Set theory 3. Symbolic logic 4. Logic, Symbolic and mathematical
ISBN 978-1-56881-466-7; 1-56881-466-6

LC 2010-14077

"This book offers an introduction to modern ideas about infinity and their implications for mathematics. It unifies ideas from set theory and mathematical logic, and traces their effects on mainstream mathematical topics of today, such as number theory and combinatorics." Publisher's note

Includes bibliographical references

512   Algebra

Havil, Julian

The **irrationals**; a story of the numbers you can't count on. Julian Havil. Princeton University Press 2012 298 p. (alk. paper) $29.95 **512**

1. Mathematicians 2. Irrational numbers 3. Mathematics -- History
ISBN 0691143420; 9780691143422

LC 2012931844

This book "tells the story of irrational numbers and the mathematicians who have tackled their challenges, from antiquity to the twenty-first century. Along the way, [author Julian Havil] explains why irrational numbers are surprisingly difficult to define -- and why so many questions still surround them." (Publisher's note)

Livio, Mario

The **equation** that couldn't be solved; how mathematical genius discovered the language of symmetry. Simon & Schuster 2005 353p il $26.95 **512**

1. Symmetry 2. Mathematicians
ISBN 0-7432-5820-7

LC 2005-44123

"Even the mathematically fainthearted can learn a great deal about symmetry from this book." Sci Books Films

Includes bibliographical references

Singh, Simon

Fermat's enigma; the epic quest to solve the world's greatest mathematical problem. foreword by John Lynch. Anchor Books 1998 315p il pa $13.95 **512**

1. Number theory 2. Mathematicians 3. College teachers
ISBN 0-385-49362-2

First published 1997 in the United Kingdom with title: Fermat's last theorem

"This vivid account is fascinating reading for anyone interested in mathematics, its history, and the passionate quest for solutions to unsolved riddles." SLJ

Includes bibliographical references

512.7   Number theory

Derbyshire, John

Prime obsession; Bernhard Riemann and the greatest unsolved problem in mathematics. Plume 2004 422p il pa $16 **512.7**

1. Number theory 2. Mathematics
ISBN 978-0-452-28525-5; 0-452-28525-9

First published 2003 by Joseph Henry Press

The author "first takes readers through . . . mathematical fundamentals in order to give them a good understanding of Riemann's discovery and its consequences. Interspersed with the hardcore math, other chapters profile Riemann the man and trace the history of mathematics in relation to his still-unproven hypothesis. Derbyshire shows how after 150 years, the world's greatest minds still haven't found a solution." Libr J

512.9   Foundations of algebra

Mackenzie, Dana

The **universe** in zero words; the story of mathematics as told through equations. Dana Mackenzie. Princeton University Press 2012 224 p. ill. (some col.) (hardcover) $27.95 **512.9**

1. Equations 2. Mathematics -- History
ISBN 0691152829; 9780691152820

LC 2011936364

This book "tells the history of twenty-four . . . equations that have shaped mathematics, science, and society -- from the elementary . . . to the sophisticated . . . and from the famous . . . to the arcane . . . [Dana] Mackenzie . . . explains what each equation means, who discovered it (and how), and how it has affected our lives." (Publisher's note)

Includes bibliographical references (p. 219-221) and index.

513   Arithmetic

Bellos, Alex

Here's looking at Euclid; a surprising excursion through the astonishing world of math. Free Press hardcover ed.; Free Press 2010 319p il $25; ebook $11.99 **513**

1. Number concept
ISBN 978-1-4165-8825-2; 978-1-4165-9634-9 ebook

LC 2009-36815

The author "offers a lively romp through many different fields of mathematics as he incorporates ancient discoveries and modern developments alike. Topics include geometry, number theory, the development of sudoku, numerous aspects of pi and its calculation, statistics, probability and its application to gambling, and many other historical tidbits." Libr J

Includes bibliographical references

513.5 Numeration systems

Aczel, Amir D., 1950-2015

Finding zero; a mathematician's odyssey to uncover the origins of numbers. Amir D. Aczel. Palgrave Macmillan 2015 256 p. (hardback) $26 **513.5**

1. Numerals 2. Zero (The number)
ISBN 1137279842; 9781137279842

LC 2014024462

This book, by Amir D. Aczel, tells the "story of how and where we got . . . numerals. The history begins with the early Babylonian cuneiform numbers, followed by the later Greek and Roman letter numerals. Then Aczel asks the key question: where do the numbers we use today, the so-called Hindu-Arabic numerals, come from? It is this search that leads him to explore uncharted territory, to go on a grand quest into India, Thailand, Laos, Vietnam, and ultimately into the wilds of Cambodia." (Publisher's note)

"The story brims with local color, as well as insights into the history of mathematics and philosophy." Pub Wkly

Includes bibliographical references

Thaller, Bernd

Numbers; their tales, types, and treasures. by Alfred S. Posamentier & Bernd Thaller. Prometheus Books 2015 400 p. illustrations (pbk.) $19 **513.5**

1. Numbers 2. Mathematics 3. Counting 4. Number concept 5. Arithmetic -- Foundations
ISBN 1633880303; 9781633880306

LC 2015011662

This book by Alfred S. Posamentier and Bernd Thaller is designed to "teach you everything you ever wondered about numbers--and more. [It answers] how and why did human beings first start using numbers at the dawn of history? Would numbers exist if we Homo sapiens weren't around to discover them? What's so special about weird numbers like pi and the Fibonacci sequence?" (Publisher's note)

"Overall the book is extremely well written and entertaining. Its rich, satisfying variety encompasses Piaget, multicultural references, Bertrand Russell, number patterns, and historical surprises. Summing Up: Highly recommended. All readers." Choice

Includes bibliographical references and index

515 Analysis

Ash, Avner

Elliptic tales; curves, counting, and number theory. Avner Ash, Robert Gross. Princeton University Press 2012 253 p. (hardcover) $29.95 **515**

1. Number theory 2. Cubic equations 3. Elliptic curves 4. Curves, Elliptic 5. Elliptic functions
ISBN 0691151199; 9780691151199

LC 2011044712

This book explains a major unsolved problem "in contemporary mathematics—the Birch and Swinnerton-Dyer Conjecture. . . . The key to the conjecture lies in elliptic curves, which are cubic equations in two variables. These equations may appear simple, yet they arise from some very deep—and often very mystifying—mathematical ideas. Using only basic algebra and calculus while presenting numerous eye-opening examples, Ash and Gross make these ideas accessible to general readers." (Barnes and Noble)

Includes bibliographical references and index.

Ouellette, Jennifer

The **calculus** diaries; how math can help you lose weight, win in Vegas, and survive a zombie apocalypse. [illustrations by Jason Torchinsky] Penguin Books 2010 318p il pa $15 **515**

1. Calculus
ISBN 978-0-14-311737-7; 0-14-311737-8

LC 2010-25843

The author "shows how she learned to apply calculus to everything from gas mileage to dieting, from the rides at Disneyland to shooting craps in Vegas." Publisher's note

Includes bibliographical references

516 Geometry

Apostol, Tom M., 1923-2016

New Horizons in Geometry; Tom M. Apostol and Mamikon A. Mnatsakanian. Cambridge University Press 2012 520 p. $75 **516**

1. Calculus 2. Geometry
ISBN 088385354X; 9780883853542

In this book, Tom Apostol and Mamikon A. Mnatsakanian introduce "Mamikon's sweeping-tangent theorem," which "relies on a continuous transformation of a unit tangent to a curve, and then explore its consequences. The authors use this powerful method, which does not fit into the canon of either Euclidean geometry or calculus, to unfold much of classical geometry and to . . . solve problems usually requiring calculus." (Choice)

Lehmann, Ingmar

The **secrets** of triangles; a mathematical journey. by Alfred S. Posamentier and Ingmar Lehmann. Prometheus Books 2012 387 p. ill. (hardcover) $26 **516**

1. Geometry 2. Triangle 3. Trigonometry
ISBN 1616145870; 9781616145873

LC 2012013635

This book offers "mathematical insights, intriguing relationships, and surprising results focused on the triangle." Topics include "noteworthy points, special lines, and concentric circles as related to triangles. Ultimately the book is a . . . compendium of results that" may surprise the reader with their simultaneous simplicity and complexity. (Choice)

Includes bibliographical references (p. 367-368) and index.

O'Rourke, Joseph

How to fold it; the mathematics of linkages, origami, and polyhedra. Cambridge University Press 2011 177p il $80; pa $27.99 **516**

1. Origami 2. Mathematics
ISBN 978-0-521-76735-4; 0-521-76735-0; 978-0-521-14547-3 pa; 0-521-14547-3 pa

LC 2011001236

The author explains "folding problems starting from high school algebra and geometry and introducing more advanced concepts in tangible contexts as they arise. He shows how variations on these basic problems lead directly to the frontiers of current mathematical research and offers ten . . . unsolved problems for the enterprising reader." Publisher's note

516.2   Euclidean geometry

Berlinski, David

★ The **king** of infinite space; Euclid and his Elements. David Berlinski. Basic Books 2013 172 p. illustrations (hardcover; alk. paper) $24   **516.2**
1. Geometry 2. Mathematics, Greek 3. Geometry -- History
ISBN 046501481X; 9780465014811
LC 2012042492

This book by David Berlinski looks at the ancient mathematician Euclid "and the world of axioms and theorems he created--a geometric world that became the basis for much of modern math, from analytic geometry to the idea of curved space-time. To Berlinski, Euclid's fourth-century B.C., 13-volume 'Elements' is a manifestation of his 'intense demand for an idealized world.'" (Publishers Weekly)

Kaplan, Ellen

Hidden harmonies; the lives and times of the Pythagorean theorem. [by] Robert Kaplan and Ellen Kaplan. Bloomsbury Press 2011 290p il $25   **516.2**
1. Pythagorean theorem 2. Mathematics -- History
ISBN 978-1-59691-522-0; 1-59691-522-6
LC 2010-19959

The authors discuss "the famous theorem that relates the sides of a right triangle. Going through many of the apparently hundreds of proofs of it, the Kaplans sinuously weave personalities into the history of proving Pythagoras correct. . . . Showing the theorem's endless versatility, the Kaplans and their logic- and symbol-permeated text will engage those who delight in doing the math." Booklist

Includes bibliographical references

Livio, Mario

The **golden** ratio; the story of phi, the world's most astonishing number. Broadway Bks. 2002 294p hardcover o.p. pa $14.95   **516.2**
1. Geometry
ISBN 0-7679-0815-5; 0-7679-0816-3 pa
LC 2002-23084

The author examines the history and myths of phi, the "golden ratio" of 1.6180339887 that has been related to phenomena as diverse as the arrangements of petals on roses and the breeding patterns of rabbits.

"Overall, an enjoyable work, amply supported by index, extensive references, and ten appendixes presenting mathematical elaborations of text material." Choice

Includes bibliographical references

519.2   Probabilities

Devlin, Keith J.

The **unfinished** game; Pascal, Fermat, and the seventeenth-century letter that made the world modern. [by] Keith Devlin. Basic Books 2008 191p il (Basic ideas) $24.95   **519.2**
1. Theologians 2. Probabilities 3. Mathematicians 4. Writers on religion
ISBN 978-0-465-00910-7; 0-465-00910-7
LC 2008-12222

"This informative book is a lively, quick read for anyone who wonders about the science of predicting what's next and how deeply it affects our lives." Publ Wkly

Includes bibliographical references

Mazur, Joseph

Fluke; the math and myth of coincidences. Joseph Mazur. Basic Books 2016 288 p. illustrations (hardcover) $26.99   **519.2**
1. Chance 2. Mathematics -- Popular works 3. Coincidence 4. Simultaneity (Physics) 5. Coincidence theory (Mathematics)
ISBN 9780465060955
LC 2015043288

In this book, "mathematician Joseph Mazur takes a second look at the seemingly improbable, sharing with us an entertaining guide to the most surprising moments in our lives. He takes us on a tour of the mathematical concepts of probability, such as the law of large numbers and the birthday paradox, and combines these concepts with lively anecdotes of flukes from around the world." (Publisher's note)

"An ideal book . . . for the lay reader who is curious about the nature of coincidence." Booklist

Includes bibliographical references and index

Mlodinow, Leonard

The **Drunkard's** walk; how randomness rules our lives. Pantheon Books 2008 252p il $24.95   **519.2**
1. Chance 2. Probabilities
ISBN 978-0-375-42404-5; 0-375-42404-0
LC 2007-42507

"Mlodinow will help readers sort out Mark Twain's 'damn lies' from meaningful statistics and the choices we face every day." Publ Wkly

Includes bibliographical references

Santos, Aaron

How many licks? or, How to estimate damn near anything. Running Press 2009 175p il pa $14.95   **519.2**
1. Probabilities
ISBN 978-0-7624-3560-9; 0-7624-3560-7

"No matter how you feel about math, Santos' puzzle-solving prowess shows you just how much you can do when you put on your thinking cap." Am Profile

Smith, Gary

What the luck? the surprising role of chance in our everyday lives. Gary Smith. Overlook Press 2016 304 p. illustrations (ebook) $50; $28.95   **519.2**
1. Chance 2. Statistics 3. Probabilities
ISBN 9781468313918; 1468313754; 9781468313758
LC 2016036451

This book, by Gary Smith, explores the role of regression to the mean in our day to day lives. Smith "explains--in clear, understandable, and witty prose--how a statistical understanding of luck can change the way we see just about every aspect of our lives...and can help us learn to rely less on random chance, and more on truth." (Publisher's note)

"For anyone interested in statistics, fantasy sports players, and those curious about the role of chance." LJ

Includes bibliographical references (pages 269-282) and index.

519.3   Game theory

Highfield, Roger

★ **Supercooperators**; altruism, evolution, and why we need each other to succeed. [by] Martin A. Nowak, with Roger Highfield. Free Press 2011 330p $27   **519.3**
1. Evolution 2. Game theory 3. Cooperative societies 4. Evolution (Biology) -- Mathematical models

ISBN 978-1-4391-0018-9; 1-4391-0018-7

LC 2010-35517

"Nowak aims to tackle the mysteries of nature with paper, pencil and computer. By looking at phenomena as diverse as H.I.V. infection and English irregular verbs, he has formally defined five distinct mechanisms that have helped give rise to cooperative behavior, from the first molecules that joined to self-replicate, to the first cells that formed multicellular organisms, all the way to human societies, which exhibit a degree of cooperation unmatched in all creation. In Nowak's view, figuring out how cooperation comes about and breaks down, as well as actively pursuing the 'snuggle for existence,' is the key to our survival as a species." N Y Times Book Rev

Includes bibliographical references

519.5   Statistical mathematics

Everitt, Brian

★ The **Cambridge** dictionary of statistics; [by] B.S. Everitt, A. Skrondal. 4th ed.; Cambridge University Press 2010 468p il $59   **519.5**
1. Reference books 2. Statistics -- Dictionaries
ISBN 978-0-521-76699-9

LC 2010-502891

First published 1998

"This field-specific dictionary explains nearly 4000 terms, concepts, and models relevant to fields employing theoretical, applied, scientific, and survey-related probability methods." Libr J

Reinhart, Alex, 1991-

Statistics done wrong; the woefully complete guide. by Alex Reinhart. No Starch Press 2015 176 p. illustrations (pbk.) $24.95   **519.5**
1. Errors 2. Statistics 3. Statistics -- Methodology 4. Missing observations (Statistics)
ISBN 1593276206; 9781593276201

LC 2015002128

This book, by Alex Reinhart, "is a pithy, essential guide to statistical blunders in modern science that will show you how to keep your research blunder-free. You'll examine embarrassing errors and omissions in recent research, learn about the misconceptions and scientific politics that allow these mistakes to happen, and begin your quest to reform the way you and your peers do statistics." (Publisher's note)

"Overall, this concise guide aims at helping the scientific community better understand the strengths and weaknesses of the research process. A comprehensive bibliography is included, as are numerous references for the statistical misconceptions that are addressed." Choice

Silver, Nate

The **signal** and the noise; why so many predictions fail--but some don't. Nate Silver. Penguin Press 2012 534 p. $27.95   **519.5**
1. Statistics 2. Forecasting 3. Theory of knowledge 4. Knowledge, Theory of 5. Forecasting -- History 6. Forecasting -- Methodology 7. Bayesian statistical decision theory
ISBN 159420411X; 9781594204111

LC 2012027308

This book, by political forecaster Nate Silver, "examines the world of prediction, investigating how we can distinguish a true signal from a universe of noisy data. Most predictions fail, . . . because most of us have a poor understanding of probability and uncertainty. . . . Silver visits the most successful forecasters in a range of areas. . . . He explains

and evaluates how these forecasters think and what bonds they share." (Publisher's note)

Includes bibliographical references (p. 459-514) and index

Smith, Gary

Standard deviations; flawed assumptions, tortured data, and other ways to lie with statistics. Gary Smith. Overlook Duckworth 2014 304 p. illustrations (hardback) $28.95 **519.5**
1. Economics 2. Statistics 3. Standard deviations
ISBN 146830920X; 9781468309201

LC 2014017052

In this book, economics professor Gary Smith "walks us through the various tricks and traps that people use to back up their own . . . theories. Sometimes, the unscrupulous deliberately try to mislead us. Other times, the well-intentioned are blissfully unaware of the mischief they are committing. Today, data is so plentiful that researchers spend precious little time distinguishing between good, meaningful indicators and total rubbish." (Publisher's note)

"We believe these stories if they seem reasonable and love them if they're provocative—see Freakonomics, whose authors have admitted some mistakes."We are too easily seduced by explanations for the inexplicable," writes the author in this amusing, informative account of how many arguments are backed by meaningless statistics." Kirkus

Includes bibliographical references and index

Wheelan, Charles

Naked statistics; stripping the dread from the data. Charles Wheelan. W W Norton & Co Inc 2013 304 p. (hardcover) $26.95   **519.5**
1. Statistics
ISBN 0393071952; 9780393071955

LC 2012034411

Wheelan "has provided an intuitive presentation of statistical concepts without getting bogged down by extensive data lists or computation. The author begins by generally introducing each idea with an idealized situation to illustrate that statistical setting and its impact on effective interpretation, and then moves on to current real-world settings to legitimize his discussion. He also clearly discusses subtleties that can be encountered, showing how data users must be careful to avoid oversimplifying the implications of a given result. The presentation is non-threatening, yet readers will find it a suitably thoughtful consideration of statistical ideas." Choice

Includes bibliographical references and index

520   Astronomy and allied sciences

The **astronomy** book; DK Publishing ; [Jacqueline Mitton, consultant editor ; David W. Hughes [and others], contributors] DK Publishing 2017 352 p. color illustrations (Big ideas simply explained) (hardcover) $25   **520**
1. Stars 2. Planets 3. Astronomy 4. Telescopes 5. Astrophysics 6. Constellations
ISBN 0241225930; 1465464182; 9780241225936; 9781465464187

LC 2017446518

This book, from DK Publishing, is "an essential guide to milestone developments in astronomy, telling the story of our ideas about space, time, and the physics of the cosmos. . . . From planets and stars to black holes and the Big Bang, take a journey through the wonders of the universe. . . . [The book features] topics from the Copernican Revolution to the mind-boggling theories of recent science." (Publisher's note)

Astronomy photographer of the year; prize-winning images by top astrophotographers. Firefly Books 2015 287 p. (bound) $39.95 **520**

1. Astronomy 2. Space photography 3. Astronomical photography 4. Astronomy -- Pictorial works 5. Astronomical photography -- Competitions

ISBN 1770854738; 9781770854734

LC 2015458652

This book is a "collection of images from the Astronomy Photographer of the Year competition. Organized by the Royal Observatory, the photographs capture an astounding range of astronomical phenomena both within our solar system and far into deep space. The book features four sections: Earth and Space, Our Solar System, Deep Space, and Overall Winners." (Publisher's note)

"Recommended strongly for anyone with an interest in astronomy or photography, this work would also make for a terrific coffee-table book." Library Journal

Bartusiak, Marcia

The **day** we found the universe. Pantheon Books 2009 337p il $27.95 **520**

1. Astronomy -- History

ISBN 978-0-375-42429-8; 0-375-42429-6

LC 2008-34377

"This is a superb book that interweaves the fascinating story of a major scientific quest with a cast of characters, situations, painstaking observations, and imaginative thinking that reminds us all of the human side of scientific endeavors and the ways in which the universe itself continuously surprises us." Sci Books Films

Includes bibliographical references

Consolmagno, Guy

Turn left at Orion; hundreds of night sky objects to see in a home telescope-- and how to find them. Guy Consolmagno, Dan M. Davis ; illustrated by the authors ; cover and title page, Mary Lynn Skirvin ; additional illustrations by Karen Kotash Sepp, Todd Johnson, and Anne Drogin. 4th edition Cambridge University Press 2011 255 p. illustrations (pbk, spiral) $34.99 **520**

1. Astronomy 2. Constellations

ISBN 9780521153973; 0521153972

LC 2011027048

Originally published 1989

This is a "guidebook to the night sky, providing all the information you need to observe a whole host of celestial objects. . . . Large-format eyepiece views, positioned side-by-side, show objects exactly as they are seen through a telescope, and with improved directions, updated tables of astronomical information and an expanded night-by-night Moon section, it has never been easier to explore the night sky on your own." (Publisher's note)

Includes bibliographical references and index

Couper, Heather

The **history** of astronomy; [by] Heather Couper & Nigel Henbest; foreword by Arthur C. Clarke. Firefly Books 2007 285p il $59.95; pa $29.95 **520**

1. Astronomy -- History

ISBN 978-1-55407-325-2; 1-55407-325-1; 978-1-55407-537-9 pa; 1-55407-537-8 pa

LC 2008-272095

This "history is pieced together through astronomer interviews and visits to historically important astronomy sites around the world. . . . This

is a copiously illustrated, straightforwardly written volume that will appeal to readers with and without an astronomy background. In addition to covering astronomy through the ages, the authors do an admirable job explaining current astronomical discoveries and personalities." Choice

Dickinson, Terence

NightWatch ; a practical guide to viewing the universe; foreword by Timothy Ferris; illustrations by Adolf Schaller, Victor Costanzo, Roberta Cooke, Glenn LeDrew; principal photography by Terence Dickinson. 4th ed.; Firefly Books 2006 192p il $35 **520**

1. Astronomy

ISBN 978-1-55407-147-0; 1-55407-147-X

LC 2006-491527

Ferris, Timothy

Seeing in the dark; how backyard stargazers are probing deep space and guarding earth from interplanetary peril. Simon & Schuster 2002 379p il hardcover o.p. pa $14 **520**

1. Astronomy 2. Astronomers

ISBN 0-684-86579-3; 0-684-86580-7 pa

LC 2002-20693

"This book should turn many novices on to astronomy and captivate those already fascinated by the heavens." Publ Wkly

Miller, Arthur I.

Empire of the stars; obsession, friendship, and betrayal in the quest for black holes. Houghton Mifflin 2005 364p il $26 **520**

1. Astronomers 2. Mathematicians 3. Black holes (Astronomy) 4. Astrophysicists 5. Writers on science 6. Nobel laureates for physics

ISBN 0-618-34151-X

LC 2004-60909

This history of the discovery of black holes focuses on the bitter rivalry between Indian astrophysicist Subrahmanyan Chandrasekhar and Cambridge astrophysicist Sir Arthur Eddington.

"Astronomy buffs and readers fascinated by the history of science will find this a compelling read." Publ Wkly

Includes bibliographical references

Oxford Dictionary of Astronomy; edited by Ian Ridpath. 3rd edition Oxford University Press 2018 **520**

1. Reference books 2. Astronomy -- Dictionaries

ISBN 9780191851193

"Compiled with the help of a team of expert contributors under the editorship of renowned author and broadcaster Ian Ridpath, the third edition of this dictionary covers everything from space exploration and the equipment involved to astrophysics, cosmology, and the concept of time. The dictionary also includes biographical entries on eminent astronomers, as well as worldwide coverage of observatories and telescopes. Supplementary material is included in the appendices, such as tables of Apollo lunar landing missions, the constellations, and planetary data, and numerous other tables and diagrams complement the entries." (Publisher's note)

Plait, Philip C.

Death from the skies! these are the ways the world will end . . . [by] Philip Plait. Viking 2008 326p il $25.95 **520**

1. End of the world

ISBN 978-0-670-01997-7; 0-670-01997-6

LC 2008-22943

"The book is extremely informative: Plait explains not only what can destroy the planet but also how it would happen. It's a crash course in astronomy as well as a cautionary tale about the (possibly brief) future of our world." Booklist

Raymo, Chet

An **intimate** look at the night sky. Walker & Co. 2001 242p il $25; pa $16 **520**

1. Astronomy

ISBN 0-8027-1369-6; 0-8027-7670-1 pa

"A delightful, inspiring introduction to astronomy." Booklist

Includes bibliographical references

Roy, Jean-Rene

A **question** and answer guide to astronomy; Carol Christian, Space Telescope Science Institute, Baltimore, USA, Jean-Rene Roy, Laval University, Quebec, Canada. Second edition Cambridge University Press 2017 xiv, 344 p.p color illustrations (pbk.; alk. paper) $29.99 **520**

1. Astronomy -- Miscellanea 2. Astronomy -- Popular works 3. Astronomy -- Amateurs' manuals

ISBN 9781108214025; 131661526X; 9781316615263

LC 2016040127

This guide book, by Pierre-Yves Bely, Carol Christian and Jean-Rene Roy, "answers . . . questions [on astronomy], making it a practical reference for anyone who has ever wondered what is out in the cosmos, where it all comes from, and how it all works. Richly illustrated in color throughout, it gives simple yet rigorous explanations in non-technical language, summarizing current astronomical knowledge, without overlooking the important underlying scientific principles." (Publisher's note)

"This book includes thorough, well-written answers to 244 questions that cover just about all aspects of astronomy." Choice

Includes bibliographical references (pages 325-332) and index

Sagan, Carl

Cosmos. Random House 2002 365p $35 **520**

1. Astronomy

ISBN 0-375-50832-5

LC 2002-69744

A reissue of the title first published 1980

Based on the author's television series of the same name, this volume covers "the 10- to 20-billion-year history of the universe, from the big bang and subsequent evolution of molecular material through the evolution of human culture." Libr J {review of 1980 edition}

Includes bibliographical references

Pale blue dot; a vision of the human future in space. Ballantine Books 1997 360p pa $14.95 **520**

1. Outer space -- Exploration

ISBN 978-0-345-37659-6; 0-345-37659-5

First published 1994 by Random House

"In a tour of our solar system, galaxy and beyond . . . Sagan meshes a history of astronomical discovery, a cogent brief for space exploration and an overview of life. . . . His exploration of our place in the universe is illustrated with photographs, relief maps and paintings, including high-resolution images made by Voyager 1 and 2, as well as photos taken by the Galileo spacecraft, the Hubble Space Telescope and satellites orbiting Earth." Publ Wkly

Includes bibliographical references

Scagell, Robin

Complete Guide to Stargazing; Robin Scagell. Firefly Books Ltd 2015 320 p. illustrations (some color) (paperback) $39.95 **520**

1. Astronomy -- Encyclopedias 2. Astronomy -- Popular works

ISBN 1770854746; 9781770854741

This book, by Robin Scagell, "is a comprehensive introduction to [the] increasingly popular leisure pursuit [of stargazing.] . . . It explains how and why the sky changes during the night and through the seasons. It gives practical advice on what equipment to choose and describes what you can expect to see. There are also plenty of tips for observing just with the naked eye." (Publisher's note)

"Featuring clear and thorough explanations, this is a worthwhile resource for the beginning stargazer."

Schaaf, Fred

The **50** best sights in astronomy and how to see them; observing eclipses, bright comets, meteor showers, and other celestial wonders. John Wiley 2007 280p il pa $19.95 **520**

1. Astronomy

ISBN 978-0-471-69657-5; 0-471-69657-9

LC 2006-36221

The author "begins with some basic information and terminology (altazimuth system, for example, or right ascension) and then plunges right in with the most easily accessible astronomical sight, the starry sky above our heads. For each sight, he not only explains what it is and the best conditions under which to observe it, he also tells us about its historical, mythological, or scientific importance and explores how these far-off wonders can have a very real effect on our humble home world. This could so easily have been a dry-as-dust tome, but Schaaf's enthusiasm overflows every page." Booklist

Includes bibliographical references

Schilling, Govert

Deep Space; Beyond the Solar System to the End of the Universe and the Beginning of Time. Govert Schilling. Black Dog & Leventhal Pub 2014 224 p. color illustrations $29.95 **520**

1. Astronomy 2. Outer space

ISBN 1579129781; 9781579129781

In this book author Govert Schilling "explores the mysteries of space that lie beyond our solar system on this mind-bending trip to nebulae, galaxies, black holes, and the edge of the observable universe. The book concludes at the edge of the cosmological horizon with a look at dark matter, dark energy, and theories of extraterrestrial life and the Multiverse." (Publisher's note)

"A well-conceived, absorbing survey of the wonders of the cosmos that truly reinforces the author's point that "space is big. Unimaginably big." Recommended for space enthusiasts and astronomy aficionados." LJ

Schneider, Howard

Backyard guide to the night sky; Howard Schneider ; foreword by Sandy Wood. National Geographic 2009 21 cm. color illustrations $21.95 **520**

1. Astronomy

ISBN 9781426202810; 1426202814

"Ten chapters cover everything a beginning stargazer will need to know, from understanding the phases of the moon to picking Mars out of a planetary lineup to identifying the kinds of stars twinkling in the constellations. Throughout the book, star charts and tables present key facts in an easy-to-understand format, sidebars and fact boxes present illuminating anecdotes and fun facts." (Publisher's note)

Includes bibliographical references (pages 276-277) and index

Sobel, Dava

A **more** perfect heaven; how Copernicus revolutionized the cosmos. Walker Pub. 2011 273p il map $25   **520**

1. Astronomy 2. Astronomers 3. Solar system

ISBN 978-0-8027-1793-1

LC 2011024772

"Dava Sobel excels in telling the story of Nicholas Copernicus and his almost-shelved masterpiece, On the Revolutions. Along the way, she brings the social and political milieu of the times into sharp relief providing context for the sheer audacity of his insights into planetary motion and his reticence in pursuing their dissemination." Sci Books Films

Includes bibliographical references

Tirion, Wil

★ **Stars** & planets; the most complete guide to the stars, planets, galaxies, and solar system. Ian Ridpath and Wil Tirion. 5th edition Princeton University Press 2017 400 p. illustrations (some color) (paperback) $22.95   **520**

1. Stars 2. Planets 3. Astronomy

ISBN 9780691177885; 0691177880

LC 2017937756

"In this newly updated and expanded edition of their classic work, Ian Ridpath and Wil Tirion illuminate the night sky as never before, providing novice stargazers and professional astronomers alike with the most informative, user-friendly, comprehensive, and authoritative celestial field guide available. . . . [It] features the latest information on stars, a revised section on planets that incorporates recent research on exoplanets . . . and new photographs." (Publisher's note)

"The entire sky is presented in hemisphere maps, but each individual constellation is given its own map and description. The constellation pages include descriptions of bright stars, a brief mythology and history of the constellation, and often an inset with a color image of an important object or other description of interest to observers. There are several excellent Moon maps, too, which can be used to identify the major craters visible to observers." Choice

Trefil, James

Space atlas; mapping the universe and beyond. James Trefil ; includes "The moon fifty years later" by Buzz Aldrin. 2nd edition National Geographic 2018 352 p. illustrations hardcover $50   **520**

1. Stars -- Atlases 2. Galaxies -- Atlases 3. Solar system -- Atlases 4. Astronomy -- Charts, diagrams, etc

ISBN 9781426219696

"In this guided tour of our planetary neighborhood, the Milky Way and other galaxies, and beyond, detailed maps and fascinating imagery from recent space missions partner with clear, authoritative scientific information. Starting with the sun and moving outward into space, acclaimed science writer and physicist James Trefil illuminates each planet, the most important moons, significant asteroids, and other objects in our solar system. Looking beyond, he explains what we know about the Milky Way and other galaxies--and how we know it, with clear explanations of the basics of astrophysics, including dark matter and gravitational waves. For this new edition, and to celebrate the 50th anniversary of his moonwalk, astronaut and American hero Buzz Aldrin offers a new special section on Earth's moon and its essential role in space exploration past and future." (Publisher's note)

Trotta, Roberto

The **edge** of the sky; all you need to know about the all-

there-is; (using only the ten hundred most-used words in our tongue) Roberto Trotta. Basic Books, a member of the Perseus Books Group 2014 112 p. illustrations (hardcover) $16.99 **520**

1. Astronomy -- Popular works 2. Cosmology -- Popular works

ISBN 0465044719; 9780465044719; 9780465044900

LC 2014020067

This book, by Roberto Trotta, "tells the story of the most important discoveries and mysteries in modern cosmology. . . . The book's lexicon is limited to the thousand most common words in the English language. . . . Through the eyes of a fictional scientist . . . hunting for dark matter . . ., [the author] explores the most important ideas about our universe . . . in language simple enough for anyone to understand." (Publisher's note)

"The book barely qualifies as a book at all, just squeaking past booklet status. An entertaining exercise, in the end, for those student-people who like to ponder the All-There-Is while testing the always-inadequate limits of language." Kirkus

521   Astronomy

Goodstein, David L.

Feynman's lost lecture; the motion of planets around the sun. {by} David L. Goodstein and Judith R. Goodstein. Norton 1996 191p il $35; pa $19.95   **521**

1. Authors 2. Universe 3. Physicists 4. Astrophysics 5. Solar system 6. Writers on science 7. Nobel laureates for physics

ISBN 0-393-03918-8; 0-393-31995-4 pa

LC 95-38719

This "book consists of four chapters. The first and largest is a brief history of the establishment of the Copernican cosmology, which Feynman gave as a lecture to the freshman class at Caltech. Feynman then revisits the work of Isaac Newton and the watershed proof of the Scientific Revolution that separated the ancient world from the modern. There is also a chapter with some wonderful reminiscences of Feynman." Libr J

Includes bibliographical references

522   Techniques, procedures, apparatus, equipment, materials

Dickinson, Terence

The **backyard** astronomer's guide; [by] Terence Dickinson & Alan Dyer. 3rd ed; Firefly Books 2008 368p il $49.95 **522**

1. Astronomy

ISBN 978-1-55407-344-3; 1-55407-344-8

First published 1991 by Camden House

The authors provide guidance "on the right types of telescopes and other equipment; photographing the stars through a telescope; and star charts, software and other references. They cover daytime and twilight observing, planetary and deep-sky observing, and . . . more." Publisher's note

Includes bibliographical references

Kerrod, Robin

Hubble; the mirror on the universe. [by] Robin Kerrod & Carole Stott. 3rd ed. updated, rev. and expanded.; Firefly Books 2011 224p il pa $29.95   **522**

1. Hubble Space Telescope 2. Outer space -- Exploration

ISBN 978-1-55407-972-8; 1-55407-972-1

LC 2011292195

First published 2003

"Kerrod provides an excellent overview of Hubble's accomplishments (along with a history of the evolution of the telescope), thought-fully organizing the spellbinding images from space, and clearly and avidly explaining exactly which phenomena they depict." Booklist

Sobel, Dava

★ The **glass** universe; Dava Sobel. Viking 2016 336 p. **522**

1. Harvard College Observatory 2. Astronomy -- History -- 19th century 3. Astronomy -- History -- 20th century 4. Women in astronomy -- Massachusetts -- History 5. Women mathematicians -- Massachusetts -- History

ISBN 9780670016952

LC 2016029496

Carnegie Medal Longlist: Nonfiction (2017)

"In the mid-nineteenth century, the Harvard College Observatory began employing women as calculators, or 'human computers,' to interpret the observations their male counterparts made via telescope each night... As photography transformed the practice of astronomy, the ladies turned from computation to studying the stars captured nightly on glass photographic plates. The 'glass universe' of half a million plates that Harvard amassed over the ensuing decades--through the generous support of Mrs. Anna Palmer Draper, the widow of a pioneer in stellar photography--enabled the women to make extraordinary discoveries that attracted worldwide acclaim." (Publisher's note)

"With grace, clarity, and a flair for characterization, Sobel places these early women astronomers in the wider historical context of their field for the very first time." Pub Wkly

Includes bibliographical references and index

522.686   Particle methods of observation

Bowen, Mark

The **telescope** in the ice; inventing a new astronomy at the South Pole. Mark Bowen. St. Martin's Press 2017 viii, 424 p.p (hardcover) $27.99 **522.686**

1. Astronomy 2. Neutrinos 3. IceCube South Pole Neutrino Observatory

ISBN 1137280085; 9781137280084

LC 2017026874

This book, by Mark Bowen, "is about the building of IceCube, which Scientific American has called the 'weirdest' of the seven wonders of modern astronomy. It's the inside story of the people who built the instrument, the mistakes they made, the blind alleys they went down, the solutions they found, their conflicts, and their teamwork. It's a success story." (Publisher's note)

Includes bibliographical references (pages 401-415) and index

523   Specific celestial bodies and phenomena

The **planets**; Heather Couper, Robert Dinwiddie, John Farndon, Nigel Henbest, David W. Hughes, Giles Sparrow, Carole Stott, Colin Stuart. Dorling Kindersley 2014 256 p. color illustrations **523**

ISBN 1465424644; 9781465424648

LC 2014451572

This book, by Heather Couper, Robert Dinwiddie, John Farndon, Nigel Henbest, David W. Hughes, Giles Sparrow, Carole Stott, and Colin Stuart, offers "an awe-inspiring journey through the Solar System, from Earth to Mars and beyond. Viewed layer by layer, planets and other objects in the Solar System are taken out of the night sky and presented on

a white background, revealing every detail of their surface and internal anatomy in astonishing detail." (Publisher's note)

"This handy volume packed with the latest scientific observational analysis is a must-have for fans of planetary science." LJ

Tirion, Wil

2019 guide to the night sky; a month-by-month guide to exploring the skies above North America. Storm Dunlop and Wil Tirion. Firefly Books Ltd 2018 96 p. color illustrations $14.95 **523**

1. Astronomy 2. Astronomers 3. Astronomy -- Popular works 4. Astronomy -- Amateurs' manuals 5. Astronomy -- Observers' manuals

ISBN 9780228101055

This book, by Storm Dunlop and Wil Tirion, helps "amateur astronomers . . . view the sky over the course of the year and not miss a thing. It is also a compact and comprehensive introduction to astronomy. . . . With its maps, centered on latitude 40 degrees North, . . . [the book] will help backyard astronomers in the United States and Canada see how the visible stars change over the year, and ensure that they catch the exciting sky events that occur." (Publisher's note for 2018 edition)

523.01   Astrophysics

Tyson, Neil deGrasse, 1958-

★ **Astrophysics** for People in a Hurry; Neil deGrasse Tyson. W W Norton & Co Inc 2017 222 p. (hardcover) $18.95 **523.01**

1. Outer space 2. Astrophysics 3. Universe 4. Cosmology 5. Space and time

ISBN 9780393609400; 0393609391; 9780393609394

LC 2017005442

In this book author Neil deGrasse Tyson answers questions like "what is the nature of space and time? How do we fit within the universe? How does the universe fit within us? Tyson brings the universe down to Earth succinctly and clearly, with sparkling wit, in tasty chapters consumable anytime and anywhere in your busy day." (Publisher's note)

"Substituting down-to-earth wit for unnecessary jargon, Tyson presents ideas in clean, straightforward language and allows for the awesome nature of the universe to impress itself on readers unadorned." Kirkus

Includes bibliographical references and index.

523.1   The universe, galaxies, quasars

Aczel, Amir D.

God's equation; Einstein, relativity, and the expanding universe. Delta Trade Paperbacks 2000 236p il pa $12 **523.1**

1. Cosmology 2. Physicists 3. Relativity (Physics) 4. Nobel laureates for physics

ISBN 978-0-385-33485-3; 0-385-33485-0

First published 1999 by Four Walls Eight Windows

"Though Aczel's analysis of Einstein's work requires familiarity with advanced mathematics, that analysis makes up only a minor portion of his book, and most readers will appreciate the author's inclusion of the great physicist's letters to astronomer Erwin Freundlich." Publ Wkly

Includes bibliographical references

Bell, Jim, 1965-

The **space** book; from the beginning to the end of time,

250 milestones in the history of space & astronomy. Jim Bell. Sterling 2013 528 p. color illustrations; maps (hardcover) $29.95   **523.1**
   1. Universe 2. Cosmology 3. Physics -- History 4. Cosmology -- History
   ISBN 9781402780714; 1402780710
                                                        LC 2013372035
   This book by Jim Bell "presents 250 of the most groundbreaking astronomical events, from the formation of galaxies to the recent discovery of water ice on Mars. . . . Open the book to any page to discover some new wonder or mystery about the Universe around us." (Publisher's note)
   "This is a fine coffee-table book, suitable for either deep study or a few moments' perusal. Recommended for readers with a casual interest in the history of astronomy and the universe, or for sparking such an interest in others." LJ
   Includes bibliographical references (p. 518-525) and index

Benson, Michael

   Cosmigraphics; picturing space through time. Michael Benson. Harry N. Abrams 2014 320 p. illustrations, maps $50   **523.1**
   1. Maps 2. Astronomy 3. Cosmology
   ISBN 1419713876; 9781419713873
                                                        LC 2014930552
   Los Angeles Times Book Prize Finalist: Science and Technology (2014)
   This book by Michael Benson tells the "story of the discovery and description of the universe in a new way. Selecting artful and profound illustrations and maps, many hidden away in the world's great science libraries and virtually unknown today, he chronicles more than 1,000 years of humanity's ever-expanding understanding of the size and shape of space itself." (Publisher's note)
   "Perfect for astronomy lovers and of great interest to those who enjoy the histories of art, book making, cartography, philosophy, or theology."

Cham, Jorge

   We have no idea; a guide to the unknown universe. Jorge Cham ; Daniel Whiteson. Riverhead Books 2017 354 p. illustrations (hardcover) $28   **523.1**
   1. Universe 2. Cosmology 3. Cosmology -- Popular works
   ISBN 9780735211537; 9780735211513
                                                        LC 2016049070
   This book, by Jorge Cham and Daniel Whiteson, "explore[s] the biggest unknowns in the universe, why these things are still mysteries, and what a lot of smart people are doing to figure out the answers (or at least ask the right questions). While they're at it, they helpfully demystify many complicated things we do know about, from quarks and neutrinos to gravitational waves and exploding black holes." (Publisher's note)
   "Cham and Whiteson mesh comics, lighthearted infographics, and lively explanations to painlessly introduce curious readers to complex concepts in easily digestible chapters. This fun guide is just the ticket for science fans of any age." Pub Wkly
   Includes bibliographical references (pages [343]-346) and index.

Clark, Stuart

   The **Unknown** Universe; A New Exploration of Time, Space, and Modern Cosmology. by Stuart Clark. W W Norton & Co Inc 2016 288 p. illustrations $27.95   **523.1**
   1. Universe 2. Cosmology 3. Big bang theory
   ISBN 1681771535; 9781681771533

   This book, by Stuart Clark, is a "guide to the universe and how our latest deep-space discoveries are forcing us to revisit what we know—and what we don't. On March 21, 2013, the European Space Agency released a map of the afterglow of the Big Bang. Taking in 440 sextillion kilometres of space and 13.8 billion years of time, it is physically impossible to make a better map: we will never see the early universe in more detail." (Publisher's note)
   "Since satisfying results have yet to turn up, Clark's book ends on a cliffhanger, but readers will be entirely pleased with the experience." Kirkus
   Includes bibliographical references (pages 292-293) and index.

Dauber, Philip M.

   The **three** big bangs; comet crashes, exploding stars, and the creation of the universe. [by] Philip M. Dauber, Richard A. Muller. Perseus Books 1997 207p il pa $15   **523.1**
   1. Cosmology 2. Supernovas 3. Catastrophes (Geology)
   ISBN 978-0-201-15495-5; 0-201-15495-1
   First published 1996 by Addison-Wesley
   The authors discuss the origins of the universe and of life on Earth.
   "Dauber and Muller have not only chosen three 'hot topics' in . . . astronomy but also have masterfully woven the underlying scientific strands together. They paint a colorful picture of the theories and techniques of modern astronomy." Choice
   Includes bibliographical references

Forshaw, Jeff

   Universal; a guide to the cosmos. Brian Cox & Jeff Forshaw. Da Capo Press 2017 ix, 280 p.p ills., maps (chiefly color) (hardcover) $35   **523.1**
   1. Cosmology 2. Solar system 3. Big bang theory 4. Solar system -- Origin
   ISBN 9780306822704; 9780306822711
                                                        LC 2017930821
   This book, by Brian Cox and Jeff Forshaw, takes readers "on an epic journey of scientific exploration. It reveals how we can all come to grips with some of the most fundamental questions about our Earth, Sun, and solar system--and the star-filled galaxies beyond. How big is our solar system? How quickly is space expanding? How big is the universe? What is it made of? Some of these questions can be answered on the basis of observations you can make in your own backyard." (Publisher's note)
   "Curious readers will appreciate how Cox and Forshaw celebrate the scientific process as heartily as they embrace the wonder of the universe." Pub Wkly
   Includes bibliographical references and index.

Frank, Adam

   About time; cosmology and culture at the twilight of the Big Bang. Free Press 2011 xxi, 406p il $26   **523.1**
   1. Cosmology 2. Space and time 3. Big bang theory 4. Life -- Origin
   ISBN 978-1-4391-6959-9; 1-4391-6959-4; 978-1-4391-6961-2 ebook
                                                        LC 2011011345
   "Frank offers a unique and fascinating look at complex concepts with an accessible style that is both matter-of-fact and thoroughly entertaining." Publ Wkly
   Includes bibliographical references

   Light of the stars; alien worlds and the fate of the Earth. Adam Frank. W W Norton & Co Inc 2018 272 p. (hardcover)

$26.95 **523.1**

1. Cosmology -- Popular works 2. Human ecology -- Popular works
3. Earth (Planet) -- Popular works 4. Exobiology -- Popular works
ISBN 9780393609011

LC 2017061640

This book, by Adam Frank, "tells the story of humanity's coming of age as we awaken to the possibilities of life on other worlds and their sudden relevance to our fate on Earth. . . . Frank traces the question of alien life and intelligence from the ancient Greeks to the leading thinkers of our own time, and shows how we as a civilization can only hope to survive climate change if we recognize what science has recently discovered." (Publisher's note)

Includes bibliographical references and index

Alien worlds and the fate of the Earth

Galfard, Christophe

The **Universe** in Your Hand; A Journey Through Space, Time, and Beyond. by Christophe Galfard. St. Martin's Press 2016 400 p. $27.99 **523.1**

1. Cosmology
ISBN 1250069521; 9781250069528

LC 2016005257

In this book, author Christophe Galfard "employs . . . direct language to show us, not explain to us, the theories that underpin everything we know about our universe. To understand what happens to a dying star, we are asked to picture ourselves floating in space in front of it. To get acquainted with the quantum world, we are shrunk to the size of an atom and then taken on a journey." (Publisher's note)

"Readers looking to expand their knowledge of physics and cosmology will find everything they need here." Pub Wkly

Includes bibliographical references and index.

Geach, James

Galaxy; Mapping the Cosmos. by James Geach. University of Chicago Press 2014 256 p. color illustrations $35 **523.1**

1. Galaxies 2. Astronomy
ISBN 1780233639; 9781780233635

In this book, "astronomer James Geach tells the rich stories of both the evolution of galaxies and our ability to observe them, offering a fascinating history of how we've come to realize humanity's tiny place in the vast universe. Taking us on a compelling tour of the state-of-the-art science involved in mapping the infinite, Geach offers a first-hand account of both the science itself and how it is done, describing what we currently know as well as that which we still do not." (Publisher's note)

"Advanced researchers may be frustrated by the purposeful lack of higher-level mathematics, but the casual reader will appreciate how well Geach presents a clear narrative of the science." Choice

Gott, J. Richard

Welcome to the universe; an astrophysical tour. Neil deGrasse Tyson, Michael A. Strauss, and J. Richard Gott. Princeton University Press 2016 472 p. ill. (mostly col.) hbk $39.95 **523.1**

1. Stars 2. Cosmology 3. Relativity (Physics) 4. Stars -- Popular works 5. Cosmology -- Popular works 6. Relativity (Physics) -- Popular works
ISBN 9780691157245; 0691157243

LC 2016013487

"Describing the latest discoveries in astrophysics, the informative and entertaining narrative propels you from our home solar system to the outermost frontiers of space. How do stars live and die? Why did Pluto lose its planetary status? What are the prospects for intelligent life else-

where in the universe? How did the universe begin? Why is it expanding and why is its expansion accelerating? Is our universe alone or part of an infinite multiverse?" (Publisher's note)

"An accessible and comprehensive overview of our universe by three eminent astrophysicists, based on an introductory course they have taught at Princeton University." Kirkus

Includes bibliographical references and index

Greene, Brian R.

The **fabric** of the cosmos; space, time, and the texture of reality. Knopf 2004 569p il $28.95; pa $15.95 **523.1**

1. Cosmology
ISBN 0-375-41288-3; 0-375-72720-5 pa

LC 2003-58918

"Frogs in bowls, falling eggs, loaves of bread, pennies on balloons, ping pong balls in molasses, and babushka dolls are just some of the analogies used to explain complex concepts cleverly. After reading this book, you will never look at a starry night sky the same way again." Libr J

Includes bibliographical references

Gribbin, John

13.8; the quest to find the true age of the universe and the theory of everything. John Gribbin. Yale University Press 2016 256 p. 16 plates; illustrations $30 **523.1**

1. Cosmology 2. Quantum theory 3. Space and time 4. Relativity (Physics) 5. Cosmochronology
ISBN 0300218273; 9780300218275

LC 2015513118

In this book, author John Gribbin "presents his own version of the Holy Grail of physics, the search that has been going on for decades to find a unified "Theory of Everything" that combines these ideas into one mathematical package. . . . With his inimitable mixture of science, history, and biography, Gribbin shows how . . . these two great theories are very compatible. . . . The answer lies, intriguingly, with the age of the universe: 13.8 billion years." (Publisher's note)

"In order to bring lay readers up to speed, Gribbin first reprises the crucial developments, beginning in the 19th century, that have led scientists to their current understanding. An exciting chronicle of a monumental scientific accomplishment by a scientist who participated in the measur i ng of the age of the universe." Kirkus

Includes bibliographical references and index

Halpern, Paul

Edge of the universe; a voyage to the cosmic horizon and beyond. by Paul Halpern. John Wiley & Sons 2012 236 p. (cloth) $27.95 **523.1**

1. Universe 2. Big bang theory 3. Dark energy (Astronomy) 4. Cosmology -- Popular works
ISBN 0470636246; 9780470636244

LC 2012002028

This book offers a "look at the mysteries that lurk at the edge of the known universe and beyond." Author Paul Halpern "explains what we know about the Big Bang, the accelerating universe, dark energy, dark flow, and dark matter to examine some of the theories about the content of the universe and why its edge is getting farther away from us faster." (Publisher's note)

Includes bibliographical references and index

Hawking, Stephen, 1942-2018

Black holes and baby universes and other essays; [by] Stephen Hawking. Bantam Bks. 1993 182p hardcover o.p. pa

$18 **523.1**

1. Cosmology 2. Science -- Philosophy

ISBN 0-553-37411-7 pa

LC 93-8269

A collection of essays and speeches ranging from autobiographical sketches to theoretical discussions of black holes, relativity and quantum mechanics.

The author "sprinkles his explanations with a wry sense of humor and a keen awareness that the sciences today delve not only into the far reaches of the cosmos, but into the inner philosophical world as well." N Y Times Book Rev

A **brief** history of time; {by} Stephen Hawking. Updated and expanded tenth anniversary ed; Bantam Bks. 1998 212p il $27.95; pa $16.95 **523.1**

1. Cosmology

ISBN 0-553-10953-7; 0-553-38016-8 pa

LC 98-21874

First published 1988

The author describes concepts about space and time, black holes, the origin and nature of the universe, the uncertainty principle, and the unification of physics. This edition includes a new introduction and a new chapter about wormholes and time travel

★ A **briefer** history of time; [by] Stephen Hawking and Leonard Mlodinow. Bantam Dell 2005 162p il $25 **523.1**

1. Cosmology

ISBN 0-553-80436-7

LC 2005-42949

First published 1988 with title: A brief history of time

The authors describe concepts about space and time, black holes, the origin and nature of the universe, the uncertainty principle, and the unification of physics. It also discusses string theory, dark matter, and dark energy.

"Hawking and Mlodinow provide one of the most lucid discussions of this complex topic ever written for a general audience. Readers will come away with an excellent understanding of the apparent contradictions and conundrums at the forefront of contemporary physics." Publ Wkly

Includes bibliographical references

Hirshfeld, Alan, ca. 1956-

Starlight Detectives; How Astronomers, Inventors, and Eccentrics Discovered the Modern Universe. by Alan Hirshfeld. Bellevue Literary Press 2014 400 p. illustrations, portraits $19.95 **523.1**

1. Astronomy 2. Astronomers

ISBN 1934137782; 9781934137789

This book, by Alan Hirshfeld, focuses on the history of astronomy. "From William Bond, who turned his home into a functional observatory, to John and Henry Draper, a father and son team who were trailblazers of astrophotography and spectroscopy, to geniuses of invention such as Léon Foucault, and George Hale, who founded the Mount Wilson Observatory, Hirshfeld reveals the incredible stories-- and the ambitious dreamers-- behind the birth of modern astronomy." (Publisher's note)

"Although the story fizzles toward the end, this is a well-written and enjoyable title for astronomers—professional and amateur alike—as well as science history fans." LJ

Kaku, Michio

Parallel worlds; a journey through creation, higher dimensions, and the future of the cosmos. Doubleday 2005 428p il

hardcover o.p. pa $15.95 **523.1**

1. Cosmology 2. String theory 3. Big bang theory

ISBN 0-385-50986-3; 1-4000-3372-1 pa

LC 2004-56039

"This is a riveting popular treatment of the string revolution in physics written by a pioneering theorist in the field. Kaku expounds comprehensibly on why astrophysicists love strings and branes and the way they resolve various vexatious cosmological paradoxes." Booklist

Krauss, Lawrence M.

A **universe** from nothing; Lawrence M. Krauss ; with a foreword by Christopher Hitchens and an afterword by Richard Dawkins. Free Press 2012 224p (hardback) $24.99 **523.1**

1. Universe 2. Cosmology 3. Physics -- Philosophy

ISBN 145162445X; 9781451624458

LC 2011032519

In this book, "theoretical physicist Lawrence Krauss . . . reveals that modern science 'is' addressing the question of why there is something rather than nothing. . . . Krauss takes us back to the beginning of the beginning, presenting the most recent evidence for how our universe evolved--and the implications for how it's going to end. . . . It looks at the most basic underpinnings of existence" and provides an "entry into the debate about the existence of God and everything that exists." (Publisher's note)

Lightman, Alan P., 1948-

Searching for stars on an island in Maine; Alan Lightman. Pantheon Books 2017 240 p. (hard cover; alk. paper) $24.95 **523.1**

1. Cosmology 2. Metaphysics 3. Phenomenology 4. Cosmology -- Miscellanea

ISBN 9781101871867

LC 2017014750

This book, by Alan Lightman, "is an inspiring, lyrical meditation on religion and science that explores the tension between our yearning for permanence and certainty, and the modern scientific discoveries that demonstrate the impermanent and uncertain nature of the world. . . . What he gives us is a profound inquiry into the human desire for truth and meaning, and a journey along the different paths of religion and science that become part of that quest." (Publisher's note)

"Lightman's illuminating language and crisp imagery aim to ignite a sense of wonder in any reader who's ever pondered the universe, our world, and the nature of human consciousness." Pub Wkly

Merali, Zeeya

A **big** bang in a little room; the quest to create new universes. Zeeya Merali. Basic Books 2017 320 p. illustrations $27.99 **523.1**

1. Cosmology 2. Astrophysics

ISBN 0465065910; 9780465065912

LC 2016036546

This book, by Zeeya Merali, "takes us into the lab to answer some of life's biggest questions: How was the universe created? And could we create our own? . . . As startling as it sounds, modern physics suggests that within the next two decades, scientists may be able to perform this seemingly divine feat—to concoct an entirely new baby universe, complete with its own physical laws, star systems, galaxies, and even intelligent life." (Publisher's note)

"A rich and wonderful cosmological history that illuminates the scientific possibility of the nearly unthinkable." Kirkus

Includes bibliographical references and index

Mitton, Simon

Heart of darkness; unraveling the mysteries of the invisible universe. Jeremiah P. Ostriker, Simon Mitton. Princeton University Press 2013 299 p. (Science essentials) (alk. paper) $27.95 **523.1**

1. Cosmology 2. Dark matter (Astronomy) 3. Cosmology -- Popular works 4. Dark energy (Astronomy) -- Popular works 5. Dark matter (Astronomy) -- Popular works

ISBN 0691134308; 9780691134307

LC 2012950892

This book by Jeremiah P. Ostriker and Mitton explores the history of cosmology. "From humankind's early attempts to comprehend Earth's place in the solar system, to astronomers' exploration of the Milky Way galaxy . . . to the detection of the primordial fluctuations of energy from which all subsequent structure developed, this book explains the physics and the history of how the current model of our universe arose and has passed every test hurled at it by the skeptics." (Publisher's note)

Includes bibliographical references (p. 291-293) and index

Randall, Lisa

Dark Matter and the Dinosaurs; The Astounding Interconnectedness of the Universe. by Lisa Randall. HarperCollins 2015 256 p. illustrations, charts $29.99 **523.1**

1. Asteroids 2. Dinosaurs 3. Outer space

ISBN 0062328476; 9780062328472

This book, particle physicist Lisa Randall "uses her research into dark matter to illuminate the startling connections between the furthest reaches of space and life here on Earth. Sixty-six million years ago, an object the size of a city descended from space to crash into Earth, creating a devastating cataclysm that killed off the dinosaurs, along with three-quarters of the other species on the planet. What was its origin?" (Publisher's note)

"Writing in a deceptively chatty narrative style, Randall provides a fascinating window into the ex c itement of discovery and the rigor required to test and elaborate new hypotheses. A top-notch science book from a leading researcher." Kirkus

Rees, Martin J.

Just six numbers; the deep forces that shape the universe. {by} Martin Rees. Basic Bks. 2000 173p il hardcover o.p. pa $14.95 **523.1**

1. Cosmology 2. Big bang theory

ISBN 0-465-03673-2 pa

LC 00-268248

First published 1999 in the United Kingdom

"A brief, readable, and profoundly instructive account of where cosmological knowledge stands at this moment." New Yorker

Includes bibliographical references

Scharf, Caleb

The **Copernicus** complex; our cosmic significance in a universe of planets and probabilities. Caleb Scharf. Scientific American/Farrar, Straus & Giroux 2014 288 p. illustrations (hardback) $26 **523.1**

1. Universe 2. Astronomy 3. Life -- Origin 4. Life 5. Cosmology 6. Space and time

ISBN 0374129215; 9780374129217; 9780374709464

LC 2014008035

In this book, author "Caleb Scharf takes us on a scientific adventure, from tiny microbes within the Earth to distant exoplanets, probability theory, and beyond, arguing that there is . . . a third way of viewing our place in the cosmos. Bringing us to the cutting edge of scientific discovery, Scharf shows how the answers to fundamental questions of existence will come from embracing the peculiarity of our circumstance without denying the Copernican vision." (Publisher's note)

"Scharf covers a lot of ground, and his entertaining, accessible approach offers valuable insight not just into science, but also into the way our assumptions can make a difficult task, like finding life in the universe, even harder." Pub Wkly

Includes bibliographical references and index

The **zoomable** universe; an epic tour through cosmic scale, from almost everything to nearly nothing. Caleb Scharf ; illustrations by Ron Miller ; and 5W Infographics. Scientific American/Farrar, Straus & Giroux 2017 xi, 206 p.p color illustrations (hardcover) $28 **523.1**

1. Cosmology 2. Astrophysics 3. Cosmology -- Popular works 4. Astrophysics -- Popular works 5. Inflationary universe -- Popular works 6. Large scale structure (Astronomy) -- Popular works

ISBN 9780374279745; 0374715718; 9780374715717

LC 2017001222

This book, by Caleb Scharf, illustrated by Ron Miller, is "an epic tour through all known scales of reality, from the largest possible magnitude to the smallest. Drawing on cutting-edge science, they begin at the limits of the observable universe, a scale spanning 10^{27} meters—about 93 billion light-years. And they end in the subatomic realm, at 10^{-35} meters, where the fabric of space-time itself confounds all known rules of physics." (Publisher's note)

"A beautifully illustrated survey of the universe and its constituent parts, from quarks to galaxies and beyond. . . .A superb composite of scientific knowledge that will no doubt inspire readers of all ages to learn more about our enigmatic universe." Kirkus

Includes bibliographical references (pages 195-204).

Singh, Simon

Big bang: the origins of the universe. Fourth Estate 2005 532p il $27.95 **523.1**

1. Cosmology 2. Big bang theory

ISBN 0-00716-220-0

The author "presents a brief history of the origins of the universe. . . . He begins with a historical overview of how scientific thought changed from mythology to cosmology, then moves to the debate between the steady state model of an eternal universe and the Big Bang theory, which saw the universe as beginning at a unique moment that was followed by rapid extension. . . . This readable book provides an accessible overview of this complex scientific theory." Libr J

Smoot, George

Wrinkles in time; witness to the birth of the universe. [by] George Smoot and Keay Davidson; with a new preface. Harper Perennial 2007 331p il pa $14.95 **523.1**

1. Cosmology

ISBN 978-0-06-134444-2; 0-06-134444-3

LC 2008-530705

First published 1993 by William Morrow

"Smoot and Davidson present a historical review of cosmology that takes the reader from the work of Galileo to the recent . . . work on 'COBE' (the Cosmic Background Explorer satellite). An excellent nontechnical study of research into what makes the universe the way it is, the book provides a detailed discussion of the search for and the eventual discovery of what are called the 'wrinkles in time' from the viewpoint of the authors' own experiences in the field." Choice [review of 1993 edition]

Includes bibliographical references

Startalk; everything you ever need to know about space travel, sci-fi, the human race, the universe, and beyond. with Neil deGrasse Tyson. National Geographic 2016 304 p. color illustrations hbk $30   **523.1**
1. Cosmology 2. Human beings 3. Earth sciences 4. Outer space -- Exploration
ISBN 1426217277; 9781426217272

LC 2016019357

This is a companion volume to Neil deGrasse Tyson's podcast and TV show of the same name. "Featuring vivid photography, thought-provoking sidebars, enlightening facts, and fun quotes from science and entertainment luminaries like Bill Nye and Dan Aykroyd, StarTalk reimagines science's most challenging topics--from how the brain works to the physics of comic book superheroes--in a relatable, humorous way that will delight fans and new readers alike." (Publisher's note)

Tegmark, Max

Our mathematical universe; my quest for the ultimate nature of reality. Max Tegmark. Alfred A. Knopf 2014 432 p. illustrations (hardback) $30   **523.1**
1. Physics 2. Cosmology 3. Mathematics 4. Plurality of worlds
ISBN 0307599809; 9780307599803; 9780307744258

LC 2013016020

In this book, author Max Tegmark "leads us ... through the physics, astronomy and mathematics that are the foundation of his work, most particularly his hypothesis that our physical reality is a mathematical structure and his theory of the ultimate multiverse. He ... shares with us some of the often surprising triumphs and disappointments that have shaped his life as a scientist." (Publisher's note)

"Lively and lucid, the narrative invites general readers into debates over computer models for brain function, over scientific explanations of consciousness, and over prospects for finding advanced life in other galaxies." Booklist

Tucker, Wallace H.

Chandra's cosmos; dark matter, black holes, and other wonders revealed by NASA's premier X-ray observatory. Wallace H. Tucker. Smithsonian Books 2017 266 p. color illustrations $29.95   **523.1**
1. Astronomy 2. X-ray astronomy 3. Chandra X-ray Observatory (U.S.)
ISBN 9781588345875

LC 2016016560

In this book, by Wallace H. Tucker, "on July 23, 1999, the Chandra X-Ray Observatory, the most powerful X-ray telescope ever built, was launched aboard the space shuttle Columbia. Since then, Chandra has given us a view of the universe that is largely hidden from telescopes sensitive only to visible light. ... Tucker uses a series of short, connected stories to describe the telescope's exploration of the hot, high-energy face of the universe." (Publisher's note)

"It's one astonishment after another in this invaluable, imagination-stirring overview of cutting-edge astrophysics." Booklist.

Includes bibliographical references (pages 239-254) and index.

Tyson, Neil deGrasse

Origins ; fourteen billion years of cosmic evolution; {by} Neil deGrasse Tyson, Donald Goldsmith. W.W. Norton 2004 345p il $27.95   **523.1**
1. Cosmology 2. Evolution 3. Life -- Origin
ISBN 0-393-05992-8

LC 2004-12201

"Amateur astronomers—in fact, any reader who enjoys popular science—will find fascinating information presented in clear but never patronizing language." Libr J

Includes bibliographical references

The **universe**; leading scientists explore the origin, mysteries, and future of the cosmos. edited by John Brockman. HarperCollins 2014 379 p. (paperback) $15.99   **523.1**
1. Universe 2. Astrophysics
ISBN 0062296086; 9780062296085

This book, edited by John Brockman, part of the "Best of Edge" series, "brings together the world's best-known physicists and science writers--including Brian Greene, Walter Isaacson, Nobel Prize-winner Frank Wilczek, Benoit Mandelbrot, and Martin Rees--to explain the universe in all wondrous splendor." (Publisher's note)

Universe; general editor, Martin Rees. Rev. ed. DK Pub. 2012 528 p. color illustrations $50   **523.1**
1. Astronomy 2. Cosmology -- Popular works
ISBN 0756698413; 9780756698416

LC 2011277855

This book, by Martin Rees, "takes you on the ultimate guided tour of the cosmos. Full of . . . images reflecting recent advances in space imagery, you'll go on a journey from our solar system all the way to the farthest limits of space. . . . [The book includes] information on the nature of the universe, the study of cosmology, Earth's motion, modern telescopes, astrophotography, and even a comprehensive star atlas." (Publisher's note)

Universe

DK Smithsonian universe

Weintraub, David A.

How old is the universe? Princeton University Press 2011 370p il $29.95   **523.1**
1. Universe 2. Cosmology 3. Solar system 4. Earth -- Age
ISBN 978-0-691-14731-4

LC 2010-9117

"This is no-nonsense science writing that will be enjoyed for years: David Weintraub is an expert guide, laying out the evidence in just the right amount of detail." New Sci

523.2   Planetary systems

Baker, David

The **50** most extreme places in our solar system; [by] David Baker and Todd Ratcliff. Belknap Press 2010 290p il $27.95   **523.2**
1. Solar system 2. Extreme environments
ISBN 0-674-04998-5; 978-0-674-04998-7

LC 2010-06126

"Descriptions of physical phenomena are given around themes such as 'Surface and Interior' and 'Extreme Climates.'" (Sci Books Films) Glossary. Bibliography. Index.

The authors "discuss phenomena like the potential for diamond rain on Uranus and Neptune and the hardiness of extremophile life forms. As planetary scientists, they write clearly about the most extreme physical aspects of solar system bodies such as planets, moons, and comets, but deftly mix in more familiar comparisons from planet Earth as well." Choice

Includes bibliographical references

Benson, Michael

Otherworlds; visions of our solar system. Michael Benson. Abrams 2017 160 p. illustrations (hardcover) $29.95 **523.2**

1. Planets 2. Solar system 3. Space photography 4. Solar system -- Pictorial works 5. Solar system -- Photographs from space

ISBN 1419724452; 9781419724459

LC 2016949534

This book by Michael Benson and Joseph Michalski "is a record of humanity's planetary exploration and a tribute to the. . . solar system in . . . high-resolution landscape images, processed by Benson to capture how the planets would look if we could visit them and see them with our own eyes. [Readers] start in low Earth orbit and then move on to the Moon and our planetary neighbors, Mars and Venus . . . then explore Mercury and the Sun before . . .Jupiter, Saturn, Uranus, and Neptune [and] Pluto." (Publisher's note)

Chown, Marcus

Solar system; a visual exploration of the planets, moons, and other heavenly bodies that orbit our sun. written by Marcus Chown. Black Dog & Leventhal Publishers 2011 224 p. color illustrations hbk $29.95   **523.2**

1. Astronomy 2. Solar system

ISBN 9781579128852; 1579128858

"Every planet and moon is introduced with a big, beautiful, full-page image and a databox that shows the orbit and position of the planet or moon in relation to surrounding bodies, as well as the diameter, mass, volume, surface temperature, atmospheric makeup, and orbital period of the planet; a scale comparison graphic; and a planet cross-section for the eight planets." (Publisher's note)

Daniels, Patricia

The **new** solar system; ice worlds, moons, and planets redefined. foreword by Robert Burnham. National Geographic Society 2009 223p il map $35   **523.2**

1. Solar system

ISBN 978-1-4262-0462-3; 1-4262-046-20

LC 2009-10117

This is "a sumptuously illustrated book describing the history, composition, and exploration of the solar system. Aimed at a general audience, the text is highly readable and contains numerous side notes providing fascinating anecdotes and facts about the planets, the sun, and astronomers." Choice

Includes bibliographical references

Lang, Kenneth R.

The **Cambridge** guide to the solar system; Kenneth R. Lang. 2nd edition Cambridge University Press 2011 500 p. ill. (some col.) $69.99   **523.2**

1. Solar system

ISBN 0521198577 ; 9780521198578

LC 2011411432

This book, by Kenneth R. Lang, presents a "comprehensive, up-to-date description of the planets, their moons, and recent exoplanet discoveries. . . . Examples include water on the Moon, volcanism on Mercury's previously unseen half, vast buried glaciers on Mars, geysers on Saturn's moon Enceladus, lakes of hydrocarbons on Titan, encounter with asteroid Itokawa, and sample return from comet Wild 2. The book is further enhanced by hundreds of striking new images of the planets and moons." (Publisher's note)

North, Chris

How to Read the Solar System; A Guide to the Stars and Planets. Chris North and Paul Abel ; foreword by Brian May. Pegasus Books 2015 320 p. illustrations hc $26.95   **523.2**

1. Astronomy 2. Solar system

ISBN 9781605986715; 1605986712

Authors Paul Abel and Chris North "look at all the major players, including our more familiar cosmic neighbors--the Sun, the planets and their moons--as well as the occasional visitors to our planet--asteroids, meteors and comets--in addition to distant stars and what might lie beyond our Solar System." (Publisher's note)

'The authors comprehensively cover all the basics, making this book a great primer for readers who are just getting started in their reading on the subject. . . . [T]his chatty, non-technical discussion is perfect for the armchair or budding astronomer who wants a bit of background and history spread widely across the field." Pub Wkly

523.24   Extrasolar systems

Trefil, James

Exoplanets; diamond worlds, super-earths, pulsar planets, and the new search for life beyond our solar system. Michael Summers, James Trefil. Smithsonian Books 2017 224 p. illustrations (some color) $29.95; (ebook) $29.95   **523.24**

1. Planets 2. Extrasolar planets 3. Life on other planets 4. Extraterrestrial beings

ISBN 9781588345943; 9781588345950

LC 2016018596

In this book, "astronomer Michael Summers and physicist James Trefil explore these remarkable recent discoveries: planets revolving around pulsars, planets made of diamond, planets that are mostly water, and numerous rogue planets wandering through the emptiness of space. . . . [They] argue that the incredible richness and complexity we are finding necessitates a change in our questions and mental paradigms." (Publisher's note)

"These revelations, how they were made, imaginative voyages to five un-Earthly types of planets, and their implications for life and intelligence elsewhere than on Earth are concisely illuminated by astrophysicists Summers and Trefil in this marvelously fascinating and wonderfully accessible illustrated book." Booklist

523.4   Planets, asteroids, trans-Neptunian objects of solar system

Brown, Mike

How I killed Pluto and why it had it coming; Mike Brown. Spiegel & Grau 2010 xiii, 267p 1 ill. (pbk.) $15.00; (alk. paper) o.p.; (alk. paper) o.p.; (ebook) $12.99   **523.4**

1. Planets 2. Astronomers 3. Solar system 4. Pluto (Dwarf planet) 5. Discoveries in science 6. Pluto (Planet) 7. College teachers 8. Eris (Dwarf planet) 9. Discoveries in science -- Anecdotes

ISBN 9780385531108; 0385531087; 9780385531085; 9780385531092

LC 2010015074

This book relates the story of astronomer Mike Brown's research that led to the demotion of Pluto as a planet. "The solar system most of us grew up with included nine planets, with Mercury closest to the sun and Pluto at the outer edge. Then, in 2005, astronomer Mike Brown made the discovery of a lifetime: a tenth planet, Eris, slightly bigger than Pluto. But instead of adding one more planet to our solar system, Brown's find ignited a firestorm of controversy that culminated in the demotion of Pluto from real planet to the newly coined category of 'dwarf' planet.

Suddenly Brown was receiving hate mail from schoolchildren and being bombarded by TV reporters—all because of the discovery he had spent years searching for and a lifetime dreaming about." (Publisher's note)

"Deftly pulling readers along on his journey of discovery and destruction, Brown sets the record straight and strongly defends his science with a conversational, rational, and calm voice that may change the public's opinion of scientists as poor communicators." Publ Wkly

Kessler, Andrew

Martian summer; robot arms, cowboy spacemen, and my 90 days with the Phoenix Mars Mission. Pegasus 2011 340p il $27.95   **523.4**
1. Space flight to Mars 2. Phoenix Mars Mission (U.S.) 3. Mars (Planet) -- Exploration
ISBN 978-1-60598-176-5; 1-60598-176-1

The author chronicles the three months he spent in Mission Control for NASA's Phoenix Mars Mission, a project that lead to the discovery of liquid water on Mars, as well as a giant frozen ocean trapped beneath the planet's north pole

"The author provides some fascinating glimpses of the real work of a space mission: planning activities for the lander, dealing with peremptory orders from NASA and JPL, interpreting the sometimes ambiguous data and occasionally letting one's hair down for a party." Kirkus

Levenson, Thomas

The **hunt** for Vulcan; ...and how Albert Einstein destroyed a planet, discovered relativity, and deciphered the universe. Thomas Levenson. Random House Inc 2015 256 p. illustrations $26   **523.4**
1. Relativity (Physics) 2. Vulcan (Hypothetical planet) 3. Relativity
ISBN 0812998987; 9780812998986

LC 2015018989

This book, by Thomas Levenson, tells the "all-but-forgotten story of Isaac Newton, Albert Einstein, and the search for a planet that never existed. For more than fifty years, the world's top scientists searched for the 'missing' planet Vulcan, whose existence was mandated by Isaac Newton's theories of gravity. Countless hours were spent on the hunt . . . and some of the era's most skilled astronomers even claimed to have found it. There was just one problem: It was never there." (Publisher's note)

"Though brief, Levenson's narrative is a well-structured, fast-paced example of exemplary science writing. A scintillating popular account of the interplay between mathematical physics and astronomical observations." Kirkus

Includes bibliographical references

Weintraub, David A.

Is Pluto a planet? a historical journey through the solar system. Princeton University Press 2007 254p il $27.95   **523.4**
1. Planets 2. Pluto (Dwarf planet) 3. Solar system
ISBN 0-691-12348-9; 978-0-691-12348-6

LC 2006-929630

Weintraub "provides a very interesting and thought-provoking history concerning the whole idea of planets, and I recommend the book highly to anyone interested in the solar system." Sci Books Films

Includes bibliographical references

523.43   Mars

Hubbard, Scott

Exploring Mars; chronicles from a decade of discovery.

Scott Hubbard ; foreword by Bill Nye. University of Arizona Press 2011 xix, 194 p.p (hardcover) $45   **523.43**
1. Space flight to Mars 2. Mars (Planet) -- Exploration 3. United States. National Aeronautics and Space Administration 4. Space flight to Mars -- History
ISBN 0816521115; 0816528969; 9780816521111; 9780816528967

LC 2011036184

This book presents author Scott Hubbard's "perspective on the logistical issues -- technical, scientific, and political -- that . . . [he] faced as NASA's 'Mars Czar' during a reorganization of its Mars Exploration Program. Covering the period between . . . 1999 and the launch of the Mars Odyssey spacecraft in April 2001, Hubbard details the . . . process of simultaneous planning and approval seeking for multiple missions as far as a decade in advance." (Library Journal)

Jenner, Nicky

4th rock from the Sun; the story of Mars. Nicky Jenner. Bloomsbury Sigma 2017 272 p. illustrations (chiefly color) (hardcover) $27.00   **523.43**
1. Mars (Planet) -- Geology 2. Mars (Planet) -- Exploration 3. Mars (Planet)
ISBN 9781472922519; 9781472922496; 1472922492

In this book author Nicky Jenner "examines Mars in its entirety--its nature, attributes, and impact on the 3rd Rock's culture; its environmental science and geology; and its potential for human colonization. Writing in an engaging manner, Nicky Jenner provides a comprehensive and spellbinding guide to the Red Planet." (Publisher's note)

"Science writer Jenner illuminates the significance of Mars to humankind, covering geology, pop culture, history, and more." Pub Wkly

Morton, Oliver

Mapping Mars; science, imagination, and the birth of a world. Picador 2002 357p il maps $30; pa $16   **523.43**
1. Mars (Planet)
ISBN 0-312-24551-3; 0-312-42261-X pa

The author "traces scientists' efforts to map and understand the surface of Mars. . . . Morton writes eloquently and displays a breadth of knowledge not often found in science writing." Publ Wkly

Includes bibliographical references

523.5   Meteors, solar wind, zodiacal light

Bevan, A. W. R.

Meteorites ; a journey through space and time; [by] Alex Bevan and John de Laeter. Smithsonian Institution Press 2002 215p il maps $35.95   **523.5**
1. Meteorites
ISBN 1-58834-021-X

LC 2001-49551

"Informative and visually appealing, this title meets any library's need for a basic source on meteorites." Booklist

Includes bibliographical references

Cokinos, Christopher

The **fallen** sky; an intimate history of shooting stars. Jeremy P. Tarcher/Penguin 2009 518p $27.95   **523.5**
1. Meteorites
ISBN 978-1-58542-720-8; 1-58542-720-9

LC 2009-17493

"In 1894, fifteen years before his storied expedition to the North

Pole, Robert Peary crossed a treacherous expanse of ice in Greenland in search of another prize: a massive meteorite laden with rare metals from outer space. In this hefty, industrious book, Cokinos retraces Peary's steps, and those of other meteor 'obsessives,' in an idiosyncratic hunt of his own." New Yorker

Includes bibliographical references

523.6   Comets

Sagan, Carl

Comet; [by] Carl Sagan and Ann Druyan. Random House 1985 398p il hardcover o.p. pa $23   **523.6**

1. Comets 2. Halley's comet

ISBN 0-345-41222-2

LC 85-8308

"The authors explore the myth and science of comets in a lavishly illustrated, slightly oversize volume that is both fascinating and authoritative." Booklist

Includes bibliographical references

523.7   Sun

Golub, Leon

Nearest star; the surprising science of our sun. {by} Leon Golub & Jay M. Pasachoff. Harvard Univ. Press 2001 267p il $29.95; pa $16.95   **523.7**

1. Sun

ISBN 0-674-00467-1; 0-674-01006-X pa

LC 00-63213

Golub and Pasachoff set out to review what is currently known about the sun. Bibliography. Index.

This is "a brilliant, richly illustrated survey." Booklist

Includes bibliographical references

Nordgren, Tyler

Sun, moon, Earth; The History of Solar Eclipses from Omens of Doom to Einstein and Exoplanets. Tyler Nordgren. Basic Books 2016 256 p. ill. (some color), col. maps (hardcover) $26.99; (ebook) $18.99   **523.7**

1. Solar eclipses

ISBN 9780465060924; 9780465096466

LC 2016013888

In this book, "astronomer Tyler Nordgren illustrates how this most seemingly unnatural of natural phenomena was transformed from a fearsome omen to a tourist attraction. From the astrologers of ancient China and Babylon to the high priests of the Maya, [this book] takes us around the world to show how different cultures interpreted these dramatic events." (Publisher's note)

"A charming natural history of eclipses and a guide to witnessing the awe-inspiring event yourself." Kirkus

Includes bibliographical references and index

523.78   Eclipses

Baron, David, 1964-

American eclipse; a nation's epic race to catch the shadow of the moon and win the glory of the world. David Baron. Liveright Publishing Corporation 2017 xii, 330 p.p ills. (some color), maps (hardcover) $27.95   **523.78**

1. Solar eclipses 2. Astronomy -- History 3. Eclipses -- History 4. United States -- Civilization -- 1865-1918 5. Science -- United States -- History -- 19th century 6. Science -- United States -- History -- 20th century 7. Astronomy -- United States -- History -- 19th century 8. Astronomy -- United States -- History -- 20th century

ISBN 9781631490163; 9781631490170

LC 2017009679

This book, by David Baron, "focuses on a single eclipse, that of 1878. Baron ('The Beast in the Garden') highlights the experiences of three observers of that event: Maria Mitchell, James Craig Watson, and Thomas Edison. Other individuals and scientific details are woven into the narrative as it moves the central figures toward the day of the eclipse. Throughout, the book depicts the United States as a young country striving to achieve parity with Europe on the intellectual stage." (Library Journal)

"With a wealth of choice details about their lives, Baron brilliantly presents these three pioneers, their ambitions, and their struggles." Booklist

Includes bibliographical references (pages [289]-308) and index.

Dvorak, John

Mask of the Sun; The Science, History, and Forgotten Lore of Eclipses. John Dvorak. Pegasus Books Ltd. 2017 336 p. ills. (some color), maps (hardcover) $27.95   **523.78**

1. Solar eclipses 2. Saros cycle 3. Solar eclipses -- History

ISBN 9781681773308; 9781681773858; 1681773309

LC 2017449069

This book, by John Dvorak, discusses "the importance of the number 177 and why the ancient Romans thought it was bad to have sexual intercourse during an eclipse (whereas other cultures thought it would be good luck). . . . Eclipses are an amazing phenomena—unique to Earth—that have provided the key to much of what we now know and understand about the sun, our moon, gravity, and the workings of the universe." (Publisher's note)

"This book provides an excellent overview of how eclipses work and how people have interpreted them through time." LJ

Includes bibliographical references (pages 247-264) and index.

523.8   Stars

Bartusiak, Marcia

Black hole; how an idea abandoned by Newtonians, hated by Einstein, and gambled on by Hawking became loved. Marcia Bartusiak. Yale University Press 2015 256 p. (clothbound; alk. paper) $27.50   **523.8**

1. Discoveries in science 2. Black holes (Astronomy) 3. Science -- Social aspects

ISBN 030021085X; 9780300210859

LC 2014038950

This book, by Marcia Bartusiak, "tells the story of the fierce black hole debates and the contributions of Einstein and Hawking and other leading thinkers who completely altered our view of the universe. . . . This book celebrates the hundredth anniversary of general relativity, uncovers how the black hole really got its name, and recounts the scientists' frustrating, exhilarating, and at times humorous battles over the acceptance of one of history's most dazzling ideas." (Publisher's note)

"Superior science writing that eschews the usual fulsome biographies of eccentric geniuses, droll anecdotes and breathless prognostication to deliver a persistently fascinating portrait of an odd but routine feature of the cosmos." Kirkus

Includes bibliographical references and index

Fletcher, Seth

Einstein's shadow; a black hole, a band of astronomers, and the quest to see the unseeable. Seth Fletcher. HarperCollins 2018 288 p. $26.99 **523.8**

1. Astronomy 2. Relativity (Physics) 3. Black holes (Astronomy)
ISBN 0062312022; 9780062312020

This book, by Seth Fletcher, "follows a team of elite scientists on their historic mission to take the first picture of a black hole, putting Einstein's theory of relativity to its ultimate test and helping to answer our deepest questions about space, time, the origins of the universe, and the nature of reality. . . . 'Einstein's Shadow' is a tale of great minds on a mission to change the way we understand our universe--and our place in it." (Publisher's note)

Impey, Chris

Einstein's monsters; the life and times of black holes. Chris Impey. W W Norton & Co Inc 2019 304 p. (hardcover) $26.95 **523.8**

1. Astronomy 2. Gravitation 3. Black holes (Astronomy) 4. Gravitation -- Popular works 5. Black holes (Astronomy) -- Popular works
ISBN 9781324000938

LC 2018019192

In this book, astronomer Chris Impey explores the "science of black holes and their role in understanding the history and future of our universe. . . . He blends this history with a poignant account of the phenomena scientists have witnessed while observing black holes: stars swarming like bees around the center of our galaxy; black holes performing gravitational waltzes with visible stars; the cymbal clash of two black holes colliding, releasing ripples in space-time." (Publisher's note)

Includes bibliographical references and index

Kaler, James B.

Extreme stars; at the edge of creation. Cambridge Univ. Press 2001 236p il maps $40 **523.8**

1. Stars
ISBN 0-521-40262-X

LC 00-58522

"Each chapter covers extreme stars of a different kind, including the faintest, the coolest, the brightest, the largest, the smallest, the youngest, the oldest, and the strangest. . . . {Kaler} piques the curiosity of the novice, while encouraging knowledgeable readers to think about stars from a different perspective. There is a wealth of information, much of it not available elsewhere at this semipopular level." Choice

Pretorius, Frans

The **little** book of black holes; Steven S. Gubser and Frans Pretorius. Princeton University Press 2017 200 p. $19.95 **523.8**

1. Physics 2. Black holes (Astronomy)
ISBN 0691163723; 9780691163727

LC 2017024783

This book in the Science Essentials series, by Steven S. Gubser and Frans Pretorius, explores "the physics of black holes. . . . After introducing the basics of the special and general theories of relativity, this book describes black holes both as astrophysical objects and theoretical 'laboratories' in which physicists can test their understanding of gravitational, quantum, and thermal physics." (Publisher's note)

"A comprehensive overview of the science of black holes, among the most mysterious, powerful, and mesmerizing entities in the universe."

Kirkus Reviews

Scharf, Caleb

Gravity's engines; how bubble-blowing black holes rule galaxies, stars, and life in the cosmos. Caleb Scharf. Scientific American/ Farrar, Straus and Giroux 2012 ix, 252 p.p (hardback) $26 **523.8**

1. Gravity 2. Cosmology 3. Black holes (Astronomy)
ISBN 0374114129; 9780374114121

LC 2011047089

Author Caleb Scharf presents a "journey through the endlessly colorful place we call our galaxy and reminds us that the Milky Way sits in a special place in the cosmic zoo--a 'sweet spot' of properties. Is it coincidental that we find ourselves here at this place and time? Could there be a deeper connection between the nature of black holes and their role in the universe and the phenomenon of life?" (Publisher's note)

Includes bibliographical references and index.

The **Stars**; The Definitive Visual Guide to the Cosmos. DK Publishing. Dk Pub 2016 256 p. illustrations (chiefly color) $30 **523.8**

1. Cosmology
ISBN 1465453407; 9781465453402

"Packed with 3-D artworks of each constellation and incredible new imagery from the Hubble Space Telescope, ground-based observatories worldwide, and more, this . . . guide features the most fascinating objects known to astronomy, from glittering star-birth nebulae to supermassive black holes." (Publisher's note)

Tirion, Wil

The **Cambridge** star atlas; Wil Tirion. 4th edition Cambridge University Press 2011 86 p. col ill, col maps $39.99 **523.8**

1. Stars 2. Stars -- Atlases
ISBN 9780521173636 ; 0521173639

LC 2012589778

This star atlas, by Wil Tirion "is ideal for both beginning astronomers and more experienced observers worldwide. The clear, full-color maps show stars, clusters and galaxies visible with binoculars or a small telescope. The atlas also features constellation boundaries and the Milky Way, and lists objects that are interesting to observe." (Publisher's note)

Tyson, Neil deGrasse

Death by black hole; and other cosmic quandaries. Norton 2007 384p $24.95; pa $15.95 **523.8**

1. Cosmology 2. Space biology 3. Religion and science 4. Black holes (Astronomy) 5. Solar system
ISBN 978-0-393-06224-3; 0-393-06224-4; 978-0-393-33016-8 pa; 0-393-33016-8 pa

LC 2006-22058

"A wonderfully informed viewpoint on the slowly expanding boundaries of human knowledge." Boston Globe

Includes bibliographical references

White, Vivian

The **Total** Skywatcher's Manual; 275+ Skills and Tricks for Exploring Stars, Planets & Beyond. by Astronomical Society of the Pacific. Simon & Schuster 2015 272 p. color illustrations $29 **523.8**

1. Astronomy
ISBN 161628871X; 9781616288716

This astronomy book "will help you choose the best telescope, identify constellations and objects in the night sky, search for extraterrestrial phenomena, plan star parties, capture beautiful space imagery and much more. . . . With fully illustrated star charts, gorgeous astrophotography and step-by-step project instruction, this family friendly book is the only guide you'll ever need to navigate the nightsky." (Publisher's note)

"Enhanced by gorgeous photos and colorful diagrams, this excellent volume will encourage users to 'engage with and appreciate the extraordinary laboratory unfolding' above them." LJ

523.9 Satellites and rings; eclipses, transits, occultations

Wulf, Andrea

Chasing Venus; the race to measure the heavens. Andrea Wulf. Alfred A. Knopf 2012 xxvi, 304 p.p (hardback) $26.95 **523.9**
1. Astronomy 2. Scientists 3. Venus (Planet) 4. Venus (Planet) -- Transit 5. Astronomy -- History -- 18th century 6. Geodetic astronomy -- History -- 18th century
ISBN 0307700178; 0307958612; 9780307700179; 9780307958617
LC 2011049136

This book "is concerned with Venus's 1761 and 1769 transits, when the international science community dispatched a remarkable set of expeditions to remote parts of the world to observe and measure the planet's passages across the sun. Their primary objective was to use newly acquired observational data to improve knowledge of the distance between Earth and the Sun and the solar system's dimensions. Many of the traveling scientists underwent great travails, and several died." (Library Journal)

526 Mathematical geography

Alder, Ken

The **measure** of all things; the seven-year odyssey and hidden error that transformed the world. Free Press 2002 422p $27; pa $15 **526**
1. Geography 2. Astronomers 3. Metric system
ISBN 0-7432-1675-X; 0-7432-1676-8 pa
LC 2002-70267

"In 1792, two astronomers set out from Paris in opposite directions to measure the meridian and thereby define the length of the meter. Alder's marvelous account of their quest is a dramatic tale of revolution, science, and human error." Libr J
Includes bibliographical references

Danson, Edwin

Weighing the world; the quest to measure the Earth. Oxford University Press 2005 289p il $29.95 **526**
1. Surveying 2. Earth 3. Science -- History
ISBN 978-0-19-518169-2; 0-19-518169-7
LC 2004-66284

The author "enlivens data about geodetic surveying, transforming them into greatly interesting dramas of science." Booklist
Includes bibliographical references

Felt, Hali

Soundings; the remarkable woman who mapped the ocean floor. Hali Felt. Henry Holt and Co. 2012 340 p. (hardback) $30.00 **526**
1. Women cartographers 2. Oceanography -- History 3. Submarine

topography 4. Cartographers -- United States -- Biography 5. Geomorphologists -- United States -- Biography 6. Women cartographers -- United States -- Biography
ISBN 0805092153; 9780805092158
LC 2011044178

This book presents a "biography of a groundbreaking geologist who discovered 'a rift valley running down the center of the Atlantic,' essentially transforming 20th-century geophysics despite . . . gender bias and scientific rivalries. . . . From the 1950s through the '70s, Marie Tharp (1920-2006) mapped the entire ocean floor, an accomplishment honored by the Library of Congress in 1997, when she was named 'one of the four greatest cartographers' of the 20th century." (Kirkus Reviews)

Ferreiro, Larrie D.

Measure of the Earth; the enlightenment expedition that reshaped our world. Basic Books 2011 353p il map $28 **526**
1. Geodesy 2. Scientific expeditions 3. Geodesy -- Europe -- History 4. Scientific expeditions -- Europe -- History -- 18th century
ISBN 978-0-465-01723-2; 0-465-01723-1; 978-0-465-02345-5 ebook; 0-465-02345-2 ebook
LC 2011007173

This book "reads like a script from an Indiana Jones adventure film. . . . [It is] very well written and will interest any reader as it gives insight into the 18th Century and introduces some fascinating and unforgettable characters." Sci Books Films
Includes bibliographical references

Nicastro, Nicholas

Circumference; Eratosthenes and the ancient quest to measure the globe. St. Martin's Press 2008 223p il map $23.95 **526**
1. Astronomers 2. Measurement 3. Weights and measures 4. Geographers 5. Writers on science
ISBN 978-0-312-37247-7; 0-312-37247-7
LC 2008-25773

"Nicastro delivers the deeply human story of a multitalented genius whose tenure as the head of Alexandria's famed library occasioned remarkable achievements in literature, history, linguistics, and philosophy despite the political turmoil that periodically rocked the Ptolemaic world." Booklist
Includes bibliographical references

Raymo, Chet

Walking zero; discovering cosmic space and time along the Prime Meridian. Walker & Co. 2006 194p il maps $22.95 **526**
1. Longitude 2. Great Britain -- Description and travel
ISBN 0-8027-1494-3; 978-0-8027-1494-7
LC 2006-282372

This is the author's "expression of his personal exploration of space, time, and scientific history, inspired partly by his walking the footpaths of southeast England in close proximity to the 0 degrees longitude line. . . . This work is a thought-provoking, highly enlightening discussion of some of the most fascinating concepts in physics, astronomy, and geology, among other subjects." Sci Books Films
Includes bibliographical references

Reinhartz, Dennis

The **Art** of the Map; An Illustrated History of Map Elements and Embellishments. by Dennis Reinhartz. Sterling Pub Co Inc 2012 240 p. ill. (hardcover) $40 **526**
1. Maps 2. Map drawing
ISBN 1402765924; 9781402765926
This book, by Dennis Reinhartz, offers an "illustrated history of the golden age of cartography, from the sixteenth through the nineteenth

centuries, explor[ing] not only the embellishments on maps but also what they reveal about the world in which they were created. Here there be monsters . . . ; ships actual and archetypical; newly discovered flora such as corn and tobacco; fauna ranging from buffalo to unicorns; [and] godlike beings and fantasy-like depictions of native peoples." (Publisher's note)

Sobel, Dava

★ **Longitude**; the true story of a lone genius who solved the greatest scientific problem of his time. with a new foreword by Neil Armstrong. Hardcover anniversary ed., [10th anniversary ed., 2005 anniversary ed.]; Walker & Co. 2005 184p il $19   **526**

     1. Longitude 2. Mechanical engineers 3. Clock and watch makers
     ISBN 0-8027-1462-5; 978-0-8027-1462-6
     First published 1995

"In 1714, Britain's Parliament offered the modern equivalent of $12 to anybody who could develop a means of determining longitude at sea. While the likes of Isaac Newton and Edmund Halley sought to calculate longitude by celestial measurement, John Harrison, an uneducated clockmaker, solved the problem with his invention of the chronometer. Science writer Sobel tells this story in a way that enables readers 'to see the globe anew.'" Libr J

     Includes bibliographical references

Winchester, Simon

The **map** that changed the world; William Smith and the birth of modern geology. illustrations by Soun Vannithone. HarperCollins Pubs. 2001 329p il map $26; pa $13.95   **526**

     1. Geologists 2. Stratigraphic geology 3. Civil engineers 4. Writers on science
     ISBN 0-06-019361-1; 0-06-093180-9 pa

                         LC 2001-16603

"In the early years of the nineteenth century, William Smith created the first geological map of Great Britain, a time-consuming, solitary project that helped establish geology as one of the 'fundamental fields of study.'. . . Winchester tells Smith's story, including the dramatic ups and downs of his personal life. . . . This is just the kind of creative nonfiction that elevates a seemingly arcane topic into popular fare." Booklist

529   Chronology

Falk, Dan

In search of time; the science of a curious dimension. Thomas Dunne Books, St. Martin's Press 2008 329p il $25.95; pa $15.99   **529**

     1. Time 2. Science and civilization
     ISBN 978-0-312-37478-5; 0-312-37478-X; 978-0-312-60351-9 pa; 0-312-60351-7 pa

                         LC 2008-24875

"The book's scope is audaciously broad. Relying on reportage and humour to offset writing that is occasionally prolix, Falk deftly weaves together elements of religion, anthropology, philosophy, and physics into an engaging narrative." Quill Quire

     Includes bibliographical references

Galison, Peter Louis

Einstein's clocks and Poincare's maps; empires of time. by Peter Galison. Norton 2003 389p il $23.95   **529**

     1. Time 2. Physicists 3. Mathematicians 4. Relativity (Physics) 5. Nobel laureates for physics
     ISBN 0-393-02001-0

                         LC 2002-155114

"Gallison shows how Einstein's work was influenced by French cartographer Henri Poincaré and by the physicist's own experience working in a Bern patent office, where the numerous patent requests for devices designed to coordinate distant clocks may have prompted further inquiry into the problem of simultaneity, which lies at the heart of relativity. Few books have ever made Einstein's theories more accessible—or more engrossing—for general readers." Booklist

     Includes bibliographical references

Garfield, Simon

Timekeepers; how the world became obsessed with time. Simon Garfield. Canongate 2016 349 p. illustrations (hardcover) $25   **529**

     1. Time 2. Clocks and watches 3. Time perception
     ISBN 9781782113201; 9781782113195

                         LC 2016435902

This book, by Simon Garfield, presents stories that "explore our obsessions with time. An Englishman arrives back from Calcutta but refuses to adjust his watch. Beethoven has his symphonic wishes ignored. A moment of war is frozen forever. The timetable arrives by steam train. A woman designs a ten-hour clock and reinvents the calendar. Roger Bannister becomes stuck in the same four minutes forever. . . . And a prince attempts to stop time in its tracks." (Publisher's note)

"Exhibiting dry wit and fizzing with insatiable curiosity, Garfield collects enough eccentric characters, places, and ideas to entertain every reader." Pub Wkly

     Includes bibliographical references (pages 332-335) and index

Sims, Michael

Apollo's fire; a day on Earth in nature and imagination. Viking 2007 xxiv, 296p $24.95   **529**

     1. Days 2. Time 3. Astronomy
     ISBN 978-0-670-06328-4; 0-670-06328-2

                         LC 2007-6024

The author "takes a single day and guides readers through the history of what we know, and what we've imagined, about sunrises, clouds and other natural phenomena. . . . His delightful tour of day and night skies will inspire many readers to look up with a marveling new perspective." Publ Wkly

     Includes bibliographical references

529.2   Intervals of time

Burdick, Alan

Why time flies; a mostly scientific investigation. by Alan Burdick. Simon & Schuster 2017 320 p. illustrations (hardcover; alk. paper) $28; (ebook) $20.99   **529.2**

     1. Space and time 2. Time measurements -- Popular works
     ISBN 9781416540274; 9781416540281; 9781451677010

                         LC 2016025791

In this book, author Alan Burdick "takes readers on a personal quest to understand how time gets in us and why we perceive it the way we do. In the company of scientists, he visits the most accurate clock in the world (which exists only on paper); discovers that "now" actually happened a split-second ago; finds a twenty-fifth hour in the day; lives in the Arctic to lose all sense of time; and, for one fleeting moment in a neuroscientist's lab, even makes time go backward." (Publisher's note)

"A highly illuminating intellectual investigation." Kirkus

     Includes bibliographical references and index

530   Physics

Ananthaswamy, Anil

The **edge** of physics; a journey to Earth's extremes to unlock the secrets of the universe. Houghton Mifflin Harcourt 2010 322p il $25   **530**
1. Physics 2. Cosmology
ISBN 978-0-618-88468-1; 0-618-88468-8

LC 2009-20225

"A meticulous, accessible update of the latest ideas and instruments that contribute to the clarification of an increasingly puzzling universe." Kirkus

Includes bibliographical references

Baggott, Jim

Mass; the quest to understand matter from Greek atoms to quantum fields. Jim Baggott. Oxford University Press 2017 xvi, 346 p.p illustrations (hardback) $27.95   **530**
1. Matter 2. Relativity (Physics) 3. Particles (Nuclear physics) 4. Mass (Physics) 5. Matter -- Properties
ISBN 9780198759713

LC 2016960645

In this book author Jim Baggott explains "the nature of matter, the origin of mass, and its implications for our understanding of the material world. Ranging from the Greek philosophers Leucippus and Democritus, and their theories of atoms and void, to the development of quantum field theory and the discovery of a Higgs boson-like particle, . . . [Bagott] explores our changing understanding of the nature of matter, and the fundamental related concept of mass." (Publisher's note)

"Baggott smartly renders particle physics, typically a dense and opaque topic for the nonexpert, clear and captivating. Not only will readers grasp the building blocks of the standard model, they will forever look at mass differently." Pub Wkly

Includes bibliographical references (pages 317-324) and index.

Balibar, Sebastien

The **atom** and the apple; twelve tales from contemporary physics. translated by Nathanael Stein. Princeton University Press 2008 190p il $24.95   **530**
1. Physics
ISBN 978-0-691-13108-5

LC 2008-18027

This "is a delightful ramble through many areas of science as well as through the experiences, opinions, passions and frustrations of a leading research physicist. . . . It is a very refreshing read that will do much to bring an understanding of scientific culture to the reader." Times Higher Ed

Includes bibliographical references

Buchanan, Mark

Nexus ; small worlds and the groundbreaking science of networks. Norton 2002 235p $25.95; pa $14.95   **530**
1. System analysis 2. Patterns (Mathematics)
ISBN 0-393-04153-0; 0-393-32442-7 pa

LC 2002-518

The author "introduces readers to the dynamics of networks and shows how these networks affect behaviors in both the natural and the social world. . . . {Buchanan} finds the same patterns taking shape in food chains, in the neuronal networks of insects, in the architecture of the Internet and in the cultural backgrounds of elite CEOs. . . . Buchanan's ability as an affable, easygoing storyteller makes up for myriad digressions, and the narrative is, at times, spellbinding." Publ Wkly

Includes bibliographical references

The **Cambridge** companion to Newton; edited by I. Bernard Cohen and George E. Smith. Cambridge Univ. Press 2002 500p il $65; pa $23   **530**
1. Physicists 2. Mathematicians 3. Writers on science
ISBN 0-521-65177-8; 0-521-65696-6 pa

LC 2001-37836

This is "the best available brief overview of Newton's contributions to mechanics, cosmology, optics, mathematics, alchemy, and theology. The contributors have produced 16 well-written and admirably focused chapters. Some will be challenging for nonspecialist readers, but even those that discuss mechanics in detail are so well organized and clearly written that they amply repay close attention." Choice

Includes bibliographical references

Close, F. E.

Nothing; a very short introduction. [by] Frank Close. Oxford University Press 2009 157p (Very short introductions) pa $11.95   **530**
1. Physics -- Philosophy
ISBN 978-0-19-922586-6; 0-19-922586-9

LC 2009-281157

First published 2007 in the United Kingdom with title: The void

This history of "nothing" covers the "history of the vacuum: how the efforts to make a better vacuum led to the discovery of the electron; the ideas of Newton, Mach, and Einstein on the nature of space and time; the mysterious aether and how Einstein did away with it; and the . . . [idea] that the vacuum is filled with the Higgs field." Publisher's note

Includes bibliographical references

Czerski, Helen

Storm in a teacup; the physics of everyday life. Helen Czerski. W W Norton & Co Inc 2017 288 p. (ebook) $50; $26.95   **530**
1. Physics 2. Physics -- Miscellanea
ISBN 9780393248975; 0393248968; 9780393248968

LC 2016046555

This book, by Helen Czerski, "provides the tools to alter the way we see everything around us by linking ordinary objects and occurrences, like popcorn popping, coffee stains, and fridge magnets, to big ideas like climate change, the energy crisis, or innovative medical testing. She guides us through the principles of gases . . . , gravity . . . , size . . . , and time." (Publisher's note)

"Light but genuinely informative writing for readers who have forgotten their high school science." Kirkus

Includes bibliographical references and index

Darling, David J.

Gravity's arc; the story of gravity, from Aristotle to Einstein and beyond. [by] David Darling. J. Wiley 2006 278p $24.95   **530**
1. Gravity
ISBN 0-471-71989-7; 978-0-471-71989-2

LC 2005-30772

This is a "historical review of the human understanding of gravity from the ancient Greeks to the 21st century. Included are examinations of Greek philosophers and their debates, medieval and Arabic developments, Galileo, Tycho, Kepler, Newton, Eotvos, [and] Einstein. . . . The writing style is clear and reader friendly. . . . Read this book to learn about gravity and experience a model scientific exposition for the scientist and general reader alike." Sci Books Films

Includes bibliographical references

Einstein, Albert

The **ultimate** quotable Einstein; collected and edited by Alice Calaprice; with a foreword by Freeman Dyson. Princeton University Press 2011 xxviii, 578p il $24.95; ebook $24.95 **530**

1. Quotations

ISBN 978-0-691-13817-6; 0-691-13817-6; 978-1-4008-3596-6 ebook

LC 2010002855

This collection of Einstein's quotes includes "sections titled 'On and to Children' and 'On Race and Prejudice,' and a brief selection of Einstein's wry verses. The comments are few on the matters of physics and mathematics, concentrating more on personal, social, political, philosophical, and educational subjects." Choice

Includes bibliographical references

Feynman, Richard Phillips

★ **Six** easy pieces; essentials of physics explained by its most brilliant teacher. [by] Richard P. Feynman; originally prepared for publication by Robert B. Leighton and Matthew Sands; introduction by Paul Davies. Basic Books 2005 xxix, 144p il pa $13.95 **530**

1. Atoms 2. Physics 3. Gravitation 4. Quantum theory 5. Energy conservation

ISBN 978-0-465-02392-9

First published 1995 by Helix Bks.

This book reprints six chapters from Feynman's Lectures on Physics. "In these six chapters, Feynman introduces the general reader to the following: atoms, basic physics, the relationship of physics to other topics, energy, gravitation, and quantum force." Publisher's note

Goldberg, Dave

A **user's** guide to the universe; surviving the perils of black holes, time paradoxes, and quantum uncertainty. [by] Dave Goldberg and Jeff Blomquist. Wiley 2010 296p il $24.95 **530**

1. Physics

ISBN 978-0-470-49651-0; 0-470-49651-7

Surveys the major discoveries of modern physics, from relativity to the Large Hadron Collider. The authors discuss subjects such as special relativity, quantum mechanics, randomness, time travel, and the expanding universe. Illustrated with cartoons

"With a large measure of humor and a minimum of math (one equation), physics professor Goldberg and engineer Blomquist delve into the fascinating physics topics that rarely make it into introductory classes. . . . This nearly-painless guide is . . . involved and scientific, aimed at science hobbyists rather than science-phobes." Publ Wkly

Includes bibliographical references

Gray, Theodore

Reactions; an illustrated exploration of elements, molecules, and change in the universe. Theodore Gray ; photographs by Nick Mann. Black Dog & Leventhal Publishers, Hachette Book Group 2017 216 p. (hardcover) $29.99 **530**

1. Chemistry 2. Molecules 3. Chemical elements 4. Molecular structure

ISBN 0316391220; 9780316391221

LC 2017020093

This book, by Theodore Gray, "demonstrat[es] how molecules interact in ways that are essential to our very existence. The book begins with a brief recap of elements and molecules and then goes on to ex-

plain important concepts the characterize a chemical reaction, including Energy, Entropy, and Time. It is then organized by type of reaction." (Publisher's note)

Hiltzik, Michael

Big science; Ernest Lawrence, the cyclotron, and the birth of the military-industrial complex. by Michael Hiltzik. Simon & Schuster 2015 528 p. 24 plates; illustration (hardcover; alk. paper) $30 **530**

1. Cyclotrons 2. Physicists -- Biography 3. Physicists -- United States -- Biography

ISBN 1451675755; 9781451675757; 9781451675764; 9781451676037

LC 2014017463

This book, by Michael Hiltzik, presents "the untold story of how science went 'big,' built the bombs that helped win World War II, and became dependent on government and industry--and the forgotten genius who started it all, Ernest Lawrence. . . .Ernest Orlando Lawrence's cyclotron would revolutionize nuclear physics, but that was only the beginning of its impact. It would change our understanding of the basic building blocks of nature." (Publisher's note)

Hrabovsky, George

The **theoretical** minimum; what you need to know to start doing physics. Leonard Susskind, George Hrabovsky. Basic Books 2013 256 p. illustrations (hardcover) $26.99 **530**

1. Physics

ISBN 046502811X; 9780465028115; 9780465031740

LC 2012953679

This book by "physicist Leonard Susskind and hacker-scientist George Hrabovsky offer[s] a first course in physics and associated math for the ardent amateur. Challenging, lucid, and concise, . . . [it] provides a tool kit for amateur scientists to learn physics at their own pace." (Publisher's note)

"Excellent as an introduction to theoretical physics for the educated layperson, the book will also be useful to students and physicists for its elegant summary of the complete structure of classical mechanics. Summing Up: Highly recommended." Choice

Kakalios, James

The **physics** of everyday things; the extraordinary science behind an ordinary day. James Kakalios. Crown Publishers 2017 245 p. illustrations (hardcover) $26 **530**

1. Science -- Miscellanea 2. Physics -- Popular works 3. Physics -- Miscellanea 4. Science in popular culture

ISBN 0770437737; 9780770437732; 9780770437749

LC 2016046355

This book, by James Kakalios, "takes us on a . . . journey into the subatomic marvels that underlie so much of what we use and take for granted. Breaking down the world of things into a single day, Kakalios engages our curiosity about how our refrigerators keep food cool, how a plane manages to remain airborne, and how our wrist fitness monitors keep track of our steps. Each explanation is coupled with a story revealing the interplay of the astonishing invisible forces that surround us." (Publisher's note)

"Kakalios makes physics relatable, this time demonstrating how profoundly its principles enable our way of life." Kirkus

Includes bibliographical references and index.

Krauss, Lawrence Maxwell

★ **Fear** of physics; a guide for the perplexed. [by] Lawrence M. Krauss. Rev ed; Basic Books 2007 257p il pa

$29.95 **530**

1. Physics
ISBN 978-0-465-00218-4; 0-465-00218-8

LC 2007-04700

First published 1993

This overview describes what physics is and the work of physicists. "The writing style genuinely keeps the reader interested. . . . This book is a great resource if you want insight into what physics really is and what physicists do." Sci Books Films

Includes bibliographical references

Levi, Mark

Why cats land on their feet; and 76 other physical paradoxes and puzzles. Mark Levi. Princeton University Press 2012 x, 190 p.p ill. (pbk.; alk. paper) $19.95 **530**

1. Puzzles 2. Science -- Miscellanea
ISBN 0691148546; 9780691148540

LC 2011045728

This book by Mark Levi presents "a compendium of paradoxes and puzzles that readers can solve using their own physical intuition. . . . Levi introduces each physical problem, sometimes gives a hint or two, and then fully explains the solution. Here readers can test their critical-thinking skills against a whole assortment of puzzles and paradoxes. . . . This . . . collection also features an appendix that explains all physical concepts used in the book." (Publisher's note)

Includes bibliographical references and index

Ohanian, Hans C.

Einstein's mistakes; the human failings of genius. W.W. Norton & Company 2008 394p il $24.95 **530**

1. Physics 2. Physicists 3. Nobel laureates for physics
ISBN 978-0-393-06293-9; 0-393-06293-7

LC 2008-13155

This "clearly written, fascinating, and exciting book is a gem." Sci Books Films

Includes bibliographical references

Pickover, Clifford A.

The **physics** book; from Olbers' paradox to Schrodinger's cat: from the big bang to quantum resurrection, 250 milestones in the history of physics. Clifford A. Pickover. Sterling Pub Co Inc 2011 527 p. (alk. paper) $29.95 **530**

1. Physics -- History 2. Physics -- Dictionaries
ISBN 1402778619; 9781402778612

LC 2010051365

This book, by Clifford A. Pickover, is "a richly illustrated chronology of physics, containing 250 short, entertaining, and thought-provoking entries. In addition to exploring such engaging topics as dark energy, parallel universes, the Doppler effect, the God particle, and Maxwell's demon, the book's timeline extends back billions of years to the hypothetical Big Bang and forward trillions of years to a time of 'quantum resurrection.'" (Publisher's note)

"This attractive reference by biophysicist, biochemist, and science writer Pickover is composed of lucid one-page explanations of physics concepts, alternating with full-page color illustrations." LJ

Includes bibliographical references and index

Randall, Lisa

Warped passages; unravelling the mysteries of the Universe's hidden dimensions. Ecco 2005 499p il $27.95 **530**

1. Particles (Nuclear physics) 2. Physics -- Philosophy
ISBN 0-713-99699-4; 9780060531089

LC 2004-56376

The author "brings much of the excitement of her field to life as she describes her quest to understand the structure of the universe." Publ Wkly

Includes bibliographical references

Rovelli, Carlo

★ **Seven** Brief Lessons on Physics; Carlo Roveli ; translated by Simon Carnell and Erica Segre. Penguin Group USA 2016 96 p. illustrations $18 **530**

1. Gravity 2. Physics 3. Quantum theory 4. Relativity (Physics) 5. Black holes (Astronomy)
ISBN 0399184414; 9780399184413

LC 2016001513

This book, by Carlo Rovelli, is an "introduction to modern physics, offering . . . explanations of Einstein's general relativity, quantum mechanics, elementary particles, gravity, black holes, the complex architecture of the universe, and the role humans play in this weird and wonderful world. He takes us to the frontiers of our knowledge: to the most minute reaches of the fabric of space, back to the origins of the cosmos, and into the workings of our minds." (Publisher's note)

"An intriguing meditation on the nature of the universe and our attempts to understand it that should appeal to both scientists and general readers." Kirkus

Simonyi, Károly, 1916-2011

A **cultural** history of physics; Károly Simonyi ; translated by David Kramer. CRC Press 2012 622 p. (alk. paper) $59.00 **530**

1. Physics 2. Science -- History 3. Science and the humanities 4. Physics -- History
ISBN 1568813295; 9781568813295

LC 2010009407

In this book, "Hungarian scientist and educator Károly Simonyi" describes "the experimental methods and theoretical interpretations that created scientific knowledge, from ancient times to the present day, within the cultural environment in which it was formed." He "explores the interplay of science and the humanities to convey the wonder and excitement of scientific development throughout the ages." (Barnes and Noble)

Includes bibliographical references and index.

530.01 Philosophy and theory

Cole, K. C.

The **hole** in the universe; how scientists peered over the edge of emptiness and found everything. Harcourt 2001 274p il hardcover o.p. pa $14 **530.01**

1. Physics
ISBN 0-15-601317-7 pa

LC 00-44947

Cole discusses the history of nothing, "combining the history of zero (a mathematical nothing) with that of the vacuum (a physical nothing). . . . Until Einstein showed that light needed no tangible medium through which to travel, theorists filled the vacuum with 'ether'—the 'enfant terrible' of substances, as Einstein put it. It was subsequently banished." Atl Mon

Includes bibliographical references

530.092   Physicists

Kaiser, David

How the hippies saved physics; science, counterculture, and the quantum revival. David Kaiser. 1st ed. W.W. Norton 2011 xxvi, 372 p.p ill. (hardcover) $26.95   **530.092**
1. Counterculture 2. Quantum theory 3. Physicists -- Biography 4. Counter culture 5. Counterculture -- United States 6. Fundamental Fysiks Group (Berkeley, Calif.)
ISBN 0393076369; 9780393076363

LC 2010053415

This book by David Kaiser looks at "a coterie of physicists who, during the 1970s, embraced New Age fads and sometimes went on to make dramatic discoveries. . . . They explored complex, hitherto ignored areas such as Bell's theorem and quantum entanglement while annoying the establishment by exploring their links to the paranormal. The end result was a transformation in cutting-edge physics and major discoveries in quantum information science, now a thriving industry." (Kirkus Reviews)

"This entertaining, worthwhile read is as much about the nature of society at the dawn of the New Age as it is about quantum physics." Choice

Includes bibliographical references

Schulmann, Robert

An **Einstein** encyclopedia; Alice Calaprice, Daniel Kennefick, and Robert Schulmann. Princeton University Press 2015 376 p. ills., maps, portraits, charts (hardcover; alk. paper) $39.95   **530.092**
1. Physicists 2. Physicists -- Biography -- Encyclopedias 3. Relativity (Physics) -- History -- Encyclopedias 4. Physics -- History -- 20th century -- Encyclopedias
ISBN 0691141746; 9780691141749

LC 2015008233

This book, by Daniel Kennefick, Robert Schulmann, and Alice Calaprice, is a "guide to Albert Einstein's life and work for students, researchers, and browsers alike. [It] contains entries on Einstein's birth and death, family and romantic relationships, honors and awards, educational institutions where he studied and worked, citizenships and immigration to America, hobbies and travels, plus the people he befriended and the history of his archives and the Einstein Papers Project." (Publisher's note)

"This is an extremely well-organized and user-friendly reference title, thoroughly researched and accessible to the general public, students, and scholars alike. Highly recommended for public and academic libraries." Booklist

Includes bibliographical references and index

530.1   Theories and mathematical physics

Baggott, Jim

The **quantum** story; [by] Jim Baggott. Oxford University Press 2011 469p il $29.95   **530.1**
1. Quantum theory 2. Quantum theory -- History
ISBN 978-0-19-956684-6; 0-19-956684-4

In this history of quantum theory, Baggott examines "how, over the space of three decades, Einstein, Bohr, Heisenberg, and others formulated and refined the theory. . . . To take us from the story's beginning to the present day, Baggott organizes his narrative around forty turning-point moments of discovery." (Publisher's note)

"Quantum theory—challenging, disconcerting and heavy on math—

is not going to be pinned down and dissected for lay readers without a lot of kicking and screaming. Baggott succeeds, however, imbuing the narrative with important context, his own communicable enthusiasm and the instances of dense theoretical exposition mediated by historical and biographical storytelling. His survey runs roughly chronologically, starting with Max Planck's contention that energy is composed of a definite number of equal finite packages, through Einstein, Bohr, Heisenberg, Dirac, Feynman, Hawking et al. the author then looks at the Standard Model and the more amorphous superstring theory." Kirkus

Includes bibliographical references and index

Bodanis, David

E =mc2; a biography of the world's most famous equation. Walker & Company 2005 337p il $25   **530.1**
1. Physicists 2. Space and time 3. Force and energy 4. Nobel laureates for physics
ISBN 0-8027-1463-3

First published 2000

The author relates the story of "Einstein's formulation of the equation in 1905 and its association ever after with relativity and nuclear energy. Parallel with the science, Bodanis populates his tale with dramatic lives." Booklist [review of 2000 edition]

Bolles, Edmund Blair

Einstein defiant; genius versus genius in the quantum revolution. Joseph Henry Press 2004 348p il $27.95   **530.1**
1. Physicists 2. Quantum theory 3. Nobel laureates for physics
ISBN 0-309-08998-0

LC 2003-23735

"This carefully researched book achieves a nice balance between science and history. The author provides enough scientific information to illuminate the unfolding drama for nonscientists and constructs a marvelously choreographed tale of how just about every physicist of note in the last century contributed to the debate." Sci Books Films

Includes bibliographical references

Carroll, Sean M.

★ **From** eternity to here; the quest for the ultimate theory of time. [by] Sean Carroll. Dutton 2009 438p il $25   **530.1**
1. Space and time
ISBN 978-0-525-95133-9; 0-525-95133-4

LC 2009-23828

"Understanding time requires an acquaintance with entropy, relativity, cosmology, thermodynamics and statistical mechanics, which Carroll enthusiastically delivers at great length. Not for the scientifically disinclined, but determined readers will come away with a rewarding grasp of a complex subject." Kirkus

Includes bibliographical references

Close, F. E.

The **infinity** puzzle; quantum field theory and the hunt for an orderly universe. [by] Frank Close. Basic Books 2011 435p il $28.99   **530.1**
1. Infinite 2. Quantum theory
ISBN 978-0-465-02144-4; 978-0-465-02803-0 ebook

LC 2011022966

Close "offers a compelling history and sociology of modern particle theory. We discover the motivations and achievements of a rich cast of brilliant individuals, and get enough of the science to grasp what they were trying to do. Where Close really shines is in exposing the fraught process of recognition in science, focusing on key players such as Pakistani theoretical physicist Abdus Salam and the man after whom the famous boson is named, British physicist Peter Higgs." Nature

Includes bibliographical references

Einstein, Albert

The **meaning** of relativity; 5th ed; Princeton University Press 2005 xxiv, 166p il pa $16.95   **530.1**

1. Relativity (Physics)

ISBN 0-691-12027-7

LC 2004-111082

First published 1922. Translated by Edwin Plimpton Adams, Ernst G. Straus and Bruria Kaufman

"Though few can understand it, most readers in physics and librarians in charge of science collections know this book as one of the landmarks of modern knowledge. . . . The book is not intended for general reading. Instead it is addressed to . . . those whose training enables them to understand the mathematical expressions of relativity." N Y Public Libr. New Tech Books

★ A **stubbornly** persistent illusion; the essential scientific works of Albert Einstein. [edited, with commentary, by Stephen Hawking] Running Press 2007 468p il $29.95   **530.1**

1. Relativity (Physics) 2. Physics -- Philosophy

ISBN 978-0-7624-3003-1; 0-7624-3003-6

LC 2007-935658

The editor presents with introductions writings by Albert Einstein on relativity, the history of physics and philosophy.

"Hawking adds a brief but effective introduction to each section, making this gem of a collection really shine." Publ Wkly

Includes bibliographical references

Ford, Kenneth W.

101 quantum questions; what you need to know about the world you can't see. [by] Kenneth W. Ford. Harvard University Press 2011 291p il   **530.1**

1. Quantum theory

ISBN 9780674050990

LC 2010-34791

"Ford explains the essential concepts of quantum reality, our small-fast world, full of uncertainty and probability, where all matter can exist in more than one state simultaneously. Ford brings interesting and entertaining anecdotal and historical material into his answers, organizing and shaping his book around 15 subjects. By using humor and straight talk to answer questions that often bedevil the nonscientist who attempts to grasp this knotty subject, Ford has created an entertaining read and an excellent companion piece to more detailed popular treatments of modern physics." Publ Wkly

Includes bibliographical references

Gilder, Louisa

The **age** of entanglement; when quantum physics was reborn. Alfred A. Knopf 2008 443p il $27.50   **530.1**

1. Quantum theory

ISBN 978-1-4000-4417-7; 1-4000-4417-0

LC 2008-11796

This is "the story of quantum mechanics and its lively cast of supporters. . . . Gilder's history is rife with curious characters and dramatizes how difficult it was for even these brilliant scientists to grasp the paradigm-changing concepts of quantum science." Publ Wkly

Includes bibliographical references

Greene, B. (Brian), 1963-

★ The **hidden** reality; parallel universes and the deep laws of the cosmos. [by] Brian Greene. Alfred A. Knopf 2011 370p

il $29.95   **530.1**

1. Cosmology 2. Quantum theory 3. Relativity (Physics) 4. Physics -- Philosophy 5. General relativity (Physics)

ISBN 0-307-26563-3; 978-0-307-26563-0

LC 2010-42710

The Hidden Reality aims to show how major developments in different branches of fundamental theoretical physics—relativistic, quantum, cosmological, unified, computational—have all led us to consider one or another variety of parallel universe. Index.

The author "explores the possibility that there is not one big uncharted universe, but many. Those universes take the form of Swiss cheese, suds in a bubble bath, passageways right out of 'Star Trek,' and realms right next to us. The danger of writing a mind-blower like 'The Hidden Reality' is that, if the author isn't careful, it can become mind-numbing to read. A caution here upfront: There are points where Greene walks perilously close to that precipice. Black holes, parallel universes, the idea that we and our world may have doppelgängers in different dimensions are heady concepts. For some, such conjecture is religious heresy; for others, it aims to answer the ultimate questions as to how and why we are here, with science, not faith, forming a necessary and—so far—inadequate, bridge to explore the mystery. What Greene . . . does exceedingly well is to lay out the prevailing theories, advanced by the brightest human minds, as to how the whole of everything may be ordered." Christ Sci Monit

Includes bibliographical references

Gribbin, John R.

Schrodinger's kittens and the search for reality; solving the quantum mysteries. {by} John Gribbin. Little, Brown 1995 261p il hardcover o.p. pa $14.95   **530.1**

1. Light 2. Reality 3. Physicists 4. Quantum theory 5. Nobel laureates for physics

ISBN 0-316-32819-7 pa

LC 95-75652

In this sequel to In search of Schrödinger's cat, Gribbin attempts to "explain recent experimental and theoretical findings about the . . . nature of the submicroscopic world of the atom. The 'Copenhagen interpretation' of quantum mechanics offered by Niels Bohr and his colleagues has prevailed for almost 70 years, but there {are} now . . . competing interpretations. Gribbin reviews this . . . {field and} indicates his personal preference for one of the new theoretical models." Libr J

Includes bibliographical references

Hawking, Stephen, 1942-2018

★ The **grand** design; [by] Stephen Hawking and Leonard Mlodinow. Bantam Books 2010 198p il $28; ebook $28   **530.1**

1. Universe 2. Cosmology 3. String theory 4. Quantum theory 5. Life -- Origin 6. Science -- Philosophy

ISBN 978-0-553-80537-6; 0-553-80537-1; 978-0-553-90707-0 ebook; 0-553-90707-7 ebook

"The three central questions of philosophy and science: Why is there something rather than nothing? Why do we exist? Why this particular set of laws and not some other? . . . Along with Caltech physicist Mlodinow . . . Hawking deftly mixes cutting-edge physics to answer those key questions. . . . This is an amazingly concise, clear, and intriguing overview of where we stand when it comes to divining the secrets of the universe." Publ Wkly

Includes bibliographical references

The **nature** of space and time; [by] Stephen Hawking and Roger Penrose. [New ed.]; Princeton University Press 2010 145p il (Isaac Newton Institute series of lectures) pa $14.95;

ebook $14.95 **530.1**

1. Astrophysics 2. Quantum theory 3. Space and time

ISBN 978-0-691-14570-9 pa; 978-1-4008-3474-7 ebook

First published 1996

This volume "takes the form of a debate between Hawking and Penrose at Cambridge in 1994. At the center of the discussion is a pair of powerful theories: the quantum theory of fields and the general theory of relativity. The issue is how—if at all—one can merge the two into a quantum theory of gravity. . . . A substantial background in theoretical physics is needed for full comprehension." Libr J

Includes bibliographical references

★ The **universe** in a nutshell; [by] Stephen Hawking. Bantam Bks. 2001 216p il $35 **530.1**

1. Quantum theory

ISBN 0-553-80202-X

LC 2001-35757

Hawking "explains the basic laws of physics that govern the universe, beginning with a brief history of the concept of relativity, and then he is off and running to explore time, space, the future, and the possibility of time travel, among other fundamental rules of the universe's road. Admirers of Hawking's previous book will continue to appreciate his ability not only to air fresh, provocative ideas but also to say what he means clearly and without watering down his material or condescending to his audience—he even injects humor into his narrative. The profuse, beautifully rendered illustrations contribute greatly to the reader's understanding of his points." Booklist

Kakalios, James

The **amazing** story of quantum mechanics; a math-free exploration of the science that made our world. Gotham Books 2010 318p il $26 **530.1**

1. Quantum theory

ISBN 978-1-59240-479-7; 1-59240-479-0

LC 2010-29568

"Though the book does not quite live up to the subtitle's promise of a 'math-free' text, readers need no more than basic algebra to accompany comic-book heroes into well-illustrated explanations of quantum packets of light energy, of the wave functions of particles, and even of the angular spin inherent in both energy and matter. These basic principles illuminate the solid-state physics of semiconductors, the atomic magnetism of MRIs, and the nanotechnology of high-capacity storage batteries. And all of this conceptual heavy lifting comes with entertaining episodes from DC Comics and H. G. Wells' fiction. Physics has never been more fun!" Booklist

Includes bibliographical references

Kumar, Manjit

★ **Quantum**; Einstein, Bohr and the great debate about the nature of reality. W.W. Norton 2010 448p il $27.95 **530.1**

1. Quantum theory

ISBN 978-0-393-07829-9; 0-393-07829-9

LC 2009-51249

"A staggering account of the scientific revolution that still challenges our notions of reality. . . . Kumar evokes the passion and excitement of the period and writes with sparkling clarity and wit. Expertly delineates complex scientific issues in nontechnical language, using telling detail to weave together personal, political and scientific elements." Kirkus

Includes bibliographical references

Lloyd, Seth

★ **Programming** the universe; a quantum computer scien-

tist takes on the cosmos. Knopf 2006 221p il $25.95 **530.1**

1. Quantum theory 2. Microcomputers

ISBN 1-4000-4092-2; 978-1-4000-4092-6

LC 2005-50408

"Exploring big questions in accessible, comprehensive fashion, Lloyd's work is of vital importance to the general-science audience." Booklist

Includes bibliographical references

Nadis, Steve

The **shape** of inner space; string theory and the geometry of the universe's hidden dimensions. Shing-tung Yau and Steve Nadis; illustrations by Xianfeng (David) Gu and Xiaotian (Tim) Yin. Basic Books 2010 xix, 377 p.p $30 **530.1**

1. Geometry 2. String theory 3. Fourth dimension 4. Hyperspace 5. String models

ISBN 978-0-465-02023-2; 0-465-02023-2; 9780465020232; 0465020232

LC 2010009956

"It is a testimony to [Yau's] careful prose (and no doubt to the skills of co-author Steve Nadis) that this book so compellingly captures the essence of what pushes string theorists forward in the face of formidable obstacles. It gives us a rare glimpse into a world as alien as the moons of Jupiter, and just as fascinating. . . . Yau and Nadis have produced a strangely mesmerizing account of geometry's role in the universe." New Scientist

Includes bibliographical references (p. 331-343) and index

Rigden, John S.

★ **Einstein** 1905; the standard of greatness. Harvard University Press 2005 173p il $21.95; pa $14.95 **530.1**

1. Physicists 2. Quantum theory 3. Nobel laureates for physics

ISBN 0-674-01544-4; 0-674-02104-5 pa

LC 2004-54049

"The book is a delight to read, with a lot of interesting, useful information." Choice

Includes bibliographical references

Smolin, Lee

The **trouble** with physics; the rise of string theory, the fall of a science, and what comes next. Houghton Mifflin Co. 2006 392p il $26 **530.1**

1. String theory 2. Science -- Methodology

ISBN 978-0-618-55105-7; 0-618-55105-0

LC 2006-07235

"This is a well-written, critical profile of the theoretical physics community, free of equations, from the perspective of a member." Libr J

Includes bibliographical references

Susskind, Leonard

The **black** hole war; my battle with Stephen Hawking to make the world safe for quantum mechanics. Little, Brown 2008 470p il $27.99; pa $15.99 **530.1**

1. Physicists 2. Quantum theory 3. Space and time 4. Relativity (Physics) 5. Black holes (Astronomy) 6. People with disabilities 7. College teachers 8. Writers on science

ISBN 978-0-316-01640-7; 0-316-01640-3; 978-0-316-01641-4 pa; 0-316-01641-1 pa

LC 2007-48355

The author "delves into the related and disturbingly dangerous subject of black holes. Here, he describes disagreements that he and his Dutch friend, Gerard d'Hooft, had with the famous British mathematician/physicist Stephen Hawking on his predictions regarding the interaction of objects with black holes. This book provides an anecdotal, highly readable discussion of the background to black holes and the consequences of their existence." Choice

Includes glossary

Thorne, Kip S.

Black holes and time warps; Einstein's outrageous legacy. Norton 1994 619p il hardcover o.p. pa $18.95　　**530.1**
　　1. Physics 2. Astrophysics 3. Relativity (Physics) 4. Black holes (Astronomy)
　　ISBN 0-393-31276-3 pa

LC 93-2014

This book is "about black holes, white holes, wormholes, parallel universes, time travel, 10-dimensional space-time, the origin and fate of the universe and a lot of other subjects dear to science fiction fans." N Y Times Book Rev

Includes bibliographical references

Toomey, David M.

The **new** time travelers; a journey to the frontiers of physics. [by] David Toomey. W. W. Norton 2007 391p il $28　**530.1**
　　1. Space and time
　　ISBN 978-0-393-06013-3; 0-393-06013-6

LC 2007-11307

This book on the physics of time travel "illustrates dimension-bending concepts with space-time diagrams, M. C. Escher drawings, and the plot of H.G. Wells' Time Machine. Toomey gets a grip on bending the fourth dimension by historically chronicling physicists who have theorized about time travel .... If you dream of getting outside your personal light cone, Toomey shows how it might be imagined." Booklist

Includes bibliographical references

Wertheim, Margaret

Physics on the fringe; Smoke rings, circlons, and alternative theories of everything. Margaret Wertheim. Walker & Company 2011 336 p. il　　　　　　　　　　　**530.1**
　　1. Physics
　　ISBN 0802715133; 9780802715135

This book "describes work done by amateur . . . [scientists], people rejected by the academic establishment and rejecting orthodox academic beliefs. . . . Margaret Wertheim's . . . leading character is Jim Carter. . . . Carter's . . . belief in a theory of the universe [is] based on endless hierarchies of circlons. Circlons are mechanical objects of circular shape. . . . He verified the behavior of circlons by doing experiments with smoke rings at his home." (New York Review of Books)

The author "offers a look into the hearts and minds of the 'outsider' physicists: solitary figures who, usually with little or no formal training, strive to explain our world. Wertheim builds the book around the affable Jim Carter, explorer, self-taught physicist, trailer park owner, and proponent of circlon synchronicity, with atoms shaped like tiny circles of coiled spring. . . . This sympathetic portrayal of one outsider's work offers an entry point into a fascinating corner of pseudoscience." Publ Wkly

Includes bibliographical references

Wolfson, Richard

Simply Einstein; relativity demystified. Norton 2003 261p il $24.95　　　　　　　　　　　　　　　**530.1**
　　1. Relativity (Physics)
　　ISBN 0-393-05154-4

LC 2002-2984

"Wolfson's economical and vivid tutorial should open doors for lay readers encountering Einstein's principles for the first time. His popular style, with a minimum of math, should make this a must-have book for Einstein buffs as well." Publ Wkly

Includes bibliographical references

530.11　Relativity theory

Ferreira, Pedro G.

The **perfect** theory; a century of geniuses and the battle over general relativity. Pedro G. Ferreira. Houghton Mifflin Harcourt 2014 304 p. (hardback) $28　　　　**530.11**
　　1. Relativity (Physics) 2. Physicists -- Biography 3. Physics -- History 4. Science and civilization -- History
　　ISBN 0547554893; 9780547554891

LC 2013021741

In this book on Albert Einstein's theory of relativity, author Pedro G. Ferreira "shares the story of general relativity's revival and application to previously unobservable objects like quasars and black holes. Ferreira's book is also about the people who find joy and excitement in discovering the secrets of the universe. . . . International collaboration made confirmation of [Einstein's] theory possible, while overturning some initial conclusions." (Publishers Weekly)

"Ferreira does not downplay relativity's complexity and avoids the easy route of oversimplifying it into a cosmic magic show. The result is one of the best popular accounts of how Einstein and his followers have been trying to explain the universe for decades." Kirkus

Includes bibliographical references and index

Gleick, James, 1954-

Time travel; A History. James Gleick. Pantheon Books 2016 352 p. illustrations (ebook) $65.00; (hard cover; alk. paper) $26.95　　　　　　　　　　　　　　**530.11**
　　1. Time travel 2. Space and time 3. Time travel -- Popular works 4. Space and time -- Popular works
　　ISBN 9780307908803; 9780307908797

LC 2016002323

This book, by James Gleick, "is a mind-bending exploration of time travel: its subversive origins, its evolution in literature and science, and its influence on our understanding of time itself. The story begins at the turn of the previous century, with the young H. G. Wells writing and rewriting the fantastic tale that became his first book and an international sensation: The Time Machine." (Publisher's note)

"Ultimately, readers discern behind the modern mania for the phenomenon a human craving for immortality that—particularly in a secular age—fosters this mania. Both piquant and profound." Booklist

Includes bibliographical references (pages [317]-322) and index.

Gribbin, John

Einstein's Masterwork; 1915 and the General Theory of Relativity. John Gribbin. Icon Books Ltd 2015 240 p. illustrations (ebook) $50.00; (hardcover) $27.95　　　　　**530.11**
　　1. Relativity (Physics)
　　ISBN 1681772124; 1848318529; 9781848318526; 9781681772653; 9781681772127

This book by John Gribbin reveals "the origins of Einstein's General Theory. . . . In 1915, Albert Einstein presented his masterwork to the Prussian Academy of Sciences—a theory of gravity, matter, space and time: the General Theory of Relativity. . . . It describes the evolution of the universe, black holes, the behavior of orbiting neutron stars, and why clocks run slower on the surface of the earth than in space. It even suggests the possibility of time travel." (Publisher's note)

"Walter Isaacson goes deeper into his life and Dennis Overbye into his work, but readers will find this shorter biography entirely satisfactory." Kirkus

Includes bibliographical references (pages 208-212) and index.

Krauss, Lawrence M.

The **Greatest** Story Ever Told--So Far; Why Are We Here? by Lawrence M. Krauss. Pocket Books 2017 336 p. illustrations (ebook) $18.99; $27   **530.11**

    1. Life (Biology)

    ISBN 9781476777634; 1476777616; 9781476777610

                   LC 2017004042

This book, by Lawrence M. Krauss, "leads us to the furthest reaches of space and time, to scales so small they are invisible to microscopes, to the birth and rebirth of light, and into the natural forces that govern our existence. His unique blend of rigorous research and engaging storytelling invites us into the lives and minds of the remarkable, creative scientists who have helped to unravel the unexpected fabric of reality—with reason rather than superstition and dogma." (Publisher's note)

"An admirable complement to the author's previous book and equally satisfying for those willing to read carefully." Kirkus

Muller, Richard A., 1944-

Now; The Physics of Time. Richard A. Muller. W W Norton & Co Inc 2016 368 p. illustrations (hardcover) $27.95; (ebook) $50   **530.11**

    1. Entropy 2. Space and time 3. Physics -- Philosophy

    ISBN 9780393285239; 0393285235; 9780393285246

                   LC 2016012496

This book by Richard A. Muller "points out that the standard Big Bang theory explains the ongoing expansion of the universe as the continuous creation of new space. [Muller] argues that time is also expanding and that the leading edge of the new time is what we experience as "now." This thought-provoking vision has remarkable implications for some of our biggest questions, not only in physics but also in philosophy—including the ongoing debate about the reality of free will." (Publisher's note)

"Not for the faint of heart or mathematically averse, but Muller is a masterful guide within this survey of cosmology." Kirkus

Musser, George

Spooky action at a distance; the phenomenon that reimagines space and time--and what it means for black holes, the big bang, and theories of everything. George Musser. Scientific American/Farrar, Straus & Giroux 2015 304 p. illustrations (hardcover) $26   **530.11**

    1. Space and time 2. Relativity (Physics) 3. Space and time -- Philosophy

    ISBN 0374298513; 9780374298517

                   LC 2015010155

This book, by George Musser, "sets out to answer . . . [questions about space and time,] offering a provocative exploration of nonlocality and a celebration of the scientists who are trying to explain it. Musser guides us on an epic journey into the lives of experimental physicists observing particles acting in tandem, astronomers finding galaxies that look statistically identical, and cosmologists hoping to unravel the paradoxes surrounding the big bang." (Publisher's note)

"Clarity and humor illuminate Musser's writing, and he adroitly captures the excitement and frustration involved in investigating the mysteries of our universe." Pub Wkly

Includes bibliographical references and index

Rovelli, Carlo

The **order** of time; Carlo Rovelli ; translated by Erica Segre and Simon Carnell. Riverhead Books 2018 224 p. (hardcover) $20   **530.11**

    1. Time 2. Cosmology 3. Space and time 4. Presentism (Philosophy)

    ISBN 9780735216105

                   LC 2017060293

This book, by Carlo Rovelli, translated by Erica Segre and Simon Carnell, Rovelli "explains how the theory of quantum gravity attempts to understand and give meaning to the resulting extreme landscape of this timeless world. Weaving together ideas from philosophy, science and literature, he suggests that our perception of the flow of time depends on our perspective, better understood starting from the structure of our brain and emotions than from the physical universe." (Publisher's note)

Includes bibliographical references and index

530.12   Quantum mechanics (Quantum theory)

Ananthaswamy, Anil

Through two doors at once; the elegant experiment that captures the enigma of our quantum reality. Anil Ananthaswamy. Dutton, an imprint of Penguin Random House LLC 2018 290 p. $27   **530.12**

    1. Reality 2. Quantum theory 3. Wave theory of light 4. Reality -- Popular works 5. Quantum theory -- Popular works 6. Wave theory of light -- Popular works

    ISBN 1101986093; 9781101986097

                   LC 2018008272

This book, by Anil Ananthaswamy, presents "the intellectual adventure story of the 'double-slit' experiment, showing how a sunbeam split into two paths first challenged our understanding of light and then the nature of reality itself--and continues to almost 200 years later. . . . With his extraordinarily gifted eloquence, . . . Ananthaswamy travels around the world and through history, down to the smallest scales of physical reality we have yet fathomed." (Publisher's note)

"An engaging and accessible history of a fascinating and baffling experiment that remains inconclusive to this day. Recommended for those interested in the subject or anyone wishing to delve further into the double-slit experiment." Library Journal

Includes bibliographical references and index

Becker, Adam

What is real? the unfinished quest for the meaning of quantum physics. Adam Becker. Basic Books 2018 ix, 370 p.p illustrations (hardcover) $32   **530.12**

    1. Quantum theory 2. Wave mechanics 3. Relativity (Physics) 4. Quantum theory -- History

    ISBN 9781541617018; 9780465096053; 0465096050

                   LC 2017043844

This book, by Adam Becker, is "the untold story of the heretical thinkers who dared to question the nature of our quantum universe. Every physicist agrees quantum mechanics is among humanity's finest scientific achievements. But ask what it means, and the result will be a brawl. For a century, most physicists have followed Niels Bohr's Copenhagen interpretation and dismissed questions about the reality underlying quantum physics as meaningless." (Publisher's note)

"With his crisp voice, Becker lucidly relates the complicated history of quantum foundations." Pub Wkly

Includes bibliographical references and index

Clegg, Brian

The **quantum** physics bible; the definitive guide to 200 years of subatomic science. Brian Clegg. Firefly Books Ltd 2017 320 p. illustrations (chiefly color) (paperback) $19.95 **530.12**

1. Atomic theory 2. Quantum theory 3. Physics -- Popular works 4. Quantum theory -- Popular works

ISBN 9781770859920; 1770859926

LC 2017448764

This book in the Subject Bible series, by Brian Clegg, "explains the complexities of quantum physics in bite-sized 'lessons' that make it clear and accessible to all readers. . . . Throughout the book, there are timelines and profiles about the scientists who developed the theories and made important discoveries in quantum physics, including Dmitri Rutherford, Albert Einstein, Heike Kamerlingh Onnes, . . . Isama Akasaki, Stephen Hawking, Enrico Fermi, and Max Born." (Publisher's note)

Cox, Brian

The **quantum** universe; (and why anything that can happen, does) [by] Brian Cox [and] Jeff Forshaw. Da Capo Press 2012 256p **530.12**

1. Physics 2. Quantum theory 3. Science -- Methodology

ISBN 9780306819643; 9780306820601; 0306819643

LC 2011942393

In this book, "Brian Cox and Jeff Forshaw approach the world of quantum mechanics . . . and make fundamental scientific principles accessible . . . to everyone. The subatomic realm has a reputation for weirdness, spawning any number of profound misunderstandings." This book "asks what observations of the natural world made it necessary, how it was constructed, and why we are confident that, for all its apparent strangeness, it is a good theory." (Publisher's note)

Crease, Robert P.

The **quantum** moment; how Planck, Bohr, Einstein, and Heisenberg taught us to love uncertainty. Robert P. Crease, Alfred Scharff Goldhaber. W W Norton & Co Inc 2014 352 p. illustrations (hardcover) $29.95 **530.12**

1. Quantum theory 2. Physics -- Popular works 3. Quantum theory -- Popular works

ISBN 0393067920; 9780393067927

LC 2014011427

This book, by Robert P. Crease and Alfred Scharff Goldhaber, offers "the fascinating story of how quantum mechanics went mainstream. . . . The authors--one a philosopher, the other a physicist--draw on their training and six years of co-teaching to dramatize the quantum's rocky path from scientific theory to public understanding. Together, they and their students explored missteps and mistranslations, jokes and gibberish, of public discussion about the quantum." (Publisher's note)

"Though the authors acknowledge that many of those appropriating the jargon of quantum physics have no clue as to its scientific meaning, readers will learn to appreciate the imaginative process that transforms quantum formulas into new metaphors for understanding the human condition. An exhilarating romp for the intellectually adventurous!" Booklist

Includes bibliographical references and index

Parker, Barry R.

Quantum legacy; the discovery that changed our universe. {by} Barry Parker. Prometheus Bks. 2002 282p il $29 **530.12**

1. Quantum theory

ISBN 1-57392-993-X

LC 2002-67966

The author describes the theory of quantum mechanics, its practical applications, and the work of such scientists as Max Planck, Albert Einstein, Niels Bohr, Werner Heisenberg, Erwin Schrodinger, and Richard Feynman

Includes bibliographical references (p. 269-273) and index

530.13   Statistical mechanics

Halpern, Paul

Einstein's dice and Schrödinger's cat; how two great minds battled quantum randomness to create a unified theory of physics. Paul Halpern, PhD. Basic Books 2015 288 p. illustrations (hardcover) $27.99 **530.13**

1. Quantum theory 2. Quantum chaos 3. Physics -- Philosophy 4. Unified field theories 5. Quantum theory -- Philosophy

ISBN 0465075711; 9780465075713

LC 2014041325

In this book, author "Paul Halpern tells the little-known story of how [Albert] Einstein and [Erwin] Schrödinger searched, first as collaborators and then as competitors, for a theory that transcended quantum weirdness. This story of their quest--which ultimately failed--provides readers with new insights into the history of physics and the lives and work of two scientists whose obsessions drove its progress." (Publisher's note)

"Einstein's life feels familiar and true; Schrödinger emerges as someone scarred by envy and not a little opportunistic--e.g., when he composed a 'statement of support for the Anschluss.' Halpern ably explores the clashing personalities and worldviews that had physics in churning ferment during the early part of the 20th century." Kirkus

Includes bibliographical references and index

530.143   Quantum field theory

Rovelli, Carlo

Reality is not what it seems; the journey to quantum gravity. Carlo Rovelli ; translated by Simon Carnell and Erica Segre. Riverhead Books, an imprint of Penguin Random House LLC 2017 288 p. illustrations $26; (ebook) $65 **530.143**

1. Quantum theory 2. Quantum gravity

ISBN 0735213925; 9780735213920; 9780735213944

LC 2016036293

This book, by theoretical physicist Carlo Rovelli, translated by Simon Carnell and Erica Segre, addresses questions such as "what are the elementary ingredients of the world? Do time and space exist? And what exactly is reality? . . . Rovelli has spent his life exploring these questions. He tells us how our understanding of reality has changed over the centuries and how physicists think about the structure of the universe today." (Publisher's note)

"Rovelli's work is challenging, but his excitement is contagious and he delights in the possibilities of human understanding." Pub Wkly

Includes bibliographical references and index

530.4   States of matter

Frankel, Felice

On the surface of things; images of the extraordinary in science. [by] Felice Frankel and George M. Whitesides. Harvard University Press 2007 160p il pa $26.50 **530.4**

1. Optical images 2. Surfaces (Physics)
ISBN 978-0-674-02688-9
First published 1997 by Chronicle Bks.

Text and photographs explore the way light interacts with various surfaces.

"Materials science bears an unfortunate reputation for dullness, dealing as it does with the stuff of everyday life. A ramble through the pages of this poetic volume, however, exposes the field's underlying luster." Sci Am [review of 1997 ed.]

Includes bibliographical references

530.8   Measurement

Barrow, John D.

The **constants** of nature; from Alpha to Omega--the numbers that encode the deepest secrets of the universe. Pantheon Books 2002 352p il $26; pa $15   **530.8**
1. Measurement
ISBN 0-375-42221-8; 1-4000-3225-3 pa

LC 2002-75975

"Barrow traces scientists' evolving understanding of natural constants, like the speed of light, in this erudite and enthralling work of popular science." Publ Wkly

Includes bibliographical references

Robinson, Andrew

The **story** of measurement. Thames & Hudson 2007 224p il map $34.95   **530.8**
1. Measurement
ISBN 978-0-500-51367-5; 0-500-51367-8

LC 2007-921450

"Robinson has the knack to explain any number of complex concepts lucidly and with simplicity, without being condescending. . . . He has produced a highly readable book." Times Lit Suppl

Includes bibliographical references

531   Classical mechanics

Chown, Marcus

The **ascent** of gravity; the quest to understand the force that explains everything. Marcus Chown. W W Norton & Co Inc 2017 256 p. $26.95   **531**
1. Gravity 2. Gravitation
ISBN 1681775379; 9781681775371

In this book, author Marcus Chown "takes us on an unforgettable journey from the recognition of the 'force' of gravity in 1666 to the discovery of gravitational waves in 2015. And, as we stand on the brink of a seismic revolution in our worldview, he brings us up to speed on the greatest challenge ever to confront physics." (Publisher's note)

"Adults and teens interested in science history and exciting new physics and astronomy discoveries will thoroughly enjoy." (LJ)

535   Light and related radiation

Ball, Philip

Invisible; the dangerous allure of the unseen. Philip Ball. The University of Chicago Press 2014 336 p. illustrations (cloth; alk. paper) $27.50   **535**

1. Invisibility
ISBN 022623889X; 1847922899; 9781847922892; 9780226238890

LC 2014035709

In this book, Philip Ball explores "the history of the idea of the invisible. He examines both the why and the how of invisibility, pondering the concept's allure and the opportunity it gives individuals to seize 'power, wealth, or sex,' as well as the intriguing ways that myth, magic, and science intersect in its study. In the Middle Ages, magic books were 'scarcely complete without a spell of invisibility,' but scientists began to test such spells experimentally by the 18th Century." (Publishers Weekly)

Pendergrast, Mark

Mirror mirror; a history of the human love affair with reflection. Basic Books 2003 404p il $27.50; pa $17   **535**
1. Mirrors
ISBN 0-465-05470-6; 0-465-05471-4 pa

LC 2003-2544

"Those with a historical and scientific bent may profitably read this book for insight into the manufacture of mirrors—along with descendents the telescope and microscope—down through the ages. . . . Whether for pleasure or profit, this well-written, entertaining book, packed with historical information, should be read!" Choice

Includes bibliographical references

535.6   Color

Eckstut, Arielle

The **Secret** Language of Color; Science, Nature, History, Culture, Beauty and Joy of Red, Orange, Yellow, Green, Blue, and Violet. Joann Eckstut and Arielle Eckstut. Black Dog & Leventhal Pub 2013 240 p. color illustrations $29.95   **535.6**
1. Color 2. Vision 3. Physics
ISBN 1579129498; 9781579129491

LC 2014397031

This book, by Joann Eckstut and Arielle Eckstut, is "organized into chapters that begin with . . . [an] explanation of the physics and chemistry of color. . . . In these chapters we learn about how and why we see color, the nature of rainbows, animals with color vision far superior and far inferior to our own, how our language influences the colors we see, and much more." (Publisher's note)

"The book's dynamic design and short entries make it easy to skim, but it's likely that those intending just a casual perusal will find themselves engrossed by this terrifically entertaining and informative volume." Pub Wkly

Includes bibliographical references (p. [234]-235) and index.

536   Heat

Shachtman, Tom

Absolute zero and the conquest of cold. Houghton Mifflin 1999 261p hardcover o.p. pa $14   **536**
1. Thermodynamics 2. Low temperatures -- Research
ISBN 0-395-93888-0; 0-618-08239-5 pa

LC 99-33305

The author "analyzes the social impact of the chill factor, explains the science of cold and tells the curious tales behind inventions like the thermometer, the fridge and the thermos flask." N Y Times Book Rev

Includes bibliographical references

537   Electricity and electronics

Bodanis, David

Electric universe; the shocking true story of electricity. Crown Publishers 2004 308p hardcover o.p. pa $31   **537**
1. Electricity 2. Force and energy
ISBN 1-4000-4550-9; 0-307-33598-4 pa

LC 2004-11275

"As a storyteller, author David Bodanis is wonderful. . . . This book is directed at a general audience, but it should be required reading for all scientific professionals." Sci Books Films

Includes bibliographical references

538.7   Geomagnetism and related phenomena

Mitchell, Alanna

The **spinning** magnet; the force that created the modern world--and could destroy it. Alanna Mitchell. Dutton, an imprint of Penguin Random House, LLC 2018 ix, 323 p.p (hardcover) $28   **538.7**
1. Magnetism 2. Geomagnetism 3. Electromagnetism 4. Magnetic fields 5. Earth (Planet) -- Mantle 6. Solar radiation -- Health aspects
ISBN 9781101985168; 9781101985182

LC 2017034554

This book, by Alanna Mitchell, presents the "history of the science of electromagnetism and the Earth's magnetic field--right up to the latest indications that the North and South Poles may soon reverse, with apocalyptic results. . . . When the poles switch, . . . the Earth is unprotected from solar radiation storms that would, among other disturbances, wipe out much and possible all of our electromagnetic technology." (Publisher's note)

"This immersion in magnetism is an invaluable contribution to the popular science shelf." Booklist

Includes bibliographical references and index

539.2   Radiation (Radiant energy)

Blatner, David

Spectrums; our mindboggling universe from infinitesimal to infinity. David Blatner. Walker & Co. 2012 183 p. (hardback) $25   **539.2**
1. Size 2. Science 3. Measurement 4. Spectrum analysis
ISBN 0802717705; 9780802717702

LC 2012010727

This book, by David Blatner, asks "how can we understand the world of the atom or the size of our galaxy? How do we grasp a billionth of a second or a billion years? . . . Blatner re-introduces us to six fundamental spectrums in the world around us: numbers, size, light, sound, heat, and time. Offering fascinating glimpses of hidden realities, full of comparisons, facts, and anecdotes." (Publisher's note)

Jorgensen, Timothy J.

Strange glow; the story of radiation. Timothy J. Jorgensen. Princeton University Press 2016 512 p. illustrations (alk. paper) $35   **539.2**
1. Radiation 2. Radiobiology
ISBN 9780691165035

LC 2015959168

In this book, author Timothy J. Jorgensen "explores how our knowledge of and experiences with radiation in the last century can lead us to smarter personal decisions about radiation exposures today. Jorgensen introduces key figures in the story of radiation—from Wilhelm Roentgen, the discoverer of x-rays, and pioneering radioactivity researchers Marie and Pierre Curie, to Thomas Edison and the victims of the recent Fukushima Daiichi nuclear power plant accident." (Publisher's note)

"Jorgensen's easy-to-follow and enthusiastic style will appeal to readers who are interested in the study of radiation yet have plenty of time on their hands to get to the information they seek." LJ

Includes bibliographical references (pages 411-464) and index.

539.7   Atomic and nuclear physics

Aczel, Amir D.

Present at the creation; the story of CERN and the Large Hadron Collider. [by] Amir Aczel. Harmony Books 2010 271p il $25.99; ebook $12.99   **539.7**
1. Large Hadron Collider (France and Switzerland) 2. CERN
ISBN 978-0-307-59167-8; 978-0-307-59168-5 ebook

LC 2010-14835

Aczel "has produced an excellent review of past, current, and possible future theories of particle physics and how they relate to the field of cosmology. He uses the Large Hadron Collider (LHC), the most energetic particle accelerator ever built, as a focal point for a discussion of these theories." Choice

Includes bibliographical references

Carroll, Sean

The **particle** at the end of the Universe; how the hunt for the Higgs boson leads us to the edge of a new world. Sean Carroll. Penguin Group USA 2012 352 p. $27.95   **539.7**
1. Higgs bosons 2. Dark matter (Astronomy)
ISBN 0525953590; 9780525953593

In this book "Sean Carroll takes readers behind the scenes of the Large Hadron Collider at CERN to meet the scientists and explain . . . the Higgs boson [particle], the key to understanding why mass exists. . . . The fact is, while we have now essentially solved the mass puzzle, there are things we didn't predict and possibilities we haven't yet dreamed. A doorway is opening into the mind boggling, somewhat frightening world of dark matter." (Publisher's note)

Includes bibliographical references and index.

Feynman, Richard Phillips

QED; the strange theory of light and matter. [by] Richard Feynman. Princeton Univ. Press 1985 158p (Alix G. Mautner memorial lectures) $55; pa $15.95   **539.7**
1. Light 2. Electrons 3. Quantum theory
ISBN 0-691-08388-6; 0-691-02417-0 pa

LC 85-42685

The author attempts to describe the interaction between light and electrons

"Feynman describes with accuracy, insight, self-deprecating humor, and clarity the centerpiece of modern elementary particle theory—quantum electrodynamics. . . . 'QED' will challenge the mind." Christ Sci Monit

Goldberg, Dave

The **Universe** in the Rearview Mirror; How Hidden Symmetries Shape Reality. Dave Goldberg. Dutton 2013 336 p. illustrations $27.95   **539.7**

1. Physics 2. Universe 3. Reality 4. Symmetry 5. Cosmology
ISBN 0525953663; 9780525953661

LC 2013016178

Author Dave Goldberg examines "space, time and everything in between showing that our elegant universe--from the Higgs boson to antimatter to the most massive group of galaxies--is shaped by hidden symmetries that have driven all our recent discoveries about the universe and all the ones to come." (Publisher's note)

An "informative, math-free, and completely entertaining look at the concept of symmetry in physics." Pub Wkly

Includes bibliographical references and index

Greene, Brian R.

★ The **elegant** universe; superstrings, hidden dimensions, and the quest for the ultimate theory. [by] Brian Greene. Vintage Books 2000 448p il pa $15.95   **539.7**
1. Cosmology 2. String theory
ISBN 0-375-70811-1; 978-0-375-70811-4

LC 99-42018

First published 1999 by Norton

The author "makes the terribly complex theory of strings accessible to all. He possesses a remarkable gift for using the everyday to illustrate what may be going on in dimensions beyond our feeble human perception." Publ Wkly

Includes bibliographical references

Lederman, Leon

Beyond the god particle; Leon M. Lederman, Christopher T. Hill. Prometheus Books 2013 340 p. ill hc $24.95 **539.7**
1. Matter 2. Particles (Nuclear physics) 3. Higgs bosons
ISBN 9781616148010

LC 2013022346

The coauthors "discuss the 2012 discovery of the Higgs boson particle . . . and what's next for subatomic particle physics research. This is essentially a sequel to The God Particle, in which the titular term for Higgs boson was coined. Both descriptive and prescriptive, this new book presents enjoyable overviews of discoveries of the physical world, from molecules to atoms and subatomic particles, including a clear description of the need for huge machines to provide energy to accelerate tiny particles. . . . The authors aim to offer "coulds and shoulds," and do, including a directive thoroughly to study strong interactions in particle physics." Booklist

Includes bibliographical references and index

Levin, Janna

Black hole blues and other songs from outer space; Janna Levin. Alfred A. Knopf 2016 241 p. $26.95   **539.7**
1. Black holes (Astronomy) 2. Gravitational waves
ISBN 030794848X; 0307958191; 9780307948489;
9780307958198

LC 2015046692

This book, by Janna Levin, is the "authoritative story of the headline-making discovery of gravitational waves. . . . An experimental ambition that began as an amusing thought experiment, a mad idea, became the object of fixation for the original architects--Rai Weiss, Kip Thorne, and Ron Drever. Striving to make the ambition a reality, the original three gradually accumulated an international team of hundreds." (Publisher's note)

"A superb alignment of author and subject: Levin is among the best contemporary science writers, and LIGO is arguably the most compelling experiment on the planet." Kirkus

Includes bibliographical references and index

Lincoln, Don

The **large** hadron collider; the extraordinary story of the Higgs boson and other stuff that will blow your mind. by Don Lincoln. Johns Hopkins University Press 2014 240 p. illustrations (hardcover; alk. paper) $29.95   **539.7**
1. Higgs bosons 2. Scientific apparatus and instruments 3. Large Hadron Collider (France and Switzerland)
ISBN 1421413515; 9781421413518

LC 2013040921

In this book, author "Don Lincoln shares an insider's account of the [Large Hadron Collider's] operational history. Lincoln devotes an entire chapter to the Higgs boson and Higgs field, using several extended analogies to help explain the importance of these concepts to particle physics. In the final chapter, he describes what the discovery of the Higgs boson tells us about our current understanding of basic physics." (Publisher's note)

"Readers will be fascinated by the project's sheer mechanical challenges and the failure that caused it to be shut down and rebuilt before being operated at its design power. This engaging story will be appreciated by readers interested in the frontiers of science. Summing Up: Highly recommended. All levels/libraries." Choice

Includes bibliographical references and index

Malley, Marjorie Caroline

Radioactivity; a history of a mysterious science. [by] Marjorie C. Malley. Oxford University Press 2011 xxi, 267p il map $21.95   **539.7**
1. Radioactivity
ISBN 978-0-19-976641-3

LC 2010038979

"Malley presents a timely tale about the discovery of radioactivity, the development of our knowledge of the physical universe, and the way radioactivity has changed our world. . . . [She] manages to make the periodic table and the giants involved in its creation interesting. . . . Malley does a wonderful job of demonstrating how scientific discovery functions, as opposed to the usual approach in which facts and figures are given as tidbits along a chronology." Libr J

Includes bibliographical references

Nelson, Craig

The **age** of radiance; the epic rise and dramatic fall of the atomic era. Craig Nelson. Scribner 2014 416 p. illustrations (hardcover) $29.99   **539.7**
1. Radiation 2. Radioactivity 3. Nuclear energy 4. Nuclear physics 5. Nuclear weapons
ISBN 145166043X; 9781451660432; 9781451660449

LC 2013042192

This book, by Craig Nelson, is a "history of the Atomic Age. . . . From the discovery of X-rays in the 1890s, through the birth of nuclear power in an abandoned Chicago football stadium, to the bomb builders of Los Alamos, . . . Nelson illuminates a pageant of fascinating historical figures: Marie and Pierre Curie, Albert Einstein, Niels Bohr, Franklin Roosevelt, J. Robert Oppenheimer, Harry Truman, Curtis LeMay, John F. Kennedy, Robert McNamara, Ronald Reagan, and Mikhail Gorbachev." (Publisher's note)

"An engaging history that raises provocative questions about the future of nuclear science." Kirkus

Includes bibliographical references and index

Seife, Charles

Sun in a bottle; the strange history of fusion and the science of wishful thinking. Viking 2008 294p il map $25.95 **539.7**

1. Nuclear fusion
ISBN 978-0-670-02033-1; 0-670-02033-8

LC 2008-13135

"Ever since the first hydrogen bomb tests in the 1950s, scientists have hoped to reproduce the sun's magic in a controlled fashion, unlocking an unlimited source of energy. But the dream has been elusive. With great explanatory skill, Seife . . . explains how fusion works and why it is so hard to get power out of it. Seife reviews the parade of hubristic and sometimes comic or outright dishonest claims that fusion scientists have made over the decades." Sci News

Includes bibliographical references

Stewart, Ian

Why beauty is truth; a history of symmetry. Basic Books 2007 290p il $26.95 **539.7**

1. Symmetry
ISBN 978-0-465-08236-0; 0-465-08236-X

LC 2006-38274

"Beginning with the early struggles of the Babylonians to solve quadratics, Stewart guides his readers through the often-tangled history of symmetry, illuminating for nonspecialists how a concept easily recognized in geometry acquired new meanings in algebra. . . . An exciting foray for any armchair physicist!" Booklist

Includes bibliographical references

539.72   Particle physics

Butterworth, Jon

Atom land; a guided tour through the strange (and impossibly small) world of particle physics. Jon Butterworth. Workman Pub Co 2018 288 p. $19.95 **539.72**

1. Quantum theory 2. Nuclear physics 3. Particles (Nuclear physics)
ISBN 1615193731; 9781615193738

"Welcome to Atom Land, the impossibly small world of quantum physics. With award-winning physic[ist] Jon Butterworth as your guide, you'll set sail from Port Electron in search of strange new terrain. Each discovery will expand the horizons of your trusty map--from the Hadron Island to the Isle of Quarks and beyond. Just beware of Dark Energy and other sea monsters!" (Publisher's note)

Randall, Lisa

Higgs discovery; the power of empty space. Lisa Randall. Ecco Solo/HarperCollins 2013 99 p. illustrations pbk $9.99 **539.72**

1. Physics 2. Higgs bosons
ISBN 0062300474; 9780062300478

LC 2015300802

"On July 4, 2012, physicists at the Large Hadron Collider in Geneva madehistory when they discovered an entirely new type of subatomic particle that many scientists believe is the Higgs boson. For forty years, physicists searched for this capstone to the Standard Model of particle physics--the theory that describes both the most elementary components that are known in matter and the forces through which they interact. This particle points to the Higgs field, which provides the key to understanding why elementary particles have mass. . . . Lisa Randall explains the science behind this monumental discovery, its exhilarating implications, and the power of empty space." (Publisher's note)

Still, Ben

Particle physics brick by brick; atomic and subatomic physics explained.... in Lego. Ben Still. Firefly Books Ltd 2018 176 p. $24.95 **539.72**

1. Matter 2. Physics 3. LEGO toys
ISBN 0228100127; 9780228100126

This book, by Ben Still, "explains how and with what the universe came to be. It introduces the Standard Model of Physics, the 'rule book' of physics which has been proven correct again and again since its mid-20 century development. Today, it is the gaps in the model that keep physicists busy. . . . Particle Physics Brick by Brick is a succinct introduction for anyone that wants to gain a basic understanding of the atomic world, its elements and how they interact." (Publisher's note)

540   Chemistry and allied sciences

Cobb, Cathy

Creations of fire; chemistry's lively history from alchemy to the atomic age. [by] Cathy Cobb and Harold Goldwhite. Perseus Pub. 2001 475p il pa $20.95 **540**

1. Chemistry -- History
ISBN 0-7382-0594-X; 978-0-7382-0594-6

LC 2001-99001

First published 1995 by Plenum Press

This history "begins with chemistry in the Stone Age and ends with current areas of interest such as superheavy elements and the polymerase chain reaction. Along the way, the coverage includes alchemy, cold fusion, and . . . topics like the contributions of Lise Meitner and Marie Lavoisier. . . . This book's light and often humorous style makes it especially appealing to the general reader." Libr J

Includes bibliographical references

The joy of chemistry; the amazing science of familiar things. [by] Cathy Cobb & Monty L. Fetterolf. Prometheus Books 2005 393p il hardcover o.p. pa $19 **540**

1. Chemistry
ISBN 1-591-02231-2; 1-591-02771-3 pa

LC 2004-20144

The authors cover "the material of a general chemistry course along with organic, inorganic and analytical chemistry and biochemistry; there's even a chapter on forensic chemistry. . . . They explain everything from flatulence (the chemical composition of intestinal gas) to pizza cheese (why mozzarella rather than, say, parmesan?)." Publ Wkly

Includes bibliographical references

Coffey, Patrick

Cathedrals of science; the personalities and rivalries that made modern chemistry. Oxford University Press 2008 379p il $29.95 **540**

1. Chemists 2. College teachers 3. Chemistry -- History 4. Science -- Ethical aspects 5. Nobel laureates for chemistry
ISBN 978-0-19-532134-0; 0-19-532134-0

LC 2007-48304

The author writes about the careers of such chemists as Gilbert Lewis, Irving Langmuir, Fritz Haber, Glenn Seaborg, Harold Urey, Linus Pauling, and Dorothy Wrinch.

This is "is an engaging, well-written, balanced account of 13 chemists who built modern chemistry." Choice

Includes bibliographical references

CRC Handbook of Chemistry and Physics; W. M. Haynes, editor-in-chief. 95th edition CRC Press 2014 various pagings $169.95 **540**

1. Reference books 2. Physics -- Tables 3. Chemistry -- Tables
ISBN 1482208679; 9781482208672
First published 1913. Periodically revised

A "reference book containing much-used information on mathematics, chemistry, and physics, including tables, physical constants of chemical elements and compounds, definitions, formulae, etc." AAAS Sci Book List for Young Adults

Includes bibliographical references

A dictionary of chemistry; edited by Richard Rennie and Jonathan Law. 7th edition Oxford University Press 2016 577 p. illustrations pbk $19.95 **540**

1. Chemistry -- Dictionaries
ISBN 0198722826; 9780198722823

'Fully revised and updated, the seventh edition of this popular dictionary is the ideal reference resource for students of chemistry, either at school or at university. With over 5000 entries--over 175 new to this edition--it covers all aspects of chemistry, from physical chemistry to biochemistry. The seventh edition boasts broader coverage in areas such as nuclear magnetic resonance, polymer chemistry, nanotechnology and graphene, and absolute configuration." (Publisher's note)

Greenberg, Arthur

From alchemy to chemistry in picture and story. Wiley-Interscience 2007 xxiii, 637p il $69.95 **540**

1. Chemistry -- History
ISBN 978-0-471-75154-0; 0-471-75154-5

LC 2006-33564

According to the author, this "is a combination of his two previous books, A Chemical History Tour and The Art of Chemistry, with some additions and revisions. . . . One could open the book at almost any page to learn something about the remarkable history of the chemical sciences." Sci Books Films

Includes bibliographical references

★ **Lange's** handbook of chemistry; James G. Speight. 17th edition McGraw-Hill 2016 $199 **540**

1. Chemistry 2. Chemistry -- Tables
ISBN 9781259586095; 125958609X
First published 1934. Periodically revised

"Lange's Handbook of Chemistry, 17th Edition, is divided into six sections--general information and conversion tables, spectroscopy, inorganic chemistry, organic chemistry, petroleum and petroleum products, biomass and biofuels, and environmental science. Existing tables have been thoroughly overhauled and new tables have been added that cover the properties of coal, minerals, natural gas, oil shale, and petroleum." (Publisher's note)

541 Chemistry

Atkins, Peter William, 1940-

Reactions; the private life of atoms. by Peter Atkins. Oxford University Press 2011 191 p. **541**

1. Chemical reactions
ISBN 9780199695126; 0199695121

LC 2011275047

The author "provides detailed descriptions of the reactions that occur in everyday life, using language that, while elevated, will be ac-

cessible for the armchair scientist. Each chapter focuses on a particular type of reaction, including: precipitation, neutralization, combustion, reduction, oxidation separately and in combination, catalysis, and more." Publ Wkly

Gray, Theodore

Molecules; The Elements and the Architecture of Everything. Theodore Gray; photography by Nick Mann. Black Dog & Leventhal Pub 2014 240 p. color illustrations $29.95 **541**

1. Molecules 2. Chemical elements
ISBN 1579129714; 9781579129712

This book by Theodore Grey "begins with an explanation of how atoms bond to form molecules and compounds, as well as the difference between organic and inorganic chemistry. He then goes on to explore the vast array of materials molecules can create." (Publisher's note)

"Readers who wish to learn more about chemistry would be better served with another work that isn't so strongly focused on photography. Those already familiar with the topic are sure to enjoy the images." LJ

546 Inorganic chemistry

Aldersey-Williams, Hugh, 1959-

Periodic tales; a cultural history of the elements, from arsenic to zinc. Ecco 2011 428p il $29.99 **546**

1. Periodic law 2. Chemical elements
ISBN 978-0-06-182472-2; 0-06-182472-0

"Because Aldersey-Williams's ultimate subject is human civilization rather than simply the elements, he gives himself room to expound on just about everything, treating the components of the table as though they were 'sorted by an anthropologist.' So his book is organized (loosely) into five sections: power (elements hoarded as riches or used to exert control); fire (elements that can best be understood by what happens when they are burned); craft (elements used to create and the cultural meaning we ascribe to them); beauty (elements used to 'colour our world'); and earth (elements that have marked the place where they were discovered in a notable way). It's an ambitious project. . . . [The book] is swollen with names, places, and long-forgotten (or simply unknown to most of us) figures, with zigzagging detours into almost every subject imaginable. It is almost more of a question of what the book does not touch upon than what it does." Boston Globe

Includes bibliographical references

Bernstein, Jeremy

Plutonium; a history of the world's most dangerous element. National Academies Press 2007 194p il map $27.95 **546**

1. Plutonium
ISBN 978-0-309-10296-4; 0-309-10296-0

LC 2006-38466

"Bernstein's book should play a useful role by helping to demystify plutonium and by encouraging interested members of the public and Congress to start constructing a more rational policy to deal with the dangers posed by this manmade element." Am Sci

Includes bibliographical references

Challoner, Jack

The **Elements**; The New Guide to the Building Blocks of Our Universe. Sterling Pub Co Inc. 2012 160 p. illustrations (chiefly color) $19.95 **546**

1. Atoms 2. Chemical elements
ISBN 023300436X; 1780971257; 9780233004365; 9781780971254

This book by Jack Challoner presents "both a concise, visual introduction to basic concepts about the atom and a short history of the elements and development of the periodic table, as well as a profile for each element organized by the appropriate color-coded periodic table grouping. Challoner has created an . . . up-to-date collection of profiles on the elements and how they affect our daily lives." (Library Journal)

Gray, Theodore

★ The **elements**; a visual exploration of every known atom in the universe. photographs by Theodore Gray and Nick Mann. Black Dog & Leventhal Publishers 2009 240p il $29.95 **546**

1. Periodic law 2. Chemical elements 3. Chemical elements -- Pictorial works

ISBN 1579128149; 9781579128142

LC 2009-34931

This is a collection of "photographic representations of the 118 elements in the periodic table. . . . [The book also contains] facts, figures, and stories of the elements as well as data on the properties of each, including atomic weight, density, melting and boiling point, valence, electronegativity, and the year and location in which it was discovered." (Publisher's note) Index.

This is a collection of "photographic representations of the 118 elements in the periodic table. . . . Organized in order of appearance on the periodic table, each element is represented by a spread that includes a . . . full-page, full-color photograph that most closely represents it in its purest form. . . . [Also included are] facts, figures, and stories of the elements as well as data on the properties of each, including atomic weight, density, melting and boiling point, valence, electronegativity, and the year and location in which it was discovered." Publisher's note

Includes bibliographical references

Kean, Sam

★ The **disappearing** spoon; and other true tales of madness, love, and the history of the world from the periodic table of the elements. Little, Brown and Co. 2010 391p $24.99 **546**

1. Chemical elements

ISBN 978-0-316-05164-4; 0-316-05164-0

LC 2009-40754

"Kean's traipse among the elements leads him through a warren of subjects, as he examines how these basic building blocks have factored prominently in astronomy, biology, literature, history, politics, and even cryptozoology. With the anecdotal flourishes of Oliver Sacks and the populist accessibility of Malcolm Gladwell, but without the latter's occasional facileness, he makes even the most abstract concepts graspable for armchair scientists. His keen sense of humor is a particular pleasure." Entertainment Wkly

Includes bibliographical references

Rigden, John S.

Hydrogen; the essential element. Harvard Univ. Press 2002 280p il $28; pa $15.95 **546**

1. Hydrogen 2. Science -- History

ISBN 0-674-00738-7; 0-674-01252-6 pa

LC 2001-51708

The author chronicles "how one enduring conundrum—that of explaining the element hydrogen—has challenged two centuries of brilliant scientists. . . . In the process, he clarifies for general readers the nature of the scientific enterprise, in which elegant theories must meet the test of empirical verification." Booklist

Includes bibliographical references

Zoellner, Tom

Uranium; war, energy, and the rock that shaped the world. Viking 2009 337p $26.95; pa $16 **546**

1. Uranium

ISBN 978-0-670-02064-5; 0-670-02064-8; 978-0-14-311672-1 pa; 0-14-311672-X pa

LC 2008-29023

This is an overview of the radioactive mineral.

"Zoellner vividly conveys both the potential benefits and the harm that uranium holds for human civilization. . . . Policymakers and citizens alike need to read 'Uranium.'" Washington Post Book World

Includes bibliographical references

547 Organic chemistry

Gorman, Hugh S.

The **story** of N; a social history of the nitrogen cycle and the challenge of sustainability. by Hugh S. Gorman. Rutgers University Press 2012 xiii, 241 p.p (Studies in modern science, technology, and the environment) (hardcover; alk. paper) $49.95 **547**

1. Nitrogen 2. Climate change 3. Sustainability 4. Nitrogen cycle 5. Sustainable development 6. Nitrogen -- Environmental aspects 7. Nature -- Effect of human beings on

ISBN 0813554381; 9780813554389; 9780813554396

LC 2012009901

In this book, author Hugh S. "Gorman analyzes the notion of sustainability from a fresh perspective--the integration of human activities with the biogeochemical cycling of nitrogen--and provides a supportive alternative to studying sustainability through the lens of climate change and the cycling of carbon." (Publisher's note)

Includes bibliographical references (p. 209-233) and index

549 Mineralogy

Bonewitz, Ronald

Rocks and minerals; Ronald Louis Bonewitz. 1st American ed. DK Publishing 2012 352 p. col. ill. (DK Smithsonian nature guide) $14.95 **549**

1. Rocks 2. Minerals

ISBN 0756690420 ; 9780756690427

LC 2012470083

"[P]acked full of stunning images that reveal intricate details and unique characteristics of each rock and mineral. . . . Us[es] close-up photographs of every specimen and profiles containing examples from all over the world [and] brings revealing key facets and details perfect for quick identification." (Publisher's note)

Chaline, Eric

Fifty minerals that changed the course of history; Eric Chaline. Firefly Books 2012 223 p. ill. (chiefly col.), ports. $29.95 **549**

1. Minerals 2. Mines and mineral resources

ISBN 1554079845; 9781554079841

This book by Eric Chaline is a "guide to the minerals that have had the greatest impact on human civilization. These are the materials used from the Stone Age to the First and Second Industrial Revolutions to the Nuclear Age and include metals, ores, alloys, salts, rocks, sodium, mercury, steel and uranium. The book also includes minerals used as currency, as jewelry and as lay and religious ornamentation when combined with gem minerals like diamonds, amber, coral, and jade." (Publisher's note)

Includes bibliographical references and index.

Chesterman, Charles W.

★ The **Audubon** Society field guide to North American rocks and minerals; scientific consultant, Kurt E. Lowe. Knopf 1979 850p il $19.95   **549**

   1. Rocks 2. Minerals

   ISBN 0-394-50269-8

                           LC 78-54893

   "Pocket guide providing color photos and descriptions of some 232 mineral species and forty types of rocks. Includes guide to mineral environments, glossary, bibliography, and indexes by name and locality." Ref Sources for Small & Medium-sized Libr. 5th edition

Harlow, George E.

Gems & Crystals; From One of the World's Great Collections. by George E. Harlow and Anna S. Sofianides. Sterling Pub Co Inc 2015 232 p. illustrations (chiefly color) (hardcover) $27.95   **549**

   1. Gems 2. Crystals

   ISBN 9781454917113; 1454917113

   This book, by George E. Harlow and Anna S. Sofianides, "showcases the . . . [American Museum of Natural History's] renowned collection and unlocks the science behind the dazzling properties of each gemstone species. Nearly 150 key varieties of gems and minerals are profiled, with information on their history, lore, and sources, as well as the relationships among the bewildering variety of crystals, minerals, rocks, and gemstones." (Publisher's note)

   "Recommended both for its reference value and as a coffee-table book, this title will appeal to geologists and lovers of the lapidary arts." LJ

   Includes bibliographical references (pages 201-205) and index.

Johnsen, Ole

Minerals of the world. Princeton Univ. Press 2002 439p il (Princeton field guides) pa $24.95   **549**

   1. Crystals 2. Minerals

   ISBN 0-691-09537-X

                           LC 2001-97695

   Originally published in hardcover with title: Photographic guide to minerals of the world

   The author "provides descriptive information for the identification of more than 500 minerals. . . . This book follows the standard mineralogy textbook approach in which the mineral sections are arranged according to mineral composition and structure. . . . The book's suitability as a field guide is completed by the addition of hundreds of excellent color photographs and drawings. . . . The content material is solid, and superb illustrations on high-quality paper make for an attractive volume." Choice

Klein, Cornelis

Manual of mineral science; [by] Cornelis Klein, Barbara Dutrow. 23rd ed; Wiley 2007 xxi, 675p il $150.95   **549**

   1. Minerals

   ISBN 978-0-471-72157-4; 0-471-72157-3

                           LC 2007-273750

   First published 1848 under the authorship of James D. Dana. Periodically revised. Variant title: Manual of mineralogy

   This is a standard introductory reference book for the use of students and collectors. It covers physical, chemical, determinative, and descriptive mineralogy, discusses mineral occurrence, association, and use, and includes both a subject and mineral index

Includes bibliographical references

Pough, Frederick H.

★ A **field** guide to rocks and minerals; photographs by Jeff Scovil. 5th ed; Houghton Mifflin 1996 396p il hardcover o.p. pa $20   **549**

   1. Rocks 2. Minerals

   ISBN 0-395-72778-2; 0-395-91096-X pa

                           LC 94-49005

   First published 1953

   This illustrated guide utilizes traditional identification methods and includes discussions of crystallography, mineralogy and home laboratory techniques.

   Includes bibliographical references

550   Earth sciences

Childs, Craig

Apocalyptic planet; field guide to the everending Earth. Craig Childs. Pantheon Books 2012 xvii, 343 p.p $27.95 **550**

   1. Earth 2. End of the world 3. Earth -- History -- Popular works

   ISBN 0307379094; 9780307379092

                           LC 2012006012

   In this book "[Craig] Childs makes clear that ours is not a stable planet, that it is prone to sudden, violent natural disasters and extremes of climate. Alternate futures, many not so pretty, are constantly waiting in the wings. Childs refutes the idea of an apocalyptic end to the earth and finds clues to its more inevitable end in some of the most physically challenging places on the globe." (Publisher's note)

   Includes bibliographical references (p. 331-343)

★ **Earth**; the definitive visual guide. editors-in-chief, James F. Luhr and Jeffrey E. Post. Revised and updated ed. DK Publishing 2013 528 p. ill. (chiefly col.) (hbk.) $50   **550**

   1. Earth 2. Earth (Planet) 3. Earth (Planet) -- Pictorial works

   ISBN 1465414371; 9781465414373

                           LC 2013444093

   First published 2003

   This book, edited by James F. Luhr, presents "insight into the forces and processes that formed our environment and which continue to influence its evolution. With thousands of . . . photographs and unique visual catalogues of the features and phenomena that take place on Earth -- such as rocks, minerals, and mountains to tropical rain forests and the different types of clouds -- [it] contains the most up-to-date ideas on how our world works." (Publisher's note)

   "Specially commissioned new 3-D digital artwork provides a striking, informative guide to the features of our planet, explains the scientific processes that govern our world, and looks at the complex relationship between humans and the natural environment." Publisher's note

Hazen, Robert M.

★ The **story** of Earth; the first 4.5 billion years, from stardust to living planet. Robert M. Hazen. Viking 2012 306 p.   **550**

   1. Evolution 2. Earth -- Age 3. Earth sciences 4. Earth -- Internal structure 5. Earth

   ISBN 0670023558; 9780670023554

                           LC 2011043713

   This book on the history of Earth, by Robert M. Hazen, argues that "'Earth's living and nonliving spheres' have co-evolved over the past four billion years. . . . Describing the 'discoveries of organisms in places long considered inhospitable [to life] - in superheated volcanic vents, acidic pools, Arctic ice and stratospheric dust,' he argues for the dating of the origin of life more than a billion years earlier than estimates based on Nobel Prize winner Harold Urey's groundbreaking experiments." (Kirkus Reviews)

Rudwick, Martin J. S.

Earth's deep history; how it was discovered and why it matters. Martin J. S. Rudwick. University of Chicago Press 2014 392 p. (cloth; alkaline paper) $30 **550**
1. Natural history 2. Religion and science 3. Earth sciences -- History 4. Natural history -- History
ISBN 022620393X; 9780226203935

LC 2014010242

This book, by Martin J. S. Rudwick, "begins in the seventeenth century with Archbishop James Ussher, who famously dated the creation of the cosmos to 4004 BC. His narrative then turns to the crucial period of the late eighteenth and early nineteenth centuries, when inquisitive intellectuals, who came to call themselves 'geologists,' began to interpret rocks and fossils, mountains and volcanoes, as natural archives of Earth's history." (Publisher's note)

"Rudwick's descriptions of the personalities and ideas in the development of "deep history" are fascinating, well written, and novel. His effective dismissal of 'young Earth creationism' in the appendix is classic." Choice
Includes bibliographical references and index

Shubin, Neil H., 1960-

The **universe** within; discovering the common history of rocks, planets, and people. Neil Shubin. Pantheon Books 2012 240 p. $25.95 **550**
1. Geology 2. Universe 3. Human body 4. Petrology 5. Earth -- Origin
ISBN 0307378438; 9780307378439

LC 2012007541

This book by Neil Shubin addresses "how . . . the events that formed our solar system billions of years ago [are] embedded inside each of us. . . . Starting . . . with fossils, [Shubin] turns his gaze skyward, showing us how the entirety of the universe's fourteen-billion-year history can be seen in our bodies. As he moves from our very molecular composition . . . to the workings of our eyes, Shubin makes clear how the evolution of the cosmos has profoundly marked our own bodies." (Publisher's note)
Includes bibliographical references and index.

Williams, David B.

Stories in stone; travels through urban geology. Walker 2009 260p il **550**
1. Urban geology
ISBN 978-0-8027-1622-4

LC 2009-5609

The author "describes the mineralogy and history of some of the world's most common building materials. . . . Each chapter showcases a different stone. By describing how the stones formed and how they are used, this book reveals that natural and cultural history may lie no farther than the building next door." Sci News
Includes bibliographical references

551 Geology, hydrology, meteorology

Flannery, Tim, 1956-

Here on Earth; a natural history of the planet. [by] Tim Flannery. Atlantic Monthly Press 2011 316p il **551**
1. Evolution 2. Earth sciences 3. Earth 4. Earth -- Origin 5. Evolution -- History 6. Earth sciences -- History
ISBN 080211976X; 9780802119766

The author "expands on the proposition that humans inherently exhaust their resources, triggering all manner of ecological and societal trauma. To evaluate the idea, he ranges over the entirety of human existence, remarking within each subtopic he raises--for example, the Aborigines' relation to Australian ecosystems--the ramifications of human use of available natural resources." Booklist
Includes bibliographical references

Lambert, David

The **field** guide to geology; [by] David Lambert and the Diagram Group. New ed.; Checkmark Books 2006 304p il map $39.95; pa $16.95 **551**
1. Geology
ISBN 0-8160-6509-8; 978-0-8160-6509-7; 0-8160-6510-1 pa; 978-0-8160-6510-3 pa

LC 2006-48533

First published 1988

This is an "overview of the processes that forged the planet and the technologies that have revolutionized the way that scientists investigate Earth's systems." Publisher's note
Includes bibliographical references

Whitehouse, David

Into the Heart of Our World; A Journey to the Center of the Earth: a Remarkable Voyage of Scientific Discovery. by David Whitehouse (Author) W W Norton & Co Inc 2016 288 p. illustrations (some color) $27.95 **551**
1. Geology 2. Planets 3. Earthquakes 4. Plate tectonics 5. Earth -- Internal structure
ISBN 1605989592; 9781605989594

In this book, by David Whitehouse, "The journey to the centre of the earth is a voyage like no other we can imagine. . . . Our planet appears tranquil from outer space. And yet the arcs of volcanoes, the earthquake zones and the auroral glow rippling above our heads are a testimony to something remarkable happenings within the earth's core. For thousands of years, these phenomena were explained in legend and myth. Only in recent times has the brave new science of seismology emerged." (Publisher's note)

"Whitehouse takes readers on a richly rewarding journey through space and time in this scientific travelogue." Kirkus

551.2 Volcanoes, earthquakes, thermal waters and gases

Feldman, Jay

★ **When** the Mississippi ran backwards; empire, intrigue, murder, and the new Madrid earthquakes. Free Press 2005 307p il maps $27 **551.2**
1. Mississippi River valley 2. Earthquakes -- United States
ISBN 0-7432-4278-5

LC 2004-57537

"Through four historical figures, Feldman recreates the frontier world of 1811-12, when the New Madrid earthquakes devastated the lower Ohio and mid-Mississippi valleys. . . . Synthesizing lives and times, Feldman composes a fluent, coherent narrative that culminates in the War of 1812." Booklist
Includes bibliographical references

Gates, Alexander E.

★ **Encyclopedia** of earthquakes and volcanoes; [by] Alexander E. Gates, Ph.D and David Ritchie. 3rd ed.; Facts on File 2007 346p il map (Facts on File science library) pa $21.95; $75 **551.2**

1. Reference books 2. Volcanoes -- Encyclopedias 3. Earthquakes -- Encyclopedias

ISBN 9780816071203; 0-8160-6302-8

LC 2005-46619

First published 1994

"The book's entries cover information on key environmental issues, economic dilemmas, ethical concerns, advances in research and technology, organizations, and individuals who have left their mark on the fields of volcanology and seismology." Publisher's note

Includes bibliographical references

Oppenheimer, Clive

Eruptions that shook the world. Cambridge University Press 2011 392p il map $30 **551.2**

1. Volcanoes

ISBN 978-0-521-64112-8

LC 2011004246

The author "pieces together our volcanic past by connecting major historic and prehistoric eruptions to the course of human civilization. . . . A fascinating work that will engage not just volcano experts but also those with an interest in history, climatology, archaeology, and geochronology." Libr J

Includes bibliographical references

Scarth, Alwyn

Vesuvius ; a biography. Princeton University Press 2009 342p il map $29.95 **551.2**

1. Volcanoes 2. Vesuvius (Italy)

ISBN 978-0-691-14390-3; 0-691-14390-0

LC 2009-925151

"Vesuvius has been central to Western civilization's unfolding understanding of volcanoes. While the detailed descriptions of historic eruptions here are valuable, if repetitious, the real strength of the book lies in the quotations from primary sources. These range from Pliny the Younger's description of the C.E. 79 eruption that destroyed Pompeii and Herculaneum, to medieval and Counter-Reformation reactions invoking the supernatural (after a brief naturalistic approach in the Renaissance), to the beginnings of a modern scientific understanding of volcanoes in the late 18th century with the work of Sir William Hamilton, the British envoy in Naples. The chronology concludes with current concerns about the safety of the increasing population around Vesuvius." Libr J

Includes bibliographical references

Winchester, Simon

Krakatoa ; the day the world exploded, August 27, 1883. HarperCollins Pubs. 2003 416p il maps $25.95; pa $13.95 **551.2**

1. Volcanoes

ISBN 0-06-621285-5; 0-06-083859-0 pa

"As a rich blend of science and history, this book is highly recommended for most public and academic libraries." Libr J

551.21 Volcanoes

Thompson, Dick

Volcano cowboys; the rocky evolution of a dangerous science. St. Martin's Press 2000 326p il map $26.95; pa $14.95 **551.21**

1. Volcanoes 2. Mount Saint Helens (Wash.)

ISBN 0-312-20881-2; 0-312-28668-6 pa

LC 00-26158

This describes the work of U.S. Geological Survey scientists in predicting volcanic eruptions, focusing on the eruptions of Mount St. Helens in 1980 and Mount Pinatubo in 1991

"An informative book about science's communication with the lay public." Booklist

Includes bibliographical references

551.22 Earthquakes

Dvorak, John

Earthquake Storms; The Fascinating History and Volatile Future of the San Andreas Fault. by John Dvorak. W W Norton & Co Inc 2014 352 p. illustrations $27.95 **551.22**

1. Faults (Geology) 2. California -- History 3. Earthquakes -- California

ISBN 1605984957; 9781605984957

LC 2014395154

Author John Dvorak "treats Californians and other tectonics enthusiasts to an enjoyable history of the Golden State's earthquakes alongside a bracing look at potential future ones. Dates, locations, magnitudes, and damage figures are all embedded in these stories of quakes and in the stories of those who studied them, like Andrew Lawson, the University of California geology professor who named the San Andreas Fault in 1895, and Charles Richter, developer of the eponymous magnitude scale." (Publishers Weekly)

"Although almost entirely focused on California, this is a fine popular primer on the subject, lucidly written and no more technical than necessary." Kirkus

Fountain, Henry

The **great** quake; how the biggest earthquake in North America changed our understanding of the planet. Henry Fountain. Crown 2017 vii, 277 p.p illustrations, maps (hardback) $28 **551.22**

1. Earthquakes 2. Natural history -- Alaska 3. Alaska Earthquake, Alaska, 1964 4. Geologists -- United States -- Biography 5. Prince William Sound Region (Alaska) -- History -- 20th century 6. Seismology -- Alaska -- Prince William Sound Region -- History -- 20th century 7. Earthquakes -- Alaska -- Prince William Sound Region -- History -- 20th century 8. Earthquake damage -- Alaska -- Prince William Sound Region -- History -- 20th century 9. Prince William Sound Region (Alaska) -- Environmental conditions -- History -- 20th century

ISBN 9781101904060; 9781101904077

LC 2016059373

This book, by Henry Fountain, "is a riveting narrative about the biggest earthquake in North American recorded history--the 1964 Alaska earthquake that demolished the city of Valdez and swept away the island village of Chenega--and the geologist who hunted for clues to explain how and why it took place. . . . [The author] combines history and science to bring the quake and its aftermath to life in vivid detail." (Publisher's note)

"A veteran science journalist illuminates the significance of the biggest earthquake ever recorded in North America." Kirkus

Includes bibliographical references (pages 248-269) and index.

Miles, Kathryn

Quakeland; on the road to America's next devastating earthquake. Kathryn Miles. Dutton 2017 viii, 357 p.p (hardcover) $28 **551.22**

1. Earthquakes -- United States 2. Earthquake prediction -- United States

ISBN 9780525955184; 9780698411463

LC 2017011994

In this book, by Kathryn Miles, "a journey around the United States in search of the truth about the threat of earthquakes leads to spine-tingling discoveries, unnerving experts, and ultimately the kind of preparations that will actually help guide us through disasters. It's a road trip full of surprises." (Publisher's note)

"Miles's fascinating volume is an eye-opener, demonstrating how this new knowledge impacts long-held beliefs about earthquakes, their occurrences, and their behavior." LJ

Includes bibliographical references and index

551.3   Surface and exogenous processes and their agents

Fredston, Jill

Snowstruck; in the grip of avalanches. [by] Jill Fredston. Harcourt 2005 342p il $24; pa $14 **551.3**

1. Avalanches 2. Survival skills 3. Mountaineers 4. Safety educators 5. Biography, Individual 6. Snow and ice climbing

ISBN 0-15-101249-0; 0-15-603254-6 pa; 978-0-15-101249-7; 978-0-15-603254-4 pa

LC 2005-20454

This is a memoir by the avalance expert Jill Fredston. Fredston forecasts "where and when [avalanches] will strike, deliberately triggering them with explosives, teaching potential victims how to stay alive, and leading rescue efforts when tragedy strikes." (Publisher's note)

"As avalanche experts, . . . [the author and her husband] are often called upon to forecast, trigger, and teach about avalanches as well as rescue survivors—or, sadly, more often to recover remains. Fredston's decades of experience distilled into this instructive and personal narrative will leave readers with a newfound appreciation for the force, the fury, and the cold sorrow of avalanches." Libr J

Gosnell, Mariana

Ice; the nature, the history, and the uses of an astonishing substance. Knopf 2005 560p il $30 **551.3**

1. Ice

ISBN 0-679-42608-6

LC 2005-45126

The author "opens with a description of the sound and sight of a small lake freezing, expanding from there to discuss the seasonal advance and retreat of ice, as on the Great Lakes or Lake Baikal. Taking the next natural step, the persistence of ice through the summer, brings Gosnell to the 1800s origin of glaciology in Louis Agassiz's study of Mont Blanc's Mer de Glace, and subsequently into the contemporary specialty of ice cores in ice-age research. En route through the science, which Gosnell condenses from the technical literature, the author imparts eclectic information through excerpts from poems, adventure and disaster stories, and discussions of ice sports and diversions." Booklist

Pollack, H. N.

A world without ice; [by] Henry Pollack. Avery 2009 287p il map $26; pa $16 **551.3**

1. Ice 2. Glaciers 3. Greenhouse effect

ISBN 978-1-58333-357-0; 978-1-58333-407-2 pa

LC 2009-30326

"Seldom has a scientist written so well and so clearly for the lay reader. Pollack's explanations of how researchers can tell that the climate is warming faster than normal are free of the usual scientific jargon and understandable. All readers concerned about global warming and students writing papers on the topic will want this excellent and important volume." Libr J

Includes bibliographical references

551.41   Geomorphology

Streever, Bill

Heat; adventures in the world's fiery places. Bill Streever. Little, Brown, and Co. 2013 368 p. (hardback) $26.99 **551.41**

1. Fire 2. Heat 3. Arid regions -- Description and travel

ISBN 0316105333; 9780316105330

LC 2012020861

In this book, Bill Streever "explores any place hot or anything that creates heat, like Death Valley, forest fires, coal, oil, nuclear bombs, cooking, and volcanoes. . . . In this . . . companion to 'Cold,' Streever is able to mix the pop science, personal experiences, and historic asides into a . . . commentary on a subject that few people think about." (Publishers Weekly)

551.432   Mountains

Messner, Reinhold

Mountains; Mapping the Earth's Extremes. Stefan Dech, Reinhold Messner, and Nils Sparwasser. Thames & Hudson Inc. 2016 241 p. color illustrations (hardcover) $55 **551.432**

1. Earth 2. Geology 3. Mountain mapping 4. Image processing -- Digital techniques 5. Mountains -- Discovery and exploration

ISBN 9780500518892; 9781938340055; 0500518890

LC 2016931310

This book, by Stefan Dech, Reinhold Messner, and Nils Sparwasser, "marks a new milestone in Earth observation and Alpine exploration. For the first time, a special recording process and a technique developed at the German Aerospace Center (DLR) allow the satellite recording of three-dimensional views from 300 miles above with a resolution in the range of a few meters. Photorealistic images are created in this manner from perspectives denied even to mountaineers and helicopter pilots." (Publisher's note)

"This exceptional and beautiful book effectively combines technology, geography, and human adventure in such a way that the reader is compelled to return to it again and again—rereading passages and reviewing the images." Choice

551.45   Plane and coastal regions

Goodell, Jeff

The water will come; rising seas, sinking cities, and the remaking of the civilized world. Jeff Goodell. Little, Brown & Co. 2017 340 p. illustrations (hc) $28 **551.45**

1. Floods 2. Sea level 3. Climate change 4. Climatic changes 5. Flood forecasting 6. Sea level -- Forecasting

ISBN 9780316260220; 9780316260206; 9780316260244

LC 2017947000

This book, by Jeff Goodell, describes how "across the globe, scientists and civilians alike are noticing rapidly rising sea levels, and higher and higher tides pushing more water directly into the places we live. . . . [It] is the definitive account of the coming water, why and how this will happen, and what it will all mean." (Publisher's note)

"A frightening, scientifically grounded, and starkly relevant look at how climate change will affect coastal cities." Kirkus

Includes bibliographical references (pages 303-330) and index.

Rush, Elizabeth

Rising; dispatches from the new American shore. Elizabeth Rush. Milkweed Editions 2018 320 p. (hardcover) $26 **551.45**

1. Climate 2. Climate change 3. Coasts -- Climatic factors -- United States 4. Sea level -- Climatic factors -- United States 5. Coast changes -- Climatic factors -- United States

ISBN 9781571313676

LC 2017059870

In this book, author Elizabeth Rush "guides readers through some of the places where . . . [climate] change has been most dramatic, from the Gulf Coast to Miami, and from New York City to the Bay Area. For many of the plants, animals, and humans in these places, the options are stark: retreat or perish in place. Weaving firsthand accounts from those facing this choice, . . . [this book] privileges the voices of those usually kept at the margins." (Publisher's note)

Includes bibliographical references

551.46   Oceanography and submarine geology

Ballard, Robert D.

The **eternal** darkness; a personal history of deep-sea exploration. {by} Robert D. Ballard with Will Hively. Princeton Univ. Press 2000 388p il maps $55; pa $18.95   **551.46**

1. Underwater exploration

ISBN 0-691-02740-4; 0-691-09554-X pa

LC 99-43072

Ballard "blends his personal experiences exploring hydrothermal vents and shipwrecks with stories of earlier deep-sea pioneers, focusing especially on the technology. . . . Ballard's volume is easy to read and will be an excellent addition to collections at all levels on oceanography, history of science, and exploration." Libr J

Includes bibliographical references

Carson, Rachel, 1907-1964

The **sea** around us. Oxford Univ. Press 2003 274p il maps $45   **551.46**

1. Ocean 2. Oceanography

ISBN 0-19-514701-4

LC 2002-29299

This is a reissue of the title first published 1951

This is a new edition of a "work originally published in 1951 and revised in 1961." (Sci Books Films)

Casey, Susan

The **wave**; in pursuit of the rogues, freaks and giants of the ocean. Doubleday 2010 326p il map $27.95   **551.46**

1. Surfing 2. Ocean waves

ISBN 978-0-7679-2884-7; 0-7679-2884-9

LC 2010-10193

Casey "estimates that freak waves might have a hand in sinking about two dozen large ships every year. She embarked on a five-year odyssey to meet the people who know these monsters best—from salvagers working a graveyard of ships off the South African coast to a convention of wave scientists, from researchers and mariners who have

battled these beasts to surfers who roam the world in search of the ultimate thrill. Reading the 'The Wave' is almost like riding one, paddling in the expositional surf of vivid imagery and colorful description, thrown at you in ever-escalating surges." Cleveland Plain Dealer

Includes bibliographical references

Day, Trevor

Oceans; illustrations by Richard Garratt. rev ed; Facts on File 2008 318p il map (Ecosystem) $70   **551.46**

1. Ocean 2. Oceanography

ISBN 0-8160-5932-2; 978-0-8160-5932-4

LC 2006-100769

First published 1999

This volume describes the oceans of the world with regard to their geography, geology, history, chemistry, biology, ecology, exploration, relationship to the atmosphere, economic resources, and management.

Includes glossary and bibliographical references

Earle, Sylvia A.

The **world** is blue; how our fate and the ocean's are one. National Geographic 2009 303p il map $26   **551.46**

1. Oceanography 2. Marine biology 3. Marine ecology 4. Marine pollution 5. Human influence on nature

ISBN 978-1-4262-0541-5; 1-4262-0541-4

LC 2009-23972

The author "illustrates, in ways both humorous and discomforting, how our cavalier attitude toward the ocean and its inhabitants is causing our slow but certain destruction. Even more importantly, Earle offers solutions and discusses ongoing actions that have been taken to reverse this frightening cycle of obliteration. Even those who do not consider themselves environmentalists will find themselves easily caught up in Earle's heroic fight to save our 'blue world.'" Choice

Includes bibliographical references (p. 286-303)

Hohn, Donovan

Moby-Duck; The True Story of 28,800 Bath Toys Lost at Sea. Donovan Hohn. Viking 2011 402p. map (pbk) $16   **551.46**

1. Journalism 2. Oceanography

ISBN 0-670-02219-5; 978-0-670-02219-9; 9780143120506

LC 2010-33608

"When the writer Donovan Hohn heard of the mysterious loss of thousands of bath toys at sea, he figured he would interview a few oceanographers, talk to a few beachcombers, and read up on Arctic science and geography... Hohn's accidental odyssey pulls him into the secretive arena of shipping conglomerates, the daring work of Arctic researchers, the lunatic risks of maverick sailors, and the shadowy world of Chinese toy factories." (Publisher's note)

A "thoroughly engaging environmental/travel title that crosses partisan divides with its solid research and apolitical nature." Booklist

Nichols, C. Reid

Encyclopedia of marine science; [by] C. Reid Nichols and Robert G. Williams. Facts on File 2009 626p il map (Facts on File science library) $85   **551.46**

1. Reference books 2. Marine sciences -- Encyclopedias

ISBN 978-0-8160-5022-2; 0-8160-5022-8

LC 2007-45166

"The expert contributors have packed these pages with top-notch information that will be invaluable to students and reference librarians." SLJ

Includes bibliographical references

Roberts, Callum

The **ocean** of life; the fate of man and the sea. Callum Roberts. Viking 2012 405 p. paperback $17; hardcover o.p. **551.46**

1. Ocean 2. Ocean mining 3. Human ecology 4. Climate change 5. Marine ecology 6. Ocean -- History 7. Ocean and civilization

ISBN 9780143123484; 9780670023547; 067002354X

LC 2012000252

This book by Callum Roberts addresses how the ocean "has been used as a dumping ground while being indiscriminately overharvested." It also looks at "noise pollution, invasive species, plastic pollution, and the effects of climate change on reefs and sea levels as well as ocean acidification. . . . Roberts . . . provides . . . arguments against some of the technological 'fixes' some scientists have proposed." (Choice: Current Reviews for Academic Libraries)

Includes bibliographical references and index.

Stow, Dorrik A. V.

★ **Oceans** ; an illustrated reference; [by] Dorrik Stow. University of Chicago Press 2006 256p il map $55 **551.46**

1. Ocean 2. Oceanography 3. Marine biology

ISBN 0-226-77664-6

LC 2004-55333

This "reference work presents a thorough overview of the physical, geological, chemical, and biological properties of the world's oceans. . . . [The author's] up-to-date and well-organized volume would make a valuable introduction to a huge field of knowledge." Libr J

Includes bibliographical references

Ulanski, Stan L.

The **Gulf** Stream; tiny plankton, giant bluefin, and the amazing story of the powerful river in the Atlantic. [by] Stan Ulanski. University of North Carolina Press 2008 212p il map $28; pa $22 **551.46**

1. Gulf Stream

ISBN 978-0-8078-3217-2; 0-8078-3217-0; 978-0-8078-8709-7 pa; 0-8078-8709-9 pa

LC 2008-4746

This "book provides the layperson a synopsis of the physical origin, general biology, and rich exploration history of the Gulf Stream. Ulanski . . . offers a concise, engaging blend of science and history for anyone interested in learning about the general flow dynamics, the intricate food webs, and the human use and exploitation of this vital western-boundary current of the North Atlantic Ocean." Choice

Includes bibliographical references

Winchester, Simon

Atlantic; great sea battles, heroic discoveries, titanic storms, and a vast ocean of a million stories. Harper 2010 495p il map $27.99 **551.46**

1. Atlantic Ocean

ISBN 978-0-06-170258-7; 0-06-170258-7

LC 2010-15229

"Writing the history of the Atlantic Ocean — from tectonic labor pains to its lead role in modern European and American history — might be one of the more difficult tasks Simon Winchester has set for himself. . . . Luckily, the author comes armed with a knowledge almost as vast and deep as his subject, as well as a clever yet functional organizational scheme that divides his oceanic biography Atlantic into the seven ages of a man's life as proposed by Shakespeare. A formidable writer and storyteller, Winchester still gets distracted by the occasional unworthy anecdote or superfluous specificity, but for all the densely packed infor-

mation in this work, the one thing it never becomes, quite appropriately, is dry." Entertainment Wkly

551.464 Tides

Aldersey-Williams, Hugh, 1959-

The **tide**; The Science and Stories Behind the Greatest Force on Earth. Hugh Aldersey-Williams. W W Norton & Co Inc 2016 368 p. illustrations (ebook) $50; (hardcover) $27.95 **551.464**

1. Tides

ISBN 9780393243109; 9780393241631

LC 2016018456

This book, by Hugh Aldersey-Williams, is an "exploration into the science and history behind the most mysterious, primal, and powerful force on earth: the tide. . . . He visits the Bay of Fundy in Nova Scotia, where the tides are the strongest in the world; arctic Norway, home of the raging tidal whirlpool known as the maelstrom; and Venice, to investigate efforts to defend the city against flooding caused by the famed acqua alta." (Publisher's note)

"An engaging exploration of the profound historical relationship between science and culture, written in a lively style with clear scientific explanations." Kirkus

Includes bibliographical references and index

551.48 Hydrology

Montgomery, David R.

★ The **rocks** don't lie; a geologist investigates Noah's flood. David R. Montgomery. W.W. Norton 2012 320 p. (hardcover) $26.95 **551.48**

1. Geology 2. Noah's ark 3. Creationism 4. Paleohydrology 5. Paleolimnology

ISBN 0393082393; 9780393082395

LC 2012015146

In this book, geologist David R. Montgomery "offers a . . . critique of creationist worldviews (including Noah's flood) . . . , reflecting on both ancient and modern debates . . . . He admits that geologists have often stifled dissent and stubbornly rejected the idea that massive floods could have ever occurred, discounting such ideas as myths though there have, in fact, been many throughout human history." (Library Journal)

Includes bibliographical references and index

551.5 Meteorology

Buckley, Bruce

Weather ; a visual guide; [by] Bruce Buckley, Edward J. Hopkins [and] Richard Whitaker. Firefly Books 2004 303p il maps $29.95; pa $27.95 **551.5**

1. Weather 2. Meteorology

ISBN 1-55297-957-1; 978-1-55297-957-0; 1-55407-430-4 pa; 978-1-55407-430-3 pa

LC 2004-303909

This is "a comprehensive academic resource with information and glorious color photographs on virtually every aspect of weather." SLJ

Dewdney, Christopher

18 miles; the epic drama of our atmosphere and its weather.

by Christopher Dewdney. ECW Press 2018 320 p. illustrations $17.95   **551.5**

1. Climate 2. Weather 3. Meteorology 4. Atmosphere 5. Climatology 6. Weather forecasting

ISBN 1770413464; 9781770413467

In this book, author "Chris Dewdney reveals to us the invisible rivers in the sky that affect how our weather works and the structure of clouds and storms and seasons, the rollercoaster of climate. Dewdney details the history of weather forecasting and introduces us to the eccentric and determined pioneers of science and observation whose efforts gave us the understanding of weather we have today." (Publisher's note)

"Equal parts science, historical journey, and whimsical reflection that traces to Dewdney's childhood fascination with meteorology, this book marks an accessible and enjoyable entry into a field more often characterized by dry, uninspired texts." Pub Wkly

Includes bibliographical references (pages 243-248) and index

Logan, William Bryant

Air; the restless shaper of the world. William Bryant Logan. W.W. Norton & Co. 2012 416 p. (hardcover) $26.95   **551.5**

1. Air 2. Atmosphere 3. Air pollution 4. Environmental protection 5. Air -- Social aspects

ISBN 039306798X; 9780393067989

LC 2012013823

This environmental book by William Bryant Logan discusses air. "Air sustains the living. Every creature breathes to live, exchanging and changing the atmosphere. . . . Ignorance of the air is costly. The artist Eva Hesse died of inhaling her fiberglass medium. Thousands were sickened after 9/11 by supposedly 'safe' air." The author describes the scope of the atmospheric ecosystem and the importance of its preservation. (Publisher's note)

"For everyone who has wondered just how a 747 manages to get off the ground, luxuriated in the intoxicating aroma of a bed of roses, or marveled at a tropical sunset, Logan's meticulously researched and engagingly presented treatise is a breath of, well, fresh air." Booklist

Includes bibliographical references and index

McGuire, Bill

Waking the giant; how a changing climate triggers earthquakes, tsunamis, and volcanoes. Bill McGuire. Oxford University Press 2012 xiv, 303 p.p (acid-free paper) $29.95 **551.5**

1. Climate change 2. Natural disasters 3. Tsunamis 4. Earthquakes 5. Volcanic eruptions 6. Climatic changes -- Environmental aspects

ISBN 0199592268; 9780199592265

LC 2011278933

This book by Bill McGuire describes how "an astonishing transformation over the last 20,000 years has seen . . . not only a huge temperature hike but also the Earth's crust bouncing and bending in response to the melting of the great ice sheets and the filling of the ocean basins. . . . McGuire argues that now that human activities are driving climate change as rapidly as anything seen in post-glacial times, the sleeping giant beneath our feet is stirring once again." (Publisher's note)

Includes bibliographical references (p. 271-282) and index

Williams, Jack

★ The **AMS** weather book; the ultimate guide to America's weather. University of Chicago Press 2009 316p il map $35   **551.5**

1. Climate 2. Weather 3. Meteorology

ISBN 0-226-89898-9; 978-0-226-89898-8

LC 2008-35916

This book "provides a clearly written, profusely illustrated narra-

tive guide to weather that affects the US. . . . Topics in this 12-chapter volume range from how rainbows are formed and what makes the wind blow, to climate change and how weather satellites work. In addition, Williams highlights profiles of meteorologists and other scientists influential in weather prediction and research, including many women and minorities. This work, with its attractive, easy-to-understand graphics, offers a useful, engaging basic introduction to a wide variety of weather-related topics." Choice

Includes glossary

Wohlleben, Peter, 1964-

The **weather** detective; rediscovering nature's secret signs. Peter Wohlleben ; translated by Ruth Ahmedzai Kemp. Penguin Group USA 2018 208 p. $20   **551.5**

1. Nature 2. Gardens 3. Weather

ISBN 1524743747; 9781524743741

In this book, translated by Ruth Ahmedzai Kemp, author "Peter Wohlleben uses his long experience and deep love of nature to help decipher the weather and our local environments in a completely new and compelling way. . . . At what temperature do bees stay home? Why do southerly winds in winter often bring storms? How can birdsong or flower scents help you tell the time? These are among the many questions Wohlleben poses in his newly translated book." (Publisher's note)

"An inviting and easily understandable look at weather and natural phenomena that will appeal to weather, nature, and gardening buffs, and all who want a better understanding of nature's processes." Library Journal

551.51   Composition, regions, dynamics of atmosphere

Kean, Sam

Caesar's last breath; decoding the secrets of the air around us. Sam Kean. Little, Brown & Co. 2017 viii, 373 p.p illustrations (hardcover) $28   **551.51**

1. Chemistry 2. Philosophy -- History 3. Air 4. Atmosphere

ISBN 9780316465199; 9780316381642

LC 2016954781

This book, by Sam Kean, "takes us on a journey through the periodic table, around the globe, and across time to tell the story of the air we breathe, which, it turns out, is also the story of earth and our existence on it. . . . Tracing the origins and ingredients of our atmosphere, Kean reveals how the alchemy of air reshaped our continents, steered human progress, powered revolutions, and continues to influence everything we do." (Publisher's note)

"A witty book that turns the science of the stuff we breathe into a delightful romp through history." Kirkus

Includes bibliographical references (pages 357-362) and index.

Marder, Michael

Dust; Michael Marder. Bloomsbury Academic 2016 xii, 129 p.p illustrations (pbk.; alk. paper) $16.95   **551.51**

1. Dust 2. Spraying and dusting 3. Allergens 4. Particles 5. Cosmic dust 6. Sweeping and dusting

ISBN 1628925582; 9781628921717; 9781628925586

LC 2015024508

In this book, by Michael Marder, "no matter how much you fight against it, dust pervades everything. It gathers in even layers, adapting to the contours of things and marking the passage of time. In itself, it is also a gathering place, a random community of what has been and what is yet to be, a catalog of traces and a set of promises: dead skin cells and plant pollen, hair and paper fibers, not to mention dust mites who make it their home." (Publisher's note)

Includes bibliographical references and index

551.55 Atmospheric disturbances and formations

Emanuel, Kerry A.

Divine wind; the history and science of hurricanes. [by] Kerry Emanuel. Oxford Univ. Press 2005 285p il $45 **551.55**

1. Hurricanes

ISBN 0-19-514941-6

LC 2004-13078

This is a study of hurricanes.

"A gripping popular treatment of peril, that will have great resonance in light of recent disasters." Booklist

Includes bibliographical references

Miles, Kathryn

Superstorm; nine days inside Hurricane Sandy. Kathryn Miles. Dutton, Penguin Group USA 2014 368 p. color illustrations, color map (hardback) $27.95 **551.55**

1. Disaster relief 2. Hurricane Sandy, 2012 3. Weather broadcasting -- United States 4. Hurricanes -- United States -- History -- 21st century

ISBN 0525954406; 9780525954408

LC 2014031087

This book, by Kathryn Miles, profiles the events of Hurricane Sandy in 2012 and offers "the first complete moment-by-moment account of the largest Atlantic storm system ever recorded. . . . Sandy was not just enormous, it was also unprecedented. . . . journalist Kathryn Miles takes readers inside the maelstrom, detailing the stories of dedicated professionals at the National Hurricane Center and National Weather Service." (Publisher's note)

"Miles spends a lot of time talking not just about the storm's severity and significance (there hadn't been anything quite like it before) but also about the people who saw the early warning signs but didn't understand what they meant (one weather-forecasting center was warned the storm was coming, but the forecasted storm seemed so impossible that they dismissed the warnings as a computer anomaly). A fascinating and often moving account of a widely talked about disaster." Booklist

Includes bibliographical references and index

Sandlin, Lee

★ **Storm** kings; the untold history of America's first tornado chasers. Lee Sandlin. Pantheon Books 2013 xxv, 266 p., [16] p. of platesp ill., maps (hardcover) $26.95 **551.55**

1. Tornadoes 2. Storm chasers

ISBN 0307378527; 9780307378521

LC 2012027314

This book, by Lee Sandlin, "explores America's fascination with and unique relationship to tornadoes. . . . Drawing on memoirs, letters, eyewitness testimonies, and archives, Sandlin brings to life the forgotten characters and scientists who changed a nation--including James Espy, America's first meteorologist, and Colonel John Park Finley, who helped place a network of weather 'spotters' across the country." (Publisher's note)

Sobel, Adam

Storm surge; Hurricane Sandy, our changing climate, and extreme weather of the past and future. by Adam Sobel. HarperCollins 2014 336 p. 8 plates; color ills., maps $27.99 **551.55**

1. Weather 2. Hurricanes 3. Climate change 4. Hurricane Sandy,

2012

ISBN 0062304763; 9780062304766

In this book, atmospheric scientist Adam Sobel, "takes us through the devastating and unprecedented events of Hurricane Sandy, using it to explain our planet's changing climate, and what we need to do to protect ourselves and our cities for the future. Was Hurricane Sandy a freak event-- or a harbinger of things to come? Was climate change responsible?" (Publisher's note)

"In 28 absorbing and instructive chapters, Sobel recounts the full history of the hurricane, including its warning signs and an explanation of the weather anomalies that forced Sandy to make a sudden left turn into the New Jersey coastline. He also explores the debate about how much climate change played a role in Sandy's devastating impact and examines how we can better respond to other extreme weather events. Must reading for earth-science and weather buffs and anyone living along the vulnerable passageways of potential future hurricanes." Booklist

551.56 Atmospheric electricity and optics

Bogard, Paul

The **end** of night; searching for natural darkness in an age of artificial light. Paul Bogard. Little, Brown and Co. 2013 336 p. $27 **551.56**

1. Sky 2. Light 3. Night 4. Light pollution 5. Lighting -- Social aspects 6. Night -- Psychological aspects 7. Lighting -- Physiological aspects

ISBN 0316182907; 9780316182904

LC 2012027287

Author Paul Bogard presents a "blend of environmental and cultural history . . . about light pollution. As he travels the world looking for dark spaces that best reveal the night skies, Bogard considers our affinity for artificial light, the false sense of security it provides, and its implications. He studies the skies of Las Vegas and Paris, Walden Pond and Mantua, Italy. He walks with lighting designers, naturalists, and astronomers while pondering the best way to embrace the night." (Booklist)

"In this artful blend of environmental and cultural history, Bogard manages to make a book about light pollution pure reading pleasure." Booklist

Includes bibliographical references

551.57 Hydrometeorology

Barnett, Cynthia

★ **Rain**; a natural and cultural history. Cynthia Barnett. Crown Publishers 2014 368 p. (hardcover) $25 **551.57**

1. Rain 2. Weather 3. Droughts 4. Rain and rainfall 5. Physical geography 6. Rainfall anomalies

ISBN 0804137099; 9780804137096; 9780804137119

LC 2014034180

This book by Cynthia Barnett "begins four billion years ago with the torrents that filled the oceans, and builds to the storms of climate change. It weaves together science--the true shape of a raindrop, the mysteries of frog and fish rains--with the human story of our ambition to control rain, from ancient rain dances to the 2,203 miles of levees that attempt to straitjacket the Mississippi River." (Publisher's note)

Barnett "explores every facet of the substance. A seamless blending of personal narrative with scientific and cultural explanations makes the book both informative and entertaining." LJ

Includes bibliographical references and index

Hamblyn, Richard

The **invention** of clouds; how an amateur meteorologist forged the language of the skies. Picador 2002 292p il pa $15   **551.57**

1. Clouds 2. Chemists 3. Meteorology 4. Meteorologists

ISBN 0-312-42001-3; 978-0-312-42001-7

LC 2002-25152

First published 2001 by Farrar, Straus and Giroux

This is a study of Luke Howard, an unknown amateur scientist who in 1802 "gave a lecture in which he named and defined the different types of clouds-cirrus, cumulus, stratus and their various hybrid forms. . . . [His taxonomy] gave scientists a standardised way to record and compare observations and begin to form theories." Economist

Includes bibliographical references

551.6   Climatology and weather

DeBuys, William Eno

A **great** aridness; climate change and the future of the American southwest. [by] William deBuys. Oxford University Press 2011 369p il map   **551.6**

1. Droughts 2. Water supply 3. Southwestern States 4. Climate -- Environmental aspects

ISBN 978-0-19-977892-8

LC 2011033298

The author discusses "the untenable water situation in the Southwest. . . . While he focuses on the environmental science of heat and aridity, he also acknowledges the uncertain nature of climate variability itself. . . . With wide-eyed wonder and the clearest of prose, deBuys explains why we should care about these places, the people he portrays, and the conundrums over land and water he illuminates." Booklist

Includes bibliographical references

Dow, Kirstin, 1963-

The **atlas** of climate change; mapping the world's greatest challenge. Kirstin Dow and Thomas E. Downing. 3rd edition University of California Press 2011 128 p. col. ill., col. maps pbk $24.95   **551.6**

1. Atlases 2. Climate 3. Reference books

ISBN 9780520268234

LC 2011922284

First published 2006

"This atlas examines the causes of climate change and considers its possible impact on subsistence, water resources, ecosystems, biodiversity, health, coastal megacities, and cultural treasures. It reviews historical contributions to greenhouse gas levels, progress in meeting international commitments, and local efforts to meet the challenge of climate change." Publisher's note

Includes bibliographical references

Dumanoski, Dianne

The **end** of the long summer; why we must remake our civilization to survive on a volatile Earth. Crown Publishers 2009 311p $25   **551.6**

1. Climate -- Environmental aspects

ISBN 978-0-307-39607-5; 0-307-39607-X

LC 2009-281272

An environmental journalist discusses the possible ecological consequences beyond global warming resulting from modern human activity and describes the possibility of massive instability and climate swings, including a possible return to ice ages of the past.

"A passionate, precise account of climate change and a persuasive strategy for dealing with 'Nature's return to center stage as a critical player in human history.'" Kirkus

Includes bibliographical references

Fleming, James Rodger

Fixing the sky; the checkered history of weather and climate control. [by] James Rodger Fleming. Columbia University Press 2010 325p il (Columbia studies in international and global history) $27.95   **551.6**

1. Global warming 2. Weather control 3. Human influence on nature 4. Climatic changes

ISBN 978-0-231-14412-4

LC 2010-15482

This book "should be read by all who want a better understanding of global climate change and the debate over geoengineering our environment." Sci Books Films

Includes bibliographical references

Fry, Juliane L.

The **encyclopedia** of weather and climate change; a complete visual guide. [authors, Juliane L. Fry ... et al.] University of California Press 2010 512 p. col. ill., col. maps   **551.6**

1. Reference books 2. Weather -- Encyclopedias 3. Climatology -- Encyclopedias 4. Meteorology -- Encyclopedias 5. Climatic changes -- Encyclopedias

ISBN 0520261011; 9780520261013

LC 2009943908

"Major sections fall under the following headings: Engine, Action, Extremes, Watching, Climate, and Change. Chapters within the sections begin with a broad overview of a particular topic, then move on to greater detail. The regional climate guide, focusing on 43 specific locations around the world, is particularly noteworthy. . . . The profuse illustrations carry the information; this title could be just the thing for visual learners." Libr J

Includes index.

Goodell, Jeff

How to cool the planet; geoengineering and the audacious quest to fix Earth's climate. Houghton Mifflin Harcourt 2010 262p $26   **551.6**

1. Greenhouse effect 2. Climate -- Environmental aspects

ISBN 978-0-618-99061-0; 0-618-99061-5

LC 2009-46565

"There is no trace of climate alarmism or political advocacy here. Goodell takes a detailed look at the range of hard choices humanity faces and explores how complicated moral and ethical considerations will dictate our response. Goodell is also a skilled writer. He splices complicated ideas into pithy turns of phrase." Business Week

Includes bibliographical references

Linden, Eugene

The **winds** of change; climate, weather, and the destruction of civilizations. Simon & Schuster 2006 302p il map $26   **551.6**

1. Climate 2. Weather 3. Social change

ISBN 0-684-86352-9; 978-0-684-86352-8

LC 2005-54434

"Relatively restrained in tone, and consequently more persuasive by its sobriety, Linden's presentation of scientists' theories on historical climate change will provoke readers concerned about the implications of global warming for modern civilization." Booklist

Lynas, Mark, 1973-

★ **Six** degrees; our future on a hotter planet. National Geographic 2008 335p $26   **551.6**

1. Environmental influence on humans 2. Greenhouse effect 3. Climate -- Environmental aspects

ISBN 978-1-4262-0213-1

LC 2007-30864

First published 2007 in the United Kingdom

"In 2001, the Intergovernmental Panel on Climate Change released a landmark report projecting average global surface temperatures to rise between 1.4 degrees and 5.8 degrees Celsius (roughly 2 to 10 degrees Fahrenheit) by the end of this century. Based on this forecast, author Mark Lynas outlines what to expect from a warming world, degree by degree." Publisher's note

Includes bibliographical references

Marshall, George

Don't Even Think About It; Why Our Brains Are Wired to Ignore Climate Change. George Marshall. St. Martin's Press 2014 272 p. $27; (ebook) $39.00   **551.6**

1. Climate change -- Public opinion

ISBN 1620401339; 9781620401330; 9781620401347

This book by George Marshall examines why "people have difficulty accepting climate change, even when presented with mountains of evidence. He draws heavily upon interviews with scientists and policy makers, as well as with individuals who have faced the ravages of severe flood or drought. . . . Marshall concludes by pointing out that multiple interpretations of climate change contain the central reason we can ignore it." (Publishers Weekly)

"His work is a much-needed kick in the pants for policymakers, grassroots environmentalists, and the public to induce us to develop effective motivational tools to help us take action to face the reality of climate change before it's too late." Booklist

Includes bibliographical references (pages 243-246) and index.

Pearce, Fred

With speed and violence; why scientists fear tipping points in climate change. Beacon Press 2007 xxvi, 278p $24.95; pa $15   **551.6**

1. Greenhouse effect 2. Climate -- Environmental aspects

ISBN 978-0-8070-8576-9; 0-8070-8576-6; 978-0-8070-8577-6 pa; 0-8070-8577-4 pa

LC 2006-19901

"Important reading for policymakers, climate-change skeptics and anyone planning a future beyond the next decade." Kirkus

Includes bibliographical references

Redniss, Lauren

Thunder & Lightning; Weather Past, Present, Future. Lauren Redniss. Random House Inc 2015 272 p. color illustrations $35   **551.6**

1. Weather 2. Meteorology

ISBN 0812993179; 9780812993172

This book, by Lauren Redniss, focuses on weather. It "roams from the driest desert on earth to a frigid island in the Arctic, from the Biblical flood to the defeat of the Spanish Armada. Redniss visits the headquarters of the National Weather Service, recounts top-secret rainmaking operations during the Vietnam War, and examines the economic impact of disasters like Hurricane Katrina." (Publisher's note)

"This book is not simply a collection of oddments and odd fellows, but rather a genuine demonstration of weather as a phenomena and how it is fantastical on both the symbolic and systematized levels." Kirkus

Includes bibliographical references

Weart, Spencer R.

★ The **discovery** of global warming; Spencer R. Weart. Rev. and expanded ed. Harvard University Press 2008 x, 230 p.p il pbk $21   **551.6**

ISBN 9780674031890

LC 2008013675

The author "reports the history of global warming theory, including the internal conflicts plaguing the research community and the role government has had in promoting climate studies. . . . Without resorting to fear-mongering, Weart gives an informed history and offers his readers solutions to consider." Publ Wkly

551.63 Weather forecasting and forecasts, reporting and reports

Cullen, Heidi

The **weather** of the future; heat waves, extreme storms, and other scenes from a climate-changed planet. HarperCollins 2010 329p il map $25.99; pa $15.99   **551.63**

1. Forecasting 2. Climate -- Environmental aspects

ISBN 978-0-06-172688-0; 0-06-172688-5; 978-0-06-172694-1 pa; 0-06-172694-X pa

"A lively and troubling but not entirely doomsday scenario of our warmer future, which will hopefully persuade readers to pay greater attention." Kirkus

Includes bibliographical references

551.69 Geographic treatment of climate

Tape, Ken D.

The **changing** arctic landscape; Ken D. Tape. University of Alaska Press 2010 viii, 56p ill. (some col.), col. maps (cloth; alk. paper) $35.00   **551.69**

1. Alaska 2. Arctic regions 3. Climate change 4. Alaska -- Climate 5. Alaska -- Environmental conditions -- Pictorial works 6. Climatic changes -- Environmental aspects -- Alaska -- Pictorial works

ISBN 9781602230804; 1602230803

LC 2009035478

It was the author's intent to demonstrate "how the work of several generations of earth scientists can be integrated into a picture of arctic Alaska landscapes that are responding to both natural and human influences. Decades-old photos from pioneering studies of the geology, vegetation, glaciers, and landforms of Brooks Range and North Slope were used to select specific environments for change detection. . . . The author concludes that the changes are consisted with a warming climate, but the argument for warming is not as solid as the argument for the changes themselves." (Environment)

Includes bibliographical references and index.

551.7 Historical geology

Bjornerud, Marcia

Reading the rocks; the autobiography of the earth. Basic Books 2005 237p $26   **551.7**

1. Geology

ISBN 0-8133-4249-X

LC 2004-22738

"This wonderful book should be examined by anyone with a curiosity about the natural history of our planet and how one science in particular has done such an impressive job of deciphering key mysteries of its origin and evolution." Sci Books Films

Includes bibliographical references

Childs, Craig

Atlas of a lost world; travels in ice age America. Craig Childs. Pantheon Books 2018 288 p. (hardback) $28.95 **551.7**

1. Ice age 2. Fossil mammals 3. Prehistoric peoples 4. Glacial epoch -- North America 5. Paleo-Indians -- North America 6. Mammals, Fossil -- North America 7. Prehistoric peoples -- North America 8. Paleoecology -- North America -- Pleistocene

ISBN 9780307908650

LC 2017033037

This book, by Craig Childs, "chronicles the last millennia of the Ice Age, the violent oscillations and retreat of glaciers, the clues and traces that document the first encounters of early humans, and the animals whose presence governed the humans' chances for survival. A blend of science and personal narrative reveals how much has changed since the time of mammoth hunters, and how little. [R]eaders will see the Ice Age, and their own age, in a whole new light." (Publisher's note)

Fortey, Richard A.

★ **Earth**; an intimate history. by Richard Fortey. Knopf 2004 429p il hardcover o.p. pa $19   **551.7**

1. Stratigraphic geology

ISBN 0-375-40626-3; 0-375-70620-8 pa

LC 2004-46470

The author "relates his walks in places that visually reveal the deep earth (Vesuvius, Hawaii, the Grand Canyon) as well as sites, which, if not so spectacular, contain puzzling elements that provoked great interpretive controversies. . . . The Alps, the Scottish Highlands, Newfoundland, the Deccan Traps of India—these are among Fortey's destinations as he explains the theory of plate tectonics, showing how the theory came to be, as well as the continents and oceans whose skein of connections it explains. This is a marvelously inviting presentation." Booklist

Includes bibliographical references

Macdougall, J. D.

Frozen earth; the once and future story of ice ages. [by] Doug Macdougall. University of California Press 2004 256p il $24.95; pa $15.95   **551.7**

1. Ice Age

ISBN 0-520-23922-9; 0-520-24824-4 pa

LC 2004-8502

The author "presents the scientific history behind ice ages, emphasizing the roles of four great scientists in the field: Louis Agassiz, James Croll, Milutin Milankovitch, and Harlan Bretz. . . . Macdougall's account promotes a welcome reasoning attitude toward ice-age research and its relevance to global warming." Booklist

Includes bibliographical references

Nature's clocks; how scientists measure the age of almost everything. University of California Press 2008 271p il $40; pa $17.95   **551.7**

1. Geochronometry 2. Geological time 3. Radiocarbon dating 4. Radioisotopes in geology

ISBN 978-0-520-24975-2; 978-0-520-26161-7 pa

LC 2007-46955

"Rich in historical titbits, this book is a delightful study of how scientists figured out analytical techniques that revealed the history of the Earth." New Sci

Includes bibliographical references

Richet, Pascal

A **natural** history of time; translated by John Venerella. University of Chicago Press 2007 471p il $29   **551.7**

1. Geological time 2. Earth -- Age

ISBN 978-0-226-71287-1; 0-226-71287-7

LC 2006-33992

Original French edition, 1999

"How old is the Earth? Mr. Richet sets out to explore humanity's attempts to answer this most perplexing of questions, which acted as a spur and a baffle to human ingenuity for 2,500 years. . . . The book is translated from the French—capably, considering how much scientific terminology it contains, but not gracefully—and . . . can be rough going. Still, 'A Natural History of Time' more that repays the effort it requires. Not only does it shed light on key advances in the history of science, from the ancient Greeks to the X-ray, it reminds us of the real heroism and nobility of the scientific enterprise." N Y Sun

552   Petrology

Coenraads, Robert Raymond

Rocks and fossils; a visual guide. [by] Robert R. Coenraads. Firefly Books 2005 304p il $29.95   **552**

1. Rocks 2. Fossils 3. Minerals

ISBN 1-55407-068-6

In this "introduction to geology and paleontology . . . [the author presents the] facts of how fossils are formed, how rocks are formed, and how plate tectonics work. . . . A science work perfectly suited for general use." Booklist

Pellant, Chris

Rocks and Minerals; A Photographic Field Guide. St. Martin's Press 2015 192 p. color illustrations $18   **552**

1. Rocks 2. Minerals

ISBN 1472909933; 9781472909930

In this photographic to rocks and minerals, "a general introduction is followed by a detailed exploration of the three groups of rocks: igneous, metamorphic and sedimentary, including their formation and occurrence, main characteristics and economic uses. . . . The second part of the book begins with an introduction to minerals, including gemstones, explaining their classification, occurrence, formation and characteristics, identification and economic uses." (Publisher's note)

"Students, nature photographers, and budding geologists will find this book both easy to use and highly informative." LJ

553.4   Metals and semimetals

Williams, Susan

Spies in the Congo; America's Atomic Mission in World War II. Susan Williams. PublicAffairs 2016 432 p. illustrations, map (hardcover) $28.99   **553.4**

1. Espionage 2. World War, 1939-1945 -- North Africa

ISBN 9781610396547; 9781610396554

LC 2016936154

This book, by Susan Williams, is the "true story of the unsung heroism of a handful of good men—and one woman—in colonial Africa who risked their lives in the fight against fascism and helped deny Hitler his atomic bomb." (Publisher's note)

"While there are numerous books on the Manhattan Project, this is the first to focus on operations related to the origins of the uranium used." LJ

Includes bibliographical references (pages 313-327), filmography (page 329) and index.

553.6   Other economic materials

Kurlansky, Mark

Salt ; a world history. Penguin Books 2003 484p il map pa $16   **553.6**
1. Salt
ISBN 0-14-200161-9

LC 2004-270006

First published 2002 by Walker & Co.

"Throughout his engaging, well-researched history, Kurlansky sprinkles witty asides and amusing anecdotes. A piquant blend of the historic, political, commercial, scientific and culinary, the book is sure to entertain as well as educate." Publ Wkly

Includes bibliographical references

Welland, Michael

Sand; the never-ending story. University of California Press 2009 343p il map $24.95   **553.6**
1. Sand
ISBN 978-0-520-25437-4

LC 2008-9084

The author "discusses the science, geology, and cultural significance of sand as a critical ingredient in so many aspects of our lives. Learn about arenophiles, sand forensics, extraterrestrial sand, Udden-Wentworth scale, Bagnold formula, and how sand shapes our environment... . Anyone who has walked on a beach, run up a sand dune, or built a sand castle will be fascinated by this excellent book." Libr J

Includes bibliographical references

553.7   Water

Fagan, Brian

Elixir; a history of water and humankind. Brian Fagan. 1st U.S. ed. Bloomsbury Press 2011 384 p. ill., maps $28 **553.7**
1. Water supply 2. Human ecology 3. Drinking water 4. Water 5. Water -- History 6. Water and civilization -- History 7. Water -- Social aspects -- History
ISBN 9781608190034; 160819003X

LC 2010032082

Author Brian Fagan presents "anecdotes and historical episodes showing how pre-industrial people . . . properly appreciated water, from the San hunters of the Kalahari, who see the whole world as a sometimes grudging source of the substance, to John Wesley Powell's efforts to create political divisions in the American West not based on surveyors' straight lines but on natural watersheds." (Kirkus Reviews)

"Supplying intriguing historical background, Fagan well informs those pondering freshwater's role in contemporary environmental problems." Booklist

Includes bibliographical references and index.

Kandel, Robert S.

Water from heaven; the story of water from the big bang to the rise of civilization, and beyond. [by] Robert Kandel. Columbia Univ. Press 2003 311p il maps $29.95; pa $24 **553.7**
1. Water
ISBN 0-231-12244-6; 0-231-12245-4 pa

LC 2002-31229

Original French edition, 1998

"While dense with facts and figures, Kandel's aquatic history is riveting, an exhaustive and complex examination of our most precious chemical compound." Publ Wkly

Includes bibliographical references

Solomon, Steven

Water; the epic struggle for wealth, power, and civilization. Harper 2010 596p il map   **553.7**
1. Water 2. World history 3. Water and civilization 4. Water-supply -- Government policy
ISBN 0060548304; 9780060548308

LC 2009-27500

This is "a narrative account of how water has shaped human society from the ancient past to the present." (Publisher's note) Bibliography. Index.

"Solomon's unprecedented inquiry into the history, science, and politics of water use provides fascinating and ample testimony to the need to place a higher value on water and its preservation." Booklist

Includes bibliographical references

553.8   Gems

Gem; The Definitive Visual Guide. DK, with foreword by Aja Raden. DK Publishing 2016 440 p. color illustrations (ebook) $65; (hardcover) $50   **553.8**
1. Gems 2. Precious metals 3. Precious stones
ISBN 1465453563; 9781465462121; 9781465453563

This book from publisher DK, with foreword by Aja Raden, offers a "guide to precious and semiprecious stones, organic gems, and precious metals. . . . From diamonds to sapphires to obsidian, this compendium profiles all the key gemstones and other precious materials and . . . [shows] the jewels in their different cuts, colors, and uses. . . . The stories, myths, and legends that surround the most celebrated gems and . . . [jewels] from around the world are [also] revealed." (Publisher's note)

Hart, Matthew

Diamond ; a journey to the heart of an obsession. Walker & Co. 2001 276p il maps $26   **553.8**
1. Diamonds
ISBN 0-8027-1368-8

LC 2001-26348

Hart's "account of the glittering business of mining and marketing diamonds is also a story of avarice, theft, aesthetics, monopoly, and war. A thoroughly entrancing book." Booklist

Includes bibliographical references

Oldershaw, Cally

★ Firefly guide to gems. Firefly Bks. 2004 224p il map $14.95   **553.8**
1. Gems 2. Precious stones
ISBN 1-55297-814-1

This book "opens with extensive introductory material including history, various properties, and lore. Then, each gem is presented with text and charts of specific chemical properties. While most gems are discussed on a single page, some that are well known have longer articles." SLJ

553.82   Diamonds

Bergstein, Rachelle

Brilliance and Fire; a biography of diamonds. Rachelle Bergstein. HarperCollins 2016 400 p. illustrations (chiefly color) (ebook) $27.99; $29.99   **553.82**

1. Diamonds 2. Precious stones 3. Diamond industry and trade -- History

ISBN 9780062323798; 0062323776; 9780062323774

LC 2016023889

Author "Rachelle Bergstein's cultural biography of the diamond illuminates the enticing, often surprising story of our society's enduring obsession with the hardest gemstone—and the people who have worked tirelessly to ensure its continued allure.... [This book] offers a glittering history of the world's most coveted gemstone and its greatest champions and most colorful enthusiasts." (Publisher's note)

"Bergstein's book is an informative, well-written, and entertaining window onto another way of life." Kirkus

Includes bibliographical references (pages 323-352) and index.

557   Earth sciences of North America

Morton, Mary Caperton

Aerial geology; a high-altitude tour of North America's spectacular volcanoes, canyons, glaciers, lakes, craters, and peaks. Mary Caperton Morton. Timber Press 2017 303 p. (hardcover) $34.95   **557**

1. Nature 2. Landforms 3. Geology -- North America 4. Landforms -- North America 5. Landforms -- North America -- Pictorial works

ISBN 1604697628; 9781604697629

LC 2016057866

This book, by Mary Caperton Morton, explores North America's 100 most spectacular geological formations. Crisscrossing the continent from the Aleutian Islands in Alaska to the Great Salt Lake in Utah and to the Chicxulub Crater in Mexico,... Morton brings you on a fantastic tour, sharing aerial and satellite photography, explanations on how each site was formed, and details on what makes each landform noteworthy." (Publisher's note)

Includes bibliographical references and index

559.9   Earth sciences of extraterrestrial worlds

Sykes, Bryan

DNA USA; a genetic portrait of America. Bryan Sykes. Liveright Pub. Corp. 2012 369 p.   **559.9**

1. Genetics 2. Genealogy 3. Chromosomes 4. DNA fingerprinting 5. United States -- Population 6. Human genetics -- Popular works 7. Human population genetics -- United States -- Popular works

ISBN 0871404125; 9780871404121

LC 2011053182

In this book, "America's gorgeous mosaic emerges from its DNA in this ... treatise on genetics and genealogy. Oxford geneticist [Bryan] Sykes ... traveled across the United States collecting DNA samples, recording family histories.... The resulting 'chromosomal portraits,' painted by analyzing markers that correlate with African, European, or Asian-Native American populations, reveal DNA tell-tales of unsuspected centuries-old migrations and mixings: Mexican-American Cath-

olics descended from Spanish Jews; white Southerners with substantial African-American ancestry; possible journeys from Europe to North America 10,000 years ago, Sykes gives ... explanations of new genetic techniques and their startling success at tracing familial ties across continents and millennia." (Publishers Weekly)

Includes bibliographical references and index

560   Paleontology

Eldredge, Niles

Extinction and Evolution; What Fossils Reveal About the History of Life. by Niles Eldredge ; introduction by Carl Zimmer. Firefly Books Ltd 2014 256 p. colour illustrations $45   **560**

1. Evolution 2. Extinction (Biology)

ISBN 1770853596; 9781770853591

This book "recounts the work and discoveries of Niles Eldredge, one of the world's most renowned paleontologists, whose research overturned Charles Darwin's theory of evolution as a slow and inevitable process.... [It] chronicles how Eldredge made his discoveries and traces the history of life through the lenses of paleontology, geology, ecology, anthropology, biology, genetics, zoology, mammalogy, herpetology, entomology and botany." (Publisher's note)

"Though the text and photo captions are plagued by an assortment of typographical errors, the fossils and theories could not be presented in a more attractive, readable format. This handsome book should appeal to anyone with even the slightest curiosity about how life evolved on this planet. Highly recommended for all science collections." LJ

Fortey, Richard A.

★ **Fossils**; the key to the past. [by] Richard Fortey. 3rd ed; Smithsonian Institution Press 2002 232p il maps $55; pa $27.50   **560**

1. Fossils

ISBN 1-58834-023-6; 1-58834-048-1 pa

LC 2001-49439

First published 1982 by Van Nostrand Reinhold

In this volume, fossils "from earliest Precambrian forms onward are discussed, emphasizing evolutionary trends and extinctions, and relationships with habitat environments and geologic processes, such as volcanism and meteorite impacts, are evaluated.... Aspects of preservation, discovery, collection, and identification are discussed." Choice {review of 1991 edition}

Includes bibliographical references

Trilobite! eyewitness to evolution. by Richard Fortey. Knopf 2000 284p il $26; pa $14   **560**

1. Fossils 2. Evolution

ISBN 0-375-40625-5; 0-375-70621-6 pa

LC 00-34908

The author's "unabashed trilobite-centric view of the evolution of life on Earth is full of personal anecdotes and asides, but it's also full of excellent science." Libr J

Includes bibliographical references

Prothero, Donald R., 1954-

The **story** of life in 25 fossils; tales of intrepid fossil hunters and the wonders of evolution. Donald R. Prothero. Columbia University Press 2015 432 p. illustrations (cloth; alk. paper) $35   **560**

1. Fossils 2. Paleontology 3. Life -- Origin 4. Evolution (Biology)

ISBN 0231171900; 9780231171908

LC 2015003667

This book, by Donald R. Prothero, "describes twenty-five famous, beautifully preserved fossils in a gripping scientific history of life on Earth. Recounting the adventures behind the discovery of these objects and fully interpreting their significance within the larger fossil record, Prothero creates a riveting history of life on our planet." (Publisher's note)

"Of particular appeal to those who enjoy the writings of Stephen Jay Gould but ideal for anyone interested in the origins of life on earth." Library Journal

Includes bibliographical references and index

Rea, Tom

Bone wars; the excavation and celebrity of Andrew Carnegie's dinosaur. University of Pittsburgh Press 2001 276p il hc o.p.; pa $16 **560**

1. Fossils 2. Dinosaurs 3. Philanthropists 4. Metal industry executives

ISBN 0-8229-4173-2; 9780822958468

LC 2001-3336

This describes the history of the excavation of the dinosaur fossil Diplodocus carnegii in 1899 which was financed by Andrew Carnegie

"Rea pieces together countless bits of information to construct an overall picture of this period of scientific discovery." Booklist

Includes bibliographical references

Taylor, Paul D.

A **history** of life in 100 fossils; Paul D. Taylor & Aaron O'Dea. Smithsonian Books, in association w/the Natural History Museum, London 2014 224 p. color illustrations $34.95 **560**

1. Fossils 2. Natural history 3. Paleontology 4. Life -- Origin 5. Plants, Fossil 6. Animals, Fossil 7. Fossil hominids 8. Evolution (Biology) 9. Evolutionary paleobiology 10. Fossils -- Pictorial works

ISBN 1588344827; 9781588344823

LC 2014940275

This book "showcases 100 key fossils that together illustrate the evolution of life on earth. Iconic specimens have been selected from the renowned collections of the two premier natural history museums in the world, the Smithsonian Institution, Washington, and the Natural History Museum, London. The fossils have been chosen not only for their importance in the history of life, but also because of the visual story they tell." (Publisher's note)

"From single-celled foraminifera to gigantic steppe mammoths, this volume presents a sweeping panorama of ancient life and is recommended for nonspecialists interested in paleontology or evolutionary biology." LJ

Includes bibliographical references (page 223) and index

Thompson, Ida

★ The **Audubon** Society field guide to North American fossils; with photographs by Townsend P. Dickinson; visual key by Carol Nehring. Knopf 1982 846p il maps flexible bdg $19.95 **560**

1. Fossils

ISBN 0-394-52412-8

LC 81-84772

"This softbound field guide to fossils is divided into a section of color photographs followed by a section of detailed descriptions. It covers 420 fossils of marine and freshwater invertebrates, insects, plants, and vertebrates that are likely to be found by the amateur." Malinowsky.

Best Sci & Technol Ref Books for Young People

Travels with the fossil hunters; edited by Peter Whybrow. Cambridge Univ. Press 2000 211p il $40 **560**

1. Fossils 2. Scientists

ISBN 0-521-66301-6

LC 99-30134

A collection of essays by paleontologists from London's Natural History Museum describing their work in such places as China, India, the Sahara, Latvia, and Antarctica

"The essayists give enough details of their quests to explain their presence in these places and keep science buffs entertained. . . . Heightening the impact of the stories is an abundance of beautiful, colorful photos of the places, the people, and the fossils." SLJ

560.43 Trace fossils

Martin, Anthony J.

The **evolution** underground; burrows, bunkers, and the marvelous subterranean world beneath our feet. Anthony J. Martin. W W Norton & Co Inc 2017 400 p. color illustrations (ebook) $50; $28.95 **560.43**

1. Evolution 2. Paleontology 3. Cave dwellers

ISBN 9781681773759; 1681773120; 9781681773124

LC 2017005020

"Some 66 million years ago, a massive asteroid hit the Earth, causing a huge wave of extinctions. As a result, writes paleontologist Martin (Geosciences/Emory Univ.; Dinosaurs Without Bones: Dinosaur Lives Revealed by Their Trace Fossils, 2014, etc.), 'all of the dinosaurs that did not have the good sense to be birds died.' Many of the critters that did survive the cataclysm had the good sense to dwell under the surface, where they had some measure of protection from the elements. Just so, Martin writes in a closing reverie, when Mount St. Helens went up in a plume of ash and fire 36 years ago, only 14 of the 55 mammal species o n the mountain survived—and guess which ones? Yep: burrowing rodents, along with a tiny shrew. Martin, known for having discovered an ancient burrowing dinosaur, examines the world underground and the evolutionary advantages attendant in knowing how to get around down there (and, as he notes, even some birds burrow)." Kirkus

"A spry exercise in popular science." Kirkus

Includes bibliographical references (pages 305-391) and index.

560.75 Fossil collecting

Williams, Paige

The **dinosaur** artist; obsession, betrayal, and the quest for earth's ultimate trophy. Paige Williams. Hachette Books 2018 432 p. (hardcover) $28 **560.75**

1. Geopolitics 2. Fossils -- Collectors and collecting

ISBN 9780316382502; 9780316382533; 9781549194931

LC 2018937293

This book, by Paige Williams, is "about humans' relationship with natural history and a seemingly intractable conflict between science and commerce. A story that stretches from Florida's Land O' Lakes to the Gobi Desert, 'The Dinosaur Artist' illuminates the history of fossil collecting--a murky, sometimes risky business, populated by eccentrics and obsessives, where the lines between poacher and hunter, collector and smuggler, enthusiast and opportunist, can easily blur." (Publisher's note)

567 Fossil cold-blooded vertebrates

Ewing, Susan

Resurrecting the shark; a scientific obsession and the mavericks who solved the mystery of a 270-million-year-old fossil. Susan Ewing. Pegasus Books 2017 282 p. illustrations (chiefly color) (hardcover) $27.95   **567**

1. Sharks 2. Fossils 3. Helicoprion 4. Sharks, Fossil

ISBN 9781681773438; 9781681773926; 1681773430

In this book, author Susan Ewing "shares the century-long story of scientific investigation that resulted in the discovery of Helicoprion. Ewing brings to life the personalities of those who wrestled with these fossils to reveal 'the beautiful, frustrating, addictive, rewarding way' that research works." (Publishers Weekly)

"A weird creature from deep time comes alive in this engaging account of Helicoprion, the "buzz saw" shark, which patrolled the seas . . . some 270 to 280 million years ago." LJ

Includes bibliographical references (pages 259-276) and index.

567.9 Reptiles

Barrett, Paul

Dinosaurs; How They Lived and Evolved. Darren Naish, Paul Barrett. Smithsonian Books 2016 224 p. color ill., color maps (hardcover) $29.95   **567.9**

1. Dinosaurs

ISBN 9781588345820

LC 2016937682

This book by Darren Naish and Paul Barrett traces "the evolution, anatomy, biology, ecology, behavior, and lifestyle of a variety of dinosaurs. [The authors] . . . also remind us that dinosaurs are far from extinct: they present evidence supporting the evolution of dinosaurs to birds that exist today as approximately ten thousand different species. Throughout their narrative Naish and Barrett reveal state-of-the-art new findings shaping our understanding of dinosaurs." (Publisher's note)

"For those who enjoy science but haven't thought about dinosaurs in a while, this volume brings these creatures to mind in a whole new way." LJ

Includes bibliographical references (page 219) and index.

Brusatte, Stephen

★ The **rise** and fall of the dinosaurs; a new history of a lost world. Stephen Brusatte. William Morrow 2018 416 p. (hardcover) $29.99   **567.9**

1. Fossils 2. Dinosaurs

ISBN 9780062490421

LC 2017038066

This book, by Stephen Brusatte, "reveals . . . the dinosaurs' extraordinary, 200-million-year-long story as never before. . . . Brusatte . . . masterfully tells the complete, surprising, and new history of the dinosaurs, drawing on cutting-edge science to dramatically bring to life their lost world and illuminate their enigmatic origins, spectacular flourishing, astonishing diversity, cataclysmic extinction, and startling living legacy." (Publisher's note)

"His explanations of how sauropods became so large, the reasons for the dominance of Tyrannosaurus rex, the evolution of flying ability in some dinosaurs, and the factors leading to the demise of most of these creatures are carefully crafted and presented. Brusatte is not shy about saying what is not yet known, while making it clear that this is a truly exciting period, in which new fossils are being uncovered at a dizzying pace." Pub Wkly

Includes bibliographical references and index

★ **Dinosaurs**; edited by John J. Meier. H.W. Wilson Co. 2011 221p il (Reference shelf) pa $55   **567.9**

1. Dinosaurs

ISBN 978-0-8242-1107-3

LC 2011007540

A collection of articles discussing dinosaurs "from their origins and evolution to their much-debated extinction. . . . Coverage includes . . . background information distilled from the fossil record as well as more speculative and theoretical material." Publisher's note

Includes bibliographical references

Horner, John R.

How to build a dinosaur; extinction doesn't have to be forever. [by] Jack Horner and James Gorman. Dutton 2009 246p il $25.95   **567.9**

1. Dinosaurs 2. Evolution

ISBN 978-0-525-95104-9; 0-525-95104-0

LC 2008-48042

"Dinosaurs could walk the earth again within five years, says paleontologist Jack Horner. It won't happen the way it did in Jurassic Park, the novel and movie inspired in part by Horner's work. No active DNA from history's big lizards is likely ever to be found, he says. But birds carry dinosaur DNA. As embryos, they sprout the beginnings of teeth, claws, and a lizard tail before certain genes cancel and redirect that growth. Horner's dream these days is to bring out a chicken's inner dinosaur by turning off those controlling secondary genes. . . . The great value of How to Build a Dinosaur is that it illuminates how the work of paleontologists has changed in the past few decades." Week

Includes bibliographical references

Lacovara, Ken

Why Dinosaurs Matter; Kenneth Lacovara ; illustrations by Mike Lemanski. TED Books / Simon & Schuster 2017 169 p. color illustrations (hardcover) $16.99   **567.9**

1. Dinosaurs 2. Paleontology 3. Human beings 4. Extinction (Biology)

ISBN 1501120107; 9781501120107

In this book, paleontologist Kenneth Lacovara "offers the latest ideas about the shocking and calamitous death of the dinosaurs and ties their vulnerabilities to our own. . . . [This book] is compelling and engaging--a great reminder that our place on this planet is both precarious and potentially fleeting. 'As we move into an uncertain environmental future, it has never been more important to understand the past.'" (Publisher's note)

"As paleontologist Lacovara has dug up the bones of some mighty dinosaurs . . . he's just the man to tell us what dinosaurs can tell us about ourselves." LJ

Includes bibliographical references (pages 163-169).

Paul, Gregory S.

The **Princeton** field guide to dinosaurs. Princeton University Press 2010 320p il map (Princeton field guides) $35 **567.9**

1. Dinosaurs

ISBN 978-0-691-13720-9; 0-691-13720-X

LC 2010-14916

"Though not a field guide to stuff in your backpack, this exciting addition to dinosaur reference is essential for high school through university libraries and is highly recommended for all students of dinosaurs." Libr J

Includes bibliographical references

Pim, Keiron

Dinosaurs the grand tour; everything worth knowing about dinosaurs from Aardonyx to Zuniceratops. Keiron Pim with field notes by Jack Horner ; illustrated by Fabio Pastori. The Experiment 2014 352 p. illustrations (some color) (hardcover) $24.95   **567.9**

1. Fossils 2. Dinosaurs
ISBN 9781615192120; 1615192123

LC 2014018581

This book on dinosaurs, by Keiron Pim and Jack Horner provides "a chronological survey of the group by genus/species from their first appearances in the fossil record in the Triassic through the Jurassic and their final extinction at the end of the Cretaceous. They include information on the initial and later discoveries of parts or whole skeletons and information on many famous dinosaur collectors." (Choice: Current Reviews for Academic Libraries)

"This book provides detailed analyses of more than 300 different dinosaurs, grouped by the period (Triassic, Jurassic, or Cretaceous) in which they lived. Information is provided for each dinosaur on name pronunciation, the creature's diet and weight, where bones have been found, and when it lived. . . . This is a good, inexpensive choice for those who want the most up-to-date, comprehensive information on dinosaurs, and it is suitable for school and public libraries." Booklist

Includes bibliographical references and index

Sampson, Scott D.

Dinosaur odyssey; fossil threads in the web of life. University of California Press 2009 332p il map $29.95   **567.9**

1. Fossils 2. Dinosaurs
ISBN 978-0-520-24163-3; 0-520-24163-0

LC 2009-6150

"This book draws scientifically accurate pictures in a style that is accessible to researchers and general readers alike." Libr J

Includes bibliographical references

567.91   Specific dinosaurs and other archosaurs

Hone, David

The **Tyrannosaur** chronicles; the biology of the tyrant dinosaurs. David Hone. Bloomsbury Sigma 2016 304 p. illustrations (some color) (hardcover) $27   **567.91**

1. Dinosaurs
ISBN 9781472911254; 1472911253

This book, by David Hone, "tracks the rise of these dinosaurs, and presents the latest research into their biology, showing off more than just their impressive statistics--tyrannosaurs had feathers, and fought and even ate one another. Indeed, David Hone tells the evolutionary story of the group through their anatomy, ecology, and behavior, exploring how they came to be the dominant terrestrial predators of the Mesozoic--and more recently, one of the great icons of biology." (Publisher's note)

"Hone provides a solid meal to feed the popular fascination with these tyrant lizards, easily digestible but made from ingredients that, at least in paleontological terms, are quite fresh." Pub Wkly

Includes bibliographical references (pages 281-289) and index.

569   Fossil mammals

Lister, Adrian

Mammoths; giants of the ice age. [by] Adrian Lister and Paul Bahn; foreword by Jean M. Auel. Rev ed; University of California Press 2007 192p il $29.95   **569**

1. Mammoths
ISBN 978-0-520-25319-3; 0-520-25319-1

LC 2007-26369

First published 1994 by Macmillan

This book integrates "research to piece together the story of mammoths, mastodons, and their relatives, icons of the Ice Age." Publisher's note

Includes glossary and bibliographical references

569.67   Mammoths

McKay, John J.

Discovering the mammoth; a tale of giants, unicorns, ivory, and the birth of a new science. John J. McKay. Pegasus Books 2017 xiii, 241 p.p illustrations, map (hardcover) $27.95 **569.67**

1. Mammoths 2. Paleontology -- History 3. Woolly mammoth 4. Fossils -- Social aspects
ISBN 1681774240; 9781681774817; 9781681774244

This book, by John J. McKay, deals with "the fascinating saga of solving the mystery of . . . [the mammoth] who once roamed the north country--and has captivated our collective imagination ever since. . . . [It] brings together dozens of original documents and illustrations, some ignored for centuries, to show how this odd assortment of characters solved the mystery of the mammoth and, in doing so, created the science of paleontology." (Publisher's note)

"McKay masterfully weaves an intricate story of the events, politics, people, and scientific development associated with the 'rediscovery' of mammoths." Booklist

Includes bibliographical references (pages 211-234) and index.

569.9   Humans and related genera

Johanson, Donald C.

Lucy's legacy; the quest for human origins. [by] Donald Johanson and Kate Wong. Harmony Books 2009 309p il map $25   **569.9**

1. Human origins
ISBN 978-0-307-39639-6; 0-307-39639-8

LC 2008-39907

"In 1974 paleontologist Donald C. Johanson found a female skeleton 3.2 million years old that exhibited both ape and human characteristics. Johanson and Kate Wong . . . recount the stunning discovery of Lucy, and then they venture far beyond that to bring readers up-to-date on what has been unearthed since and the implications of these new finds for what it means to be human. . . . Conversational, knowledgeable, flowing logically from one topic to the next, the book is packed with information of the kind that will be especially intriguing to general readers." Sci Am

Includes bibliographical references

Pyne, Lydia

Seven skeletons; the evolution of the world's most famous human fossils. Lydia Pyne. Viking 2016 288 p. illustrations, map (hardcover) $28   **569.9**

1. Human origins 2. Fossil hominids 3. Human evolution
ISBN 9780525429852

LC 2016008398

This book, by Lydia Pyne, "explores how seven . . . famous fossils of our ancestors have the social cachet they enjoy today. Drawing from archives, museums, and interviews, Pyne builds a cultural history for each celebrity fossil—from its discovery to its afterlife in museum exhibits to its legacy in popular culture." (Publisher's note)

"Pyne's tales complement and flesh out the well-known narratives already associated with these fossils; her work impressively blends the humanities and science to greatly enrich both." Pub Wkly

Includes bibliographical references and index

Sang-Hee Lee

Close encounters with humankind; a paleoanthropologist investigates our evolving species. Sang-Hee Lee with Shin-Young Yoon. W W Norton & Co Inc 2018 304 p. illustrations (hardcover) $26.95   **569.9**
    1. Evolution 2. Fossil hominids 3. Paleoanthropology 4. Human evolution
    ISBN 9780393634822; 9780393634839; 0393634825

This book, by Sang-Hee Lee and Shin-Young Yoon, "explores some of our greatest evolutionary questions from new and unexpected angles. Through a series of entertaining, bite-sized chapters, we gain fresh perspectives into our first hominin ancestors and ways to challenge perceptions about the traditional progression of evolution. . . . Lee's surprising conclusions shed new light on our beginnings and connect us to a far-away past." (Publisher's note)

"Lee, professor of anthropology at the University of California, Riverside, approaches an array of topics in the field of human evolution with candor, clarity, and brevity." Pub Wkly

Includes bibliographical references (pages 265-286) and index.

Sarmiento, Esteban

The **last** human; a guide to twenty-two species of extinct humans. created by G.J. Sawyer and Viktor Deak; text by Esteban Sarmiento, G.J. Sawyer, Richard Milner; with contributions by Donald C. Johanson, Meave Leakey, and Ian Tattersall. Yale University Press 2006 256p il map $45   **569.9**
    1. Evolution 2. Human beings 3. Fossil hominids
    ISBN 978-0-300-10047-1; 0-300-10047-7

"This is fascinating stuff, not least because it drives home just how much of our knowledge about the past is based on inference." New Sci

Includes bibliographical references

Walter, Chip

Last ape standing; the seven-million year story of how and why we survived. Chip Walter. Walker & Co. 2013 240 p. $17; $26   **569.9**
    1. Evolution 2. Human origins 3. Fossil hominids 4. Human evolution 5. Primates -- Evolution
    ISBN 9781620405215; 080271756X; 9780802717566
                                        LC 2012037484

In this book, Chip Walter considers human evolution. He "argues that neotony, 'the retention of juvenile features in the adult animal,' is most responsible for differences between humans and other hominids. . . . In the end, Walter posits that the next evolutionary step might be Cyber sapiens: immortal superhuman hybrids of humans and machines." (Publishers Weekly)

"An exceptionally well-written overview of man's evolutionary history as well as an accessible guide to the underappreciated field of paleoanthropology." Booklist

Includes bibliographical references and index

569.986   Neanderthals

Bahrami, Beebe

Café Neandertal; excavating our past in one of Europe's most ancient places. Beebe Bahrami. Counterpoint Press 2017 300 p. illustrations, map (hardback) $26   **569.986**
    1. Archeology 2. Neanderthals 3. Archaeologists 4. Excavations (Archeology) -- Europe 5. Dordogne (France) -- Antiquities 6. Neanderthals -- France -- Dordogne 7. Archaeologists -- France -- Dordogne 8. Dordogne (France) -- Description and travel 9. Excavations (Archaeology) -- France -- Dordogne
    ISBN 9781619027770
                                        LC 2017004034

This book, by Beebe Bahrami, "follows and participates in the work of archaeologists who are doing some of the most comprehensive and global work to date on the research, exploration, and recovery of our ancient ancestors. . . . Neck-deep in Neanderthal dirt, Bahrami takes us to the front row of the heated debates about our long-lost cousins." (Publisher's note)

"Written with all the flair and enthusiasm of an experienced writer eager to share her love of her subject." Kirkus.

Includes bibliographical references and index

570   Biology

Carroll, Sean B.

The **Serengeti** Rules; The Quest to Discover How Life Works and Why It Matters. by Sean B. Carroll. Princeton University Press 2016 280 p. illustrations, map $24.95   **570**
    1. Ecology 2. Science 3. Developmental biology
    ISBN 0691167427; 9780691167428
                                        LC 2015038116

In this book, "biologist and author Sean Carroll tells the stories of the pioneering scientists who sought the answers to . . . simple yet profoundly important questions, and shows how their discoveries matter for our health and the health of the planet we depend upon. One of the most important revelations about the natural world is that everything is regulated." (Publisher's note)

"Carroll superbly animates biological principles while providing important insights." Pub Wkly

Includes bibliographical references and index.

Dawkins, Richard, 1941-

Brief Candle in the Dark; My Life in Science. by Richard Dawkins. HarperCollins 2015 416 p. 24 plates; color illustrations $27.99   **570**
    1. Scientists 2. Intellectual life 3. Religion and science
    ISBN 0062288431; 9780062288431

In this book, author Richard Dawkins "offers a candid look at the events and ideas that encouraged him to shift his attention to the intersection of culture, religion, and science. He also invites the reader to look more closely at the brilliant succession of ten influential books that grew naturally out of his busy life, highlighting the ideas that connect them and excavating their origins." (Publisher's note)

"Though the narrative could have used some pruning, the author provides an entertaining portrait of his life and times, including the quaint cus t oms still in practice at Oxford. An impressive overview of Dawkins' life's work, written with the freshness of youthful vigor." Kirkus

De Queiroz, Alan

The **monkey's** voyage; how improbable journeys shaped

the history of life. Alan de Queiroz. Basic Books 2013 368 p. illustrations; maps (hardcover) $27.99 **570**
1. Plants 2. Animals 3. Biogeography 4. Plants -- Dispersal 5. Animals -- Dispersal
ISBN 0465020518; 9780465020515

LC 2013036248

In this book, biologist Alan De Queiroz "describes the radical new view of how fragmented distributions came into being: frogs and mammals rode on rafts and icebergs, tiny spiders drifted on storm winds, and plant seeds were carried in the plumage of sea-going birds to create the map of life we see today. In other words, these organisms were not simply constrained by continental fate; they were the makers of their own geographic destiny." (Publisher's note)

Includes bibliographical references and index

A **dictionary** of biology; editor, Robert S. Hine. 7th edition Oxford University Press 2015 662 p. illustrations pbk $19.95 **570**
1. Biology -- Dictionaries
ISBN 9780198714378 ; 0198714378

"With more than 5,500 clear and concise entries, it provides comprehensive coverage of biology, biophysics, and biochemistry. Over 250 new entries include terms such as Broca's area, comparative genomic hybridization, mirror neuron, and Pandoravirus. Appendices include classifications of the animal and plant kingdoms, the geological time scale, major mass extinctions of species, model organisms and their genomes, Nobel prizewinners, and a new appendix on evolution." (Publisher's note)

Dunn, Rob

Never home alone; from microbes to millipedes, camel crickets, and honeybees, the natural history of where we live. Rob Dunn. Basic Books 2018 336 p. (hardcover) $30 **570**
1. Biology -- Popular works 2. Natural history -- Popular works
ISBN 9781541645769

LC 2018015934

"In 'Never Home Alone,' biologist Rob Dunn introduces us to the nearly 200,000 species living with us in our own homes, from the Egyptian meal moths in our cupboards and camel crickets in our basements to the lactobacillus lounging on our kitchen counters. You are not alone. Yet, as we obsess over sterilizing our homes and separating our spaces from nature, we are unwittingly cultivating an entirely new playground for evolution." (Publisher's note)

Includes bibliographical references and index

Wilson, Edward O., 1929-

★ **Letters** to a Young Scientist; by Edward O. Wilson. Liveright 2013 256 p. $21.95 **570**
1. Science -- Vocational guidance 2. Observation (Scientific method) 3. Science 4. Biologists -- United States -- Correspondence 5. Naturalists -- United States -- Correspondence
ISBN 0871403773; 9780871403773

LC 2012051412

In this book, author Edward O. Wilson "draws on the experiences of a long career to offer encouraging advice to those considering a life in science. . . . After a prologue in which the author assures would-be scientists of their importance in our technoscientific world, he groups 20 letters into five sections. . . . In Part II, 'The Creative Process,' Wilson discusses the nature of science, the scientific method, how scientists think creatively and what it takes to succeed." (Kirkus Reviews)

570.1 Philosophy and theory

Bulletproof feathers; how science uses nature's secrets to design cutting-edge technology. edited by Robert Allen. University of Chicago Press 2010 192p il $35 **570.1**
1. Robots 2. Bionics
ISBN 978-0-226-01470-8

LC 2009037097

This book "is a fascinating introduction to the field of biomimetics, or bionics. Biomimetics refers to efforts to understand the design and complexity of natural, biological systems and the application of this knowledge to achieve useful new technologies. . . . This book, beautifully illustrated with many real-world examples and explanatory diagrams, will be a joy to read for any fan of science and technology." Choice

Includes bibliographical references

Leroi, Armand Marie

★ The **lagoon**; how Aristotle invented science. Armand Marie Leroi ; with translations from the Greek by Simon MacPherson and original illustrations by David Koutsogiannopoulos. Viking 2014 512 p. illustrations, map (hbk) $29.95 **570.1**
1. Biology -- History
ISBN 0670026743; 9780670026746

LC 2014021366

Kirkus Prize Finalist: Nonfiction (2014)

In this book, by Armand Marie Leroi, the author "recovers Aristotle's science. He revisits Aristotle's writings and the places where he worked. He goes to the eastern Aegean island of Lesbos to see the creatures that Aristotle saw, where he saw them. . . . He shows how Aristotle's science is deeply intertwined with his philosophical system and reveals that he was not only the first biologist, but also one of the greatest." (Publisher's note)

"Leroi credits Aristotle with the most basic tenet of empirical science--to understand the world, look first and then try to explain what you see--but resists crediting him with textually unsupported prescience, which highlights beautifully the fact that ideas can be self-consistent, elegant, yet entirely wrong." Pub Wkly

Includes bibliographical references and index

Lovelock, James

The **ages** of Gaia; a biography of our living earth. Norton 1988 xx, 252p il hardcover o.p. pa $13.95 **570.1**
1. Biosphere 2. Life (Biology) 3. Gaia hypothesis 4. Biology -- Philosophy
ISBN 0-393-31239-9 pa

LC 87-36567

"Gaia is the Greek goddess of the earth. For James Lovelock she is the embodiment of a hypothesis: the earth is not merely the abode of life but is a single living organism. He proposes that all living species are components of that organism, as cells are components of the human body." N Y Times Book Rev

Includes bibliographical references

Margulis, Lynn

What is life? foreword by Niles Eldredge. University of California Press 2000 288p il pa $24.95 **570.1**
1. Life (Biology) 2. Life -- Origin 3. Biological diversity 4. Biology -- Philosophy
ISBN 0-520-22021-8

LC 00-25833

First published 1995 by Simon & Schuster

"Continuing Margulis's contention that organelles within cells, such as mitochondria, were originally free-living organisms that fused with others to form complex cells and bodies, the authors extend this concept to the Earth as a superorganism. Although following traditional evolutionary pathways, the authors argue that life has played a role in its own evolution." Choice

Includes bibliographical references

Thomas, Lewis

The **lives** of a cell; notes of a biology watcher. Viking 1974 153p hardcover o.p. pa $13   **570.1**
1. Biology -- Philosophy
ISBN 0-14-004743-3 pa

In this collection of twenty-nine short essays "the author does not confine his scientist's eye to a microscope. He takes a much wider view of the world, looking at insect behavior and the possibility of intelligent life in outer space or bird songs and the evolution of language. He also offers a modest proposal for saving ourselves from nuclear self-destruction." Time

Includes bibliographical references

Turner, J. Scott

Purpose and Desire; What Makes Something "Alive" and Why Modern Darwinism Has Failed to Explain It. by J. Scott Turner. HarperOne, an imprint of HarperCollins Publishers 2017 xvi, 332 p.p illustrations (hardcover) $27.99   **570.1**
1. Evolution 2. Social Darwinism 3. Homeostasis 4. Evolution (Biology) 5. Life (Biology) -- Philosophy 6. Life (Biology) -- Philosophy -- History
ISBN 9780062651587; 9780062651563; 0062651560
LC 2017019588

In this book, author J. Scott Turner "argues that modern Darwinism's materialist and mechanistic biases have led to a scientific dead end, unable to define what life is—and only an openness to the qualities of 'purpose and desire' will move the field forward. . . . Turner draws on the work of Claude Bernard, a contemporary of Darwin revered among physiologists as the founder of experimental medicine." (Publisher's note)

"A n unsettling but highly thought-provoking book." Kirkus
Includes bibliographical references (pages 303-320) and index.

Yoon, Carol Kaesuk

Naming nature; the clash between instinct and science. W.W. Norton 2009 344p il $27.95   **570.1**
1. Names 2. Biology -- Classification
ISBN 978-0-393-06197-0; 0-393-06197-3
LC 2009-14332

This is "a wondrous history of taxonomy—the science of ordering and naming living things—and how it has disconnected us from the natural world. . . . Yoon is an outstanding science writer who takes a seemingly dull topic and rivets unsuspecting readers to the page. Superb." Kirkus

Includes bibliographical references

570.9 History, geographic treatment, biography

Gerald, Michael C.

The **Biology** Book; From the Origin of Life to Epigenetics, 250 Milestones in the History of Biology. by Michael C. Gerald, with Gloria E. Gerald. Sterling Pub Co Inc 2015 528 p. color illustrations $29.95   **570.9**

1. Biology
ISBN 1454910682; 9781454910688

This book on biology, by Michael C. Gerald, "introduce[s] readers to every major subdiscipline, including cell theory, genetics, evolution, physiology, thermodynamics, molecular biology, and ecology. With information on such varied topics as paleontology, pheromones, nature vs. nurture, DNA fingerprinting, bioenergetics, and so much more, this lively collection will engage everyone who studies and appreciates the life sciences." (Publisher's note)

"Well suited to reference collections in secondary schools; also an optimal pick for general readers with an interest in biology or the history of science." LJ

Jackson, Tom

Biology; an illustrated history of life science. Tom Jackson. Shelter Harbor Press 2017 144 p. $24.95   **570.9**
1. Biology 2. Molecules 3. Life sciences
ISBN 1627950931; 9781627950930

This book in the 100 Discoveries that Changed History series, by Tom Jackson, is an "essential guide to biology. . . . [It] examines how we have uncovered the secrets of life, the most complex process in the Universe. From the workings of molecules to the way entire oceans or continents of lifeforms interact, biology seeks to understand how it is that something can be alive, how it fends off death and how it leaves more life in its wake." (Publisher's note)

571 Internal biological processes and structures

Roach, Mary, 1959-

Packing for Mars; the curious science of life in the void. W.W. Norton 2010 334p il   **571**
1. Space biology
ISBN 0-393-06847-1; 978-0-393-06847-4
LC 2010-17113

This book examines space travel and life without gravity. (Publisher's note)

The author "explores the organic aspects of the space program, such as the dangerous bane of space motion sickness and the challenges of space hygiene. . . . She devotes one chapter to space food and another to zero-gravity elimination, which is a serious matter, even with a term like 'fecal popcorning.' An impish and adventurous writer with a gleefully inquisitive mind and a standup comic's timing, Roach celebrates human ingenuity (the odder the better), and calls for us to marshal our resources, unchain our imaginations, and start packing for Mars." Booklist

Includes bibliographical references

Toomey, David

Weird Life; The Search for Life That Is Very, Very Different from Our Own. David Toomey. 1st ed. W W Norton & Co Inc 2013 288 p. ill pbk $15.95; (hardcover) $25.95   **571**
1. Life 2. Ecology 3. Organisms 4. Life (Biology) 5. Adaptation (Biology) 6. Extreme environments 7. Life on other planets 8. Curiosities and wonders
ISBN 9780393348262; 0393071588; 9780393071580
LC 2012042391

This book looks at living organisms. The "author begins by describing 'extremophiles,' which thrive in wildly harsh conditions: chemical hot springs, inside sea ice, . . . or at the ocean's bottom. Having dealt with creatures that, however weird, exist, he proceeds to even stranger life that may exist on Earth, the planets, elsewhere throughout the universe, and in the minds of writers and philosophers. Along the way, he addresses surprisingly difficult questions, such as how to define life."

(Kirkus)

"Toomey manages to make this panoply of life forms at once strange and familiar, and in doing so will entrance his readers." LJ

Includes bibliographical references and index.

571.2 Plants and microorganisms

Chalker-Scott, Linda

How plants work; the science behind the amazing things plants do. Linda Chalker-Scott. Timber Press 2015 235 p. color illustrations (Science for Gardeners) $19.95   **571.2**
    1. Plants 2. Gardening 3. Plant physiology
    ISBN 9781604693386

LC 2014032414

This book, by Linda Chalker-Scott, "brings the stranger-than-fiction science of the plant world to vivid life. She uncovers the mysteries of how and why plants do the things they do, and arms the home gardener with fascinating knowledge that will change the way they garden." (Publisher's note)

571.7 Biological control and secretions

Foster, Russell G.

Rhythms of life; the biological clocks that control the daily lives of every living thing. Yale University Press 2004 276p il $30; pa $18   **571.7**
    1. Biological rhythms
    ISBN 0-300-10574-6; 978-0-300-10574-2; 0-300-10969-5 pa; 978-0-300-10969-6 pa

LC 2004-105609

The authors "survey the biological clocks that dictate circadian rhythms, the daily cycles that affect creatures from cockroaches to humans. . . . Biology buffs will marvel at the fascinating material." Publ Wkly

Includes bibliographical references

571.8 Reproduction, development, growth

Carroll, Sean B.

Endless forms most beautiful; the new science of evo devo and the making of the animal kingdom. with illustrations by Jamie W. Carroll, Josh P. Klaiss, Leanne M. Olds. W.W. Norton & Co. 2005 350p il $25.95   **571.8**
    1. Evolution
    ISBN 0-393-06016-0

LC 2004-29388

The author's "highly detailed and well-illustrated technical discussions are enriched by his appreciation for the philosophical, aesthetic, and ethical implications of the biological wonders he decodes, adding up to a vital and enjoyable introduction to a field with profound implications." Booklist

Includes bibliographical references

Haycock, David Boyd

Mortal coil; a short history of living longer. Yale University Press 2008 308p il   **571.8**
    1. Aging 2. Longevity 3. Death 4. Medicine -- Philosophy 5. Immortality (Philosophy)

ISBN 0-300-11778-7; 9780300117783

LC 2007-35341

This book "explores the medical, scientific, and philosophical theories behind the quest for the prolongation of human life. [According to Haycock], it was a conundrum that intrigued Sir Francis Bacon and underpinned the scientific revolution; ideas of ultimate perfectibility, indefinite progress, and worldly rather than heavenly immortality fed directly into the spirit of the Enlightenment and even further into the nineteenth and twentieth centuries. In today's world of genetic research, cryonics, and nanotechnology, we still seek the same elusive philosopher's stone." (Publisher's note) Index.

This book is "fully successful in managing to drum up excitement for the future of human development while steering clear of propaganda." PopMatters

Includes bibliographical references

572 Biochemistry

Finkel, Elizabeth

The **Genome** Generation; by Elizabeth Finkel. Melbourne University Publishing 2012 256 p. $32.95   **572**
    1. Genomes 2. Evolution 3. Medical technology
    ISBN 0522856470; 9780522856477

This book, by Elizabeth Finkel, covers revolutionary genetic developments in areas as diverse as medicine, agriculture, and evolution. From Botswana to Boston and from Australia to Mexico, the contributors to this work reveal what it means to be part of the genome generation. [It answers questions] such as What have we learned about evolution? How has it changed the way we practice medicine, grow crops, and breed livestock? and Is the genomic revolution an overhyped flop?" (Publisher's note)

McFadden, Johnjoe

Life on the Edge; The Coming of Age of Quantum Biology. Jim Al-Khalili and Johnjoe Macfadden. Random House Inc 2015 368 p. illustrations, map $28   **572**
    1. Life -- Origin 2. Quantum theory
    ISBN 0307986810; 9780307986818

LC 2015018948

In this book on quantum biology by Jim Al-Khalili and Johnjoe McFadden, "by explaining the fundamentals of quantum mechanics, and exploring recent theories and findings, they aim to convince the reader that quantum effects are more than simply the deep substrate on which biology exists--without recourse to a single equation." (New Scientist)

"Of interest to readers curious about the inner workings of life; suitable for public and undergraduate academic libraries." LJ

Morton, Oliver

★ **Eating** the sun; how plants power the planet. HarperCollins 2008 457p il $28.95   **572**
    1. Photosynthesis
    ISBN 978-0-00-716364-9; 0-00-716364-9

LC 2008-23433

First published 2007 in the United Kingdom

This book "is a work of flowing prose that makes vivid why our leafy nub of cosmic dust, swirling around an average star, is an extraordinarily beautiful and rare place to reside in the universe." Christ Sci Monit

Includes bibliographical references

Wilcox, Christie

Venomous; How Earth's Deadliest Creatures Mastered Biochemistry. Christie Wilcox. Scientific American/Farrar, Straus and Giroux 2016 256 p. illustrations (hardcover) $26 **572**

1. Biochemistry 2. Poisonous animals 3. Venom

ISBN 9780374283377; 9780374712211

LC 2016001951

In this book, "biologist Christie Wilcox investigates and illuminates the animals of our nightmares. . . . She reveals just how venoms function and what they do to the human body. With Wilcox as our guide, we encounter a jellyfish with tentacles covered in stinging cells that can kill humans in minutes; a two-inch caterpillar with toxic bristles that trigger hemorrhaging; and a stunning blue-ringed octopus capable of inducing total paralysis." (Publisher's note)

"Whether she's discussing snakes and pufferfish or Komodo dragons and spiders—not to mention octopuses, snails, platypuses, and bees—Wilcox relates technical biochemical and physiological information in a manner that is accessible and enjoyable. " Pub Wkly

Includes bibliographical references and index

572.8 Biochemical genetics

Arney, Kat

Herding Hemingway's Cats; Understanding How Our Genes Work. Kat Arney. St. Martin's Press 2016 288 p. (hardcover) $27 **572.8**

1. Genetics

ISBN 1472910044; 9781472910042

This book, by Kat Arney, is "a survey of recent research and thinking on genes. What are genes, asks science writer Arney, and what do they do? . . . Genetic knowledge has the power to save us, she writes at the beginning of the book. Of course, it's not nearly that simple, but by the end of the book, Arney has arrived at a simplified definition of a gene." (Kirkus Reviews)

"A robust, bouncy, pellucid introduction to DNA and genetics." Kirkus

Includes bibliographical references (pages [263]-279) and index.

Carroll, Sean B.

The **making** of the fittest; DNA and the ultimate forensic record of evolution. with illustrations by Jamie W. Carroll and Leanne M. Olds. W.W. Norton & Co. 2006 301p il map $25.95 **572.8**

1. DNA 2. Evolution

ISBN 978-0-393-06163-5; 0-393-06163-9

LC 2006-17197

The author presents "discoveries gathered from DNA evidence that confirm Charles Darwin's theory of evolution 'beyond any reasonable doubt.' . . . Readers will gain insight into the evolutionary process and expand their knowledge of how the 'fittest' species were made, from fish that live in subfreezing water to birds that communicate via ultraviolet colors." Libr J

Includes bibliographical references

Cobb, Matthew

Life's Greatest Secret; The Race to Crack the Genetic Code. Matthew Cobb. Basic Books 2015 464 p. 16 plates; illustrations $29.99 **572.8**

1. DNA 2. Genetic code 3. Life -- Origin

ISBN 0465062679; 9780465062676

Author Matthew Cobb presents "the story of the discovery and cracking of the genetic code, the thing that ultimately enables a spiraling molecule to give rise to the life that exists all around us. Cobb gives the full and rich account of the cooperation and competition between the eccentric characters--mathematicians, physicists, information theorists, and biologists--who contributed to this revolutionary new science." (Publisher's note)

"Like Cobb's other titles, this scholarly work reflects extensive research and draws upon primary documents. Upper-level students and researchers in biology or the history of science are best equipped to appreciate this detailed book. Other readers should consider Michel Morange's A History of Molecular Biology." LJ

Francis, Richard C.

Epigenetics; the ultimate mystery of inheritance. W.W. Norton 2011 234p il $25.95 **572.8**

1. Genetics 2. Adaptation (Biology)

ISBN 978-0-393-07005-7; 0-393-07005-0

LC 2011-00696

The author "sets out to dethrone the notion that genes are the 'directors' of the 'plays' that are our lives, orchestrating our development and determining our risk for disease and sundry physical and behavioral traits. Yes, genes are important, writes the author, but they are subject to regulation by forces that can turn them on or off, sometimes for a lifetime, sometimes across generations. These forces can come via the cell housing of the genes, other parts of the body or the environment, in each instance initiating the actions of chemicals that bind (or unbind) one or more parts of a gene, preventing (or activating) its transcription. This is an 'epigenetic' process—epigenetics is the science that studies the ways in which DNA can undergo long-term regulatory changes that do not involve mutations of the genes themselves. To illustrate, Francis provides a dizzying array of examples." Kirkus

Includes bibliographical references

Heine, Steven J.

DNA is not destiny; the remarkable, completely misunderstood relationship between you and your genes. Steven J. Heine. W W Norton & Co Inc 2017 344 p. (hardcover) $26.95 **572.8**

1. Genetics 2. Genetic engineering 3. Genes -- Popular works 4. Human genetics -- Popular works 5. Molecular genetics -- Popular works 6. Genetic engineering -- Popular works

ISBN 9780393244090; 9780393244083

LC 2017000693

In this book, "cultural psychologist Steven Heine argues that the first thing we'll do upon receiving our DNA test results is to misinterpret them completely. We've become accustomed to breathless media coverage about newly discovered 'cancer' or 'IQ' or 'infidelity' genes, each one promising a deeper understanding of what makes us tick. But as Heine shows, most of these claims are oversimplified and overhyped misinterpretations of how our DNA really works." (Publisher's note)

"An accessible contribution to what the author calls 'genetic literacy' and a satisfyingly hard-edged work of popular science." Kirkus

Includes bibliographical references (pages [271]-331) and index.

Kean, Sam

The **violinist's** thumb; and other lost tales of love, war, and genius, as written by our genetic code. Sam Kean. Little, Brown and Co. 2012 ix, 401 p.p (hardback) $25.99 **572.8**

1. DNA 2. Genetics 3. Human genome 4. Behavior genetics 5. Human genetics -- Miscellanea

ISBN 0316182311; 9780316182317

LC 2012007029

In this book, author Sam Kean "attempts to take the mystery out of DNA by explaining its structure, its historical impact, and how the science of genetics continues to influence our lives. A good portion of the book examines how modern genetic breakthroughs have helped to explain our evolutionary and historical past. . . . The latter part of the book concentrates on what the future may hold as computer technology and our base of genetic knowledge expands." (Library Journal)

Includes bibliographical references and index.

Segrè, Gino

Ordinary geniuses; Max Delbruck, George Gamow, and the origins of genomics and big bang cosmology. Gino Segrè. Viking 2011 xxi, 330 p.p $27.95 **572.8**

1. Physicists -- United States -- Biography 2. Molecular biologists -- United States -- Biography

ISBN 9780670022762; 0670022764

LC 2011009309

The author "explores the extraordinary lives and scientific accomplishments of two far-from-ordinary men, Max Delbrück and George Gamow. . . . An exuberant dual biography that integrates developments in quantum physics, cosmology and genetics since the 1920s with the lives of these two scientists." Kirkus

Includes bibliographical references (p. 309-318) and index

Sulston, John

The **common** thread; a story of science, politics, ethics, and the human genome. [by] John Sulston, Georgina Ferry. Joseph Henry Press 2002 310p il $24.95 **572.8**

1. Human Genome Project

ISBN 0-309-08409-1

LC 2002-14007

The author gives an "account of the excitement, hard work, vision, and daring needed to move from worm biology to recommending sequencing of the human genome, while senior and influential colleagues argued vigorously against it. He speaks forcefully of the necessity of keeping the sequence public and freely available. . . . {This title is} recommended for almost any library, particularly those with readers willing to go beyond sound bites and media hype." Libr J

Includes bibliographical references

Wagner, Andreas

Arrival of the fittest; the hidden mechanism of evolution. Andreas Wagner. Current 2014 304 p. illustrations $27.95 **572.8**

1. Evolution 2. Natural selection 3. Evolutionary genetics

ISBN 1591846463; 9781591846468

LC 2014009774

In this book "evolutionary biologist Andreas Wagner draws on over fifteen years of research to present the missing piece in [Charles] Darwin's theory. Using experimental and computational technologies that were heretofore unimagined, he has found that adaptations are not just driven by chance, but by a set of laws that allow nature to discover new molecules and mechanisms in a fraction of the time that random variation would take." (Publisher's note)

"A book of startling congruencies, insightful flashes and an artful enthusiasm that delivers knowledge from the inorganic page to our organic brains." Kirkus

Includes bibliographical references and index

Watson, James D., 1928-

★ The **annotated** and illustrated double helix; James D. Watson ; edited by Alexander Gann & Jan Witkowski. Simon & Schuster 2012 345 p. (hardcover) $30 **572.8**

1. DNA 2. Genetic Code 3. Molecular Biology

ISBN 1476715491; 9781476715490; 9781476715506; 9781476715513

LC 2012037483

This book, by James D. Watson, Alexander Gann and Jan Witkowski, was "published to mark the 50th anniversary of the Nobel Prize for Watson and Crick's discovery of the structure of DNA, an annotated and illustrated edition of . . . his 1968 memoir, 'The Double Helix,' the brash young scientist James Watson chronicled the drama of the race to identify the structure of DNA, a discovery that would usher in the era of modern molecular biology." (Publisher's note)

"Numerous appendices include a chapter about his Nobel Prize experiences, the first letters about the double helix, a previously unpublished chapter, and reviews of the original edition. Watson strikes a balance between science for the layman and science for the scientist, resulting in a memoir that will hold the interest of a broad, scientifically-minded audience." Pub Wkly

Includes bibliographical references and index

573.7 Musculoskeletal system

Winchester, Simon

Skulls; An Exploration of Alan Dudley's Curious Collection. Black Dog & Leventhal Pub 2012 240 p. $29.95 **573.7**

1. Skull

ISBN 1579129129; 9781579129125

This book by Simon Winchester focuses on the "story of skulls, both human and animal, from every perspective imaginable: historical, biographical, cultural, and iconographic. . . . At the center of 'Skulls' is a . . . never-before-seen-in-any-capacity visual array of the skulls of more than 300 animals. . . . The skulls are from the collection of Alan Dudley, a British collector and owner of what is probably the largest and most complete private collection of skulls in the world." (Publisher's note)

573.8 Nervous and sensory systems

Iacoboni, Marco

Mirroring people; the new science of how we connect with others. Farrar, Straus and Giroux 2008 308p il $25 **573.8**

1. Nervous system

ISBN 978-0-374-21017-5; 0-374-21017-9

LC 2007-47322

The author introduces "readers to the world of mirror neurons and what they imply about human empathy, which, the author says, underlies morality. . . . Iacoboni's expansive style and clear descriptions make for a solid introduction to cutting-edge neurobiology." Publ Wkly

Includes bibliographical references

575.5 Roots and leaves

Vogel, Steven, 1940-2015

The **life** of a leaf; Steven Vogel. The University of Chicago Press 2012 xi, 303 p.p (hardcover; alkaline paper) $35 **575.5**

1. Leaves 2. Leaves -- Growth 3. Leaves -- Physiology

ISBN 0226859398; 9780226859392

LC 2011037295

In this book, Steven Vogel "demonstrates how a scientist can unite micro and macro perspectives in looking at the natural world. Using the leaf of a plant as his model system of life, he explores aspects of structure, function, and physiology while embedding specific questions in a broader evolutionary context. Thus, as we learn how a leaf . . . uses various strategies to maintain appropriate water balance, we also learn why these strategies are important." (Publishers Weekly)

Includes bibliographical references (pages 287-293) and index

576   General and external biological phenomena

Dawkins, Richard

The **selfish** gene; 30th anniversary ed; Oxford University Press 2006 xxiii, 360p il pa $15.95   **576**

1. Genetics 2. Evolution

ISBN 978-0-19-929115-1; 0-19-929115-2 pa

LC 2007-271478

First published 1976

The author examines evolution and contends that genes that benefit individual members of a species will be passed on to future generations, rather than those which may benefit the entire group

Includes bibliographical references

576.5   Genetics

Doudna, Jennifer A.

A **crack** in creation; gene editing and the unthinkable power to control evolution. Jennifer A. Doudna, Samuel H. Sternberg. Houghton Mifflin Harcourt 2017 xx, 281 p.p illustrations (hardcover) $28.00   **576.5**

1. Evolution 2. Genetics -- Research 3. Genetic Code 4. United States 5. CRISPR-Cas Systems 6. Gene Editing -- history 7. Genetic Research -- history

ISBN 9780544716964; 9780544716940

LC 2016058472

In this book "writing with fellow researcher Samuel Sternberg, [author Jennifer] Doudna shares the thrilling story of her discovery, and passionately argues that enormous responsibility comes with the ability to rewrite the code of life. With CRISPR, she shows, we have effectively taken control of evolution. What will we do with this unfathomable power? [The] biologist grapples with her role in the biggest scientific discovery of our era: a cheap, easy way of rewriting genetic code, with nearly limitless promise and peril." (Publisher's note)

"Doudna . . . and Sternberg . . . explain the basics of the potentially revolutionary CRISPR technology, the events leading up to Doudna's discovery of that technology, and the ethical dilemmas posed by the newfound ability to alter any living being's genetic composition." Pub Wkly

Includes bibliographical references (pages 250-269) and index

Endersby, Jim

A **guinea** pig's history of biology. Harvard University Press 2007 499p il $27.95; pa $18.95   **576.5**

1. Genetics 2. Heredity 3. Biology -- History

ISBN 978-0-674-02713-8; 0-674-02713-2; 978-0-674-03227-9 pa; 0-674-03227-6 pa

LC 2007-20824

"This book would be of interest to anyone fascinated or intrigued by genetics or biological research, as well as any professional or lay student of history and science." Sci Books Films

Includes bibliographical references

Henig, Robin Marantz

★ The **monk** in the garden: how Gregor Mendel and his pea plants solved the mystery of inheritance. Houghton Mifflin 2000 292p il $24; pa $14   **576.5**

1. Geneticists

ISBN 0-395-97765-7; 0-618-12741-0 pa

LC 00-24341

The author explores "Mendel's personality and experiments. The latter lasted but a few years in the 1850s and 1860s, ending when Mendel became the abbot of his monastery in what is now Brno in the Czech Republic. Henig crisply conveys how the laws of inheritance that Mendel derived from his statistical analysis remained unnoticed until several botanists who discovered them independently in 1900 also learned that Mendel found them first. This biography itself rediscovers a scientist often mentioned but insufficently known." Booklist

Knight, Jeffrey A.

★ **Genetics** & inherited conditions; editor, Jeffrey A. Knight. Salem Press 2010 3v il (Salem health) set $395 **576.5**

1. Reference books 2. Genetics -- Encyclopedias 3. Medical genetics -- Encyclopedias

ISBN 978-1-587-65650-7; 1-587-65650-7

LC 2010-5289

First published 1999 with title: Encyclopedia of genetics

"The subjects covered include all aspects of genetics, such as diseases, biology, genetic engineering, social issues, and more. . . . Articles covering diseases and syndromes include such information as definition, risk factors, etiology and genetics, symptoms, screening and diagnosis, treatment and therapy, and prevention and outcomes. For other types of articles, essays are preceded by a brief summary of the significance of the topic and definitions of key terms." Booklist

Includes bibliographical references

Monosson, Emily

Unnatural selection; how we are changing life, gene by gene. Emily Monosson. Island Press 2014 232 p. (cloth; alk. paper) $30   **576.5**

1. Pollution 2. Natural selection 3. Pesticides and wildlife

ISBN 1610914988; 1610914996; 9781610914987; 9781610914994

LC 2014939900

This book by Emily Monosson presents "evidence of how human activities drive evolution for the unintended benefit of certain organisms . . . . In part 1, she uses case studies to investigate the anthropogenic selective pressures that cause unnatural selection in pest and disease organisms. . . . . In part 2, she investigates the impacts of pollutants on natural selection of organisms in the wild." (Choice: Current Reviews for Academic Libraries)

Watson, James D., 1928-

DNA; the story of the genetic revolution. by James D. Watson, with Andrew Berry and Kevin Davies. Revised and updated ed. Alfred A. Knopf 2017 xiv, 487 p.p illustrations (some color) (paperback) $29.95   **576.5**

1. DNA fingerprinting 2. Genetic engineering 3. Science -- Popular works 4. DNA -- Popular works 5. Genetics -- Popular works

ISBN 9780385351201; 9780385351188

LC 2016058413

This book, by James D. Watson, with Andrew Berry and Kevin Davies, "charts the greatest scientific journey of our time, from the discovery of the double helix to today's controversies to what the future may hold. Updated to include new findings in gene editing, epigenetics, agricultural chemistry, as well as . . . on personal genomics and cancer research. This is the most comprehensive and authoritative exploration of DNA's impact . . . on our society and our world." (Publisher's note)

"A masterful summary of genetic science past, present, and future, from one of its prime movers." Kirkus

Includes bibliographical references and index

Zimmer, Carl

She has her mother's laugh; the powers, perversions, and potential of heredity. Carl Zimmer. Dutton, an imprint of Penguin Random House LLC 2018 544 p. (hardcover) $30 **576.5**
1. Genetics 2. Heredity 3. Heredity -- genetics
ISBN 9781101984598

LC 2017046101

"New York Times columnist and science writer Carl Zimmer presents a profoundly original perspective on what we pass along from generation to generation. . . . Weaving historical and current scientific research, . . . Zimmer ultimately unpacks urgent bioethical quandaries arising from new biomedical technologies, but also long-standing presumptions about who we really are and what we can pass on to future generations." (Publisher's note)

Includes bibliographical references and index

576.8   Evolution

Aliens; the world's leading scientists on the search for extraterrestrial life. edited and with an introduction by Jim Al-Khalili. First U.S. edition Picador 2017 232 p. (hardcover) $25 **576.8**
1. Human-alien encounters 2. Extraterrestrial beings 3. Interstellar communication 4. Life on other planets 5. Search for Extraterrestrial Intelligence (Study group; U.S.)
ISBN 9781250109651; 9781250109637

LC 2016058284

In this collection of essays edited by Jim Al-Khalili "scientists from around the world weigh in on the latest advances in the search for intelligent life in the universe and discuss just what that might look like. Included here are essays from a broad spectrum of the scientific community: cosmologists, astrophysicists, NASA planetary scientists, and geneticists, to name just a few, discussing the latest research and theories relating to alien life." (Publisher's note)

"Al-Khalili's collection is efficient and factual but never dry; it's an excellent primer on various concepts and aspects of potential alien life, and the consequences of such an earth-shattering discovery." Pub Wkly

Includes bibliographical references.

Ayala, Francisco Jose, 1934-

Darwin's gift to science and religion. Joseph Henry Press 2007 237p il map $24.95 **576.8**
1. Evolution 2. Creationism 3. Naturalists 4. Natural selection 5. Travel writers 6. Writers on science 7. Evolution (Biology) 8. Intelligent design (Teleology)
ISBN 0-309-10231-6; 978-0-309-10231-5

LC 2007-05821

"With the publication in 1859 of On the Origin of Species by Means of Natural Selection, Charles Darwin established evolution. . . . [Francisco Ayala offers] explanations of the science [and] reviews the history that led us to ratify Darwin's theories." (Publisher's note)

"This elegant book provides the single best introduction to Darwin and the development of evolutionary biology now available." Publ Wkly

Includes bibliographical references

Barnosky, Anthony D.

Dodging extinction; power, food, money and the future of life on Earth. Anthony D. Barnosky. University of California Press 2014 256 p. (cloth; alk. paper) $29.95 **576.8**

1. Human ecology 2. Mass extinctions 3. Human influence on nature 4. Extinction (Biology) 5. Conservation of natural resources
ISBN 0520274377; 9780520274372

LC 2013048773

In this book, by Anthony D. Barnosky, "weaves together evidence from the deep past and the present to alert us to the looming Sixth Mass Extinction and to offer a practical, hopeful plan for avoiding it. . . . He presents compelling evidence that unless we rethink how we generate the power we use to run our global ecosystem, where we get our food, and how we make our money, we will trigger what would be the sixth great extinction on Earth, with dire consequences." (Publisher's note)

"The author is an optimist who suggests a way through the present crisis: implement reasonable and responsible resource management and sustainable agricultural and energy practices along with habitat restoration and conservation biology. It can be done. This is a must read for college students and a well-informed citizenry. Summing Up: Essential. All levels/libraries." Choice.

Includes bibliographical references and index

Billings, Lee

Five billion years of solitude; the search for life among the stars. by Lee Billings. Current 2013 304 p. $27.95 **576.8**
1. Universe 2. Life -- Origin 3. Extrasolar planets 4. Life on other planets
ISBN 1617230065; 9781617230066

LC 2013017672

This book presents an "overview of the still-evolving field of 'exoplanetary' research (discovery and characterization of planets orbiting other stars). Early dreams that we would locate and visit intelligent, technologically sophisticated beings elsewhere in space have been tempered as declining governmental funding has restricted our planet hunting." (Library Journal)

"A great outline of the subject, bringing what's often treated as science fiction down to Earth, where it can be understood." Kirkus

Includes bibliographical references and index

Brannen, Peter

The **ends** of the world; volcanic apocalypses, lethal oceans, and our quest to understand Earth's past mass extinctions. Peter Brannen. Ecco, an imprint of HarperCollins Publishers 2017 x, 322 p.p illustrations (chiefly color) (hardcover) $27.99 **576.8**
1. Climate change 2. Mass extinctions 3. Paleoclimatology 4. Climatic changes
ISBN 9780062364807; 9780062364821; 0062364804

In this book, author Peter Brannen "dives into deep time, exploring Earth's past dead ends, and in the process, offers us a glimpse of our possible future. Many scientists now believe that the climate shifts of the twenty-first century have analogs in . . . five [mass] extinctions. . . . Brannen examines the fossil record . . . and introduces us to the researchers . . . [who] are piecing together what really happened at the crime scenes of the Earth's biggest whodunits." (Publisher's note)

"If readers have time for only one book on the subject, this wonderfully written, well-balanced, and intricately researched (though not too dense) selection is the one to choose." LJ

Includes bibliographical references (pages 293-308) and index.

Catling, David C.

Astrobiology; a very short introduction. David C. Catling. Oxford University Press 2013 142 p. illustrations (Very short introductions) (pbk.) $11.95 **576.8**
1. Space biology 2. Life on other planets 3. Exobiology
ISBN 0199586454; 9780199586455

LC 2013940856

In this book "David C. Catling introduces [astrobiology] through our understanding of the factors that allowed life to arise and persist on our own planet, and for the signs we are looking for in the search for extraterrestrial life. Astrobiologists seek to understand the origin and evolution of life on Earth in order to illuminate and guide the search for life on other planets." (Publisher's note)

A "very good treatment of astrobiology. In eight chapters and just about 130 pages, it covers the full gamut of the discipline, which really only came about in the 1990s. Importantly, in spite of the necessary requirement of brevity, Catling . . . does not neglect key historical elements in his topical discussions." Choice

Includes bibliographical references and index

Costa, James T.

Darwin's backyard; how small experiments led to a big theory. James T. Costa. W W Norton & Co Inc 2017 xviii, 441 p.p illustrations (hardcover) $27.95 **576.8**
1. Biography 2. Evolution (Biology) -- History 3. Natural history -- Experiments 4. Down House (Bromley, London, England) 5. Natural history -- Experiments -- Handbooks, manuals, etc.
ISBN 9780393239898; 9780393249156; 0393239896
LC 2017017865

This book, by James T. Costa, "takes readers on a journey from [Charles] Darwin's childhood through his voyage on the HMS Beagle where his ideas on evolution began. . . . Using his garden and greenhouse, . . . Darwin tested ideas of his landmark theory of evolution with an astonishing array of hands-on experiments . . . without specialized equipment. . . . From the experiments' results, he plumbed the . . . evidence for the revolutionary arguments of On the Origin of Species." (Publisher's note)

"An instructive and entertaining look at Darwin's 'experimentising' and how it can be readily duplicated using mostly simple household tools." Kirkus

Includes bibliographical references (pages 379-418) and index.

Coyne, Jerry A.

★ **Why** evolution is true. Viking 2009 xx, 282p il map $27.95 **576.8**
1. Evolution
ISBN 978-0-670-02053-9
LC 2008-33973

Presents the threads of modern work in genetics, paleontology, geology, molecular biology, and anatomy that demonstrate the stamp of the evolutionary processes first proposed by Darwin.

"Readers looking to understand the case for evolution and searching for a response to many of the most common creationist claims should find everything they need in this powerful book, which is clearer and more comprehensive than the many others on the subject." Publ Wkly

Includes bibliographical references

Darwin, Charles

The **Beagle** letters; edited by Frederick Burkhardt; with an introduction by Janet Browne. Cambridge University Press 2008 xxx, 470p il map $32 **576.8**
1. Evolution 2. Beagle Expedition (1831-1836)
ISBN 978-0-521-89838-6; 0-521-89838-2
LC 2009-417801

"The complete correspondence both to and from Charles Darwin during his five years circumnavigating the globe on the HMS Beagle, beginning in 1831, documents his growth as a naturalist and offers a picture of life in the England he left behind. . . . It is fascinating to watch Darwin attempt to come to grips with the huge amount of data he collected and make sense of the patterns he observed. We get an intimate look at an adventurous young Darwin, so unlike his more familiar, sedentary older self who would write On the Origin of Species." Publ Wkly

Includes bibliographical references

The **Darwin** reader; edited by Mark Ridley. 2nd ed; Norton 1996 315p il pa $21.30 **576.8**
1. Evolution 2. Natural selection
ISBN 0-393-96967-3
LC 95-50297

First published in the United Kingdom with title: The essential Darwin; first Norton edition published 1987

This collection presents excerpts from Darwin's most important works including Origin of the species, The descent of man and Coral reef. Illustrations are taken from the original editions

Includes bibliographical references

On the origin of species; David Quammen, general editor. Illustrated ed.; Sterling Pub. 2008 544p il $35 **576.8**
1. Heredity 2. Evolution 3. Human origins 4. Natural selection
ISBN 978-1-4027-5639-9
LC 2008-6902

Illustrated edition of the book first published 1859 with title: The origin of species by means of natural selection

"As a milestone not only in the history of science but also in cultural history, On the Origin of Species belongs in every library, high school and above. . . . [Quammen] offers a gloriously illustrated and richly annotated volume, which testifies to the book's enduring legacy. Throughout the text, relevant sidebars from other of Darwin's writings, including his Autobiography, field notes from the HMS Beagle, and his myriad letters, are presented for their insight. Illustrations include historical images, such as sketches, woodcuts, and portraits of people and places, but also included are contemporary photographs of the flora and fauna that Darwin described." Libr J

Includes bibliographical references

★ The **origin** of species by means of natural selection, or, The preservation of favored races in the struggle for life. Modern Library 1993 689p $21.95 **576.8**
1. Heredity 2. Evolution 3. Human origins 4. Natural selection
ISBN 0-679-60070-1
LC 93-3598

First published 1859. Variant title: The origin of species by means of natural selection

The classic exposition of the "theory of evolution by natural selection. Darwin argues that every species develops or evolves from a previous one and that all life is a continuing pattern. His objects of study were the variations from generation to generation in domestic plants and animals. . . . While subsequent investigation has superseded some of Darwin's arguments, Origin of Species remains one of the most influential books ever published." Reader's Ency. 4th edition

Davies, P. C. W.

The **eerie** silence; renewing our search for alien intelligence. [by] Paul Davies. Houghton Mifflin Harcourt 2010 241p il $27 **576.8**
1. Life on other planets 2. Extraterrestrial beings 3. Unidentified flying objects
ISBN 978-0-547-13324-9; 0-547-13324-3
LC 2010-3088

"After 50 years of scanning the skies for signs of extraterrestrial intelligence, astronomers have only silence to report — an eerie silence, Davies argues. Part history of the search, part road map for its future and (large) part mind-stretching exercise, the book provides Davies' perspective on profound questions that have implications far beyond alien hunting." Sci News

Includes bibliographical references

Dawkins, Richard

★ The **ancestor's** tale; a pilgrimage to the dawn of evolution. with additional research by Yan Wong. Houghton Mifflin 2004 673p il $28; pa $16.95 **576.8**

1. Evolution

ISBN 0-618-00583-8; 0-618-61916-X pa

LC 2004-59864

The author "sets out on a pilgrimage tracing the history of the human species back to the very origins of life, marking along the way 39 rendezvous points where the human genealogical path crosses that of other terrestrial species. . . . Lively and daring, a book certain to draw even casual readers deep into the adventure—and controversy—of science." Booklist

Includes bibliographical references

The **greatest** show on Earth; the evidence for evolution. Free Press 2009 470p il map $30 **576.8**

1. Evolution

ISBN 978-1-4165-9478-9; 1-4165-9478-7

LC 2009-25330

"A pleasure in the face of so much scientific ignorance—biology rendered accessible and relevant to the utmost degree." Kirkus

Includes bibliographical references

★ **Evolution**; the first four billion years. edited by Michael Ruse [and] Joseph Travis; with a foreword by Edward O. Wilson. Belknap Press of Harvard University Press 2009 979p il map $39.95 **576.8**

1. Evolution

ISBN 9780674031753

LC 2008-30270

"If ever there were an education in a book, there's one in this massive volume." Booklist

Includes bibliographical references

Fortey, Richard A.

★ **Life**; a natural history of the first four billion years of life on earth. [by] Richard Fortey. Knopf 1998 346p il $32.59; pa $15 **576.8**

1. Evolution 2. Life -- Origin

ISBN 0-375-40119-9; 0-375-70261-X pa

LC 97-49466

First published 1997 in the United Kingdom with subtitle: an unauthorized biography

This work is "written for readers with no science. It will help them understand the specialized and often technical books on evolution that make headlines but leave most people wondering why." N Y Times Book Rev

Includes bibliographical references

Gould, Stephen Jay, 1941-2002

The **structure** of evolutionary theory. Belknap Press 2002 xxii, 1433p il $39.95 **576.8**

1. Evolution 2. Evolution (Biology) 3. Punctuated equilibrium (Evolution)

ISBN 0-674-00613-5

LC 2001-43556

This is a summation of the author's "life work, building on Dar-

winism to provide a . . . synthesis of how {in Gould's view} evolution has shaped the living world. . . . Gould says of his book that it 'cycles through the three central themes of Darwinian logic at three scales—by brief mention of a framework in (the introduction), by full exegesis of Darwin's presentation in Chapter 2, and by lengthy analysis of the major differences and effects in historical (part 1) and modern critiques (part 2) of these three themes in the rest of the volume.'" (N Y Rev Books) Index.

This is a "history and analysis of classical and twentieth-century evolutionary theory." Booklist

Includes bibliographical references

Grasset, Léo

How the Zebra Got Its Stripes; Darwinian Stories Told Through Evolutionary Biology. Léo Grasset, translated by Barbara Mellor. Pegasus Books 2017 256 p. illustrations (some color) (hardcover) $26.95 **576.8**

1. Evolution

ISBN 1681774143; 9781681774763; 9781681774145

This book, by Léo Grasset, translated by Barbara Mellor, "explains the intricacies of the animal kingdom through the lens of evolutionary biology. Why do giraffes have such long necks? Why are zebras striped? And why does the clitoris of the female hyena exactly resemble and in most respects function like the male's penis? Deploying the latest scientific research and his own extensive observations in Africa, Léo Grasset offers answers to these questions and many more in a book of post-Darwinian." (Publisher's note)

"Grasset's approach underlies a personal commitment to popularizing interesting facets of life-forms, using selected African fauna as a vehicle to entertain and inform the general public." Choice

Includes bibliographical references (pages 125-143) and index.

Johnson, Paul, 1928-

Darwin; portrait of a genius. Paul Johnson. Viking 2012 176 p. $25.95 **576.8**

1. Biography 2. Evolution 3. Social Darwinism 4. Naturalists -- England -- Biography

ISBN 0670025712; 9780670025718

LC 2012003433

In this book, Paul Johnson presents a biography of Charles Darwin. He "summarizes the key events of Darwin's formative days, then devotes the meat of the book to his development of the theory and the publication of 'The Origin of Species.' . . . Johnson also points to what he considers two central flaws in Darwin's work: a too-literal acceptance of Malthus' theories and insufficient understanding of anthropology." He also discusses social Darwinism. (Kirkus Reviews)

Jones, Steve

Darwin's ghost; the origin of species updated. Random House 2000 xxix, 377p il hardcover o.p. pa $15.95 **576.8**

1. Evolution 2. Natural selection

ISBN 0-345-42277-5 pa

LC 99-53246

First published 1999 in the United Kingdom with title: Almost like a whale

Jones "has updated Charles Darwin's On the origin of species (1859) so that the fact of organic evolution is both understandable and relevant to today's general reader. . . . Very informative and cogently argued, this book is an important addition to the natural history literature." Libr J

Includes bibliographical references

Kaufman, Marc

First contact; scientific breakthroughs in the hunt for life beyond Earth. Simon & Schuster 2011 213p il $26; ebook $12.99   **576.8**

1. Life on other planets

ISBN 978-1-4391-0900-7; 978-1-4391-3030-8 ebook

LC 2010-44630

Kaufman "takes us from beneath the surface of our planet, where scientists hunt for and study 'extremophile' microbes that alter our views of what is necessary for life to exist, to observatories and labs searching deep space for extraterrestrial signals or exoplanets, planets outside the solar system. Not only does the book suggest the breadth of the effort, it reveals how each aspect reveals ideas and science never before suspected. . . . [The author] does what excellent science reporters do—he translates at times difficult concepts into language those of us who barely passed 'Bonehead Chemistry' can understand." Seattle Post-Intelligencer

Includes bibliographical references

Keller, Michael

Charles Darwin's On the Origin of Species; a graphic adaptation. [by] Michael Keller; art by Nicolle Rager Fuller. Rodale 2009 192p il $19.99; pa $14.99   **576.8**

1. Naturalists 2. Graphic novels 3. Travel writers 4. Writers on science 5. Heredity -- Graphic novels 6. Evolution -- Graphic novels 7. Human origins -- Graphic novels 8. Natural selection -- Graphic novels

ISBN 978-1-60529-697-5; 1-60529-697-X; 978-1-60529-948-8 pa; 1-60529-948-0 pa

LC 2009-11387

"The first part of this book gives the background and context in which Darwin developed his theory of natural selection. Arriving home in 1836 after five years of exploration aboard the Beagle, he is asked to explain what he learned. Thus the structure of this graphic novel is established. Through his voice, readers learn about his discoveries and observations, his correspondence with other scientists who helped him formulate his theories, as well as his personal life. The second section highlights the salient points of the original On the Origin of Species." (School Library Journal)

"The graphic novel follows Origin's original chapters, combining snippets of Darwin's text with quotes from letters, illustrative examples from his time and from the present, and occasional invented dialog. Fuller's images of people seem clumsy, but her full-color plants, animals, charts, maps, and scientific accoutrements are attractive and effective. . . . [This] version well conveys both the science and the wonder of Origin." Libr J

Kirschvink, Joseph

A **new** history of life; the radical new discoveries about the origins and evolution of life on earth. Peter Ward & Joe Kirschvink. Bloomsbury Press 2015 416 p. illustrations (alk. paper) $30   **576.8**

1. Life sciences 2. Life -- Origin 3. Evolution (Biology)

ISBN 160819907X; 9781608199075

LC 2014029828

Authors Peter Ward and Joe Kirschvink "show that many of our long-held beliefs about the history of life are wrong. First, the development of life was not a stately, gradual process. Second, life consists of carbon, but three other molecules have determined how it evolved: oxygen, carbon dioxide, and hydrogen sulfide. Third, ever since Darwin we have thought of evolution in terms of species. Yet it is the evolution of ecosystems-from deep-ocean vents to rainforests-that has formed the living world." (Publisher's note)

Includes bibliographical references and index

Kolbert, Elizabeth

★ The **sixth** extinction; an unnatural history. Elizabeth Kolbert. First edition. Henry Holt and Co 2014 336 p. illustrations, map (hardback) $28   **576.8**

1. Extinction (Biology) 2. Environmental degradation 3. Human influence on nature 4. Mass extinctions 5. Environmental disasters

ISBN 0805092994; 9780805092998

LC 2013028683

Carnegie Medal Shortlist: Nonfiction (2015)

Pulitzer Prize: General Nonfiction (2015)

Kirkus Prize Finalist: Nonfiction (2014); National Book Critics Circle Finalist: Nonfiction (2014)

Los Angeles Times Book Prize: Science and Technology (2014)

"In 'The Sixth Extinction,' [author] Elizabeth Kolbert draws on the work of scores of researchers in half a dozen disciplines, accompanying many of them into the field: geologists who study deep ocean cores, botanists who follow the tree line as it climbs up the Andes, marine biologists who dive off the Great Barrier Reef. She introduces us to a dozen species, some already gone, others facing extinction." (Publisher's note)

"Kolbert . . . weaves a relatable element into the at-times heavily scientific discussion, bringing the sites of past and present extinctions vividly to life with fascinating information that will linger with readers long after they close the book. A highly significant eye-opener rich in facts and enjoyment." Kirkus

Includes bibliographical references and index

Larson, Edward J.

Evolution ; the remarkable history of a scientific theory. Modern Library 2004 337p il (Modern Library chronicles) $21.95; pa $14.95   **576.8**

1. Evolution

ISBN 0-679-64288-9; 0-8129-6849-2 pa

LC 2003-64888

This is an "overview of evolutionary thought from ancient speculations to the emergence of a neo-Darwinian synthesis. It focuses on those essential facts, events, and ideas that have contributed to the successes of scientific evolutionism. . . . Larson is to be commended for stressing the value of both scientific inquiry and the evolutionary framework. This outstanding book is highly recommended for all academic and public libraries." Libr J

Includes bibliographical references

Lister, Adrian

★ **Darwin's** fossils; the collection that shaped the theory of evolution. Adrian Lister. Smithsonian Books 2018 160 p. (pbk.) $19.95   **576.8**

1. Fossils 2. Evolution 3. Evolution (Biology) 4. Fossils -- Catalogs and collections

ISBN 9781588346179

LC 2017046415

This book, by Adrian Lister, "is an accessible account of [Charles] Darwin's pioneering work on fossils, his adventures in South America, and his relationship with the scientific establishment. . . . [The] book brings Darwin's fossils, many of which survive in museums and institutions around the world, together for the first time. . . . [It also] reveals how Darwin's discoveries played a crucial role in the development of his groundbreaking ideas." (Publisher's note)

"Richly illustrated with photos from the fossil collection and line drawings produced when Darwin was alive, Lister's work is an essential acquisition for every library prizing quality books on evolution." (Booklist)

Includes bibliographical references and index

Lloyd, Christopher

The **Story** of the World in 100 Species; Christopher Lloyd. SDC Publications 2016 416 p. color ill., color maps (paperback) $30.00 **576.8**

1. Ecology 2. Evolution

ISBN 9781408876381; 1408876388

This book, by Christopher Lloyd, "leads us on an extraordinary journey, from the birth of life to the present day, as he explains, in a jargon-free way, the phenomenon we call 'life on Earth.' . . . [It] explore[s] the creatures that evolved in the murky deep and crept up on the shore to become pioneers of life on land. He then investigates the world 'after humans' and how the coevolution of humans . . . has transformed the planet." (Publisher's note)

"Lloyd shares the history of each of his entrants with casual enthusiasm and a sense of wonder, in articles that stand alone well for readers interested in browsing and which together give a sense of biodiversity as a source of joy." Pub Wkly

Includes bibliographical references (pages 402-403) and index.

Losos, Jonathan B.

Improbable destinies; fate, chance, and the future of evolution. Jonathan B. Losos ; illustrated by Marlin Peterson. Riverhead Books 2017 xv, 368 p.p illustrations (hardcover) $28 **576.8**

1. Evolution 2. Natural selection 3. Science -- Popular works 4. Mutation (Biology) 5. Evolution (Biology)

ISBN 9780399184932; 9780399184925

LC 2016054594

In this book, author "Jonathan Losos reveals what the latest breakthroughs in evolutionary biology can tell us about one of the greatest ongoing debates in science. . . . He illustrates how experiments with guppies, fruit flies, bacteria, foxes, and field mice, along with his own work with anole lizards on Caribbean islands, are rewinding the tape of life to reveal just how rapid and predictable evolution can be. " (Publisher's note)

"A cheerful, delightfully lucid primer on evolution and the predictive possibilities within the field." Kirkus

Includes bibliographical references (pages [343]-353) and index.

Mayr, Ernst

What evolution is. Basic Bks. 2001 318p il maps hardcover o.p. pa $16 **576.8**

1. Evolution

ISBN 0-465-04426-3 pa

LC 2001-36562

"A wise and illuminating examination, by an illustrious evolutionary biologist, that sorts out the complexities of evolution." N Y Times Book Rev

Includes bibliographical references

McCalman, Iain, 1947-

Darwin's armada; four voyages and the battle for the theory of evolution. W.W. Norton & Co. 2009 422p il map **576.8**

1. Botanists 2. Evolution 3. Biologists 4. Naturalists 5. Essayists 6. Travel writers 7. Writers on science

ISBN 0-393-06814-5; 978-0-393-06814-6

LC 2009-16055

"This geographically expansive account of the rise of evolutionary theory traces the lives and travels of four titans of nineteenth-century biology: Darwin, the botanist Joseph Hooker, the physiologist Thomas Huxley, and Alfred Russel Wallace, a fearless globetrotter whose dangerous and often unpleasant journeys in the Amazon and the Malay Archipelago were the source of biological epiphanies and tens of thousands of specimens. Though these stories have been told before, McCalman's central conceit—that the four naturalists, who all travelled at length in the Southern Hemisphere, share a 'special bond of the salt'—supplies a fresh, antipodean perspective." New Yorker

Includes bibliographical references

Mesler, Bill

A **Brief** History of Creation; Science and the Search for the Origin of Life. by Bill Mesler and H. James Cleaves II. W W Norton & Co Inc 2015 336 p. illustrations $27.95 **576.8**

1. Biology 2. Creation 3. Theology 4. Evolution

ISBN 0393083551; 9780393083552

LC 2015024251

This book, by Bill Mesler and H. James Cleaves II, is the "epic story of the scientists through the ages who have sought answers to life's biggest mystery: How did it begin? . . . [They] examine historical discoveries in the context of philosophical debates, political change, and our evolving understanding of the complexity of biology. The story they tell is rooted in metaphysical arguments, in a changing understanding of the age of the Earth, and even in the politics of the Cold War." (Publisher's note)

"This lively, accessible book is recommended for science enthusiasts interested in origin of life issues and the history of science." LJ

Newitz, Annalee

Scatter, adapt, and remember; how humans will survive a mass extinction. Annalee Newitz. Doubleday 2013 320 p. illustrations, maps (hardcover; alk. paper) $26.95 **576.8**

1. Human beings 2. Survival skills 3. Extinction (Biology) 4. Survival

ISBN 0385535910; 9780385535915

LC 2012042409

LA Times Book Prize Finalist: Science & Technology (2013)

In this book, author Annalee Newitz "explains that although global disaster is all but inevitable, our chances of long-term species survival are better than ever. [She] focuses on humanity's long history of dodging the bullet, as well as on new threats that we may face in years to come. Most important, it explores how scientific breakthroughs today will help us avoid disasters tomorrow." (Publisher's note)

"Humans may be experts at destroying the planet, but we are no slouches at preserving it, either, and Newitz's shrewd speculations are heartening." Kirkus

Includes bibliographical references and index

Novacek, Michael J.

Terra; our 100-million-year-old ecosystem--and the threats that now put it at risk. [by] Michael Novacek. Farrar, Straus and Giroux 2007 xxiv, 451p il map $27 **576.8**

1. Ecology 2. Evolution 3. Environmental degradation 4. Human influence on nature

ISBN 978-0-374-27325-5; 0-374-27325-1

LC 2007-9126

The author takes a "look at what humans have done over time and in more recent years. Combining paleontology, evolutionary biology, and environmental science, he shows how these three perspectives can bring us to a better understanding of the 'mass extinction event' that threatens this planet if changes aren't implemented now." Libr J

Includes bibliographical references

Nye, Bill, 1955-

Undeniable; evolution and the science of creation. Bill Nye

with Corey Powell. St Martin's Press 2014 320 p. illustrations (hardcover; alk. paper) $25.99　　　**576.8**
1. Evolution 2. Creationism 3. Natural history 4. Religion and science 5. Creationism -- Popular works 6. Evolution (Biology) -- Popular works 7. Natural history -- Philosophy -- Popular works
ISBN 1250007135; 9781250007131

LC 2014027163

"Revealing the mechanics of evolutionary theory, the scientist, engineer and inventor presents a compelling argument for the scientific unviability of creationism and insists that creationism's place in the science classroom is harmful not only to our children, but to the future of the greater world as well." Publisher's Note

"The straightforward, accessible language and clear explanations make this ideal reading to understand life's origins, especially for those new to the evidence of evolution." LJ

Includes bibliographical references and index

Rutherford, Adam, ca. 1975-

Creation; how science is reinventing life itself. Adam Rutherford. Current 2013 288 p. (hardback) $27.95　　**576.8**
1. Life -- Origin 2. Genetic engineering 3. Biogenesis -- Popular Works
ISBN 1617230057; 9781617230059

LC 2013013441

Author Adam Rutherford's book brings "genomics and synthetic biology to life in this accessible overview of the past and future of the fields. In the first half," Rutherford "describes what we know about cellular biology, while the second portion explores where and how we might apply our growing knowledge base in the future. He argues that the theory of evolution does not aim to explain the origin of life, but he also insists that in order to know where we're going, we have to know where we're from, and one of the best ways to do that is to trace evolution at the cellular level." (Publisher's note)

Includes bibliographical references and index

Sasselov, Dimitar

The **life** of super-Earths; Dimitar Sasselov. Basic Books 2012 xvi, 202 p.p ill.　　　**576.8**
1. Exobiology 2. Extrasolar planets 3. Life on other planets 4. Life -- Origin 5. Synthetic biology
ISBN 9780465021932; 9780465023400

LC 2011036888

This book discusses the research supporting the claim for extraterrestrial life beyond Earth. Author Dimitar "Sasselov (Astronomy/Harvard Univ.) reviews the hard evidence in favor . . . before proceeding to explain discoveries and simulations that suggest we are not alone. No telescope has directly observed an extra-solar planet, but the author delivers a[n] . . . explanation of how instruments and, since 2009, a satellite are detecting subtle changes in a star's light or movement that reveal not only the presence of planets (600 so far) but their size, orbits and a hint of their composition. Sasselov maintains that the minority of 'super-earths' possess conditions favorable to life: proper temperature, protective atmosphere, volcanism and tectonic movements." (Kirkus)

Includes bibliographical references and index

Stott, Rebecca

★ **Darwin's** ghosts; the secret history of evolution. Rebecca Stott. Spiegel & Grau 2012 xviii, 396 p.p　　**576.8**
1. Evolution 2. Naturalists 3. Biology -- History 4. Scientists -- Biography 5. Naturalists -- Biography 6. Evolution (Biology) -- History
ISBN 1400069378; 9781400069378

LC 2011041951

This book "draws for readers stories of the people who came before [Charles] Darwin and who presented ideas that were precursors to the theory of evolution. . . . Many of the thinkers and ideas presented in this book . . . Darwin was not aware of until after the publication of 'On the Origin of Species.' After receiving a critical letter, he compiled a list of his scientific predecessors to be included in the foreword of later editions . . . including Aristotle, Al-Jahiz, Leonardo da Vinci, and Denis Diderot." (Library Journal)

Includes bibliographical references (p. [357]-376) and index

Switek, Brian

Written in stone; evolution, the fossil record and our place in nature. Brian Switek. 1st ed. Bellevue Literary Press 2010 320p il pa $17.95　　　**576.8**
1. Fossils 2. Evolution 3. Fossil hominids 4. Human evolution
ISBN 1-934137-29-4 pa; 978-1-934137-29-1 pa

This is a "history of evolutionary discovery." (Publisher's note) Index.

The author "presents a popular account of fossil discoveries, historical debates related to evolution, and how the unearthing of these missing links is filling in the gaps in evolutionary history. . . . Armchair scientists and general readers interested in evolution will enjoy this informative book." Libr J

Wall, Michael

Out there; a scientific guide to alien life, antimatter, and human space travel (for the cosmically curious) Michael Wall, PhD (senior writer, Space.com) Grand Central Publishing 2018 304 p. (hardcover) $27　　　**576.8**
1. Life on other planets 2. Extraterrestrial beings 3. Outer space -- Exploration
ISBN 9781538729373

LC 2018022905

This book, by Michael Wall, "is arranged in a simple question-and-answer format. . . . Dr. Wall covers questions far beyond alien life, venturing into astronomy, physics, and the practical realities of what long-term life might be like for we mere humans in outer space, such as the idea of lunar colonies, and even economic implications. Dr. Wall also shares the insights of some of the leading lights in space exploration today." (Publisher's note)

Ward, Peter Douglas

Life as we do not know it; the NASA search for (and synthesis of) alien life. Peter D. Ward. Viking 2005 xxvii, 292p ill. hardcover o.p. (pbk.) $15.00; o.p.　　　**576.8**
1. Science 2. Solar system 3. Life (Biology) 4. Life on other planets 5. Life -- Origin
ISBN 9780143038498; 0670034584

LC 2005056299

This book "sets a research agenda aimed at unraveling science's most profound questions: What is life, and where does it exist? To that query, he adds this philosophical discussion: What is humanity's role in life's unfolding on Earth and in the rest of the Solar System? . . . [Author Peter] Ward begins with a generally agreed-upon set of criteria — life metabolizes, has complexity and organization, reproduces, develops, evolves, and is autonomous — but then proposes the controversial hypothesis that this definition should include viruses. . . . Ward leaves no solar-system world unvisited. He quickly dismisses Mercury but spends a number of pages discussing the possibility of life floating high in the sulfuric-acid-laced clouds of Venus. . . . Mars gets the most attention outside of Earth." (National Space Society)

The author "believes researchers might be taking the wrong approach by looking only for earthly DNA-based life forms. Truly alien life, he argues, might have completely different origins. . . . The science is neatly laid out, and readers willing to follow his daring, scientifically based speculations will find their imaginations spurred." Publ Wkly

Includes bibliographical references (p. [257]-278) and index

Wesson, Rob

Darwin's first theory; exploring Darwin's quest to find a theory of the Earth. Rob Wesson. Pegasus Books Ltd. 2017 384 p. illustrations, maps (hardcover) $29.95 **576.8**
1. Geodynamics -- History 2. Voyages around the world 3. Geology -- History -- 19th century
ISBN 9781681773773; 9781681773162; 1681773163

This book, by Rob Wesson, "leads the reader on an adventure through the landscape that absorbed and inspired Charles Darwin. . . . As he follows Darwin's path—literally and intellectually—Wesson experiences the land as Darwin did, engages with his observations, and tackles the same questions Darwin had about our ever-changing Earth." (Publisher's note)

"In this recovery of Darwin's early adulthood, Wesson reminds readers that the great naturalist began his scientific career as a geologist framing his first daring hypotheses in geological, not biological, terms." Booklist

Includes bibliographical references (pages 385-439) and index.

Wilson, David Sloan

★ **Evolution** for everyone; how Darwin's theory can change the way we think about our lives. Delacorte Press 2007 390p $24 **576.8**
1. Evolution
ISBN 978-0-385-34021-2; 0-385-34021-4

LC 2006-23685

"Rather than catalog its successes, denounce its detractors or in any way present evolutionary theory as the province of expert tacticians like himself, Wilson invites readers inside and shows them how Darwinism is done, and at lesson's end urges us to go ahead, feel free to try it at home. The result is a sprightly, absorbing and charmingly earnest book that manages a minor miracle, the near-complete emulsifying of science and the 'real world,' ingredients too often kept stubbornly, senselessly apart." N Y Times Book Rev

Includes bibliographical references

Young, Christian C.

★ **Evolution** and creationism; a documentary and reference guide. [by] Christian C. Young and Mark A. Largent. Greenwood Press 2007 298p il $85 **576.8**
1. Evolution 2. Creationism
ISBN 978-0-313-33953-0; 0-313-33953-8

LC 2007-10682

"This reference work provides over 40 of the most important documents to help readers understand the [evolution versus creationism] debate in the eyes of the people of the time. Each document is from a major participant in the debates from the predecessors of Darwin to the judges of the influential court cases of the present day." Publisher's note

Includes bibliographical references

576.82   Theories of evolution

Fuller, Randall, 1963-

The **book** that changed America; how Darwin's theory of evolution ignited a nation. Randall Fuller. Viking 2017 304 p.

illustrations (hardcover) $27; (ebook) $65 **576.82**
1. Evolution 2. Evolution (Biology) -- United States -- History -- 19th century
ISBN 9780525428336; 9780698186675

LC 2016010344

This book, by Randall Fuller, focuses on a unique "moment in American history when the ideas of Charles Darwin reshaped American notions about nature, religion, science and race. . . . Fuller takes us back to . . . 1860, with the story of the influence of Charles Darwin's just-published On the Origin of Species on five American intellectuals, including Bronson Alcott, Henry David Thoreau, the child welfare reformer Charles Loring Brace, and the abolitionist Franklin Sanborn." (Publisher's note)

"A fresh, invigorating history of philosophical and political struggles." Kirkus

Includes bibliographical references and index

576.839   Extraterrestrial life

Preston, Louisa

Goldilocks and the water bears; the search for life in the universe. Louisa Preston. St. Martin's Press 2016 288 p. illustrations $27 **576.839**
1. Astronomy 2. Astrophysics 3. Space sciences 4. Life on other planets
ISBN 1472920090; 9781472920096; 9781472920089

This book in the Bloomsbury Sigma series, by Louisa Preston, deals with "astrobiology[, which] is the study of life in the universe from its origins to its evolution into intelligent sentient beings. All life as we know it is carbon-based, . . . and as far as we are aware, exists only on Earth. . . . We can learn much about the possibilities of extraterrestrial life . . . by exploring organisms still present in harsh environments on Earth that mimic those on other worlds." (Publishers's note)

"Preston's accessible writing style, enthusiasm, and optimism succeed at informing as well as tickling readers' imaginations." Pub Wkly

576.84   Evolutionary cycles

Thomas, Chris D.

Inheritors of the Earth; how nature is thriving in an age of extinction. Chris D. Thomas. Public Affairs 2017 viii, 300 p.p illustrations, maps (hardcover) $28 **576.84**
1. Evolution 2. Biodiversity 3. Human influence on nature 4. Species -- Popular works 5. Biodiversity -- Popular works 6. Evolution (Biology) -- Popular works 7. Resilience (Ecology) -- Popular works 8. Nature -- Effect of human beings on -- Popular works
ISBN 9781610397278; 9781610397285

LC 2017941303

In this book, biologist Chris Thomas shows that although human beings have permanently damaged the natural world, they are also "helping nature grow and change. Human cities and mass agriculture have created new places for enterprising animals and plants to live, and our activities have stimulated evolutionary change in virtually every population of living species." (Publisher's note)

Includes bibliographical references (pages 256-282) and index.

577   Ecology

Burdick, Alan

★ **Out** of Eden; an odyssey of ecological invasion. Farrar, Straus & Giroux 2005 324p il $25; pa $14   **577**

1. Ecology 2. Biological invasions

ISBN 0-374-21973-7; 0-374-53043-2 pa

LC 2005-922517

National Book Award Finalist: Nonfiction (2005)

"A sober report, Burdick's work still sounds an alarm for readers concerned with the way humans alter nature." Booklist

Carroll, Sean

The **Big** Picture; On the Origins of Life, Meaning, and the Universe Itself. by Sean Carroll. Penguin Group USA 2016 496 p. illustrations $28   **577**

1. Universe 2. Quantum theory

ISBN 0525954821; 9780525954828

LC 2015050590

In this book, by Sean Carroll, "readers learn the difference between how the world works at the quantum level, the cosmic level, and the human level--and then how each connects to the other. Carroll's presentation of the principles that have guided the scientific revolution from Darwin and Einstein to the origins of life, consciousness, and the universe is dazzlingly unique." (Publisher's note)

"Carroll is the perfect guide on this wondrous journey of discovery. A brilliantly lucid exposition of profound philosophical and scientific issues in a language accessible to lay readers." Kirkus

Includes bibliographical references and index.

Christopher, Thomas

Garden revolution; How Our Landscapes Can Be a Source of Environmental Change. Larry Weaner and Thomas Christopher. Timber Press 2016 328 p. color illustrations $39.95 **577**

1. Gardening 2. Landscape ecology

ISBN 9781604696165

LC 2015036650

This book, by Larry Weaner and Thomas Christopher, "shows how an ecological approach to planting can lead to beautiful gardens that buck much of conventional gardening's counter-productive, time-consuming practices. Instead of picking the wrong plant and then constantly tilling, weeding, irrigating, and fertilizing, Weaner advocates for choosing plants that are adapted to the soil and climate of a specific site and letting them naturally evolve over time." (Publisher's note)

"With accompanying stunning color photographs, the authors invite readers into a world of new landscape possibilities with an eye toward natural beauty and sustainability." Pub Wkly

Includes bibliographical references and index

Egan, Dan

★ The **death** and life of the Great Lakes; Dan Egan. W W Norton & Co Inc 2017 xix, 364 p.p illustrations, map (hardcover) $27.95   **577**

1. Great Lakes 2. Lake ecology 3. Great Lakes (North America) -- Environmental conditions

ISBN 0393246434; 9780393246438; 9780393246445

LC 016039546

LA Times Book Prize: History (2017)

This book, by Dan Egan, "provides a chilling account of how sea lamprey, zebra and quagga mussels and other invaders have made their way into the [Great] Lakes, decimating native species and largely destroying the age-old ecosystem. And because the lakes are no longer iso-lated, the invaders now threaten water intake pipes, hydroelectric dams and other infrastructure across the country." (Publisher's note)

"Egan . . . effectively calls attention to the inherent fragility of the Great Lakes in this thought-provoking investigation, providing a modern history of the lakes . . . and the problems that have plagued them." Pub Wkly

Includes bibliographical references (pages [325]-347) and index.

Roston, Eric

The **carbon** age; how life's core element has become civilization's greatest threat. Distributed to the trade by Macmillan 2008 309p il $25.99   **577**

1. Carbon 2. Atmosphere

ISBN 978-0-8027-1557-9; 0-8027-1557-5

LC 2008-2754

"The first half traces carbon's history from the beginning of the universe, the Big Bang, and the nucleosynthesis (the formation of the elements) through the life cycle of stars, and then covers the development of life and dynamics of the 'natural' carbon cycle of Earth. The second section spans the last 150 years and delves into the impact of humans on the climate in creating what Roston calls the 'industrial carbon cycle.' Without using a great deal of scientific jargon, Roston leads us patiently and clearly through this complex issue." Libr J

Includes bibliographical references

Wills, Christopher

Green Equilibrium; The Vital Balance of Humans and Nature. Christopher Wills. Oxford University Press 2013 320 p. $34.95   **577**

1. Ecology 2. Evolution 3. Ecosystem health 4. Biotic communities 5. Ecosystem management 6. Nature -- Effect of human beings on 7. Human beings -- Effect of environment on

ISBN 0199645701; 9780199645701

LC 2012277418

In this book, Christopher Wills "recounts visits to diverse wildlife reserves around the world, illustrated with his photographs, while discussing many aspects of evolution. The author describes a green equilibrium as balance among organisms that maintains a local ecosystem. No paradise, it includes predation, disease, and starvation." Humans' effects, both positive and negative, on ecosystems are considered. (Library Journal)

Includes bibliographical references (p. 247-267) and index

577.2   Specific factors affecting ecology

Global weirdness; severe storms, deadly heat waves, relentless drought, rising seas, and the weather of the future. produced by Climate Central. Pantheon Books 2012 214 p. ill. $22.95   **577.2**

1. Meteorology 2. Climate change 3. Global warming 4. Climatic changes 5. Weather forecasting 6. Global environmental change 7. Climatic changes -- Forecasting 8. Climatic changes -- Mathemathical models 9. Greenhouse gases -- Environmental aspects

ISBN 0307907309; 9780307907301

LC 2011047699

This book, "[p]roduced by Climate Central, . . . summarizes . . . everything we know about the science of climate change; explains what is likely to happen to the climate in the future; and lays out in practical terms what we can and cannot do to avoid further shifts. Sixty . . . entries tackle such questions as: Is climate ever 'normal'? . . . [and w]hat risks

does climate change pose for human health?" (Publisher's note)
Includes bibliographical references (p. 201-214).

Montaigne, Fen
  Fraser's penguins; a journey to the future in Antarctica.
Henry Holt and Co. 2010 288p il map $26   **577.2**
  1. Penguins 2. Human influence on nature 3. Ecologists 4.
Climate -- Environmental aspects 5. Antarctica -- Description and
travel
  ISBN 978-0-8050-7942-5; 0-8050-7942-4
                                               LC 2010-07151
  The author "spent five months tracking penguins through the breeding season on the northwestern Antarctica peninsula with the scientist
Bill Fraser, and his book is a bittersweet account of the stark beauty of
the continent and the climate change that threatens its delicate ecosystem. . . . Montaigne poetically portrays the daunting Antarctic landscape
and gives readers an intimate perspective on its rugged, audacious, and
charming penguin and human inhabitants." Publ Wkly
  Includes bibliographical references

577.27 Effects of humans on ecology

Vince, Gaia
  Adventures in the anthropocene; a journey to the heart of
the planet we made. Gaia Vince. Milkweed Editions 2014 448
p. illustrations, map (alk. paper) $30   **577.27**
  1. Global warming 2. Environmental health 3. Pollution control
industry 4. Global environmental change 5. Global environmental
change -- Social aspects
  ISBN 1571313575; 9781571313577
                                               LC 2014017309
  In this book, science journalist and author Gaia Vince "chronicles a
two-year journey around the globe to evaluate warnings that we face an
ecological tipping point. . . . Despite [the] dim picture, the author found
grounds for optimism on her travels. . . . In China and India, she chronicles government efforts to address atmospheric pollution and looming
water shortages. Her main interest, however, is the inventiveness of
people at the local level dealing with these problems." (Kirkus Reviews)
  "There is no avoiding the complexity and severity of the situations
Vince delineates, but she aims for positivity as she celebrates the wonders of nature and reminds us that we are a superbly adaptive species."
Booklist
  Includes bibliographical references and index

577.276 Air pollution

Nuccitelli, Dana
  Climatology versus pseudoscience; exposing the failed predictions of global warming skeptics. Dana Nuccitelli. Praeger,
an imprint of ABC-CLIO, LLC 2015 xiii, 212 p.p illustrations
(alk. paper) $48   **577.276**
  1. Climate 2. Climate change 3. Global warming 4. Climatic
changes
  ISBN 1440832013; 9781440832017
                                               LC 2014046795
  This book, by Dana Nuccitelli, "explains the science of climate
change in plain language and shows that the 2 to 4 percent of climate
scientists who are skeptical that humans are the main cause of global
warming are a fringe minority—and have a well-established history of
being wrong." (Publisher's note)

"The book includes the best available short account of the history of
climate science and describes climate change models and controversies
in brief but incisive and well-illustrated detail." Choice.
  Includes bibliographical references (pages 189-204) and index

577.3 Ecology of specific environments

Fortey, Richard
  The **wood** for the trees; one man's long view of nature.
Richard Fortey. Alfred A. Knopf 2016 320 p. ill. (some color),
maps (ebook) $65; (hardcover) $28.95   **577.3**
  1. Forests and forestry -- England 2. Chiltern Hills (England) --
History 3. Phenology -- England -- Chiltern Hills 4. Old growth
forests -- England -- Chiltern Hills
  ISBN 9781101875766; 9781101875759
                                               LC 2015048791
  This book, by Richard Fortey, is a "'biography' of four acres of
woodland, evoking a cosmos of living and inanimate things and imagining its millennia of existence. A few years ago, . . . Fortey purchased
four acres of woodland in the Chiltern Hills of Oxfordshire, England. .
. . Fortey, along with the occasional expert friend, investigates the forest top to bottom, discovering a new species and explaining the myriad
connections that tie us to nature and nature to itself." (Publisher's note)
  "An eloquent, eccentric, and precise nature memoir." Kirkus
  Includes bibliographical references and index

Haskell, David G., 1969-
  The **forest** unseen; a year's watch in nature. David George
Haskell. Viking 2012 268 p   **577.3**
  1. Seasons 2. Nature study 3. Philosophy of nature 4. Natural
history -- Tennessee 5. Forests and forestry -- Tennessee 6. Seasons
-- Tennessee 7. Nature observation -- Tennessee 8. Old growth
forests -- Tennessee 9. Old growth forest ecology -- Tennessee
  ISBN 9780670023370
                                               LC 2011037552
  In this book, "biologist David Haskell uses a one-square-meter
patch of old-growth Tennessee forest as a window onto the entire natural world. Visiting it almost daily for one year to trace nature's path
through the seasons, he brings the forest and its inhabitants to . . . life.
Each of this book's short chapters begins with a simple observation: a
salamander scuttling across the leaf litter; the first blossom of spring
wildflowers. From these, Haskell spins a . . . web of biology and ecology, explaining the science that binds together the tiniest microbes and
the largest mammals and describing the ecosystems that have cycled for
thousands- sometimes millions-of years." (Publisher's note)
  Includes bibliographical references and index

Preston, Richard
  The **wild** trees; a story of passion and daring. Random
House 2007 294p il map $25.95; pa $16   **577.3**
  1. Redwood 2. Botanists 3. College teachers
  ISBN 978-1-4000-6489-2; 1-4000-6489-9; 978-0-8129-7559-8
pa; 0-8129-7559-6 pa
                                               LC 2006-48646
  The author tells the story of Steve Sillett, Marie Antoine and other
naturalists and researchers who climb and explore giant redwoods in
northern California
  "There is something so elementally boyish in searching out the biggest and tallest, poring over maps and measurements, dubbing these
trees with names lifted from J.R.R. Tolkein's Middle Earth. . . . Preston
knows how to fold the science into the seams of his narrative, and his dry
humor crops up, pleasurably, at the edges of his observations." Cleve-

land Plain Dealer

LC 2016029007

In this book, author "Nancy Lawson describes why and how to welcome wildlife to our backyards. Through engaging anecdotes and inspired advice, profiles of home gardeners throughout the country, and interviews with scientists and horticulturalists, Lawson applies the broader lessons of ecology to our own outdoor spaces." (Publisher's note)

"This gorgeously written, well-argued title will help backyard gardeners see all creatures, from insects to elk, as visitors to be welcomed rather than pests to be removed." LJ

Includes bibliographical references

577.34   Rain forest ecology

Lowman, Margaret

Life in the treetops; adventures of a woman in field biology. [by] Margaret D. Lowman. Yale Univ. Press 1999 219p il maps hardcover o.p. pa $13.95   **577.34**

1. Botanists 2. Women scientists
ISBN 0-300-07818-8; 978-0-300-07818-3; 0-300-08464-1 pa; 978-0-300-08464-1 pa

LC 98-48691

Lowman "gives a funny, unassuming and deeply idiosyncratic chronicle of her trials and triumphs as a field biologist of tree canopies and other ecosystems in Australia, New England, Belize, Panama and elsewhere." N Y Times Book Rev

Includes bibliographical references

Followed by It's a jungle up there! (2006)

Royte, Elizabeth

The **Tapir's** morning bath; mysteries of the tropical rain forest and the scientists who are trying to solve them. Houghton Mifflin 2001 328p maps $25; pa $14   **577.34**

1. Rain forest ecology 2. Panama -- Description
ISBN 0-395-97997-8; 0-618-25758-6 pa

LC 2001-24989

Royte discusses time spent with scientists studying the ecology of Barro Colorado, an island in the Panama Canal.

This is "a superb introduction to tropical ecology and theoretical biology, as well as original and thoroughly engaging travel writing." Publ Wkly

Includes bibliographical references

577.5   Ecology of miscellaneous environments

Barilla, James

★ **My** Backyard Jungle; The Adventures of an Urban Wildlife Lover Who Turned His Yard into Habitat and Learned to Live With It. James Barilla. Yale University Press 2013 376 p. $28   **577.5**

1. Wildlife conservation 2. Human-animal relationships 3. Habitat (Ecology) 4. Urban ecology (Biology) 5. Animals and civilization
ISBN 0300184018; 9780300184013

LC 2012040298

In this book, James Barilla "takes readers on his personal journey to explore human and animal relationships in shared habitats around the world. To begin with, he had his own property in Columbia, SC, certified by the National Wildlife Federation as a wildlife habitat. . . . Going between his backyard and distant locations, his chapters cover topics from idealized children's toys . . . to the illegal wildlife trade." (Library Journal)

Includes bibliographical references (pages 349-353) and index

Lawson, Nancy

The **humane** gardener; nurturing a backyard habitat for wildlife. Nancy Lawson. Princeton Architectural Press 2017 223 p. color illustrations (alk. paper) $24.95   **577.5**

1. Wildlife 2. Garden ecology 3. Gardening to attract wildlife
ISBN 9781616896171; 9781616895549

Schilthuizen, Menno

Darwin comes to town; how the urban jungle drives evolution. Menno Schilthuizen. Picador 2018 304 p. (hardcover) $27   **577.5**

1. Evolution 2. Urban ecology 3. Human influence on nature 4. Evolution (Biology) 5. Urban ecology (Biology) 6. Nature -- Effect of human beings on
ISBN 9781250127822

LC 2017059153

In this book, author Menno Schilthuizen "takes us around the world for an up-close look at just how stunningly flexible and swift-moving natural selection can be. . . . [The book] draws on eye-popping examples of adaptation to share a stunning vision of urban evolution in which humans and wildlife co-exist in a unique harmony. It reveals that evolution can happen far more rapidly than [Charles] Darwin dreamed." (Publisher's note)

Includes bibliographical references and index

577.57   Soil ecology

Montgomery, David R.

Growing a revolution; bringing our soil back to life. David R. Montgomery. W W Norton & Co Inc 2017 316 p. (hardcover) $26.95   **577.57**

1. Soil ecology 2. Sustainable agriculture 3. Soil biology 4. Soil science 5. Soil restoration 6. Sustainable agriculture
ISBN 9780393608335; 9780393608328

LC 2016055810

The book, by David R. Montgomery, "introduces us to farmers around the world at the heart of a brewing soil health revolution that could bring humanity's ailing soil back to life remarkably fast. [It] draws on visits to farms in the industrialized world and developing world to show that a new combination of farming practices can deliver innovative, cost-effective solutions to problems farmers face today." (Publisher's note)

"Relevant to farmers, backyard gardeners, and everyone who cares about our future, this is a clarion call that should not be ignored." Booklist

Includes bibliographical references and index

577.6   Aquatic ecology

Douglas, Marjory Stoneman

The **Everglades**; river of grass. illustrated by Robert Fink; [update by Michael Grunwald] 60th anniversary ed; Pineapple Press 2007 447p $19.95   **577.6**

1. Everglades (Fla.)
ISBN 978-1-56164-394-3

LC 2007-28384

First published 1947 by Rinehart

A natural history of South Florida focusing on the unique ecosystem of the Everglades. Discusses environmental changes, scientific research, and political responses to conservation efforts.

Includes bibliographical references

577.7 Marine ecology

Ellis, Richard

The **empty** ocean; plundering the world's marine life. written and illustrated by Richard Ellis. Island Press 2003 367p il hardcover o.p. pa $25; pa $37.50   **577.7**

    1. Marine ecology 2. Endangered species

    ISBN 1-55963-974-1; 1-55963-637-8 pa; 9781559636377

"Rather than writing the 'Silent Spring' of the oceans, [Ellis] has produced a book that is likely to provide the inspiration and source materials for such a badly needed work . . . It is also a splendid example of history illuminating ecology, with well-chosen facts that enable us to picture a largely invisible catastrophe." N Y Times Book Rev

Includes bibliographical references

578 Natural history of organisms and related subjects

Weidensaul, Scott

    ★ **Return** to wild America; a yearlong journey in search of the continent's natural soul. North Point Press 2005 xx, 394p il map $26; pa $15   **578**

    1. Artists 2. Illustrators 3. Ornithologists 4. Writers on nature 5. Natural history -- North America

    ISBN 0-8654-7688-8; 0-8654-7731-0 pa

        LC 2005-47720

Fifty years after the publishing of Roger Tory Peterson's and James Fisher's Wild America, the author retraces Peterson and Fisher's steps "from Newfoundland's craggy coastline, down the East Coast, into Mexico and up the West Coast to Alaska. . . . This engrossing state-of-nature memoir, making a vibrant case for preserving America's wild past for future Americans, promises to become a classic in its own right." Publ Wkly

Includes bibliographical references

578.4 Adaptation

Forbes, Peter

Dazzled and deceived; mimicry and camouflage. Yale University Press 2009 283p il map $27.50   **578.4**

    1. Camouflage (Biology)

    ISBN 978-0-300-12539-9; 0-300-12539-9

        LC 2009-23577

"Forbes has produced a colorful look at camouflage in nature and battle, with a focus on the two world wars. . . . [The book] straddles the worlds of evolutionary biology, art, and military strategy with a world-class cast of characters, among them Charles Darwin, Pablo Picasso, Vladimir Nabokov, Theodore Roosevelt, and Winston Churchill. A pivotal character is Abbott Handerson Thayer, the eccentric New England painter who studied the animals near his summer home in Dublin, N.H., and is one of the few artists to have a scientific law (Thayer's Law of Concealing Coloration) named after him." Boston Globe

Includes bibliographical references

Morris, Patrick

Life; extraordinary animals, extreme behaviour. [by] Martha Holmes and Mike Gunton; [with] Rupert Barrington ... [et al.] University of California Press 2010 311p il map   **578.4**

    1. Animal behavior 2. Adaptation (Biology)

    ISBN 0-520-26537-8; 978-0-520-26537-0

        LC 2009-31158

First published 2009 in the United Kingdom

"In 2009, to commemorate the 200th anniversary of Charles Darwin's birth, the BBC premiered the ten-episode television documentary Life to great acclaim. . . . Written by the documentary's producers, this impressive companion volume showcases species of fish, amphibians, reptiles, insects, birds, mammals, and plants that have developed unique or unusual strategies for solving 'the eternal problems of life': finding food, escaping predators, attracting mates, and raising young. . . . Even the most casual reader will be awed by the beauty, complexity, and ingenuity of nature as celebrated here." Libr J

Simon, Matt

The **wasp** that brainwashed the caterpillar; evolution's most unbelievable solutions to life's biggest problems. Matt Simon ; illustrated by Vladimir Stankovic. Penguin Books 2016 272 p. illustrations (hardcover) $20   **578.4**

    1. Evolution 2. Adaptation (Biology) 3. Zoology -- Popular works 4. Parasitism 5. Predation (Biology) 6. Animals -- Adaptation

    ISBN 9780143128687; 014312868X

        LC 2016001823

Alex Award (2017)

This book, by Matt Simon, presents an account of several unusual evolutionary adaptations within the animal kingdom. The author "introduces you to the creatures that have it figured out, the ones that joust with their mustaches or choke sharks to death with snot, all in a wild struggle to survive and, of course, find true love." (Publisher's note)

"This is not an in-depth look at evolutionary processes; each entry in the parade of creatures is brief. Simon's wit, combined with the genuine eccentricity of his subjects, make this a fun and accessible book." Pub Wkly

Includes bibliographical references

578.6 Miscellaneous nontaxonomic kinds of organisms

Hamilton, Garry

Super species; the creatures that will dominate the planet. Firefly Books 2010 271p il $35   **578.6**

    1. Nonindigenous pests 2. Biological invasions

    ISBN 978-1-55407-630-7; 1-55407-630-7

        LC 2011286604

"Well researched and written, with an abundance of excellent photos, this work provides an outstanding, balanced look at this group of species." Choice

Includes bibliographical references

578.68 Rare and endangered species

Flach, Tim

    ★ **Endangered**; Tim Flach ; text by Professor Jonathan Baillie, Sam Wells. Abrams, in association with Blackwell & Ruth 2017 335 p. $65   **578.68**

    1. Rare animals -- Pictorial works 2. Endangered species --

Pictorial works
ISBN 9781419726514

LC 2016960608

This book, with photographs by Tim Flach and text by Jonathan Baillie, is "the result of an extraordinary multiyear project to document the lives of threatened species. . . . Traveling around the world[,] . . . Flach has constructed a powerful visual record of remarkable animals and ecosystems facing harsh challenges. Among them are primates coping with habitat loss, . . . and numerous bird species taken as pets." (Publisher's note)

Includes bibliographical references.

578.7 Organisms characteristic of specific kinds of environments

Burt, William

Marshes; the disappearing Edens. Yale University Press 2007 179p il $35   **578.7**
1. Marshes
ISBN 978-0-300-12229-9; 0-300-12229-2

LC 2006-26961

This book combines photographs of marsh life with information about wetland habitat in North America.

"This well-structured, readable book will be valuable for students, teachers, researchers, and sundry readers interested in a unique kind of wetland. Reading this book is an excellent way to understand marshes as wild places." Choice

Includes bibliographical references

Carson, Rachel

Under the sea wind; introduction by Linda Lear; illustrations by Howard Frech. Penguin Books 2007 xx, 184p il (Penguin classics) pa $15   **578.7**
1. Marine biology
ISBN 978-0-14-310496-4

LC 2006-50707

First published 1941 by Simon & Schuster

A series of narratives describe the birds and sea creatures that inhabit the Eastern coasts of North America.

Includes bibliographical references

Cramer, Deborah

Smithsonian ocean; our water, our world. Smithsonian Books 2008 295p il map $39.95   **578.7**
1. Marine biology 2. Marine ecology
ISBN 978-0-06-134383-4; 0-06-134383-8

LC 2008-15633

"With its hundreds of beautiful photographs, the volume is visually enchanting. It is also a vividly, accurately, and clearly written survey of the state of our understanding . . . of the history and current condition of the ocean." Sci Books Films

Includes bibliographical references

Crist, Darlene Trew

World ocean census; a global survey of marine life. [by] Darlene Trew Crist, Gail Scowcroft, James M. Harding, Jr. Firefly Books 2009 256p il map $40   **578.7**
1. Marine animals 2. Marine biology 3. Science -- Methodology 4. Census of Marine Life (Project)
ISBN 978-1-55407-434-1; 1-55407-434-7

The authors "have produced a highly readable text with stunning

photos that should fully engage the public imagination." Publ Wkly
Includes bibliographical references

DeStefano, Stephen

Coyote at the kitchen door; living with wildlife in suburbia. Harvard University Press 2010 196p il $24.95   **578.7**
1. Coyotes 2. Urbanization 3. Suburban life 4. Wildlife conservation
ISBN 978-0-674-03556-0; 0-674-03556-9

The author "examines the expanding field of 'urban ecology' in this pithy volume. Urban ecologists study changes in human-animal interactions caused by factors like sprawl, traffic, and noise pollution, in an attempt to understand why some species (the mountain lion, say) are badly disrupted by human developments, while others, such as the coyote, appear to be thriving—turning up in more and more Eastern back yards. DeStefano cites some alarming facts . . . but, having experienced the benefits of a suburban childhood, he refuses to reduce his thinking to a view in which wilderness preservation is the only solution." New Yorker

Includes bibliographical references

Kirby, Richard R.

Ocean drifters; a secret world beneath the waves. Firefly Books 2011 192p il $29.95   **578.7**
1. Marine plankton
ISBN 978-1-55407-982-7; 1-55407-982-9

LC 2011284690

"Kirby (Marine Inst. Research Fellow, Plymouth Univ., UK), who has published widely in scientific journals, combines in this book his area of expertise-plankton-with magnificent color photography of each species. He details the importance of the ocean's plankton layer to the health of the globe and its effects on sea and human life in the photos' descriptions...Recommended for readers interested in the smaller denizens of the natural world, the ocean, or microphotography." (Library Journal)

Koslow, J. Anthony

The silent deep; the discovery, ecology, and conservation of the deep sea. [by] Tony Koslow. University of Chicago Press 2007 270p il map $35   **578.7**
1. Marine ecology 2. Marine resources 3. Conservation of natural resources
ISBN 978-0-226-45125-1; 0-226-45125-9

LC 2006-22282

"This important book should be read by everyone who cares about Earth's future." Choice

Includes bibliographical references

Rice, Stanley A.

Encyclopedia of biodiversity; author, Stanley A Rice. Facts On File 2012 598 p. $95   **578.7**
1. Biology -- Encyclopedias 2. Evolution -- Encyclopedias 3. Biodiversity -- Encyclopedias
ISBN 0816077266; 9780816077267

LC 2010050557

This biology and evolutionary science encyclopedia, by Stanley A. Rice, provides "information about groups of organisms (from bacteria to mammals) and about ecological concepts and processes (such as biogeography and ecological succession). . . . Tables at the end of each entry . . . allow . . . readers to see how environmental conditions and biodiversity have changed through evolutionary time." (Publisher's note)

"The text is suitable for high school students but advanced enough for adult readers, too. Although there are many encyclopedias on ecology, resources, and science, this one presents important biodiversity topics in one volume, providing a handy overview for term papers and class presentations." LJ

Includes bibliographical references and index

Sardet, Christian

Plankton; wonders of the drifting world. Christian Sardet ; edited by Rafael D. Rosengarten and Theodore Rosengarten ; translated from the French by Christian Sardet and Dana Sardet ; prologue by Mark Ohman. University of Chicago Press 2015 224 p. illustrations (chiefly color) (cloth; alkaline paper) $45 **578.7**

1. Marine biology 2. Marine ecology 3. Plankton -- Pictorial works

ISBN 022618871X; 9780226188713

LC 2014034445

This book by Christian Sardet "transports readers into the currents, where jeweled chains hang next to phosphorescent chandeliers, spidery claws jut out from sinuous bodies, and gelatinous barrels protect microscopic hearts. The creatures¿ vibrant colors pop against the black pages, allowing readers to examine every eye and follow every tentacle. Jellyfish, tadpoles, and bacteria all find a place in the book, representing the broad scope of organisms dependent on drifting currents." (Publisher's note)

"A fascinating book that will cause readers to think deeply about plankton and its importance to human and animal life. A biology or general science background is not necessary to read this book; the reader needs only a desire to learn more about these intriguing organisms." LJ

Includes bibliographical references and index

Wolfe, David W.

Tales from the underground; a natural history of subterranean life. Perseus Bks. 2001 221p il hardcover o.p. pa $18 **578.7**

1. Soil microbiology

ISBN 0-7382-0679-2 pa

The author discusses the ecology of life in the soil and the earth's rocky crust, including Darwin's experiments with earthworms, Lewis and Clark's first encounter with prairie dogs, the use of genetic tools, and the possible role of primitive underground microbes in evolution.

Wolfe "explains in a straightforward, readable style that there is probably as much biodiversity and even as much biomass below ground as above." New Sci

Includes bibliographical references

579   Natural history of microorganisms, fungi, algae

Ben-Barak, Idan

The invisible kingdom; from the tips of our fingers to the tops of our trash, inside the curious world of microbes. Basic Books 2009 204p $24 **579**

1. Microbiology

ISBN 978-0-465-01887-1; 0-465-01887-4

LC 2009-19655

The author "gives an enthusiastic tour of single-celled life. . . . He touches on myriad microbes in a range of environments, from the abyss of the sea to the inside of humans, explaining how they defend themselves, eat, move, and reproduce." Booklist

Includes bibliographical references

Dunn, Rob

The wild life of our bodies; predators, parasites, and partners that shape our evolution. Harper 2011 290p $26.99 **579**

1. Evolution 2. Parasites 3. Human ecology 4. Microorganisms

ISBN 978-0-06-180648-3; 0-06-180648-X

LC 2010-43564

The author "shares the view of modern human life as a paradise lost, but the loss he laments is not merely of a vague sense of being one with nature. What we have sacrificed, he argues, is a physical connection with the species that shaped our bodies from our physique to the immune system. As humans became urban and industrial, we also separated ourselves from other species. Pets aside, we have laboured to rid our houses and cities of creatures — not just visible predators and pests but also the microbes on our countertops and hands. Some of these steps were sensible acts of self-preservation, but others were driven by an ideology of humans as separate from nature. Dunn . . . catalogues the dangers of that ideology." New Scientist

Includes bibliographical references

Montgomery, David R.

The hidden half of nature; the microbial roots of life and health. David R. Montgomery and Anne Bikle. W W Norton & Co. 2016 320 p. (hardcover) $26.95 **579**

1. Health 2. Farm produce 3. Soil microbiology 4. Conservation of natural resources

ISBN 9780393244403

LC 2015027979

In this book, authors David R. Montgomery and Anne Bikle study "how microbes are transforming the way we see nature and ourselves— and could revolutionize agriculture and medicine. . . . They are abruptly plunged further into investigating microbes when Biklé is diagnosed with cancer. . . . The authors also discover startling insights into the similarities between plant roots and the human gut." (Publisher's note)

"Recommended for general readers wishing to learn more about gardening, sustainability, and nutrition, as well as students and scholars of geology, microbiology, botany, the history of science, public health, agriculture, and nutrition." LJ

Includes bibliographical references and index

Yong, Ed

★ **I** Contain Multitudes; The Microbes Within Us and a Grander View of Life. Ed Yong. HarperCollins 2016 256 p. color illustrations (hardcover) $27.99 **579**

1. Microbiology 2. Microorganisms

ISBN 9780062368591; 0062368591

This book, by Ed Yong, offers an "informative and vastly entertaining examination of the most significant revolution in biology since Darwin—a 'microbe's-eye view' of the world that reveals a marvelous, radically reconceived picture of life on earth. . . . Many people think of microbes as germs to be eradicated, but those that live with us—the microbiome—build our bodies, protect our health, shape our identities, and grant us incredible abilities." (Publisher's note)

"The author excels at objectively navigating the large body of research related to the microbiome without overselling its curative potential or sacrificing any of the deliciously icky details, and he delivers some of the finest science writing out there in language that will appeal to a wide audience." Kirkus

Includes bibliographical references (pages 299-338) and index

579.2   Viruses and subviral organisms

Roossinck, Marilyn J.

Virus; An Illustrated Guide to 101 Incredible Microbes. Marilyn J. Roossinck. Princeton University Press 2016 272 p.

color ill., color maps (cloth) $35.00   **579.2**
1. Viruses 2. Microbiology 3. Microorganisms
ISBN 9780691166964

LC 2016931621

This illustrated book by Marilyn J. Roossinck "offers an unprecedented look at 101 incredible microbes that infect all branches of life on Earth--from humans and other animals to insects, plants, fungi, and bacteria. . . . Readers can learn about the history of . . . [virology], how viruses are named, how their genes work, how they copy and package themselves, how they interact with their hosts, how immune systems counteract viruses, and how viruses travel from host to host." (Publisher's note)

"A visually appealing resource that will be useful for virologists while simultaneously appealing to the layperson curious about the fascinating and vital role these organisms play in the ecosystem." LJ

Includes bibliographical references and index.

579.3   Prokaryotes (Bacteria)

Tetro, Jason
The **Germ** Files; The Surprising Ways Microbes Can Improve Your Health and Life (And How to Protect Yourself from the Bad Ones) by Jason Tetro. Random House Inc 2016 288 p. illustrations $19   **579.3**
1. Bacteria 2. Microbiology 3. Microorganisms 4. Germ theory of disease
ISBN 0385685777; 9780385685771

This book, by Jason Tetro, "is a one-stop source of the most up-to-date, life-changing information on our relationship with microbes, presented in concise and highly readable items grouped by theme. Areas covered include health, hygiene, sex, childcare, nutrition and dieting." (Publisher's note)

"Written in an engaging, fluid style that is nonacademic, this book also imparts a plethora of in-depth information." LJ

Zimmer, Carl
Microcosm; E. coli and the new science of life. Pantheon Books 2008 243p il $25.95   **579.3**
1. Bacteria
ISBN 978-0-375-42430-4; 0-375-42430-X

LC 2007-37155

The author "renders an absorbing picture of what E. coli says about the history and future of life." Booklist

Includes bibliographical references

579.6   Mushrooms

McKnight, Kent H.
A **field** guide to mushrooms, North America; [by] Kent H. McKnight and Vera B. McKnight; illustrations by Vera B. McKnight. Houghton Mifflin 1987 429p il hardcover o.p. pa $21   **579.6**
1. Mushrooms
ISBN 0-395-91090-0 pa

LC 86-27799

"More than 500 species [of mushrooms] are described and depicted. . . . Edibility of each species is noted and signified by marginal pictograms both in the text and on the colorplates. . . . Appended: a genial chapter of recipes by Anne Dow, glossary, selected references, and index." Booklist

580   Natural history of plants and animals

Goodall, Jane, 1934-
Seeds of Hope; Wisdom and Wonder from the World of Plants. Jane Goodall with Gail Hudson. 1st ed. Grand Central Pub. 2013 384 p. (hardcover) $26.99   **580**
1. Plants 2. Philosophy of nature 3. Hope 4. Trees 5. Human-plant relationships
ISBN 1455513229; 9781455513222

LC 2012045482

This book, by Jane Goodall with Gail Hudson, "examines the critical role that trees and plants play in our world. . . . She introduces us to botanists around the world, as well as places where hope for plants can be found, such as The Millennium Seed Bank, where one billion seeds are preserved. She shows us the secret world of plants with all their mysteries and potential for healing our bodies as well as Planet Earth." (Publisher's note)

Kassinger, Ruth
★ A **Garden** of Marvels; How We Discovered That Flowers Have Sex, Leaves Eat Air, and Other Secrets of Plants. Ruth Kassinger. HarperCollins Publishers 2014 416 p. illustrations $25.99   **580**
1. Botany 2. Gardens 3. Botanists 4. Gardening 5. Botany -- Humor 6. Botanists -- United States -- Anecdotes 7. Women gardeners -- United States -- Anecdotes
ISBN 0062048996; 9780062048998

LC 2014002824

In this book, author Ruth Kassinger "sets out to understand the basics of botany in order to become a better gardener. She retraces the progress of the first botanists who banished myths and misunderstandings and discovered that flowers have sex, leaves eat air, roots choose their food, and hormones make morning glories climb fence posts. She also visits modern gardens, farms, and labs to discover the science behind extraordinary plants." (Publisher's note)

"[A]n informal, entertaining account of how early researchers discovered how plants work and what scientists are still learning about plants today." Kirkus

Includes bibliographical references and index

Laurent, Anna
Botanical art from the golden age of scientific discovery; Anna Laurent. University of Chicago Press 2017 224 p. color illustrations (cloth; alk. paper) $60   **580**
1. Plants -- Pictorial works 2. Botany -- Charts, diagrams, etc. 3. Botanical illustration -- History 4. Botany -- Charts, diagrams, etc
ISBN 9780226321073

LC 2016014267

This book on botanical illustration, by Anna Laurent, "gives the humble wall chart its due, reproducing more than two hundred of them in dazzling full color. Each wall chart is accompanied by captions that offer accessible information about the species featured, the scientists and botanical illustrators who created it, and any particularly interesting or innovative features the chart displays." (Publisher's note)

"This major accomplishment of bringing attention to this singular blending of science, art, and nature will be of interest to a wide range of readers including botanists, illustrators, gardeners, and anyone who has looked at a flower with pleasure and admiration." LJ

Includes bibliographical references and index

Mabey, Richard
The **cabaret** of plants; forty thousand years of plant life and

the human imagination. by Richard Mabey. W W Norton & Co Inc 2016 400 p. color illustrations (hardcover) $29.95 **580**
1. Botany -- History
ISBN 9780393239973

LC 2015033568

This book, by Richard Mabey, "explores dozens of plant species that for millennia have challenged our imaginations, awoken our wonder, and upturned our ideas about history, science, beauty, and belief. Going back to the beginnings of human history, Mabey shows how flowers, trees, and plants have been central to human experience not just as sources of food and medicine but as objects of worship, actors in creation myths, and symbols of war and peace, life and death." (Publisher's note)

"What Mabey does best is invite readers to think about plants in a radical new way, even posing the question as to whether a plant's sensory abilities—electrostatic charges, chemical communication through pheromones and bio- a coustic sound waves—actually constitute intelligence. An unusual and vastly entertaining journey into the world of mysterious plant life as experienced by a gifted nature writer." Kirkus

Includes bibliographical references and index

Mancuso, Stefano

The **revolutionary** genius of plants; a new understanding of plant intelligence and behavior. Stefano Mancuso. Pocket Books 2018 240 p. $30 **580**
1. Plants 2. Plant physiology
ISBN 1501187856; 9781501187858

In this book, author and scientist Stefano Mancuso reveals the "sophisticated ability of plants to innovate, to remember, and to learn, offering us creative solutions to the most vexing technological and ecological problems that face us today. Despite not having brains or central nervous systems, plants perceive their surroundings with an even greater sensitivity than animals. They efficiently explore and react promptly to potentially damaging external events." (Publisher's note)

"This quick, accessible read will appeal to anyone with an interest in how plants continue to surprise us." Library Journal

Marder, Michael

The **philosopher's** plant; an intellectual herbarium. Michael Marder ; with drawings by Mathilde Roussel. Columbia University Press 2014 288 p. illustrations (pbk.; alk. paper) $24.95 **580**
1. Botany 2. Philosophy 3. Botany -- History 4. Botany -- Philosophy 5. Plants -- Adaptation 6. Human-plant relationships
ISBN 0231169035; 9780231169028; 9780231169035

LC 2014010349

This book, by Michael Marder and illustrated by Mathilde Roussel, explores how "philosophers have used germination, growth, blossoming, fruition, reproduction, and decay as illustrations of abstract concepts. . . . Choosing twelve botanical specimens that correspond to twelve significant philosophers, . . . [the author] recasts the development of philosophy through the evolution of human and plant relations." (Publisher's note)

Includes bibliographical references and index

580.973   Botany – History – United States

Johnson, Victoria

American Eden; David Hosack, botany, and medicine in the garden of the early republic. Victoria Johnson. Liveright Publishing Corporation 2018 480 p. (hardcover) $29.95 **580.973**

1. Medical botany 2. Botanical gardens 3. Botany, Medical -- United States 4. Medical botanists -- United States
ISBN 9781631494192

LC 2018002489

National Book Award Finalist: Nonfiction (2018)

This biography, by Victoria Johnson, tells the story of physician Dr. David Hosack who dreams of building "America's first botanical garden. . . . [H]e was educated in Europe and returned to America inspired by his newfound knowledge. He assembled a plant collection so spectacular and diverse that it amazes botanists today, conducted some of the first pharmaceutical research in the United States, and introduced new surgeries to America." (Publisher's note)

Includes bibliographical references and index

581.4   Adaptation

Dunn Chace, Teri

Seeing seeds; discover the unexpected beauty in seedheads, pods, and fruit. Robert Llewellyn and Teri Dunn Chace. Timber Press 2015 284 p. color illustrations $29.95 **581.4**
1. Fruit 2. Seeds 3. Seeds -- Pictorial works
ISBN 1604694920; 9781604694925

LC 2015006910

This book by Teri Dunn Chace and Robert Llewellyn reveals "there is much more to a seed than the plant it will someday become: seeds, seedheads, pods, and fruits have their own astounding beauty that rivals, and sometimes even surpasses, the beauty of flowers. In these stunning pages you'll gain an understanding of how seeds are formed and dispersed, why they look the way they do, and how they fit into the environment." (Publisher's note)

Includes bibliographical references and index

Hanson, Thor

The **triumph** of seeds; how grains, nuts, kernels, pulses, and pips, conquered the plant kingdom and shaped human history. Thor Hanson. Basic Books, a member of the Perseus Books Group 2015 304 p. illustrations (hardcover; alk. paper) $26.99 **581.4**
1. Seeds
ISBN 0465055990; 9780465048724; 9780465055999

LC 2014047078

In this book, author Thor Hanson explains that "[w]e live in a world of seeds. From our morning toast to the cotton in our clothes, they are quite literally the stuff and staff of life, supporting diets, economies, and civilizations around the globe. . . . Spanning the globe, . . . from gardens and flower patches to the spice routes of Kerala, this is a book of knowledge, adventure, and wonder." (Publisher's note)

"Hanson argues that evolutionary intelligence finds the right balance--evolution acts like a gardener, saving the most successful experiments." Choice

Includes bibliographical references and index

581.6   Miscellaneous nontaxonomic kinds of plants

Angier, Bradford

Field guide to edible wild plants; revisions by David K. Foster; illustrations by Arthur J. Anderson; additional illustrations by Jacqueline Mahannah, Michelle L. Meneghini, and Kristen E. Workman. 2nd ed.; Stackpole Books 2008 282p il

pa $21.95　　　　　　　　　　　　　　　**581.6**
1. Edible plants
ISBN 978-0-81173-447-9; 0-81173-447-1

LC 2007-40125

First published 1974

"Plants are arranged alphabetically by one of their common names. Each entry includes genus, family affiliation, other common names, a lengthy plant description (including many interesting facts about the plant), notes on distribution, and a statement concerning edibility and preparation of the plant parts." Libr J

Foster, Steven

★ **Peterson** field guide to medicinal plants and herbs of eastern and central North America; Steven Foster and James A. Duke ; photographs by Steven Foster. Houghton Mifflin Harcourt 2014 456 p. col. ill. (Peterson field guides) $21　**581.6**
1. Medical botany 2. Plants -- Identification
ISBN 0547943989; 9780547943985

In this book, authors "Steven Foster and James A. Duke have used recent advances in the study of medicinal plants and their combined experience of over 100 years to completely update the 'Peterson Field Guide to Medicinal Plants.' The clear and concise text identifies the key traits, habitats, uses, and warnings for more than 530 of the most significant medicinal plants in the eastern and central United States and Canada including both native and alien species." (Publisher's note)

"A hefty handbook to haul over marsh and meadow, but invaluable to searchers and researchers alike.—" LJ

Includes bibliographical references (p. 422-425) and indexes

Stewart, Amy

★ The **drunken** botanist; the plants that create the world's great drinks. Amy Stewart. Algonquin Books of Chapel Hill 2013 400 p. $19.95　　　　　　　　　**581.6**
1. Edible plants 2. Alcoholic beverages 3. Cocktails 4. Plants, Edible 5. Plants, Useful
ISBN 1616200464; 9781616200466

LC 2012041725

This book by Amy Stewart "explores the botanical beginnings of our favorite drinks. . . . Each plant description includes history, propagation, and usage details. Stewart includes sidebars with recipes, field guides, planting instructions, a description of the role of bugs in getting from seed to plant to table, and in-depth historical details. She includes archaeological finds such as the presence of barley beer on clay pot fragments dated to 3400 B.C.E." (Library Journal)

Turner, Nancy J.

★ The **North** American guide to common poisonous plants and mushrooms; [by] Nancy J. Turner and Patrick von Aderkas. Timber Press 2009 375p il $29.95　　　　　　**581.6**
1. Mushrooms 2. Poisonous plants
ISBN 0-88192-929-8; 978-0-88192-929-4

LC 2008-35095

First published 1991 with title: Common poisonous plants and mushrooms of North America

"The book is split into four main categories: mushrooms, wild plants, ornamental and crop plants, and houseplants. Each plant entry includes a . . . photograph to aid the task of identification, a description of the plant, notes on where they commonly occur, and a description of their toxic properties." Publisher's note

Includes bibliographical references

Van Wyk, Ben-Erik

★ **Food** plants of the world; an illustrated guide. Timber Press 2005 480p il $39.95　　　　　　　**581.6**
1. Edible plants
ISBN 0-88192-743-0; 978-0-88192-743-6

LC 2005-44048

For a fuller review, see: Booklist, Feb. 15, 2005

This is an "illustrated guide to more than 350 commercially important plants that are sources of cereals, nuts, fruits, vegetables, drinks, herbs, and spices." Choice

Includes bibliographical references

581.634　　Medicinal plants

Toll, Maia

The **illustrated** herbiary; guidance and rituals from 36 bewitching botanicals. Maia Toll. Storey Publishing 2018 176 p. (hardcover with 9 cardstock sheets in a bound-in envelope; alk. paper) $19.95　　　　　　　　　**581.634**
1. Occultism 2. Medical botany 3. Herbs -- Therapeutic use 4. Medicinal plants 5. Plants -- Symbolic aspects
ISBN 9781612129686

LC 2018002245

"The symbolism of plants . . . has fascinated us for centuries. [In this book] contemporary herbalist Maia Toll adds her distinctive spin to this tradition with profiles of the mysterious personalities of 36 herbs, fruits, and flowers. Combining a passion for plants with imagery reminiscent of tarot, enticing text offers reflections and rituals to tap into each plant's power for healing, self-reflection, and everyday guidance." (Publisher's note)

" This will not replace more traditional herbal guides, but it will appeal to those looking for fun new ways of considering plants." Publishers' Weekly

581.7　　Plant ecology, plants characteristic of specific environments

Pretty tough plants; 135 resilient, water-smart choices for a beautiful garden. by the experts at Plant Select. Timber Press 2017 256 p. color illustrations (pbk.) $24.95 **581.7**
1. Plants -- Hardiness 2. Drought-tolerant plants 3. Plants -- Drought tolerance
ISBN 9781604698039; 9781604697353

LC 2016054536

This book, by the experts at Plant Select, "highlights 135 of Plant Select's top [hardy] plant picks. Each profile features a color photograph and specific details about the plant's size, best features, and bloom season, along with cultural needs, landscape features, and design ideas. The plant list includes perennials and annuals, groundcovers, grasses, shrubs, and trees." (Publisher's note)

"This is a beautiful and helpful book that advances a lively trend in intentional and sustainable landscaping." Pub Wkly

Includes bibliographical references and index.

582   Plants noted for specific vegetative characteristics and flowers

Darcey, Cheralyn

Flowerpaedia; 1000 flowers and their meanings. Cheralyn Darcey. Red Wheel/Weiser 2018 264 p. $17.95   **582**
1. Plants 2. Flowers
ISBN 1925429466; 9781925429466

This book "is a handy and engaging A-Z reference guide of over 1000 flowers, researched and compiled by botanical explorer Cheralyn Darcey. Readers will delight in understanding what each flower means--emotionally, spiritually, and symbolically--and the dictionary format allows people to search by the feeling or emotion they wish to convey or change. . . . Included is an index of each flower's precise botanical name for easy and exact identification." (Publisher's note)

"This is an exceptionally well crafted book that will do well on the reference shelf." Booklist

582.1   Herbaceous and woody plants, plants noted for their flowers

Symonds, George W. D.

The **shrub** identification book; the visual method for the practical identification of shrubs, including woody vines and ground covers. photos by A. W. Merwin. William Morrow & Company 1963 379p il pa $22   **582.1**
1. Shrubs
ISBN 978-0-688-05040-5; 0-688-05040-9
First published 1963 by Barrow

"Part I gives pictorial keys for thorns, leaves, flowers, fruit, twigs and bark of broad-leaved upright shrubs. Part II contains 200 master pages arranged under four categories, with data on habitat, blooming period, etc., accompanying the photographs." Wilson Libr Bull

Includes bibliographical references

582.13   Plants noted for their flowers

Spellenberg, Richard

National Audubon Society field guide to North American wildflowers, western region; 2nd ed rev; Knopf 2001 862p il map $19.95   **582.13**
1. Wild flowers
ISBN 0-375-40233-0

LC 2001-269242

First published 1979

"More than 940 . . . full-color images show the wildflowers of western North America close-up and in their natural habitats. . . . Images are grouped by flower color and shape and keyed to . . . descriptions that reflect current taxonomy." Publisher's note

Thieret, John W.

National Audubon Society field guide to North American wildflowers: eastern region; revising author, John W. Thieret; original authors, William A. Niering and Nancy C. Olmstead. Knopf 2001 879p il map (National Audubon Society field guide series) $19.95   **582.13**
1. Wild flowers
ISBN 0-375-40232-2

LC 2001-269241

First published 1979 under the authorship of William A. Niering and Nancy C. Olmstead

"Covers the area east of the Rockies and east of the Big Bend area of Texas to the Atlantic. Color photographs together with family and species descriptions make this a most useful field guide." Sci News {review of 1979 edition}

582.16   Trees

Dove, Tony

Essential native trees and shrubs for the eastern United States; the guide to creating a sustainable landscape. Tony Dove, Ginger Woolridge. Charlesbridge 2018 336 p. (reinforced for library use) $35   **582.16**
1. Shrubs 2. Trees -- United States 3. Plants -- United States 4. Endemic plants -- East (U.S.) 5. Trees -- East (U.S.) -- Identification 6. Shrubs -- East (U.S.) -- Identification
ISBN 9781623545031

LC 2017016789

This book, by Tony Dove and Ginger Woolridge, "offers suggestions on species selection based on a plant's performance, aesthetic appeal, and wide range of adaptability. . . . [It] is organized for fast and confident tree and shrub selections for specific landscape applications, and is full of vivid four-color photographs, graphs, and practical tips." (Publisher's note)

"Dove, who has more than 50 years' experience in garden management, and landscape designer Woolridge have thoughtfully photographed and annotated approximately 700 trees and shrubs, noting the characteristics that make them ideal for Eastern U.S. landscapes." LJ

Includes bibliographical references and index

Hugo, Nancy Ross

★ **Seeing** trees; Nancy Ross Hugo ; photography by Robert J. Llewellyn. 1st ed; Timber Press 2011 242p. col. ill.   **582.16**
1. Trees
ISBN 9781604692198

LC 2010052455

National Outdoor Book Awards: Nature and the Environment (2011)

This book, "[f]ocusing on widely grown trees, . . . describes the rewards of careful and regular tree viewing, outlines strategies for improving your observations, and describes some of the most visually interesting tree structures, including leaves, flowers, buds, leaf scars, twigs, and bark. . . . [P]rofiles of ten familiar species -- including such beloved trees as white oak, southern magnolia, white pine, and tulip poplar -- show you how to recognize and understand many of their most compelling (but usually overlooked) physical features." (Publisher's note)

Includes bibliographical references and index.

Johnson, Hugh

The **world** of trees; consultant editor, John Grimshaw; preface by Thomas Pakenham. University of California Press 2010 400p il map $34.95   **582.16**
1. Trees
ISBN 978-0-520-24756-7
First published 1973 with title: The international book of trees

"The first section of the book provides general information on how trees grow, the life cycle of trees, their classification, and morphological characteristics. Next comes a compendium of more than 600 taxa of trees, divided into conifers and broadleaves. Beautiful color photographs, including portraits and landscape scenes, grace every page. The last section includes a guide to choosing trees for the landscape and a chart comparing the ornamental traits of trees throughout the seasons." Am Gardener

Kingsbury, Noël

The **glory** of the tree; an illustrated history. by Noel Kingsbury ; photography by Andrea Jones. Firefly Books Ltd 2014 288 p. colour illustrations $39.95   **582.16**

1. Trees

ISBN 1770852654; 9781770852655

This book, written by Noel Kingsbury, with photography by Andrea Jones, "describes 90 species of tree that collectively span the millennia of evolution and cross the globe. Organized into six categories -- Antiquity, Ecology, Sacred, Utility, Food and Ornament -- the trees are presented in short chapters that touch on botany, history, culture and more." (Publisher's note)

Sibley, David

★ The **Sibley** guide to trees; written and illustrated by David Allen Sibley. Alfred A. Knopf 2009 xxxviii, 426p il map $39.95   **582.16**

1. Trees -- North America

ISBN 978-0-375-41519-7

LC 2009-927625

This "is an outstanding book that should be available in all public libraries, schools, colleges, universities, and homes. The text is comprehensive and the illustrations are pertinent, accurate, and clear." Sci Books Films

Wohlleben, Peter, 1964-

The **Hidden** Life of Trees; What They Feel, How They Communicate—Discoveries from a Secret World. by Peter Wohlleben. Greystone Books 2016 288 p. illustrations (ebook) $24.99; $24.95   **582.16**

1. Trees 2. Forests and forestry

ISBN 9781771642491; 1771642483; 9781771642484

In this book, author Peter Wohlleben "draws on groundbreaking scientific discoveries to describe how trees are like human families: tree parents live together with their children, communicate with them, support them as they grow, share nutrients with those who are sick or struggling, and even warn each other of impending dangers. Wohlleben also shares his deep love of woods and forests, explaining the amazing processes of life, death, and regeneration he has observed in his woodland." (Publisher's note)

"In this spirited exploration, he guarantees that readers will never look at these life forms in quite the same way again." LJ

Includes bibliographical references (pages 252-260) and index.

583   Dicotyledons

Anderson, Edward F.

★ The **cactus** family; with a foreword by Wilhelm Barthlott; and a chapter on cactus cultivation by Roger Brown. Timber Press 2001 776p il maps $99.95   **583**

1. Cactus

ISBN 0-88192-498-9; 978-0-88192-498-5

LC 00-60700

This reference work on cactaceae covers 125 genera and 1810 species

"While more than 1,000 photographs overall illustrate the extraordinary diversity and beautiful flowers of cacti, the main section—an alphabetically arranged reference—will arguably rank as the definitive work readers will use to examine and identify cactus genera, species,

and subspecies." Booklist

Includes bibliographical references

Pappalardo, Joe

Sunflowers; the secret history; the unauthorized biography of the world's most beloved weed. Overlook Press 2008 256p il $22.95   **583**

1. Sunflowers

ISBN 978-1-58567-991-1; 1-58567-991-7

A "look at a flower so ubiquitous that its critical role in cultural development since the dawn of time often goes overlooked. A glib, upbeat writer and fiercely determined researcher, Pappalardo intrepidly investigates everything from the sunflower's genetic history and recent bioengineering discoveries to its influence on global economies from the U.S. to Uganda." Booklist

590   Animals

Jones, Richard

House Guests, House Pests; A Natural History of Animals in the Home. by Richard Jones. St. Martin's Press 2015 288 p. illustrations $28   **590**

1. Household pests

ISBN 1472906233; 9781472906236

In this book, author Richard Jones notes that from "bats in the belfry to beetles in the cellar, moths in the wardrobe and mosquitoes in the bedroom, humans cannot escape the attentions of the animal kingdom. . . . [He] poses questions such as where these animals came from, can we live with them, can we get rid of them, and should we?" (Publisher's note)

Stewart, Tracey

Do unto animals; a friendly guide to how animals live, and how we can make their lives better. Tracey Stewart ; illustrated by Lisel Ashlock. Artisan 2015 200 p. color illustrations (alk. paper) $19.95   **590**

1. Animal welfare 2. Human-animal relationship 3. Pets 4. Livestock 5. Animal communication 6. Animals -- Habitations 7. Human-animal relationships

ISBN 9781579656232; 1579656234

LC 2015010995

In this book, "through hundreds of charming illustrations, a few homemade projects, and her humorous, knowledgeable voice, [Tracey] Stewart provides insight into the secret lives of animals and the kindest ways to live with and alongside them. [Its] part practical guide, part memoir of her life with animals, and part testament to the power of giving back." (Publisher's note)

"Rich in informed insights on animal behavior, augmented by creative craft projects, and alluring with clever watercolor illustrations, Stewart's passionate and practical guide to living with domestic pets, backyard critters, and farm animals artfully combines sensible advice with grassroots advocacy." Booklist

Includes bibliographical references and index

590.2   Animals – Miscellany

Cooke, Lucy

The **truth** about animals; stoned sloths, lovelorn hippos, and other tales from the wild side of wildlife. Lucy Cooke. Ba-

sic Books 2018 352 p. $28 **590.2**
1. Animal behavior 2. Animals -- Miscellanea
ISBN 0465094643; 9780465094646

In this book, author Lucy Cooke "takes us on a worldwide journey to meet everyone from a Colombian hippo castrator to a Chinese panda porn peddler, all to lay bare the secret--and often hilarious--habits of the animal kingdom. Charming and at times downright weird, this modern bestiary is perfect for anyone who has ever suspected that virtue might be unnatural." (Publisher's note)

590.73 Collections and exhibits of living mammals

Charman, Isobel
The **zoo**; the wild and wonderful tale of the founding of London Zoo, 1826-1851. Isobel Charman. Pegasus Books 2017 349 p. illustrations (hardcover) $27.95 **590.73**
1. Zoos -- History 2. London (England) -- History 3. Zoo animals 4. Wildlife conservation 5. London Zoo (London, England) -- History
ISBN 9781681773568; 9781681774015; 1681773562

This book, by Isobel Charman, is about the founding of the London Zoo. "It is the story of the first zoo in history, a weird and wonderful oasis in the heart of . . . Dickensian London, and of the incredible characters, both human and animal, that populated it--from Charles Darwin and Queen Victoria to Obaysch the celebrity hippo. . . . This is a story of Victorian grandeur, of science and empire, and of adventurers and charlatans." (Publisher's note)

"A deeply researched, terrifically entertaining exploration of the London Zoo 'through the eyes of some of the people who made it happen.'" Kirkus

Includes bibliographical references and index.

French, Thomas
Zoo story; life in the garden of captives. Hyperion 2010 288p $24.99 **590.73**
1. Zoos 2. Lowry Park Zoo
ISBN 978-1-4013-2346-2

The author "chronicles the rise of Lowry Park from one of the worst zoos in the country to one of the best. . . . This behind-the-scenes look will both entertain and enlighten animal lovers. It is a story that needs to be told, and French does it superbly." Libr J

Includes bibliographical references

590.75 Museum activities and services

Milgrom, Melissa
Still life; adventures in taxidermy. Houghton Mifflin Harcourt 2010 285p $25 **590.75**
1. Taxidermy
ISBN 978-0-618-40547-3

LC 2009-13511

"An animated initiation to the realm of taxidermy—its cultural significance, its hybrid status between art, craft and science, and the obsessive, idiosyncratic personalities who practice it. . . . Brimming with respect and immersive vitality." Kirkus

591 Specific topics in natural history of animals

Wildlife of the world; contributors Jamie Ambrose [and nine others] DK Publishing 2015 480 p. illustrations, color maps $50 **591**
1. Animals 2. Animals -- Pictorial works
ISBN 1465438041; 9781465438041

LC 2015458474

This book, by DK Publishing, foreword by Don E. Wilson and produced in association with the Smithsonian Institution,"takes you on a journey through some of the most scenic and rich animal habitats--from the Amazon rain forests to the Himalayas, the Sahara to the South Pole--meeting the most important animals in each ecosystem along the way. . . . An additional eighty-page illustrated reference section on the animal kingdom explains the animal groups and profiles additional species." (Publisher's note)

"A chart at the beginning of each section indicates the number of species in each order, class, or phylum. . . . [T]his is an important, gorgeous, accessible introduction to hundreds of species and their habitats throughout the world at a very small price." Booklist

591.38 Evolution

Quammen, David, 1948-
★ The **tangled** tree; a radical new history of life. David Quammen. Simon & Schuster 2018 xvi, 461 p.p illustrations (hardcover) $30 **591.38**
1. Genetics 2. Evolution 3. Phylogeny 4. Evolution (Biology) -- History 5. Phylogeny -- Molecular aspects
ISBN 9781476776620; 9781476776644; 1476776628

LC 2018004356

In this book, author David Quammen "explains how recent discoveries in molecular biology can change our understanding of evolution and life's history, with powerful implications for human health and even our own human nature. In the mid-1970s, scientists began using DNA sequences to reexamine the history of all life. Perhaps the most startling discovery to come out of this new field . . . is horizontal gene transfer (HGT), or the movement of genes across species lines." (Publisher's note)

"A consistently engaging collection of vivid portraits of brilliant, driven, quarrelsome scientists in the process of dramatically altering the fundamentals of evolution, illuminated by the author's insightful commentary." Kirkus

Includes bibliographical references (pages 391-439) and index.

591.47 Protective and locomotor adaptations, color

Emlen, Douglas J.
Animal weapons; the evolution of battle. by Douglas J. Emlen ; illustrated by David J. Tuss. Henry Holt & Co. 2014 288 p. 16 plates; color illustrations (hardcover) $30 **591.47**
1. Weapons 2. Animal defenses 3. Military art and science 4. Animal weapons 5. Defensive (Military science)
ISBN 0805094504; 9780805094503

LC 2014004772

This book, by Douglas J. Emlen, is the "story behind the stunning, extreme weapons we see in the animal world--teeth and horns and claws--and what they can tell us about the way humans develop and use arms and other weapons. . . . He looks at everything from our armor and camouflage to the evolution of the rifle and the structures human populations have built across different regions and eras to protect their homes and communities." (Publisher's note)

"Emlen's excellent writing will draw in readers intrigued by astonishingly powerful weapons, both in the wild and in the military, and how they have evolved owing to selective pressures. Though Philip Street's Animal Weapons describes a greater variety of animal defenses, Emlen's book is a more compelling read because it focuses on the parallels between animal and humans in this regard." LJ

Includes bibliographical references and index

591.479 Locomotor adaptation

Cheshire, James

Where the animals go; tracking wildlife with technology in 50 maps and graphics. James Cheshire, Oliver Uberti. W W Norton & Co Inc 2017 174 p. illustrations, maps (hardcover) $39.95   **591.479**
1. Remote sensing 2. Animals -- Dispersal 3. Tracking and trailing 4. Remote-sensing maps 5. Wildlife monitoring -- Remote sensing 6. Animals -- Dispersal -- Remote sensing 7. Tracking and trailing -- Technological innovations
ISBN 9780393634020

LC 2017002269

This book, by James Cheshire and Oliver Uberti, offers "a comprehensive, data-driven portrait of how creatures like ants, otters, owls, turtles, and sharks navigate the world. Based on pioneering research by scientists at the forefront of the animal-tracking revolution, . . . [it] tell[s] fascinating stories of animal behavior. . . . [The book brings] broad perspective and intimate detail to our understanding of the animal kingdom." (Publisher's note)

Includes bibliographical references

591.5 Behavior

Bekoff, Marc

Wild justice; the moral lives of animals. [by] Marc Bekoff and Jessica Pierce. University of Chicago Press 2009 188p il $26; pa $17   **591.5**
1. Animal behavior 2. Animal intelligence 3. Animal psychology 4. Motivation in animals 5. Social behavior in animals
ISBN 0-226-04161-1; 0-226-04163-8 pa; 978-0-226-04161-2; 978-0-226-04163-6 pa

LC 2008-40173

Bekoff and Pierce argue "that animals exhibit a broad repertoire of moral behaviors, including fairness, empathy, trust, and reciprocity. Underlying these behaviors is a complex and nuanced range of emotions, backed by a high degree of intelligence and surprising behavioral flexibility. . . . [The authors draw the] conclusion that there is no moral gap between humans and other species: morality is an evolved trait that we unquestionably share with other social mammals." (Publisher's note)

The authors "discuss recent scientific studies documenting that great apes, monkeys, wolves, coyotes, hyenas, dolphins, whales, elephants, rats, and mice are capable of a wide range of moral behavior. They strongly urge the scientific and philosophical communities to recognize that these animals can act as moral agents within the context of their own social groups. This provocative and well-argued view of animal morality may surprise some readers as it challenges outdated assumptions about animals." Libr J

Includes bibliographical references and index

Benyus, Janine M., 1958-

The **secret** language of animals; A Guide to Remarkable Behavior. by Janine M. Benyus ; illustrations by Juan Carlos Barberis. Black Dog & Leventhal Pub 2014 480 p. illustrations $22.95   **591.5**
1. Animal behavior 2. Wildlife watching 3. Zoo animals -- Behavior
ISBN 1579129684; 9781579129682

LC 98028743

In this book, "biologist Janine Benyus takes us inside the animal kingdom and shows us the whys and the hows behind the distinctive behavior of creatures great and small in their natural environments. Divided geographically into five sections—Africa, Asia, North America, the oceans, and the poles—the book examines and describes the behavior, body language, and patterns of communication of 20 different animals." (Publisher's note)

"The narrative is extremely accessible, and readers of all ages will enjoy learning something new about their favorite zoo animals." Booklist

Includes bibliographical references (p. 444-455) and index

Braitman, Laurel

Animal madness; how anxious dogs, compulsive parrots, and elephants in recovery help us understand ourselves. Laurel Braitman. Simon & Schuster 2014 384 p. (hardback) $28   **591.5**
1. Mental illness 2. Animal behavior 3. Comparative psychology 4. Animal psychology
ISBN 1451627009; 9781451627008

LC 2014000791

This book by Laurel Braitman "draws evidence from across the world to show how humans and other animals are astonishingly similar when it comes to their feelings and the ways in which they lose their minds. . . . Nonhuman animals can lose their minds. And when they do, it often looks a lot like human mental illness." (Publisher's note)

"Braitman's gradual accretion of reasons to believe in animal emotional states that we can relate to, including the loopy ones, gives pause and sparks curiosity." Kirkus

Fagan, Brian

The **intimate** bond; how animals shaped human history. Brian Fagan. Bloomsbury Press 2014 304 p. illustrations, maps (alk. paper) $28   **591.5**
1. Working animals -- History 2. Human-animal relationships -- History
ISBN 1620405725; 9781620405727

LC 2014027152

Animals, and our ever-changing relationship with them, have left an indelible mark on human history. From the dawn of our existence, animals and humans have been constantly redefining their relationship with one another, and entire civilizations have risen and fallen upon this curious bond we share with our fellow fauna. Brian Fagan unfolds this fascinating story from the first wolf who wandered into our prehistoric ancestors' camp and found companionship, to empires built on the backs of horses, donkeys, and camels, to the industrial age when some animals became commodities, often brutally exploited, and others became pets, nurtured and pampered, sometimes to absurd extremes." McMillan Palgrave

"History, anthropology, and cultural studies enthusiasts will enjoy this excellent, intelligent book, as will animal lovers of all stripes." LJ

Includes bibliographical references and index

Foster, Charles

Being a Beast; Adventures Across the Species Divide. Charles Foster. Henry Holt & Co. 2016 256 p. (hardcover) $28 **591.5**
1. Animal behavior 2. Human-animal relationships -- History
ISBN 1627796339; 9781627796330

In this book author Charles Foster "explores what it's really like to be an animal--by living like them. He lived alongside badgers for weeks, sleeping in a sett in a Welsh hillside and eating earthworms. He caught fish in his teeth while swimming like an otter; rooted through London garbage cans as an urban fox; was hunted by bloodhounds as a red deer. And he followed the swifts on their migration route over the Strait of Gibraltar, discovering himself to be strangely connected to the birds." (Publisher's note)

"This approach, along with his willingness to address and avoid the temptation for anthropomorphism, makes his book interesting and informative." Pub Wkly

Includes bibliographical references (pages [219]-226) and index.

Grandin, Temple

★ **Animals** in translation; using the mysteries of autism to decode animal behavior. [by] Temple Grandin and Catherine Johnson. Scribner 2010 356p $28; ebook $18.99 **591.5**
1. Autism 2. Animal behavior
ISBN 978-1-4391-8710-4; 978-1-4391-3084-1 ebook
First published 2005

"This fascinating book will teach readers to see as animals see, to be a little more visual and a little less verbal, and, as a unique analysis of animal behavior, it belongs in all libraries." Booklist

Includes bibliographical references

Kalaugher, Liz

Furry Logic; The Physics of Animal Life. Matin Durrani, Liz Kalaugher. St. Martin's Press 2017 304 p. illustrations (some color) (ebook) $53; $27.00 **591.5**
1. Zoology 2. Biophysics 3. Animal behavior 4. Molecular biology 5. Animal behavior -- Juvenile literature
ISBN 9781472914101; 1472914090; 9781472914095
LC 2016497302

In this book in the Bloomsbury Sigma series, by Matin Durrani and Liz Kalaugher, each of the "six chapters tackles a separate branch of physics and, through more than 30 animal case studies, examines each creature's key features before describing the ways physics is at play in its life, how the connection between physics and animal behavior was discovered, and what remains to be found out." (Publisher's note)

"Another offbeat factoid—in a book full of them—is the way that elephants raise one foot from the ground in order to use their other three to triangulate vibrations. Light science reading that informs while it entertains—good for dipping into and out of." Kirkus

Masson, J. Moussaieff

When elephants weep; the emotional lives of animals. {by} Jeffrey Moussaieff Masson and Susan McCarthy. Delacorte Press 1995 xxiii, 291p il hardcover o.p. pa $15.95 **591.5**
1. Animal behavior 2. Animal intelligence
ISBN 0-385-31428-0 pa
LC 94-23819

The authors gather "the evidence to date for the existence of emotions and, hence, something approaching human consciousness in animals. . . . Masson and McCarthy do a commendable job of synthesizing the material they tackle . . . making it efficiently readable." Booklist

Includes bibliographical references

Morell, Virginia

Animal wise; the thoughts and emotions of our fellow creatures. Virginia Morell. Random House Inc 2013 304 p. $26 **591.5**
1. Animal behavior 2. Thought and thinking 3. Cognition in animals 4. Human-animal communication
ISBN 0307461440; 9780307461445
LC 2012031503

LA Times Book Prize Finalist: Science & Technology (2013)

This book, by Virginia Morell, "explores the frontiers of research on animal cognition and emotion. . . . [The book] takes us . . . into the inner world of animals, from ants to elephants to wolves, and from sharp-shooting archerfish to pods of dolphins that rumble like rival street gangs. . . . She probes the moral and ethical dilemmas of recognizing that even 'lesser animals' have cognitive abilities such as memory, feelings, personality, and self-awareness." (Publisher's note)

Smoller, Jordan

The **other** side of normal; how biology is providing the clues to unlock the secrets of normal and abnormal behavior. Jordan Smoller. HarperCollins 2012 390 p. **591.5**
1. Psychology 2. Human behavior 3. Mental illness 4. Behavior genetics 5. Abnormal psychology 6. Psychobiology 7. Norm (Philosophy) 8. Biological psychiatry
ISBN 0061492191; 9780061492198; 9780061492204
LC 2011040827

In this book, "[t]he author uses the 2010 announcement by the American Psychiatric Association of provisional plans to revise the Diagnostic and Statistical Manual of Mental Disorders as an opportunity to revisit the hot-button issue of what constitutes mental disease. In his opinion, one of the shortcomings of the DSM is its creation of 'categories from constellations of symptoms' without understanding how they connect to the 'functional organization of the mind and brain.'" (Kirkus)

Includes bibliographical references

Stange, Karlene

The **spiritual** nature of animals; a country vet explores the wisdom, compassion, and souls of animals. Karlene Stange, DVM. New World Library 2017 291 p. (paperback) $16.95 **591.5**
1. Human-animal relationships 2. Animal psychology 3. Animals -- Religious aspects 4. Veterinary medicine -- Anecdotes
ISBN 9781608685158; 9781608685165
LC 2017025307

In this book author Karlene Stange "chronicles her amazing exploration through the teachings of various religious and cultural traditions, as well as her encounters with the magnificent Rocky Mountain terrain and the quirky characters -- both animal and human--who inhabit it." (Publisher's note)

Includes bibliographical references (pages 253-270) and index.

Waal, F. B. M. de (Frans B. M.), 1948-

★ **Are** We Smart Enough to Know How Smart Animals Are? Frans de Waal. W W Norton & Co Inc 2016 352 p. illustrations $27.95 **591.5**
1. Psychology 2. Animal intelligence
ISBN 0393246183; 9780393246186
LC 2015049994

This book by Frans de Waal "based on research involving crows, dolphins, parrots, sheep, wasps, bats, whales, and of course chimpanzees and bonobos, . . . explores both the scope and the depth of animal intelligence. He offers a firsthand account of how science has stood traditional behaviorism on its head by revealing how smart animals really are, and how we've underestimated their abilities for too long." (Publisher's note)

"This insightful and fascinating work by a scientist who has been at the forefront of new thinking about primates and what it means to be human is highly recommended. De Waal fans and general readers interested in the field of animal cognition will be delighted." Library Journal

Weiner, Jonathan

Time, love, memory; a great biologist and his quest for the origins of behavior. Knopf 1999 300p il $27.50; pa $14   **591.5**
1. Behavior genetics 2. Biophysicists 3. Neuroscientists 4. College teachers
ISBN 0-679-44435-1; 0-679-76390-2 pa
        LC 98-43128

An exploration of the work of "one of the unsung pioneers of molecular biology: brash, eccentric physicist-turned-biologist Seymour Benzer. By studying tiny genetic mutations in the fruit fly, Benzer seeks to shed light on the question of whether genes determine behavior. Weiner . . . presents an elegant scientific detective story." Publ Wkly

Includes bibliographical references

Wohlleben, Peter, 1964-

The **inner** life of animals; love, grief, and compassion; surprising observations of a hidden world. Peter Wohlleben ; foreword by Jeffrey Moussaieff Masson ; translation by Jane Billinghurst. Greystone Books 2017 x, 277 p.p (hardcover) $24.95   **591.5**
1. Animal behavior 2. Animal intelligence 3. Animal psychology 4. Emotions in animals
ISBN 9781771643016; 9781771643023; 1771643013

"Writing nontechnically but with obvious depth of knowledge, . . . [Peter Wohlleben] invites readers to imagine that animals have many of the same feelings we do. . . . 'Basically,' he writes, 'emotions are linked to the unconscious part of the brain. If animals lacked consciousness, all that would mean is that they would be unable to have thoughts.'" (Kirkus)

"Wohlleben (The Hidden Life of Trees, 2016) offers an insightful consideration of the emotional and cognitive lives of animals." Booklist

Includes bibliographical references (pages 251-262) and index.

591.53   Predation

Levin, Rachel

Look big; and other tips for surviving animal encounters of all kinds. Rachel Levin, illustrated by Jeff Östberg. Ten Speed Press 2018 143 p. (trade pbk.; alk. paper) $14.99   **591.53**
1. Animal attacks 2. Survival skills 3. Wilderness survival 4. Pests -- Control 5. Human-animal relationships 6. Animal attacks -- Prevention
ISBN 0399580379; 9780399580376
        LC 2017024044

This book, by Rachel Levin, illustrated by Jeff Östberg, is "helpful illustrated field guide to fending off 50 of our most feared--or frustrating--wild animals, including survival techniques, wildlife etiquette, and other essential advice. . . . [This] is a must-have survival guide for outdoor, urban, and suburban adventurers alike. If you have ever feared the approach of a grizzly, the spray of a skunk, or an army of cockroaches in the kitchen, this book is for you." (Publisher's note)

Includes bibliographical references and index

591.56   Behavior relating to life cycle

Bondar, Carin

Wild Sex; The Science Behind Mating in the Animal Kingdom. by Carin Bondar Ph. D. W.W. Norton & Co Inc. 2016 400 p. $27.95   **591.56**
1. Sexual behavior in animals
ISBN 1681771667; 9781681771663

This book, by Carin Bondar Ph. D., is a "guide to the reproductive habits of creatures great and small. . . . She looks at the evolution of sexual organs (and how they've shaped social hierarchies), tactics of seduction, and the mechanics of sex. She investigates a wide range of topics, from whether animals experience pleasure from sex to what happens when females hold the reproductive power." (Publisher's note)

"A fascinating peek into the intimate behavior of our animal cousins that provides new insight into the benefits of being human." Kirkus

Includes bibliographic references (pages 295-366) and glossary.

Prum, Richard O.

The **evolution** of beauty; how Darwin's forgotten theory of mate choice shapes the natural world--and us. Richard O. Prum. Doubleday 2017 428 p. illustrations (some color) (alk. paper) $30   **591.56**
1. Evolution 2. Animal courtship 3. Human evolution 4. Sexual selection 5. Courtship in animals 6. Evolutionary theories 7. Sexual selection in animals
ISBN 9780385537223; 9780385537216
        LC 2016050808

Pulitzer Prize Finalist: General Nonfiction (2018)

In this book, author Richard Prum explains how Charles Darwin's "long-neglected theory of sexual selection in which the act of choosing a mate for purely aesthetic reasons--for the mere pleasure of it--is an independent engine of evolutionary change. Mate choice can drive ornamental traits from the constraints of adaptive evolution, allowing them to grow ever more elaborate." (Publisher's note)

"Prum's prose is simple and enjoyable enough for the Darwinian-challenged to understand while based in enough scientific evidence to engage those who might disagree with the ideas presented." LJ

Includes bibliographical references (pages [387]-404) and index.

Safina, Carl

Beyond words; what animals think and feel. Carl Safina. Henry Holt & Co. 2015 480 p. 16 plates; illustrations (hardcover) $32   **591.56**
1. Animal behavior 2. Animal intelligence 3. Animal psychology 4. Whales -- Psychology 5. Wolves -- Psychology 6. Elephants -- Psychology 7. Psychology, Comparative
ISBN 0805098887; 9780805098884
        LC 2014045385

This book, by Carl Safina, "offers an intimate view of animal behavior to challenge the fixed boundary between humans and nonhuman animals. . . . [It] brings forth . . . insight into the unique personalities of animals through extraordinary stories of animal joy, grief, jealousy, anger, and love. The similarity between human and nonhuman consciousness, self-awareness, and empathy calls us to re-evaluate how we interact with animals." (Publisher's note)

"With forays into neurology and diverse animal-behavior studies, Safina reveals that ours is just one of many powerful minds at work on Earth and that we share many profound traits with our fellow animals. By turns mesmerizing, thrilling, and tragic, Safina's enlightening inquiry into animal intelligence calls for a new, compassionate perspective before we unwittingly drive our precious animal kin into extinction."

Booklist
Includes bibliographical references and index

Wilcove, David S.

No way home; the decline of the world's great animal migrations. with illustrations by Louise Zemaitis. Island Press/ Shearwater Books 2008 253p il map $24.95   **591.56**
1. Environmental degradation 2. Animals -- Migration
ISBN 978-1-55963-985-9; 1-55963-985-7

LC 2007-26205

"Absorbing and thought provoking, [this work] deserves to be widely read and used to promote conservation action." Science
Includes bibliographical references

591.563   Family behavior

Bondar, Carin

Wild moms; motherhood in the animal kingdom. Dr. Carin Bondar. Pegasus Books 2018 xi, 271 p.p illustrations (chiefly color) (hardcover) $27.95   **591.563**
1. Mammals 2. Zoology 3. Animal behavior 4. Parental behavior in animals
ISBN 9781681776651; 9781681777214; 1681776650

In this book, author "Carin Bondar takes readers on an enthralling tour of the animal kingdom as she explores the phenomenon of motherhood in the wild. . . . Bondar answers . . . questions about the animal kingdom: How do moms in the animal kingdom cope with crying babies and potty training? How does breastfeeding work in the wild. . . . If children with disabilities do not fit into Darwin's theory of evolution?" (Publisher's note)

"Well-researched and with a large bibliography, Bondar's study celebrates the idea that motherhood may be the most important job ever created by evolution." Booklist

Includes bibliographical references (pages 231-256) and index.

591.59   Communication

Katz, Jon

Talking to animals; how you can understand animals and they can understand you. Jon Katz. Atria Books 2017 240 p. (hardcover; alk. paper) $26   **591.59**
1. Human-animal communication 2. Human-animal relationships
ISBN 9781476795478; 9781476795492

LC 2016032799

In this book, author Jon Katz "marshals his experience to offer us a deeper insight into animals and the tools needed for effectively communicating with them. By better understanding animal instincts, recognizing they are not mere reflections of our own human emotions and neuroses, we can help them live happily in our shared world." (Publisher's note)

"Katz's honest, straightforward, and sometimes searing prose will speak to those who love animals, and might well convert some who do not." Booklist

591.6   Miscellaneous nontaxonomic kinds of animals

Quammen, David

Monster of God; the man-eating predator in the jungles of history and the mind. Norton 2003 513p maps $26.95; pa $15.95   **591.6**
1. Dangerous animals 2. Predatory animals 3. Endangered species
ISBN 0-393-05140-4; 0-393-32609-8 pa

LC 2003-7812

"Rich with personal stories that clarify humanity's true place in the universe, this book will leave the reader eager for more. . . . This has all the makings of a science book of the year. Highly recommended." Libr J
Includes bibliographical references

591.65   Harmful animals

Simon, Matt

Plight of the living dead; what the animal kingdom's real-life zombies reveal about nature -- and ourselves. Matt Simon. Penguin Books 2018 256 p. (paperback) $16   **591.65**
1. Parasites 2. Predation (Biology)
ISBN 9780143131410

LC 2018004526

In this book, author "Matt Simon documents his journey through the bizarre evolutionary history of mind control. Along the way, he visits a lab where scientists infect ants with zombifying fungi, joins the search for kamikaze crickets in the hills of New Mexico, and travels to Israel to meet the wasp that stings cockroaches in the brain before leading them to their doom." (Publisher's note)

"Simon's work is easily the most fun one could ever expect to have reading about the mind-controlling insects, insidious fungi, and parasites living alongside humanity." Publishers Weekly

Includes bibliographical references

591.68   Rare and endangered animals

DeBuys, William

The last unicorn; a search for one of Earth's rarest creatures. William DeBuys. Little, Brown & Co. 2015 368 p. $18   **591.68**
1. Saola 2. Laos -- Description and travel 3. Nakai-Nam Theun National Biodiversity Conservation Area (Laos) 4. Saola -- Laos -- Nakai-Nam Theun National Biodiversity Conservation Area 5. Endangered species -- Laos -- Nakai-Nam Theun National Biodiversity Conservation Area 6. Wildlife conservation -- Laos -- Nakai-Nam Theun National Biodiversity Conservation Area
ISBN 0316232874; 9780316232869; 9780316232876

LC 2014020923

In this book, William DeBuys "recounts his journey to the Nakai-Nam Theun region of Laos in search of the saola, an endangered antelopelike creature that has rarely been seen by man. . . . The creature recalls the mythical unicorn as it has largely evaded discovery, leaving scientists to piece together information based on bone samples, hunter accounts, and photographic evidence." (Library Journal)

"Recommended for readers of popular science, travel, and autobiography." LJ

Dinerstein, Eric

The kingdom of rarities; Eric Dinerstein. Island Press 2013 312 p. (cloth; alk. paper) $29.95   **591.68**
1. Ecology 2. Rare animals 3. Rare vertebrates
ISBN 1610911954; 1610911962; 9781610911955; 9781610911962

LC 2012025535

In this book, Eric Dinerstein "demonstrates that while rarity is a phenomenon of nature, few scientists have sought to study the more 'uncommon' species in a given ecosystem, and therefore may be missing key issues to better understand the natural world. He has cumulated over 40 years of his studies and experiences to highlight how rare species have developed intricate and complex webs, and how their existence has profound impacts on the ecosystem(s) in which they live." (Choice)

Includes bibliographical references and index

Girling, Richard

The **Hunt** for the Golden Mole; All Creatures Great & Small and Why They Matter. Richard Girling. Counterpoint Press 2014 312 p. illustrations $26   **591.68**

1. Hunting 2. Rare animals 3. Moles (Animals) 4. Golden moles -- Somalia 5. Extinct animals -- Somalia 6. Biodiversity -- South Africa 7. Nature conservation -- South Africa 8. Hunting -- Moral and ethical aspects

ISBN 1619024500; 9781619024502

LC 2014022506

This book, "taking as its narrative engine the hunt for an animal that is legendarily rare, Richard Girling writes [a] . . . history of humankind's interest in hunting and collecting--what prompts us to do this? What good might come of our need to catalog all the living things of the natural world?" (Publisher's note)

"Though Girling presents a sobering assessment of the state of the world's fauna, he does so with the dramatic flair of a novelist and eye for detail of a travel journalist. The result is a page-turning, thought-provoking treatise on a desperate environmental crisis." Booklist

Includes bibliographical references and index

Mezrich, Ben

Woolly; the true story of the quest to revive one of history's most iconic extinct creatures. Ben Mezrich ; epilogue by Dr. George Church ; afterword by Stewart Brand. Atria Books 2017 293 p. (hardcover) $26   **591.68**

1. Woolly mammoth 2. Extinct animals -- Cloning 3. Extinct animals -- Genetics 4. Extinct mammals 5. Animal genetic engineering 6. Animal diversity conservation

ISBN 9781501135576; 9781501135552; 9781501135569

LC 2017010876

In this book, by Ben Mezrich, "a group of young scientists, under the guidance of [geneticist Dr. George Church, . . . works to . . . [sequence] the DNA of a frozen woolly mammoth harvested from above the Arctic circle, and splicing elements of that sequence into the DNA of a modern elephant. Will they be able to turn the hybrid cells into a functional embryo and bring the extinct creatures to life in our modern world?" (Publisher's note)

"Making complex genetic engineering intelligible, Mezrich successfully channels the enthusiasms of the scientists he so vividly portrays." Booklist

Includes bibliographical references (pages 273-275) and index.

O'Connor, M. R.

Resurrection Science; Conservation, De-extinction and the Precarious Future of Wild Things. M.R. O'Connor. St. Martin's Press 2015 266 p. $25.99   **591.68**

1. Climate change 2. Extinction (Biology)

ISBN 113727929X; 9781137279293

LC 2015004485

This book, by M.R. O'Connor, "explores the extreme measures scientists are taking to try and save them, from captive breeding and genetic management to de-extinction. In stories of sixteenth-century galleon excavations, panther-tracking in Florida swamps, ancient African rain-forests, Neanderthal tool-making, and cryogenic DNA banks, O'Connor investigates the philosophical questions of an age in which we 'play god' with earth's biodiversity." (Publisher's note)

"A book as thought-provoking as it is fascinating." Booklist

Includes bibliographical references and index.

Shapiro, Beth

How to Clone a Mammoth; The Science of De-extinction. Beth Shapiro. Princeton University Press 2015 256 p. illustrations (some color) $24.95   **591.68**

1. Genetic engineering 2. Extinction (Biology)

ISBN 0691157057; 9780691157054

LC 2014049574

This book, by Beth Shapiro, "walks readers through the astonishing and controversial process of de-extinction. From deciding which species should be restored, to sequencing their genomes, to anticipating how revived populations might be overseen in the wild, . . . [the author] vividly explores the extraordinary cutting-edge science that is being used--today--to resurrect the past." (Publisher's note)

"The beauty of this work is in its honesty: Shapiro, who is invested in this science as a practitioner, does not attempt to woo the masses. She takes the ethical concerns head on, not as an advocate but as an honest broker." Choice

Wray, Britt

Rise of the Necrofauna; The Science, Ethics, and Risks of De-extinction. Britt Wray ; foreword by George Church. Greystone Books 2017 ix, 293 p.p illustrations (hardcover) $26.95   **591.68**

1. Extinct animals 2. Endangered species 3. Wildlife reintroduction -- Moral and ethical aspects 4. Extinct animals -- Cloning -- Moral and ethical aspects 5. Animal diversity conservation -- Moral and ethical aspects 6. Extinct vertebrates -- Cloning -- Moral and ethical aspects 7. Rare animals -- Genetic engineering -- Moral and ethical aspects 8. Endangered species -- Genetic engineering -- Moral and ethical aspects

ISBN 9781771641630; 9781771641647; 1771641649

This book, by Britt Wray, "introduces us to renowned futurists like Stewart Brand and scientists like George Church, who are harnessing the powers of CRISPR gene editing in the hopes of 'reviving' extinct passenger pigeons, woolly mammoths, and heath hens. . . . Wray delves into the larger questions that come with this incredible new science, reminding us that de-extinction could bring just as many dangers as it does possibilities." (Publisher's note)

Includes bibliographical references (pages 269-283) and index.

591.7 Animal ecology, animals characteristic of specific environments

Heinrich, Bernd

Life everlasting; the animal way of death. Bernd Heinrich. Houghton Mifflin Harcourt 2012 xiv, 236 p.p   **591.7**

1. Death 2. Zoology 3. Animal behavior 4. Animal communication 5. Life cycles (Biology) 6. Animal ecology 7. Animal life cycles 8. Animals -- Psychological aspects

ISBN 9780544002265; 0547752660; 9780547752662

LC 2012010583

This book "explores the taboos and relevance of scavengers, the 'life-giving links that keep nature's systems humming along smoothly.' After a friend asked if he could be buried on the author's woodland property in Maine, he reexamined his curiosity with the natural world . . . [Bernd] Heinrich presents five major sections outlining how bodies and plants are recycled and broken down: small to large . . . north to south . . . plant undertakers . . . watery deaths . . . and changes (metamorphosis and death rituals). Above all, temperature affects how and what breaks down carrion as the flies and insects of summer are replaced by various birds in the winter. The author also tracks how trees decompose, a process that often begins before they die". (Kirkus Reviews)

Summer world; a season of bounty. Ecco 2009 253p il $26.95   **591.7**
1. Summer 2. Animals
ISBN 978-0-06-074217-1; 0-06-074217-8
A discussion of animal survival in the hot season explores the ways in which animals make the most of the summer's short span by efficiently compacting most of their procreative and survival activities.
"Heinrich presents natural science at its engaging best." Kirkus
Includes bibliographical references

Hoyt, Erich
Creatures of the deep; in search of the sea's monsters and the world they live in. Erich Hoyt. Firefly Books 2014 288 p. color illustrations $39.95   **591.7**
1. Ocean bottom 2. Marine biology 3. Abysses 4. Abyssal zone 5. Faune marine 6. Marine animals
ISBN 1770852816; 9781770852815
    LC 2014901153
In this book author "Erich Hoyt gives readers a glimpse of the amazing variety of creatures found in the deepest parts of the ocean. Weaving together details from the latest scientific research about sharks, giant squid, dragonfish, huge tube worms, clams and tiny microbes of the deep-sea vents, Hoyt embarks on a magical journey roaming across the abyssal plains and descending into deep-sea trenches more than 20,000 feet down." (Publisher's note)
"From the surface-dwelling manta ray to the marine spider of the hadal zone (appropriately named for Hades), Hoyt describes life cycles and family trees of marine flora and fauna, as well as the scientific community's efforts to understand them. Startling facts abound, and Hoyt's enthusiasm for his subject shows on every page." Pub Wkly
Includes bibliographical references and index

Naskrecki, Piotr
The **smaller** majority; the hidden world of the animals that dominate the tropics. Belknap Press of Harvard University Press 2005 278p il $35   **591.7**
1. Invertebrates 2. Tropics 3. Animals -- Pictorial works
ISBN 0-674-01915-6; 978-0-674-01915-7
    LC 2005-46060
"Naskrecki's exuberant, expert knowledge of this microscopic world has been distilled down to the most arresting details. Crisp, enjoyable prose, clearly explains complex biological processes." Publ Wkly
Includes bibliographical references

591.77 Marine animals

Honeyborne, James
★ **Blue** planet II; a new world of hidden depths. James Honeyborne and Mark Brownlow, with foreword by Sir David Attenborough. Trafalgar Square 2018 312 p. $39.95   **591.77**
1. Marine animals 2. Marine biology 3. Underwater exploration
ISBN 1849909679; 9781849909679

This book, by James Honeyborne and Mark Brownlow, with foreword by Sir David Attenborough, "which accompanies an epic seven-part series, is a ground-breaking new look at the richness and variety of underwater life across our planet. With 300 breathtaking photographs and stills from the BBC Natural History Unit's spectacular footage, each chapter brings to life a different habitat of the oceanic world." (Publisher's note)
"BBC producers Honeyborne and Brownlow share a substantial and awe-inspiring behind-the-scenes look at their popular 2017 documentary series. They thoroughly record the great diversity in marine life that team members encountered while filming around the world." Pub Wkly

591.9 Animals by specific continents, countries, localities

Bambaradeniya, Channa N. B.
The **illustrated** atlas of wildlife; [by] Channa Bambaradeniya [et al.] University of California Press 2009 288p il map $39.95   **591.9**
1. Atlases 2. Biogeography 3. Reference books
ISBN 978-0-520-25785-6; 0-520-25785-5
    LC 2008-40625
"This gorgeous book, featuring detailed, customized maps and more than 800 photographs . . . and original artworks, presents a spectacular visual survey of wild animals across the globe and describes in detail their habitats, physical characteristics, diet, and behavior. . . . [It also includes] conservation and preservation data, information about human impact upon the world's complex ecosystems, and chronicles of the evolution and adaptation of animals over the ages." Education Digest
Includes glossary and bibliographical references

592 Specific taxonomic groups of animals

Attenborough, David
Life in the undergrowth. Princeton University Press 2006 288p il $29.95   **592**
1. Invertebrates
ISBN 0-691-12703-4
    LC 2005-934727
"This wonderful exploration of invertebrates exceeds the requirements for a great nature book through the strength of its photographs and the quality of its prose." Publ Wkly

593.53 Jellyfish

Berwald, Juli
Spineless; the science of jellyfish and the art of growing a backbone. Juli Berwald ; illustrations by Rachel Ivanyi. Riverhead Books 2017 336 p. illustrations (hardcover) $27 **593.53**
1. Jellyfishes 2. Marine biology
ISBN 9780735211261; 9780735211278
    LC 2017005838
In this book, author Juli Berwald describes how "she traveled the globe to meet the biologists who devote their careers to jellies, hitched rides on Japanese fishing boats to see giant jellyfish in the wild [and] raised jellyfish in her dining room. . . . She discovers that jellyfish science is more than just a quest for answers. It's a call to realize our collective responsibility for the planet we share." (Publisher's note)
"Combining humor and passion, science textbook writer Berwald investigates the strange world of the jellyfish in this captivating and in-

formative science memoir." Pub Wkly

Includes bibliographical references (pages 311-325) and index.

594   Mollusks and molluscoids

Harasewych, M. G.

The **book** of shells; a life-size guide to identifying and classifying six hundred seashells. [by] M.G. Harasewych & Fabio Moretzsohn. University of Chicago Press 2010 655p il map $55   **594**

1. Shells 2. Mollusks 3. Reference books
ISBN 978-0-226-31577-5; 0-226-31577-0

LC 2009-34321

This book "provides an excellent introduction to the major classes of sea-living mollusks worldwide. Students and the lay enthusiast will find the 600 entries accessible and engaging. . . . A table lists the family, shell-size range, distribution, abundance, depth, habitat, feeding habit, and the presence or absence of an operculum. A color range map, genus and species and common name, a paragraph-long description of the species, a listing of related species, a color life-size illustration, and, for small shells, a larger, more detailed image complete the information." Booklist

Includes bibliographical references

Montgomery, Sy

The **soul** of an octopus; a joyful exploration into the wonder of consciousness. Sy Montgomery. Atria Books 2015 272 p. color illustrations (hardback) $26   **594**

1. Octopuses 2. Animal intelligence 3. Octopuses -- Behavior
ISBN 1451697716; 9781451697711

LC 2014038751

National Book Award Finalist: Nonfiction (2015)

In this book, author "Sy Montgomery explores the emotional and physical world of the octopus--a surprisingly complex, intelligent, and spirited creature--and the remarkable connections it makes with humans. Montgomery chronicles this growing appreciation of the octopus, but also tells a love story." (Publisher's note)

"Along with an abundance of fascinating octopus lore, Montgomery illuminates her own quest to understand the creatures better and paints vivid portraits of the people who are similarly drawn to them. Her affection for her subjects, both human and cephalopod, shines through." LJ

Includes bibliographical references and index

Scales, Helen

Spirals in Time; The Secret Life and Curious Afterlife of Seashells. by Helen Scales. St. Martin's Press 2015 304 p. 8 plates; color illustrations $27   **594**

1. Shells
ISBN 1472911369; 9781472911360

In this book, marine biologist Helen Scales "shows how seashells have been sculpted by the fundamental rules of mathematics and evolution; how they gave us color, gems, food, and new medicines. After surviving multiple mass extinctions millions of years ago, molluscs and their shells still face an onslaught of anthropogenic challenges. . . But rather than dwelling on all that is lost, Scales emphasizes that seashells offer an accessible way to reconnect people with nature." (Publisher's note)

"Aiming to inspire a sympathetic public, Scales tells the story of mollusks and reveals their importance in human economy and culture. Never dull or overly technical, this book is a welcome introduction to mollusks and seashells." Booklist

Williams, Wendy

Kraken; the curious, exciting, and slightly disturbing science of squid. Abrams Image 2011 223p il $21.95   **594**

1. Squids
ISBN 978-0-8109-8465-3

LC 2010032489

This book "traces sightings of the giant squid throughout the centuries. . . . Discussion of the anatomy, physiology, reproduction, evolution, and taxonomy of Architeuthis is provided, along with accounts of the author's visits to various scientific laboratories and descriptions of research studies being conducted on the animal. . . . This serves as a good introduction to the subject for general readers and an inspiration to young people interested in marine biology." Libr J

Includes filmography and bibliographical references

595   Arthropods

Fortey, Richard

Horseshoe crabs and velvet worms; the story of the animals and plants that time has left behind. by Richard Fortey. Alfred A. Knopf 2012 320 p. ill. (some col.) $28.95   **595**

1. Botany 2. Zoology 3. Paleontology 4. Worms 5. Plant conservation 6. Arthropoda -- Conservation 7. Invertebrates -- Conservation 8. Limulus polyphemus -- Conservation
ISBN 9780307263612

LC 2011039941

This book by Richard Fortey introduces "the reader to organisms that seemingly have undergone little change since their ancient origins. . . . Evolution has never stopped, and Fortey discusses changes that occur at the molecular level in response to predation pressure and other changing environmental conditions. He starts his journey by witnessing the spectacular spawning of horseshoe crabs, the closest living relatives of his specialty, the trilobites." (Choice: Current Reviews for Academic Libraries)

"Informative, engrossing and delightful." Kirkus

595.4   Chelicerates

Beccaloni, Jan

Arachnids. University of California Press 2009 320p il $39.95   **595.4**

1. Mites 2. Ticks 3. Spiders
ISBN 978-0-520-26140-2; 0-520-26140-2

LC 2009-18657

"This book is overflowing with scientific data and crystal-clear images of strange insects that are certain to make your skin crawl. Free of myths and misconceptions, this book delivers the real facts on the diverse arachnid family which includes a wide variety of scorpions, ticks, mites, and over 38,000 species of spiders. They vary from bizarre to beautiful and a few are even deadly but all are interesting and sure to spark your imagination." Shutterbug

Includes bibliographical references

595.7   Insects

Capinera, John L.

Field guide to grasshoppers, crickets, and katydids of the United States; [by] John L. Capinera, Ralph D. Scott, and

Thomas J. Walker. Cornell University Press 2004 249p il maps hardcover o.p. pa $29.95 **595.7**

1. Crickets 2. Grasshoppers

ISBN 0-8014-4260-5; 0-8014-8948-2 pa

LC 2004-10727

"The highlight is certainly the 50 pages of Scott's color illustrations. . . . For those who want to know what's plaguing them when locusts descend, this is the book." Publ Wkly

Includes bibliographical references

Eisner, Thomas

For love of insects. Belknap Press of Harvard University Press 2003 448p il $35; pa $19.95 **595.7**

1. Insects

ISBN 0-674-01181-3; 0-674-01827-3 pa

LC 2003-44399

"Ranging from a caterpillar who feeds on flowers while disguising as one by affixing petals to his back, to a beetle who can resist a pull 200 times his own weight, the book is full of little known information about how insects feed, fight, and reproduce." Univ Press Books for Public and Second Sch Libr, 2006

Includes bibliographical references

Holldobler, Bert

The **leafcutter** ants; civilization by instinct. [by] Bert Hölldobler and Edward O. Wilson. Norton 2010 160p il pa $19.95 **595.7**

1. Ants

ISBN 978-0-393-33868-3

LC 2010-16202

The authors "introduce the general reader to earth's most evolved animal society. With the colony's queen as its reproductive organ; the various ages and types of workers as the brain, heart, and other organs; and the communication among the ants similar to the communication of nerves and ganglia, a leafcutter ant colony can be truly considered as a superorganism." Booklist

Includes bibliographical references

The **superorganism**; the beauty, elegance, and strangeness of insect societies. [by] Bert Hölldobler and Edward O. Wilson; line drawings by Margaret C. Nelson. W.W. Norton & Company 2009 xxi, 522p il $55 **595.7**

1. Insects

ISBN 978-0-393-06704-0; 0-393-06704-1

LC 2008-38547

"This study covers mathematical analysis as well as field data, but in a straightforward manner that guides readers from one remarkable fact or concept to the next, inspiring wonder at the origin of our own societies." Publ Wkly

Includes bibliographical references

MacNeal, David

Bugged; the insects who rule the world and the people obsessed with them. David MacNeal. St. Martin's Press 2017 x, 308 p.p illustrations (hardcover) $25.99 **595.7**

1. Insects 2. Spiders 3. Entomology

ISBN 9781250095510; 9781250095503

LC 2017006880

This book, by David MacNeal, Illustrated by Michael Kennedy, "introduces a cast of bug-lovers--from a woman facilitating tarantula sex and an exterminator nursing bedbugs (on his own blood), to a kingpin of the black market insect trade and a 'maggotologist'--2ho obsess over

the crucial role insects play in our everyday lives." (Publisher's note)

"MacNeal delivers a joy-filled dose of science, reminding readers that the strange and alien creatures in our midst are not to be feared, but celebrated." Pub Wkly

Includes bibliographical references (pages 279-298) and index

Milne, Lorus Johnson

★ The **Audubon** Society field guide to North American insects and spiders; [by] Lorus and Margery Milne; visual key by Susan Rayfield. Knopf 1980 989p il $19.95 **595.7**

1. Insects 2. Spiders

ISBN 0-394-50763-0

LC 80-7620

The authors "have based their field guide on 702 excellent color photographs (75 of which are of spiders and other arachnids). In addition to some general information, the text (two thirds of the book) is made up of brief comments on each kind of arthropod pictured." Choice

Includes glossary

Raffles, Hugh

Insectopedia. Pantheon Books 2010 465p il **595.7**

1. Insects 2. Human-animal relationships

ISBN 0375423869; 9780375423864

LC 2009-24302

"For as long as humans have existed, insects have existed, too. Wherever we've traveled, they've traveled, too. Yet we hardly know them. . . . Organizing his book alphabetically with one entry for each letter, weaving together brief vignettes, meditations, and extended essays, Raffles embarks on an . . . exploration of history and science, anthropology and travel, economics, philosophy, and popular culture to show us how insects have triggered our obsessions, stirred our passions, and beguiled our imaginations." (Publisher's note) Index.

"In addition to the fine writing, Raffles includes many intriguing drawings and illustrations, as well as a fascinating Notes section. Because of his manner of organization, there is little reason to read the book in order; you can simply open it anywhere and discover a new way to reflect on not only insects but people." Seattle Times

Includes bibliographical references

Schmidt, Justin O.

The **sting** of the wild; Justin O. Schmidt. Johns Hopkins University Press 2016 280 p. color illustrations (hardcover; alk. paper) $24.95 **595.7**

1. Insect pests 2. Poisonous animals 3. Poisonous arthropoda

ISBN 1421419289; 1421419297; 9781421419282; 9781421419299

LC 2015026989

In this book, author Justin O. Schmidt "takes us on a journey inside the lives of stinging insects, seeing the world through their eyes as well as his own. He explains how and why they attack and reveals the powerful punch they can deliver with a small venom gland and a 'sting,' the name for the apparatus that delivers the venom. We learn which insects are the worst to encounter and why some are barely worth considering." (Publisher's note)

"Schmidt's tales will prove infectiously engaging even to entomophobes." Pub Wkly

Includes bibliographical references and index

Van Dokkum, Pieter, 1972-

Dragonflies; Magnificent Creatures of Water, Air, and Land. Pieter van Dokkum. Yale University Press 2015 176 p. color illustrations (alk. paper) $35 **595.7**

1. Dragonflies 2. Dragonflies -- United States 3. Dragonflies -- United States -- Pictorial works
ISBN 030019708X; 9780300197082

LC 2014025844

This book, by Pieter van Dokkum, "begins . . . when an alien-looking larva crawls out of the water and transforms into a fully formed dragonfly. In the following chapters we witness dew-covered dragonflies sparkling in the morning sun, then a pair of mating dragonflies moving through the air. . . . In the final chapter, one generation dies as the next prepares to leave the water and begin its own winged journey." (Publisher's note)

"A lovely volume to pair with Forrest L. Mitchell and James L. Lasswell's A Dazzle of Dragonflies, van Dokkum's vivid compilation of photographs is a treat for nature lovers. The accompanying text is poetically written and a fascinating introduction to the distinct characteristics of these creatures."LJ

Includes bibliographical references and index

Waldbauer, Gilbert

What good are bugs? insects in the web of life. Harvard University Press 2003 384p il hardcover o.p. pa $17.50 **595.7**
1. Insects
ISBN 0-674-01027-2; 0-674-01632-7 pa

LC 2002-27335

This "is an excellent work about the beneficial insects, that vast majority of insect species of which we are generally unaware. . . . The author is an excellent writer and provides many interesting examples." Choice

Includes bibliographical references

Zuk, Marlene

Sex on six legs; lessons on life, love, and language from the insect world. [by] Marlene Zuk. Houghton Mifflin Harcourt 2011 262p $25 **595.7**
1. Insects 2. Sexual behavior in animals
ISBN 978-0-15-101373-9

LC 2010025829

"Despite the title, . . . the book gives clear accounts of a wide range of research beyond sex: insect personalities, wasp facial recognition, fruit flies artificially bred for intelligence, slave-making ants, hitchhiking blister beetles and much more." Sci News

Includes bibliographical references

595.736   Termites

Margonelli, Lisa

Underbug; an obsessive tale of termites and technology. Lisa Margonelli. Scientific American / Farrar, Straus & Giroux 2018 320 p. (hardcover) $27 **595.736**
1. Insects 2. Termites
ISBN 9780374282073

LC 2017059906

In this book, journalist and author Lisa Margonelli, "investigates the environmental and economic impact termites inflict on human societies. . . . Margonelli introduces us to the enigmatic creatures that collectively outweigh human beings ten to one and consume $40 billion worth of valuable stuff annually--and yet, in Margonelli's telling, seem weirdly familiar." (Publisher's note)

"Margonelli has written a book as entertaining as it is informative." Publishers' Weekly

Includes bibliographical references and index

595.76   Beetles

Lewis, Sara

Silent sparks; the wondrous world of fireflies. Sara Lewis. Princeton University Press 2016 240 p. ill. (chiefly color), col. map (hardcover; alk. paper) $29.95 **595.76**
1. Fireflies
ISBN 9780691162683

LC 2015037057

In this book, "noted biologist and firefly expert Sara Lewis dives into the fascinating world of fireflies and reveals the most up-to-date discoveries about these beloved insects. From the meadows of New England and the hills of the Great Smoky Mountains, to the rivers of Japan and mangrove forests of Malaysia, this beautifully illustrated and accessible book uncovers the remarkable, dramatic stories of birth, courtship, romance, sex, deceit, poison, and death among fireflies." (Publisher's note)

"A delightful book sure to charm nature lovers of all ages." Kirkus

Includes bibliographical references and index

595.77   Flies (Diptera) and fleas

McAlister, Erica

The **secret** life of flies; Erica McAlister. Firefly Books Ltd 2017 248 p. color illustrations (hardcover) $29.95 **595.77**
1. Flies 2. Insects 3. Flies -- Popular works 4. Diptera -- Popular works
ISBN 9781770858091; 1770858091

This book, by Erica McAlister, "dispels common misconceptions about flies and reveals how truly extraordinary, exotic and important are these misunderstood creatures. . . . In clear language, McAlister explains Diptera taxonomy and forensic entomology, and describes the potential of flies to transform their relationship with humans from one of disease vector to partner in environmental preservation." (Publisher's note)

Includes bibliographical references (pages 242-244) and index.

595.78   Moths and butterflies

Beadle, David

★ **Peterson** field guide to moths of southeastern North America; Seabrooke Leckie and David Beadle. Houghton Mifflin Harcourt 2018 ix, 652 p.p (trade paper) $29 **595.78**
1. Moths 2. Insects 3. Butterflies 4. Moths -- North America -- Identification 5. Moths -- North America -- Pictorial works 6. Moths -- Southern States -- Identification 7. Moths -- Southern States -- Pictorial works
ISBN 054425211X; 9780544252110

LC 2017051335

This book in the Peterson Field Guides series, by Seabrooke Leckie and David Beadle, presents details on more than 1,800 common moth species found in southeastern North America. "With helpful tips and techniques for observing moths, range maps and graphs showing when and where to see them, and keys to identifying even the tough species, the . . . [book] provides everything an amateur or experienced moth-watcher needs." (Publisher's note)

"A profoundly beautiful guide that will not be surpassed anytime soon. All libraries should have a copy."

Includes bibliographical references and index

Brock, James P.

★ **Kaufman** field guide to butterflies of North America;

[by] Jim P. Brock and Kenn Kaufman; with the collaboration of Rick and Nora Bowers and Lynn Hassler. Houghton Mifflin 2006 391p il map pa $19.95 **595.78**
1. Butterflies
ISBN 0-618-76826-2; 978-0-618-76826-4

LC 2006-287515

First published 2003 with title: Butterflies of North America

"Each species is listed by common name and scientific name and receives a several-sentence description, including flight time and larval food plants. All except very local or accidental species also are shown on range maps. The illustrations are opposite the written description, with most species pictured in multiple images. . . . The illustrations are created by digital enhancement of photographs. . . . An essential purchase for all libraries." Booklist [review of 2003 edition]

Leach, William

Butterfly people; an American encounter with the beauty of the world. William R. Leach. Pantheon Books 2012 416 p. $32.50 **595.78**
1. Butterflies 2. Entomologists -- United States 3. Butterflies -- United States -- History -- 19th century 4. Entomologists -- United States -- History -- 19th century 5. Industrial revolution -- United States -- History -- 19th century
ISBN 0375422935; 9780375422935

LC 2012000389

This book, by William R. Leach, "is [a] . . . chronicle of nineteenth-century America's infatuation with butterflies, and the story of the naturalists who unveiled the mysteries of their existence. . . . Leach focuses on the correspondence and scientific writings of half a dozen pioneering lepidopterists who traveled across the country and throughout the world, collecting and studying unknown and exotic species." (Publisher's note)

Includes bibliographical references and index

Oberhauser, Karen S.

The **monarch** butterfly; biology & conservation. edited by Karen S. Oberhauser & Michelle J. Solensky. Cornell University Press 2004 248p il maps (A Comstock book) $39.95 **595.78**
1. Monarch butterflies 2. Wildlife conservation
ISBN 0-8014-4188-9

LC 2004-884

"Covered is every facet of monarch breeding, migration, and overwintering, as well as population modeling and management. . . . The text is clearly written, and the mathematical formulas included in certain chapters are not essential to understanding the main ideas. The most up-to-date and comprehensive publication on monarch butterfly biology, this will be an important reference tool." Libr J

Includes bibliographical references

Orenstein, Ronald

Butterflies. Firefly Books Ltd 2015 288 p. color illustrations $45 **595.78**
1. Butterflies
ISBN 1770855807; 9781770855809

This book on butterflies, by Ronald Orenstein, "reveals a rare and close up look at the odd beauty and behavior of some of the strangest of these tiny creatures. Despite their large numbers, the world of these particularly weird insects exists largely hidden from our view. Included in the book are some of the most interesting species from North and South America, Europe, the Caribbean, Australia, New Zealand and beyond." (Publisher's note)

"Though one might quibble with the infrequent identification of plant life in the photographs, or perhaps wish for exact-size measurements of pictured species to be included in the captions, this gorgeous book reveals a wonder on nearly every page and will enthrall natural history enthusiasts both amateur and expert alike." LJ

Pyle, Robert Michael

★ The **Audubon** Society field guide to North American butterflies; visual key by Carol Nehring and Jane Opper. Knopf 1981 916p il $19.95 **595.78**
1. Butterflies
ISBN 0-394-51914-0

LC 80-84240

This guide "introduces more than 600 species of North American butterfly, including those native to the Hawaiian Islands. A section of brilliant color plates (more than 1,000 of them) featuring butterflies in their natural habitats, follows a general introduction and notes on text organization and use." Booklist

595.789 Butterflies

Marren, Peter

Rainbow dust; three centuries of butterfly delight. Peter Marren. University of Chicago Press 2017 320 p. illustrations (cloth; alk. paper) $30 **595.789**
1. Butterflies
ISBN 9780226395883

LC 2016014269

This book, by Peter Marren, "explores this idea of butterflies—the why behind the mysterious power of these insects we do not flee, but rather chase. . . . Floating around the globe and through the whole gamut of human thought, from art and literature to religion and science, . . . [the book] is a cultural history rather than merely a natural one, a tribute to butterflies' power to surprise, entertain, and obsess us." (Publisher's note)

"An erudite, engaging book that will find the broadest readership among nature lovers on the other side of the Atlantic." Kirkus

Includes bibliographical references and index

595.79 Hymenoptera

Moffett, Mark W.

Adventures among ants; a global safari with a cast of trillions. University of California Press 2010 280p il $29.95 **595.79**
1. Ants 2. Ants -- Ecology 3. Ants -- Behavior
ISBN 978-0-520-26199-0; 0-520-26199-2

LC 2009-40610

"This superb book by a first-class writer with an unsurpassed feel for ants begins at the ground level as we come face to face with the creatures, move into their minds, and begin to understand what makes them tick. Moffett organizes his text around six ant lifestyles, each represented by an insect that dominates its habitat: Indian Marauder ants, African army ants, African Weaver ants, Amazon slavemaking ants, Neotropical leaf cutter ants, and the Argentine ant, a global invader. . . . This marvelous volume illustrated with the author's closeup photographs will delight biologists, naturalists, and general readers with a natural history bent." Libr J

Includes bibliographical references

Seeley, Thomas D.

Honeybee democracy. Princeton University Press 2010

273p $29.95   **595.79**
1. Bees 2. Democracy 3. Honeybee -- Behavior
ISBN 978-0-691-14721-5

LC 2010-10265

Seeley's "enthusiasm and admiration for honeybees is infectious. His accumulated research seems truly masterly, doing for bees what E. O. Wilson did for ants." N Y Times Book Rev

Includes bibliographical references

Wilson, Joseph S.

The **bees** in your backyard; a guide to North America's bees. Joseph S. Wilson & Olivia Messinger Carril. Princeton University Press 2016 288 p. color illustrations (paperback) $29.95   **595.79**
1. Beekeeping 2. Bees -- North America 3. Honeybee -- North America 4. Bumblebees -- North America 5. Bee culture -- North America 6. Bees -- North America -- Identification
ISBN 9781400874156; 9780691160771

LC 2015007075

This book, by Joseph S. Wilson and Olivia Messinger Carril, "features more than 900 stunning color photos of the bees living all around us--in our gardens and parks, along nature trails, and in the wild spaces between. It describes their natural history, including where they live, how they gather food, their role as pollinators, and even how to attract them to your own backyard." (Publisher's note)

595.799 Apoidea

Frey, Kate

The **bee**-friendly garden; Kate Frey and Gretchen LeBuhn. Ten Speed Press 2016 224 p. color illustrations (trade pbk.) $19.99   **595.799**
1. Bees 2. Gardening 3. Honey plants 4. Gardening to attract wildlife
ISBN 9781607747635

LC 2015025815

In this book, "garden designer Kate Frey and bee expert Gretchen LeBuhn provide everything you need to know to create a dazzling garden that helps both the threatened honeybee and our own native bees. No matter how small or large your space, and regardless of whether you live in the city, suburbs, or country, just a few simple changes to your garden can fight the effects of colony collapse disorder and the worldwide decline in bee population that threatens our global food chain." (Publisher's note)

"Frey and LeBuhn's accessible and inspiring advice, if correctly followed by growers around the world, could profoundly help restore diminishing bee populations to thriving good health, which is essential to our crops and our well-being." Booklist

Includes bibliographical references (page 184) and index.

597 Cold-blooded vertebrates

Balcombe, Jonathan

What a Fish Knows; The Inner Lives of Our Underwater Cousins. by Jonathan Balcombe. Farrar, Straus & Giroux 2016 304 p. color illustrations $27   **597**
1. Fishes 2. Animal behavior
ISBN 0374288216; 9780374288211

LC 2015048629

This book on fish, by Jonathan Balcombe, "draws on the latest sci-

ence to present a fresh look at these remarkable creatures in all their breathtaking diversity and beauty. Fishes conduct elaborate courtship rituals and develop lifelong bonds with shoalmates. They also plan, hunt cooperatively, use tools, curry favor, deceive one another, and punish wrongdoers." (Publisher's note)

"This is a lively and surprising work that makes a strong argument for sport and food fishing reform." LJ

Includes bibliographical references and index.

Behnke, Robert J.

Trout and salmon of North America; illustrated by Joseph R. Tomelleri; foreword by Thomas McGuane; introduction by Donald S. Proebstel; edited by George Scott. Free Press 2002 359p il maps $40   **597**
1. Trout 2. Salmon
ISBN 0-7432-2220-2

LC 2002-69256

"Along with full and clearly written scientific explanations, statistics and analysis, the author provides anecdotal and historical details that make this not just a field guide, but a fascinating read for those interested in the natural world." Publ Wkly

Includes bibliographical references

Compagno, Leonard J. V.

Sharks of the world; [by] Leonard Compagno, Marc Dando, Sarah Fowler. Princeton University Press 2005 368p il map (Princeton field guides) hardcover o.p. pa $29.95   **597**
1. Sharks
ISBN 0-691-12071-4; 0-691-12072-2 pa

LC 2004-111901

First published in the United Kingdom with title: Field guide to the sharks of the world

The authors cover "over 450 species, including many as-yet-unnamed species and some that are only known from a single specimen. Each is illustrated with both a line drawing and a beautifully rendered color painting; in most cases a ventral view of the head and illustrations of the teeth are included. . . . Packed with information, this is an invaluable guide for anyone interested in this fascinating group." Choice

Includes bibliographical references

Ebert, David A.

A **pocket** guide to sharks of the world; David A. Ebert, Sarah Fowler, Marc Dando. Princeton University Press 2015 256 p. illustrations, map (Princeton pocket guides) (paper) $19.95   **597**
1. Sharks
ISBN 0691165998; 9780691165998

LC 2014951471

This book, by David A. Ebert, Sarah Fowler, and Marc Dando, "is the first field guide to identify, illustrate, and describe the world's 501 shark species. Its compact format makes it handy for many situations, including recognizing living species, fishery catches, or parts sold at markets. The book also contains useful sections on identifying shark teeth and the shark fins most commonly encountered in the fin trade." (Publisher's note)

"This well-organized, well-written guide is ideal for scholars, professionals, and enthusiasts. Leonard Compagno et al's Sharks, while slightly older, is an engaging introduction for beginners." LJ

Gilbert, Carter Rowell

★ **National** Audubon Society field guide to fishes, North America; [by] Carter R. Gilbert, James D. Williams. rev ed,

2nd ed, fully rev; Alfred A. Knopf 2002 607p il maps pa $19.95 **597**

1. Fishes -- North America
ISBN 0-375-41224-7

LC 2002-20773

First published 1983 with title: The Audubon Society field guide to North American fishes, whales, and dolphins

This guide covers over 600 freshwater and saltwater species in detail, with notes on 771 more species.

Page, Lawrence M.

★ **Peterson** field guide to freshwater fishes of North America north of Mexico; [by] Lawrence M. Page, Brooks M. Burr; illustrations by Eugene C. Beckham III . . . [et al.]; maps by Griffin E. Sheehy. 2nd ed.; Houghton Mifflin Harcourt 2011 663p il map pa $21 **597**

1. Fishes -- North America
ISBN 978-0-547-24206-4; 0-547-24206-9

LC 2010-49219

First published 1991 with title: A field guide to freshwater fishes: North America north of Mexico

This guide to identifying different species of freshwater fish in North America includes "maps and information showing where to locate each species of fish—whether that species can be found in miles-long stretches of river or small pools that cover only dozens of square feet." Publisher's note

Includes glossary and bibliographical references

Pepperell, Julian G.

Fishes of the open ocean; a natural history & illustrated guide. illustrated by Guy Harvey. University of Chicago Press 2010 266p il map $35 **597**

1. Fishes
ISBN 978-0-226-65539-0; 0-226-65539-3

LC 2009032290

This book "details the biology and brief ecology of various open-ocean fishes. The first half of the book details the importance of pelagic fish in the oceans, the food web of oceanic life, and the relationship between form (fish shape) and function, along with a historical perspective of interactions between fish and humans. The second half of the book illustrates the distribution range, migratory patterns and behavior, reproductive patterns, and trophic information of various fishes. . . . the book is not exhaustive in detail, it provides a very useful overall description of various fishes and their life in the oceans." Choice

Includes bibliographical references

Schultz, Ken

Ken Schultz's field guide to saltwater fish. Wiley 2004 274p il pa $17.95 **597**

1. Fishes
ISBN 0-471-44995-4

LC 2003-15773

"Arranged alphabetically by species, each entry covers the identification, size/age, distribution, habitat, life history/behavior, and feeding habits of each fish." Publisher's note

Smith, C. Lavett

National Audubon Society field guide to tropical marine fishes of the Caribbean, the Gulf of Mexico, Florida, the Bahamas, and Bermuda. Knopf 1997 720p il maps $19.95 **597**

1. Tropical fish
ISBN 0-679-44601-X

LC 97-7690

This illustrated guide to tropical fishes describes nearly 1,200 species and includes color photographs, classification and identification information.

597.176   Freshwater fishes

Voigt, Emily

The **dragon** behind the glass; a true story of power, obsession, and the world's most coveted fish. Emily Voigt. Scribner 2016 336 p. illustrations, maps (alk. paper) $26 **597.176**

1. Fishes 2. Black market 3. Endangered species 4. Scleropages formosus
ISBN 9781451678949; 9781451678956; 9781451678963

LC 2015040075

Carnegie Medal Longlist: Nonfiction (2017)

This book, by Emily Voigt, is a "journey into the bizarre world of the Asian arowana or 'dragon fish'—the world's most expensive aquarium fish. . . . Treasured as a status symbol believed to bring good luck, the Asian arowana is bred on high-security farms in Southeast Asia. . . . In the United States, however, it's protected by the Endangered Species Act and illegal to bring into the country—though it remains the object of a thriving black market." (Publisher's note)

"A fresh, lively look at an obsessive desire to own a piece of the wild." Kirkus

Includes bibliographical references and index

597.3   Selachii, Holocephali, fleshy-finned fishes

Weinberg, Samantha

A **fish** caught in time; the search for the coelacanth. HarperCollins Pubs. 2000 xx, 220p il map hardcover o.p. pa $13 **597.3**

1. Coelacanth
ISBN 0-06-093285-6 pa

LC 99-44800

First published 1999 in the United Kingdom

"In 1938, a fish believed to be extinct for 70 million years was caught off the South African coast, triggering the 'greatest scientific find of the century.' The search for the coelacanth . . . is a fascinating story, and Weinberg . . . tells it well." Libr J

Includes bibliographical references

597.33   Lamnidae

Carrier, Jeffrey C.

Sharks of the shallows; coastal species in Florida and the Bahamas. Jeffrey C. Carrier, photographs by Andy Murch, Jillian Morris, and Duncan Brake. Johns Hopkins University Press 2017 xii, 195 p.p (hardcover; alk. paper) $34.95 **597.33**

1. Marine animals 2. Marine biology 3. Sharks -- Bahamas -- Identification 4. Sharks -- Florida -- Identification
ISBN 1421422948; 9781421422947

LC 2016044752

In this book "biologist Jeffrey C. Carrier reveals the captivating lives of . . . [sharks] and describes how they have survived for over 400 million years. . . . Carrier explains fascinating phenomena, including the reason for the bizarre shape of the hammerhead, . . . what lies behind sharks' remarkable capability to learn and remember, and why many scientists believe that they are equipped with the most sophisticated sensory systems in the animal kingdom." (Publisher's note)

"Carrier writes in an engaging style that non-technical readers can easily comprehend. Detailed photographs provide intriguing, informative perspectives." Choice Reviews

Includes bibliographical references (pages 171-187) and index

597.8 Amphibians

Moore, Robin

In search of lost frogs; The Campaign to Discover the World's Rarest Amphibians. Robin Moore. Firefly Books Ltd 2014 256 p. illustrations, color portraits $35   **597.8**
  1. Frogs 2. Rare animals
  ISBN 1770854649; 9781770854642

In this book, author Robin Moore "seeks to raise the profile of frogs in the consciousness of a public largely unaware that in recent years 'amphibians have been at the forefront of the largest mass extinction.' Moore spearheaded an international effort to search for species feared to be extinct. Following Moore on his global odyssey and riding the rollercoaster of his hopes, disappointments and triumphs brings the reader closer to his beloved frogs." (Publishers Weekly)

"This is a superb resource for general readers and for specialists with advanced training in herpetology. It not only makes fascinating reading but also provides numerous, excellent color photos of rare frogs and salamanders. Summing Up: Highly recommended. All readership levels and libraries." Choice

597.9 Reptiles

Attenborough, David

Life in cold blood. Princeton University Press 2008 288p il $29.95   **597.9**
  1. Reptiles 2. Amphibians
  ISBN 978-0-691-13718-6; 0-691-13718-8

LC 2007-938089

"The writing is crisp and lively, the examples are up to date, and the photography is beautiful. . . . This is a very interesting book, which provides many examples of organisms some of us often overlook." Am Biology Teacher

Firefly Encyclopedia of Reptiles and Amphibians; edited by Chris Mattison. Firefly Books Ltd 2015 272 p. color illustrations, maps (hardcover) $49.95   **597.9**
  1. Reptiles 2. Amphibians
  ISBN 1770855939; 9781770855939

This encyclopedia, edited by Chris Mattison, "covers every family [of reptile and amphibian], ranging from large, predatory constrictors and crocodilians to miniature tree frogs and salamanders. This third edition adds 32 extra pages to incorporate numerous important updates based on the latest scientific findings and interpretations." (Publisher's note)

"Some 320 color photographs complement topical essays, evenly split into 'amphibian' and 'reptile' parts, which together weave what Mattison calls the 'threads' of taxonomy and other key themes regarding these complex creatures." LJ

Includes bibliographical references (pages 259-261) and index.

★ **Peterson** field guide to reptiles and amphibians of eastern and central North America; Robert Powell, Roger Conant,

and Joseph T. Collins ; illustrated by Isabelle Hunt Conant, Tom R. Johnson, and Errol D. Hooper Jr. ; maps by Travis W. Taggart. 4th edition Houghton Mifflin Harcourt 2016 494 p illustrations $21.99   **597.9**
  1. Reptiles -- Canada -- Identification 2. Amphibians -- Canada -- Identification 3. Reptiles -- United States -- Identification 4. Amphibians -- United States -- Identification
  ISBN 9780544129979
  4th edition

"The new edition of this definitive guide reflects 25 years' worth of changes in our knowledge of reptiles and amphibians. It includes descriptions of 122 newly recognized or recently established non-native species, updated maps, and new figures and photos. Color illustrations and drawings show key details for accurate identification. More than 100 color photographs and 322 color distribution maps accompany the species descriptions. Clear and concise species accounts provide key characteristics, similar species, habitats, and ranges, as well as subspecies, voice descriptions, and conservation status." (Publisher's note)

Includes bibliographical references (pages 456-457) and index

Stebbins, Robert C.

★ A **field** guide to Western reptiles and amphibians; text and illustrations by Robert C. Stebbins. 3rd ed newly rev; Houghton Mifflin 2003 533p il map (Peterson field guide series) pa $22   **597.9**
  1. Reptiles 2. Amphibians
  ISBN 0-395-98272-3

LC 2002-27561

First published 1966

This "covers all the species of reptiles and amphibians found in western North America. More than 650 full-color paintings and photographs show key details for making accurate identifications. . . . Color range maps give species' distributions. . . . [Includes] information on conservation efforts and survival status." Publisher's note

Includes bibliographical references

597.92 Turtles

Safina, Carl

Voyage of the turtle; in pursuit of the Earth's last dinosaur. Holt 2006 383p il map $27.50; pa $17   **597.92**
  1. Turtles
  ISBN 978-0-8050-7891-6; 0-8050-7891-6; 978-0-8050-8318-7 pa; 0-8050-8318-9 pa

LC 2005-55023

"This is a well-written natural history/conservation narrative. General readers will enjoy the book and hopefully will become excited to learn more about critical environmental issues." Sci Books Films

Includes bibliographical references

Spotila, James R.

Sea turtles; a complete guide to their biology, behavior, and conservation. Johns Hopkins University Press 2004 227p il $24.95   **597.92**
  1. Sea turtles
  ISBN 0-8018-8007-6

LC 2004-8935

"The author is eloquent in his appeal for the conservation of sea turtles. The best single book on the subject." Booklist

Includes bibliographical references

597.96   Snakes

Campbell, Jonathan

The **venomous** reptiles of the Western Hemisphere; by Jonathan A. Campbell and William W. Lamar, with contributions by Edmund D. Brodie III [et al.] Comstock Pub. Associates 2004 2v il maps (Comstock books in herpetology) set $149.95
597.96

1. Reptiles 2. Poisonous animals
ISBN 0-8014-4141-2

LC 2003-7834

The authors "describe two species of lizards (the Gila monster and the beaded lizard) and 190 species of dangerously venomous snakes of North, Central and South America. Provided are . . . accounts of each species—from the smallest to the largest—complete with descriptions, habitats, and geographic distribution." Libr J
Includes bibliographical references

Ernst, Carl H.

Snakes of the United States and Canada; [by] Carl H. Ernst, Evelyn M. Ernst. Smithsonian Books 2003 668p il map $70
597.96

1. Snakes
ISBN 1-58834-019-8

LC 2002-26924

"This current and comprehensive volume contains all the information currently available on the 131 species of snakes living in North America." Libr J
Includes bibliographical references

Ernst, Evelyn M.

Venomous reptiles of the United States, Canada, and northern Mexico; Carl H. Ernst and Evelyn M. Ernst. Johns Hopkins University Press 2011 424 p. ill. (some col.), maps (v. 2; alk. paper) $75
597.96

1. Reptiles 2. Poisonous animals 3. Animals -- North America 4. Heloderma -- North America 5. Poisonous snakes -- North America
ISBN 0801898757; 0801898765; 9780801898754; 9780801898761

LC 2010036966

This book presents a reference guide to the venomous reptiles of North America. "The first volume contains species accounts of the venomous lizards and elapid and viperid snakes found north of Mexico's twenty-fifth parallel. Volume 2 of this definitive work covers the twenty-one species of the genus Crotalus found in the United States, Canada, and . . . northern Mexico." (Publisher's note)
"A current, vital addition to herpetology collections." LJ
Includes bibliographical references and index

Mattison, Christopher

★ The **new** encyclopedia of snakes. Princeton University Press 2007 272p il map $35
597.96

1. Reference books 2. Snakes -- Encyclopedias
ISBN 0-691-13295-X; 978-0-691-13295-2

LC 2007-922951

First published 1995 by Facts on File with title: The encyclopedia of snakes

This encyclopedia "covers all aspects of snake biology and habitat. This is not a field guide aimed at snake identification. . . . But the work contains a wealth of information about our scaled friends, including patterns of distribution and matters relating to evolution and morphology, feeding, reproduction, and defensive strategies. . . . This captivating work will appeal to students and snake lovers everywhere." Libr J
Includes bibliographical references

O'Shea, Mark

Venomous snakes of the world. Princeton University Press 2005 160p il map $29.95
597.96

1. Snakes 2. Poisonous animals
ISBN 0-691-12436-1

LC 2005-920576

"Fascinating photographs and descriptions will make this title a favorite." Univ Press Books for Public and Second Sch Libr, 2006
Includes bibliographical references

Rubio, Manny

Rattlesnake; portrait of a predator. Smithsonian Institution Press 1998 xxvii, 239p il $49.95
597.96

1. Rattlesnakes
ISBN 1-56098-808-8

LC 98-22935

This book contains "more than 120 color photographs of various North American rattlesnakes. . . . The text discusses many aspects of rattlesnake evolution, anatomy and physiology, and ecology, including several chapters on interactions between snakes and people." Sci Books Films
Includes bibliographical references

598   Birds

Ackerman, Jennifer

★ The **Genius** of Birds; by Jennifer Ackerman. Penguin Group USA 2016 352 p. illustrations $28
598

1. Birds 2. Animal intelligence 3. Birds -- Behavior 4. Birds -- Psychology
ISBN 1594205213; 9781594205217

In this book, author Jennifer Ackerman "explores the newly discovered brilliance of birds and how it came about. As she travels around the world to the most cutting-edge frontiers of research . . . Ackerman not only tells the story of the recently uncovered genius of birds but also delves deeply into the latest findings about the bird brain itself that are revolutionizing our view of what it means to be intelligent." (Publisher's note)

"Ackerman (Ah-Choo! The Uncommon Life of Your Common Cold; Sex Sleep Eat Drink Dream: A Day in the Life of Your Body) documents the amazing and almost unbelievable abilities of birds to migrate great distances, remember where thousands of food items are stored, and adapt to nonnative areas. Also described are the virtuoso skills of birdsong (some creatures are capable of hundreds of vocalizations) and the artistry of nest builders, such as bowerbirds, which favor artificial blue objects. . . . Highly recommended for all interested in natural history, behavior, and ecotravel." LJ

Alderfer, Jonathan

National Geographic birding essentials; all the tools, techniques, and tips you need to begin and become a better birder. [by] Jonathan Alderfer and Jon L. Dunn. National Geographic 2007 224p il pa $15.95
598

1. Bird watching
ISBN 978-1-4262-0135-6; 1-4262-0135-4

LC 2007-30960

This "book offers data on how to begin and how to improve your bird-watching skills. Chapters deal with the pleasures of birding, getting started, where and when birds are found, how common or rare they are at different seasons, parts of a bird, how to identify them, and variations in birds. . . . With a helpful glossary, this is an essential volume for all bird-watchers." Booklist

Includes bibliographical references

★ The **atlas** of bird migration; tracing the great journeys of the world's birds. general editor Jonathan Elphick; foreword by Thomas E. Lovejoy. Firefly Books 2007 176p il map hardcover o.p. pa $24.95   **598**
1. Birds -- Migration

ISBN 978-1-55407-248-4; 1-55407-248-4; 978-1-55407-971-1 pa; 1-55407-971-3 pa

First published 1995 by Random House

"The first section is a primer on bird migration and habitat usage patterns, consisting of short, illustrated essays on topics like the evolution of migration, the mechanics of flight, birds' navigational methods and how human development affects migration patterns. Succeeding sections examine different families of migrating birds according to geographical distribution, and each has carefully designed maps that show birds' seasonal ranges and migratory routes. The use of color to describe, clarify, distinguish and compare migration patterns is exceptional, and clear explanations of complicated topics (e.g., how birds fly) make it an excellent text for middle and high school students as well as adults." Publ Wkly

Attenborough, David

The **life** of birds. Princeton Univ. Press 1998 320p il $29.95   **598**
1. Birds

ISBN 0-691-01633-X

LC 98-30705

"Well illustrated with color photographs, Attenborough's latest goes a long way to converting all readers into bird lovers." Booklist

Includes bibliographical references

Barnes, Simon

The **meaning** of birds; Simon Barnes. Pegasus Books 2018 323 p. illustrations (hardcover) $26.95   **598**
1. Birds -- Social aspects 2. Human-animal relationships 3. Birds

ISBN 9781681776958; 9781681776262; 168177626X

"From the mocking-birds of the Galapagos who guided Charles Darwin toward his evolutionary theory, to the changing patterns of migration that alert us to the reality of contemporary climate change, Simon Barnes explores both the intrinsic wonder of what it is to be a bird--and the myriad ways in which birds can help us understand the meaning of life." (Publisher's note)

"This is an entertaining peek into the world of birds and birding that is sure to delight nature lovers." Booklist

Birkhead, Tim

Bird sense; what it's like to be a bird. by Tim Birkhead. Walker & Company 2012 265 p. $25   **598**
1. Nightingales 2. Birds -- Behavior 3. Senses and sensation in animals 4. Birds -- Physiology 5. Birds -- Psychology

ISBN 0802779662; 9780802779663

LC 2011043684

This book attempts to answer the question "what would an avian existence be like?" Zoologist Tim Birkhead examines "a bird's basic senses. . . . Birkhead describes, for example, ducks that keep half of their brain awake during sleep so they can still spot predators. Then there are the great grey owls that pinpoint their rodent prey using asymmetric ears." (New Scientist)

Includes bibliographical references and index.

The **Most** Perfect Thing; Inside (and Outside) a Bird's Egg. by Tim Birkhead. St. Martin's Press 2016 304 p. illustrations (some color) $27   **598**
1. Eggs

ISBN 1632863693; 9781632863690

This book, by Tim Birkhead, "is about how eggs in general are made, fertilized, developed, and hatched. The eggs of most birds spend just 24 hours in the oviduct; however, that journey takes 48 hours in cuckoos, which surreptitiously lay their eggs in the nests of other birds. From the earliest times, the study of birds' ovaries and ova (eggs) played a vital role in the quest to unravel the mysteries of fertilization and embryo development in humans." (Publisher's note)

"Birkhead manages to contain what could have become an unwieldy topic, and readers with little familiarity in guillemot eggs specifically will still find the material fascinating." Pub Wkly

Includes bibliographical references (pages [221]-265) and index.

★ **Ten** thousand birds; ornithology since Darwin. Tim Birkhead, Jo Wimpenny, Bob Montgomerie. Princeton University Press 2014 544 p. ill (some color), color maps   **598**
1. Birds 2. Evolution 3. Ornithologists 4. Evolution (Biology) 5. Ornithology -- History -- 19th century 6. Ornithology -- History -- 20th century 7. Ornithology -- History -- 21st century

ISBN 9780691151977; 0691151970

LC 2013939390

This book, by Tim Birkhead, "provides a . . . history of modern ornithology, tracing how the study of birds has been shaped by a succession of visionary and often-controversial personalities, and by the unique social and scientific contexts in which these . . . individuals worked. . . . It describes how in the early 1900s pioneering individuals such as Erwin Stresemann, Ernst Mayr, and Julian Huxley recognized the importance of studying live birds in the field." (Publisher's note)

An "engaging, readable history of ornithology, replete with dozens of color and black-and-white illustrations and vivid, frequently humorous descriptions of the people who advanced ornithology because of, and often in spite of, their personalities. The charming and witty work fills the needs of academic scientists and researchers as well as serious birders." Choice

Includes bibliographical references (pages 467-496) and index

Bull, John L.

★ The **National** Audubon Society field guide to North American birds, Eastern region; [by] John Bull and John Farrand, Jr.; revised by John Farrand, Jr.; visual key by Amanda Wilson and Lori Hogan. rev ed; Knopf 1994 797p il maps pa $19.95   **598**
1. Birds -- North America

ISBN 0-679-42852-6

LC 94-7768

Companion volume to National Audubon Society field guide to North American birds, Western region, by Miklos D. F. Udvardy

First published 1977

This pictorial guide to 508 eastern species arranges birds by color and shape to simplify identification. It also includes information on bird-watching and conservation status

Includes bibliographical references

Clark, William S.

★ A **field** guide to hawks of North America; {by} William S. Clark and Brian K. Wheeler; illustrations by Brian K.

Wheeler. 2nd ed; Houghton Mifflin 2001 316p il maps $30; pa $22 **598**

1. Hawks

ISBN 0-395-67068-3; 0-395-67067-5 pa

LC 2001-2477

First published 1987

"Accounts are presented for all 39 of North America's diurnal raptors, including eagles, falcons, and vultures. Each species account reviews details of plumages and molts, useful identification features, patterns of flight, and general behavior. . . . The guide also provides size data (weight, length, and wingspread) for all species, as well as the etymology of common and scientific names. Basically, the reference is essential for any student of raptors and useful for serious birders in general." Am Ref Books Annu, 2002

Includes bibliographical references

Floyd, Ted

Smithsonian field guide to the birds of North America; [by] Ted Floyd; edited by Paul Hess and George Scott; designed by Charles Nix; maps by Paul Lehman; photographs by Brian E. Small . . . [et al.] HarperCollins Publishers 2008 512p il map pa $24.95 **598**

1. Birds -- North America

ISBN 978-0-06-112040-4; 0-06-112040-5

LC 2008-1395

"Ideal for beginners, but also has formidable resources for experienced birders. . . . Perfect for field use. Birders of any experience level will be happy with this volume on their bookshelf." Publ Wkly

Includes bibliographical references

Hanson, Thor

Feathers; the evolution of a natural miracle. Basic Books 2011 336p il **598**

1. Birds 2. Feathers

ISBN 0-465-02013-5; 978-0-465-02013-3

LC 2011003272

Hanson "presents the natural history of feathers, applying the findings of paleontologists, ornithologists, biologists, engineers and art historians to answer questions about the origin of feathers, their evolution and their uses throughout the ages." (Publisher's note) Index.

"Divided into sections that cover such categories as evolution, insulation, flight and adornment, 'Feathers' stretches from the ancient mists of the late Jurassic to the laboratories of today's Smithsonian Museum, where 'snarge'—science slang for what's produced when a bird meets a plane—is analyzed for data. In between, you learn that a falcon thrown out of an airplane can dive at a speed of 242 miles per hour, that the word pen is itself derived from the Latin word for feather and that the most valuable cargo on the Titanic wasn't gold or jewels but more than 40 cases of plumes intended for women's hats, a fashion craze that nearly caused the extinction of several species and led to the formation of the Audubon Society, as well as America's first National Wildlife Refuge, Florida's Pelican Island. Mr. Hanson may be a scientist but he writes like a man who believes in the value of story. . . . [He] offers more than a fanciful, associative style. He is a very good explainer of serious biology." Wall Street J

Includes bibliographical references

Haupt, Lyanda Lynn

Mozart's starling; Lyanda Lynn Haupt. Little, Brown & Co. 2017 x, 277 p.p illustrations (paperback) $16.99; (hardcover) $27 **598**

1. Birdsongs 2. Music -- History and criticism 3. Human-animal relationships 4. Starlings -- Social aspects

ISBN 9780316370905; 9780316269568; 9780316370899

LC 2016954839

This book, by Lyanda Lynn Haupt, "explores the unlikely and remarkable bond between one of history's most cherished composers and one of earth's most common birds. The intertwined stories of Mozart's beloved pet and Haupt's own starling provide an unexpected window into human-animal friendships, music, the secret world of starlings, and the nature of creative inspiration." (Publisher's note)

"This hard-to-put-down, charming blend of science, biography, and memoir illuminating the little-known story of the composer and his beloved bird is enlivened by the immediacy of Haupt's tales of Carmen, and brimming with starling information, travelogues, and historical details about Mozart's Vienna." Booklist

Includes bibliographical references (pages 267-276).

Hayward, Neil

Lost among the birds; Accidentally Finding Myself in One Very Big Year. Neil Hayward. Bloomsbury USA 2016 416 p. (hardback) $28 **598**

1. Bird watching 2. Bird watchers -- Anecdotes 3. Bird watching -- Anecdotes 4. Birds -- Counting -- Anecdotes

ISBN 9781632865793

LC 2015045570

In this book, by Neil Hayward, "birding was a lifelong passion. It was only among the birds that Neil found a calm that had eluded him in the confusing world of humans. But this time he also found competition. His growing list of species reluctantly catapulted him into a Big Year--a race to find the most birds in one year." (Publisher's note)

"Readers will be intrigued and inspired." Booklist

Karlson, Kevin T.

Birding by Impression; A Different Approach to Knowing and Identifying Birds. by Kevin Karlson, Dale Rosselet. Houghton Mifflin Harcourt 2015 304 p. color illustrations $30 **598**

1. Bird watching 2. Birds -- Identification

ISBN 0547195788; 9780547195780

This book, by Kevin Karlson and Dale Rosselet, offers a "highly visual guide to identifying birds in the field based on the important, unchanging features of size, shape, structure, and behavior. . . . Using this approach, birders can quickly assess all birds and distinguish new and uncommon species from familiar ones. They can then examine more detailed field marks to fine-tune the identification." (Publisher's note)

"This is not a guide for use in the field but a work to study when readers want to have a broader understanding of the differences among similar species. Roger Tory Peterson would be pleased that the institute that bears his name sponsored this work. This reference belongs in all libraries with natural-history collections." Booklist

Kaufman, Kenn

Kaufman field guide to birds of North America; with the collaboration of Rick and Nora Bowers and Lynn Hassler Kaufman. Houghton Mifflin 2005 392p il map pa $18.95 **598**

1. Birds -- North America

ISBN 0-618-57423-9; 978-0-618-57423-0

First published 2000 with title: Birds of North America

For this identification guide "Kaufman selected over 2000 digitally edited photographs, enhanced to improve contrast, color, and the like. The excellent result will appeal to beginning birders perhaps intimidated by illustrations. . . . Kaufman's text is simple and uncluttered, a plus for novices." Libr J

Kiser, Joy M.

America's other Audubon; Joy M. Kiser. Princeton Architectural Press 2012 191 p. (hardcover; alk. paper) $45.00 **598**
1. Birds 2. Nature study 3. Animal painting and illustration 4. Birds in art 5. Birds -- North America -- Pictorial works 6. Ornithological illustration -- North America 7. Ornithologists -- United States -- Biography
ISBN 1616890592; 9781616890599

LC 2011039605

This book is a reprinted collection of "almost unknown late 19th-century color paintings of birds' nests and eggs by an obscure Ohio family. Begun by Genevieve Jones, who died young, it was eventually completed by her brother Howard, mother Virginia, and friend Eliza Schulze. . . . The accompanying detailed notes and paintings of the eggs are more in the nature of a scientific contribution at a time when there were no guides to such." (Library Journal)

Leahy, Christopher W.

The **birdwatcher's** companion to North American birdlife; illustrations by Gordon Morrison. Princeton University Press 2004 1039p il hardcover o.p. pa $19.95 **598**
1. Birds -- North America
ISBN 0-691-09297-4; 0-691-11388-2 pa

LC 2003-66383

First published 1982 by Hill & Wang

"This alphabetical compendium of ornithology offers entries ranging from single-line definitions of avian terminology ('Erne') to 12-page essay-style articles ('Systemics') that concentrate primarily on the US and Canada. Entries include a substantial number of biographies and black-and-white drawings. . . . Comprehensive entries on conservation, evolution of birdlife, optical equipment, and human threats to birdlife provide welcome up-to-date information. . . . Leahy's style is by turns serious and scholarly or personal and whimsical, appropriate to a comprehensive reference for both novice and expert birders. There is no recent comparable work." Choice

Includes bibliographical references

Lederer, Roger J.

Beaks, bones, and bird songs; How the Struggle for Survival Has Shaped Birds and Their Behavior. Roger J. Lederer. Timber Press 2016 282 p. illustrations, maps (hardcover) $24.95 **598**
1. Birds -- Behavior 2. Birds -- Evolution
ISBN 9781604696486

LC 2015045261

This book, by Roger J. Lederer, "guides the reader through the myriad, and often almost miraculous, things that birds do every day to merely stay alive. . . . Lederer shares how and why birds use their sensory abilities to see ultraviolet, find food without seeing it, fly thousands of miles without stopping, change their songs in noisy cities, navigate by smell, and much more." (Publisher's note)

"This is an exceptional overview of the life, adaptations, and impressive skill sets of wild birds." LJ

Includes bibliographical references (pages 245-261) and index.

Marzluff, John M.

Welcome to subirdia; sharing our neighborhoods with wrens, robins, woodpeckers, and other wildlife. John M. Marzluff ; illustrations by Jack DeLap. Yale University Press 2014 320 p. illustrations (cloth; alk. paper) $30 **598**
1. Birds 2. Bird watching 3. Habitat (Ecology) 4. Urban animals 5. Birds -- Habitat 6. Bird watchers -- Anecdotes 7. Bird watching -- Washington (State) -- Seattle 8. Birds -- Washington (State) -- Seattle -- Identification
ISBN 0300197071; 9780300197075

LC 2014012257

In this book, author John M. Marzluff "reveals how our own actions affect the birds and animals that live in our cities and towns, and he provides ten specific strategies everyone can use to make human environments friendlier for our natural neighbors." (Publisher's note)

"Readers visit ten cities around the world and marvel at the simplicity of the author's ten rules for saving the situation. And readers are left with an optimistic list of deeply rewarding projects accessible to anyone. This is therapy for people who worry. Beautifully illustrated in black-and-white by Jack Delap, with accuracy and touches of humor. For scientists, bird lovers, philosophers—and everyone else. Summing Up: Highly recommended. All levels/libraries." Choice

Includes bibliographical references and index

Montgomery, Sy

Birdology; lessons learned from a pack of hens, a peck of pigeons, cantankerous crows, fierce falcons, hip hop parrots, baby hummingbirds, and one murderously big cassowary. Free Press 2010 260p il $25 **598**
1. Birds
ISBN 978-1-4165-6984-8; 1-4165-6984-7

LC 2009-31303

"Montgomery assists a hummingbird rehabilitator in the delicate raising of two tiny orphans, and meets the 'most dangerous bird on earth,' the enormous, razor-clawed cassowary in Australia, one bird whose dinosaur ancestry is blazingly apparent. She also writes from unexpected perspectives about falcons, crows, pigeons, chickens, and parrots. . . . Inspired equally by all that we share with birds—similarities in intelligence, emotion, language, and music—and all that is mysterious (birds 'remain fundamentally wild'), Montgomery expresses profound appreciation for the living web of life in a book that both bird lovers and readers new to bird lore will find evocative, enlightening, and uplifting." Booklist

Includes bibliographical references

National Audubon Society

Bird; the definitive visual guide. Audubon; [senior editor, Peter Frances; contributors, BirdLife International, David Burnie] DK Pub. 2007 512p il map $50 **598**
1. Birds
ISBN 978-0-7566-3153-6; 0-7566-3153-X

LC 2007-282186

"From flyleaf to fore edge, the visuals are astounding. . . . An enclosed CD with bird calls and songs adds yet another dimension to a glorious work." Libr J

National Geographic complete birds of North America; edited by Jonathan Alderfer with Jon L. Dunn ; maps by Paul Lehman ; contributing authors, Jessie H. Barry ... [and 24 others] National Geographic 2014 743 p. color illustrations, color map $40 **598**
1. Birds -- North America
ISBN 1426213735; 9781426213731

LC 2014451569

This book, edited by Jonathan Alderfer, "is an astonishing resource that covers every bird species found in North America as well as all the seasonal visitors. Entries are organized by family group, the taxonomic organization newly updated to match current American Ornithologists' Union guidelines. Within a family, each separate bird entry has dozens of tips and illustrations on species' gender, age group, behavior, habitat, nesting and feeding habits, and migration routes." (Publisher's note)

"The introductory material is brief, as are the bibliography and website list (which omits the National Audubon Society). The binding is supple; that of the first edition is too tight. Summing Up: Highly recommended. All academic and public libraries." Choice

Includes bibliographical references and index

Pete Dunne on bird watching; a beginner's guide to finding, identifying, and enjoying birds. Pete Dunne ; featuring photographs by Scott Whittle. Second edition Stackpole Books 2015 308 p illustrations $19.95 **598**
1. Birds 2. Bird watching
ISBN 9780811715768

"Birding is one of the most popular and fastest-growing outdoor activities, but it can seem intimidating for beginners who don't know where, when, or how to search for birds. Fortunately, Pete Dunne, one of the most popular and respected writers in the field, has written a guide that will help even the most casual observers identify the skills and tools they need to develop their interest in birding." (Publisher's note)

Peterson, Roger Tory, 1908-1996
★ **Peterson** field guide to birds of Eastern and Central North America; [by] Roger Tory Peterson, with contributions from Michael DiGiorgio [et al.] 6th ed; Houghton Mifflin Harcourt 2010 445p il map (Peterson field guide series) $19.95 **598**
1. Birds -- North America
ISBN 978-0-547-15246-2; 0-547-15246-9
LC 2009-37681

First published 1934 with title: A field guide to the birds

This guide to birds found east of the Rocky Mountains contains colored illustrations painted by the author, with a description of each species on the facing page. Views of young birds and seasonal variations in plumage are included.

Peterson field guide to birds of North America; with contributions from Michael DiGiorgio . . . [et al.] Houghton Mifflin Co. 2008 527p il map (Peterson field guide series) $26 **598**
1. Birds -- North America
ISBN 0-618-96614-5; 978-0-618-96614-1
LC 2007-39803

First published 1934 with title: A field guide to the birds. Previously published in two separate parts as A field guide to western birds (1990) and A field guide to the birds of eastern and central North America (2002)

This guide to birds found in North America contains colored illustrations painted by the author, with a description of each species on the facing page. Views of young birds and seasonal variations in plumage are included. The book also includes a URL to video podcasts.

"This field guide is of high quality and should be in millions of birders' and other nature lovers' backpacks." Sci Books Films

★ **Peterson** field guide to birds of Western North America; with contributions from Michael DiGiorgio [et al.] 4th ed; Houghton Mifflin Harcourt 2010 493p il map (Peterson field guide series) pa $19.95 **598**
1. Birds -- North America
ISBN 978-0-547-15270-7; 0-547-15270-1
LC 2009-39158

First published 1941 with title: A field guide to western birds

This guide illustrates over 600 species of birds on 176 color plates. In addition, over 588 range maps are included.

The **Princeton** encyclopedia of birds; edited by Christopher Perrins. Princeton University Press 2009 656p il map pa $35 **598**
1. Reference books 2. Birds -- Encyclopedias
ISBN 978-0-691-14070-4; 0-691-14070-7

First published 1985 by Facts on File with title: The encyclopedia of birds. Previous edition published 2003 by Firefly Bks. with title: Firefly encyclopedia of birds

The editor "combines the work of 150 contributors and more than 1000 great color photographs, maps, and other illustrations to produce a stunning book that informs both amateurs and experts. Coverage includes form and function, distribution, diet, breeding biology, and conservation and environment." Libr J

Includes bibliographical references

Robbins, Jim
The **wonder** of birds; what they tell us about ourselves, the world, and a better future. Jim Robbins. Spiegel & Grau 2017 xviii, 331 p.p illustrations (hardcover) $28 **598**
1. Birds 2. Science -- Popular works 3. Human-animal relationships
ISBN 9780812993530; 9780679645672
LC 2016049366

This book, by Jim Robbins, "illuminates qualities unique to birds that demonstrate just how invaluable they are to humankind--both ecologically and spiritually. . . . Exploring . . . scientific research and our oldest cultural beliefs, Robbins moves these astonishing creatures from the background of our lives to the foreground, . . . showing us that we must fight to save imperiled bird populations and the places they live, for the sake of both the planet and humankind." (Publisher's note)

"In this deeply felt and well-supported argument for avians' value to humankind, science writer Robbins . . . hits the full trifecta for engrossing and satisfying nature writing." Pub Wkly

Includes bibliographical references (pages 307-311) and index.

Sibley, David
★ **Sibley** Birds East; field guide to birds of eastern North America. written and illustrated by David Allen Sibley. 2nd edition Alfred A. Knopf 2016 438 p illustrations paperback $19.95 **598**
1. Birds 2. Bird watching
ISBN 9780307957917

"Compact and comprehensive, this guide features 650 bird species, plus regional populations, found east of the Rocky Mountains. Entries include stunningly accurate illustrations--more than 4,601 in total--with descriptive captions pointing out the most important field marks. Each entry has been updated to include the most current information concerning frequency, nesting, behavior, food and feeding, voice description, and key identification features. Here too are more than 601 updated maps drawn from information contributed by 110 regional experts across the continent, and showing winter, summer, year-round, migration, and rare ranges." (Publisher's note)

★ **Sibley** Birds West; field guide to birds of western North America. written and illustrated by David Allen Sibley. 2nd edition Alfred A. Knopf 2016 477 p illustrations **598**
1. Birds 2. Bird watching
ISBN 9780307957924

"Compact and comprehensive, this guide features 715 bird species, plus regional populations, found west of the Rocky Mountains. Entries include stunningly accurate illustrations--more than 5,046 in total--with descriptive captions pointing out the most important field marks. Each entry has been updated to include the most current information concerning frequency, nesting, behavior, food and feeding, voice description, and key identification features. Here too are more than 652 updated maps drawn from information contributed by 110 regional experts across the continent, and showing winter, summer, year-round, migration, and rare ranges." (Publisher's note)

★ The **Sibley** guide to birds; written and illustrated by David Allen Sibley. Second edition Alfred A. Knopf 2014 598 p illustrations $40 **598**
   1. Birds
   ISBN 9780307957900

Presents a new identification guide to North American birds with paintings of hundreds of species and information on bird calls, stages of growth, shapes, markings, ranges, migration routes, breeding locations, and habitats.

"Published to universal acclaim in 2000, Sibley expands the first edition of his guide by over 50 pages, with more than 100 species added. . . . More than 600 paintings are new, the range maps revised, and information on habitat, behavior, and food preferences--largely lacking previously--enhance this superb guide." LJ

★ The **Sibley** field guide to birds of Eastern North America; written and illustrated by David Allen Sibley. Knopf 2003 431p il pa $19.95 **598**
   1. Birds -- North America
   ISBN 0-679-45120-X
          LC 2002-114931

"All the qualities to be expected in a field guide are here. . . . Image reproduction is crisp, colors are distinct, shading shows well, and despite the very small size, range map colors are clear. . . . Sibley has accomplished the difficult task of condensing . . . [The Sibley guide to birds] to practical field size." Libr J

★ The **Sibley** guide to bird life & behavior; illustrated by David Allen Sibley; edited by Chris Elphick, John B. Dunning, Jr., David Allen Sibley. Knopf 2001 588p il maps hardcover o.p. pa $39.95 **598**
   1. Birds -- North America
   ISBN 9781400043866; 0-679-45123-4; 1-4000-4386-7 pa
          LC 2001-33903

This companion volume to The Sibley guide to birds provides "information about birds' lives and behavior. . . . Part 1 ('The World of Birds') discusses basic avian biology, including form, distribution, population, and conservation, in about 100 pages. Part 2 ('Bird Families of North America'), to which over 40 ornithologists contributed, uses a standard format to describe taxonomy, foraging, breeding, range, nests, eggs, longevity, conservation, and more." Libr J

★ **Sibley's** birding basics; written and illustrated by David Allen Sibley. Knopf 2002 154p il pa $15.95 **598**
   1. Birds 2. Bird watching
   ISBN 0-375-70966-5
          LC 2002-20768

Sibley "explores general aspects of birding such as getting started, misidentification, voice, understanding feathers, age variation, ethics and conservation, taxonomy, and finding birds. If being a field naturalist is a craft, then this book is essential in helping to develop and understand the required skills." Libr J

Stokes, Donald

The **new** Stokes field guide to birds; western region. Donald Stokes, Lillian Stokes. Little, Brown and Co. 2013 574 p.

$19.99 **598**
   1. Birds -- North America 2. Birds -- Handbooks, manuals, etc.
   ISBN 0316213926; 9780316213929
          LC 2012945368

This guide offers information about North American birds, devoted to the western region. "Much of the data is directly taken from the earlier 1996 editions," but there are "many new photos and inclusions. . . . The tiny range maps include not only the year-round, summer, and winter ranges, but migration routes as well." (Library Journal)

Strycker, Noah

The **thing** with feathers; the surprising lives of birds and what they reveal about being human. Noah Strycker. Riverhead Books, a member of Penguin Group (USA) 2014 304 p. illustrations (hardback) $27.95 **598**
   1. Birds -- Behavior 2. Human-animal relationship 3. Bird watching -- Anecdotes
   ISBN 1594486352; 9781594486357
          LC 2013030320

Written by Noah Strycker, "'The Thing with Feathers' explores the astonishing homing abilities of pigeons, the good deeds of fairy-wrens, the influential flocking abilities of starlings, the deft artistry of bowerbirds, the extraordinary memories of nutcrackers, the lifelong loves of albatross, and other mysteries--revealing why birds do what they do, and offering a glimpse into our own nature." (Publisher's note)

"Strycker . . . here combines the latest in ornithological science with snippets of history and his own vast experience in the field to hatch a thoroughly entertaining examination of bird behavior." Booklist

Includes bibliographical references and index

Swash, Andy

The **world's** rarest birds; Erik Hirschfeld, Andy Swash & Robert Still ; with contributions by Nick Langley ... [et al.] ; and illustrations by Tomasz Cofta. Princeton University Press 2013 360 p. ill. (chiefly col.), col. maps (WILDGuides) $45 **598**
   1. Birds 2. Extinct animals 3. Endangered species 4. Extinct birds 5. Birds -- Conservation 6. Rare birds -- Identification 7. Rare birds -- Geographical distribution
   ISBN 0691155968; 9780691155968
          LC 2012945960

This book, by Erik Hirschfeld, Andy Swash & Robert Still, "depicts the most endangered birds in the world and provides the latest information on the threats each species faces and the measures being taken to save them. Today, 571 bird species are classified as critically endangered or endangered, and a further four now exist only in captivity. . . . [It] has introductory chapters that explain the threats to birds, the ways threat categories are applied, and the distinction between threat and rarity." (Publisher's note)

"The scope, depth and organization is exemplary. The links to regularly updated information through the QR codes means the book's value will continue." LJ

Tudge, Colin

The **bird**; a natural history of who birds are, where they came from, and how they live. Crown Publishers 2009 462p il $30 **598**
   1. Birds
   ISBN 978-0-307-34204-1

First published 2008 in the United Kingdom with title: Consider the birds

"The author writes with clarity and cheerful wit about the physics and mechanics of flight, evolution and the archaeological record [of birds] . . . [Tudge] covers the avian landscape like a tarp, from amusing anecdotes about bird behavior, to a critique of behavioralism, to the abuse of Darwin's theories, to the complex structure of avian taxonomy. . . . Entertaining, charming and knowledgeable." Kirkus

Includes bibliographical references

Weidensaul, Scott

Of a feather; a brief history of American birding. Harcourt, Inc. 2007 358p il $25; pa $15 **598**

1. Bird watching 2. Bird watching -- United States
ISBN 0-15-101247-4; 0-15-603355-0 pa; 978-0-15-101247-3; 978-0-15-603355-8 pa

LC 2007-07364

This narrative history of birding in America "begins in colonial America, where new arrivals from Europe 'made awed note of the continent's teeming skies and waterways.'" (N Y Times Book Rev) Index.

The author's "vivid descriptions of his own experiences should send many a reader out of doors to look for the small, contained miracle that is a bird." Publ Wkly

Includes bibliographical references

Zickefoose, Julie

Baby Birds; An Artist Looks into the Nest. Julie Zickefoose. Houghton Mifflin Harcourt 2016 352 p. color illustrations $28 **598**

1. Birds 2. Nest building
ISBN 0544206703; 9780544206700

In this book, by Julie Zickefoose, "more than 400 watercolor paintings show the breathtakingly swift development of seventeen different species of wild birds. Sixteen of those species nest on Julie's wildlife sanctuary, so she knows the birds intimately, and writes about them with authority. Julie shares a lifetime of insight about bird breeding biology, growth, and cognition." (Publisher's note)

"This is not a field guide; rather, it is for learning about baby birds and savoring watercolor paintings of them in more contemplative settings. It will appeal to lovers of nature art and bird-watching enthusiasts." Library Journal

Includes bibliographical references (pages 326-327) and index

The **bluebird** effect; uncommon bonds with common birds. Julie Zickefoose. Houghton Mifflin Harcourt Co. 2012 355 p. **598**

1. Naturalists 2. Bird watching 3. Birds -- Behavior 4. Wildlife rehabilitation 5. Human-animal relationships 6. Birds -- United States
ISBN 9780547003092

LC 2011036692

This book by bird rehabilitator Julie Zickefoose presents an "account of her rescues of cardinals, robins and more than 20 other bird species. . . . The birds are a disparate lot: the starlings with their imitations of car alarms and barking dogs; the potentially home-wrecking chickadees; the lean and sinewy ospreys; the barn sparrows that haunt the eaves of large home-improvement stores." (Kirkus Reviews)

Includes bibliographical references and index

598.072   Birds – Research

Strycker, Noah

Birding without borders; an obsession, a quest, and the biggest year in the world. by Noah Strycker. Houghton Mifflin Harcourt 2017 336 p. ill. (some color), color maps (hbk.)

$27 **598.072**

1. Ecotourism 2. Bird watching
ISBN 0544558146; 9780544558144

LC 2017039303

This book, by Noah Strycker, follows the author's 365-day travel in 2015 to observe different birds around the world. "[W]ith a backpack, binoculars, and a series of one-way tickets, he traveled across forty-one countries and all seven continents, eventually spotting 6,042 species--by far the biggest birding year on record. . . . [The author] offers a hopeful message that even as many birds face an uncertain future, more people than ever are working to protect them." (Publisher's note)

"Even readers who wouldn't know a marvellous spatuletail from a southern ground hornbill will be awed by Strycker's achievement and appreciate the passion with which he pursues his interest. " Pub Wkly.

598.156   Birds – Life cycle

Beehler, Bruce M.

North on the wing; travels with the songbird migration of spring. Bruce M. Beehler, illustrated by John T. Anderton. Smithsonian Books 2018 256 p. (hardcover) $24.95 **598.156**

1. Songbirds 2. Birds -- Migration 3. Birds -- Migration -- United States
ISBN 9781588346131

LC 2017034701

This book, by Bruce M. Beehler, illustrated by John T. Anderton, is "the story of an ornithologist's journey to trace the spring migration of songbirds from the southern border of the United States through the heartland and into Canada. . . . [The] book engages readers in the wonders of spring migration and serves as a call for the need to conserve, restore, and expand bird habitats to preserve them for future generations of both birds and humans." (Publisher's note)

"This debut will satisfy a variety of readers; those interested in bird-watching, natural and American history, and travelogs will find Beehler's story especially appealing." LJ

Includes bibliographical references and index

598.177   Sea birds

Nicolson, Adam

★ The **seabird's** cry; the lives and loves of the planet's great ocean voyagers. Adam Nicolson. Henry Holt & Co. 2018 400 p. (hardcover) $32 **598.177**

1. Sea birds 2. Birds -- Behavior 3. Sea bird populations 4. Sea birds -- Ecology 5. Sea birds -- Behavior 6. Sea birds -- Effect of human beings on
ISBN 9781250134189

LC 2017031320

This book on seabirds, by Adam Nicolson, "demonstrates that wonder about the natural world can be deepened by increasing one's knowledge of it and that emotional wisdom can be reinforced by the acquisition of practical information. He blends insightful ethological observations with elements of the mythical and peppers his delivery of practical, premodern knowledge with poetic imagery." (Publishers Weekly)

"Marveling at lives lived in some of the harshest places on the planet, Nicolson writes lyrically of birds most of us only briefly notice when visiting a rocky shoreline, beings possessing extraordinary forms of understanding we have never shared." Booklist

Includes bibliographical references and index

598.47   Penguins

Jones, Mark

Penguins; the ultimate guide. Tui De Roy, Mark Jones, Julie Cornthwaite. Princeton University Press 2014 240 p. color illustrations, col. maps (cloth) $35   **598.47**
1. Penguins
ISBN 0691162999; 9780691162997

LC 2013956959

This book by Tui de Roy, Mark Jones, and Julie Cornthwaite "provides a unique look at [penguins] and the cutting-edge science that is helping us to better understand them. Featuring more than 400 breathtaking photos, this is the ultimate guide to all 18 species of penguins, including those with retiring personalities or nocturnal habits that tend to be overlooked and rarely photographed." (Publisher's note)

"Most highly recommended for all interested, whether the lay public or scientists, in natural history and Antarctic and sub-Antarctic places." LJ

598.7   Miscellaneous orders of land birds

Davies, Nick, 1953-

Cuckoo; Cheating by Nature. by Nick Davies. St. Martin's Press 2015 320 p. 8 plates; illustrations $27   **598.7**
1. Cuckoos 2. Birds -- Nests
ISBN 1620409526; 9781620409527

In this book, scientist Nick Davies asks "how does the cuckoo get away with laying its eggs in the nests of other birds and tricking them into raising young cuckoos rather than their own offspring? . . . Davies and his colleagues studied adult cuckoo behavior, cuckoo egg markings, and cuckoo chick begging calls to discover exactly how cuckoos trick their hosts." (Publisher's note)

"He describes experiments involving recorded bird calls, radio transmitters, and egg substitutions, and he reports findings that suggest how predators and prey continue to adapt. Readers may gain some respect, if not affection, for a hard-to-understand bird." Booklist

Orenstein, Ronald

Hummingbirds; by Ronald I. Orenstein ; photographs by Michael Fogden and Patricia Fogden. Firefly Books Ltd 2014 256 p. color illustrations (paperback) $24.95; $35   **598.7**
1. Hummingbirds
ISBN 9780228100768; 1770854002; 9781770854000

LC 2014497430

This book, by Ronald I. Orenstein, "covers all aspects of hummingbird natural history, their relationship with the plants on which they feed, the miracle of their flight, their elaborate social life and nesting behavior, and their renowned feats of migration." (Publisher's note)

"Of optional interest to naturalists, nature buffs, and birders." LJ

Shunk, Stephen A.

Peterson Reference Guide to Woodpeckers of North America; Stephen Shunk. Houghton Mifflin Harcourt 2016 320 p. ill. (some color), color maps (hardcover) $35   **598.7**
1. Woodpeckers 2. Natural history
ISBN 9780618739950; 0618739955

This book, by Stephen Shunk, offers "a complete guide to the natural history, ecology, and conservation of North America's 23 woodpecker species. . . . It explores their unique anatomy and their fascinating and often comical behaviors; it covers each species' North American conservation status; and it showcases over 250 stunning photographs

of woodpeckers in their natural habitats, plus easy-to-read figures and range maps." (Publisher's note)

"A colorful guide to the 'carpenters' within the world of birds." LJ
Includes bibliographical references (pages 264-293) and index.

598.8   Perching birds (Passeriformes)

Young, Jon

What the robin knows; how birds reveal the secrets of the natural world. Jon Young ; with science and audio editing by Dan Gardoqui. Houghton Mifflin Harcourt 2012 xxviii, 241 p.p (paperback) $14.95   **598.8**
1. Birdsongs 2. Bird watching 3. Philosophy of nature 4. Nature observation 5. Songbirds -- Behavior 6. Natural history -- New Jersey
ISBN 9780544002302; 0547451253; 9780547451251

LC 2012002403

In this book naturalist Jon Young teaches "three basic premises: the robin, junco, and other songbirds know everything important about their environment, be it backyard or forest; by tuning in to their vocalizations and behavior, we can acquire much of this wisdom for our own pleasure and benefit; and the birds' companion calls and warning alarms are just as important as their songs. Birds are the sentries—and our key to understanding the world beyond our front door. Unwitting humans create a zone of disturbance that scatters the wildlife. Respectful humans who heed the birds acquire an awareness that radically changes the dynamic. We are welcome in their habitat." (Publisher's note)

Includes bibliographical references and index.

598.9   Falconiformes, Caprimulgiformes, owls

Macdonald, Helen, 1970-

★ **H** is for Hawk; Helen Macdonald. Grove Press 2015 320 p. (hardcover) $26   **598.9**
1. Grief 2. Hawks 3. Falconry
ISBN 9780802123411; 0802123414

LC 2014472504

Carnegie Medal Shortlist: Nonfiction (2016)
National Book Critics Circle Award Finalist: Autobiography (2015)

In this memoir, "following the sudden death of her father, [Helen] Macdonald . . . tried staving off deep depression with a unique form of personal therapy: the purchase and training of an English goshawk, which she named Mabel. Although a trained falconer, the author chose a raptor both unfamiliar and unpredictable, a creature of mad confidence that became a means of working against madness." (Kirkus Reviews)

"Macdonald, a trained falconer, rediscovers a favorite book of her childhood, T.H. White's The Goshawk (1951), in which White, author of The Once and Future King, recounts his mostly failed but illuminating attempts at training a goshawk. . . . The book moves from White's frustration at training his bird to Macdonald's sure, deliberate efforts to get Mabel to fly to her." Pub Wkly

Includes bibliographical references

Mikkola, Heimo

Owls of the world; a photographic guide. Heimo Mikkola. 2nd edition Firefly Books 2013 528 p. col. ill., col. maps $49.95   **598.9**
1. Owls
ISBN 9781770852747

This book is "a complete guide to identifying the world's owls. Photographers spend hours waiting to capture them and birders seek them out with determination, but owls have been tough to identify--until now. . . .Owls are shown as adults from a perspective that clearly shows markings which assist in identification. Photographs of similar-looking species are included where identification is particularly difficult." (Publisher's note)

Includes bibliographical references (p. 504) and index

Taylor, Marianne

Owls; [text by Marianne Taylor ; photos by Markus Varesvuo ... et al.] Cornell University Press 2012 224 p. col. ill. (hardcover) $35   **598.9**
1. Owls
ISBN 0801451817; 9780801451812

LC 2012023191

This book, by Marianne Taylor, presents an introduction to various species of owls. "From tiny Elf and Pygmy Owls through the familiar Tawny and Barn Owls to the giant Eagle and Fish Owls, these fierce hunters of dawn, dusk and night have long held a fascination for people around the world. This . . . book, covering all owl species found in the northern hemisphere, looks closely at how owls live their lives, and how best to recognize them." (Publisher's note)

Includes bibliographical references (p. 220) and index.

Unwin, Mike

The **enigma** of the owl; an illustrated natural history. Mike Unwin and David Tipling ; foreword by Tony Angell. Yale University Press 2017 288 p. illustrations (chiefly color) (alk. paper) $40   **598.9**
1. Owls 2. Animals -- Pictorial works 3. Owls -- Pictorial works
ISBN 9780300222739

LC 2016942340

This book, by Mike Unwin and David Tipling, with foreword by Tony Angell, "celebrates owls from every corner of the world and offers abundant details on fifty-three of the most striking and interesting species, from the tiny Elf Owl of southwestern American deserts to the formidable Blakiston's Fish Owl, the largest of all owls." (Publisher's note)

"Visually stunning and scientifically sound, this title will appeal to owl enthusiasts as well as the casual browser." Booklist

Includes bibliographical references (page 282) and index.

599   Mammals

Drew, Liam

I, mammal; the story of what makes us mammals. Liam Drew. Bloomsbury Sigma 2018 336 p. illustrations (hardcover) $27   **599**
1. Animals 2. Mammals 3. Zoology 4. Evolution 5. Developmental biology
ISBN 9781472922892; 9781472922922; 1472922891

In this book, author Liam Drew "delves into ancient biological history to understand what it means to be mammalian. . . . [He] explores the different characteristics that distinguish mammals from other types of animals. He charts the evolution of milk, warm blood and burgeoning brains, and examines the emergence of sophisticated teeth, exquisite ears, and elaborate reproductive biology, plus a host of other mammalian innovations." (Publisher's note)

"With wit and passion, Drew, a freelance writer and former neurobiologist, explores what it means to be a mammal by taking an evolutionary look at how and where mammals arose." Pub Wkly

Includes bibliographical references (pages 321-328) and index.

Elbroch, Mark

Mammal tracks & sign; a guide to North American species. Stackpole Bks. 2003 779p il maps $44.95   **599**
1. Mammals 2. Animal tracks
ISBN 0-8117-2626-6

LC 2002-10549

The author "brings an ideal combination of practical experience and careful research to this work. . . . A definitive treatment, Elbroch's book will set the standard for years to come and is essential to anyone interested in tracking this continent's mammals." Libr J

Includes bibliographical references

★ The **Peterson** field guide to animal tracks; [by] Mark Elbroch and Olaus J. Murie. 3rd ed.; Houghton Mifflin Company 2005 (The Peterson field guide series) hardcover o.p. pa $19.95   **599**
1. Animal tracks
ISBN 978-0-618-51742-8; 978-0-618-51743-5 pa

LC 2005-13108

First published 1954

"Murie's handbook is recognized as the classic work on the subject. . . . The illustrated guide describes the tracks, droppings, and marks left on bones and leaves by an army of wild animals-bats, bears, rabbits, reptiles, moles, weasels, and others. A fascinating collection of miscellaneous information about the habits of these creatures is part of the descriptive text." Wynar. Ref Books in Paperback. 2d edition

Owens, Mark

Secrets of the savanna; twenty-three years in the African wilderness unraveling the mysteries of elephants and people. [by] Mark and Delia Owens. Houghton Mifflin 2006 230p il map $26; pa $14.95   **599**
1. Elephants 2. Wildlife conservation
ISBN 978-0-395-89310-4; 0-395-89310-0; 978-0-618-87250-3 pa; 0-618-87250-7 pa

LC 2005-23842

Sequel to The eye of the elephant

"This book, full of adventure and a few hair-raising moments, deserves a wide readership." Libr J

Includes bibliographical references

Whitaker, John O.

★ **National** Audubon Society field guide to North American mammals; rev ed; Knopf 1996 937p il maps pa $19.95 **599**
1. Mammals
ISBN 0-679-44631-1

LC 95-81456

First published 1980

This field guide describes 390 species of mammals of North America and includes keys for identification, range maps, information on tracks and anatomy, and 375 color photos

599.2   Marsupials and monotremes

Flannery, Tim F.

Chasing kangaroos; a continent, a scientist, and a search for the world's most extraordinary creature. Grove Press 2007 258p il map hardcover o.p. pa $14   **599.2**
1. Kangaroos 2. Australia -- Description and travel
ISBN 978-0-8021-1852-3; 0-8021-1852-6; 978-0-8021-4371-6

pa; 0-8021-4371-7 pa

LC 2006-52628

First published 2004 in Australia with title: Country

"In a time where pride in one's country is a rarity, Flannery has written a love letter to his. . . . Just as much as Chasing Kangaroos is about the evolution of a creature, it's also Flannery's acknowledgement of Australia's inherent uniqueness, a uniqueness he begs is not casually lost in the growing conformity of the global landscape." Paste

599.5   Cetaceans and sea cows

Folkens, Pieter A.

National Audubon Society guide to marine mammals of the world; illustrated by Pieter A. Folkens; written by Randall R. Reeves [et al.] Knopf 2002 527p il maps $26.95   **599.5**
1. Marine mammals
ISBN 0-375-41141-0

LC 2001-38103

"Just about everything one could hope for in a guide can be found in this info-packed yet extremely user-friendly tome. . . . A liberal dose of superb, high-quality action color photographs shows the creatures in their natural surroundings." SLJ

Includes bibliographical references

Hoare, Philip

The **whale**; in search of the giants of the sea. Ecco 2010 453p il map $27.99   **599.5**
1. Whales 2. Whaling
ISBN 978-0-06-197621-6; 0-06-197621-0

First published 2009 in the United Kingdom with title: Leviathan; or, The whale

A "chronicle of the tragic interaction between humans and whales. Using Herman Melville's life and 'Moby-Dick' as touchstones, Hoare traces the whaling industry from its origins in 18th century New England to the present." Los Angeles Times

Includes bibliographical references

Hoyt, Erich

Encyclopedia of whales, dolphins and porpoises; Erich Hoyt ; principal photography by Brandon Cole ; illustrations by Uko Gorter. Firefly Books Ltd 2017 300 p. illustrations (some color) (hardcover) $49.95   **599.5**
1. Whales 2. Dolphins 3. Marine mammals 4. Marine mammals -- Encyclopedias
ISBN 9781770859418; 1770859411

LC 2017300268

In this book, "author and whale researcher Erich Hoyt takes readers into the field for an intimate encounter with some 90 species of cetaceans that make their homes in the world's oceans. Drawing on decades of firsthand experience and a comprehensive familiarity with the current revolution in cetacean studies, Hoyt provides unique insights into the life histories of these compelling marine mammals." (Publisher's note)

Includes bibliographical references (page 297) and index.

Pyenson, Nick

Spying on whales; the past, present, and future of earth's most awesome creatures. Nick Pyenson. Penguin Group USA 2018 336 p. $27   **599.5**
1. Whales 2. Mammals
ISBN 0735224560; 9780735224568

In this book, author Nick Pyenson dives "into the secret lives of whales, from their evolutionary past to today's cutting edge of science. . . . Pyenson's research has given us the answers to some of our biggest questions about whales. He takes us deep inside the Smithsonian's unparalleled fossil collections, to frigid Antarctic waters, and to the arid desert in Chile, where scientists race against time to document the largest fossil whale site ever found." (Publisher's note)

Rothenberg, David

Thousand mile song; whale music in a sea of sound. Basic Books 2008 287p il $27.50   **599.5**
1. Whales
ISBN 978-0-465-07128-9; 0-465-07128-7

LC 2007-48161

"Biologists know that whale songs, which may carry for hundreds of miles, change over time and are passed on from one generation to the next, but they don't fully understand what these complex sounds are for. . . . [The author] proposes that music played by humans can help us find answers. He tested this theory by playing his clarinet into an underwater speaker and recording the whales' responses on an underwater hydrophone. His intriguing book includes sonograms and a CD demonstrating that the orcas, belugas and humpbacks he played for seemed to interact with his music. . . . His paean to the beautiful music these great mammals make should lend further support to attempts to save the whales at a time when they are increasingly threatened." Publ Wkly

Includes bibliographical references

599.53   Dolphins and porpoises

Casey, Susan

Voices in the Ocean; A Journey into the Wild and Haunting World of Dolphins. Susan Casey. Random House Inc 2015 320 p. 16 plates; illustrations $27.95   **599.53**
1. Dolphins 2. Human-animal relationship
ISBN 0385537301; 9780385537308

LC 2015011763

This book by Susan Casey offers a "look into the mysterious world of dolphins and their conflicted history with man. For two years Casey traveled the world, and now she has written a thrilling book about the other intelligent life on the planet. Since the dawn of recorded history, humans have felt a kinship with the sleek and beautiful dolphin, an animal whose playfulness, sociability, and intelligence seems like an aquatic mirror of mankind." (Publisher's note)

"This book does not provide scientific background as does Justin Gregg's Are Dolphins Really that Smart? but will interest general and YA readers, as well as nature lovers, who will lose their eagerness to visit dolphin shows and may be motivated toward further reading on the subject." LJ

Hargrove, John

Beneath the surface; killer whales, SeaWorld, and the truth beyond Blackfish. John Hargrove with Howard Chua-Eoan. Palgrave Macmillan 2015 272 p. 8 plates; color illustrations (alk. paper) $26   **599.53**
1. Whales 2. Animal rights 3. Marine aquariums 4. Sea World 5. Killer whale 6. Aquatic animal welfare 7. Captive marine mammals 8. Killer whale -- Habitat
ISBN 1137280107; 9781137280107

LC 2014039895

This book by authors John Hargrove and Howard Chua-Eoan "paints a compelling portrait of these highly intelligent and social creatures, including [Hargrove's] favorite whales Takara and her mother Kasatka, two of the most dominant orcas in SeaWorld. And he includes vibrant descriptions of the lives of orcas in the wild, contrasting their freedom in the ocean with their lives in SeaWorld." (Publisher's note)

"Hargrove, with coauthor Chua-Eoan, blends natural history and corporate indictment into an emotional story about a man changing sides in the argument over human domination of the animal world. Recommended for animals-rights collections in public libraries." Booklist

Kirby, David

Death at SeaWorld; Shamu and the dark side of killer whales in captivity. David Kirby. St. Martin's Press 2012 469 p. (hardcover) $26.99   **599.53**
   1. Amusement parks 2. Captive marine mammals 3. Marine mammals -- Behavior 4. Sea World 5. Killer whale 6. Animal attacks 7. Marine biologists 8. Aquatic animal welfare 9. Humane Society of the United States
   ISBN 1250002028; 9781250002020; 9781250008312
                       LC 2012009433

In this book, investigative journalist David Kirby examines the marine mammal theme park SeaWorld. "SeaWorld trainer Dawn Brancheau's death in 2010 after being attacked by a killer whale made headlines, but the story goes deeper. Marine biologist and animal advocate Naomi Rose had already spent two decades challenging SeaWorld's captivity of killer whales as dangerous to both whales and humans." (Library Journal)

Montgomery, Sy

Journey of the pink dolphins; an Amazon quest. Simon & Schuster 2000 317p il maps hardcover o.p. pa $16   **599.53**
   1. Dolphins 2. Amazon River valley
   ISBN 0-7432-0026-8 pa
                       LC 99-45840

The author "recounts her Amazonian adventures in search of the botos, the famously elusive freshwater pink dolphins, a quest that yields not only invaluable scientific observations but profound insights into the significance of myth." Booklist
   Includes bibliographical references

Neiwert, David

Of orcas and men; what killer whales can teach us. David Neiwert. The Overlook Press 2015 320 p. illustrations $27.95   **599.53**
   1. Killer whales 2. Human-animal relationship 3. Killer whale 4. Human-animal relationships
   ISBN 1468308653; 9781468308655
                      LC 2015010796

This book, by David Neiwert, is a "history of orcas, and an exploration of their relationship with human beings. . . . Beginning with their role in myth and contemporary popular culture, Neiwert shows how killer whales came to capture our imaginations, and brings to life the often catastrophic environmental consequences of that appeal." (Publisher's note)

"This narrative is perhaps a bit long but accessible and persuasive. The author authoritatively presents his facts and will likely inspire readers to share what they've learned from his call to action to ensure the orcas' survival. His tone isn't alarmist or strident, but his message is urgent. A wide-ranging, interesting book that should be required reading for school-aged environmentalists." Kirkus
   Includes bibliographical references and index

599.638   Giraffe and okapi

Peterson, Dale

  ★ **Giraffe** reflections; text by Dale Peterson ; photographs by Karl Ammann. University of California Press 2013 221 p. (cloth; alk. paper) $39.95   **599.638**
   1. Animals -- Pictorial works 2. Giraffe
   ISBN 0520266854; 9780520266858
                    LC 2012038611

Author Dale Peterson's book features a book on endangered giraffes. The book presents "a natural and cultural history of the world's tallest and second-biggest land animals, describing in detail their biology and behavior. He offers a new perspective on the giraffes' place in our world, and argues for the stronger protection of these imposing yet endangered creatures and their elusive forest relatives, the okapis." (Publisher's note)
   Includes bibliographical references and index

599.64   Bovids

Castelló, José R.

Bovids of the world; Antelopes, Gazelles, Cattle, Goats, Sheep, and Relatives. Jose R. Castello ; foreword by Brent Huffman and Colin Groves. Princeton University Press 2016 664 p. ill. (chiefly color), maps (pbk.; alk. paper) $35 **599.64**
   1. Bovidae 2. Bovidae -- Classification 3. Bovidae -- Identification
   ISBN 9780691167176
                    LC 2015035946

This Princeton Field Guide, by Jose R. Castello, with foreword by Brent Huffman and Colin Groves, covers "all 279 bovid species, including antelopes, gazelles, cattle, buffaloes, sheep, and goats. From the hartebeest of Africa and the takin of Asia to the muskox of North America, bovids are among the world's most spectacular animals and this stunningly illustrated and easy-to-use field guide is an ideal way to learn more about them." (Publisher's note)

"Although the great majority of bovid species reside in hard-to-reach Africa, this volume may inspire a new generation of conservationists and raise awareness of beautiful, endangered bovids and their perilous situations." Choice Reviews
   Includes bibliographical references and index

Rinella, Steven

American buffalo; in search of a lost icon. Spiegel & Grau 2008 277p il map (paperback) $17; $24.95   **599.64**
   1. Bison
   ISBN 9780385521697; 978-0-385-52168-0; 0-385-52168-5
                  LC 2008-13624

"In 2005, [Rinella] won an Alaska state lottery permit making him one of 24 hunters allowed to kill one wild buffalo each to thin out the Copper River herd in the Wrangell-Saint Elias National Park. The book's core is Rinella's entertaining and often harrowing account of that hunting trip into Alaska's frozen south-central wilderness, where he bagged his first buffalo. But entwined throughout that story line is an engaging back story — a stampede of facts and factoids, legends and lore, hard-core science and staggering history of North America's largest land animal. Everything you ever wanted to know about the buffalo — or didn't — going back to Pleistocene days." USA Today
   Includes bibliographical references

599.67   Elephants

Ammann, Karl

Elephant reflections; photographs by Karl Ammann; text by Dale Peterson. University of California Press 2009 272p il $39.95   **599.67**

1. Elephants

ISBN 978-0-520-25377-3; 0-520-25377-9

LC 2008-42391

"Ammann's photographs capture an astonishing range of elephant behavior, but Peterson's text—with its scope, synthesis of history and observation, précis of the ivory trade and conservation—is what distinguishes this book. He spins the history of elephant research into mini-mysteries of how scientists struggled to understand elephants' secretive behaviors. . . . The photographs and text complement each other beautifully in their respective odes to the 'improbable' physicality of the elephant's body." Publ Wkly

Includes bibliographical references

Anthony, Lawrence, 1950-2012

The **elephant** whisperer; my life with the herd in the African wild. [by] Lawrence Anthony with Graham Spence. Thomas Dunne Books/St. Martin's Press 2009 368p il $24.99 **599.67**

1. Elephants 2. Wildlife refuges

ISBN 978-0-312-56578-7

LC 2009-23815

This is the author's "robust portrait of Thula Thula, the game land he owns, in cooperation with a number of Zulu tribes, in Zululand—5,000 acres of raw landscape that is thought to have been part of the exclusive hunting grounds of the Zulu king. No longer, since Anthony now runs it as a conservationist lodge, but it continues to produce colorful tales of wild discovery. Most prominent are the many fascinating stories that surround his adoption of the elephants, an unruly bunch he endeavors to make at home on the reserve. With a combination of intuition and experience, the author intelligently discusses many aspects of elephant behavior." Kirkus

599.75   Cat family

Adamson, Joy

Born free; a lioness of two worlds. Pantheon Bks. 1987 220p il hardcover o.p. pa $14.95   **599.75**

1. Lions 2. Kenya -- Description and travel

ISBN 0-375-71438-3 pa

LC 86-42972

A reissue of the title first published 1960

This is the "story of a lioness who bridged the gulf between two worlds, that of the jungle and of man. The author and her husband, a Kenya game warden, reared a cub to kill and fend for herself when she was returned to the jungle. At the same time they were able to preserve the bond of confidence and affection established with her as a pet." Cincinnati Public Libr

Hunter, Luke

Wild cats of the world; by Luke Hunter. St. Martin's Press 2015 240 p. ill. (chiefly color), maps $40   **599.75**

1. Cats 2. Wild cats

ISBN 1472912195; 9781472912190

This book, by Luke Hunter, "explores the spectacular Cat Family in unprecedented depth. Drawing on thousands of scientific papers and direct observations in the field, each species is profiled at length, cover-

ing all aspects of felid behaviour and ecology. The book is profusely illustrated with colour plates, black-and-white sketches showing important aspects of cat life, and accurate images of every species' skull." (Publisher's note)

"The authoritative and accessible text is accompanied by charming drawings and documentary photographs, including some showing the capturing and killing of prey. Location maps, size data, and conservation status introduce each species' information." Booklist

Includes bibliographical references (page 235) and index.

Sunquist, Fiona

The **wild** cat book; Fiona Sunquist and Mel Sunquist ; with photos by Terry Whittaker and others. University of Chicago Press 2014 v, 268 p.p color illustrations (cloth) $35 **599.75**

1. Wild cats 2. Photography of animals 3. Felidae

ISBN 0226780260; 9780226780269

LC 2013048755

In this book, authors and "cat experts Fiona and Mel Sunquist introduce us to the full panoply of the purring, roaring feline tribe. Illustrated throughout with Terry Whittaker's . . . color photographs as well as unique photos from biologists in the field--some the highest quality images ever captured of exceptionally rare species--'The Wild Cat Book'. . . also serves as a valuable and accessible reference on cat behavior and conservation." (Publisher's note)

"An extensive bibliography for each species provides sources of additional information for interested readers. The clearly written text and attractive layout of photographs make this book a valuable resource for both academic and public libraries." Choice

Includes bibliographical references (pages 245-259) and index

Williams, Jim

Path of the puma; the remarkable resilience of the mountain lion. Jim Williams with Joe Glickman ; foreword by Douglas Chadwick. Patagonia 2018 288 p. color illustrations $24.95   **599.75**

1. Wildlife conservation 2. Puma -- Rocky Mountains 3. Puma -- Dispersal -- America

ISBN 9781938340727; 9781938340734

LC 2018945772

In this book, by Jim Williams and Joe Glickman, "during a time when most wild animals are experiencing decline in the face of development and climate change, the intrepid mountain lion . . . has experienced reinvigoration as well as expansion of territory. What makes this cat . . . so resilient and resourceful? And what can conservationists and wildlife managers learn from them about the web of biodiversity that is in desperate need of protection?" (Publisher's note)

"The many spectacular landscape photographs are a treasure on their own and worth the cover price. A handsome book that is well-balanced, instructive, and authoritative." Kirkus

599.756   Tiger

Park, Sooyong (Filmmaker)

Great Soul of Siberia; Passion, Obsession, and One Man's Quest for the World's Most Elusive Tiger. Sooyong Park. Greystone Books 2015 340 p. 16 plates; ills.; maps; ports. $27.95   **599.756**

1. Tigers 2. Wildlife conservation

ISBN 1771641134; 9781771641135

Author "Sooyong Park tracks three generations of Siberian tigers living in remote southeastern Russia. Reminiscent of the way Timothy

Treadwell . . . immersed himself in the lives of bears, Park sets up underground bunkers to observe the tigers, living thrillingly close to these beautiful but dangerous apex predators. At the same time, he draws from twenty years of experience and research to focus on the Siberian tigers' losing battle against poaching and diminishing habitat." (Publisher's note)

"Living in solitary confinement during the brutal winter months, waiting patiently for Bloody Mary to appear, Park felt he had gained access to 'the intimate depths of nature,' and he shares this intimacy with readers. A heartfelt memoir that reflects the author's respect and love for a wild and pitiless world." Kirkus

Vaillant, John

The **tiger**; a true story of vengeance and survival. Alfred A. Knopf 2010 329p il map $26.95; pa $15   **599.756**

1. Tigers 2. Tiger hunting 3. Tigers -- Behavior 4. Human-animal relationships 5. Siberia (Russia) -- Description and travel 6. Russian Far East (Russia) -- Description and travel

ISBN 978-0-307-26893-8; 0-307-26893-4; 978-0-307-38904-6 pa; 0-307-38904-9 pa; 978-0-307-59379-5 ebook; 0-307-59379-7 ebook

LC 2010-04068

"What makes 'The Tiger' a grand addition to the animal-pursuit subgenre is the sensitive way in which Vaillant . . . evokes his cat. Few writers have taken such pains to understand their monsters, and few depict them in such arresting prose." N Y Times Book Rev

Includes bibliographical references

599.77   Dog family

Flores, Dan

Coyote America; Dan Flores. Basic Books 2016 288 p. illustrations (hardcover) $27.5   **599.77**

1. Coyotes 2. Animals -- North America 3. Coyote -- North America -- History

ISBN 9780465052998; 0465052991

LC 2015043370

This book, by Dan Flores, "is both an environmental and a deep natural history of the coyote. It traces both the five-million-year-long biological story of an animal that has become the "wolf" in our backyards, as well as its cultural evolution from a preeminent spot in Native American religions to the hapless foil of the Road Runner." (Publisher's note)

"Flores's mix of edification and entertainment is a welcome antidote to a creature so often viewed with fear." Pub Wkly

Includes bibliographical references (pages 249-256) and index.

Lopez, Barry Holstun

★ **Of** wolves and men; with photographs by John Bauguess; including a new afterword by the author and expanded bibliography. 1st Scribner Classics ed.; Scribner Classics 2004 323p il $45   **599.77**

1. Wolves

ISBN 0-7432-4936-4

LC 2004-45429

First published 1978

The author "infuses his natural history of the long relationship between wolves and humankind with both myth and science, then revisits the controversial subject of wolf reintroduction." Booklist

Includes bibliographical references

Smith, Douglas W.

★ **Decade** of the wolf; returning the wild to Yellowstone. [by] Douglas W. Smith & Gary Ferguson. Lyons Press 2005 212p il maps (paperback) $16.95; $23.95; pa $16.95 **599.77**

1. Wolves 2. Endangered species 3. Yellowstone National Park

ISBN 9780762779055; 1-59228-700-X; 1-59228-886-3 pa

LC 2005-40767

"Well illustrated with black-and-white and color photographs, this intimate history of the return of the top predator to Yellowstone will find an eager audience." Booklist

Includes bibliographical references

Thomas, Elizabeth Marshall, 1931-

The **hidden** life of dogs; Elizabeth Marshall Thomas. Mariner Books 2010 xxiii, 168 p.p illustrations (pbk.) $13.95   **599.77**

1. Dogs -- Behavior 2. Dogs -- Psychology

ISBN 0547416857; 9780547416854

LC 2010483554

"In this . . . account, based on thirty years of living with and observing dogs, we meet Misha, a friend's husky, whom [author Elizabeth Marshall] Thomas followed on his daily rounds of more than 130 square miles, and who ultimately provided the simple and surprising answer to the question What do dogs want most? Not food, not sex, but other dogs." (Publisher's note)

"Although Thomas draws on her knowledge of philosophy and the theory of animal consciousness, this book never bogs down in theory and remains very readable. A title worth considering for libraries where there is client interest." LJ

Includes bibliographical references (p. [167]-168)

599.773   Canis lupus and Canis rufus

Blakeslee, Nate

★ **American** wolf; a true story of survival and obsession in the West. Nate Blakeslee. Crown Publishers 2017 300 p. (hardcover) $28   **599.773**

1. Wolves 2. Mammals 3. Yellowstone National Park 4. Wolves -- Yellowstone National Park 5. Endangered species -- Yellowstone National Park 6. Mammal populations -- Yellowstone National Park 7. Wildlife management -- Yellowstone National Park 8. Nature -- Effect of human beings on -- Yellowstone National Park

ISBN 9781101902806; 9781101902783

LC 2017008953

This book, by Nate Blakeslee, "tells the. . . story of . . . O-Six, a charismatic alpha female [wolf] named for the year of her birth. Uncommonly powerful, with gray fur and faint black ovals around each eye, O-Six is a kind and merciful leader, a fiercely intelligent fighter, and a doting mother. She is beloved by wolf watchers, particularly renowned naturalist Rick McIntyre, and becomes something of a social media star, with followers around the world." (Publisher's note)

"The fight between federal and state control of Yellowstone's wolves is embodied in O-Six's story, told with great immediacy and empathy in a tale that reads like fiction. This one will grab readers and impel them into the heart of the conflict." Booklist.

Includes bibliographical references (pages 273-289) and index.

Busch, Robert

The **wolf** almanac; a celebration of wolves and their world. Robert H. Busch ; foreword by Rick Bass. 3rd edition The Lyons Press 2018 303 p illustrations   **599.773**

1. Wolves
ISBN 9781493033751

LC 2017057201

Includes bibliographical references (pages [269]-285) and index

"The Wolf Almanac is the most widely respected compendium on wolves. With hundreds of full-color photos, graphs, charts, maps, and more, The Wolf Almanac covers every aspect of the wolf kingdom, from the animal's evolution, to its anatomy, physiology, behavior, social dynamics, and interactions with other species. Important updates about wolf conservation and reintroductions are included." (Publisher's note)

Dutcher, Jim

The **wisdom** of wolves; lessons from the Sawtooth pack. Jim & Jamie Dutcher, with foreword by Marc Bekoff. National Geographic 2018 224 p. (hardback) $26 **599.773**
1. Gray wolf 2. Animal behavior 3. Human-animal relationships 4. Wildlife photography 5. Gray wolf -- Behavior -- Idaho -- Sawtooth Wilderness 6. Human-animal relationships -- Idaho -- Sawtooth Wilderness 7. Social behavior in animals -- Idaho -- Sawtooth Wilderness
ISBN 9781426218866

LC 2017033893

In this book, authors Jim and Jamie Dutcher "reflect on the virtues they observed in wolf society and behavior. Each chapter exemplifies a principle, such as kindness, teamwork, playfulness, respect, curiosity, and compassion. Their heartfelt stories combine into a thought-provoking meditation on the values shared between the human and the animal world." (Publisher's note)

"Wolf lovers will appreciate the follow-up to the original movies, and animal and wildlife lovers, especially in wolf territory, will be drawn to this latest addition on an ever-popular topic." Booklist

Peterson, Brenda

Wolf nation; the life, death, and return of wild American wolves. Brenda Peterson. Da Capo Press 2017 x, 292 p.p illustrations (hardcover) $27 **599.773**
1. Wolves 2. Wildlife conservation 3. Wolves -- Control -- United States 4. Wolves -- United States -- History 5. Wildlife management -- United States 6. Wolves -- Conservation -- United States 7. Wolves -- Reintroduction -- United States
ISBN 9780306824937; 9780306902550; 0306824930

LC 2017288504

This Merloyd Lawrence book, by Brenda Peterson, "tells the 300-year history of wild wolves in America. . . . The earliest Americans revered them. Settlers zealously exterminated them. Now, scientists, writers, and ordinary citizens are fighting to bring them back to the wild. Peterson . . . makes the powerful case that without wolves, not only will our whole ecology unravel, but we'll lose much of our national soul." (Publisher's note)

"In eloquent language, Peterson brings us to the truisms that not only does wilderness need wolves, but wolves must thrive to make the world whole again." Booklist

Includes bibliographical references (pages 259-279) and index.

599.78 Bears

Croke, Vicki

★ The **lady** and the panda; the true adventures of the first American explorer to bring back China's most exotic animal. [by] Vicki Constantine Croke. Random House 2005 372p il $25.95; pa $14.95 **599.78**

1. Explorers 2. Giant panda
ISBN 0-375-50783-3; 0-375-75970-0 pa

LC 2004-51356

"This well-written, exhaustively researched and documented book should be on every library's shelves." Libr J

Includes bibliographical references

Nicholls, Henry

The **way** of the panda; the curious history of China's political animal. Pegasus Books 2011 319p il map $25 **599.78**
1. Giant panda 2. Wildlife conservation 3. China -- Foreign relations
ISBN 978-1-60598-188-8; 1-60598-188-5
First published 2010 in the United Kingdom

"When the Chinese government brings Giant Pandas to the negotiating table, the stakes change. Whole populations and their leaders clamor for access to these animals, as if they were toddlers reaching for toys. Washington, London and Moscow have all succumbed to this awesome (a chorus of 'Awwwwwww!' accompanies every panda appearance) force. That is only one reason that Henry Nicholls refers to the Giant Panda as a political animal in his charmingly written 'The Way of the Panda.' At times everything concerning the creatures seems to have a political angle: not only their value as state gifts (with heavy strings attached) but also their precise scientific classification; their mating habits and offspring; and the efforts to ensure their preservation. The author compares the history of the panda in the modern world to that of China itself, complete with a 'great leap forward' in the 1960s, when the captive breeding of pandas first became possible." Wall Street J

Includes bibliographical references

599.8 Primates

Goodall, Jane

★ **In** the shadow of man; photographs by Hugo van Lawick; [with a new preface; foreword by Richard Wrangham] Mariner Books 2009 xxx, 302p il map pa $15.95 **599.8**
1. Chimpanzees
ISBN 978-0-547-33416-5

LC 2009044848

First published 1971

The author describes the chimpanzee group she studied during ten years of field observation in the Gombe Stream Chimpanzee Reserve in Tanzania.

Includes bibliographical references

Through a window; my thirty years with the chimpanzees of Gombe. [with a new preface and a new afterword] Houghton Mifflin Harcourt 2010 xx, 337p il map pa $15.95 **599.8**
1. Chimpanzees
ISBN 978-0-547-33695-4; 0-547-33695-0

LC 2009045230

First published 1990

This continuation of In the shadow of man "tells two stories: first of how the chimps of Gombe in Tanzania have grown, changed and died, and second, how Goodall and her dedicated group of Tanzanian observers have survived the rigours of the past thirty years. It is beautifully written, and evokes both sympathy and understanding of these animals." Times Lit Suppl

Includes bibliographical references

Redmond, Ian

The **primate** family tree; the amazing diversity of our closest relatives. foreword by Jane Goodall. Firefly Books 2008 176p il map $35; pbk $24.95 **599.8**

1. Primates

ISBN 978-1-55407-378-8; 1-55407-378-2; 9781554079643

The Primate Family Tree "is beautifully designed, and the contents are well organized and will be interesting to all. . . . This is a very attractive, interesting, and informative publication." Sci Books Films

Includes bibliographical references

Sapolsky, Robert M.

A **primate's** memoir. Scribner 2001 304p pa $14; $25 **599.8**

1. Baboons 2. Baboons -- Behavior -- Africa, East -- Anecdotes

ISBN 0-7432-0241-4 pa; 0-7432-0247-3

LC 00-63522

This is an account of the author's experiences observing baboons in Kenya

"One closes Sapolsky's book a lot more knowledgeable about plenty of baboon-related matters. But mostly one has already begun to miss the company of this sometimes cranky but always impassioned, learned and winningly irreverent man." N Y Times Book Rev

★ **World** atlas of great apes and their conservation; edited by Julian Caldecott and Lera Miles; foreword by Kofi A. Annan. University of California Press, in association with UNEP-WCMC 2005 456p il map $45 **599.8**

1. Apes 2. Atlases 3. Biogeography 4. Reference books 5. Wildlife conservation

ISBN 0-520-24633-0; 978-0-520-24633-1

LC 2006-272653

"Each great ape specie is given a separate chapter that contains information on behavior and ecology, communication and tool use, threats and conservation, and exceptionally detailed distribution maps. What sets this book apart is the section that details each country in which apes are found and exactly what conservation efforts are underway." Univ Press Books for Public and Second Sch Libr, 2006

Includes bibliographical references

599.88   Great apes and gibbons

Fossey, Dian

★ **Gorillas** in the mist. Houghton Mifflin 1983 326p il hardcover o.p. pa $14 **599.88**

1. Gorillas

ISBN 0-618-08360-X pa

LC 82-23332

This book "recounts some of the events of the thirteen years that I have spent with the mountain gorillas in their natural habitat and includes data from the fifteen years of continuing field study. . . . The region inhabited by the gorillas is some twenty-five miles long and varies in width from six to twelve miles. Two thirds of the conservation area lies in Zaire (formerly known as the Democratic Republic of the Congo) in the Parc National des Virungas; about 30,000 acres of conservation area lie in Rwanda and are known as the Parc National des Volcans. The small remaining northeastern portion of the mountain gorillas' habitat lies in Uganda and is known as the Kigezi Gorilla Sanctuary." (Preface) Bibliography. Index.

This book "recounts some of the events of the thirteen years that I have spent with the mountain gorillas in their natural habitat and in-

cludes data from the fifteen years of continuing field study." Preface

Includes bibliographical references

Stanford, Craig B.

Planet without apes; Craig B. Stanford. Belknap Press of Harvard University Press 2012 262 p. ill. (hardcover) $25.95 **599.88**

1. Apes 2. Endangered species 3. Extinct animals

ISBN 0674067045; 9780674067042

LC 2012023985

This book, by Craig B. Stanford, "warns that extinction of the great apes--chimpanzees, bonobos, gorillas, and orangutans--threatens to become a reality within just a few human generations. We are on the verge of losing the last links to our evolutionary past, and to all the biological knowledge about ourselves that would die along with them. The crisis we face is tantamount to standing aside while our last extended family members vanish from the planet." (Publisher's note)

"Stanford has brilliantly distilled scientific research, African and Asian economic issues, and ethical concerns surrounding the exploitation of these intelligent, highly social creatures into a powerful plea for primate protection." LJ

Includes bibliographical references and index

599.885   Chimpanzees

Crocker, John

★ **Following** Fifi; my adventures among wild chimpanzees: lessons from our closest relatives. John Crocker, MD ; foreword by Jane Goodall. Pegasus Books 2017 xv, 269 p.p $27.95 **599.885**

1. Comparative psychology 2. Chimpanzees -- Behavior 3. Gombe Stream National Park (Tanzania) 4. Physicians -- United States -- Biography

ISBN 1681775689; 9781681775685

In this book, author John Crocker "shares how his time spent with our closest animal cousins has helped him better understand his patients with ADD, anxiety, and depression, and how primate traits hardwired into our own natural behavior help chimpanzees protect their community, raise their young, and survive. Finally, chronicling his return to Gombe thirty-six years later with his own son, he reflects on how his experience with the chimps has come full circle." (Publisher's note)

"A sympathetic personal journey that explores the many profound similarities between humans and the creatures with whom we share 96 percent of our DNA, this book will make a great addition to public and college libraries alike." Library Journal

599.9   Humans

Fabian, Ann

The **skull** collectors; Ann Fabian. The University of Chicago Press 2010 xi, 270 p.p ill. **599.9**

1. Anthropometry 2. Race relations 3. Craniology -- History

ISBN 978-0-226-23348-2; 0-226-23348-0

LC 2009047712

This book tells the "story of [naturalist Samuel] Morton, his contemporaries, and their search for a scientific foundation for racial difference. From cranial measurements and museum shelves to heads on stakes, bloody battlefields, and the 'rascally pleasure' of grave robbing, [author Ann] Fabian paints a . . . picture of scientific inquiry in service of an agenda of racial superiority, and of a society coming to grips with both the deadly implications of manifest destiny and the mass slaughter of the Civil War. . . . Fabian also . . . traces the continuing implications of this history, from lingering traces of scientific racism to debates over the return of the remains of Native Americans that are held by museums to this day." (Publisher's note)

Includes bibliographical references and index

Olson, Steve

Mapping human history; discovering the past through our genes. Houghton Mifflin 2002 292p il $25; pa $14   **599.9**

1. Human beings 2. Physical anthropology

ISBN 0-618-09157-2; 0-618-35210-4 pa

LC 2001-51880

National Book Award Finalist: Nonfiction (2002)

The author "traces the history of human civilization in five regions of the world—Africa, the Middle East, Asia, Australia, and Europe and the Americas, plus a final chapter on Hawaii—to explain how physical differences originated and to provide evidence of our essential sameness." Publ Wkly

Includes bibliographical references and index

599.93   Genetics, sex and age characteristics, evolution

Johanson, Donald C.

From Lucy to language; [by] Donald Johanson & Blake Edgar; principal photography, David L. Brill. Rev., updated, and expanded; Simon and Schuster 2006 288p il map $65 **599.93**

1. Human origins 2. Fossil hominids

ISBN 0-7432-8064-4; 978-0-7432-8064-8

LC 2007-270098

First published 1996

This is a "photographic showcase of the essential physical evidence of human origins. . . . Permitting a face-to-face encounter with human ancestors, this work furnishes essential information, [and] an incomparable visual experience." Booklist

Includes bibliographical references

Ridley, Matt

Genome; the autobiography of a species in 23 chapters. HarperCollins Pubs. 2000 344p hardcover o.p. pa $14.95   **599.93**

1. Genomes 2. Genetics

ISBN 0-06-019497-9; 978-0-06-089408-5 pa; 0-06-089408-3 pa

LC 99-40933

Ridley presents a "summation of our ever increasing understanding of the roles that genes play in disease, behavior, sexual differences, and even intelligence. More important, though, he addresses not only the ethical quandaries faced by contemporary scientists but the reductionist danger in equating inheritability with inevitability." New Yorker

Includes bibliographical references

Tattersall, Ian

Masters of the planet; Ian Tattersall. Palgrave Macmillan 2012 272p.   **599.93**

1. Biology 2. Evolution 3. Human origins

ISBN 9780230108752

LC 2011034415

This book examines the evolution of humans. "When homo sapiens made their entrance 100,000 years ago they were confronted by a wide range of other early humans - homo erectus, who walked better and used fire; homo habilis who used tools; and of course the Neander-

thals, who were brawny and strong. . . . [Author Ian Tattersall] explores how the physical traits and cognitive ability of homo sapiens distanced them from the rest of nature. Even more importantly, 'Masters of the Planet' looks at how our early ancestors acquired these superior abilities; it shows that their strange and unprecedented mental facility is not, as most of us were taught, simply a basic competence that was refined over unimaginable eons by natural selection. Instead, it is an emergent capacity that was acquired quite recently and changed the world definitively." (Publisher's note)

Includes bibliographical references and index.

Wade, Nicholas

Before the dawn; recovering the lost history of our ancestors. Penguin Press 2006 312p il map $24.95   **599.93**

1. Evolution 2. Social change

ISBN 1-59420-079-3; 978-1-59420-079-3

LC 2005-55293

"This is highly recommended for readers interested in how DNA analysis is rewriting the history of mankind." Publ Wkly

Includes bibliographical references

Wilson, Edward O., 1929-

★ The **social** conquest of earth; Edward O. Wilson. W. W. Norton & Co 2012 viii, 330 p.p   **599.93**

1. Evolution 2. Human origins 3. Human behavior 4. Natural selection 5. Human evolution -- Philosophy 6. Social evolution -- Philosophy 7. Evolution (Biology) -- Philosophy

ISBN 0871404133; 9780871404138

LC 2011052680

This book by Edward O. Wilson provides an "explanation of why humans rule the Earth. After a respectful nod to the old favorites (big brains, tools, language, fire), the author maintains that these merely provide the background to our overpowering 'eusociality'; we are the world's most intensely social creatures, living in complex societies of mutually dependent individuals. . . . Group selection--as opposed to kin selection . . . --is the author's big idea." (Kirkus Reviews)

Includes bibliographical references and index.

600   TECHNOLOGY

600   Technology (Applied sciences)

Bobick, James

The **handy** technology answer book; Naomi Balaban and James Bobick. Visible Ink Press 2016 451 p. $21.95   **600**

1. Technology 2. Genetic engineering 3. Questions and answers 4. Technology -- Miscellanea

ISBN 9781578595631

LC 2015029037

This Handy Answer Book, by Naomi Balaban and James Bobick, "explains how technology has revolutionized the way people live, work, and play. It covers a broad range of fields, including medicine, mining, buildings, transportation, the military, and agriculture, and how they have been changed by technology." (Publisher's note)

"This book will serve well its intended audience of general patrons of public libraries as well as students using K-12 school libraries." Choice

Includes bibliographical references (pages 425-432) and index

Doorley, Rachelle

Tinkerlab; a hands-on guide for little inventors. Rachelle

Doorley. Roost Books 2014 xv, 219 p.p color illustrations (pbk.; alk. paper) $21.95 **600**
1. Inventions 2. Creative activities 3. Playrooms 4. Creative activities and seat work
ISBN 161180065X; 9781611800654

LC 2013027910

This book, by Rachelle Doorley, offers "55 playful experiments that encourage tinkering, curiosity, and creative thinking. . . . [It offers] hands-on activities that explore art, science, and more . . . for children two and up. . . . In addition to offering a host of activities that parents and teachers can put to use right away, this book also includes a buffet of recipes . . . and a detailed list of materials to include in the art pantry." (Publisher's note)

"Young children will relish the projects provided here. From paper houses to marble runs to marker explosions, Doorley's designs have more of an engineering essence than those found in the standard arts and crafts book, and they will also take more preparation, but early educators, in particular, will delight in the volume's possibilities. For all budding inventors." LJ

Includes bibliographical references (page 216)

Harman, Jay

The **shark's** paintbrush; biomimicry and how nature is inspiring innovation. Jay Harman. White Cloud Press 2013 326 p. ill $26.95 **600**
1. Biomimicry 2. Sustainable development
ISBN 1935952846; 9781935952848

LC 2012015185

This book, by Jay Harman, describes how, "in a world of depleted natural resources, entrepreneurs and scientists are turning to nature to inspire future products that are more energy- and cost-efficient. Biomimicry, the science of employing nature to advance sustainable technology, is arguably one of the hottest new business concepts." Harman "shows business leaders and aspiring entrepreneurs how we can reconcile creating more powerful, lucrative technologies with maximizing sustainability." (Publisher's note)

"A useful update on recent developments in biomimicry and an intriguing case for innovative green technology that goes beyond sustainability." Kirkus

Macaulay, David

The **Way** Things Work Now; From Levers to Lasers, Windmills to Wi-fi, a Visual Guide to the World of Machines. [by] David Macaulay with Neil Ardley. Houghton Mifflin Harcourt 2016 400 p. illustrations hbk $35 **600**
1. Machinery 2. Inventions 3. Technology
ISBN 9780544824386; 0544824385
Originally published 1988 and 1998 as The Way Things Work and The New Way Things Work

"Famously packed with information on the inner workings of everything from windmills to Wi-Fi, this extraordinary and humorous book both guides readers through the fundamental principles of machines, and shows how the developments of the past are building the world of tomorrow. This sweepingly revised edition embraces all of the latest developments, from touchscreens to 3D printer." (Publisher's note)

"Macaulay's brilliantly designed, engagingly informal diagrams and cutaways bring within the grasp of even casual viewers a greater understanding of the technological wonders of both past and present." Kirkus

601.12 Technology – Forecasting

Weinersmith, Kelly

Soonish; ten emerging technologies that'll improve and/or ruin everything. Kelly and Zach Weinersmith. Penguin Press 2017 358 p. illustrations (chiefly color) (hardcover; alk. paper) $30 **601.12**
1. Technology -- Popular works 2. Technological innovations -- Forecasting 3. Technological forecasting -- Humor 4. Technological forecasting -- Popular works 5. Technological forecasting -- Pictorial works
ISBN 9780399563836; 9780399563829

LC 2017008654

In this book, authors Zach Weinersmith and Dr. Kelly Weinersmith "give us a snapshot of what's coming next--from robot swarms to nuclear fusion powered-toasters. By weaving their own research, interviews with the scientists who are making these advances happen, and Zach's trademark comics, the Weinersmiths investigate why these technologies are needed, how they would work, and what is standing in their way." (Publisher's note)

"With infectious enthusiasm, the Weinersmiths serve up the perfect combination for curious, critical minds. Popular-science writing has rarely been so whip-smart, captivating, or hilarious (albeit occasionally terrifying)." Booklist

Includes bibliographical references and index

607 Education, research, related topics

Creighton, Margaret

The **electrifying** fall of Rainbow City; Spectacle and Assassination at the 1901 World's Fair. Margaret Creighton. W W Norton & Co Inc 2016 352 p. illustrations (hardcover) $28.95 **607**
1. Exhibitions 2. Buffalo (N.Y.) 3. Buffalo (N.Y.) -- Social conditions -- 20th century 4. Buffalo (N.Y.) -- Social life and customs -- 20th century 5. Scandals -- New York (State) -- Buffalo -- History -- 20th century 6. Exhibitions -- Social aspects -- New York (State) -- Buffalo -- History -- 20th century 7. Spectacular, The -- Social aspects -- New York (State) -- Buffalo -- History -- 20th century
ISBN 9780393247503

LC 2016018256

This book, by Margaret Creighton, focuses on "The Pan American Exposition in Buffalo, New York, meant to herald the twentieth century. . . . The Exposition opened with fanfare; its wonders, both strange and magnificent, dazzled the public. Then tragedy struck. In the early autumn of 1901, an assassin stalked the fairgrounds, waiting for President William McKinley. That was shocking enough, but there were more surprises in store." (Publisher's note)

"An excellent and entertaining history for all readers." LJ
Includes bibliographical references and index

Tirella, Joseph

Tomorrow-land; the 1964-65 World's Fair and the transformation of America. Joseph Tirella. Lyons Press, an imprint of Globe Pequot Press 2014 197 p. illustrations $26.95 **607**
1. Exhibitions 2. United States -- Politics and government -- 20th century 3. Social change -- United States -- History -- 20th century 4. United States -- Social conditions -- 20th century 5. United States -- Social life and customs -- 20th century 6. Political culture -- United States -- History -- 20th century 7. Technological

innovations -- United States -- History -- 20th century
ISBN 0762780355; 9780762779840; 9780762780358

LC 2013015055

This book, by Joseph Tirella, tells the "story of New York's second World's Fair in the context of its tumultuous times. Robert Moses, the city's . . . master builder . . . who had a hand in the construction of the first World's Fair in 1939, maneuvered his way to power for the entire 1964-1965 version. His ultimate goal was to turn the fair's grounds in Flushing Meadow Park in Queens into a rival for the jewel in Manhattan's crown, Central Park." Kirkus Reviews

"A model of accessible narrative, showing the author's immersion in archival research, this book will be appreciated most by those who love reading about Sixties or New York City history or, of course, world's fairs." LJ

Includes bibliographical references and index

609   History, geographic treatment, biography

1001 Inventions; the enduring legacy of Muslim civilization. Salim T. S. Al-Hassani, chief editor. National Geographic 2012 352 p. illustrations (chiefly color) (paperback) $28   **609**
1. Islamic civilization 2. Technological innovations 3. Inventions -- History 4. Islam and science -- History 5. Muslim scientists -- History 6. Technology and civilization -- History
ISBN 9781426209345; 1426209347

LC 2011294410

This book, by Salim T. S. Al-Hassan, "takes readers on a journey through years of forgotten Islamic history to discover one thousand fascinating scientific and technological inventions still being used throughout the world today. Take a look at all of the discoveries that led to the great technological advances of our time; engineering, early medicinal practices, and the origins of cartography are just a few of the areas explored in this book." (Publisher's note)

"With striking full-color illustrations, this book eloquently serves as a celebration of Muslim contributions to human knowledge and innovation." LJ

Includes bibliographic references (p. 331 - 335) and index

Ashton, Kevin

How to fly a horse; the secret history of creation, invention, and discovery. Kevin Ashton. Doubleday 2015 336 p. (hardback) $27.95   **609**
1. Success 2. Inventions 3. Creative ability 4. Success -- History 5. Inventions -- History 6. Creative ability -- History
ISBN 0385538596; 9780385538596

LC 2014030841

This book, by Kevin Ashton, "leads us on a journey through humanity's greatest creations to uncover the surprising truth behind who creates and how they do it. . . . Ashton showcases the seemingly unremarkable individuals, gradual steps, multiple failures, and countless ordinary and usually uncredited acts that lead to our most astounding breakthroughs." (Publisher's note)

Harford, Tim

50 inventions that shaped the modern economy; Tim Harford. Riverhead Books 2017 321 p. (hardcover) $28   **609**
1. Economic conditions 2. Inventions -- History 3. Technological innovations 4. Economic history 5. Inventions -- Economic aspects -- History 6. Technological innovations -- Economic aspects -- History

ISBN 9780735216143; 9780735216136

LC 2017013776

This book, by Tim Harford, "paints an epic picture of change in an intimate way by telling the stories of the tools, people, and ideas that had far-reaching consequences for all of us. From the plough to artificial intelligence, from Gillette's disposable razor to IKEA's Billy bookcase, . . . Harford recounts each invention's own curious, surprising, and memorable story." (Publisher's note)

"And while the essays stand on their own, he has a broader point to make. 'Inventions shape our lives in unpredictable ways,' he writes, 'and while they're solving a problem for someone, they're often creating a problem for someone else.' Harford's contagious delight in his subject reminds readers not to take for granted the impact of objects and ideas so familiar they're easy to overlook." Kirkus.

North, Ryan

How to invent everything; a survival guide for the stranded time traveler. Ryan North ; illustrations by Lucy Bellwood. Riverhead Books 2018 464 p. illustrations (hardback) $27   **609**
1. Inventions 2. Time travel 3. Discoveries in science 4. Survival -- Fiction 5. Time travel -- Fiction
ISBN 9780735220140

LC 2018003730

In this book, author "Ryan North shows you how to invent all the modern conveniences we take for granted--from first principles. This illustrated manual contains all the science, engineering, art, philosophy, facts, and figures required for even the most clueless time traveler to build a civilization from the ground up. . . . 'How to Invent Everything' will make you smarter, more competent, and completely prepared to become the most important and influential person ever." (Publisher's note)

"North's "survival guide" is a fun, thoughtful, and thoroughly accessible reference for curious readers, students, and world-builders, as well as wayward time travelers." Pub Wkly

Popular mechanics magazine.

The **wonderful** future that never was; flying cars, mail delivery by parachute, and other predictions from the past. Gregory Benford and the editors of Popular mechanics. Hearst Communications 2010 207p il $24.95   **609**
1. Forecasting 2. Technological innovations 3. Inventions -- History
ISBN 978-1-58816-822-1

LC 2010-3998

"Profusely illustrated (there's something on nearly every page), the book is endlessly fascinating, a collage of snapshots of the present the way people saw it when it was still the distant future." Booklist

609.2   Biography

Kendall, Joshua

★ **America's** obsessives; the compulsive energy that built a nation. Joshua Kendall. GCP 2013 304 p. (hardcover) $27   **609.2**
1. Success 2. Compulsive behavior 3. United States -- Biography 4. Scholars -- United States -- Biography 5. Inventors -- United States -- Biography 6. Successful people -- United States -- Biography 7. Motivation (Psychology) -- United States -- Case studies 8. Compulsive behavior -- Social aspects -- United States -- Case studies
ISBN 1455502383; 9781455502387; 9781611138320

LC 2012051196

Author Joshua Kendall "profiles a 'ticker-tape parade of American icons' in an effort to understand how their 'obsessions and compulsions. . . fueled their stratospheric success.' Across a range of disciplines, from sexuality to sports, these seven legendary figures revolutionized their fields, and they all likely had obsessive-compulsive personality disorder (OCPD)." Subjects include Thomas Jefferson, Henry Heinz, Melvil Dewey, Alfred Kinsey, Charles Lindbergh, and Ted Williams. (Publishers Weekly)

Includes bibliographical references and index

Vare, Ethlie Ann

Patently female; from AZT to TV dinners: stories of women inventors and their breakthrough ideas. [by] Ethlie Ann Vare, Greg Ptacek. Wiley 2002 220p il $27.95   **609.2**
1. Women inventors
ISBN 0-471-02334-5

LC 2001-26950

Sequel to: Mothers of invention (1988)

The authors "detail how women's ideas like the cotton gin, automatic sewing machine and even the Brooklyn Bridge have often been attributed to men and how history books and museums like the Smithsonian and the National Inventors Hall of Fame have ignored women's achievements." Publ Wkly

Includes bibliographical references

610   Medicine and health

Adler, Robert E.

Medical firsts; from Hippocrates to the human genome. Wiley 2004 232p il $24.95   **610**
1. Medicine -- History
ISBN 0-471-40175-7

LC 2003-14212

"Adler ably combines good storytelling, clear and cogent scientific explanations [and] a respect for science over superstition." Publ Wkly

Includes bibliographical references

Anderson, Julie

The **art** of medicine; over 2,000 years of images and imagination. [by] Julie Anderson, Emm Barnes, and Emma Shackleton; foreword by Antony Gormley. Ilex Press 2011 256 p. $50.00   **610**
1. Medicine in art 2. Medicine -- History 3. Medical illustration 4. Medical illustration -- History 5. Medicine -- History -- Pictorial works
ISBN 0226749363; 9780226749365

LC 2011019933

This book on visual representations of medicine "offers a . . . gallery of rarely seen paintings, artifacts, drawings, prints, and extracts from manuscripts and manuals to provide . . . visual insight into our knowledge of the human body and mind, and how both have been treated with medicine. Julie Anderson, Emm Barnes, and Emma Shackleton take readers on a . . . journey through the history of medical practice, exploring contemporary biomedical images, popular art, and caricature." (Publisher's note)

Includes bibliographical references and index

The **Cambridge** illustrated history of medicine; edited by Roy Porter. Cambridge Univ. Press 1996 400p il maps hardcover o.p. pa $35   **610**
1. Medicine -- History

ISBN 0-521-44211-7; 0-521-00252-4 pa

LC 95-38000

This is a history of medicine from antiquity to the present. In ten "chapters, Roy Porter and his collaborators examine the changing form of medicine and . . . {the} technical successes that it has achieved." Sci Am

Includes bibliographical references

Current medical diagnosis and treatment; edited by Maxine A. Papadakis and Stephen J. McPhee ; associate editor Michael W. Rabow. McGraw-Hill illustrations   **610**
1. Medicine

Annual. First published 1974 as a successor to Current diagnosis & treatment. Editors vary

"Provides concise information on the diagnosis and treatment of diseases and disorders for medical practitioners. Uses common medical terminology, but is generally understandable to the layperson." N Y Public Libr Book of How & Where to Look It Up

★ **Dorland's** illustrated medical dictionary; 32nd ed; Elsevier/Saunders 2011 xxvii, 2147p il $51.95   **610**
1. Reference books 2. Medicine -- Dictionaries
ISBN 978-1-4160-6257-8

LC 2011-9789

First published 1900. Periodically revised

This standard reference includes terms used in medicine, surgery, dentistry, pharmacy, chemistry, nursing, veterinary science, biology, and medical biology. Pronunciation, derivation, and definitions are given.

"This is considered one of the most comprehensive medical dictionaries in print." N Y Public Libr Book of How & Where to Look It Up

Includes bibliographical references

Groopman, Jerome E.

★ **How** doctors think; [by] Jerome Groopman. Houghton Mifflin Co. 2007 307p il $26   **610**
1. Medicine 2. Diagnosis 3. Physicians
ISBN 978-0-618-61003-7; 0-618-61003-0

LC 2006-35718

This book is comprised of a series of "essays that explore the rational and irrational factors that influence medical decision-making. By turns inspired and dismaying, it explains how even the best doctor can draw the wrong conclusion, and why that same doctor might also come up with a brilliant diagnosis that has eluded his peers. Uncertainty hovers over the practice of medicine, which Dr. Groopman, a clear writer and a humane thinker, presents as an art as well as a science, despite the spectacular advances in medical technology." N Y Times (Late N Y Ed)

Includes bibliographical references

Your medical mind; how to decide what is right for you. [by] Jerome Groopman and Pamela Hartzband. Penguin Press 2011 308p $27.95   **610**
1. Medicine 2. Decision making 3. Physician-patient relationship
ISBN 978-1-59420-311-4

LC 2011019808

The authors "present readers with a fascinating look into medical decision making. Through detailed portraits of socially and ethnically diverse real-life individuals who must make medical choices, the authors show how patients' family history, culture, profession, and attitudes toward medicine and technology can shape their decisions about treatment. . . . This engaging, insightful, and illuminating book should be read by general audiences as well as medical and health-care professionals, who are often baffled by the choices their patients make." Libr J

Includes bibliographical references

Mukherjee, Siddhartha

The **laws** of medicine; field notes from an uncertain science. Siddhartha Mukherjee. Simon & Schuster 2015 96 p. (hardcover) $16.99   **610**

1. Medicine 2. Science -- Philosophy

ISBN 9781476784847; 1476784841

This book, by Siddhartha Mukherjee, discusses "philosophy on the little-known principles that govern medicine--and how understanding these principles can empower us all. . . . Is medicine a 'science'? Sciences must have laws—statements of truth based on repeated experiments that describe some universal attribute of nature. But does medicine have laws like other sciences?" (Publisher's note)

"This mininarrative, packed with complex ideas translated into easily accessible language and an engaging style, leaves the readers time to ponder the author's ideas at greater length, and the result is a fascinating and illuminating trek through a beautiful mind. A splendid exploration of how medicine might be transformed." Kirkus

Orbinski, James

An **imperfect** offering; humanitarian action in the twenty-first century. Walker & Co. 2008 431p il $27   **610**

1. War relief 2. Medical assistance 3. Médecins Sans Frontières (Organization)

ISBN 978-0-8027-1709-2; 0-8027-1709-8

"Orbinski was president of Doctors Without Borders when it received the Nobel Peace Prize in 1999, and this book echoes and expands on his acceptance speech. He argues that humanitarian action must be free of political influence, must not become a tool of war and must not be silent in the face of human-rights violations. . . . An important, consciousness-raising work." Kirkus

Includes bibliographical references

Parker, Steve

Kill or cure; an illustrated history of medicine. Steve Parker. Dorling Kindersley 2013 400 p. illustrations; portraits (hbk.) $30   **610**

1. Popular medicine 2. Medicine -- History 3. Medicine, Popular 4. Medicine -- History -- Popular works

ISBN 1465408428; 9781465408426

LC 2013474432

This illustrated reference book, by Steve Parker, relates "compelling stories behind mankind's never-ending quest to cure every disease. . . . Beginning with early healers, chance discoveries, technological advancement, and 'wonder' drugs, . . . [the volume] highlights information about human anatomy, surgical instruments, and medical breakthroughs while telling the dramatic tale of medical progress." (Publisher's note)

Includes bibliographical references (page 392) and index

Pogrebin, Letty Cottin

How to be a friend to a friend who's sick; Letty Cottin Pogrebin. PublicAffairs 2013 304 p. (hardcover) $24.99   **610**

1. Sick 2. Caregivers 3. Helping behavior 4. Diseases -- Psychological aspects 5. Care of the sick -- Psychological aspects

ISBN 1610392833; 9781610392839

LC 2012049749

"Throughout her recent bout with breast cancer, Letty Cottin Pogrebin became fascinated by her friends' and family's diverse reactions to her and her illness: how awkwardly some of them behaved; how some misspoke or misinterpreted her needs; and how wonderful it was when people read her right. She began talking to her fellow patients and dozens of other veterans of serious illness, seeking to discover what sick people wished their friends knew." (Publisher's note)

"A useful refresher course on navigating the complicated territory of compassionate companionship." Kirkus

Includes bibliographical references and index

Schweitzer, Albert, 1875-1965

Out of my life and thought; an autobiography. Albert Schweitzer ; foreword by Jimmy Carter ; new foreword by Lachlan Forrow ; translated by Antje Bultmann Lemke. Johns Hopkins University Press 2009 xx, 272 p.p ill. (paperback) $27   **610**

ISBN 0801894123; 9780801894121

LC 2009925674

This book presents Albert Schweitzer's "autobiography, first published in 1933" in which he "discusses his research into primitive Christianity and his search for the historical Jesus; his love of Bach, 'poet and painter in sound'; his fancy for rebuilding old church organs. His philosophy, which he called 'Reverence for Life,' blends mysticism and rationalism, with an impulse to release the 'active ethic' he sees latent in Christianity." (Publishers Weekly)

Includes bibliographical references (p. 257-260) and index

Shapiro, Nina

Hype; a doctor's guide to medical myths, exaggerated claims and bad advice - how to tell what's real and what's not. Nina Shapiro, M.D., with Kristin Loberg. St. Martin's Press 2018 304 p. (hardcover) $26.99   **610**

1. Popular medicine 2. Medical misconceptions

ISBN 9781250149305

LC 2017055072

This book, by Nina Shapiro, with Kristin Loberg, "look[s] at the real science behind our most common beliefs and assumptions in the health sphere. . . . covers everything from exercise to supplements, diets to detoxes, alternative medicine to vaccines, and medical testing to media coverage. Shapiro tackles popular misconceptions such as toxic sugar and the importance of drinking eight glasses of water a day." (Publisher's note)

Includes bibliographical references and index

Szczeklik, Andrzej

Kore; on sickness, the sick, and the search for the soul of medicine. Andrzej Szczeklik ; translated by Antonia Lloyd-Jones ; with an introduction by Adam Zagajewski. Counterpoint 2012 320 p. (hardback; alk. paper) $26   **610**

1. Sick 2. Soul 3. Medicine 4. Humanities 5. History of Medicine 6. Philosophy, Medical 7. Physician-Patient Relations

ISBN 161902019X; 9781619020191; 9781619021389

LC 2012042867

In this book, translated by Antonia Lloyd-Jones, author Andrzej Szczeklik "insists that only with a curiosity thoroughly at home in both [science and the humanities] . . . can one expect to discover what we should mean about sickness and about the soul. . . . Anecdotes drawn from a personal immersion in art, music, and literature are woven with reports on experimental medicine and daily clinical experience." (Publisher's note)

Includes bibliographical references and index

Teresi, Dick

The **undead**; organ harvesting, the ice-water test, beating heart cadavers; how medicine is blurring the line between life and death. Dick Teresi. Pantheon Books 2012 256 p.   **610**

1. Death 2. Brain death 3. Medical ethics 4. Physicians -- Attitudes 5. Transplantation of organs, tissues, etc. -- Ethical aspects 6. Attitude to Death 7. Death -- Autobiography 8. Persistent

Vegetative State 9. Tissue and Organ Harvesting
ISBN 9780375423710

LC 2011032025

"In this . . . look at how doctors determine the moment of death, skeptical science writer . . . [Dick] Teresi . . . relishes ripping into the 1968 Harvard team that formulated new criteria for determining death: 'loss of personhood,' or brain death. Doctors, Teresi says, can now 'declare a person dead in less time than it takes to get a decent eye exam' by testing reflexes: 'a flashlight in the eyes, ice water in the ears, and then an attempt to gasp for air' when the respirator is disconnected. Teresi interviews scientists who question the finality of brain death when the heart is still beating, and even the concept that personhood is located solely in the brain. . . . Teresi charges that the brain-death revolution is driven by the $20 billion-a-year organ transplant business." (Publishers Weekly)

Includes bibliographical references and index

610.1   Medicine -- philosophy

Meadows, Susannah

The **other** side of impossible; ordinary people who faced daunting medical challenges and refused to give up. Susannah Meadows. Random House 2017 302 p. (hardback) $28 **610.1**
  1. Mind and body 2. Creative nonfiction 3. Alternative medicine 4. Medicine -- Philosophy 5. Alternative medicine -- Philosophy
ISBN 9780812986457; 9780812996470

LC 2016044332

This book, by Susannah Meadows, "tells the real-life stories of seven families who persisted when traditional medicine alone wasn't enough. Their adventures take us to the outer frontiers of medical science and cutting-edge complementary therapies, as Meadows explores research into the mind's potential to heal the body, the possible role food may play in reversing disease, the power of agency, perseverance, and hope--and more." (Publisher's note)

"Encouraging, honest information and real-life cases that show the role food can play in healing the body." Kirkus

Includes bibliographical references pages [275]-285 and index.

Rakel, David

The **compassionate** connection; the healing power of empathy and mindful listening. David Rakel. W W Norton & Co Inc 2018 304 p. (hardcover) $25.95 **610.1**
  1. Compassion 2. Mind and body 3. Interpersonal relations 4. Healing -- Psychological aspects 5. Interpersonal relations -- Health aspects 6. Interpersonal communication -- Health aspects
ISBN 9780393247749

LC 2017056375

In this book Dr. David Rakel "introduces the concept of bio-psycho-spiritual authentic awareness, . . . an innovative approach to enhancing health in others and strengthening relationships through the art of connecting. These tools guide us to improve our connections--whether between doctor and patient, husband and wife, parent and child, or boss and employee--and live with clarity, wisdom, and good health." (Publisher's note)

Includes bibliographical references and index

610.28   Auxiliary techniques and procedures; apparatus, equipment, materials

Gawande, Atul

  ★ The **checklist** manifesto; how to get things right. Met-

ropolitan Books 2010 209p $24.50

610.28

  1. Lists 2. Medical care -- Quality control
ISBN 9780805091748

LC 2009-46888

"We live in a world of great and increasing complexity, where even the most expert professionals struggle to master the tasks they face. Longer training, ever more advanced technologies—neither seems to prevent grievous errors. But in [this book], . . . Gawande finds a remedy in the . . . simplest of techniques: the checklist. First introduced decades ago by the U.S. Air Force, checklists have enabled pilots to fly aircraft of mind-boggling sophistication. Now innovative checklists are being adopted in hospitals around the world. . . . Gawande takes us from Austria, where an emergency checklist saved a drowning victim who had spent half an hour underwater, to Michigan, where a cleanliness checklist in intensive care units virtually eliminated a type of deadly hospital infection. He explains how checklists actually work to prompt striking and immediate improvements." (Publisher's note) Index.

"Few medical writers working today can transmit the gore-drenched terror of an operation that suddenly goes wrong—a terror that has a special resonance when it is Dr. Gawande himself who makes the initial horrifying mistake. And few can make it as clear as he can what exactly is at stake in the effort to minimize calamities." N Y Times (Late N Y Ed)

Includes bibliographical references

Topol, Eric

The **creative** destruction of medicine; Eric Topol. Basic Books 2012 xi, 303p.p **610.28**
  1. Medical technology 2. Access to health care 3. Technological innovations 4. Internet 5. Health Communication 6. Biomedical Technology 7. Diffusion of Innovation 8. Medical Informatics Applications 9. Delivery of Health Care -- trends
ISBN 9780465025503; 9780465029341

LC 2011041162

This book offers information about "how academic healthcare organizations . . . can collaborate with for-profit companies to accelerate technological progress in medicine. . . . The author says that no single innovation will have a more profound effect than the conversion of biological data. . . . Dr. [Eric] Topol focuses much of his attention on the development of 'theranostics,' or the integrated use of treatments and diagnostics . . . to better guide therapy." (Wall Street Journal)

Includes bibliographical references and index.

Wachter, Robert

The **digital** doctor; hope, hype, and harm at the dawn of medicine's computer age. by Robert Wachter. McGraw-Hill 2015 330 p. illustrations (hardback; alk. paper) $30 **610.28**
  1. Medical technology 2. Physician-patient relationship 3. Clinical Medicine 4. Clinical Competence 5. Medical Informatics 6. Physician-Patient Relations
ISBN 0071849467; 9780071849463

LC 2015001206

This book, by Robert Wachter, "examines healthcare at the dawn of its computer age. It tackles the hard questions, from how technology is changing care at the bedside to whether government intervention has been useful or destructive. And it does so with clarity, insight, humor, and compassion. Ultimately, it is a hopeful story." (Publisher's note)

"Wachter writes about the complexity of health-care IT systems, patient access and contributions to their office notes, IBM's Watson (the Jeopardy-champion supercomputer), and intelligent, biosensing underwear. Maybe the best take on modern medicine's 'man versus machine' debate is provided by Warner Slack, a physician and informatics expert: 'Any doctor who could be replaced by a computer should be.'"

610.3   Medicine -- dictionaries

Magill's medical guide; medical editors: Bryan C. Auday, Ph.D., Gordon College, Michael A. Buratovich, Ph.D., Spring Arbor University, Geraldine F. Marrocco, Ed.D., APRN, CNS, ANP-BC, Yale University School of Nursing, Paul Moglia, Ph.D., South Nassau Communities Hospital. Seventh edition Salem Press 2014 5 volumes ill   **610.3**
1. Medicine -- Encyclopedias
ISBN 9781619252141; 1619252147
First published 1995
This medical reference book "covers diseases, disorders, treatments, procedures, specialties, anatomy, biology, and issues in an A-Z format, with sidebars addressing recent developments in medicine and concise information boxes for all diseases and disorders." (Publisher's note)
Includes bibliographical references and index.

Mosby's medical dictionary; editor, Marie T. O'Toole. 10th edition Elsevier 2016 1942 p. ill. (chiefly col.) hbk $43.95   **610.3**
1. Medicine 2. Medicine -- Dictionaries
ISBN 9780323414258; 0323414257
"Over 56,000 entries offer detailed definitions, as well as the latest information on pathophysiology, treatment and interventions, and nursing care.More than 2,450 color photographs and line drawings demonstrate and explain complex conditions and abstract concepts.Strict, common-sense alphabetical organization makes it easy to find key terms and definitions." (Publisher's note)

Taber's cyclopedic medical dictionary; editor, Donald Venes ... [et. al.] 22nd ed F.A. Davis 2013 2846 p. col. ill. (indexed) $42.95   **610.3**
1. Medical care 2. Medicine -- Dictionaries
ISBN 080362977X; 9780803629783; 9780803629790; 9780803629776
LC 2012034064
First published 1940. Periodically revised
"In hand, online, or on your mobile device--anywhere and everywhere, 'Taber's 22' is the all-in-one, go-to source in the classroom, clinical, and beyond. Under the editorial direction of Donald Venes, MD, MSJ, a team of expert consulting editors and consultants, representing nearly every health care profession, ensures that the content reflects the most current healthcare information." (Publisher's note)
This work gives "definitions of medical terms and words. Pronunciation is given for all but very common terms and the etymology of most words is included. Appendixes include such information as emergency treatment, dietetic charts, Latin and Greek nomenclature, and normal reference laboratory values." Guide to Ref Books
Includes bibliographical references and index

610.69   Medical personnel and relationships

Berger, Zackary
Talking to your doctor; a patient's guide to communication in the exam room and beyond. Zackary Berger. "Rowman & Littlefield Publishers, Inc. 2013 208 p. illustrations (cloth; alk. paper) $34   **610.69**
1. Communication 2. Patient participation 3. Physician-patient relationship 4. Physician and patient 5. Communication in medicine
ISBN 1442220503; 9781442220508

LC 2013014172
This book, by Zackary Berger, "helps readers navigate the new, more promising waters of doctor-patient collaboration, starting at the simplest and most human interaction --the conversation between two people in a room-- and ending with the benefits that can be obtained by cultivating an effective partnership. While patients need to take control of the visit and set their agenda, the latest research shows that doctors and patients need to connect on a more emotional level as well." (Publisher's note)
"Every visit to the doctor's office is an opportunity for a new beginning and an important dialogue about remaining healthy or feeling better. Patients should feel comfortable about expressing their concerns, and physicians need to listen carefully. Berger's book lays a strong foundation for constructing solid relationships between patients and their physicians." Booklist
Includes bibliographical references and index

Fischer-Wright, Halee
Back to balance; the art, science, and business of medicine. Halee Fischer-Wright. Greenleaf Book Group Llc 2017 248 p. $25.95   **610.69**
1. Medical care -- United States 2. Physician-patient relationship
ISBN 1633310140; 9781633310148
In this book, author Halee Fischer-Wright presents a unique prescription for fixing America's health care woes. . . . The problem, Fischer-Wright asserts, is that we have lost our focus on strengthening the one thing that has always been at the heart of effective health care: namely, strong relationships between patients and physicians, informed by smart science and enabled by good business, that create the trust necessary to achieve the outcomes we all want." (Publisher's note)
"A motivational and elucidating appeal for health system reform and a return to patient-centered medical care." Kirkus

Michelson, Leslie D.
The **patient's** playbook; how to save your life and the lives of those you love. by Leslie D. Michelson. Alfred A. Knopf 2015 336 p. (hardback) $24.95   **610.69**
1. Medical care 2. Decision making 3. Patient advocacy 4. Patient education 5. Self-care, Health 6. Medicine -- Decision making 7. Medical errors -- Prevention
ISBN 038535228X; 9780385352284
LC 2015014325
This book, by Leslie D. Michelson, seeks to "show you how to choose the right doctor, coordinate the best care, and get to the No-Mistake Zone in medical decision making. . . . [The book] is an essential guide to the most effective techniques for getting the best from a broken system: sourcing excellent physicians, selecting the right treatment protocols, researching with precision, and structuring the ideal support team." (Publisher's note)
"In a fluid, informative, and educated manner, Michelson delivers an impassioned call to arms for patients and caregivers to be their best advocate, ready to organize, question, and ask for second opinions." LJ

Ofri, Danielle
What doctors feel; how emotions affect the practice of medicine. Danielle Ofri. Beacon Press 2013 232 p. (alk. paper) $24.95   **610.69**
1. Physicians 2. Physician-patient relationship 3. Empathy -- Personal Narratives 4. Emotions -- Personal Narratives 5. Physicians -- psychology -- Personal Narratives 6. Interprofessional Relations -- Personal Narratives 7. Physician-Patient Relations -- Personal Narratives 8. Attitude of Health Personnel -- Personal Narratives
ISBN 0807073326; 9780807073322

LC 2012049349

Here, Dr. Danielle Ofri offers a "take on the inner life of medical professionals, describing not only her own bumpy path from med student to M.D., but also the difficulty of maintaining empathy for patients over the years. 'Emotional layers' in medicine are more subtle and pervasive than anyone wants to believe, and they often become the 'dominant players in medical decision-making,' she argues." (Publishers Weekly)

Includes bibliographical references

Reilly, Brendan

One doctor; close calls, cold cases, and the mysteries of medicine. Brendan Reilly. Atria Books 2013 352 p. $28 **610.69**
1. Physician-patient relationship 2. Physician's Role -- Personal Narratives 3. Physician-Patient Relations -- Personal Narratives
ISBN 1476726299; 9781476726298; 9781476726366

LC 2013006739

In this book, phyisican Brendan Reilly "relates his most challenging cases, beginning in the present--when he sees 19 ER patients on an average day--before backtracking to his early career at Dartmouth in 1985. That year, Reilly struggled to identify the cause of an eccentric and lovable patient's delirium. By the time he figured it out, the patient--Fred--had died." (Publishers Weekly)

Reilly's "book is about more than the joy of saving lives and the sadness of losing them—it's an intimate exploration of modern medicine and the human condition." Pub Wkly

Includes bibliographical references and index

610.695   Physicians

Epstein, Ronald

Attending; medicine, mindfulness, and humanity. Ronald Epstein. Scribner 2017 288 p. (hardcover; alk. paper) $26; (ebook) $19.99   **610.695**
1. Meditation 2. Alternative medicine 3. Physicians -- Psychology 4. Mindfulness 5. Physicians -- psychology 6. Physician-Patient Relations
ISBN 9781501121715; 9781501121722; 9781501121739

LC 2016024695

This book, by Ronald Epstein, is "about mindfulness and medical practice, a groundbreaking, intimate exploration of how doctors think and what matters most--safe, effective, patient-centered, compassionate care--from the foremost expert in the field. . . . Dr. Epstein introduces a revolutionary concept: by looking inward, health care practitioners can grow their capacity to provide high-quality care and the resilience to be there when their patients need them." (Publisher's note)

"While focusing primarily on health-care professionals, Epstein presents for general readers a concise guide to his view of what mindfulness is, its value, and how it is a skill that anyone can work to acquire." LJ

Includes bibliographical references and index

610.730   Organizations and management

Makary, Marty

Unaccountable; what hospitals won't tell you and how transparency can revolutionize health care. by Marty Makary. Bloomsbury Press 2012 246 p. ill. (hardback) $26 **610.730**
1. Medical records 2. Health care reform -- United States 3. Medical errors 4. Patient education 5. Medical personnel and patient 6. Medical care -- Quality control 7. Health facilities --

Public relations
ISBN 1608198367; 9781608198368

LC 2012007740

In this book, surgeon Marty Makary "suggests that providing patients with more access to their own medical information, as well as to the volume and safety records of facilities and doctors, would improve the overall quality of health care and save money. . . . He takes on what he believes is the health-care profession's inept self-regulation, poor communication caused by fear of speaking up, obfuscation of available statistics, and nonprofit hospital CEO compensation." (Library Journal)

Includes bibliographical references and index

610.9   Medicine--history

Mattern, Susan P.

Prince of medicine; Galen in the Roman world. Susan P. Mattern. Oxford University Press 2013 368 p. $29.95 **610.9**
1. Medicine -- History 2. Roman World 3. History, Ancient 4. History of Medicine 5. Physicians -- Biography
ISBN 019976767X; 9780199767670

LC 2012035656

Susan P. Mattern presents a "biography of Galen of Pergamum (circa 130-212 C.E.), a Greek who practiced medicine and philosophy in the Roman-dominated Mediterranean, first rising to fame at home in Asia Minor before becoming preeminent in Rome during the reign of Marcus Aurelius." (Library Journal)

Includes bibliographical references and index

610.92   Biography

Sweet, Victoria

God's hotel; a doctor, a hospital, and a pilgrimage to the heart of medicine. Victoria Sweet. Riverhead Books 2012 384 p. ill. (hardback) $27.95 **610.92**
1. Medicine 2. Hospitals 3. Physicians 4. MEDICAL -- Essays 5. Laguna Honda Hospital (San Francisco, Calif.) -- History 6. Hospital care -- California -- San Francisco -- Anecdotes
ISBN 1594488436; 9781594488436

LC 2011049340

This book offers a "portrait of a . . . physician on a quest to understand the heart, as well as the art, of medicine. Laguna Honda Hospital, the last remaining almshouse in the United States--a therapeutic community that houses and cares for the chronically ill or impoverished--offers . . . [author and physician Victoria] Sweet . . . a[n] . . . education in ministering to the body, heart, and soul." (Library Journal)

Includes bibliographical references

611   Human anatomy, cytology, histology

Balaban, Naomi E.

The handy anatomy answer book; [by] Naomi E. Balaban and James E. Bobick. Visible Ink Press 2008 362p il pa $21.95 **611**
1. Physiology 2. Human anatomy
ISBN 978-1-57859-190-9

"This book can provide an excellent way to read and self-test for health and human biology classes. Adults wanting to know more about the subjects covered will also find a wealth of useful and accessible information." Voice Youth Advocates

Gray's anatomy; the anatomical basis of clinical practice. editor-in-chief, Susan Standring. 41st edition Elsevier 2015 1562 p. ill. (some col.) hbk $228.99   **611**
1. Anatomy
ISBN 9780702052309; 0702052302

LC 2015027527

A comprehensive standard reference work with illustrations, descriptions and definitions.

Includes bibliographical references and index

Roach, Mary

Stiff; the curious lives of human cadavers. Norton 2003 303p il $23.95; pa $13.95   **611**
1. Dead 2. Dissection 3. Human experimentation in medicine
ISBN 0-393-05093-9; 0-393-32482-6 pa

LC 2002-152908

"For those who are interested in the fields of medicine or forensics and are aware of some of the procedures, this book makes excellent reading." SLJ

Includes bibliographical references

Rutherford, Adam, ca. 1975-

★ A **brief** history of everyone who ever lived; the human story retold through our genes. Adam Rutherford ; foreword by Siddhartha Mukherjee. The Experiment 2017 xiv, 401 p.p (hardcover) $25.95   **611**
1. Genetics 2. Human genome 3. DNA -- history 4. Genomics -- history 5. Biological Evolution 6. Human beings -- Origin 7. Genome, Human -- genetics
ISBN 1615194045; 9781615194049

LC 2017022566

National Book Critics Circle Award Finalist: Nonfiction (2017)

This book, by Adam Rutherford and Siddhartha Mukherjee, "will upend your thinking on Neanderthals, evolution, royalty, race, and even redheads. (For example, we now know that at least four human species once roamed the earth.) Plus, here is the remarkable, controversial story of how our genes made their way to the Americas--one that's still being written, as ever more of us have our DNA sequenced." (Publisher's note)

"An enthusiastic history of mankind in which DNA plays a far greater role than the traditional "bones and stones" approach, followed by a hopeful if cautionary account of what the recent revolution in genomics foretells."--Kirkus Reviews

Includes bibliographical references and index

612   Human physiology

Ashcroft, Frances

The **spark** of life; electricity in the human body. Frances Ashcroft ; illustrations by Ronan Mahon. Norton 2012 339 p. ill.   **612**
1. Biology 2. Physiology 3. Electrophysiology 4. Human physiology 5. Electrophysiology -- Popular works
ISBN 0393078035; 9780393078039

LC 2012021264

This book, by Frances Ashcroft, presents an "exploration of the surprising role that electricity plays in our bodies. What happens during a heart attack? Can someone really die of fright? What is death, anyway? How does electroshock treatment affect the brain? What is consciousness? The answers to these questions lie in the electrical signals constantly traveling through our bodies, driving our thoughts, our movements, and even the beating of our hearts." (Publisher's note)

Includes bibliographical references and index

Doherty, Paul

And then you're dead; what really happens if you get swallowed by a whale, are shot from a cannon, or go barreling over Niagara. Cody Cassidy and Paul Doherty, PhD. Penguin Books 2017 xiii, 235 p.p (paperback) $16   **612**
1. Death 2. Curiosities and wonders 3. Human anatomy 4. Human physiology 5. Accidents -- Humor
ISBN 9780143108443; 9781101991954; 0143108441

LC 2016040949

This book answers "what would happen if you took a swim outside a deep-sea submarine wearing only a swimsuit? How long could you last if you stood on the surface of the sun? How far could you actually get in digging a hole to China? [Authors] Paul Doherty . . . and . . . Cody Cassidy explore the real science behind these and other fantastical scenarios, offering insights into physics, astronomy, anatomy, and more along the way." (Publisher's note)

"With bite-size morsels of astonishing science and the perfect combination of smart-alecky writing and black humor, this page-turner will surely debunk any misapprehension that science is dull." Booklist

Includes bibliographical references.

Francis, Gavin

Adventures in human being; a grand tour from the cranium to the calcaneum. Gavin Francis. Basic Books, a member of the Perseus Books Group 2015 272 p. (hardback) $26.99   **612**
1. Human body 2. Physiology 3. Human anatomy 4. Human physiology
ISBN 0465079687; 9780465079681

LC 2015015371

"Drawing on his experiences as a surgeon, ER specialist, and family physician, Francis blends stories from the clinic with episodes from medical history, philosophy, and literature to describe the body in sickness and in health, in life and in death. When assessing a young woman with paralysis of the face, Francis reflects on the age-old difficulty artists have had in capturing human expression. A veteran of the war in Iraq suffers a shoulder injury that Homer first described three millennia ago in the Iliad. And when a gardener pricks her finger on a dirty rose thorn, her case of bacterial blood poisoning brings to mind the comatose sleeping beauties in the fairy tales we learn as children." Publisher's Note.

"His skill as a writer and an observer of human nature become obvious when he is able to make a chapter entitled "Large Bowel & Rectum" thoroughly engaging. Francis writes with humility and makes the point that being a good medical practitioner is not "about dramatically saving lives, but quietly, methodically, trying to postpone death." Pub Wkly.

Includes bibliographical references and index

The **Human** body; an illustrated guide to its structure, function, and disorders. editor-in-chief, Charles Clayman. Dorling Kindersley 1995 240p il $30   **612**
1. Physiology 2. Human anatomy
ISBN 1-56458-992-7

LC 94-37165

"This absolutely stunning book succeeds immeasurably as a guide to the human body." Sci Books Films

Hutchinson, Alex

★ **Endure;** mind, body, and the curiously elastic limits of human performance. Alex Hutchinson ; foreword by Malcolm Gladwell. William Morrow 2018 320 p. (hardback) $27.99   **612**

1. Sports 2. Mind and body 3. Physical fitness 4. Sports -- Physiological aspects
ISBN 9780062499868

LC 2017035195

In this book, author "Alex Hutchinson reveals that a wave of paradigm-altering research over the past decade suggests the seemingly physical barriers you encounter as set as much by your brain as by your body. This means the mind is the new frontier of endurance. . . . He carefully disentangles the delicate interplay of mind and body by telling the riveting stories of men and women who've pushed their own limits in extraordinary ways." (Publisher's note)

"The science shines (though, occasionally, it's a hefty lift), and it can be fun: the human body at rest produces about 100 watts of heat, but bicycling boosts that figure to 1,000 watts, and running a six-minute mile generates 1,500 watts. 'When it comes to pushing our limits, we're just getting started,' Hutchinson writes. Persuasive and motivating." Booklist

Lieberman, Daniel, 1964-

The **story** of the human body; evolution, health, and disease. Daniel Lieberman. Pantheon Books 2013 464 p. illustrations $27.95   **612**

1. Evolution 2. Human body 3. Adaptation (Biology)
ISBN 0307379418; 9780307379412

LC 2013011811

This book, by Daniel E. Lieberman, presents the "story of human evolution consisting of five biological transformations (walking upright, eating a variety of different foods, accumulating physical traits aligned to hunting and gathering, gaining bigger brains with larger bodies, and developing unique capacities for cooperation and language) and two cultural ones (farming and reliance on machines)." (Booklist)

"Lieberman's discussion of type 2 diabetes, heart disease, and breast cancer are as clear as any yet published, and he offers a well-articulated case for why an evolutionary perspective can greatly enrich the practice of medicine." Pub Wkly

Includes bibliographical references and index

612.022   Control processes

Damasio, Antonio

The **strange** order of things; life, feeling, and the making of the cultures. Antonio Damasio. Pantheon Books 2017 336 p. (hard cover; alk. paper) $27.95   **612.022**

1. Neurosciences 2. Homeostasis
ISBN 0307908755; 9780307908759

LC 2017019925

This book, by Antonio Damasio, "is a pathbreaking investigation into homeostasis, the condition of that regulates human physiology within the range that makes possible not only the survival but also the flourishing of life. . . . Damasio makes clear that we descend biologically, psychologically, and even socially from a long lineage that begins with single living cells." (Publisher's note)

"Damasio's sophisticated and complex theory on the role of feelings in the emergence of culture incorporates hard science, neuroscience, and even philosophy." Library Journal

Includes bibliographical references and index

612.044   Exercise and sports

Fitzgerald, Matt

How bad do you want it? mastering the psychology of mind over muscle. Matt Fitzgerald ; foreword by Samuele Marcora, PhD. VeloPress 2015 xiii, 282 p.p (pbk.; alk. paper) $18.95   **612.044**

1. Physical fitness 2. Sports -- Psychological aspects 3. Endurance sports 4. Endurance sports -- Physiological aspects 5. Endurance sports -- Psychological aspects
ISBN 1937715418; 9781937715410

LC 2015048381

This book, by Matt Fitzgerald, "examines more than a dozen pivotal races to discover the surprising ways elite athletes strengthen their mental toughness. . . . Their own words reinforce what the research has found: strong mental fitness lets us approach our true physical limits. . . . Each chapter explores the how and why of an elite athlete's transformative moment, revealing powerful new psychobiological principles you can practice to flex your own mental fitness." (Publisher's note)

Includes bibliographical references (pages 267-271) and index

612.1   Specific functions, systems, organs

Amidon, Stephen

The **sublime** engine; a biography of the human heart. [by] Stephen Amidon and Thomas Amidon. Rodale 2011 242p $24.99   **612.1**

1. Heart
ISBN 978-1-60529-584-8

LC 2010-30227

This book "presents a multifaceted picture of the heart's influences on mythology, science, and popular culture through the ages. In six lyrically written chapters, they trace humanity's perennial fascination with the heart through the eyes of history's greatest artists and medical explorers, beginning with the Greeks and fancifully ending with a peek into the future of cardiological innovation." Booklist

Includes bibliographical references

George, Rose

★ **Nine** pints; a journey through the money, medicine, and mysteries of blood. Rose George. Metropolitan Books/ Henry Holt & Co. 2018 368 p. illustrations (hardcover) $30 **612.1**

1. Blood 2. Medicine
ISBN 9781627796378

LC 2018013647

In this book, author Rose George presents "an eye-opening exploration of blood. . . . She takes us from ancient practices of bloodletting to the breakthrough of the 'liquid biopsy,' which promises to diagnose cancer and other diseases with a simple blood test. . . . She probes the lucrative business of plasma transfusions. . . . And she looks to the future, as researchers seek to bring synthetic blood to a hospital near you." (Publisher's note)

"The author packs her book with the kinds of provocative, witty, and rigorously reported facts and stories sure to make readers view the integral fluid coursing through our veins in a whole new way. An intensive, humanistic examination of blood in all its dazzling forms and functions." Kirkus

Includes bibliographical references and index

Jauhar, Sandeep

Heart; a history. Sandeep Jauhar. Farrar, Straus & Giroux

2018 288 p. (hardcover) $27   **612.1**

1. Heart 2. Cardiology 3. Heart diseases 4. Cardiologists
ISBN 9780374168650

LC 2017055262

In this book, author Sandeep Jauhar, "tells the story of the thing that makes us tick. For centuries, the human heart seemed beyond our understanding: an inscrutable shuddering mass that was somehow the driver of emotion and the seat of the soul. . . . Jauhar shows . . . [that] it was only recently that we demolished age-old taboos and devised the transformative procedures that have changed the way we live." (Publisher's note)

612.3   Digestive system

Collen, Alanna

10% human; how your body's microbes hold the key to health and happiness. Alanna Collen. Harper 2015 336 p. color illustrations (hardback) $26.99   **612.3**

1. Health 2. Biology 3. Viruses 4. Microbial metabolism 5. Intestines -- Microbiology 6. Microorganisms -- Therapeutic use
ISBN 0062345982; 9780062345981; 9780062345998

LC 2015004721

In this book, author "Alanna Collen draws on the latest scientific research to show how our personal colony of microbes influences our weight, our immune system, our mental health, and even our choice of partner. She argues that so many of our modern diseases--obesity, autism, [and] mental illness . . . have their root in our failure to cherish our most fundamental and enduring relationship: that with our personal colony of microbes." (Publisher's note)

"Collen never claims that she has uncovered the answers to modern health woes, but she points out the markers that may one day lead to such answers. Everything you wanted to know about microbes but were afraid to ask." Kirkus

Price, Catherine

Vitamania; our obsessive quest for nutritional perfection. Catherine Price. The Penguin Press 2015 336 p. (hardback) $27.95   **612.3**

1. Vitamins 2. Nutrition 3. Dietary supplements 4. Food -- United States 5. Vitamins -- History 6. Food -- United States -- Psychological aspects 7. Nutrition -- United States -- Psychological aspects 8. Dietary supplements -- Social aspects -- United States 9. Vitamins in human nutrition -- Social aspects -- United States
ISBN 1594205043; 9781594205040

LC 2014036657

In this book, author Catherine Price "offers a lucid and lively journey through our cherished yet misguided beliefs about vitamins, and reveals a straightforward, blessedly anxiety-free path to enjoyable eating and good health. . . . Her travels to vitamin manufacturers and food laboratories and military testing kitchens--along with her deep dive into the history of nutritional science--provide a witty and dynamic narrative." (Publisher's note)

"Price's sharp wit, skillful and vivid translation of science into story, and valiant inquisitiveness (she insists on tasting synthetic vitamins and gets buzzed on the military's caffeinated meat sticks) make for an electrifying dissection of our vitamin habit in contrast to our irrevocable need for naturally nutrient-rich food." Booklist

Includes bibliographical references and index

Roach, Mary, 1959-

★ **Gulp**; adventures on the alimentary canal. Mary Roach.

W W Norton 2013 336 p.   **612.3**

1. Alimentary canal -- Popular works 2. Digestive organs -- Popular works 3. Gastrointestinal system -- Popular works
ISBN 9780393081572

LC 2012050391

In this book, science writer Mary Roach explores "the alimentary canal. Roach asks the questions that some readers may have always wondered: Does saliva have curative properties? Do pets taste food differently than their owners do? Could Jonah have survived three days in a whale's stomach? . . . As she investigates these questions, Roach encounters many an eccentric scientist who has worked tirelessly to unlock the mysteries of saliva, gastrointestinal gases, and mastication." (Library Journal)

"Roach's approach is grounded in science, but the virtuosic author rarely resists a pun, and it's clear she revels in giving readers a thrill... Adventurous kids and doctors alike will appreciate this fascinating and sometimes ghastly tour of the gastrointestinal system." Pub Wkly

Includes bibliographical references

612.4   Hematopoietic, lymphatic, glandular, urinary systems

Epstein, Randi Hutter

Aroused; the history of hormones and how they control just about everything. Randi Hutter Epstein. W W Norton & Co Inc 2018 336 p. (hardcover) $26.95   **612.4**

1. Hormones 2. Endocrinology 3. Hormones -- history 4. Hormones -- physiology
ISBN 9780393239607

LC 2017061090

This book, by Randi Hutter Epstein, presents "a guided tour through the strange science of hormones and the age-old quest to control them. Metabolism, behavior, sleep, mood swings, the immune system, fighting, fleeing, puberty, and sex: these are just a few of the things our bodies control with hormones. . . . 'Aroused' introduces the leading scientists who made life-changing discoveries about the hormone imbalances that ail us." (Publisher's note)

Includes bibliographical references and index

History of hormones and how they control just about everything

612.6   Reproduction, development, maturation

Dolnick, Edward

The **seeds** of life; from Aristotle to Da Vinci, from shark's teeth to frog's pants, the long and strange quest to discover where babies come from. Edward Dolnick. Basic Books 2017 320 p. illustrations (hardcover) $28   **612.6**

1. Reproduction 2. Life sciences 3. Science -- Popular works 4. Human reproduction -- History 5. Human reproduction -- Mythology 6. Human reproduction -- Social aspects ISBN 0465082955; 9780465082957

LC 2016054195

Kirkus Prize Finalist: Nonfiction (2017)

This book, by Edward Dolnick, deals with "how a series of blundering geniuses and brilliant amateurs struggled for two centuries to discover where, exactly, babies come from. Taking a page from investigative thrillers, . . . [the author] looks to these early scientists as if they were detectives hot on the trail of a bedeviling and urgent mystery." (Publisher's note)

"The best sort of science history, explaining not only how great men made great discoveries, but why equally great men, trapped by prejudices and what seemed to be plain common sense, missed what was in front of their noses." Kirkus

Includes bibliographical references and index

Eliot, Lise

Pink brain, blue brain; how small differences grow into trouplesome gaps--and what we can do about it. Houghton Mifflin Harcourt 2009 420p il $25   **612.6**

1. Child development 2. Sex differences (Psychology)
ISBN 978-0-618-39311-4

LC 2009-14746

"This is an important book and highly recommended for parents, teachers, and anyone who works with children." Libr J

Includes bibliographical references

Jensen, Frances E.

The **teenage** brain; a neuroscientist's survival guide to raising adolescents and young adults. Frances E. Jensen ; with Amy Ellis Nutt. Harper 2014 384 p. illustrations (hardback) $27.99   **612.6**

1. Parenting 2. Neurosciences 3. Adolescent psychology 4. Brain -- Growth 5. Parent and teenager 6. Developmental neurobiology 7. Developmental psychobiology
ISBN 0062067842; 9780062067845; 9780062067852; 9780062067869

LC 2014009600

In this book, by Frances E. Jensen, with Amy Ellis Nutt, "drawing on her research knowledge and clinical experience, [a] neurologist and mother of two boys" . . . offers a revolutionary look at the science of the adolescent brain, providing . . . insights that translate into practical advice for both parents and teenagers." (Publisher's note)

"Recommended for readers who enjoyed Laurence Steinberg's Age of Opportunity, this title applies new science to the frustrating dilemma of how to live with teenage kids." LJ

Katz, Rebecca

The **longevity** kitchen; satisfying, big-flavor recipes featuring the top 16 age-busting power foods [120 recipes for vitality and optimal health] Rebecca Katz with Mat Edelson ; photography by Leo Gong. Ten Speed Press 2013 256 p. color illustrations (hardback) $29.99   **612.6**

1. Health 2. Cookbooks 3. Longevity 4. Natural foods 5. Physical fitness 6. Natural foods -- Recipes 7. Longevity -- Nutritional aspects 8. Older people -- Health and hygiene
ISBN 1607742942; 9781607742944

LC 2012035097

This cookbook presents a "collection of 125 delicious whole-foods recipes showcasing 16 antioxidant-rich power foods, developed by wellness authority Rebecca Katz to combat and prevent chronic diseases such as diabetes, heart disease, high blood pressure, inflammation, arthritis, and other conditions that plague American adults, enabling readers to live longer, healthier lives." (Publisher's note)

"The authors' introductions to each recipe can be tiresomely silly, so readers should skip straight to the ingredient list and start cooking up something healthy and delicious." Pub Wkly

Includes bibliographical references and index

Kim, Susan

Flow; the cultural story of menstruation. [by] Elissa Stein and Susan Kim. St. Martin's Griffin 2009 270p $27.99 **612.6**

1. Menstruation

ISBN 978-0-312-37996-4

LC 2009-17046

"There is probably no better book for moms who want their daughters to respect themselves in every aspect, and for female preteens and teens who would never say a word about their moms reading a book about menses but surely would like several sneak peeks into its pages." Booklist

Includes bibliographical references

Martin, Robert

How we do it; the evolution and future of human reproduction. Robert Martin. Basic Books 2013 xii, 304 p.p (hardcover) $27.99   **612.6**

1. Evolution 2. Reproduction 3. Human fertility 4. Human evolution 5. Human reproduction 6. Evolution (Biology)
ISBN 0465030157; 0465037844; 9780465030156; 9780465037841

LC 2012278031

In this book, "primatologist Robert Martin draws on forty years of research to locate the roots of everything from our sex cells to the way we care for newborns. He examines the procreative history of humans as well as that of our primate kin to reveal what's really natural when it comes to making and raising babies, and distinguish which behaviors we ought to continue--and which we should not." (Publisher's note)

"The author explains potentially complicated topics in a marvelously clear manner; although the focus is clearly evolutionary, he does not shy from considering practical implications." Choice

Includes bibliographical references and index

Nilsson, Lennart

A **child** is born; [photography], Lennart Nilsson; text, Lars Hamberger; translated from the Swedish by Linda Schenck. 4th ed, completely rev and updated; Delacorte Press 2003 239p il $35; pa $21   **612.6**

1. Pregnancy 2. Childbirth 3. Embryology
ISBN 0-385-33754-X; 0-385-33755-8 pa

LC 2003-43854

Original Swedish edition, 1965; first United States edition, 1966

An illustrated look at male and female reproductive anatomy and physiology, the processes of ovulation and fertilization, fetal development, and labor and delivery.

Roach, Mary, 1959-

Bonk; the curious coupling of science and sex. Norton 2008 319 p. il   **612.6**

1. Sex (Biology)
ISBN 0393064646; 9780393064643

LC 2007-51990

This is an overview of the research on sexual physiology.

"Tucked between the jokes and anecdotes, you will find lessons on impotence, orgasm, unusual and unusually brave scientists, and the sexual behaviour of other species, including a hilarious description of porcupine sex." New Sci

Includes bibliographical references (p. 307-319)

Weil, Andrew

Healthy aging; a lifelong guide to your physical and spiritual well-being. Alfred A. Knopf 2005 293p $27.95 **612.6**

1. Aging
ISBN 0-375-40755-3

LC 2005-45183

The author "explores common Western beliefs and attitudes about aging and urges readers to develop healthier perspectives. The 60-year-old author assesses the growing and lucrative field of anti-aging medicine, takes the position that aging is not reversible, and offers many ways for readers to prevent conditions and illnesses that limit mortality and ensure well-being into the later years. . . . The real value is Weil's courageous stand, one likely to meet resistance in a culture devoted to external indicators of eternal youth." Publ Wkly

Includes bibliographical references

Williams, Florence

Breasts; a natural and unnatural history. Florence Williams. W.W. Norton & Co. 2012 338 p. ill. (hardcover) $25.95 **612.6**
1. Breast 2. Breast cancer 3. Human ecology 4. Cancer -- Environmental aspects 5. Breast -- History 6. Breast -- Psychological aspects
ISBN 0393063186; 9780393063189

LC 2011053153
This book is a "comprehensive 'environmental history' of the only human body part without its own medical specialty, [in which] . . . [Florence] Williams . . . the reader along a journey extending from the evolution of human breasts from sweat glands, through cosmetic breast enhancements, the science and politics of breastfeeding, and possible links between pollutants and breast cancer in both women and men." (Publishers Weekly)

Includes bibliographical references

612.67   Aging

DeClaire, Joan

Enlightened aging; building resilience for a long, active life. Eric B. Larson, MD, and Joan DeClaire. Rowman & Littlefield 2017 xvi, 218 p.p (cloth; alk. paper) $34   **612.67**
1. Aging 2. Advice literature 3. Older people -- Health and hygiene 4. Aging -- Physiological aspects
ISBN 9781442274372; 9781442274365

LC 2017001674
This book, by Eric B. Larson and Joan DeClaire, "offers practical advice for growing old with resilience and foresight. More than just canned advice, Enlightened Aging proposes a path to resilience--one that's proven to help many stave off disability until very old age. The steps on this path include pro-activity, acceptance, and building and maintaining good physical, mental, and social health." (Publisher's note)

"This can-do guide gives commonsense, doable advice on how to proactively create a path to a meaningful life." Booklist

Includes bibliographical references and index

Sagan, Dorion

Cracking the aging code; Josh Mitteldorf and Dorion Sagan. Flatiron Books 2016 336 p. (hardback) $27.99 **612.67**
1. Aging 2. Aging -- Physiological aspects
ISBN 9781250061706

LC 2016001602
In this book, "theoretical biologist Josh Mitteldorf and award-winning writer and ecological philosopher Dorion Sagan reveal that evolution and aging are even more complex and breathtaking than we originally thought. Using meticulous multidisciplinary science, as well as reviewing the history of our understanding about evolution, this book makes the case that aging is not something that 'just happens,' nor is it the result of wear and tear or a genetic inevitability." (Publisher's note)

"A thoughtful examination of the role of aging and death in supporting life." Kirkus

Includes bibliographical references (pages 309-318) and index.

612.68   Longevity factors

Day, Jane

The **longevity** plan; seven life-transforming lessons from ancient China. John D. Day and Jane Ann Day with Matthew LaPlante. HarperCollins 2017 288 p. color illustrations (hardcover) $25.99   **612.68**
1. Aging 2. Longevity 3. China -- Social conditions 4. Age 5. Centenarians 6. China -- Social life and customs
ISBN 0062319817; 9780062319838; 9780062319814
This book, by Dr. John D. Day and Jane Ann Day with Matthew LaPlante, presents [John's] "story of his time living in Longevity Village in China, and the seven lessons he learned there that lead to a happy, healthy, long life. . . . Dr. Day shares his . . . proven program to help you feel sharper, more motivated, productive, and pain-free. 'The Longevity Plan' is not only a fascinating travelogue but also a practical, accessible, and groundbreaking guide to a better life." (Publisher's note)

"Practical, applicable health guidance validated by a remarkable collective of revered Chinese elders." Kirkus

Includes bibliographical references (pages 267-278) and index.

612.8   Nervous system

Aftel, Mandy

Fragrant; the secret life of scent. Mandy Aftel. Riverhead Books 2014 288 p. illustrations (hardback) $27.95   **612.8**
1. Perfumes 2. Cosmetics 3. Odors 4. Smell 5. Jasmine 6. Cinnamon 7. Ambergris 8. Frankincense 9. Mints (Plants)
ISBN 1594631417; 9781594631412

LC 2014018554
In this book by Mandy Aftel "through five major players in the epic of aroma, she explores the profound connection between our sense of smell and the appetites that move us. Cinnamon, queen of the Spice Route, touches our hunger for the unknown. Mint, homegrown the world over, speaks to our affinity for the familia. Frankincense, an ancient incense ingredient, taps into our longing for transcendence. And exquisite jasmine exemplifies our yearning for beauty." (Publisher's note)

"Targeted toward those new to the perfume world, this book is strongly recommended for casual readers interested in the basics of scent and perfumery." LJ

Alter, David

Staying sharp; 9 keys for a youthful brain through modern science and ancient wisdom. Henry Emmons, MD And David Alter, PhD. Touchstone, a imprint of Simon & Schuster, Inc. 2015 288 p. (hardcover) $25   **612.8**
1. Brain 2. Intellect 3. Brain -- Care and hygiene
ISBN 1476758948; 9781476758947; 9781501116810

LC 2015000723
Authors Henry Emmons and David Alter "demonstrate how to blend the best of modern science and Eastern holistic medicine together to form a powerful drug-free program to maintain a youthful mind and a happy life. [They] have taken their expertise and translated the fundamentals of brain science into an easily accessible collection of the nine key lessons proven to preserve and strengthen mental acuity." (Publisher's note)

"The authors, who have worked together for over 25 years, dub their approach an intersection of Eastern tradition and Western science. Some readers may be skeptical, but for those open to new ways of thinking and acting, this book will provide a valuable start." Pub Wkly

Biever, John A.

The **wandering** mind; understanding disassociation, from daydreams to disorders. John A. Biever and Maryann Karinch. Rowman & Littlefield Publishers 2012 xv, 167 p.p (hardcover) $35; (ebook) $34.99 **612.8**

1. Mental illness 2. Dissociation (Psychology) 3. Consciousness 4. Mental health

ISBN 1442216158; 1442216174; 9781442216150; 9781442216174 pdf

LC 2012013303

In this book by John A. Biever and Maryann Karinch, Biever "describes daydreaming, fantasy-prone personalities, and charismatic leaders. He differentiates dissociate identity disorder (DID) from dissociative fugue, dissociative amnesia, depersonalization disorders, and false memories, using examples from the literature as well as his own case studies." (Choice)

Includes bibliographical references (p. 155-156) and index.

Buonomano, Dean

Brain bugs; how the brain's flaws shape our lives. W. W. Norton & Co. 2011 310p $25.95 **612.8**

1. Brain 2. Memory

ISBN 978-0-393-07602-8

LC 2011014934

The author explains "that as the human brain has evolved over the past 100,000 years, it has added layer upon layer of networked neural connections to cope with a rapidly changing world. But, he writes, the brain's most detrimental malfunctions are often traceable to its most ancient structures—those that compose the limbic system.... Drawing on real-world examples and current research in neuroscience, Buonomano guides the reader through the unexpected ways in which our lives are influenced by the messiness of our busiest, most intricate, and often most error-prone organ." The Scientist

Includes bibliographical references

Burnett, Dean

Idiot brain; What Your Head Is Really Up To. Dean Burnett. W W Norton & Co Inc 2016 336 p. (hardcover) $26.95 **612.8**

1. Brain 2. Memory 3. Consciousness 4. Neurosciences 5. Brain -- Popular works 6. Memory -- Popular works 7. Consciousness -- Popular works 8. Neurosciences -- Popular works

ISBN 9780393253788

LC 2016009451

In this book, "neuroscientist Dean Burnett celebrates blind spots, blackouts, insomnia, and all the other downright laughable things our minds do to us, while also exposing the many mistakes we've made in our quest to understand how our brains actually work." (Publisher's note)

"Burnett manages to both entertain and inform in engaging ways that would benefit the performance of the most humorless pedant." Kirkus

Includes bibliographical references and index

Carter, Rita

The **human** brain book; Rita Carter, Susan Aldridge, Martyn Page, Steve Parker ; consultants Chris Frith, Utal Frith Melanie Shulman. DK Publishing 2014 264 p color illustrations hc $40 **612.8**

1. Brain 2. Human anatomy 3. Brain -- Physiology

ISBN 9781465416025 ; 1465416021

LC 2013444872

Written by Rita Carter, this second edition uses "the latest findings from neuroscience with new brain imaging techniques, as well as developments on infant brains, telepathy, and brain modification, this new edition of DK's 'The Human Brain Book' covers brain anatomy, function, and disorders. . . . With its . . . 22-page atlas, illustrated with MRI scans, and an interactive DVD, 'The Human Brain Book' is a . . . resource for . . . human biology, anatomy, and neuroscience." (Publisher's note)

"Using computer-generated three-dimensional images, graphics, and clear explanatory text presented in brief sections, the follow-up to The Human Body Book (2007) examines each aspect of the brain's structure and functions...This is a valuable resource for any high-school, college, and public library collection. Libraries should be aware that it comes with a DVD." Booklist

DeSalle, Rob

The **brain**; big bangs, behaviors, and beliefs. Rob DeSalle and Ian Tattersall ; illustrated by Patricia J. Wynne. Yale University Press 2012 xiv, 354 p.p ill. (clothbound; alk. paper) $29.95 **612.8**

1. Brain 2. Evolution 3. Nervous system 4. Cognition 5. Neurophysiology 6. Brain -- Evolution

ISBN 0300175221; 9780300175226

LC 2011044329

This book by Rob DeSalle and Ian Tattersall presents a "step-by-step account of the evolution of the brain and nervous system." The authors "explain how the cognitive gulf that separates us from all other living creatures could have occurred. They discuss the development and uniqueness of human consciousness, how human and nonhuman brains work, the roles of different nerve cells, the importance of memory and language in brain functions, and much more." (Publisher's note)

Includes bibliographical references (p. 327-336) and index

Doidge, Norman

The **brain's** way of healing; remarkable discoveries and recoveries from the frontiers of neuroplasticity. Norman Doidge, M.D. Viking 2015 432 p. (hardback) $29.95 **612.8**

1. Neuroplasticity 2. Brain -- Physiology 3. Brain 4. Healing

ISBN 067002550X; 9780670025503

LC 2014038471

This book by Norman Doidge shows "how the amazing process of neuroplastic healing really works. It describes natural, non-invasive avenues into the brain provided by the forms of energy around us--light, sound, vibration, movement--which pass through our senses and our bodies to awaken the brain's own healing capacities without producing unpleasant side effects. Doidge explores cases where patients alleviated years of chronic pain or recovered from debilitating strokes or accidents." (Publisher's note)

"A fascinating study on brain science that shows the way to major therapeutic discoveries." LJ

Includes bibliographical references and index

Gazzaniga, Michael S.

The **consciousness** instinct; unraveling the mystery of how the brain makes the mind. Michael S. Gazzaniga. Farrar, Straus & Giroux 2018 288 p. (cloth) $28 **612.8**

1. Consciousness 2. Mind and body 3. Neurosciences 4. Brain 5. Cognitive neuroscience

ISBN 9780374715502

LC 2017038333

In this book, author and "neuroscience pioneer Michael S. Gazzaniga puts the latest research in conversation with the history of human thinking about the mind, giving a big-picture view of what science has revealed about consciousness. . . . New research suggests the brain is actually a confederation of independent modules working together. Understanding how consciousness could emanate from such an organization will help . . . close the gap between brain and mind." (Publisher's note)

"Gazzaniga's accessible, well-organized arguments are bound to provoke deep metathoughts, and readers should find his treatise delightful." Pub Wkly

Includes bibliographical references and index

Human; the science behind what makes us unique. Ecco 2008 447p $27.50   **612.8**
1. Brain 2. Human beings 3. Consciousness
ISBN 978-0-06-089288-3; 0-06-089288-9

LC 2008-297703

"A savvy, witty guide to neuroscience today." Kirkus
Includes bibliographical references

Tales from Both Sides of the Brain; a life in neuroscience. Michael S. Gazzaniga. HarperCollins 2015 432 p. illustrations, portraits $28.99   **612.8**
1. Brain 2. Neurosciences
ISBN 0062228803; 9780062228802

This book, by Michael S. Gazzaniga, "tells the impassioned story of his life in science and his decades-long journey to understand how the separate spheres of our brains communicate and miscommunicate with their separate agendas. . . . He paints a vivid portrait not only of his discovery of split-brain theory, but also of his comrades in arms--the many patients, friends, and family who have accompanied him on this wild ride of intellectual discovery." (Publisher's note)

"For those familiar with the groundbreaking studies that make up the field's backbone, however, the book is a rare opportunity to relive the history of cognitive neuroscience through Gazzaniga's knowledgeable and relatable perspective. Summing Up: Recommended. Upper-division undergraduates and above." Choice

Godfrey-Smith, Peter

Other Minds; the octopus, the sea, and the deep origins of consciousness. by Peter Godfrey-Smith. Farrar, Straus & Giroux 2016 272 p. illustrations (some color) (cloth) $27 **612.8**
1. Cephalopods 2. Nervous system 3. Cephalopoda -- Behavior
ISBN 9780374537197; 9780374227760; 0374227764

LC 2016016696

This book, by Peter Godfrey-Smith, discusses the evolution of the cephalopod mind. "Drawing on the latest scientific research and his own scuba-diving adventures, Godfrey-Smith probes the many mysteries that surround the lineage. How did the octopus, . . . become so smart? What is it like to have eight tentacles that are so packed with neurons that they virtually 'think for themselves'? What happens when some octopuses abandon their hermit-like ways and congregate." (Publisher's note)

"He makes the case that cephalopods demonstrate a type of intelligence that is largely "alien" to our understanding of the concept but is no less worthy of wonder. He also ponders how and why such intelligence developed in such short-lived creatures (they generally live only a few years). Godfrey-Smith doesn't provide definitive answers to his questions, but the journey he leads is both thoroughly enjoyable and informative." Pub Wkly

Includes bibliographical references and index.

Holmes, Bob

Flavor; the science of our most neglected sense. Bob Holmes. W W Norton & Co Inc 2017 310 p. (hardcover) $26.95   **612.8**
1. Taste 2. Flavor 3. Taste buds 4. Senses and sensation
ISBN 9780393244427; 9780393244434

LC 2016046897

This book, by Bob Holmes, is "a journey into the surprising science behind our flavor senses. . . . Considering every angle of flavor from our neurobiology to the science and practice of modern food production, Holmes takes readers on a journey to uncover the broad range of factors that can affect our appreciation of a fine meal or an exceptional glass of wine." (Publisher's note)

"As Holmes runs through terrific experiments and describes strange technologies, he makes food science fun and approachable." Pub Wkly
Includes bibliographical references and index

Kaku, Michio

The **future** of the mind; the scientific quest to understand, enhance, and empower the mind. Dr. Michio Kaku, professor of Theoretical Physics, City University of New York. Doubleday 2014 400 p. illustrations $28.95   **612.8**
1. Mind and body 2. Neurosciences 3. Neuropsychology 4. Brain-computer interfaces 5. Cognitive neuroscience 6. Brain -- Mathematical models
ISBN 038553082X; 9780385530828

LC 2013017338

In this book, "theoretical physicist [Michio] Kaku . . . explores fantastical realms of science fiction that may soon become our reality. His futurist framework merges physics with neuroscience to model how our brains construct the future, and is loosely applied to demonstrations that 'show proof-of-principle' in accomplishing what was previously fictional: that minds can be read, memories can be digitally stored, and intelligences can be improved to great extents." (Publishers Weekly)

Kaku "delivers ingenious predictions extrapolated from good research already in progress." Kirkus
Includes bibliographical references

Kounios, John, 1956-

The **Eureka** factor; aha moments, creative insight, and the brain. John Kounios and Mark Jung-Beeman. Random House Inc 2015 288 p. illustrations $28   **612.8**
1. Intuition 2. Cognitive styles 3. Thought and thinking 4. Insight 5. Cognition -- Physiological aspects 6. Higher nervous activity -- Measurement 7. Thought and thinking -- Physiological aspects
ISBN 1400068541; 9781400068548

LC 2014022220

First edition.

In this book, neuroscientists John Kounios and Mark Jung-Beeman "explain how insights arise and what the scientific research says about stimulating more of them. They discuss how various conditions affect the likelihood of your having an insight, when insight is helpful and when deliberate methodical thought is better suited to a task, what the relationship is between insight and intuition, and how the brain's right hemisphere contributes to creative thought." (Publisher's note)

"An excellent title for those interested in neuroscience or creativity, or those who enjoy reading about brain research." LJ

Kurzweil, Ray, 1948-

How to create a mind; the secret of human thought revealed. Ray Kurzweil. Viking 2012 336 p. $27.95   **612.8**
1. Brain 2. Consciousness 3. Artificial intelligence 4. Self-consciousness (Awareness) 5. Brain -- Localization of functions
ISBN 0670025291; 9780670025299

LC 2012027185

In this book, "[Ray] Kurzweil . . . provides insight into how the human brain functions, while speculating on the possibilities and philosophical implications of creating a nonbiological mind. Underlying this analysis is the Pattern Recognition Theory of Mind, a process in the neocortex, the seat of higher brain functions such as perception, memory, and language and, by extension, consciousness." (Publishers Weekly)

Includes bibliographical references and index.

Linden, David J.

Touch; the science of hand, heart, and mind. David J. Linden. Viking 2015 261 p. illustrations (hardback) $28.95 **612.8**
1. Touch 2. Emotions -- Physiological aspects 3. Touch -- Physiological aspects 4. Touch -- Psychological aspects
ISBN 0670014877; 9780670014873

LC 2014038475

This book by David J. Linden "combines anecdotes, stories, history, and neuroscience research" to explore touch in humans. "Chapters address how we sense what we actively touch, how we sense things that come in contact with our skin (other people as well as substances), how touch interacts with emotions in intimate forms of touching, and how our touch sensors can cause problems or be fooled." (Library Journal)

"An exciting book for those interested in learning more about the sense of touch and how the brain performs." LJ

Includes bibliographical references and index"||"Includes bibliographical references and index

McAuliffe, Kathleen

This is your brain on parasites; How Tiny Creatures Manipulate Our Behavior and Shape Society. Kathleen McAuliffe. Houghton Mifflin Harcourt 2016 288 p. (hardback) $27 **612.8**
1. Parasites 2. Microbiology 3. Nervous system -- Diseases 4. Parasitology
ISBN 9780544192225

LC 2016002949

This book, by Kathleen McAuliffe, is an "investigation of the myriad ways that parasites control how other creatures—including humans—think, feel, and act. These tiny organisms can only live inside another animal, and as McAuliffe reveals, they have many evolutionary motives for manipulating their host's behavior. Far more often than appreciated, these puppeteers orchestrate the interplay between predator and prey." (Publisher's note)

"McAuliffe presents her collected research—often from small, nearly anecdotal studies—less as fact than in a spirit of exploration." Pub Wkly

Includes bibliographical references and index.

Mlodinow, Leonard

Elastic; flexible thinking in a time of change. Leonard Mlodinow. Pantheon Books 2018 272 p. (hardback) $28.95 **612.807**
1. Neurosciences 2. Decision making 3. Cognitive psychology 4. Neurosciences -- Research 5. Neurology -- Technological innovations
ISBN 9781101870921

LC 2017015377

In this book, author "Leonard Mlodinow takes us on an illuminating journey through the mechanics of our minds as we navigate the rapidly changing landscapes around us. Out of the exploratory instincts that allowed our ancestors to prosper . . . , humans developed a cognitive style that Mlodinow terms elastic thinking, a unique set of talents that include neophilia . . . , schizotypy . . . imagination and idea generation, and divergent and integrative thinking." (Publisher's note)

"With elements of self-help and business writing and including entertaining anecdotes and turns of phrase, this fantastically accessible science writing about the brain can be enjoyed by anyone. Of particular interest to those wishing to understand how to cope with the pace of change in the modern world." LJ

Palca, Joe

Annoying; the science of what bugs us. [by] Joe Palca and Flora Lichtman. Wiley 2011 272p $25.95 **612.8**
1. Physiology 2. Neuropsychology
ISBN 978-0-470-63869-9

LC 2010-54046

Palca and Lichtman "skitter all over the map in pursuit of their subject, and at first their progress seems peculiarly random, like one of those robotic vacuums. But in the end they do indeed cover every part of the terrain: from physics and psychology to aesthetics, genetics and even treatment for the miserably, terminally annoyed." N Y Times (Late N Y Ed)

Includes bibliographical references

Randall, David K.

Dreamland; adventures in the strange science of sleep. David K. Randall. W.W. Norton 2012 304 p. $25.95; (hardcover) $25.95 **612.8**
1. Sleep 2. Dreams 3. Sleepwalking
ISBN 039308020X; 9780393080209

LC 2012014932

This book offers an "examination of the science behind the little-known world of sleep. . . . [David K.] Randall explores the research that is investigating those dark hours that make up nearly a third of our lives. Taking readers from military battlefields to children's bedrooms, [the book] shows that sleep isn't as simple as it seems. Why did the results of one sleep study change the bookmakers' odds for certain Monday Night Football games? Do women sleep differently than men? And if you happen to kill someone while you are sleepwalking, does that count as murder?" (Publisher's note)

Includes bibliographical references

Sacks, Oliver, 1933-2015

★ The **river** of consciousness; Oliver Sacks. Alfred A. Knopf 2017 x, 237 p.p (hardcover; alk. paper) $27 **612.8**
1. Consciousness 2. Neuropsychology 3. Creative ability
ISBN 9780385352574; 9780385352567

LC 2017000815

This book, by Oliver Sacks, presents "a collection of essays that displays . . . Sacks's passionate engagement with the most compelling and seminal ideas of human endeavor: evolution, creativity, memory, time, consciousness, and experience. . . . [It] reveals his ability to make unexpected connections, his sheer joy in knowledge, and his unceasing, timeless project to understand what makes us human." (Publisher's note)

"The essays are all enlightening, entertaining, and a pleasure to read and are of value to scholars and lay readers alike." Choice

Includes bibliographical references (pages 219-228) and index.

Sapolsky, Robert M.

★ **Behave**; the biology of humans at our best and worst. Robert M. Sapolsky. Penguin Press 2017 790 p. illustrations (hardback) $35 **612.8**
1. Biology 2. Human behavior 3. Neurobiology 4. Animal behavior 5. Neurophysiology
ISBN 9780735222786; 9781594205071; 1594205078

LC 2016056755

LA Times Book Prize: Science & Technology (2017)

This book, by Robert M. Sapolsky, "starts by looking at the factors that bear on a person's reaction in the precise moment a behavior occurs, and then hops back in time from there, in stages, ultimately ending up at the deep history of our species and its evolutionary legacy. Sapolsky builds on this understanding to wrestle with some of our deepest and thorniest questions relating to tribalism and xenophobia, hierarchy and competition, morality and free will, and war and peace." (Publisher's note)

"An exemplary work of popular science, challenging but accessible." Kirkus

Includes bibliographical references (pages 721-773) and index.

Satel, Sally

Brainwashed; The Seductive Appeal of Mindless Neuroscience. Sally Satel and Scott O. Lilienfeld. Perseus Books Group 2013 256 p. $26.99   **612.8**
1. Mind and body 2. Neurosciences
ISBN 0465018777; 9780465018772
LA Times Book Prize Finalist: Science & Technology (2013)

In this book, "a psychiatrist and a clinical psychologist . . . argue against the use of brain scans as the basis for marketing efforts, addiction treatment, lie detection, and decisions in criminal trials. . . . The authors explain how particular mental states cannot be pinned directly onto active brain regions. They assert that a comprehensive understanding of behavior requires consideration of not only brain activity but also psychological, social, and cultural influences." (Library Journal)

Suskind, Dana

Thirty Million Words; How to Build Your Child's Brain. Dana Suskind. Penguin Group USA 2015 320 p. $28   **612.8**
1. Child rearing 2. Child development 3. Parent-child relationship
ISBN 0525954872; 9780525954873
LC 2015016306

In this book, author "Dana Suskind, explains why the most important--and astoundingly simple--thing you can do for your child's future success in life is to talk to him or her, reveals the recent science behind this truth, and outlines precisely how parents can best put it into practice." (Publisher's note)

"Parents, other caregivers, and early childhood educators will be moved and inspired by this work." LJ

Walker, Matthew

★ **Why** we sleep; unlocking the power of sleep and dreams. Matthew Walker, PhD. First edition Scribner 2017 viii, 352 p.p illustrations hardcover $27   **612.8**
1. Dreams 2. Sleep disorders 3. Sleep -- Popular works 4. Sleep 5. Sleep -- Physiological aspects
ISBN 9781501144318; 1501144316
LC 2017033123

This book, by Matthew Walker PhD, "gives us a new understanding of the vital importance of sleep and dreaming. Within the brain, sleep enriches our ability to learn, memorize, and make logical decisions. It recalibrates our emotions, restocks our immune system, fine-tunes our metabolism, and regulates our appetite. Dreaming mollifies painful memories and creates a virtual reality space in which the brain melds past and present knowledge to inspire creativity." (Publisher's note)

Includes bibliographical references.

Williams, Caroline

My plastic brain; one woman's yearlong journey to discover if science can improve her mind. Caroline Williams. Prometheus Books 2018 320 p. (hardback) $24   **612.8**
1. Neurosciences 2. Neuroplasticity 3. Brain -- Physiology 4. Brain -- Regeneration
ISBN 9781633883918
LC 2017047080

In this book, "Caroline Williams spends a year exploring 'neuroplasticity'--the brain's ability to reorganize itself by forming new neural connections--to find out whether she can make meaningful, lasting changes to the way her brain works. A science journalist . . . , she volunteers herself as a test subject, challenging researchers to make real changes to the function and performance of her brain. She seeks to improve on everyday weaknesses." (Publisher's note)

Includes bibliographical references and index

612.82   Central nervous system

Buonomano, Dean

Your brain is a time machine; the neuroscience and physics of time. Dean Buonomano. W W Norton & Co Inc 2017 293 p. illustrations (hardcover) $26.95   **612.82**
1. Time 2. Brain -- Physiology 3. Time perception
ISBN 9780393247954; 9780393247947
LC 2016046898

In this book author Dean Buonomano "draws on evolutionary biology, physics, and philosophy to present his influential theory of how we tell, and perceive, time. The human brain, he argues, is a complex system that not only tells time but creates it; it constructs our sense of chronological flow and enables 'mental time travel'-simulations of future and past events. These functions are essential not only to our daily lives but to the evolution of the human race." (Publisher's note)

"Fascinating throughout and a pleasing vehicle by which to think about thinking—and the passing hours." Kirkus

Includes bibliographical references (pages 237-278) and index.

Eagleman, David

The **brain**; the story of you. David Eagleman. Pantheon Books 2015 218 p. color illustrations (hardback) $28.95 **612.82**
1. Self 2. Brain 3. Reality 4. Neurosciences
ISBN 1101870532; 9781101870532
LC 2015023281

This book, by David Eagleman, is "a journey into the questions at the mysterious heart of our existence. What is reality? Who are 'you'? How do you make decisions? Why does your brain need other people? How is technology poised to change what it means to be human? In the course of his investigations, Eagleman guides us through the world of extreme sports, criminal justice, facial expressions, genocide, brain surgery, gut feelings, robotics, and the search for immortality." (Publisher's note)

"This is a straightforward, stimulating companion book to the PBS series on the subject." Pub Wkly

Includes bibliographical references (pages 204-213).

Masley, Steven

The **better** brain solution; how to start now-at any age-to reverse and prevent insulin resistance of the brain, sharpen cognitive function, and avoid memory loss. Steven Masley, M.D. Alfred A. Knopf 2018 xiv, 367 p.p (hardback) $27.95 **612.82**
1. Nutrition 2. Health self-care 3. Brain -- Popular works 4. Nutrition -- Popular works 5. Mental health -- Popular works 6. Self-care, Health -- Popular works
ISBN 9781524732394; 1524732389; 9781524732387
LC 2017016326

In this book, author "Steven Masley . . . [focuses on] the two urgent epidemics we are facing now--escalating rates of disabling memory loss and rapidly increasing rates of diabetes and pre-diabetes. . . . Masley offers a program that, in the fight against diabetes, memory loss, and cognitive decline, can reverse insulin resistance, enhance cognitive performance, and stop cognitive decline before it is too late." (Publisher's note)

"Masley's book will appeal to anyone interested in a well-substantiated guide to mental health." Pub Wkly

Includes bibliographical references (pages 341-345) and index.

Ros, Hana

Neurocomic; Hana Ros; illustrated by Matteo Farinella. Nobrow Press 2014 144 p. illustrations $24.95   **612.82**

    1. Brain 2. Psychology 3. Neurosciences

    ISBN 1907704701; 9781907704703

This book by Hana Ros, illustrated by Matteo Farinella, is a "journey through the human brain: a place of neuron forests, memory caves, and castles of deception. Along the way, you'll encounter Boschean beasts, giant squid, guitar-playing sea slugs, and the great pioneers of neuroscience. Hana Ros and Matteo Farinella provide an insight into the most complex thing in the universe." (Publisher's note)

"The information relayed is sufficiently genuine for the book to be a neophyte's primer on brain science, and the manner of its presentation is certainly exciting enough to sustain interest." Booklist

Sigman, Mariano

The **secret** life of the mind; how your brain thinks, feels, and decides. Mariano Sigman. Little, Brown & Co. 2017 277 p. illustrations (hardcover) $27   **612.82**

    1. Neurosciences 2. Brain -- Popular works 3. Science -- Popular works 4. Neurosciences -- Popular works

    ISBN 9780316434744; 9780316549622

    LC 2017939488

In this book, author Mariano Sigman "draws on research in physics, linguistics, psychology, education, and beyond to explain why people who speak more than one language are less prone to dementia; how infants can recognize by sight objects they've previously only touched; how babies, even before they utter their first word, have an innate sense of right and wrong; and how we can 'read' the thoughts of vegetative patients by decoding patterns in their brain activity." (Publisher's note)

"An exploration of recent discoveries in neuroscience and the ways in which we perceive and interpret the world." Kirkus

Includes bibliographical references (pages 247-263) and index.

612.823   Emotions, conscious mental processes, intelligence

Adam, David

The **genius** within; unlocking our brain's potential. David Adam. Pegasus Books 2018 326 p. illustrations (hardcover) $27.95   **612.823**

    1. Medicine 2. Neurosciences 3. Cognition 4. Cognitive neuroscience

    ISBN 9781681776743; 9781681777016; 168177674X

In this book, author "David Adam explores the groundbreaking neuroscience of cognitive enhancement that is changing the way the brain and the mind works--to make it better, sharper, more focused and . . . more intelligent. He considers how we measure and judge intelligence, taking us on a fascinating tour of the history of brain science and medicine, from gentlemen scientist brain autopsy clubs to case studies of mental health patients with extraordinary savant abilities." (Publisher's note)

"Adam provides readers with a lucidly written and enticing look at cutting-edge neuroscience discoveries that may eventually benefit us all." Booklist

Includes bibliographical references (pages 317-326).

613   Personal health and safety

Auerbach, Paul

★ **Enviromedics**; the impact of climate change on human health. Jay Lemery and Paul Auerbach. Rowman & Littlefield 2017 xiii, 214 p.p (cloth; alk. paper) $33   **613**

    1. Climate change 2. Environmental health 3. Environmental literature 4. Climate Change 5. Environmental Health

    ISBN 9781442243187

    LC 2017015582

In this book, authors Jay Lemery and Paul Auerbach examine the impact of climate change on human health. "By weighing in from a physician's perspective, . . . [the authors] clarify the science, dispel the myths, and help readers understand the threats of climate change to human health. No better argument exists for persuading people to care about climate change than a close look at its impacts on our physical and emotional well-being." (Publisher's note)

Includes bibliographical references and index.

Boston Women's Health Book Collective

★ **Our** bodies, ourselves; [by the] Boston Women's Health Book Collective. 40th anniversary ed.; Touchstone 2011 928p il pa $26; ebook $12.99   **613**

    1. Women -- Psychology 2. Women -- Health and hygiene

    ISBN 978-1-4391-9066-1 pa; 1-4391-9066-6 pa; 978-1-4391-9665-6 ebook; 1-4391-9665-6 ebook

    LC 2011022749

First published 1971

This encyclopedia of women's health covers such topics as body image, food, alcohol and drugs, holistic healing, psychotherapy, occupational health, violence, relationships and sexuality, sexual health and controlling fertility, childbearing, aging and politics of women and health.

This is "the bible for women's health; an outstanding resource that belongs in all health collections." Libr J

Brewer, Stephen C.

The **Canyon** Ranch guide to men's health; a doctor's prescription for male wellness. Stephen C. Brewer. SelectBooks, Inc. 2016 256 p. illustrations (hardbound book; alk. paper) $24.95   **613**

    1. Exercise 2. Nutrition 3. Heart diseases 4. Men -- Health and hygiene 5. Heart -- Diseases 6. Medicine and psychology

    ISBN 9781590793626

    LC 2015026737

This book, by Stephen C. Brewer, "is a sustainable, real-world approach to men's health. The book is divided into four sections designed to target a specific phase on your journey to well-being. In-depth detail is tailored to target five specific age groups and then subdivided by function. The guide takes a comprehensive look at every aspect of men's health from sexual health to cardiovascular and prostate." (Publisher's note)

"This accessible handbook is equal parts factual and friendly, and it will help men conquer their health fears and make wise choices for healthy, long lives." Pub Wkly

Columbia University/Health Service

The **Go** ask Alice book of answers; a guide to good physical, sexual, and emotional health. [by] Columbia University's Health Education Program. Holt & Co. 1998 345p pa $15.95　　　**613**

1. Adolescence 2. Sex education 3. Youth -- Health and hygiene
ISBN 0-8050-5570-3

LC 98-3318

"The title within the title refers to a Web site maintained by Columbia University Health Services. Set up to answer questions about relationships, sex, physical and mental health, nutrition, and related matters, the site eventually was opened to the general public as a quick-reference forum. The book's seven chapters round up queries the site has received and responses to them from Columbia-associated health educators." Booklist

Includes bibliographical references

Dietert, Rodney

The **human** superorganism; How the Microbiome Is Revolutionizing the Pursuit of a Healthy Life. Rodney Dietert. Dutton 2016 352 p. (hardcover) $28　　　**613**

1. Health 2. Microbiology 3. Microbiota
ISBN 9781101983904

LC 2015041110

This book, by Rodney Dietert, "makes a sweeping, paradigm-shifting argument. It demolishes two fundamental beliefs that have blinkered all medical thinking until very recently: 1) Humans are better off as pure organisms free of foreign microbes; and 2) the human genome is the key to future medical advances. The microorganisms that we have sought to eliminate have been there for centuries supporting our ancestors." (Publisher's note)

"Dietert makes a fascinating case for an exciting, emerging field that offers a new way of thinking about the human body and health." Pub Wkly

Includes bibliographical references and index

Dusenbery, Maya

Doing harm; the truth about how bad medicine and lazy science leave women dismissed, misdiagnosed, and sick. Maya Dusenbery. HarperOne 2017 400 p. (hardback) $27.99 **613**

1. Health education 2. Women -- Health and hygiene 3. Sexism in medicine 4. Women -- Health and hygiene -- Research 5. Women -- Health and hygiene -- Sociological aspects
ISBN 9780062470805

LC 2017019560

In this book, author "Maya Dusenbery brings together scientific and sociological research, interviews with doctors and researchers, and personal stories from women across the country to provide the first comprehensive, accessible look at how sexism in medicine harms women today. . . . [She] explores the deep, systemic problems that underlie women's experiences of feeling dismissed by the medical system." (Publisher's note)

"For readers interested in a feminist critique of health care, especially in the treatment of women." LJ

Includes bibliographical references

García, Héctor, 1981-

Ikigai; the Japanese secret to a long and happy life. Héctor García and Francesc Miralles ; translated by Heather Cleary. Penguin Books 2017 194 p. illustrations (hardcover) $20 **613**

1. Happiness 2. Longevity -- Japan 3. Longevity 4. Quality of life
ISBN 9780143130727; 9781524704551

LC 2017005811

In this book, by Héctor García and Francesc Miralles, translated by Heather Cleary, "the authors interviewed the residents of the Japanese

village with the highest percentage of 100-year-olds. 'Ikigai' reveals the secrets to their longevity and happiness: how they eat, how they move, how they work, how they foster collaboration and community, and . . . how they find the ikigai that brings satisfaction to their lives." (Publisher's note)

"Throughout, the book persuasively shows that small changes can help readers find more joy and purpose in their lives." Pub Wkly

Includes bibliographical references

Grigore, Adina

Skin cleanse; the simple, all-natural program for clear, calm, happy skin. Adina Grigore. HarperWave 2015 237 p. illustrations (hardback) $24.99　　　**613**

1. Health 2. Skin -- Care 3. Nutrition 4. Self-care, Health 5. Detoxification (Health) 6. Skin -- Care and hygiene
ISBN 0062332554; 9780062332554

LC 2014044382

This book by Adina Grigore "helps readers diagnose and understand the underlying causes of their individual skin problems and offers all-natural recipes--using inexpensive ingredients that can be found at the grocery store to treat them effectively. From learning about how diet and lifestyle factors affect the quality of your skin to examining what is in the dozens of products we use every day, Grigore helps you take control over what goes on your skin." (Publisher's note)

Guiliano, Mireille

French women don't get facelifts; the secret of aging with style and attitude. Mireille Guiliano. Grand Central Life & Style 2013 272 p. (hardcover) $25　　　**613**

1. Women -- France 2. Women -- Health and hygiene 3. Aging -- Psychological aspects 4. Older women -- France -- Attitudes 5. Older women -- Health and hygiene -- France
ISBN 1455524115; 9781455524112

LC 2013017824

Author Mireille Guiliano's book "presents an insightful guide to the French way of aging with style, grace, and attitude. She encourages midlife women to adopt French-inspired remedies for aging woes, such as antiaging foods, regular exercise, sufficient sunlight, proper skin care, and plenty of water . . . . The author provides a list of superfoods paired with easy-to-follow recipes, a straightforward skin-care routine, product recommendations, and ways to stay physically active." (Library Journal)

Hamblin, James

If our bodies could talk; A Guide to Operating and Maintaining a Human Body. James Hamblin. Doubleday 2016 400 p. color illustrations (hardcover) $26.95　　　**613**

1. Health -- Popular works
ISBN 9780385540971; 9780385540988; 9781101970829; 9780385540988

LC 2016956917

This book, by James Hamblin, "explores the human stories behind health questions that never seem to go away—and which tend to be mischaracterized and oversimplified by marketing and news media. He covers topics such as sleep, aging, diet, and much more: Can I 'boost' my immune system? Does caffeine make me live longer? Do we still not know if cell phones cause cancer? How much sleep do I actually need? Is there any harm in taking a multivitamin? Is life long enough?" (Publisher's note)

"He does a stellar job with nutrition, covering supplements, multivitamins, energy drinks, and gluten. He calls out medical misinformation and marketing myths. He is troubled... by how money, politics, and industry distort scientific data and muddle health policy. Educational, entertaining, and a bit eccentric." Booklist

Includes bibliographical references (page 371).

Jacobs, Jennifer

Do You Really Need That Pill? How to Avoid Side Effects, Interactions, and Other Dangers of Overmedication. Jennifer Jacobs. Skyhorse Publishing 2018 192 p. (paperback) $14.99 **613**

1. Medical ethics 2. Medication abuse
ISBN 1510715649; 9781510715646

This book by Jennifer Jacobs "shows readers how to avoid the dangers of over-medication. The first half of the book describes the harmful effects of taking too many drugs, including drug-drug interactions, medication errors, [and] unintentional overdoses. The second half discusses the benefits and harm caused by many of the most popular drugs used to treat diseases such as high blood pressure, diabetes, [and] high cholesterol. Finally, readers will learn how to discuss their concerns about too many medications with their health care providers." (Publisher's note)

"This is a cautious book, offering peer-reviewed treatment options." LJ

Northrup, Christiane

Goddesses never age; the secret prescription for radiance, vitality, and well-being. Christiane Northrup, M.D. Hay House, Inc. 2015 408 p. illustration (hardback) $25.99 **613**

1. Aging 2. Women -- Health and hygiene 3. Physical fitness
ISBN 1401945163; 9781401945169
LC 2014029338

This book, by Christiane Northrup, "in chapters that blend personal stories and practical exercises with the latest research on health and aging, . . . lays out the principles of ageless living, from rejecting processed foods to releasing stuck emotions, from embracing our sensuality to connecting deeply with our Divine Source." (Publisher's note)

Roizen, Michael F.

This is your do-over; the 7 secrets to losing weight, living longer, and getting a second chance at the life you want. Michael F. Roizen and Ted Spiker. Scribner 2015 358 p. illustrations (hardback) $26 **613**

1. Health 2. Weight loss 3. Vitality 4. Rejuvenation 5. Self-care, Health
ISBN 1501103334; 9781501103339; 9781501103346
LC 2014049798

In this book author Michael Roizen "provides the tools you need to halt bad health and start living at your peak vitality. In this book, he addresses all the areas that contribute to total-body wellness, including nutrition, exercise, sex, stress, sleep, and the brain. Using concrete strategies available to anyone of any age, Dr. Roizen shows you how to reset your health with his seven simple secrets to earning a Do-Over." (Publisher's note)

Smith, Rick

Toxin toxout; getting harmful chemicals out of our bodies and our world. Bruce Lourie, Rick Smith. St. Martin's Press 2014 304 p. (hardcover) $25.99 **613**

1. Pesticides 2. Environmental health 3. Detoxification (Health) 4. Environmentally induced diseases -- Nutritional aspects
ISBN 1250051339; 9781250051332
LC 2013049688

This book presents a "guide to the toxins in our everyday environment and how best to avoid them or get them out of our bodies. . . . The authors . . . focus on providing practical advice on how to avoid toxins (the short answer is to buy organic and natural products) and eliminate those that have accumulated from our bodies. . . . Toward the end of their book, [Bruce] Lourie and [Rick] Smith discuss some of the broader implications of their findings." (CCPA Monitor)

"In a collegial, straightforward style, Lourie and Smith quiz doctors and researchers, converse with wellness activists, visit organic stores and companies and, most interestingly, engage in a variety of experiments to track how the more than 80,000 synthetic chemicals in use today got into our bodies and what it will take to get them out." Booklist

Includes bibliographical references and index

Tanzi, Rudolph E.

Super genes; the hidden key to total well-being. Deepak Chopra, M.D. & Rudolph E. Tanzi, Ph.D. Harmony 2015 336 p. illustrations (hardback) $26 **613**

1. Heredity 2. Health self-care 3. Nature and nurture 4. Genes -- Popular works 5. Self-care, Health -- Popular works
ISBN 9780804140133; 9780804140157
LC 2015028562

This book, by Deepak Chopra and Rudolph E. Tanzi, "present[s] a bold new understanding of our genes and how simple changes in lifestyle can boost genetic activity. . . . You will always have the genes you were born with, but genes are dynamic, responding to everything we think, say, and do. Suddenly they've become our strongest allies for personal transformation." (Publisher's note)

"Chopra's name, along with his trademark blend of concrete suggestions with spiritual principles, will guarantee popularity." Booklist

Vonn, Lindsey

Strong Is the New Beautiful; Embrace Your Natural Beauty, Eat Clean, and Harness Your Power. by Lindsey Vonn. HarperCollins 2016 256 p. color illustrations (ebook) $26.99; $27.99 **613**

1. Women -- Health and hygiene
ISBN 9780062400604; 0062400584; 9780062400581

In this book, author Lindsey Vonn "lays out the never-before-seen training routines and her overall philosophy that have helped her become the best female skier in the world—tailored for women of all shapes and sizes. Lindsey backs up her fitness program with advice on what to eat and how to work out, and kicks readers into high-gear, helping bolster their self-confidence and build a better body image, with the tips and tricks she's learned as a pro." (Publisher's note)

"Vonn has created an inspiring narrative, along with a seductive means of getting healthy and fit." Pub Wkly

613.2 Dietetics

Abbott, Christmas

The **Badass** Body Diet; The Breakthrough Diet and Workout for a Tight Booty, Sexy Abs, and Lean Legs. Christmas Abbott. HarperCollins 2015 384 p. color illustrations $27.99 **613.2**

1. Diet 2. Exercise
ISBN 0062390953; 9780062390950

In this book, author "Christmas Abbott shows how to attain the body of your dreams with a targeted eating strategy and total-body workout plan that will whip glutes and hips--and every problem area--into top shape. She dispels the myth of the health benefits of a "pear shape" body, teaches readers how to spot-reduce excess fat with targeted meal plans and recipes that zap cellulite, and galvanizes them with a quick and simple workout plan." (Publisher's note)

"Abbott's unadorned focus on fitness should appeal to any woman seeking to improve her body, regardless of body type." Pub Wkly

Avena, Nicole M.

What to feed your baby and toddler; a month-by-month guide to support your child's health and development. Nicole M. Avena, PhD with recipes by Charity Ferreira. Ten Speed Press 2018 224 p. (paperback) $16.99   **613.208**

1. Infants -- Nutrition 2. Children -- Nutrition 3. Children -- Health and hygiene 4. Baby foods 5. Child development 6. Toddlers -- Nutrition 7. HEALTH & FITNESS -- Children
ISBN 9780399580239

LC 2018010055

In this book physician "Nicole M. Avena presents an essential guide for new parents on feeding babies during their critical first two years. Answering common questions about picky eaters, food allergies, diversifying baby's appetite, . . . feeding baby at daycare or when with another caregiver, and food safety, this comprehensive guide offers easy monthly meal plans and baby-friendly, nutrient-rich recipes designed to support your baby's developmental milestones." (Publisher's note)

"Specific nutritional information and straightforward, fun-to-eat recipes make this a great primer for new parents." Library Journal

Includes bibliographical references and index

Barrett, Pearl

★ **Trim** healthy mama trim healthy table; more than 300 all-new healthy and delicious recipes from our homes to yours. Pearl Barrett and Serene Allison. First edition Harmony Books 2017 559 p. color illustrations (hardcover; alk. paper) $32.50   **613.2**

1. Cooking 2. Health 3. Nutrition 4. Weight loss 5. Reducing diets -- Recipes
ISBN 0804189986; 9780804189989; 9780804189996

LC 2017030325

This book, by Pearl Barrett and Serene Allison, "contains all their best tips, tricks and encouragement for families, whether large or small. Serene and Pearl shamelessly share cunning ways to get picky eaters gobbling down veggies and other healthy foods they usually detest. You will learn how to painlessly use whole, unprocessed foods, including blood-sugar friendly carbs, fats, proteins, fruits and vegetables to create meals even the fussiest kids (and husbands) will love." (Publisher's note)

Trim health table

Brown, Harriet

Body of truth; how science, history, and culture drive our obsession with weight--and what we can do about it. Harriet Brown. Da Capo Lifelong Books 2015 273 p. (hardback) $25.99   **613.2**

1. Body image 2. Body weight 3. Weight loss 4. Reducing diets -- Evaluation 5. Weight loss -- Social aspects 6. Weight loss -- Psychological aspects
ISBN 0738217697; 9780738217697

LC 2014043431

In this book author Harriet Brown "systematically unpacks what's been offered as 'truth' about weight and health. Starting with the four biggest lies, Brown shows how research has been manipulated; how the medical profession is complicit in keeping us in the dark; how big pharma and big, empty promises equal big, big dollars; how much of what we know (or think we know) about health and weight is wrong. And how all of those affect all of us every day, whether we know it or not." (Publisher's note)

"A solid general overview of the scientific and cultural issues surrounding fatness and weight loss with an excellent starter bibliography."

LJ

Includes bibliographical references and index

Buettner, Dan

The **Blue** Zones solution; eating and living like the world's healthiest people. Dan Buettner. National Geographic 2015 320 p. illustrations (hardcover; alk. paper) $26   **613.2**

1. Diet 2. Health 3. Nutrition 4. Functional foods
ISBN 1426211929; 9781426211928

LC 2014044932

Author "Dan Buettner . . .lays out a proven plan to maximize your health based on the practices of the world's healthiest people. Buettner reveals how to transform your health using smart eating and lifestyle habits gleaned from new research on the diets, eating habits, and lifestyle practices of the communities he's identified as 'Blue Zones'--those places with the world's longest-lived, and thus healthiest, people." (Publisher's note)

"Readers seeking a healthier lifestyle will appreciate this warm and encouraging book." LJ

Includes bibliographical references and index

Campbell, T. Colin

The **China** study; the most comprehensive study of nutrition ever conducted and the startling implications for diet, weight loss and long-term health. T. Colin Campbell, PhD, Thomas M. Campbell II, MD. BenBella Books, Inc. 2016 xxx, 451 p.p illustrations, map (paperback) $17.95   **613.2**

1. Nutrition 2. Diet therapy 3. Vegetarianism 4. Eating customs 5. Diet in disease 6. Nutritionally induced diseases
ISBN 9781942952831; 9781941631560; 9781944648770; 1941631568

LC 2016461145

This book, by T. Colin Campbell, PhD, and Thomas M. Campbell II, MD., "includes the latest undeniable evidence of the power of a plant-based diet, plus updated information about the changing medical system and how patients stand to benefit from a surging interest in plant-based nutrition." (Publisher's note)

"The current revised edition of The China Study is an update to the first edition (CH, Jun'05, 42-5895). The new work offers the same message, but with added emphasis and some updating." Choice

Includes bibliographical references (pages 389-438) and index

Carroll, Aaron

The **bad** food bible; how and why to eat sinfully. Aaron Carroll, MD. Houghton Mifflin Harcourt 2017 xxxiv, 234 p.p illustrations (hardcover) $25   **613.2**

1. Health 2. Nutrition 3. Weight loss 4. Eating customs 5. Nutrition -- Popular works
ISBN 0544952561; 9780544952577; 9780544952560

LC 2017044244

In this book, author "Aaron Carroll mines the latest evidence to show that many 'bad' ingredients actually aren't unhealthy, and in some cases are essential to our well-being. . . . There's usually only one thing experts can agree on: some ingredients . . . are bad for you, full stop. But as . . . Carroll explains, these over simplifications are both wrong and dangerous: if we stop consuming some of our most demonized ingredients altogether, it may actually hurt us." (Publisher's note)

Includes bibliographical references (pages 203-226) and index.

Davis, Brenda

Becoming vegan; the complete reference on plant-based nutrition. Brenda Davis, RD, Vesanto Melina, MS, RD. Book

Publishing Company 2014 ix, 611 p.p color illustrations (pbk.) $29.95 **613.2**

1. Veganism 2. Nutrition 3. Veganism -- Health aspects
ISBN 1570672970; 9781570672972

LC 2014018034

Authors "Brenda Davis and Vesanto Melina specifically designed this fully referenced, comprehensive edition to meet the needs of health professionals, academic librarians, and curriculum developers as well as lay readers with a deep interest in nutrition.

The authors explore the health benefits of vegan diets compared to other dietary choices; explain protein and amino acid requirements at various stages of life; describe fats and essential fatty acids and their value in plant-based diets." (Publisher's note)

"The book also carefully considers specific issues surrounding veganism during pregnancy and lactation, infancy, childhood, the teen years, and adulthood and provides practical advice for athletes and for those seeking to maintain a healthy weight. The science behind the recommendations is well documented with extensive chapter references. Summing Up: Highly recommended. All nutrition collections." Choice

Includes bibliographical references (pages 449-532) and index

Duyff, Roberta Larson

American Dietetic Association complete food and nutrition guide; Roberta Larson Duyff. 4th ed. rev. and updated John Wiley & Sons Inc 2012 708 p. ill. (paper) $24.95 **613.2**

1. Diabetes 2. Nutrition
ISBN 9780470912072; 0470912073

LC 2012382537

This book, by Roberta Larson Duyff, "covers the basics on nutrition, managing weight, and healthy eating. It also provides easy steps and how-tos for selecting, preparing, and storing foods safely to get the most nutrition and flavor for your dollar, and more. Comprehensive, accessible, and easy-to-use, this valuable reference shows how to make healthy food choices to fit any lifestyle." (Publisher's note)

"The author's goal is 'to answer the whats, hows, and whys about food and nutrition' for wellness. This new edition . . . is divided into six sections covering food choices for wellness; the basics of nutrition; food selection and safety; special needs for various life stages; food choices for some selected health problems; and a selected list of resources." Choice

Includes bibliographical references and index

Friedman, Howard S.

The **longevity** project; surprising discoveries for health and long life from the eight-decade study. [by] Howard S. Friedman and Leslie R. Martin. Hudson Street Press 2010 248p $25.95 **613.2**

1. Longevity
ISBN 978-1-594630-75-0; 1-594630-75-5

LC 2010-22833

"Analyzing the data from the Terman study and following up on the 1500 participants, . . . [the authors] investigate why some people live until old age while others die or become ill prematurely. Unlike most studies, this work looks at key psychological factors, habits, and patterns that affect health and longevity over time. Some of the authors' conclusions about achieving longevity are surprising. Factors such as the study participants' sociability, conscientiousness, happiness, and religious involvement were analyzed to show which patterns lead over time to an increased life span. The authors have provided a well-written and easy-to-follow analysis of this interesting study." Libr J

Includes bibliographical references

Hartwig, Melissa

Food Freedom Forever; Letting Go of Bad Habits, Guilt, and Anxiety Around Food. Melissa Hartwig. Houghton Mifflin Harcourt 2016 288 p. (hardcover) $27; (ebook) $27 **613.2**

1. Nutrition 2. Weight loss 3. Diet therapy 4. Health self-care
ISBN 9780544838291; 9780544838307; 0544838297

LC 2016462353

This book, by Melissa Hartwig, "offers real solutions for anyone stuck in the exhausting cycle of yo-yo dieting and the resulting stress, weight gain, uncontrollable cravings, and health complaints. . . . Hartwig defines true 'food freedom' as being in control of the food you eat, instead of food controlling you. . . . [Her plan] will help you . . . create the kind of food freedom that stays with you for the rest of your life." (Publisher's note)

"The prospect of food freedom is appealing, and Hartwig's conversational style and no-nonsense stance make her plan seem doable. This is sure to be a popular purchase." Booklist

The **whole30**; the 30-day guide to total health and food freedom. Melissa Hartwig and Dallas Hartwig ; with Chef Richard Bradford ; photography by Alexandra Grablewski. Houghton Mifflin Harcourt 2015 ix, 421 p.p color illustrations (hardcover) $30 **613.2**

1. Diet 2. Nutrition 3. Weight loss 4. Nutrition -- Popular works 5. Food habits -- Popular works 6. Weight loss -- Popular works 7. Diet therapy -- Popular works 8. Self-care, Health -- Popular works
ISBN 0544609719; 9780544609716

LC 2015007139

This book, by Melissa Hartwig and Dallas Hartwig, is a "step-by-step plan to break unhealthy habits, reduce cravings, improve digestion, and strengthen your immune system. . . . [It] features more than 100 chef-developed recipes, like Chimichurri Beef Kabobs and Halibut with Citrus Ginger Glaze, designed to build your confidence in the kitchen and inspire your taste buds. The book also includes real-life success stories, community resources, and an extensive FAQ." (Publisher's note)

"For those interested in trying the Whole30, this book is an invaluable guide that shouldn't be overlooked."

Heller, Marla

The **everyday** DASH diet cookbook; over 150 fresh and delicious recipes to speed weight loss, lower blood pressure, and prevent diabetes. by Marla Heller, MS, RD ; with Rick Rodgers. Grand Central Life & Style 2013 214 p. (hardback) $26 **613.2**

1. Cookbooks 2. Hypertension -- Prevention 3. Reducing diets -- Recipes 4. Salt-free diet -- Recipes 5. Diabetes -- Diet therapy -- Recipes 6. COOKING -- Health & Healing -- Heart 7. Hypertension -- Diet therapy -- Recipes
ISBN 1455528064; 9781455528066

LC 2012045485

This cookbook looks at the "research-based DASH (dietary approaches to stop hypertension) diet," which "emphasizes 'real foods' and minimizes processed sugars, salt, cholesterol, and fats. Writing with veteran cookbook author [Rick] Rodgers . . . , leading DASH expert [Marla] Heller . . . offers easy recipes (e.g., crunchy broccoli slaw, rosemary pork chops with balsamic glaze) for readers living a healthy lifestyle." (Library Journal)

Includes bibliographical references and index

Hever, Julieanna

The **Vegiterranean** Diet; The New and Improved Mediterranean Eating Plan--with Deliciously Satisfying Vegan Recipes for Optimal Health. by Julieanna Hever. Da Capo Lifelong

Books 2014 288 p. illustrations $17.99   **613.2**
1. Mediterranean cooking
ISBN 0738217891; 9780738217895

LC 2015304766

This Mediterranean diet cookbook, by Julieanna Hever, offers "comprehensive nutrition info, shopping lists with everyday ingredients, more than 40 delicious, budget-friendly recipes, flexible meal plans (great for families, too!), [and] strategies for overall health." (Publisher's note)

"Readers may recognize Hever from her Veria Living show What Would Julieanna Do? and appearances on programs such as The Dr. Oz Show. The author's strong media presence, combined with early accolades from established vegan chefs and advocates such as Colleen Patrick-Goudreau, increase the likelihood of demand. Readers seeking nutritional guidance will be pleased with the range of coverage." LJ

Hyman, Mark
Food; what the heck should I eat? Mark Hyman. Little, Brown & Co. 2018 320 p. $28   **613.2**
1. Nutrition 2. Diet therapy 3. Eating customs
ISBN 0316338869; 9780316338868

In this book, author Mark Hyman "takes a close look at every food group and explains what we've gotten wrong, revealing which foods nurture our health and which pose a threat. From grains to legumes, meat to dairy, fats to artificial sweeteners, and beyond, Dr. Hyman debunks misconceptions and breaks down the fascinating science in his signature accessible style. He also explains food's role as powerful medicine capable of reversing chronic disease." (Publisher's note)

Jacobson, Howard
Proteinaholic; how our obsession with meat is killing us and what we can do about it. Garth Davis, M.D. HarperOne 2015 384 p. (hardback) $27.99   **613.2**
1. Diet in disease 2. Proteins in human nutrition 3. Meat
ISBN 9780062279309; 9780062279316

LC 2015020233

In this book, by Garth Davis, a "surgeon specializing in weight loss delivers a paradigm-shifting examination of the diet and health industry's focus on protein, explaining why it is detrimental to our health, and can prevent us from losing weight. . . . This . . . book reveals the truth about the dangers of protein and shares a proven approach to weight loss, health, and longevity." (Publisher's note)

"This title is easy to understand and, despite its infomercial-like tone, gives sound information that will motivate readers to improve their health." LJ

Leake, Lisa
100 days of real food; how we did it, what we learned, and 100 easy, wholesome recipes your family will love. by Lisa Leake. HarperCollinsPublishers 2014 360 p. color illustrations $29.99   **613.2**
1. Health 2. Cookbooks 3. Natural foods 4. Cooking -- Natural foods
ISBN 0062252550; 9780062252555

LC 2015303205

In this book, author Lisa Leake "draws from her hugely popular website to offer simple, affordable, family-friendly recipes and practical advice for eliminating processed foods from your family's diet. . . . Illustrated with 125 photographs and filled with step-by-step instructions, this hands-on cookbook and guide includes [a]dvice for navigating the grocery store and making smart purchases, [t]ips for reading ingredient labels, [and] 100 quick and easy recipes." (Publisher's note)

Includes bibliographical references and index

Lee, Janet
The **supplement** handbook; a trusted expert's guide to what works & what's worthless for more than 100 conditions. Mark Moyad, MD, MPH; with Janet Lee, LAc. Rodale 2014 ix, 502 p.p (paperback) $24.99   **613.2**
1. Dietary supplements
ISBN 1623360358; 9781623360351

LC 2014035702

This handbook on supplements, by Mark Moyad, will "guide you through the proven (or debunked) treatment options for more than 100 common conditions--everything from arthritis, heartburn, and high cholesterol to fibromyalgia, migraines, and psoriasis. Dr. Moyad provides clear guidelines, sifting through conflicting information for a definitive answer you can use today." (Publisher's note)

"This book explains what supplements are, what they can and can't do, and when to use them. It also tells readers how to evaluate the information that is available about supplements.The bulk of the book discusses specific medical conditions, with recommendations for supplements based on evidence from research." Booklist

Ludwig, David
Always hungry? conquer cravings, retrain your fat cells, and lose weight permanently. David Ludwig. Grand Central Life & Style 2016 384 p. illustrations (hardback) $28 **613.2**
1. Hunger 2. Weight loss 3. Self-care, Health 4. Metabolism -- Regulation 5. Reducing diets -- Recipes
ISBN 1455533866; 9781455533862

LC 2015032645

This book, by David Ludwig, "explains why traditional diets don't work, and presents a radical new plan to help you lose weight without hunger, improve your health, and feel great. [It] turns dieting on its head with a three-phase program that ignores calories and targets fat cells directly. The recipes and meal plan include luscious high fat foods (like nuts and nut butters, full fat dairy, avocados, and dark chocolate), savory proteins, and natural carbohydrates." (Publisher's note)

"Ludwig's meal plans and recipes are excellent. This quality book on the basics of losing weight will appeal to all types of readers." Library Journal

Includes bibliographical references and index

Mann, Traci
Secrets from the eating lab; the science of weight loss, the myth of willpower, and why you should never diet again. Traci Mann, PhD. HarperWave 2015 272 p. illustrations (hardback) $26.99   **613.2**
1. Diet 2. Weight loss 3. Eating habits 4. Weight loss -- Social aspects 5. Reducing diets -- Social aspects 6. Weight loss -- Psychological aspects 7. Reducing diets -- Psychological aspects
ISBN 0062329235; 9780062329233

LC 2014049872

In this book, author Traci Mann "challenges assumptions--including those that make up the very foundation of the weight loss industry--about how diets work and why they fail. The result of more than two decades of research, it offers cutting-edge science and exciting new insights into the American obesity epidemic and our relationship with eating and food." (Publisher's note)

"Mann cites study after study to make her case; titles her last chapter, 'Final Words: Diet Schmiet'; and declares that no single eating plan will ever make the pounds melt away forever. 'The fragility of willpower' and 'a culture of ubiquitous temptations' conspire against the best-laid plans. Her bottom-line recommendation: 'reach your leanest livable weight.' Sold." Booklist

Mercola, Joseph M., 1954-

Effortless healing; 9 simple ways to sidestep illness, shed excess weight, and help your body fix itself. Joseph Mercola. Random House Inc 2015 323 p. illustrations (hardback) $26 **613.2**

1. Nutrition 2. Health self-care

ISBN 0553417975; 9780553417975; 9781781805091

LC 2014022046

In this book, "online health pioneer, natural medicine advocate, and . . . author Dr. Joseph Mercola reveals the nine simple secrets to a healthier, thinner you." His advice includes "avoiding certain meat and fish, but enjoying butter. . ., eating sauerkraut (and other fermented foods) to improve your immune system and your mood . . ., [and] walking barefoot outside to decrease system-wide inflammation (and because it just feels great)." (Publisher's note)

Moss, Michael

★ **Salt,** sugar, fat; how the food giants hooked us. Michael Moss. Random House Inc 2013 480 p. (hardcover) $28 **613.2**

1. Obesity 2. Junk food -- Marketing 3. Food industry -- United States 4. Food industry and trade -- United States 5. Nutrition -- Economic aspects -- United States 6. Food habits -- Economic aspects -- United States

ISBN 1400069807; 9780679604778; 9781400069804

LC 2012033034

Pulitzer prize winner Michael Moss offers an exposé of the U.S. food industry. He "explains the two-faced science of salt, sugar, and fat, which impart tantalizing tastes and luscious mouth-feel that light up the same neural circuits that narcotics do . . . while causing epidemic obesity, cardiovascular disease, and diabetes. But he also crafts an . . . insiders' view of the food industry, where these ingredients are the main weapons in a brutally competitive war for stomach-share." (Publishers Weekly)

Nesheim, Malden

Why calories count; from science to politics. Marion Nestle and Malden Nesheim. University of California Press 2012 288 p. (California studies in food and culture) (hardback; alk. paper) $29.95 **613.2**

1. Diet 2. Nutrition 3. Weight loss 4. Eating customs 5. Food -- Caloric content 6. Politics 7. Marketing 8. Food Industry 9. Energy Intake -- physiology 10. Obesity -- prevention & control

ISBN 9780520262881

LC 2011044785

This book "assists readers in evaluating diet claims, formulating strategies to lose, gain, or maintain weight, and learning how to make healthy food choices. [Marion] Nestle . . . and [Malden] Nesheim . . . focus on the history of the calorie and its relationship to body weight, the science behind metabolism, how to estimate calories in a given portion, and . . . the role of big business in creating calorie-laden food." (Library Journal)

Includes bibliographical references and index.

Netzer, Corinne T.

The **complete** book of food counts; Corinne T. Netzer. Dell 2012 903 p. (pbk.) $8.99 **613.2**

1. Diet therapy 2. Low-calorie diet 3. Nutrition -- Tables 4. Food -- Composition -- Tables 5. Brand name products -- Composition -- Tables

ISBN 0440245613; 9780440245612

LC 2014415863

Written by Corinne T. Netzer, "this vital reference provides all the essential counts you need to know for generic and brand-name foods-

-as well as the latest gourmet and health foods and a variety of ethnic cuisines. Whether it's fresh or frozen, fast-food or slow-cooked, 'The Complete Book of Food Counts' is an A to Z guide to the choices in your supermarket aisles, at your local farmer's market, or served in your favorite restaurants!" (Publisher's note)

Phillips, Robert

★ **Fast** food genocide; how processed food is killing us and what we can do about it. Joel Fuhrman, M.D. ; with research and contributions by Robert B. Phillips. HarperOne 2017 342 p. (hardback) $27.99 **613.22**

1. Junk food 2. Processed foods -- Health aspects 3. Diet 4. Nutrition 5. Junk food -- Health aspects

ISBN 9780062571212

LC 2017040958

This book, by Joel Fuhrman with Robert B. Phillips, "draws on twenty-five years of clinical experience and research to confront our fundamental beliefs about the impact of what we eat. . . . Fast food kills, but it also perpetuates bigotry and derails the American dream of equal opportunity and happiness for all. . . . [Here,] Dr. Fuhrman offers a life-changing, scientifically sound approach that can alter American history and perhaps save your life in the process." (Publisher's note)

Includes bibliographical references and index.

Prescott, Matthew

Food is the solution; what to eat to save the world; 80+ recipes for a greener planet and a healthier you. Matthew Prescott. Flatiron Books 2018 272 p. $29.99 **613.2**

1. Cooking 2. Vegetarianism 3. Vegetarian cooking 4. Veganism 5. Vegan cooking 6. Sustainable living

ISBN 1250144450; 9781250144454

LC 2018935045

In this book, author Matthew Prescott, 'shows how our plates have the power to heal the world. . . . [The book also] shows how anyone can help solve the world's major issues--environmental problems chief among them--simply by incorporating more plants into their diets. Featuring investigative reporting, compelling infographics, and essays from notable contributors . . . , 'Food Is the Solution' will inspire us all to put more plants on our plates." (Publisher's note)

Includes bibliographical references and index

Tara, Sylvia

The **secret** life of fat; the science behind the body's least understood organ and what it means for you. Sylvia Tara. W W Norton & Co Inc 2016 288 p. illustrations (ebook) $50; (hardcover) $26.95 **613.2**

1. Metabolism 2. Body weight

ISBN 9780393244847; 9780393244830; 0393244830

LC 2016027841

This book, by Sylvia Tara, "reveals that fat is much smarter than we think. . . . You may not love your fat, but your body certainly does. In fact, your body is actually endowed with many self-defense measures to hold on to fat. . . . Tara expertly illustrates the complex role that genetics, hormones, diet, exercise, and history play in our weight, and . . . sets you on the path to beat the bulge once and for all." (Publisher's note)

"This genuinely enlightening book will be a revelation to those engulfed in self-blame and shame about their weight. Hopefully, individualized weight loss will become the way of the future, leading to effective new treatments for those desperately seeking them." Pub Wkly

Includes bibliographical references (pages 211-224) and index.

Taubes, Gary

The **case** against sugar; by Gary Taubes. Alfred A. Knopf 2016 368 p. illustrations (ebook) $65; (hardback) $26.95   **613.2**

1. Sugar 2. Nutrition 3. Sugar-free diet 4. Sugar-free diet -- Case studies 5. Sugar -- Physiological effect -- Popular works 6. Nutritionally induced diseases -- Popular works
ISBN 9780451493996; 9780307701640

LC 2016018147

This book, by Gary Taubes, is "a groundbreaking, eye-opening exposé that makes the convincing case that sugar is the tobacco of the new millennium: backed by powerful lobbies, entrenched in our lives, and making us very sick. . . . Taubes delves into Americans' history with sugar: its uses as a preservative, as an additive in cigarettes, the contemporary overuse of high-fructose corn syrup. He explains what research has shown about our addiction to sweets." (Publisher's note)

"Readers will hate to love this book, since it will cause them to thoroughly rethink the place of sugar in their diets." Pub Wkly

Includes bibliographical references and index

Wansink, Brian

Slim by design; mindless eating solutions for home, school, grocery stores, restaurants, and more. Brian Wansink. William Morrow 2014 320 p. color illustrations, color map $26.99   **613.2**

1. Diet 2. Architectural design
ISBN 0062136526; 9780062136527

LC 2015304142

In this book "author Brian Wansink introduces groundbreaking solutions for designing our most common spaces--schools, restaurants, grocery stores, and home kitchens, among others--in order to make positive changes in how we approach and manage our diets. Wansink presents compelling research conducted at the Food and Brand Lab at Cornell University by way of cartoons, drawings, charts, graphs, floor plans, and more." (Publisher's note)

"Every plant or office manager, school lunch supervisor, restaurateur, and parent should have this book." LJ

613.25   Weight-losing diet

Cruikshank, Tiffany

Meditate your weight; the 21-day retreat to optimize your metabolism and feel great. Tiffany Cruikshank. Harmony 2016 336 p. (hardback) $22   **613.25**

1. Meditation 2. Metabolism 3. Weight loss 4. Metabolism -- Regulation 5. Weight loss -- Psychological aspects
ISBN 9780804187961

LC 2015033619

This book, by Tiffany Cruikshank, "helps you explore and release what's weighing you down physically, emotionally, and mentally—the mental blocks, thoughts, habits, and behaviors that stand in your way— to make it easier to think more clearly, make better choices, and maximize metabolism. As you lighten up on the inside, you'll lighten up on the outside." (Publisher's note)

Includes bibliographical references (pages 305-311) and index.

Kingsford, Eliza

Brain-powered weight loss; the 11-step behavior-based plan that ends overeating and leads to dropping unwanted pounds for good. Eliza Kingsford, Executive Director of Wellspring Weight Loss Programs, with Debora Yost. Rodale 2017 232 p.

$26.99   **613.25**

1. Weight loss 2. Diet -- Psychological aspects 3. Weight loss -- Psychological aspects
ISBN 162336809X; 9781623368098

LC 2017004359

This book, by Eliza Kingsford, "shows that more than 90 percent of people who go on diet programs (even healthy ones) fail or eventually regain because they have a dysfunctional relationship with food. Changing this relationship by changing the way you think about and behave around food is what it takes to permanently achieve weight-loss success. Kingsford's 11-step first-of-its-kind program enlists dozens of mind-altering and behavior-changing exercises and techniques." (Publisher's note)

"This book is easily recommended to anyone who has ever tried, and failed, to lose weight through methods that emphasized the body at the expense of the mind." Pub Wkly.

Includes bibliographical references and index.

Parker, Louise

The **Louise** Parker Method; Lean for Life. Louise Parker. Octopus Pub Group 2016 224 p. color illustrations $24.99   **613.25**

1. Exercise 2. Nutrition 3. Weight loss 4. Mind and body
ISBN 1784721751; 9781784721756

LC 2016052784

In this book, personal trainer Louise Parker "shares her unique four-pronged approach to lasting success that has made her method the mecca for worldwide clients demanding the most intelligent, focused and practical solution to permanent weight loss and habit change. The book details four simple pillars that promise you can drop two dress sizes in six weeks without a chia seed in sight." (Publisher's note)

"Parker's guide is gorgeous from cover to cover, teeming with photos of Parker herself in various modes of life." Pub Wkly

613.28   Specific nutritive elements

Wolf, Robb

Wired to eat; turn off cravings, rewire your appetite for weight loss, and determine the foods that work for you. Robb Wolf. Harmony Books 2017 xii, 388 p.p (hardcover) $26.99   **613.28**

1. Nutrition 2. Weight loss 3. Low-carbohydrate diet 4. Reducing diets 5. Reducing diets -- Recipes 6. Low-carbohydrate diet -- Recipes
ISBN 9780451498571; 9780451498564

LC 2016053468

This book, by Robb Wolf, "offers an eating program, based on groundbreaking research, that will rewire your appetite for weight loss and help you finally determine the optimal foods for your diet and metabolism. . . . There are more than 70 delicious recipes, detailed meal plans, and shopping lists to aid you on your journey. Wolf also includes meal plans for people who suffer with autoimmune diseases, as well as advice on eating a ketogenic diet." (Publisher's note)

Includes bibliographical references (pages 354-373) and index.

613.6   Personal safety and special topics of health

Bailey, Elizabeth

Safe kids, smart parents; what parents need to know to keep their children safe. Rebecca Bailey, Ph.D. with Elizabeth Bailey

; introduction by Terry Probyn. Simon & Schuster 2013 224 p. (trade paper; alk. paper) $15 **613.6**

1. Children 2. Safety education 3. Parenting 4. Children -- Protection 5. Critical thinking in children 6. Children -- Crimes against -- Prevention

ISBN 1476700443; 9781476700441

LC 2012047452

This book is a guide to children's safety. It is "divided into two sections, one intended for parents and guardians, the other written especially for children. The message in both is the same: the need for parents and children (whether toddlers or teens) to be aware of their environment and vigilant. The authors emphasize the difficult reality that, these days, children must be taught to be wary of all strangers, even those who appear to be in trouble and are requesting help." (Kirkus Reviews)

Canterbury, Dave

Bushcraft 101; a field guide to the art of wilderness survival. Dave Canterbury. Adams Media 2014 256 p. (pb) $16.99 **613.6**

1. Camping 2. Wilderness survival 3. Camping -- Handbooks, manuals, etc 4. Outdoor life -- Handbooks, manuals, etc 5. Outdoor recreation -- Handbooks, manuals, etc 6. Wilderness survival -- Handbooks, manuals, etc 7. Camping -- Equipment and supplies -- Handbooks, manuals, etc

ISBN 1440579776; 9781440579776

LC 2014012976

This book, by Dave Canterbury, "gets you ready for your next backcountry trip with advice on making the most of your time outdoors. Based on the 5Cs of Survivability--cutting tools, covering, combustion devices, containers, and cordages--this valuable guide offers only the most important survival skills to help you craft resources from your surroundings and truly experience the beauty and thrill of the wilderness." (Publisher's note)

Dorn, Michael

Staying alive; how to act fast and survive deadly encounters. Michael Dorn, Stephen Satterly, Dr. Sonayia Shepherd, Chris Dorn. Barrons Educational Series, Inc. 2014 292 p. illustrations $14.99 **613.6**

1. Survival skills 2. Survival

ISBN 1438004087; 9781438004082

LC 2013031901

In this book, authors Michael Dorn, Stephen Satterly, Dr. Sonayia Shepherd, and Chris Dorn "take the successful strategies that have been used to avert planned school shootings, bombings, and other deadly events and demonstrate how those techniques can be utilized by the average person. . . . With an in-depth look at mass casualty attacks across the centuries, . . . [it] offers everything the average person needs to know in order respond to, and recover from, a crisis." (Publisher's note)

"A chilling and comprehensive crisis-preparedness guide." LJ

Includes bibliographical references and index

Gervasi, Lori Hartman

Fight like a girl-- and win; defense decisions for women. St. Martin's Griffin 2007 285p pa $14.99 **613.6**

1. Safety education 2. Self-defense for women

ISBN 978-0-312-35772-6; 0-312-35772-9

LC 2007-17216

"Although the author has a black belt in karate, she maintains that 90 percent of self-defense is awareness and common sense. She helps readers set up absolute rules and boundaries, sharpen their observation skills, and trust in their intuition. Physical fitness is stressed, and resources are provided for further training." Libr J

Includes bibliographical references

Kostigen, Thomas M.

National Geographic extreme weather survival guide; understand, prepare, survive, recover. by Thomas M. Kostigen. Random House Inc 2014 384 p. illustrations, maps (pbk.; alk. paper) $30 **613.6**

1. Extreme weather 2. Survival skills 3. Weather 4. Severe storms 5. Natural disasters 6. Emergency management -- Handbooks, manuals, etc

ISBN 142621376X; 9781426213762

LC 2014005362

This book, by Thomas M. Kostigen, "tells you how to plan ahead and prepare, respond to emergencies, and survive the worst-case scenarios. From the risks of building on changing coastlines to the safety kit you should have packed up at home, from the telltale signs of a hurricane on the horizon to how to power up when the grid goes down--this will be the one book to carry with you through all kinds of bad weather." (Publisher's note)

"Readers intending to use this as a reference will want to purchase a copy to keep at home. Libraries may wish to purchase for the book's excellent photographs, along with the browsable short sections and checklists. A young readers' version, Extreme Weather: Surviving Tornadoes, Sandstorms, Hailstorms, Blizzards, Hurricanes, and More! is available through National Geographic Kids." LJ

Includes bibliographical references and index

Extreme weather survival guide

Marquis, Sarah

Wild by nature; from Siberia to Australia, three years alone in the wilderness on foot. Sarah Marquis. Thomas Dunne Books/St. Martin's Press 2016 272 p. color illustrations, maps (hardcover) $26.99 **613.6**

1. Hiking 2. Wilderness survival

ISBN 9781250081971

LC 2015039458

This travel memoir, by Sarah Marquis, "takes you on the trail of her ten-thousand-mile solo hike across the remote Gobi desert from Siberia to Thailand, at which point she was transported by boat to complete the hike at her favorite tree in Australia. Against nearly insurmountable odds and relying on hunting and her own wits, Sarah Marquis survived the Mafia, drug dealers, . . . temperatures from subzero to scorching, . . . and a life-threatening abscess." (Publisher's note)

"Her tales of whom she meets and what she sees are as bracing as she is. Straightforward and forthright, this is adventure writing as it was meant to be." Booklist

Moore, Alexis

Cyber self-defense; expert advice to avoid online predators, identity theft, and cyberbullying. Alexis Moore and Laurie J. Edwards. Lyons Press 2014 272 p. illustration (paperback) $16.95 **613.6**

1. Computer crimes 2. Computer security 3. Internet -- Safety measures 4. Cyberbullying 5. Online identity theft -- Prevention

ISBN 1493005693; 9781493005697

LC 2014027221

This book, by Alexis Moore and Laurie J. Edwards, offers advice for online personal security. It "introduces the ten most common personality profiles of cyberstalkers—such as Attention-Getting, Jealous, Manipulative, Controlling, and Narcissistic—and their threatening online behaviors. . . . Case studies illustrate how that particular cybercriminal operates, and . . . offer[] tips to prevent and/or recover from each type of cybercrime." (Publisher's note)

Includes bibliographical references and index

Rawles, James Wesley

Tools for survival; what you need to survive when you're on your own. James Wesley Rawles. Plume 2014 368 p. (paperback) $18   **613.6**

1. Self-reliance 2. Survival skills 3. Alternative lifestyles 4. Survival 5. Self-reliant living
ISBN 0452298121; 9780452298125

LC 2014032904

This book, by James Wesley Rawles, provides "essential survival advice from the world's preeminent expert in preparedness. . . . [He] details the tools needed to survive anything from a short-term disruption to a long-term, grid-down scenario." (Publisher's note)

Wiseman, John

SAS survival handbook; the ultimate guide to surviving anywhere. John "Lofty" Wiseman. 3rd edition William Morrow 2014 672 p. illustrations pbk $21.99   **613.6**

1. Survival skills 2. Wilderness survival
ISBN 0062378074; 9780062378071

LC 2014956877

"The ultimate guide to surviving anywhere, now updated with more than 100 pages of additional material. Revised to reflect the latest in survival knowledge and technology, and covering new topics such as urban survival and terrorism, the internationally bestselling SAS Survival Handbook is the definitive resource for all campers, hikers, and outdoor adventurers." (Publisher's note)

Zeisler, Avital

Weapons of fitness; the women's ultimate guide to fitness, self-defense, and empowerment. Avital Zeisler. Avery 2015 240 p. $20   **613.6**

1. Self-defense for women 2. Women -- Physical fitness 3. Physical fitness
ISBN 1583335692; 9781583335697

LC 2014044613

This book, by Avital Zeisler, offers a "self-defense and fitness book for women by a ballerina-turned-self-defense expert. . . . After ballerina Avital Zeisler was savagely attacked as a young woman, she . . . took action to train with experts in self-defense from around the world. Seeking a method specific to women and using Krav Maga as a base, she created her own self-defense program: the Soteria Method." (Publisher's note)

613.69   Survival

Canterbury, Dave

Advanced bushcraft; an expert field guide to the art of wilderness survival. Dave Canterbury. Adams Media 2015 256 p. illustrations (paperback) $16.99   **613.69**

1. Wilderness survival 2. Camping -- Handbooks, manuals, etc 3. Outdoor life -- Handbooks, manuals, etc 4. Outdoor recreation -- Handbooks, manuals, etc 5. Wilderness survival -- Handbooks, manuals, etc 6. Camping -- Equipment and supplies -- Handbooks, manuals, etc
ISBN 1440587965; 9781440587962

LC 2015008301

This book, by Dave Canterbury, "goes beyond bushcraft basics to teach you how to survive in the backcountry with little or no equipment.

. . . He covers crucial survival skills like tracking to help you get even closer to wildlife, crafting medicines from plants, and navigating without the use of a map or compass. He also offers ways to improvise and save money on bushcraft essentials like fire-starting tools and packs." (Publisher's note)

Sprinkle, Timothy

Lost and stranded; expert advice on how to survive being alone in the wilderness. Timothy Sprinkle. Skyhorse Publishing 2017 xvii, 275 p.p illustrations (paperback) $17.99 **613.69**

1. First aid 2. Outdoor life 3. Wilderness survival
ISBN 9781510727700; 9781510727724; 1510727701

In this book, "author Timothy Sprinkle breaks down the perils that can befall hikers, hunters, and other outdoor enthusiasts. There are animal encounters, weather events (lightning strikes), parasites (giardia), biting insects (bees/wasps), winter hazards (avalanches), natural disasters (forest fires), hypothermia, dehydration, disorientation, and much, much more to worry about." (Publisher's note)

613.7   Physical fitness

American College of Sports Medicine

★ **Complete** guide to fitness & health; Barbara Bushman, editor. Human Kinetics 2011 396p il pa $21.95   **613.7**

1. Health 2. Exercise 3. Physical fitness
ISBN 978-0-7360-9337-8; 0-7360-9337-0

LC 2011-6563

"Contributions from a range of academics (many affiliated with the ACSM) distill the current thinking on nutrition and exercise for all ages and for adults with chronic conditions such as arthritis and diabetes. They discuss how to determine your current levels of fitness, create a graduated fitness plan and coordinate it with proper eating habits, and measure your progress and maintain your optimum level. Chapters include recommendations for those with special health and medical conditions, such as diabetes, high cholesterol, high blood pressure, and arthritis. . . . Anyone who is serious about getting in shape will want this guide." Libr J

Includes bibliographical references

Bercovici, Jeff

Play on; the new science of elite performance at any age. Jeff Bercovici. Houghton Mifflin Harcourt 2018 288 p. (hardback) $27   **613.7**

1. Sports for older people 2. Aging -- Physiological aspects 3. Older people -- Physical fitness 4. Sports sciences 5. Exercise for older people 6. Physical fitness for older people
ISBN 9780544809987

LC 2017050323

"Season after season, today's sports superstars seem to defy the limits of physical aging. . . . How much of the difference is genetic destiny and how much can be attributed to better training, medicine and technology? Is athletic longevity a skill that can be taught, or a mental discipline that can be mastered? . . . Journalist Jeff Bercovici spent extensive time with professional . . . athletes, coaches and doctors to find the answers to these questions." (Publisher's note)

"Bercovici smartly separates science from quackery—avoiding GMO foods won't help, he argues, but taking creatine will—while offering colorful reportage on sports trainers, physiologists, and gurus, and using his own achy frame to road test their wares, from -286 °F cryotherapy chamber to an exercise/torture device called the Versaclimber." Pub Wkly

Includes bibliographical references and index

Bonifonte, Philip

T'ai chi for seniors; how to gain flexibility, strength, and inner peace. New Page Bks. 2004 213p il pa $16.99 **613.7**

1. Tai chi

ISBN 1-564-14697-9

LC 2003-60207

The author describes the ancient Chinese exercise that focuses "on easy, gentle movements that increase aerobic capacity, decrease blood pressure and stress, and improve balance and joint function. Along with a short history of various tai chi styles philosophies, the text features breathing techniques, warm-up exercises, movement forms, and meditation exercises with modifications for those with limited mobility." Libr J

Broad, William J.

The **science** of yoga; William J. Broad. Simon & Schuster 2012 xxxi, 298p ill. **613.7**

1. Exercise 2. Hatha yoga 3. Yoga -- History

ISBN 9781451641424; 9781451641431; 9781451641448

LC 2011020408

This book, "[f]ive years in the making, . . . draws on more than a century of . . . research to present the first impartial evaluation of a practice thousands of years old. It celebrates what's real and shows what's illusory, describes what's uplifting and beneficial and what's flaky and dangerous--and why. Broad illuminates how yoga can lift moods and inspire creativity. He exposes moves that can cripple and kill. . . . [The book] presents a . . . body of evidence that raises questions about whether humans have latent capabilities for entering states of suspended animation and unremitting sexual bliss. 'The Science of Yoga' takes us on a . . . tour of unknown yoga that goes from old archives in Calcutta to the world capitals of medical research, from storied ashrams to spotless laboratories, from sweaty yoga studios with master teachers to the cozy offices of yoga healers." (Publisher's note)

Budig, Kathryn

Aim true; love your body, eat without fear, nourish your spirit, discover true balance! Kathryn Budig. William Morrow 2016 336 p. (paperback) $24.99 **613.7**

1. Self 2. Yoga 3. Health 4. Exercise 5. Hatha yoga 6. Physical fitness 7. Women -- Health and hygiene

ISBN 0062419714; 9780062419712

LC 2015034599

In this book author Kathyrn Budig "extends her empowering message beyond the [yoga] mat. Whether your goal is to love who you are right now, reshape the way you view food, develop a meditation practice, or discover new ways to embrace the great balancing act that is life, this holistic approach to yoga, diet, and mindfulness has something for you." (Publisher's note)

"In an age that increasingly commercializes the ancient practice of yoga, Budig's wholesome, down-to-earth outlook is welcome, sure to aid readers of all shapes and sizes in establishing healthy food and exercise patterns while practicing self-love and acceptance." Publisher's Weekly

Contreras, Bret

Strong curves; a woman's guide to building a better butt and body. Victory Belt Pub. 2013 320 p. color illustrations $34.95 **613.7**

1. Exercise 2. Women -- Health and hygiene

ISBN 1936608642; 9781936608645

Written by Bret Contreras, "'Strong Curves' offers an extensive fitness and nutrition guide for women seeking to improve their physique,

function, strength, and mobility. . . . Each page is packed with information decoding the female anatomy, providing a better understanding as to why most fitness programs fail to help women reach their goals." (Publisher's note)

Cordoza, Glen

Becoming a supple leopard; the ultimate guide to resolving pain, preventing injury, and optimizing athletic performance. by Kelly Starrett, Glen Cordoza. Victory Belt Pub. 2013 400 p. color illustrations $59.95 **613.7**

1. Human locomotion 2. Physical education

ISBN 1936608588; 9781936608584

This book, by Kelly Starrett with Glen Cordoza, "maps out a detailed system comprised of more than two hundred techniques and illuminates common movement errors that cause injury and rob you of speed, power, endurance, and strength. Whether you are a professional athlete, a weekend warrior, or simply someone wanting to live healthy and free from restrictions, . . . [this book] will teach you how to maintain your body and harness your genetic potential." (Publisher's note)

Cucuzzella, Mark

Run for your life; how to run, walk, and move without pain or injury and achieve a sense of well-being and joy. Mark Cucuzzella. Alfred A. Knopf 2018 384 p. (hardback) $26.95 **613.7**

1. Running 2. Sports medicine 3. Physical fitness 4. Running -- Training 5. Running injuries -- Prevention 6. Running -- Physiological aspects

ISBN 9781101946305

LC 2017056684

In this book Dr. Mark Cucuzzella "explains the simple mechanics of how our bodies have evolved and adapted to run. Despite our natural ability and our human need to run, each year more than half of all runners suffer injuries. Pain and discouragement inevitably follow. Cucuzzella's book outlines the proven, practical techniques to avoid injury and reach the goal of personal fitness and overall health." (Publisher's note)

Includes bibliographical references and index

Dawn, Karena

Tone it up; balanced and beautiful; 5-day reset for your body, mind, and spirit. Katrina Scott and Karena Dawn. HarperCollins 2018 256 p. $27.99 **613.7**

1. Physical fitness 2. Self-help techniques 3. Women -- Physical fitness 4. Exercise for women. 5. Physical fitness for women. 6. Women -- Health and hygiene.

ISBN 0062843486; 9780062843487

LC 2018055738

This book, by Katrina Scott and Karena Dawn, "is a guide to focusing on the amazing woman that is you, with a 5-day plan to Refresh, Motivate, Inspire, Energize, and last but not least, Relax. Filled with daily fitness routines, delicious recipes, wisdom to transform your mindset, and all the love and advice of the TIU community, Karena and Katrina make it easier than ever to reach your goals and feel great." (Publisher's note)

Durant, John

Spartan Fit; 30 Days. Transform Your Mind. Transform Your Body. Commit to Grit. by Joe De Sena and John Durant. Houghton Mifflin Harcourt 2016 256 p. illustrations $24 **613.7**

1. Physical fitness

ISBN 0544439600; 9780544439603

This book, by Joe De Sena and John Durant, presents "a complete

30-day workout and diet plan to help you reach peak performance. . . . De Sena designed the Spartan races to test overall conditioning: strength, flexibility, endurance, and speed. His signature take-no-prisoners approach to achieving physical and mental fitness has taken the endurance world by storm and inspired millions." (Publisher's note)

"This book is ideal for workout enthusiasts who want to push themselves to the limit." Pub Wkly

Includes bibliographical references (page 201) and recipes.

Epstein, David

The **sports** gene; inside the science of extraordinary athletic performance. David Epstein. Current 2013 352 p. $26.95 **613.7**

1. Athletes 2. Genetics 3. Human genetics 4. Sports -- Physiological aspects

ISBN 1591845114; 9781591845119

LC 2013013443

In this book, David Epstein investigates the connection between genetics and athletic ability. "Drawing on interviews with athletes and scientists, he points out that 'a nation succeeds in a sport not only by having many people who practice prodigiously at sport-specific skills, but also by getting the best all-around athletes into the right sports in the first place.'" (Publishers Weekly)

"[T]his book is essential reading for sports fans interested in the science of sports, and for readers (not scholars) interested in the science of human differences." LJ

Includes bibliographical references and index

Grossman, Gail Boorstein

Restorative yoga for life; Gail Boorstein Grossman, E-RYT, CYKT. Adams Media Corp 2014 254 p. color illustrations (pb) $19.99 **613.7**

1. Rest 2. Yoga 3. Hatha yoga 4. Relaxation

ISBN 1440575207; 9781440575204

LC 2014026432

This book, by Gail Boorstein Grossman, "teaches you how to practice restorative yoga--a form of yoga that focuses on physical and mental relaxation through poses aided by props. . . . While restorative yoga is beneficial for your entire body, Gail also shows you how to treat more than twenty ailments, such as headaches, digestive issues, and anxiety, through specific yoga poses and sequences." (Publisher's note)

Hanoch, Doron

The **yoga** lifestyle; Using the Flexitarian Method to Ease Stress, Find Balance, and Create a Healthy Life. Doron Hanoch. Llewellyn Publications 2016 384 p. illustrations $19.99 **613.7**

1. Health 2. Hatha yoga 3. Vegetarianism 4. Stress management 5. Vegetarians 6. Medicine, Ayurvedic

ISBN 9780738748665

LC 2016002999

This book, by Doron Hanoch, "expands on the concept of the flexitarian diet to help you build an entire flexitarian lifestyle. Integrating yoga, Ayurveda, breathing practices, meditation, nutrition, and recipes—the flexitarian method takes a holistic approach to cultivating health and joy. Presenting techniques that can be utilized immediately, this book helps you become flexible in mind and body so that you can adapt to the needs and changes of today's world." (Publisher's note)

"It is clear from this thoughtful guide that Hanoch has the determination and know-how to introduce readers from all walks of life to a happier and healthier mode of living." Pub Wkly

Includes bibliographical references

Hesson, James L.

Weight training for life; 9th ed.; Wadsworth/Cengage Learning 2010 178p il $59.95 **613.7**

1. Weight lifting

ISBN 978-0-495-55909-2; 0-495-55909-1

LC 2010291364

First published 1985 by Morton

"The text contains hundreds of full-color photos demonstrating exercises and proper techniques. It also contains forms for writing goals, planning a personal weight-training program, and recording circumference, strength, and muscle endurance measurements." Publisher's note

Includes bibliographical references

Isacowitz, Rael

Pilates; Rael Isacowitz. 2nd ed Human Kinetics 2014 373 p. illustrations $22.95 **613.7**

1. Pilates method

ISBN 1450434169; 9781450434164

LC 2013019507

This book, by Rael Isacowitz, is a "comprehensive guide on Pilates. . . . In this second edition, [a] world-renowned Pilates expert . . . shows you the same repertoire that he has used to train multiple Olympians as well as an elite group of professional instructors who work with celebrities and athletes around the world." (Publisher's note)

Includes bibliographical references and index

Krasno, Jeff

Wanderlust; A Modern Yogi's Guide to Discovering Your Best Self. Jeff Krasno, Sarah Herrington, and Nicole Lindstrom. St. Martin's Press 2015 304 p. illustrations (chiefly color) $24.99 **613.7**

1. Yoga 2. Self-perception

ISBN 1623363500; 9781623363505

LC 2015023375

This book by Jeff Krasno, Sarah Herrington, and Nicole Lindstrom "a road map for the millions of people engaged in cultivating their best selves. For the 20 million people who grab their yoga mats in the United States every week, this book gives a completely unique way to understand 'yoga'--not just as something to do in practice, but as a broader principle for living." (Publisher's note)

"A reader can, in effect, experience the festival's essence through the book, which includes yoga routines, meditation guidance, blank pages for guided journaling and drawing, and recipes for conscious eating. The richly illustrated volume is a souvenir, a sampler of yoga lifestyle activities, and, perhaps, a vicarious trip for those who have yet to go in search of their own 'true north.'" Pub Wkly

Kunitz, Daniel

Lift; Fitness Culture, from Naked Greeks and Acrobats to Jazzercise and Ninja Warriors. Daniel Kunitz. Harper Wave 2016 336 p. (hardback) $26.99 **613.7**

1. Exercise 2. Physical fitness 3. Sports -- History 4. Exercise -- Social aspects 5. Physical fitness -- Social aspects 6. Physical education and training -- Social aspects

ISBN 9780062336187

LC 2016004087

This book by Daniel Kunitz explores "the ways in which human exercise and physical ideals have changed over time—and what we can learn from our past. . . . Humans have been conditioning our bodies . . . for a variety of reasons: to imitate gods, to be great warriors, to build nations, . . . to achieve physical perfection. . . . Behind each of these goals is a story and method of exercise that . . . sheds light on aspects of . . .

multi-faceted fitness culture of today." (Publisher's note)

"Kunitz includes his own challenges with fitness along the way, making this a book not just for those interested in the roots of fitness, but for anyone who struggles to live healthily." Pub Wkly

Includes bibliographical references ([291] - 304) and index.

Lacerda, Daniel

2,100 Asanas; the complete yoga poses. Daniel Lacerda, Founder of Mr. Yoga, Inc. Black Dog & Leventhal 2015 736 p. color illustrations (hardback) $35 **613.7**
  1. Hatha yoga 2. Yoga 3. Exercise
  ISBN 9781631910104

LC 2015026283

This book, by Daniel Lacerda, "is a . . . meticulously crafted catalog of yoga poses and modifications. . . . Each photograph features an expert yogi performing the pose to perfection. . . . The book is organized into eight major types of poses-standing, seated, core, quadruped, backbends, inversions, prone, and supine-and further broken down by families of poses that progress from easiest to more challenging." (Publisher's note)

"For readers with an interest in yoga, from beginners to advanced experts." Library Journal

Liebman, Hollis

1,500 stretches; the complete guide to flexibility and movement. Hollis Liebman. Black Dog & Leventhal 2017 736 p. (hardcover) $35 **613.7**
  1. Stretching exercises
  ISBN 0316440353; 9780316440356; 9780316473682

LC 2017940502

Liebman, Hollis Lance

Encyclopedia of Exercise Anatomy; by Hollis Liebman. Firefly Books Ltd 2014 392 p. color illustrations $49.95 **613.7**
  1. Exercise
  ISBN 1770854436; 9781770854437

LC 2015301045

This book on exercise, by Hollis Liebman, "enables the reader to tailor a personalized and professional program that will meet specific needs. A runner can dip into yoga to improve his breathing; a muscle builder can shape her legs with cycling workouts; a gymnast can combine yoga with core stability and strength exercises, and a woman over 50 can design a program that fits into her busy life." (Publisher's note)

"This useful title, which will also work well as a circulating item, presents that something extra for fitness enthusiasts who want to become serious about their conditioning." LJ

McClusky, Mark

Faster, higher, stronger; how sports science is creating a new generation of superathletes, and what we can learn from them. Mark McClusky. Hudson Street Press 2014 288 p. (alk. paper) $25.95 **613.7**
  1. Sports science 2. Sports medicine 3. Athletes -- Training 4. Sports sciences 5. Athletes -- Training of
  ISBN 1594631530; 9781594631535

LC 2014021223

This book, by Mark McClusky, explores how "today, it's impossible to separate the achievements of athletes from the scientists who support them. . . . [This volume] brings readers behind the scenes with a new generation of athletes, coaches, and scientists whose accomplishments are changing our understanding of human physical achievement and completely redefining the limits of the human body." (Publisher's note)

"All of this trickles down to amateur athletics as well, and McClusky

does a good job of relating cutting-edge science to people wanting to run their 5K a little faster or shave a few strokes off their golf handicap." Booklist

Includes bibliographical references and index

Pagano, Joan

Strength training exercises for women; exercises for women. Joan Pagano. DK Publishing 2014 336 p. color illustrations $22.95 **613.7**
  1. Weight lifting 2. Women -- Health and hygiene 3. Muscle strength 4. Exercise for women 5. Weight training for women 6. Physical fitness for women
  ISBN 1465415807; 9781465415806

LC 2014397527

"Packed with more than 200 visual step-by-step exercises designed to burn calories, strengthen the core, and tone the body, 'Strength Training for Women' is a must-have for core-conscious women who want to target key areas of their body and maintain all-round strength and fitness." (Publisher's note)

Pohlman, Dean

Yoga fitness for men; build strength, improve performance, increase flexibility. Dean Pohlman. Alpha Books 2018 192 p. color illustrations $19.99 **613.7**
  1. Hatha yoga 2. Physical fitness 3. Men -- Health and hygiene
  ISBN 9781465473486

LC 2017956773

This book, by Dean Pohlman, "will teach you how to execute the yoga postures you need for greater endurance, flexibility, balance, and strength. Workouts and multi-week programs are tailored to your specific performance and health goals, such as increased core strength, rotational power, or back pain relief. You'll find that incorporating yoga into your training will help you get stronger, play harder, and feel better." (Publisher's note)

Reynolds, Gretchen

The first 20 minutes; surprising science reveals how we can exercise better, train smarter, live longer. Gretchen Reynolds. Hudson Street Press 2012 xvii, 266 p.p **613.7**
  1. Health 2. Exercise 3. Physical fitness 4. Exercise -- Popular Works 5. Exercise -- Physiological aspects 6. Physical Fitness -- Popular Works 7. Exercise -- physiology -- Popular Works 8. Physical education and training -- Physiological aspects
  ISBN 1594630933; 9781594630934

LC 2012000321

This book by Gretchen Reynolds offers "findings about the mental and physical benefits of exercise, personal stories from scientists and laypeople alike, as well as researched-based prescriptions for readers, . . . show[ing] what kind of exercise—and how much—is necessary to stay healthy, get fit, and attain a smaller jeans size. Inspired by Reynolds's . . . 'Phys Ed' column for 'The New York Times,' this book explains how exercise affects the body in distinct ways and provides the tools readers need to achieve their fitness goals, whether that's a faster 5K or staying trim." (Publisher's note)

Schuler, Lou

Strong; Nine Workout Programs for Women to Burn Fat, Boost Metabolism, and Build Strength for Life. by Lou Schuler and Alwyn Cosgrove. Avery, an imprint of Penguin Random House 2015 304 p. illustrations (hardback) $27.95 **613.7**
  1. Exercise 2. Weight lifting 3. Women -- Health and hygiene 4. Exercise for women 5. Weight training for women

ISBN 9781583335758

LC 2015015248

In this book, fitness author Lou Schuler and strength coach Alwyn Cosgrove "present a comprehensive strength and conditioning plan to help women burn fat and build muscle by getting them off the machines and revolutionizing how they work out." (Publisher's note)

"This book is thoughtful, precise, and well-geared to providing women of all ages and fitness backgrounds with the knowledge and tools necessary for building strength." Pub Wkly

Stanley, Jessamyn

Every body yoga; let go of fear, get on the mat, love your body. Jessamyn Stanley. Workman Pub Co 2017 232 p. color illustrations $16.95; (ebook) $16.95   **613.7**
1. Yoga 2. Exercise 3. Hatha yoga
ISBN 0761193111; 9780761193111; 9781523500208

LC 2017009009

This book, by Jessamyn Stanley, is "a book for readers already doing yoga, looking to refresh their practice or find new ways to stay motivated. It's a how-to book: Here are easy-to-follow directions to 50 basic yoga poses and 10 sequences to practice at home, all photographed in full color. It's a book that challenges the larger issues of body acceptance and the meaning of beauty." (Publisher's note)

"This touching work is a must for those new to yoga, no matter their age or body type." Pub Wkly

Starrett, Kelly

Ready to run; unlocking your potential to run naturally. Simon & Schuster 2014 288 p. $29.95   **613.7**
1. Running 2. Athletes -- Wounds and injuries
ISBN 1628600098; 9781628600094

"The harsh effects of too much sitting and too much time wearing the wrong shoes has left us shackled to lower back problems, chronic knee injuries, and debilitating foot pain. In this book [by Kelly Starrett and T. J. Murphy], you will learn the 12 standards that will prepare your body for a lifetime of top-performance running." (Publisher's note)

Taubes, Gary

Why we get fat and what to do about it. Alfred A. Knopf 2011 257p $24.95   **613.7**
1. Obesity 2. Weight loss 3. Low-carbohydrate diet
ISBN 978-0-307-27270-6; 0-307-27270-2

LC 2010-34248

The author "assures readers that overweight and obesity are not character flaws but a disorder of fat accumulation; most of the book deals with this issue in detail. This brave, paradigm-shifting man uses logic and the primary literature to unhinge the nutritional mantra of the last 80 years that an imbalance of 'calories in versus calories out' leads to weight change." Choice

Includes bibliographical references

Wertheim, L. Jon

4-minute fit; the weight loss solution for the time-crunched, deskbound, and stressed-out. Siphiwe Baleka, "America's Fittest Trucker", with L. Jon Wertheim. Touchstone 2017 xiii, 224 p.p illustrations (paperback) $16.99   **613.7**
1. Exercise 2. Metabolism 3. Weight loss 4. Physical fitness 5. Exercise -- Popular works 6. Weight loss -- Popular works
ISBN 9781501129834; 9781501129773

LC 2016038003

This book, by Siphiwe Baleka, with L. Jon Wertheim, is a "a revolutionary metabolism-spiking program for anyone who feels they don't

have enough time, equipment, or money to get in shape and lose those extra pounds. . . . Baleka's program is geared not only for those who drive eighteen-wheelers, but also for anyone who travels for work, has a job that involves a lot of sitting, or doesn't think they have enough time to exercise and eat better." (Publisher's note)

613.704   Special topics of physical fitness

Marcum, Andrea

Close to om; stretching yoga from your mat to your life. Andrea Marcum. St. Martin's Griffin 2018 x, 214 p.p illustrations (chiefly color) (paperback) $19.99   **613.704**
1. Yoga 2. Hatha yoga 3. Mindfulness (Psychology)
ISBN 9781250127594; 9781250127600; 1250127599

This book, by Andrea Marcum, "promotes and teaches mindfulness in both your yoga practice and your everyday life. . . . [It] offers a guide to teach all three aspects of yoga showcasing Marcum's signature unique style, this program combines the teaching of poses with the exploration of yoga philosophy and insight into meditation and mindfulness." (Publisher's note)

"L.A. yoga teacher Marcum brings her reflective, challenging yoga perspective and practice to the page in this inspiring guide for both beginners and seasoned practitioners." Pub Wkly

Includes bibliographical references and index.

613.71   Exercise and sports activities

Copeland, Misty, 1982-

Ballerina body; dancing and eating your way to a leaner, stronger, and more graceful you. Misty Copeland, with Charisse Jones ; movement and dance photography by Henry Leutwyler, food photography by Amy Roth. Grand Central Life & Style 2017 xii, 226 p.p illustrations (some color) (Hardcover) $30   **613.71**
1. Ballet 2. Eating habits 3. Physical fitness 4. Nutrition 5. Ballet dancing 6. Reducing diets 7. Ballet dancers -- Nutrition 8. Ballet dancers -- Training of
ISBN 9781455596300; 9781455569878

LC 2016033443

In this book author Misty Copeland attempts to "show women how to find the motivation to get healthier and stronger, and how to reshape their bodies to be lean and flexible, with step-by-step advice, meal plans, workout routines, and words of inspiration. Celebrating the importance of healthy fats and a fitness regimen based on ballet exercises, Misty shares her own time-tested exercises and an eating plan focusing on healthy fats, both of which keep her in top shape." (Publisher's note)

Green, Louise

Big fit girl; embrace the body you have. Louise Green ; foreword by Jess Weiner. Greystone Books 2017 xi, 236 p.p illustrations $16.95   **613.71**
1. Women -- Physical fitness
ISBN 1771642122; 9781771642125

This book, by Louise Green, "describes how the fitness industry fails to meet the needs of plus-size women and thus prevents them from improving their health and fitness. By telling her own story of how she stopped dieting, got off the couch, and unleashed her inner athlete—as well as showcasing similar stories from other women—Green inspires other plus-size women to do the same." (Publisher's note)

"Green, an athlete and personal trainer who founded a plus-size fitness boot camp, has written an inspiring and useful book for women who see their size as an impediment to getting fit and healthy." Pub Wkly.

Includes bibliographical references (pages 225-226) and index.

613.794   Sleep

Huffington, Arianna Stassinopoulos, 1950-

The **sleep** revolution; transforming your life, one night at a time. Arianna Huffington. Harmony 2016 400 p. (hardback) $26   **613.794**

1. Sleep 2. Sleep deprivation 3. Sleep -- Health aspects
ISBN 9781101904008

LC 2015039918

This book, by Arianna Huffington, is an "exploration of sleep from all angles, from the history of sleep, to the role of dreams in our lives, to the consequences of sleep deprivation, and the new golden age of sleep science that is revealing the vital role sleep plays in our every waking moment and every aspect of our health – from weight gain, diabetes, and heart disease to cancer and Alzheimer's." (Publisher's note)

"So compelling and informative is Huffington's book that everyone should read it and sleep!" Booklist

Includes bibliographical references (pages [315]-375) and index.

Reiss, Benjamin

Wild nights; how taming sleep created our restless world. Benjamin Reiss. Basic Books 2017 305 p. (hardcover) $28   **613.794**

1. Sleep 2. Sleep disorders 3. Sleep -- History
ISBN 9780465061952; 9781541698758

LC 2016043568

In this book author Benjamin Reiss, "finds answers in sleep's hidden history--one that leads to our present, sleep-obsessed society, its tacitly accepted rules, and their troubling consequences. . . . Reiss weaves together insights from literature, social and medical history, and cutting-edge science to show how and why we have tried and failed to tame sleep." (Publisher's note)

"This is a captivating examination and Reiss gives readers much to ponder long into the night." Pub Wkly

Includes bibliographical references (pages 273-291) and index.

613.835   Cannabis

Dolce, Joe

Brave new weed; adventures into the uncharted world of cannabis. Joe Dolce. HarperCollins 2016 288 p. (ebook) $24.99; (hardcover) $25.99   **613.835**

1. Marijuana 2. Cannabis 3. Cannabis -- Utilization 4. Cannabis -- Social aspects
ISBN 9780062499943; 9780062499912; 0062499912

LC 2016288356

In this book, author Joe Dolce "adventures into the fascinating 'brave new world' of cannabis, tracing its history and possible future as he investigates the social, medical, legal, and cultural ramifications of this surprisingly versatile plant. . . . We all think we know what cannabis is and what we use it for. But do we? Our collective understanding of this surprising plant has been muddled by politics and morality; what we think we know isn't the real story." (Publisher's note)

"This is an interesting overview of the world of marijuana, and Dolce's easygoing narrative style holds lots of appeal for an ever-growing audience." Booklist

Includes bibliographical references (pages 267-275).

613.9   Birth control, reproductive technology, sex hygiene, sexual techniques

Comfort, Alex, 1920-2000

The **joy** of sex; The Ultimate Revised Edition. Alex Comfort, Susan Quilliam. Rev. ed. Crown Publishers 2008 288 p. ill. (some col.) (hc) $29.95   **613.9**

1. Sex 2. Sex education 3. Sex -- Psychological aspects
ISBN 9780307452030; 0307452034

LC 2008017531

"An international bestseller since it was first published in 1972, Dr. Alex Comfort's classic work dared to celebrate the joy of human physical intimacy with such authority and candor that a whole generation felt empowered to enjoy sex. . . . Substantial revisions from sex expert and relationship psychologist Susan Quilliam include new information on [k]ey scientific discoveries in the fields of psychology, physiology, and sexology." (Publisher's note)

Includes bibliographical references and index

Kerner, Ian

She comes first; The Thinking Man's Guide to Pleasuring a Woman. Ian Kerner. ReganBooks 2004 228 p. (ebook) $15.99; $22.99   **613.9**

1. Sex 2. Sex education 3. Oral sex 4. Female orgasm 5. Sex instruction for men
ISBN 9780061792649; 0060538252; 9780060538255

LC 2004041787

This book, by Ian Kerner, "offers a radical new philosophy for pleasuring women. . . . An indispensable aid to a healthier, more fulfilling sex life for her and him, [it] offers techniques and philosophy that have already earned raves from the likes of bestselling author and Loveline co-host Dr. Drew Pinsky." (Publisher's note)

"Dispelling the widely held myth of genital penetration as the apogee of sexual pleasure, Kerner, who holds a doctorate in clinical sexology, offers this witty, well-researched manual for 'consistently leading women to orgasm' through cunnilingus." Pub Wkly

Includes bibliographical references (p. [225]-226)

Nagoski, Emily

Come as you are; the surprising new science of women's sexual wellbeing. Emily Nagoski, Ph.D. Simon & Schuster 2015 400 p. (hardcover) $16   **613.9**

1. Sex education 2. Sexual hygiene 3. Women -- Sexual behavior 4. Women -- Health and hygiene 5. Sexual health 6. Sex instruction for women
ISBN 1476762090; 9781476762098; 9781476762104

LC 2014017773

This book, by Dr. Emily Nagoski, is an "exploration of why and how women's sexuality works. . . . Cutting-edge research across multiple disciplines tells us that the most important factor for women in creating and sustaining a fulfilling sex life, is not what you do in bed or how you do it, but how you feel about it. Which means that stress, mood, trust, and body image are not peripheral factors in a woman's sexual wellbeing; they are central to it." (Publisher's note)

"An essential purchase for consumer health and women's health collections. This book will empower women to fully understand why their sexual desire is so different from men's." LJ

Includes bibliographical references

Smiler, Andrew P.

Dating and sex; A Guide for the 21st Century Teen Boy. by Andrew P. Smiler. Magination Press 2016 288 p. (pbk.) $14.95   **613.9**

1. Teenage boys -- Sexual behavior 2. Sex education -- Juvenile literature 3. Dating (Social customs) -- Juvenile literature 4. Interpersonal attraction -- Juvenile literature 5. Sex instruction for teenagers -- Juvenile literature
ISBN 1433820455; 9781433820458

LC 2015019582

This book by Andrew P. Smiler provides teenage boys "with the knowledge they need to understand dating, relationships, and sex. It goes beyond basic descriptions of biological processes with a progressive, practical approach that relies on secular ethics and emphasizes sexual health and personal responsibility. The book . . . provides a framework for dating and sex that fits their values and identity." (Publisher's note)

Includes bibliographical references and index

Vernacchio, Al

For goodness sex; changing the way we talk to teens about sexuality, values, and health. Al Vernacchio, with Brooke Lea Foster. HarperWave 2014 272 p. (hardback) $25.99   **613.9**

1. Sex education 2. Teenagers -- Sexual behavior 3. Sexual ethics 4. Parent and teenager 5. Sex instruction for teenagers
ISBN 0062269518; 9780062269515

LC 2014019134

This book by Al Vernacchio offers a "progressive, effective, and responsible approach to sex education for parents and teens that challenges traditional teaching models and instead embraces 21st century realities by promoting healthy sexuality, values, and body image in young people." The book contains "examples from the classroom, exercises and quizzes, and a wealth of sample discussions and crucial information." (Publisher's note)

Weschler, Toni

Taking charge of your fertility; the definitive guide to natural birth control, pregnancy achievement, and reproductive health. Toni Weschler, MPH. 20th anniversary edition William Morrow/HarperCollins 2015 536 p. illustrations pbk $25.99   **613.9**

1. Birth control 2. Human fertility
ISBN 9780062326034; 0062326031

Includes bibliographical references and index

This book, by Toni Weschler, is "a thoroughly revised and expanded edition of the leading book on fertility and women's reproductive health. Since [it was first published] two decades ago, Toni Weschler has taught a whole new generation of women how to become pregnant, avoid pregnancy naturally and gain better control of their gynecological and sexual health by taking just a couple minutes a day using the proven Fertility Awareness Method." (Publisher's note)

613.907   Education

Roffman, Deborah

Talk to me first; everything you need to know to become your kids' "go-to" person about sex. by Deborah Roffman. 1st ed. Da Capo Lifelong 2012 xii, 281 p.p (pbk.; alk. paper) $14.99   **613.907**

1. Parenting 2. Conversation 3. Sex education 4. Parent and child 5. Parent and teenager 6. Sexual ethics for teenagers 7. Sex

instruction for children 8. Sex instruction for teenagers
ISBN 0738215082; 9780738215082; 9780738215877

LC 2012006068

This book presents a "guide for parents contemplating how to talk to their children about [sex]. . . . [Deborah] Roffman discusses a laundry list of commonly used statements about sex and doesn't shy away from more sensitive material such as abstinence, gay and transgendered kids, sexually transmitted infections and rape. Throughout, she emphasizes the importance of positive, direct interaction with children." (Kirkus Reviews)

Includes bibliographical references (p. 245-251) and index.

613.96   Sexual techniques

Graham, Jessica

Good sex; getting off without checking out. Jessica Graham. North Atlantic Books 2017 xv, 285 p.p (trade paper; alk. paper) $16.95   **613.96**

1. Sex education 2. Family life education 3. Sex instruction
ISBN 9781623172350; 1623172349; 9781623172343

LC 2017036252

In this book, author "Jessica Graham demonstrates that a deep spiritual life and an extraordinary sex life are not mutually exclusive in this keenly personal and unflinchingly frank guide to finding mindfulness in sex without losing the fun and adventure. Not only a tool kit for creating a rich and deeply satisfying sex life, this . . . book conveys the deeper message of how combining meditation with sex can bring about profound spiritual awakenings." (Publisher's note)

Includes bibliographical references

614   Forensic medicine; incidence of injuries, wounds, disease; public preventive medicine

Balko, Radley, 1975-

★ The **cadaver** king and the country dentist; a true story of injustice in the American South. Radley Balko and Tucker Carrington. PublicAffairs 2017 416 p. (hardcover) $28   **614**

1. Trials (Rape) 2. Judicial error 3. Trials (Homicide) 4. Trials (Rape) -- Mississippi 5. Judicial error -- Mississippi 6. Trials (Murder) -- Mississippi 7. Criminal justice, Administration of -- Mississippi
ISBN 9781610396912

LC 2017009508

This book, by Radley Balko and Tucker Carrington, "tells the haunting story of how the courts and Mississippi's death investigation system--a relic of the Jim Crow era--failed to deliver justice for its citizens. The authors argue that bad forensics, structural racism, and institutional failures are at fault, raising sobering questions about our ability to and willingness to address these crucial issues." (Publisher's note)

"hrough the intensive scrutiny of how the men were speedily tried, convicted, and then released after years in prison, the authors uncover an unholy alliance of racist cops and prosecutors with questionable death investigations and misapplied forensics. This work should spark both admiration and outrage—and, one hopes, reform." Booklist

Includes bibliographical references and index

Bass, William M.

Death's acre; inside the legendary forensic lab the Body Farm where the dead do tell tales. [by] Bill Bass and Jon Jefferson; foreword by Patricia Cornwell. Putnam 2003 304p il

670

$24.95; pa $15 **614**

1. Forensic anthropology
ISBN 0-399-15134-6; 0-425-19832-4 pa

LC 2003-46908

"The author explains the process of decomposition and how bones give clues to identify: approximate age, sex, height, and race, all of which are needed to bring the forensic scientist one step closer to putting a name to a corpse. He describes some of the cases he has been involved with and laughs at himself when he shares stories of mistakes and assumptions. Young adults will gain insight into the forensic process and appreciate Bass's dedication to the truth and his work." SLJ

Blum, Deborah

The **poisoner's** handbook; murder and the birth of forensic medicine in Jazz Age New York. Penguin Press 2010 319p pa $16; $25.95 **614**

1. Toxicology 2. Forensic sciences 3. Poisons and poisoning 4. Poisoning 5. Forensic toxicology 6. Forensic sciences -- History 7. Crime -- New York (N.Y.) -- History -- 20th century
ISBN 0-14-311882-X pa; 1-59420-243-5; 978-0-14-311882-4 pa; 978-1-59420-243-8

LC 2009-26461

This "history of the development of forensics in New York City . . . spans the years from 1915 to 1936." (N Y Times Book Rev) Index.

"Blum effectively balances the fast-moving detective story with a clear view of the scientific advances that her protagonists brought to the field. Caviar for true-crime fans and science buffs alike." Kirkus

Includes bibliographical references

Melinek, Judy

Working stiff; two years, 262 bodies, and the making of a medical examiner. Judy Melinek, MD and T.J. Mitchell. First Scribner hardcover ed Scribner 2014 272 p. (hardback) $25 **614**

1. Forensic sciences 2. Medical jurisprudence 3. Forensic pathologists -- New York (State) -- New York -- Biography 4. Medical examiners (Law) -- New York (State) -- New York -- Biography
ISBN 1476727252; 9781476727257; 9781476727264

LC 2014017610

This book, by Judy Melinek and T. J. Mitchell, offers a "memoir of a young forensic pathologist's 'rookie season' as a NYC medical examiner, and the cases--hair-raising and heartbreaking and impossibly complex--that shaped her as both a physician and a mother. . . . [It] offers a firsthand account of daily life in one of America's most arduous professions, and the unexpected challenges of shuttling between the domains of the living and the dead." (Publisher's note)

"Though some sections call for a strong stomach, armchair detectives and would-be forensic pathologists will find Melinek's well-written account to be inspiring and engaging." Pub Wkly

614.4   Incidence of and public measures to prevent disease

Conis, Elena

Vaccine nation; America's changing relationship with immunization. Elena Conis. University of Chicago Press 2015 344 p. (cloth; alkaline paper) $27.50 **614.4**

1. Vaccination 2. Immunization 3. Vaccination -- United States -- History -- 20th century
ISBN 0226923762; 9780226923765

LC 2014009846

This book by Elena Conis "opens in the 1960s, when government scientists--triumphant following successes combating polio and smallpox--considered how the country might deploy new vaccines against what they called the 'milder' diseases, including measles, mumps, and rubella. In the years that followed, Conis reveals, vaccines fundamentally changed how medical professionals, policy administrators, and ordinary Americans came to perceive the diseases they were designed to prevent." (Publisher's note)

"This fascinating book is for those interested in the history of medicine and in the relationship between medicine and American culture. Scholars, public health officials, and some general readers will find Conis's thesis—that changing social attitudes about the role of government in health, the place of individual freedoms, and an individual's duty to a larger society shaped how citizens thought about vaccines—to be cogent and carefully argued." LJ

Includes bibliographical references and index

Encyclopedia of plague and pestilence; from ancient times to the present. George Childs Kohn, editor. 3rd ed; Facts On File 2008 529p il map (Facts on File library of world history) $85 **614.4**

1. Reference books 2. Epidemics -- Encyclopedias
ISBN 978-0-8160-6935-4; 0-8160-6935-2

LC 2006-41296

First published 1995

This encyclopedia provides "descriptions of more than 700 epidemics, listed alphabetically by location of the outbreak. Each . . . entry includes when and where a particular epidemic began, how and why it happened, whom it affected, how it spread and ran its course, and its outcome and significance." Publisher's note

Includes bibliographical references

Fryer, Bronwyn

The **end** of epidemics; the looming threat to humanity and how to stop it. Jonathan D. Quick, MD, with Bronwyn Fryer. St. Martin's Press 2018 xii, 290 p.p illustrations, map (hardcover) $26.99 **614.4**

1. Epidemics 2. Communicable diseases -- Prevention 3. Epidemics -- Prevention
ISBN 9781250117786; 9781250117779

LC 2017037542

This book, by Jonathan D. Quick and Bronwyn Fryer, "examines the eradication of smallpox and devastating effects of influenza, AIDS, SARS, and Ebola. Analyzing local and global efforts to contain these diseases and citing firsthand accounts of failure and success, Dr. Quick proposes a new set of actions which he has coined 'The Power of Seven,' to end epidemics before they can begin." (Publisher's note)

Includes bibliographical references and index

Kinch, Michael

Between hope and fear; a history of vaccines and human immunity. Michael Kinch. W W Norton & Co Inc 2018 360 p. $27.95 **614.4**

1. Vaccines -- History 2. Vaccination -- History 3. Immunization -- History
ISBN 1681777517; 9781681777511

LC 2018080363

This book, by Michael Kinch, is a "smart and compelling examination of the science of immunity . . . and the real-world outcomes of failing to vaccinate. . . . [It] tells the remarkable story of vaccine-preventable infectious diseases and their social and political implications. While detailing the history of vaccine invention, Kinch reveals the ominous reality that our victories against vaccine-preventable diseases are not permanent--and could easily be undone." (Publisher's note)

"Kinch (radiation oncology, Washington Univ.; director, Ctr. for Research Innovation in Business; Prescription for Change), ostensibly writing to refute the dangerous rise of antivaccinators, provides readers with an interdisciplinary cornucopia of meticulously researched information on the intersection of history, disease, and vaccine invention." LJ

McNeill, William H. (William Hardy), 1917-2016

Plagues and peoples; William H. McNeill. Anchor Press 1998 340 p. map $17   **614.4**
    1. Epidemics -- History 2. Civilization -- History
    ISBN 9780385121224; 0385121229

                    LC 89027689

This book, by William Hardy McNeill, offers an interpretation "of world history as seen through the extraordinary impact . . . . of disease on cultures. From the conquest of Mexico by smallpox as much as by the Spanish, to the bubonic plague in China, to the typhoid epidemic in Europe, the history of disease is the history of humankind. With the identification of AIDS in the early 1980s, another chapter has been added to this chronicle of events." (Publisher's note)

Offit, Paul A.

★ **Deadly** choices; how the anti-vaccine movement threatens us all. Basic Books 2010 270p il $27.50   **614.4**
    1. Vaccination 2. Vaccination of children 3. Vaccination of children -- Complications
    ISBN 0-465-02149-2; 978-0-465-02149-9

                    LC 2010-22446

Offit examines the history of the anti-vaccine movement, opening with the "introduction of smallpox vaccination in 19th-century England and continuing to present-day anti-vaccine activism in the United States." (Sci Books Films) Bibliography. Index.

This "is a thorough dismantling of antivaccine notions and a sober warning about the resurgence of deadly childhood infections stemming from declining vaccination rates. Worried parents, especially, will find this a lucid, compelling riposte to antivaccine fear-mongering." Publ Wkly

Includes bibliographical references

Oldstone, Michael B. A.

Viruses, plagues, and history; past, present, and future. by Michael B.A. Oldstone. Rev and updated ed; Oxford University Press 2010 383p il map $17.95   **614.4**
    1. Viruses 2. Epidemics 3. Communicable diseases
    ISBN 978-0-19-532731-1; 0-19-532731-4

                    LC 2009-03550

First published 1998

Oldstone "focuses his tale on a few of the most famous viruses humanity has battled, beginning with some we have effectively defeated, such as smallpox, polio, and measles. . . . [He] then describes the fascinating viruses that have captured headlines in more recent years: Ebola and other hemorrhagic fevers, which literally turn their victims' organs to a bloody pulp; the Hantavirus outbreaks in the southwestern United States and elsewhere; mad cow disease, a frightening illness made worse by government mishandling and secrecy; and, of course, AIDS." Publisher's note

Includes bibliographical references (p. 343-369) and index. (BLCM)

Quammen, David, 1948-

★ **Spillover**; animal infections and the next human pandemic. David Quammen. W.W. Norton & Co. 2012 587 p.

(hardcover) $28.95   **614.4**
    1. Epidemics 2. Animals -- Diseases 3. Animals as carriers of disease
    ISBN 0393066800; 9780393066807

                    LC 2012029300

This book by David Quammen "sums up . . . what we know about some of the world's scariest scourges: Ebola, AIDS, pandemic influenza--and what we can do to thwart the 'NBO,' the Next Big One. The author discusses zoonoses, infectious diseases that originate in animals and spread to humans. . . . They persist because they are endemic in a reservoir population through a process of mutual adaptation." (Kirkus Reviews)

Includes bibliographical references and index

Sears, Robert W.

The **vaccine** book; making the right decision for your child. Robert W. Sears. 2nd ed. Little, Brown & Co. 2011 335 p. (Sears parenting library) pbk $16   **614.4**
    1. Vaccination 2. Children -- Health and hygiene 3. Vaccination of children 4. Immunization of children
    ISBN 9780316180528; 0316180521

                    LC 2011293797

In this book, author Robert W. Sears "devotes each chapter in the book to a disease/vaccine pair and offers a comprehensive discussion of what the disease is, how common or rare it is, how serious or harmless it is, the ingredients of the vaccine, and any possible side effects from the vaccine." (Publisher's note)

"The first 12 chapters discuss each vaccination in the childhood series, providing explanation of the relative disease, how the vaccine is made and points to assess a child's at-risk level when considering if the vaccine is necessary. Sears does offer guidance for those who are indecisive, offering his opinion based on clinical experience and 13 years of research taken from product inserts, pediatric reference books, articles and databases. Additional chapters illuminate more controversial aspects of the debate, such as how vaccine safety is researched and what the findings are, side effects and how to minimize them, common myths and questions." Pub Wkly

Includes bibliographical references and index

614.5   Incidence of and public measures to prevent specific diseases and kinds of diseases

Allen, Arthur

★ The **fantastic** laboratory of Dr. Weigl; how two brave scientists battled typhus and sabotaged the Nazis. Arthur Allen. W.W. Norton & Co. Inc 2014 400 p. illustrations, maps (hardcover) $26.95   **614.5**
    1. Typhus 2. Zoologists 3. World War, 1939-1945 -- Poland 4. Anti-Nazi movement -- Poland 5. Scientists -- Poland -- Biography 6. Typhus fever -- Poland -- History 7. World War, 1939-1945 -- Underground movements -- Poland
    ISBN 039308101X; 9780393081015

                    LC 2014003246

This book by Arthur Allen describes how "In the 1920s, [zoologist Rudolf] Weigl had created the first typhus vaccine . . . . giving him cover during the Nazi's violent occupation of Lviv. His lab soon flourished as a hotbed of resistance. Weigl hired otherwise doomed mathematicians, writers, doctors, and other thinkers, protecting them from atrocity. Among the scientists saved by Weigl, who was a Christian, was a gifted Jewish immunologist named Ludwik Fleck." (Publisher's note)

"Allen is unflinching in his retelling of this monstrous era, but he manages to avoid writing a depressing narrative. Instead, Weigl, Fleck and their vaccines illuminate the inherent social complexities of science and truth and reinforce the overriding good of man." Kirkus

Includes bibliographical references and index

Barry, John M.

The **great** influenza; the epic story of the deadliest plague in history. Viking 2004 546p il $29.95; pa $16   **614.5**
1. Influenza
ISBN 0-670-89473-7; 0-14-303649-1 pa

LC 2003-57646

In this account of the 1918 influenza pandemic, the author "explores how the deadly confluence of biology (a swiftly mutating flu virus that can pass between animals and humans) and politics (President Wilson's all-out war effort in WWI) created conditions in which the virus thrived, killing more than 50 million worldwide and perhaps as many as 100 million in just a year." Publ Wkly

Includes bibliographical references

Cantor, Norman F.

In the wake of the plague; the Black death and the world it made. 1st Perennial ed.; Perennial/HarperCollins 2002 245p il map pa $13.95   **614.5**
1. Plague
ISBN 0-06-001434-2

LC 2001-51819

First published 2001 by Free Press

"By animating history and demonstrating our times' connections to even as remote an event as the Black Death, Cantor's erudite excursion proves most engrossing." Booklist

Includes bibliographical references

Foege, William H., 1936-

House on fire; the fight to eradicate smallpox. University of California Press/Milbank Memorial Fund 2011 218p il map (California/Milbank books on health and the public) $29.95   **614.5**
1. Smallpox
ISBN 978-0-520-26836-4

LC 2010-41703

"Foege's emphasis on the personal does enliven the myriad statistics he presents. But he seems a reluctant memoirist, uncomfortable with the spotlight, and as a consequence, the story gets bogged down, at times, by Foege's need to mention (and compliment) every colleague with whom he ever collaborated. Still, though Foege is anything but self-congratulatory, it is impossible to read 'House on Fire' without admiring him and feeling grateful for the gift he gave to mankind." Boston Globe

Includes bibliographical references

Halperin, Daniel

Tinderbox; How the West Sparked the AIDS Epidemic and How the World Can Finally Overcome It. Craig Timberg and Daniel Halperin. Penguin Press HC 2012 421 p. ill. (hardback) $29.95   **614.5**
1. Imperialism 2. AIDS (Disease) 3. Communicable diseases -- History 4. Epidemiology -- Africa -- History 5. Pakistan -- History 6. Colonialism -- Africa 7. Western World -- Africa 8. India -- History -- Partition, 1947 9. HIV Infections -- etiology -- Africa 10. India -- Foreign relations -- Pakistan 11. Pakistan -- Foreign relations -- India 12. HIV Infections -- epidemiology -- Africa 13. Acquired Immunodeficiency Syndrome -- etiology -- Africa 14. Acquired Immunodeficiency Syndrome -- epidemiology -- Africa

ISBN 159420327X; 9781594203275

LC 2011040206

It was the authors' intent to "trace the history, growth and spread of HIV and present what will in the minds of many be a controversial approach to addressing the disease. . . . The key factor in the spread of the disease was the expansion of European colonialism in Africa. . . . [Craig] Timberg and [Daniel] Halperin examine how to confront it." (Kirkus Reviews)

Includes bibliographical references and index.

Holt, Nathalia

Cured; how the Berlin patients defeated HIV and forever changed medical science. Nathalia Holt. Dutton, published by the Penguin Group 2014 336 p. $27.95   **614.5**
1. Gene therapy 2. HIV infections 3. Gene therapy -- Germany -- Berlin -- History 4. HIV infections -- Treatment -- Germany -- Berlin
ISBN 0525953922; 9780525953920

LC 2013037181

In this book, HIV researcher Nathalia Holt "offers increasing hope for a cure by spotlighting the two male 'Berlin Patients' . . . who chemically bombarded and expunged the HIV virus from their bodies. The author tracks the enduring histories of these men--German-born Christian Hahn and Timothy Brown, an American. . . . Holt also profiles HIV specialists Heiko Jessen, Bruce Walker and David Ho." (Kirkus Reviews)

"[I]n this accessible and fascinating account, Holt . . . juggles genetic mysteries, research perils, the agonies of these two reserved and sensitive men diagnosed with what was considered a death sentence, and the dogged doctors who successfully treated them during the later stages of AIDS epidemic." Pub Wkly

Includes bibliographical references

Johnson, Steven

The **ghost** map; the story of London's most terrifying epidemic--and how it changed science, cities, and the modern world. Riverhead 2006 299p il map $26.95   **614.5**
1. Cholera 2. Physicians 3. Writers on medicine
ISBN 1-59448-925-4; 978-1-59448-925-9

LC 2006-23114

"From Snow's discovery of patient zero to Johnson's compelling argument for and celebration of cities, this makes for an illuminating and satisfying read." Publ Wkly

Includes bibliographical references

Kelly, John

The **great** mortality; an intimate history of the Black Death, the most devastating plague of all time. HarperCollins Publishers 2005 364p hardcover o.p. pa $14.95   **614.5**
1. Plague
ISBN 0-06-000692-7; 0-06-000693-5 pa

LC 2004-54213

"Western Europe is the primary focus of Kelly's compact history, which is 'intimate' in that it highlights many particular persons' passages through the crucible years, 1348-49. . . . Kelly proceeds chronologically, beginning with the plague's prehistory in north central Asia and its spread through China before empire-building Mongols brought it west. . . . This sweeping, viscerally exciting book contributes to a literature of perpetual fascination: the chronicles of pestilence." Booklist

Includes bibliographical references

Kolata, Gina

Flu; the story of the great influenza pandemic of 1918 and

the search for the virus that caused it. Simon & Schuster 2001
330p il pa $15   **614.5**
1. Influenza 2. Epidemiology 3. Influenza -- History -- 20th
century
ISBN 0-7432-0398-4; 978-0-7432-0398-2

LC 00-64861

First published 1999 by Farrar, Straus & Giroux
"Clearly explaining both the science and the social toll of the pandemic, Kolata writes an admirable history and soberly spells out how
the U.S. government is prepared—or unprepared—for a similar public
health threat today." Publ Wkly
Includes bibliographical references

Murphy, Monica, 1970-
Rabid; a cultural history of the world's most diabolical
virus. Bill Wasik and Monica Murphy. Viking 2012 240 p.
$25.95   **614.5**
1. Rabies 2. Diseases in literature 3. Communicable diseases --
History 4. Rabies -- Treatment -- History 5. Rabies -- Epidemiology
-- History
ISBN 0670023736; 9780670023738

LC 2011043903

This book "chart[s] four thousand years in the history, science, and
cultural mythology of rabies. . . . A disease that spreads avidly from
animals to humans, rabies has served throughout history as a symbol of
savage madness, of inhuman possession. And today, its history can help
shed light on the wave of emerging diseases, from AIDS to SARS to
avian flu, that we now know to originate in animal populations." (Publisher's note)

Pisani, Elizabeth
The **wisdom** of whores; bureaucrats, brothels, and the business of AIDS. W. W. Norton & Co. 2008 372p $25.95 **614.5**
1. Sexual behavior 2. AIDS (Disease) -- Prevention
ISBN 978-0-393-06662-3; 0-393-06662-2

LC 2007-51396

The author discusses various aspects of international
AIDS prevention.
This is "an eye-opening look at who gets AIDS how, when and
where. . . . Delivers a strong, well-told and believable message." Kirkus
Includes bibliographical references

Quammen, David, 1948-
Ebola; the natural and human history of a deadly virus. David Quammen. W W Norton & Co Inc 2014 128 p. map (paperback) $13.95   **614.5**
1. Ebola virus 2. Public health 3. Disease Reservoirs -- Popular
Works 4. Disease Outbreaks -- history -- Popular Works 5. Ebola
virus -- pathogenicity -- Popular Works 6. Hemorrhagic Fever,
Ebola -- history -- Popular Works
ISBN 0393351556; 9780393351552

LC 2014038144

In this book author David Quammen examines how "Ebola has
emerged sporadically, each time to devastating effect. It can kill up to
90 percent of its victims. In between these outbreaks, it is untraceable,
hiding deep in the jungle. The search is on to find Ebola's elusive host
animal. And until we find it, Ebola will continue to strike." (Publisher's note)
"This book will appeal to a wide range of readers. Those who have
not previously read Spillover but want to learn more about Ebola will
find much to interest them here. Summing Up: Recommended. All lev-
els/libraries." Choice

Includes bibliographical references

Shah, Sonia
The **fever**; how malaria has ruled humankind for 500,000
years. Sarah Crichton Books/Farrar, Straus, and Giroux 2010
307p $26   **614.5**
1. Malaria 2. Malaria -- History
ISBN 0-374-23001-3; 978-0-374-23001-2

LC 2010-2374

This is a chronicle of the illness and its influence on human lives.
(Publisher's note) Index.
"This fascinating, mordant pop-sci account tells us why malaria is
one of the world's greatest scourges, killing a million people every year
and debilitating another 300 million, and why we have remained complacent about it. . . . [This] is an absorbing account of human ingenuity
and progress, and of their heartbreaking limitations." Publ Wkly
Includes bibliographical references

Tayman, John
The **Colony**; John Tayman. Scribner 2006 421p il maps
$27.50   **614.5**
1. Leprosy 2. Hawaii -- History
ISBN 0-7432-3300-X

LC 2005-47767

This is a "history of the leper colony at the Hawaiian island Molokai.
. . . Tayman's crisp, flowing writing and inclusion of personal stories and
details make this an utterly engrossing look at a heartbreaking chapter in
Hawaiian history." Booklist

614.523   Measles

Wadman, Meredith
The **vaccine** race; science, politics, and the human costs
of defeating disease. Meredith Wadman. Viking 2017 448 p.
illustrations (ebook) $65; (hardback) $30   **614.523**
1. Rubella -- Vaccination 2. Rubella vaccines -- History 3. Human
experimentation in medicine 4. United States 5. History, 20th
Century 6. Human Experimentation -- history 7. Measles-Mumps-
Rubella Vaccine -- history
ISBN 9780698177789; 9780525427537

LC 2016044189

This book, by Meredith Wadman, presents an account of the science
behind the race to develop vaccines against rubella and other diseases
in the 1960s, along with "the political roadblocks that nearly stopped
the scientists. She describes the terrible dilemmas of pregnant women
exposed to German measles and recounts testing on infants, prisoners,
orphans, and the intellectually disabled, which was common in the era."
(Publisher's note)
"This is an exemplary piece of medical journalism, and Wadman
makes strikingly clear the human costs of medical developments as well
as the roles of politics and economics." Pub Wkly
Includes bibliographical references and index

614.574   Borrelia infections

Pfeiffer, Mary Beth
Lyme; the first epidemic of climate change. Mary Beth Pfeiffer. Island Press 2018 256 p. (cloth; alk. paper) $28 **614.574**
1. Climate 2. Lyme disease 3. Public health
ISBN 1610918444; 9781610918442

LC 2017958888

In this book, author "Mary Beth Pfeiffer shows how we have contributed to . . . [the spread of Lyme disease], and how modern medicine has underestimated its danger. She tells the heart-rending stories of families destroyed by a single tick bite, of children disabled, and of one woman's tragic choice after an exhaustive search for a cure. Pfeiffer also warns of the emergence of other tick-borne illnesses that make Lyme more difficult to treat and pose their own grave risks." (Publisher's note)

615 Pharmacology and therapeutics

Griffith, H. Winter

Complete Guide to Prescription & Nonprescription Drugs; H. Winter Griffith, revised and updated by Stephen W. Moore. Tarcherperigree   **615**
1. Drugs 2. Pharmacology
Annual

This is a "guide to all major prescription and nonprescription drugs, featuring revised, up to date FDA information and an A-Z list of illnesses for easy reference. [It] includes coverage of dosage and length of time before drug takes effect; side effects, special precautions; interactions with other food and drugs; standards for use by different age groups, and more." (Publisher's note)

O'Neil, Maryadele J.

★ The **Merck** index; an encyclopedia of chemicals, drugs, and biologicals. Maryadele J. O'Neil, editor; Patricia E. Heckelman, senior associate editor; Cherie B. Koch, associate editor; Kristin J. Roman, assistant editor; Catherine M. Kenny, editorial assistant; Maryann R. D'Arecca, administrative assistant. 14th ed.; Merck 2006 various paging il $125   **615**
1. Reference books 2. Drugs -- Dictionaries 3. Materia medica -- Dictionaries
ISBN 0-911910-00-X; 978-0-911910-00-1
First published 1889. Periodically revised

"Technical descriptions of the preparation, properties, uses, commercial names, and toxicity of drugs and medicines." N Y Public Libr Book of How & Where to Look It Up

Offit, Paul A.

★ **Do** You Believe in Magic? The Sense and Nonsense of Alternative Medicine. by Paul A. Offit. HarperCollins 2013 336 p. (hardcover) $26.99   **615**
1. Holistic medicine 2. Alternative medicine
ISBN 0062222961; 9780062222961

In this book, Paul A. Offit reveals that "half of Americans believe in the 'magic' of alternative medicine, fueling a $34 billion-a-year business that offers treatments that are at best placebos, and at worst deadly. He blasts untested, unregulated, overhyped remedies--like anti-autism creams and bogus cancer cures using 'antineoplastons'--and dares to berate celebs like" Mehmet Oz, Andrew Weil, Deepak Chopra, and Suzanne Somers. (Publishers Weekly)

PDR for nonprescription drugs. Physicians Desk Reference Inc 2014 360 p. $59.95   **615**
1. Pharmacology 2. Nonprescription drugs
ISBN 1563638274; 9781563638275

This book, by the editorial staff of the Physicians' Desk Reference, "offers . . . [a] guide to hundreds of the most commonly used OTC medications, including analgesics, cough and cold preparations, fever reducers, allergy medications, and more. Organized for easy use, . . . [the

volume] offers comprehensive drug information such as usage, dosage, warnings and precautions, side effects, ingredients, and more." (Publisher's note)

Physicians' desk reference. Physicians Desk Reference Inc   **615**
1. Pharmacology
Annual. First published 1947. Title varies

"Latest available information intended for physicians on over 2,000 products. Covers dosage, contraindications, precautions, side effects, and undesirable interactions. The information is furnished by the manufacturers of the various products. Product identification in color." N Y Public Libr Book of How & Where to Look It Up

615.107 Research

Goldacre, Ben

Bad Pharma; How Drug Companies Mislead Doctors and Harm Patients. Ben Goldacre. Faber & Faber 2013 448 p. $28   **615.107**
1. Drug industry 2. Drugs -- Testing 3. Drugs --Testing 4. Drugs --Quality control 5. Clinical trials --Moral and ethical aspects 6. Drugs --Testing --Moral and ethical aspects 7. Pharmaceutical industry --Moral and ethical aspects
ISBN 0865478007; 9780865478008

LC 2012038902

In this book, physician Ben Goldacre "reveals how pharmaceutical companies mislead doctors and hurt patients. They 'sponsor' trials, which tend to yield favorable results, while negative results often remain unreported. He also reports that drug companies spend twice as much on marketing and advertising as on researching and developing new drugs." (Booklist)

Includes bibliographical references and index.

615.3 Organic drugs

Orr, Stephen

The **new** American herbal; Stephen Orr. Clarkson Potter 2014 384 p. color illustrations $27.50   **615.3**
1. Herbs 2. Herb gardening 3. Herbals 4. Herbs -- Handbooks, manuals, etc 5. Herbs -- Utilization -- Handbooks, manuals, etc
ISBN 0449819930; 9780449819937

LC 2013043040

"With more than 900 entries, each accompanied by brand new photography and helpful growing advice, 'The New American Herbal' takes the study of herbs to [a] . . . new level. [author Stephen] Orr covers the entire spectrum of herbaceous plants, from culinary to ornamental to aromatic and medicinal, presenting them in an easy to use A to Z format packed with recipes, DIY projects, and . . . examples of garden design highlighting herbal plantings."

Pursell, J. J.

The **herbal** apothecary; 100 medicinal herbs and how to use them. JJ Pursell ; with photos by Shawn Linehan. Timber Press 2016 292 p. color illustrations (hardcover) $34.95 **615.3**
1. Medical botany 2. Herbs -- Therapeutic use -- Handbooks, manuals, etc 3. Materia medica, Vegetable -- Handbooks, manuals, etc
ISBN 9781604695670; 9781604696622

LC 2015009786

This book, by J. J. Pursell, with photos by Shawn Linehan, "provides an accessible and comprehensive introduction to medicinal plants, explaining how they work and how to use them safely. Incorporating traditional wisdom and scientific information, . . . [it also] includes advice on growing and foraging for healing plants and recommendations for plant-based formulations to fight common ailments." (Publisher's note)

"It is not a quick read, but will quickly become indispensable for understanding a neglected field that is ripe with great benefits." Pub Wkly

Includes bibliographical references and index

One hundred medicinal herbs and how to use them

615.32   Drugs derived from plants and microorganisms

Chevallier, Andrew

Encyclopedia of herbal medicine; Andrew Chevallier, FNIMH. DK Publishing 2016 336 p. color illustrations (ebook) $65; $40.00   **615.32**
1. Medical botany 2. Materia medica, Vegetable -- Encyclopedias 3. Medicinal plants -- Encyclopedias
ISBN 9781465456755; 1465449817; 9781465449818

LC 2016285124

This book, by Andrew Chevallier, features "550 key herbs and their uses as natural remedies for nearly 200 common ailments. . . . [This] is the definitive home reference to healing with the world's oldest form of medicine. From ginger to lavender and thyme to dandelion, learn about the chemistry of plants and how and why they work as medicines within the body." (Publisher's note)

"Though this selection should not be used as a medical reference on its own, it goes into enough depth for average readers looking for home remedies." LJ

Includes bibliographical references (page 322) and indexes

615.321   Drugs derived from plants

Essential oils; Neal's Yard Remedies. Alpha Books 2016 256 p. color illustrations (alk. paper) $19.95; (ebook) $59.85   **615.321**
1. Naturopathy 2. Aromatherapy 3. Essences and essential oils
ISBN 9781465454379; 9781465458155

LC 2016930604

This book is an "an introductory guide to essential oils and aromatherapy from the experts at Neal's Yard Remedies, a trusted source for natural health and beauty products. . . . Featuring comprehensive profiles of 88 essential oils, all-natural remedies for common ailments, aromatic recipes for home and beauty, and helpful guidance for blending, storing, and using essential oils." (Publisher's note)

"This updated text is an ideal introduction for readers who want to learn about the many uses for essential oils and a solid resource for those who already use them." LJ

615.5   Therapeutics

Bland, Jeffrey S.

The **disease** delusion; conquering the causes of chronic illness for a healthier, longer, and happier life. HarperCollins 2014 409 p. illustrations $26.99   **615.5**
1. Chronic diseases 2. Diseases -- Causes
ISBN 0062290738; 9780062290731

"In 'The Disease Delusion,' Dr. [Jeffrey] Bland explains what Func-

tional Medicine is and what it can do for you. While advances in modern science have nearly doubled our lifespans in only four generations, our quality of life has not reached its full potential. Outlining the reasons why we suffer chronic diseases from asthma and diabetes to obesity, arthritis and cancer to a host of other ailments, Dr. Bland offers achievable, science-based solutions." (Publisher's note)

Borins, Mel

A **doctor's** guide to alternative medicine; what works, what doesn't, and why. Mel Borins, MD. ; foreword by Dr. Bernie Siegel. Lyons Press 2014 336 p. (paperback) $19.95   **615.5**
1. Alternative medicine
ISBN 1493005952; 9781493005956

LC 2014015122

In this book, doctor Mel Borins uses "the latest scientific research and double-blind studies to educate patients and physicians alike on which alternative treatments work, which don't, and why. . . . Written in clear, accessible language for the layperson while providing citations to full studies for the medical professional, the book covers traditional healing and herbal remedies, physical therapies, psychological therapies, and natural health products." (Publisher's note)

Fondin, Michelle S.

The **wheel** of healing with ayurveda; an easy guide to a healthy lifestyle. Michelle S. Fondin. New World Library 2015 288 p. illustrations (paperback) $15.95   **615.5**
1. Lifestyles 2. Ayurvedic medicine 3. Medicine, Ayurvedic -- Popular works
ISBN 1608683524; 9781608683529

LC 2015001783

This book, by Michelle S. Fondin, presents a guide to "Ayurveda, the 'science of life,' is a complete wellness system that includes all that we associate with medical care--prevention of disease, observation, diagnosis, and treatment--as well as self-care practices that are generally absent from Western medicine. This truly holistic approach considers not just diet, exercise, and genetics but also relationships, life purpose, finances, environment, and past experiences." (Publisher's note)

"A strong beginning text for those seeking wellness beyond the bounds of traditional medicine." LJ

Includes bibliographical references and index

The **Gale** encyclopedia of alternative medicine; Laurie J. Fundukian, editor. 4th ed Gale / Cengage Learning 2014 2848 p. 4v (set; hbk.; alk. paper) $714   **615.5**
1. Reference books 2. Alternative medicine -- Encyclopedias 3. Internal Medicine -- Encyclopedias 4. Complementary Therapies -- Encyclopedias -- English
ISBN 1573027308; 9781573027304

LC 2013045439

"The four volumes contain more than 800 entries, approximately 400 color images, and many informative illustrations and charts pertaining to herbs and flowers, therapies and procedures, nutrition, and diseases and conditions. More than 50 new entries were added" for the fourth edition. (Publisher's note)

Includes bibliographical references and index

Low Dog, Tieraona

Healthy at home; get well and stay well without prescriptions. Tieraona Low Dog, M.D. National Geographic 2014 335 p. (hardback) $26   **615.5**
1. Naturopathy 2. Diet therapy 3. Health self-care 4. Self-care, Health

ISBN 1426212585; 9781426212581

LC 2013034581

This book, by Tieraona Low Dog, "helps you take charge of health care guided by a physician expert in natural healing, herbal medicine, and home remedies. . . . [The author] guides us in identifying, responding to, and caring for all the most common ailments, so that when it's time to take care at home, you have a doctor's advice on how." (Publisher's note)

"Accessible and reliable, this title will appeal to readers interested in alternative medicine and those who enjoyed the author's other books (Life Is Your Best Medicine: A Woman's Guide to Health, Healing, and Wholeness at Every Age; National Geographic Guide to Medicinal Herbs: The World's Most Effective Healing Plants). Recommended." LJ

Murray, Michael T.

The **encyclopedia** of natural medicine; Michael T. Murray, Joseph E. Pizzorno. 3rd ed Atria Books 2012 x, 1219 p.p ill. (trade paper; alk. paper) $29.99   **615.5**
1. Naturopathy 2. Alternative medicine 3. Naturopathy -- Encyclopedias
ISBN 1451663005; 9781451663006; 9781451663013; 9781451687347

LC 2012023268

First published 1991

In this book, authors "Michael Murray and Joseph Pizzorno focus on promoting health and treating disease with nontoxic, natural therapies. This . . . book . . . shows you how to improve your health through a positive mental attitude, a healthy lifestyle, a health-promoting diet, and supplements, along with plenty of practical tips. Murray and Pizzorno present an evidence-based approach to wellness, based on firm scientific findings." (Publisher's note)

Includes bibliographical references and index

Speid, Lorna

Clinical trials; what patients and healthy volunteers need to know. Oxford University Press 2010 186p il pa $19.95 **615.5**
1. Drugs -- Testing
ISBN 978-0-19-973416-0

LC 2010-9154

"If informed consent is the gold standard for clinical-trial participants, this book raises the bar to become the platinum standard. A must-have for anyone—healthy or sick—who is considering volunteering." Booklist

Includes bibliographical references

Weil, Andrew, 1942-

Mind over meds; know when drugs are necessary, when alternatives are better-- and when to let your body heal on its own. Andrew Weil, MD. Little, Brown & Co. 2017 xiv, 289 p.p (hardcover) $29   **615.5**
1. Medication abuse 2. Alternative medicine
ISBN 9780316269704; 9780316352970

LC 2016950776

In this book, "Dr. Andrew Weil alerts readers to the problem of over-medication, and outlines when medicine is necessary, and when it is not. Dr. Weil examines how we came to be so drastically overmedicated, presents science that proves drugs aren't always the best option, and provides reliable integrative medicine approaches to treating common ailments like high blood pressure, allergies, depression, and even the common cold." (Publisher's note)

"Weil's (Univ. of Arizona; Spontaneous Happiness, Healthy Aging) revolutionary book casts a critical eye on modern medicine, examining the very serious risks that medicine can carry." LJ

Includes bibliographical references (pages 239-277) and index.

615.7 Pharmacokinetics

Backes, Michael

Cannabis Pharmacy; the practical guide to medical marijuana. Michael Backes. Black Dog & Leventhal Pub 2014 272 p. illustrations, map $22.95   **615.7**
1. Marijuana 2. Alternative medicine
ISBN 157912951X; 9781579129514

This book, by Michael Backes, offers "evidence-based information on using cannabis for ailments and conditions, plus a comprehensive guide to the most popular varieties. . . . [It] begins with the history of medical marijuana and an explanation of how cannabis works with the body's own endocannabinoid system. . . . [It then] goes on to explore in detail 27 of the most popular cannabis varieties . . . and the medical conditions for which patients have reported effectiveness." (Publisher's note)

"Suitable as an at-home reader for patients (and their families) considering medicinal marijuana as a treatment option." LJ

Blaser, Martin J.

★ **Missing** microbes; how the overuse of antibiotics is fueling our modern plagues. Dr. Martin Blaser. Henry Holt & Co. 2014 288 p. illustrations (hardback) $28   **615.7**
1. Bacteria 2. Antibiotics 3. Drug resistance in microorganisms
ISBN 0805098100; 9780805098105; 9780805098112

LC 2013042578

Los Angeles Times Book Prize Finalist: Science and Technology (2014)

"In 'Missing Microbes,' Dr. Martin Blaser invites us into the wilds of the human microbiome where for hundreds of thousands of years bacterial and human cells have existed in a peaceful symbiosis that is responsible for the health and equilibrium of our body. . . . Taking us into both the lab and deep into the fields where these troubling effects can be witnessed firsthand, Blaser . . . provides cutting edge evidence for the adverse effects of antibiotics." (Publisher's note)

A "masterful work of preventive health and superb science writing." Booklist

Includes bibliographical references (pages 221-256) and index

Kramer, Peter D.

★ **Ordinarily** well; the case for antidepressants. Peter D. Kramer. Farrar, Straus & Giroux 2016 336 p. (hardback) $27   **615.7**
1. Drug therapy 2. Antidepressants 3. Depression (Psychology) 4. Psychotropic drugs 5. Antidepressants -- History 6. Antidepressants -- Effectiveness
ISBN 9780374280673

LC 2015036472

In this book, Peter D. Kramer "examines the growing controversy about the popular medication [of antidepressants]. A practicing doctor who trained as a psychotherapist and worked with pioneers in psycho-pharmacology, Kramer combines moving accounts of his patients' dilemmas with an eye-opening history of drug research to cast antidepressants in a new light." (Publisher's note)

"Kramer (Listening to Prozac), a psychiatrist and professor at Brown Medical School, makes an energetic and personal case for the role of antidepressants in easing crippling depression. Starting with the history of psychotherapy, when "infinite patience was the norm" in treatment for depression, Kramer delves into the breakthrough use of imipramine for treatment in the mid-1950s that helped "redefine the disorder" and "invigorate" psychopharmacology. . . . Kramer shows that the tools may be imperfect, but people battling severe depression are " lucky to have them." PW

Kuhn, Cynthia

Buzzed; the straight facts about the most used and abused drugs from alcohol to ecstasy. Cynthia Kuhn, Ph.D., Scott Swartzwelder, Ph.D., Wilkie Wilson, Ph.D., Duke University and Duke University School of Medicine ; with Leigh Heather Wilson and Jeremy Foster. 4th edition W.W. Norton & Company 2014 385 p. pbk $19.95   **615.7**

1. Drugs 2. Drug abuse

ISBN 0393344517; 9780393344516

LC 2014011441

This book, by Cynthia Kuhn, Scott Swartzwelder, Wilkie Wilson, with Leigh Heather Wilson and Jeremy Foster, is "the fourth edition of the essential, accessible source for understanding how drugs work and their effects on body and behavior. . . . It includes new information about biological and behavioral changes in addiction, the prescription-drug abuse epidemic, distinctive drug effects on the adolescent brain, and trends from synthetic cannabinoids to e-cigarettes." (Publisher's note)

"[S]urveys the most used and abused drugs from caffeine to heroin to methamphetamine. In both quick-reference summaries and in-depth analysis, it reports on how these drugs enter the body, how they manipulate the brain, their short-term and long-term effects, the different highs they produce, and the circumstances in which they can be deadly." Publisher's note

Includes bibliographical references and index

Rosen, William

Miracle cure; the creation of antibiotics and the birth of modern medicine. William Rosen. Viking 2017 358 p. illustrations (hardcover) $28   **615.7**

1. Antibiotics 2. Antibacterial agents -- History

ISBN 9780698184107; 9780525428107

LC 2016029488

This book, by William Rosen, is the "epic history of how antibiotics were born, saving millions of lives and creating a vast new industry known as Big Pharma. . . . Rosen captures this revolution with all its false starts, lucky surprises, and eccentric characters. He explains why, given the complex nature of bacteria—and their ability to rapidly evolve into new forms—the only way to locate and test potential antibiotic strains is by large-scale, systematic, trial-and-error experimentation." (Publisher's note)

"An encyclopedic reference for researchers and practitioners but also accessible for general readers due to Rosen's lively depiction of the people, places, and politics that color the history of the fight against infectious disease." Kirkus

Includes bibliographical references (pages 327-342) and index.

Shroder, Tom

Acid test; LSD, Ecstasy, and the power to heal. Tom Shroder. Blue Rider Press, a member of Penguin Group (USA) 2014 448 p. (hardback) $27.95   **615.7**

1. LSD (Drug) 2. Hallucinogens 3. Ecstasy (Drug) 4. Mental illness 5. Post-traumatic stress disorder 6. Mental illness -- Treatment 7. LSD (Drug) -- Therapeutic use 8. Ecstasy (Drug) -- Therapeutic use 9. Hallucinogenic drugs -- Therapeutic use 10. Mentally ill -- United States -- Biography 11. Post-traumatic stress disorder -- Treatment 12. Post-traumatic stress disorder -- Patients -- United States -- Biography

ISBN 0399162798; 9780399162794

LC 2014016115

This book, by Tom Shroder, focuses on "LSD and MDMA (better known as Ecstasy) [and how they] have proven . . . effective in treating anxiety disorders such as PTSD yet . . . remain illegal. . . . [It] covers the first heady years of experimentation in the fifties and sixties, through the backlash of the seventies and eighties, when the drug subculture exploded and uncontrolled use of street psychedelics led to a PR nightmare that created the drug stereotypes of the present day." (Publisher's note)

'Shroder both informs readers about the drugs' shadowy pasts and provides insight into the future of mental health." Pub Wkly

Slater, Lauren

Blue dreams; the science and the story of the drugs that changed our minds. Lauren Slater. Little, Brown 2018 416 p. $28   **615.7**

1. Hallucinogens 2. Psychotropic drugs

ISBN 9780316370646; 9780316552530

LC 2017947288

This book, by Lauren Slater, "offers the explosive story of the discovery and development of psychiatric medications, as well as the science and the people behind their invention, told by a riveting writer and psychologist who shares her own experience with the highs and lows of psychiatric drugs." (Publisher's note)

"Slater offers many insights here, and her moving personal story truly illuminates the triumphs and shortcomings of psychotropic drugs." Pub Wkly

615.788   Psychotropic drugs

Pollan, Michael, 1955-

★ **How** to change your mind; what the new science of psychedelics teaches us about consciousness, dying, addiction, depression, and transcendence. Michael Pollan. Penguin Press 2018 xii, 465 p.p (hardcover) $28   **615.788**

1. Hallucinogens 2. Mental illness -- Drug therapy 3. Psychotherapy patients -- Biography 4. Hallucinogenic drugs -- Therapeutic use

ISBN 9781594204227; 9780525558941; 1594204225

LC 2018006190

This book, by Michael Pollan, is the "gripping account of a journey to an exciting and unexpected new frontier in our understanding of the mind, the self, and our place in the world. The true subject of Pollan's 'mental travelogue' is not just psychedelic drugs but also the eternal puzzle of human consciousness and how, in a world that offers us both struggle and beauty, we can do our best to be fully present and find meaning in our lives." (Publisher's note)

"This nuanced and sophisticated exploration, which asks big questions about meaning-making and spiritual experience, is thought-provoking and eminently readable." Pub Wkly

Includes bibliographical references and index.

615.8   Specific therapies and kinds of therapies

Howick, Jeremy

Doctor you; introducing the hard science of self-healing. Jeremy Howick. Quercus 2018 xvi, 301 p.p (hardcover) $26.99   **615.8**

1. Mind and body 2. Mental healing 3. Health self-care 4. Self-care, Health

ISBN 163506077X; 1635060788; 9781635060775;

9781635060782

LC 2017050365

In this book, Doctor "Jeremy Howick draws on the latest peer-reviewed medical studies to arm readers with scientific evidence that will empower them to make sensible choices about what drugs to take, what drugs to give their children, and when (and when not) to simply let the body do its thing. . . . [The book] will change the way you think about your health, your body, and your approach to medicine." (Publisher's note)

"Among other things, he urges people to hang out with healthy folks, choose an empathetic doctor with a good bedside manner, volunteer, and, before getting invasive surgery, look for 'systemic reviews' of treatments and get second opinions. Sometimes, patients may be better off with a cup of ginger tea than with another prescription. This is sound, commonsense advice in an era of what Howick calls 'too much medicine.'" Booklist

Includes bibliographical references (pages 239-301)

Quest, Penelope

Reiki for life; the complete guide to reiki practice for levels 1, 2 & 3. Jeremy P. Tarcher/Penguin 2010 310p il pa $16.95   **615.8**
    1. Reiki (Healing system)
    ISBN 978-1-58542-790-1

LC 2009-51213

This book covers "basic routines, details about the power and potential of each level, special techniques for enhancing Reiki practice, and . . . direction on the use of Reiki toward spiritual growth. Penelope Quest also compares the origins and development of Reiki in the West and the East, revealing methods specific to the original Japanese Reiki tradition." Publisher's note

Includes bibliographical references

Tanzi, Rudolph E.

The **healing** self; Deepak Chopra, M.D. and Rudolph E. Tanzi, Ph.D. Harmony Books 2018 304 p. (hc) $26   **615.8**
    1. Well-being 2. Mind and body 3. Stress management 4. Integrative medicine 5. Integrative medicine -- Popular works 6. Mind and body therapies -- Popular works
    ISBN 0451495527; 9780451495525

LC 2017030783

This book, by Deepak Chopra, M.D. and Rudolph E. Tanzi, Ph.D, "closely examines how we can best manage chronic stress and inflammation, which are immerging as the primary detriments of well-being. Moreover, Chopra and Tanzi turn their attention to a host of chronic disorders such as hypertension, heart disease, type 2 diabetes, and Alzheimer's Disease, known to take years and sometimes decades to develop before the first symptoms appear." (Publisher's note)

615.852   Religious and psychic therapies

Taylor, Madisyn

Unmedicated; the four pillars of natural wellness. Madisyn Taylor. Atria"||"Beyond Words 2018 xxxviii, 165 p.p (hardcover) $22   **615.852**
    1. Naturopathy 2. Health self-care 3. Alternative medicine 4. Mind and body therapies -- Methodology 5. Anxiety disorders -- Alternative treatment 6. Depression, Mental -- Alternative treatment
    ISBN 9781501176906; 9781582706573; 9781582706580

LC 2017033107

This book, by Madisyn Taylor, "is her thoughtful account of how she broke free from binding mental chains and physical ailments to be happy, healthy, and productive; it is also a guide for you to apply her practical techniques to your own healing journey. Madisyn offers a daily program of easy-to-follow actions based on four pillars that will build a lifelong foundation for health: clear your mind; strengthen your body; nurture your spirit; and find your tribe." (Publisher's note)

"Taylor . . . shares her story of her own overreliance on medications that numbed her to her full potential in this instructive take on holistic medicine." Pub Wkly

616   Diseases

Biddle, Wayne

A **field** guide to germs; 2nd Anchor Books ed; Anchor Bks. (NY) 2002 209p il pa $13.95   **616**
    1. Microbiology 2. Germ theory of disease
    ISBN 1-400-03051-X

LC 2002-511927

First published 1995 by Holt & Co.

"Relaying essential information about the 100 most prevalent, powerful, or literarily famous microbiological malefactors in dictionary-encyclopedia style, Biddle injects social and political history into the exposition to provide fuller understanding of germs, their roles in society, their histories, and their current statuses. . . . Eminently entertaining, the book yet has the serious purpose of showing how concerns other than science and the relief of human suffering have affected the course of medical history." Booklist {review of 1995 edition}

Includes bibliographical references

Collins, Francis S.

The **language** of life; DNA and the revolution in personalized medicine. Harper 2010 332p il $26.99   **616**
    1. Medical genetics 2. Genetic screening
    ISBN 978-0-06-173317-8; 0-06-173317-2

LC 2009-25832

"This readable book . . . can help anyone understand more about how genetics and our DNA contribute to our health." Libr J

Includes bibliographical references

Groopman, Jerome E.

The **anatomy** of hope; how people prevail in the face of illness. [by] Jerome Groopman. Random House 2004 248p hardcover o.p. pa $14.95   **616**
    1. Hope 2. Physician-patient relationship
    ISBN 0-375-50638-1; 0-375-75775-9 pa

LC 2003-46692

The author "discovered that hope could actually cause physiological change, blocking pain and improving respiratory, circulatory, and motor function. He shares personal experiences from his own life and his patients' case histories that illustrate the power and importance of hope. . . . An excellent narrative for public libraries." Libr J

Includes bibliographical references

Kaplan, Gary

Total recovery; Solving the mystery of chronic pain and depression. Dr. Gary Kaplan, DO, with Donna Beech. Rodale 2014 250 p. (hardcover) $26.99   **616**
    1. Chronic pain 2. Depression (Psychology) 3. Depression, Mental 4. Chronic pain -- Complications
    ISBN 162336275X; 9781623362751

LC 2013046868

"In 'Total Recovery,' Dr. Gary Kaplan argues that we've been thinking about disease all wrong. Drawing on dramatic patient stories and cutting-edge research, the book reveals that chronic physical and emotional pain are two sides of the same coin. New discoveries show that disease is not the result of a single event but an accumulation of traumas. Every injury, every infection, every toxin, and every emotional blow generates the same reaction: inflammation." (Publisher's note)

Includes bibliographical references and index

Kenneally, Christine

The **invisible** history of the human race; how DNA and history shape our identities and our futures. Christine Kenneally. Viking 2014 368 p. (hardback) $27.95   616
1. DNA 2. Genetics 3. Human beings 4. Pedigree 5. DNA -- history 6. Genetics -- history 7. Human Migration -- history
ISBN 0670025550; 9780670025558

LC 2014021679

In this book, "Christine Kenneally draws on cutting-edge research to reveal how both historical artifacts and DNA tell us where we come from and where we may be going. While some books explore our genetic inheritance and popular television shows celebrate ancestry, this is the first book to explore how everything from DNA to emotions to names and the stories that form our lives are all part of our human legacy." (Publisher's note)

"Those interested in learning basic human genetics or seeking a more accurate story of eugenics might prefer Ricki Lewis's Human Genetics: The Basics or Paul A. Lombardo's A Century of Eugenics in America. For appreciating genealogy and family history in a new light, Kenneally's work shines." LJ

Includes bibliographical references and index

Lewis, Moshe

Understanding pain; an introduction for patients and caregivers. Naheed Ali and Moshe Lewis. Rowman & Littlefield 2015 376 p. (cloth; alk. paper) $38   616
1. Physiology 2. Psychology 3. Pain -- Treatment 4. Pain -- Popular Works 5. Age Factors -- Popular Works 6. Pain Management -- Popular Works 7. Attitude to Health -- Popular Works
ISBN 1442233605; 9781442233607

LC 2014042262

In this book authors Naheed Ali and Moshe Lewis "walk readers through the various types of pain, the causes and symptoms, as well as the methods of treatment currently available. From prescription medication to acupuncture and massage therapy, various approaches may work for some but not for others. Here, the authors provide a comprehensive introduction to the subject, covering self-care as well as caring for others in pain, and addressing alternative as well as traditional methods of pain management." (Publisher's note)

"Medical doctors Lewis and Ali (author of books about diabetes, obesity, Alzheimer's, and arthritis) deliver a hefty overview of the history, causes, symptoms, and treatment of pain... Fortunately, they provide a glossary at the end, along with such helpful resources as names and addresses of nationally recognized clinics. As for their advice, much of it seems quite basic: exercise, reduce stress, eat a well-balanced diet... Still, the millions of Americans who suffer from acute pain (less than six months) or chronic pain (more than six months) and the doctors, friends, and family who look out for them will find much good information here." Booklist

Includes bibliographical references and index

Moalem, Sharon

Survival of the sickest; a medical maverick discovers why we need disease. [by] Sharon Moalem, with Jonathan Prince.

William Morrow 2007 267p $25.95   616
1. Diseases 2. Genetics 3. Evolution 4. Natural selection
ISBN 978-0-06-088965-4; 0-06-088965-9

LC 2006-50128

The author "uses numerous examples to show how analyzing history might help explain why a certain genetic trait that seems useless—even harmful—to us now made perfect sense in our ancestors' environment. He also introduces such recent research topics as host manipulation, noncoding DNA, and epigenetics. The particularly coherent writing style makes complex ideas accessible to people without a science background. With the book's emphasis on evolution's goals of survival and reproduction, readers will gain insights into why evolution may have selected for certain traits and why having that insight may better our lives." Libr J

Murphree, Rodger H.

Treating and beating fibromyalgia and chronic fatigue syndrome; a step-by-step program proven to help you feel good again. by Rodger H. Murphree. Cardinal Pub Group 2014 544 p. $21.95   616
1. Fibromyalgia 2. Chronic fatigue syndrome
ISBN 0972893873; 9780972893879

In this book on fibromyalgia and chronic fatigue syndrome, Dr. Rodger H. Murphree "explains in easy to understand terms how and why using scientifically researched and clinically proven natural vitamins, minerals, amino acids, and other over the counter supplements, corrects the problems associated with these illnesses." (Publisher's note)

Parks, Tim

Teach us to sit still; a skeptic's search for health and healing. Rodale Books 2011 322p il   616
1. Chronic pain 2. Mind and body
ISBN 1609611586; 9781609611583

LC 2011-08512

First published 2010 in the United Kingdom

"In a hallmark of conversion narratives, the original mania reproduces itself as a mirror image: in the old days, hyperbolically anxious; in the new, hyperbolically anxious to enumerate the old anxiety. To his credit, Parks doesn't pretend otherwise. Moreover, his personal account, never preachy, engages some serious matters about contemporary life, notably what it's like to be a patient, as nearly all of us, sooner or later, are or will be." N Y Times Book Rev

Rochman, Bonnie

The **gene** machine; how genetic technologies are changing the way we have kids--and the kids we have. Bonnie Rochman. Scientific American / Farrar, Straus & Giroux 2017 272 p. (hardcover) $26   616
1. Medical genetics 2. Genetic engineering 3. Genetic Testing -- methods 4. Genetic Engineering -- trends 5. Genetic Diseases, Inborn -- prevention & control
ISBN 9780374160784; 9780374713966

LC 2016035006

In this book on genetic technologies, author Bonnie Rochman "tells the stories of scientists working to unlock the secrets of the human genome; genetic counselors and spiritual advisers guiding mothers and fathers through life-changing choices; and, of course, parents (including Rochman herself) grappling with revelations that are sometimes joyous, sometimes heartbreaking, but always profound." (Publisher's note)

"Journalist Rochman takes a calm, thorough, and nonsensationalist look at core bioethical questions . . . as well as the ethical spaces where what can be done and what should be done come into conflict."

Pub Wkly
Includes bibliographical references and index

Twelve breaths a minute; end-of-life essays. edited by Lee Gutkind; foreword by Karen Wolk Feinstein; introduction by Francine Prose. Southern Methodist University Press 2011 267p (Medical humanities) $23.95 **616**
1. Death 2. Caregivers 3. Terminal care 4. Terminally ill
ISBN 978-0-87074-571-3; 0-87074-571-9

LC 2010-45874

"A collection of creative nonfiction essays about end-of-life issues. How depressing, a friend said. I thought the same thing until I read one and then another and then another. Sad, yes. But depressing? No. 'Twelve Breaths a Minute,' a book commissioned by the Jewish Healthcare Foundation as part of its ongoing end-of-life initiative, is uplifting. The 23 essays, chosen from among more than 400 submissions, also are beautifully written. The writers are the sons, daughters and parents who have had to deal with the deaths of family, as well as members of the medical profession who have had to balance the oath to save lives with the desires of a patient to die without extraordinary medical measures. Sometimes they are both." Pittsburgh Post-Gazette

Wood, David
★ **What** have we done; The Moral Injury of Our Longest Wars. David Wood. Little, Brown & Co./Hachette Book Group 2016 304 p. $28.00; (ebook) $84 **616**
1. Ethics 2. Human behavior 3. War and civilization
ISBN 9780316264150; 9780316269797

LC 2016932416

This book, by David Wood, "examines the far more pervasive yet less understood experience of those we send to war: moral injury, the violation of our fundamental values of right and wrong that so often occurs in the impossible moral dilemmas of modern conflict. [It features] portraits of combat veterans and leading mental health researchers, along with Wood's personal observations of war and the young Americans deployed in Iraq and Afghanistan." (Publisher's note)

"This powerful book is essential reading for anyone seeking to understand the life of a soldier after they return home from war." LJ

Includes bibliographic references and index.

616.02 Special topics of diseases

Anthes, Emily
Frankenstein's cat; cuddling up to biotech's brave new beasts. Emily Anthes. 1st ed. Scientific American / Farrar, Straus and Giroux 2013 256 p. (hardcover) $26 **616.02**
1. Biotechnology 2. Transgenic animals
ISBN 0374158592; 9780374158590

LC 2012029045

This book, by Emily Anthes, "takes us from petri dish to pet store as she explores how biotechnology is shaping the future of our furry and feathered friends. . . . [Visiting] a 'frozen zoo' where scientists are storing DNA from the planet's most exotic creatures, she discovers how we can use cloning to protect endangered species, craft prosthetics to save injured animals, and employ genetic engineering to supply farms with disease-resistant livestock." (Publisher's note)

"[A] quick, often surprising review of current advances, giving accessible treatment to a weighty subject and employing clear descriptions of complex science." Booklist

Includes bibliographical references and index.

Brody, Jane E.
Jane Brody's guide to the great beyond; a practical primer to help you and your loved ones prepare medically, legally, and emotionally for the end of life. [by] Jane Brody. Random House 2009 xxiv, 287p il $26 **616.02**
1. Death 2. Terminal care 3. Terminally ill
ISBN 978-1-4000-6654-4

LC 2008-16583

"With bulleted lists itemizing what needs to be done and how to do it, short portraits and anecdotes throughout, Brody covers the importance of preparation; the necessity of an advance directive and why a living will is not enough; funeral plans; living with a bad prognosis and dealing with uncertainty; caregiving; hospice; communicating with doctors; assisted dying; organ donation and autopsy; and legacies. An instructive, inspiring and reassuring work full of compassion and humor (along with several cartoons from various New Yorker illustrators), this volume belongs on every family's bookshelf." Publ Wkly

Brown, Theresa
The **shift**; one nurse, twelve hours, four patients' lives. Theresa Brown. Algonquin Books of Chapel Hill 2015 204 p. $24.95 **616.02**
1. Nurses 2. Patients 3. Medical care 4. Cancer -- Nursing 5. Interpersonal relations 6. Intensive Care Units -- Pennsylvania -- Popular Works 7. Critical Care Nursing -- Pennsylvania -- Popular Works 8. Nurse-Patient Relations -- Pennsylvania -- Popular Works 9. Nursing Staff, Hospital -- Pennsylvania -- Popular Works 10. Intensive Care Units -- Pennsylvania -- Personal Narratives 11. Critical Care Nursing -- Pennsylvania -- Personal Narratives 12. Interprofessional Relations -- Pennsylvania -- Popular Works 13. Nurse-Patient Relations -- Pennsylvania -- Personal Narratives 14. Nursing Staff, Hospital -- Pennsylvania -- Personal Narratives 15. Interprofessional Relations -- Pennsylvania -- Personal Narratives
ISBN 161620320X; 9781616203207

LC 2015010992

In this book, author "Theresa Brown invites us to experience not just a day in the life of a nurse but all the life that happens in just one day on a hospital's cancer ward. . . . In Brown's skilled hands . . . we are given an unprecedented view into the individual struggles as well as the larger truths about medicine in this country, and by shift's end, we have witnessed something profound about hope and healing and humanity." (Publisher's note)

"At its best, Brown's memoir increases empathy for nurses, who work hard and often must care for difficult patients and cope with a caste system that gives them less respect than MDs. This account also raises important ethical questions, such as just how fully informative healthcare workers should be when the prognosis isn't good." Booklist

Butler, Katy
Knocking on Heaven's Door; the path to a better way of death. Katy Butler. Simon & Schuster 2013 336 p. illustrations $25 **616.02**
1. Death 2. Right to die 3. Terminal care -- Decision making 4. Euthanasia -- Moral and ethical aspects 5. Adult children of aging parents -- Family relationships
ISBN 1451641974; 9781451641974

LC 2013017659

In this book, "when doctors refused to disable the pacemaker that caused her eighty-four-year-old father's heart to outlive his brain, Katy Butler . . . embarked on a quest to understand why modern medicine was depriving him of a humane, timely death. After his lingering death, Katy's mother, nearly broken by years of nonstop caregiving, defied her doctors, refused open-heart surgery, and insisted on facing death the old-fashioned way: bravely, lucidly, and head on." (Publisher's note)

"With candidness and reverence, Butler examines one of the most challenging questions a child may face: how to let a parent die with dignity and integrity when the body has stopped functioning." Kirkus

Includes bibliographical references

Casarett, David

Shocked; adventures in bringing back the recently dead. David Casarett. Current 2014 304 p. $27.95   **616.02**
1. Cardiac resuscitation 2. Science -- Popular works 3. Resuscitation -- Popular Works
ISBN 1591846714; 9781591846710

LC 2014004313

This book, by David Casarett, explores how "not too long ago, there was no coming back from death. But now, with revolutionary medical advances, death has become just another serious complication. . . . [The author] chronicles his exploration of the cutting edge of resuscitation and reveals just how far science has come." (Publisher's note)

"This book may work for readers of Mary Roach's Stiff, in which the author's interest is more theoretical." LJ

Includes bibliographical references and index

Fersko-Weiss, Henry

★ **Caring** for the dying; the doula approach to a meaningful death. by Henry Fersko-Weiss. Conari Press, an imprint of Red Wheel/Weiser, LLC 2017 xiv, 222 p.p (hardcover) $24.95   **616.02**
1. Terminal care 2. Terminally ill 3. Doulas 4. Terminally ill -- Care
ISBN 9781573246965; 9781633410367

LC 2016041229

In this book, by Henry Fersko-Weiss, "the end-of-life doula model is adapted from the work of birth doulas and helps the dying to find meaning in their life. . . . The approach calls for around-the-clock vigil care, so the dying person and their family have the emotional and spiritual support they need along with guidance on signs and symptoms of dying. It also covers the work of reprocessing a death with the family afterward and the early work of grieving." (Publisher's note)

"Experiences from the author's many years as an end-of-life doula illustrate the concepts presented and provide examples that readers can apply and adapt to their own situations." LJ

First aid manual; the step-by-step guide for everyone. American College of Emergency Physicians ; medical editor-in-chief, Gina M. Piazza, DO, FACEP. DK Publishing 2014 288 p. color illustrations $14.95   **616.02**
1. First aid 2. Medicine -- Handbooks, manuals, etc. 3. First aid in illness and injury -- Handbooks, manuals, etc
ISBN 9781465419507

LC 2014430333

This book, edited by Gina M. Piazza, "looks at more than 100 different conditions, from splinters and sprained ankles to strokes and unconsciousness, and shows exactly what to do with step-by-step photographic sequences. Every condition is clearly explained, outlining causes, symptoms and signs, and action plans." (Publisher's note)

American College of Emergency Physicians first aid manual

Gibney, Mike

Something to chew on; challenging controversies in food and health. Mike Gibney. University College Dublin Press 2012 xiv, 177 p.p (paperback) $38.95   **616.02**

1. Food 2. Nutrition 3. Food supply 4. Public health 5. Genetic engineering
ISBN 1906359679; 9781906359676

LC 2012405919

This book, by Mike Gibney, discusses the scientific perspective on many of "the worldwide controversies dominating the popular press in relation to the modern food chain. It deals with the topics of organic food, GM foods, obesity, growing old, the integrity of food research, global warming, global malnutrition, consumer perception of food-borne risk, our gut bacteria, and how nutrition during pregnancy primes us for health in later life." (Publisher's note)

Lamas, Daniela J.

You can stop humming now; a doctor's stories of life, death, and in between. Daniela J Lamas. Little, Brown & Co. 2018 256 p. $28   **616.02**
1. Medical care 2. Medical ethics 3. Emergency medicine
ISBN 9780316393171

LC 2017947289

In this book, author Daniela J. Lamas explores the question "what it means to be saved by modern medicine . . . through intimate accounts of patients and their families. A grandfather whose failing heart has been replaced by a battery-operated pump; a salesman who found himself a kidney donor on social media--these moving narratives paint a detailed picture of the fragile border between sickness and health." (Publisher's note)

"This thoughtful, reflective, and beautifully rendered book examines the costs of modern medicine. Readers who enjoy books by Oliver Sacks and Atul Gawande, or Paul Kalanithi's When Breath Becomes Air will find this volume moving and provocative." LJ

Volandes, Angelo E., 1971-

The **conversation**; a revolutionary plan for end-of-life care. Angelo Volandes. Bloomsbury 2015 256 p. illustrations (hardback) $26   **616.02**
1. Terminal care 2. Palliative treatment 3. Older people -- Medical care 4. Advance Directives 5. Advance Care Planning 6. Terminal Care -- methods 7. Palliative Care -- methods 8. Physician-Patient Relations
ISBN 1620408546; 9781620408544

LC 2014028386

This book, by Angelo Volandes, "through the stories of seven patients and seven very different end-of-life experiences, . . . demonstrates that what people with a serious illness, who are approaching the end of their lives, need most is not new technologies but one simple thing: The Conversation." (Publisher's note)

"Written with passion and clarity, this book moves beyond others on the topic by including empirical evidence of how to make such conversations about end-of-life care most effective." LJ

Includes bibliographical references and index

Zitter, Jessica Nutik

★ **Extreme** measures; finding a better path to the end of life. Jessica Nutik Zitter. Avery 2017 352 p. Hardcover $27   **616.02**
1. Terminal care 2. Popular medicine 3. Terminally ill -- Care
ISBN 1101982551; 9781101982556

LC 2016056303

This book, by Jessica Nutik Zitter, charts the author's "journey from wanting to be one kind of hero to becoming another--a doctor who prioritizes the patient's values and preferences in an environment where the default choice is the extreme use of technology. . . . In her work Zitter has learned what patients fear more than death itself: the prospect of dy-

ing badly." (Publisher's note)
Includes bibliographical references (pages 312-324) and index.

616.029 Palliative and terminal care

Harrington, Samuel
At peace; choosing a good death after a long life. Samuel Harrington, MD. Grand Central Life & Style 2018 xix, 282 p.p (hardcover) $26 **616.029**
1. Terminal care 2. Terminally ill -- Care 3. Geriatrics -- Popular works 4. Terminal care -- Popular works 5. Terminally ill -- Popular works
ISBN 9781538711538; 1478917415; 9781478917410
LC 2017034568
In this book, author Samuel Harrington, "outlines specific active and passive steps that older patients and their health-care proxies can take to ensure loved ones live their last days comfortably at home and/or in hospice when further aggressive care is inappropriate. . . . [Harrington] describes the terminal patterns of the six most common chronic diseases; . . . when to seek hospice care; and how to deal with dementia and other special issues." (Publisher's note)
Includes bibliographical references and index

Monte, Tom
Unexpected recoveries; seven steps to healing body, mind, and soul when serious illness strikes. Tom Monte. Square One Publishers 2017 256 p. (pbk.; alk. paper) $17.95 **616.029**
1. Healing 2. Chronic diseases 3. Terminally ill 4. Chronically ill 5. Sick -- Psychology 6. Catastrophic illness
ISBN 9780757004001
LC 2016043898
This book, by Tom Monte, "combines modern medical know-how, ancient healing practices, and a healing diet to provide a comprehensive and practical guidebook for physical, emotional, and spiritual recovery. It takes aim at such conditions as cancer, heart disease,. . . and more. . . . Also included are a helpful resource section, a twenty-one-day menu planner, and over sixty kitchen-tested recipes." (Publisher's note)
"The easy-to-follow format, combined with compelling and dramatic patient recovery stories, makes for an appealing read." Pub Wkly
Includes bibliographical references and index

616.042 Genetic diseases (Hereditary diseases)

Kolata, Gina
Mercies in disguise; a story of hope, a family's genetic destiny, and the science that rescued them. Gina Kolata. St. Martin's Press 2017 viii, 262 p.p $25.99 **616.042**
1. Prion diseases 2. Medical genetics 3. Genetic engineering 4. Genetic disorders 5. Genetic screening -- Moral and ethical aspects
ISBN 1250064341; 9781250064349
LC 2016044044
In this book, "author Gina Kolata tells the story of the Baxleys, an almost archetypal family in a small town in South Carolina. A proud and determined clan, many of them doctors, they are struck one by one with an inscrutable illness. They finally discover the cause of the disease after a remarkable sequence of events that many saw as providential." (Publisher's note)
"Kolata's book reads like a medical thriller and readers will be caught up in the lives of the protagonists." Pub Wkly.
Includes bibliographical references and index.

Mukherjee, Siddhartha
★ The **gene**; an intimate history. Siddhartha Mukherjee. Scribner 2016 592 p. illustrations (some color) (hardcover) $30 **616.042**
1. Genetics 2. Heredity 3. Genes 4. Genetics -- history
ISBN 9781476733500; 9781476733524
LC 2015039962
In this book, author Siddhartha Mukherjee "has a written a biography of the gene. . . . Weaving science, social history, and personal narrative to tell us the story of one of the most important conceptual breakthroughs of modern times, Mukherjee animates the quest to understand human heredity and its surprising influence on our lives, personalities, identities, fates, and choices." (Publisher's note)
"Sobering, humbling, and extraordinarily rich reading from a wise and gifted writer who sees how far we have come—but how much farther we have to go to understand our human nature and destiny." Kirkus
Includes bibliographical references and index

616.044 Chronic diseases

Mangalik, Aroop
Dealing with doctors, denial, and death; a guide to living well with serious illness. Aroop Mangalik. Rowman & Littlefield 2017 xiv, 260 p.p (hardcover) $33 **616.044**
1. Creative nonfiction 2. Physician-patient relationship 3. Chronic diseases -- Patients -- Care 4. Medical ethics 5. Physician and patient 6. Chronically ill -- Care 7. Chronically ill -- Treatment 8. Chronically ill -- Family relationships
ISBN 9781442272804; 9781442272811
LC 2016025054
In this book, author Aroop Mangalik, "looks at the ways in which we are accustomed to treating illness at all costs, even at the expense of the quality of a patient's life. He considers our culture of denial, the medical profession's role in over treating patients and end of life care, and the patient's options and role in these decisions. The goal is to help patients and families make informed decisions that may help the seriously ill live better with their illnesses." (Publisher's note)
"Mangalik provides invaluable information everyone can use to be prepared to face the inevitability of death and celebrate each life." Booklist
Includes bibliographical references (pages 243-252) and index.

616.07 Pathology

Biss, Eula
★ **On** immunity; an inoculation. Eula Biss. Graywolf Press 2014 216 p. (alk. paper) $24 **616.07**
1. Immunity 2. Immunization
ISBN 1555976891; 9781555976897
LC 2014935701
National Book Critics Circle Finalist: Criticism (2014)
In this book, author Eula Biss "addresses a chronic condition of fear--fear of the government, the medical establishment, and what is in your child's air, food, mattress, medicine, and vaccines. She finds that you cannot immunize your child, or yourself, from the world. . . . Biss investigates the metaphors and myths surrounding our conception of immunity and its implications for the individual and the social body." (Publisher's note)
Includes bibliographical references

Franscell, Ron

Morgue; a life in death. Dr. Vincent Di Maio and Ron Franscell ; foreword by Dr. Jan Garavaglia. St. Martin's Press 2016 288 p. illustrations (hardback) $26.99   **616.07**
1. Physicians -- Biography 2. Pathologists -- New York (State) -- Brooklyn -- Biography
ISBN 1250067146; 9781250067142

LC 2016001125

In this book, Dr. Vincent Di Maio "guides us into the inner sanctum, through the cases that have made him famous, from the exhumation of assassin Lee Harvey Oswald and the racially charged shooting of Florida teen Trayvon Martin, to the unmasking of a serial baby-killer and the mysterious death of troubled genius Vincent van Gogh." (Publisher's note)

"Di Maio and Franscell deliver a well-paced, thoughtful, and absorbing work that will fascinate crime buffs and scholars alike." Pub Wkly

Pagana, Timothy J.

Mosby's diagnostic and laboratory test reference; Kathleen Deska Pagana, Timothy J. Pagana, and Theresa N. Pagana. 13th edition Mosby Inc. 2016 1040 p. pbk $57.95   **616.07**
1. Medicine 2. Diagnosis 3. Laboratories
ISBN 0323399576; 9780323399579

First published 1992. Frequently revised

This medical handbook, by Kathleen Deska Pagana, Timothy J. Pagana, and Theresa N. Pagana, provides "concise test entries are arranged alphabetically and reflect the latest in research and diagnostic testing. Each test entry includes vital information such as type of test, alternate or abbreviated test names, test explanation, normal and abnormal findings, possible critical values, contraindications, potential complications, interfering factors, and patient care." (Publisher's note)

Sanders, Lisa

Every patient tells a story; medical mysteries and the art of diagnosis. Broadway 2009 xxvii, 276p $25   **616.07**
1. Diagnosis
ISBN 0-7679-2246-8; 978-0-7679-2246-3

LC 2008-41478

The author "discusses how doctors deal with diagnostic dilemmas. . . . Sanders not only collects difficult cases, she reflects on what each means for both patient and struggling physician. . . . Readers who enjoy dramatic stories of doctors fighting disease will get their fill, and they will also encounter thoughtful essays on how doctors think and go about their work, and how they might do it better." Publ Wkly

Includes bibliographical references

Zuk, M.

Riddled with life; friendly worms, ladybug sex, and the parasites that make us who we are. Harcourt 2007 328p il $25   **616.07**
1. Diseases 2. Parasites 3. Pathology 4. Human ecology 5. Adaptation (Biology)
ISBN 978-0-15-101225-1; 0-15-101225-3

LC 2006-28642

"Zuk has an amazing gift for turning experiments and facts into stories. . . . She is urging the public to take a new look at disease, though it's one that's well supported by the research. There are moments where she's speculating ahead of the science a bit, but those moments are clearly marked. Riddled with Life will change the way you look at public and private health." PopMatters

Includes bibliographical references

616.075   Diagnosis and prognosis

Hatch, Steven

Snowball in a blizzard; a physician's notes on uncertainty in medicine. Steven Hatch. Basic Books, a member of the Perseus Books Group 2016 320 p. illustrations (ebook) $18.99; (hc) $27.99   **616.075**
1. Diagnosis 2. Medical policy 3. Uncertainty 4. Health Policy
ISBN 9780465098576; 9780465050642

LC 2015041457

In this book, author Steven Hatch "argues that instead of ignoring . . . uncertainty [in medicine], we should embrace it. By digging deeply into a number of rancorous controversies, from breast cancer screening to blood pressure management, Hatch shows us how medicine can fail--sometimes spectacularly--when patients and doctors alike place too much faith in modern medical technology." (Publisher's note)

"Hatch's book may prove to be a tough sell because its conclusions contradict human impulses, but it is worthwhile reading for both doctors and patients." Pub Wkly

Includes bibliographical references and index

Medical symptoms; a visual guide: the easy way to identify medical problems. Dk Pub 2018 256 p. $19.95   **616.075**
1. Diseases 2. Diagnosis 3. Popular medicine
ISBN 1465459146; 9781465459145

This book is "a simple, visual symptom checker that helps you match your symptoms and health problems to possible conditions, and quickly directs you to the correct treatment. . . . Head-to-toe visual diagnostic guides help you identify suspected conditions or injuries based on symptoms. . . . Once you've narrowed it down, a cross-reference takes you to easy-to-follow descriptions of the condition at the back of the book." (Publisher's note)

616.079   Immunity

Carver, Catherine

Immune; how your body defends and protects you. Catherine Carver. Bloomsbury Sigma 2017 304 p. illustrations (hardcover) $27   **616.079**
1. Immunity 2. Immune system
ISBN 9781472915115; 9781472915146; 1472915119

This book, by Catherine Carver, "explores the incredible arsenal that lives within us--how it knows what to attack and what to defend, and how it kills everything from the common cold to the plague bacterium. We see what happens when the immune system turns on us, and conversely how impossible life is without its protection. We learn how diseases try to evade the immune system, how they exploit vulnerabilities and even subvert it to their own advantage." (Publisher's note)

"This book is jam-packed with hard-core science, and Carver engages readers with her cheeky, playful style and the inclusion of fascinating human-interest anecdotes." LJ

Includes bibliographical references (pages 285-295) and index.

616.08   Psychosomatic medicine

O'Sullivan, Suzanne

Is it all in your head? True Stories of Imaginary Illness. by Suzanne O'Sullivan. Other Press 2016 352 p. (ebook) $12.99; (hardcover) $26.95   **616.08**
1. Psychosomatic medicine -- Case studies 2. Medicine,

Psychosomatic -- Case studies
ISBN 9781590517963; 9781590517956

LC 2015049009

This book, by Suzanne O'Sullivan, takes readers "on a journey through the world of psychosomatic illness, where we meet patients such as Rachel, a promising young dancer now housebound by chronic fatigue syndrome, and Mary, whose memory loss may be her mind's way of protecting her from remembering her husband's abuse. O'Sullivan reveals the hidden stresses behind their mysterious symptoms, approaching a sensitive topic with patience and understanding." (Publisher's note)

"If empathy is bolstered by understanding, then this book will bring such sentiments to a rarely understood condition. It will engage readers' heads, but also quite possibly enter their hearts." Pub Wkly

616.1   Specific diseases

Forrester, James

The **Heart** Healers; The Misfits, Mavericks, and Rebels Who Created the Greatest Medical Breakthrough of Our Lives. James S. Forrester. St. Martin's Press 2015 400 p. 16 plates; illustrations $27.99   **616.1**

1. Heart diseases 2. Medicine -- Research
ISBN 1250058392; 9781250058393

LC 2015017977

In this book author "James Forrester tells the story of the mavericks and rebels who defied the accumulated medical wisdom of the day to begin conquering heart disease. Forrester tells the story of these rebels and the risks they took with their own lives and the lives of others to heal the most elemental of human organs - the heart. The result is a compelling chronicle of a disease and its cure, a disease that is still with us, but one that is slowly being worn away." (Publisher's note)

"Forrester brings history to life and explains complex procedures for lay readers in this excellent book for readers interested in medical history and those who want to understand modern medical procedures." LJ

Khan, Joel

The **whole** heart solution; halt heart disease now with the best alternative and traditional medicine. Joel Kahn, MD, Preventive Cardiologist and Clinical Professor of Medicine at Wayne State University School of Medicine. The Reader's Digest Association, Inc. 2013 308 p. (alk. paper) $24.99 **616.1**

1. Heart diseases 2. Holistic medicine 3. Heart -- Diseases -- Alternative treatment
ISBN 1621451437; 9781621451433; 9781621451518

LC 2013040399

In this book, holistic doctor Joel Kahn "reveals more than 75 simple, low-cost things you can do right away—from drinking your veggies to opening your windows to walking barefoot—to make yourself heart attack proof." (Publisher's note)

Includes bibliographical references (pages 293-302) and index.

616.12   Diseases of heart

Fuhrman, Joel

The **end** of heart disease; the eat to live plan to prevent and reverse heart disease. Joel Fuhrman, MD. HarperOne 2016 448 p. illustrations (hardback) $28.99   **616.12**

1. Heart diseases -- Prevention 2. Heart -- Diseases -- Prevention -- Popular works 3. Heart -- Diseases -- Diet therapy -- Popular

works 4. Heart -- Diseases -- Nutritional aspects -- Popular works
ISBN 9780062249357

LC 2015033616

This book, by Joel Fuhrman, MD, "presents a scientifically proven, practical program to prevent and reverse heart disease—coinciding with the author's new medical study. . . . [It] shows us how we can significantly lower cholesterol and blood pressure, reduce weight, heal obstructive coronary artery disease, and even eradicate advanced heart disease —all without the need for dangerous procedures like angioplasty or bypass surgery." (Publisher's note)

"It's obvious Furhman's zeal is genuine as he passionately tries to convince the general public to make smarter choices." Booklist

Includes bibliographical references (pages [383]-422) and index.

616.2   Diseases of respiratory system

Ackerman, Jennifer

Ah-choo! the uncommon life of your common cold. Twelve 2010 245p $22.99   **616.2**

1. Cold (Disease)
ISBN 978-0-446-54115-2; 978-0-446-57401-3 ebook

LC 2010-4794

The author "parses the variety and durability of the cold, its wellknown miseries, paradoxes (a highly active immune system may actually make you sicker with a cold), and myriad mysteries (why do poorer people get more colds? what roles do stress and sleep play? is our clean obsession making us more susceptible to sickness?) with the thoroughness of a scientist, the doggedness of a journalist, and the verve of a thriller writer. . . . There's a nifty collection of comforting recipes as well, including a nonalcoholic hot toddy (and a delicious sounding boozy one, too), banana pudding, and yes, chicken soup." Publ Wkly

Includes bibliographical references

616.3   Diseases of digestive system

Ali, Naheed

Understanding celiac disease; an introduction for patients and caregivers. Naheed Ali. Rowman & Littlefield Pub Inc 2014 332 p. (cloth; alk. paper) $38   **616.3**

1. Celiac disease 2. Celiac Disease
ISBN 1442226552; 9781442226555

LC 2014016086

"Celiac disease is being diagnosed more and more frequently, as people recognize their digestive issues may be linked to their gluten intake and sensitivity to various foods that include gluten. Here, Ali, in typical fashion, reviews the biology of celiac disease, its various symptoms, causes, and outcomes, and includes information about treatment, prevention, and living well with celiac." Publisher's note.

"Those who want a more technical description of celiac disease will find this book useful; readers looking for a basic overview and understanding of the condition and how to live with it may want to consider David L. Burns's 100 Questions & Answers About Celiac Disease and Sprue or Celiac Disease by Sylvia Llewelyn Bower, et al." LJ

Includes bibliographical references and index

Lacy, Brian E.

Making sense of IBS; a physician answers your questions about irritable bowel syndrome. Brian E. Lacy, Ph.D., M.D. The Johns Hopkins University Press 2013 xii, 380 p.p illustrations (pbk.; alk. paper) $21.95   **616.3**

1. Irritable bowel syndrome 2. Irritable colon
ISBN 1421411156; 9781421411156

LC 2013006074

This book, by Brian E. Lacy, discusses irritable bowel syndrome. "Today more than ever before, physicians are able to diagnose this complex disorder, understand and explain its origins, and develop a treatment plan that effectively meets the individual needs of a patient. . . . [The author] explains normal digestion, the causes of IBS, how IBS is diagnosed, and what to expect with treatment." (Publisher's note)

Includes bibliographical references and index

Making sense of irritable bowel syndrome

Steinhart, A. Hillary

Crohn's & colitis diet guide; Includes 175 Recipes. by Dr. Hillary Steinhart and Julie Cepo. Robert Rose 2014 336 p. illustrations $24.95   **616.3**

1. Diet 2. Chronic diseases 3. Digestive system
ISBN 077880478X; 9780778804789

Second edition

This book on Crohn's disease and ulcerative colitis, by Dr. Hillary Steinhart and Julie Cepo, "provides all the necessary guidelines regarding the specific foods that might cause problems, as well as delicious and nutritious recipes that can be enjoyed without compromising this difficult condition." (Publisher's note)

"The guide is written in easy-to-understand language, provides answers to commonly asked questions and many useful illustrations, although there are no photos of the recipes. Steinhart and Cepo are both knowledgeable, and clearly interested in helping those with IBD lead healthier lives. They have produced an invaluable guide that is highly recommended for those with IBD and those who care for them." Pub Wkly

---

616.4   Diseases of endocrine, hematopoietic, lymphatic, glandular systems; diseases of male breast

American Diabetes Association

American Diabetes Association complete guide to diabetes; 5th ed.; American Diabetes Association 2011 499p il pa $22.95   **616.4**

1. Diabetes
ISBN 978-1-58040-330-6

LC 2010-41272

First published 1996

This book describes types of insulin and the best ways to use them, insulin pumps and injection-free insulin techniques in research, new oral diabetes medications and therapies, the use of carbohydrate counting techniques as a meal planning tool as well as information on diabetes in the workplace, school, and day care.

Includes bibliographical references

Ask the experts; expert answers about your diabetes from the pages of Diabetes forecast. American Diabetes Association. American Diabetes Association 2014 159 p. (pbk.) $12.95   **616.4**

1. Diabetes -- Miscellanea
ISBN 1580405398; 9781580405393

LC 2013046542

This book, by the editors of the American Diabetes Association, provides advice for managing diabetes, "written by physicians, nurse practitioners, physician assistants, dietitians, diabetes educators, and other experts in the diabetes research and clinical communities. . . . Un-

like most self-care titles for people with diabetes, the unique format . . . creates an open forum for people to ask the specific and individualized questions that normally don't get answered." (Publisher's note)

Flippin, Royce

The **diabetes** reset; the revolutionary plan to reverse, control, and avoid Type 2 diabetes. George King, M.D. with Royce Flippin. Workman Publishing Company, Inc. 2014 326 p. illustrations (alk. paper) $25.95   **616.4**

1. Diet 2. Diabetes 3. Exercise 4. Weight loss 5. Self-care, Health 6. Non-insulin-dependent diabetes -- Alternative treatment
ISBN 076117592X; 9780761175926

LC 2014034312

This book, by Dr. George King, presents "a plan that will let readers avoid, control, and even reverse type 2 diabetes. The program begins with losing weight—and shows why losing only 5% of body weight makes a life-changing difference. It explains how a good's night sleep can significantly lower blood glucose levels. . . . It disentangles the carbohydrate confusion, reveals how to decrease the body's inflammatory response, and explains the importance of moderate exercise." (Publisher's note)

"While the promise of a "reset" may set off some red flags for skeptics, readers searching for a hopeful look at life with Type 2 diabetes or a step-by-step guide to making lifestyle changes will be attracted to this book." LJ

Includes bibliographical references and index

Mayo Clinic, the essential diabetes book; how to prevent, control & live well with diabetes. medical editor, M. Regina Castro, M.D. 2nd ed Time Home Entertainment, Inc. 2014 vii, 223 p.p color illustrations (pbk.) $19.95   **616.4**

1. Diabetes
ISBN 0848743393; 9780848743390

LC 2014933598

This book, edited by M. Regina Castro, presents a guidebook to diabetes, including discussion of how to manage "the pre-diabetes stage . . . ; types of diabetes; symptoms and risk factors; treatments and strategies for managing your blood sugar; avoiding serious complications; advances in insulin delivery [and more.]" (Publisher's note)

"This title covers: the pre-diabetes stage - taking charge to prevent diabetes; types of diabetes; symptoms and risk factors; treatments and strategies for managing your blood sugar; avoiding serious complications; advances in insulin delivery and new medications; and recipes." Publisher's note

Rubin, Richard R.

The **Johns** Hopkins guide to diabetes; for patients and families. Christopher D. Saudek, M.D., Richard R. Rubin, Ph.D., CDE, Thomas W. Donner, M.D. Johns Hopkins University Press 2014 xi, 488 p.p illustrations (pbk.; alk. paper) $22.95   **616.4**

1. Diabetes 2. Therapeutics 3. Diabetes -- Treatment -- Handbooks, manuals, etc
ISBN 1421411792; 1421411806; 9781421411798; 9781421411804

LC 2013015256

Written by Christopher D. Saudek, Richard R. Rubin, and Thomas W. Donner, "'The Johns Hopkins Guide to Diabetes' is a comprehensive and easy-to-read guide to this complex condition, answering questions such as: What are the differences between Type 1 and Type 2 diabetes? How are the different forms of this disease treated? Can gestational diabetes become a permanent condition? Can diabetes ever be managed successfully with diet and exercise alone?" (Publisher's note)

Wright, Hillary

The **prediabetes** diet plan; how to reverse prediabetes and prevent diabetes through healthy eating and exercise. Hillary Wright, MEd, RD. Ten Speed Press 2013 ix, 245 p.p (trade paperback) $15.99 **616.4**

   1. Preventive medicine 2. Diabetes -- Diet therapy 3. Physical fitness 4. Diabetes -- Prevention 5. Prediabetic state -- Patients -- Diet therapy

   ISBN 1607744627; 9781607744627

                       LC 2013018751

This book by Hillary Wright tells how, "While diabetes cannot be cured, prediabetes can be reversed, so it is critical to take action at an early stage. In straightforward, jargon-free language, 'The Prediabetes Diet Plan' explains insulin resistance (the underlying cause of prediabetes and type 2 diabetes) and offers a comprehensive strategy of diet and lifestyle change, which has been proven more effective than medication." (Publisher's note)

"This excellent introduction for readers recently diagnosed with (or at risk for) prediabetes will also interest readers with other forms of insulin resistance." LJ

Includes bibliographical references and index

616.5 Diseases of integument

Yosipovitch, Gil

Living with itch; a patient's guide. Gil Yosipovitch, M.D., and Shawn G. Kwatra, M.D. Johns Hopkins University Press 2013 160 p. color illustrations (A Johns Hopkins Press health book) (pbk.; alk. paper) $16.95 **616.5**

   1. Skin -- Diseases 2. Itching -- Popular works 3. Dermatology -- Popular works 4. Skin -- Diseases -- Popular works

   ISBN 1421412330; 9781421412337

                       LC 2013016433

In this book, authors Gil Yosipovitch and Shawn G. Kwatra "explain the cascade of physiological events that causes us to experience itch. They describe the many skin diseases, from atopic dermatitis (eczema) to psoriasis, and conditions like chronic kidney disease, lymphoma, HIV, and neuropathies that cause itch. . . . Patient and parent narratives illustrate how people cope with itch and how, with medical and social support, itch can be managed." (Publisher's note)

"Although there is no simple cure, the book offers hope as well as treatment options, useful charts, and links to online resources. Those seeking support, information, and relief will benefit from this forthright guide." LJ

Includes bibliographical references (page 135) and index

616.6 Diseases of urogenital system

Kang, Mandip S.

The **doctor's** kidney diets; a nutritional guide to managing and slowing the progression of chronic kidney disease. Mandip S. Kang, MD, FASN. Square One Publishers 2015 208 p. (pbk.) $17.95 **616.6**

   1. Kidneys -- Diseases 2. Self-care, Health 3. Kidneys -- Diseases -- Diet therapy 4. Kidneys -- Diseases -- Nutritional aspects

   ISBN 9780757003738

                       LC 2015018370

This book, by Dr. Mandip S. Kang, "is divided into two parts. Part

One provides a clear overview of kidney function, kidney disease, and the role that nutrition plays in the treatment of kidney problems. The doctor then reviews the special dietary considerations of individuals with CKD, including the need to limit certain nutrients, fluids, and other dietary components." (Publisher's note)

"This well-written manual is essential for anyone diagnosed with kidney disease, or their caregivers, and is a needed addition for all consumer health collections." LJ

Includes bibliographical references and index

616.7 Diseases of musculoskeletal system

Pizzorno, Lara

Your bones; how you can prevent osteoporosis & have strong bones for life-naturally. Lara Pizzorno, MA, LMT ; with Jonathan V. Wright, MD. Praktikos Books 2013 xiii, 496 p.p illustrations (some color) (pbk.) $12 **616.7**

   1. Osteoporosis 2. Preventive medicine 3. Osteoporosis -- Prevention -- Popular works 4. Osteoporosis -- Diet therapy -- Popular works 5. Osteoporosis -- Exercise therapy -- Popular works 6. Osteoporosis -- Nutritional aspects -- Popular works

   ISBN 160766013X; 9781607660132

                       LC 2012047340

Written by Lara Pizzorno, "'Your Bones' contains everything you need to know for healthy bones in one book, providing scientifically based advice which highlights natural prevention and treatment strategies. This updated and expanded edition includes many new studies on the dangers of the bisphosphonate drugs and an in depth discussion of two new drugs with potential adverse effects." (Publisher's note)

"Consumer health collections looking for another book about the natural ways to prevent osteoporosis would do well to choose this title. Those looking for recipes or photos of recommended exercises need to look elsewhere." LJ

Includes bibliographical references and index

Thomas, Donald E.

The **lupus** encyclopedia; a comprehensive guide for patients and families. Donald E. Thomas, Jr., M.D., FACP, FACR. Johns Hopkins University Press 2013 912 p. illustrations (A Johns Hopkins Press health book) (pbk.; alk. paper) $34.95 **616.7**

   1. Systemic lupus erythematosus 2. Systemic lupus erythematosus -- Encyclopedias

   ISBN 1421409836; 1421409844; 9781421409832; 9781421409849

                       LC 2012042648

This book on the topic of lupus, by doctor Donald E. Thomas, "is an authoritative compendium that provides detailed explanations of every body system potentially affected by the disease, along with practical advice about coping. People with lupus, their loved ones, caregivers, and medical professionals-- all will find here an invaluable resource." (Publisher's note)

"This book supplies a caring, comprehensive guide to understanding and coping with lupus." LJ

Includes bibliographical references and index

616.8 Diseases of nervous system and mental disorders

Bowling, Allen C.

Optimal health with multiple sclerosis; a guide to integrating lifestyle, alternative, and conventional medicine. Allen C. Bowling, MD, PhD, Physician Associate, Colorado Neurological Institute, Englewood, Colorado and Clinical Professor of Neurology, University of Colorado, Aurora, Colorado. Demos Medical Publishing, LLC 2014 402 p. (alk. paper) $24.95　　　**616.8**

1. Multiple sclerosis 2. Alternative medicine 3. Multiple sclerosis -- Treatment 4. Multiple sclerosis -- Alternative treatment

ISBN 1936303701; 9781936303700

LC 2014027383

This book, by doctor Allen C. Bowling, provides "evidence-based information on the relevance, safety, and effectiveness of various alternative and lifestyle medicine approaches to MS treatment and the best ways to safely integrate them with conventional medicine. . . . [It] provides the accurate and unbiased information people with MS, their friends and family, health care professionals, and educators need to make responsible decisions and achieve the very best outcome." (Publisher's note)

Includes bibliographical references and index

Cahalan, Susannah

Brain on fire; my month of madness. by Susannah Cahalan. Free Press 2012 264 p. illustrations $25　　　**616.8**

1. Encephalitis 2. Brain -- Diseases 3. Autoimmune diseases 4. Diagnostic errors -- United States -- Case studies 5. Encephalitis -- Patients -- United States -- Biography 6. Autoimmune diseases -- Patients -- United States -- Biography 7. Frontal lobes -- Diseases -- Patients -- United States -- Biography 8. Limbic system -- Diseases -- Patients -- United States -- Biography

ISBN 145162137X; 9781451621372

LC 2012012670

This book chronicles how "when she was twenty-four years old, [Susannah] Cahalan had a seizure that was accompanied by delusions, paranoia, hallucinations, and violent mood swings. Over the course of a month, she was hospitalized with an autoimmune disease that caused her body to attack her brain. She remembers almost nothing of this month. . . . She began researching what happened to her and recreating, in words, her month of madness." (Voice of Youth Advocates)

"Cahalan expertly weaves together her own story and relevant scientific and medical information about autoimmune diseases, which are about two-thirds environmental and one-third genetic in origin. So, she writes, an external trigger, such as a sneeze or a toxic apartment, probably combined with a genetic predisposition toward developing aggressive antibodies to create her problem. A compelling health story." Booklist

Includes bibliographical references

Ehrnstrom, Colleen

End the Insomnia Struggle; A Step-by-Step Guide to Help You Get to Sleep and Stay Asleep. Colleen Ehrnstrom ; Alisha L. Brosse. New Harbinger Pubns Inc 2016 256 p. (paperback) $24.95　　　**616.8**

1. Sleep 2. Insomnia 3. Self-help techniques

ISBN 9781626253452; 9781626253445; 9781626253438; 1626253439

This book, by Colleen Ehrnstrom and Alisha L. Brosse, "offers a comprehensive, medication-free program that can be individually tailored for anyone who struggles with insomnia. Integrating the physiology of sleep, and proven-effective approaches from cognitive behavioral therapy for insomnia (CBT-I) and acceptance and commitment therapy (ACT), this book provides step-by-step guidance for developing your own treatment plan according to your particular challenges with insom-

nia." (Publisher's note)

"Of interest to anyone who suffers from insomnia or has a family member who does." LJ

Includes bibliographical references.

Estep, Preston

The **mindspan** diet; reduce Alzheimer's risk, minimize memory loss, and keep your brain young. Preston Estep, III. Ballantine Books 2016 304 p. illustrations (hardcover; alk. paper) $27　　　**616.8**

1. Diet therapy 2. Alzheimer's disease 3. Alzheimer's disease -- Diet therapy

ISBN 9781101886120

LC 2016003594

This book, by Preston Estep, III, presents a "plan for curbing memory loss and improving cognitive longevity that will forever change how you think about diet and aging. . . . Complete with food recommendations, shopping lists, advice on reading nutrition labels, and more than seventy delicious recipes, [it] shows that you can enjoy the richest flavors life has to offer and remain lean, healthy, and cognitively intact for a very long life." (Publisher's note)

"Presenting a sensible regimen that people can follow easily, this recommended diet book with useful information about aging is for most consumer health collections." LJ

Includes bibliographical references and index

Ingram, Jay

The **End** of Memory; A Natural History of Aging and Alzheimer's. by Jay Ingram. St. Martin's Press 2015 304 p. $26.99　　　**616.8**

1. Alzheimer's disease

ISBN 125007648X; 9781250076489

LC 2015019167

In this book on Alzheimer's, "science author Jay Ingram writes a biography of this disease that attacks the brains of patients. He charts the history of the disease from before it was noted by Alois Alzheimer through to the twenty-first century, explains the fascinating science of plaques and tangles, recounts the efforts to understand and combat the disease, and introduces us to the passionate researchers who are working to find a cure." (Publisher's note)

Highly readable and informative, this work is strongly recommended for readers interested in medicine, scientific research or pathology." Library Journal

Jebelli, Joseph

★ **In** pursuit of memory; the fight against Alzheimer's. Joseph Jebelli. Little, Brown & Co. 2017 xv, 301 p.p illustrations (hardcover) $28　　　**616.8**

1. Alzheimer's disease 2. Alzheimer's disease patients 3. Alzheimer's disease -- Popular works 4. Alzheimer's disease -- Patients -- Care 5. Alzheimer's disease -- Patients -- Biography 6. Alzheimer's disease -- Patients -- Family relationships

ISBN 9780316360777; 9780316360791; 0316360791

LC 2017946259

In this book, author Joseph Jebelli "follows every lead for a cure with the panache of a detective novelist, giving readers much to hope for despite the devastation Alzheimer's has left in its wake. Based on his meticulous and wide-ranging research, he makes a convincing argument that Alzheimer's will be defeated in the decades to come. Jebelli analyzes every facet of Alzheimer's with personal empathy and scientific rigor, a combination that makes for enthralling reading." (Kirkus)

"Jebelli analyzes every facet of Alzheimer's with personal empathy and scientific rigor, a combination that makes for enthralling reading." Kirkus

Includes bibliographical references (pages 253-288) and index.

Kapsambelis, Niki

The **inheritance**; a family on the front lines of the battle against Alzheimer's disease. Niki Kapsambelis. Simon & Schuster 2017 xviii, 344 p.p ills., genealogical tables (hardback) $26   **616.8**
1. Alzheimer's disease 2. Alzheimer's disease patients 3. Alzheimer's disease -- Patients -- United States -- Biography 4. Alzheimer's disease -- Patients -- Rehabilitation -- Popular works 5. Alzheimer's disease -- Patients -- Family relationships -- United States -- Case studies
ISBN 9781451697223; 9781451697322; 9781451697339
LC 2016033463

This book, by Niki Kapsambelis, tells the story of Alzheimer's through the humanizing lens of . . . [the DeMoes,] made extraordinary by both their terrible circumstances and their bravery. Their tale is intertwined with the dramatic narrative history of the disease, the cutting-edge research that brings us ever closer to a possible cure, and the accounts of the extraordinary doctors spearheading these groundbreaking studies." (Publisher's note)

"An educational and emotional chronicle that should resonate with a wide variety of readers." Kirkus

Includes bibliographical references (pages 301-333) and index.

Kosik, Kenneth S.

Outsmarting Alzheimer's; what you can do to reduce your risk. Kenneth S. Kosik, MD, with Alisa Bowman. The Reader's Digest Association, Inc. 2015 320 p. illustrations (hardback) $24.99   **616.8**
1. Dementia 2. Nervous system 3. Health self-care 4. Alzheimer's disease 5. Self-care, Health 6. Alzheimer's disease -- Prevention
ISBN 9781621452447
LC 2015025509

This book, by Kenneth S. Kosik, "is an easy-to-follow, research-based guide to the simple, low-cost choices that give the reader the power to reduce the risk of developing Alzheimer's disease and dementia. . . . [This book] gives you 80 simple lifestyle prescriptions in the six key areas with the most scientific evidence for protecting your brain health: Social Smarts, Meal Smarts, Aerobics Smarts, Resilience to Stress Smarts, Train Your Brain Smarts, and Sleep." (Publisher's note)

"Kosik offers a very reasonable and feasible program, aimed at both avoiding Alzheimer's disease and achieving overall enhanced physical and mental well-being." Pub Wkly

Includes bibliographical references and index

Kozol, Jonathan, 1936-

The **theft** of memory; losing my father one day at a time. Jonathan Kozol. Crown Publishers 2015 320 p. (hardback) $26   **616.8**
1. Brain 2. Father-son relationship 3. Alzheimer's disease patients 4. Neurologists -- Biography 5. Fathers and sons -- Biography 6. Alzheimer's disease -- Biography
ISBN 0804140979; 9780804140973; 9780804140997
LC 2014041699

In this memoir, author Jonathan Kozol tells "the story of his father's life and work as a nationally noted specialist in disorders of the brain and his astonishing ability, at the onset of Alzheimer's disease, to explain the causes of his sickness and then to narrate, step-by-step, his slow descent into dementia." (Publisher's note)

"The author's approach is shrewd yet warmly empathetic; he is curious about how the mind's gradual breakdown exposes its machinery, and raptly attuned to the emotional effects of these changes on his parents and himself. The result is a clear-eyed and deeply felt meditation on the aspects of family that age does not ravage." Pub Wkly

Includes bibliographical references and index

Kuhn, Daniel

Alzheimer's early stages; first steps for families, friends and caregivers. 2nd ed; Hunter House 2003 306p hardcover o.p. pa $15.95   **616.8**
1. Alzheimer's disease
ISBN 0-89793-398-2; 0-89793-397-4 pa
LC 2002-151932

First published 1999

This book covers "the importance of getting a diagnosis, risk factors (including the role of depression), early symptoms, treatment and prevention, and information on physical health, safety concerns, caring for the caregiver, and financial and end-of-life planning—all illustrated with brief, first-person narratives. Of special interest are chapters on relationships, including telling others about the diagnosis, and the . . . section on current available treatments. . . . Intelligently written with numerous references to professional and consumer literature, this book is an excellent choice for Alzheimer's and consumer health collections." Libr J

Includes bibliographical references

Lang, Anthony E.

★ **Parkinson's** disease; a complete guide for patients and families. [by] William J. Weiner, Lisa M. Shulman, Anthony E. Lang. 2nd ed.; Johns Hopkins University Press 2007 278p il $55; pa $17.95   **616.8**
1. Parkinson's disease
ISBN 0-8018-8545-0; 978-0-8018-8545-7; 0-8018-8546-9 pa; 978-0-8018-8546-4 pa
LC 2006-18814

First published 2001

This book contains "information for managing this complex condition, including details on the use of medications, diet, exercise, complementary therapies, and surgery." Publisher's note

Lemonick, Michael D.

The **perpetual** now; a story of amnesia, memory, and love. Michael D. Lemonick. Doubleday 2016 304 p. illustrations (some color) (ebook) $65; (hardback) $27.95   **616.8**
1. Encephalitis 2. Brain -- Diseases 3. Brain damage -- Patients -- Biography 4. Encephalitis -- Patients -- Biography
ISBN 9780385539678; 9780385539661
LC 2016017750

This biography of Lonni Sue Johnson, by Michael D. Lemonick, "is the moving story of this exceptional woman, and the groundbreaking revelations about memory, learning, and consciousness her unique case has uncovered. . . . Johnson was a renowned artist who . . . contracted encephalitis. The disease burned through her hippocampus like wildfire, leaving her severely amnesic, living in a present that rarely progresses beyond ten to fifteen minutes." (Publisher's note)

"An absolutely memorable book." Kirkus

Includes bibliographical references (pages 281-282).

Mainardi, Diogo

The **fall**; a father's memoir in 424 steps. by Diogo Mainardi ; translated from the Portuguese by Margaret Jull Costa. Other Press 2014 176 p. illustrations (hardback) $20   **616.8**

1. Cerebral palsy 2. Father-son relationship 3. Fathers and sons -- Biography 4. Paralysis, Spastic, in children -- Biography
ISBN 1590517008; 9781590517000; 9781590517017

LC 2014005571

This memoir by Diogo Mainardi is "424 short passages [that] match the number of steps taken by [his] son Tito as he walks, with great difficulty, alongside his father through the streets of Venice, the city where a medical mishap during Tito's birth left him with Cerebral Palsy. Mainairdi begins to draw on his knowledge of art and history, seeking to better explain a tragedy that was entirely avoidable." (Publisher's note)

"Tito emerges as collaborator in the book—not as a cause or a type or a symbol but as a happy, well-adjusted, well-loved individual with a life well worth living. A singularly compelling memoir." Kirkus

Owen, Adrian

Into the Gray Zone; A Neuroscientist Explores the Border Between Life and Death. Adrian Owen. Scribner 2017 xi, 304 p.p (hardcover) $28   **616.8**
1. Brain -- Diseases 2. Brain damage -- Patients 3. Persistent vegetative state 4. Persistent vegetative state -- Moral and ethical aspects
ISBN 9781501135200; 9781501135224; 1501135201

This book, by Adrian Owen, focuses on "the so-called 'gray zone' between full consciousness and brain death. People in this middle place have sustained traumatic brain injuries or are the victims of stroke or degenerative diseases. . . . Many are oblivious to the outside world, and their doctors believe they are incapable of thought. But a sizeable number are experiencing something different: intact minds adrift deep within damaged brains and bodies." (Publisher's note)

"An exploration of the current medical research on brain health and the consciousness of patients who suffer catastrophic head trauma." Kirkus

Includes bibliographical references (pages 263-281) and index.

Palfreman, Jon

Brain storms; the race to unlock the mysteries of Parkinson's disease. Jon Palfreman. Scientific American/Farrar, Straus & Giroux 2015 272 p. illustrations (hardback) $26   **616.8**
1. Parkinson's disease 2. Parkinson Disease -- Personal Narratives
ISBN 0374116172; 9780374116170

LC 2015003861

This book, by Jon Palfreman, named a Publisher's Weekly Top 10 Science Book form Fall 2015, "chronicles how scientists have worked to crack the mystery of [Parkinson's Disease,] what was once called the shaking palsy, from the earliest clinical descriptions of tremors, gait freezing, and micrographia to the cutting edge of neuroscience, and charts the victories and setbacks of a massive international effort to best the disease." (Publisher's note)

"In this illuminating book, Palfreman reminds patients that exercise and a positive attitude help, and he urges them to participate in clinical trials and take to task drug companies reluctant to initiate huge trials for what they dismiss as a non-life-threatening disease." Kirkus

Ropper, Allan H.

Reaching down the rabbit hole; a renowned neurologist explains the mystery and drama of brain disease. Dr. Allan H. Ropper and Brian David Burrell. St. Martin's Press 2014 272 p. (hardback) $25.99   **616.8**
1. Neurosciences 2. Nervous system 3. Brain -- Diseases 4. Neurology -- Anecdotes 5. Brain -- Diseases -- Anecdotes 6. Neurologists -- Massachusetts -- Boston -- Biography
ISBN 1250034981; 9781250034984

LC 2014017011

In this book, authors Dr. Allan H. Ropper and Brian David Burrell "take the reader behind the scenes at Harvard Medical School's neurology unit to show how a seasoned diagnostician faces down bizarre, life-altering afflictions." (Publisher's note)

Sacks, Oliver W.

Uncle Tungsten; memories of a chemical boyhood. [by] Oliver Sacks. Knopf 2001 337p il hardcover o.p. pa $14 **616.8**
1. Physicians 2. Neurologists 3. Writers on science 4. Writers on medicine
ISBN 0-375-40448-1; 0-375-70404-3 pa

LC 2001-33738

"Sacks' first scientific love was chemistry, and he presents an avid history of the field within a memoir that pays tribute to his uncle, who welcomed Sacks into his lab, thus encouraging his passion for chemistry and learning." Booklist

Small, Gary

2 weeks to a younger brain; Gary Small, Gigi Vorgan. Humanix Books 2015 308 p. illustrations (hardback; alk. paper) $24.95   **616.8**
1. Brain 2. Self-improvement
ISBN 1630060305; 9781630060305; 9781630060312

LC 2014958068

This book, by Gary Small and Gigi Vorgan, "translates the latest brain science into practical strategies and exercises that yield quick and long-lasting benefits. It will not only improve your memory, but will also strengthen your physical health by reducing your risk for diabetes, heart disease, and stroke. The latest research confirms that there is a lot we can do to boost our memory and keep our brains young." (Publisher's note)

Includes bibliographical references (pages 245-282) and index

What if it's not Alzheimer's? a caregiver's guide to dementia. edited by Gary Radin and Lisa Radin ; foreword by Murray Grossman, MD EdD. Prometheus Books 2014 340 p. illustrations (paperback) $19   **616.8**
1. Dementia 2. Caregivers -- Handbooks, manuals, etc. 3. Caregivers -- Handbooks, manuals, etc 4. Dementia -- Nursing -- Handbooks, manuals, etc 5. Dementia -- Patients -- Care -- Handbooks, manuals, etc
ISBN 161614968X; 9781616149680

LC 2014015843

This book, edited by Gary Radin and Lisa Radin, is a "comprehensive guide dealing with frontotemporal degeneration (FTD), one of the largest groups of non-Alzheimer's dementias. . . . The first part defines and explores FTD as an illness distinct from Alzheimer's disease. . . . In the following section on caregiver resources, the contributors identify professional and government assistance programs along with private resources and legal options." (Publisher's note)

"While there is some overlap among the individual chapters, this guide presents a wealth of medical information, written in terms the interested layperson can understand, as well as practical advice. One of the few books to discuss FTD specifically, this is an invaluable resource for patients, family, and friends, as well as health-care providers." LJ

Includes bibliographical references and index

Winter, W. Chris

The **sleep** solution; Why Your Sleep is Broken and How to Fix It. W. Chris Winter, MD. New American Library 2017 272 p. illustrations $26   **616.8**

1. Sleep 2. Sleep disorders 3. Sleep -- Popular works 4. Sleep disorders -- Popular works

ISBN 9780399583605

LC 2016034735

This book, by W. Chris Winter, MD, "will help anyone achieve healthy sleep and eliminate pills, pain, and fatigue. If you want to fix your sleep problems, Internet tips and tricks aren't going to do it for you. You need to really understand what's going on with your sleep—both what your problems are and how to solve them." (Publisher's note)

"This highly recommended title will appeal to those who have trouble sleeping—and who hasn't?" LJ

Includes bibliographical references (pages 253-258) and index.

616.84 Manifestations of nervous system diseases

Thomson, Helen

Unthinkable; an extraordinary journey through the world's strangest brains. Helen Thomson. HarperCollins 2018 288 p. $27.99 **616.84**

1. Brain 2. Neurosciences 3. Brain -- Diseases

ISBN 006239116X; 9780062391162

In this book, author Helen Thomson describes her work "tracking down incredibly rare brain disorders. . . . She tells the stories of nine extraordinary people she encountered along the way. From the man who thinks he's a tiger to the doctor who feels the pain of others just by looking at them to a woman who hears music that's not there, their experiences illustrate how the brain can shape our lives in unexpected and, in some cases, brilliant and alarming ways." (Publisher's note)

"Thomson has a gift for making the complex and strange understandable and relatable." Library Journal

616.849 Miscellaneous symptoms

Nicholls, Henry

Sleepyhead; the neuroscience of a good night's rest. Henry Nicholls. Basic Books 2018 368 p. (hardcover) $30 **616.849**

1. Sleep apnea 2. Chronic fatigue syndrome 3. Sleep -- Physiological aspects

ISBN 9781541672567; 9781541672574

LC 2018939612

In this book writer Henry Nicholls "uses his own experience with chronic narcolepsy as a gateway to better understanding the . . . relatively uncharted world of sleep disorders. We meet insomniacs who can't get any sleep . . . and sleep apnea victims who nearly suffocate in their sleep. We learn the underlying difference between morning larks and night owls; why our sleeping habits shift as we grow older; and the evolutionary significance of REM sleep and dreaming." (Publisher's note)

616.85 Miscellaneous diseases of nervous system and mental disorders

Adam, David

The **man** who couldn't stop; OCD and the true story of a life lost in thought. David Adam. Farrar, Straus and Giroux 2015 336 p. (hardcover) $26 **616.85**

1. Obsessive-compulsive disorder

ISBN 0374223955; 9780374223953; 9780374710514

LC 2014017387

This book, by David Adam, is an "intimate look at the power of

intrusive thoughts, how our brains can turn against us, and living with obsessive compulsive disorder. . . . Adam explores the weird thoughts that exist within every mind, and how they drive millions of us toward obsession and compulsion." (Publisher's note)

"For all the impressive marshaling of information, it is Adam's own story of his struggles with the condition, which his infant daughter forced him to confront instead of uneasily accepting, that is the most captivating aspect of this impressive work." Booklist

Includes bibliographical references

Alpern, Gerald

Vets for vets; harnessing the power of vets to heal. Gerald Alpern. Psychological Development Publications 2016 xix, 187 p.p (hardcover) $24.99 **616.85**

1. Veterans -- Mental health 2. Post-traumatic stress disorder

ISBN 1622179277; 9781622179275

This book, by Gerald Alpern, "is based on decades of work with veterans. It provides innovative new and practical treatment techniques for veterans. Each chapter offers the three targeted groups of readers (i.e family and friends of vets, mental health professionals and vets themselves) insights and practical tools for healthy transition from warrior to citizen." (Publisher's note)

"A compassionate and eye-opening approach to healing mentally and emotionally wounded soldiers." Kirkus

Bass, Ellen

The **courage** to heal; a guide for women survivors of child sexual abuse. by Ellen Bass and Laura Davis. 20th anniversary edition; 4th revised edition; Collins Living 2008 xxxiv, 606p pa $22.95 **616.85**

1. Child sexual abuse 2. Adult child sexual abuse victims 3. Women -- Psychology

ISBN 978-0-06-128433-5; 0-06-128433-5

LC 2008-11616

First published 1988

"This book offers help and encouragement to women who were sexually abused in childhood. Through moving firstperson narratives, it illustrates how to come to terms with the past and work constructively towards the future. Along the way it describes the effects of sexual abuse, maps the stages survivors pass through, and offers practical guidance on dealing with self-defeating behaviors and building self-esteem. . . . Compassionate and supportive." Libr J

Includes bibliographical references

Begley, Sharon

Can't just stop; An Investigation of Compulsions. Sharon Begley. Simon & Schuster 2017 304 p. (hardcover) $27.00; (ebook) $18.99 **616.85**

1. Obsessive-compulsive disorder -- Popular works

ISBN 9781476725826; 9781476725840

LC 2016016745

This book, by Sharon Begley, examines "the science behind both mild and extreme compulsive behavior—using fascinating case studies to understand its deeper meaning and reveal the truth about human compulsion. . . . She explores the role of compulsion in our fast paced culture, the brain science behind it, and strange manifestations of the behavior throughout history." (Publisher's note)

"Due to Begley's dense explanations of brain science, the book requires close attention at times, but her captivating, accessible anecdotes of individual cases lead to unforgettable scenarios." Kirkus

Boyes, Alice

The **anxiety** toolkit; strategies for fine-tuning your mind and moving past your stuck points. Alice Boyes. Perigee 2015 240 p. (paperback) $16   **616.85**

1. Anxiety 2. Psychology 3. Anxiety -- Popular works 4. Anxiety -- Treatment -- Popular works

ISBN 0399169253; 9780399169250

LC 2014040065

In this book, author "Alice Boyes translates powerful, evidence-based tools used in therapy clinics into tips and tricks you can employ in everyday life. Whether you have an anxiety disorder, or are just anxiety-prone by nature, you'll discover how anxiety works, strategies to help you cope with common anxiety 'stuck' points and a confidence that - anxious or not - you have all the tools you need to succeed in life and work." (Publisher's note)

Boyes's tone is friendly but never saccharine, and endlessly practical. Her tips and exercises, drawn from cognitive behavioral therapies that she herself has administered, should make a valuable reference for anxiety sufferers, and an ideal companion to readers undergoing psychotherapy themselves." Pub Wkly

Bulik, Cynthia M.

Midlife eating disorders; your journey to recovery. Cynthia M. Bulik, Ph. D. Walker & Company 2013 352 p. $17 **616.85**

1. Eating disorders 2. Middle aged persons 3. Middle-aged persons 4. Middle age -- Psychological aspects

ISBN 080271269X; 9780802712691

LC 2012037481

In this book, clinical psychologist and director of the University of North Carolina Eating Disorders Program Cynthia M. Bulik "reviews the causes, features, and age-appropriate treatments of midlife eating disorders from anorexia nervosa to binge eating, bulimia nervosa, and purging. She explores some of the challenges facing adults with eating problems, including parenting, intimacy, pregnancy, and breastfeeding." (Booklist)

"[Bulik] discusses treatment options, finding compassionate care, and the importance of support from health professionals as well as family and friends. The book has extensive notes as well as a resource list of American and British organizations." LJ

Includes bibliographical references and index

Collins, Judy

Cravings; how I conquered food. Judy Collins. Nan A. Talese 2017 288 p. illustrations (some color) (ebook) $65; (hardback) $26   **616.85**

1. Compulsive eating -- United States -- Biography 2. Bulimia -- Patients -- United States -- Biography 3. Singers -- United States -- Biography 4. Eating disorders -- Patients -- United States -- Biography

ISBN 9780385541329; 9780385541312

LC 2016009368

This memoir is "a no-holds-barred account of folk legend Judy Collins's harrowing struggle with compulsive overeating and of the journey that led her to a solution. Since childhood Judy Collins has had a tumultuous, fraught relationship with food. Her issues with overeating nearly claimed her career and her life. . . . She tried nearly every diet plan that exists, often turning to alcohol to dull the pain of yet another failed attempt to control her . . . insatiable cravings." (Publisher's note)

"Collins's radiant memoir shines a light on her almost deadly struggles while vividly celebrating her new life free from cravings and sharing hope with everyone who suffers from food addiction." Pub Wkly

Includes bibliographical references and index

Denevi, Timothy

Hyper; a personal history of ADHD. Timothy Denevi. Simon & Schuster 2014 304 p. (hardback) $26   **616.85**

1. Attention deficit disorder 2. Attention-deficit-disordered adults -- Biography 3. Attention-deficit hyperactivity disorder -- Complications

ISBN 1476702578; 9781476702575; 9781476702582

LC 2013042085

This book, by Timothy Denevi, is a "memoir about what it's like to be a child with ADHD. . . . [U]sing his own experience as a springboard, Denevi also reveals the origins of ADHD, from the late nineteenth century when hyperactivity was attributed to defective moral conscience, demons, or head trauma, through the twentieth century when food additives, bad parenting, and even government conspiracies were blamed, to the most recent genetic research." (Publisher's note)

"A well-written, easy-to-read journey of one man's experience living with ADHD and the history of the disorder. Parents may see their children in Denevi's story, and adults may see themselves in the childhood accounts that are shared here. A great addition to a large developmental disabilities collection." LJ

Includes bibliographical references (pages 261-274)

Dittrich, Luke

★ **Patient** H.M. a story of memory, madness and family secrets. Luke Dittrich. Random House 2016 320 p. illustrations (hardback) $28   **616.85**

1. Memory 2. Memory Disorders 3. Memory, Long-Term 4. Epilepsy -- surgery 5. Amnesia, Anterograde

ISBN 9780812992731

LC 2015048638

This book, by Luke Dittrich, describes how "in 1953, a twenty-seven-year-old factory worker named Henry Molaison . . . received a radical new version of the then-common lobotomy. . . . The operation failed to eliminate Henry's seizures, but it did have an unintended effect: Henry was left profoundly amnesic, unable to create long-term memories. Over the next sixty years, Patient H.M., as Henry was known, became the most studied individual in the history of neuroscience." (Publisher's note)

"Though long, there's not a wasted word in the book, which should make readers glad we live in the age of Prozac and not the scalpel. A mesmerizing, maddening story and a model of journalistic investigation." Kirkus

Donvan, John

★ **In** a different key; the story of autism. John Donvan and Caren Zucker. Crown Publishers 2016 688 p. (hardback) $30   **616.85**

1. Autism 2. Mental health 3. People with disabilities 4. Autism spectrum disorders 5. Autism spectrum disorders -- History

ISBN 0307985679; 9780307985675; 9780307985705

LC 2015024706

Pulitzer Prize Finalist: General Nonfiction (2017)

This book on autism by authors John Donovan and Caren Zucker "tells the extraordinary story of this often misunderstood condition, and of the civil rights battles waged by the families of those who have it. Unfolding over decades, it is a beautifully rendered history of ordinary people determined to secure a place in the world for those with autism—by liberating children from dank institutions, campaigning for their right to go to school, challenging expert opinion on what it means to have autism." (Publisher's note)

"This book will not educate researchers with new information on autism. It will, however, introduce a human aspect to the chronology. Parents of autistic children will recognize themselves in many of these stories but also learn more about the truth behind them. Autistic individuals will take away lessons to forgive the past and to recognize the vast spectrum of difference—not just among those on the autism spectrum but among all people, who are always learning and growing." LJ

Frost, Randy O.

Stuff. Houghton Mifflin Harcourt 2010 290p $27 **616.85**
1. Compulsive hoarding 2. Collectors and collecting 3. Obsessive-compulsive disorder
ISBN 978-0-15-101423-1; 0-15-101423-X
LC 2009-28273
"Writing with authority and compassion, the authors tell the stories of diverse men and women who acquire and accumulate possessions to the point where their apartments or homes are dangerously cluttered with mounds of newspapers, clothing and other objects. . . . An absorbing, gripping, important report." Kirkus
Includes bibliographical references

Gambaro, Jill, 1959-

The **truth** about carpal tunnel syndrome; finding answers, getting well. Jill Gambaro. Rowman & Littlefield Pub Inc 2014 151 p. (cloth; alk. paper) $34 **616.85**
1. Stress (Physiology) 2. Occupational health and safety 3. Carpal tunnel syndrome 4. Overuse injuries -- Miscellanea 5. Carpal tunnel syndrome -- Treatment
ISBN 1442225793; 9781442225794
LC 2013051337
Written by Jill Gambaro, "'The Truth About Carpal Tunnel Syndrome' is a . . . patient account of this controversial injury. Using layman's terms, the book describes why it's so difficult to treat, how the author learned to manage hers, and how the medical and legal systems work in conflict to those suffering such injuries. Offering hope to sufferers and their loved ones, this book captures the reality of carpal tunnel syndrome." (Publisher's note)
Includes bibliographical references and index

Grandin, Temple, 1947-

★ The **autistic** brain; thinking across the spectrum. Temple Grandin and Richard Panek. Houghton Mifflin Harcourt 2013 256 p. (hardcover) $28 **616.85**
1. Autism 2. Neurosciences 3. Autism -- Research 4. Psychology, Pathological 5. Autism spectrum disorders 6. Autistic people -- Mental health
ISBN 0547636458; 9780547636450
LC 2013000662
This book, by Temple Grandin and Richard Panek, presents an "account of the latest science of autism. . . . Autism studies have moved from the realm of psychology to neurology and genetics, and there is far more hope today than ever before thanks to groundbreaking new research into causes and treatments. Now Temple Grandin reports from the forefront of autism science, bringing her singular perspective to a thrilling journey into the heart of the autism revolution." (Publisher's note)

Guyenet, Stephan J.

The **Hungry** Brain; outsmarting the instincts that make us overeat. Stephan J. Guyenet ; illustrated by Shizuka N. Aoki. St. Martin's Press 2017 304 p. illustrations (ebook) $60; $27.99 **616.85**
1. Eating disorders 2. Compulsive eating 3. Obesity -- Psychological aspects
ISBN 9781250081230; 125008119X; 9781250081193
This book, by Stephan J. Guyenet, illustrated by Shizuka N. Aoki,

"takes readers on an eye-opening journey through cutting-edge neuroscience that has never before been available to a general audience. 'The Hungry Brain' delivers profound insights into why the brain undermines our weight goals and transforms these insights into practical guidelines for eating well and staying slim." (Publisher's note)
"This fun, insightful, and important text will appeal to both science lovers and fitness fanatics." Pub Wkly
Includes bibliographical references (pages 241-278) and index

Hallowell, Edward M.

Driven to Distraction; Recognizing & Coping With Attention Deficit Disorder From Childhood to Adulthood. by Edward M. Hallowell and John Ratey. Rev. and updated ed. Anchor Books 2011 382 p. $15.95 **616.85**
1. Attention deficit disorder
ISBN 0307743152; 9780307743152
LC 2011292194
The authors of this book, Edward M. Hallowell and John Ratey, "explore the varied forms ADHD takes, from hyperactivity to daydreaming. They dispel common myths, offer helpful coping tools, and give a thorough accounting of all treatment options as well as tips for dealing with a diagnosed child, partner, or family member. But most importantly, they focus on the positives that can come with this 'disorder'—including high energy, intuitiveness, creativity, and enthusiasm." (Publisher's note)
Includes bibliographical references and index

Higashida, Naoki

Fall down 7 times get up 8; a young man's voice from the silence of autism. Naoki Higashida ; translated by Ka Yoshida and David Mitchell. Random House 2017 xxiii, 206 p.p illustrations **616.85**
1. Autism 2. Autistic people 3. Autistic people -- Psychology 4. Autistic people -- Japan -- Biography
ISBN 9780812997408; 9780812997392
LC 2017004105
This book, by Naoki Higashida, translated by KA Yoshida and David Mitchell, is "an extraordinary self-portrait of life as a young adult with autism. . . . [Higashida] shares his thoughts and experiences as a twenty-four-year-old man living each day with severe autism. In short, powerful chapters, Higashida explores school memories, family relationships, the exhilaration of travel, and the difficulties of speech." (Publisher's note)
"In a mix of short essays . . . Higashida explores aspects of his atypicality, most of it pointing to the fact that he is indeed atypical, indeed unlike most other people, in the depth of his emotional and intellectual strength." Kirkus

Kinsman, Kat, 1972-

Hi, anxiety; Life With a Bad Case of Nerves. Kat Kinsman. Dey Street 2016 240 p. (ebook) $24.99; (hardcover) $25.99 **616.85**
1. Anxiety in women -- Popular works 2. Depression, Mental -- Popular works 3. Women -- Psychology -- Popular works 4. Depression, Mental -- Treatment -- Popular works
ISBN 9780062369703; 9780062369680; 9780062369697
LC 2016030635
In this book writer and commentator Kat Kinsman "expands on the high profile pieces she wrote for CNN.com about depression, and . . . anxiety. Taking us back to her adolescence, when she was diagnosed with depression at fourteen. . . . With her mother also gripped by depression and health issues throughout her life, . . . [Kinsman] came to live in a constant state of unease—that she would fail, that she would never find love . . . that she would end up just like her mother." (Publisher's note)

"An insightful look at an often misunderstood disorder that doesn't have an immediate cure, this book should appeal to anyone who has struggled with anxiety or loves someone who has." LJ

Kluger, Jeffrey

The **Narcissist** Next Door; Understanding the Monster in Your Family, in Your Office, in Your Bed--in Your World. Jeffrey Kluger. Riverhead Books 2014 288 p. $27.95   **616.85**
> 1. Narcissism
> ISBN 1594486360; 9781594486364

LC 2014006297

This book, by Jeffrey Kluger, is an "exploration of narcissism, how to recognize it, and how to handle it. . . . Kluger frames the surprising new research on narcissism and explains the complex, exasperating personality disorder. He reveals how narcissism and narcissists affect our lives at work and at home, on the road, and in the halls of government; what to do when we encounter narcissism; and how to neutralize its effects before it's too late." (Publisher's note)

"In addition to being informative and engaging, Kluger's account provides some effective tools for dealing with potential narcissists." Pub Wkly

Lask, Bryan

Can I tell you about eating disorders? a guide for friends, family and professionals. Bryan Lask and Lucy Watson ; illustrated by Fiona Field. Jessica Kingsley Publishers 2015 56 p. illustrations (alk. paper) $14.95   **616.85**
> 1. Eating disorders 2. Eating disorders -- Juvenile literature
> ISBN 1849054215; 9781849054218

LC 2014025450

In this book, by Bryan Lask and Lucy Watson, "[m]eet Alice - a teenage girl with anorexia nervosa. Alice invites readers to learn about anorexia nervosa and how it makes her see herself differently from how other people see her. She also introduces readers to Beth who has bulimia nervosa, Sam who has selective eating problems, Francesca who has functional dysphagia and Freddie who has food avoidance emotional disorder." (Publisher's note)

Eating disorders; a parents' guide. Rachel Bryant-Waugh and Bryan Lask. Routledge 2013 xv, 180 p.p illustrations (pbk.) $26.95   **616.85**
> 1. Eating disorders in children 2. Eating disorders in adolescence 3. Eating disorders in children -- Popular works 4. Eating disorders in adolescence -- Popular works
> ISBN 0415501563; 9780203375228; 9780415501569; 9780415814775

LC 2012034666

This book, by Rachel Bryant-Waugh and Bryan Lask, "is dedicated to clarifying the subject of eating disorders. Combining an accessible and straightforward introduction to the subject with practical advice, this book represents the first step towards recognising, understanding and dealing with the problem." (Publisher's note)

Ledoux, Joseph

Anxious; using the brain to understand and treat fear and anxiety. by Joseph LeDoux. Penguin Group USA 2016 468 p. illustrations $18   **616.85**
> 1. Anxiety 2. Anxiety -- Treatment
> ISBN 0143109049; 9780143109044

LC 2015460672

In this book, author Joseph LeDoux "explains that anxiety is fear in the absence of obvious danger. . . . The author stresses that fear is the end product of brain structures that generate no feelings by themselves but detect danger and orchestrate defensive responses that ensure the organism's survival. Technical advances have given neuroscientists precise tools to investigate these structures, and psychologists have been active in the process as well." (Kirkus Reviews)

"Life is dangerous, and professor of neuroscience LeDoux is an expert on the way the brain gathers, stores, and processes data about danger." Booklist

Lintala, Janet

The **un**-prescription for Autism; a natural approach for a calmer, happier, and more focused child. Janet Lintala with Martha W. Murphy ; foreword by Elizabeth Mumper ; illustrations by Jill Seale. AMACOM, American Management Association 2016 304 p. (paperback) $18.95   **616.85**
> 1. Autism 2. Autistic children 3. Asperger's syndrome 4. Autism spectrum disorders 5. Asperger's syndrome -- Patients -- Care 6. Asperger's syndrome -- Patients -- Biography
> ISBN 9780814436639

LC 2015038238

In this book, "Dr. Janet Lintala, founder of the Autism Health center and an autism mom herself, shares the natural protocols used in her practice to dramatically improve the function and well-being of children on the spectrum. Drawing on the latest research developments, as well as personal and clinical experience, she targets the underlying issues . . . associated with the behavior, bowel, and sleep problems so common to autism." (Publisher's note)

"In prose that is easy to understand and sometimes humorous, Lintala relates going through the protocols with her own son as well as patients." LJ

Includes bibliographical references and index

Lock, James

Help your teenager beat an eating disorder; James Lock, Daniel Le Grange. Guilford Pubn 2015 310 p. $18.95 **616.85**
> 1. Parenting 2. Eating disorders 3. Eating disorders in adolescence
> ISBN 146251748X; 9781462517480

LC 200416664

In this book, authors James Lock and Daniel Le Grange "explain what you need to know about eating disorders, which treatments work, and why it is absolutely essential to play an active role in your teen's recovery--even though parents have often been told to take a back seat. Learn how to monitor your teen's eating and exercise, manage mealtimes, end weight-related power struggles, and partner successfully with health care providers." (Publisher's note)

Matlen, Terry

The **queen** of distraction; how women with ADHD can conquer chaos, find focus, and get more done. Terry Matlen, MSW ; foreword by Sari Solden, MS LMFT. New Harbinger Publications, Inc. 2014 200 p. (paperback) $16.95   **616.85**
> 1. Women -- Mental health 2. Attention deficit disorder 3. Women -- Life skills guides 4. Mothers -- Life skills guides 5. Women -- Mental health -- Popular works 6. Attention-deficit disorder in adults -- Popular works 7. Attention-deficit disordered adults -- Life skills guides
> ISBN 1626250898; 9781626250895

LC 2014015747

This book "presents practical skills to help women with ADHD achieve focus and balance in all areas of life. . . . Psychotherapist Terry Matlen delves into the feminine side of ADHD—the elements of this condition that are particular to women, such as: relationships, skin sensitivities, meal-planning, parenting, and dealing with out-of-control hormones. In addition, the book offers helpful tips and strategies to get your symptoms under control." (Publisher's note)

"Whether or not one actually suffers from ADHD, this work is helpful for regaining focus and control over the events of everyday." LJ

Includes bibliographical references

McBride, Karyl

Will I ever be good enough? healing the daughters of narcissistic mothers. Free Press 2008 243p il $24   **616.85**

1. Narcissism 2. Self-acceptance 3. Mother-daughter relationship
ISBN 978-1-4165-5132-4; 1-4165-5132-8

LC 2008-14676

In this book aimed at women whose mothers have narcissistic personality disorder, "McBride presents specific steps toward recovery that daughters of any age can use as they grieve for the love and support they didn't receive, set healthy boundaries with their mothers and access an 'internal mother' as a source of self-comforting. The author provides parenting tips as well as advice on maintaining healthy love relationships and friendships—all of which tend to be weak points of the daughters of narcissistic mothers." Publ Wkly

Includes bibliographical references

Milliken, Kirsten

PlayDHD; Kirsten Milliken. BookBaby 2016 146 p. illustrations (some color) $19.84; (ebook) $5.99   **616.85**

1. Play therapy 2. Attention deficit disorder
ISBN 0997004509; 9780997004502; 9780997004519

This book, by Kirsten Milliken, "focuses on how developing a more playful mindset and habit of engaging in playful activities can actually help you to manage symptoms and excel with ADHD. . . . Play is actually what you need to better manage your difficulties with attention. ADHD is a serious problem. But your approach to it doesn't have to be." (Publisher's Note)

"This book is a must for those with ADHD and their loved ones." Pub Wkly

Morris, David J.

The **evil** hours; a biography of post-traumatic stress disorder. David J. Morris. Houghton Mifflin Harcourt 2015 336 p. (hardback) $27   **616.85**

1. War 2. Post-traumatic stress disorder 3. Post-traumatic stress disorder -- United States 4. Post-traumatic stress disorder -- Patients -- United States -- Biography
ISBN 0544086619; 9780544570320; 9780544086616

LC 2014034487

This book, by David J. Morris, offers "a moving, eye-opening exploration of PTSD. . . . Through interviews with individuals living with PTSD, forays into the scientific, literary, and cultural history of the illness, and memoir, Morris crafts a . . . work that will speak not only to those with the condition and to their loved ones, but also to all of us struggling to make sense of an anxious and uncertain time." (Publisher's note)

"Though its incidence among combat veterans has brought post-traumatic stress disorder to the fore, the National Institute of Mental Health estimates that one in every 30 American adults suffers from the condition. Seasoned war correspondent Morris, also a former marine infantry officer with PTSD, here draws on personal experience, interviews, and scientific studies to present the big picture." LJ

Nathan, Debbie

Sybil exposed; the extraordinary story behind the famous multiple personality case. Free Press 2011 xxi, 297p il $26;

ebook $12.99   **616.85**

1. Artists 2. Painters 3. Mentally ill 4. Multiple personality
ISBN 978-1-4391-6827-1; 978-1-4391-6829-5 ebook

LC 2011009164

The author "claims that the subject of the 1973 international bestseller, Sybil by Flora Schreiber, and the blockbuster film that followed, was a deliberate fabrication that not only fooled a mass popular audience but shaped the practice of psychiatry, opening the door to mass hysteria and misdiagnosis. . . . A nuanced, not-entirely-unsympathetic account of the women who perpetrated a sensational literary fraud." Kirkus

Includes bibliographical references

Petersen, Andrea

On edge; a journey through anxiety. Andrea Petersen. Crown 2017 305 p. (hardcover) $27   **616.85**

1. Mental illness 2. Abnormal psychology 3. Anxiety disorders -- Treatment 4. Anxiety -- Patients -- Biography
ISBN 9780553418576; 9780553418583; 9780553418590

LC 2016050111

In this book, author Andrea Petersen, looks at the "biology of anxiety and the groundbreaking research that might point the way to new treatments. She compares psychoactive drugs to non-drug treatments, including biofeedback and exposure therapy. And she explores the role that genetics and the environment play in mental illness, visiting top neuroscientists and tracing her family history." (Publisher's note)

"Sensitive and frank personal views on anxiety backed by substantial research and analysis of the evolution of treatment methods and drugs to alleviate symptoms." Kirkus

Includes bibliographical references and index

Raine, Adrian

The **anatomy** of violence; the biological roots of crime. Adrian Raine. 1st ed. Pantheon Books 2013 xv, 478 p.p ill. (some col.) (hardcover) $35   **616.85**

1. Genetics 2. Violence 3. Mind and body 4. LAW -- General 5. Violence -- Physiological aspects 6. Violence -- Psychological aspects
ISBN 0307378845; 9780307378842

LC 2012036952

This book, by Adrian Raine, researches "the biological roots of violence. . . . Raine documents from genetic research that the seeds of sin are sown early in life, giving rise to abnormal physiological functioning that cultivates crime. Drawing on classical case studies of well-known killers in history . . . Raine illustrates how impairments to brain areas controlling our ability to experience fear, make good decisions, and feel guilt predispose us to violence." (Publisher's note)

Includes bibliographical references (pages 375-453) and index.

Robison, John Elder

Switched on; a memoir of brain change and emotional awakening. John Elder Robison. Spiegel & Grau 2015 320 p. (hardback) $28   **616.85**

1. Asperger's syndrome 2. Autism -- Treatment 3. Asperger's syndrome -- Patients -- Treatment 4. Asperger's syndrome -- Patients -- United States -- Biography
ISBN 9780812996890; 9780812996906

LC 2015014112

In this memoir, author John Elder Robison "wrote . . . 'Look Me in the Eye,' a memoir about growing up with Asperger's syndrome. Amid the blaze of publicity that followed, he received a unique invitation: Would John like to take part in a study led by one of the world's foremost neuroscientists, who would use an experimental new brain therapy known as TMS, or transcranial magnetic stimulation, in an effort to understand and then address the issues at the heart of autism?" (Publisher's note)

"Fascinating for its insights into Asperger's and research, this engrossing record will make readers reexamine their preconceptions about this syndrome and the future of brain manipulation." Booklist

Includes bibliographical references

Ronson, Jon

The **psychopath** test; Jon Ronson. Riverhead Books 2011 275 p.　　　　　　　　　**616.85**

1. Research 2. Abnormal psychology 3. Mentally ill -- Institutional care 4. Psychopaths

ISBN 978-1-59448-801-6; 1-59448-801-0

　　　　　　　　　　　　　　　　　　　　LC 201103133

This book provides an "exploration of psychiatry's attempts to understand and treat psychopathy, [in which] British journalist Ronson . . . reveals that psychopaths are more common than we'd like to think. Visiting Broadmoor Psychiatric Hospital, where some of Britain's worst criminal offenders are sent, Ronson discovers the difficulties of diagnosing the complex disorder when he meets one inmate who says he feigned psychopathy to get a lighter sentence, and instead has spent 12 years in Broadmoor. The psychiatric community's criteria for diagnosing psychopathy . . . is a checklist developed by the Canadian prison psychologist Robert Hare. Using Hare's rubric, which includes 'glibness,' 'grandiose sense of self-worth,' and 'lack of remorse,' Ronson sets off to interview possible psychopaths, many of them in positions of power, from a former Haitian militia leader to a power-hungry CEO." (Publishers Weekly)

Includes bibliographical references (p. [273]-275).

Sacks, Oliver, 1933-2015

The **mind's** eye. Alfred A. Knopf 2010 263p il $26.95　　　　　　　　　　　　　　　**616.85**

1. Perception 2. Nervous system 3. Vision disorders 4. Communicative disorders 5. Neurology 6. Face perception 7. Cognition disorders

ISBN 978-0-307-27208-9; 0-307-27208-7

　　　　　　　　　　　　　　　　　　　　LC 2010-12791

Sacks "offers case histories of six individuals adjusting to major changes in their vision. A renowned pianist has lost the ability to read music scores and must cope with the fear of an ever-shrinking life as her vision worsens. A prolific writer develops 'word blindness' and is unable to read even what he himself writes, forcing him to develop memory books in his mind, adaptations that he later incorporates into his fiction writing. Sacks recalls his own struggle to cope with a tumor in his eye that left him unable to perceive depth. He includes diary entries and drawings of his harrowing experience. . . . [A] riveting exploration of how we use our vision to perceive and understand the world and our place in it and how our brains teach us to 'see' those things we need to lead a complete, fulfilled life." Booklist

Includes bibliographical references

Schreiber, Flora Rheta

Sybil. Warner Books 1995 460p il pa $7.99　**616.85**

1. Multiple personality

ISBN 978-0-446-35940-5; 0-446-35940-8

First published 1973 by Regnery Pub.

This is the "true story of Sybil I. Dorsett, a battered child possessed by 16 different personalities. . . . The author skillfully evokes Sybil's patient work during 11 years of psychoanalysis and her eventual success in integrating these selves into a unified personality." Libr J

Senator, Susan

Autism Adulthood; Strategies and Insights for a Fulfilling Life. Susan Senator. Skyhorse Publishing 2016 320 p. $26.99　　　　　　　　　　　　　　　　**616.85**

1. Autistic people 2. People with disabilities

ISBN 151070423X; 9781510704237

This book by Susan Senator "features thirty interviews with autistic adults, their parents, caregivers, researchers, and professionals. Each vignette reveals firsthand a family's challenge, their circumstances, their thought processes, and their unique solutions, and plans of action. Sharing the wisdom that emerges from parents' and self-advocates' experiences, Senator adds her own observations and conclusions based on her long-term experience with autism." (Publisher's note)

"Straightforward and to the point, Senator's book addresses many parents' worst fears and inspires them to step up and create a situation and a community that can support their child in their absence. This is a must-read for any parent with a child on the autism spectrum as well as caregivers, siblings, and extended family. Suitable for any library with parenting and autism collections." Library Journal

Smith, Daniel

Monkey mind; a memoir of anxiety. Daniel B. Smith. 1st Simon & Schuster hardcover Simon & Schuster 2012 viii, 212 p.p (hardcover) $25　　　　　　　　　　　　　**616.85**

1. Anxiety 2. Journalists 3. Interpersonal relations 4. Anxiety disorders 5. Mentally ill -- United States -- Biography

ISBN 1439177309; 9781439177303; 9781439177327

　　　　　　　　　　　　　　　　　　　　LC 2011025971

In this memoir, "afflicted journalist and editor [Daniel] Smith uses humor . . . as he explains the excess of thought and emotion also known as 'Monkey Mind' in Buddhism." After college "graduation, he embarks on his first romance and lands a fact-checking job at the Atlantic. . . . Reading the harsh comments posted online about his article and tracking his thoughts and behavior for triggers helps him reroute his psychological circuitry and win his ex back." (Publishers Weekly)

Smith, R. Garth

ASD, the complete autism spectrum disorder health & diet guide; The complete Autism Spectrum Disorder health & diet guide. by R. Smith, Susan Hannah, Elke Sengmueller. Firefly Books Ltd 2014 408 p. illustrations $24.95　　　**616.85**

1. Autism 2. Autistic children 3. Children -- Health and hygiene

ISBN 0778804739; 9780778804734

This book on autism spectrum disorder (ASD), by R. Smith, Susan Hannah, and Elke Sengmueller, "will be a valuable resource for parents, caregivers and health professionals as well, with its combination of years of practical experience and a range of skills and knowledge. . . . 175 recipes and gluten-free/cassein-free meal plans help to build a nutritious, varied and tasty diet that may improve gastrointestinal and ASD symptoms for some children." (Publisher's note)

"With sections for all parts of the day, there are plenty of recipes to work through for even the pickiest/limited eater. This should be required reading for anyone wanting to best address healthy options for Autistic people." Pub Wkly

Solomon, Andrew

The **noonday** demon; an atlas of depression. Scribner 2001 569p $28; pa $16　　　　　　　　　　**616.85**

1. Depression (Psychology)

ISBN 0-684-85466-X; 0-684-85467-8 pa

　　　　　　　　　　　　　　　　　　　　LC 2001-18884

National Book Award: Nonfiction (2001)

"The author draws on his own life story and other sources for a deeply moving and provocative exploration of depression." Booklist

Includes bibliographical references

Stewart, Alison

Junk; Digging Through America's Love Affair With Stuff. by Alison Stewart. Chicago Review Press 2016 304 p. illustrations (ebook) $26.99; $26.99   **616.85**

1. Antiques 2. Space debris 3. Personal belongings 4. Collectors and collecting

ISBN 9781613730584; 1613730551; 9781613730553

LC 2015050224

In this book, by Alison Stewart, "junk has become ubiquitous in America today. . . . Stewart rides along with junk removal teams from around the country such as Trash Daddy, Annie Haul, and Junk Vets. She goes backstage to a taping of Antiques Roadshow, and learns what makes for compelling junk-based television with the executive producer of Pawn Stars. And she even investigates the growing problem of space junk." (Publisher's note)

"Absorbing and enjoyably compelling research on the packrat conundrum in our society." Kirkus

Includes bibliographical references (pages 279-284).

Stossel, Scott

My age of anxiety; fear, hope, dread, and the search for peace of mind. Scott Stossel. Alfred A. Knopf 2014 416 p. (hardcover) $27.95   **616.85**

1. Anxiety 2. Anxiety -- Chemotherapy 3. Anxiety disorders -- Epidemiology 4. Tranquilizing drugs -- Social aspects

ISBN 0307269876; 9780307269874; 9780307390608

LC 2013006336

This book, by Scott Stossel, presents an "account of the author's struggles with anxiety, and of the history of efforts by scientists, philosophers, and writers to understand the condition. . . . He ranges from the earliest medical reports of Galen and Hippocrates, through later observations by Robert Burton and Soren Kierkegaard, to the investigations by great nineteenth-century scientists, such as Charles Darwin, William James, and Sigmund Freud." (Publisher's note)

"[T]he author's beautiful prose and careful research combine to make this book informative, thoughtful and fun to read. Powerful, eye-opening and funny." Kirkus

Includes bibliographical references

Styron, William, 1925-2006

Darkness visible; a memoir of madness. Random House 1990 84p hardcover o.p. pa $11   **616.85**

1. Depression (Psychology) 2. Authors 3. Essayists 4. Novelists 5. Depression (Psychology) -- Personal narratives

ISBN 0-679-73639-5 pa

LC 90-53141

This is an account of the author's experience of suicidal depression and his recovery.

"The book's virtues—considerable—are twofold. First, it is a pitiless and chastened record of a nearly fatal human trial far commoner than assumed—and then a literary discourse on the ways and means of our cultural discontents." Publ Wkly

Van der Kolk, Bessel A., 1943-

The **body** keeps the score; brain, mind, and body in the healing of trauma. Bessel A. van der Kolk. Viking 2014 464 p. illustrations $27.95   **616.85**

1. Stress (Psychology) 2. Post-traumatic stress disorder 3. Stress Disorders, Post-Traumatic -- therapy 4. Stress Disorders, Post-Traumatic -- physiopathology

ISBN 0670785938; 9780670785933

LC 2014021365

In this book, author Bessel A. van der Kolk "transforms our understanding of traumatic stress, revealing how it literally rearranges the brain's wiring specifically areas dedicated to pleasure, engagement, control, and trust. He shows how these areas can be reactivated through innovative treatments including neurofeedback, mindfulness techniques, play, yoga, and other therapies." (Publisher's note)

"This valuable work for psychologists, therapists, and public health professionals walks the line between academic medical text and popular nonfiction. More important, it offers hope for the millions of sufferers and their families seeking meaningful treatment and relief from the ongoing pain of trauma." LJ

Includes bibliographical references and index

Wansink, Brian

Mindless eating; why we eat more than we think. Bantam Books 2006 276p il hardcover o.p. pa $14   **616.85**

1. Eating habits

ISBN 978-0-553-80434-8; 0-553-80434-0; 978-0-553-38448-2 pa; 0-553-38448-1 pa

LC 2006-47532

The author "explores some of the psychological aspects of overeating to explain why we in fact consume more than we believe we do. . . . Wansink's dual approach emphasizing food knowledge and self-knowledge offers a sensible route to permanent weight loss." Booklist

Includes bibliographical references

Wilson, Sarah

First, we make the beast beautiful; a new journey through anxiety. Sarah Wilson. Dey Street 2018 312 p. (hardcover) $25.99   **616.85**

1. Anxiety 2. Phobias 3. Mental health 4. Mental healing 5. Spiritual healing 6. Anxiety -- Prevention 7. Anxiety -- Alternative treatment

ISBN 0062836781; 9780062836786; 9780062836809

In this book, author Sarah Wilson, "charts . . . [her] epic journey to make peace with [anxiety,] her lifetime companion, and to learn to see it as a guide, rather than as an enemy. With intensive focus and investigatory skills, Wilson examines the triggers and treatments, the fashions and fads. She reads widely and interviews fellow sufferers, mental health experts, philosophers, and even the Dalai Lama, processing all she learns through the prism of her own experiences." (Publisher's note)

"Amusing, practical, and filled with delightful asides, this book will appeal to anxiety-prone readers, who will find much to calm them in these pages." Pub Wkly

616.852   Neuroses

Bailey, Lily

Because we are bad; OCD and a girl lost in thought. Lily Bailey. HarperCollins 2018 272 p. $26.99   **616.852**

1. Neuroses 2. Compulsive behavior 3. Obsessive-compulsive disorder

ISBN 0062696165; 9780062696168

This memoir, by Lily Bailey, is "about her childhood battle with debilitating obsessive compulsive disorder, and her hard-won journey to recovery. . . . [Bailey] recounts a childhood consumed by obsessive compulsive disorder. . . . [The book] is an illuminating and uplifting look into the mind and soul of an extraordinary young woman, and a startling portrait of OCD that allows us to see and understand this condition as never before." (Publisher's note)

Stern, Amanda

Little panic; dispatches from an anxious life. Amanda Stern. Grand Central Pub. 2018 400 p. (hardcover) $27   **616.852**

1. Anxiety 2. Panic disorders -- Patients 3. American authors -- 21st century -- Biography

ISBN 9781538711910; 9781538711927; 9781549168505

LC 2017963706

In this memoir, author Amanda Stern shares that "growing up in the 1970s and 80s in New York, . . . [she] experiences the magic and madness of life through the filter of unrelenting panic. Plagued with fear that her friends and family will be taken from her if she's not watching-- . . . Amanda treats every parting as her last. . . . [Stern offers] a deep, personal, and comedic account of the trials and errors of seeing life through a very unusual lens." (Publisher's note)

616.86   Substance abuse (Drug abuse)

Beattie, Melody

Beyond codependency; and getting better all the time. Hazelden Foundation 1989 252p pa $15.95   **616.86**

1. Drug abuse 2. Applied psychology

ISBN 0-89486-583-8

The author discusses "the process of recovering from the self-defeating behaviors adopted as survival tactics by adult children of families rendered dysfunctional by parental alcoholism or similar traumas." Publ Wkly

Includes bibliographical references

★ **Codependent** no more; how to stop controlling others and start caring for yourself. 2nd ed.; Hazelden 1992 250p pa $15.95   **616.86**

1. Drug abuse 2. Codependency 3. Health self-care

ISBN 0-89486-402-5

LC 2004-351623

First published 1987

This guide offers advice on how to overcome codependency, aimed at the spouses and other caretakers of people who abuse drugs or alcohol.

Includes bibliographical references

Jamison, Leslie

★ The **recovering**; intoxication and its aftermath. Leslie Jamison. Little, Brown and Co. 2018 534 p. (hardcover) $30   **616.86**

1. Substance abuse 2. Alcoholics -- Rehabilitation 3. Drug addicts -- Rehabilitation 4. Addicts -- Rehabilitation 5. Recovering addicts -- Case studies 6. Recovering alcoholics -- Case studies

ISBN 9780316259606; 0316259616; 9780316259613

LC 2017946582

This book, by Leslie Jamison, "turns our understanding of the traditional addiction narrative on its head, demonstrating that the story of recovery can be every bit as electrifying as the train wreck itself. Leslie Jamison deftly excavates the stories we tell about addiction--both her own and others'--and examines what we want these stories to do and what happens when they fail us." (Publisher's note)

"The bracing, unflinching, and beautifully resonant history of a writer's addiction and hard-won reclamation." Kirkus

Includes bibliographical references (pages 461-520) and index.

616.89   Mental disorders

Adamec, Christine

When your adult child breaks your heart; coping with mental illness, substance abuse, and the problems that tear families apart. Joel L. Young, MD., Christine Adamec. Lyons Press, an imprint of Globe Pequot Press 2013 251 p. (pbk.) $19.95   **616.89**

1. Mental illness 2. Substance abuse 3. Self-care, Health 4. Parent and adult child 5. Parents of mentally ill children -- Psychology

ISBN 0762792973; 9780762792979

LC 2013023047

"Behind nearly every adult who is accused of a crime, . . . addicted to drugs or alcohol, or . . . severely mentally ill . . . , there is . . . one extremely stressed-out parent." This book by Joel L. Young, with Christine Adamec, "presents families with quotations and scenarios from real suffering parents . . . , practical advice, and tested strategies for coping. It also discusses the fact that parents of adult children may themselves need therapy and medications." (Publisher's note)

"The book offers practical advice, stories, and resources—and, perhaps most importantly, comfort for any parent facing one of the biggest parenting challenges." Pub Wkly

Includes bibliographical references and index

Bollas, Christopher

When the Sun Bursts; The Enigma of Schizophrenia. by Christopher Bollas. Yale University Press 2015 240 p. 1 illustration $28   **616.89**

1. Schizophrenia

ISBN 0300214731; 9780300214734

This book on schizophrenia, by Christopher Bollas, "asserts that schizophrenics can be helped by much more humane treatments, and that they have a chance to survive and even reverse the process if they have someone to talk to them regularly and for a sustained period, soon after their first breakdown. . . . [Bollas] offers his interpretation of how schizophrenia develops, typically in the teens, as an adaptation in the difficult transition to adulthood." (Publisher's note)

"A vastly informative, coherent, and valuable assessment; useful and accessible for both mental health professionals and laypeople—even those who don't share the author's unique perspectives and treatment alternatives." Kirkus

Burns, Tom

★ **Our** Necessary Shadow; The Nature and Meaning of Psychiatry. Tom Burns. W.W. Norton & Co Inc. 2014 384 p. $27.95   **616.89**

1. Psychiatry 2. Medicine -- History

ISBN 1605985708; 9781605985701

"This is the first attempt in a generation to explain the whole subject of psychiatry. . . . Tom Burns reviews the historical development of psychiatry, throughout alert to where psychiatry helps, and where it is imperfect. What is clear is that mental illnesses are intimately tied to what makes us human in the first place and the drive to relieve the suffering they cause is even more human." (Publisher's note)

"There are fine chapters on neuroscience and pharmaceuticals . . . , and Burns covers antipsychiatry movements, the insanity defense, and the impact of war." LJ

Includes bibliographical references (p. 306-309) and index

Earley, Pete

Resilience; two sisters and a story of mental illness. Jessie Close with Pete Earley. Grand Central Publishing 2015 320 p.

16 plates; illustrations (hardback) $27 **616.89**
1. Mentally ill -- Family relationships 2. Sisters 3. Psychoses 4. Manic-depressive illness
ISBN 1455548820; 9781455530229; 9781455548804; 9781455548828
LC 2014024743

This book, by Jessie Close with Pete Earley, is the memoir of actress Glenn Close's sister after "Jessie first started to exhibit symptoms of severe bipolar disorder. . . . Glenn was always by her side throughout. . . . It wasn't until [Jessie's son] Calen entered McLean's psychiatric hospital that Jessie herself was diagnosed. Fifteen years and twelve years of sobriety later, Jessie is a stable and productive member of society." (Publisher's note)

"Close's story alternates with brief corroborative vignettes written by her sister in a belabored and grim memoir that will nonetheless reach its intended audience thanks to the author's famous sister and their shared nonprofit group geared toward mental health, Bring Change 2 Mind." Pub Wkly

Frances, Allen
★ **Saving** Normal; An Insider's Revolt Against Out-of-control Psychiatric Diagnosis, DSM-5, Big Pharma, and the Medicalization of Ordinary Life. Allen Frances. HarperCollins 2013 xx, 314 p.p (hardcover) $27.99 **616.89**
1. Psychiatry 2. Mental health 3. Mental illness
ISBN 0062229257; 9780062229250

This book, by Allen Frances, "warns that mislabeling everyday problems as mental illness has shocking implications for individuals and society. . . . We also shift responsibility for our mental well-being away from our own naturally resilient and self-healing brains . . . into the hands of 'Big Pharma,' who are reaping multi-billion-dollar profits." (Publisher's note)

Greenberger, Dennis
Mind over mood; change how you feel by changing the way you think. Dennis Greenberger and Christine A. Padesky. Guilford Press 2016 341 p. (pbk.; alk. paper) $26.95 **616.89**
1. Human behavior 2. Cognitive therapy 3. Mood (Psychology) 4. Affective disorders -- Treatment 5. Cognitive therapy -- Popular works
ISBN 1462520421; 9781462520428
LC 2015025241

Authors Dennis Greenberger and Christine A. Padesky present this book with "steps you can take to overcome emotional distress--and feel happier, calmer, and more confident. The second edition contains numerous new features: expanded content on anxiety; chapters on setting personal goals and maintaining progress; happiness rating scales; gratitude journals; innovative exercises focused on mindfulness, acceptance, and forgiveness." (Publisher's note)

"Recommended for dedicated readers willing to spend an hour a day working on new skills." LJ

Includes bibliographical references and index

Jamison, Kay Redfield
Robert Lowell, Setting the River on Fire; A Study of Genius, Mania, and Character. by Kay Redfield Jamison. Random House Inc 2017 544 p. $29.95 **616.89**
1. American poets
ISBN 0307700275; 9780307700278
LC 2016028281
Pulitzer Prize Finalist: Biography (2018)
This book, by Kay Redfield Jamison, is a biography "of one of the

major American poets of the twentieth century. . . . In his Pulitzer Prize-winning poetry, Robert Lowell (1917-1977) put his manic-depressive illness into the public domain. . . . Jamison brings her expertise to bear on his story, illuminating the relationship between bipolar illness and creativity, and examining how Lowell's illness and the treatment he received came to bear on his work." (Publisher's note)

"A deeply informed investigation of a poet's suffering and creative triumph." Kirkus

Kalb, Claudia
Andy Warhol was a hoarder; inside the minds of history's great personalities. Claudia Kalb. National Geographic Books 2016 320 p. illustrations (hardback) $24 **616.89**
1. Celebrities 2. Mental health 3. Fame -- Psychological aspects 4. Celebrities -- Psychology -- Biography
ISBN 1426214669; 9781426214660
LC 2015024370

In this book, author "Claudia Kalb gives readers a glimpse into the lives of high-profile historic figures through the lens of modern psychology, weaving groundbreaking research into biographical narratives that are deeply embedded in our culture. From Marilyn Monroe's borderline personality disorder to Charles Darwin's anxiety, Kalb provides . . . insight into a broad range of maladies, using historical records and interviews with leading mental health experts." (Publisher's note)

"In all, Kalb's well-written exercise in applying modern psychiatric theory to historical figures, from Marilyn Monroe to Albert Einstein to Charles Darwin, certainly makes for some very entertaining armchair speculation." Booklist

Includes bibliographical references

Kandel, Eric R., 1929-
The **disordered** mind; what unusual brains tell us about ourselves. Eric R. Kandel. Farrar, Straus & Giroux 2018 336 p. (hardcover) $30 **616.89**
1. Mental health 2. Mental illness 3. Neuropsychiatry -- methods 4. Mental Processes -- physiology 5. Mental Disorders -- physiopathology 6. Psychophysiologic Disorders -- physiopathology
ISBN 9780374287863
LC 2017049274

In this book author Eric R. Kandel "confronts one of the most difficult questions we face: How does our mind, our individual sense of self, emerge from the physical matter of the brain? . . . By studying disruptions to typical brain functioning and exploring their potential treatments, we will deepen our understanding of thought, feeling, behavior, memory, and creativity. Only then can we grapple with the big question of how billions of neurons generate consciousness itself." (Publisher's note)

"Emphasizing advances in the fields of genetics, brain imaging, and animal research, Kandel writes about decision-making, sense of self, emotion, mood, addiction, and gender identity." Booklist

Includes bibliographical references and index

Lieberman, Jeffrey A.
Shrinks; the untold story of psychiatry. Jeffrey Lieberman, MD, Ogi Ogas. Little, Brown & Co. 2015 352 p. illustrations (hardcover) $28 **616.89**
1. Psychiatry 2. Psychoanalysis
ISBN 0316278866; 9780316278980; 9780316278867
LC 2014956581

This book by Jeffrey A. Lieberman "offers a broad historical perspective of how the mental health profession acquired its notoriously pseudoscientific reputation through chapters mining the processes of diagnosis and treatment, including a generous section highlighting the trailblazing career of Sigmund Freud. . . . Lieberman also discusses psychiatry's historic role regarding issues of sexual orientation, the treatment of PTSD and the riddles involved in diagnosing schizophrenia." (Kirkus Reviews)

"A lively defense of psychiatry that extols brain science and pharmaceutical treatment. A contrasting approach is found in Philip Thomas's Psychiatry in Context; critical of routine overuse of pharmaceuticals, Thomas makes a case for understanding the unique experience of each patient, even in schizophrenia." LJ

Lowe, Jaime

Mental; lithium, love, and losing my mind. Jaime Lowe. Blue Rider Press 2017 320 p. (hardback) $28   **616.89**

1. Lithium -- Therapeutic use 2. Manic-depressive illness -- Treatment 3. Manic-depressive illness -- Chemotherapy -- Biography 4. Manic-depressive persons -- United States -- Biography

ISBN 9780399574498

LC 2017021267

This book, by Jaime Lowe, is "a riveting memoir and a fascinating investigation of the history, uses, and controversies behind lithium, an essential medication for millions of people struggling with bipolar disorder. . . . Lowe shares and investigates her story of episodic madness, as well as the stability she found while on lithium. She interviews scientists, psychiatrists, and patients to examine how effective lithium really is and how its side effects can be dangerous." (Publisher's note)

"...this readable, moving, and accessible account of her episodic madness and lithium-maintained stability ... will keep readers engrossed with her often painful, sometimes funny story, whose well-researched information on this age-old malady complements her enlightening journey." (Booklist)

Marchant, Jo

Cure; a journey into the science of mind over body. by Jo Marchant. Crown Publishers 2016 320 p. (hardback) $26   **616.89**

1. Mental healing 2. Alternative medicine 3. Mind and body therapies

ISBN 9780385348157; 9780385348171

LC 2015024707

This book, by Jo Marchant, presents a "look at the new science behind the mind's surprising ability to heal the body. . . . We learn how meditation protects against depression and dementia, how social connections increase life expectancy and how patients who feel cared for recover from surgery faster. We meet Iraq war veterans who are using a virtual arctic world to treat their burns and children whose ADHD is kept under control with half the normal dose of medication." (Publisher's note)

"A balanced, informative review of a controversial subject." Kirkus

Includes bibliographical references (pages 257-286) and index.

Montross, Christine

Falling into the fire; a psychiatrist's encounters with the mind in crisis. Christine Montross. Penguin Press 2013 256 p. $16   **616.89**

1. Mentally ill 2. Human behavior 3. Mental illness 4. Medical personnel 5. Physician-patient relationship 6. Behavior -- Personal Narratives 7. Mental Disorders -- therapy -- Personal Narratives 8. Physician-Patient Relations -- Personal Narratives 9. Attitude of Health Personnel -- Personal Narratives 10. Mental Disorders -- psychology -- Personal Narratives 11. Mentally Ill Persons -- psychology -- Personal Narratives

ISBN 0143125710; 9780143125716; 9781594203930

LC 2013007699

This book "is psychiatrist Christine Montross's thoughtful investigation of the gripping patient encounters that have challenged and deepened her practice. . . . Each case study presents its own line of inquiry, leading Montross to seek relevant psychiatric knowledge from diverse sources. A doctor of uncommon curiosity and compassion, Montross discovers lessons in medieval dancing plagues, in leading forensic and neurological research, and in moments from her own life." (Publisher's note)

"Diagnoses rest upon a physician's knowledge and judgment but also clinical intuition. We are all fragile and vulnerable creatures. Compassion counts." Booklist

Includes bibliographical references and index

Porter, Roy

Madness; a brief history. Oxford Univ. Press 2002 241p il hardcover o.p. pa $12.95   **616.89**

1. Psychiatry 2. Mental illness

ISBN 0-19-280267-4 pa

LC 2001-52329

This is a study on the many ways madness has been perceived and misperceived from antiquity to modern times. The author "also discusses topical issues, including the relationship between lunacy and creativity, the drive to institutionalize, which peaked in the mid-20th century; the rise and demise of psychoanalysis; and the development of the antipsychiatry movement. This book combines the appeal of history as narrative with the intellectual stimulation derived from cogent analysis." Libr J

Includes bibliographical references

Scull, Andrew

Madness in civilization; a cultural history of insanity, from the Bible to Freud, from the madhouse to modern medicine. Andrew Scull. Princeton University Press 2015 432 p. 32 plates; illustrations (cloth) $39.50   **616.89**

1. Social conditions 2. Mental illness -- History

ISBN 0691166153; 9780691166155

LC 2014956046

This book, by Andrew Scull, explores the cultural history of insanity. "From the Bible to Sigmund Freud, from exorcism to mesmerism, from Bedlam to Victorian asylums, from the theory of humors to modern pharmacology, the book explores the manifestations and meanings of madness, its challenges and consequences, and our varied responses to it." (Publisher's note)

"Scull is sharp on every point, but some of his best moments come when he explains the introduction of psychoanalysis into pop culture in the postwar period, thanks in good part to Hollywood, and when he takes a sidelong look at both the drug-dependent psychiatry of today and its discontents, such as Scientology. To be read as both corrective and supplement to Foucault, Szasz, and Rieff. Often brilliant and always luminous and rewarding." Kirkus

Searls, Damion

The **inkblots**; Hermann Rorschach, His Iconic Test, and the Power of Seeing. Damion Searls. Crown Publishing 2017 416 p. (hardcover) $28.00   **616.89**

1. Rorschach Test 2. Psychiatrists -- Switzerland

ISBN 9780804136549; 9780804136563

LC 2016028995

This book, by Damion Searls, narrates how in 1917, while working "in a remote Swiss asylum, psychiatrist Hermann Rorschach devised an experiment to probe the human mind. For years he had grappled with the theories of Freud and Jung while also absorbing the aesthetic of a new generation of modern artists. . . . Rorschach himself was a visual artist, and his test, a set of ten carefully designed inkblots, quickly made its way to America, where it took on a life of its own." (Publisher's note)

"Searls shows persuasively how the creation and reinvention of ink-blots has reflected psychologists' scientific and cultural perspectives." Kirkus

Includes bibliographical references and index

Sederer, Lloyd I.

The **family** guide to mental health care; Lloyd I Sederer, MD ; foreword by Glenn Close. W.W. Norton & Co Inc. 2013 xxii, 312 p.p (hardcover) $25.95   **616.89**

1. Mental health services 2. Families of terminally ill 3. Mental illness -- United States 4. Mental health services -- United States 5. Families of the mentally ill -- Counseling of

ISBN 0393707946; 9780393707946

LC 2013007244

This book, by Lloyd I. Sederer, offers advice for families navigating the U.S. mental health care system. "More than fifty million people a year are diagnosed with some form of mental illness. . . . Family members and friends are often the first to realize when someone has a problem. . . . From understanding depression, bipolar illness and anxiety to eating and traumatic disorders, schizophrenia, and much more, readers will learn what to do and how to help." (Publisher's note)

Includes bibliographical references and index.

Slater, Lauren

Prozac diary. Penguin Bks. 1999 203p pa $15   **616.89**

1. Mental illness 2. Psychotropic drugs

ISBN 0-14-026394-2; 978-0-14-026394-7

LC 97-35727

First published 1998 by Random House

The author "was among the first patients to be given Prozac, and she has now been on it, almost without interruption, for ten years. She credits the drug with enabling her, after an incapacitating adolescence, not only to taste and see but to complete a doctorate; marry; and, as director of a clinic, be useful. But she also ponders what it means to one's sense of self to be more or less permanently under the influence of a personality (and libido) altering drug." New Yorker

Torrey, E. Fuller (Edwin Fuller), 1937-

Surviving schizophrenia; a manual for families, consumers, and providers. E. Fuller Torrey. 3rd ed; HarperCollins 2013 488 p. illustrations $16.99   **616.89**

1. Mentally ill 2. Schizophrenia

ISBN 0062268856; 9780062268853

Written by E. Fuller Torrey, "Since its first publication in 1983, 'Surviving Schizophrenia' has become the standard reference book on the disease and has helped thousands of patients, their families, and mental health professionals. In clear language, this . . . book describes the nature, causes, symptoms, treatment, and course of schizophrenia and also explores living with it from both the patient's and the family's point of view." (Publisher's note)

Waldman, Ayelet

A **Really** Good Day; How Microdosing Made a Mega Difference in My Mood, My Marriage, and My Life. Ayelet Waldman. Random House Inc 2017 256 p. (ebook) $65; $25.95   **616.89**

1. Hallucinogens -- Therapeutic use 2. Manic-depressive illness -- Treatment

ISBN 9780451494108; 0451494091; 9780451494092

LC 2016023416

This book, by Ayelet Waldman, presents an "account of the author's

experiment with microdoses of LSD in an effort to treat a debilitating mood disorder, of her quest to understand a misunderstood drug, and of her search for a really good day. . . . She also explores the history and mythology of LSD, the cutting-edge research into the drug, and the byzantine policies that control it." (Publisher's note)

"This great read will attract open-minded psychology buffs, contemporary biography readers, and those keen to hear a new voice discuss issues associated with so-called illicit drugs in America." LJ

Includes bibliographical references (pages 223-229).

Washington, Harriet A.

Infectious madness; the surprising science of how we catch mental illness. Harriet A. Washington. Little, Brown & Co./Hachette Book Group 2015 304 p. illustrations $28   **616.89**

1. Psychology 2. Mental illness

ISBN 0316277800; 9780316277808

LC 2015935999

Author Harriet Washington "presents the new germ theory, which posits not only that many instances of Alzheimer's, OCD, and schizophrenia are caused by viruses, prions, and bacteria, but also that with antibiotics, vaccinations, and other strategies, these cases can be easily prevented or treated." (Publisher's note)

"Recommended for fans of science journalism and readers interested in the next 'hot topic' in biological psychiatry." LJ

Whitaker, Robert

Anatomy of an epidemic; magic bullets, psychiatric drugs, and the astonishing rise of mental illness in America. Crown Publishers 2010 404p il $26   **616.89**

1. Psychiatry 2. Mental illness 3. Psychotropic drugs

ISBN 978-0-307-45241-2; 0-307-45241-7

LC 2009-49467

This is the "first book to investigate the long-term outcomes of patients treated with psychiatric drugs, and Whitaker finds that, overall, the drugs may be doing more harm than good. Adhering to studies published in prominent medical journals, he argues that, over time, patients with schizophrenia do better off medication than on it. Children who take stimulants for ADHD, he writes, are more likely to suffer from mania and bipolar disorder than those who go unmedicated. Intended to challenge the conventional wisdom about psychiatric drugs, 'Anatomy' is sure to provoke a hot-tempered response, especially from those inside the psychiatric community." Salon

Includes bibliographical references

616.9   Other diseases

Fallon, Brian

Conquering Lyme disease; science bridges the great divide. Brian A. Fallon and Jennifer Sotsky ; with Carl Brenner, Carolyn Britton, Marina Makous, and Jenifer Nields. Columbia University Press 2018 384 p. (alk. paper) $30   **616.9**

1. Lyme disease 2. Tick-borne diseases 3. Lyme Disease

ISBN 9780231183840

LC 2017031085

This book, by Brian A. Fallon and Jennifer Sotsky, "[explains] that, despite the vexing 'Lyme Wars,' there is cause for both doctors and patients to be optimistic. . . . [The book] gives an up-to-the-minute overview of the science that is transforming the way we address this complex illness. It argues forcefully that the expanding plague of Lyme and other tick-borne diseases can be confronted successfully and may soon even be reversed." (Publisher's note)

Aimed at specialists, Fallon and Sotsky's heady volume presents the multidisciplinary cadre aiming to restore Lyme patients 'to their former well-being and good grace.'" Pub Wkly

Includes bibliographical references and index

Finlay, B. Brett

Let Them Eat Dirt; Saving Your Child from an Oversanitized World. B. Brett Finlay ; Marie-Claire Arrieta. Workman Pub Co 2016 304 p. (ebook) $26.95; (hardcover) $26.95 **616.9**

1. Microbiota 2. Microorganisms 3. Children -- Health and hygiene

ISBN 9781616206710; 9781616206499; 1616206497

LC 2016018794

In this book, microbiologists Brett Finlay and Marie-Claire Arrieta "explain how the trillions of microbes that live in and on our bodies influence childhood development; why an imbalance of those microbes can lead to obesity, diabetes, and asthma, among other chronic conditions; and what parents can do--from conception on--to positively affect their own behaviors and those of their children." (Publisher's note)

"Solid, easily assimilated evidence showing how microbes are an integral part of a child's healthy life." Kirkus

Includes bibliographical references (pages 263-274) and index.

Horowitz, Richard I.

Why can't I get better? solving the mystery of lyme and chronic disease. Richard Horowitz, M.D. St. Martin's Press 2013 544 p. (hardback) $29.99 **616.9**

1. Diagnosis 2. Lyme disease 3. Chronic diseases 4. Symptoms
ISBN 1250019400; 9781250019400

LC 2013013336

This book, by doctor Richard Horowitz, is "about diagnosing, treating and healing Lyme, and peeling away the layers that lead to chronic disease. . . . [He] covers in detail Lyme's leading symptoms and co-infections, including immune dysfunction, sleep disorders, chronic pain and neurodegenerative disorders–providing a . . . health care model . . . for physicians and health care providers to effectively treat Lyme and other chronic illnesses." (Publisher's note)

"Less self-help and more educational, this work is recommended for health sciences professionals and medically literate audiences, not necessarily for introductory or casual readers.—" LJ

Includes bibliographical references) and index

Ingels, Darin

The **Lyme** solution; a 5-part plan to fight the inflammatory auto-immune response and beat Lyme disease. Darin Ingels and Amy Myers. Penguin Group USA 2018 384 p. $27 **616.9**

1. Naturopathy 2. Lyme disease 3. Autoimmune diseases
ISBN 0735216304; 9780735216303

LC 2018000933

This book, by Darin Ingels and Amy Myers, "shares [a] revolutionary approach to treating and healing acute and chronic Lyme. . . . [It] offers a simple, five-step plan, including: the most effective early treatment and prevention measures to avoid contracting the disease or stop it in its tracks." "Publisher's note)

Masterson, Karen M.

The **malaria** project; the U.S. government's secret mission to find a miracle cure. Karen Masterson. New American Library 2014 406 p. 16 plates; ills. $26.95 **616.9**

1. Malaria 2. Human experimentation in medicine 3. Malaria -- history -- United States 4. History, 20th Century -- United States 5. Malaria -- drug therapy -- United States 6. Antimalarials -- history

-- United States 7. Government Programs -- history -- United States 8. Human Experimentation -- history -- United States

ISBN 0451467329; 9780451467324

LC 2014018351

This book, by Karen M. Masterson, "is the story of America's secret mission to combat malaria during World War II—a campaign modeled after a German project which tested experimental drugs on men gone mad from syphilis. . . . The project tasked dozens of the country's top research scientists and university labs to find a treatment to remedy half a million U.S. troops incapacitated by malaria." (Publisher's note)

Includes bibliographical references and index

McKenna, Maryn

Superbug; the fatal menace of MRSA. Free Press 2010 271p $26 **616.9**

1. Methicillin-Resistant Staphylococcus aureus
ISBN 978-1-4165-5727-2; 1-4165-5727-X

LC 2009-37793

"McKenna suggests that vaccines might be the answer, but it seems a distant hope — and too late for the patients whose heartbreaking stories she tells. A meticulously researched, frightening report on a deadly pathogen." Kirkus

Includes bibliographical references

Preston, Richard

The **demon** in the freezer; a true story. Random House 2002 240p hardcover o.p. pa $7.99 **616.9**

1. Smallpox 2. Biological warfare
ISBN 0-375-50856-2; 0-345-46663-2 pa

The author explains "the chemical properties of the smallpox virus; how a single infected person . . . can set off an epidemic; and what this horrendous disease can be like. . . . We learn how the disease was eliminated by an international vaccination campaign in the 1970's; why there are reasons to believe that the Soviet Union grew staggering quantities of the virus, allegedly in part to arm intercontinental missiles; and how the virus might now be used by others as a 'strategic weapon.'" N Y Times Book Rev

Weintraub, Pamela

Cure Unknown; inside the Lyme epidemic. Pamela Weintraub. Revised ed. St. Martin's Press 2013 456 p. ill $17.99 **616.9**

1. Lyme disease
ISBN 1250044561; 9781250044563

This book, by Pamela Weintraub, is an "investigation into Lyme disease--the science, history, medical politics, and patient experience. . . . In this nuanced picture of the intense controversy and crippling uncertainty surrounding Lyme disease, Pamela Weintraub sheds light on one of the angriest medical disputes raging today." (Publisher's note)

"When Pamela Weintraub, a science journalist, learned that her oldest son tested positive for Lyme disease, she thought she had found an answer to the symptoms that had been plaguing her family for years. . . . Almost everything about Lyme disease turned out to be deeply controversial, from the microbe causing the infection, to the length and type of treatment and the kind of practitioner needed." Publisher's note

Includes bibliographical references and index

Cure unknown; inside the Lyme epidemic. St. Martin's Press 2008 xxiv, 408p $27.95 **616.9**

1. Lyme disease
ISBN 978-0-312-37812-7; 0-312-37812-2

LC 2008-7816

The author "deftly weaves top-notch research and reporting on this malevolent infection . . . with the personal narrative of a family's encounters with ignorance and bias while fighting a tenacious, disabling illness. The result is a compelling read that is also important journalism." Discover

Includes bibliographic references

616.95 Sexually transmitted diseases, zoonoses

Sexually transmitted disease; an encyclopedia of diseases, prevention, treatment, and issues. Jill Grimes, MD, editor ; Kristyn Fagerberg, MD and Lori Smith, MD, coeditors. Greenwood 2013 2 volumes (xxxiii, 784 p.)p illustrations $189   **616.95**
1. Reference books   2. Sexually transmitted diseases -- Encyclopedias
ISBN 1440801347; 9781440801341

LC 2013016319

This encyclopedia, edited by Jill Grimes, MD, "contains over 230 entries that span the history and wide range of topics regarding [sexually transmitted diseases], from the birth of condoms over 3,000 years ago through discovery of the infectious agents and the invention of effective vaccines to the legal and societal implications of STDs." (Publisher's note)

"Many entries include boxed case studies, black-and-white photographs, or diagrams to supplement the text. Volume 1 features a time line, from 400 BCE to 2012, offering historical context." Booklist

Includes bibliographical references and index

616.97 Diseases of immune system

Blum, Susan

Your immune system recovery plan; a doctor's 4-step program to feel better now. by Susan S. Blum, MD, MPH ; with Michele Bender. Simon & Schuster 2013 384 p. illustrations (hardcover) $27.99   **616.97**
1. Immune system 2. Health self-care 3. Autoimmune diseases -- Treatment 4. Self-care, Health
ISBN 1451694970; 1451694997; 9781451694970; 9781451694994

LC 2012031929

In this book, by Susan S. Blum, with Michele Bender, the author "shares her . . . four-step program to treat, reverse, and prevent autoimmune conditions and repair your immune system. . . . The program she used to treat her own serious autoimmune condition and help countless patients reverse their symptoms, heal their immune systems, and prevent future illness" is outlined in full detail. (Publisher's note)

"By cycling back to the nonnegotiable role of food (for example, Blum expresses frustration with people who think low-calorie packaged snacks are healthy and states that most people are guilty of "food amnesia") and examining the effects of infections on specific conditions, Blum encourages readers to play detective, find the root causes of their problem, and take control of recovery." Pub Wkly

Includes bibliographical references and index

Mace, Nancy L.

★ The **36**-Hour Day; A Family Guide to Caring for People Who Have Alzheimer Disease, Related Dementias and Memory Loss. [by] Nancy L. Mace, Peter V. Rabins. 5th ed Johns Hopkins University Press 2011 353 p. hc $45   **616.97**
1. Alzheimer's disease

ISBN 1421402793; 9781421402796

This book, by Nancy L. Mace and Peter V. Rabins, is "the definitive guide for people caring for someone with dementia. Now in a new and updated edition, this best-selling book features thoroughly revised chapters on the causes of dementia, managing the early stages of dementia, the prevention of dementia, and finding appropriate living arrangements for the person who has dementia when home care is no longer an option." (Publisher's note)

Myers, Amy

The **autoimmune** solution; prevent and reverse the full spectrum of symptoms and diseases. Amy Myers, MD. HarperOne 2015 416 p. illustrations (hardback) $27.99   **616.97**
1. Popular medicine 2. Autoimmune diseases 3. Autoimmune diseases -- Popular works
ISBN 0062347470; 9780062347473; 9780062347480

LC 2014017620

In this book, by Amy Myers, "a renowned leader in functional medicine . . . offers her medically proven approach to prevent a wide range of inflammatory-related symptoms and diseases, including allergies, obesity, asthma, cardiovascular disease, fibromyalgia, lupus, IBS, chronic headaches, and Hashimoto's thyroiditis." (Publisher's note)

"Americans who suffer from psoriasis, type 1 diabetes, and other autoimmune diseases and want to treat them without conventional medicine will find many alternative ideas in this guide from medical doctor Myers." Booklist

Sicherer, Scott H.

Food allergies; a complete guide for eating when your life depends on it. Scott H. Sicherer ; foreword by Maria Laura Acebal ; introduction by Hugh A. Sampson. Johns Hopkins University Press 2013 279 p. ill. (hdbk.; alk. paper) $45   **616.97**
1. Food allergy 2. Food allergy -- Diet therapy
ISBN 1421408449; 1421408457; 1421408988; 9781421408446; 9781421408453; 9781421408989

LC 2012025274

In this book, Scott H. Sicherer "addresses the full spectrum of food allergies, from mild to life threatening, from single foods to food families, clearing up misconceptions along the way. He explains how exposure to foods can bring about an allergic response, describes the symptoms of food allergy, and illuminates how food allergies develop. He also recommends tests for diagnosing both food allergies and chronic health problems caused by food allergies." (Publisher's note)

"This book is practical and informative without being overwhelming." LJ

Includes bibliographical references and index

Velasquez-Manoff, Moises

An **Epidemic** of Absence; A New Way of Understanding Allergies and Autoimmune Diseases. by Moises Velasquez-Manoff. Simon & Schuster 2012 vii, 385 p.p ill.   **616.97**
1. Health 2. Immune system 3. Parasitic diseases
ISBN 1439199388; 9781439199381

LC 2012289041

Author Moises Velasquez-Manoff looks at "worm theory"--deliberate infection with parasitic worms--in development to treat autoimmune disease. It explains why farmers' children so rarely get hay fever, why allergy is less prevalent in former Eastern Bloc countries, and how one cancer-causing bacterium may be good for us. It probes the link between autism and a dysfunctional immune system. It investigates the newly apparent fetal origins of allergic disease--that a mother's inflammatory response imprints on her unborn child, tipping the scales toward allergy."

(Publisher's note)

Includes bibliographical references (p. 313-356) and index.

616.99   Tumors and miscellaneous communicable diseases

Aaronson, Naomi

Pilates for breast cancer survivors; a guide to recovery, healing, and wellness. Naomi Aaronson, Ann Marie Turo. Demos Medical Publishing, LLC 2014 176 p. illustrations $21.95   **616.99**

1. Breast cancer 2. Pilates method 3. Cancer patients 4. Relaxation Therapy -- Popular Works 5. Breathing Exercises -- Popular Works 6. Exercise Movement Techniques -- Popular Works 7. Breast Neoplasms -- rehabilitation -- Popular Works

ISBN 1936303574; 9781936303571

LC 2014020932

This book, by Naomi Aaronson and Ann Marie Turo, presents a guide to Pilates exercises for breast cancer survivors. "No matter where you are in treatment, what side effects you may be experiencing, or your general fitness level, Pilates is a safe and effective way to help you regain flexibility, power, and endurance while relieving treatment side effects such as lymphedema, fatigue, depression, peripheral neuropathy, osteoporosis, and upper extremity impairment." (Publisher's note)

"Strengthening the body and spurring recovery through pilates seems like a win-win. For patient health and fitness collections." LJ

Includes bibliographical references and index

Ahuja, Nita

Johns Hopkins patients' guide to colon and rectal cancer; Nita Ahuja, Brenda S. Nettles. Jones & Bartlett Learning 2013 166 p. illustrations (alk. paper) $27.95   **616.99**

1. Colon cancer 2. Rectum cancer 3. Rectum -- Cancer -- Popular works 4. Colon (Anatomy) -- Cancer -- Popular works

ISBN 0763774286; 9780763774288

LC 2012023015

This book, by Nita Ahuja and Brenda S. Nettles, "is a concise patient guide on treating and coping with colorectal cancer. . . . The Johns Hopkins Patients' Guides are designed to alleviate your anxiety, empower you with information, and enable you to fully understand your treatment options. . . . The information is there to help lighten your burden and to assist you in becoming an active participant in your care." (Publisher's note)

Ali, Naheed

Understanding lung cancer; an introduction for patients and caregivers. Naheed Ali. Rowman & Littlefield Publishers, Inc. 2014 363 p. (cloth; alk. paper) $38   **616.99**

1. Caregivers 2. Lung cancer 3. Cancer patients 4. Caregivers -- Popular works 5. Lung -- Cancer -- Popular works

ISBN 1442223235; 9781442223233

LC 2013036194

In this book, Dr. Naheed Ali "helps readers to understand what lung cancer is, how it develops, its different forms, and how both patients and caregivers can approach healing and treatment. Offering a clear background on the disease and its development, this work will help lung cancer sufferers and their friends and family better cope with and understand the diagnosis." (Publisher's note)

Includes bibliographical references and index

Fullbright, Colleen Dolan

How to help your friend with cancer; by Colleen Dolan

Fullbright. American Cancer Society/Health Promotion 2014 112 p. illustrations (paperback) $12.95   **616.99**

1. Cancer patients 2. Helping behavior 3. Cancer -- Psychological aspects

ISBN 1604432241; 9781604432244

LC 2014030700

This book, by Colleen Dolan Fullbright, "provides insight into a friend's cancer experience in each part of the journey, answering questions such as 'What do caregivers cite as their number one need?' and 'What does a cancer patient fear most when active treatment is over?' It contains suggestions for expressing concern and helping in practical ways throughout a friend's cancer experience, from diagnosis, through treatment, and after active treatment." (Publisher's note)

Includes bibliographical references and index

Funk, Kristi

Breasts; the owner's manual; every woman's guide to reducing cancer risk, making treatment choices, and optimizing outcomes. Kristi Funk, MD. W Publishing 2018 416 p. (hardback) $26.99   **616.99**

1. Women -- Diseases 2. Breast cancer -- Treatment 3. Breast cancer -- Prevention 4. Breast -- Care and hygiene 5. Breast -- Cancer -- Treatment 6. Breast -- Cancer -- Prevention 7. Breast -- Cancer -- Risk factors

ISBN 9780785218722

LC 2018000692

This book, by Kristi Funk, presents "guidelines on how to improve your breast health, lower your risk of getting cancer, optimize your outcomes if you're faced with a diagnosis, and make informed medical choices after treatment. . . . 'Breasts: The Owner's Manual' not only provides a clear path to breast health, but a road that leads straight to your healthiest self. As someone who has faced breast cancer, I suggest you follow it." (Publisher's note)

Gazella, Karolyn A.

The definitive guide to thriving after cancer; a five-step integrative plan to reduce the risk of recurrence and build lifelong health. Lise N. Alschuler, ND, FABNO and Karolyn A. Gazella. Ten Speed Press 2013 224 p. (trade pbk.) $15.99   **616.99**

1. Health 2. Diet therapy 3. Cancer patients 4. Cancer -- Prevention 5. Cancer -- Diet therapy

ISBN 160774564X; 9781607745648

LC 2013014557

In this book, authors Lise N. Alschuler and Karolyn A. Gazella "teach you not just how to survive, but also how to thrive after cancer by integrating the best of conventional, natural, and alternative cancer prevention therapies to support and enhance your body's five critical pathways. With simple, empowering daily actions that you can start today, it is the only program that provides the comprehensive approach needed for optimal health and recurrence prevention." (Publisher's note)

"For cancer survivors and caregivers who need a well-organized, comprehensible manual for healthy living after cancer and who don't already have the previous titles by these authors." LJ

Gubar, Susan, 1944-

Memoir of a debulked woman; enduring ovarian cancer. Susan Gubar. W.W. Norton & Co. 2012 288 p.   **616.99**

1. Ovaries -- Cancer -- Patients 2. Ovaries -- Cancer -- Treatment 3. Women -- United States -- Biography 4. Cancer -- Psychological aspects 5. Ovaries -- Cancer -- Patients -- United States -- Biography

ISBN 9780393073256

LC 2011053073

This book presents an "account of the author's ovarian cancer treatment and a staunch protest against the state of contemporary approaches to the disease. In telling her personal story, feminist scholar Gubar . . . remains the academic, looking for understanding not just in the medical literature but also in Frida Kahlo's art . . . and other women's writings." (Kirkus Reviews)

Includes bibliographical references

Hutton, Andrea

Bald Is Better With Earrings; A Survivor's Guide to Getting Through Breast Cancer. Andrea Hutton. HarperCollins 2015 224 p. $17.99 **616.99**

1. Cancer patients 2. Breast cancer -- Treatment
ISBN 0062375652; 9780062375650

This book is author Andrea Hutton's "answer for women diagnosed with breast cancer: a straightforward handbook, leavened with humor and inspiration, to shepherd them though the experience. Warm and down-to-earth, Hutton explains what to expect and walks you through this intense and emotional process: tests, surgery, chemo, losing your hair and shaving your head, being bald, radiation treatments." (Publisher's note)

"Readers will be equally overwhelmed and overjoyed by Hutton's prescriptions. This book could be a lifesaver for breast cancer club members." LJ

Jacobs, Hollye

The **Silver** Lining; A Supportive and Insightful Guide to Breast Cancer. text by Hollye Jacobs, RN, MS, MSW; photography by Elizabeth Messina. Pocket Books 2014 288 p. ill. (some col.) $35 **616.99**

1. Breast cancer 2. Cancer patients 3. Cancer -- Patients -- Attitudes
ISBN 147676350X; 9781476763507

LC 2013019103

Author Hollye Jacobs "offers an unabashedly candid account of her experience with breast cancer. Each chapter . . . focuses on a particular point in the breast cancer journey and discusses how to handle challenges . . . including: diagnosis; relaying the news; . . . surgery; chemotherapy; the isolating nature of the disease; radiation; nutritional and other therapies to ease treatment; discovering the new normal; and redefining your life post-treatment." (Publishers Weekly)

"With her humorous and approachable style, Jacobs has written an essential title for patients facing a cancer diagnosis." LJ

Kalanithi, Paul, 1977-2015

★ **When** breath becomes air; Paul Kalanithi. Random House 2016 256 p. 1 illustration (hardback) $25 **616.99**

1. Surgeons 2. Lung cancer 3. Husband and wife 4. Neurosurgeons -- Biography 5. Lungs -- Cancer -- Patients -- United States -- Biography
ISBN 081298840X; 9780812988406

LC 2015023815

Pulitzer Prize Finalist: Biography or Autobiography (2017)

In this memoir, author Paul Kalanithi tells how "at the age of thirty-six, on the verge of completing a decade's worth of training as a neurosurgeon, [he] was diagnosed with stage IV lung cancer. [It] chronicles Kalanithi's transformation from a naïve medical student . . . into a neurosurgeon at Stanford working in the brain, the most critical place for human identity, and finally into a patient and new father confronting his own mortality." (Publisher's note)

"This eloquent, heartfelt meditation on the choices that make life worth living, even as death looms, will prompt readers to contemplate their own values and mortality." Booklist

Leaf, Clifton

The **truth** in small doses; why we're losing the war on cancer-and how to win it. Clifton Leaf. 1st S&S hardcover ed Simon & Schuster 2013 512 p. illustrations (hbk.; alk. paper) $27 **616.99**

1. Cancer 2. Medicine -- Research 3. Drug Discovery -- History
ISBN 1476739986; 9781476739984; 9781476739991; 9781476740003

LC 2013005817

This book, by Clifton Leaf, offers a "history of the war on cancer. . . . [The author] began to investigate why we had made such limited progress fighting this terrifying disease. The result is a gripping narrative that reveals why the public's immense investment in research has been badly misspent." (Publisher's note)

"Leaf believes that the system must be revamped now, arguing that free exchange of information and a major upgrade in preventative medicine are the keys to improvement. An important evaluative study meriting serious public discussion." Kirkus

Includes bibliographical references and index

Leifer, John

After you hear it's cancer; a guide to navigating the difficult journey ahead. John Leifer ; with Lori Lindstrom Leifer. Rowman & Littlefield 2015 320 p. (cloth; alk. paper) $36 **616.99**

1. Cancer patients 2. Cancer -- Popular works 3. Cancer -- Patients -- Popular works 4. Cancer -- Treatment -- Popular works
ISBN 1442246251; 9781442246256

LC 2015000013

This book, by John Leifer, "guides cancer patients along their journey where no one knows the duration or the destination. Divided into the three parts of being a cancer patient¿the diagnosis, initial treatment, and on to survivorship¿the book will help the newly diagnosed cancer patient navigate a complex health care system, make astute decisions at difficult junctures, and manage the emotional turbulence that can rock his or her world." (Publisher's note)

"Recommended for medically literate cancer patients who want to make well-informed decisions about their treatments." LJ

Includes bibliographical references and index

Mukherjee, Siddhartha

★ The **emperor** of all maladies. Scribner 2010 571p il $30; ebook $14.99 **616.99**

1. Cancer
ISBN 978-1-4391-0795-9; 1-4391-0795-5; 978-1-4391-8171-3 ebook; 1-4391-8171-3 ebook

LC 2010-24114

The author explores how cancer has been perceived throughout history.

"Mukherjee's formidable intelligence and compassion produce a stunning account of the effort to disrobe the 'emperor of maladies.'" Publ Wkly

Includes bibliographical references

Port, Elisa

★ The **new** generation breast cancer book; how to navigate your diagnosis and treatment options--and remain optimistic--in an age of information overload. Elisa Port, MD, FACS, Chief of Breast Surgery at Mount Sinai Medical Center and Co-director of the Dubin Breast Center. Ballantine Books 2015 320 p. (paperback) $20 **616.99**

1. Breast cancer -- Diagnosis 2. Breast cancer -- Treatment 3. Breast -- Cancer 4. Women -- Health and hygiene 5. Breast --

Cancer -- Treatment
ISBN 1101883154; 9781101883150

LC 2015022841

This book, by Elisa Port, offers a "definitive guide to managing breast cancer in the information age¿a comprehensive resource for diagnosis, treatment, and peace of mind. The breast cancer cure rate is at an all-time high, and so is the information, to say nothing of the misinformation, available to patients and their families. . . . Dr. Elisa Port describes every possible test and every type of doctor visit, providing a comprehensive, empathetic guide." (Publisher's note)

"Over the years there have been many excellent texts for patients from physicians in the field. Port's title is as up-to-date as one can get, with lots to offer people facing a cancer diagnosis or hoping to support someone with the disease." LJ

Prijatel, Patricia

Surviving triple negative breast cancer; hope, treatment, and recovery. Patricia Prijatel. Oxford University Press 2013 256 p. (hardback; alk. paper) $7.95   **616.99**
1. Breast cancer 2. Cancer patients 3. Breast cancer -- Treatment 4. Breast -- Cancer -- Treatment -- Popular works 5. Breast -- Cancer -- Patients -- United States -- Biography
ISBN 1616518898; 9780195387629

LC 2012012425

This book, by health journalist Patricia Prijatel, "delivers . . . information on . . . [triple-negative breast cancer]; the role of genetics, family history, and race; how to navigate treatment options; understanding a pathology report; and a plethora of strategies to reduce the risk of recurrence. . . . Woven throughout the book are stories of women who have faced TNBC, . . . who went through a variety of medical treatments and then got on with life." (Publisher's note)

Includes bibliographical references and index.

Ross, Theodora

A **cancer** in the family; take control of your genetic inheritance. Theodora Ross. Avery 2016 304 p. illustration (hardback) $25   **616.99**
1. Cancer 2. Genetics 3. Families -- History 4. Cancer -- Genetic aspects 5. Oncologists -- United States -- Biography
ISBN 1101982837; 9781101982839

LC 2015026294

This book, by Theodora Ross, "shows readers how to spot the patterns of inherited cancer, how to get tested for cancer-causing genes, and what to do if you have one. With a foreword by Siddartha Mukherjee, prize winning author of 'The Emperor of All Maladies,' this will be the first authoritative, go-to for people facing inherited cancer, this book empowers readers to face their genetic heritage without fear." (Publisher's note)

"Recommended for readers seeking appropriate information on hereditary cancers, including their causes, and risk management as well as those beyond the target audience who are interested in sound writing on medical topics." Library Journal

Roth, Andrew J.

Managing prostate cancer; a guide for living better. Andrew J. Roth. Oxford University Press 2016 368 p. (paperback) $21.95   **616.99**
1. Prostate gland -- Cancer 2. Men -- Health and hygiene 3. Physician and patient 4. Prostate -- Cancer -- United States 5. Men -- Health and hygiene -- United States 6. Prostate -- Cancer -- Psychological aspects
ISBN 019933692X; 9780199336920

LC 2015016699

This book, by Andrew J. Roth, "provides the emotional skills and strategies necessary to help patients deal with the challenges a prostate cancer diagnosis brings to everyday life. These tools, which Dr. Roth terms 'Emotional Judo,' effectively teach patients to identify what their fears are rooted in, how to distinguish the rational and irrational aspects of their thoughts and behaviors, make healthier choices to promote a more positive approach." (Publisher's note)

"Roth offers a first-rate overview of how best to respond to a diagnosis of prostate cancer." Booklist

Includes bibliographical references and index

Schwalbe, Will

★ The **end** of your life book club; Will Schwalbe. 1st ed. Alfred A. Knopf 2012 viii, 336 p.p (hardcover) $25.00; (paperback) $15.00; (ebook) $25.00   **616.99**
1. Terminally ill 2. Books and reading 3. Mother-son relationship 4. Families of terminally ill 5. Cancer -- Patients -- United States -- Biography 6. Cancer -- Patients -- Family relationships -- United States
ISBN 0307594033; 9780307594037; 9780307739780; 9780307961112

LC 2012018989

In this book by Will Schwalbe, after his mother is "diagnosed with a form of advanced pancreatic cancer" the pair "start a 'book club' that brings them together as her life comes to a close. . . . Their list jumps from classic to popular, from poetry to mysteries, from fantastic to spiritual. The issues they discuss include questions of faith and courage as well as everyday topics such as expressing gratitude and learning to listen." (Publisher's note)

Scott, Walter J.

Lung cancer; a guide to diagnosis and treatment. Walter J. Scott. 2nd ed. Addicus Books 2012 vii, 110 p.p ill. (pbk.) $19.95   **616.99**
1. Lung cancer
ISBN 1886039097; 9781886039094

LC 2011042503

"The completely revised second edition has been updated to include a discussion of the movement towards customized chemotherapy; treatment options for early-stage lung cancer including minimally invasive surgery; and the most promising treatments, among them multimodality therapy--a combination of surgery, chemotherapy, and radiation." Publisher's note

Includes bibliographical references and index

Sikka, Madhulika

A **breast** cancer alphabet; Madhulika Sikka. Crown Publishers 2014 224 p. $19   **616.99**
1. Breast cancer 2. Cancer patients 3. Breast -- Cancer -- Miscellanea
ISBN 0385348517; 9780385348515

LC 2013003652

In this book, Madhulika Sikka "has gathered together her reflections and discoveries of being in 'Cancerland' in an A-to-Z guidebook to the entire process of cancer diagnosis, treatment and life afterward. The author examines the process of coping with the waves of feelings one will experience (anxiety, guilt, indignity and others), the need for pampering and the odds of a diagnosis--one in eight women in the United States will get breast cancer." (Kirkus Reviews)

"Whether discussing turbans and other headwear, omnipresent anxiety, or the relief that pillows can provide from post-surgery pain, Sikka's voice is calm and earnest, poetic and descriptive, and occasionally even uplifting." Pub Wkly

Includes bibliographical references

Silver, Marc

Breast cancer husband; how to help your wife (and yourself) through diagnosis, treatment, and beyond. foreword by Frederick P. Smith. Rodale 2004 319p pa $14.95   **616.99**
  1. Caregivers 2. Breast cancer
  ISBN 1-579-54833-4
                            LC 2004-7914
"Silver's prose is funny, tender, and filled with rock-solid advice." Libr J

Smith, Claire Bidwell, 1978-

The **rules** of inheritance; a memoir. Claire Bidwell Smith. Hudson Street Press 2012 298 p.   **616.99**
  1. Bereavement 2. Autobiographies 3. Self-realization 4. Women -- United States -- Biography 5. Bereavement -- Psychological aspects 6. Daughters -- United States -- Biography 7. Psychotherapists -- United States -- Biography 8. Women psychotherapists -- United States -- Biography 9. Children of cancer patients -- United States -- Biography
  ISBN 1594630887; 9781594630880
                          LC 2011025136
This memoir by Claire Bidwell Smith describes "a young woman who loses her family but finds herself in the process. . . . Smith is just fourteen years old when both of her charismatic parents are diagnosed with cancer. With an impatience typical of youth, Claire throws herself at anything she thinks might help her cope with the weight of this harsh reality: boys, alcohol, traveling, and the anonymity of cities like New York and Los Angeles. By the time she is twenty-five years old they are both gone and Claire is very much alone in the world." (Publisher's note)

Stark, Lizzie

  ★ **Pandora's** DNA; tracing the breast cancer genes through history, science, and one family tree. Lizzie Stark. Chicago Review Press 2014 336 p. (hardback) $26.95   **616.99**
  1. Mastectomy 2. Breast cancer 3. Cancer -- Genetic aspects 4. BRCA genes 5. Breast -- Cancer -- Genetic aspects 6. Mastectomy -- Patients -- United States -- Biography
  ISBN 1613748604; 9781613748602
                          LC 2014018310
In this book, Lizzie Stark "uses her family's experience to frame a larger story about the so-called breast cancer genes, exploring the morass of legal quandaries, scientific developments, medical breakthroughs, and ethical concerns that surround the BRCA mutations, from the troubling history of prophylactic surgery . . . to the landmark lawsuit against Myriad Genetics, which held patents on the BRCA genes every human carries." (Publisher's note)
"The book is a must-read for women questioning whether to be tested for the BRCA mutations and for women considering their options after testing positive. A gutsy, deeply revealing account that more than fulfills the promise of the subtitle." Kirkus
Includes bibliographical references and index

Waldman, Elisha

  ★ **This** narrow space; a pediatric oncologist, his Jewish, Muslim, and Christian patients, and a hospital in Jerusalem. Elisha Waldman. Schocken Books 2018 245 p. (hardback) $25.95   **616.99**
  1. Autobiographies 2. Cancer in children 3. Physicians -- Biography 4. Oncologists -- Jerusalem -- Biography 5. Cancer in children -- Social aspects -- Jerusalem 6. Bet ha-holim 'Hadasah' (Jerusalem) -- Employees -- Biography
  ISBN 0805243321; 9780805212648; 9780805243321
                          LC 2017031186
In this memoir, pediatric oncologist Elisha Waldman shares her seven-year experience "in Jerusalem treating children--Israeli Jews, Muslims, and Christians, and Palestinian Arabs from the West Bank and Gaza--who had all been diagnosed with cancer. . . . Navigating the baffling Israeli bureaucracy, the ever-present threat of full-scale war, and the cultural clashes that sometimes spilled into his clinic, Waldman learned to be content with small victories." (Publisher's note)

Walsh, Patrick C.

  ★ **Dr.** Patrick Walsh's guide to surviving prostate cancer; Patrick C. Walsh and Janet Farrar Worthington. 4th edition Grand Central Life & Style 2018 524 p illustrations $20.99   **616.99**
  1. Prostate gland -- Cancer 2. Prostate -- Cancer
  ISBN 9781538727478
This book, by Patrick C. Walsh and Janet Farrar Worthington, "offers a message of hope to every man facing . . . [prostate cancer.] Prostate cancer is a different disease in every man, which means that the right treatment varies for each man. Readers will discover their risk factors, simple changes that can reduce the risk of developing the disease, treatment options, and more." (Publisher's note)

Wapner, Jessica

The **Philadelphia** chromosome; a mutant gene and the quest to cure cancer at the genetic level. Jessica Wapner ; foreword by Robert A. Weinberg, PhD. The Experiment, LLC 2013 320 p. ill. (some col.) (pbk.) $25.95   **616.99**
  1. Chromosomes 2. Gene therapy 3. Philadelphia Chromosome -- United States
  ISBN 1615190678; 9781615190676; 9781615191659
                          LC 2012047686
This book by Jessica Wapner "describes the path from the first description of a chromosomal abnormality in cancer cells to the successful deployment of a gene-targeted medicine against what had previously been a lethal leukemia. Along the way, she pays homage to various scientific underdogs. . . . In the last chapter, Wapner surveys the current landscape of cancer research, noting hurdles to continued progress such as difficulties in sequencing tumors." (Science)
"Wapner weaves together the basic and applied science with the stories of the dedicated researchers, the broader supporting superstructure of modern medicine and the process of bringing pharmaceuticals to market. An absorbing, complex medical detective story." Kirkus
Includes bibliographical references and index

Will my cancer come back? staying healthy after treatment. edited by Julia H. Rowland, PhD, Julie K. Silver, MD. American Cancer Society 2015 240 p. (paperback) $19.95 **616.99**
  1. Cancer patients 2. Cancer -- Diet therapy 3. Cancer -- Treatment 4. Cancer -- Exercise therapy 5. Cancer -- Psychological aspects
  ISBN 160443211X; 9781604432114
                          LC 2014030908
"Although no one can predict whether cancer will recur in any one individual, certain behaviors reduce the risk of cancer recurrence for cancer survivors as a group." Edited by Julia H. Rowland and Julie K. Silver, "This book looks at the scientific evidence behind these behaviors; the chapters included cover diet and nutrition, physical activity, social support, psychological interventions, coping strategies, and everything in between."

617   Surgery, regional medicine, dentistry, ophthalmology, otology, audiology

Doherty, Gerard M.

Current Diagnosis and Treatment Surgery; Gerard M. Doherty. 14th edition McGraw-Hill 2015 1395 p. illustrations pbk $93   **617**

1. Surgery 2. Medicine 3. Diagnosis
ISBN 9780071792110; 0071792112

First published 1977. Periodically revised

This book, by Gerard M. Doherty, provides "evidence-based, point-of-care information on 1000 diseases and disorders most often treated by surgeons. . . . [It includes] coverage of general surgery and all sub-specialties you need to be versed in, including otolaryngology, plastic and reconstructive surgery, gynecology, orthopedics, urology, and pediatrics." (Publisher's note)

Fitzharris, Lindsey

The **butchering** art; Joseph Lister's quest to transform the grisly world of Victorian medicine. Lindsey Fitzharris. Scientific American / Farrar, Straus & Giroux 2017 286 p. (hardcover) $27   **617**

1. Surgery -- History 2. Surgeons -- Great Britain -- Biography 3. Surgery -- Great Britain -- History -- 19th century
ISBN 9780374117290; 9780374715489

LC 2016059275

PEN/E.O. Wilson Prize for Literary Science Writing (2018)

This book, by Lindsey Fitzharris, "reveals the shocking world of nineteenth-century surgery on the eve of profound transformation. . . . These medical pioneers . . . were baffled by the persistent infections that kept mortality rates stubbornly high. . . . Fitzharris dramatically recounts [Joseph] Lister's discoveries in gripping detail, culminating in his audacious claim that germs were the source of all infection—and could be countered by antiseptics." (Publisher's note)

"Fitzharris captures the chaos, personalities, and bumpy evolution of surgery during the Victorian period." Booklist

Includes bibliographical references (pages 235-266) and index.

Gawande, Atul

Complications ; a young surgeon's notes on an imperfect science. Metropolitan Bks. 2002 269p $24   **617**

1. Surgery
ISBN 0-8050-6319-6

LC 2001-55884

National Book Award Finalist: Nonfiction (2002)

The author describes the work of a trainee surgeon. The pieces "range from edgy accounts of medical traumas to sobering analyses of doctors' anxieties and burnout. . . . These exquisitely crafted essays, in which medical subjects segue into explorations of much larger themes, place Gawande among the best in the field." Publ Wkly

Includes bibliographical references

Van de Laar, Arnold

Under the knife; a history of surgery in 28 remarkable operations. Arnold van de Laar. St. Martin's Press 2018 368 p. $29.99   **617**

1. Surgery -- History 2. Medicine -- History
ISBN 9781250200105

LC 2018019684

In this book, surgeon Arnold van de Laar tells the "history of surgery through 28 famous operations--from Louis XIV and Einstein to JFK and Houdini. . . . [The book] offers . . . insights into medicine and history

via the operating room. What happens during an operation? How does the human body respond to being attacked by a knife, a bacterium, a cancer cell or a bullet? And . . . what are the limits of surgery?" (Publisher's note)

"Beyond his interesting review of surgical history, van de Laar also offers insight into the thought process and philosophy of those who cut to heal." Booklist

Includes bibliographical references and index

617.1   Injuries and wounds

Fainaru, Steve

League of Denial; The NFL, Concussions and the Battle for Truth. Mark Fainaru-Wada and Steve Fainaru. Random House Inc 2013 416 p. illustrations (chiefly color) $27   **617.1**

1. Brain -- Concussion 2. National Football League 3. Sports medicine -- United States 4. Football injuries -- United States
ISBN 0770437540; 9780770437541

LC 2012276088

"Both ESPN investigative reporters, the authors reveal how the NFL, over a period of nearly two decades, sought to cover up and deny mounting evidence of the connection between football and brain damage. This narrative moves between the NFL trenches, America's research labs and the boardrooms where the NFL went to war against science; it examines how the league used its power and resources to attack independent scientists and elevate its own flawed research." Publisher's note

"The narrative is fast-paced and almost cinematic in the way it describes the culture of the gridiron, and in the picture it provides of the NFL research labs where scientists drew their conclusions, and the NFL boardrooms where football executives decided to go to war." Pub Wkly

★ The **long** distance runner's guide to injury prevention and treatment; how to avoid common problems and deal with them when they happen. edited by Brian J. Krabak, Grant S. Lipman, and Brandee L. Waite. Skyhorse Publishing 2017 424 p. illustrations Paperback $22.99   **617.1**

1. Long-distance runners 2. Long-distance running 3. Running injuries -- Treatment 4. Running injuries -- Prevention 5. Running -- Physiological aspects
ISBN 9781510717909; 1510717900

LC 2017021922

This book, edited by Brian J. Krabak, Grant S. Lipman, and Brandee L. Waite, "is a vital source to help those who love to run understand some of the most common causes of injuries, and learn how to best avoid and treat athletic ailments. In this book, expert editors and long-time runners Brian Krabak and Grant Lipman combine valuable insights, tips, and tactics from more than a dozen medical professionals who specialize in treating endurance athletes." (Publisher's note)

Includes bibliographical references (pages 353-407) and index.

Yaeger, Don

Any given Monday; sports injuries and how to prevent them for athletes, parents, and coaches; based on my life in sports medicine. James R. Andrews with Don Yaeger. Scribner 2013 288 p. (hardcover; alk. paper) $25   **617.1**

1. Sports medicine 2. Athletes -- Wounds and injuries 3. Sports injuries
ISBN 1451667086; 9781451667080; 9781451667097; 9781451667103

LC 2012028374

This book, by James R. Andrews and Don Yaeger, presents a "sport-by-sport guide to injury prevention and treatment, written specifically for the parents, grandparents, and coaches of young athletes. From identifying eating disorders to preventing career-ending ACL tears and concussions, 'Any Given Monday' . . . reveals how young athletes can maximize their talent and maintain a lifetime of health both on the field and off." (Publisher's note)

"While it is unlikely that many will read this cover to cover, it makes a great pass-around for parents and grandparents and demands to be read by youth coaches, trainers, and sports administrators, who, hopefully, will heed Andrews' call for change." Booklist

Sports injuries and how to prevent them for athletes, parents, and coaches

617.4   Surgery by systems and regions

Esty, Mary Lee

Conquering Concussion; by Mary Lee Esty, C. M. Shifflett. Round Earth Publishing 2014 310 p. 8 plates; color illustrations $24.95   **617.4**
  1. Brain -- Concussion 2. Brain -- Wounds and injuries
  ISBN 0965342506; 9780965342506

This book on concussion, by Mary Lee Esty and C. M. Shifflett, "presents history, new research, treatments, and 20 years of clinical case histories. These are real stories about real people struggling with post-concussion symptoms: terrible fatigue, headache and body pain, emotional swings, mental fog, insomnia, weight gain and balance problems. . . . It features neurotherapy, but presents additional therapies that can aid recovery." (Publisher's note)

"Clear figures, photos and illustrations; a glossary; and a list of supplemental resources make the book even more user-friendly.An eye-opener for anyone concerned about concussion—which the authors persuasively argue should include everyone." Kirkus

Kean, Sam

The **tale** of the dueling neurosurgeons; the history of the human brain as revealed by true stories of trauma, madness, and recovery. Sam Kean. Little, Brown & Co. 2014 407 p. illustrations (hardcover) $27   **617.4**
  1. Physicians 2. Neurosciences 3. Brain -- Diseases 4. Brain Diseases -- Popular Works 5. Brain -- Physiology -- Popular Works 6. Physicians -- History -- Popular Works 7. Neurosciences -- History -- Popular Works 8. Neurologic Manifestations -- Popular Works
  ISBN 9780316286480 (international); 0316182346; 9780316182348

LC 2014004910

In this book, author "Sam Kean travels through time with stories of neurological curiosities: phantom limbs, Siamese twin brains, viruses that eat patients' memories, blind people who see through their tongues. . . . Kean explores the brain's secret passageways and recounts the forgotten tales of the ordinary people whose struggles, resilience, and deep humanity made neuroscience possible." (Publisher's note)

"Entertaining and quotable, Kean's writing is sharp, and each individual story brings the history of neuroscience to life. Compulsively readable, wicked scientific fun." Kirkus

Includes bibliographical references and index

Krug, Louise

Louise; amended. Louise Krug. Black Balloon Pub. 2012 192 p. (trade paper; alk. paper) $14   **617.4**
  1. Brain -- Wounds and injuries

ISBN 1936787016; 9781936787012

LC 2011938591

This memoir by Louise Krug describes "A beautiful young woman from Kansas [who] is about to embark on the life of her dreams--California! Glossy journalism! French boyfriend!--only to suffer a brain bleed that collapses the right side of her body, leaving her with double vision, facial paralysis, and a dragging foot. . . . The memoir presents not only Louise's perspective, but also the reaction of her loved ones. . . in fictional interludes." (Publisher's note)

Marsh, Henry, 1954-

Do No Harm; Stories of Life, Death and Brain Surgery. Henry Marsh. St. Martin's Press 2015 304 p. $25.99   **617.4**
  1. Surgeons 2. Brain -- Surgery
  ISBN 125006581X; 9781250065810

LC 2015002573

This book by Henry Marsh "provides unforgettable insight into the countless human dramas that take place in a busy modern hospital. Above all, it is a lesson in the need for hope when faced with life's most difficult decisions. Marsh reveals the fierce joy of operating, the profoundly moving triumphs, the harrowing disasters, the haunting regrets, and the moments of black humor that characterize a brain surgeon's life." (Publisher's note)

"One of the best books ever about a life in medicine, Do No Harm boldly and gracefully exposes the vulnerability and painful privilege of being a physician." Booklist

Snyder, Rich, d. 1993

What you must know about dialysis; the secrets to surviving and thriving on dialysis. Rich Snyder. Square One Publishers 2013 197 p. (pbk.) $17.95   **617.4**
  1. Chronic disease 2. Kidneys -- Diseases 3. Hemodialysis -- Patients 4. Hemodialysis -- Popular works
  ISBN 0757003494; 9780757003493

LC 2012028692

In this book, "osteopathic physician and nephrologist [Rich] Snyder . . . arms patients with . . . information to aid in coping with chronic kidney conditions that require dialysis or a kidney transplant. . . . Focusing primarily on controlling fluid intake and blood pressure, Snyder discusses a dietary regimen, diet supplements, and caring for emotional and spiritual as well as physical well-being." (Publishers Weekly)

Includes bibliographical references and index

Stoler, Diane Roberts

Coping with concussion and mild traumatic brain injury; a guide to living with the challenges associated with post concussion syndrome and brain trauma. Diane Roberts Stoler, Ed.D., and Barbara Albers Hill. Avery 2013 400 p. illustrations (alk. paper) $18   **617.4**
  1. Brain -- Concussion 2. Brain -- Wounds and injuries 3. Brain damage 4. Brain damage -- Psychological aspects
  ISBN 1583334769; 9781583334768

LC 2013016860

This book, by Diane Roberts Stoler and Barbara Albers Hill, is a "guide for improving memory, focus, and quality of life in the aftermath of a concussion. Often presenting itself after a head trauma, concussion-- or mild traumatic brain injury (mTBI)-- can cause chronic migraines, depression, memory, and sleep problems that can last for years, referred to as post concussion syndrome (PCS)." (Publisher's note)

"Filled with practical advice on understanding and living with concussion and TBI, this well-written and well-organized volume is an excellent resource for patients who have suffered from this condition and for their family members." LJ

Includes bibliographical references and index

Westaby, Stephen

Open heart; a cardiac surgeon's stories of life and death on the operating table. Stephen Westaby. Basic Books 2017 x, 287 p.p illustrations (hardcover) $27 **617.4**

1. Surgeons 2. Heart -- Surgery 3. Heart -- Surgery -- Anecdotes 4. Heart surgeons -- United States -- Biography

ISBN 9781541698093; 9780465094837

LC 2016058151

This book, by Stephen Westaby, "reflects on over 11,000 surgeries, showing us why the procedures have never become routine and will never be. With astonishing compassion and candor, Dr. Westaby recounts the . . . stories from his operating room: we meet a pulseless man who lives with an electric heart pump, an expecting mother who refuses surgery unless the doctors let her pregnancy reach full term, and a baby who gets a transplanted heart-only to die once it's in place." (Publisher's note)

"Intense and sometimes-stunning stories of the heart, delivered from the heart." Booklist

617.5   Regional medicine

Deyo, Richard A.

Watch your back! how the back pain industry is costing us more and giving us less, and what you can do to inform and empower yourself in seeking treatment. Richard A. Deyo MD. ILR Press, an imprint of Cornell University Press 2014 232 p. (Culture and politics of health care work) (cloth; alk. paper) $21.95 **617.5**

1. Backache 2. Backache -- Treatment 3. Back -- Diseases -- Treatment

ISBN 0801453240; 9780801453243

LC 2014006972

In this book, Dr. Richard A. Deyo "proposes an approach to managing back pain . . . that empowers the individual and leads more directly to effective care. . . . [It] exposes [the] flaws in the current approach to back pain, along with the profit motives and conflicts of interest behind many of them. The book dramatizes the problems with stories of prominent individuals who encountered high-tech pitfalls, then found low-tech solutions suited to their lifestyles and the nature of their back pain." (Publisher's note)

"Concise, clearly written, and evidence based, Deyo's work would be invaluable to those facing the onset of back pain and the dizzying range of treatment choices, as well as to practitioners and policy makers." LJ

Includes bibliographical references and index

Laskas, Jeanne Marie, 1958-

Concussion; Jeanne Marie Laskas. Random House Inc 2015 288 p. 8 plates; illustrations (acid-free paper) $16 **617.5**

1. Brain -- Concussion 2. National Football League 3. Sports injuries 4. Head -- Wounds and injuries

ISBN 0812987578; 9780812987577

LC 2015020171

Author Jeanne Marie Laskas presents the "story of Dr. Bennet Omalu, the pathologist who made one of the most significant medical discoveries of the twenty-first century, a discovery that challenges the existence of America's favorite sport and puts Omalu in the crosshairs of . . . the [National Football League]. Omalu discovered in [Mike] Webster's brain . . . proof that Iron Mike's mental deterioration was . . . a disease caused by blows to the head that could affect everyone playing [football]." (Publisher's note)

"Effectively sobering. Suffice it to say that Pop Warner parents will want to armor their kids from head to toe upon reading it." Kirkus

617.6   Dentistry

Artemis, Nadine, 1971-

Holistic dental care; the complete guide to healthy teeth and gums. Nadine Artemis ; foreword by Victor Zeines. North Atlantic Books 2013 xvii, 130 p.p color illustrations (pbk.) $16.95 **617.6**

1. Health self-care 2. Dentistry -- Popular works 3. Dental Care -- Popular Works 4. Oral Hygiene -- Popular Works 5. Holistic Health -- Popular Works

ISBN 1583947205; 9781583947203; 9781583947210

LC 2013014011

This book, by Nadine Artemis, is "a comprehensive guide to natural, do-it-yourself oral care, [which] . . . introduces simple, at-home dental procedures that anyone can do. Highlighted with fifty-three full-color photos and illustrations, this book offers dental self-care strategies and practices that get to the core of the problems in our mouths--preventing issues from taking root and gently restoring dental health." (Publisher's note)

Includes bibliographical references (p. 115-121) and index

Best-Boss, Angie

Your child's teeth; a complete guide for parents. Evelina Weidman Sterling, Angie Best-Boss. Johns Hopkins University Press 2013 296 p. illustrations (hardcover; alk. paper) $40 **617.6**

1. Children -- Dental care 2. Pedodontics

ISBN 1421410621; 142141063X; 9781421410623; 9781421410630

LC 2012047776

In this book, authors Evelina Weidman Sterling and Angie Best-Boss "team up with pediatric dentists and oral health experts to answer parents' many questions about children's teeth. Topics include: how thumb sucking and pacifiers affect teeth, how to brush your young children's teeth, . . . how to help special needs children get proper dental care, how medical problems affect teeth, how fluoride rinses and dental sealants work, how a root canal is done." (Publisher's note)

"Untypical, too, but much appreciated are Day's admissions of difficult times and how to overcome them. A super (and superquirky) memoir." Booklist

Otto, Mary

Teeth; the story of beauty, inequality, and the struggle for oral health in America. Mary Otto. New Press 2017 x, 291 p.p (hc; alk. paper) $26.95 **617.6**

1. Dental care 2. Medical policy 3. Teeth -- Diseases 4. Dental hygiene

ISBN 9781620972816; 9781620971444

LC 2016041484

This book, by Mary Otto, "looks inside America's mouth, revealing unsettling truths about our unequal society. . . . [It] takes readers on a disturbing journey into America's silent epidemic of oral disease, exposing the hidden connections between tooth decay and stunted job prospects, low educational achievement, social mobility, and the troubling state of our public health. . . . [It] exposes for the first time the extent and meaning of our oral health crisis." (Publisher's note)

"A focused, well-researched depiction of the dental industry's social and cultural relevance and its dire need for reform." Kirkus

Includes bibliographical references (pages 263-280) and index.

617.8   Otology and audiology

Bouton, Katherine

★ **Shouting** won't help; why I - and 50 million other Americans - can't hear you. Katherine Bouton. Sarah Crichton Books/Farrar, Straus, and Giroux 2013 288 p. (hardcover; alk. paper) $26 **617.8**

1. Deaf 2. Hearing impaired 3. Deafness 4. Deaf women -- New York (State) -- New York -- Biography

ISBN 0374263043; 9780374263041

LC 2012029096

This book, by Katherine Bouton, describes the author's personal experiences struggling with hearing loss. "For twenty-two years, Katherine Bouton had a secret that grew harder to keep every day. . . . She had gone profoundly deaf in her left ear; her right was getting worse. . . . Using her experience as a guide, Bouton examines the problem [of hearing loss] personally, psychologically, and physiologically." (Publisher's note)

Includes bibliographical references and index

617.9   Operative surgery and special fields of surgery

Cole-Adams, Kate

Anesthesia; the gift of oblivion and the mystery of consciousness. Kate Cole-Adams. Counterpoint Press 2017 400 p. $28 **617.9**

1. Consciousness 2. Anesthesia -- History 3. Anesthesia 4. Anesthesia -- history 5. Consciousness -- drug effects 6. Unconsciousness -- chemically induced

ISBN 9781619029507

LC 2017034798

This book, by Kate Cole-Adams, "is the story of the time in between, an exploration of that most crucial and baffling gift of modern medicine: the disappearing act that enables us to undergo procedures that would otherwise be impossibly, often fatally, painful. . . . [The author] weaves her own personal experiences with surgery and its aftermath with the explorations and personal accounts of others, doctors and patients alike." (Publisher's note)

" While the author raises more questions than she answers, and some readers may be put off by her less-that-straightforward style, these are thought-provoking questions, and Cole-Adams presents a lyrical journey through the vital question of what it means to be human." (Kirkus)

Includes bibliographical references and index

Przybylo, Henry Jay

Counting backwards; a doctor's notes on anesthesia. Henry Jay Przybylo. W W Norton & Co Inc 2018 xiii, 240 p.p (hardcover) $25.95 **617.9**

1. Anesthesia 2. Anesthesiologists 3. Anesthesiology -- Anecdotes 4. Anesthesiologists -- United States -- Biography

ISBN 9780393254440; 9780393254433

LC 2017018049

This book, by Henry Jay Przybylo, "delivers an unforgettable account of the [anesthesia] procedure's daily dramas and fundamental mysteries. Przybylo has administered anesthesia more than 30,000 times in his career . . . on newborn babies, screaming toddlers, sullen teenagers, even a gorilla. With compassion and candor, he weaves his experiences into an intimate exploration of the nature of consciousness, the politics of pain relief, and the wonder of modern medicine." (Publisher's note)

"Przybylo offers a rare and thoughtful look behind the scenes of this crucial yet arcane specialization." Pub Wkly

Includes bibliographical references (pages 231-240).

618.1   Gynecology and obstetrics

Allmen, Tara

Menopause confidential; A Doctor Reveals the Secrets to Thriving Through Midlife. Tara Allmen, MD. HarperOne 2016 256 p. (hardback) $26.99 **618.1**

1. Menopause -- Popular works 2. Middle-aged women -- Health and hygiene -- Popular works

ISBN 9780062447265

LC 2016028325

This book, by Tara Allmen, is "an authoritative guide to understanding . . . the hormonal changes and health issues women experience in midlife and beyond. . . . [It provides] information and practical advice on . . . the symptoms and hormonal changes of perimenopause and menopause, . . . various remedies, both allopathic and natural, to improve symptoms and empower women to make individual choices, . . . [and] practical tips and reliable resources for living a healthy life." (Publisher's note)

"Board-certified gynecologist and nationally certified menopause practitioner Allmen offers a comprehensive health guide for women over 40." LJ

Includes bibliographical references (pages [233]-239) and index.

Anstett, Patricia

Breast cancer surgery and reconstruction; What's Right for You. Patricia Anstett ; with photography by Kathleen Galligan. Rowman & Littlefield 2016 224 p. illustrations (cloth; alk. paper) $35 **618.1**

1. Breast cancer 2. Plastic surgery 3. Breast -- Surgery 4. Surgery, Plastic

ISBN 9781442242623

LC 2016003294

This book, by Patricia Anstet, "offers a glimpse into the big picture of the various stages and types of breast reconstruction using stories and photos of real women. It offers a true picture of what breast reconstruction entails, and offers hope to those facing it." (Publisher's note)

"This important, well-reported guide should empower women with breast cancer to figure out their own best treatment." Booklist

Includes bibliographical references and index

Boggs, Belle

★ The **art** of waiting; On Fertility, Medicine, and Motherhood. Belle Boggs. Graywolf Press 2016 224 p. (alk. paper) $16 **618.1**

1. Motherhood 2. Infertility

ISBN 9781555977498

LC 2016931135

In this book, author Belle Boggs "recounts her realization that she might never be able to conceive. She searches the apparently fertile world around her--the emergence of thirteen-year cicadas, the birth of eaglets near her rural home, and an unusual gorilla pregnancy at a local zoo--for signs that she is not alone. Boggs also explores other aspects of fertility and infertility." (Publisher's note)

"Readers struggling with infertility may find reassurance and comfort in Boggs's experiences; their loved ones will gain insight into the painful experience of infertility. All readers will appreciate the engaging prose and thought-provoking information." LJ

Eig, Jonathan

★ The **birth** of the pill; how four crusaders reinvented sex and launched a revolution. Jonathan Eig. W W Norton & Co Inc 2014 416 p. (hardcover) $27.95   **618.1**

1. Oral contraceptives

ISBN 0393073726; 9780393073720

LC 2014019355

This book on this history of birth control, by Jonathan Eig, "revolves around four principal characters:... feminist Margaret Sanger, who was a champion of birth control, ... Katharine McCormick, who owed her fortune to her wealthy husband, ... scientist Gregory Pincus, who was dismissed by Harvard in the 1930s as a result of his experimentation with in vitro fertilization, ... and the telegenic John Rock, a Catholic doctor from Boston." (Publisher's note)

Includes bibliographical references and index

Greer, Germaine

The **change**; women, aging and the menopause. Ballantine 1993 422p pa $23   **618.1**

1. Aging 2. Menopause 3. Self-realization 4. Women -- Psychology

ISBN 0-449-90853-4; 978-0-449-90853-2

First published 1991 in the United Kingdom

This is a discussion of menopause in Western society. Greer looks at medical, psychological and social aspects of the cessation of menstruation and the aging process. She views the climateric as an important turning-point in a woman's life.

"In a wise, witty and inspiring book, Greer rebukes doctors, psychiatrists—and women themselves—who blame the aging female for her menopausal distress.... Greer dispels all manner of myths and misconceptions about menopause." Publ Wkly

Includes bibliographical references

Love, Susan M.

Dr. Susan Love's Breast Book; Susan M. Love, M.D. ; with Elizabeth Love and Karen Lindsey ; illustrations by Marcia Williams. 6th edition Da Capo Lifelong Books 2015 704 p. illustrations pbk $24   **618.1**

1. Breast 2. Breast cancer

ISBN 9780738218212; 0738218219

LC 2015458675

This book covers breast development, plastic surgery, common problems, and breast cancer diagnosis, treatment, and screening.

"New to this edition is the use of 'liquid biopsy,' blood tests that trace metastases, and ways of lessening the side effects of chemotherapy and radiation." LJ

Includes bibliographical references and index

Potter, Daniel A.

What to do when you can't get pregnant; the complete guide to all the options for couples facing fertility issues. by Daniel A. Potter, MD, and Jennifer S. Hanin, MA ; foreword by Pamela Madsen. Da Capo Press, a member of the Perseus Books Group 2013 xxii, 329 p.p illustrations (paperback) $18.99   **618.1**

1. Infertility 2. Reproductive technology 3. Infertility -- Treatment

-- Popular works 4. Human reproductive technology -- Popular works

ISBN 0738216917; 9780738216911

LC 2013372225

This book, by doctor Daniel A. Potter and journalist Jennifer S. Hanin, is a "guide to all the options for couples facing fertility issues, now revised and updated. . . . Drawing on the latest science, Potter and Hanin offer sound advice for choosing the right doctor, asking the right questions, and living a healthy, fertile lifestyle." (Publisher's note)

"This solid, up-to-date resource supplants Debra Fulghum Bruce and Samuel Thatcher's Making a Baby: Everything You Need To Know To Get Pregnant. Recommended for most consumer health collections." LJ

Silverstone, Alicia, 1976-

The **kind** mama; a simple guide to supercharged fertility, a radiant pregnancy, a sweeter birth, and a healthier, more beautiful beginning. Alicia Silverstone. Rodale 2014 354 p. color illustrations (paperback) $23.99   **618.1**

1. Pregnancy 2. Women -- Health and hygiene 3. Infants -- Nutrition 4. Pregnancy -- Nutritional aspects 5. Childbirth -- Psychological aspects 6. Infertility, Female -- Diet therapy

ISBN 1623360404; 9781623360405

LC 2013049183

"In 'The Kind Mama,' Alicia Silverstone has created a comprehensive and practical guide empowering women to take charge of their fertility, pregnancy, and first 6 months with baby. Drawing on her own experience, as well as that of obstetricians, midwives, nutritionists, holistic health counselors, and others, Silverstone offers advice on getting one's 'baby house' in order through nutrient-rocking foods that heal and nourish." (Publisher's note)

"In addition to her birth story, Silverstone discusses morning sickness, circumcision (not recommended) and the family bed (create a safe sleep sanctuary for the whole family). In "For Gentlemen Only" sections, she doles out useful tips for dads on how to be supportive partners. Health-conscious moms-to-be will enjoy and learn from this heart-centered guide." Pub Wkly

Streicher, Lauren F., 1956-

The **essential** guide to hysterectomy; advice from a gynecologist on your choices before, during, and after surgery. Lauren F. Streicher, M.D. M. Evans 2013 xiv, 466 p.p illustrations (pbk.; alk. paper) $22.95   **618.1**

1. Hysterectomy 2. Women -- Health and hygiene 3. Patient education 4. Hysterectomy -- Popular works

ISBN 1590772113; 9781590772119

LC 2012043565

In this book, author "Lauren Streicher . . . reveals the following: What your doctor isn't telling you; robotic hysterectomy and why it is becoming so popular; new nonsurgical ways to control heavy bleeding; the latest on hormone therapy, including bioidentical hormones; how to decrease your risk of uterine or ovarian cancer without removing your uterus or ovaries; new methods for treating fibroids; and a comprehensive guide to websites and resources." (Publisher's note)

618.2   Obstetrics

Epstein, Randi Hutter

Get me out; a history of childbirth from the Garden of Eden to the sperm bank. W.W. Norton 2010 302p il $24.95 **618.2**

1. Childbirth

ISBN 978-0-393-06458-2

LC 2009-34751

The author "provides a sharp, sassy history of childbirth. The book is as much a study in sociology as historical snapshot of human birthing practices and gynecological advances, with particular emphasis on developments in the late 19th- and 20th-century United States. . . . The author's engaging sarcasm . . . lends this chronicle a welcome punch and vitality often absent from medical histories." Kirkus

Includes bibliographical references

Mayo Clinic guide to a healthy pregnancy; [by the pregnancy experts at Mayo Clinic ; medical editors, Roger Harms, Myra Wick] Good Books 2011 509 p. ill. (chiefly ill.) (pbk.) $19.95 **618.2**
1. Pregnancy 2. Childbirth 3. Prenatal care
ISBN 1561487171; 9781561487172

LC 2011920078

This book, by Roger Harms and Myra Wick, presents a centralized reference to pregnancy, prenatal care and childbirth. "Features include week-by-week updates on baby's growth and month-by-month changes for mom, a 40-week pregnancy calendar, a symptoms guide, and a review of important pregnancy decisions. In this illustrated book you'll also receive advice on how to get pregnant, meal planning, exercise, medication use and parenthood." (Publisher's note)

The **mommy** docs' ultimate guide to pregnancy and birth; [by] Yvonne Bohn, Allison Hill, Alane Park with Melissa Jo Peltier. Da Capo Lifelong 2011 526p il pa $15.95 **618.2**
1. Pregnancy 2. Childbirth 3. Infants -- Care
ISBN 978-0-7382-1460-3

"Chapters are arranged from preparing for pregnancy to first, second, and third trimesters; birth; and early days at home. Additional chapters handle complications of early pregnancy, high-risk pregnancies, and 'frequently asked questions . . . and frequently repeated myths.' They offer reassurance for a healthy pregnancy even for those with health conditions such as hypertension or diabetes. Throughout, the authors deliver practical tips and emotional support for coping with both complicated and uncomplicated pregnancies as well as the things that can go wrong, such as miscarriages or infertility. . . . A great resource for anyone seeking information on pregnancy, childbirth, and the first weeks after birth." Libr J

Includes bibliographical references

Murkoff, Heidi
★ **What** to expect when you're expecting; by Heidi Murkoff and Sharon Mazel ; foreword by Charles J. Lockwood, MD. 5th edition Workman Pub. Co. 2016 644 p. illustrations hardcover $29.95 **618.2**
1. Pregnancy 2. Childbirth
ISBN 0761189246; 9780761189244

LC 2015044527

"The revised fifth edition of 'America's pregnancy bible' has completely updated medical information, including the latest on prenatal screening, a brand-new section on postpartum birth control, and effects of current lifestyle trends, such as juice bars, raw diets, e-cigarettes, and omega-3 fatty acids, on pregnant women." LJ

The **pregnancy** encyclopedia; all your questions answered. consultant editor, Paula Amato, M.D. ; editor-in-chief, Dr. Chandrima Biswas, consultant obstetrician. DK Publishing 2016 351 p. color illustrations (hbk) $40 **618.2**
1. Infants 2. Pregnancy 3. Childbirth 4. Pregnancy -- Popular works 5. Childbirth -- Popular works 6. Obstetrics -- Popular

works 7. Newborn infants -- Popular works
ISBN 1465443789; 9781465443786

LC 2016304347

This book "is an engaging and accessible question-and-answer guide to some of the most commonly asked questions about pregnancy, packed with full-color photographs and illustrations. . . . Top experts in the field offer encyclopedic coverage of the topics relating to pregnancy and birth, from fertility and family planning to nutrition and exercise to lifestyle changes, planning for the future, and more." (Publisher's note)

"This book will be a very useful resource. It has a detailed index and a glossary to help readers find what they need. This is an excellent addition to public and consumer-health library collections." Booklist

Romm, Aviva Jill
The **natural** pregnancy book; your complete guide to a safe, organic pregnancy and childbirth with herbs, nutrition, and other holistic choices. Aviva Jill Romm ; foreword by Ina May Gaskin. Ten Speed Press 2014 xvi, 288 p.p (paperback) $17.99 **618.2**
1. Pregnancy 2. Holistic medicine 3. Pregnancy -- Popular works 4. Holistic medicine -- Popular works 5. Alternative medicine -- Popular works
ISBN 1607744481; 9781607744481; 9781607744498

LC 2014008356

Written by Aviva Jill Romm, this is "A revised and updated edition of the classic handbook for women seeking a safe, organic, eco-friendly, and natural pregnancy, featuring an integrative-based approach with new medical, herbal, and nutritional information. . . . Dr. Romm takes a holistic approach, emphasizing natural remedies wherever possible and providing up-to-date advice on herbs that promote wellness during pregnancy." (Publisher's note)

Includes bibliographical references and index

Rope, Kate
Strong as a mother; how to stay healthy, happy, and (most importantly) sane from pregnancy to parenthood; the only guide to taking care of you! Kate Rope. St. Martin's Griffin 2018 400 p. (pbk.) $18.99 **618.2**
1. Pregnancy 2. Postpartum depression 3. Pregnancy -- Health aspects 4. Pregnant women -- Health and hygiene
ISBN 9781250105585

LC 2017059644

This book, by Kate Rope, "is a practical and compassionate guide to preparing for a smooth start to motherhood. . . . Topics includes; prioritizing emotional health, . . . [setting] boundaries and asking for help, . . . [making] choices about feeding and childcare . . . [getting] good sleep, . . . [creating] strong relationship with your partner, . . . [and] self care." (Publisher's note)

Rowland, Kelly, 1981-
Whoa, baby! a guide for new moms who feel overwhelmed and freaked out (and wonder what the #*$& just happened) Kelly Rowland ; and Tristan Emily Bickman, MD with Laura Moser. Da Capo Lifelong Books 2017 xv, 176 p.p illustrations (hardcover) $25 **618.2**
1. Pregnancy 2. Childbirth 3. Women -- Health and hygiene 4. Parenting -- Popular works 5. Pregnancy -- Popular works 6. Childbirth -- Popular works 7. Women -- Health and hygiene -- Popular works
ISBN 9780738234144; 9780738219424

LC 2016043406

This book, by Kelly Rowland, Tristan Emily Bickman and Laura

Moser, "offers first-time moms an honest and humorous look at all the odd changes and often gross repercussions that accompany childbirth. . . . [It] addresses the issues such as swelling, constipation, hemorrhoids, incontinence, and more unfortunates relevant to the birthing experience." (Library Journal)

Schuler, Judith

★ **Your** pregnancy week by week; Glade B. Curtis, M.D., M.P.H., OB/GYN and Judith Schuler, M.S. 8th edition DaCapo Lifelong 2016 463 p. illustrations pbk $15.99   **618.2**
1. Fetus 2. Pregnancy
ISBN 9780738218939; 0738218936

LC 2016303069

First published 1989 by Fisher Books

This book, by Glade B. Curtis and Judith Schuler, "provides everything expectant parents need for a healthy, happy pregnancy, including descriptions of the fetus's development each week, up-to-date information about medical tests and procedures, safe weekly exercises to help expectant moms stay in shape, and helpful hints for the father-to-be." (Publisher's note)

Sears, William

The **healthy** pregnancy book; month by month, everything you need to know from America's baby experts. Williams Sears, MD, and Martha Sears, RN, with Linda Holt, MD, and BJ Snell, PhD, CNW. Little, Brown & Co. 2013 xviii, 446 p.p illustrations $17   **618.2**
1. Pregnancy 2. Women -- Health and hygiene 3. Childbirth
ISBN 0316187437; 9780316187435

LC 2013946521

In this book, author William Sears and Martha Sears "address emotional and physical changes that take place during pregnancy, baby's brain development, healthy pregnancy habits, pregnancy superfoods, optimal weight gain, fitness, managing stress, sleep, choosing the right healthcare provider, birthing choices, the transition into parenthood, engaging personal stories, and more." (Publisher's note)

Includes bibliographical references (pages 425-427) and index

Simkin, Penny

The **Birth** Partner; A Complete Guide to Childbirth for Dads, Doulas & All Other Labor Companions. HougHton Mifflin Harcourt 2013 396 p. illustrations $18.95   **618.2**
1. Pregnancy 2. Childbirth 3. Pregnancy -- Popular works
ISBN 155832819X; 9781558328198

LC 891763

"Since the original publication of 'The Birth Partner,' new mothers' mates, friends, and relatives and doulas (professional birth assistants) have relied on Penny Simkin's guidance in caring for the new mother from the last few weeks of pregnancy through the early postpartum period. Fully revised in its fourth edition, 'The Birth Partner' remains the definitive guide for preparing to help a woman through childbirth and the essential manual to have at hand during the event." (Publisher's note)

Vincent, Peggy

Baby catcher; chronicles of a modern midwife. Scribner 2002 336p $26; pa $13   **618.2**
1. Midwives
ISBN 0-7432-1933-3; 0-7432-1934-1 pa

LC 2001-54988

This is an account of a midwife specializing in home births who "over the course of 40 years, brought some 2,000 babies into the world. . . . A solid writer, Vincent doesn't preach the virtues of unmedicated

birthing; she just lays consistent stories of women doing it—Christian Science moms, Muslim moms, spiritualist moms, lesbian moms, teen moms and just plain ordinary moms." Publ Wkly

618.3   Diseases, disorders, management of pregnancy, childbirth, puerperium

Ilse, Sherokee

The **prenatal** bombshell; help and hope when continuing or ending a precious pregnancy after an abnormal diagnosis. Stephanie Azri and Sherokee Ilse. Rowman & Littlefield 2015 254 p. (cloth; alk. paper) $37   **618.3**
1. Pregnancy 2. Prenatal care 3. Bereavement -- Personal Narratives 4. Decision Making -- Personal Narratives 5. Abortion, Induced -- Personal Narratives 6. Patient Education as Topic -- Personal Narratives 7. Prenatal Diagnosis -- psychology -- Personal Narratives
ISBN 1442239425; 9781442239425

LC 2014040890

Authors Stephanie Azri and Sherokee Ilse present this "companion guide through the journey from diagnosis and beyond once you've decided to either continue or end your precious pregnancy. Issues such as managing the pregnancy, delivery, termination, creating memories, future babies, and the long term impact of such a traumatic experience are all covered in detail. The lived experiences of other women who have gone through this journey are also included to provide hope, support, and guidance through difficult times." (Publisher's note)

"The book's underlying message for parents is to look clearly at what is happening and to accept, not try to deny, the difficult emotions that it will bring. This book is an excellent vehicle for coming to grips with a very difficult situation." Pub Wkly

Includes bibliographical references and index

618.4   Childbirth

Gaskin, Ina May

Ina May's guide to childbirth. Bantam Books 2003 348p il pa $14.95   **618.4**
1. Natural childbirth
ISBN 0-553-38115-6

LC 2002-29901

Gaskin "explains that the female body is well designed for normal birth and provides techniques for dealing with the discomforts of labor. A whole chapter devoted to women's birthing experiences supports her stance. More than a childbirth guide, this comprehensive book provides insight into the sociological and historical aspects of the natural childbirth movement." Libr J

Includes bibliographical references

Leboyer, Frédérick, 1918-2017

Birth without violence; Frédérick Leboyer; new translation by Yvonne Fitzgerald and the author. 3rd ed Healing Arts Press 2009 xiii, 130 p.p ill. (pbk.) $14.95   **618.4**
1. Childbirth 2. Natural childbirth
ISBN 1594772975; 9781594772979

LC 2009001028

Original French edition, 1974; first English translation published 1975 by Knopf

This book, by Frédérick Leboyer, translated by Yvonne Fitzgerald, advocates that "babies are born complete human beings with the ability to experience a full range of emotions. First published in 1974, it revolutionized the way we perceive the process of birth. . . . Examining alternatives to technocentric approaches to childbirth, this new edition . . . shows us how we can ease the transition from womb to world without trauma or fear." (Publisher's note)

A new edition of the book that "revolutionized the way we perceive the process of birth, urging us to consider birth from the infant's point of view." It shows how to "ease the transition from womb to world without trauma or fear." (Publisher's note)

Silbernagel, Shantel

The **Many** Faces of Home Birth; 25 Honest, Firsthand Accounts from Parents Around the World. by Shantel Silbernagel. Skyhorse Publishing 2017 188 p. $17.99   **618.4**
  1. Childbirth 2. Home birth
  ISBN 1510724974; 9781510724976

LC 2017041965

This book, by Shantel Silbernagel, "provid[es] a rare glimpse into the private moments of twenty-five unique and modern home births from around the world. With honesty, humor, and confidence, these personal narratives and shared experiences leave readers with the understanding that home birth isn't just for one type of woman." (Publisher's note)

618.6   Normal puerperium

Serrallach, Oscar

The **postnatal** depletion cure; a complete guide to rebuilding your health and reclaiming your energy for mothers of newborns, toddlers, and young children. Dr. Oscar Serrallach. Grand Central Life & Style 2018 304 p. (hardcover edition) $81   **618.6**
  1. Motherhood 2. Postnatal care 3. Women -- Health and hygiene 4. Postnatal care -- Popular works 5. Postnatal care -- Treatment -- Popular works
  ISBN 9781478970309

LC 2017046606

This book, by Dr. Oscar Serrallach, is "filled with trustworthy advice [and] protocols for successful recovery. . . . [It] is a guide to help any mother restore her energy, replenish her body, and reclaim her sense of self. Most mothers have experienced pain, forgetfulness, indecision, low energy levels, moodiness, or some form of baby brain. And it's no wonder: The process of growing a baby depletes a mother's body in substantial ways." (Publisher's note)

"A practical volume that will be of use to mothers everywhere." Library Journal

Includes bibliographical references

618.7   Puerperal diseases

Friedmann, Jessica

Things that helped; on postpartum depression. Jessica Friedmann. Farrar, Straus & Giroux 2018 272 p. (paperback) $16   **618.7**
  1. Mental illness 2. Postpartum depression 3. Depression (Psychology) 4. Depression in women -- Patients -- Australia 5. Postpartum depression -- Patients -- Australia
  ISBN 9780374274801

LC 2017038315

This memoir in essays, details "Australian writer Jessica Friedmann's recovery from postpartum depression. In each essay she focuses on

a separate totemic object--from pho red lips to the musician Anohni--to tell a story that is both deeply personal and culturally resonant. Drawing on critical theory, popular culture, and her own experience, Friedmann's wide-ranging essays touch on class, race, gender, and sexuality, as well as motherhood, creativity, and mental illness." (Publisher's note)

Includes bibliographical references

618.92   Pediatrics

Barnett, Kristine

The **spark**; raising a genius. Kristine Barnett. Random House 2013 272 p. illustrations $25   **618.92**
  1. Autism 2. Genius 3. Parents of autistic children 4. Autism in children -- Case studies 5. Autistic children -- Rehabilitation 6. Mothers of autistic children -- Case studies
  ISBN 0812993373; 9780679645245; 9780812993370

LC 2012032774

This book, by Kristine Barnett is a "memoir that attempts to answer the question, how do we determine the differences between gifted and disabled? . . . Her son Jake received a diagnosis [of autism] at the age of 2, which set off a series of standard educational responses. . . . Barnett took an approach that instead focused on what she would refer to as his 'spark.' . . . Her success with Jake is unimpeachable: He is a 'prodigy in math and science.'" (Kirkus Reviews)

"Barnett even runs a day-care center, takes in foster kids, and starts a sports program for autistic kids. Jake is unusual, but so is his superhuman mom." Booklist

Bashe, Patricia Romanowski, 1949-

Asperger Syndrome; The Oasis Guide: Advice, Inspiration, Insight, and Hope, from Early Intervention to Adulthood. Patricia Romanowski Bashe. 3rd ed Random House Inc 2014 592 p. illustrations $17   **618.92**
  1. Autism 2. Asperger's syndrome
  ISBN 0385344651; 9780385344654
  First published 2001

This book, by Patricia Romanowski Bashe, offers a "comprehensive, authoritative guide to Asperger syndrome. This fully revised, updated, and expanded edition captures the latest in research, strategies, and parenting wisdom, and delivers it all in the empathetic, practical, and hopefilled style 'The OASIS Guide' is famous for." (Publisher's note)

"This edition includes new developments made in AS research over the past four years, new thinking on diagnosis and evaluation, the latest approaches to medication and social skills development, and tips on navigating the maze of interventions, therapies, and special education." Publisher's note

Includes bibliographical references

The **big** book of symptoms; A-Z guide to your child's health. American Academy of Pediatrics ; [edited by] Steven P. Shelov, MD, MS, FAAP, Shelly Vaziri Flais, MD, FAAP. American Academy of Pediatrics 2014 260 p. illustrations $16.95   **618.92**
  1. Diagnosis 2. Children -- Health and hygiene
  ISBN 1581108400; 9781581108408

LC 2013945504

Edited by Steven P. Shelov and Shelly V. Flais, "This book is designed to help you distinguish minor everyday concerns with more serious conditions, and to suggest a reasonable course of action. Organized into 2 sections, an A to Z directory of the 100 or so most common childhood symptoms and an illustrated first aid manual, 'Symptoms' will help parents determine the best way to help their sick child." (Publisher's note)

"In July 2011, the American Academy of Pediatrics (AAP) published My Child Is Sick: Expert Advice for Managing Common Illnesses and Injuries by Barton D. Schmitt, whose bulleted and numbered triage system was more helpful. While any AAP title is worthy of consideration for libraries, those owning Schmitt's can pass on this." LJ

Camarata, Stephen M.

Late-talking children; a symptom or a stage? Stephen M. Camarata. The MIT Press 2014 256 p. (hardcover; alk. paper) $19.95   **618.92**

1. Child development 2. Children -- Language 3. Language disorders in children 4. Language disorders in children -- Diagnosis 5. Developmentally disabled children -- Education

ISBN 0262027798; 9780262027793

LC 2014003809

In this book, author Stephen Camarata "describes in accessible language what science knows about the characteristics and causes of late talking. He explains that late talking is only one of a constellation of autism symptoms. Although all autistic children are late talkers, not all late-talking children are autistic." (Publisher's note)

"Camarata, while wanting to support parents, sometimes has an alarmist tone, even when referring to colleagues. The text, therefore, is more appropriate for academic audiences and scientific readers than the distressed parent. Undergraduate libraries and colleges with speech therapy programs will want to consider." LJ

Includes bibliographical references and index

Chansky, Tamar E.

Freeing your child from anxiety; practical strategies to overcome fears, worries, and phobias and be prepared for for life--from toddlers to teens. Tamar Chansky, Ph.D. ; illustrations by Phillip Stern. Harmony Books 2014 viii, 468 p.p illustrations (paperback) $16.99   **618.92**

1. Anxiety 2. Child psychology 3. Anxiety in children

ISBN 0804139806; 9780804139809

LC 2013050665

This book, by Tamar Chansky, "contains easy, fun, and effective tools for teaching children to outsmart their worries and take charge of their fears. This revised and updated edition also teaches how to prepare children to withstand the pressure in our competitive test-driven culture." (Publisher's note)

Includes bibliographical references (pages 449-450) and index

Chicoine, Brian

The **guide** to good health for teens & adults with Down syndrome; [by] Brian Chicoine & Dennis McGuire. Woodbine House 2010 391p il pa $29.95   **618.92**

1. Down syndrome

ISBN 978-1-890627-89-8

LC 2010-18783

"This excellent book provides a wealth of information for DS caregivers. . . . The authors describe diagnosis, treatment, and prevention of common health conditions impacting DS people and cover mental and emotional issues that can affect physical health. Sexuality and birth control are discussed, as is abuse prevention. The book also includes information on residential options as well as coverage of end of life issues." Libr J

Includes bibliographical references

Cohen, Scott W.

Eat, sleep, poop; a common sense guide to your baby's first year--essential information from an award-winning pediatrician and new dad. Scribner 2010 291p il pa $16   **618.92**

1. Infants -- Care

ISBN 978-1-4391-1706-4; 1-4391-1706-3

LC 2009-37966

"Cohen is great at identifying parental concerns, and he responds with reassuring answers, providing just enough information to assuage worries. Of the multitude of baby guides out there, this is, hands down, one of the best in years." Libr J

Includes bibliographical references

Dawson, Geraldine

A **parent's** guide to high-functioning autism spectrum disorder; how to meet the challenges and help your child thrive. Sally Ozonoff, Geraldine Dawson, James C. McPartland. The Guilford Press 2015 308 p. (paperback) $18.95   **618.92**

1. Autism 2. Autistic children 3. Asperger's syndrome 4. Parents of autistic children 5. Asperger's syndrome -- Popular works 6. Autism spectrum disorders -- Popular works

ISBN 1462517471; 9781462517473; 9781462517954

LC 2014026326

In this book on high-functioning autism spectrum disorder (ASD), authors Sally Ozonoff, Geraldine Dawson, and James C. McPartland "show how you can work with your child's unique impairments--and harness his or her capabilities. Vivid stories and real-world examples illustrate ways to help kids with ASD relate more comfortably to peers, learn the rules of appropriate behavior, and succeed in school. You'll learn how ASD is diagnosed and what treatments and educational supports really work." (Publisher's note)

Includes bibliographical references and index

Estreich, George

The **Shape** of the Eye; A Memoir. George Estreich. Penguin Group USA"||"Jeremy P. Tarcher/Penguin 2013 336 p. $16.95   **618.92**

1. Heredity 2. Down syndrome 3. Children with disabilities 4. Authors, American -- Biography 5. Stay at home fathers -- Biography 6. Down syndrome -- Patients -- Biography 7. Children with disabilities -- Biography 8. Down syndrome -- Patients -- Family relationships 9. Parents of children with disabilities -- Biography

ISBN 0399163344; 9780399163340

LC 2013009657

"In this . . . memoir, George Estreich, a poet and stay-at-home dad, tells his daughter's story, reflecting on her inheritance--from the literal legacy of her genes, to the family history that precedes her, to the Victorian physician John Langdon Down's diagnostic error of 'Mongolian idiocy.' Against this backdrop, Laura takes her place in the Estreich family as a unique child, quirky and real, loved for everything ordinary and extraordinary about her." (Publisher's note)

"An elegantly written, luminous, and profoundly human portrait of pain and sorrow, hope and cautious optimism." Booklist

Includes bibliographical references (pages [299]-314)

Foss, Ben

The **dyslexia** empowerment plan; a blueprint for renewing your child's confidence and love of learning. by Ben Foss. Ballantine Books 2013 336 p. (hardback) $27   **618.92**

1. Parents 2. Dyslexia 3. Child psychology 4. Dyslexic children -- Rehabilitation 5. Parents of children with disabilities

ISBN 0345541235; 9780345541239

LC 2013023931

In this book, author Ben Foss "describes dyslexia as a characteristic and a disability that should be accommodated in the same way as blindness or mobility issues. Foss reframes the use of film, audiobooks, and material read aloud as ear-reading, in contrast to the eye-reading that is the educational standard. He hopes that parents can learn to explain their child's needs in a way that will win them essential support, and that they can help their child build self-esteem." (Publishers Weekly)

Includes bibliographical references and index

French, Thomas

Juniper; The Girl Who Was Born Too Soon. Kelley French, Thomas French. Little, Brown & Co. 2016 336 p. illustrations $26   **618.92**

1. Parents 2. Premature infants

ISBN 0316324426; 9780316324427

LC 2016933403

In this memoir, by Kelley French and Thomas French, "a micro preemie fights for survival. . . . Juniper French was born four months early, at 23 weeks gestation. She weighed 1 pound, 4 ounces, and her twiggy body was the length of a Barbie doll. . . . Premature babies like Juniper, born at the edge of viability, trigger the question: Which is the greater act of love--to save her, or to let her go?" (Publisher's note)

"A fierce and fact-filled love story with few holds barred." Kirkus

Gnaulati, Enrico

Back to normal; why ordinary childhood behavior Is mistaken for ADHD, bipolar disorder, and Autism Spectrum Disorder. Enrico Gnaulati. Beacon Press 2013 256 p. (alk. paper) $26.95   **618.92**

1. Mental health 2. Child psychology 3. Adolescent psychology 4. Adolescent 5. Medicalization 6. Diagnostic Errors 7. Child Behavior -- psychology 8. Mental Disorders -- diagnosis 9. Behavioral Symptoms -- diagnosis

ISBN 0807073342; 9780807073346; 9780807073353

LC 2013009182

This book, by clinical psychologist Enrico Gnaulati, is a "definitive account of why our kids are being dramatically overdiagnosed-- and how parents and professionals can distinguish between true psychiatric disorders and normal childhood reactions to stressful life situations. . . . Gnaulati tells detailed stories of wrongly diagnosed kids, . . . with information about the developmental, temperamental, and environmentally driven symptoms that . . . can mimic a psychiatric disorder." (Publisher's note)

"Gnaulati makes a strong case that an incorrect diagnosis of behavioral problems can be stigmatizing and that prescription drugs frequently have overlooked, negative side effects. A valuable guide for parents and educators that includes tips on choosing a therapist and parenting strategies." Kirkus

Includes bibliographical references and index

Harris, Sandra L.

Essential first steps for parents of children with autism; helping the littlest learners. by Lara Delmolino & Sandra L. Harris. 1st edition Woodbine House 2014 154 p. illustrations (Topics in autism) $21.95   **618.92**

1. Autism 2. Parents of autistic children 3. Autistic children

ISBN 1606131893; 9781606131893

LC 2013038047

The authors "offer a detailed, authoritative guide that discusses everything from early indicators of autism to likely behaviors (including

those rooted in sensory issues), how-to's for increasing communication and social skills, and family support. Case studies and reviews of promising research and interventions make this the go-to guide for parents of autistic children." LJ

Includes bibliographical references and index

Siblings of Children With Autism; A Guide for Families. [by] Sandra L. Harris and Beth A. Glasberg. Woodbine House 2012 163 p. illustrations $21.95   **618.92**

1. Autism 2. Siblings 3. Autistic children 4. Autistic children -- Family relationships

ISBN 1606130749; 9781606130742

LC 20031239

This book, by Sandra L. Harris and Beth A. Glasberg, "takes a fresh look at what it's like to grow up as the brother or sister of a child with autism--the basics of sibling relationships at all ages and how autism can affect these dynamics. Parents get important advice about balancing responsibilities for each child, encouraging their kids to share feelings, explaining autism to other children, and initiating play and interaction between siblings." (Publisher's note)

Jackson, Luke

Freaks, geeks and asperger syndrome; a user guide to adolescence. foreword by Tony Attwood. Kingsley, J. 2002 217p il pa $17.95   **618.92**

1. Autism 2. Asperger's syndrome 3. Adolescent psychology 4. Autistic youth 5. Asperger's syndrome -- Patients 6. Asperger's syndrome -- Patients -- Family relationships

ISBN 1-8431-0098-3

LC 2002-70930

"In this terrific book that is sure to inspire other adolescents with the same condition, 13-year-old Jackson offers a teenager's perspective on what it's like to live with Asperger's. He also writes about his younger brother, who has a more severe condition on the ASD spectrum." Libr J

Includes bibliographical references

Sex, drugs and Asperger's syndrome (ASD) a user guide to adulthood. Luke Jackson ; foreword by Tony Attwood. Jessica Kingsley Publishers 2016 208 p. (alk. paper) $25   **618.92**

1. Adulthood 2. Autistic people -- Life skills guides 3. Autistic youth -- Life skills guides 4. Asperger's syndrome -- Patients -- Family relationships

ISBN 9781849056458

LC 2015027315

This book, by Luke Jackson, is an "unabridged and sparkling sequel to his . . . user guide to adolescence 'Freaks, Geeks and Asperger Syndrome.' . . . With devastating clarity, Luke focuses on the pitfalls involved in navigating the transition to adulthood, and the challenges of adult life. He covers everything from bullying and drugs to socialising, sex, negotiating relationships, and finding and keeping your first job." (Publisher's note)

"Jackson's personal and brutally honest take on being an adult with ASD is eye-opening and refreshing. A valuable read for teens and adults with ASD as well as parents, siblings, employers, teachers, caregivers, friends, and partners of those on the spectrum." LJ

Jassey, Jonathan

The **newborn** sleep book; a simple, proven method for training your new baby to sleep through the night. Dr. Lewis Jassey and Dr. Jonathan Jassey. Perigee Trade 2014 224 p. (paperback) $15   **618.92**

1. Sleep 2. Infants -- Health and hygiene 3. Infants -- Sleep

ISBN 0399167986; 9780399167980

LC 2014011339

This book by Lewis Jassey and Jonathan Jassey provides advice on getting newborn babies to sleep through the night by strictly regulating feeding times despite an infant's hunger. "The Jassey Way uses a feeding schedule that allows newborns (and their parents) a full night's sleep at a younger age than other sleep training techniques." (Publisher's note)

"Parent testimonials and numerous checklists are appended to this manageable plan." Pub Wkly

Includes bibliographical references

Keene, Nancy

★ **Childhood** leukemia; a guide for families, friends & caregivers. Nancy Keene. Childhood Cancer Guides 2018 xvi, 476 p.p illustrations (pbk.; alk. paper) $29.95   **618.92**
1. Leukemia 2. Cancer in children 3. Childhood Leukemia
ISBN 9781941089040

LC 2017031837

This book, by Nancy Keene, presents a guide for families, friends and caregivers about childhood leukemia. The book contains the information and support parents need during this difficult time, including: New treatments such as immunotherapy, tailoring drugs dosages to children's genetic profiles, and ways to deal with side effects, . . . tips for forming a partnership with the medical team, [and] poignant and practical stories from family members." (Publisher's note)

"In its fifth edition, Keene's revised resource includes five brand-new chapters, 20 updated sections, and material on CAR T-cell immunotherapy (a recently approved treatment)" LJ

Includes bibliographical references and index

Latson, Jennifer

The **boy** who loved too much; a true story of pathological friendliness. Jennifer Latson. Simon & Schuster 2017 x, 290 p.p (hardcover) $26   **618.92**
1. Domestic relations 2. Friendship in children 3. Friendship in children -- Case studies 4. Williams syndrome -- Patients -- Case studies 5. Social interaction in children -- Case studies
ISBN 9781476774060; 9781476774046; 9781476774053

LC 2016043207

This book, by Jennifer Latson, is "the poignant story of a boy's coming-of-age complicated by Williams syndrome, a genetic disorder that makes people biologically incapable of distrust. . . . Twelve-year-old Eli D'Angelo has a genetic disorder that obliterates social inhibitions, making him irrepressibly friendly, indiscriminately trusting, and unconditionally loving toward everyone he meets. . . . Latson follows Eli over three critical years of his life." (Publisher's note)

"A well-researched, perceptive exploration of a rare genetic disorder seen through the eyes of a mother and son." Kirkus

Includes bibliographical references (pages [281]-290).

Lazebnik, Claire

Overcoming Autism; Finding the Answers, Strategies and Hope That Can Transform a Child's Life. by Lynn Kern Koegel and Claire LaZebnik. Penguin Group USA 2014 398 p. $17   **618.92**
1. Child rearing 2. Autistic children 3. Parents of autistic children 4. Autism in children
ISBN 0143126547; 9780143126546

LC 2013046676

This book, by Lynn Kern Koegel and Claire LaZebnik, is "a fully revised and updated edition of the definitive guide to reducing symptoms of autism spectrum disorder. . . . This revised edition has also been expanded to clarify the importance of community support to affected families and the effect of societal acceptance on a child's life." (Publisher's note)

"The book has the feel of a reference work with a structure that uses questions to open each section. More accessible and straightforward than most books detailing treatments, including Bryna Siegel's Helping Children with Autism Le'tn, this book is strongly recommended." LJ

Leach, Penelope

Your Baby and Child From Birth to Age Five; Penelope Leach ; photographs by Camilla Jessel. Alfred A. Knopf 2010 559 p. color illustrations $23.95   **618.92**
1. Parenting 2. Child development
ISBN 0375712038; 9780375712036

LC 2010022848

This book, by Penelope Leach, "encompasses the latest research and thinking on child development and learning, and reflects the realities of today's changing lifestyles and new approaches to parenting. . . . Dr. Leach describes--in easy-to-follow stages, from birth through starting school--what is happening to your child, what he or she is doing, experiencing and feeling." (Publisher's note)

"In addition to physical growth and progress, Leach addresses the psychosocial needs of children. She also includes parent concerns and responses similar to those found in Workman's 'What To Expect' series. Public and academic libraries would do well to stock the new version of this primer on children and their development for circulation as well as for the reference shelf." LJ

Linden, Dana Wechsler

Preemies; the essential guide for parents of premature babies. Dana Wechsler Linden, Emma Trenti Paroli, and Mia Wechsler Doron. 2nd ed Gallery Books 2010 xxii, 633 p.p ill. $26.99   **618.92**
1. Infants -- Care 2. Premature infants 3. Infants -- Health and hygiene 4. Premature infants -- Care 5. Pregnancy -- Complications 6. Birth weight, Low -- Complications
ISBN 1416572325; 9781416572329

LC 2011289347

"'Preemies, Second Edition' is the only parents' reference resource of its kind--delivering up-to-the-minute information on medical care in a warm, caring, and engaging voice. Authors Dana Wechsler Linden and Emma Trenti Paroli are parents who have 'been there.' Together with neonatologist Mia Wechsler Doron, they answer the dozens of questions that parents will have at every stage." (Publisher's note)

This guide "covers risk factors, the first day, the first week, surgery, taking the baby home and many other topics. Each section contains personal observations from parents of preemies, insightful comments from 'the doctor's perspective' and information on procedures, equipment, common problems and other issues." Publ Wkly

Newman, Judith

★ **To** Siri with love; A mother, her autistic son, and the kindness of machines. Judith Newman. HarperCollins 2017 xi, 228 p.p $26.99   **618.92**
1. Autism 2. Autistic children 3. Parent-child relationship
ISBN 0062413627; 9780062413628

This book, by Judith Newman, "is a collection of funny, poignant, and uplifting stories about living with an extraordinary child who has helped a parent see and experience the world differently. From the charming (Gus weeping with sympathy over the buses that would lie unused while the bus drivers were on strike) . . . to the profound (how an automated 'assistant' helped a boy learn how to communicate with the rest of the world)." (Publisher's note)

Includes bibliographical references (pages 223-228).

Porto, Anthony

The **pediatrician's** guide to feeding babies and toddlers; practical answers to your questions on nutrition, starting solids, allergies, picky eating, and more. Anthony Porto, M.D. and Dina DiMaggio, M.D. Ten Speed Press 2016 256 p. illustrations (paperback) $18.99   **618.92**

  1. Child rearing 2. Bottle feeding 3. Breast feeding 4. Infants -- Nutrition 5. Food habits 6. Children -- Nutrition 7. HEALTH & FITNESS -- Children

ISBN 9781607749011; 9781607749028

LC 2015031409

This book, by Anthony Porto, M.D. and Dina DiMaggio, M.D, is a "comprehensive manual that takes the guesswork out of feeding [babies and toddlers]. . . . With recipes, parenting stories, and recommendations based on the latest pediatric guidelines, this book will allow you to approach mealtime with confidence so you can spend more time enjoying your new family." (Publisher's note)

"Parents will find the chapters useful to read through as their children reach each stage, and well enough organized to use as a reference when particular concerns come up." Pub Wkly

Includes bibliographical references and index

Prizant, Barry M.

Uniquely human; a different way of seeing autism. Barry Prizant, Ph.D. ; with Tom Fields-Meyer. Simon & Schuster 2015 272 p. (hardcover) $26   **618.92**

  1. Autism 2. Psychotherapy 3. Autism in children

ISBN 9781476776231; 9781476776248

LC 2014035241

This book, by Barry Prizant with Tom Fields-Meyer, challenges "autism therapy [that] typically focuses on ridding individuals of 'autistic' symptoms. . . . Now Dr. Barry M. Prizant offers a new . . . paradigm: the most successful approaches to autism don't aim at fixing a person by eliminating symptoms, but rather seeking to understand the individual's experience and what underlies the behavior." (Publisher's note)

"This positive volume should reassure parents and caregivers of kids with autism and any other disability that their kids are not broken, but, indeed, special." Booklist

Includes bibliographical references and index.

Rapp, Emily

The **still** point of the turning world; Emily Rapp. The Penguin Press 2013 272 p. (hardcover) $25.95   **618.92**

  1. Tay-Sachs disease 2. Parents of children with disabilities

ISBN 1594205124; 9781594205125

LC 2012039516

This book, by Emily Rapp, is a memoir of a mother struggling to parent her terminally ill child. "Ronan was diagnosed at nine months old with Tay-Sachs disease, a rare and always-fatal degenerative disorder. . . . Rapp and her husband were forced to re-evaluate everything they thought they knew about parenting. They would have to learn to live with their child in the moment; to find happiness in the midst of sorrow; to parent without a future." (Publisher's note)

Saline, Sharon

What your ADHD child wishes you knew; working together to empower kids for success in school and life. Dr. Sharon Saline ; foreword by Laura Markham. TarcherPerigee 2018 272 p. (paperback) $17   **618.92**

  1. Parent-child relationship 2. Attention deficit disorder 3. Children with mental disabilities 4. Parent and child 5. Attention-deficit-disordered children 6. Attention-deficit hyperactivity disorder 7. Attention-deficit hyperactivity disorder -- Social aspects

ISBN 9780143132394

LC 2018017661

In this book, psychologist Sharon Saline, with foreword by Laura Markham, "presents a proven roadmap to help ADHD kids succeed in school and life. . . . Saline shares the words and inner struggles of children and teens living with ADHD--and a blueprint for achieving lasting success by working together. . . . Saline's advice and real-world examples reveal how parents can shift the dynamic and truly help kids succeed." (Publisher's note)

Saul, Richard

ADHD does not exist; the truth about attention deficit and hyperactivity disorder. Richard Saul. HarperWave 2013 336 p. (hardback) $25.99   **618.92**

  1. Psychology 2. Hyperactivity 3. Mental health 4. Attention deficit disorder 5. Attention-deficit hyperactivity disorder

ISBN 006226673X; 9780062266736

LC 2013030794

In this book, "behavioral neurologist Dr. Richard Saul draws on five decades of experience treating thousands of patients labeled with Attention Deficit and Hyperactivity Disorder--one of the fastest growing and widely diagnosed conditions today--to argue that ADHD is actually a cluster of symptoms stemming from over 20 other conditions and disorders." (Publisher's note)

Includes bibliographical references and index

Schwarz, Alan

ADHD nation; children, doctors, big pharma, and the making of an American epidemic. Alan Schwarz. Scribner 2016 338 p. (hardback) $28   **618.92**

  1. Ritalin 2. Hyperactive children -- United States 3. Attention-deficit hyperactivity disorder -- United States 4. Diagnostic errors -- United States

ISBN 1501105914; 9781501105913

LC 2016018493

This book about ADHD in America by Alan Schwarz examines "this cultural and medical phenomenon: The father of ADHD, Dr. Keith Conners, spends fifty years advocating drugs like Ritalin before realizing his role in . . . 'a national disaster of dangerous proportions'; a troubled young girl and a studious teenage boy get entangled in the growing ADHD machine and take medications that backfire horribly; and big Pharma egregiously over-promotes the disorder and earns billions." (Publisher's note)

"In this powerful, necessary book, Schwarz exposes the dirty secrets of the growing ADHD epidemic." Kirkus

Includes bibliographical references and index

Sears, William

The **allergy** book; solving your family's nasal allergies, asthma, food sensitivities, and related health and behavioral problems. by Robert Sears, MD, FAAP, William Sears, MD FRCP. Little, Brown & Co. 2015 352 p. $16   **618.92**

  1. Allergy 2. Food allergy

ISBN 0316324809; 9780316324809

LC 2014954181

This book, by doctors Robert and William Sears, is "a comprehensive guide to treating and preventing nasal allergies, asthma, food allergies and intolerances, and more. Allergies are one of the most common ailments, causing children to miss school and parents to miss work. Left untreated or unresolved, stuffy noses, itchy skin, and irritated bellies can lead to chronic asthma, eczema, inflammatory bowel disease, and neurological disorders." (Publisher's note)

"The authors warn readers about hidden sources of allergens (eggs can turn up in canned soups and in salad dressings), and discuss healthy eating, favoring fruits and vegetables over gluten-filled foods. Even allergy-free people will benefit from checking out the Searses' easy-to-read, clearly laid-out guidebook." Booklist

Sheffer, Edith

Asperger's children; the origins of autism in Nazi Vienna. Edith Sheffer. W W Norton & Co Inc 2018 288 p. (hardcover) $27.95   **618.92**

1. Autism 2. National socialism 3. Asperger's syndrome 4. Asperger's syndrome in children -- Patients -- Austria -- Vienna -- History 5. Asperger's syndrome in children -- Austria -- Vienna -- History -- 1930-1940 6. Asperger's syndrome in children -- Diagnosis -- Austria -- Vienna -- 20th century
ISBN 9780393609646

LC 2018003422

This book, by Edith Sheffer, is the "first comprehensive history of the links between autism and Nazism. . . . [The book] uncovers how a diagnosis common today emerged from the atrocities of the Third Reich. With vivid storytelling and wide-ranging research, 'Asperger's Children' will move readers to rethink how societies assess, label, and treat those diagnosed with disabilities." (Publisher's note)

Includes bibliographical references and index

Shetreat-Klein, Maya

The **Dirt** Cure; Growing Healthy Kids With Food Straight from Soil. Maya Shetreat-Klein. Pocket Books 2016 384 p. $26   **618.92**

1. Food industry 2. Children -- Nutrition
ISBN 1476796971; 9781476796970

Author Maya Shetreat-Klein examines the "contents of children's food, how it's seriously harming their bodies and brains, and what we can do about it. [She] explains how food is constantly changing kids' bodies, brains, and even genes--for better or for worse. She also shares success stories from her practice and tips as a working mother of three on stocking healing foods (from veggies to chocolate!), reading labels, and getting even picky eaters into the new menu." (Publisher's note)

"The text is full of scientific information presented in a fun and informative way, giving concrete evidence that good food can transform one's life." Pub Wkly

Includes bibliographical references (pages 333-358) and index.

Sicherer, Scott H.

Understanding and managing your child's food allergies. Johns Hopkins University Press 2006 312p il $45; pa $18.95   **618.92**

1. Parenting 2. Food allergy
ISBN 0-8018-8491-8; 978-0-8018-8491-7; 0-8018-8492-6 pa; 978-0-8018-8492-4 pa

LC 2006-5261

This "book provides parents with practical advice for managing a child's environment at home, at school, or out in the world at large. In Part 2, 'Diagnosing a Food Allergy,' the practice of taking a detailed medical history is espoused and case studies serve to bring the issue home. An action plan for anaphylaxis, a life-threatening type of allergic reaction, as well as a chapter on food allergy resources are included." Libr J

Includes bibliographical references

Sleep; what every parent needs to know. American Academy of Pediatrics ; [edited by] Rachel Moon, MD, FAAP. American Academy of Pediatrics 2013 250 p. ill. $16.95 **618.92**

1. Sleep 2. Parenting 3. Sleep therapy
ISBN 1581107811; 9781581107814

LC 2012953639

This book, edited by Rachel Moon, "incorporates the expertise of more than 20 pediatricians and covers numerous issues regarding how to create and maintain healthy sleep habits in children. . . . The book is divided into two sections: Ages, Stages and Phases and Childhood Sleep Challenges. Part one guides readers from the first year of life through adolescence, with chapters along the way about toddlers, preschoolers, and school-age kids." (Publisher's note)

Suskind, Ron

Life, animated; a story of sidekicks, heroes, and autism. by Ron Suskind. Kingswell 2014 358 p. illustrations, some color (hardback) $26.99   **618.92**

1. Autism 2. Communication 3. Animated films 4. Parents of autistic children 5. Autistic children
ISBN 1423180364; 9781423180364

LC 2014006760

"This is the real-life story of Owen Suskind, the son of the Pulitzer Prize-winning journalist Ron Suskind and his wife, Cornelia. An autistic boy who couldn't speak for years, Owen memorized dozens of Disney movies, turned them into a language to express love and loss, kinship, brotherhood.The family was forced to become animated characters, communicating with him in Disney dialogue and song; until they all emerge, together, revealing how, in darkness, we all literally need stories to survive." (Publisher's note)

"The Disney effect may be distinctive to this experience, but the family dynamic should resonate with a much wider readership." Kirkus

Taking Charge of ADHD; The Complete, Authoritative Guide for Parents. Russell A. Barkley, PHD. 3rd ed The Guilford Press 2013 363 p. pbk $19.95; hc $55   **618.92**

1. Child psychology 2. Adolescent psychology 3. Attention deficit disorder 4. Child rearing 5. Attention-deficit hyperactivity disorder
ISBN 1462508510; 1462507891; 9781462507894; 9781462508518
First published 1995

Presents "science-based information . . . about attention-deficit/hyperactivity disorder (ADHD) and its treatment. It also presents a proven eight-step behavior management plan specifically designed for 6- to 18-year-olds with ADHD. Updated throughout with current research and resources, the third edition includes the latest facts about medications and about what causes (and doesn't cause) ADHD." Publisher's note

Includes bibliographical references and index

Thurow, Roger

The **first** 1,000 days; a crucial time for mothers and children-and the world. Roger Thurow. PublicAffairs 2016 304 p. (hardback) $26.99   **618.92**

1. Pregnancy 2. Infants -- Nutrition 3. Children -- Health and hygiene 4. Infants -- Nutrition -- Case studies 5. Infants -- Health and hygiene -- Case studies
ISBN 9781610395854

LC 2015050285

This book, by Roger Thurow, focuses on women who "were participating in an unprecedented international initiative designed to transform their lives, the lives of their children, and ultimately the world. The 1,000 Days movement, a response to recent, devastating food crises and new research on the economic and social costs of childhood hunger and stunting, is focused on providing proper nutrition during the first 1,000 days of children's lives, beginning with their mother's pregnancy." (Publisher's note)

"You may find yourself cheering and crying with the families you meet. 1,000 Days is a valuable addition to larger public and academic libraries, and for any library where mothers and healthcare providers can share the information." Booklist

Includes bibliographical references and index.

Trainor, Kathleen

Calming your anxious child; words to say and things to do. Kathleen Trainor. Johns Hopkins University Press 2016 264 p. (hardcover; alk. paper) $45   **618.92**
1. Anxiety -- Treatment 2. Parent-child relationship 3. Parent and child -- Popular works 4. Anxiety in children -- Popular works 5. Anxiety disorders -- Treatment -- Popular works
ISBN 1421420090; 1421420104; 9781421420097; 9781421420103

LC 2015034014

In this book, "Dr. Kathleen Trainor builds on cognitive behavioral therapy to provide practical steps for guiding parents through the process of helping their children manage their anxieties. . . . Dr. Trainor's method involves identifying the anxieties and the behaviors, rating them, agreeing on what behaviors to work on changing, identifying strategies for changing behaviors, noting and charting progress, offering incentives, and reinforcing progress." (Publisher's note)

"Anxiety can be a tough condition to beat, but parents with the organizational skills to stick to the Trainor approach will in all likelihood achieve improvement. A solid offering." LJ

Includes bibliographical references and index

Turbo, Richard

★ **Caring** for your baby and young child; birth to age 5. Steven P. Shelov, editor-in-chief; Tanya Remer Altmann, medical editor; Robert E. Hannemann, associate medical editor; Richard Turbo, writer. 6th edition Bantam 2014 917 p. illustrations (paperback) $23   **618.92**
1. Child care 2. Infants -- Care 3. Child development
ISBN 0553393820; 9780553393828

LC 2014013096

This book, edited by Steven P. Shelov, Tanya Remer Altmann, Robert E. Hannemann, with writings by Richard Turbo, is an infant and early child care handbook "covering everything from preparing for childbirth to toilet training to nurturing your child's self-esteem. Whether it's resolving common childhood health problems or detailed instructions for coping with emergency medical situations, this new and revised edition . . . has everything you need." (Publisher's note)

Understanding the NICU; what parents of preemies and other hospitalized newborns need to know. [edited by] Jeanette Zaichkin, RN, MN, NNP-BC, David Loren, MD, FAAP, Gary Weiner, MD, FAAP. American Acemdy of Pediatrics 2016 260 p. illustrations $16.95   **618.92**
1. Neonatal intensive care 2. Newborn infants -- Hospital care 3. Premature infants -- Hospital care
ISBN 9781610020480

LC 2015960373

This book, edited by Jeanette Zaichkin, Gary Weiner, and David Loren, "will guide you through your NICU journey, help you communicate with members of the NICU team, and learn about your baby's condition so that you can ask questions and participate as a valuable partner in your baby's care. It will also provide important information about how to care for your baby after you leave the hospital and head home with your little one." (Publisher's note)

"Over 380,000 babies are born prematurely each year. This is an important acquisition for all collections." LJ

Wedge, Marilyn

A **Disease** Called Childhood; Why ADHD Became an American Epidemic. by Marilyn Wedge. Penguin Group USA 2015 272 p. $26.95   **618.92**
1. Attention deficit disorder
ISBN 1583335633; 9781583335635

LC 2014045248

This book, by Marilyn Wedge, presents a "look at the rise of ADHD in America, arguing for a better paradigm for diagnosing and treating our children. . . . Wedge examines how myriad factors have come together, resulting in a generation addictied to stimulant drugs, and a medical system that encourages diagnosis instead of seeking other solutions." (Publisher's note)

"While Wedge offers options not every medical professional or concerned parent will swallow willingly, her affable a pproach and compassionate universal concern for the wellness of children are evident throughout. In an important read for open-minded parents, Wedge offers fresh perspectives and practical approaches to the continuing ADHD conundrum." Kirkus

618.928   Pediatric neurology

Taylor, Lori Ashley

Dragonfly; a daughter's emergence from autism: a practical guide for parents. Lory Ashley Taylor, with foreword by Jennifer O'Toole. Skyhorse Publishing 2018 336 p. $27.99 **618.928**
1. Autism 2. Autistic children
ISBN 1510732179; 9781510732179

This book, by Lory Ashley Taylor, with foreword by Jennifer O'Toole, "provides anecdotal and practical guidance for parents of children with autism spectrum disorder. The author discusses intervention strategies, therapies such as Applied Behavioral Analysis (ABA), and different medical tests. She explains Autism terminology like hyperresponsivesness and stimming. A classroom teacher herself, she recommends educational accommodations and supports." (Publisher's note)

618.97   Geriatrics

Serani, Deborah

Depression in later life; Deborah Serani. Rowman & Littlefield Pub Inc 2016 286 p. illustrations (cloth; alk. paper) $35   **618.97**
1. Depression (Psychology) 2. Older people -- Psychology 3. Depression in old age -- Popular works
ISBN 144225582X; 9781442255821

LC 2015045280

This book, by Deborah Serani, "introduces readers to depression among the aging and elderly. It looks at both sufferers who've been diagnosed in their younger years as well as those with a new diagnosis, and reviews the symptoms, the diagnostic process, treatment options including alternative and holistic approaches, and long term care for those experiencing mild, moderate, or severe depression." (Publisher's note)

"Though the author uses a lot of technical jargon, overall this is a valuable resource that can help improve the quality of life for a highly at-risk group." Booklist

Includes bibliographical references and index

620 Engineering and allied operations

Khan, Amina

Adapt; How Humans Are Tapping into Nature's Secrets to Design and Build a Better Future. Amina Khan. St. Martin's Press 2017 344 p. (hardcover) $26.99   **620**

1. Nature 2. Adaptation (Biology) 3. Biotechnology 4. Engineering design

ISBN 9781250060402; 9781466865631

LC 2016049027

In this book author Amina Khan "presents fascinating examples of how nature effortlessly solves the problems that humans attempt to solve with decades worth of the latest and greatest technologies, time, and money. Humans are animals too, and animals are incredibly good at doing more with less. [She] shares the weird and wonderful ways that nature has been working smarter and not harder, and how we can too to make billion dollar cross-industrial advances in the very near future." (Publisher's note)

"These well-crafted tales of bio-inspired innovation will entrance general readers and warrant the close attention of scientists and technologists." Kirkus

Includes bibliographical references (pages 321-330) and index.

Molotch, Harvey Luskin

Where stuff comes from; how toasters, toilets, cars, computers, and many other things come to be as they are. [by] Harvey Molotch. Routledge 2003 324p il $35; pa $29.95 **620**

1. Engineering

ISBN 0-415-94400-7; 0-415-95042-2 pa

LC 2003-1191

The author examines "the complicated, dynamic relationships between inventor, society, corporation, regulator, shopkeeper, community, family and customer. . . . Myriad links, he argues, ultimately produce and constantly change what we want, buy, keep and throw away; thus, neither consumers nor producers are to be blamed for our numerous possessions. . . . Molotch's description of systemic person-product complexes could work to end blame-the-consumer guilt-mongering in the popular discourse." Publ Wkly

Includes bibliographical references

Petroski, Henry

The essential engineer; why science alone will not solve our global problems. Alfred A. Knopf 2010 274p il $26.95 **620**

1. Engineering 2. Technological innovations 3. Technology and civilization

ISBN 978-0-307-27245-4; 0-307-27245-1

LC 2009-21216

"Petroski presents a book-length argument for the place of engineering in humanity's future, especially when it comes to ensuring that future in the face of climate change, natural disasters, dwindling oil supplies and other global problems. . . . Scientists get the credit for everything from the moon landing to the construction of the Large Hadron Collider, he complains, when in reality those and myriad other projects large and small couldn't have been achieved without the creative, intelligent and rigorous input of engineers." Washington Post Book World

Includes bibliographical references

Success through failure; the paradox of design. Princeton

University Press 2006 235p il hardcover o.p. pa $21.95 **620**

1. Design 2. Engineering

ISBN 978-0-691-12225-0; 0-691-12225-3; 978-0-691-13642-4 pa; 0-691-13642-4 pa

LC 2005-34126

An "engaging and readable book. . . . Petroski uses countless interesting case histories to show how failure motivates technological advancement." IEEE Spectrum

Includes bibliographical references

Petroski, Henry, 1942-

★ **To** forgive design; understanding failure. Henry Petroski. Belknap Press of Harvard University Press 2012 xii, 410 p.p ill.   **620**

1. Design 2. Engineering 3. Structural failures 4. System failures (Engineering)

ISBN 0674065840; 9780674065840

LC 2011044194

This book, by Henry Petroski, "looks not only at how people contribute to the failure of engineering designs but also at how analyzing those failures can improve subsequent models. He considers many different types of failures, from several infamous bridge collapses to carefully designed intentional failures, which are engineered specifically to prevent greater failures." (Library Journal)

"Even the layman will find Petroski's study to be accessible, informative, and interesting." Pub Wkly

Includes bibliographical references and index.

620.009 History, geographic treatment, biography

Brain, Marshall

The **engineering** book; From the Catapult to the Curiosity Rover: 250 Milestones in the History of Engineering. Marshall Brain. Sterling Pub Co Inc 2015 528 p. illustrations (some color) (hardcover) $29.95   **620.009**

1. Engineering 2. Encyclopedias and dictionaries

ISBN 1454908092; 9781454908098

This book, by Marshall Brain, the "creator of the 'How Stuff Works' series and a professor at the Engineering Entrepreneurs Program at NCSU provides a detailed look at 250 milestones in the discipline [of engineering]. He covers the various areas, including chemical, aerospace, and computer engineering, from ancient history to the present." (Publisher's note)

"Despite some problems, this book is a solid introduction to its topic and can serve to generate interest in the applied sciences and engineering. For report use, however, it lacks the depth that high-school students and older readers would expect, thus it's recommended for middle schoolers only." LJ

Winchester, Simon

★ The **perfectionists**; how precision engineers created the modern world. Simon Winchester. HarperCollins 2018 xii, 395 p.p illustrations (hardcover) $29.99   **620.009**

1. Engineering -- History 2. Machine design -- History 3. Technological innovations -- History 4. Metrology

ISBN 9780062652553; 9780062652577; 0062652559

In this book, author Simon Winchester "traces the development of technology from the Industrial Age to the Digital Age to explore the single component crucial to advancement--precision. . . . The rise of manufacturing could not have happened without an attention to precision. . . . Winchester . . . introduces the scientific minds that helped usher in modern production: John Wilkinson, Henry Maudslay, Joseph Bramah, Jesse Ramsden, and Joseph Whitworth." (Publisher's note)

"Winchester (The Professor and the Madman) smoothly mixes history, science, and biographical sketches to pay homage to the work of precision engineers, . . . Winchester's latest is a rollicking work of pop science that entertains and informs." Pub Wkly

Includes bibliographical references (pages [369]-374) and index.

620.1   Engineering mechanics and materials

Freinkel, Susan
    Plastic; a toxic love story. Houghton Mifflin Harcourt 2011 324p $27   **620.1**
        1. Plastics
        ISBN 978-0-547-15240-0
                                                    LC 2010-43019
    "At first a godsend, [plastic] reduced dependence on shrinking natural resources, such as the shell of the hawksbill turtle (combs) or elephants' ivory (billiard balls and piano keys.) Ultimately it democratized materialism, making everything available to everybody, cheaply. Now, the partner we've found in plastic 'can rightly inspire both our deepest admiration and our strongest disgust.' To describe its history, wonders and dangers, journalist Freinkel reviews eight products: the comb, the chair, the Frisbee, the IV bag, the disposable lighter, the grocery bag, the soda bottle and the credit card. You will not look casually at any of them again." Cleveland Plain Dealer

    Includes bibliographical references

Johnson, Les
    Graphene; the superstrong, superthin, and superversatile material that will revolutionize the world. by Les Johnson and Joseph E. Meany, PhD. Prometheus Books 2018 269 p. (pbk.) $19   **620.1**
        1. Carbon 2. Graphite 3. Graphene
        ISBN 9781633883253
                                                    LC 2017032965
    In this book, scientists Les Johnson and Joseph E. Meany "explain how graphene was developed, discuss the problems in scaling up production for large-scale commercial use, and forecast the potentially transformative effects of incorporating graphene into everyday life. Recent research developments include adding graphene to Silly Putty to make extremely sensitive and malleable medical sensors." (Publisher's note)

    Includes bibliographical references and index

Miodownik, Mark
    Stuff matters; exploring the marvelous materials that shape our manmade world. Mark Miodownik. Houghton Mifflin Harcourt 2014 272 p. illustrations (hardback) $26   **620.1**
        1. Materials 2. Physical sciences 3. Materials science -- Popular works
        ISBN 0544236041; 9780544236042
                                                    LC 2013047575
    In this book, author Mark Miodownik "entertainingly examines the materials he encounters in a typical morning, from the steel in his razor and the graphite in his pencil to the foam in his sneakers and the concrete in a nearby skyscraper. He offers a compendium of the most astounding histories and marvelous scientific breakthroughs in the material world." (Publisher's note)

    "At a time when science is maligned, first-rate storyteller Miodownik entertains and educates with pop-culture references, scholarly asides, and nods to everyone from the Six Million Dollar Man to the Lumière

brothers. A delight for the curious reader." Booklist

Waldman, Jonathan
    Rust; the longest war. Jonathan Waldman. Simon & Schuster 2015 304 p. 8 unnumbered pages of plates (hardcover) $26.95   **620.1**
        1. Engineering 2. Structural steel 3. Corrosion and anticorrosives 4. Corrosion and anti-corrosives -- History 5. Corrosion and anti-corrosives -- Anecdotes
        ISBN 1451691599; 9781451691597; 9781451691603
                                                    LC 2014043291
    In this book on rust and corrosion author "Jonathan Waldman travels from Key West, Florida, to Prudhoe Bay, Alaska, to meet the colorful and often reclusive people who are fighting our mightiest and unlikeliest enemy. The result is a fresh and often funny account of an overlooked engineering endeavor that is as compelling as it is grand, illuminating a hidden phenomenon that shapes the modern world." (Publisher's note)

    "A brilliantly written and fascinating close-up look at one of nature's most neglected threats to man-made structures and machines." Booklist

620.191   Soils and related materials

Beiser, Vince
    The **world** in a grain; the story of sand and how it transformed civilization. Vince Beiser. Riverhead Books 2018 304 p. (hardcover) $28   **620.191**
        1. Sand 2. Technology and civilization
        ISBN 9780399576423
                                                    LC 2017053122
    This book, by Vince Beiser, "is the compelling true story of [sand,] the hugely important and diminishing natural resource that grows more essential every day, and of the people who mine it, sell it, build with it-and sometimes, even kill for it. It's also a provocative examination of the serious human and environmental costs incurred by our dependence on sand, which has received little public attention." (Publisher's note)

    "Beiser is a diligent researcher, and his sources and interviews build a strong case in this entirely absorbing if troubling read to argue that the many grains of sand, often associated with abundance, are in fact, finite." Library Journal

    Includes bibliographical references and index

621   Applied physics

Alley, Richard B., 1957-
    Earth; the operators' manual. W.W. Norton 2011 479p il $27.95   **621**
        1. Energy development 2. Renewable energy resources 3. Greenhouse effect
        ISBN 978-0-393-08109-1
                                                    LC 2010-54016
    The author "presents a primer on combatting global warming. The book begins with a history of how fuel—from trees, whale oil, and petroleum—has been instrumental to civilization and how we tend to exhaust our sources. He goes on to explain how scientists study climate change and why the evidence is convincing, and ends with a call to action and an overview of possible solutions. . . . This optimistic book ought to convince even the most obstinate climate-change denier." Publ Wkly

    Includes bibliographical references

Marks' standard handbook for mechanical engineers; Ali M. Sadegh, William M. Worek. 12th edition McGraw-Hill 2017 1509 p il $154   **621**

1. Mechanical engineering -- Handbooks, manuals, etc.

ISBN 9781259588501

First published 1916 under the editorship of Lionel S. Marks with title: Mechanical engineers' handbook. Periodically revised. Editors vary

This volume presents concisely the basic scientific and technical data of mechanical engineering, covering theory, basic mechanism, standard practice, often-needed mathematical formulae and technical data

Includes bibliographical references

621.3 Electrical, magnetic, optical, communications, computer engineering; electronics, lighting

American electricians' handbook; Terrell Croft, Frederic P. Hartwell, Wilford I. Summers [editors] 16th ed McGraw-Hill 2013 1712 p ill. $90   **621.3**

1. Electrical engineering -- Handbooks, manuals, etc. 2. Electric engineering -- Handbooks, manuals, etc

ISBN 0071798803; 9780071798808

This handbook, edited by Terrell Croft, Frederic P. Hartwell, and Wilford I. Summers, is "the definitive industry reference for information on designing, installing, operating, and maintaining electrical systems and equipment. The Sixteenth Edition is revised to comply with the 2011 National Electrical Code and the 2012 National Electrical Safety Code, and covers current energy-efficient technologies, such as photovoltaics and induction lighting." (Publisher's note)

"The Sixteenth Edition is revised to complywith the 2011 National Electrical Code and the 2012 National Electrical Safety Code, and covers current energy-efficient technologies, such as photovoltaics and induction lighting. Detailed photos, diagrams, charts, tables, and calculations are included throughout." Publisher's note

National electrical code handbook 2017; [edited by] Mark W. Earley, P.E., Christopher D. Coache, Mark Cloutier, Gil Moniz, Derek Vigstol. 14th edition National Fire Protection Association 2016 1306 p $191   **621.3**

1. Electrical engineering -- Handbooks, manuals, etc.

ISBN 9781455912841

First published 1978. Periodically revised

This book, edited by Mark W. Earley, Christopher D. Coache, Mark Cloutier, and Gil Moniz, is a professional handbook on the electrical safety codes published by the National Fire Protection Association. It "explains the reasoning behind NFPA 70®: NEC concepts, provides real-world examples, and gives you the background behind Code revisions, so you can work with authority." (Publisher's note)

This "is a nationally accepted guide to the safe installation of electrical conductors and equipment, and is, in fact, the basis for all electrical codes used in the United States." Ref Sources for Small & Medium-sized Libr. 5th edition

Roach, Craig

Simply electrifying; the technology that transformed the world, from Benjamin Franklin to Elon Musk. Craig R. Roach. BenBella Books, Inc. 2017 xvii, 462 p.p (trade cloth; alk. paper) $26.95   **621.3**

1. Electricity -- History 2. Inventors -- Biography 3. Electrical engineering -- History

ISBN 9781944648275; 1944648267; 9781944648268

LC 2017004508

This book, by Craig R. Roach, "brings to life the 250-year history of electricity through the stories of the men and women who used it to transform our world: Benjamin Franklin, James Watt, Michael Faraday, Samuel F.B. Morse, Thomas Edison, Samuel Insull, Albert Einstein, Rachel Carson, Elon Musk, and more. In the process, it reveals . . . the complete, thrilling, and often-dangerous story of electricity's historic discovery, development, and worldwide application." (Publisher's note)

"Simply Electrifying provides a comprehensive history of this life-changing discovery and is a fascinating and deeply engaging look at how we live today and where we may be headed in the future." Booklist

Includes bibliographical references (pages 378-394) and index

Shulman, Seth

★ The **telephone** gambit; chasing Alexander Graham Bell's secret. W. W. Norton & Co. 2008 256 p il $24.95 **621.3**

1. Inventors 2. Telephone 3. Teachers of the deaf 4. Telecommunications executives

ISBN 978-0-393-06206-9; 0-393-06206-6

LC 2007-30904

The author argues that Alexander Graham Bell is not the true inventor of the telephone.

This book "does a neat job of painting, in rapid brush strokes, a portrait of the thrilling era of innovation in which Bell lived and also of the interesting circumstances of his life. . . . [He] also manages to lace his work with just enough technology to tell his story without losing the interest of any low-tech readers." Christ Sci Monit

Includes bibliographical references

Standard Handbook for Electrical Engineers; Surya Santoso, H. Wayne Beaty. 17th edition McGraw-Hill 2018 1633 p ill $199   **621.3**

1. Green technology 2. Electrical engineering -- Handbooks, manuals, etc.

ISBN 9781259642586

First published 1908. Periodically revised

"This fully revised, industry-standard resource offers practical details on every aspect of electric power engineering. The book contains in-depth discussions from more than 100 internationally recognized experts. Generation, transmission, distribution, operation, system protection, and switchgear are thoroughly explained." (Publisher's note)

621.31 Generation, modification, storage, transmission of electric power

Fletcher, Seth

Bottled lightning; superbatteries, electric cars, and the new lithium economy. Hill and Wang 2011 260p $26   **621.31**

1. Lithium 2. Electronics 3. Electric batteries

ISBN 978-0-8090-3053-8; 0-8090-3053-5

LC 2010-47695

"Provides an entertaining, surprisingly eventful history of human efforts to harness energy in the form of battery power . . . . A fine, readable work of popular science." Kirkus

Includes bibliographical references

621.319   Transmission

The **complete** guide to wiring; current with 2017-2020 electrical codes. 7th edition Cool Springs Press 2017 335 p. color illustrations $24.99   **621.319**
1. Electric wiring 2. Houses -- Maintenance and repair 3. Electric wiring, Interior -- Amateurs' manuals 4. Dwellings -- Electric equipment -- Amateurs' manuals 5. Dwellings -- Maintenance and repair -- Amateurs' manuals
ISBN 9780760353578
First published 1998 by Cowles Creative Pub.
"The modern home can include dozens of electronic components unknown just a few years ago, and this book provides essential information on wiring for those devices. It includes information on security systems, home theaters and surround-sound systems, computer networks, and a host of kitchen amenities like espresso machines to grind-and-brew coffee machines." (Publisher's note)
Includes bibliographical references and index

Litchfield, Michael

Wiring complete; includes the latest in Wi-Fi, smart-house technology. Michael McAlister & Michael Litchfield. Third edition The Taunton Press, Inc 2017 284 p. (paperback) $24.95   **621.319**
1. Electric wiring 2. Electric household appliances 3. Electric wiring, Interior 4. Dwellings -- Electric equipment
ISBN 9781631868382; 1631868381
LC 2017014083
This book, by Michael Litchfield and Michael McAlister, "covers everything homeowners need to know about practically any wiring scenario imaginable, from simple switches to outdoor lighting. . . . This second edition . . . has been updated to the latest electrical code (NEC, 2017). And there's more detailed coverage of today's hot topics, including: expanded sections on receptacles, switches, and lighting, . . . [and] details on the changing world of multimedia wiring." (Publisher's note)
Includes bibliographical references and index

Richter, H. P.

Wiring simplified; Based on the 2017 National Electrical Code. F.P. Hartwell, W.C. Schwan, H.P. Richter. 45th edition Park Publishing, Inc. 2017 256 p. $14.95   **621.319**
1. Electric wiring 2. Houses -- Maintenance and repair
ISBN 097929455X; 9780979294556
"This 45th edition--part of a series continuously published for more than 80 years and based on the 2017 National Electrical Code—is a handy instruction manual that has been used by generations of readers to learn the 'why' as well as the 'how-to' of wiring practices. Encouraging readers to tackle jobs small and large, the guide covers everything from repairing a table lamp to wiring a whole house." (Publisher's note)

621.32   Lighting

Brox, Jane

Brilliant; the evolution of artificial light. Houghton Mifflin Harcourt 2010 360p $25   **621.32**
1. Lighting
ISBN 978-0-547-05527-5; 0-547-05527-7
LC 2009-35441
The author "examines our relationship with light, our attempts to harness it to brighten places we cannot see, and its impact on American psychology and culture. . . . This well-written, well-researched, and

thought-provoking book has much to offer. The general reader with an interest in the (social) history of technology will find it . . . a source of inspiration for considering technology's impact on our lives." Libr J
Includes bibliographical references

621.381   Electronics

Horowitz, Paul

The **art** of electronics; Paul Horowitz, Harvard University, Winfield Hill, Rowland Institute. Cambridge University Press 2015 1223 p. illustrations (hardback) $120   **621.381**
1. Electronic circuits 2. Electronics -- Handbooks, manuals, etc. 3. Electrical engineering -- Handbooks, manuals, etc. 4. Electronics 5. Electronic circuit design
ISBN 9780521809269
LC 2015002303
This book, by Paul Horowitz and Winfield Hill, "is the thoroughly revised and updated third edition of the . . . authoritative book on electronic circuit design. In addition to new or enhanced coverage of many topics, the third edition includes 90 oscilloscope screenshots illustrating the behavior of working circuits, [and] dozens of graphs giving highly useful measured data of the sort that is often buried or omitted in datasheets but which you need when designing circuits." (Publisher's note)
Includes bibliographical references and index

Platt, Charles

Make; more electronics: journey deep into the world of logic chips, amplifiers, sensors, and randomicity. Charles Platt. Oreilly & Associates Inc 2014 357 p. $34.99   **621.381**
1. Electronics 2. Electrical engineering
ISBN 1449344046; 9781449344047
This book, by Charles Platt, "picks up where 'Make: Electronics' left off: you'll work with components like comparators, light sensors, higher-level logic chips, multiplexers, shift registers, encoders, decoders, and magnetic sensors. . . . With step-by-step instructions, and hundreds of color photographs and illustrations, this book will help you use -- and understand -- intermediate to advanced electronics concepts and techniques." (Publisher's note)

Schultz, Mitchel E.

Grob's basic electronics; Mitchel E. Schultz. 12th edition McGraw-Hill 2015 1232 p il $218.10   **621.381**
1. Electricity 2. Electronics
ISBN 9780073373874
LC 2014042490
First published 1959 under the authorship of Bernard Grob. Periodically revised
An introductory text on the fundamentals of electricity and electronics for technicians in radio, television, and industrial electronics.
Includes glossary

621.384   Specific topics in general radio

The **ARRL** handbook for radio communications. American Radio Relay League various pagings il   **621.384**
1. Radio -- Handbooks, manuals, etc.

I   S   B   N

Annual. Began publication 1926. Editions 1 through 61 published with title: The Radio amateur's handbook. Editions 62 through 79 published with title: The ARRL handbook for radio amateurs

"Chapters cover fundamentals and changing technology in the field and include many tables, circuit diagrams, photographs, and occasional references." Guide to Ref Books. 11th edition

Silver, H. Ward

Ham radio for dummies; by H. Ward Silver. John Wiley & Sons Inc 2013 xvi, 358 p.p illustrations $24.99   **621.384**
1. Amateur radio stations 2. Radio -- Handbooks, manuals, etc. 3. Radio -- Amateurs' manuals
ISBN 1118592115; 9781118592113

LC 2013938107

This book, by H. Ward Silver, offers "first step[s] for learning about ham radio. . . . This hands-on beginner guide reflects the operational and technical changes to amateur radio over the past decade and provides you with updated licensing requirements and information, changes in digital communication (such as the Internet, social media, and GPS), and how to use e-mail via radio." (Publisher's note)

Includes bibliographical references and index

621.388   Television

Abramson, Albert

The **History** of Television 1880 to 1941. McFarland & Company, Inc. 2009 354 p. $49.95   **621.388**
1. Inventions -- History 2. Television -- History 3. Television
ISBN 0786440864; 9780786440863

LC 8643091

"A sole inventor of television does not exist. Instead, it came about through a remarkable interaction of several hundred scientists. Interviews with the scientists whose imagination and enterprise combined to make television a reality, extensive archival research worldwide, and rare photos make this book [by Albert Abramson] the one definitive history and the only authoritative account." (Publisher's note)

The **history** of television, 1942 to 2000; foreword by Christopher H. Sterling. McFarland & Co. 2003 309p il hardcover o.p. pa $75   **621.388**
1. Television -- History
ISBN 0-7864-1220-8; 978-0-7864-3243-1 pa; 0-7864-3243-8 pa

LC 2002-326

"No reference work available in print right now matches the attention to detail that is obvious here. A significant work on how the machinery of television has evolved, this . . . should stand as the authority for years to come." Libr J

Includes bibliographical references

621.389   Security, sound recording, related systems

Zen and the art of recording; Mixerman. Hal Leonard Books 2014 291 p. $24.99   **621.389**
1. Sound recordings 2. Popular music -- Writing and publishing 3. Popular music -- Production and direction 4. Sound recording industry -- Vocational guidance 5. Sound recordings -- Production and direction -- Vocational guidance
ISBN 1480387436; 9781480387430

LC 2014035146

In this book, author Mixerman "distills the inescapable technical realities of recording down to understandable and practical terms. Whether musician or self-taught recordist, whether at home or in a full-blown studio complex, you'll discover a definitive blueprint for recording within

the current realities of the business, without ever losing focus on the core consideration--the music itself." (Publisher's note)

621.43   Internal-combustion engines

★ **Small** engines and outdoor power equipment; a care & repair guide for lawn mowers, snowblowers & small gas-powered implements. edited by Peter Hunn. Cool Springs Press 2014 144 p. color illustrations (pbk) $19.99 **621.43**
1. Household equipment and supplies -- Maintenance and repair 2. Small gasoline engines -- Maintenance and repair 3. Gardening -- Equipment and supplies -- Maintenance and repair
ISBN 1591865875; 9781591865872

LC 2013028515

"Small engine repair and maintenance is well covered here, starting with an introduction to common engine types, with interior systems and components clearly illustrated. Tools needed and safety considerations are carefully detailed, followed by a lengthy troubleshooting chart. A section on annual maintenance is accompanied by large photos and step-by-step instructions; it's followed by basic repairs, which focus on common issues. The book finishes with more difficult repairs that involve interior systems, such as rebuilding or replacing parts." LJ

621.48   Nuclear engineering

Smith, Gar

Nuclear roulette; the truth about the most dangerous energy source on earth. Gar Smith ; foreword by Jerry Mander and Ernest Callenbach. Chelsea Green Pub. 2012 xxx, 279 p.p (hardcover) $29.95   **621.48**
1. Nuclear energy 2. Nuclear power plants 3. Nuclear power plants -- Accidents 4. Nuclear power plants -- Risk assessment 5. Nuclear power plants -- Natural disaster effects
ISBN 1603584773; 9781603584340; 9781603584357; 9781603584777

LC 2012027407

Author Gar Smith argues that "nuclear power is not clean, cheap, or safe. . . . While some critiques are familiar-nuclear power is too costly, too dangerous, and too unstable-others are surprising: Nuclear Roulette exposes historic links to nuclear weapons, impacts on Indigenous lands and lives, and the ways in which the Nuclear Regulatory Commission too often takes its lead from industry, rewriting rules to keep failing plants in compliance." (Publisher's note)

Includes bibliographical references (p. [233]-267) and index

621.56   Low-temperature technology

Jackson, Tom

Chilled; How Refrigeration Changed the World and Might Do So Again. Tom Jackson. St. Martin's Press 2015 272 p. (hardcover) $27   **621.56**
1. Refrigeration 2. Technology -- History
ISBN 9781472911438; 1472911431

This book on refrigeration by Tom Jackson examines "how experts through the ages have attempted to understand the elemental laws that govern our universe and then to allow for the possibility of manipulating temperature. Aristotle, Fahrenheit, Joule, and many lesser-known scientists make appearances, as do the early icebox and refrigeration prospectors who created a global market for preserving food through controlled chilling as opposed to salting, pickling, or canning." (Booklist)

"Jackson's spirited explanations of centuries-old scientific experiments relating to the transmutation of gases into water, finding absolute zero, and identifying chemical elements—to name a few—will be most appreciated by readers with a strong interest in the physical sciences." Booklist

Includes bibliographical references (page [268]) and index.

621.9   Tools

Horne, Richard

3D printing for dummies; Kalani K. Hausman and Richard Horne. John Wiley & Sons Inc 2014 368 p. illustrations (pbk.) $29.99 **621.9**

1. Three-dimensional printing 2. Industrial arts -- Handbooks, manuals, etc.

ISBN 1118660757; 9781118660751

LC 2013952422

This handbook, by Kalani K. Hausman and Richard Horne, "examines each type of 3D printing technology available today and gives artists, entrepreneurs, engineers, and hobbyists insight into the amazing things 3D printing has to offer. You'll discover methods for the creation of 3D printable objects using software, 3D scanners, and even photographs with the help of this timely 'For Dummies guide.'" (Publisher's note)

Rigsby, Mike

A **beginner's** guide to 3D printing; 14 simple toy designs to get you started. Mike Rigsby. Chicago Review Press 2014 291 p. illustrations (paperback) $17.95 **621.9**

1. Computer-aided design 2. Three-dimensional printing 3. Computer-aided design software 4. SketchUp 5. CAD--CAM systems 6. Rapid prototyping

ISBN 1569761973; 9781569761977

LC 2014026069

In this book on 3D printing, "engineer Mike Rigsby leads readers step-by-step through fourteen simple toy projects, each illustrated with screen caps of Autodesk 123D Design, the most common free 3D software available. The projects are later described using Sketchup, another free popular software package." (Publisher's note)

Beginner's guide to three-D printing

621.908   Hand tools

Davy, Phil

The **tool** book; a tool lover's guide to more than 200 hand tools. writers, Phil Davy, Luke Edwardes-Evans, Jo Behari, Matthew Jackson ; foreword by Nick Offerman. DK Publishing 2018 256 p. $30 **621.908**

1. Tools 2. Carpentry tools

ISBN 1465468544; 9781465468543

LC 2017276784

In this book, by Phil Davy, "explore tools from every angle, with detailed patent drawings, exploded diagrams, and step-by-step illustrations of tools in action with the science behind the techniques. Gallery pages display different types of hammers, spades, or chisels, while expert advice tells you what to look for when choosing a tool, and how to use it and care for it best." (Publisher's note)

Tool book

622   Mining and related operations

Carter, Bill

Boom, Bust, Boom; A Story About Copper, the Metal That Runs the World. Bill Carter. Simon & Schuster 2012 288 p. $26 **622**

1. Copper 2. Copper mines and mining

ISBN 1439136440; 9781439136447

This book by Bill Carter is "a sweeping account of civilization's complete dependence on copper and what it means for people, nature, and our global economy. Copper is a miraculous and contradictory metal, essential to nearly every human enterprise. . . . Yet . . . copper mining causes irrevocable damage to the Earth . . . . and the mines themselves have significant effects on the economies and wellbeing of the communities where they are located." (Publisher's note)

Includes bibliographical references and index.

Prud'homme, Alex

Hydrofracking; Alex Prud'homme. Oxford University Press 2013 184 p. (What everyone needs to know) (pbk.; alk. paper) $16.95 **622**

1. Hydraulic fracturing 2. Environmental protection 3. Hydraulic fracturing -- Popular works 4. Shale gas reservoirs -- Popular works 5. Gas wells -- Hydraulic fracturing -- Popular works 6. Oil wells -- Hydraulic fracturing -- Popular works

ISBN 0199311250; 9780199311255; 9780199311262

LC 2013028962

"A timely addition to Oxford's What Everyone Needs to Know series, 'Hydrofracking' tackles this contentious topic, exploring both sides of the debate and providing a clear guide to the science underlying the technique. In . . . question-and-answer format, Alex Prud'homme . . . [covers] key points, from the economic and political benefits of fracking to the health dangers and negative effects on the environment." (Publisher's note)

"Most useful are the point/counterpoint discussions on the pros and cons of fracking." Choice

Includes bibliographical references and index

623.4   Ordnance

Gun digest 2019; edited by Jerry Lee. F & W Media Inc 2018 560 p. illustrations $36.99 **623.4**

1. Guns 2. Firearms industry

ISBN 9781946267344

Annual

This guidebook, edited by Jerry Lee, "has been regarded by the shooting industry, hunters, competitive shooters, collectors, and hobbyists everywhere as the shooter's No. 1 resource. . . . With in-depth articles about today's most fascinating guns, both old and new, testfire stories on the industry's hot-off-the-line guns, insights on fine collectibles and custom creations, and up to date reports on new optics, guns, ammo, and reloading equipment, this book has something for everyone." (Publisher's note)

Hodge, Nathan

A **nuclear** family vacation; travels in the world of atomic weaponry. [by] Nathan Hodge and Sharon Weinberger. Bloomsbury 2008 324p $24.99 **623.4**

1. Arms control 2. Nuclear weapons 3. Nuclear engineering

ISBN 978-1-59691-378-3; 1-59691-378-9

LC 2008-2013

This "is a book that is both entertaining and informative. Hodge and Weinberger are shrewd and observant nuclear tour guides who are knowledgeable about their subject without being didactic." Am Sci

Includes bibliographical references

Sheinkin, Steve

Bomb; the race to build and steal the world's most dangerous weapon. Steve Sheinkin. Roaring Brook Press 2012 266 p. ill. (hc) $19.99   **623.4**

1. Nuclear warfare 2. Nuclear weapons 3. World War, 1914-1918 -- Chemical warfare 4. Atomic bomb -- History 5. Operation Freshman, 1942 6. Atomic bomb -- Germany -- History 7. World War, 1939-1945 -- Secret service -- Soviet Union 8. World War, 1939-1945 -- Secret service -- Great Britain 9. World War, 1939-1945 -- Commando operations -- Norway -- Vemork

ISBN 1596434872; 9781596434875

           LC 2011044096

John Newbery Honor Book (2013); National Book Award Finalist: Young People's Literature (2012)

YALSA Award for Excellence in Nonfiction for Young Adults (2013)

Robert F. Sibert Informational Book Medal (2013)

Author Steve Sheinkin's "story unfolds in three parts, covering American attempts to build the [atomic] bomb, how the Soviets tried to steal American designs and how the Americans tried to keep the Germans from building a bomb. It was the eve of World War II, and the fate of the world was at stake . . . all along the way spies in the United States were feeding sensitive information to the KGB." (Kirkus Reviews)

Includes bibliographical references (p. [243]-259) and index

Weapons & warfare; editor, John Powell. 2nd ed.; Salem Press 2010 3v il map set $395   **623.4**

1. Reference books 2. Military weapons 3. Military art and science

ISBN 978-1-58765-594-4

           LC 2009-50491

First published 2001

"Volume 1, Ancient & Medieval, . . . covers warfare from prehistoric times to approximately 1500; Volume 2, Modern, covers 1500 to the present. The organization is chronological by geographic region, and both volumes open with essays discussing weapons and forces used in that era of history, how and why those tools of warfare have evolved or been discontinued, and the military achievement of the forces, weapons, uniforms and armor, military organizations, and doctrine strategy and tactics. In the third volume, Culture and Concepts, essays cover social aspects of war, technological achievements used in warfare, and morality of behavior during war. . . . This useful overview of warfare's evolution will be appreciated by students as well as general readers." Libr J

623.7   Communications, vehicles, sanitation, related topics

Cockburn, Andrew

Kill Chain; Drones and the Rise of the High-tech Assassins. by Andrew Cockburn. Henry Holt & Co. 2015 320 p. illustrations $28   **623.7**

1. Drone aircraft 2. Military art and science 3. National security -- United States

ISBN 0805099263; 9780805099263

           LC 2014029340

This book, by Andrew Cockburn, is a "narrative on the history of drone warfare. . . . Taking the reader inside the well-guarded world of national security, the book reveals the powerful interests - military, CIA and corporate - that have led the drive to kill individuals by remote control. Most importantly of all, the book describes what has re-

ally happened when the theories underpinning the strategy -- and the multi-billion dollar contracts they spawn -- have been put to the test." (Publisher's note)

"Despite some problems, this is an informative and easy-to-read book for those interested in this hot topic. Perhaps a drone will drop it off at your front door." LJ

623.74   Vehicles

Whittle, Richard

Predator; The Secret Origins of the Drone Revolution. Richard Whittle. Henry Holt & Co. 2014 352 p. illustrations $30   **623.74**

1. Drone aircraft 2. Aerospace engineering 3. Military art and science 4. Drone aircraft -- United States -- History 5. Aerospace industries -- California, Southern -- History 6. Drone aircraft -- United States -- Design and construction

ISBN 0805099646; 9780805099645

           LC 2014014070

This book, by Richard Whittle, is the "untold story of the birth of the Predator drone, a wonder weapon that transformed the American military, reshaped modern warfare, and sparked a revolution in aviation. . . . The remarkable cast of characters responsible for developing the Predator includes a former Israeli inventor, . . . two billionaire brothers, . . . a pair of fighter pilots, . . . a cunning Pentagon operator, . . . and a secretive Air Force organization known as Big Safari." (Publisher' snote)

"Military and aviation aficionados will learn from and enjoy this in-depth work that employs a readable, journalistic style." LJ

Includes bibliographical references and index

623.8   Nautical engineering and seamanship

Naranjo, Ralph

The **Art** of Seamanship; Evolving Skills, Exploring Oceans, and Handling Wind, Waves, and Weather. McGraw-Hill 2014 544 p. illustrations $50   **623.8**

1. Sailing 2. Navigation

ISBN 0071493425; 9780071493420

           LC 2015300840

In this book, "Around-the-world sailor Ralph Naranjo . . . delivers a . . . reference for anything that comes up while on the water, sharing all the knowledge today-s sailors need to -hand, reef, and steer'--an enduring reference to the collective skills of the bluewater sailor. Naranjo's vast knowledge is supported by real-life examples of sailing mishaps, sample itineraries, vibrant photos, as well as first-hand accounts and sidebars from top sailors and marine experts." (Publisher's note)

Ujifusa, Steven

A **man** and his ship; America's greatest naval architect and his quest to build the S.S. United States. Steven Ujifusa. Simon & Schuster 2012 x, 437 p., [32] p. of platesp ill. (hc; alk. paper) $29.99   **623.8**

1. Ocean liners 2. United States -- Military history 3. World War, 1939-1945 -- Naval operations 4. United States (Steamship) 5. Gibbs & Cox -- History -- 20th century 6. Naval architects -- United States -- Biography 7. Ocean liners -- United States -- History -- 20th century

ISBN 9781451645071; 9781451645088

           LC 2011049883

Author Steven Ujifusa tells the story of William Francis Gibbs, who, in 1915, "completed plans for the world's largest and fastest superliner . . . Setting up his own company in 1922, Gibbs made his name building modest liners for American companies . . . As World War II loomed, Gibbs became the leading designer for the U.S. Navy and Merchant Marine. It took the Cold War and energetic lobbying to achieve Gibbs' dream . . . Launched in 1952 to national acclaim, the SS United States was a technological triumph; rival liners never matched her speed, reliability or safety." (Kirkus)

Includes bibliographical references and index

623.88 Seamanship

Bigon, Mario

The **Morrow** guide to knots; for sailing, fishing, camping, climbing. Mario Bigon and Guido Regazzoni ; translated from the Italian by Maria Piotrowska. W. Morrow 1982 255 p. color illustrations $16.99   **623.88**

1. Knots and splices 2. Life skills -- Handbooks, manuals, etc.

ISBN 0688012256; 0688012264; 9780688012267

LC 82006308

"Included . . . are a section on decorative knots, a cross-reference list of the many applications of knots, and a detailed glossary." Written by Mario Bigon and Guido Regazzoni and edited by Kennie Lyman, "'The Morrow Guide to Knots' is a . . . reference tool for all sportsmen and campers, homeowners, and youngsters as well." (Publisher's note)

Bibliography: p. 252

Chapman piloting & seamanship; edited by Elbert S. Maloney, Peter A. Janssen, and Jonathan Eaton. Sterling Pub Co Inc 2013 919 p. color illustrations $60   **623.88**

1. Boats and boating 2. Navigation -- Handbooks, manuals, etc.

ISBN 1588169618; 9781588169617

LC 2013018755

This book, edited by Elbert S. Maloney, Peter A. Janssen, and Jonathan Eaton, is the 67th edition of "a single comprehensive reference that combines the best traditions of seamanship with cutting-edge practices, gear, and technology. . . . [It includes] how-to maintenance information for . . . engines; a complete integration of the tools and techniques of electronic navigation . . . with . . . unsurpassed treatment of traditional chart-and-compass piloting skills." (Publisher's note)

Pawson, Des

The **handbook** of knots; Expanded ed.; DK 2004 176p il pa $17   **623.88**

1. Rope 2. Knots and splices

ISBN 0-7566-0374-9; 978-0-7566-0374-8

LC 2004-274491

First published 1998

"This is a step-by-step guide to tying and using more than 100 knots. . . . There's a chapter on rope construction, rope materials, and properties of ropes and their main uses. It's very informative and put together concisely." BAYA Book Rev [review of 1998 edition]

Rousmaniere, John

The **Annapolis** Book of Seamanship; John Rousmaniere ; illustrated by Mark Smith. 4th edition Simon & Schuster 2014 403 p. illustrations hbk $49.99   **623.88**

1. Sailing 2. Navigation

ISBN 9781451650198; 1451650191

LC 2014412287

"Completely revised and updated to address changes in technology

and safety standards, this new edition is the definitive guide to the art and science of sailing." (Publisher's note)

623.89 Navigation

Cutler, Thomas J.

Dutton's nautical navigation; [by] Thomas J. Cutler; with the U.S. Naval Institute Navigation Board. 15th ed; Naval Inst. Press 2004 447p il map $55   **623.89**

1. Navigation

ISBN 1-557502-48-X

LC 2003-11183

First published 1926 under the authorship of Benjamin Dutton with title: Navigation and nautical astronomy. Variant title: Dutton's navigation & piloting

This guide for the coastal and seagoing mariner focuses on piloting, celestial navigation, radio navigation and dead reckoning

624.1 Structural engineering and underground construction

Agrawal, Roma

Built; the hidden stories behind our structures. Roma Agrawal. St. Martin's Press 2018 320 p. $28   **624.1**

1. Building 2. Structural engineering

ISBN 1635570220; 9781635570229

In this book, "structural engineer Roma Agrawal explains how construction has evolved from the mud huts of our ancestors to skyscrapers of steel that reach into the sky. She unearths how humans have tunneled through solid mountains; how we've walked across the widest of rivers, and tamed nature's precious water resources. . . . 'Built' offers a fascinating window into a subject that makes up the foundation of our everyday lives." (Publisher's note)

"A unique addition to public library collections on technology and engineering." LJ

624.2 Bridges

Blockley, D. I.

Bridges; the science and art of the world's most inspiring structures. Oxford University Press 2010 312p il $29.95 **624.2**

1. Bridges

ISBN 978-0-19-954359-5

"In this fascinating exploration for lay readers, Blockley lucidly explains both the basic forces at work on every bridge—tension, compression, and shear—and the structural elements combating those forces: beams, arches, trusses, and suspension cables. . . . Bold, insightful statements help make this a remarkable work." Publ Wkly

Includes bibliographical references

625.1 Railroads

Train; the definitive visual history. DK Publishing. DK Publishing 2014 320 p. illustrations (some color) $40   **625.1**

1. Railroads 2. Engineering 3. Railroads -- History 4. Locomotives -- History 5. Railroads -- History -- Pictorial works 6. Locomotives -- History -- Pictorial works

ISBN 1465422293; 9781465422293

LC 2012287667

This book from DK Publishing is a "celebration of all things train and track, with stories of key innovators, designers, and iconic rail journeys. Iconic trains, such as the Orient Express and Mallard are showcased in 'virtual tours' that reveal the anatomy of these legendary engines. This guide provides a truly international view of trains through time, from English steam to Japanese electric." (Publisher's note)

625.2   Railroad rolling stock

Jensen, Joel

Steam ; an enduring legacy; the railroad photographs of Joel Jensen. introduction by Scott Lothes; essay by John Gruber; afterword by Jeff Brouws. W. W. Norton & Company 2011 160p il $50   **625.2**

1. Steam engines 2. Railroads -- Pictorial works
ISBN 978-0-393-08248-7; 0-393-08248-2

"Jensen has been photographing trains and rail stations west of the Mississippi River for some 25 years, and this long-overdue collection of his work features black-and-white shots that capture the bygone majesty and sense of history inspired by these steam-powered machines, preserved and operated in the latter-day era by dedicated rail-fans. Besides the 150 photos, there are essays by John Gruber and Scott Lothes—both of the Center for Railroad Photography and Art—examining the economics and cultural importance of trains in America." BookPage

Solomon, Brian, 1966-

The **field** guide to trains; Locomotives and Rolling Stock. Brian Solomon. Voyageur Press 2016 208 p. illustrations (some color) (flexi; alk. paper) $24.99   **625.2**

1. Locomotives 2. Railroad trains 3. Railroad cars -- History 4. Railroad cars 5. Diesel locomotives 6. Locomotives -- History
ISBN 9780760349977

LC 2015047962

This book, in the Voyageur Field Guides series by Brian Solomon, provides "information on locomotives and cars. . . . The book is divided by diesel-electric locomotives, self-propelled passenger trains, passenger cars, freight cars, rail transit, and preserved equipment at museums and excursion steam locomotives. It also touches on historic diesels, vintage trams, maintenance trains, snowplow engines, and circus trains." (Publisher's note)

"This book will be a useful guide for anyone interested in learning more about railroading today." Booklist

Includes bibliographical references and index

627   Hydraulic engineering

Hiltzik, Michael A.

Colossus; Hoover Dam and the making of the American century. Free Press 2010 496p il map $30   **627**

1. Hoover Dam (Ariz. and Nev.) 2. Civil engineers
ISBN 978-1-4165-3216-3; 1-4165-3216-1

LC 2009-33833

In this account of the Hoover Dam story, Hiltzik "explains the technological and physical difficulties posed by the dam project, but he also fixes the endeavor in its time and captures the personalities of the people involved. . . . The author is at his best in a masterly portrayal of Frank Crowe, the central figure in the dam's construction. A born engineer who demanded much from his workmen, Crowe had to solve a myriad of problems on the fly as he confronted the unexpected difficulties of an unprecedented project in an unprecedented location. . . . One of the nice things about nonfiction such as 'Colossus' is that the stories don't need to be believable; they just need to be true." Wall Street J

Includes bibliographical references and index

Matson, Tim, 1943-

Earth ponds; the country pond maker's guide to building, maintenance, and restoration. Tim Matson. 3rd ed Countryman Press 2012 150 p. ill. $21.95   **627**

1. Ponds 2. Water supply engineering
ISBN 9781581571479; 158157147X

This book, by Tim Matson, is "the bible of pond-making in a fully redesigned 30th-anniversary edition. . . .For thirty years now . . . [this book] has guided an entire generation of pond makers on everything from site planning to soil sampling to drainage and wildlife management. It's a complete overview of the country pond. Illustrations guide the pond builder through every step of the process; chapters carefully describe the issues and decisions in a wonderfully personal way." (Publisher's note)

Includes bibliographical references

628.4   Waste technology, public toilets, street cleaning

Humes, Edward

Garbology; our dirty love affair with trash. Edward Humes. Avery 2012 277 p.   **628.4**

1. Pollution 2. Consumption (Economics) 3. United States -- Social life and customs 4. Refuse and refuse disposal -- United States 5. Salvage (Waste, etc.) -- China 6. Environmental engineering -- United States
ISBN 1583334343; 9781583334348

LC 2012001701

In this book, "Edward Humes . . . [makes the case] that the United States—the world's largest generator of trash—will soon confront a new crisis of garbage. . . . Humes spotlights a turning point in the history of American garbage: the postwar rise of consumer culture, birthed by a new generation of advertisers who saw their mission in life as persuading Americans to throw away perfectly good things in order to buy bigger, better replacements. . . . Humes argues that an economy whose health depends on how much disposable stuff people buy is driving us toward a precipice. Making and trashing all those things will generate economic activity and jobs, to be sure, but the waste-driven model of mass consumption also eats up tremendous amounts of increasingly scarce resources." (Bookforum)

Includes bibliographical references and index

628.5   Pollution control technology and industrial sanitation engineering

Sengo, Zenaida

Air plants; the curious world of Tillandsias. Zenaida Sengo ; photographs by Caitlin Atkinson. Timber Press, Inc. 2014 224 p. color illustrations $19.95   **628.5**

1. House plants 2. Ornamental plants 3. Epiphytes 4. Tillandsia
ISBN 1604694890; 9781604694895

LC 2014009480

This book, by Zenaida Sengo, illustrated by Caitlin Atkinson, "shows how simple and rewarding it is to grow, craft, and design with these modern beauties. Decorating with air plants is made easy with .

. . photographs that showcase ideas for using them mounted on walls, suspended from the ceiling, as living bows and jewelry, as screens, and in unique containers, like leather pouches, dishes, and baskets." (Publisher's note)

"The coverage of air-plant display, design, and decor is dazzling as Sengo offers guidance in using these "virtually weightless" plants in ceiling suspensions and wall displays and even as wearable, living art. This comprehensive guide is an invaluable resource that delights the eye with the dizzying variety and beauty of air plants and the possibilities for inventive installments." Booklist

628.9 Other branches of sanitary and municipal engineering

National Fire Protection Association

Fire protection handbook; Arthur E. Cote, editor-in-chief; Casey C. Grant, John R. Hall, Jr., Robert E. Solomon, asoociate editors; Pamela A. Powell, managing editor. 20th ed; National Fire Protection Assn. 2008 2v il $233.75   **628.9**

1. Fire prevention
ISBN 978-0-87765-758-3; 0-87765-758-0

LC 2007-928644

First published 1896. Periodically revised. Title varies

"A handbook of approved practice in the fields of fire prevention and fire protection. Will be useful to owners and superintendents of buildings, and to architects and engineers interested in designing safe buildings and planning for their protection against fire." Carnegie Libr of Pittsburgh

Walliser, Jessica

Attracting beneficial bugs to your garden; a natural approach to pest control. Jessica Walliser. Timber Press 2014 240 p. col. ill. $24.95   **628.9**

1. Gardening 2. Beneficial insects 3. Garden pests -- Biological control
ISBN 1604693886; 9781604693881

LC 2013015303

Written by Jessica Walliser, "'Attracting Beneficial Bugs to Your Garden' is a book about bugs and plants, and how to create a garden that benefits from both. In addition to information on companion planting and commercial options for purchasing bugs, there are 19 detailed bug profiles and 39 plant profiles." (Publisher's note)

"While the subject matter and close-up photographs of insects eating insects may make some readers squirm, dedicated gardeners will discover enough solid information and genuine motivation to finally put down their bug spray." Booklist

Includes bibliographical references and index

629.1 Aerospace engineering

Branson, Richard

Reach for the skies; ballooning, birdmen, and blasting into space. Current 2011 343p il $26.95   **629.1**

1. Aeronautics -- History
ISBN 978-1-61723-003-5

LC 2010-52340

"The Virgin Atlantic Airlines founder and billionaire adventurer celebrates the exploits of airborne daredevils—his own prominently among them—in this lively history of aviation pioneers. Branson ranges from the Montgolfier brothers' 1783 invention of the hot-air balloon to to-

day's nascent space tourism industry . . . highlighting men and women who risked their money and lives to advance aerial technology or just put on a good show. It's a colorful assemblage of engineers, test pilots, barnstormers, and fighter aces. . . . Branson's enthusiasm for avant-garde flight and his firsthand understanding of its rigors make this a rousing—sometimes even elevating—read." Publ Wkly

Includes bibliographical references

629.13 Aeronautics

Alexander, David E.

Why don't jumbo jets flap their wings? flying animals, flying machines, and how they are different. Rutgers University Press 2009 278p il $26.95   **629.13**

1. Aeronautics 2. Animal flight
ISBN 978-0-8135-4479-3; 0-8135-4479-3

LC 2008-35425

Alexander discusses the mechanics and physics of how animals and aircraft fly.

"Anyone interested in the flight of birds or insects or the flight of various types of aircraft will find this volume fascinating. . . . [This book] is very well written and approaches complex topics in a manner that readers at any level of expertise will find understandable and interesting." Sci Books Films

Includes glossary and bibliographical references

Butler, Susan

East to the dawn; the life of Amelia Earhart. Da Capo Press 1999 489p il map pa $15.95   **629.13**

1. Air pilots 2. Missing persons 3. Women air pilots 4. Memoirists
ISBN 978-0-306-81837-0

First published 1997 by Addison-Wesley

In this biography of the pilot and women's rights advocate "Butler shows a mastery of aviation history, and considerable sophistication about the technology of flight and navigation . . . The mountain of new material it marshals guarantees 'East to the Dawn' a permanent place on the shelf of Amelia Earhart references." N Y Times Book Rev

Includes bibliographical references

Goldstone, Lawrence

★ **Birdmen**; The Wright Brothers, Glenn Curtiss, and the Battle to Control the Skies. Lawrence Goldstone. Random House Inc 2014 448 p. illustrations $28   **629.13**

1. Aeronautics -- History
ISBN 034553803X; 9780345538031

LC 2014001424

This book, by Lawrence Goldstone, tells the "story of the . . . feud between . . . great air pioneers, the Wright brothers and Glenn Curtiss. . . . On one side, a pair of tenacious siblings who together had solved the centuries-old riddle of powered, heavier-than-air flight. On the other, an audacious motorcycle racer whose innovative aircraft became synonymous in the public mind with death-defying stunts. For more than a decade, they battled each other in court, at air shows, and in the newspapers." (Publisher's note)

"A superbly crafted retelling of a story familiar to aviation buffs, here greatly strengthened by fresh perspectives, rigorous analyses, comprehensible science, and a driving narrative." LJ

Includes bibliographical references (pages 401-404) and index

Grant, R. G.

Flight; 100 years of aviation. DK Pub. 2002 440p il hard-

cover o.p. pa $24.95   **629.13**
1. Aeronautics -- History
ISBN 0-7894-8910-4; 0-7566-1902-5 pa

      LC 2002-73935

"The impressive illustrations include over 300 gorgeous, full-color profiles of the world's major military and civilian aircraft and space vehicles." Libr J

Gubert, Betty Kaplan

   Distinguished African Americans in aviation and space science; {by} Betty Kaplan Gubert, Miriam Sawyer, and Caroline M. Fannin. Oryx Press 2002 319p il (Distinguished African Americans series) $64.95   **629.13**
1. Astronauts 2. African American pilots
ISBN 1-57356-246-7

      LC 2001-34821

This profiles 80 men and 20 women in aviation and space science covering 80 years of the 20th century

"Libraries should not hesitate to add this title to their collections." Booklist

Includes bibliographical references

Hampton, Dan

   The **flight**; Charles Lindbergh's daring and immortal 1927 transatlantic crossing. Dan Hampton. William Morrow & Co 2017 xii, 317 p.p illustrations, maps (hardcover) $28.99 **629.13**
1. Aeronautics -- Flights -- History 2. Air pilots -- United States -- Biography 3. Transatlantic flights
ISBN 0062464396; 9780062464392; 9780062464415

      LC 2017033695

This book, by Dan Hampton, "is a long-overdue, flyer's-eye narrative of [Charles] Lindbergh's legendary journey. A decorated fighter pilot . . . , Hampton draws on his unique perspective to bring alive the danger, uncertainty, and heroic accomplishment of Lindbergh's crossing. Hampton's deeply researched telling also incorporates a trove of primary sources, including Lindbergh's own personal diary and writings, as well as family letters and untapped aviation archives." (Publisher's note)

"A celebration of a heroic feat sure to interest fans of aviation history." Kirkus

Includes bibliographical references (pages [281]-298) and index.

Haynsworth, Leslie

   Amelia Earhart's daughters; the wild and glorious story of American women aviators from World War II to the dawn of the space age. {by} Leslie Haynsworth and David Toomey. Morrow 1998 322p il hardcover o.p. pa $14   **629.13**
1. Air pilots 2. Women air pilots 3. Women astronauts 4. Cosmetics industry executives
ISBN 0-380-72984-9 pa

      LC 98-8727

This "study of American women aviators concentrates almost exclusively on the WASPs of World War II and the would-be female astronauts of the early 1960s." Booklist

Includes bibliographical references

Lindbergh, Charles

   The **spirit** of St. Louis; [by] Charles A. Lindbergh. Scribner 1998 562p il hardcover o.p. pa $20   **629.13**
1. Spirit of St. Louis (Airplane) 2. Aeronautics -- Flights
ISBN 0-684-85277-2; 0-7432-3705-6 pa

      LC 98-33556

First published 1953

This is an account of the first solo transatlantic flight from New York to Paris, as well as a detailed description of the preparation for the flight which in turn mirrors aviation of the 1920's.

Mortimer, Gavin

   Chasing Icarus; the seventeen days in 1910 that forever changed American aviation. Walker & Co 2009 305p il $26   **629.13**
1. Aeronautics -- History
ISBN 978-0-8027-1711-5

The author "argues that three aeronautic events in 1910 vouchsafed the primacy of U.S. aviation and the triumph of heavier-than-air flight. Interweaving the events—Walter Wellman's failed attempt to cross the Atlantic in his dirigible, America; the International Balloon Cup Race, which embarked from St. Louis; and the country's first international aircraft contest, held above the Belmont Park racetrack in New York—Mortimer effectively places the reader at the vital center of all three. . . . A singular contribution to early aviation history." Libr J

Includes bibliographical references

Ryan, Jason

   Race to Hawaii; the 1927 Dole Air Derby and the thrilling first flights that opened the Pacific. Jason Ryan. Chicago Review Press Inc. 2018 320 p. (cloth) $26.99   **629.13**
1. Aeronautics -- Hawaii -- History -- 20th century 2. Airplane racing -- United States -- History -- 20th century 3. Transpacific flights -- History -- 20th century
ISBN 9780912777252

      LC 2017057554

This book, by Jason Ryan, "chronicles the thrilling first flights during the Golden Age of Aviation, a time when new airplanes traveled farther and faster but were also unreliable, fragile, and hampered by primitive air navigation equipment. The US Navy tried first, sending flying boats winging toward the islands. Next came Army Air Corps aviators and a civilian pilot, who informally raced each other to Hawaii." (Publisher's note)

"Ryan builds suspense skillfully and makes heroes out of the men and one woman who vied in the derby." Booklist

Includes bibliographical references

Smithsonian atlas of world aviation; charting the history of flight from the first balloons to today's most advanced aircraft. [compiled by] Dana Bell. HarperCollins 2008 230p il map $39.95   **629.13**
1. Reference books 2. Historical atlases 3. Aeronautics -- History
ISBN 978-0-06-125144-3; 0-06-125144-5

      LC 2007-47574

"Bell's writing . . . adds immeasurably to the value of this atlas: it is articulate, clear, informative, and, above all, accurate." SLJ

Includes bibliographical references

629.130 Biography of flight

Jackson, Joe

   Atlantic fever; Lindbergh, his competitors, and the race to cross the Atlantic. Joe Jackson. Farrar, Straus and Giroux 2012 x, 525 p.p   **629.130**
1. Aeronautics -- History 2. Air pilots -- Biography 3. Aeronautics -- Competitions 4. Transatlantic flights -- History -- 20th century 5. Aeronautics -- Competitions -- History -- 20th century

ISBN 0374106754; 9780374106751

LC 2011046068

In this book, Joe Jackson "places Lindbergh's historic flight of May 20-21, 1927, in the dramatic framework of the 'Great Atlantic Air Race,' which began eight years earlier when Franco-American hotelier Ramond Orteig sponsored a $25,000 prize to the first aviator to cross the Atlantic. . . . Jackson traces the futile attempts to win the Orteig Prize until the spring of 1927, when a bevy of pilots stepped forth to compete for the honor no matter the cost. Jackson's compelling portraits of these contenders . . . place Lindbergh's successful bid in perspective. The reader is reminded that 'Lindy' was the last contestant to arrive in New York but the first to depart, owing to the simplicity of his effort compared with the technical, funding, and personnel complexities of his rivals' preparations." (Libr J)

Includes bibliographical references and index

629.132 Mechanics of flight; flying and related topics

Hampton, Dan

Chasing the demon; a secret history of the quest for the sound barrier, and the band of American aces who conquered it. Dan Hampton. HarperCollins 2018 400 p. $28.99   **629.132**
1. Aeronautics 2. High speed aeronautics 3. Supersonic aerodynamics 4. High-speed aeronautics -- Research -- United States 5. Aerodynamics, Supersonic -- Research -- United States
ISBN 0062688723; 9780062688729

LC 2018024770

In this book, "aviation historian Dan Hampton, tells the "true story of mankind's quest for Mach 1. Here, of course, is . . . Captain Chuck Yeager, who made history flying the futuristic Bell X-1 faster than the speed of sound on October 14, 1947. Officially Yeager was the first to achieve supersonic flight, but drawing on new interviews with survivors of the program, . . . Hampton presents evidence that a fellow American--George Welch . . . met the demon first." (Publisher's note)

"Author of the New York Times best-selling Viper Pilot and a decorated military pilot well acquainted with flying supersonic fighter jets, Hampton chronicles the U.S. effort to break the sound barrier, starting with the founding of the U.S. Air Force in 1947 and ending with Capt. Chuck Yeager's triumph on October 14, 1947." LJ

Includes bibliography and index.

Vanhoenacker, Mark

Skyfaring; a journey with a pilot. Mark Vanhoenacker. Alfred A. Knopf 2015 368 p. (hardback) $25.95   **629.132**
1. Airplanes -- Piloting 2. Aeronautics -- Popular works 3. Airplanes -- Piloting -- Popular works
ISBN 038535181X; 9780385351812

LC 2014041159

In this book, Mark Vanhoenacker explores his experiences as a pilot. He "recalls how he came to become a long-haul pilot, abandoning postgraduate work at Cambridge University. . . .The author describes in detail his classroom instruction together with various exams for his Boeing 747-type rating before entering the cockpit as a licensed pilot." Vanhoenacker draws on "autobiography, avionics, history, geography, physics, and poetry" to explain his experiences of flight. (Library Journal)

"The author loves travel and encountering new cities and situations, and his job makes this possible for him. This is a delightful and entertaining work, a genuine pleasure to read, and likely to be enjoyed by all. Highly recommended. Summing Up: Highly recommended. All levels." Choice

629.133 Aircraft types

Botting, Douglas

Dr. Eckener's dream machine; the great Zeppelin and the dawn of air travel. Holt & Co. 2001 331p il maps $27.50; pa $16   **629.133**
1. Airships 2. Aeronautics -- Flights 3. Graf Zeppelin (Airship) 4. Aircraft industry executives
ISBN 0-8050-6458-3; 0-8050-6459-1 pa

LC 2001-24770

Botting discusses the history of the Zeppelin, a rigid airship designed by a Prussian army officer, Ferdinand Count von Zeppelin, and the career of Hugo Eckener, who promoted and flew the dirigible

"A truly exciting book, filled with colorful characters and plenty of derring-do and laced with just the right amount of sadness and tragedy." Booklist

Includes bibliographical references

Chiles, James R.

The **god** machine; from boomerangs to black hawks, the story of the helicopter. Bantam Dell 2007 354p il hardcover o.p. pa $16   **629.133**
1. Helicopters
ISBN 978-0-553-80447-8; 978-0-553-38352-2 pa

LC 2007-28575

This "is an engaging blend of pop science and pop culture." Publ Wkly

Includes bibliographical references

629.2 Motor land vehicles, cycles

Lessing, Hans-Erhard

Bicycle design; an illustrated history. Tony Hadland and Hans-Erhard Lessing ; with contributions from Nick Clayton and Gary W. Sanderson. The MIT Press 2014 xiii, 564 p.p illustrations (hardcover; alk. paper) $34.95   **629.2**
1. Bicycles -- History 2. Bicycles -- Parts -- History 3. Bicycles -- Design and construction -- History
ISBN 0262026759; 9780262026758

LC 2013023698

This book, by Tony Hadland and Hans-Erhard Lessing, with contributions from Nick Clayton and Gary W. Sanderson, gives a "comprehensive account of the bicycle's technical and historical evolution, from the earliest velocipedes . . . to modern racing bikes, mountain bikes, and recumbents. It traces the bicycle's development in terms of materials, ergonomics, and vehicle physics, as carried out by inventors, entrepreneurs, and manufacturers." (Publisher's note)

Includes bibliographical references (pages 29-548) and index

629.22 Types of vehicles

Harley-Davidson; the complete history. by Darwin Holmstrom. Motorbooks 2016 240 p. illustrations (chiefly color) (hc w/jacket) $50   **629.22**
1. Motorcycles 2. Harley-Davidson motorcycle
ISBN 0760350000; 9780760350003

LC 2016937974

This book on the history of Harley-Davidson by Darwin Holmstrom "celebrates these iconic motorcycles. . . . Pages in the book reveal historic images as well as modern photos from the top motorcycle photographers working today. Additionally, there are chapters from some of the most celebrated motorcycle writers of all time--Peter Egan, Kevin Cameron, Ed Youngblood, Allan Girdler, Steve Anderson, and many more." (Publisher's note)

629.222   Gasoline-powered, oil-powered, man-powered vehicles

The **Beaulieu** encyclopedia of the automobile; editor in chief, Nick Georgano; foreword by Lord Montagu of Beaulieu. Fitzroy Dearborn Pubs. 2000 2v il set $325   **629.222**
1. Reference books 2. Automobiles -- Encyclopedias
ISBN 1-57958-293-1

LC 2001-316285

"The most comprehensive automobile encyclopedia available today." Am Libr

Cagle, Gregory A.
Scenes from an automotive wonderland; remarkable cars spotted in postwar Europe. by Gregory A. Cagle; foreword by Jeff Lane. McFarland & Company, Inc., Publishers 2018 viii, 231 p.p (softcover; alk. paper) $39.95   **629.222**
1. Automobiles 2. Photography 3. Photography of automobiles 4. Automobiles -- Europe -- Pictorial works 5. Automobiles -- Europe -- History -- 20th century
ISBN 1476671788; 9781476671789

LC 2017055037

This book, by Gregory A. Cagle, "features 105 specimens of auto exotica, captured with Cagle's Iloca Rapid-B 35mm camera--not showpieces in museums but daily drivers in their natural habitats. In the background can be glimpsed, here and there, the mood of postwar Europe. The story behind each photo is told, with dates and locations, information and history about the cars and some of their owners, along with Cagle's personal anecdotes." (Publisher's note)

"Cagle makes it easy to feel the excitement and enthusiasm he felt as a young boy. Any car spotter will enjoy this book, and may find a 26 horsepower favorite. The book is presented in a pleasant, easily readable format and contains a useful index and excellent bibliography." Choice Reviews

Includes bibliographical references (pages 215-224) and index

Car; the definitive visual history of the automobile. [senior project editor, Kathryn Hennessy ; US editor, Beth Landis Hester] DK Pub. 2011 360 p. ill. (chiefly col.) (hbk.) $40   **629.222**
1. Automobiles -- History 2. Automobiles -- Pictorial works 3. Automobiles -- History -- Chronology
ISBN 0756671671; 9780756671679

LC 2011282325

This book, edited by Kathryn Hennessy and Beth Landis, "tracing the history of the automobile, from the first prototypes to the super cars of today, . . . covers the technological developments and manufacture of cars, the cultural backdrop against which the various models arose, and the enduring impact the car has had on society as an object of curiosity, symbol of luxury, and item of necessity." (Publisher's note)

Classic Car; DK. DK Publishing 2016 320 p. color photographs $40; (ebook) $65   **629.222**
1. Automobiles -- History 2. Antique and classic cars
ISBN 1465453393; 9781465453396; 9781465459077

This book by DK Publishing is "a visual guide to the most iconic classic cars of every decade from the 1940s to the 1980s, featuring more than 1,300 photographs. . . . From the Aston Martin DB5 to the Chevrolet Corvette, . . . [the book] is packed with the marques and models of every decade from the 1940s to the 1980s. Virtual tours offer close-up views of iconic models, and comprehensive catalogs showcase key features with detailed profiles and specifications." (Publisher's note)

"Obviously, this is a book to savor, to be pored over time and again." Booklist

Drive; the definitive history of driving. edited by Giles Chapman, with foreword by Jodie Kidd. DK Publishing 2018 360 p. $40   **629.222**
1. Automobiles -- History 2. Transportation -- History 3. Automobile driving -- History 4. Automobiles -- History -- Chronology 5. Automobile driving -- History -- Chronology 6. Transportation, Automotive -- History -- Chronology
ISBN 0241317665; 1465469249; 9780241317662; 9781465469243

LC 2018302277

This book, edited by Giles Chapman, with foreword by Jodie Kidd, "explores the early glamour of driving, motor sport, and car design, and looks at how the automobile has shaped the modern world. . . . [It] tracks trends in auto manufacturing and the public's changing tastes in cars: whether it's Golden Era sports cars such as the MG, Alfa Romeo, Jaguar, and Chevrolet, muscle cars like the Mustang, hot rods, custom cars, the hippie-standard VW, or modern-day hybrid cars." (Publisher's note)
Definitive history of driving
DK Smithsonian drive
Smithsonian drive

Gross, Ken
Dream cars; innovative design, visionary ideas. Sarah Schleunung, Ken Gross. Random House Inc 2014 134 p. color illustrations (hardback) $40   **629.222**
1. Antique and classic cars 2. Automobiles -- Design and construction 3. Product design -- Exhibitions 4. High Museum of Art -- Catalogs 5. Automobiles -- Drawings -- Exhibitions 6. Antique and classic cars -- Exhibitions 7. Experimental automobiles -- Exhibitions
ISBN 0847842630; 9780847842636

LC 2014000794

This book, by Sarah Schleunung and Ken Gross, "presents some of the world's most breathtaking concept cars built between 1934 and 2001, a series of visionary designs that influenced the automotive industry and challenged notions of what is possible both aesthetically and technologically." (Publisher's note)
Includes bibliographical references and index

Ingrassia, Paul
Engines of change; a history of the American dream in fifteen cars. Paul Ingrassia. 1st Simon & Schuster hc ed. Simon & Schuster 2012 xx, 395 p., [32] p. of platesp ill. (some col.) (hardcover) $30.00; (paperbook) $18.00   **629.222**
1. Popular culture -- United States 2. Automobiles -- United States -- History 3. Automobiles -- Social aspects -- United States -- History
ISBN 1451640633; 9781451640632; 9781451640649; 9781451640656

LC 2012002303

This book, by Paul Ingrassia, offers a cultural history of automobiles in the United States. "From the assembly lines of Henry Ford to the open roads of Route 66, from the lore of Jack Kerouac to the sex appeal of the

Hot Rod, America's history is a vehicular history. . . . Ingrassia offers a[n] . . . epic in fifteen automobiles, . . . as well as the personalities and tales behind them." (Publisher's note)

Includes bibliographical references (p. 373-375) and index.

Klara, Robert

The **Devil's** Mercedes; the bizarre and disturbing adventures of Hitler's limousine in America. Robert Klara. Thomas Dunne Books, St. Martin's Press 2017 342 p. illustrations (hardcover) $26.99   **629.222**

    1. Mercedes automobiles 2. Limousines -- History 3. Mercedes automobiles -- History -- 20th century

ISBN 9781466878587; 9781250069726; 1250069726

LC 2016058801

This book, by Robert Klara, focuses on two Mercedes Grosser 770K Model 150 automobiles in the U.S. that were allegedly linked to Nazi leader Adolf Hitler. "Klara uncovers the forgotten story of how Americans responded to these rolling relics of fascism on their soil. The limousines made headlines, drew crowds, made fortunes and ruined lives." (Publisher's note)

"An entertaining story of the irresistible cult of a creepy car." Kirkus

Includes bibliographical references (pages [245]-334) and index.

Parissien, Steven

The **life** of the automobile; a history of the motor car. Steven Parissien. Thomas Dunne Books 2014 448 p. (hardback) $27.99   **629.222**

    1. Automobiles -- History

ISBN 1250040639; 9781250040633

LC 2013045750

This book, by Steven Parissien, "is the first comprehensive world history of the car. . . . The author examines the advances of the interwar era, the Golden Age of the 1950s, and the iconic years of the 1960s to the decades of doubt and uncertainty following the oil crisis of 1973, the global mergers of the 1990s, the bailouts of the early twenty-first century, and the emergence of the electric car." (Publisher's note)

"This elegant and authoritative work demonstrates the historical links among people, machines, and cultures on a global scale." LJ

Includes bibliographical references and index

Swift, Earl

Auto Biography; A Classic Car, an Outlaw Motorhead, and 57 Years of the American Dream. by Earl Swift. HarperCollins 2014 368 p. illustrations (some color) $26.99   **629.222**

    1. American dream 2. Criminals -- Fiction 3. Automobiles -- Fiction

ISBN 0062282662; 9780062282668

This book, by Earl Swift, "follows an outlaw auto dealer as he struggles to save a rusted '57 Chevy--a car that has already passed through twelve pairs of hands before his--while financial ruin, government bureaucrats and the FBI close in on him. . . . [H]assled by a growing assortment of challengers, the Chevy's thirteenth owner--an orphan, grade-school dropout and rounder, a felon arrested seventy-odd times, and a man who's been written off as a ruin himself--embarks on a mission to save the car." (Publisher's note)

"A big, weird, heartfelt book about a badass who could give a damn whether you root for him or not." Kirkus

Includes bibliographical references

629.225   Work vehicles

Tractor; the definitive visual history. Jemima Dunne (ed.) DK Publishing 2015 256 p. illustrations (chiefly color) $30   **629.225**

    1. Agricultural machinery 2. Tractors -- Pictorial works 3. Tractors -- History

ISBN 1465435999; 9781465435996

LC 2015288087

This book, edited by Jemima Dunne and the Dorling Kindersley company, "showcases the complete history of farm machinery--from steam and vintage tractors to the latest combine harvesters. . . . Packed with images and tractor data on more than 200 iconic machines, . . . [the book] explores the entire range of tractors and farming machines from around the world." (Publisher's note)

"There is also a chapter on 'How Tractors Work: Tractor Technology,' a glossary, and an index. While the photographs are the obvious draw, the narrative is surprisingly informative and well-researched. Suitable for public libraries, this book will do well in the circulating collection." Booklist

629.227   Cycles

Hallett, Richard

Bike deconstructed; a grand tour of the modern bicycle. Richard Hallett. Princeton Architectural Press 2014 192 p. color illustrations (alk. paper) $29.95   **629.227**

    1. Bicycles 2. Bicycles -- Parts 3. Bicycles -- Design and construction -- History

ISBN 1616892285; 9781616892289

LC 2013029264

In this book, author Richard Hallett "dismantles the modern bicycle to uncover the origin, design, and evolution of every integral part. Through stunning photography, accessible writing, and clear diagrams, Hallett examines every aspect of the bike in detail-- from the anatomy of the drive chain to the geometry of the main frame, and from spoke weaving patterns to the effect of fork rake on steering and stability." (Publisher's note)

"The author includes historical background for many topics, as well as the advantages and disadvantages of different materials used in terms of weight, strength, and flexibility. A fascinating work of interest to a wide audience." Choice

Zinn, Lennard

Zinn & the art of road bike maintenance; the world's best-selling bicycle repair and maintenance guide. Lennard Zinn ; illustrated by Todd Telander and Mike Reisel. 5th edition Velo-Press 2016 28 cm illustrations pbk $26.95   **629.227**

    1. Bicycles -- Maintenance and repair

ISBN 9781937715373; 193771537X

LC 2015039577

"From basic repairs like how to fix a flat tire to advanced overhauls of drivetrains and brakes, Zinn's clearly illustrated guide makes every bicycle repair and maintenance job easy for everyone. Zinn's friendly step-by-step guide explains the tools you'll need and how to know you've done the job right. The two-color interior is easy to read—even in a dimly-lit garage or workshop. Hundreds of hand-drawn illustrations and exploded parts diagrams show just the right level of detail to lead you through every bicycle repair task." (Publisher's note)

Includes bibliographical references (page 447) and indexes

629.28   Tests, driving, maintenance, repair

Downs, Todd

Essential road bike maintenance handbook; Todd Downs with Brian Fiske. Rodale 2014 ix, 166 p.p illustrations (pbk.) $14.99   **629.28**

1. Bicycles -- Maintenance and repair 2. Bicycles -- Maintenance and repair -- Handbooks, manuals, etc
ISBN 1623361664; 9781623361662

            LC 2012474514

This book, by Todd Downs with Brian Fiske, "distills the core fundamentals and serves as a guide to repairing and maintaining one's bike, focusing specifically on instructions with step-by-step photos, troubleshooting tips, links to videos, and helpful sidebar material. The book is clearly organized . . . so that readers can find quickly and efficiently the information they need." (Publisher's note)

Henderson, Bob

The **Haynes** bicycle book; the Haynes repair manual for maintaining and repairing your bike. by Bob Henderson. 3rd edition Haynes North America 2013 224 p. ill. (chiefly col.) pbk $29.95   **629.28**

1. Cycling 2. Bicycles -- Maintenance and repair
ISBN 9781620920404; 1620920409

            LC 2013930927

This bicycle manual, by Bob Henderson, presents information on "how to set up your bike, routine maintenance, troubleshooting, and easy-to-follow repair procedures for road, mountain, hybrid, cruiser and BMX bikes." (Publisher's note)

McCormick, Danielle

Essential car care for women; Jamie Little and Danielle McCormick. Seal Press 2013 192 p. color illustrations (pbk.) $16   **629.28**

1. Automobiles -- Maintenance and repair 2. Automobiles -- Maintenance and repair -- Amateurs' manuals
ISBN 1580054366; 9781580054362

            LC 2011045604

In this guidebook, authors Jamie Little and Danielle McCormick "offer the indispensable, hard-won advice women need to buy, sell, and care for their cars with confidence. . . . [They] explain what an alternator, regulator, distributor, and timing belt are; how to change a tire, recharge a flat battery, check the oil, and assess tire pressure; what to do when a car breaks down or when an accident occurs; how to buy a car without being taken advantage of; and more." (Publisher's note)

"This is a good update for Julie Sussman & Stephanie Glakas-Tenet's Dare To Repair Your Car. As it lacks an overwhelming amount of mechanical instruction, this book proves useful and approachable. It will appeal to high school to adult audiences, male or female, though guys may be leery of the pink cover. Very strongly recommended." LJ

Ramsey, Dan

Teach yourself visually car care & maintenance; by Dan Ramsey and Judy Ramsey. Visual / Wiley 2009 210p il (Visual read less, learn more) pa $24.95   **629.28**

1. Automobiles -- Maintenance and repair
ISBN 978-0-470-37727-7

            LC 2009-920042

This book covers "how to change oil and other fluids; rotate tires; replace fuel pumps, air filters, and batteries; and . . . more." Publisher's note

Includes glossary

Vanderbilt, Tom

Traffic; why we drive the way we do (and what it says about us) Alfred A. Knopf 2008 402p $24.95   **629.28**

1. City traffic 2. Automobile drivers
ISBN 978-0-307-26478-7

            LC 2008-11507

"This may be the most insightful and comprehensive study ever done of driving behavior and how it reveals truths about the types of people we are." Booklist

Includes bibliographical references

629.295   Vehicles for extraterrestrial surfaces

Manning, Rob

Mars Rover Curiosity; an inside account from curiosity's chief engineer. Rob Manning, William L. Simon. Smithsonian Books 2014 240 p. illustrations $29.95   **629.295**

1. Space vehicles 2. Mars (Planet) -- Exploration 3. United States. National Aeronautics and Space Administration
ISBN 1588344738; 9781588344731

            LC 2014941274

This book on the Mars rover Curiosity by Rob Manning and William L. Simon "tells of bringing the groundbreaking spacecraft to life. Manning and his team at NASA's Jet Propulsion Laboratory, tasked with designing a lander many times larger and more complex than any before, faced technical setbacks, fights over inadequate resources, and the challenges of leading an army of brilliant, passionate, and often frustrated experts." (Publisher's note)

"It will be an enjoyable read for anyone interested in Mars, the exploration of Mars, or how NASA designs its missions. Summing Up: Highly recommended. Lower- and upper-division undergraduates; general readers." Choice

629.4   Astronautics

Cassutt, Michael

The **astronaut** maker; how one mysterious engineer ran human spaceflight for a generation. Michael Cassutt. Chicago Review Press Incorporated 2018 480 p. illustrations (hardback) $30   **629.4**

1. Aeronautics 2. Engineers -- United States 3. Aerospace engineers -- United States -- Biography 4. Government executives -- United States -- Biography 5. United States. National Aeronautics and Space Administration -- Management -- History 6. United States. National Aeronautics and Space Administration -- Officials and employees -- Biography
ISBN 9781613737002

            LC 2017060552

This book, by Michael Cassutt, "takes readers inside NASA to learn the real story of how [George W. S.] Abbey rose to power, from young pilot and wannabe astronaut to engineer, bureaucrat, and finally director of the Johnson Space Center. . . . He was in mission control the night of the Apollo 13 accident and organized the recovery effort. Abbey also led NASA's recruitment of women and minorities as space shuttle astronauts and was responsible for hiring Sally Ride." (Publisher's note)

Includes bibliographical references and index

Clegg, Brian

Final Frontier; The Pioneering Science and Technology of Exploring the Universe. Brian Clegg. St. Martin's Press 2014

304 p. $26.99 **629.4**

1. Science 2. Technology 3. Outer space -- Exploration 4. Astronautics -- Popular works 5. Interplanetary voyages -- Popular works 6. Outer space -- Exploration -- Popular works
ISBN 1250039436; 9781250039439

LC 2014010056

In this book, by Brian Clegg, "we discover the massive challenges that face explorers, both human and robotic, to uncover the current and future technologies that could take us out into the galaxy and take a voyage of discovery where no one has gone before-- but one day someone will." (Publisher's note)

"This fine work belongs in all college libraries. Summing Up: Highly recommended." Choice

Includes bibliographical references and index

Dean, Margaret Lazarus

Leaving orbit; notes from the last days of american spaceflight. Margaret Lazarus Dean. Graywolf Press 2015 240 p. (alk. paper) $16 **629.4**

1. Astronautics -- United States 2. United States. National Aeronautics and Space Administration
ISBN 155597709X; 9781555977092

LC 2014960047

This book, by Margaret Lazarus Dean, winner of the Graywolf Press Nonfiction Prize, presents an "elegy to the waning days of human spaceflight as we have known it. In the 1960s, humans took their first steps away from Earth, and for a time our possibilities in space seemed endless. But in a time of austerity and in the wake of high-profile disasters . . . that dream has ended." (Publisher's note)

"Dean deftly captures the thrill and discovery of American space exploration, as well as the disappointment and outrage she believes everyone should feel at its ending." Pub Wkly

Launius, Roger D.

The **Smithsonian** history of space exploration; from the ancient world to the extraterrestrial future. Roger D. Launius. Smithsonian Books 2018 400 p. illustrations (hardcover) $40 **629.4**

1. Space flight to Mars 2. Astronautics -- History 3. Outer space -- Exploration -- History 4. Manned space flight -- History
ISBN 9781588346377; 1588346374

LC 2018017014

This book, by Roger D. Launius, "examines space exploration's origins in the pioneering work undertaken by the ancients of Greece, Rome, and China, and moves through the great discoveries of Renaissance thinkers including Copernicus, Galileo, and Kepler. It offers new insight into well-known moments such as the launch of Sputnik 1 and the Apollo Moon landing and explores the unexpected events and hidden figures of space history." (Publisher's note)

"Part history, part nostalgia, part cutting-edge science, this entertaining book reminds us of the magnitude of space flight--and hints at what's to come." Kirkus

Includes bibliographical references and index

Milestones of space; eleven iconic objects from the Smithsonian National Air and Space Museum. Michael J. Neufeld, [editor] Smithsonian National Air & Space Museum in assoc. w/Zenith Press 2014 176 p. illustrations (mostly color) (hardback) $30 **629.4**

1. Astronautics 2. United States. National Aeronautics and Space Administration 3. National Air and Space Museum -- Catalogs 4. Astronautics -- United States -- Equipment and supplies -- Pictorial

works
ISBN 0760344442; 9780760344446

LC 2013045152

This book, edited by Michael J. Neufeld, "select curators of the Smithsonian National Air and Space Museum present a . . . photographic celebration of some of the most groundbreaking artifacts that played key parts in giving humanity its first steps into the cosmos. Focusing on the most iconic objects and technology . . . , this book extensively profiles eleven of the NASM's most important breakthroughs in space technology." (Publisher's note)

Includes bibliographical references (page 172) and index

Teitel, Amy Shira

Breaking the Chains of Gravity; The Story of Spaceflight Before Nasa. Amy Shira Teitel. St. Martins Press 2016 304 p. 8 plates; illustrations $27 **629.4**

1. Space flight 2. United States. National Aeronautics and Space Administration
ISBN 1472911172; 9781472911179

LC 2015046643

"NASA's history is a familiar story, culminating with the agency successfully landing men on the moon in 1969, but its prehistory is an important and rarely told tale. America's space agency drew together some of the best minds the non-Soviet world had to offer." Written by Amy Shira Teitel, "'Breaking the Chains of Gravity' looks at the evolving roots of America's space program." (Publisher's note)

"Aircraft and rocketry geeks will find the most to love in this jet-powered history, but it's a great primer for anyone interested in the origins of space travel." LJ

Tyson, Neil deGrasse, 1958-

Space chronicles; facing the ultimate frontier. Neil deGrasse Tyson ; edited by Avis Lang. W.W. Norton 2012 364 p. ill. $26.95 **629.4**

1. Space flight -- Forecasting 2. Astronautics -- United States 3. Astronautics and state -- United States 4. United States. National Aeronautics and Space Administration 5. Astronautics 6. Space flight 7. Outer space -- Exploration 8. United States -- National Aeronautics and Space Administration
ISBN 0393082105; 9780393082104

LC 2011032481

In this book, Neil DeGrasse Tyson "delivers . . . [an] argument for space exploration even in the face of a disastrous economy. In this collection of articles and talks, the author investigates what space travel means to us as a species and, more specifically, what NASA means to America. . . . 'When science does advance, when discovery does unfold . . . ,' he writes, 'they happen as an auxiliary benefit and not as a primary goal of NASA's geopolitical mission statement.'" (Kirkus Reviews)

"Tyson is an articulate popularizer of astrophysics. . . . His writing style, while necessarily a bit technical, is as engaging as his screen presence." LJ

629.43 Unmanned space flight

Stern, Alan, 1957-

Chasing new horizons; inside the epic first mission to Pluto. Alan Stern and David Grinspoon. Picador 2018 320 p. (hardcover) $28 **629.43**

1. Space flight 2. Pluto (Planet) 3. Planets -- Exploration 4. Pluto probes 5. Space flight to Pluto 6. New Horizons (Spacecraft) 7. Pluto (Dwarf planet) -- Exploration

ISBN 9781250098962

LC 2017060114

This book, by Alan Stern and David Grinspoon, tells "the . . . inside story of the greatest space exploration project of our time, New Horizons' mission to Pluto. . . . On July 14, 2015, . . . more than 3 billion miles from Earth, a small NASA spacecraft called New Horizons screamed past Pluto at more than 32,000 miles per hour, focusing its instruments on the long mysterious icy worlds of the Pluto system, and then . . . continued on its journey out into the beyond." (Publisher's note)

"Armchair space explorers and budding scientists will relish this inspiring aerospace adventure." LJ

Zimmerman, Robert

The **universe** in a mirror; the saga of the Hubble Telescope and the visionaries who built it. Princeton University Press 2008 287p il $29.95   **629.43**
1. Hubble Space Telescope
ISBN 978-0-691-13297-6; 0-691-13297-6

LC 2007-943159

"Must reading for armchair astrophysicists." Booklist
Includes bibliographical references

629.44 Auxiliary spacecraft

Aldrin, Buzz, 1930-

Mission to Mars; my vision for space exploration. by Buzz Aldrin and Leonard David. National Geographic 2013 272 p. $26   **629.44**
1. Outer space -- Exploration 2. Mars (Planet) -- Exploration
ISBN 1426210175; 9781426210174

LC 2012953599

In this book, by Buzz Aldrin and Leonard David, Aldrin "speaks out as a vital advocate for the continuing quest to push the boundaries of the universe as we know it. As a pioneering astronaut who first set foot on the moon during mankind's first landing of Apollo 11--and as an aerospace engineer who designed an orbital rendezvous technique critical to future planetary landings--Aldrin has a vision, and in this book he plots out the path he proposes, taking humans to Mars by 2035." (Publisher's note)

"Aldrin makes a daring proposal for further space exploration in this exciting glimpse of the new new frontier." Pub Wkly

Miller, Ron

Space stations; the art, reality, and science of working in space. Gary Kitmacher, Ron Miller, and Robert Pearlman. Smithsonian Books 2018 240 p. color illustrations (hardcover) $34.95   **629.44**
1. Space stations 2. Outer space -- Exploration 3. Space stations -- History 4. Space stations -- Popular works 5. Outer space -- Exploration -- Popular works
ISBN 9781588346322

LC 2018004838

This book, by Gary Kitmacher, Ron Miller, and Robert Pearlman, "takes the reader deep into the heart of past, present, and future space stations, both real ones and those dreamed up in popular culture. This . . . book explains the development of space stations from the earliest fictional visions through historical and current programs--including Skylab, Mir, and the International Space Station--and on to the dawning possibilities of large-scale space colonization." (Publisher's note)

"Covering technical breakthroughs as well as Star Trek and comic book references, their work will win high marks from space buffs and sf fans alike." Booklist
Includes bibliographical references and index

White, Rowland

Into the Black; the extraordinary untold story of the first flight of the space shuttle Columbia and the men who flew her. Rowland White. Simon & Schuster 2016 464 p. ill. (some color), maps (hardcover) $29.99   **629.44**
1. Columbia (Spacecraft) 2. Outer space -- Exploration
ISBN 9781501123634; 9781501123627; 1501123629

LC 2016006784

This book, by Rowland White, "using interviews, NASA oral histories, and recently declassified material, . . . pieces together the dramatic untold story of the Columbia mission and the brave people who dedicated themselves to help the United States succeed in the age of space exploration. On April 12, 1981, NASA's Space Shuttle Columbia blasted off from Cape Canaveral." (Publisher's note)

"Bolstering technological insights with personal information from his interviews with astronauts and engineers, White produces a space history aerospace enthusiasts will very much enjoy." Booklist
Includes bibliographical references (pages 403-412) and index.

629.45 Manned space flight

Ackmann, Martha

The **Mercury** 13: the untold story of thirteen American women and the dream of space flight. Random House 2003 239p il hardcover o.p. pa $13.95   **629.45**
1. Women astronauts 2. Project Mercury
ISBN 0-375-50744-2; 0-375-75893-3 pa

LC 2002-37118

"Mercury 13 is both an outstanding work of research and an exceptionally readable and well-told story. Readers will gain new perspectives on space, medicine, women, and American culture, and will appreciate the magnitude of what was lost when the women were grounded." SLJ
Includes bibliographical references

Kaku, Michio

The **future** of humanity; terraforming Mars, interstellar travel, immortality, and our destiny beyond Earth. Michio Kaku. Random House Inc 2018 352 p. $28.95   **629.45**
1. Space colonies 2. Outer space -- Exploration
ISBN 0385542763; 9780385542760

This book, by Michio Kaku, "traverses the frontiers of astrophysics, artificial intelligence, and technology to offer a stunning vision of man's future in space. . . . Kaku explores . . . the process by which humanity may gradually move away from the planet and develop a sustainable civilization in outer space. He reveals how cutting-edge developments in robotics, nanotechnology, and biotechnology may allow us to terraform and build habitable cities on Mars." (Publisher's note)

"Kaku's writings have garnered a reputation for combining hard science with clever speculation, and his latest book continues that winning trend. A breathtaking voyage through what is almost certainly the next major period in the history of humanity." (Booklist)

Kluger, Jeffrey

★ **Apollo** 8; the thrilling story of the first mission to the Moon. Jeffrey Kluger. Henry Holt & Co. 2017 307 p. illustrations (some color) (hardback) $30   **629.45**
1. Space flight 2. Apollo project 3. Moon -- Exploration 4. Project Apollo (U.S.) 5. Space flight to the moon

ISBN 9781627798310; 9781627798327

LC 2016046157

This book by Jeffrey Kluger "takes [readers] from Mission Control to the astronaut's homes, from the test labs to the launch pad. The race to prepare an untested rocket for an unprecedented journey paves the way for the hair-raising trip to the moon. Then, on Christmas Eve, a nation that has suffered a horrendous year of assassinations and war is heartened by an inspiring message from the trio of astronauts in lunar orbit." (Publisher's note)

"Readers will relish Kluger's multisensory prose, and the whole gamut of space flight comes alive in the details. Moreover, extensive interviews lend authenticity to the dialogue and character sketches." Pub Wkly

Includes bibliographical references and index

Koppel, Lily

The **Astronaut** Wives Club; A True Story. Lily Koppel. Grand Central Pub. 2013 384 p. (hardcover) $28   **629.45**
1. United States -- History 2. Astronauts' spouses -- Biography 3. Astronautics -- United States -- History 4. Astronauts' spouses -- Texas -- Houston -- Biography 5. Women -- Texas -- Houston -- Social life and customs -- 20th century
ISBN 1455503258; 9781455503254

LC 2012045976

This book, by Lily Koppel, profiles the lives of U.S. astronauts' wives during the 1960s and onward. "As America's Mercury Seven astronauts were launched on death-defying missions, television cameras focused on the brave smiles of their young wives. Overnight, these women were transformed from military spouses into American royalty... They formed the Astronaut Wives Club, meeting regularly to provide support and friendship." (Publisher's note)

Kranz, Eugene F.

Failure is not an option; mission control from Mercury to Apollo 13 and beyond. {by} Gene Kranz. Simon & Schuster 2000 415p il $26   **629.45**
1. Space flight 2. Astronautics -- United States 3. United States -- National Aeronautics and Space Administration
ISBN 0-7432-0079-9

LC 00-27720

"A welcome contribution to the history of space flight. More than any previous book, it gives the view of that history as lived by the brotherhood of Mission Control. The writing, like Kranz himself, is brisk, unadorned and informative, but warmed from time to time by characteristic expressions of irony and humor." N Y Times Book Rev

Mailer, Norman, 1923-2007

Of a fire on the moon; Norman Mailer. Random House Trade Paperbacks 2004 463 p. (acid-free paper) $16   **629.45**
1. Apollo project 2. Space flight to the moon 3. Project Apollo (U.S.) 4. Astronauts -- United States 5. United States -- Civilization -- 1945-
ISBN 0553390619; 9780553390612

LC 2014415502

This book, by Norman Mailer, is a "chronicle of the Apollo 11 mission..., America's reach for greatness in the midst of the Cold War... [This volume] compiles the reportage [Norman] Mailer published between 1969 and 1970 in 'Life' magazine: gripping firsthand dispatches from inside NASA's clandestine operations in Houston and Cape Kennedy; technical insights into the magnitude of their awe-inspiring feat; and prescient meditations that place the event in human context." (Publisher's note)

Nelson, Craig

Rocket men; the triumph and tragedy of the first Americans on the moon. Viking 2009 404p il $27.95   **629.45**
1. Apollo project 2. Space flight to the moon 3. Astronautics -- United States
ISBN 978-0-670-02103-1

LC 2008-51175

"A thorough recounting—as full in human terms as in scientific and technical detail—of NASA's first manned Moon landing.... The definitive account of a watershed in American history." Kirkus

Includes bibliographical references

Piantadosi, Claude A.

Mankind beyond Earth; the history, science, and future of human space exploration. Claude A. Piantadosi. Columbia University Press 2012 336 p. (cloth; alk. paper) $35   **629.45**
1. Interplanetary voyages 2. Outer space -- Exploration 3. Outer space -- Exploration -- Popular works 4. Manned space flight -- History -- Popular works 5. Astronautics -- United States -- Forecasting -- Popular works
ISBN 0231162421; 9780231162425; 9780231531030

LC 2012017631

In this book, Claude A. Piantadosi "offers a brief history of human space exploration; a discussion of various strategies for extending human excursions to asteroids, the Moon (again), Mars, the outer planets of the Sun, and even targets beyond the solar system; and a rigorous examination of the very special and expensive conditions needed for human survival on such trips." (Library Journal)

Includes bibliographical references and index

Potter, Christopher

The **Earth** gazers; on seeing ourselves. Christopher Potter. Pegasus Books 2018 456 p. illustrations (some color) (hardcover) $28.95   **629.45**
1. Astrophysics 2. Space flight 3. Space sciences 4. Manned space flight -- Popular works
ISBN 9781681776361; 9781681777047; 1681776367

This book, by Christopher Potter, tells the "history of the space program and of the ways in which it transformed our view of the earth and changed the lives of the astronauts who walked in space and on the moon. It is the story of the often blemished visionaries who inspired that journey into space: Charles Lindbergh, Robert Goddard and Wernher Von Braun, and of the courageous pilots who were the first humans to escape the Earth's orbit." (Publisher's note)

"Potter (You Are Here: A Portable History of the Universe) pens this excellent account of the people and events that brought about the first photographs of the earth taken from outer space." LJ

Pyle, Rod

Destination moon; the Apollo missions in the astronauts' own words. HarperCollins Publishers 2005 192p il $24.95; pa $14.95   **629.45**
1. Space flight to the moon 2. Project Apollo
ISBN 0-06-087349-3; 0-06-087350-7 pa

LC 2005-51350

This "survey of the Apollo moon program includes a brief summary of each flight and attempted flight of the great effort, from the fatal fire on Pad 34 in 1967 to the landing of a scientist on the moon in Apollo 17 in 1972.... Space collections of all sizes should welcome Pyle's book, and smaller ones will find it invaluable." Booklist

Wohlforth, Charles

Beyond Earth; Our Path to a New Home in the Planets. Charles Wohlforth and Amanda R. Hendrix, Ph.D. Pantheon Books 2016 320 p. hardcover $27.95   **629.45**

1. Astronautics 2. Space colonies 3. Titan (Satellite) 4. Interplanetary voyages 5. Manned space flight 6. Space flight -- Physiological effect 7. Space flight -- Psychological aspects

ISBN 9780804197977

LC 2016009498

This book by Charles Wohlforth and Amanda R. Hendrix offers an "account of the developments . . . that have transformed the dream of space colonization into something that may well be achievable. . . . [It] is grounded not only in the human capacity for invention . . . but also in the bureaucratic, political, and scientific realities. . . . The authors . . . [claim] that . . . Titan . . . offers the most realistic . . . prospect of life without support from Earth." (Publisher's note)

"On the whole, the fictional chapters are entertaining, chilling, and put the science in a more human context. The two halves work together to create a striking, reality-based possible future that's seen through the lens of current knowledge." Pub Wkly

Wolfe, Tom

★ The **right** stuff. Picador 2008 352p pa $16   **629.45**

1. Astronauts 2. Astronautics -- United States

ISBN 0-312-42756-5; 978-0-312-42756-6

First published 1979 by Farrar, Straus & Giroux

This volume chronicles "the handful of adrenaline-junkie military test pilots who became the Mercury astronauts. Their story is juxtaposed against that of Chuck Yeager, the ace of aces pilot who broke the sound barrier but couldn't apply to the space program because he lacked a college degree. . . . A terrific read from beginning to end." Libr J

629.454   Circumterrestrial and lunar flights

Kurson, Robert

★ **Rocket** men; the daring odyssey of Apollo 8 and the astronauts who made man's first journey to the Moon. Robert Kurson. Random House Inc 2018 x, 372 p.p illustrations (some color) (hardback) $28   **629.454**

1. Space flight to the moon 2. Outer space -- Exploration 3. Apollo 8 (Spacecraft) 4. Project Apollo (U.S.)

ISBN 9780812988727; 9780812988703

LC 2017009386

In this book about the Apollo 8 mission, author "Robert Kurson puts the focus on the three astronauts and their families: the commander, Frank Borman, a conflicted man on his final mission; idealistic Jim Lovell, who'd dreamed since boyhood of riding a rocket to the Moon; and Bill Anders, a young nuclear engineer and hotshot fighter pilot making his first space flight." (Publisher's note)

"An exuberant history of a major turning point in early American spaceflight, possibly 'the riskiest and most thrilling of all the Apollo missions.'" Kirkus

Includes bibliographical references (pages [351]-356) and index.

629.47   Astronautical engineering

Guthrie, Julian

How to make a spaceship; A Band of Renegades, an Epic Race, and the Birth of Private Spaceflight. by Julian Guthrie. Penguin Group USA 2016 448 p. illustrations (ebook) $65;

$28   **629.47**

1. Space flight

ISBN 9780698405851; 1594206724; 9781594206726

This book, by Julian Guthrie, is about "the historic race that reawakened the promise of manned spaceflight. Alone in a Spartan black cockpit, test pilot Mike Melvill rocketed toward space. He had eighty seconds to exceed the speed of sound. . . . The spectacle defied reason, the result of a competition dreamed up by entrepreneur Peter Diamandis, whose vision for a new race to space required small teams to do what only the world's largest governments had done before." (Publisher's note)

"Guthrie well captures the high-risk, buccaneering spirit of privately financed spaceflight." Booklist

629.8   Automatic control engineering

Bascomb, Neal

The **new** cool; a visionary teacher, his FIRST robotics team, and the ultimate battle of smarts. Crown Publishers 2010 337p il $25; ebook $12.99   **629.8**

1. Robots 2. FIRST (Organization)

ISBN 978-0-307-58889-0; 978-0-307-58891-3 ebook

LC 2010-21646

The author "charts the marathon play-by-play teamwork of a group of fourth-year Southern California students from Dos Pueblos High School Engineering Academy as they competed in a robot-building contest. Since 2002, physics teacher and mentor Amir Abo-Shaeer has administered an experimental science curriculum culminating in a team entry in 'FIRST' (For Inspiration and Recognition of Science and Technology), a worldwide robotics competition created by Dean Kamen. . . . Aside from a mind-numbing plethora of physics terminology, Bascomb skillfully translates the exhilarating challenge to the page via intricately descriptive, expertly paced sketches of the group and their combined handiwork. A nail-biting thrill ride for techies and armchair engineers." Kirkus

Includes bibliographical references

Davis, Joshua

Spare parts; four undocumented teenagers, one ugly robot, and the battle for the American dream. Joshua Davis. Farrar Straus & Giroux 2014 240 p. illustrations (hardcover) $25   **629.8**

1. Robots -- Competitions 2. Mexicans -- United States 3. Mexican Americans -- Economic conditions 4. Robotics -- Competitions -- United States 5. Phoenix (Ariz.) -- Social life and customs 6. Mexican American boys -- Education -- United States 7. Remote submersibles -- Competitions -- United States

ISBN 0374183376; 9780374183370; 9780374534981

LC 2014018569

This book, by Joshua Davis, profiles how "In 2004, four Latino teenagers arrived at the Marine Advanced Technology Education Robotics Competition. . . . They were born in Mexico but raised in Phoenix, Arizona. . . . No one had ever suggested . . . that they might amount to much--but two inspiring science teachers had convinced these impoverished, undocumented kids from the desert who had never even seen the ocean that they should try to build an underwater robot." (Publisher's note)

"Davis pulls no punches as he describes the grim sociopolitical atmosphere that allows the oppression of talented people for no morally acceptable reason. The four young inventors and their struggles helped spur the DREAMers movement, and their story will also be told in a forthcoming Hollywood movie. This is important reading." Booklist

Dufty, David F.

How to build an android; the true story of Philip K. Dick's robotic resurrection. David F. Dufty. 1st US ed. H. Holt 2012 272 p. ill. (hbk.) $26.00   **629.8**

1. Robots 2. Artificial intelligence 3. Roboticists -- Biography 4. Androids -- Popular works 5. Robotics -- Popular works 6. Artificial intelligence -- Popular works

ISBN 0805095519; 9780805095517

LC 2011043674

This book by David F. Dufty tells "the story of the roboticists who created a fully functioning android replica of renowned writer Philip K. Dick." (Kirkus Reviews) "Dufty focuses on two main developers . . . David Hanson . . . who created Phil's head only to later lose it on an airplane, and Andrew Olney, a computer programmer who was obsessed with science fiction books as a youngster. Dufty examines how their differing outlooks influenced the project." (Publishers Weekly)

Long, John

Darwin's devices; what evolving robots can teach us about the history of life and the future of technology. John Long. Basic Books 2012 273 p.   **629.8**

1. Biology -- Simulation methods 2. Evolution -- Study and teaching 3. Robots -- Design and construction 4. Technological innovations -- Forecasting 5. Evolutionary robotics 6. Technological forecasting 7. Evolution (Biology) -- Simulation methods

ISBN 0465021417; 9780465021413; 9780465029280

LC 2011051804

The author "traces his path from a doctoral student studying the evolution of fish vertebrae to his present position as director of Vassar's Interdisciplinary Robotics Laboratory. . . . [John] Long explains how a blunder in an early version of his doctoral thesis led to his later work with robots. . . . Long's first self-propelled robot had a fairly simple design--an embedded minicomputer, one light sensor and a backbone built to mimic varying structural aspects of a marlin vertebrae. . . . More complex robots allowed him to model predator/prey relationships and target acquisition more realistically, and he was able to consider broader issues such as the relationship between goal-directed behavior and animal intelligence." (Kirkus)

Includes bibliographical references and index

Mindell, David A.

Our Robots, Ourselves; Robotics and the Myths of Autonomy. David A. Mindell. Penguin Group USA 2015 272 p. illustrations $27.95   **629.8**

1. Robots 2. Technological innovations

ISBN 0525426973; 9780525426974

Author "David Mindell offers a . . . behind-the-scenes look at the cutting edge of robotics today, debunking commonly held myths and exploring the rapidly changing relationships between humans and machines. Drawing on firsthand experience, extensive interviews, and the latest research from MIT and elsewhere, Mindell takes us to extreme environments--high atmosphere, deep ocean, and outer space--to reveal where the most advanced robotics already exist." (Publisher's note)

"An expansively researched and enjoyably accessible treatment of robotic automation, recommended for readers of popular science and those with an interest in artificial intelligence and automation." LJ

630   Agriculture and related technologies

Berry, Wendell

Bringing it to the table; on farming and food. introduction

by Michael Pollan. Counterpoint 2009 234p pa $14.95   **630**

1. Family farms 2. Sustainable agriculture 3. Agriculture -- United States

ISBN 978-1-58243-543-5

LC 2009-24437

"The essays [included] address such concerns as: How does organic measure up against locally grown? What are the differences between small and large farms, and how does that affect what you put on your dinner table? What can you do to support sustainable agriculture?" Publisher's note

Includes bibliographical references

Levatino, Audrey

Woman-powered farm; manual for a self-sufficient lifestyle from homestead to field. Audrey Levatino. The Countryman Press 2015 343 p. color illustrations (pbk.) $24.95   **630**

1. Women farmers 2. Farm management

ISBN 1581572417; 9781581572414

LC 2015006642

In this book, by Audrey Levatino with photography by Michael Levatino, the author "shares her experiences of running a farm and offers invaluable advice on how to get started, whether you have hundreds of acres or a simple lot for an urban community garden. [The book is] filled with personal anecdotes and stories from other women farmers, from old hands to brand new ones, from agricultural icons like Temple Grandin, to her own sister." (Publisher's note)

"A comprehensive volume on farming for women beginning to contemplate the industry, whether as a hobby or for a living. Personal anecdotes and a friendly tone don't overshadow the wealth of information in this book." LJ

Includes bibliographical references and index

630.68   Agriculture management

Lanier, Karen

The **woman** hobby farmer; female guidance for growing food, raising livestock, and building a farm-based business. Karen Lanier. CompanionHouse Books 2017 240 p. (softcover) $24.99   **630.68**

1. Women farmers

ISBN 1620082608; 9781620082607

LC 2017013667

This book, by Karen Lanier, is "dedicated to hobby farming from a female perspective. Written for women, by a woman, this insightful volume is packed with stories and advice from women hobby farmers and looks at female-specific farming challenges as well as issues that all farmers face." (Publisher's note)

Includes bibliographical references and index

630.9   Agriculture – History

Genoways, Ted

This blessed earth; a year in the life of an American family farm. Ted Genoways. W W Norton & Co Inc 2017 226 p. illustrations (hardcover) $26.95   **630.9**

1. Farm life -- United States 2. Agriculture -- United States 3. Farmers -- Economic conditions 4. Family farms -- Nebraska -- Case studies

ISBN 9780393356458; 9780393292572; 9780393292589; 0393292576

LC 2017025062

This book, by Ted Genoways, describes how "Rick Hammond grew up on a small ranch, and for forty years he has raised cattle and crops on his wife's fifth-generation homestead in York County, Nebraska. . . [But] their small family farm—and their entire way of life—are under siege. . . . Following the Hammonds from harvest to harvest, Ted Genoways explores this rapidly changing landscape of small, traditional farming operations, mapping as it unfolds day to day." (Publisher's note)

"By following a single family through time, the book captures the complex reality of farmers in America today both in terms of the future of the industry and of their everyday lives. It is an unvarnished portrait striking for both its depth and humanity." Pub Wkly

Includes bibliographical references (pages [225]-226).

630.973   Agriculture – History – United States

Letters to a young farmer; on food, farming, and our future. Stone Barns Center for Food & Agriculture ; Martha Hodgkins, editor ; illustrations by Chris Wormell. Princeton Architectural Press 2017 176 p. illustrations (alk. paper) $19.95   **630.973**
1. Farm life -- United States 2. Agriculture -- United States 3. Agricultural literature -- United States
ISBN 9781616895303

LC 2016013820

In this book, edited by Martha Hodgkins and illustrated by Chris Wormell, "esteemed writers, farmers, chefs, activists, and visionaries address the highs and lows of farming life, as well as larger questions of how our food is produced and consumed. . . . Barbara Kingsolver speaks to the tribe of farmers . . . with love, admiration, and regret. Dan Barber traces the rediscovery of lost grains and foodways. Michael Pollan bridges the chasm between agriculture and nature." (Publisher's note)

"Longtime advocates of sustainable agriculture join with new voices for a comradely take on the challenging future of farming." Kirkus.

Includes bibliographical references.

631.5   Cultivation and harvesting

Dirr, Michael A.

The **Reference** Manual of Woody Plant Propagation; by Michael A. Dirr and Charles W. Heuser, Jr. Varsity Press 2009 410 p. illustrations $49.95   **631.5**
1. Horticulture 2. Plant propagation
ISBN 1604690046; 9781604690040

LC 2009497202

"Over 1,100 species and their propagation requirements by seeds, cuttings, grafting and budding, and tissue culture are discussed in exhaustive detail. Essentially a recipe book for making more trees and shrubs, this reference is a high-level how-to." (Publisher's note)

Jenkins, McKay

Food Fight; by Mckay Jenkins. Penguin Group USA 2017 336 p. $26; (ebook) $65   **631.5**
1. Genetically modified foods
ISBN 1594634602; 9781594634604; 9780698409835

LC 2016054194

In this book, "environmental writer McKay Jenkins traveled across the country . . . and discovered that the GMO controversy is more complicated than meets the eye. He interviewed dozens of people on all sides of the debate. . . . The result is a comprehensive, nuanced examination of the state of our food system and a much-needed guide for consumers to help them make more informed choices about what to eat for their next meal." (Publisher's note)

"Highlighting the pros and cons of this contentious topic, Jenkins gives conscientious readers plenty to chew on." Pub Wkly

Includes bibliographical references and index.

631.584   Organic farming

Gillam, Carey

★ **Whitewash**; the story of a weed killer, cancer, and the corruption of science. Carey Gillam. Island Press 2017 xiv, 305 p.p (cloth; alk. paper) $30   **631.584**
1. Agriculture -- United States 2. Pesticides -- Environmental aspects
ISBN 1610918320; 9781610918329

LC 2017940669

This book, by Carey Gillam, "uncovers one of the most controversial stories in the history of food and agriculture, exposing new evidence of corporate influence. Gillam introduces readers to farm families devastated by cancers which they believe are caused by the chemical, and to scientists whose reputations have been smeared for publishing research that contradicted business interests." (Publisher's note)

Includes bibliographical references (pages 255-293) and index.

631.6   Clearing, drainage, revegetation

Fukuoka, Masanobu

Sowing seeds in the desert; natural farming, global restoration, and ultimate food security. Masanobu Fukuoka ; edited by Larry Korn. Chelsea Green Pub. 2012 168 p. (hardback) $22.50   **631.6**
1. Sustainable agriculture 2. Agricultural innovations 3. Agriculture -- Environmental aspects 4. Revegetation 5. Desert reclamation 6. Desertification -- Control
ISBN 9781603584180; 1603584188; 9781603584197

LC 2012007330

This book "calls on modern-day farmers to reconsider their methods and heed the needs of the land. . . . [Masanobu Fukuoka] illuminates regional disparities in environmental and agricultural thought and practice. . . . In clarifying popular misconceptions about organic and natural farming, he advises that we must not focus on cash crops. . . . Only by the co-existence of myriad micro-organisms and vegetation will we be able to preserve and maintain our land." (Publishers Weekly)

Includes bibliographical references.

631.8   Fertilizers, soil conditioners, growth regulators

Pleasant, Barbara

★ The **complete** compost gardening guide; banner batches, grow heaps, comforter compost, and other amazing techniques for saving time and money, and producing the most flavorful, nutritious vegetables ever. [by] Barbara Pleasant & Deborah L. Martin. Storey Pub. 2008 319p il map $29.95; pa $19.95   **631.8**
1. Compost 2. Gardening
ISBN 978-1-58017-703-0; 978-1-58017-702-3 pa

LC 2007-49729

The authors "provide both a reference guide and an introduction to composting. The first section . . . includes a number of interesting facts, definitions, and even recipes (e.g., for Miracle Leaf Mold). The second section, on compost gardening techniques, examines easy methods of composting with piles, bins, and cans as well as more elaborate approaches involving pits and trenches. It also discusses the use of earthworms in composting. Finally, the third section treats in detail the kinds of plants that will do well in a composter's garden. . . . Essential reading for any gardener interested in composting, this should find its way into many public libraries with active gardening communities and academic and special libraries with an interest in horticulture and gardening." Libr J

632 Plant injuries, diseases, pests

Dickinson, Richard

Weeds of North America; Richard Dickinson and France Royer. University of Chicago Press 2014 797 p. illustrations (chiefly color) (pbk.; alk. paper) $35 **632**

1. Weeds 2. Weeds -- North America -- Identification 3. Weeds -- North America -- Handbooks, manuals, etc
ISBN 022607644X; 9780226076447

LC 2013038953

This book, by Richard Dickinson and France Royer, "is the first to cover North American weeds at every stage of growth. The book is organized by plant family, and more than five hundred species are featured. Each receives a two-page spread with images and text identification keys. Species are arranged within family alphabetically by scientific name, and entries include vital information on seed viability and germination requirements." (Publisher's note)

"This comprehensive identification guide will aid in weed ecology and control." LJ

Includes bibliographical references and index

Mabey, Richard

Weeds; in defense of nature's most unloved plants. Harper-Collins 2011 324p il $25.99; ebook $12.99 **632**

1. Weeds
ISBN 978-0-06-206545-2; 978-0-06-206547-6 ebook

LC 2011010483

First published 2010 in the United Kingdom

"This lively, erudite work invites readers to take a new look at the lowly and unloved weed. Mabey explains how weeds have cunningly evolved to survive natural disasters, human devastation, climate change, and almost every attempt to eradicate them. He weaves together a complex, fascinating tale of history and botany that travels from the first farm fields of Mesopotamia to the bomb craters of the London Blitz and the lowly industrial outfields of our modern cities." Publ Wkly

Includes bibliographical references

Orlando, Richard

Weeds in the urban landscape; where they come from, why they're here, and how to live with them. Richard Orlando. North Atlantic Books 2018 400 p. (pbk.) $24.95 **632**

1. Weeds 2. Urban gardening 3. Urban gardening -- West (U.S.) 4. Weeds -- Control -- West (U.S.) 5. Weeds -- West (U.S.) -- Identification
ISBN 9781623172114

LC 2017043940

This book, by Richard Orlando, is "a comprehensive identification guide to 189 common weeds in the urban environment, explaining their

families and characteristics, with strategies for managing their presence in the garden and fields. This engaging field guide . . . traces the history of weeds . . . and explains their role in the evolution of agriculture and human civilizations as well as their many uses for medicine, food, animal fodder, and soil enhancement." (Publisher's note)

Includes bibliographical references and index

Stewart, Amy

Wicked bugs; the louse that conquered Napoleon's army & other diabolical insects. etchings and drawings by Briony Morrow-Cribbs. Algonquin Books of Chapel Hill 2011 271p il $18.95 **632**

1. Mites 2. Ticks 3. Spiders 4. Insect pests
ISBN 978-1-56512-960-3

LC 2011-3629

"Ranging from verdant South American jungles to Manhattan's cold concrete canyons, Stewart amusingly but analytically profiles the baddest bugs around in quick but attention-grabbing snapshots of little creatures that pack a lot of punch. Bed bugs and bookworms, rat fleas and filth flies all come under Stewart's curious gaze as she exposes their evil habits and lethal charms. No alarmist setting out to stoke preexisting phobias, Stewart shares her natural fascination with the insect world to help readers recognize both the threats and the wonders that could be lurking in corner crevices or come wafting in on the next gentle breeze." Booklist

Includes bibliographical references

633.1 Cereals

Yafa, Stephen

Grain of truth; the real case for and against wheat and gluten. Stephen Yafa. Avery 2015 304 p. illustrations (hardcover) $25.95 **633.1**

1. Wheat 2. Gluten-free diet 3. Gluten 4. Wheat-free diet
ISBN 1594632499; 9781594632495

LC 2015005944

In this book, author Stephen Yafa "sets the record straight, breaking down the botany of the wheat plant we've hijacked for our own use, the science of nutrition and digestion, the effects of mass production on our health, and questions about gluten and fiber-- all to point us towards a better, richer diet." (Publisher's note)

"Well researched and accessible, this title is recommended for libraries where people look for Michael Pollan's titles (Cooked; Food Rules; The Omnivore's Dilemma). Worth considering for any collection with copies of William Davis's Wheat Belly or David Perlmutter's Grain Brain." LJ

Includes bibliographical references and index

633.5 Fiber crops

Fine, Doug

Hemp bound; dispatches from the front lines of the next agricultural revolution. Doug Fine. Chelsea Green Publishing Company 2014 192 p. (pbk.) $14.95 **633.5**

1. Hemp 2. Agriculture -- United States 3. Hemp industry
ISBN 1603585435; 9781603585439; 9781603585446

LC 2013048926

"In 'Hemp Bound: Dispatches from the Front Lines of the Next Agricultural Revolution,' . . . author Doug Fine embarks on a . . . journey to meet the men and women who are testing, researching, and pioneering hemp's applications for the twenty-first century. . . . Fine learns how . . . possible it is for this misunderstood plant to help us end dependence on fossil fuels, heal farm soils damaged [by] growing monocultures, and bring . . . taxable revenue into the economy." (Publisher's note)

"A short, sweet, logical and funny argument for the potential of one of the world's most dynamic cash crops." Kirkus

Includes bibliographical references and index

633.79 Marijuana

Cervantes, Jorge

The **Cannabis** Encyclopedia; The Definitive Guide to Cultivation & Consumption of Medical Marijuana. Jorge Cervantes. Van Patten Publishing 2015 596 p. color illustrations, map $50   **633.79**

   1. Marijuana 2. Herbs -- Therapeutic use
   ISBN 1878823345; 1878823396; 9781878823342;
   9781878823397

Author Jorge Cervantes presents this "guide to medical marijuana cultivation and consumption. It explains all the essential techniques to grow indoors, outdoors and in greenhouses. All gardening practices are well-researched and illustrated with easy step-by-step examples and instructions. More than 2,000 . . . color images illustrate this 596-page book." (Publisher's note)

"Essential where patrons grow, or are interested in growing, their own cannabis." LJ

Stein, David

Grow your own; understanding, cultivating, and enjoying cannabis. Nichole Graf, Micah Sherman, David Stein and Liz Crain. Tin House Books 2017 193 p. illustrations (chiefly color) (hardcover) $26.95   **633.79**

   1. Cannabis -- Propagation 2. Marijuana -- Propagation
   ISBN 9781941040584; 9781941040591; 1941040586

This book, by Nichole Graf, Micah Sherman, David Stein and Liz Crain, "provides all the background and instruction you need to set up a grow space, raise your plants, and harvest your buds. It will teach you how to choose a strain based on its flavors and effects, how to to manage insects and molds without the use of pesticides, and how to mix just the right soil. . . . [It] will also give you a primer on the myriad ways to enjoy cannabis." (Publisher's note)

"The stylish presentation of the book and its useful information give it broad appeal among open-minded gardeners and 420-friendly readers." Pub Wkly

634 Orchards, fruits, forestry

Begos, Kevin

Tasting the past; the science of flavor and the search for the original wine grapes. Kevin Begos. Algonquin Books of Chapel Hill 2018 288 p. (hardcover; alk. paper) $26.95 **634**

   1. Vineyards 2. Wine and wine making -- History 3. Viticulture 4. Grapes -- History 5. Grapes -- Varieties
   ISBN 9781616205775

                LC 2017046783

In this book, by Kevin Begos, "discover the hidden life of wine. After a chance encounter with an obscure Middle Eastern red, . . . Begos embarks on a ten-year journey to seek the origins of wine. What he unearths is a whole world of forgotten grapes, each with distinctive tastes and aromas, as well as the archaeologists, geneticists, chemists--even a

paleobotanist--who are deciphering wine down to molecules of flavor." (Publisher's note)

Includes bibliographical references

Bowling, Barbara L.

Homegrown berries; successfully grow your own strawberries, raspberries, blueberries, blackberries, and more. Barbara L. Bowling. Timber Press, Inc. 2014 224 p. color illustrations $19.95   **634**

   1. Berries 2. Gardening 3. Ornamental berries
   ISBN 1604693177; 9781604693171

                LC 2014009483

This book, by Barbara L. Bowling, is a guidebook to growing berries in home gardens. This volume "covers the entire process, from planting to picking that first nutritious, luscious fruit. You'll learn the best varieties for your region, how to fit them into your landscape, and how to maintain them for peak harvest year after year." (Publisher's note)

"From "Berry Basics" to the listings of recommended cultivars by region, suggested reading, and resources, this comprehensive guide will inspire and instruct everyone interested in homegrown berries." Booklist

Successfully grow your own strawberries, raspberries, blueberries, blackberries, and more

Deardorff, David

What's wrong with my fruit garden? 100% organic solutions for berries, trees, nuts, vines, and tropicals. David Deardorff and Kathryn Wadsworth. Timber Press 2014 312 p. color illustrations $24.95   **634**

   1. Gardening 2. Fruit culture 3. Fruit-culture 4. Organic gardening 5. Fruit -- Diseases and pests -- Control 6. Fruit trees -- Wounds and injuries -- Diagnosis
   ISBN 1604693584; 9781604693584; 9781604694888

                LC 2013009257

Written by David Deardorff and Kathryn Wadsworth, "'What's Wrong With My Fruit Garden?' offers a path toward a healthy garden packed with fresh fruit. In addition to learning how to diagnose a plant problem through clear visual keys, you will also learn the most effective organic solutions for every problem. Detailed plant portraits include information on growth; seasonality; temperature, light, and soil requirements; and planting techniques." (Publisher's note)

"Deardorff and Wadsworth arm the gardener with needed strategies that lessen the risk of failure and encourage robust growth." Pub Wkly

Includes bibliographical references and index

Happy cactus; cacti, succulents, and more. John Pilbeam. DK Publishing 2018 144 p. $14.99   **634**

   1. Cactus 2. Desert plants 3. Succulent plants
   ISBN 1465474536; 9781465474537

This book, by John Pilbeam, "unearth[s] the secrets of different cacti and succulents, with profiles on more than 50 popular varieties--from the cute, flowering pincushion cactus to the wacky prickly pear, discover what makes your plant unique and how it might behave when treated with a little bit of love. Find out where to put it, when to water it, what to feed it, what to look out for, and how to encourage its distinctive traits, from flower stalks to fast growth." (Publisher's note)

"The book's chipper tone perfectly matches its friendly visual design, with plants pictured at the center of the page accompanied by informative speech bubbles. Experienced cacti growers will know this basic stuff, but those newly interested in cacti and succulents will be well served by this book." Pub Wkly

Ralph, Ann

Grow a little fruit tree; simple pruning techniques for small-space, easy-harvest fruit trees. by Ann Ralph. Storey Publishing 2015 168 p. color illustrations (pbk.; alk. paper) $16.95 **634**

1. Pruning 2. Fruit trees -- Pruning

ISBN 1612120547; 9781603428897; 9781612120546

LC 2014025665

With this book, by Ann Ralph, "grow your own apples, plums, cherries, and peaches in even the smallest backyard! . . . Ralph reveals a simple yet revolutionary secret that keeps an ordinary fruit tree much smaller than normal. These great little trees take up less space, require less care, offer easy harvest, and make a fruitful addition to any home landscape." (Publisher's note)

"Every gardener who has previously felt too intimidated to cultivate his or her own mini orchard will find enough well-seasoned advice and inspiration here to begin planting a fruit tree or two during the next growing season."

Simple pruning techniques for small-space, easy-harvest fruit trees

634.8 Grapes

Cox, Jeff

From vines to wines; the complete guide to growing grapes and making your own wine. by Jeff Cox. Storey Publishing 2015 264 p. illustrations (pbk.; alk. paper) $18.95 **634.8**

1. Vineyards 2. Wine and wine making 3. Viticulture 4. Viticulture -- United States

ISBN 1612124380; 9781612124384

LC 2014033708

In this book, by Jeff Cox, "every aspect of growing flawless grapes and making extraordinary wine is covered in this classic guide. Fully illustrated instructions clearly show you how to choose and prepare a vineyard site; build effective trellising systems; select, plant, prune, and harvest the right grapes for your climate; press, ferment, age, and bottle wine; and judge wine for clarity, color, aroma, and taste." (Publisher's note)

"A must-have for anyone interested in making their own wine." LJ

634.9 Forestry

Connors, Philip

Fire season; field notes from a wilderness lookout. Ecco 2011 246 p. (trade) $24.99 **634.9**

1. Authors 2. Solitude 3. New Mexico 4. Forest fires 5. Essayists 6. Fire lookouts 7. Newspaper editors 8. Writers on nature 9. Fire lookout stations 10. Gila National Forest (N.M.)

ISBN 0061859362; 9780061859366

The content of this book is based on author "Philip Connors[' time] . . . spent . . . in a seven-by-seven foot fire-lookout tower, ten thousand feet above the ground in one of the remotest territories of New Mexico. One of the least developed parts of the country, the first region designated as an official wilderness area in the world, the section he tends is also one of the most fire-prone, suffering more than thirty thousand lightning strikes each year. . . . Connors' time up on the peak is filled with drama—there are fires large and small; spectacular midnight lightning storms and silent mornings awakening above the clouds; surprise encounters with long-distance hikers, smokejumpers, bobcats, black bears, and an abandoned, dying fawn." (Blackstone Audio)

"For almost a decade, former Wall Street Journal reporter Connors has spent half a year keeping vigil over 20,000 square miles of desert, forest, and mountain chains from atop a tower 10,000 feet above sea level. One of a handful of seasoned, seasonal fire-watchers in New Mexico's Gila National Forest, Connors introduces us to his wilderness in this ruminative, lyrical, occasionally suspenseful account." Publ Wkly

Egan, Timothy

★ The **big** burn; Teddy Roosevelt and the fire that saved America. Houghton Mifflin Harcourt 2009 324p il map $27 **634.9**

1. Governors 2. Presidents 3. Forest fires 4. Vice-presidents 5. Conservationists 6. Forest conservation 7. Nature conservation 8. Foresters 9. Nobel laureates for peace 10. United States -- Forest Service 11. Forest conservation -- United States 12. Forest fires -- United States -- History 13. National parks and reserves -- United States 14. Forest conservation -- United States -- History 15. Nature conservation -- United States -- History 16. National parks and reserves -- United States -- History

ISBN 978-0-618-96841-1; 0-618-96841-5

LC 2009-21881

"This is history that is well researched, vividly set into the context of the early twentieth century, and written with such skill in character development and pacing that readers will be lost in a vivid reimagining of those surreal days in 1910 when an ecological event unfolded with the spectacle of a modern summer blockbuster." Orion

Includes bibliographical references (p. [287]-305) and index.

MacLean, Norman

Young men & fire. University of Chicago Press 1992 301p pl maps $19.95 **634.9**

1. Forest fires 2. Fire fighters 3. Large print books 4. United States -- Forest Service

ISBN 0226500616; 9780226500614

LC 92-11890

"On Aug. 5, 1949, 16 Forest Service smoke jumpers landed at a fire in remote Mann Gulch, Mont. Within an hour, 13 were dead or irrevocably burned, caught in a 'blowup'--a rare explosion of wind and flame. . . . [A]n engrossing account of human fallibility and natural violence." Pub Wkly

635 Garden crops (Horticulture)

Allaby, Michael

The **gardener's** guide to weather and climate; How to Understand the Weather and Make It Work for You. Michael Allaby. Timber Press, Inc. 2015 336 p. color illustrations, maps $29.95 **635**

1. Climate 2. Weather 3. Gardening 4. Crops and climate

ISBN 1604695544; 9781604695540

LC 2014040762

This book by Michael Allaby offers "practical advice on adapting your garden to create optimum conditions for plants. You'll learn how weather works, how to predict different conditions, and how to make the best of meteorological highs and lows. And you'll discover fascinating insights into climate change, cloud formation, jet streams, and much more." (Publisher's note)

"Color illustrations enhance the value of this book for the reference shelf; it's probably best read in winter by those seeking the really big picture for their gardens." Pub Wkly

Balick, Michael J.

Rodale's 21st-century herbal; a practical guide for healthy living using nature's most powerful plants. Michael J. Balick ; foreword by Andrew Weil. Rodale 2013 498 p. color illustrations (hardcover) $35　　**635**

1. Herbs -- Therapeutic use 2. Encyclopedias and dictionaries 3. Herbs 4. Herbals 5. Herb gardening 6. Organic gardening
ISBN 1609618041; 9781609618049

LC 2013022312

Written by Michael J. Balick, "'Rodale's 21st-Century Herbal' first explores the historical relationship between people and herbal plants and how it has evolved over time. In the second part, readers will delve into an A-to-Z encyclopedia of 180 of the most useful herbs from around the globe. . . . The final section highlights how herbs create a 'fuller' life and features herbal cooking techniques, ways to use herbs for beauty and the bath, ideas for daily herbal use." (Publisher's note)

Bellamy, Andrea

Small-space vegetable gardens; growing great edibles in containers, raised beds, and small plots. Andrea Bellamy. Timber Press, Inc. 2014 224 p. color illustrations $19.95　　**635**

1. Small farms 2. Vegetable gardening 3. Farms, Small
ISBN 1604695471; 9781604695472

LC 2014009485

This book, by Andrea Bellamy, offers advice on growing vegetable gardens in limited spaces. The author "explains the basics of growing a bounty of edibles in a minimal amount of space . . . [and] shares all the knowledge she's gained from years of gardening small: how to find and assess a space, and how to plan and build a garden." (Publisher's note)

"Recommended for readers interested in gardening on a smaller scale or growing food where lack of physical space is challenging." LJ

Includes bibliographical references and index

Growing great edibles in containers, raised beds, and small plots

Biodynamic gardening; DK Publishing. Dk Publishing 2015 253 p. color illustrations $22.95　　**635**

1. Gardening 2. Organic farming
ISBN 1465429867; 9781465429865

DK Publishing offers this "resource for learning more about the biodynamic method of organic gardening. This clear, practical guide gives you tried-and-true advice on biodynamic gardening and tips on this ultra-green, organic gardening method. Full-color photographs and easy-to-understand charts and graphs are helpful tools in organizing information in a way anyone can understand and use in biodynamic gardening." (Publisher's note)

"For people with an interest in environmentally aware gardening and a willingness to experiment with nontraditional methods." LJ

Bradley, Fern Marshall

Saving vegetable seeds; by Fern Marshall Bradley. Storey Publishing 2014 91 p. illustrations (pbk.; alk. paper) $8.95　　**635**

1. Seeds 2. Vegetable gardening 3. Vegetables -- Seeds 4. Vegetables -- Seeds -- Harvesting
ISBN 1612123635; 9781612123639; 9781612123646

LC 2014011272

"This illustrated, step-by-step guide shows you how to save seeds from 20 of the most popular vegetable garden plants, including beans, carrots, peas, peppers, and tomatoes. You'll learn how each plant is pollinated (key to determining how the seed should be saved), how to select the seeds to collect, and how to process and store collected seeds." (Publisher's note)

"Five stages—plant maintenance for producing top-quality seeds, harvesting, cleaning and drying, packaging and storing, and testing for

viability—are thoroughly explored for each crop, including lettuce, radishes, cucumbers, and more. Wonderfully user-friendly, this will be in demand." Booklist

Buck, Leslie

Cutting back; my apprenticeship in the gardens of Kyoto. Leslie Buck. Timber Press 2017 279 p. (hardcover) $24.95 **635**

1. Pruning 2. Apprentices 3. Kyoto (Japan) 4. Apprentices -- Japan -- Kyoto 5. Pruning -- Study and teaching -- Japan -- Kyoto 6. Gardens, Japanese -- Study and teaching -- Japan -- Kyoto
ISBN 9781604698046; 9781604697933

LC 2016045504

Author Leslie Buck reflects on her "impulsive decision to put her personal life on hold to pursue her passion. Leaving behind a full life of friends, love, and professional security, she became the first American woman to learn pruning from one of the most storied landscaping companies in Kyoto. But she learns the most important lessons from her fellow gardeners: how to balance strength with grace, seriousness with humor, and technique with heart." (Publisher's note)

"This is an absorbing read about the formative interplay of humans, cultures, and gardens." Pub Wkly

Campbell, Stu

How to mulch; save water, feed the soil, and suppress weeds. Stu Campbell and Jennifer Kujawski. Storey Publishing 2015 96 p. (Storey basics) (pbk.; alk. paper) $8.95　　**635**

1. Soils 2. Gardening 3. Mulching
ISBN 1612124445; 9781612124445; 9781612124452

LC 2014029013

This book, by Stu Campbell and Jennifer Kujawski, part of the "Storey basics" series, "shows you exactly how to mulch for any situation, covering sheet mulching, feeding mulches, and living mulches for use in the yard, garden, and home landscape. It even includes a quick-reference chart of mulch types and a section on mulching for success with specific vegetables." (Publisher's note)

"Campbell's sound, experienced advice, supported by excellent illustrations, makes this handbook an indispensable one for both veteran and novice gardeners." Booklist

Chongue, Jason

Plant society; create an indoor oasis for your urban space. Jason Chongue. Chronicle Books Llc 2018 192 p. $22.99 **635**

1. House plants 2. Indoor gardening 3. Container gardening
ISBN 174379343X; 9781743793435

This book, by Jason Chongue, "is your 101 guide on how to love and keep indoor plants. . . . Covering everything from basic plant care and re-potting, to plants suited to pets and propagating, this book will help remove your fear of gardening and inspire you to create you own indoor oasis. It includes profiles of 25 ideal tropical indoor plants, organised from the most low-maintenance species through to the more exotic and labor-intensive plants." (Publisher's note)

"Urban dwellers and stylists with an affinity for indoor gardening will find this useful guide most appealing." Pub Wkly

Coombes, Allen J.

The A to Z of plant names; a quick reference guide to 4000 garden plants. Allen J. Coombes. 1st ed. Timber Press 2012 312 p. $19.95　　**635**

1. Popular plant names 2. Botany -- Nomenclature 3. Botany -- Great Britain -- Dictionaries 4. Botany -- North America -- Dictionaries 5. Plants -- Great Britain -- Nomenclature -- Dictionaries 6. Plants -- North America -- Nomenclature -- Dictionaries

ISBN 1604691964; 9781604691962

LC 2011029271

This guide to plant names "features the botanic names of the plants that gardeners really grow. Additional information includes suggested pronunciation, the common name, the derivation of the scientific name, the number of species currently accepted, the type of plant and the distribution." (Publisher's note)

Includes bibliographical references (p. 311-312).

Cranshaw, Whitney

Garden insects of North America; the ultimate guide to backyard bugs. Whitney Cranshaw and David Shetlar. Princeton University Press 2017 704 p. (pbk.; alk. paper) $35 **635**

1. Insects -- North America -- Identification 2. Arthropoda -- North America -- Identification 3. Agricultural pests -- North America -- Identification 4. Garden pests -- North America -- Identification

ISBN 0691167443; 9780691167442

LC 2017013286

This book, by Whitney Cranshaw and David Shetlar, "covers the hundreds of species of insects and mites associated with fruits and vegetables, shade trees and shrubs, flowers and ornamental plants, and turfgrass . . . and much more. This new edition also provides a greatly expanded treatment of common pollinators and flower visitors, the natural enemies of garden pests, and the earthworms, insects, and other arthropods that help with decomposing plant matter in the garden." (Publisher's note)

Includes bibliographical references and index

Culp, David L.

The **layered** garden design lessons for year-round beauty from Brandywine Cottage; design lessons for year-round beauty from Brandywine Cottage. David L. Culp ; with Adam Levine ; photographs by Rob Cardillo. Timber Press 2012 312 p. illustrations $34.95 **635**

1. Gardens 2. Gardening 3. Garden design 4. Gardens -- Pennsylvania -- Design 5. Gardening -- Pennsylvania -- Anecdotes

ISBN 1604692367; 9781604692365

LC 2012007640

This gardening guidebook, by David L. Culp, "starts with a basic lesson in layering -- how to choose the correct plants by understanding how they grow and change throughout the seasons, how to design a layered garden, and how to maintain it. To illustrate how layering works, Culp takes you on a personal tour through each part of his celebrated garden: the woodland garden, the perennial border, the kitchen garden, the shrubbery, and the walled garden." (Publisher's note)

"In the tradition of classics like Beverly Nichols's Merry Hall, this is a marvelous account of how one gardener created his garden and a sense of place. It's an essential title in the 'how I did it' genre of garden writing." LJ

Includes bibliographical references and index

Damrosch, Barbara

The **garden** primer; illustrations by Linda Heppes Funk, Ray Maher, and Carol Bolt. 2nd ed.; Workman Pub. 2008 820p il map $28.95; pa $18.95 **635**

1. Gardening

ISBN 978-0-7611-4856-2; 978-0-7611-2275-3 pa

LC 2007-51425

First published 1988

This is a "book for the new gardener that clearly explains the basics of garden planning, plant care, and equipment. Detailed chapters on the different categories of plants—annuals, perennials, vegetables, fruits, lawns, shrubs, roses, vines, trees, wildflowers, and even house plants—give general advice on how to use and care for these varieties. A valuable book for public libraries." Libr J

Includes bibligoraphical references

Deardorff, David C.

What's wrong with my plant (and how do I fix it?) a visual guide to easy diagnosis and organic remedies. [by] David Deardorff and Kathryn Wadsworth. Timber Press 2009 451p il pa $24.95 **635**

1. Plant diseases 2. Ornamental plants 3. Natural pesticides

ISBN 978-0-88192-961-4; 0-88192-961-1

LC 2009-19447

"The book allows readers to select a suitable starting point that describes a plant's symptom—for example, wilting leaves or holes in the stems—and answer simple questions that eventually lead to a solution to the problem. . . . The book is divided into three parts. The first features clear keys that help identify the cause. . . . Once the problem is identified, the reader just goes to the suggested page in the second section, which contains a hierarchy of remedies. The third section, also referenced by individual page numbers in the previous two, contains excellent pictures of symptoms to help confirm the diagnosis of the problem and offer remedies. . . . [This book] is an important reference that will help gardeners successfully diagnose their own plant problems and make educated decisions about how to solve them." Am Gardener

Includes bibliographical references

What's wrong with my vegetable garden? 100% organic solutions for all your vegetables, from artichokes to zucchini. David Deardorff and Kathryn Wadsworth. Timber Press 2012 p. cm. color illustrations (pbk.) $24.95 **635**

1. Organic gardening 2. Vegetable gardening 3. Vegetables -- Diseases and pests -- Control

ISBN 9781604691849; 9781604692839; 1604691840

LC 2011018443

This book on gardening, by David Deardorff and Kathryn Wadsworth, "teaches you how to keep your vegetables healthy so they're less susceptible to attack, and when problems do occur, it shows you how to recognize the problem and find the right organic solution. Among the book's highlights are . . . detailed portraits of the most commonly grown vegetables, . . . illustrated problem-solving guides, . . . [and] discussions of the most effective organic solutions." (Publisher's note)

"With this attractive book, organic gardeners will find it easy to grow vegetables and diagnose and organically treat common problems. Recommended." LJ

Includes bibliographical references and index

Elliott, Shaye

Welcome to the farm; how-to wisdom from the Elliott homestead. Shaye Elliott. Lyons Press 2017 xx, 313 p.p color illustrations (pbk.) $21.95 **635**

1. Gardening 2. Urban agriculture 3. Agriculture -- Popular works 4. Country life -- Popular works

ISBN 9781493026012; 9781493030422

LC 2016057686

This book, by Shaye Elliott, provides a "guide to growing the very best food right in your own backyard. . . . [The author] takes readers on a journey that teaches them how to harvest baskets full of organic produce, milk a dairy cow . . ., plant a homestead orchard, can jams and jellies, ... [and explores] the beginning stages of small-area farming and utilizing whatever amount of space they have available for optimal and delicious food production." (Publisher's note)

"The book is filled with useful tips on how to save seeds, how to make herbal teas, and how to decide if dairy farming is the right choice for you." Pub Wkly

The **gardener's** year. Dorling Kindersley 2015 317 p. color illustrations $24.95   **635**
1. Gardening 2. Horticulture 3. Gardens
ISBN 1465424571; 9781465424570

LC 2015430167

This book from publisher DK features "gardening tips for a wide variety of garden projects, covering flowers and plants, fruits, vegetables and herbs, and trees and shrubs. Its vibrant galleries of what and when to plant, photo sequences of key techniques, and season-by-season approach make it accessible for even the most inexperienced of gardeners." (Publisher's note)

"This is a great book for daydreaming over. Experienced gardeners may take away a few new ideas." Library Journal

Gardiner, Mary M.

Good garden bugs; everything you need to know about beneficial predatory insects. Mary M. Gardiner, Ph.D. Quarry Books 2015 176 p. color illustrations $24.99   **635**
1. Agricultural pests 2. Beneficial insects 3. Predatory insects 4. Garden pests -- Biological control
ISBN 1592539092; 9781592539093

LC 2014049089

This book, by Mary M. Gardiner, "is an easy-to-follow reference to beneficial insects that provide pest control, allowing your garden to grow full and bountiful. Aphids, caterpillars, grubs, and slugs are not only creepy-crawlies; They can wreak havoc on your garden and plants. But fear not! You don't need dangerous chemicals to enjoy a lively, healthy garden. The secret? More lady beetles, fewer aphids! Wildlife in your garden--especially insects--can be natural pesticide alternatives." (Publisher's note)

Includes bibliographical references and index

Grow All You Can Eat in Three Square Feet; by DK Publishing. DK Pub 2015 256 p. color illustrations $22.95   **635**
1. Gardening
ISBN 1465429808; 9781465429803

This book, for "small-space gardeners," is "packed with information on window boxes, potted plants, patio gardening, raised beds, small square-foot gardening, container gardening, and everything else related to growing your own small garden." (Publisher's note)

"While the title may be overly optimistic, this book is useful for beginning and experienced gardeners alike because of the multiple projects and sample gardens that are provided. However, Andrea Bellamy's Small-Space Vegetable Gardens offers expanded contextual material and provides specific growing instructions for additional edible plants." LJ

Harrison, Lorraine

Heirloom Plants; A Complete Compendium of Heritage Vegetables, Fruits, Herbs & Flowers. by Lorraine Harrison and Thomas Etty. Chicago Review Press 2016 224 p. illustrations (some color) $29.99   **635**
1. Gardening
ISBN 1613735758; 9781613735756

This book, by Lorraine Harrison and Thomas Etty, "includes information on almost 500 exciting cultivars to be grown and harvested, along with detailed profiles and cultivation tips for each plant. In addition to edibles, the book also has chapters on antique herbs and flowers,

from Cup and Saucer vines to Sweet William carnations to Empress of India nasturtiums." (Publisher's note)

"This encyclopedic delineation of 'directories' of vegetable, fruit, herbs, and flowers offers practical help to the gardener who's interested in preserving heirloom cultivars and turning a green-thumb hobby into an all-out mission." Pub Wkly

Includes bibliographic references (pages 218-219) and index.

Hurwitz, Jane

Butterfly gardening; the North American butterfly association guide. Jane Hurwitz. Princeton University Press 2018 288 p. (pbk.) $29.95   **635**
1. Gardening 2. Butterflies
ISBN 9780691170343

LC 2017958516

This book, by Jane Hurwitz, serves as a "guide to creating a garden that attracts and sustains butterflies. . . . [It covers] all the practical details needed to create a vibrant garden habitat that fosters butterflies. It tells you which plants support which butterflies, depending on where you live; it describes what different butterflies require in the garden over the course of their lives; and it shows you how to become a butterfly watcher as well as a butterfly gardener." (Publisher's note)

Jabbour, Niki

Groundbreaking food gardens; 73 plans that will change the way you grow your garden. by Niki Jabbour. Storey Pub. 2014 272 p. col. ill. (pbk.; alk. paper) $19.95   **635**
1. Fruit 2. Vegetables 3. Edible plants 4. Vegetable gardening 5. Food crops 6. Edible landscaping
ISBN 161212061X; 9781603428446; 9781612120614

LC 2013030517

In this book, author Niki Jabbour "has collected 73 plans for novel and inspiring food gardens from her favorite superstar gardeners, including Amy Stewart, Amanda Thomsen, Barbara Pleasant, Dave DeWitt, and Jessi Bloom. You'll find a garden that provides salad greens 52 weeks a year, another that supplies your favorite cocktail ingredients, one that you plant on a balcony, one that encourages pollinators, one that grows 24 kinds of chile peppers, and dozens more." (Publisher's note)

"Every plan is accompanied by full-color illustrations, growing tips, and tweakable lists of crop possibilities. The abundance of creative advice here will help perk up the gardens of both novice and professional growers." Booklist

Seventy-three plans that will change the way you grow your garden

Niki Jabbour's veggie garden remix; 224 new plants to shake up your garden and add variety, flavor, and fun. Niki Jabbour. Storey Publishing 2018 232 p. illustrations (pbk.; alk. paper) $19.95   **635**
1. Vegetables 2. Vegetable gardening
ISBN 9781612126715; 9781612126708

LC 2017034219

In this book, author Niki Jabbour, "invites you to shake up your vegetable garden with an intriguing array of 224 plants from around the world. . . . Jabbour encourages you to start with what you know and expand your repertoire to try related plants, many of which are delicacies in other cultures. Jabbour presents detailed growing information for each plant, along with fun facts and plant history." (Publisher's note)

"Loaded with lush photos throughout, this attractive book will appeal to gardeners and gourmands alike." Pub Wkly

Joffe, Daron

Citizen farmers; the biodynamic way to grow healthy food, build thriving communities, and give back to the Earth. by Daron "Farmer D" Joffe ; with Susan Puckett ; photography by Rinne Allen. Stewart, Tabori & Chang, an imprint of Abrams 2014 224 p. color illustrations $24.95 **635**

   1. Gardening 2. Organic gardening 3. Sustainable agriculture 4. Sustainable living 5. Biodynamic agriculture
   ISBN 1617691011; 9781617691010

LC 2013945633

IACP Cookbook Award Winner: Food Matters (2015)

   In this book, Daron "Farmer D" Joffe "teaches us to not only create sustainable gardens but also to develop a more holistic, community-minded approach to how our food is grown and how we live our lives in balance with nature. . . . [T]he book is . . . packed with advice on establishing a biodynamic garden, composting, soil composition and replenishment, controlling pests and disease, cooperative gardening practices, and even creating delicious meals." (Publisher's note)

   Includes bibliographical references (pages 218-219) and index

Joy, LaManda

   Start a community food garden; the essential handbook. LaManda Joy. Timber Press, Inc. 2014 224 p. illustrations $24.95 **635**

   1. Community gardens 2. Food crops 3. Vegetables
   ISBN 160469484X; 9781604694840

LC 2014020842

   This book, by LaManda Joy, offers a guide to community gardening and "covers every step of the process: fundraising, community organizing, site sourcing, garden design and planning, finding and managing volunteers, and managing the garden through all four seasons. A section dedicated to the basics of growing was designed to be used by community garden leaders as an educational tool for teaching new members how to successfully garden." (Publisher's note)

   "A valuable reference for building a strong foundation for anyone new to organizing or community gardening." LJ

Karsten, Joel

   Straw bale gardens complete; Joel Karsten. Cool Springs Press 2015 176 p. color illustrations (sc) $24.99 **635**

   1. Gardens 2. Garden design
   ISBN 1591869072; 9781591869078

LC 2014955422

   This book by Joel Kartsen "contains all of the original information that has set the gardening world on fire. But it also goes much deeper, with nearly 50 pages of all-new advice and photos on subjects such as growing in a tight urban setting, making your straw bale garden completely organic, and using new fertilizers and conditioning products. There is even information on using straw bale techniques to grow veggies in other organic media for anyone who has a hard time finding straw." (Publisher's note)

Leendertz, Lia

   My Tiny Veg Plot; Grow Your Own in Surprisingly Small Places. Lia Leendertz. Trafalgar Square 2017 160 p. $24.95; (ebook) $14.57 **635**

   1. Urban gardening 2. Container gardening 3. Vegetable gardening
   ISBN 1910496057; 9781910496053; 9781910904015

LC 2017006261

   This book on growing your own vegetables, by Lia Leendertz, "offers solutions and inspirations for . . . tricky spots that we frequently overlook, and highlights some unusual growing spaces such as a minuscule balcony in England, an innovative installation of hexagonal polytunnels full of salad leaves in Amiens, France, and an ingenious self-sufficient growing system that provides a wealth of vegetables in an old swimming pool in Phoenix, Arizona." (Publisher's note)

   "Leendertz's suggestions are delectable—and doable." Pub Wkly

LeHoullier, Craig

   Epic tomatoes; How to Select and Grow the Best Varieties of All Time. by Craig LeHoullier. Storey Publishing 2015 255 p. color illustrations (hbk.; alk. paper) $29.95 **635**

   1. Tomatoes
   ISBN 161212464X; 9781612122083; 9781612124643

LC 2014029010

   In this book, author Craig LeHoullier "offers everything a tomato enthusiast needs to know about growing more than 200 varieties of tomatoes — from sowing seeds and planting to cultivating and collecting seeds at the end of the season. He also offers a comprehensive guide to the various pests and diseases of tomatoes and explains how best to avoid them." (Publisher's note)

   "The many charming illustrations and color photos include images of vintage seed packets and ads, and the appendix offers lists of resources and sources, all immensely useful for growers of America's most popular home crop." Booklist

   Includes bibliographical references and index

Markham, Brett L.

   Mini farming; self sufficiency on a 1/4 acre. rev. and expanded; Skyhorse Pub. 2010 227p il pa $16.95 **635**

   1. Farms 2. Agriculture 3. Self-reliance
   ISBN 978-1-60239-984-6

LC 2009041561

   "An excellent guide for gardeners wanting to eliminate most of their grocery bills. Markham's approach combines his own experience with the best practices from several raised-bed methods. Advice includes how to select vegetables that are calorie-dense and budget friendly, how to raise poultry, how to build both a plucker and a thresher, and how to preserve food." Libr J

   Includes bibliographical references

McCrate, Colin

   High-yield vegetable gardening; grow more of what you want in the space you have. by Colin McCrate and Brad Halm. Workman Pub Co. 2015 319 p. illustrations $18.95 **635**

   1. Vegetable gardening
   ISBN 1612123961; 9781612123967

   In this book, authors Colin McCrate and Brad Halm "show how you can make your food garden much more productive, no matter how big or small it is. You'll learn their secrets for preparing the soil, selecting and rotating your crops, and mapping out a specific customized plan to make the most of your space and your growing season." (Publisher's note)

   "With worksheets, charts, and tables galore, the volume also includes an extensive collection of links for people who prefer to do their record keeping, an essential tool of the high-yield garden arsenal, on a computer. Appendixes and a list of suppliers round out this rich, thoughtful resource." LJ

   Includes bibliographical references (pages 307-308) and index.

Pleasant, Barbara

   Homegrown pantry; a gardener's guide to selecting the best varieties & planting the perfect amounts for what you want to eat year round. by Barbara Pleasant. Storey Publishing 2017 319 p. color illustrations (pbk.; alk. paper) $22.95 **635**

   1. Food -- Preservation 2. Vegetables -- Preservation 3. Fruit 4. Herbs 5. Food crops 6. Vegetables

ISBN 9781612125787; 9781612125794

LC 2016055527

This book, by Barbara Pleasant "picks up where beginning gardening books leave off, with in-depth profiles of the 55 most popular crops--including beans, beets, squash, tomatoes, and much more--to keep your pantry stocked throughout the year. Each vegetable profile highlights how many plants to grow for a year's worth of eating, and which storage methods work best for specific varieties." (Publisher's note)

"Pleasant delivers a guidebook of soul-saving coherence, practicality, thoroughness, and deeply seated wisdom, and reconnects our imagination to our soil to our labor to our mouths." Booklist

Starter vegetable gardens. Storey Pub. 2010 179p il pa $19.95   **635**

1. Vegetable gardening
ISBN 978-1-60342-529-2

LC 2009-49114

"From simple bag gardens to bountiful food cornucopias, each garden plan is . . . laid out with precise lists of materials and plants based on detailed landscape plans suitable for small city gardens as well as larger suburban backyards. Along with year-by-year overviews that allow gardeners to anticipate growth and adapt to changes, Pleasant provides essential cultivation and maintenance techniques." Booklist

★ **Rodale's** ultimate encyclopedia of organic gardening; the indispensable green resource for every gardener. edited by Fern Marshall Bradley, Barbara W. Ellis, and Ellen Phillips, with Deborah L. Martin. newly revised and updated Rodale Press 2018 706 p $27.99   **635**

1. Organic gardening
ISBN 9781635650983

"Rodale's Ultimate Encyclopedia of Organic Gardening has been the go-to resource for gardeners for more than 50 years, and the best tool novices can buy to start applying organic methods to their fruit and vegetable crops, herbs, trees and shrubs, perennials, annuals, and lawns. This thoroughly revised and updated version highlights new organic pest controls, new fertilizer products, improved gardening techniques, the latest organic soil practices, and new trends in garden design." (Publisher's note)

Russell, Stephen

The **essential** guide to cultivating mushrooms; by Stephen Russell. Storey Publishing 2014 232 p. color illustrations (pbk.; alk. paper) $24.95   **635**

1. Mushrooms 2. Edible plants 3. Edible mushrooms
ISBN 1612121462; 9781612121468; 9781612124636

LC 2014015198

This book, by Stephen Russell, "shows you how to cultivate mushrooms in your own home, producing shiitakes, oysters, lion's manes, maitakes, and portabellas for your kitchen or for a small business. Beginners will learn the best way to use a mushroom kit, as well as how to maintain the sterile procedures and controlled environment that cultivation requires." (Publisher's note)

"Thorough and clearly written with helpful photos on nearly every page, this guide is a must for anyone who wants to move beyond premade growing kits. With Russell's emphasis on building basic skills, advice for avoiding common mistakes, and sections on troubleshooting, the book will be a valuable resource for those interested in growing a variety of gourmet mushrooms." LJ

Schwartz, Bobbie

Garden renovation; transform your yard into the garden of your dreams. Bobbie Schwartz. Timber Press 2017 259 p. illustrations (chiefly color) (pbk.) $24.95   **635**

1. Gardening 2. Garden design 3. Gardens -- Design
ISBN 9781604698329; 1604696125; 9781604696127

LC 2016055618

This book, by Bobbie Schwartz, "will help you turn a problem-filled yard into a paradise. . . . Schwartz draws on her years of experience as a garden designer to teach gardeners how to evaluate their yards, determine what to keep and what to remove, choose the right plants and design plans for successful remodels, and know when to hire help. A gallery of before-and-after photos provides ideas and inspiration for turning a tired garden into an enlivening retreat." (Publisher's note)

Includes bibliographical references and index

Slatalla, Michelle

Gardenista; The Definitive Guide to Stylish Outdoor Spaces. by Michelle Slatalla. Artisan 2016 408 p. color illustrations (hardback, paper over board) $40; (ebook) $40   **635**

1. Garden design 2. Outdoor living spaces 3. Gardens -- Design
ISBN 9781579656522; 9781579657352

LC 2016012874

This book by Michelle Slatalla "contains lushly photographed tours of 12 enviable gardens; planting guides for a variety of climates and color palettes; in-depth case studies on more than a dozen outdoor structures (from yoga studios to chicken coops); do-it-yourself projects; easy-to-implement design ideas; 'The Gardenista 100,' a guide to timeless everyday objects for the outdoors; plus advice from landscape professionals." (Publisher's note)

"The end result is a display of outdoor living space that integrates plants, color, balance, design, and also functionality." Pub Wkly

Smith, Edward C.

★ The **vegetable** gardener's bible; discover Ed's high-yield W-O-R-D system for all North American gardening regions. 2nd ed., [Fully updated 10th anniversary ed.]; Storey Pub. 2009 351p il map $34.95; pa $24.95   **635**

1. Organic gardening 2. Vegetable gardening
ISBN 978-1-60342-476-9; 978-1-60342-475-2 pa

LC 2009-23862

First published 2000

The author "explains everything novice and experienced gardeners need to know to grow vegetables and herbs using his system of wide, deep, raised beds. He gives detailed instructions on siting, preparing, and planning a vegetable garden, then goes on to cover choosing plant varieties, starting seed, and growing plants. Smith discusses compost creation, companion planting, crop rotation, succession planting, and ecologically friendly methods of dealing with plant diseases and pests." Libr J

Includes bibliographical references

Speichert, C. Greg

Encyclopedia of water garden plants; [by] Greg Speichert & Sue Speichert; foreword by Ann Lovejoy. Timber Press 2004 386p il $49.95   **635**

1. Freshwater plants 2. Landscape gardening
ISBN 0-88192-625-6

LC 2003-16619

"The authors devote separate chapters to hardy waterlilies, tropicals, lotus, marginal plants, irises, waterlily-like plants (such as water snowflakes), floaters, and submerged plants. . . . This is the most comprehensive guide to all types of water plants and would make an excellent addition to gardening collections." Libr J

Step-by-step projects for self-sufficiency; grow edibles, raise animals, live off the grid, do it yourself. Cool Spring Press. Cool Springs Press 2017 352 p. color illustrations (hc) $30 **635**
1. Sustainable agriculture 2. Agriculture -- Handbooks, manuals, etc 3. Self-reliant living -- Handbooks, manuals, etc
ISBN 9780760357552; 9781591866886
LC 2016045690

In this book, by the editors of Cool Spring Press, "step-by-step instructions and photos will guide you through how to make over 60 complete projects. After all, DIY projects are more fun (and generally easier) when you approach them with helpful aides and tools you made yourself." (Publisher's note)

"For those interested in a self-sufficient lifestyle, this collection has something for everyone." LJ

Stross, Amy
The **suburban** micro-farm; modern solutions for busy people. Amy Stross. Chelsea Green Pub Co. 2018 356 p. $34.95 **635**
1. Small farms 2. Organic gardening -- United States 3. Vegetable gardening -- United States
ISBN 0997520833; 9780997520835

In this book, "author Amy Stross talks straight about why the suburbs might be the ideal place for a small farm. . . . [The book] will show you how to grow your own fruits, herbs, and vegetables even on a limited schedule. From seed to harvest, this book will keep you on track so you feel a sense of accomplishment for your efforts." (Publisher's note)

Swift, Vivian
Gardens of awe and folly; a traveler's journal of the meaning of life and gardening. Vivian Swift. St. Martins Press 2016 176 p. color illustrations (alk. paper) $28 **635**
1. Gardens 2. Voyages and travels
ISBN 9781632860279; 1632860279
LC 2015019652

This book, by Vivian Swift, offers "a charming stroll through some public gardens. Swift . . . plainly loves the experience of gardens: the plentitude and solitude they offer, the colors and the scents, the tea rooms that provide the opportunity to relax and reflect. She . . . proves an engaging guide to gardens in locales ranging from Key West and post-Katrina New Orleans to Paris . . . and Marrakech." (Kirkus Reviews)

"A breezy, whimsical book that does its best to approximate the renewal one might feel upon visiting a garden." Kirkus

Wulf, Andrea
The **brother** gardeners; botany, empire and the birth of an obsession. Andrea Wulf. Vintage 2010 368 p. il map $17.95 **635**
1. Gardens 2. Horticulture 3. Horticulturists 4. Plant collectors 5. Gardening -- Great Britain -- History
ISBN 0307454754; 9780307454751
LC 200855080

Author Andrea Wulf "conveys the allure and cultural importance of the garden. Spanning nearly 100 years and several continents, Wulf begins her cultural investigation with the creation of the first manmade hybrid by devout Christian gardener Thomas Fairchild. She also introduces egomaniacal Swedish botanist Carl Linnaeus, who scandalized British society with his sexual system of classification. There is New World farmer John Bartram, who braved storms and steep mountains to discover new plants." (Publishers Weekly)

"As Wulf fills her readily accessible book with adventures aboard Captain Cook's ship, petty rivalries and outsized personalities, she provides an entertaining account of kooky botanists traveling the world and explores how gardening neutralized class lines, how horticulture and botany brought wealth and power, and how the English garden had a profound impact on modern landscape gardening, elevating the humble pursuit into the highest art." Pub Wkly

Yglesias, Caren
Desert gardens of Steve Martino; Caren Yglesias; photographs by Steve Gunther. Monacelli Press 2018 240 p. col. ill. (alk. paper) $50 **635**
1. Gardening 2. Landscape architecture
ISBN 9781580934916
LC 2017962354

This book, by Steve Martine, presents a "survey of twenty-one gardens . . . [that] is sure to inspire gardeners, landscapers, and admirers of California and the Southwest. For more than thirty years, Martino has been committed to the development and advancement of landscape architecture in the Southwest. . . . A recurring theme of his work is the dramatic juxtaposition of man-made elements with ecological processes of the region." (Publisher's note)

"A beautifully made book that will appeal to gardeners and designers interested in the Southwest." LJ

Ziegler, Lisa Mason
Vegetables love flowers; companion planting for beauty and bounty. Lisa Mason Ziegler. Cool Springs Press 2018 176 p. (sc) $21.99 **635**
1. Flowers 2. Gardening 3. Vegetables 4. Companion planting
ISBN 9780760357583
LC 2017043293

This book, by Lisa Mason Ziegler, "walks you through the ins and outs of companion planting, from how it works to which plants go together and how to grow the best garden for your climate. Alongside gorgeous garden photography, you'll also learn about: Seed-starting, growing, and harvesting, [h]ow to make garden flower bouquets, with 'recipes' for various arrangements, [and h]ow to attract beneficial creatures to pollinate your garden and prey on its pest." (Publisher's note)

"Ziegler's business specializes in cut flowers, and she recommends combinations and tips for this use as well. General garden care is also addressed, including soil amendments, organic fertilizers and pest control, garden design, irrigation, and more. An appendix illustrates a variety of bed designs." Booklist

635.022 Gardening – Photographs

Woods, Christopher
Gardenlust; a botanical tour of the world's best new gardens. Christopher Woods. Timber Press 2018 416 p. (hardcover) $40 **635.022**
1. Gardens 2. Garden design 3. Landscape gardening 4. Gardens -- Pictorial works
ISBN 9781604697971
LC 2018019654

In this book, "intrepid plant expert Christopher Woods spotlights 50 modern gardens that push boundaries and define natural beauty in significant ways. Featuring both private and public gardens, this journey makes its way from the Americas and Europe to Australia and New Zealand, with stops in Asia, Africa, and the Arabian Peninsula. . . . "As inspiring as it is insightful, Gardenlust will delight your passion for garden inspiration--and the many places it grows." (Publisher's note)

" A recommended purchase for public libraries that have patrons interested in gardening as well as those who combine gardening and travel." Booklist

Includes bibliographical references and index

635.09　Gardening – History

McDowell, Marta

All the presidents' gardens; Madison's cabbages to Kennedy's roses; how the White House grounds have grown with America. Marta McDowell. Timber Press, Inc. 2016 328 p. illustrations (chiefly color), $29.95　　**635.09**
1. Gardens 2. White House (Washington, D.C.) 3. Gardens -- Washington (D.C.) -- History 4. Horticulture -- Washington (D.C.) -- History 5. White House Gardens (Washington, D.C.) -- History
ISBN 1604695897; 9781604695892

LC 2015029811

This book, by Marta McDowell, "tells the untold history of the White House Grounds, starting with the seed-collecting, plant-obsessed George Washington and ending with Michelle Obama's kitchen garden. Filled with fascinating details about Lincoln's goats, Ike's putting green, Jackie's iconic roses, Amy Carter's tree house, and information on the plants whose favor has come and gone over the years." (Publisher's note)

"Photographs, line drawings, paintings, maps, and other documents add to the interesting stories. Short biographies of the 14 head gardeners, a lengthy chart of the plants in the gardens, and two bibliographies add to this delightful and elucidating work." Booklist

Includes bibliographical references and index

635.097　Gardening – North America

Bonine, Paul

Gardening in the Pacific Northwest; the complete homeowner's guide. Paul Bonine and Amy Campion. Timber Press 2017 320 p. (pbk.) $24.95　　**635.097**
1. Gardening 2. Garden design 3. Landscape gardening
ISBN 9781604693331

LC 2017949320

This book, "by regional gardening experts Paul Bonine and Amy Campion, is comprehensive, enthusiastic, and accessible to gardeners of all levels. It features information on site and plant selection, soil preparation and maintenance, and basic design principles. Plant profiles highlight the region's best perennials, shrubs, trees, and vines. Color photographs throughout show wonderful examples of Northwest garden style." (Publisher's note)

"It's an almost entirely new book, now officially encompassing not only the traditional coastal Pacific Northwest but also the arid zone from the Cascades east to Idaho, a move that is certain to broaden this book's appeal." Booklist

635.65　Garden legumes

Malone, Hilary

The **Power** of Pulses; Saving the World With Peas, Beans, Chickpeas, Favas & Lentils. by Dan Jason, Hilary Malone, and Alison Malone Eathorne. Douglas & McIntyre 2016 240 p. $24.95　　**635.65**
1. Vegetable gardening 2. Cooking -- Vegetables

ISBN 1771621028; 9781771621021

LC 2016026118

This book, by Dan Jason, Hilary Malone, and Alison Malone Eathorne, "provides tips on how North American home gardeners can grow and save their own delicious, vividly hued heirloom beans, peas, chickpeas, lentils and favas. As well as being incredibly versatile in the kitchen, pulses are also rich in fiber, high in vitamin B, gluten-free and remarkably low on the glycemic index—contributing to good health." (Publisher's note)

"This is a perfect book for gardeners, vegetarians, and others looking to expand beyond their tried-and-true pulses." Booklist

635.7　Aromatic and sweet herbs

Hildebrand, Caz

Herbarium; Caz Hildebrand. Thames & Hudson 2016 224 p. (hardcover) $29.95　　**635.7**
1. Herbs 2. Cooking -- Herbs
ISBN 9780500518939

LC 2016931264

This book, by Caz Hildebrand, "explores the histories, associations, and uses of 100 herbs, as well as providing ideas for how each herb can be used to improve both food and well-being. Each entry features a specially commissioned illustration with texts that include the botanical name, place of origin, varieties, and areas where the herb is most commonly grown." (Publisher's note)

"The point of the book is that the earth is filled with these horticultural gifts, which are plentiful, useful, beneficial, beautiful, and, most importantly, right there in front of you." Pub Wkly

635.9　Flowers and ornamental plants

American Horticultural Society encyclopedia of plants & flowers; editor-in-chief, Christopher Brickell. Rev ed DK Publishing 2011 744 p. col. ill., maps $60　　**635.9**
1. Horticulture 2. Ornamental plants 3. Plants -- Encyclopedias
ISBN 0756668573; 9780756668570

LC 2011290703

First published 1989 in the United Kingdom with title: The Royal Horticultural Society gardeners' encyclopedia of plants and flowers

"Packed with 8,000 plants for every climate . . . from trees, shrubs, perennials, annuals, biennials, bulbs, water plants, and cacti, the 'AHS Encyclopedia of Plants & Flowers' is a . . . reference for . . . gardeners. This fully revised and updated edition features a brighter, clearer design and improved navigation--cataloging plants by color, season, and size--that makes the book more intuitive for the reader." (Publisher's note)

Armitage, Allan M.

Armitage's garden perennials; 2nd ed., fully rev. and updated; Timber Press 2011 347p il $49.95　　**635.9**
1. Reference books 2. Perennials -- Encyclopedias
ISBN 978-1-60469-038-5

LC 2011293867

First published 2000

This is an "illustrated compilation of 136 genera of garden-worthy perennials. Alphabetical entries feature illuminating descriptions of plant habits and forms, along with essential cultural advice. Armitage recommends countless varieties that can be depended on to perform well or are particularly lovely specimens. Appropriate U.S.D.A. zones and regions where the plants will thrive are noted, too. With its accessible writing style, abundant color photographs, and final section listing plants suggested for specific conditions or purposes, Armitage's latest work should be considered an essential addition to gardening collections." Booklist

Armitage's native plants for North American gardens. Timber Press 2006 451p il $49.95   635.9
   1. Ornamental plants
   ISBN 0-88192-760-0; 978-0-88192-760-3
                    LC 2005-22495
This book provides "information on more than 630 native species and cultivars of perennials, biennials, and annuals that are readily available to mainstream gardeners. . . . With more than 400 color photos, this is an essential reference book for nursery people and horticulturalists, home gardeners, and all libraries." Libr J
   Includes bibliographical references

Armitage's vines and climbers. Timber Press 2010 212p il $29.95   635.9
   1. Climbing plants 2. Ornamental plants
   ISBN 978-1-60469-039-2
                    LC 2009-32437
This book is "written with authority, in simple language, with humor. Anyone trying to build a gardening library should think about adding this one." Philadelphia Inquirer
   Includes bibliographical references

Bainbridge, David A.
Gardening with less water; low-tech, low-cost techniques for using up to 90% less water in your garden. by David A. Bainbridge. Storey Publishing 2015 128 p. color illustrations (pbk.; alk. paper) $14.95   635.9
   1. Xeriscaping
   ISBN 9781612125824; 9781612125831
                    LC 2015036487
This book "offers simple, inexpensive, low-tech techniques for watering your garden much more efficiently -- using up to 90% less water for the same results. With illustrated step-by-step instructions, [author] David Bainbridge shows you how to install buried clay pots and pipes, wicking systems, and other porous containers that deliver water directly to a plant's roots with no or minimal evaporation." (Publisher's note)
   "Beyond soaker hoses, the title offers a varied range of scalable options for growers of all types committed to the exploration and use of optimal water-sparing techniques." LJ

Baldwin, Debra Lee
Succulents simplified; growing, designing, and crafting with 100 easy-care varieties. Debra Lee Baldwin. Timber Press 2013 272 p. color illustrations $24.95   635.9
   1. Succulent plants 2. Succulent plants -- Varieties
   ISBN 1604693932; 9781604693935
                    LC 2012038829
This book, by Debra Lee Baldwin, "is a complete primer on choosing, growing and designing with succulents. Along with gorgeous photos packed with design ideas, Debra offers her top 100 plant picks and explains how to grow and care for succulents no matter where you live. Step-by-step projects, including a cake-stand centerpiece, special-occasion bouquets, a vertical garden, and a succulent topiary sphere, will inspire you to express your individual style." (Publisher's note)
   "This fresh and entertaining volume certainly deserves a green thumbs up." LJ
   Includes bibliographical references and index

Bender, Richard W.
Bountiful bonsai; create instant indoor container gardens with edible fruits, herbs and flowers. Richard Bender. Tuttle Pub. 2015 128 p. (pbk.) $14.95   635.9
   1. Bonsai 2. Indoor gardening
   ISBN 480531270X; 9784805312704
                    LC 2013040431
This book, by Richard Bender, "presents a radical new approach that applies bonsai techniques to everyday container gardening, instantly turning houseplants and herbs into beautiful and unusual bonsai sculptures!" (Publisher's note)

Benzakein, Erin
Floret Farm's cut flower garden; grow, harvest & arrange stunning seasonal blooms. by Erin Benzakein with Julie Chai ; photographs by Michèle M. Waite. Chronicle Books Llc 2017 308 p. color illustrations (hardcover; alk. paper) $29.95 635.9
   1. Flower arrangement 2. Cut flowers
   ISBN 9781452145761; 9781452150932
                    LC 2016011482
This book, by Erin Benzakein with Julie Chai, "is equal parts instruction and inspiration—a book overflowing with lush photography of magnificent flowers and breathtaking arrangements organized by season. This beautiful guide to growing, harvesting, and arranging gorgeous blooms year-round gives readers vital tools to nurture a stunning flower garden and use their blossoms to create showstopping arrangements." (Publisher's note)

Branhagen, Alan
Native plants of the Midwest; a comprehensive guide to the best 500 species for the garden. Alan Branhagen. Timber Press 2016 440 p. (hardcover) $39.95; (ebook) $39.95   635.9
   1. Middle West 2. Native plants 3. Endemic plants -- Middle West 4. Native plants for cultivation -- Middle West
   ISBN 9781604695939; 9781604697773
                    LC 2016009571
This book, by Alan Branhagen, "features the best native plants in the heartland and offers clear and concise guidance on how to use them in the garden. Plant profiles for more than 500 species of trees, shrubs, vines, perennials, ground covers, bulbs, and annuals contain the common and botanical names, growing information, tips on using the plant in a landscape, and advice on related plants." (Publisher's note)
   "As more people are incorporating more natives in their landscapes for their own pleasure, pollinators, and birds, this book will be used by novice and experienced gardeners alike." Booklist
   Includes bibliographical references and index

Brown, George E.
Essential pruning techniques; trees, shrubs, and conifers. by George E. Brown ; revised and enlarged by Tony Kirkham ; with photography from Andrea Jones and a new foreword by Hugh Johnson. [Third edition] Timber Press 2017 404 p. color illustrations (hardcover) $49.95   635.9
   1. Pruning 2. Trees -- Pruning 3. Shrubs -- Pruning 4. Conifers -- Pruning
   ISBN 9781604692884
                    LC 2016017684
In this book on pruning "Tony Kirkham—the head of the arboretum and gardens at the Royal Botanic Gardens, Kew—shares his decades of knowledge and expertise and expands on the groundbreaking work done by George E. Brown. Step-by-step photographs clearly show the general principles of pruning, and profiles of 379 woody plants include advice

on habit, attributes, reasons for pruning, and the best time to prune." (Publisher's note)

Includes bibliographical references (page 385) and index.

Calvo, Janit

The **gardening** in miniature prop shop; handmade accessories for your tiny living world. Janit Calvo ; with photographs by Kate Baldwin. Timber Press 2017 247 p. color illustrations (pbk.) $19.95   **635.9**

1. Miniature gardens 2. Garden ornaments and furniture 3. Garden structures 4. Gardens, Miniature
ISBN 9781604698091; 9781604697018

LC 2016045507

This book, by Janit Calvo, with photographs by Kate Baldwin, discusses miniature gardening, "the next big thing for the crafters and gardeners already captivated by gardening small. Organized by playful themes—including gardens around the world, holidays, and fantasy gardens—it's a fun-filled guide to creating one-of-a-kind gardens and the accessories that make them shine. Thirty-seven projects are included with fully illustrated, step-by-step instructions." (Publisher's note)

"Fairy gardens and miniature gardens are extremely popular right now, and this book offers a guide to creating one (or many) of your own." Booklist

Includes bibliographical references (pages 239-240) and index

Carey, Jenny Rose

Glorious shade; dazzling plants, design ideas, and proven techniques for your shady garden. Jenny Rose Carey. Timber Press 2017 323 p. color illustrations (pbk.) $24.95   **635.9**

1. Gardening 2. Gardening in the shade 3. Shade-tolerant plants
ISBN 9781604696813; 9781604698060

LC 2016036949

This book, by Jenny Rose Carey, "celebrates the benefits of shade and shows you how to make the most of it. This information-rich, hard-working guide is packed with everything you need to successfully garden in the shadiest corners of a yard. You'll learn how to determine what type of shade you have and how to choose the right plants for the space. The book also shares the techniques, design and maintenance tips that are key to growing a successful shade garden." (Publisher's note)

"As much as Glorious Shade strives to help the amateur gardener, the text is also a professional botanist's primer on how to talk about plants to a lay audience and have them listen." Choice

Includes bibliographical references (pages 311-312) and index.

Christopher, Thomas

Essential perennials; the complete reference to 2700 perennials for the home garden. Ruth Rogers Clausen and Thomas Christopher ; photographs by Alan L. Detrick and Linda Detrick. Timber Press, Inc. 2015 452 p. color illustrations $39.95 **635.9**

1. Perennials 2. Flower gardening 3. Perennials -- Handbooks, manuals, etc
ISBN 1604693169; 9781604693164

LC 2014020896

"Perennials are the mainstay of any garden. But how do you choose from the thousands available, and care for the ones you already have? Essential Perennials helps you decide exactly which plants will bring you the beauty you want and will thrive in the conditions you can provide. Trusted garden experts Ruth Rogers Clausen and Thomas Christopher focus on what every gardener needs to know. For each plant you'll find information on flower color; season of bloom; foliage characteristics; height and width; light requirements; and hardiness and heat sensitivity. You'll also learn cultural tips, the most outstanding cultivars for each

species, and whether a plant has any special requirements or potential problems." Publisher's Note.

"This update to Clausen's lauded Perennials in American Gardens (1989) is enthusiastically recommended for both academic and public libraries and is an essential purchase for libraries where there is an interest in gardening." Booklist

Colletti, Maria

Terrariums; gardens under glass; designing, creating, and planting modern indoor gardens. by Maria Colletti. Cool Springs Press 2015 176 p. illustrations, color (sc) $24.99 **635.9**

1. Terrariums 2. Indoor gardening 3. Glass gardens
ISBN 9781591866336

LC 2015012059

In this book, author Maria Colletti "makes designing your very own interior gardens easy with step-by-step photos of over twenty of her own designs. Get all of the information you need on the 'it' plants of today--tillandsias (air plants), orchids, mosses, cacti, and succulents, along with 'traditional' terrarium ferns." (Publisher's note)

"Colletti includes plant ideas and design schemes for ecosystems such as the tropical terrarium (lots of air plants), the woodland (ferns and mosses), or the desert (succulents, cacti), all illustrated with abundant color photos. In all cases the basic premise is the same: a thriving ecosystem that sits on the dining table, rendering the joy of watching nature in progress in a small world you created." Pub Wkly

Cullina, William

Native trees, shrubs & vines; a guide to using, growing, and propagating North American woody plants. William Cullina. HougHton Mifflin Harcourt 2002 xi, 354 p.p color illustrations $40   **635.9**

1. Native plants 2. Cultivated plants 3. Ornamental plants 4. Ornamental woody plants -- Canada 5. Native plants for cultivation -- Canada 6. Ornamental woody plants -- United States 7. Native plants for cultivation -- United States
ISBN 0618098585; 9780618098583

LC 2002022586

This book, by William Cullina, "is a comprehensive reference to almost one thousand native woody plants. A . . . guide for naturalists, restorationists, nursery owners, landscape architects, and designers as well as gardeners, it points out that ecological gardening offers specific benefits to the individual as well as the environment." (Publisher's note)

"Cullina's writing is a pleasure to read beautifully descriptive, informative, and personal. His useful, authoritative work is highly recommended for North American libraries." LJ

Includes bibliographical references (p. 338-339) and index
Native trees, shrubs, and vines

Dash, Mike

Tulipomania; the story of the world's most coveted flower and the extraordinary passions it aroused. Crown 2000 273p hardcover o.p. pa $13.95   **635.9**

1. Tulips 2. Netherlands -- History
ISBN 0-609-80765-X pa

LC 99-39186

"The centerpiece of this story is a stunning two months, December 1636 and January 1637, when fortunes were made and lost in the Netherlands—in tulip bulb futures trading. Stripped to its basics, this would be a dry case study in an economics textbook. But Dash adds depth to the tale by including relevant bits of botany, sociology and history, as well as glimpses of the personalities involved in the creation of the tulip market." Publ Wkly

Includes bibliographical references

Deardorff, David

What's wrong with my houseplant? save your indoor plants with 100% organic solutions. David Deardoff, Kathryn Wadsworth. Timber Press 2016 292 p. color illustrations (hardcover) $34.95   **635.9**

1. House plants 2. Indoor gardening 3. Organic gardening
ISBN 9781604695908; 9781604696332

LC 2015013389

This book, by David Deardoff and Kathryn Wadsworth, "shows you how to keep indoor plants healthy by first teaching you how to identify the problem. This hardworking guide includes plant profiles for 148 plants organized by type, visual keys to the most of common problems, and the related organic solutions that will lead to a healthy plant. This easy-to-navigate book is for anyone who loves and has struggled with their indoor plants—it will turn even the brownest thumbs green!" (Publisher's note)

"Clearly and expertly written, the finder is easy to follow whether readers are looking to add plants inside their homes or salvaged the ones they already have." Pub Wkly

Includes bibliographical references and index

Dewees, Jason

Designing with palms; Jason Dewees ; photographs by Caitlin Atkinson. Timber Press 2018 368 p. color illustrations (hardcover) $50   **635.9**

1. Gardening 2. Landscape architecture 3. Palms 4. Landscape design
ISBN 1604695439; 9781604695434

LC 2017046009

In this book, "palm expert Jason Dewees, with photographs by Caitlin Atkinson details every major aspect of designing and caring for palms. This definitive guide shares essential information on planting, irrigation, nutrition, pruning, and transplanting. A gallery of the most important species showcases the range of options available, and stunning photographs by Caitlin Atkinson spotlight examples of home and public landscapes that make excellent use of palms." (Publisher's note)

"A visually fascinating tour of several parts of the US where palms are a major part of a garden landscape awaits the reader of this book. Some technical details, such as how to tell a palm from an "imposter," are necessary first. Morphological and anatomical characteristics of true palms are made textually clear and accompanied by beautiful photographs." Choice

Includes bibliographical references (pages 349-250) and index

Dirr, Michael A.

Dirr's encyclopedia of trees and shrubs; Michael A. Dirr. Timber Press 2011 951 p. col. ill. $79.95   **635.9**

1. Trees 2. Shrubs 3. Ornamental plants 4. Ornamental trees -- Encyclopedias 5. Ornamental shrubs -- Encyclopedias
ISBN 0881929018; 9780881929010

LC 2011007951

This reference book, by Michael A. Dirr, focuses on trees and shrubs. "From majestic evergreens to delicate vines and flowering shrubs, Dirr features thousands of plants and all the essential details for identification, planting, and care, plus full-color photographs showing a tree's habit in winter, distinctive bark patterns, fall color, and more." (Publisher's note)

"With beautiful, artistic photographs and succinct text, this volume is nearly as attractive as one of the gorgeous blossoming shrubs discussed within. . . . The chatty descriptions incorporate information often limited to tables—disease resistance, size, shape, and zone hardiness as

well as some history and taxonomy. These descriptions are accompanied by high-quality photographs." Booklist

Includes bibliographical references and index

Dirr's trees and shrubs for warm climates; an illustrated encyclopedia. by Michael A. Dirr. Timber Press 2002 446p il map $69.95   **635.9**

1. Trees 2. Shrubs 3. Ornamental plants 4. Landscape gardening
ISBN 0-88192-525-X

LC 2001-35810

"This volume, in conjunction with Dirr's Hardy Trees and Shrubs, completes [the author's] coverage of the woody ornamentals cultivated in North America. In a witty and informative style, Dirr presents botanic, cultural, and landscaping details on over 400 species. Entries are accompanied by magnificent color photos." Libr J

Manual of woody landscape plants; their identification, ornamental characteristics, culture, propagation and uses. Michael A. Dirr ; illustrations by Bonnie Dirr ... [et al.] 6th ed; Stipes Pub. 2009 1325 p. illustrations, map   **635.9**

1. Ornamental plants 2. Landscape gardening
ISBN 9781588748706; 1588748685; 9781588748683

LC 2009905492

This book, by Michael A. Dirr, is the sixth edition of the guide to woody landscape gardening. "It features expanded descriptions of former entries, over 2,000 new species and cultivars, trademark names and patent numbers, as well as all species, subspecies and variety names verified using the GRIN taxonomic data base (germplasm resources information network) and other sources." (Publisher's note)

Duffield, Mary Rose

Plants for dry climates; how to select, grow, and enjoy. {by} Mary Rose Duffield and Warren D. Jones. rev ed; Perseus Pub. 2001 216p il pa $27.50   **635.9**

1. Gardening 2. Desert plants
ISBN 1-55561-251-2

LC 2001-280011

First published 1981

The authors "explore strategies for gardening in dry or arid climates. . . . They cover climate conditions and predesign concerns such as possible planting restrictions by neighborhood covenants, the use of professional landscaping services, costs, and maintenance. A detailed plant guide identifies more than 300 species best suited to arid gardens, explaining conditions in which they thrive or are compromised." Libr J

Includes bibliographical references

Ellis, Barbara W.

Covering ground; unexpected ideas for landscaping with colorful, low-maintenance ground covers. Storey Pub. 2007 224p il map $29.95; pa $19.95   **635.9**

1. Grasses 2. Climbing plants 3. Ornamental plants
ISBN 1-58017-664-X; 978-1-58017-664-4; 1-58017-665-8 pa; 978-1-58017-664-4 pa

LC 2007-335

"Divided into three main sections, the book addresses why one should consider using ground covers, types of plants for different areas, and planting, growing, and propagating. . . . Suitable for all gardening collections, this easy and fun read is essential for the home gardener looking for low-maintenance or problem-area ground covers." Libr J

Gardiner, Jim

The **Timber** Press encyclopedia of flowering shrubs; Jim

Gardiner. Timber Press 2011 p. cm.   **635.9**
1. Shrubs 2. Gardening 3. Garden design 4. Flowering shrubs -- Encyclopedias 5. Flowering shrubs -- Pictorial works
ISBN 9780881928235

LC 2011020264

This book, by Jim Gardiner, is a reference work for gardening with flowering shrubs. "Rich attributes . . . make flowering shrubs the most rewarding of garden plants, but this vast group with its scores of tempting plants . . . requires careful navigation. Leading expert on woody plants Jim Gardiner has distilled several decades of knowledge and experience into . . . [a] pictorial reference of hardy shrubs that excel in temperate-zone gardens." (Publisher's note)

Includes bibliographical references and index

Gray, Mary

Potted; make your own stylish garden containers. Annette Goliti Gutierrez and Mary Gray. Timber Press 2017 227 p. color illustrations (pbk.) $19.95   **635.9**
1. Container gardening 2. Plant containers -- Design and construction
ISBN 9781604698084; 9781604696974

LC 2016036945

This book, by Annette Goliti Gutierrez and Mary Gray, "empowers you to create your own show-stopping containers made from everyday materials such as concrete, plastic, metal, terracotta, rope, driftwood, and fabric. The 23 step-by-step projects are affordable, made from accessible materials, and most importantly, gorgeous. They include new spins on old favorites, . . . along with never-before-seen ideas." (Publisher's note)

"Gutierrez and Gray combine design prowess and essential plant knowledge for a winning how-to." Booklist

Includes bibliographical references and index

Greenlee, John

The **American** meadow garden; creating a natural alternative to the traditional lawn. photography by Saxon Holt. Timber Press 2009 278p il $34.95   **635.9**
1. Grasses 2. Landscape gardening
ISBN 978-0-88192-871-6; 0-88192-871-2

LC 2009-19438

"Meadow gardening is an exciting, fresh approach to horticulture. By taking advantage of native plant life and soil conditions, gardeners can create an ecologically friendly yard that requires less water and mowing. Greenlee . . . focuses on the conditions of regional types of American grasslands, emphasizing throughout that gardeners must first understand local ecology (using professional help where necessary) to be successful. With Holt's photographs, this is a large and colorful showcase of Greenlee's extensive knowledge and great passion for gardening." Libr J

Includes bibliographical references

Heibel, Tara

Rooted in design; Sprout Home's guide to creative indoor planting. Tara Heibel and Tassy de Give ; photography by Ramsay de Give and Maria Lawson. Ten Speed Press 2015 224 p. illustrations (chiefly color) (hardcover) $25   **635.9**
1. House plants 2. Indoor gardening
ISBN 1607746972; 9781607746973; 9781607746980

LC 2014036284

This book, by Tara Heibel and Tassy de Give, is a "guide to creatively integrating indoor plants with home decor. . . . [They] offer expert advice for choosing plant varieties and pairing them with unique design

ideas. Sharing practical tips honed through hundreds of plant design classes, Heibel and DeGive tell readers everything they need to know to care for their one-of-a-kind green creations." (Publisher's note)

"While the authors concentrate more on design than the practicalities of indoor gardening, they do address many common issues, such as watering and lighting. Buried in the last few pages is a plant directory that answers questions of what plants work best in low light and with varying levels of water and soil." Pub Wkly

Helm, Bennett

The **water** gardener's bible; Ben Helm, Kelly Billing. Rodale 2008 192 p. color illustrations; maps (pbk.) $21.95 **635.9**
1. Water gardens
ISBN 1594866589; 9781594866586

LC 2007045129

In this book, authors Ben Helm and Kelly Billing explain how "installing a beautiful water garden has become a feasible undertaking for the average homeowner. . . . The pages are crammed with specifics about pond biology and chemistry, beneficial bacteria, fish health, nuisance algae, and electrical and child safety—all that is necessary to duplicate the sights, sounds, and sanctuary of a babbling brook, splashing fountain, or cascading waterfall right in the backyard." (Publisher's note)

Includes bibliographical references and index

Hitchmough, James

Sowing beauty; Designing Flowering Meadows from Seed. James Hitchmough. Timber Press 2017 364 p. (hardcover) $39.95   **635.9**
1. Meadows 2. Gardening 3. Meadow gardening
ISBN 9781604696325

LC 2016036943

Author James Hitchmough "is well-regarded in the design world for his exuberant, colorful, and flower-filled meadows. His signature style can be seen in prominent places like London's Olympic Park and the Botanic Garden at the University of Oxford. . . . [This book] shows you how to recreate Hitchmough's masterful, romantic style." (Publisher's note)

"This is a hopeful and expansive book for the gardener who can see a field as a canvas." Pub Wkly

Includes bibliographical references and index

Iwai, Terutoshi

Miniature bonsai; the complete guide to super-mini bonsai. Terutoshi Iwai ; translated by Leeyong Soo. Tuttle Pub 2017 80 p. color illustrations (hardcover) $16.95   **635.9**
1. Bonsai 2. Gardens, Miniature
ISBN 9781462919451; 9784805314388; 4805314389

This book, by Terutoshi Iwai, "reveals the Japanese art of super-mini bonsai gardening. As rewarding as full-scale bonsai cultivation is, mini bonsai is affordable, straightforward to learn and kind to your busy schedule. It's a complete gardening experience—a plant raised from seed or cutting, carefully potted, grown and maintained over time—a world of green in a pot no bigger than a demitasse or a thimble." (Publisher's note)

"An excellent introduction to the practice and deserves a spot on a shelf with conventional bonsai-gardening books." Booklist

Keville, Kathi

The **aromatherapy** garden; growing fragrant plants for happiness and well-being. Kathi Keville. Timber Press 2016 276 p. color illustrations $24.95   **635.9**
1. Gardening 2. Aromatherapy 3. Fragrant gardens 4. Aromatic plants -- Therapeutic use

ISBN 9781604695496

LC 2015029697

This book, by Kathi Keville, "explains how fragrant plants can be as therapeutic as they are intoxicating, and how easy it is to add this captivating element to gardens large and small. . . . Revealed here are the scents, secrets, and science behind plant aromatherapy, and how to optimize its full benefits. Detailed plant profiles will help you create a beautiful source of restorative aromas, oils, sachets, teas, and more." (Publisher's note)

"With such rich descriptions, readers will long for the actual aroma." Pub Wkly

Kukielski, Peter E.

Roses without chemicals; 150 disease-free varieties that will change the way you grow roses. Peter E. Kukielski. Timber Press, Inc. 2015 256 p. color illustrations $19.95   **635.9**

1. Roses 2. Gardening 3. Roses -- Varieties -- North America 4. Roses -- Disease and pest resistance -- North America

ISBN 1604693541; 9781604693546

LC 2014020741

In this book on rose gardening, author Peter E. Kukielski "highlights 150 . . . tough, new varieties, rating them for disease resistance, flowering, and fragrance. He also tells which perform best in each region and teaches simple cultivation techniques that will result in gorgeous, easy-care gardens filled with healthy roses." (Publisher's note)

"This valuable guide for gardeners wanting to try roses that are less disease-prone is recommended for public libraries and horticultural collections." LJ

Martin, Tovah

The **indestructible** houseplant; 200 beautiful plants that everyone can grow. Tovah Martin ; photography by Kindra Clineff. Timber Press 2015 288 p. color illustrations (alk. paper) $22.95   **635.9**

1. Plants 2. Interior design 3. House plants

ISBN 1604695013; 9781604695014

LC 2014042918

In this book author Tovah Martin "shows that anyone can grow healthy houseplants. It all boils down to a simple set of skills and--here's the crucial part--picking the right plants. These tough but beautiful plants can thrive in less-than-ideal conditions, and they're easy to find. You'll also learn how to pot, repot, water, and fertilize; pick up some great ideas for fun, funky containers; and benefit from Tovah's tips on how to display your plants." (Publisher's note)

"The green-thumb-challenged will give Martin a standing ovation for this much-needed book created for "windowsill-gardener wannabees" desiring plants to "survive tough love" and "transform" lives. New England-based Martin appreciates interest in an indoor gardening approach requiring minimal time investment." Booklist

Includes bibliographical references and index

The **new** terrarium; creating beautiful displays for plants and nature. [by] Tovah Martin and Kindra Clineff. Clarkson Potter/Publishers 2009 176p il $25   **635.9**

1. Terrariums

ISBN 978-0-307-40731-3; 0-307-40731-4

LC 2008-27713

"With beguiling photographs by Kindra Clineff, this attractive volume contains everything you need to know about growing plants under glass." N Y Times Book Rev

The **unexpected** houseplant; 220 extraordinary choices for every room in your home. Tovah Martin ; photography by Kindra Clineff. 1st ed. Timber Press 2012 328 p. col. ill. (paperback) $22.95; (ebook) $22.95   **635.9**

1. House plants 2. Indoor gardening 3. Container gardening

ISBN 160469243X; 9781604692433; 1604694262; 9781604694260

LC 2011045164

It was author Tovah Martin's intent to demonstrate "how correctly chosen plants placed in creative containers can enhance indoor living space. Martin shows how imagination and use of fundamental ground rules for growing and proper placement should result in an indoor horticultural paradise year round. Martin covers over 220 plants, ranging from exotic to conventional. . . .Growth requirements, propagation advice, problems, and attributes of plants are outlined." (Library Journal)

Includes bibliographical references and index.

McGowan, Alice

Bulbs in the basement, geraniums on the windowsill; how to grow and overwinter 165 tender plants. [by] Alice McGowan, Brian McGowan. Storey Pub. 2008 208p il pa $17.95 **635.9**

1. Perennials 2. Greenhouses 3. Ornamental plants

ISBN 978-1-60342-042-6; 1-60342-042-8

LC 2008-22440

"After offering readers a brief history of gardening with 165 plants, the McGowans give advice on choosing a container, on container combinations, and on the best type of soil to use. They stress the importance of the correct temperature and give instructions on setting up a site. There's a color photograph of each plant, along with information on its shape, color, and foliage, what the genus comprises, and design ideas. There also are instructions on how to use the guide, as well as suggested reading." Booklist

Includes bibliographical references

McIndoe, Andy

The **creative** shrub garden; eye-catching combinations for year-round interest. Andy McIndoe. Timber Press 2014 248 p. color illustrations $29.95   **635.9**

1. Shrubs 2. Gardening 3. Ornamental shrubs

ISBN 9781604694345

LC 2013040985

This book, by Andy McIndoe, "shows you how to make the most of the many benefits of shrubs—including their hardiness, year-long beauty, size, and low-maintenance nature—by making them the main element in a garden design. McIndoe teaches you the basics first, with tips on choosing shrubs based on a garden's size, determining soil and climate needs, and pruning and maintenance." (Publisher's note)

"A plant directory; alphabetical guide for planting and maintaining various shrubs, including container planting; suggested readings; and an index round out this comprehensive text sure to please gardeners who love perennials." Booklist

Includes bibliographical references and index

Michener, David C.

Peony; the best varieties for your garden. David C. Michener and Carol A. Adelman. Timber Press 2017 248 p. color illustrations (hardcover) $27.95   **635.9**

1. Plants 2. Gardening 3. Perennials 4. Peonies 5. Peonies -- Varieties

ISBN 9781604695205

LC 2017046303

This book, by David C. Michener and Carol A. Adelman, "features growing advice for one of the most beautiful and popular flowering plants. You'll learn the history of the plant, discover the different types of peonies available, and enjoy profiles of the best 194 varieties. Growing information includes details on climate, soil, light, planting, and water needs." (Publisher's note)

"Gardeners who already know and love peonies will find use in this book, as will those just getting started." Booklist

Includes bibliographical references and index

Miniature terrariums; tiny glass container gardens using easy-to-grow plants and inexpensive glassware. by Fourwords; translated by Leeyong Soo. Tuttle Publishing 2018 96 p. $17.99   **635.9**

1. Terrariums 2. Miniature gardens 3. Container gardening
ISBN 480531477X; 9784805314777

LC 2018085984

Translated by Leeyong Soo, "coming to you from Japan, where simplicity is all things is paramount, this book is full of ideas for creating the perfect little Japanese garden using repurposed glass containers--a lab flask, a wine glass, a mason jar, or an inexpensive glass box or hanging bulb. . . . Included are tips for selecting your containers and arranging your soils, stones and plants so that your tiny garden stays healthy and beautiful in its glass home for many years to come." (Publisher's note)

The **New** Southern Living Garden Book; The Ultimate Guide to Gardening. by The Editors of Southern Living Magazine. Oxmoor House 2015 768 p. $34.95   **635.9**

1. Gardening
ISBN 0848742982; 9780848742980

This book is a "definitive source on gardening from the brand Southern gardeners have turned to for nearly 50 years. Completely redesigned and updated for the first time in 10 years, the new edition features over 1,700 beautiful color photographs and over 7,000 featured plants. Enhanced features include a monthly garden checklist, a Q&A section to tackle everyday problems, and garden design solutions." (Publisher's note)

O'Sullivan, Penelope

The **homeowner's** complete tree & shrub handbook; the essential guide to choosing, planting and maintaining perfect landscape plants. photography by Karen Bussolini. Storey Pub. 2007 408p il map $39.95; pa $29.95   **635.9**

1. Trees 2. Shrubs 3. Ornamental plants
ISBN 978-1-58017-571-5; 978-1-58017-570-8 pa

LC 2007-10718

This guide to planting trees and shrubs discusses planning the landscape and buying, planting and caring for trees and shrubs. Includes descriptions of 348 trees and shrubs.

"The real jewel of this volume is the extensive AZ directory of nearly 350 trees and shrubs, many offering more than one season of interest. There is even a handy pronunciation guide for every plant name." Libr J

Includes webliography and bibliographical references

Ondra, Nancy J.

Grasses; versatile partners for uncommon garden design. Nancy J. Ondra ; photography by Saxon Holt. Storey Books 2002 143 p. illustrations, map $19.95   **635.9**

1. Grasses 2. Gardening 3. Ornamental plants 4. Ornamental grasses
ISBN 158017423X; 9781580174237

LC 2001049845

This book, by Nancy J. Ondra, with photographs by Saxon Holt, "is

a complete introduction to using ornamental grasses in combination with perennials, annuals, shrubs, and other garden plants. [The volume includes] full-color photos [that] illuminate complete plans for 24 gardens featuring grasses." (Publisher's note)

"Supported by Saxon Holt's captivating color photographs, Ondra elevates grasses from garden understudies to starring roles." Booklist

Penick, Pam

The **water**-saving garden; how to grow a gorgeous garden with a lot less water. by Pam Penick. Ten Speed Press 2016 240 p. color illustrations (trade pbk.) $19.99   **635.9**

1. Gardening 2. Xeriscaping 3. Water conservation 4. Drought-tolerant plants
ISBN 9781607747932

LC 2015025964

This book, by Pam Penick, offers "a guide to growing beautiful gardens in drought-prone areas utilizing minimal water for maximum results. . . . [It] provides gardeners and homeowners with a diverse array of techniques and plentiful inspiration for creating outdoor spaces that are so beautiful and inviting, it's hard to believe they are water-thrifty. Including a directory of 100 plants appropriate for a variety of drought-prone regions of the country." (Publisher's note)

"With the growing popularity of permaculture and sustainable cultivation techniques, Penick's how-to offers gardeners at all levels of experience much timely advice on working with one of the Earth's most precious natural resources." Booklist

The **plant** finder; the right plants for every garden. senior consultants, Tony Rodd and Geoff Bryant. Firefly Books 2007 992p il map $49.95   **635.9**

1. Gardening 2. Ornamental plants 3. Landscape gardening
ISBN 978-1-55407-265-1; 1-55407-265-4

LC 2007-298960

This book "gives basic descriptions and growing conditions for more than 5,000 plants, with a focus on the temperate zones. . . . Beginning gardeners as well as plant fanatics may find this comprehensive volume an indispensable midwinter reference for yearly garden planning, as well as a useful outdoor planting companion come spring." Publ Wkly

Pleasant, Barbara

The **complete** houseplant survival manual; essential know-how for keeping (not killing) more than 160 indoor plants. photography by Rosemary Kautzky. Storey Pub. 2005 365p il pa $24.95   **635.9**

1. House plants
ISBN 1-58017-569-4

LC 2005-14205

"Following an enlightening introduction that discusses the history, uses, and benefits that houseplants bestow, the manual is divided into three main sections. The first two are plant directories offering in-depth plant profiles of first flowering, then foliage, houseplants. The third is an extensive compilation of houseplant-care topics, from acclimatization to watering. With vivid color photographs, precise illustrations, appendixes listing helpful resources, definitions, and a cross-reference chart of botanical and common names, this is a must-have manual for anyone who shares home or office space with potted plants." Booklist

Silver, Johanna

The **bold** dry garden; Lessons from the Ruth Bancroft Garden. Johanna Silver ; photographs by Marion Brenner. Timber Press 2016 236 p. color illustrations (hardcover) $34.95 **635.9**

1. Gardens 2. Xeriscaping 3. Landscape gardening 4. Landscape

gardening -- Water conservation 5. Ruth Bancroft Garden (Walnut Creek, Calif.)

ISBN 9781604696707

LC 2016001680

This book, by Johanna Silver, with photographs by Marion Brenner, helps you "celebrate and recreate the beauty of The Ruth Bancroft Garden! Ruth Bancroft is a dry gardening pioneer. Her lifelong love of plants led to the creation of one of the most acclaimed public gardens, The Ruth Bancroft Garden in Walnut Creek, California. . . . [This book] offers unparalleled access to the garden and the extraordinary woman responsible for it." (Publisher's note)

"Replete with brilliant color photography, this hopeful book will win over anyone who doubts that a desolate landscape can support thriving life." Pub Wkly

Includes bibliographical references and index

Sterman, Nan

Hot color in the dry garden; inspiring designs and vibrant plants for year-round beauty. Nan Sterman. Timber Press 2018 320 p. (pbk.) $24.95 **635.9**

1. Gardening 2. Xeriscaping 3. Drought-tolerant plants

ISBN 9781604694574

LC 2017046300

This book, by Nan Sterman, "provides home gardeners with a joyful, color-filled way to exuberantly garden in low-water conditions. Garden expert . . . Sterman highlights inspiring examples of brilliant gardens filled with water-smart plants. Gardeners will find advice for adding color to the garden, information about designing for structure and texture, and a plant directory that features drought-tolerant plants that dazzle." (Publisher's note)

Includes bibliographical references and index

Tychonievich, Joseph

Rock gardening; Reimagining a Classic Style. Joseph Tychonievich. Timber Press, Inc. 2016 296 p. color illustrations (hardcover) $34.95; (ebook) $34.95 **635.9**

1. Rock plants 2. Rock gardens

ISBN 9781604695878; 9781604697780

LC 2016009686

This book on rock gardening, by Joseph Tychonievich, focuses on "the art of growing alpines and other miniature plants in the company of rocks in order to recreate the look of a rugged mountaintop. . . . [This book] brings this traditional style to a new generation of gardeners. It includes a survey of gorgeous rock gardens from around the world, the techniques and methods specific to creating and maintaining a rock garden, and profiles of the top 50 rock garden plants." (Publisher's note)

"This useful work targets a wide range of garden enthusiasts and/or horticulturalists. While comparable to the North American Rock Garden Society's Rock Garden Design and Construction, this stands on its own merits." LJ

Includes bibliographical references and index

Weathington, Mark

Gardening in the South; the complete homeowner's guide. Mark Weathington. Timber Press 2017 320 p. (pbk.) $24.95 **635.9**

1. Gardening 2. Advice literature 3. Ornamental plants 4. Gardening -- Southern States 5. Plants, Ornamental -- Southern States

ISBN 9781604695915

LC 2016036944

This gardening guidebook, by Mark Weathington, "features information on site and plant selection, soil preparation and maintenance, and

basic design principles. Plant profiles highlight the region's best perennials, annuals, trees, shrubs, and bulbs. Color photographs throughout show wonderful examples of southern garden style." (Publisher's note)

Includes bibliographical references and index

Wiley, Keith

Designing and planting a woodland garden; plants and combinations that thrive in the shade. Keith Wiley. Timber Press, Inc. 2014 280 p. color illustrations $34.95 **635.9**

1. Gardening 2. Woodland gardening 3. Shade-tolerant plants 4. Woodland garden plants

ISBN 1604693851; 9781604693850

LC 2014011045

In this book, author and gardener Keith Wiley "offers comprehensive information on hundreds of woodland plants and details how to use them in a well-designed garden. Information on planting a woodland garden includes design tips and instruction on how to create shade in a garden. Plant profiles for woodland trees, shrubs, perennials, bulbs, ferns, and grasses include complete growing information, along with the botanical and common name and zone requirements." (Publisher's note)

"The helpful garden designs and diagrams (such as how to plant a tree), along with hundreds of color photographs, facilitate choosing perennials, shrubs, trees, bulbs, tubers, and ferns. Gardeners, who are dreamers, writes Wiley, can dream that, once established, this magical garden will in fact grow itself." PW

635.965   House plants

Claffey, Bree

Indoor green; living with plants. Bree Claffey. Thames & Hudson 2017 208 p. color illustrations (hardcover) $39.95 **635.965**

1. House plants 2. Indoor gardening

ISBN 9780500500538

LC 2016941848

In this book "author Bree Claffey journeys into the interior worlds of fellow plant lovers to explore the enduring attraction of houseplants. From the ever-reliable peace lily and beguiling fiddle leaf fig to the elusive Chinese money plant, . . . [this book] makes it obvious that even the humblest greenery can transform a home." (Publisher's note)

"This enlivening exploration will inspire even the most timid of indoor plant lovers, providing a fresh look at an affordable type of gardening that both beautifies a home and expands the soul." Pub Wkly

Includes bibliographical references (page 206) and index.

635.987   Organic gardening

Whitman, John

Fresh from the garden; An Organic Guide to Growing Vegetables, Berries, and Herbs in Cold Climates. John Whitman. University of Minnesota Press 2017 536 p. illustrations (hc; alk. paper) $49.95 **635.987**

1. Herbs 2. Berries 3. Organic gardening 4. Vegetable gardening 5. Berries -- Canada 6. Herb gardening -- Canada 7. Berries -- Snowbelt States 8. Organic gardening -- Canada 9. Vegetable gardening -- Canada 10. Herb gardening -- Snowbelt States 11. Organic gardening -- Snowbelt States 12. Vegetable gardening -- Snowbelt States

ISBN 9780816698394; 9780816698417

LC 2016027971

This book on organic gardening, by John Whitman, "describes various methods of planting to make the most of different sites, whether in containers, raised beds, or on level ground, and takes into consideration the abbreviated growing season and longer summer days. He discusses the merits of starting from seed indoors or outdoors, the making and uses of compost, and measures for keeping a garden healthy, from mulching and fertilizing to crop rotation and winter protection." (Publisher's note)

"An excellent handbook deserving a larger audience than it may receive." Booklist

636   Animal husbandry

Ehringer, Gavin

Leaving the wild; the unnatural history of dogs, cats, cows, and horses. Gavin Ehringer. Pegasus Books 2017 xii, 356 p.p (hardcover) $27.95   **636**

1. Dogs -- Breeding 2. Domestic animals 3. Horses -- Breeding 4. Human-animal relationships 5. Animal breeding 6. Cats -- Breeding 7. Cattle -- Breeding 8. Domestic animals -- History
ISBN 9781681776064; 9781681775562; 1681775565

This book, by Gavin Ehringer, "explores the ever-evolving relationship between humans and domesticated animals. . . . [In this book] you'll meet cows cloned from steaks, a Quarter horse stallion valued at $7.5 million, Chinese dogs that glow in the dark, and visit a Denver cat show featuring naked cats and other cuddly mutants." (Publisher's note)

"Solid, well-reported popular science for animal lovers." Kirkus

Francis, Richard C.

Domesticated; evolution in a man-made world. Richard C. Francis. W W Norton & Co Inc 2015 400 p. illustrations (hardcover) $27.95   **636**

1. Evolution 2. Human-animal relationship 3. Animals and civilization 4. Domestic animals -- History
ISBN 0393064603; 9780393064605

LC 2014046934

In this book, author Richard C. Francis "investigates the nature of domestication, focusing mostly on the biological rather than anthropological factors responsible for a wide array of human/animal partnerships. He ranges widely across species, including house pets, livestock, and pack animals, discussing the types of genetic changes that commonly occur during the process of domestication and the developmental implications such changes have." (Publishers Weekly)

"The cited literature is extensive and an excellent source for those wishing to pursue specific topics further. This treatise will be valuable to a wide readership, from animal lovers to a large array of professionals. Summing Up: Highly recommended. All readers." Choice

Includes bibliographical references and index

Galaxy, Jackson

Catification; designing a happy and stylish home for your cat (and you!) Jackson Galaxy, Kate Benjamin. Tarcher 2014 304 p. color illustrations (paperback) $21.95   **636**

1. Cats 2. Interior design 3. Cats -- Housing 4. Interior decoration 5. Cats -- Equipment and supplies
ISBN 0399166017; 9780399166013

LC 2014019022

This book, by Jackson Galaxy and Kate Benjamin, "shows cat owners everywhere how to make their homes both cat-friendly and chic. . . . [It] includes more than twenty fun DIY projects, from kitty beds and litter boxes to catios (cat patios) that will be sure to make readers-- and their cats-- purr in approval." (Publisher's note)

"If you have cats, you need this book." LJ

Grandin, Temple

★ **Animals** make us human; creating the best life for animals. [by] Temple Grandin and Catherine Johnson. Houghton Mifflin Harcourt 2009 342p $26   **636**

1. Animal behavior
ISBN 978-0-15-101489-7; 0-15-101489-2

LC 2008-34892

"Packed with fascinating insights, unexpected observations and a wealth of how-to tips, Grandin's peppy work ably challenges assumptions about what makes animals happy." Publ Wkly

★ **Temple** Grandin's guide to working with farm animals; safe, humane livestock handling practices for the small farm. by Temple Grandin. Storey Publishing 2017 181 p.   **636**

1. Domestic animals 2. Livestock
ISBN 9781612127446; 9781612127453; 9781612127606

LC 2016055528

In this book, Temple Grandin "extends her expert guidance to small-scale farming operations. Grandin's fascinating explanations of how herd animals think . . . and how to analyze their behavior, will help you handle your livestock more safely and effectively. You'll learn to become a skilled observer of animal movement and behavior, and detailed illustrations will help you set up simple and efficient facilities for managing a small herd of 3 to 25 cattle or pigs, or 5 to 100 goats or sheep." (Publisher's note)

"Grandin gets to the finest points of animal husbandry, providing perceptive insights into animals' physical strengths, weaknesses, and emotional capabilities. Augmented by finely wrought illustrations that delineate pastures, pens, chutes, and handling facilities, Grandin's guidebook is an essential resource for anyone involved with livestock management on any scale." Booklist.

Includes bibliographical references and index

The **Merck** veterinary manual; 11th edition Merck & Co. 2016 3325 p $65   **636**

1. Veterinary medicine
ISBN 9780911910612

"This completely revised and redesigned new edition of the veterinary classic uses a two-column format and color throughout for easy-to-read text and tables. Hundreds of color images enhance and illustrate the text. In addition to extensive revisions and updates, this edition includes a new section on public health and zoonoses, expanded coverage of fish and aquaculture, new chapters on backyard poultry, toxicologic workplace hazards, smoke inhalation, and additional coverage of numerous new and emerging topics in veterinary medicine." (Publisher's note)

636.088   Animals for specific purposes

Link, Tim

Talking with dogs and cats; joining the conversation to improve behavior and bond with your animals. Tim Link. New World Library 2015 240 p. (pbk.; alk. paper) $14.95 **636.088**

1. Cats 2. Dogs 3. Animal communication 4. Pets -- Behavior 5. Pets -- Psychology 6. Human-animal communication
ISBN 1608683222; 9781608683222

LC 2015004274

In this book, author and "animal communicator Tim Link's approach respects the personality and feelings of animals, and his simple, accessible methods can facilitate the understanding and communication that all animal lovers crave. If you've ever wondered what your animal was trying to tell you with a bark, meow, or tweet, this is the book for you." (Publisher's note)

"For readers who enjoyed Amelia Kinkade's Straight from the Horse's Mouth, Link's easygoing attitude and sincerity will be a welcome addition to those interested in alternative forms of animal communication." LJ

Includes bibliographical references

Pierce, Jessica

Run, Spot, run; the ethics of keeping pets. Jessica Pierce. University of Chicago Press 2016 256 p. (cloth; alk. paper) $26 **636.088**

1. Animal welfare 2. Pets -- Ethical aspects 3. Human-animal relationships 4. Pets -- Moral and ethical aspects 5. Animal welfare -- Moral and ethical aspects 6. Human-animal relationships -- Moral and ethical aspects
ISBN 9780226209890

LC 2015038627

In this book, Jessica Pierce, "a lover of pets herself (including, over the years, dogs, cats, fish, rats, hermit crabs, and more), . . . understands the joys that pets bring us. But she also refuses to deny the ambiguous ethics at the heart of the relationship, and through a mix of personal stories, philosophical reflections, and scientifically informed analyses of animal behavior and natural history, she puts pet-keeping to the test. Is it ethical to keep pets at all?" (Publisher's note)

"A thoughtful book that should spark debate, with the author stressing that bringing a companion animal into one's life is an ethical commitment that should not to be taken lightly." Kirkus

Includes bibliographical references and index

636.089   Veterinary medicine

Black's veterinary dictionary; edited by Edward Boden and Anthony Andrews. 22nd ed A. & C. Black 2015 790 p. il $52 **636.089**

1. Veterinary medicine 2. Veterinary medicine -- Dictionaries
ISBN 0713663626; 140817572X; 9781408175729

First published 1928 by Macmillan with title: Black's veterinary cyclopedia

This book, edited by Edward Boden and Anthony Andrews, "is an essential reference tool for all with a professional or leisure interest in the care of animals. . . . For the 22nd edition much new and updated information has been included, reflecting the numerous developments that have taken place in animal care and husbandry, and welfare. There is greatly expanded coverage of topics relating to popular breeds of dog and cat, and the inheritable conditions that might affect their health." (Publisher's note)

Fincham-Gray, Suzanne

My patients and other animals; a veterinarian's stories of love, loss, and hope. Suzanne Fincham-Gray. Spiegel & Grau 2018 288 p. (hardback) $27 **636.089**

1. Veterinary medicine 2. Human-animal relationships 3. Veterinarians -- Biography
ISBN 9780812998184

LC 2017025329

In this memoir, veterinarian Suzy Fincham-Gray "sheds light on the universal experience of loving, healing, and losing our beloved pets, and the many ways they change our lives. . . . She writes about some of the most emotionally challenging and rewarding cases of her career. . . . She

describes the satisfaction of diagnosing and treating difficult diseases and the universal experience of loving a pet, and--inevitably--raises questions about their end-of-life care." (Publisher's note)

636.1   Horses

Forrest, Susanna

The **age** of the horse; an equine journey through human history. Susanna Forrest. Atlantic Monthly Press 2017 xi, 418 p.p illustrations (some color) (hardcover) $27 **636.1**

1. Horses -- History 2. Animals and civilization
ISBN 9780802189516; 9780802126511; 0802126510

LC 2017003334

This book, by Susanna Forrest, "is a breathtaking exploration of the enduring connection between humans and Equus caballus. . . . [The author] presents a unique, sweeping panorama of the animal's prominent role in societies around the world and across time. . . . [She] draws from an immense range of archival documents as well as literature and art to illustrate how our evolution has coincided with that of horses." (Publisher's note)

"In clear, introspective prose that underscores the astonishing depth of her research, Forrest tracks human history through the eyes of our equine companions." Booklist

Includes bibliographical references (pages 371-398) and index.

Hill, Cherry

How to think like a horse; the essential handbook for understanding why horses do what they do. Cherry Hill. Storey Publishing 2006 ix, 181 p.p ill. (chiefly col.) $19.95 **636.1**

1. Horses -- Behavior 2. Human-animal relationship 3. Horsemanship 4. Human-animal communication
ISBN 1580178359; 1580178367; 9781580178358

LC 2005027792

In this book, by Cherry Hill, "horse trainer and instructor Cherry Hill believes that every human/horse relationship benefits from a greater human understanding of what motivates horses, how they experience the world, what makes them happy, and what worries them. Journey through the equine mind with Hill as she explores what makes a horse tick." (Publisher's note)

Includes bibliographical references (p. 178) and index

Philipps, David

Wild Horse Country; The History, Myth, and Future of the Mustang. by David Philipps. W W Norton & Co Inc 2017 xxxix, 316 p.p illustrations, map (hardcover) $27.95 **636.1**

1. Horses -- History 2. Mustang 3. West (U.S.) -- History
ISBN 9780393635300; 9780393247138; 0393247139

LC 2017018261

This book, by David Philipps, "is the grand story of the horse: from its prehistoric debut in North America to its reintroduction by Spanish conquistadors and its spread through the epic battles between native tribes and settlers during the days of the Wild West. Philipps explores how wild horses became so central to America's sense of itself, and he delves into the hold that wild horses have had on the American imagination." (Publisher's note)

"A fine, readable work of advocacy journalism . . . that deserves to inform discussion about the mustang issue as it plays out in courts and in Congress." Kirkus

Includes bibliographical references (pages [299]-304) and index.

Raulff, Ulrich, 1950-

Farewell to the horse; a cultural history. Ulrich Raulff ; translated by Ruth Ahmedzai Kemp. Liveright Publishing Corp., a Division of W.W. Norton & Co. 2018 464 p. (hardcover) $35 **636.1**
   1. Horses -- History 2. Human-animal relationships -- History
ISBN 9781631494321

LC 2017047848

This book, by Ulrich Raulff, translated by Ruth Ahmedzai Kemp, is "a surprising, lively, and erudite history of horse and man. . . . Raulff chronicles the dramatic story of this most spectacular creature, thoroughly examining how they've been muses and brothers in arms, neglected and sacrificed in war yet memorialized in paintings, sculpture, and novels--and ultimately marginalized on racetracks and in pony clubs." (Publisher's note)

"A top-notch addition to the library of any cultured equestrian; highly readable from start to finish." Kirkus

Includes bibliographical references and index

Richards, Susan

Chosen by a horse; a memoir. Soho Press 2006 248p $20 **636.1**
   1. Horses
ISBN 1-56947-419-2

LC 2005-52337

"Richards adopts an emaciated mare and her foal, overriding the small voice telling her that she already has three horses to care for and a herniated disk. Her experience with her new charges proves profoundly instructive in terms of how love can foster growth of the human spirit and help in overcoming pain and loss. The abused mare, Lay Me Down, proves to be one of those rare creatures that remain gentle despite years of mistreatment, responding profoundly to the kind treatment that is part of everyday life for Richards' animals. Fascinated by the affection this animal accords a stranger, Richards notes the mare's courage and slowly begins to emulate it in her own life, opening up to a love affair and its aftermath." Booklist

Rousseau, Élise

★ **Horses** of the world; Élise Rousseau ; illustrated by Yann Le Bris ; translated by Teresa Lavender Fagan. Princeton University Press 2017 536 p. illustrations (chiefly color) (hardcover; alk. paper) $39.95 **636.1**
   1. Horses 2. Zoology 3. Animals -- Anatomy 4. Horses -- Encyclopedias 5. Horse breeds -- Identification
ISBN 9780691167206

LC 2016042566

This book, in the Princeton Field Guides series, by Élise Rousseau, illustrated by Yann Le Bris, translated by Teresa Lavender Fagan, "is a comprehensive . . . overview of 570 breeds of domestic and extant wild horses, including hybrids between the two and between domestic breeds and other equids, such as zebras. This beautifully illustrated and detailed guide covers the origins of modern horses, anatomy and physiology, variation in breeds, and modern equestrian practices." (Publisher's note)

"Cleverly designed and handsomely illustrated, this single-volume encyclopedia of horse breeds will serve nicely both on the reference shelf and as a desktop companion for equine enthusiasts." Booklist

Includes bibliographical references and index

Shatner, William, 1931-

Spirit of the horse; a celebration in fact and fable. William Shatner with Jeff Rovin. Thomas Dunne Books 2017 viii, 292 p.p (hardcover) $26.99 **636.1**
   1. Horses 2. Human-animal relationships 3. Horses -- Folklore 4. Horses in literature 5. Actors -- Canada -- Biography 6. Horses -- Literary collections
ISBN 9781250130020; 9781250130037

LC 2017001073

In this book, author William Shatner "speaks from the heart about the remarkable effect horses have had on his life and on the lives of others. From his first horse, . . . to his favorite horses, acquired after many years of learning what to look for, this book draws from Shatner's own experience and pairs it with a wealth of classic horse stories. . . . The result is a celebration that captures the unparalleled connection between humans and horses." (Publisher's note)

"Shatner puts forth a lovely look at the influence and importance of horses." Booklist

Storey's horse-lover's encyclopedia; an English and Western A-to-Z guide. edited by Deborah Burns. Storey Bks. 2001 471p il $37.50; pa $24.95 **636.1**
   1. Horses
ISBN 1-58017-336-5; 1-58017-317-9 pa

LC 00-46329

"The alphabetically arranged entries vary in length from a few sentences to a few pages, with the most thorough coverage going to extensive topics like breeding, foot care, and feeding. Most entries consist of one or two paragraphs and provide a good definition of the term at hand." Libr J

Williams, Wendy

The **horse**; the epic history of our noble companion. Wendy Williams. Scientific American/Farrar, Straus & Giroux 2015 320 p. illustrations (some color) (hardcover) $26 **636.1**
   1. Horses 2. Human-animal relationships -- History 3. Horses -- History 4. Horses -- Evolution
ISBN 0374224404; 9780374224400

LC 2015003860

In this book, author Wendy Williams "chronicles the 56-million-year journey of horses as she visits with experts around the world, exploring what our biological affinities and differences can tell us about the bond between horses and humans, and what our longtime companion might think and feel. . . . Williams charts the course that leads to our modern Equus-from the protohorse to the Dutch Warmbloods, Thoroughbreds, and cow ponies of the twenty-first century." (Publisher's note)

"Williams's book educates, entertains, and enthralls; it's part scientific discovery, part social commentary, and part history lesson, while always focusing on the relationship between horses and humans. This accessible profile of equines through the ages pays homage to an animal that had a crucial role in the modernization of the world." Pub Wkly

Includes bibliographical references and index

636.2 Cattle and related animals

Branch, John

The **last** cowboys; a pioneer family in the new West. John Branch. W W Norton & Co Inc 2018 288 p. $26.95 **636.2**
   1. Ranch life 2. Family life 3. Cowboys -- Fiction
ISBN 0393292347; 9780393292343

This book, by John Branch, "chronicles three years in the life of the . . . [Wright family], each culminating in rodeo's National Finals in Las Vegas. Will Bill and Evelyn be able to hold the family together as rodeo injuries pile up and one of their sons goes off on a religious mission? Will their son Cody . . . make it to the finals one last time--and compete with his own son? And will the younger generation . . . be able to continue the family's ways in the future?" (Publisher's note)

Lewis, Celia

The **illustrated** guide to cows; how to choose them. [Celia Lewis] ; with a foreword by the Prince of Wales. St Martins Pr 2014 160 p. color illustrations $25   **636.2**
   1. Beef cattle 2. Dairy cattle
   ISBN 1408181355; 9781408181355

LC 2011278365

Written by Celia Lewis, "'The Illustrated Guide to Cows' covers the 58 most familiar breeds of cattle in Europe and North America. Breed profiles are written in engaging text that covers the history of each breed, its main characteristics and how to look after them, and each one has been beautifully illustrated by the author." (Publisher's note)

"Lewis concludes with instructions on milking, dairy production, tanning, and more. This guide, with its abundance of friendly illustrations, is an informative and fun homage to an animal of great importance." Pub Wkly
   Chickens

Young, Rosamund

The **secret** life of cows; Rosamund Young. Penguin Group USA 2018 160 p. $23   **636.2**
   1. Organic farming 2. Cattle -- Behavior 3. Livestock industry
   ISBN 0525557318; 9780525557319

In this book, author Rosamund Young "distills a lifetime of organic farming wisdom, describing the surprising personalities of her cows and other animals. At her famous Kite's Nest Farm in Worcestershire, England, the cows (as well as sheep, hens, and pigs) all roam free. They make their own choices about rearing, grazing, and housing. Left to be themselves, the cows exhibit temperaments and interests as diverse as our own." (Publisher's note)

636.4   Swine

Estabrook, Barry

Pig tales; an omnivore's quest for sustainable meat. Barry Estabrook. W. W. Norton & Company 2015 320 p. illustration (hardcover) $26.95   **636.4**
   1. Pigs 2. Meat industry
   ISBN 039324024X; 9780393240245

LC 2014048321

This book, by Barry Estabrook, offers an "investigation of the commercial pork industry and an inspiring alternative to the way pigs are raised and consumed in America. . . . [The author] shows how these creatures are all too often subjected to lives of suffering in confinement and squalor, sustained on a drug-laced diet just long enough to reach slaughter weight, then killed on mechanized disassembly lines. But it doesn't have to be this way." (Publisher's note)

"An enjoyable and erudite read, the book will appeal to a broad audience. It includes detailed notes; photos and illustrations would have been welcome." Choice

Jenkins, Steve

Happily ever Esther; two men, a wonder pig, and their life-changing mission to give animals a home. Steve Jenkins, Derek Walter, and Caprice Crane. Grand Central Publishing 2018 240 p. (hardcover) $27   **636.4**
   1. Pigs 2. Animal sanctuaries 3. Human-animal relationships 4. Farm life -- Canada -- Anecdotes 5. Swine as pets -- Canada -- Anecdotes 6. Animal sanctuaries -- Canada -- Anecdotes 7.

Domestic animals -- Care -- Canada -- Anecdotes
   ISBN 9781538728147

LC 2017046608

In this book, authors Steve Jenkins, Derek Walter, and Caprice Crane, recount how "their lives turned upside down when they adopted their pig-daughter Esther--the so-called micro pig who turned out to be a full-sized commercial pig growing to a whopping 600 pounds. . . . The book ends with them moving to a new farm, and starting a new wonderful life where they will live on the Happily Ever Esther Farm Sanctuary to care for other animals and just live happily ever after." (Publisher's note)

Montgomery, Sy

The **good** good pig; the extraordinary life of Christopher Hogwood. Ballantine Books 2006 228p il $21.95; pa $13.95   **636.4**
   1. Pigs
   ISBN 0-345-48137-2; 978-0-345-48137-5; 0-345-49609-4 pa; 978-0-345-49609-6 pa

LC 2005-57094

This is a "description of the 14-year life of a 750-pound pet pig who was named after the conductor [Christopher Hogwood]. Anyone who has ever loved a pet can enjoy reading about the relationship between Montgomery and her Christopher." Sci Books Films

636.5   Chickens and other kinds of domestic birds

Johnson, Samantha

How to build chicken coops; everything you need to know. Samantha Johnson and Daniel Johnson. Voyageur Press 2015 176 p. color illustrations (sc) $19.99   **636.5**
   1. Chickens 2. Animal housing 3. Chickens -- Housing
   ISBN 0760347336; 9780760347331

LC 2014039439

This book, by Samantha Johnson and Daniel Johnson, provides instruction on raising chickens and building chicken coops, but "is not just a collection of plans, but a compendium of the background and insider information for chicken owners. How much space will you need? What is dust bathing? How many nest boxes and windows will your coop need? How much will it cost? What steps do you need to take to keep your chickens safe from predators?" (Publisher's note)

"This book is ideal for high school students or adults who need an introduction on raising chickens and coop building." LJ

Lawler, Andrew

Why did the chicken cross the world? the epic saga of the bird that powers civilization. Andrew Lawler. Atria Books 2014 336 p. (hardback) $26   **636.5**
   1. Chickens 2. Civilization -- History 3. Animals and civilization 4. Human-animal relationships 5. Chickens -- History 6. Animals and civilization -- History 7. Human-animal relationships -- History
   ISBN 1476729891; 9781476729893

LC 2014031979

In this book, author Andrew Lawler "delivers a sweeping history of the animal that has been most crucial to the spread of civilization across the globe—the chicken. . . . Beginning with the recent discovery in Montana that the chicken's unlikely ancestor is T. rex, . . . [it] track[s] the chicken from its original domestication in the jungles of Southeast Asia some 10,000 years ago to postwar America, where it became the most engineered of animals." (Publisher's note)

"Recommended for readers of popular nonfiction as well as those with a specific interest in accessible scientific and anthropological studies." LJ

Includes bibliographical references and index

Litt, Robert

The **new** rules of the roost; organic care and feeding for the family flock. Robert Litt, Hannah Litt. Workman Pub Co 2018 248 p. $29.95   **636.5**

1. Poultry 2. Chickens 3. Organic farming
ISBN 1604698454; 9781604698459

This book, by Robert and Hannah Litt, "addresses the real problems that crop up when keeping chickens long term. The Litts cover a wide range of topics including organic health remedies and disease prevention, pest management, organic nutrition, the best breeds for specific needs, and the simplest options for daily maintenance and feeding." (Publisher's note)

McKenna, Maryn

Big chicken; the incredible story of how antibiotics created modern agriculture and changed the way the world eats. Maryn McKenna. National Geographic 2017 400 p. (hardback) $27   **636.5**

1. Chickens 2. Antibiotics 3. Drug resistance in microorganisms 4. Poultry -- Marketing 5. Chickens -- Marketing 6. Chickens -- Microbiology 7. Antibiotics in animal nutrition
ISBN 9781426217661

LC 2017011586

In this book, "Maryn McKenna documents how antibiotics transformed chicken from local delicacy to industrial commodity--and human health threat--uncovering the ways we can make America's favorite meat safer again. . . . Rich with scientific, historical, and cultural insights, this spellbinding cautionary tale shines a light on one of America's favorite foods--and shows us the way to safer, healthier eating for ourselves and our children." (Publisher's note)

"In this well-written expose, McKenna (Superbug) dissects the controversy of the routine use of antibiotics to fatten chicken, which has lead to the rise of drug-resistant bacteria. ... Throughout, McKenna offers spot-on commentary on the dangerous additives in chickens and concludes on a relatively hopeful note." PW

Includes bibliographical references (pages 323-389) and index.

Rude, Emelyn

Tastes Like Chicken; A History of America's Favorite Bird. by Emelyn Rude. W W Norton & Co Inc 2016 272 p. illustrations (ebook) $50; $27.95   **636.5**

1. Poultry 2. Chickens 3. Eating customs 4. Cooking (Chicken)
ISBN 9781681771984; 1681771632; 9781681771632

A fowl introduction -- The early bird -- A healing broth -- The general chicken merchants -- Of chicken and champagne -- The poor man's chicken -- America's egg basket -- Calories and constituents -- The kosher chicken wars -- Celia Steele's modest endeavor -- They saw in hens a way -- A chicken for every grill -- A nugget worth more than gold -- The tale of the colonel and the general -- The modern chicken -- the end and the beginning.

In this book, author Emelyn Rude "details the ascendancy of chicken from its humble origins to its centrality on grocery store shelves and in restaurants and kitchens. Along the way, she reveals startling key points in its history, such as the moment it was first stuffed and roasted by the Romans, how the ancients' obsession with cockfighting helped the animal reach Western Europe, and how slavery contributed to the ubiquity of fried chicken today." (Publisher's note)

"Readers of food histories such as Mark Kurlansky's Cod will appreciate this engaging, well-researched, and thorough history of America's changing food preferences." LJ

Includes bibliographical references (pages 201-263) and index.

636.7   Dogs

Achterberg, Cara Sue

Another good dog; one family and fifty foster dogs. Cara Sue Achterberg. W W Norton & Co Inc 2018 304 p. $25.95   **636.7**

1. Dogs 2. Animal welfare 3. Dog owners -- Biography
ISBN 1681777932; 9781681777931

LC 2018109824

This memoir, by Cara Sue Achterberg, is "about what happens when you foster fifty dogs in less than two years--and how the dogs save you as much as you save them. . . . The stories of these remarkable dogs . . . and the joy they bring to Cara and her family . . . fill the pages of this touching and inspiring new book that reveals the wonderful rewards of fostering." (Publisher's note)

"Witty and full of love, her memoir beautifully captures the personalities of the dogs she's helped save and recounts the concurrent struggles in her family life, particularly watching her teenagers fly the nest. This easy read is a must for animal lovers and those interested in volunteering with animals and a good choice for reluctant readers." Booklist

Anderson, Teoti

The **ultimate** guide to dog training; puppy training to advance techniques plus 50 problem behaviors solved. by Teoti Anderson. I-5 Press 2014 239 p. color illustrations (alk. paper) $19.95   **636.7**

1. Dogs -- Behavior 2. Dogs -- Training
ISBN 1621870901; 9781621870906

LC 2014015365

This dog training guide "encompasses every topic from the puppy's first lessons and house-training to advance training methods and retraining rescue dogs, rebellious teens, and seniors. . . . Dog trainer and behavior expert Teoti Anderson offers straightforward advice and easy-to-follow instructions for each topic, all based on her success-oriented positive-training methods." (Publisher's note)

The **art** of raising a puppy; the Monks of New Skete ; [photographs by the Monks of New Skete] Little, Brown & Co. 2011 x, 341 p.p illustrations (hbk.) $26   **636.7**

1. Dogs -- Care 2. Animal rescue 3. Puppies 4. Puppies -- Training
ISBN 0316083275; 9780316083270

LC 2011002744

"This new edition of 'The Art Of Raising a Puppy' features new photographs throughout, along with updated chapters on play, crating, adopting dogs from shelters and rescue organizations, raising dogs in an urban environment, and the latest developments in canine health and canine behavioral theory." (Publisher's note)

Includes bibliographical references (p. [329]-331) and index

Bendersky, Jorge

DIY dog grooming, from puppy cuts to best in show; everything you need to know, step by step. Jorge Bendersky. Quarry Books 2013 160 p. illustrations (chiefly color) $24.99 **636.7**

1. Dogs -- Care 2. Dogs -- Grooming
ISBN 1592538886; 9781592538881

LC 2013038975

This book, by Jorge Bendersky, "will show you how to take the best care of your dog, regardless of breed, temperament, or age. Practical step-by-step photos will take you through everything you need to know to bathe and trim your dog, plus care for her nails, ears, teeth, and more. Learn how to train her to relax and enjoy grooming." (Publisher's note)

Blackwell, Lewis

The **life** and love of dogs; Lewis Blackwell. Abrams 2014 216 p. color illustrations $50   **636.7**

1. Dogs -- Pictorial works 2. Human-animal relationship
ISBN 1419713930; 9781419713934

LC 2014930772

This book, by Lewis Blackwell, "offers hundreds of incredible images by acclaimed photographers from around the world. A textual exploration of our unique relationship with dogs-- including a surprising analysis of the qualities that make a dog attractive in our eyes, a detailed look at how the breeds we see today are a product of our own needs and desires, and more." (Publisher's note)

"Readers who have enjoyed Blackwell's other books will delight in this beautiful, contemplative analysis of dogs as a species and as human companions." LJ

Bradshaw, John (Author)

Dog sense; how the new science of dog behavior can make you a better friend to your pet. John Bradshaw. Basic Books 2011 xxiv, 324 p.p il $25.99   **636.7**

1. Dogs -- Behavior 2. Dogs -- Psychology 3. Human-animal relationship 4. Animal intelligence 5. Human-animal relationships
ISBN 0465019447; 9780465019441

LC 2010054337

The author discusses "how humans can live in harmony with their canine friends, explaining why positive reinforcement is a more effective way to control behavior and how to weigh a dog's unique personality against the stereotypes of its breed." (Publisher's note) Bibliography. Index.

"Pet owners and those interested in the animal mind will learn from this balanced, well-referenced guide to the science of canine behavior.—" LJ

Includes bibliographical references and index

Burch, Mary R.

Citizen canine; ten essential skills every well-mannered dog should know. Kennel Club Books 2010 256p il pa $14.95   **636.7**

1. Dogs -- Training
ISBN 978-1-593786-44-1

LC 2009-28847

"Often a component of therapy dog assessment, the Canine Good Citizen (CGC) test has become a popular way to document a dog's manners. . . . [The author] outlines the ten test items and demonstrates how to teach your dog these skills. . . . This well-indexed guide is essential reading for dog owners, whether the goal is obedience training, therapy dog work, or simply polite pets." Libr J

Coile, D. Caroline

Encyclopedia of dog breeds; 3rd edition Barron's Educational Series 2015 392p il $29.99   **636.7**

1. Reference books 2. Dogs -- Encyclopedias
ISBN 9780764167294

First published 1998

"More than 150 breed descriptions are grouped along American Kennel Club divisions: the sporting group, the hound group, the working

group, and so on. . . . Breed descriptions are organized into subsections entitled 'History,' 'Temperament,' 'Upkeep,' 'Health,' and 'Form and Function.'" Booklist

★ **Decoding** Your Dog; The Ultimate Experts Explain Common Dog Behaviors and Reveal How to Prevent or Change Unwanted Ones. by American College of Veterinary Behaviorists ; edited by Debra Horwitz, John Ciribassi, and Steve Dale. Houghton Mifflin Harcourt 2014 384 p. illustrations $27   **636.7**

1. Dogs -- Behavior 2. Dogs -- Training
ISBN 0547738919; 9780547738918

LC 2014395601

This book, edited by Debra Horwitz, John Ciribassi, and Steve Dale, is a "dog behavior guide. . . . Experts analyze problem behaviors, decipher the latest studies, and correct common misconceptions and outmoded theories. The book includes: effective, veterinary-approved positive training methods [and] expert advice on socialization, house-training, diet, and exercise." (Publisher's note)

"A fascinating and detailed exploration of the reasons behind common dog behaviors and of how to interpret dogs' communication signals in order to train them to be happy, healthy, obedient companions." LJ

Eldredge, Debra

Dog owner's home veterinary handbook; [by] Debra M. Eldredge . . . [et al.] 4th ed; Wiley Pub. 2007 xxviii, 628p il $34.99   **636.7**

1. Dogs -- Diseases
ISBN 978-0-4700-6785-7; 0-4700-6785-3

LC 2007-16275

First published 1980

"The authors discuss all of the major organ systems with descriptions of normal functions and infectious and parasitic diseases. Writing in easy-to-understand terms, they identify emergency situations and explain first-aid care. . . . It contains information on Lyme disease and other recently recognized problems." Libr J [review of 1992 edition]

Franklin, Jon

★ The **wolf** in the parlor; the eternal connection between humans and dogs. Henry Holt 2009 283p $25   **636.7**

1. Dogs
ISBN 978-0-8050-9077-2; 0-8050-9077-0

LC 2009-2227

Building on evolutionary science, archaeology, behavioral science, and the firsthand experience of watching his own dog evolve from puppy to family member, Franklin posits that man and dog are more than just inseparable; they are part and parcel of the same creature.

"Among a plethora of books on breeding, disciplining, loving and lamenting the loss of man's best friend, this thoughtful discourse is a best of breed." Publ Wkly

Goldberg, Marc

Let dogs be dogs; understanding canine nature and mastering the art of living with your dog. The Monks of New Skete and Marc Goldberg. Little, Brown & Co. 2017 xiii, 272 p.p illustrations (hardcover) $28   **636.7**

1. Dogs -- Training 2. Human-animal relationships 3. Dogs -- Philosophy 4. Human-animal relationships -- Religious aspects -- Christianity
ISBN 9780316269612; 9780316387934

LC 2017939186

In this book, authors Marc Goldberg and the Monks of New Skete, "distill decades of experience in a comprehensive 'foundational' guide for dog owners. . . . [They] reveal how canine nature manifests itself in various behaviors, some potentially disruptive to domestic accord, and show how in addressing these behaviors you can strengthen the bond with your dog as well as keep the peace." (Publisher's note)

"This mix of philosophy and practical tips will help owners build a stronger bond with their animals to curb unwanted behaviors." Booklist

The **good** dog; true stories of love, loss, and loyalty. [edited by] David DiBenedetto & the editors of Garden & Gun. Harper-Wave 2014 336 p. illustrations $25.99 **636.7**
1. Dogs 2. Pets 3. Human-animal relationship 4. Dogs -- Anecdotes 5. Human-animal relationships -- Anecdotes
ISBN 0062242350; 9780062242358
LC 2014015874
This book presents a "collection of true stories celebrating the unique relationship between humans and their canine companions, penned by some of today's top writers, including Jon Meacham, Roy Blount, Jr, Dominique Browning, and P.J. O'Rourke." (Publisher's note)

"Other contributors include Ace Atkins, Rick Bragg, Roy Blount Jr., Jon Meacham and Julia Reed. Bird lovers may blanch at feather-in-the-mouth hunting tales, but this selection of vignettes is varied, entertaining and frequently heartwarming." Kirkus

Grossi, Craig
★ **Craig** & Fred; a Marine, a stray dog, and how they rescued each other. Craig Grossi. William Morrow 2017 272 p. $25.99 **636.7**
1. Working dogs 2. Human-animal relationships 3. United States. Marine Corps -- Biography 4. Dogs
ISBN 0062693387; 9780062693389
This book, by Craig Grossi, is the "true story of a US Marine, the stray dog he met on an Afghan battlefield, and how they saved each other and now travel America together. . . . In 2010, Sergeant Craig Grossi was doing intelligence work for Marine RECON—the most elite fighters in the Corps—in a remote part of Afghanistan. While on patrol, he spotted a young dog. . . . After eating a piece of beef jerky Craig offered—against military regulations—the dog began to follow him." (Publisher's note)

Death, violence, and fear are a constant in the battlefield, but Grossi manages to find humor in the midst of horror and life after loss...Positive, encouraging, and inspirational. --Kirkus (December 15, 2017)

Herriot, James
James Herriot's dog stories. St. Martin's Press 1986 xxxiii, 426p il $23.95; pa $7.99 **636.7**
1. Dogs
ISBN 0-312-43968-7; 0-312-92558-1 pa
LC 86-6637
Herriot "has gathered 50 recollections of canines, some of them sentimental, a few tragic and at least one—the story of a terrier male who abruptly becomes attractive to other males—as odd as anything in the Decameron. Herriot recalls that in his student days domestic animals were customarily listed in descending order of importance: horse, ox, sheep, pig, dog. In the latest work, he has brought his favorites to the front and given them a new leash on life." Time

Horowitz, Alexandra
★ **Being** a dog; Following the Dog Into a World of Smell. Alexandra Horowitz. Scribner 2016 336 p. (ebook) $18.99; (alk. paper) $27.00 **636.7**
1. Nose 2. Dogs -- Psychology 3. Dogs -- Sense organs 4. Smell

5. Perception in animals
ISBN 9781476796048; 9781476795997
LC 2016006968
In this book author Alexandra Horowitz, "explains how dogs perceive the world through their most spectacular organ--the nose--and how we humans can put our under-used sense of smell to work in surprising ways. . . . Horowitz sets off on a quest to make sense of scents, combining a personal journey of smelling with a tour through the cutting edge and improbable science behind the olfactory powers of the dog, . . . revealing the spectacular biology of the dog snout." (Publisher's note)

"Both dog lovers and pop science readers will want to stick their noses in this book, and they may find themselves using their noses, like Horowitz and dogs everywhere, to experience the world more vividly." Pub Wkly

Includes bibliographical references and index

Inside of a dog; what dogs see, smell, and know. Scribner 2009 353p $27 **636.7**
1. Dogs -- Psychology
ISBN 1-4165-8340-8; 978-1-4165-8340-0
LC 2008-45842
This book examines "the sensations and thought processes of dogs." (N Y Times Book Rev)
Includes bibliographical references

Kaplan, Laurie
Help Your Dog Fight Cancer; Empowerment for Dog Owners, Turn Despair into Confidence, Become Your Best Friend's Best Advocate. Laurie Kaplan ; edited by Alice Villalobos. Jangen Press 2016 258 p. ill. (some col.) (paperback) $29.99 **636.7**
1. Cancer 2. Dogs -- Care 3. Veterinary medicine
ISBN 0975479431; 9780975479438
LC 2004107152
This book, by Laurie Kaplan, edited by Alice Villalobos, discusses "Canine cancer causes and prevention . . . , the most common types of cancer in dogs, diagnostic tests and treatment options . . . , [and] communicating clearly with your veterinarian and making informed decisions . . . about testing and treatment." (Publisher's note)

"A unique contribution to the field of animal care, this work is highly recommended for most public libraries." LJ

Katz, Jon
★ **Katz** on dogs; a commonsense guide to training and living with dogs. Villard 2005 xxviii, 240p il $24.95 **636.7**
1. Dogs -- Training
ISBN 1-4000-6403-1
LC 2005-46209
Katz's "commonsense approach and skill as a storyteller make this an appealing, informative book." Libr J
Includes bibliographical references

Kavin, Kim
The **Dog** Merchants; Inside the Big Business of Breeders, Pet Stores, and Rescuers. by Kim Kavin. W W Norton & Co Inc 2016 336 p. $27.95 **636.7**
1. Dogs -- Breeding
ISBN 1681771403; 9781681771403
This book, by Kim Kavin, "is the first book to explain the complex and often surprisingly similar business practices that extend from the American Kennel Club to local shelters, from Westminster champions to dog auctions. . . . Kavin reveals how dog merchants create markets

for dogs, often in defiance of the usual rules of supply and demand. She takes an investigative approach and meets breeders and rescuers at all levels." (Publisher's note)

"A scathing indictment of an industry run amok; belongs on every pet lover's bookshelf." Kirkus

Includes bibliographic references (pages 273-296) and index.

Kerasote, Ted

Merle's door; lessons from a freethinking dog. Harcourt, Inc. 2007 398p $25   **636.7**
  1. Dogs
  ISBN 978-0-15-101270-1

                      LC 2006-38041

"In telling Merle's story, Kerasote also explores the science behind canine behavior and evolution, weaving in research on the human-canine bond and musing on the way dogs see the world. Merle is a true character, yet Merle is also Everydog. An absolute treasure of a book." Booklist

Includes bibliographical references

Pukka's Promise; The Quest for Longer-lived Dogs. Ted Kerasote. Houghton Mifflin Harcourt 2013 464 p. $28 **636.7**
  1. Dogs 2. Animals -- Longevity 3. Dog owners -- Anecdotes
  ISBN 0547236263; 9780547236261

                      LC 2012289472

This book, by Ted Kerasote, discusses dogs as pets and their health and longevity, "questioning our conventional wisdom and emerging with vital new information that will surprise even the most knowledgeable dog lovers. . . . Interviewing breeders, veterinarians, and leaders of the animal-welfare movement, Kerasote pulls together the latest research to help us rethink the everyday choices we make for our companions." (Publisher's note)

Kress, Rory

The **doggie** in the window; how one dog led me from the pet store to the factory farm to uncover the truth of where puppies really come from. Rory Kress. Sourcebooks 2018 368 p. (paperback; alk. paper) $15.99   **636.7**
  1. Pets 2. Dogs -- Breeding 3. Human-animal relationships 4. Pet shops -- United States 5. Dog industry -- United States 6. Dogs -- Breeding -- United States
  ISBN 9781492651826

                      LC 2017046006

This book, by Rory Kress, "is a story of hope and redemption. It upends the notion that purchased dogs are a safer bet than rescues, examines how internet puppy sales allow customers to get even farther from the truth of dog breeding, and offers fresh insights into one of the oldest bonds known to humanity. With Izzie's help, we learn the real story behind the dog in the window--and how she got there in the first place." (Publisher's note)

Includes bibliographical references

McConnell, Patricia

For the love of a dog; understanding emotion in you and your best friend. Ballantine Books 2006 332p il hardcover o.p. pa $15.95   **636.7**
  1. Dogs
  ISBN 0-345-47714-6; 978-0-345-47714-9; 0-345-47715-4 pa; 978-0-345-47715-6 pa

                      LC 2006-45200

"This is not a book on how to train dogs, but McConnell's examination of cases from her veterinary practice, backed up by her scientific study of animal behavior, will help readers better understand their closest companions." Booklist

Meet the breeds; a guide to more than 200 AKC breeds. American Kennel Club. 5th edition Companionhouse Books 2016 238 p illustrations $19.95   **636.7**
  1. Dog breeds
  ISBN 9781621871170

                      LC 2017303181

Presents information on dog breeds, including size, color, life expectancy, grooming, activity level, and temperament.

Millán, César, 1969-

Cesar Millan's lessons from the pack; stories of the dogs who changed my life. Cesar Millan ; with Melissa Jo Peltier. National Geographic 2017 234 p. illustrations (hardcover; alk. paper) $24.95   **636.7**
  1. Dogs 2. Human-animal relationships 3. Dogs -- Behavior 4. Dogs -- Training 5. Dogs -- Psychology
  ISBN 1426216130; 9781426216138; 9781426216190

                      LC 2016044868

In this book author "Cesar Millan uses decades of experience to reveal the many ways that dogs and people can enrich each other's lives, sharing eight essential life lessons imparted by a group of very special dogs he's trained over the years. Each chapter, drawing on celebrity and noncelebrity clients alike, spotlights the essential traits that allow these animals to make the best of their situations--from authenticity to acceptance--and reveals how we can embrace these values to enrich our own lives." (Publisher's note)

"Famed dog behavior expert Millan goes from teacher to student in this touching and informative tribute to the dogs he's loved and learned from." Booklist

Includes bibliographical references (pages 227-228).

Monks of New Skete

How to be your dog's best friend; the classic training manual for dog owners. {by} the Monks of New Skete. completely rev and updated, 2nd ed; Little, Brown 2002 336p il $25.95 **636.7**
  1. Dogs -- Training
  ISBN 0-316-61000-3

                      LC 2002-102894

First published 1978

This guide to dog training focuses on important aspects of the canine-human relationship, including discipline and choosing a breed that fits the owner's personality and lifestyle

This book's "unique value lies in the monks' insights and thoughts about the human-canine bond. . . . Without devolving into New Age psychobabble, the monks make philosophical and spiritual observations that no dog lover could resist." Publ Wkly

Includes bibliographical references

Myles, Eileen

Afterglow; a dog memoir. Eileen Myles. Grove Press 2017 210 p. illustrations (hardcover) $24   **636.7**
  1. Pets 2. Pit bull terriers 3. Pet owners -- Psychology 4. Human-animal relationships
  ISBN 9780802188786; 9780802127099; 0802127096

                      LC 2017008720

This book, by Eileen Myles, "launches a heartfelt and fabulist investigation into the true nature of the bond between pet and pet-owner. Through this lens, we witness Myles's experiences with intimacy and spirituality, celebrity and politics, alcoholism and recovery, fathers and family history, as well as the fantastical myths we spin to get to the heart of grief." (Publisher's note)

"Poetic, heartrending, soothing, and funny, this is a mind-expanding contemplation of creation, the act and the noun, and the creatures whose deaths we presume will precede ours but whose lives make our own better beyond reason." Booklist

★ The **new** complete dog book; official breed standards and profiles for over 200 breeds. the American Kennel Club. Fox Chapel Publishing 2017 919 p.   **636.7**
   1. Dogs 2. Dog breeds 3. Dogs -- Standards -- United States
   ISBN 9781621871736

LC 2017020403

"In print since 1929, this 900-plus page resource, produced by the American Kennel Club with assistance from members of the national breed clubs, covers the official standards for more than 200 breeds... New to this edition is a helpful chapter with "Green Light" and "Red Flag" tips for finding a responsible breeder." Library Journal

O'Grey, Eric

Walking with Peety; the dog who saved my life. Eric O'Grey with Mark Dagostino. Grand Central Publishing 2017 xv, 299 p.p color illustrations (hardcover) $26   **636.7**
   1. Dogs 2. Human-animal relationships 3. Overweight persons -- Biography 4. Diabetics -- United States -- Biography 5. Overweight persons -- United States -- Biography
   ISBN 9781538712535; 9781478971160; 1478971169

LC 2017020075

In this book, by Eric O'Grey with Mark Dagostino, "after a lifetime of failed diet attempts, and the onset of type 2 diabetes due to his weight, Eric went to a new doctor, who surprisingly prescribed a shelter dog. And that's when Eric met Peety: an overweight, middle-aged, and forgotten dog who, like Eric, had seen better days. The two adopted each other and began an incredible journey together, forming a bond of unconditional love that forever changed their lives." (Publisher's note)

"This feel-good, easy-to-read book, coauthored with Dagostino and lightly sprinkled with scripture, is sure to inspire many readers." Booklist

Includes bibliographical references.

Orlean, Susan

★ **Rin** Tin Tin. Simon & Schuster 2011 324p il $26.99; ebook $12.99   **636.7**
   1. Working dogs 2. Rin-Tin-Tin (Dog)
   ISBN 978-1-4391-9013-5; 978-1-4391-9015-9 ebook

LC 2011024476

This book discusses the "story of Lee Duncan (1893-1960), a young American soldier and dog-lover who found the German shepherd puppy that became Rin Tin Tin (Rinty) in France, got the dog home and spent the rest of his life training and promoting Rinty, breeding other German shepherds. . . . [The author] also provides the biography of Duncan, as well as Bert Leonard, writer and producer, and she includes interviews with Duncan's daughter, the current keeper of the latest Rinty and scores of others. The author tells the story of silent films (where Rinty began his career), the transition to talkies and to color, the rise of television, the popularity of dog ownership in America (especially of German shepherds and collies--because of Lassie) and the evolving tastes of American youth." (Kirkus)

"A terrific dog's tale that will make readers sit up and beg for more." Kirkus

Includes bibliographical references

Pierson, Melissa Holbrook

The **secret** history of kindness; learning from how dogs learn. Melissa Holbrook Pierson. W W Norton & Co Inc 2015 320 p. (hardcover) $26.95   **636.7**
   1. Kindness 2. Dogs -- Training 3. Positive psychology 4. Dogs -- Psychology 5. Dog trainers -- Psychology 6. Dogs -- Training -- Philosophy
   ISBN 0393066193; 9780393066197

LC 2014045932

This book, by Melissa Holbrook Pierson, is an "intimate, surprising look at man's best friend and what the leading philosophies of dog training teach us about ourselves. . . . Pierson draws surprising connections in her exploration of how kindness works to motivate all animals, including the human one." (Publisher's note)

"A well-researched and thorough examination of current methods of dog training based on psychology; useful to those who want a deeper, beyond-the-basics understanding of the techniques." LJ

Includes bibliographical references

Rosenfelt, David

Dogtripping; 25 rescues, 11 volunteers, and 3 RVs on our canine cross-country adventure. David Rosenfelt. St. Martin's Press 2013 288 p. color illustrations (hardcover) $25.99 **636.7**
   1. Dogs 2. Moving 3. Human-animal relationship 4. Dog adoption 5. Dogs -- Biography 6. Human-animal relationships 7. Authors, American -- 21st century -- Biography
   ISBN 1250014697; 9781250014696

LC 2013009168

This book, by David Rosenfelt, is an "account of a cross-country move from California to Maine, and the beginnings of a dog rescue foundation. When . . . Rosenfelt and his family moved from Southern California to Maine, he thought he had prepared for everything. . . . But traveling with twenty-five dogs turned out to be a bigger ordeal than he anticipated, despite the RVs, the extra kibble, volunteers, and camping equipment." (Publisher's note)

"Spirited and absolutely absorbing reading for fans of canine capers." Booklist

Rutherford, Clarice

How to raise a puppy you can live with; [by] Clarice Rutherford, David H. Neil. 4th ed., rev. & updated; Alpine Blue Ribbon Books 2005 153p il pa $11.95   **636.7**
   1. Dogs -- Training
   ISBN 1-57779-076-6

LC 2005-41038

First published 1981

This book features "practical advice on puppy selection, development, training, and problem-solving." Libr J

Includes bibliographical references

Schenone, Laura

The **dogs** of Avalon; the race to save animals in peril. Laura Schenone. W W Norton & Co Inc 2017 x, 324 p.p illustrations (hardcover) $26.95   **636.7**
   1. Dogs 2. Animal welfare 3. Dog rescue -- Ireland 4. Greyhounds -- Ireland 5. Animal rescue -- Ireland
   ISBN 0393073580; 9780393073584; 9780393248784

LC 2017013983

This book, by Laura Schenone, "introduces us to the strong-willed Marion Fitzgibbon. When Fitzgibbon becomes head of the Irish Society for the Prevention of Cruelty to Animals and focuses on the cause of the greyhound, she faces an entrenched racing industry protected by money and power. She . . . create[s] an international network to find these animals homes, confront the racing industry, and provide safe havens where animals can live in peace." (Publisher's note)

"An engrossing account of greyhounds, their owners, and their champions." Kirkus

Includes bibliographical references

Stilwell, Victoria

Train your dog positively; understand your dog and solve common behavior problems including separation anxiety, excessive barking, aggression, housetraining, leash pulling, and more! Victoria Stilwell. Ten Speed Press 2013 248 p. illustrations $14.99   **636.7**

    1. Dogs -- Behavior 2. Dogs -- Training

ISBN 1607744147; 9781607744146

LC 2012045637

In this book, author "Victoria Stilwell provides a comprehensive toolbox designed to help dog owners overcome the most persistent, annoying and dangerous behavior problems in their dogs. Far from being merely another dog training manual, however, it also serves as [a] . . . roadmap for understanding where our dogs come from, how they experience the world and what we need to teach them most effectively." (Publisher's note)

    Includes bibliographical references and index

Sutherland, Amy

Rescuing Penny Jane; One Shelter Volunteer, Countless Dogs, and the Quest to Find Them All Homes. by Amy Sutherland. HarperCollins 2017 288 p. illustrations $26.99; (ebook) $25.99   **636.7**

    1. Volunteer work 2. Animal shelters 3. Human-animal relationships

ISBN 006237723X; 9780062377234; 9780062377265

LC 2017006986

This book, by Amy Sutherland, "introduces readers to dogs like Alfred, a loony, gorilla-sized Goldendoodle, intent on jumping on absolutely everyone at the shelter; Rugby, the crippled pit bull—mix puppy who was found abandoned on a roadside; and Brody, an overly exuberant and misunderstood German shepherd mix. Then there are the author's own adopted dogs: Penny Jane . . . and Walter Joe." (Publisher's note)

"An inside look at the experiences of shelter dogs that is sure to appeal to dog and animal lovers." Kirkus

Thomas, Elizabeth Marshall

The **social** lives of dogs; the grace of canine company. illustrated by Jared Taylor Williams. Simon & Schuster 2000 253p hardcover o.p. pa $13.95   **636.7**

    1. Dogs

ISBN 0-7434-2236-8 pa

LC 99-87357

Thomas discusses how dogs interact with various members of the household, including other dogs and pets of other species

The author "draws upon her extensive knowledge of the behavior and treatment of feral dogs in East Africa to explain the domestication of the dog. Appendixes containing advice on controlling dogs' behavior and on keeping parrots as pets conclude this entertaining and informative book." Libr J

Toutonghi, Pauls

Dog Gone; a lost pet's extraordinary journey and the family who brought him home. Pauls Toutonghi. Alfred A. Knopf, a division of Penguin Random House LLC 2016 272 p. illustra-

tions, map (hardcover) $25   **636.7**

    1. Dogs 2. Rescue work 3. Dog owners 4. Human-animal relationships

ISBN 9781101947012; 1101947012; 1101971010

LC 2015034739

This book, by Pauls Toutonghi, tells a "true story of a lost dog's journey and a family's furious search to find him before it is too late. . . . Saturday, October 10, 1998. Fielding Marshall is hiking on the Appalachian Trail. His beloved dog—a six-year-old golden retriever mix named Gonker—bolts into the woods. Just like that, he has vanished. And Gonker has Addison's disease. If he's not found in twenty-three days, he will die." (Publisher's note)

"This book offers a poignant reminder of the important role dogs often fill as they help their human companions traverse difficult life passages." LJ

Warren, Cat

What the dog knows; the science and wonder of working dogs. Cat Warren. Simon & Schuster 2013 352 p. $26.99 **636.7**

    1. Working dogs 2. Search dogs -- Anecdotes

ISBN 1451667310; 9781451667318

LC 2013012006

This book, by Cat Warren, focuses on working dogs. She "interviews cognitive psychologists, historians, medical examiners, epidemiologists, and forensic anthropologists, as well as the breeders, trainers, and handlers who work with and rely on these . . . animals daily. Along the way, she discovers story after story that proves the . . . capabilities—as well as the . . . limits—of working dogs and their human partners." (Publisher's note)

"Warren writes with verve and provides rare insight into our working partnership with canines." Kirkus

Zheutlin, Peter

Rescue road; one man, thirty thousand dogs, and a million miles on the last hope highway. Peter Zheutlin. Sourcebooks, Inc. 2015 236 p. illustrations (paperback) $14.99   **636.7**

    1. Dogs 2. Animal rescue 3. Dog rescue 4. Animal welfare

ISBN 9781492614074

LC 2015012970

This book, by Peter Zheutlin, presents "the extraordinary story of one man who has driven more than 1 million miles to rescue thousands of dogs from hunger, abuse and neglect and give them a second chance at life and love . . . from Houston's impoverished Fifth Ward--where thousands of strays roam the streets--and high-kill animal shelters in Louisiana, to joyous scenes of adopters embracing their new pups in the Northeast." (Publisher's note)

"An unabashedly sentimental and affecting portrait of a modern-day animal-loving hero."

636.737   Herding dogs

Dohner, Janet Vorwald

★ **Farm** dogs; a comprehensive breed guide to 93 guardians, herders, terriers, and other canine working partners. Janet Vorwald Dohner. Storey Publishing 2016 351 p. illustrations (chiefly color) (hardcover; alk. paper) $36.95   **636.737**

    1. Working dogs 2. Terriers 3. Herding dogs 4. Livestock protection dogs

ISBN 1612126006; 9781612125923; 9781612126005

LC 2016014115

This book, by Janet Vorwald Dohner, "describes 93 breeds of livestock guardian dogs, herding dogs, terriers, and traditional multipurpose farm dogs, highlighting the tasks each dog is best suited for and describing its physical characteristics and temperament. She also offers an accessible history of how humans bred dogs to become our partners in work and beyond, providing a thorough introduction to these highly intelligent, independent, and energetic breeds." (Publisher's note)

This guide is an in-depth look at the history of dog breeds that have been an invaluable part of farmwork for centuries. . . . This is a beautiful, well-organized, and comprehensive title." Booklist

Includes bibliographical references (pages 336-337) and index

636.755   Terriers

Dickey, Bronwen

Pit bull; the battle over an American icon. by Bronwen Dickey. Alfred A. Knopf 2016 352 p. illustrations (hardcover) $26.95   **636.755**

1. Dogs -- Breeding 2. Pit bull terriers
ISBN 9780307961761; 0307961761

LC 2015033292

This book, by Bronwen Dickey, offers an "illuminating story of how a popular breed of dog became the most demonized and supposedly the most dangerous of dogs—and what role humans have played in the transformation. . . . Dickey offers us a clear-eyed portrait of this extraordinary breed, and an insightful view of Americans' relationship with their dogs." (Publisher's note)

"This exceptional, thoroughly researched, and expertly written work is a must for all libraries." LJ

Includes bibliographical references

636.8   Cats

Bradshaw, John, 1950-

Cat sense; how the new feline science can make you a better friend to your pet. John Bradshaw. Basic Books 2013 336 p. (hardcover) $27.99   **636.8**

1. Cats 2. Pets 3. Animal intelligence 4. Cat owners 5. Cats -- Behavior 6. Cats -- Psychology 7. Human-animal relationships
ISBN 0465031013; 9780465031016

LC 2013020749

In this book, author John Bradshaw takes readers "further into the mind of the domestic cat . . . using cutting-edge scientific research to dispel the myths and explain the true nature of our feline friends. Tracing the cat's evolution from lone predator to domesticated companion, Bradshaw shows that although cats and humans have been living together for at least eight thousand years, cats remain independent, predatory, and wary of contact with their own kind." (Publisher's note)

"Bradshaw teases out a better understanding of what our cats want (and need) from their owners. . . . This fascinating book will be a bible for cat owners." Booklist

Includes bibliographical references and index

The **cat** encyclopedia. DK Publishing 2014 320 p. color illustrations, col. maps $40   **636.8**

1. Cats -- Encyclopedias 2. Animals -- Encyclopedias
ISBN 1465419594; 9781465419590

"Offering everything you need to know about cats in one easy-reference volume, 'The Cat Encyclopedia' features stunning photographs of cat breeds from around the world combined with expert advice on kitten and cat care, and a celebration of cats in art and culture. 'The Cat

Encyclopedia' is packed with information on the characteristics, origins, and behaviors of each type of cat, and includes beautifully photographed profiles of the world's cat breeds." (Publisher's note)

The **complete** cat breed book; consultant editor, Kim Dennis-Bryan. DK Publishing 2013 256 p. color illustrations $22   **636.8**

1. Cats 2. Pets 3. Cat breeds
ISBN 1465408517; 9781465408518

LC 2012554447

"Combining cat breeds, behavior, and training tips in one easy volume, 'The Complete Cat Breed Book' is an essential reference to the basics of choosing and looking after a cat. Packed with practical advice on cat maintenance, from handling and grooming to nutrition, exercise, and health, current and prospective cat owners will discover the best cat breed for their lifestyle." (Publisher's note)

Includes index

DK the complete cat breed book

Cox, Tom

Close encounters of the furred kind; New Adventures with My Sad Cat & Other Feline Friends. Tom Cox. Thomas Dunne Books, St. Martin's Press 2016 256 p. illustrations (hardcover) $24.99   **636.8**

1. Cats 2. Cats -- England -- Norfolk -- Anecdotes
ISBN 9781250077325

LC 2016003326

This book by Tom Cox "is the follow-up to The Good, The Bad, and the Furry, . . . it tells the story of Tom Cox's life with his charismatic cats--The Bear, Shipley, Ralph, and recent recruit Roscoe. . . . Readers who became attached to The Bear's magical, owlish persona during his previous adventures will become more so here as he proves, once again, that he's a cat with endless secrets and significantly more than nine lives." (Publisher's note)

"Cox is endlessly funny, speaking for his cats and poking good-natured fun at every human he encounters, including himself." Booklist

Ellis, Sarah

The **trainable** cat; a practical guide to making life happier for you and your cat. John Bradshaw and Sarah Ellis. Basic Books 2016 352 p. illustrations (hardcover) $27.99   **636.8**

1. Cats 2. Cats -- Behavior 3. Cats -- Training
ISBN 0465050905; 9780465050901; 9780465096497

LC 2016019146

This book, by John Bradshaw and Sarah Ellis, "show[s] that not only can cats be trained, but they absolutely must be in order to strengthen the bond between pet and owner, reduce their anxiety, and maximize their happiness. . . . Once we understand our beloved pet's journey from wild predator to domesticated animal, we can train them to overcome their natural inhibitions, fears, and anxieties." (Publisher's note)

"Cat lovers will appreciate the sensible advice and in-depth explanations of feline behavior." Pub Wkly

Includes bibliographical references and index

Galaxy, Jackson

★ **Total** cat mojo; the ultimate guide to life with your cat. Jackson Galaxy with Mikel Delgado and Bobby Rock. TarcherPerigee Book 2017 xviii, 365 p.p illustrations (paperback) $17   **636.8**

1. Cats 2. Pets 3. Animal behavior 4. Cats -- Health
ISBN 9781524705268; 9780143131618

LC 2017026753

This book, by Jackson Galaxy, is a "comprehensive guide . . . to cat behavior and basic cat care, rooted in understanding cats better. From getting kittens off to the right start socially, to taking care of cats in their senior years, and everything in between, this book addresses the head-to-toe physical and emotional needs of cats--whether related to grooming, nutrition, play, or stress-free trips to the vet." (Publisher's note)

"Filled with arcane facts, humorous stories, good black-and-white illustrations, and downright excellent advice, this manual begins with an in-depth look at what "mojo" means to our pets, and how owners of cats can help them achieve their confident lives." Booklist

Hart, Benjamin L.

Your ideal cat; insights into breed and gender differences in cat behavior. Benjamin L. Hart, DVM, PhD, and Lynette A. Hart, PhD. Purdue University Press 2013 x, 147 p.p illustrations (pbk.; alk. paper) $15   **636.8**
    1. Cats 2. Animal behavior 3. Cat breeds 4. Cats -- Behavior
    ISBN 1557536481; 9781557536488
                            LC 2012034713

Written by Benjamin L. Hart and Lynette A. Hart, this "book takes the process of selecting a cat to the next level by offering data-based behavioral profiles of a wide range of cat breeds. Developed over a lifetime of research and through extensive interviews with eighty veterinary experts, the profiles are presented in easy-to-use graphical form." (Publisher's note)

Includes bibliographical references (pages 135-140) and index

Herriot, James

James Herriot's cat stories; with illustrations by Lesley Holmes. St. Martin's Press 1994 161p $17.95   **636.8**
    1. Cats
    ISBN 0-312-11342-0
                            LC 94-20131

A "collection of favorite cat tales from Herriot's veterinary practice. Retired after over 50 years in practice, Herriot continues to entertain young and old alike with his storytelling ability. His current collection includes 'Alfred, the Sweet-Shop Cat,' 'Boris and Mrs. Bond's Cat Establishment,' 'Moses Found Among the Rushes,' and others." Libr J

Johnson-Bennett, Pam

Catwise; America's Favorite Cat Expert Answers Your Cat Behavior Questions. Pam Johnson-Bennett. Penguin Books 2016 352 p. $18   **636.8**
    1. Cats -- Behavior
    ISBN 9780143129561
                         LC 2016000873

This book by Pam Johnson-Bennett answers "150 questions most often asked by puzzled cat owners. . . . Here, in one complete authoritative guide, those elusive mysteries are solved. . . . [It] combines the questions that come up most often with answers to help you solve your cat's behavior problems (or head them off before they start), or simply improve the relationship you have with your cat." (Publisher's note)

"The book is an excellent choice for someone planning to adopt a kitten as well as for experienced cat owners with senior cats." Pub Wkly

Myron, Vicki

Dewey; a small-town library cat who touched the world. Grand Central Publisher 2008 277p il $19.99   **636.8**
    1. Cats
    ISBN 978-0-446-40741-0; 0-446-40741-0
                       LC 2008-4498

The story of Dewey Readmore Books, the beloved library cat of Spencer, Iowa.

"Myron's beguiling, poignant, and tender tale of survival, loyalty, and love is an unforgettable study in the mysterious and wondrous ways animals, and libraries, enrich humanity." Booklist

Tucker, Abigail

The **lion** in the living room; How House Cats Tamed Us and Took Over the World. Abigail Tucker. Simon & Schuster 2016 256 p. (ebook) $19.99; (hardcover; alk. paper) $26.00 **636.8**
    1. Cats -- History 2. Human-animal relationships
    ISBN 9781476738253; 9781476738239
                        LC 2016000722

This book narrates how, "to better understand these furry strangers in our midst, [author] Abby Tucker travels to meet the breeders, activists, and scientists who've dedicated their lives to cats. She visits the labs where people sort through feline bones unearthed from the first human settlements, treks through the Floridian wilderness in search of house cats on the loose, and hangs out with [feline celebrity] Lil Bub." (Publisher's note)

"Tucker's informative interviews with werewolf cat breeders, cat lobbyists, and Internet star Little Bub's owner round out a thoughtful look at the illogical human love of felines." Pub Wkly

Includes bibliographical references and index

636.9   Other mammals

Westoll, Andrew

The **chimps** of Fauna Sanctuary; a true story of resilience and recovery. Houghton Mifflin Harcourt 2011 268p il $25   **636.9**
    1. Chimpanzees 2. Wildlife refuges 3. Animal rescue 4. Fauna Foundation 5. Chimpanzees -- Behavior 6. Animal experimentation -- Moral and ethical aspects
    ISBN 978-0-547-32780-8; 0-547-32780-3
                        LC 2010049783

"This is both an inspiring and a disturbing book. It is inspiring because of the devotion of caregivers to welfare of the chimps; it is disturbing because of the callous treatment to which chimps in research are subjected." Sci Books Films

Includes bibliographical references

637   Processing dairy and related products

Caldwell, Gianaclis

Mastering artisan cheesemaking; the ultimate guide for home-scale and market producers. Gianaclis Caldwell ; foreword by Ricki Carroll. Chelsea Green Publishing 2012 vi, 345 p.p color illustrations $40   **637**
    1. Cooking 2. Cheesemaking
    ISBN 1603583327; 9781603583329
                        LC 2012023148

This cheese-making book, by Gianaclis Caldwell, "thoroughly explains the art and science that allow milk to be transformed into epicurean masterpieces. Caldwell offers a deep look at the history, science, culture, and art of making artisan cheese on a small scale, and includes detailed information on equipment and setting up a home-scale operation." (Publisher's note)

"Recipes are offered and explained in very easy terms. A complete package." Booklist

Includes bibliographical references (pages 327-328) and index

English, Ashley

Home dairy with Ashley English; all you need to know to make cheese, yogurt, butter & more. Lark Crafts 2011 135p il (Homemade living) $19.95   **637**
1. Dairy products
ISBN 978-1-60059-627-8

LC 2010020669

"English is no slouch at demystifying the intricacies of home dairy; from the simplicities of churning out your own delectable butter to pressing your very first gouda, the author covers it all in clean, unpretentious, step-by-step instruction. Excellent for those looking to take a slight step off the grid." Kirkus

Includes bibliographical references

Kurlansky, Mark, 1948-

★ **Milk!** a 10,000-year food fracas. Mark Kurlansky. Bloomsbury Publishing 2018 400 p. (hardcover) $29   **637**
1. Dairy products 2. Milk -- History 3. Dairy products -- History
ISBN 1632863820; 9781632863829

LC 2017039795

This book, by Mark Kurlansky, "[is his] first global food history since the bestselling 'Cod' and 'Salt;' [it outlines] the fascinating cultural, economic, and culinary story of milk and all things dairy--with recipes throughout. . . . Tracing the liquid's diverse history from antiquity to the present, he details its curious and crucial role in cultural evolution, religion, nutrition, politics, and economics." (Publisher's note)

"A fascinating and comprehensive book that will keep readers engaged and entertained. The recipes, especially those on the historical side, are a unique and complimentary addition. Will appeal to both foodies and readers of world history. Highly recommended." LJ

Includes bibliographical references and index

Lucero, Claudia

One-hour cheese; ricotta, mozzarella, chèvre, paneer--even burrata, fresh and simple cheeses you can make in an hour or less! by Claudia Lucero, founder of Urban Cheesecraft and Creator of DIY Cheese Kit. Workman Pub. Company, Inc. 2014 260 p. color illustrations (alk. paper) $14.95   **637**
1. Cheesemaking
ISBN 0761177485; 9780761177487

LC 2014001166

In this cookbook Claudia Lucero "shows step by step—with every step photographed—exactly how to make sixteen fresh cheeses at home, using easily available ingredients and tools, in an hour or less. The approach is basic and based on thousands of years of cheesemaking wisdom: Heat milk, add coagulant, drain, salt, and press. Simple variations produce delicious results across three categories—Creamy and Spreadable, Firm and Chewy, and Melty and Gooey." (Publisher's note)

"A fantastic introduction for novices who want simple, delicious, DIY cheese." LJ

Includes bibliographical references and index

The **Oxford** companion to cheese; edited by Catherine Donnelly ; foreword by Mateo Kehler. Oxford University Press 2016 xx, 849 p.p illustrations (Oxford companions) (hardcover; alk. paper) $65   **637**
1. Cheese 2. Cheesemaking 3. Cheese -- Encyclopedias
ISBN 9780199330881

LC 2016034026

This book in the Oxford Companions series, edited by Catherine Donnelly, "is the first major reference work dedicated to cheese, containing 855 A-Z entries on cheese history, culture, science, and production.

. . . [It] also reflects a fascination with the microbiology and chemistry of cheese, featuring entries on bacteria, molds, yeasts, cultures, and co-agulants used in cheesemaking and cheese maturing." (Publisher's note)

"Overall, this book is extremely useful for those looking to know more about the art and science of cheese making. Highly recommended for foodies and also those involved in food and nutrition studies." Booklist

Includes bibliographical references and index.

638   Insect culture

The **bee** book; Fergus Chadwick, Steve Alton, Emma Sarah Tennant, Bill Fitzmaurice, Judy Earl. DK Publishing 2016 221 p. illustrations (some color) $25   **638**
1. Beekeeping 2. Bees 3. Honeybee 4. Bumblebees 5. Bee culture
ISBN 1465443835; 9781465443830

LC 2015458993

This book "shows you step-by-step how to create a bee-friendly garden, get started in beekeeping, and harness the power of honey for well-being. Fully illustrated with full-color photographs throughout, this . . . guide covers everything you need to know to start your own backyard hive, from setup to harvest. Practical beekeeping techniques are explained with clear step-by-step sequences, photos, and diagrams." (Publisher's note)

"This is a charming, information-rich book that should lead readers to appreciate bees and welcome them into their gardens and wild places and even encourage some to keep honeybees." Booklist

Black, Scott Hoffman

Gardening for butterflies; How You Can Attract and Protect Beautiful, Beneficial Insects. the Xerces Society (Scott Hoffman Black, Brianna Borders, Candace Fallon, Eric Lee-Mader, Matthew Shepherd) ; foreword by Robert Michael Pyle. Timber Press 2016 287 p. color illustrations $24.95   **638**
1. Gardening 2. Butterflies 3. Butterfly gardening
ISBN 9781604695984

LC 2015029810

This book, "by the experts at the Xerces Society, introduces you to a variety of colorful garden guests who need our help, and shows you how to design a habitat where they will thrive. This optimistic call to arms is packed with everything you need to create a beautiful, beneficial, butterfly-filled garden." (Publisher's note)

"This book will help even those without green thumbs support the much-needed effort to assist and protect pollinators." Booklist

Includes bibliographical references (pages 269-274) index.

Flottum, Kim

★ The **backyard** beekeeper; an absolute beginner's guide to keeping bees in your yard and garden. Kim Flottum. Quarry Books 2018 240 p. color illustrations $24.99   **638**
1. Beehives 2. Beekeeping 3. Honeybee 4. Bee culture
ISBN 9781631593321

LC 2017050221

Written by Kim Flottum, 'The Backyard Beekeeper,' now revised and expanded in its 4th edition, "makes the time-honored and complex tradition of beekeeping an enjoyable and accessible backyard pastime that will appeal to urban and rural beekeepers of all skill levels." (Publisher's note)

"Flottum (editor, Bee Culture magazine) brings beekeeping into the backyard with this handbook on keeping hives and harvesting their products. New material on natural beekeeping and "extreme urban bee-keeping" will satisfy most readers." LJ

Goulson, Dave

A **Buzz** in the Meadow; The Natural History of a French Farm. Dave Goulson. Picador 2015 288 p. $25   **638**

1. Farms 2. France 3. Insects
ISBN 1250065887; 9781250065889

In this book, author Dave "Goulson returns to tell the tale of how he bought a derelict farm in the heart of rural France. Over the course of a decade, on thirty-three acres of meadow, he created a place for his beloved bumblebees to thrive. But other creatures live there too, myriad insects of every kind, many of which Goulson had studied before in his career as a biologist." (Publisher's note)

"Unexpectedly, Goulson also moves beyond his home to reflect on the work of biologists of the past and present, particularly when considering the critical state of the world's pollinators, for whom he issues a gentle call to arms. The book is, therefore, less a meditative reflection of wildlife in the country and more an artful blend of E. O. Wilson and Barry Lopez, with a continental flair. Backyard naturalists, regardless of their locale, will delight in the amiable company of this witty and thoughtful guide." Booklist

Hanson, Thor

Buzz; the nature and necessity of bees. Thor Hanson. Basic Books, an imprint of Perseus Books, a subsidiary of Hachette Book Group 2018 304 p.   **638**

1. Bees -- Popular works
ISBN 9780465052615; 9780465098804

LC 2018012761

In this book, "[author] Thor Hanson takes us on a journey that begins 125 million years ago, when a wasp first dared to feed pollen to its young. From honeybees and bumbles to lesser-known diggers, miners, leafcutters, and masons, bees have long been central to our harvests, our mythologies, and our very existence. They've given us sweetness and light, the beauty of flowers, and as much as a third of the foodstuffs we eat. And, alarmingly, they are at risk of disappearing." (Publisher's note)

"According to conservation biologist Hanson, populations of many species of bees are in decline due to habitat loss, herbicides, pesticides, and introduced pathogens. Despite this news, the author is surprisingly optimistic that we can reform and protect our bees, citing recent research and improved agricultural practices." Booklist

Includes bibliographical references and index

Jones, Richard A.

★ The **beekeeper's** bible; bees, honey, recipes & other home uses. by Richard A. Jones and Sharon Sweeney-Lynch. Stewart, Tabori & Chang 2011 413 p.   **638**

1. Bee culture 2. Bee products 3. Cooking (Honey)
ISBN 9781584799184

LC 2010041458

Includes bibliographical references (p. 241-254) and index

Nordhaus, Hannah

The **beekeeper's** lament; how one man and half a billion honey bees help feed America. Harper Perennial 2011 269p il pa $14.99   **638**

1. Bees 2. Beekeeping 3. Beekeepers
ISBN 978-0-06-187325-6; 0-06-187325-X

"Nordhaus centers her account on John Miller, a migratory beekeeper who hauls truckloads of bees from crop to crop to help farmers who don't have natural pollinators. Honey bees are crucial to American

agriculture, pollinating crops of 90 different fruits and vegetables. We would lose our almond crops almost entirely without bees, for example. Nordhaus meticulously details this process, demonstrating how modern apiculture affects everyone from keeper to bee to farmer to consumer. . . . [She] provides an almost overwhelming amount of information in a relatively short amount of space, but it's a fascinating read from cover to cover, and Miller makes a genuinely likable American hero." Stamford Advocate

Sammataro, Diana

The **beekeeper's** handbook; Diana Sammataro and Alphonse Avitabile ; foreword by Dewey M. Caron. Comstock Pub. Associates 2011 x, 308 p.p illustrations (pbk.; alk. paper) $29.95   **638**

1. Beekeeping 2. Bee culture -- Handbooks, manuals, etc
ISBN 0801476941; 9780801449819; 9780801476945

LC 2010050047

This book, by Diana Sammataro and Alphonse Avitabile, is a "guide to the hobby and profession of beekeeping. Featuring clear descriptions and authoritative content, this handbook provides step-by-step directions accompanied by more than 100 illustrations for setting up an apiary, handling bees, and working throughout the season to maintain a healthy colony of bees and a generous supply of honey. This book explains the various colony care options and techniques." (Publisher's note)

Includes bibliographical references and index

639   Hunting, fishing, conservation, related technologies

Dray, Philip

The **fair** chase; the epic story of hunting in America. Philip Dray. Basic Books 2018 416 p. (hardcover) $30   **639**

1. Sports -- United States 2. Hunting -- United States -- History
ISBN 9780465061723

LC 2018005078

This book, by Philip Dray, "tells the story of hunting in America, showing how this sport has shaped our national identity. . . . Hunting is one of America's most sacred-but also most fraught-traditions. It was promoted in the 19th century as a way to reconnect 'soft' urban Americans with nature and to the legacy of the country's path finding heroes. . . . But the sport's popularity also caused class, ethnic, and racial divisions." (Publisher's note)

"While steering clear of taking sides in the matter of recreational hunting, Dray provides a lively h i story that can be enjoyed by hunters and conservationists alike." Kirkus

Includes bibliographical references and index

Greenlaw, Linda

The **lobster** chronicles; life on a very small island. Hyperion 2002 238p $22.95; pa $13.95   **639**

1. Lobster fisheries 2. Isle au Haut (Maine)
ISBN 0-7868-6677-2; 0-7868-8591-2 pa

In this companion to The hungry ocean, the author gives "up swordfishing to return to her parents' home on Isle Au Haut off the coast of Maine and fish for lobster. . . . She intersperses her narrative with plenty of eccentrics who live on her tiny island. . . . Self-speculation and uncertainties . . . nicely balance her delightfully cocky essays of island life." Publ Wkly

Swift, Earl

Chesapeake requiem; a year with the waterman of vanishing Tangier Island. Earl Swift. HarperCollins 2018 464 p.

$28.99   **639**

1. Islands 2. Lifestyles 3. Aquaculture

ISBN 0062661396; 9780062661395

This book "is an intimate look at . . . [Tangier Island's] past, present and tenuous future, by an acclaimed journalist [Earl Swift] who spent much of the past two years living among Tangier's people, crabbing and oystering with its watermen, and observing its long traditions and odd ways. What emerges is the poignant tale of a world that has, quite nearly, gone by--and a leading-edge report on the coming fate of countless coastal communities." (Publisher's note)

639.2   Commercial fishing, whaling, sealing

Cook, Langdon

Upstream; searching for wild salmon, from river to table. Langdon Cook. Ballantine Books 2017 314 p. illustrations, map (hardback) $27   **639.2**

1. Salmon 2. Salmon fisheries 3. Nutrition 4. Salmon stock management 5. Salmon -- Pacific Coast (U.S.) 6. Salmon fishing -- Pacific Coast (U.S.) 7. Salmon fisheries -- Pacific Coast (U.S.)

ISBN 9781101882900; 9781101882887

LC 2017012853

In this book author Langdon Cook, looks "at how . . . [salmon] have nourished humankind through the ages and why their destiny is so closely tied to our own. Cook journeys up and down salmon country, from the glacial rivers of Alaska to the rainforests of the Pacific Northwest to California's drought-stricken Central Valley. . . . Reporting from remote coastlines . . . He follows today's commercial pipeline from fisherman's net to corporate seafood vendor." (Publisher's note)

"The Pacific salmon is a great American fish, and by writing about it with such care and curiosity, Cook establishes its ecological importance and tells a great American story." Booklist

Includes bibliographical references (pages 313-314) and index.

Dolin, Eric Jay

Leviathan; the history of whaling in America. W.W. Norton & Company 2007 479p il $27.95   **639.2**

1. Whaling -- History

ISBN 978-0-393-06057-7; 0-393-06057-8

LC 2007-06113

The author "chronicles the long history of whaling in North America, from the voyages of Capt. John Smith, who, like many after him, 'found this Whale-fishing a costly conclusion,' to the last voyage of the Wanderer, a whaler that set sail from the once-teeming port of New Bedford, Mass., in 1924 and promptly wrecked in the shallows before a crowd of curious onlookers. . . . Anyone whose knowledge of whaling begins and ends with 'MobyDick' will get a solid education from Mr. Dolin, who fills in the historical record and sets the stage for the glory years when men like Melville set out from Nantucket, New Bedford, Sag Harbor and dozens of other ports on voyages lasting as long as four years." N Y Times (Late N Y Ed)

Includes bibliographical references

Kurlansky, Mark

The **last** fish tale; the fate of the Atlantic and survival in Gloucester, America's oldest fishing port and most original town. Riverhead Books 2009 xxix, 269p il map pa $16 **639.2**

1. Commercial fishing 2. Gloucester (Mass.)

ISBN 978-1-59448-374-5

First published 2008 by Ballantine Books

The author "provides a delightful, intimate history and contem-

porary portrait of the quintessential northeastern coastal fishing town: Gloucester, Mass., on Cape Anne. Illustrated with his own beautifully executed drawings, Kurlansky's book vividly depicts the contemporary tension between the traditional fishing trade and modern commerce, which in Gloucester means beach-going tourists." Publ Wkly

Includes bibliographical references

639.34   Fish culture in aquariums

Bailey, Mary

The **Ultimate** Encyclopedia of Aquarium Fish & Fish Care; A definitive guide to identifying and keeping freshwater and marine fishes. by Mary Bailey and Gina Sandford. Natl Book Network 2015 256 p. color illustrations $13.99   **639.34**

1. Fishes 2. Aquariums

ISBN 1780193416; 9781780193410

This book, by Mary Bailey and Gina Sandford, is a "comprehensive manual on planning, building, stocking and maintaining all types of aquaria, fully illustrated with 700 photographs and diagrams." (Publisher's note)

Mills, Dick

Aquarium fish. DK 2004 72p il (101 essential tips) pa $5   **639.34**

1. Fishes 2. Aquariums

ISBN 0-7566-0611-X; 978-0-7566-0611-4

LC 2004-303366

Reprint of paperback printed by DK Pub. in 1996

This book offers advice on choosing fish for aquariums, aquarium equipment, decoration, feeding, and health care, and describes various species of tropical, coldwater, freshwater, and marine fishes.

"Accurate, clear, and concise writing is enhanced with wonderful color photographs on each page." Voice Youth Advocates [review of 1996 edition]

639.9   Conservation of biological resources

Jacobsen, Rowan

The **living** shore; rediscovering a lost world. illustrated by Mary Elder Jacobsen. Bloomsbury 2009 167p il map $20   **639.9**

1. Oysters 2. Commercial fishing 3. Puget Sound region (Wash.)

ISBN 978-1-59691-684-5; 1-59691-684-2

LC 2009-8903

A marine scientist, together with Rowan and a conservancy group interested in habitat restoration, suggests a possible blueprint for cleaning up our oceans by observing an isolated pocket of oysters living on the western side of Vancouver Island.

"Lovely science writing, and a smart look into where the work of ecological restoration is headed." Kirkus

Includes bibliographical references

Varty, Boyd

Cathedral of the wild; an African journey home. Boyd Varty. Random House Inc 2014 304 p. illustrations (acid-free paper) $27   **639.9**

1. Game reserves 2. Africa -- Social conditions 3. Londolozi Game Reserve (South Africa) -- History 4. Wildlife conservation -- South Africa -- Londolozi Game Reserve -- History

ISBN 1400069858; 9781400069859

LC 2013022706

Author Boyd Varty presents a "memoir of his life in [Londolozi Game Reserve in South Africa]. At Londolozi, Varty gained the confidence that emerges from living in Africa. It was there that young Boyd and his equally adventurous sister learned to track animals, raised leopard and lion cubs, followed their larger-than-life uncle on his many adventures filming wildlife, and became one with the land. An intense spiritual quest takes him across the globe and back again." (Publisher's note)

An "intense, insightful memoir that brings together several wise observations about the relationship between nature and humanity." Pub Wkly

Includes bibliographical references and index

639.97 Specific kinds of animals

Bradley, Carol

Last chain on Billie; how one extraordinary elephant escaped the big top. Carol Bradley. St. Martin's Press 2014 336 p. (hardcover) $25.99 **639.97**

1. Circus 2. Elephants 3. Animal rescue 4. Animal welfare 5. Animal rescue -- United States 6. Animal welfare -- United States 7. Elephants -- United States -- Anecdotes 8. Circus animals -- United States -- Anecdotes 9. Captive elephants -- United States -- Anecdotes

ISBN 1250025699; 9781250025692

LC 2014008568

This book, by Carol Bradley, "charts the history of elephants in America, the . . . story of the Elephant Sanctuary and the . . . tale of a resilient elephant who defied the system. . . . Left in the wild, Billie the elephant would have spent her days surrounded by family. . . . Instead, traders captured her as a baby and shipped her to America, where she learned . . . the full repertoire of elephant tricks. . . . But behind the scenes she lived a life of misery." (Publisher's note)

"Graphic details of animal abuse may offend some readers, but the overall story is worth enduring those passages.A moving and informative account of the plight of trained elephants in the U.S. and the efforts of those who have created an asylum for them." Kirkus

Mills, J. A.

Blood of the tiger; a story of conspiracy, greed, and the battle to save a magnificent species. J.A. Mills. Beacon Press 2015 272 p. illustrations (hardback) $27.95 **639.97**

1. Tiger trade -- China

ISBN 0807074969; 9780807074961

LC 2014015760

This book, by J.A. Mills, "takes readers on a wild ride to save one of the world's rarest animals from a band of Chinese billionaires. . . . There may be only three thousand wild tigers left in the entire world. More shocking is the fact that twice that many-- some six thousand-- have been bred on farms, not for traditional medicine but to supply a luxury-goods industry that secretly sells tiger-bone wine, tiger-skin décor, and exotic cuisine enjoyed by China's elite." (Publisher's note)

"The author provides a list of resources for readers inspired to take action, in addition to a substantial set of notes. A telling inside view of 20 years in international tiger conservation work, including the successes, failures and the work that is still required." Kirkus

Includes bibliographical references and index

Raffin, Michele

The **birds** of Pandemonium; life among the exotic and the endangered. by Michele Raffin. Algonquin Books of Chapel Hill 2014 240 p. 16 plates; color illustrations $24.95 **639.97**

1. Birds -- Protection 2. Wildlife conservation 3. Pandemonium Aviaries 4. Birds -- Conservation -- California

ISBN 1616201363; 9781616201364

LC 2014023612

In this book, author "Michele Raffin steps outside into the bewitching bird music that heralds another day at Pandemonium Aviaries. . . . Pandemonium, the home and bird sanctuary that Raffin shares with some of the world's most remarkable birds, is a conservation organization dedicated to saving and breeding birds at the edge of extinction, with the goal of eventually releasing them into the wild. . . . Their amazing stories make up the heart of this book." (Publisher's note)

"Animal lovers will likely forgive the author her stylistic lapses and read appreciatively of her many strong works." LJ

640 Home and family management

Alink, Merissa

Little house living; the make-your-own guide to a frugal, simple, and self-sufficient life. Merissa Alink. Gallery Books 2015 320 p. color illustrations $26.99 **640**

1. Home economics 2. Household budgets 3. Housekeeping

ISBN 1501104268; 9781501104268; 9781501104282

LC 2015024538

Author Merissa A. Alink presents this "homemaking book, inspired by Laura Ingalls Wilder's 'Little House on the Prairie,' featuring creative, fun ways to live . . . life simply and frugally. With over 130 practical, simple DIY recipes, . . . full-color photographs, and [Alink's] trademark charm in personal stories and tips, 'Little House Living' is the epitome of heartland warmth and prairie inspiration." (Publisher's note)

"With chapters on Body and Beauty, Household, Children and Pets, and Make-Ahead Mixes, plus additional stories, Alink brings a bit of Wilder's life into the present." LJ

Bried, Erin

How to sew a button; and other nifty things your grandmother knew. Ballantine Books 2009 xxii, 278p il pa $15 **640**

1. Handicraft 2. Life skills 3. Home economics

ISBN 978-0-345-51875-0; 0-345-51875-6

LC 2009036046

"These anecdotes and tutorials gleaned from subject experts and grandmothers who were children during the Great Depression cover a broad swath of homemaking skills. Instead of systematic how-tos, Bried presents these lessons as a means to improve the quality of the reader's life. Excellent information, but definitely written to a female audience." Libr J

English, Ashley

The **Essential** Book of Homesteading; The Ultimate Guide to Sustainable Living. Ashley English. Lark Books 2017 vii, 360 p.p color illustrations (Homemade living) (hardcover) $24.95 **640**

1. Urban homesteading 2. Bee culture 3. Poultry farms 4. Dairy processing 5. Sustainable living 6. Canning and preserving 7. Agriculture -- United States

ISBN 9781454710202; 1454710209

This book explores "the modern homesteading movement. Whether it's turning a lawn into a vegetable garden, getting a flock of chickens, or transforming cucumbers into pickles, people everywhere are taking charge of their own food supply. Ashley English, a major figure in the return to homesteading, gives newcomers . . . tips for successfully over-seeing food production in their own homes." (Publisher's note)

"Overall, a detail-laden volume ideal for hobbyists and serious DI-Yers." Booklist

Stewart, Martha, 1941-

Martha Stewart's Homekeeping Handbook; the essential guide to caring for eveything in your home. Martha Stewart. Clarkson Potter 2006 744 p. illustrations $45   **640**

1. Home economics
ISBN 0517577003; 9780517577004

LC 2006050267

This book, by Martha Stewart, offers the author's "expertise in home maintenance and care. . . . With charts, sidebars, illustrated techniques, and personal anecdotes from . . . decades of experience caring for . . . homes–this is far more than just a compendium of ways to keep your house clean. It covers everything from properly executing a living room floor plan to setting a formal table . . . , to polishing your silver and caring for family heirlooms." (Publisher's note)

Sundeen, Mark

The **unsettlers**; In Search of the Good Life in Today's America. Mark Sundeen. Riverhead Books 2016 336 p. (ebook) $65; $26   **640**

1. Simplicity 2. Alternative lifestyles 3. Sustainable development 4. Sustainable living -- United States 5. Self-reliant living -- United States 6. Alternative lifestyles -- United States 7. United States -- Civilization -- 21st century
ISBN 9781101618059; 9781594631580

LC 2016026360

This book, by Mark Sundeen, focuses on the "search for the simple life in today's America. On a frigid April night, . . . [an] opera singer, five months pregnant, and her husband, a former marine biologist, disembark an Amtrak train in La Plata, Missouri, . . . and pedal off into the night, bound for a homestead they've purchased. . . Meanwhile, a horticulturist . . . and her husband . . . have turned to urban farming to revitalize the blighted city they both love." (Publisher's note)

"An engaging read for those with an interest in sustainable living, urban farming, and homesteading." LJ

Introduction -- Missouri -- Detroit -- Montana -- Epilogue.

Tracy, Brian

Eat that frog! 21 great ways to stop procrastinating and get more done in less time. by Brian Tracy. Berrett-Koehler Publishers 2006 128 p. $15.95   **640**

1. Time management 2. Procrastination
ISBN 1576754227; 9781576754221

LC 0013189

Second Edition
This book, by Brian Tracy, "provides the 21 most effective methods for conquering procrastination and accomplishing more. This new edition is revised and updated throughout, and includes brand new information on how to keep technology from dominating our time." (Publisher's note)

Includes index

640.43 Time management

Lightman, Alan P., 1948-

In praise of wasting time; Alan Lightman. Simon & Schuster 2018 128 p. $16.99   **640.43**

1. Creative ability 2. Creative thinking 3. Social psychology
ISBN 1501154362; 9781501154362

LC 2018080071

This book by Alan Lightman "investigates the creativity born from allowing our minds to freely roam, without attempting to accomplish anything and without any assigned tasks. . . .[He] documents the rush and heave of the modern world, suggests the technological and cultural origins of our time-driven lives, and examines the many values of 'wasting time'--for replenishing the mind, for creative thought, and for finding and solidifying the inner self." (Publisher's note)

640.73 Evaluation and purchasing guides

Pogue, David

Money; Essential Tips and Shortcuts (That No One Bothers to Tell You) About Beating the System. by David Pogue. St. Martin's Press 2016 256 p. illustrations (ebook) $60; $19.99   **640.73**

1. Money 2. Personal finance
ISBN 9781250081421; 1250081416; 9781250081414

LC 2016033301

This book, by David Pogue, "proves that information is money. Each of his 150 simple tips and tricks includes a ballpark estimate of the money you could make or save. Okay, you won't use every tip in the book— but if you did, you'd come ahead by $61,195 a year." (Publisher's note)

Rossen, Jeff

Rossen to the rescue; secrets to avoiding scams, everyday dangers, and major catastrophes. Jeff Rossen. Flatiron Books 2017 x, 245 p.p (hardcover) $24.99   **640.73**

1. Advice literature 2. Consumer protection 3. Crime prevention 4. Consumer education 5. Home accidents -- Prevention
ISBN 125011943X; 9781250119445; 9781250119438

LC 2017027321

This book, by Jeff Rossen, "includes daring experiments, expert advice, and game plans for handling all the wild cards in life--big and small--while sharing personal, and sometimes embarrassing, anecdotes that he couldn't tell on television. Overflowing with never-before-seen tips and tricks, this book is filled with enough hacks to keep you and your family safe and it just might save your life." (Publisher's note)

"In Rossen's brisk handbook of practical tips, expert advice, and life hacks, the Today Show reporter helps the average person navigate life's sticky situations." Pub Wkly

Includes bibliographical references and index.

641 Food and drink

101 classic cookbooks; 501 classic recipes. Marvin J. Taylor, Clark Wolf, The Fales Library, New York University. Rizzoli 2012 688 p. $50   **641**

1. Cookbooks 2. American cooking
ISBN 0847837939; 9780847837939

LC 2012940384

This "collection, edited by [Marvin J.] Taylor . . . and food consultant [Clark] Wolf, offers signature recipes from 20th-century classics such as Fannie Farmer's 'The Boston Cooking-School Cook Book,' James Beard's 'American Cookery,' and Mark Bittman's 'How To Cook Everything.' Books are organized chronologically in entries that explain each title's historical significance and include bibliographic information, images of the first edition, and a list of notable recipes." (Library Journal)

The **backyard** homestead; edited by Carleen Madigan. Storey Pub. 2009 367p il pa $18.95 **641**

1. Vegetable gardening 2. Food -- Preservation

ISBN 978-1-60342-138-6

LC 2009-01338

"Madigan presents the information in clear chapters, starting with vegetables, herbs, and fruit and nut trees; moving on through growing grains and grinding them into flour; and then tackling keeping chickens, cows, pigs, and more. The last chapter, 'Food from the Wild,' delves into beekeeping, foraging for berries and mushrooms, and making your own maple syrup. None of the information is particularly in-depth—if you decide to pursue something, you'll likely want to get another book on that one subject. But as an inspiration and an introduction to the various possibilities, it's perfect." Epicurious

Includes bibliographical references

Bourdain, Anthony

A **cook's** tour; global adventures in extreme cuisines. Ecco 2002 274p il pa $14.99 **641**

1. Food 2. Cooking

ISBN 0-06-001278-1

LC 2002-23507

First published 2001 by Bloomsbury Press

This is an "account of the author's global search for the 'perfect mix of food and context' that takes the reader to the culinary corners of the earth: from Vietnam (a live cobra heart) and Japan (poisonous blowfish) to England (roasted bone marrow) and Scotland (deep-fried Mars bar)." N Y Times Book Rev

Bourdain, Anthony, 1956-2018

Appetites; a cookbook. Anthony Bourdain, Laurie Woolever. HarperCollins 2016 304 p. (hardcover) $37.50 **641**

1. Cooking 2. Cookbooks

ISBN 0062409956; 9780062409959

This cookbook, by Anthony Bourdain and Laurie Woolever, "boils down forty-plus years of professional cooking and globe-trotting to a tight repertoire of personal favorites—dishes that everyone should (at least in Mr. Bourdain's opinion) know how to cook. . . . After years of traveling more than 200 days a year, he now enjoys entertaining at home." (Publisher's note)

"In what might be his most accessible book yet, Bourdain reveals his 'Ina Garten–like need to feed the people around me' with a terrific collection of recipes for family and friends." Pub Wkly

Coffey, Bennett

Chocolate every day; 85+ Plant-based Recipes for Cacao Treats That Support Your Health and Well-being. Bennett Coffey and Kyleen Keenan. Penguin Group USA 2018 224 p. $27 **641**

1. Desserts 2. Cookbooks 3. Cooking -- Chocolate

ISBN 0735216045; 9780735216044

In this cookbook, Bennett Coffey and Kyleen Keenan. "show chocolate for what it really is: a delicious and incredibly potent, antioxidant powerhouse filled with vitamins and nutrients. Their decadent recipes do away with the refined sugar, dairy, and gluten found in traditional chocolate treats, and instead rely on raw cacao and high-quality, unprocessed ingredients to create snacks and desserts you can actually feel good about eating." (Publisher's note)

"With fruit and nut ingredients, such as orange zest for chocolaty orange scones, pomegranate seeds for chocolate bark, and peanut butter and honey frosting for chocolate cupcakes, this book is filled with dozens of wonderful flavor combinations." Pub Wkly

Fisher, M. F. K. (Mary Frances Kennedy), 1908-1992

The **art** of eating; M.F.K. Fisher ; with an introduction by Clifton Fadiman ; an appreciation by James A. Beard ; and a retrospective essay by Joan Reardon. Wiley Pub. 2004 xxxiv, 749 p.p $24.95 **641**

1. Cooking 2. Eating habits 3. Gastronomy

ISBN 0764542613; 9780764542619

LC 2003026124

James Beard Cookbook Hall of Fame (1990)

IACP Culinary Classics Book Award (2012)

This book, by Mary Frances Kennedy Fisher, is a "50th anniversary paperback reprint . . . [of the author's collected best writings on food and cooking. M. F. K.] Fisher (1908-1992) was one of this country's earliest food writers. . . . The 784-page collection brings together five works originally published under separate titles. . . . There are also recipes scattered throughout." (Publisher's note)

Fraioli, James O.

The **Canon** Cocktail Book; Recipes from the Award-Winning Bar. by Jamie Boudreau and James O. Fraioli. Houghton Mifflin Harcourt 2016 352 p. (ebook) $28; $28 **641**

1. Bars 2. Cocktails

ISBN 9780544631595; 054463103X; 9780544631038

This book, by Jamie Boudreau and James O. Fraioli, focuses on "Seattle bar Canon. . . . offers 100 cocktail recipes ranging from riffs on the classics, like the Cobbler's Dream and Corpse Reviver, to their lineup of original house drinks, such as the Truffled Old Fashioned and the Banksy Sour. In addition to tips, recipes, and formulas for top-notch cocktails, syrups, and infusions, Boudreau breaks down the fundamentals and challenges of opening and running a bar." (Publisher's note)

"This terrific resource is sure to send armchair bartenders scurrying to their shakers." Pub Wkly

Gaines, Joanna

★ **Magnolia** table; a collection of recipes for gathering. Joanna Gaines. HarperCollins 2018 336 p. hardcover $29.99 **641**

1. Cookbooks 2. Southern cooking

ISBN 0062863428; 9780062820150

LC 2018020559

"'Magnolia Table' is infused with Joanna Gaines' warmth and passion for all things family, prepared and served straight from the heart of her home, with recipes inspired by dozens of Gaines family favorites and classic comfort selections from the couple's new Waco restaurant, Magnolia Table. . . . [It] includes 125 classic recipes-[,] . . . presenting a modern selection of American classics and personal family favorites." (Publisher's note)

Garten, Ina

Barefoot Contessa at home; everyday recipes you'll make over and over again. photographs by Quentin Bacon. Clarkson Potter 2006 p. cm. **641**

1. Menus. 2. Cookery.

ISBN 1400054346

Garten "follows her surefire formula: uncomplicated but elegant recipes for the home cook whose priority is spending time with friends and family, not in the kitchen. From breakfast to dessert, the Food Network star organizes this volume by meal, with an easy-to-navigate recipe list at the top of each section." (Publishers Weekly)

LC 2006014257

Barefoot in Paris; easy French food you really can make

at home \ Ina Garden ; photographs by Quentin Bacon ; Food Stuyleing by Rori Trovato ; Prop Styling by Miguel Flores-Vianna. Clarkson Potter\Publishers 2004 p. cm **641**
    ISBN 1-400-04935-0 (hardcover)
    Provides recipes for simple dishes from France, using fresh, quality ingredients to concoct new twists on traditional French favorites, including steak au poivre, and creme brulee.

LC 2004-3280

Jordan, Christy
    Sweetness; Southern recipes to celebrate the warmth, the love, and the blessings of a full life. Christy Jordan. Workman Pub Co 2016 304 p. (paperback) $16.95 **641**
    1. Desserts 2. Southern cooking
    ISBN 0761189424; 9780761189428
    This Southern cookbook, by Christy Jordan, "shares 197 recipes for sweet things to eat and drink—recipes that are deeply delicious, rich with tradition, often reaching through generations, and designed with today's hectic schedules in mind. Because life is just better when you add a little sweetness." (Publisher's note)
    "Filled with family stories and cheerful advice, this cookbook is a reasonably priced volume of easy-to-make sweets." LJ

Kaminsky, Peter
    The **sweet** spot; dialing back sugar and amping up flavor. Bill Yosses and Peter Kaminsky. Penguin Group USA 2017 272 p. $35 **641**
    1. Baking 2. Cooking 3. Desserts
    ISBN 0804189013; 9780804189019

LC 2017044672

    In this book former White House pastry chef, Bill Yosses, "upends the notion of 'healthy' desserts and shares an inspiring collection of delectable sweets that reveal the magic that happens when you bake with less sugar. . . . From Kabocha Persimmon Pie and Matcha Green Tea Roll with Blackberry Pastry Cream, to Lemon Kaffir Semifreddo and Popped Quinoa Chocolate Cookies, Bill's treats show us that desserts don't have to be a source of penance to be exquisite and indulgent." (Publisher's note)
    "Notes throughout the collection—with information such as how to work with dried fruit and what to do with leftover yolks—add value to any baker's arsenal. Yoses, with Kaminsky, has produced a thoughtful, inspiring title to bake through the seasons." Publishers Weekly

Kamp, David
    The **United** States of Arugula; how we became a gourmet nation. Broadway Books 2006 392p il $26 **641**
    1. Dining 2. Gastronomy 3. Cookery, American
    ISBN 0-7679-1579-8

LC 2006-42599

    In this book, David Kamp "details the development of fine dining in the U.S. and proves healthy, even exotic food movements are having an effect on our diet. . . . Historically, the rich always had high-end restaurants; the rest contented themselves with recipes in the ladies' sections of newspapers and magazines. But thanks to 'the Big Three'--James Beard, Julia Child and Craig Claiborne-America had an eating revolution." (Publishers Weekly)
    The author "details the development of fine dining in the U.S. and proves healthy, even exotic food movements are having an effect on our diet. . . . This cultural history makes for an engrossing read, documenting the dramas and rivalries of the food industry." Publ Wkly
    Includes bibliographical references

Kingsolver, Barbara, 1955-
    ★ **Animal,** vegetable, miracle; a year of food life. [by] Barbara Kingsolver, with Steven L. Hopp and Camille Kingsolver; original drawings by Richard A. Houser. HarperCollins Publishers 2007 370p il $26.95; pa $15.99 **641**
    1. Farm life 2. Eating customs 3. Appalachian region 4. Agriculture and energy
    ISBN 978-0-06-085255-9; 0-06-085255-0; 978-0-06-085256-6 pa; 0-06-085256-9 pa

LC 2006-53516

    "This is a serious book about important problems. Its concerns are real and urgent. It is clear, thoughtful, often amusing, passionate and appealing. It may give you a serious case of supermarket guilt, thinking of the energy footprint left by each out-of-season tomato, but you'll also find unexpected knowledge and gain the ability to make informed choices about what—and how—you're willing to eat." Washington Post Book World
    Includes bibliographical references

Krissoff, Liana
    Canning for a New Generation; Bold, Fresh Flavors for the Modern Pantry. by Liana Krissoff ; photographs by Rinne Allen. Harry N Abrams Inc 2016 400 p. $27.50 **641**
    1. Canning and preserving
    ISBN 1617691852; 9781617691850
    This book on canning, by Liana Krissoff, "is filled with fresh and new ways to preserve nature's bounty throughout the year. Organized by season and illustrated with beautiful photographs, it offers detailed instructions and recipes for making more than 150 canned, pickled, dried, and frozen foods, as well as 50 inventive recipes for dishes using these foods. Basic information on canning techniques and lively sidebars round out this refreshing take on a classic cooking tradition." (Publisher's note)

Lappé, Anna, 1973-
    Diet for a hot planet; the climate crisis at the end of your fork and what you can do about it. with a forward by Bill McKibben. Bloomsbury 2010 xxi, 313p il **641**
    1. Food supply 2. Food industry 3. Eating customs 4. Greenhouse effect
    ISBN 1-59691-659-1; 978-1-59691-659-3

LC 2010-17363

    The author "argues that food is 'the integrating lens' for the innumerable responses to climate change. At three meals or more per day, Lappe writes, we are faced with either supporting or resisting industrial food production. So-called conventional food production and distribution—ecologically and economically fragile—contributes to nearly one-third of total human-caused global warming and paradoxically creates hunger out of plenty. Organic, local, plant-based foods, on the other hand, have the potential to not only mitigate but ultimately repair this damage. Lappe bolsters her support for a local, organic diet with a substantial bibliography of peer-reviewed science, studies, policies and interviews." Kirkus
    Includes bibliographical references

Lumb, Marianne
    Kitchen knife skills; techniques for carving, boning, slicing, chopping, dicing, mincing, filleting. Marianne Lumb. Book Sales 2018 176 p. $12.99 **641**
    1. Knives 2. Cooking 3. Kitchen utensils
    ISBN 0785835989; 9780785835981
    In this book, by Marianne Lumb, "good knife skills are the most

important ingredient in every recipe--knowing the right knife to use for each task, and how to use it, will make your cooking faster, safer, stylish and fun. Whether you are dicing an onion, filleting a fish, shucking an oyster or slicing melba toast, this book will tell you which knife to use and the correct method of preparation to enable professional results." (Publisher's note)

O'Neill, Laura

Van Leeuwen Artisan Ice Cream; by Laura O'Neill, Benjamin Van Leeuwen, Peter Van Leeuwen, Olga Massov. HarperCollins 2015 256 p. illustrations (chiefly color) (hardcover) $29.99 **641**

1. Cookbooks 2. Ice cream, ices, etc.
ISBN 9780062329585; 0062329588

This ice cream cookbook, by Laura O'Neill, Benjamin Van Leeuwen, Peter Van Leeuwen, and Olga Massov, "includes . . . recipes for every palate and season, from beloved favorites like Vanilla to adventurous treats inspired by a host of international culinary influences, such as Masala Chai with Black Peppercorns and Apple Crumble with Calvados and Crème Fraîche." (Publisher's note)

"This engagingly written cookbook is a recommended purchase for all libraries." LJ

Oliver, Jamie, 1975-

Jamie's dinners; with photographs by David Loftus and Chris Terry and illustrations by Marion Deuchars. Hyperion 2004 **641**

1. Cookery.
ISBN 1-4013-0194-0

Rushdie, Sameen

Sameen Rushdie's Indian cookery; Sameen Rushdie ; foreword by Salman Rushdie. St. Martin's Press 2018 272 p. $16 **641**

1. Cookbooks 2. Indian cooking
ISBN 1250102812; 9781250102812

In this cookbook in the Picador Cookstr Classics series, author Sameen Rushdie "offers a marvelous array of meat, poultry and fish dishes, together with vegetable creations which will give heart to cooks at the end of their vegetarian repertoire. She explains where to find fresh ingredients and how to store, prepare and use them, and makes it clear which recipes are most suitable for the end of a busy day." (Publisher's note)

Sivrioglu, Somer

Anatolia; Adventures in Turkish Cooking. by Somer Sivrioglu and David Dale. Murdoch Books, an imprint of Allen & Unwin 2016 359 p. color illustrations $59.95 **641**

1. Turkish cooking 2. Cookbooks 3. Cooking, Turkish
ISBN 1743360495; 9781743360491
IACP Cookbook Award: International (2016)

This book, by Somer Sivrioglu and David Dale, "is a richly illustrated, entertaining and informative exploration of the regional cooking culture of Turkey. . . . More than 150 dishes are featured, and images of the recipes are complemented by specially commissioned photographs shot on location in Turkey. Feature spreads on local Turkish chefs and producers and their specialities add a fascinating layer of interest and flavour." (Publisher's note)

The **story** of food; an illustrated history of everything we eat. DK Publishing, Inc. DK Publishing 2018 360 p. $35 **641**

1. Eating customs 2. Diet -- History 3. Food -- History 4. Food habits 5. Food preferences

ISBN 146547336X; 9781465473363

LC 2018288104

This book, from DK Publishing, highlights the "cultural impact of the foods we eat, explores the early efforts of humans in their quest for sustenance, and tells the fascinating stories behind individual foods. With profiles of the most culturally and historically interesting foods of all types, from nuts and grains, fruits and vegetables, and meat and fish, to herbs and spices, this . . . historical reference provides the facts on all aspects of each food's unique story." (Publisher's note)

Young, Catherine

The **Beetlebung** Farm cookbook; a year of cooking on Martha's Vineyard. by Chris Fischer, with Catherine Young. Little, Brown & Co. 2015 320 p. color illustrations; color map $35 **641**

1. American cooking 2. Martha's Vineyard (Mass.)
ISBN 0316404071; 9780316404075

LC 2014957428

This book, by Chris Fischer, presents a "year of fresh, simple, seasonal cooking. . . . Beetlebung Farm, his grandparents' five-acre parcel in the town of Chilmark, [Martha's Vineyard] is both Fischer's inspiration and the source for the fine raw materials he showcases. These recipes express the unique understanding of ingredients that comes from a life spent hauling in lobster pots, cultivating vegetables, tracking game in the woods, and butchering his own meat." (Publisher's note)

"This superb collection is a must-have for every cook interested in simple yet flavorful food that's guaranteed to please." Pub Wkly

641.01   Philosophy and theory

Harrison, Jim, 1937-2016

A **really** big lunch; the roving gourmand on food and life. Jim Harrison ; with an introduction by Mario Batali. Grove Press, an imprint of Grove Atlantic 2017 xii, 275 p.p illustrations (hardcover) $26 **641.01**

1. Cooking 2. Gastronomy
ISBN 9780802189448; 9780802126467

LC 2016056292

This collection of essays, by Jim Harrison, is "a celebration of eating well and drinking even better as a recipe for the good life . . . The author waxes wickedly funny over matters of art, politics, spirituality, sex, and the commingling of all of them. His advice: 'Your meals in life are numbered and the number is diminishing. Get at it.' If this is the last we get from Harrison, it serves as a fitting memorial." (Kirkus Reviews)

"With an introduction from Harrison's longtime friend Mario Batali, this makes a great addition to popular food and wine collections and will be a savory treat for Harrison fans." Booklist

Mohammadi, Kamin

Bella figura; how to live, love, and eat the Italian way. Kamin Mohammadi. Alfred A. Knopf 2018 304 p. (hardback) $26.95 **641.01**

1. Gastronomy 2. Italian cooking 3. Italy -- Description and travel 4. Cooking, Italian 5. Gastronomy -- Italy 6. Travel writers -- England -- Biography
ISBN 9780385354011

LC 2017055692

This book by Kamin Mohammadi "is a mantra for savoring the beauty and color of every day that Italians have followed for generations, a guide to the slow life for busy people, a story of finding love (and self-love) in unlikely places, and an evocative account of a year living an

Italian life." (Publisher's note)

Wilson, Bee

First bite; how we learn to eat. Bee Wilson ; with illustrations by Annabel Lee. Basic Books, a member of the Perseus Books Group 2015 352 p. illustrations (hardcover) $27.99   **641.01**

1. Gastronomy 2. Eating customs 3. Food preferences
ISBN 9780465064984

LC 2015027683

In this book, "food writer Bee Wilson draws on the latest research from food psychologists, neuroscientists, and nutritionists to reveal that our food habits are shaped by a whole host of factors: family and culture, memory and gender, hunger and love. . . . The way we learn to eat holds the key to why food has gone so disastrously wrong for so many people. But Wilson also shows that both adults and children have immense potential for learning new, healthy eating habits." (Publisher's note)

"This work will appeal to food scientists, parents wishing to know the roots of their children's meal choices, and curious readers in general." LJ

Includes bibliographical references and index

641.013   Gastronomy

Frank, Dana

Wine food; new adventures in drinking and cooking. Dana Frank and Andrea Slonecker. Ten Speed Press 2018 256 p. (hardcover) $25   **641.013**

1. Food 2. Cooking 3. Wine and wine making 4. Food and wine pairing
ISBN 9780399579592

LC 2017058757

In this cookbook, Dana Frank and Andrea Slonecker, "deliver 75 recipes for brunches, salads, vegetable dishes, picnics, weeknight dinners, and feasts with friends, all inspired by delicious, affordable wines that go with them beautifully. Each recipe opens with a succinct overview of the wine style that inspired it, describing the grapes and naming the countries the wine comes from, followed by a brief explanation of how it complements the flavors and textures in the recipe." (Publisher's note)

"One of the many new books that emphasize wholesome meals using ingredients that can be found at large supermarkets or specialized grocery stores, this work is recommended for complete cookbook collections or where wine and food pairings are popular." Library Journal

Includes bibliographical references and index

Kramer, Jane

The **reporter's** kitchen; Jane Kramer. St Martins Pr 2017 304 p. $26.99   **641.013**

1. Food writing 2. Food -- Social aspects
ISBN 1250074371; 9781250074379

LC 2017024876

This book, by Jane Kramer, is a "collection of definitive chef profiles, personal essays, and gastronomic history that is at once deeply personal and humane. . . . [It] follows Jane [Kramer] everywhere, and throughout her career. . . . [This book] is an important record of culture distilled through food around the world." (Publisher's note)

"Eloquent and charmingly loquacious, Kramer's essays are sharp and insightful. A joyous feast of food, travel, and human relationships." Kirkus Reviews

641.2   Beverages (Drinks)

Acitelli, Tom

The **audacity** of hops; the history of America's craft beer revolution. Tom Acitelli. Chicago Review Press 2013 416 p. (pbk.) $19.95   **641.2**

1. Beer 2. Brewing 3. Microbreweries 4. Beer -- United States
ISBN 1613743882; 9781613743881

LC 2013002264

This book by Tom Acitelli is a "look at craft beer from the 1960s onward, from its birth out of the home brewing movement to ultimately revitalize an industry—and the drinking habits of millions. The author traces craft brewing's passage from an unorthodox business decision to a potentially logical investment. His book provides the histories of dozens of breweries, from familiar names to more obscure, long-shuttered institutions, and takes in numerous industry-wide controversies." (Library Journal)

Includes bibliographical references and index

Alworth, Jeff

The **beer** bible; the essential beer lover's guide. Jeff Alworth. Workman Publishing 2015 656 p. illustrations (alk. paper) $19.95   **641.2**

1. Beer
ISBN 0761168117; 9780761168119

LC 2015024777

IACP Cookbook Award Winner: Wine, Beer and Spirits (2016)

This book, by Jeff Alworth, "is the ultimate reader- and drinker-friendly guide to all the world's beers. . . . Divided into four major families¿ales, lagers, wheat beers, and tart and wild ales¿there¿s everything a beer drinker wants to know. . . . Each style is a chapter unto itself, delving into origins, ingredients, description and characteristics, substyles, and tasting notes, and ending with a recommended list of the beers to know in each category." (Publisher's note)

"Beer enthusiasts will welcome this guide that feels like one is spending time with a well-versed drinking pal." LJ

Includes bibliographical references and index

Bauer, Bryce T.

The **new** rum; a modern guide to the spirit of the Americas. Bryce T. Bauer. W W Norton & Co Inc 2018 224 p. $24.95   **641.2**

1. Rum 2. Cocktails 3. Alcoholic beverages
ISBN 1682680002; 9781682680001

In this book, "author Bryce T. Bauer charts the historical and cultural journey of the spirit of the Americas from its origins in the Caribbean, to its long- held status as a cheap vacation drink, to today's inspiring craft revival. This rum-spiked travelogue also includes a producer-focused drinks guide, covering dozens of the world's most innovative and iconic producers." (Publisher's note)

Beaumont, Stephen

The **world** atlas of beer; The Essential Guide to the Beers of the World. Sterling Epicure 2012 256 p. (hardcover) $30   **641.2**

1. Beer 2. Brewing
ISBN 1402789610; 9781402789618

This book presents the "global history of beer. . . . Color photographs accompany the text, which offers information on buying and drinking beer, as well as a geographic survey of beers around the world. Other topics covered include the various types of beer, brewing methods and technologies, trends, brands, and more." (Booklist)

Broom, Dave

The **World** Atlas of Whisky; More Than 200 Distilleries Explored and 750 Expressions Tasted. by Dave Broom. Octopus Pub Group 2014 336 p. $39.99 **641.2**

1. Whiskey

ISBN 1845339428; 9781845339425

IACP Cookbook Award Finalist: Food and Beverage/Reference/Technical (2015)

In this whisky guidebook, author Dave Broom "explores over 200 distilleries and examines over 400 expressions. Detailed descriptions of the Scottish distilleries can be found here, while Ireland, Japan, the USA, Canada and the rest of the world are given exhaustive coverage. There are tasting notes on single malts from Aberfeldy to Tormore, Yoichi (and coverage of the best of the blends)." (Publisher's note)

"A perfect complement to Dominic Roskrow's expansive The World's Best Whiskies, which includes distiller interviews." LJ

Kolpan, Steven

Exploring wine; The Culinary Institute of America's Complete Guide to Wines of the World. Steven Kolpan, Brian H. Smith, Michael A. Weiss. 3rd ed Wiley 2010 792 p. col. ill., col. maps (cloth) $70 **641.2**

1. Wine and wine making

ISBN 0471770639; 9780471770633

LC 2009014016

This book, by Steven Kolpan, Brian H. Smith, and Michael A. Weiss, "thoroughly demystifies wine, from the basics of wine production to the nuances of wine lists, wine marketing, and wine service. Completely revised and updated, this new edition of the critically acclaimed guide features more comprehensive coverage of the wine regions of the world, grape varietals, winemaking, purchasing, tasting, service, and pairing." (Publisher's note)

"This new edition of the critically acclaimed guide features more comprehensive coverage of the wine regions of the world, grape varietals, winemaking, purchasing, tasting, service, and pairing." Publisher's note

Includes bibliographical references and index

Winewise; your complete guide to understanding, selecting, and enjoying wine. Steven Kolpan, Brian H. Smith, and Michael A. Weiss, The Culinary Institute of America. Revised edition Houghton Mifflin Harcourt 2014 376 p. illustrations, maps $35 **641.2**

1. Wine and wine making

ISBN 0544334620; 9780544334625

LC 2014016316

This book, by Steven Kolpan, Brian Smith, and Michael Weiss, offers an "essential consumer guide to wine [that] features all the most current information for today's wine landscape. The authors, longtime wine educators at The Culinary Institute of America, have added all the latest and most relevant information to their award-winning book, including new picks for the best regional producers, off-the-beaten-path finds, and bargain bottles." (Publisher's note)

"Brevity is the soul of keeping a reader's attention, and a lot of ground is covered here by breaking out the material into hundreds of short entries grouped across 17 chapters. . . . Back-of-book gems include best practices for at-home wine tastings, a list of value wines, and full permission to enjoy wine from a box." Pub Wkly

Liem, Peter

★ **Champagne**; the essential guide to the wines, producers, and terroirs of the iconic region. Peter Liem, with Kate

Leahy. Ten Speed Press 2017 321 p. illustrations (hardback) $80 **641.2**

1. Champagne (France) 2. Wine and wine making -- France 3. Champagne (Wine) 4. Wine and wine making -- France -- Champagne-Ardenne

ISBN 9781607748434; 1607748428; 9781607748427

LC 2017022013

James Beard Award: Reference, History, and Scholarship (2018)

This book, by Peter Liem, is "groundbreaking guide to the modern wines of Champagne--a region that in recent years has undergone one of the most dramatic transformations in the wine-growing world. This luxurious box set includes a pullout tray with a complete set of seven vintage vineyard maps by Louis Larmat, a rare and indispensable resource that beautifully documents the region's terroirs." (Publisher's note)

"In writing that pairs authoritative knowledge with an inviting tone, the author guides readers through the history of champagne, the process of producing the wine, the geography of the Champagne region, and the major manufacturers." LJ

Includes bibliographical references and index

Old, Marnie

Wine; a tasting course. Marnie Old. DK Publishing 2013 256 p. color ills, color maps (hardcover) $25 **641.2**

1. Wine and wine making 2. Wine tasting

ISBN 1465405887; 9781465405883

LC 2013454888

IACP Cookbook Award Finalist: Food and Beverage/Reference/Technical (2015)

This book, by Marnie Old, "[offers] a visual tour of wine styles, explaining the big-picture concepts, and encouraging readers to recognize the connections between wines. . . . [Old] challenges all the stuffy orthodoxies about wine, and teaches that best way to learn is through tasting." (Publisher's note)

Proulx, Annie, 1935-

Cider; making, using & enjoying sweet & hard cider. Annie Proulx & Lew Nichols. 3rd ed; Storey Pub. 2003 iv, 219 p.p illustrations $14.95 **641.2**

1. Cider 2. Brewing 3. Apples

ISBN 1580175201; 9781580175203

LC 2003272271

In this brewing cookbook, Annie Proulx and Lew Nichols "take you step-by-step through the cidermaking process, covering everything from the various types of apple presses to how to filter, fine, rack, and store your cider. They also provide recipes for making six types of cider---still, sparkling, champagne, barrel, French, and flavored---and advise you on which apples to use to achieve particular flavor qualities." (Publisher's note)

Risen, Clay

American Whiskey, Bourbon & Rye; A Guide to the Nation's Favorite Spirit. by Clay Risen. Sterling Pub Co Inc 2013 304 p. color illustrations $24.95 **641.2**

1. Whiskey 2. Alcoholic beverages

ISBN 1402798407; 9781402798405

This book, by Clay Risen, is a "guide devoted solely to US-made whiskey, rye, and bourbon. Arranged alphabetically by distillery and/or brand, it offers histories, ratings, and tasting notes for over 200 whiskeys. Each main account includes the name and address of the maker, including website URL and contact information, along with its various products." (Publisher's note)

"Risen . . . deftly combines history and assessment in this informative volume that covers more than 200 of the titular spirits." LJ

Includes bibliographical references (pages 281-284) and index

Tardi, Alan

Champagne, uncorked; the house of Krug and the timeless allure of the world's most celebrated drink. Alan Tardi. PublicAffairs 2016 296 p. illustrations (chiefly color) (hardcover) $26.99   **641.2**

1. Alcohol 2. Wine and wine making 3. Champagne (Wine)

ISBN 161039688X; 9781610396882; 9781610396899

LC 2016007400

In this book author "Alan Tardi journeys into the heartland of the world's most beloved wine. Anchored by the year he spent inside the prestigious and secretive Krug winery in Reims, the story follows the creation of the superlative Krug Grande Cuvée. Tardi also investigates the evocative history, quirky origins, and cultural significance of Champagne." (Publisher's note)

"Tardi deftly melds the process of creating champagne with the story of the winery from its earliest days. The result is fascinating, all the more so for the rich side stories captured in endnotes." LJ

Includes bibliographical references (page 263).

Wallace, Benjamin

The **billionaire's** vinegar; the mystery of the world's most expensive bottle of wine. Crown Publishers 2008 319p $24.95; pa $14.95   **641.2**

1. Wine and wine making

ISBN 978-0-307-33877-8; 0-307-33877-0; 978-0-307-33878-5 pa; 0-307-33878-9 pa

LC 2007-31645

"This is a gripping story, expertly handled by Benjamin Wallace who writes with wit and verve, drawing the reader into a subculture strewn with eccentrics and monomaniacs. . . . Full of detail that will delight wine lovers. It will also appeal to anyone who merely savours a great tale, well told." Economist

Includes bibliographical references

Zraly, Kevin

Windows on the World Complete Wine Course; Kevin Zraly. 30th anniv ed Sterling Epicure 2014 368 p. il $27.95 **641.2**

1. Wine and wine making

ISBN 1454913649; 9781454913641

Annual. First published 1985

IACP Cookbook Award Finalist: Wine, Beer and Spirits (2015)

Zraly's "definitive . . . bestselling guide to wine receives a complete update. As always, [Kevin] Zraly deftly takes the mystery out of wine, recommending hundreds of new wines . . . and providing the latest information on vintage wines. But this thoroughly redesigned edition also presents a beautiful tribute to the renowned restaurant, Windows on the World, where Zraly's course began." (Publisher's note)

"Zraly deftly takes the mystery out of choosing wine, explains the basics, and suggests hundreds of new wines to try. . . . [T]his thoroughly redesigned edition also presents a beautiful tribute to Windows on the World, the renowned restaurant where Zraly's course began. User-friendly smartphone tags and audio guides are featured throughout." Publisher's note

641.22   Wine

Bosker, Bianca

Cork dork; A Wine-Fueled Adventure Among the Obses-

sive Sommeliers, Big Bottle Hunters, and Rogue Scientists Who Taught Me to Live for Taste. Bianca Bosker. Penguin Books 2017 352 p. $17   **641.22**

1. Wine and wine making -- Social aspects

ISBN 9780143128090

LC 2016029203

This book, by Bianca Bosker, "takes the reader inside elite tasting groups, exclusive New York City restaurants, a California mass market wine 'factory,' and even a neuroscientist's fMRI machine as Bosker attempts to answer the most nagging question of all: what's the big deal about wine?" (Publisher's note)

"An interesting look at those with an unquenchable thirst for those unique bottles of vinicultural perfection." Booklist

Includes bibliographical references

Johnson, Hugh, 1939-

Hugh Johnson on wine; good bits from 55 years of scribbling. Hugh Johnson. Mitchell Beazley 2017 288 p. (hardcover) $24.99   **641.22**

1. English authors 2. Alcoholic beverages -- History 3. Wine and wine making

ISBN 1784722626; 9781784722623

This book looks back at author Hugh Johnson's decades "of wine writing. Beginning in the 1960s, the book takes a chronological journey through . . . Johnson's writing . . . [and] the evolution of wine production, tasting and drinking over the last sixty years. It [discusses] the fundamental shift in our understanding of wine, and our subsequent enjoyment of it. From early tastings in Bordeaux . . . [through] the 2014 discussion of the the ever-increasing ABV strength of wine." (Publisher's note)

"Every page presents careful thought and nuanced presentation. This work is highly recommended to beginners learning about wine and for established professionals. Johnson's writing is a joy to read." Choice

Larousse wine; the definitive reference for wine lovers. Hamlyn. Hamlyn 2017 654 p. (hardcover) $60   **641.22**

1. Alcoholic beverages 2. Wine and wine making

ISBN 9780600635093; 0600635090

This book, by Hamlyn, presents a "comprehensive coverage of the wine-producing regions of the world. . . . Each section begins with it a beautiful color illustration of the area, with the major districts, rivers, and cities highlighted. A short history and analysis of each region follows, with a discussion of the types of wines produced in each district, the specific oenological properties that make the region unique, and the appellations of the area." (Publisher's note)

"A sumptuous treat for every level of oenophile, and a good choice for public libraries looking to update older titles." Booklist

Neiman, Ophelie

Wine isn't rocket science; a quick & easy guide to understanding, buying, tasting, & pairing every type of wine. Ophélie Neiman ; illustrations by Yannis Varoutsikos ; translated by Nysa Kline. First English-language edition Black Dog & Leventhal Publishers 2017 272 p. color illustrations, maps (hardcover) $24.99   **641.22**

1. Wine and wine making 2. Wine tasting

ISBN 9780316440240; 9780316431309; 0316431303

LC 2017289068

This book, by Ophelie Neiman, illustrated by Yannis Varoutsikos, offers "information presented in an easy, illustrated style, and chock-full of the fool-proof and reliable knowledge of a seasoned oenophile. . . . From how grapes are grown, harvested and turned into wine, to judging the color, aroma, and taste of the world's most popular varietals, to understanding terroir and feeling confident ordering and serving wine at any occasion, this book explains it all." (Publisher's note)

"This book is a terrific introduction to an often intimidating subject." Pub Wkly

The **Oxford** companion to wine; edited by Jancis Robinson ; assistant editor, Julia Harding ; advisory editor, viticulture: Richard E. Smart ; advisory editors, oenology: Valérie Lavigne & Denis Dubourdieu. Oxford University Press 2015 xlvii, 859 p.p color illustrations, maps (hardcover) $65   **641.22**
   1. Wine and wine making
   ISBN 9780198705383; 0198705387
                                      LC 2015941385

This book, edited by Jancis Robinson with Julia Harding, part of the publisher's "Oxford Companions" series, is the fourth edition of the work, which "presents almost 4,000 entries on every wine-related topic imaginable, from regions and grape varieties to the owners, connoisseurs, growers, and tasters in wine through the ages; from viticulture and oenology to the history of wine, from its origins to the present day." (Publisher's note)

"This hefty volume is certain not just to answer both broad and obscure questions on viniculture, but also to pique the interest of the reader who dips into its pages." LJ

Includes bibliographical references

641.23 Brewed and malted beverages

Huckelbridge, Dane
The **United** States of beer; a freewheeling history of the all-American drink. Dane Huckelbridge. HarperCollins 2016 289 p. illustrations (hbk.) $25.99   **641.23**
   1. Beer 2. Brewing 3. United States -- Civilization
   ISBN 0062389750; 9780062389756
                                        LC 2016302473

This book, by Dane Huckelbridge, offers a "cultural history [that] charts the . . . complex story of our favorite alcoholic drink, showing how America has been under the influence of beer at almost every stage. From the earliest Native American corn brew (called chicha) to the waves of immigrants who brought with them their unique brewing traditions, to the seemingly infinite varieties of craft-brewed suds found on tap today, beer has claimed an outsized place in our culture." (Publisher's note)

"The author's breezy style is a perfect match for his subject." LJ
Includes bibliographical references (pages [271]-277) and index.

641.3 Food

Adarme, Adrianna
The **year** of cozy; 125 Recipes, Crafts, and Other Homemade Adventures. Adrianna Adarme. Rodale Books 2015 259 p. color illustrations (trade hardcover) $24.99   **641.3**
   1. Cooking 2. Handicraft 3. Comfort food 4. Do-it-yourself work
   ISBN 1623365104; 9781623365103
                                        LC 2015034972

This book, by Adrianna Adarme, presents "recipes and projects. . . . Organized by the months of the year and by categories as 'Live,' 'Do,' and 'Make,' [it] offers ideas for activities, recipes, and DIY projects that make the little moments in life just as exciting as the big. Adarme gives

us special (but totally doable) things we can do for others and ourselves. From quick recipes to easy crafts, she focuses on simple, inexpensive undertakings that have a big reward: happiness." (Publisher's note)

Barber, Dan
  ★ The **third** plate; field notes on the future of food. by Dan Barber. The Penguin Press 2014 496 p. illustrations (hardback) $29.95   **641.3**
   1. Agriculture 2. Natural foods 3. Eating customs 4. Seasonal cooking
   ISBN 1594204071; 9781594204074
                                        LC 2013039966

James Beard Foundation Award Winner: Writing and Literature (2015)

This book, by Dan Barber, advocates for "an integrated system of vegetable, grain, and livestock production that is fully supported--in fact, dictated--by what we choose to cook for dinner. The third plate is where good farming and good food intersect. While the third plate is a novelty in America, Barber demonstrates that this way of eating is rooted in worldwide tradition." (Publisher's note)

"In this bold and impassioned analysis, Barber insists that chefs have the power to transform American cuisine to achieve a sustainable and nutritious future." Kirkus

Includes bibliographical references and index

Bittman, Mark
The **food** matters cookbook; 500 revolutionary recipes for better living. Simon & Schuster 2010 645p $35; ebook $16.99   **641.3**
   1. Food 2. Health 3. Cooking 4. Nutrition
   ISBN 978-1-4391-2023-1; 978-1-4391-4123-6 ebook
                                        LC 2010-28623

The author "provides a rational approach to eating that not only improves health but also helps the environment. Extolling the benefits of a plant-heavy diet, Bittman offers more than 500 healthful recipes that feature unprocessed fruits, vegetables, legumes, nuts, and whole grains and reduce all types of meat to backup players. In addition, he shares five basic principles for sane eating that are easy to implement and understand as well as an unusually helpful pantry section and handy charts for substituting produce and seafood by season. . . . Practical and balanced, this collection will shape the way we cook at home for years to come." Publ Wkly

Blount, Roy
Save room for pie; food songs and chewy ruminations. Roy Blount, Jr. Sarah Crichton Books/Farrar, Straus & Giroux 2016 304 p. (hardcover) $26   **641.3**
   1. Food 2. Wit and humor 3. Food -- Anecdotes 4. Food in literature
   ISBN 9780374175207
                                        LC 2015036049

In this book, the author and comedian Roy Blount Jr. "applies his much-praised wit and charm to a rich and fundamental topic: food. As a lifelong eater, Blount always got along easy with food. . . . But food doesn't exist in a vacuum; there's the global climate and the global economy to consider, not to mention Blount's chronic sinusitis, which constricts his sense of smell, and consequently his taste buds." (Publisher's note)

"Eminently quotable, informative, and entertaining, Blount makes for a genial host, regaling the reader with story after story." Pub Wkly
Includes bibliographical references

Britton, Sarah

My| new roots; Sarah Britton. Clarkson Potter/Publishers
2015 256 p. color illustrations $29.99   **641.3**
1. Plants 2. Cooking 3. Cooking (Natural foods)
ISBN 0804185387; 9780804185387

LC 2014018135

This book by Sarah Britton "is the ultimate guide to revitalizing
one's health and palate, one delicious recipe at a time: no fad diets or
gimmicks here. Whether readers are newcomers to natural foods or are
already devotees, they will discover how easy it is to eat healthfully and
happily when whole foods and plants are at the center of every plate."
(Publisher's note)

Chaplin, Amy

★ At home in the whole food kitchen; celebrating the art of
eating well. Amy Chaplin. Roost Books, an imprint of Shambhala Publications, Inc. 2014 386 p. color illustrations hbk
$35   **641.3**
1. Cookbooks 2. Cooking -- Natural foods 3. Natural foods
ISBN 1611800854; 9781611800852

LC 2013043411

James Beard Foundation Award: Vegetable Focused and Vegetarian
(2015)

IACP Cookbook Award Finalist: Julia Child First Book (2015)

IACP Cookbook Award: Health & Special Diet (2015)

This natural foods cookbook, by Amy Chaplin, offers a "vegetarian
cookbook with all the tools you need to be at home in your kitchen,
cooking in the most nourishing and delicious ways--from the foundations of stocking a pantry and understanding your ingredients, to preparing elaborate seasonal feasts." (Publisher's note)

"After introducing whole food pantry essentials ranging from ancient grains to superfoods, [Chaplin] presents mostly vegan and gluten-
free recipes. . . . [She] also offers lifestyle advice, weighing in on the
benefits of cleansing and eating organic." LJ

Includes bibliographical references and index

Crosby, Guy

The| science of good cooking; master 50 simple concepts to
enjoy a lifetime of success in the kitchen. the editors at America's Test Kitchen and Guy Crosby ; illustrations by Michael
Newhouse and John Burgoyne. America's Test Kitchen 2012
486 p. $40   **641.3**
1. Food 2. Cooking 3. Cookbooks
ISBN 1933615982; 9781933615981

LC 2012012807

This book by the editors of America's Test Kitchen and Guy Crosby,
part of the Cook's Illustrated Cookbooks series, "brings science to the
stove. . . . In addition to explaining how food science works (and why
you should care), 'The Science of Good Cooking' shows you the science. This book brings you into the test kitchen with 50 . . . experiments
engineered to illustrate (and illuminate) the science at work." (Publisher's note)

Darlington, Tenaya

Dibruno Bros. House of Cheese; by Tenaya Darlington ;
photographs by Jason Verney. 1st ed. Running Press 2013 256
p. (hardcover) $25.00   **641.3**
1. Cheese
ISBN 0762446048; 9780762446049

LC 2012942524

In this book, Tenaya Darlington "draws on the offerings at long-established Philadelphia cheese monger Di Bruno Bros. and the expertise

of its staff to highlight a range of cheeses according to such personalities as 'mountain men,' 'vixens,' 'quiet types,' and 'pierced punks.' . . .
The description of each cheese briefly captures its history and its flavor,
complemented with suggestions for beverage pairings and accompaniments." (Library Journal)

David, Laurie

The family cooks; 100+ recipes to get your family craving
food that's simple, tasty, and incredibly good for you. Laurie
David ; foreword by Katie Couric. Rodale Books 2014 277 p.
color illustrations (hardback) $27.99   **641.3**
1. Nutrition 2. Cooking -- Natural foods 3. Families -- Nutrition
4. Cooking (Natural foods)
ISBN 1623362504; 9781623362508

LC 2014003505

IACP Cookbook Award Finalist: Children, Youth and Family (2015)

In this cookbook, author Laurie David "inspires parents and kids to
take control of what they eat by making it themselves. With her longtime
collaborator, Kirstin Uhrenholdt, David offers more than 100 recipes
that are simple, fast, 'low in the bad stuff and high in the good stuff,'
and designed to bring kids into the cooking process. The authors also
demystify cooking terms and break down basic prep techniques, creating stress-free meals that foster health, togetherness, and happy palates."
(Publisher's note)

"Written primarily for busy families with children, David's attractive guide to reclaiming the family dinner will also appeal to young
couples and professionals trying to shop smarter and eat less-processed
meals at home." LJ

Family cooks, one hundred plus recipes to get your family craving
food that's simple, tasty, and incredibly good for you

100+ recipes to get your family craving food that's simple, tasty, and
incredibly good for you

Del Mar Sacasa, María

The quinoa [keen-wah] cookbook; Maria del Mar Sacasa. HarperWave 2015 193 p. color illustrations (hardback)
$23.99   **641.3**
1. Quinoa 2. Cooking 3. Cooking (Quinoa)
ISBN 0062411217; 9780062411211

LC 2015009849

In this book by Maria del Mar Sacasa readers "will find more than
seventy-five recipes that utilize quinoa in unexpected, creative, and delicious ways. From Nutty Quinoa Granola to Breakfast Coconut Quinoa; Roasted Peppers with Lamb-Quinoa Stuffing to Matzo Ball–Style
Quinoa Soup; Charred Romaine Greek Salad with Quinoa-Crusted Feta
to Quinoa, Sweet Potato, and Walnut Veggie Burgers; Quinoa, Cashew,
and Orange Blossom Brittle." (Publisher's note)

DiSpirito, Rocco

Rocco's healthy & delicious; more than 200 (mostly) plant
based recipes for everyday life. by Rocco Dispirito. Harper
Wave 2017 400 p. $29.99   **641.3**
1. Cooking 2. Health 3. Nutrition 4. Vegan cooking 5. Cooking
(Natural foods)
ISBN 0062378120; 9780062378125; 9780062378156

LC 2017012595

In this book, by Rocco Dispirito, "readers will find simple, everyday
recipes for meals, snacks, desserts, smoothies and more. Start your day
with Pomegranate Chia Oatmeal or a Strawberry Pistachio Breakfast
Bar. Power up with a Chopped Salad with Avocado Crema or Coconut Cilantro Chicken Soup. Feast over Cauliflower Rice Risotto or Thai
Curry Veggie Burgers. Indulge in Coconut Macaroons and No Bake

Chocolate Chip Cookies. All of these recipes are plant-based, and most importantly: delicious." (Publisher's note)

Foer, Jonathan Safran

Eating animals. Little, Brown and Company 2009 341p $25.99; pa $14.99 **641.3**
1. Vegetarianism
ISBN 978-0-316-06990-8; 978-0-316-06988-5 pa
LC 2009-34434

The novelist presents a critique of the food industry and explores arguments in favor of humane agriculture and vegetarianism.

"A blend of solid—and discomforting—reportage with fierce advocacy that will make committed carnivores squeal." Kirkus

Includes bibliographical references

Forte, Sara

The **sprouted** kitchen; a tastier take on whole foods. Sara Forte ; photography by Hugh Forte. Ten Speed Press 2012 241 p. color illustrations (hbk.) $25 **641.3**
1. Cookbooks 2. Cooking -- Natural foods 3. Cooking (Cereals) 4. Cooking (Natural foods) 5. Sugar-free diet -- Recipes
ISBN 1607741148; 1607741156; 9781607741145; 9781607741152
LC 2012008143

This cookbook by Sara Forte "features 100 of her most mouthwatering recipes. Illustrated by her photographer husband, Hugh Forte, [it] celebrates the simple beauty of seasonal foods with original recipes--plus a few favorites from her popular Sprouted Kitchen food blog. The collection features tasty snacks on the go like Granola Protein Bars, gluten-free brunch options like Cornmeal Cakes with Cherry Compote, dinner party dishes like Seared Scallops on Black Quinoa." (Publisher's note)

Tastier take on whole foods

The **sprouted** kitchen bowl and spoon; simple and inspired whole foods recipes to savor and share. Sara Forte ; photography by Hugh Forte. Ten Speed Press 2015 256 p. color illustrations $25 **641.3**
1. Salads 2. Cooking -- Natural foods 3. Cooking (Natural foods)
ISBN 1607746557; 9781607746553
LC 2014036843

In this cookbook "author Sara Forte turns her attention to bowl food, which combines vegetables, whole grains, and lean proteins in one vessel to make a simple, complete, and nutritious meal. . . . Sara offers delicious, produce-forward recipes for every meal, such as Golden Quinoa and Butternut Breakfast Bowl; Spring Noodles with Artichokes, Pecorino, and Charred Lemons; Turkey Meatballs in Tomato Sauce; and Cocoa Nib Pavlovas with Mixed Berries." (Publisher's note)

"Vegetarians and flexitarians will find plenty to love here, as will vegans, though they'll have fewer choices. Readers interested in healthy bowl foods may also like Ruth Tal and Jennifer Houston's Fresh: New Vegetarian and Vegan Recipes from Fresh Restaurants." LJ

Ganeshram, Ramin

Future Chefs; recipes by tomorrow's cooks across the nation and the world. Ramin Ganeshram ; photography by Jean Paul Vellotti. Rodale 2014 xi, 276 p.p color illustrations (paperback) $24.99 **641.3**
1. Cooking 2. Teenagers -- United States 3. Cooking -- United States 4. Teenage cooks -- United States
ISBN 1623362067; 9781623362065
LC 2014025322

IACP Cookbook Award Winner: Children, Youth and Family (2015)

This cookbook, by Ramin Ganeshram, is a "curated collection of 150 recipes drawn from the experience and kitchens of young cooks all over America. . . . Whether they've taken to it because of necessity, inspiration, or sheer passion, these are kids, teens, and tweens who are very serious about food." (Publisher's note)

Future chefs

Hamilton, Gabrielle

★ **Prune**; Gabrielle Hamilton. Random House Inc 2014 576 p. illustrations (chiefly color) (hardback) $45 **641.3**
1. French cooking 2. American cooking 3. Prune (Restaurant)
ISBN 0812994094; 9780812994094
LC 2014003617

This cookbook, by Gabrielle Hamilton, is "filled with signature recipes from her celebrated New York City restaurant Prune. . . . A self-trained cook turned James Beard Award–winning chef, . . . Hamilton opened Prune on New York's Lower East Side fifteen years ago. . . . A deeply personal and gracious restaurant, in both menu and philosophy, Prune uses the elements of home cooking and elevates them in unexpected ways." (Publisher's note)

" Recipes range from a complex cold pork with tuna sauce to a simple butter-and-sugar sandwich. . . . Despite the book's address to fellow restaurateurs, skilled home chefs can find a number of ways to profit from a fair number of Hamilton's creations." Booklist

Hamshaw, Gena

Choosing raw; making raw foods part of the way you eat. Gena Hamshaw. Da Capo Lifelong, a member of the Perseus Books Group 2014 276 p. color illustrations (paperback) $19.99 **641.3**
1. Veganism 2. Cooking -- Natural foods 3. Cooking (Natural foods)
ISBN 0738216879; 9780738216874
LC 2014017394

This book, by Gena Hamshaw, "addresses the questions and concerns for any newcomer to veganism; makes a plant-based diet with many raw options feel easy instead of intimidating; provides a starter kit of delicious recipes; and offers a mainstream, scientifically sound perspective on healthy living." (Publisher's note)

"Among vegan cookbooks, this volume will appeal most to those who are interested in better understanding a vegan diet and curious about raw foods. Cooks looking for vegan recipes without the raw focus have lots of other great recent titles to choose from, such as The Oh She Glows Cookbook by and Isa Does It by Isa Chandra Moskowitz." LJ

Includes bibliographical references and index

Helwig, Jenna

Baby-led feeding; a natural way to raise happy, independent eaters. Jenna Helwig with Natalia Stasenko. Houghton Mifflin Harcourt 2018 208 p. (trade paper) $16.99 **641.3**
1. Parenting 2. Infants -- Nutrition 3. Children -- Nutrition 4. Baby foods -- Popular works 5. Infants -- Weaning -- Popular works
ISBN 9780544963405
LC 2017051889

In this book, "author and food editor at 'Parents' magazine Jenna Helwig gives an easy-to-follow introduction to . . . [baby-led feeding]. With more than 100 ideas and recipes, this bright, photo-driven book includes chapters on the benefits of this approach, when and how to get started, essential safety and nutrition guidelines, frequently asked questions, basic fruit and vegetable prep, more complex finger foods, and family meals." (Publisher's note)

Hemphill, Ian

The **spice** & herb bible; Ian Hemphill with recipes by Kate Hemphill. 2nd ed; Robert Rose 2014 800 p. color illustrations (bound) $49.95   **641.3**
1. Herbs 2. Spices 3. Cooking -- Herbs 4. Cookbooks 5. Cooking (Herbs) 6. Cooking (Spices)
ISBN 0778804968; 9780778804963

LC 2014472224

James Beard Foundation Award Nominee: Reference and Scholarship (2015)

This cookbook, by Ian Hemphill, with recipes by Kate Hemphill, "is a fascinating and authoritative guide. Hemphill describes a wide range of global herbs and spices used in modern kitchens either alone or in wonderful blends. He completely demystifies the art of combining herbs and spices and home cooks can meet and enjoy a world of flavors previously found only at internationally inspired restaurants." (Publisher's note)

"This truly beautiful and quite comprehensive volume will appeal to lovers of food, amateur and professional chefs, and everyone in between. While other works may address similar information, the author gives a personal touch to this one, which creates an uncommon warmth." LJ

Hoffmann, James

The **world** atlas of coffee; from beans to brewing--coffees explored, explained, and enjoyed. by James Hoffmann. Firefly Books Ltd 2014 256 p. color illustrations; maps $35   **641.3**
1. Coffee 2. Coffeehouses 3. Coffee industry
ISBN 1770854703; 9781770854703

This book on coffee, by James Hoffmann, "presents the bean in full-color photographs and concise, informative text. It shows the origins of coffee -- where it is grown, the people who grow it; and the cultures in which coffee is a way of life -- and the world of consumption -- processing, grades, the consumer and the modern culture of coffee." (Publisher's note)

"An unusual offering that will be of value in collections serving agriculture, business, and nutrition students." LJ

Kass, Sam

Eat a little better; great flavor, good health, better world. Sam Kass. Clarkson Potter/Publishers 2018 287 p. (hardcover) $32.50   **641.3**
1. Cooking 2. Nutrition 3. Seasonal cooking 4. Health
ISBN 0451494946; 9780451494948

LC 2017019841

In this cookbook, chef Sam Kass "shares his philosophy and methods to help make it easy to choose, cook, and eat delicious foods without depriving yourself of agency or pleasure. He knows that going organic, local, and so forth all the time is just not realistic for most people, and that's ok--it's all about choosing and doing a little better, and how those choices add up to big change." (Publisher's note)

Katzinger, Jennifer

Gluten-free & vegan pie; more than 50 sweet and savory pies to make at home. Jennifer Katzinger ; photographs by Charity Burggraaf. Sasquatch Books 2013 xvii, 140 p.p color illustrations (alk. paper) $23.95   **641.3**
1. Pies 2. Veganism 3. Cookbooks 4. Gluten-free diet 5. Vegetarian cooking 6. Gluten-free diet -- Recipes
ISBN 1570618682; 9781570618680

LC 2012050141

This book, by Jennifer Katzinger with photographs by Charity Burggraaf, offers "more than 55 gluten-free and vegan pie recipes.... Baking

your favorite pies without dairy, eggs, gluten, or animal products calls for a different approach to both fillings and dough. Here you'll find techniques and tips for mixing and working with dough that doesn't contain butter or lard, and for luscious fillings that contain neither cream nor egg." (Publisher's note)

"Katzinger presents a breadth of pastry doughs, press-in crusts, and sweet and savory fillings that can be used to make pies, turnovers, cobblers, crisps, galettes, tarts, and more." LJ

Lakshmi, Padma, 1970-

The **Encyclopedia** of Spices and Herbs; An Essential Guide to the Flavors of the World. by Padma Lakshmi. HarperCollins 2016 352 p. color illustrations $39.99; (ebook) $37.99 **641.3**
1. Herbs 2. Spices
ISBN 0062375237; 9780062375230; 9780062375247

LC 2016042330

This book, by Padma Lakshmi, "brings together the world's spices and herbs in a vibrant, comprehensive alphabetical guide. This definitive culinary reference book is illustrated with rich color photographs that capture the essence of a diverse range of spices and their authentic flavors." (Publisher's note)

"Cooks will appreciate Lakshmi's explanations of what goes into spice blends such as Chinese five spice powder, curries, dukkah, and garam masala. Full-color photographs appear every few pages, showing spices and herbs in various states, from just-harvested to finely ground." LJ

Includes bibliographical references (pages 325-326) and index.

★ **Larousse** gastronomique; the world's greatest culinary encyclopedia. with the assistance of the Gastronomic Committee, president Joël Robuchon. Clarkson Potter Publishers 2009 1206p il map $90   **641.3**
1. French cooking 2. Reference books 3. Food -- Encyclopedias 4. Cooking -- Encyclopedias
ISBN 978-0-307-46491-0

Original French edition published 1938 under the authorship of Prosper Montagné; first United States edition 1961

"The alphabetical entries range in length from a few sentences to several pages. They cover types of food (Apples, Locusts); cooking techniques (Braising, Grilling); famous chefs (Auguste Escoffier, Alice Waters); culinary jobs (Maître d'hôtel, Sommelier); countries (China, Greece); and tools of the trade (Knife, Saucepan).... This is an essential resource for most library reference collections as well as a wonderful book to browse." Booklist

Le, Stephen

One hundred million years of food; what our ancestors ate and why it matters today. Stephen Le. Picador 2015 320 p. (hardcover) $26   **641.3**
1. Nutrition 2. Food -- History 3. Natural foods 4. Prehistoric peoples -- Food
ISBN 9781250050410

LC 2015029501

This book, by Stephen Le, offers a "tour through the evolution of the human diet, and how we can improve our health by understanding our complicated history with food.... Travelling around the world to places as far-flung as Vietnam, Kenya, India, and the US, Stephen Le introduces us to people who are growing, cooking, and eating food using both traditional and modern methods, striving for a sustainable, healthy diet." (Publisher's note)

"An intriguing viewpoint on how dietary practices have changed over time, but further research is needed to support some of Le's healthy living recommendations." Library Journal

McLagan, Jennifer

Odd bits; how to cook the rest of the animal. photography by Leigh Beisch. Ten Speed Press 2011 248p il $35 **641.3**
1. Cooking -- Meat
ISBN 978-1-58008-334-8

LC 2011-11575

A "unique, informative, and readable cookbook. The ingredients used for the 100 recipes include lungs, necks, spleens, tongues, cheeks, testicles, and feet, as well as a few more common cuts (ribs, brisket, and shanks). In her introduction, McLagan traces the history of eating meat and why in earlier times the odd bits were considered the prime parts. In the last 75 to 100 years, most of these parts have been discarded or used for cat and dog food in the United States. McLagan encourages readers with a detailed and clear discussion of how to choose, prepare, and cook them. She draws the line at eyeballs and notes that lungs are not sold in the United States." Libr J

Medrich, Alice

★ **Flavor** flours; Alice Medrich with Maya Klein. Artisan Boioks 2014 368 p. Illustrations $35 **641.3**
1. Flour 2. Baking 3. Cookbooks
ISBN 1579655130; 9781579655136

LC 2014004631

James Beard Foundation Award Winner: Baking and Dessert (2015)
IACP Cookbook Award Finalist: Baking: Savory or Sweet (2015)

In this cookbook, author "Alice Medrich applies her baking precision and . . . palate to flavor flours--wheat-flour alternatives including rice flour, oat flour, corn flour, sorghum flour, teff, and more. The resulting (gluten-free!) recipes show that baking with alternate flours adds an extra dimension of flavor." (Publisher's note)

Mitchell, Andie

Eating in the middle; Andie Mitchell. Clarkson Potter 2016 240 p. color illustrations $27.99 **641.3**
1. Diet 2. Eating habits 3. Food 4. Health 5. Nutrition
ISBN 9780770433277; 0770433278

LC 2015034879

In this cookbook, author Andie Mitchell "gives readers the dishes that helped her reach her goals and maintain her new size. In 80 recipes, she shows how she eats: mostly healthy meals that are packed with flavor, like Lemon Roasted Chicken with Moroccan Couscous and Butternut Squash Salad with Kale and Pomegranate, and then the 'sometimes' foods, the indulgences such as Peanut Butter Mousse Pie with Marshmallow Whipped Cream." (Publisher's note)

"Mitchell's middle ground philosophy is woven into the chatty, bloggish storytelling, and abundant recipe notes describe her journey away from emotional eating and toward a practical, balanced approach to food, but this cookbook is not a diet book." Pub Wkly

★ **Nutritious** delicious; turbocharge your favorite recipes with 50 everyday superfoods. America's Test Kitchen. America's Test Kitchen 2018 x, 318 p.p $29.99 **641.3**
1. Cookbooks 2. Cooking -- Natural foods 3. Natural foods 4. Cooking (Natural foods)
ISBN 9781945256110

LC 2017030625

"A simple approach to amping up the nutrition in our cooking, . . . [this book] focuses on 50 everyday superfoods among vegetables and fruit, grains, and proteins, and uses them as the basis for building more nutrient-packed versions of the dishes we love for every meal of the day. (Publisher's note)

"This is a wonderful, useful guide to healthy eating." Pub Wkly

Olmsted, Larry

Real food/fake food; Why You Don't Know What You're Eating and What You Can Do about It. Larry Olmsted. Algonquin Books of Chapel Hill 2016 336 p. illustrations $27.95 **641.3**
1. Fraud 2. Nutrition 3. Food additives 4. Artificial foods 5. Consumer education 6. Fraud -- Popular works 7. Nutrition. -- Popular works 8. Food additives -- Popular works 9. Food -- Quality -- Popular works 10. Artificial foods -- Popular works 11. Food substitutes -- Popular works 12. Consumer education -- Popular works
ISBN 9781616204211

LC 2016018797

This book by Larry Olmsted discusses "why real food matters and empowers consumers to make smarter choices. Olmsted brings readers into the unregulated food industry, revealing the shocking deception . . . from high-end foods . . . to everyday staples. . . . It's a massive bait . . . in which counterfeiting is rampant and in which the consumer . . . pays the price. . . . He travels to the sources of the real stuff to help us recognize what to look for, eat, and savor." (Publisher's note)

"A provocative yet grounded look at the U.S. food industry. Though the prospect of finding quality food products may prove increasingly challenging for most consumers, Olmsted provides encouraging tips to help navigate the many obstacles." Kirkus

Includes bibliographical references (pages 293-315).

Pierson, Stephanie

The **brisket** book; a love story with recipes. photographs by Roger Sherman. Andrews McMeel Publishing 2011 208p il $29.99 **641.3**
1. Cooking -- Meat
ISBN 978-1-4494-0697-4

LC 2011-921500

"The book is both humorous and serious: from a section called Found in Translation—how to order brisket in sixteen languages—to The Last Brisket, a joke by David Minkoff. Pierson shares cooking tips, chef interviews, information on beef cuts, different cooking techniques and more than 30 brisket recipes. It took Stephanie a year to select and test the recipes that are included in the book. They come from notable chefs, cookbook authors, cowboys, pit masters and home cooks." KosherEye

Rathbone, Olivia

The **Occidental** Arts and Ecology Center cookbook; fresh-from-the-garden recipes for gatherings large and small. The OAEC Collective with Olivia Rathbone ; foreword by Alice Waters. Chelsea Green Publishing 2015 416 p. illustrations (chiefly color) (hardcover) $40 **641.3**
1. Cookbooks 2. Vegetable gardening 3. Cooking -- Natural foods 4. Kitchen gardens 5. Cooking (Natural foods)
ISBN 9781603585132

LC 2014043698

IACP Cookbook Award: Food Matters (2016)

This cookbook, by the OAEC Collective with Olivia Rathbone, and with foreword by Alice Waters, "shows readers how to cook based on what is available in the garden. . . . [It] incorporates ingredients from all seasons, including weeds, flowers, herbs, nuts, fruits, mushrooms, and other forages. The recipes also include the quantities and measurements necessary to cook for a crowd--making each dish perfect to cook at home, or to share at parties, potlucks, and community events." (Publisher's note)

" Vegetarians---and even omnivores who appreciate the diversity of veg-focused cuisine—will find much to love in this book from the Mother Garden." Booklist

Includes bibliographical references pages (385-389) and index.

Rodale, Maria

Scratch; Home Cooking for Everyone Made Simple, Fun, and Totally Delicious. by Maria Rodale. St. Martin's Press 2016 384 p. color illustrations $35; (ebook) $27.99 **641.3**
1. Cooking
ISBN 1623366437; 9781623366438; 9781623366445

This cookbook, by Maria Rodale, "is full of comfort food recipes that aren't focused on any one healthy trend, but are instead innately healthy. . . . Besides sharing her family's favorite recipes, Maria's book also gives you a peek into her life as a Rodale, with personal family portraits and stories." (Publisher's note)

"This down-to-earth, totally accessible cookbook will take any cook from breakfast to dessert." Pub Wkly

Rosenblum, Mort

Chocolate ; a bittersweet saga of dark and light. North Point Press 2005 290p il $24; pa $14 **641.3**
1. Chocolate
ISBN 0-86547-635-7; 0-86547-730-2 pa
LC 2004-54734

The author "unveils chocolate's history and its various incarnations, including in his fresh and insightful discussions the origins of mole; the differences between, say, Hershey's kisses and Valrhona's products; the invention of Nutella; and the small boutique chocolate artisans found nearly everywhere. . . . A compelling and tasty read." Booklist

Sacks, Stefanie

What the fork are you eating? an action plan for your pantry and plate. Stefanie Sacks, MS, CNS, CDN. Jeremy P. Tarcher/Penguin, a member of Penguin Group, (USA) 2014 400 p. (paperback) $16.95 **641.3**
1. Nutrition 2. Natural foods 3. Food additives 4. Grocery shopping
ISBN 039916796X; 9780399167966
LC 2014027015

In this book, by Stefanie Sacks, "we learn exactly what the most offensive ingredients in our food are and how we can remove (or at least minimize) them in our diets. Sacks gives us an aisle-by-aisle rundown of how to shop for healthier items and create simple, nutritious, and delicious meals, including fifty original recipes." (Publisher's note)

"While Sacks writes in a similar style to Marion Nestle and Michael Pollan, her book is more accessible and practical for people seeking the motivation and tools to follow a healthier lifestyle, emphasizing that even very small changes in diet can make a big difference in health. Although some readers may object to the mildly offensive language she deploys as part of her no-nonsense shtick, this is a valuable guide to evaluating, choosing, and preparing food for wellness." LJ

Includes bibliographical references and index

Schatzker, Mark

The Dorito effect; the surprising new truth about food and flavor. Mark Schatzker. Simon & Schuster 2015 272 p. (hardcover) $27 **641.3**
1. Nutrition 2. Food industry -- United States 3. Junk food 4. Food portions 5. Reducing diets
ISBN 1476724210; 9781476724218; 9781476724232
LC 2014044543

This book by Mark Schatzker "examines the state of the American food industry and its role in the rising obesity epidemic. He contends that foods such as tomatoes are losing flavor owing to modern agricultural practices; meanwhile, 'things' such as chips and fast food have become highly flavored to taste more appealing. . . .Schatzker makes his case for curing this problem by seeking out several foods that were specifically cultivated for their taste." (Library Journal)

"This is a provocative new take on American eating." Booklist

Tea; history, terroirs, varieties. edited by Kevin Gascoyne, Francois Marchand, Jasmin Desharnais, and Hugo Americi. Firefly Books 2014 271 p. color ills., color maps (pbk.) $24.95 **641.3**
1. Tea 2. Tearooms 3. Tea industry 4. Thé 5. Cooking (Tea) 6. Tea -- History 7. Cuisine (Thé) 8. Thé -- Histoire
ISBN 1770853197; 9781770853195
LC 2014415257

This book on tea, edited by Kevin Gascoyne, Francois Marchand, Jasmin Desharnais, and Hugo Americi, is "concise and authoritative with dozens of photographs and images of the teas themselves, revealing the surprising variety of color and opacity of each variety. The book is an escorted tour of the world's tea-growing countries -- China, Japan, Taiwan, India, Sri Lanka, Nepal, Vietnam and East Africa." (Publisher's note)

"While there is no shortage of tea-related tomes, this definitive guide will appeal to die-hard tea enthusiasts interested in learning about the modern, global industry as well as the history and enjoyment of this ubiquitous beverage." LJ

Includes bibliographical references (page 269) and index

The **tea** book. Dk Pub 2015 224 p. $22 **641.3**
ISBN 1465436065; 9781465436061

This book "is your world tour of the art of tea. Visit tea plantations from India to Kenya and explore maps of the world's most important growing regions. Learn to recognize tea-leaf varietals and spot the best types from each region. Recreate a Japanese tea ceremony with a guide to storied traditions and practical implements. Discover the health benefits of green tea. Craft the perfect Chai tea." (Publisher's note)

White, Dana Angelo

First bites; superfoods for babies and toddlers. Dana Angelo White, MS, RD, ATC. Published by the Penguin Group 2015 192 p. (paperback) $14.95 **641.3**
1. Toddlers 2. Infants -- Nutrition 3. Infants -- Health and hygiene 4. Baby foods 5. Toddlers -- Nutrition
ISBN 0399172467; 9780399172465
LC 2014040028

Author Dana Angelo White presents this book " introducing 50 superfoods into baby and toddler diets, with tips and recipes to show parents how to raise healthy eaters for life. Recipes are designed to help to foster healthy eating habits and create a diet filled with 50 fresh, minimally processed superfoods that are just as delicious as they are healthy." (Publisher's note)

"Most parents eventually conclude that little ones can eat whatever healthy dish you are enjoying (just smash up or blend), but White's focus on the known 50 superfoods will get everyone off to a great start. Bon Appetit!" LJ

World cheese book; edited by Juliet Harbutt. DK Publishing 2015 352 p. il map (pbk.) $25 **641.3**
1. Cheese 2. Cooking -- Cheese 3. Cooking (Cheese)
ISBN 1465436057; 9781465436054
LC 2015413323

This book, edited by Juliet Harbutt, is a "comprehensive guide to cheese and covers more world cheeses, with more photography, than any other book on the subject. Discover the flavor profile, shape, and texture of just about every imaginable cheese in this exhaustive, at-a-glance reference." (Publisher's note)

"A must for cheese connoisseurs, this title will delight with its extensive detail and full-color, up-close pictures. The tasting and enjoyment notes for each entry will guide the new cheese enthusiast." LJ

Includes bibliographical references

Wrangham, Richard W.

Catching fire; how cooking made us human. [by] Richard Wrangham. Basic Books 2009 309p $26.95 **641.3**
1. Fire 2. Cooking 3. Eating customs 4. Prehistoric peoples
ISBN 978-0-465-01362-3

LC 2009-1742

This "is a plainspoken and thoroughly gripping scientific essay that presents nothing less than a new theory of human evolution. . . . [This book] contains serious science yet is related in direct, no-nonsense prose. It is toothsome, skillfully prepared brain food." N Y Times (Late N Y Ed)

Includes bibliographical references

Ying, Chris

The **wurst** of Lucky peach; a treasury of encased meat. Chris Ying and the editors of Lucky peach. Clarkson Potter/ Publishers 2016 240 p. illustrations (chiefly color) (hardcover) $26 **641.3**
1. Sausages
ISBN 9780804187770

LC 2015038559

In this book, Chris Ying and the editors of Lucky Peach present "a cookbook as a scrapbook, stuffed with curious local specialties, like cevapi, a caseless sausage that's traveled all the way from the Balkans to underneath the M tracks in Ridgewood, Queens; a look into the great sausage trails of the world, from Bavaria to Texas Hill Country and beyond; and the ins and outs of making your own sausages, including fresh chorizo." (Publisher's note)

"Refreshingly enthusiastic about their subject material (and damning when the situation calls for it), the team has done a great favor for the world's carnivores." Pub Wkly

641.302   Health foods

Hill, McKel

Nutrition Stripped; 100 Whole-Food Recipes Made Deliciously Simple. by McKel Hill. HarperCollins 2016 304 p. color illustrations (ebook) $22.99; $23.99 **641.302**
1. Cooking
ISBN 9780062419934; 0062419927; 9780062419927

This book, by McKel Hill, "based on the popular Nutrition Stripped blog, featur[es] more than 100 exciting and good-for-you recipes and color photography throughout. . . . Drawing inspiration from nature, the turning of the seasons, the world of plants, nutrient dense foods and hidden gems in the world of superfoods, Hill celebrates simplicity, and shares her vast professional knowledge and expertise." (Publisher's note)

"Best known for the anti-inflammatory turmeric milk recipe on her healthy living site, Nutrition Stripped, Hill offers elixirs and more in her first cookbook. But this is more than a cookbook; it's a healthy living guide." Booklist

Lillien, Lisa

Hungry girl clean & hungry; all-natural recipes for clean eating in the real world. Lisa Lillien. St. Martin's Griffin 2016 348 p. illustrations (trade pbk.) $19.99 **641.302**
1. Cookbooks 2. Cooking -- Natural foods 3. Cooking (Natural foods) 4. Women -- Health and hygiene
ISBN 9780312676773

LC 2015048585

This cookbook, by Lisa Lillien, "gives mainstream America delicious, satisfying, and clean recipes, using healthy ingredients found in supermarkets everywhere. The best part? The recipes are so easy, anyone can make 'em! Featuring 90 vegetarian recipes, 108 gluten-free recipes, 56 recipes in 30 minutes or less, [and] 43 recipes with 5 ingredients or less." (Publisher's note)

"Most readers will simply rejoice at the fact that pumpkin spice waffles, barbecue meatloaf, and fudgy flourless chocolate cake are now legit diet foods." Pub Wkly

Seo, Danny

Naturally, delicious; 100 Recipes for Healthy Eats That Make You Happy. Danny Seo. Pam Krauss Books 2016 240 p. color illustrations (hardcover) $30 **641.302**
1. Cookbooks 2. Cooking -- Natural foods 3. Cooking (Natural foods)
ISBN 9781101905302

LC 2015038829

This cookbook by Danny Seo "will show home cooks that preparing healthy, delicious food on a daily basis doesn't have to feel like an expensive, time-consuming chore. By following Danny's emphasis on clever kitchen hacks, kitchen efficiency strategies, and eye-catching presentations, readers will be able to create simple, delicious meals with minimal effort and time, making eating healthfully and well a sustainable practice anyone can introduce to their everyday routine." (Publisher's note)

"Overall, this is an interesting approach to good-for-you food without sacrificing flavor and appeal." Pub Wkly

Ward, Tess

The **naked** cookbook; Tess Ward ; photography by Columbus Leth. Ten Speed Press 2016 128 p. (hardcover) $24.99 **641.302**
1. Cookbooks 2. Cooking -- Natural foods 3. Health 4. Cooking (Natural foods)
ISBN 1607749947; 9781607749943

LC 2015039084

This cookbook, by Tess Ward, with photography by Columbus Leth, offers "a transformative approach to healthy eating that strips back one's diet to simple, clean, and pure foods that cleanse, restore, and nourish the body, featuring 60 recipes and a chapter on detoxing. . . . This is not a deprivation diet but an achievable lifestyle where food is enjoyed and celebrated in its purest form." (Publisher's note)

641.35   Vegetables

Dinki, Nikki

Meat on the side; Delicious Vegetable-Focused Recipes for Every Day. Nikki Dinki ; photographs by Ellen Silverman. St. Martin's Griffin 2016 288 p. color illustrations (hardback) $27.99 **641.35**
1. Cooking -- Vegetables 2. Cooking (Vegetables)
ISBN 9781250067166

LC 2015043188

This cookbook, by Nikki Dinki, presents "100 recipes to put meat in the passenger seat. You won't miss the beef in these Eggplant Meatballs; you'll marvel that pasta can be made from a parsnip using just a peeler; and you'll never want traditional nachos again after trying Nikki's Cabbage Nachos." (Publisher's note)

"For those who like flexible recipes that can be both meaty and meatless, this cookbook provides excellent choices." LJ

641.36   Meat

Venezia, Ray

The **everyday** meat guide; a neighborhood butcher's advice book. Ray Venezia with Chris Peterson. Chronicle Books Llc 2016 184 p. illustrations $19.95   **641.36**
1. Meat 2. Cooking -- Meat
ISBN 9781452142883

LC 2015008240

This book "condenses [Ray] Venezia's expert advice from 25 years behind the butcher block, giving every weeknight shopper and grill enthusiast the need-to-know information on meat grades, best values, and common cuts for poultry, pork, lamb, veal, and beef. [It] includes easy-to-follow illustrations and instructions for the questions butchers are most often asked, plus a handy photo gallery for quick identification at the market." (Publisher's note)

"Venezia clearly and succinctly leads consumers through the butcher shop, from poultry—including ducks, geese, turkey, and, of course, chicken—right up to beef." LJ

641.4   Food preservation and storage

Barrow, Cathy

Mrs. Wheelbarrow's practical pantry; recipes and techniques for year-round preserving. Cathy Barrow ; photographs by Christopher Hirsheimer and Melissa Hamilton. W.W. Norton & Co. Inc. 2014 432 p. color illustrations (hardcover) $35   **641.4**
1. Cooking 2. Canning and preserving
ISBN 0393240738; 9780393240733

LC 2014017291

IACP Cookbook Award Winner: Single Subject (2015)

In this book, author "Cathy Barrow presents a beautiful collection of essential preserving techniques for turning the fleeting abundance of the farmers' market into a well-stocked pantry full of canned fruits and vegetables, jams, stocks, soups, and more. Beyond the core techniques of water-bath canning, advanced techniques for pressure canning, salt-curing meats and fish, smoking, and even air-curing pancetta are broken down." (Publisher's note)

"Barrow offers a well-rounded look at home preserving and this book will appeal to those looking to expand their pantry." LJ

Includes bibliographical references and index

Complete book of home preserving; 400 delicious and creative recipes for today. edited by Judi Kingry and Lauren Devine. R. Rose 2006 448 p. 32 plates; color illustrations $22.95   **641.4**
1. Fruit -- Preservation 2. Canning and preserving 3. Vegetables -- Preservation 4. Cooking (Fruit) 5. Cooking (Vegetables)
ISBN 0778801314; 077880139X; 9780778801313; 9780778801399

LC 2007701974

This cookbook, edited by Judi Kingry and Lauren Devine, sponsored by the Ball Home Canning Products company, "includes comprehensive directions on safe canning and preserving methods plus lists of required equipment and utensils. [The book includes both] specific instructions for first-timers and handy tips for the experienced." (Publisher's note)

Costenbader, Carol W.

The **big** book of preserving the harvest; {foreword by Joanne Lamb Hayes} rev ed; Storey Bks. 2002 347p il pa $18.95   **641.4**
1. Canning and preserving
ISBN 1-58017-458-2

LC 2002-21172

First published 1997

In addition to recipes this book provides instructions for food preservation techniques, including canning, drying, freezing, the preparation of jams and jellies, pickles, relishes and chutneys, vinegars and seasonings, and cold storage. Includes a section on gift giving, directions on building a food dehydrator, a table of equivalents, and a conversion chart to metric measures

Includes bibliographical references

Field, Rick

The **Art** of preserving; authors, Lisa Atwood, Rebecca Courchesne, Rick Field ; photographer, France Ruffenach. Weldon Owen 2010 239 p. col. ill. (pbk) $19.95   **641.4**
1. Food -- Preservation 2. Canning and preserving
ISBN 9781740899789; 9781616283834; 1616283831

This book, by Lisa Atwood, Rick Field, and Rebecca Courchesne, "[p]acked with . . . recipes for preserves, from Apricot Jam to Pickled Fennel with Orange Zest to Preserved Lemons, . . . provides a wealth of ideas for making the most of the harvest. Additional recipes showcase the many ways that preserved foods can be used in finished dishes, from savory starters to flavorful main courses to sweet desserts." (Publisher's note)

Foolproof preserving; a guide to small batch jams, jellies, pickles, condiments, and more. by the editors at America's Test Kitchen. America's Test Kitchen 2016 310 p. color illustrations (paperback) $26.95   **641.4**
1. Condiments 2. Canning and preserving 3. Jam
ISBN 9781940352510

LC 2015045561

This book, by the editors and staff of America's Test Kitchen, presents instructions on "the art of preserving produce by canning and preserving. . . . This detailed guide to home preserving is perfect for novice canners and experts alike and offers more than 100 foolproof recipes across a wide range of categories, from sweet jams and jellies to savory jams, vegetables, condiments, pickles, whole fruits, and more." (Publisher's note)

"An exceptional resource for novice canners, though preserving veterans will find plenty here to love as well." LJ

Macdonald, Emma

Artisan Preserving; Over 100 Recipes for Jams, Chutneys and Relishes, Pickles, Sauces and Cordials, and Cured Meats and Fish. by Emma Macdonald. Osprey Pub Co 2014 224 p. color illustrations $29.95   **641.4**
1. Canning and preserving
ISBN 1848991959; 9781848991958

This book, by Emma Macdonald, "is a one-stop resource for all of your preserving needs. . . . Learn the lost arts of curing, drying, pickling, bottling/canning, crystalizing and jellying; make all kinds of jams, jellies, pickles, chutneys, relishes, cordials, fruit liqueurs, sauces, ketchups, confits and salamis, fruit curds, cheeses and butters, and dried fruits and veggies." (Publisher's note)

"This chic, thoughtful overview of many types of food preservation has the potential to become a staple for novice and veteran cooks alike." LJ

Mackenzie, Jennifer

The **complete** book of pickling; 250 recipes from pickles & relishes to chutneys & salsas. Robert Rose 2009 335p il pa $24.95   **641.4**

1. Canning and preserving
ISBN 978-0-77880216-7; 0-7788-0216-7

This is a "terrific collection of 250 pickles, sauces, chutneys and relishes. . . . Even readers without an appreciation for the tang of a good pickle will appreciate MacKenzie's 50 chutneys, including variations such as Sangria Citrus, classic cranberry and peach, pineapple ginger and spiced tomato; six chili sauces; 18 salsas; and homemade ketchup." Publ Wkly

West, Kevin

Saving the season; the essential guide to home canning, pickling, and preserving. by Kevin West. Alfred A. Knopf 2013 544 p. (hardback) $35   **641.4**

1. Fruit -- Preservation 2. Canning and preserving
ISBN 0307599485; 9780307599483

LC 2012037844

In this book, Kevin West "explores the various preserves available through the four seasons. Each base recipe includes variations to please any palate; the recipe for Black Mission Fig Jam offers directions to flavor it with Syrah, Madeira, or Smoky Black Tea. . . . Appendixes of peak seasons by region and tables of fruit varieties provide extensive information for cooks in any region. More than just recipes, the book also contains stories of the author's travels." (Library Journal)

Includes bibliographical references and index

641.42   Canning

The **all** new ball book of canning and preserving; Over 350 of the Best Canned, Jammed, Pickled, and Preserved Recipes. Jarden Home Brands. Oxmoor House 2016 368 p. illustrations $22.95   **641.42**

1. Fruit -- Preservation 2. Canning and preserving 3. Vegetables -- Preservation
ISBN 0848746783; 9780848746780

LC 2015958285

This book on canning and preserving "covers water bath and pressure canning, pickling, fermenting, freezing, dehydrating, and smoking. Straightforward instructions and step-by-step photos ensure success for beginners, while practiced home canners will find more advanced methods and inspiring ingredient twists." (Publisher's note)

"These 200-plus recipes prove that jellies and chutneys, salsas and syrups contain enough seasoning magic to flavor any meal. The book also shows how thoroughly the experts at Ball approach the subject." Booklist

641.5   Cooking

Acheson, Hugh

The **chef** and the slow cooker; Hugh Acheson ; photographs by Andrew Lee. Clarkson Potter/Publishers 2017 256 p. (hardcover) $29.99   **641.5**

1. Cookbooks 2. Electric cooking, Slow
ISBN 9780451498540; 9780451498557

LC 2017005293

This cookbook, by Hugh Acheson, with photographs by Andy Lee, "brings a chef's mind to the slow cooker, with 100 recipes showing readers how an appliance generally relegated to convenience cooking can open up many culinary doors. Hugh celebrates America's old countertop stalwart with fresh, convenient slow cooker recipes with a chef's twist, dishes like brisket with soy, orange, ginger, and star anise, or pork shoulder braised in milk with fennel and raisins." (Publisher's note)

"Georgia restaurateur and James Beard Best Chef–winner Acheson (A New Turn in the South) transforms the venerable slow cooker into a versatile countertop workhorse capable of high-end culinary feats." Pub Wkly

Adjonyoh, Zoe

Zoe's Ghana kitchen; traditional Ghanaian recipes remixed for the modern kitchen. Zoe Adjonyoh. Mitchell Beazley 2017 256 p. color illustrations (hardcover) $29.99   **641.5**

1. Cookbooks 2. Food -- Ghana 3. Ghanaian cooking 4. Cooking, Ghanaian
ISBN 9781784721633; 1784721638

In this book, author Zoe Adjonyoh, "takes traditional Ghanaian recipes and re-mixes them for the modern kitchen. From Pan-roasted Cod with Grains of Paradise and Nkruma (Okra) Tempura to Coconut and Cassava Cake and Cubeb Spiced Shortbread, Ghanaian food is always fun, always relaxed and always tasty! These fabulous Ghanaian dishes are homemade favorites, focusing on traditional flavors with Zoe's twist." (Publisher's note)

"African cuisine remains largely unexplored in the West, and this excellent and appealing volume offers the warmest of welcomes." Pub Wkly

Ahern, Shauna James

Gluten-free girl every day; Shauna James Ahern, with Daniel Ahern ; photography by Penny De Los Santos. John Wiley & Sons, Inc. 2013 319 p. col. ill. (cloth) $29.99   **641.5**

1. Cookbooks 2. Gluten-free diet 3. Gluten-free diet -- Recipes
ISBN 111811521X; 9781118115213

LC 2012030520

James Beard Award (2014)

This cookbook, by Shauna James Ahern, was the winner of a James Beard Foundation cookbook award. "Vegetables in season are the key to these healthy, relatively simple recipes, along with whole grains, beans, and a few key spices and homemade sauces. . . . [The book] also includes practical tips on how to stock a gluten-free pantry, as well as helpful insights into how to bake gluten-free." (Publisher's note)

Alford, Jeffrey

Beyond the Great Wall; recipes and travels in the other China. [by] Jeffrey Alford and Naomi Duguid; studio photography by Richard Jung; location photographs by Jeffrey Alford and Naomi Duguid. Artisan 2008 376p il map $40   **641.5**

1. Chinese cooking 2. Tibet (China) -- Description and travel
ISBN 978-1-57965-301-9

LC 2007-28556

The authors "explore the food and peoples of the outlaying regions of present-day China, historically home to those not ethnically Chinese. Part travel guide and part cookbook, this collection looks at the cultural survival and preservation of food in smaller societies including that of the Tibetan, Mongol, Tuvan and Kirghiz peoples, among others. . . . A handsome and engaging collection suitable for travelers and cooks alike, this book will delight anyone with an interest in this part of the world." Publ Wkly

Includes bibliographical references

Ali, Laila, 1977-

Food for life; delicious & healthy comfort food from my table to yours! Laila Ali ; with Leida Scheintaub. St. Martin's Press 2017 312 p. (hardcover) $29.99   **641.5**
1. Cooking 2. Cooking -- Natural foods 3. Comfort food
ISBN 125013109X; 9781250131096

LC 2017045756

In this cookbook, Laila Ali "shares more than 100 of . . . [her] favorite recipes. Whether you're new to cooking, busy feeding a family, or ready to eat healthier, . . . [the book] will be your guidebook! In 'Food for Life,' you'll find real-life recipes to bring simple, healthy, hearty, and satisfying food to the table, such as: Stovetop Ratatouille, Oven-'Fried' Chicken, West Coast Southern Greens, . . . [and] Heavenly Lemon Yogurt Cake." (Publisher's note)

Includes bibliographical references and index

Allibhoy, Omar

Spanish made simple; foolproof Spanish recipes for every day. Omar Allibhoy ; photographs by Martin Poole. Quadrille Publishing 2017 207 p. color illustrations (hardcover) $24.99   **641.5**
1. Desserts 2. Spanish cooking 3. Cookbooks 4. Cooking, Spanish
ISBN 9781849497602; 1849497605

This cookbook, by Omar Allibhoy, "guides you through the basics of 100 key Spanish dishes. All of the ingredients are available from grocery stores and you don't need to be an expert cook. Spanish cooking is characterized by deep flavors, vibrant color, and minimal ingredients--so you will learn to make a paella that packs a punch, cook up a tapas feast for friends, and even whip up a delectable Spanish dessert in minutes." (Publisher's note)

"Vivid full-color photos round out this superb introduction to Spanish cooking." Pub Wkly

The **America's** Test Kitchen healthy family cookbook; a new, healthier way to cook everything from America's most trusted test kitchen. the editors at America's test kitchen ; photography, Daniel J. Van Ackere, Carl Tremblay. America's Test Kitchen 2010 viii, 520 p.p ill. (chiefly col.) (looseleaf) $34.95   **641.5**
1. Cookbooks 2. American cooking 3. Cooking, American 4. Families -- Health and hygiene
ISBN 1933615567; 9781933615561

LC 2011278441

This cookbook, produced by the editors at America's Test Kitchen, "[p]resents advice on cooking techniques, equipment, food preparation, and selection of ingredients, along with more than 750 recipes for healthy dishes, including appetizers, soups, meats, fish, vegetables, sauces, breads, and desserts." (Publisher's note)

"[A] well-tested collection of more than 750 recipes that employ vetted techniques and abundant flavor to create dishes that are as healthy as they can be, given what they are, without sacrificing a pleasurable eating experience." Pub Wkly

The **America's** Test Kitchen new family cookbook; all-new edition of the best-selling classic with 1,100 new recipes. the editors at America's Test Kitchen. America's Test Kitchen 2014 928 p. col. ill. $40   **641.5**
1. Cookbooks 2. American cooking 3. Cooking, American
ISBN 1936493853; 9781936493852

LC 2014009517

"The 'America's Test Kitchen New Family Cookbook' contains more than 1,100 new recipes accompanied by new photography and a brand-new package. The result is a comprehensive but approachable tome that every cook will want in the kitchen, for many years to come. . . . This new edition is hardcover (rather than ringbound) and features a fresh design with four-color food photography throughout." (Publisher's note)

American Institute for Cancer Research

The **new** American plate cookbook; recipes for a healthy weight and a healthy life. American Institute for Cancer Research. University of California Press 2005 306p il $24.95   **641.5**
1. Cooking
ISBN 0-520-24234-3

LC 2004-17993

The recipes in this book are "built around vegetables and whole grains, with an emphasis on brown rice, wheat pasta, and other healthful foods, rather than protein. . . . Recipes are appealing and easy to make and cover every course of a meal. Well-known dishes are reworked, e.g., New England Clam Chowder, to help with the transition to healthier eating." Libr J

Anderson, Pam

How to cook without a book; recipes and techniques every cook should know by heart. Broadway Bks. 2000 290p $25   **641.5**
1. Cooking
ISBN 0-7679-0279-3

LC 99-43776

"Former executive editor of Cook's magazine and author of The Perfect Recipe, Anderson wants to teach Americans a new way to cook without relying on recipes. It's somewhat surprising, then, to discover that this book is full of recipes. However, readers may cotton to Anderson's method: each chapter consists of a simple technique, basic recipe, variations, key points and a little mnemonic device used to recall the technique. The techniques are, for the most part, terrific time-savers." Pub Wkly

Andrews, Colman

Country cooking of Ireland; photographs by Christopher Hirsheimer; foreword by Darina Allen. Chronicle 2009 383p il map $50   **641.5**
1. Irish cooking
ISBN 978-0-8118-6670-5

The author "provides new perspectives on the often maligned Irish cuisine. The breathtakingly beautiful photographs are alone enough to convince, but Andrews, calling Irish cuisine one of the most exciting food stories in the world today, lets the dishes make his case. Robust soups such as butternut and apple and roast pork belly start the mouth juices flowing. Andrews offers a culinary feast with everything from nested eggs and steak-and-kidney pie to Arlington chicken liver pâté and battered sausages. . . . Andrews has done the near impossible in elevating a cuisine thought to be humble and drab into tantalizing fare that will have worldwide appeal." Publ Wkly

Includes bibliographical references

Arokiasamy, Christina

The **Malaysian** Kitchen; 150 Recipes for Simple Home Cooking. by Christina Arokiasamy. Houghton Mifflin Harcourt 2017 352 p. color illustrations (ebook) $35; $35   **641.5**
  1. Malaysia 2. Asian cooking
  ISBN 9780544810020; 0544809998; 9780544809994
                        LC 2017007022

This cookbook, by Christina Arokiasamy, presents "Malaysian recipes for the American home cook. . . . This cuisine borrows from the traditions of Thailand, India, China, and Portugal for dishes as varied as Chili Prawns, Salmon Tandoori, Hainanese Chicken Rice, and Grilled Lamb with Rosemary Pesto." (Publisher's note)

"A mouthwatering introduction to Malaysian cooking, this book offers home cooks a wealth of delicious everyday meals sure to delight." Pub Wkly

Includes bibliographical references (pages 330-331) and index.

Aron, Jules

★ **Vegan** cheese; simple, delicious plant-based recipes. Jules Aron. The Countryman Press, a division of W W Norton & Co. 2017 190 p. color illustrations (hardcover) $24.95 **641.5**
  1. Vegetarian cooking 2. Cooking -- Natural foods 3. Vegan cooking 4. Dairy substitutes 5. Cheese -- Varieties
  ISBN 9781581575392; 9781581574036
                        LC 2017003596

This cookbook, by Jules Aron, offers "60 dairy-free and delicious cheeses to make at home. . . . Aron shares the tricks of the trade for making sauces, cheese you can grate or slice, and soft spreadable options, using homemade nut milks, vegetables, and natural helpers like lemon juice, probiotics, agar-agar, and nutritional yeast. Her flavorful creations are enhanced with herbs and spices, and run from incredibly easy to more complex, mimicking familiar cheeses." (Publisher's note)

"Aron's book is a useful, fun, and necessary addition to both the beginner and advanced vegan cook's repertoire." Pub Wkly

Bajaj, Ashok

Rasika; Flavors of India. stories by Ashok Bajaj ; recipes by Vikram Sunderam ; coauthored by David Hagedorn. HarperCollins 2017 xxv, 310 p.p color illustrations (hardcover) $34.99   **641.5**
  1. Cooking 2. India -- Food 3. Cooking, Indic 4. Ethnic restaurants -- Washington (D.C.)
  ISBN 9780062435545; 9780062435552; 0062435558

This cookbook, by Ashok Bajaj, Vikram Sunderam and David Hagedorn, presents "innovative recipes and reinvented classics of modern Indian cuisine. Using traditional techniques as jumping-off points, Rasika incorporates local, seasonal ingredients to reinterpret dishes from one of the world's richest and most varied cuisines. . . . Rasika showcases the cuisine of one of Washington, DC's most popular and critically acclaimed restaurants." (Publisher's note)

"Innovative yet familiar, this collection offers many excellent, appetizing recipes home cooks are sure to embrace." Pub Wkly

Includes bibliographical references (page 299) and index.

Bastianich, Lidia Matticchio

Lidia cooks from the heart of Italy; by Lidia Matticchio Bastianich and Tanya Bastianich Manuali, with David Nussbaum; full-page photographs by Christopher Hirsheimer; other photographs by Lidia Matticchio Bastianich. Alfred A. Knopf 2009 411p il $35   **641.5**
  1. Italian cooking
  ISBN 978-0-307-26751-1; 0-307-26751-2
                        LC 2009-22021

"Bastianich and daughter Tanya take readers on a culinary tour of Italy's 12 regions. Grouped by those areas, the recipes are simple enough for novice cooks. Included are appetizers, soups, salads and side dishes, condiments, pastas and risottos/rice, vegetarian main courses (aside from pasta), fish and seafood, meat and poultry, and desserts. In addition, there are stories about the history of the dishes." Libr J

Lidia's celebrate like an Italian; 220 foolproof recipes that make every meal a party. Lidia Matticchio Bastianich and Tanya Bastianich Manuali ; photographs by Steve Giralt. Alfred A. Knopf 2017 xxvii, 383 p.p color illustrations (hardcover; alk. paper) $35   **641.5**
  1. Parties 2. Cookbooks 3. Italian cooking 4. Cooking, Italian
  ISBN 9780385349499; 9780385349482
                        LC 2017010180

This cookbook, by Lidia Matticchio Bastianich and Tanya Bastianich Manuali, illustrated by Steve Giralt, presents "220 fantastic recipes for entertaining with that distinctly Bastianich flare. From Pear Bellinis to Carrot and Chickpea Dip, from Campanelle with Fennel and Shrimp to Berry Tiramisu--these are dishes your guests will love. . . . Here, too, are Lidia's suggestions for hosting a BBQ, . . . choosing the perfect wine, setting an inviting table, and much more." (Publisher's note)

★ **Lidia's** family table; Lidia Matticchio Bastianich, with David Nussbaum ; photographs by Christopher Hirsheimer. Random House Inc 2004 419 p. col. ill. $35   **641.5**
  1. Cookbooks 2. Italian cooking
  ISBN 1400040353; 9781400040353
                        LC 2004022411

In this cookbook, author and television chef "Lidia Bastianich, . . . gives us her most generous, instructive, and creative cookbook. The emphasis here is on cooking for the family, and her book is filled with unusually delicious basic recipes for everyday eating Italian-style, as well as imaginative ideas for variations and improvisations." (Publisher's note)

"Step-by-step photographs illustrate kitchen techniques, and charming photos of the author's grandchildren and other family scenes add to the appeal of this engaging, immensely practical book." LJ

Batali, Mario

Italian grill; [by] Mario Batali with Judith Sutton; photography by Beatriz da Costa; art direction by Lisa Eaton and Douglas Riccardi. Ecco 2008 246p il $29.95   **641.5**
  1. Italian cooking 2. Barbecue cooking
  ISBN 978-0-06-145097-6; 0-06-145097-9

A collection of eighty recipes for grilled Italian food is divided into categories for antipasti, pizza, meat, fish, and vegetables, and includes information on grilling basics, different heat-source options, and differences in grilling equipment.

"This is an essential collection for any serious backyard cook." Publ Wkly

Bayless, Rick

Fiesta at Rick's; fabulous food for great times with friends. [by] Rick Bayless with Deann Groen Bayless; photographs by Paul Elledge. W. W. Norton 2010 348p il $35   **641.5**
  1. Menus 2. Entertaining 3. Mexican cooking
  ISBN 978-0-393-05899-4
                        LC 2010-13128

"The book loosely packages recipes around fiestas, from a luxury guacamole and cocktail party for 12 to classic mole for 24, complete with game-plan checklists. . . . The hardest thing about using this book isn't finding the ingredients (today, practically every small town has a great Mexican grocery), it's keeping yourself from eating everything before the guests arrive." N Y Times Book Rev

Behr, Edward

The **Food** and Wine of France; Eating and Drinking from Champagne to Provence. by Edward Behr. Penguin Group USA 2016 320 p. $28   **641.5**
1. Eating customs 2. French cooking
ISBN 1594204527; 9781594204524

In this book, "food writer Edward Behr investigates French cuisine and what it means, in encounters from Champagne to Provence. He tells the stories of French artisans and chefs who continue to work at the highest level. Many people in and out of France have noted for a long time the slow retreat of French cuisine, concerned that it is losing its important place in the country's culture and in the world culture of food." (Publisher's note)

"What resonates is that whether a cuisine is defined by its ingredients, techniques, or even the logistical structure of its menu, it is perhaps the story and the telling that remain most important." LJ

Berry, Mary, 1935-

Cooking with Mary Berry; Mary Berry. DK Publishing 2016 256 p. color illustrations $25   **641.5**
1. Cookbooks 2. English cooking
ISBN 1465459510; 9781465459510

LC 2017287009

This book, by Mary Berry, "covers a broad selection of recipes—brunch ideas, soups, salads, appetizers, mains, sides, and desserts—drawing on Mary's more than 60 years in the kitchen. Many, like her French Onion Soup, Steak Diane, and Cinnamon Rolls, are familiar classics, but all have been adapted to follow Mary's prescription for dishes that are no-fuss, practical, and foolproof." (Publisher's note)

"This is a basic, go-to volume, with the flair that Berry's growing U.S. fan base will expect." Booklist

Besh, John

Cooking from the heart; my favorite lessons learned along the way. John Besh. Andrews McMeel Pub., LLC 2013 320 p. $40   **641.5**
1. Cooking 2. Cookbooks
ISBN 1449430562; 9781449430566

LC 2013936654

In this book "James Beard Award-winning chef John Besh shares the lessons he learned from his mentors through 140 accessible recipes and cooking lessons. . . . From Germany's Black Forest to the mountains of Provence, each chapter highlights . . . memories and . . . recipes--the framework for his love of food." (Publisher's note)

The **best** of America's test kitchen 2018; best recipes, equipment reviews, and tastings. America's Test Kitchen. Random House Inc 2017 336 p.   **641.5**
1. Cooking
ISBN 1945256036; 9781945256035

This book, by America's Test Kitchen, provides a compilation of "some 150 of the 'best' recipes tried and tested by the show's cooks, including steps, photographs, and detailed instructions, along with tips and tricks from the kitchen (equipment suggestions, shortcuts, and more). . . . Each recipe also comes with a detailed narrative explaining just about

every element that goes into its creation." (Library Journal)

"Each recipe also comes with a detailed narrative explaining just about every element that goes into its creation, while the index makes it easy to search by meal and main ingredient for the perfect dish. A must for any home cook." (LJ)

The **best** recipe; by the editors of Cook's illustrated ; illustrations by John Burgoyne ; photography by Carl Tremblay. Boston Common Press 1999 575 p. illustrations $29.95   **641.5**
1. Cooking 2. Cookbooks
ISBN 0936184388; 9780936184388

LC 2002512594

"'The Best Recipe' is a collection of the editors' picks from the pages of 'Cook's Illustrated.' The recipes have been edited, organized, and annotated with in-depth descriptions of how we developed the 'best' recipe. And they appear alongside dozens of equipment ratings and taste tests of supermarket foods, as well as more than 200 illustrations demonstrating the most efficient food preparation methods." (Publisher's note)

Better homes and gardens

Better homes and gardens new cook book; 15th ed.; J. Wiley 2010 660p il $29.95   **641.5**
1. Cooking
ISBN 978-0-470-55686-3

LC 2010-25417

First published 1930 with title: My Better Homes and Gardens cook book. Periodically revised

"A standard cookbook . . . with staple recipes and types of cooking." N Y Public Libr. Book of How & Where to Look It Up

★ **Better** Homes and Gardens New Cook Book; Better Homes and Gardens. 16th edition HougHton Mifflin Harcourt 2014 658 p. color illustrations (loose leaf) $29.99   **641.5**
1. Cooking 2. Cookbooks 3. Canning and preserving
ISBN 0544307070; 9780544307070

LC 2014012314

This Better Homes and Gardens cookbook is "the fully updated and revised [16th] edition. . . . [It] includes more than 1,200 recipes, 1,000 color photos, and more tips and how-to information than ever. . . . Along with the best recipes for favorite foods, this indispensable volume offers information on new cooking trends and fresh ideas, a new fruit and vegetable guide with ID photos, and expanded coverage of canning." (Publisher's note)

★ **Betty** Crocker cookbook; everything you need to know to cook today. 10th ed.; Wiley 2005 575p il $29.95; pa $17.95   **641.5**
1. Cooking
ISBN 0-7645-6877-9; 978-0-7645-6877-0; 0-7645-8374-3 pa; 978-0-7645-8374-2 pa

LC 2006-281166

First published with this title 1969 by Golden Press. Periodically revised. Publisher varies. Variant title: Betty Crocker's new cookbook

"This book gives easily readable and understandable recipes. Also has a glossary of cooking terms in back, as well as nutritional guidelines and 'special helps.'" N Y Public Libr. Book of How & Where to Look It Up

Bharadwaj, Monisha

The **Indian** cooking course; techniques, masterclasses, ingredients, 300 recipes. Monisha Bharadwaj ; photography by

Gareth Morgans. Kyle Books 2016 496 p. color illustrations (hardcover) $39.95 **641.5**

1. Indian cooking

ISBN 1909487465; 9781909487468

LC 2016942418

This cookbook, by Monisha Bharadwaj, "explores the myriad regional varieties of authentic, healthy, and exotic Indian recipes. With chapters broken down into Rice, Breads, Meat, etc., Monisha covers a varied range of dishes, with techniques and step-by-step masterclasses to help you recreate more than 450 classic and popular recipes." (Publisher's note)

"This is a must-have for almost any public-library cookbook collection." Booklist

Bianco, Chris

Bianco; pizza, pasta, and other food I like. Chris Bianco. Ecco, an imprint of HarperCollinsPublishers 2017 xi, 212 p.p illustrations (chiefly color) (hardcover) $34.99 **641.5**

1. Pizza 2. Italian cooking

ISBN 0062224379; 9780062224385; 9780062224378

This book, by Chris Bianco, "brings . . . the fundamentals of pizza making, from the basics of flour and water to the philosophy behind Bianco's cooking. The book features recipes for his signature pies as well as strategies and techniques for translating chef's methods to the home kitchen. . . . It also features recipes for market salads, tasting plates, and dessert options, as well as the staff meals." (Publisher's note)

"Thanks to Bianco's focus on simple recipes and outstanding ingredients, home cooks get appealing, classic dishes great for any day of the week." Pub Wkly

Bittman, Mark

★ **How** to cook everything; 2,000 simple recipes for great food. illustrations by Alan Witschonke. 2nd ed.; J. Wiley 2008 1044p il $35 **641.5**

1. Cooking

ISBN 978-0-76-457865-6; 0-76-457865-0

LC 2008-18984

First published 1998 by Macmilllan

The author presents "more than 1000 basic recipes and simple and inventive variations. The enormous breadth of recipes along with Bittman's engaging, straightforward prose will appeal to cooks looking for reliable help with kitchen fundamentals." Publ Wkly

Includes bibliographical references

How to Cook Everything Fast; A Better Way to Cook Great Food. Mark Bittman ; illustrations by Olivia de Salve Villedieu. Houghton Mifflin Harcourt 2014 1056 p. illustrations $35 **641.5**

1. Cooking 2. Cookbooks 3. Quick and easy cooking

ISBN 0470936304; 9780470936306

LC 2014427729

In this book, author Mark Bittman "provides a game plan for becoming a better, more intuitive cook while you wake up your weekly meal routine with 2,000 main dishes and accompaniments that are simple to make, globally inspired, and bursting with flavor. . . . Time management-- the essential principle of fast cooking-- is woven into revolutionary recipes that do the thinking for you." (Publisher's note)

"Bittman's latest is fantastic for busy, novice, and noncooks. It's also a practical tool for anyone who aspires but struggles to cook more often." LJ

★ **How** to cook everything vegetarian; simple meatless

recipes for great food. Mark Bittman ; photography by Burcu Avsar & Zach DeSart ; illustrations by Alan Witschonke. Tenth anniversary edition Houghton Mifflin Harcourt 2017 830 p. color illustrations (hardcover) $35 **641.5**

1. Cookbooks 2. Vegetarian cooking

ISBN 9781118455647; 9780544186941; 1118455649

LC 2017051874

This cookbook, by Mark Bittman, presents "the ultimate guide to meatless meals. . . . This new edition has been completely reviewed and revised to stay relevant to today's cooks: New recipes include more vegan options and a brand-new chapter on smoothies, teas, and more. Charts, variations, and other key information have been updated." (Publisher's note)

"Bittman's evenhanded tone and his ability to cover a gamut of recipes . . . render this book as relevant today as it was when it first appeared, and confirm its status as an indispensable resource." Pub Wkly

Mark Bittman's Kitchen express; 404 inspired seasonal dishes you can make in 20 minutes or less. Simon & Schuster 2009 233p $26 **641.5**

1. Quick and easy cooking

ISBN 978-1-4165-7566-5

LC 2008-54823

"Bittman here offers a sampling of 404 inspiring recipes. . . . The no-sweat recipes are divided into four sections: summer, fall, winter and spring, capitalizing on the freshest ingredients of each season while whittling down the prep time of ordinarily elaborate dishes like coq au vin and ricotta cheesecake to 10 minutes or less. The book includes a drilldown of how best to stock your kitchen, and given the impromptu nature of the book, the substitution grid proves indispensable." Publ Wkly

Mark Bittman's kitchen matrix; more than 700 simple recipes & techniques to mix & match for endless possibilities. Mark Bittman. Pam Krauss Books 2015 304 p. illustrations (hardback) $35 **641.5**

1. Cooking 2. Cookbooks

ISBN 0804188017; 9780804188012

LC 2015020733

IACP Cookbook Award Nominee: Compilations (2016)

This book, by Mark Bittman, "anthologizes his popular Matrix series in a boldly graphic new cookbook that emphasizes creativity, improvisation, and simplicity as the keys to varied cooking. . . . Accompanied by striking photographs and brief, straightforward instructions, these thematic matrices show how simple changes in preparation and ingredient swaps in a master recipe can yield dishes that are each completely different from the original, and equally delicious." (Publisher's note)

"This unconventional cookbook can help proficient cooks develop ideas for creating their own recipe variations." LJ

The **VB6** cookbook; 320 all-new recipes that help you eat healthy vegan meals all day and delicious flexitarian dinners at night. Mark Bittman ; photographs by Quentin Bacon. Clarkson Potter 2014 272 p. color illustrations $29.95 **641.5**

1. Veganism 2. Cookbooks 3. Vegetarian cooking 4. Vegan cooking 5. Reducing diets -- Recipes

ISBN 0385344821; 9780385344821

LC 2013050637

"When [author Mark] Bittman committed to a vegan before 6:00 pm diet, he quickly realized that everything about it became easier if he cooked his own meals at home. In The VB6 Cookbook he makes this proposition more convenient than you could imagine. Drawing on a varied and enticing pantry of vegan staples strategically punctuated with 'treat' foods . . . , he has created a versatile repertoire of recipes that makes following his plan simple, satisfying, and sustainable." (Publisher's note)

"Rather than overload readers with prescriptive rules, unfamiliar ingredients, and complicated preparations, Bittman gives them a memorable charge (eat more plants, less meat and processed foods) and tools to help them follow it." LJ

Blais, Richard

So good; 100 recipes from my kitchen to yours. Richard Blais with Mary Goodbody ; photography by Evan Sung. Houghton Mifflin Harcourt 2017 255 p. illustrations (hardcover) $30   **641.5**

    1. Cooking 2. Cookbooks

    ISBN 9780544663312; 9780544663091; 0544663314

                 LC 2017017426

This cookbook, by Richard Blais, features "elevated homestyle recipes and personal stories which invite you behind the scenes and into his own kitchen for the first time. Some recipes might look familiar, like spaghetti and meatballs, but have a secret, flavor-boosting ingredient, and others feature clever but unexpected techniques, like his fried chicken which is first marinated in pickle juice." (Publisher's note)

"Home cooks interested in upping their game will want to give this one a look." Pub Wkly

The **Blue** Apron cookbook; 165 essential recipes and lessons for a lifetime of home cooking. from the Blue Apron Culinary Team ; photography by John Kernick. HarperCollins Publishers 2017 400 p. $39.99   **641.5**

    1. Cooking 2. Cooking (Natural foods)

    ISBN 0062562762; 9780062562760

                 LC 2017018933

This book, from the Blue Apron culinary team, "excites, educates, and inspires. With the help of 800 stunning color photographs and unparalleled step-by-step instruction, amateur home cooks will grow into competent home chefs, perfecting and creating variations of classics ranging from roast chicken to risottos, pastas, soups, salads, and desserts." (Publisher's note)

Bracken, Peg

The **I** hate to cook book; with a new foreword by Jo Bracken; drawings by Hilary Knight. 50th anniversary ed.; Grand Central Pub. 2010 207p $22.99; ebook $10.99   **641.5**

    1. Cooking 2. Quick and easy cooking

    ISBN 978-0-446-54592-1; 978-0-446-56894-4 ebook

                 LC 2009-1249

First published 1960 by Harcourt, Brace

"This book's strident title belies both its usefulness and its popularity. Peg Bracken faced the burden of being a full-time writer, a full-time mother and a full-time housewife. To buy herself a bit more time for other pursuits, she and her friends collected a host of easy, stress-free recipes. What's truly wonderful is Bracken's droll delivery and the more than 200 recipes that run the gamut from appetizers to desserts." Washington Post

Brennan, Kathy

Keepers; two home cooks share their tried-and-true weeknight recipes and the secrets to happiness in the kitchen. Kathy Brennan and Caroline Campion ; photographs by Christopher Testani. Rodale Books 2013 256 p. color illustrations (hardcover) $26.99   **641.5**

    1. Menus 2. Cookbooks 3. American cooking 4. Quick and

easy cooking 5. Cooking, American 6. Low budget cooking 7. Cooking -- Philosophy 8. Kitchens -- Management

    ISBN 1609613546; 9781609613549

                 LC 2013005481

IACP Cookbook Award (2014)

In this cookbook, chefs Kathy Brennan and Caroline Campion "offer 120 appealing, satisfying recipes ideal for weeknight meals. There's an array of master recipes for classic dishes with options for substitutions, updated old favorites, one-pot meals, 'international' dishes, super-fast ones, and others that reheat well or can be cooked in individual portions." (Publisher's note)

Britton, Sarah

Naturally nourished; Healthy, Delicious Meals Made with Everyday Ingredients. Sarah Britton. Clarkson Potter/Publishers 2017 240 p. color illustrations (hardcover) $29.99; (ebook) $65   **641.5**

    1. Vegetarian cooking 2. Nutrition 3. Cooking (Natural foods)

    ISBN 9780804185400; 9780804185417

                 LC 2016008218

This book, by Sarah Britton, "streamlines vegetarian cooking. . . . Her mains, sides, soups, salads, and snacks all call for easy cooking techniques and ingredients found in any grocery store. With callouts to vegan and gluten-free options and ideas for substitutions, this beautiful cookbook shows readers how to cook smart, not hard." (Publisher's note)

"Britton's approachable guide to healthy eating will appeal to many readers." LJ

Includes bibliographical references and index

Brown, Alton, 1962-

Everydaycook; Alton Brown. Random House Inc. 2016 256 p. color illustrations (ebook) $65; (hardcover) $35 **641.5**

    1. Cookbooks

    ISBN 1101885718; 9781101885727; 9781101885710

This book by cooking show host Alton Brown discusses how he got into cooking and why he wrote the book. "I was sitting around trying to organize my recipes, and I realized that I should put them into a personal collection. One thing led to another, and here's EveryDayCook. There's still plenty of science and hopefully some humor in here . . . , but unlike in my other books, a lot of attention went into the photos . . . . As for the recipes, . . . they're pretty darned tasty." (Publisher's note)

Brown, Leanne

★ **Good** and cheap; eat well on $4/day. Leanne Brown. Workman Publishing 2015 208 p. color illustrations (alk. paper) $16.95   **641.5**

    1. Cooking 2. Household budgets 3. Low budget cooking

    ISBN 0761184996; 9780761184997

                 LC 2015011072

IACP Cookbook Award Finalist: Food Matters (2015)

IACP Cookbook Award: Judge's Choice (2015)

This book, by Leanne Brown, is a "cookbook filled with delicious, healthful recipes created for everyone on a tight budget. . . . While studying food policy as a master's candidate at NYU, Leanne Brown asked a simple yet critical question: How well can a person eat on the $4 a day given by SNAP, the U.S. government's Supplemental Nutrition Assistance Program informally known as food stamps? The answer is surprisingly well." (Publisher's note)

"Brown estimates the cost per serving for all dishes, including potato leek pizzas, dark and spicy chili, and peanut chicken and broccoli with coconut rice." LJ

Includes bibliographical references and index

Brownson, JeanMarie

Dinner at home; 140 recipes to enjoy with family and friends. JeanMarie Brownson. Surrey Books an Agate Surrey imprint 2015 282 p. color illustrations (hardback) $29.95 **641.5**

    1. American cooking 2. Cookbooks 3. Cooking, American -- Midwestern style

ISBN 1572841788; 9781572841789

        LC 2015031410

IACP Cookbook Award: Children, Youth and Family (2016)

This cookbook, by JeanMarie Brownson, "features inventive and easy-to-make recipe ideas, along with gorgeous full-color photography. . . . Readers will enjoy the seasonal menus for special occasions such as Anniversary Dinner, Ultimate Father's Day, and Sunday Brunch, as well as themed meals like Manhattan Cocktail Party, Saturday Night Beer Tasting, and Wish We Were in Ireland Supper." (Publisher's note)

Brule, Jennifer

Learn to cook 25 Southern classics 3 ways; Traditional, Contemporary, International. Jennifer Brulé. University of North Carolina Press 2016 248 p. color illustrations (cloth; alk. paper) $30 **641.5**

    1. Cookbooks 2. Southern cooking 3. International cooking 4. Cooking, American -- Southern style

ISBN 9781469629124

        LC 2016012031

This cookbook by Jennifer Brulé features "step-by-step instructions designed to teach basic cooking techniques. Brulé shows cooks how to whisk, chop, slice, simmer, saute, fry, bake, and roast their way to seventy-five wonderfully tasty dishes. The contemporary versions incorporate especially wholesome elements, such as unrefined grains and healthier fats, while the international versions offer popular global tastes." (Publisher's note)

"An ingenious cookbook that will appeal to cooks of all stripes." Booklist

Bryant, George

The **paleo** kitchen; finding primal joy in modern cooking. George Bryant and Juli Bauer. Victory Belt Publishing Inc 2014 327 p. color illustrations $34.95 **641.5**

    1. Cookbooks 2. Paleo cooking

ISBN 1628600101; 9781628600100

This cookbook, by George Bryant and Juli Bauer, "bring[s] a myriad of bold and delectable gluten & grain-free Paleo recipes straight from their kitchens to yours in their new cookbook. . . . [It] boasts over 100 brand new recipes consisting of appetizers, entrées, side dishes, and decadent desserts that are sure to invigorate and please the fearless caveman palate." (Publisher's note)

Includes bibliographical references (page 314) and index

Buffett, Lucy

Gumbo love; recipes for Gulf Coast cooking, entertaining, and savoring the good life. Lucy Buffett ; foreword by Thomas McGuane. Grand Central Life & Style 2017 xxxi, 303 p.p color illustrations (hardcover) $30 **641.5**

    1. Cooking 2. Entertaining 3. Gulf Coast (U.S.) 4. Cooking -- Gulf States 5. Cooking, American -- Southern style

ISBN 1455566446; 9781455566440; 9781478973003

        LC 2016056560

This cookbook by Lucy Buffett "includes recipes from all over the Gulf Coast. The dishes incorporate Caribbean, Cajun, Cuban, Mexican, Old Florida, and Creole influences. Lucy proves through her collection of recipes that the Gulf Coast has its own distinct flavors and traditions that make it a coastal destination year after year." (Publisher's note)

"Restaurateur Buffett (Lulu's Kitchen) packs Gumbo Love with stories and recipes reflecting her love of the Gulf Coast." Pub Wkly

Buford, Bill

Heat; an amateur's adventures as kitchen slave, line cook, pasta-maker, and apprentice to a Dante-quoting butcher in Tuscany. Knopf 2006 318p $25.95 **641.5**

    1. Cooks 2. Italian cooking 3. Television personalities 4. Restaurateurs 5. Cookbook writers

ISBN 1-4000-4120-1; 978-1-4000-4120-6

        LC 2005-57868

"Mr Buford also has a biographer's gift of bringing characters to life. . . . [He] fills his book with people as pungent and spicy as the food." Economist

Calderone, Athena

  ★ **Cook** beautiful; Athena Calderone ; photography by Johnny Miller. Abrams 2017 288 p. $35 **641.5**

    1. Cooking

ISBN 1419726528; 9781419726521

        LC 2016960601

James Beard Award: Photography (2018)

This book, by Athena Calderone, "reveals the secrets to preparing and presenting unforgettable meals. As the voice and curator behind EyeSwoon, an online lifestyle destination for food, entertaining, fashion, and interior design, Athena cooks with top chefs, hosts incredible dinners, and designs stunning tablescapes, while emphasizing the importance of balancing the visual elements of each dish with incredible flavors." (Publisher's note)

Cayne, Alison

The **Haven's** Kitchen cooking school; recipes and inspiration to build a lifetime of confidence in the kitchen. Alison Cayne. Artisan 2017 374 p. illustrations (hardcover) $35 **641.5**

    1. Cooking 2. Seasonal cooking 3. Quick and easy cooking 4. Cookbooks 5. Haven's Kitchen (Firm) 6. Seasonal cooking -- United States

ISBN 9781579657871; 9781579656737

        LC 2016038079

This cookbook, by Alison Cayne, shows that cooking has never been simpler-or more delicious. "Each of the book's nine chapters centers on a key lesson: in the eggs chapter, readers will learn about timing and temperature while poaching, frying, and scrambling; in the soups chapter, they will learn to layer flavors through recipes. . . . Beautiful photographs show both the finished dishes and the how-to techniques, and helpful illustrations offer further guidance." (Publisher's note)

"This book will remain a staple in kitchens long after readers have mastered the basics of boiling an egg and searing a steak." Pub Wkly

Includes bibliographical references and index

Chang, David

Momofuku; [by] David Chang and Peter Meehan; photographs by Gabriele Stabile. Clarkson Potter 2009 303p il $40 **641.5**

    1. Asian cooking

ISBN 978-0-307-45195-8

"Chang's Virginia upbringing, upscale restaurant experience and love of certain Korean and Japanese flavors result in the kind of dishes that will jam your eyeballs into the back of your head, like brussels sprouts with bacon and kimchi puree. This fawningly produced book . .

. is fueled by Chang's hard-core attitude and punctuated with a 'Hell's Kitchen' season's worth of unprintable words. The dude's intense, and he wants you to know it. The food is intense, too, especially as the recipes increase in difficulty as the chapters move up the Momofuku restaurant scale, from Noodle Bar to Ssam Bar to Ko." N Y Times Book Rev

Chang, Joanne

Baking with less sugar; recipes for desserts using natural sweeteners and little-to-no white sugar. by Joanne Chang ; photographs by Joseph De Leo. Chronicle Books LLC 2015 224 p. color illustrations $25   **641.5**
1. Baking
ISBN 145213300X; 9781452133003

LC 2014023855

In this cookbook on baking with less sugar, author Joanne Chang "warmly shares her secrets for playing up delicious ingredients and using natural sweeteners, such as honey, maple syrup, and fruit juice. In addition to entirely new go-to recipes, she's also revisited classics from 'Flour' and her lines-out-the-door bakeries to use minimal refined sugar." (Publisher's note)

Chapple, Justin

Just cook it! 145 built-to-be-easy recipes that are totally delicious. Justin Chapple. Houghton Mifflin Harcourt 2018 288 p. (paper over board) $30   **641.5**
1. Cooking 2. Quick and easy cooking
ISBN 9780544968837

LC 2017051913

This cookbook presents "delicious, fun, and easy recipes and tips for everyday cooking from Justin Chapple, Food & Wine's test kitchen whiz and TODAY show regular. . . . [It offers] a collection of 125 mouth-watering recipes like Avocado Pizza with Dukka and Stovetop Mac-n-Cheese with Bacon Breadcrumbs, with Justin's signature time-saving tips and hacks throughout." (Publisher's note)

"Folksy introductions to each recipe, good tips (go ahead and wash mushrooms—quickly), and favorite dishes—red-curry peanut soup, classic meat-loaf sandwiches and tomato jam, chocolate-peanut pie, Reuben toast with poached eggs—done simply and well make this a must-have." Booklist

Chitnis, Christine

Little bites; 100 healthy, kid-friendly snacks. Christine Chitnis and Sarah Waldman ; photographs by Christine Chitnis. Roost Books 2015 x, 277 p.p color illustrations (paperback) $24.95   **641.5**
1. Cookbooks 2. Snack foods 3. Children -- Nutrition
ISBN 161180177X; 9781611801774

LC 2014022055

This cookbook, by Christine Chitnis and Sarah Waldman, "offers 100 wholesome, seasonal, vegetarian snacks perfect for active families. When you're on the go with little ones, snacks are essential. Whether it's an energetic pick-me-up after school or a nutritional boost at the playground, the 100 wholesome snacks in this book will help everyone get through the day." (Publisher's note)

Includes bibliographical references and index

Christensen, Ashley

Poole's; Recipes and Stories from a Modern Diner. Ashley Christensen and Kaitlyn Goalen ; photography by Johnny Autry. Ten Speed Press 2016 304 p. illustrations (some color) (ebook) $65; (hardcover) $35   **641.5**
1. Cookbooks 2. Southern cooking 3. Poole's (Restaurant) 4.

Cooking, American, -- Southern style
ISBN 9781607746881; 9781607746874

LC 2016018885

This book, by Ashley Christensen with Kaitlyn Goalen, with photographs by Johnny Autry, "is also the story of how Christensen opened a restaurant, and in the process, energized Raleigh's downtown. By fostering a network of farmers, cooks, and guests, and taking care of her people by feeding them well, she built a powerful community around the restaurant. The cookbook is infused with Christensen's generous spirit and belief that great cooking is fundamental to good living." (Publisher's note)

"Mouthwatering Southern foods beckon to readers from the pages of this attractive restaurant cookbook, which recalls other excellent titles such as Frank Stitt's Southern Table. Highly recommended." LJ

Clair, Jennifer

Six basic cooking techniques; culinary essentials for the home cook. Jennifer Clair, photographs by Meredith Heuer. Small Press United 2018 112 p. $19.95   **641.5**
1. Sauces 2. Cooking -- Meat 3. Cooking -- Technique 4. Cooking -- Vegetables
ISBN 0998979201; 9780998979205

LC 2018045284

In this book, culinary instructor Jennifer Clair details "the six essential skills needed to create a strong foundation so that any home cook can maximize his/her culinary potential, [from how to handle a chef's knife,] cooking meats of perfection, making delicious pan sauces, roasting vegetables blanching green vegetables, to cooking leafy greens. . . . [This] is an intimate guide that offers home cooks confidence and leaves them with an 'I can do it' attitude." (Publisher's note)

"This quick course in how-to's can also serve as a refresher course." Booklist

Clark, Melissa

Cook this now; 120 easy and delectable dishes you can't wait to make. Hyperion 2011 396p il $29.99   **641.5**
1. Cooking
ISBN 978-1-4013-2398-1

LC 2011010420

"Clark presents readers with 120 recipes organized by season and month. With a candid opening essay on weekly trips to her local NYC farmers' market in the dead of winter—think frosty fingers, and ice-topped milk—Clark sets the course for this down-to-earth, realistic guide to cooking throughout the year, finding and highlighting seasonal gems in mains, side dishes, and desserts. . . . Even with a multitude of cooking-by-season titles in the marketplace, the author's inspiring use of fresh ingredients and flexible attitude toward cooking make this a solid addition to any kitchen cookbook shelf." Publ Wkly

Dinner; changing the game. Melissa Clark ; Eric Wolfinger (Photographer) Clarkson Potter/Publishers 2017 400 p. color illustrations (hardcover) $35; (ebook) $65   **641.5**
1. Dinners 2. Cookbooks 3. Cooking
ISBN 9780553448238; 9780553448245

LC 2016013021

This cookbook, by Melissa Clark, illustrated by Eric Wolfinger, "is all about options: inventive, unfussy food with unexpected flavor. Clark's mission is to help anyone—whether a novice with just a single pan or the experienced home cook—figure out what to make any night of the week without settling on fallbacks. These inherently simple recipes can turn anyone into a better and more confident cook." (Publisher's note)

"Sharp, easy-to-follow instructions and helpful spreads on subjects such as cooking grains and using canned and dried beans round out this excellent volume." Pub Wkly

★ **Dinner** in an instant; 75 modern recipes for your pressure cooker, multicooker, + Instant Pot®. Melissa Clark. Clarkson Potter/Publishers 2017 159 p. (hardback) $22   **641.5**
   1. Quick and easy cooking
   ISBN 1524762962; 9781524762964

LC 2017021737

This book, by Melissa Clark, "gives home cooks recipes for elevated dinners that never sacrifice convenience. Beloved for her flawless recipes, Melissa Clark turns her imagination to the countertop appliances that have won American hearts from coast to coast. Recipes include Fresh Coconut Yogurt, Japanese Beef Curry, Osso Buco, Smoky Lentils, Green Persian Rice with Tahdig, and Lemon Verbena Crème Brulee." (Publisher's note)

In the kitchen with a good appetite. Hyperion 2010 444p il $27.50   **641.5**
   1. Cooking
   ISBN 978-1-4013-2376-9

LC 2010-5760

""A Good Appetite," Melissa Clark's weekly feature in the New York Times Dining Section, is about dishes that are easy to cook and that speak to everyone, either stirring a memory or creating one. Now, Clark takes the same freewheeling yet well-informed approach that has won her countless fans and applies it to one hundred and fifty delicious, simply sophisticated recipes." (Publisher's note)
   Includes bibliographical references

Coe, Andrew

A **square** meal; A Culinary History of the Great Depression. Jane Ziegelman and Andrew Coe. Harper 2016 336 p. illustrations (hardback) $26.99   **641.5**
   1. American cooking -- History 2. Great Depression, 1929-1939 3. United States -- History -- 20th century 4. Depressions -- 1929 -- United States 5. Cooking, American -- History -- 20th century 6. United States -- Social conditions -- 1933-1945 7. Diet -- United States -- History -- 20th century 8. Crises -- United States -- History -- 20th century 9. Food supply -- United States -- History -- 20th century 10. Social change -- United States -- History -- 20th century 11. Home economics -- United States -- History -- 20th century 12. United States -- Environmental conditions -- History -- 20th century
   ISBN 9780062216410; 9780062216427

LC 2016016051

This book by Jane Ziegelman and Andrew Coe offers "an in-depth exploration of the greatest food crisis the nation has ever faced--the Great Depression--and how it transformed America's culinary culture. . . . [It] examines the impact of economic contraction and environmental disaster on how Americans ate then--and the lessons and insights those experiences may hold for us today. [It] features 25 black-and-white photographs." (Publisher's note)

"Coe and Ziegelman have written an engaging social history illustrated throughout with historically authentic recipes. Even if the period cuisine doesn't make the reader's mouth water, the vivid recreation of American eating at a historical crossroads is engrossing." Pub Wkly
   Includes bibliographical references and index

Colwin, Laurie

Home cooking; a writer in the kitchen. Laurie Colwin ; illustrated by Anna Shapiro. Vintage Books 2010 x, 193 p.p ill. $15.95   **641.5**
   1. Cooking 2. Cookbooks

ISBN 0307474410; 9780307474414

LC 2010455796

James Beard Cookbook Hall of Fame (2012)

This autobiographical cookbook, "is [author] Laurie Colwin's manifesto on the joys of sharing food and entertaining. From the humble hotplate of her one-room apartment to the crowded kitchens of bustling parties, Colwin regales us with tales of meals gone both magnificently well and disastrously wrong." (Publisher's note)

The **complete** vegetarian cookbook; a fresh guide to eating well with 700 foolproof recipes. by the editors at America's test kitchen. America's Test Kitchen 2015 463 p. illustrations (chiefly color) $29.95   **641.5**
   1. Vegetarian cooking
   ISBN 1936493969; 9781936493968

LC 2014042807

This book presents "a collection of. . .vegetarian recipes covering hearty vegetable mains, rice and grains, beans and soy as well as soups, appetizers, snacks, and salads. More than 300 recipes are fast (start to finish in 45 minutes or less), 500 are gluten-free, and 250 are vegan and are all highlighted with icons on the pages." (Publisher's note)

Cook's illustrated (Periodical)

The **best** International recipe; a home cook's guide to the best recipes in the world. by the editors of Cook's Illustrated. America's Test Kitchen 2007 579p il $35   **641.5**
   1. Cooking
   ISBN 978-1-933615-17-2; 1-933615-17-6

This volume contains more than 300 recipes from around the world. Each has been tested to ensure success. Includes explanations of ingredients and what to look for, and in some cases, what you can substitute without compromising flavor. Specialty equipment is also discussed. Core techniques are highlighted throughout the book.

The **new** best recipe; by the editors of Cook's illustrated; photography, Carl Tremblay, Daniel J. Van Ackere; illustrations, John Burgoyne. 2nd ed.; America's Test Kitchen 2004 1028p il $35   **641.5**
   1. Cooking
   ISBN 978-0-936184-74-6; 0-936184-74-4
   First published 1999 by Boston Common Press

A compendium of more than 1,000 recipes. "Twenty-two chapters cover appetizers to desserts. Even the simplest tasks, such as blanching vegetables or peeling an egg, are explained and illustrated in detail. More involved techniques include brining poultry and roasting a turkey. . . . Well organized and extremely clear." Publ Wkly

Cooking light cooking that counts; the Editors of Cooking Light. Oxmoor House 2017 288 p. color illustrations $21.95   **641.5**
   1. Cooking 2. Weight loss
   ISBN 0848749502; 9780848749507

LC 2016955288

This book by the editors of Cooking Light "delivers sustainable 1,200-1,500 calorie-controlled meal plans packed with tasty food in an easy-to-use format. Unlike other weight-loss plans that rely on processed meals and preportioned snacks, the Cooking Light solution emphasizes delicious meals prepared with whole, natural foods and teaches proper portion sizes to ensure you lose weight and keep it off, for life." (Publisher's note)

Coscarelli, Chloe

Chloe flavor; saucy, spicy, crunchy, vegan. Chloe Coscarelli ; photographs by Christina Holmes ; foreword by Michael & Liz Symon. Clarkson Potter/Publishers 2018 288 p. (hardcover) $27.99 **641.5**

    1. Vegan cooking 2. Cooking -- Vegetables
    ISBN 045149962X; 9780451499622

LC 2017021732

This cookbook, by Chloe Coscarelli, with photographs by Christina Holmes, presents recipes that are bold in taste, loud in color, unabashedly unique, and, above all, easy to make. With dishes like Smoky Grits & Greens, Mango-Guacamole Crunch Burgers, and Sea Salted Chocolate Chunk Cookies, this food is for fun, friends, and family--and it's all about the flavor. Vegans will delight in Chloe's creations and carnivores won't miss the meat one bit." (Publisher's note)

"For those who want to try vegan cooking, this is the perfect cookbook." Pub Wkly

Craig, Caroline

The **little** book of lunch; 100 recipes & ideas to reclaim the lunch hour. Caroline Craig, Sophie Missing ; photography by David Loftus. Regan Arts 2015 207 p. color illustrations $24.95 **641.5**

    1. Luncheons
    ISBN 1941393225; 9781941393222

LC 2014955542

This book about lunch, by Caroline Craig and Sophie Missing, is a "beautiful, internationally acclaimed guide to turning your midday meal into a masterpiece—featuring 100 easy, inexpensive, delicious recipes designed to be made ahead of time with just a few ingredients." (Publisher's note)

Crandall, Russell

Paleo takeout; restaurant favorites without the junk. Russ Crandall. Simon & Schuster 2015 320 p. color illustrations (paperback) $34.95 **641.5**

    1. Cookbooks 2. Paleo cooking
    ISBN 162860087X; 9781628600872

This paleo cookbook, by Russ Crandall, offers "over 200 weeknight-friendly dishes that taste so good, you'll finally throw out that emergency stack of takeout menus hiding in your kitchen drawer. . . . [The author] re-creates everyone's favorite takeout meals using wholesome ingredients and some seriously inventive techniques." (Publisher's note)

Crapanzano, Aleksandra

The **London** cookbook; Recipes from the Restaurants, Cafes, and Hole-in-the-Wall Gems of a Modern City. Aleksandra Crapanzano ; photography by Sang An. Ten Speed Press 2016 320 p. illustrations (mostly color) (ebook) $65; (hardcover; alk. paper) $35.00 **641.5**

    1. Cookbooks 2. English cooking 3. Restaurants -- England -- London 4. Cooking, English 5. Cooking -- England -- London
    ISBN 9781607748144; 9781607748137

LC 2016012459

This book, by Aleksandra Crapanzano, with photographs by Sang An, "explores London's incredibly diverse cuisine through an eclectic mix of dishes, from The Cinnamon Club's Seared Aubergine Steaks with Sesame and Tamarind to the River Cafe's Tagliatelle with Lemon, and from Tramshed's Indian Rock Chicken Curry to Nopi's Sage and Cardamom Gin." (Publisher's note)

"Crapanzano perfectly captures all that's exciting about the people, places, and foods that make up London's modern culinary scene. Af-

ter reading this cookbook, home cooks may find themselves planning a London vacation." LJ

Includes bibliographical references and index

Cunningham, Marion

The **Fannie** Farmer cookbook; illustrated by Lauren Jarrett. 13th ed; Knopf 1996 874p il $30 **641.5**

    1. Cooking
    ISBN 0-679-45081-5

LC 97-162330

First published 1896 under the authorship of Fannie Merritt Farmer. Periodically revised

This standard cookbook focuses on the selection, preparation, and serving of a wide variety of foods

Dalí; Les Dîners de Gala. by Salvador Dalí. Taschen America Llc 2016 321 p. $59.99 **641.5**

    1. Cooking 2. Surrealism
    ISBN 3836508761; 9783836508766

LC 2017003964

"This reprint features all 136 recipes over 12 chapters, specially illustrated by Dalí, and organized by meal courses, including aphrodisiacs. The illustrations and recipes are accompanied by Dalí's extravagant musings on subjects such as dinner conversation." (Publisher's note)

David, Elizabeth

A **book** of Mediterranean food; decorated by John Minton. 2nd rev. ed.; New York Review Books 2002 203p il (New York Review Books classics) pa $14.95 **641.5**

    1. Mediterranean cooking
    ISBN 978-1-59017-003-8; 1-59017-003-2

LC 2002-749

First published 1950 in the United Kingdom

This is a "mixture of recipes, culinary lore, and frank talk. In bleak postwar Great Britain, when basics were rationed and fresh food a fantasy, David set about to cheer herself—and her audience—up with dishes from the south of France, Italy, Spain, Portugal, Greece, and the Middle East." Publisher's note

French provincial cooking. Grub Street 2008 519p il $34.95 **641.5**

    1. French cooking
    ISBN 978-1-904943-71-6; 1-904943-71-3

LC 2008-411778

First published 1960 in the United Kingdom

This book "should be approached and read as a series of short stories, as well as written and evocative as the best literature. The voice is highly personal and opinionated, sometimes sharp but always true and always entertaining. This book is a long essay on French cuisine, offering background stories and sketches of recipes very different from the prescriptive type of recipes that most modern readers might be used to today." Living France

Italian food; rev ed; Penguin Books 1999 xxxiii, 376p pa $16 **641.5**

    1. Italian cooking
    ISBN 978-0-14-118155-4; 0-14-118155-9

LC 99-200031

First published 1958 in the United Kingdom

"David studies and analyzes cooking the way a scholar analyzes literature, and, as a result, her titles are far more than just cookbooks. Along with the recipes, of which there are many, she explains at length the histories of the dishes and offers splendid advice on serving wine with the meals." Libr J

Includes bibliographical references

Summer cooking; illustrated by Adrian Daintrey. New York Review Books 2002 234p il (New York Review Books classics) pa $12.95   **641.5**

1. British cooking

ISBN 978-1-59017-004-5; 1-59017-004-0

LC 2002-744

First published 1955 in the United Kingdom

"Don't let the unsophisticated subject fool you into expecting only cheese sandwiches and potato salads. For all its simplicity, 'Summer Cooking' is a wonderfully subversive volume — every bit as unexpected and enchanting to read today as it must have been 50 years ago, when England was just stirring from its wartime fast and garlic was an ingredient still capable of provoking controversy. . . . David earned her place in gastronomic history by being one of the first writers to suggest that thoughtful food and cooking itself could be a means of escape. Now, 15 years after her death, that voice remains a singular note in the chorus of her contemporaries and acolytes, neither frankly amiable like Julia Child, nor seductively literate like M.F.K. Fisher, nor playfully mod like Nigella Lawson. No matter how trivial the point, David speaks her mind." Salon.com

Davies, Katie Quinn

What Katie Ate; Recipes and Other Bits and Pieces. photography by Katie Quinn Davies. Penguin Group USA 2012 304 p. col. ill. $40   **641.5**

1. Cookbooks 2. Cooking

ISBN 0670026182; 9780670026180

LC 2012289524

James Beard Foundation Award: Photography (2013)

In this book, food photographer Katie Quinn Davies "shares her favorite simple dishes with a . . . collection of recipes and . . . images. . . . Showcasing her extraordinary eye, this debut cookbook is a unique combination of food diary and how-to, with tips and tricks, photographs, recipes, and stories. . . . Featured dishes range from Wild Mushrooms on Toast with Parmesan and Herbs to Roasted Pork Tenderloin with Apple, Prune & Pine Nut Stuffing and Cider Cream Gravy." (Publisher's note)

"Davies built her fan base with a blog that chronicles her meals and work, and her debut book gives readers a tangible record—part recipe collection, part scrapbook, laden with sumptuous color and extravagant, full-page layouts." Pub Wkly

Davison, Julia Collin

★ **Cooking** at home with Bridget & Julia; the TV hosts of America's Test Kitchen share their favorite recipes for feeding family and friends. Bridget Lancaster, Julia Collin Davison, and the editors at America's Test Kitchen. America's Test Kitchen 2017 xv, 304 p.p color illustrations (alk. paper) $35   **641.5**

1. Cooking 2. Holiday cooking 3. Italian cooking 4. Entertaining

ISBN 1945256168; 9781945256165

LC 2017018306

This book presents "a winning collection of 150 recipes hand selected by Julia Collin Davison and Bridget Lancaster, the well-known and beloved stars of our public television shows. Here, for the first time, they get personal and pull back the curtain on their lives, their families, and the recipes they like to cook when they are off camera." (Publisher's note)

De Laurentiis, Giada, 1970-

Happy cooking; Giada De Laurentiis. Pam Krauss Books 2015 320 p. color illustrations $35   **641.5**

1. Family 2. Cooking

ISBN 0804187924; 9780804187923; 9780804187930

LC 2015022028

Author Giada de Laurentis presents "nearly 200 new recipes and helpful advice on everything from hosting a potluck or open house to what to pack along for lunch every day. Drawing on the time-saving tips and healthy eating strategies that keep her functioning at the highest possible level in her roles as working mom, restaurateur, and tv personality, she has assembled a year-round roadmap to vibrant good health and delicious eating." (Publisher's note)

Dickerman, Sara

The **food** lover's cleanse; 140 delicious, nourishing recipes that will tempt you back into healthful eating. by Sara Dickerman. HarperCollins 2015 341 p. color illustrations $35 **641.5**

1. Diet 2. Cooking

ISBN 0062390236; 9780062390233

In this book, by Sara Dickerman, "you'll find four different two-week cleanse plans, one for each season, and 140 fabulous recipes that use fresh, flavorful, unprocessed ingredients. High in fruits, vegetables, and whole grains . . . the program emphasizes eating mindfully, controlling portion size, and curbing grazing impulses. Empty calories are replaced with filling protein- or fiber-rich snacks." (Publisher's note)

"Dickerman's approachable guide to whole foods-centric, occasionally meatless healthy eating can help readers curb their postholiday guilt and adopt sustainable life changes. For vegetarians and vegans, Mark Bittman's The VB6 Cookbook is a better choice." Library Journal

Digregorio, Sarah

Adventures in slow cooking; 120 slow-cooker recipes for people who love food. Sarah DiGregorio. HarperCollins 2017 256 p. $24.99   **641.5**

1. Cooking 2. Cookbooks

ISBN 006266137X; 9780062661371

LC bl2017041532

In this book, "food writer [Sarah DiGregorio] revamps the slow cooker for the modern home cook, providing ingenious ideas and more than 100 delicious recipes for maximizing this favorite time-saving kitchen appliance and making it easier than ever to use. . . . 'Adventures in Slow Cooking' provides a repertoire of delicious food for any time of day. Inside you'll find ideas for flavorful sweet and savory slow cooker dishes." (Publisher's note)

"Essential for most collections, this is an exciting and refreshingly unbiased guide to slow cooking." (Library Journal)

DiSpirito, Rocco

Now eat this! 150 of America's favorite comfort foods, all under 350 calories. Ballantine Books 2010 xxiii, 246p il pa $22; ebook $22   **641.5**

1. Cooking 2. Low-calorie diet

ISBN 978-0-345-52090-6 pa; 0-345-52090-4 pa; 978-0-307-76753-0 ebook; 0-307-76753-1 ebook

LC 2009-52470

"Lower-calorie brownies, gravy, spaghetti and meatballs, and beef stroganoff will delight readers who have been avoiding favorite foods." Libr J

Donofrio, Jeanine

The **Love** and Lemons Cookbook; An Apple-to-zucchini

Celebration of Impromptu Cooking. by Jeanine Donofrio. Penguin Group USA 2016 320 p. color illustrations $35   **641.5**

1. Cooking -- Vegetables 2. Quick and easy cooking
ISBN 1583335862; 9781583335864

LC 2016006543

This cookbook, by Jeanine Donofrio, "features more than one hundred simple recipes that help you turn your farmers market finds into delicious meals. . . . Organized by ingredient, [it] teaches readers how to make beautiful food with what's on hand. . . . The book also features resources to show readers how to stock their pantry, gluten-free and vegan options for many of the recipes, as well as ideas on mixing and matching ingredients, so that readers always have something new to try." (Publisher's note)

"Celebrating spontaneity in cooking with plant-based inspiration, this imaginative recipe collection will please cooks who take their cue from ingredients as much as from recipes." Pub Wkly

Drummond, Ree

The **pioneer** woman cooks; come and get it!; simple, scrumptious recipes for crazy busy lives. by Ree Drummond. HarperCollins 2017 400 p.   **641.5**

1. Quick and easy cooking
ISBN 006222526X; 9780062225269

This cookbook, by Ree Drummond, "includes more than 120 of my best solutions for tasty, wholesome meals (with minimal fuss!) for breakfast, lunch, dinner, and snacks. (And let's not forget the glue that holds it all together: desserts! There are some dandies in here, friends.) With a mix of categories and flavors that will please everyone, this book has everything you need to whip up delicious, downhome recipes that you can get on the table without a lot of stress." (Publisher's note)

Duclos, Andrea

The **plantiful** table; easy, from-the-earth recipes for the whole family. Andrea Duclos. Experiment, LLC 2015 311 p. color illustrations (cloth) $24.95   **641.5**

1. Vegetarian cooking
ISBN 1615192476; 9781615192472

LC 2015003784

This cookbook, by Andrea Duclos, presents "Over 125 full-flavored, plant-based dishes sure to please even the pickiest kids and the hungriest adults. . . . Throughout, Drea gives kid-friendly tips so that one meal can feed everyone. Plus, she takes the guesswork out of reviving leftovers. So, from Drea's family to yours—large or small, all-vegan or not—here are hearty meals straight from the earth, perfect for your happy home, every day!" (Publisher's note)

Duguid, Naomi

Taste of Persia; A Cook's Travels Through Armenia, Azerbaijan, Georgia, Iran, and Kurdistan. by Naomi Duguid. Artisan, a division of Workman Publishing Company, Inc. 2016 400 p. color ill., color maps (ebook) $35; (hardback, with dust jacket) $35   **641.5**

1. Middle Eastern cooking 2. Cooking, Iranian 3. Cooking, Kurdish 4. Cooking, Armenian 5. Cooking, Azerbaijani 6. Cooking, Georgian (South Caucasian)
ISBN 9781579657277; 9781579655488

LC 2016012875

This book, by Naomi Duguid, focuses on "the Persian culinary region. . . . Nearly 125 recipes, framed with stories and photographs of people and places, introduce us to a culinary paradise where ancient legends and ruins rub shoulders with new beginnings—where a wealth of history and culinary traditions makes it a compelling place to read about

for cooks and travelers and for anyone hankering to experience the food of a wider world." (Publisher's note)

"This gorgeous and compelling title will transport home cooks and armchair travelers to another time and place." LJ

Includes bibliographical references (pages 375-379) and index.

Dunlop, Fuchsia

Land of fish and rice; Recipes from the Culinary Heart of China. Fuchsia Dunlop. W W Norton & Co Inc 2016 368 p. (hardcover) $35   **641.5**

1. Cookbooks 2. Chinese cooking 3. Cooking, Chinese
ISBN 9780393254389

LC 2016013124

This cookbook by Fuchsia Dunlop "draws on years of study and exploration to present the recipes, techniques, and ingredients of the Jiangnan kitchen. You will be inspired to try classic dishes such as Beggar's Chicken and sumptuous Dongpo Pork, as well as fresh, simple recipes such as Clear-Steamed Sea Bass and Fresh Soybeans with Pickled Greens." (Publisher's note)

"The Jiangnan is an exquisite 'crucible of Chinese gastronomy,' and Dunlop's scholarly homage to the region will captivate the culinary imagination." Pub Wkly

Includes bibliographical references and index

Durand, Faith

The **Kitchn** cookbook; Sara Kate Gillingham-Ryan and Faith Durand ; photographs by Leela Cyd. Clarkson Potter/Publishers 2014 304 p. color illustrations $32.50   **641.5**

1. Cooking 2. Kitchens
ISBN 0770434436; 9780770434434; 9780770434441

LC 2014029477

James Beard Foundation Award Winner: General Cooking (2015)

In this book by Sara Kate Gillinghma and Faith Durand "comes 150 recipes and a cooking school with 50 essential lessons, as well as a guide to organizing your kitchen--plus storage tips, tool reviews, inspiration from real kitchens, maintenance suggestions, 200 photographs, and much more." (Publisher's note)

Dusoulier, Clotilde

The **French** market cookbook; vegetarian recipes from my Parisian kitchen. by Clotilde Dusoulier. Clarkson Potter Publishers 2013 224 p. (pbk.) $22.50   **641.5**

1. French cooking 2. Vegetarian cooking 3. Cooking, French
ISBN 0307984826; 9780307984821

LC 2012554926

In this book author Clotilde Dusoulier "takes [readers] through the seasons in 82 recipes--and explores the love story between French cuisine and vegetables. [Recipes include] carrots are lightly spiced with star anise and vanilla in a soup made with almond milk; tomatoes are jazzed up by mustard in a gorgeous tart; winter squash stars in golden Corsican turnovers; and luscious peaches bake in a cardamom-scented custard." (Publisher's note)

"Organized by season and peppered with tips on how to select and store vegetables, this cookbook will excite readers looking for substantial vegetarian meals they can feel good about eating." LJ

The **Eat** Like a Man Guide to Feeding a Crowd; how to cook for family, friends, and spontaneous parties. by Ryan D'Agostino ; foreword by Bryan Voltaggio ; introduction by David Granger and Mario Batali. Chronicle Books 2015 224 p. illustrations (chiefly color) (alk. paper) $30   **641.5**

1. Entertaining 2. Quantity cooking

ISBN 1452131848; 9781452131849

LC 2014031085

This cookbook, by Ryan D'Agostino, "is the ultimate resource for guys who want to host big crowds and need the scaled-up recipes, logistical advice, and mojo to pull it off whether they're cooking breakfast for a houseful of weekend guests, producing an epic spread for the playoffs, or planning the backyard BBQ that trumps all. With tantalizing photos and about 100 recipes for lazy breakfasts, afternoon noshing, dinner spreads, and late-night binges." (Publisher's note)

"Well, men may not need this follow-up volume, timed for Father's Day, but they just might want it. Maintaining a formula similar to the original, 80 recipes from a distinguished line-up of chefs are offered, interspersed with brief essays from Esquire authors." Pub Wkly

Eckhardt, Robyn

Istanbul & beyond; exploring the diverse cuisines of Turkey. Robyn Eckhardt, photographs by David Hagerman. Houghton Mifflin Harcourt 2017 352 p. color illustrations (hardback) $35 **641.5**

1. Cookbooks 2. Turkish cooking 3. Cooking, Turkish
ISBN 9780544444348; 9780544444317

LC 2017016108

In this cookbook, author Robyn Eckhardt and photographer David Hagerman, "take readers on an unforgettable epicurean adventure, beginning in Istanbul, home to one of the world's great fusion cuisines. From there, they journey to the lesser-known provinces, opening a vivid world of flavors influenced by neighboring Syria, Iran, Iraq, Armenia, and Georgia." (Publisher's note)

"This collection will delight and inspire home cooks who are unfamiliar with the region's food but are looking to broaden their culinary horizons." Pub Wkly

Includes bibliographical references (page 343).

Edge, John T.

The **potlikker** papers; a food history of the modern South. John T. Edge. Penguin Press 2017 x, 370 p.p illustrations (hardcover) $28 **641.5**

1. Southern cooking 2. American cooking -- History 3. Food -- Southern States -- History 4. Cooking, American -- Southern style
ISBN 9781594206559; 9780698195875

LC 2016029615

This book, by John T. Edge, shares the "people's history of the modern South, told through its food. Beginning with the pivotal role cooks and waiters played in the civil rights movement, . . . Edge narrates the South's fitful journey from a hive of racism to a hotbed of American immigration. He shows why working-class Southern food has become a vital driver of contemporary American cuisine." (Publisher's note)

"Edge's research and command of prose make this a necessary history." Booklist

Includes bibliographical references and index

Erickson, Meredith

Kristen Kish cooking; recipes and techniques. Kristen Kish with Meredith Erickson ; photographs by Kristin Teig. Clarkson Potter/Publishers 2017 288 p. (hard cover) $40 **641.5**

1. Cooking 2. Cooking -- Technique 3. Creative ability in cooking
ISBN 0553459767; 9780553459760

LC 2016055343

This book, by Kristen Kish, is "a cookbook with more than 80 recipes that celebrate impeccable technique and bridge her Korean heritage, Michigan upbringing, Boston cooking years, and more. . . . Her recipes are surprising yet refined, taking the expected—an ingredient or a tech-

nique, for example—and using it in a new way to make dishes that are unique and irresistible." (Publisher's note)

The **essential** New York times grilling cookbook; more than 100 years of sizzling food writing and recipes. edited by Peter Kaminsky ; foreword by Mark Bittman ; other contributors include Craig Claiborne, Pierre Franey, Florence Fabricant, Steven Raichlen, Molly O'Neill, Julia Moskin, and many more. Sterling Epicure 2014 400 p. illustrations (some color) $24.95 **641.5**

1. Cookbooks 2. Barbecue cooking 3. Barbecuing
ISBN 1402793243; 9781402793240

LC 2013026602

Edited by Peter Kaminsky, this book shows how "Over the past 100 years, the 'New York Times' has published thousands of articles on barbecuing and grilling, along with mouthwatering recipes--and this unique collection gathers the very best. These essential pieces are worth savoring not only for their time-tested advice and instruction, but also for the quality of the storytelling: even non-cooks will find them a delight to read." (Publisher's note)

"A fascinating look at how various innovators, personalities, and cultural trends have shaped the evolution of grilling and barbecue." LJ

Includes bibliographical references and index

Estrine, Darryl

Harvest to heat; cooking with America's best chefs, farmers, and artisans. [by] Darryl Estrine and Kelly Kochendorfer; foreword by Alice Waters. Taunton Press 2010 295p il $40 **641.5**

1. Cooking
ISBN 978-1-60085-254-1

LC 2010-11943

"The authors match farmers and artisans with chefs and restaurants across the country to present 100 original recipes from, e.g., Eric Ripert (Le Bernardin, New York), Paul Kahan (Blackbird, Chicago), and Vitaly Paley (Paley's Place, Portland, OR), for the home cook, for starters and salads, main courses, sides, and desserts. . . . Each recipe is accompanied by a description of the farmer or artisan who provided the main ingredients. Sustainable food is in, and this book will encourage home cooks to follow the tenets of the movement." Libr J

Fairchild, Barbara

The **Bon** appetit cookbook. Wiley 2006 xxiv, 792p il $34.95 **641.5**

1. Cooking
ISBN 0-7645-9686-1; 978-0-7645-9686-5

LC 2005-5181

"Mirroring the magazine on which it is based, this collection of 1,200 recipes is accessible, applicable to most home cooks' lives and a pleasure to cook from." Publ Wkly

The **Bon** appetit fast easy fresh cookbook. J. Wiley 2008 xxix, 770p il $34.95 **641.5**

1. Cooking
ISBN 978-0-470-22630-8

LC 2007-44562

This cookbook "presents hundreds of quick and simple recipes from the magazine's popular 'Fast Easy Fresh' feature. An introductory 'Shopping Guide' covers buying and storing produce, meat, and fish, and dozens of sidebars and boxes provide more information on ingredients and techniques. . . . Sure to appeal to any busy cook as well as the magazine's numerous fans, this is highly recommended." Libr J

Falk, Daina

The **hungry** fan's game day cookbook; 165 recipes for eating, drinking & watching sports. Daina Falk. Oxmoor House 2016 256 p. color illustrations (paperback) $22.95   **641.5**
1. Cooking 2. Cookbooks 3. Sports spectators
ISBN 0848745833; 9780848745837

LC 2016943633

This cookbook, by Daina Falk, "celebrates game day cooking at its best, from pulled pork sandwiches at the tailgate to sky-high stadium chili at home. . . . [In this collection,] Daina presents more than 100 crowd-pleasing recipes to jazz up your tailgate and score points with any home game-watching guest." (Publisher's note)

"Regardless of culinary preferences or skill level, every hungry sports fan can find something appealing in this go-to guide for game days all year long." Pub Wkly

Fearnley-Whittingstall, Hugh

River Cottage every day; photography by Simon Wheeler. Ten Speed Press 2011 415p il $32.50   **641.5**
1. British cooking 2. Cooking -- Natural foods
ISBN 978-1-60774-098-8

LC 2010-46949

First published 2009 in the United Kingdom

"An advocate of a back-to-basics approach to cooking and sustainable agriculture, . . . [the author] delivers thoughtful insight and colorful narratives that celebrate the joy of good family food, which will inspire and compel readers into the kitchen, book in hand. Simple ingredients become brilliant when combined in fresh and easy recipes like Baked Breakfast Cheesecake, Curried Fish Pie, breads, boxed lunches, and frittatas." Libr J

River Cottage Veg; 200 Inspired Vegetable Recipes. Hugh Fearnley-Whittingstall. Random House Inc. 2013 416 p. (hardcover) $35   **641.5**
1. Cookbooks 2. Vegetarian cooking
ISBN 1607744724; 9781607744726

This book, by Hugh Fearnley-Whittingstall, offers "a comprehensive collection of 200+ recipes that embrace vegetarian cuisine as the centerpiece of a meal. . . . In this . . . illustrated cookbook, you'll find handy weeknight one-pot meals, pure and simple raw dishes, and hearty salads as well as a chapter of meze and tapas dishes to mix and match." (Publisher's note)

Fernald, Anya

Home cooked; 100 essential recipes for a new way to cook. Anya Fernald with Jessica Battilana. Ten Speed Press 2016 304 p. color illustrations (hardback) $35   **641.5**
1. Cooking 2. Family life
ISBN 9781607748403; 9781607748410

LC 2015033515

Authors Anya Fernald and Jessica Battilana present this "recipe collection and how-to guide for preparing base ingredients that can be used to make simple, weeknight meals, while also teaching skills like building and cooking over a fire, and preserving meat and produce, written by a sustainable food expert and founder of Belcampo Meat Co." (Publisher's note)

"Fernald's approach advances the importance of celebration, traditional ways of food and farm, and viable food production techniques." Pub Wkly

Includes bibliographical references and index

Fertel, Rien

The **one** true barbecue; fire, smoke, and the pitmasters who cook the whole hog. by Rien Fertel ; photographs by Denny Culbert. Touchstone 2016 288 p. ill.(chiefly color), map (hardcover; alk. paper) $25   **641.5**
1. Barbecue cooking 2. Southern cooking 3. Cooks -- Southern States -- Biography 4. Barbecuing -- Southern States -- History 5. Southern States -- Social life and customs
ISBN 9781476793979

LC 2015033791

In this book, author Rien Fertel "chronicles the uniquely southern art of whole hog barbecue—America's original barbecue—through the professional pitmasters who make a living firing, smoking, flipping, and cooking 200-plus pound pigs." (Publisher's note)

"Fertel is well-aware that the ground he covers isn't entirely new, but food fans and lovers of Americana alike will go wh o le hog for this loving paean to a distinct tradition." Kirkus

Includes bibliographical references and index

Fertig, Judith

The **back** in the swing cookbook; recipes for eating and living well every day after breast cancer. Barbara C. Unell and Judith Fertig ; foreword by Rachel S. Beller ; photography by Sara Remington. Andrews McMeel Pub., LLC 2012 261 p. col. ill. $29.99   **641.5**
1. Cookbooks 2. Breast cancer 3. Breast -- Cancer -- Prevention 4. Breast -- Cancer -- Diet therapy -- Recipes
ISBN 1449418325; 9781449418328

LC 2011944354

IACP Cookbook Award (2013)

This cookbook, by Barbara C. Unell and Judith Fertig, "is . . . full of 150 feel-good recipes that are easy to prepare, with fresh ingredients specifically designed to help breast cancer survivors get back in the swing of joyful, healthy living. . . . In addition to . . . food and drinks, . . . [it] include[s] . . . friendly nuggets on topics ranging from genetics, lifestyle choices, and the environment to the influence of all three on living a full and happy life." (Publisher's note)

Firth, Henry

Bosh! simple recipes * amazing food * all plants. Ian Theasby and Henry David Firth. HarperCollins 2018 288 p. $27.50   **641.5**
1. Cooking 2. Cookbooks 3. Vegan cooking
ISBN 0062820680; 9780062820686

In this cookbook, Ian Theasby and Henry David Firth "share more than 100 of their favorite go-to breakfasts, crowd-pleasing party pieces, hearty dinners, sumptuous desserts, and incredible sharing cocktails. The book is jam-packed with fun, unpretentious and mega satisfying recipes, easy enough to be rustled up any night of the week. It's enough to convince the staunchest of carnivores to give plants a whirl." (Publisher's note)

"An excellent choice for established and aspiring vegans who crave meaty flavors and substantial recipes."

Flanagan, Shalane

Run fast, eat slow; nourishing recipes for athletes. by Shalane Flanagan and Elyse Kopecky. St. Martin's Press 2016 242 p. color illustrations $24.99; (ebook) $19.99   **641.5**
1. Cooking 2. Nutrition
ISBN 162336681X; 9781623366810; 9781623366827

This cookbook, by Shalane Flanagan and Elyse Kopecky, "proves food can be indulgent and nourishing at the same time. Finally here's a cookbook for runners that shows fat is essential for flavor and performance and that counting calories, obsessing over protein, and restrictive dieting does more harm than good." (Publisher's note)

Includes bibliographical references (pages 220-222) and index.

Flay, Bobby, 1964-

Bobby Flay fit; 200 recipes for a healthy lifestyle. Bobby Flay with Stephanie Banyas and Sally Jackson. Clarkson Potter/Publishers 2017 256 p. color illustrations (hardcover) $23.50 **641.5**

1. Health 2. Cookbooks 3. Low-calorie diet 4. Cooking
ISBN 9780385345941; 9780385345934

LC 2016044398

This cookbook, by Bobby Flay with Stephanie Banyas and Sally Jackson, "shares smoothies and juices, breakfast bowls, snacks to fuel workouts, hearty salads, nourishing soups, satisfying dinners, and lightened-up desserts. With fitness tips and a look into the chef's daily healthy routines, this cookbook is for those who want to eat right without overhauling their pantries or sacrificing taste." (Publisher's note)

"The book does an excellent job of addressing different dining styles—it's easy to pick full breakfasts, lunches, and dinners from dedicated chapters, or to assemble a meal-sized assortment of snacks, sides, and small plates." LJ

Brunch @ Bobby's; 140 Recipes for the Best Part of the Weekend. Bobby Flay with Stephanie Banyas and Sally Jackson ; photographs by Ben Fink. Clarkson Potter/Publishers 2015 256 p. color illustrations $29.99 **641.5**

1. Brunches 2. Brunch @ Bobby's (Television program)
ISBN 0385345895; 9780385345897

LC 2014012752

This cookbook, by celebrity chef Bobby Flay, "includes 140 recipes starting with the lip-smacking cocktails, both spiked and virgin, . . . along with hot and iced coffees and teas. He then works his way through eggs; pancakes, waffles, and French toast (including flavored syrups and spreads); pastries (a first) and breads; salads and sandwiches; and side dishes. . . . This is how Bobby does brunch." (Publisher's note)

"These bold, flavorful moves from Flay's breakfast playbook will leave readers salivating." Pub Wkly

Fong, Henry

Nom nom paleo; food for humans. Michelle Tam + Henry Fong. Andrews McMeel Publishing 2013 277 p. color illustrations (hbk.) $35 **641.5**

1. Paleo cooking 2. Cooking (Natural foods) 3. Gluten-free diet -- Recipes 4. High-protein diet -- Recipes 5. Prehistoric peoples -- Nutrition
ISBN 1449450334; 9781449450335

LC 2013942801

James Beard Foundation Award Nominee: Focus on Health (2015)

This cookbook, by Michelle Tam and Henry Fong, presents "more than 100 fool-proof Paleo and gluten-free recipes, and over 900 step-by-step photographs and cartoons. . . . Building blocks such as Paleo Sriracha, Magic Mushroom Powder, and Paleo Mayonnaise lay the flavor foundation for many of the dishes in the rest of the book." (Publisher's note)

Includes bibliographical references (page 268) and index
Nomnom paleo

Foose, Martha Hall

My two Souths; Blending the Flavors of India into a Southern Kitchen. Asha Gomez, Martha Hall Foose ; photography by Evan Sung. Running Press 2016 288 p. color illustrations $35; (ebook) $16.99 **641.5**

1. Indian cooking 2. Southern cooking
ISBN 9780762457830; 9780762458295; 9780762458295

LC 2016941856

This book, by Asha Gomez with Martha Hall Foose, with photographs by Evan Sung, takes you on a culinary journey with Chef Gomez, "from her small village in the Kerala region of southern India to her celebrated restaurants in Atlanta, and on into your kitchen. Her singular recipes are rooted in her love of Deep-South cooking, as well as the Southern Indian flavors of her childhood home." (Publisher's note)

"Guaranteed to spice up your dinner routine, Gomez's debut enlivens Indian and Southern foods." LJ

★ **Screen** doors and sweet tea; recipes and tales from a Southern cook. Clarkson Potter/Publishers 2008 248p il $32.50 **641.5**

1. Southern cooking
ISBN 0-307-35140-8; 978-0-307-35140-1

LC 2007031646

"Born and raised in Mississippi, Foose cooks Southern food with a contemporary flair: Sweet Potato Soup is enhanced with coconut milk and curry powder; Blackberry Limeade gets a lift from a secret ingredient¿cardamom; and her much-ballyhooed Sweet Tea Pie combines two great Southern staples¿sweet tea and pie, of course¿to make one phenomenal signature dessert. The more than 150 original recipes are not only full of flavor, but also rich with local color and characters." (Publisher's note)

Foung, Jessica Goldman

Sodium girls limitless low-salt cookbook; Jessica Goldman ; photography by Matt Armendariz. Wiley 2012 256 p. (pbk.) $24.99 **641.5**

1. Cookbooks 2. Food -- Sodium content 3. Salt-free diet -- Recipes
ISBN 1118123778; 9781118123775

LC 2011040042

This is a cookbook by blogger Jessica Goldman Foung, who documents her experiences with living a low-sodium lifestyle on her blog Sodium Girl. Here, "she shares . . . recipes (some new, some from her blog, and some from celebrity chefs) and useful advice, such as how to cut salt from your favorite recipes, including buffalo wings and Bloody Marys. Also provided is information on handling diet-challenging situations and environments (e.g., restaurant outings, trips abroad, college dining halls)." (Library Journal)

Friedman, Andrew

Knives at dawn; the American quest for culinary glory at the legendary Bocuse d'Or competition. Free Press 2009 304p $26 **641.5**

1. Cooking -- Competitions
ISBN 978-1-4391-5307-9

LC 2009-35271

"A vibrant portrait of the world's most significant cooking competition, the Bocuse d'Or, in Lyon, France. . . . [The author] dynamically illustrates the colorful personalities, ego-battering conflicts, career-defining aspirations, politicking, precision planning, naked missteps and the final judges' decisions regarding the 2009 U.S. team's shot for the culinary gold medal. . . . The book is infused with the muscular, meticulous gusto of a sportswriter covering the Olympics. Edge-of-your-seat food writing of the highest caliber." Kirkus

Includes bibliographical references

Fuentes, Laura

The **best** homemade kids' lunches on the planet; make lunches your kids will love with over 200 deliciously nutritious lunchbox ideas. Laura Fuentes. Fair Winds Press 2014 240 p. color illustrations $24.99   **641.5**

1. Cookbooks 2. School children -- Food 3. Lunchbox cooking
ISBN 1592336086; 9781592336081

LC 2013049151

This cookbook dedicated to school child lunches, written by Laura Fuentes, "[f]ull of recipes to suit every age and stage, . . . shows you how simple and easy it is to prepare food that'll be the envy of the lunch table. . . . There are even entire lunchbox meals that are gluten-, soy-, and/or nut-free." (Publisher's note)

The **best** homemade kids' snacks on the planet; more than 200 healthy homemade snacks you and your kids will love. Laura Fuentes. Quarto Pub Group USA 2015 240 p. illustrations $24.99   **641.5**

1. Snack foods 2. Eating habits
ISBN 1592336612; 9781592336616

LC 2014047820

In this book by Laura Fuentes readers will "find more than 200+ great ideas for solving the snack conundrum. Recipes and ideas you can whip up in minutes, without fuss in the kitchen, or fuss from your kid! So whether you're packing snacks for your purse, the school bag, the sports bag, or the can't-make-it-until-dinner whining hour, you'll find quick and healthy ideas everyone in your family will love." (Publisher's note)

"Stocked with good ideas, these recipes will give families (not just the kids!) nutritional snacking options." LJ

Fuhrman, Joel

Eat to live quick and easy cookbook; 131 delicious recipes for fast and sustained weight loss, reversing disease, and lifelong health. Joel Fuhrman, M.D. HarperOne, an imprint of HarperCollins Publishers 2017 vii, 294 p.p color illustrations (hardback) $22.99   **641.5**

1. Weight loss 2. Eating customs 3. Quick and easy cooking 4. Cookbooks 5. Nutrition 6. Reducing diets -- Recipes
ISBN 9780062684967; 0062684957; 9780062684950

LC 2017013630

In this cookbook author Joel Fuhrman asks "too busy to shop? Too tired to cook? Not sure what's healthy? [He presents] 131 super delicious, easy-to-prepare, incredibly healthy recipes." (Publisher's note)

"Most recipes take only minutes to assemble; vegans, nonvegans, and raw foodies also will find suitable options." Pub Wkly

Galarza, Daniela

Beyond the plate; top food blogs from around the world. foreword by Adam Sachs ; text by Daniela Galarza. Prestel 2017 200 p. color illustrations, map (hardcover) $29.95 **641.5**

1. Cookbooks 2. Cooks 3. Food -- Blogs 4. Cooking -- Blogs
ISBN 9783791382777

LC 2016037475

This book, by Daniela Galarza, "bring[s] together 30 of the best food blogs from around the world. . . . Blogs such as My Darling Lemon Thyme, Indian Simmer, Local Milk, Lady & Pups, and Eat in My Kitchen, among others, effortlessly guide readers through the latest global food trends from curry noodle soups to sweet tahini pastries. . . . Brimming with vibrant photographs, . . . this first-of- its-kind cookbook features two recipes from each blogger." (Publisher's note)

"Beautiful, full-page food photos tantalize throughout, while recipes cover a vast range of trends and techniques." Booklist

Gand, Gale

Gale Gand's brunch! Clarkson Potter/Publishers 2009 208p il $27.50   **641.5**

1. Cooking
ISBN 978-0-307-40698-9

LC 2008-36988

Gand "starts with an enticing assortment of drinks (e.g., white hot chocolate and a three-alarm Bloody Mary), then a chapter on brunch's eggy foundations—omelets, stratas, frittatas, quiches and crêpes, each with appetizing variations—that will please any brunch crowd. In subsequent chapters, Gand hits the sweet and savory high points, from pancakes and doughnuts to onion tarts and cheddar grits. . . . Accessible instructions, basic preparation tips and make-ahead hints ensure that both beginners and those who think cooking brunch is too bothersome will find this volume to be inspiring." Publ Wkly

Garten, Ina

Barefoot Contessa family style; easy ideas and recipes that make everyone feel like family. photographs by Maura McEvoy; food styling by Rori Trovato. Potter 2002 240p il $35   **641.5**

1. Cooking
ISBN 0-609-61066-X

LC 2002-74979

This is "simple, elegant home cooking with good ingredients and a minimum of fuss. It takes a certain amount of chutzpah to include ordinary chicken noodle soup and mashed potatoes and gravy in a cookbook, but Garten pulls it off with heart and style." Publ Wkly

Barefoot Contessa, how easy is that? Ina Garten. 1st ed.; Clarkson Potter 2010 p. cm. $35   **641.5**

1. Cooking 2. Barefoot Contessa (East Hampton, N.Y.: Store)
ISBN 978-0-307-23876-4

LC 2010-2025

"Ina proves once again that it doesn't take complicated techniques, special equipment, or stops at more than one grocery store to make wonderful dishes for your family and friends. Her newest must-have cookbook is all about saving time and avoiding stress while having fun in the kitchen. These are not recipes with three ingredients thrown together in five minutes; instead home cooks will find fantastic Barefoot Contessa recipes that are easy to make but still have all that deep, delicious flavor Ina is known for—and that makes a meal so satisfying." (Publisher's note)

Cook like a pro; Ina Garten. Clarkson Potter/Publishers 2018 272 p. (hardcover) $35   **641.5**

1. Cooking 2. Cookbooks 3. Barefoot Contessa (Store)
ISBN 9780804187046

LC 2018006753

In this cookbook in the Barefoot Contessa Cookbook series, Ina Garten "shares some of her most irresistible recipes and very best 'pro tips,' from the secret to making her custardy, slow-cooked Truffled Scrambled Eggs to the key to the crispiest and juiciest Fried Chicken Sandwiches. Ina will even show you how to make an easy yet showstopping pattern for her Chocolate Chevron Cake--your friends won't believe you decorated it yourself!" (Publisher's note)

Cooking for Jeffrey; A Barefoot Contessa Cookbook. Ina Garten. Clarkson Potter/Publishers 2016 256 p. color illustrations (hardcover) $35   **641.5**

1. Cookbooks 2. Quick and easy cooking
ISBN 9780307464897

LC 2016025974

This cookbook by Ina Garten, "is filled with the recipes . . . [her husband] and their friends request most often. . . . Traditional dishes that she's updated, such as Brisket with Onions and Leeks, and Tsimmes, . . . and new favorites, like Skillet-Roasted Lemon Chicken and Roasted Salmon Tacos, . . . salads, including Maple-Roasted Carrot Salad and Kale Salad. . . . Ina has included a chapter devoted to bread and cheese, with recipes and tips." (Publisher's note)

"True to form, this culinary love letter is as warm and comforting as Garten's dishes." Pub Wkly

Make it ahead; Ina Garten ; photographs by Quentin Bacon ; garden photographs by John M. Hall. Clarkson Potter 2014 272 p. color illustrations (hardback) $35 **641.5**
    1. Cooking 2. Cookbooks 3. Make-ahead cooking 4. Barefoot Contessa (Store)
    ISBN 0307464881; 9780307464880; 9780770434496
                LC 2014004486

This cookbook, by Ina Garten, focuses on make-ahead practices in cooking. "Each recipe includes clear instructions for what you can do ahead of time, and how far in advance, so you can cook with confidence and eliminate last-minute surprises. . . . With beautiful photographs and hundreds of invaluable make-ahead tips, this is your new go-to guide for preparing meals that are stress-free yet filled with those fabulously satisfying flavors." (Publisher's note)

"Throughout, her tips and tricks, from a sidebar to one page, will simply help transform the cooking and the entertaining; she'll recommend storing pasta sauce in plastic freezer bags as well as spotlight the 10 make-ahead tips for parties. A quieter, simpler, more accessible version of Martha Stewart in the kitchen. Make-ahead meals appended." Booklist

Garutti, Randy
    Shake Shack; recipes & stories. Randy Garutti and Mark Rosati ; introduction by Danny Meyer ; photographs by Christopher Hirsheimer and Melissa Hamilton. Clarkson Potter/Publishers 2017 240 p. illustrations (hardcover) $26 **641.5**
    1. Hamburgers 2. Restaurants 3. Cookbooks 4. Milkshakes 5. Frankfurters 6. French fries 7. Shake Shack (Restaurant chain)
    ISBN 9780553459814; 9780553459821
                LC 2016055794

This cookbook, by Randy Garutti and Mark Rosati, contains "70 recipes and plenty of stories, fun facts, and pro tips for the home cook and ShackFan, as well as 200 photographs. Follow Shake Shack's journey around the world; make your own ShackBurgers, crinkle-cut fries, and hand-spun frozen custard shakes at home; and get a glimpse into the culture, community, and inner workings of this global phenomenon." (Publisher's note)

"Garutti and Rosati . . . unveil a must-read chronicle for fans of Danny Meyer's famous eatery." Pub Wkly

Gentry, Ann
    The **Real** Food Daily cookbook; really fresh, really good, really vegetarian. [by] Ann Gentry with Anthony Head. Ten Speed Press 2005 232p $24.95 **641.5**
    1. Vegetarian cooking
    ISBN 1-58008-618-7
                LC 2005-16245

The author presents "what she has learned about seasonal, organic, macrobiotic and vegan cooking. Gentry doesn't break new ground—sandwiches made with tempeh instead of meat, and nut cheeses like cashew cheddar will be familiar to most vegans—but she provides clear and comprehensive directions on how to make them more interesting and flavorful. . . . Gentry explains the basics without preaching or conde-

scending to readers, and discusses nutritional benefits without unnecessary jargon." Publ Wkly

Gerson, Fany
    My sweet Mexico; recipes for authentic breads, pastries, candies, beverages, and frozen treats. Ten Speed Press 2010 215p il $30 **641.5**
    1. Desserts 2. Mexican cooking
    ISBN 978-1-58008-994-4
                LC 2010-14469

The author "has dutifully catalogued the confections of her native Mexico. . . . American readers who have only encountered the occasional tres leches cake in a Mexican restaurant will be stunned by the breadth and depth of recipes here, ranging from coffee-flavored corn cookies to guava caramel pecan rolls and hibiscus ice pops, all culled from Gerson's family, friends, and generous strangers. . . . Gerson's vivid descriptions, exacting instruction, and obvious passion for her subject matter make this volume a substantial read about the most tempting indulgences." Publ Wkly

    Includes bibliographical references

Goin, Suzanne
    ★ **Sunday** suppers at Lucques; [by] Suzanne Goin with Teri Gelber; photographs by Shimon and Tammar. Knopf 2005 398p il $35 **641.5**
    1. French cooking
    ISBN 1-4000-4215-1
                LC 2004-58604

The author "writes with passion and humor, and while her recipes are sophisticated and sometimes complicated, they are written with the home cook in mind." Libr J

Goldberg, Dan
    Cuba! Recipes and Stories from the Cuban Kitchen. written by Dan Goldberg, Andrea Kuhn, and Jody Eddy. Ten Speed Press 2016 256 p. color illustrations (hardcover; alk. paper) $30 **641.5**
    1. Cookbooks 2. Cuban cooking 3. Caribbean cooking 4. Cooking, Cuban
    ISBN 9781607749868; 9781607749875
                LC 2016011291

This cookbook written by Dan Goldberg, Andrea Kuhn, and Jody Eddy "explores the magic of this country through recipes and stories. . . . Goldberg and Kuhn . . . with renowned food writer Jody Eddy, bring the best of Cuban food to home kitchens with more than 75 meticulously tested recipes. From Cuban-Style Fried Chicken . . . to Squid-ink Empanadas. . . . This cookbook offers a unique opportunity to bring a little slice of Cuba into your home and onto your plate." (Publisher's note)

"Photographer Goldberg, art director Kuhn, and food writer Eddy made three visits to Havana and its environs over a five-year period, feasting on the local cuisine and meeting the proud cooks and farmers of the area. They now report back on their sightseeing, with scores of photos and 75 recipes in tow." Pub Wkly

    Includes bibliographical references and index

Goldstein, Joyce
    Jam session; a fruit-preserving handbook. Joyce Goldstein. Ten Speed Press 2018 264 p. color illustrations (hardcover) $24.99 **641.5**
    1. Cookbooks 2. Jam (Preserves) 3. Food -- Preservation 4. Jam 5. Jelly 6. Seasonal cooking
    ISBN 9780399579615

LC 2018001021

This book, by Joyce Goldstein, "is the lushly photographed and selective guide to making all-natural fruit preserves, organized by type of fruit and seasonal availability, with descriptions of the best varieties for preserving plus master recipes and contemporary variations for each type of fruit. . . . Goldstein includes straightforward, no-fail instructions for canning fruit preserves, along with serving ideas for using preserves for much more than toast." (Publisher's note)

"Goldstein's accessible guide presents an excellent option for those seeking to create and enjoy their own preserves." LJ

The **new** Mediterranean Jewish table; Old World recipes for the modern home. Joyce Goldstein. University of California Press 2016 468 p. (cloth; alk. paper) $39.95　　**641.5**
1. Jewish cooking 2. Mediterranean cooking 3. Cooking, Mediterranean
ISBN 9780520284999

LC 2015043306

This book, by Joyce Goldstein, is a "guide to Jewish home cooking. . . . It is . . . filled with . . . seasonal recipes . . . that embrace fresh fruits and vegetables; grains and legumes; small portions of meat, poultry, and fish; and a healthy mix of herbs and spices. It is also the story of how Jewish cooks successfully brought the local ingredients, techniques, and traditions of their new homelands into their kitchens." (Publisher's note)

"Thorough research and excellent recipes make Goldstein's latest an instant classic, worthy of shelf space alongside complementary works by Claudia Roden and Joan Nathan." LJ

Includes bibliographical references and index

Good housekeeping (Periodical)

★ The **Good** Housekeeping cookbook; 1,275 recipes from America's favorite test kitchen. edited by Susan Westmoreland. 125th anniversary ed.; Hearst Books 2010 752p il $35 **641.5**
1. Cooking
ISBN 978-1-58816-813-9

LC 2010-18437

Provides over 1,200 traditional and contemporary American recipes and offers information on cooking techniques, tools, ingredients, food handling, nutrition, canning, freezing, and holiday celebrations.

"Quick recipes and simple dessert preparations, like Fire-Roasted Nectarines and Coffee Granita, will please anyone pressed for time, but the encyclopedic inclusion of recipes for everything from Egg Salad, Lobster Bisque, and Chocolate Souffle to Pad Thai, Salmon with Mustard-Dill Sauce, and Muffuletta is its true benefit, making it a cookbook readers will grow with." Publ Wkly

Goodall, Tiffany

The **ultimate** student cookbook; from chicken to chili. photography by Claire Peters. Firefly Books 2010 160p il pa $14.95　　**641.5**
1. Cooking 2. Quick and easy cooking
ISBN 978-1-55407-602-4

The author "outlines basic kitchen equipment, pantry ingredients, and food hygiene. Writing for the student with no cooking experience, she offers step-by-step photos that will make cooking a breeze. Goodall discusses basics like how to cook noodles, rice, and potatoes and presents dishes like wraps, salads, soups, chili, pizza, kebabs, and cakes. Two alcoholic drinks are included. Highly recommended for the numerous photographs and the variety of recipes." Libr J

The **gourmet** cookbook; more than 1000 recipes. edited by Ruth Reichl. Houghton Mifflin 2004 1040p $40　　**641.5**
1. Cooking
ISBN 0-618-37408-6

LC 2004-47873

Recipes culled from issues of Gourmet magazine include "concoctions like Coq au Vin, Beef Wellington, Coulibiac, Chop Suey, Bananas Foster, and Black Forest Cake. . . . Every chapter begins with an overview of its subject; each recipe has an introduction; and many dishes feature helpful 'cook's notes,' which give tips for food preparation, technique and storage." Publ Wkly

Gourmet today; more than 1000 all-new recipes for the contemporary kitchen. edited by Ruth Reichl. Houghton Mifflin Harcourt 2009 1008p il $40　　**641.5**
1. Cooking
ISBN 978-0-618-61018-1

LC 2009-19781

The editor "offers a diverse range of recipes that reflect the ever-changing American palate and the many cultures that have influenced it. Alongside Stilton cheese puff are recipes for babaghanouj, bangers and mash, Armenian lamb pizza, arepas with black beans and feta, and Vietnamese fried spring rolls. Informative sidebars provide details on a huge array of topics, from what salt to use when to preserving fish. . . . Comprehensive, appetizing and thoroughly tested, this mammoth collection is the book no kitchen should be without." Publ Wkly

Greenspan, Dorie

Around my French table; more than 300 recipes from my home to yours. photographs by Alan Richardson. Houghton Mifflin Harcourt 2010 530p il $40　　**641.5**
1. French cooking
ISBN 978-0-618-87553-5; 0-618-87553-0

LC 2010-14232

"A part-time Paris resident for more than a decade, Greenspan focuses on what French people really eat at home: easy-to-prepare yet flavorful dishes that are suitable for just about any time of day. From Bacon and Eggs and Asparagus Salad to Chicken in a Pot to Veal Chops with Rosemary Butter, her offerings are hardy, mostly uncomplicated, and superbly appetizing. She also provides sidebars on a wide range of topics, including whether or not to wash raw chicken, several ways of cooking beets, mussels, and more." Publ Wkly

★ **Everyday** Dorie; the way I cook. Dorie Greenspan ; photographs by Ellen Silverman. Houghton Mifflin Harcourt 2018 368 p. (hardcover) $35　　**641.5**
1. Cooking 2. Cookbooks
ISBN 9780544826984

LC 2017061484

This book, by Dorie Greenspan, photographs by Ellen Silverman, "invites readers into her kitchen to savor the dishes that she makes all the time. . . . Each one has a small surprise that makes it special. Mustard and walnuts in the cheese puffs. Cherry tomatoes stuffed into red bell peppers and oven-charred. Cannellini beans in cod en papillote. The dishes are practical, made with common ingredients from the supermarket, farmers' market, or pantry." (Publisher's note)

"Greenspan (Around My French Table), five-time James Beard Award winner, shares her favorite day-to-day recipes in this standout cookbook." Pub Wkly

Gregory-Smith, John

Orange blossom & honey; magical Moroccan recipes from

the Souks to the Sahara. John Gregory-Smith ; food photography by Martin Poole ; location photography by Alen Kechane. Kyle Books 2018 192 p. color illustrations $29.99 **641.5**

1. Cookbooks 2. Moroccan cooking
ISBN 9781909487901

LC 2018936324

This cookbook, by John Gregory Smith, "takes you on a culinary journey across Morocco, from the souks of Marrakesh, through the Sahara, and onto the wind-swept shores of the Atlantic. In researching this book, John travelled into the heart of the High Atlas Mountains to learn the secrets of traditional lamb barbecue, then journeyed north, through the city of Fes, where the rich dishes of the Imperial Courts are still prepared in many homes." (Publisher's note)

Griffin, Brooke

Skinny suppers; 125 lightened up, healthier meals for your family. Brooke Griffin. William Morrow, an Imprint of HarperCollins Publishers 2016 320 p. color illustrations (hardcover) $29.99 **641.5**

1. Low-calorie diet 2. Quick and easy cooking 3. Low-calorie diet -- Recipes
ISBN 9780062419156

LC 2015034595

This cookbook, by Brooke Griffin, offers "125 suppers and sides (including 25 fan favorites) like Philly Cheesesteak Stuffed Peppers, Supreme Pizza Pasta Casserole, Un-Sloppy Janes, and Loaded Nacho Soup. These are recipes you can feel good about—they're satisfying, lower in fat and calories, and, most important, delicious! Plus, most are under 350 calories per serving and take less than 30 minutes from prep to table." (Publisher's note)

"Having this cookbook on hand will be like having your own personal cheerleader in the kitchen." Booklist

Griffith, Dotty

The **Enchilada** Queen Cookbook; Enchiladas, Fajitas, Tamales, and More Classic Recipes from Texas-Mexico Border Kitchens. Sylvia Casares with Dotty Griffith. St. Martin's Griffin 2016 240 p. illustrations (chiefly color) (ebook) $60; (hardcover) $27.99 **641.5**

1. Mexican American cooking
ISBN 9781250082923; 9781250082916

LC 2016033309

How I Became the Enchilada Queen -- Border Cuisine -- The Foundation -- Enchilada Queen Sauces -- Enchilada Queen Wisdom -- Salsas, Appetizers, and Snacks -- A la Parilla -- Enchilada Queen Homestyle -- Tamale Tutorial -- Enchilada Queen Sides -- Enchilada Queen Sweet Endings -- Sipping with the Enchilada Queen.

This cookbook, by Sylvia Casares with Dotty Griffith, explains that "the heart of great Tex-Mex cooking comes from home kitchens along the Rio Grande. . . . Casares gives you the best of the best, including tricks and simple techniques to turn any dish from appetizing to amazing. You'll learn how to make her Holy Trinity spice paste; why you should use certain key shortcuts, such as chicken bouillon, in some dishes; and how to do her tortilla-changing Texas Two-Step marinating technique." (Publisher's note)

"A satisfying combination of autobiography and popular Mexican foods." LJ

The **grilling** book; the definitive guide from Bon Appetit. edited by Adam Rapoport ; photography by Peden + Munk.

Andrews McMeel Pub., LLC 2013 432 p. color illustrations $45 **641.5**

1. Cookbooks 2. Barbecue cooking
ISBN 1449427529; 9781449427528

LC 2012952341

This cookbook, edited by Adam Rapoport, focuses on grilling. "Offering more than 350 foolproof recipes, dozens of luscious full-color photographs, crystal clear illustrations, and plenty of plainspoken, here's-how-to-do-it guidelines, [it] welcomes you to everything that is sensational (and sensationally simple) about grilling." (Publisher's note)

Gur, Janna

The **book** of New Israeli food; a culinary journey. photography, Eilon Paz; contributing writers Rami Hann . . . [et al.] Schocken Books 2008 303p il $35 **641.5**

1. Israeli cooking
ISBN 978-0-8052-1224-2; 0-8052-1224-8
First published 2007 in Israel

"Beautiful and comprehensive, this book will become an immediate favorite with anyone with even a passing interest in Israeli cuisine." Publ Wkly

Hair, Jaden

The **steamy** kitchen cookbook; 101 Asian recipes simple enough for tonight's dinner. photography by Jaden Hair. Tuttle Pub. 2009 160p il $27.95 **641.5**

1. Asian cooking
ISBN 978-0-8048-4028-6

LC 2009-17461

The author, a food blogger, "shares recipes drawn from her mother's kitchen, other food bloggers, and her own delightful archives. Her focus is mostly simple Asian dishes (from China, Vietnam, Japan, and Thailand), with several more complicated ones thrown into the mix. . . . For home cooks of all levels of experience seeking to expand their repertoire of Asian recipes, Hair has written an extremely accessible cookbook that blends great recipes with mouthwatering photographs she took." Libr J

Hart, Alice

Good veg; ebullient vegetables, global flavors; a modern vegetarian cookbook. Alice Hart. Experiment 2017 xiii, 321 p.p color illustrations (New vegetarian) (cloth) $24.95 **641.5**

1. Vegetarian cooking 2. Cookbooks
ISBN 9781615192878; 9781615192861

LC 2016045768

This book, by Alice Hart, "showcases ebullient vegetables, fruits, and grains—in inventive, reliable dishes to sustain you (and family and friends) all day, through every season. Hart's food surprises and thrills through contrasts (think crisp and soft, sweet and sour, chile heat and refreshing herb)." (Publisher's note)

"The 200 colorful creations presented here represent a veritable master class in meat-free cookery and would be a worthy addition to any cook's shelf, no matter vegetarian or omnivore." Booklist

Hasselbrink, Kimberley

Vibrant food; celebrating the ingredients, recipes, and colors of each season. written and illustrated by Kimberley Hasselbrink. Ten Speed Press 2014 224 p. colored illustrations (hardback) $25 **641.5**

1. Seasonal cooking 2. Color of food 3. Food -- Pictorial works
ISBN 1607745410; 9781607745419

LC 2013040310

IACP Cookbook Award Finalist: Health & Special Diet (2015)

In this book, author Kimberley Hasselbrink "invites you to look at ingredients differently and let their colors inspire you: the shocking fluorescent pink of a chard stem, the deep reds and purples of baby kale leaves, the bright shades of green that emerge in the spring, and even the calm yellows and whites of so many winter vegetables. Thinking about produce in terms of color can reinvigorate your relationship with food." (Publisher's note)

"This enjoyable title would be a nice addition to the shelves of voracious seasonal cookbook readers, but it does not do enough to distinguish itself for most cooks, other than readers of the author's blog, to seek it out specifically." LJ

Hazan, Marcella, 1924-2013

Ingredienti; Marcella's Guide to the Market. by Marcella Hazan and Victor Hazan. Simon & Schuster 2016 256 p. illustrations $20   **641.5**

1. Cookbooks 2. Italian cooking 3. Grocery shopping
ISBN 145162736X; 9781451627367

This book by Marcella Hazan and Victor Hazan presents a guide "on how to shop for the best ingredients and prepare the most delicious meals.... Her husband and ... collaborator ... translated and transcribed these vignettes on how to buy and what to do with the fresh produce used in Italian cooking.... Her clear, practical guidance in acquiring the components of good cooking is helpful wherever you choose to shop—in supermarkets, farmers' markets, ... or online." (Publisher's note)

"This little volume offers a treasury of lifetime observations to serious, inquisitive cooks." Booklist

Includes bibliographical references.

Marcella says . . . Italian cooking wisdom from the legendary teacher's master classes, with more than 120 of her irresistible new recipes. HarperCollins Publishers 2004 390p il $29.95   **641.5**

1. Italian cooking
ISBN 0-06-620967-6

LC 2004-42892

The author shares lessons in Italian cooking, discussing techniques, ingredients and planning and preparing Italian dishes

Headley, Brooks

Superiority Burger cookbook; the vegetarian hamburger is now delicious. Brooks Headley ; with Julia Goldberg, Gabe Rosner, Matthew Silverstein, and Matt Sweeney ; photographs by Sunny Shokrae. W W Norton & Co 2018 224 p. illustrations (hardcover) $29.95   **641.5**

1. Cooking 2. Cookbooks 3. Sandwiches 4. Vegetarian cooking 5. Hamburgers 6. Meat substitutes 7. Superiority Burger (Restaurant)
ISBN 9780393253986

LC 2018015069

In this cookbook, by Brooks Headley, "you'll find out why Superiority Burger in New York City's East Village is the hottest ticket in North America and the surrounding continents.... The book is divided into six flavorful sections--Sandwiches, Cool Salads, Warm Vegetables, Soups and Stews, Sweets, and Pantry Recipes--and reveals the recipes for some of the restaurant's favorites: the Sloppy Dave, Burnt Broccoli Salad, ... and ... the now legendary Superiority Burger." (Publisher's note)

Includes bibliographical references and index

Henry, Diana

A **Change** of Appetite; where healthy meets delicious. Diana Henry. Octopus Pub Group 2014 336 p. color illustrations $34.99   **641.5**

1. Cookbooks 2. Asian cooking 3. Middle Eastern cooking
ISBN 1845338928; 9781845338923

LC 2014412876

James Beard Foundation Award Nominee: Focus on Health (2015)

"What happened when one of today's best-loved food writers had a change of appetite? Here are the dishes that Diana Henry created when she started to crave a different kind of diet--less meat and heavy food, more vegetable-, fish-, and grain-based dishes--often inspired by the food of the Middle East and Far East, but also drawing on cuisines from Georgia to Scandinavia." (Publisher's note)

"Broken down by season, the book offers a nice mix of food from around the world that will not take a toll on the digestive system." Pub Wkly

Includes bibliographical references (page 328-329) and index

How to eat a peach; menus, stories, and places. Diana Henry. Octopus Pub Group 2018 224 p. $34.99   **641.5**

1. Menus 2. Cooking 3. Entertaining
ISBN 1784724114; 9781784724115

LC 2018064231

This book, by Diana Henry, presents "24 menus and 100 recipes . . . that reflect places Diana loves, and dishes that are real favorites. . . . The menus are introduced with personal essays in Diana's now well-known voice- about places or journeys or particular times and explain the choice of dishes. Each menu is a story in itself, but the recipes can also stand alone." (Publisher's note)

Plenty; good, uncomplicated food for the sustainable kitchen. Diana Henry. Mitchell Beazley 2017 320 p. color illustrations (hardcover) $29.99   **641.5**

1. Cooking 2. Seasonal cooking 3. Sustainable living
ISBN 1784723002; 9781784723002

This cookbook, by Diana Henry, "is packed with 300 recipes from around the world. A section on using less expensive cuts of meat will inspire you to create new favorites such as Roast Pork Shoulder with Baked Squash. . . . There are also great ideas for using the best value fish. . . . Leftovers are also at the heart of this book, and Diana offers an abundance of ideas for transforming roasts and other big family meals." (Publisher's note)

"A very timely book—sure to appeal to many cooks." LJ

Simple; by Diana Henry. Octopus Pub Group 2016 320 p. $32.99   **641.5**

1. Cookbooks 2. Quick and easy cooking
ISBN 1784722049; 9781784722043

This cookbook by Diana Henry features "ingenious ideas such as no-hassle starters and sauces that will lift any dish. From Turkish Pasta with Caramelized Onions, Yoghurt and Dill and Paprika-baked Pork Chops with Beetroot, . . . to Parmesan-roasted Cauliflower with Garlic and Thyme, [Henry] takes the kind of ingredients we are most likely to find in our cupboard and fridge . . . and provides recipes that will become your friends for life." (Publisher's note)

"Those looking to enliven their daily toast, eggs, pastas, and salads will find particularly fabulous choices here, along with other delicious mains and desserts." LJ

Hesser, Amanda

The **essential** New York Times cook book; classic recipes for a new century. W.W. Norton 2010 932p il $40   **641.5**

1. Cooking
ISBN 978-0-393-06103-1; 0-393-06103-5

LC 2010-33311

The author "spent six years combing the Times's vast recipe archive, cooking her way through more than 1000 recipes to assemble this indispensible tome culled from 150 years of the paper's food columns. This daunting compendium features both noteworthy classics (Osso Buco) and modern recipes (Smoked Mashed Potatoes) that have been tested and, in some cases, updated for the contemporary cook. Chapters begin with a time line and are arranged by type of food (e.g., soups, vegetables, cakes) then chronologically within the chapter, making for a fascinating historic overview of the interests of American cooks." Libr J

Includes bibliographical references

Food52 a new way to dinner; A Playbook of Recipes and Strategies for the Week Ahead. by Amanda Hesser and Merrill Stubbs ; photography by James Ransom. Ten Speed Press 2016 288 p. color illustrations (ebook) $65; (hardcover; alk. paper) $35   **641.5**
1. Dinners 2. Cookbooks 3. American cooking 4. Seasonal cooking 5. Cooking, American 6. Dinners and dining
ISBN 9780399578014; 9780399578007
LC 2016022690

In this cookbook by Amanda Hesser and Merrill Stubbs, with photographs by James Ransom, "Amanda and Merrill mix, match, and riff to create new dinners, lunches, and even desserts throughout the week. Blistered tomatoes are first served as a side, then become sauce for spaghetti with corn. Tuna, poached in olive oil on a Sunday, gets paired with braised peppers and romesco for a fiery dinner, with spicy mayo for a hearty sandwich, and . . . [then added to] a pack-and-go salad." (Publisher's note)

"Expect much buzz surrounding this cookbook..." LJ
Includes bibliographical references and index

Hirsheimer, Christopher
Canal house cooks every day; Melissa Hamilton, Christopher Hirsheimer. Andrews McMeel Pub., LLC 2012 359 p. col. ill. $45   **641.5**
1. Cooking 2. Cookbooks
ISBN 1449421474; 9781449421472
LC 2012936742

James Beard Foundation Award: General Cooking (2013)

This book, by Melissa Hamilton and Christopher Hirsheimer, was the 2013 James Beard Foundation Award winner for General Cooking. "The delicious, easy-to-prepare recipes celebrate the everyday practice of simple cooking and the enjoyment of eating. . . . In addition to the recipes, this wonderful cookbook includes menus for all the great holidays throughout the year, plus twelve intimate essays . . . that introduce each month and capture the feeling and vibe of that special time of the year." (Publisher's note)

Hood, Ann
Kitchen yarns; notes on life, love, and food. Ann Hood. W W Norton & Co Inc 2018 256 p. (hardcover) $24.95   **641.5**
1. Cooking 2. Cookbooks 3. Novelists, American -- 20th century -- Biography
ISBN 9780393249507
LC 2018027425

"In this warm collection of personal essays and recipes, best-selling author Ann Hood nourishes both our bodies and our souls. From her Italian American childhood through singlehood, raising and feeding a growing family, divorce, and a new marriage to food writer Michael Ruhlman, . . . Hood has long appreciated the power of a good meal. . . . [She] tracks her lifelong journey in the kitchen with twenty-seven heartfelt essays, each accompanied by a recipe (or a few)." (Publisher's note)

Howard, Vivian (Vivian S.), 1978-
Deep run roots; Stories and Recipes from My Corner of the South. Vivian Howard. Little, Brown & Co. 2016 576 p. color illustrations (ebook) $120; $40   **641.5**
1. Cookbooks 2. Southern cooking
ISBN 9780316269490; 9780316381109
LC 2016931447

This cookbook, by Vivian Howard, "imparts the true tale of Southern food: rooted in family and tradition, yet calling out to the rest of the world. . . . Recipes include family favorites like Blueberry BBQ Chicken, Creamed Collard-Stuffed Potatoes, Fried Yams with Five-Spice Maple Bacon Candy, Chicken and Rice, and Country-Style Pork Ribs in Red Curry-Braised Watermelon." (Publisher's note)

"This tribute to her family roots is destined to become an enduring classic." Pub Wkly

Hunt, Lindsay Maitland
Healthyish; a cookbook with seriously satisfying, truly simple, good-for-you (but not too good-for-you) recipes for real life. Lindsay Hunt. Abrams 2017 255 p. $29.99   **641.5**
1. Cooking for one 2. Quick and easy cooking
ISBN 1419726560; 9781419726569
LC 2016960984

This cookbook, by Lindsay Hunt, "offers 131 satisfying recipes with straightforward instructions, using as few pots and pans as possible, and ingredients that won't break the bank. Not to mention, you can find the ingredients at your everyday grocery store. . . . Emphasizing balanced eating rather than fad diet tricks, Hunt includes guilt-free recipes for every meal of the day, from breakfast to snacks to dinner." (Publisher's note)

"Whether you like to leave cooking till the last minute or enjoy whipping up a big batch of something to eat throughout the week, this book will serve you well." LJ

Hyland, Matthew
Emily; the cookbook. Emily Hyland and Matt Hyland. Ballantine Books 2018 240 p. color illustrations (hardcover; alk. paper) $30   **641.5**
1. Pizza 2. Cookbooks 3. Hamburgers 4. Cooking
ISBN 9781524796839
LC 2018018964

In this cookbook, Emily Hyland and Matt Hyland "share their delicious and doable recipes--wood-fired oven or fancy equipment required. . . . You'll be shown how to re-create such crowd-pleasing favorites as their famous round pizza, the iconic Detroit pan pizza, and their legendary EMMY Burger. . . . Packed with full-color photos and handy tips, 'EMILY: The Cookbook' is a fabulous find for people who want new ways to entertain, feed, and wow their friends and family." (Publisher's note)

"The husband-and-wife culinary team behind the New York City restaurants Emily and Emmy Squared serve up more than 100 recipes in their excellent debut collection." Pub Wkly

Includes bibliographical references and index

Hyman, Gwen
Urban Italian; simple recipes and true stories from a life in food. [by] Andrew Carmellini, and Gwen Hyman; photographs by Quentin Bacon. Bloomsbury 2008 311p il $35   **641.5**
1. Italian cooking
ISBN 978-1-59691-470-4

The author "presents spectacular recipes while opening a window onto his life with food, from his Italian-American boyhood and cooking school to revelations while traveling in Italy and being a top New York chef. . . . The recipes, which come from all over Italy and mix regional Italian and American influences, are arranged classically, from antipasti to dolci." Publ Wkly

Iyer, Raghavan

660 curries; the gateway to the world of Indian cooking. by Raghavan Iyer. Workman Pub. 2008 809p il $32.50; pa $22.95   **641.5**

1. Indian cooking 2. Cooking -- Curry
ISBN 978-0-7611-4855-5; 0-7611-4855-8; 978-0-7611-3787-0 pa; 0-7611-3787-4 pa

LC 2008-1288

"A wide-ranging guide to the curries of the Indian subcontinent, including Pakistan, Nepal, and Sri Lanka. Iyer explains that Indian curries are not based on a can of curry powder and that the term 'curry' refers to any dish simmered in or covered with a fragrant, spicy (though not necessarily hot) sauce or gravy. The hundreds of recipes include appetizer curries such as Skewered Chicken with Creamy Fenugreek Sauce, main-course curries like Yogurt-Marinated Lamb with Ginger and Garlic, and 'contemporary curries' such as Wild Salmon with Chiles, Scallions, and Tomato; there are also recipes for 'curry cohorts'—rice, bread, and other accompaniments." Libr J

Jaffrey, Madhur

At home with Madhur Jaffrey; simple, delectable dishes from India, Pakistan, Bangladesh, and Sri Lanka. Alfred A. Knopf 2010 301p il $35; ebook $35   **641.5**

1. Asian cooking
ISBN 978-0-307-26824-2; 978-0-307-59440-2 ebook

LC 2010-19678

This is a "cookbook of easily prepared, thoughtful, and unusual dishes from India, Pakistan, Bangladesh, and Sri Lanka. Anyone looking to explore Indian cooking for the first time will find this volume uniquely helpful." Booklist

Jenkins, Nancy Harmon

The **new** Mediterranean diet cookbook; a delicious alternative for lifelong health. with a foreword by Marion Nestle. Bantam Books 2009 496p $26.95   **641.5**

1. Low-fat diet 2. Mediterranean cooking
ISBN 978-0-553-38509-0; 0-553-38509-7

LC 2008-40982

First published 1994 with title: The Mediterranean diet cookbook
Jenkins' "knowledge of these cuisines is both personal and informed. . . . An essential purchase." Libr J
Includes bibliographical references

Jennings, Matthew

Homegrown; Cooking from My New England Roots. Matt Jennings with Jessica Battilana ; photographs by Huge Galdones. Artisan 2017 ix, 340 p.p color illustrations (hardcover) $35   **641.5**

1. American cooking 2. Cooking, American -- New England style
ISBN 1579656749; 9781579656744; 9781579658144

LC 2016058708

This cookbook, by Matt Jennings, "honors the iconic foods of his heritage and celebrates the fresh ingredients that have come to define his renowned, inventive approach to cooking. . . . With over 100 vibrant, ingredient-driven recipes, . . . [it] shines a spotlight on a trailblazing chef and pays homage to America's oldest cuisine." (Publisher's note)
"His debut cookbook is a treasury of ingenious takes on New Eng-

land and American classics, with some challenging but most well within reach." LJ
Includes bibliographical references and index.

Jinich, Pati

Mexican today; new and rediscovered recipes for contemporary kitchens. Pati Jinich ; photography by Ellen Silverman. Houghton Mifflin Harcourt 2016 320 p. color illustrations (paper over board) $30   **641.5**

1. Mexican cooking 2. Mexican American cooking 3. Cooking, Mexican
ISBN 0544557247; 9780544557246

LC 2015042717

In this Mexican cookbook, chef Pati Jinich "shares easy, generous dishes, both traditional ones and her own new spins. Some are regional recipes she has recovered from the past and updated, like Miners' Enchiladas with fresh vegetables and cheese or Drunken Rice with Chicken and Chorizo, a specialty of the Yucatán." (Publisher's note)
"Many of her recipes can be made in advance or in less than 30 minutes and rely on easy-to-find ingredients. A highlight of this cookbook is its playful variations such as baked huevos rancheros casserole." LJ

Jones, Anna

A **modern** way to eat; 200+ Satisfying Vegetarian Recipes. by Anna Jones. Ten Speed Press 2014 352 p. color illustrations (hardback) $35   **641.5**

1. Cookbooks 2. Vegetarian cooking
ISBN 1607748037; 9781607748038

LC 2014035561

This book, by Anna Jones, offers a "modern vegetarian cookbook packed with quick, healthy, and fresh recipes that explore the full breadth of vegetarian ingredients--grains, nuts, seeds, and seasonal vegetables--from Jamie Oliver's London-based food stylist and writer Anna Jones." (Publisher's note)
"Attuned to the latest dietary trends, this excellent vegetarian cookbook blends the cozy, clever charm of Sophie Dahl's Very Fond of Food with the varied textures and flavors from Yotam Ottolenghi's Plenty and the quick, bonus meal ideas (e.g., one soup: 1,000 variations, ten ways with avocado on toast) of Mark Bittman's "How To Cook Everything" series."LJ

Jones, Heather K.

Skinnytaste Fast and Slow; Knockout Quick-Fix and Slow Cooker Recipes. by Gina Homolka and Heather K. Jones. Random House Inc 2016 304 p. color illustrations (ebook) $65; $30   **641.5**

1. Cooking
ISBN 9780553459616; 0553459600; 9780553459609

LC 2016427943

"With Skinnytaste Fast and Slow, you can get a nutritious, flavor-packed, figure-friendly meal—complete with a flourless chocolate brownie made in a slow cooker—on the table any night of the week. Gina Homolka, founder of the widely adored blog Skinnytaste, shares 140 dishes that come together in a snap—whether in a slow cooker or in the oven or on the stovetop." (Publisher's note)
"With its attractive design and easy everyday dishes, Homolka's latest may strike advanced cooks as too basic, but these recipes are excellent for novices. Expect demand." LJ

Jones, Judith

The **pleasures** of cooking for one. Alfred A. Knopf 2009 273p il $27.95   **641.5**

1. Cooking
ISBN 978-0-307-27072-6

LC 2009-12307

Counsels readers on how to enjoy a solitary culinary life by preparing meals in accordance with one's own preferences, outlining a range of basic through sophisticated recipes that work in weekly menus and make use of leftovers.

This is a "civilized, unfussy guide to cooking—and cooking well—for solitary diners. . . . [The author] doesn't skip desserts, entertaining or self-indulgence, and best of all, her whole book benefits from the diverse and cumulative gleanings of work with many of the great cooks and cookbook writers (including Julia Child, of course) of the latter half of the 20th century." Publ Wkly

Includes bibliographical references

Joulwan, Melissa

Well fed; Paleo recipes for people who love to eat. by Melissa Joulwan ; foreword by Melissa and Dallas Hartwig ; photos by David Humphreys ; design by Kathleen Shannon. Greenleaf Book Group Llc 2012 160 p. ill. (chiefly col.) $29.95 **641.5**

1. Cookbooks 2. Paleo cooking 3. Reducing diets 4. High-protein diet -- Recipes 5. Prehistoric peoples -- Nutrition
ISBN 061557226X; 9780615572260

This paleo-diet cookbook, by Melissa Joulwan, "explains how to get in the habit of a Weekly Cookup so that you have ready-to-go food for snacks and meals every day. It will also show you how to make Hot Plates, a mix-and-match approach to combining basic ingredients with spices and seasonings. . . . The recipes are as simple as possible, without compromising taste." (Publisher's note)

Kamozawa, Aki

Ideas in food; great recipes and why they work. [by] Aki Kamozawa and H. Alexander Talbot. Clarkson Potter 2010 320p il $25
641.5

1. Cooking 2. Chemistry
ISBN 978-0-307-71740-5; 978-0-307-71974-4 ebook

LC 2010-17633

"The authors break down the science behind correctly and deliciously preparing everything from bread, pasta, and eggs (including soft scrambled eggs; hardboiled eggs, and brown butter hollandaise sauce) to homemade butter and yogurt. Most recipes fall into the 'Ideas for Everyone' category, which composes about the first three-quarters of the book; the final section is 'Ideas for Professionals,' which explores trendy molecular gastronomy topics like liquid nitrogen-used to make popcorn gelato-and carbon dioxide, a necessary tool for making coffee onion rings. Straightforward prose and anecdotes with personality keep this from being a dry food science tome. And accessible recipes for such dishes as a simple roast chicken, green beans almondine, and root beer-braised short ribs mean it never gets too lofty." Publ Wkly

Includes bibliographical references

Kassoff, Anya

Simply vibrant; all-day vegetarian recipes for colorful plant-based cooking. Anya Kassoff, photography by Masha Davydova. Roost 2018 328 p. (hardcover; alk. paper) $35
641.5

1. Cookbooks 2. Cooking -- Vegetables 3. Seasonal cooking 4. Vegetarian cooking
ISBN 9781611803846

LC 2016057919

This cookbook, by Anya Kassoff, "offers a modern way to eat--breaking the boundaries between sweet and savory with intuitively

nourishing foods. Start your day with 'Creamy Steel Cut Oats with Rainbow Chard and Pine Nuts,' throw together a rainbow-colored salad for lunch or make black rice sushi for a quick snack, and later, feed your sweet tooth and your body with 'Sweet Potato Chocolate Brownies.' This is fresh, fun, delightful whole food." (Publisher's note)

"She offers a wealth of recipes, all of which promise to stimulate both taste buds and retinas." Booklist

Katz, Rebecca

The **cancer**-fighting kitchen; nourishing big-flavor recipes for cancer treatment and recovery. [by] Rebecca Katz with Mat Edelson. Celestial Arts 2009 222p il $32.50 **641.5**

1. Cooking for the sick 2. Cancer -- Diet therapy
ISBN 978-1-58761-344-9

LC 2009-14359

"Katz's experience with cancer patients and their long, often frustrating recovery lends authority to her wise, common-sense approach, suitable for cooks of all skill levels." Publ Wkly

Includes bibliographical references

Katzen, Mollie

The **heart** of the plate; vegetarian recipes for a new generation. Mollie Katzen ; photographs and illustrations by Mollie Katzen. Houghton Mifflin Harcourt 2013 464 p. $34.99 **641.5**

1. Cookbooks 2. Vegetarian cooking 3. International cooking 4. Cooking (Natural foods)
ISBN 0547571593; 9780547571591

LC 2013010180

This cookbook by Mollie Katzen promotes vegetables, focusing "on their natural flavors rather than rich accompaniments such as butter, cream, and cheese." The recipes "combine everyday vegetables in appetizing ways." Chapters on soups, salads, grains, burgers, pasta, and desserts are included. (Publishers Weekly)

The **Moosewood** Cookbook; 40th Anniversary Edition. by Mollie Katzen. Random House Inc 2014 231 p. illustrations $19.99
641.5

1. Cooking 2. Vegetarian cooking
ISBN 1607747391; 9781607747390

LC 2014015685

This cookbook, by Mollie Katzen, originally published in 1974, "has inspired generations to cook simple, healthy, and seasonal food. . . . Katzen hand-wrote, illustrated, and locally published a spiral-bound notebook of recipes for vegetarian dishes inspired by those she and fellow cooks served at their small restaurant co-op in Ithaca, N.Y. . . . [It] continues to be a seminal, timely, and wholly personal work." (Publisher's note)

Keller, Thomas

★ **Ad** Hoc at home. Artisan Books 2009 359p il $50 **641.5**
1. Cooking
ISBN 978-1-57965-377-4

LC 2009-13258

For this cookbook, the author focuses on "family-style meals for the home cook in this accessible and dazzlingly beautiful book based on the fare served at his Ad Hoc restaurant, in Napa, Calif. . . . [He provides] a thorough primer on the foundations of cooking, offering clear and easy-to-follow instructions on techniques such as butchering and trussing chickens and tying a pork loin. . . . Dishes such as braised beef short ribs, buttermilk fried chicken, and fig-stuffed roast pork loin highlight a vast array of offerings that range from crab cakes to shortbread cookies." Publ Wkly

Kennedy, Diana

From my Mexican kitchen; techniques and ingredients. photographs by Michael Calderwood; and styled by the author. Clarkson Potter 2003 320p il $40   **641.5**
   1. Mexican cooking
   ISBN 0-609-60700-6

                               LC 2002-70405

The author "explains how to produce authentic enchiladas, tacos, tamales, sopes, panuchos, and other Mexican classics. Kennedy also provides a guide to wild greens, items rarely seen outside provincial markets. Her advice on freezing excess quantities of cuitlacoche (corn fungus) will reward fans of that uncommon mushroom. This is an indispensable addition to any library cookbook collection." Booklist

Kimball, Christopher, 1951-

Milk Street; the new home cooking. Christopher Kimball. Little, Brown & Co. 2017 xxv, 310 p.p (hardback) $40 **641.5**
   1. Cooking 2. Gastronomy
   ISBN 9780316437288

                               LC 2017937767

This cookbook, by Christopher Kimball, "delivers more than 125 new recipes arranged by type of dish: from grains and salads, to a new way to scramble eggs, to simple dinners and twenty-first-century desserts. . . . These recipes are more than just good recipes. They teach a simpler, bolder, healthier way to cook that will change your cooking forever. And cooking will become an act of pure pleasure, not a chore." (Publisher's note)

"Overall, with its testing notes, short ingredient lists, and firm directions (each recipe has a "don't" section), this volume is a trustworthy and easy-to-use collection of international flavors from one of the nation's best cooking teachers." Booklist

Kiros, Tessa

Food from many Greek kitchens. Andrews McMeel Pub. 2011 333p il $35   **641.5**
   1. Greek cooking
   ISBN 978-1-4494-0652-3

                               LC 2010943021

First published 2010 in Australia

"For each recipe, [the author] gives the title in English and Greek and offers an introduction to the dish and thorough instruction. From Baklava to Keftedes Fried Meatballs to Pita Bread, the accessible dishes are accompanied by beautiful photography. Greek cookbooks written for the beginner are rare, so this book is a gem. It provides a good foundation and is sure to be a gateway to more advanced Greek cooking." Lirb J

Ko, Genevieve

Home cooking with Jean-Georges; [by] Jean-Georges Vongerichten with Genevieve Ko. Clarkson Potter/Publishers 2011 256p il $40   **641.5**
   1. Cooking
   ISBN 978-0-307-71795-5; 0-307-71795-X

                             LC 2010-53808

"After working 18-hour days six days a week, Vongerichten buys a weekend country home and rediscovers the joys of unfussy cooking. He shares recipes for the meals he and his family enjoy in this pleasingly accessible volume. Chicken liver and pancetta crostini, swiss chard braised in shiitake butter, shortbread are among the recipes that cover salads, fish and seafood, meat, desserts, and brunch. All focus on flavor yet rely on a minimal number of ingredients that don't take a lot of time and effort to prepare. . . . Dotted with culinary reminiscences both personal and professional, this book shows Vongerichten at his simple best and offers his many fans the opportunity to cook and enjoy his favorite meals without being chained to the kitchen for hours." Publ Wkly

Koenig, Leah

Modern Jewish cooking; recipes & customs for today's kitchen. Leah Koenig ; photographs by Sang An. Chronicle Books 2014 352 p. color illustrations (hardcover) $35 **641.5**
   1. Cookbooks 2. Jewish cooking
   ISBN 1452127484; 9781452127484

                               LC 2014012075

This cookbook, by Leah Koenig, with photographs by Sang An, "shares 175 recipes showcasing handmade, seasonal, vegetable-forward dishes. Classics of Jewish culinary culture--such as latkes, matzoh balls, challah, and hamantaschen--are updated with smart techniques and vibrant spices." (Publisher's note)

"The beautiful photography, pleasing layout on heavy paper, and excellent recipes make this a fine gift book as well as a suitable purchase for cookbook collections, especially in communities with large Jewish populations." LJ

Krieger, Ellie

You have it made! delicious, healthy do-ahead meals. Ellie Krieger ; photography by Quentin Bacon. Houghton Mifflin Harcourt 2016 352 p. chiefly color illustrations (paper over board) $30   **641.5**
   1. Quick and easy cooking 2. Make-ahead cooking
   ISBN 9780544579309

                               LC 2015028798

This cookbook, by Ellie Krieger, is "devoted to . . . make-ahead meals. . . . Her recipes . . . can all be prepared ahead of time, making putting food on the table that much easier. Each recipe includes instructions for refrigerating and/or freezing as well as storing and reheating directions. With exciting dishes like the Pumpkin Spice Overnight Oats in Jars and the Herbed Salmon Salad, you'll be able to have meals ready days in advance." (Publisher's note)

"Healthy cooking often requires many steps and a reliance on daily visits to farmers' markets, but Krieger's new collection makes truly nourishing food more accessible to the average household." Pub Wkly

Ladner, Mark

The **Del** Posto cookbook; by Mark Ladner. Grand Central Pub 2016 239 p. color illustrations (ebook) $150; $50 **641.5**
   1. Italian cooking
   ISBN 9781455569298; 1455561541; 9781455561544

                               LC 2016047628

This cookbook, by Mark Ladner, "redefines what excellent Italian Cooking in America can be. With a focus on regional Italian ingredients and tradition, Ladner has chosen recipes that bring together flavors from the old country, but in sophisticated new ways, like: Fried Calamari with Spicy Caper Butter Sauce; Red Wine Risotto with Carrot Puree; Monkfish Piccata, Veal Braciole, and Ricotta-Chocolate Tortino." (Publisher's note)

"In addition to a thorough index, Ladner provides a welcome rarity: an allergen guide, three pages of charts listing all the recipes and the common allergens they include." Pub Wkly

Lagasse, Emeril, 1959-

Essential Emeril; favorite recipes and hard-won wisdom from a life in the kitchen. by Emeril Lagasse. Oxmoor House 2015 304 p. color illustrations $29.95   **641.5**
   1. Cooking

ISBN 0848744780; 9780848744786

LC 2015944368

In this cookbook, chef Emeril Lagasse "presents his favorite recipes, best-kept cooking secrets, and behind-the-scenes stories from his life in the kitchen. Discover more than 130 iconic dishes . . . each tested and perfected for today's home cook. . . . Anecdotes reveal the inspiration behind each recipe, with cameos from A-list names including Mario Batali, Roy Choi, and Nobu Matsuhira, alongside memories of family, friends, and early influences such as Julia Child and Charlie Trotter." (Publisher's note)

"More advanced than some of his other titles, Lagasse's latest showcases his skill. Emeril fans will savor these delicious and iconic dishes." LJ

Lang, Adam Perry

Serious barbecue; smoke, char, baste, and brush your way to great outdoor cooking. [by] Adam Perry Lang, with J.J. Goode and Amy Vogler. Hyperion Books 2009 390p il $35   **641.5**
    1. Barbecue cooking
    ISBN 978-1-4013-2306-6

LC 2009-1765

The author's "definition of barbecue includes grilling as well as 'low and slow cooking,' and he presents a wide variety of tasty recipes here, along with a detailed introduction to barbecue basics and many useful sidebars on techniques and other tips. Highly recommended for all collections." Libr J

Lawson, Nigella, 1960-

How to Eat; The Pleasures and Principles of Good Food. Nigella Lawson. John Wiley 2002 474 p. $35   **641.5**
    1. Cooking 2. Cookery
    ISBN 0471257508; 9780471257509

This cookbook, by celebrity chef Nigella Lawson, is an "all-purposed cookbook, brimming with easygoing mealtime strategies and 350 mouthwatering recipes, from a truly sublime Tarragon French Roast Chicken to a totally decadent Chocolate Raspberry Pudding Cake." (Publisher's note)

Nigella express; good food, fast. photographs by Lis Parsons. Hyperion 2007 390p il $35   **641.5**
    1. Cooking
    ISBN 978-1-4013-2243-4; 1-4013-2243-3

"Recipes in this book run the gamut from retro crepe suzettes to modern favorites like quesadillas and smoothies; and from orange French toast for breakfast to cocktail nibbles for a party. In the interest of speed Lawson uses prepared ingredients, but they're the ones many of us use already, like mayonnaise from a jar or frozen puff pastry. And if her tastes are sometimes nostalgically British (Eton mess, roly poly pudding) she also has a whole chapter on quick Tex-Mex food." WeightWatchers.com

Simply Nigella; feel good food. Nigella Lawson ; photographs by Keiko Oikawa. Flatiron Books 2015 416 p. color illustrations (hardcover) $35   **641.5**
    1. Cooking 2. Well-being 3. Comfort food
    ISBN 1250073758; 9781250073754

LC 2015036267

This cookbook by Nigella Lawson "taps into the rhythms of our cooking lives with recipes that are uncomplicated and relaxed yet always satisfying. From quick and calm workday dinners (Miso Salmon; Cauliflower & Cashew Nut Curry) to stress-free ideas when feeding a crowd (Chicken Traybake with Bitter Orange & Fennel) to the instant joy of bowlfood for cozy nights on the sofa (Thai Noodles with Cinnamon and Shrimp), here is food guaranteed to make everyone feel good." (Publisher's note)

"Home cooks who love planning relaxed meals by whim will be well served by Lawson's latest, which offers a winning selection of recipes for all occasions." Library Journal

Le, Stephanie

Easy Gourmet; Awesome Recipes Anyone Can Cook. by Stephanie Le. St. Martin's Press 2014 240 p. color illustrations $21.99   **641.5**
    1. Cooking 2. Cookbooks 3. Quick and easy cooking
    ISBN 1624140629; 9781624140624

This cookbook, by Stephanie Le, "is full of updated modern twists on your favorite classics like Chicken and Waffles, Maple-Glazed Duck, Miso Cod and Quinoa, and Sriracha Hot Wings. Her must-have recipes cover every meal and everything in between, all paired with stunning photography and clean, modern design." (Publisher's note)

"Simple recipes, attractive photographs, an easy-to-read layout, and a functional lie-flat binding make this a great choice for young and aspiring cooks, small families, and anyone looking for easy meal ideas." LJ

Lederman, Matthew

Forks over knives family; Every Parent's Guide to Raising Healthy, Happy Kids on a Whole-Food, Plant-Based Diet. Alona Pulde, MD, Matthew Lederman, MD, With Marah Stets, And Brian Wendel ; Recipes by Darshana Thacker. Touchstone Books 2016 320 p. color illustrations (hardcover) $25.99   **641.5**
    1. Veganism 2. Cookbooks 3. Natural foods 4. Children -- Nutrition 5. Cooking -- Natural foods 6. Cooking (Natural foods) 7. Veganism -- Health aspects 8. Natural foods -- Health aspects
    ISBN 9781476753324; 9781476753331

LC 2016011411

This book in the Forks Over Knives series by Alona Pulde, Matthew Lederman, Marah Stets, and Brian Wendel, with recipes by Darshana Thacker, offers "a complete guide to a whole-food, plant-based lifestyle for your entire family, with more than 125 delicious kid-friendly recipes and tips for raising a whole-foods-loving child in a junk-food-laden world." (Publisher's note)

"Doctors Pulde and Lederman capably build on the philosophy laid out in their previous book (The Forks Over Knives Plan) that 'a whole-food, plant-based diet is the optimum choice a person can make.' " Pub Wkly

Includes bibliographical references and index

Lee, Cecilia Hae-Jin

Quick and easy Korean cooking; more than 70 everyday recipes. photographs by Julie Toy and Cecilia Hae-Jin Lee. Chronicle Books 2009 168p il pa $22.95   **641.5**
    1. Korean cooking
    ISBN 978-0-8118-6146-5

LC 2008-33629

"Quality, accessible, authentic Korean cookbooks are hard to come by. Ably filling that gap is [this book]. . . . It's filled with more than 70 recipes, most of which only call for about six ingredients. If you're skeptical that such simple recipes can produce the flavor bombs that are Korean dishes, know that three recipes were tested, and all worked perfectly as written. Each one was lively with the flavors of garlic, chiles, soy sauce, and sesame." Village Voice

Lee, Jennifer Tyler

The **52** new foods challenge; a family cooking adventure

for each week of the year. by Jennifer Tyler Lee. Penguin Group USA 2014 316 p. $20   **641.5**

1. Cooking 2. Parenting

ISBN 1583335560; 9781583335567

IACP Cookbook Award Finalist: Children, Youth and Family (2015)

In this book, author Jennifer Tyler Lee "gives parents practical tips to dramatically change the way their families eat. Her helpful advice . . . will show parents how to start eating healthy every week of the year. Each week offers a healthy new food to try, from artichokes to zucchini, and includes easy recipes and fun activities to work on as a family-- from learning to cook together to enjoying the farmers' market to even experimenting with growing your own food." (Publisher's note)

"A fun way to engage children in creating meals and trying new things." LJ

Lee, Matthew

★ The **Lee** Bros. southern cookbook; stories and recipes for southerners and would-be southerners. [by] Matt Lee and Ted Lee; color photography by Gentl & Hyers. W.W. Norton 2006 589p il $35   **641.5**

1. Southern cooking

ISBN 978-0-393-05781-2; 0-393-05781-X

LC 2006-22745

This "cookbook begins with a collection of drink recipes, from sweet tea to potent planters' punch. To accompany these beverages, the Lee brothers array a long series of snack and party foods. A section on preserves and pickles documents some rarely seen regional treats, such as Jerusalem artichoke relish. Meats, seafood, sweets, and breads round out the book. Every recipe has a story attached, and the large format makes for easy reading." Booklist

Leidich, Shari Koolik

Two Moms in the Raw; simple, clean, irresistible recipes for your family's health. Shari Koolik Leidich ; photography by Iain Bagwell. Rux Martin/Houghton Mifflin Harcourt 2015 288 p. color illustrations (hardback) $22   **641.5**

1. Cookbooks 2. Quick and easy cooking 3. Cooking -- Natural foods 4. Raw foods 5. Cooking (Natural foods) 6. Raw food diet -- Recipes 7. Two Moms in the Raw (Firm)

ISBN 0544253256; 9780544253254

LC 2014036934

This raw, cooked and gluten-free cookbook, by Shari Koolik Leidich, offers "130-plus dishes, like Brunchy Poached Eggs on Spinach with Roasted Red Pepper Sauce, or Plum and Tatsoi Salad. . . . Indulgent snacks like Creamy Olive and Artichoke Dip and Butternut-Lemongrass Soup satisfy cravings, and chicken and fish . . . come bolstered with plenty of raw produce and grains. Desserts ditch processed sugar in favor of natural sweeteners and power nutrients." (Publisher's note)

"Home cooks may be daunted by her inclusive list of basic "exotics"—including gomaiso, ashwagandha, coconut aminos, and psyllium husks—but her kid-friendly 'coconutty' chicken breasts and raw key lime pie bring a fun nutritional boost to the family table." Pub Wkly

Includes bibliographical references (page 276) and index

Leite, David

The **new** Portuguese table; exciting flavors from Europe's western coast. photographs by Nuno Correia. Clarkson Potter 2009 256p il $32.50   **641.5**

1. Portuguese cooking

ISBN 978-0-307-39441-5; 0-307-39441-7

LC 2008-51283

The author "begins by outlining Portugal's diverse regional cuisines

and then describes traditional ingredients. From there it is a straightforward listing of appetizers, soups, fish, meat, poultry, vegetable/egg/rice dishes, breads, sweets, liqueurs, and condiments, with approximately 150 recipes overall. . . . Full of delicious-sounding recipes, this title is sure to appeal to adventurous cooks wanting to try a new ethnic cuisine and will also be popular with Portuguese American communities." Libr J

Notes on a Banana; A Memoir of Food, Love, and Manic Depression. by David Leite. HarperCollins 2017 272 p. $26.99   **641.5**

1. Mental illness 2. Portuguese Americans

ISBN 0062414372; 9780062414373

LC 2017007293

This memoir, by David Leite, is a "story of family, food, mental illness, and sexual identity. Born into a family of Azorean immigrants, David Leite grew up in the 1960s in a devoutly Catholic, blue-collar, food-crazed Portuguese home in Fall River, Massachusetts. A clever and determined dreamer with a vivid imagination and a flair for the dramatic, . . . David also struggled with the emotional devastation of manic depression." (Publisher's note)

"In this coming-of-age story and chronicle of self-acceptance, Leite impressively finds honesty and humor in the darkest of circumstances, making this a strong debut memoir. A brave and moving tale of food, family, and psychology." Kirkus

Levine, Sarabeth

Sarabeth's good morning cookbook; Breakfast, Brunch, and Baking. by Sarabeth Levine. Random House Inc 2015 282 p. color illustrations $40   **641.5**

1. Baking 2. Brunches 3. Breakfasts

ISBN 0847846385; 9780847846382

In this cookbook, author Sarabeth Levine "shares her most beloved breakfast and brunch recipes. . . . A comprehensive guide to morning meals, this . . . book covers the dishes everyone desires. Sarabeth's signature pancakes and muffins are quick enough for weekdays, while her quiches and coffee cakes are guaranteed to impress weekend guests. In addition to her sophisticated twists on the standards, Sarabeth surprises with such innovative breakfast treats as morning cookies." (Publisher's note)

Lewis, Edna

★ The **taste** of country cooking; [with a foreword by Alice Waters] 30th anniversary ed.; Knopf 2006 xxi, 268p il $22.95   **641.5**

1. Southern cooking

ISBN 0-307-26560-9; 978-0-307-26560-9

First published 1976

"Recipes are categorized by the four seasons and are ones . . . [the author] grew up with in a small Virginia farming community (personal reminiscences about her family life appear throughout the text)." Booklist

Liddon, Angela

The **oh** she glows cookbook; over 100 vegan recipes to glow from the inside out. Angela Liddon. Avery, a member of Penguin Group (USA) 2016 352 p. color illustrations (print; alk. paper) $27   **641.5**

1. Veganism 2. Cookbooks 3. Vegetarian cooking 4. Vegan cooking

ISBN 9781583335741; 1583335749

LC 2016009038

This cookbook, by Angela Liddon, presents collected recipes taken from the author's "blog, ohsheglows.com, to spread the word about her journey to health and the powerful transformation that food can make. . . . [This book] is packed with more than 100 delicious recipes such as go-to breakfasts, protein-packed snacks, hearty entrées, and decadent desserts." (Publisher's note)

"Liddon's authentic voice and candidly shared successes will motivate nonvegans to try healthy recipes." LJ

Includes bibliographical references and index

Lim, Allen

Feed zone portables; a cookbook of on-the-go food for athletes. Biju Thomas & Allen Lim. VeloPress 2013 xv, 271 p.p color illustrations (hardback) $24.95   **641.5**

1. Cookbooks 2. Athletes -- Nutrition 3. Snack foods
ISBN 1937715000; 9781937715007

LC 2013003073

In this cookbook, author "[Allen] Lim joined professional chef Biju Thomas to make eating delicious and practical. . . . Their groundbreaking 'Feed Zone Cookbook' brought the favorite recipes of the pros to everyday athletes. In [this,] their new cookbook . . . , Chef Biju and Dr. Lim offer 75 all-new portable food recipes for cyclists, runners, triathletes, mountain bikers, climbers, hikers, and backpackers." (Publisher's note)

Link, Donald

Real Cajun; rustic home cooking from Donald Link's Louisiana. [by] Donald Link with Paula Disbrowe; photographs by Chris Granger. Clarkson Potter Publishers 2009 255p il $35   **641.5**

1. Cooking -- Louisiana
ISBN 978-0-307-39581-8; 0-307-39581-2

LC 2008-36989

"Link shares the fare he ate growing up on the bayou, as well as what he cooks for family, friends and funerals. Some recipes are aspirationally insane—fried chicken and andouille gumbo, or 'game day' choucroute with sausage, tasso and duck confit—while others I simply aspire to make, like a fried oyster and bacon sandwich (bacon recipe included), and Link's outstanding boudin, which he also uses as a heart-stopping beignet filling. The tone is easygoing, the explanations clear." N Y Times Book Rev

Lohman, Sarah

Eight Flavors; The Untold Story of American Cuisine. Sarah Lohman. Simon & Schuster 2016 288 p. illustrations (ebook) $18.99; $26.99   **641.5**

1. American cooking -- History 2. Eating customs -- United States -- History
ISBN 9781476753980; 1476753954; 9781476753959

LC 2016040059

This book, by Sarah Lohman, shows "that American food is united by eight flavors: black pepper, vanilla, curry powder, chili powder, soy sauce, garlic, MSG, and Sriracha. . . . Lohman sets out to explore how these influential ingredients made their way to the American table. . . . [She] introduces the explorers, merchants, botanists, farmers, writers, and chefs whose choices came to define the American palate." (Publisher's note)

"A tantalizing look at flavors of the American table that foodies will absolutely devour." Kirkus

Includes bibliographical references (pages 257-260) and index.

Lukins, Sheila

The **Silver** Palate cookbook; Julee Rosso & Sheila Lukins with Michael McLaughlin ; photographs by Patrick Tregenza and Susan Goldman ; illustrations by Sheila Lukins. Workman Pub Co 2007 xi, 452 p.p col. ill. (pbk) $22.95   **641.5**

1. Cookbooks 2. American cooking 3. Cooking
ISBN 9780761145981; 9780761145974; 0761145974

LC 2007276244

James Beard Cookbook Hall of Fame (1992)
IACP Culinary Classics Book Award (2014)

This cookbook, by Julee Rosso & Sheila Lukins, is a 25th anniversary edition that "brings a new passion for food and entertaining into American homes. Its 350 . . . dishes make every occasion special, and its recipes, featuring vibrant, pure ingredients, are a pleasure to cook. Brimming with kitchen wisdom, cooking tips, information about domestic and imported ingredients, menus, quotes, and lore, this . . . book feels as fresh and exciting as the day it was first published." (Publisher's note)

Lundy, Ronni

Victuals; An Appalachian Journey, with Recipes. Ronni Lundy ; photographs by Johnny Autry. Clarkson Potter/Publishers 2016 320 p. illustrations (some color) (hardback) $32.50; (ebook) $65   **641.5**

1. American cooking 2. Appalachian Region 3. Cooking, American 4. Cooking -- Appalachian Region, Southern 5. Appalachian Region, Southern -- Social life and customs
ISBN 9780804186742; 9780804186759

LC 2016013454

This book, by Ronni Lundy, "explores the diverse and complex food scene of the Mountain South through recipes, stories, traditions, and innovations. Each chapter explores a specific defining food or tradition of the region--such as salt, beans, corn (and corn liquor). The essays introduce readers to their rich histories and the farmers, curers, hunters, and chefs who define the region's contemporary landscape." (Publisher's note)

"Fans of locally sourced foods and Southern cooking will find a lot to like here, as Lundy does a terrific job of showcasing Appalachia's breadth and depth." Pub Wkly

Madison, Deborah

★ **In** my kitchen; A Collection of New and Favorite Vegetarian Recipes. by Deborah Madison. Ten Speed Press 2017 296 p. (hardcover; alk. paper) $32.50   **641.5**

1. Cookbooks 2. Cooking -- Vegetables 3. Cooking
ISBN 9780399578885

LC 2016038957

This book, by Deborah Madison, "is a vegetable-forward cookbook organized alphabetically and featuring recipes like Roasted Jerusalem Artichoke Soup with Sunflower Sprouts; Fennel Shaved with Tarragon and Walnuts; and Olive Oil, Almond, and Blood Orange Cake. With dozens of tips for building onto, scaling back, and creating menus around, Deborah's recipes have a modular quality that makes them particularly easy to use." (Publisher's note)

"One glance will quickly show why the dishes here are Madison's go-to meals, and they will soon become readers' favorites as well." Pub Wkly

Includes bibliographical references and index

The **new** vegetarian cooking for everyone; Deborah Madison. Ten Speed Press 2014 665 p. $40   **641.5**

1. Cookbooks 2. Vegetarian cooking
ISBN 1607745534; 9781607745532

LC 2013046540

Originally published: New York; Broadway Books, 1997

This cookbook, by Deborah Madison, "originally published in 1997,

.... has endured as one of the world's most popular vegetarian cookbooks, winning both a James Beard Foundation award and the IACP Julia Child Cookbook of the Year Award. Now, . . . [this edition] picks up where that culinary legacy left off, . . . including a new introduction, more than 200 new recipes, and comprehensive, updated information on vegetarian and vegan ingredients." (Publisher's note)

★ **Vegetarian** cooking for everyone; 10th anniversary ed; Broadway Books 2007 742p il $40   **641.5**
  1. Vegetarian cooking
  ISBN 978-0-7679-2747-5; 0-7679-2747-8
                                     LC 2007-10075
  First published 1997
  Following information on ingredients and techniques, the recipes focus "mainly on vegetables and grains, aiming at flavor and variety, both often arrived at via assorted ethnic approaches." Publ Wkly

Makan, Chetna

The **Cardamom** Trail; Chetna Bakes With Flavours of the East. by Chetna Makan. Octopus Pub Group 2016 240 p. color illustrations $29.99   **641.5**
  1. Spices 2. Indian cooking
  ISBN 1784721298; 9781784721299
  In this cookbook, by Chetna Makan, "Indian influences will transform your baking from the familiar to the exotic, from the ordinary to the extraordinary. Discover rare but precious traditional bakes from India, as well as new spice-infused recipes. Delve into the history of Indian herbs and spices and learn how to match foods and flavors." (Publisher's note)
  "Infuse the vibrant flavors of India into your baked goods with this beautiful volume of recipes redolent with herbs, spices, and surprising ingredients." Booklist

The **make**-ahead cook; 8 smart strategies for dinner tonight. by the editors at America's Test Kitchen. America's Test Kitchen 2014 328 p. illustrations (chiefly color) $26.95   **641.5**
  1. Dinners 2. Cookbooks 3. Dinners and dining 4. Make-ahead cooking
  ISBN 1936493845; 9781936493845
                                   LC 2014014386
  This cookbook, by the editors at America's Test Kitchen, "reinvents make-ahead cooking so that you can cook when you want and still eat well every night of the week. While most make-ahead cookbooks focus only on stocking your freezer, this book takes a new approach, with 8 strategies that show you how a little advance work and planning can reap huge benefits." (Publisher's note)
  "Indispensable for busy families and anyone who has limited time to cook during the week." LJ

Mallmann, Francis

Seven fires; grilling the Argentine way. [by] Francis Mallmann, with Peter Kaminsky. Artisan 2009 278p il $35 **641.5**
  1. Outdoor cooking 2. Barbecue cooking 3. Argentine cooking
  ISBN 978-1-57965-354-5
                                   LC 2008-37367
  "Mallmann cooks with the elegant purity achieved only after attaining a mastery of complicated food. . . . He also reconnects us to the primal simplicity and visceral pleasure of cooking over a fire—though his recipes can be made over charcoal or in a grill pan, too." N Y Times Book Rev

Mason, Taymer

Caribbean vegan; meat-free, egg-free, dairy-free authentic island cuisine for every occasion. by Taymer Mason. Expanded second edition The Experiment 2016 311 p. color illustrations (pbk.) $24.95   **641.5**
  1. Vegan cooking 2. Caribbean cooking 3. Cooking, Caribbean
  ISBN 9781615193615; 9781615193608
                                   LC 2016020831
  This cookbook, by Taymer Mason, "shares 75 all-new recipes, including Caribbean Sushi, Brule Jol (avocado salad), and Breadfruit Ravioli with Calabaza Squash Filling. Plus, she explains the key kitchen skills she learned growing up: how to cut breadfruit, make your own cassava flour, choose a ripe coconut, and more." (Publisher's note)
  "Mason invites home cooks to sample a rich array of dishes, from callaloo fritters to . . . guava bread pudding with coconut rum sauce." LJ
  Includes bibliographical references and index

Massaad, Barbara Abdeni

Man'oushé; inside the Lebanese street corner bakery. Barbara Abdeni Massaad ; photography by Barbara Abdeni Massaad and Raymond Yazbeck. Interlink Books, An imprint of Interlink Publishing Group, Inc. 2014 200 p. color illustrations $30   **641.5**
  1. Cookbooks 2. Lebanese cooking 3. Cooking, Lebanese
  ISBN 1566569281; 9781566569286
                                   LC 2013032109
  This cookbook, by Barbara Abdeni Massaad, "is dedicated entirely to the art of creating the perfect man'oushé. With over 70 simple recipes, it offers you a way to enjoy these typical [Lebanese] pies traditionally baked in street corner bakeries in the comfort of your own home." (Publisher's note)
  "A reasonably adept home baker will find Massaad's recipes easy to follow. . . . The book's full-color photographs bring into focus not just the foods but also the lively characters who constitute a remarkably diverse nation." Booklist

McDonnell, Imen

The **Farmette** cookbook; recipes and adventures from my life on an Irish farm. Imen McDonnell. Roost Books 2016 361 p. color illustrations (hardcover; alk. paper) $35   **641.5**
  1. Ireland 2. Country life 3. Irish cooking 4. Cooking, Irish 5. Country life -- Ireland
  ISBN 9781611802047
                                   LC 2015026646
  This cookbook "documents Imen McDonnell's extraordinary Irish country cooking journey, which began the moment she fell in love with an Irish farmer and moved across the Atlantic to County Limerick. This book's collection of 150 recipes and colorful stories chronicles nearly a decade-long adventure of learning to feed a family (and several hungry farmers) while adjusting to her new home (and nursing a bit of homesickness)." (Publisher's note)
  "An outstanding debut, with just the right amount of sentimentality." LJ

McFadden, Joshua

★ **Six** seasons; a new way with vegetables. Joshua McFadden with Martha Holmberg ; foreword by Barbara Damrosch and Eliot Coleman. Artisan 2017 397 p. illustrations (chiefly color) (hardcover) $35   **641.5**
  1. Seasonal cooking 2. Cooking -- Vegetables 3. Cookbooks
  ISBN 9781579657789; 9781579656317
                                   LC 2016038070
  James Beard Award: Vegetable-Focused Cooking (2018)
  This book, by Joshua McFadden with Martha Holmberg, highlights

"the evolving attributes of vegetables throughout their growing seasons. . . . Each chapter begins with recipes featuring raw vegetables at the start of their season. As weeks progress, McFadden turns up the heat--grilling and steaming, then moving on to sautés, pan roasts, braises, and stews. His ingenuity is on display in 225 revelatory recipes that celebrate flavor at its peak." (Publisher's note)

"McFadden's debut cookbook is an invaluable resource for all things veggie." Booklist

McGuire, Larry

★ **Elizabeth** Street Cafe; breakfast lunch dinner sweets. Tom Moorman, Larry McGuire, with Julia Turshen. Phaidon Press Limited 2017 240 p. $39.95 **641.5**
1. Restaurants 2. Cooking, Vietnamese
ISBN 0714873950; 9780714873954

"Elizabeth Street Café – a celebrated eatery with a devoted following – features French-inspired Vietnamese cooking. Chefs Tom Moorman and Larry McGuire share 100 recipes of beautiful and delicious Vietnamese fare and French baked goods – from Spicy Breakfast Fried Rice and Eggs to Green Jungle Curry Noodles, and Palm Sugar Ice Cream to Toasted Coconut Cream Puffs." (Publisher's note)

Meehan, Peter

WD ~50; the cookbook. Wylie Dufresne with Peter Meehan ; photography by Eric Medsker. Ecco, an imprint of HarperCollins Publishers 2017 343 p. color illustrations (hardcover) $75 **641.5**
1. Cooking 2. Restaurants -- New York (State) -- New York
ISBN 9780062318534; 9780062318541; 0062318535

"The first cookbook from one of the world's most groundbreaking chefs and a pioneering restaurant on the Lower East Side—the story of Wylie Dufresne's wd~50 and the dishes that made it famous." (Publisher's note)

"Dufresne himself is a rock star of the kitchen, and his recipes here are clever and inspirational." Pub Wkly

Miglore, Kristen

Food52 genius recipes; 100 recipes that will change the way you cook. Kristen Miglore ; photography by James Ransom. Ten Speed Press 2015 272 p. color illustrations (hardback) $35 **641.5**
1. Cooking
ISBN 1607747979; 9781607747970

LC 2014034413
IACP Cookbook Award Winner: Compilations (2016)
This cookbook presents what author "Kristen Miglore calls genius recipes. Passed down from the cookbook authors, chefs, and bloggers who made them legendary, these foolproof recipes rethink cooking tropes, solve problems, get us talking, and make cooking more fun. Every week, Kristen features one such recipe and explains just what's so brilliant about it in the James Beard Award-nominated Genius Recipes column on Food52. Here, in this book, she compiles 100 of the most essential ones." (Publisher's note)

"Miglore's addition to Food52's growing list of cookbooks is a treat for readers who enjoy casual gourmet food." LJ
Genius recipes

Miller, Laura

Raw, vegan, not gross; all vegan and mostly raw recipes for people who love to eat. Laura Miller. Flatiron Books 2016 215 p. color illustrations (hardback) $25.99 **641.5**
1. Veganism 2. Cookbooks 3. Vegetarian cooking 4. Raw foods

5. Vegan cooking
ISBN 1250066905; 9781250066909

LC 2016014385
This cookbook, by Laura Miller, "offers more than a hundred entirely vegan and mostly raw recipes for all people who want to eat deliciously. . . . [It seeks to] engage your taste buds with strengthening breakfasts . . . , easy weeknight dinners . . . , crowd-pleasing party food . . . , irresistible drinks & desserts . . . , and many more nutritious, satisfying dishes that are as beautiful and fun to make as they are healthful." (Publisher's note)

Moore, Russell

This is Camino; Russell Moore and Alison Hopelain with Chris Colin and Maria Zizka ; photographs by Yoko Takahashi. Ten Speed Press 2015 272 p. color illustrations (hardcover) $35 **641.5**
1. California 2. Restaurants 3. American cooking 4. Camino (Restaurant) 5. Cooking, American -- California style 6. Cooking -- California -- San Francisco
ISBN 1607747286; 9781607747284

LC 2015013757
This cookbook, by Russell Moore and Alison Hopelain, is "about the unique, fire-based cooking approach and ingredient-focused philosophy of Camino restaurant in Oakland, CA, with approximately 100 recipes." (Publisher's note)

"A compelling look at an innovative restaurant. Aspiring chefs and advanced cooks may also enjoy Suzanne Goin's The A.O.C. Cookbook and Nancy Silverton's The Mozza Cookbook (also from California restaurants)." LJ

Moosewood Restaurant cooks at home; fast and easy recipes for any day. the Moosewood Collective. Simon & Schuster 1994 416 p. ill. $25 **641.5**
1. Cookbooks 2. Vegetarian cooking 3. Cooking -- Natural foods 4. Moosewood Restaurant 5. Cooking (Natural foods)
ISBN 0671679929; 0671879545; 9780671679927

LC 93039126
James Beard Award (1995)
Written by the Moosewood Collective, this book features "over 150 carefully honed and tested recipes calling for the best ingredients, accompanied by time-saving tips and planning suggestions, add up to a delicious whole-foods cuisine that is versatile and healthful and can be prepared with a minimum of effort." (Publisher's note)

Moosewood restaurant favorites; the 250 most-requested, naturally delicious recipes from one of America's best-loved restaurants. The Moosewood Collective. St. Martin's Press 2013 416 p. ill. (chiefly col.) (hardback) $29.99 **641.5**
1. Veganism 2. Vegetarian cooking 3. Cooking -- Vegetables 4. Cooking -- Natural foods 5. Moosewood Restaurant
ISBN 1250006252; 9781250006257

LC 2013013841
This book focuses on "Moosewood Restaurant, founded in 1973. . . . [It] contains 250 of their most requested recipes completely updated and revised to reflect the way they're cooked now--increasingly vegan and gluten-free, benefitting from fresh herbs, new varieties of vegetables, and the wholesome goodness of newly-rediscovered grains." (Publisher's note)

"This collection of some of Moosewood's cooks' and customers' most admired recipes has something for just about everyone." Booklist

The **Moosewood** Restaurant table; 250 brand-new recipes from the natural foods restaurant that revolutionized eating in America. The Moosewood Collective ; food photography by Al Karevy ; food styling by Patti Harville. St. Martin's Griffin 2017 xii, 402 p.p color illustrations (hardcover) $35   **641.5**
1. Vegetarian cooking 2. Vegan cooking 3. Pescatarian cooking 4. Moosewood Restaurant 5. Cooking (Natural foods) 6. Gluten-free diet -- Recipes
ISBN 9781466885974; 9781250074331

LC 2017032064

This cookbook, by The Moose Collective, photographed by Al Karevy, presents "over 250 brand new, never-before-published recipes. With the restaurant now in its fifth decade, the Moosewood chefs continue to remain faithful to the farm-to-table philosophy that has governed the restaurant since its founding, while also keeping an eye on today's gastro-trends. . . . Of course, a Moosewood cookbook wouldn't be complete without desserts like Turkish Coffee Brownies." (Publisher's note)

"Throughout, recipes are concise and confident, accompanied by helpful preparation tips and serving ideas. Whether vegetarian or not, home cooks looking for fresh inspiration will appreciate this book built on years of experience." Booklist

Morales, Bonnie Frumkin

Kachka; a return to Russian cooking. Bonnie Frumkin Morales with Deena Prichep ; photography by Leela Cyd. Flatiron Books 2017 389 p. color illustrations (hardcover) $40 **641.5**
1. Cookbooks 2. Russian cooking 3. Cooking, Russian 4. Kachka (Restaurant)
ISBN 9781250089205; 9781250087607

LC 2017022390

This cookbook, by Bonnie Frumkin Morales with Deena Prichep, "covers the vivid world of Russian cuisine. More than 100 recipes show how easy it is to eat, drink, and open your heart in Soviet-inspired style, from the celebrated restaurant that is changing how America thinks about Russian food. The recipes in this book set a communal table with nostalgic Eastern European dishes . . . and give new and exciting twists to current food trends like pickling . . . and bone broths." (Publisher's note)

"This fantastic cookbook from the chef at Kachka in Portland, Ore., is by turns funny, moving, informative, and appetite-whetting." Pub Wkly

Morgan, Jeff

The **covenant** kitchen; food and wine for the new Jewish table. Jeff Morgan and Jodie Morgan. Schocken Books, OU Press 2015 262 p. color illustrations (hardback) $35 **641.5**
1. Kosher food 2. Jewish cooking 3. Food and wine pairing
ISBN 0805243259; 9780805243253

LC 2014025769

Authors Jeff Morgan and Jodie Morgan present "the ultimate kosher cookbook for food lovers, with more than one hundred mouthwatering recipes complete with suggested wine pairings, from the veteran cookbook authors and owners of the acclaimed Covenant Winery in California. [It] includes informative sidebars on how to select the right wine for any occasion, on the requirements for kosher food preparation, and on how to prepare the basics." (Publisher's note)

"This hip, fresh cookbook is just the thing for foodies desiring to keep kosher while elevating their repertoire of dishes for the benefit of themselves or their dinner guests—and there's plenty to interest cooks who lack a kosher kitchen as well." LJ

Morimoto, Masaharu, 1955-

Mastering the Art of Japanese Home Cooking; Masaharu Morimoto. HarperCollins 2016 288 p. color illustrations $45.00   **641.5**
1. Cookbooks 2. Japanese cooking
ISBN 0062344382; 9780062344380

LC 2016048973

This book, by Masaharu Morimoto, "introduces readers to the healthy, flavorful, surprisingly simple dishes favored by Japanese home cooks. Chef Morimoto reveals the magic of authentic Japanese food—the way that building a pantry of half a dozen easily accessible ingredients allows home cooks access to hundreds of delicious recipes, empowering them to adapt and create their own inventions." (Publisher's note)

"Soups, stir-fry, and noodles each have their own chapter and a section on the underappreciated art of simmering features fish simmered with sake, soy sauce, and sugar, as well as slow-cooked pork belly with beer-teriyaki glaze. The 177 color photos range from utilitarian instruction on flipping a Japanese omelet to an artistic interpretation of rice grains clustered in the hand of the chef." Pub Wkly

Includes bibliographical references (pages 261-262) and index.

Morris, Julie

Superfood Kitchen; Cooking with Nature's Most Amazing Foods. Sterling Pub Co Inc 2012 256 p.   **641.5**
1. Cookbooks 2. Nutrition 3. Cooking -- Natural foods
ISBN 145490352X; 9781454903529

This cookbook, by Julie Morris, presents "dishes . . . entirely composed of plant-based, nutrient-dense, and whole foods that energize, nourish, and taste delicious. Each recipe . . . combines natural ingredients that deliver . . . antioxidants, essential fatty acids (like omega-3), minerals, vitamins, and more. The . . . superfood meals--from Goldenberry Pancakes to Quinoa Spaghetti with Cashew Cream Sauce and Chard--will make you feel as good as they taste." (Publisher's note)

Moskowitz, Isa Chandra

The **superfun** times vegan holiday cookbook; Entertaining for Absolutely Every Occasion. Isa Chandra Moskowitz. Little, Brown & Co. 2016 448 p. color illustrations (ebook) $96; $32   **641.5**
1. Cookbooks 2. Vegan cooking 3. Holiday cooking
ISBN 9780316344586; 9780316221894

LC 2016941207

This cookbook, by Isa Chandra Moskowitz, provides "tasty vegan recipes for Cinnamon Apple Crepes, Cheeseburger Pizza, Biscuits and Gravy, Churro Biscotti, and so much more. . . . Isa provides everything you need to get your party started, from finger food and appetizers to casseroles, roasts, and dozens of special sides. Then comes a throng of cakes, cookies, cobblers, loaves, pies, and frozen treats to make you feel like the best . . . vegan cook in the world." (Publisher's note)

"Readers of the author's other books (Vegan with a Vengeance) will want this, but all cooks looking for next-level flavor vegan dishes will enjoy as well." LJ

Vegan pie in the sky; 75 out-of-this-world recipes for pies, tarts, cobblers & more. [by] Isa Chandra Moskowitz & Terry Hope Romero. Da Capo Lifelong 2011 223p il pa $17 **641.5**
1. Pies 2. Vegetarian cooking
ISBN 978-0-7382-1274-6

The authors focus on "dessert in this collection of 75 egg, dairy and animal-free pies, cheesecakes, cobblers and tarts. . . . The duo deserves plaudits for their user-friendly approach as well as their ability to keep scarcer ingredients to a minimum. Bakers who fear they won't be able to recreate these will be happy to discover that once they've mastered a crust or two they'll be able to whip together a Strawberry Field Hand Pie, Chocolate Mousse Tart, or even a Coconut Cream with confidence." Publ Wkly

Moulton, Sara

Sara Moulton's Home Cooking 101; How to Make Everything Taste Better. by Sara Moulton. Oxmoor House 2016 368 p. color illustrations $35   **641.5**
    1. American cooking
ISBN 0848744411; 9780848744410

LC 2015956841

This cookbook, by Sara Moulton, "is packed with essential techniques, expert tips, and practical advice to sharpen your sense of taste and cultivate confidence in the kitchen. . . . Sara guide[s] readers through the fundamentals, then offers 150 hit recipes to illustrate, step-by-step, the time-tested methods that make each so delicious. You'll learn to navigate your stove, season like a pro, and add umami to a dish while discovering new ideas for weeknight dinners." (Publisher's note)

"Busy home cooks will find much to savor in this approachable, elegant collection of recipes." Pub Wkly

Includes indexes.

Myers, Amy

The **autoimmune** solution cookbook; over 150 delicious recipes to prevent and reverse the full spectrum of inflammatory symptoms and diseases. Amy Myers, M.D. HarperOne 2018 336 p. (hardback) $29.99   **641.5**
    1. Cookbooks 2. Autoimmune diseases -- Diet therapy 3. Autoimmune diseases -- Diet therapy -- Recipes
ISBN 0062853546; 9780062853547

LC 2018010173

"The companion cookbook to the revolutionary New York Times bestseller 'The Autoimmune Solution,' filled with more than 150 nutritious, easy-to-prepare, every day recipes to heal symptoms of inflammation and autoimmune disorders, including Graves' Disease, Psoriasis, Fibromyalgia, Lupus, Celiac disease, Hashimoto's thyroiditis, and Multiple sclerosis." (Publisher's note)

Nathan, Joan

★ **King** Solomon's table; a culinary exploration of Jewish cooking from around the world. Joan Nathan ; photographs by Gabriela Herman. Alfred A. Knopf 2017 xxviii, 382 p.p color illustrations (hardcover; alk. paper) $35   **641.5**
    1. Jewish cooking 2. Cookbooks
ISBN 9780385351140; 9780385351157

LC 2016047294

In this cookbook, by Joan Nathan, with photographs by Gabriela Herman, "the biblical King Solomon is said to have sent emissaries on land and sea to all corners of the ancient world, initiating a mass cross-pollination of culinary cultures that continues to bear fruit today. With Solomon's appetites and explorations in mind, in these pages . . . Nathan . . . gathers together more than 170 recipes, from Israel to Italy to India and beyond." (Publisher's note)

"This is a cookbook to be read and savored for its stories as much as its recipes. Nathan, with her passionate and unceasing search for Jewish cooking traditions, has made an important contribution to Jewish history and culture." Pub Wkly

Includes bibliographical references and index

Quiches, kugels, and couscous; my search for Jewish cooking in France. Alfred A. Knopf 2010 387p il $39.95; ebook

$40   **641.5**
    1. French cooking 2. Jewish cooking 3. Jews -- France
ISBN 978-0-307-26759-7; 978-0-307-59450-1 ebook

LC 2010-20280

"Nathan's multi-layered, narrative approach makes this treasury of tempting flavors an entertaining and compelling read." Publ Wkly

Includes bibliographical references

Nathan, Zoe

Breakfast at Huckleberry; recipes, stories, and secrets from our kitchen. by Zoe Nathan ; with Laurel Almerinda and Josh Loeb ; photographs by Matt Armendariz. Chronicle Books 2014 288 p. illustrations (chiefly color) $35   **641.5**
    1. Baking 2. Cookbooks 3. Breakfasts 4. Huckleberry (Restaurant)
ISBN 1452123527; 9781452123523

LC 2013037996

This cookbook, by Zoe Nathan, with Laurel Almerinda and Josh Loeb, "collects more than 115 recipes and more than 150 color photographs, including how-to sequences for mastering basics such as flaky dough and lining a cake pan. [The Los Angeles-based restaurant] Huckleberry's recipes span from sweet (rustic cakes, muffins, and scones) to savory (hot cereals, biscuits, and quiche)." (Publisher's note)

"Filled with entertaining behind-the-scenes stories and technical tips relayed in plain English, this cookbook will thrill meticulous bakers and Huckleberry's devotees." LJ

Neely, Pat

Down home with the Neelys; a Southern family cookbook. [by] Patrick Neely and Gina Neely; with Paula Disbrowe. Alfred A. Knopf 2009 278p il $27.95   **641.5**
    1. Barbecue cooking 2. Southern cooking
ISBN 978-0-307-26994-2; 0-307-26994-9

LC 2008-54393

This cookbook written by "husband-and-wife television personalities with their own Tennessee chain of barbecue joints . . . [is] full of 120 recipes that pull back the curtain on their award-winning seasonings, sauce, and fixings. Emphasizing their personal story and family recipes, this cookbook is brimming with down-home personality . . . and dishes that are 'simple, stylish, and not too fussy.'" Publ Wkly

New American Heart Association cookbook

The **new** American Heart Association cookbook; 8th ed.; Clarkson Potter 2010 xxi, 696p il $35   **641.5**
    1. Cooking 2. Low-cholesterol diet 3. Heart diseases -- Diet therapy
ISBN 978-0-307-40757-3

LC 2009-44692

First published 1973 with title: American Heart Association cookbook

"Each recipe comes with a breakdown of calories, protein content, carbohydrates, cholesterol, fats (broken down by saturated, polyunsaturated and monounsaturated) and sodium content, along with a table of dietary exchange. . . . This book remains a basic in many heart-conscious kitchens." Publ Wkly

★ The **new** essentials cookbook; a modern guide to better cooking. America's Test Kitchen. America's Test Kitchen 2018 496 p. color illustrations (hardcover) $40   **641.5**
    1. Cooking 2. Cookbooks
ISBN 9781945256042

LC 2018017355

In this cookbook from America's Test Kitchen, "you'll find the perfect roast chicken and a killer banana bread but also a Turkish-inspired tomato soup, luscious Chinese braised short ribs, and a set of wholesome grain bowls. A chapter on weeknight dinners offers smart paths to great flavor--from Bucatini with Peas, Kale, and Pancetta that cooks in one pot to a pizza that bakes in a skillet--including plenty of vegetarian options." (Publisher's note)

"The latest, super useful, approachable, and photo-laden cookbook from the team behind America's Test Kitchen will nudge curious but hesitant home cooks toward everyday recipes that are a little more complicated, and a lot more rewarding, than garden-variety easy fare." Booklist

The **New** York Times Jewish cookbook; more than 825 traditional and contemporary recipes from around the world. edited by Linda Amster; introduction by Mimi Sheraton. St. Martin's Press 2003 xxvi, 614p $35   **641.5**
1. Jewish cooking
ISBN 978-0-312-29093-1; 0-312-29093-4

                   LC 2002-68358
"Included here are hundreds of recipes from Jewish communities all over the world, reflecting Mimi Sheraton's introductory comment that Jewish food is 'the world's oldest fusion cuisine.' Recipes range from Persian Chicken Soup with Chickpea Dumplings to Alain Ducasse's Rib-Eye Steaks with Peppered Cranberry Marmalade to Fresh Corn and Red Pepper Blini. All the classics are here, too, and there's a separate chapter on 'Trimmings,' including an array of condiments and garnishes. . . . This is an essential purchase." Libr J

Nosrat, Samin
   ★ **Salt,** fat, acid, heat; mastering the elements of good cooking. by Samin Nosrat, illustrated by Wendy MacNaughton. Simon & Schuster 2017 473 p. color illustrations (hardcover; alk. paper) $35   **641.5**
1. Cooking 2. Cookbooks
ISBN 9781476753850; 9781476753836; 9781476753843

                   LC 2016040649
James Beard Award: General (2018)
This cookbook, by Samin Nosrat, illustrated by Wendy MacNaughton, "will teach and inspire a new generation of cooks how to confidently make better decisions in the kitchen and cook delicious meals with any ingredients, anywhere, at any time. . . . With charming narrative, illustrated walkthroughs, and a lighthearted approach to kitchen science, Samin demystifies the four elements of good cooking for everyone." (Publisher's note)

"This exceptional debut is sure to inspire greater confidence in readers and enable them to create better meals on their own." Pub Wkly
Includes bibliographical references (pages 441-444) and index.

Oliver, Jamie, 1975-
   Jamie Oliver's comfort food; The Ultimate Weekend Cookbook. by Jamie Oliver. HarperCollinsPublishers 2014 406 p. color illustrations, portraits $34.99   **641.5**
1. Cooking 2. Cookbooks
ISBN 0062305611; 9780062305619

                   LC 2015460582
This book, by celebrity chef Jamie Oliver, "brings together 100 ultimate comfort food recipes from around the world. . . . Recipes include everything from mighty moussaka, delicate gyoza with crispy wings, steaming ramen and katsu curry to super eggs Benedict, scrumptious sticky toffee pudding and tutti frutti pear tarte tatin." (Publisher's note)

   Jamie Oliver's cookbook Christmas; for the best Christmas ever. Jamie Oliver. Flatiron Books 2017 405 p. (hardcover)

$35   **641.5**
1. Christmas cooking
ISBN 1250146267; 9781250146250; 9781250146267

                   LC 2017032269
This cookbook, by Jamie Oliver, "is packed with all the classics you need for the big day and beyond, as well as loads of delicious recipes for edible gifts, party food, and new ways to love those leftovers. It's everything you need for the best Christmas ever. Inside you'll find all the classics as well as tasty alternatives." (Publisher's note)
Cookbook Christmas
Jamie Oliver's Christmas cookbook

Olsson, Nina
   ★ **Bowls** of goodness; vibrant vegetarian recipes full of nourishment. recipes and photography by Nina Olsson. Kyle Books 2017 192 p. $27.95   **641.5**
1. Vegetarian cooking
ISBN 1909487694; 9781909487697

                   LC 2017938382
"Inspired by home cooking and ingredients from around the world, Nina Olsson's eclectic mix of recipes—which are all vegetarian, and often vegan and gluten-free too—are based on her hugely popular blog, nourishatelier.com, and showcase plant based bowl food at its best. They include such indulgent and delectable dishes as Cosmic Green Smoothie, Loyal Lentil Chili, Laksa Lux Bowl, Watermelon Poke Bowl, and Almond-filled Dumplings in Blackberry Sauce." (Publisher's note)

Ortega, Simone
   1080 recipes; [by] Simone and Ines Ortega; illustrations, Javier Mariscal. Phaidon 2007 975p il $39.95   **641.5**
1. Spanish cooking
ISBN 978-0-7148-4836-5; 0-7148-4836-0
First published 1977 in Spain
"Something like the Joy of Cooking for the Spanish home cook, . . . [this book] includes recipes for both traditional regional fare and dishes inspired by a variety of other cuisines. . . . An essential purchase." Libr J

Oseland, James
   Saveur; The New Classics Cookbook: More Than 1,000 of the World's Best Recipes for Today's Kitchen. James Oseland. Simon & Schuster 2014 624 p. illustrations (some color) $40   **641.5**
1. Cooking 2. Cookbooks
ISBN 1616287357; 9781616287351
James Beard Foundation Award Nominee: General Cooking (2015)
IACP Cookbook Award Finalist: General (2015)
This cookbook, by James Oseland, presents several selections from the culinary magazine "Saveur." It "features more than 1,000 well-curated global recipes in an essential collection for home cooks everywhere. This . . . selection celebrates the brand's authority, heritage, and depth of worldwide culinary knowledge." (Publisher's note)

"Highly recommended for most collections and home cooks who'd like a contemporary, all-purpose kitchen reference." LJ

Ottolenghi, Yotam
   ★ **Jerusalem;** a cookbook. Yotam Ottolenghi, Sami Tamimi. Ten Speed Press 2012 318 p. (hardcover) $35.00 **641.5**
1. Cookbooks 2. Jewish cooking 3. Israeli cooking 4. Cooking, Middle Eastern 5. Jerusalem -- Description and travel
ISBN 1607743949; 9781607743958; 9781607743941

                   LC 2012017560
James Beard Foundation Award: International (2013).

This is a cookbook of recipes from Jerusalem. "London chefs and business partners [Yotam] Ottolenghi and [Sami] Tamimi both grew up in Jerusalem (the former in the Jewish west, the latter in the Arab east). Drawing on their childhood experiences for inspiration, they've updated traditional recipes (e.g., Falafel, Tabbouleh, Lamb Shawarma) to suit the lifestyles and preferences of modern home cooks." (Library Journal)

Nopi; the cookbook. Yotam Ottolenghi, Ramael Scully ; with Tara Wigley. Ten Speed Press 2015 352 p. color illustrations (hardback) $40 **641.5**
1. Cookbooks 2. Mediterranean cooking 3. Middle Eastern cooking 4. Nopi (Restaurant) 5. Cooking, Mediterranean 6. Cooking, Middle Eastern
ISBN 9781607746232; 9781607746249
LC 2015017809

This book, by Yotam Ottolenghi, Ramael Scully, with Tara Wigley, offers "a cookbook from acclaimed London restaurant Nopi, by . . . author Yotam Ottolenghi and Nopi head chef Ramael Scully. Pandan leaves meet pomegranate seeds, star anise meets sumac, and miso meets molasses in this collection of 120 new recipes from Yotam Ottolenghi's restaurant." (Publisher's note)

"Although Ottolenghi's latest will challenge readers in ways its predecessors did not, it reliably delivers unique recipes with flavor combinations unmatched in their inventiveness." LJ

Ottolenghi; the cookbook. Yotam Ottolenghi and Sami Tamimi. Ebury 2008 288 p. col. ill. (hardcover) $35 **641.5**
1. Cookbooks 2. Mediterranean cooking 3. Cooking 4. Ottolenghi (Restaurant)
ISBN 9781607744184; 160774418X
LC 2014397522

This cookbook, by Yotam Ottolenghi and Sami Tamimi, "features 140 recipes culled from the popular Ottolenghi restaurants and inspired by the diverse culinary traditions of the Mediterranean. . . . The recipes reflect the authors' upbringings in Jerusalem yet also incorporate culinary traditions from California, Italy, and North Africa, among others." (Publisher's note)

"This vibrant and bold collection lives up to the authors promise that 'cooking can be enjoyable, simple, and fulfilling, yet look and taste amazing.'" Pub WKly

Ottolenghi simple; Yotam Ottolenghi, with Tara Wigley and Esme Howarth ; photographs by Jonathan Lovekin. Ten Speed Press 2018 320 p. color illustrations $35 **641.5**
1. Cookbooks 2. Quick and easy cooking 3. Make-ahead cooking
ISBN 9781607749165
LC 2018020229

In this cookbook, "author and chef Yotam Ottolenghi presents 130 streamlined recipes packed with his signature Middle Eastern-inspired flavors, all simple in at least (and often more than) one way: made in 30 minutes or less, with 10 or fewer ingredients, in a single pot, using pantry staples, or prepared ahead of time for brilliantly, deliciously simple meals." (Publisher's note)

"Ottolenghi's many fans will want this book, but it will also appeal to home cooks looking for exciting, approachable recipes." LJ

Includes bibliographical references and index

Oz, Daphne, 1986-
The **Happy** Cook; 125 Recipes for Eating Every Day Like It's the Weekend. Daphne Oz. HarperCollins 2016 336 p. color illustrations (ebook) $30.99; $32.50 **641.5**
1. Cooking

ISBN 9780062426918; 0062426907; 9780062426901
LC 2016037715

Daphne Oz "takes the intimidation out of cooking and shows you how to savor life fully every day with this gorgeous cookbook featuring more than 125 easy, healthy, and delicious timesaving recipes. . . . [It] is filled with friendly advice, expert tips, inspiring ideas, and best of all, 125 simple yet fabulous recipes, all using just a handful of ingredients, that will transform the most nervous or reluctant novice into a happy, confident home cook." (Publisher's note)

"Tips, variations, and sidebars will guide inexperienced cooks to consider shortcuts and alternatives (try refrigerated piecrust, or include horseradish for its healing properties)." Booklist

Page, Karen
The **flavor** bible; the essential guide to culinary creativity, based on the wisdom of America's most imaginative chefs. [by] Karen Page and Andrew Dornenburg; photographs by Barry Salzman. Little, Brown and Company 2008 380p il $35 **641.5**
1. Cooking
ISBN 978-0-316-11840-8; 0-316-11840-0
LC 2007-33064

"The authors first discuss the four basic tastes and the roles played by weather, the season of the year, and other environmental factors in cooking. The rest of the book is an extensive alphabetic guide to different culinary ingredients. . . . . Rather than just another collection of recipes, this is a unique resource that both beginning cooks and serious chefs will find wonderfully inspiring and immensely useful." Libr J

Paltrow, Gwyneth, 1972-
It's all easy; delicious weekday hacks for the super-busy home cook. Gwyneth Paltrow with Thea Baumann ; photographs by Ditte Isager. Life & Style 2016 288 p. illustrations (chiefly color) (hardcover) $35 **641.5**
1. Cookbooks 2. Quick and easy cooking
ISBN 9781455584215
LC 2015044440

In this cookbook, by Gwyneth Paltrow with Thea Baumann and photographs by Ditte Isager, the author shares "more than 125 of her favorite recipes that can be made in the time it would take to order takeout (which often contains high quantities of fat, sugar, and processed ingredients). All the dishes are surprisingly tasty, with little or no sugar, fat, or gluten." (Publisher's note)

"Paltrow's recipes offer refreshing ways for home cooks to regain balance in their lives and on their plates in face of today's on-the-go lifestyle."

Pascal, Cybele
The **whole** foods allergy cookbook; two hundred gourmet & homestyle recipes for the food allergic family. Vital Health Pub. 2006 213p pa $18.95 **641.5**
1. Cooking 2. Diet therapy 3. Food allergy
ISBN 1-890612-45-6; 978-1-890612-45-0
LC 2005-931263

"Each and every dish offered is free of dairy, eggs, wheat, soy, peanuts, tree nuts, fish, and shellfish. . . . [The book includes] recipes for breakfast pancakes, breads, and cereals; lunch soups, salads, spreads, and sandwiches; dinner entrées and side dishes; dessert puddings, cupcakes, cookies, cakes, and pies; and even after-school snacks ranging from trail mix to pizza and pretzels. Included is a resource guide to organizations that can supply information and support, as well as a shopping guide for hard-to-find items." Publisher's note

Includes bibliographical references

Paskin, Layo

The **Palomar** cookbook; Layo Paskin and Tomer Amedi ; photography by Helen Cathcart. Clarkson Potter/Publishers 2016 256 p. color illustrations (ebook) $65; (hardcover; alk. paper) $35   **641.5**
   1. Mediterranean cooking 2. Middle Eastern cooking 3. Cooking, Israeli
   ISBN 9780451496621; 9780451496614

                        LC 2016031350

In this cookbook by Layo Paskin and Tomer Amedi, "From Beet Carpaccio with Burnt Goat Cheese and Date Syrup to Pork Belly Tajine with Ras el Hanout and Israeli couscous, these innovative dishes explore delicious ingredients like za'atar, labneh, pomegranate syrup, and tahini in everything from sharable mezze to dessert." (Publisher's note)

"This inventive and deeply appealing book will introduce the wonders of Israeli cooking to a wide new audience." Pub Wkly

Patalsky, Kathy

Healthy happy vegan kitchen; Kathy Patalsky. Houghton Mifflin Harcourt 2015 352 p. color illustrations (trade paper) $25   **641.5**
   1. Health 2. Veganism 3. Cookbooks 4. Vegan cooking 5. Cooking (Natural foods)
   ISBN 0544379802; 9780544379800

                        LC 2014014408

This cookbook by Kathy Patalsky presents "vegan recipes from the the author behind the blog HealthyHappyLife.com. Along with the inventive recipes, the book also includes guides to help 'veganize' your kitchen, cooking techniques for vegan staples, and wellness tips, making it the perfect book for both long-time vegans and newcomers alike." (Publisher's note)

"Headnotes and information on the author's own vegan journey offer encouragement and background for anyone interested in embracing the meatless life or simply incorporating meatless meals into their diet." Pub Wkly

Peltre, Beatrice

My French family table; Recipes for a Life Filled with Food, Love, and Joie de Vivre. Béatrice Peltre. Roost Books, an imprint of Shambhala Publications, Inc. 2016 392 p. color illustrations (hardcover; alk. paper) $35   **641.5**
   1. French cooking 2. Cooking, French
   ISBN 9781611801361

                        LC 2015026649

This cookbook, by Beatrice Peltre, "offers a beautiful assortment of over 120 recipes for naturally gluten-free dishes that feature whole grains, colorful produce, and distinctive spices. Every meal is an inspired work of love." (Publisher's note)

"Peltre's latest shows how cooking for gluten-free eaters doesn't have to be stressful. Highly recommended for foodies, flexitarians, and confident home cooks who are new to gluten-free cooking." LJ

Pepin, Jacques

The **apprentice** ; my life in the kitchen. Houghton Mifflin 2003 318p il $26   **641.5**
   1. Cooks 2. Cooking 3. Television personalities 4. Cookbook writers
   ISBN 0-618-19737-0

                        LC 2002-192158

"Pépin relates how his interest in food and culinary techniques developed into passions for cooking and teaching. He does this deftly, neatly capturing personalities and events with clear, concise writing."

Libr J

Essential Pepin; more than 700 all-time favorites from my life in food. Houghton Mifflin Harcourt 2011 685p il $40   **641.5**
   1. French cooking
   ISBN 978-0-547-23279-9

                        LC 2011-16057

Pepin "offers more than 700 of his best French and French-accented dishes from decades of cooking and teaching. They're simple without being dumbed down; approachable yet still adventurous. Whether he's explaining how to make Escoffier quenelles with mushroom sauce; black sea bass gravlax; chicken livers sautéed with vinegar; duck cassoulet; artichoke hearts with tarragon and mushrooms; or tarte tatin, he makes it seem doable and shares tidbits of wisdom to boost confidence and kitchen knowledge. His head notes are brief but informative, warm but not cloying. Pepin's own line drawings accompany the recipes, and they are, appropriately, at once homey and sophisticated. A DVD teaching a variety of cooking techniques accompanies the book, promising to make even the more challenging recipes less intimidating. For serious cooks and beginners alike, this is an instant classic." Publ Wkly

Heart & soul in the kitchen; Jacques Pepin ; photography by Tom Hopkins Studio. Houghton Mifflin Harcourt 2015 ix, 435 p.p illustrations $35   **641.5**
   1. Cooking
   ISBN 0544301986; 9780544301986

                        LC 2015490299

This book, by author Jacques Pépin "is an intimate look at the celebrity chef and the food he cooks at home with family and friends—200 recipes in all. There are the simple dinners Jacques prepares for his wife, like the world's best burgers (the secret is ground brisket). There are elegant dinners for small gatherings. . . . And there are the dishes for backyard parties, including grilled chicken tenderloin in an Argentinean chimichurri sauce." (Publisher's note)

"Readers can expect effortless, entertaining-worthy fare...along with humorous and informative anecdotes from Pépin's storied career... Highly recommended for fans of the chef and most public libraries." LJ

Jacques Pepin celebrates; by Jacques Pépin with Claudine Pépin; photographs by Christopher Hirsheimer; illustrations by Jacques Pépin. Knopf 2001 458p il $40   **641.5**
   1. Cooking 2. Entertaining
   ISBN 0-375-41209-3

                        LC 2001-29929

"In this companion to a new PBS series, Pépin builds on a broad definition of celebrations—encompassing holidays, special occasions, and simply nice weather—to present a collection of typically solid French recipes and numerous useful tips and techniques. . . . More valuable than the recipes . . . are the many notes on chopping, garnishing, carving and so forth." Publ Wkly

Perelman, Deb

★ The **smitten** kitchen cookbook; Deb Perelman. Alfred A. Knopf 2012 p. cm.   **641.5**
   1. Cooking 2. Kitchens 3. Cookbooks
   ISBN 9780307595652

                        LC 2012007711

This book is a cookbook by "Deb Perelman of Smitten Kitchen-home cook, photographer, and celebrated food blogger." The book is "all about approachable, uncompromised home cooking. Here you'll find better uses for your favorite vegetables: asparagus blanketing a pizza; ratatouille dressing up a sandwich; cauliflower masquerading as pesto. . . . Deb tells you her favorite summer cocktail; how to lose your fear of cooking for a crowd; and the essential items you need for your own kitchen." (Publisher's note)

★ **Smitten** kitchen every day; triumphant and unfussy new favorites. Deb Perelman. Alfred A. Knopf 2017 330 p. (hardback) $35   641.5
 1. Cooking
 ISBN 9781101874813

LC 2017010179

This book, by Deb Perelman, "presents more than one hundred impossible-to-resist recipes--almost all of them brand-new, plus a few favorites from her website--that will make you want to stop what you're doing right now and cook. These are real recipes for real people--people with busy lives who don't want to sacrifice flavor or quality to eat meals they're really excited about." (Publisher's note)

"Blogger and cookbook author Perelman (The Smitten Kitchen Cookbook) found she had to modify her approach to mealtime to accommodate a young, hungry family. This cookbook is her attempt to inspire herself and others to take a relaxed yet celebratory approach to feeding our families. The result is a joyous cookbook filled with delectable, creative possibilities for every meal." PW

Peternell, Cal
 A **Recipe** for Cooking; by Cal Peternell. HarperCollins 2016 352 p. $29.99; (ebook) $27.99   641.5
 1. Cooking
 ISBN 0062427865; 9780062427861; 9780062427878

LC 2016046678

This cookbook, by Cal Peternell, "gives you everything you need to cook for big get-togethers, holiday feasts, family occasions, and for a special dinner for two. He organizes the recipes by season to help cooks plan their meals from first bite to last—how a meal should start, what should be the main attraction, what should be served alongside, and how to choose the perfect finish." (Publisher's note)

"Cookbooks for relaxed entertaining are making a comeback." LJ

★ **Twelve** Recipes; Cal Peternell. 1st ed HarperCollins 2014 304 p. ill. (chiefly col.) hbk $26.99   641.5
 1. Cooking 2. Cookbooks
 ISBN 0062270303; 9780062270306

LC 2015303204

IACP Cookbook Award: General (2015)

"Based on the life-altering course of instruction [author Cal Peternell] prepared and honed through many phone calls with his son, 'Twelve Recipes' is [an] . . . introduction to the kitchen. Peternell focuses on the core foods and dishes that comprise a successful home cook's arsenal, each building skill upon skill--from toast, eggs, and beans, to vinaigrettes, pasta with tomato, and rice, to vegetables, soup, meats, and cake."

"Marked by Peternell's zeal for good, simple food, this title takes a very different approach from cooking handbooks that emphasize science or technical precision." LJ

Peterson, James
 Cooking. Ten Speed Press 2007 534p il $40   641.5
 1. Cooking
 ISBN 978-1-580-08789-6; 1-580-08789-2

LC 2007-21065

This book "opens with a fairly brief description of ten basic cooking techniques and then moves on to Recipes To Learn By, organized by course or main ingredient. Many of the recipes are traditional French

standbys, from Celeriac Rémoulade to Beef à la Mode, although there are dishes inspired by Thai, Mexican, and other cuisines as well. . . . Essentially an intensive course for home cooks in the classic techniques that underlie good cooking, this is recommended for all cookery collections." Libr J

Glorious French food; a fresh approach to the classics. Wiley 2002 xxv, 742p il map $45   641.5
 1. French cooking
 ISBN 0-471-44276-3

LC 2001-46972

The author presents "50 classic recipes as the starting point for his wide-ranging exploration of French food and techniques; each recipe serves both to demonstrate a variety of techniques and as the inspiration for a diverse collection of other recipes related to it in one way or another. . . . Each chapter includes boxes and charts on improvising with different ingredients and flavors. The suggested variations for individual recipes, often mini-essays in themselves, open up dozens of other possibilities. Peterson is both passionate and knowledgeable about his subject, and his . . . book is an essential purchase." Libr J

Includes bibliographical references

Phillips, Carolyn
 All under heaven; Recipes from the 35 Cuisines of China. written and illustrated by Carolyn Phillips ; introduction by Ken Hom. Ten Speed Press 2016 524 p. illustrations, map (hardcover; alk. paper) $40   641.5
 1. Cookbooks 2. Chinese cooking 3. Cooking, Chinese
 ISBN 9781607749820

LC 2015029244

This cookbook by Carolyn Phillips is "a comprehensive, contemporary portrait of China's culinary landscape and the geography and history that has shaped it. . . . With hundreds of recipes--from simple Fried Green Onion Noodles to Lotus-Wrapped Spicy Rice Crumb Pork--written with clear, step-by-step instructions, [it] serves as both a handbook for the novice and a source of inspiration for the veteran chef." (Publisher's note)

"Those who enjoy the thoroughly researched cookbooks of experts such as Claudia Roden (The New Book of Middle Eastern Food) will appreciate Phillips's comprehensive treatment, which includes historical information, an extensive ingredient glossary, suggested menus, and useful advice." LJ

Includes bibliographical references and index

Pierson, Joy
 Vegan holiday cooking from Candle Cafe; celebratory menus and recipes from New York's premier plant-based restaurants. Joy Pierson, Angel Ramos, and Jorge Pineda. Ten Speed Press 2014 176 p. color illustrations (hardback) $22.99 641.5
 1. Veganism 2. Cookbooks 3. Holiday cooking 4. Candle Cafe 5. Vegan cooking 6. Candle 79 (Restaurant)
 ISBN 1607746476; 9781607746478; 9781607746485

LC 2014005259

"This collection of vegan holiday recipes—the first of its kind from award-winning chefs—elevates plant-based fare to a new level. With fresh, inventive menus for Thanksgiving, Christmas, New Year's Eve, Lunar New Year, Super Bowl Sunday, Valentine's Day, Passover, Easter, Cinco de Mayo, and Independence Day, this cookbook blends favorite traditions with a modern sensibility. Tantalizing dishes include Sweet Potato Latkes with Almond Crème Fraîche for Passover; Porcini-Crusted Seitan with Glazed Cipollini Onions and Mushroom Gravy for Thanksgiving; and Red, White, and Blue Margaritas for the Fourth of July.

Now home cooks can entertain in the spirit of New York's premier vegan restaurants, Candle Cafe, Candle 79, and Candle Cafe West. With forewords by Alicia Silverstone and Laura and Woody Harrelson, plus sumptuous photography throughout, this festive cookbook invites vegans and omnivores alike to gather around the holiday table and enjoy." Publisher's Note

"You'll be proud to serve and eat these vegan foods, and party hosts won't be tempted to hide them at the end of their holiday buffet." LJ

Pollan, Michael, 1955-

★ Cooked; a natural history of transformation. Michael Pollan. Penguin Press 2013 480 p. (hardback) $27.95 **641.5**
1. Cooking 2. Food industry -- United States 3. Cooks
ISBN 1594204217; 9781594204210

LC 2012039705

In this book, author Michael Pollan shows that "taking back control of cooking may be the single most important step anyone can take to help make the American food system healthier and more sustainable. Reclaiming cooking as an act of enjoyment and self-reliance, learning to perform the magic of these everyday transformations, opens the door to a more nourishing life." (Publisher's note)

"The author mixes journalistic encounters with tales of skilled, often relentlessly obsessive cooks who demonstrated the art of transforming the products of nature into tasty food and then tried, with spotty success, to teach him to do the same. Four sections describe this transformation with the four classical elements: fire, water, air and earth." Kirkus

Includes bibliographical references

Pomeroy, Naomi

Taste & technique; Recipes to Elevate Your Home Cooking. Naomi Pomeroy with Jamie Feldman. Ten Speed Press 2016 400 p. color illustrations (ebook) $65; (hardcover; alk. paper) $40 **641.5**
1. Cooking
ISBN 9781607749004; 9781607748991

LC 2016016387

In this cookbook, author Naomi Pomeroy "shares her hard-won knowledge, passion, and experience along with nearly 140 recipes that outline the fundamentals of cooking. By paring back complex dishes to the building-block techniques used to create them, Naomi takes you through each recipe step by step, distilling detailed culinary information to reveal the simple methods chefs use to get professional results." (Publisher's note)

"Her debut cookbook offers home cooks a superb arsenal of methods and elegant, do-able dishes designed to increase competence, confidence, and cooking pleasure." Pub Wkly

Includes bibliographical references and index

The **professional** chef; the Culinary Institute of America. 8th ed; Wiley 2006 1215p il map $70 **641.5**
1. Cooking 2. Restaurants
ISBN 978-0-7645-5734-7; 0-7645-5734-3

LC 2004-27110

First published 1962

"The nation's most prestigious training school for food careerists concentrates the essence of its course work within a comprehensive volume that competent students must master. Every aspect of the restaurant business is addressed, from nutrition and portion sizing to fiscal and human resource management. Sections on equipment, from major appliances to handheld tools, show the bond between chef and technology. Chapters on world cooking identify the most typical cooking processes and give examples of commonly appearing ingredients in each style.

Recipes record classic preparations that form the foundation for myriad elaborations and personalization to move cooking from mere technique to high art. Although beyond the need of most home cooks, this massive tome is a necessary reference-collection purchase for any library whose community includes food-service-training programs." Booklist

Prueitt, Elisabeth

Tartine all day; modern recipes for the home cook. Elisabeth Prueitt ; with Jessica Washburn and Maria Zizka ; photographs by Paige Green. Lorena Jones Books, an imprint of Ten Speed Press 2017 373 p. color illustrations (hardback) $40 **641.5**
1. Cookbooks 2. American cooking 3. Tartine (Bakery) 4. Cooking, American -- California style
ISBN 9780399578823; 9780399578830

LC 2016049912

This book is author "Elisabeth Prueitt's gift to home cooks everywhere who crave an all-in-one repertoire of wholesome, straight-forward recipes for the way they want to eat morning, noon, and night. As the family cook in her own household, Prueitt understands the challenge of making daily home cooking healthy, delicious, and enticing for all--without wearing out the cook." (Publisher's note)

"Although uncomplicated, her recipes are full of surprising ingredients and techniques . . . . Anyone who cooks through this book will come away with new favorite recipes and a deeper understanding of nonwheat flours." LJ

Psilakis, Michael

How to roast a lamb; new Greek classic cooking. [by] Michael Psilakis with Brigit Binns & Ellen Shapiro; foreword by Barbara Kafka; photography, Christopher Hirsheimer & Melissa Hamilton. Little, Brown and Company 2009 288p il $35 **641.5**
1. Greek cooking 2. Mediterranean cooking
ISBN 978-0-316-04121-8

LC 2008-54932

This "cookbook is an emotional autobiography in narrative and recipe form. It's also an introduction to the marvels of Hellenic cuisine. Psilakis, beginning with childhood favorites, moves from simple home cooking to complex restaurant fare. The bulk of the dishes—precise and lavishly illustrated—are easy enough to replicate (although some of his Anthos creations require dozens of ingredients and could take all day to make)." Time Out N Y

Punyaratabandhu, Leela

★ Bangkok; Recipes and stories from the heart of Thailand. Leela Punyaratabandhu ; photography by David Loftus. Ten Speed Press 2017 359 p. illustrations (chiefly color) (hardcover; alk. paper) $35 **641.5**
1. Thai cooking 2. Bangkok (Thailand) 3. Cooking, Thai 4. Bangkok (Thailand) -- Description and travel
ISBN 9780399578311; 9780399578328

LC 2016051340

This book, by Leela Punyaratabandhu, is a "personal ode to Bangkok, the top-ranked travel destination in the world. Every year, more than 16 million visitors flock to Thailand's capital city, and leave transfixed by the vibrant culture and unforgettable food they encounter along the way. Thai cuisine is more popular today than ever, yet there is no book that chronicles the real food that Thai people eat every day—until now." (Publisher's note)

"Punyaratabandhu is a gifted storyteller, and her work is an outstanding addition to the Thai cooking canon." Pub Wkly

Purviance, Jamie

Weber's greatest hits; 125 classic recipes for every grill. Jamie Purviance ; photography by Ray Kachatorian. Houghton Mifflin Harcourt 2017 318 p. color illustrations (paperback) $24.99 **641.5**

1. Cookbooks 2. Barbecue cooking 3. Barbecuing

ISBN 0544952375; 9780544951631; 9780544952379

In this cookbook, by Jamie Purviance, "Weber rated, debated, and curated its entire recipe collection, with help from its most enthusiastic fans. Here in one gorgeous package are the ultimate go-to recipes for every occasion. The book includes all-new photography, fun stories from Weber's rich and often hilarious history, and special features such as the Top Ten Grilling Dos and Don'ts." (Publisher's note)

"Accompanied by all-new photographs and practical tips, these easy dishes will interest just about everyone." LJ

Raichlen, Steven

★ The **barbecue!** bible; photography by Ben Fink. 10th anniversary edition; Workman Pub. 2008 556p il **641.5**

1. Barbecue cooking

ISBN 978-0-7611-4944-6; 978-0-7611-4943-9

First published 1998

"Redesigned inside and out for its 10th anniversary, The Barbecue! Bible now includes full-color photographs illustrating food preparation, grilling techniques, ingredients, and of course those irresistible finished dishes. A new section has been added with answers to the most frequently asked grilling questions, plus Steven's proven tips, quick solutions to common mistakes, and more." (Publisher's note)

Raij, Alex

The **Basque** book; a love letter in recipes from the kitchen of Txikito. Alex Raij with Eder Montero and Rebecca Flint Marx ; photography by Penny De Los Santos. Ten Speed Press 2016 304 p. color illustrations (hardcover; alk. paper) $29.99 **641.5**

1. Basque cooking 2. Basque Provinces (France and Spain) 3. Cooking, Basque

ISBN 9781607747611; 9781607747628

LC 2015041924

This Basque cookbook, by Alex Raij with Eder Montero and Rebecca Flint Marx, with photography by Penny De Los Santos, "share[s] more than one hundred recipes from [the authors' New York City restaurant] Txikito—all inspired by the home cooking traditions of the Basque Country—that will change the way you cook." (Publisher's note)

"Part cookbook, part travelog, this richly descriptive title is a pleasure to read and recalls evocative, landscape photography-rich works such as Giorgio Locatelli's Made in Sicily." LJ

Includes bibliographical references and index

Ramineni, Shubhra

Entice with spice; easy Indian recipes for busy people. photography by Masano Kawana; styling by Christina Ong and Magdalene Ong. Tuttle Pub. 2010 160p il map $27.95 **641.5**

1. Indic cooking

ISBN 978-0-8048-4029-3

LC 2009-49092

This is a "cookbook full of traditional Indian recipes adapted for busy American kitchens. Beginning with thorough explanations, from terminology to spice mixtures, she provides time-saving suggestions and tips for preparing ingredients. . . . This may be the Indian cookbook that American foodies have been waiting for." Publ Wkly

Ramsay, Gordon, 1966-

Gordon Ramsay's fast food; more than 100 delicious, super-fast, and easy recipes. by Gordon Ramsay. Sterling 2012 208 p. col. ill. $24.95 **641.5**

1. Cookbooks

ISBN 1402797877; 9781402797873

In this cookbook, celebrity chef Gordon Ramsay "serves up a feast of doable ideas: more than 100 recipes and 15 great menus for putting food on the table each and every day. Many of the dishes take only 15 minutes to prepare and cook; none takes longer than half an hour--and you can put together an entire meal in only 30-45 minutes. Ramsay also offers time-saving shortcuts, plus info on how to stock your pantry." (Publisher's note)

Rea, Andrew

★ **Eat** what you watch; a cookbook for movie lovers. Andrew Rea ; photography by Scott Gordon Bleicher. Dovetail Press 2017 131 p. $25 **641.5**

1. Cooking 2. Motion pictures

ISBN 0998739952; 9780998739953

LC 2017952443

In this book, by Andrew Rea, "many of our favorite movies come with a side of iconic food moments. . . . [This book] recreates these iconic food scenes and many more. With recipes from more than 40 classic and cult films, Eat What You Watch is the perfect gift for both movie buffs and home cooks who want to add some cinematic flair to their cooking repertoire." (Publisher's note)

Recipes from an Italian summer; [translation by Mary Consoni; photographs by Joel Meyerowitz, Andy Sewell; illustrations by Jeffrey Fisher] Phaidon Press Limited 2010 431p il $39.95 **641.5**

1. Italian cooking

ISBN 978-0-714857732

This collection, "from the editors behind The Silver Spoon cookbook, is comprised of a glorious 400+ pages of recipes for picnics, barbecues, light suppers and summer entertaining (with the chapters thus organized, along with chapters on salads, desserts and ice cream/ beverages). It's a compilation of dishes from popular Italian vacation regions. . . . The dishes are simple yet glorious in that Italian way (meaning without good ingredients first press olive oil, farmers market greens, real Parmigiano-Reggiano, there's little point in making many of the recipes)." L A Wkly

Redzepi, Nadine Levy

★ **Downtime**; deliciousness at home. Nadine Levy Redzepi ; photographs by Ditte Isager ; styled by Christine Rudolph. Pam Krauss Books/Avery 2017 304 p. $35 **641.52**

1. Cookbooks 2. European cooking

ISBN 0735216061; 9780735216068

In this cookbook, author Nadine Levy Redzepi "has developed a stripped-down repertoire of starters, mains, and desserts that can always accommodate a few more at the table. . . . Each recipe is studded with tips to help cooks build confidence and expertise as they cook, as well as restaurant-ready techniques that contribute precision, flavor, and plate appeal to even down-to-earth preparations." (Publisher's note)

Reichl, Ruth, 1948-

My kitchen year; 136 recipes that saved my life. Ruth Reichl. Random House Inc. 2015 336 p. color illustrations (hardcover) $30 **641.5**

1. Seasonal cooking

ISBN 9781400069989; 140006998X

LC 2014029197

This book, by Ruth Reichl, describes the author's experiences re-learning to appreciate cooking after she lost her job as a food magazine editor. It "follows the change of seasons--and Reichl's emotions--as she slowly heals through the simple pleasures of cooking. While working 24/7, Reichl would 'throw quick meals together' for her family and friends. Now she has the time to rediscover what cooking meant to her." (Publisher's note)

"Reichl has written some classics in food literature, including Tender at the Bone (1998); therefore, much attention will be accorded her latest book." Booklist

Ridge, Brent

The **Beekman** 1802 heirloom dessert cookbook; 100 delicious heritage recipes from the farm and garden. by Brent Ridge, Josh Kilmer-Purcell, and Sandy Gluck. Rodale Books 2013 272 p. (hardback) $32.50   **641.5**
1. Farm produce 2. American cooking 3. Farm life -- United States 4. Desserts 5. Cooking, American 6. Farm life -- New York (State) -- Upstate New York 7. Farm produce -- New York (State) -- Upstate New York
ISBN 1609615735; 9781609615734

LC 2013010502

This book, by Josh Kilmer-Purcell, Brent Ridge, and Sandy Gluck, " will show off the delicious and decadent recipes that the Beekman Boys have collected from across the generations of their family, from Brent's grandmother's Fourth of July Fruitcake to Josh's mother's Hot Chocolate Dumplings. Each recipe will be accompanied by a personal memory from the authors or a story about how that recipe came to be." (Publisher's note)

Riggs, Taylor

Real food, real simple; 80 delicious paleo-friendly, gluten-free recipes in 5 steps or less. Taylor Riggs. Page Street Pub. Co. 2017 192 p. illustrations (pbk.) $21.99   **641.5**
1. Cookbooks 2. Gluten-free diet 3. Quick and easy cooking
ISBN 1624143377; 1624143512; 9781624143373; 9781624143519

LC 2016940924

This book, by Taylor Riggs, "makes preparing whole, nutrient-dense foods as easy as one, two, three, four, five with delicious recipes that are gluten-free, Paleo-friendly and exceptionally healthy. . . . Riggs, Registered Dietitian Nutritionist and founder of Simply Taylor, shares 80 incredible recipes that encompass her healthy lifestyle manifesto in five steps or less. Her recipes showcase complex and intriguing flavors but are surprisingly easy to make." (Publisher's note)

"It's a terrific introduction to paleo and gluten-free cooking for novices and experts interested in expanding their repertoires with new dishes that come together quickly and easily." Pub Wkly

Robertson, Robin

Robin Robertson's vegan without borders; easy everyday meals from around the world. Robin Robertson. Andrews McMeel Pub., LLC 2014 304 p. illustrations $40   **641.5**
1. Cooking 2. Veganism
ISBN 1449447082; 9781449447083

LC 2014930776

Author Robin Robertson presents a cookbook of her "favorite dishes from the great cuisines of the world and shows how cooking vegan makes borders disappear. Whether the recipe hails from Ecuador or Ethiopia, these plant-based dishes invite you to travel the culinary world and

sample 150 of Robin's all-time favorites." (Publisher's note)

"Robertson's existing fans will be joined by many new ones on this tasty whirlwind tour of the globe." LJ

Vegan planet; more than 425 irresistible recipes with fantastic flavors from home and around the world. Robin Robertson. The Harvard Common Press 2014 xii, 532 p.p (pbk.) $19.95   **641.5**
1. Veganism 2. Vegan cooking 3. International cooking
ISBN 1558328319; 9781558328310

LC 2013022919

This vegan cookbook, by Robin Robertson, "is back in a thoroughly revised edition. . . . [U]pdates cover such things as: the newly expanded range of whole grains that are available; super greens, such as kale and chard, that are rising in popularity; new facts concerning which cooking oils are healthiest and most earth-friendly; and new saucing and flavoring ideas from the global pantry." (Publisher's note)

Includes bibliographical references and index

Roden, Claudia

Arabesque ; a taste of Morocco, Turkey, and Lebanon. Knopf 2006 341p il $35   **641.5**
1. Turkish cooking 2. Lebanese cooking 3. Moroccan cooking
ISBN 0-307-26498-X; 978-0-307-26498-5

LC 2006-45258

First published 2005 in the United Kingdom

The author "has chosen more than 150 recipes from Morocco, Turkey, and Lebanon, some newly discovered, some variations on more familiar dishes, and a selection of favorite classic dishes. Each section opens with a fascinating insider's guide, providing both cultural and culinary history as well as information on specific ingredients and techniques. . . . An essential purchase." Libr J

The **book** of Jewish food; an odyssey from Samarkand to New York. Claudia Roden. Knopf 1996 668 p. il $45 **641.5**
1. Cookbooks 2. Jewish cooking 3. Jewish civilization
ISBN 0394532589; 9780394532585

LC 96028758

James Beard Award (1997)

This cookbook, written by Claudia Roden, "traces the development of both Ashkenazic and Sephardic Jewish communities and their cuisine over the centuries. The 800 . . . recipes, many never before documented, represent treasures garnered by Roden through nearly 15 years of traveling around the world." (Publisher's note)

Includes bibliographical references and index

The **food** of Spain. Ecco Press 2011 $39.99   **641.5**
1. Spanish cooking
ISBN 978-0-06-196962-1

Roman, Alison

★ **Dining** in; highly cookable recipes. Alison Roman ; photographs by Michael Graydon and Nikole Herriott. Clarkson Potter/Publishers 2017 304 p. $30   **641.52**
1. Cooking 2. Cookbooks
ISBN 9780451496997

LC 2017026507

This cookbook, by Alison Roman, photographs by Michael Graydon and Nikole Herriott, "features 125 recipes for simple, of-the-moment dishes that are full of quickie techniques. . . . Roman's recipes set today's trends and will show up as tomorrow's classics: vegetable-forward with quality ingredients, punctuated by standout flavors like hot honey browned butter, preserved lemon, za'atar, and garlicky walnuts." (Publisher's note)

Rombauer, Irma von Starkloff

★ **Joy** of cooking; [by] Irma S. Rombauer, Marion Rombauer Becker, Ethan Becker; illustrated by John Norton. 75th anniversary ed.; Scribner 2006 1132p il $30 **641.5**

1. Cooking

ISBN 978-0-7432-4626-2; 0-7432-4626-8

LC 2006-51231

First published 1931

This is the "backbone for any library's cookery reference collection, its nearly 4,000 recipes defining essential American home cooking." Booklist

Rose, Evelyn

100 Best Jewish Recipes; Evelyn Rose with Judi Rose. Interlink Pub Group Inc 2015 208 p. color illustrations $30 **641.5**

1. Cookbooks 2. Jewish cooking

ISBN 156656073X; 9781566560733

"100 Best Jewish Recipes is comprised of the highlights from Evelyn Rose's culinary life, which spanned several decades and earned her the recognition as one of the world's foremost Jewish food writers. Packed with mouthwatering ideas for both family meals and those special occasions when you want to impress without spending hours in the kitchen, this book contains 100 fail-safe recipes for which the author is justly celebrated." (Publisher's note)

"Condensing the world's vast tradition of Jewish cookery to just 100 dishes presents a formidable challenge. The late Evelyn Rose spent a lifetime scouring Europe, Africa, and Asia and documenting the foods consumed in those continents' Jewish communities. Duck breast glazed with ginger, honey, and soy recalls the seasonings of Chinese food. Sephardi-style pizza evokes Armenian or Turkish lahmacun, and further topping it with kosher salami transforms it almost into American pepperoni pizza.... Because Jewish holidays have so many food traditions supplementing religious ones, Rose gives advice on dishes to celebrate the eight major festivals that Jews observe. An excellent addition to most library collections." Booklist

Rosenthal, Mitchell

Cooking my way back home; recipes from San Francisco's Town Hall, Anchor & Hope, and Salt House. Mitchell Rosenthal with Jon Pult, foreword by wolfgang Puck ; photography by Paige Green. Ten Speed Press 2011 vii, 263 p.p col. ill. (hbk.) $35 **641.5**

1. Cookbooks 2. American cooking 3. Southern cooking 4. Salt House (Restaurant) 5. Anchor & Hope (Restaurant) 6. Cooking, American -- Southern style 7. Cooking, American -- California style 8. Town Hall (Restaurant; San Francisco, Calif.)

ISBN 158008592X; 9781580085922

LC 2011011631

This cookbook, by Mitchell Rosenthal with Jon Pult, "blends Southern-inspired comfort food with urban sophistication and innovation, for exciting results. Reflecting on the classics (Shrimp Étouffée), updating regional specialties (Poutine), elevating family favorites (Chopped Liver), and reveling in no-holds-barred, all-out indulgences (Butterscotch Chocolate Pot de Crème) are what's on order in this collection of 100 .. . recipes." (Publisher's note)

Includes bibliographical references

Roux, Michel

The **French** kitchen; recipes from the master of French cooking. by Michel Roux Jr. Simon & Schuster 2016 352 p. $40 **641.5**

1. French cooking

ISBN 1681880601; 9781681880600

LC 2015057875

In this cookbook, by Michel Roux Jr., "you'll find 200 classics recipes . . . to master French cooking. No topic is breezed over: and with chapters for soup, terrines and pâtés, eggs and cheese, fish and shellfish, chicken, duck and game birds, meat, vegetables and salads, desserts, bread and croissants, and stocks and sauces." (Publisher's note)

"Today, chefs of all statures are adored, revered for their kitchen talent, devotion to the "cause," and painstaking meticulousness in this art and craft of food. Yet not all can translate those competencies into a collection of recipes for the home cook to follow. Roux, of London's Michelin-starred La Gavroche, can..." Booklsit

Ruhlman, Michael

Ratio; the simple codes behind the craft of everyday cooking. Scribner 2009 xxv, 224p il $27 **641.5**

1. Cooking

ISBN 978-1-416-56611-3; 1-416-56611-2

LC 2008-32679

"While Ruhlman was attending the Culinary Institute of America for a book project, a chef showed him a copy of the golden rules, which boiled down the elements of (French) cooking into ratios.... [In this volume] Ruhlman guides readers through the ratios for a variety of doughs, batters, stocks, sauces, custards and sausages, explaining their chemical and culinary basis in clear, earnest prose and providing tasteful recipes that lay out the technique for each formula." N Y Times Book Rev

Ruhlman's twenty; the ideas and techniques that will make you a better cook. Michael Ruhlman ; photographs by Donna Turner Ruhlman. Chronicle Books 2011 367 p. col. ill. (alk. paper) $40 **641.5**

1. Cooking 2. Cookbooks

ISBN 9780811876438

LC 2011036735

James Beard Award (2012)

IACP Award (2012)

This cookbook "distills [author Michael] Ruhlman's decades of cooking, writing, and working with the world's greatest chefs into twenty essential ideas from ingredients to processes to attitude that are guaranteed to make every cook more accomplished. Whether cooking a multi-course meal, the juiciest roast chicken, or just some really good scrambled eggs, Ruhlman reveals how a cook s success boils down to the same twenty concepts." (Publisher's note)

"Thorough, clearly explained, and stunningly beautiful, this collection will appeal to cooks of all levels." Pub Wkly

Includes bibliographical references and index

Saltsman, Amelia

The **Santa** Monica Farmers' Market Cookbook; seasonal foods, simple recipes, and stories from the market and farm. Amelia Saltsman ; foreword by Deborah Madison. Blenheim 2007 216 p. col. ill. $22.95 **641.5**

1. Markets 2. Cookbooks 3. Farm produce 4. Santa Monica (Calif.) 5. Cooking 6. Santa Monica Farmers' Market (Santa Monica, Calif.)

ISBN 0979042909; 9780979042904

LC 2007901323

This cookbook, by Amelia Saltsman, is "a celebration of the [Santa Monica Farmers' Market].... What s the difference between white and green zucchini? What are amaranth, sapote, and ramps? With Amelia as your guide, you'll learn the answers to these questions and more. You'll also find advice on how to select and store produce, stories about farmers and their crops, chef and farmer cooking tips, and more than 100 of Amelia's simple, tempting recipes." (Publisher's note)

Includes bibliographical references (p. 205-206) and index

Saltz, Joanna

Delish; eat like every day's the weekend. Joanna Saltz and the editors of Delish. Houghton Mifflin Harcourt 2018 416 p. (paper over board) $30   **641.5**
1. Cooking 2. Cookbooks 3. Quick and easy cooking 4. Entertaining
ISBN 9781328498861

LC 2018012229

This cookbook, by Joanna Saltz and the editors of Delish, presents "recipes that are as fun to watch as they are to make. . . . [The book provides] more than 275 recipes and ideas that are meant to be devoured, not perfected--including Quesadilla Cake, Chicken Fried Cauliflower, and Cookie Dough Cheesecake--plus their best tips, tricks, and indispensable advice." (Publisher's note)

Samuelsson, Marcus, 1970-

Marcus off duty; the recipes I cook at home. Marcus Samuelsson with Roy Finamore ; photography by Paul Brissman. Houghton Mifflin Harcourt 2014 352 p. illustrations (chiefly color) (paper over board) $35   **641.5**
1. Cooking 2. Cookbooks
ISBN 0470940581; 9780470940587

LC 2014018169

James Beard Foundation Award Nominee: General Cooking (2015)

This book, by chef Marcus Samuelsson, "serves up the dishes he makes at his Harlem home for his wife and friends. The recipes blend a rainbow of the flavors he experienced in his travels-- Ethiopian, Swedish, Mexican, Caribbean, Italian, and Southern soul. His eclectic, casual food includes dill-spiced salmon; coconut-lime curried chicken; mac, cheese, and greens; chocolate pie spiced with Indian garam masala; and for kids, peanut noodles with slaw." (Publisher's note)

"Highly recommended for adventurous and well-traveled home cooks, as well as fans of Susan Feniger's Street Food." LJ

Red Rooster Cookbook; The Story of Food and Hustle in Harlem. Marcus Samuelsson ; photographs by Bobby Fisher ; text with April Reynolds ; recipes and text with Roy Finamore ; illustrations by Rebekah Maysles and Leon Johnson. Houghton Mifflin Harcourt 2016 384 p. color illustrations (paper over board) $37.50   **641.5**
1. Restaurants 2. American cooking 3. Harlem (New York, N.Y.) 4. International cooking 5. Red Rooster (Restaurant) 6. Food -- New York (State) -- New York 7. Cooking -- New York (State) -- New York
ISBN 9780544639775

LC 2016037226

This cookbook, by Marcus Samuelsson, presents "Southern comfort food and multicultural recipes. . . . When . . . Samuelsson opened Red Rooster on Malcolm X Boulevard in Harlem, he envisioned more than a restaurant. It would be the heart of his neighborhood and a meet-and-greet for both the downtown and the uptown sets, serving Southern black and cross-cultural food." (Publisher's note)

"Fisher's food and street photography colorfully captures the character of Samuelsson's dishes as well as the characters that inhabit his neighborhood." Pub Wkly

The **soul** of a new cuisine; a discovery of the foods and flavors of Africa. foreword by Desmond Tutu. Wiley 2006 xxii, 344p il map $40   **641.5**
1. African cooking
ISBN 0-7645-6911-2

For this African cookbook, the author "traveled to Africa and even took cooking lessons in Ethiopia, the country of his birth. Samuelsson emphasizes that this is not the definitive cookbook of an area with over 800 languages and dialects, but an overview of what he saw and ate in his travels. . . . This is a unique cookbook about a little-known cuisine, including travel essays and enhanced by beautiful color photographs that depict the food and the people of Africa. A necessary acquisition for international cookery collections." Libr J

Includes bibliographical references

Sanfilippo, Diane

Practical paleo; a customized approach to health and a whole-foods lifestyle. Diane Sanfillipo, with photography by Bill Staley. Victory Belt Pub. 2012 416 p. col. ill. $39.95 **641.5**
1. Cookbooks 2. Paleo cooking
ISBN 1936608758; 9781936608751

This Paleo cookbook, by Diane Sanfilippo, illustrated by Bill Staley, "explains why avoiding both processed foods and foods marketed as 'healthy'--like grains, legumes, and pasteurized dairy--will improve how you look and feel and lead to lasting weight loss. . . . [This book] is jam-packed with over 120 easy recipes, all with special notes about common food allergens including nightshades and FODMAPs. Meal plans are also included." (Publisher's note)

Sauvage, Jeanne

Gluten-free wish list; sweet & savory treats you've missed the most. Jeanne Sauvage ; photographs by Eva Kolenko. Chronicle Books Llc 2015 256 p. color illustrations (hardcover) $29.95   **641.5**
1. Cookbooks 2. Gluten-free diet 3. Baking 4. Gluten-free diet -- Recipes
ISBN 9781452138336

LC 2015000533

This gluten-free cookbook, by Jeanne Sauvage, with photographs by Eva Kolenko, includes "recipes for pizza crust, bagels, and all of the other wheat-laden staples folks miss most after eliminating gluten from their diets. Here author Jeanne Sauvage proves that gluten-free should never be anything less than delicious." (Publisher's note)

"For those looking to expand their specialty cooking section or who are thinking of going gluten-free themselves, this book would seem to be the ticket. For all cookbook collections." LJ

Includes bibliographical references and index

Scala Quinn, Lucinda

Mad hungry family; 120 Essential Recipes to Feed the Whole Crew. Lucinda Scala Quinn. Artisan, a division of Workman Publishing Company, Inc. 2015 272 p. color illustrations $27.95; (ebook) $27.95   **641.5**
1. Cooking 2. Cookbooks
ISBN 9781579656645; 9781579657130

LC 2015037712

In this book, author Lucinda Scala Quinn has collected the "recipes that send her family stampeding to the kitchen table—from flat roast chicken to second-day spaghetti pancakes—and peppered them with tips, tricks, and solutions learned over a lifetime of cooking both professionally and for her family of five. Here are survival strategies for nothing-in-the-fridge crises, feeding unexpected guests, getting Thanksgiving dinner on the table before your family revolts, and more." (Publisher's note)

"Quinn's Mad Hungry books are fantastic for novice cooks who like simple, everyday recipes without heavy-handed diet and lifestyle advice. Her latest doesn't disappoint." LJ

Seal, Rebecca

Lisbon; recipes from the heart of Portugal. Rebecca Seal; photography by Steven Joyce. Hardie Grant Books 2017 253 p. color illustrations (hardcover) $35   **641.5**

1. Cookbooks 2. Lisbon (Portugal) 3. Portuguese cooking 4. Cooking, Portuguese

ISBN 1784881031; 9781784881030

This cookbook, by Rebecca Seal with photography by Steven Joyce, focuses on Portuguese cuisine and culture. "Full of history, great food, and bursting with character, Portugal's capital is one of Europe's most charming cities. . . . Seal shares her favorite recipes, inspired by her travels. Set on seven hills, Lisbon features world-class beaches, city views, and wild forests. And the food is as diverse as the surroundings." (Publisher's note)

"These photos along with Seal's enticing anecdotes about her introduction to these dishes make the final result part cookbook, part travelogue—a book as likely to result in vacation planning as meal planning." Pub Wkly

Shepherd, Sue

The **2**-step low-FODMAP eating plan; How To Build a Custom Diet that Relieves the Symptoms of IBS, Lactose Intolerance, and Gluten Sensitivity. Sue Shepherd. Experiment 2016 288 p. (pbk.) $19.95   **641.5**

1. Diet therapy 2. Digestive system 3. Irritable colon -- Diet therapy -- Recipes 4. Malabsorption syndromes -- Diet therapy -- Recipes

ISBN 9781615193158

LC 2015042268

In this book, Dr. Sue Shepherd "presents a reliable approach to identify what foods you can enjoy, and eliminate only those that cause symptoms [of your digestive disorder]. . . . With menu plans for adults, kids, vegetarians and vegans, anyone can do it. Dr. Shepherd also delivers a guide to shopping and how to approach food labels, travel information and tips for eating out, and over 80 crave-worthy recipes." (Publisher's note)

"This superlative guide, as deeply informative and accessible as it is hunger-inducing and eye-catching, will benefit not only those with IBS, celiac, and lactose intolerance, but health-cognizant gourmands as well." Pub Wkly

Shulman, Martha Rose

Mediterranean harvest; vegetarian recipes from the world's healthiest cuisine. Martha Rose Shulman. Rodale 2007 p. cm.   **641.5**

1. Vegetarian cookery. 2. Cookery, Mediterranean.

ISBN 9781594862342 (hardcover); 1594862346 (hardcover)

LC 2007031561

Includes bibliographical references and index.

"Shulman's (Entertaining Light) expertise with vegetarian and Mediterranean cooking shines through, especially in the practical information provided after many recipes, such as tips on prepping ahead of time and how to ensure high-quality leftovers. The end matter includes online ingredient sources, helpful for those living outside of major cities, as well as a breakdown of recipes by region." (Library Journal)

The **silver** spoon. Phaidon Press 2005 1263p il $39.95 **641.5**

1. Italian cooking

ISBN 978-0-7148-4531-9; 0-7148-4531-0

Original Italian edition, 1950

"The book contains recipes for everything from basic sauces and marinades to salads, game, fish and baked goods, with each section color-coded for easy browsing. Recipes emphasize fresh ingredients and are to-the-point, typically summed up in a paragraph sans photo illustrations. Those who know their way around a kitchen will appreciate the brevity. . . . Almost all of the ingredients called for can be found in a typical supermarket. . . . Globe-trotting gourmands will appreciate the menu and 'signature dish' contributions by famous Italian chefs that round out the book. The most exhaustive Italian cookbook in recent memory, this volume offers something for every cook, regardless of their skill level, and deserves to be a fixture in American kitchens." Publ Wkly

The **simple** art of vegetarian cooking; templates and lessons for making delicious meatless meals every day. Martha Rose Shulman. Rodale Books 2014 270 p. color illustrations (hardback) $32.50   **641.5**

1. Cookbooks 2. Vegetarian cooking 3. Quick and easy cooking

ISBN 162336129X; 9781623361297

LC 2013049184

"In 'The Simple Art of Vegetarian Cooking,' . . . Martha Rose Shulman offers a . . . method for creating delicious plant-based meals every day. . . . It teaches the reader how to cook basic dishes via templates--master recipes with simple guidelines for creating an essential dish, such as a frittata or an omelet, a stir-fry, a rice bowl, a pasta dish, a soup--and then how to swap in and out key ingredients as desired based on seasonality and freshness." (Publisher's note)

The **very** best of recipes for health; 250 recipes and more from the popular feature on NYTimes.com. Martha Rose Shulman. Rodale 2010 xvi, 352 p.p col. ill. (hardcover) $37.50   **641.5**

1. Cookbooks 2. Cooking -- Natural foods 3. Health 4. Nutrition 5. Cooking (Natural foods)

ISBN 9781605295732; 1605295736

LC 2010021608

This cookbook, by Martha Rose Shulman, "shows how to fill your refrigerator, freezer, and cabinets with healthy staples such as beans, grains, extra virgin olive oil, tuna, eggs, yogurt, and tomato sauce, so that you are prepared to cook delicious dishes like Asparagus and Herb Frittata, Quinoa Salad with Lime Ginger Dressing and Shrimp, or Pizza Marinara with Tuna and Capers in minutes." (Publisher's note)

Silverton, Nancy

Mozza at home; More than 150 Crowd-Pleasing Recipes for Relaxed, Family-Style Entertaining. by Nancy Silverton with Carolynn Carreño ; photographs by Christopher Hirsheimer. Alfred A. Knopf 2016 432 p. (hardcover) $35   **641.5**

1. Entertaining 2. Italian cooking 3. Pizzeria Mozza 4. Cooking, Italian

ISBN 9780385354325

LC 2015029125

In this cookbook, author Nancy Silverton "shares her renewed passion and provides nineteen menus packed with easy-to-follow recipes that can be prepared in advance (with no fancy restaurant equipment needed!) and are perfect for entertaining. Organized by meal, each menu provides a main dish along with a complementary selection of appetizers and side dishes." (Publisher's note)

"The exceptional foods of Nancy Silverton's wildly popular Los Angeles restaurants now come to delight home kitchens. Silverton's recipes reflect her attention to detail, her sophistication, and her creative imagination." Booklist

Simmons, Gail

Bringing it home; favorite recipes from a life of adventurous eating. Gail Simmons with Mindy Fox ; foreword by Tom Colicchio ; photographs by Johnny Miller. Life & Style 2017 249 p. (hardcover) $30   **641.5**

1. Cooking 2. Television programs
ISBN 9781455542215; 9781455542208

LC 2017020073

In this cookbook, Gail "Simmons shares her best recipes and food experiences. From her travels, exploring global flavors and keeping detailed diaries, to her 'Top Chef' culinary adventures with the world's most notable chefs, she is always asking: 'How can I bring this dish home to my own kitchen?' Her goal is to make fabulous recipes using accessible ingredients and smart, simple cooking techniques for successful family meals and easy entertaining." (Publisher's note)

"Top Chef judge and food-media powerhouse Simmons serves up 100 recipes drawn from her journeys in the culinary world. The recipes, which consist of Simmons's personal favorites inspired by food memories and famous mentors, aim to elevate the home cook's 'everyday cooking game.'" PW.

Includes bibliographical references and index

Simonds, Nina

★ **Spices** of life; simple and delicious recipes for great health. Nina Simonds ; photographs by Tina Rupp. 1st ed.; Random House Inc 2005 383 p. col. ill. $24.95   **641.5**

1. Cookbooks 2. Cooking -- Herbs 3. Quick and easy cooking 4. Spices 5. Cooking (Herbs)
ISBN 0375411607; 9780375411601

LC 2004021089

IACP Cookbook Award (2006)

James Beard Award (2006)

In this cookbook, author and chef "Nina Simonds offers us more than 175 . . . recipes, along with practical tips for a sensible lifestyle, that demonstrate that health-giving foods not only provide pleasure but can make a huge difference in our lives. With her emphasis on the tonic properties of a wide variety of foods, herbs, and spices, this book also brings us up to date on the latest scientific research" (Publisher's note)

Simonds' book is "full of straightforward but practical recipes, and peppered with loads of health information." Pub Wkly

Includes bibliographical references (p. 362-364) and index

Slonecker, Andrea

Beer bites; tasty recipes and perfect pairings for brew lovers. Christian DeBenedetti and Andrea Slonecker ; photographs by John Lee. Chronicle Books Llc 2015 168 p. color illustrations $24.95   **641.5**

1. Beer 2. Cooking 3. Food and beer pairing
ISBN 145213524X; 9781452135243

LC 2014032763

This cookbook, by Christian DeBenedetti and Andrea Slonecker, "n serves up 65 globe-roaming and simple recipes from appetizers to snacks and main courses that go beyond typical pub grub with recommendations of beer styles and widely available must-try brews for each dish. Beer Bites is ideal for the growing cadre of craft beer lovers eager to explore the basics and nuances of beer and food pairings." (Publisher's note)

This superb collection features of recipes that are sure to be hits at any gathering. Highly recommended for all cooking collections." Library Journal

Smith, Michelle

The **Whole** Smiths good food cookbook; delicious real food recipes to cook all year long. Michelle Smith. Houghton Mifflin Harcourt 2018 288 p. (hardback) $30   **641.5**

1. Diet therapy 2. Eating customs 3. Cooking -- Natural foods 4. Nutrition -- Popular works 5. Food habits -- Popular works 6. Diet therapy -- Popular works 7. Self-care, Health -- Popular works 8. Cooking (Natural foods) -- Popular works
ISBN 1328915093; 9781328915092

LC 2017051915

"This cookbook, [by Michelle Smith], the first ever fully endorsed and supported by Whole30, offers a collection of 150 recipes to keep Whole30 devotees going strong. Many recipes like Spaghetti Squash Chicken Alfredo are fully Whole30-compliant, and all are gluten-free, but you"l also find recipes with a careful reintroduction of grains, like the tortillas in the Chile Enchilada Bake." (Publisher's note)

Sobel, Adam

Street vegan; recipes and dispatches from the Cinnamon Snail food truck. Adam Sobel ; photographs by Kate Lewis. Clarkson Potter/Publishers 2015 272 p. $25   **641.5**

1. Veganism 2. Vegan cooking 3. Street food -- New York (State) -- New York
ISBN 0385346190; 9780385346191; 9780385346207

LC 2014047446

This cookbook, by Adam Sobel, presents "[m]eatless meals revamped by the Cinnamon Snail, the vegan food truck with a cult following. . . . Adam brings his food straight to your kitchen, along with stories of the challenges of working on a food truck while still finding ways to infuse food with imagination, love, and a pinch of perspective." (Publisher's note)

Spieler, Marlena

Paris; authentic recipes celebrating the foods of the world. recipes and text Marlena Spieler; photographs Jean-Blaise Hall; general editor Chuck Williams. Oxmoor House 2004 191p il map (Williams-Sonoma foods of the world) $24.95   **641.5**

1. French cooking
ISBN 978-0-8487-2854-8

Illustrated with full-color photographs. "Dozens of stories reveal the secrets of making long-cherished foods and profile people, places, and influences that have shaped the Parisian food scene. More than 45 recipes allow you to sample traditional dishes, such as Boeuf en Daube, Steak withe Shallot Sauce, or Raspberry Charlotte, as well as such innovations as Duck Breasts with Port and Figs or Strawberry Soup." Publisher's note

Spring, Justin

The **gourmands'** way; six Americans in Paris and the birth of a new gastronomy. Justin Spring. Farrar, Straus & Giroux 2017 433 p. illustrations (hardcover) $30   **641.5**

1. Food writing 2. French cooking 3. Cooks -- Biography 4. Food writing -- France -- Paris 5. Cooks -- United States -- Biography 6. Food writers -- United States -- Biography
ISBN 9780374711740; 9780374103156

LC 2017001319

This book, by Justin Spring, is "a biography of six writers on food and wine whose lives and careers intersected in mid-twentieth-century France. . . . The six are A. J. Liebling, Alice B. Toklas, M.F.K. Fisher,

Julia Child, Alexis Lichine, and Richard Olney. . . . Justin Spring focuses on the most joyful, exciting, formative, and dramatic moments of these six lives, many of which were intimately connected to the exploration and discovery of fine French food and drink." (Publisher's note)

"A literary meal both luscious and lively—and essential to understanding our vacillating love affair with the French." Kirkus

Includes bibliographical references and index

Stabiner, Karen

Generation chef; Risking It All for a New American Dream. Karen Stabiner. Avery, an imprint of Penguin Random House, LLC 2016 320 p. $26   **641.5**
1. Cooks 2. Restaurants 3. Entrepreneurs
ISBN 9781583335802

LC 2016026428

This book by Karen Stabiner tells "the story of Jonah Miller, who at age twenty-four attempts to fulfill a lifelong dream by opening the Basque restaurant Huertas in New York City. . . . Miller, a rising star who has been named to the 30-Under-30 list of both Forbes and Zagat, quits his job as a sous chef, creates a business plan, lines up investors, leases a space, hires a staff, and gets ready to put his reputation and his future on the line." (Publisher's note)

"Stabiner takes the reader beyond the shiny surface of food celebrity and Instagrammed plates to expose the beating hearts of those who get up every day to create something inspiring for strangers to consume." Pub Wkly

Stewart, Martha

Martha Stewart's cooking school; lessons and recipes for the home cook. by Martha Stewart with Sarah Carey; photographs by Marcus Nilsson; portraits by Ditte Isager. Clarkson Potter 2008 504p il $45   **641.5**
1. Cooking 2. Entertaining
ISBN 978-0-307-39644-0; 0-307-39644-4

LC 2008-531117

This "cookbook is the result of what Stewart refers to as her 'mission to teach the methods of home cooking.' Chapters are organized by technique, from 'How To Make White Stock' to 'How To Make Pâte à Choux.' Master recipes are followed by others that build on them, and there are hundreds of color photographs, including many step by steps for essential techniques. The illustrated 'Basics' section that opens the book covers equipment, knife skills, herbs and spices, 'the onion family,' and citrus fruits. Charts, buying guides, and sidebars are featured throughout, along with dozens of tips on ingredients, special techniques, and more." Libr J

Streiff, Fritz

The **art** of simple food; notes, lessons, and recipes from a delicious revolution. [by] Alice Waters, with Patricia Curtan, Kelsie Kerr & Fritz Streiff ; illustrations by Patricia Curtan. Clarkson Potter 2007 405p il $35   **641.5**
1. Quick and easy cooking
ISBN 978-0-307-33679-8; 0-307-33679-4

LC 2007-300393

"After a useful discussion of ingredients and equipment come chapters on techniques, such as making broth and soup. Each of these includes three or four recipes that rely on the technique described. . . . The final third of the book divides many more recipes traditionally into salads, pasta and so forth. Waters taps an almost endless supply of ideas for appealing and fresh yet low-stress dishes." Publ Wkly

Sunset the great outdoors cookbook; Adventures in Cooking Under the Open Sky. by The Editors of Sunset Magazine. Time Home Entertainment Inc. 2014 254 p. color illustrations $24.95   **641.5**
1. Outdoor cooking
ISBN 0376028076; 9780376028075

LC 2013939860

IACP Cookbook Award Winner: Compilations (2015)

This cookbook "draws on the long tradition of cooking and living in the great outdoors. Discover the tradition and evolution of outdoor cooking in the West with stories, quotes, and historical photos. . . . With 200+ fresh recipes and 150+ full-color photos, this book has everything readers need to experience the ultimate outdoor cooking adventure - from menu planning and packing tips, to easy step-by-step cooking techniques." (Publisher's note)

Swanson, Heidi

Super natural every day; well-loved recipes from my natural foods kitchen. Heidi Swanson. Ten Speed Press 2011 p. cm. pa $23   **641.5**
1. Cooking -- Natural foods
ISBN 978-1-58008-277-8

LC 2010-43749

'A collection of 100 vegetarian recipes for nutritious, weekday-friendly dishes from the blogger behind 101 Cookbooks'--

Swift, Sally

The **Splendid** table's how to eat supper; recipes, stories, and opinions from public radio's award-winning food show. [by] Lynne Rossetto Kasper and Sally Swift. Clarkson Potter/Publishers 2008 338p il $35   **641.5**
1. Dining 2. Cooking
ISBN 978-0-307-34671-1

LC 2007-24749

"This superb book should grace the shelves of even the most infrequent of cooks." Publ Wkly

Tanis, David

David Tanis market cooking; recipes and revelations ingredient by ingredient. David Tanis ; photographs by Evan Sung. Artisan, a division of Workman Publishing Company, Inc. 2017 478 p. color illustrations (hardcover) $40   **641.5**
1. Cooking 2. Farm produce
ISBN 9781579656287; 9781579658205; 1579656285

LC 2017000348

This book, by David Tanis, "is about seeking out the best ingredients, learning the qualities of each, and the methods and recipes that showcase what makes them special—pulling from all the world's great cuisines. Sections on universal ingredients—such as alliums (garlic, onion, shallots, leeks, etc.)—offer some of the simplest yet most satisfying recipes in the world." (Publisher's note)

"With this elegant collection of vegetable-based dishes, chef and New York Times columnist Tanis (One Good Dish) makes the task of meal planning a little easier." LJ

Heart of the artichoke and other kitchen journeys. Artisan 2010 344p il $35   **641.5**
1. Menus 2. Cooking 3. Entertaining
ISBN 978-1-57965-407-8

LC 2010-4538

The author "begins with 14 'Kitchen Rituals' (ordinary pleasures perfect for one or two people) such as Jalapeño Pancakes and raw artichokes for lunch. Menus are arranged by season and feature, e.g., Fork-Mashed Potatoes and Spring Lamb with Rosemary. There are also menus for a long table (for a large crowd) such as A Perfect Suckling Pig. Simple recipes, eloquent writing, and Tanis's great reputation make this an essential purchase." Libr J

A **platter** of figs and other recipes; foreword by Alice Waters; photographs by Christopher Hirsheimer. Artisan 2008 294p il $35   **641.5**

1. Menus 2. Cooking 3. Entertaining
ISBN 978-1-57965-346-0; 1-57965-346-4

LC 2007-49384

This volums is "both a meditation on the powerful rites of cooking and serving a meal and a gentle but serious education in doing both. . . . With 24 menus distributed over the course of a year, Tanis emphasizes seasonality with ingredients (blueberry-blackberry crumble in summer; celery root mashed potatoes in winter) and with the types of dishes provided for each menu (as with a divine, warming lobster risotto as part of a menu for a cold spring day). Anecdotes from his peripatetic life of enjoying good food around the world, from Venice to Morocco to New Mexico, add another intimate dimension and help the book appear written just for the reader by a kind, patient friend." Publ Wkly

Includes bibliographical references

Tarlow, Andrew

Dinner at the Long Table; Andrew Tarlow and Anna Dunn. Ten Speed Press 2016 336 p. color illustrations (ebook) $65.00; (hardcover) $40   **641.5**

1. Dinners 2. Cookbooks 3. Cooking
ISBN 9781607748472; 9781607748465

LC 2016012177

This cookbook by Andrew Tarlow and Anna Dunn "brings Tarlow's keen eye for combining design and taste to a collection of seventeen seasonal menus ranging from small gatherings to blow-out celebrations. The menus . . . include recipes like a leisurely ragu, followed by fruit and biscotti; paella with tomato toasts, and a Catalan custard; fried calamari sandwiches and panzanella; or a lamb tajine with spiced couscous, pickled carrots, and apricots in honey." (Publisher's note)

"With nine outer-borough eateries and shops in his portfolio, Tarlow, more than anyone, has been responsible for defining Brooklyn's artisinal food scene." Pub Wkly

Tausend, Marilyn

Cocina de la familia; more than 200 authentic recipes from Mexican-American home kitchens. {by} Marilyn Tausend with Miguel Ravago. Simon & Schuster 1997 415p hardcover o.p. pa $20   **641.5**

1. Mexican American cooking
ISBN 0-684-85259-4 pa

LC 97-26979

This cookbook includes recipes for "Green Enchiladas with Spinach and Tofu, Chicken with Spicy Prune Sauce made with Coca-Cola, and Mexican Beef Chow Mein, {as well as} more traditional Mexican fare like Guacamole and Braised Chicken with Rice and Vegetables." Publ Wkly

Includes bibliographical references

Taylor, Kathryne

Love real food; more than 100 feel-good vegetarian favorites to delight the senses and nourish the body. Kathryne Taylor. Rodale 2017 xxvii, 243 p.p color illustrations (hardcover) $27.50   **641.5**

1. Cookbooks 2. Natural foods 3. Vegetarian cooking
ISBN 9781623367411; 9781623367428

LC 2017007675

In this book, author Kathryne Taylor "offers over 100 approachable and outrageously delicious meatless recipes complete with substitutions to make meals special diet-friendly (gluten-free, dairy-free, and egg-free) whenever possible. Her book is designed to show everyone-vegetarians, vegans, and meat-eaters alike--how to eat well and feel well." (Publisher's note)

"Taylor, creator of the vegetarian food blog Cookie and Kate (cookieandkate.com), debuts an approachable collection that will coax even reluctant cooks toward healthy eating." LJ

Terry, Bryant

Vegan Soul kitchen; fresh, healthy, and creative African American cuisine. Da Capo Press 2009 223p il pa $18.95   **641.5**

1. Southern cooking 2. African American cooking
ISBN 978-0-7382-1228-9; 0-7382-1228-8

LC 2008-46945

Includes bibliographical references

"In this electric, eclectic collection of vegan soul food, West Coast chef Bryant Terry . . . manages not only to demystify classic southern cooking, he makes it healthier and more accessible. With a low-key approach, commonly sourced ingredients and recipes worthy of any palette, Terry avoids the didacticism and rigidity of other vegan cookbooks. An impressive amount of information for each recipe, including entertainment recommendations, is also provided." (Publishers Weekly)

Theroux, Jessica

Cooking with Italian grandmothers; recipes and stories from Tuscany to Sicily. introduction by Alice Waters. Welcome Books 2010 296p $25.99   **641.5**

1. Italian cooking
ISBN 978-1-59962-089-3

LC 2010-21657

"American chef Jessica Theroux spent a year traveling throughout Italy, cooking and talking with Italian grandmothers, learning their secrets and listening to their stories. The result is a charming and authentic collection of recipes, techniques, anecdotes, and photographs that celebrate the rustic and sustainable culinary traditions of Italy's most experienced home cooks." (Publisher's note)

Thiessen, Tiffani, 1974-

Pull up a chair; recipes from my family to yours. Tiffani Thiessen with Rachel Holtzman. Houghton Mifflin Harcourt 2018 336 p. (paper over board) $30   **641.5**

1. Cooking 2. Cookbooks
ISBN 9781328710307

LC 2017059617

"The 125 recipes in this debut cookbook[, by Tiffani Thiessen,] are the kind that bring people together. Whether it's Stuffed French Toast or her husband, Brady's Favorite Short Rib Enchiladas for family-friendly meals, Curried Deviled Eggs or Boozy Date Milkshakes for special-occasion treats, or Mom's Cream Cheese Pie--because you can't forget dessert!" (Publisher's note)

"Thiessen's simple recipes and presentation truly inspire meals to reconnect and celebrate with friends and family." Publishers' Weekly

Thomas, Anna

Love soup; 160 all-new vegetarian recipes from the author of The Vegetarian Epicure. illustrations by Annika Huett. W. W.

Norton & Company 2009 528p il $35; pa $22.95 **641.5**

1. Soups 2. Vegetarian cooking

ISBN 978-0-393-06479-7; 978-0-393-33257-5 pa

LC 2009-19632

The author presents 160 "enticing recipes that may just charm even a die-hard carnivore. Soups are organized by season and range from hearty selections like rustic leek and potato, and minestrone for a crowd, to lighter summer options including tomato and fennel soup with blood orange and sweet corn. . . . Recipes for breads, dips and spreads, salads and a collection of desserts, as well as sample menus at the start of each chapter, make it easy to plan a full meal." Publ Wkly

Vegan, vegetarian, omnivore; dinner for everyone at the table. Anna Thomas ; photography by Victoria Pearson. W W Norton & Co Inc 2016 496 p. color illustrations (hardcover) $35 **641.5**

1. Cookbooks 2. Vegetarian cooking 3. Cooking

ISBN 9780393083019

LC 2015043951

This cookbook, by Anna Thomas with photography by Victoria Pearson, "shows us how to cook for today's table, with over 150 recipes for all tastes, and menus for every occasion. For a casual evening with friends, Farro with Lentils and Lavender served with Ratatouille from the Charcoal Grill makes a beautiful vegan supper—and also pairs wonderfully with garlic-and-herb rubbed lamb chops for the omnivores." (Publisher's note)

"Armed with nearly 200 of Thomas's versatile recipes, hosts can feel confident cooking one menu for all their guests." LJ

Thomas, Deepa

★ **Deepa's** secrets; slow-carb, new Indian cuisine. by Deepa Thomas ; foreword by Curt Ellis. Skyhorse Publishing 2017 229 p. illustrations (some color) (hardcover) $24.99 **641.5**

1. Cookbooks 2. Indian cooking 3. Low-carbohydrate diet -- Recipes 4. Cooking, Indic

ISBN 1510718982; 9781510718999; 9781510718982

James Beard Award: Health and Special Diets (2018)

This book, by Deepa Thomas with foreword by Curt Ellis, "introduces breakthrough slow carb and gut-healing recipes that are simple and nutrient-packed, without sacrificing its rich South Asian flavors. On a mission to demystify and make healthy an 'exotic' cuisine, Deepa shares shortcuts and techniques that will make 'New Indian' everyday fare." (Publisher's note)

"Engaging personal stories combined with artfully scattered notes and hints make this book reminiscent of the earliest Moosewood Cookbook in its tone and inviting narrative." Pub Wkly

Thompson, David

Thai food; with photography by Earl Carter. Ten Speed Press 2002 673p $40 **641.5**

1. Thai cooking

ISBN 978-1-580-08462-8; 1-580-08462-1

LC 2002-18117

"The first section of the book provides detailed cultural and social history and a guide to the regions and regional cuisines of Thailand. Then a detailed glossary of ingredients and a guide to techniques introduce the hundreds of recipes. These are grouped into chapters on relishes, soups, curries, salads, and sides, followed by one of menus with recipes. . . . [This] culinary history/cookbook is unique and will be an important purchase for any Asian cookery collection." Libr J

Includes bibliographical references

Thorisson, Mimi

French country cooking; Meals and Moments from a Village in the Vineyards. Mimi Thorisson ; photographs by Oddur Thorisson. Clarkson Potter/Publishers 2016 336 p. illustrations (chiefly color) (hardcover) $40 **641.5**

1. Cookbooks 2. French cooking 3. Cooking, French 4. Wineries -- France 5. Cooking -- France -- Médoc

ISBN 9780553459586

LC 2016004585

This cookbook by blogger Mimi Thorisson contains recipes inspired by people living in the village that Thorisson's family moved into in Médoc, France. It includes "White Asparagus Soufflé, Wine Harvest Pot au Feu, Endives with Ham, and Salted Butter Chocolate Cake. Featuring evocative photographs taken by Mimi's husband, Oddur Thorisson, and illustrated endpapers, this cookbook is a charming jaunt to an untouched corner of France that has thus far eluded the spotlight." (Publisher's note)

"Francophiles and armchair travelers who loved Dorie Greenspan's Around My French Table and David Lebovitz's My Paris Kitchen will gladly add this classic title to their collections." LJ

Includes bibliographical references and index

Thug Kitchen; eat like you give a f*ck. by Thug Kitchen. Rodale 2014 212 p. color illustrations (hardback) $24.99 **641.5**

1. Vegetarian cooking 2. Cooking -- Vegetables 3. Cooking (Vegetables)

ISBN 1623363586; 9781623363581

LC 2014036430

In this cookbook "Thug Kitchen wants to show everyone how to take charge of their plates and cook up some real f*cking food. . . . [T]hey're throwing down more than 100 recipes for their best-loved meals, snacks, and sides for beginning cooks to home chefs. . . . Plus they're going to arm you with all the info and techniques you need to shop on a budget and go and kick a bunch of ass on your own." (Publisher's note)

Tourles, Stephanie L.

Raw energy; 124 raw food recipes for energy bars, smoothies, and other snacks to supercharge your body. [by] Stephanie Tourles. Storey Pub. 2009 271p il pa $16.95 **641.5**

1. Snack foods 2. Vegetarian cooking 3. Cooking -- Natural foods

ISBN 978-1-60342-467-7

LC 2009-28675

"This delightful addition is easily accessible even to readers looking to make small changes in their diets. . . . [The author] shares a list of ingredients with pictures of each item. A list of kitchen equipment is also provided to accompany these recipes for shakes, bars, and soups, some of which require the use of a juicer or dehydrator. For libraries that don't have any books on the topic, this is an excellent introduction." Libr J

Includes bibliographical references

Trang, Corinne

Essentials of Asian cuisine; fundamentals and favorite recipes. black-and-white photographs by Corinne Trang; color photographs by Christopher Hirscheimer. Simon & Schuster 2003 592p il hardcover o.p. pa $34.99 **641.5**

1. Asian cooking

ISBN 0-7432-0312-7; 1-4391-9108-5 pa

LC 2002-30490

"Authoritative and thoroughly researched, this will be invaluable as both a reference and a cookbook." Libr J

Includes bibliographical references

Tsai, Ming

Blue Ginger; East-meets-West cooking with Ming Tsai. by Ming Tsai and Arthur Boehm. Potter 1999 275p $32.50 **641.5**
1. Cooking 2. Asian cooking
ISBN 0-609-60530-5
LC 99-36393
"Chapters divide the 125-plus recipes into soups, dim sum, rice and noodles, poultry, meat, seafood, elaborate side dishes and desserts, with mail-order sources. . . . Instructions are clearly written and often include tips for wine and food pairings and advice on ingredient substitutions and techniques." Publ Wkly

Turner, Kristy

But I could never go;-vegan!- 125 recipes that prove you can live without cheese, it's not all rabbit food, and your friends will still come over for dinner. by Kristy Turner, photographs by Chris Miller. The Experiment 2014 xi, 308 p.p color illustrations (pbk.) $23.95 **641.5**
1. Veganism 2. Cookbooks 3. Vegetarian cooking 4. Vegan cooking
ISBN 1615192107; 9781615192106; 9781615192113
LC 2014020051
This vegan cookbook, by Kristy Turner, with photographs by Chris Miller, "deliciously refutes every excuse you've ever heard with 125 bursting-with-flavor vegan recipes for every meal of the day--including dessert! . . . You'll find you can get enough protein, fit in at a potluck, learn to love cauliflower, and enjoy pizza, nachos, brownies, and more--without any animal products at all." (Publisher's note)
"Vegan foodies and foodies considering becoming vegan will be eager to break out their farro, sriracha, and liquid smoke, and have fun in the kitchen." LJ

Turshen, Julia

Feed the resistance; recipes + ideas for getting involved. Julia Turshen with contributions from Jocelyn Delk Adams, Maya-Camille Broussard, Anthony Thosh Collins and Chelsea Luger, Erika Council, Devita Davison, Cheryl Day, Von Diaz, Yana Gilbuena, Mikki Halpin, Hawa Hassan, Jocelyn Jackson, Callie Jayne, Jordyn Lexton, Preeti Mistry, People's Kitchen Collective, Stephen Satterfield, Nik Sharma, Shakirah Simley, Bill Smith and Antonio Lopez, Bryant Terry, Tunde Wey, and Caleb Zigas. Chronicle Books Llc 2017 143 p. (hc; alk. paper) $14.95 **641.5**
1. Cooking 2. Human rights 3. Advocacy (Political science)
ISBN 9781452168388; 9781452168432
LC 2017024414
"From favorite cookbook author Julia Turshen comes this practical and inspiring handbook for political activism--with recipes. . . . These dishes foster community and provide sustenance for the mind and soul, including a dozen of the healthy, affordable recipes Turshen is known for, plus over 15 more recipes from a diverse range of celebrated chefs." (Publisher's note)

Small victories; Recipes, Advice + Hundreds of Ideas for Home Cooking Triumphs. Julia Turshen ; photographs by Gentl + Hyers. Chronicle Books LLC 2016 303 p. color illustrations (hardcover; alk. paper) $35; (ebook) $36.39 **641.5**
1. Cooking
ISBN 9781452143095; 9781452148762
LC 2015039651
This book presents "more than 400 recipes and variations from Julia

Turshen, writer, go-to recipe developer, [and] co-author for best-selling cookbooks. . . . The process of truly great home cooking is demystified via more than a hundred lessons called out as 'small victories' in the funny, encouraging headnotes; these are lessons learned by Julia through a lifetime of cooking thousands of meals." (Publisher's note)
"Home cooks aiming to produce delicious, unpretentious fare or those who enjoyed such cookbooks as Deb Perelman's The Smitten Kitchen Cookbook or Kristen Miglore's Food52 Genius Recipes would do well to add this to their shelves." LJ

Valladolid, Marcela, 1978-

Casa Marcela; recipes and food stories of my life in the Californias. Marcela Valladolid ; foreword by Geoffrey Zakarian ; photography by Coral Von Zumwalt. Houghton Mifflin Harcourt 2017 xix, 265 p.p color illustrations (hardcover) $30 **641.5**
1. California 2. Mexican American cooking 3. Cookbooks 4. Cooking, Mexican
ISBN 054480855X; 9780544808577; 9780544808553
This book, by Marcela Valladolid, is "a reflection of her experience growing up in Tijuana and traveling back and forth to San Diego to see family and friends and for school. This book captures a culture centered around food, loved ones, and gatherings with mouthwatering recipes and in vibrant photography, all shot at Valladolid's home. Mexican food really is simple at its core, if you have some extra time for slow roasting meats or to prepare a few salsas, and the results are sure to impress." (Publisher's note)
"In Valladolid's latest cookbook, the Food Network host warmly welcomes readers into her new southern California home." Pub Wkly

Vetri, Marc

Il viaggio di Vetri; a culinary journey. [by] Marc Vetri with David Joachim; wine notes by Jeff Benjamin; photography by Douglas Takeshi Wolfe. Ten Speed Press 2008 289p il $40 **641.5**
1. Italian cooking
ISBN 978-1-58008-888-6; 1-58008-888-0
LC 2008-21667
"More than a cookbook, this . . . is a guide through the particular Italian cuisine and culture on which . . . [the author] has based his career. . . . Amateur chefs may have only dreamed of having a culinary journey like Vetri's, but with this book he has given them a reliable key to turning dream into reality." Publ Wkly

Vinton, Sherri Brooks

Eat it up! 150 Recipes to Use Every Bit and Enjoy Every Bite of the Food You Buy. Sherri Brooks Vinton. Da Capo Lifelong Books, a member of the Perseus Books Group 2016 256 p. (pbk.) $18.99 **641.5**
1. Cooking 2. Food conservation 3. Food waste -- Prevention
ISBN 9780738218182
LC 2015045183
In this cookbook, author Sherri Brooks Vinton "helps you make the most out of the food you bring home. These 150 delicious recipes mine the treasure in your kitchen—the fronds from your carrots, leaves from your cauliflower, bones from Sunday's roast, even the last lick of jam in the jar are put to good, tasty use." (Publisher's note)
"A sterling resource for the ecologically minded cook." Booklist
Includes bibliographical references and index

Voltaggio, Bryan

Home; recipes to share with family and friends. Bryan Voltaggio. Little, Brown & Co. 2015 272 p. color illustrations (hardcover) $35 **641.5**

1. Entertaining 2. American cooking
ISBN 0316323888; 9780316323888

LC 2014944089

This cookbook is author "Bryan Voltaggio's tribute to the American comfort food he enjoyed growing up, elevated with sophisticated and irresistible new recipes. Voltaggio brings an authentic love for seasonal, farm-to-table cooking and a playful and distinctive approach to classic dishes in his first solo cookbook. Many of the recipes celebrate his Middle-Atlantic roots in inventive ways." (Publisher's note)

"This is a celebrity chef cookbook that readers will want to use, not relegate to the coffee table." LJ

Waters, Alice

In the green kitchen; techniques to learn by heart. photographs by Hirsheimer & Hamilton. Clarkson Potter/Publishers 2010 151p il $28 **641.5**

1. Slow food movement 2. Vegetarian cooking 3. Cooking -- Natural foods
ISBN 978-0-307-33680-4; 0-307-33680-8

LC 2010-278664

The author "showcases basic cooking techniques every cook can and should master along with recipes using each method in this slim and attractive book. Derived from a Slow Food Nation event she helped organize, where notable chefs and foodies provided demonstrations on foundational procedures, Waters highlights a set of techniques that are universal to all cuisines. She covers the most basic of the basics, from stocking the pantry and washing lettuce to boiling pasta and wilting greens.... Ideal for the cooking novice, this gem of a book captures the expertise of world-class chefs in an accessible, straightforward manner." Publ Wkly

Weight Watchers 50th anniversary cookbook; 280 delicious recipes for every meal. St. Martin's Griffin 2013 335 p. $29.99 **641.5**

1. Cookbooks 2. Weight loss
ISBN 1250036402; 9781250036407

This cookbook of updated recipes "supplements the new Weight Watchers 360 program. Emphasizing retro comfort foods like chicken cordon bleu, cheddar corn pudding, and Boston cream pie, the book aims to dispel notions that diet food can't be crave-worthy. Each recipe includes nutritional analysis and a 'PointsPlus' value based on the amount of protein, carbohydrates, fat, and fiber per serving. Using the secondary index, readers can easily choose recipes by points value." (Library Journal)

Weil, Andrew

The **healthy** kitchen; recipes for a better body, life, and spirit. {by} Andrew Weil and Rosie Daley; photographs by Sang An, Amy Haskell, and Eric Studer. Knopf 2002 xxxvii, 325p il $24.95; pa $16.95 **641.5**

1. Cooking 2. Natural foods
ISBN 0-375-41306-5; 0-375-71031-0 pa

LC 2001-50391

This is "a stimulating invitation to healthy, pleasurable eating." Publ Wkly

Weinstein, Bruce

The **Great** Big Pressure Cooker Book; 500 easy recipes for every day and every machine. Bruce Weinstein and Mark Scarborough ; photographs by Tina Rupp. Clarkson Potter/Pub-

lishers 2015 512 p. 16 plates; color illustrations $25 **641.5**

1. Cookbooks 2. Quick and easy cooking 3. Pressure cooking
ISBN 0804185328; 9780804185325

LC 2014022862

This cookbook by Bruce Weinstein and Mark Scarbrough " has recipes for every device, stovetop and electric, no matter the manufacturer. Whether you're seeking an adventurous array of spices, found in dishes such as Cherry Chipotle Pulled Chicken or Smashed Sweet Potatoes with Pineapple and Ginger, or pure comfort food, like French Toast Bread Pudding or Classic Pot Roast and Potatoes, you'll find the perfect recipe." (Publisher's note)

Weir, Joanne

Sunset kitchen gypsy; Joanne Weir. Time Home Entertainment 2015 288 p. illustrations $35 **641.5**

1. Food 2. Cooking 3. Creation (Literary, artistic, etc.)
ISBN 0848746031; 9780848746032

LC 2014954434

Author Joanne Weir "shares the spark that led to her love of cooking, how she learned to taste and develop a palate, the meal that would forever change her life, her years working with Alice Waters at Chez Panisse during the beginning of the farm-to-table movement, and her continued travels teaching cooking classes the world over. Throughout, she offers the cherished dishes and lessons that have shaped her culinary journey." (Publisher's note)

"A compelling read with worldly recipes and evocative writing. If you like this title, try following it with Alex Guarnaschelli's Old-School Comfort Food or Hubert Keller's Souvenirs." Library Journal

Weiss, Luisa, 1979

Classic German baking; The Very Best Recipes for Traditional Favorites, from Pfeffernüsse to Streuselkuchen. Luisa Weiss. Ten Speed Press 2016 288 p. color illustrations (hardcover; alk. paper) $35 **641.5**

1. Baking 2. German cooking 3. Cooking, German
ISBN 9781607748250

LC 2016015734

Luisa Weiss shares more than 100 recipes, "gathered from expert bakers, friends, family, and time-honored sources throughout Germany, Austria, and Switzerland. Whether you're in the mood for the simple yet emblematic Streuselkuchen, crisp and flaky Strudel, or classic breakfast Brötchen, every recipe you're looking for is here, along with detailed advice to ensure success plus delightful storytelling about the origins, meaning, and rituals behind the recipes." (Publisher's note)

"Collected from various places and people—whether it's a cookbook or from her German assistant—this cookbook presents a beautiful piece of German tradition." Pub Wkly

Includes bibliographical references and index

Wells, Patricia

★ **My** master recipes; 165 recipes to inspire confidence in the kitchen; with dozens of variations. Patricia Wells. William Morrow, an imprint of HarperCollins Publishers 2017 xxix, 466 p.p color illustrations (hardcover) $35 **641.5**

1. Cooking 2. Cookbooks
ISBN 0062424823; 9780062424822; 9780062684059

In this cookbook, author Patricia Wells, "codifies the skills she imparts in her classes. . . . Each of the recipes teaches particular techniques--blanching, searing, simmering, sweating, steaming, braising, deep-frying--with additional recipes that take your skills in directions both savory and sweet, simple and profound--giving you the knowledge and assurance to expand your cooking even further." (Publisher's note)

"Simple, seasonal dishes . . . will send gourmands to the kitchen for leisurely cooking. . . Wells's recipes are fiercely precise and personal." LJ

The **Provence** cookbook; 175 recipes and a select guide to the markets, shops, & restaurants of France's sunny south. HarperCollins 2004 338p il $29.95   **641.5**
1. French cooking
ISBN 978-0-06-050782-4; 0-06-050782-9

LC 2003-56977

Wells offers "her own recipes, along with some from her butcher, fishmonger, other merchants, neighborhood restaurants, and other sources slightly farther afield. Most of the dishes are simple, allowing the flavors of Provence's wonderfully fresh produce and other ingredients to come through. . . . Wine suggestions are included throughout—sometimes for Wells's own label, since her vineyard is now productive—and she provides addresses and other relevant details about her favorite restaurants and purveyors." Libr J

Wex, Michael
Rhapsody in schmaltz; Yiddish food and why we can't stop eating it. Michael Wex. St. Martin's Press 2016 320 p. (hardback) $26.99   **641.5**
1. Jewish cooking 2. Jews -- Social life and customs 3. Jews -- Food 4. Ashkenazim -- Social life and customs
ISBN 9781250071514

LC 2015044974

This book, by Michael Wex, "traces the pathways of Jewish food from the Bible and Talmud, to Eastern Europe, to its popular landing pads in North America today. With an eye for detail and a healthy dose of humor, Michael Wex also examines how these impact modern culture, from temple to television." (Publisher's note)

"Informative, merrily entertaining culinary and cultural history." Kirksu

Wolfert, Paula
The **slow** Mediterranean kitchen; recipes for the passionate cook. Wiley 2003 350p il $34.95   **641.5**
1. Mediterranean cooking
ISBN 0-471-26288-9

LC 2002-153265

The author offers "dishes from all the countries of the region: brodetto Pasquale (Italian Easter Lamb Soup), Expatriate Roast Chicken with Lemon and Olives from Morocco, and Catalonian Fall-Apart Lamb Shanks. Although many recipes call for braising, stewing, and other techniques of long cooking, others are not limited to those techniques, for Wolfert's definition of slow cooking also encompasses marinating and similar techniques." Libr J

Workman, Katie
Dinner solved! 100 ingenious recipes that make the whole family happy, including you. by Katie Workman. Workman Publishing 2015 384 p. (alk. paper) $17.95   **641.5**
1. Cooking
ISBN 0761181873; 9780761181873

LC 2015011304

In this cookbook, author Katie Workman "her attention to the biggest problem that every family cook faces: how to make everyone at the table happy without turning into a short-order cook. . . . Katie shows you how Asian Spareribs can start mild and sweet for less adventurous eaters—and then, in no time, become a zesty second version for spice lovers. She shakes up the usual chicken for dinner with Chicken Tikka

Masala-ish—and feeds vegetarians, too." (Publisher's note)
"Families can use this practical, mix-and-match recipe collection to lessen the stress of meal planning." LJ

The **mom** 100 cookbook; 100 recipes every mom needs in her back pocket. Katie Workman ; photographs by Todd Coleman. Workman Pub Co 2012 xxix, 366 p.p col. ill. (alk. paper) $16.95   **641.5**
1. Cooking 2. Cookbooks 3. Parenting
ISBN 0761166033; 9780761166030

LC 2012001330

This cookbook, by Katie Workman, "offers recipes, tips, techniques, attitude, and wisdom for staying happy in the kitchen while proudly keeping it homemade--because homemade not only tastes best, but is also better (and most economical) for you. . . . [It presents] 20 dilemmas every mom faces, with 5 solutions for each: including terrific recipes for the vegetable-averse, the salad-rejector, for the fish-o-phobe, or the overnight vegetarian convert." (Publisher's note)

Worrall-Thompson, Antony
The **essential** diabetes cookbook; good healthy eating from around the world. [by] Anthony Worrall Thompson, with Louise Blair. Kyle: Kyle Cathie 2010 287p il $35   **641.5**
1. Cooking 2. Diabetes -- Diet therapy
ISBN 978-1-906868-15-4

LC 2010-932221

200 recipes for diabetics that take their inspiration from cuisines around the world, including nutritional information for each recipe.
"From fish (Grilled Sea Bass with Spiced Cabbage) to crepes (Asian Surf and Turf Crêpes) to pork (Tofu, Pork, and Shellfish Hot Pot), these dishes bring life back into diabetic cooking. . . . Adventurous cooks will cheer for this diabetes cookbook." Libr J

Yeh, Molly
Molly on the range; recipes and stories from an unlikely life on a farm. Molly Yeh, creator of My name is Yeh. Rodale Books 2016 304 p. color illustrations (ebook) $23.99; (hardback) $32.50   **641.5**
1. American cooking 2. Cooking, American
ISBN 9781623366964; 162336695X; 9781623366957

LC 2016033840

This book, by food blogger Molly Yeh, "begins in the suburbs of Chicago in the 90s, when things like Lunchables and Dunkaroos were the objects of her affection; continues into her New York years, when Sunday mornings meant hangovers and bagels; and ends in her beloved new home, where she's currently trying to master the art of the hotdish." (Publisher's note)

Zakarian, Geoffrey, 1959-
My perfect pantry; Geoffrey Zakarian ; with Amy Stevenson and Margaret Zakarian ; photographs by Sara Remington. Clarkson Potter 2014 304 p. color illustrations $30   **641.5**
1. Cookbooks 2. American cooking 3. Cooking
ISBN 0385345666; 9780385345668

LC 2013050636

This cookbook, by Geoffrey Zakarian, with Amy Stevenson and Margaret Zakarian, and featuring photographs by Sara Remington, focuses on household cooking from stock pantry items. "Forget exotic condiments and specialty foods. With a working base of 50 readily available ingredients, from oats and honey to almonds and canned chickpeas, you will always have the makings of a delicious home-cooked meal." (Publisher's note)

Zakarian's "list of 50 pantry necessities includes beans, oils, pastas, sauces, and nuts. For each of these staples he proffers a trio of recipes. Color photographs enhance the text and encourage readers to pursue Zakarian's culinary vision." Booklist

641.502   Auxiliary techniques and procedures

Warner, Justin

The **Laws** of Cooking; And How to Break Them. by Justin Warner. St. Martin's Press 2015 336 p. color illustrations $35   **641.502**

1. Cooking
ISBN 1250065135; 9781250065131

LC 2015034388

This cookbook, by Justin Warner, "encourages improvisation and play. . . . By introducing eleven laws based on familiar foods, . . . [Warner] will teach you why certain flavors combine brilliantly, and then show how these combinations work in 110 more complex and inventive recipes " (Publisher's note)

"Warner's focus is on the food, and encouraging readers to stretch their palates and skills to create something truly unique. This is a refreshingly new take from an author to watch." Pub Wkly

641.509   History, geographic treatment, biography

Cherniavsky, Mark

The **cookbook** library; four centuries of the cooks, writers, and recipes that made the modern cookbook. Anne Willan ; with Mark Cherniavsky and Kyri Claflin. University of California Press 2012 xii, 328 p.p (cloth; alk. paper) $50   **641.509**

1. Cooking -- History
ISBN 0520244001; 9780520244009

LC 2011024489

Includes bibliographical references (p. 296-306) and indexes

"The Cookbook Library is an engaging, thoughtful, and well-researched history of English- and French- language cooking, using examples of antiquarian cookbooks from the author's own extensive library. Willan, a noted authority on French cooking, educator, and author/journalist, covers the years 1474-1830 and divides her chapters by century. Within each chapter, Willan gives an overview of cooking and cookbook history for the respective period, including sidebars on social customs and technical innovations." (Choice Reviews)

Prud'homme, Alex

The **French** chef in America; Julia Child's Second Act. Alex Prud'homme. Alfred A. Knopf 2016 336 p. (hardcover; alk. paper) $27.95   **641.509**

1. Cooks -- Biography 2. Cooks -- United States -- Biography
ISBN 9780385351751; 9780804168793

LC 2015043441

This book, by Alex Prud'homme, "shows us [Julia] Child in the aftermath of the publication of Mastering the Art of French Cooking, suddenly finding herself America's first lady of French food and under considerable pressure to embrace her new mantle. We see her dealing with difficult colleagues and the challenges of fame." (Publisher's note)

"Kelsey provides as much information as possible about all of the participants in these journeys and manages to keep it interesting." Pub Wkly

Includes bibliographical references and index

641.53   Light meals

Olivier, Michele

Little Bento; 32 Irresistible Bento Box Lunches for Kids. Michele Olivier. Sonoma Press 2016 178 p. color illustrations $16.99   **641.53**

1. Cookbooks 2. Japanese cooking 3. Quick and easy cooking
ISBN 1943451281; 9781943451289

This cookbook by Michele Olivier "shows parents how to turn their picky children into healthy, adventurous eaters through creative, easy-to-assemble bento box lunches. . . . [It] contains over 100 recipes and 32 photos of fully-composed, seasonally-organized bento box lunches, which include . . . comprehensive bento box ingredient lists, . . . pros and cons of various bento box options, . . . and bento meal planning tips and a weekly meal planning worksheet." (Publisher's note)

641.555   Timesaving cooking

Dinner Made Simple; 35 Everyday Ingredients, 350 Easy Recipes. Oxmoor House 2016 352 p. color illustrations (pbk.) $24.95   **641.555**

1. Dining 2. Cooking
ISBN 0848746899; 9780848746896

LC 2015958963

This cookbook, from "Real Simple Magazine," is "filled with 350 easy, quick dishes-many ready in 30 minutes or less-to help you get out of your recipe rut. With 10 ideas for every ingredient, you'll never look at a box of spaghetti, a bunch of carrots, or a ball of pizza dough the same way again." (Publisher's note)

"With plenty of ideas for meals that can be prepared in less than 30 minutes, this cookbook will satisfy busy home cooks and eaters who enjoy browsing by photo." LJ

Weinstein, Bruce

The **kitchen** shortcut Bible; more than 200 recipes to make real food fast. Bruce Weinstein, Mark Scarbrough. Little, Brown & Co. 2018 352 p. $30   **641.555**

1. Cooking 2. Cookbooks 3. Quick and easy cooking
ISBN 9780316509718

LC 2017964191

This cookbook, by Bruce Weinstein and Mark Scarbrough, is "the ultimate collection of recipes to make real food, real fast--with hundreds of ways to cook smarter, not harder. . . . [It] is for all of us who love to cook, but never seem to have enough time. Rather than a book of way-too-clever hacks, this is a collection of more than 200 ingenious recipes that supercharge your time in the kitchen without sacrificing high quality or fresh flavor." (Publisher's note)

"Basic directions and easy-to-find ingredients guarantee this book will be embraced by everyday cooks, who will welcome a respite from complicated, time-consuming, and multi-ingredient recipes." Library Journal

641.563   Cooking for health, appearance, personal reasons

Cavallari, Kristin, 1987-

True roots; a mindful kitchen with more than 100 recipes free of gluten, dairy, and refined sugar. Kristin Cavallari. St. Martin's Press 2018 272 p. $25.99   **641.563**

1. Cookbooks 2. Sugar-free diet 3. Gluten-free diet
ISBN 1623369169; 9781623369163

In this book, author Kristin Cavallari "shows you that improving the way you eat doesn't have to be difficult--a clean and toxin-free diet can and should be fun, easy, and enjoyable. She learned the hard way that dieting leads nowhere good, and that a clean lifestyle is the ticket to feeling and being healthy." (Publisher's note)

Chapman, Emma

A **beautiful** mess; weekday weekend; how to live a healthy veggie life ... and still eat treats. text and photographs by Elsie Larson and Emma Chapman. Chronicle Books 2017 208 p. color illustrations (hardcover) $24.95   **641.563**

    1. Vegetarianism 2. Vegetarian cooking 3. Cooking -- Vegetables
ISBN 9781452154718; 9781452155760

                                  LC 2016053237

In this cookbook, "Emma Chapman and Elsie Larson share their unique and approachable diet with fans and healthy eaters. . . . Their philosophy involves eating responsibly during the week--avoiding refined flours, sugars, alcohol, and dairy--and indulging on weekends. Vetted by nutritionists and divided into four parts (breakfast, meals, snacks and sweets, and drinks), each containing a weekday and weekend chapter." (Publisher's note)

Esposito, Jennifer, 1972-

Jennifer's way kitchen; easy allergen-free, anti-inflammatory recipes for a delicious life. Jennifer Esposito with Eve Adamson. Grand Central Life & Style 2017 304 p. color illustrations (hardcover) $30   **641.563**

    1. Allergy 2. Cookbooks 3. Cooking -- Natural foods 4. Cooking (Natural foods) 5. Food allergy -- Diet therapy 6. Inflammation -- Diet therapy
ISBN 9781455596713; 9781538712467

                                  LC 2017943769

This cookbook, by Jennifer Esposito, with Adamson, presents "easy-to-follow, mouthwatering recipes that will reduce inflammation-which is the single best thing anyone can do for his or her body. . . . Esposito struggled with her health her entire life and was finally diagnosed as a food-allergy sufferer with severe celiac disease. Now she opens up her kitchen to you and shares the cherished recipes that helped save her life and regain her health." (Publisher's note)

"This solid foray into allergen-free cooking is packed with information that can help those with dietary problems." Pub Wkly

Fong, Henry

Ready or not! 150+ make-ahead, make-over, and make-now recipes by Nom Nom Paleo. Michelle Tam ; Henry Fong. Andrews McMeel Pub. 2017 344 p. color illustrations (hardcover) $35   **641.563**

    1. Paleo cooking 2. Cooking (Natural foods) 3. Gluten-free diet -- Recipes 4. High-protein diet -- Recipes 5. Prehistoric peoples -- Nutrition
ISBN 9781449478292; 9781449487096; 1449478298

                                  LC 2017930875

This book, by Michelle Tam and Henry Fong, "makes healthy Paleo home cooking a breeze, no matter if there's time to prepare or just minutes to spare. Whether you're a fastidious planner or a last-minute improviser, you'll find plenty of deliciously nourishing options, from make-ahead feasts to lightning-fast leftover makeovers." (Publisher's note)

Hartwig, Melissa

The **whole30** fast & easy; 150 simply delicious everyday recipes for your Whole30. Melissa Hartwig, co-author of the

New York Times best-selling The Whole30 ; photography by Ghazalle Badiozamani. Houghton Mifflin Harcourt 2017 xix, 300 p.p color illustrations (hbk.) $30   **641.563**

    1. Cookbooks 2. Weight loss 3. Cooking -- Natural foods 4. Reducing diets -- Recipes 5. Nutrition -- Popular works 6. Food habits -- Popular works 7. Weight loss -- Popular works 8. Diet therapy -- Popular works 9. Self-care, Health -- Popular works
ISBN 9781328839398; 1328839206; 9781328839206

                                  LC 2017302891

This cookbook, by Melissa Hartwig, with photographs by Ghazalle Badiozamani, features "recipes perfect for weeknight cooking, lunches in a hurry, and hearty breakfasts that still get you out the door on time; nearly effortless skillet meals, stir-fries, sheet-pan suppers, and slow-cook and no-cook meals, most of which can be made in 30 minutes or less; [and] creative, delicious meals using widely-available ingredients found in any supermarket." (Publisher's note)

"Readers interested in preparing and serving healthier meals that come together quickly (even if they're not participating in the Whole30 program) are sure to appreciate this thoughtful collection." Pub Wkly

Hay, Donna

Life in Balance; Donna Hay. HarperCollins 2016 240 p. color illustrations $34.99   **641.563**

    1. Diet 2. Cookbooks
ISBN 1460750322; 9781460750322

This cookbook by Donna Hay "is about embracing food and all its benefits. Each chapter, from breakfast to baking, has simple recipes enriched with nature's superfoods. . . . From new ideas for power dinners to tempting grills, from super-charged breakfasts to low-carb options. . . . The only kind of diet that works, after all, is the balanced diet - the one you can sustain long term. And when your life is in balance, you feel great and it shows - from the inside out." (Publisher's note)

"Recommended for readers who dislike the idea of dieting but want to explore popular health foods." LJ

Joachim, David

The **wicked** healthy cookbook; free from animals. Chad Charno, Derek Sarno, and David Joachim ; foreword by Woody Harrelson ; photographs by Eva Kosmas Flores. Grand Central Pub 2018 320 p. $30   **641.563**

    1. Cookbooks 2. Vegetarian cooking 3. Cooking -- Natural foods
ISBN 1455570281; 9781455570287

This book, by Chad Charno, Derek Sarno, and David Joachim, "takes badass plant-based cooking to a whole new level. The chefs have pioneered innovative cooking techniques such as pressing and searing mushrooms until they reach a rich and delicious meat-like consistency. Inside, you'll find informative sidebars and must-have tips on everything from oil-free and gluten-free cooking (if you're into that) to organizing an efficient kitchen." (Publisher's note)

"This varied assortment will appeal mostly to herbivores wishing to comfort their inner carnivore." Publishers' Weekly

Meyer, Linda

Great vegan bbq without a grill; amazing plant-based ribs, burgers, steaks, kabobs and more smokey favorites. Linda Meyer, Alex Meyer. Page Street Pub. Co. 2018 192 p. (pbk.) $21.99   **641.563**

    1. Vegan cooking 2. Barbecue cooking
ISBN 1624144969; 1624144977; 9781624144967; 9781624144974

                                  LC 2017946105

This cookbook, by Linda and Alex Meyer, presents easy and convenient barbecue recipes anywhere, anytime for people with healthy vegan lifestyle. . . . [The authors] take you on a tour of America's best BBQ, inspired by their family road trips to South Carolina, Louisiana, Texas and more. They'll show you how to easily replicate the smoky flavors and textures of classic BBQ meats using a grill pan or cast iron skillet--no outdoor grill or smoker required!" (Publisher's note)

Mills, Ella

Natural Feasts; 100+ Healthy, Plant-based Recipes to Share and Enjoy with Friends and Family. by Ella Mills. Scribner 2017 286 p. color illustrations (hardcover) $24 **641.563**

    1. Vegetarian cooking 2. Gluten-free diet -- Recipes 3. Cooking (Natural foods)

    ISBN 9781501174278; 9781501174285; 1501174274

This book, by Ella Mills, "offers more than 100 exciting, accessible recipes to show how clean, gluten-free, plant-based eating is the perfect way to entertain friends and satisfy your guests. . . . When conventional medicine failed her, Ella overcame a rare, devastating illness by switching to a plant-based diet. . . . Now Ella shares her personal ideas and recipes for every foodie occasion." (Publisher's note)

"For a plant-based entertainer who wants to serve the most delicious, natural, and healthy food, this cookbook is a must purchase." Pub Wkly

Mullen, Seamus

Real food heals; eat to feel younger + stronger every day. Seamus Mullen with Genevieve Ko. Avery, an imprint of Penguin Random House 2017 319 p. color illustrations (hardback) $35 **641.563**

    1. Nutrition 2. Diet therapy 3. Paleo cooking 4. High-protein diet -- Recipes 5. Prehistoric peoples -- Nutrition

    ISBN 9780735213869; 9780735213852

                                  LC 2017012317

This cookbook, by Seamus Mullen with Genevieve Ko, presents "over 125 Paleo-inspired recipes designed to revitalize your health every day. . . . including Kefir Scrambled Eggs with Grated Garlic; Nori Rolls with Olive Oil, Tuna, Avocado, and Sprouts; and Fig Almond Cacao Nib bars. Complete with a 21-day jump-start meal plan, this unique cookbook will help everyone prepare healthy, irresistible food with big flavors every day and put them on the path to total wellness." (Publisher's note)

"Readers interested in transitioning to a healthier diet—particularly those new to the kitchen—are sure to appreciate this terrifically accessible approach." Pub Wkly

Perlmutter, David

The **grain** brain cookbook; more than 150 life-changing gluten-free recipes to transform your health. David Perlmutter. Little, Brown & Co. 2014 352 p. color illustrations (hardcover) $30 **641.563**

    1. Cookbooks 2. Gluten-free diet

    ISBN 0316334251; 9780316334259

                                  LC 2014940575

This gluten free cookbook, by David Perlmutter, builds off the author's previous work arguing "the devastating effects of wheat, sugar, and carbs on the brain. . . . [This book] presents more than 150 delectable recipes to keep your brain vibrant and your body fit, all while dramatically reducing your risk for--and treating--Alzheimer's, depression, ADHD, and epilepsy, as well as relieving everyday conditions like headaches, insomnia, and forgetfulness." (Publisher's note)

"Recommended only for libraries where Perlmutter's books are in high demand." LJ

Roll, Rich, 1972-

The **plantpower** way; whole food plant-based recipes and guidance for the whole family. Penguin Group USA 2015 319 p. color illustrations $39.95 **641.563**

    ISBN 1583335870; 9781583335871

    1. Vegetarian cooking 2. Natural foods

In this book authors Rich Roll and Julie Piatt "shares the joy and vibrant health they and their whole family have experienced living a plant-based lifestyle. Bursting with inspiration, practical guidance, and beautiful four-color photography, The Plantpower Way has more than 120 delicious, easy-to-prepare whole food recipes, including hearty breakfasts, lunches, and dinners, plus healthful and delicious smoothies and juices, and decadent desserts." (Publisher's note)

Sobon, Jackie

Vegan yack attack on the go! plant-based recipes for your fast-paced vegan lifestyle. Jackie Sobon. Quarto Publishing Group USA Inc. 2018 208 p. (hardcover book) $22.99 **641.563**

    1. Veganism 2. Cookbooks 3. Vegan cooking

    ISBN 9781631594229

                                  LC 2017059560

This cookbook by Jackie Sobon features "plant-based recipes that fit your busy lifestyle! If you're a vegan and frequently on the go, it can be hard to eat well while still maintaining your plant-based lifestyle. You need options you can make in advance, take with you, or prepare quickly and easily once you get home. [The book] has all of these scenarios covered and more." (Publisher's note)

"This cookbook is proof that vegan food can be portable, healthy, and tasty." Publishers' Weekly

Solfrini, Valentina

Naturally vegetarian; recipes & stories from my Italian family farm. Valentina Solfrini. Avery 2017 255 p. color illustrations (hardcover) $35 **641.563**

    1. Italian cooking 2. Seasonal cooking 3. Vegetarian cooking 4. Cooking, Italian

    ISBN 9781101983591; 9781101983607; 1101983590

This cookbook, by Valentina Solfrini, features "125 delicious all-vegetarian recipes from the . . . [Sofrini's] family farm in northeastern Italy. . . . [It] offer[s] readers a glimpse of a year on an Italian farm and the recipes that come with the changing of the seasons. She also shares how to stock a whole foods Italian pantry, introducing them to new ingredients . . . and the fundamental recipes and techniques for preparing and cooking fresh pasta." (Publisher's note)

"In this thoroughly enjoyable book, Solfrini, a graphic designer and blogger (Hortus Cuisine) who lives on her family's farm in central Italy, takes the reader through seasonal chapters on vegetarian Italian cooking." Pub Wkly

Walker, Danielle

Danielle Walker's against all grain; meals made simple; gluten-free, dairy-free, and paleo recipes to make anytime. by Danielle Walker. Simon & Schuster 2014 319 p. color illustrations $34.95 **641.563**

    1. Gluten-free diet

    ISBN 162860042X; 9781628600421

This cookbook, by Danielle Walker, presents "recipes that make cooking for the grain-free family both easy and enjoyable. . . . Walker takes the guesswork out of meal planning with eight weeks' worth of dinner ideas, complete with full shopping lists and recipes for using up leftovers. Whether we're moms, students, or business owners, at the end of the day we all want fresh, home-cooked meals that are easy to prepare." (Publisher's note)

Weil, Andrew, 1942-

Fast Food, Good Food; More Than 150 Quick and Easy Ways to Put Healthy, Delicious Food on the Table. Andrew Weil. Little, Brown & Co. 2015 304 p. color illustrations $30   **641.563**

1. Health 2. Cooking

ISBN 0316329428; 9780316329422

LC 2015931944

IACP Cookbook Award Winner: Health & Special Diet (2016)

The recipes in author Andrew Weil's cookbook "showcase fresh, high-quality ingredients and hearty flavors, like Buffalo Mozzarella Bruschetta, Five-Spice Winter Squash Soup, Greek Style Kale Salad, Pappardelle with Arugula Walnut Pesto, Pan-Seared Halibut with Green Harissa, Coconut Lemon Bars, and Pomegranate Margaritas. With guidance on following an anti-inflammatory diet and mouth-wateringly gorgeous photographs, FAST FOOD, GOOD FOOD will inspire the inner nutritionist and chef in every reader." (Publisher's note)

"Weil's accessible recipes will attract flexitarians, especially those with a penchant for seafood, vegetables, whole grains, and olive oil." LJ

Winfrey, Oprah, 1954-

Food, health, and happiness; 115 on-point recipes for great meals and a better life. Oprah Winfrey. Flatiron Books 2017 240 p. color illustrations (hardcover) $35   **641.563**

1. Cookbooks

ISBN 9781250126535; 9781250126542; 9781250140173

LC 2016963619

In this book, by Oprah Winfrey, "Oprah shares the recipes that have allowed eating to finally be joyful for her. With dishes created and prepared alongside her favorite chefs, paired with personal essays and memories from Oprah herself, this cookbook offers a candid, behind-the-scenes look into the life (and kitchen!) of one of the most influential and respected celebrities in the world." (Publisher's note)

641.564   Seasonal cooking

Wiseman, Shelley

The **Farm** Cooking School; techniques and recipes that celebrate the seasons. by Ian Knauer and Shelley Wiseman; photographs by Guy Ambrosino. Motorbooks Intl 2017 256 p. $35   **641.564**

1. Cookbooks 2. Seasonal cooking 3. Cooking -- Vegetables

ISBN 0997211342; 9780997211344

This cookbook, by Ian Knauer and Shelley Wiseman, with photographs by Guy Ambrosino, "is packed with many of the same lessons you'd learn in person at [The Farm Cooking School], taught through more than 100 delicious recipes. . . . [It] is a cookbook for anyone who wants to learn to cook in tune with nature. Celebrate the seasons as you grow comfortable with the practiced techniques of our forebears." (Publisher's note)

641.568   Cooking for special occasions

All time best holiday entertaining; the editors at America's Test Kitchen. America's Test Kitchen 2017 ix, 182 p.p color illustrations (hardcover) $22.95   **641.568**

1. Entertaining 2. Holiday cooking

ISBN 9781940352992; 9781945256004

LC 2017000742

"With decades of experience turning out perfect turkeys, the experts at Cook's Illustrated are no strangers to pulling off a great holiday meal. In 'All-Time Best Holiday Entertaining,' we have gathered 75 spectacular, foolproof recipes from our extensive archives to help you confidently prepare memorably festive feasts for years to come." (Publisher's note)

"Blending classic and contemporary holiday foods, this slim volume from the editors at America's Test Kitchen (ATK) puts 75 starters, centerpieces, sides, and sweets at readers' fingertips." LJ

Rosenstrach, Jenny

How to celebrate everything; Recipes & Rituals for Birthdays, Holidays, Family Dinners & Every Day in Between. Jenny Rosenstrach. Ballantine Books 2016 336 p. color illustrations (hardback) $30   **641.568**

1. Dinners 2. Cookbooks 3. Entertaining 4. Holiday cooking 5. Families 6. Dinners and dining

ISBN 9780804176309

LC 2016001416

This cookbook by Jenny Rosenstrach is "a warm and inviting guide to turning birthdays, holidays, and everyday occasions into cherished traditions, with more than 100 time-tested recipes. . . . [It includes] complete menus for Thanksgiving, Christmas, and New Year's Eve and, of course, dozens of Rosenstrach's signature family dinners: Grilled Soy-Glazed Pork Chops, Harissa Roasted Chicken, [and] Crispy Chickpeas with Yogurt Sauce." (Publisher's note)

"This book is a delicious and delightful ode to the ways family and food intertwine, reinforcing each other." Booklist

641.578   Outdoor cooking

Ly, Linda

The **new** camp cookbook; Linda Ly ; photography by Will Taylor. Voyager Press an imprint of The Quarto Group 2017 224 p. illustrations (hc; alk. paper) $25   **641.578**

1. Outdoor cooking

ISBN 9780760359372; 0760352011; 9780760352014

LC 2016054283

This book, by Linda Ly, with photography by Will Taylor, is "for day trippers, adventurers, campers, and anyone who enjoys cooking outdoors. You'll find organizational advice and cooking techniques, from planning your meals, packing a cooler, and stocking a camp pantry to building a fire, grilling in foil packs, and maintaining heat in a dutch oven. The recipes are presented by meal: breakfast, lunch, snacks, sweets, and all-out feasts." (Publisher's note)

Includes bibliographical references (page 218) and index

Master of the grill; foolproof recipes, top-rated gadgets, gear, & ingredients plus clever test kitchen tips & fascinating food science. by the editors at America's Test Kitchen. America's Test Kitchen 2016 464 p. illustrations (chiefly color) (paperback) $29.95   **641.578**

1. Outdoor cooking 2. Barbecue cooking 3. Barbecuing

ISBN 9781940352541

LC 2015040405

This cookbook, edited by America's Test Kitchen, "features a wide variety of kitchen-tested recipes. . . . Everyone should know how to make — the juiciest burgers, barbecue chicken that's moist not tough, tender grill-smoked pork ribs, the greatest steak. . . . Learn how to make Cowboy Steaks, Alabama BBQ Chicken, and Kansas City Sticky Ribs.

... Covers the pros and cons of gas and charcoal grills and which might be right for you, as well as the tools you'll use with them." (Publisher's note)

"The recipes are presented thoughtfully and often accompanied by step-by-step photos guiding readers through processes such as trimming asparagus and arranging coals. This is a fabulous addition to the ATK canon." Pub Wkly

641.587   Steam and pressure cooking

Multicooker perfection; cook it fast or cook it slow-you decide. by the editors at America's Test Kitchen. America's Test Kitchen 2018 192 p. (paperback) $22.99   **641.587**
1. Cookbooks 2. Slow cooking 3. Pressure cooking 4. Cooking 5. Electric cooking, Slow
ISBN 9781945256288

LC 2017055683

This cookbook, by the editors of America's Test Kitchen, provides "a collection of foolproof recipes tested and developed to work in any multicooker and conform to your schedule. Make each recipe 'fast' using the pressure-cook setting or let dinner cook while you're out by preparing it 'slow' on the slow-cook setting. These crowd-pleasing recipes are perfectly suited for cooking at the touch of a button, from soups and stews." (Publisher's note)

641.589   Specific utensils

Food processor perfection; 75 amazing ways to use the most powerful tool in your kitchen. by the editors at America's Test Kitchen. America's Test Kitchen 2017 182 p. color illustrations (Test Kitchen handbook) (paperback) $19.95   **641.589**
1. Cooking 2. Cookbooks 3. Food processors 4. Food processor cooking
ISBN 9781940352916; 9781940352909

LC 2016051195

This book, by America's Test Kitchen, "unleashes the potential of what a food processor can do with an eye-opening collection of 75 kitchen-tested recipes to make your cooking easier, faster, and better. . . . It will transform how you use this appliance, streamline everyday cooking and baking, and open doors to projects you would never have considered tackling by hand." (Publisher's note)

"This is a solid guide for those in search of no-fuss, easy-to-follow recipes that maximize food processor use." Pub Wkly

641.59   Cooking characteristic of specific geographic environments, ethnic cooking

Acheson, Hugh

A **New** Turn in the South; Southern Flavors Reinvented for Your Kitchen. Hugh Acheson. Clarkson Potter 2011 299 p. color illustrations $35   **641.59**
1. Cookbooks 2. American cooking 3. Southern cooking 4. Cooking, American -- Southern style
ISBN 0307719553; 9780307719553

LC 2010052632

James Beard Award (2012)

In this cookbook, by Hugh Acheson, "you'll find libations, seasonal vegetables that take a prominent role, salads and soups, his prized sides,

and fish and meats--all of which turn Southern food on its head every step of the way. Hugh's recipes include: Oysters on the Half Shell with Cane Vinegar and Chopped Mint Sauce; . . . Chanterelles on Toast with Mushrooms; . . . Braised and Crisped Pork Belly with Citrus Salad; . . . and Lemon Chess Pies with Blackberry Compote." (Publisher's note)

Acquista, Angelo

The **Mediterranean** Family Table; 125 Simple, Everyday Recipes Made With the Most Delicious and Healthiest Food on Earth. by Acquista Angelo, M.D. and Laurie Anne Vandermolen. HarperCollins 2015 336 p. color illustrations $29.99   **641.59**
1. Diet 2. Mediterranean cooking
ISBN 006240718X; 9780062407184

In this book, Dr. Acquista Angelo "combines his medical experience and Sicilian roots to outline the guiding principles of the Mediterranean diet and takes it one step further with a collection of easy, wholesome, and delicious recipes the entire family will love." (Publisher's note)

"For those interested in changing their life through diet, Acquista is an infectiously positive coach, and his recipes make a fine playbook." Pub Wkly

Adimando, Stacy

★ **Nopalito**; a Mexican kitchen. Gonzalo González Guzmán, with Stacy Adimando ; photography by Eva Kolenko. Ten Speed Press 2017 256 p. illustrations (chiefly color) (ebook) $65; (hardback) $30   **641.59**
1. Cookbooks 2. Mexican cooking 3. Cooking, Mexican 4. Nopalito (Restaurant)
ISBN 9780399578298; 9780399578281

LC 2016030890

James Beard Award: International (2018)

This cookbook, from Gonzalo Guzman and Stacy Adimando, with photographs by Eva Kolenk, "includes fundamental techniques of Mexican cuisine, insights into Mexican food and culture, and favorite recipes from Nopalito such as Crispy Red Quesadillas with Braised Pork and Pork Rinds; Toasted Corn with Crema, Ground Chile, and Queso Fresco; Tamales with Red Spiced Sunflower Seed Mole; and Salsa-Dipped Griddled Chorizo and Potato Sandwiches." (Publisher's note)

"The author's welcoming affect and sure hand offer much-needed balance to these rewarding but sometimes challenging recipes." Pub Wkly

Includes bibliographical references and index

Alford, Jeffrey

★ **Hot,** sour, salty, sweet; a culinary journey through Southeast Asia. Jeffrey Alford and Naomi Duguid ; studio photographs by Richard Jung ; location photographs by Jeffrey Alford and Naomi Duguid. Artisan 2000 346 p. col. ill. $45 **641.59**
1. Cookbooks 2. Southeast Asian cooking 3. Cookery, Southeast Asian
ISBN 1579651143; 9781579651145

LC 00022092

In this cookbook, written by Jeffrey Alford and Naomi Duguid, "more than 175 recipes for spicy salsas, welcoming soups, grilled meat salads, and exotic desserts are accompanied by evocative stories about places and people. The recipes and stories are . . . illustrated throughout with more than 150 full-color food and travel photographs." (Publisher's note)

"Part travel essay and part culinary exploration, this is a perfect choice for both adventurous cooks and armchair travelers." LJ

Includes bibliographical references (p. 325-327) and index

Alger, Kajsa

Susan Feniger's street food; Susan Feniger, Kajsa Alger, and Liz Lachman. Random House Inc. 2012 224 p. $27.50 **641.59**
1. Salads 2. Cooking 3. Asian cooking 4. Street food 5. International cooking
ISBN 0307952584; 9780307952585

LC 2011041175

Author Susan Feniger "shares 83 of her favorite recipes with home cooks, giving them a taste of these . . . dishes. On her globe-trotting adventures, with cooking and eating as the only shared language, Susan has forged friendships with rice farmers in Vietnam, women baking flat-bread in Turkey, and nomadic cheesemakers in Mongolia. . . . [Recipes are featured, such as] Saigon Chicken Salad, . . . Thai Drunken Shrimp with Rice Noodles, or sweet-savory Korean Glazed Short Ribs with Sesame and Asian Pear." (Publisher's note)

Balla, Nicolaus

★ **Bar** Tartine; techniques & recipes. Nicolaus Balla and Cortney Burns ; photographs by Chad Robertson. Chronicle Books 2014 256 p. hbk $40 **641.59**
1. Cookbooks 2. Restaurants 3. Bar Tartine (San Francisco, Calif.) 4. Cooking, American -- California style
ISBN 1452126461; 9781452126463

LC 2014011157

James Beard Foundation Award: Cooking from a Professional Point of View (2015)

IACP Cookbook Award: Chefs and Restaurants (2015)

"Chefs Balla and Burns, at their much-praised Bar Tartine, in San Francisco, have transformed the craft of drying all sorts of herbs, flowers, vegetables, fruits, and meats into an art form. They share their methods for creating dehydrated delicacies, be it via oven-drying, sun-drying, or a food dehydrator, and offer a selection of recipes that utilize those ingredients." (Publishers Weekly)

"Many of these techniques are doable for home cooks, though it's hard to imagine amateurs making their own bottarga (which involves drying cured sacs of fish roe for five to seven weeks)." LJ

Barr, Luke

Provence, 1970; M.F.K. Fisher, Julia Child, James Beard, and the Reinvention of American Taste. Luke Barr. Clarkson Potter 2013 320 p. (alkaline paper) $26 **641.59**
1. Cooks 2. French cooking 3. Provence (France) -- Biography 4. Cooking, American -- Philosophy 5. Cooking, American -- History -- 20th century 6. Provence (France) -- Social life and customs -- 20th century
ISBN 0307718344; 9780307718341

LC 2013007782

This book discusses winter 1970, when "culinary icons M.F.K. Fisher, Julia Child, James Beard, Simone Beck, and Richard Olney all found themselves in Provence, France. This period was a turning point both for these figures and for the culture of food. . . . [Luke] Barr, Fisher's great-nephew, pieces together the events of that winter from diaries and letters, chronicling the dinner parties that took place and the food that was eaten." (Library Journal)

Includes bibliographical references and index

Bastianich, Lidia Matticchio

Lidia's commonsense Italian cooking; 150 delicious and simple recipes everyone can master. by Lidia Matticchio Bastianich and Tanya Bastianich Manuali ; photographs by Marcus Nilsson. Alfred A. Knopf 2013 304 p. color illustrations hbk $35 **641.59**

1. Cookbooks 2. Italian cooking
ISBN 0385349440; 9780385349444

LC 2013005067

In this cookbook, it was the authors' intent to "creat[e] a new sort of Italian cooking for American kitchens that crosses time-honored boundaries and looks to fashion a more relaxed . . . cuisine." Recipes include "potatoes baked in beer, eggplant and rice parmigiana, and veggie 'meatballs.' Traditionally unadorned pasta carbonara gets some sliced artichokes in its cream-and-egg sauce. Desserts include an apple cake, cookies, and several variations of rice pudding." (Booklist)

Includes bibliographical references and index

Lidia's Italian-American kitchen; by Lidia Matticchio Bastianich; photographs by Christopher Hirsheimer. Knopf 2001 xxvi, 432p il $35 **641.59**
1. Italian cooking
ISBN 0-375-41150-X

LC 2001-45009

"Bastianich has a warm, engaging style, and she's a teacher as well as a chef: throughout, she provides thoughtful head-notes and sidebars along with useful boxes on cooking with wine, 'resting' soup, and other such practicalities." Libr J

Bayless, Rick

Rick Bayless's Mexican kitchen; capturing the vibrant flavors of a world-class cuisine. [by] Rick Bayless with Deann Groen Bayless and JeanMarie Brownson; photographs by Maria Robledo; illustrations by John Sandford. Scribner 1996 448p il $35 **641.59**
1. Mexican cooking
ISBN 0-684-80006-3

LC 96-218444

This cookbook "includes more than 200 tantalizing recipes and is packed with information on Mexican ingredients and cooking techniques, regional cuisine, and history. . . . A serious guide to an often underestimated cuisine, this is important as both a reference and a cookbook." Libr J

Includes bibliographical references

Besh, John

My New Orleans; the cookbook; 200 of my favorite recipes & stories from my hometown. by John Besh. Andrews McMeel Universal 2009 374 p. ill. (chiefly col.) $45 **641.59**
1. Cookbooks 2. Cooking -- Louisiana 3. New Orleans (La.) -- Social life and customs 4. Cooking, Cajun 5. Cooking, Creole 6. Cooking -- Louisiana -- New Orleans 7. Cooking, American -- Louisiana style
ISBN 0740784137; 9780740784132

LC 2009920846

IACP Cookbook Award (2010)

In this cookbook, by John Besh, "archival, four-color, location photography along with ingredient information make the Big Easy easy to tackle in home kitchens. Cooks will salivate over the 200 recipes that honor and celebrate everything New Orleans. . . . From Mardi Gras, to the shrimp season, to the urban garden, to gumbo weather, boucherie (the season of the pig), and everything tasty in between, Besh gives a sampling of New Orleans." (Publisher's note)

Bishara, Rawia

Levant; new Middle Eastern cooking from Tanoreen. Rawia Bishara. Kyle Books 2018 223 p. $34.95 **641.59**
1. Cooking 2. Cookbooks 3. Middle Eastern cooking 4. Cooking,

Middle Eastern
ISBN 1909487724; 9781909487727

LC 2018931966

In this book, author Rawia Bishara, "offers more than 100 [Middle Eastern] recipes that represent a new modern style. These are the very best of the dishes she has developed over the last twenty years in her New York City restaurant for the contemporary palate. Relying on a traditional pantry (including olive oil, tahini, za'atar, sumac), she updates classic flavour profiles to dazzling effect." (Publisher's note)

Olives, lemons & za'atar; the best middle eastern home cooking. Rawia Bishara. Kyle Books 2014 224 p. (hardcover) $29.95   **641.59**
    1. Cookbooks 2. Middle Eastern cooking
    ISBN 1906868840; 9781906868840

LC 2013952643

This cookbook by Rawia Bishara is "Organized by Breakfasts, Mezze, Salads, Soups and Stews, Main Courses (including vegetarian, fish, chicken, lamb and beef), Sides, Pickles and Sauces, and Desserts.... A dish like Egyptian Rice with Lamb and Pine Nuts shows this cookbook goes beyond Nazareth, and is more of a bible of Middle Eastern food." (Publisher's note)

"Themes of food, family, and personal growth flow throughout this gorgeous cookbook, which balances both simple and challenging recipes." LJ

Brock, Sean

★ **Heritage;** Sean Brock with contributions by Marion Sullivan and Jeff Allen ; photographs by Peter Frank Edwards. Artisan 2014 336 p. illustrations (chiefly color) hbk $40 **641.59**
    1. Cookbooks 2. American cooking 3. Southern cooking
    ISBN 1579654630; 9781579654634

LC 2014005022

IACP Cookbook Award Winner: Julia Child First Book (2015)
James Beard Foundation Award Winner: American Cooking (2015)
IACP Cookbook Award Finalist: Chefs and Restaurants (2015)
IACP Cookbook Award Finalist: American (2015)

This cookbook, by Sean Brock, "offers all of his inspired recipes. With a drive to preserve the heritage foods of the South, Brock cooks dishes that are ingredient-driven and reinterpret the flavors of his youth in Appalachia and his adopted hometown of Charleston. The recipes include all the comfort food (think food to eat at home) and high-end restaurant food (fancier dishes when there's more time to cook) for which he has become so well-known." (Publisher's note)

"The recipes (e.g., butter-bean chowchow; pork belly with herbed farro, pickled elderberries, chanterelles, and sumac; buttermilk pie with cornmeal crust) range from simple to sophisticated, and some call for unusual preparations. . . . Within chapters, Brock profiles producers who supply his restaurants, explains various ingredient categories, and touches on topics from industrial agriculture to the origins of bourbon to 19th-century books on food and drink." LJ

Carrillo Arronte, Margarita

★ **Mexico;** The Cookbook. Margarita Carrillo Arronte. Phaidon Inc Ltd 2014 704 p. color illustrations hbk $49.95   **641.59**
    1. Cookbooks 2. Mexican cooking
    ISBN 0714867527; 9780714867526

This book Margarita Carrillo Arronte by "features an unprecedented 700 recipes from across the entire country, showcasing the rich diversity and flavors of Mexican cuisine. [It includes] notes on recipe origins, ingredients, and techniques, along with contributions from top chefs such as Enrique Olvera and Hugo Ortega." (Publisher's note)

"Full-color photos of food, landscapes, and people round out this hefty and appealing collection. For those interested in learning how to make authentic Mexican cuisine, Arronte has provided the definitive guide." Pub Wkly

Includes bibliographical references and index

Chambers, Veronica

Between Harlem and Heaven; Afro Asian American cooking for big nights, weeknights and every day. J.J. Johnson and Alexander Smalls ; with Veronica Chambers. Flatiron Books 2018 269 p. (hardcover) $37.50   **641.59**
    1. Cooking 2. Cookbooks 3. African American cooking 4. Asian American cooking
    ISBN 1250108713; 9781250108715

LC 2018000426

In this cookbook, authors J.J. Johnson and Alexander Smalls, with Veronica Chambers, "take us on a culinary journey through space and time that started more than 400 years ago, on the shores of West Africa. . . . [The] book branches far beyond 'soul food' to explore the melding of Asian, African, and American flavors. The Afro Asian flavor profile is a window into the intersection of the Asian diaspora and the African diaspora." (Publisher's note)

Cook, Steven

★ **Zahav;** a world of Israeli cooking. Michael Solomonov and Steven Cook ; produced by Dorothy Kalins ; photography by Mike Persico. Houghton Mifflin Harcourt 2016 368 p. color illustrations (hardcover) $35   **641.59**
    1. Cookbooks 2. Israeli cooking 3. Cooking, Israeli
    ISBN 9780544373280

LC 2015004346

This Israeli cookbook, by Michael Solomonov and Steven Cook, "showcases the melting-pot cooking of Israel, especially the influences of the Middle East, North Africa, the Mediterranean, and Eastern Europe [sold at the Philadelphia-based restaurant Zahav]. Solomonov's food includes little dishes called mezze, such as the restaurant's insanely popular fried cauliflower; a hummus so ethereal that it put Zahav on the culinary map; and a pink lentil soup with lamb meatballs." (Publisher's note)

"Readers with an adventurous palate and an open mind will be richly rewarded by this terrific debut." Pub Wkly

Cramby, Jonas

Tex-Mex from Scratch; Jonas Cramby. Sterling Pub Co Inc. 2015 144 p. color illustrations $24.95   **641.59**
    1. Mexican cooking 2. Barbecue cooking
    ISBN 145491629X; 9781454916291

In this book by Jonas Cramby "along with 70 mouthwatering recipes--from antojitos like shrimp taquitos to sweet Helado de Cajeta (caramel ice cream) to top it all off¿this collection takes you through all the basics. Learn how to prepare your own tortillas, assemble the best taco, knock together the perfect guacamole, and make your own barbecue smoker." (Publisher's note)

"Texas BBQ is a treat for armchair cooks and can broaden regional collections. Cramby, whose daughters are named Dixie Margarita and Lone Star, has an infectious passion for Tex-Mex food and a talent for food photography. Of his available and forthcoming titles, Tex-Mex from Scratch offers the best value." LJ

Currence, John

Pickles, pigs & whiskey; recipes from my three favorite food groups and then some. John Currence. Andrews McMeel

Pub., LLC 2013 259 p. col. ill. $40 **641.59**
1. Cookbooks 2. American cooking 3. Southern cooking
ISBN 1449428800; 9781449428808

LC 2013940033

This cookbook, by John Currence, presents "130 recipes organized by 10 different techniques, . . . [including] Pickled Sweet Potatoes, Whole Grain Guinness Mustard, Deep South 'Ramen' with a Fried Poached Egg, Rabbit Cacciatore, Smoked Endive, Fire-Roasted Cauliflower, and Kitchen Sink Cookie Ice Cream Sandwiches. Each recipe has a song pairing with it." (Publisher's note)

"Recipes for mint julep redux, deep South "ramen" with fried poached eggs, hill country cioppino, and bourbon-pecan pie with tonka bean ice cream, showcase some of the most exciting trends in Southern food and drink." LJ

Deetz, Kelley Fanto

Bound to the fire; how Virginia's enslaved cooks helped invent American cuisine. Kelley Fanto Deetz. University Press of Kentucky 2017 177 p. illustrations (hardcover; acid-free paper) $29.95 **641.59**
1. African American cooking -- History 2. Plantation life -- Virginia -- History 3. Slaves -- Virginia -- Social life and customs 4. Cooking, American -- History 5. Slaves -- Virginia -- Biography 6. Virginia -- Race relations -- History 7. Slaves -- Virginia -- Social conditions 8. African American cooks -- Virginia -- History 9. African American cooks -- Virginia -- Biography 10. African Americans -- Food -- Virginia -- History
ISBN 9780813174754; 9780813174747; 9780813174730

LC 2017029779

"Kelley Fanto Deetz draws upon archaeological evidence, cookbooks, plantation records, and folklore to present a nuanced study of the lives of enslaved plantation cooks from colonial times through emancipation and beyond. She reveals how these men and women were literally 'bound to the fire' as they lived and worked in the sweltering and often fetid conditions of plantation house kitchens." (Publisher's note)

"Scholarly yet readable, Deetz's book honors these American ancestors by reclaiming their rightful places and stories." Booklist

Includes bibliographical references and index

Deuki Hong

Koreatown; a cookbook. Deuki Hong and Matt Rodbard ; photographs by Sam Horine. Clarkson Potter/Publishers 2015 272 p. color illustrations (hardcover) $30 **641.59**
1. Korean cooking 2. Korean Americans 3. Cooking, Korean
ISBN 9780804186131; 0804186138

LC 2015009587

This cookbook, by Deuki Hong and Matt Rodbard, is based on the authors' "love affair with the grit and charm of Korean cooking in America. Koreatowns around the country are synonymous with mealtime feasts and late-night chef hangouts, and Deuki Hong and Matt Rodbard show us why with stories, interviews, and over 100 delicious, super-approachable recipes." (Publisher's note)

"Hong, with coauthor Robard, celebrates Korean cooking in America, and his recipes cover a wide spectrum of meat, seafood, and vegetable offerings." Booklist

Disbrowe, Paula

Down south; soulful recipes and slow-simmered recollections. Donald Link with Paula Disbrowe. Clarkson Potter 2014 256 p. color illustrations (hardback) $35 **641.59**
1. Southern States 2. American cooking 3. Cooking, Cajun 4. Cooking, American -- Southern style

ISBN 0770433189; 9780770433185

LC 2013020280

IACP Cookbook Award Winner: American (2015)

In this cookbook author Donald Link, with Paula Disbrowe, "combines his talents to unearth true down home Southern cooking so everyone can pull up a seat at the table and sample some of the region's finest flavors. Along the way, he introduces all sorts of characters and places, including pitmaster Nick Pihakis of Jim 'N Nick's BBQ, Louisiana goat farmer Bill Ryal, beloved Southern writer Julia Reed, a true Tupelo honey apiary in Florida, and a Texas lamb ranch with a llama named Fritz." (Publisher's note)

Dixon, Kirsten

The **Tutka** Bay Lodge cookbook; coastal cuisine from the wilds of Alaska. by Kirsten Dixon and Mandy Dixon ; photography by Tyrone Potgieter. Alaska Northwest Books 2014 224 p. color illustrations (hardcover) $29.99 **641.59**
1. Alaska 2. American cooking 3. Cooking -- Alaska 4. Tutka Bay Lodge (Alaska) 5. Cooking, American -- Pacific Northwest style
ISBN 1941821154; 9781941821152

LC 2014017785

IACP Cookbook Award Winner: E-Cookbook (2015)

This cookbook, by Kirsten Dixon and Mandy Dixon, offers "personal stories, evocative photographs, and recipes that are purposefully simple and designed for the home cook. . . . This recipe collection represents the cuisine at Tutka Bay Lodge, the Dixons' seaside lodge nestled within the curve of a quiet cove at the entrance to Tutka Bay, a deep seven-mile fjord in Kachemak Bay, Alaska." (Publisher's note)

Duguid, Naomi

★ **Burma**; rivers of flavor. Naomi Duguid. Artisan 2012 372 p. col. ill. $35 **641.59**
1. Myanmar 2. Cookbooks 3. Asian cooking 4. Food -- Burma 5. Cooking (Spices) 6. Cooking, Burmese 7. Burma -- Social life and customs
ISBN 1579654134; 9781579654139

LC 2011052121

IACP Cookbook Award (2013)

"Located at the crossroads between China, India, and the nations of Southeast Asia, Burma has long been a land that absorbed outside influences into its everyday life. . . . Interspersed throughout the 125 recipes are intriguing tales from the author's many trips to this fascinating but little-known land." (Publisher's note)

"A colorful immersion into the daily market and table of the Burmese people, this volume is an invitation to celebrate the Burmese people and their transformation." Pub Wkly

Includes bibliographical references and index

Dunlop, Fuchsia

Every grain of rice; simple Chinese home cooking. Fuchsia Dunlop ; photography by Chris Terry. W W Norton & Co Inc 2013 351 p. illustrations (hardcover) $35 **641.59**
1. Cookbooks 2. Chinese cooking 3. Cooking, Chinese
ISBN 0393089045; 9780393089042

LC 2012004741

James Beard Award (2014)

In this book, author "Fuchsia Dunlop trained as a chef in China's leading Sichuan cooking school and possesses the rare ability to write recipes for authentic Chinese food that you can make at home. Following her two seminal volumes on Sichuan and Hunan cooking, . . . [this cookbook] is inspired by the vibrant everyday cooking of southern China, in which vegetables play the starring role, with small portions of meat and fish." (Publisher's note)

Dupree, Nathalie

Mastering the art of Southern cooking; Nathalie Dupree & Cynthia Graubart ; photographs by Rick McKee ; with a foreword by Pat Conroy. Gibbs Smith 2012 720 p. col. ill. $45   **641.59**

    1. Cookbooks 2. American cooking 3. Southern cooking 4. Cooking, American -- Southern style

    ISBN 1423602757; 9781423602750

                        LC 2012017365

    James Beard Foundation Award: American Cooking (2013)

    "Through more than 600 recipes and hundreds of step-by-step photographs, Dupree and Graubart make it easy to learn the techniques for creating the South's fabulous cuisine. . . . Traditional Southern recipes and ingredients are also given modern twists to make them relevant for today's healthy lifestyle." (Publisher's note)

    Includes bibliographical references and index

Eddy, Jody

North; the new Nordic cuisine of Iceland. Gunnar Karl Gíslason and Jody Eddy ; foreword by René Redzepi. Ten Speed Press 2014 352 p. color illustrations (hardback) $40 **641.59**

    1. Cooking 2. Iceland 3. Restaurants 4. Cooking, Icelandic

    ISBN 1607744988; 9781607744986

                        LC 2014003525

    IACP Cookbook Award: Judge's Choice (2015)

    IACP Cookbook Award Finalist: International (2015)

    This book, by Gunnar Karl Gíslason and Jody Eddy, offers a "look into the food and culture of Iceland. . . . Perhaps no Icelandic restaurant is as well-loved and critically lauded as . . . Gíslason's Restaurant Dill, which opened in Reykjavík's historic Nordic House in 2009. 'North' is Gíslason's wonderfully personal debut: equal parts recipe book and culinary odyssey, it offers an unparalleled look into a star chef's creative process." (Publisher's note)

    "Many of the recipes reflect the natural resources of Iceland, for example, the sea-salt employed is Icelandic and the fact that so many recipes involve pickled items is a direct product of the necessity of storing food items in a harsh climate. . . . There are many recipes, though, for which the chef does not need to have access to Iceland." Pub Wkly

Foose, Martha Hall

A **southerly** course; recipes & stories from close to home. Martha Hall Foose. Clarkson Potter 2011 256 p. col. ill. $32.50   **641.59**

    1. Cookbooks 2. American cooking 3. Southern cooking 4. Cookery, American -- Southern style

    ISBN 0307464288; 9780307464286

                        LC 2010022969

    This cookbook, by Martha Hall Foose, "delves deep into Mississippi Delta flavors and foodways. . . . In her signature style, she pairs each recipe with an anecdote or words of advice. . . . Martha's beloved Southern cuisine is a fresh take on homey favorites fiercely protected by the locals, including Skillet Fried Corn, Sweet Pickle Braised Pork Shoulder, and Blackberry Jelly Roll." (Publisher's note)

    "Offering meditations on subjects like congealed salads and family china, Foose has all the savvy of a local tour guide, leading the way through her native state with poetry and wit." Pub Wkly

Friedman, Andrew, 1967-

Classico e moderno; Michael White and Andrew Friedman. Ballantine Books 2013 448 p. (hardcover; alk. paper)

$50   **641.59**

    1. Italian cooking 2. Cooking, Italian

    ISBN 0345530527; 9780345530523

                        LC 2013009625

    In this book by Michael White and Andrew Friedman, "White brings his passion for authentic Italian cuisine to the home kitchen, with recipes--nearly 250--that cover both the traditional and contemporary dishes of the region. White shares such iconic dishes as Meatballs Braised in Tomato Sauce; Pasta and Bean Soup; Cavatelli with Lamb Ragù and Bell Peppers; and Roasted Pork Leg with Rosemary and Black Pepper." (Publisher's note)

    Includes bibliographical references and index

Galimberti, Gabriele

In her kitchen; stories and recipes from grandmas around the World. Gabriele Galimberti. Clarkson Potter/Publishers 2014 248 p. color illustrations, maps $30   **641.59**

    1. Cooking 2. Grandmothers 3. International cooking 4. Galimberti, Gabriele -- Travel

    ISBN 0804185557; 9780804185554

                        LC 2013050635

    James Beard Foundation Award Winner: Photography (2015)

    In this book, author Gabriele Galimberti presents "beautiful portraits of grandmothers from all over the world with their signature recipes. . . . These vibrant and intimate profiles and photographs pay homage to grandmothers and their cooking everywhere. From a Swedish housewife and her homemade lox and vegetables to a Zambian villager and her Roasted Spiced Chicken, this collection features a global palate." (Publisher's note)

    "While drawing on some academic sources, this book is written in lively narrative prose that is more appropriate for general readers than scholars." LJ

Grimes, Dixie

The **B.T.C.** old-fashioned grocery cookbook; recipes and stories from a Southern revival. Alexe van Beuren ; with recipes by Dixie Grimes. Clarkson Potter 2014 240 p. color illustrations hbk $29.99   **641.59**

    1. Cookbooks 2. Southern cooking 3. B.T.C. Old-Fashioned Grocery 4. Water Valley, Miss. -- Social life and customs

    ISBN 0385345003; 9780385345002

                        LC 2013019690

    "'The B.T.C. Old-Fashioned Grocery Cookbook' shares 120 of the store's best recipes, giving home cooks everywhere a taste of the food that brought a community together." (Publisher's note)

    "Water Valley, Miss., is a small, rural village saved from obscurity by being just 25 minutes from the campus town of Oxford, and by being fortunate enough to be the home of chef Grimes and self-made business woman van Beuren. . . . Van Beuren's unadorned prose keeps the character studies pure, with a refreshingly minimal amount of folksiness, while Grimes's 120 recipes alternate between classic and surprising." Pub Wkly

    Includes bibliographical references and index

Helou, Anissa

Mediterranean street food; stories, soups, snacks, sandwiches, barbecues, sweets, and more, from Europe, North Africa, and the Middle East. Anissa Helou. William Morrow 2006 277 p. ill. $19.99   **641.59**

    1. Cookbooks 2. Mediterranean cooking 3. Cookery, Mediterranean

    ISBN 0060891513; 9780060891510

                        LC 2001051451

In this cookbook by Anissa Helou, readers will "join her on a fascinating adventure around the Mediterranean, where eating on the street is a way of life. . . . With . . . black-and-white photographs from Anissa's travels and more than eighty-five fast, flexible, flavorful recipes, . . . [this book] offers home cooks the chance to experience the tastes of distant lands without leaving the kitchen." (Publisher's note)

Includes bibliographical references and index

Hiroko Shimbo

Hiroko's American kitchen; cooking with Japanese flavors. Hiroko Shimbo ; photography by Frances Janisch. Andrews McMeel Pub., LLC 2012 215 p. col. ill. $24.99 **641.59**
1. Cookbooks 2. Japanese cooking 3. Cooking, Japanese
ISBN 1449409784; 9781449409784

LC 2012936725
IACP Cookbook Award (2013)

This cookbook, by Hiroko Shimbo, presents "125 . . . recipes that highlight the best of Japanese cuisine. . . . The recipes are organized in chapters, each using one of two stocks or four sauces. By preparing and storing these easily made items, with a minimum of time and fuss you can enjoy a wide variety of delicious dishes every day. These are recipes . . . are prepared and served in dishes that are familiar to American tastes and dining habits." (Publisher's note)

Hoyer, Daniel

Mayan cuisine; recipes from the Yucatan region. Daniel Hoyer ; photographs by Marty Snortum. Gibbs Smith 2008 224 p. ill. (chiefly col.) $34.95 **641.59**
1. Cookbooks 2. Mayan cooking 3. Maya cooking 4. Cooking -- Mexico -- Yucatán (State)
ISBN 1423601319; 9781423601319

LC 2007033541
In this cookbook, author "Daniel Hoyer brings us the authentic recipes of the . . . [Maya of the Yucatan Region,] along with his personal experiences that make the historical and cultural background of this people accessible and enjoyable." Recipes include "Sweet Corn and Cilantro Cream Soups, Yucatan BBQ Shrimp, Smoked Pork Loin, Jicama-Orange Salad, and Chicken in Red Chile and Pumpkinseed Sauce." (Publisher's note)

"Hoyer is encouraging and enthusiastic, offering salient tips for key techniques like working with tamale wrappers and charring tomatoes, as well as sources for hard-to-locate ingredients." Pub Wkly

Humm, Daniel

I love New York; ingredients and recipes; a moment in New York cuisine. Daniel Humm and Will Guidara. Ten Speed Press 2013 512 p. col. ill. $50 **641.59**
1. Local foods 2. American cooking 3. New York (State) 4. Cooking, American 5. Cooking -- New York (State) -- New York
ISBN 1607744406; 9781607744405

LC 2012026491
IACP Cookbook Award (2014)

Chef Daniel Humm and restaurant manager Will Guidara present a "cookbook showcasing the foods, ingredients, and culinary history of New York. . . . [They take] an in-depth look at the region's centuries-old farming traditions along with nearly 150 recipes that highlight its outstanding ingredients. . . . Included among these dishes designed explicitly for the home cook are reinterpretations of New York classics." (Publisher's note)

The **immigrant** cookbook; recipes that make America great. collected and edited by Leyla Moushabeck. Interlink Pub Group Inc 2017 224 p. (hardcover) $35 **641.59**
1. Cooking 2. Cookbooks 3. American cooking 4. Cooking, American 5. International cooking 6. Cooks -- United States -- Biography 7. Immigrant business enterprises -- United States -- Biography
ISBN 9781566560382; 1566560381

LC 2018028229
This cookbook, by Leyla Moushabeck, "offers a culinary celebration of the many ethnic groups that have contributed to America's vibrant food culture. This beautifully photographed cookbook features appetizers, entrees, and desserts some familiar favorites, some likely to be new encounters by renowned chefs from Africa, Asia, Latin America, the Middle East, and Europe." (Publisher's note)

"A great collection that benefits from the incredible accomplishments of its contributors, and its excellent cause." Booklist

Iyer, Raghavan

Indian cooking unfolded; a master class in Indian cooking, with 100 easy recipes using 10 ingredients or less. by Raghavan Iyer ; photography by TK. Workman Publishing 2013 340 p. color illustrations (alk. paper) $19.95 **641.59**
1. Cookbooks 2. Indian cooking 3. Cooking, Indic
ISBN 0761165215; 9780761165217

LC 2013004247
This cookbook, by Raghavan Iyer, focuses on Indian cooking. "The book's 100 authentic recipes use only ingredients readily available at the local supermarket. Taking into account time restraints, each dish can be quickly assembled and will give home cooks the confidence to create knockout Tandoori Chicken, Coconut Squash with Chiles, Turmeric Hash Browns, Saffron-Pistachio Ice Cream Bars, and Mango Bread Pudding with Chai Spices." (Publisher's note)

Includes bibliographical references and index

Jaffrey, Madhur

An **invitation** to Indian cooking; Madhur Jaffrey ; with a new preface by the author. Ecco Press/Alfred A. Knopf 1999 285, 15 p.p ill hardcover o.p.; paperback $16.95 **641.59**
1. Cookbooks 2. Indian cooking 3. Cooking, Indic
ISBN 0880016647; 9780375712111; 0375712119

LC 98030321
First published 1973
James Beard Cookbook Hall of Fame (2006)
IACP Culinary Classics Book Award (2014)

This cookbook, by Madhur Jaffrey, "originally published in 1973, introduced the richly fascinating cuisine of India to America--and changed the face of American cooking. Now, as Indian food enjoys an upsurge of popularity in the United States, a whole new generation of readers and cooks will find all they need to know about Indian cooking in Madhur Jaffrey's . . . book." (Publisher's note)

Jamison, Bill

The **border** cookbook; authentic home cooking of the American Southwest and Northern Mexico. {by} Cheryl Alters Jamison and Bill Jamison. Harvard Common Press 1995 500 p. ill. pbk $21.95; hardcover o.p. **641.59**
1. Cookbooks 2. American cooking 3. Cooking 4. Mexican cooking 5. Cooking -- Southwestern style
ISBN 9781558321038; 9781558321021; 1558321039

LC 95010799
James Beard Award (1996)

In this "James Beard Book Award-winning cookbook, authors Cheryl Alters Jamison and Bill Jamison combine the best of Mexican and Southwest cooking, bringing together this large region's Native American, Spanish, Mexican, and Anglo culinary roots into one big, exuberant book. . . . In over 300 recipes they explore the common elements and regional differences of border cooking." (Publisher's note)

Joachim, David

Cooking light global kitchen; the world's most delicious food made easy. David Joachim. Oxmoor House 2014 319 p. color illustrations (hardcover) $29.95   **641.59**
 1. Cooking 2. Cookbooks
 ISBN 9780848739980; 0848739981
             LC 2013956992
This cookbook, by David Joachim and the editors of 'Cooking Light Magazine,' "brings a world of flavor, texture, and enticing aromas to your everyday meals. In this book, the sometimes intimidating topic of preparing your favorite ethnic-inspired dishes is made easy, approachable, and, most importantly, doable for home cooks of any skill level, by using ethnic ingredients easy-to-find in your local grocery store!" (Publisher's note)

Rustic Italian food; Marc Vetri with David Joachim ; beverage notes by Jeff Benjamin ; photography by Kelly Campbell ; foreword by Mario Batali. Ten Speed Press 2011 291 p. col. ill. $35   **641.59**
 1. Sauces 2. Cookbooks 3. Italian cooking 4. Cooking -- Pasta products 5. Cooking, Italian
 ISBN 158008589X; 9781580085892
             LC 2011015301
In this cookbook, "Philadelphia chef Marc Vetri celebrates the handcrafted cuisine of Italy, advocating a hands-on, back-to-the-basics approach to cooking. . . . [It presents] an education in kitchen fundamentals, with detailed, step-by-step instructions for making terrines, dry-cured salami, and cooked sausage; a thorough guide to bread and pasta making; and a primer on classic Italian preserves and sauces." (Publisher's note)
"Advanced cooks looking to master bread and pasta will value Vetri's patient, masterful explanation of underlying techniques." LJ

Jones, Catherine Cheremeteff

A **year** of Russian feasts; Catherine Cheremeteff Jones ; illustrations by Barbara Stott McCoy. Jellyroll Press 2002 192 p. ill. $16.95   **641.59**
 1. Russian cooking 2. Religious holidays 3. Russian Orthodox Church 4. Cooking, Russian 5. Food habits -- Russia (Federation) 6. Russia (Federation) -- Social life and customs
 ISBN 0971601305; 9780971601307
             LC 2001129493
This cookbook, by Catherine Cheremeteff Jones, illustrated by Barbara Stott McCoy, "explains to Western readers the regularly recurring Russian Orthodox feasts, those traditional dishes associated with them, and the holidays' significance in the life of the church and the people. In Orthodoxy, prior to feasting comes fasting, so Jones' first recipes exemplify ascetic vegetarian dishes. Then it's on to the celebrations . . .; beet soups, meat-stuffed dumplings, sweetly spiced and aromatic Easter bread, and many variations on potatoes." (Booklist)

Kennedy, Diana

The **essential** cuisines of Mexico. Potter 2000 526p $35   **641.59**
 1. Mexican cooking

ISBN 0-609-60355-8
             LC 00-23156
The author has gathered "the recipes from her first cookbook, the groundbreaking Cuisines of Mexico (1972), as well its two successors, The Tortilla Book (1975) and Mexican Regional Cooking (1978) . . . in this new collection. She's revised the recipes and simplified some, and there are also 30 or so new recipes. Kennedy's books became classics long ago; this compilation of her early works is an essential purchase." Libr J
Includes bibliographical references

Khanna, Vikas

Return to the rivers; recipes and memories of the Himalyan River Valleys. Vikas Khanna, Andrew Blackmore-Dobbyn. Lake Isle Press 2013 444 p. color illustrations, map (hardback; alk. paper) $35   **641.59**
 1. Himalaya Mountains
 ISBN 1891105531; 9781891105531
             LC 2013951725
IACP Cookbook Award Finalist: Culinary Travel (2015)
This book, by Vikas Khanna and Andrew Blackmore-Dobbyn, "is an incredible collection of recipes, photos, and memories as a means to preserve and share the sacred foodways, values, and simple gifts of friendship that the Himalayan people bestowed Khanna. Exploring the regions the great Himalayas directly touch upon – Bhutan, Nepal, Tibet, Northern India, Myanmar, Western China, Pakistan – Khanna was met with immeasurable kindness and hospitality." (Publisher's note)

Kijac, Maria Baez

The **South** American table; the flavor and soul of authentic home cooking from Patagonia to Rio de Janeiro, with 450 recipes. Maria Baez Kijac ; foreword by Charlie Trotter. Houghton Mifflin Harcourt 2003 478 p. ill., 1 map (alk. paper) $29.95   **641.59**
 1. Cookbooks 2. Latin American cooking 3. Cookery, Latin American 4. Cookery -- South America 5. South America -- Social life and customs
 ISBN 9781558322486; 1558322485
             LC 2003011100
This South American-themed cookbook, by Maria Baez Kijac, "reflects a true mix of history and cultures, melding the bounty of the New World (tomatoes, potatoes, corn, beans, hot peppers) and the cooking traditions of its indigenous peoples with the influences and culinary heritage of the Conquistadors, African slaves, and immigrants from Italy, Germany, China, and elsewhere." (Publisher's note)
Author Kijac "offers a thorough volume that is part reference book and part cookbook. Long chapters about the geography of South America and its pre-Columbian civilizations, as well as a history of cooking in South America precede the hundreds of recipes. A glossary of South American ingredients as well as a dictionary of ingredients are included as well. The recipes are wonderful, if overwhelming in number." Pub Wkly

Kochilas, Diane

The **glorious** foods of Greece. Morrow 2000 496p map $40   **641.59**
 1. Greek cooking
 ISBN 0-688-15457-3
             LC 00-28158
This cookbook includes over 400 recipes from various "regions, starting with the Peloponnesus and the Ionian Islands, moving on to Macedonia, the islands of the Aegean, and Crete, and finishing up in

the city of Athens. . . . Kochilas also provides extensive historical background, cultural as well as culinary, along with detailed descriptions and explanations of ingredients." Libr J

Includes bibliographical references and index

Koehler, Jeff

Spain; Recipes and Traditions from the Verdant Hills of the Basque Country to the Coastal Waters of Andalucía. by Jeff Koehler ; location photographs by Jeff Koehler , plated food photographs by Kevin Miyazaki. Chronicle Books 2013 352 p. color illustrations (hardback) $40   **641.59**

1. Spanish cooking 2. Cooking, Spanish
ISBN 0811875016; 9780811875011

LC 2013026594

This book of Spanish recipes, by food writer Jeff Koehler, is "organized by food type rather than local. . . . A tasty section on tapas covers classics like dates wrapped in bacon, as well as more intense options, such as Galician octopus with paprika on potatoes. . . . In addition to the food itself, Koehler explores a variety of the country's food-related traditions." (Publishers Weekly)

Kostow, Christopher, 1976-

★ A **new** Napa cuisine; Christopher Kostow ; photography by Peden + Munk. Ten Speed Press 2014 304 p. illustrations (hardback) $50   **641.59**

1. American cooking 2. Napa Valley (Calif.) 3. Cooking, American -- California style 4. Napa Valley (Calif.) -- Description and travel
ISBN 1607745941; 9781607745945

LC 2014010462

James Beard Foundation Award Nominee: Photography (2015)
IACP Cookbook Award: Cookbook of the Year (2015)
IACP Cookbook Award: Global Design (2015)

This cookbook on Napa, California, by Christopher Kostow, "celebrates the local artisans, products, growers, and wilds that have played a role in the creation of a nascent style of cooking specific to this small American valley. Through tales of designing china with local ceramicists or discovering wild edibles along the creek while walking his dog; planting seeds both literal and figurative--Kostow's story is a personal and engaging one." (Publisher's note)

"This sort of food lies beyond even the most ambitious amateur, but culinary students will appreciate the challenge of seeing where their art and craft are headed, and the restaurant's patrons will love documentation of a once-in-a-lifetime dinner." Booklist

Lawson, Nigella, 1960-

At my table; a celebration of home cooking. Nigella Lawson. Flatiron Books 2018 288 p. (hardcover) $35   **641.59**

1. Cookbooks 2. Mediterranean cooking 3. Quick and easy cooking 4. Cooking 5. Cooking, English 6. Cooking, Mediterranean
ISBN 1250154286; 9781250154286

LC 2018000297

In this cookbook, author Nigella Lawson, "shares recipes of the meals that she loves to cook for friends and family. Warm, comforting, and inspiring, . . . [the cookbook] offers a collection of recipes that are simple to prepare, giving you an opportunity to enhance your culinary skills and create a variety of delicious dishes--featuring a host of new ingredients to enrich classic flavors and tastes." (Publisher's note)

Lebovitz, David

★ **My** Paris kitchen; recipes and stories. David Lebovitz. Ten Speed Press 2014 345 p. ill. (chiefly col.) (hardback) $35   **641.59**

1. French cooking 2. Paris (France) -- Civilization 3. Paris (France) -- Description and travel 4. Food habits -- France 5. Paris (France) -- Social life and customs
ISBN 1607742675; 9781607742678

LC 2013032561

IACP Cookbook Award Finalist: International (2015);
James Beard Foundation Award Nominee: International (2015)
IACP Cookbook Award Finalist: Literary Food Writing (2015)

"In 'My Paris Kitchen,' [author] David [Lebovitz] remasters the classics, introduces lesser-known fare, and presents 100 sweet and savory recipes that reflect the way modern Parisians eat today. You'll find Soupe à l'oignon, Cassoulet, Coq au vin, and Croque-monsieur, as well as Smoky barbecue-style pork, Lamb shank tagine, Dukkah-roasted cauliflower, Salt cod fritters with tartar sauce, and Wheat berry salad with radicchio, root vegetables, and pomegranate." (Publisher's note)

"French food personalized and demystified for the home cook in the best way." Pub Wkly

Includes bibliographical references and index

Lee, Edward

Buttermilk graffiti; a chef's journey to discover America's new melting-pot cuisine. Edward Lee. Artisan, a Division of Workman Publishing Co., Inc. 2018 304 p. (hardcover; alk. paper) $27.50   **641.59**

1. International cooking 2. American cooking -- History 3. Cooks -- United States -- Biography
ISBN 1579657389; 9781579657383

LC 2017051428

In this book, author Edward Lee explores how "American food [has become] the story of mash-ups. . . . Lee decided to hit the road and spent two years uncovering fascinating narratives from every corner of the country. . . . [The book features] sixteen adventures, sixteen vibrant new chapters in the great evolving story of American cuisine. And forty recipes, created by Lee, that bring these new dishes into our own kitchens." (Publisher's note)

Lee, Matt

The **Lee** Bros. Charleston kitchen; Matt Lee and Ted Lee. Clarkson Potter 2012 240 p. col. ill., col. maps $35   **641.59**

1. Cookbooks 2. American cooking 3. Southern cooking 4. Cooking, American -- Southern style 5. Cooking -- South Carolina -- Charleston
ISBN 0307889734; 9780307889737

LC 2012013331

IACP Cookbook Award (2014)

This cookbook, by Matt Lee and Ted Lee, features recipes for Southern U.S. cuisine. "The 100 offerings represent a mix of the classic and the newfangled. There's peach leather, a Charleston chew dating back to the 19th century, which requires two days of sun-drying. And then there's a totally nontraditional tomato and watermelon gazpacho with shrimp." Chapters "cover drinks, snacks, soups, vegetables, fish, meat, and desserts." (Publishers Weekly)

"The brothers also provide two excellent addendums: a comprehensive bibliography of Charleston cookbooks dating back to 1756 and directions for a walking or driving tour featuring eateries from which many of their recipes were derived." Pub Wkly

Includes bibliographical references (p. 232-[235]) and index

Lewis, Edna, 1916-2006

The **gift** of Southern cooking; recipes and revelations from two great Southern cooks. by Edna Lewis and Scott Peacock. Knopf 2003 352p il $29.95   **641.59**

1. Southern cooking 2. Cookery, American -- Southern style

ISBN 0-375-40035-4

LC 2002-73153

This is a collection of recipes by Edna Lewis, author of The Taste of Country, and Scott Peacock, the chef at Watershed in Decatur, Alabama. "Together they share their secrets for such Southern basics as pan-fried chicken, . . . creamy grits, . . . and genuine Southern biscuits. . . . {According to the authors}, the way everything is put together—with the condiments and relishes and preserves and wealth of vegetables all spread out on the table—is what makes the meal uniquely Southern. . . . {The book includes} twenty-two seasonal menus, from A Spring Country Breakfast for a Late Sunday Morning and A Summer Dinner of Big Flavors to An Alabama Thanksgiving and A Hearty Dinner for a Cold Winter Night." (Publisher's note) Index.

"If you care—and I mean really care—about coleslaw, pan-fried chicken, trout, . . . greens simmered in pork stock and Southern-style ketchups, relishes and vinegars, this is a book you shouldn't be without." N Y Times Book Rev

Lo, Eileen Yin-Fei

Mastering the art of Chinese cooking; Eileen Yin-Fei Lo ; photographs by Susie Cushner ; brush calligraphy by San Yan Wong. Chronicle Books 2009 384 p. col. ill. $50   **641.59**
    1. Cookbooks 2. Chinese cooking 3. Cooking, Chinese
ISBN 0811859339; 9780811859332

LC 2010027670

IACP Cookbook Award (2010)

This cookbook, by Eileen Yin-Fei Lo, offers "a series of lessons [to] build skill, knowledge, and confidence as Lo guides the home cook step by step through the techniques, ingredients, and equipment that define Chinese cuisine. With more than 100 classic recipes and technique illustrations throughout, . . . [It] makes . . . this ancient cuisine utterly accessible." (Publisher's note)

"[V]isually stunning—with brush calligraphy, decorative borders, and full-page color photographs—as well as a comprehensive and educational guide that fulfills the promise of how to master Chinese cooking." Pub Wkly

Miller, Adrian

Soul food; the surprising story of an American cuisine, one plate at a time. by Adrian Miller. University of North Carolina Press 2013 344 p. (cloth; alk. paper) $30   **641.59**
    1. American cooking 2. African American cooking 3. African American cooking -- History 4. Cooking, American -- Southern style
ISBN 146960762X; 9781469607627

LC 2013002823

In this book author Adrian Miller "delves into the influences, ingredients, and innovations that make up the soul food tradition. Focusing each chapter on the culinary and social history of one dish--such as fried chicken, chitlins, yams, greens, and 'red drinks'--Miller uncovers how it got on the soul food plate and what it means for African American culture and identity." (Publisher's note)

"An engaging, tradition-rich look at an often overlooked American cuisine--certainly to be of interest to foodies from all walks of life." Kirkus

Includes bibliographical references and index

The **new** Filipino kitchen; stories and recipes from around the globe. edited by Jacqueline Chio-Lauri ; photos by Rowena Dumlao-Giardina ; foreword by John Birdsall. Surrey Books, an imprint of Agate Publishing 2018 248 p. color illustrations (hardcover) $28   **641.59**
    1. Cookbooks 2. Philippine cooking 3. Philippines -- Social life and customs 4. Cooking, Philippine
ISBN 157284258X; 9781572842588

LC 2018007796

This book, edited by Jacqueline Chio-Lauri with photos by Rowena Dumlao-Giardina, "collects 30 recipes and stories from expat Filipinos, all of whom have taken their favorite dishes with them, preserving their food memories and, if necessary, tweaking their recipes to work in a new environment or, in the case of some chefs, a more modern context." (Publisher's note)

"Standouts include White House executive chef Cristeta Comerford's Ani Pambihirang Lutoni Nanay and escabeche-inspired fried snapper (an homage to her mother Nana Pate) and in-flight chef Novel Omamalin's sylvana dessert. A gentle, inspiring, and exciting introduction to a savory world still new to many U.S. readers." Booklist

Nguyen, Andrea

Asian dumplings; mastering gyoza, spring rolls, samosas, and more. Andrea Quynhgiao Nguyen ; photography by Penny De Los Santos. Ten Speed Press 2009 234 p. col. ill. (hardcover) $30   **641.59**
    1. Dumplings 2. Asian cooking 3. Cooking, Asian
ISBN 1580089755; 9781580089753

LC 2010286323

This cookbook, by Andrea Quynhgiao Nguyen, focuses on preparing Asian style dumplings. "Plump pot stickers, spicy samosas, and tender bāo (stuffed buns) are enjoyed by the million every day in dim sum restaurants, streetside stands, and private homes worldwide. Wrapped, rolled, or filled; steamed, fried, or baked--Asian dumplings are also surprisingly easy to prepare, as [the author] . . . demonstrates." (Publisher's note)

Includes bibliographical references (p. 227-228) and index

★ The **pho** cookbook; easy to adventurous recipes for Vietnam's favorite soup and noodles. Andrea Quynhgiao Nguyen ; studio photography by John Lee ; location photography by Karen Shinto. Ten Speed Press 2017 160 p. color illustrations (hardcover; alk. paper) $22   **641.59**
    1. Soups 2. Vietnamese cooking 3. Cookbooks 4. Noodle soups 5. Cooking, Vietnamese
ISBN 9781607749585; 9781607749592

LC 2016022687

James Beard Award: Single Subject (2018)

This cookbook in the Easy to Adventurous, Recipes or Vietnam's Favorite Soup and Noodles series, by Andrea Quynhgiao Nguyen, shares various recipes of the Vietnamese broth and noodle soup pho. "Options range from quick weeknight cheats to impressive weekend feasts with broth and condiments from scratch, as well as other pho rice noodle favorites. [It offers] . . . versatile recipes, including snacks, salads, companion dishes, and vegetarian and gluten-free options." (Publisher's note)

Nguyen, Luke

The **food** of Vietnam; Luke Nguyen. Hardie Grant Books 2013 367 p. $50   **641.59**
    1. Cookbooks 2. Vietnamese cooking 3. Vietnam -- Description and travel
ISBN 1742706207; 9781742706207

A journey to discover food & heritage -- Saigon & south -- From coast to countryside -- Salt water people -- Princes & paupers -- The dragon & the turtle -- Mountain people -- Basic recipes -- Glossary -- Index

This cookbook and travel memoir, by Luke Nguyen, "follows his trip from northern Vietnam down to the south, through marketplaces and kitchens of strangers and family alike to find the best recipes Vietnam has to offer. Luke records his experiences with the people he meets and the places he visits along the way, breathing life into the classic recipes of Vietnam, from pho to banh mi and everything in between." (Publisher's note)

Oliver, Jamie, 1975-

Jamie's Italy; Jamie Oliver ; photographs by David Loftus and Chris Terry. Hyperion 2006 319 p. il $34.95   **641.59**
1. Cookbooks 2. Italian cooking
ISBN 1401301959; 9781401301958

LC 2006445348

This cookbook by Jamie Oliver focuses on Italian cuisine. "Italy and its wonderful flavors have always had a major influence on Jamie Oliver's food and cooking. . . . [Here] he travels this famously gastronomic country paying homage to the classic dishes of each region and searching for new ideas to bring home. The result is a . . . collection of Italian recipes, old and new." (Publisher's note)

Olney, Richard

Lulu's Provencal table; the food and wine from Domaine Tempier Vineyard. by Richard Olney; foreword by Alice Waters; photographs by Gail Skoff. Grub Street 2013 364 p. il (hc) $29.95   **641.59**
1. Cookbooks 2. Vineyards 3. French cooking 4. Domaine Tempier 5. Domaine Tempier Vineyard 6. Cookery, French -- Provencal style
ISBN 9781909166189; 1909166189
First published 1994

This book, by Richard Olney, describes how the author "moved to Provence[, France] in 1961 and had the good fortune to befriend Lulu and Lucien Peyraud, the owners of the noted Domaine Tempier vineyard in Provence, not far from Marseilles. . . . [The book provides] Olney's descriptions of the regional food served as the vineyard meals at the domaine. Then he lovingly transcribes Lulu's recipes." (Publisher's note)

Simple French food; Richard Olney ; new foreword by Mark Bittman ; foreword by James Beard ; introduction by Patricia Wells ; drawings by Richard Olney. Houghton Mifflin Harcourt 2014 455 p. ill. (hbk.) $24.99   **641.59**
1. Cookbooks 2. French cooking 3. Cooking, French 4. Cooking, French -- Provencal style
ISBN 0544242203; 9780544242203

LC 2014012324

IACP Culinary Classics Book Award (2013)

"This new edition of [Richard Olney's] classic cookbook includes a fresh cover, new interior design, and a foreword by Mark Bittman. . . . Olney's 175 recipes are so straightforward that cooks will be inspired to go right into the kitchen: herb omelets, fish with zucchini, lamb shanks with garlic, and many more. He also shares techniques (several featuring his own illustrations), such as fermenting vinegar, in line with the back-to-basics trend in cooking." (Publisher's note)

Pelaez, Ana Sofia

The Cuban table; a celebration of food, flavors, and history. Ana Sofia Pelaez ; photographs by Ellen Silverman. St. Martin's Press 2014 336 p. illustrations (hardback) $35   **641.59**
1. Cookbooks 2. Cuban cooking 3. Cooking, Cuban

ISBN 1250036089; 9781250036087

LC 2014026974

James Beard Foundation Award Nominee: International (2015)

This cookbook, by Ana Sofia Pelaez, with photographs by Ellen Silverman, "is a comprehensive, contemporary overview of Cuban food, recipes and culture as recounted by serious home cooks and professional chefs, restaurateurs and food writers. . . . Here you'll find documented recipes for everything from iconic Cuban sandwiches to rich stews with Spanish accents and African ingredients, accompanied by details about historical context and insight into cultural nuances." (Publisher's note)

"Let's hope Pelaez and Silverman undertake more collaborations. Their thorough and respectful treatment of their subject results in a compelling cookbook that conveys a strong sense of place." LJ

Includes bibliographical references and index

Phan, Charles

★ The slanted door; modern Vietnamese food. Charles Phan with Janny Hu ; photography by Ed Anderson. Ten Speed Press 2014 288 p. ill. (chiefly col.) (hardcover) $40   **641.59**
1. Vietnamese cooking
ISBN 1607740540; 9781607740544

LC 2014015943

IACP Cookbook Award: Photography (2015)
IACP Cookbook Award Finalist: Chefs and Restaurants (2015)

"Charles Phan opened The Slanted Door in San Francisco in 1995, inspired by the food of his native Vietnam. . . . The Slanted Door is a love letter to the restaurant, its people, and its food. Featuring stories in addition to its most iconic recipes,The Slanted Door both celebrates a culinary institution and allows home cooks to recreate its excellence." (Publisher's note)

"Phan's cuisine illustrates the synthesis that is Vietnam's culinary heritage: Chinese ingredients and traditions blended with French techniques. The Slanted Door's bar also mixes extensive lists of innovative cocktails, and these, along with Phan's cooking, are here documented." Booklist

Vietnamese home cooking; Charles Phan with Jessica Battilana ; photography by Eric Wolfinger. Ten Speed Press 2012 xxix, 222 p.p col. ill. $35   **641.59**
1. Cookbooks 2. Vietnamese cooking 3. Cooking, Vietnamese
ISBN 1607740532; 9781607740537; 9781607743859

LC 2012014119

IACP Cookbook Award (2013)

In this cookbook, chef Charles Phan "introduces traditional Vietnamese cooking to home cooks by focusing on fundamental techniques and ingredients. . . . With solid instruction and encouraging guidance, perfectly crispy imperial rolls, tender steamed dumplings, delicately flavored whole fish, and meaty lemongrass beef stew are all deliciously close at hand." (Publisher's note)

Phillips, Michael

The Chelsea Market cookbook; 100 recipes from New York's premier indoor food market. by Michael Phillips with Rick Rodgers. Stewart, Tabori & Chang 2013 223 p. color illustrations $29.95   **641.59**
1. Cookbooks 2. American cooking 3. Cooking, American 4. International cooking 5. Chelsea Market (New York, N.Y.)
ISBN 1617690376; 9781617690372

LC 2013009924

IACP Cookbook Award (2014)

This book, by Michael Phillips and Rick Rodgers, "collects the most interesting and famous recipes from the [Chelsea New York City] market's eclectic vendors and celebrity food personalities. Archival images, gorgeous food photography, and cooking and entertaining tips and anecdotes accompany the 100 recipes, ranging from Buddakan's Hoisin Glazed Pork Belly, to Sarabeth's Velvety Cream of Tomato Soup, to Ruthy's Rugelach." (Publisher's note)

Plum, Camilla

The **Scandinavian** Kitchen; Camilla Plum ; photography by Anne-Li Engstrom. Natl Book Network 2011 272 p. col. ill. hardcover o.p. $35   **641.59**
1. Cookbooks 2. Scandinavian cooking 3. Cooking, Scandinavian
ISBN 1906868476; 9781906868475

This cookbook, by Camilla Plum, "shares Scandinavian tastes, broken down by group of ingredient, easy to recreate in your own kitchen. Scandinavian cooking achieves a delicate balance between extravagance and the humble, producing a wealth of seasonal daily food, and more luxurious festive food." (Publisher's note)

"Plum, a leading Danish food writer, broadcaster, and cookbook author, extols the virtues of Scandinavian cuisine in this beautiful and fascinating collection. More of a guide to Scandinavian agriculture and its bounty than a full-fledged cookbook, this work showcases the diverse ingredients that make up the Scandinavian diet, including the wide array of both fresh and preserved fish, meat, and vegetables. Recipes are numerous but feel almost secondary." Pub Wkly

Psilakis, Michael

Live to eat; cooking the Mediterranean way. Michael Psilakis with Kathleen Hackett ; photography and design Hirsheimer & Hamilton. Little, Brown & Co. 2017 xvii, 219 p.p color illustrations (hardcover) $30   **641.59**
1. Mediterranean cooking 2. Cookbooks 3. Cooking, Mediterranean
ISBN 9780316308199; 9780316380133
LC 2016934518

This book, by Michael Psilakis, "offers a simple strategy for healthy cooking, highlighting the ease, deliciousness, and proven benefits of the Mediterranean diet. . . . Cooking the Mediterranean way means deliciousness, not deprivation: a nearly endless array of satisfying weeknight meals for your family can start with just seven easy-to-find staples, from Greek yogurt to simple tomato sauce." (Publisher's note)

Randall, Alice

Soul food love; 100 years of cooking and eating in one Black family, with recipes. Alice Randall and Caroline Randall Williams ; photographs by Penny De Los Santos. Clarkson Potter/Publishers 2015 224 p. illustrations (chiefly color)   **641.59**
1. Cookbooks 2. African American cooking
ISBN 9780804137935
LC 2014014423

NAACP Image Award: Outstanding Literary Work - Instructional (2016)

In this cookbook, by Alice Randall and Caroline Randall Williams, with photographs by Penny De Los Santos, "a mother-daughter duo reclaims and redefines soul food by mining the traditions of four generations of black women and creating 80 healthy recipes to help everyone live longer and stronger." (Publisher's note)

"The Wind Done Gone author Randall and daughter, poet Randall Williams, write about the history of black cooking in America and offer recipes that are both traditional and nutritious." LJ

Ray, Rachael, 1968-

Everyone is Italian on Sunday; Rachael Ray. Atria Paperback 2015 408 p. color illustrations (hardcover; alk. paper) $39.99   **641.59**

1. Cookbooks 2. Italian cooking 3. Cooking, Italian
ISBN 9781476766072
LC 2014043645

This Italian cookbook, by Rachael Ray, brings "together signature recipes for the traditional Italian staples that [the author] grew up with and still cooks for her family and friends today. From arancini to saffron gnocchetti sardi, from small bites to hearty meals, from her sister's favorite Italian desserts to her husband's Italian ingredient-inspired cocktails, here is a treasury of delicious dishes to prepare with love and devour with gusto." (Publisher's note)

"For those who are looking for a new angle , this cookbook satisfies in spades." Pub Wkly

Richards, Todd

Soul; a culinary evolution in 150 recipes. Todd Richards. Oxmoor House 2018 368 p. illustrations $35   **641.59**
1. Cooking 2. Cookbooks 3. Southern cooking
ISBN 9780848754419
LC 2017960063

In this cookbook, chef Todd Richards "shares his personal culinary exploration of soul food. . . . The chapters in . . . [this book] are organized by featured ingredients: Collards, Onions, Berries, Lamb, Seafood, Corn, Tomatoes, Melons, Stone Fruit, Eggs and Poultry, Pork and Beef, Beans and Rice, and Roots. Each one begins with a traditional recipe and progresses alongside Richards' exploration of flavor combinations and techniques." (Publisher's note)

"Lovers of Southern cuisine will find grits, corn, shrimp, and peaches showcased, but in unexpected, delightful ways (grilled peach toast with pimiento cheese; and peach salsa, chicken liver pâté on zucchini bread)." Pub Wkly

Richardson, Alan

The **breath** of a wok; unlocking the spirit of Chinese wok cooking through recipes and lore. Grace Young and Alan Richardson ; with text and recipes by Grace Young. Simon & Schuster 2004 240 p. ill. (some col.) $37.50   **641.59**
1. Cookbooks 2. Wok cooking 3. Cooking, Chinese 4. Food habits -- China
ISBN 0743238273; 9780743238274
LC 2003070403

IACP Cookbook Award (2005)

This cookbook, written by Grace Young and Alan Richardson, "brings the techniques and flavors of old-world wok cooking into today's kitchen, enabling anyone to stir-fry with wok hay. . . . The 125 recipes are a testament to the versatility of the wok, with stir-fried, smoked, pan-fried, braised, boiled, poached, steamed, and deep-fried dishes." (Publisher's note)

Includes bibliographical references and index

Roden, Claudia

The **new** book of Middle Eastern food; rev ed; Knopf 2000 513p il $35   **641.59**
1. Middle Eastern cooking 2. Cookery, Middle Eastern
ISBN 0-375-40506-2
LC 00-708864

Originally published 1968 in the United Kingdom; first United States edition published 1972 with title: A book of Middle Eastern food

This volume "includes 800 recipes and variations, as well as historical background, an introduction to essential ingredients and regional dietary practices, folktales, and a vast amount of other information." Libr J

Includes bibliographical references

Rodriguez, Jessamyn Waldman

The **Hot** Bread Kitchen cookbook; artisanal baking from around the world. Jessamyn Waldman Rodriguez and the Bakers of Hot Bread Kitchen with Julia Turshen. Clarkson Potter/Publishers 2015 301 p. (hardcover) $35 **641.59**

1. Bread 2. Cookbooks 3. International cooking
ISBN 9780804186179

LC 2014048697

This cookbook, by Jessamyn Waldman Rodriguez and the Bakers of Hot Bread Kitchen with Julia Turshen, "Hot Bread Kitchen is a bakery that employs and empowers immigrant women, providing them with the skills to succeed in the culinary industry. The tasty corollary of this . . . is a line of authentic breads you won't find anywhere else . . . [but] these ethnic gems can now be made at home." (Publisher's note)

'Hot Bread Kitchen's first cookbook foray is essential reading for serious foodies, bakers and anyone inspired by the bakery's philanthropic mission." LJ

Includes bibliographical references and index

Ronnen, Tal

Crossroads; extraordinary recipes from the restaurant that is reinventing vegan cuisine. Tal Ronnen with Scot Jones and Serafina Magnussen with JoAnn Cianciulli. Artisan 2015 304 p. color illustrations $35 **641.59**

1. Veganism 2. Cookbooks 3. Vegetarian cooking 4. Vegan cooking 5. Cooking, Mediterranean
ISBN 1579656366; 9781579656362

LC 2015010988

IACP Cookbook Award Nominee: Chefs and Restaurants (2016)

In this cookbook, chef Tal Ronnen with Scot Jones and Serafina Magnussen with JoAnn Cianciulli, "teaches readers to make his recipes and proves that the flavors we crave are easily replicated in dishes made without animal products. With accessible, unfussy recipes, [the book] . . . takes plant-based eating firmly out of the realm of hippie health food and into a cuisine that fits perfectly with today's modern palate." (Publisher's note)

"Vegan cooking taken to a new level of refinement. Epicures and professionals should take note." LJ

Rouxel, Sebastien

★ **Bouchon** Bakery; Thomas Keller, with Sebastien Rouxel and Matt McDonald ; along with Susie Heller, Michael Ruhlman, and Amy Vogler ; photographs by Deborah Jones. Artisan 2012 399 p. col. ill. $50 **641.59**

1. Baking 2. Pastry 3. Cookbooks 4. Bouchon Bakery
ISBN 1579654355; 9781579654351

LC 2012000695

IACP Cookbook Award (2013)

This cookbook, by Thomas Keller, was the winner of the 2013 IACP Cookbook Award for Food Photography & Styling. "[I]n this . . . amalgam of American and French baked goods, you'll find recipes for the beloved TKOs and Oh Ohs (Keller's takes on Oreos and Hostess's Ho Hos) and all the French classics he fell in love with as a young chef apprenticing in Paris: the baguettes, the macarons, the mille-feuilles, the tartes aux fruits." (Publisher's note)

"[T]his lovely volume is a must-have for cooks who want to take baking to the next level." Pub Wkly

Includes index

Santibañez, Roberto

Truly Mexican; Essential Recipes and Techniques for Authentic Mexican Cooking. [by] Roberto Santibanez, with J.J.

Goode and Shelley Wiseman. John Wiley & Sons, Inc. 2011 264 p. col. ill. $35 **641.59**

1. Cookbooks 2. Mexican cooking 3. Sauces 4. Cooking, Mexican
ISBN 0470499559; 9780470499559

LC 2010013151

This cookbook, by Roberto Santibanez, is "[a]n introduction to Mexican cooking. [It] covers the main ingredients as well as how they're best prepared--from toasting tortillas to roasting tomatoes--and offers a few simple kitchen commandments that make great results a given. Recipes cover main dishes, sides, salsas, guacamoles, moles, adobos, and more." (Publisher's note)

"[T]he author's expertise is conveyed in a straightforward and inspiring tone that will instill confidence in cooks eager to prepare Mexican meals at home, regardless of previous experience or skill level." Pub Wkly

Sherman, Sean

★ The **Sioux** chef's indigenous kitchen; by Sean Sherman with Beth Dooley. University of Minnesota Press 2017 256 p. (hardback) $34.95 **641.59**

1. Indian cooking 2. Indians of North America -- Food
ISBN 9780816699797

LC 2017020954

James Beard Award: American (2018)

This book, by Sean Sherman with Beth Dooley, offers tips on "creating boldly seasoned foods that are vibrant, healthful, at once elegant and easy. Sherman dispels outdated notions of Native American fare. . . . [This book] is a rich education and a delectable introduction to modern indigenous cuisine of the Dakota and Minnesota territories, with a vision and approach to food that travels well beyond those borders." (Publisher's note)

"Oglala Lakota chef Sherman has set out to educate the U.S. about its indigenous fruits and vegetables. Starting from his base in the northern Midwest and Great Plains and extending into Navajo lands, he ably demonstrates just how tasty and sophisticated the produce of the nation's heartland can be." Booklist

★ The **Silver** Spoon; 2nd English edition Phaidon Press 2011 1504 p. ill. (chiefly col.), map hbk $49.95 **641.59**

1. Italian cooking
ISBN 0714862568; 9780714862569

LC 2011293278

This classic Italian cookbook "features over 2,000 revised recipes and is illustrated with 400 brand new, full□color photographs. A comprehensive and lively book, its uniquely stylish and user□friendly format makes it accessible and a pleasure to read. The new updated edition features new introductory material covering such topics as how to compose a traditional Italian meal, typical food traditions of the different regions, and how to set an Italian table." (Publisher's note)

"Globe-trotting gourmands will appreciate the menu and 'signature dish' contributions by famous Italian chefs that round out the book. The most exhaustive Italian cookbook in recent memory, this volume offers something for every cook, regardless of their skill level, and deserves to be a fixture in American kitchens." Pub Wkly

Speck, Maria

Ancient grains for modern meals; Mediterranean whole grain recipes for barley, farro, kamut, polenta, wheat berries & more. Maria Speck ; photography by Sara Remington. Ten Speed Press 2011 ix, 210 p.p col. ill. (hardback) $29.99 **641.59**

1. Cookbooks 2. Cooking -- Grains 3. Alternative grains 4. Grain 5. Cooking (Cereals) 6. Cooking, Mediterranean

ISBN 1580083544; 9781580083546

LC 2010045867

IACP Cookbook Award (2012)

This cookbook, by Maria Speck, presents recipes for alternative, traditional grains including "farro, barley, polenta, and wheat berries." It contains "rustic but elegant dishes--Creamy Farro with Honey-Roasted Grapes, Barley Salad with Figs and Tarragon-Lemon Dressing, Lamb Stew with Wheat Berries in Red Wine Sauce, and Purple Rice Pudding with Rose Water Dates." (Publisher's note)

Includes bibliographical references and index

Sterling, David

★ **Yucatán**; recipes from a culinary expedition. by David Sterling. University of Texas Press 2014 576 p. ill. (chiefly col.), col. map (hardbound; alk. paper) $60   **641.59**

1. Maya cooking 2. Yucatan (Mexico) 3. Cooking -- Yucatan Peninsula 4. Mayas -- Social life and customs 5. Yucatán Peninsula -- Description and travel 6. Yucatán Peninsula -- Social life and customs

ISBN 0292735812; 9780292735811

LC 2013021911

James Beard Foundation Award Winner: Cookbook of the Year (2015)

James Beard Foundation Award Winner: International (2015)

This book, by David Sterling, "takes you on a gastronomic tour of the [Yucatan] peninsula in this unique cookbook. . . . Throughout the journey, Sterling serves up over 275 authentic, thoroughly tested recipes. . . . He also discusses pantry staples and basic cooking techniques and offers substitutions for local ingredients that may be hard to find elsewhere." (Publisher's note)

"Some recipes are multiday affairs, but they're clearly written and intended for home cooks. An introductory index provides an invaluable reference to unique Mesoamerican ingredients." LJ

Includes bibliographical references and index

Stone, Robyn

Add a Pinch cookbook; Robyn Stone, photographs by Helene Dujardin. Clarkson Potter/Publishers 2017 240 p. color illustrations (hardcover) $25; (ebook) $65   **641.59**

1. Cooking 2. Cookbooks 3. Southern cooking 4. Quick and easy cooking 5. Cooking -- Southern States 6. Cooking, American -- Southern style

ISBN 9780553496413; 9780553496420

LC 2016044983

In this cookbook, by Robyn Stone, photographs by Helene Dujardin and foreword by Ree Drummond, "fresh ingredients take center stage in slow cooker meals, casseroles and one-dish suppers, salads, soups, and desserts that have deep, satisfying flavors but are a cinch to make. Smart swaps like Greek yogurt for mayo in pimento cheese and cauliflower 'rice' put a modern spin on these dishes. With 75 color photographs and lots of sidebars, this is the new Southern cooking handbook." (Publisher's note)

"Vegetables include the gratifyingly regional, such as butter beans, okra, and collard greens, in approachable preparations, and a classic condiment whose time might finally have arrived: suitable-for-canning, authentic chow chow." Pub Wkly

Swanson, Heidi

Near & far; recipes inspired by home and travels. Heidi Swanson. Ten Speed Press 2015 336 p. color illustrations (hardcover; alk. paper) $29.99   **641.59**

1. International cooking

ISBN 1607745496; 9781607745495

LC 2014047586

In this cookbook author Heidi Swanson "describes the fragrance of flatbreads hot off a Marrakech griddle, soba noodles and featherlight tempura in Tokyo, and the taste of wild-picked greens from the Puglian coast. Recipes such as Fennel Stew, Carrot & Sake Salad, Watermelon Radish Soup, Brown Butter Tortelli, and Saffron Tagine use healthy, whole foods ingredients and approachable techniques." (Publisher's note)

"Highly recommended for anyone who loves unassuming and easy gourmet cooking. Fans of David Tanis (One Good Dish) and Alice Waters (The Art of Simple Food) will love this." LJ

Includes bibliographical references and index

Near and far

Terry, Bryant

Afro-vegan; farm-fresh African, Caribbean & Southern flavors remixed. Bryant Terry ; photography by Paige Green. Ten Speed Press 2014 215 p. ill. (chiefly col.), col. map (hardback) $27.50   **641.59**

1. Veganism 2. Caribbean cooking 3. African American cooking 4. Vegan cooking 5. Cooking, African 6. Cooking, Caribbean 7. Cooking, American -- Southern style

ISBN 1607745313; 9781607745310

LC 2013048560

"With more than 100 modern and delicious dishes that draw on [author Bryant] Terry's personal memories as well as the history of food that has traveled from the African continent, Afro-Vegan takes you on an international food journey. Accompanying the recipes are Terry's insights about building community around food, along with suggested music tracks from around the world and book recommendations." (Publisher's note)

Includes bibliographical references and index

Thielen, Amy

The **New** Midwestern table; 200 heartland recipes. Amy Thielen. Clarkson Potter/Publishers 2013 399 p. color illustrations (hardback) $35   **641.59**

1. Cookbooks 2. Midwestern cooking 3. Cooking, American -- Midwestern style

ISBN 0307954870; 9780307954879

LC 2012047058

James Beard Award (2014)

This cookbook, by Amy Thielen, "reveals all that she's come to love--and learn--about the foods of her native Midwest, through updated classic recipes and numerous encounters with spirited home cooks. . . . [The book also contains] 150 color photographs capturing these fresh-from-the-land dishes and the striking beauty of the terrain." (Publisher's note)

Twitty, Michael, 1977-

★ The **cooking** gene; a journey through African-American culinary history in the Old South. Michael W. Twitty. Amistad 2017 464 p. color illustrations hardcover $28.99; paperback $16.99   **641.59**

1. Southern cooking 2. African American cooking 3. African American cooking -- History 4. Cooking, American -- Southern style -- History 5. African Americans -- Food -- Southern States -- History

ISBN 0062379275; 9780062379290; 9780062379283; 0062379291; 9780062379276

LC 2017003374

James Beard Award: Book of the Year (2018); James Beard Award: Writing (2018)

Author Michael W. Twitty, "offers a fresh perspective on our most divisive cultural issue, race, in this illuminating memoir of Southern cuisine and food culture that traces his ancestry . . . through food, from Africa to America and slavery to freedom. . . . From the tobacco and rice farms of colonial times to plantation kitchens and . . . cotton fields, Twitty tells his family story through the foods that enabled his ancestors' survival across three centuries." (Publisher's note)

"Drawing on a wealth of documentary digging, personal interviews, and plenty of time in the kitchen, Twitty ably joins past and present, puzzling out culinary mysteries along the way. . . . An exemplary, inviting exploration and an inspiration for cooks and genealogists alike."

Includes bibliographical references

Van Aken, Norman

New World kitchen; Latin American and Caribbean cuisine. Norman Van Aken, with Janet Van Aken ; photographs by Tim Turner. Ecco 2003 xiv, 322 p.p ill. (some col.) $34.95 **641.59**

1. Cookbooks 2. Caribbean cooking 3. Latin American cooking 4. Cooking, Caribbean 5. Cooking, Latin American

ISBN 0060185058; 9780060185053

LC 2002027158

This cookbook, by Norman Van Aken with Janet Van Aken, "explores the rich influence of Latin American cuisine on the American palate. From the African-influenced Creole cuisines of Cuba, Puerto Rico, and Jamaica to South American flavors from Brazil, Peru, and Argentina to the distinct tastes of Mexico, Van Aken works his particular magic on this luscious cornucopia and emerges with a wealth of brilliant recipes." (Publisher's note)

"Combined with Van Aken's many thoughtful sidebars and notations, the sophistication of these recipes make this a treat for serious home cooks." Pub Wkly

Includes bibliographical references and index

Von Bremzen, Anya

Mastering the art of Soviet cooking; a memoir of love and longing. by Anya von Bremzen. Crown Publishers 2013 352 p. $26 **641.59**

1. Russian cooking 2. Russia -- History -- 1917-1991, Soviet Union 3. Food habits -- Soviet Union 4. Moscow (Russia) -- Biography 5. Russian Americans -- Biography 6. Soviet Union -- Social life and customs 7. Women cooks -- Soviet Union -- Biography 8. Food writers -- United States -- Biography 9. Cooking, Russian -- History -- 20th century 10. Russia (Federation) -- Social conditions -- 1991-

ISBN 0307886816; 9780307886811

LC 2013007787

This book by Anya von Bramzen presents "a memoir of life in Soviet Russia. The book is subdivided by decade, and von Bremzen . . . weaves her own memories together with stories from her grandmother and mother, beginning in 1910. The common denominator--and recurring touchstone--is food. . . . Von Bremzen concludes with nine recipes." (Library Journal)

"With anecdotes, history and recipes, the author delivers a lively, precisely detailed cultural chronicle." Kirkus

Includes bibliographical references

Paladares; recipes inspired by the private restaurants of Cuba. Anya von Bremzen ; recipe development and photography by Megan Fawn Schlow. Abrams 2017 351 p. illustrations (chiefly color) (hardcover) $40 **641.59**

1. Cooking 2. Cuban cooking 3. Cooking, Cuban 4. Food habits -- Cuba

ISBN 9781683351450; 9781419727030; 1419727036

LC 2016961368

In this book, author "Anya von Bremzen brings a unique perspective to the stories that Cuba's chefs, restaurateurs, farmers, and food historians share with her. She eavesdrops on passionate arguments about black beans and tamales; pries Daiquirí secrets from legendary El Floridita . . . ; guides us to vibrant agros (markets) and visionary organic farms." (Publisher's note)

Wadi, Sameh

The **new** mediterranean cookbook; incredible dishes inspired by cooking traditions spanning three continents. Sameh Wadi. Page Street Pub. Co. 2015 224 p. color illustrations (pbk.) $28 **641.59**

1. Mediterranean cooking

ISBN 1624140955; 1624141048; 9781624140952; 9781624141041

LC 2014950215

In this Mediterranean cookbook, chef Sameh Wadi "offers a collection of recipes that represent an exceptional look into his rich heritage, the culinary foundation that has propelled him to the top of the American restaurant scene. . . . He takes influences from everything from Mediterranean street food to top gourmet offerings and gives you the best of the Mediterranean, one recipe at a time." (Publisher's note)

Wells, Patricia

Patricia Wells at home in Provence; recipes inspired by her farmhouse in France. Patricia Wells ; photographs by Robert Freson. Fireside 1999 355 p. col il (paperback) $24 **641.59**

1. Cookbooks 2. French cooking 3. Provence (France) -- Description 4. French cooking -- Provencal style

ISBN 9780684815695; 9780684863283; 0684863286

LC 00266924

James Beard Award (1997)

In this French cookbook, Patricia Wells, "the award-winning journalist and author invites readers to share the passion, the joy, and, best of all, the cooking of her adopted home. Provence is uniquely blessed with natural beauty as well as some of the world's most appealing foods and liveliest wines. . . . Here are 175 recipes from Patricia's farmhouse kitchen." (Publisher's note)

Willan, Anne

The **country** cooking of France; by Anne Willan ; photographs by France Ruffenach. Chronicle Books 2007 390 p. ill. (chiefly col.), col. map $50 **641.59**

1. Cookbooks 2. French cooking 3. Cooking, French

ISBN 0811846466; 9780811846462

LC 2007004773

James Beard Award (2008)

This cookbook, by Anne Willan, "combines years of hands-on experience with extensive research to create a brand new classic. More than 250 recipes range from the time-honored La Truffade, with its crispy potatoes and melted cheese, to the Languedoc specialty Cassoulet de Toulouse, a bean casserole of duck confit, sausage, and lamb." (Publisher's note)

Wolfert, Paula

Couscous and other good food from Morocco; Introd. by Gael Green. Color photos. by Bill Bayer. Drawings by Sidonie Coryn. Harper & Row 1973 xv, 351 p.p illus. (part col.) $19.99 **641.59**

1. Cookbooks 2. Moroccan cooking 3. Cooking, Moroccan

ISBN 0060147210; 0060913967; 9780060913960

LC 72009165

James Beard Cookbook Hall of Fame (2008)

IACP Culinary Classics Book Award (2013)

"Since it was first published in 1973, 'Couscous and Other Good Food from Morocco' has established itself as the classic work on one of the world's great cuisines, and in 2008 it was inducted into the James Beard Cookbook Hall of Fame. From the magnificent bisteeyas . . . to endless varieties of couscous, [author] Paula Wolfert reveals not only the riches of the Moroccan kitchen but also the variety and flavor of the country itself." (Publisher's note)

Bibliography: p. 342

The **food** of Morocco; Paula Wolfert ; photographs by Quentin Bacon ; drawings by Mark Marthaler. Ecco 2011 518 p. ill. (chiefly col.), col. maps $45 **641.59**

1. Cookbooks 2. Moroccan cooking 3. Cooking, Moroccan

ISBN 0061957550; 9780061957550

LC 2011278431

James Beard Award (2012)

This cookbook, by Paula Wolfert, "provides food lovers with the definitive guide to the food of Morocco. Lavishly photographed and packed with tantalizing recipes to please the modern palate, . . . [the book] provides helpful preparation techniques for chefs, home cooks, and any serious student of the culinary arts and culture." (Publisher's note)

Deftly balancing authenticity with ease of preparation, . . . Wolfert is an eager and encouraging host, walking readers through the various regions and their signature dishes as well as the handful of ingredients that make the cuisine so distinctive." Pub Wkly

Includes bibliographical references and index

Mediterranean clay pot cooking; traditional and modern recipes to savor and share. Paula Wolfert. John Wiley & Sons 2009 xviii, 334 p.p ill. (chiefly col.) (cloth) $34.95 **641.59**

1. Cookbooks 2. Clay pot cooking 3. Mediterranean cooking 4. Cooking, Mediterranean

ISBN 076457633X; 9780764576331

LC 2008055912

In this cookbook, author Paula Wolfert, "shares her inimitable passion for detail and insatiable curiosity about cultural traditions and innovations. . . . Here, the self-confessed clay pot 'junkie'--having collected in her travels ceramic pots of all sorts . . . shares recipes as vibrant as the Mediterranean itself along with the delightful stories behind the earthy pots, irresistible dishes, and outstanding cooks she has met along the way." (Publisher's note)

"Wolfert is a true cook's author, and . . . this book is not for the casual home cook. But for those willing to tackle them, Wolfert's clay pot dishes do indeed merit the hype." Pub Wkly

Includes bibliographical references and index

Wong, Lee Anne

Dumplings All Day Wong; A Cookbook of Asian Delights from a Top Chef. by Lee Anne Wong. St. Martin's Press 2014 256 p. color illustrations $22.99 **641.59**

1. Cookbooks 2. Dumplings 3. Asian cooking

ISBN 1624140599; 9781624140594

LC 2013922991

This book, by celebrity chef Lee Anne Wong, "will have you creating one-of-a-kind dumplings that wow your family and friends. Folds such as Potstickers, Gyozas, Shumai, Har Gow, Wontons and more, along with countless fillings and different cooking methods such as steaming, pan-frying, baking or deep-frying, allow you to create awe-inspiring dumplings in innumerable ways." (Publisher's note)

"This excellent dumpling cookbook highlights a wealth of flavors

and techniques and advocates a from-scratch approach. The simpler dumplings in Bee Yin Low's Easy Chinese Recipes would make a great starting point for novices." LJ

641.594   Cooking – Europe

Bastianich, Lidia Matticchio

Lidia's favorite recipes; 100 foolproof Italian dishes, from basic sauces to irresistible entrées. by Lidia Matticchio Bastianich and Tanya Bastianich Manuali ; photographs by Marcus Nilsson. Alfred A. Knopf 2012 240 p. color illustrations $24.95 **641.594**

1. Cookbooks 2. Italian cooking 3. Cooking, Italian

ISBN 0307595668; 9780307595669

LC 2012023455

This book by Lidia Matticchio Bastianich and Tanya Bastianich Manuali presents "the recipes for dishes that [have been] raved and written about over and over--the best, the most comforting, and the most delicious dishes in [Lidia's] repertoire. With new information about the affordability, seasonality, and nutritional value of the ingredients, this book shows there is no question why these dishes are the easiest and most enjoyable to bring to the family table." (Publisher's note)

"More compact than Bastianich's other titles, this practical collection is perfect for families as well as readers who enjoyed Viana La Place and Evan Kleiman's Cucina Rustica." LJ

Lidia's mastering the art of Italian cuisine; everything you need to know to be a great Italian cook. by Lidia Mattichio Bastianich, with Tanya Bastianich Manuali. Alfred A. Knopf 2015 480 p. (hardcover) $37.50 **641.594**

1. Italian cooking 2. Cooking, Italian

ISBN 0385349467; 9780385349468

LC 2015001871

Author Lidia Mattichho Bastianich presents this "guide to Italian cooking, coauthored with her daughter, Tanya [Bastianich Manuali]--covering everything from ingredients to techniques to tools, plus more than 400 delectable recipes. Lidia introduces us to the full range of standard ingredients--meats and fish, vegetables and fruits, grains, spices and condiments--and how to buy, store, clean, and cook with them." (Publisher's note)

"The book completes its course with a charming chapter on Italian culture and language, as well as an extensive glossary of food terms. With this passionate treatise on Italian food and culture, readers dreaming of la dolce vita may find armchair travels enough to satisfy their hunger." Pub Wkly

Mastering the art of italian cuisine

Bjork, Katrin

From the north; a simple and modern approach to authentic Nordic cooking. Katrin Bjork. Page Street Pub. Co. 2018 192 p. (pbk.) $21.99 **641.594**

1. Cooking 2. Cookbooks 3. Scandinavian cooking

ISBN 1624145302; 1624145310; 9781624145308; 9781624145315

LC 2017952212

In this cookbook, "Katrín Björk celebrates the flavors of her childhood with fresh ingredients and unique twists. Her modern techniques make traditional Nordic cooking simple and approachable, no matter how far south your kitchen. . . . With helpful tips on how to select the freshest fish, preserve ingredients safely and bake the rustic bread essential to any Nordic meal, it's easy to make these dishes your own."

(Publisher's note)

Bottura, Massimo, 1962-

Never Trust a Skinny Italian Chef; Massimo Bottura. Phaidon Inc Ltd 2014 296 p. color illustrations $59.95 **641.594**

    1. Cooking 2. Italian cooking

    ISBN 0714867144; 9780714867144

James Beard Foundation Award Nominee: Cooking from a Professional Point of View (2015)

This cookbook by Massimo Bottura is "a tribute to [his] twenty☐five year career and the evolution of Osteria Francescana, his three Michelin star restaurant based in Modena, Italy. Divided into four chapters, each one dealing with a different period, the book features 50 recipes and stories explaining Bottura's inspirations (including the music and art that motivates him), ingredients, and techniques." (Publisher's note)

"Quirky dishes such as a deconstructed mortadella sandwich made with mortadella foam; bread, butter, and anchovies; and a compression of pasta and beans make this a fun collection to peruse, but one unlikely to inspire home cooks. Professionals, however, will relish the opportunity for guided experimentation with Italian classics." Pub Wkly

Clark, Melissa

Franny's; simple seasonal Italian. by Andrew Feinberg, Francine Stephens, Melissa Clark. Artisan 2013 ix, 366 p.p ill. (some col.) (hardcover) $35.00 **641.594**

    1. Cooking 2. Cookbooks 3. Cooking, Italian 4. Cooking -- New York (State) -- Brooklyn

    ISBN 1579654649; 9781579654641

                              LC 2012028954

In this book, Andrew Feinberg and Francine Stephens, owners of the Brooklyn, New York restaurant Franny's, offer recipes "for everything from soups, salads, and fritti to fish, vegetables, and cocktails." For more complicated recipes, "the authors provide straightforward step-by-step instructions accompanied by photos that demonstrate the proper technique." (Publishers Weekly)

Includes index.

De Laurentiis, Giada, 1970-

Giada's Italy; my recipes for la dolce vita. Giada De Laurentiis. Clarkson Potter 2018 288 p. (hardback) $35 **641.594**

    1. Cooking 2. Cookbooks 3. Italian cooking 4. Cooking, Italian

    ISBN 9780307987228

                              LC 2017049489

In this cookbook, author Giada De Laurentiis "invites fans and home cooks to get to know the flavors and stories that have inspired her life's work. Here, she shares recipes for authentic Italian dishes as her family has prepared them for years while infusing them with her signature fresh flavors to make them her own." (Publisher's note)

Dusoulier, Clotilde

Tasting Paris; 100 recipes to eat like a local. Clotilde Dusoulier. Clarkson Potter/Publishers 2018 256 p. (hard cover) $30 **641.594**

    1. Cookbooks 2. French cooking 3. Cooking, French

    ISBN 9780451499141

                              LC 2017025780

This book, by Clotilde Dusoulier, "features new and classic French recipes and cooking techniques that will demistify the art of French cooking and transport your dinner guests to Paris.Whether you have experienced the charm of Paris many times or dream of planning your first trip, here you will find the food that makes this city so beloved." (Publisher's note)

"Chapters are organized by time of day, so that one for afternoon treats, for instance, proffers light sweets, which are differentiated from dinner desserts. The setup can be a bit confusing at first, but it does ultimately lend reading this volume the same feel as of discovering something new while strolling down a city street." Pub Wkly

Hercules, Olias

Mamushka; A Cookbook. Olia Hercules. Weldon Owen 2015 240 p. color illustrations $35 **641.594**

    1. Cooking 2. Ukraine 3. Eastern Europe

    ISBN 1616289619; 9781616289614

This cookbook by Olia Hercules is a "celebration of the food, flavors, and heritage of Eastern Europe--from the Black Sea to Baku, Kiev to Kazakhsta--[and] features over 100 recipes for fresh, delicious, and unexpected dishes from this dynamic yet underappreciated region. [It] showcases the cuisine from Ukraine and beyond, weaving together vibrant food with descriptive narratives and stunning lifestyle photography." (Publisher's note)

Hercules's unexpected Ukranian, Azerbaijani, Russian, and Armenian comfort foods can help home cooks transition to colder months." LJ

Hoffman, Susanna

The **olive** and the caper; adventures in Greek cooking. by Susanna Hofman ; in collaboration with Victoria Wise. Workman Pub. Co. 2004 xvii, 589 p.p ill. (some col.) $19.95 **641.594**

    1. Greek cooking 2. Greece -- Social life and customs 3. Cooking, Greek 4. Food habits -- Greece

    ISBN 0761134689; 1563058480; 9781563058486

                              LC 2004040862

This book, by Susanna Hofman, combines "recipes and adventure. . . Including 325 recipes developed in collaboration with Victoria Wise, . . . [it] celebrates all things Greek: Chicken Neo-Avgolemeno. Fall-off-the-bone Lamb Shanks. . . . Siren-like sweets, from world-renowned Baklava to uniquely Greek preserves. . . . In addition, it . . . has dozens of lively essays throughout the book--about the origins of Greek food, about village life, history, language, [and] customs." (Publisher's note)

"With its fascinating trove of information, this work will please armchair cooks and traveling foodies. For those willing to surrender to its searingly bright palate of flavors, it's a boon to the kitchen, too. Photos, illus. (July)Forecast: With the Olympics in Athens next month, interest should be strong." Pub Wkly

Includes bibliographical references and index

How to eataly; a guide to buying, cooking, and eating Italian food. Written by Eataly, Foreword by Mario Batali, Lidia Bastianich, Joseph Bastianich and Oscar Farinetti. Rizzoli International Publications 2014 304 p. illustrations (chiefly color) $35 **641.594**

    1. Cookbooks 2. Italian cooking

    ISBN 0847843351; 9780847843350

                              LC 2014941649

This cookbook, by Eataly, with a foreword by Mario Batali, Lidia Bastianich, Joseph Bastianich and Oscar Farinetti, offers "the secrets to Italian cooking, straight from the source—the wildly popular food emporium that is founded in Italy. . . . Learn how to assemble an antipasto platter, how to eat breakfast like an Italian, and how to use pantry flavor boosters like capers and anchovies." (Publisher's note)

Italian Comfort Food; by The Editors of Saveur. Simon & Schuster 2015 224 p. color illustrations $35 **641.594**

    1. Italian cooking

    ISBN 1616289643; 9781616289645

This cookbook, by The Editors of Saveur, "features 100 recipes from the magazine's archives and editors. . . . With classic and brand new recipes, this cookbook presents the flavors, ingredients and techniques you need for Italian comfort food. This masterful selection illuminates SAVEUR's authority, heritage, and culinary wealth." (Publisher's note)

Kahan, Paul

★ **Cheers** to the Publican, repast and present; recipes and ramblings from an American beer hall. Paul Kahan and Cosmo Goss with Rachel Holtzman ; photographs by Peden + Munk ; poems by Jason Pickleman. Lorena Jones Books, an imprint of Ten Speed Press 2017 xi, 324 p.p (hardcover) $40 **641.594**
1. Cookbooks 2. Restaurants 3. Cooking, American 4. Cooking, European 5. Publican (Restaurant; Chicago, Ill.)
ISBN 0399578560; 9780399578564

LC 2017013468

This book, by Paul Kahan and Cosmo Goss with Rachel Holtzman, focuses on the "destination restaurant, The Publican. . . . The Publican, often named one of Chicago's most popular restaurants, conjures a colonial American beer hall with its massive communal tables, high-backed chairs, deep beer list, and Kahan's hallmark style of crave-worthy heartland cooking that transcends the expected and is eminently cookable." (Publisher's note)

Includes bibliographical references and index

Kochilas, Diane

Ikaria; lessons on food, life, and longevity from the Greek island where people forget to die. Diane Kochilas ; photographs by Vassillis Stenos. Rodale 2014 306 p. color illustrations (hardback) $35 **641.594**
1. Longevity 2. Greek cooking 3. Greece -- Description and travel 4. Cooking, Greek 5. Ikaria (Greece; Municipality) 6. Food -- Greece -- Ikaria (Municipality) 7. Cooking -- Greece -- Ikaria (Municipality)
ISBN 1623362954; 9781623362959

LC 2014032164

IACP Cookbook Award Winner: International (2015)

This book, by Diane Kochilas, is "[p]art cookbook, part travelogue, filled with gorgeous photography, stunning recipes, and interviews with locals. . . . We'll learn about the life-giving benefits of delicious salads both raw and cooked, the gorgeous breads and savory pies that are a part of every meal, the bean dishes that are passed down through generations, and the seafood that is at the root of the Ikarian culinary culture." (Publisher's note)

Includes bibliographical references and index

Loomis, Susan Herrmann

In a French kitchen; tales and traditions of everyday home cooking in France. Susan Herrmann Loomis. Gotham Books 2015 320 p. $26.95 **641.594**
1. French cooking 2. Cooking, French 3. Food habits -- France
ISBN 1592408869; 9781592408863

LC 2014035856

In this book, expat Susan Herrmann Loomis "demystifies . . . the seemingly effortless je ne sais quoi behind a simple French meal. One by one, readers are invited to meet the busy people of Louviers and surrounding villages and towns of Loomis's adopted home, from runway-chic Edith, who has zero passion for cooking--but a love of food that inspires her to whip up an array of mouthwatering dishes--to Nathalie, who becomes misty-eyed as she talks about her mother's Breton cooking." (Publisher's note)

"Loomis also shares scores of recipes from her own repertoire and those of her friends, including a 12-month meal plan based on fresh, seasonal ingredients. A tempting and helpful guide to delectable food." Kirkus

Mendes, Nuno

My Lisbon; a cookbook from Portugal's city of light. Nuno Mendes. Ten Speed Press 2018 372 p. (hardback) $35 **641.594**
1. Cookbooks 2. Portuguese cooking 3. Cooking, Portuguese 4. Cooking -- Portugal -- Lisbon
ISBN 9780399581717

LC 2017049818

"In this groundbreaking cookbook, Lisbon native and internationally renowned chef Nuno Mendes reveals the alluring food of one of the great undiscovered culinary centers of Europe. Sharing recipes inspired by the dishes that he grew up eating, Mendes takes you to his beloved Lisbon, revealing the secrets for re-creating the city's most vibrant dishes." (Publisher's note)

"Pitch-perfect and mouthwatering, this book is a joy from start to finish." Pub Wkly

Includes bibliographical references and index

Minchilli, Elizabeth

Eating Rome; living the good life in the Eternal City. Elizabeth Minchilli. St. Martin's Griffin 2015 256 p. illustrations (trade pbk.) $24.99 **641.594**
1. Rome (Italy) 2. Italian cooking 3. Cooking, Italian 4. Restaurants -- Italy -- Rome 5. Grocery shopping -- Italy -- Rome 6. Dinners and dining -- Italy -- Rome
ISBN 1250047684; 9781250047687

LC 2014044288

This book, by Elizabeth Minchilli, "is a personal . . . look at some of the city[of Rome]'s monuments to food culture. Join her as she takes you on a stroll through her favorite open air markets; stop by the best gelato shops; order plates full of carbonara and finish the day with a brilliant red Negroni." (Publisher's note)

"Minchilli is biased toward family-run specialty shops in certain neighborhoods, and she reflects on the changing culinary scene with the rise of the Roman brunch and the closing of many traditional spots." Pub Wkly

Moulle, Jean Pierre

French roots; two cooks, two countries, and the beautiful food along the way. Jean-Pierre Moullé and Denise Lurton Moullé. Ten Speed Press 2014 272 p. color illustrations (hardcover) $35 **641.594**
1. Cooks 2. California 3. French cooking 4. Cooking, French 5. Cooks -- United States -- Biography
ISBN 160774547X; 9781607745471

LC 2014023823

IACP Cookbook Award Finalist: Julia Child First Book (2015)

This book, by Jean-Pierre Moullé and Denise Lurton Moullé, "is the story of their lives told through the food they cook-- beginning with the dishes of old-world France, the couple's birthplace, and focusing on the simple, pared-down preparations of French food common in the postwar period. The story then travels to the San Francisco Bay Area in the 1970s, where Jean-Pierre was appointed executive chef at Chez Panisse when California cuisine was just emerging." (Publisher's note)

"Readers who have an active imaginary life in France will relish poring over this cookbook's extensive narrative. Fans of Chez Panisse will enjoy pairing it with titles from other chef alums, such as David Tanis and David Lebovitz." LJ

Necchio, Valeria

Veneto; recipes from an Italian country kitchen. Valeria Necchio. Guardian Faber Publishing 2017 288 p. color illustrations (hardcover) $29.95   **641.594**

1. Cookbooks 2. Italian cooking 3. Cooking -- Italy -- Veneto 4. Cooking, Italian -- Northern style 5. Cooking, Italian -- Venetian style

ISBN 9781783351091; 9781783351084; 178335108X

In this book, "food-writer, cook, and photographer Valeria Necchio shares the food and flavors at the heart of the Veneto region in North Eastern Italy. 'Veneto' includes lovingly written recipes that capture the spirit of this beautiful and often unexplored region, and Valeria's memories of the people and places that make the Veneto so special." (Publisher's note)

"Necchio writes in lovely elegiac prose about her small hometown . . . and the recipes themselves are clear and appealing, no matter from which time in the author's life they originate." Pub Wkly

Nolen, Jeremy

German cooking now; 100 recipes for family-style meals. by Jeremy and Jessica Nolen with Drew Lazor ; photographs by Jason Varney. Chronicle Books LLC 2014 248 p. color illustrations (hardcover) $40   **641.594**

1. Cookbooks 2. German cooking 3. Cooking, German

ISBN 9781452128061; 1452128065

LC 2014000717

This cookbook, by Jeremy and Jessica Nolen with Drew Lazor, with photography by Jason Varney, "celebrates fresh vegetables, grains, herbs, and spices as obsessively as it does pork, pretzels, and beer. Chefs Jeremy and Jessica Nolen share recipes from their family table, inspired by their travels in Germany." (Publisher's note)

"Despite its traditional leanings, this German cookbook is refined and chic, with very clear instructions." LJ

Includes bibliographical references (page 228) index

River Cafe London; thirty years of recipes and the story of a much-loved restaurant. Ruth Rogers, Rose Gray, Sian Wyn Owen, Joseph Trivelli, Matthew Donaldson, Jean Pigozzi, Stephanie Nash, Anthony Michael. Alfred A. Knopf 2018 320 p. (hardcover; alk. paper) $40   **641.594**

1. Cooking 2. Cookbooks 3. Quick and easy cooking 4. River Cafe (London, England) 5. Cooking, Italian -- Tuscan style

ISBN 9780525521303

LC 2017044066

In this book "Ruth [Rogers] and her restaurant's head chefs, Joseph Trivelli and Sian Wyn Owen, invite you to join them in marking 30 years of memories and good food--the simple, high-quality Italian cooking that River Cafe has been providing since 1987. Here are 120 recipes for incomparable antipasti, primi, secondi, contorni, and dolci, . . . as well as 30 new classics from their menus today. . . . [It] also incorporates Ruth's memories of the restaurant's storied history. "(Publisher's note)

Thorisson, Mimi

A **kitchen** in France; a year of cooking in my farmhouse. Mimi Thorisson ; photographs by Oddur Thorisson. Clarkson Potter/Publishers 2014 304 p. illustrations (print edition; alkaline paper) $40   **641.594**

1. Cookbooks 2. French cooking 3. Country life -- France 4. Cooking, French 5. Cooking -- France -- Médoc 6. Seasons -- France -- Médoc 7. Médoc (France) -- Biography 8. Farmhouses -- France -- Médoc 9. Seasonal cooking -- France -- Médoc 10. Médoc (France) -- Description and travel 11. Médoc (France) --

Social life and customs

ISBN 080418559X; 9780804185592

LC 2013049107

IACP Cookbook Award Finalist: Photography (2015)

This cookbook, by Mimi Thorisson, "chronicles the family's seasonal meals and life in an old farmhouse, all photographed by her husband, Oddur. Mimi's convivial recipes--such as Roast Chicken with Herbs and Crème Fraîche, Cèpe and Parsley Tartlets, Winter Vegetable Cocotte, Apple Tart with Orange Flower Water, and Salted Butter Crème Caramel--will bring the warmth of rural France into your home." (Publisher's note)

"And while the appeal of this collection rests firmly on its recipes, the incredible photographs capture life in the French countryside. Sidebars on everything from dried grapevines and wine to garlic and visits the butcher add little details that transport the reader to this bucolic, idyllic world where Thorisson is the perfect host."

Waters, Alice, 1944-

My pantry; Alice Waters ; illustrations by Fanny Singer. Pam Krauss Books 2015 144 p. illustrations $24.99 **641.594**

1. Cooking 2. Grocery shopping 3. Spices 4. Cooking, French

ISBN 080418528X; 9780804185288; 9780804185295

LC 2014042977

Author Alice Waters, with Fanny Singer, "invites readers to step not into the kitchen at Chez Panisse, but into her own, sharing how she shops, stores, and prepares the pantry staples and preserves that form the core of her daily meals. Ranging from essentials like homemade chicken stock, red wine vinegar, and tomato sauce to the unique artisanal provisions that embody Alice's unadorned yet delightful cooking style, she shows how she injects even simple meals with nuanced flavor." (Publisher's note)

"The truly ambitious may make their own simple, unaged cheeses. Not everyone has access to the sorts of ingredients available in Waters' Mediterranean climate, but creative cooks can adapt local produce in season to Waters' techniques." Booklist

Weiss, Jeffrey

Charcuteria; the soul of Spain. Jeffrey Weiss. Surrey Books 2013 460 p. (hardcover) $39.95   **641.594**

1. Cooking -- Meat 2. Spanish cooking 3. Cooking (Meat) 4. Cooking, Spanish

ISBN 1572841524; 9781572841529

LC 2013018755

This cookbook, by Jeffrey Weiss, "is the first book to introduce authentic Spanish butchering and meat-curing techniques to America. Included are more than 100 traditional Spanish recipes, straightforward illustrations providing easy-to-follow steps for amateur and professional butchers, and gorgeous full-color photography of savory dishes, Iberian countrysides, and centuries-old Spanish cityscapes." (Publisher's note)

Wells, Patricia

The **French** kitchen cookbook; recipes and lessons from Paris and Provence. Patricia Wells ; photographs by Jeff Kauck. HarperCollinsPublishers 2013 312 p. color illustrations $35   **641.594**

1. French cooking 2. Cooking, French 3. Cooking -- France -- Paris 4. Cooking -- France -- Provence

ISBN 0062088912; 9780062088918

LC 2013013311

In this cookbook, chef Patricia Wells "invites home cooks into her life in France, making the fresh and delicious recipes from her popular classes. . . . Here are some of her best recipes for appetizers, desserts, and everything in between, dishes inspired by the vibrant Provençal countryside and the bustle of Parisian life." (Publisher's note)

Wright, Caroline

Catalan food; culture & flavors from the Mediterranean. Daniel Olivella and Caroline Wright. Clarkson Potter/Publishers 2018 272 p. (hardcover) $30   **641.594**

    1. Cooking 2. Cookbooks 3. Spanish cooking 4. Cooking, Spanish -- Catalonian style

    ISBN 9780451495884

                        LC 2017048094

In this cookbook, "Catalan cuisine authority Daniel Olivella serves historical narratives alongside 80 carefully curated Spanish food recipes, like tapas, paella, and seafood, that are simple and fresh. . . . [T]he recipes are intended to be cooked leisurely and with love--the Catalan way. . . . 'Catalan Food' brings heritage into any home cook's kitchen, where Catalonia's cuisine was born." (Publisher's note)

641.595   Cooking – Asia

Chang, Joanne

Myers + Chang at home; recipes from the beloved Boston eatery. Joanne Chang with Karen Akunowicz ; preface by Christopher Myers ; photographs by Kristin Teig. Houghton Mifflin Harcourt 2017 320 p. color illustrations (hardcover) $32   **641.595**

    1. Cooking 2. Cookbooks 3. Myers+Chang 4. Cooking, Chinese -- Taiwan style

    ISBN 9780544836730; 9780544836471; 0544836472

                        LC 2017018562

This cookbook, by Joanne Chang and Karen Akunowicz, includes "Dan Dan Noodle Salad, Triple Pork Mushu Stir-fry, or Grilled Corn with Spicy Sriracha Butter. This is food people crave and will want to make again and again. Paired with . . . [Chang and Christopher Myers's] favorite recipes, the photography perfectly captures the spirit of the [Myers+Chang] restaurant, making this book a keepsake for devoted fans." (Publisher's note)

"Readers will feel confident re-creating these flavorful foods, even the ones that aren't ultrasimple." LJ

Chattman, Lauren

Maangchi's real Korean cooking; authentic dishes for the home cook. Maangchi with Lauren Chattman ; photographs by Maangchi. Houghton Mifflin Harcourt 2015 320 p. color illustrations (hardcover) $30   **641.595**

    1. Cooking 2. Korean cooking 3. Cooking, Korean

    ISBN 054412989X; 9780544129894; 9780544465756

                        LC 2015004571

In this book on Korean cooking, author Maangchi " shows how to cook all the country's best dishes, from few-ingredient dishes (Spicy Napa Cabbage) to those made familiar by Korean restaurants (L.A. Galbi, Bulgogi, Korean Fried Chicken) to homey one-pots like Bibimbap." (Publisher's note)

"Like Robert Danhi's Easy Thai Cooking and Bee Yin Low's Easy Chinese Recipes, this encouraging and instructional cookbook demystifies Asian home cooking. First-timers to Korean restaurants and grocery stores will be grateful for Maangchi's introductory chapters." LJ

Erway, Cathy

The **food** of Taiwan; recipes from the beautiful island. Cathy Erway ; photography by Pete Lee. Houghton Mifflin

Harcourt 2015 256 p. color illustrations (paper over board) $30   **641.595**

    1. Cookbooks 2. Taiwanese cooking 3. Food -- Taiwan 4. Taiwan -- Description and travel 5. Cooking, Chinese -- Taiwanese style

    ISBN 0544303016; 9780544303010

                        LC 2014016524

This book, by Cathy Erway, photography by Pete Lee, "offers an insider's look at Taiwanese cooking--from home-style dishes to authentic street food. . . . Recipes range from the familiar, such as Pork Belly Buns, Three Cup Chicken, and Beef Noodle Soup, to the exotic, like the Stuffed Bitter Melon, Oyster Noodle Soup, and Dried Radish Omelet." (Publisher's note)

"A fabulous addition to any collection." LJ

Ghayour, Sabrina

Persiana; recipes from the Middle East & beyond. by Sabrina Ghayour. Interlink Books, an imprint of Interlink Publishing Group, Inc. 2015 240 p. $35   **641.595**

    1. Cookbooks 2. Middle Eastern cooking 3. International cooking 4. Cooking, Middle Eastern

    ISBN 1566569958; 9781566569958

                        LC 2014021227

This book, by Sabrina Ghayour, is "a celebration of the food and flavors from the regions near the Southern and Eastern shores of the Mediterranean Sea, with over 100 recipes for modern and accessible Middle Eastern dishes, including Lamb & Sour Cherry Meatballs; . . . Blood Orange & Radicchio Salad; . . . and Spiced Carrot, Pistachio & Coconut Cake with Rosewater Cream." (Publisher's note)

"Though the decidedly 70's font and presentation wears a little thin, this is an outstanding collection that will surely win readers over and inspire many a meal." Pub Wkly

Goodwin, Jason

Yashim Cooks Istanbul; by Jason Goodwin. Argonaut Books 2016 224 p. illustrations $35   **641.595**

    1. Turkish cooking

    ISBN 0957254016; 9780957254015

This book, by Jason Goodwin, "covers the full spectrum of Turkish cookery, from simple meze and vegetable dishes to meat, fish and puddings. Good in the kitchen, good on the table, it will draw the reader into the extraordinary atmosphere of old Istanbul. Step back into Yashim's world, where the flavors and colors of Istanbul come to life." (Publisher's note)

Greeley, Alexandra

Nong's Thai kitchen; 84 classic and contemporary recipes that are healthy and delicious. Nongkran Daks and Alexandra Greeley. Tuttle Publishing 2015 160 p. color illustrations (pbk.) $14.95   **641.595**

    1. Cookbooks 2. Thai cooking 3. Cooking, Thai

    ISBN 0804843317; 9780804843317

                        LC 2014030057

In this cookbook, author Nongkran Daks "shares her secrets for creating Thai cuisine's most beloved dishes at home--using ingredients that can be found in most grocery stores. Daks teams up with veteran food writer Alexandra Greeley to show readers how to prepare classic Thai recipes." (Publisher's note)

"Chef in suburban Washington, D.C., Daks offers recipes for all manner of Thai dishes to re-create at home. Ever-popular satay can be grilled indoors or out, and the spicy peanut-coconut sauce that makes satay almost universally appreciated turns out to be easy to reproduce from ingredients available in most well-stocked supermarkets." Booklist

Ha, Robin

Cook Korean! a comic book with recipes. Robin Ha. Ten Speed Press 2016 176 p. color illustrations (paperback) $19.99 **641.595**

1. Cookbooks 2. Korean cooking 3. Cooking, Korean -- Comic books, strips, etc

ISBN 9781607748878

LC 2015047866

This cookbook and graphic novel by Robin Ha "is the ideal introduction to cooking Korean cuisine at home. Ha's colorful and humorous one- to three-page comics fully illustrate the steps and ingredients needed to bring more than sixty traditional (and some not-so-traditional) dishes to life. . . . You'll learn how to create everything from easy kimchi (mak kimchi) and soy garlic beef over rice (bulgogi dupbap) to seaweed rice rolls (gimbap) and beyond." (Publisher's note)

"Like Maangchi's Real Korean Cooking, this highly recommended collection is a solid introduction for readers who feel daunted by Korean cooking and ingredients." LJ

Includes bibliographical references and index

Helou, Anissa

Feast; food of the Islamic world. Anissa Helou. HarperCollins 2018 544 p. color illustrations, color map $60 **641.595**

1. Cooking 2. Cookbooks 3. Cooking, Indic 4. Islamic cooking 5. Cooking, North African 6. Cooking, Middle Eastern 7. Cooking -- Islamic countries.

ISBN 9780062363039; 0062363034

In this book, author "Anissa Helou . . . shares her extraordinary range of beloved, time-tested recipes and stories from cuisines throughout the Muslim world. . . . With sweeping knowledge and vision, Helou delves into the enormous variety of dishes associated with Arab, Persian, Mughal (or South Asian), and North African cooking." (Publisher's note)

"Renowned chef Helou takes readers on a culinary tour of the Muslim world, showcasing more than 300 recipes from the Middle East, Africa, and Indonesia, while exploring the history and tradition of Islamic cuisine." LJ

Jaffrey, Madhur

★ **Vegetarian** India; a journey through the best of Indian home cooking. Madhur Jaffrey. Alfred A. Knopf 2015 448 p. illustrations (hardcover; alk. paper) $35 **641.595**

1. Vegetarianism 2. Indian cooking 3. Cooking, Indic 4. Vegetarian cooking

ISBN 1101874864; 9781101874868

LC 2014048953

IACP Cookbook Award Winner: Single Subject (2016)

Author Madhur Jaffrey "shares the delectable, healthful, vegetable- and grain-based foods enjoyed around the Indian subcontinent. Jaffrey travels from north to south, and from the Arabian Sea to the Bay of Bengal, collecting recipes for the very tastiest dishes along the way. She visits the homes and businesses of shopkeepers, writers, designers, farmers, doctors, weavers, and more, gathering their stories and uncovering the secrets of their most delicious family specialties." (Publisher's note)

"Jaffrey's fresh compilation features extraordinary variety and achieves approachability without oversimplification. Highly recommended for vegetarians and Indian food enthusiasts." LJ

Joo, Judy

Korean food made simple; Judy Joo ; With Vivian Jao ; Photography by Jean Cazals. Houghton Mifflin Harcourt 2016 288 p. (hardback) $30 **641.595**

1. Cookbooks 2. Korean cooking 3. Cooking, Korean

ISBN 9780544663305

LC 2015049784

This cookbook, by Judy Joo, with Vivian Jao, and photography by Jean Cazals, "brings Korean food to the masses, proving that it's fun and easy to prepare at home. . . . The book has over 100 recipes including well-loved dishes like kimchi, sweet potato noodles (japchae), beef and vegetable rice bowl (bibimbap), and Korean fried chicken, along with creative, less-traditional recipes." (Publisher's note)

"Cooks looking to make a first foray into Korean cooking or those wishing to enhance their knowledge will delight in Joo's uncommon approach and her tasty creations." Pub Wkly

Kian Lam Kho

Phoenix claws and jade trees; essential techniques of authentic Chinese cooking. Kian Lam Kho ; photographs by Jody Horton. Clarkson Potter 2015 368 p. color illustrations $35 **641.595**

1. Chinese cooking 2. China -- Social life and customs 3. Cooking, Chinese

ISBN 0385344686; 9780385344685

LC 2014046694

IACP Cookbook Award Winner: Julia Child First Book (2016); IACP Cookbook Award Nominee: Culinary Travel (2016)

This cookbook by Kian Lam Kho "offers a unique introduction to Chinese home cooking, demystifying it by focusing on its basic cooking methods. In outlining the differences among various techniques--such as pan-frying, oil steeping, and yin-yang frying--and instructing which one is best for particular ingredients and end results, culinary expert Kian Lam Kho provides a practical, intuitive window into this unique cuisine." (Publisher's note)

"Kho rounds out his excellent book with recipes and lessons on smoking as well as cold and sweet dishes. This extraordinary collection is a must-have for anyone interested in Chinese cuisine." Pub Wkly

Includes bibliographical references and index

Kim, Bill

Korean BBQ; master your grill in seven sauces. by Bill Kim with Chandra Ram ; photography by Johnny Autry. Ten Speed Press 2017 240 p. (hardcover; alk. paper) $28 **641.595**

1. Korean cooking 2. Outdoor cooking 3. Barbecue cooking 4. Barbecuing 5. Cooking, Korean

ISBN 0399580786; 9780399580789

LC 2017040334

This book, by Bill Kim with Chandra Ram, with photographs by Johnny Autry, is "a casual and practical guide to grilling with Korean-American flavors. . . . Kim teaches the fundamentals of the Korean grill through flavor profiles that can be tweaked according to the griller's preference, then gives an array of knockout recipes. Starting with seven master sauces . . . you'll soon be able to whip up a whole array of recipes." (Publisher's note)

"Although some of the recipes may seem daunting, Kim provides even the most basic cook with a guide to understanding their way around a grill." LJ

Includes bibliographical references and index

Maffei, Yvonne

My halal kitchen; Global Recipes, Cooking Tips, and Lifestyle Inspiration. by Yvonne M. Maffei. Surrey, an Agate imprint 2016 224 p. color illustrations (hardback) $29.95 **641.595**

1. Middle Eastern cooking 2. Islamic cooking 3. Cooking, Middle Eastern 4. Food -- Religious aspects -- Islam

ISBN 1572841745; 9781572841741

LC 2016001808

This book, by Yvonne M. Maffei, "celebrates halal cooking and shows readers how easy it can be to prepare halal meals. Her cookbook collects more than 100 recipes from a variety of culinary traditions, proving that halal meals can be full of diverse flavors. Home cooks will learn to make classic American favorites and comfort foods, as well as international dishes that previously may have seemed out of reach: Coq without the Vin, Shrimp Pad Thai, Chicken Tamales, and many more." (Publisher's note)

"An approachable introduction to halal home cooking for Muslim and non-Muslim families alike." LJ

Includes bibliographical references and index

Matar, Marlene

The **Aleppo** cookbook; Celebrating the Legendary Cuisine of Syria. by Marlene Matar. Interlink Books 2014 288 p. color illustrations $40   **641.595**
1. Syrian cooking 2. Middle Eastern cooking 3. Cooking, Syrian 4. Cooking -- Syria -- Aleppo
ISBN 9781566569866

LC 2014032555

This book on Syrian cooking, by Marlene Matar, "unlocks the secrets to this distinctive cuisine. . . [It is] filled with practical guidance on Middle Eastern cooking techniques as well as step-by step explanations of over 200 irresistible recipes, such as Chili and Garlic Kebab, Syrian Fishcakes, Lamb Stuffed Eggplants, Semolina and Butter pudding, and the queen of the mezze table, Red Pepper and Walnut Spread." (Publisher's note)

"This introduction to Middle Eastern cooking techniques will equally satisfy beginners or experienced fans of the regional fare." Pub Wkly

Meehan, Peter

Lucky Peach 101 easy Asian recipes; Peter Meehan and the editors of Lucky Peach ; Photographs by Gabriele Stabile. Clarkson Potter/Publishers 2015 272 p. color illustrations $35   **641.595**
1. Asian cooking 2. Southeast Asian cooking 3. Cooking, Asian
ISBN 0804187797; 9780804187794

LC 2015015729

Author Peter Meehan "present[s] a compendium of recipes that hit the sweet spot between craveworthy and stupid simple and are destined to become favorites. Your friends and lovers will marvel as you show off your culinary worldliness, whipping up meals with fish-sauce-splattered panache and all the soy-soaked, ginger-scalliony goodness you could ever want--all for dinner tonight." (Publisher's note)

"Readers will also appreciate the surprising lack of prep for many dishes; few require chopping and dicing multitudes of vegetables or sourcing ingredients that are difficult to find in the U.S. This is an outstanding, practical guide sure to inspire even the most discouraged home cook." Pub Wkly

Phillips, Carolyn

The **dim** sum field guide; a taxonomy of dumplings, buns, meats, sweets, and other specialties of the Chinese teahouse. written and illustrated by Carolyn Phillips. Ten Speed Press 2016 169 p. illustrations (hardcover; alk. paper) $14.99; (ebook) $44.97   **641.595**
1. Dumplings 2. Chinese cooking 3. Dim sum 4. Cooking, Chinese -- Cantonese style
ISBN 1607749564; 9781607749561; 9781607749578

LC 2015036911

In this book, author Carolyn Phillips "demystifies the rich, nuanced culinary institution of teahouse snacks. . . . With entries for all the dim sum classics--including siu mai, xiaolongbao, char siu, roast duck, and even sweets like milk tarts and black sesame rolls--this handy reference is perfect for bringing on-the-go to your next dim sum outing." (Publisher's note)

Ricker, Andy, 1964-

★ **Pok** Pok. Andy Ricker with J.J. Goode ; photography by Austin Bush. First edition Ten Speed Press 2017 265 p. color illustrations (hardcover) $35   **641.595**
1. Cooking 2. Cookbooks 3. Cooking, Thai 4. Pok Pok (Restaurant) 5. Food and beer pairing 6. Thailand -- Social life and customs
ISBN 1607747731; 9781607747734

LC 2017025853

This cookbook, by Andy Ricker with J.J. Goode, photographed by Austin Bush, features "50 recipes for Thai drinking food--an entire subset of Thai cooking that is largely unknown in the United States yet boasts some of most craveable dishes in the Thai canon, inspired by . . . Ricker's decades in Thailand and his beloved restaurant, Whiskey Soda Lounge." (Publisher's note)

Shaya, Alon

Shaya; an odyssey of food, my journey back to Israel. Alon Shaya with Tina Antolini. Alfred A. Knopf 2018 440 p. (hardcover; alk. paper) $35   **641.595**
1. Cooking 2. Cookbooks 3. Mediterranean cooking 4. Cooking, Israeli
ISBN 9780451494160

LC 2017010159

This cookbook, by Alon Shaya with Tina Antolini, "is a memoir of a culinary sensibility that begins in Israel and wends its way from the U.S.A. (Philadelphia) to Italy (Milan and Bergamo), back to Israel (Jerusalem) and comes together in the American South, in the heart of New Orleans. It's a book that tells of how food saved the author's life and how . . . the author's celebrated cuisine . . . came to be." (Publisher's note)

"This is a must-read book for up-and-coming chefs, and a worthy addition to the chef-memoir genre." Pub Wkly

Sodha, Meera

Fresh India; 130 quick, easy, and delicious vegetarian recipes for every day. Meera Sodha ; photography by David Loftus. Flatiron Books 2018 302 p. color illustrations (hardcover) $35   **641.595**
1. Cooking 2. Indian cooking 3. Vegetarian cooking 4. Cooking, Indic
ISBN 1250123836; 9781250123831; 9781250123848

LC 2018000170

In this cookbook, Meera Sodha reveals a whole new side of Indian food that is fresh, delicious, and quick to make at home. . . . Meera leads home cooks on a culinary journey through its many flavorful dishes that will delight vegetarians and those simply looking to add to their recipe repertoire alike. Here are surprising recipes for every day made using easy-to-find ingredients. Mushroom and Walnut Samosas, Oven-Baked Onion Bhajis, and Beet and Paneer Kebabs." (Publisher's note)

Made in India; recipes from an Indian family kitchen. Meera Sodha. St. Martin's Press 2015 319 p. color illustrations $35   **641.595**
1. Indian cooking 2. India -- Social life and customs
ISBN 1250071011; 9781250071019

In this cookbook author Meera Sodha presents "over 130 delicious recipes collected from three generations of her family. On the menu is everything from hot chapatis to street food (chili paneer; beet and feta samosas), fragrant curries (spinach and salmon, or perfect cinnamon lamb curry) to colorful side dishes (pomegranate and mint raita; kachumbar salad), and mouthwatering desserts (mango, lime, and passion fruit jello; pistachio and saffron kulfi)." (Publisher's note)

"Sodha offers helpful sections explaining how each Indian ingredient tastes and the best ways to use it, and how to fix a dish that's too spicy or salty. The power of this book lies in its simplicity—both in terms of ingredients and technique." Publisher's Weekly

Srulovich, Itamar

Honey & Co. the cookbook. Itamar Srulovich, Sarit Packer. Little, Brown & Co. 2015 304 p. color illustrations $35   **641.595**

1. Cooking 2. Restaurants 3. Middle Eastern cooking
ISBN 0316284300; 9780316284301

LC 2014953286

In this cookbook by Itamar Srulovich and Sarit Packer, "recipes include spreads and dips, exquisitely balanced salads, one-pan dishes, simple fragrant soups, rich Persian entrees, the tagines of North Africa, the Sofritos of Jerusalem, and the herb-infused stews of Iran. HONEY & CO. brings the flavors of the Middle East to life in a wholly accessible way, certain to entice and satisfy in equal measure." (Publisher's note)

"This restaurant cookbook is representative of the hottest trends and has enough variety to be suitable for everyday use." LJ

Syhabout, James

Hawker Fare; stories & recipes from a refugee chef's Isan Thai & Lao roots. James Syhabout with John Birdsall ; foreword by Roy Choi ; preface by Anthony Bourdain ; photography by Eric Wolfinger. Ecco, an Imprint of HarperCollins Publishers 2018 xvii, 349 p.p color illustrations (hardback) $39.99   **641.595**

1. Cookbooks 2. Thai cooking 3. Asian cooking 4. Cooking, Lao 5. Hawker Fare (Restaurant) 6. Cooking, Thai -- Northeastern style
ISBN 9780062656100; 9780062656094

LC 2017038047

This cookbook, by James Syhabout with John Birdsal, presents "simple recipes for cooking home-style Thai and Lao dishes. . . . Each chapter opens with stories from Syhabout's roving career, starting with his mother's work as a line cook in Oakland, and moving into the turning point of his culinary life, including his travels as an adult in his parents' homelands." (Publisher's note)

"Syhabout's outstanding debut is a combination immersive deep dive into authentic Thai and Lao cuisine and personal memoir of Syhabout's journey to chefdom and owner of the restaurants Commis and Hawker Fare in the San Francisco Bay Area." Pub Wkly

Tila, Jet

101 Asian dishes you need to cook before you die; discover a new world of badass flavors in authentic recipes. Jet Tila ; foreword by Alton Brown. Page Street Pub. Co. 2017 192 p. color illustrations (pbk.) $21.99   **641.595**

1. Cooking 2. Asian cooking 3. Cooking, Asian
ISBN 1624143822; 1624144039; 9781624143823; 9781624144035

LC 2016961788

In this book, chef Jet Tila, "brings his years of experience and hard-earned knowledge together in this breakthrough book. Step inside Jet's kitchen and learn the secrets to making your favorite Asian dishes taste better than takeout. . . . And if you haven't made your own Sriracha yet,

Jet's killer recipe will change your life. All in all, you get Jet's 101 best Asian recipes to impress your friends and family." (Publisher's note)

"Readers of all skill levels and heat tolerances will appreciate Tila's instructions, which emphasize flavor without calling for hours of prep or multiple trips to specialty stores." Pub Wkly

West, Da-Hae

K-food; Korean home cooking and street food. Da-Hae West, Gareth West. Octopus Pub Group 2016 240 p. color illustrations (hardcover) $24.99   **641.595**

1. Cookbooks 2. Korean cooking
ISBN 9781784721596; 178472159X

This cookbook, by Da-Hae West and Gareth West, offers instruction on Korean cuisine "from a run-down on the basics of Korean cooking, including now readily available sauces, pastes and other ingredients, through chapters on kimchi and the etiquette of the famous Korean BBQ, to recipes for everything from the irresistible Bulgogi Burger and spicy, sticky spare ribs to Panjeon (seafood pancakes) and corn on the cob with kimchi butter." (Publisher's note)

"Korean cookbooks are very popular right now—this one will satisfy adventurous cooks looking for contemporary recipes." LJ

Ying, Chris

The **Mission** Chinese Food Cookbook; Danny Bowien and Chris Ying. HarperCollins 2015 336 p. color illustrations (hardcover) $34.99   **641.595**

1. Cookbooks 2. Restaurants 3. Chinese cooking
ISBN 9780062243416; 0062243411

This cookbook, by Danny Bowien and Chris Ying, "tracks the fascinating, meteoric rise of the [Mission Chinese Food] restaurant and its chef. Each chapter in the story—from the restaurant's early days, to an ill-fated trip to China, to the opening of the first Mission Chinese in New York—unfolds as a conversation between Danny and his collaborators, and is accompanied by detailed recipes for the addictive dishes that have earned the restaurant global praise." (Publisher's note)

"To hear Bowien in his own words is a treat, and his debut cookbook is not to be missed. Like Gabrielle Hamilton's Prune, this will thrill foodies and aspiring chefs." LJ

Zhou, Xiaojing, 1952-

Chinese soul food; a friendly guide for homemade dumplings, stir-fries, soups, and more. Hsiao-Ching Chou ; photography by Clare Barboza. Sasquatch Books 2018 256 p. color illustrations (hardcover; alk. paper) $24.95   **641.595**

1. Wok cooking 2. Chinese cooking 3. Cooking, Chinese
ISBN 9781632171245; 1632171236; 9781632171238

LC 2017041434

This book, by Hsiao-Ching Chou, photography by Clare Barboza, "draws cooks into the kitchen with recipes that include sizzling potstickers, stir-fries that are . . . easy to make, saucy braises, and soups that bring comfort with a sip. These are dishes that feed the belly and speak the universal language of 'mmm!' You'll find approachable recipes and plenty of tips for favorite homestyle Chinese dishes, such as red-braised pork belly . . . [and] braised-beef noodle soup." (Publisher's note)

"This is a fun guide to creating favorite restaurant recipes at home." Pub Wkly

Includes bibliographical references and index

641.597   Cooking – North America

Acheson, Hugh

The **broad** fork; recipes for the wide world of vegetables and fruits. Hugh Acheson ; photographs by Rinne Allen. Clarkson Potter/Publishers 2015 336 p. color illustrations $35   **641.597**

> 1. Farm produce 2. American cooking 3. Seasonal cooking 4. Southern cooking 5. Cooking, American -- Southern style
> ISBN 038534502X; 9780385345026
>
> LC 2014023531

This book, by Hugh Acheson, is "a seasonal cookbook of 200 recipes designed to make the most of your farmers' market bounty, your CSA box, or your grocery produce aisle. . . . Beautifully written, this book brings fresh produce to the center of your plate. It's what both your doctor and your grocery bill have been telling you to do, and Hugh gives us the knowledge and the inspiration to wrap ourselves around produce in new ways." (Publisher's note)

Ahern, Shauna James

Gluten-Free Girl American classics reinvented; Shauna James Ahern and Daniel Ahern ; photography by Lauren Volo. Houghton Mifflin Harcourt 2015 320 p. color illustrations (paper over board) $29.99   **641.597**

> 1. Cookbooks 2. American cooking 3. Gluten-free diet 4. Cooking, American 5. Gluten-free diet -- Recipes
> ISBN 0544219880; 9780544219885
>
> LC 2015007133

IACP Cookbook Award Nominee: Health & Special Diet (2016)

This cookbook, by Shauna James Ahern and Daniel Ahern, with photography by Lauren Volo, offers "a collection of comfort-food classics that are all . . . gluten-free. Cinnamon Rolls with Cream Cheese Frosting, Chicken-Fried Steak, New England Clam Chowder--the country's most beloved dishes, reinvented. Of course, it wouldn't be true comfort food without dessert, and Shauna aptly provides plenty of delicious recipes for sweets lovers." (Publisher's note)

"Those who feel limited on a gluten-free diet will rejoice in this extensive and appetizing collection of family favorites that can once again be on the menu." Pub Wkly

The **America's** test kitchen do-it-yourself cookbook; 100+ foolproof kitchen projects for the adventurous home cook. by the editors at America's test kitchen ; photography by Anthony Tieuli. America's Test Kitchen 2012 viii, 360 p.p $26.95   **641.597**

> 1. Cookbooks 2. American cooking 3. Cooking, American
> ISBN 193649308X; 9781936493081
>
> LC 2012022144

In this book, the editors of the television cooking show America's Test Kitchen "walk home cooks step-by-step through more than 100 of their favorite D.I.Y. kitchen projects. . . . This book delivers a wide variety of projects, from jams and pickles like Grandma used to make to artisanal cheeses and cured meats that you usually have to pay top dollar for at a specialty shop." (Publisher's note)

Batali, Mario, 1960-

America--farm to table; simple, delicious recipes celebrating local farmers. Mario Batali and Jim Webster ; food photography by Quentin Bacon ; farm photography by Christine Birch Ferrelli and Lara Cerri. Grand Central Life & Style 2014 302 p. color illustrations (hardback) $35   **641.597**

> 1. Farms 2. Local foods 3. Farm produce 4. American cooking 5. Cooking, American 6. Local foods -- United States 7. Farms, small -- United States
> ISBN 1455584681; 9781455584680; 9781455584697
>
> LC 2014011984

In this book "author and . . . chef Mario Batali pays homage to the American farmer-from Maine to Los Angeles-in stories, photos, and recipes. . . . Batali asked his chef friends from Nashville, Tennessee, to San Francisco, to tell him who their favorite farmers were, and those farmers graciously shared their personal stories along with their top-of-the-line produce and products." (Publisher's note)

"No particular ingredient is sacred; all ingredients are celebrated in the unique farmer-chef-home-cook collaboration." Booklist

Mario Batali Big American cookbook; 250 favorite recipes from across the USA. Mario Batali with Jim Webster ; photographs by Quentin Bacon. Grand Central Life & Style 2016 512 p. color illustrations (hardcover) $40   **641.597**

> 1. American cooking 2. Cooking, American 3. Local foods -- United States
> ISBN 1455584711; 9781455584710; 9781455569663
>
> LC 2016022712

This cookbook, by celebrity chef Mario Batali, presents "over 250 simple recipes celebrating the treasures of the state fairs and the dishes of the local rotary clubs and ethnic groups. Batali has interpreted these regional gems with the same excitement and passion that he has approached traditional Italian food." (Publisher's note)

"Boosting recipes with color photographs, Batali makes every dish look like great fun, and it's impossible not to share his enthusiasm." Booklist

Bayless, Rick, 1953-

Authentic Mexican; regional cooking from the heart of Mexico. Rick Bayless with Deann Groen Bayless ; illustrations by John Sandford. William Morrow 1987 384 p. color illustrations; map $35   **641.597**

> 1. Mexican cooking 2. Cooking, Mexican
> ISBN 0061373265; 0688043941; 9780061373268
>
> LC 86012706

This Mexican cookbook, by Rick Bayless, "offers the full range of dishes, from poultry, meat, fish, rice, beans, and vegetables to eggs, snacks made of corn masa, tacos, turnovers, enchiladas and their relatives, tamales, and moles, ending with desserts, sweets, and beverages. . . . Menu suggestions and timing and advance-preparation tips make these dishes perfectly convenient for today's working families. And traditional and contemporary variations accompany each recipe." (Publisher's note)

Bibliography: p. [357]-361

Mexican everyday; Rick Bayless, with Deann Groen Bayless ; color photographs by Christopher Hirsheimer. 1st ed.; Norton 2005 336 p. col. ill. (hbk.) $29.95   **641.597**

> 1. Mexican cooking 2. Cooking, Mexican
> ISBN 039306154X; 9780393061543
>
> LC 2005023129

This Mexican cookbook, by Rick Bayless, "is a collection of 90 full-flavored recipes—like Green Chile Chicken Tacos, Shrimp Ceviche Salad, Chipotle Steak with Black Beans—that meet three criteria for 'everyday' food: 1) most need less than 30 minutes' involvement; 2) they have the fresh, clean taste of simple, authentic preparations; and 3) they are nutritionally balanced, full-featured meals—no elaborate side dishes required." (Publisher's note)

"Befitting the Mexican origins of these dishes, Bayless uses a wide variety of chiles, especially the deeply flavorful poblano. With virtually every recipe in the book, Bayless adds "riffs" that offer imaginative variations on the main recipe's techniques." Booklist

Mexico ; one plate at a time; {by} Rick Bayless, with Jeanmarie Brownson and Deann Groen Bayless; color photographs by Bentl & Hayers; Mexican location photographs by James Baigrie. Scribner 2000 x, 374 p.p color illustrations $35   **641.597**

1. Mexican cooking 2. Cookery, Mexican
ISBN 068484186X; 9780684841861

LC 00058327

In this book, author Rick Bayless "takes us . . . through Mexican markets, street stalls and home kitchens to bring us the great dishes of Mexico, one 'plate' at a time. . . . To complete the journey into the Mexican mindset, Rick, with help from his testers, ends each 'plate' with a question-and-answer section. . . . Rick draws from his years of living in Mexico, pulling us into the Mexican kitchen, to teach us how to create authentic Mexican dishes in our American kitchens." (Publisher's note)

"There are helpful questions and answers at the end of each section, based on questions generated by recipe testers, an addition that may be unique to the cookbook genre. There is much here for both neophytes and experienced cooks. Highly recommended for all public libraries." LJ

Includes bibliographical references and index

More Mexican everyday; simple, seasonal, celebratory. Rick Bayless, with Deann Groen Bayless and David Tamarkin ; photographs by Hirsheimer and Hamilton. W.W. Norton & Co. Inc. 2015 384 p. color illustrations (hardcover) $35 **641.597**

1. Mexican cooking 2. Seasonal cooking 3. Cooking, Mexican
ISBN 0393081141; 9780393081145

LC 2015005985

This Mexican cookbook, by Rick Bayless, "teaches home cooks how to build tasty meals with a few ingredients in a short amount of time. . . . He explains fully the classic techniques that create so many much-beloved Mexican meals, from tacos and enchiladas to pozole and mole. Home cooks under his guidance will be led confidently to making these their go-to recipes night after night." (Publisher's note)

"Recipes conclude with quick summaries of ingredients to ease shopping. An effective starting point for the would-be home Mexican cook." Booklist

Brioza, Stuart

State Bird Provisions; a cookbook. Stuart Brioza + Nicole Krasinski ; with JJ Goode. Ten Speed Press 2017 368 p. (hardback) $40   **641.597**

1. Restaurants 2. American cooking 3. State Bird Provisions (Restaurant) 4. Cooking, American -- California style
ISBN 9781607748441

LC 2017026602

In this book, "chefs Stuart Brioza and Nicole Krasinski use dim sum style carts to offer guests small but finely crafted dishes ranging from Potato Chips with Crème Fraiche and Cured Trout Roe, to Black Butter-Balsamic Figs with Wagon Wheel Cheese Fondue, to their famous savory pancakes (such as Chanterelle Pancakes with Lardo and Maple Vinegar), along with a menu of more substantial dishes such as their signature fried quail with stewed onions." (Publisher's note)

"This earnest debut book... has all the elements of a great restaurant cookbook: artful photographs, enlightening recipes, and a compelling story of triumph in the face of hardship." (LJ)

Includes bibliographical references and index

Cook's Country eats local; 150 regional recipes you should be making no matter where you live. by the editors at America's Test Kitchen. America's Test Kitchen 2015 320 p. (alk. paper) $26.95   **641.597**

1. American cooking 2. Cooking, American
ISBN 1936493993; 9781936493999

LC 2015005574

This cookbook provides "150 Regional Recipes. . . . From Maine's hearty Joe Booker Stew to pineapple-packed Hawaiian Fried Rice, this collection of recipes brings bold local flavors and tried-and-true cooking techniques home¿no matter where that may be. Home cooks will discover little-known specialties and revamped classics in each of the four chapters: New England and the Mid-Atlantic, Appalachia and the South, The Midwest and Great Plains, Texas and the West." (Publisher's note)

"For families and home cooks seeking foolproof classic fare for potlucks, picnics, tailgates, and other occasions." LJ

Includes bibliographical references and index

Diaz, Von

Coconuts and collards; recipes and stories from puerto rico to the deep south. Von Diaz. University Press of Florida 2018 192 p. (cloth; alk. paper) $28   **641.597**

1. American cooking 2. Southern cooking 3. Caribbean cooking
ISBN 9780813056654

LC 2017947181

This cookbook, by Von Diaz "celebrates traditional recipes while fusing them with Diaz's own family history and a contemporary Southern flair. Diaz discovers the connections between the food she grew up eating in Atlanta and the African and indigenous influences in so many Puerto Rican dishes. . . . Diaz innovates for modern palates, updating and lightening recipes and offering vegetarian alternatives." (Publisher's note)

Edna Lewis; at the table with an American original. edited by Sara B. Franklin. University of North Carolina Press 2018 272 p. (cloth; alk. paper) $28   **641.597**

1. Cooks 2. Cookbooks 3. Southern cooking 4. African American cooks 5. Cookbooks -- History and criticism 6. Cooking, American -- Southern style
ISBN 9781469638553

LC 2017036473

This collection of essays, edited by Sara B. Franklin, is about "Edna Lewis, . . . [who] wrote some of America's most resonant, lyrical, and significant cookbooks, including the now classic 'The Taste of Country Cooking.' Lewis cooked and wrote as a means to explore her memories of childhood on a farm in Freetown, Virginia, a community first founded by black families freed from slavery. . . . Franklin provides an illuminating introduction to Lewis." (Publisher's note)

Includes bibliographical references and index

Erickson, Renee

A **boat,** a whale, and a walrus; a year of menus. by Renee Erickson with Jess Thomson. Sasquatch Books 2014 320 p. illustrations (some color) (alk. paper) $40   **641.597**

1. American cooking 2. Seasonal cooking 3. Cooking, American -- Pacific Northwest style
ISBN 1570619263; 9781570619267

LC 2014021808

IACP Cookbook Award Finalist: Photography (2015)

This cookbook, by chef Renee Erickson, is "for anyone who loves the fresh seasonal food of the Pacific Northwest. Defined by the bounty of the Puget Sound region, as well as by French cuisine, [it] is filled with seasonal, personal menus like Renee's Fourth of July Crab Feast, Wild Foods Dinner, and a fall pickling party." (Publisher's note)

"If a trip to Seattle isn't possible, this book provides the next best way to enjoy Erickson's beautiful seafood." LJ

Includes bibliographical references and index

Gartland, Ashley

Heartlandia; heritage recipes from the Country Cat. by Adam and Jackie Sappington with Ashley Gartland. Houghton Mifflin Harcourt 2015 304 p. (hardcover) $30 **641.597**
1. Restaurants 2. Portland (Or.) 3. American cooking 4. Cooking, American 5. Country Cat Dinner House & Bar (Portland, Ore.)
ISBN 9780544363779; 0544363779

LC 2014036933

This cookbook "is based on husband-and-wife team Adam and Jackie Sappington's acclaimed Portland restaurant, The Country Cat Dinner House & Bar.... Some of the ... dishes include Autumn Squash Soup with Apple Cider and Brown Butter, Red Wine-Braised Beef with Wild Mushroom Steak Sauce, and Crispy Fried Oysters with Smoky Bacon and Green Apple Ragout.... The sweets are just as enticing... . Additional chapters include one for drinks and another for pickles and preserves." (Publisher's note)

"A beautiful restaurant cookbook to have on hand in colder months, when you'll crave comforting meals." LJ

Guarnaschelli, Alex, 1969-

★ The **home** cook; recipes to know by heart. Alex Guarnaschelli. Clarkson Potter/Publishers 2017 368 p. (hard cover) $35 **641.597**
1. Cookbooks 2. Cooking, American
ISBN 9780307956583

LC 2016045628

This book, by Alex Guarnaschelli, is an "all-in-one cooking bible for a new generation with 300 recipes for everything from simple vinaigrettes and roast chicken to birthday cake and cocktails.... For generations raised on vibrant, international flavors and supermarkets stocked with miso paste, harissa, and other bold condiments and ingredients, here are 300 recipes to replace their parents' Chicken Marbella." (Publisher's note)

Humm, Daniel

The **NoMad** cookbook; Daniel Humm, Will Guidara, and Leo Robitschek. Ten Speed Press 2015 552 p. color illustrations, map (hardcover) $100 **641.597**
1. Cooking 2. Cocktails 3. NoMad Hotel (New York, N.Y.)
ISBN 9781607748229

LC 2015007694

This book, by Daniel Humm, Will Guidara, and Leo Robitschek, is a "uniquely packaged cookbook.... What appears to be a traditional cookbook is in fact two books in one: upon opening, readers discover that the back half contains false pages in which a smaller cocktail recipe book is hidden. The result is a wonderfully unexpected collection of both sweet and savory food recipes and cocktail recipes." (Publisher's note)

"Superb in both substance and scope, this collection offers a feast for the senses that will be savored at length." Pub Wkly

Langholtz, Gabrielle

America; the cookbook. Gabrielle Langholtz. Phaidon Inc Ltd 2017 767 p. $49.95 **641.597**
1. Cooking 2. American cooking

ISBN 0714873969; 9780714873961

This cookbook, by Gabrielle Langholtz, "document[s] comprehensively--and celebrate[s]--the remarkable diversity of American cuisine and food culture. A thoroughly researched compendium of 800 home-cooking recipes for delicious and authentic American dishes, 'America: The Cookbook' explores the country's myriad traditions and influences, regional favorites and melting-pot fusion--the culinary heritage of a nation, from appetizers to desserts and beyond." (Publisher's note)

"Rather than simply offering a rote recitation of well-worn classics, Langholtz artfully includes recipes that show America's kaleidoscopic culinary landscape." (Pub Wkly)

O'Brady, Tara

Seven spoons; my favorite recipes for any and every day. Tara O'Brady. Ten Speed Press 2015 296 p. color illustrations (hardback) $27.50 **641.597**
1. Cooking 2. Canadians 3. Cooking, Canadian
ISBN 1607746379; 9781607746379

LC 2014036366

In this cookbook, Tara O'Brady "shares stories and recipes from her Canadian home.... Recipes like Roasted Carrots with Dukkah and Harissa Mayonnaise, Braised Beef Short Ribs with Gremolata, and Plum Macaroon Cake are wholesome, hearty, and showcase the myriad culinary influences at work in O'Brady's kitchen.... Impeccable food photography and a lavish package round out this beautiful, personal collection." (Publisher's note)

"Recommended for fans of O'Brady's blog (sevenspoons.net) and readers who'd like a globally influenced home cooking collection." LJ

Includes bibliographical references and index

Presilla, Maricel E.

★ **Gran** cocina latina; the food of Latin America. Maricel E. Presilla ; photography by Gentl & Hyers/Edge ; illustrations by Julio Figueroa. Norton & Company 2012 vii, 901 p., [32] p. of plates ill. (some col.) (hardcover) $45 **641.597**
1. Cookbooks 2. Latin American cooking 3. Cooking, Mexican 4. Cooking, Caribbean 5. Cooking, Latin American
ISBN 0393050696; 9780393050691

LC 2012017701

James Beard Foundation Award: Cookbook of the Year (2013)

Author Maricel E. Presilla, "who runs a restaurant in Hoboken, N.J., and holds a doctorate in medieval Spanish history, offers this bible of Latin American food." It "covers dishes from Mexico, Argentina, and the Hispanic Caribbean.... Presilla includes more than 500 recipes for everything from tropical roots to empanadas and meat dishes of every kind." (Publishers Weekly)

Puckett, Susan

Turnip greens & tortillas; a Mexican chef spices up the southern kitchen. Eddie Hernandez and Susan Puckett ; photographs by Angie Mosier. Houghton Mifflin Harcourt 2018 320 p. (hbk) $30 **641.597**
1. Cooking 2. Cookbooks 3. Mexican cooking 4. Cooking, Mexican
ISBN 9780544618824

LC 2017051352

In this cookbook, chef Eddie Hernandez, with Susan Puckett, presents Southern and Mexican recipes. Eddie "lands on the commonalities of Southern and Mexican food, with dishes like Memphis barbecue pork tacos, chicken pot pie served in a 'bowl' of a puffed tortilla, turnip greens in 'pot likker' spiked with chiles, or the 'Eddie Palmer,' sweet tea with a jab of tequila. Eddie never hesitates to break with purists to make food taste better." (Publisher's note)

"A stellar debut imbued with Hernandez's infectious excitement for cooking." LJ

Rodgers, Rick

The **essential** James Beard cookbook; 400 recipes that shaped the tradition of American cooking. James Beard with Rick Rodgers. St. Martin's Press 2012 380 p. illustrations (hardback) $35   **641.597**

     1. Cookbooks 2. American cooking 3. Cooking, American
ISBN 0312642180; 9780312642181

LC 2012028372

This cookbook is a "compilation of some of [chef James] Beard's best recipes" and "spans the breadth of his culinary achievement. In true American fashion, he draws from French, Italian, Indian, African, and other cuisines and adapts them to American kitchens and techniques, often simplifying otherwise complex dishes, such as cassoulet, without compromising flavor. Betty Fussell contributes a perceptive essay on Beard's complicated life and his teaching talents." (Booklist)

"Home cooking has evolved considerably since Beard's cookbooks were first published, so it's wonderful to see his recipes reprinted in this functional collection." LJ

Rollins, Kent

A **taste** of cowboy; ranch recipes and tales from the trail. Kent Rollins with Shannon Rollins ; photographs by Shannon Keller Rollins. Houghton Mifflin Harcourt 2015 248 p. color illustrations (hardback) $30   **641.597**

     1. Cowhands 2. American cooking 3. Ranch life -- West (U.S.)
4. Cooking, American -- Western style 5. Cowboys -- West (U.S.)
-- Social life and customs
ISBN 0544275004; 9780544275003

LC 2014036936

In this cookbook, author Kent Rollins takes readers "into his frontier world with simple food anyone can do. Kent offers labor-saving breakfasts like Egg Bowls with Smoked Cream Sauce. For lunch or dinner, there's 20-minute Green Pepper Frito Pie, hands-off, four-ingredient Sweet Heat Chopped Barbecue Sandwiches, or mild and smoky Roasted Bean-Stuffed Poblano Peppers." (Publisher's note)

"Though Rollins offers sage advice on choosing and caring for cast-iron cookware, readers won't need to worry about building a fire, since these recipes have been adjusted to allow followers to recreate cowboy fare in the comfort of their own kitchens. However, Rollins remains true to his methods by incorporating a wide variety of boxed, canned, and prepared ingredients such as creamed soups and processed cheese. Rollins's campfire stories and DIY cures for ailments such as arthritis (honey in your coffee) and spider bites (tape a penny on it) give warmth and personality to a book that even city slickers will enjoy spending time with." PW

Rosen, Ali

Bring it! tried and true recipes for potlucks and casual entertaining. Ali Rosen. Running Press 2018 239 p. $25 **641.597**

     1. American cooking 2. Seasonal cooking 3. Quick and easy cooking 4. Cooking, American
ISBN 0762462728; 9780762462728

LC 2017955766

This cookbook, by Ali Rosen, "is the ultimate source for potluck, picnic, or dinner party-worthy dishes that combine simple prep with big taste! The word 'potluck' may inspire memories of church dinners and mystery covered dishes. . . . Inside 'Bring It!,' you will find dozens of impressive-looking recipes that come together easily, and are perfect for

carrying to any occasion." (Publisher's note)

Selengut, Becky

How to taste; the curious cook's handbook to seasoning and balance, from umami to acid and beyond--with recipes. Becky Selengut. Sasquatch Books 2018 240 p. (hardcover; alk. paper) $22.95   **641.597**

     1. Spices 2. American cooking 3. Flavor 4. Cooking (Spices) 5. Cooking, American
ISBN 9781632171054

LC 2017041100

This cookbook, by Becky Selengut, "outlines the underlying principles of taste, and then takes a deep dive into salt, acid, bitter, sweet, fat, umami, bite (heat), aromatics, and texture. You'll find out how temperature impacts your enjoyment of the dishes you make as does color, alcohol, and more. The handbook goes beyond telling home cooks what ingredients go well together or explaining cooking ratios." (Publisher's note)

Includes bibliographical references and index

Sewall, Jeremy

The **New** England kitchen; fresh takes on seasonal recipes. Jeremy Sewall, Erin Byers Murray, Baron Seaver. Rizzoli International Publications 2014 255 p. color illustrations (hardcover) $39.95   **641.597**

     1. New England 2. American cooking
ISBN 0789327473; 9780789327475

LC 2014942046

James Beard Foundation Award Nominee: American Cooking (2015)

In this New England cookbook, chef Jeremy Sewall "adapts the region's fresh, simple flavors into refined dishes for the home cook. More than one hundred delectable recipes highlight the area's celebrated farms and fisheries to incorporate distinct flavors throughout the year. . . . The book also includes profiles of a New England farmer, fishermen, and an artisanal beer brewer to capture the new revolutionary spirit." (Publisher's note)

Tellez, Lesley

Eat Mexico; recipes from Mexico City's streets, markets and fondas. Lesley Tellez. Kyle Books 2015 192 p. color illustrations (hardcover; alk. paper) $24.95   **641.597**

     1. Mexican cooking 2. Mexico City (Mexico)
ISBN 1909487279; 9781909487277

LC 2014960085

This book by Lesley Tellez is "a culinary love letter to one of the biggest cities in the world--a chaotic, vibrant place where residents eat from sidewalk grills and stands, and markets and casual restaurants serve up fresh, hot food daily. Tellez takes you through [Mexico City's] most classic dishes, offering recipes from her favorite haunts on the streets, in city markets, and in small, homestyle fondas." (Publisher's note)

Thompson-Anderson, Terry, 1946-

Texas on the Table; people, places, and recipes celebrating the flavors of the Lone Star State. by Terry Thompson-Anderson ; photos by Sandy Wilson. University of Texas Press 2014 452 p. illustrations (chiefly color) (cl.; alk. paper) $45 **641.597**

     1. Texas 2. American cooking 3. Southern cooking 4. Cooking -- Texas 5. Terroir -- Texas 6. Cooking, American -- Southwestern style
ISBN 0292744099; 9780292744097

LC 2013048386

James Beard Foundation Award Nominee: American Cooking (2015)

This cookbook, by Terry Thompson-Anderson, "presents 150 new and classic recipes, along with stories of the people—farmers, ranchers, shrimpers, cheesemakers, winemakers, and chefs—who inspired so many of them and who are changing the taste of Texas food. The recipes span the full range from finger foods and first courses to soups and breads, salads, seafood, chicken, meat (including wild game), sides and vegetarian dishes, and sweets." (Publisher's note)

Werner, Eric

Hartwood; bright, wild flavors from the edge of the Yucatan. Eric Werner and Mya Henry. Artisan 2015 301 p. illustrations (chiefly color) (alk. paper) $40   **641.597**
1. Mexican cooking 2. Yucatan (Mexico) 3. Maya cooking 4. Cooking, Mexican 5. Hartwood (Restaurant; Tulum, Mexico)
ISBN 157965620X; 9781579656201
LC 2015013061

IACP Cookbook Award Winner: Culinary Travel (2016)

This cookbooks is also the "the story of [authors] Eric Werner and Mya Henry, an intrepid young couple who gave up their restaurant jobs in New York City to start anew in the one-road town of Tulum, Mexico. Here they built Hartwood, one of the most exciting and inspiring restaurants in the world. Werner's passion for dazzling flavors and natural ingredients is expertly translated into recipes anyone can cook at home." (Publisher's note)

"Vibrant flavors dominate this warm and welcoming collection, bringing the local tastes of the Yucatán region into the home kitchen." Pub Wkly

Includes bibliographical references and index

Wilson, Maya

The **Alaska** from scratch cookbook; seasonal. scenic. homemade. Maya Wilson. St. Martin's Press 2018 272 p. $27.99   **641.597**
1. Cookbooks 2. American cooking 3. Seasonal cooking
ISBN 1635650631; 9781635650631
LC 2018037016

This cookbook, by Maya Wilson celebrates "Alaska and its ocean-to-table, homemade food culture. . . . [The] book is filled with 75 delicious, family-friendly recipes that are based on the seasonality of Alaska. There's an abundance of wild berries, so summer recipes are full of them, and to get through the cold winters, she includes hearty soups and pot pies. Her recipes . . . are created for busy families like hers." (Publisher's note)

641.598 Cooking – South America

Acurio, Gastón

Peru; the cookbook. Gastón Acurio. Phaidon Inc Ltd 2015 400 p. color illustrations (hardcover) $49.95   **641.598**
1. Peru 2. Cooking
ISBN 0714869201; 9780714869209

This Peruvian cookbook, by Gastón Acurio, offers "500 traditional home cooking recipes from the country's most acclaimed and popular chef. . . . [The author] guides cooks through the full range of Peru's vibrant cuisine from popular classics like quinoa and ceviche, and lomo saltado to lesser known dishes like amaranth and aji amarillo." (Publisher's note)

"In chef and restaurant owner Acurio's first foray into English-language cookbooks, the cuisine of Peru shines. The color-coded sections book break down the usual Western groupings of dishes (appetizers, first course, etc.) with a more Peruvian sensibility in mind." Pub Wkly

Castanho, Thiago

Brazilian Food; Thiago Castanho, Luciana Bianchi. Firefly Books Ltd 2014 256 p. illustrations; portraits (col) $39.95   **641.598**
1. Cookbooks 2. Brazilian cooking
ISBN 177085472X; 9781770854727

This cookbook, by Thiago Castanho and Luciana Bianchi, "explores the best of Brazilian food and its traditions. Along with three award-winning guest chefs, . . . [the authors] selected more than 100 recipes that adventurous cooks will want to try at home, even if they have never been to Brazil." (Publisher's note)

"With beautiful, splashy photos of the recipes, markets, food producers and even street artists at work, this book is elevated above a simple collection of recipes. It's an ode to the author's foodscape, and his passion for it is infectious. Readers who have never heard of manteiga de garrafa or tried pickled peppers will be excited about Castanho's recipes and may be inspired to visit Brazil." Pub Wkly

Kaminsky, Peter

Mallmann on fire; Francis Mallmann with Peter Kaminsky and Donna Gelb. Artisan 2014 320 p. color illustrations $40   **641.598**
1. Cookbooks 2. Outdoor cooking 3. Frying 4. Broiling 5. Barbecuing 6. Cooking, Argentine 7. Cooking -- Patagonia (Argentina and Chile)
ISBN 9781579655372; 1579655378
LC 2014004632

This cookbook, by Francis Mallmann with Peter Kaminsky and Donna Gelb, "takes us grilling in magical places . . . , each locale inspiring new discoveries as revealed in 100 recipes for meals both intimate and outsized. We encounter legs of lamb and chicken hung from strings, coal-roasted delicata squash, roasted herbs, a parrillada of many fish, and all sorts of griddled and charred meats, vegetables, and fruits, plus rustic desserts cooked on the chapa and baked in wood-fired ovens." (Publisher's note)

"Though the author targets serious outdoor cooks, his title is suitable for amateurs and armchair travelers. Not all of the recipes require a fire, and those that do can usually be adapted to the stovetop." LJ

Includes index

641.6 Cooking specific materials

Anthony, Michael, 1968-

V Is for Vegetables; Inspired Recipes & Techniques for Home Cooks: From Artichokes to Zucchini. Michael Anthony. Little, Brown & Co. 2015 384 p. color illustrations $40 **641.6**
1. Diet 2. Cooking -- Vegetables
ISBN 0316373354; 9780316373357
LC 2015931409

In this cookbook author Michael Anthony "celebrates the act of cooking vegetables he loves. Anthony shows how unlocking the secrets of vegetables can be as simple as roasting a beet, de-knobbing a Jerusalem artichoke, peeling a gnarly celery root, slicing a bright radish, washing a handful of just-picked greens." (Publisher's note)

"With its distinctive recipes, this title can augment and supplement collections that already include classics such as James Peterson's Vegetables, Revised and Deborah Madison's Vegetable Literacy." Library Journal

Bevill, Amanda

World spice at home; New Flavors for 75 Favorite Dishes. Amanda Bevill and Julie Kramis Hearne. Sasquatch Books 2014 240 p. color illustrations (alk. paper) $24.95 **641.6**

1. Spices 2. Cooking 3. Cookbooks 4. Cooking (Spices)
ISBN 1570619077; 9781570619076

LC 2014011114

This cookbook, by Amanda Bevill and Julie Kramis Hearne, "brings the world's exotic spices to your home kitchen to breath new life into favorite, familiar, and traditional dishes with wonderful new flavors. Transform a grilled ribeye steak using an Arabic baharat spice blend; add drama to your carrot cake using Kashmiri garam masala. Spices add gratifying dimension to foods, and while the spice blends come from around the world, these recipes are friendly and familiar." (Publisher's note)

"Bevill and Kramis Hearnes's spice blends, which contain 7–14 spices (compared to 40-plus in some ethnic cookbooks), taste superior to many premade and shelf-weary equivalents. Their approachable recipes offer home cooks a gentle introduction to new flavorings." LJ

Includes bibliographical references and index

Byres, Tim

Smoke; new firewood cooking; how to build flavor with fire, on the grill and in the kitchen. Tim Byres. Rizzoli International Publications 2013 255 p. ill. (chiefly col.) $40 **641.6**

1. Cookbooks 2. Barbecue cooking
ISBN 0847839796; 9780847839797

LC 2012950104

James Beard Award (2014)

This cookbook, by Tim Byres, was the winner of the 2014 James Beard Award in the General Cooking Category. "Byres . . . gives innovative ideas for easy ways to use smoke in your everyday kitchen arsenal of flavors--such as smoking safely on the stovetop with woodchips, putting together relishes and salsas made with smoked peppers and other vegetables, grilling with wood planks, and using smoke-cured meats to add layers of flavor to a dish." (Publisher's note)

Carreño, Carolynn

Meat; everything there is to know; recipes and stories from America's gretest Butcher. Pat LaFrieda and Carolynn Carreño. Atria Books 2014 256 p. color illustrations (hardback) $39.99 **641.6**

1. Meat industry 2. Cooking -- Meat 3. Cooking (Meat)
ISBN 1476725993; 9781476725994; 9781476726007; 9781476726014

LC 2014000898

IACP Cookbook Award Finalist: Single Subject (2015)

"In 'Meat,' [author] Pat [LaFrieda] introduces you to cuts beyond chops and tenderloins--including inexpensive and unusual cuts--so you can venture outside your everyday selections. With detailed, step-by-step photos, he provides instruction in the best butchering skills for the home cook, such as needling, frenching, rolling, and tying." (Publisher's note)

"LaFreida's emphasis is in educating readers on the various animals, diagramming cuts, and showing how to best utilize them. Tips like how to break down a chicken or cut pockets in veal or pork chops for stuffing make this a valuable reference that will give readers a greater appreciation for not only their favorite cuts of meat, but their butcher as well." Pub Wkly

Includes bibliographical references and index

Chernila, Alana

Eating from the ground up; recipes for simple, pefect vegetables. Alana Chernila ; photographs by Johnny Autry. Clarkson Potter/Publishers 2018 271 p. (alk. paper) $28 **641.6**

1. Cookbooks 2. Seasonal cooking 3. Cooking -- Vegetables 4. Vegetables 5. Cooking (Vegetables)
ISBN 0451494997; 9780451494993

LC 2017013871

This book, by Alana Chernila, with photographs by Johnny Autry, "teaches you how to showcase the unique flavor and texture of each vegetable, truly bringing out the best in every root and leaf. The answers lie in smart techniques and a light touch. Here are dishes so simple and quick that they feel more intuitive than following a typical recipe. . . . No matter the vegetable, the central lesson is: don't mess with a good thing." (Publisher's note)

Cole, Tyson

Uchi ; the cookbook; by Tyson Cole and Jessica Dupuy; foreword by Lance Armstrong. Umaso Publishing 2011 268p $39.95 **641.6**

1. Sushi 2. Japanese cooking 3. Cooking -- Seafood 4. Uchi (Austin, Tex.: Restaurant)
ISBN 978-0-292-77129-1; 0-292-77129-0

"Every now and then a cookbook comes along that is such a great read and has such dazzling photography that I can't put it down. Uchi, the Cookbook is one of those." Texas Monthly

Cook's illustrated (Periodical)

The **best** chicken recipes; by the editors of Cook's illustrated; photography, Keller + Keller, Carl Tremblay, and Daniel J. Van Ackere; illustrations, John Burgoyne. America's Test Kitchen 2008 422p il $35 **641.6**

1. Cooking -- Poultry
ISBN 978-1-933615-23-3; 1-933615-23-0

This volume "offers more than 300 recipes for chicken, along with a primer called 'Chicken 101,' information on techniques (including step-by-step illustrations), and ratings of equipment and ingredients." Libr J

The **cook's** illustrated meat book; the game-changing guide that teaches you how to cook meat and poultry with 425 bulletproof recipes. the editors of America's Test Kitchen. America's Test Kitchen 2014 504 p. illustrations (some color) $40 **641.6**

1. Cookbooks 2. Cooking -- Meat 3. Cooking (Meat)
ISBN 1936493861; 9781936493869

LC 2014016170

This cookbook "begins with a 27-page master class in meat cookery, which covers shopping, . . . storing, . . . and seasoning meat. . . . 425 bulletproof and rigorously tested recipes for beef, pork, lamb, veal, and poultry provide plenty of options for everyday meals and special occasion dinners and you'll learn new (and better) ways to cook favorites such as Pan-Seared Thick-Cut Steak, Juicy Pub-Style Burgers, Weeknight Roast Chicken, Barbecued Pulled Pork, and more." (Publisher's note)

"That said, carnivores with an obsession for perfection will likely have found their new bible in this comprehensive collection." Pub Wkly

Fraioli, James O.

Culinary birds; the ultimate poultry cookbook. Chef John Ash, James O. Fraioli. Running Press 2013 319 p. color illustrations (hardcover) $30 **641.6**

1. Cookbooks 2. Cooking -- Poultry 3. Cooking (Poultry)
ISBN 0762444843; 9780762444847

LC 2013938633

James Beard Award (2014)

This cookbook, by John Ash and James O. Fraioli, "offers more than 170 savory ways to enjoy poultry. . . . Because it is important to know where your bird comes from, [the book also] . . . provides a brief history of poultry, the rise of factory farms, and the progression of the sustainability movement." (Publisher's note)

Includes index

Giller, Megan

Bean-to-bar chocolate; America's craft chocolate revolution: the origins, the makers, and the mind-blowing flavors. Megan Giller. Storey Publishing 2017 240 p. (paper over board; alk. paper) $19.95 **641.6**

1. Chocolate 2. Cooking -- Chocolate 3. Cocoa 4. Cooking (Chocolate)
ISBN 9781612128214

LC 2017011628

In this book, "[a]uthor Megan Giller invites fellow chocoholics on a fascinating journey through America's craft chocolate revolution. Learn what to look for in a chocolate bar and how to successfully pair chocolate with coffee, beer, spirits, cheese, and bread. This comprehensive celebration of chocolate busts some popular myths . . . and introduces you to more than a dozen of the hottest artisanal chocolate makers in the US today." (Publisher's note)

"A timely snapshot of trends in American artisanal chocolate, this title will strengthen dessert collections."

Includes bibliographical references and index

Grescoe, Taras

Bottomfeeder; how to eat ethically in a world of vanishing seafood. Bloomsbury USA 2008 327p $24.99; pa $16 **641.6**

1. Seafood 2. Marine resources 3. Conservation of natural resources 4. Cooking -- Seafood
ISBN 978-1-59691-225-0; 1-59691-225-1; 978-1-59691-625-8 pa; 1-59691-625-7 pa

LC 2007-49843

The author, a food and travel writer, presents an account of his experiences eating fish and seafood around the world and looks at the ecological ramifications of our diet. He argues that we need to redesign our relationship with seafood.

This is "a comprehensive, lively and illuminating guide." Nation
Includes bibliographical references

Grigson, Jane

Charcuterie and French pork cookery; Jane Grigson. Grub Street 2001 347 p. ill. $34.95 **641.6**

1. French cooking 2. Cooking -- Pork 3. Cookery (Pork) 4. Cooking, French
ISBN 1902304888; 9781902304885

LC 2008426563

IACP Culinary Classics Book Award (2013)

This book, by Jane Grigson, "first published in 1969 but unavailable for many years, . . . is a guidebook and a recipe book. She describes every type of charcuterie available for purchase and how to make them yourself. She describes how to braise, roast, pot-roast and stew all the cuts of pork, how to make terrines, how to cure your own ham and make your own sausages." (Publisher's note)

Guggiana, Marissa

Primal cuts; cooking with America's best butchers. Marissa Guggiana ; foreword by Dario Cecchini ; introduction by Andrew Zimmern. Welcome Books 2012 287 p. col. ill. (hardcover) $40 **641.6**

1. Cookbooks 2. Cooking -- Meat 3. Carving (Meat, etc.) 4. Cooking (Meat) 5. Meatcutting -- United States
ISBN 1599621150; 9781599621159

LC 2012018389

This cookbook describes how "Marissa Guggiana, food activist, writer, and fourth generation meat purveyor traveled the country to discover 50 of our most gifted butchers and share their favorite dishes, personal stories, and cooking techniques. From the Michelin star chef to the small farmer who raises free-range animals--butchers are the guide for this unique visual cookbook, packed with tons of their most prized recipes and good old-fashioned know-how." (Publisher's note)

Guittard, Amy

Guittard Chocolate cookbook; irresistible family recipes and stories from San Francisco's bean-to-bar chocolate company. Amy Guittard ; photographs by Antonis Achilleos. Chronicle Books Llc 2015 177 p. color illustrations $25 **641.6**

1. Cooking 2. Chocolate 3. Cooking, Chocolate
ISBN 1452135339; 9781452135335

LC 2014033173

Author "Amy Guittard presents tried-and-true favorite recipes from five generations of Guittards [San Francisco's oldest continuously family-owned chocolate company], ranging from start-your-day-right Chocolate Cherry Scones to fudgey Mocha Cookies and deep, dark Chocolate Caramel Pecan Bundt Cake. Leave it to the people who really know chocolate to make a collection of recipes that are sure to make every chocolate lover long for one bite more." (Publisher's note)

Higgins, Katie

Chocolate-covered Katie; over 80 delicious recipes that are secretly good for you. Katie Higgins. Life & Style 2015 207 p. color illustrations (trade pbk.) $20 **641.6**

1. Desserts 2. Cooking -- Chocolate 3. Chocolate desserts 4. Cooking (Chocolate)
ISBN 1455599700; 9781455599707

LC 2014017846

In this cookbook, Katie Higgins "shares over 80 never-before-seen recipes, such as Chocolate Obsession Cake, Peanut Butter Pudding Pops, and Ultimate Unbaked Brownies, that use only real ingredients, without any unnecessary fats, sugars, or empty calories. These desserts prove once and for all that health and happiness can go hand-in-hand-you can have your dessert and eat it, too!" (Publisher's note)

Iyer, Raghavan

Smashed, mashed, boiled, and baked-and fried, too! A Celebration of Potatoes in 75 Irresistible Recipes. Raghavan Iyer. Workman Publishing 2016 256 p. color illustrations (ebook) $17.95; (alk. paper) $16.95 **641.6**

1. Cooking -- Potatoes 2. Potatoes 3. Cooking (Potatoes)
ISBN 9780761189732; 9780761185475

LC 2016023744

This book, by Raghavan Iyer, "pays tribute to . . . the amazing potato. Its recipes, inspired by a diversity of cuisines and accompanied by enticing full-color photographs, feature scrumptious starters, like Ecuadorean Llapingachos and Sweet Potato Samosas. Hearty mains: Canadian Lamb-Potato Tortière, Moroccan Potato Stew with Saffron Biscuits, Potato Lasagna. Plus rich gratins, a boundary-defying Mojito Potato-Pomegranate Salad, luscious sauces and condiments, and even desserts." (Publisher's note)

Jacoby, Kate

Vedge; 100 plates, large and small, that place vegetables in the spotlight. Rich Landau and Kate Jacoby. The Experiment 2013 256 p. (cloth) $24.95 **641.6**

1. Veganism 2. Cooking -- Fruit 3. Vegetarian cooking 4. Cooking -- Vegetables 5. Vegan cooking 6. Cooking (Fruit) 7. Cooking (Vegetables) 8. Vedge (Restaurant; Philadelphia, Pa.)

ISBN 1615190856; 9781615190850

LC 2013012098

In this cookbook, chefs Rich Landau and Kate Jacoby "share their passion for ingenious vegetable cooking. The more than 100 recipes here--such as Fingerling Potatoes with Creamy Worcestershire Sauce, Pho with Roasted Butternut Squash, Seared French Beans with Caper Bagna Cauda, and Eggplant Braciole--explode with flavor but are surprisingly straightforward to prepare." (Publisher's note)

Kafka, Barbara

★ **Vegetable** love; a book for cooks. [by] Barbara Kafka with Christopher Styler; photographs by Christina Cornish. Artisan 2005 708p il $35 **641.6**

1. Vegetables 2. Cooking -- Vegetables

ISBN 1-57965-168-2

LC 2005-47818

The author "has triumphed with an outstanding, indispensable cookbook that not only summons the reader to get into the kitchen and cook but also constitutes a valuable and comprehensive reference tool." Booklist

Includes bibliographical references

Khong, Rachel

All about eggs; everything we know about the world's most important food. Rachel Khong and the editors of Lucky peach ; photographs by Tamara Shopsin and Jason Fulford. Clarkson Potter 2017 256 p. color illustrations (hard cover; alk. paper) $26 **641.6**

1. Eggs 2. Cooking -- Eggs 3. Cookbooks 4. Eggs as food 5. Cooking (Eggs)

ISBN 9780804187756; 9780804187763

LC 2016048977

This book, Rachel Khong and the editors of Lucky peach, with photographs by Tamara Shopsin and Jason Fulfor, "celebrates everything an egg can be and do. Whether illuminating the progress of an egg through a chicken, or teaching you how to poach the perfect egg,[it] bursts with facts to deploy at your next cocktail party—then serves up a killer deviled egg recipe to serve while you're doing it." (Publisher's note)

"In usual Lucky Peach style, this well-rounded, informative cookbook has a hip vibe and quirky illustrations." Pub Wkly

Includes bibliographical references and index

La Place, Viana

Verdura; vegetables, Italian style. Viana La Place. Grub Street 2010 320 p. il (pbk) $24.95 **641.6**

1. Cookbooks 2. Cooking -- Vegetables 3. Italian cooking 4. Cookery (Vegetables)

ISBN 1906502781; 9781906502782

LC 2010537034

Originally published: New York: Morrow, 1991. London: Macmillan, 1994

This cookbook, by Viana La Place, offers "300 irresistible recipes [that] represent the best of the Italian approach to vegetable preparation, an earthy yet spirited technique that celebrates fresh ingredients simply treated. . . . Contending that eating well-prepared vegetables helps us

to appreciate life's natural cycles, [the volume] . . . presents recipes for antipastos, salads, soups, sandwiches, pasta, risottos, pizzas, and much more." (Publisher's note)

Includes bibliographical references (p. 307) and index

Lobel, Stanley

The **meat** bible; all you need to know about meat and poultry from America's master butchers. by Stanley Lobel ... [et al.]; with Mary Goodbody and David Whiteman; photographs by Lucy Schaeffer. Chronicle Books 2009 319p il $40 **641.6**

1. Cooking -- Meat 2. Cooking -- Poultry

ISBN 978-0-8118-5826-7; 0-8118-5826-X

LC 2008-33441

"Recipes number 135, well photographed and indexed." Publ Wkly

Madison, Deborah

Vegetable literacy; exploring the affinities and history of the vegetable families, with 300 recipes. Deborah Madison. 1st ed. Ten Speed Press 2013 416 p. col. ill. (hardcover) $40.00 **641.6**

1. Cooking (Vegetables) 2. Food crops -- Identification

ISBN 9781607741916; 1607741911

LC 2012030968

Includes bibliographical references (page 395) and index.

Masonis, Todd

Making chocolate; from bean to bar to s'more. Todd Masonis, Greg D'Alesandre, Lisa Vega & Molly Gore ; photographs by Eric Wolfinger. Clarkson Potter/Publishers 2017 366 p. color illustrations (hardcover) $40 **641.6**

1. Chocolate 2. Cooking -- Chocolate 3. Cacao beans 4. Cooking (Cocoa)

ISBN 9780451495358; 9780451495365; 0451495357

LC 2017005182

This book, by Todd Masonis, Greg D'Alesandre, Lisa Vega and Molly Gore, with photographs by Eric Wolfinger, is a "complete guide to making chocolate from scratch. From the simplest techniques and technology . . . to the science and mechanics of making chocolate from bean to bar, . . . [the book] holds everything the founders and makers behind San Francisco's beloved chocolate factory [Dandelion Chocolate] have learned since the day they first cracked open a cocoa bean." (Publisher's note)

Mast, Rick

Mast Brothers Chocolate; a family cookbook. Rick Mast & Michael Mast ; foreword by Thomas Keller ; photography by Tuukka Koski. Little Brown & Co 2013 276 p. illustrations, some color (hbk.) $40 **641.6**

1. Desserts 2. Cookbooks 3. Cooking -- Chocolate 4. Chocolate 5. Cooking (Chocolate) 6. Mast Brothers Chocolate

ISBN 0316234842; 9780316234849

LC 2013938865

IACP Cookbook Award (2014)

In this cookbook, authors Rick Mast and Michael Mast "share their unique story and recipes for classic American desserts like chocolate cookies and cakes, brownies, bars, milkshakes, and even home-made whoopie pie. There are mouthwatering savory dishes as well, like Pan-seared Scallops with Cocoa Nibs and Cocoa Coq au Vin." (Publisher's note)

Moonen, Rick

Fish without a doubt; the cook's essential companion. [by] Rick Moonen and Roy Finamore; photographs by Ben Fink. Houghton Mifflin Co. 2008 496p il $35   **641.6**

1. Cooking -- Fish 2. Cooking -- Seafood
ISBN 978-0-618-53119-6; 0-618-53119-X

LC 2007-52084

In this cookbook that covers the preparing of sustainable fish, the authors "show how to clean, bone, and portion both finfish and shellfish. Recipes are organized by cooking method—broiling, poaching, roasting, grilling, steaming, [and] frying. . . . Succeeding chapters cover such fish basics as chowders, fish cakes, and salads. . . . Both the book's organization and its comprehensive coverage make this a necessary addition to any cookbook collections." Booklist

Music, Debra

Theo Chocolate; recipes & sweet secrets from Seattle's favorite chocolate maker. Debra Music and Joe Whinney with Leora Bloom. Sasquatch Books 2015 256 p. (alk. paper) $24.95   **641.6**

1. Chocolate 2. Cookbooks 3. Theo Chocolate 4. Chocolate candy 5. Chocolate desserts
ISBN 1570619972; 9781570619977

LC 2015011364

This book, by Debra Music and Joe Whinney with Leora Bloom, presents "sweet and savory chocolate recipes, along with the fascinating story of how North America's first organic and Fair Trade chocolate factory came to be (and why they are so passionate about how their chocolate is made)." (Publisher's note)

"Though light on technical instruction, this book contains a compelling range of sweet and savory recipes." Library Journal

Includes bibliographical references and index

Ottolenghi, Yotam

★ **Plenty** more; vibrant vegetable cooking from London's Ottolenghi. Yotam Ottolenghi. Ten Speed Press 2014 352 p. color illustrations (hardcover) $35   **641.6**

1. Cookbooks 2. Vegetarian cooking 3. Cooking (Vegetables) 4. Ottolenghi (Restaurant)
ISBN 1607746212; 9781607746218

LC 2014017924

IACP Cookbook Award Finalist: Chefs and Restaurants (2015)

James Beard Foundation Award Nominee: Vegetable Focused and Vegetarian (2015)

In this vegetarian cookbook, author Yotam Ottolenghi "continues to explore the diverse realm of vegetarian food with a wholly original approach. Organized by cooking method, more than 150 dazzling recipes emphasize spices, seasonality, and bold flavors." It also includes "120 vegetarian dishes organized by cooking method." (Publisher's note)

While the recipes "require time and finesse . . . they are often revelatory, introducing textures and flavor combinations that readers won't find elsewhere." LJ

Peterson, James

Meat; a kitchen education. Ten Speed Press 2010 326p il $35   **641.6**

1. Cooking -- Meat
ISBN 978-1-58008-992-0; 1-58008-992-5

LC 2010-21759

"Though his introduction addresses vegans, admonishing all to 'follow your conscience' about the consumption of animals, the rest of [Peterson's] text advocates only the use of the best lamb, rabbit, beef, and chicken available. Thoroughly review the first two chapters; in them Peterson sets forth the proper ways to sauté, grill, braise, and poach (among other methods), illustrates such fundamental preparation methods as julienning a leek and sectioning a turnip, and identifies the flavors associated with different international cuisines. Next, the fun: 175 recipes and, more important, instructions and sidebars to ensure that expensive roasts and whole birds emerge with great taste." Booklist

Phipps, Catherine

Citrus; 150 Recipes Celebrating the Sweet and the Sour. Catherine Phipps ; photography by Mowie Kay. Quadrille 2017 255 p. illustrations (hardcover) $29.99   **641.6**

1. Citrus fruits 2. Cookbooks 3. Cooking (Citrus fruits)
ISBN 9781849499002; 1849499004

This citrus cookbook "offers 150 inspiring recipes that celebrate these wonderful fruits. Through fresh salads, soups, seafood, Asian and Mediterranean-influenced meat dishes, preserves and pickles, to the world of sweet pies, cakes, and cocktails, Catherine Phipps explores the myriad uses of oranges and lemons, and all things in between." (Publisher's note)

"Evoking the nostalgic scent and global flavor of citrus, Phipps presents a rich collection that includes preserves, starters, soups, meals, desserts, candies, and drinks that can be mixed and matched based on the season and variety of fruit available." LJ

Pollinger, Ben

School of fish; Ben Pollinger. Simon & Schuster 2014 439 p. colored illustrations (hardback) $35   **641.6**

1. Cooking -- Seafood 2. Cooking (Seafood)
ISBN 145166513X; 9781451665130; 9781451665147

LC 2014000760

IACP Cookbook Award Finalist: General (2015)

In this cookbook, chef Ben Pollinger "distills years of experience working in some of the world's best restaurants in this no-nonsense book that demystifies the art of cooking seafood. With more than 100 recipes organized by technique from the easiest to the most advanced, Pollinger takes you through the ins and outs of baking, roasting, braising, broiling, steaming, poaching, grilling, frying, sautéing, and of course seasoning." (Publisher's note)

Presilla, Maricel E.

Peppers of the Americas; the remarkable capsicums that forever changed flavor. Maricel E. Presilla ; photographs by Romulo Yanes. Ten Speed Press 2017 x, 341 p.p color illustrations (hardcover) $35   **641.6**

1. Peppers 2. Cookbooks 3. Cooking (Peppers) 4. Peppers -- America
ISBN 9780399578939; 9780399578922; 0399578927

LC 2017011484

This book, by Maricel E. Presilla, with photography by Romulo Yanes, offers "a beautiful culinary and ethnobotanical survey of the punch-packing ingredient central to today's multi-cultural palate, with more than 40 pan-Latin recipes from a three-time James Beard Award-winning author and chef-restaurateur. . . . This stunning visual reference to peppers now seen on menus, in markets, and beyond, showcases nearly 200 varieties." (Publisher's note)

"Presilla is both 'botanical sleuth' and chef, presenting a scholarly and stunning visual guide to peppers in this definitive guide." Pub Wkly

Includes bibliographical references (pages 331-333) and index.

Raichlen, Steven

Project smoke; by Steven Raichlen. Workman Publishing

2016 336 p. (alk. paper) $22.95   **641.6**
1. Cooking 2. Barbecue cooking 3. Smoked foods 4. Smoking (Cooking) 5. Cooking (Smoked foods)
ISBN 9780761181866

LC 2015044528

This cookbook, by Steven Raichlen, "a step-by-step guide to cold-smoking, hot-smoking, and smoke-roasting, and a collection of 100 innovative recipes for smoking every kind of food, from starters to desserts. . . . Illustrated throughout with full-color photographs, it's a book that inspires hunger at every glance, and satisfies with every recipe tried." (Publisher's note)

"An excellent how-to for those fired up about smoke." Booklist

Rule, Cheryl Sternman

Yogurt culture; a global look at how to make, bake, sip, and chill the world's creamiest, healthiest food. Cheryl Sternman Rule ; photography by Ellen Silverman. Houghton Mifflin Harcourt 2015 352 p. color illustrations (paper over board) $22   **641.6**
1. Cookbooks 2. Dairy products 3. Cooking (Yogurt)
ISBN 0544252322; 9780544252325

LC 2014039690

This cookbook, by Cheryl Sternman Rule, with photography by Ellen Silverman, "presents 115 flavorful recipes, taking yogurt farther than the breakfast table, lunchbox, or gym bag. . . . In chapters like Flavor, Slurp, Dine, and Lick, [the author] pairs yogurt not just with fruit but with meat, not just with sugar but with salt, not just with herbs but with fragrant spices whose provenance spans the globe." (Publisher's note)

"This excellent cookbook belongs in most collections, along with Arto de Hartounian's The Yogurt Cookbook." LJ

Seaver, Barton

For cod and country. Sterling Epicure 2011 294p il $30   **641.6**
1. Cooking -- Seafood
ISBN 978-1-4027-7775-2

A "a user's manual for any seafood lover who wants to eat sustainably—and very well. Seaver's book vibrates with personality, practical advice, photographs (both evocative and how-to), and stovetop wisdom: never be shy about adding butter, but go easy on the black pepper. With the help of step-by-step photographs, he demonstrates seafood-savvy techniques, everything from how to fillet a bass to how to open an oyster without severing one of your arteries. He also provides a list of substitutions for overexploited species: Use Pacific cod in place of Atlantic cod; sablefish instead of Chilean sea bass; squid instead of octopus." Atlantic

Selengut, Becky

Good fish; 100 sustainable seafood recipes from the Pacific Coast. Becky Selengut. Sasquatch Books 2018 336 p. (pbk.; alk. paper) $29.95   **641.6**
1. American cooking 2. Cooking -- Seafood 3. International cooking 4. Cooking (Seafood) 5. Cooking, American -- Pacific Northwest style
ISBN 9781632171078

LC 2017041101

In this book, "chef and seafood advocate Becky Selengut helps simplify sustainable seafood choices for consumers . . . [and] includes lingcod, Pacific cod, wahoo (or ono), mahi-mahi, and herring. From shellfish to finfish to 'littlefish' (think sardines), there are 100 recipes for 20 varieties of 'good fish.' . . . There are also cooking techniques . . , practical tips for buying and caring for seafood, and the most current sustainability information." (Publisher's note)

Includes bibliographical references and index

Slater, Nigel

Ripe; a cook in the orchard. Nigel Slater ; photography by Jonathan Lovekin. Ten Speed Press 2012 591 p. col. ill. (hardback) $40   **641.6**
1. Cookbooks 2. Gardening 3. Cooking -- Fruit 4. Cooking (Fruit)
ISBN 1607743329; 9781607743323

LC 2011043551

James Beard Foundation Award: Single Subject (2013)

This cookbook, by food writer Nigel Slater, "focuses on sweet and savory applications for fruits grown in his London garden. Organized alphabetically, the fruit-focused chapters offer historical and varietal information, gardening tips, and suggested flavor pairings, followed by simple recipes like Baked Peaches with Maple Syrup and Vanilla, Slow-Cooked Quinces with Cassis, and Roast Leg of Pork with Spiced Rhubarb." (Library Journal)

Speck, Maria

Simply ancient grains; fresh and flavorful whole grain recipes for living well. by Maria Speck. Ten Speed Press 2015 272 p. color illustrations (hardcover) $27.50   **641.6**
1. Cookbooks 2. Cooking -- Grains 3. Grain 4. Cooking (Cereals) 5. Heirloom varieties (Plants)
ISBN 1607745887; 9781607745884

LC 2014036879

This cookbook, by Maria Speck and photography by Erin Kunkel, presents recipes for cooking Ancient grains. "From black rice to red quinoa to golden Kamut berries, ancient grains are showing up on restaurant menus and store shelves in abundance. . . . [The author] makes cooking with these fascinating and nourishing staples easy and accessible with sumptuous recipes for breakfast, lunch, dinner, and dessert." (Publisher's note)

"Speck simplifies cooking with grains without sacrificing flavor. Her recipes—including minted barley and fennel stew with marinated feta, New England cider mussels with fresh cranberries and bulgur, and walnut spelt biscotti with olive oil—are deliciously nourishing and not to be missed." LJ

Includes bibliographical references and index

Stein, Rick

Rick Stein's complete seafood; a step-by-step reference with over 150 recipes and 550 photographs. Rick Stein [photography by James Murphy] Ten Speed Press 2004 264 p. col. ill. $27.99   **641.6**
1. Cookbooks 2. Cooking -- Fish 3. Cooking -- Seafood 4. Cooking (Fish) 5. Cooking (Seafood) 6. Cookery, International
ISBN 1580085687; 1580089143; 9781580089142

LC 2006298920

James Bead Award (2005)

This cookbook, by Rich Stein, "offers an almost limitless repertoire [of seafood recipes], with detailed instructions and extensive charts. Hundreds of photographs and illustrations show how to scale and gut fish for the grill, bake whole fish in a salt or pastry casing, hot-smoke fish, prepare live crabs, and clean and stuff squid, along with other essential techniques." (Publisher's note)

Vegetables from an Italian garden; season-by-season recipes. Phaidon 2011 431p il $39.95   **641.6**
1. Vegetable gardening 2. Cooking -- Vegetables
ISBN 978-0-7148-6117-3; 0-7148-6117-0

This book, assembled by the editors at Phaidon Press, "is divided into four chapters, following the four seasons. Each chapter has its own colored ribbon, which makes it easy to go to the season you want to cook from. . . . Each season starts with an explanation of the vegetables available that season. There is a short history of the vegetable, then an explanation of how to select and buy them, along with stunning photos by Andy Sewell. Following this is a description of how and when to plant these vegetables in your own garden. The scrumptious recipes are taken from all parts of Italy. Well written and clear, they let you jump in and start cooking." Super Chef

Viljoen, Marie

Forage, harvest, feast; a wild-inspired cuisine. Marie Viljoen. Chelsea Green Publishing 2018 480 p. (plc) $40 **641.6**
    1. Edible plants 2. Seasonal cooking 3. Cooking -- Vegetables 4. Wild plants, Edible 5. Cooking (Wild foods)
    ISBN 9781603587501

LC 2018007866

"In this groundbreaking collection of nearly 500 wild food recipes, celebrated New York City forager, cook, kitchen gardener, and writer Marie Viljoen incorporates wild ingredients into everyday and special occasion fare. . . . [Viljoen] offers deliciously compelling recipes for everything from cocktails and snacks to appetizers, entrées, and desserts, as well as bakes, breads, preserves, sauces, syrups, ferments, spices, and salts." (Publisher's note)

" As long as readers heed Viljoen's explanations—typically related to sourcing, preparation or, in the case of ramps, sustainability—they'll be set. The book's imaginative yet practical recipes make it one of the best resources of its type. It's a terrific entry point for would-be foragers, as well as experts interested in making the most of their bounty." Pub Wkly

Vinton, Sherri Brooks

Put 'em up! a comprehensive home preserving guide for the creative cook, from drying and freezing to canning and pickling. Storey Pub. 2010 303p il pa $19.95 **641.6**
    1. Cooking -- Fruit 2. Cooking -- Vegetables 3. Fruit -- Preservation 4. Vegetables -- Preservation
    ISBN 978-1-60342-546-9

LC 2010009609

"Vinton provides an excellent introduction to multiple food preservation methods. Organized first by technique, then by fruit or vegetable, this volume contains many easy-to-follow options for prepared and preserved foods." Libr J

Includes bibliographical references

Wells, Patricia

Vegetable harvest; vegetables at the center of the plate. William Morrow 2007 324p il $34.95 **641.6**
    1. Cooking -- Vegetables
    ISBN 978-0-06-075244-6; 0-06-075244-0

LC 2006-43723

"After surveying the bounty of her backyard garden, Wells became inspired to build meals around vegetables rather than starting with meat, fish or poultry. She tripled the number she served at each meal and tried different cooking methods, looking for the best-tasting, most wholesome ways of cooking each type. She includes nutritional information and an equipment list for each recipe, and selectively offers wine suggestions, translations of French food idioms, and nuggets of folklore connected to the dish or main ingredient. . . . This collection is highly recommended for cooks and gardeners alike." Publ Wkly

641.64   Fruits

Bir, Sara

The **fruit** forager's companion; ferments, desserts, main dishes, and more from your neighborhood and beyond. Sara Bir. Chelsea Green Publishing 2018 400 p. (pbk.) $29.95 **641.64**
    1. Forage plants 2. Cooking -- Natural foods 3. Cooking (Fruit)
    ISBN 9781603587167; 9781603587174

LC 2017058242

This book, by Sara Bir, "is a how-to guide with nearly 100 recipes devoted to the secret, sweet bounty just outside our front doors and ripe for the taking, from familiar apples and oranges to lesser-known pawpaws and mayhaws. . . . Bir . . . primes readers on foraging basics, demonstrates gathering and preservation techniques, and presents a suite of recipes including habanero crabapple jelly, lime pickle, pawpaw lemon curd, and fermented cranberry relish." (Publisher's note)

" Even if readers don't have a lemon or apple tree in the backyard, they're sure to find some useful advice, as Bir does an outstanding job of illustrating how to get the most out of simple, often neglected or discarded ingredients." Pub Wkly

641.65   Vegetables

Bloomfield, April

A **Girl** and Her Greens; Hearty Meals from the Garden. HarperCollins 2015 272 p. color illustrations $34.99 **641.65**
    ISBN 006222588X; 9780062225887

LC 2015490298

This cookbook by April Blomfield "reflects the lighter side of the renowned chef whose name is nearly synonymous with nose-to-tail eating. In recipes such as Pot-Roasted Romanesco Broccoli, Onions with Sage Pesto, and Carrots with Spices, Yogurt, and Orange Blossom Water, April Bloomfield demonstrates the basic principle of her method: that unforgettable food comes out of simple, honest ingredients, an attention to detail, and a love for the sensual pleasures of cooking and eating." (Publisher's note)

"Bloomfield's latest is an excellent companion to its popular predecessor, offering a second helping of narrative-rich recipes and Sun Young Park's charming illustrations." LJ

Eatingwell Vegetables. Houghton Mifflin Harcourt 2016 516 p. color illustrations $35 **641.65**
    1. Cooking 2. Vegetables
    ISBN 0544715284; 9780544715288

This book, from the editors of "EatingWell" magazine, "guides both vegetable lovers and novices through the world of produce, including must-know basics, shopping notes, growing advice, and cooking tips on 100 common and less common vegetables, from arugula to yucca." (Publisher's note)

"Food trends such as the cauliflower pizza crust and raw kale salads also get their due. Throughout, bonus tips for growing cucumbers and "stale-ing" bread offer added value. This is a useful addition to a veg-centric cook's collection." Pub Wkly

Lang, Rebecca

The **Southern** vegetable book; A Root-to-Stalk Guide to the South's Favorite Produce. Rebecca Lang. Oxmoor House 2016 256 p. color illustrations (hardcover) $27.95 **641.65**
    1. Southern cooking 2. Cooking -- Vegetables
    ISBN 0848746880; 9780848746889

This cookbook, by Rebecca Lang, "brings you to the table to celebrate the versatility of vegetables with Southern flair. . . . The classic vegetables that we all know and love are represented, but lesser-known but equally-celebrated ones, such as Jerusalem artichokes and ramps, also make an appearance. The recipes in the book pay homage to classic Southern dishes while offering modern interpretations for the home cook, whether you call the South home or not." (Publisher's note)

" Many recent cookbooks feature creative vegetable preparations... this one has a distinct Southern twist." LJ

Mangini, Cara

The **Vegetable** Butcher; How to Select, Prep, Slice, Dice, and Masterfully Cook Vegetables from Artichokes to Zucchini. Cara Mangini. Workman Pub Co 2016 352 p. color illustrations (hardcover) $29.95   **641.65**

1. Cookbooks 2. Cooking -- Vegetables
ISBN 9780761180524; 0761180524

LC 2016004215

In this cookbook, by Cara Mangini, "the skills of butchery meet the world of fresh produce. . . . In step-by-step photographs, [a] 'vegetable butcher' . . . shows how to break down a butternut squash, cut a cauliflower into steaks, peel a tomato properly, chiffonade kale, turn carrots into coins and parsnips into matchsticks, and find the meaty heart of an artichoke. Additionally, more than 150 original, simple recipes put vegetables front and center." (Publisher's note)

"Blending practical aspects found in such manuals as Jacque Pepin's New Complete Techniques with the varied recipes familiar to titles such as Michael Anthony's V Is for Vegetables, Mangini's debut will augment most vegetable cooking collections." LJ

Wilkinson, Matt

Mr. Wilkinson's vegetables; a cookbook to celebrate the garden. Matt Wilkinson. Black Dog & Leventhal Pub. 2013 287 p. $27.95   **641.65**

1. Cooking -- Vegetables
ISBN 157912934X; 9781579129347

In this cookbook, "Melbourne, Australia-based chef [Matt] Wilkinson takes a 'veg-first approach' to cooking, building dishes around fresh, seasonal produce. In 25 chapters named for vegetables, he shares inspiring and beautifully photographed recipes that range from rustic (braised eggplant, tomato and meatballs) to playful ('Shepherd's Pie' croquettes) to unconventional (frozen vanilla syrup-coated fennel)." (Library Journal)

641.654   Greens

Squires, Kathleen

The **book** of greens; a cook's compendium of 40 varieties, from arugula to watercress, with over 150 recipes. Jenn Louis and Kathleen Squires, photographs by Ed Anderson. Ten Speed Press 2017 328 p. (ebook) $65; (hardcover; alk. paper) $35   **641.654**

1. Cookbooks 2. Cooking -- Vegetables 3. Cooking (Greens)
ISBN 9781607749851; 9781607749844

LC 2016036277

This cookbook, by Jenn Louis and Kathleen Squires, with photographs by Ed Anderson, offers "more than 150 recipes for simple, show-stopping fare, from snacks to soups to mains (and even breakfast and dessert) that will inspire you to reach for new greens at the farmers' market, or use your old standbys in totally fresh ways. Organized alphabetically by green, each entry features information on seasonality, nutrition, and prep and storage tips." (Publisher's note)

"For the CSA-produce subscribers and enthusiastic farmers market shoppers who find themselves staring cluelessly at piles of unknown greens each week, Louis and Squires's book is a boon." Pub Wkly

Includes bibliographical references and index

641.658   Mushrooms

Selengut, Becky

Shroom; mind-bendingly good recipes for cultivated and wild mushrooms. Becky Selengut. Andrews McMeel Pub., LLC 2014 205 p. color illustrations $35   **641.658**

1. Cooking -- Mushrooms
ISBN 1449448267; 9781449448264

LC 2014931303

This cookbook by Becky Selengut focuses on mushrooms. "She answers common questions about buying, cleaning . . ., storing, and eating mushrooms. . . . Each chapter includes five recipes that are presented in order from easy to advanced, with suggested wine pairings." Recipes include "banh mi sandwiches with red curry roasted portobellos and pickled vegetables [and] silken scrambled eggs with shaved Alba white truffles." (Library Journal)

"A delight to read and cook from, this is one of the most welcoming and unintimidating mushroom books to hit shelves in ages." LJ

641.66   Meat

Burgers; 125 Mouthwatering Recipes and Tips. edited by Jane Francisco. Hearst Books 2016 127 p. color illustrations (hardcover) $16.95   **641.66**

1. Cooking 2. Cookbooks 3. Hamburgers 4. Cooking (Meat)
ISBN 9781618372017; 1618372017

LC 2016427269

In this hamburger cookbook, edited by Jane Francisco and the Good Housekeeping publishing company, "you'll discover something exciting and delicious—including Texas Chicken Burgers, Rosemary-Cabernet Sliders, Greek Lamb Burgers, Salmon Burgers with Cajun Rémoulade Sauce, and Portobello Pesto Burgers." (Publisher's note)

"A reasonably priced cookbook for burger lovers working with a modest budget." LJ

Recipes from an Italian butcher; roasting, stewing, braising. The Silver Spoon Kitchen. Phaidon Press Limited 2017 303 p. illustrations (chiefly color) (hardcover) $49.95   **641.66**

1. Cooking -- Meat 2. Italian cooking 3. Cooking (Meat) 4. Cooking, Italian
ISBN 9780714874975; 0714874973

LC 2017449201

This book, from The Silver Spoon Kitchen, "showcases simple, hearty dishes that are true to this tradition, from chicken cacciatore and braised beef with Barolo to osso buco and Roman lamb. With more than 150 recipes, most published for the first time in English, it's comprehensive and authoritative, demystifying the different cuts, cooking methods, and techniques unique to each meat type--along with the side dishes that best complement them." (Publisher's note)

641.665   Poultry

Flores, Eva Kosmas

Adventures in chicken; 150 Amazing Recipes from the

Creator of AdventuresInCooking.com. Eva Kosmas Flores. Houghton Mifflin Harcourt 2016 288 p. color illustrations (paper over board) $30 **641.665**

1. Cookbooks 2. Cooking (Chicken)
ISBN 9780544558205

LC 2015038041

This cookbook by Eva Kosmas Flores is aimed at "home cooks who want to push their cooking to the next level with the best versions of classics like Chicken Marsala with Balsamic Caramelized Onions and Pork Belly or innovative temptations such as Korean Barbecue Drumsticks with Ginger-Pear Sauce. There are sections on chicken cooking techniques, how to make perfect stock, and more." (Publisher's note)

"An aptly titled book that takes everyday chicken to the ends of the earth." Booklist

Henry, Diana

A **Bird** in the Hand; Chicken Recipes for Every Day and Every Mood. by Diana Henry. Mitchell Beazley 2015 224 p. color illustrations $19.02 **641.665**

1. Cooking (Chicken)
ISBN 1845338960; 9781845338961

This chicken cookbook, by Diana Henry, presents a "collection of recipes for every day and every mood.... From quick Vietnamese lemon grass and chilli chicken thighs and a smoky chicken salad with roast peppers and almonds, through to a complete feast with pomegranate, barley and feta stuffed roast chicken with Georgian aubergines, there is no eating or entertaining occasion that isn't covered in this book." (Publisher's note)

"Whether herbaceous, aromatic, sweet, or spicy, these new chicken dishes promise to reinvigorate even the tiredest taste buds." LJ

641.673 Cheese

Greenspan, Eric

The **great** grilled cheese book; grown up recipes for a childhood classic. Eric Greenspan. Ten Speed Press 2018 152 p. (hardcover; alk. paper) $16.99 **641.673**

1. Cookbooks 2. Sandwiches 3. Quick and easy cooking 4. Cooking (Cheese)
ISBN 9780399580741

LC 2017049573

This cookbook, by Eric Greenspan, features "fifty chef-created recipes--some classic, some boundary pushing--for America's favorite sandwich, the grilled cheese.... Featuring both common and elevated ingredients like brie cheese, poppy seed bread, olive tapenade, fig marmalade, smoked salmon, candied bacon, bourbon-glazed ham, and raisin walnut bread, these are recipes that invite you into new and uncharted grilled cheese territory." (Publisher's note)

"Highly recommended for anyone looking to up their grilled cheese game." Library Journal

Includes bibliographical references and index

641.675 Eggs

Ruhlman, Michael

★ **Egg**; a culinary exploration of the world's most versatile ingredient. Michael Ruhlman ; photography by Donna Turner Ruhlman. Little Brown & Co 2014 xix, 235 p.p col. ill. $40 **641.675**

1. Cooking -- Eggs

ISBN 0316254061; 9780316254069

LC 2013948058

James Beard Foundation Award Nominee: Single Subject (2015)

In this cookbook Michael Ruhlman "explains why the egg is the key to the craft of cooking.... He starts with perfect poached and scrambled eggs and builds up to brioche and Italian meringue. Along the way readers learn to make their own mayonnaise, pasta, custards, quiches, cakes, and other preparations that rely fundamentally on the hidden powers of the egg." (Publisher's note)

"Ruhlman's regard for this simple ingredient is evident as he describes the multiple functions it serves and then offers up recipes for a wide array of appetizing dishes." Pub Wkly

641.691 Game

Canterbury, Dave

The **Bushcraft** field guide to trapping, gathering, and cooking in the wild; Dave Canterbury, New York Times bestselling author of Bushcraft. Adams Media 2016 264 p. (pbk.) $16.99 **641.691**

1. Camping 2. Wilderness survival 3. Cooking (Game) -- Technique 4. Cooking (Wild foods) -- Technique 5. Camping -- Handbooks, manuals, etc 6. Hunting -- Handbooks, manuals, etc 7. Wilderness survival -- Handbooks, manuals, etc
ISBN 1440598525; 9781440598524

LC 2016024921

This book, by Dave Canterbury, " provides you with all you need to know about packing, trapping, and preparing food for your treks and wilderness travels. Whether you're headed out for a day hike or a week-long expedition, you'll find everything you need to survive--and eat well--out in the wild." (Publisher's note)

641.692 Fish

Seaver, Barton

Two if by sea; Delicious Sustainable Seafood. Barton Seaver. Sterling Pub Co Inc 2016 304 p. color illustrations (hardcover) $30 **641.692**

1. Cooking -- Seafood
ISBN 1454917873; 9781454917878

This seafood cookbook, by Barton Seaver, "offers more than 150 new mouthwatering recipes, including entrees, salads, appetizers, soups, pastas, stews, sides, and sauces.... Each of Seaver's fresh-tasting, casual (and always delicious) recipes features seafood that hasn't been overfished or caught in an environmentally destructive way." (Publisher's note)

"From a quick weeknight meal of canned shrimp and pasta to a show-stopping stew for guests, the ideas here will fit any bill. Essential for seafood lovers." LJ

Thompson, Jennifer Trainer

Fresh Fish; A Fearless Guide to Grilling, Shucking, Searing, Poaching & Roasting Seafood. by Jennifer Trainer Thompson. Workman Pub Co 2016 352 p. illustrations (chiefly color) **641.692**

1. Cooking -- Fish 2. Cooking -- Seafood
ISBN 1612128084; 9781612128085

LC 2015041612

This book on seafood, by Jennifer Trainer Thompson, "offers simple step-by-step instructions for all of the essential cooking methods, including baking, pan-frying, braising, broiling, steaming, poaching, roasting, marinating, and grilling — along with 175 mouthwatering recipes that bring out the best in everything from fish fillets and whole fish to shrimp, mussels, lobster, clams, calamari, and more." (Publisher's note)

"A capable, reasonably priced all-purpose seafood cookbook that focuses primarily on recipes."

641.694 Mollusks

Jacobsen, Rowan

The **Essential** Oyster; A Salty Appreciation of Taste and Temptation. by Rowan Jacobsen. St. Martin's Press 2016 304 p. color illustrations $35 **641.694**

1. Oysters

ISBN 1632862565; 9781632862563

This book, by Rowan Jacobsen, "is the definitive book for oyster-lovers everywhere, featuring stunning portraits, tasting notes, and back-stories of all the top oysters, as well as recipes from America's top oyster chefs and a guide to the best oyster bars." (Publisher's note)

"A handful of recipes from top chefs round out the book, chased down with a dirty oyster-brine martini." Pub Wkly

641.7 Specific cooking processes and techniques

Blonder, Greg

Meathead; the science of great barbecue and grilling. text and photos by Meathead Goldwyn ; with Greg Blonder, Ph.D. A Rux Martin Book, Houghton Mifflin Harcourt 2016 400 p. illustrations (chiefly color) (hardback) $35 **641.7**

1. Cookbooks 2. Barbecue cooking 3. Barbecuing

ISBN 9780544018464

LC 2015049143

This cookbook, by Meathead Goldwyn with Greg Blonder, offers a "definitive guide to the concepts, methods, equipment, and accessories of barbecue and grilling. The founder and editor of the world's most popular BBQ and grilling website, AmazingRibs.com, Meathead applies the latest research to backyard cooking more than 100 thoroughly tested recipes." (Publisher's note)

"This highly recommended food-science focused guide to grilling and barbecue will satisfy amateurs and professionals alike." LJ

Science of great barbecue and grilling

Carroll, Joe

Feeding the fire; recipes and strategies for better barbecue and grilling. Joe Carroll with Nick Fauchald. Artisan Books 2015 264 p. illustrations $29.95 **641.7**

1. Cookbooks 2. Barbecue cooking 3. Barbecuing

ISBN 1579655572; 9781579655570

LC 2014035876

This grilling cookbook, by Joe Carroll with Nick Fauchald, "teaches the hows and whys of live-fire cooking: how to create low and slow fires, how to properly grill chicken (leave it on the bone), why American whiskey blends so nicely with barbecued meats (both are flavored with charred wood), and how to make the best sides to serve with meat (keep it simple)." (Publisher's note)

"With dishes like smoked and grilled hot dogs, charred corn with compound cream cheese, and butcher's steaks with garlic butter, this cookbook is a master class in minimal and well-prepared barbecue." LJ

Cook it in cast iron; kitchen-tested recipes for the one pan that does it all. by the editors at America's Test Kitchen. America's Test Kitchen 2016 304 p. color illustrations (alk. paper) $26.95 **641.7**

1. Skillet cooking

ISBN 9781940352480

LC 2015037708

This cookbook, by the editor's of America's Test Kitchen, "will show you everything you need to know about cast-iron cookware and the many (and often surprising) dishes you can cook and bake in this multitasker of a pan, from the classic dishes everyone knows and loves like steak, perfect fried eggs, and cornbread, to innovative and inspiring recipes like skillet apple pie, pizza, and cinnamon swirl bread." (Publisher's note)

"The editors of Cook's Country undertake a comprehensive exploration of the classic cast iron skillet, as well as the panoply of meals it can provide." Pub Wkly

Includes bibliographical references and index

Cook's illustrated (Periodical)

Best skillet recipes; a best recipe classic. by the editors of Cook's illustrated; photography, Keller + Keller, Carl Tremblay, and Daniel J. Van Ackere; illustrations, John Burgoyne. America's Test Kitchen 2009 335p il $35 **641.7**

1. Cooking

ISBN 978-1-933615-41-7; 1-933615-41-9

This cookbook celebrates the "versatility of that ordinary workhorse, the 12-inch skillet. An indispensable tool for eggs, pan-seared meats and sautéed vegetables, the skillet can also be used for stovetop-to-oven dishes such as All-American Mini Meatloaves; layered dishes such as tamale pie and Tuscan bean casserole; and even desserts such as hot fudge pudding cake. . . . Whether or not you properly appreciate your skillet, this book will at least teach you to wield it gracefully." Publ Wkly

Davis, Timothy Charles

The **hot** chicken cookbook; the fiery history and red-hot recipes of Nashville's beloved bird. Timothy Charles Davis. Spring House Press 2015 128 p. ill. (chiefly color), portrait (pbk.; alk. paper) $19.95 **641.7**

1. Cooking (Chicken) 2. Nashville (Tenn.)

ISBN 9781940611198

LC 2015951464

In this book, by Timothy Charles Davis, "Nashville-style Hot Chicken is the Music City's claim to culinary fame. . . . Davis, a chef, writer, and Nashville resident, traces the dish's origins back to the late 1930's at Prince's Hot Chicken Shack, a story of love gone wrong, and follows the trail to its white-hot buzz of today." (Publisher's note)

"Reading Davis's cookbook, it's easy to understand why hot chicken has a cult following. A fascinating exploration of food culture and highly recommended." LJ

Fine cooking roasting; favorite recipes & essential tips for chicken, beef, veggies & more. editors and contributors of Fine cooking. The Taunton Press, Inc. 2014 153 p. colored illustrations $14.95 **641.7**

1. Cooking 2. Roasting (Cooking)

ISBN 1627108076; 9781627108072

LC 2014024594

IACP Cookbook Award Finalist: Compilations (2015)

This roasting cookbook, by the editors of Fine Cooking magazine "serves up the best recipes and techniques so home cooks can successfully produce bold-flavored, juicy meat and vegetable dishes time and again. . . . You will easily learn the age-old art of: Slow roasting, Quick searing, Braising, [and] Simmering." (Publisher's note)

Roasting

Kaminsky, Peter

Charred & scruffed; Bold New Techniques for Explosive Flavor On and Off the Grill. Adam Perry Lang with Peter Kaminsky. Artisan 2012 xiv, 266 p.p col. ill.   **641.7**

1. Barbecue cooking 2. Barbecuing
ISBN 9781579654658

LC 2011031786

In this book, chef Adam Perry Land "employs his extensive culinary background to refine and concentrate the flavors and textures of barbecue and reimagine its possibilities. Adam's new techniques, from roughing up meat and vegetables ('scruffing') to cooking directly on hot coals ('clinching') to constantly turning and moving the meat while cooking ('hot potato'), produce crust formation and layers of flavor." (Publisher's note)

Includes index

Mackay, Jordan

Franklin barbecue; a meat-smoking manifesto. Aaron Franklin and Jordan Mackay ; photography by Wyatt McSpadden. Ten Speed Press 2015 224 p. illustrations (chiefly color) (hardcover) $29.99   **641.7**

1. Barbecue cooking 2. Barbecuing
ISBN 1607747200; 9781607747208

LC 2014036177

IACP Cookbook Award Nominee: Single Subject (2016)

This cookbook, by Aaron Franklin and Jordan Mackay, "is a definitive resource for the backyard pitmaster, with chapters dedicated to building or customizing your own smoker; finding and curing the right wood; creating and tending perfect fires; sourcing top-quality meat; and of course, cooking mind-blowing, ridiculously delicious barbecue, better than you ever thought possible." (Publisher's note)

Franklin "spends most of the book exploring the general mechanics and intangibles behind creating a delicious brisket."

Mills, Mike

Praise the lard; recipes and revelations from a legendary life in barbecue. Mike Mills and Amy Mills ; photographs by Ken Goodman. Houghton Mifflin Harcourt 2017 324 p. illustrations (hardcover) $25   **641.7**

1. Cookbooks 2. Barbecue cooking 3. Barbecuing
ISBN 9780544702493; 9780544702509

LC 2016051671

This book, by Mike Mills and Amy Mills, with photographs by Ken Goodman, "dispenses all the secrets of the [Mills] family's lifetime of worshipping at the temple of barbecue. At the heart of the book are almost 100 recipes from the family archives: Private Reserve Mustard Sauce, Ain't No Thang but a Chicken Wing, Pork Belly Bites, and Prime Rib on the Pit, Tangy Pit Beans, and Blackberry Pie." (Publisher's note)

"Mike and daughter Amy offer advice on achieving barbecue excellence in the home setting." Booklist

Noyes, Brian

Red Truck Bakery cookbook; gold-standard recipes from America's favorite rural bakery. Brian Noyes with Nevin Martell, photographs by Andrew Thomas Lee. Clarkson Potter/Publishers 2018 224 p. $25   **641.7**

1. Pies 2. Baking 3. Desserts 4. Cookbooks 5. Southern cooking 6. Cupcakes 7. Red Truck Bakery

ISBN 9780804189613

LC 2018002249

This cookbook, by Brian Noyes with Nevin Martell, photographs by Andrew Thomas Lee, is "full of fresh flavors, a sprinkle of homespun comfort, and a generous pinch of Americana, the recipes range from Southern classics like Flaky Buttermilk Biscuits and Mom's Walnut Chews, to local favorites like the Shenandoah Apple Cake and Appalachian Pie with Ramps and Morels. Between the keepsake recipes are charming stories of the bakery's provenance." (Publisher's note)

Raichlen, Steven

Project fire; cutting-edge techniques and sizzling recipes from the caveman porterhouse to salt slab brownie s'mores. Steven Raichlen. Workman Publishing 2018 336 p. (alk. paper) $22.95   **641.7**

1. Cooking 2. Barbecue cooking 3. Barbecuing
ISBN 9781523502769

LC 2018011117

This cookbook, by Steven Raichlen, presents "100 boldly flavored recipes that will help you turbocharge your game at the grill. Here's how to reinvent steak with reverse-seared beef tomahawks, dry-brined filets mignons, ember-charred porterhouses, and T-bones tattooed with grill marks and enriched, the way the pros do it, with melted beef fat. . . . [This book] proves that live-fire, and understanding how to master it, makes everything taste better." (Publisher's note)

Ruhlman, Michael

Ruhlman's how to braise; foolproof techniques and recipes for the home cook. Michael Ruhlman. Little, Brown & Co. 2015 147 p. color illustrations (hardcover) $25   **641.7**

1. Braising (Cooking)
ISBN 0316254134; 9780316254137

LC 2014941487

This cookbook, by Michael Ruhlman, focuses on braising. "Among the recipes featured . . . are Moroccan Lamb Tagine, Classic Yankee Pot Roast, Mexican Pork and Posole Stew with Dried Chilis, Braised Fennel, and a Corned Beef and Cabbage Braise." (Publisher's note)

"... Ruhlman (How to Roast) notes, 'There is pleasure to be had in the aroma of floured meat sizzling in hot fat.' Anyone who shares that sentiment will want to dive into this handy guide, and anyone without a Dutch oven would be well advised to purchase one along with the book." Pub Wkly

Stevens, Molly

★ **All** about braising; the art of uncomplicated cooking. Molly Stevens ; color photographs by Gentl & HyersEdge ; black-and-white illustrations by Yevgeniy Solovyev ; wine notes and selections by Tim Gaiser. 1st ed; W W Norton & Co Inc 2004 481 p. ill. (some col.) $35   **641.7**

1. Cookbooks 2. Braising (Cooking)
ISBN 0393052303; 9780393052305

LC 2004017907

James Beard Foundation Award (2005)
IACP Award (2005)

This book, by Molly Stevens, offers a cookbook dedicated to braising. "Written to instruct a cook at any level . . . , [it includes] 125 . . . recipes for meat, poultry, seafood, and vegetables, ranging from quick-braised weeknight dishes to slow-cooked weekend braises." It also includes "a thorough explanation of the principles of good braising with helpful advice on the best cuts of meat, the right choice of fish and vegetables, and the right pots." (Publisher's note)

"[T]he book contains interesting tasting notes and cultural information, and Stevens's lengthy instructions will be particularly valuable to beginners." Pub Wkly

Includes bibliographical references and index

Stone, Tuffy

Cool smoke; the art of great barbecue. by Tuffy Stone ; photographs by Ken Stone. St. Martin's Griffin 2018 304 p. (hardcover) $29.99   **641.7**

1. Outdoor cooking 2. Barbecue cooking 3. Barbecuing
ISBN 9781250137845

LC 2017055075

This cookbook, by Tuffy Stone, with photographs by Ken Stone, is a "complete guide to barbeque [cooking]. . . . Inside you'll find a wealth of barbecue information including: how to choose the right cooker, the best way to trim a cut of meat, how to prepare your own brines, rubs, and sauces, insider tips and hints for taking on the competition circuit, [and] over 100 creative, delicious recipes to make you a barbecue master." (Publisher's note)

Symon, Michael

Michael Symon's playing with fire; BBQ and more from the grill, smoker, and fireplace. Michael Symon with Douglas Trattner. Clarkson Potter/Publishers 2018 240 p. (hard cover) $30   **641.7**

1. Cooking -- Meat 2. Barbecue cooking 3. Barbecuing 4. Cooking (Meat)
ISBN 0804186588; 9780804186582

LC 2017034644

This cookbook presents barbecue and live-fire grilling recipes from Michael Symon. "The 72 finger-licking, lip-smacking recipes here draw inspiration from his favorites, including dry ribs from Memphis, wet ribs from Nashville, brisket from Texas, pork steak from St. Louis, and burnt ends from Kansas City--to name just a few--as well as the unique and now signature Cleveland-style barbecue he developed to showcase the flavors of his hometown." (Publisher's note)

"With just 42 main-dish recipes spread across the first 167 pages, the gaps are filled with an overabundance of 'pitmaster profiles,' in which barbecue chefs from across the country are briefly interviewed and their own eateries promoted. Meanwhile, Ed Anderson's color photography of savory cuts encrusted with dry rub or slathered with sauce is nearly enough to make Cleveland synonymous with mouthwatering. This is an excellent guide to live-fire cooking." Pub Wkly

641.76   Barbecuing, broiling, grilling

Bittman, Mark, 1950-

★ **How** to grill everything; simple recipes for great flame-cooked food. Mark Bittman ; photography by Chritina Holmes. Houghton Mifflin Harcourt 2018 vii, 568 p.p color illustrations (hardback) $30   **641.76**

1. Cookbooks 2. Barbecue cooking 3. Barbecuing
ISBN 9780544790827; 9780544790308

LC 2017051933

"Here's how to grill absolutely everything--from the perfect steak to cedar-plank salmon to pizza--explained in Mark Bittman's trademark simple, straightforward style. Featuring 1,000 recipes and variations, plus Bittman's practical advice on all the grilling basics, this book is an exploration of the grill's nearly endless possibilities. Recipes cover every part of the meal, including appetizers, seafood, meat and poultry, vegetables . . . , and even desserts." (Publisher's note)

"Regardless of one's grilling experience, fans of outdoor cooking will find this volume to be essential." Pub Wkly

Carruthers, John

Eat street; the ManBQue guide to making street food at home. John Carruthers, John Scholl, Jesse Valenciana. Running Press 2016 328 p. color illustrations (paperback) $23 **641.76**

1. Cooking -- Meat 2. Barbecue cooking 3. Barbecuing 4. International cooking 5. Street food -- United States
ISBN 9780762458691; 0762458690

LC 2015959425

This book, by John Carruthers, Jesse Valenciana, and John Scholl, "presents 200 recipes for . . . street food. Starting with the setups, [readers] discover how to get the most out of everything from flat-top griddles to outdoor brick ovens to earthenware pots. Then dig into the greatest hand-held grub from around the world: Philly Cheese Steaks, Pork Belly Gyoza Dumplings, Arepas, and more." (Publisher's note)

"Recommend this humorous, unconventional cookbook to readers who like meaty and fried comfort foods with a healthy dose of sarcasm." LJ

641.8   Cooking specific kinds of dishes and preparing beverages

Alexander, William

52 loaves; one man's relentless pursuit of truth, meaning, and a perfect crust. Algonquin Books of Chapel Hill 2010 339p il $23.95   **641.8**

1. Bread
ISBN 978-1-56512-583-4

LC 2009-49656

Charts the author's attempts to bake the perfect loaf of bread, including growing, harvesting, and milling his own wheat.

"Bakers will delight in his often humorous mission as he relates leaving out salt, growing his own wheat, discovering parchment paper, and splashing water into the oven in an effort to create steam. . . . This humorous memoir is recommended for anyone who has ever tried to bake a loaf." Libr J

Includes bibliographical references

Alford, Jeffrey

Flatbreads and flavors; a baker's atlas. Jeffrey Alford and Naomi Duguid. Morrow 1995 xvi, 441 p.p ill. (some col.) $21.99   **641.8**

1. Bread 2. Cookbooks 3. International cooking
ISBN 0061673269; 0688114113; 9780061673269

LC 94030892

James Beard Award (1996)

In this cookbook, "Jeffrey Alford and Naomi Duguid have found an internationally shared and nourishing element of culture and cuisine: flatbreads, humankind's simplest, oldest, and most remarkably varied form of bread. . . . In addition, they provide 150 recipes for traditional accompaniments to the flatbreads, from chutneys and curries, salsas and stews." (Publisher's note)

Includes bibliographical references (p. 421-425) and index

The **America's** test kitchen family baking book; [by] the editors at America's Test Kitchen; photography, Daniel J. Van Ackere, Carl Tremblay, Keller + Keller. America's Test Kitchen 2008 544p il $34.95   **641.8**

1. Baking 2. America's test kitchen (Television program)
ISBN 978-1-933615-22-6; 1-933615-22-2

"Expert bakers and novices scared of baking's requisite exactitude can all learn something from this hefty, all-purpose home baking volume." Publ Wkly

Anderson, Pam

Perfect one-dish dinners; all you need for easy get-togethers. photographs by Judd Pilossof. Houghton Mifflin Harcourt 2010 266p il $32   **641.8**

1. Entertaining 2. One-dish cooking

ISBN 978-0-547-19595-7

LC 2010-21447

This is an "accessible, engaging collection of meals based around a singular dish. Grouped into four sections—summer salads and grilled platters; casseroles; the roasting pan; and stews—Anderson smartly mixes classics like Osso Bucco, Paella, and Lasagna with riffs on standards like Coq Au Vin (here with white wine and spring vegetables) and a Spanish beef stew (with bell peppers, chickpeas, saffron, paprika, and orange). . . . Whether readers are new to cooking or simply looking for new ideas for meals, Anderson's winning collection is sure to encourage and inspire." Publ Wkly

Andres, Jose

Tapas; a taste of Spain in America. [by] José Andrés with Richard Wolffe. Clarkson Potter 2005 256p il $35   **641.8**

1. Appetizers 2. Spanish cooking

ISBN 1-4000-5359-5

LC 2004-27466

The author presents some of the small-plate dishes "he serves at his tapas restaurants, including traditional favorites recreated with American ingredients. . . . Recipes are organized by ingredient, from olives and olive oil to citrus to fish, shellfish, and meat, and they are mouthwatering: Oven-Roasted Potatoes and Oyster Mushrooms, for example, or Lobster with Pimentón and Olive Oil." Libr J

Includes bibliographical references

Baking illustrated; a best recipe classic. by the editors of Cook's illustrated; illustrations, John Burgoyne; photography, Carl Tremblay, Keller + Keller, Daniel Van Ackere. America's Test Kitchen 2004 515p il $35   **641.8**

1. Baking

ISBN 0-936184-75-2

"Test kitchen cooks analyzed brand-name baking ingredients and equipment and . . . make 'best buy' recommendations. . . . The test summaries preceding each recipe include both successes and failures; the resulting recipes (more than 350) cover everything from the simplest quick breads to more complex yeast breads and cookies and pastries. . . . This is the best instructional book on baking this reviewer has seen." Libr J

Bauer, Jeni Britton

Jeni's splendid ice creams at home. Artisan 2011 217p il $23.95   **641.8**

1. Ice cream, ices, etc.

ISBN 978-1-57965-436-8; 1-57965-436-3

LC 2010-39453

"This inspiring collection of seasonal ice cream recipes from Ohio-based ice cream whiz Bauer stands apart for its creative, unconventional flavors like Sweet Basil & Honeyed Pine Nut and Sweet Potato with Torched Marshmallows." Libr J

Beranbaum, Rose Levy

The **cake** bible; edited by Maria D. Guarnaschelli; photo-

graphs by Vincent Lee; foreword by Maida Heatter. Morrow 1988 555p il   **641.8**

1. Cake

ISBN 0-688-04402-6; 978-0-688-04402-2

LC 8801369

This collection of cake recipes includes "discussions on ingredients and equipment and concludes with a . . . section on the chemistry of cake baking and on making . . . professional wedding cakes." (Libr J) Bibliography. Index.

Includes bibliographical references

The **best** one-dish suppers; a best recipe classic. by the editors of Cook's Illustrated; photography, Keller + Keller, Carl Tremblay, and Daniel J. Van Ackere; illustrations, John Burgoyne. America's Test Kitchen 2011 342p il $35   **641.8**

1. One-dish cooking 2. Quick and easy cooking

ISBN 978-1-933615-81-3

"This volume presents recipes (180 of them, further clarified by 169 illustrations) for supremely simple meals (including many versions of tempting classics) prepared in one cooking vessel. There are dinners that can be made in just a sheet pan, a single pot, a dutch oven, or a slow cooker, plus stews and chilis, casseroles, and stir-frys. . . . This book could easily become a go-to resource for busy home cooks." Publ Wkly

Boyle, Tish

The **cake** book; the definitive guide to making great cakes with nearly 200 recipes. Tish Boyle ; photography by John Uher. Houghton Mifflin Harcourt 2006 376 p. ill. (some col.) $39.95   **641.8**

1. Cake 2. Cookbooks 3. Cake decorating

ISBN 0471469335; 9780471469339

LC 2005021384

This cake cookbook, written by Tish Boyle, "includes recipes ranging from pound cakes and coffee cakes to meringue, mousse, and ice cream cakes to fillings, frostings, and more. Throughout, color and black-and-white photographs and drawings show you important techniques and spectacular end results. A difficulty rating with each recipe helps you decide which to make, depending on how much time--or ambition--you have." (Publisher's note)

"Well written, easy to read, and beautifully photographed." LJ

Colicchio, Tom

'wichcraft; craft a sandwich into a meal--and a meal into a sandwich. [by] Tom Colicchio with Sisha Ortúzar; text by Rhona Silverbush; photographs by Bill Bettencourt. Clarkson Potter/Publishers 2009 208p il $27.50   **641.8**

1. Sandwiches

ISBN 978-0-609-61051-0

LC 2008-27803

The authors offer "an entire cookbook featuring the sandwiches served at . . . [their] New York restaurant, 'wichcraft. . . . This book's table of contents alone will have grab-and-go eaters and sophisticated gastronomes alike salivating." Booklist

The **Complete** book of pasta and noodles; by the editors of Cook's illustrated; preface by Christopher Kimball; illustrations by Judy Love; photographs by Daniel J. van Ackere. Potter 2000 483p il hardcover o.p. pa $19.95   **641.8**

1. Cooking -- Pasta products

ISBN 0-609-80930-X pa

LC 99-40076

This work brings "together information and recipes covering pasta's worldwide range from North America's beloved macaroni and cheese through Italy's sophisticated sauces, across China's exotic rice noodles, and up to Japan's modest Zen noodles in broth. . . . Content and organization combine to make this a superior cooking reference book for libraries." Booklist

Corriher, Shirley

BakeWise; the hows and whys of successful baking with over 200 magnificent recipes. [by] Shirley O. Corriher. Scribner 2008 532p $40   **641.8**
1. Baking
ISBN 978-1-4165-6078-4; 1-4165-6078-5

LC 2008-32681

This "collection of more than 200 recipes offers amateur and expert bakers alike clear, numbered steps and a plethora of information on ingredients, equipment and method. Invaluable troubleshooting sections solve pesky problems on everything from pale and crumbly cookies to fallen soufflés. . . . Astute references to a variety of chefs, cookbook authors and restaurants add a knowing punch to this solid collection that's sure to please bakers of all skill levels." Publ Wkly

DeMasco, Karen

The **craft** of baking; cakes, cookies, & other sweets with ideas for inventing your own. [by] Karen DeMasco & Mindy Fox; photographs by Ellen Silverman. Clarkson Potter Publishers 2009 256p il $35   **641.8**
1. Cake 2. Candy 3. Baking 4. Cookies 5. Desserts
ISBN 978-0-307-40810-5; 0-307-40810-8

"In the first sections, [DeMarco] covers ingredients and techniques accessible even to novice bakers. Then come her 'new modern-day treats,' created with 'traditional recipes and familiar home baking techniques,' e.g., Lemon Olive Cake (an interesting variation on the traditional lemon cake using butter and extra virgin olive oil). Sources are listed for hard-to-find items. Owing to DeMasco's well-respected culinary pedigree, home bakers will want this." Libr J

Desaulniers, Marcel

Death by chocolate cakes; an astonishing array of chocolate enchantment. recipes with Brett Bailey and Kelly Bailey; photography by Duane Winfield. Morrow 2000 216p il $35 **641.8**
1. Cake 2. Cooking -- Chocolate
ISBN 0-688-16297-5

LC 00-56247

This "cookbook features indulgent showstoppers, from Happy All the Time Cakes to Excessively Expressive Espresso Ecstasy, each one shown in a full-page color photograph. Although many of the recipes are complicated, instructions are detailed and clear; there are no headnotes per se to introduce these creations, but 'The Chef's Touch' section at the end of each recipe provides tips and some background." Libr J

Includes bibliographical references

Fine cooking appetizers; 200 recipes for small bites with big flavor. from the editors and contributors of Fine cooking. Taunton Press 2010 252 p. col. ill. $19.95   **641.8**
1. Cookbooks 2. Appetizers
ISBN 1600853307; 9781600853302

LC 2010028598

"In [this collection] the editors of Fine Cooking have gathered a tempting--and satisfying--range of recipes on favorite topics. . . . As always, clear instructions, full-color photos, plus tips and techniques help you get delicious results." This cookbook features 200 recipes for appetizers. (Publisher's note)

The **Gourmet** cookie book; the single best recipe from each year 1941-2009. Houghton Mifflin Harcourt 2010 161p il $18   **641.8**
1. Cookies
ISBN 978-0-547-32816-4

LC 2010-18882

This cookbook "features one recipe for every year Gourmet magazine was in business. . . . The recipes are grouped by decade, from the ration-era pluck of the 1940s (honey refrigerator cookies and Scotch oat crunchies), when the magazine was published out of a penthouse in the Plaza Hotel, to the twisted classics of the oughts (cranberry turtle bars and glittering lemon sandwich cookies). The wistful headnotes offer historical insight into our past tastes and aspirations." N Y Times Book Rev

Haedrich, Ken

★ **Pie** ; 300 tried-and-true recipes for delicious homemade pie. The Harvard Common Press 2004 639p il $37.95; pa $24.95   **641.8**
1. Baking
ISBN 1-558-32253-1; 1-558-32254-X pa

LC 2004-3635

Haedrich's "zeal and solid expertise make this book a worthy addition to the baker's bookshelf." Publ Wkly

Heatter, Maida

Maida Heatter's cookies; by Maida Heatter ; illustrations by Melanie Marder Parks. Cader Books"||"Andrews McMeel 1997 xii, 308 p.p illustrations $19.99   **641.8**
1. Baking 2. Cookies
ISBN 0836237331; 1449401155; 9781449401153

LC 97031043

This book is a "classic cookie collection from Maida Heatter, James Beard Lifetime Hall of Fame member. . . . [It] offers 225 classic cookie recipes for drop cookies, bar cookies, icebox cookies, rolled cookies, hand-formed cookies, dessert crackers, ice creams, sauces, and more, accompanied by two-color, line-drawn illustrated pages." (Publisher's note)

Hellmich, Mittie, 1960-

Ultimate bar book; the comprehensive guide to over 1,000 cocktails. by Mittie Hellmich ; illustrations by Arthur Mount. Chronicle Books 2006 474 p. ill. (jacket) $19.95   **641.8**
1. Cocktails 2. Bartending
ISBN 0811843513; 9780811843515

LC 2005030720

This alcoholic mixed-drinks guidebook, by Mittie Hellmich, features "essential-to-know topics such as barware, tools, and mixing tips. . . . Illustrations show precisely what type of glass should be used for each drink. With dozens of recipes for garnishes, rims, infusions, and syrups; punches, gelatin shooters, hot drinks, and non-alcoholic beverages." (Publisher's note)

Includes bibliographical references and indexes

Hensperger, Beth

The **best** quick breads; 150 recipes for muffins, scones, shortcakes, gingerbreads, cornbreads, coffeecakes, and more. Beth Hensperger. Harvard Common Press 2000 256p pa $22.95   **641.8**
1. Bread
ISBN 1-55832-171-3

LC 00-36962

First published 1994 by Chronicle Books with title: The art of quick breads

This book includes about 150 recipes. "In addition to quick loaves, both sweet and savory, there are waffles, dumplings, biscuits, popovers, and a variety of other easy baked goods, along with some tasty accompaniments, such as the Fruit Salsa for her Hopi Blue Corn Hotcakes." Libr J

Hirigoyen, Gerald

Pintxos; small plates in the Basque tradition. [by] Gerald Hirigoyen with Lisa Weiss; photography by Maren Caruso. Ten Speed Press 2009 201p il $24.95   **641.8**

1. Cooking 2. Basque cooking
ISBN 978-1-58008-922-7; 1-58008-922-4

LC 2008-43518

Lebovitz, David

The **perfect** scoop; ice creams, sorbets, granitas, and sweet accompaniments. David Lebovitz ; photography by Lara Hata. Ten Speed Press 2007 256 p. il (pbk) $18.99; (hbk) $24.99   **641.8**

1. Desserts 2. Cookbooks 3. Ice cream, ices, etc.
ISBN 9781580082198; 9781580088084; 158008219X

LC 2006037610

This cookbook, by David Lebovitz, offers a "guide to the pleasures of homemade ice creams, sorbets, granitas, and more. With an emphasis on intense and sophisticated flavors and a bountiful helping of the author's expert techniques, this collection of frozen treats ranges from classic . . . to comforting . . . , contemporary . . . to cutting edge." (Publisher's note)

"The author's 25 years of experience as a frozen-dessert maker are put to excellent use in this wittily written, detailed volume. Step-by-step photos and advice on selecting an ice cream machine will reassure ice cream amateurs." Pub Wkly

Matheson, Christie

Flour; spectacular recipes from Boston's Flour Bakery + Cafe. by Joanne Chang, with Christie Matheson ; photographs by Keller + Keller. Chronicle Books 2010 319 p. col. ill. (hbk.) $35   **641.8**

1. Flour 2. Baking 3. Cookbooks 4. Baked products 5. Flour Bakery + Cafe 6. Baking -- Massachusetts -- Boston 7. Cooking -- Massachusetts -- Boston
ISBN 081186944X; 9780811869447

LC 2011377998

This baking cookbook, by Joanne Chang with Christie Matheson, features Boston, Massachusetts-based "Flour Bakery-owner Joanne Chang's repertoire of baked goods. . . . Almost 150 Flour recipes such as Milky Way Tart and Dried Fruit Focaccia are included, plus Joanne's essential baking tips." (Publisher's note)

Medrich, Alice

Chewy gooey crispy crunchy melt-in-your-mouth cookies. Artisan Books 2010 384p il $25.95   **641.8**

1. Cookies
ISBN 978-1-57965-397-2

LC 2010-19491

"Medrich presents a compendium of exciting and enticing cookie recipes that reflects every aspect of our widening culinary landscape. . . . The recipes are organized by texture, hence the title, but there's also a section grouping cookies into categories like those containing whole grains, those that keep at least two weeks, ridiculously quick and easy cookies, and cookies to make with kids. This book has redesigned and

reframed the often-overlooked cookie and is a boon to the modern, conscious baker." Publ Wkly

Mix shake stir; cocktails for the home bar: recipes from Danny Meyer's acclaimed New York City restaurants. foreward by Danny Meyer. Little, Brown 2009 223p il $29.99   **641.8**

1. Cocktails
ISBN 978-0-316-04512-4; 0-316-04512-8

LC 2008-934947

Restauranteur Meyers "delivers a terrific collection of 140 tempting recipes for cocktails created by bartenders in his award-winning dining establishments. Included are old favorites like the Ritz as well as new classics like the Winter Mojito, and the book's clear instructions and luscious photographs will inspire even nondrinkers to pick up a cocktail shaker. As a bonus, basic tips on mixing drinks, recipes for simple syrups and garnishes, and a concise collection of recipes for bar snacks are offered." Libr J

Nevins, Jerry

Sloshies; 102 boozy cocktails straight from the freezer. Jerry Nevins of Snow & Co. Workman Publishing Co. 2017 152 p. (hardcover; alk. paper) $14.95   **641.8**

1. Cocktails 2. Alcoholic beverages 3. Blenders (Cooking) 4. Slushies (Beverages)
ISBN 9780761189466; 9781523500574; 0761189467

LC 2017024296

This book, by Jerry Nevins, illustrated by Edward McGowan, "features more than 100 innovative refreshers guaranteed to jazz up (and cool down) backyard parties, barbecues, or any gathering with family and friends. And they are so easy to make: Based on a simple granita technique, sloshies require little to no special equipment. Just mix the ingredients, stick them in the freezer, and wait until they're slushy." (Publisher's note)

Ojakangas, Beatrice

The **Best** Casserole cookbook ever; by Beatrice Ojakangas; photographs by Susie Cushner. Chronicle Books 2008 640 p. col. ill. (alk. paper) $24.95   **641.8**

1. Baking 2. Cookbooks 3. Casserole cooking
ISBN 0811856240; 9780811856249

LC 2007042019

This cookbook, by Beatrice Ojakangas, with photography by Susie Cushner, is dedicated to baking casseroles. "From a breakfast of Eggs Florentine to a dinner of Pork Chops with Apple Stuffing, soon even the most casserole-wary cook will be dishing about these delights. Yummy treats like Parmesan and Sun-Dried Tomato Quiche and Strawberry Rhubarb Crisp are just right for parties. Even appetizers are reinvented in casserole form!" (Publisher's note)

Parsons, Brad Thomas

Bitters; a spirited history of a classic cure-all, with cocktails, recipes, and formulas. Brad Thomas Parsons ; photographs by Ed Anderson. Ten Speed Press 2011 231 p. col. ill. $24.99   **641.8**

1. Cocktails 2. Alcohol -- History 3. Alcoholic beverages 4. Bitters
ISBN 1580083595; 9781580083591

LC 2011017774

IACP Award (2012)
James Beard Award (2012)

A brief history of bitters -- A bitters boom -- Making your own bitters -- Setting up your bar -- Bitters hall of fame -- Old-guard cocktails

-- New-look cocktails -- Bitters in the kitchen

This book, by Brad Thomas Parsons with photography by Ed Anderson, "traces the history of the world's most storied elixir, [bitters,] from its earliest 'snake oil' days to its near evaporation after Prohibition to its ascension as a beloved (and at times obsessed-over) ingredient on the contemporary bar scene." (Publisher's note)

Includes bibliographical references and index

Pasta, atlante dei prodotti tipici/English

Encyclopedia of pasta; translated by Maureen B. Fant; with a foreword by Carol Field. University of California Press 2009 xxi, 374p il map (California studies in food and culture) $29.95   **641.8**

1. Italian cooking 2. Reference books 3. Cooking -- Pasta products 4. Pasta products -- Encyclopedias

ISBN 978-0-520-25522-7

LC 2009-10522

This book provides "a complete history of pasta in Italy, showcasing more than 300 types of pasta—from bucatini and gnocchetti to tortellini and ziti. . . . Each entry is nicely displayed in a box and includes an overview of each pasta type: the primary ingredients, preparation techniques, the different names for each kind of pasta, how it is served, the region where it is found, and the author's remarks. . . . This wonderful resource is destined to become the definitive book on pasta. It succeeds both as a scholarly achievement and as an entertaining and authentic overview of Italian history and geography." Libr J

Includes bibliographical references

Peterson, James

Baking. Ten Speed Press 2009 378p il $40   **641.8**

1. Baking

ISBN 978-1-58008-991-3

"This workhorse of a guidebook . . . is a worthy baking school between covers. . . . The work features over 300 recipes, mostly classics based in the French tradition. The five chapters—Cakes; Pies, Tarts and Pastries; Cookies; Breads, Quick Breads, and Bread-based Desserts; and Custards, Soufflés, Fruit Curds and Mousses—include a comprehensive overview, sidebars on techniques and recipes designed to teach techniques that can be used in more than the recipe listed." Publ Wkly

Robertson, Chad

Tartine; by Elisabeth M. Prueitt and Chad Robertson ; foreword by Alice Waters ; photographs by France Ruffenach. Chronicle Books 2006 223 p. ill. (chiefly col.) $35   **641.8**

1. Pastry 2. Desserts 3. Cookbooks 4. Tartine (Bakery)

ISBN 0811851508; 9780811851503

LC 2006004651

In this cookbook, "pastry chef Elisabeth Prueitt and . . . baker Chad Robertson share not only their fabulous recipes, but also the secrets and expertise that transform a delicious homemade treat into a great one." Recipes featured include "moist Brioche Bread Pudding; luscious Banana Cream Pie; [and] the sweet-tart perfection of Apple Crisp. . . . Practical advice comes in the form of handy Kitchen Notes. These "hows" and "whys" convey the authors' know-how." (Publisher's note)

Tartine bread; photographs by Eric Wolfinger. Chronicle Books 2010 304p il $40   **641.8**

1. Bread

ISBN 978-0-8118-7041-2

"This 'baker's guidebook' is divided into four parts: Basic Country Bread; Semolina and Whole-Wheat Breads; Baguettes and Enriched Breads; and Day-Old Bread. Robertson's basic recipe is explained in depth with numbered steps, and consists of making a natural leaven and baking in a cast-iron cooker. The author's passionate tone and tales of baking apprenticeships, along with top-notch step-by-step photos, elevate the title from mere manual to enjoyable read." Publ Wkly

Sax, Richard

★ **Classic** home desserts; a treasury of heirloom and contemporary recipes from around the world. Richard Sax ; photography by Alan Richardson. Houghton Mifflin Harcourt 2010 648 p. col il $35   **641.8**

1. Desserts 2. Cookbooks 3. International cooking

ISBN 0618057080; 9780618057085

LC 2010025552

IACP Cookbook Award (1995)
James Bead Award (1995)

This dessert cookbook, by Richard Sax with photography by Alan Richardson, winner of the James Beard Award and the Julia Child Award, offers "350 of the best and most beloved home desserts. Everything the cook longs for is here: cobblers and crisps, cakes and cookies, puddings and soufflés, pies and pastries, ice creams and sauces." (Publisher's note)

Includes bibliographical references and index

Schreiber, Cory

Rustic fruit desserts; crumbles, buckles, cobblers, pandowdies, and more. [by] Cory Schreiber and Julie Richardson; photography by Sara Remington. Ten Speed Press 2009 164p il $22   **641.8**

1. Desserts 2. Cooking -- Fruit

ISBN 978-1-58008-976-0; 1-58008-976-3

LC 2008-49349

"A seasonal mini-bible that goes beyond basics." N Y Times Book Rev

Tosi, Christina, 1981-

Momofuku Milk Bar; Christina Tosi. 1st ed.; Clarkson Potter 2011 p. cm. $35   **641.8**

1. Baking 2. Desserts 3. Momofuku Milk Bar

ISBN 978-0-307-72049-8

LC 2011007720

"Momofuku Milk Bar finally shares the recipes for these now-legendary riffs on childhood flavors and down-home classics—all essentially derived from ten mother recipes—along with the compelling narrative of the unlikely beginnings of this quirky bakery's success. It all started one day when Momofuku founder David Chang asked Christina to make a dessert for dinner that night. Just like that, the pastry program at Momofuku began, and Christina's playful desserts helped the restaurants earn praise from theNew York Times and the Michelin Guide and led to the opening of Milk Bar, which now draws fans from around the country and the world." (Publisher's note)

Walter, Carole

Great cookies; secrets to sensational sweets. Carole Walter ; photographs by Duane Winfield. 1st ed; Clarkson Potter 2003 418 p. col. ill. $35   **641.8**

1. Cookbooks 2. Cookies

ISBN 0609609696; 9780609609699

LC 2003007633

IACP Cookbook Award Winner (2004)

This cookbook, by Carole Walter with photography byDuane Winfield, is "packed with more than 200 . . . recipes and more than 150 . . . photographs [of cookies,] . . . from traditional favorites like Snickerdoodles, Oatmeal Raisin, and Favorite Lemon Squares to future stars of the cookie jar like the trail mix-inspired Teton Trailers and chewy, chocolaty Midnight Macaroons." (Publisher's note)

Includes bibliographical references (p. 404) and index

Wells, Patricia

Salad as a meal; healthy main-dish salads for every season. Patricia Wells ; photography by Jeff Kauck. William Morrow 2011 360 p. illustrations $34.99   **641.8**

1. Salads

ISBN 006123883X; 9780061238833

LC 2010027043

This book, by Patricia Wells is a "definitive guide to creating delicious and hearty salads for any occasion—including more than 150 recipes and gorgeous color photographs. . . . You can experience a whole world in a salad—with tender greens, savory meat, seafood, and vegetable accompaniments, and versatile dressings—and salad-friendly sides such as homemade bread and home-cured olives." (Publisher's note)

"Given Wells's high profile and the book's useful focus, this can't miss wherever cookbooks are popular." LJ

Zabar, Tracey

One sweet cookie; celebrated chefs share favorite recipes. photography by Ellen Silverman. Rizzoli 2011 191p il $30   **641.8**

1. Cookies

ISBN 978-0-8478-3666-6

LC 2011927545

"When cookie-obsessed baker Zabar couldn't convince friends to participate in a cookie swap, she orchestrated a virtual exchange, the result of which is this outstanding collection of recipes from more than 50 well-known New York City chefs. . . . [It features] contributions from Dorie Greenspan, Michael Laiskonis, Maury Rubin, Laurent Tourondel, and others." Libr J

Includes bibliographical references

641.81 Side dishes, sauces, garnishes

Baker, Lucy

Fat witch bake sale; 67 recipes from the beloved Fat Witch Bakery for your next bake sale or party. Patricia Helding with Lucy Baker. Rodale Books 2014 184 p. color illustrations (hardback) $22.99   **641.81**

1. Baking 2. Baked products 3. Fat Witch Bakery

ISBN 1623362261; 9781623362263

LC 2014038513

This cookbook, by Patricia Helding, presents a "collection of yummy brownies, blondies, barks, bars, and more . . . along with tips and tricks for packaging and selling them at your next bake sale. Here are mouthwatering recipes for Pecan Caramel Brownies; Red Velvet Brownies; Five Layer Chocolate Bars; Jelly Blondies; Cinnamon Bars; Pumpkin Oatmeal Bars; Coconut Macadamia Cookies; uniquely grownup flavors like Fruitcake Brownies and Rum Raisin Spice Bars; and even gluten-free treats." (Publisher's note)

Beranbaum, Rose Levy

★ The **baking** Bible; Rose Levy Beranbaum. Houghton Mifflin Harcourt 2014 576 p. color illustrations (hardback) $40   **641.81**

1. Baking 2. Cookbooks

ISBN 1118338618; 9781118338612

LC 2014016319

IACP Cookbook Award: Baking: Savory or Sweet (2015)

"With all-new recipes for the best cakes, pies, tarts, cookies, candies, pastries, breads, and more, this magnum opus draws from [author] Rose [Levy Beranbaum's] passion and expertise in every category of baking. As is to be expected from the woman who's been called 'the most meticulous cook who ever lived,' each sumptuous recipe is truly foolproof--with detail-oriented instructions that eliminate guesswork, 'plan-aheads,' ingenious tips, and highlights for success." (Publisher's note)

"Berenbaum successfully bridges the gap between popular home baking collections and professional texts." LJ

★ **Rose's** baking basics; Rose Levy Beranbaum ; photography by Matthew Septimus. Houghton Mifflin Harcourt 2018 400 p. (paper over board) $35   **641.81**

1. Pies 2. Baking 3. Pastry 4. Cooking 5. Cookbooks 6. Bread 7. Cookies

ISBN 9780544816220

LC 2017058732

In this cookbook, by Rose Levy Beranbaum, "you will be able to easily make perfect brownies, banana bread, holiday pies, birthday cakes, homemade bread, and more, with recipes including: Chocolate Sheet Cake with Ganache Frosting, Peanut Butter and Jelly Thumbprints, Beer Bread, Apple Walnut Muffins, Peach Cobbler, Milk Chocolate Caramel Tart, and more. Throughout, Rose shares her unique tips and methods for unlocking the secrets to the best flavors and foolproof results." (Publisher's note)

"Instructions for creating related toppings and fillings such as classic ganache, along with solutions for problems during the baking process, will help guide new bakers to create treats such as basic chocolate cupcakes, apple cinnamon coffee cake, and butter biscuits. Lavish step-by-step photographs and storing information accompany each recipe." - Library Journal

Black, Sarah

One dough, ten breads; making great bread by hand. Sarah Black ; photography by Lauren Volo. Houghton Mifflin Harcourt Publishing Co. 2016 224 p. color illustrations (hardcover) $25   **641.81**

1. Bread 2. Baking

ISBN 9780470260951

LC 2015004574

This bread cookbook, by Sarah Black with photography by Lauren Volo, offers an "introduction to making bread by hand, from one easy dough to ten classic loaves to infinite possibilities. . . . instructor Sarah Black starts with the simplest 'plain white' dough, then makes small changes to ingredients, proportions, and shapes to take the reader through ten 'foundation' breads." (Publisher's note)

"Black, who believes "getting your hands in the dough is the best way to learn about bread," provides easy-to-follow directions for 10 types of bread, each created from one dough and with less than 30 minutes of active time." Pub Wkly

Day, Cheryl

Back in the Day Bakery, made with love; more than 100 recipes and make-it-yourself projects to create and share. Cheryl Day and Griffith Day. Artisan Books 2015 312 p. color illustrations $24.95   **641.81**

1. Baking 2. Cookbooks 3. Cake 4. Pies 5. Back in the Day Bakery (Savannah, Ga.)

ISBN 1579655564; 9781579655563

LC 2014035874

This baking cookbook, by Cheryl Day and Griffith Day, "features more than 100 . . . recipes, including some of the[ir] bakery's most requested treats, such as Star Brownies and the Cakette Party Cake, as well as savories like Chive Parmigiano-Reggiano Popovers and Rosemary Focaccia. Cheryl and Griff share their baking techniques and also show readers how to put together whimsical decorations, like a marshmallow chandelier and a best-in-show banner." (Publisher's note)

"Though the Days are wordy at times, the narrative is instructive and warming. The inclusion of crafts like a marshmallow chandelier and a "keepsake cake topper" seems jarring rather than jovial, the only off note. This is a terrific sequel, and fans of Southern baking (not to mention baking in general) will want to add it to their collection." Pub Wkly

Includes bibliographical references and index

Daykin, Rosie

Butter baked goods; nostalgic recipes from a little neighborhood bakery. Rosie Daykin ; photography by Janis Nicolay. Alfred A. Knopf 2015 272 p. color illustrations (hardcover) $29.95 **641.81**
    1. Baking 2. Cooking 3. Cake 4. Pastry 5. Baked products
    ISBN 1101875089; 9781101875087

                      LC 2014039534

This cookbook by Rosie Daykin "has simple instructions written in an accessible and easy-to-follow style, plus tips on how to stock your pantry and your toolbox with everything that you'll need to get started. Rosie's baking is not about trickery . . . but about great-tasting, homemade treats that celebrate life's milestones: birthdays, Thanksgiving, Christmas, Easter, baby showers, bridal showers, or just that gloomy afternoon when you need a little pick-me-up." (Publisher's note)

"Daykin's enchanting collection of traditional goodies made from scratch (with plenty of butter, sugar, and heavy cream) can help home bakers improve their skills and expand their repertoire."

Food52 baking; 60 sensational treats you can pull off in a snap. by the editors of Food52 ; photography by James Ransom. Ten Speed Press 2015 172 p. color illustrations (hardback) $22.99 **641.81**
    1. Baking 2. Desserts
    ISBN 1607748010; 9781607748014

                      LC 2015027663

This cookbook "curated by the editors of Food52, [shows how] you can have homemade treats far superior to the store-bought variety, even when it feels like you're too busy to turn on the oven. From Brown Butter Cupcake Brownies to 'Cuppa Cuppa Sticka' Peach and Blueberry Cobbler, these sixty reliable, easy-to-execute recipes won't have you hunting down special equipment and hard-to-find ingredients." (Publisher's note)

"A troubleshooting guide collects tips scattered through the book, explaining how to stale fresh bread in a hurry, how to pit cherries without a cherry pitter, and how to package cookies for the mail. This title may just become that one baking book kept out on the counter for use time and time again." Pub Wkly

Forkish, Ken

Flour water salt yeast; the fundamentals of artisan bread and pizza. Ken Forkish ; photographs by alan Weiner. Ten Speed Press 2012 265 p. col. ill. (hardback) $35 **641.81**
    1. Bread 2. Pizza 3. Baking 4. Cookbooks
    ISBN 160774273X; 9781607742739; 9781607742746

                      LC 2012012080

IACP Cookbook Award (2013)
James Beard Foundation Award: Baking and Dessert (2013)

This book, by Ken Forkish, is "[d]ivided into four sections ('The Principles of Artisan Bread,' 'Basic Bread Recipes,' 'Levain Bread Recipes,' and 'Pizza Recipes'), with recipes broken down by breads made with store-bought yeast, breads made with long-fermented simple doughs, and doughs made with pre-ferments. . . . [The] book presents recipes accessible to novices, while providing a different approach for making dough to experienced bakers." (Publishers Weekly)

Fromartz, Samuel

  ★ **In** search of the perfect loaf; a home baker's odyssey. Samuel Fromartz. Viking 2014 256 p. illustrations (hardback) $26.95 **641.81**
    1. Bread
    ISBN 0670025615; 9780670025619

                      LC 2014004522

In this memoir, journalist Samuel Fromartz "was offered the assignment of a lifetime: to travel to France to work in a boulangerie. So began his quest to hone not just his homemade baguette . . . but his knowledge of bread, from seed to table. For the next four years, Fromartz traveled across the United States and Europe, perfecting his sourdough in California, his whole grain rye in Berlin, and his country wheat in the South of France." (Publisher's note)

"Richly detailed history and lively anecdotes make this book a consummate celebration of the deceptively simple loaf of bread." Kirkus

Includes bibliographical references and index

Goldman, Duff

Duff Bakes; Duff Goldman. HarperCollins 2014 304 p. color illustrations $27.50 **641.81**
    1. Cake 2. Baking 3. Pastry 4. Cookies
    ISBN 0062349805; 9780062349804

This book, by celebrity baker Duff Goldman, is a "full-color baking book filled with more than 100 recipes for irresistible must-bake favorites, from cakes to cookies to brownies to muffins to breads. . . . [It] includes chapters on different types of pastry dough, a variety of cookies, brownies, muffins, bread, biscuits, pies, cakes and cake decorating, gluten-free and vegan desserts, and much more." (Publisher's note)

"Rounded out with plenty of salient tips on everything from selecting the right blowtorch (hit the hardware store) to getting cheesecake out of a cake pan (briefly warm the bottom over the stove top), Goldman and Gonzalez's thoughtful instructions are sure to inspire and embolden readers." Pub Wkly

Haedrich, Ken

The **harvest** baker; 150 sweet & savory recipes clebrating the fresh-picked flavors of fruits, herb & vegetables. Ken Haedrich ; photography by Johnny Autry. Storey Publishing 2017 303 p. color illustrations (pbk.; alk. paper) $19.95 **641.81**
    1. Bread 2. Baking 3. Pastry 4. Cookbooks
    ISBN 9781612127682; 9781612127675

                      LC 2016059746

"Author Ken Haedrich serves up 150 delicious baked goods that are full of fresh fruits, vegetables, and herbs and go far beyond zucchini bread and carrot cake. From Bacon, Cheddar, and Fresh Corn Muffins to Fresh Fennel and Italian Sausage Pizza, Spaghetti Squash and Parmesan Quiche, and Brown Sugar Rhubarb Tart Squares, these scrumptious recipes add nutrition plus amazing flavor to every meal of the day." (Publisher's note)

"Renowned author and teacher Haedrich (Dinner Pies) returns with a new collection of hearty baked goods featuring garden and farm fresh produce." LJ

Hertzberg, Jeff

Holiday and celebration bread in five minutes a day; sweet and decadent baking for every occasion. Zoë François and Jeff Hertzberg, M.D. ; photographs by Sarah Kieffer and Zoë François. St. Martin's Press 2018 400 p. (hardcover) $35 **641.81**
    1. Bread 2. Baking 3. Holiday cooking
ISBN 9781250077561

LC 2018017182

This cookbook, by Zoë François and Jeff Hertzberg, presents quick and easy bread baking methods for the holiday season. "The book is chock-full of fragrant, yeasted treats made for celebrations and special occasions. . . . [It] has color photos of every bread and includes step-by-step collages." (Publisher's note)

Kulaga, Agatha

Ovenly; sweet and salty recipes from New York's most creatvie bakery. Agatha Kulaga & Erin Patinkin ; photography by Winona Barton-Ballentine. Harlequin Nonfiction 2014 240 p. color illustrations (alk. paper) $29.95 **641.81**
    1. Bread 2. Baking 3. Baked products 4. Ovenly (Bakery)
ISBN 0373892950; 9780373892952

LC 2014005173

This cookbook by Erin Patinkin and Agatha Kulaga is based on "Ovenly . . . an award-winning bakery headquartered in Greenpoint, Brooklyn. Since 2010, their innovative baked goods have found their way into cafés, restaurants and stores nationwide." (Publisher's note)

"Complemented by an attractive design and step-by-step photographs of important techniques, this is a satisfying everyday baking collection—perfect for readers who like substantial baked goods with a salty streak." LJ

McDowell, Erin Jeanne

The **fearless** baker; simple secrets for baking like a pro. Erin Jeanne McDowell. Houghton Mifflin Harcourt 2017 384 p. $30 **641.81**
    1. Baking 2. Cookies 3. Cookbooks
ISBN 0544791436; 9780544791435

In this cookbook, author Erin Jeanne McDowell "shares insider tips and techniques that make desserts taste as good as they look. With recipes from flourless cocoa cookies and strawberry-filled popovers (easy), through apple cider pie and black-bottom crème brûlée (medium), . . . and 'Why It Works,' 'Pro Tip,' and make-ahead sidebars with each recipe, this exciting, carefully curated collection will appeal to beginning and experienced bakers alike." (Publisher's note)

"Comprehensive tips on baking and decorating cakes and pies accompany tempting recipes, including for pound cupcakes made with honey-caramel glaze, mocha cake with a coffee and white chocolate ganache, and a simple cider caramel apple pie. Her clearly written recipes and tips, explained in a friendly, encouraging voice, will inspire confidence in experienced and novice bakers alike." (Pub Wkly)

Peacock, Julie

The **soup** club cookbook; feed your friends, feed your family, feed yourself. Courtney Allison, Tina Carr, Caroline Laskow, and Julie Peacock. Clarkson Potter Publishers 2014 240 p. illustrations (mostly color) (paperback) $25 **641.81**
    1. Soups 2. One-dish cooking 3. One-dish meals
ISBN 0770434622; 9780770434625; 9780770434632

LC 2014009496

In this book, authors Courtney Allison, Tina Carr, Caroline Laskow, and Julie Peacock "share not only their formula for starting a soup club--which gives you at least three meals every month when you don't have to worry about dinner--but also 150 fantastic recipes for soups and sides and storing tips for stretching those meals across the week." (Publisher's note)

Peterson, James

★ Sauces; classical and contemporary sauce making. James Peterson. 4th edition Houghton Mifflin Harcourt 2017 xxi, 666 p.p color illustrations $60 **641.81**
    1. Sauces 2. Cookbooks
ISBN 0544819829; 9780544819825

LC 2017449213

James Bead Award (1992)

This cookbook, by James Peterson, is the "former winner of the prestigious James Beard Cookbook-of-the-Year award and the ultimate reference for saucemaking. . . . With more 325 recipes in all, [it] includes all-new chapters on Asian sauces and pasta sauces, plus new recipes that cater to lighter, contemporary tastes. Includes a 32-page color insert with more than 100 color photos of sauce-making techniques." (Publisher's note)

Includes bibliographical references and index

Robertson, Chad

Tartine Book No. 3; modern, ancient, classic, whole. Chad Robertson. Chronicle Books 2013 336 p. color illustrations $40 **641.81**
    1. Baking 2. Cookbooks 3. Alternative grains 4. Pastry 5. Cooking (Bread) 6. Tartine (Bakery)
ISBN 1452114307; 9781452114309

LC 2012276745

This book, by Chad Robertson, the third cookbook published "from Tartine Bakery & Cafe. . . . is a revolutionary, and altogether timely, exploration of baking with whole grains. The narrative of Chad Robertson's search for ancient flavors in heirloom grains is interwoven with 85 recipes for whole-grain versions of Tartine favorites." (Publisher's note)

"Acclaimed baker and Tartine Bakery cofounder Robertson's third cookbook is as visually impressive as its predecessors. . . . Its recipes, however, are far more challenging, providing spare instructions and assuming considerable technical knowledge. Robertson breaks up chapters of intriguing and innovative breads, crispbreads, and pastries (e.g., sprouted quinoa kamut bread, lemon-poppy-kefir pound cake) with accounts of baking-related travels in Denmark, Sweden, Germany, Austria, France, and Mexico." LJ

Smith, Ed

On the side; a sourcebook of inspiring side dishes. Ed.Smith. St. Martin's Press 2018 352 p. $28 **641.81**
    1. Cooking 2. Cookbooks 3. Gastronomy
ISBN 140887315X; 9781408873151

This book, by Ed Smith, discusses how "our side dishes have the potential to be as inspirational as the main event itself. . . . Here it's the 'two veg' rather than the meat which are given the spotlight: you'll find 140 inspiring recipes and insightful tips to make your pulses, roots, vegetables and greens dazzle in their own right." (Publisher's note)

Symon, Michael

Michael Symon's 5 in 5 for every season; 150 quick dinners, sides, and holiday dishes. Michael Symon, with Douglas Trattner ; photographs by Jennifer May. Clarkson Potter 2015 255 p. color illustrations $19.99 **641.81**
    1. Cooking 2. Seasons 3. Holiday cooking 4. Dinners and dining 5. Side dishes (Cooking) 6. Quick and easy cooking
ISBN 0804186561; 9780804186568

LC 2015006128

This cookbook by Michael Symon "delivers 165 quick, easy, fresh recipes organized by season with an entire section devoted to making the holidays simpler than ever. Each chapter features inspired main courses as well as recipes for sides and 5 fun ways to celebrate the season, including no-bake summer fruit desserts and spiked drinks to warm up with in winter." (Publisher's note)

Volger, Lukas

Bowl; vegetarian recipes for ramen, pho, bibimbap, dumplings, and other one-dish meals. Lukas Volger; photography by Michael Harlan Turkell. Houghton Mifflin Harcourt 2016 256 p. color illustrations (paperback) $25   **641.81**
    1. Soups 2. Asian cooking 3. Vegetarian cooking 4. Stews 5. Cooking, Asian 6. One-dish meals
    ISBN 0544325281; 9780544325289

LC 2015037777

This cookbook tells how author Lukas Volger's "ramen explorations led him from a simple bowl of miso ramen to a glorious summer ramen with corn broth, tomatoes, and basil. From there, he went on to the Vietnamese noodle soup pho, with combinations like caramelized spring onions, peas, and baby bok choy. Volger also includes many tips, techniques, and indispensable base recipes perfected over years of cooking, including broths, handmade noodles, sauces, and garnishes." (Publisher's note)

"A go-to cookbook for Asian-inspired vegetarian soups, noodle bowls, and dumplings." Library Journal

Volland, Susan

Mastering Sauces; The Home Cook's Guide to New Techniques for Fresh Flavors. by Susan Volland. W W Norton & Co Inc 2015 464 p. 16 plates; color illustrations $39.95   **641.81**
    1. Sauces
    ISBN 0393241858; 9780393241853

LC 2015017677

This cookbook, by Susan Volland, "presents sauce-making in a whole new way. . . . In addition to over 150 recipes that reflect today's tastes for seasonal produce, international ingredients, and alternative dietary choices, there are dozens of tips and tables suggesting ways to adapt and customize sauces." (Publisher's note)

"This is an excellent culinary reference with a thoroughness that recalls titles such as Shirley Corriher's Cookwise and Karen Page and Andrew Dornenburg's The Flavor Bible. Highly recommended, along with Martha Holmberg's Modern Sauces." LJ

Weber, Kathleen

Della Fattoria bread; Kathleen Weber ; with Amy Albert and Amy Vogler ; photographs by Ed Anderson. Workman Publishing Company, Inc. 2014 336 p. illustrations $29.95 **641.81**
    1. Bread 2. Della Fattoria (Bakery)
    ISBN 1579655319; 9781579655310

LC 2014004630

James Beard Foundation Award Nominee: Baking and Dessert (2015)

This book, by Kathleen Weber, "is filled with . . . bread-baking secrets . . . and features recipes for all levels of bakers. Beginners can learn to bake yeasted breads using pans. Advanced bakers can jump right into making free-form loaves of naturally leavened breads in all shapes and flavors. Other chapters include recipes for enriched breads like brioche and challah; pre-fermented breads, including baguettes; and crackers, breadsticks, naan, and more." (Publisher's note)

"Highly recommended for serious home bakers, especially those

looking to move on from easier titles such as Jeff Hertzberg and Zoe Francois's Artisan Bread in Five Minutes a Day." LJ
    Includes an index

641.813   Soups

Manning, Ivy

Easy soups from scratch with breads to match; 70 recipes to pair and share. Ivy Manning ; photographs by Dina Avila. Chronicle Books 2017 175 p. color illustrations (hc; alk. paper) $24.95   **641.813**
    1. Bread 2. Soups 3. Quick and easy cooking
    ISBN 9781452156729; 145215502X; 9781452155029

LC 2016032627

This cookbook, by Ivy Manning, with photographs by Dina Avila, "shows home cooks how to . . . [cook soups] under an hour. . . . [The book] makes it simple to create delicious, nourishing soups and warm, toothsome breads for any day of the week with straight-forward, time-saving recipes. With 70 soups and breads to mix and match, soup lovers can choose from cozy classics . . . [to] international flavors." (Publisher's note)

641.815   Bread and bread-like foods

Dodge, Abigail Johnson

The everyday baker; recipes & techniques for foolproof baking breads, pastries, cakes, pies, cookies, and more. Abigail Johnson Dodge. Taunton Press, Inc. 2015 624 p. color illustrations $40   **641.815**
    1. Bread 2. Baking 3. Desserts
    ISBN 9781621138105

LC 2015032688

IACP Cookbook Award Winner: Baking: Savory or Sweet (2016)

This cookbook, by Abigail Johnson Dodge, is a "resource for anyone who likes, loves, or lives to bake. This definitive collection serves as a delicious roadmap through a baker's sweet and savory kitchen and includes over 176 foolproof, innovative recipes all featuring must-know tips and techniques, comprehensive instructions, 80 stunning photographs of the finished dishes, and almost 1,000 step-by-step photographs designed to revolutionize the home baking experience." (Publisher's note)

"Filled with step-by-step photographs of essential techniques and precise recipes that include both weight and volume measurements, her book will help home bakers of all skill levels feel more confident when making easy and advanced treats." LJ

Emberling, Amy

Zingerman's Bakehouse; by Amy Emberling and Frank Carollo ; photographs by Antonis Achilleos. Chronicle Books 2017 255 p. illustrations (some color) (hc; alk. paper) $29.95   **641.815**
    1. Bread 2. Baking 3. Zingerman's Bakehouse
    ISBN 9781452157009; 1452156581; 9781452156583

LC 2016057669

In this book, by Amy Emberling and Frank Carollo, "Zingerman's Bakehouse in Ann Arbor, has fed a fan base across the United States and beyond with their chewy-sweet brownies and gingersnaps, famous sour cream coffee cake, and fragrant loaves of Jewish rye, challah, and sourdough. It's no wonder Zingerman's is a cultural and culinary institution. Now, for the first time, to celebrate their 25th anniversary, the Zinger-

man's bakers share 65 meticulously tested, carefully detailed recipes "
(Publisher's note)

"All home bakers will recognize its merit, made visible in precise recipes . . . stunning photographs, and deeply reflective storytelling." LJ

Kaminsky, Peter

Bien Cuit; Zachary Golper, Peter Kaminsky. Regan Arts 2015 324 p. illustrations (chiefly color) $50   641.815
   1. Bread 2. Baking
   ISBN 9781941393413; 1941393411

LC 2015938343

IACP Cookbook Award Nominee: Baking: Savory or Sweet (2016)

This cookbook, by Zachary Golper and Peter Kaminsky "introduces a new approach to a proudly old-fashioned way of baking bread. In the oven of his Brooklyn bakery, Chef Zachary Golper creates loaves that are served in New York's top restaurants and sought by bread enthusiasts around the country. His secret: long, low-temperature fermentation, which allows the dough to develop deep, complex flavors." (Publisher's note)

"This essential addition for serious bread enthusiasts, especially those who work exclusively by hand, will also interest novice and intermediate bakers, but they should be prepared to read recipes several times, use metric measurements and specialty flours, and budget considerable time." Library Journal

Lahey, Jim

The **Sullivan** Street Bakery cookbook; Jim Lahey with Maya Joseph ; photography by Squire Fox. W W Norton & Co Inc 2017 240 p. chiefly color illustrations (hardcover) $35   641.815
   1. Baking 2. Cookbooks 3. Cooking, Italian 4. Sullivan Street Bakery
   ISBN 0393247287; 9780393247282; 9780393247299

LC 2017029427

This cookbook, by Jim Lahey with Maya Joseph, provides "a clear, illustrated guide to making sourdough and the Italian-inspired café dishes from one of Manhattan's best bakeries. . . . The bread at Sullivan Street Bakery, crackling brown on the outside and light and aromatic on the inside, is inspired by the dark, crusty loaves that James Beard Award-winning baker . . . Lahey discovered in Rome." (Publisher's note)

"A terrific addition to the bread-making canon." Pub Wkly

Includes bibliographical references and index.

Lawson, Nigella, 1960-

How to be a domestic goddess; baking and the art of comfort cooking. Nigella Lawson ; photography by Petrina Tinslay. Hyperion 2001 viii, 374 p.p color illustrations $35   641.815
   1. Baking
   ISBN 0786867973; 9780786867974

LC 2001024170

This cookbook, by celebrity chef Nigella Lawson, "is not about being a goddess, but about feeling like one. . . . Filled with over 220 gorgeously illustrated recipes, this book understands our anxieties, feeds our fantasies, and puts cakes, pies, pastries, preserves, puddings, breads, and cookies back in our own kitchens." (Publisher's note)

"Timed to launch with her television series Nigella Bites on the E! channel and Style networks this fall, this book will bask in the warm, fuzzy and competent glow of Lawson's renown. She'll be a hit in the U.S.; her book will get ample promo and fly off the shelves." Pub Wkly

Includes bibliographical references (p. 364-365) and index

Lin, Irvin

Marbled, swirled & layered; 150 Recipes and Variations for Artful Bars, Cookies, Pies, Cakes, and More. Irvin Lin ; photography by Linda Xiao. Houghton Mifflin Harcourt 2016 352 p. color illustrations (paper over board) $30; (ebook) $30   641.815
   1. Baking 2. Cookbooks
   ISBN 9780544453739; 9780544454132

LC 2015038040

In this book, by Irvin Lin, with photographs by Linda Xiao, "bakers of all levels will enjoy recipes ranging from easy brownies and bars to brunch-worthy muffins and morning buns to show-stopping cakes and tarts: cinnamon spiral icebox cookies, pistachio-swirl brownies, triple-chocolate pie, multicolored 'Neapolitan' layer cake, and more. Lin offers variations to suit any taste (more than 150 recipes total) plus baking and decorating tips." (Publisher's note)

"Lin's outstanding first book can help all home bakers to expand their repertoire and think more creatively about flavor combinations." LJ

Meyer, Claus

Meyer's Bakery; bread and baking in the Nordic kitchen. Claus Meyer. Mitchell Beazley 2017 296 p. (hardcover) $29.99   641.815
   1. Bread 2. Baking
   ISBN 9781784722715; 1784722715

In this book, Claus Meyer "shares his knowledge of bread and baking and the simple idea that bread made with lots of whole grain and slow fermentation is one of the healthiest things we can eat--and that everyone can learn how to make it. Through detailed, delicious recipes, step-by-step sequences, in-depth information on ingredients and trouble-shooting sections, this book provides all the help you need on your journey to becoming a better baker." (Publisher's note)

Moore, Christine

Little Flower baking; Christine Moore with Cecilia Leung ; photographs by Staci Valentine. Prospect Park Books 2016 288 p. color illustrations (alk. paper) $35   641.815
   1. Baking 2. Cookbooks 3. American cooking 4. Cooking, American 5. Little Flower (Restaurant)
   ISBN 9781938849602

LC 2015042873

This cookbook, by Christine Moore with Cecilia Leung, with photographs by Staci Valentine, offers "one of California's most acclaimed bakers is sharing her very best recipes, all adapted and carefully tested for the home cook. Extensively photographed . . . , it inspires home cooks to make her rustically beautiful, always delicious cookies, cakes, pastries, savory baked goods, breads, rolls, bars, puddings, and so much more." (Publisher's note)

"Recipes are written clearly enough, even for kitchen novices, and she includes a helpful prologue of baking and ingredient tips. This one's a must-read for serious bakers." Booklist

A **new** way to bake; classic recipes updated with better-for-you ingredients from the modern pantry. from the kitchens of Martha Stewart. Clarkson Potter 2017 320 p. (hardback; alk. paper) $26   641.815
   1. Baking 2. Cookbooks
   ISBN 9780307954718

LC 2016008583

This book, from the editors of Martha Stewart living, "has 130 foolproof recipes that showcase the many ways these newly accessible ingredients can transform traditional cookies, pies, cakes, breads, and more. Chocolate chip cookies gain greater depth with earthy farro flour, pancakes become protein powerhouses when made with quinoa, and lemon squares get a wonderfully crumbly crust and subtle nutty flavor thanks to coconut oil. Superfoods are right at home in these baked goods." (Publisher's note)

"This is a healthier, yet no less tasty collection to rely on." Pub Wkly.

Scheft, Uri

Breaking breads; A New World of Israeli Baking--Flatbreads, Stuffed Breads, Challahs, Cookies, and the Legendary Chocolate Babka. Uri Scheft with Raquel Pelzel. Artisan Books 2016 351 p. color illustrations (ebook) $35; (hardback, paper over board; alk. paper) $35   **641.815**
1. Baking 2. Israeli cooking 3. Bread
ISBN 9781579657284; 157965682X; 9781579656829
                                                                      LC 2016027530

In this book, author Uri Scheft "takes the combined influences of his Scandinavian heritage, his European pastry training, and his Israeli and New York City homes to provide sweet and savory baking recipes that cover European, Israeli, and Middle Eastern favorites. Scheft sheds new light on classics like challah, babka, and ciabatta . . . and introduces his take on Middle Eastern daily breads like kubaneh and jachnun." (Publisher's note)

"An essential modern Middle Eastern baking collection featuring delights such as shakshuka focaccia and chocolate rugelach." LJ

Includes bibliographical references and index.

641.82   Main dishes

Bastianich, Joseph

Healthy pasta; the sexy, skinny, and smart way to eat your favorite food. Joseph Bastianich and Tanya Bastianich Manuali. Alfred A. Knopf 2015 185 p. color illustrations (hardcover) $26.95   **641.82**
1. Cookbooks 2. Cooking -- Pasta products 3. Cooking (Pasta)
4. Cooking, Italian
ISBN 0385352247; 9780385352246
                                                                      LC 2014025460

This cookbook by Joseph Bastianich and Tanya Bastianich Manuali presents "100 recipes, each under 500 calories per serving, that are as good for you as they are delectable. This wonderfully informative, easy-to-use cookbook provides simple ways to make pasta an integral part of a healthy and well-balanced lifestyle, even if you're gluten-free." (Publisher's note)

"Though their sexiness is debatable, these recipes are tasty, practical, and in line with current dietary trends. Recommended for pasta lovers in search of healthier everyday recipes." LJ

Beddia, Joe

Pizza camp; recipes from Pizzeria Beddia. Joe Beddia ; photography by Randy Harris. Abrams 2017 223 p. illustrations (chiefly color) (hardcover) $29.95   **641.82**
1. Pizza 2. Cookbooks
ISBN 9781683350194; 9781419724091
                                                                      LC 2016942236

This book, by Joe Beddia, "is the ultimate guide to achieving pizza nirvana at home, from the chef who is making what Bon Appetit magazine calls 'the best pizza in America.' Joe Beddia's pizza is old school—it's all about the dough, the sauce, and the cheese. And after perfecting his pie-making craft at Pizzeria Beddia in Philadelphia, he's offering his methods and recipes in a cookbook that's anything but old school."

(Publisher's note)

Carluccio, Antonio, 1937-2017

Pasta; The Essential New Collection from the Master of Italian Cookery. Antonio Carluccio. Chronicle Books Llc 2015 224 p. color illustrations $29.95   **641.82**
1. Italian cooking 2. Cooking -- Pasta products
ISBN 1849496641; 9781849496643

This cookbook by Antonio Carluccio "combines his inimitable knowledge with his expert taste buds to provide over 100 original and irresistible pasta recipes in this definitive book. The book begins with an instructional masterclass, teaching the reader everything they will need to know about pasta--how to cook it and how to marry it with the perfect sauce--with accompanying step-by-step photography." (Publisher's note)

"This is a superb addition to shelves already groaning with Italian cookbooks. Pasta lovers will want to give this one some serious consideration." Pub Wkly

Forkish, Ken

The **elements** of pizza; Ken Forkish ; photography by Alan Weiner. Ten Speed Press 2016 256 p. color illustrations (hardcover; alk. paper) $30   **641.82**
1. Pizza
ISBN 9781607748380
                                                                      LC 2015032247

In this cookbook, Ken Forkish "breaks down each step of the pizza-making process, from choosing a dough to shaping your pie to selecting cheeses and toppings that will work for your home kitchen setup. Forkish offers more than a dozen different dough recipes. . . . His clear, expert instructions will have you shaping pies and loading a pizza peel with the confidence of a professional pizzaiolo. And his innovative, seasonal topping ideas will surprise and delight any pizza lover." (Publisher's note)

"Committed bakers will find plenty here to keep ovens hot and families' plates filled with honest versions of one of the nation's most beloved foods." Booklist

Includes bibliographical references and index

Green, Aliza

Making artisan pasta; how to make a world of handmade noodles, stuffed pasta, dumplings, and more. [Aliza Green ; with photography by Steve Legato] Quarry Books 2012 176 p. col. ill. (pbk.) $24.99   **641.82**
1. Cookbooks 2. Cooking -- Pasta products 3. Noodles 4. Cooking (Pasta)
ISBN 1592537324; 9781592537327
                                                                      LC 2011031326

This cookbook offers "chef Aliza Green's pasta expertise and encyclopedic knowledge of all things culinary, plus hundreds of . . . photos by acclaimed food photographer Steve Legato, [so that readers can] learn how to use the best ingredients and simple, classic techniques to make fresh, homemade pasta in . . . [their] own kitchen." (Publisher's note)

"The book contains many useful extras such as nutrition information, resources, and a glossary, but those who want to serve a homemade sauce along with their pasta fresca may need to consult another resource." LJ

Includes bibliographical references (p. 168-169) and index

Joachim, David

Mastering pasta. Ten Speed Press 2015 272 p. color illustrations hardcover $29.99   **641.82**
1. Cookbooks 2. Italian cooking

ISBN 1607746077; 9781607746072

LC 2014020868

"Vetri's personal stories of travel and culinary discovery in Italy appear alongside his easy-to-follow, detailed explanations of how to make and enjoy fresh handmade pasta. Whether you're a home cook or a professional, you'll learn how to make more than thirty different types of pasta dough, from versatile egg yolk dough, to extruded semolina dough, to a variety of flavored pastas—and form them into shapes both familiar and unique. In dishes ranging from classic to innovative, Vetri shares his coveted recipes for stuffed pastas, baked pastas, and pasta sauces. He also shows you how to make light-as-air gnocchi and the perfect dish of risotto." Publisher's Note.

"This lavish pasta cookbook has lots of science-based information and an overview of 15 types of wheat flours. Perfect for dedicated pasta lovers looking to hone their skills." LJ

Louis, Jenn

Pasta by hand; a collection of Italy's small pasta shapes and dumplings. Jenn Louis ; photographs by Ed Anderson. Chronicle Books LLC 2015 208 p. illustrations (hardback) $25 **641.82**

1. Cookbooks 2. Cooking -- Pasta products 3. Dumplings 4. Pasta products 5. Cooking (Pasta)
ISBN 1452121885; 9781452121888

LC 2014032602

IACP Cookbook Award Nominee: Single Subject (2016)

This cookbook, by Jenn Louis, with photographs by Ed Anderson, "includes more than 65 recipes for hand-shaped traditional pastas and dumplings, along with deeply satisfying sauces to mix and match. Louis shares her recipes and expertise in hand-forming beloved shapes such as gnocchi, orecchiette, gnudi, and spatzli as well as dozens of other regional pasta specialties." (Publisher's note)

"The luxurious sauce recipes in the last chapter are worth the price of admission alone and feature traditional ragús of lamb, rabbit, porcini, tomato, beef, and wild boar. This single-focus cookbook is written with both authority and a passion for 'some of the most soulful Italian food we can eat.'" Pub Wkly

Marchetti, Domenica

The **glorious** pasta of Italy; by Domenica Marchetti. Chronicle Books 2011 280 p. col. ill. (alk. paper) $30 **641.82**

1. Cookbooks 2. Italian cooking 3. Cooking -- Pasta products 4. Cooking, Italian
ISBN 0811872599; 9780811872591

LC 2011030010

This pasta-centered Italian cookbook, by Domenica Marchetti, "draws from her Italian heritage to share 100 classic and modern recipes. Step-by-step instructions for making fresh pasta offer plenty of variations on the classic egg pasta, while a glossary of pasta shapes, a source list for unusual ingredients, and a handy guide for stocking the pantry with pasta essentials encourage the home cook to look beyond simple spaghetti." (Publisher's note)

One pot; 120-plus easy recipes for your stockpot, skillet, slow cooker, and more. from the kitchens of Martha Stewart Living. Clarkson Potter/Publishers 2014 256 p. color illustrations $26 **641.82**

1. Cooking 2. Quick and easy cooking 3. Stews 4. One-dish meals 5. Electric cooking, Slow
ISBN 0307954412; 9780307954411

LC 2013050638

In this book "editors of 'Martha Stewart Living' present a brand-new collection of 120 recipes--organized by vessel--to help you do just that,

all while adding savory new dishes to your weekly rotation. With chapters devoted to your essential cooking vessels--stockpot, skillet, slow cooker, and more--this book is [designed] to streamline your meals." (Publisher's note)

"Useful for weeknight home cooking, this survey of one-pot preparations features consistent, classic recipes and vibrant photographs. Readers interested in the slow-cooking chapters will also enjoy Andrew Schloss's Cooking Slow." LJ

Parachini, Chris

Roberta's; Carlo Mirarchi, Brandon Hoy, Chris Parachini and Katherine Wheelock, art direction by Ryan Rice. Clarkson Potter 2013 287 p. color illustrations $35 **641.82**

1. Pizza 2. Cookbooks 3. Restaurants 4. Roberta's (Restaurant)
ISBN 0770433715; 9780770433710

LC 2013004300

The authors of this cookbook, Carlo Mirarchi, Brandon Hoy, Chris Parachini and Katherine Wheelock, "share recipes, photographs, and stories meant to capture the experience of [the Brooklyn-based pizza restaurant] Roberta's for those who haven't been, and to immortalize it for those who've been there since the beginning." (Publisher's note)

Segan, Francine

Pasta modern; new & inspired recipes from Italy. Francine Segan. Stewart, Tabori & Chang 2013 208 p. $35 **641.82**

1. Italian cooking 2. Cooking -- Pasta products
ISBN 1617690627; 9781617690624

LC 2013935989

In this book, author Francine Segan "challenges the notion that pasta must be traditional or old-world. . . .Segan details . . . unusual pasta dishes from Italy's food bloggers, home cooks, artisan pasta makers, and vanguard chefs.... Tips and anecdotes culled from Segan's Italian travels enhance the easy-to-follow directions, and a glossary of more than 50 . . . dried pastas showcases shapes to revive any pasta lover's repertoire." (Publisher's note)

"Meticulously researched, thoughtfully curated, and artfully designed, this unique collection will inspire readers to try new preparations and flavors." LJ

Tanis, David

One good dish; by David Tanis. Artisan 2013 256 p. $25.95 **641.82**

1. Cookbooks 2. One-dish meals
ISBN 1579654673; 9781579654672

LC 2013006289

Author David Tanis "turns his focus to an eclectic array of simple, casual meals that satisfy and are appropriate to be eaten at any time of day. Tanis's whimsy runs from bread, snacks, and condiments to vegetables, griddled foods, desserts, and more. Waffle-iron grilled cheese, gorgonzola and walnut crostini; and ham and gruyere bread pudding are highlights among the rustic offering of bread entries." (Publishers Weekly)

641.822   Noodle and pasta dishes

Henry, Colu

Back pocket pasta; inspired dinners to cook on the fly. Colu Henry. Clarkson Potter/Publishers 2017 240 p. color illustrations (ebook) $65; (hardcover) $28 **641.822**

1. Cookbooks 2. Quick and easy cooking 3. Cooking -- Pasta products 4. Cooking (Pasta)
ISBN 9780553459753; 9780553459746

LC 2016010616

This cookbook, by Colu Henry, "shows how a well-stocked kitchen and a few seasonal ingredients can be the driving force behind delicious, simply prepared meals. . . . For instance, if you know that you have a tin of anchovies, a hunk of parmesan, and panko bread crumbs, you can pick up fresh kale to make Tuscan Kale 'Caesar' Pasta. Or if you have capers, red pepper flakes, and a lemon, you can make Linguine with Quick Chili Oil." (Publisher's note)

"Sensible suggestions for maintaining a well-stocked pantry and refrigerator make it easy to have supplies on hand, and her 'Set Up Your Station' chapter includes staging a few tools in advance of the work week." Pub Wkly

641.824   Meat and cheese pies

Bruni, Frank

A **meatloaf** in every oven; two chatty cooks, one iconic dish and dozens of recipes--from Mom's to Mario Batali's. by Frank Bruni and Jennifer Steinhauer ; illustrations by Marilyn Pollack Naron. GCP Life & Style 2017 272 p. color illustrations (hardcover) $24; (ebook) $72   **641.824**
   1. Cookbooks 2. Meat loaf 3. Cooking -- Meat
   ISBN 9781455563050; 9781478943686

LC 2016025917

This book, by Frank Bruni and Jennifer Steinhauer, illustrated by Marilyn Pollack Naron, presents 50 meatloaf recipes, "from the best classic takes to riffs by world-famous chefs like Bobby Flay and Mario Batali; from Italian polpettone to Middle Eastern kibbe to curried bobotie; from the authors' own favorites to those of prominent politicians. Bruni and Steinhauer address all the controversies . . . surrounding a dish that has legions of enthusiastic disciples." (Publisher's note)

"Liberally peppered with Bruni and Steinhauer's snappy dialogue, this is a terrific collection that deserves a look from meatloaf lovers of all ages." Pub Wkly

Rodino, Heather

★ **Todd** English's rustic pizza; handmade artisan pies from your own kitchen. Todd English & Heather Rodino. St. Martin's Castle Point 2017 214 p. (hardcover) $24.99   **641.824**
   1. Pizza 2. Cookbooks
   ISBN 9781250147677; 9781250165183

LC 2017947564

In this book, by Todd English with Heather Rodino, Todd "brings his pizza-making secrets to home cooks! 'RUSTIC PIZZA' will give step-by-step instructions on making pizza dough, sauces, and toppings along with Todd's insider secrets on how to achieve truly great pizza with a home oven." (Publisher's note)

641.83   Salads

Caldesi, Giancarlo

Around the world in 120 salads; fresh, healthy, delicious. Katie & Giancarlo Caldesi ; photography by Helen Cathcart. Kyle Books 2017 208 p. color illustrations (paperback) $24.95   **641.83**
   1. Salads 2. Eating habits 3. Cookbooks
   ISBN 9781909487611

LC 2016956952

In this cookbook authors Katie Caldesi and Giancarlo Caldesi "show how salads are perfect for any time of day and occasion – Watermelon,

Feta & Mint for a refreshing breakfast, meat, fish and vegetable-based mains for a complete meal plus recipes for starters and side salads where salad plays a supporting role. They even cover sweet salads such as Roast Black Fruit Salad or Raspberries & Redcurrants with Whipped Ricotta for a healthier alternative to an indulgent dessert." (Publisher's note)

"Sharing an impressive range of artfully composed salads from around the world, they deftly explain how to craft an exciting meal from varied ingredients, flavors, and textures." LJ

Includes bibliographical references (page 204) and index.

Food52 mighty salads; 60 new ways to turn salad into dinner- and make-ahead lunches, too. editors of Food52 ; photography by James Ransom. Ten Speed Press 2017 xiii, 145 p.p color illustrations (hardcover; alk. paper) $22.99   **641.83**
   1. Salads 2. Cookbooks
   ISBN 9780399578052; 9780399578045

LC 2016050225

"Make way for Mighty Salads, in which the editors of Food52 present sixty salads hefty with vegetables, meats, grains, beans, fish, seafood, pasta, and bread. Think shrimp and radicchio tossed in a bacon vinaigrette, a make-ahead jumble of white beans with charred lemon and fennel, slow-roasted duck and apples scattered across spicy greens. It's comforting food made captivating by simply charring one ingredient or marinating another—shaving some, or roasting a bunch." (Publisher's note)

"Sixty recipes . . . emphasize variety, drawing on flavorful components such as fresh herbs and toasted nuts for vibrancy and zest." LJ

Romero, Terry Hope

Salad samurai; 100 cutting-edge, ultra-hearty, easy-to-make salads you don't have to be vegan to love. Terry Hope Romero. Da Capo Lifelong 2014 180 p. col. ill. (pbk.) $19.99 **641.83**
   1. Salads 2. Veganism 3. Cookbooks 4. Vegan cooking
   ISBN 0738214876; 9780738214870

LC 2014002618

This vegan cookbook, by Terry Hope Romero, offers a "guide to real salad bushido: a hearty base, a zesty dressing, and loads of seriously tasty toppings. . . . Based on whole food ingredients and seasonal produce, these versatile meatless, dairy-free dishes are organized by season for a full year of memorable meals." (Publisher's note)

Rosen, Ilene

Saladish; a crunchier, grainier, herbier, heartier, tastier way with vegetables. Ilene Rosen with Donna Gelb. Artisan, a division of Workman Publishing Co., Inc. 2018 208 p. (hc; alk. paper) $24.95   **641.83**
   1. Salads 2. Cooking 3. Cooking -- Vegetables 4. Salad greens 5. Salad vegetables
   ISBN 9781579656959

LC 2017036051

In this cookbook, author Ilene Rosen "shares 100 fresh and creative recipes, organized seasonally, from the intoxicatingly aromatic (Toasty Broccoli with Curry Leaves and Coconut) to the colorfully hearty (Red Potatoes with Chorizo and Roasted Grapes). Each chapter includes a fun party menu, a timeline of preparation, and an illustrated tablescape to turn a saladish meal into an impressive dinner party spread." (Publisher's note)

"Highly recommended for fans of grain bowls, meal-sized salads, and meatless meals." Library Journal

641.84 Sandwiches and related dishes

García, Lorena

Lorena Garcia's new taco classics; Lorena Garcia. Celebra 2015 368 p. color illustrations $29.95   **641.84**

   1. Mexican cooking 2. Latin American cooking 3. Tacos

   ISBN 0451476913; 9780451476913

          LC 2015008294

In this cookbook, "breaking down each new-style taco into its elements, [author Lorena Garcia] shows you how to create each delicious layer--from the shell to the fillings to the toppings, including slaws, salads, and sauces. These flavor-packed recipes are made for pairing and sharing, depending on your craving or occasion." (Publisher's note)

"Traditionalists will appreciate the inclusion of tamales with green tomatillo and pulled chicken and tostadas al pastor, as well as tips on making the best chile de arbol sauce. This book is approachable enough for the novice, and packed with must-try dishes for everyday dining as well as special occasions. Readers might want to buy two copies, since the first one's going to be stained and tattered in no time." Pub Wkly

Kord, Tyler

A **super** upsetting cookbook about sandwiches; Tyler Kord ; photography by Noah Fecks ; artwork by William Wegman. Clarkson Potter/Publishers 2016 191 p. (hardcover) $22.99   **641.84**

   1. Cookbooks 2. Sandwiches

   ISBN 0804186413; 9780804186414

          LC 2015028505

This book, by Tyler Kord, with photography by Noah Fecks and artwork by William Wegman, presents "careless ruminations on sandwich philosophy, love, self-loathing, pay phones, getting drunk in the shower, Tom Cruise, food ethics, and what it's like having the names of two different women tattooed on your body. Most of these ruminations also happen to be truly excellent recipes." (Publisher's note)

Mena, Juan Carlos

Tacopedia; Deborah Holtz ; Juan Carlos Mena. Phaidon Press Limited 2015 317 p. illustrations (chiefly color) (paperback) $29.95   **641.84**

   1. Mexican cooking 2. Cookbooks 3. Tacos -- Mexico 4. Cooking, Mexican

   ISBN 9780714870472; 0714870471

          LC 2015472830

   IACP Cookbook Award: Reference and Technical (2016)

This book, by Deborah Holtz and Juan Carlos Mena, "will appeal to hip taco lovers, food truck enthusiasts, and serious followers of Mexican cuisine, both young, and young at heart." (Publisher's note)

Parks, Richard

Guerrilla Tacos; recipes from the streets of L.A. Wesley Avila with Richard Parks III. Ten Speed Press 2017 272 p. (hardback) $30   **641.84**

   1. Cooking 2. Cookbooks 3. American cooking 4. Tacos 5. Guerilla Tacos 6. Cooking, American -- California style

   ISBN 9780399578632

          LC 2017024762

This book, by Wesley Avila and Richard Parks III, presents "50 [taco] base recipes . . . grounded in authenticity but never tied down to tradition. . . . [Avila] uses ingredients like kurobata sausage and sea urchin, but his bestselling taco is made from the humble sweet potato. From basic building blocks to how to balance flavor and texture, with comic-inspired illustrations and stories throughout, Guerrilla Tacos is

the final word on tacos from the streets of L.A." (Publisher's note)

   Includes bibliographical references and index

Stupak, Alex

Tacos; recipes and provocations. Alex Stupak and Jordana Rothman ; photographs by Evan Sung. Clarkson Potter 2015 240 p. color illustrations (hardback) $32.50   **641.84**

   1. Cooking -- Meat 2. Mexican cooking 3. Tacos 4. Tortillas 5. Cooking, Mexican

   ISBN 0553447297; 9780553447293

          LC 2015006214

   IACP Cookbook Award Winner: Chefs and Restaurants (2016); IACP Cookbook Award Nominee: Julia Child First Book (2016); IACP Cookbook Award Nominee: International (2016)

"TACOS is a deep dive into the art and craft of one of Mexico's greatest culinary exports. We start by making fresh tortillas from corn and flour, and variations that look to innovative grains and flavor infusions. Next we master salsas, from simple chopped condiments to complex moles that simmer for hours and have flavor for days. Finally we explore fillings, both traditional and modern--from a pineapple-topped pork al pastor to pastrami with mustard seeds." Publisher's Note

641.85 Preserves and candy

Curl, Jami

Candy is magic; real ingredients, modern recipes. Jami Curl ; photography by Maggis Kirkland ; illustrations by Michelle Ott. Ten Speed Press 2017 312 p. illustrations (hardcover) $35   **641.85**

   1. Candy 2. Confectionery 3. Cookbooks

   ISBN 0399578390; 9780399578403; 9780399578397

          LC 2016047716

This cookbook by Jami Curl "offers more than 200 achievable recipes using real, natural ingredients for everything from flavor-packed fruit lollipops to light-as-air marshmallows. She begins with the foundations of candy; how to create delicious syrups, purees, and 'magic dusts' that are the building blocks for making lollipops, caramels, marshmallows, and gummy candy." (Publisher's note)

"Curl's enthusiasm for her craft makes this cookbook a pleasure to read; she is the ideal coach for would-be candy makers." Pub Wkly Annex

   Includes bibliographical references (pages 291-295) and index.

641.86 Desserts

Adams, Jocelyn Delk

Grandbaby cakes; modern recipes, vintage charm, soulful memories. Jocelyn Delk Adams. Surrey Books, An Agate Imprint 2015 224 p. $22.95   **641.86**

   1. Cake 2. Baking

   ISBN 1572841737; 9781572841734

          LC 2015013216

   NAACP Image Award Nominee: Outstanding Literary Work - Instructional (2016)

This cookbook is author Jocelyn Delk Adams's "love note to her family, thanking those who came before and passing on this touching tradition with 50 brilliant cakes. Adams creates sophisticated flavor combinations based on [her grandmother] Big Mama's gorgeous centerpiece cakes, giving each recipe something familiar mixed with something new." (Publisher's note)

"Adams's cake recipes are familiar yet unlike any you'll find in similar cookbooks. An instant classic, this title belongs in most baking collections." LJ

Ansel, Dominique

Dominique Ansel; the secret recipes. foreword by Daniel Boulud. Simon & Schuster 2014 272 p. color illustrations (hardback) $35   **641.86**

1. Pastry 2. Cookbooks
ISBN 1476764190; 9781476764191

LC 2014024377

This cookbook, by Dominique Ansel, "shares the secret to transforming the most humble ingredients into the most extraordinary, tempting, and satisfying pastries imaginable.... [The book] reveals the stories and recipes behind his most sought-after creations and teaches lovers of dessert everywhere how to make magic in their own kitchens." (Publisher's note)

"Ansel's essays will delight his fans, as well as foodies who enjoy learning about the creative processes of famous chefs. Those new to French pastry will prefer collections with more recipes and instruction." LJ

Austin, Maggie

Maggie Austin cake; artistry and technique. Maggie Austin ; photography by Kate Headley. Houghton Mifflin Harcourt 2017 304 p. color illustrations $35   **641.86**

1. Cake 2. Baking 3. Cookbooks 4. Cake decorating
ISBN 0544765354; 9780544765351

In this cookbook, former ballerina Maggie Austin, who turned to baking, "shares a collection of her edible works of art and the methods behind their creation, with a 'theme and variations' organization that shows how mastering any single technique can open the door to endless creativity. Each is broken down into clear instructions and illustrated with step-by-step photos that are easy to follow whether you're a professional baker or an amateur enthusiast." (Publisher's note)

"Filled with technical know-how and sumptuous photographs, this book will tempt all cake lovers." LJ.

Beddall, Catherine

The **magic** of gingerbread; 16 Beautiful Projects to Make and Eat. written and photographed by Catherine Beddall. Peter Pauper Press, Inc. 2016 176 p. illustrations (chiefly color) (hardcover; alk. paper) $22.99   **641.86**

1. Gingerbread
ISBN 1441319808; 9781441319807

LC 2016003632

In this book, pastry artist Catherine Beddall "shares her secrets for creating classic gingerbread houses and a bounty of other gingerbread whimsies, including a gingerbread space rocket, robot, and chess set!" (Publisher's note)

Includes bibliographical references

Ben-Ishay, Melissa

★ **Cakes** by Melissa; life is what you bake it: 120+ recipes for cakes, icings, fillings, and toppings for endless flavor combinations from the creative force behind Baked by Melissa. Melissa Ben-Ishay ; photography by Ashley Sears. HarperCollins 2017 291 p. $26.99   **641.86**

1. Cake 2. Baking 3. Cookbooks
ISBN 0062681273; 9780062681270

This book, by Melissa Ben-Ishay, "is a . . . collection of easy and imaginative cakes from the creative force behind the delicious bite-size cupcake brand Baked by Melissa. . . . It offers Melissa's fresh takes on traditional cakes and inventive ideas to make dessert in any form extra sweet. The cookbook will encourage home bakers to be creative and spontaneous in their baking, even including fill-in-the-blank ingredient sheets to individualize their special treats." (Publisher's note)

Bilderback, Leslie

No-churn ice cream; over 100 simply delicious no-machine frozen treats. Leslie Bilderback. St. Martin's Griffin 2015 168 p. color illustrations (trade pbk.) $22.99   **641.86**

1. Cookbooks 2. Ice cream, ices, etc.
ISBN 1250054389; 9781250054388

LC 2015007286

This dessert cookbook, by Leslie Bilderback, gives instruction for ice-cream making. "What if you could make your own ice cream at home without all of the fuss, for a fraction of the cost of buying it, and without any special equipment? . . . [This book] is a mouthwatering collection of shortcuts and classic culinary techniques that help you achieve delicious, artisanal results." (Publisher's note)

"Supplemented by Bilderback's professional pastry knowledge, this easy yet informative ice cream cookbook will appeal to a wide audience. Highly recommended for college students, apartment dwellers, and anyone lacking kitchen equipment or space." LJ

Bittman, Mark, 1950-

★ **How** to Bake Everything; Simple Recipes for the Best Baking. Mark Bittman. Houghton Mifflin Harcourt 2016 704 p. illustrations (hardcover) $35; (ebook) $35   **641.86**

1. Baking 2. Cookbooks
ISBN 9780470526880; 9780544798861; 0470526882

LC 2016449439

This cookbook by Mark Bittman offers "the simplest way to bake everything, from American favorites (Crunchy Toffee Cookies, Baked Alaska) to of-the-moment updates (Gingerbread Whoopie Pies). It explores global baking, too: Nordic ruis, New Orleans beignets, Afghan snowshoe naan. The recipes satisfy every flavor craving thanks to more than 2,000 recipes and variations." (Publisher's note)

"This compendium is the next best thing to having the master himself in the kitchen, and should be a staple for all public library collections." Booklist

Boyle, Tish

Flavorful; 150 irresistible desserts in all-time favorite flavors. Tish Boyle ; photography by Andrew Meade. Houghton Mifflin Harcourt 2015 384 p. color illustrations (hardcover) $35   **641.86**

1. Baking 2. Desserts 3. Cookbooks
ISBN 1118523555; 9781118523551

LC 2015004678

IACP Cookbook Award Nominee: Baking: Savory or Sweet (2016)

This baked goods and desserts cookbook, by Tish Boyle with photography by Andrew Meade, describes how "pastry chefs . . . [use] vanilla, berry and cherry, apple, citrus, cheese, nuts, caramel, coffee, and chocolate. . . . Author Tish Boyle has translated this list of go-to ingredients into a stunning collection of more than 150 recipes for baked goods and other desserts, with a chapter dedicated to each singular flavor." (Publisher's note)

"Reliable and technically informative, Boyle's latest functions like nine single-subject titles in one. Highly recommended for readers who enjoy classic dessert collections such as Sherry Yard's The Secrets of Baking and Flo Braker's The Simple Art of Perfect Baking." LJ

Includes bibliographical references

Byrn, Anne

American cake; From Colonial Gingerbread to Classic Layer, the Stories and Recipes Behind More Than 125 of Our Best-Loved Cakes. Anne Byrn. Rodale 2016 352 p. illustrations (chiefly color) (trade hardcover; acid-free paper) $29.99 **641.86**

1. Cookbooks 2. Cake decorating 3. Cake -- United States -- History 4. Cake
ISBN 9781623365431

LC 2016029092

This cookbook by Anne Byrn takes "a journey through America's past to present with more than 125 authentic recipes for our best-loved and beautiful cakes and frostings. Tracing cakes chronologically from the dark, moist gingerbread of New England to the elegant pound cake, the hardscrabble Appalachian stack cake, . . . Hawaiian Chantilly, and the modern California cakes. . . . Byrn shares . . . stories, and a behind-the-scenes look into what cakes we were baking back in time." (Publisher's note)

"These well researched and written pages go far beyond the average baking guide." Pub Wkly

Includes bibliographical references (pages 325-329) and index.

American cookie; The Snaps, Drops, Jumbles, Tea Cakes, Bars & Brownies That We Have Loved for Generations. Anne Byrn. Random House Inc 2018 336 p. $24.99 **641.86**

1. Baking 2. Cookies 3. Desserts 4. Cookies -- United States -- History.
ISBN 1623365457; 9781623365455

LC 2018180646

In this cookbook, author Anne Byrn, "takes us on a journey through America's baking history. . . . [S]he provides an incredibly detailed historical background alongside each recipe. . . . Each of the 100 recipes, from Katharine Hepburn Brownies and Democratic Tea Cakes to saltwater taffy and peanut brittle, comes with a lesson that's both informative and enchanting." (Publisher's note)

"The introduction sets the stage, outlining the basic ingredients and supplies required for the recipes. Sidebars offer baking suggestions and historical notes, and each recipe is introduced with a brief anecdote about its origins." Library Journal

Cook, Steven

★ **Federal** Donuts; by Michael Solomonov, Steven Cook, Tom Henneman, Bob Logue, Felicia D'Ambrosio. Houghton Mifflin Harcourt 2017 224 p. $16.99 **641.86**

1. Doughnuts 2. Cooking 3. Restaurants
ISBN 0544969049; 9780544969049

This book, by Michael Solomonov, Steven Cook, Tom Henneman, Bob Logue, and Felicia D'Ambrosio, "is at once an ode to an American passion and a collection of recipes for the cult-favorite hits. With a wad of cash in hand and a dream, Solomonov and Cook meet a Craigslist stranger in a parking lot and buy a used 'donut robot.' It would do all the rest, right? Regrets, partially raw donuts, and long lines ensue, but soon the partners work out the kinks and develop an exquisite dough." (Publisher's note)

Includes bibliographical references (pages 220-221) and index.

Ferroni, Lara

Doughnuts; 90 simple and delicious recipes to make at home. Lara Ferroni. Sasquatch Books 2018 208 p. (hardcover; alk. paper) $19.95 **641.86**

1. Baking 2. Cookbooks 3. Doughnuts
ISBN 9781632171252

LC 2017041913

This cookbook, by Lara Ferroni, "makes it easy to create doughnuts in your own kitchen. Be prepared to be tempted by favorite classics like old-fashioned sour cream, maple-bacon bars, or red velvet, and new delights such as pineapple fritters, dulce de leche, and rainbow cake. There are also variations for vegan and gluten-free versions in this expanded edition, now with 30 new recipes. Your family and friends will not be disappointed!" (Publisher's note)

"Especially helpful are confidence-building tips on such things as when to use doughnut pans vs. flat baking sheets, frying times, and shaping doughnuts. Ferroni's is a charming, easy-to-follow manual of fried dough confections." Pub Wkly

Includes bibliographical references and index

Food52 Ice Cream and Friends; 60 Recipes and Riffs for Sorbets, Sandwiches, No-Churn Ice Creams, and More. editors of Food52 ; photography by James Ransom. Ten Speed Press 2017 xii, 161 p.p color illustrations (hardcover) $22.99 **641.86**

1. Ice cream, ices, etc. 2. Cookbooks 3. Frozen desserts
ISBN 9780399578038; 9780399578021; 0399578021

LC 2017288552

This book, by the editors of Food52, presents a "collection of 60 recipes, riffs, toppings, and serving ideas for ice creams of all styles. . . . There are surprising flavors—think cinnamon roll ice cream, coffee frozen custard, and grilled watermelon cremolada—and spins on enduring favorites, such as spiced fudgesicles, cherry-mint snow cones, and even a chocolate-hazelnut baked Alaska." (Publisher's note)

"Impressive in its variety, the book blends all-new and reader-contributed recipes . . ." LJ

Gerson, Fany

Mexican ice cream; beloved recipes and stories. Fany Gerson ; photography by Justin Walker and Fernando Gomez Carbajal. Ten Speed Press 2017 173 p. color illustrations (hardcover; alk. paper) $22 **641.86**

1. Desserts 2. Mexican cooking 3. Ice cream, ices, etc. 4. Frozen desserts 5. Cooking, Mexican 6. Desserts -- Mexico 7. Ice cream, ices, etc
ISBN 9781607747789; 9781607747772

LC 2016051341

This book, by Fany Gerson, "showcases the incredibly diverse flavors of Mexican ice cream while exploring the cultural aspects of preparing and consuming ice cream in Mexico. Gerson uses unique ingredients to create exciting and fresh flavors like Red Prickly Pear Ice Cream, Oaxacan-style Lime Sorbet, Avocado-Chocolate Ice Cream, and Rice-Almond Ice Cream with Cinnamon." (Publisher's note)

"[Gerson's] extensive expertise underpins this inspiring cookbook, which collects classic and modern recipes for sorbets, ice creams, and accompaniments." LJ

Includes bibliographical references and index

Greenspan, Dorie

★ **Baking** chez moi; recipes from my paris home to your home anywhere. Dorie Greenspan ; photographs by Alan Richardson. Houghton Mifflin Harcourt 2014 496 p. ill. (chiefly col.) (hardback) $40 **641.86**

1. Baking 2. Desserts 3. French cooking
ISBN 0547724241; 9780547724249

LC 2014016312

James Beard Foundation Award Nominee: Baking and Dessert (2015)

IACP Cookbook Award Finalist: International (2015)

IACP Cookbook Award Finalist: Baking: Savory or Sweet (2015)

In this cookbook, author Dorie Greenspan "explores the fascinating world of French desserts, bringing together a charmingly uncomplicated mix of contemporary recipes, including original creations based on traditional and regional specialties, and drawing on seasonal ingredients, market visits, and her travels throughout the country." (Publisher's note)

"Combining everyday desserts with doable versions of extremely popular treats (think macarons, éclairs, and crackle-top cream puffs), Greenspan's new collection is an instant classic." LJ

★ **Dorie's** cookies; Dorie Greenspan, photographed by Davide Luciano. Houghton Mifflin Harcourt 2016 528 p. color illustrations (ebook) $35; (paper over board) $35 **641.86**

1. Cookies

ISBN 9780547614854; 9780547614847

LC 2015042719

This cookbook, by Dorie Greenspan, presents "cookies for every taste and occasion. . . . There are company treats like Portofignos, with chocolate dough and port-soaked figs, and lunch-box Blueberry Buttermilk Pie Bars. They Might Be Breakfast Cookies are packed with goodies—raisins, dried apples, dried cranberries, and oats— while Almond Crackle Cookies have just three ingredients. [And] there are dozens of choices for the Christmas cookie swaps." (Publisher's note)

"Accomplished bakers will be challenged and inspired by the breadth of recipes and the many suggestions Greenspan offers throughout the book to modify recipes. This is a cookbook to read, bake, and eat your way through." Pub Wkly

Greenstein, Elaine

A **Jewish** baker's pastry secrets; George Greenstein with Elaine Greenstein, Juia Greenstein, and Isaac Bleicher. Ten Speed Press 2015 202 p. (hardback) $29.99 **641.86**

1. Pastry 2. Jewish cooking 3. Cooking, European

ISBN 1607746735; 9781607746737

LC 2015025814

In this cookbook, author George Greenstein "crafts master dough recipes for Jewish holiday baking and European classics. . . . Greenstein's expert guidance for making doughs like bundt, babka, strudel, gugelhopf, stollen, pressburger, puff pastry, and Danish create a jumping-off point for more than 200 variations of classic pastries. . . . The book also offers an in-depth guide to ingredients and equipment, . . . as well as basic recipes for fillings, icings, and glazes." (Publisher's note)

Includes bibliographical references (pages 197) and index

Harris, Miriam

Magpie; Sweets and Savories from Philadelphia's Favorite Pie Boutique. by Holly Ricciardi, with Miriam Harris. Running Press 2015 256 p. color illustrations (hardcover) $27.50 **641.86**

1. Pies 2. Cookbooks

ISBN 9780762454532; 0762454539

LC 2015937006

This cookbook, by Holly Ricciardi, with Miriam Harris, "serves up Magpie [Artisan Pie Boutique's] . . . seasonal menu for home bakers everywhere: the fruity, creamy, and nutty pies; hand pies, pot pies, and quiches; and even pie shakes and pie 'fries,' all fine-tuned to exacting standards and with lots of step-by-step instruction for that all-important crust." (Publisher's note)

"Versatile enough to be used year-round, this pie cookbook will complement most baking collections." LJ

Holiday cookies; prize-winning family recipes from the Chicago Tribune for cookies, bars, brownies and more. Chicago Tribune"||"Surrey Books 2014 222 p. color illustrations (hard cover) $24.95 **641.86**

1. Baking 2. Cookies 3. Holiday cooking

ISBN 1572841648; 9781572841642

LC 2014026785

IACP Cookbook Award Finalist: Compilations (2015)

This book by the staff of the "Chicago Tribune" "is a comprehensive collection of the best holiday cookies as curated from nearly three decades worth of reader submissions. These delicious recipes represent an eclectic mix of traditional and modern recipes from diverse cultural background and skill levels, such as Tropical Nuevo Latino Cookies, Dorie's Dark and Stormies, and Grandma Grump's Peanut Butter Drizzles." (Publisher's note)

"A timely cookie collection that's big on variety and nostalgia." LJ

Jaronsky, Shelly

The **cookies** & cups cookbook; let's all agree to eat dessert first; 100 recipes to make your life sweet, plus 25 recipes for the weirdos who like to eat dinner. by Shelly Jaronsky. Gallery Books 2016 320 p. (trade pbk.) $23.99 **641.86**

1. Cookies 2. Desserts

ISBN 9781501102516

LC 2015027541

This cookbook, by Shelly Jaronsky, "features . . . sweet treats 100% guaranteed to make you want to eat dessert first. . . . With recipes ranging from the deliciously decadent (her S'mores Fudge Bars will make you seriously reconsider everything you thought you knew about baked goods) to the deceptively simple (her Favorite Chocolate Chip Cookie will become an instant staple in your baking repertoire), [it] truly has something for everyone." (Publisher's note)

"Jaronsky, the creator of the website Cookies & Cups, presents over 125 selections with sweets in the front. Her casual tone and concise recipes with numbered steps are inviting for those new to the kitchen." Pub Wkly

Kalman, Maira

Cake; a cookbook. Maira Kalman and Barbara Scott-Goodman. Penguin Press 2018 93 p. (hardback) $25 **641.86**

1. Cake 2. Baking

ISBN 1101981547; 9781101981542

LC 2017025262

"Renowned artist and author Maira Kalman and food writer Barbara Scott-Goodman bring us a beautifully illustrated book dedicated to their mutual love of cakes. Kalman's enchanting illustrations, in her inimitable style, and Scott-Goodman's mouthwatering recipes complement each other perfectly, making Cake a joyful whimsical celebration of a timeless dessert." (Publisher's note)

"Illustrator and author Kalman (And the Pursuit of Happiness) and Scott-Goodman (The Beach House Cookbook) charmingly write about the importance of cake in daily life." Pub Wkly

Kave, Allison

First prize pies; Shoo-fly, candy apple & other deliciously inventive pies for every week of the year (and more) Allison Kave. Stewart, Tabori & Chang 2014 224 p. color illustrations $29.95 **641.86**

1. Pies 2. Cookbooks

ISBN 161769102X; 9781617691027

LC 2013945638

In this cookbook, author "Allison Kave made pies as a hobby, until one day her boyfriend convinced her to enter a Brooklyn pie-making contest.... [Now] people can't get enough of her Bourbon Ginger Pecan pie, her whimsical Root Beer Float Pie, her addictive Chocolate Peanut Butter Pretzel Pie. . . . Organized by month, the book includes pies for every sweet tooth, from inventive pies like Chocolate Lavender Teatime to old-school comfort pies like Candy Apple." (Publisher's note)

Includes bibliographical references and index

Kieffer, Sarah

The **Vanilla** Bean baking book; recipes for irresistible everyday favorites and reinvented classics. Sarah Kieffer. Avery, an imprint of Penguin Random House, LLC 2016 336 p. color illustrations (ebook) $65; (print) $27.00 **641.86**
   1. Desserts 2. Cookbooks 3. Cake
   ISBN 9780698198425; 9781583335840

LC 2016016459

This cookbook, by Sarah Kieffer, presents "100 recipes for delicious treats and desserts from the founder of the Saveur Award–winning 'Vanilla Bean' baking blog. . . . From everyday favorites such as Lemon Bread and Peanut Butter Cookies to inventive twists on classics such as Burnt Honey Buttercream Cake with Chocolate, Coffee Blondies, and Apple-Blackberry Turnovers, these irresistible treats will delight and inspire." (Publisher's note)

"Familiar and timeless without being superfluous, this highly recommended, well-executed baking book will thrill home bakers who like to keep things simple." LJ

Includes bibliographical references (page 321) and index.

Lane, Christina

Dessert for Two; Small Batch Cookies, Brownies, Pies, and Cakes. Christina Lane. W W Norton & Co Inc 2015 240 p. color illustrations $24.95 **641.86**
   1. Desserts 2. Cookbooks 3. Cooking for two
   ISBN 1581572840; 9781581572841

This cookbook, by Christina Lane, offers "well-loved desserts and scales them down to make only two servings. . . . Cakes are baked in small pans and ramekins. Pies are baked in small pie pans or muffin cups. Cookie recipes are scaled down to make 1 dozen or fewer. . . . Now you can have your own personal-sized cake and eat it, too." (Publisher's note)

Ludwinski, Lisa

Sister Pie; the recipes and stories of a big-hearted bakery in Detroit. Lisa Ludwinski ; photographs by E.E. Berger. Ten Speed Press 2018 256 p. (hardcover) $25 **641.86**
   1. Pies 2. Pastry 3. Cooking 4. Cookbooks 5. Sister Pie Bakery
   ISBN 9780399579769

LC 2018003428

In this cookbook Lisa Ludwinski, owner of Detroit's Sister Pie bakery, features "75 of her most-loved recipes for sweet and savory pies--such as Toasted Marshmallow-Butterscotch Pie and Sour Cherry-Bourbon Pie--and other bakeshop favorites, the 'Sister Pie' cookbook pays homage to Motor City ingenuity and all-American spirit. Illustrated throughout with 75 drool-worthy photos and Ludwinski's charming line illustrations, and infused with her plucky, punny style." (Publisher's note)

McDermott, Kate

Art of the pie; A Practical Guide to Homemade Crusts, Fillings, and Life. Kate McDermott, photographed by Andrew Scrivani. Countryman Press, a division of W W Norton & Co. 2016 352 p. color illustrations (hardcover) $35 **641.86**
   1. Pies 2. Baking 3. Cookbooks
   ISBN 9781581573275

LC 2016017593

This cookbook, by Kate McDermott, photographed by Andrew Scrivani, gives "detailed instructions for making, rolling, and baking crusts. A pie needs filling, too, and [McDermott] does not neglect a single detail when describing her ingredients, methods, and tricks for making the filling and finishing off the pie. Recipes include: Blackberry Pie for Julia Child,The Best Peach Pie in the World, and Old-Fashioned Rhubarb Pie."(Publisher's note)

"It's really all about the standards... McDermott excels, giving readers an informative guide they'll be referring to for years to come." Pub Wkly

Medrich, Alice

Holiday cookies; the ultimate chewy, gooey, crispy, crunchy treats. Alice Medrich. Artisan 2017 110 p. color illustrations (Artisanal kitchen) (paper-over-board) $12.95 **641.86**
   1. Cookies 2. Holiday cooking
   ISBN 9781579658267; 1579658040; 9781579658045

LC 2017005079

This cookbook in the Artisanal Kitchen series, by Alice Medrich, "provides . . . recipes for cookies, bars, and savories of all textures, from simple holiday classics like Vanilla Bean Tuiles and Great Grahams to the more decadent Caramel Cheesecake Bars and Chunky Hazelnut Meringues. There are even some delicious savories that can double as hors d'oeuvres at the holiday buffet like Crunchy Seed Cookies and Salted Peanut Toffee Cookies." (Publisher's note)

Includes bibliographical references (pages 106-107) and index

Moore, Kathy

Delicious dump cakes; 50 Super Simple Desserts to Make in 15 Minutes or Less. Roxanne Wyss and Kathy Moore ; photographs by Staci Valentine. St. Martin's Griffin 2016 128 p. color illustrations (trade pbk.) $19.99 **641.86**
   1. Cake 2. Baking 3. Cobblers (Cooking)
   ISBN 9781250082633

LC 2015049003

In this cookbook, by Roxanne Wyss and Kathy Moore, "you'll find a wide array of cakes and desserts that require minimal utensils to prepare. For nearly all of the recipes, simply open readily available cans or a package of cake mix and layer in the pan. Never again will you have to struggle with complex steps or deal with lots of dirty dishes." (Publisher's note)

"Whatever readers' level of experience or inexperience in the kitchen, this cookbook will have them serving up delicious desserts in a flash." LJ

Naturally sweet; Bake All Your Favorites with 30% to 50% Less Sugar. by the editors at America's Test Kitchen. America's Test Kitchen 2016 336 p. color illustrations $26.95; (ebook) $25.99 **641.86**
   1. Baking 2. Desserts 3. Sugar-free diet
   ISBN 9781940352589; 9781940352596

LC 2016009055

This cookbook by the editors of America's Test Kitchen, tackles the "challenge of creating foolproof, great-tasting baked goods that contain less sugar and rely only on natural alternatives to white sugar.... Changing the sugar in a recipe can have disastrous results: Baked goods turn out dry . . . [and] inedible.... [This book] address these issues . . . with 120 foolproof, great-tasting recipes . . . that reduce the overall sugar content by at least 30%." (Publisher's note)

"Cooks with a powerful sweet tooth should scoop up this well-researched recipe book for healthier takes on classic sweet treats." Booklist

Nederlanden, Elisabet der

Holiday cookies; showstopping recipes to sweeten the season. Elisabet der Nederlanden ; photography by Erin Scott. Ten Speed Press 2017 161 p. color illustrations (hardcover) $20   **641.86**
1. Cookies 2. Cookbooks 3. Confectionery 4. Holiday cooking
ISBN 9780399580253; 9780399580260

LC 2017015950

This cookbook, by Elisabet der Nederlanden, "is packed with 50 recipes, each gorgeously photographed and meticulously tested, along with dozens of decorating and packaging ideas. Filled with . . . favorites like Giant Molasses Spice Cookies and Hazelnut Sandwich Cookies; confections like Peppermint Bark, Smoked Almond and Cacao Nib Brittle, and Dark Chocolate-Hazelnut Fudge; and detailed instructions for gorgeous gingerbread houses, cookie place cards, and edible ornaments." (Publisher's note)

"Home cooks determined to step up their cookie-making this holiday season will find many satisfying choices, along with useful decorating and packaging tips, and a few decorative projects." LJ

Includes bibliographical references and index

Ottolenghi, Yotam

Sweet; desserts from London's Ottolenghi. Yotam Ottolenghi, Helen Goh with Tara Wigley. Ten Speed Press 2017 363 p. illustrations (chiefly color) (hardcover)   **641.86**
1. Desserts 2. Confectionery 3. Pastry 4. Cooking, Middle Eastern 5. Ottolenghi (Restaurant)
ISBN 9781607749158; 9781607749141; 1607749149

LC 2017022017

This cookbook, by Yotam Ottolenghi and Helen Goh, presents "a collection of over 110 recipes for sweets, baked goods, and confections. . . . Sweet is entirely filled with delicious baked goods, desserts, and confections starring [Yotam] Ottolenghi's signature flavor profiles and ingredients including fig, rose petal, . . . and cinnamon. A baker's dream, Sweet features simple treats such as Chocolate, Banana, and Pecan cookies and Rosemary Olive Oil Orange Cake." (Publisher's note)

"Modern, creative, appealing, and, most importantly, fun—this is Ottolenghi at the top of his game." Pub Wkly

Parks, Stella

★ **BraveTart**; Iconic American Desserts. Stella Parks ; foreword by J. Kenji López-Alt ; photography by Penny De Los Santos. W W Norton & Co Inc 2017 395 p. illustrations (chiefly color) (hardcover) $35   **641.86**
1. Desserts 2. American cooking 3. Cookbooks
ISBN 9780393239867; 9780393634273; 0393239861

LC 2017007009

James Beard Award: Baking and Desserts (2018)

This book, by Stella Parks, "is a celebration of classic American desserts. Whether down-home delights like Blueberry Muffins and Glossy Fudge Brownies or supermarket mainstays such as Vanilla Wafers and Chocolate Chip Cookie Dough Ice Cream, your favorites are all here. These meticulously tested recipes bring an award-winning pastry chef's expertise into your kitchen." (Publisher's note)

"Parks, a senior editor at Serious Eats and the creator of the Bravetart blog, has written a cookbook that is as interesting to read as it is to cook from." Pub Wkly

Includes bibliographical references (pages 363-379) and index

Payard, Francois

Payard cookies; François Payard with Anne E. McBride ; photography by Rogørio Voltan. Houghton Mifflin Harcourt 2015 272 p. color illustrations (hardcover) $30   **641.86**
1. Cookies 2. French cooking 3. Cooking, French
ISBN 0544512987; 9780544512986

LC 2014044010

Author "François Payard shares his favorite cookie recipes—the bestsellers at his popular New York City patisseries and cafés, the recipes he learned from his father, and the ones he makes at home. They range from the simplest sablés (butter cookies) to the most picture-perfect macarons, with everything in between." (Publisher's note)

"Experienced bakers will have no trouble with Payard's pleasing and precise cookie recipes." LJ

The **perfect** cake; your ultimate guide to classic, modern, and whimsical cakes. the editors at America's Test Kitchen. America's Test Kitchen 2018 432 p. (hardback) $35 **641.86**
1. Cake 2. Desserts 3. Cake decorating
ISBN 9781945256264

LC 2017049045

This book, by the editors at America's Test Kitchen, "is the definitive guide to any cake you crave from Classic Pound Cake to enjoy anytime to a stunning and impressive Blueberry Jam Cake with brilliant jam stripes and ombré frosting. In addition to foolproof recipes are features that make towering 24-layer Hazelnut- Chocolate Crêpe Cake as approachable as Applesauce Snack Cake." (Publisher's note)

Includes bibliographical references and index

The **perfect** cookie; your ultimate guide to foolproof cookies, brownies & bars. the editors at America's Test Kitchen. America's Test Kitchen 2017 ix, 438 p.p color illustrations (hardcover) $35   **641.86**
1. Cookies 2. Cookbooks 3. Bars (Desserts) 4. Brownies (Cooking)
ISBN 9781940352954; 9781940352961

LC 2017008692

This cookbook, by the editors of America's Test Kitchen, offers "250 cookie, brownie, and bar recipes. . . . A chapter on rolled, shaped, and pressed cookies features unusual combinations of flavor and texture. . . . Twenty types of brownies and blondies, including fudge brownies and butterscotch meringue bars, ... [and a] selection of bar cookie recipes, which include reliable recipes for classics such as lemon bars and cheesecake bars, [are also featured]." (Publishers Weekly)

"The editors at America's Test Kitchen pack decades of baking experience into this impressive volume of 250 recipes for cookies, brownies, bars, and no-bake confections." LJ

Ptak, Claire

The **Violet** Bakery cookbook; Claire Ptak. Ten Speed Press 2015 272 p. color illustrations (hardcover) $29.99   **641.86**
1. Baking 2. Desserts 3. Violet Bakery (London, England)
ISBN 1607746719; 9781607746713

LC 2014036768

This book, by Claire Ptak, is a "design-forward cookbook for sweet and savory baked goods from London's popular Violet Bakery that focuses on quality ingredients, seasonality, and taste (as opposed to science) as the keys to creating satisfying, delightful homemade pastries, tarts, sweets, and more. . . . Over 100 recipes include nourishing breakfasts, midday snacks, desserts to share, fruit preserves, and stylish celebration cakes." (Publisher's note)

"Highly recommended for fans of baking books such as Elisabeth

Prueitt and Chad Robertson's Tartine and Zoe Nathan's Huckleberry. Aspiring pastry chefs will find inspiration in Ptak's impressive career highlights." LJ

Purchese, Darren

Lamingtons & lemon tart; best-ever cakes, desserts & treats from a modern sweets maestro. Darren Purchese. Hardie Grant Books 2017 262 p. color illustrations (hardcover) $40 **641.86**
    1. Cake 2. Desserts 3. Cookbooks
    ISBN 9781743791868; 1743791860

In this cookbook, author Darren Purchese, who is renowned for his high-end dessert creations, "turns his eye to the classics, cast with his trademark flair for the home cook who might be ambitious, but also wants to feel that the recipes are within their grasp. . . . He includes a selection of his favorite modern creations, from Caramelized white chocolate mousse to Explosive raspberry wagon wheels; Lemon meringue pie éclair; . . . and his . . . Popcorn and honeycomb rubble." (Publisher's note)

Richardson, Julie

Vintage cakes; timeless cupcakes, flips, rolls, layer, angel, snack, chiffon, and icebox cakes for today's sweet tooth. Julie Richardson ; photography by Erin Kunke. Ten Speed Press 2012 166 p. col. ill. (hbk.) $24 **641.86**
    1. Cake 2. Cookbooks
    ISBN 1607741024; 9781607741022
                    LC 2011041262

This cookbook by Julie Richardson focuses on cakes. She "consulted classic cookbooks, submissions from family and friends, and vintage recipes dating back to the 1920s. . . . Richardson includes familiar (e.g., Wacky, Texas Sheet, Red Velvet, Caramel, and Watergate cakes) and lesser-known classics and a few originals, all updated to suit modern palates." (Library Journal)

Includes bibliographical references (p. 157) and index

Robicelli, Allison

Robicelli's; A Love Story, With Cupcakes: With 50 Decidedly Grown-up Recipes. by Allison Robicelli and Matt Robicelli. Penguin Group USA 2013 320 p. $35 **641.86**
    1. Baking 2. Family 3. Cupcakes
    ISBN 0670785873; 9780670785872

Authors Allison Robicelli and Matt Robicelli present a "guide to gourmet cupcakes, featuring grown-up flavors (figs! whiskey! fried chicken!) and the delicious story of a family saved by a love of sweets. Nixing cutesy, pastel-colored dollops of fluff for real ingredients and rich French buttercreams, the husband and wife team have reinvented the cupcake craze for a more sophisticated palate." (Publisher's note)

"Photos are lick-the-page enticing and proof that home bakers are going to enjoy the best bleeping cupcakes their side of the Brooklyn Bridge." Pub Wkly

Seneviratne, Samantha

Sugar and spice; Samantha Seneviratne ; photography by Erin Kunkel. Ten Speed Press 2015 240 p. (hardcover) $27.50 **641.86**
    1. Pastry 2. Cookies 3. Cooking (Spices)
    ISBN 1607747464; 9781607747468
                    LC 2015005473

In this book, author Samantha Senevirante presents a "collection of more than eighty unique, unexpected, and uniformly delicious recipes for spice-centric sweets. [It is] filled with fascinating histories, origin stories, and innovative uses for the world's most enticing spices--including vanilla, cinnamon, peppercorns, and cardamom." (Publisher's note)

"Marked by a sense of the exotic, Seneviratne's recipes will lure many home cooks, including fans of Alice Medrich's Pure Dessert and Claudia Fleming's The Last Course." LJ

Shulman, Martha Rose

★ The **art** of French pastry; Jacquy Pfeiffer ; with Martha Rose Shulman ; photographs by Paul Strabbing. Alfred A. Knopf 2013 432 p. (hardback) $85 **641.86**
    1. Baking 2. Pastry 3. French cooking 4. Cooking, French
    ISBN 0307959368; 9780307959355
                    LC 2013017643

In this cookbook, pastry chef Jacquy Pfeiffer provides "an intimate knowledge of the fundamentals of pastry. . . . By teaching you how to make everything from pâte à choux to pastry cream, Pfeiffer builds on the basics until you have an understanding of the science behind the ingredients used, how they interact with one another, and what your hands have to do to transform them into pastry." (Publisher's note)

"Anyone studying to be a professional baker will profit from Pfeiffer's guidance, and the amateur cook can vastly improve family desserts." Booklist

Thomas, Claire

Sweet Laurel; recipes for whole food, grain-free desserts. Laurel Gallucci and Claire Thomas. Clarkson Potter/Publishers 2018 256 p. $28 **641.86**
    1. Baking 2. Desserts 3. Low-fat diet 4. Nutrition 5. Sweet Laurel Bakery 6. Low-fat diet -- Recipes
    ISBN 9781524761455
                    LC 2017031551

This cookbook, by Laurel Gallucci and Claire Thomas, is aimed at making "eating paleo, gluten-free, and dairy-free diets a lot sweeter for home bakers. From the beginning, Sweet Laurel [bakery] has been about making sweet things simple. The recipes here are indulgent yet healthful. They use just a few quality ingredients to create delicious desserts that benefit your body; all of these treats are paleo, and many are vegan and raw." (Publisher's note)

Tosi, Christina, 1981-

Milk Bar Life; Sweet and Savory Recipes to Make Right Now. Christina Tosi. Clarkson Potter 2015 256 p. color illustrations $35 **641.86**
    1. Cooking 2. Eating habits 3. Desserts 4. Momofuku Milk Bar
    ISBN 0770435106; 9780770435103
                    LC 2014041740

In this cookbook author Christina Tosi "bakes one-bowl treats, grills with skills, and embraces simple, nostalgic--and often savory--recipes made from supermarket ingredients. For anyone addicted to crack pie®, compost cookies®, and cake truffles, here are their savory counterparts--such as Kimcheezits with Blue Cheese Dip, Burnt Honey–Butter Kale with Sesame Seeds, and Choose Your Own Adventure Chorizo Burgers." (Publisher's note)

Weinstein, Bruce

All-time favorite sheet cakes & slab pies; easy to make, easy to serve. Bruce Weinstein and Mark Scarbrough ; photographs by Eric Medsker. St. Martin's Griffin 2017 ix, 211 p.p (trade pbk.) $24.99 **641.86**
    1. Cake 2. Pies 3. Baking 4. Quick and easy cooking
    ISBN 9781250117588; 9781250117595
                    LC 2017018871

In this cookbook, by Bruce Weinstein and Mark Scarbrough, "sheet cakes and slab pies have long been a staple at holidays, family reunions, and potlucks everywhere. Now [the] authors . . . are reinventing these American originals with their new book. . . . With over 100 recipes inside you'll find the perfect dessert for every occasion. In addition to the cakes and pies there are also recipes for cheesecakes, Danish, coffee cakes, and more." (Publisher's note)

"This laid-back approach to baking is sure to entice home bakers of all levels to get out that sheet pan and invite a hungry crowd." Pub Wkly

Wright, Caroline

Mix + Match Cakes; Mix & Match Your Way to 100 Amazing Combinations. by Caroline Wright (Author) Workman Pub Co 2016 192 p. $17.95   **641.86**
1. Cake 2. Baking 3. Desserts
ISBN 0761182039; 9780761182030

LC 2013036826

This book, by Caroline Wright, "is a full-color visual cookbook— photos in the front, recipes in the back—and the first step in every baker's cake adventure. It includes valuable baking tips, vegan and gluten-free variations, plus how to tweak the recipes to make sheet cakes, Bundt cakes, and cupcakes, too." (Publisher's note)

"Baking purists may turn up their spatulas, but this is a kid-friendly title that's downright fun for adults, too."

641.865   Pastries

Berry, Mary, 1935-

Baking with Mary Berry; cakes, cookies, pies, and pastries from the British queen of baking. Mary Berry. DK Publishing 2015 192 p. color illustrations (paperback) $19.95 **641.865**
1. Baking 2. Cookbooks
ISBN 1465453237; 9781465453235

This baking cookbook, by Mary Berry, "draws on Mary's more than 60 years in the kitchen, with tips and step-by-step instructions for bakers just starting out and full-color photographs of finished dishes throughout. The recipes follow Mary's prescription for dishes that are no fuss, practical, and foolproof—from breakfast goods to cookies, cakes, pastries, and pies, to special occasion desserts such as cheesecake and soufflés, to British favorites that will inspire." (Publisher's note)

"The recipes themselves are clear and concise and the offerings wide ranging, everything from the usual, brownies and lemon meringue pie, to the unusual, almond and apricot tartlets to the exotic, figgy-seeded bites. A solid guide, not just for fans of the show—but it's those fans (and their numbers are growing in the U.S.) who will be clamoring for copies." Booklist

Johnstone, Christi Farr

Smart cookie; transform store-bought cookies into amazing treats. Christi Farr Johnstone ; [edited by] Jordana Tusman. Running Press 2014 192 p. color illustrations $16   **641.865**
1. Cookies
ISBN 0762452528; 9780762452521

LC 2013958111

This book, by Christi Farr Johnstone, "includes 50 simple and fun cookie creations made entirely from easy-to-find store-bought ingredients-- no baking required! Projects include rainbows, monster pops, balloons, robots, ladybugs, and much more, with lots of ideas for tips, techniques, packaging, and displays. From birthdays to graduations and baby showers to Christmas, there is a cookie in this book for any and all occasions." (Publisher's note)

"Johnstone's charming decorated cookies require minimal time and equipment and no baking. This is her debut title and a great resource for kid-friendly decorating projects and last-minute party favors." LJ

Lebo, Kate

Pie school; lessons in fruit, flour and butter. by Kate Lebo. Sasquatch Books 2014 227 p. color illustrations (paperback) $24.95   **641.865**
1. Pies 2. Cookbooks 3. Baking
ISBN 1570619107; 9781570619106

LC 2014021810

This book, by Kate Lebo, with photography by Rina Jordan, offers "recipes for fifty perfect pies. Included are apple (of course), five ways with rhubarb, lemon chiffon, several blueberry pie variations, galettes, and more. . . . In addition to recipes, Lebo invites readers to ruminate on the social history, the meaning, and the place of pie in the pantheon of favorite foods." (Publisher's note)

"An informed and rather romantic take on the art of the handmade pie." LJ

Includes bibliographical references and index

Weinstein, Bruce

A **la** mode; 120 recipes in 60 pairings; pies, tarts, cakes, crisps, and more topped with ice cream, gelato, frozen custard, and more. Bruce Weinstein and Mark Scarbrough. St. Martin's Griffin 2016 224 p. color illustrations (trade pbk.) $24.99   **641.865**
1. Cake 2. Pies 3. Desserts 4. Ice cream, ices, etc
ISBN 1250072131; 9781250072139

LC 2016000033

This book, by Mark Scarbrough and Bruce Weinstein, "offers not just solid dessert recipes, from raspberry oat bars to bear claws, from chocolate pecan pie to a white chocolate pavlova, but also gives you the unforgettable pairings that make these desserts smash hits: apple cranberry pie with Camembert ice cream, chocolate sheet cake with salt caramel frozen custard, and espresso cream jelly roll with mascarpone ice cream." (Publisher's note)

"This isn't your average ice cream cookbook. Rather than providing just a few suggested accompaniments, Weinstein and Scarbrough (The Great Big Pressure Cooker Book) pair each of the 60 ice cream recipes with a complementary dessert. They also forego a master ice cream base in favor of multiple ice cream types and techniques. . . . As with Jeni Britton Bauer's Jeni's Splendid Ice Cream Desserts, this cookbook is a playful collection of unusual ice cream pairings." LJ

641.87   Preparing beverages

Arnold, Dave

★ **Liquid** intelligence; the art and science of the perfect cocktail. Dave Arnold ; photography by Travis Huggett. 1st ed W W Norton & Co Inc 2014 416 p. color illustrations (hardcover) $35   **641.87**
1. Cocktails 2. Bartending 3. Measuring instruments
ISBN 0393089037; 9780393089035

LC 2014022332

IACP Cookbook Award: Jane Grigson Award (2015)
James Beard Foundation Award: Beverage (2015)

This book, by Dave Arnold, "is the beginning of a new method of making drinks, a problem-solving approach grounded in attentive observation and creative techniques. Readers will learn how to extract the sweet flavor of peppers without the spice, why bottling certain drinks beforehand beats shaking them at the bar, and why quinine powder and succinic acid lead to the perfect gin and tonic." (Publisher's note)

"Professional bartenders will drink up this remarkable manual, and amateurs will find Arnold's step-by-step guide to gathering requisite hardware both achievable and fun." Booklist

Includes bibliographical references and index

Conigliaro, Tony, 1971-

The **cocktail** lab; unraveling the mysteries of flavor and aroma in drink, with recipes. Tony Conigliaro. Ten Speed Press 2013 224 p. color illustrations (hardback) $29.99   **641.87**

1. Bartending 2. Alcoholic beverages 3. Cocktails
ISBN 1607745674; 9781607745679

LC 2013004969

James Beard Award (2014)

In this book, bartender Tony Conigliaro presents a "collection of 60 revolutionary cocktails, all grounded in the classics but utilizing technologies and techniques from the molecular gastronomy movement. . . . Tony presents his best and boldest creations: drinks like the Vintage Manhattan, Dirty Martini by the Sea, and Cosmo Popcorn." (Publisher's note)

Includes bibliographical references (pages 217-218) and index

Del Mar Sacasa, María

Summer cocktails; margaritas, mint juleps, punches, party snacks, and more. Maria del Mar Sacasa. Quirk Books 2015 160 p. color illustrations (hardcover) $22.95   **641.87**

1. Cocktails 2. Cookbooks
ISBN 1594747857; 9781594747854

LC 2014944415

This book, by Maria del Mar Sacasa, "features more than 100 seasonal recipes for punches and pitchers, frosty drinks, classics and throwbacks, and more. Craft your beverages from the bottom up with underpinnings straight from your summer garden, including Strawberry-Rosemary Shrub, Rhubarb Syrup, or Tomatillo and Coriander Tequila. Plus, round out the perfect party with savory snacks to match your cool drinks." (Publisher's note)

"With clear instructions and bright color photographs it's easy to make a Pulparindo or a Pimm's your new summer staple, while handy guides to tools and prep techniques round out this essential primer." LJ

Fauchald, Nick

★ **Death** & Co; modern classic cocktails. David Kaplan, Nick Fauchald, Alex Day ; photographs by William Hereford ; illustrations by Tim Tomkinson. Ten Speed Press 2014 320 p. ill. (some col.) (hardcover) $40   **641.87**

1. Bars 2. Cocktails 3. Bartending 4. Death & Co. (Bar; New York, N.Y.)
ISBN 1607745259; 9781607745259

LC 2014004245

James Beard Foundation Award Nominee: Beverage (2015)

IACP Cookbook Award Finalist: Global Design (2015)

This book, by David Kaplan, Nick Fauchald, and Alex Day, is a "guide to the contemporary craft cocktail movement. . . . [M]ore than just a collection of recipes, [it] is also a complete cocktail education, with information on the theory and philosophy of drink making, a complete guide to buying and using spirits, and step-by-step instructions for mastering key bartending techniques." (Publisher's note)

"There's a clear, unpretentious spirits primer for those who have been bluffing their way through in-vogue varieties of rum, tequila, and whiskey; other sections tackle bitters, ice, glassware, and additional details without dictating. More than half the book is devoted to 450-plus recipes for classics, variations, and riffs." LJ

Includes bibliographical references and index

Helwig, Jenna

Smoothie-licious;   power-packed smoothies and juices the whole family will love. Jenna Helwig. Houghton Mifflin Harcourt Publishing Co. 2015 159 p. color illustrations $14.99   **641.87**

1. Health 2. Beverages 3. Natural foods 4. Smoothies (Beverages)
ISBN 0544370082; 9780544370081

LC 2015431117

Author "Jenna Helwig shows how to make 75 smoothies and whole-fruit juices that are both healthy and delicious. Kids will love the bright colors and playful names like Peanut Berry Blast and Mexican Frozen Hot Chocolate; parents will love that they feature nutrient-dense seeds, dark greens and fresh fruit, and use no refined sugars." (Publisher's note)

McDonnell, Duggan

Drinking the devil's acre; a love letter to San Francisco and her cocktails. Duggan McDonnell ; photographs by Luke Abiol. Chronicle Books 2015 256 p. $24.95   **641.87**

1. Cocktails 2. San Francisco (Calif.) 3. Bars (Drinking establishments) -- California -- San Francisco -- History
ISBN 1452135258; 9781452135250

LC 2014044040

This book by Duggan McDonnelp is a "mix of barman's memoir and literary journalism, with layers of spirited history and liquid wisdom. A tender tale of love for delicious drink, and for one's city, a book for anyone with a passion for history, cocktails, San Francisco, and the wanderlust of travel." (Publisher's note)

"Not just another cocktail recipe book but a great read peppered with drinks to be made. Highly recommended where books on cocktails are popular." LJ

Includes bibliographical references and index

Meehan, Jim

★ **Meehan's** bartender manual; Jim Meehan ; photography by Doron Gild.; illustrations by Gianmarco Magnani. Ten Speed Press 2017 ix, 477 p.p illustrations (hardcover) $40   **641.87**

1. Cocktails 2. Bartending 3. Cocktails -- Handbooks, manuals, etc.
ISBN 9781607748625; 9781607748632

LC 2017024758

James Beard Award: Beverage (2018)

This book "is acclaimed mixologist Jim Meehan's magnum opus. . . . This groundbreaking work chronicles Meehan's storied career in the bar business through practical, enlightening chapters that mix history with professional insight. Meehan's deep dive covers the essential topics, including the history of cocktails and bartending, service, hospitality, menu development, bar design, spirits production, drink mixing technique, and the tools you'll need to create a well-stocked bar." (Publisher's note)

". . . divulges the recipes for 100 classic and fanciful cocktails and gives away intel that is vital not only for would-be bartenders but for anyone who dreams of owning and operating their own establishment." Pub Wkly

Includes bibliographical references (pages 464-468) and index.

Morgenthaler, Jeffrey

Bar Book; Elements of Cocktail Technique. Jeffrey Morgenthaler with Martha Holmberg ; photographs by Alanna Hale. Chronicle Books Llc 2014 288 p. color illustrations (hc)

$30   641.87

1. Cocktails 2. Bartending 3. Alcoholic beverages
ISBN 9781452113845; 145211384X

IACP Cookbook Award Finalist: Wine, Beer and Spirits (2015)

"Written by renowned bartender and cocktail blogger Jeffrey Morgenthaler, 'The Bar Book' is the only technique-driven cocktail handbook out there.... More than 60 recipes illustrate the concepts explored in the text, ranging from juicing, garnishing, carbonating, stirring, and shaking to choosing the correct ice for proper chilling and dilution of a drink." (Publisher's note)

"Straightforward directions are matched with beautifully clear photographs that make homemade grenadine, limoncello, and ginger beer look enticingly simple. The author also demystifies shaking, muddling, and presentation." LJ

Muldoon, Sean

The **Dead** Rabbit drinks manual; secret recipes and barroom tales from two Belfast boys who conquered the cocktail world. Jack McGarry, Sean Muldoon, Ben Schaffer ; photography by Brent Herrig. Houghton Mifflin Harcourt 2015 288 p. color illustrations (hardcover) $27   **641.87**

1. Bars 2. Cocktails 3. Dead Rabbit Grocery and Grog (New York, N.Y.)
ISBN 9780544373204

LC 2014043215

This book is a "cocktail collection from ... Dead Rabbit Grocery & Grog in Lower Manhattan.... [A]long with its inventive recipes, [it] also details founder Sean Muldoon and bar manager Jack McGarry's inspiring rags-to-riches story that began in Ireland and has brought them to the top of the cocktail world.... Dead Rabbit's award-winning drinks ... range from fizzes to cobblers to toddies, each with its own historical inspiration." (Publisher's note)

"Like the best Irish bartender, this book is warm, welcoming, full of great stories, and dedicated to excellent drinks." LJ

Reiner, Julie

The **craft** cocktail party; amazing drinks for every occasion. Julie Reiner with Kaitlyn Goalen ; photographs by Daniel Krieger. Grand Central Life & Style 2015 240 p. color illustrations (hardcover) $26   **641.87**

1. Cocktails
ISBN 1455581593; 9781455581597; 9781455581603

LC 2014049853

This book of cocktails, by Julie Reiner, "provides inspiration for the rest of us, not only the cocktail geeks.... Recipes are organized around seasonality and occasion, with different events and themes appropriate to the specific time of the year. Each section will include a mixture of holiday-inspired drinks, classic cocktails, and innovative new drinks, all along with fun cocktail lore." (Publisher's note)

Simonson, Robert

A **proper** drink; The Untold Story of How a Band of Bartenders Saved the Civilized Drinking World. Robert Simonson. Ten Speed Press 2016 352 p. (hardcover; alk. paper) $27   **641.87**

1. Bars 2. Bartenders 3. Cocktails -- History 4. Bartenders -- Biography 5. Bars (Drinking establishments)
ISBN 9781607747543

LC 2016014120

This book by Robert Simonson tells the "story of the contemporary craft cocktail revival.... Simonson interviewed more than 200 key players from around the world ... --bars, bartenders, patrons, and visionar-

ies--who in the last 25 years have changed the course of modern drinkmaking. The book also features a curated list of about 40 cocktails--25 modern classics, plus an additional 15 to 20 rediscovered classics and classic contenders--to emerge from the movement." (Publisher's note)

"No matter which side of the bar readers are on, they're sure to work up a powerful thirst." Pub Wkly

Includes bibliographical references and index

★ **Three**-ingredient cocktails; an opinionated guide to the most enduring drinks in the cocktail canon. Robert Simonson ; photographs by Colin Price. First edition Ten Speed Press 2017 166 p. color illustrations (hardcover) $18.99   **641.87**

1. Cocktails 2. Bartending 3. Alcoholic beverages
ISBN 0399578544; 9780399578540

LC 2017016197

This book, by Robert Simonson, with photography by Colin Price, "is a concise history of the best classic cocktails, and a curated collection of the best three-ingredient cocktails of the modern era. Organized by style of drink and variations, the book features 75 delicious recipes for cocktails both classic (Japanese Cocktail, Bee's Knees, Harvey Wallbanger) and contemporary (Remember the Alimony, Little Italy, La Perla)." (Publisher's note)

Sultan, Tim

Sunny's nights; lost and found at a bar on the edge of the world. Tim Sultan. Random House 2016 288 p. illustrations, map $27   **641.87**

1. Bars 2. Bartending -- New York (State) -- New York 3. Red Hook (N.Y.) -- Social life and customs 4. Brooklyn (New York, N.Y.) -- Social life and customs 5. Bartenders -- New York (State) -- New York -- Biography
ISBN 1400067278; 9781400067275

LC 2015019985

This memoir, by Tim Sultan, is a "portrait of the dream experience we're all searching for every time we walk into a bar, and an enchanting memoir of an unlikely and abiding friendship. The first time he saw Sunny's Bar, in 1995, Tim Sultan was lost, thirsty for a drink, and intrigued by the single bar sign among the forlorn warehouses lining the Brooklyn waterfront. Soon enough, Sultan has quit his office job to bartend fulltime for Sunny Balzano, the bar's owner." (Publisher's note)

"An indelible portrait of an unusual man and a nearly forgotten part of NYC."

Tanguay, Paul

The **Tippling** bros. a lime and a shaker. Tad Carducci and Paul Tanguay, the Tippling bros., with Alia Akkam ; foreword by Doug Frost ; photography by Lauren Volo. Houghton Mifflin Harcourt 2015 256 p. color illustrations $18.99   **641.87**

1. Cocktails 2. Cookbooks
ISBN 054430232X; 9780544302327

LC 2014023051

This mixed drink cookbook, by Tad Carducci and Paul Tanguay, with Alia Akkam, illustrated by Lauren Volo, offers "Mexican cocktail culture and vibrant mezcal- and tequila-based recipes from renowned drinks experts The Tippling Bros.... Their 72 exciting recipes go past the classic margarita and include traditional, craft, and spicy drinks." (Publisher's note)

"A title that is sure to have readers looking for opportunities to try the recipes contained within. Highly recommended for any collection in which books on cocktails are prevalent." LJ

641.874   Alcoholic beverages

Jones, Carey

The **Brooklyn** bartender; a modern guide to cocktails and spirits. Carey Jones ; photographs by Lucy Schaeffer. Black Dog & Leventhal Publishers 2016 304 p. (hardcover; alk. paper) $24.99   **641.874**

1. Cocktails 2. Brooklyn (New York, N.Y.) 3. Liqueurs
ISBN 9780316390255

LC 2015050472

This book, by Carey Jones, "gathers 300 of the most innovative and exciting cocktail recipes from . . . Brooklyn. . . . Organized by spirit, the recipes allow readers to replicate bartenders' signature drinks, from the ornate juleps and cobblers of Maison Premiere to the party-friendly 'Frozemonade' at Extra Fancy to the namesake gin cocktail of Clover Club." (Publisher's note)

"Even the staunchest teetotaler will work up quite a thirst while perusing what is easily one of the best cocktail books this year." Pub Wkly

Parsons, Brad Thomas

Amaro; The Spirited World of Bittersweet, Herbal Liqueurs, with Cocktails, Recipes, and Formulas. Brad Thomas Parsons ; photography by Ed Anderson. Ten Speed Press 2016 280 p. color illustrations (hardcover; alk. paper) $26   **641.874**

1. Cocktails 2. Cookbooks 3. Wine and wine making 4. Bitters 5. Sweetness (Taste) 6. Bitterness (Taste)
ISBN 9781607747482

LC 2016012981

In this book by Brad Thomas Parsons with photographs by Ed Anderson, "the European tradition of making bittersweet liqueurs--called amari in Italian--has been around for centuries. But it is only recently that these herbaceous digestifs have moved . . . and become a key ingredient on cocktail lists in the country's best bars and restaurants. . . . [The book includes] more than 100 recipes for amaro-centric cocktails, DIY amaro, and even amaro-spiked desserts." (Publisher's note)

"Bitter flavors may not be for everyone, but Parsons succeeds at opening up exciting possibilities to try at home or seek out at bars." LJ

Includes bibliographical references and index

Winter drinks; 70 essential cold-weather cocktails. editors of PUNCH. Ten Speed Press 2018 160 p. (hardcover) $19.99   **641.874**

1. Beverages 2. Cocktails
ISBN 9780399581663

LC 2018006298

This book "offers the ultimate collection of cold-weather cocktails, both classic and modern. Curated by the PUNCH editorial team with the help of its network of top bartenders, each recipe has been tested and adapted to contemporary tastes, alongside creative tweaks that offer new ways to incorporate the season's flavors into foolproof drinks." (Publisher's note)

"For those looking for ways to celebrate during the dead of winter, this is a smart and handy go-to guide." Publishers' Weekly

641.877   Nonalcoholic brewed beverages

Easto, Jessica

Craft coffee; a manual; brewing a better cup at home. by Jessica Easto with Andreas Willhoff. Surrey Books, an Agate Imprint 2017 272 p. illustrations (trade cloth) $19.95 **641.877**

1. Coffee 2. Reference books 3. Coffee making paraphernalia 4.

Coffee brewing -- Handbooks, manuals, etc.
ISBN 9781572848047; 1572842334; 9781572842335

LC 2017019958

This book, by Jessica Easto with Andreas Willhoff, "is a comprehensive guide to improving your brew at home. The book provides all the information readers need to discover what they like in a cup of specialty coffee. . . . From the science of extraction and brewing techniques to choosing equipment and deciphering coffee bags, Craft Coffee focuses on the issues . . . that home coffee brewers negotiate." (Publisher's note)

"Clearly written and comprehensive, this book belongs in every home barista's tool kit." Booklist

Includes bibliographical references and index.

642   Meals and table service

Battista, Maggie

Food gift love; more than 100 recipes to make, wrap, and share. Maggie Battista, founder of Eat Boutique ; photography Heidi Murphy. Houghton Mifflin Harcourt 2015 255 p. (paper over board) $25   **642**

1. Gifts 2. Cookbooks 3. Snack foods 4. Gift baskets
ISBN 9780544387676

LC 2015004480

This book, by Maggie Battista, presents a "food-gift guide for crafty cooks and food-DIY fans. . . . [It] features 100 memorable, edible gifts for any occasion with simple, delicious recipes, detailed wrapping instructions, and stunning photography. . . . [It includes diverse projects from] simple homemade infused salts and sugars to instant-gratification gifts like fresh ricotta and flavored butters." (Publisher's note)

"An exquisite book for browsing and inspiration. Best for readers with plenty of time to cook and wrap their edible, special-occasion treasures." LJ

Colwin, Laurie

More home cooking; a writer returns to the kitchen. Laurie Colwin. HarperPerennial 2000 224 p. $12.99   **642**

1. Cookbooks 2. Food 3. Cookery 4. Cooking 5. Entertaining
ISBN 0060955317; 9780060955311

James Beard Cookbook Hall of Fame (2012)

This book, "like its predecessor, 'Home Cooking,' is an expression of [author] Laurie Colwin's lifelong passion for cuisine. In this . . . mix of recipes, advice, and anecdotes, she writes about often overlooked food items such as beets, pears, black beans, and chutney. . . . Colwin also discusses the many pleasures and problems of cooking at home in essays such as 'Desserts That Quiver,' 'Turkey Angst,' and 'Catering on One Dollar a Head.'" (Publisher's note)

Hanel, Marnie

The **picnic**; recipes and inspiration from basket to blanket. Marnie Hanel, Andrea Slonecker, and Jen Stevenson. Artisan 2014 192 p. color illustrations $19.95   **642**

1. Picnics
ISBN 1579656080; 9781579656089

LC 2014036496

IACP Cookbook Award Winner: General (2016)

This book, by Marnie Hanel, Andrea Slonecker, and Jen Stevenson, "shares everything you need to plan an effortless outdoor get-together: no-fail recipes, helpful checklists, and expert advice. With variations on everyone's favorite deviled eggs, 99 uses for a Mason jar, . . . rules for scoring lawn games, and refreshing drinks to mix up in crowd-friendly batches, let 'The Picnic' take the stress out of your next party and leave only the fun." (Publisher's note)

"A fresh look at outdoor entertaining that's just in time for spring and summer. Highly recommended." LJ

Includes an index

Isabella, Maria

★ **Chefs** & Company; 75 top chefs share more than 180 recipes to wow last-minute guests. Maria Isabella ; foreword by Ted Allen ; photography by Ken Goodman. Page Street Publishing 2017 464 p. (pbk.) $35   **642**

1. Cooking
ISBN 1624144551; 162414456X; 9781624144554; 9781624144561

LC 2017930480

This book, by Maria Isabella, presents a "collection of recipes offer[ing] a rare and exciting glimpse into the private home kitchens of 75 culinary superstars. . . . For example, Curtis Stone whips up delicious Charcoal-Grilled Rib Eye Steaks & Boccolini, while Stephanie Izard prepares a fabulous Stir-Fried Eggplant and Sesame Cucumber Salad. For her choice, Naomi Pomeroy makes a mouthwatering Pasta Amatriciana." (Publisher's note)

Rosenstrach, Jenny

Dinner; the playbook; a 30-day plan for mastering the art of the family meal. Jenny Rosenstrach. Ballantine Books Trade Paperbacks 2014 240 p. illustrations (chiefly color) (pbk.) $20   **642**

1. Dinners 2. Eating customs 3. Cooking 4. Families 5. Dinners and dining
ISBN 0345549805; 9780345549808

LC 2013033023

In this book author Jenny Rosenstrach "shares her story, offering weekly meal plans, tons of organizing tips, and eighty-plus super-simple, kid-vetted recipes. She and her husband, Andy, would cook thirty new dishes in a single month--and her kids would try them all. Was it nuts for two working parents to take on this challenge? Yes. But did it transform family dinner from stressful grind to happy ritual? Completely." (Publisher's note)

"Families and novice cooks who accept Rosenstrach's challenge will definitely find a few "keepers" here to add to their repertoire." LJ

Sims, Molly, 1973-

★ **Everyday** chic; my secrets for entertaining, organizing, and decorating at home. Molly Sims with Tracy O'Connor. Dey Street Books 2017 296 p. (tp) $24.99   **642**

1. Entertaining 2. Home economics 3. Interior design 4. Housekeeping
ISBN 0062439634; 9780062439635

LC 2017038316

This book, by Molly Sims, "shares her secrets for effortless entertaining, feeding friends and family, and making your house a home—with just the right amount of her signature supermodel style. . . . Juggling a career and a growing household—and trying to look stylish while doing it—is a challenge for anyone! Molly knows this, and as her family has grown, she has had to be resourceful and savvy, finding fun and stylish solutions that work for her busy life." (Publisher's note)

Includes bibliographical references.

642.4   Meals for social and public occasions

Hudson, Kate

Pretty Fun; Creating and Celebrating a Lifetime of Tradition. Kate Hudson. HarperCollins 2017 272 p. $26.99   **642.4**

1. Cooking 2. Entertaining 3. Family traditions
ISBN 0062685767; 9780062685766

LC 2017044234

This book, by Kate Hudson, "shares her philosophy behind gatherings, how to be in the moment, make them uniquely yours, embracing occasions to just be together. A beautiful, fun, and nourishing guide filled with dozens of dazzling color photos, fabulous recipes for healthy and even some more indulgent snacks and beverages, and infused with Kate's mindful and healthy approach to life, [this book] will help you plan a year of special events." (Publisher's note)

Reed, Julia

Julia Reed's south; Spirited Entertaining and High-Style Fun All Year Long. Julia Reed, Paul Costello ; [edited by] Sandy G. Rizzoli International Publications, Inc. 2016 224 p. color illustrations (hardcover) $50   **642.4**

1. Entertaining
ISBN 9780847848287

LC 2015958266

In this book, author Julia Reed "offers up a feast of options for holiday cocktails, spring lunches, formal dinners, and even a hunt breakfast. Eleven seasonal events feature delicious, easy-to-prepare recipes, ranging from fried chicken to Charlotte Russe and signature cocktails or wine-pairings—she introduces her talented friends (rum makers, potters, fabric designers, bakers) along the way." (Publisher's note)

643   Housing and household equipment

101 Saturday morning projects; organize, decorate, rejuvenate. The Reader's Digest Association. Reader's Digest Association 2010 144 p. col. ill. $14.95   **643**

1. Self-instruction 2. Storage in the home 3. Houses -- Remodeling 4. Do-it-yourself work 5. Storage in the home -- Amateurs' manuals 6. Dwellings -- Remodeling -- Amateurs' manuals 7. Dwellings -- Maintenance and repair -- Amateurs' manuals
ISBN 1606520180; 9781606520185

LC 2009038049

This book "is a storehouse of practical ideas and projects for keeping things running smoothly around your home or apartment. From storage ideas to plumbing fixes, these sensible projects provide easy-to-follow answers to keeping your home and yard in tip-top shape-with no project taking more than four hours." (Publisher's note)

Black & Decker Corp.

The **complete** photo guide to home improvement; [created by the editors of Creative Publishing International, Inc., in cooperation with Black & Decker] Creative Pub. International 2009 560p il $35   **643**

1. Houses -- Remodeling 2. Houses -- Maintenance and repair
ISBN 978-1-58923-452-9; 1-58923-452-9

LC 2008-45755

First published 2001

This home improvement guide covers such topics as flooring, ceilings and walls, windows and doors, and remodeling different rooms including kitchens, bathrooms, and basements.

This "guide is basic, easy to follow, and completely illustrated. The organization is sensible and information easy to find." Libr J

The **complete** photo guide to home repair. Creative Pub. International 2008 559p il $35 **643**
1. Houses -- Maintenance and repair
ISBN 978-1-58923-417-8; 1-58923-417-0

LC 2008-16520

First published 1999
"Features more than 200 . . . home repair projects, including common wiring, plumbing, interior and exterior repairs." Publisher's note

The **book** of home how-to; complete photo guide to home repair & improvement. Black+Decker. Cool Springs Press 2014 600 p. color illustrations (hardback) $35 **643**
1. Houses -- Maintenance and repair 2. Dwellings -- Maintenance and repair -- Amateurs' manuals
ISBN 9781591865988

LC 2013047686

This book, by the editors of Cool Springs Press, offers a "fully-loaded, ridiculously overpacked reference book for every home project you can dream of; the compilation of our longstanding expertise; the home how-to book to crush all others. . . . This book is an A-to-Z encyclopedia with precise how-to instructions and clear photos packed onto every page." (Publisher's note)
"For libraries that lack the titles it pulls from, this compilation is a recommended addition. The photos and instructions are quite strong, and the lack of topical arrangement is awkward but not insurmountable." LJ

Bray, Ilona M.
Nolo's essential guide to buying your first home; [by] Ilona Bray, Alayna Schroeder & Marcia Stewart. 6th edition Nolo 2016 430p il $24.99 **643**
1. Houses -- Buying and selling
ISBN 9781413323450

LC 2016026455

First published 2007. Frequently revised
Provides information on selecting the right house, the right mortgage, the right agent, the right inspections and more. CD-ROM contains a "Homebuyer's Toolkit" with forms and other resources.
Includes bibliographical references

Bryson, Bill
At home; a short history of private life. Doubleday 2010 497p il $28.95 **643**
1. Rooms 2. Houses
ISBN 978-0-7679-1938-8; 0-7679-1938-6

LC 2010-04008

The author takes readers on a tour of his house, a rural English parsonage, showing how each room has figured in the evolution of private life.
"It takes a very particular kind of thoughtfulness, as well as a bold temperament, to stuff all this research into a mattress that's supportive enough to loll about on while pondering the real subject of this book—the development of the modern world. . . . Bryson is fascinated by everything, and his curiosity is infectious." N Y Times Book Rev
Includes bibliographical references

Complete do-it-yourself manual; by Editors Of Family Handyman. Simon & Schuster 2014 528 p. color illustrations $35 **643**
1. Self-instruction 2. House construction

ISBN 1621452018; 9781621452010
This book is a "manual for home improvements. . . . Written in a style of text that addresses readers in a very accessible, conversational tone for easy, user-friendly assistance with every do-it-yourself task. All instructions and materials have been updated to address current codes (electrical, plumbing and building), and revised to indicate the very latest in materials, tools, and technology." (Publisher's note)
"A worthy competitor to this old standby is Black and Decker's The Complete Photo Guide to Home Repair , but the Complete Do-It-Yourself Manual is still more comprehensive and detailed. Recommended for all libraries." LJ

The **complete** guide to finishing basements; projects and practical solutions for converting basements into livable space. by Editors of Cool Springs Press. Cool Springs Press 2013 239 p. color illustrations (softcover) $24.99 **643**
1. Basements 2. Houses -- Remodeling 3. Basements -- Remodeling -- Amateurs' manuals
ISBN 1591865883; 9781591865889

LC 2013009481

This book "covers every aspect of designing and planning a basement conversion/remodeling project. . . . It deals comprehensively with adapting home mechanical systems to basement conditions. The many featured projects include finishing a bathroom stub-out, installing an all-new basement bathroom, insulating, repairing foundation walls, installing sump pumps, dehumidification strategies, as well as many other projects designed for livability." (Publisher's note)

Crook, David
The **Wall** Street Journal complete home owner's guidebook; make the most of your biggest asset in any market. Three Rivers Press 2008 260p il pa $14.95 **643**
1. Real estate investment 2. Houses -- Buying and selling
ISBN 978-0-307-40592-0; 0-307-40592-3

LC 2008-25355

This is a "look at the pros and cons of owning a home—rather than renting one from a bank via a mortgage—along with its ultimate costs. . . . For those aspiring to own a home and those trying to manage the affordability of their biggest asset, this is a must read." Publ Wkly
Includes bibliographical references

Do it yourself kitchens; stunning spaces on a shoestring budget. Wiley 2011 192p **643**
1. Kitchens
ISBN 9781118031629
"Ranked by budget, from $1000 up to $10,000, sample kitchen makeovers showcased here illustrate a range of possibilities. With spending breakdowns, stunning before-and-after shots, and lots of tips that make big differences, this book has wide appeal. For each makeover there are detailed instructions for selected projects, such as installing fixtures, resurfacing, and tiling. This is not in-depth how-to, but ideas and inspiration. Each sample kitchen is brimming with creativity and innovation." Libr J

German, Roger
Remodeling a basement; Rev. ed.; Taunton Press 2010 170p il (Taunton's build like a pro) pa $19.95 **643**
1. Basements 2. Houses -- Remodeling
ISBN 978-1-60085-292-3

LC 2009-33545

First published 2004
"Beginning with solving moisture problems, then renovating space, this book walks the reader through a logical process for repair and re-

modeling, with easy-to-follow instruction and illustrations. Design ideas and the latest building code data are also included." Libr J

Home Depot, Inc.

Home improvement 1-2-3; 3rd ed., Newly expanded and rev.; Home Depot Books 2008 607p il $34.95   **643**
1. Interior design 2. Houses -- Remodeling 3. Houses -- Maintenance and repair
ISBN 978-0-696-23850-5

        LC 2008-924090
First published 1995
This book offers illustrated instructions for home remodeling, decorating, and repair.

Litchfield, Michael W.

Renovation; [by] Michael Litchfield; Chip Harley, technical editor. The Taunton Press, Inc. 2012 615 p. color illustrations $50   **643**
1. Houses -- Remodeling
ISBN 1600854923; 9781600854927

        LC 2005110
This book, in its fourth edition, "contains the collective wisdom of hundreds of contractors, architects and tradespeople who shared their first-hand experience with [author] Mike Litchfield as he interviewed and photographed them on job sites across North America. . . . [It] contain[s] extensively revised chapters on planning; doors, windows and skylights; electrical wiring; and energy conservation." (Publisher's note)

O'Connor, Kevin

The **best** homes from This old house; Kevin O'Connor ; photographs by Michael Casey. Stewart, Tabori & Chang 2011 225 p. color illustrations $35   **643**
1. House construction 2. Domestic architecture 3. Architecture, Domestic -- United States 4. Dwellings -- Remodeling -- United States 5. Dwellings -- United States -- Maintenance and repair
ISBN 1584799358; 9781584799351

        LC 2011018212
Author Kevin O'Connor "chronicle[s] 10 of the finest transformations rendered by the craftsmen and artists from the past decade of filming the show ['This Old House']. Never before have completed projects from This Old House been displayed in such detail. From interiors to exteriors, with insights from every step of the process, the works presented in this book will give devotees of 'This Old House' something they've never had before—the rarely shown finished spaces." (Publisher's note)

Reader's Digest Association, Inc.

Complete do-it-yourself manual; with the editors of Family handyman. rev and updated; Reader's Digest 2005 528p il $35   **643**
1. Houses -- Maintenance and repair
ISBN 0-7621-0579-8

        LC 2004-50945
First published 1973 with title: Reader's Digest complete do-it-yourself manual
This manual for homeowners covers topics such as power tools, plumbing, landscaping, and storage projects with photos, diagrams and illustrations
"Intriguing sidebars on wood refinishers (the fastest drying versus the safest), the financial benefits of renting specialty tools for a large drywall project and other subjects round out this must-have guide." Publ Wkly

New fix-it-yourself manual; by Reader's Digest. The Reader's Digest Association, Inc. 1996 448 p. color illustrations $35   **643**
1. Self-instruction 2. Furniture -- Repairing 3. Electric household appliances -- Maintenance and repair 4. Do-it-yourself work 5. Furniture -- Repairing -- Amateurs' manuals 6. Household appliances -- Maintenance and repair -- Amateurs' manuals 7. Household appliances, Electric -- Maintenance and repair -- Amateurs' manuals
ISBN 0895778718; 9780895778710

        LC 96015189
This book is a "reference guide for every homeowner, guaranteed to help you maintain and improve your home while saving time and money. Covering everything from replacing faulty faucets and showerheads to curing the quirks of an air conditioner, this book provides step-by-step illustrated instructions, plus a comprehensive chapter on tools. Includes more than 3,000 instructional photographs, illustrations, charts, and diagrams." (Publisher's note)

Soles, Clyde

The **fire** smart home handbook; preparing for and surviving the threat of wildfire. Clyde Soles ; foreword by Molly Mowery. Lyons Press 2014 288 p. illustrations (some color) (pbk.) $19.95   **643**
1. Wildfires 2. Houses -- Safety measures 3. Wildfires -- United States -- Prevention and control 4. Dwellings -- Fires and fire prevention -- United States
ISBN 0762796901; 9780762796908

        LC 2013050242
Written by Clyde Soles, "this highly detailed and practical guide will help you live safely in the wildfire zone and save you time and money along the way, providing various methods of risk mitigation along with the financial level of each action. . . . This book will help you create a survivable space that will not only enhance the scenery but may increase the value of your home." (Publisher's note)
"While not everyone has to worry about wildfire, some of this advice applies to fire preparedness in most any home." Pub Wkly

Sussman, Julie

Dare to repair; a do-it-herself guide to fixing (almost) anything in the home. {by} Julie Sussman and Stephanie Glakas-Tenet; illustrations by Yeorgos Lampathakis. HarperCollins Pubs. 2002 253p il pa $14.95   **643**
1. Houses -- Maintenance and repair
ISBN 0-06-095984-3

        LC 2002-27625
The authors "show women how to perform a number of the most common repairs, including unclogging drains and toilets, replacing electrical switches and outlets, leveling appliances, lighting pilot lights, unsticking windows, and installing a door peephole. . . . This is a wonderful book that should be purchased by every public library." Libr J

★ **Ultimate** guide; home repair and improvement; technical editor for updated edition: Charles T. Byers. Updated edition Creative Homeowner 2016 599 p illustrations $29.99 **643**
1. Dwellings -- Remodeling -- Handbooks, manuals, etc. 2. Dwellings -- Maintenance and repair -- Handbooks, manuals, etc.
ISBN 9781580117838
Home emergencies -- Safety & security -- Remodeling guide -- Tools -- Fasteners & adhesives -- Masonry -- Electrical -- Plumbing -- Insulation -- Heating -- Cooling -- Ventilation -- Floors & stairs -- Walls & ceilings -- Trimwork -- Cabinets & counters -- Shelving & storage

-- Roofing -- Siding -- Windows & doors -- Decks, patios & walks -- Unfinished space -- Canadian code

"The most complete home improvement manual on the market, this book offers more than 2,300 photos, 800 drawings, and understandable, practical text. Readers will find essential instruction on plumbing and electrical repairs, heating and cooling, roofing and siding, cabinets and countertops, and more. Information is also provided on tools, materials, and basic skills, plus 325 step-by-step projects with how-to photo sequences." (Publisher's note)

Wilson, Bee

Consider the fork; a history of how we cook and eat. Bee Wilson ; with illustrations by Annabel Lee. Basic Books 2012 xxiii, 327 p.p (hardback) $26.99 **643**
1. Food writing 2. Eating habits 3. Eating customs 4. Cooking -- History 5. Kitchen utensils -- History 6. Dinners and dining -- History
ISBN 9780465021765; 9780465033324

LC 2012016283

Author Bee Wilson presents an "evolution of cooking around the world, revealing the hidden history of everyday objects we often take for granted. Knives . . . predate the discovery of fire, whereas the fork endured centuries of ridicule before gaining widespread acceptance . . . Blending history, science, and anthropology, Wilson reveals how our culinary tools and tricks came to be, and how their influence has shaped modern food culture." (Publisher's note)

Includes bibliographical references and index.

Wing, Charlie

★ **How** your house works; a visual guide to understanding and maintaining your home. Charlie Wing. Expanded and updated third ed. Wiley 2018 216 p illustrations $27.95 **643**
1. Buildings -- Mechanical equipment 2. Dwellings -- Maintenance and repair
ISBN 9781119467618

LC 2018008701

"The revised and updated third edition of How Your House Works is a hands-on guide that gives you the low-down on why your faucet is leaking, your dishwasher is overflowing, or your furnace is on the fritz. This comprehensive book is your reference to virtually everything in your house with richly illustrated explanations of electrical systems, heating and air conditioning, plumbing, major household appliances, foundation, framing, doors, and windows. This must-have book answers most questions homeowners face when repairs are needed or when a new house or addition is in your future." (Publisher's note)

643.12   Selecting, buying, selling homes

Scott, Drew

Dream home; the Property Brothers' ultimate guide to finding & fixing your perfect house. Jonathan Scott, Drew Scott ; photography by David Tsay. Houghton Mifflin Harcourt Publishing Company 2016 304 p. color illustrations (paper over board) $30 **643.12**
1. Houses -- Remodeling 2. Houses -- Buying and selling 3. House buying 4. Dwellings -- Inspection 5. Dwellings -- Remodeling
ISBN 0544715675; 9780544715677

LC 2015037674

Authors Jonathan Scott and Drew Scott present this "comprehensive source, covering the ins and outs of buying, selling, and renovating a house, with hundreds of full-color photos throughout. The brothers

cover numerous topics including the hidden costs of moving, savvy negotiating tactics, and determining your home must-haves. Other handy features include a calendar of key dates for finding the best deals on home products and a cheat sheet of worth-it fix-its." (Publisher's note)

"Dream Home is full of ideas and is a good source for anyone looking to buy, sell, or renovate a property. " Booklist

643.52   Bathrooms

Bathroom upgrades; editors of Fine Homebuilding. The Taunton Press, Inc. 2016 220 p. (ebook) $17.99; $24.95 **643.52**
1. Bathrooms -- Remodeling 2. Bathrooms -- Remodeling -- Amateurs' manuals
ISBN 9781631868078; 9781631866548

LC 2016027698

"This completely new edition from the editors of 'Fine Homebuilding' will provide all the advice you need to remodel a bathroom of any size or shape, on any budget. Our pros will take you through every step of the process from choosing the best materials for your bathroom and designing to get the most storage and daylight in your room, through tiling a tub surround, to building a floating vanity and installing a toilet." (Publisher's note)

"Considerations of design and accessibility are illustrated, along with bathroom storage, fixtures, surface options, and more. The helpful pros and cons comparisons aide with planning decisions." LJ

643.7   Renovation, improvement, remodeling

★ **Popular** mechanics how to fix anything; essential home repairs anyone can do. Popular Mechanics. Hearst Books, an imprint of Sterling Publishing, Inc. 2018 190 p. $19.95 **643.7**
1. Plumbing 2. Houses -- Maintenance and repair 3. Dwellings -- Maintenance and repair -- Amateurs' manuals
ISBN 1618372602; 9781618372604

LC 2017276920

This book, by Popular Mechanics, "is the handy and reliable go-to guide for the most common household problems offering a primer on plumbing, unexpected hacks like using a golf tee to fill a stripped screw hole, instructions for tuning up the garage door, and so much more. . . . [The book] answers questions about the trickiest fix-its, including how to deal with a recurring ceiling cracks or get rid of that stench from the kitchen sink." (Publisher's note)

""Know your stuff" highlights tools, materials, and their appropriate uses, whether fillers, painter's knives, or screws. The "essential tool" call-outs spotlight particular instruments that are critical to have on hand. And captioned, step-by-step color photographs bring clarity to specific tasks." Booklist

Susanka, Sarah

Not so big remodeling; tailoring your home for the way you really live. by Sarah Susanka and Marc Vassallo. Taunton Press 2012 329 p. illustrations (chiefly color) $24.95 **643.7**
1. Houses -- Remodeling
ISBN 1600858244; 9781600858246

LC 2008046632

In this book, authors Sarah Susanka and Marc Vassallo "demonstrate how carefully chosen tweaks and simple additions can make a home seem much larger and more inviting. . . . [They] show readers how to think like an architect, so they can accurately assess their home's short-comings, apply 'Not So Big' principles to their remodeling plan, and phase in their project incrementally over time." (Publisher's note)

645   Household furnishings

Montano, Mark

The **big**-ass book of home decor; photographs by Auxy Espinoza. Stewart, Tabori & Chang 2010 271p il pa $22.50 **645**
1. Interior design
ISBN 978-1-58479-825-5

LC 2009-36376

The author "presents over 100 projects for decorating, creating, and repurposing furniture and decorative accessories. He offers clearly written instructions illustrated with color photographs of the steps. The wealth of inspiring projects that require only basic skills—e.g., decoupage, spray paint, glue gun—will make this a popular choice for both experienced and inexperienced crafters." Libr J

Petersik, Sherry

Lovable livable home; how to add beauty, get organized, and make your house work for you. Sherry and John Petersik of Young House Love. Artisan 2015 336 p. color illustrations (alk. paper) $27.50 **645**
1. Houses 2. Interior design 3. Interior decoration 4. Dwellings -- Remodeling
ISBN 1579656226; 9781579656225

LC 2015010991

In this book authors Sherry Petersik and John Peterski " set out to prove that just because you have kids or pets doesn't mean you're sentenced to floors overrun with toys or furniture covered in plastic. Through never-before-seen makeovers in the Petersiks¿ own house, doable DIY projects, and a gallery of other inspiring spaces, Lovable Livable Home shows how beautiful homes can be functional too." (Publisher's note)

"The clever ideas developed by these amateurs that adapt to the needs of busy families will motivate others to tackle their own spaces." LJ

Includes bibliographical references and index

646   Sewing, clothing, management of personal and family life

Stowell, Lauren

The **American** duchess guide to 18th century dressmaking; how to hand sew georgian gowns and wear them with style. Lauren Stowell and Abby Cox. Page Street Pub. Co. 2017 240 p. (pbk.) $24.99 **646**
1. Sewing 2. Dressmaking 3. Clothing and dress -- History -- 18th century
ISBN 1624144535; 1624144543; 9781624144530; 9781624144547

LC 2017942125

In this book, by Lauren Stowell and Abby Cox, "learn how to make four of the most iconic 18th century silhouettes--the English Gown, Sacque Gown, Italian Gown and Round Gown--using the same hand sewing techniques done by historic dressmakers. From large hoops to full bums, wool petticoats to grand silk gowns, ruffled aprons to big feathered hats, this manual has project patterns and instructions for every level of 18th century sewing enthusiast." (Publisher's note)

646.2   Sewing and related operations

Bednar, Nancy

The **encyclopedia** of sewing machine techniques; [by] Nancy Bednar, JoAnn Pugh-Gannon. Sterling Pub. 2007 336p il pa $24.95 **646.2**
1. Sewing
ISBN 1-4027-4293-2; 978-1-4027-4293-4
First published 1999

Among the techniques covered in this illustrated step-by-step guide are beading, fringing, pintucks, and puffing.

Bull, Jane

Get set, sew; the beginner's sewing machine book. Jane Bull. Dk Pub 2015 125 p. color illustrations (hardcover) $20 **646.2**
1. Sewing 2. Handicraft
ISBN 1465435875; 9781465435873

LC 2015472670

This handicraft book, by Jane Bull, "is a clear, fresh, enjoyable introduction to sewing on a machine. Jane's friendly, jargon-free instructions and step-by-step photos will walk you through everything you need to know to learn how to use a sewing machine. Master sewing machine basics one at a time, then put newly learned skills to work with 20 simple sewing projects to make--including creative and original bags, accessories, cushions, and toys." (Publisher's note)

Creative Publishing International, Inc.

★ The **complete** photo guide to sewing; 1200 full-color how-to photos. [created by the editors of Creative Publishing International] Rev. + expanded ed.; Creative Pub. International 2009 352p il pa $24.99 **646.2**
1. Sewing
ISBN 978-1-58923-434-5; 1-58923-434-0

LC 2008-31264

First published 1999

"Sections include choosing the right tools and notions, using conventional machines and sergers, fashion sewing, tailoring, and home décor projects. Included are step-by-step instructions for basic projects like pillows, tablecloths, and window treatments." Publisher's note

The **complete** photo guide to window treatments; [edited by Linda Neubauer] 2nd ed; Creative Publisher International 2011 320p il pa $24.99 **646.2**
1. Draperies
ISBN 978-1-58923-607-3

LC 2010046925

First published 2007

"Fabric recommendations and materials lists introduce each style of window treatment, with clear, step-by-step instructions. Organization is consistent and well thought out, making this an easy manual to follow." Libr J

Includes bibliographical references

First time sewing; the absolute beginner's guide. by the editors of Creative Publishing international. Creative Publishing international, a member of Quayside Publishing Group 2014 127 p. (pbk.) $19.99; (ebook) $19.99 **646.2**
1. Sewing 2. Machine sewing
ISBN 1589238044; 9781589238046; 9781627880091

LC 2015430813

This book, by the editors of Creative Publishing international, is a "guide that . . . teaches you how to sew using hand stiches as well as sewing machines. Filled with detailed descriptions of materials and tools, the easy step-by-step instructions for all the basic sewing techniques will have you creating projects like aprons, pillows, and even pants and shorts in no time." (Publisher's note)

Gardiner, Wendy

The **sewing** machine accessory bible; get the most out of your machine from using basic feet to mastering specialty feet. [by] Wendy Gardiner & Lorna Knight. Griffin: St. Martin's 2011 128p il pa $22.99   **646.2**

1. Sewing machines

ISBN 978-0-312-67658-2

This book focuses "on sewing machine accessories—feet, needles, and other attachments. . . . [The authors] briefly cover the basics of sewing machines, but they focus on the specialized feet that come with the machine. A photo of a sewing machine foot is included at the top left corner of each spread, allowing for quick and easy identification. There's also information about how to use each foot—what it's for and how to sew with it. Beginners will find this book especially handy." Libr J

Handmade interiors; DK Publishing. DK Publishing 2015 304 p. color illustrations $40   **646.2**

1. Furniture 2. Interior design

ISBN 1465427082; 9781465427083

This book by DK Publishing "shows you how to create your own soft furnishings, such as cushions and curtains, and transform every room in the house. Clear step-by-step pictures show how to create your version of the inspiration pieces shown, while advice on fabrics and suggested variations are provided to help you tailor each project to your own unique space and budget." (Publisher's note)

"This book will soon become a well-worn reference." LJ

Ishida, Sanae

Sewing happiness; A Year of Simple Projects for Living Well. Sanae Ishida. Sasquatch Books 2016 225 p. illustrations $22.95   **646.2**

1. Sewing 2. Autobiography 3. Machine sewing

ISBN 9781570619953

LC 2015040697

In this book, "twenty simple sewing projects are tied together with a thread of memoir that tells the story of how sewing brought Sanae Ishida profound happiness. Each seasonal project, specially designed to promote health, creativity, relationships and more, provides gentle inspiration to live your best life." (Publisher's note)

"The instructions are thorough, the tips and advice are generous, and the overall presentation is thoughtful." LJ

Includes bibliographical references

Lee, Linda

Sewing edges and corners. Taunton Press 2000 134p il pa $19.95   **646.2**

1. Sewing

ISBN 1-56158-418-5

LC 00-29919

The author offers about 40 corner and edge techniques for garments and home decorating projects

"Readers appreciate the clarity of Lee's instructions, since each step is numbered, photographs and other illustrations ease difficult tasks, and sidebars ensure the comfortableness of the sewing." Booklist

Lindsay, Virginia

Sewing to sell; the beginner's guide to starting a craft business; bonus, 16 starter projects; how to sell locally & online. Virginia Lindsay. C&T Publishing 2014 152 p. color illustrations (soft cover) $25.95   **646.2**

1. Sewing 2. Arts and crafts movement 3. Selling -- Handbooks, manuals, etc 4. Small business -- Management -- Handbooks, manuals, etc 5. Handicraft industries -- Management -- Handbooks, manuals, etc 6. Home-based businesses -- Management -- Handbooks, manuals, etc

ISBN 1607059037; 9781607059035

LC 2014013070

Author Virginia Lindsay presents "a book that's half-helpful suggestions for those who want to start a home-based sewing business and half a selection of 16 sewing patterns that can be used to make projects to sell. The first section contains valuable information on everything from identifying potential customers to taking good photos for online sales and setting prices for craft shows." (Publishers Weekly)

"Most appropriate for crafters who need a very basic guide to selling their handmade goods. Those looking to take their business to the next level will benefit from Kari Chapin's Grow Your Handmade Business and The Handmade Marketplace, which provide a more comprehensive view of operating a craft-based enterprise." LJ

Includes bibliographical references

Lubin, Clementine

A **beginner's** guide to overlockers, sergers & coverlockers; 50 lessons and 15 projects to get you started. Clementine Lubin. Random House Inc 2018 160 p. $19.95   **646.2**

1. Sewing 2. Needlework

ISBN 1782214909; 9781782214908

This practical and comprehensive book, by [Clementine Lubin], helps you master all the functions and applications of your overlocker and coverlocker, from the simplest to the most complex. There are 50 beautifully photographed step-by-step lessons and 15 lovely projects to apply your knowledge and help you realize your sewing goals. You can make a dress, a T-shirt, a shoulder bag, a playsuit and more." (Publisher's note)

New complete guide to sewing; step-by-step techniques for making clothes and home accessories. Reader's Digest. Reader's Digest Association 2011 384 p. ill. (some col.) $35   **646.2**

1. Sewing 2. Tailoring 3. Dressmaking 4. Household linens

ISBN 1606522086; 9781606522080

LC 2010029616

This book is the "ultimate stitch-and-seam reference book for both beginners and seasoned sewers. . . . In this updated edition, sewers will find 20 new modern projects from Simplicity patterns; Instructions for making smart trousers, traditional curtains, a light summer dress, kids' clothes, a beach towel, patchwork bag, and more." (Publisher's note)

The **new** sewing essentials; Updated and rev. ed.; Creative Publishing International 2008 144p il pa $16.99   **646.2**

1. Sewing

ISBN 978-1-58923-432-1; 1-58923-432-4

First published 1984 by Random House with title: Sewing essentials

This guide to sewing clothes and other items includes information on equipment, patterns, fabrics, and techniques.

Paganelli, Jennifer

Happy home; twenty-one sewing and craft projects to pretty up your home. by Jennifer Paganelli ; with Dolin O'Shea ; photographs by Tim Geaney. Chronicle Books 2012 175 p. illustrations $27.50   **646.2**

    1. Sewing 2. Interior design 3. Machine sewing 4. House furnishings

    ISBN 0811874451; 9780811874458

                                      LC 2011018891

    In this book, author Jennifer Paganelli "shows readers how to whip up twenty-one beautiful accessories to transform their space into a sunny, happy home. Each project showcases Jennifer's . . . style—from luxe drapery to cheery tablecloths and napkins. Featuring simple step-by-step instructions, a comprehensive glossary of techniques, pattern sheets tucked into a handy front pocket, and lush color photos, this book makes it exceptionally easy to pretty up every room in the house." (Publisher's note)

Sandqvist, Anton

    Heavy duty sewing; making backpacks and other stuff. Anton Sandqvist. Motorbooks Intl 2018 128 p. $19.99   **646.2**

    1. Sewing 2. Needlework

    ISBN 0711239258; 9780711239258

    This craft book, by Anton Sandqvist, "is all about using needle and thread, a sewing machine and stiff materials to make your own practical, hardwearing functional objects. . . . [It] teaches you all about leather and how to repair your own belongings. You then have the chance to put these techniques into practice by turning your hand at ten cool projects for countryside, town and travel." (Publisher's note)

    "With awe-inspiring photos of mountain ranges and other Nordic landscapes throughout, Sandqvist encourages adventuresome sewers with projects that are practical and a lifestyle that's aspirational." Pub Wkly

Shore, Debbie

    Half yard gifts; easy sewing projects using left-over pieces of fabric. Debbie Shore. Search Press 2015 96 p. color illustrations (paperback) $19.95   **646.2**

    1. Gifts 2. Sewing

    ISBN 9781782211501; 1782211500

    This book "is the latest title from sewing guru Debbie Shore, and the next book in her best-selling half yard series. . . . It contains 22 projects to sew and give away, each made using less than half a yard of fabric. The book contains gifts for all your family and friends: the projects range from pincushions, bags and paperweights to aprons for budding chefs, kneeling pads for gardeners and tool belts for DIY-enthusiasts." (Publisher's note)

    "Gift sewing is popular, and there's a wide range of projects here. Sewists looking for cute, feminine gift designs will enjoy." LJ

Smith, Alison

    The **sewing** book; An Encyclopedic Resource of Step-by-Step Techniques. Alison Smith. DK Pub. 2009 400 p. illustrations (some color) (ebook) $65; $40   **646.2**

    1. Sewing

    ISBN 9780756657185; 0756642809; 9780756642808

    This book, by Alison Smith, "is the only sewing book you'll ever need. Every tool and every technique you require for making your own home furnishings or clothing is closely and sharply photographed, carefully annotated, and clearly explained." (Publisher's note0

Staples, Heidi

    Sew organized for the busy girl; tips to make the most of your time & space; 23+ quick and clever sewing projects you'll

love. by Heidi Staples. C&T Publishing, Inc. 2015 112 p. illustrations (some color) (softcover) $22.95   **646.2**

    1. Sewing 2. Time management 3. House furnishings

    ISBN 1607059797; 9781607059790

                               LC 2014031103

    This book, by Heidi Staples, describes how to "fit sewing into your busy lifestyle with practical tips that will help you put hours back on the clock! . . . Revive your creative life and make the most of your time with easy-to-implement advice. Stitch up 23 projects, ranging from handcrafted quilts to home decor, children's gifts, and attractive storage cases." (Publisher's note)

    "Staples's suggestions range from useful (gathering items related to an ongoing project into a project bag) to a little silly (using a weekly "family meeting" to declare your need for some sewing time), but the chronically disorganized—and those seeking a better system—will appreciate her low-stress, creative approach." LJ

Yaker, Rebecca

    Little one-yard wonders; by Rebecca Yaker and Patricia Hoskins. Storey Publishing 2014 360 p. color illustrations (One-yard wonders series) (paper w/concealed wire-o and patterns; alk. paper) $29.95   **646.2**

    1. Handicraft 2. Children's clothing 3. Machine sewing 4. Children's paraphernalia

    ISBN 1612121241; 9781612121246

                               LC 2013045043

    Written by Rebecca Yaker and Patricia Hoskins, "[t]his newest addition to the best-selling One-Yard Wonders series features 101 . . . projects for babies and kids, each using just one yard of fabric and many requiring just a few hours to complete. Step-by-step illustrated instructions, . . . close-up photographs, and pattern pieces included in a bound-in envelope make it easy and fun to create all kinds of adorable items." (Publisher's note)

    "This title is a treasure trove of handmade kid's stuff, and sewists of all skill levels will find ideas and inspiration in this lighthearted collection." LJ

    One-yard wonders; look how much you can make with just one yard of fabric! Rebecca Yaker and Patricia Hoskins ; photography by John Gruen ; photo styling by Raina Kattelson. Storey Pub. 2009 303 p. ill. (some col.) $24.95   **646.2**

    1. Sewing 2. Interior design 3. Clothing and dress 4. Machine sewing 5. House furnishings

    ISBN 1603424490; 9781603424493

                               LC 2009023721

    This book, by Rebecca Yaker and Patricia Hoskins, "presents a delightful array of simple, stylish projects that can be made with just a single yard of fabric - from apparel to accessories, from plush toys to pet beds, from baby items to bags, and from home decor to 'Happy Birthday' banners. Projects have a hip, contemporary flair, and most can be completed in a few hours." (Publisher's note)

    "This is a fundamental crafts book appropriate for most crafts collections." Booklist

646.21   Construction of home furnishings

Ellis, Cassandra

    Home sewn; projects and inspiration for every room. Cassandra Ellis. Random House Inc. 2016 160 p. color illustrations (hardcover) $24.99   **646.21**

    1. Sewing 2. Handicraft

ISBN 9781101906958; 1101906952

LC 2015030531

This craft book, by Cassandra Ellis, "features distinctive sewing projects dedicated to living, resting, eating, and sharing. Use quality materials—from rustic linen to leather—to create simple ottomans, pendant light shades, a voile bed skirt, and more. With dreamy lifestyle photography and ideas for every room." (Publisher's note)

Pillows, curtains, & shades; step by step. DK ; project editor: Anne Hildyard. DK Publishing 2017 224 p. color illustrations (paperback) $15.95 **646.21**
1. Sewing 2. Draperies 3. House furnishings 4. Household linens 5. Textile fabrics in interior decoration
ISBN 9781465455758; 9781465464521; 1465455752

LC 2017304824

This book, from DK, presents "25 easy projects to elevate your home decor without the expensive price tag. Sew curtains, make Roman blinds, design bed runners, and more. You'll learn how to make everything from professional curtains and cushion covers to seating, bedding, and blinds with guided step-by-step instructions and clear photography." (Publisher's note)

"Aimed at experienced sewers, this painstaking guidebook encourages readers to save money by tackling decorating projects, providing clear and complete steps along with details photographs for 25 domestic projects." Pub Wkly

646.4   Clothing and accessories construction

Adams, Anne
Bags and totes; 10 easy, fashionable projects anyone can sew. Liz Johnson and Anne Adams, founders & managing editors of Sew4Home. Fons & Porter 2016 127 p. color illustrations (Sew4home) (paperback) $22.99 **646.4**
1. Sewing 2. Handbags -- Design and construction 3. Tote bags -- Design and construction
ISBN 9781440245046; 1440245045

This book in the Sew4home series, by Liz Johnson and Anne Adams, shows "you how to create ten hip projects, from clutches and shoulder bags to a slick yoga mat sling and a vintage kids' book bag. No paper patterns required! . . . You'll find step-by-step instructions and sewing tutorials. Learn to make ruffles, fussy cut fabric, add an inset zipper, and other design details to give your bag a professional finish." (Publisher's note)

"The tutorials are detailed and walk beginners through each step, with tips and illustrations provided as needed." LJ

Armstrong, Helen Joseph
Patternmaking for fashion design; technical illustrator, Vincent James Maruzzi; fashion illustrator, Kathryn Hagen. 4th ed; Pearson Prentice Hall 2006 xxi, 805p il $104.40 **646.4**
1. Dressmaking -- Patterns
ISBN 978-0-13-194893-9; 0-13-194893-8

LC 2005-283500

First published 1987 by Harper & Row

"Covers the three steps in the development of design patterns—dart manipulation, added fullness, and contouring—with a central theme that all designs are based on one, or more of these three major patternmaking and design principles." Publisher's note

Includes bibliographical references

Butler, Amy
Amy Butler's style stitches; 12 Easy Ways to 26 Wonderful Bags. by Amy Butler. Chronicle Books 2010 182 p. illustrations $29.95 **646.4**
1. Sewing 2. Handbags 3. Fancy work
ISBN 0811866696; 9780811866699

LC 2009025698

This book on handbag sewing, by Amy Butler, "offers 12 basic patterns with enough variations to achieve 26 unique looks. Ranging from chic clutches and delicate wristlets to pretty hobo bags and handy coin purses, with instructions for altering dimensions, straps, and embellishments to get the desired look, each project incorporates Butler's fresh, modern style and attention to detail." (Publisher's note)

Hirsch, Gretchen
Gertie's ultimate dress book; a modern guide to sewing fabulous vintage styles. Gretchen Hirsch. STC Craft 2016 236 p. color illustrations (hardcover) $35 **646.4**
1. Sewing 2. Dressmaking
ISBN 9781617690754

LC 2015948555

This book, by Gretchen Hirsch, with photography by Karen Pearson, "is packed with all the information and patterns you could ever need to create a wardrobe filled with stunning vintage frocks. The book begins with all the essential techniques for dressmaking and includes instructions and patterns for 23 dresses for a variety of occasions." (Publisher's note)

"Though these garments are less suitable for everyday wear than the ones featured in her previous book, Gertie Sews Vintage Casual, the retro-style dresses will appeal to sewists interested in customizing their own 1950s style frock." LJ

Includes bibliographical references (page 230) and index.

A **modern** guide to sportswear styles of the 1940s and 1950s; Gretchen Hirsch. STC Craft/A Melanie Falick Book 2014 223 p. ills; folded patterns $35 **646.4**
1. Sewing 2. Fashion 3. Women's clothing
ISBN 1617690740; 9781617690747

LC 2014930803

Author "Gretchen 'Gertie' Hirsch celebrates the classic casual styles that icons like Katharine Hepburn, Audrey Hepburn, and Rosie the Riveter made famous--think wide-legged trousers, fitted capri pants, beach rompers, shorts, knit tops, jeans, and day dresses. In Part I, Hirsch introduces key techniques for sportswear construction--from working with knit fabrics to the intricacies of pant-making--and in Part II, she showcases a 30-plus-piece vintage-inspired casual wardrobe." (Publisher's note)

"The audience for Hirsch's second book will likely be wider than that for her first, since casualwear is more accessible than retro-cocktail dresses. Though a few pieces veer toward the costumey, women will find that the garments in this collection fall well within contemporary workplace and casual styles but with a clever, retro flair." LJ

Kim, Sue
Boutique bags; classic style for modern living - 19 projects 76 bags. Sue Kim. C&T Publishing, Inc. 2015 160 p. illustrations, color (soft cover) $24.95 **646.4**
1. Handbags 2. Handicraft
ISBN 1607059851; 9781607059851

LC 2014038488

This handicraft book, by Sue Kim, offers "19 fashionable projects [for making handbags], from a metal-framed clutch to a ruffled carryall, you'll have a match for every outfit. Learn to sew darts, ruffles, and other design elements for a professional finish. Make multiples of your favorites and see for yourself how a simple change in fabric offers a whole new look." (Publisher's note)

"Sewists who enjoy bags designed by Lexie Barnes, Amy Butler, or Sara Lawson will enjoy Kim's stylish designs." LJ

Mallalieu, Nicole

The **better** bag maker; an illustrated handbook of handbag design--techniques, tips, and tricks. Nicole Claire Mallalieu. Stash Books, an imprint of C&T Publishing 2014 192 p. color illustrations (soft cover) $26.95 **646.4**

1. Sewing 2. Handbags
ISBN 1607058057; 9781607058052

LC 2013034373

In this book, by Nicole Claire Mallalieu, "accomplished bag maker, Nicole Mallalieu, reveals her high-end techniques, shortcuts, and secrets for professional design and finishes. The 10 featured projects teach a range of expert skills from adjusting the proportion of the pattern to constructing pockets, straps, flaps, and bases." (Publisher's note)

"While these plans are useful, the technique tutorials are the highlight here—they contain information that can be applied to many bag patterns, not just the ones in this collection. Sewists of every ability level will appreciate having a wealth of bag-making information in a single volume." LJ

Includes bibliographical references (page 191)

Mitnick, Sarai

The **Colette** sewing handbook; inspired styles and classic techniques for the new seamstress. Sarai Mitnick. Krause Publications 2011 176 p. color illustrations $29.99 **646.4**

1. Sewing 2. Dressmaking 3. Dressmaking -- Patterns
ISBN 1440215456; 9781440215452

LC 2011275711

This book, by Sarai Mitnick, presents "simple fundamentals [that] can help you perfect any sewing project. . . . [It] includes five beautiful patterns for modern classic pieces, including a scalloped-hem skirt, flutter-sleeve blouse, sweetheart neck sheath dress, asymmetrical flounce dress, and a lined dress with gathered sleeves. Each project will help you put the fundamentals into practice as you sew." (Publisher's note)

"Though the book is intended for beginners, it is appropriate for sewers of all levels who appreciate a well-tailored garment." LJ

Quindt, Svetlana

The **costume** making guide; creating armor & props for cosplay. Svetlana Quindt , AKA Kamui Cosplay. Impact 2016 128 p. color illustrations (paperback) $22.99 **646.4**

1. Cosplay 2. Costume 3. Costume design
ISBN 1440345163; 9781440345166; 9781440345258

In this book, author Svetlana Quindt [brings] "your cosplay dreams to life. . . . Internationally known cosplayer Kamui Cosplay (a.k.a. Svetlana Quindt) shows you how to easily create elaborate costumes and successful props out of items available at your local arts and craft or hardware stores: turn foam into a realistic axe, create a breastplate from scratch and use a glue gun to modify just about anything." (Publisher's note)

"Cosplay armor and props are the focus of Quindt's guide, which takes crafters through the steps of designing, fitting, and creating custom pieces." LJ

Smith, Alison

Dressmaking; The Complete Step-by-Step Guide to Making your Own Clothes. Alison Smith. DK Publishing 2015 224 p. color illustrations (paperback) $15.95 **646.4**

1. Sewing 2. Dressmaking 3. Clothing and dress 4. Tailoring (Women's)
ISBN 1465429816; 9781465429810

LC 2015300522

This book, by Alison Smith, "covers everything one needs to know to make, alter, and customize clothes. Sewers will discover what supplies to buy and how to use them, the best fabrics to choose based on drape and weave, how to understand patterns and alter them, and the essential general techniques to master — plus patterns and detailed step-by-step instructions are provided for a skirt, dress, shirt, tee, jacket, and pair of pants — including suggested variations!" (Publisher's note)

Veblen, Sarah

The **complete** photo guide to perfect fitting; Sarah Veblen. Creative Pub. International 2012 224 p. color illustrations (pbk.) $24.99 **646.4**

1. Dressmaking 2. Patternmaking 3. Dressmaking -- Pattern design -- Pictorial works 4. Clothing and dress measurements -- Pictorial works 5. Clothing and dress -- Alteration -- Pictorial works
ISBN 1589236084; 9781589236080

LC 2011023810

This book, by Sarah Veblen, "is the ultimate reference for fitting test garments and transferring accurate adjustments to patterns! . . . Rather than making commonly accepted changes to a commercial pattern, the method presented in this guide focuses on the way a test garment fits the body. The fabric is manipulated to improve the fit, and then those specific changes are made to the pattern." (Publisher's note)

646.42 Construction of undergarments and hosiery

Powell, Pamela

Lingerie Design; A Complete Course. Pamela Powell. Chronicle Books Llc 2016 304 p. $65 **646.42**

1. Lingerie -- Design and construction
ISBN 178067791X; 9781780677910

LC 2017002164

"In this book, Pamela Powell takes a very practical approach, showing how to design and construct lingerie, sleepwear, and foundation garments. Step-by-step illustrations demonstrate the basic slopers and show how to manipulate them into different styles. Advice is given about how to work with the specialty fabrics used in the industry including woven, knit, power stretch, and bias-cut fabrics." (Publisher's note)

"Lingerie sewing is increasingly popular among experienced garment sewists, and this guide provides a wealth of information for both home sewists who want to make custom-fit lingerie and designers interested in costuming." LJ

646.45 Construction of outerwear

Tsukiori, Yoshiko

Stylish wraps sewing book; ponchos, capes, coats and more - fashionable warmers that are easy to sew. Yoshiko Tsukiori ; translated from Japanese by Sanae Ishida. Tuttle Publishing 2017 80 p. illustrations (some color) (paperback) $15.95 **646.45**

1. Sewing
ISBN 0804846952; 9780804846950; 9781462919246

This book, by Yoshiko Tsukiori, "provides five free full-sized patterns that can be used to create 22 timeless wraps to keep the chill off—and look great in the process. All the sewing designs can be made in a few hours for a fraction of what you would pay in a store. And it is easy to mix and match different fabrics and styles to suit your wardrobe and mood." (Publisher's note)

646.478   Costumes

Conahan, Gillian

The **hero's** closet; sewing for cosplay and costuming. Gillian Conahan ; photographs by Karen Pearson. Abrams 2017 207 p. illustrations (some color) (paperback) $24.95 **646.478**
1. Sewing 2. Cosplay 3. Costume
ISBN 9781419723964
LC 2016945899

This book, by Gillian Conahan, "offers detailed, step-by-step instructions that cover the basics of sewing costumes (which often require skills not found in standard sewing guides) to help even the most novice sewists create the costumes of their dreams. . . . Gillian Conahan walks readers through finding inspiration online and through their fandom; shares insight into translating character art into real-world garments; and offers advice on . . . techniques." (Publisher's note)

646.7   Management of personal and family life

Becker-Phelps, Leslie

Love; The Psychology of Attraction. by DK (Author) DK Pub 2016 224 p. color illustrations, charts $19.95 **646.7**
1. Courtship 2. Dating (Social customs) 3. Interpersonal relations 4. Love -- Psychological aspects
ISBN 1465429891; 9781465429896

This book "explores the nature of intimate relationships. . . . The book is divided into five chapters, beginning with 'You' and ending with 'Together,' with all the complexities of seeking and dating in between. Specific topics include determining whether a second date is appropriate and deciding whether and when to become physically intimate with a new partner. Interactive exercises guide couples onto the road to harmony." (Publishers Weekly)

"This is one of the most straightforward guides to dating available." LJ

Blake, Jenny

Life after college; the complete guide to getting what you want. Jenny Blake. Running Press 2011 293 p. (pbk.) $17 **646.7**
1. Personal finance 2. College graduates 3. Life skills -- Handbooks, manuals, etc. 4. Professional developmen -- Handbooks, manuals, etc. 5. College graduates -- Employment 6. Young men -- Life skills guides 7. Young women -- Life skills guides 8. Young adults -- Life skills guides 9. College graduates -- Life skills guides
ISBN 0762441275; 9780762441273
LC 2010940614

The book is "full of . . . advice to encourage young adults who are on the precipice of a new life, a life that can be tenuous and daunting. It covers money, relationships (both romantic and familial), friends, health, fun and relaxation, life planning, and personal and professional growth." (Library Journal)

Bowe, Whitney

The **beauty** of dirty skin; the surprising science to looking and feeling radiant from the inside out. Whitney Bowe, MD with Kristin Loberg. Little, Brown & Co. 2018 viii, 278 p.p $28 **646.7**
1. Skin -- Care 2. Skin -- Diseases 3. Personal grooming 4. Skin -- Diseases -- Diet therapy 5. Skin -- Care and hygiene -- Popular works 6. Skin. -- Care and hygiene -- Popular works 7. Skin. -- Diseases -- Diet therapy -- Popular works
ISBN 0316509825; 9780316509824
LC 2017959143

This book, by Whitney Bowe, with Kristin Loberg, presents "the connection between a healthy gut and radiant, clear skin, with a 21-day program to maximize skin health and beauty. . . . Bowe shows readers that skin health is much more than skin deep. . . . [S]he explains how the spectrum of skin disorders . . . are manifestations of irregularities rooted in the gut." (Publisher's note)

Includes bibliographical references (pages 253-265) and index

Cullinane, Jan

The **new** retirement; the ultimate guide to the rest of your life. [by] Jan Cullinane and Cathy Fitzgerald. Rev. and updated ed.; Rodale 2007 484p pa $19.95 **646.7**
1. Retirement
ISBN 978-1-59486-479-7; 1-59486-479-9
LC 2007-15947

First published 2004

This guide provides "information about particular locales, financial planning and tax considerations, lifelong learning opportunities, leisure and volunteer activities, and working after retirement." Publisher's note

Includes bibliographical references

Hinden, Stan

How to retire happy; the 12 most important decisions you must make before you retire. Stan Hinden. McGraw-Hill 2013 xx, 261 p.p (pbk.; acid-free paper) $20 **646.7**
1. Retirement 2. Retirement income 3. Retirement income -- United States 4. Retirement -- United States -- Planning 5. Retirement -- Economic aspects -- United States
ISBN 0071800697; 9780071800693
LC 2012039679

This book, by financial reporter Stan Hinden, "helps you make the right decisions to ensure a happy, healthful retirement. It delivers all the expert advice you need in an easy-to-understand step-by-step style." (Publisher's note)

Johansen, Signe

How to hygge; the Nordic secrets to a happy life. Signe Johansen. St. Martin's Press 2017 192 p. color illustrations $19.99; (ebook) $60 **646.7**
1. Well-being 2. Happiness -- Scandinavia 3. Scandinavia -- Civilization
ISBN 1250122031; 9781250122032; 9781250122049
LC 2016059131

This book, by chef and author Signe Johansen, "is a fresh, informative, lighthearted, fully illustrated how-to guide to hygge. It's a combination of recipes, helpful tips for cozy living at home, and cabin porn: essential elements of living the Danish way--which, incidentally, encourages a daily dose of 'healthy hedonism.'" (Publisher's note)

"Readers interested in simplifying their homes and lives are sure to find plenty of practical recipes and suggestions here that they can implement immediately." Pub Wkly

Includes bibliographical references (pages 202-204) and index.

Lofas, Jeannette

Stepparenting; Rev. and updated.; Citadel Press 2004 241p pa $12.95 **646.7**

1. Parenting 2. Stepparents 3. Stepchildren
ISBN 0-8065-2652-1; 978-0-8065-2652-2

LC 2004-556219

First published 1985 by Zebra Books

"Acknowledging the difficulty of a stepparent's role, this standout title guides readers through carefully forming a stepfamily, with straightforward coverage of the usual issues (e.g., etiquette, praising positive behavior)." Libr J

Massey, Lorraine

Curly girl; the handbook. by Lorraine Massey with Michele Bender. Workman Pub. Co. 2010 xi, 188 p.p ill. (chiefly col.) (alk. paper) $13.95 **646.7**

1. Hair 2. Hair -- Care and hygiene
ISBN 076115678X; 9780761156789

LC 2011004311

This book, by Lorraine Massey, "is packed with unique and failproof hair-care methods, inspiration, and an empowering pro-curl attitude. It's all here: daily routines for Botticelli, fractal, and wavy curls; Lorraine's no-more-shampoo epiphany—handle your hair as gently as you do your best cashmere sweater; homemade lotions and potions." (Publisher's note)

Soukup, Ruth

Unstuffed; Ruth Soukup. Zondervan 2016 219 p. (softcover) $16.99 **646.7**

1. Simplicity 2. Conduct of life 3. Simplicity -- Religious aspects -- Christianity
ISBN 0310337690; 9780310337690

LC 2015031891

In this book, author Ruth Soukup, "through personal stories, Biblical truth, and practical action plans, . . . will inspire and empower each of us to finally declutter not just our home, but our mind and soul as well. 'Unstuffed' is real, honest, and gets right down to the question we are all facing--how can we take back our lives from the stuff that is weighing us down?" (Publisher's note)

"Commonsense suggestions, personal anecdotes, and Soukup's Christian perspective give the book a friendly, nonthreatening feel. Hopefully delving into the why as well as the how may allow some of us to break the 'stuff' cycle." Booklist

Thomas, Mathilde

The French beauty solution; time-tested secrets to look and feel beautiful inside and out. by Mathilde Thomas. Gotham Books 2015 263 p. illustrations (hardback) $26.95 **646.7**

1. Skin -- Care 2. Health self-care 3. Personal grooming 4. Personal appearance 5. Women -- Health and hygiene 6. Beauty, Personal 7. Self-care, Health 8. Skin -- Care and hygiene
ISBN 1592409512; 9781592409518

LC 2015003934

In this book, author Mathilde Thomas "shares the simple, natural, time-tested beauty secrets she learned growing up in France that any woman can use to look younger, healthier, and more radiant without harsh products or drastic procedures. . . . [It] covers everything from how to use natural ingredients such as oil and honey to wash your face; what foods to eat for healthier hair, skin, and nails; and the amazing properties of grapes and grapeseed oil." (Publisher's note)

Ziegler, Sheryl

Mommy burnout; how to reclaim your life and raise healthier children in the process. Sheryl Ziegler. HarperCollins 2018 320 p. $26.99 **646.7**

1. Motherhood 2. Burn out (Psychology) 3. Mothers -- Psychology
ISBN 0062683683; 9780062683687

This book, by Sheryl Ziegler, is "the ultimate must-read handbook for the modern mother: a practical, and positive tool to help free women from the debilitating notion of being the 'perfect mom,' filled with funny and all too relatable true-life stories and realistic suggestions to stop the burnout cycle, and protect our kids from the damage burnout can cause." (Publisher's note)

"Although this book is well researched and broad in scope of topics, it's written for a singular audience—the heterosexual, middle-class mother. Beyond this limitation, the harrowing descriptions of how women are suffering are anxiety-inducing in their own right and may make the reader opt to put down the book and call her therapist." Booklist

646.782 Spousal relationship

Dunn, Jancee

How not to hate your husband after kids; Jancee Dunn. Little, Brown & Co. 2017 288 p. $27; (ebook) $81 **646.782**

1. Parenting 2. Communication in marriage
ISBN 9780316267106; 9780316267083

LC 2016946111

This book, by Jancee Dunn, "tackles the last taboo subject of parenthood: the startling, white-hot fury that new (and not-so-new) mothers often have for their mates. . . . Part memoir, part self-help book with actionable and achievable advice, 'How Not To Hate Your Husband After Kids' is an eye-opening look at how the man who got you into this position in this first place is the ally you didn't know you had." (Publisher's note)

"A highly readable account of how solid research and personal testing of self-help techniques saved a couple's marriage after the birth of their child." Kirkus

647 Management of public households (Institutional housekeeping)

Ripert, Eric

On the line; [by] Eric Ripert, Christine Muhlke. Artisan 2008 239p il $35 **647**

1. Restaurants 2. Le Bernardin (New York, N.Y.: Restaurant)
ISBN 978-1-57965-369-9; 1-57965-369-3

LC 2008-05930

"A behind-the-scenes look at the famed New York restaurant Le Bernardin. . . . Chef Ripert and New York Times writer Muhlke recount the restaurant's history, from its founding in 1986 by Gilbert and Maguy Le Coze, through Ripert's joining the team in 1991, to the present day. This thorough guide to how the restaurant operates teaches about various kitchen stations, tools of the trade, key personnel and their duties, how new dishes are born and what it's like to spend a night 'on the line.' . . . [Some recipes are included.] A huge treat for industry insiders, fans of Le Bernardin and foodies everywhere." Publ Wkly

647.9   Specific kinds of public households and institutions

Gordon, Joanne

Onward; how Starbucks fought for its life without losing its soul. [by] Howard Schultz with Joanne Gordon. Rodale 2011 350p il $25.99   **647.9**

   1. Leadership 2. Coffee industry 3. Starbucks Coffee International (Firm)

   ISBN 978-1-60529-288-5

LC 2011003239

"Throughout this book, readers get a very intimate look at the conviction that drives leaders, the resiliency of employees, the passion that customers feel about a brand, and the global community that one brand can inspire. Whether or not you are a coffee lover or have a fondness for the Starbucks experience, Onward details tremendous leadership lessons from which everyone can learn." T + D

Ottolenghi, Yotam

   ★ **Plenty**; vibrant vegetable recipes from London's Ottolenghi. by Yotam Ottolenghi. Chronicle Books 2011 287p il $35   **647.9**

   1. Cooking -- Vegetables 2. Ottolenghi (Restaurant)

   ISBN 978-1-4521-0124-8

LC 2011036741

Includes bibliographical references

"Ottolenghi, acclaimed British restaurateur and author of the Guardian's New Vegetarian column, offers a vibrant and versatile collection of mouth-watering dishes that elevate vegetables from paltry side-dish status to superstar prominence. He combines previously published recipes with an array of new offerings that spotlight everything from root vegetables and mushrooms to legumes and grains. Highlights include leek fritters, lentils with broiled eggplant, quinoa and grilled sourdough salad, and a stunningly gorgeous salad he calls tomato party that combines multicolored tomatoes, couscous, and several herbs." (Publishers Weekly)

647.95   Eating and drinking places

Cate, Martin

Smuggler's Cove; Exotic Cocktails, Rum, and the Cult of Tiki. by Martin Cate and Rebecca Cate. Random House Inc 2016 352 p. $30   **647.95**

   1. Cocktails

   ISBN 1607747324; 9781607747321

LC 2016012487

In this book, authors Martin Cate and Rebecca Cate "take you on a colorful journey into the lore and legend of tiki: its birth as an escapist fantasy for Depression-era Americans; how exotic cocktails were invented, stolen, and re-invented; Hollywood starlets and scandals; and tiki's modern-day revival." (Publisher's note)

"Even the most serious single-malt sipper will be charmed by this richly illustrated ode to escapism." LJ

Includes bibliographical references (pages 340-341) and index.

Friedman, Andrew, 1967-

Chefs, drugs and rock & roll; how food lovers, free spirits, misfits and wanderers created a new American profession. Andrew Friedman. HarperCollins 2018 480 p. $27.99 **647.957**

   1. American cooking 2. Cooks -- United States 3. Restaurants -- United States -- History

   ISBN 0062225855; 9780062225856

This book, by Andrew Friedman, "transports readers back in time to witness the remarkable evolution of the American restaurant chef in the 1970s and '80s. . . . [The book] treats readers to an unparalleled 360-degree re-creation of the business and the times through the perspectives not only of the groundbreaking chefs but also of line cooks, front-of-house personnel, investors, and critics who had front-row seats to this extraordinary transformation." (Publisher's note)

"An easy-going history that will be devoured by foodies and cooking fans as well as those interested in American cultural history." LJ

Freedman, Paul

Ten restaurants that changed America; Paul Freedman ; introduction by Danny Meyer. Liveright Publishing Corp., a division of W W Norton & Co Inc 2016 560 p. illustrations (chiefly color) (ebook) $50; (hardcover) $35   **647.95**

   1. Restaurants -- United States -- History

   ISBN 9781631492464; 9780871406804

LC 2016029340

In this book on American restaurants, food historian Paul Freedman "uses each restaurant to tell a wider story of race and class, immigration and assimilation. Freedman also treats us to a scintillating history of the then-revolutionary Schrafft's, a chain of convivial lunch spots that catered to women, and that bygone favorite, Howard Johnson's, which pioneered midcentury, on-the-road dining, only to be swept aside by McDonald's." (Publisher's note)

"This will appeal widely, engaging readers with both a casual or scholarly interest in food history and its influence on American culture in the late 19th and 20th centuries." LJ

Includes bibliographical references and index

Wizenberg, Molly

Delancey; a man, a woman, a restaurant, a marriage. Molly Wizenberg. Simon & Schuster 2014 256 p. illustrations (hardback) $25.00; (trade paperback) $15.99   **647.95**

   1. Marriage 2. Restaurants 3. Married people 4. Delancey (Pizzaria; Seattle, Wash.) 5. Food writers -- United States -- Biography 6. Pizzerias -- Washington (State) -- Seattle 7. Restaurateurs -- United States -- Biography

   ISBN 9781451655094; 9781451655117; 9781451655124

LC 2013034429

In this memoir, author Molly Wizenberg "recounts how opening a restaurant sparked the first crisis of her young marriage. . . . [W]hen Brandon decided to open a pizza restaurant, Molly was supportive. . . . The restaurant, Delancey . . . became a success, and Molly tried to convince herself that she was happy in their new life until--in the heat and pressure of the restaurant kitchen--she realized that she hadn't been honest with herself or Brandon." (Publisher's note)

"Wizenberg candidly describes her fears and doubts, as well as her struggles with trying to be a supportive wife." LJ

648   Housekeeping

Friedman, Virginia M.

Field guide to stains; how to identify and remove virtually every stain known to man. by Virginia M. Friedman, Melissa Wagner, and Nancy Armstrong. Quirk Bks. 2003 280p il pa $14.95   **648**

   1. Cleaning

   ISBN 1-931686-07-6

LC 2002-104065

This guide to identifying and removing over 100 stains features sections on sauces, fruits and vegetables, office products, and yard and garage stains. It also includes information on when and where certain stains are most likely to occur

Good Housekeeping Simple Household Wisdom; 425 Easy Ways to Clean & Organize Your Home. Sterling Pub Co Inc 2016 216 p. color illustrations $19.95   **648**
   1. Home economics 2. House cleaning
   ISBN 161837169X; 9781618371690

This book, edted by Good Housekeeping, is "filled with fabulous photographs of every room, plus genius tips, savvy shortcuts, and quick fixes for tidying, decluttering, organizing, adding style, and more. . . . [It] is your go-to guide for turning a house into the home you'll love even more." (Publisher's note)

"Part housekeeping handbook, part inspiration board, and part product guide, this work offers the practical advice expected from Good Housekeeping (GH) magazine with a bright, modern feel." LJ

Kerr, Jolie
   My boyfriend barfed in my handbag ... and other things you can't ask Martha; Jolie Kerr. Penguin Group 2014 256 p. $15   **648**
   1. House cleaning
   ISBN 0142196932; 9780142196939

                    LC 2013022730

In this book, author Jolie Kerr "offers a . . . guide to cleaning up life's little emergencies. Life is filled with spills, odors, and those oh-so embarrassing stains you just can't tell your parents about. And let's be honest: no one is going to ask Martha Stewart what to do when your boyfriend barfs in your handbag. . . . Jolie takes on questions ranging from the basic-- how do I use a mop? -- to the esoteric-- what should I do when bottles of homebrewed ginger beer explode in my kitchen?" (Publisher's note)

Kondo, Marie
   ★ The **life**-changing magic of tidying up; the Japanese art of decluttering and organizing. Marie Kondo ; translated from Japanese by Cathy Hirano. Ten Speed Press 2014 213 p. (hardcover) $16.99   **648**
   1. Home economics 2. House cleaning 3. Housekeeping
   ISBN 1607747308; 9781607747307

                    LC 2014017930

This book is a "guide to decluttering your home from Japanese cleaning consultant Marie Kondo. . . . Most methods advocate a room-by-room or little-by-little approach, which doom you to pick away at your piles of stuff forever. The KonMari Method, with its revolutionary category-by-category system, leads to lasting results." (Publisher's note)

Mendelson, Cheryl
   Laundry; the home comforts book of caring for clothes and linens. Cheryl Mendelson ; illustrated by Harry Bates. Scribner 2005 xvi, 400 p.p $24.99   **648**
   1. Laundry 2. Home economics
   ISBN 0743271459; 0743271467; 9780743271455; 9780743271462

                    LC 2005051602

This book, edited by Cheryl Mendelson and illustrated by Harry Bates, is a "comprehensive, entertaining, and inspiring book on the art of laundering. Culled from the bestselling 'Home Comforts,' with revised and updated information and a new introduction, . . . [it] is an indispensable guide to caring for all the cloth in one's home." (Publisher's note)

   Includes bibliographical references (p. [371]-380) and index

Platt, Stacey
   What's a disorganized person to do? Artisan 2010 277p il pa $16.95   **648**
   1. House cleaning 2. Storage in the home
   ISBN 978-1-57965-372-9

                    LC 2009-13493

The author "offers quick tips (e.g., storing sterling silver with chalk to prevent tarnish), instructions (e.g., folding silk scarves correctly), and one-hour projects (e.g., taking back the junk drawer) that anyone can immediately put into practice. Guidelines for organizing office space are designed for those who like to file and those who prefer to pile, and detailed steps for vacation packing and cross-country moving are also included. The employment of one idea alone is worth the price of the book." Libr J

   Includes bibliographical references

648.5   Housecleaning

Ewer, Cynthia Townley
   Cut the Clutter; by Cynthia Ewer. DK Publishing 2016 240 p. color illustrations $16.95   **648.5**
   1. House cleaning
   ISBN 1465453059; 9781465453051

                    LC 2016387148

This book, by Cynthia Ewer, is "a guide to conquering clutter and cleaning your home. . . . Step-by-step instructions, household routines, and quick tips make these daunting tasks easier to tackle, and will leave you with more time and energy for the good things in life." (Publisher's note)

The book delves into the nitty-gritty of list-making, menu planning, and the cycles of cleaning. It's best used as a reference guide for specific chores... rather than as a method to follow strictly. This practical guide will be a solid resource for young adults and new parents." Pub Wkly

Magnusson, Margareta
   ★ The **gentle** art of Swedish death cleaning; how to free yourself and your family from a lifetime of clutter. text and drawings by Margareta Magnusson. Scribner 2018 ix, 117 p.p illustrations (hardcover) $18.99   **648.5**
   1. Orderliness 2. House cleaning 3. Estate planning 4. Self-help techniques 5. Hoarders 6. Storage in the home 7. Sweden -- Social life and customs
   ISBN 9781501173257; 9781501173240

                    LC 2017061728

In the book, artist Margareta Magnusson, "instructs readers to embrace minimalism. Her radical and joyous method for putting things in order helps families broach sensitive conversations, and makes the process uplifting rather than overwhelming. . . . [She] suggests which possessions you can easily get rid of (unworn clothes, unwanted presents, more plates than you'd ever use) and which you might want to keep (photographs, love letters, a few of your children's art projects)." (Publisher's note)

"Striking a balance of gentle encouragement, philosophical musing, and pragmatism, her recommendations are wholly practical and warmly convey her hope for a positive outcome." LJ

648.8   Storage

Carlson, Julie
   Remodelista; the organized home; simple, stylish storage

ideas for all over the house. Julie Carlson and Margot Guralnick ; with the editors of Remodelista ; photographs by Matthew Williams ; creative direction by Alexa Hotz. Artisan 2017 224 p. (hardcover) $24.95 **648.8**

> 1. Orderliness 2. Interior design 3. Storage in the home 4. Interior decoration -- Themes, motives
> ISBN 9781579658151; 9781579656935

LC 2017013398

This book, by Julie Carlson and Margot Guralnick, encourages us to "buy fewer (and better) things. . . . Readers will learn strategies for conquering their homes' problem zones (from the medicine cabinet to the bedroom closet) and organizing tricks and tools that can be deployed in every room (embrace trays; hunt for unused spaces overhead; decant everything). Interviews with experts, ranging from kindergarten teachers to hoteliers, offer even more ingenious ideas to steal." (Publisher's note)

"This practical guide . . . translates the less-is-more impulse into efficient and aesthetically pleasing organizing suggestions." Pub Wkly

649 Child rearing; home care of people with disabilities and illnesses

Agnew, Connie L.

Twins! pregnancy, birth, and the first year of life. [by] Connie L. Agnew, Alan H. Klein, and Jill Alison Ganon; illustrations by Victor Robert. 2nd ed.; Collins 2005 360p il pa $18.95 **649**

> 1. Twins
> ISBN 0-06-074219-4; 978-0-06-074219-5

LC 2005-45585

First published 1997

An overview of the physical, medical, emotional, and psychological issues involved in having twins. Fetal and embryonic development, nutrition, and exercise are among the topics covered. Includes interviews with parents of twins.

Includes bibliographical references

Bowers, Mark

8 keys to raising the quirky child; how to help a kid who doesn't (quite) fit in. Mark Bowers ; foreword by Babette Rothschild. W W Norton & Co Inc. 2015 320 p. (pbk.) $19.95 **649**

> 1. Parenting 2. Child rearing 3. Autistic children 4. Exceptional children 5. Parents of autistic children 6. Parents of exceptional children
> ISBN 0393709205; 9780393709209

LC 2015004622

This book, by Mark Bowers, "defines quirky markers and offers strategies for parents to understand their children's brains and behaviors; to know what is developmentally appropriate, and what isn't; to understand how to reach their kids; and to help facilitate their social functioning in the world." (Publisher's note)

"Frustrated parents who believe their child is well-described by the 'quirky' profile will find Bowen's attitude supportive, his psychological explanations of their child's motivations satisfying, and his specific strategies for helping these kids accept breadth of experience and build social competency usable and encouraging." Pub Wkly.

Includes bibliographical references and index

Brazelton, T. Berry

Touchpoints birth to 3; your child's emotional and behavioral development. revised with Joshua Sparrow. 2nd ed.; Da Capo Lifelong Books 2006 xxvi, 500p il pa $17.95 **649**

> 1. Child rearing 2. Child psychology 3. Child development
> ISBN 978-0-7382-1049-0; 0-7382-1049-8

LC 2008-274711

First published 1992 by Addison-Wesley with title: Touchpoints

The author "defines 'touchpoints' as the periods of development and regression which every child experiences while growing up. He describes the first six years of life and the touchpoints of that period. . . . Worried new parents will be put at ease after reading this book. Brazelton is knowledgeable, warm, and kind, and his book is a pleasure to read." Libr J

Includes bibliographical references

Brooks, Robert B.

Raising resilient children; fostering strength, hope, and optimism in your child. {by} Robert Brooks, Sam Goldstein. Contemporary Bks. 2001 317p hardcover o.p. pa $14.95 **649**

> 1. Child rearing 2. Parent-child relationship
> ISBN 0-8092-9765-5 pa

LC 00-60316

The authors "synthesize research on children's coping skills; define and describe resilience (the capacity to cope and feel competent); and offer specific strategies for nurturing resilience in children." Booklist

Includes bibliographical references

Brown, Christia Spears

Parenting beyond pink and blue; how to raise your kids free of gender stereotypes. Christia Spears Brown, PhD. Ten Speed Press 2014 240 p. illustrations (pbk) $14.99 **649**

> 1. Parenting 2. Gender role 3. Sex differences (Psychology) 4. Stereotype (Social psychology)
> ISBN 160774502X; 9781607745020

LC 2014001259

This book, by developmental psychologist Christia Spears Brown, is "a guide that helps parents focus on their children's unique strengths and inclinations rather than on gendered stereotypes to more effectively bring out the best in their individual children, for parents of infants to middle schoolers. . . . [It] addresses all the issues that contemporary parents should consider--from gender-segregated birthday parties and schools to sports, sexualization, and emotional intelligence." (Publisher's note)

Brown "argues that children are 'free to flourish' when gender is deemphasized and covers both the neuroscience and cultural influences of sex in language that is accessible and at times even humorous." LJ

Includes bibliographical references and index

Cohen, Lawrence J.

Playful parenting; a bold new way to use play in raising your children. Ballantine Bks. 2001 307p $23.95; pa $14 **649**

> 1. Play 2. Games 3. Parenting
> ISBN 0-345-43897-3; 0-345-44286-5 pa

LC 00-66809

"According to Cohen, children of all ages have an ongoing need for connectedness, security and attachment; playful interaction with parents is an important way to develop such bonds. Through play, parents can help their kids develop greater confidence, express bottled up or difficult feelings, recover from daily emotional upheavals, negotiate agreements, express love and—not least—have fun." Publ Wkly

Dawson, Peg

Smart but scattered; the revolutionary 'executive skills' approach to helping kids reach their potential. [by] Peg Dawson [and] iRichard Guare. Guilford Press 2009 vi, 314 p.p illustrations $53 **649**

1. Parenting 2. Life skills 3. Parent and child 4. Child development 5. Executive ability in children 6. Children -- Life skills guides
ISBN 1593859872; 9781593854454; 9781593859879

LC 2008026078

This parenting book, by Peg Dawson and Richard Guare, "shows that many kids who have the brain and heart to succeed lack or lag behind in crucial 'executive skills'--the fundamental habits of mind required for getting organized, staying focused, and controlling impulses and emotions. Learn easy-to-follow steps to identify your child's strengths and weaknesses, use activities and techniques proven to boost specific skills, and problem-solve daily routines." (Publisher's note)

"As the first books on the subject to speak directly, comprehensively, and universally to parents, both titles are recommended for parenting collections in public and school libraries; Dawson and Guare's work should be considered essential." LJ

Includes bibliographical references (p. 303-309) and index

Deak, JoAnn

Girls will be girls; a parent's guide to cultivating confident, competent and connected daughters. by JoAnn Deak with Teresa Barker. Hyperion 2002 287p $23.95; pa $14.95 **649**

1. Girls 2. Teenagers 3. Child rearing
ISBN 0-7868-6768-X; 0-7868-8657-9 pa

LC 2001-39247

"Deak discusses the differences between fathers and daughters and mothers and daughters and also some of the more common problems faced by teens, such as body image and peer pressure." Publ Wkly

Eanes, Rebecca

Positive parenting; an essential guide. Rebecca Eanes ; foreword by Dr. Laura Markham. TarcherPerigee 2016 xx, 183 p.p (pbk.) $15 **649**

1. Parenting 2. Family life 3. Parent-child relationship 4. Parent and child
ISBN 0143109227; 9780143109228

LC 2016009096

In this parenting guidebook, Rebecca Eanes "shares her hard-won wisdom for overcoming limiting thought patterns and recognizing emotional triggers, as well as advice for connecting with kids at each stage, from infancy to adolescence. This heartfelt, insightful advice comes not from an 'expert,' but from a learning, evolving parent." (Publisher's note)

Includes bibliographical references (pages 177-178)

Ezzo, Gary

★ **On** becoming baby wise; giving your infant the gift of nighttime sleep. by Gary Ezzo and Robert Buckman. Hawksflight & Assoc Inc 2012 279 p. illustrations $13.95 **649**

1. Infants -- Care 2. Parent-child relationship
ISBN 1932740139; 9781932740134

This book, by Gary Ezzo and Robert Buckman, is a "newborn parenting manual for naturally synchronizing your baby's feeding time, waketime and nighttime sleep cycles, so the whole family can sleep through the night. The authors demonstrate how order and stability are mutual allies of every newborn's metabolism and how parents can take advantage of these biological propensities. In particular, they note how an infant's body responds to the influences of parental routine or the lack thereof." (Publisher's note)

Fonseca, Christine

Raising the shy child; a parent's guide to social anxiety; advice for helping kids make friends, speak up, and stop worrying. Christine Fonseca. Prufrock Press, Inc. 2015 xvi, 223 p.p illustrations (pbk.) $16.95 **649**

1. Shyness 2. Parenting 3. Child rearing 4. Social phobia 5. Bashfulness in children 6. Social phobia in children
ISBN 1618213989; 9781618213983

LC 2014048544

This book, by Christine Fonseca, "takes a fresh look at social anxiety disorder, coupling the latest in research trends with evidence-based strategies and real-world stories to untangle the complexities of this disorder. . . . [It] uses a combination of real-world examples and stories from adults and children with social anxiety disorder to show parents and educators how to help children find a path through their fear and into social competence." (Publisher's note)

"Parents who have seen educators minimize their child's struggles as normal shyness, felt herded into one-size-fits-all solutions, or struggled to comprehend apparently nonsensical behavior from bright children will find this comprehensive resource grounding and practical." Pub Wkly

Includes bibliographical references (pages 213 -222)

Foster, Joanne

Beyond intelligence; secrets of raising happily productive kids. Dona Matthews, Joanne Foster. House of Anansi Press Inc. 2014 280 p. (pbk.; alk. paper) $15.95 **649**

1. Intellect 2. Parenting
ISBN 1770894772; 9781770894778; 9781770894785

LC 2014935195

In this book, authors Dona Matthews and Joanne Foster "show that intelligence is not fixed rather, it can be increased. Through myriad anecdotes from personal experience and case studies, they reveal how parents can identify a child's abilities, foster creativity, and bolster effort and persistence. They also address how to prevent or alleviate emotional and social problems, and how to embrace failures as learning opportunities." (Publisher's note)

"Parents who have read other child rearing books may recognize but still appreciate the information and advice provided here: listen to, understand, and nurture children in order to foster their growth." LJ

Gold, Tammy

Secrets of the nanny whisperer; a practical guide for finding and achieving the gold standard of care for your child. by Tammy Gold. Perigee 2015 288 p. (paperback) $16 **649**

1. Child care services 2. Nannies -- Recruiting 3. Child care services -- United States 4. Nannies -- Employment -- United States 5. Nannies -- Selection and appointment -- United States
ISBN 0399169881; 9780399169885

LC 2014040010

This book by Tammy Gold focuses on the hiring and managing of child care workers. "In Part 1, the author explains the value of the nanny-family match and outlines how to best pursue the nanny relationship for long-term success. Part 2 equips readers with a Family Needs Assessment and the author's eponymous 'Gold Standard' hiring process, including screenings, in-home trials, and background checks. Part 3 focuses on managing the nanny relationship and resolving conflicts." (Library Journal)

"While many families view their nanny as a part of the family, Gold reminds readers that this is ultimately an employment relationship. She dispenses exceptional advice that will help families avoid common pitfalls and is especially strong when illustrating scenarios from the nanny's point of view. From her needs assessment to interview questions to problem-solving language, Gold's examples and crisp narrative gives readers one-stop shopping for nanny know-how. A required purchase."

Well done." LJ

Hartzell, Mary

Parenting from the inside out; how a deeper self-understanding can help you raise children who thrive. Daniel J. Siegel and Mary Hartzell. Jeremy P. Tarcher/Penguin, a member of Penguin Group (USA) 2014 xxiv, 311 p.p (paperback) $17 **649**

1. Parenting 2. Self-perception 3. Parent-child relationship 4. Parent and child
ISBN 039916510X; 9780399165108

LC 2013037883

In this book, by Daniel J. Siegel and Mary Hartzell, "explore the extent to which our childhood experiences shape the way we parent. Drawing on stunning new findings in neurobiology and attachment research, they explain how interpersonal relationships directly impact the development of the brain, and offer parents a step-by-step approach to forming a deeper understanding of their own life stories, which will help them raise compassionate and resilient children." (Publisher's note)

Includes bibliographical references and index

Huggins, Kathleen

The **nursing** mother's companion; Kathleen Huggins ; foreword by Ruth A. Lawrence. Harvard Common Press 2010 x, 358 p.p illustrations (pbk.; alk. paper) $16.95 **649**

1. Breast feeding 2. Breastfeeding -- Popular works
ISBN 1558327207; 9781558327191; 9781558327207

LC 2010005981

This book "has been among the best-selling books on breastfeeding for 25 years, and is respected and recommended by professionals and well loved by new parents for its encouraging and accessible style. Kathleen Huggins equips breastfeeding mothers with all the information they need to overcome potential difficulties and nurse their babies successfully from the first week through the toddler years, or somewhere in between." (Publisher's note)

Includes bibliographical references (p. 341-347) and indexes

Hurley, Katie

The **happy** kid handbook; how to raise joyful children in a stressful world. Katie Hurley. Tarcher 2015 320 p. (paperback) $16.95 **649**

1. Happiness 2. Parenting 3. Child rearing 4. Happiness in children
ISBN 9780399171819

LC 2015022156

This book, by Katie Hurley, "shows parents how happiness is the key to raising confident, capable children.... Happiness is about parenting the individual, because not every child is the same.... By exploring the differences among introverts, extroverts, and everything in between, this definitive guide to parenting offers parents the specific strategies they need to meet their child exactly where he or she needs to be met from a social-emotional perspective." (Publisher's note)

"Her book is highly recommended for people who seek a parenting orientation rather than a method but still want a substantial toolbox of specific activities to use in understanding and connecting with their children." Pub Wkly

Includes bibliographical references and index

Karp, Harvey

The **happiest** baby guide to great sleep; simple solutions for kids from birth to 5 years. by Harvey Karp. William Morrow 2012 367 p. illustrations; charts $15.99 **649**

1. Sleep 2. Parenting
ISBN 0062113313; 0062113321; 9780062113313; 9780062113320

In this book on regulating young children's sleep patterns, "[Harvey] Karp lays a number of myths to rest in his latest book, including the idea that babies, who have shorter sleep cycles than adults, can't learn better sleep habits before three months of age. In fact, he gets right to work giving parents tips and tools to help their newborns develop good sleeping patterns, and then moves on to older babies and toddlers." (Publishers Weekly)

"While the advice is sound, the book is embarrassingly long while the author belabors the obvious, and the pace is insufferable. Despite the critique, patrons may likely request." LJ

The **happiest** baby on the block; the new way to calm crying and help your baby sleep longer. Bantam Bks. 2002 267p il $21.95; pa $13.95 **649**

1. Child rearing 2. Parent-child relationship 3. Infants -- Care
ISBN 0-553-80255-0; 0-553-38146-6 pa

LC 2001-56734

To calm a crying baby the author "recommends a series of five steps designed to imitate the uterus. These steps include swaddling, side/stomach position, shhh sounds, swinging and sucking. The book includes detailed advice on the proper way to swaddle a child, the difference between a gentle rocking versus shaking and more." Publ Wkly

Kazdin, Alan E.

The **Everyday** Parenting Toolkit; The Kazdin Method for Easy, Step-by-step, Lasting Change for You and Your Child. Alan E. Kazdin. Houghton Mifflin Harcourt 2013 208 p. $25 **649**

1. Child rearing 2. Parent-child relationship 3. Parenting
ISBN 0547985541; 9780547985541

LC 2012537349

Here, Alan E. Kazdin "offers practical strategies to help parents manage everyday behavioral problems. His science-based method may surprise some readers, particularly those who favor a more authoritarian approach. The core of the book focuses on the 'ABC's': antecedents, behavior, and consequences. According to Kazdin, parents can effect desired behavior in their children by offering choices and speaking in pleasant tones." (Publishers Weekly)

Includes bibliographical references (p. [178]-181) and index

Kennedy, Janet Krone

The **good** sleeper; the essential guide to sleep for your baby--and you. Janet Krone Kennedy, PhD. Holt Paperbacks 2015 304 p. (paperback) $16 **649**

1. Sleep 2. Infants -- Care 3. Naps (Sleep) 4. Infants -- Sleep 5. Parent and infant
ISBN 0805099433; 9780805099430

LC 2014019607

This book, by Janet Krone Kennedy, offers a "straightforward method for training infants to become great sleepers for life.... For something so important, there's too much conflicting information about how best to get your baby to sleep through the night and nap successfully during the day. This book is a straightforward, no-nonsense answer to one of the biggest challenges new parents face when they welcome a brand new baby home." (Publisher's note)

"Proposing 'authoritative parenting' (rather than attachment parenting), Kennedy is making an argument about more than infant rest... This approach is sure to draw strong reactions from the mommy-blogosphere, whether it's ire from moms who like to sleep in the same bed as baby, or praise from exhausted parents who will no doubt be eager to try Kennedy's program." Pub Wkly

Kennedy-Moore, Eileen, 1964-

Smart parenting for smart kids; nurturing your child's true potential. Eileen Kennedy-Moore, Mark S. Lowenthal. John Wiley & Sons inc. 2011 xii, 306 p.p (pbk.) $16.95   **649**
    1. Child rearing 2. Academic achievement 3. Parent-child relationship 4. Gifted children 5. Parents of gifted children
    ISBN 0470640057; 9780470640050

LC 2010043005

Author Eileen Kennedy-Moore discusses child-rearing and offers "a perceptive guide to help smart children succeed academically and socially." The author offers suggestions for parents on how they can "help lead their children to new intellectual and emotional growth. Near the end of each chapter are suggestions for how parents can model healthy behaviors for their kids. . . . This . . . look at raising smart children will help parents teach their kids that there's more to life than academic achievement." (Kirkus Reviews)

Includes bibliographical references and index.

La Leche League International

The **Womanly** art of breastfeeding; 7th rev ed; Plume 2004 463p il pa $18   **649**
    1. Breast feeding
    ISBN 978-0-452-28580-4; 0-452-28580-1

LC 2004-557599

First published 1956. Periodically revised

This guide explains the benefits of breastfeeding and offers advice on avoiding problems, breastfeeding and working mothers, family life, and weaning.

Includes bibliographical references

Lahey, Jessica

The **gift** of failure; how the best parents learn to let go so their children can succeed. Jessica Lahey. Harper 2015 304 p. (hardback) $26.99   **649**
    1. Parenting 2. Failure (Psychology) 3. Parental overprotection 4. Self-reliance in children 5. Parenting -- United States 6. Child rearing -- United States 7. Early childhood education -- United States
    ISBN 0062299239; 9780062299239

LC 2014039146

This book, by Jessica Lahey, "focuses on the critical school years when parents must learn to allow their children to experience the disappointment and frustration that occur from life's inevitable problems so that they can grow up to be successful, resilient, and self-reliant adults. . . . Even though . . . parents see themselves as being highly responsive to their children's well being, they aren't giving them the chance to experience failure." (Publisher's note)

"Lahey's conversational tone, combined with research and narratives from both children and parents, delivers in-depth insight into the value of mistakes. With chapters on specific age groups (middle schoolers and high schoolers) and hot-button issues, such as household chores, homework, and friendships, any parent who needs assistance reining in the supermom tendencies will find sound advice here." LJ

Lev, Arlene Istar

The **complete** lesbian & gay parenting guide; Berkeley trade pbk. ed.; Berkley Books 2004 379p pa $17   **649**
    1. Parenting 2. Gay parents
    ISBN 0-425-19197-4; 978-0-425-19197-2

LC 2004-57080

"This book addresses the concerns of transgendered parents, as well as those of lesbian and gay parents. . . . [The author] knows how to tackle relevant issues, e.g., dealing with the homophobia that children of GLBT parents will inevitably encounter. Humorous and replete with valuable narratives." Libr J

Includes bibliographical references

Lickona, Thomas

How to raise kind kids; and get respect, gratitude, and a happier family in the bargain. Thomas Lickona. Penguin Books 2018 336 p. (paperback) $17   **649**
    1. Kindness 2. Parenting 3. Moral education 4. Education -- Parent participation
    ISBN 9780143131946

LC 2017058211

In this book, psychologist Thomas Lickona. "shares with parents the vital tools they need to bring peace and foster cooperation at home. Kindness doesn't stand on its own. It needs a supporting cast of other essential virtues--like courage, self-control, respect, and gratitude. . . . [The book] will help you give and get respect . . . and improve the dynamic of your relationship with your children while putting them on the path to a happier and more fulfilling life." (Publisher's note)

Includes bibliographical references and index

Markham, Laura

Peaceful parent, happy kids; how to stop yelling and start connecting. Laura Markham. Perigee Books 2012 274 p. $16   **649**
    1. Parenting 2. Child rearing 3. Parent-child relationship 4. Parent and child
    ISBN 0399160280; 9780399160288

LC 2012031273

This book, by Laura Markham, is "a groundbreaking guide to raising responsible, capable, happy kids. . . . [This] guide will help parents better understand their own emotions--and get them in check--so they can parent with healthy limits, empathy, and clear communication to raise a self-disciplined child. Step-by-step examples give solutions and kid-tested phrasing for parents of toddlers right through the elementary years." (Publisher's note)

"In this compassionate yet practical text, Markham deftly leads parents down a gentler, kinder path to raising emotionally intelligent and happier children." Pub Wkly

Includes bibliographical references and index

Medina, John, 1956-

Brain rules for baby; how to raise a smart and happy child from zero to five. John Medina. 2nd ed; updated Pear Press 2014 323 p. ill pbk $15.95   **649**
    1. Child psychology 2. Parent-child relationship 3. Parenting 4. Child rearing 5. Child development
    ISBN 0983263388; 9780983263388

Medina "presents the best of the refereed literature to examine how infants process information at the molecular, cellular, and behavioral levels. . . . Covering such topics as pregnancy, relationships, and 'moral' babies, the book will educate even the most learned parents. Medina's humorous, conversational style makes this an absolute pleasure to read." LJ

Miller, Lisa

The **Spiritual** Child; The New Science on Parenting for Health and Lifelong Thriving. by Lisa Miller. St. Martin's Press 2015 400 p. $27.99   **649**

1. Parenting 2. Spiritual life 3. Child development
ISBN 125003292X; 9781250032928

LC 2015005940

In this book, author Lisa Miller "presents the next big idea in psychology: the science and the power of spirituality. . . . Combining cutting-edge research with broad anecdotal evidence from her work as a clinical psychologist to illustrate just how invaluable spirituality is to a child's mental and physical health, Miller translates these findings into practical advice for parents, giving them concrete ways to develop and encourage their children's . . . well-being." (Publisher's note)

"If the plights of Marin and Kurt had been introduced earlier, Miller could have established more emotional connection with her readers, who would then be more engaged with the science she presents. New science or a leap of faith? Either way, nurturing spirituality in your children may save them a world of pain." Kirkus

Murkoff, Heidi

★ **What** to Expect the First Year; by Heidi Murkoff with Sharon Mazel. 3rd edition Workman Pub. Co. 2014 704 p. illustrations pbk $16.95 **649**
1. Child rearing 2. Infants -- Care
ISBN 0761181504; 9780761181507

LC 8740647

This book, by Heidi Murkoff, "is the world's best-selling, best-loved guide to the instructions that babies don't come with, but should. And now, it's . . . completely updated. Keeping the trademark month-by-month format that allows parents to take the potentially overwhelming first year one step at a time, . . . [it's] packed with even more practical tips, realistic advice, and relatable, accessible information than before." (Publisher's note)

★ **What** to expect the second year; from 12 to 24 months. [by] Heidi Murkoff and Sharon Mazel; foreword by Mark D. Widome. Workman Pub Co 2011 512p il $24; pa $15.95 **649**
1. Toddlers 2. Child rearing
ISBN 978-0-7611-6364-0; 978-0-7611-5277-4 pa

This is a "look at the toddler from 12 to 24 months. In 15 chapters the authors cover feeding, sleeping, learning, playing, health and safety, injuries and developmental disorders, discipline, and other issues with a meaty center section on behavior. . . . Murkoff offers sound advice and reassurance that will help parent and toddler stay grounded during this whirlwind period of growth and change." Publ Wkly

Neifert, Marianne R.

Great expectations; the essential guide to breastfeeding. [by] Marianne Neifert. Sterling 2009 312p il pa $14.95 **649**
1. Breast feeding
ISBN 978-1-4027-5817-1

LC 2009-5248

"The author combines detailed, readable medical explanations with practical tips for success and addresses potential challenges honestly rather than glossing over them with bland reassurances. Each chapter seems designed to stand alone, making it easy for time-pressed mothers to find the information they need without reading the entire book." Libr J

Palmer, Sara

Just one of the kids; raising a resilient family when one of your children has a physical disability. Kay Harris Kriegsman, Ph.D., and Sara Palmer, Ph.D. Johns Hopkins University Press 2013 240 p. (hardcover; alk. paper) $49 **649**
1. Children with physical disabilities 2. Parents of children with disabilities 3. Children with disabilities -- Family relationships

ISBN 1421409305; 1421409313; 9781421409306; 9781421409313

LC 2012035771

This book, by psychologists Kay Harris Kriegsman and Sara Palmer, presents a guide for parents of children with physical disabilities. "The authors show families how to be pragmatic and inclusive when solving problems and setting expectations. The real family stories and personal experiences of the authors, one of whom has such a disability, create an intimate and nonjudgmental tone with a degree of optimism." (Library Journal)

"A valuable resource for families looking for encouragement as they try to create an inclusive environment for their child with a physical disability." LJ
Includes bibliographical references and index

Phelan, Thomas W.

★ **1-2-3 magic;** effective discipline for children 2-12. Thomas W. Phelan, PhD. Sourcebooks 2016 288 p. illustrations (hardcover; alk. paper) $24.99 **649**
1. Parenting 2. Child rearing 3. Children -- Conduct of life 4. Discipline of children
ISBN 9781492629887; 9781492631828; 149262988X

LC 2015021612

This book, by Thomas W. Phelan, Ph.D. "compiles two decades of research and experience into an easy-to-use program designed for parents striving to connect more deeply with their children and help them develop into healthy, capable teenagers and adults. [Readers will] find tools to use in virtually every situation, as well as real-life stories from parents who have successfully navigated common parenting challenges such as reluctance to do chores, talking back, and refusing to go to bed." (Publisher's note)

Phelan's 1-2-3 is the gold standard of child discipline for good reason. All libraries should update to the new edition and purchase in sufficient quantities." Library Journal
Includes bibliographical references and index

Pitman, Teresa

Sweet sleep; nighttime and naptime strategies for the breastfeeding family. Diane Wiessinger and [three others] Ballantine Books 2014 512 p. illustrations (paperback; acid-free paper) $20 **649**
1. Parenting 2. Breast feeding 3. Sleeping customs 4. Sleep 5. Breastfeeding 6. Breastfeeding -- Safety measures
ISBN 0345518470; 9780345518477

LC 2014019411

Written by Diane Wiessinger, Diana West, Linda J. Smith, and Teresa Pitman, "'Sweet Sleep' includes extensive information on creating a safe sleep space, helping children learn to sleep on their own and defusing criticism of your family's choices. . . . This book is nothing but supportive of whatever your choices are about nursing and sleeping." (BookPage)

"The core of the book offers detailed, practical advice on bed sharing and breast-feeding, with basic guidelines for safe bed sharing outlined in seven steps." Pub Wkly
Includes bibliographical references and index

The **womanly** art of breastfeeding; by Diane Wiessinger, Diana West, and Teresa Pitman. Ballantine Books 2010 xxiv, 550 p.p illustrations (pbk.) $20 **649**
1. Breast feeding 2. Breastfeeding
ISBN 0345518446; 9780345518446

LC 2010014031

This guide to breastfeeding, by Diane Wiessinger, Diana West, and

Teresa Pitman, "has been retooled, refocused, and updated for today's mothers and lifestyles. Working mothers, stay-at-home moms, single moms, and mothers of multiples will all benefit from the book's range of nursing advice, stories, and information—from preparing for breastfeeding during pregnancy to feeding cues, from nursing positions to expressing and storing breast milk." (Publisher's note)

Includes bibliographical references (p. [499]-535) and index

Richey, Mary Anne

The **impulsive,** disorganized child; solutions for parenting kids with executive functioning difficulties. James W. Forgan, Ph.D., & Mary Anne Richey. Prufrock Press Inc. 2015 xiv, 258 p.p illustrations (pbk.) $17.95   **649**
1. Self-control 2. Child rearing 3. Children with mental disabilities 4. Child psychology 5. Self-control in children 6. Executive functions (Neuropsychology) 7. Children with mental disabilities -- Care
ISBN 1618214012; 9781618214010

LC 2015001880

This book, by James W. Forgan and Mary Anne Richey, "helps parents pinpoint weak executive functions in their children, then learn how to help their kids overcome these deficits with practical, easy solutions. Children who can't select, plan, initiate, or sustain action toward their goals are children who simply struggle to succeed in school and other aspects of life." (Publisher's note)

"The advice presented has practical context and gives specifics for action. Using the "SMART" model (goals should be: specific, measurable, attainable, realistic, and timely), kids can join their parents in improving impulse control and organization." LJ

Includes bibliographical references

Sears, William

The **baby** book; everything you need to know about your baby from birth to age two. William Sears, MD, Martha Sears, RN, Robert Sears, MD, and James Sears, MD. 3rd ed Little, Brown & Co. 2013 xiv, 770 p.p ill., charts (pbk.) $21.99 **649**
1. Infants -- Care 2. Infants -- Development 3. Newborn infants -- Care
ISBN 0316198269; 9780316198264

LC 2012953605

Written by William Sears, Martha Sears, Robert Sears, and James Sears, this book "presents a practical, contemporary approach to parenting that reflects the way we live today. Focusing on the essential needs of babies--eating, sleeping, development, health, and comfort--it addresses the questions of greatest concern to parents. The Searses acknowledge that there is no one way to parent a baby." (Publisher's note)

"The authors teach new parents how to bond with their babies through seven fundamental behaviors, including breastfeeding, 'babywearing' and setting proper boundaries. . . . From tips for a healthy birth, getting your baby to sleep and feeding him the 'right fats,' to information about early health concerns, the major steps in infant development and troublesome but typical toddler behavior, the authors of this comprehensive volume . . . are assured and reassuring experts." Publ Wkly

Includes bibliographical references and index

Siegel, Daniel J.

No-drama discipline; the whole-brain way to calm the chaos and nurture your child's developing mind. Daniel J. Siegel, M.D., Tina Payne Bryson, Ph.D. Bantam Books 2014 288 p. illustrations (hardback) $26   **649**
1. Parenting 2. Child rearing 3. Child development
ISBN 0345548043; 9780345548047

LC 2014008270

Written by Daniel J. Siegel and Tina Payne Bryson, "'No-Drama Discipline' provides an effective, compassionate road map for dealing with tantrums, tensions, and tears--without causing a scene." It includes "strategies that help parents identify their own discipline philosophy--and master the best methods to communicate the lessons they are trying to impart." (Publisher's note)

"With lucid, engaging prose accompanied by cartoon illustrations, Siegel and Bryson help parents teach and communicate more effectively." Pub Wkly

The **whole**-brain child; 12 revolutionary strategies to nurture your child's developing mind. Daniel J. Siegel, Tina Payne Bryson. Delacorte Press 2011 xiii, 176 p.p illustrations $24   **649**
1. Parenting 2. Child rearing 3. Child development
ISBN 0553807919; 9780553807912; 9780553907254

LC 2010052988

In this book, authors Daniel J. Siegel and Tina Payne Bryson "demystify the meltdowns and aggravation, explaining the new science of how a child's brain is wired and how it matures. . . . By applying these discoveries to everyday parenting, you can turn any outburst, argument, or fear into a chance to integrate your child's brain and foster vital growth." (Publisher's note)

"Siegel and Bryson reveal that an integrated brain with parts that cooperate in a coordinated and balanced manner creates a better understanding of self, stronger relationships, and success in school, among other benefits. With illustrations, charts, and even a handy 'Refrigerator Sheet,' the authors have made every effort to make brain science parent-friendly." Pub Wkly

Smith, David H.

★ The **silent** garden; a parent's guide to raising a deaf child. Paul W. Ogden, David H. Smith. Third edition Gallaudet University Press 2016 xi, 354 p.p (paperback) $34.95 **649**
1. Deaf children 2. Parent-child relationship 3. Deaf children -- Education 4. Deaf children -- Family relationships
ISBN 1563686767; 9781563686764

LC 2016026123

"Authors Paul W. Ogden and David H. Smith, who are both deaf, present examples and research that guide parents through often unfamiliar territory. From coping mechanisms for parents to advice on creating healthy home environments, the authors cover a range of topics that impact day-to-day actions and decision-making." (Publisher's note)

"In this third edition of this esteemed text, coauthors Ogden . . . and Smith . . . deliver a foundational approach to raising deaf and hard-of-hearing children, emphasizing that 'being deaf is not about hearing but about communication.'" LJ

Spock, Benjamin

Dr. Spock on parenting; sensible advice from America's most trusted child care expert. Simon & Schuster 1988 318p hardcover o.p. pa $16.95   **649**
1. Parenting
ISBN 0-7434-2683-5 pa

LC 88-15792

"The author presents a personal critique on parenting, often bordering on the autobiographical. . . . He discusses in depth and with great conviction contemporary and traditional parent concerns, such as divorce, discipline, sex education, and the father's role." Libr J

Dr. Spock's baby and child care; by Benjamin Spock. Gal-

lery Books 2012 xx, 1130 p.p illustrations $19.99 **649**
1. Child care 2. Child rearing 3. Infants -- Care
ISBN 1439189285; 9781439189283

LC 2012382318

Author Benjamin Spock offers "advice on age-old topics such as caring for a new baby, as well as accidents, illness, and injuries, [and] this revised edition also covers: medical opinion on immunizations . . . obesity and nutrition . . . [and] cultural diversity, and non-traditional family structures." (Publisher's note)

Dr. Spock's the first two years; the emotional and physical needs of children from birth to age two. edited by Martin T. Stein. Pocket Bks. 2001 153p pa $13.95 **649**
1. Child care 2. Child rearing 3. Child development
ISBN 0-7434-1122-6

In these articles culled from Redbook and Parenting Spock's advice to parents is that they should "trust themselves" and "expands on this idea in his reply to the question, 'What has eroded so many parents' self-asssurance in asking for reasonably good behavior?'" Libr J

Dr. Spock's the school years; the emotional and social development of children. edited by Martin T. Stein. Pocket Bks. 2001 283p pa $15.95 **649**
1. Child care 2. Child rearing 3. Child development
ISBN 0-7434-1123-4

This volume collects Spock's essays published in Redbook and Parenting. They address "our contemporary culture's tendency to over-schedule children." Libr J

Wiseman, Rosalind, 1969-
Masterminds and wingmen; helping our boys cope with schoolyard power, locker-room tests, girlfriends, and the new rules of Boy World. Rosalind Wiseman. Harmony Books 2013 384 p. illustrations $25 **649**
1. Masculinity 2. Boys -- Psychology 3. Adolescent psychology 4. Parent and teenager 5. Teenage boys -- Psychology
ISBN 0307986659; 9780307986658

LC 2013372427

This book offers information "for every parent--or anyone who cares about boys--to know. Collaborating with a large team of middle- and high-school-age editors, Rosalind Wiseman has created an unprecedented guide to the life your boy is actually experiencing--his on-the-ground reality. Not only does Wiseman challenge you to examine your assumptions, she offers innovative coping strategies aimed at helping your boy develop a positive, authentic, and strong sense of self." (Publisher's note)

"Wiseman's sound and steady assistance provides a calm response to every twist and turn on the multifaceted road of parenthood. . . . A wealth of sensible information for parents of boys." Kirkus

Includes bibliographical references (pages 365-366) and index

Wright, Julie
The **happy** sleeper; the science-backed guide to helping your baby get a good night's sleep-newborn to school age. Heather Turgeon, Julie Wright ; illustrations by Jack Sheehy. Jeremy P. Tarcher/Penguin 2014 368 p. illustrations (paperback) $16.95 **649**
1. Sleep 2. Child rearing 3. Infants -- Sleep 4. Children -- Sleep
ISBN 0399166025; 9780399166020

LC 2014035240

This book, by Heather Turgeon and Julie Wright, presents a guide for infant sleeping habits. The authors "show parents how to be sensitive and nurturing, but also clear and structured so that babies and young children develop the self-soothing skills they need to fall asleep independently . . . , sleep through the night . . . , take healthy naps . . . , [and] grow into natural, optimal sleep patterns for day and night." (Publisher's note)

"Different approaches are given for kids up to age six, making this a manual that will grow with the child. Turgeon and Wright's compassionate but firm system reminds parents that even the smallest infants are already learners, and to be more cognizant of what they want to teach." Pub Wkly

Includes bibliographical references and index

649.1 Child rearing

Alpert, Karen
I Want My Epidural Back; Adventures in Mediocre Parenting. by Karen Alpert. HarperCollins 2016 x, 309 p.p illustrations $19.99 **649.1**
1. Parenting -- Humor
ISBN 0062427083; 9780062427083

LC 2016440757

This book, by Karen Alpert, "is a celebration of mediocre parents and how awesome they are and how their kids love them just as much as children with perfect parents. . . . Alpert's honest but hilarious observations, stories, quips and pictures will have you nodding your head and peeing in your pants. Or on the toilet if you're smart and read it there." (Publisher's note)

"Alpert is honest, humbling, and crass in this irreverent account on parenting." Pub Wkly

Ash, Jennifer
The **expectant** father; facts, tips, and advice for dads-to-be. Armin A. Brott, Jennifer Ash. 4th edition Abbeville Press 2015 333 p. **649.1**
1. Fathers 2. Pregnancy -- Popular works
ISBN 9780789212122

LC 2015009011

"This information-packed, month-by-month guide incorporates the expertise of top practitioners in their fields, from obstetricians and birth-class instructors to psychologists and sociologists. It also draws from Brott's own experience as a father of three and from the real-world experiences of the thousands of dads he's interviewed." (Publisher's note)

Includes bibliographical references and index

Faber, Adele
★ **How** to Talk So Kids Will Listen and Listen So Kids Will Talk; Adele Faber, Elaine Mazlish ; ill. by Kimberly Ann Coe. 30th anniversary edition Scribner Classics 2012 345 p. illustrations hbk $26 **649.1**
1. Parenting 2. Communication 3. Parent-child relationship
ISBN 1451663870; 9781451663877

First published 1980 by Rawson, Wade Publishers

This book on parenting, by Adele Faber and Elaine Mazlish, "includes fresh insights and suggestions as well as the author's time-tested methods to solve common problems and build foundations for lasting relationships." (Publisher's note)

The authors "keep true to the style of the original, while also updating their text with new scenarios and including feedback and letters they have received from readers over the years. Praised for its down-to-earth and respectful approach to communication, this book helps parents acknowledge their child's feelings, engage their cooperation, and encourage autonomy." LJ

Includes bibliographical references and index

Glickman, Elaine Rose

Your kid's a brat and it's all your fault; nip the attitude in the bud--from toddler to tween. Elaine Rose Glickman. Tarcher 2016 320 p. (paperback) $16   **649.1**

1. Parenting 2. Parent-child relationship 3. Emotionally disturbed children 4. Parent and child 5. Pampered child syndrome 6. Problem children -- Behavior modification

ISBN 9780399173127

LC 2015045423

In this book, author "Elaine Rose Glickman tells parents that—when it comes to their bratty kids—the buck stops with them! . . . Divided into three sections—'Your Budding Brat' for toddlers and preschoolers, 'Your Bratty Child' for grade-schoolers, and 'Your Bratty Tween'—this book is packed with wisdom and tips culled from the trenches of child-rearing." (Publisher's note)

"Most parents will find this humorous guide refreshing and truly helpful." Booklist

How do I explain this to my kids? parenting in the age of Trump. introduction and commentary by Dr. Ava Siegleredited by Sarah Swong and Diane Wachtell. New Press 2017 xii, 170 p.p illustrations (pbk.; alk. paper) $15.95   **649.1**

1. Parenting 2. Child rearing -- United States 3. Political culture -- United States

ISBN 9781620973561

LC 2017018179

This book, edited by Sarah Swong and Diane Wachtell, with introduction by Dr. Ava Siegler, "brings together moving first-person accounts by parents including novelist Mira Jacob, Pulitzer Prize winner Viet Thanh Nguyen, scholar Robin D.G. Kelley, . . . and others, who recount their best efforts to parent effectively in the . . . . [wake of the 2016 presidential election.] . . . The second half of the book features advice from leading child psychologist Ava Siegler." (Publisher's note)

Includes bibliographical references

Ingall, Marjorie

Mamaleh knows best; What Jewish Mothers Do to Raise Successful, Creative, Empathetic, Independent Children. Marjorie Ingall. Harmony Books 2016 245 p. (hardback) $25; (ebook) $65   **649.1**

1. Parenting 2. Parent-child relationship 3. Child rearing -- Religious aspects -- Judaism

ISBN 080414141X; 9780804141413; 9780804141420

LC 2016010796

This book by Marjorie Ingall "shares Jewish secrets for raising self-sufficient, ethical, and accomplished children. [Ingall] offers abundant examples showing how Jewish mothers have nurtured their children's independence, fostered discipline, . . . stressed education, and maintained a sense of humor. These . . . strategies have proven successful in a wide variety of settings. . . . . But you don't have to be Jewish to cultivate the same qualities in your own children." (Publisher's note)

"Ingall's engaging guide will help parents, Jewish or not, navigate the jagged terrain of child-rearing with a hearty dose of confidence and laughter." Pub Wkly

Includes bibliographical references (pages 232-235) and index.

Janis-Norton, Noel

Calmer, easier, happier screen time; for parents of toddlers to teens: a guide to getting back in charge of technology. Noël

Janis-Norton. Yellow Kite 2017 xiv, 257 p.p (paperback) $15.99   **649.1**

1. Parenting 2. Internet and children 3. Computers and children 4. Child rearing 5. Information technology 6. Technology and children 7. Computers and civilization 8. Adjustment (Psychology) in children 9. Children -- Effect of technological innovations on

ISBN 9781473622760; 147362276X

In this book, author Noël Janis-Norton "adapts her proven parenting strategies to . . . [the] most complex of areas. Using the latest scientific research to show just how addictive the digital world can be for the developing brain of a child, she using the calmer, easier, happier techniques to help parents wean their children away from their electronic devices and get back in charge." (Publisher's note)

Lewis, Lisa

Feed the baby hummus; pediatrician-backed secrets from cultures around the world. Lisa Lewis, MD. Familius 2018 256 p. (alk. paper) $18.99   **649.1**

1. Parenting 2. Infants -- Care

ISBN 9781945547799

LC 2017958506

This book, by Lisa Lewis, "teaches parents to confidently incorporate various multicultural practices into their own caretaking plan. . . . Lewis offers the wisdom and proven caretaking practices of the cultures of the world, drawn from her own training, research, travel, and clinical experience. . . . . 'Feed the Baby Hummus' offers a variety of cross-cultural parenting information and baby care guidance from a trusted source." (Publisher's note)

Mogel, Wendy

Voice lessons for parents; what to say, how to say it, and when to listen. Wendy Mogel, PhD. Scribner 2018 xvi, 302 p.p (hardcover) $27   **649.1**

1. Parenting 2. Parent-child relationship 3. Parent and child 4. Interpersonal communication

ISBN 9781501142390; 9781501142413; 1501142399

This book, by Wendy Mogel, "offers an essential guide to the new art of talking to children, showing how a change in tone and demeanor can transform the relationship between parent and child. Most parents are perfectly fine communicators--unless they're talking to their children. Then, too often, their pitch rises and they come across as pleading, indignant, wounded, outraged. In tone and body language they signal, I can't handle it when you act like a child." (Publisher's note)

Includes bibliographical references (pages 283-288) and index.

Morgenstern, Julie

Time to parent; organizing your life to bring out the best in your child and you. by Julie Morgenstern. Henry Holt & Co. 2018 352 p. (trade paperback) $18   **649.1**

1. Parenting 2. Time management

ISBN 9781627797436

LC 2018001408

In this book on parenting, author "[Julie] Morgenstern's bite-size, achievable goals and skill levels are simple to digest. Backed by scientific data and personal experience, the book is full of straightforward advice presented in an intriguing way...A multi-part, common-sense approach to parenting that addresses a wide variety of the issues parents face in their complex lives." (Kirkus Reviews)

"Morgenstern's many fans will appreciate the organizational insights she brings to the parenting arena as well as the concrete ideas for finding more time for family and self-care." Library Journal

Morin, Amy

13 things mentally strong parents don't do; raising self-assured children and training their brains for a life of happiness, meaning, and success. Amy Morin. William Morrow, an imprint of HarperCollins Publishers 2017 342 p. (hardcover) $26.99 **649.1**

   1. Parenting 2. Child rearing 3. Self-confidence in children
   ISBN 0062565737; 9780062565730; 9780062565747

LC 2017031138

This book, by Amy Morin, "gives adults--parents, teachers, and other mentors--the tools they need to become mental strength trainers. . . . [It] combines case studies, practical tips, specific strategies, and concrete and proven exercises to help children of all ages--from preschoolers to teenagers--build mental muscle and develop into healthy, strong adults." (Publisher's note)

"Her combination of common sense backed by research—amply cited—will help parents make a midcourse correction. While the title focuses on the negative, the book itself accentuates the positive." Pub Wkly

Includes bibliographical references (pages 333-342).

Raeburn, Paul

The **game** theorist's guide to parenting; how the science of strategic thinking can help you deal with the toughest negotiators you know--your kids. Paul Raeburn and Kevin Zollman. Scientific American/Farrar, Straus & Giroux 2016 240 p. (hardcover) $25 **649.1**

   1. Parenting 2. Game theory 3. Negotiation 4. Game theory -- Social aspects
   ISBN 9780374160012

LC 2015036381

In this book, authors Paul Raeburn and Kevin Zollman "pair up to highlight tactics from the worlds of economics and business that can help parents. . . . [They] show that some of the same strategies successfully applied to big business deals and politics—such as the Prisoner's Dilemma and the Ultimatum Game—can be used to solve such titanic, age-old parenting problems as dividing up toys, keeping the peace on long car rides, and sticking to homework routines." (Publisher's note)

"Tantalizing perspectives on cultivating sharing, honesty, and cooperation via game theory." Kirkus

Includes bibliographical references and index

Walker, Bridget Flynn

Anxiety Relief for Kids; On-the-Spot Strategies to Help Your Child Overcome Worry, Panic & Avoidance. by Bridget Flynn Walker PhD ; foreword by Michael A. Tompkins PhD ABPP. New Harbinger Publications, Inc. 2017 203 p. (paperback) $16.95 **649.1**

   1. Anxiety -- Treatment 2. Parenting 3. Worry in children 4. Anxiety in children 5. Self-confidence in children 6. Defense mechanisms (Psychology)
   ISBN 9781626259553; 9781626259546; 9781626259539; 1626259534

This book, by Bridget Flynn Walker PhD, "provides quick solutions based in evidence-based CBT and exposure therapy—two of the most effective treatments for anxiety disorders. You'll find a background and explanation of the different types of anxiety disorders, in case you aren't sure whether or not your child has one. You'll also learn to identify your child's avoidant and safety behaviors . . . as well as anxiety triggers that set your child off." (Publisher's note)

Includes bibliographical references (pages 201-203).

Willingham, Emily

The **informed** parent; a science-based resource for your child's first four years. Tara Haelle and Emily Willingham, Ph.D. Perigee Books 2016 336 p. (paperback) $20 **649.1**

   1. Parenting 2. Child rearing 3. Child development 4. Pregnancy 5. Parenthood 6. Infants -- Care 7. Families -- Health and hygiene
   ISBN 9780399171062

LC 2015046759

This book, by Tara Haelle and Emily Willingham, Ph.D, offers the "latest scientific research on home birth, breastfeeding, sleep training, vaccines, and other key topics—to help parents make their own best-informed decisions. . . . The ultimate resource for today's science-minded generation, [this book] was written for readers who prefer facts to "friendly advice," and who prefer to make up their own minds, based on the latest findings as well as their own personal preferences." (Publisher's note)

"For anyone headed into parenthood, this is a must-read, as it answers so many questions new parents are bound to ask. Easy-to-read, up-to-date information on the latest research into pregnancy, childbirth, and early childhood." Kirkus

Zaske, Sara

Achtung baby; an American mom on the German art of raising self-reliant children. Sara Zaske. Picador 2018 ix, 239 p.p (hardcover) $26 **649.1**

   1. Parenting 2. Self-reliance 3. Children -- Conduct of life 4. Parent and child 5. Parenting -- Germany 6. Self-reliance in children 7. Parenting -- United States
   ISBN 9781250160188; 9781250160171

LC 2017032099

This book, by Sara Zaske, "reveals that today's Germans know something that American parents don't (or have perhaps forgotten) about raising kids with 'selbstandigkeit' (self-reliance),and provides practical examples American parents can use to give their own children the freedom they need to grow into responsible, independent adults." (Publisher's note)

"An entertaining, informative, and enlightening narrative on the German methods of parenting that will have many in the U.S. reconsidering how they're raising their children." Kirkus

Includes bibliographical references (pages 211-225) and index.

649.122   Care of infants

Cross, Claire

The **baby** book; pregnancy, birth, baby & childcare from 0 to 3. writers Shaoni Bhattacharya, Claire Cross, Carol Dyce, Kate Ling, Susannah Marriott, Karen Sullivan, and Jo Wiltshire. DK Publishing 2016 320 p. color illustrations (paperback) $24.95 **649.122**

   1. Parenting 2. Pregnancy 3. Child rearing
   ISBN 1465444785; 9781465444783

LC 2015458963

This book, by Shaoni Bhattacharya, Claire Cross, Carol Dyce, Kate Ling, Susannah Marriott, Karen Sullivan, and Jo Wiltshire, "is a guide to caring for your child — from pregnancy through age three. . . . [The book] . . . provides everything you need to know as a parent — from pregnancy superfoods and labor tips to first check-ups and breastfeeding secrets — while presenting this part of life as something you should celebrate, not fear." (Publisher's note)

"While books on this subject are abundant, readers will be naturally drawn to the warm style and sheer beauty of the DK titles. Libraries can't go wrong with this acquisition." LJ

649.123   Care of preschool children

Seldin, Tim

How to raise an amazing child the Montessori way; Tim Seldin. Second edition DK Publishing 2017 208 p. color illustrations (paperback) $19.95   **649.123**
1. Parenting 2. Child rearing 3. Montessori method of education
ISBN 9781465466792; 9781465462305; 1465462309
LC 2017302243

This book, by Tim Seldin, is "a parent's guide to building independence, creativity, and confidence in their children using Montessori learning techniques. . . . This edition . . . [includes] information about the neuroscience of child development and shares advice about screen time in the digital age, coparenting, other family changes, and gentle discipline methods." (Publisher's note)

"Child psychiatrist Seldin, president of the Montessori Foundation, here adapts key Montessori principles for the home environment, maintaining the core tenets of 'kindness, partnership, and respect.'"LJ

Includes bibliographical references (page 208) and index.

649.3   Feeding children

Altmann, Tanya Remer

What to feed your baby; a pediatrician's guide to the eleven essential foods to guarantee veggie-loving, no-fuss, healthy-eating kids. Tanya Altmann. HarperOne 2016 336 p. (paperback) $17.99   **649.3**
1. Eating customs 2. Infants -- Nutrition 3. Food habits
ISBN 9780062404947
LC 2015033614

In this book, pediatrician Tanya Altmann "provides the latest nutritional recommendations and best practices for feeding babies and young children. The simple, fool-proof program focuses on serving eleven foundation foods: eggs, prunes, avocado, fish, yogurt/cheese/milk, nuts, chicken/beans, fruit, green veggies, whole grains, and water." (Publisher's note)

"This clear, thorough guide will take the angst and confusion out of feeding time for parents and youngsters alike." Pub Wkly

Includes bibliographical references (pages 311-314) and index.

649.33   Breast feeding

Grayson, Jennifer

Unlatched; the evolution of breastfeeding and the making of a controversy. Jennifer Grayson. HarperCollins 2016 336 p. (ebook) $14.99; $15.99   **649.33**
1. Breast feeding 2. Infants -- Nutrition
ISBN 9780062423405; 0062423398; 9780062423399
LC 2016027825

"Growing up, journalist Jennifer Grayson thought nothing of the fact that she was bottle-fed. But when she became a mother, Grayson considered the impact of missing out on this profound connection. Her book is a worldwide search for answers about the first, most fundamental experience of newborn life. . . . [It also] uncovers astonishing cultural, corporate, political, and technological factors at the heart of our contemporary breastfeeding disconnection." (Publisher's note)

"Persuasive arguments backed by scientific research that clearly demonstrate the benefits of breast-feeding for as long as possible." Kirkus

Includes bibliographical references (pages 301-324).

Seals-Allers, Kimberly

The **big** letdown; Kimberly Seals Allers. St. Martin's Press 2017 304 p. (ebook) $60; (hardback) $25.99   **649.33**
1. Parenting 2. Breast feeding 3. Breastfeeding 4. Breastfeeding -- Social aspects 5. Breastfeeding -- Economic aspects
ISBN 9781250026972; 9781250026965
LC 2016044039

This book, by Kimberly Seals Allers, "uncovers the multibillion-dollar forces battling to replace mothers' milk and the failure of the medical establishment to protect infant health. Weaving together research and personal stories with original reporting on medicine, big pharma, and hospitals, . . . Allers shows how mothers and babies have been abandoned by all the forces that should be supporting families from the start-and what we can do to help." (Publisher's note)

"Easily digested research and personal stories in support of breastfeeding and its importance to mothers and their children." Kirkus

Includes bibliographical references (pages 269-280) and index.

Shortall, Jessica

Work. Pump. Repeat. The New Mom's Survival Guide to Breastfeeding and Going Back to Work. Jessica Shortall. Harry N Abrams Inc 2015 208 p. $19.95   **649.33**
1. Breast feeding 2. Working mothers
ISBN 9781419718700; 1419718703
LC 2015934789

Author Jessica Shortall presents this "book to give women what they need to know beyond the noise of the "Mommy Wars" and judgment on breastfeeding choices. Jessica Shortall shares the nitty-gritty basics of surviving the working world as a breastfeeding mom, offering a road map for negotiating the pumping schedule with colleagues, navigating business travel, and problem-solving when forced to pump in less-than-desirable locales." (Publisher's note)

649.58   Reading and related activities

Newman, Nancy

Raising passionate readers; 5 easy steps to success in school and life. Nancy Newman. Tribeca View Press 2014 222 p. $16.95   **649.58**
1. Literacy 2. Children -- Books and reading
ISBN 0615847544; 9780615847542
LC 2013951969

In this book, by Nancy Newman, "bridging the gap between scientists and busy parents by combining the latest scientific research with what she has learned as a teacher and mother, . . . [the author] offers a simple, practical, and joyful approach that boosts children's literacy skills and instills an enduring love of reading." (Publisher's note)

"While the subject literature has not changed much over the years, it is still widely accepted that reading is the greatest indicator of future academic success. Recommended for collections needing an update on the topic." LJ

649.62   Toilet training

Ockwell-Smith, Sarah

Ready, set, go! a gentle parenting guide to calmer, quicker

potty training. Sarah Ockwell-Smith. Tarcher Perigee 2017
208 p. (pbk.) $16 **649.62**

1. Parenting 2. Toilet training
ISBN 9780143131908

LC 2018011129

This book, by Sarah Ockwell-Smith, "provides step-by-step advice
for a compassionate and emotionally aware process [of toilet training]--
one that focuses on positive connection rather than relying on gimmicks,
pressure, or rewards (which usually backfire). Topics include: signs your
child is ready, and how to begin; preparing your child emotionally . . .
[and] practical stories and tips from parents." (Publisher's note)

"There is little new here, but potty training is of perennial interest to parents, and newbies may find this a solid starter manual."
Library Journal

649.64   Behavior modification, discipline, obedience

Ockwell-Smith, Sarah

Gentle discipline; using emotional connection--not punish-
ment--to raise confident, capable kids. Sarah Ockwell-Smith.
TarcherPerigee 2017 xxiv, 246 p.p illustrations (paperback)
$16 **649.64**

1. Parenting 2. Child rearing 3. Advice literature 4. Discipline of
children 5. Emotions -- Social aspects
ISBN 9780143131892; 9781524705756; 0143131893

LC 2017015635

This book, by Sarah Ockwell-Smith, provides "a practical guide that
presents an alternative to shouting, shaming, and blaming--to give kids
the skills they need to grow and thrive. . . . Citing the latest research
in child development, psychology and neuroscience, . . . [it] debunks
common myths about punishments, rewards, . . . and more, and presents practical, connection-based techniques that really work." (Publisher's note)

"Ockwell-Smith, a parenting blogger, presents a primer on placing
empathy and respect for children at the center of parenting." Pub Wkly

Includes bibliographical references and index.

Pearlman, Catherine

Ignore It! how selectively looking the other way can decrease behavioral problems and increase parenting satisfaction.
Catherine Pearlman. TarcherPerigee 2017 256 p. (paperback)
$16 **649.64**

1. Parenting 2. Conflict management 3. Children -- Family
relationships
ISBN 9781524704001; 9780143130338; 0143130331

LC 2017015621

This book, by Catherine Pearlman, "teaches frustrated, stressed-out
parents that selectively ignoring certain behaviors can actually inspire
positive changes in their kids. . . . Dr. Pearlman's four-step process returns the joy to child rearing. Combining highly effective strategies with
time-tested approaches, she teaches parents when to selectively look the
other way to withdraw reinforcement for undesirable behaviors." (Publisher's note)

"Fun to read and written in a parent-to-parent voice, this is a welcome reintroduction of well-tested child-raising methods and should be
required reading for all parents." Pub Wkly

Includes bibliographical references (pages 247-254) and index.

649.7   Moral and character training of children

Borba, Michele

Unselfie; why empathetic kids succeed in our all-about-me
world. Michele Borba. Touchstone 2016 288 p. (hardback)
$25 **649.7**

1. Empathy 2. Child rearing 3. Interpersonal relations
ISBN 9781501110030

LC 2015049137

This book, by Michele Borba, "offers a 9-step program to help parents cultivate empathy in children, from birth to young adulthood—and
explains why developing a healthy sense of empathy is a key predictor
of which kids will thrive and succeed in the future. . . . Borba offers a
framework for parenting that yields the results we all want: successful,
happy kids who also are kind, moral, courageous, and resilient." (Publisher's note)

"Her thought- provoking and practical book may very well tip over
the parenting priority applecart—and rightly so." Pub Wkly

Includes bibliographical references and index.

Prosek, Jen

Raising Can-Do Kids; Giving Children the Tools to Thrive
in a Fast-Changing World. Richard Rende, Jen Prosek. Penguin
Group USA 2015 272 p. $24.95 **649.7**

1. Parenting 2. Child development
ISBN 0399168966; 9780399168963

This book by Richard Rende and Jen Prosek attempts to "make a
link between the essential qualities that make great entrepreneurs tick
and what we know about how children learn and grow, offering parents
proven ways to raise kids who embrace the uncertain, challenging adventure that is growing up in today's (and tomorrow's) changing world.
Each chapter is devoted to a quality ¿ including curiosity, inventiveness, optimism, opportunity-seeking, compassion, and service." (Publisher's note)

"The authors' suggestions and insights cover a wide spectrum of
child-raising situations and should, when properly applied, deliver lasting results." Kirkus

649.8   Home care of people with disabilities and illnesses

American Cancer Society complete guide to family caregiving;
the essential guide to cancer caregiving at home. by Julia A.
Bucher, Peter S. Houts, Terri Ades. American Cancer Soci-
ety/Health Promotions 2011 354 p. illustrations (pbk.; alk.
paper) $24.95 **649.8**

1. Cancer patients 2. Caregivers -- Handbooks, manuals, etc. 3.
Caregivers 4. Cancer -- Palliative treatment 5. Cancer -- Patients
-- Home care
ISBN 094423500X; 9780944235003

LC 2010015968

This book, by Julia A. Bucher, Peter S. Houts, and Terri Ades, "offers manageable solutions to the many conditions and situations caregivers may face. From physical and emotional conditions, to dealing with
health care providers and insurance carriers this resource helps teach
caregivers to take care of their own needs as well as those of the person
with cancer." (Publisher's note)

Includes bibliographical references and index

650.1   Personal success in business

Bolles, Richard, 1927-2017

★ **What** color is your parachute? 2017; a practical manual for job-hunters and career-changers. by Richard N. Bolles. Ten Speed Press 2016 355 p. hbk $29.99   **650.1**

1. Job hunting 2. Cover letters 3. Resumes (Employment)
ISBN 9780399578212; 0399578218
First published 1972; revised annually

"This revised and updated edition combines classic elements like the famed Flower Exercise with updated tips on social media and search tactics. Bolles demystifies the entire job-search process, from resumes to interviewing to networking, expertly guiding job-hunters toward their dream job." (Publisher's note)

Burkus, David

Friend of a friend... understanding the hidden networks that can transform your life and your career. David Burkus. Houghton Mifflin Harcourt 2018 256 p. (hardback) $27   **650.1**

1. Social networking 2. Vocational guidance 3. Business communication 4. Business networks
ISBN 9780544971264

LC 2017045593

In this book about business networking, author David Burkus "digs deep to find the unexpected secrets that reveal the best ways to grow your universe. Based upon entertaining case studies and scientific research, this practical and revelatory guide shares what the best networkers really do...and it looks a lot less like collecting business cards and making random introductions and a lot more like fostering authentic connections and seeking out diverse new voices." (Publisher's note)

"This work offers thought-provoking case studies and practical guidelines on a popular but generally misunderstood topic. Of interest to social scientists, business professionals, and job seekers alike." LJ

Includes bibliographical references and index

Cast, Carter

The **right**--and wrong--stuff; how brilliant careers are made and unmade. Carter Cast. PublicAffairs 2017 288 p. (hardcover) $28   **650.1**

1. Success 2. Executive ability 3. Career development
ISBN 1610397096; 9781610397094

LC 2017042061

This book, by Carter Cast, "is a candid, unvarnished guide to the bumpy road to success. The shocking truth is that 98 percent of us have at least one career-derailment risk factor, and half to two-thirds actually go off the rails. And the reason why people get fired, demoted, or plateau is because they let the wrong stuff act out, not because they lack talent, energy, experience, or credentials." (Publisher's note)

"This relatable career manual should inspire plenty of white-collar professionals to work on serious self-accounting, take responsibility for their own mistakes, and form support teams of friends, managers, and mentors." Publishers Weekly

Includes bibliographical references and index

Chideya, Farai

The **episodic** career; how to thrive at work in the age of disruption. Farai Chideya. Atria Books 2016 288 p. (hardback) $26   **650.1**

1. Job hunting 2. Vocational guidance 3. Job hunting -- United States -- History -- 21st century 4. Vocational guidance -- United States -- History -- 21st century
ISBN 1476751501; 9781476751504

LC 2015029936

This book, by Farai Chideya, "explores the landscape of employment in America. Profiling the rich, the poor, and people from every strata in between, Chideya seeks to understand the many kinds of work we do--for example, not just job fields, but whether we seek to build institutions or seek social change while earning money. In addition, Chideya provides a self-diagnostic tool to help you find your work/life 'sweet spot.'" (Publisher's note)

"A fun, useful, and informative book for any stage of the career path. Recommended for public libraries and career collections." LJ

Includes bibliographical references and index.

Dufu, Tiffany

Drop the Ball; achieving more by doing less. Tiffany Dufu ; foreword by Gloria Steinem. St. Martin's Press 2017 304 p. (ebook) $60; $25.99   **650.1**

1. Work-life balance 2. Leadership in women 3. African American women -- Biography
ISBN 9781250071750; 1250071739; 9781250071736

LC 2016037631

In this book, author Tiffany Dufu "recounts how she learned to re-evaluate expectations, shrink her to-do list, and meaningfully engage the assistance of others—freeing the space she needed to flourish at work and to develop deeper, more meaningful relationships at home... . [Dufu] urges women to embrace imperfection, to expect less of themselves and more from others— . . . [in order to] create the type of rich, rewarding life we all desire." (Publisher's note)

Evans, Dave

Designing your life; how to think like a designer and build a well-lived, joyful life. William Burnett and David J. Evans. Alfred A. Knopf 2016 304 p. (hardcover) $26.95   **650.1**

1. Design 2. Quality of life 3. Vocational guidance 4. Decision making 5. Self-realization 6. Design -- Social aspects
ISBN 1101875321; 9781101875322

LC 2016008862

In this book authors "Bill Burnett and Dave Evans show . . . how design thinking can help . . . create a life that is both meaningful and fulfilling. The same design thinking responsible for amazing technology, products, and spaces can be used to design and build your career and your life, a life of fulfillment and joy, constantly creative and productive, one that always holds the possibility of surprise." (Publisher's note)

"With useful fact-finding exercises, an empathetic tone, and sensible advice, this book will easily earn a place among career-finding classics." Pub Wkly

Goulston, Mark

Just listen; discover the secret to getting through to absolutely anyone. foreword by Keith Ferrazzi. American Management Association 2009 234p il $24.95   **650.1**

1. Business communication 2. Interpersonal relations
ISBN 978-0-8144-1403-3

LC 2009-14386

This is "a primer on dealing with hard-to-reach people in virtually every scenario—defiant executives, angry employees, families in turmoil, warring couples—through use of well-honed psychological techniques. . . . Chapter summaries feature action steps preparing readers to encounter similar scenarios, yielding a guide that is as entertaining as it is useful." Publ Wkly

Hansen, Morten T.

Great at work; How Top Performers Do Less, Work Better

& Achieve More. Morten T. Hansen. Simon & Schuster 2018 320 p. (hbk.) $29.99 **650.1**

1. Labor productivity 2. Self-help techniques 3. Self-management (Psychology)

ISBN 1476765626; 9781476765624

This book, by Morten Hansen, "[is] an authoritative, practical guide to individual performance--based on analysis from an exhaustive, groundbreaking study. . . . [He] reveals the answers in his 'Seven Work Smarter Practices' that can be applied by anyone looking to maximize their time and performance." (Publisher's note)

"Based on this work, Hansen identifies the seven key factors that make people work smarter, not harder: do less, then obsess; redesign your work; don't just learn, loop; have passion and purpose; be a forceful champion; fight over ideas but unite on decisions; and use disciplined collaboration." Booklist

Harris, Carla A.

Strategize to win; the new way to start out, step up, or start over in your career. Carla A. Harris. Hudson Street Press 2014 256 p. (hardback) $25.95 **650.1**

1. Career changes 2. Vocational guidance 3. Career development 4. Success in business

ISBN 1594633053; 9781594633058

LC 2014031571

This book, by Carla A. Harris, "offers a new way to conceptualize career strategies and gives us proven tools for successful change. . . . [The author] gives readers the tools they need to get started; get 'unstuck' from bad situations; redirect momentum; and position themselves to manage their careers no matter the environment." (Publisher's note)

"Advice to those in the 'Starting Over' phase covers knowing when it's time to jump ship and recognizing what factors motivate one, whether it's increased compensation, improved chances for advancement, or escaping current unfair treatment. She also provides an informative chapter on repositioning oneself, which many will find especially insightful. Most professionals should be able to find something of value, whether they're just starting out, ready to move on, or somewhere in between." Pub Wkly

Hill, Napoleon

Think and grow rich; the landmark bestseller--now revised and updated for the 21st century. rev. and expanded by Arthur R. Pell. 1st Jeremy P. Tarcher/Penguin ed.; Jeremy P. Tarcher/Penguin 2005 302p pa $10 **650.1**

1. Success 2. Entrepreneurship

ISBN 1-585-42433-1

LC 2005-44133

First published 1937 by The Ralston Society

A motivational guide to achieving wealth and success, drawing upon stories of successful millionaires as examples.

Jacobs, Bert

Life is good; the book. Bert Jacobs and John Jacobs. National Geographic 2015 271 p. color illustrations (hardback) $25 **650.1**

1. Optimism 2. Happiness 3. Life Is Good (Firm) 4. Clothing trade -- United States 5. Businesspeople -- United States -- Conduct of life

ISBN 9781426215636

LC 2015020909

This book, by Bert Jacobs and John Jacobs, "celebrates the power of optimism: the driving force behind their beloved, socially conscious clothing and lifestyle brand. Following the chronology of their personal and professional journeys, Bert and John share their unique ride—from their scrappy upbringing outside Boston to the unlikely runaway success of their business. The brothers illuminate ten key superpowers accessible to us all [including:] openness, courage, [and] simplicity." (Publisher's note)

"An outstanding book for all ages. One cannot browse through it without smiling and feeling that, despite everything, life is good." LJ

Includes bibliographical references (pages 269-270).

Johnson, Jaclyn

WorkParty; how to create & cultivate the career of your dreams. Jaclyn Johnson. Gallery Books 2018 256 p. (hardback) $25.99 **650.1**

1. Success in business 2. Women -- Employment 3. Sex discrimination in employment 4. Job satisfaction 5. Businesswomen -- United States 6. Success in business -- United States 7. Women -- Employment -- United States 8. Sex discrimination against women -- United States

ISBN 9781501190834; 9781501190841

LC 2018014251

In this book, author Jaclyn Johnson, "shows how she turned distrust into determination, frustration into fuel, and heartache into hard work--and how you can, too. With stories from leading female entrepreneurs including Christene Barberich . . . , Alli Webb, . . . , Morgan Debaun . . . , Jen Gotch . . . , Rebecca Minkoff, and Kendra Scott, you will learn the tips and tricks from the best in the business while cultivating the passion and happiness you need to succeed." (Publisher's note)

Kerpen, Dave

The **art** of people; 11 Simple People Skills That Will Get You Everything You Want. Dave Kerpen. Crwon Business 2016 276 p. $27 **650.1**

1. Communication 2. Industrial psychology 3. Interpersonal relations 4. Psychology, Industrial 5. Interpersonal communication

ISBN 0553419404; 9780553419405

LC 2015016366

In this book, author Dave Kerpen argues "the key to getting ahead is being the person others like, respect, and trust. Because no matter who you are or what profession you're in, success is contingent less on what you can do for yourself, but on what other people are willing to do for you. Here, through 53 bite-sized, easy-to-execute, and often counterintuitive tips, you'll learn to master the 11 People Skills that will get you more of what you want at work, at home, and in life." (Publisher's note)

Knapp, Jake

Make time; how to focus on what matters every day. Jake Knapp and John Zeratsky. Currency 2018 304 p. $27 **650.1**

1. Time management 2. Self-realization 3. Work-life balance

ISBN 9780525572428

LC 2017059817

This book, by Jake Knapp and John Zeratsky, offers "the most effective tactics [for restructuring one's life to free up time] into a four-step daily framework that anyone can use to systematically design their days. 'Make Time' is not a one-size-fits-all formula. Instead, it offers a customizable menu of bite-size tips and strategies that can be tailored to individual habits and lifestyles." (Publisher's note)

Includes bibliographical references and index

Kotter, John P., 1947-

Buy-in; saving your good idea from being shot down. [by] John P. Kotter and Lorne A. Whitehead. Harvard Business Review Press 2010 192p **650.1**

1. Creative ability 2. Public relations
ISBN 978-1-4221-5729-9

LC 2010016497

"This book explains how to protect a good idea and win support for it. The authors welcome naysayers, nitpickers, and handwringers into the room during the discussion, because they show you in this book how to respond to the unfair attacks to find success. Readers learn about the four attack strategies—death by delay, confusion, fear mongering, and character assassination—and how to show respect for all and use simple, clear, and common-sense responses. . . . This book helps you gain the upper hand by giving you practical responses to more than 24 generic attacks that people often use to shoot down good ideas." T + D

Kramer, Andrea S.

Breaking through bias; communication techniques for women to succeed at work. Andrea S. Kramer and Alton B. Harris. Bibliomotion, Inc. 2016 256 p. (hardcover; alk. paper) $27.95 **650.1**
1. Vocational guidance 2. Business communication 3. Women in the workplace 4. Sex discrimination 5. Women -- Communication 6. Vocational guidance for women 7. Stereotypes (Social psychology) 8. Communication in management -- Sex differences 9. Communication in organizations -- Sex differences
ISBN 9781629561042

LC 2015040059

This book, by Andrea S. Kramer and Alton B. Harris, "explains that it is the stereotypes about women, men, work, leadership, and family that hold women back, and it presents an integrated set of communication techniques that women can use to avoid the discriminatory consequences of these stereotypes." (Publisher's note)

"In addition to providing intelligent guidance, it reminds us all that we have a long way to go when it comes to achieving gender equality in the workplace." Booklist

Includes bibliographical references and index

Kreamer, Anne

Risk /reward; why intelligent leaps and daring choices are the best career moves you can make. by Anne Kreamer. Random House Inc. 2015 224 p. (hardback) $26 **650.1**
1. Career changes 2. Success in business 3. Risk-taking (Psychology) 4. Risk management 5. Career development
ISBN 1400067987; 9781400067985

LC 2014046074

In this book, author Anne Kreamer "makes the compelling case that embracing risk is essential to managing a twenty-first-century career. Risk-taking isn't just for entrepreneurs, nor does it require working on a figurative tightrope. Rather, Kreamer says, conscious, consistent, and modest risk-taking can help us become more able to recognize opportunity when it appears, and more likely to seize the chance to make the right change at the right moment." (Publisher's note)

"Well-written with intriguing findings, this quick and relevant read is recommended for public libraries and career collections." LJ

Includes bibliographical references

Kwong, David

Spellbound; seven principles of illusion to captivate audiences and unlock the secrets of success. David Kwong. Harper Business 2017 xiv, 251 p.p illustrations (hardcover) $27.99 **650.1**
1. Success in business 2. Persuasion (Psychology) 3. Illusion (Philosophy) 4. Magicians -- Miscellanea
ISBN 9780062448477; 0062448463; 9780062448460

This book, by David Kwong, "reveals how to bridge the gap between perception and reality to increase your powers of persuasion and influence. . . . Kwong has astounded corporate CEOs, TED talk audiences, and . . . other hyper-rational people, making them see, believe, and even remember what he wants them to. . . . Successful leaders --like Steve Jobs, Warren Buffett, and Ted Turner--are masters of control and command who understand how to sway opinions and achieve goals." (Publisher's note)

"Without revealing major secrets of his craft, Kwong gives laypeople a taste of what lies behind the sleight of hand and misdirection wielded by magicians from Houdini to David Copperfield." Pub Wkly

Includes bibliographical references (pages 229-239) and index.

Licht, Aliza

Leave Your Mark; Land Your Dream Job. Kill it in Your Career. Rock Social Media. Aliza Licht. Grand Central Publishing 2015 259 p. (hardback) $26 **650.1**
1. Success 2. Vocational guidance 3. Social media 4. Career development
ISBN 1455584142; 9781455584147

LC 2014049281

In this book, author Aliza Licht, "shares advice, inspiration, and a healthy dose of real talk. . . . She delivers personal and professional guidance for people just starting their careers and for people who are well on their way. With a particular emphasis on communicating and building your personal brand." (Publisher's note)

Lidsky, Isaac

Eyes wide open; overcoming obstacles and recognizing opportunities in a world that can't see clearly. Isaac Lidsky. TarcherPerigee 2017 viii, 305 p.p (hardback) $26 **650.1**
1. Blind 2. Success 3. Self-realization 4. Self-actualization (Psychology)
ISBN 9780143129578

LC 2016048498

In this book, author Isaac Lidsky "draws on his experience of achieving immense success, joy, and fulfillment while losing his sight to a blinding disease to show us that it isn't external circumstances, but how we perceive and respond to them, that governs our reality." (Publisher's note)

"This master class in counting one's blessings will stay with readers long after the final page is turned." Pub Wkly

Includes bibliographical references and index

Mohr, Tara

Playing big; find your voice, your mission, your message. by Tara Sophia Mohr. Gotham Books 2014 304 p. (hardcover) $27 **650.1**
1. Success 2. Women -- Psychology 3. Self-help techniques 4. Success in business 5. Self-actualization (Psychology)
ISBN 1594206074; 9781594206078

LC 2014021945

This book by Tara Mohr "provides real, practical tools to help women quiet self-doubt, identify their callings, 'unhook' from praise and criticism, unlearn counterproductive good girl habits, and begin taking bold action. The book offers tools to help every woman play bigger--whether she's an executive, community volunteer, artist, or stay-at-home mom." (Publisher's note)

"Recommended for women who have good ideas but are unsure of themselves or how to implement their innovative concepts. A useful book for public libraries and those with strong feminist or career collections." LJ

Includes bibliographical references

Mulcahy, Diane

The **gig** economy; The Complete Guide to Getting Better Work, Taking More Time Off, and Financing the Life You Want. Diane Mulcahy. AMACOM 2016 240 p. (hardcover) $22.00; (ebook) $16.95 **650.1**

1. Vocational guidance 2. Part-time employment 3. Quality of work life 4. Career development 5. Flexible work arrangements
ISBN 9780814437339; 9780814437346

LC 2016023117

This book on the gig economy, by Diane Mulcahy, presents a "guide to this uncertain but ultimately rewarding world. Succeeding in it starts with shifting gears to recognize that only you control your future. Next is leveraging your skills, knowledge, and network to create your own career trajectory--one immune to the whims of an employer." (Publisher's note)

"The book is filled with helpful step-by-step instructions, sound examples of good and bad approaches, and financial reality checks." Booklist

Includes bibliographical references

Newport, Cal

Deep work; rules for focused success in a distracted world. Cal Newport. Grand Central Publishing 2016 304 p. (hardback) $28 **650.1**

1. Attention 2. Distraction (Psychology) 3. Success 4. Cognition 5. Distraction 6. Mental work
ISBN 9781455586691

LC 2015032646

This book, by Cal Newport, "instead of arguing distraction is bad, . . . celebrates the power of its opposite. Dividing this book into two parts, he first makes the case that in almost any profession, cultivating a deep work ethic will produce massive benefits. He then presents a rigorous training regimen, presented as a series of four 'rules,' for transforming your mind and habits to support this skill." (Publisher's note)

"It's tempting to blow off the message as the complaints of an admitted non-technophile, but Newport's disarming self-awareness... and emphasis on a meaningful work practice that's 'rich with productivity and meaning' makes for an excellent lesson in focusing on quality rather than quantity at work." Pub Wkly

Includes bibliographical references and index

Palmieri, Jennifer

Dear madam president; an open letter to the women who will run the world. Jennifer Palmieri. Grand Central Publishing 2018 192 p. (hardcover) $20 **650.108**

1. Self-realization 2. Leadership in women 3. Women -- Conduct of life
ISBN 9781538713440; 9781538713457; 9781538713525; 9781549169823; 9781549169908

LC 2017963453

This book, by Jennifer Palmieri, "is filled with forward-thinking, practical advice for all women who are determined to seize control of their lives. . . . Palmieri argues that our feelings--confusion, love, hate, acceptance--can now open the country up to reimagining women in leadership roles. And that is what Palmieri takes on in this book-redefining expectations for women looking to lead and creating a blueprint for women candidates and leaders to follow." (Publisher's note)

Power, Katherine

The **career** code; Must-Know Rules for a Strategic, Stylish, and Self-Made Career. Hillary Kerr, Katherine Power. Abrams Image 2016 168 p. illustrations $19.95 **650.1**

1. Success in business
ISBN 9781419718021

LC 2015949324

In this book, authors Hillary Kerr and Katherine Power "bring you the Everygirl's guide for creating your own professional success, on every level, flawlessly. . . . Chapters include advice on résumé building, dressing for the job you want, and how to effectively communicate at work—even with the most difficult colleagues—all done with the Who What Wear girls' practical and polished signature style." (Publisher's note)

"This savvy, smart guide will benefit professionals at all career stages." LJ

RoAne, Susan

How to work a room; the ultimate guide to making lasting connections, in person and online. Susan RoAne. William Morrow 2014 xxviii, 370 p.p illustrations (pbk.) $15.99 **650.1**

1. Public relations 2. Business etiquette 3. Business entertaining 4. Interpersonal relations
ISBN 0062295349; 9780062295347

LC 2007935900

This book, by Susan RoAne, "is the fully revised and updated edition of the ground-breaking self-help book on improving communicating and socializing skills in business and life. [It] lays down the fundamentals for savvy socializing, whether at a party, a conference, or even communicating online." (Publisher's note)

Includes bibliographical references (p. [349]-354) and index

Samit, Jay

Disrupt you! master personal transformation, seize opportunity, and thrive in the era of endless innovation. Jay Samit. Flatiron Books 2015 304 p. (hardback) $27.99 **650.1**

1. Decision making 2. Success in business 3. Creative ability in business 4. Technological innovations -- Economic aspects
ISBN 1250059372; 9781250059376

LC 2015017121

In this book, author Jay Samit "describes the unique method he has used to invent new markets and expand established businesses. . . . Incorporating stories from his own experience and anecdotes from other innovators and disruptive businesses-including Richard Branson, Steve Jobs, Elon Musk, YouTube, Circ du Soleil, Odor Eaters, Iams, Silly Putty, and many more-Samit shows how personal transformation can reap entrepreneurial and professional rewards." (Publisher's note)

"Throughout, Samit incorporates elements of his own success story as well as those of prominent figures such as actor Jim Carrey, Benihana founder Hiroaki Aoki, and Zappos CEO Tony Hsieh. Samit closes with a motivational 'Self-Disruptor's Manifesto.' For readers seeking to get more out of their lives and careers, Samit is a wise teacher with valuable lessons to impart." Pub Wkly

Shell, G. Richard

Springboard; launching your personal search for success. G. Richard Shell. Portfolio/Penguin 2013 320 p. $26.95 **650.1**

1. Success 2. Vocational guidance 3. Satisfaction 4. Job satisfaction 5. Self-realization
ISBN 1591845475; 9781591845478

LC 2013017451

Author G. Richard Shell "offers a guide to a more fruitful life. . . . The reader learns about developing his or her own definition of success. . . . Citing research on happiness and wealth, as well as anecdotes and spiritual wisdom, Shell concludes that meaningful work--i.e., work that uses your talents, 'ignites you emotionally,' and is financially rewarding, in addition to building health and strong relationships--is the true measure of success." (Publishers Weekly)

Includes bibliographical references and index

Smith, Larry R., 1943-

No fears, no excuses; what you need to do to have a great career. Larry Smith. Houghton Mifflin Harcourt 2016 272 p. (hardback) $26   **650.1**

1. Self-realization 2. Vocational guidance 3. Career development

ISBN 9780544663336

LC 2015037676

This book, by Larry Smith, offers "a provocative new approach to discovering your true calling in life and achieving not just a good career, but a great one. . . . In his straightforward, no-nonsense approach, Smith itemizes and dismisses all the usual excuses, fears, and worries that people hide behind when trying to find their true direction." (Publisher's note)

"This compelling book offers a highly readable blueprint for career success. Readers willing to invest the time and effort required to finding their true direction and achieving their goals will appreciate." LJ

Steib, Mike

The **career** manifesto; discover your calling and create an extraordinary life. Mike Steib. TarcherPerigee 2018 xi, 274 p.p illustrations (hardcover) $18   **650.1**

1. Vocational guidance 2. Personnel management 3. Career development

ISBN 9781101993194; 9780143129349

LC 2017044388

This book, by Mike Steib, "presents an inspiring . . . approach to finding your passion and purpose and then jumpstarting a dream career to achieve those, by asking three essential questions: What do you want your impact to be? What are the potential pathways that move you towards your purpose? How can you hold yourself accountable for your goals? . . . [This book] is the essential way to build . . . an effective plan to excel at whatever job, project or career goal. (Publisher's note)

"His book lays out a sound and logical approach, with easily applicable and customizable advice aplenty." Pub Wkly

Includes bibliographical references and index

Sull, Donald

Simple Rules; How to Thrive in a Complex World. by Donald Sull, Kathleen Eisenhardt. Houghton Mifflin Harcourt 2015 256 p. $27   **650.1**

1. Conduct of life

ISBN 0544409906; 9780544409903

LC 2014044513

This book, by by Donald Sull and Kathleen Eisenhardt, is "a hands-on tool to achieve some of our most pressing personal and professional objectives, from overcoming insomnia to becoming a better manager or a smarter investor. Simple rules can help solve some of our most urgent social challenges. . . . Drawing on more than a decade of rigorous research, the authors provide a clear framework for developing effective rules and making them better over time." (Publisher's note)

"Feeling info-ed out? Sull, a senior lecturer at the MIT Sloan School of Management and a global expert on market strategy and execution, and Eisenhardt, professor of strategy and organization at Stanford University, offer a framework for the creation of a few simple rules to manage it all." LJ

Tracy, Brian

Master your time, master your life; The Breakthrough System to Get More Results, Faster, in Every Area of Your Life. Brian Tracy. TarcherPerigee 2016 240 p. (hardback) $22   **650.1**

1. Success 2. Time management 3. Self-realization 4. Self-actualization (Psychology)

ISBN 9780399183812

LC 2016021429

In this book "international speaker, productivity expert, and bestselling author Brian Tracy explains why tackling the right project at the right time is of the utmost importance. By using our time in the appropriate way in the most important areas of our lives we will accomplish much more, faster and more easily than we ever thought possible!" (Publisher's note)

"Angled mostly for those in the twenty- to thirtysomething crowd, this book will be valuable to those looking to be more productive." LJ

Vaden, Rory

Procrastinate on purpose; 5 permissions to multiply your time. Rory Vaden. Perigee Trade 2014 236 p. illustrations (hardback) $24.95   **650.1**

1. Time management 2. Labor productivity

ISBN 0399170626; 9780399170621

LC 2014040004

This book, by Rory Vaden, offers a "high-energy approach and can-do spirit to the most nagging problem in our professional lives: stalled productivity. Millions are overworked, organizationally challenged, or have a motivation issue that's holding them back. Vaden presents a simple yet powerful paradigm that will set readers free to do their best work--on time and without stress and anxiety." (Publisher's note)

Includes bibliographical references and index

Verveer, Melanne

Fast forward; how women can achieve power and purpose. Melanne Verveer and Kim K. Azzarelli ; foreword by Hillary Rodham Clinton. Houghton Mifflin Harcourt 2015 256 p. 8 plates; color illustrations (hardback) $24   **650.1**

1. Success 2. Businesswomen 3. Work-life balance 4. Women executives 5. Success in business 6. Women in the professions 7. Women in economic development

ISBN 0544527194; 9780544527195; 9780544664357

LC 2015019683

This book by Melanne Veveer and Kim K. Azzarelli, "through interviews with a network of more than seventy trailblazing women, . . . shows women how to accelerate their growing economic power and combine it with purpose to find both success and meaning in their lives. Through clear, practical advice and personal stories of women around the world -- including Hillary Clinton, Geena Davis, Christine Lagarde, and Diane von Furstenberg -- Fast Forward shows every woman how to know her power." (Publisher's note)

Waller, David

★ The **reputation** game; the art of changing how people see you. David Waller, Rupert Younger. Oneworld Publications 2017 xvii, 283 p.p $27   **650.1**

1. Reputation

ISBN 1786070715; 9781786070715

In this book, "through pioneering research and interviews with a host of major figures ranging from Jay-Z and LinkedIn co-founder Reid Hoffman to Bernie Madoff and Man Booker prize-winning Hilary Mantel, [authors David] Waller and [Rupert] Younger reveal the key mechanisms that make and remake our reputations, providing the essential guide to the most important game in business and in life." (Publisher's note)

Includes bibliographical references (pages 271-272) and index.

Wasmund, Shaa

Do less, get more; how to work smart and live life your way. Shaa Wasmund. Portfolio Penguin 2015 218 p. $27.95 **650.1**

1. Success 2. Time management 3. Success in business
ISBN 1591847168; 9781591847168

LC 2015295904

This book, by Sháá Wasmund, argues that "when you stop trying to do so much, you get so much more done. . . . [The author] reveals that when we embrace a 'less is more' attitude, we can appreciate all the good things we already have and find the courage to prune the nonessentials. And then we can find the space in which to pursue exciting new opportunities." (Publisher's note)

"Wasmund ultimately brings her reader to a place where they believe, along with her, that the 'things that will create your best life are perfectly attainable if you are willing to stop doing what's not important and start prioritizing what is.' Sage and sane advice." Booklist

Includes bibliographical references (pages 216-217)

Do < get >

Webb, Caroline

How to have a good day; harnessing the power of behavioral science to transform our working lives. Caroline Webb. Crown Business 2016 368 p. (hardback) $26 **650.1**

1. Neuropsychology 2. Job satisfaction 3. Industrial psychology 4. Psychology, Industrial 5. Performance -- Psychological aspects 6. Job satisfaction -- Psychological aspects
ISBN 9781447276517; 9780553419634

LC 2015026815

In this book, "economist and former McKinsey partner Caroline Webb shows readers how to use recent findings from behavioral economics, psychology, and neuroscience to transform our approach to everyday working life. Advances in these behavioral sciences are giving us ever better understanding of how our brains work, why we make the choices we do, and what it takes for us to be at our best." (Publisher's note)

Includes bibliographical references and index.

Williams, Joan, 1952-

What works for women at work; four patterns working women need to know. Joan C. Williams, Rachel Dempsey ; [foreword by] Anne-Marie Slaughter. NYU Press 2014 384 p. (hardback) $24.95 **650.1**

1. Gender role 2. Work environment 3. Women -- Employment 4. Women -- Psychology 5. Sex role in the work environment
ISBN 1479835455; 9781479835454

LC 2013029819

This book, by Joan C. Williams and Rachel Dempsey, "is a comprehensive and insightful guide for mastering office politics as a woman. . . . Distilling over 35 years of research, Williams and Dempsey offer four crisp patterns that affect working women: Prove-It-Again!, the Tightrope, the Maternal Wall, and the Tug of War. Each represents different challenges and requires different strategies—which is why women need to be savvier than men to survive and thrive in high-powered careers." (Publisher's note)

"[F]illed with street-smart advice and plain old savvy about the way life works in corporate America." Booklist

Includes bibliographical references and index

650.12 Financial success

Aarons-Mele, Morra

★ **Hiding** in the bathroom; an introvert's roadmap to getting out there (when you'd rather stay home) Morra Aarons-Mele. Dey Street Books 2017 287 p. $25.99 **650.12**

1. Anxiety 2. Success in business 3. Introverts -- Vocational guidance
ISBN 0062666088; 9780062666086

This book, by Morra Aarons-Mele, is "a breakthrough introverts' guide that broadens the conversation sparked by Quiet and moves away from the 'Lean In' approach, offering wisdom and practical tips to help readers build strong relationships and achieve their own definition of professional success. . . . [The book] empowers professionals of all ages and levels to take control and build their own versions of success." (Publisher's note)

Includes bibliographical references (page 283-287).

650.13 Personal improvement and success in business relationships

Green, Alison

Ask a manager; how to navigate clueless colleagues, lunch-stealing bosses, and the rest of your life at work. Alison Green. Random House Inc 2018 304 p. $16 **650.13**

1. Work environment 2. Self-help techniques 3. Industrial psychology
ISBN 0399181814; 9780399181818

LC 2018288338

In this book, author Alison Green "tackles the tough discussions you may need to have during your career. You'll learn what to say when coworkers push their work on you--then take credit for it, you accidentally trash-talk someone in an email then hit 'reply all,' you're being micromanaged--or not being managed at all, . . . your boss seems unhappy with your work, your cubemate's loud speakerphone is making you homicidal [and] you got drunk at the holiday party." (Publisher's note)

" All of her advice boils down to the idea that you should be professional (even when others are not) and that communicating in a straightforward manner with candor and kindness will get you far, no matter where you work." Booklist

Porath, Christine

Mastering civility; A Manifesto for the Workplace. Christine Porath. Grand Central Publishing 2016 240 p. forms (hardcover) $25.00 **650.13**

1. Employee morale 2. Work environment 3. Courtesy in the workplace 4. Interpersonal relations 5. Organizational behavior
ISBN 9781455568987

LC 2016028809

In this book, author Christine Porath "shows how people can enhance their influence and effectiveness with civility. Combining scientific research with fascinating evidence from popular culture and fields such as neuroscience, medicine, and psychology, this book provides managers and employers with a much-needed wake-up call, while also reminding them of what they can do right now to improve the quality of their workplaces." (Publisher's note)

"This book will arm readers with the tools they need to move from defeat to empowerment and prompt change in the workplace." Pub Wkly

Includes bibliographical references and index

Sutton, Robert I.

The **asshole** survival guide; how to deal with people who treat you like dirt. by Robert I. Sutton. Houghton Mifflin Harcourt 2017 214 p. (hardcover) $28   **650.13**

1. Human behavior 2. Social psychology 3. Psychological abuse 4. Interpersonal conflict 5. Interpersonal relations 6. Organizational behavior 7. Bullying in the workplace

ISBN 9781328695925; 9781328695918; 1328695913

LC 2017012053

This book, by Robert I. Sutton, "shifts focus from building civilized workplaces to providing relief for anybody who feels plagued and pushed around by assholes. . . . Sutton starts with diagnosis—what kind of asshole problem, exactly, are you dealing with? From there, he provides field-tested, evidence-based, and sometimes surprising strategies for dealing with assholes—avoiding them, outwitting them, disarming them, sending them packing, and developing protective psychological armor." (Publisher's note)

Includes bibliographical references (pages 190-206) and index.

650.14 Success in obtaining jobs and promotions

Aujla, Dev

50 ways to get a job; an unconventional guide to finding work on your terms. Dev Aujla, with foreword by Lodro Rinzler. TarcherPerigee, an imprint of Random House LLC 2018 256 p. (paperback) $15   **650.14**

1. Job hunting 2. Vocational guidance

ISBN 9780143131533

LC 2017033682

"This book reveals career expert Dev Aujla's tried-and-tested method for job seekers at every stage of their career. Filled with anecdotes and advice from professionals ranging from a wilderness guide to an architect, it includes quick-step exercises that help you avoid the common pitfalls of navigating a modern career. . . . [The book] will keep you poised, on-track, and motivated right up to landing your dream career." (Publisher's note)

Includes bibliographical references and index

Berger, Lauren

All work, no pay; finding an internship, building your resume, making connections, and gaining job experience. Lauren Berger. Ten Speed Press 2012 xii, 194 p.p $12.99   **650.14**

1. Job hunting 2. Internship programs 3. Employees -- Training 4. Vocational guidance

ISBN 1607741687; 9781607741688

LC 2011034540

This book is a "guide [that] reveals insider secrets to scoring the perfect internship, building invaluable connections, boosting transferable skills, and ultimately moving toward your dream career." Topics include "internship opportunities," writing "effective resumes and cover letters," and "network[ing] like a pro." (Publisher's note)

Includes bibliographical references and index.

Citrin, James M.

The **career** playbook; essential advice for today's aspiring young professional. by James M. Citrin. Random House Inc 2015 241 p. illustrations $14   **650.14**

1. Job hunting 2. Success in business 3. Vocational guidance

ISBN 0553446967; 9780553446968

LC 2015288094

This book, by James M. Citrin, "offers recent graduates and aspiring

young professionals actionable advice for excelling. From his practical tips on generating valuable introductions, nailing interviews, and negotiating compensation to strategic advice on the arc of a career, the importance of relationships, how to cultivate a mentor, and knowing when to change jobs or industries, Citrin provides an invaluable guide to the most urgent questions." (Publisher's note)

Kay, Andrea

This is how to get your next job; an inside look at what employers really want. Andrea Kay ; foreword by Richard Nelson Bolles. American Management Association 2013 245 p. (pbk.) $16   **650.14**

1. Job hunting 2. Vocational guidance 3. Career development 4. Employment interviewing

ISBN 0814432212; 9780814432211

LC 2012051814

In this book, Andrea Kay "offers practical advice for the job seeker based on her expertise as a career consultant. The first chapter, 'You Are What You Seem,' lists 17 characteristics employers look for, such as consistent, stable behavior; clear, critical thinking; and initiative. Her approach highlights multiple ways to reassess strengths and weaknesses and offers readers the opportunity to glean the employer's perspective." (Library Journal)

Mackay, Harvey

Use your head to get your foot in the door; job search secrets no one else will tell you. Portfolio 2010 329p il $25.95; pa $16   **650.14**

1. Job hunting

ISBN 978-1-59184-321-4; 1-59184-321-9; 978-1-59184-343-6 pa; 1-59184-343-X pa

LC 2009039791

"This collection of job search tips by Mackay . . . [comes] complete with humorous examples and 'Quickie' one-page stories that illustrate his main points. Don't let the cover or any worry about his sense of humor dissuade you: this is a very useful book. The short chapters with descriptive titles make it easy to navigate, and Mackay offers tips—from changing your attitude to getting hired—both for those currently employed but wishing to position themselves better in their current companies and for those who are out of work." Libr J

Includes bibliographical references

Raskin, Donna

The **dirty** little secrets of getting your dream job; Don Raskin. Regan Arts 2016 192 p. illustrations (paperback) $22.95   **650.14**

1. Job hunting 2. Vocational guidance

ISBN 1942872763; 9781942872764

LC 2015951639

This book, by Don Raskin, "offers all the necessary tools for navigating the tough job market and securing your dream job. Don Raskin owns and operates . . . an advertising and marketing agency in New York City. During his twenty-five years at the agency he has interviewed hundreds of new college graduates for positions within his agency and has placed a strong emphasis on entry-level recruitment for positions in creative, account management, traffic, and production." (Publisher's note)

Selingo, Jeffrey J.

There Is Life After College; What Parents and Students Should Know About Navigating School to Prepare for the Jobs of Tomorrow. by Jeffrey J. Selingo. HarperCollins 2016 288 p. $25.99   **650.14**

1. College graduates -- Vocational guidance
ISBN 006238886X; 9780062388865

LC 2015046199

This book, by Jeffrey J. Selingo, "offers students, parents, and even recent graduates the practical advice and insight they need to jumpstart their careers. . . . Selingo answers key questions—Why is the transition to post-college life so difficult for many recent graduates? How can graduates market themselves to employers that are reluctant to provide on-the-job training? . . . —and offers a practical step-by-step plan every young professional can follow." (Publisher's note)

"Levelheaded advice for students and parents on the best path to take from high school to employment." Kirkus

Includes bibliographical references and index.

Yate, Martin

Knock 'em dead cover letters; cover letters and strategies to get the job you want. Martin Yate, CPC. 12th edition Adams Media 2016 pbk $15.99 **650.14**

1. Resumes (Employment) 2. Applications for positions
ISBN 1440596182; 9781440596186

LC 2016020841

In this book, author Martin Yate "shows you how to dramatically increase your chances of landing an interview with a dynamic cover letter. Using his 25+ years of experience, he has built a practical, easy-to-follow approach to creating every type of letter you will use in a job search. Inside this book, you'll find all-new examples of cover letters and learn how to use his proven methods." (Publisher's note)

Knock 'em dead resumes; Resumes that knock 'em dead. Martin Yate, CPC. Adams Media Corp 2014 320 p. (pb) $14.99 **650.14**

1. Resumes (Employment) 2. Résumés (Employment)
ISBN 1440579075; 9781440579073

LC 2014019106

In this book on resume writing, author Martin Yate "shows you how to beat the competition. Using his 25+ years of experience, he has built a practical, easy-to-follow approach to writing killer resumes. This new edition of the perennially bestselling guide includes cutting-edge advice on the latest and most effective resume-writing tactics and has completely new sample resumes." (Publisher's note)

652.1 Penmanship

Trubek, Anne

The **history** and uncertain future of handwriting; Anne Trubek. St. Martin's Press 2016 192 p. illustrations (some color) (hardcover) $26 **652.1**

1. Handwriting
ISBN 1620402157; 9781620402153

LC 2016005079

In this book, author Anne Trubek "uncovers the long and significant impact handwriting has had on culture and humanity--from the first recorded handwriting on the clay tablets of the Sumerians some four thousand years ago and the invention of the alphabet as we know it, to the rising value of handwritten manuscripts today. Each innovation over the millennia has threatened existing standards and entrenched interests." (Publisher's note)

"An absorbing and concise book that will engage readers who are curious about communications." LJ

Includes bibliographical references (pages 157-166) and index.

652.3 Keyboarding

Casillo, Anthony

Typewriters; iconic machines from the golden age of mechanical writing. by Anthony Casillo ; foreword by Tom Hanks ; photography by Bruce Curtis and Anthony Casillo. Chronicle Books LLC 2017 207 p. color illustrations (hardcover) $40 **652.3**

1. Typewriters 2. Office equipment and supplies 3. Typewriters -- History
ISBN 9781452154886; 9781452155746

LC 2016044392

This book, by Anthony Casillo, with photographs by Bruce Curtis, presents "a visual homage to the golden age of the typewriter. From the world's first commercially successful typewriter . . . to the iconic electric models of the 1960s, eighty vintage devices are profiled in elegant photographs and fascinating text that highlights the design modifications, intricate details, and peculiar quirks that make each typewriter unique." (Publisher's note)

Includes bibliographical references and index.

657 Accounting

Shim, Jae K.

Accounting handbook; by Joel G. Siegel, Jae K. Shim, Nick Dauber, and Anique A. Qureshi. 6th edition Barrons Educational Series Inc 2015 1062 p. $39.99 **657**

1. Accounting 2. Accounting -- Handbooks, manuals, etc
ISBN 0764166573; 9780764166570

LC 2014009657

This reference book, by Joel G. Siegel, Jae K. Shim, Nick Dauber, and Anique A. Qureshi, is an accounting handbook. "An opening overview of financial accounting describes financial statements and presents details on financial reporting requirements and compliance, and U.S. GAAP (Generally Accepted Accounting Principles) and IFRS (International Financial Reporting Standards). Chapters that follow cover cost management, as well as taxation forms and their preparation." (Publisher's note)

Includes bibliographical references and index

658 General management

Collins, James C.

Good to great; why some companies make the leap, and others don't. {by} Jim Collins. HarperBusiness 2001 300p il $27.50 **658**

1. Leadership 2. Management
ISBN 0-06-662099-6

LC 2001-24818

"Starting with every company that ever appeared in the Fortune 500, Collins identifies 11 great ones and looks for similarities among them, and what he finds will both surprise and fascinate anyone involved in management." Booklist

Includes bibliographical references

Drucker, Peter F.

The **Drucker** lectures; essential lessons on management, society, and economy. edited and with an introduction by Rick Wartzman. McGraw-Hill 2010 266p $29.95; ebook

$29.95   **658**

1. Management
ISBN 978-0-07-170045-0; 0-07-170045-5; 978-0-07-175950-2
ebook; 0-07-175950-6 ebook

LC 2010484567

This book presents thirty-three of Peter F. Drucker's speeches and talks delivered at professional gatherings and in the classroom.

"From his concern with continuous and full employment in the 1950s to globalization, nonprofit management, and the future of the corporation in the early 2000s, these lectures reflect a Drucker that many scholars and practitioners knew, but they also reveal new insights into the currency . . . of his thinking." Choice

Includes bibliographical references

Horstman, Mark

The **effective** manager; Mark Horstman. John Wiley & Sons Inc. 2016 208 p. (hardback) $28   **658**

1. Management 2. Executive ability 3. Personnel management 4. Teams in the workplace 5. Supervision of employees 6. Teams in the workplace -- Management
ISBN 1119244609; 9781119244608

LC 2016018227

This book, by Mark Horstman, "is a hands-on practical guide to great management at every level. . . . First, you'll identify what 'effective management' actually looks like: can you get the job done at a high level? Do you attract and retain top talent without burning them out? Then you'll dig into the four critical behaviors that make a manager great, and learn how to adjust your own behavior to be the leader your team needs." (Publisher's note)

Michelli, Joseph A.

Driven to delight; delivering world-class customer experience the Mercedes-Benz way. Joseph Michelli. McGraw-Hill 2016 304 p. illustrations (alk. paper) $27   **658**

1. Customer services 2. Automobile industry 3. DaimlerChrysler 4. Mercedes automobiles 5. Automobile industry and trade -- Germany -- Management 6. Automobile industry and trade -- Customer services -- Germany
ISBN 007180630X; 9780071806305

LC 2015029398

In this book, author Joseph Michelli "shares the greatest customer-driven insights behind one of the most iconic brand names in the world: Mercedes-Benz USA. . . . It reveals the action plan Mercedes-Benz USA used to catapult the company to first place rankings in national customer satisfaction studies while at the same time growing sales and profits." (Publisher's note)

Thompson, Mark

Now, build a great business! 7 ways to maximize your profits in any market. [by] Mark Thompson and Brian Tracy; foreword by Frances Hesselbein. American Management Association 2011 xxii, 228p $24.95   **658**

1. Marketing 2. Leadership
ISBN 978-0-8144-1697-6; 0-8144-1697-7

LC 2010030612

The authors "offer easy, tried-and-true ways to think about and plan organizational growth, especially in tough economic times. In seven steps (with a chapter devoted to each), the authors identify sustainable strategies for attracting customers and recruiting better leaders. They share seven simple questions that leaders ask themselves and provide helpful checklist exercises on a variety of key topics including creating a great business plan, designing an effective marketing plan, and creating

a good customer experience." Publ Wkly

Travis, Nigel

The **challenge** culture; why the most successful organizations run on pushback. Nigel Travis. PublicAffairs, an imprint of Perseus Books, a subsidiary of Hachette Book Group 2018 288 p. (hardcover; alk. paper) $28   **658**

1. Corporate culture 2. Businessmen -- United States -- Biography
ISBN 9781541762145

LC 2018010002

In this book, the chairman of Dunkin' Brands, Nigel Travis "reflects on the unique, results-oriented discipline he's developed over decades of leadership, which provides a blueprint for any organization to achieve prosperity. . . . He argues that the best way for organizations to succeed in today's environment is to embrace challenge and encourage pushback. . . . Travis shows how to establish a culture that welcomes challenge . . . and ensures a prosperous future." (Publisher's note)

Includes bibliographical references and index

Wall Street journal

The **Wall** Street Journal essential guide to management; lasting lessons from the best leadership minds of our time. Harper Business 2010 xxvii, 207p pa $16.99   **658**

1. Management
ISBN 978-0-06-184033-3

LC 2010-2879

The author "lays out in helpful order and understandable prose what he considers the best practices for a good manager to follow; especially instructive are his discussions of 'six different styles that leaders use to motivate others.' . . . For serious consideration for any library business collection." Booklist

Includes bibliographical references

Webb, Maynard G., 1955-

Dear founder; letters of advice for anyone who leads, manages, or wants to start a business. Maynard Webb, with Carlye Adler. St. Martin's Press 2018 352 p. (hardcover) $28.99 **658**

1. Leadership 2. Entrepreneurship 3. New business enterprises
ISBN 9781250195647

LC 2018013472

This book, by Maynard Webb, with Carlye Adler, presents various "sound advice on an array of business topics, from turning your idea into a reality to building a culture, to reaching key financial goals. This book is an indispensable guide to navigating the realities, risks, and rewards of being your own boss--and founding the company of your dreams." (Publisher's note)

"This recommended book provides honest guidance about the work that goes into a new company, delivered in digestible chunks for the entrepreneur on the go." LJ

Wooldridge, Adrian

Masters of management; how the business gurus and their ideas have changed the world--for better and for worse. HarperBusiness 2011 446p $29.99   **658**

1. Management
ISBN 978-0-06-177113-2; 9780061771132

LC 2011015690

First published 1996 by Times Bks. with title: The witch doctors

"The core of the book is a solid examination of the effects of entrepreneurship, globalization, and the free-agency economy on corporate governance. Wooldridge offers a balanced look at how business schools have spawned a guru industry that offers a gamut of theories on learning, innovation, and strategy. Peter Drucker, Tom Peters, and the 'Journo-Gurus' (Thomas Friedman, Malcolm Gladwell, and Chris Anderson) receive focused attention as the main influences in contemporary theory. . . . This is one of the best overviews of management theory in the 20th century. It is written in a clear and accessible style that will appeal to both MBA students and the general reader." Libr J

658.02   Management of enterprises of specific sizes and scope

Sarillo, Nick, 1963-

A **slice** of the pie; how to build a big little business. Nick Sarillo. Portfolio 2012 272 p. $26.95   **658.02**
1. Small business 2. Entrepreneurship 3. Business planning 4. Success in business 5. Industrial management 6. Employees -- Training of 7. New business enterprises
ISBN 1591844584; 9781591844587

LC 2012019321

In this book, Nick Sarillo, "founder and CEO of Nick's Pizza & Pub, offers a personal account of being a small business owner, sharing his perspectives, challenges he's faced and overcome, and the way he's transformed his company into a thriving success. More than a mere autobiography, it's also the story of his company and the people he works with. Sarillo expounds on the paths that he has chosen and why, what those choices have produced, and where the results have led." (Publishers Weekly)

Strauss, Steven D.

The **small** business bible; everything you need to know to succeed in your small business. Steven D. Strauss. Wiley 2012 xiii, 578 p.p (pbk.) $22.95   **658.02**
1. Small business 2. New business enterprises 3. New business enterprises -- United States 4. Small business -- United States -- Finance 5. Small business -- United States -- Management
ISBN 1118135946; 9781118135945

LC 2011042848

This book, by Steven D. Strauss, is a "comprehensive guide to small business success. . . . It shows you what really works (and what doesn't!) and includes scores of tips, insider information, stories, and proven secrets of success. . . . This Third Edition includes entirely new chapters devoted to social media, mobility and apps, and new trends in online discounting and group buying that are vital to small business owners everywhere." (Publisher's note)

658.022   Small enterprises

Downs, Paul

Boss Life; Surviving My Own Small Business. Paul Downs. Penguin Group USA 2015 368 p. black and white illustrations $26.95   **658.022**
1. New business enterprises 2. Cabinetmakers -- United States 3. Small business -- United States -- Management 4. New business enterprises -- United States -- Management
ISBN 0399172335; 9780399172335

LC 2015016068

This book, by Paul Downs, "paints an honest portrait of a real business, with a real boss, a real set of employees, and the real challenges they face. Fresh out of college in 1986, Downs opened his first business, a small company that builds custom furniture. In 1987, he hired his first employee. That's when things got complicated. As his enterprise began

to grow, he had to learn about management, cash flow, taxes, and so much more." (Publisher's note)

"This is an invaluable look into operational details for anyone considering starting a business or caught up in the struggle of owning and running one." Booklist

658.1   Organization and financial management

Barringer, Bruce

Launching a Business; The First 100 Days. Bruce Barringer. Business Expert Pr 2013 254 p. illustrations (Entrepreneurship and small business management collection) $43.95   **658.1**
1. Management 2. Entrepreneurship 3. New business enterprises
ISBN 1606493973; 9781606493977

This book by Bruce R. Barringer "focuses on the tasks that a new business owner must complete in the first 100 days of launching a business. . . . Examples include securing the proper business licenses and permits, setting up a bookkeeping system, negotiating a lease, buying insurance, entering into contracts with vendors, recruiting and hiring employees, making the first sale, and so on." (Publisher's note)

"[Offers] tactical advice on things important during early launch of a business that an experienced founder should know but a novice likely will not." Choice

Bennett, Jessica

Feminist Fight Club; An Office Survival Manual for a Sexist Workplace. by Jessica Bennett. HarperCollins 2016 336 p. illustrations $24.99; (ebook) $23.99   **658.1**
1. Sexism 2. Work environment
ISBN 0062439782; 9780062439789; 9780062439796

LC 2016288019

This book, by Jessica Bennett, "is a . . . guide to navigating subtle sexism at work, providing real-life career advice and humorous reinforcement for a new generation of professional women. . . . Bennett offers a new vocabulary for the sexist workplace archetypes women encounter everyday—such as the Manterrupter who talks over female colleagues in meetings or the Himitator who appropriates their ideas—and provides practical hacks for navigating other gender landmines in today's working world." (Publisher's note)

"Bennett is on a mission to reform today's workplaces, and this manifesto just might be the weapon modern women are looking for." Booklist

Includes bibliographical resources (pages 279-294).

Debaise, Colleen

★ **Start** a successful business; expert advice to take your startup from idea to empire. Colleen DeBaise. AMACOM 2018 272 p. (pbk.) $19.95   **658.1**
1. Business planning 2. Strategic planning 3. New business enterprises
ISBN 0814439187; 9780814439180

LC 2017039547

"From brainstorming to crowdfunding to building partnerships, . . . [this] book, [by Colleen DeBaise] walks new and aspiring founders through seven crucial stages: Come up with a brilliant business idea, select the best structure and strategy for your startup, figure out funding, get the word out-and get customers, dig deep to discover their wants and needs, become an exceptional leader, [and] prepare to go global." (Publisher's note)

"This is a great first alternative to Michael Porter and Harvard Business Review publications and a lot more accessible." Booklist

Duffy, Scott

Launch! the critical ninety days from idea to market. Scott Duffy. Portfolio Hardcover 2013 240 p. (hardback) $26.95 **658.1**

1. New products 2. Entrepreneurship 3. New business enterprises
ISBN 1591846064; 9781591846062

LC 2013039077

In this book, entrepreneur Scott Duffy "has developed a practical approach for turning your big idea into a thriving venture by focusing on the crucial period of 90 days immediately before, during, and after starting your business. Based on his own experiences, . . . Duffy . . . emphasizes the personal side of entrepreneurship, including balancing finances, relationships, and your health." (Publisher's note)

"A breezy handbook for entrepreneurs on how to launch a new business, product or service. . . . Solid advice for novice risk-takers." Kirkus
Includes bibliographical references and index

Guillebeau, Chris, 1979-

The **$100** startup; how to fire your boss and create a new future. by Chris Guillebeau. Crown Business 2012 xviii, 285 p.p illustrations (hbk.) $23 **658.1**

1. Entrepreneurship 2. Vocational guidance 3. New business enterprises 4. New business enterprises -- Management
ISBN 0307951529; 9780307951526

LC 2012003093

This book, by Chris Guillebeau, seeks to show "how to lead of life of adventure, meaning and purpose--and earn a good living. . . . [The author presents] the most valuable lessons from those who've learned how to turn what they do into a gateway to self-fulfillment. It's all about finding the intersection between your 'expertise'-- even if you don't consider it such--and what other people will pay for." (Publisher's note)

Johnson, Victoria M.

Grant writing 101; everything you need to start raising funds today. McGraw-Hill 2011 269p pa $20; ebook $20 **658.1**

1. Fund raising 2. Grants-in-aid
ISBN 978-0-07-175018-9 pa; 978-0-07-175018-9 ebook

LC 2010039599

This guide to grant writing offers "ten tactics for writing a compelling proposal; tips for finding the best grantor for your needs; important components of various types of grants; [and] next steps for when you're approved." Publisher's note

Karlgaard, Rich

Team Genius; The New Science of High-Performing Organizations. Rich Karlgaard and Michael S. Malone. HarperCollins 2015 304 p. $27.99 **658.1**

1. Management 2. Teams in the workplace
ISBN 006230254X; 9780062302540

This book by Rich Karlgaard and Michael S. Malone "shows managers and executives that the planning, design, and management of great teams no longer have to be a black art. It explores solutions to essential questions that could spell the difference between success and obsolescence. Do you know how to reorganize your subpar teams to turn them into top performers? Can you identify which of the top-performing teams in your company are reaching the end of their life span?" (Publisher's note)

"Gems of insight and wisdom are offered here, such as the need for balance between creative and analytical skills to maintain a team's for-

ward momentum, but not all readers will persevere to find and employ them. For fans of business history and theory." LJ

Kawasaki, Guy

The **art** of the start 2.0; the time-tested, battle-hardened guide for anyone starting anything. by Guy Kawasaki. Penguin Group USA 2015 326 p. illustrations $29.95 **658.1**

1. Success in business
ISBN 1591847842; 9781591847847

This book, by Guy Kawasaki, is a "guide to launching and making your new product, service, or idea a success. . . . Guy understands the seismic changes in business over the last decade: . . . Many of the basics of getting established have become easier, cheaper, and more democratic. Business plans are no longer necessary. Social media has replaced PR and advertising as the key method of promotion." (Publisher's note)

"An excellent guide packed with valuable information for students, would-be entrepreneurs, and practicing entrepreneurs." LJ

Kidder, David S.

The **Startup** playbook; secrets of the fastest-growing startups from their founding entrepreneurs / David S. Kidder. David S. Kidder. Chronicle Books 2013 292 p. $29.99 **658.1**

1. Entrepreneurs 2. Entrepreneurship 3. New business enterprises 4. New business enterprises -- Management
ISBN 1452105049; 9781452105048

LC 2012019684

This book by David S. Kidder "shares the hard-hitting experiences of some of the world's most influential entrepreneurs and CEOs, revealing their most closely held advice. Face-to-face interviews with 40 founders give readers key insights into what it took to build PayPal, LinkedIn, AOL, TED, Flickr, and many others into household names. Special sections include topics ranging from how to select the right idea to pursue to finding funding and overcoming inevitable obstacles." (Publisher's note)

Schramm, Carl J.

★ **Burn** the business plan; what great entrepreneurs really do. Carl J. Schramm. Simon & Schuster 2018 xiii, 272 p.p $28 **658.1**

1. Entrepreneurship 2. Business planning 3. New business enterprises 4. New business enterprises -- Management
ISBN 9781476794358

LC 2017015637

This book, by Carl J. Schramm, "tells stories of successful entrepreneurs in a variety of fields. It shows how knowledge, passion, determination, and a willingness to experiment and innovate are vastly more important than financial skill. This is an important, motivating look at true success that dispels the myths and offers invaluable real-world advice on how to achieve your dreams." (Publisher's note)

Includes bibliographical references and index

Wasserman, Noam

The **founder's** dilemmas; anticipating and avoiding the pitfalls that can sink a startup. Noam Wasserman. Princeton University Press 2012 p. cm. **658.1**

1. Management 2. Entrepreneurship 3. New business enterprises 4. New business enterprises -- Management
ISBN 9780691149134

LC 2011037954

This book, by Noam Wasserman, is part of the Kauffman Foundation Series on Innovation and Entrepreneurship. "Often downplayed in the . . . starting up a new business venture is . . . [the question] should they go it alone, or bring in cofounders, hires, and investors to help build the business? . . . Bad decisions at the inception of a promising venture lay the foundations for its eventual ruin. . . . Wasserman reveals the common pitfalls founders face and how to avoid them." (Publisher's note)

Includes bibliographical references and index

658.11   Initiation of business enterprises

Buelow, Beth L.

The **Introvert** Entrepreneur; Amplify Your Strengths and Create Success on Your Own Terms. by Beth Buelow. Penguin Group USA 2015 272 p. $15.95; (ebook) $16.99   **658.11**
    1. Entrepreneurship 2. Success in business
    ISBN 0399174834; 9780399174834; 9781101992647

In this book, author Beth Buelow "shows readers how to harness their natural gifts (including curiosity, independence, and a love of research) and counteract their challenges (such as an aversion to networking and self-promotion). She addresses a wide range of topics . . . informed by interviews with introverts who have created successful businesses without compromising their core personality." (Publisher's note)

"This is a thoughtful, kind, and helpful guide for all those who are looking to strike out on their own, but concerned that their need for alone time may get in the way." Pub Wkly

Includes bibliographical references (pages 245-248) and index.

658.15   Financial management

Goldfayn, Alex

The **revenue** growth habit; the simple art of growing your business by 15% in 15 minutes per day. Alex Goldfayn. Wiley 2015 256 p. illustrations (hardback) $25   **658.15**
    1. Management 2. Strategic planning 3. Revenue management
    ISBN 1119084067; 9781119084068

LC 2015013431

In this book, author Alex Goldfayn "shows how to grow your organization by 15% or more in 15 minutes or less per day without spending a penny of your money. . . . [He] shows how to request and collect testimonials and how to communicate these testimonials to grow your business. You will discover how to write powerful case studies, ask for (and get!) referrals, grow your lists, and send a revenue-growing newsletter." (Publisher's note)

McKeever, Mike

How to write a business plan; Mike P. McKeever. 13th edition Nolo 2016 pbk $34.99   **658.15**
    1. Small business 2. Business planning 3. New business enterprises
    ISBN 9781413323191; 1413323197

LC 2016026296

"This bestselling, newly updated book contains clear, step-by-step instructions to make realistic financial projections, develop effective marketing strategies and refine your overall business goals. . . . Updated 13th Edition includes the latest laws and banking regulations that could affect businesses and their investors, plus an expanded collection of resources for putting together the best plan." (Publisher's note)

Rice, Condoleezza, 1954-

Political risk; how businesses and organizations can anticipate global insecurity. Condoleezza Rice and Amy Zegart. Twelve 2018 336 p. (hardcover) $30   **658.15**
    1. Financial risk 2. World politics 3. Decision making 4. Risk

management -- Political aspects
    ISBN 9781455542352

LC 2017054476

This book, by Condoleezza Rice and Amy B. Zegart, is "an examination of the rapidly evolving state of political risk, and how to navigate it. . . . Drawing on lessons from the successes and failures of companies across multiple industries as well as examples from aircraft carrier operations, NASA missions, and other unusual places, [the book] offers a first-of-its-kind framework that can be deployed in any organization, from startups to Fortune 500 companies." (Publisher's note)

Includes bibliographical references and index

658.3   Personnel management (Human resource management)

Elton, Chester

All in; how the best managers create a culture of belief and drive big results. Adrian Gostick and Chester Elton. Free Press 2012 viii, 243 p.p (hbk.) $25   **658.3**
    1. Leadership 2. Executive ability 3. Personnel management 4. Corporate culture 5. Employee motivation 6. Organizational behavior
    ISBN 1451659822; 9781451659825

LC 2011045590

Author Adrian Gostick answers today's leadership questions, such as why are managers "able to get their employees to commit wholeheartedly to their culture and give that extra push that leads to outstanding results? . . . [The author presents] a simple seven-step road map for creating a culture of belief: define a burning platform; create a customer focus; develop agility; share everything; partner with your talent; root for each other; and establish clear accountability." (Publisher's note)

Includes bibliographical references and index.

Hallowell, Edward M.

Shine; using brain science to get the best from your people. Harvard Business Review Press 2011 197p il $26.95   **658.3**
    1. Management 2. Job satisfaction 3. Interpersonal relations 4. Motivation (Psychology)
    ISBN 978-1-59139-923-0; 1-59139-923-8

LC 2010024950

"Edward Hallowell draws on brain science, performance research, and his own experience helping people maximize their potential to present a . . . process for getting the best from your people." Publisher's note

Includes bibliographical references

Kelly, Matthew

The **dream** manager. Hyperion 2007 158p $19.95 **658.3**
    1. Employee morale 2. Personnel management 3. Motivation (Psychology)
    ISBN 978-1-4013-0370-9; 1-4013-0370-6

LC 2007-13597

This "business fable extols the virtues of helping those working for and with you to achieve their dreams. In this way . . . managers can boost morale and control turnover. . . . This one's sure to appeal to business readers." Libr J

Tracy, Brian

Full engagement! inspire, motivate, and bring out the best in your people. American Management Association 2011 226p $22   **658.3**
    1. Employee morale 2. Personnel management 3. Motivation

(Psychology)
ISBN 978-0-8144-1689-1; 0-8144-1689-6

LC 2010048293

The author "shows managers how they can supercharge their employees' efforts." Publisher's note

658.312   Conditions of employment, performance rating, utilization of personnel

Richards, Shola

Making work work; The Positivity Solution for Any Work Environment. Shola Richards. Sterling Ethos 2016 256 p. (hardback) $19.95   **658.312**
   1. Self-realization 2. Work environment 3. Self-help techniques 4. Self-actualization (Psychology)
ISBN 9781454918721

LC 2016016626

In this book, author Shola Richards " focuses on inspiring current and future leaders to start a movement that will banish on-the-job bullying, put meaning back into work, and enhance coworkers' happiness and engagement. Richards, whose popular blog has a worldwide following, explains why inaction is insane, [and]why we must move forward with positivity," (Publisher's note)

"Most books about creating a better work climate center on the role of management... Richard's focus on leading change from across title ranks will be appreciated by people at any stage of their careers who are seeking a more spirit-enriching workplace." LJ

Includes bibliographical references and index

658.4   Executive management

Barsh, Joanna

Grow wherever you work; straight talk to help with your toughest challenges. Joanna Barsh. McGraw-Hill Education 2017 272 p. (hardback) $26   **658.4**
   1. Leadership 2. Self-improvement 3. Executive ability
ISBN 1260026469; 9781260026467

LC 2017039530

"This hands-on guide on leadership, [by Joanna Barsh], helps you grow through the challenges you face--not despite them. You'll learn how to: handle rising pressure and recover from colossal mistakes, . . . get people on board with you and your mission, deal with office villains like a superhero, take uncomfortable risks and dare to challenge, . . . know when it's time to find another position." (Publisher's note)

"The essential coach's handbook for anyone in a position of leadership: engaging, wise, and extremely practical. A must-read for students of business, organizational communication, and psychology." LJ

Bock, Laszlo

Work rules! insights from inside Google that will transform how you live and lead. Laszlo Bock. Twelve 2015 416 p. illustrations (hardback) $30   **658.4**
   1. Leadership 2. Management 3. Google (Firm) 4. Corporate culture 5. Google (Firm) -- Management
ISBN 1455554790; 9781455554799

LC 2014020843

This book by Laszlo Bock explains "how Google hires and manages its employees. . . . The company aims to 'keep people in an environment of freedom, creativity, and play.' However, there are rules underlying this culture, and values underlying these rules, to each of which Bock

devotes one of the book's 14 chapters. Its bedrock is trust in the fundamental goodness of people." (Library Journal)

"Bock makes a persuasive case for ceding power to individual employees and teams. For visionary managers." LJ

Includes bibliographical references and index

Bolman, Lee G.

How great leaders think; the art of reframing. Lee G. Bolman, Terrence E. Deal. Jossey-Bass 2014 228 p. (hardback) $30   **658.4**
   1. Leadership 2. Thought and thinking 3. Organizational change
ISBN 1118140982; 9781118140987

LC 2014013595

This book "uses compelling, contemporary examples to show how more complex thinking is the key to better leadership.[Authors Lee] Bolman and [Terrence] Deal's influential four-frame model of leadership and organizations . . . offers leaders an accessible guide for understanding four major aspects of organizational life: structure, people, politics, and culture." (Publisher's note)

Catmull, Ed

Creativity, Inc. overcoming the unseen forces that stand in the way of true inspiration. Ed Catmull, President of Pixar and Disney Animation, with Amy Wallace. Random House Inc 2014 368 p. illustrations (chiefly color) (hardback) $28 **658.4**
   1. Corporate culture 2. Creative ability in business 3. Pixar (Firm) 4. Organizational effectiveness
ISBN 0812993012; 9780812993011

LC 2013036026

This book, by co-founder of Pixar Animation Studios Ed Catmull, "is a book for managers who want to lead their employees to new heights, a manual for anyone who strives for originality, and the first-ever, all-access trip into the nerve center of Pixar Animation" into the meetings, postmortems, and 'Braintrust' sessions where some of the most successful films in history are made. It is, at heart, a book about how to build a creative culture." (Publisher's note)

Chan, Ronald W.

Behind the Berkshire Hathaway curtain; lessons from Warren Buffett's top business leaders. John Wiley & Sons 2010 178p il $24.95; ebook $16.99   **658.4**
   1. Success 2. Business 3. Management 4. Executive ability 5. Financiers 6. Berkshire Hathaway Inc.
ISBN 978-0-470-56062-4; 0-470-56062-2; 978-0-470-64297-9 ebook

LC 2010281776

"Chan shares some of the business philosophies, strategies, and mindsets learned from exclusive interviews with leaders of Buffett's Berkshire Hathaway, including David Sokol of MidAmerican Energy, Cathy Baron Tamraz of Business Wire, Brad Kinstler of See's Candies, and Maria Gottschalk of Pampered Chef. The detailed stories of these executives' early career decisions bring to life practical lessons for personal and professional success." T + D

Chapman, Bob

Everybody matters; the extraodinary power of caring for your people like family. by Bob Chapman and Raj Sisodia. Penguin Group USA 2015 260 p. charts $27.95   **658.4**
   1. Employees 2. Job satisfaction 3. Work environment
ISBN 1591847796; 9781591847793

LC 2015303330

In this book, authors Bob Chapman and Raj Sisodia "show how any organization can reject the traumatic consequences of rolling layoffs, dehumanizing rules, and hypercompetitive cultures. Once you stop treating people like functions or costs, disengaged workers begin to share their gifts and talents toward a shared future. Uninspired workers stop feeling that their jobs have no meaning. Frustrated workers stop taking their bad days out on their spouses and kids." (Publisher's note)

"Chapman is convincing in his appeal for a more human approach to management in all kinds of organizations. This inspirational read is recommended for all types of business collections." LJ

Includes bibliographical references (pages 249-253) and index.

Conant, Douglas R.

Touchpoints; creating powerful leadership connections in the smallest of moments. [by] Douglas R. Conant, Mette Norgaard. Jossey-Bass 2011 xxxi, 173p (Warren Bennis signature series) $26.95; ebook $12.99   **658.4**

1. Leadership

ISBN 978-1-1180-0435-7; 978-1-1180-7554-8 ebook

LC 2011008907

"In an engaging personal style, Doug Conant, the CEO of Campbell Soup Company, discusses a leadership philosophy that he and leadership development expert Mette Norgaard refer to as 'TouchPoints'—those daily encounters with staff, co-workers, or colleagues that leaders can use to 'touch' others in meaningful ways, such as influencing, inspiring, or providing clarity. The book highlights ways to develop that ability and ways to practice leadership in the moment." T + D

Covey, Sean

The **4** disciplines of execution; achieving your wildly important goals. Chris McChesney, Sean Covey, Jim Huling. 1st Free Press hardcover ed. Free Press 2012 xxvi, 326 p.p ill. (hbk.) $28   **658.4**

1. Leadership 2. Responsibility 3. Executive ability 4. Organization 5. Goal -- Psychology 6. Goal setting in personnel management

ISBN 145162705X; 9781451627053

LC 2012001672

Authors Chris McChesney and Sean Covey provide "a simple repeatable, and proven formula for executing on your most important strategic priorities in the midst of the whirlwind. . . . Leaders can produce breakthrough results, even when executing the strategy requires a significant change in behavior from their teams [through] focusing on the wildly important, acting on lead measures, keeping a compelling scoreboard, [and] creating a cadence of accountability." (Publisher's note)

Includes bibliographical references and index

Davidds, Yasmin

★ **Your** own terms; a woman's guide to taking charge of any negotiation. Yasmin Davidds, PsyD with Ann Bidou. American Management Association 2015 256 p. illustrations (pbk.; alk. paper) $16.95   **658.4**

1. Negotiation 2. Businesswomen 3. Negotiation in business

ISBN 9780814436028

LC 2015009457

This book, by Yasmin Davidds, with Ann Bidou, "helps women strike a balance, merging our natural strengths (collaboration, relationship building, listening) with a firm grasp of established tactics. Guidelines, stories, and exercises illuminate the psychology of negotiation and reveal how women can: control how they are perceived; eliminate self-sabotaging beliefs and behaviors; discover their personal negotiation style; . . . and set the bar high and negotiate to get there." (Publisher's note)

"This is that rare guide that matches big-picture strategy with specific advice, worksheets, and scripts. It's indispensable for women looking to effectively negotiate a salary, career move, or new opportunity with confidence and ease." Pub Wkly

Includes bibliographical references and index

Doerr, John

Measure what matters; how Google, Bono, and the Gates Foundation rock the world with OKRs. John Doerr, with foreword by Larry Page. Portfolio/Penguin 2018 xii, 306 p.p (hardcover) $27   **658.4**

1. Management 2. Entrepreneurship 3. Business planning 4. Performance 5. Goal (Psychology) 6. Organizational effectiveness

ISBN 9780525536222

LC 2018002727

In this book "legendary venture capitalist John Doerr reveals how the goal-setting system of Objectives and Key Results (OKRs) has helped tech giants from Intel to Google achieve explosive growth--and how it can help any organization thrive. . . . Doerr shares a broad range of first-person, behind-the-scenes case studies, with narrators including Bono and Bill Gates, to demonstrate the focus, agility, and explosive growth that OKRs have spurred at so many great organizations." (Publisher's note)

Includes bibliographical references (pages 289-295) and index

Duke, Annie

Thinking in bets; making smarter decisions when you don't have all the facts. Annie Duke. Portfolio/Penguin 2018 276 p. (hardback) $26   **658.4**

1. Decision making 2. Strategic planning 3. Management games

ISBN 0735216355; 9780735216358

LC 2017042666

In this book, "poker champion turned business consultant Annie Duke teaches you how to get comfortable with uncertainty and make better decisions as a result. . . . [Duke] draws on examples from business, sports, politics, and (of course) poker to share tools anyone can use to embrace uncertainty and make better decisions." (Publisher's note)

Includes bibliographical references (pages 241-266) and index

Erwin, Michael

Lead Yourself First; Inspiring Leadership Through Solitude. Raymond M. Kethledge and Michael S. Erwin ; with a foreword by Jim Collins. Bloomsbury USA 2017 xxi, 214 p.p (hardcover) $27   **658.4**

1. Solitude 2. Leadership 3. Leadership -- Case studies

ISBN 1632866315; 9781632866318; 9781632866332

LC 2016044432

This book, by Raymond M. Kethledge and Michael S. Erwin, is "a guide to the role of solitude in good leadership, including profiles of historical and contemporary figures who have used solitude to lead with courage, creativity, and strength. Throughout history, leaders have used solitude as a matter of course. . . . To find solitude today, a leader must make a conscious effort. This book explains why the effort is worthwhile and how to make it." (Publisher's note)

"This book is a rare gem, offering an optimistic message that there remain powerful leaders intent on being courageous and moral, and on finding 'transcendent meaning' in their vocation." Pub Wkly

Includes bibliographical references (pages 192-204) and index.

Ferrazzi, Keith

Never eat alone and other secrets to success; one relationship at a time. Keith Ferrazzi with Tahl Raz. 1st ed.; Random

House Inc 2014 379 p. $27   **658.4**

1. Interpersonal relations
ISBN 0385346654; 9780385346658

LC 2004061757

In this book, author Keith Ferrazzi "lays out the specific steps—and inner mindset—he uses to reach out to connect with the thousands of colleagues, friends, and associates on his Rolodex. . . . Ferrazzi's form of connecting to the world around him is based on generosity, helping friends connect with other friends. Ferrazzi distinguishes genuine relationship-building from the crude, desperate glad-handling usually associated with 'networking.'" (Publisher's note)

"In addition to variations on the theme of hard work, Ferrazzi offers counterintuitive perspectives that ring true: 'vulnerability... is one of the most underappreciated assets in business today'; 'too many people confuse secrecy with importance.' No one will confuse this book with its competitors" Pub Wkly

Gallo, Carmine

Talk like TED; the 9 public speaking secrets of the world's top minds. Carmine Gallo. St. Martin's Press 2014 288 p. illustrations (hardcover; alk. paper) $24.99   **658.4**

1. Public speaking 2. Business presentations
ISBN 1250041120; 9781250041128

LC 2013031049

In this book about public speaking, author Carmine Gallo "identifies the common elements that make TED Talks so successful. He offers nine secrets, including mastering the art of storytelling, being passionate about the subject matter, speaking conversationally, using humor, . . . and keeping presentations to 18 minutes. Gallo divides the lessons into three parts, focusing on the emotional, novel, and memorable." (Booklist)

"The author . . . includes successful outlines and guides to using both audio-visual aides and effective body language. Dramatic composition and vigorous presentation make this a powerful tool to improve mastery of speaking skills." Kirkus

Includes bibliographical references and index

Goleman, Daniel, 1946-

Primal Leadership; Unleashing the Power of Emotional Intelligence. Daniel Goleman, Richard Boyatzis, Annie McKee. 2nd edition Harvard Business Review Press 2013 336 p. $22   **658.4**

1. Emotions 2. Management
ISBN 1422168034; 9781422168035

LC 2013018294

This book, by Daniel Goleman, Richard Boyatzis, and Annie McKee, "established 'emotional intelligence' in the business lexicon-- and made it a necessary skill for leaders. . . . This refreshed edition, with a new preface by the authors, vividly illustrates the power . . . of leadership that is self-aware, empathic, motivating, and collaborative in a world that is ever more economically volatile and technologically complex." (Publisher's note)

Granet, Keith, 1956-

The **business** of creativity; how to build the right team for success. Keith Granet. Princeton Architectural Press 2016 224 p. illustrations (some color) (ebook) $40; (hardback) $40   **658.4**

1. Business planning 2. Creative ability in business
ISBN 9781616895532; 9781616893941

LC 2016018288

In this book "management consultant of the design world, Keith Granet reveals more of his clear-eyed insights about running a creative business in this follow-up to his book 'The Business of Design.' . . . Granet's advice, quickly summarized as 'know what you do best and focus on that,' applies to any organization, small or large, commercial or nonprofit. He delves into the skill sets and people needed to grow a business . . . in an engaging and easy-to-implement manner." (Publisher's note)

"This excellent handbook for the design community also offers important insights for other creative entrepreneurs." Booklist

Johnson, Whitney

Disrupt yourself; putting the power of disruptive innovation to work. by Whitney Johnson. Bibliomotion 2015 208 p. illustrations (hardback) $24.95   **658.4**

1. Strategic planning 2. Success in business 3. Organizational change 4. Career changes 5. Disruptive technologies
ISBN 1629560529; 9781629560526

LC 2015019271

"As president and cofounder of Rose Park Advisors' Disruptive Innovation Fund with Clayton Christensen, Whitney Johnson used the theory of disruptive innovation to invest in publicly traded stocks and private early-stage companies. In [this book], she helps you understand how the frameworks of disruptive innovation can apply to your particular path." (Publisher's note)

"Johnson astutely highlights the value of constraints, the dangers of entitlement, and the necessity of changing plans when circumstances call for it. Her chapter on learning from failure contains particularly wise advice that everyone should embrace. In Johnson's closing chapter, she emphasizes the value of a "discovery-driven career" and the possibilities it offers. Savvy and often counterintuitive, this superb book offers the tools, mind-set guidance, and rationale for avoiding complacency and embracing a new career path." Pub Wkly

Klubeck, Martin

Why organizations struggle so hard to improve so little; overcoming organizational immaturity. Martin Klubeck, Michael Langthorne, and Donald Padgett. Praeger Pub 2010 xvi, 222 p.p ill. (hardcover; alk. paper) $34.95; (ebook) $49.00   **658.4**

1. Organizational change 2. Organizational behavior
ISBN 0313380228; 0313380236; 9780313380228; 9780313380235

LC 2009046410

This book by Martin Klubeck, Michael Langthorne, and Donald Padgett "explains the difficulties and dangers of organizational immaturity, then provides proven, effective tools and ideas for achieving change within the limitations of an immature organization. With this guide, leaders and other stakeholders will be able to determine the maturity level of an organization, get beyond prevailing myths about how change gets derailed, and identify potential areas for improvement." (Publisher's note)

Includes bibliographical references and index.

Kouzes, James M.

The **truth** about leadership; the no-fads, heart-of-the-matter facts you need to know. [by] James M. Kouzes, Barry Z. Posner. Jossey-Bass 2010 xxv, 197p $24.95; ebook $16.99   **658.4**

1. Leadership 2. Executive ability
ISBN 978-0-470-63354-0; 978-0-470-87243-7 ebook

LC 2010018715

"It's hard to think of a better introduction for a new manager—or back-to-basics review for a veteran." Conference Board Rev

Includes bibliographical references

Kowitz, Braden

Sprint; How to Solve Big Problems and Test New Ideas in Just Five Days. by Jake Knapp (Author), John Zeratsky (Author), Braden Kowitz (Author) Simon & Schuster 2016 288 p. illustrations $28 **658.4**
1. Success 2. Management 3. Decision making 4. Problem solving
ISBN 150112174X; 9781501121746

This book, by Jake Knapp and John Zeratsky, presents "a unique five-day process for solving tough problems, proven at more than a hundred companies. Entrepreneurs and leaders face big questions every day: What's the most important place to focus your effort, and how do you start? What will your idea look like in real life? . . . Now there's a surefire way to answer these important questions: the sprint." (Publisher's note)

"This workbook is a solid guide to getting unstuck and generating your next great idea." Pub Wkly

Lanik, Martin

The **leader** habit; master the skills you need to lead in just minutes a day. Martin Lanik. AMACOM, American Management Association 2018 xiv, 238 p.p (hardcover) $25 **658.4**
1. Success 2. Leadership 3. Self-improvement 4. Self-help techniques
ISBN 0814439349; 9780814439340
LC 2017051455

This book, by Martin Lanik, "spotlights 22 essential leadership abilities, breaking them down into a series of small, learnable behaviors. . . . Drawn from a study of hundreds of leaders across the globe, the book's simple formula focuses on developing one skill at a time: sell the vision, delegate well, innovate often, empower others, overcome resistance, build strategic relationships, focus on customers, listen actively, negotiate effectively, and more." (Publisher's note)

"Ultimately, the book provides a refreshing counterpoint to the standard idea that some people are simply gifted with good leadership skills, instead shifting the emphasis to daily attention. An engaging program that demystifies leadership skills with bite-sized exercises." Kirkus Reviews

Includes bibliographical references and index

Martin, Roger L.

Creating great choices; a leader's guide to integrative thinking. by Jennifer Riel and Roger L. Martin. Harvard Business Publishing Press 2017 xvii, 242 p.p illustrations (hbk; alk. paper) $32 **658.4**
1. Decision making 2. Problem solving 3. Thought and thinking 4. Contradiction 5. Leadership -- Psychological aspects
ISBN 9781633692978; 1633692965; 9781633692961
LC 2017012026

This book, by Jennifer Riel and Roger L. Martin, "includes fresh stories of successful integrative thinkers that will demystify the process of creative problem solving, as well as practical tools and exercises to help readers engage with the ideas. And it lays out the authors' four-step methodology for creating great choices, which can be applied in virtually any context." (Publisher's note)

"This book provides a refreshing and novel twist on the underlying cognitive processes of great decision-making." Choice

Includes bibliographical references (pages [221]-226) and index

Meyer, Jennifer

Decision quality; Value Creation from Better Business Decisions. Carl Spetzler, Hannah Winter, Jennifer Meyer. John Wiley & Sons, Inc. 2016 237 p. (hardback) $30 **658.4**
1. Decision making
ISBN 9781119144670; 1119144671
LC 2015043777

This book, by Carl Spetzler, Hannah Winter, and Jennifer Meyer, "empowers you to make the best possible choice and get more of what you truly want from every decision. . . . [They] show you how to frame a problem or opportunity, create a set of attractive alternatives, identify relevant uncertain information, clarify the values that are important in the decision, apply tools of analysis, and develop buy-in among stakeholders.' (Publisher's note)

Mueller, Jennifer

Creative change; Why We Resist It . . . How We Can Embrace It. Jennifer Mueller. Houghton Mifflin Harcourt 2017 256 p. (hardcover) $28.00; (ebook) $28 **658.4**
1. Creative thinking 2. Change (Psychology) 3. Creative ability in business
ISBN 9780544703094; 9780544882034; 9780544703131
LC 2016036403

This book, by Jennifer Mueller, reveals "that many business leaders chronically reject creative solutions and often embrace the familiar, even as they profess commitment to innovation. . . . It's not just CEOs, but educators, scientists, and many, many others who often struggle to accept new and creative ideas even when desired. . . . Could people love but also hate creative ideas? Could the mindset we use to evaluate ideas turn this love or hate on or off—in an instant?" (Publisher's note)

"This enlightening book not only shows why people reject creativity but provides solutions on how to switch one's thinking and truly welcome it." Pub Wkly

Includes bibliographical references and index

Peshawaria, Rajeev

Too many bosses, too few leaders; the art of being a true leader. Free Press 2011 xxii, 222p $26; ebook $12.99 **658.4**
1. Leadership
ISBN 978-1-4391-9774-5; 978-1-4391-9776-9 ebook

"Peshawaria's book ought to become required reading for all business people—from students to executives." Publ Wkly

Includes bibliographical references

Peters, Thomas J.

The **little** big things; 163 ways to pursue excellence. [by] Tom Peters. HarperStudio 2010 xxix, 538p $24.99; ebook $11.99 **658.4**
1. Management
ISBN 978-0-06-189408-4; 978-0-06-196350-6 ebook
LC 2009051160

The author "combines observations he has gleaned from his travels, current news items, conversations, and followers of his blog in a compact guide that aims to help readers realize effective projects, customer contentment, employee engagement, and business profitability. No doubt, Peters is on target as he advises readers to appreciate the angry customer, work on their last impressions, make sure that the restroom is clean, and 160 other ways to guarantee success. Each suggestion contains a rationale, example, and method of implementation, all in two pages apiece." Libr J

Peters, Tom

The **excellence** dividend; meeting the tech tide with work that wows and jobs that last. Tom Peters. Vintage Books 2018

496 p. (trade pbk.) $17   **658.4**
1. Strategic planning 2. Organizational change 3. Organizational behavior 4. Organizational effectiveness 5. Automation -- Economic aspects
ISBN 9780525434627

LC 2017031994

In this book, author Tom Peters "offers brilliantly simple, actionable guidelines for success that any business leader can immediately implement. He provides a roadmap for your organization and for you as an individual to thrive amidst the tech tsunami, and he has a lot of fun doing it. 'The Excellence Dividend' is an important new book from one of today's greatest business thinkers." (Publisher's note)

Pimsleur, Julia

Million Dollar Women; The Essential Guide for Female Entrepreneurs Who Want to Go Big. Julia Pimsleur. Simon & Schuster 2015 256 p. illustrations (hbk) $28   **658.4**
1. Success 2. Businesswomen 3. Entrepreneurship 4. Fund raising 5. New business enterprises 6. Women-owned business enterprises
ISBN 0349406316; 1476790299; 9781476790299

LC 2015011025

In this book author Julia Pimsleur "introduces you to seven women who, instead of 'leaning in,' simply left corporate America and 'marched in' to the world of entrepreneurship. They have raised capital, developed powerful networks, and generated multimillion-dollar companies from scratch." (Publisher's note)

"A useful book on angel investing and funding opportunities, primarily aimed at women entrepreneurs. Recommended for public libraries with strong business collections." LJ

Includes bibliographical references

Pinson, Linda

Anatomy of a business plan; the step-by-step guide to building your business and securing your company's future. Linda Pinson. 8th edition Out of Your Mind...and Into the Marketplace 2008 372 p. $22.95   **658.4**
1. Business planning 2. New business enterprises 3. New business enterprises -- Planning
ISBN 0944205550; 9780944205556

This book, by Linda Pinson, "provides any entrepreneur the tools to create a well-constructed business plan. All steps are included—from initial considerations to envisioning the organizational structure to creating a growth-powering marketing plan and building for the future with airtight financial documents. The book offers proven, step-by step advice for developing and packaging the components of the plan and keeping them up to date." (Publisher's note)

Port, Michael

Steal the show; from speeches to job interviews to deal-closing pitches, how to guarantee a standing ovation for all the performances in your life. Michael Port. Houghton Mifflin Harcourt 2015 272 p. (hardback) $27   **658.4**
1. Communication 2. Job interviews 3. Business communication 4. Business presentations 5. Employment interviewing 6. Interpersonal communication
ISBN 9780544555181

LC 2015017313

In this book on presentations, author Michael Port "draws on his experience as an actor and as a highly successful corporate speaker and trainer to teach readers how to make the most of every presentation and interaction. He demonstrates how the methods of successful actors can

help you connect with, inspire, and persuade any audience." (Publisher's note)

"Required reading for anyone preparing for a job interview, serving in a leadership position, or speaking to the public." LJ

Raz, Tahl

The **CEO** next door; what it takes to get to the top, and succeed. Elena L. Botelho, Kim R. Powell, Tahl Raz. Currency 2017 288 p. $28   **658.4**
1. Executives 2. Executive ability 3. Career development 4. Success in business 5. Chief executive officers -- Case studies
ISBN 9781101906491

LC 2017035471

This book, by Elena L. Botelho and Kim R. Powell, "offer[s] career advice for everyone who aspires to get ahead. Based on research insights illustrated by real life stories from CEOs and boardrooms, they tell us how to: Fast-track our career by deploying the career catapults used by those who get to the top quickly . . . [and a]void the 5 hazards that most commonly derail those promoted into a new role." (Publisher's note)

"Botelho and Powell have created a thought-provoking look at successful leadership without the typical bluster." Pub Wkly

Includes bibliographical references and index

Sandberg, Sheryl, 1969-

Lean in; for graduates. Sheryl Sandberg, with Nell Scovell. Alfred A. Knopf 2014 432 p. (hardback) $24.95   **658.4**
1. Leadership 2. Self-improvement 3. Women -- Employment 4. Women executives 5. Leadership in women 6. Women -- Vocational guidance 7. College graduates -- Employment
ISBN 0385353677; 9780385353670

LC 2014002390

"In 'Lean In,' Sheryl Sandberg examines why women's progress in achieving leadership roles has stalled, explains the root causes, and offers . . . solutions that can empower women to achieve their full potential. . . . She describes specific steps women can take to combine professional achievement with personal fulfillment and demonstrates how men can benefit by supporting women in the workplace and at home." (Publisher's note)

"An expanded version of Facebook COO Sandberg's 2013 best-seller, this time with additional material aimed specifically at women just entering the workforce. . . . Sandberg recruits a considerable number of women, and a couple of men, to add their voices to hers." Kirkus

Includes bibliographical references and index

Scott, Kim

Radical candor; be a kick-ass boss without losing your humanity. Kim Scott. St. Martin's Press 2017 xxi, 246 p.p illustrations (hardcover) $26.99   **658.4**
1. Leadership 2. Executive ability 3. Personnel management 4. Corporate culture
ISBN 9781250103505

LC 2016044291

This book, by Kim Scott, "offers a guide to those bewildered or exhausted by management, written for bosses and those who manage bosses. Taken from years of the author's experience, and distilled clearly giving actionable lessons to the reader; it shows managers how to be successful while retaining their humanity, finding meaning in their job, and creating an environment where people both love their work and their colleagues." (Publisher's note)

"Informational and clear, this is necessary reading for anyone who's having trouble coming to terms with an underperforming workforce." Pub Wkly

Snow, Shane

Dream teams; working together without falling apart. Shane Snow. Portfolio/Penguin 2018 304 p. (hardcover) $27 **658.4**

1. Cooperativeness 2. Teams in the workplace 3. Interpersonal relations 4. Interpersonal conflict 5. Small groups -- Psychological aspects

ISBN 9780735217799

LC 2018014633

This book, by Shane Snow, "reveals the counterintuitive reasons why so many partnerships and groups break down--and why some break through. . . . Snow takes us on an adventure through history, neuroscience, psychology, and business, exploring what separates groups that simply get by together from those that get better together. . . . 'Dream Teams' is a landmark work that will change the way we think about people, progress, and collaboration." (Publisher's note)

"Entrepreneur, journalist, and author Snow (Smartcuts, 2014) explains how the composition of teams can make or break ideas, progress, and even the outcomes of battles. Using a combination of historical events (like the Battle of New Orleans, against the British, with General Andrew Jackson at the helm) and psychological research, Snow's narrative and perspective are clear: to become stronger, work must be collective in certain ways." Booklist

Solovic, Susan

The **one**-percent edge; small changes that guarantee relevance and build sustainable success. Susan Solovic with Ray Manley. AMACOM Books 2018 256 p. (hardcover) $24.95 **658.4**

1. Customer services 2. Success in business 3. Organizational change

ISBN 9780814438800

LC 2017027592

In this book, author Susan Solovic, with Ray Manley, "explains how to continually grow, improve, and move the business forward. With hundreds of strategies, examples, and a six-step process, [this book] explains how to: put energy into profitable areas and trim dead weight; raise prices by selling value instead of things; access new markets by adapting products or services; [and] hire the right team players." (Publisher's note)

Stauth, Cameron

The **code** of trust; an American counterintelligence expert's five rules to lead and succeed. Robin Dreeke and Cameron Stauth ; foreword by Joe Navarro. St. Martin's Press 2017 xi, 371 p.p (hardcover) $25.99 **658.4**

1. Trust 2. Leadership 3. Success in business 4. Corporate culture 5. Organizational behavior 6. Interpersonal communication

ISBN 1250093465; 9781250093462; 9781250093479

LC 2017006882

This book, by Robin Dreeke and Cameron Stauth, "is based on the system Dreeke devised, tested, and implemented during years of field work at the highest levels of national security. Applying his system first to himself, he rose up through federal law enforcement, and then taught his system to law enforcement and military officials throughout the country, and later to private sector clients." (Publisher's note)

"Smart, empowering, and easy to follow, Dreeke's manual should become a classic business—and personal—primer on the art of building trust." Pub Wkly

Taylor, William

Practically radical; not-so-crazy ways to transform your company, shake up your industry, and challenge yourself. [by] William C. Taylor. William Morrow 2011 xxi, 293p $27.99; pa $14.99 **658.4**

1. Leadership 2. Business enterprises

ISBN 978-0-06-173461-8; 0-06-173461-6; 978-0-06-203522-6 pa; 0-06-203522-3 pa

LC 2010028021

The author "takes us on an inside look at 25 companies that have grown ever more adaptive to not merely survive but thrive in today's challenging environment. . . . An engaging and briskly written read, this will captivate and benefit business people interested in change and innovation." Publ Wkly

Includes bibliographical references

Webb, Amy

The **signals** are talking; why today's fringe is tomorrow's mainstream. Amy Webb. PublicAffairs 2016 336 p. illustrations (ebook) $18.99; (hardcover) $27.99 **658.4**

1. Forecasting 2. Strategic planning 3. Business forecasting 4. Technological innovations

ISBN 9781610396677; 9781610396660

LC 2016028425

This book, by Amy Webb, "reveals a systemic way of evaluating new ideas . . . , distinguishing what is a real trend from the merely trendy. This book helps us hear which signals are talking sense, and which are simply nonsense, so that we might know today what developments—especially those seemingly random ideas at the fringe as they converge and begin to move toward the mainstream—that have long-term consequence for tomorrow." (Publisher's note)

"Webb provides a logical way to sift through today's onslaught of events and information to spot coming changes in your corner of the world." Kirkus

Includes bibliographical references and index

Wheeler, Michael

The **art** of negotiation; how to improvise agreement in a chaotic world. by Michael Wheeler. Simon & Schuster 2013 320 p. (hardcover; alk. paper) $26 **658.4**

1. Negotiation 2. Business planning 3. Negotiation in business

ISBN 1451690428; 9781451690422; 9781451690439

LC 2013005793

This book, by Michael Wheeler, "hows how master negotiators thrive in the face of chaos and uncertainty. Wheeler illuminates the improvisational nature of negotiation, drawing on his own research and his work with Program on Negotiation colleagues. He explains how the best practices of diplomats such as George J. Mitchell, dealmaker Bruce Wasserstein, and Hollywood producer Jerry Weintraub apply to everyday transactions." (Publisher's note)

658.452 Oral communication

McGowan, Bill

Pitch Perfect; How to Say It Right the First Time, Every Time. by Bill McGowan. HarperCollins 2014 288 p. illustrations $27.99 **658.452**

1. Communication

ISBN 0062273221; 9780062273222

In this book, Bill McGowan "teaches you how to get your message across and get what you want with pitch perfect communication. . . . Saying the right thing the right way can make the difference between sealing the deal or losing the account, getting a promotion, or getting a pink slip. It's essential to be pitch perfect--to get the right message across to the right person at the right time." (Publisher's note)

"In this engaging, enlightening, and full-of-practical-advice text, McGowan calls out poor public speaking doctrine and replaces it with examples of better ways to persuade and communicate." LJ

658.5　Management of production

Kolko, Jon

Well-designed; how to use empathy to create products people love. Jon Kolko. Harvard Business Review Press 2014 224 p. (hardback) $28　　**658.5**

1. Design 2. Empathy 3. New products 4. Product design 5. Consumer behavior 6. Marketing research

ISBN 9781625274793; 1625274793

LC 2014032507

This book, by Jon Kolko, presents advice for product design, "demonstrating how . . . [to] conceive and build successful, emotionally resonant products again and again. . . . You need to deeply understand customer needs and feelings, and this understanding must be reflected in the product. . . . We see how leading companies use a design process of storytelling and iteration that evokes positive emotions, changes behavior, and creates deep engagement." (Publisher's note)

"Passion and energy are left out of the writer's equation, and the pale, gray typeface and bland charts lack the pizzazz the subject calls for. Because of these deficiencies, the book is recommended with reservations for graduate design and marketing students, faculty, and practitioners. Summing Up: Recommended. With reservations. Graduate students, faculty, and practitioners." Choice

Tenner, Edward

The **efficiency** paradox; what big data can't do. Edward Tenner. Alfred A. Knopf 2018 320 p. (hardback) $27.95 **658.5**

1. Big data 2. Industrial efficiency 3. Artificial intelligence 4. Serendipity

ISBN 9781400034888; 9781400041398

LC 2017032040

This book, by Edward Tenner, "questions our ingrained assumptions about efficiency, persuasively showing how relying on the algorithms of digital platforms can in fact lead to wasted efforts, missed opportunities, and above all an inability to break out of established patterns. . . . Tenner offers a smarter way of thinking about efficiency." (Publisher's note).

658.8　Management of marketing

Burcher, Nick

Paid, owned, earned; maximizing marketing returns in a socially connected world. Nick Burcher. Kogan Page 2012 xiv, 279 p.p　　**658.8**

1. Marketing 2. Mass media 3. Social media 4. Digital media 5. Internet marketing 6. Online social networks 7. Marketing -- Management

ISBN 074946562X; 9780749465629; 9780749465636

LC 2011038487

This book by Nick Burcher "defines the constituents of each area of paid, owned and earned media and shows how they are linked together. The complexity of media that now sees multiple channels accessed through multiple devices has created major challenges for today's marketing and advertising professionals. [Burcher] proposes a blueprint for how to think and navigate across this space." (Publisher's note)

Includes bibliographical references and index

Kim, W. Chan

Blue ocean shift; beyond competing; proven steps to inspire confidence and seize new growth. W. Chan Kim and Renee Mauborgne. Hachette Books 2017 xi, 322 p.p illustrations (hardcover) $28　　**658.8**

1. Marketing 2. Entrepreneurship 3. Success in business 4. New products 5. Market segmentation

ISBN 0316314048; 9780316440066; 9780316314046

This book, by W. Chan Kim and Renee Mauborgne, guides "you step-by-step through how to take your organization from a red ocean crowded with competition to a blue ocean of uncontested market space. By combining the insights of human psychology with practical market-creating tools and real-world guidance, Kim and Mauborgne deliver the definitive guide to shift yourself, your team, or your organization to new heights of confidence, market creation, and growth." (Publisher's note)

"This invaluable guide will be empowering to business-minded readers." Pub Wkly

Includes bibliographical references (pages 305-307) and index.

Lindström, Martin

Small Data; The Tiny Clues That Uncover Huge Trends. Martin Lindstrom. St. Martin's Press 2016 256 p. illustrations (hardback) $25.99　　**658.8**

1. Consumers 2. Marketing 3. Brand name products 4. Consumer behavior 5. Branding (Marketing)

ISBN 9781250080684

LC 2015030202

In this book, author Martin Lindstrom "harnesses the power of 'small data' in his quest to discover the next big thing. Hired by the world's leading brands to find out what makes their customers tick, Martin Lindstrom spends 300 nights a year in strangers' homes, carefully observing every detail in order to uncover their hidden desires, and, ultimately, the clues to a multi-million dollar product." (Publisher's note)

"Lindstrom's uncanny ability to detect and decipher seemingly unrelated clues will inspire reporters and detectives as well as companies looking for ways to develop new products and ideas." Krikus

Includes bibliographical references (pages 235-239) and index.

Miles, Jason

YouTube marketing power; how to use video to find more prospects, launch your products, and reach a massive audience. by Jason Miles. McGraw-Hill 2014 xvii, 231 p.p illustrations (pbk.) $20　　**658.8**

1. Advertising 2. Internet marketing 3. YouTube (Electronic resource) 4. Internet videos 5. Internet advertising 6. Video tape advertising

ISBN 0071830545; 9780071830546

LC 2013030881

In this book, author Jason Miles "shows you how to get up and running on YouTube and offers best practices for using it to drive traffic to websites to increase sales. . . . This fast-paced but highly detailed guide reveals why companies frequently fail at YouTube marketing and how you can succeed by avoiding the same mistakes." (Publisher's note)

Schaefer, Mark W.

Return on influence; the revolutionary power of Klout, social scoring, and influence marketing. Mark Schaefer. McGraw-Hill 2012 xviii, 215 p.p (alk. paper) $25　　**658.8**

1. Social influence 2. Internet marketing 3. Online social networks 4. Social media -- Marketing

ISBN 0071791094; 9780071791090

LC 2011052315

This book, by Mark Schaefer, "is the first book to explore how brands are identifying and leveraging the world's most powerful bloggers, tweeters, and YouTube celebrities to build product awareness, brand buzz, and new sales. . . . [In it] marketing consultant and college educator Mark W. Schaefer shows you how to use the latest breakthroughs in social networking and influence marketing to achieve your goals." (Publisher's note)

Includes bibliographical references and index.

Underhill, Paco

★ **Why** we buy; the science of shopping. Updated and rev.; Simon & Schuster Pbks. 2009 306p pa $16; ebook $12.99 **658.8**

1. Shopping 2. Consumers 3. Marketing
ISBN 978-1-4165-9524-3 pa; 1-4165-9524-4 pa; 978-1-4165-6174-3 ebook; 1-4165-6174-9 ebook

LC 2010-483248

First published 1999

"Each chapter delves into a particular aspect of a store environment and its interface with customers: the importance of signage and why less is more, how men shop, . . . and clues about waiting time. Throughout, insights are peppered with one or several examples." Booklist [review of 1999 edition]

Watkins, Alexandra

Hello, my name is awesome; how to create brand names that stick. Alexandra Watkins. Berrett-Koehler Publishers 2014 112 p. (paperback) $16.95 **658.8**

1. Marketing 2. Brand name products 3. Branding (Marketing)
ISBN 1626561869; 9781626561861

LC 2014018994

In this book, the author Alexandra Watkins, a "naming consultant . . ., explains how anyone--even noncreative types--can create memorable and buzz-worthy brand names. . . . She also provides up-to-date advice, . . . and you'll see dozens of examples--the good, the bad, and the 'so bad she gave them an award.'" (Publisher's note)

"Useful for readers who are naming anything more important than a household pet." LJ

659.1   Advertising

Auletta, Ken

Frenemies; the epic disruption of the ad business (and everything else) Ken Auletta. Penguin Press 2018 368 p. (hardcover) $30 **659.1**

1. Marketing 2. Advertising -- History 3. Marketing -- History 4. Advertising agencies -- History
ISBN 9780735220867

LC 2018006195

This book "is Ken Auletta's reckoning with an industry under existential assault. He enters the rooms of the . . . [advertising] world's most important players, some of them business partners, some adversaries, many 'frenemies,' a term whose ubiquitous use in this industry reveals the level of anxiety, as former allies become competitors, and accusations of kickbacks and corruption swirl." (Publisher's note)

Includes bibliographical references and index

Turow, Joseph

The **daily** you; how the new advertising industry is defining

your identity and your world. Joseph Turow. Yale University Press 2011 xi, 234 p.p (hardback) $28.00 **659.1**

1. Advertising 2. Internet marketing 3. Consumer profiling 4. Marketing -- Technological innovations 5. Customer services -- Technological innovations
ISBN 0300165013; 9780300165012

LC 2011028202

This book presents "a warning about the impact of the 'Web 3.0' revolution . . . on individual freedom and privacy. . . . It is via this avalanche of personal data, available through networks like Facebook . . . [Joseph] Turow warns, 'the new advertising industry is defining your identity and your world.' . . . The root of the problem, Turow explains, is the disappearance of boundaries between advertising and content that shaped 20th-century media." (New Scientist)

Includes bibliographical references and index.

Wu, Tim, ca. 1973-

The **attention** merchants; Tim Wu. Alfred A. Knopf 2016 416 p. (ebook) $65; (hardback) $28.95 **659.1**

1. Consumers 2. Marketing 3. Advertising 4. Marketing -- History 5. Consumer behavior -- History 6. Advertising -- Social aspects -- History 7. Advertising -- Psychological aspects -- History
ISBN 9780385352024; 9780385352017

LC 2016010140

In this book author Tim Wu "describes the revolts that have risen against the relentless siege of our awareness, from the remote control to the creation of public broadcasting to Apple's ad-blocking OS. But he makes clear that attention merchants are always growing new heads, even as their means of getting inside our heads are changing our very nature--cognitive, social, political and otherwise--in ways unimaginable even a generation ago." (Publisher's note)

"The end result is a serious and timely study, delivered in layperson's language, that will add depth to an ongoing, urgently needed national and global conversation." Booklist

Includes bibliographical references (pages 347-385) and index.

659.144   Advertising in digital media

Todd, Bryan

Ultimate guide to Google AdWords; how to access 100 million people in 10 minutes. Perry Marshall, Mike Rhodes, Bryan Todd. Entrepreneur Media, Inc. 2017 xvi, 341 p.p (alk. paper) $24.95 **659.144**

1. Web search engines 2. Internet advertising 3. Google AdWords
ISBN 1599186128; 9781599186122

LC 2017027582

This book in the Ultimate Series, by Perry Marshall, Mike Rhodes and Bryan Todd, "introduces revised, expanded and new chapters covering Enhanced Campaigns, Google AdWord's Express, Google's Product Listing Ads, and the introduction to Google's Universal Analytics. Nuances in Big Data advertising are also revealed and expanded sections and necessary updates have been added throughout." (Publisher's note)

""Uncle Claude," as this outstanding guide affectionately calls him, pioneered results-driven advertising, so celebrating Hopkins by relating his timeless wisdom to modern-day marketing is a nice touch. An exemplary Google AdWords manual that could easily prevent costly mistakes and help boost profits." Kirkus Reviews

659.2　Public relations

Gramm, Jeff

Dear chairman; boardroom battles and the rise of share-holder activism. Jeff Gramm. Harper Business 2016 320 p. (hardcover) $29.99　　　　　　**659.2**

　　1. Stockholders 2. Corporate governance 3. Stockholders -- United States -- History 4. Corporate governance -- United States -- History 5. Corporations -- Investor relations -- United States -- History

　　ISBN 9780062369833

　　　　　　　　　　　　　　　　LC 2015038177

　　This book, by Jeff Gramm, is a "history of one of [American] capitalism's longest running tensions—the conflicts of interest among public company directors, managers, and shareholders—told through entertaining case studies and original letters from some of our most legendary and controversial investors and activists." (Publisher's note)

　　"Entertaining as well as intriguing, Gramm's work is a great read for both students of business and interested general readers." LJ

　　Includes bibliographical references and index

660.6　Biotechnology

Kurpinski, Kyle

How to defeat your own clone; and other tips for surviving the biotech revolution. [by] Kyle Kurpinski and Terry D. Johnson. Bantam Books Trade Paperbacks 2010 180p il pa $14　　　　　　**660.6**

　　1. Cloning 2. Biotechnology

　　ISBN 978-0-553-38578-6; 0-553-38578-X

　　　　　　　　　　　　　　　　LC 2009-45899

　　"Kurpinski and Johnson have written a science book that is irreverent, timely, accessible, and, best of all, compulsively readable." Publ Wkly

Piore, Adam

The **body** builders; inside the science of the engineered human. Adam Piore. HarperCollins 2017 400 p. $26.99; (ebook) $25.99　　　　　　**660.6**

　　1. Biotechnology 2. Bioengineering 3. Biomedical engineering

　　ISBN 0062347144; 9780062347145; 9780062347169

　　　　　　　　　　　　　　　　LC 2017004021

　　In this book, author Adam Piore "takes us on a fascinating journey into the field of bioengineering—which can be used to reverse engineer, rebuild, and augment human beings—and paints a vivid portrait of the people at its center. . . . Piore visits people who have regrown parts of their fingers and legs in the wake of terrible traumas, tries on a muscle suit that allows him to lift ninety pounds with his fingertips, [and] dips into the race to create 'Viagra for the brain.'" (Publisher's note)

　　"Piore writes gracefully, and with deep insight, about complex scientific endeavors that could ease human suffering but are fraught with myriad ethical perils." Pub Wkly

　　Includes bibliographical references (pages [353-366]) and index.

663　Beverage technology

Bryson, Lew

Tasting whiskey; An Insider's Guide to the Unique Pleasures of the World's Finest Spirits. by Lew Bryson. Storey Publishing 2014 256 p. (pbk.; alk. paper) $18.95　　　　　　**663**

　　1. Whiskey

　　ISBN 1612123015; 9781612123011

　　　　　　　　　　　　　　　　LC 2014023260

　　IACP Cookbook Award Finalist: Wine, Beer and Spirits (2015)

　　This book, by Lew Bryson, is a "comprehensive guide to everything there is to know about the world's whiskeys, including Scotch and bourbon as well as Tennessee, Irish, Japanese, and Canadian whiskeys. You'll learn about the types of whiskey and the distilling traditions of the regions where they are made, how to serve and taste whiskeys to best appreciate and savor them, how to collect and age whiskey for great results, and much more." (Publisher's note)

Kirk, Mimi

The **ultimate** book of modern juicing; more than 200 fresh recipes to cleanse, cure, and keep you healthy. by Mimi Kirk. W W Norton & Co Inc 2015 312 p. $24.95　　　　　　**663**

　　1. Fruit 2. Vegetables

　　ISBN 1581572603; 9781581572605

　　This book on juicing, by Mimi Kirk, "is the only book on the topic you'll ever need. Kirk has been juicing vegetables and fruits for more than 40 years, yet she doesn't look a day over 50. (And yes, those two things are connected.) She recently became more interested in how to use juicing to feel and look even better. Her discoveries—genuinely up-to-the-minute—are shared here, along with vibrant photographs of her creations." (Publisher's note)

Mitenbuler, Reid

Bourbon empire; the past and future of America's whiskey. Reid Mitenbuler. Viking Adult 2015 320 p. illustrations (hardback) $27.95　　　　　　**663**

　　1. Whiskey 2. Alcoholic beverages -- United States 3. Bourbon whiskey -- United States

　　ISBN 0670016837; 9780670016839

　　　　　　　　　　　　　　　　LC 2015001100

　　This book, by Reid Mitenbuler, "unraveling the many myths and misconceptions surrounding [Bourbon,] America's most iconic spirit, . . . traces a history that spans frontier rebellion, Gilded Age corruption, and the magic of Madison Avenue. Whiskey has profoundly influenced America's political, economic, and cultural destiny, just as those same factors have inspired the evolution and unique flavor of the whiskey itself." (Publisher's note)

　　"An illuminating, well-paced narrative that will interest students and imbibers of the wee dram, American-style." Kirkus

　　Includes bibliographical references and index

Risen, Clay

Single malt; a guide to the whiskies of scotland: includes profiles, ratings, and tasting notes for more than 330 expressions. Clay Risen. Quercus 2018 384 p. color illustrations (hardcover) $29.99　　　　　　**663**

　　1. Liquors 2. Whiskey

　　ISBN 9781681441054; 9781681441061; 9781681441078

　　　　　　　　　　　　　　　　LC 2018941147

　　This book, by Clay Risen, "is an introduction to the long history, fascinating science, and incredible diversity of malted whisky, as well as a practical drinker's guide to buying and enjoying hundreds of the greatest examples of the distiller's tradition. With maps of essential whisky regions of Scotland, profiles of each of the makers, and photographs of the bottles and tasting notes for each of the most widely available expressions. " (Publisher's note)

　　"PW Reviews 2018 August #3

Similar in tone and approach to his 2013 American Whiskey, Bourbon & Rye, New York Times deputy op-ed editor Risen covers everything in this entertaining and immersive guide to one of the world's favorite liquors. The volume is organized alphabetically, with Risen offering brief but specific tasting notes for more than 330 single malt whiskies (blends aren't covered) , along with profiles of distilleries, price ranges, and ratings." Pub Wkly

Includes bibliographical references (pages 296-298) and index

Rogers, Adam

★ **Proof**; the science of booze. Adam Rogers. Houghton Mifflin Harcourt 2014 272 p. (hardcover) $26 **663**

1. Alcohol -- History 2. Alcohol -- Research 3. Liquors 4. Distillation 5. Alcoholic beverages

ISBN 0547897960; 9780547897967

LC 2013045770

IACP Cookbook Award Winner: Wine, Beer and Spirits (2015)

In this book, author "Adam Rogers puts our alcoholic history under the microscope, from our ancestors' accidental discovery of fermented drinks to the cutting-edge laboratory research that proves why--or even if--people actually like the stuff. From fermentation to distillation to aging, 'Proof' offers a unique glimpse inside the barrels, stills, tanks, and casks that produce iconic drinks." (Publisher's note)

"The science here can be intimidating to process, but when enjoyed in leisurely sips, Rogers's cheeky and accessible writing style goes down smoothly, capturing the essence of this enigmatic, ancient social lubricant." Pub Wkly

Includes bibliographical references and index

Wood, Stephen M.

Apples to cider; how to make sweet and hard cider at home. April White with Stephen M. Wood of Farnum Hill Ciders. Quarry Books 2015 152 p. color illustrations (alk. paper) $24.99 **663**

1. Apples 2. Brewing 3. Cider

ISBN 1592539181; 9781592539185

LC 2015000551

In this book, brewers April White and Stephen M. Wood "share decades of experience and a simple philosophy: Cider is all about the apples. Whether you are a home brewer, a home winemaker, or simply a cider lover, you can join the growing community of cidermakers that are reviving this thousand-year-old craft." (Publisher's note)

"The authors detail how to set up tasting sessions to compare different ciders. They also offer instructions for making French cidre and ice cider, the apple version of ice wine. Savvy adepts can even turn cider into elegant apple champagne." Booklist

Includes bibliographical references and index

663.3 Brewed and malted beverages

The **Brew** Your Own big book of homebrewing; all-grain and extract brewing, kegging, 50+ craft beer recipes, tips and tricks from the pros. editors of Brew Your Own. Voyageur Press 2017 240 p. illustrations (paperback) $21.99 **663.3**

1. Beer 2. Brewing 3. Brewing -- Amateurs' manuals

ISBN 0760350469; 9780760350461

LC 2016033863

This book, by the editors of Brew Your Own, "is a necessity for anyone who's into homebrew. . . . It's a first-time homebrewer's best friend, explaining the entire brewing process from start to finish with step-by-step photography. . . . Whether you're looking to get into brewing, up

your game, or find inspiration for your next brew day, this book has what you need." (Publisher's note)

Includes bibliographical references (pages 232-233) and index.

663.42 Beer and ale

Hoalst-Pullen, Nancy

National Geographic atlas of beer; a globe-trotting journey through the world of beer. Nancy Hoalst-Pullen & Mark W. Patterson. National Geographic 2017 304 p. (hardcover; alk. paper) $40 **663.42**

1. Bars 2. Beer 3. Breweries 4. Beer -- Guidebooks 5. Breweries -- Guidebooks

ISBN 9781426218330

LC 2017011583

This book, by Nancy Hoalst-Pullen and Mark W. Patterson, "features more than 100 illuminating maps and 200 beautiful color photos. You'll find beer history, trends, and tasting across six continents (and how to order a beer in 14 languages!). Travel tips include the best breweries, beer festivals, and pubs in each location. Smart, compelling, and practical, this essential guide will help you discover the best beer wherever you are." (Publisher's note)

Includes bibliographical references and index

664 Food technology

Adamchak, Raoul W.

Tomorrow's table; organic farming, genetics, and the future of food. [by] Pamela C. Ronald [and] Raoul W. Adamchak. Oxford University Press 2008 208p il map $29.95 **664**

1. Organic farming 2. Genetic engineering 3. Genetically modified foods 4. Food -- Biotechnology

ISBN 9780195301755

LC 2007-7071

"The format is easy to follow and effective at highlighting . . . [the authors'] seemingly adverse positions on the subject. By the book's conclusion, their argument is elegantly presented in a logical fashion." Choice

Includes bibliographical references (p. 179-197)

Danforth, Adam

★ **Butchering** poultry, rabbit, lamb, goat, and pork; the comprehensive photographic guide to humane slaughtering and butchering. by Adam Danforth. Storey Publishing 2014 456 p. color illustrations (pbk.; alk. paper) $24.95 **664**

1. Meat 2. Animal welfare 3. Slaughtering and slaughterhouses 4. Meat animals 5. Meat cutting 6. Meat -- Preservation 7. Game and game-birds, Dressing of 8. Slaughtering and slaughter-houses

ISBN 1612121829; 9781603429313; 9781612121826; 9781612121888

LC 2013030702

James Beard Foundation Award: Reference and Scholarship (2015)

IACP Cookbook Award: Beverage/Reference/Technical (2015)

In this book, author Adam Danforth "shows you exactly how to humanely slaughter and butcher chickens and other poultry, rabbits, sheep, pigs, and goats. From creating the right pre-slaughter conditions to killing, skinning, keeping cold, breaking the meat down, and creating cuts of meat you'll recognize from the market, Danforth walks you through every step, leaving nothing to chance." (Publisher's note)

Includes bibliographical references and index

Ivanko, John D.

Homemade for Sale; How to Set Up and Market a Food Business from Your Home Kitchen. by Lisa Kivirist, John D. Ivanko. New Society Publishers 2015 240 p. illustrations (paperback) $22.95   **664**

1. Entrepreneurship 2. Home-based business
ISBN 9780865717862; 0865717869

LC 2014481269

This book, by Lisa Kivirist and John D. Ivanko, offers an "authoritative guide to conceiving and launching your own home-based food start-up. Packed with profiles of successful cottage food entrepreneurs, this comprehensive and accessible resource covers everything you need to get cooking for your customers, creating items that by their very nature are specialized and unique." (Publisher's note)

"An excellent, eminently practical resource to make a successful home-based food business a reality. Recommended for public libraries." LJ

Katz, Sandor Ellix

The **art** of fermentation; an in-depth exploration of essential concepts and processes from around the world. Sandor Ellix Katz ; foreword by Michael Pollan. Chelsea Green Pub. 2012 498 p. ill. (some col.) (hardback) $39.95   **664**

1. Fermentation 2. Canning and preserving 3. Fermented foods
ISBN 160358286X; 9781603582865; 9781603583640

LC 2011052014

James Beard Foundation Award: Reference and Scholarship (2013)

This book, by Sandor Ellix Katz, was the winner of the 2013 James Beard Foundation Book Award for Reference and Scholarship. "Readers will find detailed information on fermenting vegetables; sugars into alcohol; . . . sour tonic beverages; milk; grains and starchy tubers; beers (and other grain-based alcoholic beverages); beans; seeds; nuts; fish; meat; and eggs, as well as growing mold cultures, using fermentation in agriculture, art, and energy production, and considerations for commercial enterprises." (Publisher's note)

"Katz takes fermentation down to the molecular level while keeping it conversational and accessible to the generalist." LJ

Includes bibliographical refererences and index

López-Alt, J. Kenji

The **food** lab; better home cooking through science. J. Kenji López-Alt ; photographs by the author. W W Norton & Co Inc. 2015 938 p. color illustrations (hardcover) $49.95 **664**

1. Food 2. Cooking 3. Science 4. Food -- Analysis 5. Cooking -- Research 6. Food -- Experiments 7. Cooking -- Technique
ISBN 0393081087; 9780393081084

LC 2015016358

IACP Cookbook Award Winner: American (2016)

In this book author J. Kenji Lopez "focuses on the science behind beloved American dishes, delving into the interactions between heat, energy, and molecules that create great food. Kenji shows that often, conventional methods don't work that well, and home cooks can achieve far better results using new--but simple--techniques." (Publisher's note)

"This indispensable kitchen manual, which suggests visualizing heat capacity as a coop full of Red Bull-energized chickens, makes food science accessible." LJ

McLagan, Jennifer

★ **Bitter**; a taste of the world's most dangerous flavor, with recipes. Jennifer McLagan ; photography by Aya Brackett. Ten Speed Press 2014 272 p. color illustrations (hardback) $29.99   **664**

1. Taste 2. Cooking 3. Bitterness (Taste)
ISBN 160774516X; 9781607745167

LC 2014023824

IACP Cookbook Award Finalist: Single Subject (2015)
James Beard Foundation Award: Single Subject (2015)

In this book, author Jennifer McLagan "laments the disappearance of bitter tastes from mainstream diets and sets to reintroduce them to readers. In 100 recipes that incorporate chicories (frisee), beverages (coffee), brassicas (rutabaga), and other foods (almonds, cardoons), the author sheds light on how bitter tastes and smells affect the brain and palate." (Library Journal)

Includes bibliographical references and index

Mueller, Tom

Extra virginity; Tom Mueller. 1st ed. W. W. Norton 2011 238 p.   **664**

1. Fraud 2. Olive oil 3. Food adulteration and inspection 4. Olive -- History 5. Olive -- Folklore 6. Olive oil -- History 7. Olive oil industry -- Moral and ethical aspects
ISBN 9780393070217

LC 2011041459

In this book, author "Tom Mueller . . . [an] expert on olive oil and olive oil fraud . . . [tells] a story of globalization, deception, and crime in the food industry from ancient times to the present, and a[n] . . . indictment of today's lax protections against fake and even toxic food products in the United States. . . . [The book] is also an . . . account of the artisanal producers, chemical analysts, chefs, and food activists who are defending the extraordinary oils that truly deserve the name 'extra-virgin.'" (Publisher's note)

Robinson, Jancis

Wine grapes; a complete guide to 1,380 vine varieties, including their origins and flavors. by Jancis Robinson, Julia Harding, and Jose Vouillamoz. Ecco/HarperCollins 2012 1242 p. (hardback) $175   **664**

1. Grapes 2. Wine and wine making 3. Viticulture 4. Grapes -- Varieties
ISBN 0062206362; 9780062206367

LC 2012019224

James Beard Foundation Award: Beverage (2013)

This book by Jancis Robinson, Julia Harding, and Jose Vouillamoz provides information "about the . . . fruit that care, love, skill, and time transform into [wine]. [It] is the first complete compendium in more than a century to all grape varieties relevant to the wine lover. 'Wine Grapes' charts the relationships of the grapes . . . , discusses . . . where and how they are grown, and, most importantly, what the wines made from them will ultimately taste like." (Publisher's note)

Shetterly, Caitlin

Modified; GMOs and the Threat to Our Food, Our Land, Our Future. Caitlin Shetterly. G.P. Putnam's Sons 2016 352 p. (ebook) $65; (print) $28   **664**

1. Genetically modified foods
ISBN 9780698160224; 9780399170676

LC 2016011424

This book, by Caitlin Shetterly, "look[s] at the issue that started the biggest food fight of our time--GMOs. From a journalist and mother who learned that genetically modified corn was the culprit behind what was making her and her child sick, a must-read book for anyone trying to parse the incendiary discussion about genetically modified foods." (Publisher's note)

"Shetterly's accessible, well-researched, and damning work brings clarity to an often fuzzy debate." Pub Wkly

Winter, Ruth

A **consumer's** dictionary of food additives; 7th ed.; Three Rivers Press 2009 595p pa $17.95; ebook $17.95 **664**
1. Reference books 2. Food additives -- Dictionaries
ISBN 978-0-307-40892-1 pa; 978-0-307-45259-7 ebook
LC 2008-40601

First published 1972. Periodically revised

This guide provides "facts about the safety and side effects of more than 12,000 ingredients—such as preservatives, food-tainting pesticides, and animal drugs—that end up in food as a result of processing and curing." Publisher's note

Includes bibliographical references

666   Ceramic and allied technologies

Macfarlane, Alan

Glass ; a world history; {by} Alan Macfarlane and Gerry Martin. University of Chicago Press 2002 255p il $27.50 **666**
1. Glass
ISBN 0-226-50028-4
LC 2002-20493

The authors "make the case for the centrality of glass in the artistic renaissance and scientific revolution that took place in Western Europe from the 14th to 17th centuries. They discuss the origins of glass making and trace its development and usage across centuries and multiple cultures (Europe, the Middle East, China, India, and Japan). Their discussion combines cultural, artistic, and aesthetic viewpoints of glass within these cultures with history and developments in science. The result is a thoroughly readable, carefully argued work, filled with delightful surprises. . . . An excellent example of microhistory . . . this is required for history of science collections and recommended for large public and academic collections." Libr J

Includes bibliographical references

667   Cleaning, color, coating, related technologies

Garfield, Simon

Mauve; how one man invented a color that changed the world. Norton 2001 222p il hardcover o.p. pa $13.95 **667**
1. Chemists 2. Dyes and dyeing 3. Mauve 4. Dye industry -- Great Britain 5. Chemists -- England -- Biography
ISBN 0-393-32313-7 pa
LC 00-69533

This volume discusses how a British student, William Henry Perkin, while trying to synthesize quinine from coal tar, developed mauve, "the first mass-produced artificial dye. . . . By the turn of the 20th century, because of Perkin's novel idea, dye makers had 2,000 synthesized colors at their disposal." (N Y Times Book Rev) Index.

"The text is understandable by the average layman and is enjoyable reading for the scientist and non-scientist alike." Sci Books Films

Includes bibliographical references

Greenfield, Amy Butler

A **perfect** red; empire, espionage, and the quest for the color of desire. Amy Butler Greenfield. 1st ed; HarperCollins 2005 338p il $26.95 **667**
1. Dyes and dyeing
ISBN 0-06-052275-5
LC 2004-42376

The author "combines the investigative prowess of a detective with the intellectual reasoning of an academician to create an eminently entertaining and educational read." Booklist

Includes bibliographical references

668   Technology of other organic products

Turin, Luca

The **secret** of scent; adventures in perfume and the science of smell. Ecco 2006 207p il $23.95; pa $13.95 **668**
1. Perfumes
ISBN 0-06-113383-3; 978-0-06-113383-1; 0-06-113384-1 pa; 978-0-06-113384-8 pa
LC 2006-46273

The author "investigates the reason things smell they way they do." N Y Times Book Rev

Includes bibliographical references

Winter, Ruth

A **consumer's** dictionary of cosmetic ingredients; Complete Information About the Harmful and Desirable Ingredients Found in Cosmetics and Cosmeceuticals. Ruth Winter. Three Rivers Press 2009 567 p. $18 **668**
1. Chemicals 2. Cosmetics 3. Cosmetics -- Dictionaries
ISBN 0307451119; 9780307451118
LC 2010292417

This book, by Ruth Winter, presents "[e]verything you need to know about the safety and efficacy of cosmetics and cosmeceuticals. . . . This updated and expanded edition gives you the facts you need to protect yourself and your family from possible irritants, confusing chemical names, and the exaggerated claims of gimmicky additives. With 800 new ingredients found in toiletries, cosmetics, and cosmeceuticals . . . this alphabetically organized guide evaluates them all." (Publisher's note)

Includes bibliographical references (p. [565]-567)

674   Lumber processing, wood products, cork

The **Encyclopedia** of wood; a tree-by-tree guide to the world's most versatile resource. general editor, Aidan Walker. Facts on File 2005 192p il map $35 **674**
1. Reference books 2. Wood -- Encyclopedias
ISBN 0-8160-6181-5
LC 2004-60849

First published 1989

"A nice addition to libraries with strong interior design or DIY collections." Libr J

Includes bibliographical references

Petroski, Henry

The **pencil**; a history of design and circumstance. Knopf 1990 434p il hardcover o.p. pa $20 **674**
1. Pencils
ISBN 0-394-57422-2; 0-679-73415-5 pa
LC 89-45362

The author discusses the manufacture, design, history, and sociological significance of the pencil.

"An incredibly rich and complex history of this entirely unremarkable instrument of communication." SLJ

Includes bibliographical references

676 Pulp and paper technology

Basbanes, Nicholas A., 1943-

★ **On** paper; the everything of its two-thousand-year history. Nicholas A. Basbanes. Alfred A. Knopf 2013 448 p. $35 **676**

1. Paper 2. Paper industry 3. Paper -- History 4. Papermaking -- History 5. Paper industry -- History

ISBN 0307266427; 9780307266422

LC 2012050267

Andrew Carnegie Medal for Excellence in Nonfiction Shortlist (2014)

This book, by Nicholas A. Basbanes, presents "a consideration of all things paper: its invention that revolutionized human civilization; its thousand-fold uses (and misuses), proliferation, and sweeping influence on society; its makers, shapers, collectors, and pulpers. Basbanes writes about the ways in which paper has been used to record history, make laws, conduct business, and establish identities." (Publisher's note)

Includes bibliographical references

Grummer, Arnold E.

Trash-to-treasure papermaking. Storey Publishing 2011 207p il pa $16.95 **676**

1. Paper 2. Papermaking

ISBN 978-1-60342-547-6

LC 2010-43056

"Grummer begins with basic papermaking, then progresses to more advanced skills. Ample tips on everything from proper technique to troubleshooting problems with finished paper are included. A gallery of clever projects with directions rounds out this friendly, accessible guide to papermaking." Libr J

Includes bibliographical references

Hiebert, Helen, 1965-

The **papermaker's** companion; the ultimate guide to making and using handmade paper. Helen Hiebert. Storey Books 2000 219 p. $18.95 **676**

1. Papermaking 2. Paper, Handmade

ISBN 1580172008; 9781580172004

LC 99087351

This book by Helen Hiebert "covers absolutely everything you need to know about papermaking, from the basics to advanced techniques such as shaped sheets, embossing, laminating, and watermarking. . . . [The book] also includes thorough step-by-step instructions for processing pulp, building papermaking equipment, and making paper-based projects." (Publisher's note)

Includes bibliographical references and index.

Kurlansky, Mark, 1948-

Paper; Paging Through History. Mark Kurlansky. W.W. Norton & Company 2016 416 p. illustrations (hardcover) $27.95 **676**

1. Papermaking 2. Paper -- History 3. Papermaking -- History 4. Paper industry -- History

ISBN 9780393239614; 0393239616

LC 2016007084

Carnegie Medal Longlist: Nonfiction (2017)

This book, by Mark Kurlansky, offers "a definitive history of paper and the astonishing ways it has shaped today's world. Paper is one of the simplest and most essential pieces of human technology. For the past two millennia, the ability to produce it in ever more efficient ways has supported the proliferation of literacy, media, religion, education, commerce, and art; it has formed the foundation of civilizations, promoting revolutions and restoring stability." (Publisher's note)

"Kurlansky profiles key individuals, from inventors to master printers, writers, artists, and revolutionaries, while incisively parsing technological breakthroughs and social conundrums." Booklist

Includes bibliographical references (pages [347]-354) and index.

Monro, Alexander

The **paper** trail; an unexpected history of a revolutionary invention. Alexander Monro. Alfred A. Knopf 2016 384 p. illustrations, maps (hardback) $30 **676**

1. Paper 2. Papermaking 3. Paper industry 4. Paper -- History 5. Papermaking -- History

ISBN 9780307271662

LC 2015036988

This book, by Alexander Monro, is a "detailed history that tells the fascinating story of how paper—the simple Chinese invention of two thousand years ago—wrapped itself around our world, humankind's most momentous ideas imprinted on its surface. . . . [It] explores how the new substance was used to solidify social and political systems that influenced China even into our own time." (Publisher's note)

"The result is an engaging, lively, informative examination of a ubiquitous resource and its multimillennia influence on the world." Pub Wkly

Includes bibliographical references and index

677 Textiles

Ekarius, Carol

The **field** guide to fleece; 100 sheep breeds and how to use their fibers. by Deborah Robson and Carol Ekarius. Storey Publishing LLC 2013 231 p. color illustrations (pbk.; alk. paper) $14.95 **677**

1. Wool

ISBN 1612121780; 9781612121789

LC 2013003107

This book, by Deborah Robson and Carol Ekarius, offers a "portable reference . . . [for crafters to] quickly and easily look up any of 100 sheep breeds, the characteristics of their fleece, and the kinds of projects for which their fleece is best suited. Each breed profile includes a photo of the animal and information about its origin and conservation status, as well as the weight, staple length, fiber diameter, and natural colors of its fleece." (Publisher's note)

"This pocket-size guide is perfect for spinners and other fiber enthusiasts who want quick information on the characteristics of a wide variety of fleeces and would be a worthwhile book to have on hand at a fiber festival."

Includes bibliographical references (page 232) and index

Parkes, Clara

The **knitter's** book of yarn; the ultimate guide to choosing, using, and enjoying yarn. by Clara Parkes. 1st ed.; Potter Craft 2007 255 p. ill. (chiefly col.) ; **677**

1. Yarn 2. Knitting

ISBN 9780307352163; 0307352161

LC 2007009363

Includes bibliographical references (p. 242) and index.

Schoeser, Mary

World textiles: a concise history. Thames & Hudson 2003 224p il (World of art) pa $14.95 **677**

1. Fabrics 2. Textile industry
ISBN 0-500-20369-5

LC 2002-110919

"Arranged roughly into chronological periods, the book . . . details technique, materials, and designs and puts them in historical and cultural context. This is truly a fantastic history of textile arts. . . . The text itself is a delight to read and more comprehensive than in other comparable works." Libr J

Includes bibliographical references

681.1 Instruments for measuring time, counting and calculating machines and instruments

Marchant, Jo

Decoding the heavens; a 2,000-year-old computer--and the century-long search to discover its secrets. Da Capo Press 2009 328p il $25 **681.1**
1. Clocks and watches 2. Greece -- Antiquities
ISBN 978-0-306-81742-7; 0-306-81742-X

LC 2008-939733

First published 2008 in the United Kingdom

The author "relates the century-long struggle of competing amateurs and scientists to understand the secrets of a 2000-year-old clock-like mechanism found in 1901 by Greek divers off the coast of Antikythera, a small island near Tunisia. . . . This globe-trotting, era-spanning mystery should absorb armchair scientists of all kinds." Publ Wkly

Includes bibliographical references

682 Small forge work (Blacksmithing)

Parkinson, Peter

The **artist** blacksmith; design and techniques. Crowood Press 2002 160p il $40 **682**
1. Blacksmithing
ISBN 1-86126-428-3

"Parkinson explains the tools, materials, and equipment needed by blacksmiths as well as the most commonly used techniques. Numerous illustrations of beautiful creations (such as gates, sculptures, household items, and furniture) appear throughout this fascinating title." Libr J

683.4 Small firearms

Baum, Dan

Gun guys; a road trip. Dan Baum. 1st ed. Knopf 2013 352 p. (hardcover) $26.95 **683.4**
1. Firearms industry 2. United States -- Social conditions 3. Firearms ownership -- United States 4. Firearms owners -- United States 5. Firearms -- Social aspects -- United States
ISBN 0307595412; 9780307595416

LC 2012028767

This book, by Dan Baum, discusses gun culture in the United States. "Many Americans love guns--which horrifies and fascinates many other Americans, and much of the rest of the world. . . . [The author] grabs his licensed concealed handgun and hits the road to meet some of the 40 percent of Americans who own guns." Baum interviews gun owners and enthusiasts along with victims of gun crime. (Publisher's note)

Includes bibliographical references (pages [321]-323) and index

Firearms; an illustrated history. Dorling Kindersley, Limited. Dk Pub 2014 320 p. color illustrations $40 **683.4**
1. Guns 2. Firearms industry
ISBN 1465416056; 9781465416056

This book is a "definitive visual guide to the history of firearms and guns. . . . [It] charts the evolution and history of the gun, from the pistol, flintlock musket and rifle to the shotgun, machine gun and revolver. This book features over 300 firearms and guns spanning centuries of development, with the world's most iconic gun brands such as Colt, Smith and Wesson, Maxim and the Kalashnikov AK-47 covered with amazing photographic features." (Publisher's note)

"This is one of the best visual overviews available of the historical development of firearms, with brilliant photography and an emphasis on artistic as well as technological achievements. The material will be appreciated by readers interested in the history of technology as well as basic firearms enthusiasts." LJ

684 Furnishings and home workshops

Christiana, Asa

Build stuff with wood; make awesome projects with basic tools. Asa Christiana ; foreword by Nick Offerman. Taunton Press, Inc. 2017 202 p. illustrations (chiefly color) (paperback) $21.95 **684**
1. Woodwork 2. Furniture making
ISBN 9781631867118; 9781631868740

LC 2017007163

This book, by Asa Christiana, "is a true beginner's guide to woodworking, aimed at anyone who is interested in the craft but has little to no tools and no real idea where to start. The idea behind the book is to begin with a few portable power tools . . . build a bunch of cool projects with that basic kit, and then add skills and tools as you go. . . . In all, 14 fun projects will be presented, all built with just a few woodworking tools and off-the-shelf lumber." (Publisher's note)

"This solid, basic primer wonderfully reflects straightforward instruction with some very desirable projects." LJ

Hoadley, R. Bruce

Understanding wood; a craftsman's guide to wood technology. 2nd ed; Taunton Press 2000 280p il $39.95 **684**
1. Wood 2. Woodwork
ISBN 1-56158-358-8

LC 00-44322

First published 1980

This guide "covers the nature of wood and its properties, the basics of wood technology, and the woodworker's raw materials." Publisher's note

Includes bibliographical references

Kelsey, John

Woodworking; Techniques & Projects for the First Time Woodworker. John Kelsey. Fox Chapel Publishing 2013 111 p. ill. (chiefly col.) $14.99 **684**
1. Woodwork 2. Woodwork -- Handbooks, manuals, etc 3. Carpentry -- Handbooks, manuals, etc
ISBN 156523801X; 9781565238015

LC 2013017981

This book, by John Kelsey, is a guidebook for woodworking. "Each of the woodworking projects in this book can be completed in just a few hours. Designed to teach basic woodworking skills, they require only ordinary lumber and simple hand and power tools that you may already own. Each new project builds on what you learned before, allowing you to become more self-confident as your skills increase." (Publisher's note)

"Aimed at nine-year-olds through adults, this beautifully arranged title starts logically with wood selection and tool overviews and contains simple skill-building tasks that will develop DIYers' confidence and help them to learn technique. The quality of instruction is high, with large color photos showing each step." LJ

Warner, Pat

The **router** book. Taunton Press 2001 185p pa $19.95 **684**
1. Woodwork 2. Power tools
ISBN 1-56158-423-1

LC 2001-27149

"Warner shows readers how to get the most from their router, covering tools, accessories, and its use. Fixed-base, plunge routers, and laminate trimmers are introduced with excellent evaluations of specific models of each type." Libr J

684.1   Furniture

Blair, Barb

Furniture Makeovers; Simple Techniques for Transforming Furniture With Paint, Stains, Paper, Stencils, and More. by Barb Blair ; forward by Holly Becker ; photography by J. Aaron Greene. Chronicle Books 2013 192 p. (hardcover) $24.95 **684.1**
1. Furniture finishing
ISBN 1452104158; 9781452104157

This book looks at refinishing furniture. Author Barb Blair describes, with illustrations, 24 refinishing techniques, "ranging from . . . stripping and sanding" to "adding wallpaper. Little tips abound: use an overhead projector to display an image for tracing onto a piece of furniture; e-mail artwork to an office supply store to print instead of buying a pack of expensive transparencies for use at home." (Publishers Weekly)

Furniture makes the room; Barb Blair, founder of Knack Studios ; Photographs by Paige French. Chronicle Books 2016 190 p. color illustrations $27.95 **684.1**
1. Interior design 2. Furniture finishing 3. Furniture painting 4. Interior decoration -- Themes, motives
ISBN 1452139997; 9781452139999

LC 2015015943

This book, by Barb Blair, "goes beyond the nuts and bolts of furniture refinishing to show how to style rooms with each customized piece. For instance, she transforms a well-worn coffee table with a painted ombré design, and then reveals how to incorporate it into a bright and sunny den, a cozy reading nook, and a cheerful bedroom. With instructions for 15 before-and-after furniture projects—dressers, tables, beds, armoire, and more—in Blair's signature bold style." (Publisher's note)

Bruno, Isabelle

Reinventing Ikea; Isabelle Bruno, Christine Baillet. Abrams Image 2016 216 p. color illustrations (paperback) $24.95 **684.1**
1. Ikea (Firm) 2. Interior design 3. Furniture making 4. Furniture finishing
ISBN 1419722670; 9781419722677

LC 2016932043

This book features "70 customization projects conceived from popular Ikea products. Authors Isabelle Bruno and Christine Baillet share the

best DIY projects for every room in your home—from the bedroom to the kitchen, the living room to the office. Organized by four levels of difficulty . . . ., the projects are perfect for anyone interested in quick crafts—like a cake stand—or more involved—like constructing a kitchen island or a Mondrian-inspired desk." (Publisher's note)

Cone, Steve

Singer upholstery basics plus; complete step-by-step photo guide. Creative Pub. International 2007 155p il pa $19.95 **684.1**
1. Upholstery
ISBN 978-1-58923-329-4; 1-58923-329-8

LC 2007-7252

First published 1997 with title: Upholstery basics
"If there ever was an upholstery bible, this is it." Libr J

Dobson, Cherry

The **complete** guide to upholstery; stuffed with step-by-step techniques for professional results. St. Martin's Griffin 2009 143p il pa $24.95 **684.1**
1. Upholstery 2. Furniture -- Repairing
ISBN 978-0-312-38327-5; 0-312-38327-4

"Want to recycle your old furniture with reupholstery? This lovely manual . . . contains fine step-by-step photos and tips on technique. Master upholsterer Dobson easily walks the confident beginner through the basics." Libr J

Hingley, Brian D.

Furniture repair & restoration. Creative Homeowner 2010 175p il pa $14.95 **684.1**
1. Furniture finishing 2. Furniture -- Repairing
ISBN 978-1-58011-478-3

First published 1998 with title: Furniture repair & refinishing
"With special sections on evaluation and repair of structural issues, this volume features an array of valuable information on furniture repair and refinishing. . . . Geared toward beginners in wood restoration, the book highlights the author's professional experience, which shows through in the advice and thorough directions." Libr J

Jones, Stephanie

Upstyle your furniture; Stephanie Jones. Barrons Educational Series, Inc. 2015 160 p. color illustrations $21.99 **684.1**
1. Furniture finishing
ISBN 1438005563; 9781438005560

LC 2014932020

In this book, Stephanie Jones "compiles her techniques for furniture transformation. . . . She begins with the basics: how to select those pieces that are worth the work of transformation, and then how to decide on the style, color, and process that will make each one look its best. Using examples from her own studio to colorfully illustrate the text, Jones shows the reader the best techniques for preparing, making repairs, finishing, and embellishing each project." (Publishers Weekly)

"Overall, this is a great example of styles that will appeal to a wide range of tastes and abilities. Don't let this be the only furniture project book on the shelf, though—pair it with another that has better step-by-step illustrations, such as Christophe Pourny's The Furniture Bible." LJ

Paolini, Gregory

Arts & crafts furniture projects; Gregory Paolini. The Taunton Press 2015 170 p. color illustrations $24.95 **684.1**
1. Furniture making 2. Arts and crafts movement
ISBN 1600857817; 9781600857812

LC 2014046454

This book, by professional woodworker Gregory Paolini, "showcases nine iconic furniture projects that vary in difficulty. Timeless and always in style, Arts & Crafts is a perennial favorite and a style that works nicely with almost any home decor." (Publisher's note)

"Highly recommended for strong intermediate to more expert woodworkers who are well equipped to take on these beautiful projects, as there are no basic instructions for tool use or general techniques, though special tips appear throughout." LJ

Arts and crafts furniture projects

Pourny, Christophe

★ The **furniture** bible; everything you need to know to identify, restore and care for furniture. Christophe Pourny with Jen Renzi ; foreword by Martha Stewart. Artisan 2014 304 p. color illustrations hbk $35 **684.1**

1. Furniture finishing 2. Furniture -- Repairing
ISBN 1579655351; 9781579655358

LC 2014004628

This book, by Christophe Pourny with Jen Renzi, "teaches readers everything they need to know about the provenance and history of furniture, as well as how to restore, update, and care for their furniture--from antiques to midcentury pieces, family heirlooms or funky flea-market finds. The heart of the book is an overview of . . .[the author's] favorite techniques." (Publisher's note)

"Pourny explains how to assess damage, make repairs, and complete a final finish. A strong section on furniture care and cleaning argues that using the right methods will prolong the life of furniture. This guide will find a wide audience among those who simply want to learn about and appreciate good furniture, as well as those who are more hands-on." Pub Wkly

Includes bibliographical references and index

685 Leather and fur goods, and related products

Corral, Rodrigo

Sneakers; Rodrigo Corral, Alex French, and Howie Kahn. Penguin Group USA 2017 320 p. $24.95 **685**

1. Shoe industry 2. Fashion design 3. Shoes -- Social aspects
ISBN 0448494337; 9780448494333

This book, by Rodrigo Corral, Alex French, and Howie Kahn, "is a definitive exploration of the cultural phenomenon of sneakers, now an 85-billion-dollar-a-year industry. This gift-worthy book features 320 pages of photos and interviews with industry gurus, sports legends, and celebrities. . . . [It] is an absolute must-have for sneaker lovers and anyone who is interested in design, creative process, street culture, branding, entrepreneurship, art and fashion." (Publisher's note)

"Not a necessary purchase but a shelf-brightener where budgets allow." LJ

686 Printing and related activities

Kidd, Chip

Chip Kidd; Book one Chip Kidd ; Rizzoli International Publications 2005 304 p. **686**

1. Book design 2. Book jackets -- United States -- Design
ISBN 9780847827855; 9780847827480

LC 2005928316

This book, by Chip Kidd, "collects all of his book covers and designs for the first time, as well as hundreds of developmental sketches and concepts-annotated by Kidd and by many of the best-selling authors he's worked with over the years. The result is an important contribution to the design canon today as well as a visually dazzling (and often hilarious) insider's look at the design and publishing process." (Publisher's note)

"Stylishly designed and richly produced, this witty volume works both as a retrospective of Kidd's renowned book covers and as a memoir of his career in publishing." PW.

Lee, Marshall

Bookmaking ; editing, design, production; technical consultant Joseph Gannon. 3rd ed; Norton 2004 494p il $49.95 **686**

1. Books 2. Book industry
ISBN 0-393-73018-2

LC 2003-59672

First published 1965 by Bowker

This book describes "the business and art of transmitting an author's manuscript to readers by means of a book. The process includes editing, physical and visual design, costing, production planning, scheduling, procurement, and distribution. . . . This timeless classic should be acquired while it is still available." Choice

Includes bibliographical references

Rivers, Charlotte

Little book of book making; timeless techniques and fresh ideas for beautiful handmade books. Charlotte Rivers. Potter Craft 2014 192 p. color illustrations (hardback) $22.99 **686**

1. Book design 2. Bookbinding 3. Artists' books 4. Book designers
ISBN 0770435149; 9780770435141

LC 2013044724

This book, by Charlotte Rivers, is a "guide to 30 top bookmakers working today, plus 21 tutorials for essential techniques to make your own books. . . . Packed with wonderfully eclectic examples, this book explores the intriguing creative possibilities of bookmaking as a modern art form, including a wide range of bindings, materials, and embellishments. Featured techniques include everything from Coptic to concertina binding, as well as experimental page treatments." (Publisher's note)

686.2 Printing

Garfield, Simon

Just my type; a book about fonts. Gotham Books 2011 356p il $27.50 **686.2**

1. Printing 2. Fonts 3. Type and type-founding -- History
ISBN 978-1-59240-652-4

LC 2011379019

First published 2010 in the United Kingdom

"Conveying the richness and the personality of typefaces with love and passion, this is an accessible and entertaining introduction to the world of lettering." Blueprint

Includes biblliographical references

Kluger, Richard

★ **Indelible** ink; The Trials of John Peter Zenger and the Birth of America's Free Press. Richard Kluger. W W Norton & Co Inc 2016 368 p. illustrations (hardcover) $27.95 **686.2**

1. Freedom of the press 2. Civil rights -- United States -- History 3. Printers -- United States -- Biography 4. Trials (Seditious libel) -- New York (State) 5. Printing -- New York (State) -- History -- 18th century 6. Freedom of the press -- United States -- History -- 18th century

ISBN 9780393245462

LC 2016011040

This book by Richard Kluger presents the "untold story of the battle to legalize free expression in America. . . . When in 1733 a small newspaper . . . printed scathing articles assailing the new British governor, William Cosby, as corrupt and abusive, colonial New York was scandalized. The paper's publisher, an impoverished printer named John Peter Zenger . . . , became the endeavor's courageous fall guy." (Publisher's note)

"Event by compelling event, readers follow Zenger through the drama that eventually landed him in jail on libel charges—before a liberty-loving jury freed him with a 1735 verdict signaling a clear American commitment to the unfettered reporting that can check abuse of power." Booklist

Includes bibliographical references and index

Lupton, Ellen

Thinking with type; a critical guide for designers, writers, editors, & students. Ellen Lupton. Princeton Architectural Press 2010 224 p. color illustrations (alk. paper) $24.95 **686.2**
1. Typography 2. Type and type-founding 3. Graphic design (Typography)
ISBN 1568989695; 9781568989693

LC 2010005389

This book, by Ellen Lupton, "is the definitive guide to using typography in visual communication, from the printed page to the computer screen. This revised edition includes . . . the latest information on style sheets for print and the web, the use of ornaments and captions, lining and non-lining numerals, the use of small caps and enlarged capitals, as well as information on captions, font licensing, mixing typefaces, and hand lettering." (Publisher's note)

Includes bibliographical references and index

Spiekermann, Erik

★ **Stop** Stealing Sheep and Find out How Type Works; Erik Spiekerman. 2nd ed; Pearson P T R 2013 213 p. il (some col) $39.99 **686.2**
1. Typography 2. Graphic design 3. Type and type-founding
ISBN 0321934288; 9780321934284

LC 2014378096

"In this third edition, acclaimed type designer Erik Spiekermann brings his type classic fully up to date on mobile and web typography. . . . If you use type--and these days, almost everyone does--Spiekermann's engaging, common-sense style will help you understand how to look at type, work with type, choose the best typeface for your message, and express yourself more effectively through design." (Publisher's note)

"This updated edition uses an easygoing style to get readers from a variety of backgrounds up to speed on good use of type and general typography. The examples, images, and guidance not only are helpful to illustrate concepts, but also are up-to-date with current web and mobile trends and technologies." Choice

Includes bibliographical references and indexes

686.3 Bookbinding

Cambras, Josep

Bookbinding; techniques and projects. [translation from the Spanish, Michael Brunelle and Beatriz Cortabarria] Barron's 2007 143p il (Decorative techniques) pa $26.99 **686.3**
1. Bookbinding
ISBN 978-0-7641-6084-4; 0-7641-6084-2

LC 2007-924989

"Beginning with a historical overview, continuing to an explanation of tools and materials, Cambras showcases his expertise in chapters devoted to half a dozen techniques and the same quantity of paper-painting methods." Booklist

Diehn, Gwen

Real life journals: designing & using handmade books. Lark Books 2010 180p il (Live & learn) $24.95 **686.3**
1. Diaries 2. Bookbinding
ISBN 978-1-60059-492-2

LC 2009-32647

"Chapters on tools, covers, paper choices, and bindings are detailed and fully illustrated, but Diehn . . . goes well beyond that, making a point to include information on creating a purposeful design, enriching textual content, and binding the words to the visual elements to reflect a bookmaker's interests and personality. . . [This is] a lovely, helpful volume that will inspire and attract journalers and scrapbookers alike." Booklist

Ekrem, Erica

Bound; making 30 artful handmade books. Erica Ekrem. Lark Crafts 2015 144 p. color illustrations (paperback) $19.95 **686.3**
1. Book design 2. Bookbinding 3. Book design -- Handbooks, manuals, etc 4. Bookbinding -- Handbooks, manuals, etc
ISBN 1454708670; 9781454708674

LC 2013049059

Bookbinder Erica Ekrem "has devised creative fun for book artists of all levels. Choose from three categories: Vintage, Nature, and Leather. Make books from mason jars and seashells, a classic leather-bound photo album, and other works of art." (Publisher's note)

"This fresh look at an old art will be in demand and is highly recommended." LJ

Golden, Alisa

Making handmade books; 100+ bindings, structures & forms. Lark Crafts 2010 256p il pa $19.95 **686.3**
1. Books 2. Bookbinding
ISBN 978-1-60059-587-5

LC 2010-1546

"This volume updates and combines Golden's previous Creating Handmade Books and Unique Handmade Books to provide an introduction to the fascinating world of artists' books. The specimens highlighted are far from your traditional book—they are works of art that will challenge readers' ideas of what books can be. Though there are plenty of inspiring photographs, there is also ample direction to guide readers interested in creating their own books. Golden also intersperses tidbits of bookmaking history and lore throughout, making this guide not only pleasurable and inspiring to look at but fun to read. " Libr J

Includes bibliographical references

LaPlantz, Shereen, 1947-2003

Cover to cover; creative techniques for making beautiful books, journals & albums. Shereen LaPlantz. Sterling Pub Co Inc 2015 144 p. illustrations (some color) $19.95 **686.3**
1. Bookbinding
ISBN 1454708484; 9781454708483

This book, by Liz Shareen, "[f]irst published in 1995, . . . quickly became renowned in the bookmaking community as the definitive guide to the art. This . . . revised 20th anniversary edition . . . features updated photography and a fresh interior design. . . . After introducing all the bookbinding basics, it shows readers, step by step, how to create, fold, assemble, and stitch a wide range of books and journals . . . using a variety of materials." (Publisher's note)

688.7 Recreational equipment

Capella, Massimiliano

Barbie; The Icon. Massimiliano Capella. Natl Book Network 2016 208 p. color illustrations $65 **688.7**
1. Barbie dolls 2. Popular culture
ISBN 1943876118; 9781943876112
This book, by Massimiliano Capella, "celebrates the impact Barbie has had in culture for three generations in everything from style, to fashion, to careers, that makes her the voice of the contemporary woman, the voice of pop culture, and the image of a genuine living legend." (Publisher's note)
"This is a charming book for all ages, and older readers will especially enjoy revisiting their childhoods." Publisher's Weekly

Gathercole, Peter

Fly tying for beginners; how to tie 50 failsafe flies. Peter Gathercole. Barron's 2006 256 p. color illustrations $24.99 **688.7**
1. Fly casting 2. Fly tying 3. Fly fishing 4. Flies, Artificial
ISBN 0764158457; 9780764158452
LC 2005921781
This book, by Peter Gathercole, "shows beginners how to craft 50 professional-looking flies for trout and salmon fishing. Each fly-tying project consists of step-by-step instructions accompanied by close-up photos of the work in progress and a large photo of the finished fly. Beginners will learn how to make dry flies, wet flies, bugs, nymphs, hairwings, and streamers. They'll also get advice on which flies are best for catching which variety of fish." (Publishers note)

The **fly**-tying bible; 100 deadly trout and salmon flies in step-by-step photographs. Peter Gathercole. Barron's 2003 256 p. color illustrations $24.95 **688.7**
1. Artificial flies 2. Fly tying 3. Trout fishing 4. Salmon fishing 5. Flies, Artificial
ISBN 0764155504; 9780764155505
LC 2002109917
In this book, by Peter Gathercole, "fly-tying is a highly prized fisherman's craft, but it's also an art form, wonderfully captured in this volume's hundreds of color photos. Each of 100 fly patterns is presented in a two-page spread: an enlarged photo and textual description on the left-hand page, complemented with a set of step-by-step, clearly captioned photos on the facing page." (Publisher's note)

690 Construction of buildings

The **Art** of natural building; design, construction, resources. editors: Joseph F. Kennedy, Michael Smith, Catherine Wanek; illustrated by Joseph F. Kennedy. New Soc. Pubs. 2002 291p il pa $26.95 **690**
1. Building 2. Building materials 3. House construction
ISBN 0-86571-433-9
"The authors, who are practitioners in the natural building movement, introduce a variety of nontraditional construction options, including underground building and building with alternative materials such as adobe, recycled agricultural materials, rammed earth, and straw bale. They also address energy efficiency, design, and the desire to create a healthy environment. The final chapters include case studies." Libr J
Includes bibliographical references

Black & Decker Corp.

The **complete** guide to patios & walkways; money-saving do-it-yourself projects for improving outdoor living space. Creative Pub. International 2010 255p il pa $24.99 **690**
1. Patios
ISBN 978-1-58923-481-9
This is a guide to plan, build, repair, and maintain patios and walkways. It "stands out for its detailed photos and step-by-step, logically arranged instructions. . . . There is an original section on drainage options with projects." Libr J

The **complete** outdoor builder; from arbors to walkways; 150 DIY projects. Creative Pub. International 2009 528 p. (pbk.) $19.99 **690**
1. Masonry 2. Garden structures 3. Masonry -- Amateurs' manuals 4. Woodwork -- Amateurs' manuals 5. Building, Wooden -- Amateurs' manuals 6. Do-it-yourself work -- Amateurs' manuals 7. Outbuildings -- Design and construction -- Amateurs' manuals 8. Garden structures -- Design and construction -- Amateurs' manuals
ISBN 1589234839; 9781589234833
LC 2009028983
This book, edited by Mark Johnson, Tracy Stanley, and Jennifer Gehlhar, provides advice on adding "patios and walkways to the yard. . . . From low-cost, curb-appeal walkways to expansive, estate-quality decorative concrete patios . . . this book presents each project with step-by-step instructions and full-color photographs as well as . . . tips, tricks, and inspiration. Each project uses the most current materials, tools, common practices, codes, and construction techniques." (Publisher's note)
Includes bibliographical references and index.

Cory, Steve

Ultimate guide: porches; building techniques for adding a new porch to your home. Creative Homeowner 2011 191p il pa $16.95 **690**
1. Porches
ISBN 978-1-58011-491-2
LC 2009941175
In this manual, the author "shares numerous, clear illustrations and detailed construction information and techniques. His confident, expert instruction . . . is apparent in the projects presented here. . . . A solid addition to any home improvement collection." Libr J

Diedricksen, Derek

Microshelters; 59 creative cabins, tiny houses, tree houses, and other small structures. Derek Diedricksen. Storey Publishing 2015 255 p. illustrations (chiefly color) (pbk.; alk. paper) $18.95 **690**
1. Houses 2. Log cabins and houses 3. Outbuildings
ISBN 1612123538; 9781612123530
LC 2015009864
Author Derek Diedricksen presents this "collection of creative and inspiring ideas for tiny houses, cabins, forts, studios, and other microshelters. Created by a wide array of builders and designers around the United States and beyond, these 59 unique and innovative structures show you the limits of what is possible. Each is displayed in full-color photographs accompanied by commentary by the author." (Publisher's note)
"A handy source for tiny-house enthusiasts. Pair this with Ryan Mitchell's Tiny House Living or Jay Shafer's The Tumbleweed DIY

Book of Backyard Sheds & Tiny Houses." Library Journal

Johnston, Amy

What your contractor can't tell you; the essential guide to building and renovating. Amy Johnston. Shube Pub. 2008 208 p. $24.95   **690**

1. House construction 2. Houses -- Remodeling
ISBN 0979983800; 9780979983801

This book by Amy Johnston "is a comprehensive guide to getting the best results while building or renovating a home. . . . Chapters give detailed coverage of critical topics: design; selecting and supervising the architect and contractor; cost estimates; budget; plan specifications; contracts; dealing with town officials; and keeping track of everything along the way. For each stage of the project, there is detailed information on common pitfalls and how to avoid them." (Publisher's note)

Includes bibliographical references and index.

Kotite, Erika

She sheds; a room of your own. Erika Kotite. Cool Springs Press 2017 176 p. color illustrations (hardback) $25   **690**

1. Sheds 2. Interior design 3. Outdoor living spaces 4. Interior decoration 5. Women -- Homes and haunts
ISBN 9781591866770

LC 2016033753

This book, by Erika Kotite, "shows you how to create cozy getaways with inspiration from across the country. Start by defining the goal and purpose of your space. Will you use it for entertaining, crafting, or alone time? Then, use the gallery of over 100 photos as inspiration for your decor, paint colors, and landscaping. You'll even find fun upcycling ideas to personalize your space. Get inspired, and get started on your very own tricked-out retreat!" (Publisher's note)

Includes bibliographical references and index.

Stiles, David

Backyard Building; Treehouses, Sheds, Arbors, Gates and Other Garden Projects. Jeanie Stiles and David Stiles. W.W. Norton & Co. Inc 2014 256 p. col. ill. $19.95   **690**

1. Building 2. Garden structures 3. Life skills -- Handbooks, manuals, etc.
ISBN 1581572387; 9781581572384

This book by Jeanie Stiles and David Stiles, part of the Countryman Know How series, covers "backyard accessories, the fundamentals of tools and materials, and useful tips based on real-life questions from the couple's popular website." It features "hand-drawn illustrations to guide the reader through the building process in a user-friendly way." (Publisher's note)

Thorstensen, Ole

Making things right; the simple philosophy of a working life. Ole Thorstensen ; translated from the Norwegian by Seán Kinsella. Penguinbooks, an imprint of Penguin Random House, LLC 2018 240 p. $16   **690**

1. Building 2. Carpentry 3. Building -- Technique 4. Small business -- Norway 5. Carpenters -- Norway -- Biography 6. Dwellings -- Remodeling -- Norway -- Anecdotes
ISBN 9780143130949

LC 2017058279

This book presents "the simple yet captivating story of a loft renovation, from the moment master carpenter and contractor Ole Thorstensen submits an estimate for the job to when the space is ready for occupation. As the project unfolds, we see the construction through Ole's eyes: the meticulous detail, the pesky splinters, the problem solving, patience,

and teamwork required for its completion." (Publisher's note)

Toht, David

★ **Stanley** decks; a homeowner's guide. David Toht. The Taunton Press, Inc. 2017 234 p. (paperback) $24.95   **690**

1. Carpentry 2. Patios -- Design & construction 3. Decks (Architecture, Domestic) -- Design and construction -- Amateurs' manuals
ISBN 9781631864506

LC 2016037011

This book, by David Toht, about building a deck "takes you through every step of the way, from design and planning . . . and adding benches, planters, and other built-ins. The heart of the book is a step-by-step guide to building four different types of deck--a patio deck, a first-story deck, a raised deck, and a multi-feature deck--which include a range of decking and railing types and special features." (Publisher's note)

"This is a great go-to for deck planning and building." LJ

694   Wood construction

Purdy, Strother

Doormaking; materials, techniques, and projects for building your first door. Strother Purdy. Linden Publishing 2017 viii, 144 p.p illustrations (some color) (pbk.; alk. paper) $26.95   **694**

1. Doors 2. Woodwork 3. Handicraft 4. Wooden doors
ISBN 9781610352918

LC 2017001604

This book, by Strother Purdy "gathers all the information and guidance that both beginning and intermediate woodworkers need to be successful making their first door. . . . [It] offers project chapters that walk the reader step-by-step through the construction of eight essential doors, explaining design and material choices in specific contexts, tool options and other considerations." (Publisher's note)

Thallon, Rob

★ **Graphic** guide to frame construction; Rob Thallon. The Taunton Press 2016 xi, 243 p.p illustrations (paperback) $29.95   **694**

1. House framing 2. Framing (Building) 3. Wooden-frame buildings 4. Wooden-frame buildings -- Drawings 5. Wooden-frame buildings -- Design and construction
ISBN 9781631863721

LC 2016008479

In this updated book in the For Pros by Pros series by Rob Thallon, "whether you're setting a foundation, erecting a partition wall, or flashing a window, you'll find information on the project . . . [here]. The book's major categories include footings and foundations; beams, joist systems, and subflooring; wall framing, bracing, and sheathing; [and more]." (Publisher's note)

"An excellent companion to Scot Simpson's Complete Book of Framing, Second Edition, this work is highly recommended and a must for any building collection." LJ

Includes bibliographical references and index

695   Roof covering

Black & Decker Corp.

The complete guide to roofing, siding & trim; created by: the editors of Creative Publishing International, Inc., in cooperation with Black & Decker. Updated 2nd ed.; Creative Pub. International 2008 271p il pa $24.99 **695**

1. Roofs 2. Siding (Building materials)

ISBN 978-1-58923-418-5

LC 2008-26823

First published 2004 with title: The complete guide to roofing & siding

This guide to installing and maintaining roofing and siding includes a "section on trim work as well as a section on ecofriendly roofs. . . . The photo gallery is quite attractive and fresh, reflecting current and popular house styles. The evaluation of materials—relating to home style, maintenance, duration, and drawbacks—is particularly nice. Text is matter-of-fact and clear, with no topic overdone. A useful and usable guidebook, this is recommended for all public libraries." Libr J

The **complete** guide to roofing & siding; Choose, Install & Maintain Roofing & Siding Materials. by Editors of Creative Publishing. Creative Pub. International 2012 255 p. illustrations (chiefly color) (soft cover) $24.99 **695**

1. Houses -- Remodeling 2. Siding (Building materials) 3. Roofs -- Maintenance and repair 4. Roofing -- Handbooks, manuals, etc 5. Roofing -- Installation -- Handbooks, manuals, etc 6. Siding (Building materials) -- Handbooks, manuals, etc 7. Roofs -- Maintenance and repair -- Handbooks, manuals, etc

ISBN 158923717X; 9781589237179

LC 2011052377

This book "covers all traditional materials, from wood lap siding, brick, concrete block, stucco, stone veneer, and wooden shakes to vinyl, raised-ridge metal roofing, and fiber/cement lap siding. Less traditional roof-covering materials, such as EPDM rubber, architectural shingles, and fully bonded selvage edge and metal shingles are also featured with clear how-to photos and instructions." (Publisher's note)

696 Utilities

Black & Decker Corp.

The **complete** guide to plumbing; modern materials and current codes all new guide to working with gas pipe. Expanded 4th ed.; Creative Pub. International 2008 334p il pa $24.99 **696**

1. Plumbing

ISBN 978-1-58923-378-2; 1-58923-378-6

LC 2008-8636

First published 1998

This guide to plumbing covers fixtures, installations, repairs, materials, tools, and skills.

"The sequential directions for many common household repairs are the real asset here. Excellent photos with simple instruction for each project are also valuable. Includes a DVD with demonstrations of many of the jobs described in the book." Libr J

The **complete** guide to plumbing; faucets & fixtures - PEX - tubs & toilets - water heaters? troubleshooting & repair - much more. by Editors of Creative Publishing. Creative Pub. International 2012 335 p. color illustrations (soft cover) $24.99 **696**

1. Plumbing 2. Houses -- Remodeling 3. Plumbing -- Amateurs' manuals 4. Dwellings -- Remodeling -- Amateurs' manuals

ISBN 1589237005; 9781589237001

LC 2011052378

This book "has the answer to any home plumbing problem you're likely to find. . . . The basics of home plumbing systems are explained with clarity, and all of the most popular plumbing projects are shown with beautiful step-by-step photos. New information in this edition includes how to winterize a house and how to install a state-of-the-art, on-demand water heater." (Publisher's note)

Henkenius, Merle

Plumbing ; complete projects for the home; New expanded ed.; Creative Homeowner 2006 287p il pa $19.95 **696**

1. Plumbing

ISBN 1-58011-311-7; 978-1-58011-311-3

LC 2006-924699

First published 2002 with title: Plumbing: basic, intermediate & advanced projects

The author "shows homeowners how to tackle expensive plumbing repairs (e.g., replacing a washer in a leaky faucet). . . . The skill level of each project is rated, and photos walk users step by step through the instructions. . . . Strongly recommended for all collections." Libr J

697 Heating, ventilating, air-conditioning engineering

Ewing, Rex A.

Got sun? go solar; harness nature's free energy to heat and power your grid-tied home. [by] Rex A. Ewing and Doug Pratt. Expanded 2nd ed.; PixyJack Press 2009 191p il map pa $20 **697**

1. Wind power 2. Solar energy 3. Photovoltaic power generation

ISBN 978-0-9773724-6-1

LC 2009-19053

First published 2005

"This is an excellent primer on home application of solar energy. Written in a chatty and amusing style, the book is more informational than mechanical." Libr J

Includes bibliographical references

Thurkettle, Vincent

The **Wood** Fire Handbook; The Complete Guide to a Perfect Fire. by Vincent Thurkettle. Octopus Pub Group 2015 224 p. illustrations $16.99 **697**

1. Fire

ISBN 1845336704; 9781845336707

This wood fire handbook, by Vincent Thurkettle, "shows you that the soothing effect of dancing flames and glowing embers is a simple pleasure to have in our lives. Understanding everything that underpins the perfect wood fire makes it even more enjoyable." (Publisher's note)

"In times when utility costs can prove prohibitive, this book will enable anyone to explore the possibilities and benefits of maintaining a good fire in the hearth." Pub Wkly

698 Detail finishing

Jenkins, Alison

300 tips for painting & decorating; tips, techniques & trade secrets. Alison Jenkins. Firefly Books Ltd 2014 176 p. ill. (chiefly col.) $19.95 **698**

1. Painting 2. Interior design

ISBN 1770854525; 9781770854529

This book, by Alison Jenkins, offers "a professional decorator shares hundreds of her personal tips, techniques and trade secrets that will guide homeowners in attractive decorating and regular maintenance tasks, from repainting a ceiling to finding and fixing energy-sucking drafts. These are the how-to's, the wisdom and the time-saving shortcuts that do-it-yourself homeowners will appreciate for years to come." (Publisher's note)

"All of the tips are illustrated, if not with photographs and drawings, then with graphic design. What counts most are the author's know-how sections. . . . Great advice made accessible." Booklist

Santos, Brian

Painting and wallpapering secrets from Brian Santos, the Wall Wizard. Wiley 2011 240p il pa $21.99   **698**
1. Paperhanging 2. House painting
ISBN 978-0-470-59360-8; 0-470-59360-1

LC 2010-28548

"This guide contains useful information for wall treatments. The practical and reassuring advice includes important directions on what not to do. This is nitty-gritty do-it-yourself, with outstanding prep instruction, tool selection, well-thought-out tips and tricks, and technique photos. While inspirational wall-treatment photo books abound, . . . this is the guide you'll need to achieve those looks." Libr J

700 ARTS

700   The arts

★ **Arts** and humanities through the eras. Gale 2004 5v il set $450   **700**
1. Arts -- History 2. Civilization -- History
ISBN 0-7876-5695-X

LC 2004-10243

"Each volume consists of nine chapters covering the major branches of the humanities: architecture and design, dance, fashion, literature, music, philosophy, religion, theater, and visual arts. . . . This outstanding series offers a wealth of information; the chapters on architecture, dance, and theater alone are worth the price of each volume." Libr J
Includes bibliographical references

Cumming, Robert

Art; a visual history. by Robert Cumming. DK Publishing 2015 416 p. color illustrations $30   **700**
1. Art -- History 2. Art -- Handbooks, manuals, etc
ISBN 1465436618; 9781465436610

LC 2015473824

This book, by Robert Cumming, "is the complete visual guide to Western art, now updated and repackaged in a themed slipcase. How to tell Impressionism from Expressionism, a Degas from a Monet, early Medieval art from early Christian? [This book] explains it all — painting, sculpture, great artists, styles, and schools." (Publisher's note)

"With its solid, accessible information and hundreds of excellent, full-color reproductions, this is ideal for high school or college students as well as any art lover or museumgoer." LJ

Galitz, Kathryn Calley

The **Metropolitan** Museum of Art; masterpiece paintings. Kathryn Calley Galitz. Skira Rizzoli Publications, Inc. 2016 544 p. (hardcover) $75   **700**
1. Art museums 2. Art -- Exhibitions
ISBN 0847846598; 9780847846597

LC 2016938042

This book, by Kathryn Calley Galitz, "offers an exquisite tour,

unique in its lavish illustration, scholarship, extent, and graceful packaging. As the first large survey published in 30 years, and the first large general survey of the Met's paintings collection it is the first to celebrate the greatest and most iconic paintings of one of the largest, most important, and most beloved museums in the world." (Publisher's note)

Impelluso, Lucia

Gods and heroes in art; edited by Stefano Zuffi; translated by Thomas Michael Hartmann. Getty Mus. 2003 383p il pa $19.95   **700**
1. Reference books 2. Art and mythology -- Dictionaries 3. Classical mythology -- Dictionaries
ISBN 0-89236-702-4

LC 2002-13422

The characters of ancient Greek and Roman mythology "are each described in entries summarizing their distinctive stories, their special attributes, and the ways in which artists have depicted them. Each entry is . . . illustrated with reproductions of works of art in which the god or hero is pictured. . . . The book concludes with . . . indexes, including a list of iconographic symbols associated with the subjects, and a bibliography." Publisher's note
Includes bibliographical references

Lindquist, Sherry C. M.

Medieval monsters; terrors, aliens, wonders. Sherry C. M. Lindquist, Asa Simon Mittman ; with a preface by China Miéville. The Morgan Library & Museum in association with D Giles Limited 2018 175 p. color illustrations, color map $39.95   **700**
1. Monsters in art 2. Curiosities and wonders 3. Illumination of books and manuscripts 4. Monsters in art -- Exhibitions 5. Curiosities and wonders in art -- Exhibitions 6. Illumination of books and manuscripts, Medieval -- Themes, motives -- Exhibitions 7. Illumination of books and manuscripts, Renaissance -- Themes, motives -- Exhibitions
ISBN 1911282182; 9781911282181

LC 2017046081

This book, by Sherry C. M. Lindquist, Asa Simon Mittman, with a preface by China Miéville, "explores the cultural importance and rich variety of monstrosities in the art of the Middle Ages, with examples drawn from the Morgan Library & Museum's renowned collection of illuminated manuscripts. While presenting a lively array of strange beauties and frightful anomalies . . . the authors reveal how monsters played a central role in medieval societies." (Publisher's note)
Includes bibliographical references (pages 167-172) and index

The **muses** go to school; inspiring stories about the importance of arts in education. edited by Herbert Kohl and Tom Oppenheim. New Press 2012 xxvii, 200 p.p   **700**
1. Celebrities 2. Arts -- Study and teaching 3. Education -- Aims and objectives
ISBN 1595585397; 9781595585394

LC 2011042803

In this book, edited by Herbert Kohl and Tom Oppenheim, "autobiographical pieces with well-known artists and performers are paired with . . . essays by . . . educators to produce a . . . case for positioning the arts at the center of primary and secondary school curriculums. Spanning a range of genres from acting and music to literary and visual arts, these . . . voices make surprising connections between the arts and the development of intellect, imagination, spirit, emotional intelligence, self-esteem, and self-discipline of young people." (Publisher's note)

700.1   Philosophy and theory of the arts

Larson, Kay

Where the heart beats; John Cage, Zen Buddhism, and the inner life of artists. Kay Larson. Penguin Press 2012 474 p. (hardcover) $29.95   **700.1**
1. Zen Buddhism 2. Postmodernism 3. Zen Buddhism -- Influence
ISBN 1594203407; 9781594203404

LC 2011044714

This book, by Kay Larsen, "part biography, part cultural history," presents "reflections on [John] Cage's encounters with and absorption of Zen Buddhism. . . . Weaving threads of the teachings of Zen Buddhist writer D.T. Suzuki and Alan Watts, along with Cage's own reflections and writings on art, music, dance, and life, [Kay] Larson . . . covers Cage's growing understanding of the nature of noise and silence and the roles that each plays in music." (Publishers Weekly)

Includes bibliographical references and index

700.19   Psychological aspects of art

James, Jamie

The **glamour** of strangeness; artists and the last age of the exotic. Jamie James. Farrar, Straus & Giroux 2016 368 p. (hardback) $27   **700.19**
1. Artists 2. Identity (Psychology) 3. Alienation (Social psychology) 4. Artists -- Biography 5. Artists -- Psychology
ISBN 9780374163358

LC 2015041555

This book, by Jamie James, focuses on six "artists . . . , Walter Spies, the . . . German painter who remade his life in Bali; Raden Saleh, the Javanese painter who found fame in Europe; Isabelle Eberhardt, a Russian-Swiss writer who roamed the Sahara; . . . the American experimental filmmaker Maya Deren, who went to Haiti. . . . From France, Paul Gauguin left for Tahiti; and Victor Segalen, a naval doctor, poet, and novelist, immersed himself in . . . imperial Peking." (Publisher's note)

"Abundant primary sources inform James' sharply drawn, sympathetic portraits." Kirkus

Includes bibliographical references and index

700.411   Avant-garde arts

Ashbery, John, 1927-

John Ashbery; they knew what they wanted: poem & collages. by John Ashbery; edited by Mark Polizzotti. Rizzoli Electa 2018 128 p. $35   **700.411**
1. Collage 2. American poetry -- Collections
ISBN 9780847860562

LC 2017956512

This book, edited by Mark Polizzotti, "compiles a comprehensive selection of [American poet John] Ashbery's collage work, accompanied by a selection of collage-related poems. Like his poetry, Ashbery's collage work combines art historical and pop culture references, creating often humorous juxtapositions." (Publisher's note)

Eggers, Dave, 1970-

Ungrateful mammals; Dave Eggers ; introduction by Noah Lang. Abrams 2017 137 p. illustrations (chiefly color) (hardcover) $29.99   **700.411**
1. Mammals 2. American drawing 3. American painting 4. Avant-garde (Aesthetics) 5. Mammals -- Pictorial works 6. Drawing, American -- 21st century 7. Painting, American -- 21st century
ISBN 9781683350248; 9781419724633

LC 2017930296

This book, by Dave Eggers, is a result of his visual art efforts "to raise money for ScholarMatch, his college-access nonprofit. . . . Usually involving the pairing of an animal with humorous or biblical text, the results are wry, oddly anthropomorphic tableaus that create a very entertaining and eccentric body of work from one of today's leading culture makers." (Publisher's note)

700.9   History, geographic treatment, biography of the arts

Laing, Olivia

★ The **lonely** city; adventures in the art of being alone. by Olivia Laing. Picador 2016 336 p. illustrations (hardback) $26   **700.9**
1. Artists 2. Loneliness 3. City and town life 4. Artists -- Psychology 5. City and town life -- Psychological aspects
ISBN 1250039576 ; 9781250039576

LC 2015037147

This book, by Olivia Laing, is a "work of biography, memoir, and cultural criticism on the subject of loneliness, told through the lives of iconic artists. . . . Moving fluidly between works and lives—from Edward Hopper's Nighthawks to Andy Warhol's Time Capsules, and from Henry Darger's hoarding to the depredations of the AIDS crisis—Laing conducts an electric, dazzling investigation into what it means to be alone." (Publisher's note)

"Laing's writing becomes expansive, exploring their biographies, sharing art analysis, and weaving in observations from periods of desolation that was at times 'cold as ice and clear as glass.' " Pub Wkly

Includes bibliographical references.

700.92   Biography

Byatt, A. S. (Antonia Susan), 1936-

Peacock & vine; On William Morris and Mariano Fortuny. A.S. Byatt. Alfred A. Knopf 2016 192 p. color illustrations (hardback) $26.95   **700.92**
ISBN 9781101947470

LC 2016008946

This book, by A.S. Byatt, "opens a window into the lives, designs, and passions of Mariano Fortuny and William Morris. . . . Born a generation apart in the mid-1800s, Fortuny and Morris were seeming opposites: Fortuny a Spanish aristocrat thrilled by the sun-baked cultures of Crete and Knossos; Morris a member of the British bourgeoisie, enthralled by Nordic myths. Through their revolutionary inventions and textiles, both men inspired a new variety of art." (Publisher's note)

"Although brief, this is an inspiring homage that forges illuminating connections between two dynamos." Kirkus

Includes bibliographical references.

Kaplan, Carla

Miss Anne in Harlem; The White Women of the Black Renaissance. by Carla Kaplan. Harper 2013 512 p. $28.99 **700.92**
1. Whites 2. Harlem Renaissance 3. Women -- United States
ISBN 0060882387; 9780060882389

In this book, author Carla Kaplan "focuses on white women, collectively called 'Miss Anne,' who became Harlem Renaissance insiders.

[She] focuses on six of the unconventional, free-thinking women, some from Manhattan high society, many Jewish, who crossed race lines and defied social conventions to become a part of the culture and heartbeat of Harlem." (Publisher's note)

Ross, Clifford

The **world** of Edward Gorey; by Clifford Ross and Karen Wilkin. Abrams 1996 190p il hardcover o.p. pa $19.95 **700.92**
1. Artists 2. Authors 3. Novelists 4. Illustrators 5. Set designers 6. Children's authors
ISBN 0-8109-9083-0 pa

LC 95-47900

This book includes an "interview with Mr. Ross, {in which} Edward Gorey speaks of his likes and dislikes and aspects of his career. . . . Ms. Wilkin discusses Gorey's work as illustrator, author, stage designer, and miscellaneous creator." Atl Mon

Includes bibliographical references

701   Philosophy and theory of fine and decorative arts

Snyder, Laura J.

Eye of the beholder; Johannes Vermeer, Antoni van Leeuwenhoek, and the reinvention of seeing. Laura J. Snyder. W W Norton & Co Inc 2015 448 p. color illustrations; map (hardcover) $27.95   **701**
1. Art and science 2. Art and science -- Netherlands -- Delft -- History -- 17th century
ISBN 0393077462; 9780393077469

LC 2014038143

"In 'Eye of the Beholder,' Laura J. Snyder transports us to the streets, inns, and guildhalls of seventeenth-century Holland, where artists and scientists gathered, and to their studios and laboratories, where they mixed paints and prepared canvases, ground and polished lenses, . . . and invented the modern notion of seeing. With charm and narrative flair Snyder brings Vermeer and Van Leeuwenhoek--and the men and women around them--vividly to life." (Publisher's note)

"Though it is only speculation that these great thinkers knew each other personally, Snyder expertly brings to life their shared social milieu of artists and scientists, all seeking new ways to investigate nature. These intertwined biographies weave a story of two men whose insistence on "daring to see" revolutionized our understanding of perception itself." Booklist

Includes bibliographical references and index

704   Special topics in fine and decorative arts

Holladay, Wilhelmina Cole

A **museum** of their own; National Museum of Women in the Arts. text contributions by Philip Kopper. Abbeville Press 2008 240p il $50   **704**
1. Women artists 2. National Museum of Women in the Arts (U.S.)
ISBN 978-0-7892-1003-6; 0-7892-1003-7

LC 2008-21646

"The National Museum of Women in the Arts . . . opened in 1987. It changed the status of women artists and the life of its founder, who now tells the museum's fascinating success story in an entertainingly anecdotal, inspiring, and beautifully illustrated [book]. . . . This invaluable work of art history is enlivened by Holladay's encounters with artists . . . and gorgeous reproductions, many of works that will be new to even the most art-expert readers." Booklist

In harmony; the Norma Jean Calderwood collection of Islamic art. edited by Mary McWilliams ; with essays by Jessica Chloros and Katherine Eremin, Walter B. Denny, Penley Knipe, Oya Pancaroğlu, David J. Roxburgh, Sunil Sharma, Anthony B. Sigel, Marianna Shreve Simpson. Harvard Art Museum 2013 303 p. (Yale University Press) $75   **704**
1. Islamic art 2. Art collections 3. Islamic art -- Exhibitions 4. Art, Iranian -- Exhibitions 5. Arthur M. Sackler Museum -- Exhibitions 6. Art -- Private collections -- Massachusetts -- Cambridge -- Exhibitions
ISBN 9781891771620; 9780300176414; 0300176414

LC 2012030304

Editor Mary McWilliams' book features the Norma Jean Calderwood collection of Islamic art. The book features nine essays that "explore issues of conservation as well as the cultural and historical significance of various objects in this largely unpublished collection. Topics include the influence of calligraphic line and physical gesture on Safavid drawings; figurative imagery on Iranian ceramics; and what cobalt pigment reveals about an object's origins." (Publisher's note)

Includes bibliographical references (pages 274-290) and index

704.03   Ethnic and national groups

A **century** of African American art; the Paul R. Jones collection. edited by Amalia K. Amaki. University Museum, University of Delaware & Rutgers University Press 2004 xvi, 259 p.p illustrations (chiefly color) (paperback) $29.95   **704.03**
1. African American art 2. African American art -- 20th century -- Exhibitions 3. African American art -- 21st century -- Exhibitions 4. University of Delaware -- Art collections -- Exhibitions 5. Art -- Private collections -- Delaware -- Newark -- Exhibitions
ISBN 9780813534572; 0813534569; 0813534577

LC 2004000582

This book, edited by Amalia K. Amaki, "provides an important resource for the study of the works included in the [Paul R.] Jones collection, the artists who created them, as well as the social and historical contexts that engendered them. The volume brings together ten essays, which examine four issues in American art: portraiture and realism in relation to abstract expressionism, the implications of color, the role of narrative, and the concept of multiple originals." (Publisher's note)

"This volume will be a great addition to any art collection and is recommended for all academic and larger public libraries." LJ

Includes bibliographical references and index

The **James** T. Bialac Native American Art Collection; Selected Works. Mark Andrew White, General Editor. University of Oklahoma Press 2012 xi, 223 p.p ill. (hardcover) $49.95; (paperback) $29.95   **704.03**
1. Art collections 2. Native American art 3. Indian art -- Catalogs 4. Fred Jones Jr. Museum of Art -- Catalogs 5. Art -- Private collections -- Oklahoma -- Norman -- Catalogs
ISBN 0806143045; 9780806142999; 9780806143040

LC 2012003005

This book, published by the Fred Jones Museum of Art, presents a catalogue of the James T. Bialac Native American Art Collection of "easel paintings and three-dimensional works. . . . The collection comprises nearly four thousand items, including drawings, sculptures, prints, kachinas, jewelry, ceramics, rattles, baskets, and textiles. . . . The Bialac Collection represents indigenous cultures across North America." (Publisher's note)

Includes bibliographical references (pages 205-209) and index

★ **Native** North American art; Janet Catherine Berlo, Ruth B. Phillips. Second edition Oxford University Press 2014 410 p $62.95 **704.03**
1. Native American art and culture
ISBN 9780199947546

LC 2014004553

"This lively introductory survey of indigenous North American arts from ancient times to the present explores both the shared themes and imagery found across the continent and the distinctive traditions of each region. Focusing on the richness of artwork created in the US and Canada, Native North American Art, Second Edition, discusses 3,000 years of architecture, wood and rock carvings, basketry, dance masks, clothing and more. The expanded text discusses twentieth- and twenty-first-century arts in all media including works by James Luna, Kent Monkman, Nadia Myre, Jaune Quick-to-See Smith, Will Wilson, and many more." (Publisher's note)

Stanislaus, Grace C.

Instill & inspire; the John and Vivian Hewitt collection of African-American art. text by Grace C. Stanislaus ; foreword by Jonathan Green. University of Pittsburgh Press 2017 xiv, 152 p.p illustrations (some color) (hardback) $49.95 **704.03**
1. Art collections 2. African American art -- Collectors and collecting 3. African American art -- Catalogs 4. Art -- Private collections -- North Carolina -- Charlotte -- Catalogs 5. Harvey B. Gantt Center for African-American Arts + Culture -- Catalogs
ISBN 9780822945048

LC 2017014500

This book, by Grace C. Stanislaus, focuses on "the John and Vivian Hewitt Collection of African American Art. [It] represents fifty-eight works that celebrate the expression and passion of twenty artists, including Romare Bearden, Margaret Burroughs, Jonathan Green, Jacob Lawrence, Elizabeth Catlett, Ann Tanksley, and Henry Ossawa Tanner." (Publisher's note)

"This catalog accompanying an exhibition of the same name at the Harvey B. Gantt Center for African American Arts and Culture in Charlotte, NC, includes a succinct yet incisive essay on the history of significant collections as well as biographies about the Hewitts (and other collectors)." LJ

704.9 Iconography

Beard, Mary, 1955-

★ **How** do we look; the body, the divine, and the question of civilization. W W Norton & Co Inc 2018 240 p. $24.95 **704.9**
1. Humanity 2. Art -- History 3. Religion -- History
ISBN 1631494406; 9781631494406

In this book, author Mary Beard "explore[s] the history of art, religion, and humanity, [from prehistoric Mexico to modern Istanbul.] . . . Beard explores the power, hierarchy, and gender politics of the art of the ancient world. . . . [She also] chronicles some of the most breathtaking religious imagery ever made . . . to show how all religions . . . have faced irreconcilable problems in trying to picture the divine." (Publisher's note)

"Recommended for fans of this popular author, the Civilizations program, and those looking for brief foray into an alternative form of art appreciation." LJ

★ The **Renaissance** portrait; from Donatello to Bellini. edited by Keith Christiansen and Stefan Weppelmann ; essays by Patricia Rubin ... [et al.] Metropolitan Museum of Art --

Distributed by Yale University Press 2011 xii, 420 p.p (hc: Yale University Press) $65 **704.9**
1. Renaissance portrait painting -- Italy 2. Art, Italian -- Exhibitions 3. Portraits, Renaissance -- Italy -- Exhibitions
ISBN 0300175914; 1588394255; 1588394263; 9780300175912; 9781588394255; 9781588394262

LC 2011027471

This book, edited by Keith Christiansen and Stefan Weppelmann, "provides new research and insight into the early history of portraiture in Italy, examining in detail how its major art centers--Florence, the princely courts, and Venice--saw the rapid development of portraiture as closely linked to Renaissance society and politics, ideas of the individual, and concepts of beauty." (Publisher's note)

Includes bibliographical references and index.

706 Organizations and management of fine and decorative arts

★ **Artist's** & graphic designer's market 2018; how and where to sell your art. edited by Noel Rivera. F & W Media Inc 2017 671 p. $34.99 **706**
1. Directories 2. Art -- Marketing -- Directories
ISBN 1440352836; 9781440352836

This book, edited by Noel Rivera, is for people who "want to establish or expand a career . . . in fine art, illustration, or design. . . . Thousands of successful artists have relied on us to help develop their careers and navigate the changing business landscape. 'Artist's Market 2018' includes the most up-to-date, individually verified market contacts possible." (Publisher's note)

"Essential for most libraries. Frequent users may wish to purchase their own copy." Library Journal

708 Galleries, museums, private collections of fine and decorative arts

The **art** of music; edited by Patrick Coleman. Yale University Press 2015 318 p. (hardback) $65 **708**
1. Artists 2. Art and music 3. Creative ability
ISBN 0300215479; 9780300215472

LC 2015017781

This book, edited by Patrick Coleman, is an "illustrated and . . . interdisciplinary look at the mutual influence between music and the visual arts across cultures and eras. The book sheds new light on more familiar artists at the intersection of the visual and the musical, such as Wassily Kandinsky and Arnold Schoenberg, and presents new scholarship on less well-known examples in the arts of Asia, Africa, the Americas, and Europe." (Publisher's note)

Includes bibliographical references and index

National Gallery of Art (U.S.)

★ **National** Gallery of Art; [foreword by Earl A. Powell III] 2nd ed.; Thames and Hudson 2006 332p il (World of art) pa $18.95 **708**
1. National Gallery of Art (U.S.)
ISBN 0-500-20390-3; 978-0-500-20390-3

LC 2005-904459

First published 2004 by National Gallery of Art; Based on John Walker's National Gallery of Art, published 1984

"The collection of the National Gallery of Art in Washington includes works by the greatest masters of Western art from the twelfth century to the present. . . . [In this] look at the National Gallery's masterpieces . . . the works are illustrated in full color, and the curators have written the texts." Publisher's note

Nielsen, Christina

The **Isabella** Stewart Gardner Museum; a guide. Christina Nielsen with Casey Riley and Nathaniel Silver. Isabella Stewart Gardner Museum"||"Yale University Press 2017 ix, 205 p.p $20   **708.144**
    1. Art collections 2. Isabella Stewart Gardner Museum 3. Isabella Stewart Gardner Museum -- Guidebooks
    ISBN 0300226470; 9780300226478
                                   LC 2017939207
In this book, by Christina Nielsen with Casey Riley and Nathaniel Silver, "the Isabella Stewart Gardner Museum and its magnificent collection are enlivened through fresh insights and new photography. This updated guide . . . charts new pathways through the beloved institution's superb collection. Gardner . . . built a Venetian-inspired palazzo in Boston to share her exquisite and thought-provoking art objects from diverse cultures and eras." (Publisher's note)
    Includes index (pages 201-205)

709   History, geographic treatment, biography

The **Art** Book; Phaidon Press. Phaidon Press 2012 592 p. (hardcover) $59.95   **709**
    1. Art 2. Artists
    ISBN 0714864676; 9780714864679
This book by Phaidon Press is an "A - Z guide to artists from medieval times to the present day . . . including paintings, photographs, sculptures, video, installations and performance art. Each artist is represented on a full page with a definitive work and explanatory . . . information." The book features "examples of all periods, schools, visions and techniques." (Publisher's note)

The arts of China; Michael Sullivan with Shelagh Vainker. University of California Press 2018 376 p. $44.95   **709**
    1. Chinese art 2. Art -- History
    ISBN 0520294815; 9780520294813
"Internationally renowned and a crucial classroom text, 'The Arts of China' has been revised and expanded by the late Michael Sullivan, with Shelagh Vainker. This new, sixth, edition has an emphasis on Chinese art history, not as an assemblage of related topics, but as a continuous story. . . . [I]t reflects the latest archaeological discoveries, as well as giving increased attention to modern and contemporary art and to calligraphy throughout China's history." (Publisher's note)

Bailey, Gauvin Alexander

Art in time; a world history of styles and movements. Gauvin Alexander Bailey [and twenty four others] Phaidon Press 2014 367 p. illustrations (chiefly color) $69.95   **709**
    1. Art 2. Art -- History 3. Art movements
    ISBN 0714867373; 9780714867373
                                   LC 2014466680
This book, by Gauvin Alexander Bailey and others, "is the first book to embed art movements within the larger context of politics and history. Global in scope and featuring an innovative present□to□past arrangement, the book's accessible text looks back on the most significant art styles and movements, from the present day to antiquity." (Publisher's note)
"Regardless, this is an ambitious attempt to rethink the survey in

light of contemporary art's global turn and a valuable addition to any library." LJ

Beckett, Wendy

Sister Wendy's American collection; {by} Sister Wendy Beckett. HarperCollins Pubs. 2000 288p il $40   **709**
    1. Art appreciation 2. Art -- History
    ISBN 0-06-019556-8
                                   LC 00-40953
The author provides a "discussion of works in six of America's renowned art museums. . . . {She} includes a variety of media-- paintings, sculpture, decorative arts, armor, and other art objects-- and the individual works originate from a dizzying array of time periods and several countries." Libr J

Craven, Wayne

American art; history and culture. McGraw-Hill 2003 687p il pa $69   **709**
    1. American art
    ISBN 978-0-07-282329-5; 0-07-282329-1
                                   LC 2002-035777
    First published 1994
The author "establishes seven main stylistic periods—colonial, Federal, romantic, the American Renaissance, early modern, postwar modern, and postmodern—and then goes into great detail within each section, profiling individual artists and discussing the effects of various social, political, and technological changes on aesthetics and the role of art in daily life. . . . Coverage of American photography and twentieth-century art are particularly dynamic, but his examples and emphases prove to be insightful and creative throughout." Booklist
    Includes bibliographical references

Cuba: art and history, from 1868 to today; [edited by Nathalie Bondil; translation, Timothy Bernard et al.] Montreal Museum of Fine Arts 2008 424p il map $85   **709**
    1. Cuban art
    ISBN 3-7913-4019-0; 978-3-7913-4019-7
                                   LC 2008-396997
"This momentous, dazzling volume interweaves history, biography, and artistic expression to explicate Cuba's distinctive vibrancy and glorious creativity." Booklist
    Includes bibliographical references

Dippie, Brian W.

The **Frederic** Remington Art Museum collection. Abrams 2000 264p il $49.50   **709**
    1. Artists 2. Painters 3. Sculptors 4. West (U.S.) in art 5. Drafters
    ISBN 0-8109-6711-1
                                   LC 00-49339
This biography examines the artist's life and work and follows his evolution from illustrator to artist
"Photographs and comparative images enhance the author's discussions of Remington himself and of the individual paintings, drawings, and sculptures." Libr J
    Includes bibliographical references

Encyclopedia of Latin American & Caribbean art; edited by Jane Turner. Oxford University Press 2006 803p il (Grove library of world art) $250   **709**
    1. Reference books 2. Caribbean art -- Encyclopedias 3. Latin American art -- Encyclopedias
    ISBN 978-0-19-531075-7; 0-19-531075-6

First published 1999 by Grove's Dictionaries

"This work covers the art of every country in Central and South America and the Caribbean, from the colonial period to the present. The entries, expanded and updated from the publisher's mammoth Dictionary of Art, cover countries, artists, and artistic styles, with cross-referencing where appropriate." Libr J [review of 1999 edition]

Includes bibliographical references

Farrington, Lisa E.

Creating their own image; the history of African-American women artists. Oxford University Press 2005 354p il $55 **709**

    1. Women artists 2. African American women 3. African American artists

    ISBN 0-19-516721-X

                                    LC 2003-66171

"A richly detailed yet fluent work of trailblazing research, fresh interpretations, and cogent argument, Farrington's treatise discusses vital aesthetic as well as social and cultural issues and creates a vibrant context for such seminal artists as Augusta Savage, Faith Ringgold, Barbara Chase-Riboud, Kara Walker, and many more." Booklist

FitzGerald, Michael C.

  ★ **Picasso** and American art; [by] Michael FitzGerald; with a chronology by Julia May Boddewyn. Whitney Museum of American Art; in association with Yale University Press 2006 400p il $65 **709**

    1. Artists 2. Painters 3. American art

    ISBN 9780300114522; 0-300-11452-4

                                    LC 2006-1402

A "study of Picasso's influence on some of the most significant American artists of the 20th century. Fitzgerald moves chronologically, from the earliest Americans who engaged cubism in the teens (Max Weber, Mardsen Hartley, Man Ray, Stuart Davis), through the modernist investigations of Arshile Gorky, Willem De Kooning and Jackson Pollack, and winds up with Roy Lichtenstien's pop-art and Jasper Johns' postmodern responses to Picasso. Fitzgerald takes great pains to triangulate exhibition specifics with the work and words of each artist to document the precise nature and extent of the influence in each case. . . . There is a generous supply of images presented with the text, and they are as successful as Fitzgerald's prose in illuminating the complexities of Picasso's influence on these artists." Publ Wkly

Includes bibliographical references

Gnann, Achim

  ★ **Raphael**; Achim Gnann. University of Chicago Press 2018 448 p. $55 **709**

    1. Painters

    ISBN 3777428590; 9783777428598

This book, by Achim Gnann, focuses on Italian painter Raphael's "drawings and paintings, bringing together more than one hundred and fifty of his works, representing all his major projects in those forms and offering an overview of the various periods of his career, from his early years in Umbria through his move to Florence and on to Rome. . . . The book details his design methods, as well as his process of preparing canvas or panel paintings and frescoes." (Publisher's note)

"The inclusion of exquisite reproductions of the paintings with their preliminary drawings allows for a rich, satisfying experience." Choice Reviews

Gombrich, E. H.

  ★ The **story** of art; 16th ed rev and expanded; Phaidon Press 1995 688p il $49.95; pa $29.95 **709**

    1. Art -- History

    ISBN 0-7148-3355-X; 0-7148-3247-2 pa

                                   LC 96-140698

First published 1950

This survey of art examines artistic achievements in historical context to consider how prevailing social, political, and economic factors may have influenced the succession and popularity of certain artistic styles.

Includes bibliographical references

Gompertz, Will

  What Are You Looking at? the Surprising, Shocking & Sometimes Strange Story of 150 Years of Modern Art. Will Gompertz. Dutton 2012 432 p. (hardcover) $28.95 **709**

    1. Art -- 20th century 2. Art -- 21st century

    ISBN 0525952675; 9780525952671

                                    LC 2012027995

It was author Will "Gompertz's aim . . . to demystify modern art, to provide a basic history of each of its 'isms,' and show how these movements are interconnected." He "begins with [Marcel] Duchamp's omnipresent influence on the history of modern art and then chronicles movements that led up to and followed Duchamp's Fountain (1917), from pre-Impressionist artists Manet and Courbet to contemporary artists Banksy and Ai Weiwei." (Publishers Weekly)

The **Grove** encyclopedia of American art; editor in chief, Joan Marter. Oxford University Press 2011 5 v. ill. (some col.), map **709**

    1. American art -- Encyclopedias

    ISBN 9780195335798; 0199739269; 9780199739264; 0195335791

                                    LC 2010030274

This reference book "contains entries . . . that comprise a . . . survey . . . art history. It covers American painting, architecture, sculpture, and photography from the Pre-Columbian sources to the colonial period to the twenty-first century devoting coverage to many previously underrepresented areas of inquiry, including African American artists, Asian American artists, and Native American art, both historical and contemporary. Artists, major movements, institutions, critics, and the architecture found in major cities of the United States are covered, as are new media and methodologies, including digital art, performance art, and installation art. In addition to American artists such as John Singer Sargent, Robert Rauschenberg, Maya Lin, and Kiki Smith, attention is also paid to individuals who have had a significant impact on American art and art history through their activity in the United States, including Marcel Duchamp, Erwin Panofsky, Renzo Piano, and Max Beckmann." (Publisher's note)

Includes bibliographical references and index.

Harvey, Eleanor Jones

  The **Civil** War and American art; Eleanor Jones Harvey. Smithsonian American Art Museum 2012 xvii, 316 p.p ill. (hardcover) $65 **709**

    1. American art 2. Art collections 3. United States -- History -- 1861-1865, Civil War -- Pictorial works 4. Art, American -- 19th century -- Themes, motives -- Exhibitions 5. Art and society -- United States -- History -- 19th century -- Exhibitions 6. United States -- History -- Civil War, 1861-1865 -- Art and the war -- Exhibitions

    ISBN 0300187335; 9780300187335; 9780937311981

                                    LC 2012029342

This book, by Eleanor Jones Harvey and released by the Smithsonian American Art Museum, "looks at the range of artwork created before, during, and following the [U.S. Civil War], in the years between 1852 and 1877. [The] author . . . surveys paintings made by some of America's finest artists, including Frederic Church, Sanford Gifford, Winslow Homer, and Eastman Johnson, and photographs taken by George Barnard, Alexander Gardner, and Timothy H. O'Sullivan." (Publisher's note)

Includes bibliographical references (pages 274-293) and index.

Hauptman, Jodi

Degas; A Strange New Beauty. Jodi Hauptman ; with essays by Carol Armstrong [and 11 others] The Museum of Modern Art 2016 239 p. illustrations (chiefly color) $50   **709**
1. Engraving 2. Monotype (Engraving) -- 19th century -- Exhibitions
ISBN 1633450058; 9781633450059

LC 2015960601

This book, by Jody Hauptman, focuses on Edgar Degas. "Degas was introduced to the monotype process, a technique in which the artist draws in ink on a metal plate that is then run through a press, typically resulting in a single print. Degas embraced the medium with enormous enthusiasm, inventing a new repertoire of mark-making that included wiping, scraping, scratching, fingerprinting and rendering via removal." (Publisher's note)

"Each chapter, authored by a Degas specialist, includes helpful endnotes. A catalog of the exhibition and over 176 images are also included." LJ

Includes bibliographical references (pages 236-238)

Hughes, Robert

American visions; the epic history of art in America. Knopf 1997 635p il $65; pa $39.95   **709**
1. American art
ISBN 0-679-42627-2; 0-375-70365-9 pa

LC 96-45111

"Hughes has orchestrated a spectacular integration of facts, observations, and insights in this ambitious, lively, and gloriously illustrated volume." Booklist

Includes bibliographical references

Janson, H. W.

★ Janson's history of art; the western tradition. Penelope J.E. Davies ... [et. al] 8th ed.; Prentice Hall 2011 xxxi, 1152p il map $170.40   **709**
1. Art -- History
ISBN 978-0-205-68517-2; 0-205-68517-X

LC 2009-22617

First published 1962 by Abrams with title: History of art

A history of art from prehistoric cave paintings to video art. While the focus is primarily on Western art, brief discussions of Oriental, Near Eastern, Islamic, African and Latin American arts are included.

Includes bibliographical references

Johnson, Paul

★ Art ; a new history. HarperCollins Pubs. 2003 777p il $39.95   **709**
1. Art -- History
ISBN 0-06-053075-8

"While {Johnson's} narrative is for the most part a conventional journey through the canon, his headlong pace, quirky views and pungent prose make it anything but dull." Publ Wkly

Kettenmann, Andrea

Frida Kahlo; 1907-1954; Pain and Passion. by Andrea Kettenmann. Taschen America Llc 2015 96 p. $14.99   **709**
ISBN 383650085X; 9783836500852

This book, by Andrea Kettenmann, focuses on "Mexican artist Frida Kahlo. . . . Two events in her life were of crucial importance. When she was eighteen, a bus accident put her in hospital for a year with a smashed spinal column and fractured pelvis. It was in her sick bed that she first started to paint. Then, aged twenty-one, she married the world-famous Mexican mural artist Diego Rivera." (Publisher's note)

Khalili, Nasser D.

Islamic art and culture; a visual history. Overlook Press 2006 186p il $60   **709**
1. Islamic art 2. Islamic civilization
ISBN 1-58567-839-2; 978-1-58567-839-6

This "visual history of Islamic art introduces readers to the diverse peoples, cultures, and styles making up Islam today. Spanning 12 centuries and covering everything from miniature painting to architecture, it shows, e.g., various Qur'ans, coins, armor, and scientific instruments. . . . This is an excellent introduction to the subject that combines aptly chosen and beautifully reproduced photographs with a concise and informative text." Libr J

Includes bibliographical references

King, Ross

Art ; over 2,500 works from cave to contemporary; foreword by Ross King. DK Pub. 2008 612p il $50   **709**
1. Reference books 2. Art appreciation 3. Art -- History
ISBN 978-0-7566-3972-3; 0-7566-3972-7

LC 2008-301471

Within each time period, provides examples of significant works in painting, sculpture, drawing and other media. Highlights themes that were important at various times such as nudes, landscape, still life, and love. Includes brief biographies of some artists and a "closer look" in depth for the most significant works.

"Easy to read and use, . . . both newcomers to art and art connoisseurs will enjoy this picturesque work." Libr J

Includes glossary

Klein, Stefan

Leonardo's legacy; how Da Vinci reimagined the world. translated by Shelley Frisch. Da Capo Press 2010 291p il $26   **709**
1. Artists 2. Painters 3. Inventors 4. Scientists 5. Artists, Italian 6. Writers on science
ISBN 978-0-306-81825-7; 0-306-81825-6

LC 2010-00130

Original German edition, 2008

The author "makes a compelling case that DaVinci's ability to trigger an empathetic physical response in the viewer lay in his scientific acumen: the asymmetry of the Mona Lisa's smile, for instance, deliberately reflects the asymmetry of the human brain. While Leonardo is remembered primarily as an artist, his accomplishments as a scientist were at least as important. . . . Including a detailed chronology of the artist's life, this makes an illuminating new look at Leonardo's unique genius." Publ Wkly

Includes bibliographical references

Kleiner, Fred S.

★ Gardner's Art Through the Ages; a global history. Fred S. Kleiner. 15th edition Wadsworth 2015 2v illustrations Vol

2 $173.95; Vol 1 $173.95 **709**
1. Art -- History
ISBN 9781285839394; 9781285837840

"Easy to read and understand, the 15th edition of the most widely read art history book in the English language continues to evolve, providing a rich cultural backdrop for each of the covered periods and geographical locations, and incorporating new artists and art forms -- all reproduced according to the highest standards of clarity and color fidelity." (Publisher's note)

Langdon, Helen
Caravaggio; a life. Westview Press 2000 436p il map pa $22 **709**
1. Artists 2. Painters 3. Artists, Italian
ISBN 0-8133-3794-1; 978-0-8133-3794-4
First published 1998 in the United Kingdom

In this study of the Renaissance painter, "Langdon's masterly achievement is to integrate Caravaggio's art and life in a convincing and vividly delineated recreation of his world." Libr J
Includes bibliographical references

Little, Stephen
. . . **isms**: understanding art. Universe 2004 159p il pa $16.95 **709**
1. Art -- History
ISBN 0-7893-1209-3
LC 2004-94996

The author "identifies four types of isms: trends specific to the visual arts (perspectivism), broad cultural trends (romanticism), artist-defined movements (cubism), and retrospectively named movements (mannerism). He then moves forward chronologically, deftly defining more than 50 isms, naming key artists, and showcasing splendid examples." Booklist

Lottman, Herbert R.
Man Ray's Montparnasse. Abrams 2001 261p il $29.95 **709**
1. Artists 2. Painters 3. Photographers 4. Paris (France) -- Intellectual life
ISBN 0-8109-4333-6
LC 2001-633

Lottman presents a "snapshot of Man Ray between the two world wars, emphasizing the 1920s, with the developing Montparnasse section of Paris as the backdrop. Here are the cutting-edge dadaists and surrealists flanking Man Ray and his unerring camera eye, along with poets and artists, collectors, lovers, and other assorted characters. . . . Lottman's vivid exploration of 20th-century art events will serve the art historian and student of Paris very well in documenting an essential epoch and place." Libr J
Includes bibliographical references and index

Marin, Cheech
Chicano visions; American painters on the verge. essays by Max Benavidez, Constance Cortez, Tere Tomo. Little, Brown 2002 160p il $35; pa $19.95 **709**
1. American painting 2. Mexican Americans
ISBN 0-8212-2805-6; 0-8212-2806-4 pa
LC 2002-104645

"Marin's extraordinary collection forms the foundation for this exciting and invaluable showcase . . . {which includes works by} John Valadez, Gronk, Diane Gamboa, Patssi Valdez, Adan Hernandez, and Carlos Almaraz." Booklist

Includes bibliographical references

Muller, Melissa, 1967-
Lost lives, lost art; Jewish collectors, Nazi art theft, and the quest for justice. [by] Melissa Muller [and] Monika Tatzkow; with contributions from Thomas Blubacher and Gunnar Schnabel; foreword by Ronald S. Lauder. Vendome Press 2010 248p il $40 **709**
1. Art thefts 2. Jews -- Europe 3. Art -- Collectors and collecting 4. World War, 1939-1945 -- Destruction and pillage
ISBN 9780865652637
LC 2010-15337

The authors "cover 15 Jewish/possibly Jewish families with vast art collections looted by the Nazis. Jewish collectors either had to sell their treasures for a pittance or had them seized. The Bloch-Bauer family's story is famous, but the unknown histories of other prominent families are compellingly told here, and there is a final historical-legal commentary by expert Gunnar Schnabel on Nazi-looted art and the German laws that perpetuated these crimes. . . . Richly illustrated with excellent art reproductions and family photographs." Libr J

Nuland, Sherwin B.
Leonardo da Vinci. Viking 2000 170p il (Penguin lives series) pa $13 **709**
1. Artists 2. Painters 3. Scientists 4. Artists, Italian 5. Writers on science
ISBN 0-670-89391-9; 978-0-14-303510-7 pa; 0-14-303510-X pa
LC 00-32061

"Nuland . . . elegantly sketches Leonardo's life of constant employment by noblemen eager to enjoy the prestige he reflected on them and of even more constant curiosity, which drove him to become the greatest anatomist before Vasari. . . . A scintillating addition." Booklist

O'Riley, Michael Kampen
Art beyond the West; Michael Kampen O'Riley. 3rd edition Pearson 2012 367 p illustrations $171.07 **709**
1. Art
ISBN 9780205887897

"In this major survey of the arts of Africa, Western and Central Asia, India, Southeast Asia, China, Korea, Japan, the Pacific, and the Americas, author Michael Kampen-O'Riley presents the vast range of arts that lie outside of the Western tradition. Within a predominantly geographic and chronological framework, he explores the arts of these areas from pre-history to present day. The first dedicated survey of 'non-Western' art, Art Beyond the West is amply illustrated and accessibly written." (Publisher's note)

Paquet, Marcel, 1947-2014
Magritte; by Marcel Paquet. Taschen America Llc 2015 96 p. $14.99 **709**
ISBN 3836503573; 9783836503570

This book, by Marcel Paquet, focuses on "the influence of René Magritte. . . . His surrealistic painting turns the usual order of things ironically on its head, thus restoring mystery to a world that has lost its magic." (Publisher's note)
Contains biographical information

Petropoulos, Jonathan
The **Faustian** bargain; the art world in Nazi Germany. Oxford Univ. Press 2000 395p il $42.50 **709**
1. Art thefts 2. National socialism 3. World War, 1939-1945 -- Destruction and pillage

ISBN 0-19-512964-4

LC 99-33372

"Spotlighting five groups--art museum directors, art dealers, art journalists, art historians, and artists--Petropoulos . . . details how each of these groups either directly or indirectly facilitated the theft of countless works of art and legitimized the Nazi regime." Libr J

Includes bibliographical references (p. 281-376) and index

Robert Rauschenberg; Leah Dickerman, Achim Borchardt-Hume ; with contributions from Yve-Alain Bois [and 14 others] Museum of Modern Art 2016 412 p. illustrations (some color) (hardcover) $75 **709**

1. American art 2. Painters -- United States 3. Art, Modern -- 20th century -- Exhibitions 4. Art, American -- 20th century -- Exhibitions

ISBN 9781633450202; 9781633450219; 1633450201

LC 2016952038

This book edited by Leah Dickerman and Achim Borchardt-Hume "offers fresh perspectives on [Robert] Rauschenberg's widely celebrated 'Combines' (1954–64) and silkscreen paintings (1962–64). It also illuminates lesser-known periods within Rauschenberg's career, including his work of the early 1950s and that from the late 1960s onward. Sixteen short essays by eminent scholars and emerging new writers focus on specific moments within Rauschenberg's career." (Publisher's note)

"Lavishly illustrated, this is a sumptuously and beautifully produced catalogue of an artist who managed to speak to real-world issues by appropriating the overlooked detritus of everyday life." Pub Wkly

Includes bibliographical references and index.

Robinson, Roxana

Georgia O'Keeffe: a life. University Press of New England 1999 639p il pa $22.95 **709**

1. Artists 2. Painters

ISBN 0-87451-906-3

LC 98-30944

A reissue of the title first published 1989 by Harper & Row

"This biography, the first to draw on sources unavailable during O'Keeffe's lifetime—and the first to be granted her family's cooperation—offers a persuasive feminist analysis of the life and work of an iconic figure in American art. . . . [The author's] detailed, sensitive critique of O'Keeffe's work . . . alternates with an absorbing, intimate narrative of O'Keeffe's personal life." Publ Wkly

Includes bibliographical references

Schama, Simon

The **power** of art. Ecco 2006 448p il $50 **709**

1. Art -- History

ISBN 0-06-117610-9; 978-0-06-117610-4

LC 2007-270937

The author "presents eight remarkable artists who created their masterworks against a backdrop of personal and professional distress. From politically charged commentaries (David, Picasso, Turner and Rembrandt) to intensely personal visions of the world (van Gogh and Rothko) and the reinvention of the divine (Bernini and Caravaggio), Schama takes these masters' hallowed works off the museum wall and drags them through the mud and muck that went into their creation." Publ Wkly

Includes bibliographical references

Shackelford, George T. M.

Monet; the early years. George T. M. Shackelford. Yale University Press 2016 206 p. illustrations (hardcover; alk. paper) $50 **709**

1. Painters -- France -- Biography

ISBN 0300221851; 9780300221855

LC 2016951792

Author George T.M. Shackelford presents this "comprehensive examination of the painter's formative years, tracing the evolution of [Claude] Monet's early style and personal ambitions that drove the rest of his career. it features essays by distinguished scholars, focusing on the evolution of Monet's own distinctive mode of painting." (Publisher's note)

"It offers a fresh, coherent reassessment of Monet's early career (1858–72) before he participated in impressionistic exhibitions." Choice

Spring, Chris

South Africa; the art of a nation. John Giblin, Christopher Spring. Thames & Hudson / The British Museum 2016 255 p. illustrations (chiefly color) (hardcover) $55 **709**

1. Art and history 2. Art -- South Africa 3. South Africa -- History 4. Art, South African -- Exhibitions 5. South Africa -- Antiquities -- Exhibitions

ISBN 9780500519066

LC 2016931258

This book, by John Giblin and Chris Spring, offers "a unique insight into South Africa's history, from iconic pre-colonial artifacts to the country's vibrant contemporary art scene. . . . [It] explores this relationship between past and present, showing contemporary and historic art objects alongside each other, bearing witness to the important events in South Africa's history." (Publisher's note)

"Students and instructors looking for a well-written survey on South African art will enjoy this lavishly illustrated text, published in conjunction with the British Museum's exhibition of the same title." Choice

Includes bibliographical references (pages 238-239) and index.

Strickland, Carol

The **annotated** Mona Lisa; a crash course in art history from prehistoric to post-modern. Carol Strickland. 3rd edition Andrews McMeel Pub. 2018 222 p illustrations paperback $29.99 **709**

1. Art -- History

ISBN 9781449482138

Presents the history of art from prehistoric times to the present day, describing major artists and movements and detailing the influence of art on society through the ages.

Thompson, Erin L.

Possession; the curious history of private collectors from Antiquity to the present. Erin L. Thompson. Yale University Press 2016 224 p. illustrations $30 **709**

1. Classical antiquities 2. Collectors and collecting

ISBN 0300208529; 9780300208528

LC 2015954819

This book, by Erin L. Thompson, "shows how collecting antiquities has been a way of creating identity, informed by a desire to annex the past while providing an illicit thrill along the way. Thompson's accounts of history's most infamous collectors—from the Roman Emperor Tiberius, . . . to Queen Christina of Sweden, . . . to Sir William Hamilton . . . are as mesmerizing as they are revealing." (Publisher's note)

Includes bibliographical references (pages 183-211) and index.

Visona, Monica Blackmun

A **history** of art in Africa; [by] Monica Blackmun Visona, Robin Poynor, Herbert M. Cole; with contributions by Suzanne Preston Blier (introduction), Rowland Abiodun (preface) and

Michael D. Harris (chapter 16) 2nd ed; Pearson/Prentice Hall 2007 560p il pa $111 **709**

   1. African art

   ISBN 978-0-13-612872-4; 0-13-612872-6

                         LC 2007-15831

  First published 2000

  "Treating the subject from an art historical rather than an anthropological perspective, this groundbreaking book is organized geographically to cover the entire continent. Each of the five regional sections focuses on selected major art traditions. . . . Accompanying the text are over 700 photos and scores of maps, plans, drawings, etc." Libr J [review of 2000 edition]

  Includes bibliographical references (p. 544-551)

709.04　20th century, 1900-1999

★ **Art** deco 1910-1939; edited by Charlotte Benton, Tim Benton, and Ghislaine Wood. Bulfinch Press 2003 464p il $65 **709.04**

   1. Art deco

   ISBN 0-8212-2834-X

                       LC 2002-113762

  This exhibition catalog includes 40 essays about the Art Deco movement and its sources and expression throughout the world in such fields as architecture, ceramics, fashion, jewelry, graphic design, metalwork, glasswork, and film

  Includes bibliographical references

Barnes, Julian, 1946-

Keeping an eye open; essays on art. Julian Barnes. Alfred A. Knopf 2015 288 p. color illustrations (hardback) $30 **709.04**

   1. Art -- History 2. Art -- 20th century 3. Art, Modern -- 19th century 4. Art, Modern -- 20th century

   ISBN 9781101873373; 9781101874783; 9781101874790

                       LC 2015014317

  In this collection of essays, author Julian Barnes notes that "Flaubert believed that it was impossible to explain one art form in terms of another, and that great paintings required no words of explanation. Braque thought the ideal state would be reached when we said nothing at all in front of a painting. . . . The seventeen essays gathered here help trace the arc from Romanticism to Realism and into Modernism." (Publisher's note)

  "Barnes knows that one of the immeasurable pleasures of art is its capacity to approach us from unexpected angles and excite our senses of wonder. The same may be said of his scholarly and astute yet accessible and exciting essays." Kirkus

  Includes bibliographical references.

Chadwick, Whitney

★ **Farewell** to the muse; love, war and the women of surrealism. Whitney Chadwick. Thames & Hudson 2017 256 p. $35 **709.04**

   1. Surrealism -- History 2. World War, 1939-1945 -- Art and the war 3. Women artists -- History -- 20th century

   ISBN 0500239681; 9780500239681

  This book, by Whitney Chadwick, "charts five female friendships among the Surrealists to show how Surrealism, female friendship, and the experiences of war, loss, and trauma shaped individual women's transitions from someone else's muse to mature artists in their own right. Her vivid account includes the fascinating story of Claude Cahun and

Suzanne Malherbe in occupied Jersey, as well as the experiences of Lee Miller and Valentine Penrose at the front line." (Publisher's note)

  Includes bibliographical references (pages 242-247) and index.

Cooke, Lynne

Outliers and American vanguard art; Lynne Cooke. National Gallery of Art"||"University of Chicago Press 2018 xv, 396 p.p $65 **709.04**

   1. American art -- 19th century -- Exhibitions 2. American art -- 20th century -- Exhibitions 3. Outsider art -- United States -- Exhibitions 4. Folk art -- United States -- Exhibitions 5. Art, American -- 20th century -- Exhibitions 6. Art, American -- 21st century -- Exhibitions 7. Modernism (Art) -- United States -- Exhibitions 8. Folk art -- United States -- Influence -- Exhibitions 9. Outsider art -- United States -- Influence -- Exhibitions 10. Art and society -- United States -- History -- 20th century -- Exhibitions 11. Art and society -- United States -- History -- 21st century -- Exhibitions

   ISBN 022652227X; 0894684108; 9780226522272; 9780894684104

                       LC 2017035749

  This companion catalog, by Lynne Cooke, "offers a fantastic opportunity to consider works by schooled and self-taught creators in relation to each other and defined by historical circumstance. The art works in [this catalog] come from three distinct periods when the intersections between mainstream and outlier artists were most dynamic and productive, ushering in exhibitions of art based on various degrees of co-existence, inclusion, and assimilation." (Publisher's note)

  "Accessible for most readers without extensive art history backgrounds, and for those looking to expand their understanding of American art and artists creating from the margins." Library Journal

  Includes bibliographical references and index

Dempsey, Amy

Art in the modern era; a guide to styles, schools & movements 1860 to the present. Abrams 2002 304p il $55 **709.04**

   1. Reference books 2. Modern art -- Encyclopedias 3. Art -- 20th century -- Encyclopedias

   ISBN 0-8109-4172-4

                       LC 2001-46261

  This guide to art from 1860 to the present describes 300 schools and movements and includes a fold-out timeline

  "All major and minor movements are mentioned in this very comprehensive guide, which could easily become a standard for modern art survey courses, making it a sensible purchase for most libraries." Libr J

  Includes bibliographical references

Dickerman, Leah

★ **Dada**; Zurich, Berlin, Hannover, Cologne, New York, Paris. with essays by Brigid Doherty [et al.] National Gallery of Art in association with Distributed Art Publishers 2005 519p il $65 **709.04**

   1. Dadaism

   ISBN 1-933045-20-5

                       LC 2005-17984

  "Seven scholars and curators contribute essays that examine each of the various Dada centers in turn. . . . Each essay examines key locations (e.g., the Cabaret Voltaire), individuals, publications (including Merz magazine), and inventions (such as ready-mades and photomontage.) . . . Its comprehensive scholarship and color illustrations of many rarely seen works make this book essential for all art collections." Choice

  Includes bibliographical references

Homburg, Cornelia

Neo-impressionism and the dream of realities; painting, poetry, music. Cornelia Homburg, Paul Smith, Laura D. Corey. Yale University Press 2015 191 p. illustrations; portraits (cloth; alk. paper) $60 **709.04**

1. Impressionism (Art) 2. Symbolism in literature
ISBN 0300190832; 9780300190830

LC 2014937873

This book, by Cornelia Homburg, Paul Smith, and Laura D. Corey, "explores the creative exchange between Neo-Impressionist painters and Symbolist writers and composers in the late 1880s and early 1890s. Symbolism, with its emphasis on subjectivity, dream worlds, and spirituality, has often been considered at odds with Neo-Impressionism's approach to portraying color and light. This book repositions the relationship between these movements." (Publisher's note)

"All in all, this is a superb and much-needed assessment. Profusely and well illustrated." Choice

Ingram, Brett

★ The **secret** world of Renaldo Kuhler; Brett Ingram. Blast Books 2017 251 p. (alk. paper) $45 **709.04**

1. Outsider art -- United States
ISBN 9780922233489

LC 2017022797

This book, by Brett Ingram, "collects over 400 of [Renaldo] Kuhler's drawings chronicling the rich and tumultuous history of the fictional nation of Rocaterrania, a place Kuhler first dreamed up in his teens and developed throughout his life. . . . The book includes his extensive notes on the nation's official language, Rocaterranski, complete with its own alphabet and idioms." (Publishers Weekly)

Livingstone, Marco

Pop art; a continuing history. 2nd ed. Thames & Hudson 2000 272p il $29.95 **709.04**

1. Pop art
ISBN 978-0-500-28240-3; 0-500-28240-4

LC 00-100788

First published 1991 in the United Kingdom

With 300 color plates this volume chronicles the work of 130 artists of the Pop Art movement, including Jasper Johns, Robert Rauschenberg, Andy Warhol, and Roy Lichtenstein.

"Recommended as the best single historical survey on Pop Art." Libr J

Mansfield, Elizabeth

★ **History** of modern art; painting, sculpture, architecture, photography. H.H. Arnason, Elizabeth C. Mansfield, National Humanities Centre. 7th edition Pearson 2012 816 p illustrations $176.40 **709.04**

1. Modern art
ISBN 9780205259472
First published 1969

This book "is a visual comprehensive overview of the modern art field. It traces the trends and influences in painting, sculpture, photography and architecture from the mid-nineteenth century to the present day. The seventh edition deepens its discussions on social conditions that have affected the production and reception of modern and contemporary art." (Publisher's note)

Morris, Desmond

The **lives** of the surrealists; Desmond Morris. Thames & Hudson 2018 272 p. $39.95 **709.04**

1. Surrealism 2. Art -- History 3. Art -- Philosophy
ISBN 9780500021361

LC 2017945552

This book, by Desmond Morris, explores the "life histories of the Surrealists, known and unknown. . . . Surrealism did not begin as an art movement but as a philosophical strategy, a way of life, and a rebellion against the establishment that gave rise to the First World War. In [this book], . . . Morris concentrates on the artists as people--as remarkable individuals. What were their personalities, their predilections, their character strengths and flaws?" (Publisher's note)

Salle, David, 1952-

How to see; Looking, Talking, and Thinking about Art. David Salle. W W Norton & Co Inc 2016 256 p. (ebook) $50; (hardcover) $29.95 **709.04**

1. Art appreciation 2. Art, Modern -- 20th century 3. Art, Modern -- 21st century
ISBN 9780393248142; 9780393248135

LC 2016025215

This book, by David Salle, is a "master class in contemporary art. . . . Engaging with a wide range of Salle's friends and contemporaries—from painters to conceptual artists such as Jeff Koons, John Baldessari, Roy Lichtenstein, and Alex Katz, among others—[this book] explores not only the multilayered personalities of the artists themselves but also the distinctive character of their oeuvres." (Publisher's note)

"Sharp insights and an affable tone make this collection equivalent to a hearty discussion with a mentor—recommended for anyone interested in visual arts." Pub Wkly

709.1 Areas, regions, places in general

O'Kane, Bernard

★ **Treasures** of Islam; artistic glories of the Muslim world. Duncan Baird; Distributed in the USA by Sterling Pub. 2007 224p il map $35 **709.1**

1. Islamic art 2. Islamic civilization
ISBN 978-1-84483-483-9; 1-84483-483-2

The author "combines an overview of Islamic art and architecture with a cursory history of Islam's empires and dynasties. Beginning with a brief discussion of the earliest mosque from the seventh century, and showing how Islamic architects created a distinctive artistic tradition, O'Kane . . . follows architectural and artistic ideas to the 19th century. . . . The wealth of glorious full-color illustrations make this beautifully designed book an excellent introduction to the art of Islam." Publ Wkly

Includes bibliographical references

709.2 Biography

Henri Matisse; the cut-outs. edited by Karl Buchberg, Nicholas Cullinan, Jodi Hauptman, and Nicholas Serota. The Museum Of Modern Art 2014 298 p. illustrations (chiefly color) $60 **709.2**

1. Artists 2. Paper crafts
ISBN 0870709151; 0870709488; 9780870709159; 9780870709487

LC 2014934445

This book, edited by Karl Buchberg, Jodi Hauptman, and Nicholas Cullinan, "presents approximately 150 works in a groundbreaking reassessment of the . . . [Henri Matisse's] colorful and innovative final years. From the late 1940s on, Henri Matisse (1869-1954) worked almost exclusively with paper and scissors, cutting painted sheets into various shapes and sizes and arranging them into lively compositions, striking for their chromatic harmonies and economy of means." (Publisher's note)

"The beautifully produced catalog of this exhibition includes essays that explore Matisse's innovative process, brought to life by photographs of the artist with his assistants at work in his studio as well as a generous and representative selection of high-quality color reproductions of significant milestones from a decade of cut-out projects. Essential for art studio, history, and conservation collections. Summing Up: Essential. All readership levels." Choice

Includes bibliographical references and index

Hirst, Michael

Michelangelo; v1 Michael Hirst. Yale University Press 2011 x, 438 p.p v1 ill. (some col.) $40.00   **709.2**

1. Poets 2. Italian art 3. Mural painting and decoration 4. Artists 5. Painters 6. Sculptors 7. Architects 8. Biography, Individual
ISBN 0300118619; 9780300118612

LC 2011042294

In this book, author Michael Hirst presents a biography of Michelangelo, following "the artist from his apprenticeship in Ghirlandaio's workshop to his final move to Rome in 1534, when, at the age of 59, he left behind his native Florence, never to return. During these years he created such outstanding works as the marble 'Pietà,' the giant marble 'David,' commissioned for the cathedral in Florence, the Sistine Ceiling frescoes, and the new sacristy and library for the Medici family at San Lorenzo." (Publisher's note)

Includes bibliographical references (p. [378]-415) and index

Rothkopf, Scott

Jeff Koons; a retrospective. Scott Rothkopf. Whitney Museum of American Art 2014 303 p. illustrations (mostly color) (hb) $65   **709.2**

1. Artists
ISBN 0300195877; 9780300195873

LC 2014003418

Author "Scott Rothkopf carefully examines the evolution of [Jeff] Koons' work and his development over the past thirty-five years, offering a fresh scholarly perspective on the artist's multi-faceted career. In addition, short essays by a wide range of interdisciplinary contributors--from academics to novelists--probe provocative topics such as celebrity and media, markets and money, and technology and fabrication." (Publisher's note)

Includes bibliographical references (pages 253-271) and index

Rowland, Ingrid

The **collector** of lives; Giorgio Vasari and the invention of art. by Ingrid Rowland and Noah Charney. W. W. Norton & Company 2017 viii, 420 p.p color illustrations (hardcover) $29.95   **709.2**

1. Artists, Italian 2. Renaissance -- Italy 3. Artists -- Italy -- Biography 4. Biographers -- Italy -- Biography
ISBN 9780393248395; 9780393241310; 0393241319

LC 2017026667

This biography, by Ingrid Rowland and Noah Charney, "reveals how a Renaissance scholar reshaped the visual world. Giorgio Vasari (1511-1574) was a man of many talents--a sculptor, painter, architect, writer, and scholar--but he is best known for Lives of the Artists, the classic account that singlehandedly invented the genre of artistic biography and established the canon of Italian Renaissance art." (Publisher's note)

"Rowland and Charney do more than deliver a richly detailed life of this singular Renaissance figure. They raise intriguing questions about

how tastes and standards develop." Kirkus

Includes bibliographical references and index.

709.3   Specific continents, countries, localities

Robins, Gay

The **art** of ancient Egypt; Rev ed; Harvard University Press 2008 271p il map pa $27.95   **709.3**

1. Egyptian art 2. Egypt -- Antiquities
ISBN 978-0-674-03065-7; 0-674-03065-6

LC 2008-4264

First published 1997

"The first chapter orients the reader in the cultural, technical, and iconographic contexts needed to explore the evolution of the Egyptian artistic tradition in subsequent chapters. Beginning with the predynastic origins (5000 BCE) and concluding in the Ptolemaic Period (304-30 BCE), Robins traces the development of sculpture, painting, funerary and religious art, and architecture with over 300 illustrations, many in color." Libr J [review of 1997 edition]

Includes bibliographical references (p. 256-266)

709.38   Fine arts – Greece to 323

Boardman, John

★ **Greek** art; 5th edition Thames & Hudson 2016 320 p il map (World of art)   **709.38**

1. Greek art
ISBN 9780500204337

First published 1964 by Praeger Pubs.

"First published in the early 1960s, this history of Greek art has been enlarged and rewritten. It takes into account new finds as well as new ideas and attitudes to the subject, and emphasizes that Greek art should be seen in its proper context, not that of galleries and museums. 302 illustrations, 73 in color." (Publisher's note)

"This is a classic in the field made even more readable and useful than before. Highly recommended for all collections." Libr J

709.45   Fine arts – Italy, San Marino, Vatican City, Malta

Adams, Laurie Schneider

★ **Italian** Renaissance art; Laurie Schneider Adams. Second edition Westview Press 2013 436 p $105   **709.45**

1. Italian art
ISBN 9780813349022

Presents a survey of Italian Renaissance art, focusing on the principal works of the most important and innovative artists, along with information on women artists, Mannerism, and the late Renaissance period.

709.5   Fine arts – Asia

Brougher, Kerry

Ai weiwei; according to what? Kerry Brougher, Mami Kataoka, Charles Merewether ; edited by Kerry Brougher, Mami Kataoka, Charles Merewether. Del Monico Books 2012 176 p. ill. (some col.) (hardcover) $39.95   **709.5**

1. Artists, Chinese 2. Installations (Art) -- Exhibitions
ISBN 3791352407; 9783791352404

LC 2012949559

This book features dissident Chinese artist Ai Weiwei's work, ranging from furniture, videos, and photographs to sculpture and ceramics, [and] is published in conjunction with an exhibition . . . . Curator Mami Kataoka (Mori) summarizes the artist's life . . . and influences on his work. Two short chapters follow: Charles Merewether . . . elaborates on Ai's social concerns; Kerry Brougher . . . presents an interview with the artist." (Choice)

Includes bibliographical references (p. 142-144)

709.52   Fine arts – Japan

Clark, Timothy

Hokusai; beyond the Great Wave. edited by Timothy Clark. Thames & Hudson 2017 352 p. illustrations (chiefly color) (hardcover) $61.75   **709.52**

  1. Painters 2. Painting 3. Painting, Japanese -- Edo period, 1600-1868 -- Exhibitions 4. Color prints, Japanese -- Edo period, 1600-1868 -- Exhibitions

  ISBN 0500094063; 9780500094068

LC 2016952916

This book, by Timothy Clark, presents "Hokusai's remarkable late work, incorporating fresh scholarship on the sublime paintings and prints the artist created in the last thirty years of his life. . . . Hokusai created sublime works during the last thirty years of his life. . . . This publication . . . takes a fresh approach based on innovative scholarship: thematic groupings of late works are related to the major spiritual and artistic quests of Hokusai's life." (Publisher's note)

Includes bibliographical references (pages 334-339) and index.

711   Area planning (Civic art)

McGregor, James H.

Rome from the ground up; [by] James H.S. McGregor. Belknap Press of Harvard University Press 2005 344p il map $29.95; pa $18.95   **711**

  1. Rome -- History 2. City planning -- Rome

  ISBN 0-674-01911-3; 0-674-02263-7 pa

LC 2005-48213

The author "chronologically traces the successive periods of intense architecture and planning that helped Rome achieve strategic greatness, from the Etruscan management of the Tiber Island ford 3,000 years ago, to the city's unparalleled artistic stamp by Bramante and Michelangelo during the Renaissance, to Mussolini's monumental Fascist vision, to the precarious repairs heralding the Jubilee Year of 2000. . . . Here is a walking tour in stately, inviting prose that renders wonderfully manageable a massive history lesson for the intellectually curious and adept." Publ Wkly

Includes bibliographical references

712   Landscape architecture (Landscape design)

Buchanan, Rita

Taylor's master guide to landscaping. Houghton Mifflin 2000 384p il $40   **712**

  1. Landscape gardening

  ISBN 0-618-05590-8

LC 99-54110

Companion volume to Taylor's master guide to gardening

"Buchanan offers a comprehensive treatment of landscape design, emphasizing designing with plants and including extensive information about choosing and caring for plants, trees, shrubs, vines, and ground covers. . . . A landmark work destined to become a classic." Libr J

Cox, Madison

The **Gardener's** Garden; edited by Phaidon Editors. Phaidon Inc Ltd 2014 480 p. color illustrations $79.95   **712**

  1. Gardens 2. Gardening

  ISBN 0714867470; 9780714867472

This book is "both a collection of gardens from around the world and a resource for those seeking inspiration on garden design and planting. . . . [It features] over 250 permanent gardens by leading garden designers, horticulturalists and landscape architects, from the 14th century to the present day, and covering all key types and styles of garden." (Publisher's note)

"The density of visuals displayed with relatively little text leaves the reader a lot to digest, making it difficult at times to pinpoint the intended takeaway. Readers who can explore slowly will be transported around the world into lovely, curious, and distinctly human landscapes." Pub Wkly

Graham, Wade

American Eden; from Monticello to Central Park to our backyards: what our gardens tell us about who we are. Harper 2011 459p il $35; ebook $27.99   **712**

  1. Gardens 2. Landscape architecture

  ISBN 978-0-06-158342-1; 978-0-06-207886-5 ebook

LC 2010-24940

"Graham unveils the aesthetic, political, psychological, and ethical dimensions of the American garden. . . . Graham is able to gently mock the fashions of history while astutely observing that we are still as vulnerable to gardening fads today. After more than 250 years, the American gardening tradition has bequeathed to us treasured public parks, suburban sprawl, Kentucky bluegrass lawns in the desert, and kitchen gardens at the White House. Graham's history is a fascinating and illuminating tour of this American landscape." Publ Wkly

Includes bibliographical references

Hayward, Gordon

Stone in the garden; inspiring designs and practical projects. Norton 2001 224p il $39.95   **712**

  1. Landscape gardening

  ISBN 0-393-04779-2

LC 00-69945

"The book's first half focuses on the philosophical and design considerations of stone forms as varied as walls, paths, terraces, and even benches. The second half is more practical, covering topics such as estimating the amount of stone needed for a wall, the methods of cutting and laying stone, and building pools and fountains." Libr J

Includes bibliograhical references (p.) and index

Majerus, Marianne

Garden Design; a book of ideas. Heidi Howcroft, Marianne Majerus. Firefly Books Ltd 2015 320 p. color illustrations (hardcover) $49.95   **712**

  1. Gardens 2. Garden design

  ISBN 1770855246; 9781770855243

This book, by Heidi Howcroft and Marianne Majerus, offers "takes the reader through the entire process [of garden design]: assessing the garden situation, developing a design, installing the components, and finally, dressing the space. The . . . color photographs show an enormous variety of gardens and their elements in detail, varying from large and small, to urban and rural, covering a wide range of styles, including contemporary, modern, city, Mediterranean and natural." (Publisher's note)

"Paging through the exquisite photographs in this coffee-table book is like being given a sneak peek into some of the world's most gorgeous private outdoor spaces. It includes sections on types of paving, enclosures, garden furniture, and art. This book will inspire readers to envision what is possible even in the smallest, most improbable space." Pub Wkly

Nagel, Vanessa Gardner

Understanding garden design; the complete handbook for aspiring designers. Timber Press 2010 235p il $34.95 **712**
1. Garden design
ISBN 978-0-88192-943-0

LC 2009-53692

"Thorough and thoroughly accessible, Nagel's reasoned yet personable approach to an often intimidating subject will benefit both homeowners and design professionals." Booklist
Includes bibliographical references

Rybczynski, Witold

A **clearing** in the distance: Frederick Law Olmsted and America in the nineteenth century. Scribner 1999 480p il $28; pa $15.95 **712**
1. Travel writers 2. Urban planners 3. Landscape architects
ISBN 0-684-82463-9; 0-684-86575-0 pa

LC 99-18094

"Rybczynski, celebrated for his sparkling prose as well as for his deep knowledge of architectural history, adeptly chronicles the life of the man who 'was a landscape architect before that profession was founded.'" Booklist
Includes bibliographical references

Wulf, Andrea

Founding gardeners; the revolutionary generation, nature, and the shaping of the American nation. Knopf 2011 349p il map $30; ebook $14.99 **712**
1. Gardens 2. Gardening 3. American national characteristics 4. Statesmen -- United States
ISBN 978-0-307-26990-4; 0-307-26990-6; 978-0-307-59554-6 ebook

LC 2010-52920

The book discusses how the "leaders of the American Revolution and the early republic were engaged plantation owners keenly interested in scientific agriculture. Andrea Wulf argues that this interest, shared by other Founding Fathers, was no mere sideline activity, but rather something central to their identities as leaders and political thinkers." The author examines "the political role of horticulture/agriculture in the Constitutional Convention and the landmark battle over the Hamilton Bank Bill in 1791 that brought party political differences into the open." (Journal of American History)

The author demonstrates "that the garden, the natural world and the shape of a new nation were, for the men who launched the United States, parts of a whole. The image of the farmer-statesman is an ideal of republican government dating back to Romans. It's no accident that the men who led the Revolution and wrote the Constitution owned plantations and farms.... [Wulf is a] writer of considerable grace and breadth of vision, and 'Founding Gardeners' is an excellent portrait of the early years of the federal republic. It will delight the general reader, not just the garden buff. But for the garden enthusiast, this is a book of special interest, reminding us that a garden has a purpose, a character, a soul—that it's an expression of our relationship not just to the soil, but to a vision of the world." Cleveland Plain Dealer

712.6 Private parks and grounds

Greayer, Rochelle

Cultivating garden style; inspired ideas and practical advice to unleash your garden personality. Rochelle Greayer. Timber Press, Inc. 2014 320 p. color illustrations $35 **712.6**
1. Gardens 2. Garden design 3. Gardening 4. Gardens -- Styles
ISBN 1604694777; 9781604694772

LC 2014009479

In this book author "Rochelle Greayer shares ways to create outdoor areas that are charming, comfortable, appealing, and reflect individuality. It features twenty-three unique garden styles accompanied by advice on how to recreate the look. Simple step-by-step projects, like how to make a macramé plant hanger, help the reader personalize the space." (Publisher's note)

"The extravagant use of color photos on each page brings visual clarity to otherwise improbable schemes. Whether depicting "retro rockery," topiary, trellising, Danish or Zen features, the book offers needed guidance for designing outdoor space in a way that helps gardeners bring unique personality to their living, growing outdoor decor." Pub Wkly

Pember, Mat

The **Little** Veggie Patch Co. DIY Garden Projects; by Mat Pember and Dillon Seitchik-Reardon. Random House Inc. 2016 272 p. color illustrations $34.95 **712.6**
1. Gardening 2. Recycling 3. Handicraft
ISBN 1743790996; 9781743790991

This book, by Mat Pember and Dillon Seitchik-Reardon, "includes over 38 . . . projects for those young and old wanting to transform their outdoor living space. It is broken into 6 categories from Kids, Recycled/Upcyled, X-Factor, Vertical Gardening, Gardening basics and Kitchen, and includes a variety of projects for experienced handy folk to quirky ideas that will involve the youngest members of the family." (Publisher's note)

"Charming and hip projects emphasize recycled materials and small space gardens that will be attractive in urban settings. Highly recommended, especially where variety is desired." LJ

715 Woody plants in landscape architecture

Hobson, Jake

The **art** of creative pruning; inventive ideas for training and shaping trees and shrubs. Jake Hobson. Timber Press 2011 200 p. color illustrations $34.95 **715**
1. Pruning 2. Topiary work
ISBN 160469114X; 9781604691146

LC 2011007954

In this book, by Jake Hobson, "[n]othing brings a touch of artistry to the garden like ornamental pruning. . . . Drawing on both eastern and western styles, . . . Hobson moves beyond the traditional lollipops and animals and teaches a wholly new approach to ornamental pruning that appeals to modern sensibilities. . . . All the practical considerations are here as well, including pruning to improve a view, remedial pruning to fix problems, and pruning fruit trees to increase yield." (Publisher's note)

"Libraries already well stocked with titles such as Christopher Brickell and David Joyce's The American Horticultural Society Pruning & Training or Lewis Hill and Penelope O'Sullivan's The Pruning Answer Book will find Hobson's gorgeously illustrated, more philosophical book a good counterpart to those more nuts-and-bolts guides. Written with passion, verve, and a dash of dry wit, this title will inspire any gardener who wants to understand the how and why of creative pruning before picking up the shears and hacking off branches." LJ

Includes bibliographical references and index

How to train and shape trees and shrubs

715.1   Topiary work

Foley, Caroline

★ **Topiary,** knots and parterres; Caroline Foley. Pimpernel Press Ltd., in assoc. with the European Boxwood & Topiary Society 2017 288 p. $70   **715.12**
  1. Topiary work 2. Gardens -- History 3. Hedges -- History 4. Knot gardens -- History 5. Topiary work -- History 6. Formal gardens -- History
  ISBN 1910258180; 9781910258187

LC 2017431398

"This book, [by Caroline Foley], moves on through the formal parterres of Renaissance Italy and the more elaborate broderies of the royal French gardens (copied in palace gardens throughout Europe), the complicated conceits of the Tudors and the geometry of the Dutch school. . . . [The book also takes] a look at topiary as used by designers such as Jacques Wirtz, Piet Oudolf, Arne Maynard, Tom Stuart-Smith, Fernando Caruncho, as well as talented private garden owners." (Publisher's note)

Includes bibliographical references (page 284) and index.

720   Architecture

Cornille, Didier

Skyscrapers; who built that?; an introduction to skyscrapers and their architects. Didier Cornille. Princeton Architectural Press 2014 84 p. illustrations (alk. paper) $16.95   **720**
  1. Skyscrapers -- Juvenile literature 2. Architecture -- Juvenile literature
  ISBN 1616892706; 9781616892708

LC 2014004388

This juvenile book, by Didier Cornille, "is a colorful tour of the world's tallest buildings and the larger-than-life personalities who built them. Beginning with a brief biographical sketch of each architect, illustrator Didier Cornille imaginatively depicts the construction of eight of the world's most impressive skyscrapers." (Publisher's note)

"Though the information is a little slight, the spare illustrations easily make up for it—all of Cornille's drawings unmistakably reveal architectural components not visible in photographs, such as interior structures or foundations, and although they're very minimalistic, it's impossible not to see the structures' grandeur in each illustration. Though this resembles a picture book, the sometimes elevated language makes this better suited to middle- or even high-school students who already have an interest in architecture or graphic design." Booklist

Davies, Colin

Thinking about architecture; an introduction to architectural theory. Colin Davies. Chronicle Books Llc. 2011 160 p. ill. (paperback) $29.95; (ebook) $29.95   **720**
  1. Architecture -- Philosophy
  ISBN 185669755X; 9781856697552; 9781780670911

It was author Colin Davies' intent "to provide designers, teachers, students, and interested laypersons with a set of ideas that will enrich their conversation, their writing, and above all their thinking about ar-

chitecture." The book introduces "basic concepts such as representation, form, and space." (Publisher's note)

Rybczynski, Witold

Mysteries of the mall; and other essays. Witold Rybczynski. Farrar, Straus & Giroux 2015 336 p. (hardcover) $27 **720**
  1. Architecture -- United States 2. City planning -- United States 3. Cities and towns -- United States 4. Architecture and society -- United States 5. Cities and towns -- United States -- History
  ISBN 0374269939; 9780374269937

LC 2014046633

This collection of essays on urban planning and architecture, by Witold Rybczynski, "ranges over subjects as varied as shopping malls, Central Park, the Paris opera house, and America's shrinking cities. Along the way, he examines our post-9/11 obsession with security, the revival of the big-city library, the rise of college towns, and our fascination with vacation homes, and he visits Disney's planned community of Celebration." (Publisher's note)

"A superb book for those interested in architectural history, written in an e asygoing style by a man with encyclopedic knowledge and an obvious great love for building." Kirkus

Sudjic, Deyan, 1952-

The **language** of cities; Deyan Sudjic. Trafalgar Square 2017 240 p. (hardcover) $39.95   **720**
  1. City planning 2. Cities and towns -- Social aspects
  ISBN 9780241188040; 0241188040

"We live in a world that is now predominantly urban. So how do we define the city as it evolves in the 21st century? Drawing examples from across the globe, Deyan Sudjic decodes the underlying forces that shape our cities, such as resources and land, to the ideas that shape conscious elements of design, whether of buildings or of space." (Publisher's note)

"This title by design historian . . . and director of London's Design Museum Sudjic is the most celebratory book about cities to come along for years." LJ

Watkin, David, 1941-2018

A **history** of Western architecture; David Watkin. 6th edition Laurence King Pub 2015 736 p. ill. (some col.) pbk $45   **720**
  1. Architecture -- History
  ISBN 9781780675978; 1780675976
  First edition 1986
  Includes bibliographical references and index.

"David Watkin traces the history of western architecture from the earliest times in Mesopotamia and Egypt to the eclectic styles of the twenty-first century. The author emphasizes the ongoing vitality of the Classical language of architecture, underlining the continuity between, say, the work of Ictinus in fifth-century BC Athens and that of McKim, Mead and White in twentieth-century New York." (Publisher's note)

720.9   History, geographic treatment, biography

Architecture; the whole story. general editor, Denna Jones ; foreword by Richard Rogers & Philip Gumuchdjian. Prestel Pub. 2014 576 p. color illustrations $34.95   **720.9**
  1. Architecture 2. Architecture -- Themes, motives
  ISBN 3791349155; 9783791349152

LC 2014937907

"This latest addition to the Whole Story series offers an encyclopedic and lavishly illustrated survey of architecture throughout human history.

Sweeping in reach and exhaustive in detail, [it] is an indispensible reference for anyone interested in the evolution of our built environment. Ranging chronologically from the Neolithic period to the sustainability movement of today, it looks at hundreds of examples of structures, their designers, and their contextual significance." (Publisher's note)

"Over 1,000 images illustrate buildings, details, and an occasional cross-section or floor plan. Considering the book's worldwide focus, however, a map would have been a welcome addition. Similar comprehensive reference works, such as the two-volume Oxford Companion to Architecture, edited by Patrick Goode (CH, Mar'10, 47–3549), are more systematic but lack the vitality of Jones's work. Summing Up: Highly recommended. Lower-division undergraduates through graduate students; general readers." Choice

Includes bibliographical references and index

Boucher, Bruce

Andrea Palladio; the architect in his time. principal photography by Paolo Marton. 2nd ed; Abbeville Press 2007 324p il pa $39.95 **720.9**

1. Architects
ISBN 978-0-7892-0940-5; 0-7892-0940-3
First published 1994

"In this careful, comprehensive, stunningly illustrated survey, Boucher . . . capably illuminates Palladio's stylistic evolution. . . . Among the 300 plates are more than 100 newly commissioned photographs of building interiors and exteriors, which superbly capture Palladio's distincitve blend of simplicity and grandeur." Publ Wkly

Includes bibliographical references (p. 301-312)

Glancey, Jonathan

The **story** of architecture. Dorling Kindersley 2000 240p il hardcover o.p. pa $25 **720.9**

1. Architecture -- History
ISBN 0-7894-5965-5; 0-7894-9334-9 pa

LC 00-30434

"Devoting nearly half the text to the modern period, Glancey condenses history's panorama into a series of colorful vignettes, each described as having some contemporary relevance. Driven by a contagious enthusiasm, the narrative is enlivened by chatty, sometimes offbeat commentary." Libr J

★ A **global** history of architecture; Francis D.K. Ching, Mark Jarzombek, Vikramaditya Prakash. 3rd edition Wiley 2017 850 p illustrations $125 **720.9**

1. Architecture -- History
ISBN 9781118981337

LC 2017004046

Includes bibliographical references and index

This book "provides a comprehensive tour through the ages, spinning the globe to present the landmark architectural movements that characterized each time period. Spanning from 3,500 B.C.E. to the present, this unique guide is written by an architectural all-star team who emphasize connections, contrasts and influences, reminding us that history is not linear and that everything was 'modern architecture' in its day. This new third edition has been updated with new drawings from Professor Ching, including maps with more information and color, expanded discussion on contemporary architecture, and in-depth chapter introductions that set the stage for global views." (Publisher's note)

Hollis, Edward

The **secret** lives of buildings; from the ruins of the Parthenon to the Vegas Strip in thirteen stories. Metropolitan Books 2009 338p il $28 **720.9**

1. Buildings 2. Architecture
ISBN 978-0-8050-8785-7; 0-8050-8785-0

LC 2009-18715

This book is "built around thirteen chapters, each telling the story of a building that changed dramatically over time, either in physical terms (the Parthenon, Gloucester Cathedral) or conceptual ones (the Venetian hotel and casino in Las Vegas, which seeks to capture the image of the Most Serene Republic if not, exactly, the spirit). Hollis's stories are engrossing—his history of the Hulme housing estates in Manchester, and their role as incubator for British post-punk rock, was completely new to me—and his writing is engaging." Bookforum

Includes bibliographical references (p. 315-322)

Rybczynski, Witold

The **perfect** house: a journey with the Renaissance architect Andrea Palladio. Scribner 2002 266p il $25; pa $15 **720.9**

1. Architects 2. Architecture -- 15th and 16th centuries
ISBN 0-7432-0586-3; 0-7432-0587-1 pa

LC 2002-66838

The author offers a historical and architectural analysis of ten villas attributed to 16th century Italian architect Andrea Palladio

"With its intriguing biographical detail, precise descriptions of design elements, and engaging insights into daily life in the 16th century, Rybczynski's book is a small but lasting gift to the reader." Libr J

Includes bibliographical references

The **Seventy** wonders of the modern world; 1500 years of extraordinary feats of engineering and construction. edited by Neil Parkyn. Thames & Hudson 2002 304p il $40 **720.9**

1. Architecture 2. Curiosities and wonders
ISBN 0-500-51047-4

LC 2002-100549

Published in the United Kingdom with title: The seventy architectural wonders of our world

"Most of the featured 'wonders' date from the second half of the 20th century. The selections are divided into seven categories: churches, palaces, public buildings, towers and skyscrapers, bridges and railways, canals and dams, and statues. Each entry includes basic information on history, structural and engineering details, innovations, aesthetics, and a sidebar 'fact-file.'" Libr J

Includes bibliographical references

Storrer, William Allin

The **Frank** Lloyd Wright companion; Rev ed; University of Chicago Press 2006 492p il $99 **720.9**

1. Architects 2. Nonfiction writers
ISBN 0-226-77621-2

LC 2006-44502

First published 1993

This "volume covers more than 450 buildings designed by master architect Wright between 1886 and 1959. Storrer documents each structure with plans, drawings, photographs, and commentary. Each presentation is both complete and concise, following each stage of Wright's aesthetic development, each leap of his imagination, and each instance of technical innovation." Booklist

Wolfe, Tom

From Bauhaus to our house. Bantam Books 1999 111p il pa $15 **720.9**

1. Bauhaus -- Influence 2. Architecture -- 20th century 3. Architecture -- United States
ISBN 978-0-553-38063-7; 0-553-38063-X

First published 1981 by Farrar, Straus & Giroux

A humorous history of American architecture in the 20th century.

720.973   Architecture – United States

Howard, Hugh

Architecture's odd couple; Frank Lloyd Wright and Philip Johnson. Hugh Howard. Bloomsbury Press 2016 352 p. illustrations (some color) (hardback) $28   **720.973**

1. Architecture 2. Architecture -- United States -- History -- 20th century

ISBN 1620403757; 9781620403754

LC 2015042135

This book, by Hugh Howard, "traces the historical threads connecting [architects Frank Lloyd Wright and Philip Johnson] and offers readers a distinct perspective on the era they so enlivened with their designs. Featuring many of the structures that defined modern space--from Fallingwater to the Guggenheim, from the Glass House to the Seagram Building--this book presents an arresting portrait of modern architecture's odd couple and how they shaped the American landscape by shaping each other." (Publisher's note)

"Written with wit and flair and supported by solid research, this thoughtful and well-built book will delight architecture buffs." Booklist

Includes bibliographical references (pages 285-320) and index.

721   Architectural materials

Rybczynski, Witold

The look of architecture. Oxford Univ. Press 2001 130p il hardcover o.p. pa $9.95   **721**

1. Design 2. Architecture

ISBN 0-19-513443-5; 0-19-515633-1 pa

LC 00-53077

"The author's deeply informed enthusiasm is infectious, and his removal of architectural writing from an airily theoretical discourse to the realm of practical experience is empowering for the lay reader." Publ Wkly

Includes bibliographical references

Smith, Nathan

Color concrete garden projects; make your own planters, furniture, and fire pits using creative techniques and vibrant finishes. Nathan Smith and Michael Snyder ; photographs by Charles Coleman. Timber Press 2015 208 p. color illustrations $19.95   **721**

1. Concrete construction 2. Garden ornaments and furniture 3. Concrete construction -- Formwork 4. Garden ornaments and furniture -- Design and construction

ISBN 1604695390; 9781604695397

LC 2014048495

In this book, by Nathan Smith and Michael Snyder, "[d]iscover the countless ways you can craft with color and concrete! . . . This hands-on guide will take your outdoor space from gray to great. . . . Twenty creative step-by-step projects for furniture, planters, and art include an elegant tabletop planter, a modern birdhouse, and a charming chair for kids." (Publisher's note)

"This book has taken concrete projects to a new high; there's nothing else quite as focused on the subject. For a general concrete container book, see Malin Nilsson and Camilla Arvidsson's Concrete Garden Projects. A true standout—superior instructions and innovative design and use of pigment. A must for any DIY collection." LJ

724   Architecture from 1400

Curtis, William J. R.

Modern architecture since 1900; 3rd ed [rev, expanded, and redesigned]; Phaidon 1996 736p il $59.95; pa $39.95   **724**

1. Architecture -- 20th century

ISBN 978-0-7148-3524-2; 0-7148-3524-2; 978-0-7148-3356-9 pa; 0-7148-3356-8 pa

LC 97-112837

First published 1982

"The volume's well-detailed text is buttressed with 650 color and black-and-white illustrations. This should be a standard volume in all architecture collections." Lib J

Includes bibliographical references

Huxtable, Ada Louise

On architecture; collected reflections on a century of change. Walker 2008 478p il $35   **724**

1. Architecture -- 20th century

ISBN 978-0-8027-1707-8; 0-8027-1707-7

The author "presents her penetrating and tough-minded criticism spanning half a century. . . . Centering largely on modernism, its masters and its discontents, the volume opens with an overview of the past four decades, including startlingly powerful pieces on the late '60s urban decay and the '90s reinvention of architecture." Publ Wkly

725.76   Amusement park buildings and casinos

Pierce, Todd James

★ Three years in Wonderland; the Disney brothers, C. V. Wood, and the making of the great American theme park. Todd James Pierce. University Press of Mississippi 2016 287 p. (hardback) $30   **725.76**

1. Amusement parks -- California 2. Disneyland (Calif.) -- History

ISBN 9781628462418

LC 2015031968

This book, by Todd James Pierce, "lays out the struggles and rewards of building the world's first cinematic theme park and convincing the American public that a $17 million amusement park was the ideal place for a family vacation. The early experience of Walt Disney, Roy Disney, and C. V. Wood is one of the most captivating untold stories in the history of Hollywood." (Publisher's note)

726   Buildings for religious and related purposes

King, Ross

Brunelleschi's dome; how a Renaissance genius reinvented architecture. Penguin Books 2001 194p il pa $14   **726**

1. Artists 2. Sculptors 3. Architects 4. Church buildings 5. Santa Maria del Fiore (Cathedral: Florence, Italy)

ISBN 0-14-200015-9

LC 2001-280068

First published 2000 by Walker & Co.

"King illuminates the mysterious sources of inspiration and the secretive methods of architectural genius Filippo Brunelleschi in a fascinating chronicle of the building of his masterwork, the dome of Santa

Maria del Fiore in Florence. A remarkable saga of how one incandescent mind performed the one matchless feat that would forever transform architecture from a mechanical craft into a creative art." Booklist

Includes bibliographical references

728 Residential and related buildings

★ The **elements** of style; an encyclopedia of domestic architectural detail. general editor, Stephen Calloway ; consultant editor, Elizabeth Cromley. Firefly Books 2005 592 p. ill. (some col.) $85   **728**
1. Domestic architecture 2. Architecture -- Great Britain 3. Architecture -- United States 4. Interior architecture 5. Architecture -- Details 6. Architecture, Domestic -- Great Britain 7. Architecture, Domestic -- United States
ISBN 1554070791; 9781770850866
LC 2006276161

This book, edited by Stephen Calloway, Alan Powers, and Elizabeth Cromley, presents a "visual survey, period by period, feature by feature, of the key styles in American and British domestic architecture from the Tudor period to present day. . . . The book is designed for owners of period houses, restorers, architects, interior designers and all those interested in our architectural heritage." (Publisher's note)

Includes bibliographical references (p. 581-583) and index

The **Greenwood** encyclopedia of homes through American history; Thomas W. Paradis, general editor. Greenwood Press 2008 4v il set $399.95   **728**
1. Reference books 2. Decorative arts -- Encyclopedias 3. Domestic architecture -- Encyclopedias
ISBN 978-0-313-33496-2; 0-313-33496-X
LC 2008-2946

"The set covers ten historical eras beginning with the Colonial era and ending with the period 1986 to present. Each era is introduced by a time line and short historical essay. Other essays synthesize research under topics such as building materials, house plans, interior design, and landscaping. . . .The value of the set lies behind the pretty facade of the American home, in the contributors' exploration of the interaction of physical house and family life." Choice

Includes bibliographical references

Jordan, Wendy Adler
Universal design for the home; great looking, great living design for all ages, abilities, and circumstances. Quarry Books 2008 207p il pa $24.99   **728**
1. Domestic architecture -- Designs and plans
ISBN 978-1-59253-381-7; 1-59253-381-7
LC 2007-32663

This book "shows how a home that is accommodating to all can also have a stylish decor. . . . Color photographs and some before-and-after floor plans show how accessibility standards have been incorporated. A list of resources is provided." Libr J

McAlester, Virginia Savage
A **field** guide to American houses; the definitive guide to identifying and understanding America's domestic architecture. Virginia Savage McAlester ; with drawings by Suzanne Patton Matty and photographs by Steve Clicque. Random House Inc 2013 848 p. ill. $50   **728**
1. Architecture -- United States 2. Domestic architecture -- Guidebooks 3. United States -- Guidebooks 4. Architecture,

Domestic -- United States -- Guidebooks
ISBN 140004359X; 9781400043590
LC 2013018432

This book "covers more than 50 styles of American residential architecture, from early settlement homes of the seventeenth century to the modern 'Millennium Mansions' of the present day. Expanded and completely revised from the 1984 edition, this edition includes American house design from the last three decades and adds more than 600 new photographs and illustrations." (Booklist)

Includes bibliographical references and index

Mitchell, Ryan
Tiny house living; ideas for building and living well in less than 400 square feet. F & W Media Inc 2014 175 p. color illustrations $26.99   **728**
1. Simplicity 2. Small houses
ISBN 1440333165; 9781440333163
LC 2015490704

"This book explores the philosophies behind the tiny house lifestyle, helps you determine whether it's a good fit for you, and guides you through the transition to a smaller space. For inspiration, you'll meet tiny house pioneers and hear how they built their dwellings (and their lives) in unconventional, creative and purposeful ways. They'll invite you in, show you around their cozy abodes, and share lessons they learned along the way." (Publisher's note)

Petroski, Henry, 1942-
The **house** with sixteen handmade doors; a tale of architectural choice and craftsmanship. Henry Petroski ; with photographs by Catherine Petroski. W.W. Norton & Co. Inc. 2014 384 p. illustrations, maps (hardcover) $27.95   **728**
1. Maine 2. Domestic architecture 3. Architecture, Domestic -- Maine 4. Arrowsic (Me.) -- Buildings, structures, etc
ISBN 0393242048; 9780393242041
LC 2014006423

"When Henry Petroski and his wife Catherine bought a . . . . six-decades-old island retreat in coastal Maine, Petroski couldn't help but admire its unusual construction. An . . . expert on engineering, history, and design, he began wondering about the place's origins and evolution. . . . Sleuthing around dimly lit closets, knotty-pine wall panels, and even a secret passage . . . Petroski zooms in on the details but also steps back to examine the structure in the context of its time and place." (Publisher's note)

"Though this fascinating history of a house includes painstaking attention to woodcrafting techniques that may excite professional and amateur architects and carpenters a bit more than general readers, the book is replete with Petroski's usual fascinating details and elegant prose." Booklist

Includes bibliographical references and index

Pierce, Deborah
The **accessible** home; designing for all ages and abilities. Deborah Pierce. The Taunton Press 2012 234 p. illustrations (ebook) $23.99; (pbk.) $32.95   **728**
1. Houses -- Maintenance and repair 2. Architecture and people with disabilities 3. Universal design 4. Dwellings -- Barrier-free design
ISBN 9781621136910; 1600854915; 9781600854910
LC 2012029176

This book, by Deborah Pierce, "goes beyond ramps and grab-bars to help aging boomers, or those faced with disabilities, accomplish home accessibility on a deeper level. With a focus on closing the gap between home and homeowner, architect Deborah Pierce leads readers through the steps of universal design—from hiring the right architect to creating a pleasing space with the final details." (Publisher's note)

Susanka, Sarah

Creating the not so big house; insights and ideas for the new American home. photographs by Grey Crawford. Taunton Press 2000 258p il $34.95; pa $24.95   **728**

1. Interior design 2. Domestic architecture

ISBN 1-56158-377-4; 1-56158-605-6 pa

LC 00-44323

Susanka provides photographs and plans of houses that are designed to look bigger than their actual size

"Architect Susanka has big ideas about small design. . . . {This book promotes} well-designed, efficient, interesting modest-size homes. . . . {She} includes 25 delightful examples of houses designed by architects from around the country." Booklist

★ The **not** so big house; a blueprint for the way we really live. {by} Sarah Susanka, with Kira Obolensky. Expanded edition Taunton Press 2009 199p il col il pbk $24.95   **728**

1. Domestic architecture

ISBN 1600851509; 9781600851506

LC 2009018546

Originally published 1998

"Architect Susanka believes that the large homes being built today place too much emphasis on square footage rather than on current lifestyles. Here she shows how homes can be designed to feature 'adaptable spaces open to one another, designed for everyday use.' She describes how to examine occupants' lifestyles, how to incorporate the kitchen as the focal point of the home, how to give the illusion of space, and how, with storage, lighting, and furniture arrangement, a smaller home can be comfortably livable." (Library Journal)

Includes bibliographical references and index

Not so big solutions for your home. Taunton Press 2002 155p il pa $22.95   **728**

1. Interior design 2. Domestic architecture -- Designs and plans

ISBN 1-56158-613-7

LC 2002-7101

The author presents a compilation of 31 essays from her "Drawing Board" column in Fine Homebuilding magazine "that offer a number of solutions to household design problems both big and small. . . . Susanka offers an eclectic mix: tips on site selection, mud room design, planning to fit specific furniture, creating a family room that works, personalizing with tile, and planning window seats, pantries, TV placement, and floor plan changes." Libr J

Van Doren, Adam, 1962-

The **house** tells the story; homes of the American presidents. by Adam Van Doren ; foreword by David McCullough. David R. Godine 2015 196 p. color ill., color maps (alk. paper) $40   **728**

1. Houses 2. Presidents -- United States -- Homes 3. Dwellings in art 4. Presidents -- Dwellings -- United States -- Pictorial works

ISBN 1567925421; 9781567925425

LC 2015000579

In this book, "historian David McCullough and noted artist Adam Van Doren unite for an excursion to the celebrated homes of fifteen American presidents, past and present. The text is personal and unaffected; Van Doren visited these homes to ensure that he recorded every detail accurately, often becoming acquainted with the former presidents

themselves, always trying to portray them in the human environment they created for themselves." (Publisher's note)

"Warm, accessible, and harmonious, this book marries history with art for a uniquely American vision." Pub Wkly

Versaci, Russell

Creating a new old house; yesterday's character for today's home. Russell Versaci ; photographs by Erik Kvalsvik. The Taunton Press, Inc. 2003 218 p. color illustrations $24.95 **728**

1. Domestic architecture 2. Architecture -- United States 3. Architecture, Domestic -- United States

ISBN 1561586153; 1561587923; 9781561587926

LC 2003004993

In this book, author Russell Versaci "explores how architects, builders, and craftsmen are reinterpreting the traditional American house. Through photographs and engaging text, brief discussions of history and craftsmanship, and occasional sidelong glances at the workings of real old houses, Versaci employs his 'Pillars of Traditional Design' to explain how traditional houses go together and what gives them their unique design appeal." (Publisher's note)

Wilhide, Elizabeth

Scandinavian Home; A Comprehensive Guide to Mid Century Modern Scandinavian Designers. Elizabeth Wilhide. Chronicle Books Llc 2016 192 p. (hardcover) $29.95   **728**

1. Interior design 2. Modernism in architecture 3. Scandinavian architecture

ISBN 1849497494; 9781849497497

This book, by Elizabeth Wilhide, profiles "Scandinavian Modern . . . , the most influential and enduring design movement of the 20th century, dominating the international scene in the 1950s and continuing to shape the way we live today. Architects and designers from Denmark, Sweden, Norway, and Finland, were responsible for a range of contemporary homes, furniture, textiles, ceramics, glassware, and other products that defined an entire approach to modern post-war living." (Publisher's note)

"This solid entry point into the Scandinavian school of design has the elegance of a coffee-table book combined with the information of a reference guide." Pub Wkly

Wolfson, Elissa

Audubon birdhouse book; building, placing, and maintaining great homes for great birds. by Margaret A. Barker and Elissa Wolfson. Voyageur Press 2013 160 p. ills. (col.), col. maps (softcover) $24.99   **728**

1. Woodwork 2. Birdhouses 3. Bird attracting -- United States 4. Birdhouses -- Design and construction

ISBN 0760342202; 9780760342206

LC 2013018947

This book, by Margaret A. Barker and Elissa Wolfson, "produced in association with the National Audubon Society, . . . explains how to build and place functional . . . bird homes that are safe and appropriate for more than 20 classic North American species, from wrens to raptors. Each of the easy-to-build boxes and shelves within is accompanied by cut lists, specially created line diagrams, and step-by-step photography." (Publisher's note)

Includes bibliographical references and index

728.37   Separate houses

Susanka, Sarah

Inside the not so big house; discovering the details that bring a home to life. Sarah Susanka and Marc Vassallo ; photographs by Ken Gutmaker. Taunton Press 2005 210 p. color illustrations $21.95; (ebook) $17.99   **728.37**

1. Architecture 2. Interior design 3. Small houses 4. Interior architecture 5. Architecture -- Details 6. Room layout (Dwellings)
ISBN 1561586811; 1561589845; 9781561589845; 9781600857300

LC 2005008228

In this book, authors Sarah Susanka and Marc Vassallo "focus their lens on the tangible and sometimes intangible details that bring an otherwise ordinary home to life. Incorporating such details as dropped ceilings, built-in shelves, pocket doors, window seats, and well-placed alcoves infuses a home with the character of its owners. . . . From Rhode Island to San Diego, the 23 homes featured here illustrate exceptional attention to detail." (Publisher's note)

728.8   Large and elaborate private dwellings

Morris, Marc

Castles; their history and evolution in medieval Britain. Marc Morris. First Pegasus Books cloth ed. Pegasus Books 2017 ix, 262 p.p illustrations (hardcover) $27.95   **728.8**

1. Castles 2. British architecture 3. Medieval architecture 4. Castles -- England -- History 5. Architecture, Medieval -- Great Britain
ISBN 9781681773599; 1681773597

This book, by Marc Morris, is "a sweeping and stunning history of the most magnificent castles in Britain. Beginning with their introduction in the eleventh century, and ending with their widespread abandonment in the seventeenth, Marc Morris explores many of the country's most famous castles, as well as some spectacular lesser-known examples." (Publisher's note)

"Morris . . . imparts some fascinating information in this accessible study for readers, leading us from one noted English castle to the next without an overabundance of technical construction detail." Kirkus

Includes bibliographical references (pages 249 - 254) and index.

Wiencek, Henry

National Geographic guide to America's great houses; more than 150 outstanding mansions open to the public. by Henry Wiencek and Donna M. Lucey. National Geographic Soc. 1999 320p il pa $25   **728.8**

1. Domestic architecture 2. American architecture 3. Architecture -- United States
ISBN 0-7922-7424-5

LC 98-53013

Arranged by state, this guide includes information on past owners, furnishings, renovations, room descriptions, and excursion plans for other nearby houses of note. The text is accompanied by 170 full-color photos

736   Other plastic arts

Bolitho, Mark

The **Art** and Craft of Geometric Origami; by Mark Bolitho, with photography Brent Darby. Chronicle Books Llc 2017 128 p. $19.95   **736**

1. Origami
ISBN 1616896345; 9781616896348

This book on geometric origami, by Mark Bolitho, with photography Brent Darby, "includes twenty-seven inventive shapes, from simple one-piece pyramids to beautiful and intricate starbursts, each carefully designed and explained with illustrated step-by-step instructions. Also included are thirty-two sheets of origami paper to get you started." (Publisher's note)

"The combination of thorough, helpful instruction, geometry, and one-piece and modular models will appeal to crafters interested in trying something different with origami." (LJ)

Hayakawa, Hiroshi

Kirigami menagerie; 38 paper animals to copy, cut & fold. Sterling Pub. 2009 128p il pa $17.95   **736**

1. Paper crafts 2. Animals in art
ISBN 978-1-60059-318-5

LC 2008-50622

The author shows how to cut and fold paper shapes to make 38 different types of animals, including sheep, pandas, and dragons.

736.4   Wood

Jones, Andrew

Stickmaking handbook; Andrew Jones and Clive George. GMC Publications 2016 120 p. color illustrations (paperback) $12.95   **736.4**

1. Wood carving 2. Staffs (Sticks, canes, etc.) 3. Wood-carving
ISBN 1784940984; 9781784940980

LC 00362970

In this book, by Andrew Jones and Clive George, "the rustic art and long established craft of stickmaking is clearly explained. . . . This fantastic introduction to creating a wide range of traditional walking sticks, market sticks, crooks, and tools – from a variety of woods and other natural materials like animal horns and antlers – is presented in plain language with illustrations and hundreds of colorful photographs in a pastoral setting." (Publisher's note)

"There are few books on this traditional craft, making this title unique. Recommended as a different focus for woodworkers." LJ

736.98   Paper cutting and folding

Firchau, Louise

Paper Panda's guide to papercutting; Paper Panda & friends. Search Press 2016 152 p. illustrations (chiefly color) (paperback) $24.95   **736.98**

1. Paper crafts 2. Paper work 3. Cut-out craft
ISBN 1782213244; 9781782213246

This book, by Louise Firchau, "has Paper Panda's very distinctive stamp on it and begins with a design section which takes the reader through a very personal account of what inspires her, how she works, and how Paper Panda came about. The techniques involved in papercutting are fairly simple and easy to explain, and this is covered through step-by-step demos." (Publisher's note)

"Paper artist Firchau, known by her nom de craft Paper Panda, introduces the basics of papercutting in this lighthearted guide." LJ

736.982 Origami

Fuse, Tomoko

Tomoko Fuse's origami boxes; beautiful paper gift boxes from Japan's leading origami master. Tomoko Fuse. Tuttle Publishing 2018 95 p. illustrations (paperback) $12.99 **736.982**
1. Origami 2. Paper crafts 3. Box making
ISBN 9781462920396; 9780804850063; 0804850062

"With this origami-how-to book, [by Tomoko Fuse,] learn how to fold unique gift boxes that are as unique as the treasures they hold! . . . Step by step instructions and diagrams guide you from start to finish as you create: flat boxes in several different shapes, boxes with multifaceted tops, box tops with spiraled flourishes and so much more." (Publisher's note)

"With clearly drawn instructions and photographed finished projects, the book is an excellent introduction to an ancient art form." Pub Wkly

Morin, John

Inspired origami; projects to calm the mind and soothe the soul. John Morin and Camilla Sanderson. Running Press 2017 120 p. color illustrations (hardcover; alk. paper) $15 **736.982**
1. Origami
ISBN 9780762461752

LC 2016954810

This book on origami, by John Morin and Camilla Sanderson, "will show readers how the peaceful pastime of creating papercraft art can calm the minds of crafters of all skill levels. The book features an introduction on achieving mindfulness through origami, a history of the craft, basic rules, and all the information needed to get started." (Publisher's note)

737.4 Coins

Krause, Chester L.

Standard catalog of world coins; 1901-2000. by Chester L. Krause and Clifford Mishler. Krause Publs. il **737.4**
1. Coins
First published 1972. Periodically revised

This illustrated volume currently covers coins from throughout the world minted 1901-2000. Prices are provided for each coin in up to four grades of preservation. Includes commemorative issues.

Standard catalog of world coins, 1801-1900; Thomas Michael, senior editor & market analyst ; Tracy L. Schmidt, editor. Krause Pub. il map **737.4**
1. Coins
Annual. First published 1972

This illustrated volume covers coins from throughout the world minted 1901-2000. Prices are provided for each coin in up to four grades of preservation. Includes commemorative issues.

Yeoman, R. S.

A **guide** book of United States coins; The official red book. R.S. Yeoman; editor, Kenneth Bressett; research editor, Q. David Bowers; valuations editor, Jeff Garrett. Whitman Pub. 429p il (Official red book series) **737.4**
1. Coins 2. Reference books
Annual. First published 1946 by Whitman

This guide "known as the 'Red Book' is an outstanding reference on U.S. coins designed for use in identifying and grading coins. All issues

from 1616 to the present are covered. The guide provides historical data, statistics, values, and detailed photographs for each coin. Additional sections deal with specialties such as Civil War and Hard Times tokens, misstruck coins, and uncirculated and proof sets." Nichols. Guide to Ref Books for Sch Media Cent. 4th edition

Handbook of United States coins; the official Blue Book. by R. S. Yeoman; edited by Kenneth Bressett. Whitman Publishing 2008 various pagings il **737.4**
1. Coins
Annual. First published 1942

This companion volume to A Guide book of United States coins gives the wholesale values of U.S. coins from colonial times to the present

738.1 Techniques, procedures, apparatus, equipment, materials

Muller, Kristin

The **potter's** studio handbook; a start-to-finish guide to hand-built and wheel-thrown ceramics. Quarry Books 2007 192p il (Back yard series) pa $24.99 **738.1**
1. Pottery
ISBN 978-1-59253-373-2; 1-59253-373-6

LC 2007-16693

The author "guides beginners through advanced students in equipping a ceramic studio, handling the design, preparing the clay, constructing slab projects, throwing on a wheel, glazing, and firing. The 16 clay projects featured here include teapots, vases, and dinner plates. Readers can draw inspiration from the creative painting and underglazing examples, as well as the unusual firing techniques for color and texture." Libr J

Nelson, Glenn C.

Ceramics ; a potter's handbook; [by] Glenn C. Nelson, Richard Burkett. 6th ed; Wadsworth/Thomson Learning 2002 439p il pa $90.95 **738.1**
1. Pottery 2. Ceramics
ISBN 0-03-028937-8

LC 2001-96329

First published 1960. Periodically revised

This manual for beginner to advanced potters presents forming and decorating techniques, body and glaze recipes, and sources for raw materials and equipment.

Includes bibliographical references

Pavelka, Lisa

The **complete** book of polymer clay; step-by-step instructions, original projects, inspirational gallery. Taunton Press 2010 221p il pa $24.95 **738.1**
1. Clay 2. Modeling
ISBN 978-1-60085-128-5

LC 2009-42430

This book presents projects with complete instructions showing readers how to make pendants, curio boxes, a necklace and a bracelet.

Includes bibliographical references

Taylor, Brian

Glaze; the ultimate ceramic artist's guide to glaze and color. Kate Doody, Brian Taylor. Barrons Educational Series, Inc. 2014 320 p. color illustrations $34.99 **738.1**

1. Glazes 2. Ceramics
ISBN 0764166425; 9780764166426

LC 2014942859

In this book by Brian Taylor and Kate Doody "potters will find a wealth of guidance on the glazing process as several of today's leading ceramicists share the recipes and techniques behind their most stunning works of art--each selected specifically for its unique glaze." (Publisher's note)

"Pottery was never so alluring. Appended are a glossary, a bibliography, an Orton cone chart, a directory of ceramic materials, and teachers and artists." Booklist

738.209 History and geographic treatment of porcelain

De Waal, Edmund

The **white** road; journey into an obsession. Edmund de Waal. Farrar, Straus & Giroux 2015 416 p. illustrations (hardback) $27 **738.209**
1. Ceramics 2. Porcelain -- History
ISBN 0374289263; 9780374289263; 9780374709099

LC 2015022207

This book, by Edmund de Waal, "gives us an intimate narrative history of his lifelong obsession with porcelain, or 'white gold.' A potter who has been working with porcelain for more than forty years, de Waal describes how he set out on five journeys to places where porcelain was dreamed about, refined, collected and coveted-and that would help him understand the clay's mysterious allure." (Publisher's note)

"De Waal's passionately and elegantly elucidated story of porcelain, laced with memoir and travelogue, serves as a portal into the madness and transcendence of our covetous obsession with beauty." Booklist

Includes bibliographical references

739.2 Work in precious metals

Faber, Toby

Faberge's eggs; the extraordinary story of the masterpieces that outlived an empire. Random House 2008 302p il $30 **739.2**
1. Artists 2. Emperors 3. Empresses 4. Artisans 5. Jewelers 6. Metalworkers
ISBN 978-1-4000-6550-9; 1-4000-6550-X

LC 2007-49635

"Faber moves beyond mere description and illustration as he traces the fascinating history and sociology of these turn-of-the-century status symbols." Booklist

Includes bibliographical references

739.27 Jewelry

Burns, Cherie

Diving for starfish; the jeweler, the actress, the heiress and one of the world's most alluring pieces of jewelry. Cherie Burns. St. Martin's Press 2018 240 p. (hardcover) $26.99 **739.27**
1. Jewelry 2. Fashion accessories 3. René Boivin (Firm) 4. Brooches -- France -- History -- 20th century 5. Brooches -- Collectors and collecting -- History -- 20th century
ISBN 9781250056207

LC 2017037546

In this book, author Cherie Burns "set[s] off on a journey to find out all she could about the [starfish pin designed by jewelry designer Juliette Moutard] and the women who owned them. Her search took her around the world to Paris, London, New York, and Hollywood. 'Diving for Starfish' is the story of these marvelous pieces of jewelry and the equally dazzling women who loved them." (Publisher's note)

"Quick, fun, easy reading for devotees of high fashion and mystery fans, complete with wrong turns and false friends." Kirkus

Includes bibliographical references and index

Codina, Carles

The **complete** book of jewelry making. Lark Bks. 2000 160p il hardcover o.p. pa $19.95 **739.27**
1. Jewelry
ISBN 1-57990-188-3; 1-57990-304-5 pa

LC 00-42809

This book covers "the basics, from the ABCs of metallurgy to such complicated techniques as enameling and lacquering. . . . Most of the examples are contemporary, taken from European designers, and all blessed with great color photographs." Booklist

DeCoster, Marcia

★ **Marcia** DeCoster's beaded opulence; elegant jewelry projects with right angle weave. Lark Books 2009 128p il (Beadweaving master class) $24.95 **739.27**
1. Jewelry 2. Beadwork
ISBN 978-1-60059-292-8

LC 2008-50857

This book features jewelry projects using beading stitches with right-angle weave designs.

Haab, Sherri

The **art** of metal clay; techniques for creating jewelry and decorative objects. Rev. and expanded ed.; Watson-Guptill Publications 2010 160p il pa $24.99 **739.27**
1. Jewelry 2. Metalwork 3. Precious metal clay
ISBN 978-0-82309-932-0

LC 2009-43781

First published 2003

"An essential project book for anyone interested in learning to work with metal clay. . . . [The projects included involve] bronze and copper metal clays, etching, and enameling. An included DVD has additional projects." Libr J

Legenhausen, Courtney

Fashion jewelry; a beginner's guide to jewelry making. Courtney Legenhausen. Lark 2017 175 p. color illustrations (paperback) $21.95 **739.27**
1. Beadwork 2. Handicraft 3. Jewelry making 4. Wire craft
ISBN 9781454710325; 1454710322

This guidebook, by Courtney Legenhausen, "teaches all the basics of fashioning fun and attractive bracelets, rings, necklaces, and earrings. Detailed instructions and easy-to-follow, step-by-step photographs lay out the techniques--including jewelry stamping and applying hammered texture--and 17 projects. Even novices can make chandelier earrings, a pearl bracelet, a stone pendant, and more." (Publisher's note)

"With useful charts and resource information as well as lots of encouragement, this is a superbly well-designed and effective how-to." Booklist

McGrath, Jinks

The **complete** jewelry making course; Principles, Practice and Techniques: A Beginner's Course for Aspiring Jewelry

Makers. Jinks McGrath. Barron's 2007 144 p. color illustrations (pbk.) $21.99   **739.27**
1. Jewelry making
ISBN 0764136607; 9780764136603

LC 2006936734

This book, by Jinks McGrath, "teaches the craft of jewelry making to students looking to create professional quality items. The author covers every step of the process, from creating original design concepts to fashioning professionally finished pieces of jewelry. She lists all required tools and equipment, explains their uses, advises on safe working practices, and then guides her readers through every stage of the jewelry making process in a series of carefully structured tutorials." (Publisher's note)

Includes bibliographical references (p. 144) and index

Miller, Judith
Miller's costume jewelry. Miller's 2010 256p il $34.99   **739.27**
1. Jewelry
ISBN 978-1-84533-563-2

"The highly informative and entertaining introduction highlights the rise and continued use of costume jewelry from ancient times to the present and features many of the influences that make vintage costume jewelry so popular. The book's remainder is divided into four sections focusing on major designers, classic designers, galleries (special collections), and designers to watch. . . . This delightful book will captivate costume jewelry enthusiasts." Libr J

Young, Anastasia
The **workbench** guide to jewelry techniques. Interweave Press LLC 2009 320p il $34.95   **739.27**
1. Jewelry
ISBN 978-1-59668-169-9

LC 2009-41385

This is a "reference guide for all jewelers, amateur or professional. Includes extensive photographic illustrations of virtually all techniques needed to create quality jewelry. Also has an excellent chapter on design, and additional sections on photographing, exhibiting, marketing, and selling work." Libr J

Includes bibliographical references

740   Graphic arts

Eskilson, Stephen J.
Graphic design; a new history. [by] Stephen J. Eskilson. 2nd edition Yale University Press 2012 464 p. il (cloth; alk. paper) $65.00   **740**
1. Graphic arts -- History 2. Commerical art -- History 3. Commercial art -- History
ISBN 0300172605; 9780300172607

LC 2011025963

This book on "the history of graphic design explores its evolution from the 19th century to the present day. Author Stephen J. Eskilson demonstrates how a new era began for design arts under the influence of Victorian reformers, tracing the emergence of modernist design styles in the early 20th century, and examining the wartime politicization of regional styles." (Publisher's note)

The author focuses "on the evolution of graphic design since the 19th century as well as on what recent developments in the field of information technology mean for today's designers. . . . The result is an effective description of the political effects of design (e.g., strategies

used by illustrators of war posters) and countercultural influences (e.g., drugs and graffiti) supported beautifully by 400-plus large color reproductions." Libr J

Includes bibliographical references and index

741.09   History, geographic treatment, biography

Whistler, Catherine
Venice and drawing, 1500-1800; theory, practice and collecting. Catherine Whistler. Yale University Press 2016 xxxv, 344 p.p illustrations (hardcover) $65   **741.09**
1. Drawing 2. Italian art 3. Art -- Collectors and collecting 4. Drawing, Italian -- Italy -- Venice 5. Drawing, Italian -- Collectors and collecting
ISBN 9780300187731

LC 2015045305

This book, by Catherine Whistler, offers an "overview of drawing in Venice, from the time of Titian and Tintoretto to that of Canaletto and Tiepolo. . . . Gathering together the separate strands of theory, artistic practice, and collecting, Catherine Whistler highlights the interactions and tensions between a developing literary discourse and the practices of making and collecting graphic art." (Publisher's note)

"With its wealth of new information and its highlighting of superb examples of the craft, this book will be the gold standard for the study of Venetian drawings for years to come." Choice

Includes bibliographical references (pages 290-325)

741.092   Biography

Lester, Toby
Da Vinci's ghost; genius, obsession, and how Leonardo created the world in his own image. Toby Lester. 1st ed.; Free Press 2012 275 p.   **741.092**
1. Art criticism 2. Art -- History 3. Figure drawing
ISBN 1439189234; 9781439189238; 9781439189252 (ebook)

LC 2011027966

This book tells "the story of Vitruvian Man: Leonardo da Vinci's famous drawing of a man in a circle and a square. Deployed today to celebrate subjects as various as the nature of genius, the beauty of the human form, and the universality of the human spirit . . . it has become the world's most famous cultural icon, yet almost nobody knows anything about it. . . . Toby Lester weaves together a century-spanning saga of people and ideas. Assembled here is an eclectic cast of . . . characters . . . and, of course, in the starring role, Leonardo himself—whose ghost Lester resurrects in the . . . unfamiliar context of his own times." (Publisher's note)

Includes bibliographical references.

741.2   Techniques, procedures, apparatus, equipment, materials

Ames, Lee J.
★ **Draw** 50 outer space; the step-by-step way to draw astronauts, rockets, space stations, planets, meteors, comets, asteroids, and more. Lee J. Ames with Erin Harvey. Watson-Guptill 2017 61 p. (paperback) $9.99   **741.2**
1. Outer space -- Juvenile literature 2. Drawing -- Technique -- Juvenile literature 3. Outer space -- In art -- Juvenile literature

ISBN 0399580190; 9780399580192

LC 2017017752

This book, by Lee J. Ames with Erin Harvey, is a "step-by-step guide to sketching and rendering astronauts, planets, asteroids, comets, spaceships, space stations, and other elements related to outer space exploration is for artists of all levels." (Publisher's note)

Birch, Helen (Artist)

Freehand; sketching tips and tricks drawn from art. by Helen Birch. Chronicle Books 2013 224 p. color illustrations (pbk.) $18.95 **741.2**

1. Composition (Art) 2. Drawing -- Technique 3. Creation (Literary, artistic, etc.)

ISBN 1452119775; 9781452119779

LC 2013036430

This book, written and illustrated by Helen Birch, "breaks down basic drawing techniques . . . and reveals their practical application in dazzling examples by today's coolest artists. Over 200 innovative works of art demonstrate all the fundamentals--line, tone, composition, texture, and more--and are presented alongside friendly text explaining the simple techniques used to achieve each stylish effect." (Publisher's note)

"Employing the formula of examples + explanations = inspiration, journalist and artist Birch presents the work of dozens of practicing contemporary artists, highlighting prominent techniques so that the reader can emulate and build upon them. Illustrations can be found on nearly every page, including many close-up views that break down for the reader what is happening in the more elaborate drawings." LJ

Includes bibliographical references and index

De Reyna, Rudy

How to draw what you see; by Rudy De Reyna. Watson-Guptill 2005 175 p. illustrations (ebook) $59.97; $19.99 **741.2**

1. Drawing -- Technique

ISBN 9780307786357; 0823023753; 9780823023752

This book, by Rudy De Reyna, "shows artists how to recognize the basic shape of an object—cube, cylinder, cone, or sphere—and use that shape to draw the object, no matter how much detail it contains." (Publisher's note)

"This compact 35th anniversary edition touches on still life, landscapes, and figure drawing in pencil, charcoal, watercolor wash, acrylic, and ink. De Reyna's dedication and enthusiasm are evident on every page." LJ

Edwards, Betty

Drawing on the Right Side of the Brain; A Course in Enhancing Creativity & Artistic Confidence. Betty Edwards. 4th ed. Tarcher/Penguin 2012 xxxiii, 284 p.p ill. (hbk.) $32.95; (pbk.) $19.95; (deluxe) $29.95; (hbk.) $32.95; (pbk.) $19.95; (deluxe) $29.95 **741.2**

1. Laterality 2. Drawing -- Technique 3. Visual perception 4. Cerebral dominance

ISBN 1585429198; 1585429201; 158542921X; 9781585429196; 9781585429202; 9781585429219

LC 2012001232

"This new edition of the hugely popular and influential drawing manual first published over 30 years ago incorporates new findings from neuroscience, like the discovery of brain plasticity, together with the tried-and-true exercises included in past editions." LJ

Includes bibliographical references (p. 270-274) and index

Kaupelis, Robert

Experimental drawing; 30th anniversary ed.; Watson-Guptill 2010 192p il pa $22.99 **741.2**

1. Drawing -- Technique

ISBN 978-0-8230-1622-8; 0-8230-1622-6

LC 2009-931354

First published 1980

"This classic work is a perfect next step for artists who have mastered the basics." Libr J

Includes bibliographical references

Micklewright, Keith

Drawing ; mastering the language of visual expression. Harry N. Abrams 2005 168p il (Abrams studio) pa $29.95 **741.2**

1. Drawing -- Technique

ISBN 0-8109-9238-8

LC 2005-5862

"Using examples of master artists such as Ingres and Michelangelo as well as more contemporary work of Cezanne, Hockney, and others, different aspects of drawing are examined. Each chapter ends with 'Ideas to Explore,' in which the reader is given suggestions for practice. . . . This book is valuable for those learning the theory behind the elements of drawing and for those looking for practical instruction." Voice Youth Advocates

Includes bibliographical references

Price, Maggie

Painting with pastels; easy techniques to master the medium. North Light Books 2007 128p il pa $24.99 **741.2**

1. Pastel drawing

ISBN 978-1-58180-819-3; 1-58180-819-4

LC 2006-029048

"This book shows the reader . . . [how] to paint with pastels, from materials and techniques to painting from photographs. . . . Hand-in photos show how to hold and apply the pastel, and the twenty-two step-by-step demonstrations cover . . . preparing your surface, underpainting, figure drawing and more." Publisher's note

Scheinberger, Felix

Dare to sketch; a guide to drawing and sketching on the go. Felix Scheinberger. Watson-Guptill Publications 2017 159 p. illustrations (hardback) $24.99 **741.2**

1. Drawing 2. Art -- Technique 3. Drawing -- Technique

ISBN 9780399579561; 9780399579554

LC 2017020347

This book, by Felix Scheinberger, is "an inspirational, instructional, and visually stimulating guide to sketching and drawing. . . . [It] is filled with practical tips about which materials to use, a variety of subject matter ranging from easy to more challenging, and wisdom about overcoming creative blocks and fear of making mistakes." (Publisher's note)

"Lots of practical advice helps with everything from how to confront a blank sketchbook to the best way to catch a subject that won't sit still." LJ

Includes bibliographical references and index

Willenbrink, Mark

Drawing for the absolute beginner; a clear & easy guide to successful drawing. Mark and Mary Willenbrink. North Light Books 2006 128 p. chiefly illustrations (pbk.; alk. paper) $19.99; (ebook) $19.99 **741.2**

1. Drawing 2. Drawing -- Technique

ISBN 1581807899; 9781581807899; 9781600616013

LC 2006008900

This book, by Mark and Mary Willenbrink, "makes drawing in a realistic style easier than you may think and more fun than you ever imagined! . . . [It] cover[s] it all—from choosing materials and the correct way to hold your pencil, to expert advice on the tricky stuff, like getting proportions and perspective right, drawing reflections, and designing strong compositions." (Publisher's note)

741.235   Pastel

Creevy, Bill

The **pastel** book; materials and techniques for today's artist. by Bill Creevy. Watson-Guptill 1991 175p illustrations $32.50   **741.235**
   1. Pastel drawing
   ISBN 0-8230-3902-1; 9780823039050
This book, by Bill Creevy, is "for anyone working with pastels. . . . Defining the pastel medium broadly—color in stick form to be used for drawing and painting simultaneously—the author creates works of sensuous textures and colors, ranging from subtle to intense. He uses traditional soft and hard pastels, as well as oil pastels and oil sticks, showing the effects produced by each in step-by-step demonstrations." (Publisher's note)

Eagle, Ellen

Pastel painting atelier; essential lessons in techniques, practices, and materials. Ellen Eagle ; foreword by Maxine Hong Kingston. Watson-Guptill Publications 2013 192 p. illustrations $35; (ebook) $65   **741.235**
   1. Pastel drawing 2. Pastel drawing -- Technique
   ISBN 082300841X; 9780823008414; 9780823008421
                  LC 2012018761
This book, by Ellen Eagle, "explores pastel's rich but relatively unexamined past, reveals her own personal influences and approaches, and guides you toward the discovery and mastery of your own vision." (Publisher's note)

McKinley, Richard

Pastel pointers; top secrets for beautiful pastel paintings. Richard McKinley. North Light Books 2010 127 p. illustrations (chiefly color) (pbk.; alk. paper) $26.99; (ebook) $33.74   **741.235**
   1. Pastel drawing 2. Pastel drawing -- Technique
   ISBN 144030839X; 9781440308390; 9781440313912
                  LC 2010028709
This book on pastel painting, by Richard McKinley, "covers everything from the fundamentals to get you going (how to lay out your palette, create an underpainting, evoke luminous effects) to inspirations that will keep you growing (plein air painting, working in a series, keeping a painting journal). Whether you're a beginner or an experienced painter anxious to explore the expressive possibilities of pastel, this is your guide to making the most of the medium." (Publisher's note)
   Includes bibliographical references and index

741.5   Cartoons, graphic novels, caricatures, comics

Abel, Jessica

Drawing words & writing pictures; making comics: from manga, graphic novels, and beyond. [by] Jessica Abel & Matt Madden. First Second Books 2008 xxi, 282 p.p il $34.99 **741.5**
   1. Drawing -- Technique 2. Cartooning -- Technique 3. Comic

books, strips, etc. 4. Graphic novels -- Authorship 5. Comic books, strips, etc. -- Authorship
   ISBN 1596431318; 9781596431317
                  LC 2007044125
Authors Jessica Abel and Matt Madden present "a course on comic creation -- for college classes or for independent study -- that centers on storytelling and concludes with making a finished comic. With chapters on lettering, story structure, and panel layout, the fifteen lessons offered -- each complete with homework, extra credit activities and supplementary reading suggestions -- provide a solid introduction for people interested in making their own comics." (Publisher's note)
   This "book offers step-by-step entry into a complicated series of skills in a nonscary and approachable way." Libr J
   Includes bibliographical references (p. 261-265) and index

Mastering comics; drawing words & writing pictures continued. by Jessica Abel and Matt Madden. 1st ed. First Second 2012 xvii, 318 p.p chiefly ill. (some col.) (hardcover) $34.99   **741.5**
   1. Drawing 2. Cartoonists 3. Cartooning -- Technique 4. Comic books, strips, etc. -- Technique
   ISBN 1596436174; 9781596436176
                  LC 2011037023
Jessica Abel's book "Mastering Comics," written with her husband Matt Madden, is a "course of study for the budding cartoonist. Covering advanced topics such as story composition, coloring, and file formatting, [the book] is a vital companion to the introductory content of the first volume" entitled "Drawing Words & Writing Pictures." (Publisher's note)

Andelman, Bob

Will Eisner: A Spirited Life; 1st M Press ed. M Presss 2005 375p illustrations $14.95   **741.5**
   1. Graphic novels 2. Arts -- Biography 3. Artists -- Biography 4. Authors -- Biography 5. Literature -- Biography 6. Cartoonists -- Biography 7. Cartoonists -- United States -- Biography
   ISBN 1-59582-011-6
                  LC 2005026326
"Michael Chabon contributes a heartfelt introduction to Andelman's first-ever biography of Will Eisner (1917-2005) . . . Eisner revolutionized the field . . . from his 1940s stories featuring masked crime fighter the Spirit to his later, pioneering graphic novels but also as businessman and entrepreneur, teacher, mentor, and the inspiration of countless young artists [like Art Spiegelman]. . . . Besides verifying Eisner's impact on nearly every artist who drew comics in his wake, Andelman shows that Eisner's influence extends to such film directors as Spielberg and Tarantino." Booklist

B., David

Epileptic. Pantheon Books 2005 361p il $25; pa $18.95   **741.5**
   1. Graphic novels 2. Autobiographical graphic novels 3. Epilepsy -- Graphic novels
   ISBN 0-375-42318-4; 0-375-71468-5 pa; 9780375423185
                  LC 2004-53419
Original French edition, 2002
The author's "artwork is magnificent—gorgeously bold, impressionistic representations of the world not as it is but as he's taught himself to perceive it. . . . B.'s illustrations constantly underscore his writing's wrenching psychological depth; readers can literally see how the chaos of his childhood shaped his vision and mind." Publ Wkly

Backderf, Derf

My friend Dahmer; written & illustrated by Derf Backderf. Abrams ComicArts 2012 221 p. **741.5**

1. Comic books, strips, etc. 2. Friendship -- Graphic novels 3. High school -- Graphic novels 4. Autobiographical graphic novels
ISBN 9781419702167

LC 2011285306

Alex Award (2013)

This book is an "exploration of notorious serial killer Jeffrey Dahmer by his high-school classmate.... In this graphic novel, [Derf] Backderf interweaves his memories of Dahmer with additional information gleaned from news reports, public interviews, and the memories of other classmates and community members. The book traces Dahmer's progression from experimenting with roadkill to . . . his first human victim just post-high school." (Bulletin of the Center for Children's Books)

Barry, Lynda

What it is. Drawn & Quarterly 2008 209p il $24.95 **741.5**

1. Authorship -- Graphic novels 2. Creative writing -- Graphic novels
ISBN 978-1-897299-35-7; 1-897299-35-4

LC c2007-9047319

Independent cartoonist Lynda Barry presents an unconventional book that encourages its readers to write by using her colorful art and asking questions such as "How are monsters different? And how are they the same?" "Can/Do images exist without thinking?" "What is the difference between lying and pretending?" Each question appears with illustrated writing prompts and Barry's own ruminations on the topics. It's a workbook of sorts, but it also exists as a book to be read for itself.

"Every so often a book comes along that surpasses expectations, taking readers on an inspirational voyage that they don't want to leave. This is one such book." SLJ

Bechdel, Alison, 1960-

Are you my mother? a comic drama. Alison Bechdel. Houghton Mifflin Harcourt 2012 286 p. **741.5**

1. Cartoonists -- Biography 2. Autobiographical graphic novels 3. Mother-daughter relationship -- Graphic novels 4. Cartoonists -- United States -- Comic books, strips, etc
ISBN 0618982507; 9780618982509

LC 2012010582

In this book, "[Alison] Bechdel not only searches for keys to [her relationship with her mother] but perhaps even for surrogate mothers, through therapy, girlfriends and the writing of Virginia Woolf, Adrienne Rich, Alice Miller and others. Yet the primary inspiration in this literary memoir is psychoanalyst Donald Winnicott, whose life and work Bechdel explores along with her own." (Kirkus Reviews)

★ **Fun** home; a family tragicomic. Houghton Mifflin 2006 232p il $19.95 **741.5**

1. Artists 2. Authors 3. Novelists 4. Cartoonists 5. Graphic novels 6. Autobiographical graphic novels 7. Essayists 8. Comic book writers 9. Biography, Individual
ISBN 0-618-47794-2; 978-0-618-47794-4

LC 2005-30304

This is a memoir in graphic novel format about the author's "childhood, her father's death and their shared homosexuality.... The death was deemed an accident—a truck hit [Mr. Bechdel] as he crossed a road with an armful of garden brush—but Ms. Bechdel suspects suicide." (N Y Times (Late N Y Ed))

This "is one of the very best graphic novels ever." Booklist

Brunetti, Ivan

Cartooning; philosophy and practice. Yale University Press 2011 77p il pa $13 **741.5**

1. Cartooning -- Technique
ISBN 978-0-300-17099-3; 0-300-17099-8

LC 2010-940419

"The first half of the book is devoted to the basic terminology and materials of the medium, while the second half is devoted to an intensive and full 15-week comics course. The course should make the non-draftsperson comfortable with drawing and progressively able to translate the panels of the story from head to page. It also breaks down the drawing process so that anyone can draw a couple characters without having to fret about making realistic, Marvel-style, detailed renderings or obsessive crosshatch shading. Cartooning is set to become the next de-facto book for breaking into the comics medium." Molossus

Includes bibliographical references

Chast, Roz

★ **Can't** We Talk About Something More Pleasant? A Memoir. Roz Chast. St. Martin's Press 2014 240 p. color illustrations hc $28 **741.5**

1. Aging parents
ISBN 9781608198061; 1608198065
Kirkus Prize: Nonfiction (2014)
National Book Award Finalist: Nonfiction (2014)
National Book Critics Circle Award: Autobiography (2014)

In this memoir, author Roz Chast "brings her signature wit to the topic of aging parents. Spanning the last several years of their lives and told through four-color cartoons, family photos, and documents, and a narrative as rife with laughs as it is with tears, Chast's memoir is both comfort and comic relief for anyone experiencing the life-altering loss of elderly parents." (Publisher's note)

Chast "brings her parents and herself to life in the form of her characteristic scratchy-lined, emotionally expressive characters, making the story both more personal and universal." Pub Wkly

Chelsea, David

Perspective in action; creative exercises for depicting spatial representation from the Renaissance to the Digital Age. David Chelsea. Watson-Guptill 2017 171 p. color illustrations (paperback) $22.99 **741.5**

1. Perspective 2. Graphic novels 3. Perspective -- Comic books, strips, etc
ISBN 9781607749462

LC 2016045493

This book, by David Chelsea, "takes readers through the major perspective-related developments in history, teaching them how to re-create these same experiments by leading artists in all fields (including drawing, painting, and sculpture). Covering a wide-range of mediums (pen and ink, paint, chalk, digital art, woodwork, and more), [it] gives readers a more hands-on approach to perspective, as opposed to the usual theoretical presentations found in other books." (Publisher's note)

"Cleverly packaged in a graphic novel format, artist Chelsea's (Perspective! For Comic Book Artists) book covers all aspects of simple perspective drawing and depicts its more complex applications." LJ

★ The **complete** cartoons of the New Yorker; edited by Robert Mankoff; foreword by David Remnick. Black Dog & Leventhal 2004 655p il $60 **741.5**

1. Cartoons and caricatures 2. New Yorker (Periodical) 3. New Yorker Magazine, Inc.
ISBN 1-579-12322-8

LC 2004-46371

"Issued as part of the New Yorker's eightieth anniversary celebration, this . . . volume collects, in two formats, the cartoons that have appeared in the pages of that magazine over the course of its distinguished publishing history. . . . The book itself gathers 2,500 of the most representative cartoons for display, but two accompanying CDs contain all the cartoons (68,647, to be exact) ever published in the magazine. Arrangement is by chapter, with each covering a decade of the New Yorker's existence. . . . A testament—a tribute—to the great magazine but also an absolutely special way to spend quality time." Booklist

Crumb, R.

The **book** of Genesis; illustrated by R. Crumb. W.W. Norton 2009 un il map $24.95   **741.5**
1. Graphic novels
ISBN 978-0-393-06102-4; 0-393-06102-7

LC 2009-14303

"Originally thinking that we would do a take off of Adam and Eve, Crumb became so fascinated by the Bible's language, 'a text so great and so strange that it lends itself readily to graphic depictions,' that he decided instead to do a literal interpretation using the text word for word in a version primarily assembled from the translations of Robert Alter and the King James bible." (Publisher's note)

"This is the Bible that distressed 19th-century English philanthropist and man of letters Thomas Bowdler: not stories for sweet-faced kiddies, but sex and blood. . . . We could not expect less from the patriarch of underground comix—themselves notorious for sex and violence and deals gone sour. Indeed, Crumb's muscular, detailed black-and-white seems ideally suited to Old Testament scuffles and seaminess." Libr J

★ The **DC** comics encyclopedia; text by Alan Cowsill, Alex Irvine, Steve Korte, Matt Manning, Stephen (Win) Wiacek, Sven Wilson ; additional text by Scott Beatty, Robert Greenberger, Phil Jiminez, Nick Jones, Dan Wallace. Updated edition DK 2016 368 p color illustrations $40   **741.5**
1. DC Comics, Inc. -- Encyclopedias 2. Comic books, strips, etc. -- United States -- History and criticism -- Encyclopedias
ISBN 9781465453570

"Revamped, redesigned, and fully updated to include the New 52 and Rebirth storylines, this is the definitive and indispensable guide to the characters and worlds of the DC Comics Universe." (Publisher's note)

Delisle, Guy

★ **Pyongyang** ; a journey in North Korea; translated by Helge Dascher. Drawn & Quarterly 2005 176p il map hardcover o.p. pa $14.95   **741.5**
1. Graphic novels 2. Korea (North) -- Graphic novels
ISBN 1-896597-89-0; 1-897299-21-4 pa

"Pyongyang will appeal to multiple audiences: current events buffs, Persepolis fans and those who just love a good yarn." Publ Wkly

Eisner, Will

★ **Comics** and sequential art; principles and practices from the legendary cartoonist. W.W. Norton 2008 175p il (The Will Eisner library) pa $22.95   **741.5**
1. Drawing -- Technique 2. Graphic novels -- Authorship 3. Comic books, strips, etc. -- Authorship
ISBN 978-0-393-33126-4; 0-393-33126-1

LC 2008-20042

First published 1985 by Poorhouse Press

This book offers the author's ideas, theories, and advice about graphic storytelling and the uses to which the comic book art form can be applied.

Findakly, Brigitte

Poppies of Iraq; cowritten by Brigitte Findakly & Lewis Trondheim ; drawn by Lewis Trondheim ; colored by Brigitte Findakly ; translated by Helge Dascher. Drawn & Quarterly 2017 32 p. chiefly color illustrations (hardcover) $21.95 **741.5**
1. Women -- Iraq 2. Autobiographical graphic novels 3. Iraq -- History -- 1958-1979 -- Comic books, strips, etc. 4. Women cartoonists -- Iraq -- Biography -- Comic books, strips, etc. 5. Women cartoonists -- France -- Biography -- Comic books, strips, etc. 6. Iraq -- Social conditions -- 20th century -- Comic books, strips, etc.
ISBN 1770462937; 9781770462939

This book, translated by Helge Dascher, "is Brigitte Findakly's nuanced tender chronicle of her relationship with her homeland Iraq, co-written and drawn by her husband, the acclaimed cartoonist Lewis Trondheim. In spare and elegant detail, they share memories of her middle class childhood touching on cultural practices, the education system, Saddam Hussein's state control, and her family's history as Orthodox Christians in the Arab world." (Publisher's note)

"Each story arc is punctuated by family photos and cultural notes that help bring the family to life and make their experiences personal. Findakly is never naive or sentimental, recounting her life in Iraq with the innocence of a child but the cognizance of an adult." Booklist

Goldstein, Nancy

Jackie Ormes; the first African American woman cartoonist. University of Michigan Press 2008 225p il $35   **741.5**
1. Cartoonists 2. African American women -- Biography
ISBN 978-0-472-11624-9; 0-472-11624-X

LC 2007-35395

This book covers the life and career of Jackie Ormes, who was the first African American woman cartoonist. She wrote and drew comic strips that ran in Black newspapers such as the Pittsburgh Courier and the Chicago Defender. She was part of the Black elite in Chicago and knew other luminaries such as singer Eartha Kitt and musician/composer/conductor Duke Ellington. She was also investigated by the FBI because of her Leftist political ideas and activities. While she did such things as create Torchy paper dolls, based on her beautiful and sexy cartoon character, and cute Patty-Jo dolls, Ormes also used her comic strips to put forth her political views. This book reproduces some of her cartoons and comic strips, in both black and white and in color.

Includes bibliographical references

Guibert, Emmanuel

Alan's war. First Second 2008 304p il pa $24   **741.5**
1. Soldiers 2. Veterans 3. Graphic novels 4. Biographical graphic novels 5. Soldiers -- Graphic novels 6. World War, 1939-1945 -- Graphic novels
ISBN 978-1-59643-096-9; 1-59643-096-6

LC 2007-46190

French cartoonist Guibert met and became friends with Alan Cope and interviewed him at length to create this book. It recreates Cope's memories of being an eighteen-year-old G.I. during World War II. Unlike the war movies that focus on battles, this book focuses on more everyday, mundane memories of the day-to-day life of a soldier. Cope frankly describes a bout with crabs (genital lice), matter-of-factly tells of casual man-to-man sexual encounters among the soldiers, and gives the reader a feel for what happened back then. He also talks about postwar relationships and travels.

This is a "poignant and frank graphic memoir of young soldier who was told to serve his country in WWII and how it changed him forever. . . . Cope and Guibert forge a story that resonates with humanity." Publ Wkly

Hajdu, David

The **ten**-cent plague; the great comic-book scare and how it changed America. Farrar, Straus and Giroux 2008 434p $26 **741.5**

1. Comic books, strips, etc.
ISBN 978-0-374-18767-5; 0-374-18767-3

LC 2007-25024

"Hajdu offers captivating insights into America's early bluestocking-versus-blue-collar culture wars, and the later tensions between wary parents and the first generation of kids with the buying power to mold mass entertainment." Village Voice

Includes bibliographical references

Hart, Christopher

Cartooning for the beginner. Watson-Guptill 2000 144p il pa $19.95 **741.5**

1. Cartooning -- Technique
ISBN 0-8230-0586-0

LC 00-101905

This guide to cartooning techniques "covers the world of cartoon animals, animation, and 'edgy 'toons.'" Libr J

Hayden, Jennifer

The **Story** of My Tits; by Jennifer Hayden. Top Shelf Productions 2015 352 p. illustrations $29.99 **741.5**

1. Breast cancer -- Graphic novels
ISBN 1603090541; 9781603090544
Eisner Nominee: Best Reality-Based Work (2016)

This book is a "graphic memoir and a cancer narrative. . . . When Jennifer Hayden was diagnosed with breast cancer at the age of 43, she realized that her tits told a story. Across a lifetime, they'd held so many meanings: hope and fear, pride and embarrassment, life and death. And then they were gone. Now, their story has become a way of understanding her story." (Publisher's note)

"Using famous works of art as metaphors for her own experiences and limiting her drawings to four equally measured panels per page, Hayden's work is matter-of-fact and unsentimental without becoming cold or heartless. The pacing of her storytelling is seamless, as if she were telling the story to the reader across a kitchen table." Booklist

Howe, Sean

Marvel Comics; the untold story. by Sean Howe. Harper 2012 485 p. (hardback) $26.99 **741.5**

1. Superhero comic books, strips, etc. 2. Comic books, strips, etc. -- History 3. United States -- History -- 20th century 4. Marvel Comics Group 5. Comic books, strips, etc. -- United States -- History and criticism
ISBN 0061992100; 9780061992100

LC 2012015058

Author Sean Howe presents a book on the history of Marvel Comics. Howe "reveals the outsized personalities behind the scenes, including Martin Goodman, the self-made publisher who forayed into comics after a get-rich-quick tip in 1939 . . . and Jack Kirby, the World War II veteran who'd co-created Captain America in 1940 and, twenty years later, developed with Lee the bulk of the company's marquee characters in a three-year frenzy of creativity that would be the grounds for future legal battles and endless debates." (Publisher's note)

Includes bibliographical references and index

Jacobson, Sidney

The **9** /11 report; a graphic adaptation. by Sid Jacobson and Ernie Colón; [with a foreword by Thomas H. Kean and Lee H. Hamilton] Hill and Wang 2006 133p il $30; pa $16.95 **741.5**

1. Graphic novels 2. September 11 terrorist attacks, 2001 -- Graphic novels
ISBN 0-8090-5738-7; 978-0-8090-5738-2; 0-8090-5739-5 pa; 978-0-8090-5739-9 pa

"The book aims to make . . . [The 9/11 Commission Report] more accessable to all readers and draw in young adults. . . . This graphic adaptation is an important and necessary part of any collection." Libr J

Jones, Gerard

Men of tomorrow; geeks, gangsters and the birth of the comic book. Basic Books 2004 320p il $26; pa $15 **741.5**

1. Cartoonists 2. Comic books, strips, etc.
ISBN 0-465-03656-2; 0-465-03657-0 pa

LC 2004-9031

This book tells "the surprising story of the young Jewish misfits, hustlers and nerds who invented the superhero and the comic book industry. . . . Springing unheralded out of working-class Jewish immigrant neighborhoods in the depths of the Depression, these young men transformed an odd mix of geekdom, science fiction, and outsider yearnings into blue-eyed chisel-nosed crime-fighters and adventurers who quickly captured the mainstream imagination. . . . He chronicles how the comics sparked a frightened counterattack that nearly destroyed the industry in the 1950's and how later they surged back at an underground level, to inspire a new generation to transmute those long-ago fantasies into art, literature, blockbuster movies and graphic novels." Publisher's note

Karp, Jesse

Graphic novels in your school library; Jesse Karp ; illustrated by Rush Kress. American Library Association 2012 xi, 146 p.p ill. (alk. paper) $50 **741.5**

1. School libraries 2. Graphic novels -- Bibliography 3. Libraries -- Collection development 4. Graphic novels 5. Graphic novels in education -- United States 6. Libraries -- Special collections -- Graphic novels 7. School libraries -- Collection development -- United States
ISBN 0838910890; 9780838910894

LC 2011026353

This book, by Jesse Karp, "takes a look at the term graphic novel, how the format has become entwined in our culture, and the ways in which graphic novels can be used in the library and in the classroom. . . . Karp . . . [i]ntroduces the history . . . and the conventions of the form, . . . [p]rovides annotated lists of core titles, [and] . . . [o]ffers lesson plans that use graphic novels . . . from life skills and dating to history." (Publisher's note)

Includes bibliographical references (p. 131-132) and index

Kitchen, Denis

The **art** of Harvey Kurtzman; the mad genius of comics. by Denis Kitchen and Paul Buhle; introduction by Art Spiegelman; designed by Kitchen, Lind & Associates. Abrams Comicarts 2009 241p il $40 **741.5**

1. Cartoonists 2. Cartoons and caricatures
ISBN 978-0-8109-7296-4; 0-8109-7296-4

LC 2008-04809

"Although Kurtzman is best known for--and his greatest cultural impact stems from--his creation of MAD, comics aficionados regard him as one of the medium's most significant and influential talents. The groundbreaking war stories he created for EC Comics in the early 1950s remain unsurpassed in their genre, and while the bulk of his personal work consisted of stories he wrote and designed for other illustrators to complete, his own artwork--brash and energetic, with boldly executed brushwork--is wondrously distinctive. . . . [T]he volume's main appeal lies in the handsomely displayed wealth of Kurtzman's work, from his most acclaimed stories, reprinted in their entirety, to unpublished strips and rare preparatory drawings." (Booklist)

"Retrace the strands that led to a lot of current American satire — including The Simpsons, Saturday Night Live and The Daily Show — and sooner or later you end up at Harvey Kurtzman. A comic mastermind who created Mad Magazine and Playboy's 'Little Annie Fanny,' Kurtzman also happened to discover Robert Crumb and gave Gloria Steinem her first job. . . . [This volume] explores the life and art of the famous satirist, weaving together the story of Kurtzman's career with a collection of the artist's images and illustrations." NPR

Kneece, Mark

The **art** of comic book writing; the definitive guide to outlining, scripting, and pitching your sequential art stories. by Mark Kneece. Watson-Guptill Publications 2015 192 p. illustrations (some color) (paperback) $24.99   **741.5**
    1. Comic books, strips, etc. -- Authorship
    ISBN 9780770436971

                            LC 2015007716
This book, by Mark Kneece, is a "practical guide for beginner and advanced comic book writers that outlines the steps needed to successfully craft a story for sequential art. . . . He provides a practical set of guidelines favored by many comic book publishers and uses a unique trial and error approach to show would-be scribes the potential pitfalls they might encounter when seeking a career in comics writing." (Publisher's note)

"This guide isn't the first to discuss how to write for comics, yet it is by far the most in-depth treatment given to the subject in recent years. Although Kneece's works may not be well known, his legacy may well be this text, which will serve as a relevant resource to any program teaching comics and/or creative writing." LJ
    Includes bibliographical references and index

Lee, Stan, 1922-2018

Stan Lee's How to draw comics; from the legendary co-creator of Spider-Man, the Incredible Hulk, Fantastic Four, X-Men, and Iron Man. Watson-Guptill Publication 2010 224p il pa $24.99   **741.5**
    1. Graphic novels 2. X-Men (Fictional characters) 3. Fantastic Four (Fictional characters) 4. Drawing -- Technique 5. Comic books, strips, etc. -- Authorship
    ISBN 978-0-8230-0083-8

                            LC 2010-5781
The author "includes chapters on creating comics with computer programs and online resources and how to get work in the 21st century. The book begins with a brief history of comics, then focuses on action-adventure style, romance, humor, horror, and Japanese manga. This is the one book anyone interested in drawing comics should own." Libr J
    Includes bibliographical references

Leong, Sonia

101 top tips from professional manga artists; Sonia Leong, Hayden Scott Baron. Barrons Educational Series, Inc. 2013 176 p. $22.99   **741.5**
    1. Japanese art 2. Drawing -- Technique 3. Manga -- Study and teaching
    ISBN 1438002068; 9781438002064

                            LC 2012948428
This book, by Sonia Leong and Hayden Scott Baron, focuses on the Japanese drawing known as manga. "With additional insights from a select group of fellow professionals, this illustration-packed book covers all aspects of manga art, presenting advice and instruction on . . . everything an illustrator needs to know in order to create successful manga art for a variety of media." (Publisher's note)

"Freelance comic artist and illustrator Leong and several contributing artists provide over 100 tips grouped and organized around basic topics, highlighting key aspects of manga such as character design, backgrounds, props, software and media, and even practices of successful professionals." LJ

Lepore, Jill

★ The **Secret** History of Wonder Woman; by Jill Lepore. Alfred A. Knopf 2014 448 p. 16 plates; color illustrations (hc; alk. paper) $29.95   **741.5**
    1. Feminism in literature 2. Wonder Woman (Fictitious character) 3. Literature and society -- United States
    ISBN 0385354045; 9780385354042

                            LC 2014011064
This book, by Jill Lepore, is a "work of historical detection revealing that the origin of one of the world's most iconic superheroes hides within it a fascinating family story--and a crucial history of twentieth-century feminism. Wonder Woman, created in 1941, is the most popular female superhero of all time. . . . Lepore has uncovered an astonishing trove of documents, including the never-before-seen private papers of William Moulton Marston, Wonder Woman's creator." (Publisher's note)

"Lepore demonstrates the power of exploring popular culture as history, and her readable style, as well as the subject matter, allows her to introduce this more nuanced understanding of a complex past to a wide audience." Choice
    Includes bibliographical references and index

Mankoff, Bob

How about never--is never good for you? my life in cartoons. Bob Mankoff. Henry Holt & Co. 2014 304 p. illustrations (hardback) $32.50   **741.5**
    1. Illustrators 2. Cartoons and caricatures 3. New Yorker (New York, N.Y.; 1925) 4. Cartoonists -- United States -- Biography 5. Periodical editors -- United States -- Biography
    ISBN 080509590X; 9780805095906

                            LC 2013021129
In this memoir, cartoonist and editor Bob Mankoff "allows us into the hallowed halls of 'The New Yorker' to show us the soup-to-nuts process of cartoon creation, giving us a detailed look not only at his own work, but that of the other talented cartoonists who keep us laughing week after week. For desert, he reveals the secrets to winning the magazine's caption contest." (Publisher's note)

McCloud, Scott

Making comics; storytelling secrets of comics, manga, and graphic novels. HarperCollins 2006 264p il pa $22.95 **741.5**
    1. Graphic novels -- Drawing 2. Comic books, strips, etc. -- Authorship
    ISBN 0-06-078094-0; 978-0-06-078094-4
The author "explores practical matters, including comics devices such as panels, word balloons, and sound effects; facial expressions and body language; the creation of convincing and evocative settings; and the different tools artists can use for the job, from pencils to computers. He also delves into the framing of images in panels, the flow of panels on a page, and the relationships between words and pictures in comics. . . . This is thoughtful, fascinating, stimulating, potentially controversial,

and inspiring." Libr J

Includes bibliographical references

Reinventing comics; how imagination and technology are revolutionizing an art form. Paradox Press 2000 237p il pa $22.95 **741.5**

1. Cartoons and caricatures 2. Comic books, strips, etc.

ISBN 0-06-095350-0

LC 00-710457

The author maps out "'12 revolutions', which, he believes, need to take place for comics to survive and finally be recognized as a legitimate art form. The topics progress from the oldest of comic-related arguments (seeking respect) to the use of computer technology to renew and expand its audience. These brilliantly presented discussions concern comics as literature, comics as art, creators' rights, industry innovation, and public perception, among other topics." Libr J

★ **Understanding** comics; the invisible art. HarperPerennial 1994 215p il pa $22.95 **741.5**

1. Comic books, strips, etc.

ISBN 0-06-097625-X; 9780060976255

First published 1993 by Kitchen Sink Press

McCloud "conducts a genial, well-researched and funny tour of virtually every historical and perceptual aspect of comics, which he calls 'sequential art,' that is, art that consists of sequences of words and pictures. Beginning in the 11th century with the Bayeux tapestry, he examines pre-Columbian picture languages and the printing press, presenting a quick survey of the historical development of early sequential pictures into the specialized visual language of comics. . . . He dissects the vocabulary of the medium, cheerfully analyzing the psychological power of comics and their central role in our ultra-visual culture." (Publishers Weekly)

Includes bibliographical references

O'Neil, Dennis

The **DC** comics guide to writing comics; introduction by Stan Lee. Watson-Guptill 2001 128p il $19.95 **741.5**

1. Comic books, strips, etc. -- Authorship

ISBN 0-8230-1027-9

LC 2001-26101

"O'Neil addresses the universals of writing in a way that makes the book useful to all aspiring scripters, regardless of their knowledge of comics." Booklist

Papadatos, Alecos

Democracy; concept, Alecos Papadatos ; story, Alecos Papdatos & Abraham Kawa ; script, Abraham Kawa ; art direction & drawings, Alecos Papdatos ; colouring, Annie Di Donna. Bloomsbury 2015 236 p. color illustrations $27 **741.5**

1. Democracy 2. War stories 3. Athens (Greece) -- Fiction

ISBN 1608197190; 9781608197194

This book by Alecos Papadatos, Abraham Kawa, and Annie Di Donna "opens in 490 B.C., with Athens at war. The hero of the story, Leander, is trying to rouse his comrades for the morrow's battle against a far mightier enemy, and begins to recount his own life, having borne direct witness to the evils of the old tyrannical regimes and to the emergence of a new political system. The tale that emerges is one of daring, danger, and big ideas, of the death of the gods and the tortuous birth of democracy." (Publisher's note)

"Papadatos's lively and energetic art illuminates battles, alliances, political machinations, and vivid personalities, and Di Donna's intense coloring is gloriously rich without a touch of gaudiness. For those in-terested in further background, the extensive back matter features useful commentary on both legendary and historical figures and concepts." Pub Wkly

Radtke, Kristen

Imagine wanting only this; Kristen Radtke. Pantheon 2017 277 p. chiefly illustrations (hardback) $29.95 **741.5**

1. Loss (Psychology) 2. Cartoonists -- Graphic novels 3. Cartoonists -- United States -- Biography 4. Loss (Psychology) -- Comic books, strips, etc

ISBN 9781101870839

LC 2016034575

In this graphic memoir, by Kristen Radtke, "the sudden death of a beloved uncle and the sight of an abandoned mining town after his funeral marked the beginning moments of a lifelong fascination with ruins and with people and places left behind. Over time, this fascination deepened until it triggered a journey around the world in search of ruined places." (Publisher's note)

"A fantastic example of the graphic novel's possibilities as a literary medium, this work is visually imperfect, lyrically beautiful, and unquestionably brave." Library Journal.

Ricca, Brad

Super boys; the amazing adventures of Jerry Siegel and Joe Shuster: the creators of Superman. Brad Ricca. St Martins Pr 2013 432 p. $27.99 **741.5**

1. Superman (Fictitious character) 2. Cartoonists -- United States -- Biography 3. Comic books, strips, etc. -- United States -- History and criticism

ISBN 9781250049681; 0312643802; 9780312643805

LC 2013004046

This biography of Superman creators Jerry Siegel and Joe Shuster, by Brad Ricca, "reveals the real-life model for Lois Lane . . . and the model for Superman himself (Johnny Weissmuller, who played Tarzan). At the center of the story, of course, is Siegel and Shuster's decision to sell the Superman rights to Action Comics for a pittance--a choice they lamented the rest of their lives. The pair endured poverty, bad marriages, bad health, and a lack of recognition for their work." (Publishers Weekly)

"Ricca's comprehensive biography reveals the turmoil and creative genius that led to our most enduring superhero, the Man of Steel." Pub Wkly

Includes bibliographical references (pages 403-406) and index

Satrapi, Marjane, 1969-

★ The **complete** Persepolis. Pantheon Books 2007 341p il pa $24.95 **741.5**

1. Artists 2. Authors 3. Novelists 4. Cartoonists 5. Graphic novels 6. Autobiographical graphic novels 7. Memoirists 8. Iran -- Graphic novels

ISBN 978-0-375-71483-2

LC 2007-60106

Originally published in two separate volumes 2003-2004

Ignatz Award: Outstanding Graphic Novel (2005)

This "is the story of Satrapi's . . . childhood and coming of age within a large and loving family in Tehran during the Islamic Revolution; of the contradictions between private life and public life in a country plagued by political upheaval; of her high school years in Vienna facing the trials of adolescence far from her family; of her homecoming—both sweet and terrible; and, finally, of her self-imposed exile from her beloved homeland." Publisher's note

Small, David, 1945-

Stitches; a memoir. W.W. Norton 2009 329p il

$23.95   **741.5**

1. Artists 2. Authors 3. Illustrators 4. Graphic novels 5. Comic books, strips, etc. 6. Autobiographical graphic novels 7. Art teachers 8. Children's authors 9. Cancer -- Graphic novels 10. Family life -- Graphic novels

ISBN 978-0-393-06857-3; 0-393-06857-9

LC 2009-22526

National Book Award Finalist: Young People's Literature (2009)

David Small grew up in a dysfunctional family, with a radiologist father who was distant, an angry mother who expressed her anger in eloquent silences, and an older brother who played drums a lot to express his frustrations. When he was eleven, he had a lump, a growth, on the side of his neck. Nothing was done until he was fourteen. He thought he was going in for a minor surgery to remove the cyst from his neck; instead, there were two surgeries, and when he woke up, he had no voice—a vocal cord was removed. He later learned he had cancer, something his parents refused to discuss. After he finds his mother in bed with another woman and his father confesses that he exposed him to x-rays when he was very young, Small leaves home at age sixteen, with little except his dreams that his art could be his life. In one early scene, Small shows the indignities wrought upon his body by his father, including an enema. In another scene, young Small and his older brother look at their father's medical books and see a woman's breast and a man's penis; towards the end of the book, Small draws his grandmother stripping all her clothes off and dancing wildly after setting her house on fire. Other than these few images, Small's depictions of his horrible childhood and teen years are quiet and low-key.

"Emotionally raw, artistically compelling and psychologically devastating graphic memoir of childhood trauma." Kirkus

Spiegelman, Art, 1948-

★ **Co-Mix**; A Retrospective of Comics, Graphics, and Scraps. by Art Spiegelman. Farrar Straus & Giroux 2013 120 p. $39.95   **741.5**

1. Comic books, strips, etc.

ISBN 1770461140; 9781770461147

Harvey Nominee: Best Biographical, Historical, or Journalistic Presentation (2014)

This book, "a companion piece to a retrospective exhibition . . . collects some of [Art] Spiegelman's best work spanning nearly six decades along with biographical information and critical essays. The editors trace his career from commercial work for Playboy to his underground, experimental work, including the Raw anthology where he first serialized 'Maus'.... The book also features many of Spiegelman's controversial 1990's New Yorker covers and autobiographical comics." (Publishers Weekly)

"Maus did much to 'legitimize' comics to the wider world, but this thoughtfully curated, elegantly presented volume is an even more convincing testament to the potential of the medium." Booklist

Spiegelman, Nadja

★ **I'm** supposed to protect you from all this; a memoir. Nadja Spiegelman. Penguin Group USA 2016 320 p. (hardcover) $27   **741.5**

ISBN 9781594631924; 1594631921

LC 2016010834

This memoir, by Nadja Spiegelman, is about "mothers and daughters—and mothers as daughters—traced through four generations, from Paris to New York and back again. . . . More than . . . [the author's] famous father, Maus creator Art Spiegelman, and even more than most mothers, hers—French-born New Yorker art director Françoise Mouly—exerted a force over reality that was both dazzling and daunting." (Publisher's note)

"A fascinating, gracefully written glimpse into the complexities of family life, full of secrets, hidden wounds, and survival tips." Kirkus

Thomas, Roy

75 years of Marvel Comics; from the golden age to the silver screen. by Roy Thomas, edited by Josh Baker. Taschen America 2014 720 p. illustrations (hardcover) $200   **741.5**

1. Marvel Comics Group 2. Superhero comic books, strips, etc. -- History and criticism

ISBN 3836548453; 9783836548458

LC 2014026069

This book, by Roy Thomas and edited by Josh Baker, "presents a magnum opus of the most influential comic book publisher today, with an inside look not only at its celebrated characters, but also at the 'bullpen' of architects whose names are almost as familiar as the protagonists they brought to life. . . . This book delves into the heart of thousands of costumed characters who continue to fight the good fight in comics, movies, and toy aisles of the world." (Publisher's note)

Torres, Alissa

American widow; illustrated by Sungyoon Choi. Villard Books 2008 209p il $22   **741.5**

1. Educators 2. Graphic novels 3. Autobiographical graphic novels 4. Memoirists 5. Widows -- Graphic novels 6. September 11 terrorist attacks, 2001 -- Graphic novels

ISBN 978-0-345-50069-4

LC 2008-08396

Alissa Torres' husband Luis had just started his new job in the World Trade Center on September 10, 2001. The next day, he died in the terrorist attacks that destroyed the twin towers. Alissa was more than seven months pregnant. In this book, she recounts the personal struggles she suffered as a pregnant "terror widow," first heaped upon with sympathy, then publicly scorned. She describes the tragedies suffered by all the families who lost loved ones on September 11, 2001 and the frustrations they experienced dealing with bureaucrats as they tried to get even the smallest physical trace of their loved ones.

The author's "tragedy of errors inspires anger on her behalf, although the story is calmly and beautifully told. Choi's simple and attractive line art is set off by turquoise wash, yielding to a full-color photo at the end when Alissa embraces her life anew." Libr J

Tran, G. B. (Gia-Bao), 1976-

Vietnamerica; a family's journey. written and illustrated by GB Tran. Villard Books 2010 279 p. chiefly col. ill. $30 **741.5**

1. Artists 2. Illustrators 3. Graphic novels 4. Vietnamese Americans -- Biography 5. Cartoonists 6. Vietnamese refugees -- Graphic novels 7. Vietnamese Americans -- Graphic novels 8. Vietnam War, 1961-1975 -- Graphic novels

ISBN 0345508726; 9780345508720

LC 2011283144

"GB Tran is a young Vietnamese American artist who grew up distant from (and largely indifferent to) his family's history. Born and raised in South Carolina as a son of immigrants, he knew that his parents had fled Vietnam during the fall of Saigon. But even as they struggled to adapt to life in America, they preferred to forget the past--and to focus on their children's future. It was only in his late twenties that GB began to learn their extraordinary story. When his last surviving grandparents die within months of each other, GB visits Vietnam for the first time and begins to learn the tragic history of his family, and of the homeland they left behind." (Publisher's note)

"The comic utilizes a dizzying barrage of effects to depict the characters' confusing experience: different lettering styles, realistic action set against full-page government posters, sound effects swirling from panel to panel, action-packed panoramas breaking apart as South Vietnam collapses." Pub Wkly

Tyler, Carol

Soldier's heart; the campaign to understand my WWII veteran father - a daughter's memoir. by Carol Tyler. Fantagraphics 2015 362 p. color illustrations, color map $39.99 **741.5**
1. Father-daughter relationship 2. World War, 1939-1945 -- Biography -- Graphic novels
ISBN 160699896X; 9781606998960
Originally published as three separate volumes
Cartoonist Studio Prize (2016)
Ignatz Award: Outstanding Graphic Novel (2016)
"The phrase 'soldier's heart' is the predecessor to today's post-traumatic stress disorder (PTSD). This is the underlying theme in Tyler's . . . biography of her father's life in this book, originally released as the trilogy You'll Never Know, between 2009 and 2012. Tyler tells the story of her father, Charles, his upbringing as a plumber's son in Chicago before he enlists in the army during World War II; his war experience; after the war as he raises his family with his beloved wife, Red; and their lives into the present. The time line jumps between the current day, as Tyler deals with her own troubled marriage and raising her daughter, and the past (her own, her father's, and her mother's)." (Library Journal)

Watterson, Bill

The **complete** Calvin and Hobbes. Andrews McMeel Pub. 2005 3v il set $150 **741.5**
1. Comic books, strips, etc.
ISBN 0-7407-4847-5; 978-0-7407-4847-9
LC 2004-62709
This is a collection of the entire run of the comic strip Calvin and Hobbes, which ran from 1985 to 1995.
"This is one of the all-time great comic strips, absolutely essential for every library." Libr J

Weiner, Stephen

101 outstanding graphic novels; Stephen Weiner ; [edited by] Daniel J. Fingeroth. 3rd edition NBM Pub. 2015 80 p. (hardcover) $15.99 **741.5**
1. Graphic novels 2. Best books -- United States. 3. Graphic novels -- Bibliography
ISBN 1561639443; 9781561639441
LC 2014958652
Previously called 101 Best Graphic Novels
"The popular primer on the best graphic novels, initially called The 101 Best Graphic Novels, is back in its third updated edition. Expert librarian Stephen Weiner--with the crowdsourcing help of professionals in the field, from artists to critics to leading comic store owners--has sifted through the bewildering thousands of graphic novels now available to come up with an outstanding, not-to-be-missed 101." (Publisher's note)

Weldon, Glen

★ The **Caped** Crusade; Batman and the Rise of Nerd Culture. by Glen Weldon. Simon & Schuster 2016 336 p. color illustrations $26 **741.5**
1. Popular culture
ISBN 1476756694; 9781476756691
This book, by Glen Weldon, "explains Batman's rises and falls throughout the ages—and what his story tells us about ourselves. . . . For more than three quarters of a century, he has cycled from a figure of darkness to one of lightness and back again. . . . How we perceive Batman's character, whether he's delivering dire threats in a raspy Christian

Bale growl or trading blithely homoerotic double-entendres with partner Robin on the comics page, speaks to who we are." (Publisher's note)
Includes bibliographical references (pages [289]-305) and index.

741.56 Cartoons, caricatures, comic strips

Murphy, Cullen

Cartoon county; my father and his friends in the golden age of make-believe. Cullen Murphy. Farrar, Straus & Giroux 2017 260 p. illustrations (some color) (hardcover) $27 **741.56**
1. Comic books, strips, etc. 2. Cartoonists -- United States -- Biography 3. Illustrators -- United States -- Biography 4. Fairfield County (Conn.) -- Biography
ISBN 9780374713041; 9780374298555
LC 2017001316
This book, by Cullen Murphy, presents "a poignant history of the cartoonists and illustrators from the Connecticut School. . . . [It] brings the postwar American era alive, told through the relationship of a son to his father, an extraordinarily talented and generous man who had been trained by Norman Rockwell." (Publisher's note)
"Part memoir, part cultural history, part treasure trove of drawings and photographs, many previously unpublished—and all thoroughly delightful as a celebration of the golden age of newspaper comics." Kirkus
Includes bibliographical references and index

741.58 Cartoon animation

Ghez, Didier

They drew as they pleased; Part 1 the hidden art of Disney's musical years; 1930s. By Didier Ghez ; Foreword by John Musker. Chronicle Books 2016 207 p. illustrations (some color (hardcover) $40 **741.58**
1. Cartoonists 2. Walt Disney Productions 3. Walt Disney Productions -- History -- 20th century 4. Animated films -- United States -- History and criticism
ISBN 9781452137438; 9781452137445
LC 2015040121
Vol. 1 of 6-volume series
This book, by Didier Ghez, describes how "as the Walt Disney Studio entered its first decade and embarked on some of the most ambitious animated films of the time, Disney hired a group of 'concept artists' whose sole mission was to explore ideas and inspire their fellow animators. [This volume] . . . showcases four of these early pioneers and features artwork developed by them for the Disney shorts from the 1930s." (Publisher's note)
"This is a gem for film buffs and Disney enthusiasts looking for an absorbing title to fill out their collections." LJ
Includes bibliographical references and index

Gitlin, Marty

A **celebration** of animation; the 100 greatest cartoon characters in television history. Marty Gitlin and Joe Wos ; foreword by Tom Kenny, voice of SpongeBob SquarePants. Lyons Press 2018 xv, 296 p.p illustrations (chiefly color) (hardcover) $35 **741.58**
1. Cartoons and caricatures 2. Animated television programs 3. Cartoon characters -- Miscellanea 4. Animated television programs -- Miscellanea
ISBN 9781630762797; 1630762784; 9781630762780
LC 2017025749

This book, by Marty Gitlin and Joe Wos, "explores the best-of-the-best cartoon characters from the 1920s to the 21st century. Casting a wide net, it includes characters both serious and humorous, and ranging from silly to malevolent. But all the greats gracing this book are sure to trigger nostalgic memories of carefree Saturday mornings or after-school hours with family and friends in front of the TV set." (Publisher's note)

741.6   Graphic design, illustration, commercial art

Bang, Molly

★ **Picture** this; how pictures work. Molly Bang. Chronicle Books Llc 2016 134 p. ill. (some col.) (ebook) $23.39; $22.99   **741.6**
   1. Visual perception 2. Illustration of books 3. Visual perception -- Psychological aspects 4. Illustration of books -- Psychological aspects 5. Illustrated children's books -- Psychological aspects
   ISBN 9781452154220; 1452151997; 9781452151991
                          LC 00024402
This book, by Molly Bang, "is now revised and expanded for its 25th anniversary. Bang's powerful ideas—about how the visual composition of images works to engage the emotions, and how the elements of an artwork can give it the power to tell a story—remain unparalleled in their simplicity and genius. Why are diagonals dramatic? Why are curves calming? Why does red feel hot and blue feel cold?" (Publisher's note)

"A must-have book for anyone wanting to learn or teach about art elements and principles and their connections to (picture book) art and visual perception." Kirkus

Crumb, R.

R. Crumb: the complete record cover collection. W. W. Norton & Co. 2011 un il $27.95   **741.6**
   1. Popular music 2. Sound recordings -- Album covers
   ISBN 978-0-393-08278-4
This volume is "filled with the artist's designs for such ephemera as 'Unknown Detroit Bluesmen' or Cliff Edwards's 'I'm a Bear in a Ladies' Boudoir.' Starting in the 1970s, Mr. Crumb produced covers for reissues from labels like Yazoo, Blue Goose and Barrelhouse Records, and his love for the music is evident—a stippled Robert Johnson stares out in stark black and white, Bessie Smith sings 'Put a Little Sugar in My Bowl' and Charlie Patton gets his own mini-graphic novel. . . . (The biggest act here is Big Brother and the Holding Company, with Janis Joplin done over to fit Crumb's zaftig ideal.) In this journeyman work, however, the discipline of playing second fiddle to his favorite musicians keeps the artist's self-loathing in check without taming the ribald humor that is also a hallmark of the blues. Few Crumb projects seem like so much fun—to read about, to look at or to listen along to." Wall Street J

Hayes, Clay

Gig posters volume 1; rock show art of the 21st century. Quirk Books 2009 208p il $40   **741.6**
   1. Posters 2. Rock music
   ISBN 978-1-59474-326-9; 1-59474-326-6
                      LC 2008-938830
"There is no single style for gig posters — they are punk, grunge, new wave, neo-modern, comic, retro, parodic and satirical. Some are beautiful, others ugly; some derivative, others novel. Most are eye-catching, and some are memorable. Those that are wheat-pasted on hoardings or taped to lampposts are usually removed within days, so GigPosters has been a terrific archive of the good, the bad and the ugly. But digital versions just don't compare with the printed posters, which is why . . . [this book, compiled by the] founder of GigPosters, is such

a useful resource. The book contains posters by leaders of the art form (including Emek, Eleanor Grosch, Lil Tuffy and Luke Drozd), who offer brief commentaries about their work." N Y Times Book Rev

Heller, Steven, 1950-

Becoming a graphic & digital designer; a guide to careers in design. Steven Heller & Veronique Vienne. 5th edition John Wiley & Sons, Inc. 2015 335 p. color illustrations pbk $44.95   **741.6**
   1. Graphic arts 2. Commercial art 3. Computer graphics
   ISBN 1118771982; 9781118771983
                      LC 2015011294
"With an emphasis on portfolio requirements and job opportunities, this guide helps both students and individuals interested in entering the design field prepare for successful careers. Coverage includes design inspiration, design genres, and design education, with discussion of the specific career options available in print, interactive, and motion design. Interviews with leading designers like Michael Bierut, Stefan Sagmeister, and Mirko Ilic give readers an insider's perspective on career trajectory and a glimpse into everyday operations and inspirations at a variety of companies and firms." (Publisher's note)

Includes bibliographical references (pages 330-331) and index.

Kidd, Chip

Chip Kidd; Book 2 Chip Kidd ; introductions by Haruki Murakami, Neil Gaiman, Orhan Pamuk ; design by Mark Melnick; photography by Geoff Spear. Rizzoli International Publications 2017 318 p. (hardback) $60   **741.6**
   1. Designers 2. Book design
   ISBN 9780847860081
                      LC 2017934352
In this book, Chip Kidd "picks up where Book One left off showcasing his impressive body of work from the past decade as well as new works yet to be seen. . . . We see not just hundreds of his recent projects, but the working processes behind them--thoughts, sketches, revisions, scrapped drafts, and triumphant final versions. The bestselling authors he has worked with include the likes of Cormac McCarthy, John Updike, . . . and Elie Wiesel." (Publisher's note)

"Kidd's love of the written word and the publishing industry shines through as he details his meticulous and considered approach to book design. Some design concepts came to him in a flash, while others were developed in more iterative processes. Readers will find the scrapped ideas are often more interesting than the final designs themselves, for they provide insight into the hard work of conceptualization that goes into each book's jacket design (not to mention the corporate machinations)." PW.

Meder, Danielle

Draw fashion now; Techniques, Inspiration, and Ideas for Illustrating and Imagining Your Designs - With Fashion Paper Dolls and a Customizable, Designer-Inspired Wardrobe. Danielle Meder. Quarto Pub Group USA 2016 143 p. illustrations (some color) $22.99; (ebook) $22.99   **741.6**
   1. Fashion design 2. Fashion drawing
   ISBN 1631591207; 9781631591204; 9781631591877
                      LC 2016030336
In this book, "professional fashion illustrator Danielle Meder shares lessons she's learned over fourteen seasons of sketching fashion and style in every fashion capital, offering readers solid illustration techniques that demystify the enigma of fashion 'attitude.' Start by learning the development and rendering process of contemporary male and female figures. . . . Then, master basic sketching through rendering gar-

ments and fabrics directly on the figure." (Publisher's note)

"Fashion buffs and aspiring designers of any skill level will enjoy this fun guide." LJ

Includes bibliographical references (page 143).

Neuburger, Emily K.

Show me a story; 40 craft projects and activities to spark children's storytelling. by Emily K. Neuburger. Storey Pub. 2012 144 p. ill. (pbk.; alk. paper) $16.95; (hardcover) $26.95   **741.6**

1. Storytelling 2. Handicraft for children 3. Illustrators -- Interviews 4. Illustrated children's books

ISBN 1612121489; 9781603429887; 9781612121482

LC 2012004610

This book presents "40 creative projects and activities [designed to] encourage [children] to free their storytelling instincts." Activities for "[y]ounger children" include "making story stones and a storytelling jar . . . while older kids will enjoy word grab bags, story walks, and journaling exercises." The book is intended "[f]or everyone ages 5 to 12". (Publisher's note)

Includes bibliographical references and index.

The **poster**; 1,000 posters from Toulouse-Lautrec to Sagmeister. edited by Cees V. de Jong, Alston W. Purvis, Martijn F. Le Coultre; text by Alston W. Ourvis; intorduction by Cees W. de Jong. Abrams 2010 567p il pa $35   **741.6**

1. Posters

ISBN 978-0-8109-9588-8; 0-8109-9588-3

LC 2010-14458

"In the history of art, the poster occupies a strange no-man's-land, a middle ground at the intersection of design and commerce. However masterful they might be in terms of composition and execution, the fact remains that posters are used to sell something else—a product, an idea, a critical bit of wartime propaganda. Whether it's cookies or patriotism that is on the block, the purpose of a poster seems to rest uneasily alongside the artistic spirit that impels it. The Poster is a book that aims not to apologize for this duality, but to acknowledge it and then move on. In purely artistic terms, posters can be marvelous works of skill and imagination—powerfully designed and skillfully executed. . . . Overall, the collection succeeds admirably." PopMatters

Includes bibliographical references

Rees, Darrell

How to Be an Illustrator; by Darrel Rees. Chronicle Books LLC 2014 167 p. ill (some col) $24.95   **741.6**

1. Illustrators 2. Vocational guidance

ISBN 1780673280; 9781780673288

This book, by Darrel Rees, "offers practical help and guidance to aspiring illustrators. . . . International illustrators are interviewed, discussing how they got their break in the industry, their experiences with clients, their methods of promoting work, and more. In addition, leading art directors describe their approach to commissioning illustration, how they spot new talent, their thoughts on promotional material, and their advice to up-and-coming illustrators." (Publisher's note)

'This guide . . . shares the author's insights on everything except the artistic aspects of the occupation, i.e., business concerns such as education, job hunting, project management, billing, and promoting yourself." LJ

Includes bibliographical references

Rendgen, Sandra

Understanding the world; the atlas of infographics. Sandra

Rendgen ; ed. Julius Wiedemann. Taschen 2014 456 p. color ills; color maps $69.99   **741.6**

1. Atlases 2. Information visualization 3. Maps -- Design 4. Visual communication 5. Communication -- Graphic methods

ISBN 3836548836; 9783836548830

LC 2015588511

This book by Sandra Rendgen and Julius Wiedemann presents "more than 280 contemporary and vintage visualizations to help us understand our world, including seven fold-out spreads. Spanning the present state, and historical shaping, of society, culture, technology, economics and the environment, this is at once a showcase of . . . data design work, and a . . . digest of where and how we live." (Publisher's note)

Roeder, Katherine

David Wiesner & the art of wordless storytelling; Eik Kahng, Ellen Keiter, Katherine Roeder, David Wiesner. Santa Barbara Museum of Art 2017 112 p. illustrations (chiefly color) (hardcover; alk. paper) $29.95   **741.6**

1. Illustration of books 2. Children's literature -- Authorship 3. Art and literature -- United States -- Exhibitions 4. Illustrated children's books -- United States -- Exhibitions

ISBN 9780300226010

LC 2016041100

This book, by Eik Kahng, Ellen Keiter, Katherine Roeder, and David Wiesner, "features dozens of lavish color plates, from early work to the exquisitely wrought watercolors that are the basis of [Wiesner's] best-known books, along with pages excerpted from his forthcoming first graphic novel, Fish Girl. Also included are works by some of the artists most influential to Wiesner, including Marvel comic book legends, Surrealist and avant-garde masters, and mid-20th-century graphic artists." (Publisher's note)

"This exhibition catalog from the Santa Barbara Museum of Art offers splendid reproductions of paintings by Wiesner, whose wordless picture books have won three Caldecott Medals." Pub Wkly

Salisbury, Martin

★ The **illustrated** book jacket, 1920-1970; Martin Salisbury. Thames & Hudson 2017 199 p. color illustrations (hardcover) $39.95   **741.6**

1. Book design 2. Bookbinding 3. Book industry 4. Illustrators -- History -- 20th century 5. Book jackets -- History -- 20th century

ISBN 9780500519134

LC 2017931867

This book, by Martin Salisbury, is "a deep dive into the history of the illustrated book jacket, tracing its development across the twentieth century, reflecting some of the most iconic designs of the era. . . . Featuring talent from the US and UK, [this book] explores the pictorial dust jacket through a selection of more than 300 key works and artists that influenced the course of book jacket design." (Publisher's note)

"This volume will be of interest to professional designers and illustrators; collectors of American ephemera; and anyone interested in or studying illustration, graphic design, or American visual culture." Choice

Includes bibliographical references (page 194) and index.

Illustrating children's books; creating pictures for publication. Barron's Educational Series 2004 144p il pa $22.95   **741.6**

1. Illustrators 2. Illustration of books 3. Picture books for children

ISBN 0-76412-717-9

The author "surveys the genre's distinguished history with examples from Caldecott, Greenaway, N. C. Wyeth, Maxfield Parrish, and Howard

Pyle. . . . Through sketches and annotations, Salisbury explains how to create fantasy, fairy tale, realism, and nature drawing. Written for advanced students, the book covers storyboards and layouts, contracts, copyrights, and how to present one's work professionally. Highly recommended for all collections." Libr J

Includes bibliographical references

Schiller, Justin

Maurice Sendak; a celebration of the artist and his work. by Justin Schiller and illustrated by Maurice Sendak. Harry N. Abrams 2013 223 p. (alk. paper) $45   **741.6**

   1. Artists -- Biography

   ISBN 1419708260; 9781419708268

LC 2013007227

In this book, by Justin Schiller, "the preeminent children's book artist of the twentieth century, Maurice Sendak and his sixty-year career are celebrated in this full-color catalog of more than two hundred images being exhibited at the Society of Illustrators in New York City. [Images are] accompanied by twelve essays by such noted scholars and historians as Leonard S. Marcus, Iona Opie, Steven Heller, and Paul O. Zelinsky." (Publisher's note)

Includes bibliographical references and index

741.945   Italian drawing

Kline, Fred R.

Leonardo's holy child; the discovery of a Leonardo da Vinci masterpiece; a connoisseur's search for lost art in America; a memoir of discovery. by Fred R. Kline. Pegasus Books 2016 360 p. illustrations (some color) (hardcover) $29.95 **741.945**

   1. Art -- 15th and 16th centuries 2. Art -- Expertising

   ISBN 1605989797; 9781605989792

LC 2016387139

This book, by Fred R. Kline, "is about the discovery of one [art] piece in particular: About ten years ago, . . . a beautiful little drawing caught [the author's] eye. Attributed to Carracci, . . . but Kline's every instinct told him that the attribution was wrong. He . . . bought the drawing outright. And that was the beginning of how Kline discovered Leonardo da Vinci's model drawing for the Infant Jesus and the Infant St. John." (Publisher's note)

"Even the most casual museum goer will find something to appreciate in this fascinating account." booklist

742   Perspective in drawing

Brehm, Matthew

Drawing perspective; How to See It and How to Apply It. Paul Heaston. Barrons Educational Series, Inc. 2015 144 p. color illustrations $19.99   **742**

   1. Drawing 2. Perspective

   ISBN 9781438006598

LC 2014945484

This book, by Paul Heaston, is "a hands-on guide to perspective that's for anyone who wants to draw or paint—in any genre or medium. It's partly about learning how to draw a set of straight lines that meet at a point, but it's not filled with lots of dull, dry theory (although it does explain how it all works)." (Publisher's note)

"Dynamic layouts and simple structure make this guide fun to read and easy to comprehend." LJ

Includes bibliographical references (page 144) and index.

Norling, Ernest R.

Perspective made easy; Ernest R. Norling. Dover Publications 1999 xii, 203 p.p illustrations $10.95; (ebook) $9.95 **742**

   1. Drawing 2. Perspective 3. Drawing -- Technique

   ISBN 0486404730; 9780486404738; 9780486130002

LC 99010310

This book, by Ernest R. Norling, is "devoted entirely to clarifying the laws of perspective. . . . Beginning with clear, concise, immediately applicable discussions of the horizon, vanishing point, and the crucial relationship of eye level to perspective drawing, you'll learn how to place figures and objects in a drawing, depict interiors, create shade and shadows, and achieve all the other elements necessary for a successful perspective drawing." (Publisher's note)

743.4   Drawing human figures

Bradley, Barbara

Drawing people; how to portray the clothed figure. Barbara Bradley. North Light Books 2003 175 p. illustrations (some color) $26.99; (ebook) $33.74   **743.4**

   1. Drawing 2. Figure drawing 3. Drapery in art 4. Human figure in art 5. Drawing -- Technique

   ISBN 1581803591; 9781581803594; 9781440317798

LC 2003042043

This book, by Barbara Bradley, "provides all the information you need to render clothed human figures with energy, detail and control. Bradley begins by teaching the basics of any drawing, including proportion, perspective and value. Next, you'll learn how to overcome the special challenges posed by clothing, including fabric folds and draping effects. Bradley illustrates how they're constructed and how to draw them in different situations." (Publisher's note)

"Watson's Life Drawing Class is a rich and dynamic volume on the human form, clothed and unclothed, flabby and buff, indoors and out. Using pencil, charcoal, ink, and watercolor, Watson (Artists Sketchbook) utilizes photographs to complement lessons in balance and proportion, lighting, mood, and composition." LJ

Hart, Christopher

Human anatomy made amazingly easy. Watson-Guptill 2000 114p il pa $19.95   **743.4**

   1. Figure drawing 2. Artistic anatomy

   ISBN 0-8230-2497-0

LC 00-43514

In this work for the beginning artist "Hart simplifies the process in an accessible manual that concentrates on line and forgoes the complexity of color." Libr J

Huston, Steve

Figure drawing for artists; making every mark count. by Steve Huston. Quarto Pub Group USA 2016 192 p. $24.99   **743.4**

   1. Drawing

   ISBN 1631590650; 9781631590658

LC 2016021567

In this book, "artist Steve Huston shows beginners and pros alike the two foundational concepts behind the greatest masterpieces in art and how to use them as the basis for their own success. Embark on a drawing journey and discover how these twin pillars of support are behind everything from the Venus De Milo to Michelangelo's Sibyl to George Bellow's Stag at Sharkey's." (Publisher's note)

Loomis, Andrew, 1892-1959

Figure drawing for all it's worth; Andrew Loomis. Titan Books 2011 204 p. illustrations $39.95 **743.4**

1. Figure drawing 2. Anatomy, Artistic 3. Figure drawing -- Technique

ISBN 0857680986; 9780857680983

LC 2011381456

This book focuses on illustrator Andrew Loomis. "His hugely influential series of art instruction books have never been bettered, and Figure Drawing is the first in Titan's programme of facsimile editions, returning these classic titles to print for the first time in decades." (Publisher's note)

Parks, Carrie Stuart

Secrets to drawing realistic faces; Carrie Stuart Parks. North Light Books 2002 140 p. illustrations $23.99; (ebook) $23.99 **743.4**

1. Face in art 2. Drawing -- Technique

ISBN 1581802161; 9781581802160; 9781600614958

LC 2002023509

This book, by Carrie Stuart Parks, will help you "render strikingly realistic faces and self-portraits! . . . Proven, hands-on exercises and before-and-after examples from Parks' students ensure instant success! It's all the guidance and inspiration you need to draw realistic faces with precision, confidence and style!" (Publisher's note)

"Her useful and far-ranging discussion of materials includes an evaluation of pencils' graphite grades, kneaded and electric erasers, blending tools, and papers." Booklist

Ryder, Anthony

The **artist's** complete guide to figure drawing; a contemporary perspective on the classical tradition. Anthony Ryder. Watson-Guptill Publications 2000 160 p. illustrations $24.99; (ebook) $65 **743.4**

1. Figure drawing 2. Figure drawing -- Technique

ISBN 0823003035; 9780823003037; 9780770434748

LC 99022843

In this book, by Anthony Ryder, "amateur and experienced artists alike are guided toward [a] new way of seeing and drawing the figure with a three-step drawing method. . . . [It] starts with the block-in, an exercise in seeing and establishing the figure's shape. It then build to the contour, a refined line drawing that represents the figure's silhouette. The last step is tonal work on the inside of the contour, when light and shadow are shaped to create the illusion of form." (Publisher's note)

Vanderpoel, John H.

The **human** figure; [by] John H. Vanderpoel. Dover Publications 1958 143 p. illustrations $7.95; (ebook) $7.95 **743.4**

1. Figure drawing

ISBN 0486204324; 9780486204321; 9780486133782

LC 57014883

This book, by John H. Vanderpoel, presents a "clear, detailed presentation of thousands of fundamental features of the human figure. Every element of the body . . . is carefully and concisely pointed out in the text. Even more helpful are the 430 pencil and charcoal drawings that illustrate each feature so that you are, in effect, shown what to look for by a master teacher." (Publisher's note)

Winslow, Valerie L.

Classic human anatomy; the artist's guide to form, function, and movement. Valerie L. Winslow. Watson-Guptill Publications 2009 303 p. illustrations (some color) (hbk.) $40 **743.4**

1. Human anatomy 2. Anatomy, Artistic 3. Figure drawing -- Technique

ISBN 0823024156; 9780823024155

LC 2009280099

This book, by Valerie L. Winslow, "provides simple, insightful approaches to the complex subject of human anatomy, using drawings, diagrams, and reader-friendly text. Three major sections–the skeletal form, the muscular form and action of the muscles, and movement–break the material down into easy-to-understand pieces." (Publisher's note)

"A significant contribution to the literature of art reference." LJ

Includes glossary, bibliographical references (p. 295-296) and index

743.6   Drawing animals

Amberlyn, J. C.

How to draw dogs and puppies; a complete guide for beginners. J.C. Amberlyn. The Monacelli Press 2017 223 p. illustrations (paperback) $25 **743.6**

1. Drawing 2. Dogs in art 3. Illustrated books 4. Puppies in art

ISBN 9781580934541

LC 2016026570

This book, by J. C. Amberlyn, provides a "step-by-step guide to drawing over 100 different breeds and mixed breeds of dogs and puppies in pencil and pen-and-ink. . . . [It] includes basic information on art materials and the fundamental mechanics of drawing so that even beginners will feel confident and successful as they learn to produce highly detailed, lifelike drawings of their favorite best friends." (Publisher's note)

Hand, Diana

Draw Horses in 15 Minutes; Capture the beauty of the equine form. by Diana Hand. Octopus Pub Group 2016 112 p. illustrations $12.99 **743.6**

1. Drawing 2. Animal painting and illustration

ISBN 1781572496; 9781781572498

This book by Diana Hand "shows you how to express your love of horses through drawing. In a series of tutorials, [Hand] describes every stage from finding your model and learning the basic skills of drawing to portraying the movement and spirit of the individual horse. [The book] will inspire you to make your own expressive drawings based on the principles of equine anatomy. Furthermore, you will discover a skill you never thought you had." (Publisher's note)

"Artist Hand provides short horse drawing sessions that can function as confidence builders for wobbly beginners and offer an achievable time investment for anyone." LJ

745   Decorative arts

Akiyama, Lance

Rubber band engineer; build slingshot powered rockets, rubber band rifles, unconventional catapults, and more guerrilla gadgets from household hardware. Lance Akiyama. Quarto Pub Group USA 2016 144 p. color illustrations (paperback) $22.99 **745**

1. Handicraft 2. Rubber bands

ISBN 9781631591044; 1631591045

In this book, by Lance Akiyama, "discover unexpected ways to turn common materials into crafty contraptions that range from surprisingly simple to curiously complex. In vivid color photos, you'll be guided to create slingshot rockets, unique catapults, and even hydraulic-powered machines. Whether you build one or all 19 of these designs, you'll feel like an ingenious engineer when you're through." (Publisher's note)

"Wonderfully illustrated, with clear and straightforward instructions, these projects provide great, mischievous fun that's very much in the vein of William Gurstelle's Defending Your Castle." LJ

American Folk Art Museum

Encyclopedia of American folk art; Gerard C. Wertkin, editor; Lee Kogan, associate editor; in association with the American Folk Art Museum. Routledge 2004 xxxiii, 612p il $125 **745**

1. American folk art
ISBN 0-415-92986-5

LC 2003-18051

This volume "covers more than three centuries of folk artists and provides information about museum collections, institutions that collect and sponsor folk art, and subjects related to the various forms of folk art. Entries tend to be detailed, and in some cases, extensive. . . . The work is heavily and usefully cross-referenced. Most entries end with brief bibliographies. Although not heavily illustrated, the work offers a number of interesting color and black-and-white illustrations keyed to specific entries." Choice

Includes bibliographical references

Frisoni, Christine-Lea

The **Big** Book of a Miniature House; Create and Decorate a House Room by Room. by Christine-Lea Frisoni. GMC Publications 2015 192 p. $35 **745**

1. Doll furniture 2. Interior design 3. Miniature objects
ISBN 1861089546; 9781861089540

In this book, author Christine-Lea Frisoni "explains how to make a beautiful miniature French country house. . . . Having made the dolls' house, Christine explains how to build up the wall panels to provide deep recesses, fancy panelling and wall niches to add character - ideas that can be translated to any existing dolls' house. Instructions to make a range of French-style furniture, fittings and even flowers are included." (Publisher's note)

Wade, John

Fifty landmark cameras that changed photography; John Wade. Schiffer Pub., Ltd. 2016 256 p. (hardcover) $59.99 **745**

1. Cameras -- History 2. Cameras -- Pictorial works
ISBN 9780764350047

LC 2015954910

This book on the history of the camera, by John Wade, is "lavishly illustrated book with over 460 pictures [and] looks at the cameras that became landmarks and analyzes how and why they influenced future design – sometimes in a big, important manner, other times in a lesser but still significant way." (Publisher's note)

"This book responds to readers' indulgence; it is well written, highly informative, beautifully illustrated, and an extraordinary, wished for collector's catalog." Choice Reviews

745.1 Antiques

Miller, Judith

Miller's antiques handbook & price guide; [edited by] Judith Miller. Octopus Books various pagings il **745.1**

1. Antiques
Annual. First published 1979. Variant title: Miller's international antiques price guide
This guide includes photographs, prices and brief descriptions

of museum-quality antiques sold at auction or by dealers during the past year.

"Although this is a best-of resource, not covering attic knickknacks, it is an alluring look book with inherent educational value." Libr J

745.103   Antiques – Encyclopedias

Miller, Judith, 1951-

Miller's antiques encyclopedia; general editor, Judith Miller. Octopus Pub Group 2017 592 p. $55 **745.103**

1. Antiques -- Encyclopedias 2. Antiques -- Collectors and collecting
ISBN 1784723657; 9781784723651

LC 2004381908

This book, edited by Judith Miller, "contains valuable information for both the [antique] enthusiast and the experienced dealer. An extensive glossary explains the terms used throughout the book and clear cross-referencing leads you into related areas of interest. All the traditional areas of collecting are featured, with extensive sections on furniture, ceramics, silver and glass." (Publisher's note)

Includes bibliographical references (p. 533-535) and index

745.2   Industrial art and design

Norman, Don

The **design** of everyday things; Don Norman. Basic Books 2013 xviii, 347 p.p illustrations (pbk.) $17.99 **745.2**

1. Human engineering 2. Industrial design -- Psychological aspects
ISBN 0465050654; 9780465050659

LC 2013024417

"The Design of Everyday Things shows that good, usable design is possible. The rules are simple: make things visible, exploit natural relationships that couple function and control, and make intelligent use of constraints." Author "Don Norman hails excellence of design as the most important key to regaining the competitive edge in influencing consumer behavior." (Publisher's note)

"The revised edition updates examples; the original work preceded the Web and mobile devices. It also expands and refines the treatment of psychology, analyzing how affordances are signified to people, how emotion impacts everything people do and experience, and how culture can modulate what is 'natural' in design. Most notably, the revised edition articulates a broader view of design's goals and constraints." Choice

Includes bibliographical references (pages 321-330) and index

745.4   Pure and applied design and decoration

Albrecht, Donald

The **Work** of Charles and Ray Eames; a legacy of invention. essays by Donald Albrecht . . . {et al.} Abrams 1997 205p il hardcover o.p. pa $24.95 **745.4**

1. Design 2. Architects 3. Exhibit designers 4. Interior designers 5. Furniture designers 6. Industrial designers 7. Motion picture producers
ISBN 0-8109-1799-8; 978-0-8109-9232-0 pa; 0-8109-9232-9 pa

LC 97-4086

This overview of the work of two prominent American postwar designers features "pictures of famous furniture, toys, exhibitions, promotional material, informal snapshots, stills from films, comics, advertisements, exhibitions for the federal government, and much more. The work features six major essays, each with extensive notes, by scholars, designers, academics, and architecture/design writers." Choice

Includes bibliographical references

Miller, Judith, 1951-

Miller's arts & crafts; living with the arts & crafts style. by Judith Miller. Octopus Pub Group 2014 239 p. color illustrations $39.99 **745.4**

1. Arts and crafts movement
ISBN 1845339436; 9781845339432

This book on the arts & crafts movement, by Judith Miller, "covers furniture, ceramics, silver and metalware, glass, textiles, jewellery, books and posters, and includes fascinating profiles of key designers such as William Morris, the Stickleys, Liberty & Co, Tiffany Studios, George Ohr, Rookwood and many more. It comes with a pictorial design directory, price ranges and a wealth of essential information for collectors." (Publisher's note)

"Noteworthy for its breadth and its superb color images, this is an up-to-date resource for any art collection." LJ

745.5 Handicrafts

Chapin, Kari

★ The **handmade** marketplace; how to sell your crafts locally, globally, and online. Kari Chapin. 2nd edition Storey Publishing 2014 247 p. pbk $15.95 **745.5**

1. Handicraft 2. Internet marketing
ISBN 161212335X; 9781612123356

LC 2014004540

Chapin "provides advice on starting from the ground up, covering everything from choosing a catchy name to developing a logo and marketing strategies. There's a strong focus on using social media and blogs to promote one's business--a must in today's connected world--and Chapin gives thoughtful guidance on how to do so without overwhelming followers with your message. Online sales aren't everything, so there's also facts about selling at craft fairs and through brick-and-mortar stores." (Library Journal)

Includes bibliographical references and index

Corwin, Lena

Printing by hand; a modern guide to printing with handmade stamps, stencils, and silk screens. by Lena Corwin ; photography by Thayer Allyson Gowdy. Stewart, Tabori & Chang 2008 144 p. (alk. paper) $29.95 **745.5**

1. Handicraft 2. Stencil work 3. Silk screen printing 4. Rubber stamp printing 5. Screen process printing
ISBN 1584796723; 9781584796725

LC 2007044503

In this book, author Lena Corwin "teaches crafters everything they need to know to master stamping, stenciling, and screen printing, from making their own printing devices to trouble-shooting when plans go awry. Her . . . collection of projects ranges from stamped stationery and simple-to-sew pouches, to stenciled tote bags and furniture, to screen-printed bed linens and upholstery fabric." (Publisher's note)

Joyce, Anna

Stamp stencil paint; making extraordinary patterned projects by hand. Anna Joyce. STC Craft 2015 144 p. illustrations (some color) $27.50 **745.5**

1. Stencil work 2. Patternmaking
ISBN 9781617691775; 1617691771

LC 2014959128

In this book, author Anna Joyce "shares her signature hand-printing techniques and infectious enthusiasm for adding patterns to ready-made surfaces such as fabric, ceramics, paper, leather, furniture, walls, and more. Following beautiful step-by-step photography, crafters learn new, easy skills to stamp, stencil, and hand-paint wonderful projects for their homes, wardrobes, families, and friends." (Publisher's note)

"Crucially, sound advice about matching particular types of pigments and paints to specific surfaces is liberally dispensed." LJ

Martha Stewart living

Martha Stewart's encyclopedia of crafts; an A-to-Z guide with detailed instructions and endless inspiration. [by the editors of Martha Stewart living] Potter Craft 2009 416p il $35 **745.5**

1. Handicraft
ISBN 978-0-307-45057-9

LC 2008-33415

"In alphabetical order, from albums to wreaths, with intermediate stops at beading, jewelry making, mosaics, quilling, soap making, and more, Stewart presents easily absorbed directions for 200 projects; in each project profile, sumptuous illustrations are partnered with rich, full, stimulating discussion of materials, techniques, and tips. . . . Of primary importance to all crafts collections." Booklist

Nicholas, Kristin

Crafting a patterned home; painting, printing, and stitching projects to enliven every room. Kristin Nicholas ; photographs by Rikki Snyder. Roost Books, an imprint of Shambhala Publications, Inc. 2018 208 p. (hardcover; alk. paper) $24.95 **745.5**

1. Handicraft 2. Interior design 3. House furnishings
ISBN 9781611803495

LC 2017008660

"Create a unique space that's all your own--bold and colorful handmade projects to fill your home with pattern from color expert crafter extraordinaire Kristin Nicholas. Jump into the world of pattern--get a crash course on the types of patterns and how they are made; learn how to gain inspiration and ideas from a variety of sources; explore ways of pairing different patterns together; and make patterns of your own to embellish your home." (Publisher's note)

Pester, Sophie

Supercraft; easy projects for every weekend. Sophie Pester, Catharina Bruns. DK Publishing 2016 175 p. illustrations (chiefly color) $14.95 **745.5**

1. Handicraft
ISBN 1465449205; 9781465449207

LC 2016287005

"Supercraft is packed with DIY craft and sewing projects that use everyday materials and innovative techniques so you can upcycle your way to creating something new and stylish. Embroider a notebook, print fabric with starfruit, make a hanging garden for your bathroom, and much, much more. Each of the 52 projects in this book include everything you need to know, with step-by-step photographs and detailed instructions, and are simple enough to finish in a weekend." (Publisher's note)

"The aesthetic is fresh and contemporary, with lots of bright colors and modern art-inspired style. Numerous techniques are covered, including paper craft, painting, crochet, embroidery, weaving, origami, and sewing, making this a veritable buffet of ideas." LJ

Pigza, Jessica

Bibliocraft; the modern crafter's guide to finding inspira-

tion at the library. Jessica Pigza. STC Craft/A Melanie Falick Book 2014 208 p. illustrations (chiefly colour) $27.50 **745.5**
1. Handicraft 2. Library resources
ISBN 1617690961; 9781617690969

LC 2013945655

In this book, author Jessica Pigza "hones her literary hunting-and-gathering skills to help creatives of all types, from DIY hobbyists to fine artists, develop projects based on library resources. In Part I, she explains how to take advantage of the riches libraries have to offer—both in person and online. In Part II, she presents 20+ projects inspired by library resources." (Publisher's note)

"Though bibliophiles and fans of libraries will be drawn in by the theme of the book, crafters who haven't visited a library since childhood will be thrilled with the wealth of talented artists whose projects are featured. (Bibliophiles will also be pleased that no books are harmed in the making of these crafts.)" LJ

Samuell, Kristine

A **year** of gingerbread houses; making & decorating gingerbread houses for all seasons. by Kristine Samuell. Sterling Pub Co Inc 2015 135 p. illustrations (some color) $19.95 **745.5**
1. Gingerbread
ISBN 1454708913; 9781454708919

In this book, by Kristine Samuell, "[n]othing's more enticing for any holiday or special occasion than an awesome, lusciously decorated gingerbread house. With designs for Christmas, Halloween, Valentine's Day, and birthdays, these exquisite projects include a cottage, chalet, and two-story house. Options as customized windows, doors, chimneys, paths, trees, topiaries, and even lighting add to the charm." (Publisher's note)

"One of the best gingerbread books available, Samuell's debut is essential for serious gingerbread architects and decorators." LJ

Van't Hul, Jean

The **artful** parent; simple ways to fill your family's life with art and creativity. Jean Van't Hul. Roost Books 2013 xxi, 320 p.p color illustrations (pbk.; alk. paper) $21.95 **745.5**
1. Handicraft for children 2. Parent-child relationship 3. Child artists 4. Parent and child 5. Creative activities and seat work
ISBN 1590309642; 9781590309643

LC 2012021168

This book, by Jean Van't Hul, offers "more than 60 kids' art activities from the creator of www.ArtfulParent.com. Art making is a wonderfully fun way for young children to tap into their imagination, deepen their creativity, and explore new materials, all while strengthening their fine motor skills and developing self-confidence. . . . [This book gives] all the tools and information you need to encourage your children's creativity through art." (Publisher's note)

"Parents, teachers, and child-care providers will all find useful ideas and inspiration here." LJ

745.531   Leathers

Gethin, Rosanna

Sew luxe leather; over 20 stylish leather craft accessories. Rosanna Gethin. F & W Media Inc 2018 128 p. $22.99 **745.531**
1. Sewing 2. Handicraft 3. Leather work
ISBN 1446306763; 9781446306765

This book, by Rosanna Gethin, features a "collection of 20 luxe leather projects, [that] is perfect if you're looking for original, high quality projects made from leather, all of which can be made on a domestic

sewing machine or with hand stitching. Choose from small projects to get started such as a keyring, card case, small purse and super-useful earphone holder, right up to the ultimate leather laptop case and a really chic foldover clutch for instant style credentials." (Publisher's note)

"All are ordered by level of difficulty, easiest to most complex, and include tools, materials, and numbered directions, with accompanying color photographs." Booklist

745.54   Papers

Farrell, Patrick

Paper to petal; 75 whimsical paper flower ideas to craft by hand. Rebecca Thuss and Patrick Farrell ; Foreward by Martha Stewart. Potter Craft 2013 256 p. color illustrations (print edition) $24.99 **745.54**
1. Paper flowers
ISBN 0385345054; 9780385345057

LC 2012048675

This book on paper flowers, by Rebecca Thuss and Patrick Farrell, "walks you through the easy basics of transforming simple materials into a vibrant display of fanciful handmade blooms suitable for every occasion. . . . Customize every petal, leaf or stem to go dramatic or delicate; mimic nature or fashion your blossoms in any color you can imagine to make something uniquely personal. You'll be amazed how easy it is to produce these gorgeous flower projects." (Publisher's note)

Helfand, Jessica

Scrapbooks ; an American history; A Winterhouse edition; Yale University Press 2008 244p il $45 **745.54**
1. Scrapbooks 2. Paper crafts
ISBN 978-0-300-12635-8; 0-300-12635-2

The author "offers both an overview of the history of the creation of scrapbooks and a visual feast for readers via the integration of texts, images, and memorabilia of all types. . . . Helfand has made a brilliant selection of unusual examples by visiting numerous archives, and she weaves a narrative based on examples that she found. . . .The book is sumptuous, a superb marriage in fine design, paper, and print." Choice

Martin, Ann

The **art** of quilling paper jewelry; techniques & projects for metallic earrings & pendants. Ann Martin. Interweave 2017 144 p. color illustrations (pbk.) $22.99 **745.54**
1. Handicraft 2. Jewelry making 3. Paper quillwork
ISBN 1632505770; 9781632505774

LC 2017285411

In this book, "author and quilling enthusiast Ann Martin shows you how to turn metallic-edged papers into stunning--and sturdy--earrings and pendants. . . . Whether you're an experienced jewelry maker looking for new techniques or a quiller who wants to turn your creations into one-of-a-kind jewelry, this guide to gilded paper jewelry has what you need." (Publisher's note)

Rodabaugh, Katrina

The **paper** playhouse; awesome art projects for kids; using paper, boxes, and books. by Katrina Rodabaugh, photographs by Leslie Sopia Lindell. Quayside Pub Group 2015 144 p. color illustrations $22.99 **745.54**
1. Handicraft 2. Paper crafts
ISBN 1592539807; 9781592539802

In this book, artist Katrina Rodabaugh, with photographs by Leslie Sopia Lindell, "with simple techniques including sculpture, printmaking, bookbinding, collage, and even ideas for public art, families work through step-by-step instructions while using imagination and budding aesthetics." (Publisher's note)

"Craft projects using recycled or upcycled materials are perennially popular, and the kid-friendly angle adds a fun dimension." LJ

745.57   Rubber and plastics

Heaser, Sue

The **polymer** clay techniques book; by Sue Heaser. North Light Books 1999 128 p. color illustrations $22.99   **745.57**
1. Modeling
ISBN 1581800088; 9781581800081

With this book, by Sue Heaser, "readers can create polymer clay buttons or boxes or anything in between. Starting with the very basics (such as rolling, baking and gluing), it then moves on to more advanced methods: marbling, texturing, millefiori, bead-making, faux-stone effects and more. Feature spreads show exciting ways to combine techniques." (Publisher's note)

"The Polymer Clay Technique Book, in particular, has detailed step-by-step instructions for many techniques such as marbling, cutting, and making millefiori canes." LJ

Includes bibliographical references (p. 126) and index.

745.59   Making specific objects

Michaels, Chris Franchetti

Teach yourself visually jewelry making & beading. Wiley Publishing 2007 290p il (Visual read less, learn more) pa $24.99   **745.59**
1. Beads 2. Jewelry 3. Beadwork
ISBN 978-0-470-10150-6; 0-470-10150-4

This book explains how "to craft designs that are chic but inexpensive. With hundreds of detailed photos, this book covers tools and supplies, bead stringing and weaving, wire wrapping, and more." Publisher's note

Oppenheimer, Betty

Candlemaker's companion; a complete guide to rolling, pouring, dipping, and decorating your own candles. Completely rev and updated; Storey Bks. 2001 199p il pa $18.95 **745.59**
1. Candles
ISBN 1-58017-366-7

LC 00-53802
First published 1997

This offers a brief history of candles followed by information about wicks, waxes and additives, color and scent, and equipment. Step-by-step instructions on candlemaking techniques and decoration, and a list of suppliers

Includes bibliographical references

745.592   Toys, models, miniatures, related objects

Baker, Mark

Turned toys; Mark Baker. The Taunton Press, Inc. 2016 191 p. color illustrations $24.95   **745.592**
1. Turning 2. Woodwork 3. Wooden toy making 4. Turning (Lathe work)

ISBN 9781631866531

LC 2016021953
In this book, "woodturning expert Mark Baker shows you how to create beautiful hand-crafted toys and games for the children in your life—all while developing your skills as a woodturner. The projects range in difficulty from the cute and simple hedgehog to the detailed and complex disappearing ball trick. Other traditional childhood toys that you will learn to make include a spinning top, a lighthouse stacker, a pull-along train, and ring-turned pigs." (Publisher's note)

Davis, Todd

Handy dad; 25 awesome projects for dads and kids. by Todd Davis ; photographs by Juli Stewart and Todd Davis ; illustrations by Nik Schulz. Chronicle Books 2010 167 p. col. ill., plans (pbk.) $24.95   **745.592**
1. Handicraft 2. Toy making 3. Father-child relationship 4. Family recreation 5. Handicraft -- Design
ISBN 081186958X; 9780811869584

LC 2009026020
This book, by extreme sports athlete Todd Davis, "presents 25 awesome projects for dads to build with their kids. Busy dads can choose projects that range from simple to challenging and take anywhere from five minutes to a full weekend. Readers are given all the directions they need to grab materials that can be found around the house or at the local hardware store and get to work." (Publisher's note)

Finnanger, Tone, 1973-

Tilda's toy box; Sewing Patterns for Soft Toys and More from the Magical World of Tilda. by Tone Finnanger. F & W Media Inc. 2015 135 p. color illustrations $24.99   **745.592**
1. Soft toy making
ISBN 1446306151; 9781446306154

This book, by Tone Finnanger, "will show you how to make a wide range of beautiful soft toys and gifts for kids, plus amazing accessories for their bedrooms. Discover simple sewing patterns for adorably plump dolls with a range of outfits and accessories, cute jungle creatures like monkeys, and sea-themed creations - pirates, whales and fish--all reproduced at full-size to trace from the page." (Publisher's note)

Smith, Sally J.

Fairy houses; how to create whimsical homes for fairy folk. Sally J. Smith. Cool Springs Press 2017 192 p. (hardcover) $30   **745.592**
1. Garden structures 2. Garden ornaments and furniture 3. Nature craft 4. Miniature objects 5. Fairies -- Miscellanea
ISBN 9780760354834; 9781591866725

LC 2016033755
In this book by Sally Smith "step-by-step instructions for constructing exquisite fairy houses are revealed. [Readers] begin by flipping through an inspiration gallery, find which elements appeal to [them], and how they fit together. From there, [they]'ll learn about building materials (found and natural), on-site fairy house construction, and how to light a fairy house." (Publisher's note)

745.594   Decorative objects

Bluhm, Lisa

Creative soldered jewelry & accessories; Lisa Bluhm. Lark Crafts 2014 128 p. color illustrations $21.95   **745.594**
1. Jewelry 2. Soldering 3. Handicraft 4. Jewelry making 5. Solder and soldering

ISBN 1454708166; 9781454708162

LC 2013044513

This book, Lisa Bluhm, presents "more than 20 trendy new projects and the hottest techniques [of soldered jewelry]. Thanks to a robust basics section crafters will easily master the fundamentals of using either a soldering torch or iron, and make such gorgeous items as fashionable earrings, playful tiaras, unique frames, and pretty boudoir bottles." (Publisher's note)

"This is a practical introduction and overview of both hard and soft soldering for hobbyists. Creating fun pieces as part of the learning process is an added bonus." LJ

Creative soldered jewelry and accessories

Brown, Carrie

The **new** Christmas tree; 25 dazzling trees and over 100 handcrafted projects for an inspired holiday. Carrie Brown ; photographs by Paige Green. Artisan 2015 296 p. color illustrations (alk. paper) $29.95   **745.594**

1. Handicraft 2. Christmas trees 3. Christmas tree ornaments
ISBN 9781579655914

LC 2015010993

This book, by Carrie Brown with photographs by Paige Green, presents "one-of-a-kind trees that celebrate food, nature, fashion, folk art, typography, color, and art history. Each spectacular design is easily replicated, with step-by-step instructions for crafting coordinating ornaments, garlands, and toppers, plus advice on selecting the right tree, choosing lights, and more." (Publisher's note)

"There's no shortage of clever ideas, especially for those who'd like to produce ornaments without much fuss. Brown is at her best in suggesting simple crafts that will make an impressive statement." Pub Wkly

Includes bibliographical references and index

Brown, Stephen

Glitterville's handmade christmas; Stephen Brown. Andrews McMeel Publishing 2012 181 p. color illustrations $24.99   **745.594**

1. Christmas 2. Handicraft
ISBN 1449414559; 9781449414559

LC 2011944595

Author Stephen Brown presents "twenty new whimsical, winter-wonderful craft projects that will fill your home with sleighfuls of cheer. Hundreds of beautiful, easy-to-follow, step-by-step full-color photos and how-tos make the crafting fun and the results foolproof. From a Jolly Dolly Holly Wreath or a charming Glittery Village you can nestle into its own Sparkle Forest, to the frostiest Magic Snow and the jolliest pine-cone-bodied Glitter Gnome." (Publisher's note)

Glitterville's handmade Halloween; a glittered guide for whimsical crafting! Stephen Brown. Andrews McMeel Publishing 2012 xxiv, 178 p.p color illustrations (pbk.) $19.99   **745.594**

1. Halloween 2. Handicraft 3. Halloween decorations
ISBN 1449414524; 9781449414528

LC 2011944594

This book by Stephen Brown is "full of bright, colorful photos, step-by-step holiday how-tos, and over-the-harvest-moon decorating ideas to make your home sparkle and shine this spooktacular season. [Its designed to] delight readers as they make their way through the playfully photographed pages of the book, which include full, never-before-published instructions for making some of Glitterville's most sought-after items." (Publisher's note)

Handmade Halloween

Cetti, Livia

The **exquisite** book of paper flowers; a guide to making unbelievably realistic paper blooms. Livia Cetti. STC Craft/A Melanie Falick Book 2014 192 p. colour illustrations $24.95   **745.594**

1. Origami 2. Artificial flowers
ISBN 1617691003; 9781617691003

LC 2013945659

This book, by Livia Cetti, offers a "comprehensive how-to manual showcasing . . . techniques for creating 27 popular [tissue paper] blooms, including peonies, poppies, roses, and hibiscus. Clear instructions and . . . step-by-step photographs show crafters of all levels how to make individual flowers as well as how to combine blooms to form 20 exquisite garlands, centerpieces, wreaths, corsages, and boutonnieres." (Publisher's note)

★ **Christmas** with Southern Living 2017; inspired ideas for holiday cooking and decorating. the editors of Southern Living. Oxmoor House 2017 192 p. $29.99   **745.594**

1. Entertaining 2. Southern cooking 3. Christmas decorations
ISBN 0848752260; 9780848752262

"For 2017, Christmas with Southern Living is completely new, with all of the menu and décor ideas that you've come to expect, along with more than 100 recipes especially created for holiday cooking, baking, entertaining, and gift giving. This year's edition features five complete theme-based entertaining chapters . . . including menus and decorating ideas for every corner of your home, as well as tips and tricks on surprising ways to use leftovers, serve dishes, and more!" (Publisher's note)

Combs, Rebecca Ann

Kumihimo ; basics & beyond; 24 braided and beaded jewelry projects on the kumihimo disk. by Rebecca Combs. Kalmbach Books 2013 95 p. $21.99   **745.594**

1. Jewelry 2. Handicraft
ISBN 1627000437; 9781627000437

This book, by Rebecca Combs, "presents techniques for creating all-cord braids and beaded braids, then teaches beaders how to transform them into finished jewelry. Short demonstrations of the key techniques needed for each project are presented in easy-to-grasp portions, allowing beaders to learn and practice as they go." (Publisher's note)

Crowther, Janet

Make a statement; Katie Covington and Janet Crowther. Chronicle Books 2014 143 p. color illustrations (alk. paper) $22.95   **745.594**

1. Jewelry making 2. Fashion 3. Costume jewelry
ISBN 1452133204; 9781452133201

LC 2014004103

In this book on "statement jewelry . . . jewelry designers Janet Crowther and Katie Covington share their trade secrets for using basic techniques and easy-to-source materials to make stylish jewelry and accessories, from a gold bib necklace and geometric hoop earrings to a classic charm bracelet and elegant shoe clips." (Publisher's note)

Includes bibliographical references and index

Cupp, Lundy

Realistic Pumpkin Carving; 24 Spooky, Scary, and Spine-Chilling Designs. by Lundy Cupp. Fox Chapel Pub Co Inc 2016 96 p. illustrations (chiefly color) $12.99   **745.594**

1. Pumpkin 2. Carving (Decorative arts)
ISBN 156523894X; 9781565238947

This book, by Lundy Cupp, "will show you how to use easy-to-learn techniques to create awesome 3-D pumpkin personalities that will aston-ish your neighbors, family, and friends. . . . Learn the secrets of bring-ing expressive pumpkin characters to life by adding realistic details like teeth and eyes instead of just cutting out solid shapes. Lundy takes you step-by-step through detailed projects for both beginning and advanced carvers." (Publisher's note)

"Create the perfect pumpkin for Halloween with this stunning book. Artist Cupp presents a collection of pumpkin carving patterns. The gal-leries of brilliantly carved pumpkins, squashes, and sweet potatoes are tantalizing, and the author's level of expertise is clearly on display." LJ

Geary, Theresa Flores

The **illustrated** bead bible; terms, tips & techniques. photographs by Debra Whalen. Sterling Pub. 2008 406p il $29.95 **745.594**
  1. Beads 2. Beadwork
  ISBN 978-1-4027-2353-7; 1-4027-2353-9
LC 2007-026120

"This may be the ultimate bead reference book. The majority of the text is made up of an illustrated alphabetical encyclopedia of beads, broadly defined, and beading terms. Additional chapters include tips and techniques, charts illustrating bead characteristics, and stitch diagrams." Libr J

Includes glossary and bibliographical references

Gedeon, Jade

Beautiful bracelets by hand; seventy-five one-of-a-kind baubles, bangles and other wrist adornments you can make at home. Jade Gedeon. Page Street Pub. Co. 2014 224 p. color illustrations (pbk.) $21.99 **745.594**
  1. Bracelets 2. Handicraft
  ISBN 1624140904; 1624140920; 9781624140907; 9781624140921
LC 2014939128

In this book on bracelets, author Jade Gedeon "offers seventy-five of her favorite designs, and gives readers all the secrets for making talk-of-the-town adornments. With so many different materials and methods to choose from, you'll have multiple artistic, unique and vintage-looking bracelets to add to your collection. . . . Materials include beads, chain, cord, fabric, leather, metal, plastic and wood so you can convey a multi-tude of looks and feels." (Publisher's note)

"The majority of the bracelets in this book are so simple and easy to make that absolute beginners can duplicate them successfully. Much of the writing reads like corny catalog copy, but there's enough Gedeon to make this a worthwhile purchase, especially where beginners' jewelry-making titles are popular." LJ

Kan, Lisa

Bead metamorphosis; exquisite jewelry from custom com-ponents. Lisa Kan. Interweave A division of F+W Media, Inc. 2014 159 p. (pbk.) $25.99 **745.594**
  1. Beadwork 2. Jewelry making
  ISBN 1596688254; 9781596688254
LC 2014028517

This book, by Lisa Kan, presents "[b]eautiful bead-woven jewelry that is convertible, reversible, or interchangeable. . . . Create beautiful bead-woven earrings, necklaces, bracelets, and brooches-all of which transform by disassembling, reassembling, reversing, or interchanging separate beadwork components." (Publisher's note)

Karon, Karen

Advanced chain maille jewelry workshop; weaving with rings and scales. Karen Karon. Interweave 2014 159 p. $26.99 **745.594**
  1. Metalwork 2. Jewelry making 3. Metal-work 4. Chains (Jewelry)
  ISBN 1620336596; 9781620336595
LC 2014011104

This book, by Karen Karon, "begins by reviewing basic chain maille weaves. . . . [It] is then divided into 4 sections, each devoted to a par-ticular type of weave: new Persian weaves, Elf-based weaves, Hybrid weaves, and Scale Maille weaves that incorporate sheet metal scales into traditional weaves for a striking effect. Sprinkled throughout the illus-trated step-by-step instructions for each weave technique are valuable tips from Karen." (Publisher's note)

"For experienced jewelry makers, since basic chain maille tech-niques such as opening and closing jump rings properly are not covered. Those looking to go beyond the techniques addressed in most related books will find a wealth of information within these pages." LJ

Katz, Amy

Seed bead chic; 25 elegant projects inspired by fine jewelry. Amy Katz. Lark Jewelry & Beading 2014 128 p. illustra-tions (Lark jewelry & beading bead inspirations) (paperback) $24.95 **745.594**
  1. Jewelry 2. Beadwork 3. Jewelry making 4. Beadwork -- Patterns
  ISBN 1454708174; 9781454708179
LC 2013047476

This book by Amy Katz, "featuring a variety of stitches--including the author's newly created right-angle ladder stitch--these stunning piec-es cover everything from earrings to brooches. Photographs, diagrams, and helpful tips make the beading process simple and pleasurable!" (Publisher's note)

"Katz's projects are sophisticated in both style and technique. Jew-elry makers looking for a challenge will find one here." LJ

Papp, Csilla

Sensational soutache jewelry making; Braided Jewelry Techniques for 15 Statement Pieces. by Csilla Papp. F & W Media Inc 2016 128 p. color illustrations $24.99 **745.594**
  1. Jewelry making
  ISBN 1440243743; 9781440243745
LC 2016302298

In this book, by Csilla Papp, "you'll learn the basic techniques of soutache embroidery, and then get creative with 15 easy-to-follow proj-ects for bracelets, earrings, brooches, rings and necklaces. . . . Color and stone choice combine with elaborate braids to make these pieces distinctly yours." (Publisher's note)

"Jewelrymakers interested in experimenting with soutache, as well as fans of statement jewelry, will be drawn to Papp's intricate designs." LJ

Pester, Sophie

Homemade holiday; craft your way through more than 40 festive projects. Sophie Pester & Catharina Bruns. DK Publish-ing 2017 143 p. color illustrations $14.95 **745.594**
  1. Handicraft 2. Holiday decorations
  ISBN 9781465470737; 9781465463265; 1465463267
LC 2017449059

This book, by Sophie Pester and Catharina Bruns, presents "40 proj-ects for gifts, decorations, and homemade wrapping paper [for Christ-mas]. Save time and money with the festive craft projects. . . . Clear, step-by-step instructions guide readers to create fresh flower garlands, bake edible gift tags, make homemade bath salts, and paint authentic tree ornaments." (Publisher's note)

Sheldon, Kathy

Felt-o-ween; 40 scary-cute projects to celebrate Halloween. Kathy Sheldon. Lark Crafts 2014 132 p. illustrations (chiefly color) (alk. paper) $14.95 **745.594**

1. Halloween 2. Handicraft 3. Felt craft 4. Halloween decorations
ISBN 1454708514; 9781454708513

LC 2013039868

This book by Kathy Sheldon and Amanda Carestio "brings you 40 BOO-tiful decorations and costumes for a festive Halloween. Requiring little or no stitching, these felted projects are 100% beginner-friendly, including pumpkin candy bags, a huggable vampire stuffy, a creepy crawly wreath, and plenty of ears, headbands, and other wearables for revelers young and old." (Publisher's note)

Includes bibliographical references and index

Shore, Debbie

Sew advent calendars; count down to Christmas with 20 stylish designs to fill with festive treats. Debbie Shore. Search Press 2017 96 p. color illustrations (paperback) $19.95 **745.594**

1. Advent 2. Sewing 3. Calendars 4. Christmas decorations
ISBN 9781782214885; 1782214887

This book, by Debbie Shore, presents "20 [advent calendar] designs . . . from traditional flat-pocket calendars to hanging cones and festive pouches, for both adults and children alike, along with a treat-filled calendar for the family dog! The book contains all the techniques needed to make the calendars, and every project is shown clearly step-by-step, with helpful tips and advice throughout." (Publisher's note)

"Shore's instructions are clear enough for beginners to complete the projects successfully." LJ

Van't Hul, Jean

The **artful** year; celebrating the seasons & holidays with family arts and crafts. Jean Van't Hul. Roost 2015 351 p. color illustrations (alk. paper) $24.95 **745.594**

1. Family 2. Cooking 3. Arts and crafts movement 4. Handicraft
5. Seasonal cooking 6. Family recreation 7. Holiday decorations
ISBN 1611801494; 9781611801491

LC 2013048889

Author Jean Van't Hul presents "art activites, crafts, recipes, and more to help make each season special. By doing so, your family will create memories and mementos, you'll develop creative growth in your children and yourself, and you'll have lots of fun! The book includes: Arts and crafts, using the materials, colors, and themes of the season . . . Decorations to make as a family [and] . . . Favorite seasonal recipes that are fun for children to help make." (Publisher's note)

Includes bibliographical references and index

Watanabe, Judi

The **Complete** Photo Guide to Cardmaking; More than 800 Large Color Photos. by Judi Watanabe. Quarto Pub Group USA 2016 256 p. color illustrations $24.99 **745.594**

1. Handicraft 2. Greeting cards
ISBN 1589238826; 9781589238824

This book, by Judi Watanabe, "is the ultimate resource on card making. All paper-crafting techniques that can be employed for card making are thoroughly covered, including a comprehensive description of paper types available, folding options and techniques, coloring and image transfer methods, and adding embellishments. Inside, you'll also find methods for using a computer to design and print cards." (Pub-

lisher's note)

"Although this is a cardmaking book, scrapbookers, art journalers, and mixed-media artists will also appreciate the image-based tutorials and the abundance of inspiring photos." LJ

Williams, Tia

Mini Makers; Crafty Makes to Create With Your Kids. GMC Publications 2016 160 p. color illustrations $19.95 **745.594**

1. Handicraft 2. Handicraft for children
ISBN 1784941018; 9781784941017

This craft book, in the Little Button Diaries series by Laura Minter and Tia Williams, "provides all the inspiration and ideas you need to explore the fun and messy world of making and creating with your young children. You'll be in stitches as you paint, draw, print, cut, stick, sew, and bake your way through 23 adorable projects like a clay tea set, magnetic faces, cardboard boat, and a no-sew cape." (Publisher's note)

"Parents and caregivers will find plenty of ideas for creative play in this imaginative collection." LJ

Wiseman, Jillian

Jill Wiseman's beautiful beaded ropes; 24 wearable jewelry projects in multiple stitches. Jill Wiseman. Lark Crafts 2012 119 p. color illustrations (hardback) $27.95 **745.594**

1. Beads 2. Jewelry 3. Jewelry making 4. Beadwork -- Patterns
ISBN 1454703563; 9781454703563

LC 2012002269

Author Jill Wiseman "presents 24 beaded rope designs in this . . . entry in Lark Jewelry & Beading's popular Beadweaving Master Class series. From dainty to heavy, and from simple to outrageously textured, these . . . wearable necklace, lariat, bangle, and bracelet projects (plus a few earrings!) utilize such popular stitch techniques." (Publisher's note)

"Wiseman's designs have a lot of appeal and are easily customizable to suit individual tastes, and the variety of stitches used in the projects will pique beaders' interest." LJ

745.6 Calligraphy, heraldic design, illumination

Doh, Jenny

Creative lettering; techniques & tips from top artists. Jenny Doh. Lark Crafts 2013 144 p. color illustrations $19.95 **745.6**

1. Lettering 2. Lettering -- Technique
ISBN 1454704004; 9781454704003

LC 2012021130

In this book, edited by Jenny Doh, "[s]ixteen accomplished contributors-- including calligraphers, painters, collagists, card makers, fiber artists, and graphic designers-- give their personal perspectives on lettering. They all offer their favorite tools, how they use them, their signature technique with step-by-step instructions and photos, and an alphabet sampler of their own font." (Publisher's note)

"Artists of all skill levels can enjoy this title." LJ

More creative lettering; techniques & tips from top artists. Jenny Doh. Sterling Pub Co Inc 2015 144 p. color illustrations (paperback) $19.95 **745.6**

1. Lettering 2. Decoration and ornament
ISBN 1454708921; 9781454708926

This book, by Jenny Doh, "has gathered a variety of big names and talented up-and-coming artists, who all provide tips on their favorite forms on hand lettering and tools, along with complete alphabets and how-to projects based on their signature styles. With everything from posters and cards to signs, collages, and journals, this . . . collection will inspire readers as they create their own, personalized work." (Publisher's note)

"With lots of practical and creative applications, this book can be appreciated by a wide range of audiences." LJ

Glynn, Kathy

Hand lettering step by step; techniques and projects to express yourself creatively. by Kathy Glynn. Get Creative 6 2018 144 p. (pbk.) $19.95 **745.6**

1. Lettering 2. Handicraft 3. Calligraphy 4. Lettering -- Technique
ISBN 9781942021858

LC 2017028519

In this book "artist Kathy Glynn will help you master . . . hand lettering, brush lettering, and pointed pen calligraphy--and create work that's expressive, exquisite, and romantic. After explaining the basics, Kathy explains how to combine styles, add embellishments, and even digitize lettering. More than 20 projects include wedding invitations, temporary tattoos, address stamps, glass etching, and a custom family tree." (Publisher's note)

Godfrey-Nicholls, Gaye

Mastering calligraphy; the complete guide to hand lettering. by Gaye Godfrey-Nicholls. Chronicle Books 2013 288 p. color illustrations $40 **745.6**

1. Calligraphy
ISBN 1452101124; 9781452101125

This book, by Gaye Godfrey-Nicholls, offers a "comprehensive and up-to-date volume on this traditional craft [of caligraphy] and its contemporary practice. . . . Inside are step-by-step instructions accompanied by examples of current work, plus historical information, artist profiles, troubleshooting tips, and an extensive resource section." (Publisher's note)

"Godfrey-Nicholls, an Australia-based artist, elucidates the art of hand-lettering in this comprehensive work. The majority of the book is devoted to calligraphic hands, or different styles of writing. Each hand includes a brief history, exercises for practicing the basic shapes and strokes, foundational groups of letters arranged by type, and variations on the alphabet. Appropriate supplies are suggested for each hand." LJ

Includes bibliographical references (pages 278-281) and index

Owen, Imogen

Modern Calligraphy Workshop; The Creative Art of Pen, Brush and Chalk Lettering. Imogen Owen ; photography by Kim Lightbody. Quadrille Publishing 2017 143 p. illustrations (chiefly color) (paperback) $19.99 **745.6**

1. Calligraphy 2. Writing materials and instruments
ISBN 9781849499071; 1849499071

This book, by Imogen Owen, is "full of exquisite sample alphabets, fun exercises, and simple step-by-step projects. From modern calligraphy in ink to hand lettering in chalk on blackboard and brush lettering in paint, you will discover a variety of ingenious and unique ways to turn words and letters into projects that can be given as gifts, sent as snail mail, or used within your home decor." (Publisher's note)

"Owen, a letterpress artist and recent convert to calligraphy, presents a playful take on more traditional forms of calligraphic hand lettering." LJ

Includes bibliographical references (page 141) and index.

Rodriguez, Dina

The **big** awesome book of hand & chalk lettering; Dina Rodriguez ; [edited by] Nathalie Mornu. Alpha Books 2017 206 p. $19.95 **745.6**

1. Lettering
ISBN 1465462724; 9781465462725

LC 2016962249

This book, by Dina Rodriguez, "shows the complete beginner how to master the art of hand lettering, the composition/design of phrases on the page, and flourishes to embellish the design. It also includes chalk lettering, fun prompts for writing, and 15 projects and gift ideas, ranging from gift tags to a lettered poster to chalk-lettered signs for special events." (Publisher's note)

Shepherd, Margaret

Learn calligraphy; the complete book of lettering and design. Broadway Bks. 2001 167p il pa $16.95 **745.6**

1. Calligraphy
ISBN 0-7679-0732-9

LC 00-53016

This guide presents historical background, and advice on materials, technique, and workspace organization. Also included are recommended usages for the various alphabets. Step-by-step illustrations are provided

Thorpe, Molly Suber

Modern calligraphy; everything you need to know to get started in script calligraphy. Molly Suber Thorpe ; photography by Molly Suber Thorpe. St. Martin's Griffin 2013 vi, 184 p.p illustrations (chiefly color) (softcover) $24.99 **745.6**

1. Calligraphy 2. Writing -- Materials and instruments 3. Writing materials and instruments
ISBN 1250016320; 9781250016324

LC 2013013847

This book, by Molly Suber Thorpe, "breaks the calligraphy process down into simple steps so anyone can learn to create their own stunning wedding invitations, thank you cards, gift tags, and more. Starting with an overview of the supplies—from paper to ink to pens—you will learn how to form letters, words, and then phrases by following Molly's clear step-by-step instructions, and by practicing with the provided templates." (Publisher's note)

745.92   Floral arts

Chezar, Ariella

★ The **flower** workshop; lessons in arranging blooms, branches, fruits, and foraged materials. by Ariella Chezar, with Julie Michaels. Ten Speed Press 2016 256 p. color illustrations (hardcover; alk. paper) $25 **745.92**

1. Flower arrangement
ISBN 9781607747659

LC 2015027664

This book, by floral designer Ariella Chezar, "provides step-by-step instructions for more than forty-five stunning floral projects from simple to spectacular, but also equips you with the skills to customize arrangements at home. . . . Chezar walks you through the nuts and bolts of creating a variety of small flourishes, tonal arrangements, branch arrangements, handheld bouquets, wreathes, garlands, grand gestures, and more—all accompanied by detailed photography." (Publisher's note)

"Infused with overwhelming appreciation for nature and including quotes from others and Chezar's own poetic phrases, the book offers beauty and inspiration to flower arrangers at most levels of skill." Booklist

Includes bibliographical references and index

Cylinder, Carly

The **flower** chef; A Modern Guide to Do-It-Yourself Floral Arrangements. Carly Cylinder ; edited by Amara Holstein. Grand Central Life & Style 2016 223 p. color illustrations (hardcover) $28　　　　**745.92**

1. Flower arrangement
ISBN 1455555495; 9781455555499

LC 2015039431

This book, by Carly Cylinder, "is a modern, comprehensive guide to floral design that caters to all readers--from beginners who have never worked with flowers before, . . . to decorators, party planners and photographers looking to liven up their spaces. . . . This book teaches you everything you need to know about flower arranging including tips on how to buy and care for flowers, how to cut and prepare them, and how to use . . . decorative elements." (Publisher's note)

"This book creates a needed foundation for aspiring designers." LJ

Harampolis, Alethea

The **flower** recipe book; Alethea Harampolis and Jill Rizzo of Studio Choo. Artisan 2013 272 p. $24.95　　　　**745.92**

1. Flower arrangement
ISBN 1579655300; 9781579655303

LC 2012046704

This book, by Alethea Harampolis and Jill Rizzo, is a "flower-arranging bible for today's aesthetic. Filled with an array of stunning, easy-to-find flowers, it features 400 high-resolution photos,more than 40 step-by-step slideshows,and tappable pop-tips throughout. The arrangements run the gamut of styles and techniques: some are wild and some are structured; some are time-intensive and some are astonishingly simple." (Publisher's note)

Turner, Tiffanie

The **fine** art of paper flowers; a guide to making beautiful and lifelike botanicals. Tiffanie Turner ; photographs by Tiffanie Turner and Aya Brackett. Watson-Guptill 2017 vii, 254 p.p illustrations (hardcover) $25　　　　**745.92**

1. Paper flowers 2. Flower arrangement
ISBN 9780399578373; 9780399578380

LC 2017013232

This book, by Tiffanie Turner, illustrated by Aya Brackett, is an "art and craft guide that features complete step-by-step instructions for over 30 . . . lifelike paper flowers. . . . Turner also guides readers through making her signature giant paper peony, shares all of her secrets for special paper treatments, candy-striping, playing with color and creating botanical imperfections, and shows how to turn paper flowers into gorgeous garlands, headdresses, bouquets and more." (Publisher's note)

"Combining the skills and aptitude befitting her dual careers, she offers a study in the use of delicate papers, precision tools, wire, hot glue, and various blending brushes to create botanical imitations that one is hard-pressed to distinguish from the real thing." Pub Wkly

Underwood, Kiana

Color me floral; stunning monochromatic arrangements for every season. Kiana Underwood ; photographs by Nathan Underwood. Chronicle Books LLC 2018 240 p. (hc; alk. paper) $30　　　　**745.92**

1. Flowers 2. Flower arrangement 3. Decoration and ornament
ISBN 1452161178; 9781452161174

LC 2017020489

In this book, Kiana Underwood with Nathan Underwood, "shares her techniques for creating dazzling single-color displays using inspired ingredients, dramatic textures and vibrant colors. Organized by season,

the book includes how-tos for 40 arrangements, including: a lush green display for spring, an astonishing black bouquet for summer, a striking magenta design for fall [and] an unexpected, oh-so-pretty pink arrangement for winter." (Publisher's note)

746　Textile arts

Adams, Liza

Needle felting; from basics to bears with step-by-step photos and instructions for creating cute little bears and bunnies from natural wools. Liza Adams. Stackpole Books 2016 128 p. color illustrations (pbk.) $22.95　　　　**746**

1. Handicraft 2. Felt work 3. Textile crafts
ISBN 0811716627; 9780811716628

LC 2015045254

With this book on needle felting, by Liza Adams, "make the cutest little creatures from wool! Needle felting is all the rage, and this book shows you how to create tiny bears, rabbits, dogs, cats, fairies, dolls, cupcakes, and more." (Publisher's note)

Bardwell, Sandra

Sewing Basics; All You Need to Know about Machine and Hand Sewing. Sandra Bardwell. Murdoch 2011 272 p. $17.72　　　　**746**

1. Sewing 2. Handicraft
ISBN 1741967503; 9781741967500

Author Sandra Bardwell presents this book "covering fabrics, sewing machines, hand sewing, fitting, finishing, trouble-shooting and much more. For beginners learning how to hem and for more experienced sewers who need help dealing with difficult fabrics, 'Sewing Basics' is an invaluable reference to keep on the bookshelf for many years to come." (Publisher's note)

Clarke, Duncan

African textiles; The Karun Thakar Collection. Duncan Clarke, Bernhard Gardi, Frieder Sorbe. Prestel 2015 320 p. ill. (chiefly color), col. map $75.00　　　　**746**

1. Clothing and dress -- Africa -- History 2. Textile fabrics -- Africa -- Design -- History 3. Textile fabrics -- Private collections
ISBN 3791381636; 9783791381633

LC 2015514727

This book, by Duncan Clarke, Bernhard Gardi and Frieder Sorbe, "offers a fascinating journey through the history and culture of textiles in Africa drawn from the private collection of Karun Thakar. . . . This collection of rare and exquisite textiles from Central, Northern, and West Africa includes weavings from Ghana, Nigeria, and the Ivory Coast; embroideries, veils, and haiks from Morocco and Tunisia; and raffia fabrics from Congo." (Publisher's note)

"This book is a visual feast of weaving, pattern, and adornment. It will delight those interested in textiles, fashion, and African culture." LJ

Includes bibliographical references (page 320)

Fassett, Kaffe

Kaffe Fassett's Bold Blooms; Kaffe Fassett, Liza Prior Lucy. Harry N Abrams Inc 2016 224 p. (hardcover) $35 **746**

1. Quilts 2. Flowers in art
ISBN 1419722360; 9781419722363

This book, by Kaffe Fassett with Liza Prior Lucy, "guide and vibrant pattern collection of 25 new patchwork and needlepoint projects, from renowned color expert and quilt and fabric designer Kaffe Fassett. Drawing inspiration from the natural beauty of flowers, [it] . . . invites crafters to explore the behind-the-scenes process and fascinating design methods used to create Kaffe's bold fabrics and modern color palettes." (Publisher's note)

"Patterson's photographs enhance the artistic aspect, making the book not just a craft guide but a beautiful keepsake of its own. The whole book is just smashing." Pub Wkly

Glass, Alison

Alison Glass Appliqué; The Essential Guide to Modern Appliqué. Lucky Spool Media 2014 144 p. $28.95   **746**

ISBN 194065503X; 9781940655031

This book by Alison Glass "is for the advanced beginner interested in heirloom and slow sewing. It [offers a] way to learn about incorporating inventive textile treatments and embellishments to achieve one-of-a-kind, modern designs. All of the techniques, from old-school to cutting-edge, are clearly demonstrated with step-by-step instruction, 20 helpful illustrations, and 60 detailed, how-to photographs." (Publisher's note)

Shaw, Robert

American quilts; the democratic art. Robert Shaw. Sterling Pub Co Inc 2014 375 p. $29.95   **746**

1. Quilts 2. Needlework 3. Quilting -- History

ISBN 1454913975; 9781454913979

LC 2014042061

This book, by Robert Shaw, chronicles the growth and evolution of quilting in the U.S. . . . Shaw provide an insightful look at quilting aesthetics . . . [and] places the craft in its historical, cultural, and socioeconomic context, [by] providing a visually lush journey through American history. . . . [It also examines] key moments that had an impact on quilting culture--including Amish emigration, slavery and the Civil War." (Publisher's note)

"The story of American quilting is eloquently told here, set within a broad geographic scope, putting Shaw's expansive curatorial background to full advantage." LJ

Stewart, Martha, 1941-

Martha Stewart's encyclopedia of sewing and fabric crafts; basic techniques for sewing, appliqué, embroidery, quilting, dyeing, and printing, plus 150 inspired projects from A to Z. by Martha Stewart Living Magazine. Potter Craft 2010 400 p. illustrations (chiefly color) $35; (ebook) $65   **746**

1. Sewing 2. Handicraft 3. Textile crafts

ISBN 0307450589; 9780307450586; 9780307965516

LC 2009040548

This book, by the editors of Martha Stewart Living Magazine, "covers everything a home sewer craves: the basics of sewing by hand or machine, along with five other time-honored crafts techniques, and step-by-step instructions for more than 150 projects that reflect not only Martha Stewart's depth of experience and crafting expertise, but also her singular sense of style." (Publisher's note)

Includes index and resources (p.378-387)

White, Christine

Uniquely felt; dozens of techniques from fulling and shaping to nuno and cobweb: includes 46 creative projects. Storey Pub. 2007 311p il pa $24.95   **746**

1. Fabrics 2. Handicraft

ISBN 978-1-58017-673-6; 1-58017-673-9

LC 2007-23531

The author covers "basic feltmaking techniques as well as needle, nuno, cobweb, 3-D, and carved techniques and featuring 46 projects. . . . What makes this a title of lasting value for libraries is the depth of solid information it offers on the craft and its history, on various artists, and on related topics like setting up a feltmaking studio, teaching felt making, and leading community feltmaking projects." Libr J

Includes bibliographical references

746.1   Products and processes

Anderson, Sarah

The **spinner's** book of yarn designs; techniques for creating 80 yarns. Sarah Anderson ; foreword by Judith MacKenzie. Storey Publishing 2012 255 p. color illustrations (ebook) $27.50   **746.1**

1. Yarn 2. Spun yarns 3. Hand spinning

ISBN 1603427384; 9781603427388; 9781603429023

LC 2012039869

This book, by Sarah Anderson, "shows you how to create 80 distinctive yarn types, from classics like mohair bouclé to novelties like supercoils. . . . Anderson describes the unique architecture of each type of yarn and shares expert techniques for manipulating and combining fibers. Take your crafting to a new level and ensure that you have the best yarn available by spinning it yourself." (Publisher's note)

"Inventive, accessible, and fun, this book is an invitation to spinners of all skill levels to venture into uncharted territory and try out something new. This beautiful reference is an essential addition to any spinner's library." Pub Wkly

Includes bibliographical references (pages 248-249) and index

Boggs, Jacey

Spin art; mastering the craft of spinning textured yarn. Jacey Boggs. Interweave Press 2011 143 p. color illustrations $26.95   **746.1**

1. Yarn 2. Spinning 3. Hand spinning

ISBN 1596683627; 9781596683624

LC 2011276733

This book, by Jacey Boggs, offers a guide for craft spinning yarn. "The yarn styles explored in this comprehensive spinning guide are as well made as they are inventive. Jacey walks you through each of her techniques, with a refreshing mixture of quirky, fanciful, and unexpected designs that are always skillfully constructed." (Publisher's note)

Dixon, Anne

The **handweaver's** pattern directory; over 600 weaves for 4-shaft looms. Interweave Press 2007 254p il $34.95   **746.1**

1. Weaving

ISBN 978-1-59668-040-1

LC 2007-26351

This "guide to more than 600 different weaving patterns for four-shaft looms divides weaves into basic groups by structure (e.g., basic threadings, block drafts). Each weave is accompanied by warp threading and weaving drafts (the latter, explained in a handy extended flap), a tieup grid, closeup photos of the weave, and color photos of the actual woven fabric. Beginning weavers will appreciate the sections on weaving basics and finishing techniques as well as the glossary of common weaving terms." Libr J

Mitchell, Syne

Inventive weavng on a little loom; discover the full potential of the Rigid-Heddle loom, for beginners and beyond. Syne Mitchell. Storey Publishing 2015 295 p. color illustrations (pbk.; alk. paper) $29.95   **746.1**

1. Looms 2. Weaving 3. Handlooms 4. Hand weaving

ISBN 9781603429726; 1603429727

LC 2015019702

In this book author Syne Mitchell "covers everything rigid-heddle weavers need to know about the craft, from the basics -- how to select a loom, set it up, and get started -- to a wide variety of fun techniques that yield beautiful results. Begin by exploring a variety of weave structures, including finger-manipulated laces, tapestry, and color play." (Publisher's note)

"Notable for its full coverage of rigid heddle weaving, one of the most accessible pathways into this ancient art, this is an essential addition to weavers' bookshelves." LJ

Includes bibliographical references and index

Murphy, Marilyn

Woven to wear; 17 thoughtful designs with simple shapes. Marilyn Murphy. Interweave Press 2013 143 p. color illustrations (pbk.) $26.95   **746.1**

1. Weaving 2. Clothing and dress 3. Hand weaving
ISBN 1596686510; 9781596686519

LC 2012048056

This garment-weaver's handbook, by Marilyn Murphy, "offers guidance for weaving scarves, wraps, and more. She also provides advice for designing garments, cutting and sewing fabric, adding edgings and closures, and combining woven fabrics with other techniques. In addition, nine contributing designers share their working philosophies." (Publisher's note)

"Beginners (or experienced weavers who could use a refresher) will appreciate the thorough introduction to weaving tools and technique." LJ

Patrick, Jane

The **weaver's** idea book; creative cloth on a rigid-heddle loom. Interweave Press 2010 239p il $29.95   **746.1**

1. Weaving
ISBN 978-1-59668-175-0

LC 2009-39518

"Patrick's collection of patterns and projects explores the possibilities of weaving on a rigid heddle loom. From basic plain weaves to finger-controlled and pick-up techniques, Patrick guides weavers of all skill levels. . . . This is an excellent addition to any weaving collection." Libr J

Includes bibliographical references

746.14   Weaving

Daly, Fiona

Weaving on a little loom; techniques, patterns, and projects for beginners. Fiona Daly. Princeton Architectural Press 2018 144 p. (pbk; alk. paper) $24.95   **746.14**

1. Weaving 2. Needlework 3. Handlooms
ISBN 9781616897123

LC 2018006741

This book, by Fiona Daly, "teaches readers everything they need to know to start small-frame loom weaving, an easy and inexpensive craft that can be done at home. From setting up the loom to finishing a project, this book covers both basic and more advanced techniques, with an introduction to creating patterns such as basket and bird's eye weaves, rib, twill, and herringbone." (Publisher's note)

"Weaving, Daly explains, is not a "weekend project" but a commitment; her alluring book convinces readers it's worth the time and effort." Publishers' Weekly

746.3   Pictures, hangings, tapestries

Brosens, Koenraad

European tapestries in the Art Institute of Chicago; [by] Koenraad Brosens; with contributions by Pascal-Fran¿cois Bertrand [et al.]; Christa C. Mayer Thurman, general editor. Yale University Press 2008 407p il $75   **746.3**

1. Tapestry
ISBN 978-0-300-11960-2; 0-300-11960-7

LC 2008-930401

Brosens, "along with a distinguished group of art historians and curators, argues for the historical and artistic importance of tapestry as an art form. Designed to accompany the Art Institute of Chicago's exhibition The Divine Art: Four Centuries of European Tapestries, this is a genuinely unique text. Its pioneering scholarship is both precise in its claims and accessibly written for a wide audience. After introductory essays, the tapestries are arranged by region and then subdivided by chronology. These works range from medieval through baroque art styles. The color illustrations and the essays that analyze each tapestry are exquisite." Libr J

Includes bibliographical references

746.4   Needlework and handwork

Barbe, Karen

Colour confident stitching; how to create beautiful colour palettes. Karen Barbé. Pimpernel Press Ltd 2017 128 p. color illustrations (paperback) $24.95   **746.4**

1. Embroidery 2. Stitches (Sewing) 3. Color in art 4. Embroidery -- Technique
ISBN 9781910258651; 1910258652

This book, by Karen Barbé, "makes creating color palettes a fun and enjoyable part of the design process. It is divided into three parts: Understanding Colour; Feeling Colour and Stitching with Colour. The first two sections guide the reader through color theory as well as choosing color more instinctively. The five projects that are included will encourage the reader to explore color and build confidence through exercise and experiment." (Publisher's note)

Finnanger, Tone, 1973-

Tilda Homemade & Happy. F & W Media Inc 2014 144 p. color illustrations $22.99   **746.4**

1. Sewing 2. Handicraft 3. Interior design
ISBN 1446305902; 9781446305904

This book by designer Tone Finnanger presents a "collection of inspirational home accessories including quilts, cushions and decorative items to make Christmas even more special." These include "gold-winged reindeer and sheep, round-eyed owls, plump pigs with flower applique detail, angels, stars and darling decorative cakes . . . all in Tone's unique range of fabulous fabrics. The projects are photographed in the author's own log cabin" in Norway. (Publisher's note)

Zedenius, Fanny

Macrame; the craft of creative knotting for your home. Fanny Zedenius ; photography by Kim Lightbody. Quadrille Publishing 2017 143 p. illustrations (some color) (paperback) $16.99   **746.4**

1. Hobbies 2. Macrame 3. Handicraft 4. Macramé -- Patterns
ISBN 9781849499408; 1849499403

This book on macramé, by Fanny Zedenius, with photographs by Kim Lightbody, takes readers "through all the essentials: what you need to get started, a glossary covering 30 of the most popular knots, tips on how to create different patterns . . . , and advice on how to hang and display your makes. The book also takes readers through ombre-dyeing, fraying, and customizing with beads, and includes fully illustrated step-by-step instructions for 22 homeware projects." (Publisher's note)

"This book is an invaluable resource for igniting the imagination about an ancient craft that combines the earthy elements of rope, a few tools, and fingers." Pub Wkly

Zimmermann, Elizabeth

★ **Knitting** without tears; basic techniques and easy-to-follow directions for garments to fit all sizes. by Elizabeth Zimmermann. Scribner 1971 120 p. ill. pbk $16.95   **746.4**

1. Knitting
ISBN 0684135051; 9780684135052

LC 70140776

This book, by Elizabeth Zimmermann, "puts the fun back into knitting with easy-to-follow instructions and timeless designs. . . . This . . . book is poised to inspire a whole new generation of knitters who have yet to discover the joys and comforts of knitting." (Publisher's note)

Includes bibliography

746.42   Nonloom weaving and related techniques

Hartmann, Kat

Hot knots; fresh macrame ideas for jewelry, home and fashion. Kat Hartmann. Barrons Educational Series, Inc. 2015 128 p. illustrations $21.99   **746.42**

1. Macrame
ISBN 1438005652; 9781438005652

LC 2014956306

This book, by Kat Hartmann, "explores a variety of macramé techniques--from historical, centuries-old designs, to modern fusion knots--and guides readers through 18 cool and contemporary projects for jewelry, housewares, accessories, and more." (Publisher's note)

"Up-to-date titles about macramé are difficult to find, and while Hartmann includes nods to 1970s-era classics such as owls and plant hangers, contemporary crafters will find that macramé is both simple and versatile." LJ

746.43   Knitting, crocheting, tatting

Anderson, Susan B.

Susan B. Anderson's kids' knitting workshop; The Easiest and Most Effective Way to Learn to Knit! Susan B. Anderson. Artisan 2015 200 p. color illustrations $17.95   **746.43**

1. Knitting 2. Handicraft for children 3. Knitting -- Patterns -- Juvenile literature
ISBN 1579655904; 9781579655907

LC 2015013064

Knitter Susan B. Anderson "presents her first book targeted at a young audience. This accessible introduction to knitting in the round includes easy-to-follow illustrated tutorials on techniques from casting on and binding off to joining colors to make stripes, and 17 progressively challenging knitting projects—beginning with simple infinity scarves and hats and building to supersweet toys and decor." (Publisher's note)

Includes bibliographical references and index

Barnden, Betty

350 + knitting tips, techniques, and trade secrets; Betty Barnden. St. Martin's Griffin 2017 160 p. illustrations (chiefly color) (trade pbk.) $22.99   **746.43**

1. Knitting 2. Needlework
ISBN 9781250125132; 9781250125125

LC 2017938524

This book, by Betty Barnden, offers over 350 knitting tips and techniques. . . . Discover how to read patterns and charts, choose color and yarns, mix and match stitch patterns, and adapt designs for the perfect fit. . . . [The] book explains all the techniques you'll need in the order you'll need them, from casting on and joining in yarns, to shaping, and adding buttonholes, pockets, and embellishments." (Publisher's note)

"The variety and scope of information make this book equally useful for beginners and those doing more advanced work such as adapting or designing patterns." Booklist

Bassetti, Amanda

Arm knitting; 30 home and fashion projects for all your no-needle needs. Amanda Bassetti. Barrons Educational Series, Inc. 2015 144 p. color illustrations $17.99   **746.43**

1. Knitting 2. Handicraft
ISBN 1438007302; 9781438007304

LC 2015941220

Author Amanda Bassetti presents this guide to knitting that features "clear, step-by-step instructions and photographs . . . 30 home and fashion projects, including a winter snood, scarves, boot warmers, blankets, a chunky rug, footstool, pet bed, baby blanket, super-fast mug cozy, and more . . . [and] helpful suggestions on techniques and materials." (Publisher's note)

"Hands down (or arms up), one of the best-ever beginner craft books." Booklist

Bernard, Wendy

Up, down, all-around stitch dictionary; a collection of stitch patterns to knit top down, bottom up, back and forth, and in the round. Wendy Bernard ; photography by Thayer Allyson Gowdy. Stewart Tabori & Chang 2014 288 p. ill. (some col.) $29.95   **746.43**

1. Knitting 2. Handicraft 3. Life skills -- Handbooks, manuals, etc.
ISBN 1617690996; 9781617690990

LC 2013945660

"In the 'Up, Down, All-Around Stitch Dictionary,' designer Wendy Bernard . . . presents instructions for working 150 popular stitch patterns four different ways: top down, bottom up, back and forth, and in the round. This hefty collection, ranging from lace and cables to colorwork and fancy edgings, is loaded with . . . swatches of each pattern, plus charted and text instructions." (Publisher's note)

"As with any solid stitch dictionary, the swatches show multiple repeats of the pattern, and the color photos are clear and large enough to display detail. Charts are present as needed." LJ

Bestor, Leslie Ann

Cast on, bind off; 54 step-by-step methods. by Leslie Ann Bestor. Storey Pub. 2012 215 p. color illustrations (paper w/ partially concealed wire-o; alk. paper) $16.95   **746.43**

1. Knitting 2. Knitting -- Technique
ISBN 1603427244; 9781603427241

LC 2012002769

This book on knitting by Leslie Ann Bestor "presents more than 50 ways to cast on and bind off, creating edges that are tighter, looser, stretchier, lacier, longer-lasting, prettier. . . . Detailed instructions for each technique are combined with step-by-step photography. . . . At-a-glance charts identify the best cast on or bind off for various types of knitting, as well as cast on/bind off pairs that work well together." (Publisher's note)

Includes bibliographical references (page 209) and indexes

Bliss, Debbie

★ The **knitter's** book of knowledge; a complete guide to essential knitting techniques. Debbie Bliss ; illustrations by Cathy Brear ; photography by Kim Lightbody. Lark 2015 318 p. color illustrations (hardcover) $29.95 **746.43**

1. Needlework 2. Knitting -- Technique 3. Knitting

ISBN 145470926X; 9781454709268

This book, by Debbie Bliss, "is the distillation of her decades of experience into a single, indispensable reference. With information on everything from needles and yarns to tensioning and casting on, from basic stitches to buttonholes and beading, from cabling and entrelac to finishing embellishments, it's the ultimate guide for beginners and experienced knitters alike." (Publisher's note)

"Years in the knitwear industry have made Bliss a leading expert, but her ability to share her knowledge in a cohesive manner is special indeed." LJ

Budd, Ann

The **knitter's** handy book of patterns; basic designs in multiple sizes and gauges. Interweave Press 2002 112p pa $24.95 **746.43**

1. Knitting

ISBN 1-931499-04-7

LC 2001-59208

The patterns in this book "allow the knitter to create garments in any size from toddler to extra-large adult in any weight of yarn, from fingering to bulky. The knitter has only to knit a generous swatch with yarn and needles of her/his choice and plug the resulting gauge information into the charted instructions and schematics provided. Highly recommended for all knitting collections." Libr J

Chachula, Robyn, 1978-

Unexpected afghans; innovative crochet designs with traditional techniques. Robyn Chachula. Interweave Press 2012 159 p. illustrations (pbk.) $22.99 **746.43**

1. Crocheting 2. Afghans (Coverlets) 3. Crocheting -- Patterns

ISBN 159668299X; 9781596682993

LC 2012001563

This book, by Robyn Chachula, "presents 29 innovative interpretations of [crocheted afghan blankets.] . . . Expert designers including Kristin Omdahl, Kathy Merrick, Kimberly McAlindin, and many more, provide an abundance of fresh patterns and projects that are perfect for new and advanced crocheters as they start out beginner-friendly and become more complex, allowing a crocheter to build skills and confidence." (Publisher's note)

"With almost 30 different projects encompassing a variety of styles and techniques, this is an excellent value." LJ

Includes bibliographical references and index

Corkhill, Betsan

Crochet therapy; The Soothing Art of Savoring Each Stitch. Betsan Corkhill. Harry N Abrams Inc 2016 144 p. color illustrations $21.95 **746.43**

1. Crocheting

ISBN 1419721119; 9781419721113

LC 2016023407

This book, by Betsan Corkhill, "will inspire you to pick up a hook and take some time out of your hectic day to dive into colorful whorls of yarn. Focus, relax, and become more mindful by making more than 20 simple and colorful projects comprised of crocheted mandalas, soothing circles, and other beautiful motifs. Each repetitive pattern helps you engage with your materials, increase your well-being, and unlock your creativity." (Publisher's note)

"Corkhill's meditative projects, combined with the exercises throughout, will help crocheters reap the health and wellness benefits of mindful crafting." LJ

Crochet at home; 25 clever projects for colorful living. edited by Brett Bara. Interweave Press 2013 143 p. illustrations (chiefly color) (pbk.) $22.95 **746.43**

1. Crocheting 2. Interior design 3. Household linens 4. House furnishings 5. Crocheting -- Patterns

ISBN 1596688378; 9781596688377

LC 2012048922

In this book "editor Brett Bara and a team of crochet experts bring 25 . . . home projects to life. Explore a collection of practical, pretty pieces for your kitchen, living room, and bedroom: from a riotously colorful blanket, to a delicate bunting of crocheted snowflakes, to flower-inspired trivets that are anything but dull-and even a full-sized ottoman! Techniques such as felting, lace, and crocheting with wire will appeal to beginner and advanced crocheters alike." (Publisher's note)

Crochet to Calm; Stitch and De-Stress with 18 Simple Crochet Patterns. Editors at Interweave ; foreword by Mandy O'Sullivan. F & W Media Inc 2016 112 p. color illustrations $21.99 **746.43**

1. Crocheting

ISBN 1632504952; 9781632504951

In this book in the Craft To Calm series, by the editors at Interweave, with foreword by Mandy O'Sullivan, "you'll learn how the repetitive motion of this popular craft can not only clear your mind but also result in beautiful projects you'll be proud to show off! Best yet? All you need is a hook and a bit of yarn to get started! . . . You'll find 18 fun, easy [crochet] projects that can be completed in almost no time at all!" (Publisher's note)

"Many crafters are drawn to the relaxing properties of handwork, and crocheters seeking simple-yet-attractive projects will enjoy this collection." LJ

Crowfoot, Jane

Ultimate crochet bible; a complete reference with step-by-step techniques. Collins & Brown; Distributed in the U.S. and Canada by Sterling Pub. 2010 304p il (C & B crafts) $29.95 **746.43**

1. Crocheting

ISBN 978-1-84340-563-4

This guide begins "with an overview of the craft's origins and its requirements and necessities (for instance, hooks, needles, and knowledge of how to read a chart). Each chapter truly exposes the how-to details, not only in words but also, most important, in oversize illustrations. Included are a well-explained section of basics (for instance, how to differentiate between front and reverse sides and how to work crochet for left-handed crafters) and specific stitch categories: texture and lace, thread, Tunisian entrelac, color, beads and sequins, edgings, and professional finishing techniques." Booklist

Dassau, Jennifer

Knitting short rows; techniques for great shapes & angles. Jennifer Dassau. Interweave 2016 143 p. illustrations (chiefly color) (paperback) $24.99 **746.43**

1. Knitting -- Technique
ISBN 9781632502582; 1632502585

LC 2017287029

This book on knitting, by Jennifer Dassau, "provid[es] know-how and design inspiration. Learn to create short-rows through five easy-to-learn methods: wrap and turn knitting, the yarnover method, German short-rows, Japanese short-rows, and twin stitch shadow wraps. Master each through an illustrated step-by-step guide, discover how to choose your short-row method, and more! Then, show off your short-row skills with 17 knitting patterns for fashionable hats, cowls, mitts, shawls, and garments." (Publisher's note)

"In this collection of patterns, designer Dassau explores four different methods for knitting short rows . . . For each, she discusses the type of knitted fabric best suited to the technique, and clearly describes the process of ending the row and closing the gap created by the short row." LJ

Dosen, Stephanie

Woodland knits; over 20 enchanting patterns; a Tiny Owl Knits Collection. by Stephanie Dosen ; photographer, Tiffany Mumford. The Taunton Press, Inc. 2013 128 p. color illustrations $19.95 **746.43**
1. Knitting 2. Dress accessories 3. Knitting -- Patterns
ISBN 1627100245; 9781627100243

LC 2013026929

This book on knitting, by Stephanie Dosen, offers "delicately beautiful patterns that incorporate deer, fox, owl, and other woodland themes (plus pretty flowers and vines) and look like nothing else on the market. Here are 20 cute, contemporary projects to knit—including all the quick-to-make favorites—hats, scarves, wristlets, bags, wraps, and mitts." (Publisher's note)

Durant, Judith

Increase, decrease; by Judith Durant. Storey Publishing 2015 256 p. color illustrations (paper w/partially concealed wire-o; alk. paper) $16.95 **746.43**
1. Knitting 2. Cross-stitch 3. Stitches (Sewing) 4. Knitting -- Patterns 5. Knitting -- Technique
ISBN 1612123317; 9781612123318

LC 2014042919

Author Judith Durant presents "a comprehensive guide to 99 different methods for increasing and decreasing knitting stitches. Each method is clearly described and includes step-by-step how-to photographs, swatches showing the look of the featured stitch, and a list of best uses. You'll find the best technique for every situation, whether you want to increase from the center, shape sleeves and necklines, work shaped lace, or decrease for the top of a hat." (Publisher's note)

Durham, Teva

Loop-d-loop crochet; more than 25 novel designs for crocheters (and knitters taking up the hook) Teva Durham ; photographs by Adrian Buckmaster. Stewart, Tabori & Chang 2007 144 p. color illustrations $29.95 **746.43**
1. Crocheting 2. Crocheting -- Patterns
ISBN 1584795808; 9781584795803

LC 2006025052

In this book on crochet, author Teva Durham "presents more than 25 designs that are as up-to-the-minute, style-wise, as they are thoroughly steeped in crochet stitchwork tradition. Each of the projects, which range from purses, skirts, shawls, and sweaters for the whole family to a hammock and a pair of brocade boots, epitomizes Durham's signature design sensibility." (Publisher's note)

Includes bibliographical references (p. 142) and index

Eaton, Jan

350 + crochet tips, techniques, and trade secrets; Jan Eaton. St. Martins Griffin 2017 160 p. illustrations (chiefly color) (trade pbk.) $22.99 **746.43**
1. Crocheting
ISBN 9781250125118; 9781250125101

LC 2017938523

This book on crochet, by Jan Eaton, is a "compendium of technical know-how and troubleshooting tips. Techniques are organized in the order that you'd need them as you work through a project, from choosing the right yarn to looking after your finished garment. Step-by-step photographs, diagrams, and clear instructions guide you through each stage of your work, or you can dip in for help with a particular problem." (Publisher's note)

"A very informative book that will find steady use in virtually any craft collection." Booklist

Eckman, Edie

Around the corner crochet borders; 150 colorful, creative crocheted edgings with charts & instructions for turning the corner perfectly every time. Edie Eckman. Storey Publishing 2010 316 p. color illustrations $16.95 **746.43**
1. Crocheting 2. Decoration and ornament 3. Crocheting -- Patterns 4. Borders, Ornamental (Decorative arts)
ISBN 1603425381; 9781603425384

LC 2010001461

This book, by Edie Eckman, offers "a collection of 150 colorful crochet frames, each with detailed instructions for working around a corner. Instructions are offered both as text and as charts for working in-the-round; back-and-forth charts are also included for when that method is more appropriate. Photographs of finished borders, each turning a 90-degree corner, allow readers to see the details up close." (Publisher's note)

Crochet borders

Connect-the-shapes crochet motifs; creative techniques for joining motifs of all shapes. by Edie Eckman. Storey Publishing 2012 272 p. color illustrations (hardcover with concealed wire-o; alk. paper) $19.95 **746.43**
1. Crocheting 2. Needlework -- Patterns 3. Crocheting -- Patterns
ISBN 1603429735; 9781603429733

LC 2012013934

Author Edie Eckman presents "a book that teaches 100 original motif designs and a variety of techniques to join them. The emphasis is squarely on motifs; only a few patterns are included. Each motif, gathered in 'families' of grannies, chains, clusters, flowers, swirls, radials and more, is shown in written directions, charted, and in full-color illustrations." (Publishers Weekly)

"Eckman's eye for color and design make this an excellent addition to any crafter's crochet collection." LJ

The **crochet** answer book; solutions to every problem you'll ever face, answers to every question you'll ever ask. Edie Eckman. 2nd edition Storey Publishing 2015 408 p. illustrations $14.95 **746.43**
1. Crocheting
ISBN 1612124062 ; 9781612124063

LC 2014033696

In this book, by Edie Eckman, "you'll find helpful answers to . . . crochet questions, including . . . questions on broomstick lace, linked stitches, crochet cables, and much more. You'll also find illustrations for left-handed crocheters; up-to-the-minute information on new internet resources; and an expanded section on unusual techniques like Tunisian crochet." (Publisher's note)

Eckman "presents a definitively revised guide that reflects the latest trends. In her inimitable question-and-answer style, she features the most recently unearthed techniques (do remember: what's old is new again in this and other needlework books), like Tunisian crochet and Bruges and Clones laces. There are brief illustrations, now, for both left- and right-handed stitchers. And new yarns and new tools (or adaptive ones) are explored with helpful tips and caveats." Booklist

Herzog, Amy

Knit to flatter; by Amy Herzog. Stewart, Tabori & Chang 2013 159 p. color illustrations (alk. paper) $24.95   **746.43**
1. Knitting 2. Human body 3. Knitting -- Patterns 4. Clothing and dress measurements
ISBN 1617690171; 9781617690174

LC 2012022908

In this book, author Amy Herzon "teaches you how to assess your shape--top-heavy, bottom-heavy, or proportiona-- and then knit accordingly. With a great sense of fun and acceptance, Amy Herzog presents silhouettes and styles that work with each body shape, along with four ideal sweater patterns per category." (Publisher's note)

"Featuring a variety of models and a beauty-at-all-sizes attitude, Herzog's positive, inspiring book will help knitters create attractive garments that make them feel gorgeous." LJ

Includes bibliographical references and index

Hiatt, June Hemmons

The **principles** of knitting; methods and techniques of hand knitting. June Hemmons Hiatt ; illustrations by Jesse Hiatt. Simon & Schuster 2012 xx, 712 p.p illustrations $45   **746.43**
1. Knitting
ISBN 9781416535171; 1416535179

LC 2012418278

This book, by June Hemmons Hiatt and illustrated by Jesse Hiatt, "is the definitive book on knitting techniques, with valuable information for everyone from beginners to experienced knitters. June Hiatt presents not only a thorough, thoughtful approach to the craft, but also a passion for carrying on the art of knitting to future generations." (Publisher's note)

"This new edition of one of the great knitting references will bring Hiatt's clear explanations and comprehensive information to a new generation of knitters." LJ

Includes bibliographical references (pages 665-672) and index

Hubert, Margaret

10 Granny Squares 30 Blankets; Color Schemes, Layouts, and Edge Finishes for 30 Unique Looks. by Margaret Hubert. Quarto Pub Group USA 2015 128 p. illustrations, color (chiefly) $19.99   **746.43**
1. Crocheting
ISBN 1589238931; 9781589238930

In this book, author Margaret Hubert "shows how you can crochet 30 completely different blankets. Each square is used three times with different yarns, color schemes, motif arrangements, and edge finishes. . . You can crochet blankets that are perfect for babies, boys, girls, college kids, and grown-ups. Some are crazy, colorful, and fun; others are serene, classic, and sophisticated. Crochet them for bedrooms, family rooms, or dorms." (Publisher's note)

"Hubert is one of the crocheters responsible for rescuing granny squares from the 1970s nostalgia heap, and here she continues her quest to modernize this tried-and-true favorite." Library Journal

The **complete** photo guide to crochet. Creative Pub. International 2010 272p il pa $24.99   **746.43**
1. Crocheting
ISBN 978-1-58923-472-7

LC 2009-31798

"Reference for crocheters; includes instructions and diagrams for 200 stitch patterns, basic information about how to crochet, plus 20 patterns." Publisher's note

The **granny** square book; timeless techniques and fresh ideas for crocheting square by square. Margaret Hubert. Creative Pub. International 2011 176 p. illustrations (chiefly color) (ebook) $24.99; (spiral bound) $24.99   **746.43**
1. Crocheting 2. Crocheting -- Patterns
ISBN 9781610581646; 1589236386; 9781589236387

LC 2011013365

This book, by Margaret Hubert, "shows the evolution of the granny square, how it can be used and interpreted in different ways with different yarns, and how today's crocheter can design her own projects using the granny squares of her choice with the yarn choices of today. Just as Margaret learned from her grandmother and mother and then passed the skill down to her daughter and granddaughter, each generation finds new uses and artistic ways to interpret granny squares." (Publisher's note)

"Crocheters looking to move beyond basic granny squares, as well as new crocheters drawn to these traditional motifs, will enjoy this collection." LJ

Keim, Cecily

Teach yourself visually crochet; [by] Cecily Keim and Kim P. Werker. 2nd ed.; Wiley Publishing, Inc. 2011 333p il (Visual read less, learn more) pa $24.99   **746.43**
1. Crocheting
ISBN 978-0-470-87997-9

LC 2010-941213

First published 2006 with authors' names in reverse order

This guide to crocheting contains techniques, color photos, step-by-step instructions and tips for additional guidance.

Knight, Erika

500 crochet stitches; the ultimate crochet stitch bible. Erika Knight. St. Martin's Press 2015 287 p. illustrations (chiefly color) (paper over board) $24.99   **746.43**
1. Sewing 2. Crocheting 3. Stitches (Sewing) 4. Crocheting -- Technique
ISBN 9781250067302

LC 2015016931

This book, by Erika Knight, "is both a stitch guide and a how-to-crochet primer, all in one volume. You get all the information needed to get started, including how to choose yarn and needles, read patterns, work basic stitches, how to check gauge, increase and decrease, join pieces and finish projects and care for your crochet items." (Publisher's note)

"There are a number of crochet stitch dictionaries on the market, but most are focused on a specific type of stitch (e.g., edgings) or on motifs. This comprehensive work makes an excellent reference for crocheters of all skill levels." LJ

Marchant, Nancy

Knitting brioche; the essential guide to the brioche stitch. Nancy Marchant. North Light Books 2009 256 p. illustrations (alk. paper) $27.99   **746.43**
1. Knitting 2. Needlework 3. Knitting -- Patterns 4. Knitting -- Netherlands

ISBN 1600613012; 9781600613012

LC 2009038643

This book, by Nancy Marchant, is "devoted exclusively to brioche stitch, a knitting technique that creates a double-sided fabric. This complete guide will take you from your first brioche stitches to your first (or hundredth) project, and even to designing with brioche stitch, if you desire." (Publisher's note)

Includes bibliographical references (p. 254-255)

Knitting fresh brioche; creating two-color twists & turns: 75 stitches--12 stunning scarves & wraps. Nancy Marchant. Sixth & Spring Books 2014 240 p. illustrations (some color) (paperback) $24.95 **746.43**

  1. Knitting 2. Needlework -- Patterns 3. Knitting -- Patterns
  ISBN 1936096773; 9781936096770

LC 2014017015

This book, by Nancy Marchant, presents patterns and advice for needlework stitching with the brioche technique. The author "works brioche in two colors, forming graceful, undulating textures with increases and decreases. She explains everything from how to hold the yarn and cast on (offering multiple options) to creating the basic fabric and reading two-color charts." (Publisher's note)

"Marchant is widely recognized as the expert on brioche stitch, and her continued explorations of such knitting will appeal to experienced knitters looking for the next big trend." LJ

Includes bibliographical references and index

Meldrum, Carol

Freeform crochet with confidence; unlock the secrets of freeform crochet techniques with 30 fun projects. Carol Meldrum. Barrons Educational Series, Inc. 2015 144 p. color illustrations $18.99 **746.43**

  1. Crocheting
  ISBN 1438007000; 9781438007007

LC 2014956702

This book, by Carol Meldrum, is a "guide to playing to freeform crocheting. Each project featured in this book encourages crafters to hone their own style while taking their skills and creativity to whole new levels." (Publisher's note)

"Knowledge enough to begin a freeform project without a veteran by your side. Even more encouraging are the 30 patterns with directions, from fingerless gloves and an infinity scarf to a layered brooch and granny chic top." Booklist

Melville, Sally

Knitting pattern essentials; adapting and drafting knitting patterns for great knitwear. Sally Melville. Potter Craft 2013 224 p. color illustrations (alk. paper) $24.99 **746.43**

  1. Knitting 2. Sweaters 3. Knitting -- Patterns 4. Knitwear -- Pattern design
  ISBN 0307965570; 9780307965578; 9780307965585

LC 2012015715

This book, by Sally Melville, is a "comprehensive guide to sweater construction. . . . [Sally] reveals the secrets to creating or modifying a pattern so the finished project looks and fits exactly how you want it to. Pattern drafting has never been easier to understand as Sally breaks down each skill." (Publisher's note)

Mullett-Bowlsby, Shannon

  ★ **Complete** crochet course; the ultimate reference guide. Shannon and Jason Mullett-Bowlsby. Sterling Pub Co Inc 2018 336 p. $29.95 **746.43**

  1. Crocheting 2. Needlework 3. Decorative arts
  ISBN 1454710527; 9781454710523

This book, by Shannon and Jason Mullett-Bowlsby, "teaches you how to crochet from the very first stitch--and will keep you crocheting as you gain experience! . . . [The book] explains all the tools, materials, and techniques you need, from choosing a hook and yarn to seaming, working in the round, handling specialty stitches, and adding details." (Publisher's note)

"It's a well-organized reference, up-to-date with the different cable, ribbing, and pattern stitches that are now popular." Booklist

Newton, Deborah

Finishing school; a master class for knitters. Deborah Newton. Sixth&Spring Books 2011 164 p. color illustrations (hardback) $29.95 **746.43**

  1. Knitting 2. Knitting -- Patterns
  ISBN 1936096196; 9781936096190

LC 2011013424

In this book, knitter Deborah Newton "shares her expertise and love of finishing techniques in an on-the-page master class. Deborah patiently takes her student-readers step by step through the ins and outs of blocking, seaming, edging, and embellishments, giving them the confidence and skills to create professional-looking knitwear. In addition to Deborah's expert instructions, the book includes patterns for 12 sweaters, jackets, and scarves, many with variations." (Publisher's note)

Okun, Alanna

The **curse** of the boyfriend sweater; essays on crafting. Alanna Okun. Flatiron Books 2018 viii, 242 p.p (hardcover) $24.99 **746.43**

  1. Hobbies 2. Knitting 3. Needlework 4. Knitting -- Anecdotes 5. Knitting -- Psychological aspects 6. Knitters (Persons) -- United States
  ISBN 1250095611; 9781250095619

LC 2017045150

This memoir, by Alanna Okun, is "about life truths learned through crafting. . . . Okun knows that crafting keeps her anxiety at bay. . . . [S]he knows that even when we can't control anything else, we can at least control the sticks, string, and fabric right in front of us. Okun lays herself bare and takes readers into the parts of themselves they often keep hidden. Yet at the same time she finds humor in the daily indignities all crafters must face." (Publisher's note)

Omdahl, Kristin

The **finer** edge; crocheted trims, motifs & borders. Kristin Omdahl. Interweave Press 2013 144 p. ill. (chiefly col.) (pbk.) $22.95 **746.43**

  1. Crocheting 2. Handicraft 3. Crocheting -- Patterns
  ISBN 1596685549; 9781596685543

LC 2012029110

In this book, author Kristin Omdahl "explores crocheted edge motifs in this colorful pattern dictionary. The edgings are organized by type of construction (top-down, bottom-up, side-to-side, miscellaneous) and each contains written and charted instructions as well as a full-color swatch. Patterns for crocheted garments and accessories round out the collection and show the edgings in use on real-world projects." (Library Journal)

"Several crocheted edging/motif books have been published in the last few years. Omdahl is a big name in the field, and crocheters will appreciate this nicely curated ensemble." LJ

Includes bibliographical references and index

One-skein wonders for babies; 101 knitting projects for infants & toddlers. edited by Judith Durant. Storey Publishing 2015 288 p. (pbk.: alk. paper) $18.95   **746.43**
1. Knitting 2. Infants' clothing 3. Knitting -- Patterns
ISBN 9781612124803

LC 2015010744

This book, edited by Judith Durant, "offers 101 original knitting projects for babies and toddlers--each using just a single skein of yarn! From mittens and hats to tees, sweaters, hoodies, pants, dresses, socks, and bootees, you'll find the perfect wearable for every child and every occasion." (Publisher's note)

"This is a popular series, and the collection of projects will appeal to knitters with little ones in their lives." LJ

Radcliffe, Margaret

Circular knitting workshop; essential techniques to master knitting in the round. by Margaret Radcliffe. Storey Publishing LLC 2012 319 p. color illustrations (pbk.) $24.95   **746.43**
1. Knitting 2. Arts and crafts movement 3. Knitting -- Patterns
ISBN 1603429999; 9781603429993

LC 2011025033

Author "Margaret Radcliffe covers everything you need to know to master the art of circular knitting, presenting Fair Isle, twined, helix, tubular, and other classic techniques in detailed step-by-step photographic sequences. Thirty-five demonstration projects let you try out each technique on a mini sock, hat, bag, mitten, sweater, or vest before applying it to a larger project." (Publisher's note)

"All knitters, from novice to expert, will find something new and useful in this comprehensive guide. Essential for knitting collections." LJ

The **knitting** answer book; solutions to every problem you'll ever face; answers to every question you'll ever ask. by Margaret Radcliffe. 2nd edition Storey Publishing 2015 439 p. illustrations pbk $14.95   **746.43**
1. Knitting 2. Knitting -- Miscellanea
ISBN 9781612124056; 9781612124049; 1612124046

LC 2014033661

"Margaret Radcliffe's classic Q&A guide is better than ever! This thoroughly revised and updated new edition gives expert answers to scores of new questions that knitters have asked since the first edition was published. You'll find more than a dozen new cast ons and bind offs; new techniques for beading and knitting backwards; tips for making smooth stripes when knitting in the round and for measuring gauge on tricky fabrics, such as ribbing and lace; fresh information on interpreting patterns and adjusting patterns to fit; and much more." (Publisher's note)

Includes bibliographical references (pages 415-428) and index

The **knowledgeable** knitter; understand the inner workings of knitting and make every project a success. by Margaret Radcliffe. Storey Publishing 2014 296 p. ill. (chiefly col.) (hardcover: alk. paper) $34.95   **746.43**
1. Knitting 2. Needlework -- Patterns 3. Knitting -- Patterns
ISBN 1612124143; 9781612120409; 9781612124148

LC 2014016057

This book by Margaret Radcliffe is a "reference for any knitter seeking better results, whether the challenge is reading a pattern chart, substituting yarn, modifying a pattern, fixing a mistake, shaping a collar, or adjusting an armhole." It "covers everything from how to identify a well-written pattern to evaluating schematics, revising a pattern so it fits perfectly, and making adjustments throughout a project." (Publisher's note)

Includes bibliographical references and index

Righetti, Maggie

Crocheting in plain English; 2nd ed.; Thomas Dunne Books 2008 268p il pa $16.95   **746.43**
1. Crocheting
ISBN 978-0-312-35354-4; 0-312-35354-5

LC 2008-43913

First published 1988

This is "one of the most comprehensive and accessible guides to crochet available. This isn't a quick-start guide: Righetti provides an overview of the necessary supplies, a brief history of crochet, and information about gauge before guiding beginners through their first stitch, an ideal approach for readers who wish to understand crochet in-depth." Libr J

Includes bibliographical references

Square, Vicki

The **knitter's** companion; Expanded and updated, deluxe ed.; Interweave 2010 138p il $24.95   **746.43**
1. Knitting
ISBN 978-1-59668-314-3

First published 1996

This is "an excellent ready reference for a variety of knitting techniques, including cast-ons, bind-offs, finishing, and other basics. . . . The demonstrations on the DVDs show knitters exactly what they should be doing. Every knitting collection needs a reference; this one is affordable and accessible." Libr J

Starmore, Alice

Alice Starmore's book of Fair Isle knitting; Alice Starmore. Dover Publications 2009 199 p. ill. (some col.) (pbk.) $29.95   **746.43**
1. Knitting 2. Knitting -- Scotland -- Fair Isle -- Patterns
ISBN 0486472183; 9780486472188

LC 2009026197

In this book, author Alice Starmore "explains the traditional Fair Isle techniques of circular knitting and presents detailed tutorials on incorporating classic motifs, exploring color schemes, and creating unique patterns and designs. She shares fourteen of her own original designs, including patterns for cardigans, vests, fishermen's sweaters, hats, gloves, and mittens. More than 250 photographs, drawings, and easy-to-follow charts illustrate sources of inspiration." (Publisher's note)

Includes bibliographical references and index

Stoller, Debbie

★ **Stitch** 'n bitch; the knitter's handbook. illustrations by Adrienne Yan; fashion photography by John Dolan. Workman 2003 248p il hardcover o.p. pa $13.95   **746.43**
1. Knitting
ISBN 0-7611-3258-9; 0-7611-2818-2 pa

LC 2003-53543

"An introduction chronicles the history of knitting from the female perspective, while subsequent chapters cover topics such as yarn type, instruments, stitches, and patterns. Perhaps the most exciting bit is Stoller's 'knit as you learn' technique: with every new stitch, she presents a new pattern, thereby allowing knitters to build on their knowledge. . . . Essential for all crafts collections and perfect for a display." Libr J

Stitch 'n bitch superstar knitting; go beyond the basics. Debbie Stoller; with photography by Gabrielle Revere. Workman Pub. Co. 2010 xii, 356 p.p color illustrations (pbk.: alk.

paper) $17.95 **746.43**
1. Knitting
ISBN 0761135979; 9780761135975

LC 2010051402

This book, by Debbie Stoller, "is the only knitter's handbook to teach the full array of advanced knitting techniques and skills, such as double-knitting, knitting lace, complicated color work, beading, and more. . . . There's also a whole section on DIY—which gives a tutorial on creating your own knitting patterns." (Publisher's note)

"Essential for the well-rounded knitting collection owing to the sections on techniques and designing; a few of the patterns are destined to be popular. The Frilly Filly Scarf (see pattern, above) is simple and sophisticated." LJ

Turner, Sharon

Teach yourself visually knitting; 2nd ed.; Wiley Pub. 2010 339p il (Visual read less, learn more) pa $22.99 **746.43**
1. Knitting
ISBN 978-0-470-52832-7; 0-470-52832-X

LC 2009-941352

First published 2006

This guide to knitting contains techniques, color photos, step-by-step instructions and tips for additional guidance.

Van Impelen, Helgrid

Big knits big needles; Helgrid van Impelen. DK Publishing 2016 143 p. illustrations (chiefly color) (paperback) $14.95; (ebook) $44.85 **746.43**
1. Sweaters 2. Needlework 3. Knitting -- Patterns
ISBN 9781465453983; 1465453989; 9781465459183

LC 2016591051

This book, by Helgrid van Impelen, " includes more than 20 step-by-step projects and a tutorial section on the techniques of the basic stitches you need to know. From a belted cardigan to a hooded toggle coat, your cold-weather-wear is about to get more trendy. . . . Take your projects one step further and create matching beanies, scarves, and more with the help of 24 accessory patterns included in the book." (Publisher's note)

"Sophisticated and more rustic styles are featured and should please a variety of tastes." Booklist

746.432   Knitting

Budd, Ann

Knitter's handy book of top-down sweaters; basic designs in multiple sizes and gauges. Ann Budd. Interweave Press LLC 2012 263 p. illustrations (ebook) $22.95; (hardback) $29.95 **746.432**
1. Knitting 2. Sweaters 3. Knitting -- Patterns
ISBN 9781620330524; 1596684836; 9781596684836

LC 2012001366

This book, by Ann Budd, "offers instructions for knitting five basic sweater types: circular yoke, raglan, modified-drop shoulder, set-in sleeve, and saddle shoulder. Patterns are offered in multiple sizes and yarn gauges and for a broad age group." (Publisher's note)

"Knitters who want to design their own sweaters but don't want to figure out all the math will appreciate Budd's straightforward approach to sweater design, while knitters who are just looking for patterns will enjoy the variety of ready-to-knit patterns in this collection." LJ

Includes bibliographical references and index

New directions in sock knitting; 18 innovative designs knit-

ted from every which way. Ann Budd. F & W Media Inc 2016 167 p. illustrations (chiefly color) (paperback) $26.99 **746.432**
1. Socks 2. Knitting 3. Needlework -- Patterns
ISBN 9781620339435; 1620339439

LC 2016301981

This book, by Ann Budd, offers "eighteen designs [for sock knitting] . . . that range from traditional sock patterns to more challenging and innovative sock constructions. The socks in this collection use a variety of knitting techniques including double knitting, intarsia in the round, short-row shaping, mirrored color and texture patterns, and multi-directional knitting in both traditional and innovative ways." (Publisher's note)

"Most of the patterns are extremely detailed, but patient knitters will find the process rewarding, and the finished results are gorgeous." LJ

Sock knitting master class; innovative techniques + patterns from top designers. Ann Budd. Interweave 2011 183 p. color illustrations $26.99 **746.432**
1. Socks 2. Knitting 3. Knitting -- Patterns
ISBN 1596683120; 9781596683129

LC 2010049008

This book, by Ann Budd, "showcases methods for designing and knitting creative socks, featuring signature elements and techniques from 16 top designers. You'll learn what makes good sock design, and then dive into knitting 18 spectacular, brand-new patterns featuring the widest variety of techniques." (Publisher's note)

"This is an excellent addition to sock-knitting collections." LJ
Includes bibliographical references (p. 182) and index

Drysdale, Rosemary

Entrelac; the essential guide to interlace knitting. Rosemary Drysdale. Sixth&Spring Books 2010 160 p. color illustrations $24.95 **746.432**
1. Knitting 2. Knitting -- Patterns
ISBN 1936096005; 9781936096008

LC 2010932159

This book on entrelac knitting, by Rosemary Drysdale, "introduces both the history and how-to of this fun style, along with 20 patterns for a variety of garments, home décor items, and baby accessories. Comprehensive instructions and a wide array of swatches provide endless possibilities in lace, colorwork, and much more." (Publisher's note)

Durant, Judith

Cable left, cable right; 94 Knitted Cables. Judith Durant. Storey Publishing 2016 216 p. (pbk.: alk. paper) $16.95 **746.432**
1. Knitting 2. Cable knitting 3. Knitting -- Technique
ISBN 9781612125169

LC 2015044820

This book on kitting, by Judith Durant, "eliminates the mystery with detailed, in-depth instructions for creating 94 different styles of cable, from perfectly plain to fantastically fancy. Close-up photos and clear instructions teach you the techniques you need, including design options like braids, diamonds, and pretzels so you can make your cables truly one-of-a-kind." (Publisher's note)

"Each of the cables includes a full-color, close-up swatch illustrating clearly how the cables are formed as well as charted instructions. Helpful tips for troubleshooting—including a clever approach to remedying loose stitches before and after cables—are supplied throughout." LJ

Gaughan, Norah

Norah Gaughan's Knitted Cable Sourcebook; A Breakthrough Guide to Knitting With Cables and Designing Your Own. by Norah Gaughan; photography by Jared Flood. Harry N Abrams Inc 2016 276 p. color illustrations $29.95; (ebook) $23.32　　**746.432**

1. Knitting

ISBN 1419722395; 9781419722394; 9781613122914

LC 2016956329

This book on knitting, by Norah Gaughan, "presents more than 150 new and innovative cable stitch patterns ranging from basic to complex and offers enlightening insight into how cables are engineered, how knitters can design their own, and how knitters can mix and match cables in a knitting pattern." (Publisher's note)

Herzog, Amy

Knit wear love; foolproof instructions for knitting your best-fitting sweaters ever in the styles you love to wear. Amy Herzog. Stewart, Tabori & Chang 2015 192 p. color illustrations $24.95　　**746.432**

1. Knitting 2. Clothing and dress

ISBN 1617691399; 9781617691393

LC 2014942999

In this book about knit wear, author Amy Herzog "guides us through picking a base pattern that not only works for our inherent shape, but also suits our size and style—all with the skill of a top-notch teacher and designer and the honesty and humor of a BFF." (Publisher's note)

"This classic-in-the-making will inspire knitters to make sweaters that fit well and suit their personal style." LJ

You can knit that; foolproof instructions for fabulous sweaters. by Amy Herzog. Harry N Abrams Inc 2016 175 p. illustrations (some color) $24.95; (ebook) $18.65　　**746.432**

1. Knitting 2. Sweaters

ISBN 1419722476; 9781419722479; 9781613122938

This book, by Amy Herzog, "is a clear, simple reference book and pattern collection that gives knitters the sweater-making confidence they need. Whether you're knitting a sweater for the first time or seeking to expand your skills to knit sweaters in styles you've never tried before, this essential guide starts with basic sweater know-how and moves into instructions for knitting six must-have sweater styles." (Publisher's note)

"Herzog's expertise, combined with her ability to explain clearly the hows and whys of sweater knitting, will build confidence even in the most reluctant knitters." LJ

Includes bibliographical references.

Huff, Mary Scott

★ The **mitten** handbook; knitting recipes to make your own. Mary Scott Huff; photographs by Lesley Unruh. Abrams 2017 158 p. illustrations (some color) (paperback) $19.99　　**746.432**

1. Mittens 2. Knitting 3. Knitting -- Patterns

ISBN 9781683351399; 9781419726620

LC 2016961383

In this book, by Mary Scott Huff, illustrated by Lesley Unruh, empowers readers "to create their own mittens their own way. . . . The first [section] presents mitten elements, with a menu of choices that makes getting custom results easy. The second section covers the key aspects of construction, including how to measure for the perfect fit, yarn and gauge considerations, and which direction to knit. And the final section provides 20 complete mitten patterns." (Publisher's note)

Jurgrau, Andrea

New Heights in Lace Knitting; 17 Lace Knit Accessory Patterns. Andrea Jurgrau. F & W Media Inc 2016 144 p. illustrations (chiefly color) (ebook) $31.24; $24.99　　**746.432**

1. Knitting 2. Knitted lace

ISBN 9781632502322; 1632502313; 9781632502315

This book, by Andrea Jurgrau, "helps knitters create a beautiful collection of lace shawls and accessories and gain confidence in creating standout knitted lace. . . . [It] outlines exactly what knitters need in order to create a successful finished project. Knitters are guided through choosing the right yarns for lace, basic lace techniques, and a comprehensive how-to for adding beads to lace projects." (Publisher's note)

"Adventurous knitters will be drawn to Jurgrau's exquisite lace designs—but novices will find that these peaks are not insurmountable, thanks to an excellent introductory tutorial on lace-knitting techniques." LJ

Karlsson, Maja

Traditional Swedish knitting patterns; 40 motifs and 20 projects. Maja Karlsson; translator Carol Huebscher Rhoades. Trafalgar Square Books 2017 158 p. illustrations (chiefly color) (hardcover) $24.95　　**746.432**

1. Knitting 2. Needlework 3. Knitting -- Sweden 4. Knitting -- Patterns

ISBN 1570768218; 9781570768217

LC 2017939362

In this book, "knitting designer Maja Karlsson delved into the fascinating history of Swedish fibercrafts, and discovered a rich tradition of multi-color patterning--the perfect source of inspiration for this lovely collection of 40 uniquely Swedish motifs, applied and combined into 22 projects. Flowers, borders, geometric figures, landscapes, people, and animals, on their own or together, form the backbone of traditional Swedish stranded patterns." (Publisher's note)

Knight, Erika

750 knitting stitches; the ultimate knit stitch bible. Erika Knight. St. Martin's Griffin 2015 287 p. color illustrations (paper over board) $24.99　　**746.432**

1. Stitches (Sewing) 2. Sewing -- Technique 3. Knitting -- Technique

ISBN 9781250067180

LC 2015017155

This book, by Erika Knight, is "both a stitch guide and a how-to knit primer, all in one volume. . . . The comprehensive pattern library includes 750 knitting stitches, from simple to ornate, including knit and purl patterns, basic and complex cables, Fair Isles and intarsia designs, and rib and edging patterns. Each is fully explained with instructions and accompanied by a full-color photo of a sample knitted swatch." (Publisher's note)

"A close-up, full-color swatch is also included for each design, giving the knitter an idea of what multiple pattern repeats look like in a knitted sample. A directory of basic knitting abbreviations and a guide to knitting elementals appear in the introduction." LJ

Knitting masterclass; with over 20 technical workshops and 15 beautiful patterns. by The Knitter; edited by Juliet Bernard. Sterling Pub Co Inc 2013 160 p. color illustrations $24.95　　**746.432**

1. Knitting

ISBN 1908449020; 9781908449023

This book on knitting, edited by Juliet Bernard, presents "techniques drawn from the magazine [The Knitter's] popular Masterclass series. The 'seminars'—led by top teachers, lavishly photographed, and featuring exclusive projects—include Creating Perfect Lace, Steeking without

Fear, Confident Cables, Provisional Cast On Methods, Flawless Fair Isle, and more." (Publisher's note)

Nico, Brooke

More Lovely Knitted Lace; Contemporary Patterns in Geometric Shapes. Brooke Nico. Sterling Pub Co. Inc. 2016 128 p. illustrations (chiefly color) (paperback) $19.95   **746.432**
   1. Knitting 2. Lace and lace making 3. Needlework -- Patterns
   ISBN 9781454709183; 1454709189

This book, by Brooke Nico, "presents 16 new projects that offer a fresh and original take on lace knitting. Think sweaters, capelets, tunics and cowls, knit in yarns both thick and thin—contemporary designs that give knitters a wealth of new possibilities. Organized by overall shape—circle, square, triangle, and rectangle—these lovely garments will change the way you look at lace knitting." (Publisher's note)

"Using geometric shapes as the basic foundation of knitted designs is not a new concept, but Nico's latest book offers a fresh take." Booklist

Shida, Hitomi

Japanese knitting stitch bible; 260 exquisite patterns by Hitomi Shida. Hitomi Shida; translated with an introduction by Gayle Roehm. Tuttle Publishing 2017 160 p. illustrations (chiefly color) (pbk.) $16.95   **746.432**
   1. Knitting -- Japan 2. Knitting -- Patterns
   ISBN 9781462919406; 9784805314531

                                      LC 2017942852

In this book, Gayle Roehm translates the "work of [Hitomi] Shida, one of Japan's best-known hand-knitting designers, into English for the first time. Shida gained an international following with the Japanese publication of a book of couture knitting patterns . . . , and here presents hundreds of other patterns, adding scallops, yokes, and edgings to her offerings   For intrepid knitters looking for a challenge, the pages of stunning stitches will prove well worth the effort." (Publishers Weekly)

"For intrepid knitters looking for a challenge, the pages of stunning stitches will prove well worth the effort." Pub Wkly

Starmore, Alice

Tudor roses; by Alice Starmore. Dover Pubns 2013 175 p. color illustrations $40   **746.432**
   1. Knitting 2. Great Britain -- History -- 1485-1603, Tudors
   ISBN 1606600478; 9781606600474

This book, by Alice Starmore, is a "stunning collection of hand-knitted designs inspired by members of the Tudor dynasty. . . . [It] features charts and instructions as well as a fascinating historical background on the royal family. Glorious full-color photography spotlights the completed works." (Publisher's note)

Storey, Martin

Easy fair isle knitting; 26 Projects with a Modern Twist. Martin Storey. Trafalgar Square Books 2016 128 p. color illustrations (pbk.) $24.95   **746.432**
   1. Knitting -- Patterns
   ISBN 9781570767852

                                        LC 2016935523

"This collection of easy Fair Isle knits from renowned knitwear designer Martin Storey has 26 designs for you, your home; and your friends and family, all of which use only two colors in a row. Well within the grasp of even a novice Fair Isle knitter. Martin has included a range of softly colored cushions, some in contemporary geometric motifs and others with a more traditional theme. All in delicious color blends guaranteed to enhance a plain sofa, bed or chair." (Publisher's note)

"Knitters who are drawn to Fair Isle colorwork but aren't taken with

traditional geometric motifs will appreciate Storey's modern take on the technique." LJ

★ **Vogue** knitting; the ultimate knitting book. the editors of Vogue Knitting Magazine. revised and updated   Sixth & Spring Books 2018 351 p. illustrations (some color) (hardcover) $39.95   **746.432**
   1. Knitting 2. Needlework
   ISBN 9781942021698

                                      LC 2017033626

This book, by the editors of Vogue Knitting Magazine, "features an expanded library of cast-ons, increases, decreases, and bind-offs; in-depth sections on newly favorite [knitting] techniques such as brioche, entrelac, double knitting, and mosaic knitting; and design and construction chapters that go beyond just sweaters to encompass dozens of options for hats, mittens, socks, gloves, and more than 25 shawl shapes." (Publisher's note)

"This revised and updated edition of the classic knitting guide continues the tradition of comprehensive information presented in a clear, concise manner." LJ

Includes bibliographical references and index

Weil, Anne

Knitting without needles; by Anne Weil. Potter Craft 2015 191 p. color illustrations (ebook) $59.97; (alk. paper) $19.99   **746.432**
   1. Knitting 2. Finger weaving 3. Knitting -- Patterns 4. Knitting -- Technique
   ISBN 9780804186537; 0804186529; 9780804186520

                                      LC 2014036650

This book on knitting, by Anne Weil, "shows you how to loop yarn with your fingers or your forearms with thirty patterns that are simple to follow and produce stylish results. Best of all, many of them knit up fast—in less than an hour! " (Publisher's note)

Wood, Jennifer

Refined knits; Sophisticated Lace, Cable, and Aran Lace Knitwear. Jennifer Wood. Interweave Books 2016 156 p. illustrations (some color) $25.99   **746.432**
   1. Knitting 2. Knitting -- Patterns
   ISBN 163250068X; 9781632500687

                                      LC 2016388252

This book on cable and lace knitting patterns, by Jennifer Wood, "concentrates on these two techniques, along with incredibly unique Aran Lace which combines the two, and the results are sure to impress." (Publisher's note)

"The patterns are comprehensive, including written and charted instructions, schematics, and notes on construction as needed." LJ

Includes bibliographical references and index

746.434   Crocheting

★ **A** to Z of crochet; [editor: Sue Gardner] Martingale & Company 2008 160 p. col. ill. (pbk.) $18.99   **746.434**
   1. Crocheting 2. Crocheting -- Technique 3. Crocheting -- Handbooks, manuals, etc
   ISBN 156477998X; 9781564779984

                                      LC 2010282406

"Here's everything you ever wanted to know about crochet. This indispensable reference will guide you through everything from beginner's basics through stitches and techniques for every shape and texture

Imaginable. With step-by-step instructions and close-up photos, there's no easier way to learn to crochet!

Whether you're a new crocheter or you just want to try new techniques, this must-have resource offers all the know-how you'll ever need." Publisher's Note.

Crochet one-skein wonders for babies; 101 projects for infants & toddlers. edited by Judith Durant & Edie Eckman; photography by Geneve Hoffman. Storey Publishing 2016 288 p. color illustrations (pbk.: alk. paper) $18.95   **746.434**
   1. Crocheting 2. Infants' clothing 3. Crocheting -- Patterns
   ISBN 9781612125763; 161212576X
         LC 2015050175 This book, edited Judith Durant and Edith Eckman, is a "collection of 101 projects . . . to crochet . . . clothes, toys, and accessories for the babies and toddlers. Each project uses just one skein of yarn, many take just a few hours to complete, and plenty are suitable for beginners. Hats and caps, bootees and socks, mitts, dresses, tops and bottoms — plus blankets, bibs, soft toys, bottle cozies, diaper bags, and more." (Publisher's note)
   "Handy tips on topics such as sizing and safety are scattered throughout, featuring valuable information the crocheter will continue to use in future projects. Covering a lot of ground in one volume, this thorough collection would be a valuable addition to libraries where crochet books are in demand." Booklist

Eckman, Edie
  Beyond the square crochet motifs; 144 circles, hexagons, triangles, squares, and other unexpected shapes. Edie Eckman. Storey Publishing 2008 vi, 201 p.p illustrations (some color) (ebook) $18.95; (hardcover with concealed wire-o: alk. paper) $18.95   **746.434**
   1. Crocheting 2. Crocheting -- Patterns
   ISBN 9781603428149; 1603420398; 9781603420396
         LC 2008018090
   This book, by Edie Eckman, " opens up the door to crocheting creativity with more than 140 motifs of every shape and size. Embellish your clothing, linens, housewares, and bags with colorful patterns as you put odd yarn leftovers to good use. Step-by-step instructions and color photographs provide the building blocks to limitless possibilities. Open up your imagination and let your crochet follow." (Publisher's note)

Gullberg, Maria
  Tapestry crochet and more; A Handbook of Crochet Techniques and Patterns. Maria Gullberg. Trafalgar Square Books 2016 84 p. color illustrations (concealed spiral) $17.95 **746.434**
   1. Crocheting
   ISBN 9781570767678
         LC 2015958246
   This book, by Maria Gullberg, "is the perfect introduction to a whole new set of [crocheting] techniques that will broaden your crochet horizons. Experiment with color, shape, and structure, using ribbed, relief, double-layer, and tapestry crochet to create bags, totes, hats, wrist warmers, lace, and flowers with striking designs you almost won't believe are crocheted." (Publisher's note)
   "This concealed ring-bound book focuses on tapestry crochet but also offers several other types of projects, including granny squares and three-dimensional flowers. The look of tapestry crochet is very distinctive and is rarely represented in craft books published in the U.S." Booklist

Todhunter, Tracey
  Crochet; Techniques and Projects to Build a Lifelong Passion For Beginners Up. Tracy Todhunter. Barrons Educational Series, Inc. 2016 160 p. $18.99   **746.434**
   1. Crocheting 2. Needlework
   ISBN 9781438007595
         LC 2015951472
   This crochet resource book by Tracey Todhunter, published as part of the "Learn It! Love It!" series, features "hundreds of detailed how-to photographs, carefully annotated, . . . guest designers sharing some of their favorite crochet patterns, . . . 'quick start projects' for beginners . . . [and] clinics to help students solve project dilemmas. Find the techniques necessary to learn crochet and love it--in no time at all!" (Publisher's note)
   "The tone is straightforward but friendly, and the written and photographed instructions are thorough, making this appropriate for crafters who learn best either visually or by following written instructions." LJ

746.44   Embroidery

A-Z of Ribbon Embroidery. Search Press 2016 132 p. color illustrations $19.95   **746.44**
   1. Embroidery 2. Ribbon work
   ISBN 178221173X; 9781782211730
   In this book from Country Bump, readers "will find every stitch and technique fully explained with step by step photographs and clear instructions. Accomplished embroiderers have compiled advice on choosing ribbons, fabrics, needles and frames, as well as a host of other hints and tips. There are forty exquisite designs with full detail provided on the materials and stitches used for every element and a helpful Ribbon Embroidery Index." (Publisher's note)
   "Search Press, as always in this British series, excels, giving its readers good instructions and traditional designs, including Victorian bouquet, roses, violets, baby bears, and other animals and flowers. Occasional tips (e.g., test ribbons first for color fastness by washing) ensure that beginners are on the same page as experienced embroiderers. A fresh, instructive approach to a wonderful tradition." Booklist

A-Z of Whitework; compiled by Country Bumpkin. Search Press 2015 128 p. color illustrations $19.95   **746.44**
   1. Embroidery 2. Needlework
   ISBN 1782211799; 9781782211792
   This book is the "ultimate resource for beginning and experienced needlecrafters who want to discover the timeless appeal of whitework in its many forms. Whitework is white on white embroidery where the texture of the stitchery, whether it be delicate or bold, creates the beauty and interest. Over 1,000 step-by-step photos illustrate the creation of this beautiful traditional white-on-white embroidery which has inspired needlecrafters for centuries." (Publisher's note)
   "Traditional whitework embroidery—especially Mountmellick and cutwork—is starting to get some attention on embroidery blogs, and these classic techniques will appeal to stitchers with sophisticated tastes." LJ

Chamberlin, Ruth
  Beginner's guide to goldwork; Ruth Chamberlin. Search Press Limited 2017 80 p. color illustrations (Search Press classics) (paperback) $19.95   **746.44**
   1. Embroidery 2. Needlework 3. Gold embroidery 4. Metal thread embroidery
   ISBN 9781782214861; 1782214860

This book in the Search Press Classics series, by Ruth Chamberlin, "aims to teach the reader how to create a personal sampler--a piece of embroidery containing a mixture of designs and stitches, which shall provide a basis for future projects and enable readers to continue on their goldwork journey. . . . [The book] gently introduces beginners to the exquisite needle art of goldwork embroidery." (Publisher's note)

Christensen, Jo Ippolito

★ The **needlepoint** book; Jo Ippolito Christensen; foreword by Amy Bunger. 3rd edition Simon & Schuster 2014 560 p. ill. (some col.) (hardcover) $60 **746.44**
    1. Needlepoint 2. Canvas embroidery
    ISBN 147675408X; 9781476754086; 9781476754109
                          LC 2014023165
This is a "revised and expanded edition" of Jo Ippolito Christensen's book on needlepoint, including "a crash course on how to use new fibers; updated information on materials, as well as how to work with and care for them; dozens of new stitches; and diagrams and stitch guides for select projects included in book. Also featured are thirty-two pages of color photographs with all-new projects . . . and a new ribbon stitch chapter." (Publisher's note)

"Even though the book is a reference, the text is enjoyable to read. Sage advice from Christensen and a variety of other needle artists can be found throughout." LJ

Includes bibliographical references and index

Cross, Kate

Applique; Techniques, Projects & Pure Inspiration. Kate Cross. Search Press 2016 128 p. color illustrations $35 **746.44**
    1. Handicraft
    ISBN 1782211888; 9781782211884
This book, by Kate Cross, "is the first in a new series designed to showcase the traditional techniques, technical excellence and contemporary flair of the RSN, and provide practical guidance and inspiration. The book features an introduction to the RSN and its prestigious heritage. It reveals the history and context of appliqué and showcases galleries of inspiring appliqué work from around the world." (Publisher's note)

"Art quilters and embroiderers interested in exploring appliqué techniques will benefit from the detailed information found in this guide." LJ

Includes bibliographical references (page 127) and index.

Embroidery; a maker's guide. Victoria and Albert Museum. Thames & Hudson 2018 176 p. $24.95 **746.44**
    1. Embroidery 2. Needlework 3. Decoration and ornament
    ISBN 9780500293270
                          LC 2017944788
This book, by Victoria and Albert Museum, "contains fifteen beautiful step-by-step projects for crafters at all levels. Each one takes its cue from a different tradition, including English goldwork, . . . Japanese Kogin, and Irish whitework, as well as contemporary machine embroidery. This modern maker's guide to decorative stitching traditions around the world will expand readers' crafting horizons and become an invaluable addition to every crafting shelf." (Publisher's note)

"While the coverage isn't comprehensive, this collection provides an overview of a wide variety of techniques, and stitchers interested in global traditions of embroidery will find plenty to explore." LJ

Ganderton, Lucinda

★ **Embroidery;** Lucinda Ganderton. DK Publishing 2015 160 p. color illustrations (paperback) $15.95 **746.44**
    1. Embroidery 2. Needlework
    ISBN 1465436030; 9781465436030
                          LC 2015431417

Author Lucinda Ganderton presents "a comprehensive guide to inspire and inform sewers of all levels. Find advice on which thread, needles, or fabrics work with which techniques, and take a look at an incredible 200 stitches -- with levels of difficulty, step-by-step instructions, and ideas on where and how to use them." (Publisher's note)

" It's straightforward, simple, and easy to access, thanks not only to an appended index but also to an upfront visual table of contents. The quintessentially perfect reference." Booklist

Mornu, Nathalie

★ **Embroider** your life; techniques + motifs + inspiration: simple techniques & 150 stylish motifs to embellish your world. Nathalie Mornu. DK Publishing 2017 124 p. $16.95 **746.44**
    1. Embroidery
    ISBN 1465464859; 9781465464859
                          LC 2017933232
In this book, by Nathalie Mornu, "with 150 motifs designed by 20 of today's most popular embroidery artists selected from Instagram and Etsy, learn the simplest embroidery stitches and techniques, and see the creative ways the motifs can be used to personalize your head-to-toe wearables, accessories, and items for your home." (Publisher's note)

Embroidery is on the upswing among crafters, and Mornu's nicely organized collection is full of helpful tutorials and clever ideas. --Library Journal (October 15, 2017)

Prain, Leanne

Hoopla; the art of unexpected embroidery. photography by Jeff Christenson. Arsenal Pulp Press 2011 400p il pa $29.95 **746.44**
    1. Embroidery
    ISBN 978-1-55152-406-1
"In this combination overview of embroidery and exploration of its current trends, Prain takes a traditional approach, beginning with a cursory look at the craft's history and highlighting practicalities, such as tools and equipment, finishing techniques, and stitching resources. But it is between these lines that the author's true innovation and fun starts: specifically, with interviews with 28 working embroiderers and the same number of unusual projects to complete. . . . Projects don't disappoint, with directions as clear as the designs are funky: handkerchiefs emblazoned with microbes, a modern cuckoo clock stitched on Aida cloth, and knuckle-tattoo church gloves." Booklist

Includes bibliographical references

Reader's Digest Association

The **big** book of cross-stitch designs; over 900 simple-to-stitch decorative motifs. Reader's Digest Association 2007 320p il $29.95 **746.44**
    1. Cross-stitch 2. Needlework -- Patterns
    ISBN 0-7621-0673-5; 978-0-7621-0673-8
                          LC 2006-044634
"When editors at Reader's Digest identify a subject to publish, they explore its history, plumb the most popular techniques, then apply those learnings pragmatically. Here, cross-stitching takes on a more artistic bent, starting with the book's layout-big type fonts, step-by-step illustrations with full-color photographs of the projects—and ending with more than 900 designs." Booklist

Ringquist, Rebecca

★ **Rebecca** Ringquist's embroidery workshops; a bend-the-rules primer. Rebecca Ringquist. Stewart, Tabori & Chang 2015 160 p. illustrations $29.95 **746.44**
    1. Embroidery

ISBN 1617691410; 9781617691416

LC 2014943000

In this book on embroidery, author Rebecca Ringquist "teaches everything from the 'proper' way to form a French knot and transfer a design to a canvas to new ways to stitch three-dimensionally, work with nontraditional threads and fabrics, draw with thread freeform, and mix and match machine- and hand-stitching. Also featured are instructions for 20 innovative projects, including a cloth sampler designed especially for the book, . . . table linens, wall art, and clothing embellishments." (Publisher's note)

"Ringquist is a skilled instructor with a great deal of experience. Crafters who are intimidated by embroidery will find her free-spirited approach refreshing." LJ

Shimoda, Naoko

Artfully embroidered; motifs and patterns for bags and more. Naoko Shimoda. Interweave 2014 120 p. illustrations (chiefly color) (pbk.) $24.99   **746.44**

1. Embroidery 2. Needlework -- Patterns 3. Embroidery -- Patterns
ISBN 9781620337288; 1620337282

LC 2014036871

This book, by Naoko Shimoda, "reinvents vintage embroidery through a modern aesthetic. Traditional Japanese and western motifs are made new with color and embellishment, and 25 embroidered patterns demonstrate the beauty of the traditional designs while keeping the projects fresh and modern-looking for today's sewists." (Publisher's note)

"Shimoda is a master at combining fabric and thread for impressive effects. Sewists interested in exploring the world of embroidery will find a wealth of inspiration here, though beginners may need to consult a reference or an online tutorial to get themselves up to speed on the basics." LJ

Thomas, Mary

Mary Thomas's dictionary of embroidery stitches; by Mary Thomas and Jan Eaton. Trafalgar Square Pub. 1998 208 p. color illustrations $26.95   **746.44**

1. Embroidery 2. Embroidery -- Dictionaries
ISBN 1570761183; 9781570761188

LC 97081406

This book on embroidery, by Mary Thomas, was "[f]irst published in 1934. . . . Updated by Jan Eaton, it pictures and describes over 400 embroidery stitches arranged by usage, ranging from basic outline and border stitches to more complex detached-filling and pulled-fabric stitches." (Publisher's note)

"A comprehensive dictionary offering more than 400 stitches, this edition includes 100 new stitches, all described and pictured in full-color diagrams. Essential for public libraries and embroidery collections." LJ

Dictionary of embroidery stitches

Watson, Sarah

Pen to thread; 750+ hand-drawn embroidery designs to inspire your stitches. Sarah Watson. Interweave 2015 159 p. illustrations (some color) (pbk.) $26.99   **746.44**

1. Embroidery 2. Needlework -- Patterns 3. Embroidery -- Patterns
4. Embroidery -- Instruction and study
ISBN 1620339528; 9781620339527

LC 2016288028

This book, by Sarah Watson, "more than 750 whimsical, imaginative motifs [of embroidery.] . . . From every day objects like birdcages and backpacks to sophisticated poodles, playful mermaids, and punchy pinatas, each pattern is more charming than the next. Sarah has also included embroidery and stitching basics in case you're new to this fun and addictive hobby." (Publisher's note)

"Illustrator and fabric designer Watson brings her whimsical, hand-drawn designs to embroiderers in this collection of small and medium motifs." LJ

Includes bibliographical references and index

746.46   Patchwork and quilting

Adams, Katherine Jean

Comfort & glory; Two Centuries of American Quilts from the Briscoe Center. by Katherine Jean Adams. University of Texas Press, Briscoe Center for American History 2016 xiv, 320 p.p (cloth: alk. paper) $75   **746.46**

1. Quilts -- Texas -- History 2. University of Texas at Austin. Center for American History -- Catalogs 3. Quilts -- Texas -- Catalogs
ISBN 9781477309186

LC 2015033631

This book in the Focus on American History series, by Katherine Jean Adams, "introduces an outstanding collection of American quilts and quilt history documentation, the Winedale Quilt Collection at the Briscoe Center for American History at the University of Texas at Austin. This volume showcases 115 quilts—nearly one-quarter of the Winedale Collection—through stunning color photographs (including details) and essays about each quilt's history and construction." (Publisher's note)

"This eminently accessible and thorough title will make a wonderful addition to academic, museum, and public libraries of all sizes." LJ

Includes bibliographical references and index.

Alexander, Lissa

Oh, scrap! fabulous quilts that make the most of your stash. Lissa Alexander. Martingale 2018 96 p. $27.99   **746.46**

1. Quilts 2. Quilting 3. Patchwork 4. Quilts -- Design 5. Quilting -- Patterns 6. Patchwork -- Patterns
ISBN 1604688947; 9781604688948

LC 2017044124

In this book, author Lissa Alexander "offers page after page of tips for making dazzling scrap quilts bursting with colors, prints, and textures. Learn Lissa's secrets for deciding which fabric combinations work (and understanding why others don't). Best of all, with a dozen patterns to choose from you'll discover how to (finally!) use your unique stash to make scrap quilts that sing. Includes a preface by renowned quilt historian Barbara Brackman." (Publisher's note)

Arkison, Cheryl

Sunday morning quilts; 16 modern scrap projects: sort, store, and use every last bit of your treasured fabrics. Amanda Jean Nyberg and Cheryl Arkison. StashBooks 2012 143 p. color illustrations (pbk.) $22.95   **746.46**

1. Quilts 2. Quilting 3. Patchwork 4. Quilting -- Patterns 5. Patchwork -- Patterns
ISBN 1607054272; 9781607054276

LC 2011034028

In this book, authors Amanda Jean Nyberg and Cheryl Arkison "share a passion for scraps, and they're here to help you get creative with 16 scrappy quilt projects that include piecing, appliqué, and improvisational work. This book has ideas on how to adapt patterns for your own personal 'Sunday morning' style, plus tips for effectively cutting, storing, and organizing your scraps." (Publisher's note)

Baumgarten, Linda

Four centuries of quilts; the Colonial Williamsburg collection. Linda Baumgarten, Kimberly Smith Ivey. The Colonial Williamsburg Foundation 2014 355 p. illustrations $75 **746.46**

1. Quilts 2. Quilting -- History 3. Quilts -- Catalogs 4. Colonial Williamsburg Foundation -- Catalogs 5. Quilts -- Virginia -- Williamsburg -- Catalogs

ISBN 0300207360; 9780300207361 (Yale); 9780879352646

LC 2013049064

This book, by Linda Baumgarten and Kimberly Smith Ivey, "trace[s] the evolution of quilting styles and trends as they relate to the social, political, and economic issues of their time. The collection includes quilts made by diverse religious and cultural groups over 400 years and across continents, from the Mediterranean, England, France, America, and Polynesia." (Publisher's note)

"The catalog's arc is roughly chronological across categories (ethnic groups, quilting techniques, genres, materials, and pattern names) that reflect collection strengths. Its best feature is the authors' efforts to recover the identities of individual quilt makers." Choice

Includes bibliographical references and index

Arnett, William

Belyea, Patricia

East-meets-West quilts; explore improv with Japanese-inspired designs. Patricia Belyea. Abrams 2017 192 p. $27.50 **746.46**

1. Quilting 2. Patchwork

ISBN 9781419726590

LC 2016960609

"In this book, expert quilter Patricia Belyea offers improv instruction and shares her appealing Quilt Manifesto of five simple rules. While providing quilters with a starting point, the fifth rule of the Manifesto, 'Break any rule you like,' opens the door to creative freedom. . . . Fourteen projects combine authentic Japanese yukata cottons and contemporary fabrics; each is finished with bold hand-stitching." (Publisher's note)

" The quilts' backs prove as interesting as the fronts, and Belyea's stitching designs are innovative, too. With fresh designs and useful directions, Belyea's book is both practical and aspirational." Pub Wkly

Beyer, Jinny

The **quilter's** album of patchwork patterns; more than 4050 pieced blocks for quilters. Breckling Press 2009 488p il $49.95 **746.46**

1. Quilting

ISBN 978-1-933308-08-1

LC 2009-21009

The author "pored through newspapers, catalogs, patterns, and magazines of the 1800s and 1900s to prepare illustrations—along with grids, dates, and multiple names—of more than 4,000 quilting blocks, the foundation of this genre of stitching. Yet providing that resource wasn't enough; Beyer enhances her encyclopedic reference by featuring mini catalogs of like-minded design styles, like bow ties, airplanes, the Red Cross, and kaleidoscope blocks. She also details her sources with commentary and explains how she categorized the blocks. Worthy of any quilting (and quilter's) library." Booklist

Includes bibliographical references

Brandvig, Jera

Quilt as-you-go made vintage; 51 blocks, 9 projects, 3 joining methods. by Jera Brandvig. C&T Publishing 2017 144 p. (soft cover) $21.95 **746.46**

1. Quilts 2. Quilting -- Patterns 3. Patchwork quilts 4. Patchwork

-- Patterns 5. Machine sewing -- Technique

ISBN 9781617454721

LC 2017003179

In this book, author Jera Brandvig shares a romantic take on her easy quilting designs. Sew 9 quilt-as-you-go projects, including an elegant sampler with 51 interchangeable blocks. Choose one of three QAYG finishing methods (or stick with traditional quilting), including a new reversible-quilt method that renders a secondary patchwork design on your quilt back! No matter how busy your schedule, these timeless blocks create endless possibilities." (Publisher's note)

51 blocks, 9 projects, 3 joining methods

Gee's Bend; the architecture of the quilt. contributions by William Arnett ... [et al.] ; edited by Paul Arnett, Joanne Cubbs, Eugene W. Metcalf Tinwood Books 2006 223 p. $50 **746.46**

1. Quilts 2. Quilting 3. African American women

ISBN 0971910456; 9780971910454

This book, by William Arnett, edited by Paul Arnett, Joanne Cubbs and Eugene W. Metcalf, "is a major book and museum exhibition that will premiere at the Museum of Fine Arts, Houston (MFAH), in June 2006 before traveling to seven American museums through 2008. The book's 330 color illustrations and insightful text bring home the exciting experience to readers while displaying all the cultural heritage and craftsmanship that have gone into these remarkable quilts." (Publisher's note)

Gering, Jacquie

Quilting modern; techniques and projects for improvisational quilts. Jacquie Gering, Katie Pedersen. Interweave Press 2012 175 p. color illustrations (pbk.) $26.99 **746.46**

1. Quilts 2. Quilting 3. Patchwork 4. Patchwork -- Patterns 5. Machine quilting -- Patterns

ISBN 1596683872; 9781596683877

LC 2011039245

This book, by Jacquie Gering and Katie Pedersen, "teaches quilters how to use improvisational techniques to make graphic, contemporary quilts and quilted projects. Explore seven core techniques and multiple projects using each technique--all presented with detailed instructions. . . . New and seasoned quilting artists will love making stunning bed, wall hanging, pillowcase, and table accessory quilts with this must-have resource." (Publisher's note)

Includes bibliographical references and index

Walk; master machine quilting with your walking foot. Jacquie Gering. Lucky Spool Media 2016 160 p. illustrations (some color) (paperback) $28.95 **746.46**

1. Quilting 2. Quilts -- Design 3. Machine quilting

ISBN 1940655218; 9781940655215

This book, by Jacquie Gering, "shares a comprehensive set of walking foot quilting basics that provide a solid foundation for quilting with ease, quality and creativity. She guides you through a series of test drives with your walking foot, . . . [and] you'll learn how to prepare and mark the quilt, prevent puckers while quilting, and manage large projects. . . . [Gering] teaches over forty walking foot friendly designs . . . [such as] quilting with decorative stitches." (Publisher's note)

Includes bibliographical references (page 159).

Gilleland, Diane

All points patchwork; English paper piecing beyond the hexagon, for quilts & small projects. by Diane Gilleland. Storey Publishing 2015 224 p. color illustrations (pbk.: alk. paper) $19.95   **746.46**

1. Quilting 2. Patchwork 3. Paper work 4. Quilting -- Patterns 5. Patchwork -- Patterns

ISBN 1612124208; 9781612124209

LC 2014048235

This book on patchwork, by Diane Gilleland, focuses on the "traditional technique known as English paper piecing. . . . [It] takes you far beyond traditional hexagons with step-by-step photos showing you how to connect triangles, octagons, diamonds, jewels, triangles, tumblers, pentagons, and curved shapes. It even provides dozens of ideas for incorporating the pattern designs into clothing, pillows, quilts, and home decor items!" (Publisher's note)

"An essential reference for quilters interested in EPP." LJ

Includes bibliographical references and index

Hartman, Elizabeth

Modern patchwork; 12 quilts to take you beyond the basics. Elizabeth Hartman. StashBooks 2012 143 p. color illustrations (soft cover) $24.95   **746.46**

1. Quilts 2. Quilting 3. Patchwork 4. Patchwork quilts 5. Quilting -- Patterns

ISBN 1607055481; 9781607055488

LC 2011040928

With this book, by Elizabeth Hartman, you can "[e]xpand your patchwork skills with . . . new designs and techniques. . . . These projects are bold, bright, graphic, and designed to give modern quilters new challenges. You can learn new skills like curved seam piecing and create your best modern quilt yet. Make it fresh, make it fun, make it something you will use and cherish for years to come." (Publisher's note)

Marth, Susan R.

★ **Dresden** quilt workshop; tips, tools & techniques for perfect mini Dresden plates. Susan R. Marth. C&T Publishing, Inc. 2017 88 p. (soft cover) $24.95   **746.46**

1. Quilting 2. Patchwork 3. Patchwork quilts 4. Dresden plate quilts 5. Quilting -- Patterns

ISBN 1617455008; 9781617455001

LC 2016058062

In this book, Susan R. Marth, "step up your piecing with a small-scale version of the cherished Dresden Plate. Fall in love with the classic quilt block all over again as you learn the secret to impeccable mini Dresdens in two sizes. . . . Polish your piecing, pressing, and appliqué with proven techniques and apply those skills to 13 projects from bed-size beauties to wallhangings and table toppers." (Publisher's note)

Nyberg, Amanda Jean

No scrap left behind; 16 quilt projects that celebrate scraps of all sizes. Amanda Jean Nyberg. Stash Books, an imprint of C&T Publishing 2017 127 p. color illustrations (paperback) $26.95   **746.46**

1. Quilts 2. Patchwork 3. Quilting -- Patterns 4. Patchwork -- Patterns

ISBN 9781617453373; 9781617453366

LC 2016030821

This book, by Amanda Jean Nyberg, presents "16 satisfying quilts and projects. Sew modern quilts for everyday use that will help you return to the roots of quiltmaking, with projects designed to help you use up every last scrap. Learn sorting and storage tips to help you plan your next quilt, with projects categorized by type of scrap—squares, strings, triangles, or little snippets. You'll never look at scraps the same way again!" (Publisher's note)

Patchwork and quilting; a maker's guide. by Victoria and Albert Museum, illustrated by Eleanor Crow. Thames & Hudson 2018 176 p. $24.95   **746.46**

1. Quilts 2. Patchwork

ISBN 9780500293263

LC 2017944789

This book in the Maker's Guide series, illustrated by Eleanor Crow, offers "a practical guide to patchwork and quilting, inspired by craft traditions from across the globe. . . . [It] contains fifteen beautiful step-by-step projects for crafters at all levels. Each one takes its cue from a different tradition, including Indian kantha, . . . Japanese boro patchwork, and the block-and strip-pieced quilts of North America, as well as appliqué traditions from Hawaii and Panama." (Publisher's note)

"The combination of diverse techniques, as well as the international scope, makes this an excellent guide for crafters interested in the history and traditions of quilting." LJ

Pink, Tula

Quilts from the house of Tula Pink; 20 fabric projects to make, use and love. Tula Pink. Krause Publications 2012 144 p. color illustrations (pbk.) $24.99   **746.46**

1. Quilts 2. Quilting 3. Quilting -- Patterns

ISBN 1440218188; 9781440218187

LC 2012471570

In this book, fabric designer Tula Pink "offers 20 patterns with her signature flair for color, design and original style. Between 10 amazing quilts and 10 extra-cool companion projects, you'll be inspired to play with fabric, color and design in a way like never before!" (Publisher's note)

Includes bibliographical references and index

Tula Pink's city sampler; 100 modern quilt blocks. Tula Pink. David & Charles 2013 255 p. ill. (chiefly col.) $27.99   **746.46**

1. Quilts 2. Quilting

ISBN 1440232148; 9781440232145

In this book, author "Tula Pink gives you an inspiring quilt block collection. . . . Make a beautiful, modern quilt of your own design with the 100 original quilt blocks or try one of the 5 city-themed sampler quilts designed by Tula." (Publisher's note)

The **quilts** of Gee's Bend; William Arnett; Alvia Wardlaw; Jane Livingston; John Beardsley; foreword by Peter Marzio. Tinwood Books in association with The Museum of Fine Arts, Houston; Hi Marketing, distributor 2003 190 p. il (chiefly col) maps, ports. (chiefly col.) $50   **746.46**

1. Quilts -- History 2. African American quilts 3. Tinwood Alliance -- Exhibitions 4. African American quilts -- Alabama -- Wilcox County

ISBN 0965376648; 9780965376648

LC 2006355008

In this book, by William Arnett, Alvia Wardlaw, Jane Livingston and John Beardsley, "Gee's Bend . . . is an isolated place, one that has known extreme poverty and struggle. Its quilters of the twentieth century are showcased here. Three insightful essays on the community's history and its quilting tradition make up for a self-consciously scholarly introduction. The words of the quilters themselves follow." (Booklist) Includes bibliographical references (p. 182-183) and index

Redford, Catherine

Modern machine quilting; make a perfectly finished quilt on your home machine. Catherine Redford. Fons & Porter, an imprint of F+W Media, Inc. 2017 127 p. color illustrations (paperback) $24.99 **746.46**

1. Quilts 2. Quilting 3. Needlework 4. Machine quilting 5. Quilting -- Patterns 6. Patchwork -- Patterns 7. Machine quilting -- Patterns

ISBN 9781440246319; 1440246319

LC 2016498696

This book, by Catherine Redford, "guides you through every stage of planning, constructing, and finishing a quilt. Learn a multitude of crisp walking foot designs, including straight lines, matchstick, grids, serpentine, spirals, and more. Explore more than a dozen techniques and patterns for free-motion designs." (Publisher's note)

"While many machine quilting books focus on either walking-foot quilting or free-motion quilting, Redford includes an introduction to both techniques, providing a well-rounded overview of the possibilities offered by each." LJ

Schmidt, Denyse

Denyse Schmidt; modern quilts, traditional inspiration: 20 new designs with historic roots. Denyse Schmidt; photographs by John Gruen. Stewart, Tabori & Chang 2012 160 p. color illustrations; patterns $29.95 **746.46**

1. Quilting 2. Quilts -- Design 3. Quilting -- Patterns

ISBN 1584799005; 9781584799009

LC 2011021075

Author Denise Schmidt "pays homage to the quilters and quilts that came before her. Each of the 20 traditional quilt designs she has reinterpreted here (among them are Irish Chain, Mariner's Compass, and Orange Peel, to name a few) is introduced with a lively overview of the pattern's history. Instructions are illustrated, templates are provided at full size on a pullout pattern sheet, and a complete techniques section is included at the back of the book." (Publisher's note)

"It's wonderful to see quilting traditions treated with reverence in a modern quilting book, and the variety of designs, combined with the wealth of information on both quilting and the traditions of each design, make this an essential addition to quilting collections." LJ

Denyse Schmidt quilts; 30 colorful quilt and patchwork projects. text by Denyse Schmidt with Bethany Lyttle; photographs by Susie Cushner. Chronicle Books 2005 175 p. color illustrations $24.95 **746.46**

1. Quilting 2. Patchwork 3. Quilts -- Design 4. Quilting -- Patterns 5. Patchwork -- Patterns

ISBN 0811844420; 9780811844420

LC 2004023094

In this book on quilting, author Denyse Schmidt "reveals the secrets behind her most popular designs. Thirty projects range from the simple to the challenging, from patchwork slippers and aprons to tote bags and pillows to her beloved quilt patterns, offering something for every level of quilter. Schmidt reviews the fundamentals of quilting and provides easy-to-follow instructions, patterns, sewing tips, and an artful approach to design basics." (Publisher's note)

Stocker, Blair

Wise craft quilts; a guide to turning beloved fabrics into meaningful patchwork. Blair Stocker; foreword by Denyse Schmidt; photographs by Stephanie Congdon Barnes. Roost Books, an imprint of Shambhala Publications, Inc. 2017 192 p. illustrations (hardcover: alk. paper) $29.95 **746.46**

1. Quilts 2. Quilting 3. Patchwork 4. Textile fabrics 5. Patchwork quilts 6. Patchwork -- Patterns 7. Textile waste -- Recycling

ISBN 9781611803488

LC 2016012230

In this book "quilt designer and crafter Blair Stocker shares ways to use cherished fabrics to make quilts with more meaning. Each of the twenty-one quilts featured here gathers a special collection of fabric, outlines a new technique, and spins a story. By using special fabrics as the starting point for each project--from a wedding dress to baby's first clothes, worn denim, Tyvek race numbers, and more--the finished quilt is made even more special." (Publisher's note)

Includes bibliographical references.

Walters, Angela

Free-motion meandering; a beginners guide to machine quilting. Angela Walters. C&T Publishing, Inc. 2017 79 p. (soft cover) $21.95 **746.46**

1. Quilting 2. Patchwork 3. Needlework 4. Machine quilting 5. Decoration and ornament -- Themes, motives

ISBN 1617455202; 9781617455209

LC 2017006148

In this book, "author Angela Walters shows you that free-motion machine quilting doesn't have to be scary--with a couple designs in your pocket, you can finish almost any quilt on your home machine and enjoy the process. Practice 8 meandering stitches for beginners plus unique modifications for each, with step-by-step visuals and quilted samples. Improve your free-motion quilting, disguise mistakes, and transition between designs with ease." (Publisher's note)

Wolfe, Victoria Findlay

Modern quilt magic; 5 parlor tricks to expand your piecing skills - 17 captivating projects. Victoria Findlay Wolfe. C&T Publishing, Inc. 2017 128 p. illustrations (chiefly color) (paperback) $27.95 **746.46**

1. Quilting 2. Patchwork 3. Quilting -- Patterns 4. Patchwork -- Patterns

ISBN 9781617455087; 1617455083

LC 2016059348

In this book, by Victoria Findlay Wolfe, "grow your cache of quilter's tricks with 5 awe-inspiring patchwork techniques that are easier than you think! Learn a new piecing trick in just 15 minutes or less, and watch your skills soar to a whole new level. Say 'presto!' with partial seams for both quilts and blocks, Y-seams, mini improv piecing, and free-form curves. Test your newfound skills with 17 projects, including full-size templates for bed quilts, pillows, and more." (Publisher's note)

Wood, Sherri Lynn

Improv handbook for modern quilters; a guide to creating, quilting, and living courageously. Sherri Lynn Wood. Stewart, Tabori & Chang 2015 176 p. color illustrations $27.50 **746.46**

1. Quilts 2. Cross-stitch

ISBN 1617691380; 9781617691386

LC 2014942998

In this book author "Sherri Lynn Wood presents a flexible approach to quilting that breaks free of old paradigms. Instead of traditional instructions, she presents 10 frameworks (or scores) that create a guiding, but not limiting, structure. To help quilters gain confidence, Wood also offers detailed lessons for stitching techniques key to improvisation." (Publisher's note)

"Improv quilting may not be to everyone's taste—it can be visually jarring at times—but many who love this style are downright passionate about it, and Wood provides a comprehensive overview of improvisational techniques." LJ

746.6   Printing, painting, dyeing

Callahan, Gail

    Hand dyeing yarn and fleece; dip-dyeing, hand-painting, tie-dyeing, and other creative techniques. photography by John Polak. Storey Pub. 2010 168p il $18.95   **746.6**
    1. Wool 2. Yarn 3. Dyes and dyeing
    ISBN 1-60342-468-7; 978-1-60342-468-4

                                      LC 2009-28676

    This guide to dyeing yarn and fleece "includes instructions for designing self-striping and multicolored yarns with dip-dyeing, tie-dyeing, hand-painting, and other [techniques, as well as] . . . advice on color theory and types of dyes, including food colors and other 'grocery store' dyes." Publisher's note
    Includes bibliographical references

Corwin, Lena

    Lena Corwin's made by hand; a collection of projects to print, sew, weave, dye, knit, and otherwise create. by Lena Corwin. Stewart, Tabori & Chang 2013 176 p. illustrations (chiefly color) $29.95   **746.6**
    1. Weaving 2. Handicraft 3. Sewing 4. Knitting 5. Textile crafts 6. Dyes and dyeing 7. Textile printing
    ISBN 1617690597; 9781617690594

                                        LC 2013010186

    Author Lean Corwin "re-creates and builds upon her popular workshop series in order to reach crafters in Brooklyn and beyond. For this "best of" collection, she has chosen expert teachers and her favorite projects: Jenny Gordy introduces us to knitted socks and elegantly sewn tops and dresses; Cal Patch teaches how to make a modern embroidery sampler as well as a braided rag rug; and Corwin herself presents her favorite screen-printing." (Publisher's note)

Swearington, Jen

    Printing on fabric; techniques with screens, stencils, inks, & dyes. Jen Swearington. 1st ed. Lark Crafts 2013 160 p. (paperback) $21.95   **746.6**
    1. Textile design 2. Textile printing
    ISBN 1454703946; 9781454703945

                                          LC 2012006729

    This book, by Jen Swearington, offers "an essential and accessible guide to printing by hand on fabric. She starts by explaining how to translate design ideas into prints, from single motifs to repeating patterns. Jen then goes on to cover various methods of transfer: stencils, photo emulsion, dye baths, bleach resists, and more." (Publisher's note)

746.7   Rugs

Denny, Walter B.

    How to read Islamic carpets; Walter B. Denny. Metropolitan Museum of Art/Yale University Press 2014 143 p. color illustrations (How to read series) $25   **746.7**
    1. Islamic art 2. Rugs and carpets 3. Islamic rugs -- History 4. Islamic rugs -- Technique 5. Metropolitan Museum of Art (New York, N.Y.) 6. Islamic rugs -- New York (State) -- New York
    ISBN 030020809X; 9780300208092 (Yale University Press); 9781588395405 (The Metropolitan Museum of Art)

                                          LC 2014035553

    This book, by Walter B. Denny, part of the "How to read" series, "explores the history, design techniques, materials, craftsmanship, and socioeconomic contexts of these . . . [Islamic carpets], promoting a bet-

ter understanding and appreciation of these frequently misunderstood pieces. Fifty-five examples . . . are illustrated with new photographs and revealing details." (Publisher's note)

    "This slim, affordable book is highly recommended to both public and academic libraries of all sizes with collections on art, art history, or textile arts." LJ

    Includes bibliographical references

Rott, Ira

    Crochet animal rugs; over 20 crochet patterns for fun floor mats and matching accessories. Ira Rott. F & W Media Inc 2018 144 p. $22.99   **746.7**
    1. Crocheting 2. Needlework 3. Rugs and carpets
    ISBN 144630700X; 9781446307007

    This book, presents "seven sensational animal rug designs, by popular crochet designer Ira Rott. You will love making these unique and quirky designs that kids will simply adore. Choose from an amazing elephant, a sweet giraffe, a cuddly cat, a cheeky monkey, a sneaky crab, a friendly dinosaur and a snuggly bear, each with a coordinating pillow and accessory to crochet to continue the theme." (Publisher's note)

Tiede, Karen

    Knitting fabric rugs; 28 colorful designs for crafters of every level. Karen Tiede. Storey Publishing 2015 184 p. color illustrations (pbk.: alk. paper) $18.95   **746.7**
    1. Knitting 2. Rugs and carpets 3. Rugs 4. Knitting -- Patterns
    ISBN 1612124488; 9781612124483

                                          LC 2015008211

    Author Karen Tiede "gives you directions for making 28 different rugs, with designs that use age-old motifs, including stripes and spirals; traditional quilt patterns, such as tessellations and log cabin designs; and freeform inventions. She shows how to create a wide range of color modulations, as well as different shapes, from rectangles to circles." (Publisher's note)

    "Tiede tries to take a "knitting curmudgeon" approach à la Elizabeth Zimmerman, but unlike Zimmerman, Tiede's tone can be off-puttingly grumpy, especially when she complains about her dislike of particular colors or the physical pain that cutting and knitting with recycled fabric causes her. Still, green crafts are popular, and Tiede's techniques are tried and true, so ecoconscious knitters may be drawn in." LJ

746.9   Other textile products

Faerm, Steven

    Fashion: design course. Barron's 2010 144p il pa $23.99   **746.9**
    1. Fashion design
    ISBN 978-0-7641-4423-3

                                          LC 2009-940543

    The author "takes readers through a thorough exploration of the fashion industry, from history to inspiration to the design process to landing a job. There are also 14 practical assignments to help budding designers learn more about the industry. Teens exploring careers in fashion will enjoy the practical advice from industry insiders, and fashion-mad readers of all ages will appreciate the information about how fashion design works." Libr J

Givhan, Robin

    The **Battle** of Versailles; the night American fashion stumbled into the spotlight and made history. Robin Givhan. Flatiron Books 2015 320 p. illustrations (some color) (hardback)

$27.99 **746.9**

1. Fashion shows 2. Social change 3. Château de Versailles (Versailles, France) 4. Fashion merchandising -- Social aspects 5. Fashion shows -- France -- Versailles -- History 6. Fashion merchandising -- United States -- History
ISBN 1250052904; 9781250052902; 9781250053855

LC 2014040369

This book, by Robin Givhan, tells how, "Conceived as a fund-raiser for the restoration of King Louis XIV's palace, in the late fall of 1973, five top American designers faced off against five top French designers in an over-the-top runway extravaganza. . . . By the end of the evening, the Americans had officially taken their place on the world's stage, prompting a major shift in the way race, gender, sexuality, and economics would be treated in fashion for decades to come." (Publisher's note)

"Readers need not be fashion mavens to enjoy this entertaining episode of history, enhanced by Givhan's effortless ability to illustrate the models and designers (particularly Lambert) who changed how we dress." Kirkus

Grumbach, Didier

History of international fashion; Didier Grumbach; photo editor Isabelle d'Hauteville. Interlink Books, an imprint of Interlink Publishing Group, Inc. 2014 462 p. illustrations (chiefly color) $45 **746.9**

1. Fashion design 2. Fashion designers 3. Fashion -- History 4. Fashion design -- History 5. Fashion -- France -- History -- 20th century 6. Fashion design -- France -- History -- 20th century
ISBN 1566569761; 9781566569767

LC 2014004755

In this book, author "Didier Grumbach walks you down the runways of fashion history and unfolds the secrets of the industry with stories and accounts from those who have played an active part in its development from the 1920s to the present. . . . The heroes are Dior, Saint Laurent, Kenzo, Sonia Rykiel, Prada, Hermès, and others. Their adventures are presented in an innovative chronological--and logical--order." (Publisher's note)

"Much of this is channeled through Grumbach's own extensive experiences, beginning with his family's textile company, where he strove to create ready-to-wear that had the same quality manufacturing as haute couture." Grumbach concludes with a shrewd look at today's globalized fashion industry. Just like the best designer clothes, this exposé is both dazzling and enduring." Booklist

Includes bibliographical references (pages 436-437) and index

Linett, Andrea

The **cool** factor; Andrea Linett. Artisan 2016 208 p. color illustrations $24.95 **746.9**

1. Fashion 2. Women's clothing 3. Womens' clothing
ISBN 9781579656485

LC 2015034242

This book, by stylist Andrea Linett, "offers easy-to-implement, actionable tips that will change the way women dress. The tips are modeled by real-life style icons like Kim Gordon of Sonic Youth and Christene Barberich, founder of Refinery29, as Andrea highlights the ingenious ways in which they skillfully pile on layers, or dress up denim for work or a party." (Publisher's note)

"There's at least one tip or rule-busting—potentially game-changing—suggestion for any woman looking to cultivate a coherent wardrobe and unique style by using her eyes, judgment, and Linett's six principles." Pub Wkly

Lowit, Roxanne

Yves Saint Laurent; Roxanne Lowit. Thames & Hudson

2014 208 p. illustrations (some colour) (hardcover) $50 **746.9**

1. Fashion designers
ISBN 0500517606; 9780500517604

LC 2014930896

This biography is author "Roxanne Lowit's personal photographic history of [Yves] Saint Laurent, the man and the fashion, from 1978, the year she first met him, to the last show he gave in 2002. With contributions from YSL's muses and admirers, including Catherine Deneuve, Betty Catroux, Lucie de la Falaise, Pat Cleveland, and Valerie Steele, this book represents the backstage experience at YSL's shows as Lowit experienced them herself." (Publisher's note)

The **Mood** guide to fabric and fashion; the essential guide from the world's most famous fabric store. Harry N Abrams Inc 2015 184 p. illustrations (chiefly color) $27.50 **746.9**

1. Fabrics 2. Fashion
ISBN 1617690880; 9781617690884

LC 2014959131

This book is a "guide for home-sewers, fashion students, aspiring designers, and Project Runway fans who want to learn everything they need to know to choose and use quality fabric. Drawing upon the expertise of the Mood staff, the book teaches readers the fundamentals—from where fabric is produced to the ins and outs of its construction—and features a fabric-by-fabric guide to cottons and other plant fibers, wools, silks, knits, and other specialty fabrics." (Publisher's note)

"A pleasingly presented layperson's introduction to the world of fashion fabrics. The name recognition will be a big draw." LJ

Moses, Susan

The **art** of dressing curves; the best-kept secrets of a fashion stylist. Susan Moses. Harper Design Intl 2016 254 p. illustrations (some color) (hardcover) $35 **746.9**

1. Fashion 2. Women's clothing
ISBN 9780062362032; 0062362038

LC 2014937017

In this book, author Susan Moses, "the go-to celebrity stylist for curvy women both on and off the red carpet presents the first inspirational, confidence-building, prescriptive style guide for plus-size women who want to dress fashionably and look their beautiful best. . . . [The author] gives plus-size women the confidence and know-how to dress beautifully for their particular body shape." (Publisher's note)

Includes bibliographical references (pages 248-251).

Schuman, Emily

Cupcakes and cashmere at home; Emily Schuman. Abrams Image 2015 175 p. color illustrations $19.95 **746.9**

1. Entertaining 2. Interior design
ISBN 1419715836; 9781419715839

LC 2014942738

In this book, author Emily Schuman "expands on the personal lifestyle advice that her fans loved in her first book and on her popular blog, with a focus on interior design and entertaining at home. The book features never-before-seen content and explores Emily's accessible design philosophy for decorating and creating a fashionable personal space. In addition, the book includes DIY design projects and party planning ideas." (Publisher's note)

Thomas, Dana

Gods and Kings; The Rise and Fall of Alexander Mcqueen and John Galliano. Dana Thomas. Penguin Group USA 2015 432 p. 32 plates; portraits $29.95 **746.9**

1. Fashion designers

ISBN 1594204942; 9781594204944

LC 2015460559

In this book, author Dana Thomas "tells the true story of [Alexander] McQueen and [John] Galliano. In so doing, she reveals the revolution in high fashion in the last two decades--and the price it demanded of the very ones who saved it. They had similar backgrounds: sensitive, shy gay men raised in tough London neighborhoods, their love of fashion nurtured by their doting mothers. Both struggled to get their businesses off the ground, despite early critical success." (Publisher's note)

"This is a dark story about excess, commerce, aristocracy and fashion as high theater that is as operatic as the dizzying shows it describes. A deep dive into the provocative art of creation and the toll it exacts from those touched by its gifts."

746.92   Costume

Tetart-Vittu, Francoise

★ The **house** of worth; Chantal Trubert-Tollu. Thames & Hudson 2018 336 p.   **746.92**

1. Fashion design 2. Fashion designers
ISBN 9780500519431

LC 2017944380

"With gorgeous color images of Worth designs, paintings, and archival fashion drawings and photographs, this sumptuous book is recommended for readers interested in the history of haute couture and French fashion." Library Journal

747   Interior decoration

Becker, Holly

Decorate; 1,000 professional design ideas for every room in your home. Holly Becker & Joanna Copestick; photographs by Debi Treloar. Chronicle Books 2011 288 p. color illustrations $35   **747**

1. Interior design 2. Decoration and ornament 3. Interior decoration
ISBN 0811877892; 9780811877893

LC 2010048053

In this book by Holly Becker and Joanna Copestick "the world's top designers and leading decor experts including Kelly Wearstler, Amy Butler, Jonathan Adler, and many others come together to share over 1,000 professional tips, ideas, and solutions for every room and every budget." (Publisher's note)

Blair, Gabrielle Stanley

Design mom; how to live with kids: a room-by-room guide. Gabrielle Stanley Blair. Artisan Books 2015 288 p. color illustrations $29.95   **747**

1. Family life 2. Interior design 3. Families 4. Interior decoration 5. Interior decoration -- Human factors
ISBN 1579655718; 9781579655716

LC 2014038734

In this design book, mom Gabrielle Stanley Blair "offers a room-by-room guide to keeping things sane, organized, creative, and stylish. She provides advice on getting the most out of even the smallest spaces; simple fixes that make it easy for little ones to help out around the house; ingenious storage solutions for the never-ending stream of kid stuff; rainy-day DIY projects; and much, much more." (Publisher's note)

"Blair even finds a way to keep mass-marketed character decor out of a child's bedroom by substituting NASA photos for Buzz Lightyear pinups. This is a happy marriage of interior design book and parenting

guide." Pub Wkly

Includes bibliographical references and index

Blakeney, Justina

The **new** Bohemians; cool and collected homes. Justina Blakeney. Stewart, Tabori & Chang 2015 304 p. color illustrations $35   **747**

ISBN 1617691518; 9781617691515

LC 2014942982

In this book, author "Justina Blakeney defines the New Bohemians as creative individuals who are boutique owners and bloggers, entrepreneurs and ex-pats, artists and urban farmers. [It] explores 20 homes located primarily on the East and West coasts. Exclusive interviews with the owners, 12 DIY projects created by Blakeney and inspired by objects found in the homes, and a 'Plant-O-Pedia' offer insight into achieving this aesthetic." (Publisher's note)

"The youthful exuberance shown in these interiors will encourage amateurs to discover their own bohemian style." LJ

Bonney, Grace

Design*Sponge at home; Grace Bonney. Artisan 2011 ix, 390 p.p color illustrations $35   **747**

1. Interior design 2. Decoration and ornament 3. Interior decoration -- Amateurs' manuals
ISBN 1579654312; 9781579654313

LC 2010039458

Author Grace Bonney presents a "guide, which includes: Home tours of 70 real-life interiors featuring artists and designers . . .Fifty DIY projects, with detailed instructions for personalizing your space . . . Step-by-step tutorials on everything from stripping and painting furniture to hanging wallpaper and doing your own upholstery . . .[and] Fifty Before & After makeovers." (Publisher's note)

"A highly recommended compendium of ideas to inspire amateur decorators." LJ

Includes bibliographical references (p. 372-379) index

The **book** of decorating; a room-by-room guide to creating a home that makes you happy. Deborah Needleman, Sara Ruffin Costello, & Dara Caponigro. Simon & Schuster 2008 271 p. color illustrations (alk. paper) $32   **747**

1. Interior design 2. Interior decoration -- Handbooks, manuals, etc
ISBN 1416575464; 9781416575467

LC 2008015072

This book, by Deborah Needleman, Sara Ruffin Costello, and Dara Caponigro, "cracks the code to creating a beautiful home, bringing together inspiring rooms, how-to advice and insiders' secrets from today's premier tastemakers in an indispensable style manual. The editors take readers room by room, tapping the best ideas from domino magazine and culling insights from their own experiences." (Publisher's note)

"Different styles are shown for each in plenty of color photographs, with suggested furnishings and advice on how to mix styles. Each chapter concludes with a look at how a Domino staff member has decorated a similar room with a description of her approach to design. Recommended for large public libraries." LJ

Includes bibliographical references (p. 252-263)

Bradbury, Dominic

The **iconic** interior; private spaces of leading artists, architects, and designers. Dominic Bradbury; with photographs by Richard Powers. Abrams Books 2012 351 p. (alk. paper) $65   **747**

1. Interior design 2. Domestic architecture 3. Interior decoration

-- History -- 20th century -- Themes, motives 4. Interior decoration -- History -- 21st century -- Themes, motives
ISBN 1617690058; 9781617690051

LC 2012007221

In this book, author Dominic Bradbury "visits homes whose interiors 'sum up a design movement or define a particular style' of 20th-century interior design. Descriptions of the homes, located primarily in the United States and Europe, include text, color photographs . . . , and a brief biography of the resident or designer. The inhabitants, including Alvar Aalto, Billy Baldwin, Donna Karan, Todd Oldham, and Russel Wright, represent the epitome of 20th-century design and style." (Library Journal)

Includes bibliographical references and index

Brits, Louisa Thomsen

The **book** of hygge; The Danish Art of Contentment, Comfort, and Connection. Louisa Thomsen Brits. Plume 2017 192 p. color illustrations (ebook) $65; (hardback) $22   **747**
1. Denmark 2. Philosophy 3. Interior design 4. Human comfort -- Denmark 5. Interior decoration -- Human factors -- Denmark
ISBN 9780735214101; 9780735214095

LC 2016033681

This book, by Louisa Thomsen Brits, focuses on "Hygge (hoo-gah) . . . a Danish word but a universal feeling of being warm, safe, comforted, and sheltered. . . . When you curl up by the fire with a blanket, or have a simple meal with friends, that is hygge. When you acknowledge the sacred in the secular, or focus on people rather than things, or when you express love through small gestures, that is hygge." (Publisher's note)

"In increasingly fast-paced and competitive America, hygge has considerable appeal; readers may very well find reading Brits's compact and enjoyable book the literary version of the practice." Pub Wkly

Includes bibliographical references (page 188) and index.

Brown, Amanda

★ **Spruce**; a step-by-step guide to upholstery and design. by Amanda Brown. Storey Publishing 2013 400 p. ill. (chiefly col.) (hardcover: alkaline paper) $35   **747**
1. Upholstery
ISBN 1612121373; 9781612121376

LC 2013012590

This book, by Amanda Brown, "is the only book you'll need to learn the craft and art of upholstery from start to finish. With clear instructions illustrated by more than 900 step-by-step photographs, the five projects included here are designed to teach all of the techniques and skills you need to reupholster any piece of furniture to suit your own taste and style." (Publisher's note)

"[P]erfectly matches complete, precisely written directions with correspondingly crisp, helpful photographs." Booklist

Includes bibliographical references and index

Carlson, Julie

Remodelista; a manual for the considered home. Julie Carlson with the editors of Remodelista. Artisan 2013 400 p. color illustrations $37.50   **747**
1. Interior design 2. Houses -- Remodeling 3. Dwellings -- Remodeling 4. Interior decoration -- Themes, motives
ISBN 157965536X; 9781579655365

LC 2013006278

This interior decorating book, by Julie Carlson with the editors of Remodelista.com, "has a singular and clearly defined aesthetic: classic pieces trump designs that are trendy and transient, and well-edited spaces take precedence over cluttered environments. . . . [This guide] decodes the secrets to achieving this aesthetic, with in-depth tours and lessons from 12 enviable homes." (Publisher's note)

"An excellent source of inspiration for those interested in renovating their house or just revamping a room." LJ

Chapman, Emma

A **beautiful** mess happy handmade home; a room-by-room guide to painting, crafting, and decorating a cheerful, more inspiring space. Elsie Larson and Emma Chapman. Potter Style 2014 240 p. color illustrations (paperback) $21.99   **747**
1. Handicraft 2. Interior design 3. House furnishings 4. Interior decoration -- Amateurs' manuals
ISBN 0770434053; 9780770434052

LC 2014008902

In this book, authors Elsie Larson and Emma Chapman "overhauled each room in their first homes with DIY projects using family photos, vibrant fabrics, flea-market finds, and affordable furniture. Now, you can learn how to paint, craft, and decorate your way to a happy, bright space with distinct personality. In the same upbeat spirit and modern style found on their blog, you'll find fresh, all-new projects." (Publisher's note)

"In the introduction, the authors instruct readers to identify what features stand out in "favorite spaces" of all kinds, to make lists of how rooms might be used unconventionally (playing cards in a dining room), and to do some soul searching ("Make a list of 100 things about YOU.") The idea is to make home an expression of one's personality, a skill that the authors have clearly mastered." Pub Wkly.

Includes bibliographical references (page 237) and index

Crochet, Treena

Bungalow style; creating classic interiors in your arts and crafts home. Taunton Press 2005 186p il $29.95   **747**
1. Interior design 2. Domestic architecture 3. Houses -- Remodeling
ISBN 978-1-56158-623-3; 1-56158-623-4

LC 2004-9748

This book pictures a "variety of interior details and describes how to add or restore elements that suggest a historic flair while keeping the home comfortable and functional. Common problems such as integrating modern conveniences or gaining needed space are also addressed." Publisher's note

DeGeneres, Ellen, 1958-

Home; Ellen DeGeneres. Grand Central Life & Style 2015 304 p. color illustrations (hardcover) $35   **747**
1. Interior design
ISBN 1455533564; 9781455533558; 9781455533565

LC 2015940081

In this book, comedian Ellen DeGeneres "will, for the first time, share her passion for home design and style. . . . DeGeneres offers a personal look at every room in each of her homes. . . . An added bonus is a look at the homes of her friends and collaborators-some of the finest designers in the country. They share their advice on home design, furnishings, as well as a glimpse at their awe-inspiring rooms." (Publisher's note)

"Written with DeGeneres's typical candor and wit, this book will spark interest with her fans." LJ

Domino; your guide to a stylish home; editors of Domino, Jessica Romm Perez, Shani Silver. Simon & Schuster 2016 224 p. (hardcover) $35; (ebook) $23.99   **747**
1. Interior design 2. Interior decoration
ISBN 1501151878; 9781501151873; 9781501151880

LC 2016031819

This book, by the editors of Domino, is a "guide to discovering your personal style and creating a space you love. . . . [It] provides a trusted filter, using the friendly and authoritative voice of domino to teach readers about attainable, stylish design and how to make it uniquely your own." (Publisher's note)

Gates, Erin

Elements of style; designing a home and a life. Erin T. Gates. Simon & Schuster 2014 318 p. color illustrations (hardback) $35 **747**

1. Interior design 2. Interior decoration
ISBN 1476744874; 9781476744872

LC 2014012101

This book, by Erin T. Gates, "is a uniquely personal and practical decorating guide that shows how designing a home can be an outlet of personal expression and an exercise in self-discovery. Drawing on her ten years of experience in the interior design industry, Erin combines honest design advice and . . . photographs and illustrations with personal essays about the lessons she has learned while designing her own home and her own life—the first being: none of our homes or lives is perfect." (Publisher's note)

Giramonti, Lisa Borgnes

Novel interiors; Lisa Borgnes Giramonti. Potter Style 2014 288 p. color illustrations $35 **747**

1. Literature 2. Interior design 3. Decoration and ornament 4. Interior decoration in literature 5. Interior decoration -- Themes, motives
ISBN 0385345992; 9780385345996

LC 2013036923

In this book, author Lisa Borgnes Giramonti "inspires a new approach to decorating: by teaching us through the lens of worlds we may already know and love. With gorgeous photographs by World of Interiors photographer Ivan Terestchenko, aspirational quotes, and tailored reading lists, Novel Interiors reveals the essence and details of interiors mentioned in great literary works." (Publisher's note)

Grove, Kirsten

Simply styling; Fresh & Easy Ways to Personalize Your Home. Kirsten Grove. Sterling Pub Co Inc 2016 199 p. color illustrations $24.95 **747**

1. Interior design
ISBN 1454918225; 9781454918226

LC 2016042188

In this book, "interior stylist Kirsten Grove guides you every step of the way, . . . giving you the tools and tricks you need to create a space that captures your personality and taste. She explores options for entryways, shelves, mantels, dressers, sofas, and even difficult-to-design nooks; covers those all-important statement-making details, such as mirrors and vases; shows you how to make use of the things you already own; and provides easy-to-implement tips." (Publisher's note)

"With her blog, Simply Grove, self-taught interior stylist Grove's ideas have become quite influential, which has led to her contributing to numerous interior design publications and websites. Here, Grove explains how to achieve this popular look that she espouses of neutral-colored interiors bathed in light." LJ

Gura, Judith

The **guide** to period styles for interiors; Judith Gura. Bloomsbury, Fairchild Books, an imprint of Bloomsbury Publishing Inc. 2016 xvi, 479 p.p (alk. paper) $90 **747**

1. Interior design -- History 2. Interior decoration -- History

ISBN 9781628924718

LC 2015005290

This book, by Judith Gura, "makes it a snap to identify period styles from the 17th century to the present day. . . . Including examples and analysis on 17th-century Louis XIV through 20th-century Late Modern and each style in between, this new edition is also updated with the latest trends of the 21st century, including computer design, sustainable design, and modern office design." (Publisher's note)

"Sidebars offer information on movements, designers, and styles. Enough here has changed that libraries owning the first edition will want to consider this update." Booklist

Includes bibliographical references and index

Henderson, Emily

Styled; secrets for arranging rooms, from tabletops to bookshelves. Emily Henderson, with Angelin Borsics; photographs by David Tsay. Potter Style 2015 304 p. color illustrations $32.50 **747**

1. Interior design 2. Interior decoration -- Handbooks, manuals, etc
ISBN 0804186278; 9780804186278; 9780804186285

LC 2014045185

This book, by Emily Henderson, is a "guide to thinking like a stylist, with 1,000 design ideas for creating the most beautiful, personal, and livable rooms. . . . From editing out what you don't love to repurposing what you can't live without to arranging the most eye-catching vignettes on any surface, you'll learn how to make your own style magic." (Publisher's note)

Lee, Vinny

Kitchenalia; Furnishing and Equipping Your Kitchen With Flea Market Finds and Period Pieces. by Vinny Lee. Motorbooks Intl 2014 224 p. color illustrations $40 **747**

1. Kitchens 2. Flea markets 3. Interior design
ISBN 1909342491; 9781909342491

This book, by Vinny Lee, "is an inspiring guide to putting together a unique and creative kitchen using reclaimed and reinvented surfaces, furniture, objects and equipment. Period pieces, whether farmhouse furniture, salvaged surfaces, vintage textiles or retro cooking utensils and gadgets, are the antithesis of the mass-produced modern alternatives and have a timeless integrity. Sourcing such items from flea markets and antiques fairs is a unique and rewarding way to kit out a kitchen." (Publisher's note)

"The variety of styles makes this book an inspiring choice for those looking for ideas on decorating kitchens." LJ

Leggett, Kim

★ **City** farmhouse style; designs for a modern country life. Kim Leggett; principal photography by Alissa Saylor. Abrams 2017 222 p. $35 **747**

1. Interior design
ISBN 1419726501; 9781419726507

LC 2016960600

In this book "learn how to create country farmhouse style in your city dwelling. Author Kim Leggett is the creator of City Farmhouse, an interior design business, pop-up antiquing fairs, and vintage store. She is also a legendary 'picker' and favorite designer to celebrity clients (and country-style mavens) including Meg Ryan, Ralph Lauren, Sheryl Crow, and Phillip Sweet and Kimberly Schlapman of Little Big Town." (Publisher's note)

Lemieux, Christiane

The **Finer** Things; Timeless Furniture, Textiles, and De-

tails. Christiane Lemieux with Rumaan Alam. Potter Style 2014 416 p. color illustrations $60 **747**
1. Interior design 2. House furnishings 3. Interior decoration
ISBN 0770434290; 9780770434298; 9780770434304
LC 2013047267

In this book, by Christiane Lemieux, "quality matters. Just as a home's foundation should be built to stand the test of time, so, too, should the furniture, objects, and elements of our rooms speak to an enduring sense of beauty and comfort. They should outlast trends and our loving day-to-day use. But how does one recognize quality and judge whether something is well made?" (Publisher's note)

Includes bibliographical references and index.

Linsley, Leslie

Salvage Style; Decorate With Vintage Finds. Leslie Linsley. Hearst Books 2017 160 p. color illustrations (hardcover) $24.95 **747**
1. Antiques 2. Decoration and ornament 3. House furnishings 4. Interior decoration 5. Found objects (Art) in interior decoration
ISBN 1588169286; 9781588169280

Author Lindsey Linsley attempts to "show [readers] how to find and make the most of discarded treasures, such as old windows, barn doors, metal military desks, mailroom filing cabinets, factory lamps, and hand-forged iron hooks. Plus, the editors share best practices for bargain hunting and obtaining the most desirable cast-offs, such as antique beams and weathered barn wood." (Publisher's note)

"Crafts and design author Linsley (Nantucket: Island Living) turns her attention to using junkyard finds in home decor." LJ

Moss, Charlotte

Charlotte Moss; garden inspirations. Charlotte Moss. Rizzoli 2015 288 p. color illustrations (hardcover) $50 **747**
1. Gardens 2. Interior design
ISBN 0847844773; 9780847844777
LC 2014956849

In this book, "celebrated interior designer and renowned tastemaker Charlotte Moss turns her eye to the garden as a resource for interiors, entertaining, and good living. Charlotte Moss's greatest muse is the garden, and this book shows the myriad ways the garden provides inspiration every day--indoors and outdoors." (Publisher's note)

Needleman, Deborah

The **perfectly** imperfect home; Deborah Needleman. Clarkson Potter 2011 255 p. color illustrations $30 **747**
1. Home economics 2. Interior design 3. Interior decoration
ISBN 0307720136; 9780307720139
LC 2011020194

This book, by Deborah Needleman and illustrated by Virginia Johnson, offers home decoration advice. "Ranging from classics such as 'A Really Good Sofa' and 'Pretty Table Settings' to unusual surprises like 'A Bit of Quirk' and 'Cozifications,' the essential elements of style are treated in witty and wonderfully useful little essays. You'll learn what to look for, whether you are at a flea market or a fancy boutique-- or just mining what you already own." (Publisher's note)

"Books such as Grace Bonney's Design*Sponge at Home and Christiane Lemieux's Undecorate explain how to add a personal touch to decor, while Needleman shows how professionals approach interior design." LJ

New decorating book. John Wiley & Sons 2011 312 p. (paperback) $24.99 **747**
1. Interior design

ISBN 0470887141; 9780470887141

This book on interior design "mix[es] styles for personal expression with an awareness of budget. Organized in two parts, the first section is filled with room-by-room decorating guides and home tours to cover broad sweeps of decorating topics. The second section is organized by integral design topic: color, furniture arrangement, flooring, lighting, etc." (Publisher's note)

Petersik, Sherry

Young house love; 251 ways to paint, craft, update, organize, and show your home some love. Sherry and John Petersik. Artisan 2012 336 p. $25.95 **747**
1. Houses -- Maintenance and repair 2. Housekeeping -- Miscellanea 3. Interior decoration -- Miscellanea 4. Dwellings -- Remodeling -- Miscellanea 5. Dwellings -- Maintenance and repair -- Miscellanea
ISBN 1579654789; 9781579654788
LC 2012009849

This book by Sherry Petersik and John Petersik provides "home design ideas for every style, skill level and budget. . . . Sherry and John are home-improvement enthusiasts primed to pass on a slew of projects, tricks, and techniques to do-it-yourselfers. . . . Learn to trick out a thrift-store mirror, spice up plain old roller shades, 'hack' your Ikea table to create three distinct looks, and so much more." (Publisher's note)

Richardson, Sarah

Sarah style; Sarah Richardson. Gallery Books 2014 352 p. illustrations (hardback) $26 **747**
1. Interior design 2. Life skills -- Handbooks, manuals, etc. 3. Interior decoration -- Canada
ISBN 147678437X; 9781476784373; 9781476784380
LC 2014016081

In this book, author Sarah Richardson "walks you through each room in your home, from the master bedroom to the kids' rooms, to the kitchen, the bathroom, and everywhere in between, showing you how to turn a house into a home--Sarah style. Featuring full-page design spreads with . . . attention to detail, 'Sarah Style' is a cache of creative, unique ideas for transforming your living spaces." (Publisher's note)

"Richardson's descriptions of how she approached the design for each area and the abundance of color photographs will inspire readers to tackle their own interiors." LJ

Spencer, Lara

Flea market fabulous; designing gorgeous rooms with vintage treasures. Lara Spencer. Stewart, Tabori & Chang 2014 182 p. color illustrations $25.95 **747**
1. Flea markets 2. Interior design
ISBN 1617690953; 9781617690952
LC 2013945640

In this book, author Lara Spencer "shows readers that all it takes is planning, shopping know-how, and a little imagination to create beautiful and comfortable homes that reflect their personal style. . . . She identifies the design dilemma; comes up with a decorating plan; makes a mood board for inspiration; compiles a shopping list; scours flea markets for furniture and accessories that fit the bill; restores, repurposes, and reinvents the pieces she finds, giving them new life." (Publisher's note)

Studholme, Joa

Farrow & Ball How to Decorate; Joa Studholme and Charlotte Crosby. Octopus Pub Group 2016 256 p. color illustrations $39.99 **747**
1. Interior design 2. Decoration and ornament
ISBN 1784720879; 9781784720872

This book, by Joa Studholme and Charlotte Crosby, "provides a highly practical and inspirational guide to the successful use of paint and paper in any home, large or small, urban or country. The book brings together the expertise of Joa Studholme and Farrow & Ball's creative team to demystify the nitty-gritty of transforming a home - from deciding which colors work best in a north-facing room to creating accents with paint and making the most of a feature wall." (Publisher's note)

"The wealth of information on topics such as room accessories, color combinations, and even ceilings makes this book an invaluable tool for the novice who feels inspired to give a living space a makeover." Pub Wkly

Tanov, Erica

Design by nature; creating layered, lived-in spaces inspired by the natural world. by Erica Tanov, photographs by Ngoc Minh Ngo. Watson-Guptill 2018 232 p. (hardback) $35 **747**

1. Home economics 2. Interior design 3. Decoration and ornament 4. Interior decoration -- Themes, motives
ISBN 9780399579073

LC 2017036480

This book, by Erica Tanov, with photographs by Ngoc Minh Ngo, "teaches you how to train your eye to the beauty of the natural world, and then bring the outdoors in--incorporating patterns and motifs from nature, as well as actual organic elements, into simple ideas for everyday decorating and design." (Publisher's note)

"The book combines personal musings, essays, and artist profiles with 100 full-color photographs by Minh Ngo. It will be treasured by a diverse readership whose tastes run from British cult interior designer Ilsa Crawford to American transcendentalist Henry David Thoreau." Pub Wkly

Includes bibliographical references and index

Van der Meer, Antonia

Coastal living beach house happy; the joy of living by the water. Antonia van der Meer. Oxmoor House 2015 224 p. color illustrations (hardcover) $40 **747**

1. Houses 2. Beaches
ISBN 9780848744298; 0848744292

LC 2014953432

This book, by Antonia van der Meer, describes how "with a unique attachment to their homes, coastal dwellers and their homes exude a certain warmth and beauty found nowhere else. . . . [The author] reveals six routes to the happiness found in beach houses, exposing how the walls and windows, doors and floors, décor and architecture combine to create an atmosphere in which we can breathe easier and be our best." (Publisher's note)

"Whether looking to create an interior for a beachfront cottage or just add a coastal touch to a room, one will find an abundance of inspiring ideas in this book." LJ

Yip, Vern

Vern Yip's design wise; Your Smart Guide to a Beautiful Home. Vern Yip. Running Press 2016 286 p. color illustrations $27.50; (ebook) $14.99 **747**

1. Interior design 2. Interior decoration
ISBN 0762459859; 9780762459858; 9780762461097

LC 2016938275

This book, by Vern Yip, presents "the right formulas and measurements that can make any room feel just 'right.' And once you know these key design principles, you're free to confidently create a home that uniquely celebrates your needs and style. Vern shares his favorite insider tips, and opens his doors to show how he's made them work in his own beloved homes." (Publisher's note)

"Yip's fans and those seeking basic design advice will find much to recommend in this volume." LJ

Design wise

747.7   Decoration of specific rooms of residential buildings

Gold, Jamie

Taunton's new bathroom idea book; Jamie Gold. The Taunton Press, Inc. 2017 217 p. illustrations (paperback) $21.95 **747.7**

1. Bathrooms 2. Interior design 3. Interior decoration
ISBN 9781631868870; 9781631864056

LC 2016056526

This book, by Jamie Gold, "provides design options for all areas of the bathroom, from vanities and countertops to fixtures, flooring, and finish details. Up-to-the-minute information on new trends like digital integration in the bathroom, new materials that mimic natural materials, accessibility and aging-in-place options, and code changes that mandate water and energy conservation make this the go-to resource for all things bathroom." (Publisher's note)

"Gold . . . provides homeowners with all the basics, including when to do-it-yourself or hire a professional, the spatial clearances needed for bathroom fixtures, and the variety of decorating styles." LJ

748.2   Blown, cast, decorated, fashioned, molded, pressed glass

Chihuly; edited by Diane Charbonneau. Montreal Museum of Fine Arts; DelMonico Books, an imprint of Prestel 2013 230 p. illustrations (chiefly color) (Del Monico Books/Prestel) $65 **748.2**

1. Glass sculpture 2. Glass art -- 20th century -- Exhibitions 3. Glass art -- 21st century -- Exhibitions
ISBN 2891923685; 3791353241; 9782891923682; 9783791353241

LC 2012277913

In this book on artist Dale Chihuly, the authors "examine Chihuly's personal and artistic development, working environment and collections, and collaborative working methods, in addition to recognizing Chihuly's important achievements and contributions to craft and art history." Particular focus is given to his studio glass artwork. "Also included are Chihuly's energetic acrylic paintings and innovative burned drawings." (Choice)

The book "covers a rich set of vibrant work inspired predominantly by natural forms and makes the most of its large format. The documentation is superb, the scope is expansive, and the text is expertly presented." LJ

Includes bibliographical references

Ward, Gerald W. R.

Chihuly; through the looking glass. Gerald W.R. Ward. MFA Publications 2011 149 p. color illustrations, portraits $50 **748.2**

1. Glass sculpture 2. Site-specific installations (Art) -- Exhibitions 3. Glass art -- United States -- History -- 20th century -- Exhibitions 4. Glass art -- United States -- History -- 21st century -- Exhibitions 5. Glass sculpture -- United States -- History -- 20th century -- Exhibitions 6. Glass sculpture -- United States -- History -- 21st century -- Exhibitions
ISBN 0878467645; 0878467653; 9780878467648;

9780878467655

LC 2010941797

In this book, by Gerald W.R. Ward, "Dale Chihuly has been credited with elevating blown glass from delicate decorative object to ground-breaking fine art. . . . [It] focuses on the artist's pieces and installations in relation to the spaces that generate, shape and surround them." (Publisher's note)

Includes bibliographical references

748.5 Stained, painted, leaded, mosaic glass

Stevenson, Christine

Creative stained glass; modern designs & simple techniques. Christine Kellmann Stevenson. Lark Books 2004 128 p. illustrations (chiefly color) $14.95 **748.5**

1. Glass painting and staining 2. Glass craft

ISBN 1579904874; 1600591329; 9781600591327

LC 2003024958

This book, by Christine Kellmann Stevenson, presents "27 stained-glass projects. . . . More than 70 color photos present the techniques, all worked with easy-to-acquire, modern, and efficient tools. Try two methods of cutting, with or without making a pattern. Use overlays, plating, and patinas to color the finish, creatively combine different techniques, and see how to work with brass and copper came." (Publisher's note)

749 Furniture and accessories

Aronson, Joseph

The **encyclopedia** of furniture; by Joseph Aronson. Crown Publishers 1965 484 p. illustrations $35 **749**

1. Furniture

ISBN 0517037351; 9780517037355

LC 65024334

This book on furniture, by Joseph Aronson, "cover[s] every period and development to the present, the designers and makers, the woods and other materials, the architecture and decoration." (Publisher's note)

Kistler, Vivian Carli

The **complete** photo guide to framing & displaying artwork; 500 full-color how-to photos. Creative Pub. International 2009 192p il pa $24.99 **749**

1. Picture frames and framing

ISBN 978-1-58923-422-2; 1-58923-422-7

LC 2008-46612

In this guide, the author "teaches the do-it-yourselfer to frame like a pro. Hundreds of photos illustrate conservation matting, working with premade elements or frame-building from scratch, glazing, and hanging." Libr J

Logan, M. David

Mat, mount and frame it yourself. Watson-Guptill 2002 160p il pa $24.95 **749**

1. Decoration and ornament 2. Picture frames and framing

ISBN 0-8230-3038-5

LC 2001-93246

This describes how to mat, mount, and frame art on paper or cloth, how to determine measurements and proportions, select colors, and glaze, install, and hang framed art

"Logan does a great job of explaining everything and supplements the text with attractive photos. . . . There is something here for framers of all skill levels." Libr J

Miller, Judith

Furniture; [world styles from classical to contemporary] [foreword by David Linley] DK Publishing 2005 560p il $60 **749**

1. Furniture

ISBN 0-7566-1340-X

LC 2005-296398

The author "presents a lavish four-color and highly educational book, and the result will never lose its library-patron appeal." Booklist

Includes bibliographical references

Rybczynski, Witold

Now I sit me down; Witold Rybczynski. Farrar, Straus & Giroux 2016 256 p. illustrations (hardback) $25 **749**

1. Posture 2. Chairs -- History 3. Sitting customs -- History

ISBN 9780374223212

LC 2015041604

This book, by Witold Rybczynski, "chronicles the history of the chair from the folding stools of pharaonic Egypt to the ubiquitous stackable monobloc chairs of today. He tells the stories of the inventor of the bentwood chair, Michael Thonet, and of the creators of the first molded-plywood chair, Charles and Ray Eames. He reveals the history of chairs to be a social history--of different ways of sitting, of changing manners and attitudes, and of varying tastes." (Publisher's note)

"Rybczynski is totally engaging in this smoothly flowing, sharp, witty narrative—another winner from a top-notch writer on design." Kirkus

Includes bibliographical references and index.

751 Techniques, procedures, apparatus, equipment, materials, forms

Ganz, Nicholas

★ **Graffiti** world; street art from five continents. edited by Tristan Manco. Updated ed.; Abrams 2009 391p il $35 **751**

1. Graffiti 2. Street art 3. Mural painting and decoration

ISBN 978-0-8109-8049-5

LC 2009-922509

First published 2004

Ganz's survey of graffiti art includes "upward of 2,000 full-color photographs. . . . An ephemeral, often despised, yet irrefutably powerful mode of expression, graffiti has always been political, and although many of the street artists Ganz succinctly profiles have moved away from illegal spray painting, they have not compromised the inherent subversiveness of their work. . . . Ganz's global array captures the power and synergy of this vibrant alternative art world in which artists form crews and collectiveness to ensure that their art is seen." Booklist [review of 2004 edition]

Includes bibliographical references

751.4 Techniques and procedures

Artist's painting techniques; DK. DK Publishing 2016 304 p. color illustrations (hardcover) $30 **751.4**

1. Painting 2. Acrylic painting 3. Watercolor painting 4. Painting -- Technique

ISBN 1465450955; 9781465450951

LC 2016448564

This book from publisher DK offers a "practical guide to learning how to bring out your inner artist with a wide range of painting styles, whether you want to learn how to use acrylics, watercolors, or oil paints. With progression in mind, this master class will teach you the basic principles of painting and then inspire you to move on to new challenges and create masterpieces of your own. It explains which tools, materials, and methods should be used along the way." (Publisher's note)

"This handbook will be a foundational and popular addition to any art instruction shelf." LJ

Crilley, Mark

The **realism** challenge; drawing and painting secrets from a modern master of hyperrealism. Mark Crilley. Watson-Guptill 2015 160 p. color illustrations (paperback) $19.99   **751.4**
1. Drawing 2. Realism in art 3. Photo-realism 4. Drawing -- Technique 5. Painting -- Technique
ISBN 0385346298; 9780385346290

LC 2014024085

In this book, author "Mark Crilley takes you step-by-step through his process for producing stunning, hyperrealistic recreations of everyday items. Based on Crilley's mega-popular 'Realism Challenge' YouTube videos, The Realism Challenge contains thirty lessons demonstrating how to render mirror-like duplicates in the trompe l'oeil tradition of everything from shells, leaves, and candy bars to your very own still life arrangements." (Publisher's note)

"Those with modest artistic skills can greatly improve their ability to draw and paint realistic objects by following the tips and tricks detailed here." LJ

Includes bibliographical references and index

Marine, Carol

Daily painting; paint small and often to become a more creative, productive, and successful artist. Carol Marine. Watson-Guptill 2014 182 p. illustrations (chiefly color) (paperback) $22.99; (ebook) $65   **751.4**
1. Painting 2. Painting -- Technique
ISBN 0770435335; 9780770435332; 9780770435349

LC 2014009131

This book on painting, by Carol Marine, presents "a unique system for jump-starting artistic creativity, encouraging experimentation and growth, and increasing sales for artists of all levels, from novices to professionals. . . . The idea is simple: do art (usually small) often (how often is up to you), and if you'd like, post and sell it online. Soon you'll find that your block dissolves and you're painting work you love—and more of it than you ever thought possible!" (Publisher's note)

751.42   Use of water-soluble mediums

Kersey, Geoff

Painting successful watercolours from photographs; by Geoff Kersey. Search Press 2015 128 p. color illustrations $24.95   **751.42**
ISBN 1844489981; 9781844489985

This book, by Geoff Kersey, is for painters "who work from photographic source material. . . . Reference photographs, colour charts and preparatory sketches are shown alongside all the finished paintings in this book, with full details of the adaptations and creative processes involved. There are plenty of clear tips and advice, and an illustrated glossary of all the painting terms used." (Publisher's note)

"This guide has solid crossover potential among avid travelers, hobbyist watercolor painters, and amateur photographers." LJ

O'Connor, Birgit

Watercolor essentials; hands-on techniques for exploring watercolor in motion. North Light Books 2009 127p il $29.99   **751.42**
1. Watercolor painting -- Technique
ISBN 978-1-60061-094-3

LC 2008-36576

This guide to watercolor painting covers topics such as types of watercolor paint, painting tools and materials, using color, values, and painting techniques.

"This is an exciting, comprehensive package for the beginning watercolor artist. O'Connor . . . keys her lessons to a 70-minute DVD. Her wet and loose technique and the personal touch of the DVD make this a great choice at a good price." Libr J

751.422   Watercolor painting

Robinson, Mario Andres

Lessons in realistic watercolor; A Contemporary Approach to Painting People and Places in the Classical Tradition. Mario Andres Robinson. The Monacelli Press 2016 176 p. $25   **751.422**
1. Realism in art 2. Watercolor painting -- Technique
ISBN 9781580934459

LC 2015038871

This book, by Mario Andres Robinson, "shows us how to create beautiful, timeless, classical watercolor paintings through the use of simple, yet sophisticated, contemporary techniques every watercolorist needs to know. . . . Robinson simplifies the process and teaches artists to layer colors from light to dark and to focus on the highlighted areas first." (Publisher's note)

"Artists of intermediate skill level are best poised to benefit from these lessons." LJ

751.426   Acrylic painting

Kloosterboer, Lorena, 1962-

Painting in acrylics; the indispensable guide. Lorena Kloosterboer. Firefly Books 2014 320 p. color illustrations $35   **751.426**
1. Acrylic painting 2. Acrylic painting -- Technique
ISBN 1770854088; 9781770854086

LC 2015472146

This book, by Lorena Kloosterboer, "provides comprehensive guidance for painters of all experience. Realist painter Lorena Kloosterboer, known for her exceptional technical skill, starts with the basics and progresses to advanced techniques and professional practice." (Publisher's note)

751.45   Oil painting

Scott, Marilyn

The **Oil** Painter's Bible; A Essential Reference for the Practicing Artist. by Marylin Scott. Book Sales 2005 192 p. illustrations $14.99   **751.45**
1. Oil painting
ISBN 0785819428; 9780785819424
This book, by Marylin Scott, "is a must for anyone who has not used

oil paints before, and even those who are familiar with the medium may find some surprises among the range of techniques—and hopefully some new inspiration in the gallery of finished pictures. The book is divided into four main sections: Materials, Color, Techniques, and Subjects. Advanced techniques like glazing, impasto, knife painting, and scumbling will give even the most advanced artists inspiration." (Publisher's note)

751.7   Specific forms

Felisbret, Eric

Graffiti New York; Eric Felisbret DEAL CIA; contributions by Luke Felisbret SPAR ONE; foreword by James Prigoff. Abrams 2009 339 p. ill. (chiefly col.)   **751.7**

1. Street art 2. Artists -- United States 3. Mural painting and decoration 4. Graffiti -- New York (N.Y.) -- History 5. Graffiti -- New York (State) -- New York 6. Street art -- New York (State) -- New York 7. Mural painting and decoration, American -- New York (State) -- New York

ISBN 0810951460; 9780810951464

LC 2009011736

This book explores the history and influence of New York City as a "mecca of graffiti culture. . . . This is the city where it all began, yet few know the back story. 'Graffiti New York' fills that gap, detailing the concepts, aesthetics, ideals, and social structures that have served as a cultural blueprint for graffiti movements across the world. The book features approximately 1,000 images, complemented by texts by the authors and relevant players in the movement, as well as descriptive graphics and sidebars. [The book describes] . . . the birth of simple signature tags to today's vibrant murals, and covering the ups and downs of the movement, the culture's value system, its social framework, the various forms of graffiti, and significant artists and crews." (Publisher's Note)

759   History, geographic treatment, biography

Bosch; the 5th centenary exhibition. edited by Pilar Silva Maroto. Thames & Hudson Inc 2017 396 p. illustrations (chiefly color) (alk. paper) $45   **759**

1. Dutch art 2. Painters -- Netherlands -- Biography

ISBN 9780500970799; 0500970793

LC 2016947841

This book, edited by Pilar Silva Maroto, is "a comprehensive look at the work of Jheronimus Bosch, published to coincide with the 5th centenary of the artist's death and in conjunction with an exhibition at the Museo del Prado. . . . provides up-to-date information on the artist's life and family, examines the data available regarding his patrons, surveys his status as painter and draftsman, and investigates his visual and textual sources as well as his values and ideology." (Publisher's note)

"Primary sources enrich the historical narrative of Bosch and his art, and the complete catalogue entries provide the history of ownership and recent technological research on the physical state of each richly reproduced painting." Choice

Includes bibliographical references (pages 374-389) and index.

Kelder, Diane

The **great** book of French impressionism; 2nd Abbeville ed; Abbeville Press 2001 400p il $85   **759**

1. French painting 2. Impressionism (Art)

ISBN 978-0-7892-0688-6; 0-7892-0688-9

LC 2001-266313

First published 1980

This book "traces the development of Impressionism from its roots in landscape and Realist painting through its focus on modern urban life. . . . The works of the major Impressionists and Post Impressionists, Manet, Monet, Renoir, Degas, Toulouse-Lautrec, Seurat, and Cezanne, are featured." Publisher's note

Includes bibliographical references

King, Ross

The **judgment** of Paris; the revolutionary decade that gave the world impressionism. Walker 2006 448p il $28   **759**

1. Artists 2. Painters 3. Sculptors 4. French art 5. Illustrators 6. Impressionism (Art)

ISBN 0-8027-1466-8

LC 2005-31089

"The book serves as an entertaining if broad account of a revolutionary transformation in vision—not least of all through art." Libr J

Includes bibliographical references

★ **Leonardo** and the Last supper; Ross King. Walker & Company 2012 352 p. $28.00   **759**

1. Religious art 2. Art -- History 3. Last Supper in art 4. Italy -- Politics and government -- 1268-1559

ISBN 0802717055; 9780802717054

LC 2012005358

This book presents an account "of the political situation in 15th-century Italy and how it informs our understanding of [Leonardo da Vinci's] 'The Last Supper' . . . interspersed with analysis of history's many interpretations of the painting. . . . The book addresses such topics as the groupings of the apostles and their hand placement; readings of the painting as glorifying faith; and whether the figure next to Jesus depicts the apostle John or Mary Magdalene." (Publishers Weekly)

Michelangelo & the Pope's ceiling. Walker & Co. 2002 371p il hardcover o.p. pa $15   **759**

1. Artists 2. Painters 3. Sculptors 4. Architects 5. Mural painting and decoration 6. Italy -- History -- 0-1559 7. Vatican -- Cappella Sistina

ISBN 0-8027-1395-5; 0-14-200369-7 pa

LC 2002-38074

"This engaging narrative sets the record straight on a few points and is highly recommended for most public library collections." Libr J

Includes bibliographical references

Leal, Brigitte

The **ultimate** Picasso; {by} Brigitte Léal, Christine Piot, Marie-Laure Bernadac; preface by Jean Leymarie. Abrams 2000 535p il hardcover o.p. pa $ **759**

1. Artists 2. Painters

ISBN 0-8109-9114-4 pa

These "essays detail events in Picasso's life and the circumstances surrounding the creation of his art, his influences, and world events. This lavish, handsome book contains more than 1200 reproductions, nearly 800 in full color." SLJ

Includes bibliographical references

National Gallery of Art (U.S.)

Edouard Vuillard; [by] Guy Cogeval with Kimberly Jones [et al.] National Gallery of Art, in association with Yale University Press 2003 501p il $70   **759**

1. Artists 2. Painters

ISBN 0-300-09737-9

LC 2002-151120

"A superb display of the surprising colors, forceful textures, and mysterious atmosphere of Vuillard's paintings, accompanied by commentaries in which aesthetics, art history, and biography are perfectly balanced." Booklist

Includes bibliographical references

Roe, Sue

The **private** lives of the impressionists. HarperCollins Publishers 2006 356p il map $29.95   **759**

1. Artists, French 2. Impressionism (Art)

ISBN 0-06-054558-5; 978-0-06-054558-1

LC 2006-43621

This is a "group portrait of the revolutionary artists dubbed the impressionists for their atmospheric landscapes and forthright depictions of everyday life. Here, masterfully set against a panoramic rendering of their turbulent times, are Manet, Pissarro, Degas, Monet, Renoir, Cezanne, Sisley, Morisot, and Cassatt, each incisively defined as an individual and in terms of their complex interactions as they devoted themselves to paintings that met only with derision." Booklist

Includes bibliographical references

Sassoon, Donald

Becoming Mona Lisa; the making of a global icon. Harcourt 2001 337p il $30; pa $16   **759**

1. Artists 2. Painters 3. Scientists 4. Writers on science

ISBN 0-15-100828-0; 0-15-602711-9 pa

LC 2001-24956

This is a history of Leonardo's most famous portrait and its meanings and popularization in the centuries since it was painted

"Sassoon's knowledge of the minutiae of history and his respect for the image drive the narrative. . . . {This work is} thoroughly researched and highly readable." Libr J

Includes bibliographical references and index

Scotti, R. A.

Vanished smile; the mysterious theft of Mona Lisa. Knopf 2009 241p il map $24.95   **759**

1. Artists 2. Painters 3. Art thefts 4. Scientists 5. Writers on science

ISBN 978-0-307-26580-7; 0-307-26580-3

LC 2008-47851

The author reports on the "1911 theft of Mona Lisa. The lovely woman with the enigmatic smile was simply lifted off the wall and spirited away. The scandal was immense, the investigation feverish, the headlines screaming, and Scotti revels in every turn. Her lively, expert coverage encompasses the fascinating, many-chaptered story of Mona Lisa and ironic revelations about the frenzy among America's robber barons for old masters and the corresponding renaissance in art fraud. . . . Scotti's avid, exciting true-life mystery yields intriguing disclosures and reaffirms Mona Lisa's unique powers." Booklist

759.13   United States

Barson, Tanya

★ **Georgia** O'Keeffe; Tonya Barson. Abrams 2016 272 p. illustrations (chiefly color) (hardcover) $55   **759.13**

1. American art 2. O'Keeffe, Georgia, 1887-1986

ISBN 1419722743; 9781419722745

LC 2015958243

This book, by Tonya Barson, profiles "Georgia O'Keeffe (1887-1986), . . . one of the foundational figures of American modernism and

a pioneering woman in the arts. . . . With superb plates of more than 200 works, it ranges from well-known masterpieces to the abstractions, nature studies, and New York City scenes that have captivated new generations of art lovers. It includes essays from prominent art historians." (Publisher's note)

"For both academic and general art history collections, this genuinely valuable summation and reexamination of O'Keeffe's art and its public reception, from her earliest exhibition through today's appraisals, will be well received." LJ

Includes bibliogrphical references and index

Carter, Alice A.

The **Red** Rose girls; an uncommon story of art and love. Abrams 2000 216p il hardcover o.p. pa $19.95   **759.13**

1. Artists 2. Painters 3. Illustrators

ISBN 0-8109-9068-7 pa

LC 99-39866

"Three of the first American women artists to achieve fame and fortune in the Victorian era—Jessie Willcox Smith, Elizabeth Shippen Green and Violet Oakley—lived unconventional lives marked by a remarkable degree of collaboration. In this . . . study, Carter explores the trio's internecine artistic and romantic relations." Publ Wkly

Includes bibliographical references

Cohen-Solal, Annie

Mark Rothko; toward the light in the chapel. Annie Cohen-Solal. Yale University Press 2015 296 p. 8 plates; color illustrations (Jewish lives) (hardback) $25   **759.13**

1. Painters 2. Jewish men 3. Painters -- United States -- Biography

ISBN 030018204X; 9780300182040

LC 2014037767

Author Annie Cohen-Solal's biography on Mark Rothko, "based on considerable archival research, tells the unlikely story of how a young immigrant from Dvinsk became a crucial transforming agent of the art world. His integration into American society began with a series of painful experiences, especially as a student at Yale, where he felt marginalized for his origins and ultimately left the school. The decision to become an artist led him to a new phase in his life." (Publisher's note)

"A defining and affecting tribute to a modern master." Booklist

Includes bibliographical references and index

Elderfield, John

De Kooning: a retrospective; [by] John Elderfield; with Lauren Mahoney [et al.]; edited by David Frankel. Museum of Modern Art 2011 504p il $75   **759.13**

1. Artists 2. Painters

ISBN 978-0-87070-797-1

"A superlative exhibition. (Its catalogue is equally fantastic.)." ARTINFO

Includes bibliographical references

Fortune, Brandon Brame

Elaine de kooning; portaits. Brandon Brame Fortune, Ann Eden Gibson, Simona Cupic. DelMonico Books - Prestel 2015 160 p. illustrations, color portraits $49.95   **759.13**

1. Painters -- Biography

ISBN 3791354388; 9783791354385

LC 2014958601

This book, by Brandon Brame Fortune, "explores the portraiture of Elaine de Kooning. . . . John F. Kennedy, Frank O'Hara, Allen Ginsberg, Merce Cunningham, and Fairfield Porter were just some of the figures who sat for portraits by Elaine de Kooning. Famous for her marriage to the Abstract Expressionist Willem de Kooning, Elaine was herself a groundbreaking artist and writer who challenged many conventions during her career." (Publisher's note)

"Fortune reveals how de Kooning "simultaneously transgressed and upheld" gender stereotyping with a sensibility to the "masculine" abstract expressionist painterly style that retained a vital naturalism, which was her key contribution to the movement. Summing Up: Recommended. All readership levels." Choice

Gerdts, William H.

American impressionism; William H. Gerdts. 2nd ed; Abbeville Press 2001 368p il $85 **759.13**

1. American art 2. Impressionism (Art)

ISBN 978-0-7892-0737-1; 0-7892-0737-0

LC 2001-22419

First published 1984

"The best general source available on American Impressionism. . . . [The] book covers the major artists in the movement, including expatriates working in Europe and regional schools throughout the United States during the late 19th and early 20th centuries. . . . The well-chosen illustrations include many full-page color reproductions as well as photographs of many of the artists." Libr J

Includes bibliographical references

Kamensky, Jane

A **revolution** in color; The World of John Singleton Copley. Jane Kamensky. W W Norton & Co Inc 2016 480 p. illustrations (hardcover) $35 **759.13**

1. Artists -- United States -- Biography 2. United States -- History -- 1775-1783, Revolution 3. American loyalists -- Biography 4. Painters -- United States -- Biography 5. United States -- History -- Revolution, 1775-1783 -- Biography 6. United States -- History -- Revolution, 1775-1783 -- Social aspects

ISBN 9780393240016

LC 2016019022

This book by Jane Kamensky offers a biography of Boston-born painter John Singleton Copley, whose "brush captured the faces of his neighbors—ordinary men like Paul Revere, John Hancock, and Samuel Adams—who would become the revolutionary heroes of a new United States. . . . The artist, however, did not share his subjects' politics. Copley's nation was Britain; his capital, London. . . . He painted America's revolution from a far shore, as Britain's American War." (Publisher's note)

"There may never be a better biography of Copley than this sumptuous, exquisitely told story of a man and his time." Kirkus

Includes bibliographical references and index

Kehinde Wiley; a new republic. edited by Eugenie Tsai; with an essay by Connie H. Choi. Brooklyn Museum in association with DelMonico Books & Prestel 2015 192 p. (Prestel hardcover: alk. paper) $49.95 **759.13**

1. Painting 2. Portraits 3. Art -- 21st century

ISBN 9780872731769; 9783791354309

LC 2014034650

"Filled with reproductions of Kehinde Wiley's bold, colorful, and monumental work, this book[, edited by Eugenie Tsai, with an essay by Connie H. Choi,] encompasses the artist's various series of paintings as well as his sculptural work--which boldly explore ideas about race, power, and tradition. . . . It includes early portraits of the men Wiley observed on Harlem's streets." (Publisher's note)

" Departing from the normative format, the catalog provides commentary from 36 contributors in material disciplines, visual culture, the humanities, popular culture, and critical race discourse, to deliver a ro-

bust understanding of Wiley's treatment of black male and female portraiture and notably its absence (and contemporary reinsertion) within the Western canon." LJ

Includes bibliographical references

Levin, Gail, 1948-

Edward Hopper; the art and the artist. Gail Levin. W W Norton & Co Inc 1996 xv, 299 p.p illustrations (chiefly color) (paperback) $39.95 **759.13**

1. Painters -- United States

ISBN 0393315770; 9780393315776

This book, by Gail Levin, "presents the full range of [realist painter] Edward Hopper's work. . . . Hopper is generally considered the major twentieth-century realist. Such paintings as House by the Railroad, Early Sunday Morning, and Nighthawks seem to embody the very character of our time. . . . Levin has gone beyond the standard evaluations of the man and his work to investigate the authentic identity of the artist and the way his personality informed his art." (Publisher's note)

Includes bibliographical references (p. [72]-[74]) and index.

Livingston, Jane

The **paintings** of Joan Mitchell; with essays by Linda Nochlin, Yvette Lee. University of Calif. Press 2002 237p il $65; pa $35 **759.13**

1. Artists 2. Painters

ISBN 0-520-23568-1; 0-520-23570-3 pa

LC 2001-58514

This is a "vivid portrait of the artist. . . . Mitchell's compositions {are} gorgeously reproduced here in vibrant color." Booklist

Includes bibliographical references

Mathews, Nancy Mowll

Mary Cassatt; a life. Yale Univ. Press 1998 383p il pa $21 **759.13**

1. Artists 2. Painters 3. Artists -- United States

ISBN 0-300-07754-8

LC 98-8028

First published 1994 by Villard Bks.

This "is an evenly written, well-documented, and sympathetic—but not patronizing—biography that should be acquired by most libraries." Libr J

Includes bibliographical references

Ormond, Richard

Sargent; the watercolours. Richard Ormond and Elaine Kilmurray. GILES an imprint of D Giles Limited in association with Dulwich Picture Gallery 2017 168 p. illustrations (chiefly color) (hardcover) $44.95 **759.13**

1. Painting 2. Watercolor painting

ISBN 9781911282075; 1898519358; 1911282077; 9781898519355

LC 2017430850

This book, by Richard Ormond and Elaine Kilmurray, examines the watercolor paintings of artist John Singer Sargent. His "work in watercolor was unorthodox. . . . He ignored the celebrated panoramas of Venice and the traditional description of landscape; instead his watercolors challenged the viewer with unconventional angles, confrontational poses and geometric forms." (Publisher's note)

"This beautifully illustrated catalogue documents the exhibition of the same name organized by Dulwich Picture Gallery, a small house museum outside of London." Choice

Includes bibliographical references (pages 164-165) and index

Philadelphia Museum of Art

Thomas Eakins; organized by Darrel Sewell with essays by Kathleen A. Foster {et al.}; chronology by Kathleen Brown. Yale Univ. Press 2001 xli, 446p il $75   **759.13**
1. Artists 2. Painters 3. Sculptors 4. Art teachers
ISBN 0-300-09111-7

LC 2001-53142

"This enormous volume accompanies the largest retrospective of {Eakins' work}.... {It} includes some 120 photographs as well as examples of his work in watercolor, drawing, and sculpture. ... Several lengthy and interesting biocritical essays, themselves making up 175 pages of text, separate four sections of color plates. This is clearly the definitive monograph on one of the most significant artists America has produced." Libr J
Includes bibliographical references

Rothko; the color field paintings. foreword by Christopher Rothko; essay by Janet Bishop; picture editor, Jenny Moussa Spring. Chronicle Books LLC 2017 120 p. illustrations (chiefly color) (hardcover) $40   **759.13**
1. Color-field painting -- United States -- Themes, motives
ISBN 9781452156606; 9781452156590

LC 2016052971

This book on Mark Rothko "presents fifty large-scale artworks from the American master's color field period (1949–1970) alongside essays by Rothko's son, Christopher Rothko, and San Francisco Museum of Modern Art curator of painting and sculpture Janet Bishop. [It features] illuminating details about Rothko's life, influences, and legacy, and brim[s] with the emotional power and expressive color of his groundbreaking canvases." (Publisher's note)

"Sumptuously illustrated with reproductions of 50 paintings, this book celebrates the rich artistic legacy of American artist Mark Rothko and his signature works as a painter of abstract canvases." Pub Wkly
Includes bibliographical references

Staiti, Paul

Of Arms and Artists; The American Revolution Through Painters' Eyes. Paul Staiti. St. Martin's Press 2016 400 p. (hardcover) $30   **759.13**
1. Artists -- United States 2. United States -- History -- 1775-1783, Revolution
ISBN 9781632864659; 1632864657

LC 2016007703

Carnegie Medal Longlist: Nonfiction (2017)
This book by Paul Staiti reveals that "the lives of the five great American artists of the Revolutionary period--Charles Willson Peale, John Singleton Copley, John Trumbull, Benjamin West, and Gilbert Stuart--were every bit as eventful as those of the Founders with whom they continually interacted.... The collective stories of these five artists open a fresh window on the Revolutionary era, making more human the figures we have long honored as our Founders." (Publisher's note)

"Throughout, Staiti provides insightful, in-depth discussions of many key paintings, and the book is lavishly illustrated with illustrations and color plates. A lively, splendid history that captures the times with insight, acumen, and a juggler's finesse." Kirkus
Includes bibliographical references and index.

Wilton, Andrew

American sublime; landscape painting in the United States, 1820-1880. {by} Andrew Wilton & Tim Barringer. Princeton Univ. Press 2002 284p il $49.95; pa $35   **759.13**
1. American painting 2. Landscape painting

ISBN 0-691-09670-8; 0-691-11556-7 pa

"Wilton, of the Tate Gallery, considers the influence of Edmund Burke's theory of sublimity and the surge in scientific development on American painters, while Barringer ... discusses the profound effect on the painters' imaginations of a pristine land free of Western religious, literary, and historical associations. ... Wilton and Barringer's commentary is stimulating and important, and the exceptional plates are bliss unadulterated." Booklist
Includes bibliographical references

759.36   Austrian painting

O'Connor, Anne-Marie

The **lady** in gold; the extraordinary tale of Gustav Klimt's masterpiece, Portrait of Adele Bloch-Bauer. by Anne-Marie O'Connor. Knopf 2012 349 p.   **759.36**
1. Jews -- Austria 2. Portrait painting 3. Vienna (Austria) -- History
ISBN 9780307265647

LC 2011033578

This book explores "one of Gustav Klimt's most celebrated paintings. . . . [Anne-Marie] O'Connor traces the multifaceted history of Portrait of Adele Bloch-Bauer (1907). . . . The [book] . . . evokes the intellectually precocious and ambitious Adele's rich cultural and social milieu in Vienna, and how she became entwined with the charismatic, sexually charged, and irreverent Klimt, who may have been Adele's lover before and also during her marriage. During WWII, Adele's portrait was renamed by the Nazis as the Dame in Gold to erase her Jewish identity. O'Connor's final arguments about the tragic yet redemptive symbolism of Adele's portrait . . . while it represents the failure of the dream of Jews like Adele to assimilate, through the painting she achieves "her dream of immortality."" (Publishers Weekly)
Includes bibliographical references and index.

759.4   French painting

Danchev, Alex

Cézanne; a life. Alex Danchev. Pantheon Books 2012 xx, 488 p.p (hardback) $40   **759.4**
1. French painting 2. Artists -- Biography 3. Painters -- France -- Biography
ISBN 0307377075; 9780307377074

LC 2012007182

Author Alex Danchev presents a biography on Paul Cézanne. "One of the most influential painters of his time and beyond, Cézanne was the exemplary artist-creator of the modern age who changed the way we see the world. . . . Danchev tells the story of an artist who was originally considered a madman, a barbarian, and a sociopath. . . . [He] shows us how the beliefs Cézanne held and the life he led became the obsession and inspiration of artists, writers, poets, and philosophers from Henri Matisse and Pablo Picasso to Samuel Beckett and Allen Ginsberg." (Publisher's note)
Includes bibliographical references and index.

King, Ross

★ **Mad** enchantment; Claude Monet and the painting of the water lilies. Ross King. Bloomsbury USA 2016 416 p. ill. (some color), maps, table (hardcover) $30   **759.4**
1. French painting 2. Water lilies in art
ISBN 9781632860125

LC 2015049404

Carnegie Medal Longlist: Nonfiction (2017)

This book by Ross King tells the story behind the creation of the painting series the Water Lilies by Claude Monet. "By early 1914, French newspapers were reporting that Monet, by then 73 and one of the world's wealthiest, most celebrated painters, had retired his brushes. He had lost his beloved wife, Alice, and his eldest son, Jean. . . . And yet, despite ill health, self-doubt, and advancing age, Monet began painting again on a more ambitious scale than ever before." (Publisher's note)

"Never before has the full drama and significance of Monet's magnificent Water Lilies been conveyed with such knowledge and perception, empathy and wonder." Booklist

Includes bibliographical references

Shackelford, George T. M.

Gustave Caillebotte; the painter's eye. Mary Morton, George T.M. Shackelford; Essays by Michael Marrinan, Alexandra K. Wettlaufer, Elizabeth Benjamin, Stéphane Guégan, Sarah Kennel. "National Gallery of Art" "Kimbell Art Museum" "in association w/University of Chicago Press" 2015 283 p. ill. (chiefly color), portrait (hardback) $60   **759.4**
  ISBN 9780226263557; 9780894683930

                                                                LC 2015004438

In this book, by Mary Morton and George Shackelford, "Gustave Caillebotte (1848–94) has come to be recognized as one of the most dynamic and original artists of the impressionist movement in Paris. His paintings are favorites of museum-goers, and recent restoration of his work has revealed more color, texture, and detail than was visible before while heightening interest in all of Caillebotte's artwork." (Publisher's note)

Includes bibliographical references (pages 271-275)

Stevens, MaryAnne

Alfred Sisley; impressionist master. MaryAnne Stevens; with contributions from Kathleen Adler and Richard Shone. Yale University Press 2017 191 p. color illustrations (hardcover) $65   **759.4**
  1. Impressionism (Art)
  ISBN 9780300215571; 0300215576

                                                                LC 2016956164

This exhibition catalogue, by MaryAnne Stevens, "offers an overdue reevaluation of [Alfred] Sisley, one of Impressionism's most distinctive yet undervalued figures. An artist of unparalleled sensitivity, Sisley maintained a strong commitment to creating his works outdoors, skillfully recording the nuances within the landscapes of northern France and rendering the effects of the changing light and weather patterns along specific areas of the river Seine in a truly remarkable fashion." (Publisher's note)

"Although Sisley is included in histories of impressionism, very few single monographs have been written about him, and this one is a treasure." LJ

Includes bibliographical references (page 188) and index.

The **World** Is an Apple; The Still Lifes of Paul Cezanne. edited by Benedict Leca. Giles 2014 240 p. color illustrations $54.95   **759.4**
  1. Still-life painting
  ISBN 1907804285; 9781907804281

This book, edited by Benedict Leca, "offers a reappraisal of Paul Cézanne's achievement in the genre of still life. It examines his paintings within the context of his artistic development and professional self-fashioning, and probes the shifting scientific and critical discourses that shaped both his practice and the reception of his pictures." (Pub-

lisher's note)

"Specialists in modern and French art will especially appreciate this finely designed volume that may be considered for special and public libraries alike." LJ

759.5   Italian painting

Hales, Dianne

Mona Lisa; a life discovered. Dianne Hales. Simon & Schuster 2014 336 p. map, genealogical table (hardback) $28   **759.5**
  1. Mona Lisa (Painting) 2. Renaissance portrait painting -- Italy 3. Florence (Italy) -- History -- 1421-1737 4. Artists' models -- Italy -- Florence -- Biography
  ISBN 1451658966; 9781451658965; 9781451658972

                                                                LC 2013042086

This book on the "Mona Lisa" painting by Dianne Hales, "a blend of biography, history, and memoir, truly is a book of discovery--about the world's most recognized face, most revered artist, and most praised and parodied painting. Who was she, this ordinary woman who rose to such extraordinary fame? Why did the most renowned painter of her time choose her as his model?" (Publisher's note)

"This engaging account of a Renaissance woman will appeal to a general audience." LJ

Includes bibliographcial references (pages 293-300) and index

King, Ross

Florence; the paintings & frescoes, 1250-1743. Introductions and Essays by Ross King; Painting Descriptions by Anja Grebe. Black Dog & Leventhal 2015 708 p. chiefly col. ill, maps   **759.5**
  1. Italian art 2. Art -- History 3. Florence (Italy) -- History 4. Painting -- Italy -- Florence
  ISBN 1631910019; 9781631910012

                                                                LC 2015026785

Authors Ross King and Anje Gerbe present this "comprehensive book on the paintings and frescoes of Florence . . . with nearly 2,000 beautifully reproduced artworks from the city's great museums and churches. Every painted work that is on display in the Uffizi Gallery, The Pitti Palace, the Accademia, and the Duomo is included in the book, plus many or most of the works from 28 of the city's other magnificent museums and churches." (Publisher's note)

"Written in an easy-to-read style, this surprisingly affordable tome, given its size and lavish illustrations, will interest general readers through art historians." LJ

Includes bibliographical references

759.6   Spanish painting

Cumming, Laura

★ The **Vanishing** Velazquez; a 19th century bookseller's obsession with a lost masterpiece. by Laura Cumming. Scribner 2016 304 p. illustrations (some color) (hardcover) $28 **759.6**
  1. Art -- Attribution 2. Booksellers and bookselling 3. Portrait painting -- History 4. Portrait painting -- Attribution 5. Booksellers and bookselling -- England -- Reading
  ISBN 9781476762159; 9781476762180

                                                                LC 2015040220

In this book, by Laura Cumming, "[Diego] Velazquez (1599–1660) was the official painter of the Madrid court. . . . When Prince Charles of England—a man wealthy enough to help turn Spain's fortunes--ventured to the court to propose a marriage with a Spanish princess, he allowed just a few hours to sit for his portrait. [John] Snare believed only Velazquez could have met this challenge. But in making his theory public, Snare was ostracized." (Publisher's note)

"Snare's story is noteworthy, but it is Cumming's spirited and clever narration that makes this enigma utterly engrossing." Pub Wkly

Includes bibliographical references (pages [275]-287) and index.

Descharnes, Robert, 1926-2014

Salvador Dalí, 1904-1989; the paintings. by Robert Descharnes and Gilles Néret. Taschen America Llc 2013 780 p. illustrations (chiefly color) $19.99; (ebook) $27.07   **759.6**
1. Surrealism
ISBN 383654492X; 9783836544924; 9781599283517

LC 2015005265

This book, by Robert Descharnes and Gilles Néret, "explor[es] Dalí's grandiose and grotesque oeuvre.... Dalí (1904-1989) was one of the century's greatest exhibitionists and eccentrics—and was rewarded with fierce controversy wherever he went. He was one of the first to apply the insights of Sigmund Freud and psychoanalysis to the art of painting, approaching the subconscious with extraordinary sensitivity and imagination." (Publisher's note)

759.9   Other geographic areas

Liedtke, Walter A.

Vermeer and the Delft school; by Walter Liedtke in collaboration with Michiel C. Plomp and Axel Rüger; with contributions by Reinier Baarsen {et al.} Metropolitan Mus. of Art 2001 626p il $85   **759.9**
1. Artists 2. Painters 3. Dutch painting
ISBN 0-300-08848-5

LC 00-49550

"This is the catalog of an exhibition held at the Metropolitan Museum of Art, New York, N.Y., Mar. 8-May 27, 2001 and at the National Gallery, London, June 20-Sept. 16, 2001. It includes fifteen works by Vermeer and paintings, tapestries and drawings by other Delft artists, including Gerard Houckgeest, Emanuel de Witte, Carel Fabritius, Paulus Potter, Leonaert Bramer, Jan de Bisschop and Pieter de Hooch... . Liedtke believes that Vermeer was nurtured and goaded exclusively by Dutch art of his time and by the traditions of his hometown." N Y Rev Books

Includes bibliographical references

Lozano, Luis-Martin

Frida Kahlo. Bulfinch Press 2001 245p il $85   **759.9**
1. Artists 2. Painters
ISBN 0-8212-2766-1

LC 2001-89093

Original Mexican edition, 2000

In this "illustrated survey of Frida Kahlo's work Lozano ... explores her life and paintings in a series of essays that range from a poetic study by noted Mexican cultural critic Carlos Monsiváis to a short, prosaic piece written in 1943 by her husband, Diego Rivera, to an academic essay by Lozano himself.... Lozano uses Kahlo's own stunning images, offering high-quality reproductions of some of Kahlo's most famous works as well as some of her lesser-known pieces. Previously unseen photos of Kahlo at work in her studio are also included. The detail and clarity of the images is incredible." Libr J

Thomson, Belinda

Van Gogh paintings; the masterpieces. Thames & Hudson 2007 190p il $45   **759.9**
1. Artists 2. Painters
ISBN 978-0-500-23838-7; 0-500-23838-3

This book "offers a general survey of Van Gogh's paintings. ... [and] discusses Van Gogh's paintings in terms of a chronological and biographical progression .... Filled with beautifully written descriptive passages of the works and careful analysis of the artist's style. ... This book is a solid introduction to Van Gogh's paintings." Choice

Includes bibliographical references

759.94   European painting

Fischer, Stefan

Hieronymus Bosch; The Complete Works. by Stefan Fischer. Taschen America Llc 2016 300 p. illustrations $39.99   **759.94**
ISBN 3836538350; 9783836538350

This book, by Stefan Fischer, "presents the complete [Hieronymus] Bosch oeuvre, celebrating the artist's staggering compositional scope and most bizarre and intricate details through full-page reproductions, abundant details, and a fold-out spread drawn from The Last Judgement." (Publisher's note)

Gohr, Siegfried

★ **Magritte**; attempting the impossible. Siegfried Gohr. D.A.P./Distributed Art Publishers 2009 323 p. illustrations (chiefly color) (alk. paper) $85   **759.94**
1. Surrealism 2. Surrealism -- Belgium
ISBN 1933045930; 9781933045931

LC 2009022403

This book, by Siegfried Gohr, focuses on "Belgian painter René Magritte. .... Magritte's paintings offer a space for the viewer to contemplate the emptiness of signs and to locate that emptiness in a world we recognize--indeed, the artist relies on the props of normalcy in order to upend, invert and collapse them into the terra incognita where life leaves off and art begins." (Publisher's note)

Includes bibliographical references (p. 318-319) and indexes

Attempting the impossible

760   Printmaking and prints

Hughes, Robert

Goya. Knopf 2003 429p il $40   **760**
1. Artists 2. Etchers 3. Painters 4. Printmakers
ISBN 0-394-58028-1

LC 2002-43281

This is "a remarkably vital, delectably discursive, and deeply affecting study." Booklist

Includes bibliographical references

769.973   Prints – United States

Three centuries of American prints from the National Gallery of Art; Judith Brodie, Amy Johnston, Michael J. Lewis; With contributions by John Fagg, Adam Greenhalgh, Franklin Kelly, David M. Lubin, Leo G. Mazow, Alexander Nem-

erov, Jennifer Raab, Jennifer L. Roberts, Marc Simpson, Susan Tallman, Joyce Tsai, David C. Ward. National Gallery of Art 2016 xi, 347 p.p chiefly color illustrations (hardcover: alk. paper) $60 **769.973**
1. American prints 2. Prints -- Washington (D.C.) -- Exhibitions 3. National Gallery of Art (U.S.) -- Exhibitions 4. Prints, American -- Exhibitions
ISBN 9780500239520

LC 2015045313

This book, by Judith Brodie, Amy Johnston and Michael J. Lewis, features nearly 200 American prints from the National Gallery of Art's collection, "representing more than 100 artists, and dating from the colonial era to the present day. . . . The artists featured range from Paul Revere through James McNeil Whistler, Mary Cassatt, Winslow Homer, Louise Nevelson, Romare Bearden, Andy Warhol, Robert Rauschenberg, Chuck Close, and Kara Walker." (Publisher's note)

"An excellent contribution to current scholarship and a great resource for scholars and generalists alike." Choice Reviews

Includes bibliographical references and index

770 Photography, computer art, cinematography, videography

Adams, Ansel, 1902-1984

Ansel Adams at 100; Ansel Adams, John Szarkowski. Little, Brown & Co. 2003 191 p. (Paperback) $40 **770**
1. Photographers -- United States 2. Photography, Artistic -- Exhibitions
ISBN 9780821228654; 082122865X

LC 0069941

This book "commemorates the birth of the famous native San Franciscan photographer with 114 of [Ansel] Adams's rich, beloved images spanning his oeuvre, and some delightful photos of the artist. The book and accompanying centennial exhibit at San Francisco's Museum of Modern Art . . . , curated by John Szarkowski, director of the department of photography at New York's Museum of Modern Art, reevaluate the impact of Adams's work on photography, landscapes and the audience." (Publishers Weekly)

Arnold, Eve, 1912-2012

All about Eve; the photography of Eve Arnold. Eve Arnold. TeNeues 2012 216 p. (hardcover: alk. paper) $85 **770**
1. Portrait photography 2. Women photographers -- United States
ISBN 383279641X; 9783832796419

LC 2011943114

Eve Arnold "may be best known for her black and white images of Marilyn Monroe, but she has chronicled figures as diverse as migrant potato workers and heads of state in addition to screen icons during her assignments, which involved everything from politics, social issues, travel, to current events and a little glamour. Guided by her own words, this volume features Arnold's now iconic photographs as well as many never-before published images." (Publisher's note)

Bajac, Quentin

Photography at MOMA; 1920-1960. Quentin Bajac, Lucy Gallun, Roxana Marcoci. Museum of Modern Art 2016 392 p. $75 **770**
1. Modern art -- Exhibitions 2. Photography -- Exhibitions
ISBN 1633450139; 9781633450134

LC 2016941489

This book on photography at the Museum of Modern Art, by Quentin Bajac, Lucy Gallun, and Roxana Marcoci, "comprises a comprehensive catalogue of the collection post-1960s and brings much-needed new critical perspective to the most prominent artists working with the photographic medium of the late 20th and early 21st centuries." (Publisher's note)

Cardozo, Christopher

Edward S. Curtis; one hundred masterworks. Christopher Cardozo; with contributions by A. D. Coleman, Louise Erdrich, Eric J. Jolly, and Michael Charles Tobias. DelMonico Books/Prestel 2015 184 p. illustrations (some color) (hardcover) $65 **770**
1. Native Americans -- History 2. Photography in ethnology 3. Photographers -- United States -- Biography
ISBN 9783791354217; 9783791365800

LC 2014049053

In this book, "author Christopher Cardozo has curated a groundbreaking monograph on internationally renowned photographer Edward Curtis. Curtis's magnum opus, The North American Indian, the most extensive photographic portrait of Native Americans, is a crucial contribution to the history of America's Native peoples as well as a testament to his tireless efforts to document and express the spirit of over eighty distinct tribal groups." (Publisher's note)

One hundred masterworks

Cartier-Bresson, Henri, 1908-2004

The Decisive Moment; photography by Henri Cartier-Bresson. Steidl 2015 160 p. chiefly illustrations (hbk.) $125 **770**
1. Portrait photography 2. Photography, Artistic -- 20th century
ISBN 9783869307886; 3869307889

This book, by Henri Cartier-Bresson, was "originally published in 1952. . . . This new publication—the first and only reprint since the original 1952 edition—is a meticulous facsimile of the original book that launched the artist to international fame, with an additional booklet on the history of The Decisive Moment by Centre Pompidou curator Clément Chéroux." (Publisher's note)

Cole, Teju

Blind spot; Teju Cole; foreword by Siri Hustvedt. Random House 2017 xvi, 332 p.p color illustrations, map (hardback) $40 **770**
1. Photography 2. Creative ability 3. Travel photography 4. International travel 5. African American authors -- Travel 6. Authors -- United States -- Travel
ISBN 9780399591075; 9780399591082

LC 2016032505

In this photobook, by Teju Cole, with foreword by Siri Hustvedt, "images take center stage: one per every two pages, with short accompanying text, like the notes at a gallery show. . . . Cole made the pictures over a three-year period as he traveled the globe from Seoul to the Swiss Alps to London to Lagos and back to Brooklyn, where he makes his home." (Kirkus Reviews)

"This ambitious study deserves a spot on the shelf next to Roland Barthes's Camera Lucida and Susan Sontag's On Photography." Pub Wkly

Edward weston; 125 Photographs. Edward Weston; [edited by] Steve Crist. AMMO Books 2012 262 p. $50 **770**
1. Photography
ISBN 1934429309; 9781934429303

LC 2012933925

This book, edited by Steve Crist, "contains 125 of [Edward]

Weston's well-known images and many lesser-known gems. Additionally, a detailed introduction, along with reproductions of many unseen photographs and ephemera help round out this ultimate tribute to a legendary photographer." (Publisher's note)

Fagans, Michael

Iphone photography for everybody; Michael Fagans. Amherst Media, Inc. 2017 128 p. $19.95 **770**

1. Smartphones 2. Digital photography 3. Artistic photography

ISBN 9781682032909

LC 2017943282

In this book, [by Michael Fagans,] you'll learn to use a camera phone and apps to make far more interesting photographs. Along with some technical information, experienced professional photojournalist . . . Fagans has included insightful information about his mind-set when shooting, his approach to composition, and how he handles other creative aspects of the photography process." (Publisher's note)

Foresta, Merry A.

Irving Penn; Beyond Beauty. by Merry Foresta. Yale University Press 2015 240 p. color ill., plates, portraits $45 **770**

1. Photographers

ISBN 0300214901; 9780300214901

LC 2015934207

This book, by Merry Foresta, presents an "overview of the work of legendary American photographer Irving Penn. . . . Drawing from the extensive holdings of the Smithsonian American Art Museum, including a major gift from The Irving Penn Foundation, this . . . catalogue compiles 161 of Penn's iconic images, including a number of unpublished works." (Publisher's note)

Includes bibliographical references (pages 238) and index.

Gatcum, Chris

★ The **Beginner's** photography guide; [written by Chris Gatcum] 2nd edition DK Publishing 2016 192 p. color photos $19.95 **770**

1. Photography

ISBN 9781465449665

This book, by Chris Gatcum, is a "manual for any novice photographer who wants to unlock the potential of their new digital camera. . . . It takes you through every technique you need to create stunning images, from exposure to flash to image enhancement. Handy checklists provide a quick rundown of the equipment and camera settings for each technique, and at-a-glance comparison images show how camera settings can produce remarkably different results." (Publisher's note)

"Though perfect for novices, this manual will also be helpful to readers with prior knowledge of analog photography wishing to translate their skills to the digital realm." LJ (review of 2013 edition)

Gulbrandsen, Don

Edward Sheriff Curtis; visions of the first Americans. [photographs selected and essay by] Don Gulbrandsen. Chartwell Books"||"Compendium 2006 256 p. chiefly ill., col. map, ports. $24.99 **770**

1. Native Americans 2. Native Americans -- Biography 3. Native Americans -- Pictorial works

ISBN 0785821147; 0785826505; 9780785821144; 9780785826507

LC 2008300121

This book on Edward S. Curtis, by Don Gulbrandsen, "is a tribute to the photographer, his work, but above all to the Native Americans he photographed. Chapters on many different Native American tribes make

this collection unique." (Publisher's note)

Horenstein, Henry

Digital photography; a basic manual. Henry Horenstein with Allison Carroll. Little, Brown & Co. 2011 240 p. illustrations (some color) (pbk.) $30 **770**

1. Digital photography 2. Photography -- Digital techniques

ISBN 0316020745; 9780316020749

LC 2011018758

This book, by Henry Horenstein, is a " guide to capturing digital photographs. . . . All concepts are fully illustrated with sample work by internationally renowned professionals, representing editorial work, photojournalism, and everything in between. Topics covered include essential information for both film and digital photography, . . . as well as digital-specific information on image editing, printing methods, and even file storage." (Publisher's note)

Lowe, Paul

Digital photography complete course; written by David Taylor, Tracy Hallett, Paul Lowe, Paul Sanders. DK Publishing 2015 360 p. illustrations (chiefly color) $30 **770**

1. Photography 2. Photography -- Digital techniques

ISBN 1465436073; 9781465436078

LC 2015451543

This book "uses a combination of tutorials, step-by-step demonstrations, practical assignments, and Q&As to help you understand and use your camera to the max. Choose your own pace to work through the modules — the program is totally customizable to your schedule. As you work through the lessons, test your new knowledge and troubleshoot common issues." (Publisher's note)

"An affordable, uncomplicated way to learn about digital photography." LJ

Magnum Photos, Inc.

New York September 11; by Magnum photographers; introduction by David Halberstam. PowerHouse Bks. 2001 140p il $29.95 **770**

1. Documentary photography 2. World Trade Center terrorist attack, 2001

ISBN 1-57687-130-4

LC 2001-52330

This collection of photographs documents the attack on the World Trade Center on September 11, 2001. The book is organized essentially as a series of picture essays by individual photographers

Matter, Jordan

Dancers among us; a celebration of joy in the everyday. Jordan Matter. Workman Publishing 2012 229 p. color illustrations (alk. paper) $17.95 **770**

1. Dance in art 2. Dance -- Pictorial works 3. Dancers -- Portraits 4. Portrait photography

ISBN 0761171703; 9780761171706

LC 2012033655

This book by Jordan Matter presents photographs of "dancers leaping, laughing, reclining, and soaring in some of the most unconventional spots: in offices, crossing a busy street, high up in a leafy tree limb, and even in the shower!" The "images [are] around themes like work, play, love, exploration, and dreaming." Also included are "Matter's personal anecdotes about life, learning, and family". (Dance Magazine)

The **open** road; photography and the American road trip. David Campany. Aperture Foundation 2014 336 p. illustrations, color maps (hardcover: alk. paper) $65 **770**
1. Travel writing 2. Automobile travel 3. United States -- Description and travel 4. Photography, Artistic 5. Photographic criticism 6. United States -- Pictorial works 7. United States -- Description and travel -- Pictorial works 8. United States -- Social life and customs -- Pictorial works
ISBN 1597112402; 9781597112406

LC 2014020321

This book, edited by David Campany, "considers the photographic road trip as a genre in and of itself, and presents the story of photographers for whom the American road is muse. The book features David Campany's introduction to the genre and 18 chapters presented chronologically, each exploring one American road trip in depth through a portfolio of images and informative texts." (Publisher's note)
Includes bibliographical references

Rubin, Robert M.

Avedon's France; Old World, New Look. Robert M. Rubin and Marianne Le Galliard. Harry N Abrams Inc 2017 799 p. color illustrations (hardcover) $40 **770**
1. Documentary photography 2. France -- Description and travel 3. Photography, Artistic -- Exhibitions 4. Fashion photography -- France -- Exhibitions 5. Portrait photography -- France -- Exhibitions
ISBN 1419726005; 9781419726002

This book by Robert M. Rubin and Marianne Le Galliard "brings together a collection of spectacular photographs; selected interviews, letters, publications, and writings (including new material from the Avedon Foundation archives); and substantive essays by the authors. In addition to five portfolios of French sitters spanning a lifetime of portraiture, it looks at Avedon's apprenticeship to his mentor, Alexei Brodovitch [and] his encounters with French fashion." (Publisher's note)
Includes bibliographical references and index.

Stieglitz, Alfred

★ **Alfred** Stieglitz: the key set; the Alfred Stieglitz collection of photographs. [text by] Sarah Greenough. Abrams 2002 2v il set $150 **770**
ISBN 0-8109-3533-3

LC 2002-5066

This is a "captioned catalog of 1,642 Stieglitz photographs. . . . It contains 'the finest print of every mounted photograph in Stieglitz's possession at the time of his death.' . . . Greenough's essay examines 'what is and is not in the key set in order to clarify the evolution of Stieglitz's understanding of modernist photography. . . .' The set contains very useful, dense chronologies of Stieglitz's process and techniques (1882-1944) and of exhibitions (1888-1944), a bibliography (1875-2001), and an essay on Stieglitz's concern with reproduction printing and publishing." Choice
Includes bibliographical references

770.1 Philosophy and theory

Peterson, Bryan

Learning to see creatively; design, color, and composition in photography. Bryan Peterson. 3rd edition Amphoto Books 2015 144 p. color illustrations pbk $25.99 **770.1**
1. Photography 2. Composition (Art)
ISBN 9781607748274; 1607748274

LC 2014049147

"Fully revised with 100 percent new photography, this best-selling guide takes a radical approach to creativity by explaining that it is not just an inherent ability but a skill that can be learned and applied. Using inventive photos from his own stunning portfolio, author and veteran photographer Bryan Peterson deconstructs creativity for photographers. He details the basic techniques that go into not only taking a particular photo, but also provides insights on how to improve upon it--helping readers avoid the visual pitfalls and technical dead ends that can lead to dull, uninventive photographs." (Publisher's note)
Includes bibliographical references and index

770.23 Photography as a profession, occupation, hobby

Fordham, Demetrius

★ **If** you're bored with your camera read this book; Demetrius Fordham. ILEX 2017 128 p. illustrations (chiefly color) (paperback) $14.99 **770.23**
1. Photography 2. Digital photography 3. Photography -- Technique 4. Photography -- Themes, motives 5. Photography -- Digital techniques 6. Photography -- Vocational guidance
ISBN 9781781574317; 1781574316

"In this book, [by Demetrius Fordham], you'll find inspiring ideas and genuinely different techniques that you can use to capture anything, from artistic portraits, through to stunning street photography and unusual aboreals. This book will open your eyes, and your lens cap, to new ideas." (Publisher's note)
"Fordham, an accomplished professional photographer, shares 50 of his own personal tricks, tips, hacks, and exercises designed to refresh one's outlook." LJ

770.9 History, geographical treatment, biography

Ang, Tom

Photography; The Definitive Visual History. Tom Ang. DK Pub. 2014 480 p. color illustrations, portraits $50 **770.9**
1. Photographers 2. Photography -- History 3. Photographers -- Biography 4. Photography -- History -- Pictorial works
ISBN 1465422889; 9781465422880

LC 2014453689

This book, by Tom Ang, "lavishly celebrates the most iconic photographs and photographers of the past 200 years. Tracing the history of photography from its origins in the 1800s to the digital age, . . . [this book] is the only book of its kind to give a comprehensive account of the people, the photographs, and the technologies that have shaped the history of photography." (Publisher's note)
"While too basic for a professional or serious student, this volume will appeal to photo enthusiasts and general readers. Those wanting an extensive single-volume overview should stick with Michael R. Peres's The Focal Encyclopedia of Photography." LJ

Morris, Errol, 1948-

Believing is seeing; observations on the mysteries of photography. Penguin Press 2011 xxv, 310p il map $40 **770.9**
1. Documentary photography
ISBN 978-1-59420-301-5; 1-59420-301-6

LC 2011013101

The book "takes the reader on a walking tour of photojournalistic hot spots, from 1855 to 2006 to 2003 to 1936 to 2006 to 1863 , in that order . . . Mostly, Morris tries to clear up unsolved mysteries in the crevices of the history of photography—things like whether Walker Evans moved some knickknacks in a sharecropper's house he photographed; which of two photographs by Roger Fenton, from the Crimean War, was taken first; and how much guilt can be inferred from a digital photo of an American soldier grinning over a dead Iraqi at Abu Ghraib." (Nation)

"Morris' assiduous and profound inquiry into the relationship between reality and photography is eye-opening, mind-expanding, and essential in this age of ubiquitous digital images." Booklist

Includes bibliographical references

770.92 Biography

Alinder, Mary Street

Group f.64; Edward Weston, Ansel Adams, Imogen Cunningham, and the community of artists who revolutionized American photography. Mary Street Alinder. Bloomsbury USA 2014 416 p. 16 plates; illustrations (alk. paper) $35 **770.92**
1. Photography 2. Modernism (Aesthetics) 3. Group f.64 -- History 4. Photography -- United States -- History 5. Modernism (Art) -- West (U.S.) -- History 6. Photographers -- United States -- Biography
ISBN 1620405555; 9781620405550

LC 2014011040

"In this . . . group biography about the California photographers known as Group f.64, [Mary Street] Alinder . . . tells a distinctly West Coast story about an ambitious, broad-minded, and unusually diverse movement. Originally founded at a party in Berkeley, Calif., in 1932 by Edward Weston, Ansel Adams, Imogen Cunningham, and Willard Van Dyke, among others, Group f.64 advocated for 'straight' photography over pictorialism's painterly affectations." (Publishers Weekly)

"As she chronicles the photographers' friendships, tempestuous love lives, epic parties, scrambles to survive, passionate manifestos, heated public debates, social and environmental concerns, and hard-won exhibitions, Alinder achieves an f.64 degree of crisp and commanding detail in this landmark group portrait of the visionary photographers who succeeded in 'forever changing our way of seeing.'" Booklist

Includes bibliographical references and index

Bergey, Barry

Folk masters; a portrait of America. photographs by Tom Pich; text by Barry Bergey. Indiana University Press 2018 245 p. (cl: alk. paper) $30 **770.92**
1. Ethnic art 2. Artists -- United States 3. Folk artists -- United States -- Portraits 4. Ethnic arts -- United States -- Pictorial works 5. National Endowment for the Arts. National Heritage Fellowship
ISBN 9780253032324

LC 2017032043

This book, by Barry Bergey and photograper Tom Pich, features "one hundred of the greatest folk artists practicing in the United States. . . . Pich has traveled the country to the homes and studios of recipients of the National Endowment for the Arts' National Heritage Fellowship. . . . His portraits give us a glimpse into their art, their process, and their culture. . . . Bergey . . . provides further insight into the lives of each featured artist." (Publisher's note)

"Bergey, former director of folk and traditional arts at the National Endowment for the Arts (NEA), highlights the expansive and compelling photographs of Tom Pich, who has spent the last 25 years capturing recipients of the NEA's National Heritage Fellowship." LJ

Burrows, Larry

Vietnam; introduction by David Halberstam. Knopf 2002

243p il $50 **770.92**
1. Vietnam War, 1961-1975 -- Pictorial works
ISBN 0-375-41102-X

LC 2002-19100

This "confirms that {Burrows} was an artist as well as a journalist, capable of arousing the great tragic emotions, pity and terror." Booklist

Includes bibliographical references

Egan, Timothy

★ Short nights of the Shadow Catcher; the epic life and immortal photographs of Edward Curtis. Timothy Egan. Houghton Mifflin Harcourt 2012 384 p. ill. (hardback) $28.00 **770.92**
1. Photographers 2. Native Americans -- History 3. Native Americans -- Pictorial works 4. Photographers -- United States -- Biography
ISBN 0618969020; 9780618969029

LC 2012022390

This book by "National Book Award winner Timothy Egan" is a biography of photographer Edward Curtis that "recaptures the story of a man both entrapped by his time and ahead of it." In 1900, Curtis "made a decision that changed his life . . . . He largely abandoned his lucrative portrait studio work and began a thirty-year project to record images of Native Americans who, he believed, were doomed to extinction, [which] destroyed his marriage and left him destitute." (Barnes and Noble)

Gross, Michael, 1952-

Focus; Michael Gross. Atria Books 2016 416 p. illustrations (some color) (hardcover) $28 **770.92**
1. Photography 2. Clothing industry 3. Models (Persons) -- Biography 4. Fashion photography -- History 5. Fashion photographers -- Biography 6. Fashion merchandising -- Social aspects 7. Fashion photographers -- Conduct of life
ISBN 9781476763460

LC 2015045564

This book, by Michael Gross, "probes the lives, hang-ups, and artistic triumphs of more than a dozen of fashion photography's greatest visionaries: Richard Avedon, Irving Penn, Melvin Sokolsky, Bert Stern, David Bailey, Bill King, Deborah Turbeville, Helmut Newton, Gilles Bensimon, Bruce Weber, Steven Meisel, Corinne Day, Bob and Terry Richardson, and more." (Publisher's note)

"The subject matter will be historically significant to those who are concerned with the photo artist's role in the golden age of modern fashion photography. " LJ

Huffman, Alan

Here I Am; The Story of Tim Hetherington, War Photographer. Alan Huffman. Grove Press 2013 256 p. (hardcover) $25 **770.92**
1. War photography
ISBN 0802120903; 9780802120908

This book, by Alan Huffman, offers a biography of "Tim Hetherington (1970-2011) . . . , one of the world's most distinguished and dedicated photojournalists, whose career was tragically cut short when he died in a mortar blast while covering the Libyan Civil War. . . . Huffman recounts Hetherington's life from his first interests in photography, through his critical role in reporting the Liberian Civil War, to his tragic death in Libya." (Publisher's note)

Van Haaften, Julia

★ Berenice Abbott; a life in photography. Julia Van Haaften. W W Norton & Co Inc 2018 544 p. $49.95 **770.92**
1. Photographers -- United States -- Biography

ISBN 0393292789; 9780393292787

In this biography of American photographer Berenice Abbott, author "[Julia] Van Haaften brings this iconic public figure to life alongside outlandish, familiar characters from artist Man Ray to cybernetics founder Norbert Wiener. A teenage rebel from Ohio, Abbott escaped first to Greenwich Village and then to Paris. . . . Abbott returned to New York, where she soon fell in love with art critic Elizabeth McCausland, with whom she would spend thirty years." (Publisher's note)

"Van Haaften's expert foundational biography brings Abbott into sharp focus as a photographer able to "express deep feeling through technical mastery." Booklist

Willis, Deborah

Reflections in Black; a history of Black photographers, 1840-1999. Norton 2000 348p il $50; pa $35   **770.92**

1. African Americans in art 2. African American photographers 3. Photography -- History

ISBN 0-393-04880-2; 0-393-32280-7 pa

LC 99-55185

Companion volume to A Smithsonian traveling exhibition

"Willis sketches important figures and traces both developments in photographic techniques and the practice of photography by African Americans. . . . A beautiful and informative album." Booklist

Includes bibliographical references and index

Wilson, Robert

Mathew Brady; Portraits of a Nation. Robert Wilson. St. Martin's Press 2013 320 p. $28   **770.92**

1. United States -- History -- 1861-1865, Civil War -- Photography 2. Photographers -- United States -- Biography 3. United States -- History -- Civil War, 1861-1865 -- Photography

ISBN 1620402033; 9781620402030

LC 2013016928

In this biography of photographer Mathew Brady, author Robert Wilson "examines surviving business registers, articles, advertisements, and documents of Brady's associates and prestigious clients. . . . Wilson shows how Brady's artistic genius . . . his awareness of the commercial value and historical impact of his art; his congenial personality; and his relentless and savvy promotion of himself, his business, and his craft made him the preeminent 19th-century photographer." (Library Journal)

Includes bibliographical references and index

771   Techniques, procedures, apparatus, equipment, materials

Miotke, Jim

BetterPhoto basics; the absolute beginner's guide to taking photos like the pros. Jim Miotke. Amphoto Books 2010 239 p. color illustrations (alk. paper) $21.99; (ebook) $65   **771**

1. Photography 2. Photography -- Amateurs' manuals

ISBN 081740502X; 0817405313; 9780817405021; 9780817405311; 9780817400248

LC 2009045259

In this book, photographer Jim Miotke "shares tips and tricks to improve your photos right away, no matter what camera you're using. Too busy to read a book? No problem—flip to any page for an instant tip to use right away! Learn to compose knockout shots, make the most of indoor and outdoor light, and photograph twenty popular subjects, from sunsets and flowers to a family portrait." (Publisher's note)

Peterson, Bryan

Understanding exposure; how to shoot great photographs with any camera. Bryan Peterson. 4th edition AmPhoto Books 2016 176 p. color illustrations pbk $26.99   **771**

1. Photography 2. Photography -- Exposure

ISBN 1607748509; 9781607748502

LC 2015025905

"This latest edition of [Peterson's] very popular, user-friendly guide suitable for beginners explains exposure--the key to successful photographic images--in plain, easily understood language. Peterson breaks down complex theories into simpler concepts, offering many helpful tips and shortcuts along the way. Following an introductory chapter defining exposure, subsequent sections cover aperture, shutter speed, light, special techniques, including use of filters and multiple exposure, and electronic flash." (Library Journal)

Includes bibliographical references and index

775   Digital photography

Ang, Tom

Digital photographer's handbook; Tom Ang. 5th edition DK 2012 408 p. ill. (chiefly col.) pbk $24.95   **775**

1. Digital cameras 2. Digital photography

ISBN 0756692423; 9780756692421

LC 2012418315

The latest edition of this book has been updated with "new photographic and image-manipulation projects, up-to-the-minute information on the latest technology and equipment, with revised and updated text and new pictures." (Publisher's note0

Includes bibliographical references and index

Digital photography masterclass; Tom Ang. 2nd edition DK 2013 360 p. color illustrations hbk $30   **775**

1. Digital photography 2. Photography -- Processing

ISBN 1465408568; 9781465408563

Ang "teaches how to look at the world with a photographer's eye and offers tutorials, photographic assignments, and step-by-step image-manipulation exercises. Combining technical and artistic aspects of photography, Ang completes the volume with sections on travel, documentary, portrait, nature, sports, and architecture photography." (Library Journal)

Freeman, Michael

The **photographer's** mind; creative thinking for better digital photos. Focal Press 2011 192p il pa $29.95   **775**

1. Digital photography

ISBN 978-0-240-81517-6

The author "shares experience he has gained as a professional photographer to improve the quality of the digital pictures nearly everyone is now creating. The content is streamlined into three chapters, on intent, style, and process, that tackle both the practical and the intangible aspects of photography more thoughtfully than many similar books. Freeman is as adept at explaining composition as he is at discussing the problem of cliché or the philosophy of the sublime." Libr J

Includes bibliographical references

777   Cinematography and videography

Pincus, Ed, 1938-2013

The **filmmaker's** handbook; a comprehensive guide for the digital age. Steven Ascher & Edward Pincus; drawings by Carol

Keller and Robert Brun; original photographs by Ted Spagna and Stephen McCarthy completely revised and updated by Steven Ascher With contributions by David Leitner. Plume 2012 xii, 818 p.p (pbk.) $30; (ebook) $65   **777**
1. Cinematography 2. Motion pictures -- Production and direction 3. Digital video -- Handbooks, manuals, etc 4. Cinematography -- Handbooks, manuals, etc 5. Digital cinematography -- Handbooks, manuals, etc 6. Motion pictures -- Production and direction -- Handbooks, manuals, etc
ISBN 0452297281; 9780452297289; 9781101613801

LC 2012036572

This book, by Steven Ascher and Edward Pincus, is an "authoritative guide to producing, directing, shooting, editing, and distributing your video or film. . . . [It] is now updated with the latest advances in HD and new digital formats. For students and teachers, professionals and novices, this indispensable handbook covers all aspects of movie making." (Publisher's note)

Includes bibliographical references (pages 791-793) and index

778   Specific fields and special kinds of photography

National Geographic, the photographs. National Geographic Soc. 1994 336p il $50   **778**
1. Photojournalism 2. Documentary photography
ISBN 0-87044-986-9

LC 94-29971

"A treasury of 350 full-color photographs from the archives of the National Geographic shares a stunning array of work, reflecting the themes of The Land, Underwater, Science, The United States, and The World." (Publisher's note)

778.3   Special kinds of photography

Benson, Michael
Far out; a space-time chronicle. Abrams 2009 328p il   **778.3**
1. Space photography
ISBN 0810949482; 9780810949485

LC 2009-929096

This is a "collection of astronomical images from observatories around the world and in space." (Publisher's note) Index.

"Here are stars packed like golden sand, gas combed in delicate blue threads, piled into burgundy thunderheads and carved into sinuous rilles and ribbons, and galaxies clotted with star clusters dancing like spiders on the ceiling. . . . You can sit and look through this book for hours and never be bored, . . . or you can actually read the accompanying learned essays. Mr. Benson's prose is up to its visual surroundings, no mean feat." N Y Times (Late N Y Ed)

Includes bibliographical references

778.53   Film making and editing

Williams, Richard, 1933-
The **animator's** survival kit; A Manual of Methods, Principles and Formulas for Classical, Computer, Games, Stop Motion and Internet Animators. Richard Williams. Faber & Faber 2009 x, 382 p.p illustrations (some color) $35   **778.53**
1. Animation (Cinematography) 2. Drawing -- Technique

ISBN 0571238335; 0571238343; 086547897X; 9780571238330; 9780571238347; 9780865478978

LC 2010294449

This book, by Richard Williams, "provides the underlying principles of animation that every animator--from beginner to expert, classic animator to computer animation whiz --needs. . . . [Williams] illustrates his points with hundreds of drawings, distilling the secrets of the masters into a working system in order to create a book that will become the standard work on all forms of animation for professionals, students, and fans." (Publisher's note)

778.7   Photography under specific conditions

Rotman, Jeffrey L.
The **last** fisherman; witness to the endangered oceans. by Jeffrey L. Rotman and Yair Harel; introduction by Les Kaufman. Abbeville Press Publishers 2014 276 p. color illustrations (hardcover: alk. paper) $49.95   **778.7**
1. Overfishing 2. Underwater photography 3. Marine photography 4. Saltwater fishing -- Pictorial works
ISBN 0789211912; 9780789211910

LC 2014016848

This book, by by Jeffrey L. Rotman and Yair Harel, "with breathtaking images and compelling stories, an underwater photographer chronicles the glory, and devastation, of our changing oceans. . . . His journey mirrors our view of the oceans as places of wonder, to the fragile hunting grounds they are today." (Publisher's note)

"An excellent cautionary tale, this work offers much to celebrate, too. Highly recommended to all interested in nature, the oceans, and fishing." LJ

Includes bibliographical references and index

778.73   Underwater photography

Mustard, Alex
Underwater Photography Masterclass; by Dr. Alex Mustard. Trafalgar Square 2016 192 p. illustrations (chiefly color) $34.95   **778.73**
1. Marine biology 2. Underwater photography
ISBN 1781452229; 9781781452226

LC 2017005588

"With marine biologist Dr. Alexander Mustard as your guide you can learn all you need to know to explore the amazing creatures and landscapes that exist underwater. From information about diving equipment and cameras, to crucial advice on understanding and controlling light underwater, this book provides all the background you need before you take the plunge. Topics covered include wide-angle light, macro lighting, ambient light and macro techniques." (Publisher's note)

"This book will be invaluable for anyone seriously interested in underwater photography and those who are fascinated with creatures of the deep." LJ

Includes bibliographical references and index.

778.9   Photography of specific subjects

Shaw, John
John Shaw's nature photography field guide; by John Shaw. rev ed; AMPHOTO 2000 p. cm color illustrations   **778.9**
1. Nature photography

ISBN 0-8174-4059-3; 9780817440596

LC 00-42013

This book, by John Shaw, "contains state-of-the-art instruction on how any photographer can aim for . . . impressive results every time a camera is focused on the great outdoors. . . . Using his own exceptional work as examples, the author discusses each type of nature subject and how to approach photographing it." (Publisher's note)

"Shaw's book will be of great value to anyone wishing to make better landscapes and wildlife photographs." LJ

Watkins, Carleton Emmons

Carleton Watkins: the complete mammoth photographs; Weston Naef and Christine Hult-Lewis; with contributions by Michael Hargraves, Jack von Euw, and Jennifer A. Watts. J. Paul Getty Museum 2011 xxv, 572p il map $195   **778.9**

1. Photography 2. California -- Pictorial works
ISBN 978-1-60606-005-6; 1-60606-005-8

LC 2011-05241

" A monumental achievement in the pictorial historiography of 19th-century America, loaded with new images and data, this will be an indispensable resource for students of photography and U.S. history." Libr J

Includes bibliographical references

Wildlife Photographer of the Year; 50 Years. by Rosamund Kidman Cox. Firefly Books Ltd 2014 256 p. illustrations, portraits $49.95   **778.9**

1. Wildlife photography
ISBN 1770854622; 9781770854628

This book is a "collection of nature photography [that] features all the winning pictures from the prestigious 50th . . .Wildlife Photographer of the Year competition. . . . The photographs are chosen by an international jury for their artistic merit and originality, from categories that together represent a diversity of natural subjects. The range of styles is also diverse, as is the genre of photography, whether action, macro, underwater, landscape, or environmental reportage." (Publisher's note)

"Spare text offers readers a glimpse into how each image was made, its back story and why it deserves to be in the book. Clear the coffee table — this book has substance, beauty and will draw readers in again and again." Pub Wkly

779   Photographic images

Addario, Lynsey

Of love & war; Lynsey Addario. Penguin Press 2018 272 p. (hardback) $40   **779**

1. Photojournalism 2. War photography 3. Photographers -- United States 4. War photography -- Middle East 5. War and society -- Pictorial works 6. Photographers -- United States -- Biography 7. Africa -- Social conditions -- Pictorial works 8. PHOTOGRAPHY -- Individual Photographers -- Artists 9. Middle East -- Social conditions -- Pictorial works
ISBN 9780525560029

LC 2018006212

"Pulitzer Prize-winning photojournalist [Lynsey Addario] returns with a stunning collection of more than two hundred of her photographs from across the Middle East, South Asia, and Africa. In her distinctively powerful dramatic style, Addario documents life in Afghanistan under the Taliban, the stark truth of sub-Saharan Africa, and the daily reality of women in the Middle East, as well as much more." (Publisher's note)

Of love and war

Brandow, Todd

Edward Steichen; lives in photography. [by] Todd Brandow and William A. Ewing. W. W. Norton & Company 2008 355p il $100   **779**

1. Photographers 2. Artistic photography
ISBN 978-0-393-06626-5

LC 2007-20128

"One of the finest photography books published in many years; highly recommended for all libraries." Libr J

Includes bibliographical references (p. 309-316)

Buckland, Gail

Who shot sports; a photographic history, 1843 to the present. Gail Buckland. Alfred A. Knopf 2016 329 p. illustrations (some color) (hardcover: alk. paper) $45   **779**

1. Sports -- History 2. Photography of sports 3. Photography of sports -- History
ISBN 0385352239; 9780385352239

LC 2015038089

This book, by Gail Buckland, "brings together the work of 165 extraordinary photographers, most of their images heralded, most of their names unknown; photographs that capture the essence of athletes' mastery . . . and showing what human will, discipline, drive, and desire look like when suspended in time." (Publisher's note)

"Buckland writes with such authority that her thoughts on photography, as an art form, and her analysis of individual images in and out of the sports context make this a must-read for pop culture enthusiasts and anyone interested in photography." Pub Wkly

Includes bibliographical references and index

Carter, Graydon

Vanity Fair, the portraits; a century of iconic images. by Graydon Carter and the editors of Vanity Fair; foreword by Graydon Carter; essays by Christopher Hitchens, David Friend, and Terence Pepper. Abrams 2008 383p il $65   **779**

1. Celebrities 2. Portrait photography
ISBN 978-0-8109-7298-8; 0-8109-7298-0

LC 2008-05033

"Culled from the pages of Vanity Fair magazine by its editor, Graydon Carter, and his staff, and shot by many of the greatest photographers in the history of the medium, these pictures are engrossing less because of the people they portray than because of the breathtaking ingenuity with which each subject is captured. . . . Whether taken by Baron de Meyer, Edward Steichen or Man Ray, or by latter-day geniuses like [Annie] Leibovitz, Helmut Newton or Herb Ritts, these pictures stand as some of the finest examples of photographic craft ever to appear in the mainstream press." N Y Times Book Rev

Evans, Walker, 1903-1975

American photographs; Walker Evans; with an essay by Lincoln Kirstein. Museum of Modern Art""||"Distributed by New York Graphic Society Books 1988 205 p. chiefly illustrations $40   **779**

1. Photography 2. United States -- Pictorial works 3. Photography, Artistic 4. United States -- Social conditions -- 1918-1932 -- Pictorial works 5. United States -- Social conditions -- 1933-1945 -- Pictorial works
ISBN 0870702378; 0870702386; 087070835X; 9780870708350

LC 88062926

This book, by Walker Evans, "was a carefully prepared letterpress production, published by The Museum of Modern Art in 1938 to accompany an exhibition of photographs by Evans that captured scenes of

America in the early 1930s. . . . This version, like the fiftieth-anniversary edition produced by the Museum in 1988, captures the look and feel of the very first edition with the aid of new digital technologies." (Publisher's note)

Friedman, Elias Weiss

The **Dogist**; Photographic Encounters With 1,000 Dogs. by Elias Weiss Friedman. Workman Pub Co 2015 304 p. color illustrations $24.95   **779**

    1. Dogs 2. Animals -- Pictorial works

    ISBN 1579656714; 9781579656713

                       LC 2015036708

This book, by Elias Weiss Friedman, "is a beautiful, funny, and inspiring tribute to the beloved dogs in our lives. Every page presents dog portraits that command our attention. Whether because of the look in a dog's eyes, its innate beauty, or even the clothes its owner has dressed it in, the photos will make you ooh and aah, laugh, and fall in love." (Publisher's note)

"This delightful collection of photographs is likely to catch the eye of readers who follow Friedman's blog, Facebook page, tweets, and/ or Instagram account. Animal portraiture enthusiasts may be especially interested in this title as an exemplar of the genre." LJ

Hitchcock, Susan Tyler

National geographic rarely seen; photographs of the extraordinary. [compiled by] Susan Tyler Hitchcock; foreword by Stephen Alvarez. National Geographic Society 2015 399 p. color illustrations (hardcover: alk. paper) $40   **779**

    1. Photography 2. Nature photography 3. Travel photography 4. Landscape photography 5. Documentary photography 6. Geography -- Pictorial works

    ISBN 1426215614; 9781426215612

                       LC 2015014900

This book, by National Geographic, "features striking images of places, events, natural phenomena, and manmade heirlooms seldom seen by human eyes. It's all here: 30,000-year-old cave art sealed from the public; animals that are among the last of their species on Earth; volcanic lightning; giant crystals that have grown to more than 50 tons; the engraving inside Abraham Lincoln's pocket watch." (Publisher's note)

Leibovitz, Annie

★ **Annie** Leibovitz; Portraits 2005-2016. Phaidon Inc Ltd 2017 316 p. $89.95   **779**

    1. Photography 2. Women photographers

    ISBN 0714875139; 9780714875132

"In this new collection, Leibovitz has captured the most influential and compelling figures of the last decade in the style that has made her one of the most beloved talents of our time. Each of the photographs documents contemporary culture with an artist's eye, wit, and an uncanny ability to personalize even the most recognizable and distinguished figures." (Publisher's note)

Annie Leibovitz at work; [Sharon DeLano, editor] 2nd edition Random House 2018 237p il $49.95   **779**

    1. Portrait photography

    ISBN 9780714878294

    Originally published 2008

Leibovitz "discusses her personal approaches, trials, and discoveries as a professional photographer, pairing detailed memories and technical discussions with images of her most iconic celebrity portraits (including the Rolling Stones, Demi Moore, John Lennon, and Queen Elizabeth). The book adheres to a chronological format—from Leibovitz's earliest

black-and-white photos of the Rolling Stones and John Lennon to her conceptual color portraits from the 1980s. . . . Also included are personal and family photographs as well as her most recent photo shoots for Vanity Fair, including the Obama and Clinton campaigns." Libr J

A **photographer's** life, 1990-2005. Random House 2006 un il $75   **779**

    1. Portrait photography

    ISBN 978-0-375-50509-6; 0-375-50509-1

                       LC 2006-45765

This is a collection of Leibovitz's "work from 1990-2005. . . . [Portraits of] Johnny Cash, Nicole Kidman, Mikhail Baryshnikov, Keith Richards, Michael Jordan, Joan Didion, R2-D2, Patti Smith, Nelson Mandela, Jack Nicholson, William Burroughs, [and] George W. Bush with members of his Cabinet appear alongside pictures of Leibovitz's family and friends, reportage from the siege of Sarajevo in the early Nineties, and landscapes." Publisher's note

Life: World War 2; history's greatest conflict in pictures. edited by Richard B. Stolley. Little, Brown 2001 351p il hardcover o.p. pa $29.95   **779**

    1. World War, 1939-1945 -- Pictorial works 2. World history -- 20th century -- Pictorial works

    ISBN 0-8212-2771-8; 0-8212-5713-7 pa

                       LC 2001-93633

This "album of 665 photographs taken from the archives of Life magazine and other collections begins with the years 1919 to 1939, the two decades leading up to World War II. Editor Stolley then proceeds to chronicle the war, year by year through 1945, and ends with what he calls 'the war's aftermath,' 1946 to 2001. . . . For World War II buffs, the book is a natural treasure." Booklist

Lyon, Danny

Memories of myself; essays. Phaidon 2009 207p il $90   **779**

    1. Documentary photography

    ISBN 978-0-7148-4851-8; 0-7148-4851-4

"What happens when you hang out in brothels, derby pits, and dark alleys for forty years? For starters, you take some damn memorable photos. That's been the path of American photographer Danny Lyon, who, like a Method actor, immersed himself in the subcultures he documented. His iconic work from the '60s (pre–Easy Rider photos of bikers on the road) led to exhibitions in MoMA and the Whitney and two Guggenheim fellowships, and he's credited with pioneering the New Journalism movement in photography. In Memories of Myself . . . he shares 134 mostly unpublished pictures—of Colombian prostitutes in hair curlers, chain-smoking greasers, and Brooklyn teens playing Wiffle Ball—that are so intimate they could have come from the photo albums of the subjects themselves. This is the genius of Lyon's work: He inhabits, rather than invades, the personal space of his subjects." GQ

McCartney, Linda

Life in photographs; texts by Paul McCartney, Linda McCartney, Annie Leibovitz, Mary McCartney, Martin Harrison, Stella McCartney; edited by Alison Castle. Taschen 2011 un $69.99   **779**

    1. Portrait photography

    ISBN 978-3-8365-2728-6

This volume "offers a portrait of Beatledom from a singularly intimate point of view: that of Paul's wife of nearly three decades, the late Linda McCartney. While the couple's famous friends — Mick Jagger, Steve McQueen, Willem de Kooning — are well represented, the fly-on-the-wall shots of the McCartneys' idyllic intercontinental life ... are just as enthralling. But the real highlights are the images of Paul with John Lennon, capturing the electric chemistry and childlike joy that informed the Beatles' greatest work." Entertainment Wkly

National Geographic Society (U.S.)

★ **In** focus; National Geographic greatest portraits. National Geographic Society 2004 504p il $30   **779**
    1. Portrait photography
    ISBN 0-7922-7363-X

                             LC 2004-44953
"Comprising 280 portraits by 150 of National Geographic's celebrated photographers ... the book spans over 100 years and covers the entire globe. Organized chronologically as well as thematically and enriched with essays on the development of photographic styles through decades, it is a tasteful celebration of the medium but even more so of human diversity." Libr J

Through the lens; National Geographic greatest photographs. National Geographic Soc. 2003 504p il $30   **779**
    1. Documentary photography
    ISBN 0-7922-6164-X

                             LC 2003-52757
This is a "collection of 250 photos, mostly in color and drawn from the National Geographic Society's archive.... The society's signature blend of dramatic, rigorously composed natural shots and 'family of nations'-style culture peeps are backed by broad captions and text... . The six sections ('Europe'; 'Asia'; 'Africa & the Middle East'; 'The Americas'; 'Oceans and Isles'; 'The Universe') include the first color underwater photographs, as well as collaborative work with NASA, and prominently credit the 84 photographers whose work is featured." Publ Wkly

Parker, Kate T.

Strong is the new pretty; a celebration of girls being themselves. Kate T. Parker. Workman Publishing 2017 v, 250 p.p illustrations (some color) (hardcover) $30   **779**
    1. Self-confidence 2. Girls -- Psychology 3. Resilience (Personality trait) 4. Girls -- Pictorial works
    ISBN 1523500689; 9781523500680; 9781523500185

                             LC 2017007862
This book, by Kate T. Parker, "celebrates, through more than 175 memorable photographs, the strength and spirit of girls being 100% themselves. . . . Real beauty is about being your authentic self and owning it. . . [The book] conveys a powerful message for every girl, for every mother and father of a girl, for every coach and mentor and teacher, for everyone in the village that it takes to raise a strong and self-confident person." (Publisher's note)

"Parker shows how, whether smiling, looking tough, or helping one another out, these girls of various ages, pasts, and abilities are strong. Positively moving and totally glorious." Booklist

Sartore, Joel

★ The **photo** ark; one man's quest to document the world's animals. Joel Sartore; foreword by Harrison Ford; introduction by Douglas H. Chadwick. National Geographic 2017 399 p. color illustrations (hardcover: alk. paper) $35   **779**
    1. Endangered species 2. Wildlife photography 3. Photography of animals 4. Endangered species -- Pictorial works
    ISBN 9781426217777

                             LC 2016038616
This book, by Joel Sartore, with foreword by Harrison Ford, and

introduction by Douglas H. Chadwick, presents the lifelong project by "Sartore to make portraits of the world's animals--especially those that are endangered. His powerful message, conveyed with humor, compassion, and art: to know these animals is to save them." (Publisher's note)

"Satore more than succeeds in his goal to provide people with an opportunity to become aware of these animals, many endangered, before they disappear." Pub Wkly

Schles, Ken

The **Invisible** City; by Ken Schles. Steidl 2015 80 p. chiefly illustrations $40   **779**
    1. Photography 2. New York (N.Y.) 3. Bohemianism -- New York (N.Y.)
    ISBN 3869306912; 9783869306919
This book, by Ken Schles, is "one of the twentieth century's great depictions of nocturnal bohemian experience. Documenting his life in New York City's East Village during its heyday in the tumultuous 1980s, Schles captured its look and attitude in delirious and dark honesty." (Publisher's note)

The **Scurlock** Studio and Black Washington; picturing the promise. edited by Paul Gardulo ... [et al.] National Museum of African American History and Culture: In collaboration with the National Museum o 2009 224p il $35 **779**
    1. Scurlock Studio (Firm) 2. African Americans -- Pictorial works 3. Washington (D.C.) -- Social life and customs
    ISBN 978-1-58834-262-1; 1-58834-262-X

                             LC 2008-32847
"In 1911 Addison Scurlock opened a photography studio in Washington, D.C., and went on to chronicle the aspirations and ambitions of the black community into the 1990s.... Photographs include the famous (Marian Anderson, Duke Ellington, Ralph Bunche, W. E. B. DuBois, and Muhammad Ali) as well as the influential but perhaps less well known (business owners, churchgoers, civic leaders, members of high society). With more than 100 images, this book is a proud celebration of a vibrant community from the early to the late twentieth century." Booklist

    Includes bibliographical references

Shaughnessy, Jim

The **call** of trains; railroad photographs of Jim Shaughnessy. text by Jeff Brouws. W.W. Norton 2008 224p il $65   **779**
    1. Railroads -- Pictorial works
    ISBN 978-0-393-06592-3; 0-393-06592-8

                             LC 2008-1295
"Shaughnessy began shooting trains in downtown Troy, New York (his hometown), in the middle 1940s. He eventually took lengthy trips, first in New England and Canada, later across the Midwest to the Southwest, to photograph trains. He initially focused on the big engines but quickly extended his purview to include railway workers, railway buildings, and the countrysides through which the trains rolled. A civil engineer rather than a professional photographer, he became as skilled as any pro.... Appearing on full pages of this oversize volume, his pictures are engrossing, stunning masterpieces of photodocumentation." Booklist

    Includes bibliographical references

Stepan, Peter

★ **Photos** that changed the world; edited by Peter Stepan; with contributions by Claus Biegerd [et al.] Updated edition Prestel 2016 216 p il $19.95   **779**
    1. Photojournalism
    ISBN 9783791382371
    Originally published 2000

Stepan provides "105 images that had the lasting visual power to capture a moment that could be the image of an era held in the instant of a shutter's click for distribution to a generation. . . . The photos are well reproduced and gain from the explanations of time, place, and context included in the excellent short essays that accompany each." Libr J

Szarkowski, John

William Eggleston's Guide; essay by John Szarkowski. Museum of Modern Art"||"distributed by the MIT Press 1976 110 p. illustrations, portraits $45   **779**
1. Artistic photography 2. Photography, Artistic
ISBN 087070317X; 0870703781; 9780870703782
LC 77358661

This book of photography by William Eggleston "was the first one-man show of color photographs ever presented at The Museum of Modern Art, New York, and the Museum's first publication of color photography. . . . For this edition, . . . The Museum of Modern Art has made new color separations from the original 35 mm slides, producing a facsimile edition in which the color will be freshly responsive to the photographer's intentions." (Publisher's note)

Wegman, William

William Wegman; being human. edited by William A. Ewing; photographs by William Wegman. Chronicle Books LLC 2017 352 p. chiefly color illustrations (paperback) $24.95   **779**
1. Photography of animals 2. Dogs -- Pictorial works 3. Photography of dogs 4. Weimaraner (Dog breed) -- Pictorial works
ISBN 9781452164991
LC 2017021743

In this book, photography curator William A. Ewing "presents more than 300 images from . . . [William Wegman's] personal archive, unearthing previously unseen gems alongside the iconic images that have made Wegman--along with dressed-up dogs Man Ray, Fay Ray, and others—beloved worldwide. Presented in sixteen thematic chapters, . . . [it] foregrounds the photographer's penchant for play and his evergreen ability to create images that are at once funny, striking, and surreal." (Publisher's note)

"Culled from over three decades of Wegman's portraits of his Weimaraners . . . the more than 300 photos collected in this volume vividly illustrate the artist's witty, humanist approach to his subjects." Pub Wkly

779.092   Photographers

McCurry, Steve

Steve McCurry; The Iconic Photographs. by Steve McCurry. Phaidon Inc Ltd 2012 chiefly color illustrations   **779.092**
1. Photography
ISBN 0714865133; 9780714865133
Pictures of the Year International Book Award, Best Photography Book Award, Judges' Special Recognition, 2012

This book, by Steve McCurry, "brings together some of the most beautiful of [his] photographs from around the world, including iconic images from Southeast Asia, Africa and Europe.New edition of a previously limited edition work." (Publisher's note)

779.2   Portrait photographs

Arbus, Diane, 1923-1971

Diane Arbus; An Aperture Monograph. by Diane Arbus.

Aperture Monograph 2012 15 p. illustrations $39.95   **779.2**
1. Photography 2. Portrait photography 3. Photography, Artistic
ISBN 1597111759; 9781597111751
LC 2013456957

This book, by Diane Arbus, first published in 1972, "offered the general public its first encounter with the breadth and power of her achievements. . . . A quarter of a century has done nothing to diminish the riveting impact of these pictures or the controversy they inspire. Arbus' photographs penetrate the psyche with all the force of a personal encounter and, in doing so, transform the way we see the world and the people in it." (Publisher's note)

779.3   Nature photographs

Malin, Gray

Beaches; Gray Malin. Harry N Abrams Inc 2016 143 p. color illustrations, color map (hardcover) $40   **779.3**
1. Beaches 2. Aerial photography
ISBN 1419720899; 9781419720895
LC 2016012939

This book, by Gray Malin, documents the work of the author, "the artist of the moment for the Hollywood and fashion elite. His . . . aerial photographs of beaches around the world are shot from doorless helicopters, creating playful and stunning celebrations of light, shape, and perspective, as well as summer bliss." (Publisher's note)

779.99   Historical photographs

Frank, Robert, 1924-

The **Americans**; by Robert Frank; introduction by Jack Kerouac. Steidl 2008 180 p. chiefly illustrations $40 **779.99**
1. Documentary photography 2. United States -- Social life and customs -- 1945-1970
ISBN 386521584X; 9783865215840

This book, by Robert Frank, was "published in France in 1958, then in the United States in 1959. . . . In 83 photographs, Frank looked beneath the surface of American life to reveal a people plagued by racism, ill-served by their politicians and rendered numb by a rapidly expanding culture of consumption. Yet he also found novel areas of beauty in simple, overlooked corners of American life." (Publisher's note)

"Preceding an exhibition that will tour U.S. galleries in 2009, this volume will no doubt introduce new generations to Frank's inimitable record of daily life fifty years ago." Pub Wkly

780   Music

The **complete** classical music guide; general editor, John Burrows with Charles Wiffen and contributions from Robert Ainsley ... [et al.] DK Pub. 2012 352 p. ill. (hc) $25 **780**
1. Music 2. Musical instruments 3. Music appreciation
ISBN 0756692563; 9780756692568
LC 2012562384

This "illustrated guide is arranged by period—'early' (ie 1000-1600), baroque, classical, romantic (with additional chapters on romantic opera and national schools) and modern. Each period is introduced by an overview, and the book opens with a general guide to classical music—its elements, instruments and performance." (Classical Music)

Forney, Kristine

★ The **enjoyment** of music; Kristine Forney, Andrew Dell-Antonio, Joseph Machlis. 13th edition W. W. Norton 2018 595 p. ill. (chiefly col.), col. maps $134.90 **780**
1. Music appreciation 2. Music -- Social aspects 3. Music -- History and criticism
ISBN 9780393639032

This book "reflects how today's students learn, listen to, and live with music. . . . It emphasizes context to show how music fits in the everyday lives of people throughout history, and connects culture, performance, and technology to the lives of students today. The new edition features . . . cultural and historical context, and in-text features that encourage and develop critical thinking skills." (Publisher's note)

Includes bibliographical references and index

★ The **Harvard** dictionary of music; edited by Don Michael Randel. 4th ed; Belknap Press 2003 978p il (Harvard University Press reference library) $39.95 **780**
1. Reference books 2. Music -- Dictionaries
ISBN 0-674-01163-5

LC 2003-58262

First published 1944 under the authorship of Willi Apel

This reference "includes entries on all the styles and forms in Western music; . . . articles on the music of Africa, Asia, Latin America, and the Near East; descriptions of instruments . . . {with} historical background, and articles that reflect today's best, including popular music, jazz, and rock." Publisher's note

Hoffman, Miles

The **NPR** classical music companion; an essential guide for enlightened listening. Houghton Mifflin 2005 306p pa $15 **780**
1. Reference books 2. Music -- Dictionaries
ISBN 978-0-618-61945-0; 0-618-61945-3

LC 2006-273343

First published 1997 with title: The NPR classical music companion: terms and concepts from A to Z

This musical guide includes This musical guide includes "entries that are at least a good-size paragraph in length and liable to include, besides technical information, historical and listener's advisory material." Booklist

Lockwood, Lewis

Beethoven: the music and the life. Norton 2002 604p il music $39.95 **780**
1. Composers
ISBN 0-393-05081-5

LC 2002-75397

The author "concentrates primarily on his subject's music and development as a composer before dedicating separate chapters to biography and the historical, political, and cultural milieus. . . . All of Lockwood's narrative, including the discussion of specific compositions, will be accessible to serious music lovers with only a modest technical background. This results partly from an interesting innovation . . . 100 additional musical examples are available on a companion web site. . . . Lockwood's study offers a new and authoritative interpretation of a prodigiously gifted and complex man and artist." Libr J

Includes bibliographical references

★ The **New** Grove dictionary of music and musicians; edited by Stanley Sadie; executive editor, John Tyrrell. 2nd ed; Oxford University Press 2004 29v set $1, 500 **780**
1. Reference books 2. Music -- Dictionaries
ISBN 978-0-19-517067-2

First published 1980 in twenty volumes to supersede Grove's dictionary of music and musicians; this edition first published 2000

"Grove is not fat, it is limitless. Whether Grove is on the reference shelf or online, teachers, students, researchers, and the common reader will find it an abiding source of satisfaction." Commonweal

Includes bibliographical references

Norton Anthology of Western Music; edited by J. Peter Burkholder and Claude V. Palisca. 7th ed. W W Norton & Co Inc 2014 883 p. pa $48.30 **780**
1. Music appreciation 2. Music -- History and criticism 3. Musical analysis 4. Music collections
ISBN 0393921611; 9780393921618

LC 2009543431

This book, edited by J. Peter Burkholder and Claude V. Palisca, "feature[s] outstanding teaching pieces that reveal the sweep of history through changing genres, styles, conventions, forms, techniques, and materials. The Seventh Edition includes new twentieth- and twenty-first-century works by Adams, Bernstein, Carter, Golijov, Higdon, Revueltas, Saariaho, Strauss, and Villa-Lobos." (Publisher's note)

★ The **Oxford** companion to music; edited by Alison Latham. Oxford Univ. Press 2002 1434p il $65 **780**
1. Reference books 2. Music -- Dictionaries 3. Musicians -- Dictionaries
ISBN 0-19-866212-2

LC 2002-537302

"Among the 8000 entries are articles on composers, theorists, and some performers; instruments, forms, and terms; subjects like electronic music, individual countries, and politics and music; and some pieces (and even some famous arias). Each entry is presented in a dictionary format, with a select index of names appended and sometimes with bibliographic references. . . . The bias is still English, but the book provides cross references to American terms and includes plenty of American composers and musical subjects. A solid reference with a grand pedigree, usefully improved for home and general library use, this is highly recommended for all public libraries." Libr J

Includes bibliographical references

Ross, Alex

Listen to this. Farrar, Straus and Giroux 2010 364p il $27; ebook $12.99 **780**
1. Musical criticism 2. Music -- History and criticism
ISBN 978-0-374-18774-3; 0-374-18774-6; 978-1-4299-7761-6 ebook; 1-4299-7761-2 ebook

LC 2010-10283

"Though the bulk of the book examines classical work both historical and contemporary, Ross veers effortlessly from Mozart to Radiohead, from Kurt Cobain to Brahms, bringing a pop fan's enthusiasm to the composers and treating the rock stars seriously as musicians. . . . The triumph of 'Listen to This' is that Ross dusts off music that's centuries old to reval the passion and brilliance that's too often hidden from a contemporary audience. It's a joy for a pop fan or a classical aficionado." N Y Times Book Rev

Includes bibliographical references

Tolan, Sandy

Children of the stone; the healing power of music in a hard land. Sandy Tolan. Bloomsbury USA 2014 453 pages chiefly col. ill., maps $28   **780**

1. Intifada, 2000- 2. Music -- Study and teaching 3. Violists -- West Bank -- Biography 4. Music -- Social aspects -- West Bank 5. Music -- Instruction and study -- West Bank 6. Refugees, Palestinian Arab -- West Bank -- Education

ISBN 1608198138; 9781608198139

LC 2014032528

Author Sandy Tolan presents this stroy of "Ramzi Hussein Aburedwan, a child from a Palestinian refugee camp, confronts an occupying army, gets an education, masters an instrument, dreams of something much bigger than himself, and then, through his charisma and persistence, inspires scores of others to work with him to make that dream real. The dream: a school to transform the lives of thousands of children--as Ramzi's life was transformed--through music." (Publisher's note)

"This is an engrossing and powerful story, moving skillfully amid the failure of the never-ending battles and 'peace' talks between Israel and Palestine and the determination of one brave young man to change his world." Booklist

Includes bibliographical references and index

Walker-Hill, Helen

From spirituals to symphonies; African-American women composers and their music. Greenwood Press 2002 401p il $94.95   **780**

1. Poets 2. Singers 3. Teachers 4. Composers 5. Violinists 6. African American women

ISBN 0-313-29947-1

LC 2001-40600

This profiles the lives and works of Undine Smith Moore, Julia Perry, Margaret Bonds, Irene Britton Smith, Dorothy Rudd Moore, Valerie Capers, Mary Watkins, and Regina Harris Baiocchi.

This is "an accessible, thoughtful, and humanist study. . . . Detailed works lists and an appendix enumerating other black women composers add reference value." Libr J

Includes bibliographical references

780.2   Miscellany; texts; treatises on music scores and recordings

Calamar, Gary

Record store days; from vinyl to digital and back again. [by] Gary Calamar and Phil Gallo. Sterling 2010 238p il $19.95   **780.2**

1. Record stores 2. Music industry

ISBN 978-1-4027-7232-0

"Packed with quotes from musicians, shop owners, and fans, this volume is a treat for readers, with its inside look at the importance of vinyl in people's lives throughout the 20th century. Major vinyl shops such as Tower Records, Rhino Records, and Bleecker Bob's are profiled. Nearly every page is graced with vintage photographs and interesting sidebars filled with facts, from the format history of recorded music over the century to vinyl oddities. The authors stress the importance of record stores as community meeting places and discuss the demise of the record industry, the rise of digital music, and the comeback of vinyl thanks to bands releasing limited-edition vinyl singles." Libr J

780.26   Texts; treatises on music scores and recordings

Day, Timothy

★ **A century** of recorded music; listening to musical history. Yale Univ. Press 2000 306p il $40; pa $19   **780.26**

1. Sound recordings -- History 2. Music -- History and criticism 3. Sound -- Recording and Reproducing -- History

ISBN 0-300-08442-0; 0-300-09401-9 pa

LC 00-43490

This work provides a "narrative of the evolution of recording from cylinders (1887), shellac discs, and acoustic rerecording through the reproducing piano, electrical amplifications (1925), and magnetic tape to the long-playing record (1948) and compact disc of the 1980s. Day also discusses studio practices and the emergence of influential record producers, the role of radio and recordings in creating a mass audience, the expansion of recorded repertoire, and new ways to experience music. Recommended for all music collections." Choice

Includes bibliographical references

780.3   Music dictionaries

Bourne, Joyce

The **Oxford** Dictionary of Music; Tim Rutherford-Johnson; Michael Kennedy; Joyce Bourne. Oxford Univ Pr 2012 976 p. $49.95   **780.3**

1. Music 2. Music -- Dictionaries

ISBN 0199578109; 9780199578108

This book by Tim Rutherford-Johnson, Michael Kennedy, and Joyce Bourne, "offers broad coverage of a wide range of musical categories spanning many eras, including composers, librettists, singers, orchestras, important ballets and operas, and musical instruments and their history. Over 250 new entries have been added to this [sixth] edition to expand coverage of popular music, ethnomusicology, modern and contemporary composers, music analysis, and recording technology." (Publisher's note)

780.7   Education, research, related topics; performances

Tunstall, Tricia

Changing lives; Tricia Tunstall. Norton 2012 320 p.   **780.7**

1. Conductors (Music) 2. Music -- Study and teaching 3. Music -- Instruction and study -- Venezuela 4. Music -- Instruction and study -- United States 5. Fundación del Estado para el Sistema Nacional de las Orquestas Juveniles e Infantiles de Venezuela -- History

ISBN 9780393078961

LC 2011026504

This book tells the "story of conductor . . . Gustavo Dudamel, and the music education program, El Sistema, . . . the music education program that nurtured his musical talent, first as a young violinist and then as a budding conductor under the mentorship of its founder, José Antonio Abreu. . . . No matter the location, the overarching goal of El Sistema is unwavering: to rescue children from the depredations of poverty through music." (Publisher's note)

780.866   LGBTQ musicians

Bullock, Darryl W.

★ **David** Bowie made me gay; 100 years of LGBT music.

Darryl W. Bullock. Overlook Press 2017 358 p. $35 **780.86**
1. Gay musicians 2. Popular music -- 21st century -- History and
criticism
ISBN 1468315595; 9781468315592

This book, by Darryl W. Bullock, "cover[s] the breadth of history of
recorded music by and for the LGBT community and how those records
influenced the evolution of the music we listen to today. . . . [It] uncovers
the lives of the people who made these records, and offers a lively canter through the scarcely documented history of LGBT music-makers."
(Publisher's note)

Well-researched and brimming with intrigue, Bullock's comprehensive study not only makes the work of scores of musicians sing anew; it
also demonstrates how the pendulum of acceptance can swing from era
to era. --Kirkus (October 15, 2017)

Includes bibliographical references (pages 329-351) and index.

780.89 Ethnic and national groups

Murray, Albert
The **blue** devils of Nada; a contemporary American ap-
proach to aesthetic statement. Pantheon Bks. 1996 238p $23;
pa $12 **780.89**
1. Poets 2. Artists 3. Authors 4. Singers 5. Pianists 6.
Composers 7. Novelists 8. Blues music 9. Jazz musicians 10.
African American arts 11. Band leaders 12. Trumpet players 13.
Short story writers 14. Nobel laureates for literature
ISBN 0-679-44213-8; 0-679-75859-3 pa
LC 95-23331

In these essays Murray "presents Louis Armstrong, Count Basie,
Duke Ellington, painter Romare Bearden and Ernest Hemingway as
embodying, in their work and their lives, a peculiarly American strain
of existential improvisation and epic storytelling. His theme, variously
elaborated, is the effort of the engaged artist to document and give shape
to the rootlessness and chaos underlying contemporary life in general—
and African American life, in particular—in a way that transcends 'agit-
prop journalism.'" Publ Wkly

780.9 History, geographic treatment, biography

Crawford, Richard
America's musical life; a history. Norton 2000 976p il
hardcover o.p. pa $23.95 **780.9**
1. American music -- History and criticism
ISBN 0-393-04810-1; 978-0-393-32726-7 pa; 0-393-32726-4 pa
LC 99-47565

This survey of music in America covers "blues, jazz, swing, pop,
rock, hip hop . . . with economics and history as cultural backdrops. Well
researched and sensitively constructed, this is highly recommended."
Libr J

Includes bibliographical references

Music; the definitive visual history. DK Publishing. DK Publishing 2015 480 p. illustrations (some color) $24.95 **780.9**
1. Music -- History and criticism
ISBN 1465442464; 9781465442468
LC 2015667167

This book "guides readers through the progression of music since its
prehistoric beginnings. . . . Telling the story of musical developments,
era by era, linking musical theory, technology, and human genius into
the narrative, [it] profiles the lives of groundbreaking musicians from

Mozart to Elvis, takes an in-depth look at the history and function of
various instruments, and includes listening suggestions for each music
style." (Publisher's note)

Palisca, Claude V.
A **history** of Western music; J. Peter Burkholder, Donald
Jay Grout, Claude V. Palisca. 9th edition W.W. Norton & Co.
Inc. 2014 1009 p. illustrations hbk $144.85 **780.9**
1. Music -- History and criticism
ISBN 0393918297; 9780393918298
LC 2013035016

First published 1960
The authors survey the course of Western music from the ancient
world to modern atonalism and dodecaphony. They cover vocal and instrumental forms, notation, performance, music-printing, the development of instruments, and biographical information on composers.
Includes bibliographical references and index

Terkel, Studs, 1912-2008
And they all sang; adventures of an eclectic disc jockey.
New Press 2005 xxii, 301p $25.95; pa $16.95 **780.9**
1. Musicians
ISBN 978-1-59558-003-0; 1-59558-003-4; 978-1-59558-118-1
pa; 1-59558-118-9 pa
LC 2005-43866

In this "collection of 40 interviews, . . . Terkel recalls his venerable
radio program, The Wax Museum, which premiered shortly after the end
of WWII in 1945, profiling composers, entertainers and impresarios of
nearly every type of music. . . . Insightful and daring, Terkel always asks
the right questions, whether culturally or musically." Publ Wkly

780.92 Biography

Bernstein, Jamie
Famous father girl; a memoir of growing up Bernstein.
Jamie Bernstein. HarperCollins 2018 400 p. $28.99 **780.92**
1. Biography 2. Composers -- United States
ISBN 0062641352; 9780062641359

In this memoir, author Jamie Bernstein, "the oldest daughter of revered composer/conductor Leonard Bernstein[,] offers a rare look at her
father on the centennial of his birth. . . . [Jamie] mines the emotional
depths of her childhood and invites us into her family's private world.
. . . [The book] is an intimate meditation on a complex and sometimes
troubled man, the family he raised, and the music he composed that became the soundtrack to their entwined lives." (Publisher's note)

Boilen, Bob, 1953-
Your song changed my life; from Jimmy Page to St. Vincent, Smokey Robinson to Hozier, thirty-five beloved artists on
their journey and the music that inspired it. Bob Boilen. William Morrow, an imprint of HarperCollins Publishers 2016 288
p. illustrations (ebook) $15.99; (hardcover) $25.99 **780.92**
1. Radio broadcasting 2. Rock musicians -- United States --
Biography 3. Popular music -- History and criticism 4. Musicians
-- United States -- Biography 5. Radio broadcasters -- United States
-- Biography
ISBN 9780062344465; 9780062344441; 9780062344458;
9780062421296
LC 2015046110

This book, by Bob Boilen, is "an essential oral history of modern
music, told in the voices of iconic and up-and-coming musicians, in-

cluding Dave Grohl, Jimmy Page, Michael Stipe, Carrie Brownstein, Smokey Robinson, and Jeff Tweedy, among others--published in association with NPR Music." (Publisher's note)

"In this light, fun read, Boilen interviews a wide-enough range of musicians that there should be something in here for any music lover." LJ

Porter, Cecelia Hopkins

Five lives in music; women performers, composers, and impresarios from the baroque to the present. Cecelia Hopkins Porter. University of Illinois Press 2012 xiv, 244 p.p ill. (cloth: alk. paper) $45   **780.92**

1. Women composers -- Biography 2. Women musicians -- Biography 3. Composers -- Biography 4. Musicians -- Biography
ISBN 0252037014; 9780252037016

LC 2011051102

This book, by Cecelia Hopkins Porter, profiles women musicians through history. It "brings to light the private and performance lives of five remarkable women musicians and composers. . . . Porter probes each musician's social and economic status, her education and musical training, the cultural expectations within the traditions and restrictions of each woman's society, and other factors." (Publisher's note)

Includes bibliographical references (p. [229]-237) and index

781   Principles, forms, ensembles, voices, instruments

Mannes, Elena

The **power** of music; pioneering discoveries in the new science of song. foreword by Dr. Aniruddh Patel. Walker & Company 2011 263p il $26   **781**

1. Music and science 2. Music -- Psychological aspects
ISBN 978-0-8027-1996-6; 0-8027-1996-1

LC 2010-48255

An "investigation of how music affects people and other animals. Detailing a variety of scientific experiments, [the author] shows the effects of sound frequencies and vibrations on body organs and brain waves; her study culminates in documentation supporting music therapy. Mannes's intercontinental explorations range from songbird studies to infants' melodic preferences to the origins of the universe (one topic on which her discussions seem rather far-fetched if fascinating). Interviews with influential musicians such as Bobby McFerrin help lighten an otherwise rather dense text." Libr J

Includes bibliographical references.

781.1   Basic principles of music

Byrne, David, 1952-

★ **How** Music Works; David Byrne. Pgw 2012   **781.1**
ISBN 1936365537; 9781936365531

In this book, David Byrne "explores how profoundly music is shaped by its time and place, and he explains how the advent of recording technology in the twentieth century forever changed our relationship to playing, performing, and listening to music. Acting as historian and anthropologist, raconteur and social scientist, he searches for patterns." (Publisher's note)

Includes bibliographical references.

781.2   Elements of music

Piston, Walter

Counterpoint. Norton 1947 235p music $41.75   **781.2**
1. Counterpoint
ISBN 978-0-393-09728-3; 0-393-09728-5

This work covers the principles and techniques of counterpoint as represented in the works of 18th and 19th century composers

781.45   Conducting

Mauceri, John

Maestros and their music; the art and alchemy of conducting. John Mauceri. Alfred A. Knopf 2017 viii, 262 p.p illustrations (hardcover) $28.95   **781.45**

1. Conducting 2. Conductors (Music)
ISBN 9780451494030; 9780451494023

LC 2016055932

In this book author "John Mauceri brings a lifetime of experience to bear in an unprecedented, hugely informative, consistently entertaining exploration of his profession, rich with anecdotes from decades of working alongside the greatest names of the music world. . . . Mauceri makes clear that conducting is itself a composition: of legacy and tradition, techniques handed down from master to apprentice--and more than a trace of ineffable magic." (Publisher's note)

"Symphony-lovers will be thrilled with the behind-the-scenes details, and aspiring conductors will enjoy the rich industry insight. Those simply curious about how classical music happens will feel drawn in by Mauceri's palpable passion." Booklist

Includes bibliographical references (pages [247]-249) and index.

781.49   Recording of music

Milner, Greg

Perfecting sound forever; an aural history of recorded music. Faber and Faber 2009 416p il $35   **781.49**

1. Sound recordings 2. Musical perception 3. Music -- Computer programs 4. Sound -- Recording and reproducing 5. Sound -- Recording and reproducing -- History
ISBN 0-571-21165-8; 978-0-571-21165-4

LC 2008-55444

This is a history of recording music from 1915, the year in which "Thomas Edison proclaimed that he could record a live performance and reproduce it perfectly, shocking audiences who found themselves unable to tell whether what they were hearing was an Edison Diamond Disc or a flesh-and-blood musician. Today, [according to the author], the equation is reversed. Whereas Edison proposed that a real performance could be rebuilt with absolute perfection, Pro Tools and digital samplers now allow musicians and engineers to create the illusion of performances that never were. . . . [Milner asks the question]: Should a recording document reality as faithfully as possible, or should it improve upon or somehow transcend the music it records?" (Publisher's note) Index.

"The author begins in the late 19th century, tracing the evolution from Edison's invention of the phonograph to the contemporary use of digital music files. Broad in scope and steeped in detail, the book strikes a mostly well-maintained balance between the history of the technological development of recordings and the more approachable accounts of the people and events surrounding it." Kirkus

781.6 Traditions of music

Horowitz, Joseph

★ **Classical** music in America; a history of its rise and fall. W. W. Norton & Company 2005 606p il $39.95; pa. $19.95 **781.6**

1. Music -- United States
ISBN 0-393-05717-8; 9780393330557

LC 2004-27754

"As a comprehensive, convincing analysis of the contemporary dilemma, and a riveting portrait of the century and a half of events and personalities which brought it about, Mr Horowitz's account would be hard to beat." Economist

Includes bibliographical references

781.62 Folk music

American ballads and folk songs; [compiled by] John A. Lomax and Alan Lomax; with a foreword by George Lyman Kittredge. Dover Publications 1994 xxxix, 625p pa $21.95 **781.62**

1. Ballads 2. Folk music -- United States
ISBN 0-486-28276-7; 978-0-486-28276-3
First published 1934 by MacMillan

Treasury of authentic songs, many recorded on location by noted father-and-son folklorists. Music and lyrics for over 200 ballads about the railroads, mountain songs, chain gang songs, creole songs, songs about cocaine and whisky, reels, minstrel songs, songs of childhood and much more. Includes such time-honored favorites as John Henry, Goin Home, Frankie and Albert, Down in the Valley, Little Brown Jug, Alabama-Bound, Shortenin Bread, Skip to My Lou, Frog Went a-Courtin and a host of others. Notes about the origin of each melody, a bibliography and an index are included.

★ **Our** singing country; folk songs and ballads. collected and compiled by John A. Lomax and Alan Lomax; music editor, Ruth Crawford Seeger; introduction to the Dover edition by Judith Tick; includes bibliography by Harold W. Thompson. Dover 2000 pa $16.95 **781.62**

1. Ballads 2. Folk music -- United States
ISBN 978-0-486-41089-0 pa; 0-486-41089-7 pa
First published 1941 by MacMillan

This includes melodies and words for tunes from all parts of the United States. Songs include spirituals, hollers, game songs, lullabies, courting songs, chain-gang work songs, Cajun airs, breakdowns, and many more. Includes over 200 authentic folk songs and ballads.

Sandburg, Carl

The **American** songbag; [compiled by] Carl Sandburg; introduction by Garrison Keillor. Harcourt Brace Jovanovich 1990 xxix, 495p pa $35 **781.62**

1. Folk music -- United States
ISBN 978-0-15-605650-2 pa; 0-15-605650-X pa
A reissue of the title first published 1927

"Sandburg was not only a poet but also a noted collector and performer of American folk music. This anthology contains words and music to 290 songs that people have sung in the making of Americana." Publisher's note

Strom, Yale

The **book** of Klezmer; the history, the music, the folklore. A Cappella Bks. 2002 381p il music $28 **781.62**

1. Klezmer music
ISBN 1-55652-445-5

LC 2002-2701

This history of Klezmer music is divided into "four chapters: 'From King David to Duvid the Klezmer,' 'From the Enlightenment to the Holocaust,' 'Klezmer in the New World, 1880-1960,' and 'From Zev to Zorn: The Masters of the Culture.' The first appendix, 'Klezmer Memories in the Memorial Books,' is one of the most moving sections, featuring a collection of commentaries on klezmer music and musicians from hundreds of memorial books written by Holocaust survivors." Libr J

Includes discography and bibliographical references

Wade, Stephen

The **beautiful** music all around us; field recordings and the American experience. Stephen Wade. University of Illinois Press 2012 xvii, 477 p.p ill., music (Music in American life) (hardcover) $24.95 **781.62**

1. Sound recordings 2. Folk music -- United States 3. Archive of Folk Culture (U.S.) 4. Field recordings -- United States -- History 5. Folk music -- United States -- History and criticism
ISBN 0252036883; 9780252036880

LC 2011044092

This book, by Stephen Wade, is part of the "Music in American Life" series. It describes the "backstories of thirteen performances captured on Library of Congress field recordings between 1934 and 1942 in locations reaching from Southern Appalachia to the Mississippi Delta and the Great Plains. . . . Alongside loving and expert profiles of these performers and their locales and communities, Wade also untangles the histories of these iconic songs and tunes." (Publisher's note)

Includes bibliographical references (p. [423]-445) and index.

Ware, Charles Pickard

Slave songs of the United States; the complete 1867 collection of slave songs. [collected and compiled] by William Francis Allen, Charles Pickard Ware, and Lucy McKim Garrison; piano accompaniments by Irving Schlein; Peter Schlein, editor. Hal Leonard 2007 183p pa $15.95 **781.62**

1. Spirituals (Songs) 2. African American music 3. Folk music -- United States 4. Slavery -- United States -- Songs
ISBN 978-1-42342-262-4 pa; 1-42342-262-7 pa

"One of the first documentary collections of Negro folk songs was compiled in 1867 by William Francis Allen, Charles Pickard Ware and Lucy McKim Garrison. . . . This collection of 136 authentic folk songs of the Negro people revolutionized America's understanding of this music. The book, which contains spirituals, work songs, field hollers, soldier songs of Civil War days, and freedom songs, has become a classic of its kind. . . . In 1965, composer Irving Schlein created . . . piano settings for every song from the original edition. Chords for guitar have also been added to the musical notation." Publisher's note

Young, Rob

Electric Eden; unearthing Britain's visionary music. Faber and Faber 2011 664p il pa $25 **781.62**

1. Folk music -- Great Britain
ISBN 978-0-86547-856-5; 0-86547-856-2

LC 2011-01987

First published 2010 in the United Kingdom

"It is a commonplace that rock and R&B came out of the folk and blues revivals of the early 1960s, and Young shows, through enchanting storytelling and brilliant commentary, that a similar revival in England inspired the Beatles and Pink Floyd, Led Zeppelin and Traffic, Kate Bush and Talk Talk. Folklorists notated old songs and dances. Marxists put folk music forward as the true voice of the people. Composers like Benjamin Britten and Ralph Vaughan Williams devised rich neo-traditional pageantry. Today, the pioneers of the "acid folk" movement see this music as a model for their own." (Publisher's Note)

"Young's narrative slips fluidly forward, backward, and through the cracks of canonical music history. And he doesn't just stick to music; like Greil Marcus with a thirst for ancient paganism and postmodern urban theory, Young weaves a poetic, philosophical tapestry as rich and heady as the songs he champions." AV Club

Includes bibliographical references and discography

781.64   Western popular music

Bradley, Andy

House of hits; the story of Houston's Gold Star/SugarHill Recording Studios. by Andy Bradley and Roger Wood. University of Texas Press 2010 334p il (Brad and Michele Moore roots music series) $34.95   **781.64**
1. Popular music 2. Music industry 3. SugarHill Recording Studios (Firm)
ISBN 978-0-292-71919-4
LC 2009-44441

"A complete and well-annotated history of Gold Star/SugarHill, the oldest continuously operating recording studio in the U.S., the book is a trove of interesting stories and first-person narratives from many of the major players who made the records that are now an indelible part of the lexicon of American music." Houston Press

Includes bibliographical references

Broven, John

Record makers and breakers; voices of the independent rock 'n' roll pioneers. University of Illinois Press 2008 584p il $50   **781.64**
1. Popular music 2. Music industry
ISBN 978-0-252-03290-5; 0-252-03290-X
LC 2008-27204

"This volume is an engaging and exceptional history of the independent rock 'n' roll record industry from its raw regional beginnings in the 1940s with R & B and hillbilly music through its peak in the 1950s and decline in the 1960s. John Broven combines narrative history with extensive oral history material from numerous recording pioneers including Joe Bihari of Modern Records; Marshall Chess of Chess Records; Jerry Wexler, Ahmet Ertegun, and Miriam Bienstock of Atlantic Records; Sam Phillips of Sun Records; Art Rupe of Specialty Records; and many more." (Publisher's Note)

"The depth of factual detail is incredible, but it's presented in the style of a rich oral history. . . . It's a chronicle of the entrepreneurial American spirit, liberally punctuated by the creation of some of the most exciting and innovative music of all time." Record Collector

Includes bibliographical references (p. 545-556)

Chang, Jeff

Can't stop, won't stop; a history of the hip-hop generation. introduction by D.J. Kool Herc. St. Martin's Press 2005 546p il hardcover o.p. pa $16   **781.64**
1. Rap music
ISBN 0-312-30143-X; 0-312-42579-1 pa
LC 2004-56656

"A fascinating, far-reaching must for pop-music and pop-culture collections." Booklist
Includes bibliographical references, discography, and filmography

Charnas, Dan

The **big** payback; the history of the business of hip-hop. New American Library 2010 660p il $24.95   **781.64**
1. Hip-hop 2. Rap music 3. Music industry
ISBN 978-0-451-22929-8; 0-451-22929-0
LC 2010-16062

On this four-decade-long journey from the studios where the first rap records were made to the boardrooms where the big deals were inked, "The Big Payback" tallies the list of who lost and who won along the 40-year road to hip-hop's dominance.

This "history of the rap industry is a classic of music-business dirt-digging as well as a kind of pulp epic. . . . Tomorrow's Diddys should sleep with this book under their pillow." Rolling Stone

Doggett, Peter

★ **Electric** shock; from the gramophone to the iPhone: 125 years of pop music. Peter Doggett. Trafalgar Square 2017 728 p. $19.95   **781.64**
1. Popular music -- History and criticism 2. Sound -- Recording and Reproducing -- History
ISBN 0099575191; 9780099575191

This book, by Peter Doggett, "tells the story of popular music, from the birth of recording in the 1890s to the digital age, from the first pop superstars of the twentieth century to the omnipresence of music in our lives, in hit singles, ringtones and on Spotify. Over that time, popular music has transformed the world in which we live. . . . It has influenced our morals and social mores; it has transformed our attitudes towards race and gender, religion and politics." (Publisher's note)

This exhaustive work will be indispensable and go well alongside such books as Ed Ward's The History of Rock & Roll: Volume 1, 1920–1963 (2016) and Ann Powers' Good Booty (2017). --Booklist (October 15, 2017)

Includes bibliographical references and index.

The **Encyclopedia** of Country Music; the ultimate guide to the music. compiled by the staff of the Country Music Hall of Fame and Museum; edited by Paul Kingsbury, Michael McCall, and John W. Rumble with the assistance of Michael Gray and Jay Orr. 2nd ed. Oxford University Press 2012 xi, 626 p.p $65.00   **781.64**
1. Music industry 2. Country musicians 3. Folk music -- United States 4. Country music -- Encyclopedias
ISBN 0195395638; 9780195395631
LC 2010045104

This country music encyclopedia, edited by Michael McCall, John Rumble, and Paul Kingsbury, is a revised edition of the previous 1998 publication. "This . . . edition includes more than 1,200 A-Z entries covering nine decades of history and artistry. . . . Compiled by . . . experts at the Country Music Hall of Fame and Museum, the encyclopedia has been brought completely up-to-date, with new entries on the artists who have profoundly influenced country music in recent years." (Publisher's note)

Hermes, Will

Love goes to buildings on fire; five years in New York that changed music forever. Faber and Faber 2011 368p il $30   **781.64**
1. Popular music 2. Music -- New York (N.Y.)

ISBN 978-0-86547-980-7

LC 2011-08445

"New York City might have been dead broke, crime-ridden and garbage-infested in the 1970s, but the music sure was great. Bob Marley opened a club date for Bruce Springsteen, Bronx DJs stole power from streetlights to fiddle with turntables in new ways, Philip Glass drove classical purists nuts with his sweeping, hypnotic compositions, and The Fania All Stars remade salsa. Down at CBGB's, the Talking Heads were double-billed with the Ramones. New York City has been pumping out great music from Gershwin to Gaga, but veteran music writer Will Hermes shows in his episodic and idiosyncratic book, 'Love Goes to Buildings on Fire,' how 1973 through 1977 stood out as a time for innovation. Not only did the grimy time plant the seeds of hip-hop, it also fostered the highly influential scenes in jazz, Latino music, punk, disco, new wave and classical." Huffington Post

Includes bibliographical references

Houghton, Mick

Becoming Elektra; the true story of Jac Holzman's visionary record label. revised and expanded edition Jawbone 2017 390p il pa $19.95   **781.64**

1. Popular music 2. Music industry 3. Elektra Records (Firm) 4. Recording industry executives

ISBN 9781911036036

Originally published 2010

Includes "full-color reproductions of virtually every title in Elektra's catalog, themselves a revealing portrait of changing tastes and evolving consumer sophistication. Houghton's research is meticulous but he avoids the minutia that clogs many music books." Seattle Post-Intelligencer

McGourty, Allison

American epic; the first time America heard itself. by Bernard MacMahon and Allison McGourty with Elijah Wald. Touchstone 2017 279 p. illustrations (some color) (hardcover) $29.99   **781.64**

1. Popular music -- United States 2. Popular culture -- United States 3. Sound recording industry -- United States -- History 4. Popular music -- United States -- History and criticism 5. Popular culture -- United States -- History -- 20th century

ISBN 1501135600; 9781501135620; 9781501135606

LC 2016001493

This book, by Bernard MacMahon and Allison McGourty with Elijah Wald, is "the companion book to the groundbreaking PBS and BBC documentary series celebrating the pioneers and artists of American roots music--blues, gospel, folk, Cajun, Appalachian, Hawaiian, Native American--without which there would be no jazz, rock, country R&B, or hip hop today." (Publisher's note)

Includes bibliographical references (pages 275-277)

The **riot** grrrl collection; edited, with an introduction by Lisa Darms. Feminist Press 2013 362 p. illustrations (chiefly color) $34.95   **781.64**

1. Fanzines 2. Punk culture 3. Women's movement 4. Zines 5. Punk rock music -- Periodicals 6. Riot grrrl movement -- Periodicals

ISBN 1558618228; 9781558618220

LC 2013014331

"Against the backdrop of the culture wars and before the rise of the Internet or desktop publishing, the zine and music culture of the Riot Grrrl movement empowered young women across the country to speak out against sexism and oppression." This book, edited by Lisa Darms, "reproduces a sampling of the original zines, posters, and printed matter for the first time since their initial distribution in the 1980s and '90s,

and includes an original essay by Johanna Fateman." (Publisher's note)

"The writers' desperation, anger, and desire translate vividly into the 21st century and will resonate strongly with today's feminists, misfits, and punks." Pub Wkly

Includes bibliographical references

Roden, Steve

. . . i listen to the wind that obliterates my traces; music in vernacular photographs, 1880-1955. Dust-to-Digital 2011 un $50   **781.64**

1. Folk music 2. Popular music 3. Artistic photography 4. Musical instruments -- Pictorial works

ISBN 978-09817342-4-8

This volume is "compiled from the personal collection of interdisciplinary sound and visual artist Steve Roden. It contains a book of photographs of musicians mostly unknown and others related to the hearing of music. This beautifully hardbound book also contains two CDs containing 51 songs recorded between approximately 1914-1955, taken from 78s and acetates. The music ranges from the well known Bradley Kincaid's 1928 recording of 'Froggie Went A-Courtin' and Ukulele Ike's '(I'm Cryin' 'Cause I Know I'm) Losing You' to virtually unknown sides taken from home recordings. This is all annotated by a lengthy poetic essay by Roden that attempts to create a social and poetic context from the ephemeral, and is underscored by epigraphs from writers from James Agee, Joseph Roth, and William Wordsworth to Pär Lagerqvist and Gerhart Hauptmann." Allmusic.com

Seabrook, John

The **song** machine; inside the hit factory. by John Seabrook. W W Norton & Co Inc 2015 352 p. (hardcover) $26.95 **781.64**

1. Music industry 2. Popular music -- Writing and publishing 3. Music trade 4. Sound recording industry 5. Popular music -- Production and direction

ISBN 9780393241921

LC 2015022305

In this book, author John Seabrook explains that "songs are highly processed products. . . . [Through the] stories of artists like Katy Perry, Britney Spears, and Rihanna, as well as expert songsmiths like Max Martin, Stargate, Ester Dean, and Dr. Luke, [Seabrook] shows what life is like in an industry that has been catastrophically disrupted—spurring innovation, competition, intense greed, and seductive new products." (Publisher's note)

"Seabrook goes deeper into the career developments of Rihanna and Katy Perry, but most of the artists hold insignificant power within the international behemoth that this industry has become and even less control over their own musical progression. A revelatory ear - opener, as the music business remains in a state of significant flux." Kirkus

Includes bibliographical references and index

Smirnoff, Marc

The **Oxford** American book of great music writing; edited by Marc Smirnoff; foreword by Van Dyke Parks. University of Arkansas Press 2008 xxii, 421p il $34.95   **781.64**

1. Popular music -- History and criticism

ISBN 978-1-557-28887-5; 1-557-28887-9

LC 2008-26298

A collection of fifty-five essays taken from Oxford American magazine's Southern Music Issues from 1996 to 2007.

"With contributions from Nick Tosches, Robert Palmer, Robert Gordon, and Peter Guralnick, some of the top music writers, Smirnoff reminds us what good music writing is. This compilation is full of little gems, including Susan Straight's tender reminiscence of the music of Al Green, Tom Piazza's harrowing account of his encounter with bluegrass legend Jimmy Martin, and John Fergus Ryan's report of his time backstage with Jerry Lee Lewis in 1970. Also included are Jerry Wexler on Dusty Springfield, Roy Blount Jr. on Ray Charles, and John Jeremiah Sullivan on Chris Bell (of Big Star)." Booklist

Includes bibliographical references

Stanley, Bob

Yeah! Yeah! Yeah! the story of pop music from Bill Haley to Beyonce. Bob Stanley. W W Norton & Co Inc 2014 624 p. (hardcover) $29.95   **781.64**

1. Music appreciation 2. Popular music -- History and criticism
ISBN 9780393242690

LC 2014002223

This book, by Bob Stanley, is a "work of musical history, tracing the story of pop music through individual songs, bands, musical scenes, and styles from Bill Haley and the Comets . . . to Beyoncé's first megahit. . . . It covers the birth of rock, soul, R&B, punk, hip hop, indie, house, techno, and more, and it will remind you why you fell in love with pop music in the first place." (Publisher's note)

"The assemblage of irresistible, bite-size histories of top-of-the-charts stars is joyful, smart, and addictive, just like the best pop songs, and a must for music fans everywhere." Booklist

Includes bibliographical references and index

Watkins, S. Craig

★ **Hip** hop matters; politics, pop culture, and the struggle for the soul of a movement. Beacon Press 2005 295p $24.95; pa $16   **781.64**

1. Rap music
ISBN 0-8070-0982-2; 0-8070-0986-5 pa

LC 2004-24187

The author "presents a concise, clear history of the hip-hop movement in the US and uses it as a springboard for discussion of contemporary issues of politics, pop culture, and struggle." Choice

Includes bibliographical references

Westhoff, Ben

Dirty South; Outkast, Lil Wayne, Soulja Boy, and the Southern rappers who reinvented hip-hop. Chicago Review Press 2011 298p il pa $14.95   **781.64**

1. Rap music
ISBN 978-1-56976-606-4; 1-56976-606-1

LC 2010-53907

An "exploration of the musical and personal terrain of what has come to be known as the Southern sound of rap by such artists as Lil Wayne, Young Jeezy, and Ludacris. Westhoff convincingly details how Southern rap music—'party music, full of hypnotic hooks and sing-along choruses'—took over from dominant East Coast and West Coast rap styles by replacing 'normal rap structures and metaphor-heavy rhymes. . . in favor of chants, grunts and shouts.' In fact, the beauty of Westhoff's descriptions of the genre as a whole and various songs in particular will make old fans as well as newbies want to search out and play classic CDs such as OutKast's 'Aquemini' and 'Kings of Crunk' by Lil Jon. And Westhoff's personal trips to the home bases of each artist he presents show how the personalities of the artists reinforce their music." Publ Wkly

Includes bibliographical references

781.642   Country music

Jennings, Dana Andrew

Sing me back home; love, death, and country music. [by] Dana Jennings. Faber and Faber 2008 257p $24   **781.642**

1. Country music -- History and criticism
ISBN 978-0-86547-960-9; 0-86547-960-7

LC 2007-47955

This "quirky, endearing combination memoir, family history, music criticism, and love-of-place offering, made up of short, punchy chapters and sharp observations about country's appeal and how country has expressed the inchoate emotions of its largely rural following, essentiallypresents the music as the portrayal of a way of life and a way of being." Booklist

Includes discography and bibliographical references

Kagarise, Leon

Pure country; the Leon Kagarise archives 1961-1971. foreword by Robert Gordon; introduction and text by Eddie Dean. Process Media 2008 191p il $35   **781.642**

1. Country music -- Pictorial works
ISBN 978-1-93417-003-8

"Kagarise was an obsessive fan of 'real' country and bluegrass musics, and he amassed a giant collection of records, live tapes and ephemera, mostly during the 1960s. This volume collects many of the color slides he shot at a couple of outdoor venues in Maryland and Pennsylvania, and the views of this lost scene they provide is unparalleled. Well-known figures like Johnny Cash, George Jones and Skeeter Davis mix with more legendary unknowns (at least to proles), like the Stoneman family, with whom Kagarise had a special connection, and who he rates far above the Carter family in terms of sheer talent. The main text . . . provides a very boss thumbnail history of country music in the pre-modern era." Arthur

Russell, Tony

Country music originals; the legends & the lost. Oxford University Press 2007 258p il $29.95   **781.642**

1. Country music 2. Country musicians
ISBN 978-0-19-532509-6

LC 2007-8471

"Russell has accomplished a spectacular feat in that he has written a thorough reference book that is as pleasing to read as the best of narrative nonfiction." Publ Wkly

Includes bibliographical references

Zwonitzer, Mark

Will you miss me when I'm gone? the Carter Family and their legacy in American music. [by] Mark Zwonitzer with Charles Hirshberg. Simon & Schuster 2002 417p il hardcover o.p. pa $15   **781.642**

1. Carter family (Musical group)
ISBN 0-684-85763-4; 0-7432-4382-X pa

LC 2002-22395

The author "follows the Carter family's history from the 1891 birth of A.P. Carter, the musical founder, up through the late 1970s, offering background on the social, economic and technological developments that spawned American folk, country and rock music. . . . Zwonitzer writes with flair, weaving anecdotes into a compelling study that will intrigue historians and music lovers alike." Publ Wkly

781.643   Blues

Ferris, William
  Give my poor heart ease; voices of the Mississippi blues. [interviews by] William Ferris. University of North Carolina Press 2009 302p il $35   **781.643**
  1. Blues music 2. African Americans -- Mississippi
  ISBN 0-8078-3325-8; 978-0-8078-3325-4
                                                LC 2009-16647
  Ferris "presents transcriptions of stories he captured via films and recording devices from the 1960s and 1970s of Mississippi blues practitioners, preachers, and Parchman Prison inmates. The enclosed CD and DVD bring the package together with stories, blues songs, and gospel recordings. B.B. King and Willie Dixon are the most famous artists included, but the stories of desperately poor sharecroppers and ex-inmates are just as engrossing. The comprehensive bibliography is a great resource." Libr J
  Includes bibliographical references

Gioia, Ted
  Delta blues; the life and times of the Mississippi Masters who revolutionized American music. artwork by Neil Harpe. W. W. Norton 2008 449p il $27.95; pa $16.95   **781.643**
  1. Blues music
  ISBN 978-0-393-06258-8; 0-393-06258-9; 978-0-393-33750-1 pa; 0-393-33750-2 pa
                                                LC 2008-09412
  Gioia describes the "beginnings of the Delta sound with Charley Patton and former Parchman inmates Son House and Bukka White. He relates the stories of such obscure Delta artists as Tommy Johnson and Big Joe Williams before delivering the bulk of the book, which describes the lives and influences of Delta blues icons Robert Johnson, Muddy Waters, Howlin' Wolf, B.B. King, and John Lee Hooker. Gioia ends with a chapter about the rediscovery of Delta legends by rabid blues collectors during the 1960s and then oddly leaps to 1990s performers such as Chris Thomas King and Junior Kimbrough in the last few pages. . . . Though presenting little new information and not geared for the blues fanatic, this is an excellent introduction to Delta blues for the novice and the general reader." Libr J
  Includes bibliographical references

Lomax, Alan
  ★ The **land** where the blues began. New Press 2002 539p il pa $21.95   **781.643**
  1. Blues music 2. African American music 3. African Americans -- Mississippi
  ISBN 1-56584-739-3; 978-1-56584-739-2
                                                LC 2004-268632
  First published 1993 by Pantheon
  This is an account of the folklorist and musicologist's travels in the Mississippi Delta in the 1940s as he recorded the work of African American blues musicians.
  "If it were a novel, Alan Lomax's long-awaited account of his adventures in the Mississippi Delta would be called 'sprawling' and a 'must read.' . . . It is as delightful and hard to put down as any fictional epic." Booklist
  Includes bibliographical references, discography and filmography

781.646   Reggae

Bradley, Lloyd
  This is reggae music; the story of Jamaica's music. Grove Press 2001 572p il pa $17   **781.646**
  1. Reggae music
  ISBN 0-8021-3828-4
                                                LC 2001-33462
  First published 2000 in the United Kingdom with title: Brass culture: when reggae was king
  Presented "in a witty and engaging manner. . . . For enthusiasts, this book is fabulous." Libr J
  Includes bibliographical references

781.648   Electronica

Matos, Michaelangelo
  The **underground** is massive; how electronic dance music conquered America. Michaelangelo Matos. HarperCollins 2015 448 p. 16 plates; illustrations $25.99   **781.648**
  1. Dance music 2. Electronic music 3. Popular culture -- United States
  ISBN 0062271784; 9780062271785
                                                LC 2015563599
  This book, by Michaelangelo Matos, offers a "definitive chronicle of one of the hottest trends in popular culture--electronic dance music--from the noted authority covering the scene. . . . Drawing on a vast array of resources, including hundreds of interviews and a library of rare artifacts, from rave fanzines to online mailing-list archives, Matos reveals how EDM blossomed in tandem with the nascent Internet-message boards and chat lines connected partiers from town to town." (Publisher's note)

781.649   Rap

Westhoff, Ben
  Original gangstas; the untold story of Dr. Dre, Eazy-E, Ice Cube, Tupac Shakur, and the birth of West Coast rap. Ben Westhoff. Hachette Books 2016 viii, 422 p.p ill. (chiefly col.), portraits (hardcover) $28   **781.649**
  1. Rap musicians 2. Rap music -- History and criticism 3. Hip-hop -- California -- Los Angeles
  ISBN 9780316344869; 9780316383899; 9781478912767
                                                LC 2016941451
  This book, by Ben Westhoff, presents a "narrative history about the legendary group of artists at the forefront of West Coast hip-hop: Eazy-E, Dr. Dre, Ice Cube, Snoop Dogg, and Tupac Shakur. . . . [Westhoff] shows how N.W.A.'s shocking success lead to rivalries between members, record labels, and eventually a war between East Coast and West Coast factions. In the process, hip-hop burst into mainstream America . . . and became the most dominant musical movement." (Publisher's note)
  "Westhoff's impressive research makes this an invaluable overview of the musical influences and legal nightmares of West Coast rap's main players . . ." Pub Wkly
  Includes bibliographical references (pages 383-409) and index.

781.65   Jazz

Chinen, Nate

Playing changes; jazz for the new century. Nate Chinen. Pantheon Books 2018 288 p. (hard cover: alk. paper) $27.95   **781.65**

1. Jazz musicians 2. Jazz music -- History and criticism 3. Jazz -- 2001-2010 -- History and criticism 4. Jazz -- 2011-2020 -- History and criticism

ISBN 9781101870341

LC 2017058677

In this book, author Nate Chinen charts "the origins of jazz historicism and the rise of an institutional framework for the music. He traces the influence of commercialized jazz education and reflects on the implications of a globalized jazz ecology. . . . Woven throughout the book is a vibrant cast of characters--from the saxophonists Steve Coleman and Kamasi Washington to the pianists Jason Moran and Vijay Iyer to the bassist and singer Esperanza Spalding." (Publisher's note)

"Chinen's virtuoso jazz history will drive readers to listen to the music anew, or for the first time." Publishers' Weekly

Includes bibliographical references and index

Cooke, Mervyn

The chronicle of jazz; Mervyn Cooke. Oxford University Press 2013 272 p. illustrations (hardback: alk. paper) $39.95   **781.65**

1. Jazz ensembles 2. Jazz musicians 3. Jazz music -- History and criticism 4. Jazz -- Chronology 5. Jazz -- History and criticism

ISBN 0199341001; 9780199341009

LC 2013019617

This book, by Mervyn Cooke, "charts the evolution of jazz from its roots in Africa and the southern United States to the myriad urban styles heard around the world today. . . . Featuring hundreds of rare images, from record-cover artwork to pictures of live performances, each chronologically arranged section contains special box features on such topics as the unique tonal qualities of the bass clarinet, jazz clubs in Paris, personality sketches, and seminal gigs and albums." (Publisher's note)

"This handsome and attractive volume by music professor and writer Cooke covers the entire history of the jazz medium in one accessible and colorful resource." Booklist

Includes discography (pages 264-265), bibliographical references (page 266), and indexes

Giddins, Gary

Jazz; Gary Giddins & Scott DeVeaux. 2nd edition W W Norton & Co 2015 ML3508 ill., music pbk $159.05   **781.65**

1. Jazz music -- History and criticism

ISBN 0393937062; 9780393937060

LC 2014038121

"Enhanced with diagrams and references to specific recordings, the opening chapters walk the reader through some basic definitions and concepts required for critical listening. The authors write in a nonthreatening blend of academic and conversational language, gently guiding the novice toward deeper understanding while simultaneously offering the scholar opportunity for reflection. In the remainder of the book, the authors discuss jazz by period, providing rich detail and social, economic, and historical context." (Choice Reviews)

Visions of jazz; the first century. Oxford Univ. Press 1998 690p hardcover o.p. pa $18.95   **781.65**

1. Jazz musicians 2. Jazz music -- History and criticism

ISBN 0-19-513241-6 pa

LC 98-12199

"Alongside his virtuoso considerations of Ellington, Monk, Mingus, and the predictable greats, Giddins illuminates the contributions to be found in the likes of Al Jolson's minstrel posing and Stan Kenton's florid kitsch. His writing, like the music he loves, is joyously polyphonic, with history, legend, musicology, biography, and performance all rising out of the mix." New Yorker

Weather bird; jazz at the dawn of its second century. Gary Giddins. Oxford University Press 2004 xxiv, 632p $35 **781.65**

1. Jazz music -- History and criticism

ISBN 0-19-515607-2

LC 2004-654

"This book collects more than 140 essays, articles, and reviews that Giddins wrote from 1990 to November 2003. . . . The breadth and depth of his knowledge is extremely impressive, his ear is astounding, and his masterly style routinely achieves the near impossible in writing engagingly about something that inherently eludes description." Libr J

Gioia, Ted

The history of jazz; 2nd ed.; Oxford University Press 2011 444p il pa $19.95   **781.65**

1. Jazz music -- History and criticism

ISBN 978-0-19-539970-7; 0-19-539970-6

LC 2010-23182

First published 1997

The author "relates the story of African American music from its roots in Africa to the international respect it enjoys today. . . . This well-researched, extensively annotated volume covers the major trends and personalities that have shaped jazz. The excellent bibliography and list of recommended listening make this a valuable purchase for libraries building a jazz collection." Libr J

Includes discography and bibliographical references

Kahn, Ashley

The house that Trane built; the story of Impulse Records. Norton 2006 338p il $29.95   **781.65**

1. Jazz music 2. Jazz musicians 3. Saxophonists 4. Impulse Records (Firm)

ISBN 0-393-05879-4

LC 2005-037218

The author "offers a fascinating insider's view of the sessions that produced not only Coltrane's classics but also top-grade albums by both fiery radicals and such timeless stars as Duke Ellington, Coleman Hawkins and Benny Carter." Economist

Marsalis, Wynton, 1961-

Moving to higher ground; how jazz can change your life. [by] Wynton Marsalis with Geoffrey C. Ward. Random House 2008 181p il   **781.65**

1. Jazz music -- History and criticism

ISBN 1400060788; 9781400060788

LC 2008-16560

The author "explains in lay readers' terms how jazz works as a diverse musical genre and, more important, how an understanding and appreciation of jazz can enrich one's life. . . . This work is highly recommended." Libr J

Morgenstern, Dan

Living with jazz; a reader. edited by Sheldon Meyer. Pantheon Books 2004 712p $35   **781.65**

1. Jazz music -- History and criticism

ISBN 0-375-42072-X

LC 2004-43432

This is a compilation of "nearly half a century of Morgenstern's profiles, liner notes, record and show reviews and other musings. . . . Morgenstern reminisces about his introduction to jazz in a brief opening memoir, then segues into lengthy sections on his greatest heroes, Louis Armstrong and Duke Ellington. . . . His exuberant characterizations make this monumental volume a stimulating guide to jazz in the second half of the 20th century." Publ Wkly

Myers, Marc

Why jazz happened; Marc Myers. University of California Press 2013 267 p. (hardcover) $34.95   **781.65**
  1. Jazz music -- History and criticism   2. Jazz -- History and criticism
ISBN 0520268784; 9780520268784

LC 2012022218

This book, by Marc Myers, offers a "social history of jazz. It provides a . . . look at the many forces that shaped this most American of art forms and the many influences that gave rise to jazz's post-war styles. . . . This book views jazz's evolution through the prism of technological advances, social transformations, changes in the law, economic trends, and much more." (Publisher's note)
Includes bibliographical references and index

Sandke, Randall

Where the dark and the light folks meet; race and the mythology, politics, and business of jazz. Scarecrow Press 2010 277p (Studies in jazz) $40; ebook $40   **781.65**
  1. Jazz music -- History and criticism
ISBN 0-8108-6652-8; 0-8108-6990-X ebook; 978-0-8108-6652-2; 978-0-8108-6990-5 ebook

LC 2009-37977

The author "tackles a controversial question: Is jazz the product of an insulated African-American environment, shut off from the rest of society by strictures of segregation and discrimination, or is it more properly understood as the juncture of a wide variety of influences under the broader umbrella of American culture?" Publisher's note
Includes bibliographical references

Torgoff, Martin

Bop apocalypse; jazz, race, the beats & drugs. Martin Torgoff. Da Capo Press 2016 320 p. illustrations (hardcover) $25.99   **781.65**
  1. Beat generation   2. Drugs -- Social aspects   3. Jazz music -- History and criticism   4. Jazz -- History and criticism   5. Jazz musicians -- United States   6. Music and race -- United States -- History -- 20th century   7. Drugs -- Social aspects -- United States -- History -- 20th century
ISBN 9780306824753

LC 2016015902

This book, by Martin Torgoff, "details the rise of early drug culture in America by weaving together the disparate elements that formed this new and revolutionary segment of the American social fabric. . . . [It] is also a living history that teaches us much about the conflicts and questions surrounding drugs today, casting many contemporary issues in a new light by connecting them back to the events of this transformative era." (Publisher's note)
"A textured story of human hope and hopelessness, of artistry that blossomed in the most daunting and, in some cases, demeaning circumstances." Kirkus
Includes bibliographical references and index

Ward, Geoffrey C.

Jazz; a history of America's music. based on a documentary film by Ken Burns written by Geoffrey C. Ward; with a preface by Ken Burns. Knopf 2000 489p il $65; pa $29.95   **781.65**
  1. Jazz music
ISBN 0-679-44551-X; 0-679-76539-5 pa

LC 00-22604

The authors "have assembled a comprehensive history with a focus on the musicians and the sociology of jazz. . . . The short articles by Wynton Marsalis, Dan Morgenstern, Gerald Early, Stanley Crouch, and Gary Giddins, which are woven into the text, provide a . . . specific focus on a number of jazz's aspects." Libr J
Includes bibliographical references

781.66   Rock (Rock 'n' roll)

Almond, Steve

Rock and roll will save your life; a book by and for the fanatics among us (with bitchin' soundtrack) Random House 2010 216p $23   **781.66**
  1. Rock music -- History and criticism   2. Popular music -- History and criticism
ISBN 978-1-4000-6620-9; 1-4000-6620-4

"As a young writer plagued by self-doubt, Almond reveled in the emotional escape of music; the joy of his fanaticism is conveyed poignantly—and so completely—that we're infected with his touted salvation too. With well-placed 'interludes' or 'reluctant exegeses,' Almond peppers his pages with biting insights and funny vignettes; dismissing, for instance, Toto's 'Africa' as '. . . the lovechild of Muzak and Imperialism.' Though the language feels a bit highbrow, Almond ultimately crafts a playful and intelligent read." Paste

Browne, David

Fire and rain; the Beatles, Simon & Garfunkel, James Taylor, CSNY, and the lost story of 1970. Da Capo Press 2011 369p il $26   **781.66**
  1. Singers   2. Rock music   3. Beatles   4. Songwriters   5. Simon and Garfunkel   6. Rock music -- History and criticism   7. Crosby, Stills and Nash (Musical group)   8. Crosby, Stills, Nash and Young (Musical group)
ISBN 9780306818509; 0-306-81850-7

"Browne skillfully interleaves the stories of these musicians during this tumultuous year, making room for substantial walk-ons by other significant industry figures like Bill Graham, Peter Yarrow, Phil Spector, Rita Coolidge, Carole King and Joni Mitchell. Intimately familiar with the music, fully comprehending the cross-pollination among the artists, thoroughly awake to the dynamics of the decade's last gasp, the author expertly captures a volatile and hugely interesting moment in rock history." Kirkus
Includes bibliographical references

Buckland, Gail

Who shot rock & roll; a photographic history, 1955 to the present. Alfred A. Knopf 2009 319p il $40   **781.66**
  1. Rock music -- Pictorial works
ISBN 978-0-307-27016-0; 0-307-27016-5

LC 2009-19122

"Here are nearly 300 iconic photographs by those photographers who understood the power of the image in the formation and sustenance of rock-and-roll culture from 1955 onward. The care with which Buckland selects representative photographers and their most significant images is matched by her interpretive prowess. . . . [She] carefully but deliberately argues that the art of rock photography has been sacrificed to the paparazzi and corporate art departments. In light of this inclusive, heady and visceral collection of the genre's best, it would be hard to argue otherwise." Publ Wkly

Includes bibliographical references

Burmeister, Dennis

★ **Depeche** Mode; monument. Dennis Burmeister & Sascha Lange; translated from the German by Lucy Jones. Akashic Books 2017 432 p. (hardcover) $59.95   **781.66**

1. Biography 2. Rock music 3. Bands (Music) 4. Rock groups 5. Depeche Mode (Musical group)
ISBN 1617755931; 9781617755934; 9781617755972

LC 2017935221

In this book, Dennis Burmeister and Sascha Lange, illustrate "the success story [of the band] that began in 1981 and is still going strong after 100 million album sales. This book contains: information on all of the band's releases from 1981 to 2017; over a thousand images, including never-before-seen photos, concert posters, and album artwork; a special look at fan culture; interviews with stage managers, friends, producers, tour companions, radio hosts, and fans." (Publisher's note)

Includes bibliographical references (pages 431-432) and discography.

Cohen, Mitchell

All These Things That I've Done; My Insane, Improbable Rock Life. Matt Pinfield; Mitchell Cohen. Simon & Schuster 2016 272 p. illustrations $25   **781.66**

1. Rock music 2. Specialists
ISBN 1476793891; 9781476793894

LC 2016024686

In this book by Matt Pinfield with Mitchell Cohen, "Pinfield offers the ultimate music fan's memoir, a chronicle of the songs and artists that inspired his improbable career alongside some of the all-time greats, from The Beatles to KISS to U2 to The Killers. . . . Pinfield shares his five decades of stories from the front lines of rock and roll, exploring how . . . he became a sought-after reporter, unlikely celebrity, and the last word in popular music." (Publisher's note)

"His own recurring struggles with addiction flesh out the narrative, grounding his enthusiasm for music in an awareness of the somber side of the rock lifestyle. His encyclopedic knowledge of contemporary sounds makes the memoir as informative as it is personal." Pub Wkly

Cutler, Sam

You can't always get what you want; my life with the Rolling Stones, the Grateful Dead and other wonderful retrobates. ECW Press 2010 326p il pa $17.95   **781.66**

1. Rock music 2. Rolling Stones 3. Grateful Dead (Musical group)
ISBN 978-1-55022-932-5
First published 2008 in Australia
"Effortlessly readable, packed with entertaining, sleazy, behind-the-scenes tales. " Portland Mercury

German, Bill

Under their thumb; how a nice boy from Brooklyn got mixed up with the Rolling Stones (and lived to tell about it) Villard Books 2009 354p il $25   **781.66**

1. Rolling Stones
ISBN 978-1-4000-6622-3; 1-4000-6622-0

LC 2008-45533

"The epic tale of an obsessive teenager who launched a Rolling Stones fanzine and spent the next two decades capturing the band's

whirlwind metamorphosis from behind the scenes. . . . First-rate, first-hand account of the world's greatest rock 'n' roll band, and a disenchanted chronicle of its increasingly crass commercialization." Kirkus

Gruen, Bob

New York Dolls; the photographs of Bob Gruen. introduction by Lenny Kaye; featuring commentary by David Johansen and Sylvain Sylvain and quotes collected by Legs McNeil; afterword by Morrissey. Abrams Image 2008 158p il $24.95   **781.66**

1. Rock musicians 2. New York Dolls (Musical group)
ISBN 978-0-8109-7271-1; 0-8109-7271-9

LC 2008-13074

"Gruen met singer David Johansen, guitarists Johnny Thunders and Sylvain Sylvain, drummer Jerry Nolan and bassist Arthur 'Killer' Kane at the beginning of 1973, months after the untimely death of original drummer Billy Murcia. The book chronicles the glam-rock band's career over 230 photographs, only 30 of which have previously been seen by the public. The last picture in the book is of their 2004 reunion in London. Lenny Kaye wrote the book's foreword and interviewed the group's surviving members, Johansen and Sylvain Sylvain." Rolling Stone

Heller, Jason

Strange stars; David Bowie, pop music, and the decade sci-fi exploded. Jason Heller. Melville House Publishing 2018 xiv, 254 p.p $25.99   **781.66**

1. Popular culture 2. Popular music -- History and criticism 3. Science fiction in music 4. Popular music -- 1971-1980 -- History and criticism
ISBN 1612196977; 9781612196978

LC 2018013060

In this book, "Jason Heller recasts sci-fi and pop music as parallel cultural forces that depended on one another to expand the horizons of books, music, and out-of-this-world imagery. In doing so, he presents a whole generation of revered musicians as the sci-fi-obsessed conjurers they really were: from Sun Ra lecturing on the black man in the cosmos, to Pink Floyd jamming live over the broadcast of the Apollo 11 moon landing." (Publisher's note)

"The accessible title will have readers scouring local bookstores for old sf classics and used record bins for long-forgotten LPs such as Colonel Elliott & The Lunatics' Interstellar Reggae Drive (1973) and Zed's Visions of Dune (1979)." LJ

Includes bibliographical references, discographies (pages 237-2244) and index

Hepworth, David

Uncommon people; the rise and fall of the rock stars. David Hepworth. Henry Holt & Co. 2017 xii, 305 p.p illustrations (some color) (hardcover) $30   **781.66**

1. Biography 2. Rock musicians -- Biography 3. Rock music -- History and criticism
ISBN 9781250124135; 9781250124128; 1250124123

LC 2017036561

This book, by David Hepworth, is "an elegy to the age of the Rock Star, featuring Chuck Berry, Elvis, Madonna, Bowie, Prince, and more, uncommon people whose lives were transformed by rock and who, in turn, shaped our culture. . . . [It] zeroes in on defining moments and turning points in the lives of forty rock stars from 1955 to 1995, taking us on a journey to burst a hundred myths and create a hundred more." (Publisher's note)

"Hepworth perceptively shows how our notion of a rock star evolved over the years, as did the music itself. Despite its death-of-an-era theme, the book is really an enthusiastic, even passionate, celebration of rock stars and their music." Booklist

Includes bibliographical references (pages [283]-285) and index.

Hyden, Steven

Twilight of the gods; a journey to the end of classic rock. Steven Hyden. HarperCollins 2018 320 p. $25.99   **781.66**

1. Rock music -- Social aspects 2. Rock music -- History and criticism

ISBN 0062657127; 9780062657121

In this book, author Steven Hyden, "offers an eye-opening exploration of the state of classic rock, its past and future, the impact it has had, and what its loss would mean to an industry, a culture, and a way of life. . . . In this mix of personal memoir, criticism, and journalism, Hyden stands witness as classic rock reaches the precipice. . . . [Hyden also celebrates] his love of this incredible music that has taken him from adolescence to fatherhood." (Publisher's note)

Lang, Michael

The **road** to Woodstock; with Holly George-Warren. Ecco 2009 304p il $29.99   **781.66**

1. Woodstock Festival, 1969

ISBN 978-0-06-157655-3; 0-06-157655-7

"The author is a generous raconteur with a good memory for specifics, but what elevates this book above the level of most rock memoirs is the inclusion of voices other than Lang's—including scenesters and key Woodstock players like Jimi Hendrix, Roger Daltrey, Pete Townshend, Jerry Garcia, Abbie Hoffman, John Sebastian, Greil Marcus and Wavy Gravy. . . . Well-written, informative and tons of fun, Lang's book will be appreciated by rockers and musicologists of all ages." Kirkus

Includes bibliographical references

Margotin, Philippe

All the Songs; The Story Behind Every Beatles Release. Jean-Michel Guesdon & Philippe Margotin; preface by Patti Smith; Scott Freiman, consulting editor. Black Dog & Leventhal Pub 2013 672 p. ill, portraits (chiefly color) $50   **781.66**

1. Beatles

ISBN 1579129528; 9781579129521

In this book, by Philippe Margotin and Jean-Michel Guesdon, "every album and every song ever released by the Beatles—from 'Please Please Me' to 'The Long and Winding Road'—is dissected, discussed, and analyzed. . . . Here, we learn that one of John Lennon's favorite guitars was a 1958 Rickenbacker 325 Capri. . . . We also learn that 'Love Me Do,' recorded in Abbey Road Studios in September 1962, took 18 takes to get right, even though it was one of the first songs John and Paul ever wrote together." (Publisher's note)

"Arranged chronologically by album, the book includes for each song basic information (songwriter, track length, number of takes, etc.), a brief discussion of how it was written and recorded, and an overall assessment. . . . [N]umerous anecdotes and quotations from the group keep the book entertaining and accessible even to more casual music fans." LJ

Includes bibliographical references, discography, and indexes

The **Rolling** Stones; all the songs: the story behind every track. Philippe Margotin and Jean-Michel Guesdon; translation by Richard George Elliott. First English edition Black Dog & Leventhal Publishers 2016 703 p. illustrations (some color) (hardcover) $50   **781.66**

1. Rock music 2. Music -- Discography 3. Rolling Stones (Performer) 4. Rolling Stones 5. Rock music -- England -- History and criticism

ISBN 0316317748; 9780316432733; 9780316317740
    LC 2016564656

In this book, authors Margotin and Guesdon describe the origin of the Rolling Stones's "340 released songs, details from the recording studio, what instruments were used, and behind-the-scenes stories of the great artists who contributed to their tracks. . . . [It] begins with their 1963 eponymous debut album recorded over five days at the Regent Studio in London; through their collaboration with legendary producer Jimmy Miller . . . , [and] to their later work with Don Was." (Publisher's note)

"Like their similar books on Dylan and the Beatles, this is an entertaining reference source of music trivia and a must for the circulating collections of most public and academic libraries." Booklist

Includes bibliographical references (pages 702-703), discography, and index.

Marshall, Jim

Trust; photographs of Jim Marshall. Omnibus Press 2009 165p il $39.95   **781.66**

1. Rock music -- Pictorial works

ISBN 978-1-84772-110-5; 1-84772-110-9

Jim Marshall "devoted himself to photographing musicians. But more than just taking pictures, Marshall had a knack for capturing moments, snapshots of when the music and the individual collided, which, in turn, revealed something special or private about the artist. His pictures were often windows into the souls of those who were so revered but not always understood. . . . Dr. John sits backstage in full concert regalia, beside him a shrunken human head. Bob Dylan and Johnny Cash casually chat on the set of The Johnny Cash Show. John Coltrane looks contemplative in the backyard of his Queens, NY home. The vast majority of pictures in Trust are split among jazz, blues, and '60s rock and roll. . . . The photographs are paired with short anecdotes about the artists or stories about the images, and in doing this, Marshall lends just enough of his own story to the pictures he presents. But largely, it is Marshall's body of work that does the talking, and, in that, these photographs are revelatory." Under the Radar

McCain, Gillian

Please kill me; the uncensored oral history of punk. edited by Legs McNeil and Gillian McCain. Grove Press 2016 476 p. illustrations (ebook) $16.99; $17   **781.66**

1. Punk culture 2. Punk rock music

ISBN 9780802192769; 0802125360; 9780802125361
    LC 2016032784

Punk rock began in the United States "in the '60s with bands like the Velvet Underground and Iggy and the Stooges. McNeil and McCain {aim to} chronicle punk rock history through hundreds of interviews with the people who . . . lived it. . . . {They have} interviewed members of . . . bands like the Dictators, Television, Richard Hell and the Voidoids, and Johnny Thunder's Heartbreakers, as well as . . . the Ramones, Blondie, and the Patti Smith Group." (Booklist)

"An essential accompaniment to the first, still-thrilling punk records, this preposterously entertaining document just reeks with all the brilliance and filth of the Blank Generation." Kirkus

Includes bibliographical references (pages 475-476).

McKeen, William

Everybody had an ocean; music and mayhem in 1960s Los Angeles. William McKeen. Chicago Review Press 2017 x, 422 p.p (cloth: alk. paper) $26.99   **781.66**

1. Rock music 2. Los Angeles (Calif.) -- History 3. Music -- United States 4. Popular music -- 1961-1970 5. Music -- History & criticism 6. Rock music -- California -- Los Angeles -- 1961-1970

-- History and criticism
ISBN 9781613734940; 9781613734919

LC 2016029172

This book, by William McKeen, "chronicles the migration of the rock 'n' roll business to Southern California and how the artists flourished there. The cast of characters is astonishing—Brian and Dennis Wilson of the Beach Boys, Jan and Dean, eccentric producer Phil Spector, Cass Elliot, Sam Cooke, Ike and Tina Turner, Joni Mitchell, and scores of others—and their stories form a modern epic of the battles between innocence and cynicism, joy and terror." (Publisher's note)

"Using a synthesis of memoirs and biographies, McKeen creates a sprawling, entertaining, and sometime lurid, narrative about artists who, bursting with creative energy, converged in L.A." Booklist

Includes bibliographical references (pages 391-398), discography (pages 399-407), and index.

McMurray, Jacob

Taking punk to the masses; from nowhere to Nevermind; a visual history from the permanent collection of Experience Music Project. Fantagraphics Books 2011 253p il pa $29.99   **781.66**

1. Punk rock music

ISBN 978-1-60699-433-7

This volume "visually documents the explosion of Grunge, the Seattle Sound, within the context of the underground punk subculture that was developing throughout the U.S. in the late 1970s and 1980s. This musical journey is represented entirely through the collection of Experience Music Project, Seattle's museum of music and popular culture . . . . Featuring over 100 key artifacts from EMP's collection, Taking Punk to the Masses illustrates the evolution of punk rock from underground subculture to mainstream embrace." Publisher's note

Mohr, Tim

Burning down the Haus; punk rock, revolution, and the fall of the Berlin Wall. by Tim Mohr. Algonquin Books of Chapel Hill 2018 384 p. illustrations $28.95   **781.66**

1. Germany -- History 2. Punk culture -- History 3. Punk rock music -- History 4. Berlin (Germany) -- Social conditions -- 20th century 5. Berlin (Germany) -- Social life and customs -- 20th century 6. Punk culture -- Germany -- Berlin -- History -- 20th century 7. Punk rock music -- Social aspects -- Germany -- Berlin -- History -- 20th century

ISBN 9781616208431

LC 2018010846

This book, by Tim Mohr, "details the rebellious youth movement that helped change the world. It began with a handful of East Berlin teens who heard the Sex Pistols on a British military radio broadcast to troops in West Berlin, and it ended with the collapse of the East German dictatorship. Punk rock was a life-changing discovery. The buzz-saw guitars, the messed-up clothing and hair, the rejection of society and the DIY approach to building a new one." (Publisher's note)

"Mohr tells a frantic and exciting true story of music versus dictatorship, and the infamous wall it helped bring down." Booklist

Includes bibliographical references

Moore, Thurston

No wave; post-punk, underground, New York, 1976-1980. by Thurston Moore and Byron Coley; introduction by Lydia Lunch. Abrams Image 2008 143p il $24.95   **781.66**

1. Punk rock music 2. Experimental music

ISBN 978-0-8109-9543-7; 0-8109-9543-3

LC 2007-34093

"A treasure trove of rare photographs and oral history of a fleeting moment of New York underground that continues to reverberate 30 years later." Booklist

Reynolds, Simon

Shock and awe; glam rock and its legacy, from the seventies to the twenty-first century. Simon Reynolds. HarperCollins 2016 704 p. ill. (some color), portraits (ebook) $17.99; $18.99   **781.66**

1. Glam rock music 2. Glam rock musicians

ISBN 9780062279811; 0062279807; 9780062279804

LC 2016045701

In this book on glam rock, author Simon Reynolds "takes you on a wild cultural tour through the early Seventies, a period packed with glitzy costumes and alien make-up, thrilling music and larger-than-life personas. . . . [He] offers a fresh, in-depth look at the glam and glitter phenomenon, placing it in the wider Seventies context of social upheaval and political disillusion." (Publisher's note)

"For neo-glamsters, a blueprint for how to get things done; for oldsters, a nostalgic look into a shining, glittery era." Kirkus

Includes bibliographical references (pages 657-664) and index.

Richardson, Peter

No simple highway; a cultural history of the Grateful Dead. Peter Richardson. St. Martin's Press 2015 373 p. 16 plates; ills.; portraits (hardback) $26.99   **781.66**

1. Rock music 2. Grateful Dead (Musical group) 3. Rock musicians -- United States -- Biography 4. Rock music -- Social aspects

ISBN 1250010624; 9781250010629

LC 2014036345

This book on the rock band the Grateful Dead, by Peter Richardson, "vividly recounts the Dead's colorful history, adding new insight into everything from the Acid Tests to the band's formation of their own record label to their massive late career success, while probing the riddle of the Dead's vast and durable appeal." (Publisher's note)

Includes bibliographical references (pages 339-353) and index

Robb, John

Punk rock; an oral history. John Robb; edited by Oliver Craske; introduction by Henry Rollins. PM 2012 xv, 562 p.p illustrations $19.95   **781.66**

1. Punk culture 2. Punk rock music 3. Rock musicians -- Anecdotes 4. Punk rock musicians -- Anecdotes 5. Punk rock music -- History and criticism

ISBN 1604860057; 9781604860054

LC 2011939680

Author John Robb presents a history of punk rock music. "John Robb talks to many of those who cultivated the movement, such as John Lydon, Lemmy, Siouxsie Sioux, Mick Jones, Chrissie Hynde, Malcolm McLaren, Henry Rollins, and Glen Matlock, weaving together their accounts to create a . . . history of UK punk. . . . Over 150 interviews" are presented from groups like The Clash, the Stranglers, and The Sex Pistols on the period's "roots in the late 1960s to its enduring influence on the bands, fashion, and culture of today" are presented. (Publisher's note)

Russell, Ethan A.

Let it bleed; the Rolling Stones, Altamont, and the end of the sixties. Ethan A. Russell, with Gerard Van der Leun. Springboard Press 2009 239p il $35   **781.66**

1. Rolling Stones 2. Altamont Festival

ISBN 978-0-446-53904-3

LC 2008-53229

"In 1969, Russell was one of 16 people and the only photographer to join the Rolling Stones on their tour of America. . . . Russell's 200-plus photos, most in stark and clear black and white, range from the band rehearsing and relaxing in a bucolic setting before the tour to Mick Jagger in front of a mirror applying makeup to a closeup of Keith Richards intensely tuning up. Wide onstage shots illustrate the band's relationship with their adoring public. Including interviews and comments from many of the members of the touring group and a haunting narrative of the desolation at Altamont, Russell, with Van Der Leun . . . presents a definitive and authoritative picture of the Stones." Libr J

Savage, Jon

★ **1966**; The Year the Decade Exploded. by Jon Savage. Faber & Faber 2016 620 p. illustrations $29.95   **781.66**
    1. Popular culture 2. Nineteen sixties 3. Rock music -- 1961-1970 -- History and criticism.
    ISBN 0571277624; 9780571277629

In this book, by Jon Savage, the "pop world accelerated and broke through the sound barrier in 1966. In America, in London, in Amsterdam, in Paris, revolutionary ideas slow-cooking since the late '50s reached boiling point. . . . A unique chemistry of ideas, substances, freedom of expression and dialogue across pop cultural continents created a landscape of immense and eventually shattering creativity." (Publisher's note)

Turman, Katherine

Louder Than Hell; The Definitive Oral History of Metal. By Jon Wiederhorn and Katherine Turman. HarperCollins 2013 736 p. $32.50   **781.66**
    1. Rock musicians 2. Heavy metal (Music)
    ISBN 006195828X; 9780061958281

Written by Jon Wiederhorn and Katherine Turman, this book is an "oral history of heavy metal," which "includes hundreds of interviews with the giants of the movement, conducted over the past 25 years." It "features more than 250 interviews with some of the biggest bands in metal, including Black Sabbath, Metallica, Megadeth, Anthrax, Slayer, Iron Maiden, Judas Priest, Spinal Tap, Pantera, White Zombie, Slipknot, and Twisted Sister." (Publisher's note)

Victor, Adam

The **Elvis** encyclopedia. Overlook Duckworth 2008 598p il $65   **781.66**
    1. Actors 2. Singers 3. Rock musicians
    ISBN 978-1-58567-598-2; 1-58567-598-9

An alphabetical compendium of topics related to Elvis Presley. Includes personal and place names, movie and song titles, events, and general subjects.

"This obsessively detailed and completely entertaining chronicle . . . of every possible aspect of Elvis Preley's life is mesmerizing and deserves a wide audience." Publ Wkly

Waksman, Steve

This ain't the summer of love; conflict and crossover in heavy metal and punk. University of California Press 2009 408p   **781.66**
    1. Punk rock music 2. Heavy metal (Music)
    ISBN 0520253108; 0520257170; 9780520253100; 9780520257177

LC 2008025957

This survey of heavy metal and punk music "begins on the cusp of the '70s with the colossal arena performances of Grand Funk Rail-

road, setting up the relationship between performer and (in this case, enormous) audience, which is an ongoing point of reference. From here, Waksman uses subsequent artists to deconstruct the rock concert, moving through the performative stage antics of Alice Cooper and Iggy Pop, to the metal and hardcore bands of the early '80s. . . . The number of fanzines and interviews cited is evidence that this is a comprehensively and enthusiastically researched book. As a critical study it provides an original critique of both the genres involved, and of genre itself; the only flipside is that this ends up playing second fiddle to a damn good story." PopMatters

Includes discography and bibliographical references

Wald, Elijah

Dylan Goes Electric! Newport, Seeger, Dylan, and the Night That Split the Sixties. Elijah Wald. HarperCollins 2015 256 p. 8 plates; illustrations $26.99   **781.66**
    1. Music festivals -- Rhode Island -- Newport
    ISBN 0062366688; 9780062366689

This book, by Elijah Wald, analyzes "the day [musician Bob] Dylan 'went electric' at the Newport Folk Festival, timed to coincide with the event's fiftieth anniversary. . . . Elijah Wald explores the cultural, political and historical context of this seminal event that embodies the transformative decade that was the sixties." (Publisher's note)

"Some of this material has been covered before, but rarely has it been done so knowingly, lovingly, and felicitously. All the players, too, are here (Joan Baez, Dave Van Ronk, Johnny Cash, et al.), and, though nostalgic, the book makes a major contribution to modern musical history." Booklist

Wenner, Jann S.

50 years of Rolling Stone; Introduction by Jann S. Wenner; edited by Jodi Peckman and Joe Levy. Abrams 2017 283 p. illustrations (some color) (hbk.) $65   **781.66**
    1. Popular culture 2. Rock music -- History and criticism 3. Rock music -- Periodicals -- History 4. Rolling stone (San Francisco, Calif.) 5. Journalism -- United States -- History -- 20th century 6. Journalism -- United States -- History -- 21st century 7. Popular culture -- United States -- History -- 20th century 8. Popular culture -- United States -- History -- 21st century
    ISBN 9781683350200; 1419724460; 9781419724466

LC 2016943558

This book, with introduction by Jann S. Wenner, "documents . . . ['Rolling Stone's'] rise to prominence as the voice of rock and roll and a leading showcase for era-defining photography. From the 1960s to the present day, the book offers a decade-by-decade exploration of American music and history. Interviews with rock legends . . . and other leading image-makers" (Publisher's note).

"This gorgeous, large-scale coffee-table book is organized chronologically and includes iconic images of a vast panoply of the giants of the arts, excerpts from famous interviews and pieces, and current reflections and background context on some of the magazine's most memorable stories, with topics ranging from musicians and society to presidential campaigns, the early years of the AIDS epidemic, and the dangers of climate change." LJ

Yarm, Mark

Everybody loves our town; an oral history of Grunge. Crown Archetype 2011 567p il $25; ebook $12.99   **781.66**
    1. Rock music -- History and criticism
    ISBN 978-0-307-46443-9; 978-0-307-46445-3 ebook

LC 2011009192

A tribute to the Pacific Northwest's grunge genre draws on the observations of individuals at the forefront of the movement from Soundgarden and the Melvins to Nirvana and Pearl Jam, citing such influences as the rise of Seattle's Sub Pop record label and the death of Kurt Cobain.

"Yarm's affectionate, gossipy, detailed look at the highs and lows of the contemporary Seattle music scene is one of the most essential rock books of recent years." Kirkus

782.1 Vocal forms

Abbate, Carolyn

A **history** of opera; Carolyn Abbate and Roger Parker. W.W. Norton 2012 603 p. illustrations (hardcover) $45; (paperback) $21.95 **782.1**
1. Opera -- History 2. Opera
ISBN 9780393057218; 9780393348958

LC 2012031546

This book by Carolyn Abbate and Roger Parker chronicles the history of opera from its "birth . . . in the 17th century up through the most recent technological innovations that bring operatic performances to wider and wider audiences. While the authors cover the breadth of operatic history . . . they focus their attention on the composers whose works are most performed today: Verdi, Mozart, Puccini, Wagner, Rossini, Donizetti, Strauss, Bizet, and Handel." (Publishers Weekly)

Includes bibliographical references and index

Berger, William

Verdi with a vengeance; an energetic guide to the life and complete works of the king of opera. Vintage Bks. 2000 497p il pa $15 **782.1**
1. Composers
ISBN 0-375-70518-X

LC 00-42261

The author "provides a brief overview of the composer's life and times and examines the connections between contemporary politics and Verdi's creative output. . . . A glossary and recommended recordings, films, and soundtracks are included. Informative and eminently readable for the novice and scholar alike." Libr J

Includes discographical references (p. 431-448), bibliographical references (p. 459-463), an annotated film list (p. 464-473), and index

Bergner, Daniel

★ **Sing** for your life; a story of race, music, and family. Daniel Bergner. Little, Brown & Co. 2016 320 p. (ebook) $84; $28 **782.1**
1. Bass-baritones -- Biography 2. African American singers -- Biography 3. Bass-baritones -- United States -- Biography
ISBN 9780316300643; 9780316300674

LC 2016930855

This book, by Daniel Bergner, presents the story of African American singer Ryan Speedo Green. "At the age of twelve, Ryan was sent to Virginia's juvenile facility of last resort. . . . In 2011, at the age of twenty-four, Ryan won a nationwide competition hosted by New York's Metropolitan Opera, beating out 1,200 other talented singers. Today, he is a rising star performing major roles at the Met and Europe's most prestigious opera houses." (Publisher's note)

"While fans of opera will find this to be a captivating biography of one of the most decorated bass baritones, this highly recommended narrative is also about a man who conquers his personal demons and limitations to break racial barriers in one of the oldest cultural institutions in the world." LJ

McCarter, Jeremy

Hamilton; the revolution. Lin-Manuel Miranda, Jeremy McCarter. Grand Central Pub. 2016 287 p. illustrations (chiefly color) (hardcover) $45 **782.1**
1. Historical drama
ISBN 9781455539741; 9781455567539; 9781478938323; 9781478939351

LC 2015957946

This book, by Lin-Manuel Miranda and Jeremy McCarter, provides the libretto of the Broadway musical "Hamilton" and accounts of its creation, concept, and success. It "gives readers an unprecedented view of both revolutions, from the only two writers able to provide it. [The playwright] Miranda, along with Jeremy McCarter, a cultural critic and theater artist who was involved in the project from its earliest stages." (Publisher's note)

"A treasure trove of information, they highlight his writing process, musical influences (ranging from show tunes to pop to hip-hop), amusing anecdotes, and so much more." LJ

Mordden, Ethan

Anything goes; a history of American musical theatre. Ethan Mordden. Oxford University Press 2013 360 p. illustrations (alk. paper) $29.95 **782.1**
1. Musicals 2. Theater -- United States -- History 3. Musicals -- United States -- History and criticism
ISBN 0199892830; 9780199892839

LC 2013000208

This book by Ethan Mordden examines "the musical from the 1920s through the 1970s. . . . He also explores the changing structure of musical comedy and operetta, and the evolution of the role of the star. " (Publisher's note)

"Mordden brightly differentiates those forms, citing hundreds and analyzing dozens of examples of them in a sweeping narrative that, with plenty of sass and tang, wit and even a little snark, not to mention scholarly precision, is obviously the best-ever history of the musical and likely to remain so for a very long time." Booklist

Includes bibliographical references, discography and index

Purdum, Todd S., 1959-

Something wonderful; Rodgers and Hammerstein's Broadway revolution. Todd S. Purdum. Henry Holt & Co. 2018 400 p. $32 **782.1**
1. Musicals -- United States 2. Composers -- United States -- Biography
ISBN 162779834X; 9781627798341

In this book, by Todd S. Purdum, "even before they joined forces, Richard Rodgers and Oscar Hammerstein II had written dozens of Broadway shows, but together they pioneered a new art form: the serious musical play. Their songs and dance numbers served to advance the drama and reveal character, a sharp break from the past and the template on which all future musicals would be built." (Publisher's note)

"Purdum's anecdote-filled account is a sterling primer on the influential duo, both for newcomers to their work and to those looking to rekindle an old flame." Pub Wkly

The **Richard** Rodgers reader; edited by Geoffrey Block. Oxford Univ. Press 2002 356p il music (Readers on American musicians) $55; pa $38 **782.1**
1. Composers 2. Composers -- United States
ISBN 0-19-513954-2; 0-19-531343-7 pa

LC 2001-37505

"A fine combination of anecdote, music criticism, and biography, this is recommended for all libraries interested in American popular culture and American musical theater." Libr J

Includes bibliographical references

Rose, Michael

The **birth** of an opera; fifteen masterpieces from Poppea to Wozzeck. Michael Rose. W.W. Norton & Company 2013 480 p. (hardcover) $35   **782.1**

1. Opera 2. Composers 3. Librettists 4. Operas -- Analysis, appreciation
ISBN 0393060438; 9780393060430

LC 2012039470

This book by Michael Rose discusses "how operas are written and the personalities . . . and musical circumstances that have shaped their composition. . . . From Monteverdi and Mozart to Puccini and Berg, each chapter focuses on a well-known opera and tells the story that lies behind its creation." Rose describes "Verdi deep in Shakespearian discussion with Boito as they remodel . . . 'Otello;' and Debussy coming almost literally to blows with Maeterlinck over . . . 'Pelléas et Mélisande.'" (Publisher's note)

Includes bibliographical references and index

Sondheim, Stephen, 1930-

Finishing the hat; collected lyrics (1954-1981) with attendant comments, principles, heresies, grudges, whines and anecdotes. Knopf 2010 445p il $39.95   **782.1**

1. Songs 2. Musicals 3. Composers 4. Lyricists 5. Biography, Individual 6. Musical theater -- History 7. Popular music -- Writing and publishing
ISBN 0-679-43907-2; 978-0-679-43907-3

LC 2010-11056

"Along with the lyrics for all of his productions from 1954 to 1981—including West Side Story, Company, Follies, A Little Night Music, and Sweeney Todd—Sondheim discusses his relationship with his mentor, Oscar Hammerstein II, and his collaborations with . . . Leonard Bernstein, Arthur Laurents, Ethel Merman, Richard Rodgers, Angela Lansbury, Hal Prince, and [others]. . . . Sondheim [also seeks to] analyze his work and dissect his own songs as well as those of others." (Publisher's note) Index.

"There's so much more to 'Finishing the Hat' than witty, profound and groundbreaking lyrics. In chapters and annotations every budding lyricist and musical fan will relish, Sondheim covers everything from the history of musical theater and views of major lyricists to stories about the making of his shows and lessons in the craft of lyric writing. . . . The 80-year-old Sondheim, not surprisingly, turns out to be a remarkable writer, even when no rhymes are in sight. He's at turns funny and poignant, ornery and instructive. His honesty often stings, especially in analytical sidebars that detail the varied flaws of such heralded lyric-writing comrades as Noel Coward, Ira Gershwin, Lorenz Hart, Alan Jay Lerner and (heresy!) even Oscar Hammerstein II, his mentor." Cleveland Plain Dealer

Includes bibliographical references

Look, I made a hat; collected lyrics (1981-2011) with attendant comments, amplifications, dogmas, harangues, wafflings, diversions and anecdotes. by Stephen Sondheim. 1st ed; Alfred A. Knopf 2011 480p hardcover $45   **782.1**

1. Musicals 2. Lyricists 3. Popular song lyrics 4. Composers -- United States 5. Songs--Texts. 6. Musicals--Excerpts--Librettos.
ISBN 978-0307593412

LC 2011014604

"Picking up where he left off in Finishing the Hat, Sondheim gives us all the lyrics, along with excluded songs and early drafts, of the Pu-

litzer Prize winning Sunday in the Park with George, Into the Woods, Assassins and Passion. Here, too, is an in-depth look at the evolution of Wise Guys, which subsequently was transformed into Bounce and eventually became Road Show. Sondheim takes us through his contributions to both television and film, some of which may surprise you, and covers plenty of never-before-seen material from unproduced projects as well." (Publisher's Note)

"With this chronological continuation of Finishing the Hat, musical theater lyricist and composer Sondheim has produced another delightful book that melds lyrics, anecdotes, opinions, and whimsy...As in the previous volume, Sondheim includes descriptions about each show, as well as running commentary. Sondheim's general essays (the "harangues" and "dogmas" of the subtitle) show him at his opinionated and literate best....certainly all libraries owning the first volume will want the second." (Library Journal)

Includes bibliographical references and index.

782.4   Secular forms

Starr, Ringo, 1940-

Photograph; Ringo Starr. Genesis Publications 2015 304 p. ills., facsimiles, portraits $50   **782.4**

1. Beatles 2. Musicians
ISBN 1905662335; 9781905662333

In this collection of photographs, musician Ringo Starr "opens his archives to share memories of his childhood, The Beatles and beyond. are and unseen photographs taken by Ringo, with others reproduced from his family albums, are showcased here for fans of The Beatles and anyone passionate about modern music. Accompanied by Ringo's original manuscript of over 15,000 words, 'Photograph' gives unprecedented insight into the life of one of the world's greatest musicians." (Publisher's note)

Thomas, Richard F.

Why Bob Dylan Matters; Richard F. Thomas. Dey St. 2017 358 p. (hc) $24.99   **782.4**

1. Popular music -- Writing and publishing
ISBN 9780062685759; 0062685732; 9780062685735; 9780062685742

LC 2017041732

This book, by Richard F. Thomas, "makes a compelling case for moving [musician Bob] Dylan out of the Rock & Roll Hall of Fame and into the pantheon of Classical poets. Asking us to reflect on the question, 'What makes a classic?', Thomas offers an eloquent argument for Dylan's modern relevance, while interpreting and decoding Dylan's lyrics for readers." (Publisher's note)

"This new work doesn't simply examine Dylan's appeal or the deep meaning of his lyrics but tracks his cultural importance and ongoing relevance in today's tumbled-around world." LJ

Includes discography, bibliographical references (pages [333]-336) and index.

782.42   Songs

The **Beatles** anthology. Chronicle Bks. 2000 367p il $60; pa $35   **782.42**

1. Beatles
ISBN 0-8118-2684-8; 0-8118-3636-3 pa

LC 00-23685

The story of the Beatles as "told through quotes from John, Paul,

George, and Ringo, as well as the group's closest aides: George Martin, Neil Aspinall, and Derek Taylor. . . . The density of the text is daunting, but the book's browsability makes it as appealing to casual readers as it is indispensable to Beatlemaniacs." Libr J

Includes bibliographical references

Cohen, Rich

★ The **Sun** and the Moon and the Rolling Stones; Rich Cohen. Spiegel & Grau 2016 400 p. illustrations $30 **782.42**
1. Bands (Music) 2. Rock musicians -- England -- Biography 3. Rolling Stones
ISBN 9780804179232
LC 2015035782

This book, by Rich Cohen, is a "narrative history that will give readers a new understanding of the Rolling Stones. . . . The story begins at the beginning: the fateful meeting of Mick Jagger and Keith Richards on a train platform in 1961—and goes on to span decades, with a focus on the golden run—from the albums Beggars Banquet (1968) to Exile on Main Street (1972)—when the Stones were prolific and innovative and at the height of their powers." (Publisher's note)

"A compact and conversant history that makes the story new again, capturing the Rolling Stones in all their Faustian glory." Kirkus
Includes bibliographical references (pages 351-360) and index.

Edwards, Paul

The **concise** guide to hip-hop music; a fresh look at the art of hip-hop, from old-school beats to freestyle rap. Paul Edwards. St. Martin's Griffin 2015 240 p. (trade pbk.) $14.99 **782.42**
1. Hip-hop -- Encyclopedias 2. Rap music -- History and criticism 3. Rap (Music) -- History and criticism 4. Rap (Music) -- Analysis, appreciation
ISBN 9781250034816
LC 2014034012

This book, by Paul Edwards, "breaks down the difference between old school and new school [hip-hop music from its beginning in 1973 to the present], recaps the biggest influencers of the genre, and sets straight the myths and misconceptions of the artists and their music." (Publisher's note)

Includes bibliographical references

Gioia, Ted

Work songs; [by] Theodore Gioia. Duke University Press 2006 352p $27.95 **782.42**
1. Folk music 2. Labor -- Songs
ISBN 0-8223-3726-6; 978-0-8223-3726-3
LC 2005026241

Gioia "poignantly tells the story of work songs sung by everyone from prehistoric hunters to today's consumers. His task involved drawing on multilayered and diverse resources that include travel literature, slave narratives, historical accounts and personal journals, myths and legends, biographies, and labor union writings; the focus is on the rhythms, melodies, and lyrics of music that has accompanied such tasks as raising and lowering sails, felling trees, and weaving and sewing garments. . . . This book provides an opportunity to re-experience the history and dignity of our human toils. Highly recommended for public and academic libraries." Libr J

Includes bibliographical references

Gray, Michael

The **Bob** Dylan encyclopedia. Continuum 2006 832p il $40 **782.42**
1. Singers 2. Folk musicians 3. Songwriters
ISBN 0-82646-933-7; 978-0-82646-933-5

LC 2006-12728

This book "covers many of his songs, albums, and film work, as well as just about every personality associated with the folk singer/rock star. . . . Overall, this is an amazingly well-researched and surprisingly readable work." Libr J

Includes bibliographical references

In their lives; great writers on great Beatles songs. edited by Andrew Blauner; a note from Paul McCartney. Blue Rider Press 2017 xv, 300 p.p (hardcover) $23 **782.42**
1. Essays 2. Beatles 3. Rock music -- History and criticism
ISBN 9780735210714; 9780735210691
LC 2016053859

This collection of essays, edited by Andrew Blauner, with a note from Paul McCartney, "highlights both the Beatles' evolution as well as the span of generations their music affected. From Beatlemaniacs who grew up listening to the iconic albums on vinyl to new fans who download the songs on iTunes, each contributor explores a poignant intersection between Beatles history and personal history." (Publisher's note)

"A charming, delightful collection for Beatles fans and music fans in general." Kirkus

Lehman, David

A **fine** romance; Jewish songwriters, American songs. Nextbook/Schocken 2009 249p (Jewish encounters) $23 **782.42**
1. Composers 2. Lyricists 3. Songwriters and songwriting 4. Jews -- United States 5. Popular music -- History and criticism
ISBN 978-0-8052-4250-8; 0-8052-4250-3
LC 2009-05942

"Lehman investigates the lasting impact of 20th-century Jewish popular songwriters in America, ranging from Irving Berlin's and Jerome Kern's early efforts in the 1910s through George Gershwin, Harold Arlen, Richard Rodgers, Lorenz Hart, and Oscar Hammerstein II to Leonard Bernstein and the early 1960s. In fluid prose and expert foreshadowing and summations, the author conveys the personality of each musician or writer and recommends selected versions of his favorite songs." Libr J

Includes bibliographical references

Lynskey, Dorian

33 revolutions per minute; a history of protest songs, from Billie Holiday to Green Day. Ecco 2011 660p il pa $19.99 **782.42**
1. Political ballads and songs 2. Popular music -- 20th century 3. Popular music -- 21st century 4. Popular music -- Political aspects 5. Popular music -- History and criticism 6. Protest songs -- History and criticism
ISBN 0061670154; 9780061670152
LC 2010-24247

The author presents a history of protest music through an examination of thirty-three songs, from Strange Fruit (1939) to American Idiot (2008). Index.

The author "delves into the protest song movement from 1939 to the present. Dividing the time into discrete sections, he focuses on particular examples but also provides information on related songs. The author traces the historical context, using valuable contemporary sources and quotations from the artists. . . . Lynskey's flowing prose and well-turned phrases bring the times to life. He is especially adept at integrating the songs into the wider social milieu, which extends the appeal to cultural historians as well as music lovers." Libr J

Includes bibliographical references

Margotin, Philippe

Bob Dylan; all the songs: the story behind every track. Philippe Margotin, Jean-Michel Guesdon. Hachette Books 2015 703 p. illustrations (some color) (hardcover) $50 **782.42**

1. Composition (Music)

ISBN 9781579129859; 1579129854

LC 2015667168

This book, by Philippe Margotin and Jean-Michel Guesdon, is a "comprehensive account of Bob Dylan's work yet published with the full story of every recording session, every album, and every single released during his remarkable and illustrious 53-year career. . . . [The volume] focuses on Dylan's creative process and his organic, unencumbered style of recording." (Publisher's note)

"A Dylan fan could live inside this book for weeks. Hard-core enthusiasts will be enthralled by the details of the many outtakes." Library Journal

Mehr, Bob

Trouble boys; the true story of the Replacements. Bob Mehr. Da Capo Press 2015 520 p. illustrations (hardcover: alk. paper) $27.5 **782.42**

1. Replacements (Musical group) 2. Rock musicians -- United States -- Biography

ISBN 9780306818790; 9780306822032

LC 2015026791

This book, by Bob Mehr, is a biography of the rock band the Replacements. "Written with the participation of the group's key members, including reclusive singer-songwriter Paul Westerberg, bassist Tommy Stinson, and the family of late guitarist Bob Stinson, Trouble Boys is a deeply intimate and nuanced portrait, exposing the primal factors and forces—addiction, abuse, fear—that would shape one of the most brilliant and notoriously self-destructive groups of all time." (Publisher's note)

"Though hefty, Mehr's book is a page-turner from beginning to end and should find its way onto every music fan's bookshelf. It offers a master class on how to pen a rock biography." LJ

Includes bibliographical references and index

★ **National** anthems of the world; edited by Michael Jamieson Bristow. 11th ed.; Weidenfeld & Nicolson 2006 629p $90 **782.42**

1. National songs

ISBN 0-304-36826-1

First published 1943 in the United Kingdom with title: National anthems of the United Nations and France

This volume contains national anthems of about 198 nations, including melody and accompaniment. Words are presented in the native language with transliteration provided where necessary. English translations follow. Brief historical notes on the adoption of each anthem are included

"An essential reference resource for all libraries." Libr J

Polenberg, Richard

Hear my sad story; the true tales that inspired "Stagolee," "John Henry," and other traditional American folk songs. Richard Polenberg. Cornell University Press 2015 304 p. illustrations (cloth: alk. paper) $26 **782.42**

1. Folklore -- United States 2. Folk songs -- United States 3. Folk songs, English -- United States -- History and criticism

ISBN 9781501700026

LC 2015016652

This book, by Richard Polenberg, "describes the historical events that led to the writing of many famous American folk songs that served as touchstones for generations of American musicians, lyricists, and folklorists. Those events, which took place from the early nineteenth to the mid-twentieth centuries, often involved tragic occurrences: murders, sometimes resulting from love affairs gone wrong; [and] desperate acts borne out of poverty and unbearable working conditions." (Publisher's note)

"A well-written primer of American folk culture that should be in any serious popular music collection." LJ

Includes bibliographical references and index

Porter, Cole

Selected lyrics; Robert Kimball, editor. Library of America 2006 178p (American poets project) $20 **782.42**

1. American songs

ISBN 978-1-93108-294-5; 1-93108-294-4

LC 2006-40809

"For those hankering after a happy medium between American poetry and American Idolatry, Kimball's reading edition affords a golden opportunity to brush up on your Porter—just be sure to listen up, too, if you really want to be wowed." N Y Times Book Rev

Ritz, David

After the Dance; My Life with Marvin Gaye. Jan Gaye and David Ritz. HarperCollins 2015 304 p. 16 plates; portraits $25.99 **782.42**

1. Wives 2. Drug abuse

ISBN 0062135511; 9780062135513

NAACP Image Award Nominee: Outstanding Literary Work- Biography/Autobiography (2016)

In this book, author Jan Gaye, with David Ritz, presents a "cautionary tale about the ecstasy and dangers of loving Marvin Gaye, a performer passionately pursued by all--and a searing memoir of drugs, sex, and old school R&B from the wife of legendary soul icon Marvin Gaye." (Publisher's note) "Marvin's drug-crazed behavior became increasingly unhinged and unpredictable, right up until he was tragically shot dead in an argument with his father." (Kirkus Reviews)

"Gaye's explicitly confessional account of her doomed uphill struggle to stay with Marvin is a prime example of how obsessive celebrity worship can so easily (and dangerously) masquerade as enduring love. A fascinating, unsentimental account of a be-careful-what-you-wish-for romance." Kirkus

Southall, Brian

Sgt. Pepper's Lonely Hearts Club Band; the album, the Beatles, and the world in 1967. Brian Southall. Charlesbridge 2017 192 p. illustrations (some color) (hardcover) $30 **782.42**

1. Beatles 2. Rock music -- Pictorial works 3. Rock music -- 1961-1970 -- Pictorial works 4. Nineteen sixty-seven, A.D. -- Pictorial works 5. Beatles. Sgt. Pepper's Lonely Hearts Club Band

ISBN 9781623545260; 9781632892140

LC 2017010577

This book, by Brian Southall, "recounts the story behind the music and the cultural climate of 1967 when Sgt. Pepper's Lonely Heart Club Band debuted. [It] . . . is all about the Beatles, the music on the album, the recording process, how the disc was received at the time and how it has been acknowledged as one of the greatest albums ever recorded. . . . [It also] looks at the state of the world in 1967." (Publisher's note)

"Visually enticing, with tons of quotes and photos galore (many of which depict the Fab Four in delightfully garish hippie garb), it's ripe for browsing." LJ

Includes bibliographical references (page 191) and index.

St. James encyclopedia of hip hop culture; edited by Thomas J. Riggs. St. James Press 2018 579 p. (hardcover) $285   **782.42**
1. Hip-hop -- Encyclopedias 2. Rap music -- Encyclopedias 3. Rap (Music) -- Encyclopedias
ISBN 9781410380814

LC 2017049826

This book, edited by Thomas J. Riggs, "presents more than 200 entries that examine the history and contributions of hip hop to American and global culture. It provides academic and public libraries with a much-needed authoritative reference resource defining, exploring, and analyzing this significant aspect of culture and history." (Publisher's note)

Includes bibliographical references and index

782.421   General principles of songs

Bronson, Fred

The **Jacksons**; legacy. Jackie, Tito, Jermaine, Marlon, and Michael, Fred Bronson. Black Dog & Leventhal 2017 320 p. (hardcover) $29.99   **782.421**
1. African American musicians 2. Musicians -- United States
ISBN 0316473731; 9780316473736; 9780316473743

LC 2017943146

This book, by Fred Bronson, "is the first official book on the the Royal Family of Pop. Unrivaled access to the family archives as well as the private collections of Jackie, Marlon and Tito Jackson, combined with 12 days of exclusive interviews with the brothers, reveals the untold, unseen, and utterly unforgettable story behind the legend that is the Jacksons." (Publisher's note)

Chuck D, 1960-

★ **Chuck** D presents This day in rap and hip-hop history; Chuck D, with Duke Eatmon, Ron Maskell, Lorrie Boula, and Jonathan Bernstein; foreword by Shepard Fairey. Black Dog & Leventhal Publishers 2017 ix, 342 p.p $29.99   **782.421**
1. Rap (Music) -- History and criticism 2. Hip-hop (Music) -- History and criticism
ISBN 0316430978; 9780316430975

"Based on Chuck's long-running show on Rapstation.com, this massive compendium details the most iconic moments and influential songs in the genre's recorded history, from Kurtis Blow's 'Christmas Rappin'' to The Miseducation of Lauryn Hill to Kendrick Lamar's ground-breaking verse on "Control." Also included are key events in hip hop history, from Grandmaster Flash's first scratch through Tupac's holographic appearance at Coachella." (Publisher's note)

Kienzle, Rich

The **grand** tour; the life and music of George Jones. Richard Kienzle. HarperCollins 2016 288 p. illustrations, portraits $27.99; (ebook) $65   **782.421**
1. Country musicians -- United States -- Biography
ISBN 0062309919; 9780062309914; 9780385540964

LC 2016561296

This book, by Rich Kienzle "offers a definitive, full-bodied portrait of legendary country singer George Jones and the music that remains his legacy. Kienzle meticulously sifted through archival material, government records, recollections by colleagues and admirers, interviewing many involved in Jones's life and career. The result: an evocative portrait of this enormously gifted, tragically tormented icon called 'the Keith Richards of country.'" (Publisher's note)

"This moving biography keeps Jones's voice alive and underscores his central role in American music history." Pub Wkly

Includes bibliographical references (pages 265-279).

McNally, Dennis

A **long** strange trip; the inside history of the Grateful Dead. Dennis McNally. Broadway Bks. 2002 684 p. il $22 **782.421**
1. Biography 2. Grateful Dead (Musical group) 3. Rock musicians -- United States -- Biography 4. Rock musicians -- United States -- Interviews
ISBN 0767911857; 0767911865; 9780767911863

LC 200225561

This book, by Dennis McNally, presents "the complete history of [Grateful Dead,] one of the most long-lived and legendary bands in rock history. . . . McNally not only chronicles their experiences in a fascinatingly detailed fashion, but veers off into side trips on the band's intricate stage setup, the magic of the Grateful Dead concert experience, or metaphysical musings excerpted from a conversation among band members." (Publisher's note)

"Those looking for a detailed history of the Dead and/or such sweeping pronouncements will greatly enjoy this account of how the band has been truckin' all these years." Booklist

Includes bibliographical references

Tolokonnikova, Nadezhda, 1989-

Rules for rulebreakers; a Pussy Riot guide to revolution. Nadya Tolokonnikova. HarperOne 2018 256 p. (hardcover) $24.99   **782.421**
1. Musicians 2. Political activists 3. Advocacy (Political science) 4. Pussy Riot (Musical group) 5. Musicians -- Political activity -- Russia
ISBN 9780062741585

LC 2017059217

This book, by Nadya Tolokonnikova, "is structured around Nadya's ten rules for revolution . . . and illustrated throughout with stunning examples from her extraordinary life and the philosophies of other revolutionary rebels throughout history. . . . [This book] gives us a refreshing model for civil disobedience, and encourages our right to question every status quo and make political action exciting--even joyful." (Publisher's note)

Weisman, Eliot

The **way** it was; my life with frank sinatra. Eliot Weisman, Jennifer Valoppi. Hachette Books 2017 328 p. (hardcover) $27   **782.421**
ISBN 0316470082; 9780316470070; 9780316470087; 9780316511032; 9781478923145

LC 2017946386

This book, by Eliot Weisman and Jennifer Valoppi, is "a candid and eye-opening inside look at the final decades of Sinatra's life told by his longtime manager and friend. . . . [Sinatra] was struggling with the challenges that come with old age, as well as memory loss, depression, and antidepressents. Weisman was by his side through it all, witness to a man who had towering confidence, staggering fearlessness, and a rarely seen vulnerability that became more apparent as his final days approached." (Publisher's note)

"This is also one of the few Sinatra titles by a close friend and associate, yet Weisman doesn't shy away from sharing more than a few difficult moments, nor does he lionize a man he clearly adored." Library Journal

782.5   Vocal executants

Steinberg, Michael

Choral masterworks; a listener's guide. Michael Steinberg. Oxford University Press 2005 321p $30   **782.5**
1. Choral music
ISBN 0-19-512644-0

LC 2004-13619

"Well-written, concise introductions that record collectors, concert-goers, and chorus members alike should enjoy." Booklist

784   Instruments and their music

Hamilton-Paterson, James

Beethoven's 'eroica' the first great romantic symphony. James Hamilton-Paterson. Basic Books, an imprint of Perseus Books, a subsidiary of Hachette Book Group 2017 192 p. (hardcover) $25   **784**
1. Music -- History and criticism
ISBN 9781541697362

LC 2017956393

This book, by James Hamilton-Paterson, is "[a]n ode to Beethoven's revolutionary masterpiece, his Third Symphony. In 1805, the world of music was startled by an avant-garde and explosive new work. Intellectually and emotionally, Beethoven's Third Symphony, the 'Eroica,' rudely broke the mold of the Viennese Classical symphony and revealed a powerful new expressiveness, both personal and societal." (Publisher's note)

"Casual concertgoers and serious music aficionados alike will find much to savor in this elegant and insightful book." (Booklist)

Piston, Walter

Orchestration. Norton 1955 477p il music $56.75   **784**
1. Musical instruments 2. Instrumentation and orchestration
ISBN 978-0-393-09740-5; 0-393-09740-4

This text on writing for the orchestra begins with a discussion of individual instruments and their playing techniques. The last two sections cover analysis and specific problems of orchestration

784.19   Instruments

Wilkinson, Philip

The **history** of music in fifty instruments; written by Philip Wilkinson. Firefly Books Ltd 2014 224 p. illustrations; portraits (hardcover) $29.95   **784.19**
1. Musical instruments 2. Music -- History and criticism
ISBN 1770854282; 9781770854284

LC 2014900697

This book, by Philip Wilkinson, "outlines musical history in [50] well-written nuggets of information. Profiling one instrument at a time, it describes the history of music since the 1700s, when orchestras first took the formal shape familiar to us. The concise text explains the role of each instrument in the orchestra and its importance in the development of music in general." (Publisher's note)

"Wilkinson's history unfolds like a symphonic work with instrument makers, composers and virtuosic performers picking up these incredible creations and exposing their beauty and capability. To open it up is to be instantly hooked." Pub Wkly

784.192   Techniques and procedures for instruments themselves

Pagliaro, Michael

The **musical** instrument desk reference; a guide to how band and orchestral instruments work. Michael J. Pagliaro. Scarecrow Press 2012 189 p. (cloth: alk. paper) $65 **784.192**
1. Musical instruments 2. Wind instruments -- Construction 3. Bowed stringed instruments -- Construction
ISBN 0810882701; 9780810882706; 9780810882713

LC 2012007244

This book "begins with an 'easy-reference quick start' section on woodwinds, followed by more in-depth chapters on the flute, clarinet, saxophone, oboe, and the bassoon. For the brass instruments, there are fingering charts, an expanded in-depth study chapter, and a chapter on functioning. Nonfretted string instruments . . . are also given a chapter on producing sound and an expanded in-depth study chapter. The final chapter consists of an overview of percussion instruments." (Booklist)

785   Ensembles with only one instrument per part

Sachs, Harvey

The **Ninth**; Beethoven and the world in 1824. Random House 2010 225p il   **785**
1. Composers 2. Romanticism in music 3. Music -- Social aspects 4. Music -- Political aspects 5. Music -- History and criticism 6. Music -- Social aspects -- Europe -- History
ISBN 1-4000-6077-X; 1-58836-981-1 ebook; 978-1-4000-6077-1; 978-1-58836-981-9 ebook

LC 2009-19716

This analysis of Beethoven's seminal Ninth Symphony identifies it as a key cultural event that reflected major social upheavals, including the emergence of a dynamic Western world and changes in philosophical perspectives on individuality.

"This discussion of the cornerstone of Romantic music, whose influence extended deep into the twentieth century, is concise, thorough, and written from the heart of a great biographer, musicologist, and lover of fine music." Booklist

Includes bibliographical references

786.2   Keyboard instruments

Isacoff, Stuart

A **natural** history of the piano; the instrument, the music, the musicians--from Mozart to modern jazz, and everything in between. Alfred A. Knopf 2011 361p il   **786.2**
1. Pianos 2. Piano music -- History and criticism
ISBN 9780307266378; 978030770142-8 ebook

LC 2011011557

"Isacoff offers an encyclopedic history of the beloved instrument and profiles such masters as Beethoven, Gershwin, and Oscar Peterson in this big slice of heaven for piano lovers." Booklist

Includes bibliographical references

786.5   Organs

Whitney, Craig R.

All the stops; the glorious pipe organ and its American mas-

ters. Public Affairs 2003 xxv, 323p il $30; pa $17.95 **786.5**
1. Organs (Musical instruments)
ISBN 1-586-48173-8; 1-586-48262-9 pa

LC 2002-37025

"Whitney extolls the organ's eclectic heritage at a time when the instrument seems poised for a return to the mainstream, and his glossary of its colorful terminology will help novices tell a windchest from a bombarde." New Yorker

Includes bibliographical references

787.2   Violins

Grymes, James A.

Violins of hope; violins of the Holocaust, instruments of hope and liberation in mankind's darkest hour. James A. Grymes. Harper Perennial 2014 336 p. illustrations (paperback) $15.99   **787.2**
1. Violins 2. Holocaust, 1939-1945 3. Holocaust victims -- Biography 4. Violinists -- Europe -- Biography 5. Jewish musicians -- Europe -- Biography 6. Musical instruments -- Maintenance and repair -- History -- 20th century
ISBN 0062246836; 9780062246837; 9780062246844

LC 2013050151

National Jewish Book Award Winner: Holocaust (2014)

This book by James A Grymes "tells the remarkable stories of violins played by Jewish musicians during the Holocaust, and the Israeli violin maker dedicated to bringing these inspirational instruments back to life. Today, these instruments serve as . . . memorials to those who perished and testaments to those who survived. In this spirit, renowned Israeli violinmaker Amnon Weinstein has devoted the past twenty years to restoring the violins of the Holocaust." (Publisher's note)

787.3   Violas

Siblin, Eric

The **cello** suites; J.S. Bach, Pablo Casals, and the search for a Baroque masterpiece. Atlantic Monthly Press 2009 319p $24   **787.3**
1. Composers 2. Music appreciation 3. Cellists
ISBN 978-0-8021-1929-2; 0-8021-1929-8

The author explores the history of Bach's six suites for unaccompanied cello.

"Siblin's curiosity and passion for his subject is evident throughout, and his method of structuring the story according to the arrangement of the music is inspired. . . . Meticulous in his research, as evidenced by copious notes and resources collected over his travels to several European countries, Siblin makes convincing connections and offers possible answers to the questions surrounding the suites. In the process, he sheds considerable light on the lives of Bach and Casals." Quill Quire

Includes bibliographical references

787.4   Cellos (Violoncellos)

Todd, R. Larry

Beethoven's cello; five revolutionary sonatas and their world. Marc D. Moskovitz and R. Larry Todd. The Boydell Press 2017 xxiv, 249 p.p $39.95   **787.4**
1. Sonata 2. Cello music 3. Sonata -- 19th century 4. Chamber

music -- 19th century -- History and criticism
ISBN 1783272376; 9781783272372

LC 2017569147

This book, by Marc D. Moskovitz and R. Larry Todd, examine Ludwig van Beethoven's cello sonatas "and place them within their historical and cultural context. Also considered in a series of interludes are Beethoven's three variation sets, his cello-centric 'Triple' Concerto, and arrangements for cello and piano of other works. Two other interludes address the cellos owned by Beethoven and the changing nature of his pianos." (Publisher's note)

Includes bibliographical references (pages 203-238) and indexes

787.87   Guitars

Chapman, Richard

The **new** complete guitarist; rev American ed; DK 2003 208p il pa $20   **787.87**
1. Guitars
ISBN 0-7894-9701-8

LC 2004-271630

First published 1993 with title: The complete guitarist

This work ranges "from fundamentals such as tuning, scales, chords, picking, and strumming, to advanced techniques of various styles such as rock, blues, and jazz. . . . [It also] includes discussions on such topics as sound and amplification, choosing a guitar, studio and home recording, plus care and maintenance of the instrument. An appealing book in the style of the 'Eyewitness' series." SLJ [review of 1993 edition]

Includes bibliographical references

Chappell, Jon

Guitar All-in-one for Dummies; by Jon Chappell, Mark Phillips, and Desi Serna. 2nd edition Wiley 2014 628 p. illustrations pa. $34.99   **787.87**
1. Guitars 2. Guitars -- Study and teaching 3. Guitar 4. Guitar -- methods -- self instruction
ISBN 9781118872024; 1118872029

This book is a "complete compendium of guitar instruction, written in clear, concise For Dummies style. It covers everything from positioning and basic chords to guitar theory and playing styles, and even includes maintenance advice to keep your instrument sounding great. It's an amazing resource for newbies and veterans alike, and offers you the opportunity to stretch beyond your usual genre." (Publisher's Note)

788.52   Oboes

Butler, Marcia

The **skin** above my knee; Marcia Butler. Little, Brown & Co 2017 272 p. $27; (ebook) $81   **788.52**
1. Oboists -- Biography 2. Women musicians -- Biography
ISBN 9780316392280; 9780316272087

LC 2015960626

This memoir, by professional oboist Marcia Butler, presents "the story of a woman finding strength in her creative gifts and artistic destiny. Filled with vivid portraits of 1970's New York City, and fascinating insights into the intensity and precision necessary for a career in professional music, this is more than a narrative of a brilliant musician struggling to make it big in the big city. It is the story of a survivor." (Publisher's note)

"In the end, this is a moving account of how passion and creativity can be powerful weapons against neglect, cruelty, and self-harm."

Pub Wkly

790 Recreational and performing arts

Bennetts, Leslie

Last girl before freeway; The Life, Loves, Losses, and Liberation of Joan Rivers. Leslie Bennetts. Little, Brown & Co. 2016 432 p. illustrations (some color) $28.00; (ebook) $84 **790**

1. Comedians -- United States -- Biography
ISBN 9780316261302; 9780316269544

LC 2016938566

This biography, by Leslie Bennetts, examines how "Joan Rivers was more than a legendary comedian; she was an icon and a role model to millions, a fearless pioneer who left a legacy of expanded opportunity when she died in 2014. . . . But Rivers' career was also hugely significant in American cultural history, breaking down barriers for her gender and pushing the boundaries of truth-telling for women in public life." (Publisher's note)

"Bennetts's reporting gives readers unparalleled access to her subject, which comedy fans, and those just fascinated by superstardom, will greatly enjoy." Pub Wkly

790.1 General kinds of recreational activities

Conner, Bobbi

Unplugged play; no batteries, no plugs, pure fun. illustrations by Amy Patacchiola. Workman Pub. 2007 xxv, 401p il $27.95; pa $16.95 **790.1**

1. Play 2. Games
ISBN 978-0-7611-4114-3; 978-0-7611-4390-1 pa

LC 2007-23999

"Conner has compiled more than 710 games and activities sorted by age level. Good old-fashioned play and fun are the motto here with simple props from around the house or just an imagination. The book is separated into three major parts: 'Toddler Play,' 'Preschool Play,' and 'Grade School Play.' Each has a section on solo play, ideas for parent and child, playing with others, and birthday-party activities. Each chapter and section is loaded with ideas and suggestions for simple crafts. There is such a wealth of information in this book." SLJ

Johnson, Steven, 1968-

Wonderland; how play made the modern world. Steven Johnson. Riverhead Books 2016 336 p. illustrations (some color) (hardback) $30 **790.1**

1. Amusements 2. Technological innovations 3. Amusements -- History
ISBN 9780399184482

LC 2016035344

This book, by Steven Johnson, offers a "lushly illustrated history of popular entertainment [that] takes a long-zoom approach, contending that the pursuit of novelty and wonder is a powerful driver of world-shaping technological change. Steven Johnson argues that, throughout history, the cutting edge of innovation lies wherever people are working the hardest to keep themselves and others amused." (Publisher's note)

"This is a great book for all curious readers, especially the history-averse, who will enjoy the fast pace, topical diversity, and abundant trivia." Booklist

Includes bibliographical references (pages 287-306) and index.

791 Public performances

Austen, Jake

Darkest America; black minstrelsy from slavery to hip-hop. Yuval Taylor and Jake Austen. W. W. Norton 2012 368 p. (hardcover) $26.95 **791**

1. African Americans -- History 2. Popular culture -- United States 3. Blackface entertainers -- United States -- History 4. Hip-hop -- United States -- History 5. Minstrel shows -- United States -- History
ISBN 0393070980; 9780393070989

LC 2012007307

This book, by Yuval Taylor and Jake Austen, "investigate[s] the complex history of black minstrelsy, adopted in the mid-nineteenth century by . . . performers who played the grinning blackface fool to entertain . . . audiences. We now consider minstrelsy an embarrassing relic, but once blacks and whites alike saw it as a black art form. . . . And . . . black minstrelsy remains deeply relevant to popular black entertainment, particularly in the work of contemporary artists." (Publisher's note)

"An innovative, marvelous book about comedy, stereotypes and the struggle to steer through the sometimes-fierce internal debates over African-American identity in a society still struggling with its racial past." Kirkus

Includes bibliographical references and index

Moore, Rachel S.

The **artist's** compass; the complete guide to building a life and a living in the performing arts. Rachel Moore, President and CEO of the Los Angeles Music Center. Touchstone 2016 224 p. (hardback) $24.99 **791**

1. Success 2. Performing arts 3. Performing arts -- Economic aspects 4. Performing arts -- Vocational guidance
ISBN 9781501105951; 9781501126642

LC 2015037025

In this book, "Los Angeles Music Center CEO Rachel Moore shares how to make life as a performer more successful, secure, and sustainable by approaching a career in the arts like an entrepreneur. A former dancer in the American Ballet Theatre's corps de ballet, Moore knows firsthand what it's like to struggle and succeed as an artist. Now in an offstage role as CEO, Moore shares the hard-won lessons she's learned about making one's own success." (Publisher's note)

"Moore is qualified to become a mentor to a whole new generation of artists, and they will benefit greatly from her advice." Pub Wkly

Includes bibliographical references and index

791.3 Circuses

Daly, Michael

Topsy; The Startling Story of the Crooked Tailed Elephant, P.T. Barnum, and the American Wizard, Thomas Edison. by Michael Daly. Pgw 2013 viii, 369 p.p $27 **791.3**

1. Circus 2. Elephants
ISBN 0802119042; 9780802119049

This book, by Michael Daly, examines how "in 1903, on Coney Island, an elephant named Topsy was electrocuted, and over the past century, this bizarre, ghoulish execution has reverberated through popular culture with the whiff of urban legend. But it really happened, and many historical forces conspired to bring Topsy, Thomas Edison, and those 6600 volts of alternating current together that day. Daly weaves together a fascinating popular history, the first book on this astonishing tale." (Publisher's note)

Jensen, Dean

Queen of the air; a true story of love and tragedy at the circus. Dean Jensen. Crown Publishers 2012 336 p. $26 **791.3**
1. Circus 2. Interpersonal relations 3. Aerialists -- United States -- Biography 4. Woman circus performers -- United States -- Biography
ISBN 030798656X; 9780307986566

LC 2012018066

This book by Dean Jensen presents the "true story of renowned trapeze artist and circus performer Leitzel, Queen of the Air, the most famous woman in the world at the turn of the 20th century, and her star-crossed love affair with Alfredo Codona, of the famous Flying Codona Brothers." (Publisher's note)

Macy, Beth

★ **Truevine**; Two Brothers, a Kidnapping, and a Mother's Quest: A True Story of the Jim Crow South. Beth Macy. Little, Brown & Co. 2016 432 p. $28 **791.3**
1. Circus 2. Brothers 3. Kidnapping 4. African Americans -- Biography
ISBN 9780316337540

LC 2015959853

Carnegie Medal Longlist: Nonfiction (2017); Kirkus Prize Finalist: Nonfiction (2016)

This book, by Beth Macy, is the "true story of two African-American brothers who were kidnapped and displayed as circus freaks, and whose mother endured a 28-year struggle to get them back. The year was 1899 and the place a sweltering tobacco farm in the Jim Crow South town of Truevine, Virginia. George and Willie Muse were two little boys born to a sharecropper family. One day a white man offered them a piece of candy, setting off events that would take them around the world." (Publisher's note)

"A rambling, colorful, and thought-provoking medley of human stories intersecting with one another in carnival tents and Virginia backlands, this solid popular history has much to offer regarding issues of race, family, disability, and spectacle." LJ

791.43   Motion pictures

★ **1001** Movies You Must See Before You Die; general editor, Steven Jay Schneider; updated by Ian Haydn Smith. 7th edition Barrons 2017 960 p. illustrations hbk $35 **791.43**
1. Motion pictures
ISBN 9781438050065
Originally published 2003

"This brand-new edition of 1001 Movies You Must See Before You Die covers more than a century of movie history. Selected and authored by a team of international film critics, every profile is packed with details, plot summaries and production notes, and little-known facts relating to the film's history. Each entry offers a fresh look at some the greatest films of all time." (Publisher's note)

Arnold, Jeremy

The **essentials**; 52 must-see movies and why they matter. Jeremy Arnold; foreword by Robert Osborne. Running Press 2016 288 p. illustrations (some color) (paperback) $25; (ebook) $16.99 **791.43**
1. Motion pictures -- Appreciation 2. Motion pictures -- Reviews
ISBN 0762459468; 9780762459469; 9780762459476

LC 2015959543

This book, by Jeremy Arnold, "showcas[es] 52 Essential films from the golden age to the present. . . . These are movies that define what it means to be a classic. Readers can enjoy one film per week, for a year of stellar viewing, or indulge in their own classic movie festival." (Publisher's note)

Includes bibliographical references (pages 272-279) and index

Benson, Michael

Space odyssey; Stanley Kubrick, Arthur C. Clarke, and the making of a masterpiece. Michael Benson. Simon & Schuster 2018 512 p. (hardback) $30 **791.43**
1. 2001, a space odyssey (Motion picture)
ISBN 1501163930; 9781501163937

LC 2017051254

In this book, "author Michael Benson explains how . . . [the film '2001: A Space Odyssey] was made, telling the story primarily through the two people most responsible for the film, [Stanley] Kubrick and science fiction legend Arthur C. Clarke. Benson interviewed Clarke many times, and has also spoken at length with Kubrick's widow, Christiane; with visual effects supervisor Doug Trumbull; with Dan Richter, who played 2001's leading man-ape; and many others." (Publisher's note)

Includes bibliographical references and index

Biskind, Peter

My Lunches With Orson; Conversations Between Henry Jaglom and Orson Welles. edited by Peter Biskind. Henry Holt and Co. 2013 320 p. $28 **791.43**
1. Motion picture producers and directors -- United States 2. Motion picture producers and directors -- United States -- Anecdotes
ISBN 0805097252; 9780805097252

LC 2013000291

Here, film historian Peter Biskind has edited recordings captured when Orson Welles lunched with his friend, film director Henry Jaglom. In the montage offered, "Welles offers a montage of opinion on his career, his disappointments, and acquaintances from Marlene Dietrich and Laurence Olivier to Winston Churchill." (Library Journal)

Bogle, Donald

Bright boulevards, bold dreams; the story of Black Hollywood. One World Ballantine Books 2005 411p il $26.95; pa $15.95 **791.43**
1. African American actors 2. African Americans in motion pictures
ISBN 0345454189; 0345454197 pa

LC 2004-54781

"Starting with Madame Sul-Te-Wan's work in D.W. Griffith's 1915 The Birth of a Nation and ending with the 1960s deaths of Louise Beavers, Nat 'King' Cole and Dorothy Dandridge, Bogle tells the stories of the stars of Black Hollywood: their outfits, their love affairs and their struggles for better roles. . . . Bogle's lively style . . . and his many anecdotes will entertain and inform film students and black history buffs alike." Publ Wkly

Includes bibliographical references

Bollywood; the films! the songs! the stars! [foreword by Amitabh Bachchan] DK Publishing 2017 360 p. (hardcover) $40 **791.43**
1. Historical literature 2. Motion picture industry -- India -- Mumbai 3. Motion pictures -- India -- Mumbai -- History 4. Motion pictures -- India -- Mumbai -- History -- 20th century 5. Motion pictures -- India -- Mumbai -- History -- 21st century
ISBN 9781465463296

LC 2017299317

This book, with foreword by Amitabh Bachchan, offers "a visual tour of the glamour and color of Indian cinema. . . . [It] features film stills, plot timelines, star and producer profiles, plus historical insights, lesser-known facts, and behind-the-scenes gossip on such iconic movies as Mother India, Mughal-e-Azam, Sholay, Dilwale Dulhania Le Jayenge, and Bajirao Mastani." (Publisher's note)

Cavalier, Stephen

The **world** history of animation; Stephen Cavalier. University of California Press 2011 416 p. ill. (some col.) (cloth: alk. paper) $39.95   **791.43**

1. Animated films 2. Animation (Cinematography) 3. Animated television programs 4. Animators 5. Animated films -- History and criticism

ISBN 0520261127; 9780520261129

LC 2010931052

This book on animation by Stephen Cavalier "tells the genre's 100-year-old story around the globe, featuring key players in Europe, North America, and Asia." It is "organized chronologically and covers pioneers, feature films, television programs, digital films, games, independent films, and the web. . . . The book explains the evolution of animation techniques, from rotoscoping to refinements of cel techniques, direct film, claymation, and more." (Publisher's note)

Includes bibliographical references (p. 404-405) and index.

Conversations at the American Film Institute with the great moviemakers; the next generation. edited and with an introduction by George Stevens, Jr. Alfred A. Knopf 2012 xxiii, 737 p.p (hbk.) $39.95   **791.43**

1. Motion pictures 2. Motion picture industry 3. Motion picture producers and directors 4. Motion pictures -- Production and direction 5. Motion picture producers and directors -- United States -- Interviews

ISBN 0307273474; 9780307273475

LC 2011043741

This book presents conversations with "directors, producers, writers, actors, cameramen, composers, editors": "men and women working in pictures, beginning in 1950, when the studio system was collapsing and people could no longer depend on, or were bound by, the structure of studio life to make movies." Others, "who began to work long after the studio days were over," are featured as well. (Barnes and Noble)

Includes bibliographical references and index.

Coppola, Francis Ford, 1939-

The **Godfather** Notebook; by Francis Ford Coppola. Simon & Schuster 2016 784 p. ill. (some color), facsimiles $60   **791.43**

1. Motion picture producers and directors

ISBN 1682450740; 9781682450741

LC 2016939716

This book, by Francis Ford Coppola, "pulls back the curtain on the legendary filmmaker and the film that launched his illustrious career. Complete with an introduction by Francis Ford Coppola and exclusive photographs from on and off the set, this is a unique, beautiful, and faithful reproduction of Coppola's original notebook." (Publisher's note)

Corliss, Richard, 1944-2015

Mom in the movies; the iconic screen mothers you love (and a few you love to hate) by Richard Corliss; foreword by Debbie Reynolds and Carrie Fisher; [with editorial assistance from Turner Classic Movies] Simon & Schuster 2014 192 p. illustrations $35   **791.43**

1. Mothers 2. Women in motion pictures 3. Mothers in motion pictures

ISBN 1476738262; 9781476738260

LC 2013044850

"Turner Classic Movies and film historian Richard Corliss present 'Mom in the Movies: The Iconic Screen Mothers You Love (and a Few You Love to Hate),' the . . . fully illustrated book that shares the many ways Hollywood has celebrated, vilified and otherwise memorialized dear old Mom. . . . Here, you will meet the Criminal Moms . . . and the eccentric Showbiz Moms. . . . You'll also find Great American Moms, as warm and nourishing as apple pie." (Publisher's note)

A "comprehensive retrospective of mothers as portrayed on film from the earliest "Silent Moms" . . . to the most recent figures." LJ

D'Alessandro, Emilio

Stanley Kubrick and me; thirty years at his side. Emilio D'Alessandro with Filippo Ulivieri; translated by Simon Marsh. Arcade Publishing 2016 384 p. illustrations (some color) (hardback) $27.99   **791.43**

1. Motion picture producers and directors -- Biography 2. Motion picture producers and directors -- United States -- Biography

ISBN 9781628726695

LC 2015050645

This book, by Emilio D'Alessandro, focuses on filmmaker Stanley Kubrick. "Emilio was the silent guy in the room when the script for The Shining was discussed. He still has the coat Jack Nicholson used in the movie. He was an extra on the set of Eyes Wide Shut, Kubrick's last movie. He knew all the actors and producers Kubrick worked with; he observed firsthand Kubrick's working methods down to the smallest detail." (Publisher's note)

"Hard-core Kubrick devotees won't learn much, but this easygoing and likable memoir humanizes an eccentric titan of cinema." LJ

Dixon, Wheeler W., 1950-

A **Short** History of Film; Wheeler Winston Dixon & Gwendolyn Audrey Foster. 3rd edition Rutgers University Press 2018 449 p. illustrations (some color) $34.95   **791.43**

1. Motion picture industry 2. Motion picture industry -- History 3. Motion pictures -- History. 4. Motion picture industry -- History.

ISBN 9780813595122

LC 2012533144

"The book progresses in chronological order, decade after decade, alternating chapters between American and what Americans would consider "foreign" cinema, an arrangement that makes the discussion regimented and easy to follow. One of the more important features is the focus on women directors who may not be well known to the general public; this makes the book timely and a welcome change from older film textbooks that are more implicitly biased." (Choice Reviews)

Film noir; the encyclopedia. edited by Alain Silver . . . [et al.]; co-editor: Carl Macek; designed by Bernard Schleifer. [4th ed.]; Overlook Duckworth 2010 511p il   **791.43**

1. Mystery films 2. Motion pictures

ISBN 978-1-590201442

First published 1979

An introductory essay "lays out the history and parameters of noir in a succinct but undogmatic way, offering an intro for the new viewer as well as food for thought for the hardboiled fan. Most of the rest of the book consists of synopses of noir films, providing a brief plot summary followed by a paragraph or two detailing key aspects of each film. Important flicks like Kiss Me Deadly and Double Indemnity get a bit more space and consideration, and the authors, for the most part, avoid subjective reviews and concentrate on chasing down each film's address in the naked city of noir. . . . This new edition of the definitive text on film noir is a perfect companion for a foray into the dreamlike world of some of the most dark and mesmerizing movies ever made." PopMatters

Finch, Christopher

The **art** of Walt Disney; Christopher Finch. New edition Harry N Abrams 2011 503 p illustrations hardcover $90   **791.43**
1. Walt Disney Company
ISBN 0810998149; 9780810998148

LC 2011007947

First published 1973

"This book was the first to reveal the wealth of concept art, animation drawings, and archival material created in the course of animating films. In this newly revised edition, author Christopher Finch has thoroughly reworked every chapter to incorporate the vast achievements of The Walt Disney Company in filmmaking, theater, and theme parks, from Walt's day to the present, including all-new exciting chapters on Pixar Animation Studio and Walt Disney Animation

Fischer, Paul

★ A **Kim** Jong-Il production; the extraordinary true story of a kidnapped filmmaker, his star actress, and a young dictator's rise to power. Paul Fischer. Flatiron Books 2015 368 p. illustrations (some color) (hardcover) $27.99   **791.43**
1. Kidnapping 2. Korea (North) 3. Actresses -- Korea (South) -- Biography 4. Motion pictures -- Korea (North) -- History -- 20th century 5. Motion picture producers and directors -- Korea (South) -- Biography
ISBN 1250054265; 9781250054265

LC 2014040366

"Before becoming the world's most notorious dictator, Kim Jong-Il ran North Korea's Ministry for Propaganda and its film studios. Conceiving every movie made, he acted as producer and screenwriter. Despite this control, he was underwhelmed by the available talent and took drastic steps, ordering the kidnapping of Choi Eun-Hee (Madam Choi)-- South Korea's most famous actress--and her ex-husband Shin Sang-Ok, the country's most famous filmmaker." (Publisher's note)

"The most compelling facets of this book of astonishments are Fischer's insights into the relationships between Choi, Shin, and their diabolical captor and Fischer's canny perception of how Kim Jong-Il turned his oppressed, corrupt, and starving country into one vast theatrical production of fantasy, deceit, and terror, scripting lives of fear, ignorance, obedience, and deprivation." Booklist

Includes bibliographical references (pages 345- 353)

Frankel, Glenn

High Noon; The Hollywood Blacklist and the Making of an American Classic. Glenn Frankel. Bloomsbury 2017 xvi, 379 p.p illustrations (hardcover) $28   **791.43**
1. Communism -- United States 2. Blacklisting of entertainers 3. Motion pictures -- History and criticism 4. Motion pictures -- United States -- History -- 20th century 5. High noon (Motion picture) 6. Blacklisting of authors -- United States 7. Blacklisting of entertainers -- United States
ISBN 1620409488; 9781620409503; 9781620409480

LC 2017000380

This book, by Glenn Frankel, is "the revelatory story behind the classic movie High Noon and the toxic political climate in which it was created. . . . Starring . . . Gary Cooper and Grace Kelly, . . . High Noon was shot on a lean budget over just thirty-two days but achieved instant box-office and critical success. . . . Yet what has been often overlooked is that High Noon was made during the height of the Hollywood blacklist,

a time of political inquisition and personal betrayal." (Publisher's note)

"A comprehensive guide to both a classic film and the era that created it." Kirkus

Includes bibliographical references (pages 319-359) and index.

Gaines, Caseen

Jim Henson's the Dark Crystal; the ultimate visual history. Caseen Gaines; foreword by Cheryl Henson; introduction by Brian and Wendy Froud. Insight Editions 2017 188 p. illustrations (chiefly color) (hardcover) $45   **791.43**
1. Motion pictures -- Production and direction 2. Dark crystal (Motion picture)
ISBN 9781608878116; 1608878112

This book, by Caseen Gaines, chronicles "the entire production [of the film ['Dark Crystal'], from the initial concept based on themes close to [Jim] Henson's heart to the ingenious conceptual design, puppet construction, and logistics of the shoot itself. The book also delves into the wider world of 'Dark Crystal,' exploring the creation of comics, novels, and other official projects inspired by the film." (Publisher's note)

"A spectacular, visually thrilling celebration of The Dark Crystal's thirty-fifth anniversary." Booklist

Includes bibliographical references (page [190]).

Gleiberman, Owen

Movie freak; my life watching movies. Owen Gleiberman. Hachette Books 2016 352 p. (hardback) $28   **791.43**
1. Critics 2. Motion pictures -- History and criticism 3. Film critics -- United States -- Biography
ISBN 0316382965; 9780316382960

LC 2015039430

In this memoir, author Owen Gleiberman "paints a bittersweet portrait of his complicated and ultimately doomed friendship with Pauline Kael, the legendary New Yorker film critic who was his mentor and muse. He also offers an unprecedented inside look at what the experience of being a critic is really all about, detailing his stint at The Boston Phoenix and then, starting in 1990, at [Entertainment Weekly]." (Publisher's note)

"A story of societal change, rich in cultural as well as personal history." Kirkus

Graham, Don

Giant; Elizabeth Taylor, Rock Hudson, James Dean, Edna Ferber, and the making of a legendary American film. Don Graham. St. Martin's Press 2018 336 p. (hardcover) $27.99 **791.43**
1. Motion pictures -- History and criticism 2. Motion pictures -- Production and direction 3. Motion pictures -- United States -- History -- 20th century 4. Giant (Motion picture)
ISBN 9781250061904

LC 2017046287

"In this . . . narrative history of the making of the film ['Giant'], Don Graham chronicles the stories of [director George] Stevens, whose trauma in World War II intensified his ambition to make films that would tell the story of America; Edna Ferber, a considerable literary celebrity, who meets her match in the imposing Robert Kleberg, proprietor of the vast King Ranch; and Glenn McCarthy, an American oil tycoon; and Errol Flynn lookalike with a taste for Hollywood." (Publisher's note)

"The book also features in-depth biographies of the film's three leads, because you can't tell the story of this classic film without telling the stories of its stars, who were as tortured as their characters in their own ways. A sharp, insightful look at a legendary film." Booklist

Includes bibliographical references and index

Harris, Mark

★ **Five** Came Back; A Story of Hollywood and the Second World War. Mark Harris. Penguin Group USA 2014 480 p. illustrations $29.95 **791.43**

1. Motion picture industry 2. World War, 1939-1945 -- Motion pictures and the war 3. Motion picture producers and directors -- United States 4. Motion pictures -- United States -- History 5. Motion picture industry -- California -- Los Angeles -- History
ISBN 1594204306; 9781594204302

LC 2013039983

Los Angeles Times Book Prize Finalist: History (2014)

This book tells "the untold story of how Hollywood changed World War II, and how World War II changed Hollywood, through the prism of five film directors caught up in the war: John Ford, William Wyler, John Huston, Frank Capra, and George Stevens." (Publisher's note) "Some of the five worked together (Capra and Stevens), but others worked separately on feature-length documentaries, short subjects and films for military use only." (Kirkus Reviews)

"Narrative nonfiction that is as gloriously readable as it is unfailingly informative." Booklist

Includes bibliographical references and index

Pictures at a revolution; five movies and the birth of the new Hollywood. Penguin Press 2008 490p il $27.95 **791.43**

1. Motion pictures
ISBN 978-1-59420-152-3; 1-59420-152-8

LC 2007-32633

The author examines the five films nominated for the Academy Award for Best Picture in 1967: Bonnie and Clyde, The Graduate, Guess Who's Coming To Dinner, In the Heat of the Night, and Dr. Dolittle.

"Harris gives us a juicy, multilayered chronicle of a turning point in American culture. This is page-turning social history; someone reading this book who didn't live through those days would understand why 'the '60s' had to happen." Newsweek

Includes bibliographical references

Haskell, Molly

Steven Spielberg; A Life in Films. Molly Haskell. Yale University Press 2017 248 p. illustrations (hardcover: alk. paper) $25 **791.43**

1. Motion picture producers and directors -- Biography
ISBN 9780300186932

LC 2016938134

In this book in the Jewish Lives series, author Molly Haskell "explores the full range of [Steven] Spielberg's works for the light they shine upon the man himself. . . . Organizing chapters around specific films, the distinguished critic discusses how Spielberg's childhood in non-Jewish suburbs, his parents' traumatic divorce, his return to Judaism upon his son's birth, and other events echo in his work." (Publisher's note)

"Compact, incisive, and witty—a great starting point for those interested in Spielberg's life and art." Kirkus

Includes bibliographical references (pages 207-214) and index

Jameson, A. D.

I find your lack of faith disturbing; Star Wars and the triumph of geek culture. A. D. Jameson. Farrar, Straus & Giroux 2018 304 p. (cloth) $26 **791.43**

1. Fans (Persons) 2. Star Wars films -- History and criticism
ISBN 9780374537364

LC 2017038357

In this book, author "A. D. Jameson takes geeks and non-geeks alike on a surprising and insightful journey through the science fiction, fantasy, and superhero franchises . . . Walking us through the rise of geekdom from its underground origins to the top of the box office and bestseller lists, Jameson takes in franchises like 'The Lord of the Rings,' . . . and, in particular, 'Star Wars'--as well as phenomena like fan fiction, cosplay, and YouTube parodies." (Publisher's note)

Includes bibliographical references and index

Johnson, Mindy

Ink & paint; the women of Walt Disney's animation. Mindy Johnson. Disney Editions 2017 384 p. illustrations (chiefly color) (hardcover) $60 **791.43**

1. Animated films 2. Women animators 3. Animation (Cinematography) 4. Animation cels 5. Motion picture industry 6. Walt Disney Productions
ISBN 9781484727812; 1484727819

This book in the Disney Editions Deluxe series, by Mindy Johnson, focuses on Walt Disney's women film animators. "From the earliest origins of animated imagery, the colorful link between paper and screen was created by legions of female artists working on the slick surface of celluloid sheets. With calligraphic precision and Rembrandtesque mastery, these women painstakingly brought pencil drawings to vibrant, dimensional life." (Publisher's note)

"Award-winning historian Johnson chronicles the invaluable role women have played in animation history, especially in the creation and duration of Walt Disney Studios." Booklist

Includes bibliographical references (pages 379-383) and index.

Karp, Josh

Orson Welles's last movie; the making of The other side of the wind. Josh Karp. St. Martin's Press 2015 352 p. 8 plates; illustrations (hardback) $26.99 **791.43**

1. Motion pictures -- Production and direction 2. Other side of the wind (Motion picture)
ISBN 1250007089; 9781250007087

LC 2015002464

This book, by Josh Karp, presents a history of the "legendary but self-destructive director Orson Welles" and the production of his final film "The Other Side of the Wind." This book "is a fast-paced, behind-the-scenes account of the bizarre, hilarious and remarkable making of what has been called 'the greatest home movie that no one has ever seen.'" (Publisher's note)

"A fascinating story, much more than your typical making-of book." Booklist

Lanzmann, Claude, 1925-2018

The **Patagonian** hare; a memoir. Claude Lanzmann; translated from the French by Frank Wynne. Farrar, Straus & Giroux 2012 x, 528 p.p ill. **791.43**

1. Autobiographies 2. Journalists -- Biography 3. Motion picture producers and directors -- Biography 4. Journalists -- France -- Biography 5. Motion picture producers and directors -- France -- Biography
ISBN 0374230048; 9780374230043

LC 2011048058

This book is the memoir of the "journalist and filmmaker Claude Lanzmann. . . . Raised as a secular Jew in a family with deep communist sympathies . . . the author served in the French Resistance and narrowly missed capture by the Nazis. . . . He became editor of Jean-Paul Sartre's journal 'Le Temps Modernes' . . . and had an intense seven-year affair with Sartre's lover, Simone de Beauvoir, who was happy to take him on as her 'sixth man.' Faithfulness wasn't anyone's game then, and Lanzmann seemed to seduce nearly every woman he ever met. He also became deeply immersed in his own Jewish heritage and documentary filmmaking, ultimately resulting in his nine-hour magnum opus Shoah." (Kirkus)

Lebo, Harlan

Citizen Kane; a filmmaker's journey. Harlan Lebo. Thomas Dunne Books 2016 384 p. illustrations (ebook) $60; (hardback) $27.99   **791.43**

1. Citizen Kane (Motion picture) 2. Motion pictures -- Production and direction

ISBN 9781466889750; 9781250077530

LC 2015045237

This book, by Harlan Lebo, presents "the extraordinary story of the production of Orson Welles' classic film, using previously unpublished material from studio files and the Hearst organization, exclusive interviews with the last surviving members of the cast and crew, and what may be the only surviving copies of the 'lost' final script." (Publisher's note)

"Lebo's book is highly readable; it's dense, lucid, and page-turning. Fans of Welles and classic Hollywood will be delighted by this comprehensive, intelligent work." Pub Wkly

Includes bibliographical references (pages [309]-349) and index.

Longworth, Karina

Hollywood frame by frame; the unseen silver screen in contact sheets, 1915-1997. Karina Longworth. Princeton Architectural Press 2014 1 p. (hardback) $30   **791.43**

1. Hollywood (Calif.) 2. Motion picture industry 3. Contact printing -- United States 4. Stills (Motion pictures) -- United States 5. Motion pictures -- United States -- Pictorial works

ISBN 1616892595; 9781616892593

LC 2013051020

This book by Karina Longworth "presents hundreds of never-before-published photos from the sets of some of the greatest films of the twentieth century. Hollywood's biggest stars are caught with their guard down behind the scenes of movie classics from Some Like It Hot and Breakfast at Tiffany's to Taxi Driver and The Silence of the Lambs." (Publisher's note)

"Cinephiles will relish these moments captured from another era." LJ

Lumet, Sidney, 1924-2011

Making movies. Knopf 1995 220p hardcover o.p. pa $12   **791.43**

1. Motion pictures -- Production and direction

ISBN 0-679-75660-4 pa

LC 94-34449

In this book on the filmmaking process, "Lumet discusses writers and actors, camera and editing techniques, art direction and sound." (Libr J)

"A fascinating look at the artist at work." Libr J

Mann, William J.

Behind the screen; how gays and lesbians shaped Hollywood, 1910-1969. Viking 2001 xxiv, 422p il $29.95; pa $16   **791.43**

1. Motion picture industry 2. Homosexuality in motion pictures

ISBN 0-670-03017-1; 0-14-200114-7 pa

LC 2001-17984

In this study "Mann examines how the movie capital of the world was transformed by a host of writers, directors, designers, actors, and producers often at odds with the official codes, and mores of the times.

... Mann's book is important reading for anyone interested in the history of American film. Essential for all film and gay studies collections." Libr J

Muir, John Kenneth

The **encyclopedia** of superheroes on film and television; 2nd ed.; McFarland & Co. 2008 696p il $75   **791.43**

1. Reference books 2. Superhero films -- Encyclopedias 3. Superhero television programs -- Encyclopedias

ISBN 978-0-7864-3755-9; 0-7864-3755-3

LC 2008-19724

First published 2004

"Entries start with description and background of the hero. Live-action films are presented with reviewer comments and cast and crew. TV series also present reviewer comments and a description of the series. Episode guides include title, writer and director credits, and air dates as well as episode descriptions and guest casts. . . . A good addition to the pop-culture collection." Booklist

Includes bibliographical references

Nashawaty, Chris

Caddyshack; the making of a Hollywood Cinderella story. Chris Nashawaty. Flatiron Books 2018 304 p. (hardcover) $26.99   **791.43**

1. Comedy films 2. Motion picture industry -- United States 3. Motion pictures -- Production and direction 4. Caddyshack (Motion picture)

ISBN 9781250105950

LC 2017051033

In this book, author "Chris Nashawaty goes behind the scenes of the iconic film ['Caddyshack,'] chronicling the rise of comedy's greatest deranged minds as they form 'The National Lampoon,' . . . and ultimately blow up both a golf course and popular culture as we know it. 'Caddyshack' is at once an eye-opening narrative about one of the most interesting, surreal, and dramatic film productions there's ever been, and a rich portrait of the biggest . . . names in Hollywood." (Publisher's note)

"Nashawaty's prose is lively, and his exhaustive research is bolstered by interviews with many of the film's principle players, including the famously elusive Murray. A wonderful celebration of a passionately loved film." Booklist

Includes bibliographical references

Osborne, Robert A.

85 years of the Oscar; the official history of the Academy Awards. {by} Robert Osborne. Abbeville Press 2013 416p il $75   **791.43**

1. Academy Awards (Motion pictures)

ISBN 9780789211422

First published 1989 with title: 60 years of the Oscar. Published every five years.

This includes a history of the Academy of Motion Picture Arts and Sciences, overviews of Academy Award nominees and winners, award ceremonies, and a complete listing of nominees and winners in every category

Includes bibliographical references

Rabin, Nathan

My year of flops; the A.V. Club presents one man's journey deep into the heart of cinematic failure. Scribner 2010 264p il pa $15   **791.43**

1. Motion pictures

ISBN 978-1-4391-5312-3; 1-4391-5312-4

LC 2010-18224

"Follow Nathan Rabin on his quest 'to provide a sympathetic reappraisal of some of the most reviled films of all time,' and what do you learn? 'Pennies From Heaven'and 'Freddy Got Fingered' are better than you might think, and 'Ishtar' offers an 'exquisitely jaundiced take' on American foreign policy. Mostly, though, Mr. Rabin sits slack-jawed watching the everlasting dreadfulness of 'Mame,' 'Battlefield Earth' and 'Exit to Eden' ('the mother of all unsexy sex films'). Always glad to snark it up, Mr. Rabin can also be mournful when reflecting on how worthwhile failures like 'Heaven's Gate' diminished Hollywood's ambitions, then and now. The book, which collects columns that first appeared on The Onion's pop-culture Web site, includes more bad movies and interviews with actors caught up in the cinematic wreckage." N Y Times Book Rev

Rappaport, Helen

Victoria; the heart and mind of a young queen. Helen Rappaport. Harper Design Intl 2017 300 p. chiefly color illustrations (ebook) $27.99; $29.99   **791.43**
    1. Great Britain -- History -- Victoria, 1837-1901
    ISBN 9780062568908; 0062568892; 9780062568892
                                                    LC 2016953275
    This book, by Helen Rappaport, "delves into the private writings of the young Queen Victoria, painting a vivid picture of the personal life of one of England's greatest monarchs. . . . At only eighteen years old, Victoria ascended the throne as a rebellious teenager and gradually grew to become one of the most memorable, unshakeable and powerful women in history. The extensive writings she left behind document this personal journey and show how she triumphed over scandal and corruption." (Publisher's note)

Rough Guides (Firm)

The **Rough** Guide to film; [by] Richard Armstrong . . . [et al.] Distributed by Penguin Putnam 2007 649p il pa $27.99   **791.43**
    1. Reference books 2. Motion picture producers and directors -- Biography -- Dictionaries
    ISBN 978-1-84353-408-2; 1-84353-408-8
                                                    LC 2007-300132
    "This volume looks beyond the Hollywood mainstream to provide assistance to anyone who is browsing rental-store shelves or online DVD catalogs in search of something new. More than 800 directors from around the globe are profiled, and more than 2,000 of their most important films are briefly reviewed. . . . If you're in a hurry, you can turn to the various categorized lists of five great directors, five classic films, and five 'lesser-known gems.'" Booklist

Santopietro, Tom

The **sound** of music story; how one young nun, one handsome Austrian captain, and seven singing Von Trapp children inspired the most beloved film of all time. by Tom Santopietro. St. Martin's Press 2015 336 p. illustrations (hardcover) $28.99   **791.43**
    1. Sound of music (Motion picture)
    ISBN 9781250064462
                                                    LC 2014033795
    Includes bibliographical references and index.
    In this book on the film "The Sound of Music," Tom Santopietro "chronicles the initial faltering financial commitment of 20th Century Fox, and the torturous search for a director, a cinematographer, the actors and actresses, and other staff. . . . Although the Von Trapp family, and Austria, initially distanced themselves from the film because they

thought it inaccurately portrayed their family and the times, they later accepted . . . [it] because of what it means to people." (Publishers Weekly)
    "A fun-to-read book, perfect for musical-lovers, aspiring moviemakers, and film buffs." Booklist

Schickel, Richard, 1933-2017

Keepers; the greatest films-and personal favorites-of a moviegoing lifetime. Richard Schickel. Alfred A. Knopf 2015 320 p. (hardcover) $26.95; (ebook) $51   **791.43**
    1. Film criticism 2. Motion pictures 3. Motion pictures -- Evaluation
    ISBN 9780375424595; 9781101874714
                                                    LC 2014034997
    This book by film critic Richard Schickel offers a "history of film as he's seen—and lived—it, a tour of his favorites, a master class in what makes a film soar or flop. [His] no-holds-barred, often raucously irreverent opinions can range from panning classics, to spotlighting forgotten treasures, to defending the art of 'popular' genres such as horror, westerns, screwball comedy, and noir. Beyond his picks and pans, Schickel offers a wealth of behind-the-scenes anecdotes." (Publisher's note)
    "Schickel, who posits in his introduction that movies are about both nothing and everything, wholly succeeds in making readers care about every film he's seen." Pub Wkly

Schoenberger, Nancy

Wayne and Ford; the films, the friendship, and the forging of an American hero. Nancy Schoenberger. Nan A. Talese Doubleday 2017 240 p. illustrations (hardcover) $27.95 **791.43**
    1. Friendship 2. Historical literature 3. Western films -- History and criticism
    ISBN 9780385534857; 9780385534864
                                                    LC 2016057903
    In this book, by Nancy Schoenberger, "John Ford and John Wayne were a blockbuster Hollywood team, turning out many of the finest Western films ever made. . . . In 1939 Ford made Wayne a star in Stagecoach, and from there the two men established a close, often turbulent relationship. . . . Drawing on previously untapped caches of letters and personal documents, . . . Schoenberger dramatically narrates . . . the lasting legacy of that friendship on American culture." (Publisher's note)
    Includes bibliographical references and index

Shepard, Jim

The **tunnel** at the end of the light; essays on movies and politics. by Jim Shepard. Tin House Books 2017 xxii, 261 p.p (paperback) $15.95   **791.43**
    1. Performing arts 2. Motion pictures -- Social aspects 3. Motion pictures -- Philosophy
    ISBN 9781941040720; 9781941040737
                                                    LC 2017010540
    In this collection of essays, author Jim Shepard "weaves close readings of film with cultural criticism to explore the ways in which movies work so ubiquitously to reflect how Americans think and act. . . . [He] explores how we enter into conversations with specific genres and films--'Chinatown,' 'The Third Man,' and 'Badlands' among others--in order to construct and refine our most cherished illusions about ourselves." (Publisher's weekly)
    "This collection shows Shepard's voice to be as essential as ever, and it suggests that he should be writing similar criticism for our own fraught times." Pub Wkly
    Includes bibliographical references and index

Szostak, Phil

The **art** of Star Wars; The Last Jedi. Phil Szostak; foreword by Rian Johnson. Abrams 2017 253 p. illustrations (hardcover) $40   **791.43**

1. Star Wars films 2. Science fiction films 3. Motion pictures -- Production and direction 4. Star Wars, the last Jedi (Motion picture)
ISBN 9781419727054; 1419727052

LC 2017943326

This book, by Phil Szostak, with foreword by Rian Johnson, "takes fans on a deep dive into the development of the fantastic worlds, characters, and creatures--both old and new--of 'The Last Jedi.' Exclusive interviews with the filmmakers and with the Lucasfilm visualists provides a running commentary on this unforgettable art, and reveals the inspirations behind moviemaking magic at its finest." (Publisher's note)

Thomson, David, 1941-

The **big** screen; the story of the movies. David Thomson. 1st ed. Farrar, Straus and Giroux 2012 viii, 595 p.p (alk. paper) $35.00   **791.43**

1. Motion pictures -- Social aspects 2. Motion pictures -- United States -- History 3. Motion pictures -- Social aspects -- United States
ISBN 9780374191894; 0374191891

LC 2012009140

This book by David Thomson is "is a wide-ranging narrative about the movies and their signal role in modern life. Thomson takes us around the globe, through time, and across many media--moving from Eadweard Muybridge to Steve Jobs, from 'Sunrise' to 'I Love Lucy,' from John Wayne to George Clooney, from television commercials to streaming video--to tell the complex, gripping, paradoxical story of the movies." (Publisher's note)

Includes bibliographical references and index.

How to watch a movie; David Thomson. Alfred A. Knopf 2015 256 p. (ebook) $65; (hardcover) $24.95   **791.43**

1. Cinematography 2. Motion pictures -- Appreciation
ISBN 9781101875407; 9781101875391; 9781101910849

LC 2014046757

In this book about cinema, author David Thomson "offers his most inventive exploration of the medium yet: guiding us through each element of the viewing experience, considering the significance of everything from what we see and hear on-screen—actors, shots, cuts, dialogue, music—to the specifics of how, where, and with whom we do the viewing." (Publisher's note)

"An enjoyably deep dive into the interaction between cinema and psyche." Kirkus

Warner Bros; the making of an American movie studio. David Thomson. Yale University Press 2017 viii, 220 p.p illustrations (Jewish lives) (hardcover: alk. paper) $25 **791.43**

1. Warner Bros. 2. Motion picture industry -- History 3. Warner Bros. Pictures (1923-1967) 4. Motion picture studios -- California -- Los Angeles -- History 5. Motion picture producers and directors -- United States -- Biography
ISBN 9780300197600

LC 2016956162

This book in the Jewish Lives series, by David Thomson, "charts the rise of an unpromising film studio from its shaky beginnings in the early twentieth century through its ascent to the pinnacle of Hollywood influence and popularity. The Warner Brothers--Harry, Albert, Sam, and Jack—arrived in America as unschooled Jewish immigrants, yet they founded a studio that became the smartest, toughest, and most radical in all of Hollywood." (Publisher's note)

"An entertaining, well-documented history of the legendary studio for film scholars and fans alike." Kirkus

Includes bibliographical references (pages 193-204) and index.

The **whole** equation; a history of Hollywood. Knopf 2005 402p il hardcover o.p. pa $15   **791.43**

1. Motion picture industry -- History 2. Motion pictures -- History and criticism
ISBN 0-375-40016-8; 0-375-70154-0 pa

LC 2004-48358

"Peeling back the layers, goring sacred cows, correcting misconceptions, and revealing truth rather than reprinting legends, Thomson offers history, yes, but also a philosophical meditation on how the movie industry has inspired and influenced L.A. and America, and vice versa." Booklist

Includes bibliographical references

Turan, Kenneth

Not to be missed; 54 favorites from a lifetime of film. Kenneth Turan. PublicAffairs 2014 368 p. (hardback) $25.99; (ebook) $11.99   **791.43**

1. Motion pictures -- History and criticism 2. Motion pictures
ISBN 9781586483968; 9781610393676

LC 2014007773

This book presents Kenneth Turan's "fifty-four favorite films. . . . [It] blends cultural criticism, historical anecdote, and inside-Hollywood controversy. Turan's selection of favorites ranges across all genres. From 'All About Eve' to 'Seven Samurai' to 'Sherlock Jr.,' these are all timeless films." (Publisher's note)

"Turan's illuminating reflections do what the best essays on film always do: send us to watch the movie, whether for the first time or the 20th." Pub Wkly

Includes bibliographical references and index

Urwand, Ben

The **collaboration**; Hollywood's pact with Hitler. Ben Urwand. The Belknap Press of Harvard University Press 2013 320 p. (hardcover: alk. paper) $26.95   **791.43**

1. National socialism 2. Germany -- History -- 1933-1945 3. Motion picture industry -- History 4. National socialism and motion pictures 5. Germany -- Civilization -- American influences 6. Motion picture industry -- United States -- History -- 20th century
ISBN 0674724747; 9780674724747

LC 2013013576

This book looks at the "alliance Hollywood made with the Nazis, which allowed both to keep packing movie theaters in Germany up until the outbreak of war. Concomitant with Hollywood's golden era of the 1930s was the rise of the Nazi Party, whose chief officials admired American films. . . . The result of this complicated and slippery relationship . . . was the absolute disappearance from film of Nazis and Jews until the end of the decade." (Kirkus Reviews)

Includes bibliographical references and index

Warren, Bill

Keep watching the skies! American science fiction movies of the fifties. research associate, Bill Thomas; foreword by Howard Waldrop. 21st century ed.; McFarland & Co. 2010 1004p il $99   **791.43**

1. Reference books 2. Science fiction films
ISBN 978-0-7864-4230-0; 0-7864-4230-1

LC 2009-20594

First published in two volumes 1982-1986

Covers "nearly 300 films released between 1950 and 1962. . . . Although prominent films like Forbidden Planet, Them! The Time Machine, and The Fly receive more extensive coverage, all of the essays . . . include production, cast, and distribution credits; a plot synopsis; production details and fun background facts; discussion of the direction, acting, effects, and other prominent elements of the film; and information about public and critical reaction. Attractive photos accompany most of the essays, and posters for the best-known films are reproduced in 35 color plates. . . . Although the audience for 1950s science fiction may be dwindling, this is the kind of reference that not only informs but also creates new fans." Booklist

Includes bibliographical references

Wasson, Sam

Fifth Avenue, 5 AM; Audrey Hepburn, Breakfast at Tiffany's, and the dawn of the modern woman. HarperStudio 2010 xx, 231p il map $19.99   **791.43**

1. Actors 2. Breakfast at Tiffany's (Motion picture)
ISBN 978-0-06-177415-7

LC 2009-52439

The author "presents an irresistibly gossipy account of the production of Breakfast at Tiffany's (1961), charting the transformation of actress Audrey Hepburn into an icon of emerging sexual liberation—the good/bad girl, the lovable 'kook,' independent and sexually experienced but sufficiently charming to bring home to mother. Rich in incident and set among the glitterati of America's most glamorous era, the book reads like a novel." Kirkus

Wieland, Karin

Dietrich & Riefenstahl; Hollywood, Berlin, and a century in two lives. Karin Wieland; translated by Shelley Frisch. Liveright Publishing Corp. 2015 624 p. illustrations (hardcover) $35   **791.43**

1. Women entertainers -- Germany -- Biography 2. Motion picture actors and actresses -- Germany -- Biography 3. Women motion picture producers and directors -- Germany -- Biography
ISBN 9780871403360

LC 2015026548

National Book Critics Circle Award Finalist: Biography (2015)

This book, by Karin Wieland, translated by Shelley Frisch, named Best Book of 2015 by the "Boston Globe" and "Washington Post" newspapers, offers a dual biography of the 20th century women actresses Leni Riefenstahl and Marlene Dietrich. "Skillfully juxtaposing these two fascinating lives, Wieland brings to vivid life a time of international upheaval, chronicling radical evolutions of politics, fame, and femininity on a grand stage." (Publisher's note)

"Wieland deftly traces both lives through their many ups and downs. A sweeping, revelatory dual biography." Kirkus

Includes bibliographical references and index

791.437   Films

Klastorin, Michael

★ **Close** encounters of the third kind; the ultimate visual history. written by Michael Klastorin; foreword by Steven Spielberg. Harper Design 2017 188 p. $50   **791.437**

1. Science fiction films 2. Extraterrestrial beings
ISBN 0062692992; 9780062692993

This book on the film "Close Encounters of the Third Kind," by Michael Klastorin, "details the complete creative journey behind the making of the film and examines its cultural impact. Featuring rare and never-before-seen imagery from the archives, the book brings together a stunning collection of on-set photography, concept art, storyboards, and more to create a visual narrative of the film's journey to the big screen." (Publisher's note)

791.44   Radio

Ely, Melvin Patrick

The **adventures** of Amos 'n' Andy; a social history of an American phenomenon. University Press of Va. 2001 xxi, 322p il pa $18.50   **791.44**

1. African Americans on television 2. Amos 'n' Andy (Radio program) 3. Amos 'n' Andy (Television program)
ISBN 0-8139-2092-2

LC 2001-45538

First published 1991 by Free Press

A "historian examines one of America's greatest cultural enigmas—the amazing popularity, among blacks as well as whites, of 'Amos 'n' Andy' on radio for more than 30 years." N Y Times Book Rev

Includes bibliographical references

Schwartz, A. Brad

★ **Broadcast** hysteria; Orson Welles's War of the worlds and the art of fake news. A. Brad Schwartz. Hill & Wang 2015 352 p. illustrations (hardcover) $35   **791.44**

1. Radio broadcasting 2. War of the worlds (Radio program) 3. Science fiction radio programs -- Psychological aspects 4. Radio broadcasting -- United States -- History -- 20th century
ISBN 9780809031610; 0809031612

LC 2014040510

In this book author "A. Brad Schwartz boldly retells the story of [Orson] Welles's famed radio play and its impact. Schwartz is the first to examine the hundreds of letters sent to Orson Welles himself in the days after the broadcast, and his findings challenge the conventional wisdom. Schwartz shows that Welles's broadcast became a major scandal, prompting a different kind of mass panic as Americans debated the bewitching power of the radio." (Publisher's note)

"A gripping and informative look at the War of the World broadcast, as well as contemporary issues in the early 20th-century industry of radio. Highly recommended for students of journalism, fans of Welles, and general readers interested in radio or broadcasting." LJ

Includes bibliographical references and index

791.45   Television

Armstrong, Jennifer Keishin

Seinfeldia; how a show about nothing changed everything. Jennifer Keishin Armstrong. Simon & Schuster 2015 320 p. illustrations (some color) (ebook) $19.99; (hardcover: alk. paper) $26   **791.45**

1. Television programs 2. Seinfeld (Television program)
ISBN 9781476756127; 9781476756103

LC 2015023755

In this book, author Jennifer Keishin Armstrong "celebrates the creators and fans of . . . ['Seinfeld,'], bringing readers behind-the-scenes of the show while it was on the air and into the world of devotees for whom it never stopped being relevant, a world where . . . Joe Davola gets questioned every day about his sanity, Kenny Kramer makes his living giving tours of New York sights . . . , and fans dress up in Jerry's famous puffy shirt." (Publisher's note)

"Armstrong offers a masterly look at one of the greatest shows. The research involved makes this a boon to television scholars, but Seinfeld enthusiasts will also enjoy this funny, highly readable book." LJ

Includes bibliographical references and index

Sex and the city and us; how four single women changed the way we think, live, and love. Jennifer Keishin Armstrong. Simon & Schuster 2018 256 p. (hardcover: alk. paper) $26   791.45
1. Single women 2. Women on television 3. Sex and the city (Television program)
ISBN 9781501164828; 9781501164835

LC 2018000333

This book, by Jennifer Keishin Armstrong "is the story of how a columnist [Candace Bushnell], two gay men--Darren Star and fellow executive producer Michael Patrick King--and a writers' room full of women used their own poignant, hilarious, and humiliating stories to launch a cultural phenomenon, pushing the boundaries of television and ignited a national conversation about single women and sex in the process." (Publisher's note)

Includes bibliographical references and index

Burnett, Carol, 1933-

In such good company; Eleven Years of Laughter, Mayhem, and Fun in the Sandbox. Carol Burnett. Crown Archetype 2016 320 p. illustrations (ebook) $65; (hardback) $28   **791.45**
1. Women comedians 2. Comedy television programs 3. Carol Burnett Show (Television program: 1967-1978)
ISBN 9781101904664; 9781101904657

LC 2016008433

In this book, comedian Carol Burnett "delves into little-known stories of the guests, sketches and improvisations that made The Carol Burnett Show legendary, as well as some favorite tales too good not to relive again. While writing this book, Carol rewatched all 276 episodes and screen-grabbed her favorite video stills from the archives to illustrate the chemistry of the actors and the improvisational magic that made the show so successful." (Publisher's note)

"Burnett watched every episode afresh to research this book, and that attention to detail shows in her exhaustive accounts of major sketches. However, even nonfans will enjoy the nuggets of intrigue Burnett scatters throughout, in which she shines a light on the sexism she faced during her tenure as a leading lady of the small screen." Pub Wkly

Gaines, Chip

★ **Capital** gaines; smart things I learned doing stupid stuff. Chip Gaines. W Publishing Group, an imprint of Thomas Nelson 2017 xiii, 191 p.p (hardcover) $24.99   **791.45**
1. Television personalities 2. Conduct of life 3. Success in business
ISBN 0785216308; 9780785216308

LC 2017950989

This book, by Chip Gaines, "offers readers a ringside seat as Chip relives some of his craziest antics and the lessons learned along the way. His mentors taught him to never give up and his family showed him what it meant to always have a positive attitude despite your circumstances. Throw in a natural daredevil personality and a willingness to do (or eat!) just about anything, and you have the life and daily activity of Chip Gaines." (Publisher's note)

Includes bibliographical references (pages 187-190).

Gross, Edward

The **fifty**-year mission; the complete, uncensored, unauthor-

ized oral history of Star trek: the first 25 years. Edward Gross and Mark A. Altman; foreword by Seth MacFarlane. Thomas Dunne Books 2016 xv, 560 p.p (hardcover) $29.99   **791.45**
1. Star trek films 2. Star trek television programs 3. Science fiction television programs 4. Star trek (Television program) 5. Star Trek films -- History and criticism
ISBN 9781250089472; 9781250065841

LC 2015051257

This book, by Edward Gross and Mark A. Altman, "is a no-holds-barred oral history of five decades of 'Star Trek,' told by the people who were there. Hear from the hundreds of television and film executives, programmers, writers, creators and cast as they unveil the oftentimes shocking story of 'Star Trek's' ongoing fifty-year mission--a mission that has spanned from the classic series to the animated show, the many attempts at a relaunch through the beloved feature films." (Publisher's note)

"Breathtaking in scope and depth, this is a must-read for Star Trek lovers as well as anyone who wants a better understanding of how television and film production works." Booklist

Followed by The Fifty-Year Mission--The Next 25 Years

Slayers & vampires; the complete uncensored, unauthorized oral history of Buffy & Angel. by Edward Gross and Mark A. Altman. Tom Doherty Association 2017 524 p. (hardcover) $27.99   **791.45**
1. Television programs 2. Vampires on television 3. Horror television programs 4. Vampires -- United States 5. Angel (Fictitious character: Whedon) 6. High school students -- United States 7. Buffy, the vampire slayer (Television program) 8. Buffy the Vampire Slayer (Fictitious character)
ISBN 9781250128935; 9781250128928; 1250128927

In this book, by Edward Gross and Mark A. Altman, "two decades after its groundbreaking debut, millions of fans worldwide remain enthralled with the incredible exploits of Joss Whedon's Buffy Summers, the slayer and feminist icon who saved the world...a lot; as well as Angel, the tortured vampire with a soul who fought against the apocalyptic forces of evil. Now, go behind-the-scenes of these legendary series." (Publisher's note)

"Filled with absorbing behind-the-scenes details, Altman and Gross' illuminating celebration of Whedon's influential shows will thrill fans of Buffy and Angel and stand as invaluable primary TV history." Booklist

Kaufman, Amy

Bachelor nation; inside the world of america's favorite guilty pleasure. Amy Kaufman. Penguin Group USA 2018 320 p. $25   **791.45**
1. Single people 2. Reality television programs 3. Television programs -- Social aspects
ISBN 1101985909; 9781101985908

This book, by Amy Kaufman, offers "the first behind-the-scenes, unauthorized look into the reality television phenomenon ['The Bachelor']. . . . [Kaufman] has interviewed dozens of producers, contestants, and celebrity fans to give readers never-before-told details of the show's inner workings: what it's like to be trapped in the mansion 'bubble'; . . . and revelations about the alcohol-fueled debauchery that occurs long before the fantasy suite." (Publisher's note)

"Essential for fans of pop culture, this book could play an important role in courses on feminism and gender studies. It's also a fascinating and fun read for anyone who wants to think about how and why viewers continue to tune into shows like The Bachelor." LJ

Kelly, Megyn, 1970-

Settle for More; Megyn Kelly. HarperCollins 2016 304 p. hardcover $29.99 **791.45**

1. Women journalists -- Biography 2. Television personalities -- Biography

ISBN 9780062494603; 0062494600

LC 2016041059

This memoir by Megyn Kelly details "her rise as one of the most respected journalists working today. From the values and lessons that have shaped her career, to her time at the center of the chaotic 2016 Republican presidential primary, this book offers an inside look at an uncompromising woman's journey to the top of the news business. . . . Kelly goes behind the scenes of the stories and the storms that have made her one of the most talked about public figures in America." (Publisher's note)

Miller, James Andrew

Those guys have all the fun; inside the world of ESPN. [by] James Andrew Miller and Tom Shales. Little, Brown and Company 2011 763p il $27.99 **791.45**

1. ESPN, Inc. 2. Television broadcasting of sports

ISBN 0316043001; 9780316043007

This book "presents the history of sports channel ESPN based on interviews with . . . current and former employees, featuring announcers and analysts as well as sports stars including LeBron James, Peyton Manning, and Jeff Gordon." (Publisher's note) Index.

"Compiled from more than 550 interviews, Those Guys traces ESPN from its birth as an underdog to its current status as a money-printing behemoth. Some of the best sections deal with the early days of cable, when the network invented itself through savvy business decisions and slow-pitch-softball coverage. But it's the big libidos and bigger egos that will get the most attention. The book is packed with entertaining stories of unpleasant people and awful behavior: booze-fueled boorishness, absurdly arrogant execs, and the endlessly fascinating Olbermann. . . . Miller and Shales offer compelling behind-the-scenes tales of many major sports moments, including the Rush Limbaugh–Donovan McNabb flap and ESPN's takeover of Monday Night Football." Entertainment Wkly

Mulgrew, Kate, 1955-

Born With Teeth; A Memoir. Kate Mulgrew. Little Brown & Co 2015 320 p. illustrations $28 **791.45**

1. Actresses 2. Motherhood

ISBN 0316334316; 9780316334310

LC 2015930445

In this memoir, actress Kate Mulgrew details how "at twenty-two, just as her career was taking off, she became pregnant. Having already signed the adoption papers, she was allowed only a fleeting glimpse of her child. As her star continued to rise, her life became increasingly demanding and fulfilling, a whirlwind of passionate love affairs, life-saving friendships, and bone-crunching work. Mulgrew remained haunted by the loss of her daughter, until, two decades later, she found the courage to face the past." (Publisher's note)

"Mulgrew's enjoyable narrative is compelling as she portrays her decades of acting work, personal triumphs and heartbreaks, and her mesmerizing life." Library Journal

Mullally, Megan

The **greatest** love story ever told; an oral history. Penguin Group USA 2018 288 p. $28 **791.45**

1. Celebrities

ISBN 1101986670; 9781101986677

In this book, authors Megan Mullally and Nick Offerman "reveal the full story behind their epic romance--presented in a series of intimate conversations between the couple, including photos, anecdotes, and the occasional puzzle. . . . This is not only the intoxicating book that Mullally's and Offerman's fans have been waiting for, it might just hold the solution to the greatest threat facing our modern world: the single life." (Publisher's note)

Peisner, David

Homey don't play that! the story of In Living Color and the Black Comedy Revolution. David Peisner. Simon & Schuster 2018 400 p. $28 **791.45**

1. Comedy television programs 2. African Americans on television

ISBN 1501143328; 9781501143328

In this book, by David Peisner, "few television shows revolutionized comedy as profoundly or have had such an enormous and continued impact on our culture as 'In Living Color.' Inspired by Richard Pryor, Carol Burnett, and Eddie Murphy, Keenen Ivory Wayans created a television series unlike any that had come before it. . . . 'Homey Don't Play That' reveals the complete, captivating story of how 'In Living Color' overcame enormous odds to become a major, zeitgeist-seizing hit." (Publisher's note)

Reiss, Mike

Springfield confidential; jokes, secrets, and outright lies from a lifetime writing for the Simpsons. Mike Reiss, Mathew Klickstein with foreword Judd Apatow. HarperCollins 2018 320 p. illustrations $27.99 **791.45**

1. Comedy television programs 2. Fantasy television programs

ISBN 0062748033; 9780062748034

In this book, "four-time Emmy winner Mike Reiss--who has worked on 'The Simpsons' continuously since episode one in 1989--shares stories, scandals, and gossip about working with America's most iconic cartoon family ever. Reiss explains how the episodes are created, and provides an inside look at the show's writers, animators, actors and celebrity guests. He answers a range of questions from Simpsons fans . . . and reminisces about the making of perennially favorite episodes." (Publisher's note)

"Always honest, playful, and engaging, the book will provide fans with deep insight into the show's history but also into its daily production and future." Kirkus

Seitz, Matt Zoller

TV (the book) Two Experts Pick the Greatest American Shows of All Time. Alan Sepinwall & Matt Zoller Seitz. Grand Central Publishing 2016 432 p. (ebook) $60; (paperback) $19.99 **791.45**

1. Television programs 2. Television series -- United States -- History and criticism

ISBN 9781455537419; 9781455588190

LC 2016015540

In this book, authors Alan Sepinwall and Matt Zoller Seitz "have identified and ranked the 100 greatest scripted shows in American TV history. Using a complex, obsessively all- encompassing scoring system, they've created a Pantheon of top TV shows, each accompanied by essays delving into what made these shows great." (Publisher's note)

"The great debate: how do you pick the best show of all time? -- The inner circle -- No-doubt-about-it classics -- Groundbreakers and workhorses -- Outlier classics -- Works in progress -- A certain regard -- Miniseries -- TV-movies -- Live plays made for television." Kirkus

Shales, Tom

Live from New York; an uncensored story of Saturday

Night Live. Tom Shales and James Andrew Miller. 2nd edition Little, Brown & Co. 2015 800 p. 24 plates; illustrations $19.99   **791.45**

1. Comedy television programs 2. Saturday Night Live (TV program) 3. Saturday night live (Television program)
ISBN 031629506X; 9780316295062

LC 200272958

Authors James Andrew Miller and Tom Shales present this book on the television show "Saturday Night Live. "Trail-blazing talents recalled three turbulent decades of on-camera antics and off-camera escapades. Now a fourth decade has passed---and bestselling authors James Andrew Miller and Tom Shales have returned to Studio 8H. Over more than 100 pages of new material, they raucously and revealingly take the SNL story up to the present, adding a constellation of iconic new stars, surprises, and controversies." (Publisher's note)

Smith, Chris

The **Daily** show (the book) an oral history: as told by Jon Stewart, the correspondents, staff and guests. Chris Smith; foreword by Jon Stewart. Grand Central Publishing 2016 xviii, 459 p.p color illustrations (hardcover) $30   **791.45**

1. Television programs 2. Television and politics 3. Daily show (Television program)
ISBN 9781455565382; 1455565385

LC 2016952042

This book, by Chris Smith, with foreword by Jon Stewart, "takes the reader behind the curtain for all the show's highlights, from its origins as Comedy Central's underdog late-night program hosted by Craig Kilborn to Jon Stewart's long reign to Trevor Noah's succession, rising from a scrappy jester in the 24-hour political news cycle to become part of the beating heart of politics-a trusted source for not only comedy but also commentary." (Publisher's note)

"A lively oral history of The Daily Show focused on Jon Stewart's improbable transformation from basic-cable comic to progressive conscience." Kirkus

Stelter, Brian

Top of the morning; inside the cutthroat world of morning tv. Brian Stelter. Grand Central Pub. 2013 320 p. (hardcover) $28   **791.45**

1. Television broadcasting of news 2. Today show (Television program) 3. Good morning America (Television program)
ISBN 1455512877; 9781455512874; 9781455545360

LC 2013932327

This book looks at the struggles between the morning news television programs "Today" and "Good Morning America." It "commences with the decision of producer Jim Bell to remove struggling co-host Ann Curry from Today. As that story unfolds, Stelter periodically returns us to the earliest days of Today (1952: with Dave Garroway and chimp J. Fred Muggs) and to the beginnings of GMA in 1975." (Kirkus Reviews)

Thomson, David

Television; a biography. David Thomson. Thames & Hudson 2016 304 p. illustrations (some color) (ebook) $50; (hardcover) $34.95   **791.45**

1. Television broadcasting -- United States -- History
ISBN 9780500773727; 9780500519165

LC 2016932145

In this book, author David Thomson "brings his provocatively insightful and unique voice to the life of what was television. David Thomson surveying a Boschian landscape, illuminated by that singular glow--always 'on'--and peopled by everyone from Donna Reed to Den-

nis Potter, will be the first complete history of the defining medium of our time." (Publisher's note)

"A bracing, essential engagement with the ramifications of our lives before the small screen." Kirkus

Includes bibliographical references (pages 389-398) and index.

791.450   History, geographic treatment, biography

Lunden, Joan, 1950-

Had I Known; A Memoir of Survival. Joan Lunden. HarperCollins 2015 304 p. 16 plates; illustrations $26.99 **791.450**

1. Journalists 2. Breast cancer 3. Cancer patients
ISBN 0062404083; 9780062404084

In this memoir, journalist Joan Lunden "speaks candidly about her battle against breast cancer, her quest to learn about it and teach others, and the transformative effect it's had on her life. As Joan reveals, while her journey was not easy, it profoundly changed her in unexpected ways. Her odyssey helped Joan redefine herself, her values, and most of all, her health." (Publisher's note)

"And Lunden's fans will enjoy learning more about her life. With longtime coauthor and friend Morton, Lunden offers a chatty book with an empowering message for women with breast cancer." Booklist

Martin, Brett

Difficult men; behind the scenes of a creative revolution: from The Sopranos and The Wire to Mad Men and Breaking Bad. by Brett Martin. The Penguin Press 2013 320 p. (hardcover) $27.95   **791.450**

1. Television -- History 2. Characters and characteristics on television 3. Television series -- United States 4. Television program genres -- United States 5. Cable television -- United States -- History 6. Television broadcasting -- Social aspects -- United States
ISBN 1594204195; 9781594204197

LC 2012047001

Here, Brett Martin "names the period spanning 1999 to 2013 'the third golden age of television,'" and considers what made it possible. He looks at the rise of shows with a "serialized narrative, as opposed to the syndication-friendly stand-alone episodes common in broadcast television. A little later, shows like The Wire, The Sopranos, and Mad Men subverted network formulas to present flawed, even nihilistic antiheros wrestling with inner demons." (Publishers Weekly)

Includes bibliographical references.

Scovell, Nell

Just the funny parts; and a few hard truths about sneaking into the Hollywood boys' club. Nell Scovell. HarperCollins 2018 336 p. $27.99   **791.450**

1. Women television writers -- United States -- Biography 2. Women television producers and directors -- United States -- Biography
ISBN 0062473484; 9780062473486

This memoir, by Nell Scovell, "is a juicy and scathingly funny insider look at how pop culture gets made. For more than thirty years, writer, producer and director Scovell worked behind the scenes of iconic TV shows, including 'The Simpsons,' 'Late Night with David Letterman,'. . . Only the second woman ever to write for [Letterman's] show, Scovell used the moment to publicly call out the lack of gender diversity in late-night TV writers' rooms." (Publisher's note)

"Scovell comes across as a smart, energetic, determined woman, someone who is always shooting for greater success and who really hates it when she fails at something. A revealing and timely portrait of a professional writer and the industry in which she works." Booklist

791.456 Special aspects of television programs

Press, Joy

Stealing the show; how women are revolutionizing television. Joy Press. Atria Books 2018 336 p. (hardback) $26 **791.456**

1. Women in television broadcasting -- History 2. Television broadcasting -- United States -- History 3. Television programs -- United States -- History 4. Television and women -- United States -- History 5. Women television producers and directors -- United States

ISBN 9781501137716; 9781501137723

LC 2017032332

This book, by Joy Press, presents "a definitive look at the rise of the female showrunner--and a new golden era of television. Female writers, directors, and producers have radically transformed the television industry in recent years. . . . These extraordinary women have shaken up the entertainment landscape, making it look like an equal opportunity dream factory. But things weren't always this rosy." (Publisher's note)

"Highly recommended for those who enjoy reading about the entertainment industry, how their favorite TV shows are created, and women."

791.457 Programs

Fager, Jeff

Fifty years of 60 minutes; the inside story of television's most influential news broadcast. Jeff Fager. Simon & Schuster 2017 v, 409 p.p illustrations (chiefly color) (hardcover: alk. paper) $35 **791.457**

1. Historical literature 2. Television broadcasting of news -- United States 3. 60 minutes (Television program) 4. Broadcast journalism -- United States

ISBN 9781501135828; 9781501135804

LC 2017025966

This book, by Jeff Fager, presents "the ultimate inside story of 60 Minutes, the program that has tracked and shaped the biggest moments in post-war American history. From its almost accidental birth in 1968, 60 Minutes has set the standard for broadcast journalism. . . . Now, . . . Fager pulls back the curtain on how this remarkable journalism is done, taking the reader into the editing room with the show's brilliant producers and beloved correspondents." (Publisher's note)

"This insider perspective gives a behind-the-scenes view of how stories were developed, along with the complex interactions of the talented and competitive staff." LJ

Includes bibliographical references and index

791.5 Puppetry and toy theaters

Blumenthal, Eileen

★ **Puppetry**; a world history. Abrams 2005 272p il $65 **791.5**

1. Puppets and puppet plays

ISBN 0-8109-5587-3

LC 2004-29349

This is a "history of the puppet world, from prehistoric times to Tony-winning Broadway hit Avenue Q. . . . This would be a welcome addition to the libraries of performing arts buffs who want to learn more about a lesser known form." Publ Wkly

Includes bibliographical references

791.8 Animal performances

Hemingway, Ernest

The **dangerous** summer; introduction by James A. Michener. Scribner 1985 228p il hardcover o.p. pa $13 **791.8**

1. Bullfights 2. Spain -- Description

ISBN 0-684-83789-7 pa

LC 84-27578

"In the summer of 1959—between The Old Man and the Sea {BRD 1952} and the completion of A Moveable Feast {BRD 1964}—{Hemingway} contracted with Life magazine to write a series of articles on the personal and professional rivalry of the two greatest bullfighters since the death of Manolete in 1947: Luis Miguel Domínguín and Antonio Ordóñez. The Dangerous Summer narrated 'the gradual destruction of one person by another with all the things that led up to it and made it.'" (Natl Rev)

A look at the "personal and professional rivalry of the two greatest bullfighters since the death of Manolete in 1947: Luis Miguel Domínguín and Antonio Ordóñez. The Dangerous Summer provides an insider's view based on extensive experience, mingles memory and desire, and is essential reading for anyone interested in the subject or the author." Natl Rev

★ **Death** in the afternoon. Scribner 1999 397p il $35 **791.8**

1. Bullfights

ISBN 0-684-85922-X

LC 99-231717

First published 1932

"A loosely organized book on bullfighting in Spain. . . . Hemingway depicts the bullfight as an emblematic tragedy, a test of courage, with a bloody and not entirely predictable end. Throughout, he digresses to philosophize on life and death in exchanges with a character he calls the Old Lady." HarperCollins Reader's Ency of Am Lit. 2nd edition

792 Stage presentations

Adler, Stella

Stella Adler: the art of acting; compiled and edited by Howard Kissel. Applause Theatre Bk. Pubs. 2000 271p il $25.95 **792**

1. Acting

ISBN 1-55783-373-7

In this collection of Adler's papers Kissel "has taken tapes, transcriptions, notebooks, and other sources to reconstruct an acting course in 22 lessons. . . . The lessons are graduated from very basic matters to quite complex issues of textual analysis and decorum. Though mostly monologs, they include enough exercises and student responses to get the flavor of Adler's work. . . . This is required reading for anyone interested in theater practice." Libr J

The **Best** Men's Stage Monologues; edited by Lawrence Harbison. Smith & Kraus 210 p. **792**

1. Acting 2. Monologues

Annual. First published 1991 for the 1990 theater season under the editorship of Jocelyn Beard

This title and The Best women's stage monologues provide monologues "from contemporary dramatic luminaries. . . . Both volumes offer scenic descriptions and brief leads into the speechs and indicate the tone (dramatic, comic, or seriocomic). In the volume for women, there are no strictly comedic pieces." Libr J [review of 2000 edition]

The **Best** Women's Stage Monologues; edited by Lawrence Harbison. Smith & Kraus Pub Inc   **792**

1. Monologues

Annual. First published 1991 for the 1990 theater season under the editorship of Jocelyn Beard

Presents monologues from plays produced in the preceding year's theatrical season.

Brook, Peter

The **empty** space. Atheneum 1968 141p hardcover o.p. pa $11   **792**

1. Drama 2. Theater

ISBN 0-684-82957-6 pa

LC 68-12531

The author "distinguishes four types of theater: the Deadly Theatre (conventional), the Holy Theatre (ritualistic), the Rough Theatre (combative), and the Immediate Theatre (mutative and organic). An impassioned treatise that is also very accessible and direct." Libr J

Chekhov, Michael

To the actor; {rev and expanded ed. by Mala Powers}; Routledge 2002 lii, 222p il $75; pa $19.95   **792**

1. Acting

ISBN 0-415-25875-8; 0-415-25876-6 pa

First published 1953 by Harper & Row

"Chekhov is among a handful of master acting teachers who have profoundly influenced not only a constellation of famous stars but also shaped an acting style and sensibility. . . . This new edition contains all of Chekhov's brilliant insights, techniques, and exercises, as well as a previously unpublished chapter on the 'Psychological Gesture,' a central precept of his system." Libr J

Includes bibliographical references

Corson, Richard

Stage makeup; [by] Richard Corson, Beverly Gore Norcross, James Glavan. 10th ed.; Ally & Bacon/Pearson 2009 xx, 407p il $141.40   **792**

1. Theatrical makeup

ISBN 978-0-205-64454-4

LC 2008-53845

First published 1942 by Appleton. Periodically revised

The authors discuss the art and technique of theatrical makeup, covering such topics as facial anatomy, various methods for applying greasepaint and other makeup, and the use of beards, wigs, and prosthetic pieces.

Gillette, J. Michael

Designing With Light: An Introduction to Stage Lighting; an introduction to stage lighting. Michael Gillette, Michael J. McNamara. 6th ed. McGraw-Hill 2013 379 p. ill. (some col.) pa. $143.45   **792**

1. Stage lighting

ISBN 0073514233; 9780073514239

LC 2012034637

This book, by J. Michael Gillette and Michael J. McNamara, "is a comprehensive survey of the practical and aesthetic aspects of stage

lighting design. The authors approach stage lighting design as an art that integrates the vision of director, actor, and playwright, and as a craft that provides practical solutions for the manipulation of stage space. The sixth edition offers a wealth of new information on new trends in lighting design." (Publisher's Note)

The author "divides his standard text for undergraduate lighting design students into the two constituent elements of his craft—technology and design. He clearly and completely presents both technical and aesthetic design aspects." Libr J

Hagen, Uta, 1919-2004

Respect for acting; Uta Hagen with Haskel Frankel; foreword by David Hyde Pierce. 2nd edition Wiley 2008 226 p hardcover $22.95   **792**

1. Acting

ISBN 9780470228487

LC 2008016843

Originally published 1973

This "classic treatise on the process and craft of acting has significantly benefited actors for three decades. Juxtaposed with Hagen's aesthetic is a wealth of practical information, creative ideas, and her uniquely useful object exercises." Libr J

Lane, Stewart F.

★ **Black** Broadway; African Americans on the great white way. Stewart F. Lane. Square One Publishers 2015 288 p. illustrations (some color) (hardback) $39.95   **792**

1. African American actors 2. African American theater 3. Musicals -- United States 4. Broadway (New York, N.Y.) -- History 5. American drama -- African American authors -- History and criticism 6. African American theater -- New York (State) -- New York -- History -- 20th century 7. African Americans in the performing arts -- New York (State) -- New York -- History -- 20th century

ISBN 9780757003882; 0757003885

LC 2014006513

In this book on the history of Broadway, author "Stewart F. Lane uses words and pictures to capture this tumultuous century and to highlight the rocky road that black actors have travelled to reach recognition on the Great White Way. Like the doors of many professions, those of the theater world were shut to minorities for decades. While the Civil War may have freed the slaves, it was not until the Civil Rights Movement of the 1960s that the playing field began to level." (Publisher's note)

"This volume's superior presentation of visual theatrical elements make it essential for any theater collection." Library Journal

Includes bibliographical references

Ory, Deborah

The **art** of movement; Deborah Ory, Ken Browar, NYC Dance Project. Black Dog & Leventhal 2016 304 p. (hardcover) $50   **792**

1. Dance 2. Dancers

ISBN 0316318582; 9780316318587

LC 2016939031

This book, by Deborah Ory and Ken Browar, is a "celebration of movement and dance in hundreds of breathtaking photographs of more than 70 dancers from American Ballet Theater, New York City Ballet, Alvin Ailey American Dance Theater, Martha Graham Dance Company, Boston Ballet, Royal Danish Ballet, the Royal Ballet, and many more." (Publisher's note)

The **Oxford** companion to theatre and performance; edited by Dennis Kennedy. Oxford University Press 2010 689p $45 **792**
1. Reference books 2. Theater -- Encyclopedias 3. Performing arts -- Encyclopedias
ISBN 978-0-19-957419-3
"This is a one-volume updated version of the two-volume Oxford Encyclopedia of Theatre & Performance published in 2003. Kennedy . . . has succeeded in pulling together 2400 entries intended to educate, delight, and encourage the reader to pursue more in-depth information." Libr J

Stanislavsky, Konstantin

★ An **actor's** work; a student's diary. [by] Konstantin Stanislavski; translated and edited by Jean Benedetti. Routledge 2008 693p $35 **792**
1. Acting
ISBN 9780415422239; 0-415-42223-X
LC 2007-45357
A combined translation of Stanislavsky's An actor prepares and Building a character, which describe and illustrate the principles of method acting.
This "translation by Benedetti of Stanislavski's famous works . . . will be greeted with excitement by actors everywhere." Libr J
Includes bibliographical references

Creating a role; [by] Constantin Stanislavski; translated by Elizabeth Reynolds Hapgood; edited by Hermine I. Popper; foreword by Robert Lewis. Routledge 2003 271p pa $19.95 **792**
1. Acting
ISBN 0-87830-981-0
LC 91-228412
"Stanislavski unifies his conceptual canon and applies it to detailed preparatory work for the roles of Othello and Gogol's Inspector General." Libr J

792.02   Miscellany

Douglas, Illeana, 1965-

I blame Dennis Hopper; and other stories from a life lived in and out of the movies. Illeana Douglas. Flatiron Books 2015 304 p. illustrations (hardback) $25.99 **792.02**
1. Motion picture actors and actresses -- United States -- Biography 2. Actresses -- United States -- Anecdotes 3. Actresses -- United States -- Biography
ISBN 9781250052919
LC 2015022208
This book, by Illeana Douglas, is "a memoir about learning to survive in Hollywood. . . . Writing from the perspective of the ultimate show business fan, Douglas packs each page with hilarious anecdotes, bizarre coincidences, and fateful meetings that seem, well, right out of a plot of a movie." (Publisher's note)
"The author's warm portraits and disarming honesty infuse the memoir with an endearing sweetness and charm." Kirkus

Gillette, J. Michael

Theatrical design and production; An Introduction to Scene Design and Construction, Lighting, Sound, Costume, and Make-up. J. Michael Gillette. 7th ed. McGraw-Hill Higher Education 2012 624 p. ill. (some col.) hardcover $192.45 **792.02**
1. Theaters -- Stage setting and scenery 2. Stage management. 3. Theater--Production and direction. 4. Theaters--Stage-setting and scenery.
ISBN 0073382221; 9780073382227
LC 2012020022
This book, by J. Michael Gillette, "is a comprehensive and practical survey that examines the technical and design aspects of play production, including scene design and construction, lighting, sound, costume, and makeup. Design is presented as both an art closely integrated with the director's, actor's, and playwright's visions, and a craft that provides practical solutions for the physical manipulation of stage space." (Publisher's note)
Includes bibliographical references

Hytner, Nicholas, 1956-

Balancing acts; behind the scenes at London's National Theatre. Nicholas Hytner. Alfred A. Knopf 2017 vi, 312 p.p (hardcover) $28.95 **792.02**
1. Theater 2. Performing arts 3. Theatrical producers and directors -- Great Britain -- Biography 4. National Theatre (Great Britain) 5. Theater -- England -- London -- History -- 21st century
ISBN 9780451493415; 9780451493408; 0451493400
LC 2017016630
This memoir, by Nicholas Hytner, is about "his career directing theater, producing films and opera, and working closely with some of the world's most celebrated actors. . . . Hytner gives us a detailed behind-the-scenes look at his creative process. From reviving classic musicals and mastering Shakespeare to commissioning new plays, he shows theater making to be a necessarily collaborative exercise, and he writes insightfully about the actors and playwrights he's worked with." (Publisher's note)
"Arts leaders in general will have something to gain from Hytner's endless energy for developing new work and navigating the challenges facing today's cultural sector." Booklist

Lahr, John

Joy ride; show people and their shows. John Lahr. W.W. Norton & Co. Inc. 2015 576 p. illustrations (hardcover) $29.95 **792.02**
1. Theater -- Reviews 2. Dramatists -- Biography 3. Dramatists, American -- Biography 4. Theater -- New York (State) -- New York -- Reviews 5. Theatrical producers and directors -- United States -- Biography
ISBN 9780393246407
LC 2015013987
This book, by John Lahr, presents a collection of the author's biographical profiles and reviews from the 'New Yorker' magazine, focusing on contemporary theater. The book "throws open the stage door and introduces readers to such makers of contemporary drama as Arthur Miller, Tony Kushner, Wallace Shawn, Harold Pinter, David Rabe, David Mamet, Mike Nichols, and August Wilson." (Publisher's note)
"Faithful readers of The New Yorker will enjoy revisiting these articles. Anyone interested in the history of the American theater and contemporary drama will applaud these thoughtful and critical pieces." LJ

792.028   Acting and performance

Fischer, Jenna, 1974-

The **actor's** life; a survival guide. Jenna Fischer; foreword by Steve Carell. BenBella Books, Inc. 2017 xvi, 255 p.p illustrations (trade paper: alk. paper) $17.95 **792.028**

1. Actors 2. Acting -- Vocational guidance 3. Acting -- Handbooks, manuals, etc

ISBN 9781944648237; 9781944648220

LC 2017026414

In this book, Jenna Fischer "spells out the nuts and bolts of getting established in the [acting] profession, based on her own memorable and hilarious experiences. She tells you how to get the right headshot, what to look for in representation, and the importance of joining forces with other like-minded artists and creating your own work--invaluable advice personally acquired from her many years of struggle." (Publisher's note)

"Fischer's book is exactly what it's billed as: a helpful, essential guide that is certain to help aspirants navigate their own careers and keep hope alive while doing so." Booklist

Includes bibliographical references and index

Wasson, Sam

Improv nation; how we made a great American art. Sam Wasson. Houghton Mifflin Harcourt 2017 xiii, 449 p.p illustrations (some color) (hardcover) $28 **792.028**

1. Stand-up comedy 2. Improvisation (Acting)

ISBN 9780544557208; 9780544558250; 0544557204

In this book, author "Sam Wasson charts the meteoric rise of improv[isation] in this richly reported, scene-driven narrative that, like its subject, moves fast and digs deep. . . . With signature verve and nuance, Wasson shows why improv deserves to be considered the great American art form of the last half-century--and the most influential one today." (Publisher's note)

"While comedians today take up a large space in public life, Wasson reminds us that a lot of hard work has been done for them to get there. An entertaining book, recommended for aspiring comedians who want to historicize their practice." Kirkus

Includes bibliographical references (pages 384-435) and index.

792.09 History, geographic treatment, biography

Brockett, Oscar G.

History of the theatre; [by] Oscar G. Brockett, Franklin J. Hildy. 10th ed; Pearson 2008 688p il map $113 **792.09**

1. Theater -- History 2. Drama -- History and criticism

ISBN 978-0-205-51186-0

LC 2009-291794

First published 1968

This work traces the development of the theater from primitive times to the present, with an emphasis on European theater.

Includes bibliographical references

Levy, Reynold

They told me not to take that job; tumult, betrayal, heroics, and the transformation of Lincoln Center. Reynold Levy. PublicAffairs 2015 376 p. 8 plates; color ills., maps (hardback) $28.99 **792.09**

1. Opera 2. Centers for the performing arts -- New York (State) -- New York 3. Lincoln Center for the Performing Arts 4. Performing arts -- New York (State) -- New York -- Management

ISBN 1610393619; 9781610393614

LC 2014049065

In this book, author Reynold "Levy tells the inside story of the demise of the New York City Opera, the Metropolitan Opera's need to use as collateral its iconic Chagall tapestries in the face of mounting operating losses, and the New York Philharmonic's dalliance with Carnegie

Hall." (Publisher's note)

Includes bibliographical references and index

Riedel, Michael

Razzle Dazzle; The Battle for Broadway. Michael Riedel. Simon & Schuster 2015 464 p. 16 plates; illustrations $27 **792.09**

1. Theater 2. Musicals

ISBN 1451672160; 9781451672169

Author Michael Riedel presents this "narrative account of the people and the money and the power that re-invented an iconic quarter of New York City, turning its gritty back alleys and sex-shops into the glitzy, dazzling Great White Way--and bringing a crippled New York from the brink of bankruptcy to its glittering glory." (Publisher's note)

"While not functioning as an introduction or a detailed history of the American commercial theater, this book articulates a neglected but historically essential point of view." LJ

792.5 Opera

Osborne, Charles

The complete operas of Mozart; a critical guide. Da Capo Press 1986 349p il pa $17.95 **792.5**

1. Composers 2. Opera -- Stories, plots, etc.

ISBN 978-0-306-80190-7; 0-306-80190-6

First published 1978 by Atheneum

In this introduction to Mozart's operas, "each opera is treated as a separate chapter. . . . Each chapter begins with a separate page containing the dramatis personae and their voice range . . . the date, place, and cast for the first performance . . . the name of the librettist, and the Kochel number." Choice

The complete operas of Puccini; a critical guide. Da Capo Press 1983 279p il pa $9.95 **792.5**

1. Composers 2. Opera -- Stories, plots, etc.

ISBN 0-306-80200-7; 978-0-306-80200-3

LC 83-10142

First published 1982 by Atheneum

The author "provides general background information on all 13 Puccini operas. . . . Unencumbered by technical language, this enjoyably written book is accessible to all admirers of one of the most popular opera composers of all time." Choice

Includes bibliographical references

The complete operas of Richard Wagner. Da Capo Press 1993 288p il pa $16.95 **792.5**

1. Composers 2. Opera -- Stories, plots, etc.

ISBN 0-306-80522-7; 978-0-306-80522-6

LC 92-34417

First published 1990 in the United Kingdom

In this book, "biography—often in Wagner's own words—combined with criticism by Wagner's contemporaries, literary background, Wagner's librettos, plot summaries, descriptions of musical elements illustrated with musical examples, and Osborne's own insights form a clear picture of Wagner, his world, and the operas." Libr J

Includes bibliographical references

Sadie, Stanley

The Grove book of operas; edited by Stanley Sadie; revised by Laura Macy. 2nd ed; Oxford University Press 2009 xxiii, 740p il $39.95; pa $27.95; $27.95 **792.5**

1. Reference books 2. Opera -- Encyclopedias
ISBN 978-0-19-530907-2; 0-19-530907-3; 0-19-538711-2 pa;
9780195387117 pa

LC 2006-15323

First published 1996 by Macmillan with title: The new Grove book of operas

"A vital reference on the subject." Libr J

Includes bibliographical references

792.6　Musical plays

Bloom, Ken

Broadway musicals; the 101 greatest shows of all time. [by] Ken Bloom & Frank Vlastnik; new preface by Broadway's leading ladies; foreword by Jerry Orbach. Rev. and updated ed.; Black Dog & Leventhal 2010 344p il $40 **792.6**

1. Musicals
ISBN 978-1-57912-849-4
First published 2004

This is a history of Broadway musicals from the past 100 years. Each entry features commentary, photos and brief features on performers and creators.

Hischak, Thomas

The **Oxford** companion to the American musical; theatre, film, and television. [by] Thomas S. Hischak. Oxford University Press 2008 923p il $39.95 **792.6**

1. Reference books 2. Musicals -- Dictionaries
ISBN 9780195335330

LC 2007-52436

This is an "overview of the American musical theater on the stage, silver screen, and small screen. The 2000-plus entries are brief but detailed accounts of plots; production histories; careers of actors, dancers, musicians, lyricists, composers, choreographers, and directors; organizations; and genres (animated musicals, frontier musicals). . . . This thorough work provides enjoyable reading for anyone interested in American theatrical history in general and musicals in particular." SLJ

Includes discography and bibliographical references (p. 899-902)

Maslon, Laurence

★ **Broadway**; the American musical. Laurence Maslon; based on the documentary film by Michael Kantor; foreword by Julie Andrews. 2nd edition Applause Theatre & Cinema Books 2010 497p illustrations, maps pbk $40 **792.6**

1. Musicals -- United States
ISBN 1423491033; 9781423491033

"A companion to the six-part PBS documentary series, Broadway: The American Musical is the first comprehensive history of the musical, from its roots at the turn of the 20th century through the smashing successes of the new millennium. The in-depth text is lavishly illustrated with a treasure trove of photographs, sheet-music covers, posters, scenic renderings, production stills, rehearsal shots and caricatures, many previously unpublished." (Publisher's note)

Stempel, Larry

Showtime; a history of the Broadway musical theater. W. W. Norton & Company 2010 xx, 826p il $39.95 **792.6**

1. Musicals 2. Musicals -- New York (N.Y.)
ISBN 978-0-393-06715-6; 0-393-06715-7

LC 2010-19704

Beginning in the seventeenth-century United States, well before

Broadway existed, Stempel presents the multiple theatrical adventures that would lead from various directions to 'West Side Story' (1957) and 'Les Misérables' (1987). He examines not only minstrelsy, vaudeville, and European operetta—the musical's well-known precursors—but also the Astor Place riot of 1849, an event that publicly performed the ever-hardening divisions of class and culture among American audiences. Later, Stempel describes off-Broadway performances . . . beginning with the Works Progress Administration and the Little Theatre movement, progressing to 'Hair' (1968), which eventually transferred to Broadway, and nodding to regional theaters where many shows originated." (Journal of American History)

"Theater buffs will be delighted to find that this scholarly, definitive work is also a hugely entertaining read." Publ Wkly

Includes discography and bibliographical references

Viertel, Jack

The **secret** life of the American musical; how classic Broadway shows are built. Jack Viertel. Sarah Crichton Books 2016 336 p. (hardcover) $28 **792.6**

1. Musicals 2. Musicals -- United States -- History and criticism 3. Musicals -- United States -- Analysis, appreciation
ISBN 9780374256920; 9780374711252

LC 2015023713

This book, by Jack Viertel, "begins with an overture and concludes with a curtain call. . . . Viertel has spent three decades on Broadway, working on dozens of shows old and new as a conceiver, producer, dramaturg, and general creative force. . . . He shows us patterns in the architecture of classic shows and charts the inevitable evolution that has taken place in musical theater as America itself has evolved socially and politically." (Publisher's note)

"An enlightening trip for lovers of musicals." Kirkus

792.7　Variety shows and theatrical dancing

Apatow, Judd, 1967-

Sick in the head; conversations about life and comedy. by Judd Apatow. Random House Inc. 2015 512 p. 16 plates; illustrations (hardback) $27 **792.7**

1. Actors 2. Comedians 3. Stand-up comedy -- United States 4. Comedians -- United States -- Interviews 5. Television actors and actresses -- United States -- Interviews 6. Motion picture actors and actresses -- United States -- Interviews
ISBN 0812997573; 9780812997576

LC 2015008155

This book "gathers [filmmaker Judd] Apatow's most memorable and revealing conversations into one hilarious, wide-ranging, and incredibly candid collection that spans not only his career but his entire adult life. Here are the comedy legends who inspired and shaped him, from Mel Brooks to Steve Martin. Here are the contemporaries he grew up with in Hollywood, from Spike Jonze to Sarah Silverman. And here, finally, are the brightest stars in comedy today." (Publisher's note)

"An exceptional volume; in a field where shallowness is a hallmark, these artists reveal an unexpected depth. For all libraries." LJ

Downer, Lesley

Women of the pleasure quarters; the secret history of the geisha. Broadway Bks. 2001 288p il hardcover o.p. pa $14.95 **792.7**

1. Geishas 2. Japan -- Social life and customs
ISBN 0-7679-0490-7 pa

LC 00-49409

The author "skillfully intertwines her profiles of Kyoto personalities and tea-house customs with a fluidly written geisha history that's unabashedly aimed at a Western audience.... Written in dynamic, highly readable prose, the book is supported by exhaustive research and a lengthy bibliography." Publ Wkly

Includes bibliographical references and index

Josephson, Barney

Cafe Society; the wrong place for the right people. Barney Josephson; with Terry Trilling-Josephson; foreword by Dan Morgenstern. University of Illinois Press 2009 376p il (Music in American life) $32.95   **792.7**

1. Café Society (New York, N.Y.: Nightclub) 2. Greenwich Village (New York (N.Y.) -- Social life and customs
ISBN 978-0-252-03413-8; 0-252-03413-9

LC 2008-27205

"An epic ode to personal integrity, creative vision and entrepreneurial tenacity, shedding timely light on the germination of the civil-rights movement." Kirkus

Includes bibliographical references

Kemper, Ellie, 1980-

My squirrel days; Ellie Kemper. Simon & Schuster 2018 256 p. $26   **792.7**

1. Biography 2. Women comedians -- United States -- Biography
ISBN 1501163345; 9781501163340

In this autobiography, author "Ellie Kemper delivers a hilarious and uplifting collection of essays about one pale woman's journey from midwestern naïf to Hollywood semi-celebrity to outrageously reasonable New Yorker.... [It] is a funny, free-wheeling tour of Ellie's life--from growing up in suburban St. Louis with a vivid imagination and a crush on David Letterman to moving to Los Angeles and accidentally falling on Doris Kearns Goodwin." (Publisher's note)

Nesteroff, Kliph

The **Comedians**; Drunks, Thieves, Scoundrels, and the History of American Comedy. by Kliph Nesteroff. Grove Press 2015 432 p. 16 plates; ills; portraits $28   **792.7**

1. Comedy 2. Comedians 3. Comedy films 4. Comedy radio programs 5. Comedy television programs
ISBN 0802123988; 9780802123985

In this book, "comedy historian Kliph Nesteroff brings to life a century of American comedy with real-life characters, forgotten stars, mainstream heroes and counterculture iconoclasts. Based on over two hundred original interviews and extensive archival research, Nesteroff's groundbreaking work is a narrative exploration of the way comedians have reflected, shaped, and changed American culture over the past one hundred years." (Publisher's note)

"Both pop culture enthusiasts and entertainment scholars will relish this important history of American comedy." LJ

Seibert, Brian

What the eye hears; a history of tap dancing. Brian Seibert. Farrar, Straus & Giroux 2015 624 p. illustrations (hardback) $35   **792.7**

1. Jazz music 2. Tap dancing 3. Tap dancing -- History
ISBN 0865479534; 9780865479531

LC 2015005010

National Book Critics Circle Award Finalist: Nonfiction (2015)

Author Brian Seibert "offers an authoritative account of the great American art of tap dancing. Brian Seibert, a dance critic for The New York Times, begins by exploring tap's origins as a hybrid of the jig and clog dancing from the British Isles and dances brought from Africa by slaves. He tracks tap's transfer to the stage through blackface minstrelsy and charts its growth as a cousin to jazz." (Publisher's note)

"Drawing on primary sources of every kind, from written accounts by slave traders in the early 17th century to personal interviews conducted in the 21st, the author breaks down not merely the origins art of tap dancing itself, but the racial and gender constructs that forced the industry--and its performers--to develop in the ways they did, while acknowledging his own white male privilege." Pub Wkly

Includes bibliographical references (pages [541]-574) and index

Trav S. D.

No applause, just throw money; or, The book that made vaudeville famous; a high-class, refined entertainment. Faber and Faber 2005 328p il $25   **792.7**

1. Vaudeville
ISBN 0-571-21192-5

LC 20050-9787

This book documents the history and legacy of vaudeville in the United States.

"One of the year's best historical performing arts texts; a wonderful story wonderfully told." Libr J

Includes bibliographical references

792.8   Ballet and modern dance

Alford, Henry, 1962-

And then we danced; a voyage into the groove. Henry Alford. Simon & Schuster 2018 256 p. (hardcover) $26   **792.8**

1. Wit and humor 2. Dancers -- Biography 3. Dance -- Social aspects 4. Dance -- Humor
ISBN 9781501122255; 9781501122262

LC 2017044367

"Equal parts memoir and cultural history, from acclaimed comic stylist and professional hobbyist Henry Alford comes a hilarious journey through the world of dance that will inform, entertain and leave readers tapping their toes.... Tackling a wide range of forms (including ballet, hip-hop, jazz, ..., Zumba, swing), this grand tour takes us through the works and careers of luminaries ranging from Bob Fosse to George Balanchine, Twyla Tharp to Arthur Murray." (Publisher's note)

Craine, Debra

The **Oxford** dictionary of dance; [by] Debra Craine, Judith Mackrell. 2nd ed.; Oxford University Press 2010 502p il (Oxford paperback reference) pa $18.95   **792.8**

1. Reference books 2. Dance -- Dictionaries
ISBN 978-0-19-956344-9; 0-19-956344-6

LC 2010-930321

Based on The concise Oxford dictionary of ballet by Horst Kroegler. First published 2000

"The work covers all aspects of the diverse dance world from classical ballet to modern, from flamenco to hip-hop, from tap to South Asian dance forms and includes . . . entries on technical terms, steps, styles, works and countries, in addition to many biographies of dancers, choreographers, and companies." Publisher's note

Includes bibliographical references

Fuhrer, Margaret

American dance; the complete illustrated history. Margaret Fuhrer. Voyageur Press 2014 288 p. illustrations (chiefly color) (hardback) $45   **792.8**

1. Performance art 2. Dance -- United States 3. Dance -- United States -- History 4. Modern dance -- United States -- History
ISBN 0760345996; 9780760345993

LC 2014022261

This book by Margaret Fuhrer "explores centuries of innovation, individual genius and collaborative exploration. Some of its stories - such as Fred Astaire dancing on the ceiling or Alvin Ailey founding the trailblazing company that bears his name - will be familiar to anyone who loves dance." (Publisher's note)

"A dance sampler that should prompt readers to further explore the multifaceted history of dance and maybe take a class!" Library Journal

Homans, Jennifer

★ **Apollo's** angels. Random House 2010 643p il $35 **792.8**

1. Ballet 2. Ballet -- History
ISBN 978-1-4000-6060-3; 1-4000-6060-5

LC 201006945

This book "places ballet . . . in the larger context of the times and societies in which it evolved, flourished and flagged, only be revitalized by an infusion of fresh ideas. That revitalization could come from a ballet master like Jean-Georges Noverre, presented by Homans as an important Enlightenment figure whose ideas on reforming ballet were consonant with those of Diderot on reforming theater. Renewal came from the genius of dancers like Marie Taglioni, the incarnation of romanticism . . . . But in a closing section . . . [the author]sounds a despairing note: "ballet is dying," she declares. Not only is the creative well running dry and performances dull, but more crucially, Homans sees today's values as inimical to those of ballet." (Publishers Weekly)

"A book of this breadth is going to have its own biorhythms—chapters that engage the author's mind and heart wholly, where everything clicks and the thinking is virtually kinetic, and chapters that don't come as easily. Ms. Homans is at her best when the ideological agenda at hand aspires to discipline, precision and refinement. Her French section is masterful, as are the chapters on the rise of the ballerina, the Danish style, Imperial Russian classicism, and British ballet." Wall Street J

Includes bibliographical references

Jacobs, Laura

★ **Celestial** bodies; how to look at ballet. Laura Jacobs. Basic Books 2018 272 p. (hardback) $27 **792.8**

1. Dance 2. Ballet 3. Performing arts 4. Ballet -- History
ISBN 9780465098477

LC 2017051470

In this book, "dance critic Laura Jacobs makes the foreign familiar, providing a lively, poetic, and uniquely accessible introduction to the world of classical dance. Combining history, interviews with dancers, technical definitions, descriptions of performances, and personal stories, Jacobs offers an intimate and passionate guide to watching ballet and understanding the central elements of choreography." (Publisher's note)

"Ballet history, explanations of technique, interviews with dancers, first-person accounts of performances, and personal reflections on a variety of other related topics are presented in engaging prose, enhanced by Jessica Roux's delicate illustrations." Booklist

Includes bibliographical references and index

Kessler, Lauren

Raising the barre; big dreams, false starts, and my midlife quest to dance the Nutcracker. by Lauren Kessler. Da Capo Press A Member of the Perseus Books Group 2015 272 p. (ebook) $13.99; (Hardcover: alk. paper) $24.99 **792.8**

1. Ballet 2. Ballet dancing 3. Nutcracker (Choreographic work) 4. Authors -- United States -- Biography

ISBN 9780738218328; 9780738218311

LC 2015026258

In this book, "Lauren Kessler fell in love with ballet the first time she saw The Nutcracker, and from that day, at age five, she dreamed of becoming a ballerina. But when she was twelve, her very famous ballet instructor crushed those dreams—along with her youthful self-assurance—and she stepped away from the barre. Fast forward four decades. Lauren—suddenly, powerfully, itchingly restless at midlife—embarks on a 'Transcontinental Nutcracker Binge Tour.'" (Publisher's note)

"An amusingly shrewd memoir of following a lifelong dream." Kirkus

Includes bibliographical references and index

Minden, Eliza Gaynor

The **ballet** companion; a dancer's guide to the technique, traditions, and joys of ballet. Eliza Gaynor Minden. Touchstone Books 2005 xv, 331 p.p illustrations (some color) $29.95 **792.8**

1. Ballet 2. Ballet dancers 3. Ballet dancing -- Handbooks, manuals, etc
ISBN 9780743264075; 074326407X

LC 2005044102

This book, by Eliza Gaynor Minden "is a fresh, comprehensive, and thoroughly up-to-date reference book for the dancer. With 150 stunning photographs of ballet stars Maria Riccetto and Benjamin Millepied demonstrating perfect execution of positions and steps, this elegant volume brims with everything today's dance student needs" (Publisher's note)

"[The Author's] explanation of the differences between the six major ballet styles, along with the superb glossaries of terms and dance history timeline, make this book a valuable resource for dance studios and a great primer for dancers in the early stages of training." Publishers Weekly

Includes bibliographical references (p. [316]-317) and index

Morrison, Simon

Bolshoi confidential; secrets of the Russian ballet from the rule of the tsars to today. Simon Morrison. Liveright Publishing Corp. 2016 512 p. illustrations (ebook) $50; (hardcover) $35 **792.8**

1. Ballet -- Russia -- History 2. Ballet companies -- Russia -- History
ISBN 9780871408303; 9780871402967

LC 2016031665

This book, by Simon Morrison, presents a "new history of the Bolshoi Ballet, where visionary performances onstage compete with political machinations backstage. . . . From its disreputable beginnings in 1776 at the hand of a Faustian charlatan, the Bolshoi became a point of pride for the tsarist empire after the defeat of Napoleon in 1812. After the revolution, Moscow was transformed from a merchant town to a global capital, its theater becoming a key site of power." (Publisher's note)

"A must for ballet buffs. Not the last word on the Bolshoi, but a look backstage that is both lively and learned." Kirkus

Includes bibliographical references and index

Reynolds, Nancy

No fixed points; dance in the twentieth century. [by] Nancy Reynolds and Malcolm McCormick. Yale Univ. Press 2003 907p il $50 **792.8**

1. Dance 2. Ballet 3. Modern dance
ISBN 0-300-09366-7

LC 2003-10754

"Although everyone will be using the book for reference, Reynolds and McCormick have produced a work that is completely unlike a standard reference book; you don't just look things up in it—you read it.

Here is a coherent, reasoned and entertaining chronicle of dance performance in the West over the hundred years that are unquestionably the fullest and most complicated in the long history of this fragmented and elusive art." N Y Times

Includes bibliographical references

792.9   Stage productions

Dromgoole, Dominic, 1963-

Hamlet Globe to globe; two years, 190,000 miles, 197 countries, one play. by Dominic Dromgoole. First Grove Atlantic hardcover Grove Press 2017 390 p. color illustrations (hardcover) $27   **792.9**

     1. Globe Theatre (London, England: 1599-1644) -- History
     ISBN 080212562X; 9780802189684; 9780802125620
                            LC 2017001313
Includes index.

"Two years, 190,000 miles, 197 countries, one play. For the 450th anniversary of Shakespeare's birth the Globe Theatre in London undertook an unparalleled journey to share Hamlet with the entire world. The tour was the brainchild of Dominic Dromgoole, artistic director of the Globe, and in Hamlet Globe to Globe, Dromgoole takes readers along with him on this wildly ambitious expedition." (Publisher's note)

"Sly, witty, and delightful—a glorious Shakespearean romp." Kirkus

793.2   Parties and entertainments

Sedaris, Amy

I like you; hospitality under the influence. Warner Books 2006 303p il $27.99   **793.2**

     1. Cooking 2. Entertaining
     ISBN 978-0-446-57884-4; 0-446-57884-3
                            LC 2006-07521
"Novice party-planners will actually find some helpful hints along the way as Sedaris offers instructions and real recipes. . . . [This book] is an outrageous and deadpan delight, greatly enhanced by her deliriously kitschy illustrations and photos." Publ Wkly

793.7   Games not characterized by action

The **official** Scrabble players dictionary; 6th edition Merriam-Webster 2018 728 p.   **793.7**

     1. Scrabble (Game) -- Dictionaries
     ISBN 9780877795964; 9780877794226; 9780877796770
This is a dictionary of words which can be used in the game of Scrabble.

793.8   Magic and related activities

Gardner, Martin, 1914-2010

The **colossal** book of short puzzles and problems; combinatorics, probability, algebra, geometry, topology, chess, logic, cryptarithms, wordplay, physics and other topics of recreational mathematics. edited by Dana Richards. Norton 2006 494p il $35   **793.8**

     1. Scientific recreations 2. Mathematical recreations
     ISBN 0-393-06114-0; 978-0-393-06114-7

                            LC 2005-24080
This is a compilation of puzzles from Martin Gardner's "column, 'Mathematical Games,' which appeared for over 25 years in Scientific American. . . . [The topics] include combinatorics, probability, algebra, plane and solid geometry, topology, games, chess, logic, wordplay, and physics, among others. . . . Anyone interested in recreational mathematics should like this book. The puzzles are fascinating and the book is easily browsed. It can also serve as a good reference for (high school and college) teachers seeking interesting problems to complement routine ones in mathematics texts." Sci Books Films

Miles, Bryan

101 magic tricks; discover powerful magic for every occasion. Bryan Miles. Quarry Books 2015 208 p. colour illustrations $19.99   **793.8**

     1. Magic tricks
     ISBN 1631590723; 9781631590726
                            LC 2015025881
This book, by Bryan Miles, presents "101 Magic Tricks! Astonish and amaze everyone you know with easy-to-master tricks and illusions. Learn classic sleight of hand techniques that are simple enough for any apprentice to grasp. Conquer magical ruses that require no special equipment, and are explained with simple step-by-step instructions." (Publisher's note)

     One hundred one magic tricks
     One hundred and one magic tricks

Stone, Alex

Fooling Houdini; magicians, mentalists, math geeks, and the hidden powers of the mind. Alex Stone. Harper 2012 x, 301 p.p ill. (hardback) $26.99   **793.8**

     1. Magicians 2. Perception 3. Magic tricks 4. Autobiographies
     5. Magic -- Social aspects 6. Magicians -- United States 7. Magic -- Psychological aspects 8. Magicians -- United States -- Biography
     ISBN 0061766216; 9780061766213
                            LC 2011041927
This book by Alex Stone recounts his "quest to join the ranks of master magicians. As he navigates this . . . subculture, Stone pulls back the curtain on a community shrouded in secrecy . . . and organized around a single overriding need: to prove one's worth by deceiving others. . . . In trying to understand how expert magicians manipulate our minds to create their astonishing illusions, Stone uncovers . . . insight into human nature and the nature of perception." (Publisher's note)

793.93   Adventure games

Barbarisi, Daniel

Dueling with kings; high stakes, killer sharks, and the get-rich promise of daily fantasy sports. Daniel Barbarisi. Touchstone 2017 353 p. (hardback) $26.99   **793.93**

     1. Sports betting 2. Internet gambling 3. Fantasy sports
     ISBN 9781501146190; 1501146173; 9781501146176; 9781501146183
                            LC 2016052642
In this book author "Daniel Barbarisi quits his job as the New York Yankees beat writer for The Wall Street Journal and begins a quest: to join the top one percent of Daily Fantasy Sports ('DFS') players, the so-called 'sharks,' and figure out whether DFS is on the level--while maybe cashing in along the way." (Publisher's note)

794   Indoor games of skill

Botermans, Jack

The **book** of games; strategy, tactics & history. [by] Jack Botermans; [translated from the Spanish by Edgar Loy Fankbonner] Sterling 2008 736p il $29.95 **794**

1. Board games 2. Indoor games

ISBN 978-1-4027-4221-7; 1-4027-4221-5

LC 2007-10173

"Some 65 international games are described and demonstrated in this colorful book. Ranging from dominoes to mancala and shogi to Yut, each entry highlights the game's origins, versions, and playing rules... . Color illustrations and diagrams are used liberally to illustrate strategic moves and the variations of game boards and pieces, while photographs show the games being played.... Libraries should consider this for their circulating collections." Booklist

Kearney, Kirsten

Block city; how to build incredible worlds in minecraft. Yazur Strovoz. Abrams 2015 256 p. color illustrations (paperback) $22.50 **794**

1. Design 2. Computer games

ISBN 1419716182; 9781419716188

LC 2014945989

This book, by Yazur Strovoz, focuses on "Minecraft--a humble computer game about placing blocks--... that has captured the imagination of more than 36 million players around the world.... The most impressive and spectacular achievements in Minecraft design are its cities.... The product of thousands of hours of work by devoted Minecraft players, these virtual places are the envy of millions who aspire to master the skills to create them." (Publisher's note)

794.1   Chess

Fischer, Bobby

Bobby Fischer teaches chess; by Bobby Fisher, Stuart Margulies, Donn Mosenfelder. Bantam 1972 334p il pa $7.99 **794.1**

1. Chess

ISBN 0-553-26315-3; 978-0-553-26315-2

First published 1966 by Basic Systems, Inc.

In this book the authors give specific advice and hints aimed at both the beginning and advanced player. Each step-by-step lesson is fully illustrated.

Hallman, J. C.

The **chess** artist. Thomas Dunne Bks. 2003 334p il map $25.95; pa $13.95 **794.1**

1. Chess

ISBN 0-312-27293-6; 0-312-33396-X pa

LC 2003-46872

"Educational, fanciful, entertaining, this is a book that will make every reader see the game of chess in an entirely new—if slightly weird—light." Booklist

Includes bibliographical references

U.S. Chess Federation's official rules of chess; Tim Just, chief editor, National Tournament Director. 6th edition Random House 2014 369 p. pbk $19.99 **794.1**

1. Chess

ISBN 9780375724008; 0375724001

LC 2014009874

"This comprehensive rulebook is the only guide sanctioned and compiled by the U.S. Chess Federation (USCF), the governing body for chess in the United States. It is designed to be a useful reference for all chess players, especially tournament directors and chess club teachers." (Publisher's note)

794.6   Bowling

Manzione, Gianmarc

Pin Action; Small-time Gangsters, High-stakes Gambling, and the Teenage Hustler Who Became a Bowling Champion. by Gianmarc Manzione. W W Norton & Co Inc. 2014 336 p. 16 plates; illustrations $27.95 **794.6**

1. Bowling 2. Organized crime

ISBN 1605986453; 9781605986456

LC 2015410656

This book, by Gianmarc Manzione, explains how "in the 1960s, New York City was the center of ... a form of high-stakes gambling in which bowlers—often teenagers—faced off for thousands of dollars. ... You can bet the pressure is on ... and losses come with dire consequences. But for a few kids, the world of action bowling would turn out to be a ticket off the mean streets and onto the Professional Bowlers Association Tour. For Ernie Schlegel, it would be a chance to shed his hustler ways and become a bonafide champion." (Publisher's note)

"This well-researched account is for those who remember the glory days of bowling. Others will be fascinated by the gritty side of the sport, which few knew existed." LJ

794.7   Ball games

McCumber, David

Playing off the rail; a pool hustler's journey. Avon Books 1997 384p pa $14.95 **794.7**

1. Pool (Game) 2. Pool players

ISBN 0-380-72923-7

First published 1996 by Random House

A "look at the game of pool, which is a gambling sport not yet sanitized by what McCumber calls the 'Fellowship of Christian Athletes types.' He plays financial backer to a sharp-tongued player named Tony Annigoni, and takes him on the road across North America in search of highstakes games.... This is a terrific book." New Yorker

794.8   Electronic games

Bissell, Tom

Extra lives; why video games matter. Pantheon Books 2010 218p **794.8**

1. Video games

ISBN 0-307-37870-5; 978-0-307-37870-5

LC 2009-39602

This is a volume of essays about video games. Portions of the work originally appeared in The New Yorker, Tin House, and Kill Screen. Mr Bissell explains: "I wrote this book as a writer who plays a lot of games, and in these pages you will find one man's opinions and thoughts on what playing games feels like, why he plays them, and the questions they make him think about. In the portions of the book where I address game design and game designers, it is ... to a formally explanatory rather than technically informative end." (Author's note) Index.

The "first truly indispensable work of literary nonfiction about society's most lucrative entertainment medium. Bissell's commentary is marvelously astute and his enthusiasm for games makes even his words on the printed page feel positively backlit. Any breathless adoration for the medium he doles out, however, takes on additional weight because of his willingness to admit when a game falls on its face." Paste

A **history** of video games in 64 objects; World Video Game Hall of Fame. Dey St. 2018 ix, 341 p.p illustrations $26.99   **794.8**
1. Video games 2. Computer games 3. Electronic toys 4. Video games -- History
ISBN 0062838695; 9780062838698

LC 2017473803

"This book draws on the unique collections of The Strong museum in Rochester, New York, to chronicle the evolution of video games, from Pong to first-person shooters, told through the stories of dozens of objects essential to the field's creation and development. Drawing on the World Video Game Hall of Fame's unmatched collection of video game artifacts, this fascinating history offers an expansive look at the development of . . . video gaming." (Publisher's note)

Includes bibliographical resources (pages [317]-332) and index

Parker, Laura
  Power play; how video games can save the world. Asi Burak and Laura Parker. St. Martin's Press 2017 272 p. (ebook) $60; (hardcover) $27.99   **794.8**
1. Video games 2. Human-computer interaction 3. Video games -- Social aspects 4. Video games -- Design -- History
ISBN 9781250089342; 9781250089335

LC 2016036716

This book, by Asi Burak and Laura Parker, explores "how video games are now pioneering innovative social change around the world. As the former executive director and now chairman of Games for Change, . . . Burak has spent the last ten years supporting and promoting the use of video games for social good, in collaboration with leading organizations like the White House, NASA, World Bank, and the United Nations." (Publisher's note)

"These compelling examples of games for change are sure to engage gaming enthusiasts, activists, and game studies scholars." LJ

Includes bibliographical references and index

Parkin, Simon
  An **illustrated** history of 151 video games; a detailed guide to the most important games. by Simon Parkin. Natl Book Network 2014 255 p. color illustrations $29.99   **794.8**
1. Video games
ISBN 0754823903; 9780754823902

This book, by Simon Parkin, "charts the evolution of videogames through 151 most influential titles, with 500 photographs and screenshots." (Publisher's note)

Quinn, Zoe
  Crash override; how Gamergate (nearly) destroyed my life, and how we can win the fight against online hate. Zoë Quinn. PublicAffairs 2017 vii, 242 p.p illustrations (hardcover) $27   **794.8**
1. Autobiographies 2. Internet -- Social aspects 3. Video games -- Psychological aspects 4. Video gamers 5. Cyberbullying 6. Online hate speech 7. Women video game designers 8. Internet -- Moral and ethical aspects
ISBN 9781610398084; 9781610398909

LC 2017017273

This book, by Zoe Quinn, "offers an up-close look inside the controversy, threats, and social and cultural battles that started in the far corners of the internet and have since permeated our online lives. Through her story--as target and as activist--Quinn provides a human look at the ways the internet impacts our lives and culture, along with practical advice for keeping yourself and others safe online." (Publisher's note)

"She elevates diverse voices in her engaging, often-humorous writing. Whether readers are Internet devotees or not, Quinn's writing provides important context for our increasingly online lives." Booklist

Includes bibliographical references

795.4   Card games

Gibson, Walter Brown
  Hoyle's modern encyclopedia of card games; rules of all the basic games and popular variations. {by} Walter B. Gibson. Dolphin Bks. (NY) 1974 398p il pa $12.95   **795.4**
1. Card games
ISBN 0-385-07680-0

This guide to the rules and techniques of various card games includes special sections on pinochle, poker and solitaire

Ho, Oliver
  The **Ultimate** Book of Family Card Games; by Oliver Ho. Sterling 2010 118 p. color illustrations (hc-plc with jacket: alk. paper) $9.95   **795.4**
1. Card games 2. Card games -- Juvenile literature
ISBN 1402750412; 9781402750410

LC 2010026522

This book, by Oliver Ho, presents family card games. "Everyone loves to play cards, and this ultimate collection has all the fun favorites, including rummy, spades, war, old maid, go fish, snip snap snorem, and hearts. There are over 50 games in all, organized by type and difficulty, and complete with instructions, rules, strategies, color illustrations, and a brief note on each one's origins." (Publisher's note)

Hoyle, Edmond
  Hoyle's rules of games; descriptions of indoor games of skill and chance, with advice on skillful play: based on the foundations laid down by Edmond Hoyle, 1672-1769. edited by Albert H. Morehead and Geoffrey Mott-Smith. 3rd rev. & updated ed.; Plume 2001 362p il pa $14   **795.4**
1. Card games
ISBN 0-452-28313-2

LC 2002-278550

This guide "includes rules, strategies, and playing odds for more than 250 games." Publisher's note

Includes bibliographical references

McManus, James
  Cowboys full; the story of poker. Farrar, Straus, and Giroux 2009 516p il $30   **795.4**
1. Poker
ISBN 978-0-374-29924-8; 0-374-29924-2

LC 2009-29533

The story of poker, from its roots in China, the Middle East, and Europe to its ascent as a global—but especially an American—phenomenon, braiding history with poker's relevance to our military, diplomatic, business, and personal affairs.

"The epic story of how poker has grown from disreputable roots to become America's—and the world's—game. . . . A satisfying, useful overview." Kirkus

Includes bibliographical references (p. 471-474)

795.412 Poker

Whitehead, Colson

The **Noble** Hustle; Poker, Beef Jerky, and Death. Colson Whitehead. Random House Inc"||"Doubleday 2014 256 p. $24.95   **795.412**

1. Poker 2. Gambling 3. Las Vegas (Nev.)
ISBN 0385537050; 9780385537056

LC 2013031448

This book, by Colson Whitehead, is the story "of an amateur player who lucked into a seat at the biggest card game in town--the World Series of Poker. In 2011 'Grantland' magazine sent award-winning novelist . . . Whitehead to brave the . . . World Series of Poker in Las Vegas. It was the assignment of a lifetime, except for one hitch--he'd never played in a casino tournament before. With just six weeks to train, our . . . narrator plunged into the gritty subculture of high-stakes Texas Hold'em." (Publisher's note)

796 Athletic and outdoor sports and games

Crouse, Karen

Norwich; one tiny Vermont town's secret to happiness and excellence. Karen Crouse. Simon & Schuster 2018 276 p. (hardback) $26   **796**

1. Sports -- Social aspects 2. Olympic athletes -- Vermont -- Norwich 3. Norwich (Vt.) -- Social life and customs 4. Sports -- Vermont -- Norwich 5. Athletes -- Vermont -- Norwich 6. Sports -- Social aspects -- Vermont -- Norwich
ISBN 9781501119910; 9781501119897

LC 2017012269

This book by, Karen Crouse, presents "the extraordinary story of the small Vermont town that has likely produced more Olympians per capita than any other place in the country--and whose citizens provide a model for achieving excellence while leading a well-rounded life. . . . [After] immersing herself in the lives of Norwich Olympians . . . , Norwich, Crouse realized, wasn't just raising better athletes than the rest of America; it was raising happier, healthier kids." (Publisher's note)

"Short and sweet, this important book highlights what's wrong with youth sports by focusing on a community that gets it right." Pub Wkly

Includes bibliographical references and index

Halberstam, David

The **teammates**. Hyperion 2003 217p il $22.95   **796**
1. Baseball players 2. Sportscasters 3. Baseball managers 4. Baseball -- Biography 5. Boston Red Sox (Baseball team)
ISBN 1-401-30057-X

LC 2003-42334

"This account of good people living full lives and appreciating the experience will move readers." Booklist

Haskins, Don

★ **Glory** road; my story of the 1966 NCAA basketball championship and how one team triumphed against the odd and changed America forever. [by] Don Haskins with Daniel Wetzel. Hyperion 2006 254p il pa $14.95   **796**
1. Basketball coaches

ISBN 1-4013-0791-4

LC 2005-50349

"This is one of the best sports autobiographies in many years." Booklist

Kindred, Dave

Sound and fury; two powerful lives, one fateful friendship. Free Press 2006 368p il $27   **796**
1. Lawyers 2. Television personalities 3. Sportscasters 4. Boxers (Persons)
ISBN 0-7432-6211-5; 978-0-7432-6211-8

LC 2005-55217

This is an account of the friendship of Muhammad Ali and Howard Cosell.

"Even if the shelves are sagging with books about Ali, room should be made for this approachable, touching, and altogether fascinating buddy comedy." Booklist

Includes bibliographical references

Miller, Stephen G.

Ancient Greek athletics. Yale University Press 2004 288p il map $35   **796**
1. Athletics 2. Olympic games 3. Greece -- Civilization
ISBN 0-300-10083-3

LC 2003-16875

"Five chapters discuss the origins and history of the [Olympic] games and their sociopolitical significance, but at the core of the book are the 11 chapters that use archaeological and textual evidence . . . to reconstruct the physical reality of Greek athletics. Particularly valuable are the vivid reconstruction of the ancient Olympic program and the lucid discussion of the evidence for female athletic contests in ancient Greece." Choice

Includes bibliographical references

Murphy, Cait

A **history** of American sports in 100 objects; Cait Murphy. Basic Books, A Member of Perseus Books Group 2016 384 p. illustrations (hardcover) $29.99; (ebook) $20.99   **796**
1. Sports -- United States -- History -- Miscellanea
ISBN 9780465097746; 9780465097753

LC 2016012506

This book by Cait Murphy focuses on "what artifact best captures the spirit of American sports? The bat Babe Ruth used to hit his allegedly called shot, or the ball on which Pete Rose wrote, 'I'm sorry I bet on baseball'? Could it be Lance Armstrong's red-white-and-blue bike, now tarnished by doping . . . ? . . . The jerseys of rivals Larry Bird and Magic Johnson? Or the handball that Abraham Lincoln threw against a wall as he waited for news of his presidential nomination?" (Publisher's note)

"The backstory surrounding those championships is an eye-opening and too-little-known chapter in the history of women's sports. This is a great concept for a sports book, and it's expertly executed." Booklist

Includes bibliographical references and index

Pesca, Mike

Upon further review; the greatest what-ifs in sports history. Mike Pesca. Twelve 2018 320 p. (hardback) $28   **796**
1. Sports -- History 2. Sports -- Miscellanea 3. Sports -- Anecdotes
ISBN 9781455540365

LC 2017041897

In this book, by Mike Pesca, "the greatest sports minds [imagine] how the world would change if a play, trade, injury, or referee's call had just gone the other way. . . . [This] is a book of counterfactual sporting scenarios. In its pages the reader will find expertly reported histories, where one small event is flipped on its head." (Publisher's note)

Rhoden, William C.

$40 million slaves; the rise, fall, and redemption of the Black athlete. Crown Publishers 2006 286p il $23.95 **796**

1. Sports 2. Race discrimination 3. African American athletes
ISBN 0-609-60120-2; 978-0-609-60120-4

LC 2005-34952

"In his provocative, passionate, important and disturbing book—part memoir, part history, part journalism—William Rhoden . . . builds a historic framework that both accounts for the varieties of African-American athletic experience in the past and continues to explain them today." N Y Times Book Rev

Includes bibliographical references

Thomas, Etan

We matter; athletes and activism. Etan Thomas. Edge of Sports/Akashic Books 2018 250 p. (hardcover) $28.95 **796**

1. African American athletes 2. United States -- Race relations 3. Racial profiling in law enforcement
ISBN 9781617755910; 9781617755941; 9781617756122

LC 2017936007

"Featuring interviews by former NBA player Etan Thomas with over fifty athletes, executives, media figures, and more--and interwoven with essays and critiques by Thomas-- . . . [this book] shares the personal tales and opinions of Kareem Abdul-Jabbar, Bill Russell, Dwyane Wade, Russell Westbrook, Steve Kerr, Oscar Robertson, Mark Cuban, Michael Bennett, Carmelo Anthony, . . . [on the subject of race in the U.S.]." (Publisher's note)

"Recommended for not only high school and college students but all readers concerned with social activism and awareness. An excellent resource to spark discussions and motivate positive community expression and involvement." LJ

Wertheim, L. Jon

This is your brain on sports; The Science of Underdogs, the Value of Rivalry & What We Can Learn From the T-Shirt Cannon. L. Jon Wertheim and Sam Sommers. Crown Archetype 2016 288 p. $26 **796**

1. Sports -- Psychological aspects 2. Sports -- Miscellanea
ISBN 9780553447408

LC 2015021731

This book, by L. Jon Wertheim and Sam Sommers, "take[s] readers on a wild ride into the inner world of sports. Through the prism of behavioral economics, neuroscience, and psychology, they reveal the hidden influences and surprising cues that inspire and derail us—on the field and in the stands—and by extension, in corporate board rooms, office settings, and our daily lives." (Publisher's note)

"If sport s bring out the kooky, spooky, and creepy in us, Wertheim and Sommers give us a chance to understand ourselves and perhaps get a grip before we totally lose it." Kirkus

Includes bibliographical references

Winston, Wayne L.

Mathletics; how gamblers, managers, and sports enthusiasts use mathematics in baseball, basketball, and football. [by] Wayne Winston. Princeton University Press 2009 358p il $29.95 **796**

1. Mathematics 2. Sports -- Statistics
ISBN 978-0-691-13913-5; 0-691-13913-X

LC 2008-51678

"Sports fans will learn much from probability theory and statistical

models. . . . A rare fusion of sports enthusiasm and numerical acumen." Booklist

Includes bibliographical references (p. 343-352)

Wong, Stephen

Smithsonian baseball; inside the world's finest private collections. photographs by Susan Einstein. HarperCollins 2005 il **796**

1. Baseball -- Collectors and collecting. 2. Baseball -- Collectibles -- United States. 3. Baseball -- Collectibles -- United States -- Pictorial works.
ISBN 0-06-083851-5

"An oversized volume showcases 350 full-color photographs of twenty-one of the best private collections of baseball memorabilia, featuring numerous historical and previously unseen artifacts and providing eight expert essays on how to build a personal collection." (Publisher's note)

796.01   Sports philosophy

Afremow, Jim

The **champion's** mind; how great athletes think, train, and thrive. Jim Afremow, PhD. Rodale Books 2014 269 p. (hardback) $24.99 **796.01**

1. Physical education 2. Sports -- Psychological aspects 3. Physical education and training
ISBN 1623361486; 9781623361488

LC 2013032605

In this book, by Jim Afremow, the author "offers the same advice he uses with Olympians, Heisman Trophy winners, and professional athletes, including: tips and techniques based on high-performance psychology research, such as how to get in a 'zone,' thrive on a team, and stay humble . . . , [and] how to progress within a sport and sustain excellence long-term." (Publisher's note)

Includes bibliographical references

Rotella, Bob

How champions think in sports and in life; Dr. Bob Rotella, with Bob Cullen. Simon & Schuster 2015 304 p. (Hardcover) $26 **796.01**

1. Success 2. Athletes 3. Sports -- Psychological aspects 4. Athletes -- Attitudes 5. Athletes -- Psychology 6. Success -- Psychological aspects
ISBN 1476788626; 9781476788623

LC 2014044600

This book, by sports psychologist Bob Rotella, is a "guide to success in all aspects of life-- not just sports-- from business to relationships to personal challenges of every variety. . . . It explores how to keep the mind from holding you back, whatever your physical gifts or other talents. It's about how to make a commitment, how to persevere, how to deal with failure-- and how to train your mind to create a self-image that promotes confidence and accomplishment." (Publisher's note)

"Rotella's liberal use of sports anecdotes and an effective piece on a coach's perspective (Kentucky basketball coach John Calipari) further underscore the importance of the core set of philosophies and behaviors he promotes, although his frequent and distractive allusions to faith and religion as one of the linchpins to an athlete's or a team's success may not appeal to more secular readers. A solid motivational text for the sports-minded and those interested in the bridging of athletics and exceptionalism." Kirkus

796.04   General kinds of sports and games

Nocera, Joe

Indentured; the inside story of the rebellion against the NCAA. Joe Nocera and Ben Strauss. Portfolio 2016 384 p. illustrations (hardcover) $30 **796.04**

1. Athletes 2. College sports 3. Sports -- Economic aspects 4. National Collegiate Athletic Association 5. College sports -- United States -- Management 6. College sports -- Economic aspects -- United States 7. College athletes -- United States -- Economic conditions 8. College sports -- Moral and ethical aspects -- United States

ISBN 9781591846321

LC 2015044500

This book, by Joe Nocera and Ben Strauss, "tells the story of a loose-knit group of rebels who decided to fight the hypocrisy of the NCAA, which blathers endlessly about the purity of its 'student-athletes' while exploiting many of them: The ones who get injured and drop out because their scholarships have been revoked. The ones who will neither graduate nor go pro. The ones who live in terror of accidentally violating some obscure rule in the four-hundred-page NCAA rulebook." (Publisher's note)

"Championship-level reporting on the boundaries of sport and business." Kirkus

Includes bibliographical references and index.

796.068   Management

Kohan, Rafi

The **Arena**; Inside the Tailgating, Ticket-Scalping, Mascot-Racing, Dubiously Funded, and Possibly Haunted Monuments of American Sport. by Rafi Kohan. Liveright Publishing Corporation 2017 xi, 401 p.p color illustrations (hardcover) $27.95 **796.068**

1. Stadiums 2. Sports spectators 3. Sports spectators -- United States 4. Sports -- Social aspects 5. Stadiums -- Social aspects -- United States

ISBN 9781631491276; 9781631491283; 163149127X

LC 2017015161

This book, by Rafi Kohan, is an "exploration of the modern American sports stadium. . . . If you've ever wondered how they coordinate those fighter jet flyovers with the national anthem, how many hot dogs they serve in a day at Citi Field, how boozy pregame tailgates are kept in line, or what on earth AstroTurf is made of, look no further." (Publisher's note)

"Kohan's curiosity and empathy are infectious as he demonstrates how human this corporate aspect of sports can be. He has created an immersive, informative work that will delight and enlighten a wide range of readers." Pub Wkly

Includes bibliographical references and index.

796.07   Education, research, related topics

Davis, Seth

★ **Getting** to us; how great coaches make great teams. Seth Davis. Penguin Group USA 2018 304 p. $28 **796.07**

1. Football coaches 2. Basketball coaches 3. Coaching (Athletics)

ISBN 073522272X; 9780735222724

This book, by Seth Davis, "probes and prods the best of the best from the landscape of active coaches of football and basketball, college

and pro--from Urban Meyer, Dabo Swinney, and Jim Harbaugh to Mike Krzyzewski, Tom Izzo, Jim Boeheim, Brad Stevens, Geno Auriemma, and Doc Rivers--to get at the fundamental ingredients of greatness in the coaching sphere." (Publisher's note)

"Each chapter includes interviews with the selected coach, along with relatives, mentors, assistants, and former players as Davis relates the subject's life, career, and method. Although the coaches' styles vary from Harbaugh's in-your-face intensity to Boeheim's aloof practicality to Swinney's loquacious empathy, the nine essays fit together with what Davis views as the common keys to successful coaching." Library Journal

796.077   Coaching

Walker, Sam

The **captain** class; the hidden force that creates the world's greatest teams. Sam Walker. Random House 2017 xvii, 332 p.p (hardback) $28 **796.077**

1. Leadership 2. Sports teams 3. Coaching (Athletics)

ISBN 9780399591198; 9780812997194; 9780812997200

LC 2016054597

This book, by Sam Walker, "profiles the greatest teams in history and identifies the counterintuitive leadership qualities of the unconventional men and women who drove them to succeed. . . . [It] tells the surprising story of what makes teams exceptional. Drawing on original interviews with athletes from two dozen countries, as well as general managers, coaches, . . . Walker identifies the seven core qualities of this Captain Class. . . ." (Publisher's note)

"Written for serious sports fans in lively language that also speaks to aspiring athletes and business professionals, this book offers a compelling argument for the value of inspired leadership." Pub Wkly

Includes bibliographical references (pages 307-314) and index.

796.083   Outdoor recreation – Young people

Garlick, Hattie

Born to Be Wild; Hundreds of free nature activities for families. by Hattie Garlick. St. Martin's Press 2016 256 p. color illustrations $22 **796.083**

1. Creative activities

ISBN 147291533X; 9781472915337

This book, by Hattie Garlick, "contains easy-to-follow instructions for activities that require nothing more sophisticated than a child's imagination and access to a little outdoor space. Organized by season and then by material, it lets parents skip straight to . . . their present need. Everything you need to engage in all of its hundreds of activities can be found in your kitchen. No expensive art supplies or outward-bound kit required." (Publisher's note)

"Spring presents a wonderful opportunity to reconnect with the outdoors, and with this title nearby, even smartphone-obsessed kids will soon be clamoring to plan an outing." LJ

Includes bibliographical references and index.

796.087   People with disabilities and illnesses, gifted people

Shriver, Timothy

Fully alive; discovering what matters most. Timothy Shriver. Sarah Crichton Books 2014 304 p. 16 plates; illustrations (hardback) $27   **796.087**

1. Special Olympics 2. People with mental disabilities 3. Sports for people with mental disabilities

ISBN 0374280916; 9780374280918

LC 2014020245

In this memoir, author Timothy Shriver "shows how his teachers have been the world's most forgotten minority: people with intellectual disabilities. In these pages we meet the individuals who helped him come of age and find a deeper and more meaningful way to see the world." (Publisher's note)

"Sincere, profound and deeply satisfying." Kirkus

796.3   Ball games

Dawidoff, Nicholas

Collision Low Crossers; A Year Inside the Turbulent World of NFL Football. Nicholas Dawidoff. Little Brown & Co 2013 352 p. $87   **796.3**

1. Football 2. National Football League 3. Football -- United States 4. New York Jets (Football team)

ISBN 0316196797; 9780316196796

LC 2013030013

This book by Nicholas Dawidoff follows the football team the New York Jets throughout 2011, "operations, from the February scouting 'combine' of collegiate talent, through the May draft of college players, the torturous preseason of practices and games, and, finally, to the entire 16-game, regular season schedule and subsequent coaches' postmortem. Head coach Rex Ryan and his staff receive the primary focus." (Booklist)

Includes bibliographical references and index

796.323   Basketball

Abrams, Jonathan

Boys among men; how the prep-to-pro generation redefined the NBA and sparked a basketball revolution. Jonathan Abrams. Crown Archetype 2015 336 p. color illustrations $28 **796.323**

1. High school students 2. National Basketball Association 3. Basketball draft 4. Basketball players -- Recruiting -- United States

ISBN 0804139253; 9780804139250

LC 2015027590

This book, by Jonathan Abrams, tells the "story of the prep-to-pro generation, those basketball prodigies who from 1995 to 2005 made the jump directly from high school to the [National Basketball Association]. 'Boys Among Men' goes behind the scenes and draws on hundreds of firsthand interviews to paint insightful and engaging portraits of the most pivotal figures and events during this time." (Publisher's note)

"Especially timely considering Kobe's recent retirement announcement, this essential, well-researched book will appeal to readers interested in basketball's business side as well as the factors that have helped shape the modern NBA." Library Journal

Blais, Madeleine

In these girls, hope is a muscle. Warner Bks. 1996 266p pa $13.95   **796.323**

1. Basketball 2. Cathedral High School (Springfield, Mass.)

ISBN 0-446-67210-6; 978-0-446-67210-8

First published 1995 by Atlantic Monthly Press

"Alternately funny, exciting and moving, the book should be enjoyed not only by girls and women who have played sports but also those who wanted to but let themselves be discouraged." Publ Wkly

Colton, Larry

Counting coup; a true story of basketball and honor on the Little Big Horn. Warner Bks. 2000 420p hardcover o.p. pa $14.95   **796.323**

1. Basketball 2. Women athletes 3. Native Americans -- Social conditions 4. Hardin High School (Hardin, Mont.) -- Basketball

ISBN 0-446-52683-5; 0-446-67755-8 pa

LC 00-24987

Conroy, Pat

My losing season. Talese 2002 402p hardcover o.p. pa $14.95   **796.323**

1. Authors 2. Novelists 3. Authors, American

ISBN 0-385-48912-9; 0-553-38190-3 pa

LC 2002-66212

"A wonderfully rich, informative, and well-researched reminiscence." Libr J

Davis, Seth

When March went mad; the game that transformed basketball. Henry Holt 2009 323p il $26   **796.323**

1. Basketball 2. Indiana State University 3. Michigan State University

ISBN 978-0-8050-8810-6; 0-8050-8810-5

LC 2008-47628

The author "chronicles the 1979 NCAA basketball championship game, which featured two future legends: Earvin 'Magic' Johnson and Larry Bird. The game was a pivotal moment in the development of the sport, leading to an explosion in popularity and a change in the way the game was played and promoted. . . . An essential primer for tournament junkies, and ideal reading material for TV timeouts." Kirkus

Includes bibliographical references

Dohrmann, George

★ **Play** their hearts out; a coach, his star recruit, and the youth basketball machine. Ballantine Books 2010 422p il $26   **796.323**

1. Basketball 2. Basketball coaches 3. Basketball players

ISBN 978-0-345-50860-7; 0-345-50860-2

LC 2010-15470

The author "follows California phenom Demetrius Walker through the cycle of Amateur Athletic Union (AAU) summer league hoops, from playing for ambitious hustler and coach Joe Keller to the face of grassroots basketball, longtime coach Pat Barrett. In a constant search for the next Lebron, just as before for the next Michael Jordan, AAU coaches, with support and financing from shoe giants Nike and Adidas, woo youngsters to their summer league basketball teams with gear, shoes, and promises of a college scholarship. . . . [Dohrmann's] insights into the seamy side of youth basketball are investigative journalism at its best." Libr J

Feinstein, John

★ **Last** dance; behind the scenes at the Final Four. John Feinstein. Little, Brown 2006 369p il $25.95   **796.323**

1. Basketball

ISBN 0-316-16030-X

LC 2005-28478

The author "employs the 2005 [Final Four] weekend as the catalyst to discuss the history of the event, the key people, and, most significantly, the effect that involvement in the Final Four has had on participants' lives. . . . The anecdotes are entertaining, and the insights into the tournament's logistics fascinating, but what will linger most are the remembrances of players, especially those who ended up on the losing side." Booklist

★ The **legends** club; Dean Smith, Mike Krzyzewski, Jim Valvano, and an Epic College Basketball Rivalry. John Feinstein. Doubleday 2016 416 p. illustrations (some color) (Hard cover) $27.95 **796.323**
 1. College sports 2. Basketball teams 3. Basketball coaches 4. College basketball 5. Duke University -- Basketball -- History 6. Basketball teams -- North Carolina -- History 7. Sports rivalries -- North Carolina -- History 8. Basketball coaches -- United States -- Biography 9. North Carolina State University -- Basketball -- History 10. University of North Carolina at Chapel Hill -- Basketball -- History
 ISBN 9780385539418

LC 2015029890

This book, by John Feinstein, presents the "inside story of college basketball's fiercest rivalry among three coaching legends—University of North Carolina's Dean Smith, Duke's Mike Krzyzewski, and North Carolina State's Jim Valvano. . . . Feinstein pulls back the curtain on the recruiting wars, the intensely personal competition that wasn't always friendly, the enormous pressure and national stakes, and the battle for the very soul of college basketball allegiance in a hot-bed area." (Publisher's note)

"A text that will delight college basketball fans but also raises tacit questions about the effects of big-time athletics on a university's academic mission." Kirkus

FreeDarko presents the macrophenomenal pro basketball almanac; styles, stats and stars in today's game. Bloomsbury USA 2008 219p il $23 **796.323**
 1. Basketball 2. National Basketball Association
 ISBN 978-1-59691-561-9; 1-59691-561-7

"This is a wonderful basketball book that blends a unique perspective, arresting presentation, and superior knowledge of its subject." Booklist

Fury, Shawn
 Rise & fire; the origins, science, and evolution of the jump shot --- and how it transformed basketball forever. Shawn Fury. St. Martin's Press 2016 352 p. illustrations (hardback) $27.99 **796.323**
 1. Basketball -- History
 ISBN 9781250062161; 1250062160

LC 2015040454

This book, by Shawn Fury, "celebrates . . . [the jump shot in basketball] while tracing the history of how it revolutionized the game, shedding light on all corners of the basketball world, from NBA arenas to the playgrounds of New York City and the barns of Indiana. . . . [The author] obsesses over the jump shot, explores its fundamentals, puzzles over its complexities, marvels at its simplicity, and honors those who created some of basketball's greatest moments." (Publisher's note)

"Apart from Fury's historical account, ultimately we must return to the love letter, as it transports us back to the days when the world was just us, a basketball, and a hoop mounted in a driveway, an alley, a barn, or a deserted playground, and in our minds we became West or Robertson or Long, and it seemed we would be forever young." LJ

Includes bibliographical references and index.

Glockner, Andy
 Chasing perfection; a behind-the-scenes look at the high-stakes game of creating an NBA champion. Andy Glockner. Da Capo Press 2016 288 p. illustrations (hardback) $25.99 **796.323**
 1. Basketball teams 2. Sports -- Economic aspects 3. National Basketball Association 4. Basketball -- Philosophy 5. Basketball teams -- United States 6. Basketball -- Economic aspects -- United States 7. Basketball -- United States -- Statistical methods 8. National Basketball Association -- Forecasting -- Statistics
 ISBN 0306824027; 9780306824029

LC 2015043098

This book, by Andy Glockner, "goes behind the scenes of the multi-million dollar, high-stakes world of basketball player development, research and analysis, and the often secretive, cutting-edge methods that NBA franchises use to turn less-expensive, supporting players into vital parts of championship teams." (Publisher's note)

"Highly recommended for NBA junkies who scour box scores." LJ
 Includes bibliographical references and index

Haygood, Wil
 Tigerland; 1968-1969, a city divided, a nation torn apart, and a magical season of healing. by Wil Haygood. Alfred A. Knopf 2018 432 p. **796.323**
 1. Columbus (Ohio) -- Biography 2. Baseball -- Ohio -- Columbus -- History 3. Basketball -- Ohio -- Columbus -- History 4. East High School (Columbus, Ohio) -- History 5. Race relations -- Ohio -- Columbus -- History
 ISBN 9781524731861

LC 2018002138

"Readers of sports and American history as well as fans of Alejandro Danois's The Boys of Dunbar will find plenty of in-game action as well as historical perspective to cherish." Library Journal
 Includes bibliographical references

MacMullan, Jackie
 ★ **Basketball**; a love story. by Jackie MacMullan and Rafe Bartholomew. Crown Archetype 2018 448 p. $30 **796.323**
 1. Sports -- History 2. Basketball -- United States -- History 3. Basketball players -- United States -- Interviews
 ISBN 9781524761783

LC 2018023541

This book, by Jackie MacMullan and Rafe Bartholomew, presents "an extraordinary oral history of basketball--its eye-opening untold history, its profound deeper meaning, its transformative influence on the world--as told through an unprecedented series of candid conversations with the game's ultimate icons. . . . For the first time hundreds of legends, from Kobe [Bryant] . . . to Magic Johnson, Dr. J and Jerry West, spoke movingly about their greatest passion." (Publisher's note)

"Highly recommended for all public libraries; this work will appeal to both casual and die-hard basketball fans."

Malinowski, Erik
 Betaball; how Silicon Valley and science built one of the greatest basketball teams in history. Erik Malinowski. Atria Books 2017 390 p. (hardback) $26 **796.323**
 1. Sports 2. Basketball teams 3. National Basketball Association 4. Basketball -- Economic aspects 5. Golden State Warriors (Basketball team)
 ISBN 9781501158193; 9781501158209

LC 2017032496

This book, by Erik Malinowski, "is the definitive inside account of how the Warriors -- under the leadership of . . . Joe Lacob and . . . Peter Guber -- quickly became one of the most remarkable success stories . . . in sports or business. In just five years, the duo turned . . . [the] franchise . . . into . . . NBA's dominant force, . . . produced the best single-season record in league history, and won two championships over a three-year span." (Publisher's note)

"Much the way David Kaplan chronicled the creation of the 2016 champion Chicago Cubs in The Plan (2017), so free-lance sportswriter Malinowski has laid out the construction, piece by piece, of the power-house Golden State Warriors, who won NBA titles in 2015 and 2017, and in the 2016 regular season won a record-breaking 79 games. ... An insightful portrait of, yes, one of the all-time great NBA teams." Booklist.

McCallum, Jack

Dream team; how Michael, Magic, Larry, Charles, and the greatest team of all time conquered the world and changed the game of basketball forever. Jack McCallum. Ballantine Books 2012 xxix, 352 p.p col. ill. (hardback) $28   **796.323**
1. Olympic games 2. Basketball -- History 3. Basketball players -- United States -- Biography 4. Basketball -- United States -- History 5. Basketball teams -- United States -- History
ISBN 0345520483; 0345520505; 9780345520487; 9780345520500

LC 2012006253

In this book "sports journalist Jack McCallum delivers the . . . story of . . . the 1992 U.S. Olympic Men's Basketball Team that captivated the world. . . . He offers a . . . look at the controversial selection process. . . . [a]nd he narrates . . . the legendary July 1992 intrasquad scrimmage that pitted the Dream Teamers against one another in what may have been the greatest pickup game--and the greatest exhibition of trash talk--in history." (Publisher's note)

"...[McCallum] effectively evokes the remarkable team while placing it within the larger historical context. Basketball and Olympics fans will welcome this nostalgic trip through the recent past." Kirkus

Golden days; West's Lakers, Steph's Warriors, and the California dreamers who reinvented basketball. Jack McCallum. Ballantine Books 2017 xxv, 308 p.p (hardback: alk. paper) $28   **796.323**
1. Basketball 2. Basketball -- California -- History 3. Los Angeles Lakers (Baseketball team) -- History 4. Golden State Warriors (Basketball team) -- History
ISBN 0399179070; 9780399179075

LC 2017038872

This book, by Jack McCallum, "tells the interconnected stories of the NBA champion Golden State Warriors and the early-1970s Los Angeles Lakers, two extraordinary teams playing in extraordinary times and linked by one extraordinary man: Jerry West." (Publisher's note)

Merlino, Doug

The **hustle**; one team and ten lives in Black and White. Bloomsbury USA 2010 309p il $26   **796.323**
1. Basketball 2. School sports 3. Lakeside School (Seattle, Wash.) 4. Washington (State) -- Race relations
ISBN 978-1-60819-215-1; 1-60819-215-6

LC 2010-23030

"This book, both memoir and social analysis, is an essential read as a recent social history and personal story of America." Libr J

Reeder, Lydia

Dust bowl girls; a team's quest for basketball glory. Lydia

Reeder. Algonquin Books of Chapel Hill 2017 304 p. (hardcover) $26.95   **796.323**
1. Basketball for women 2. Basketball coaches -- Oklahoma -- Biography 3. Basketball for women -- Oklahoma -- History 4. Women basketball players -- Oklahoma -- Biography 5. Oklahoma Presbyterian College -- Basketball -- History
ISBN 1616204664; 9781616204662

LC 2016016234

This book, by Lydia Reeder, describes how "at the height of the Great Depression, Sam Babb, the charismatic basketball coach of tiny Oklahoma Presbyterian College, began dreaming. Like so many others, he wanted a reason to have hope. Traveling from farm to farm, he recruited talented, hardworking young women and offered them a chance at a better life: a free college education if they would come play for his basketball team, the Cardinals." (Publisher's note)

"Author Reeder, Babb's grandniece, had access to such primary materials as player diaries, which reveal the players' relationships to one another and their coach, and to a dust-bowl era and region marked by serious hardship." Booklist

Includes bibliographical references

Reynolds, Bill

Hope; a school, a team, a dream. Bill Reynolds. St. Martin's Press 2016 256 p. color illustrations (hardback) $26.99   **796.323**
1. Basketball 2. High schools -- Rhode Island -- Providence
ISBN 9781250080691; 125008069X

LC 2015037368

This book, by Bill Reynolds, profiles "Hope High School in Providence, Rhode Island . . . , once . . . known for its state championship basketball teams in the 1960s, but its 2012 team is much different. Disobedient, distracted, and overwhelmed by family troubles, with mismatched sneakers and a penchant for profanity and anger, these boys represent Coach Dave Nyblom's dream of a championship, however unlikely that might seem." (Publisher's note)

"A basketball book but also a candid look at inner-city life that should garner it a broad audience." Booklist

Simmons, Bill

The **book** of basketball; the NBA according to the sports guy. Ballantine/ESPN Books 2009 715p il $30; pa $18   **796.323**
1. Basketball 2. National Basketball Association
ISBN 978-0-345-51176-8; 0-345-51176-X; 978-0-345-52010-4 pa; 0-345-52010-6 pa

LC 2009-36006

The author "summarizes the history of the league, discusses his personal fandom, includes a great 'what if?' chapter (what if Michael Jordan had been drafted second by Portland instead of third by Chicago?), analyzes Most Valuable Player choices through the years, and dissects the careers of the league's all-time best players. The true NBA fan will dive into this hefty volume and won't resurface for about a week, emerging from the man cave unshaven, smelling of beer and pizza, grinning, and armed with NBA history, insight, anecdotes, statistics, and a dozen new examples of Simmons' Unintentional Comedy Scale. This is just plain fun. Expect significant demand from hoops junkies." Booklist

Includes bibliographical references

Smith, Sam

Hard Labor; the battle that birthed the billion-dollar NBA. Sam Smith. Triumph Books 2017 xv, 351 p.p illustrations (some color) (hardcover) $24.95   **796.323**

1. Basketball 2. National Basketball Association 3. Basketball -- United States -- Finance 4. National Basketball Association -- Finance 5. Basketball -- Economic aspects -- United States 6. Basketball players -- Salaries, etc. -- United States -- History
ISBN 9781629372785; 1629372781

LC 2017026712

This book, by Sam Smith, "unearths . . . [the] untold fight for players' rights and examines the massive repercussions for the NBA and sports in the United States in the 40 years since. Diving into how 'The 14' paved the way for the record-setting paydays for today's NBA players - stars and role players alike - as well as the harsh consequences faced by those involved in the lawsuit against the NBA. . . . [This book] is an essential read for both NBA and sports fans alike." (Publisher's note)

"Smith has another winner: a fascinating story well told." Booklist
Includes bibliographical references.

Smith, Tyler

★ **Called** for traveling; my nomadic life playing pro basketball around the world. Tyler Smith. Sports Publishing 2017 384 p. $24.99   **796.323**
1. Autobiography 2. Basketball players -- United States -- Biography 3. Basketball players 4. Professional basketball
ISBN 1683580761; 9781683580768

In this autobiography, author Tyler Smith, shares "a pro basketball journey that spans four continents, seven countries and twelve teams over eleven hilarious and adventurous years. . . . Smith draws readers in quickly with his humor and ability to share his clever stories that seem outrageous, but are 100 percent true. His attitude and faith are tested relentlessly through . . . the . . . reality of people around him speaking a language he could not understand." (Publisher's note)

Swidey, Neil

The **assist**; hoops, hope, and the game of their lives. PubliccAffairs 2008 358p il $26   **796.323**
1. Basketball 2. School sports 3. Basketball coaches 4. Charlestown High School (Boston, Mass.)
ISBN 978-1-58648-469-9; 1-58648-469-9

LC 2007-35826

"This is a prodigiously reported, compulsively readable book that readers (sport fans or not) will savor." Publ Wkly

Thomsen, Ian

The **soul** of basketball; the epic showdown between LeBron, Kobe, Doc, and Dirk that saved the NBA. Ian Thomsen. Houghton Mifflin Harcourt 2018 352 p. (hardcover) $27   **796.323**
1. National Basketball Association -- History 2. Basketball -- United States -- History
ISBN 9780547746517

LC 2017046213

This book, by Ian Thomsen, "tells the story of an NBA prodigy, his league and their sport in the throes of crisis during the pivotal 2010-11 season. It began . . . when uber-star LeBron James revealed that he was leaving the Cleveland Cavaliers . . . to pursue his first championship with his former opponents on the Miami Heat. . . . This is about the making of a champion. . . . [It] tells the inspiring story of LeBron's loneliest year, insecure and uncertain." (Publisher's note)

Windhorst, Brian

Return of the king; LeBron James, the Cleveland Cavaliers, and the greatest comeback in NBA history. Brian Windhorst and Dave McMenamin. Grand Central Pub 2017 xiv, 264

p.p color illustrations (hardcover) $28   **796.323**
1. Athletes -- Biography 2. Basketball -- History 3. National Basketball Association -- History 4. Cleveland Cavaliers (Basketball team) -- History
ISBN 1478971681; 9781478971689; 9781478919629

LC 2017289063

This book, by Brian Windhorst and Dave McMenamin, looks at "the inside story of LeBron James's return and ultimate triumph in Cleveland. . . . [It] takes you . . . into the middle of the intense huddles where one of the greatest stories in basketball history took place, resulting in the Cavs winning the 2016 NBA title after trailing the Golden State Warriors three games to one. You'll hear from all the characters involved . . . as they reveal stories never before told." (Publisher's note)

"This account of how a championship was built is the best NBA book in many years." Booklist

796.332   American football

Anderson, Lars

Carlisle vs. Army; Jim Thorpe, Dwight Eisenhower, Pop Warner, and the forgotten story of football's greatest battle. Random House 2007 349p il $24.95   **796.332**
1. Football 2. Generals 3. Presidents 4. Decathletes 5. Pentathletes 6. Football coaches 7. Olympic athletes 8. College presidents 9. United States Indian School (Carlisle, Pa.)
ISBN 978-1-4000-6600-1; 1-4000-6600-X

LC 2007-8410

"A forgotten football game in 1912, between Carlisle, led by Jim Thorpe and coached by the legendary Pop Warner, and Army, led by Dwight Eisenhower, becomes the launching point for a fascinating look at multiple levels of American popular culture." Booklist
Includes bibliographical references

The **Mannings**; The Fall and Rise of a Football Family. Lars Anderson. Ballantine Books 2016 368 p. color illustrations (hardcover: acid-free paper) $28   **796.332**
1. Football players 2. Football players -- United States -- Biography 3. Quarterbacks (Football) -- United States -- Biography
ISBN 1101883820; 9781101883822

LC 2016018007

This book, by Lars Anderson, is "a revealing portrait of the first family of American sports, . . . the Mannings. . . . Two generations have produced three NFL superstars: Archie Manning, the Ole Miss hero–turned–New Orleans Saint; his son Peyton, widely considered one of the greatest quarterbacks ever to play the game; and Peyton's younger brother, Eli, who won two Super Bowl rings of his own. And the oldest Manning child, Cooper—who was forced to quit playing sports." (Publisher's note)

"An expertly written impressionistic account of the first family of football that will be of wide interest." LJ
Includes bibliographical references and index

Bissinger, H. G.

★ **Friday** night lights; a town, a team, and a dream. Da Capo Press 2000 367p il pa $15.95   **796.332**
1. Football 2. Permian High School (Odessa, Tex.)
ISBN 0-306-80990-7

LC 00-40510

First published 1990 by Addison-Wesley

"It is a tricky balancing act, but Mr. Bissinger carries it off: 'Friday Night Lights' offers a biting indictment of the sports craziness that grips not only Odessa but most of American society, while at the same time providing a moving evocation of its powerful allure." N Y Times Book Rev

Burke, Monte

    Saban; the making of a coach. Monte Burke. Simon & Schuster 2015 352 p. (Hardcover) $27   **796.332**

    1. College football coaches 2. University of Alabama -- Football -- History 3. Football coaches -- United States -- Biography

    ISBN 1476789932; 9781476789934

                            LC 2015018182

Author Monte Burke presents a "biography of Nick Saban, the influential and polarizing University of Alabama football coach who not only transformed the college game but might also be the best ever at winning. Through unprecedented interviews with more than 250 friends, coworkers, rivals, former players, and others, Burke reveals the defining moments of the coach's life." (Publisher's note)

"With Saban's wins and losses over the years having been covered extensively in the media, Burke wisely focuses on the man rather than the play-by-play, and the result is a genuinely insightful look at a fierce competitor who nevertheless seems to care for his players both on and off the field." Booklist

Includes bibliographical references

Cosell, Greg

    The **games** that changed the game; the evolution of the NFL in seven Sundays. [by] Ron Jaworksi, with Greg Cosell and David Plaut. ESPN Books 2010 312p il $26; ebook $26   **796.332**

    1. Football 2. National Football League

    ISBN 978-0-345-51795-1; 978-0-345-51797-5 ebook

                            LC 2010-31008

"Filled with anecdotes, player recollections, and other wonderful details, this should be the most popular football book of the season. Terrific reading." Booklist

Dent, Jim

    Courage beyond the game; Jim Dent. Thomas Dunne Books/St. Martin's Press 2011 xi, 333 p.p ill.   **796.332**

    1. Cancer patients 2. College football 3. Football players

    ISBN 9780312652852; 9781250007001

                          LC 2011009348

This book, a 2011 "Kirkus Reviews" Best Nonfiction title, tells the story of "Freddie Steinmark [who] was an under-sized but scrappy young man when he arrived in Austin as a freshman at the University of Texas in 1967. Despite the pronouncement by many coaches that he was too small to play football at the college level, Freddie was a tenacious competitor who vowed to start every game as a varsity Longhorn. By the start of the 1969 season, Freddie was making his mark on the college gridiron and national stage as UT's star safety, but he'd also developed a crippling pain in his thigh that worried his high school sweetheart, Linda. Despite the increasingly debilitating pain, Freddie continued to play throughout the season, helping the Longhorns to rip through opponents like pulpwood. His final game was for the national championship at the end of 1969, when the Longhorns rallied to beat Arkansas in a legendary game that has become known as 'the Game of the Century.' Tragically, bone cancer took Freddie off the field when nothing else could." (Publisher's note)

Includes bibliographical references (p. [317]-318) and index.

Eatman, Nick

    Friday, Saturday, Sunday in Texas; A Year in the Life of

Lone Star Football, from High School to College to the Cowboys. Nick Eatman. HarperCollins 2016 368 p. color illustrations $26.99   **796.332**

    1. Football players -- Texas 2. Baylor Bears (Football team) 3. Dallas Cowboys (Football team) 4. Plano Senior High School (Plano, Tex.) -- Football

    ISBN 0062433318; 9780062433312

This book, by Nick Eatman, offers a "look at football in Texas--the fullest portrait ever conceived--viewed through the interwoven stories of three teams, Plano Senior High School, Baylor University, and the Dallas Cowboys, during one season. Eatman highlights the ups and downs . . . that these teams experienced over the course of the year. . . . He follows key players and coaches, including stars from Baylor and Plano, Tony Romo, Dez Bryant, . . . and Jason Witten." (Publisher's note)

"A realistic look at football as it's played in Texas." Booklist

Eisenberg, John

    The **league**; how five rivals created the NFL and launched a sports empire. John Eisenberg. Basic Books, an imprint of Perseus Books, a subsidiary of Hachette Book Group 2018 416 p. (hardcover) $30   **796.332**

    1. National Football League -- History 2. Football -- United States -- History

    ISBN 9780465048700

                          LC 2018012386

This book, by John Eisenberg, presents "the epic tale of the five owners who shepherded the NFL through its tumultuous early decades and built the most popular sport in America. . . . Eisenberg reveals that Art Rooney, George Halas, Tim Mara, George Preston Marshall, and Bert Bell . . . succeeded only because at critical junctures in the 1920s, 1930s, and 1940s each sacrificed the short-term success of his team for the longer-term good of the League." (Publisher's note)

Includes bibliographical references and index

Feinstein, John

    Next man up; a year behind the lines in today's NFL. Little, Brown 2005 502p il $25.95   **796.332**

    1. Football 2. Baltimore Ravens (Football team)

    ISBN 0-316-00964-4

Feinstein's look at the current state of the National Football League (NFL) focuses on the 2004 Baltimore Ravens' season.

"Even those who are not fanatical football fans will find that, beyond the information provided on players and coaches, there are two other engaging topics in the book: Feinstein's ruminations on how reporting and writing about football are different from reporting and writing about other sports, and his portrayal of the business side of the game through conversations with Ravens owner Steve Bisciotti. . . . Professional football fans cannot lose by reading this book. As for the rest of us, [it] provides interesting glimpses into a strange but popular cultural realm." Christ Sci Monit

Gaul, Gilbert M., 1951-

    Billion-Dollar Ball; a journey through the big-money culture of college football. Gilbert M. Gaul. Penguin Group USA 2015 272 p. (hardcover) $27.95   **796.332**

    1. College football 2. Colleges and universities -- Finance

    ISBN 9780670016730; 067001673X

                          LC 2015473475

This book, by Gilbert M. Gaul, "offers a . . . look inside the money culture of college football and how it has come to dominate a surprising number of colleges and universities. . . . College presidents have been unwilling or powerless to stop a system that has spawned a wildly profligate infrastructure of coaches, trainers, marketing gurus, and a growing cadre of bureaucrats whose sole purpose is to ensure that players remain academically eligible to play." (Publisher's note)

"Gaul's reporting is unassailable, but watch as his conclusions stir up a furor in the sports press. You don't even have to hate football to find this book valuable—and certainly worth reading." Kirkus

Gwynne, S. C.

The **Perfect** Pass; American genius and the reinvention of football. S. C. Gwynne. Scribner 2016 304 p. illustrations (ebook) $59.99; (hbk.) $27   **796.332**

1. Football coaches 2. Football -- History 3. Passing (Football) 4. Football -- Coaching 5. Football -- United States -- History
ISBN 9781508211761; 1501116193; 9781501116193
LC 2016012980

This book, by S. C. Gwynne, is the "story of how two unknown coaches revolutionized American football at every level, from high school to the NFL. Hal Mumme is one of a handful of authentic offensive geniuses in the history of American football. . . . Gwynne explores Mumme's leading role in changing football from a run-dominated sport to a pass-dominated one, the game that tens of millions of Americans now watch every fall weekend." (Publisher's note)

"That makes his subtitle all the more fitting, for undeniably, the two coaches changed the game—and brought glory to their institutions. A superb treat for all gridiron fans." Kirkus

Includes bibliographical references (pages 273-275) and index.

Keteyian, Armen

The **System**; The Glory and Scandal of Big-Time College Football. Jeff Benedict and Armen Keteyian. Random House Inc 2013 432 p. illustrations (chiefly color) (ebook) $50.85; $27.95   **796.332**

1. College football 2. College football coaches 3. Football 4. College sports -- United States 5. National Collegiate Athletic Association 6. Football -- Corrupt practices -- United States
ISBN 9780385536622; 0385536615; 9780385536615
LC 2013362311

In this book, by Jeff Benedict and Armen Keteyian, "NCAA football is big business. Every Saturday millions of people file into massive stadiums or tune in on television as 'athlete-students' give everything they've got to make their team a success. Billions of dollars now flow into the game. But what is the true cost? The players have no share in the oceans of money. And once the lights go down, the glitter doesn't shine so brightly." (Publisher's note)

"An overwhelming recommendation for all readers who love or hate college sports." LJ

Includes bibliographical references and index

Maki, Allan

Football's greatest stars; 3rd edition Firefly Books 2015 pbk $24.95   **796.332**

1. Football 2. Football players 3. National Football League
ISBN 9781770855953; 1770855955
LC 2015509094

"At the heart of Football's Greatest Stars is author Allan Maki's picks for the 50 greatest and most exciting players in the history of professional football. They're all here: from the pioneers of the game to the current stars to the legends headed to the Hall of Fame. Exciting photographs show these past and present superstars in action, and 32 franchise profiles chart the league's rise to the top of professional sports. This third edition also features a new chapter on the future greats currently rumbling on the field." (Publisher's note)

Includes bibliographical references (p. 241) and index

McIntire, Mike

Champions way; football, Florida, and the lost soul of college sports. Mike McIntire. W W Norton & Co Inc 2017 xix, 256 p.p (hardcover) $26.95   **796.332**

1. College football 2. Football players 3. Florida State Seminoles (Football team) 4. Football -- Economic aspects -- United States 5. Football -- Corrupt practices -- United States 6. College sports -- Economic aspects -- United States 7. College sports -- Corrupt practices -- United States 8. College sports -- Moral and ethical aspects -- United States
ISBN 0393292614; 9780393292626; 9780393292619
LC 2017017863

This book, by Mike McIntire, uncovers "the workings of a system that enables [college] athletes to violate academic standards and avoid criminal prosecution for actions ranging from shoplifting to drunk driving. At the heart of Champions Way is the untold story of a whistle-blower, Christie Suggs, and her wrenching struggle to hold a corrupt system to account. . . . Beyond the story of [the] Florida State [Seminoles], McIntire . . . [narrates] the history of college football." (Publisher's note)

"McIntire summarizes the history of college sports and the social and economic culture of football in American universities, particularly in the South, convincingly arguing that these transgressions are widespread." Pub Wkly

Includes bibliographical references (pages [211]-244) and index.

Parcells, Bill, 1941-

Parcells; A Football Life. Bill Parcells, Nunyo Demasio. Crown Archetype 2014 400 p. illustrations (some colored) (hardback) $30   **796.332**

1. Football coaches 2. New York Giants (Football team) 3. Football coaches -- United States -- Biography
ISBN 9780385346351; 0385346352
LC 2014027830

This book, by Bill Parcells, with Nunyo Demasio, presents an autobiography of the football coach Bill Parcells. "During his decades-long tenure as an NFL coach, he turned failing franchises into contenders. He led the ailing New York Giants to two Super Bowl victories, turned the New England Patriots into an NFL powerhouse, reinvigorated the New York Jets, brought the Dallas Cowboys back to life, and was most recently enshrined in the Pro Football Hall of Fame." (Publisher's note)

Includes bibliographical references and index

Pearlman, Jeff

Football for a buck; the crazy rise and crazier demise of the USFL. Jeff Pearlman. Houghton Mifflin Harcourt 2018 384 p. (Hardcover) $28   **796.332**

1. Anecdotes 2. Sports -- United States 3. Football -- United States -- History 4. USFL (Organization) -- History 5. USFL (Organization) -- Anecdotes 6. Football -- United States -- History -- 20th century
ISBN 9780544454385
LC 2018006360

In this book, about the United States Football League (USFL), "reporter and biographer Jeff Pearlman draws on more than four hundred interviews to unearth all the salty, untold stories of one of the craziest sports entities to have ever captivated America. . . . Pearlman transports readers back in time to this crazy, boozy, audacious, unforgettable era of the game. He shows how fortunes were made and lost on the backs of professional athletes." (Publisher's note)

Includes bibliographical references and index

Price, S. L.

Playing Through the Whistle; S. L. Price. Atlantic Monthly Press 2016 400 p. map $27   **796.332**
1. Football -- Pennsylvania -- Aliquippa -- History 2. Steel industry -- Pennsylvania -- Aliquippa -- History 3. Iron and steel workers -- Pennsylvania -- Aliquippa -- History
ISBN 0802125646; 9780802125644

In this book, by S. L. Price, "the town [of Aliquippa] didn't just make steel; it made elite football players, from Mike Ditka to Ty Law to Darrelle Revis. Pro football was born in Western Pennsylvania, and few places churned out talent like Aliquippa. Despite its troubles--maybe even because of them--Aliquippa became legendary for producing football greatness." (Publisher's note)

"From the rigidly stratified life in the 1920s and '30s during J&L's 'despotic prime,' to the brief, postwar golden age, 'a moment of civic equipoise,' to today's 'company town without a company,' where the combination of unemployment, drugs, and crime crushes hope, Price's football story is really that of America's Rust Belt in poignant miniature." Kirkus

Includes bibliographical references (pages 459-536) and index.

Roberts, Diane

Tribal; college football and the secret heart of America. by Diane Roberts. Harper 2015 256 p. illustration (hardback) $25.99   **796.332**
1. College sports 2. Football -- History 3. College football -- History 4. Football -- United States -- History 5. College sports -- United States -- History
ISBN 9780062342621

LC 2015025010

This book, by Diane Roberts, "tackles the controversies plaguing college athletics, tracing the dubious historical underpinnings of Americans' most popular sport. . . . Florida State's football team is always in the headlines, producing Heisman Trophy candidates, winning championships, and, at the same time, dealing with federal investigations into corruption and rape. Same as many big time collegiate sports programs. " (Publisher's note)

"This volume seems to be aimed at readers who already hate the sport." LJ

Ross, Charles K.

Mavericks, money, and men; the AFL, Black players, and the evolution of modern football. Charles Kenyatta Ross. Temple University Press 2016 200 p. illustrations (hardback: alk. paper) $84.5   **796.332**
1. Football -- History 2. African American athletes 3. African American football players 4. American Football League -- History 5. National Football League -- History 6. Discrimination in sports -- United States -- History
ISBN 9781439913062; 9781439913079

LC 2015031425

This book, by Charles Kenyatta Ross, "chronicles the [American Football League's] key events, including Buck Buchanan becoming the first overall draft pick in 1963, and the 1965 boycott led by black players who refused to play in the AFL-All Star game after experiencing blatant racism. He also recounts how the success of the AFL forced a merger with the NFL in 1969, which arguably facilitated the evolution of modern professional football." (Publisher's note)

"An important chapter in U.S. racial history of the 1960s. Recommended for all collections." LJ

Includes bibliographical references and index

Samaha, Albert

Never ran, never will; boyhood and football in a changing American inner city. Albert Samaha. PublicAffairs 2018 368 p. color illustrations (hardcover) $28   **796.332**
1. Football -- Social aspects 2. football teams -- New York (State) 3. Mo Better Jaguars (Football team) 4. Brownsville (New York, N.Y.) -- Social conditions 5. Football -- Social aspects -- New York (State) -- New York
ISBN 9781610398688

LC 2018000983

This book, by Albert Samaha, "tells the story of the working-class, mostly black neighborhood of Brownsville, Brooklyn; its proud youth football team, the Mo Better Jaguars; and the young boys who are often at the center of both. Oomz, Gio, Hart, and their charismatic, vulnerable friends, come together on a dusty football field. All around them their community is threatened by violence, poverty, and the specter of losing their homes to gentrification." (Publisher's note)

Includes bibliographical references and index

Savage, Phil

4th and goal every day; Alabama's relentless pursuit of perfection. Phil Savage and Ray Glier; preface by Nick Saban; foreword by Rece Davis. St. Martin's Press 2017 xxix, 304 p.p (hardback) $26.99   **796.332**
1. College sports 2. College football 3. Football coaches -- Alabama -- Biography 4. University of Alabama -- Football -- History 5. Alabama Crimson Tide (Football team) -- History
ISBN 9781250130808; 9781250130815

LC 2017016459

This book, by Phil Savage and Ray Glier, with foreword by Rece Davis, presents a "360-degree perspective on Alabama football and Coach Nick Saban's unique coaching style, . . . that has led the Crimson Tide to five Southeastern Conference titles, three consecutive College Football Playoff appearances and four national championships. . . . The book offers a close look at their player development and practice habits." (Publisher's note)

"A football lifer gives insight into how the Alabama Crimson Tide continue to be the most dominant force in college football." Kirkus

Sports Illustrated football's greatest revised and updated; [edited by] Editors of Sports Illustrated. Time Inc. Books 2017 288 p. $34.99   **796.332**
1. Football
ISBN 1683300033; 9781683300038

LC 2017941047

In this book "an all-new team of experts comes together to debate everything that makes football, football – whether it's the best players, the best on the defensive line, the cheerleaders, or the stadiums, our team of experts have ranked them. Additionally, for this revised and updated edition, we've added a 'Roundtable with the Stars' that includes some of the most legendary NFL Hall of Famers discussing whom they consider to the greatest." (Publisher's note)

St. John, Warren

Rammer jammer yellow hammer; a journey into the heart of fan mania. Crown Publishers 2004 275p $24   **796.332**
1. Football 2. Alabama Crimson Tide (Football team)
ISBN 0-609-60708-1

LC 2003-24718

"Wearing a thin veneer of journalistic detachment, St. John followed his beloved Alabama Crimson Tide football team during the 1999 season. The result is a sharp, sneaky-funny, but loving portrait of the team and its incredibly loyal fans." Booklist

Zimmerman, Paul

Dr. Z; the lost memoirs of an irreverent football writer. Paul Zimmerman. Triumph Books 2017 xvii, 280 p.p illustrations (hardback) $25.95 **796.332**

1. Autobiographies 2. Football -- United States 3. Sportswriters -- United States -- Biography

ISBN 9781629374642

LC 2017009840

This book, by Paul Zimmerman, edited by Peter King, presents a memoir from "one of the modern era's groundbreaking football minds, a man who methodically charted every play while generating copious notes, a human precursor to the data analytics websites of today. . . . Dr. Z's memoir is a rich package of personalities, stories never shared about such characters as Vince Lombardi, . . . and Johnny Unitas." (Publisher's note)

796.334   Soccer (Association football)

Abbot, Sebastian

The **away** game; the epic search for soccer's next superstars. Sebastian Abbot. W W Norton & Co Inc 2018 304 p. $26.95 **796.334**

1. Teenagers 2. Soccer -- Training

ISBN 0393292207; 9780393292206

This book, by Sebastian Abbott, "[is] the gripping story of a group of boys discovered in what may be the largest talent search in sports history. . . . Abbot follows a small group of the boys as they are discovered on dirt fields across Africa, join the glittering academy in Doha where they train, and compete for the chance to gain fame and fortune at Europe's top clubs." (Publisher's note)

"Abbot's narrative features vivid profiles, engrossing play-by-play, and a sobering lesson: bad breaks and cold business calculations sometimes trump ability in the making of champions." Pub Wkly

Anderson, Chris

The **numbers** game; why everything you know about soccer is wrong. Chris Anderson and David Sally. Penguin Books 2013 384 p. $16 **796.334**

1. Soccer 2. Mathematical analysis 3. Soccer -- Mathematical models 4. Soccer -- Statistical methods

ISBN 0143124560; 9780143124566

LC 2013011448

This book from Chris Anderson and David Sally is "about the use of analytics in soccer." Topics include "what percentage of possession determines victory," "whether it is best to focus on scoring goals or not conceding them," "how much coaches matter to a team's success," among others. (Kirkus Reviews)

Includes bibliographical references and index

Arena, Bruce, 1951-

What's wrong with US? a coach's blunt take on the state of American soccer after a lifetime on the touchline. Bruce Arena & Steve Kettmann. HarperCollins 2018 288 p. $28.99 **796.334**

1. Soccer teams 2. World Cup (Soccer) 3. Soccer -- United States

ISBN 0062803948; 9780062803948

In this book, author Bruce Arena, with Steve Kettmann, "looks back on an extraordinary career [in soccer], and forward to what the United States needs to do to compete successfully on the world stage once again. . . . Arena casts his eye on recruiting, coaching, the structure of

Major League Soccer, the integration of overseas players, and the role of money in the modern game." (Publisher's note)

"No surprise that Arena differs strongly from his predecessor, Jürgen Klinsmann, in an MLS-first approach, urging our top league to work together with U.S. Soccer for better development of American players. That and other suggestions informed by hard work and long experience will make this of interest to U.S. fans still wondering how to make things right." Booklist

Bass, Amy

One goal; a coach, a team, and the game that brought a divided town together. Amy Bass. Hachette Books 2018 320 p. (hardback) $28 **796.334**

1. Race relations 2. Soccer -- History 3. Somali refugees -- Maine 4. Somalis -- Maine -- Lewiston 5. Lewiston (Me.) -- Social conditions 6. Race relations -- Maine -- Lewiston 7. Soccer -- Maine -- Lewiston -- History 8. Lewiston High School (Lewiston, Me.) -- Soccer -- History

ISBN 9780316396547

LC 2017034578

This book, by Amy Bass, "tells the inspiring story of the soccer team . . . that united Somali refugees and multi-generation Mainers in their quest for state--and ultimately national--glory. . . . The mayor [of Lewiston] wrote a letter asking Somalis to stop coming, which became a national story. While scandal threatened to subsume the town, its high school's soccer coach integrated Somali kids onto his team, and their passion began to heal old wounds." (Publisher's note)

"Bass's effective portrayal of Lewiston as a microcosm of America's changing culture should be required reading for coaches, teachers, and those working with diverse populations." Pub Wkly

Bensinger, Ken

★ **Red** card; how the U.S. blew the whistle on the world's biggest sports scandal. Ken Bensinger. Simon & Schuster 2018 xv, 349 p.p (hardcover) $28 **796.334**

1. Soccer 2. World Cup (Soccer) 3. White collar crimes 4. Sports -- Corrupt practices 5. Soccer -- Corrupt practices

ISBN 9781501133909; 9781501133923; 150113390X

This book, by Ken Bensinger, offers a "definitive, shocking account of the FIFA scandal--the biggest international corruption case of recent years, spearheaded by US investigators, involving dozens of countries, and implicating nearly every aspect of the world's most popular sport, soccer, including its biggest event, the World Cup. . . . [The book] explores the case, and the personalities behind it, in vivid detail." (Publisher's note)

"With the flair of a novelist, Bensinger meticulously chronicles the magnitude of corruption that permeates the world's most popular sport." Pub Wkly

Conn, David

The **fall** of the house of FIFA; the multimillion-dollar corruption at the heart of global soccer. David Conn. Nation Books 2017 328 p. (hardcover) $27 **796.334**

1. Soccer 2. Historical literature 3. Sports -- Corrupt practices 4. Soccer -- Corrupt practices 5. Corporations -- Corrupt practices 6. Fédération internationale de football association

ISBN 1568585969; 9781568587721; 9781568585963

LC 2017905020

This book, by David Conn, offers "the definitive account of FIFA's rise and fall, covering in great detail the corruption allegations and the series of scandals that continued to shake the public's trust in the organization. . . . [It] situates FIFA's unraveling amidst revealing human portraits of soccer legends such as Michel Platini and Franz Beckenbauer and features an exclusive interview with former president Sepp Blatter." (Publisher's note)

"Conn's meticulous research and smooth writing style bring this unseemly chapter in FIFA history to a close, with realistic hope for the future of the most popular sport on earth." LJ

Includes bibliographical references (pages 311-312) and index.

Galeano, Eduardo, 1940-2015

Soccer in sun and shadow; by Eduardo Galeano; translated by Mark Fried. Perseus Books Group 2013 320 p. $16.99   **796.334**

1. Soccer

ISBN 1568584946; 9781568584942

LC 986769

This is a "revised and updated version" of Uruguayan author Eduardo Galeano's 1995 book about soccer. "Like so many children born in Latin America, Galeano . . . grew up wanting to play soccer. In his dreams, he was a star. During the day, however, he 'was the worst wooden leg ever to set foot on the little soccer fields of my country.' Nonetheless, his love affair with the sport continued." (Kirkus Reviews)

Honigstein, Raphael

Das Reboot; How German Soccer Reinvented Itself and Conquered the World. Raphael Honigstein. Nation Books 2015 276 p. $17.99   **796.334**

1. Germany 2. Soccer teams 3. World Cup (Soccer)

ISBN 1568585306; 9781568585307

Author "Raphael Honigstein charts the return of German soccer from the dreary functionality of the late 1990s to [Mario] Götze's moment of sublime, balletic genius and asks: How did this come about? The answer takes him from California to Stuttgart, from Munich to the Maracanã, via Dortmund and Amsterdam. Packed with exclusive interviews with key figures, including Jürgen Klinsmann, Thomas Müller, Oliver Bierhoff, and many more, Honigstein's book reveals the secrets of German soccer's success." (Publisher's note)

"Championship teams always have their books, but few are as thoughtful and edifying as this one." Booklist

Kirschbaum, Erik

Soccer without borders; Jürgen Klinsmann, Coaching the U.S. Men's National Soccer Team and the Quest for the World Cup. Erik Kirschbaum. Picador 2016 400 p. portrait (hardcover) $25   **796.334**

1. Soccer coaches 2. Soccer -- United States 3. Soccer teams -- United States 4. Soccer coaches -- Germany -- Biography

ISBN 9781250098313

LC 2016002387

This book, by Erik Kirschbaum, profiles "Jurgen Klinsmann, head coach of the U.S. men's national soccer team. . . . Erik Kirschbaum lays out Klinsmann's vision for making the U.S. men's soccer team a dominant world power for the first time in its history. . . . This book is a . . . road map for how to build a winning team in the most competitive professional sport on the globe." (Publisher's note)

"Kirschbaum provides a welcome sketch of Klinsmann, a thoughtful man of the world who has for years lived in California and who cannot be pigeonholed as merely a European trying to remake American soccer in the Old World image." Kirkus

Kuper, Simon

Soccernomics; why England loses; why Germany, Spain, and France win; and why one day Japan, Iraq, and the United States will become kings of the world's most popular sport. Si-

mon Kuper and Stefan Szymanski. Nation Books, an imprint of Perseus Books, LLC 2018 xiii, 495 p.p (2018 paperback: alk. paper) $17.99   **796.334**

1. Soccer 2. Sports 3. Ball games 4. Soccer -- Social aspects

ISBN 1568587511; 9781568584256; 9781568584812; 9781568587011; 9781568587516

LC 2018008723

This book, by Simon Kuper and Stefan Szymanski, "applies high-powered analytical tools to everyday soccer topics, looking at data and revealing counterintuitive truths about the world's most beloved game. It all adds up to a revolutionary new approach that has helped change the way the game is played." (Publisher's note)

Includes bibliographical references and index

Lloyd, Carli, 1982-

When nobody was watching; my hard-fought journey to the top of the soccer world. Carli Lloyd, with Wayne Coffey. Houghton Mifflin Harcourt 2016 256 p. color illustrations (hardcover) $26; (ebook) $26   **796.334**

1. Soccer players 2. Soccer -- United States -- History 3. Women soccer players -- United States -- Biography

ISBN 0544814622; 9780544814622; 9780544976801; 9780544814554

LC 2016036411

In this book, by soccer player Carli Lloyd, "there was a time when Carli almost quit the sport. In 2003 she was struggling, her soccer career at a crossroads. Then she found a trusted trainer, James Galanis, who saw in Carli a player with raw talent, skill, and a great dedication to the game. What Carli lacked were fitness, mental toughness, and character. Together they set to work, training day and night, fighting, grinding it out." (Publisher's note)

"This book is a remarkable portrait of the relentless drive and sacrifice required to truly be the best." Booklist

St. John, Warren

Outcasts united; a refugee team, an American town. Spiegel & Grau 2008 307p hardcover o.p. pa $15   **796.334**

1. Soccer 2. Refugees 3. Soccer coaches 4. Maintenance services executives

ISBN 978-0-385-52203-8; 0-385-52203-7; 978-0-385-52204-5 pa; 0-385-52204-5 pa

LC 2008-40697

This is a "book about an unlikely soccer program in the outlying Atlanta burb of Clarkston, Georgia. . . . Clarkston's residents woke up one morning and found that the city's housing projects had become havens of resettlement for refugee families from war-ravaged locales including Liberia, Afghanistan and Bosnia. Soccer is a pastime like sandlot baseball or touch football to the often-traumatized boys on the Fugees, a ramshackle intramural team of nine to 17-year-olds that St. John follows, along with its Jordanian founder Luma Hassan Mufleh, a Smith-educated woman whose role as volunteer coach quickly expands to extended family member and social worker. St. John's aim is to draw a portrait of small-town America in transition, and his eye for detail is compelling from start to finish." Time Out N Y

Includes bibliographical references

Thompson, Teri

American huckster; How Chuck Blazer Got Rich From-and Sold Out-the Most Powerful Cabal in World Sports. Mary Papenfuss and Teresa Thompson. HarperCollins Publishers 2016 xiv, 255 p.p color illustrations (Hardcover) $26.99   **796.334**

1. Sports -- Corrupt practices 2. Soccer -- United States -- History

3. Soccer -- Management -- Corrupt practices 4. Fédération internationale de football association
ISBN 9780062449672

LC 2015050617

This book, by Mary Papenfuss and Teresa Thompson, is the "inside account of the international soccer scandal that rocked the world and the American at its center. . . . For years, Chuck Blazer skimmed over $20 million from FIFA, stashing his money in offshore accounts and real estate holdings that included a luxury apartment in Trump Tower, a South Beach condo, and a hideaway in the Bahamas." (Publisher's note)

"This grim, always entertaining cautionary tale of greed and runaway ego is a worthy addition to any reader's collection of business fantasies gone awry." Pub Wkly

Includes bibliographical references

Vecsey, George

Eight world cups; my journey through the beauty and dark side of soccer. George Vecsey. Times Books 2014 304 p. illustrations (hardback) $28   **796.334**
1. Soccer 2. World Cup (Soccer)
ISBN 0805098488; 9780805098488

LC 2013042574

In this book, "sports columnist George Vecsey offers a personal perspective on the beautiful game. Blending witty travelogue with action on the field . . . Vecsey offers an . . . account of the last eight World Cups. He immerses himself in the great national leagues, historic clubs, and devoted fans and provides his up-close impressions of charismatic stars like Sócrates, Maradona, Baggio, and Zidane, while also chronicling the rise of the U.S. men's and women's teams." (Publisher's note)

"Vecsey's insights offer a unique look at the grace of the game as well as the underside of world soccer." LJ

Includes bibliographical references and index

Villoro, Juan

God Is Round; by Juan Villoro; illustrated by Thomas Bunstead. Simon & Schuster 2016 256 p. $16.99   **796.334**
1. Soccer 2. Soccer teams 3. Soccer players 4. World Cup (Soccer)
ISBN 1632060582; 9781632060587

This book, by Juan Villoro, illustrated by Thomas Bunstead, is an "exploration of the world's favorite sport and the passion, hopes, rivalries, superstitions, and global solidarity soccer inspires. . . . Villoro reports from the last World Cup of the twentieth century, paints portraits of contemporary soccer's most prominent stars (Lionel Messi, Cristiano Ronaldo, and Diego Armando Maradona), chats with Jorge Valdano, and teases out the contradictions of the Spanish league." (Publisher's note)

"For millions around the world, soccer is not just a game, but rather life itself and, as Villoro ably reveals, very much worth pursuing to the final whistle." Kirkus

796.34   Racket games

McPhee, John, 1931-

Levels of the game; [by] John McPhee. Farrar, Straus & Giroux 1969 149 p. $15   **796.34**
1. Tennis
ISBN 9780374515263

LC 76087219

This book, by John McPhee, is an "account of a tennis match played by Arthur Ashe against Clark Graebner at Forest Hills in 1968. [It] begins with the ball rising into the air for the initial serve and ends with the final point. McPhee provides a . . . stroke-by-stroke description while examining the backgrounds and attitudes which have molded the players' games." (Publisher's note)

796.342   Tennis (Lawn tennis)

Fisher, Marshall

A **terrible** splendor; three extraordinary men, a world poised for war, and the greatest tennis match ever played. [by] Marshall Jon Fisher. Crown Publishers 2009 336p $25 **796.342**
1. Tennis 2. Davis Cup 3. National socialism 4. Davis cup 5. Tennis players
ISBN 978-0-307-39394-4; 0-307-39394-1

LC 2008-50527

"Richly detailed . . . the story moves from one nail-biting set to the next against a backdrop of improbably high personal and political stakes." Boston Globe

Includes bibliographical references

Gallwey, W. Timothy

The **inner** game of tennis; The Classic Guide to the Mental Side of Peak Performance. W. Timothy Gallwey. Random House Inc 1997 xx, 122 p.p illustrations $17; $51 **796.342**
1. Tennis 2. Tennis -- Psychological aspects
ISBN 0679778314; 9780679778318; 9780307758859

LC 97000895

This book on tennis, by W. Timothy Gallwey, "is a revolutionary program for overcoming the self-doubt, nervousness, and lapses of concentration that can keep a player from winning. Now available in a revised paperback edition, this classic bestseller can change the way the game of tennis is played." (Publisher's note)

Hodgkinson, Mark

Fedegraphica; a graphic biography of the genius of Roger Federer. by Mark Hodgkinson. Motorbooks Intl 2016 272 p. color ill., color portraits $29.99; (ebook) $25.99 **796.342**
1. Tennis players -- Biography
ISBN 1781315299; 9781781315293; 9781781316092

This book on tennis player Roger Federer, by Mark Hodgkinson, "tells the story of how a young hothead from Basel transformed himself into a calm and poised athlete who came to dominate tennis. And who, while deep in his thirties, has continued to seek improvements, to challenge men many years younger than him and to contend for the sport's biggest prizes." (Publisher's note)

McEnroe, John

You cannot be serious; {by} John McEnroe with Jams Kaplan. Putnam 2002 342p il $25.95; pa $14 **796.342**
1. Art dealers 2. Tennis players
ISBN 0-399-14858-2; 0-425-19008-0 pa

LC 2002-23875

Tennis star McEnroe's "recollections fall into three categories: accounts of key matches, life as a jet-setting celebrity, and reflections on the emotional roller coaster that has been his personal life." Booklist

Phillips, Rowan Ricardo

The **circuit**; a tennis odyssey. Rowan Ricardo Phillips. Farrar, Straus & Giroux 2018 256 p. (hardcover) $26 **796.342**
1. Sports 2. Tennis -- Tournaments 3. Tennis players 4. ATP Tour (Organization)
ISBN 9780374123772

LC 2018017728

In this book, sports columnist Rowan Ricardo Phillips "chronicles 2017 as seen through the unique prism of its pivotal, revelatory, and historic tennis season. The annual tennis schedule is a rarity in professional sports in that it encapsulates the calendar year. And like the year, it's divided into four seasons, each marked by a final tournament: the Grand Slams." (Publisher's note)

Ryan, Mike

Tennis' greatest stars; Mike Ryan. Firefly Books Ltd 2014 216 p. illustrations, color portraits $35   **796.342**
    1. Tennis players 2. Tennis -- Tournaments
ISBN 177085293X; 9781770852938

Author Mike Ryan's book on tennis "profiles the 50 greatest and most influential players of the game and presents a historical narrative of athletic prowess, popular culture and social responsibility. [It] is packed with action photographs that celebrate the game and thoughtful essays, which cover such topics as the birth of modern tennis, the major tournaments, international play, the various court surfaces and new technologies." (Publisher's note)

"This is a good purchase for any tennis collection and is recommended for the circulating collections of public libraries." Booklist

Wallace, David Foster, 1962-2008

String theory; David Foster Wallace on tennis. by David Foster Wallace; introduction by John Jeremiah Sullivan. Library of America 2016 xv, 138 p.p illustrations $19.95   **796.342**
    1. Tennis 2. Tennis literature
ISBN 1598534807; 9781598534801
                    LC 2015951697

This book collects "David Foster Wallace's legendary writings on tennis, five tour-de-force pieces written with a competitor's insight and a fan's obsessive enthusiasm." (Publisher's note)

Includes bibliographical references

796.352   Golf

Coyne, Tom

A **course** called Scotland; searching the home of golf for the secret to its game. Tom Coyne. Simon & Schuster 2018 336 p. (Hardcover) $27   **796.352**
    1. Golf 2. Golfers 3. Golf courses 4. Golf courses -- Scotland
ISBN 9781476754284; 9781476754291
                    LC 2018015536

"From [author] Tom Coyne . . . comes the heartfelt and humorous celebration of his quest to play golf on every links course in Scotland, the birthplace of the game he loves. . . . With his signature blend of storytelling, humor, history, and insight, Coyne weaves together his journey to more than 100 legendary links courses in Scotland with compelling threads of golf history and witty insights into the contemporary home of golf." (Publisher's note)

"In this witty and charming follow-up to A Course Called Ireland, Coyne continues living a golfer's dream by playing every links course in Scotland, golf's birthplace." Pub Wkly

Feinstein, John

The **first** major; inside the story of the 2016 Ryder Cup. John Feinstein. Doubleday 2017 311 p. (hardback) $28.95 **796.352**
    1. Golf 2. Golf -- Tournaments -- Minnesota -- Chaska
ISBN 0385541090; 9780385541091
                    LC 2017021758

This book, by John Feinstein, is a "chronicle of the bitterly-fought 2016 Ryder Cup pitting a U.S. team out for revenge against the Europeans determined to keep the Cup out of American hands. . . . Feinstein takes readers behind the scenes, providing an inside view of the dramatic stories as they unfolded: veteran Phil Mickelson's two-year roller-coaster . . . [and] superstar Rory McIlroy becoming the clear-cut emotional leader of the European team." (Publisher's note)

"Golf fans will know what happened, of course, but Feinstein compellingly re-creates the excitement, sometimes shot by shot, especially in the classic McIlroy-Reed singles match, which has come to be a symbol of golf at its best, both for shotmaking and sportsmanship. A great moment in golf history, vividly captured." (Booklist)

Frost, Mark

The **match**; the day the game of golf changed forever. Mark Frost. 1st ed.; Hyperion 2007 p. cm.   **796.352**
    1. Golf -- California -- Pebble Beach -- History.
ISBN 9781401302788
                    LC 2007023325

"A chronicle of a lesser-known 1956 golf match documents how Harvie Ward and Ken Venturi competed against the leading players as a result of a bet between sponsors Eddie Lowery and George Coleman, in a competition that helped promote golf into a professional sport." (Publisher's note)

"What makes this account so fresh and so exciting for golf fans is that—unlike any other re-creation of a great moment in sports history—Frost tells a story that, being virtually unknown, carries with it genuine suspense as to the outcome. Going well beyond the simple question of who will win, however, Frost makes us see this spur-of-the-moment match for what it was: the last hurrah of amateur golf. And, best of all, he captures one of those fleeting moments in sports when competing athletes reach a kind of transcendent perfection simultaneously. Superb narrative nonfiction." Booklist

Includes bibliographical references..

Haney, Hank

The **big** miss; my years coaching Tiger Woods. Hank Haney. 1st ed. Crown Archetype 2012 262 p. $26   **796.352**
    1. Haney, Hank 2. Golf -- Coaching 3. Golfers -- United States -- Biography 4. Golf coaches -- United States
ISBN 0307985989; 9780307985989; 9780307985996
                    LC 2012003092

This memoir details Hank Haney's experiences as "American golfer [Tiger Woods's] former coach. . . . Haney assiduously monitored Woods's moods and frustrations, his silences and sulks. . . . This book is a[n] . . . account of an often-strained partnership as well as a . . . record of what it costs a man not only to dare to be the best of his generation but a champion for all the ages-- until, that was, he suffered the biggest miss of all." (New Statesman)

Rotella, Bob

Golf is not a game of perfect; Bob Rotella with Bob Cullen. Simon & Schuster 1995 224 p. $24.99; (ebook) $18.99   **796.352**
    1. Golf 2. Golf -- Psychological aspects
ISBN 068480364X; 9780684803647; 9781416563310
                    LC 95001120

This book, by Bob Rotella, is "filled with insightful stories about golf. . . . What Rotella does here . . . is to create an attitude and a mindset about all aspects of a golfer's game, from mental preparation to competition. . . . And, as some of the world's greatest golfers will attest, the results are spectacular. Golfers will improve their golf game and have more fun playing." (Publisher's note)

Wind, Herbert Warren

Five lessons; the modern fundamentals of golf. by Ben Hogan. NYT Special Services 1990 127 p. illustrations (some color) $24.99 **796.352**

1. Golf

ISBN 0671612972; 9780671723019

This book, by Ben Hogan, "outlines the building blocks of winning golf. . . . In each chapter, a different experience-tested fundamental is explained and demonstrated with clear illustrations—as though Hogan were giving you a personal lesson with the same skill and precision that made him a legend." (Publisher's note)

"The basics of hitting a ball with a club haven't changed much since this debuted, so this still offers valuable advice from one of the greats." LJ

796.357 Baseball

Barry, Dan

Bottom of the 33rd; hope and redemption in baseball's longest game. Harper 2011 255p il $26.99 **796.357**

1. Baseball 2. Baseball -- Records 3. Pawtucket Red Sox (Baseball team) 4. Rochester Red Wings (Baseball team) 5. Minor league baseball -- United States -- History

ISBN 978-0-06-201448-1; 0-06-201448-X

LC 2010-51656

"On a frigid evening in April 1981, 1,740 Pawtucket, R.I., Red Sox fans settled into their seats for a game with the Rochester Red Wings of the AAA International League. With the score tied 11 at the end of regulation, the teams played on. And on. On past 12:50 a.m., when the curfew provision, mysteriously missing from that year's edition of the rule book, would have suspended the contest; on past the 21st inning, when each team maddeningly scored a run; on past the 29th and record-tying inning; on past 4:00 a.m., the bottom of the 32nd, when the league president was finally reached and ordered the umpires to suspend the contest." Kirkus

Bissinger, H. G.

Three nights in August; strategy, heartbreak, and joy, inside the mind of a manager. [foreword by Tony La Russa] Houghton Mifflin 2005 xxi, 280p $25; pa $13.95 **796.357**

1. Baseball players 2. Baseball managers 3. St. Louis Cardinals (Baseball team)

ISBN 0-618-40544-5; 0-618-71053-1 pa

LC 2004-65134

For this book, the author "was given complete access to Tony La Russa and his St. Louis Cardinals. . . . La Russa collaborated fully, hid nothing, freely divulged his thoughts, notes, fears. The result is a fascinating look inside the day-to-day, game-by-game, inning by inning managing of a professional baseball team." N Y Times Book Rev

Includes bibliographical references

Clavin, Tom

The **DiMaggios**; Three Brothers, Their Passion for Baseball, Their Pursuit of the American Dream. Ecco 2013 320 p. $25.99 **796.357**

ISBN 006218377X; 9780062183774

This book looks at Vincent, Joe and Dominic DiMaggio. "Three brothers of 11 children born to Italian immigrants, the three boys excelled first in the Pacific Coast League for the local San Francisco Seals and then, one-by-one, they rose to play in the major leagues." Their careers during and after baseball and their personal relationships are ex-

plored. (Kirkus Reviews)

Cohen, Rich

The **Chicago** Cubs; story of a curse. Rich Cohen. Farrar, Straus & Giroux 2017 288 p. (Hardcover) $26 **796.357**

1. Baseball teams 2. Chicago Cubs (Baseball team) 3. Chicago Cubs (Baseball team) -- History

ISBN 9780374120924

LC 2017025511

This book, by Rich Cohen, is a "captivating blend of reportage and memoir exploring the history of the Chicago Cubs. . . . [Cohen] captures the story of the team, its players and crazy days. Billy Sunday and Ernie Banks, Three Finger Brown and Ryne Sandberg, Bill Buckner, the Bartman Ball, Kris Bryant, Anthony Rizzo--the early dominance followed by a 107 year trek across the wilderness." (Publisher's note)

"This is but one in what is already a succession of books on the Chicago Cubs' historic 2016 World Series championship—books that include Scott Simon's My Cubs and David Kaplan's The Plan—but it might be the best, since it's both a deeply satisfying historical account of that colorful franchise and a compelling, all-too-painful personal narrative of one longtime, besotted Cubs fan." (Booklist)

Includes bibliographical references

Cook, Kevin

Electric October; seven World Series games, six lives, five minutes of fame that lasted forever. Kevin Cook. Henry Holt & Co. 2017 x, 289 p.p illustrations (hardcover: alk. paper) $30 **796.357**

1. Baseball 2. Baseball players 3. World Series (Baseball) -- History 4. Baseball managers -- United States -- History

ISBN 9781250116574; 9781250116567

LC 2017008793

This book, by Kevin Cook, tells "[t]he story of six ordinary ballplayers whose paths crossed in the 1947 World Series--and the ways that epic October changed their lives. . . . Six men found themselves plucked from obscurity to shine on the sport's greatest stage. But their fame was fleeting. . . . Cook brings the '47 Series back to life, introducing us to men whose past offered no hint they were destined for extraordinary things." (Publisher's note)

"Cook does an excellent job of weaving articles and interviews from that time with modern sabermetrics and perspectives to make athletes and moments more relatable to fans of the current game." LJ

Includes bibliographical references (pages 263-274) and index.

Cramer, Richard Ben

Joe DiMaggio; the hero's life. Simon & Schuster 2000 546p $28; pa $16 **796.357**

1. Baseball players

ISBN 0-684-85391-4; 0-684-86547-5 pa

LC 00-49232

In this biography of the baseball player, "Cramer taps every plank in the wall that DiMaggio erected around himself and that protected him from inquiry. In the wall's hollow spots, Cramer locates the girls, finds the Mob guys, and behind the legend of grace and elegance on and off the field discovers a legend who in reality was more often than not graceless and inelegant." New Yorker

Dykstra, Lenny, 1963-

House of nails; A Memoir of Life on the Edge. Lenny Dykstra. HarperCollins 2016 340 p. illustration, portraits (ebook) $26.99; (hardcover) $27.99 **796.357**

1. Businessmen 2. Baseball players

ISBN 0062407368; 9780062407382; 9780062407368

In this memoir by baseball player Lenny Dykstra, "Lenny tells all about his tumultuous career, from battling through crippling pain to steroid use and drug addiction, to a life of indulgence and excess, then, an epic plunge and the long road back to redemption. Was Lenny's hard-charging, risk-it-all nature responsible for his success in baseball and business and his precipitous fall from grace?" (Publisher's note)

"Dykstra makes no apologies, offering 'the real truth,' but readers' opinions of him will be harsh." Kirkus

Eisenberg, John

The **streak**; Lou Gehrig, Cal Ripken Jr., and Baseball's Most Historic Record. John Eisenberg. Houghton Mifflin Harcourt 2017 xii, 299 p.p illustrations (hardcover) $26 **796.357**
1. Biography 2. Sports records 3. Baseball players -- Biography 4. Baseball -- Records -- United States 5. Baseball -- United States -- History 6. New York Yankees (Baseball team) -- History 7. Baltimore Orioles (Baseball team) -- History 8. Baseball players -- United States -- Biography
ISBN 9780544107670; 9780544103979; 0544107675

LC 2017000811

This book, by John Eisenberg, tells "the fascinating story of baseball's legendary 'Ironmen,' two players from different eras who each achieved the coveted and sometimes confounding record of most consecutive games played. . . . Cal Ripken Jr. began his career with the Baltimore Orioles at age twenty-one . . . [and] beat the historic record of playing 2,130 games in a row, a record set forty-two years before by the fabled 'Iron Horse' of the New York Yankees, Lou Gehrig." (Publisher's note)

"Eisenberg examines one of baseball's most venerated records while exploring what it all means, providing a compelling, thought-provoking history for fans of America's grand game." Kirkus

Includes bibliographical references (page 286) and index.

Feinstein, John

Where nobody knows your name; life in the minor leagues of baseball. John Feinstein. Doubleday 2014 384 p. (hardcover) $26.95 **796.357**
1. Baseball players 2. Minor league baseball 3. Minor league baseball -- United States -- History
ISBN 0385535937; 9780385535939

LC 2013030645

This book, by John Feinstein, presents a " journey through the world of minor-league baseball. . . . Focusing exclusively on the Triple-A level, one step beneath Major League Baseball, Feinstein introduces readers to nine unique men: three pitchers, three position players, two managers, and an umpire. Through their compelling stories, Feinstein pulls back the veil on a league that is chock-full of gifted baseball players, managers, and umpires." (Publisher's note)

Geist, Bill

Little League confidential; one coach's completely unauthorized tale of survival. Dell Pub 1999 217p pa $15 **796.357**
1. Baseball 2. Little League Baseball, Inc.
ISBN 0-440-50877-0
First published 1992 by Macmillan

The author "relates his decade of service as a little-league baseball coach. He admittedly distills his experiences—and those of others—into a season-long 'docudrama' journal. He tells of pompous coaches lecturing their miniplayers on the subtleties of the infield fly rule; he addresses the question of positioning a player with a personal-injury lawyer for a dad. The book is a wonderful effort filled with empathy for kids, impatience for pushy parents, and a good sense of humor." Booklist

Goodwin, Doris Kearns

Wait till next year; a memoir. Simon & Schuster 1997 261p il hardcover o.p. pa $14 **796.357**
1. Authors 2. Historians 3. Biographers 4. Nonfiction writers 5. Political commentators 6. Brooklyn Dodgers (Baseball team)
ISBN 0-684-84795-7 pa

LC 97-39766

"For self-esteem-building female role models, for baseball lore and inning-by-inning action and for a lively trip into the recent American past, you could hardly do better." N Y Times Book Rev

Halberstam, David

Summer of '49. Morrow 1989 304p il hardcover o.p. pa $14.95 **796.357**
1. Boston Red Sox (Baseball team) 2. New York Yankees (Baseball team)
ISBN 978-0-06-088426-0; 0-06-088426-6

LC 89-2886

"This book is ostensibly about the pennant race between the Yankees and Red Sox {in 1949} and the 'rivalry' between Joe DiMaggio and Ted Williams. . . . It is a study of all the elements and personalities that influenced baseball that year and beyond. Halberstam brings them together in such an enjoyable, interesting, and informative manner that a reader needn't be a baseball fan to appreciate the book." Libr J

Hample, Zack

Watching baseball smarter; a professional fan's guide for beginners, semi-experts, and deeply serious geeks. Vintage 2007 254p il pa $13.95 **796.357**
1. Baseball
ISBN 978-0-307-28032-9; 0-307-28032-2

LC 2007-296737

The author "covers basics such as what to watch for in pitchers, catchers, hitters, fielders and base runners; he also provides answers to such nagging questions as why spectators stretch in the seventh inning and why most ballplayers grab their crotches. . . . Hample hits the equivalent of a reference book home run with his witty and loose style—taking a friendly for-a-fan-by-a-fan approach that doesn't hide his enormous depth of knowledge." Publ Wkly

Hogan, Lawrence D.

Shades of glory; the Negro Leagues and the story of African-American baseball. with a foreword by Jules Tygiel. National Geographic 2006 422p il $26 **796.357**
1. Baseball 2. Negro leagues 3. African American athletes
ISBN 0-7922-5306-X; 978-0-7922-5306-8

LC 2006-273216

This book "traces the history of black baseball from the 19th century to the first great teams, such as the Cuban Giants, and on to the era of the vibrant barnstorming teams from the East Coast, Chicago, and Cuba." Publisher's note

Jaffe, Jay

The **Cooperstown** casebook; who's in the baseball hall of fame, who should be in, and who should pack their plaques. Jay Jaffe; foreword by Peter Gammons. Thomas Dunne Books 2017 xviii, 446 p.p (hardback) $25.99 **796.357**
1. Baseball -- Statistics 2. Baseball players -- Biography 3. Baseball -- United States -- History 4. National Baseball Hall of Fame and Museum
ISBN 9781250071217; 9781466882188

LC 2017012016

This book, by Jay Jaffe, explores the selection process for "the National Baseball Hall of Fame and Museum. . . . Numerous so-called 'greats' have been inducted despite having not been so great, while popular but controversial players such as all-time home run leader Barry Bonds and all-time hits leader Pete Rose are on the outside looking in. . . . Jay Jaffe shows us how to use his revolutionary ranking system to ensure the right players are recognized." (Publisher's note)

Includes bibliographical references (pages [429]-430) and index.

Jamieson, Dave

Mint condition; how baseball cards became an American obsession. Atlantic Monthly Press 2010 272p il $25 **796.357**
1. Baseball cards 2. Collectors and collecting
ISBN 978-0-8021-1939-1; 0-8021-1939-5

"For much of his book, Jamieson seems to be saying that greed and grownups have spoiled card collecting forever. But there's comfort in knowing that the cards have always appealed to baseball lovers and bottom-line business types for their own reasons. Even Jamieson holds out hope that they will find their proper place again in American kids' lives even if it's only in their closets." Minneapolis Star Tribune

Includes bibliographical references

Kenny, Brian

Ahead of the curve; Inside the Baseball Revolution. Brian Kenny. Simon & Schuster 2016 368 p. $28 **796.357**
1. Baseball -- History 2. Baseball -- Statistics 3. Baseball -- United States -- Miscellanea
ISBN 1501106333; 9781501106330

LC 2015039474

In this book, author Brian Kenny "uses stories from baseball's present and past to examine why we sometimes choose ignorance over information, and how tradition can trump logic, even when directly contradicted by evidence. Kenny wants fans to think critically, reject outmoded groupthink, and embrace the changes that have come with the 'sabermetric era.'" (Publisher's note)

"When Miguel Cabrera captured Major League Baseball's elusive Triple Crown in 2012, Kenny refused to join the adulatory journalists lauding his selection as the American League's Most Valuable Player. Convinced that two-thirds of the Crown's jewels (namely, batting average and runs batted in) poorly measure a player's performance, Kenny argues that more-sophisticated metrics established Angels outfielder Mike Trout as a more deserving MVP. . . . Recognizing Oakland's Moneyball transformation as a harbinger of things to come, Kenny predicts that as managers grow increasingly data-savvy, they will throw off the restraints of tradition when shifting infielders, setting a batting order, and using the bullpen. Perhaps unwelcome among fans who love the myth and nostalgia of the diamond, this bolt of analytical lightning will make sports talk shows crackle." Booklist

Includes bibliographical references and index

Kettmann, Steve

Baseball maverick; How Sandy Alderson Revolutionized Baseball and Revived the Mets. by Steve Kettmann. Atlantic Monthly Press 2015 320 p. illustrations (hardcover) $26 **796.357**
1. Baseball -- Coaching
ISBN 0802119980; 9780802119988

This book, by Steve Kettmann, describes how "In 2010, the New York Mets were in trouble. . . . They had recently suffered an embarrassing September collapse and two bitter losing seasons. . . . And their principle owners were embroiled in the largest financial scam in American history. To whom did they turn? Sandy Alderson, a former marine who served in Vietnam and graduated from Harvard Law." (Publisher's note)

"Kettmann has written a worthy biography of a compelling figure, but the author's desire to produce his own version of Moneyball has caused him to overstate his case." Kirkus

Knight, Molly

The **best** team money can buy; how the Los Angeles Dodgers are fighting to become baseball's new superpower. Molly Knight. Simon & Schuster 2015 336 p. 8 plates; color illustrations (hardback) $26 **796.357**
1. Baseball teams 2. Baseball players 3. Los Angeles Dodgers (Baseball team)
ISBN 1476776296; 9781476776293

LC 2015017287

Author " Molly Knight tells the story of the Dodgers¿ 2013 and 2014 seasons with detailed, previously unreported revelations. She shares a behind-the-scenes account of the astonishing sale of the Dodgers, and why the team was not overpriced, as well as what the Dodgers actually knew in advance about rookie phenom and Cuban defector Yasiel Puig and how they and teammates handled him during his first two roller-coaster seasons. We learn how close manager Don Mattingly was to losing his job." (Publisher's note)

"A must-read for fans of the Dodgers and all Los Angeles sports teams. Knight's undercover work is like none other. Dodger fanatics, this book is for you." LJ

Kurkjian, Tim

I'm fascinated by sacrifice flies; inside the game we all love. Tim Kurkjian; foreword by George F. Will. St. Martin's Press 2016 256 p. (hardback) $26.99 **796.357**
1. Baseball 2. Baseball -- United States 3. Baseball -- United States -- Miscellanea
ISBN 9781250077936

LC 2015048747

In this book, "in the aftermath of the Steroid Era that stained the game of baseball, at a time when so many players are so rich and therefore have a sense of entitlement that they haven't earned, ESPN baseball commentator Tim Kurkjian shows readers how to love the game more than ever, with incredible insight and stories that are hilarious, heartbreaking, and revealing." (Publisher's note)

"Kurkjian's celebrity and the joyous contents within the covers merit the investment." Booklist

Kurlansky, Mark

The **Eastern** stars; how baseball changed the Dominican town of San Pedro de Macoris. Riverhead Books 2010 272p $25.95 **796.357**
1. Baseball 2. San Pedro de Macorís (Dominican Republic)
ISBN 978-1-59448-750-7; 1-59448-750-2

LC 2009-41036

"In 1956, Ozzie (Osvaldo) Virgil played his first rookie season with the New York Giants, becoming the first Dominican baseball player to enter the major leagues in America. Over the next half a century, 471 Dominicans played in at least one major league game, and one in six of those players have come from the small sugar mill town of San Pedro de Macorís. . . . Kurlansky weaves a chronicle of the history of San Pedro de Macorís with the stories of young men seeking only to play baseball and escape the drudgery of working the sugarcane fields to produce a colorful social history of sport." Publ Wkly

Includes bibliographical references

Law, Keith

Smart baseball; the story behind the old stats that are ruining the game, the new ones that are running it, and the right way to think about baseball. Keith Law. William Morrow, an imprint of HarperCollins Publishers 2017 viii, 291 p.p illustrations (hardcover) $27.99 **796.357**

1. Sports -- Statistics 2. Major League Baseball 3. Baseball -- Statistics 4. Baseball -- Statistical methods 5. Major League Baseball (Organization) -- Statistics

ISBN 9780062490223; 9780062490254; 0062490222

In this book on baseball statistics, author Keith Law "demolishes a century's worth of accepted wisdom, making the definitive case against the long-established view. Armed with concrete examples from different eras of baseball history, logic, a little math, and lively commentary, he shows how the allegiance to these numbers--dating back to the beginning of the professional game--is firmly rooted not in accuracy or success, but in baseball's irrational adherence to tradition." (Publisher's note)

"This book by ESPN sportswriter and analyst Law is both a primer on how sabermetrics are changing the way fans and professionals view baseball, as well as a thorough explanation of why traditional statistics are misleading or obsolete." LJ

Leavy, Jane

Sandy Koufax; a lefty's legacy. HarperCollins Pubs. 2002 xxii, 282p $23.95; pa $13.95 **796.357**

1. Baseball players 2. Baseball players -- United States -- Biography

ISBN 0-06-019533-9; 0-06-093329-1 pa

LC 2002-68722

Leavy discusses the career of Dodgers pitcher Sandy Koufax.

The author "delivers an honest and exquisitely detailed examination of a complex man." Publ Wkly

Lewis, Michael

★ **Moneyball**; the art of winning an unfair game. Norton 2003 288p $23.95; pa $13.95 **796.357**

1. Baseball 2. Baseball executives

ISBN 0-393-05765-8; 0-393-32481-8 pa

LC 2003-5089

"With so many baseball books to choose from, it is difficult to single out a few as must-haves, but this one comes pretty close." Booklist

McGregor, Robert Kuhn, 1952-

A **Calculus** of Color; The Integration of Baseball's American League. Robert Kuhn McGregor. McFarland Publishing 2015 277 p. illustrations, portraits $39.95 **796.357**

1. Baseball -- History 2. African American baseball players

ISBN 0786494409; 9780786494408

LC 2015005733

This book, by Robert Kuhn McGregor, "examines the integration of baseball--widely viewed as a triumph--through the experiences of the American League and finds only a limited shift in racial values. The teams accepted few black players and made no effort to alter management structures, and organized baseball remained an institution governed by tradition-bound owners." (Publisher's note)

"McGregor's account makes for a compelling read. A best sports book of 2015, and one that will stand the test of time." LJ

Miller, Sam

The **Only** Rule Is It Has to Work; Our Wild Experiment Building a New Kind of Baseball Team. by Ben Lindbergh and Sam Miller. Henry Holt & Co. 2016 368 p. color illustrations $30 **796.357**

1. Baseball 2. Sports -- Statistics

ISBN 1627795642; 9781627795647

LC 2016005561

This book, by Ben Lindbergh and Sam Miller, is "the ultimate in fantasy baseball. . . . Lindbergh and Miller apply their number-crunching insights to all aspects of assembling and running a team, following one cardinal rule for judging each innovation they try: it has to work. We meet colorful figures like general manager Theo Fightmaster and boundary-breakers like the first openly gay player in professional baseball. Even José Canseco makes a cameo appearance." (Publisher's note)

"With honest and captivating prose, the authors compel readers to care about players that don't make a lot of money yet still have big league dreams and aspirations." LJ

Passan, Jeff

The **Arm**; Inside the Billion-dollar Mystery of the Most Valuable Commodity in Sports. Jeff Passan. HarperCollins 2016 368 p. illustrations $26.99 **796.357**

1. Baseball pitchers

ISBN 0062400363; 9780062400369

This book focuses on baseball pitchers. "Every year, Major League Baseball spends more than $1.5 billion on pitchers. . . . For three years, Jeff Passan, the lead baseball columnist for Yahoo Sports, has traveled the world to better understand the mechanics of the arm and its place in the sport's past, present, and future." (Publisher's note)

"As Passan interviews professionals dealing with the problem—physicians, managers, trainers, pitchers, and even epidemiologists—he reports no magical breakthroughs. But he does give readers an insider's perspective on the threat hanging over every player who takes the mound." Booklist

Posnanski, Joe

The **soul** of baseball; a road trip through Buck O'Neil's America. Morrow 2007 276p $24.95 **796.357**

1. Baseball 2. Baseball players 3. Baseball coaches 4. Baseball managers 5. United States -- Description and travel

ISBN 978-0-06-085403-4; 0-06-085403-0

An account of how the author "spent a year on the road with the iconic Negro Leagues player and manager Buck O'Neil (1911-2006), recording the magnanimous 94-year-old's encounters with scores of fans and his vast repertoire of entertaining stories." Publ Wkly

Rapp, David

Tinker to Evers to Chance; the Chicago Cubs and the dawn of modern America. David Rapp. University of Chicago Press 2018 336 p. (cloth: alk. paper) $27.50 **796.357**

1. Baseball -- History 2. Chicago Cubs (Baseball team) -- History

ISBN 9780226415048

LC 2017041630

This book, by David Rapp, recounts how "Joe Tinker, Johnny Evers, and Frank Chance came together in rough-and-tumble early twentieth-century Chicago and soon formed the defensive core of the most formidable team in big league baseball, leading the Chicago Cubs to four National League pennants and two World Series championships from 1906 to 1910." (Publisher's note)

"The compelling narrative not only details the feats these three achieved in helping establish a Cubs dynasty but also chronicles the metamorphosis of the new twentieth-century nation that embraced baseball as a game that reflected the urban strength developed in modern industry while also offering green-field comfort to city dwellers nostalgic for a rural past." Booklist

Includes bibliographical references and index

Reaves, Joseph A.

★ The **big** chair; the smooth hops and bad bounces from

the inside world of the acclaimed Los Angeles Dodgers general manager. Ned Colletti, with Joseph A. Reaves. G.P. Putnam's Sons 2017 xix, 440 p.p (Hardcover) $28 **796.357**

1. Baseball 2. Baseball managers -- United States -- Biography 3. Los Angeles Dodgers (Baseball team) -- Anecdotes 4. Sports general managers -- United States -- Biography 5. Los Angeles Dodgers (Baseball team) -- History -- 20th century 6. Los Angeles Dodgers (Baseball team) -- Management -- Biography

ISBN 0735215723; 9780735215726

LC 2017021965

This book, by Ned Colletti, with Joseph A. Reaves, "lets readers in on the real GM experience from his unique vantage point—sharing the inner workings of three of the top franchises in the sport, revealing the out-of-the-headlines machinations behind the trades, the hires and the deals; how the money really works; how the decision-making really works; how much power the players really have and why—the real brass tacks of some of the most pivotal decisions made in baseball history." (Publisher's note)

Reiter, Ben

Astroball; the new way to win it all. Ben Reiter. Crown Archetype 2018 272 p. (Hardcover: alk. paper) $27 **796.357**

1. Baseball teams 2. Baseball -- Statistics 3. Houston Astros (Baseball team) 4. Houston Astros (Baseball team) -- History 5. Houston Astros (Baseball team) -- Statistics

ISBN 9780525576648; 9780525576655

LC 2018019954

This book, by Ben Reiter, presents the inside story of how the Houston Astros baseball team won the World Series in 2017. . . . Astros general manager Jeff Luhnow and his top analyst, the former rocket scientist Sig Mejdal . . . wanted to correct . . . the biases inherent in human observation, and then roll their scouts' critical thoughts into their process. The numbers had value--but so did the gut. The strategy paid off brilliantly, and surprisingly quickly." (Publisher's note)

Includes bibliographical references and index

Ripken, Cal

Play baseball the Ripken way; the complete illustrated guide to the fundamentals. [by] Cal Ripken, Jr. and Bill Ripken with Larry Burke. Random House 2004 236p il hardcover o.p. pa $15.95 **796.357**

1. Baseball

ISBN 1-4000-6122-9; 0-8129-7050-0 pa

LC 2003-66725

"This book is the next best thing to a personal lesson with the man who broke Lou Gehrig's record of playing in 2,632 consecutive games; it's a comprehensive look at all aspects of how to play baseball that will benefit young players and adult weekend warriors." Publ Wkly

Ruck, Rob

Raceball; how the Major Leagues colonized the Black and Latin game. Beacon Press 2010 273p il $25.95 **796.357**

1. Baseball 2. Race relations 3. African American athletes 4. Hispanic American athletes 5. Major League Baseball (Organization)

ISBN 978-0-8070-4805-4; 0-8070-4805-4

LC 2010-37079

The book "blends the intertwined histories of African American and Latin baseball, and their usually ill-fated interactions with Major League Baseball (MLB). . . . [It] recasts conventional notions of baseball history by showing how, in the decades before World War I, Havana became the hub of an international baseball culture. . . . Players in the Negro leagues

banned from the major leagues commonly played winter ball in the Caribbean . . . until the early 1940s, along with many white big leaguers supplementing their incomes during the off-season. Cuban teams . . . beat the white major leaguers so frequently that MLB banned teams from playing under their own names, to avoid embarrassment." (Journal of American History)

The author "delves deeply into baseball history to explore the inextricable link between the two phenomena, starting with the struggles of black and Latin players in the segregated pre–Jackie Robinson era, continuing through the painful but inspirational period of integration and into the apex of African-American participation in the 1970s (when more than a quarter of players were black), before exploring the current state of a game dominated by Latin Americans. . . . Compellingly weaves together disparate threads of racial and sporting history." Kirkus

Includes bibliographical references

Russo, Frank

The **Cooperstown** chronicles; baseball's colorful characters, unusual lives, and strange demises. Frank Russo. Rowman & Littlefield Pub Inc 2015 304 p. illustrations (cloth: alk. paper) $40 **796.357**

1. Baseball -- History 2. Baseball teams -- History 3. Baseball players -- Biography 4. Baseball -- United States -- History 5. Baseball players -- United States -- Death 6. Baseball players -- United States -- Biography 7. Baseball players -- United States -- Social life and customs

ISBN 1442236396; 9781442236394

LC 2014019500

This book, by Frank Russo, "takes an entertaining look at the unusual lives, strange demises, and downright rowdy habits of some of the most colorful personalities in the history of baseball. Chapters profile the game's well-known tough-guys, the hard-drinking revelers, headhunting pitchers, players who took their own lives, and those who died far too young from accidents or diseases." (Publisher's note)

"Fans of baseball, in particular baseball history, will enjoy this work for the multitude of players (various teams, various years) that are documented in its pages." LJ

Includes bibliographical references and index

Sawchik, Travis

Big data baseball; math, miracles, and the end of a 20-year losing streak. Travis Sawchik. Flatiron Books 2015 256 p. (hardback) $26.99 **796.357**

1. Big data 2. Major League Baseball 3. Baseball -- Statistics 4. Pittsburgh Pirates (Baseball team) 5. Baseball -- Economic aspects -- United States 6. Baseball players -- United States -- Statistics

ISBN 1250063507; 9781250063502

LC 2015011231

In this book on statistics in baseball, author Travis Sawchik presents "the story of how the 2013 Pirates, mired in the longest losing streak in North American pro sports history, adopted drastic big-data strategies to end the drought, make the playoffs, and turn around the franchise's fortunes. It is an entertaining and enlightening underdog story that uses the 2013 Pirates season as the perfect lens to examine the sport's burgeoning big-data movement." (Publisher's note)

"Casual and hard-core baseball fans alike who enjoyed Moneyball are sure to be entertained and informed by this sort-of sequel." LJ

Simon, Scott

My Cubs; A Love Story. Scott Simon. Blue Rider Press 2017 145 p. illustrations (hardback) $23 **796.357**

1. Baseball 2. Baseball teams 3. Chicago (Ill.) -- Biography 4. Chicago Cubs (Baseball team) 5. Chicago Cubs (Baseball team) --

History 6. Baseball fans -- Illinois -- Chicago -- Biography

ISBN 9780735218031; 9780735218048

LC 2017004698

This book is "Scott Simon's personal, heartfelt reflections on his beloved Chicago Cubs, replete with club lore, memorable anecdotes, frenetic fandom and wise and adoring intimacy that have made the world champion Cubbies baseball's most tortured—and now triumphant—franchise." (Publisher's note)

"There will be many books about the Cubs' 2016 World Series win, but it's doubtful any will surpass Simon's for humor, poignancy, and, well, love." Booklist

Stout, Glenn

Fenway 1912; the birth of a ballpark, a championship season, and Fenway's remarkable first year. Houghton Mifflin Harcourt 2011 xxii, 392p il $26   **796.357**

1. Fenway Park (Boston, Mass.) 2. Boston Red Sox (Baseball team)

ISBN 978-0-547-19562-9

LC 2011016068

"While some sports histories are bone-dry and distant, Stout imbues his account with a unique vibrancy and a razor-sharp intelligence. A wonderful sports book." Booklist

Svrluga, Barry

The **grind**; inside baseball's endless season. Barry Svrluga. Blue Rider Press 2015 192 p. illustrations (hardback) $23.95   **796.357**

1. Major League Baseball 2. Baseball -- Social aspects 3. Baseball -- United States 4. Baseball -- Psychological aspects

ISBN 0399176284; 9780399176289

LC 2015016056

This book, by Barry Svrluga, explores "what's it like to live through sports' longest season, the 162-game Major League Baseball schedule? . . . [This book] captures the frustration, impermanence, and glory felt by the players, the staff, and their families from the start of spring training to the final game of the year." (Publisher's note)

"A quick and enjoyable read for any baseball lover, not just Nationals fans." LJ

Includes bibliographical references and index

Tackett, Michael

The **Baseball** Whisperer; A Small-Town Coach Who Shaped Big League Dreams. Michael Tackett. Houghton Mifflin Harcourt 2016 272 p. illustrations (hardcover) $26 **796.357**

1. Baseball 2. Baseball coaches 3. Baseball -- Iowa -- Clarinda 4. Baseball coaches -- United States -- Biography

ISBN 9780544387645

LC 2015037778

This book, by Michael Tackett, "traces the . . . story of Merl Eberly and his Clarinda A's baseball team, which he tended over the course of five decades, transforming them from a town team to a collegiate summer league powerhouse. Along with Ozzie Smith, future manager Bud Black, and star player Von Hayes, Merl developed scores of major league players. . . . In the process, Merl taught them to be men, insisting on hard work, integrity, and responsibility." (Publisher's note)

"One of baseball's most humanizing backstories." Booklist

Thorn, John

Baseball in the Garden of Eden; the secret history of the early game. Simon & Schuster 2011 365p il $26; ebook $12.99   **796.357**

1. Baseball 2. Baseball -- United States -- History

ISBN 978-0-7432-9403-4; 0-7432-9403-3; 978-1-4391-7021-2 ebook

LC 2010045155

"Thorn writes with authority, precision and humor." Minneapolis Star Tribune

Includes bibliographical references

Tygiel, Jules

Baseball's great experiment; Jackie Robinson and his legacy. [with a new afterword] 25th anniversary ed, expanded ed; Oxford University Press 2008 415p il pa $19.95   **796.357**

1. Baseball 2. Baseball players 3. Army officers 4. United States -- Race relations

ISBN 978-0-19-533928-4; 0-19-533928-2

LC 2008-273059

First published 1983

A history of the segregation and gradual integration of Afro-American athletes into major league baseball. In addition to Jackie Robinson, the author explores the careers of Larry Doby, Luke Easter, Satchel Paige, and others. Tygiel also notes the vast social and demographic changes wrought by WWII that made integration inevitable

Includes bibliographical references

Wong, Stephen

Game worn; Stephen Wong and Dave Grob, photographs by Francesco Sapienza. Smithsonian Books 2016 320 p. illustrations (some color) (hardback) $34.95   **796.357**

1. Smithsonian Institution 2. Baseball -- Collectibles -- United States 3. Baseball uniforms -- United States -- History 4. Baseball -- Collectibles -- United States -- Pictorial works 5. Baseball uniforms -- United States -- History -- Pictorial works

ISBN 9781588345714

LC 2016015599

This book by Stephen Wong and Dave Grob, with photographs by Francesco Sapienza, is the "first-of-its-kind compendium study of the world's most . . . precious baseball uniforms worn by Major League ballplayers during the twentieth century. . . . [It] features many of the most historically significant uniforms, jackets, hats, as well as other treasured baseball collectibles that tell us as much about the history and soul of America as they do about the game and the players." (Publisher's note)

"This rare look at the importance of baseball garments is a visually striking compilation that reads like a Ken Burns documentary. A book for all baseball lovers." LJ

Includes bibliographical references (pages 313-316) and index.

796.4   Weight lifting, track and field, gymnastics

Hoffer, Richard

Something in the air; American passion and defiance in the 1968 Mexico City Olympics. Free Press 2009 258p il $26   **796.4**

1. Olympic games, 1968 (Mexico City, Mex.)

ISBN 978-1-4165-8894-8; 1-4165-8894-9

LC 2009-09045

"On Oct. 16, [Tommie] Smith won the gold and [John] Carlos the bronze in the 200-meter race. There they stood on the podium, heads hanging almost humbly and gloved fists raised in a defiant black power salute. Something in the Air, Richard Hoffer's skillfully told tale of the Mexico City Olympics, revolves around this arresting image. . . . There were many other dramas played out in Mexico City—involving George

Foreman, the long jumper Bob Beamon and the high jumper Dick Fosbury, among others—and Hoffer gracefully brings them all into the same arena. More important, his jaunty but disciplined prose puts the wind at the reader's back and shows us how the leaps, lifts and dashes of 1968 made a significant impact on the civil rights movement and raised the political consciousness of athletes." N Y Times Book Rev

Includes bibliographical references

796.42   Track and field

Brown, Jeff

The **Runner's** Brain; How to Think Smarter to Run Better. Dr. Jeff Brown with Liz Neporent; foreword by Meb Keflezighi. St. Martin's Press 2015 240 p. $15.99   **796.42**

1. Performance 2. Mind and body 3. Running -- Psychological aspects
ISBN 1623363470; 9781623363475

LC 2015034962

This book, by Jeff Brown with Liz Neporent, "shows you how to unlock and capture the miraculous potential of the body's most mysterious and intriguing organ and rewire your mind for a lifetime of athletic success. The book is based on cutting-edge brain science and sports psychology that . . . [is used] in . . . private practice and as part of the medical team of several major road races including the Boston Marathon." (Publisher's note)

This accessible book is a result of Brown's own training and careful study of runners; he is intimately familiar with the considerations runners make, including the decision to compete, picking out "lucky" clothing, overcoming pre-race jitters and post-race blues, and "psych yourself up" for all types of weather. It will appeal to and aid runners of all levels and backgrounds, and perhaps those who aren't runners yet." Publisher's Weekly

Burfoot, Amby

Runner's world complete book of running; everything you need to run for weight loss, fitness, and competition. edited by Amby Burfoot. Rev. & updated ed.; Rodale; Distributed by Macmillan 2009 312p il pa $21.99   **796.42**

1. Running
ISBN 978-1-60529-579-4 pa

LC 2009-33150

First published 1997

Topics covered include: nutrition, injury prevention and treatment, shoe selection, mental readiness, and marathon preparation.

Caesar, Ed

Two hours; the quest to run the impossible marathon. Ed Caesar. Simon & Schuster 2015 256 p. maps (Hardcover) $26   **796.42**

1. Athletes 2. Marathon running 3. Marathon running -- Training
ISBN 145168584X; 9781451685848

LC 2014043224

This book, by Ed Caesar, is "about marathon running--including the current heated battle among the world's elite runners to reach the two-hour barrier--and how psychology, technology, economics, and the latest science affect the potential of human performance. . . . [The author] traces the history of the marathon as well as the science, physiology, and psychology involved in running so fast, for so long." (Publisher's note)

"Though the books are different in intent, readers might want to try David Epstein's The Sports Gene or Christopher McDougall's Born To Run." LJ

Dixon, Matt

The **well**-built triathlete; turning potential into performance. Matt Dixon. VeloPress 2014 368 p. illustrations (pbk.: alk. paper) $24.95   **796.42**

1. Triathletes
ISBN 1937715116; 9781937715113

LC 2014941073

In this book, "elite triathlon coach Matt Dixon reveals the approach he has used to turn age-group triathletes into elite professionals. . . . Dixon details the four pillars of performance that form the foundation of his highly successful purplepatch fitness program, showing triathletes of all abilities how they can become well-built triathletes and perform better year after year." (Publisher's note)

Douglas, Scott

Meb for mortals; how to run, think and eat like a champion marathoner. Meb Keflezighi with Scott Douglas. Rodale 2015 xi, 196 p.p illustrations $19.99; (ebook) $19.99   **796.42**

1. Marathon running 2. Marathon running -- Training 3. Long-distance running -- Training
ISBN 1623365473; 9781623365479; 9781623365486

LC 2016301845

This book, by Meb Keflezighi with Scott Douglas, "describes in unprecedented detail how three-time Olympian Keflezighi prepares to take on the best runners in the world. More important, the book shows everyday runners how to implement the training, nutritional, and mental principles that have guided him throughout his long career, which in addition to the 2014 Boston win includes an Olympic silver medal and the 2009 New York City Marathon title." (Publisher's note)

"The format is clean and the writing is simple and strong, all making this book a valuable tool for anyone with their sights set on running a marathon." Pub Wkly

Engle, Charlie

Running Man; A Memoir. Charlie Engle. Simon & Schuster 2016 304 p. (ebook) $19.99; (hardcover) $26   **796.42**

1. Marathon running 2. Long-distance runners
ISBN 9781476785806; 1476785783; 9781476785783

This memoir by ultra-marathon runner Charlie Engle chronicles "his globe-spanning races, his record-breaking run across the Sahara Desert, and how running helped him overcome drug addiction and an unjust stint in federal prison. After a decade-long addiction to crack cocaine and alcohol, Engle hit bottom with a near-fatal six-day binge that ended in a hail of bullets. As Engle got sober, he turned to running, which became his lifeline, his pastime, and his salvation." (Publisher's note)

"Similar to the journey of self-discovery chronicled in Rich Roll's Finding Ultra (2012), this is a fast-paced, well-written account of a man who accepts pain, pushes beyond imagined limits, and ultimately finds redemption and peace." Booklist

Finn, Adharanand

The **Way** of the Runner; A Journey into the Fabled World of Japanese Running. by Adharanand Finn. W W Norton & Co Inc 2016 326 p. $26.95   **796.42**

1. Japan 2. Running 3. Marathon running
ISBN 1681771217; 9781681771212

This book, by Adharanand Finn, focuses on "Japan, the most running-obsessed nation on earth. . . . A 135-mile relay race, or "ekiden" is the country's biggest annual sporting event. Thousands of professional runners compete for corporate teams in some of the most competitive races in the world. The legendary "marathon monks" run a thousand marathons in a thousand days to reach spiritual enlightenment. Yet so much of Japan's running culture remains a mystery to the outside world." (Publisher's note)

"An elegant, well-written pleasure even for readers with no particular interest in foot racing." Kirkus

Heminsley, Alexandra

Running like a girl; notes on learning to run. Alexandra Heminsley. Scribner 2013 224 p. (ebook) $15.99; (trade paper) $15   **796.42**

1. Running 2. Running -- Anecdotes 3. Women runners -- United States -- Biography 4. Runners (Sports) -- United States -- Biography

ISBN 9781451697179; 1451697155; 9781451697124; 9781451697155

LC 2013018909

This memoir "tells the story of . . . how [author] Alexandra [Heminsley] makes running a part of her life, and reaps the rewards: not just the obvious things, like weight loss, health, and glowing skin; but self-confidence and immeasurable daily pleasure, along with a new closeness to her father—a marathon runner—and her brother, with whom she ultimately runs her first marathon." (Publisher's note)

McDougall, Christopher

★ **Born** to run; a hidden tribe, superathletes, and the greatest race the world has never seen. Alfred A. Knopf 2009 287p $24.95   **796.42**

1. Marathon running 2. Tarahumara Indians

ISBN 0-307-26630-3; 978-0-307-26630-9

LC 2009-922861

"Implausibly difficult marathons, hundreds of miles long, and the ultra-elite competitive runners who tackle them for fun. A hidden, almost mythical, tribe in Mexico untouched by modern disease. Shoe manufacturers driven by corporate greed to sustain an industry that has created modern running injuries. An anthropological study of homo sapiens physiology and the course we took to survive while Neanderthals died out. It may seem farfetched, but Born to Run entwines all those strands and even pop-culture references into an engaging and inspirational read." PopMatters

Robbins, Liz

A **race** like no other; 26.2 miles through the streets of New York. Harper 2008 336p il map $24.99   **796.42**

1. Marathon running

ISBN 978-0-06-137313-8; 0-06-137313-3

LC 2009-275043

A narrative account of the 2007 New York City marathon interweaves the stories of professional and amateur participants, from Great Britain's world-record holder Paula Radcliffe and Latvian two-time winner Jelena Prokopcuka to South African former champion Hendrick Ramaala and a young cancer survivor running his first race.

The author "allows readers to experience the event without ever putting on a pair of running shoes." Publ Wkly

Includes bibliographical references

Wade, Becky

Run the World; My 3,500-Mile Journey Through Running Cultures Around the Globe. Becky Wade. HarperCollins 2016 288 p. illustrations (paperback) $15.99   **796.42**

1. Marathon running 2. Women athletes -- United States

ISBN 9780062416438; 006241643X

This book by Becky Wade tells "the story of her year-long exploration of diverse global running communities from England to Ethiopia—9

countries, 72 host families, and over 3,500 miles of running—investigating unique cultural approaches to the sport and revealing the secrets to the success of runners all over the world. . . . What she encountered far exceeded her expectations and changed her outlook into the sport she loved." (Publisher's note)

"Every so often a book comes along that becomes a cult classic for competitive runners but also has appeal to a broader audience... and this terrific debut is sure to join their ranks." Booklist

Includes bibliographical references (pages [267]-271).

796.422   Sprints

Moore, Richard

The **Bolt** supremacy; inside Jamaica's sprint factory. Richard Moore. Pegasus Books 2017 xii, 324 p.p illustrations (hardcover) $27.95   **796.422**

1. Running 2. Sprinters -- Biography 3. Runners (Sports) -- Jamaica -- Biography 4. Sprinting -- Jamaica -- History -- 21st century

ISBN 1681774070; 9781681774695; 9781681774077

This book, by Richard Moore, "opens the doors to a community where sprinting permeates conversations and interactions; . . . and where making it is a pass to a world of adoration and lucrative contracts. In such a society there can be the incentive for some to cheat. There are those who attribute Jamaican success to something beyond talent and hard work. . . . Peeling back the layers, Moore finally reveals the secrets of Usain Bolt and the Jamaican sprint factory." (Publisher's note)

"Fascinating reading for track fans." Booklist

Includes bibliographical references.

796.425   Non-track races

Burfoot, Amby

The **Runner's** world big book of marathon and half-marathon training; winning strategies, inpiring stories, and the ultimate training tools. Jennifer Van Allen ... [et.al.] Rodale 2012 xiii, 290 p.p illustrations $21.99; (ebook) $21.99   **796.425**

1. Marathon running 2. Marathon running -- Training

ISBN 1609616847; 9781609616847; 9781609619152; 9781609617080

LC 2012010217

This book, by Jennifer Van Allen, Bart Yasso, and Amby Burfoot, with Pam Nisevich Bede, "gives readers the core essentials of marathon training, nutrition, injury prevention, and more." (Publisher's note)

Includes bibliographical references (p. 273-278) and index

796.47   Tumbling, trampolining, acrobatics, contortion

Wall, Duncan

The **ordinary** acrobat; a journey into the wondrous world of the circus, past and present. Duncan Wall. Alfred A. Knopf 2013 336 p. (hardcover) $26.95   **796.47**

1. Circus 2. Acrobats and acrobatics 3. Circus -- History 4. Acrobats -- Biography 5. Circus performers -- Biography

ISBN 0307271722; 9780307271723

LC 2012038250

This book, by Duncan Wall, provides the "story of a young man's plunge into the . . . world of the circus--taking readers deep into circus history and its renaissance as a contemporary art form, and behind the (tented) walls of France's most prestigious circus school. When Duncan Wall . . . applied on a whim to the training program at the École Nationale des Arts du Cirque . . . [he] was, to his surprise, accepted." (Publisher's note)

796.48 Olympic games

Goldblatt, David

The **Games**; A Global History of the Olympics. by David Goldblatt. W W Norton & Co Inc 2016 464 p. $29.95 **796.48**

1. Olympic games 2. Olympic athletes

ISBN 0393292770; 9780393292770

This book, by David Goldblatt, presents the "history of . . . the Olympics. He tells the epic story of the Games from their reinvention in Athens in 1896 to the present day, chronicling classic moments of sporting achievement. . . . He goes beyond the medal counts to explore how international conflicts have played out at the Olympics, including the role of the Games in Fascist Germany and Italy, the Cold War, and the struggles of the postcolonial world for recognition." (Publisher's note)

Spivey, Nigel Jonathan

The **ancient** Olympics; [by] Nigel Spivey. Oxford University Press 2004 xxi, 273p il $28; pa $14.95 **796.48**

1. Olympic games

ISBN 0-19-280433-2; 0-19-280604-1 pa

LC 2004-46147

This book "lets us imagine both the strangeness and the glory that surrounded sports in its infancy." Christ Sci Monit

Includes bibliographical references

796.5 Outdoor life

Citro, Asia

150 + screen-free activities for kids; The Very Best and Easiest Playtime Activities from FunAtHomeWithKids.com! Asia Citro, MEd, creator of Fun at Home with Kids. Adams Media 2014 255 p. color illustrations $18.99 **796.5**

1. Outdoor recreation 2. Creative activities 3. Outdoor recreation for children 4. Creative activities and seat work

ISBN 1440576157; 9781440576157

LC 2014021922

With this book, by Asia Citro, "your family will rediscover the spirit of imaginative play! These fun activities help develop your child's creativity and skills--all without a screen in sight. Featuring step-by-step instructions and beautiful photographs, each budget-friendly project will keep your child entertained, engaged, and learning all day long." (Publisher's note)

Includes bibliographical references and index

796.51 Walking

Berger, Karen

America's great hiking trails; Appalachian, Pacific Crest, Continental Divide, North Country, Ice Age, Potomac Heritage, Florida, Natchez Trace, Arizona, Pacific Northwest, New England. Karen Berger, Photography by Bart Smith. Rizzoli International Publications 2014 335 p. color ill., color maps (hardcover: alk. paper) $50 **796.51**

1. Hiking

ISBN 0789327414; 9780789327413

LC 2014936348

This book, by Karen Berger, is a "celebration of more than 50,000 miles of America's most iconic trails. . . . Each featured trail has its own section, complete with a map and photo gallery, and the reader explores what makes it one of the most magnificent hiking experiences anywhere in the world. Trail histories accompany detailed hiker-friendly descriptions that highlight the most scenic spots, with suggestions for shorter weekend and day hikes." (Publisher's note)

Includes bibliographical references (p. 334-335)

Chamberlin, Silas

On the trail; A History of American Hiking. Silas Chamberlin. Yale University Press 2016 272 p. illustrations, maps (hardcover: alk. paper) $30 **796.51**

1. Hiking

ISBN 9780300219111

LC 2016936121

This book, by Silas Chamberlin, is the "first history of the American hiking community and its contributions to the nation's vast network of trails. . . . Delving into unexplored archives, including those of the Appalachian Mountain Club, Sierra Club, Green Mountain Club, and many others, . . . Chamberlin recounts the activities of hikers who over many decades formed clubs, built trails, and advocated for environmental protection." (Publisher's note)

"This winning, thought-provoking book offers insight into a relatively unknown aspect of environmental history." LJ

Includes bibliographical references (page 209-230) and index.

Davis, Jennifer Pharr

★ The **pursuit** of endurance; harnessing the record-breaking power of strength and resilience. Jennifer Pharr Davis. Penguin Group USA 2018 320 p. $27 **796.51**

1. Hiking 2. Physical fitness

ISBN 0735221898; 9780735221895

In this book, author Jennifer Pharr Davis "reveals the secrets and habits behind endurance as she chronicles her incredible accomplishments in the world of endurance hiking, backpacking, and trail running. . . . She distills complex rituals and histories into easy-to-understand tips and action items that will help you take perseverance to the next level." (Publisher's note)

Epic hikes of the world; Lonely Planet Publications. Lonely Planet 2018 328 p. $35 **796.51**

1. Hiking 2. Trails 3. Travel guidebooks 4. Hiking -- Guidebooks. 5. Trails -- Guidebooks.

ISBN 1787014177; 9781787014176

LC 2018146646

This book in the Lonely Planet series, presents "stories of 50 incredible hiking routes in 30 countries, from New Zealand to Peru, plus a further 150 suggestions . . . [that] will inspire a lifetime of adventure on foot. From one-day jaunts and urban trails to month-long thru-hikes, cultural rambles and mountain expeditions, each journey shares one defining feature: being truly epic. (Publisher's note)

Solnit, Rebecca

Wanderlust; a history of walking. Viking 2000 326p il hardcover o.p. pa $15 **796.51**

1. Hiking 2. Walking 3. Voyages and travels

ISBN 0-14-028601-2 pa

LC 99-41153

The author presents a "look at how the act of walking . . . has influenced our history, our science, our literature, and the very way that we see ourselves as human beings. Drawing on a multitude of diverse disciplines, Solnit illustrates that walking has led to some of the best, and worst, incidents in all of history." Booklist

Includes bibliographical references

Spira, Timothy P.

Waterfalls and wildflowers in the Southern Appalachians; thirty great hikes. Timothy P. Spira. University of North Carolina Press 2015 304 p. illustrations, maps (pbk: alk. paper) $24   **796.51**

1. Waterfalls 2. Wild flowers 3. Appalachian Region 4. Appalachian Region, Southern -- Guidebooks 5. Hiking -- Appalachian Region, Southern -- Guidebooks 6. Trails -- Appalachian Region, Southern -- Guidebooks 7. Waterfalls -- Appalachian Region, Southern -- Guidebooks 8. Wild flowers -- Appalachian Region, Southern -- Guidebooks 9. Natural history -- Appalachian Region, Southern -- Guidebooks

ISBN 1469622645; 9781469622644

LC 2014044782

Author "Tim Spira's guidebook links waterfalls and wildflowers in a spectacularly beautiful region famous for both. Leading you to gorgeous waterfalls in Virginia, North Carolina, Tennessee, South Carolina, and Georgia, the book includes many hikes in the Great Smoky Mountains National Park and along the Blue Ridge Parkway." (Publisher's note)

"Biologist's will savor this handy hiking guide to a particularly beautiful region." LJ

796.52   Walking and exploring by kind of terrain

Denny, Glen

Valley walls; a memoir of climbing and living in yosemite. Glen Denny. Yosemite Conservancy 2016 240 p. (alk. paper) $18.95   **796.52**

1. Mountaineering 2. Yosemite National Park (Calif.)

ISBN 9781930238633

LC 2015956065

This memoir, by Glen Denny, "reveals a young man's coming of age and provides a vivid look at Yosemite's early climbing culture. He relates such precarious achievements as hauling water in glass gallon jugs up the east face of Washington Column, nailing the 750-foot Rostrum in a punishing heat wave, and dangling overnight on El Capitan's Dihedral Wall in a lightning storm." (Publisher's note)

"Climbing newcomers will benefit from the glossary, but the love Denny has for the climbs, climbers, and life during this era make this a must-have for outdoor enthusiasts." LJ

Isserman, Maurice

Continental divide; a history of American mountaineering. Maurice Isserman. W W Norton & Co Inc 2016 448 p. illustrations (hardcover) $28.95   **796.52**

1. Mountains 2. Mountaineering 3. Mountaineering -- United States -- History

ISBN 0393068501; 9780393068504

LC 2016000548

In this book author "Maurice Isserman tells the history of American mountaineering through four centuries of landmark climbs and first ascents. Mountains were originally seen as obstacles to civilization; over time they came to be viewed as places of redemption and renewal. Isserman traces the evolving social, cultural, and political roles mountains played in shaping the country." (Publisher's note)

"This broad sweep of American mountaineering history will satisfy general history readers and outdoor adventurers alike." LJ

Includes bibliographical references and index

Tabor, James M.

Blind descent; the quest to discover the deepest place on earth. Random House 2010 304p $26; ebook $26   **796.52**

1. Caves 2. Explorers 3. Spelunkers 4. Structural engineers

ISBN 978-1-4000-6767-1; 978-1-58836-994-9 ebook

LC 2009-33942

"The author examines the two polar opposites at the head of each of two major cave-diving expeditions: the win-at-all-costs, classic alphamale, American Bill Stone, who led Mexican cave dives in Cheve and Huatula; and mild-mannered organization man, Ukrainian Alexander Klimchouk, who spearheaded the exploration of his country's notorious Krubera cave. Only one of these men came away with the distinction of having descended deeper into the earth's core than anyone else. Tabor expertly fashions a fly-on-the-wall narrative from the firsthand accounts of Stone, Klimchouk and their supporting casts of death-defying followers. . . . A fascinating and informative introduction to the sport of cave diving, as well as a dramatic portrayal of a significant man-vs.-nature conflict." Kirkus

Includes bibliographical references

Taylor, Joseph E.

Pilgrims of the vertical; Yosemite rock climbers and nature at risk. [by] Joseph E Taylor III. Harvard University Press 2010 368p il map $29.95   **796.52**

1. Mountaineering 2. Yosemite National Park (Calif.)

ISBN 978-0-674-05287-1; 0-674-05287-0

LC 2010-21578

Yosemite "has been a climber magnet for decades, and it was here that many of rock climbing's highly ritualized set of norms and mores evolved. . . . [This book] is at once a chronicle of how the sport evolved in Yosemite and a fascinating social history that considers climbing in the larger context of American life. . . . For the general reader, the book makes a fine introduction to the history of climbing and Yosemite's special place in its development. For climbers, 'Pilgrims of the Vertical' offers a somewhat idiosyncratic view of their sport." Wall Street J

Includes bibliographical references

796.522   Mountains, hills, rocks

Conefrey, Mick

The **Ghosts** of K2; The Epic Saga of the First Ascent. by Mick Conefrey. Oneworld Publications 2015 336 p. 8 plates; illustrations; maps $27.99   **796.522**

1. Mountaineering 2. Mountains -- Pakistan

ISBN 1780745958; 9781780745954

This book on the mountain K2, by Mick Conefrey, "describes the early attempts to reach the summit and provides a fascinating exploration of the first ascent's complex legacy. From the drug-addicted occultist Aleister Crowley to Achille Compagnoni and Lino Lacedelli, the Italian duo who finally made it to the summit, [it] charts how a slew of great men became fixated on this legendary mountain." (Publisher's note)

"An absorbing chronicle of K2's early history that all fans of mountaineering will enjoy." LJ

Jamling Tenzing Norgay

Touching my father's soul; a Sherpa's journey to the top of

Everest. [by] Jamling Tenzing Norgay with Broughton Coburn. HarperSanFrancisco 2001 316p il map hardcover o.p. pa $15.95 **796.522**

1. Mountaineering 2. Mountaineers 3. Mount Everest Expedition (1996)

ISBN 0-06-251688-4 pa

LC 00-68723

This "work has considerably more depth than an exposition of the climb. . . . The son's climb is a pilgrimage exploring his relationship to his father, his Sherpa culture, and Buddhism. It is also a fascinating look into the world of climbers and their relationship to the Sherpas who risk their lives to assist them." Booklist

Lewis-Jones, Huw

Conquest of Everest; George Lowe, Huw Lewis-Jones. Thames & Hudson Inc. 2013 240 p. (hardcover) $39.95 **796.522**

1. Mount Everest (China and Nepal)

ISBN 9780500544235

LC 2012947781

This book about Mount Everest "features a trove of original photographs and other rare materials from the George Lowe collection, many unpublished, complemented by classic images from the final ascent. Stunning landscapes, candid portraits, and action shots describe the day-by-day moments of the historic expedition as never before." (Publisher's note)

Roberts, David D., 1943-

Limits of the known; David Roberts. W W Norton & Co Inc 2018 xxi, 306 p.p maps (hardcover) $26.95 **796.522**

1. Mountaineering 2. Mountaineers -- Biography 3. Mountaineering -- History 4. Adventure and adventurers -- History 5. Mountaineers -- United States -- Biography 6. Adventure and adventurers -- United States -- Biography

ISBN 9780393609875; 9780393609868

LC 2017048507

In this book, author David Roberts "tries to make sense of why so many have committed their lives to the desperate pursuit of adventure. In the wake of his diagnosis with throat cancer, [he] seeks answers with sharp new urgency. He explores his own lifelong commitment to adventuring, as well as the cultural contributions of explorers throughout history." (Publisher's note)

"Roberts conveys the exhilaration and vitality of adventuring as well as the agony and anger of a cancer diagnosis with equal aplomb, making for a moving narrative that speaks to the glories of the human spirit and the limitations of the human body." Pub Wkly

Includes bibliographical references (pages [299]-301).

Zuckerman, Peter

Buried in the sky; the extraordinary story of the Sherpa climbers on K2's deadliest day. Peter Zuckerman and Amanda Padoan. W.W. Norton & Co. 2012 285 p. (hardcover) $26.95 **796.522**

1. Mountaineering 2. Mountains -- Pakistan 3. Sherpa (Nepalese people) 4. Outdoor life -- Accidents 5. Mountaineers -- Pakistan -- K2 (Mountain) 6. Mountaineering -- Pakistan -- K2 (Mountain) 7. Sherpa (Nepalese people) -- Social life and customs 8. Mountaineering accidents -- Pakistan -- K2 (Mountain)

ISBN 0393079880; 9780393079883

LC 2012008490

In this book, "Peter Zuckerman and Amanda Padoan explore the intersecting lives of [the Shirpas] Chhiring Dorje Sherpa and Pasang Lama, following them from their villages high in the Himalaya to the

slums of Kathmandu, across the glaciers of Pakistan to K2 Base Camp. When disaster strikes in the Death Zone, Chhiring finds Pasang stranded on an ice wall, without an axe, waiting to die. The rescue that follows has become the stuff of mountaineering legend." (Publisher's note)

Includes bibliographical references and index.

796.54 Camping

White, Dan, 1967-

Under the stars; How America Fell in Love with Camping. Dan White. Henry Holt & Co. 2016 416 p. illustrations (hardback) $28 **796.54**

1. Camping 2. Outdoor life 3. Camping -- United States 4. Outdoor life -- United States

ISBN 9781627791953

LC 2015042691

In this book, author "Dan White travels the nation to experience firsthand—and sometimes face first—how the American wilderness transformed from the devil's playground into a source of adventure, relaxation, and renewal. Whether he's camping nude in cougar country, being attacked by wildlife while 'glamping,' or crashing a girls-only adventure for urban teens, . . . White seeks to animate the evolution of outdoor recreation." (Publisher's note)

"An adventurous, informative, and irreverent look at outdoor recreation." Booklist

Includes bibliographical references and index

796.6 Cycling and related activities

Bambrick, Yvonne

The **urban** cycling survival guide; need-to-know skills and strategies for biking in the city. by Yvonne Bambrick, illustrated by Marc Ngui. ECW Press 2015 208 p. illustrations (paperback) $16.95 **796.6**

1. Cycling 2. City and town life

ISBN 9781770412187; 1770412182

This book, by Yvonne Bambrick, illustrated by Marc Ngui, "is an accessible, straight-forward pocket guide that helps cyclists new to the urban environment negotiate all the challenges, obstacles, and rules--spoken and unspoken--that come with sharing the roads . . . , from picking the bike that's right for you to smart riding strategies, tips for drivers, and bike maintenance." (Publisher's note)

"This modern guide is filled with great advice that will help people become more confident and educated bike riders. For all libraries." LJ

Bike Snob

The **enlightened** cyclist; commuter angst, dangerous drivers, and other obstacles on the path to two-wheeled transcendence. Bike Snob NYC. Chronicle Books 2012 220 p. ill. (hardback) $16.95 **796.6**

1. Cycling 2. Transportation 3. Bicycle commuting

ISBN 1452105006; 9781452105000

LC 2011041747

This book, by the anonymous urban cyclist "BikeSnobNYC," "takes on the trials and triumphs of bike commuting with snark, . . . asking the question: If we become better commuters, will that make us better people? From the deadly sins of biking to tactics for dealing with cars, pedestrians, and other cyclists, this primer on bike travel is . . . [written for] cyclists new and seasoned alike." (Publisher's note)

Byrne, David

Bicycle diaries. Viking 2009 297p il   **796.6**

1. Bicycle touring 2. Singers 3. Songwriters 4. Rock musicians
5. Urban transportation 6. Cycling -- Environmental aspects
ISBN 0670021148; 9780670021147

LC 2009-09390

This book contains accounts of Byrne's travels in New York and
other cities, mainly by bicycle.

"In these random musings over many years while cycling through
such places as Sydney, Australia; Manila, Philippines; San Francisco; or
his home of New York, the former Talking Head, artist and author . . .
offers his frank views on urban planning, art and postmodern civilization
in general. . . . Candid and self-deprecating, Byrne offers a work that is
as engaging as it is cerebral and informative." Publ Wkly

Moore, Tim

The **Cyclist** Who Went Out in the Cold; Adventures Riding
the Iron Curtain. Tim Moore. W W Norton & Co Inc 2017 368
p. illustrations, maps $26.95; (ebook) $50   **796.6**

1. Cycling 2. Bicycle touring
ISBN 168177299X; 9781681772998; 9781681773674

LC 2016057729

In this book, "Tim Moore sets out to scale a new peak of rash over-
ambition: 6,000 mile route of the old Iron Curtain on a tiny-wheeled,
two-geared East German shopping bike. Asking for trouble and getting it, Moore sets off from the northernmost Norwegian-Russian border at the Arctic winter's brutal height, bullying his plucky MIFA 900
through the endless sub-zero desolation of snowbound Finland." (Publisher's note)

"An enjoyable account of an amazing human accomplishment."
Kirkus

Gironimo! Riding the Very Terrible 1914 Tour of Italy. by
Tim Moore. W.W. Norton & Co. Inc. 2015 368 p. illustrations
$27.95   **796.6**

1. Bicycle racing 2. Bicycle touring 3. Bicycles -- History
ISBN 1605987786; 9781605987781

This book, by Tim Moore, focuses on the "1914 Giro d'Italia: The
hardest bike race in history. Eighty-one riders started and only eight finished after enduring cataclysmic storms, roads strewn with nails, and
even the loss of an eye by one competitor. . . . To truly capture the essence of what these riders endured a century ago, Tim acquires the ruined husk of a gear-less, wooden-wheeled 1914 road bike, some maps,
and an alarming period outfit." (Publisher's note)

"Readers may tire of the repeated references to the state of his "intimate parts," but, as in his previous cycling book, French Revolutions
(2002), Moore's patented combination of humor and travelogue proves
thoroughly engaging." Booklist

Petersen, Grant

Just ride; a radically practical guide to riding your bike:
equipment, health, safety, attitude. by Grant Petersen. Workman Pub. 2012 212 p. illustrations (alk. paper) $13.95 **796.6**

1. Cycling 2. Bicycles 3. Cycling -- Handbooks, manuals, etc 4.
Bicycles -- Handbooks, manuals, etc
ISBN 0761155589; 9780761155584

LC 2012001429

This book, by Grant Petersen, encourages readers to "ride like you
did when you were a kid-- just get on your bike and discover the pure joy
of riding it. . . . Petersen shares a lifetime of unexpected facts, controversial opinions, expert techniques, and his own maverick philosophy.
. . . Also includes chapters on Accessories, Upkeep, and Technicalities

as well as a final chapter titled 'Velosophy' that includes the essential,
memorable thought: Your Bike Is a Toy-- Have Fun with It." (Publisher's note)

"Smell what Petersen is cooking*. *Except for this funny idea he has
that the poncho is the ultimate cycling garment." LJ

Weiss, Eben

The **ultimate** bicycle owner's manual; the universal guide
to bikes, riding, and everything for beginner and seasoned cyclists. Eben Weiss. Black Dog & Leventhal 2016 240 p. color
illustrations (paperback) $19.99   **796.6**

1. Cycling 2. Bicycles 3. Cycling -- Handbooks, manuals, etc
4. Bicycles -- Maintenance and repair -- Handbooks, manuals, etc
ISBN 9780316352673; 9780316352680

LC 2015041449

In this book, cyclist and author Eben Weiss "makes his vast experience and practical advice available to bike 'newbies' and veterans alike.
Chapters cover Obtaining a Bike, Understanding Your Bike, Maintaining Your Bike, Operating Your Bike, Off-Road Riding, Coexisting with
Drivers, Competitive Cycling, Bike Travel, Cycling with Kids, and What
the Future Holds for Bikes in our Communities." (Publisher's note)

"A blogger and advocate of everything related to bicycling, Weiss
(The Enlightened Cyclist; Bike Snob) uses passionate, smart, and witty
prose to inspire and educate people interested in cycling." LJ

796.62   Bicycle racing

Hamilton, Tyler

The **Secret** Race; Inside the Hidden World of the Tour de
France: Doping, Cover-ups, and Winning at All Costs. Bantam
Books 2012 290 p. $28   **796.62**

1. Drug abuse 2. Bicycle racing 3. Sports -- Corrupt practices
ISBN 0345530411; 9780345530417

This book, by Tyler Hamilton and Daniel Coyle, winner of the 2012
William Hill Sports Book of the Year Award, offers a "look at the world
of professional cycling--and the doping issue surrounding this sport and
its most iconic rider, Lance Armstrong. . . . [The book] . . . takes us . . .
inside a shadowy . . . world of unscrupulous doctors, . . . team directors,
and athletes so relentlessly driven to succeed that they would do anything . . . to gain the edge they need to win." (Publisher's note)

Leonard, Max

Lanterne Rouge; The Last Man in the Tour de France. by
Max Leonard. Yellow Jersey 2014 272 p. 13 plates; color illustrations $26.95   **796.62**

1. Tour de France (Bicycle race)
ISBN 0224091999; 1605987867; 9780224091992;
9781605987866

This book about the Tour de France, by Max Leonard, "tells the
forgotten, often inspirational and occasionally absurd stories of the
last-placed rider. We learn of stage winners and former yellow jerseys
who tasted life at the other end of the bunch; the breakaway leader
who stopped for a bottle of wine and then took a wrong turn; the doper
whose drug cocktail accidentally slowed him down and the rider who
was recognized as the most combative despite finishing at the back."
(Publisher's note)

"Writer and amateur cyclist Leonard challenges what it means to
achieve greatness through the mythos of the sport's underdogs. The author provides little information about the competitors we recognize as
champions of the sport, instead populating the narrative with a strange
sort of idol worship." Kirkus

796.72 Automobile racing

Baime, A. J.

Go like hell; Ford, Ferrari, and their battle for speed and glory at Le Mans. Houghton Mifflin Harcourt 2009 304p il map $26   **796.72**

1. Sports cars 2. Automobile racing 3. Ferrari SpA 4. Ford Motor Co.

ISBN 978-0-618-82219-5; 0-618-82219-4

LC 2008-52948

"Baime tells an exciting story at a pace that manages to keep up with the drivers." Libr J

Includes bibliographical references

Busbee, Jay

Earnhardt Nation; The Full-throttle Saga of Nascar's First Family. Jay Busbee. HarperCollins 2016 352 p. illustrations (chiefly color) (hardcover) $26.99   **796.72**

ISBN 9780062367716; 0062367714

This book, by Jay Busbee, offers "portrait of the larger-than-life first family of NASCAR, the Earnhardts, and the rise of the world's fastest stock car racing organization. . . . Covering all the white-knuckle races, including the final lap at the Daytona 500 that claimed the life of the Intimidator, . . . [it] goes deep into the fast-paced world of NASCAR, its royal family's obsession with speed, and their struggle with celebrity." (Publisher's note)

"A smart look at an iconic but not necessarily admirable superstar and at what goes on behind the scenes in big-money sports."

Includes bibliographical references (pages 321-333).

Debord, Matthew

Return to Glory; the story of Ford's revival and victory in the toughest race in the world. Matthew DeBord. Atlantic Monthly Press 2017 xxi, 226 p.p illustrations, map (hardcover) $26   **796.72**

1. Ford automobile 2. Automobile racing 3. Ford GT automobile 4. Ford Motor Company

ISBN 9780802189554; 9780802126504; 0802126502

LC 2016046214

This book, by Matthew DeBord, "tells the recent story of Ford. A decade ago, CEO Alan Mulally took over the iconic company and, thanks to a financial gamble and his 'One Ford' plan, helped it weather the financial crisis and a stock price that plunged to $1 a share, without a government bailout. It was enough for the company to dream of repeating racing history. DeBord revisits the story of the 1960s and details the creation of the new GT." (Publisher's note)

"DeBord, a senior correspondent for Business Insider, takes readers inside Ford before, during and after the 2016 Le Mans race and emerges with an upbeat, feel-good business story." Pub Wkly

Hawley, Samuel Jay

Speed duel; the inside story of the land speed record in the sixties. [by] Sam Hawley. Firefly Books 2010 360p il pa $24.95   **796.72**

1. Automobile racing 2. Automobile racing drivers

ISBN 978-1-55407-633-8

"Even readers who don't know a spark plug from a gear shift will be transfixed by Hawley's white-knuckled account of the ever-escalating competition to hold the Land Speed Record in the '60s and early '70s. Drawing from countless articles, profiles, documentaries, and interviews with the men and women who were there, Hawley traces the sport's evolution from its first four-wheeled record of 39mph in 1898, to today's

jet-propelled 700mph-plus, recounting the creation, testing, and repair of legendary cars like the humble Green Monster and the charismatic Spirit of America." Publ Wkly

Includes filmography and bibliographical references

796.8 Combat sports

At the fights; American writers on boxing. edited by George Kimball & John Schulian; foreword by Colum McCann. Library of America 2011 517p $35   **796.8**

1. Boxing 2. Boxers (Sports)

ISBN 1-59853-092-5; 978-1-59853-092-6

This collection includes "work by the likes of Pete Hamill, Norman Mailer, Joyce Carol Oates, George Plimpton, David Remnick, Budd Schulberg and Gay Talese." (N Y Times Book Rev) Index.

"The book's editors accomplish several things in 'At the Fights.' They sample the work of devotees such as the incomparable A.J. Liebling and Gene Tunney on his defeat of Jack Dempsey, and of comparative outsiders such as James Baldwin and Joyce Carol Oates, whose novelistic fascination with violence, class and gender inevitably led her to ponder the boxing life. The collection plots a zigzag course through a century of boxing milestones, offering a striking range of approaches to the subject. It also throws open controversies racial, moral, legal and medical that have swirled around the sport since it first attained a sort of legitimacy. . . . [This anthology] presupposes an interest in writing as much as in boxing. Many of its contributors, such as Baldwin, Vic Ziegel, Pete Hamill, Bill Barich and Katherine Dunn, pay as much or more attention to stories tributary to fights as to the ring contests themselves. Observations in many different registers form an engrossing counterpoint as the book proceeds." San Francisco Chron

Cohen, Richard

By the sword; a history of gladiators, musketeers, samurai, swashbucklers, and Olympic champions. Random House 2002 xxiv, 519p il $29.95; pa $15.95   **796.8**

1. Fencing

ISBN 0-375-50417-6; 0-8129-6966-9 pa

LC 2002-21309

This is a worldwide history of sword fighting from Ancient Egypt to the present which considers its role in combat and sports, word origins and customs, and the fencing skills of politicians and actors

"A fascinating story told with literary verve and the pride of a long-time practitioner; highly recommended." Libr J

Includes bibliographical references

Hauser, Thomas

Boxing is-- reflections on the sweet science. The University of Arkansas Press 2010 270p pa $22.50   **796.8**

1. Boxing

ISBN 978-1-55728-942-1

LC 2010-15354

"The collection begins with a detailed biographical examination of the career of Sugar Ray Robinson, considered by many to be the greatest pound-for-pound fighter ever. It's a sadly familiar tale of poverty, ascendancy, fame, and decline, related in a respectful, objective style. The rest of the book is focused on the boxing events of 2009, from the high-profile career of Manny Pacquiao to the progress of several relatively unknown young fighters learning the trade in New York's gyms. Hauser also explores the business end of boxing, especially its painful relationship with television, but above all, he is drawn to the people of the sport: the fighters, trainers, promoters, and hangers-on. Virtually every piece is notable for its carefully drawn characters who will linger on the edges of readers' minds long after the book has been shelved." Booklist

Includes bibliographical references

Howley, Kerry

Thrown; Kerry Howley. Sarabande Books 2014 paperback $15.95   **796.8**

1. Sports -- Fiction 2. Martial arts -- Fiction 3. Graduate students -- Fiction

ISBN 1936747928; 9781936747924

LC 2014010165

"A bookish young woman insinuates herself into the lives of two cage fighters--one a young prodigy, the other an aging journeyman. . . . Acclaimed essayist Kerry Howley follows these men for three years through the bloody world of mixed martial arts as they starve themselves, break bones, fail their families and form new ones in the quest to rise from remote Midwestern fairgrounds to packed Vegas arenas." (Publisher's note)

"Howley's brilliant prose is as dexterous and doughty as the fighters she trails, torquing into philosophy, parody, and sweat-soaked poetry. At times, the narrative is difficult to follow, while the contrast between her highbrow analysis and the aggressive MMA subculture can be disorienting. Her year-long immersion in the sport, however, proves as captivating as any blood-spattered spectacle." Pub Wkly

Margolick, David

Beyond glory; Joe Louis vs. Max Schmeling, and a world on the brink. Knopf 2005 423p il $26.95   **796.8**

1. Boxing 2. Soldiers 3. Boxers (Persons)

ISBN 0-375-41192-5

LC 2005-45141

The author discusses the historical significance of the fights between Joe Louis and German boxer Max Schmeling in 1936 and 1938.

This book "will be the definitive account of Louis versus Schmeling. And it's a hell of a good read besides." Booklist

Includes bibliographical references

796.815   Oriental martial arts forms

Swanson, J. D.

Karate science; dynamic movement. J. D. Swanson, PHD. YMAA Publication Center 2017 xviii, 224 p.p illustrations (Martial Science) (print: alk. paper) $18.95   **796.815**

1. Karate 2. Karate -- Training 3. Martial arts -- Training

ISBN 9781594394591; 9781594394607

LC 2016962683

This book, by J. D. Swanson, "will help you understand the mechanics of the human body. Swanson describes these principles in incredible detail, drawing on examples from several styles of karate, as well as aikido, taekwondo, and judo. Whatever your martial background, applying this knowledge will make your techniques better, stronger, and faster." (Publisher's note)

"An informative guide for those looking to enhance their karate training." Kirkus.

Includes bibliographical references and index.

796.83   Boxing

Assael, Shaun

The murder of Sonny Liston; Las Vegas, Heroin, and Heavyweights. Shaun Assael. Blue Rider Press 2016 320 p.

illustrations (ebook) $65; (hardback) $27   **796.83**

1. Heroin abuse 2. Boxers (Sports) 3. African American athletes 4. Las Vegas (Nev.) -- History 5. African American boxers -- Biography 6. Las Vegas (Nev.) -- History -- 20th century 7. Boxers (Sports) -- United States -- Biography 8. Heroin -- Nevada -- Las Vegas -- History -- 20th century

ISBN 9780698156661; 9780399169755

LC 2016016232

This book, by Shaun Assael, is an "investigation into the mysterious death of Heavyweight Champion Sonny Liston, set against the dawn of the 1970s, when the mob was fighting to keep control of the Las Vegas Strip, Richard Nixon was launching America's first war on heroin, and boxing was in its glory days." (Publisher's note)

"Still, there is much here that will appeal to anyone interested in the intersection of crime and boxing." Booklist

Includes indexIncludes bibliographical references and index.

Butler, Brin-Jonathan

The domino diaries; my decade boxing with Olympic champions and chasing Hemingway's ghost in the last days of Castro's Cuba. by Brin-Jonathan Butler. Picador 2015 304 p. illustrations (hardback) $26   **796.83**

1. Boxing 2. Cuba -- Social life and customs 3. Boxing -- Cuba -- Anecdotes

ISBN 1250043700; 9781250043702

LC 2015012698

This book "is the culmination of [journalist Brin-Jonathan] Butler's decade spent in the trenches of Havana, trying to understand a culture perplexing to Westerners: one whose elite athletes regularly forgo multimillion-dollar opportunities to stay in Cuba and box for their country, while living in penury. Butler's fascination with this distinctly Cuban idealism sets him off on a remarkable journey, training with, befriending, and interviewing the champion boxers." (Publisher's note)

"Focusing on Dickensian characters as well as boxing, Butler's gonzo journalism should have broad appeal." LJ

Eig, Jonathan

★ Ali; a life. Jonathan Eig. Houghton Mifflin Harcourt 2017 623 p. (hardback) $30   **796.83**

1. Boxers (Sports) -- United States -- Biography

ISBN 9780544435247; 9781328505699

LC 2017044484

This book, by Jonathan Eig, looks at the life of heavyweight boxer Muhammad Ali. Eig "reveals Ali in the complexity he deserves, shedding important new light on his politics, religion, personal life, and neurological condition. 'Ali' is a story about America, about race, about a brutal sport, and about a courageous man who shook up the world." (Publisher's note)

"Eig does a fine job of covering all the bases, and though the book is occasionally overwritten, it's only out of enthusiasm for his undeniably great subject, about whom the author is now working with Ken Burns to develop a documentary. An exemplary life of an exemplary man who, despite a few missteps, deserves to be remembered long in to the future." Kirkus.

Includes bibliographical references and index.

Gildea, William

The longest fight; in the ring with Joe Gans, boxing's first African American champion. William Gildea. Farrar, Straus and Giroux 2012 245 p. ill. (hbk.): $26.00   **796.83**

1. Boxing -- Biography 2. Gans, Joe, 1874-1910 3. African American boxers -- Biography 4. Boxers (Sports) -- United States

-- Biography
ISBN 0374280975; 9780374280970

LC 2011040170

This book by William Gildea presents a biography of "Joe Gans, who in 1902 became the first African American boxing champion . . . giving special attention to the fighter's . . . championship bout against avowed racist Oscar 'Battling' Nelson. . . . Gildea gives full measure of Gans' remarkable accomplishments as an athlete . . . while also showing Gans' equally remarkable poise in the face of horrific prejudice, officially sanctioned or not, during his entire career." (Booklist)

Includes bibliographical references and index.

Kram, Mark

The **ghosts** of Manila; the fateful, brutal blood feud between Muhammad Ali and Joe Frazier. HarperCollins Pubs. 2001 232p hardcover o.p. pa $12.95   **796.83**
  1. Boxing 2. Boxers (Persons)
ISBN 0-06-095480-9 pa

LC 00-53934

This is "a fascinating blend of history and biography." Booklist

Lawton, James

A **ringside** affair; boxing's last golden age. James Lawton. St. Martin's Press 2018 304 p. $28   **796.83**
  1. Boxers (Sports) 2. Boxing -- History
ISBN 1472945638; 9781472945631

In this book, author James Lawton describes how, "for nearly three decades--throughout boxing's most engrossing era from 1977 through 2002--[he] was ringside, covering every significant bout, spending time with the likes of Muhammad Ali, Sugar Ray Leonard . . . , and many other great fighters. . . . [This book] brings that brilliant epoch back to life--and puts it in the perspective it deserves." (Publisher's note)

Liebling, A. J. (Abbott Joseph), 1904-1963

The **sweet** science; A.J. Liebling; with an introduction by Robert Anasi. North Point Press 2004 288 p. (ebook) $40; (pbk.) $16   **796.83**
  1. Boxing 2. Boxers (Sports)
ISBN 9781466801868; 0374272271; 9780374272272

LC 2004049509

This book, by A.J. Liebling, "depicts the great events of boxing's American heyday: Sugar Ray Robinson's dramatic comeback, Rocky Marciano's rise to prominence, Joe Louis's unfortunate decline. Liebling never fails to find the human story behind the fight, and he evokes the atmosphere in the arena as distinctly as he does the goings-on in the ring." (Publisher's note)

Runstedtler, Theresa

Jack Johnson, rebel sojourner; boxing in the shadow of the global color line. Theresa Runstedtler. University of California Press 2012 xxii, 348 p.p (cloth: alk. paper) $34.95   **796.83**
  1. Race relations 2. African American athletes 3. Racism in sports 4. Boxing -- United States -- History 5. African American boxers -- Biography 6. United States -- Race relations -- History 7. Boxers (Sports) -- United States -- Biography
ISBN 0520271602; 9780520271609

LC 2011027435

In this book, "[Theresa] Runstedtler . . . makes [boxer Jack] Johnson the centerpiece of what is also a study of global black-white relations during his era." The boxer "was given to living large, embarrassing white opponents, and consorting with white women at a time when Jim Crow flourished at home and the doctrine of the 'white man's burden' was en-

circling the globe. Therefore, even when he fled the United States after a Mann Act conviction, he couldn't escape racism." (Library Journal)

Includes bibliographical references and index.

796.86   Fencing

Bennett, Alexander C.

Kendo; culture of the sword. Alexander C. Bennett. University of California Press 2015 328 p. illustrations (cloth: alk. paper) $32.95   **796.86**
  1. Kendo 2. Swords 3. Swordplay -- Japan
ISBN 0520284372; 9780520284371

LC 2015004621

Author Alexander Bennett presents a "historical, cultural, and political account in English of the Japanese martial art of swordsmanship, from its beginnings in military training and arcane medieval schools to its widespread practice as a global sport today. Bennett shows how kendo evolved through a recurring process of 'inventing tradition,' which served the changing ideologies and needs of Japanese warriors and governments over the course of history." (Publisher's note)

"A highly recommended, useful resource for all readers interested in this popular sport." LJ

Includes bibliographical references and index

796.9   Ice and snow sports

Bennett, Jeff

The **complete** snowboarder; {by} Jeff Bennett, Scott Downey and Charles Arnell. 2nd ed; Ragged Mountain Press 2000 148p il pa $14.95   **796.9**
  1. Snowboarding
ISBN 0-07-135787-4

LC 00-39059

First published 1994

This offers advice on getting started in snowboarding, equipment, techniques, snowboarding areas and trails, tricks, competitions, safety, and equipment maintenance.

796.935   Alpine skiing (Downhill skiing)

Vinton, Nathaniel

The **fall** line; how American ski racers conquered a sport on the edge. Nathaniel Vinton. W W Norton & Co Inc 2015 384 p. 16 plates; illustrations (hardcover) $26.95   **796.935**
  1. Skiing 2. Winter sports -- United States 3. Skiers -- United States 4. Downhill skiing -- United States -- History
ISBN 0393244776; 9780393244779

LC 2014033594

This book, by Nathaniel Vinton, "is an authoritative portrait of a group of men and women taking mortal risks in a bid for sporting glory. A white-knuckled tour through skiing's deep traditions and least-accessible locales, . . . [The book] opens up the sexy, high-stakes world of downhill skiing-- its career-ending crashes, million-dollar sponsorship deals, international intrigue, and showdowns with nature itself." (Publisher's note)

"As the season progresses, Vinton adds rich historical context to each race venue, documenting course changes and rule revisions, while profiling past skiing greats, including Austrians Franz Klammer and Hermann Maier. The subtitle is a bit of a misnomer as this is not simply a story of American skiers but, instead, a primer on the history and current state of Alpine skiing." Booklist

796.94 Snowmobiling

O'Brien, Keith

Catching the Sky; two brothers, one family, and our dream to fly. Colten Moore, with Keith O'Brien. Simon & Schuster 2016 272 p. color illustrations (Hardcover: alk. paper) $26 **796.94**

1. Extreme sports

ISBN 9781501117244; 9781501117251; 1501117246

LC 2015044662

This book, by Colten Moore, with Keith O'Brien, presents reflections of the author and his brother's careers in ATV and snowmobile extreme sports. The author offers a "look at extreme sports, what drives people to take wild chances, and how one man, Colten, couldn't stop even after the worst possible outcome." (Publisher's note)

"Moore's well-written memoir will enthrall fans of extreme sports, the X Games, and those trying to find their way after losing a loved one." LJ

Includes bibliographical references.

796.962 Ice hockey

Gretzky, Wayne, 1961-

99; Stories of the Game. Wayne Gretzky and Kirstie McLellan Day. G.P. Putnam's Sons 2016 416 p. illustrations (some color) (ebook) $53.85; (print) $28 **796.962**

1. Hockey 2. Hockey -- History 3. Hockey players -- Canada 4. Hockey -- Anecdotes 5. Hockey players -- Canada -- Biography

ISBN 9780771083259; 9780399575471

LC 2016036048

In this book, by Wayne Gretzky and Kirstie McLellan Day, "for the first time, Gretzky discusses candidly what . . . [hockey] looks like to him and introduces . . . the people who inspired and motivated him: mentors, teammates, rivals, the famous and the lesser known. . . . He reflects on the players who inflamed his imagination when he was a kid, . . . [and shows] some of the famous moments in hockey history through the eyes of someone who regularly made that history." (Publisher's note)

"Not a complete history of the NHL, but this enjoyable book provides an overview that will educate longtime fans and relative newcomers alike." Kirkus

Hockey Hall of Fame Book of Players; edited by Steve Cameron. 2nd edition Firefly Books 2015 352 p. color illustrations pbk $29.95 **796.962**

1. Hockey players 2. Hockey -- History

ISBN 9781770855977; 1770855971

LC 2015509178

"Complete with more than 450 photos and over 70 artifacts--as well as stats, facts, quotes and other interesting stories and snapshots from each star's career--Hockey Hall of Fame Book of Players is the definitive book on the stars who have been awarded hockey's most prestigious honor." (Publisher's note)

McKinley, Michael

Hockey: a people's history. McClelland & Stewart 2006 346p il hardcover o.p. pa $37.50 **796.962**

1. Hockey

ISBN 0-7710-5769-5; 978-0-7710-5769-4; 0-7710-5771-7 pa; 978-0-7710-5771-7 pa

This history "chronicles hockey from its genesis as a winter substitute for lacrosse. A companion to a similarly titled CBC TV series, the lavishly illustrated book combines punchy boxed features celebrating individuals and hockey oddments and a detailed tracing of the game's development. . . . Essential for general sports as well as hockey-intensive collections." Booklist

Includes bibliographical references

797.1 Aquatic sports

American Canoe Association

Canoeing; outdoor adventures. editors, Pamela S. Dillon, Jeremy Oyen. Human Kinetics 2008 253p il (Outdoor adventures) pa $22.95 **797.1**

1. Canoes and canoeing

ISBN 978-0-7360-6715-7; 0-7360-6715-9

LC 2008-4392

The authors "discuss fitness basics, food and nutrition needs, and gear and equipment—from the canoe itself to life jackets, paddles, and clothing. They then cover . . . safety and survival guidelines, including weather, river hazards, capsizing, cold-water safety, and rescue protocols. . . [The DVD included contains] an introduction to paddle sports and basic safety and paddling techniques." Publisher's note

Kayaking; editors, Pamela S. Dillon, Jeremy Oyen. Human Kinetics 2009 237p il (Outdoor adventures) pa $22.95 **797.1**

1. Canoes and canoeing

ISBN 978-0-7360-6716-4; 0-7360-6716-7

LC 2008-32111

"Part I of Kayaking explains the background knowledge, fitness fundamentals, equipment and gear selection, nutritional needs, and safety and survival skills for a successful adventure. Part II helps build basic techniques, strokes, and maneuvers. . . [It includes] tips and instruction for the three most popular types of kayaking: sea, river, and whitewater. This book also includes the Quick-Start Your Kayak DVD to reinforce the paddling strokes and safety information found in the book. It features videos of kayaking maneuvers." Publisher's note

Includes bibliographical references

797.12 Types of vessels

Brown, Daniel James

★ The **Boys** in the Boat; Nine Americans and Their Epic Quest for Gold at the 1936 Berlin Olympics. Daniel James Brown. Penguin Group USA 2013 432 p. (hardcover) $28.95 **797.12**

1. Rowing 2. Olympic games, 1936 (Berlin, Ger.) 3. Rowing -- United States -- History 4. Rowers -- United States -- Biography 5. University of Washington -- Rowing -- History

ISBN 067002581X; 9780670025817

LC 2013001560

This book, by Daniel James Brown, "tells the story of the University of Washington's 1936 eight-oar crew and their . . . quest for an Olympic gold medal, a team that transformed the sport and grabbed the attention of millions of Americans. The sons of loggers, shipyard workers, and farmers, the boys defeated elite rivals first from eastern and British universities and finally the German crew rowing for Adolf Hitler in the Olympic games in Berlin, 1936." (Publisher's note)

Includes bibliographical references and index.

Rackley, Adam

Salt, sweat, tears; the men who rowed the oceans. Adam Rackley. Penguin Books 2014 272 p. 16 plates; illustrations; map (paperback) $16   **797.12**

  1. Rowing 2. Ocean travel 3. Atlantic Ocean 4. Rowers -- Biography

  ISBN 0143126660; 9780143126669

                    LC 2014010916

Author Adam Rackley presents "his story of adventure, endurance, and self-discovery. For more than seventy days, Adam Rackley and his rowing partner ate, slept and rowed in a boat seven meters long by two meters wide, in one of the world's most extreme environments." (Publisher's note)

"Told in an earnest and captivating style by first-time author Rackley will delight both armchair enthusiasts and real-life adventurers when they discover another sport for their dreams." LJ

797.124 Sailing

Sleight, Steve

The **complete** sailing manual; Steve Sleight. DK Publishing 2012 448 p. color illustrations; maps (hc) $35   **797.124**

  1. Sailing 2. Navigation 3. Sailing -- Handbooks, manuals, etc

  ISBN 0756689694; 9780756689698

                    LC 2011534511

Written by Steve Sleight, "From learning the basics of sailing, to mastering navigation and boat care, 'The Complete Sailing Manual' is the most essential reference for sailing instructors and students. Revised and updated to include all of the latest developments in equipment and safety, and to reflect the current rules, regulations, and best practices, 'The Complete Sailing Manual' is . . . for anyone interested in sailing." (Publisher's note)

797.2 Swimming and diving

Beard, Amanda

In the water they can't see you cry; a memoir. Amanda Beard; with Rebecca Paley. 1st Touchstone hardcover ed. Simon & Schuster 2012 248 p. ill. (some col.) $24.99   **797.2**

  1. Autobiographies 2. Olympic athletes 3. Depression (Psychology) 4. Swimmers -- United States -- Biography 5. Women swimmers -- United States -- Biography

  ISBN 145164437X; 9781451644371

                    LC 2012006464

This book is a memoir by Olympic swimmer Amanda Beard, with Rebecca Paley. "[S]he competed in three more Olympic games . . . and enjoyed a lucrative modeling career on the side. . . . Unaware that she was suffering from clinical depression, she . . . expressed her emotions through self-destructive behavior. . . . Only when she met her future husband . . . did Amanda realize she needed help." (Publisher's note)

Checkoway, Julie

The **three-**year swim club; the untold story of Maui's sugar ditch kids and their quest for Olympic glory. by Julie Checkoway. Grand Central Pub 2015 432 p. 16 plates; illustrations $27   **797.2**

  1. Swimming 2. Olympic games 3. Japanese Americans

  ISBN 1455523445; 9781455523443

                    LC 2015947608

This book, by Julie Checkoway, is the "story of impoverished children who transformed themselves into world-class swimmers. In 1937, a schoolteacher on the island of Maui challenged a group of poverty-stricken sugar plantation kids to . . . become Olympians. . . . The children were Japanese-American, were malnourished and barefoot and had no pool. . . . In spite of everything . . . the children outraced Olympic athletes twice their size." (Publisher's note)

"Details about training, swim times, and the team's travels occasionally overwhelm Checkoway's tense, vivid, an d inspiring narrative. Not without its flaws, but a good choice for fans of David Halberstam's The Amateurs (1985), Daniel Boyne's The Red Rose Crew (2000), and similar books." Kirkus

Graver, Dennis

Scuba diving; Dennis Graver. 5th edition Human Kinetics 2016 illustrations pbk $29.95   **797.2**

  ISBN 1492525766; 9781492525769

                    LC 2016018110

"Scuba Diving offers step-by-step instruction on preparing for and managing a dive safely with information on the latest equipment, gear selection, recommended dive locations, technologies and techniques. Dennis Graver explains the basics of diving, including managing underwater emergencies, avoiding underwater hazards and equalizing pressure in the ears, sinuses and mask." (Publisher's note)

Mullen, P. H.

Gold in the water; the true story of ordinary men and their extraordinary dream of Olympic glory. Thomas Dunne Bks. 2001 326p il hardcover o.p. pa $14.95   **797.2**

  1. Swimming 2. Olympic games, 2000 (Sydney, Australia)

  ISBN 0-312-26595-6; 0-312-31116-8 pa

                    LC 2001-31955

"Mullen chronicles the U.S. Olympic swimming team on its journey to the 2000 Summer Games in Sydney. The text moves back and forth in time, giving a sense of the athletes as people and showing what motivates someone to structure his or her whole life toward a single goal." Booklist

Nestor, James

Deep; Freediving, Renegade Science, and What the Ocean Tells Us About Ourselves. James Nestor. Houghton Mifflin Harcourt 2014 272 p. illustrations (chiefly color) $27   **797.2**

  1. Ocean 2. Skin diving

  ISBN 0547985525; 9780547985527

                    LC 2014002593

"In 'Deep,' [author James] Nestor embeds with a gang of extreme athletes and renegade researchers who are transforming not only our knowledge of the planet and its creatures, but also our understanding of the human body and mind. . . . Most illuminating of all, Nestor unlocks his own freediving skills as he communes with the pioneers who are expanding our definition of what is possible in the natural world, and in ourselves." (Publisher's note)

"[B]rimming with vivid portraits, lucid scientific explanations, gripping (and funny) first-person accounts, and urgent facts about the ocean's endangerment, Nestor's Deep is galvanizing, enlightening, and invaluable." Booklist

Includes bibliographical references and index

Shapton, Leanne

Swimming studies; Leanne Shapton. Blue Rider Press 2012 320 p. (hbk.) $30   **797.2**

1. Swimming 2. Women swimmers -- Canada -- Biography
ISBN 0399158170; 9780399158179

LC 2012011506

This memoir by Leane Shapton "explores the worlds of competitive and recreational swimming. From her training for the Olympic trials as a teenager to enjoying pools and beaches around the world as an adult, . . . Shapton offers a fascinating glimpse into the private, often solitary, realm of swimming. . . . [The book] reveals an intimate narrative of suburban adolescence, spent underwater in a discipline that continues to inspire Shapton's work as an artist and author." (Publisher's note)

Skolnick, Adam

One breath; death, freediving, and the quest to shatter human limits. by Adam Skolnick. Crown Archetype 2015 336 p. color illustrations $26   **797.2**
1. Scuba diving 2. Water safety 3. Divers -- United States -- Biography
ISBN 9780553447484; 9780553447491

LC 2015027589

In this book, by Adam Skolnick, "A handsome young American with an unmatched talent for the sport, Nick was among freediving's brightest stars. . . . So when Nick Mevoli arrived at Vertical Blue in 2013, the world's premier freediving competition, he was widely expected to challenge records and continue his meteoric rise to stardom. Instead, before the end of that fateful competition Nick Mevoli had died, a victim of the sport that had made him a star." (Publisher's note)

"A worthy addition to the growing body of literature on adventures that test the limits of nature and mankind." Kirkus

797.5 Air sports

Higgins, Matt

Bird dream; adventures at the extremes of human flight. Matt Higgins. The Penguin Press 2014 304 p. color illustrations $27.95   **797.5**
1. Flight 2. Aeronautical sports
ISBN 1594204659; 9781594204654

LC 2014005399

Written by Matt Higgins, "'Bird Dream' shows that recent decades have witnessed an unprecedented revolution in human flight. . . . Wingsuits were not new; they had fascinated men for centuries. Yet a modern design had improved safety and performance, allowing wingsuit pilots to leap from a helicopter or high cliff and soar for miles--using little more than their bodies--before deploying a parachute to reach the ground safely." (Publisher's note)

"A highflying, electrifying story of a treacherous sport in which every triumph is an eye blink away from becoming a disaster." Kirkus

Includes bibliographical references and index

798.2 Horsemanship

Letts, Elizabeth

The **eighty**-dollar champion; Snowman, the horse that inspired a nation. Ballantine Books 2011 352p $26   **798.2**
1. Horses
ISBN 978-0-345-52108-8; 978-0-345-52110-1 ebook

LC 2010050993

"In 1956, Harry De Leyer, a riding instructor at a Long Island girls' school, spent $80 on a horse that was bound for the slaughterhouse. He thought the animal might make a good horse for his students. But the horse, named Snowman by Harry's four-year-old daughter, turned out to be much more--a champion show-jumper." (Booklist)

Includes bibliographical references

798.4 Horse racing

Drape, Joe

American Pharoah; The Untold Story of the Triple Crown Winner's Legendary Rise. by Joe Drape. Hachette Books 2016 292 p. color illustrations $27   **798.4**
1. Horse racing
ISBN 0316268844; 9780316268844

This book about the racehorse American Pharoah, by Joe Drape, "is the definitive account not only of how the ethereal colt won the Kentucky Derby, Preakness, and Belmont Stakes, but how he changed lives. Through extensive interviews, Drape explores the making of an exceptional racehorse, chronicling key events en route to history." (Publisher's note)

"A captivating story woven with an affectionate yet honest portrayal of the sometimes seedy sport of kings, this work will appeal to horse-racing fans and anyone who enjoys athlete biographies." LJ

Includes bibliographical references (pages 275-278) and index.

Eisenberg, John

The **great** match race; when North met South in America's first sports spectacle. Houghton Mifflin Co. 2006 258p il $25   **798.4**
1. Horse racing
ISBN 978-0-618-55612-0; 0-618-55612-5

LC 2005-31540

The author "succeeds in creating a gripping yarn of sporting contest, portrayal of a historical moment and smart analysis of a country headed eventually for civil war." Publ Wkly

Includes bibliographical references

Hillenbrand, Laura

★ **Seabiscuit**; an American legend. Random House 2001 399p il $25.95; pa $15.95   **798.4**
1. Horse racing 2. Seabiscuit (Race horse)
ISBN 0-375-50291-2; 0-449-00561-5 pa

LC 2001-267852

"This is a remarkable tale well told by a writer who deftly blends history and sport." Economist

Includes bibliographical references

McGraw, Eliza

Here Comes Exterminator! the longshot horse, the Great War, and the making of an American hero. Eliza McGraw. St. Martin's Press 2016 336 p. illustrations (hardcover) $26.99   **798.4**
1. Horse racing -- United States -- History
ISBN 9781250065698; 1250065690

LC 2015048660

This book, by Eliza McGraw, "tells the story of how a gangling, long-shot Kentucky Derby winner named Exterminator became one of the most beloved racehorses of all time. . . . [The author] draws readers into the golden age of racing, with all its ups and downs, the ever-involving interplay of horses and people, and the beauty, grace, fear, and hope that are a daily part of life at the track." (Publisher's note)

"Unfolding without the fanfare of, say, a Seabiscuit or Man o' War, Exterminator's story, and that of the quietly competent and humane Mc-

Daniel, will still secure both horse and trainer a place in the hearts of animal lovers, and in horse racing's pantheon of champions." Booklist

Includes bibliographical references (pages [233]-314) and index.

Nack, William

Secretariat; the making of a champion. by William Nack. Da Capo Press 2002 xi, 367 p.p illustrations $16.99 **798.4**

1. Horse racing 2. Secretariat (Race horse) 3. Race horses -- United States -- Biography

ISBN 0306811332; 1401324010; 9780306811333; 9781401324018

LC 2007310325

This book, by William Nack, focuses on the horse Secretariat. "In 1973, Secretariat, the greatest champion in horse-racing history, won the Triple Crown. The only horse to ever grace the covers of Time, Newsweek, and Sports Illustrated in the same week, he also still holds the record for the fastest times in both the Kentucky Derby and the Belmont Stakes." (Publisher's note)

Ours, Dorothy

Man o' War; a legend like lightning. St Martin's Press 2006 342p il $24.95 **798.4**

1. Horse racing 2. Man o' War (Race horse)

ISBN 0-312-34099-0; 978-0-312-34099-5

LC 2006-41631

This is an account of the thoroughbred racehorse Man o' War, also known as Big Red.

This book "is clearly a labor of love, and it certifies Big Red's claim to immortality." N Y Times Book Rev

Includes bibliographical references

Squires, James D.

Horse of a different color; a tale of breeding geniuses, dominant females, and the fastest Derby winner since Secretariat. {by} Jim Squires. PublicAffairs 2002 300p il $26; pa $14 **798.4**

1. Horse racing 2. Kentucky Derby

ISBN 1-58648-117-7; 1-58648-180-0 pa

LC 2001-59602

This is the story of how the author, a former editor of the Chicago Tribune, became a breeder of thoroughbred race horses, including a horse named Monarchos, the champion of the 2001 Kentucky Derby

This "is fast paced and fun to read. It will appeal not only to horseracing fans but also to people making midlife career changes." Libr J

799.1 Fishing

Bourne, Wade

Basic fishing; A Beginner's Guide. by Wade Bourne. Skyhorse Pub. 2011 159 p. color illustrations $12.99 **799.1**

1. Fishing

ISBN 1632203383; 9781616082109; 9781632203380

LC 2011017601

This book, by Wade Bourne, is a "beginner's guide for burgeoning fishermen. . . . Bourne was taught to fish by his father. In turn, Bourne taught his children how to fish. Now he brings his expertise to . . . a step-by-step guide that masterfully breaks down the art of fishing with diagrams, vivid photographs, and lessons." (Publisher's note)

Cermele, Joe

The **total** fishing manual; 317 Essential Fishing Skills. by Joe Cermele. Welden Owen 2013 256 p. color illustrations $29 **799.1**

1. Fishing

ISBN 1616284870; 1616286296; 9781616284879; 9781616286293

This book on fishing, by Joe Cermele, "is chock full of 317 field-tested tools, techniques and tactics. . . . Whether you're a beginner, a weekend angler or a serious sport fisher this book has the information you need to hook'em." (Publisher's note)

Rosenbauer, Tom

The **Orvis** guide to the essential American flies; how to tie the most successful freshwater and saltwater patterns. Universe 2011 208p il $35 **799.1**

1. Fishing 2. Artificial flies

ISBN 978-0-7893-2269-2

LC 2011-921540

This "resource features twenty quintessential fly patterns, including the Parachute Adams, Clouser Minnow, and Woolly Bugger. [Includes] detailed chapters exploring the history of and variations on each fly, interviews with fly originators, and step-by-step tying 'recipes' and instructions." Publisher's note

Talleur, Richard W.

L.L. Bean ultimate book of fly fishing. Lyons Press 2002 344p il hardcover o.p. pa $24.95 **799.1**

1. Fishing 2. Fly casting

ISBN 1-58574-632-0; 1-59228-891-X pa

LC 2002-73191

Each chapter also published separately

The topics discussed in this book include "assembly of fly tackle; the biology of fish; natural fish foods and how to imitate them; safety techniques; bass flies; where to find bass; the eleven habits of highly effective fly casters; the basic four-part cast; the roll cast; the basics of fly tying; types of flies; the top ten most popular and successful fly patterns; and . . . more." Publisher's note

799.12 Angling

Gierach, John

All Fishermen Are Liars; by John Gierach. Simon & Schuster 2014 224 p. illustrations $24 **799.12**

1. Fishing 2. Fly fishing -- Anecdotes

ISBN 145161831X; 9781451618310

LC 2013012784

In this book, author John Gierach "travels across North America from the Pacific Northwest to the Canadian Maritimes to seek out quintessential fishing experiences. Whether he's fishing a busy stream or a secluded lake amid snow-capped mountains, Gierach insists that fishing is always the answer--even when it's not clear what the question is." (Publisher's note)

"An engaging autobiographical introduction opens the book, which includes 22 perceptive and witty essays, recalling numerous fishing trips and offering insights on fly rods and fly patterns. . . . These lyrical essays explode with descriptions of beautiful places, big fish, and beautiful fish." Booklist

Includes bibliographical references and index

799.124   Fly fishing

The **Fly** Fisher; the essence and essentials of fly fshing. edited by Jan Blumentritt, Thorsten Strüben, Maximilian Funk, and Robert Klanten. Gestalten 2017 248 p. color illustrations (hardcover) $60   **799.124**
1. Fly casting 2. Fly fishing -- Pictorial works
ISBN 9783899556742; 3899556747

This book, edited by Thorsten Struben and Jan Blumentritt, explains how "fly fishing combines connecting with nature, the defining of personal aesthetics, and physical activity. . . . [It] shows the most beautiful fishing spots, self-tied flies, and the right equipment for this increasingly popular lark of leisure." (Publisher's note)

"Beautiful watercolor renderings of fish, along with illustrations of flies and casting demonstrations, help to provide information in a gorgeous and accessible way." Choice

Gierach, John

A **fly** rod of your own; John Gierach; art by Glenn Wolff. Simon & Schuster 2017 207 p. illustrations $25   **799.124**
1. Fishing 2. Fly casting 3. Fly fishing
ISBN 1451618344; 9781451618341

LC 2016019507

In this book, author John Gierach "takes us into his world and scrutinizes the art of fly-fishing. He travels to remote fishing locations where the airport is not much bigger than a garage and a flight might be held up because a passenger is running late. He sings the praises of the skilled pilots who fly to remote fishing lodges in tricky locations and bad weather." (Publisher's note)

"A must for fisherman and outdoor enthusiasts, this book may also have wider appeal, as it is as much about travel, friendships, and navigating today's world as it is about fly-fishing." LJ.

Meyers, Charlie

The **little** red book of fly fishing; 250 tips to make you a better fisherman. Charlie Meyers and Kirk Deeter. Skyhorse Pub. 2010 xv, 201 p.p color illustrations (alk. paper) $16.95   **799.124**
1. Fly casting 2. Fly fishing
ISBN 1602399816; 9781602399815

LC 2009046448

This book, by Charlie Meyers and Kirk Deeter, "offers a simple, digestible primer on the basic elements of fly fishing: the cast, presentation, reading water, and selecting flies. In the end, this collection of 240 tips is one of the most insightful, plainly spoken, and entertaining works on this sport—one that will serve both novices and experts alike in helping them reflect and hone in their approaches to fly fishing." (Publisher's note)

Includes bibliographical references and index

Rosenbauer, Tom

The **Orvis** fly-fishing guide; Tom Rosenbauer; photographs by Tom Rosenbauer & the Orvis Company; illustrations by Bob White. Lyons Press 2007 ix, 271 p.p color illustrations $24.95; (ebook) $30.99   **799.124**
1. Fly casting 2. Fly fishing
ISBN 1592288189; 9781592288182; 9780762762422

LC 2007274210

This book, by Tom Rosenbauer, "appears in a revised edition. . . . A best-selling, fully illustrated, and comprehensive book, this large-format volume has been required reading for every angler for the past two decades. Included here are instructions for tackle selection; casting and presentation; flies and their specific uses; successful techniques on stream, pond, or ocean; and the select tackle, flies, and methods for pursuing every major gamefish." (Publisher's note)

Includes bibliographical references (p. 261-263) and index.

Whitelaw, Ian

The **history** of fly fishing in fifty flies; Ian Whitelaw; illustration by Julie Spyropoulos. Stewart Tabori & Chang, an imprint of Abrams 2015 223 p. illustrations $22.50; (ebook) $22.50   **799.124**
1. Fly casting 2. Artificial flies 3. Fly fishing -- History 4. Flies, Artificial -- History
ISBN 1617691461; 9781617691461; 9781613127834

LC 2014942977

This book, by Ian Whitelaw, with illustration by Julie Spyropoulos, "recounts the history of a sport that dates back 2,000 years, focusing on milestone flies from the first feathered hook to contemporary patterns using cutting-edge materials. Among the countless fly patterns created over the centuries, these 50 have been carefully chosen to represent the development not only of the flies themselves, but also of fly-fishing techniques—and of rods, lines, and reels." (Publisher's note)

Includes bibliographical references (pages 218-219) and index

799.173   Shark fishing

Strøksnes, Morten

Shark drunk; the art of catching a large shark from a tiny rubber dinghy in a big ocean. Morten Strøksnes; translated from the Norwegian by Tiina Nunnally. First American edition Alfred A. Knopf 2017 307 p. illustrations, map (hardcover) $26.95   **799.173**
1. Sharks 2. Shark fishing 3. Fishing -- Norway 4. Sailing -- Norway 5. True adventure stories 6. Shark fishing -- Norway 7. Greenland shark -- Norway
ISBN 9780451493491; 9780451493484

LC 2016044185

This book "is the true story of . . . the author and . . . artist Hugo Aasjord, as they embark on a wild pursuit of the famed creature--all from a tiny rubber boat. Together they tackle existential questions and encounter the world's most powerful maelstrom as they attempt to understand the ocean from every possible angle, drawing on poetry, science, history, ecology, mythology, and their own . . . observations, meanwhile pursuing the elusive Greenland shark." (Publisher's note)

"Strøksnes's erudition, salty humor, and unfussy prose yield a fresh, engrossing natural history." Pub Wkly

Includes bibliographical references (p. [295]-307).

799.2   Hunting

Rinella, Steven

The **complete** guide to hunting, butchering, and cooking big game; Big Game. Steven Rinella. Spiegel & Grau 2014 416 p. illustrations (color), maps $25   **799.2**
1. Big game hunting 2. Cooking (Game) 3. Hunting -- United States 4. Game and game-birds, Dressing of 5. Big game hunting -- United States 6. Hunting -- United States -- Equipment and supplies
ISBN 081299406X; 9780812994063

LC 2014013333

This book, by Steven Rinella, is a "comprehensive big-game hunting guide for hunters ranging from first-time novices to seasoned experts, with more than 400 full-color photographs, including work by renowned outdoor photographer John Hafner." (Publisher's note)

"Rinella doesn't offer too many tips beyond the obvious grilled steaks and jerky, though wild pig hunters will appreciate his simple but flavorful recipe for smoked ham. It's a minor flaw in a book that's terrifically informative and is sure to inspire hunters to start poring over maps and readying themselves for their next hunt." Pub Wkly

The **Complete** Guide to Hunting, Butchering, and Cooking Wild Game; Small Game and Fowl. by Steven Rinella, photography by John Hafner. Random House Inc 2015 384 p. chiefly col. ill., maps (paperback) $25 **799.2**
    1. Hunting 2. Cooking -- Game
    ISBN 9780812987058; 0812987055

This book, by Steven Rinella with photography by John Hafner, is "a comprehensive small game hunting guide for hunters ranging from first-time novices to seasoned experts. . . . [Topics addressed include] recommendations on what equipment you will need . . . , basic and advanced hunting strategies for all North American small game . . . , instructions on how to field dress and butcher your own small game animals." (Publisher's note)

"The book stands well on its own, covering the requisite gear and skills... that hunters need to develop in order to ensure a successful hunt." Pub Wkly

799.29   History, geographic treatment, biography

Rinella, Steven
    Meat eater; a natural history of an American hunter. Steven Rinella. Spiegel & Grau 2012 244 p. **799.29**
    1. Hunting 2. Food of animal origin 3. Hunting stories, American 4. Hunting -- United States -- History 5. Hunters -- United States -- Biography
    ISBN 0385529813; 9780385529815; 9780679645283
    LC 2012018129

This book by Steven Rinella "chronicles Rinella's lifelong relationship with nature and hunting through the lens of ten hunts, beginning when he was an aspiring mountain man at age ten and ending as a thirty-seven-year-old Brooklyn father who hunts in the remotest corners of North America. . . . Rinella grapples with themes such as . . . the disappearance of the hunter himself as Americans lose their connection with the way their food finds its way to their tables." (Publisher's note)

800   LITERATURE, RHETORIC & CRITICISM

801   Philosophy and theory

Kundera, Milan
    ★ The **curtain**; an essay in seven parts. translated from the French by Linda Asher. HarperCollins Publishers 2007 168p $22.95 **801**
    1. Literature -- Philosophy 2. Fiction -- History and criticism
    ISBN 978-0-06-084186-7; 0-06-084186-9
    LC 2006-43420

"The immediacy of Kundera's evocative prose and the rich tapestry he weaves compel us to pick up and read, or reread, the bountiful literary treasures of Western literature. This could be a book from which to draw

a summer reading list." Libr J

Mendelsohn, Daniel
    Waiting for the barbarians; essays from the classics to pop culture. by Daniel Mendelsohn. New York Review Books 2012 423 p. (alk. paper) $24.95 **801**
    1. Criticism 2. Classical literature 3. Popular culture -- United States 4. Literature -- History and criticism 5. Canon (Literature) 6. Literature -- Appreciation 7. Popular culture -- 21st century
    ISBN 1590176073; 9781590176078
    LC 2012012240

This book by Daniel Mendelsohn is a collection of his essays seen in "The New York Review of Books," "The New Yorker," and "The New York Times Book Review." This collection "brings together twenty-four of his recent essays . . . on a wide range of subjects. . . . Trained as a classicist, Mendelsohn moves easily from . . . considerations of the ways in which the classics continue to make themselves felt in contemporary life . . . to . . . takes on pop spectacles." (Publisher's note)

Moore, Lorrie, 1957-
    See what can be done; essays, criticism, and commentary. Lorrie Moore. Alfred A. Knopf 2018 432 p. (hardcover) $29.95 **801**
    1. Essays 2. Criticism 3. Literature, Modern -- History and criticism
    ISBN 9781524732486
    LC 2017006247

In this book, "acclaimed fiction writer [Lorrie] Moore has compiled her nonfiction writings into a marvelous collection . . . a window onto the trajectory of both late 20th-century American culture and Moore's development as a writer. Throughout, her chief virtue as a critic is shown to be a sympathetic, generous eye . . . a boon to any lover of smart cultural criticism." (Publishers Weekly)

"Deft, graceful essays from a sharply incisive writer." Kirkus

Moretti, Franco
    Distant reading; Franco Moretti. Verso 2013 254 p. illustrations, maps (hardback: alk. paper) $95 **801**
    1. Criticism 2. Literature -- History and criticism 3. Literature -- History and criticism -- Theory, etc
    ISBN 1781681120; 9781781680841; 9781781681121
    LC 2012047274

National Book Critics Circle Award Winner: Criticism (2013)

This collection of essays, by Franco Moretti, "challenges entrenched conceptions about world cultures and arts. In 'Modern European Literatu're: A Geographical Sketch,' he disputes the notion of a literature that reflects 'a European essence.' . . . In its companion piece, 'Conjectures on World Literature,' he similarly explodes the notion of a single contemporary literature that accommodates the writing of all nations." (Publishers weekly)

"Regardless of whether readers agree with Moretti's conclusions, they will find that his application of economic theory, network theory, and evolutionary models to literature and culture shows these subjects from fresh and often provocative new perspectives." Pub Wkly

Includes bibliographical references and index

801.95   Criticism

Ozick, Cynthia, 1928-
    Critics, monsters, fanatics, and other literary essays; Cynthia Ozick. Houghton Mifflin Harcourt 2016 211 p. (hardback)

$25   **801.95**
1. Criticism   2. Essays
ISBN 9780544703711

LC 2015037560

In this book, author Cynthia Ozick, "stakes the claim that, just as surely as critics require a steady supply of new fiction, novelists need great critics to build a vibrant community on the foundation of literary history. . . . She offers models of critical analysis of writers from the mid-twentieth century to today, from Saul Bellow, Bernard Malamud, and Kafka, to William Gass and Martin Amis, all assembled in provocatively named groups." (Publisher's note)

"This essay collection from novelist (Foreign Bodies) and literary critic Ozick takes a fresh look at renowned writers of the past and present." Pub Wkly.

803   Dictionaries, encyclopedias, concordances

Ayto, John

  ★ **Brewer's** dictionary of modern phrase & fable; by John Ayto & Ian Crofton. 2nd ed.; Chambers Harrap Pub. Ltd. 2010 853p $39.95   **803**
1. Allusions   2. Reference books   3. Literature -- Dictionaries
ISBN 978-0550-105-646
First published 2000 by Cassell

"Focusing on the 20th and 21st centuries, . . . [this book covers a] selection of buzzwords, catchphrases, slang, nicknames, fictional characters and . . . cultural phenomena from pop culture to politics, literature to technology." Publisher's note

Benet's reader's encyclopedia; edited by Bruce F. Murphy. 5th ed.; Collins 2008 1210p $60   **803**
1. Reference books   2. Literature -- Dictionaries
ISBN 978-0-06-089016-2

LC 2008-31430

First published 1948 under the editorship of William Rose Benet

This encyclopedia contains over 10,000 entries and covers world literature from early times to the present. Includes entries on authors, literary movements, principal characters, plot synopses, terms, awards, myths and legends, etc.

This is "an edifying staple for any literary library." Libr J

  ★ **Brewer's** dictionary of phrase & fable; edited by Susie Dent. 19th edition Brewer's 2013 1480 p $26.50   **803**
1. Reference books   2. Allusions   3. Mythology -- Dictionaries   4. Literature -- Dictionaries   5. English language -- Terms and phrases
ISBN 9780550107640
Provides definitions of typical phrases and words and explains their historical origins.

Cuddon, J. A.

The **Penguin** dictionary of literary terms and literary theory; 4th ed; Penguin 1999 1024p (Penguin reference) pa $29   **803**
1. Reference books   2. Literature -- Dictionaries
ISBN 0-14-051363-9; 978-0-14-051363-9
First published 1977 in the United Kingdom with title: A dictionary of literary terms; first United States edition published 1977 by Doubleday; this edition first published 1998 by Blackwell Publishers

"Comprehensive dictionary covering all literatures and time periods with basic definitions as currently used. Categories include technical terms, forms, genres, groups, movements, -isms, character types, phras-

es, motifs or themes, concepts, objects, and styles. Entries often indicate origin and cite examples. Numerous see and see also references." Guide to Ref Books. 11th edition

  ★ The **Oxford** dictionary of literary terms; [compiled by] Chris Baldick. 4th edition Oxford University Press 2015 392 p $18.95   **803**
1. Reference books   2. Literature -- Dictionaries   3. English language -- Terms and phrases
ISBN 9780198715443
First published 1990 with title: The concise Oxford dictionary of literary terms

"The bestselling Oxford Dictionary of Literary Terms provides clear and concise definitions of the most troublesome literary terms, from abjection to zeugma. It is an essential reference tool for students of literature in any language. Now expanded and in its fourth edition, it includes increased coverage of new terms from modern critical and theoretical movements, such as feminism, schools of American poetry, Spanish verse forms, life writing, and crime fiction." (Publisher's note)

  ★ **Oxford** dictionary of phrase and fable; edited by Elizabeth Knowles. 2nd ed.; Oxford University Press 2005 805p $40; pa $18.95   **803**
1. Allusions   2. Reference books   3. Literature -- Dictionaries
ISBN 978-0-19-860981-0; 978-0-19-920246-1 pa
First published 2000

This work seeks to define words and phrases of British cultural history. This "is a highly useful tool to help understand what phrases mean and where they come from and should definitely be added to all reference collections." Booklist

808   Rhetoric and collections of literary texts from more than two literatures

  ★ The **best** American essays. Mariner Books   **808**
1. American essays
Annual. First published 1986

Black nature; four centuries of African American nature poetry. edited by Camille T. Dungy. University of Georgia Press 2009 xxxv, 387p $69.95; pa $24.95   **808**
1. Nature poetry   2. American poetry -- African American authors
ISBN 978-0-8203-3277-2; 0-8203-3277-1; 978-0-8203-3431-8 pa; 0-8203-3431-6 pa

LC 2009-18528

"Since Bryant, Longfellow, Whitman, and Dickinson, the image of 'nature poetry' has stayed traditionally white. This collection helps complete the picture, by including a people who were chained to a foreign land and yet sustained a love for it." Orion

Includes bibliographical references

Brown, Laura

How to write anything; a complete guide. Laura Brown. W W Norton & Co Inc 2014 608 p. illustrations (hardcover) $35   **808**
1. Writing   2. Rhetoric   3. Report writing   4. English language -- Rhetoric
ISBN 0393240142; 9780393240146

LC 2013045078

This book, by Laura Brown, is "a practical guide to everything you'll ever need to write—at work, at school, and in your personal life. With more than two hundred how-to entries and easy-to-use models organized into three comprehensive sections on work, school, and personal life, [it] covers a wide range of topics that make it an essential guide for the whole family." (Publisher's note)

"Comprehensive and accessible, the work guides users through just about any situation where the written word is necessary: social media for businesses, a plea to a professor for an extension, sympathy notes, wedding toasts, letters to the editor, and more." Booklist

Includes bibliographical references and index

★ The **Chicago** manual of style; by the University of Chicago Press Editorial Staff. Seventeenth edition University of Chicago Press 2017 xvi, 1144 p.p (cloth: alk. paper) $70 **808**
1. Printing -- Style manuals 2. Authorship -- Handbooks, manuals, etc. 3. Authorship -- Style manuals 4. Authorship -- Handbooks, manuals, etc 5. Publishers and publishing -- United States -- Handbooks, manuals, etc
ISBN 9780226287058

LC 2017020712

"This seventeenth edition of 'The Chicago Manual of Style' has been prepared with an eye toward how we find, create, and cite information that readers are as likely to access from their pockets as from a bookshelf. It offers updated guidelines on electronic workflows and publication formats, tools for PDF annotation and citation management, web accessibility standards, and effective use of metadata, abstracts, and keywords." (Publisher's note)

"As ever, this manual stands as an indispensable and thoughtfully constructed English language and style resource for those compelled, by enthusiasm or responsibility, to attend to the minutiae of written expression." Pub Wkly

Includes bibliographical references (pages [991]-1013) and index.

Children's writer's & illustrator's market; edited by Alice Pope. Writer's Digest Books il **808**
1. Publishers and publishing 2. Authorship -- Handbooks, manuals, etc.
Annual. First published 1998

This reference includes listings of children's book publishers, magazines, agents, art reps, contests, clubs, conferences, awards, and grants with contact information, along with articles and interviews on a variety of subjects relating to children's writing, illustrating, and publishing

Includes bibliographical references

Evans, Harold
Do I make myself clear? why writing well matters. Harold Evans. Little, Brown and Company 2017 vi, 408 p.p illustrations (hardcover) $27 **808**
1. Journalism -- Editing 2. English language -- Grammar 3. English language -- Usage 4. English language -- Rhetoric
ISBN 9780316432290; 9780316277174

LC 2016953762

In this book, Harold Evans "brings his indispensable insight to us all in his definite guide to writing well. . . . [He] provides practical examples of how editing and rewriting can make for better communication, even in the digital age. [The book] . . . is an essential text, and one that will provide every writer an editor at his shoulder." (Publisher's note)

"Rife with specifics, and balanced between narrative and information, Evans' book belongs in the hands of any interested party looking for truth and clarity in the words around us." Booklist

Includes bibliographical references (pages 391-404).

Fish, Stanley Eugene, 1938-
Winning arguments; what works and doesn't work in politics, the bedroom, the courtroom, and the classroom. Stanley Fish. Harper 2016 212 p. (hardback) $19.99 **808**
1. Rhetoric 2. Public speaking 3. Debates and debating 4. Persuasion (Rhetoric)
ISBN 9780062226686; 9780062226655; 9780062226679

LC 2015046681

This book by Stanley Fish "guides readers through the 'greatest hits' of rhetoric. In this clever and engaging guide, Fish offers insight and outlines the crucial keys you need to win any debate, anywhere, anytime--drawn from landmark legal cases, politics, his own career, and even popular film and television." (Publisher's note)

"Fish's shrewd work can help everyone better understand the power of effective communication in everyday life." Pub Wkly

Garner, Bryan A.
Garner's Modern English Usage; by Bryan Garner. Oxford University Press 2016 1120 p. $50 **808**
1. English language -- Grammar
ISBN 0190491485; 9780190491482

This reference book, by Bryan Garner, "reflects usage lexicography at its finest. Garner explains the nuances of grammar and vocabulary with thoroughness, finesse, and wit. He discourages whatever is slovenly, pretentious, or pedantic." (Publisher's note)

Garvey, Mark
Stylized; a slightly obsessive history of Strunk & White's The elements of style. Simon & Schuster 2009 xxv, 208p il **808**
1. Poets 2. Authors 3. Rhetoric 4. Humorists 5. Novelists 6. Essayists 7. Satirists 8. College teachers 9. Children's authors 10. Nonfiction writers 11. English language -- Style 12. Authorship -- Style manuals 13. English language -- Rhetoric 14. Authorship -- Handbooks, manuals, etc.
ISBN 1-4165-9092-7; 978-1-4165-9092-7

LC 2009007166

This is a history of the composition and publication of William Strunk and E.B. White's The Elements of Style, which appeared in 1959.

"A fan's meticulously researched, bighearted tribute to a sturdy, perennial writing guide, this history of Elements of Style is complete and unreservedly affectionate." Publ Wkly

Includes bibliographical references

Gerard, Sarah
Sunshine State; essays. by Sarah Gerard. HarperCollins 2017 384 p. $15.99 **808**
1. Florida 2. American essays
ISBN 006243487X; 9780062434876

LC 2017296465

This collection of essays, by Sarah Gerard, "explores Florida as a microcosm of the most pressing economic and environmental perils haunting our society. In the collection's title essay, Gerard volunteers at the Suncoast Seabird Sanctuary, a world renowned bird refuge. There she meets its founder, who once modeled with a pelican on his arm for a Dewar's Scotch campaign but has since declined into a pit of fraud and madness." (Publisher's note)

"An intimate journey reveals a Florida few visitors would ever discover." Kirkus

Gutkind, Lee
You can't make this stuff up; the complete guide to writ-

ing creative nonfiction--from memoir to literary journalism and everything in between. Lee Gutkind. Da Capo Press/Lifelong Books 2012 xviii, 270 p.p **808**

1. Authorship 2. Creative writing 3. Creative nonfiction -- Technique 4. Exposition (Rhetoric) 5. Creative nonfiction -- Authorship 6. Reportage literature -- Technique

ISBN 9780738215549; 9780738215860

LC 2012018586

This book, by Lee Gutkind, offers advice for writing creative nonfiction. "From rags-to-riches-to-rags tell-alls to personal health sagas to literary journalism, everyone seems to want to try their hand at creative nonfiction. . . . Gutkind describes and illustrates each and every aspect of the genre, from defining a concept and establishing a writing process to the final product." (Publisher's note)

Includes bibliographical references (p. 255-259) and index

Hemingway, Ernest, 1899-1961

The **Letters** of Ernest Hemingway 1929-1931; by Ernest Hemingway, edited by Sandra Spanier and Miriam B. Mandel. Cambridge University Press 2017 730 p. $45 **808**

ISBN 052189736X; 9780521897365

This book, edited by Sandra Spanier and Miriam B. Mandel, "records the establishment of Ernest Hemingway as an author of international renown following the publication of A Farewell to Arms. Breaking new artistic ground in 1930, Hemingway embarks upon his first and greatest non-fiction work, his treatise on bullfighting, Death in the Afternoon. Hemingway, now a professional writer, demonstrates a growing awareness of the literary marketplace, successfully negotiating with publishers and agents and responding to fan mail." (Publisher's note)

The **Hodges** Harbrace handbook; Cheryl Glenn & Loretta Gray. 19th edition Wadsworth Publishing Co 2017 819 p hardcover $99.95 **808**

1. English language -- Grammar 2. English language -- Composition and exercises

ISBN 9781337279512

First published 1941 under the authorship of John C. Hodges with title: Harbrace handbook of English. Frequently revised

A guide to the fundamentals of grammar, composition, and usage

Hooks, Bell

Remembered rapture; the writer at work. Holt & Co. 1999 237p hardcover o.p. pa $13 **808**

1. Authorship 2. American literature -- African American authors

ISBN 0-8050-5910-5 pa

LC 98-7998

"The redoubtable Hooks offers a series of essays on writing, focusing on women, black writers (e.g., why there are so many black women novelists and so few in nonfiction), and what it was like to move to writer-saturated New York." Libr J

Jacob, Dianne

Will write for food; the complete guide to writing cookbooks, blogs, memoir, recipes, and more. Dianne Jacob. 3rd edition Da Capo Lifelong 2015 353 p. pbk $16.99 **808**

1. Food writing

ISBN 9780738218052; 0738218057

LC 2015003915

"The author "provides detailed, practical advice on such matters as recipe development; how to launch a blog and draw readers, pitch article and book ideas, and refine one's prose style; and where to go to network or study. Also included are writing exercises, extensive suggestions for

further reading, lists of publications and websites that accept freelancers, and perspectives drawn from interviews with dozens of well-known food writers such as Mark Bittman, Deborah Madison, and Calvin Trillin. . . . An engaging, informative handbook for hobbyists and aspiring professionals." Libr J (review of 2nd edition)

Includes bibliographical references and index

Lamott, Anne

Bird by bird; some instructions on writing and life. Pantheon Bks. 1994 xxxi, 239p $23; pa. $16 **808**

1. Authorship

ISBN 0-679-43520-4; 9780385480017

LC 94-5448

In this discussion of the craft of writing Lamott offers "examples and anecdotes that explain how she copes with self-doubt, writer's block, professional jealousy, and the discipline necessary to turn thoughts into words on a page. Her work is an honest appraisal of what it takes to be a writer and why it matters so much." Libr J

★ **MLA** Handbook; Association of America, Modern Language. 8th edition The Modern Language Association of America 2016 146 p. (pbk.: alk. paper) $15 **808**

1. Report writing 2. Research -- Methodology 3. Research -- Handbooks, manuals, etc 4. Report writing -- Handbooks, manuals, etc

ISBN 1603292624; 9781603292627

LC 2015040898

This book, by The Modern Language Association of America, "takes a fresh look at documenting sources. . . . Shorter and redesigned for easy use, the eighth edition of the MLA Handbook guides writers through the principles behind evaluating sources for their research. It then shows them how to cite sources in their writing and create useful entries for the works-cited list." (Publisher's note)

"A much more user-friendly book than previous versions, the new guide is very visually oriented and easier to use. It breaks down the pieces of a citation and shows readers where to find the publisher, author, and other necessary information for a work cited or a citation." VOYA

Includes bibliographical references and index

The **New** York times manual of style and usage; Allan M. Siegal and William G. Connolly; revised and updated by Philip B. Corbett, Jill Taylor, Patrick LaForge and Susan Wessling. 5th edition Three Rivers Press 2015 350 p $18 **808**

1. Authorship -- Handbooks, manuals, etc.

ISBN 9781101905449

First published 1962 by McGraw-Hill under the editorship of Lewis Jordan with title: Style book for writers and editors

Rules and guidelines observed by The New York Times for consistency of spelling, capitalization, punctuation, abbreviation, and preferred usage

This work "contends with the AP stylebook in authority and usefulness." Columbia J Rev

Orr, Gregory

A **primer** for poets and readers of poetry; Gregory Orr. W W Norton & Co Inc 2017 325 p. (paperback) $15.95 **808**

1. Poetics 2. Poetry -- Authorship 3. Authorship -- Handbooks, manuals, etc.

ISBN 0393253929; 9780393253924; 9780393253931

This book, by Gregory Orr, "guides young poets toward a deeper understanding of how poetry can function in their lives, while also introducing the art in an exciting new way. Structuring the presentation from life toward art, Orr urges poets to 'turn worlds into words' and then give those words a dramatic structure." (Publisher's note)

Pinker, Steven, 1954-

The **sense** of style; the thinking person's guide to writing in the 21st century. Steven Pinker. Viking Adult 2014 368 p. illustrations (hardback) $27.95   **808**

    1. Authorship   2. English language -- Grammar   3. English language -- Style

ISBN 0670025852; 9780670025855

                     LC 2014004509

In this writing guidebook, author Steven Pinker "shows how writing depends on imagination, empathy, coherence, grammatical knowhow, and an ability to savor and reverse engineer the good prose of others. He replaces dogma about usage with reason and evidence, allowing writers and editors to apply the guidelines judiciously, rather than robotically, being mindful of what they are designed to accomplish." (Publisher's note)

"A thoughtful addition for writing instruction collections; the chapter on "The Curse of Knowledge" should be mandatory reading for everyone." LJ

Includes bibliographical references and index

Plotnik, Arthur

Spunk & bite; a writer's guide to punchier, more engaging language & style. Random House 2005 263p hardcover o.p. pa $12.95   **808**

    1. Rhetoric

ISBN 0-375-72115-0; 0-375-72227-0 pa

                     LC 2005-44934

The author "demonstrates how . . . unexpected humor, loquaciousness, and apt description can jolt a writer into engaged authorship. This primer is dotted with illustrative examples that range from Shakespeare and J.K. Rowling to Dave Barry and Maeve Binchy. . . . This is an entertaining and engaging choice for writers." Libr J

Pollack, John

Shortcut; how analogies reveal connections, spark innovation, and sell our greatest ideas. John Pollack. Gotham 2014 256 p. (hardback) $27   **808**

    1. Analogy   2. Language and languages   3. Sociolinguistics   4. Creative thinking   5. Business communication   6. English language -- Business English

ISBN 1592408494; 9781592408498

                     LC 2014009895

Author John Pollack examines why "analogies are far more complex than their SAT stereotype and lie at the very core of human cognition and creativity. [Through] engaging stories, surprising examples, and a practical method to evaluate the truth or effectiveness of any analogy, 'Shortcut' will improve critical thinking, enhance creativity, and offer readers a fresh approach to resolving some of today's most intractable challenges." (Publisher's note)

"Perhaps not all readers will be fully persuaded to the impact of analogies but most, especially those with an interest in language and psychology, will come away entertained and informed." LJ

Prose, Francine

★ **Reading** like a writer; a guide for people who love books and for those who want to write them. HarperCollins Publishers 2006 273p   **808**

    1. Rhetoric   2. Creative writing   3. Books and reading   4. English language -- Rhetoric

ISBN 0-06-077704-4; 0-06-077705-2 pa; 978-0-06-077704-3;

978-0-06-077705-0 pa

                     LC 2005-58457

The author argues that "would-be writers should turn to the classics for inspiration." (N Y Times Book Rev)

This book "should be greatly appreciated in and out of the classroom. Like the great works of fiction, it's a wise and voluble companion." N Y Times Book Rev

Rabiner, Susan

Thinking like your editor; how to write serious nonfiction--and get it published. by Susan Rabiner and Alfred Fortunato. Norton 2002 284p $26.95; pa $14   **808**

    1. Authorship

ISBN 0-393-03892-0; 0-393-32461-3 pa

                     LC 2001-44551

"In part one, on submissions, the authors discuss how to put together a book proposal and, . . . whether to work through an agent or go solo. In part two, they move to the writing process. . . . Part three discusses how authors and editors (both in-house and freelance) can work together well." Publ Wkly

Strunk, William

★ The **elements** of style; with revisions, an introduction, and a chapter on writing by E.B. White. 4th ed; Allyn & Bacon 1999 105p $14.95; pa $7.95   **808**

    1. Rhetoric

ISBN 0-205-31342-6; 0-205-30902-X pa

                     LC 99-16419

First privately printed in 1918

This work provides guidelines for proper usage and composition. Misused expressions and commonly misspelled words are discussed. Includes examples.

This work is "prescriptive, conservative, and humorous; in sum, it is the best book available on how to write English prose." Nichols. Guide to Ref Books for Sch Media Cent. 4th edition

Student's guide to writing college papers; 5th edition University of Chicago Press 2019 320 p $17   **808**

    1. Dissertations   2. Report writing

ISBN 9780226430263

First published 1963 with title: Student's guide for writing college papers

This guide covers selecting a topic, collecting material, planning and writing the paper, and preparing footnotes and bibliographies.

United States/Government Printing Office

★ **Style** manual; an official guide to the form and style of Federal Government printing 2008. U.S. Government Printing Office. [30th ed.]; U.S. G.P.O. 2008 453p pa $36   **808**

    1. Printing -- Style manuals   2. Authorship -- Handbooks, manuals, etc.   3. Publishers and publishing -- Handbooks, manuals, etc.

ISBN 978-0-16-081812-7

                     LC 2009-376600

First published 1908 with title: Manual of style. Frequently revised

"A useful and extensive manual giving the practices of the Government Printing Office on copy preparation, with rules for capitalization, punctuation, abbreviations, etc., and information on foreign languages, including alphabets, with pronunciation, special rules, lists of numbers, etc." Guide to Ref Books. 11th edition

Writer's Market; edited by Robert Lee Brewer. Writer's Digest various pagings   **808**
1. Publishers and publishing 2. Authorship -- Handbooks, manuals, etc.
Annual. First published 1922
"A guide for freelance writers, covering the practical side of writing for publication, including information about book publishers; consumer magazines; trade, technical and a few professional journals; scriptwriting; syndicates; greeting card and gift markets. Provides extensive lists of contests and awards and of relevant organizations and publications. Subject index of book publishers." Guide to Ref Books. 11th edition
Includes bibliographical references

808.02   Authorship techniques, plagiarism, editorial techniques

Block, Francesca Lia
The **thorn** necklace; healing through writing and the creative process. Francesca Lia Block; foreword by Grant Faulkner. Seal Press 2018 304 p. (hardback) $26   **808.02**
1. Authorship 2. Creative writing 3. Self-help techniques 4. Authorship -- Technique 5. Creation (Literary, artistic, etc.)
ISBN 9781580057516

LC 2017043732
In this book, author Francesca Lia Block "offers an intimate glimpse of an artist at work and a detailed guide to help readers channel their own experiences and creative energy. Sharing visceral insights and powerful exercises, she gently guides us down the write-to-heal path, revealing at each turn the intrinsic value of channeling our experiences onto the page." (Publisher's note)
"With every tip, Block provides examples from classic literature and exercises for writers, such as making characters' mood boards, keeping updated lists of current obsessions, and writing scenes of backstory that may never appear in the final product. Wise and inspiring, this is a must-read for artists of all stripes." Booklist

D'Agata, John
The **lifespan** of a fact; John D'Agata and Jim Fingal. W. W. Norton 2012 160p.   **808.02**
1. E-mail 2. Journalists 3. Essay -- Authorship 4. Creative nonfiction -- Authorship
ISBN 9780393340730

LC 2011042637
In this book, "an essayist ([John] D'Agata) and his exasperated fact checker ([Jim] Fingal) debate the line between art and reality. . . . The text reproduces D'Agata's article about a teenager who leapt to his death from a Las Vegas Hotel, . . . Fingal's . . . fact-checking commentary, . . . and the authors' barbed e-exchanges on everything from the number of strip clubs in Vegas to the origins of tae kwon do and the existence of D'ata's mother's cat. . . . D'Agata cheerfully admits to embroidering the story with factoids; meanwhile, Fingal's efforts to verify them . . . required seven years and the help of medical journals, academic linguists, satellite photos, and field research." (Publishers Weekly)
Includes bibliographical references.

Favilla, Emmy J.
A **world** without "whom" the essential guide to language in the Buzzfeed age. Emmy J. Favilla, BuzzFeed Copy Chief. Bloomsbury USA 2017 vii, 392 p.p illustrations (hardcover: acid-free paper) $26   **808.02**
1. Authorship 2. English language 3. Authorship -- Style manuals

4. English language -- Style -- Handbooks, manuals, etc
ISBN 9781632867599; 9781632867575

LC 2017018955
This book, by Emmy J. Favilla, features "priceless emoji strings, sidebars, quizzes, and style debates among the most lovable word nerds in the digital media world. . . . [The book] is essential for readers and writers of virtually everything: news articles, blog posts, tweets, texts, emails, and whatever comes next . . . so basically everyone." (Publisher's note)
"Favilla's style is light and breezy, which only makes it easier to absorb the serious import of her advice. This is the rare style manual that is as entertaining as it is instructive." Pub Wkly
Includes bibliographical references (pages 371-382) and index.

Friedman, Jane
The **business** of being a writer; Jane Friedman. University of Chicago Press 2018 368 p. (pbk.: alk. paper) $25   **808.02**
1. Authorship 2. Authors and publishers 3. Literary agents 4. Authorship -- Economic aspects
ISBN 9780226393025; 9780226393162

LC 2017038268
This book, by Jane Friedman, "offers the business education writers need but so rarely receive. It is meant for early-career writers looking to develop a realistic set of expectations about making money from their work or for working writers who want a better understanding of the industry. Writers will gain a comprehensive picture of how the publishing world works . . . and will learn how they can best position themselves for success over the long term." (Publisher's note)
Includes bibliographical references and index

Kidder, Tracy
Good prose; the art of nonfiction. Tracy Kidder and Richard Todd. Random House 2013 224 p. (acid-free paper) $26   **808.02**
1. Writing 2. Biography 3. Friendship 4. Authorship 5. Prose literature -- Authorship 6. Creative nonfiction -- Authorship
ISBN 1400069750; 9780679604723; 9781400069750

LC 2012021165
Author Tracy Kidder "explores three major nonfiction forms: narratives, essays, and memoirs." She looks at "the works of a wide range of writers, novelists as well as nonfiction writers, for models and instruction." Kidder writes "about narrative strategies (and about how to find a story, sometimes in surprising places), about the ethical challenges of nonfiction, and about the realities of making a living as a writer." (Publisher's book)
Includes bibliographical references and index.

Malcolm, Janet
Forty-one false starts; essays on artists and writers. Janet Malcolm. Farrar Straus & Giroux 2013 320 p. (hardcover: alk. paper) $27   **808.02**
1. Artists 2. Authors 3. Authorship
ISBN 0374157693; 9780374157692

LC 2012034570
National Book Critics Circle Award Finalist: Criticism (2013)
This book by Janet Malcolm "brings together essays . . . that reflect her preoccupation with artists and their work. Her subjects are painters, photographers, writers, and critics. She explores Bloomsbury's obsessive desire to create things visual and literary; the 'passionate collaborations' behind Edward Weston's nudes; and the character of the German art photographer Thomas Struth, who is 'haunted by the Nazi past,' yet whose photographs have 'a lightness of spirit.'" (Publisher's note)
Includes bibliographical references

McCann, Colum, 1965-

Letters to a young writer; some practical and philosophical advice. Colum McCann. Random House Inc 2017 xix, 166 p.p illustrations (hardback) $25 **808.02**

    1. Authorship 2. Creative writing

    ISBN 9780399590818; 9780399590801

                                     LC 2016055256

    In this book, author Colum McCann "asks his readers to constantly push the boundaries of experience, to see empathy and wonder in the stories we craft and hear. . . . It charges aspiring writers to learn the rules and even break them. These fifty-two essays are ultimately a profound challenge to a new generation to bring truth and light to a dark world through their art." (Publisher's note)

    "Pithy, wise, and gently encouraging advice from an acclaimed fiction writer." Kirkus

McPhee, John, 1931-

Draft no. 4; on the writing process. John McPhee. Farrar, Straus & Giroux 2017 192 p. illustrations, maps (hardcover) $26 **808.02**

    1. Writing 2. Creation (Literary, artistic, etc.) 3. English language -- Composition and exercises 4. Authorship 5. English language -- Rhetoric

    ISBN 9780374712396; 0374142742; 9780374142742

                                       LC 2016059416

    In this book author "John McPhee shares insights he has gathered over his career and has refined while teaching at Princeton University, where he has nurtured some of the most esteemed writers of recent decades. McPhee offers definitive guidance in the decisions regarding arrangement, diction, and tone that shape nonfiction pieces, and he presents extracts from his work, subjecting them to wry scrutiny." (Publisher's note)

    "The renowned writer offers advice on information-gathering and nonfiction composition.The book consists of eight instructive and charming essays about creating narratives, all of them originally composed for the New Yorker . . . ." Kirkus

Morton, Danelle

Finishing School; The Happy Ending to That Writing Project You Can't Seem to Get Done. Cary Tennis and Danelle Morton. Penguin Group USA 2017 272 p. (ebook) $48; $16.00 **808.02**

    1. Authorship 2. Creative writing

    ISBN 9780399184710; 0399184708; 9780399184703

    "Millions of writing projects—begun with hope and a little bit of hubris—lie abandoned in desk drawers, in dated files on computer desktops, and in the far reaches of the mind. Too often, writers get tangled in self-abuse—their self-doubt, shame, yearning for perfection, and even arrogance get in the way. In . . . [this book, authors] Cary Tennis and Danelle Morton help writers overcome these emotional blocks and break down daunting projects into manageable pieces." (Publisher's note)

    "This book insightfully pinpoints the importance of time budgeting and management, and of setting reasonable expectations for completion." Pub Wkly

Scalzi, John

   ★ **Don't** live for your obituary; advice, commentary and personal observations on writing, 2008-2017. John Scalzi. Subterranean Press 2017 469 p. $40 **808.02**

    1. Authorship 2. Writing

    ISBN 1596068582; 9781596068582

    This book, by John Scalzi, "is a curated selection of that decade of advice, commentary and observations on the writing life, from one of the best-known science fiction authors working today. But more than that, it's a portrait of an era—ten years of drama, controversy and change in writing, speculative fiction and the world in general—from someone who was there when it happened and who had opinions about it all." (Publisher's note)

    Above all [Scalzi] writes accessibly and so commonsensically that this book should appeal to writers in all disciplines, and even to SF readers who have no ambitions to write themselves. --Publishers Weekly (October 2017)

Scratch; writers, money, and the art of making a living. edited by Manjula Martin. Simon & Schuster 2017 xv, 287 p.p (paperback) $16 **808.02**

    1. Authorship 2. Self-realization 3. Authors and publishers 4. Authorship -- Marketing 5. Arts -- Economic aspects 6. Work -- Psychological aspects 7. Authorship -- Vocational guidance 8. Authors, American -- 21st century -- Biography -- Anecdotes

    ISBN 9781501134593; 9781501134579

                                        LC 2016024580

    This book, edited by Manjula Martin, is a "collection of essays from today's most acclaimed authors--from Cheryl Strayed to Roxane Gay to Jennifer Weiner, Alexander Chee, Nick Hornby, and Jonathan Franzen--on the realities of making a living in the writing world. . . . [It] honestly addresses the tensions between writing and money, work and life, literature and commerce." (Publisher's note)

    "Martin's collection removes the romantic veil surrounding the production of the written word and provides some solid counseling for aspirants on what it means to offer the labors of their heart for sale in the marketplace." Pub Wkly

Shapiro, Susan

   The **byline** bible; get published in five weeks. Susan Shapiro, with foreword by Peter Catapano. Writer's Digest Books 2018 272 p. $19.99 **808.02**

    1. Authorship 2. Journalism 3. Creative nonfiction

    ISBN 1440353689; 9781440353680

    In this book author Susan Shapiro "walks you through every stage of crafting and selling short nonfiction pieces. She shows you how to spot trendy subjects, where to start, finish and edit, and divulges specific steps to submit work, have it accepted, get paid, and see your byline in your favorite publication in lightning speed. . . . This book offers everything you need to learn to write and sell your story in five weeks" (Publisher's note)

Smith, Rebecca

   The **Jane** Austen Writers' Club; inspiration and advice from the world's best-loved novelist. Rebecca Smith; illustrations by Sarah J Coleman. Bloomsbury 2016 xii, 336 p.p illustrations, map (hardcover) $27 **808.02**

    1. Authorship 2. Romance fiction -- History and criticism 3. Creative writing 4. Fiction -- Technique

    ISBN 9781408866061; 1632865882; 9781632865885

    This book, by Rebecca Smith, illustrated by Sarah J Coleman, offers a "look at the methods and devices used by the world's most beloved novelist. [Jane] Austen was a creator of immortal characters and a pioneer in her use of language and point of view; her advice continues to be relevant two centuries after her death." (Publisher's note)

    "A worthy companion for writers and readers that entertains and enlightens." Kirkus

    Includes bibliographical references (pages 325-328) and index.

Upstairs at the Strand; writers in conversation at the legendary bookstore. edited by Jessica Strand and Andrea Aguilar. W W Norton & Co Inc 2016 xi, 208 p.p (paperback) $15.95   **808.02**

1. Authorship 2. American authors 3. Creation (Literary, artistic, etc.)

ISBN 9780393352085; 9780393352092; 0393352080

LC 2015051054

This book, edited by Jessica Strand and Andrea Aguilar, features "freewheeling and behind-the-scenes conversations between renowned novelists, playwrights, and poets on how they work, think, and live, . . . [and] captures the happy collision of books and ideas in the Strand's famed reading series in its Rare Book Room." (Publisher's note)

"An array of authors edifies their fans at the home of the flourishing last survivor of Gotham's grand old Book Row." Kirkus

808.06   Rhetoric of specific kinds of writing

Aiken, Joan

The **way** to write for children. St. Martin's Griffin 1999 97p pa $9.95   **808.06**

1. Authorship 2. Children's literature -- Technique

ISBN 0-312-20048-X

LC 99-166931

First published 1982 in the United Kingdom

"In this crisp, informative and often witty survey of 'the market' Aiken is also giving the customers—teachers, librarians, parents, every one concerned with children's literature of quality-a good general idea of what is available already and of what authors are trying to do." Times Lit Suppl

Gastel, Barbara

How to write and publish a scientific paper; Barbara Gastel and Robert A. Day. Eighth edition Greenwood Press 2016 xxi, 326 p.p $35   **808.06**

1. Dissertations 2. Technical writing

ISBN 0313330271; 0313330409; 1440842809; 9780313330278; 9781440842801

LC 2015045511

Written by Barbara Gastel and Robert A. Day, "now thoroughly updated and expanded, this new edition of a classic guide offers practical advice on preparing and publishing journal articles as well as succeeding in other communication-related aspects of a scientific career." The book "Provides practical, easy-to-read, and immediately applicable guidance on preparing each part of a scientific paper." (Publisher's note)

"This highly engaging and informative work will be an excellent addition to libraries that support graduate programs in the STEM fields." Choice.

Includes bibliographical references (pages 303-309) and index.

Kephart, Beth

Handling the truth; on the writing of memoir. Beth Kephart. Gotham Books 2013 224 p. $16   **808.06**

1. Biography 2. Autobiography -- Authorship 3. Biography as a literary form

ISBN 159240815X; 9781592408153

LC 2012043517

In author Beth Kephart's book, "she thinks out loud about the form--on how it gets made, on what it means to make it, on the searing language of truth, on the thin line between remembering and imagining, and, finally, on the rights of memoirists. Drawing on proven writing

lessons and classic examples, on the work of her students and on her own memories of weather, landscape, color, and love, Kephart probes the wrenching and essential questions that lie at the heart of memoir." (Publisher's note)

Klein, Cheryl B.

★ The **magic** words; writing great books for children and young adults. Cheryl B. Klein. W W Norton & Co Inc 2016 xv, 368 p.p (pbk.) $18.95   **808.06**

1. Creative writing 2. Children's literature -- Authorship 3. Young adult fiction -- Authorship

ISBN 9780393292244; 039329224X; 9780393292251

LC 2016014423

In this book, "editor Cheryl B. Klein guides writers on an enjoyable and practical-minded voyage of their own, from developing a saleable premise for a novel to finding a dream agent. She delves deep into the major elements of fiction--intention, character, plot, and voice--while addressing important topics like diversity, world-building, and the differences between middle-grade and YA novels." (Publisher's note)

"Discursive analysis is complemented by exercises that frequently challenge readers to analyze how they introduce characters or to rewrite a dramatized scene as a narrated one." Kirkus

Includes bibliographical references (pages 347-351) and index.

Seuling, Barbara

How to write a children's book and get it published; 3rd ed; Wiley 2005 233p il pa $15.95   **808.06**

1. Authorship 2. Children's literature -- Technique

ISBN 0-471-67619-5

LC 2004-4691

First published 1984

Presents "five essential steps (from researching the current marketplace to submitting your manuscript) to publishing works for children." Libr J

Includes bibliographical references

Shulevitz, Uri

Writing with pictures; how to write and illustrate children's books. Watson-Guptill 1985 271p il hardcover o.p. pa $29.95   **808.06**

1. Picture books for children 2. Children's literature -- Technique

ISBN 0-8230-5935-9 pa

LC 85-15604

"With heavy emphasis on illustration, this detailed book guides aspiring authors/illustrators through telling the story and drawing the pictures to preparing artwork for the printer." Libr J

Includes bibliographical references

Turabian, Kate L.

★ A **manual** for writers of research papers, theses, and dissertations; Chicago Style for students and researchers. Kate L. Turabian; revised by Wayne C. Booth, Gregory G. Colomb, Joseph M. Williams, Joseph Bizup, William T. Fitzgerald, and the University of Chicago Press editorial staff. 9th edition University of Chicago Press 2018 462 p   **808.06**

1. Dissertations 2. Report writing 3. Academic writing -- Handbooks, manuals, etc 4. Dissertations, Academic -- Handbooks, manuals, etc

ISBN 9780226430577; 9780226494425

"This new edition filters decades of expertise into modern standards. While previous editions incorporated digital forms of research and writing, this edition goes even further to build information literacy, recognizing that most students will be doing their work largely or entirely online and on screens. Chapters include updated advice on finding, evaluating, and citing a wide range of digital sources and also recognize the evolving use of software for citation management, graphics, and paper format and submission." (Publisher's note)

808.1 Rhetoric in specific literary forms

Abrams, M. H. (Meyer Howard), 1912-2015

The **fourth** dimension of a poem; and other essays. M.H. Abrams; foreword by Harold Bloom. W. W. Norton & Company 2012 240 p. (hardcover) $25.95   **808.1**

1. Poetics 2. American essays 3. Poetry -- History and criticism

ISBN 0393058301; 9780393058307

LC 2012020169

This book by M. H. Abrams presents "a collection of nine new and recent essays that challenge the reader to think about poetry in new ways. In these essays . . . Abrams engages . . . with pivotal figures in intellectual and literary history, among them Kant, Keats, and Hazlitt. The centerpiece of the volume is Abrams's . . . essay 'The Fourth Dimension of a Poem' on the pleasure of reading poems aloud." (Publisher's note)

Includes bibliographical references and index.

Deutsch, Babette

Poetry handbook: a dictionary of terms; 4th ed; HarperResource 2002 203p pa $14   **808.1**

1. Reference books 2. Poetry -- Terminology 3. Poetics -- Dictionaries

ISBN 0-06-463548-1

First published 1957 by Funk & Wagnalls

"The craft of verse described in dictionary form. Terms and techniques are defined and illustrated." N Y Public Libr. Ref Books for Child Collect. 2d edition

Foster, Thomas C.

How to read poetry like a professor; a quippy and sonorous guide to verse. Thomas C. Foster. HarperCollins 2018 224 p. $15.99   **808.1**

1. Poetry -- History and criticism 2. Literature -- History and criticism

ISBN 006211378X; 9780062113788

This book, by Thomas C. Foster, "examines a wide array of poems and teaches readers: How to read a poem to understand its primary meaning. The different technical elements of poetry . . . and how to learn to see these elements as allies rather than adversaries. How to listen for a poem's secondary meaning by paying attention to the echoes that the language of poetry summons up. How to hear the music in poems--and the poetry in songs!" (Publisher's note)

Higginson, William J.

The **haiku** handbook; how to write, teach, and appreciate haiku. [by] William J. Higginson and Penny Harter; foreword by Jane Reichhold. 25th anniversary ed.; Kodansha International 2009 331p pa $18   **808.1**

1. Haiku

ISBN 978-4-770-03113-6; 4-770-03113-0

LC 2009-36628

First published 1985 by McGraw-Hill

This book "presents haiku poets writing in English, Spanish, French, German, and five other languages on an equal footing with Japanese poets. Not only are the four great Japanese masters of the haiku represented (Bashō, Buson, Issa, and Shiki) but also several major Western authors not commonly known to have written haiku. The book presents a . . . history of the Japanese haiku, including the dynamic changes throughout the twentieth century as the haiku has been adapted to suburban and industrial settings. Full chapters are offered on form, the seasons in haiku, and haiku craft, plus background on the Japanese poetic tradition, and the effect of translation on our understanding of haiku." Publisher's note

Includes bibliographical references

Hirsch, Edward, 1950-

A **Poet's** Glossary; by Edward Hirsch. Houghton Mifflin Harcourt 2014 736 p. $30   **808.1**

1. Poetry -- History and criticism 2. Poetics 3. Poetry -- Glossaries, vocabularies, etc

ISBN 0151011958; 9780151011957

LC 2014011675

In this book, author Edward Hirsch "has delved deeply into the poetic traditions of the world, returning with an inclusive, international compendium. Moving . . . from the bards of ancient Greece to the revolutionaries of Latin America, from small formal elements to large mysteries, he provides thoughtful definitions for the most important poetic vocabulary, imbuing his work with a lifetime of scholarship and the warmth of a man devoted to his art." (Publisher's note)

"Offering definitions, a discussion of poetic techniques, and an unalloyed spiritual quality to his work, Hirsch's . . . alphabetically arranged glossary includes historical explanations, quotes, interpretative material, usage in various languages, and references to additional terms for even more clarification." LJ

Hirshfield, Jane, 1953-

Ten windows; how great poems transform the world. Jane Hirshfield. Alfred A. Knopf 2015 320 p. illustrations (hardcover) $24.95   **808.1**

1. Books and reading 2. Poetry -- History and criticism

ISBN 0385351054; 9780385351058

LC 2014025430

This book, by Jane Hirshfield, is a "collection of essays on how the best poems work. . . . Closely reading poems by Dickinson, Bashō, Szymborska, Cavafy, Heaney, Bishop, and Komunyakaa, among many others, Hirshfield reveals how poetry's world-making takes place: word by charged word." (Publisher's note)

"Hirshfield writes brilliantly of paradox in poetry, of what poets and stand-up comics have in common, and how poetry "counters isolation and meaninglessness." The profound pleasure Hirshfield takes in delineating poetry's efficacy makes for a beautifully enlightening volume." Booklist

Kooser, Ted

★ The **poetry** home repair manual; practical advice for beginning poets. University of Nebraska Press 2005 163p $19.95; pa $13.95   **808.1**

1. Poetics

ISBN 0-8032-2769-8; 0-8032-5978-6 pa

LC 2004-24700

"Among the many books offering advice on writing poetry, . . . [this book] stands out for its usefulness and, at the same time, for its inspiring view of the purposes of poetry." Midwest Quarterly

Includes bibliographical references

Oliver, Mary

A **poetry** handbook. Harcourt Brace & Co. 1994 130p pa $13   **808.1**

1. Poetics
ISBN 0-15-672400-6

LC 93-49676

A "handbook for young poets on the formal aspects and structure of poetry. Oliver excels at explaining the sound and sense of poetry—from scansion to imagery, diction to voice. She stresses the importance of reading poetry, since, in order to write well, 'it is entirely necessary to read widely and deeply.' Sage advice is given in an entire chapter dedicated to revision, wherein Oliver urges poets to consider their first draft 'an unfinished piece of work' that can be polished and improved later. Written in a pleasant and lucid style, this book is a wonderful resource." Libr J

Orr, David

You, Too, Could Write a Poem; selected reviews and essays, 2000-2015. David Orr. Penguin Group USA 2017 400 p. $18; (ebook) $54
808.1
1. Poetry 2. Poetics 3. American essays
ISBN 0143128191; 9780143128199; 9780698403338

LC 2016040779

In this collection of reviews and essays by David Orr, "Orr is at his rigorous, conversational, and edifying best. Whether he is considering the careers of contemporary masters, . . . sizing up younger American poets, . . . or even turning his attention to celebrities and public figures . . . when they choose to wade into the hotly contested waters of the poetry world, Orr is never any less than fully persuasive in arguing what makes a poem or poet great—or not." (Publisher's note)

"All poetry collections should have a copy, and every librarian should be ready to put this charming volume in the hands of readers." LJ

Pinsky, Robert, 1940-

Singing School; Learning to Write (And Read) Poetry by Studying With the Masters. Robert Pinsky. W W Norton & Co Inc. 2013 160 p. $25.95
808.1
1. Poets 2. Poetry 3. Authorship 4. Poetics
ISBN 0393050688; 9780393050684

LC 2013022146

In this book, poet Robert Pinsky "focuses on how poets read poetry in order to learn how to write poetry, taking his instructive title from William Butler Yeats: 'Nor is there singing school but studying / Monuments of its own magnificence.' Pinsky has selected a . . . variety of salient poems and organized them into sections titled 'Freedom,' 'Listening,' 'Form,' and 'Dreaming Things Up.' He introduces each of the 80 selections with an illuminating bit of analysis." (Booklist)

Includes bibliographical references and index

★ **Poet's** market 2019. Writer's Digest Bks. 2018 475p **808.1**
1. Poetry -- Marketing
Annual. First published 1989

"Useful for those aspiring to publish their poems in literary journals and magazines. . . . Entries include a brief journal profile, submission requirements, and contact information. Offers advice to beginning poets on getting published, brief articles by working poets/editors, grant information, contests and awards, poetry readings, writing colonies, organizations and publications useful to poets. Indexes for chapbook publishers, publishers by subject, publishers by state, and a general index." Guide to Ref Books. 11th edition

Includes bibliographical references

The **Princeton** encyclopedia of poetry and poetics; Roland Greene, editor in chief; Stephen Cushman, general editor; Clare Cavanagh, Jahan Ramazani, Paul Rouzer, associate editors; Harris Feinsod, David Marno, Alexandra Slessarev,

assistant editors. 4th edition Princeton University Press 2012 xxxvi, 1639 p.p
808.1
1. Poetry -- Dictionaries 2. Poetics -- Dictionaries 3. Poetry -- History and criticism
ISBN 9780691133348; 9780691154916

LC 2012005602

"The go-to resource for students doing research on poetry technique and terminology, the fourth edition of The Princeton Encyclopedia of Poetry & Poetics features many new and valuable updates from the third edition, in 1993. This edition includes 250 new entries on topics such as Cognitive poetics, Fireside poets, Fractal verse, Gay poetry, Poetry of the indigenous Americas, and Poetry slam. Readers will also find expanded coverage of international poetry (characteristics of, not specific works or poets), with new entries on the poetry of China, Chile, Colombia, and Mexico." (Booklist)

Includes bibliographical references and index

808.2 Rhetoric of drama

Davis, Jeffrey

Now that's funny! the art and craft of writing comedy. Peter Desberg and Jeffrey Davis. Square One Publishers 2017 viii, 376 p.p (pbk.) $17.95
808.2
1. Comedy films 2. Comedy television programs 3. Screenwriters -- Interviews 4. Comedy films -- Authorship 5. Television comedies -- Authorship 6. Screenwriters -- United States -- Interviews 7. Television comedy writers -- United States -- Interviews
ISBN 9780757004452

LC 2016055985

In this book, authors Peter Desberg and Jeffrey Davis "provide an intimate look into the minds of twenty-four of Hollywood's funniest comedy writers, who have given us such shows as: 'Saturday Night Live,' 'Monk,' and 'Everybody Loves Raymond.' . . . How do you get to see the creative wheels turn? The authors' premise was simple: Using a Q and A format, they provided each writer with a story idea and let them run with it." (Publisher's note)

"The unique approach, combined with the in-depth interviews, makes this a solid go-to for aspiring comedy writers." Booklist

Field, Syd

★ **Screenplay**; the foundations of screenwriting. Rev. ed.; Delta Trade Paperbacks 2005 320p il pa $16
808.2
1. Motion picture plays -- Technique
ISBN 0-385-33903-8

LC 2005-48491

First published 1979

This book covers the basics of writing a screenplay, including how to build a character, set up a scene, and what to do after the screenplay is written.

Hauge, Michael

Writing screenplays that sell. HarperReference 2011 349p pa $21
808.2
1. Screenplays 2. Television scripts 3. Motion picture plays -- Technique
ISBN 9780061791437

LC 91-55005

First published 1988 by McGraw-Hill

"From renowned Hollywood story consultant Michael Hauge, considered "one of the most sought after lecturers and script consultants in the U.S." by Scriptwriter magazine, comes the ultimate concept-to-deal guide for writing and selling screenplays for movies and television—now fully revised and updated for the modern screenwriter in this all new 20th anniversary edition." (Publisher's note)

This book provides a "discussion of the craft—characters, story development, etc.—and industry; lays out the all-important details of format; then tells how to market the finished product. Hauge's volume is a detailed manual offering a step-by-step methodology, a scriptual analysis of a hit film, 'The Karate Kid,' and handy chapter summaries." Libr J

Includes bibliographical references

Inside the room; writing TV with the pros at UCLA Extension Writers' Program. edited by Linda Venis, Director, UCLA Extension Department of the Arts and Writers' Program. Gotham Books 2013 272 p. **808.2**
1. Television authorship 2. Television broadcasting 3. Television authorship -- Vocational guidance
ISBN 9781592408115

LC 2013004221

In this book, edited by Linda Venis, "accomplished writers from the . . . UCLA Extension Writers' Program provide a . . . how-to book for aspiring television writers. . . . Television writers . . . take aspiring writers through the process of writing their first spec script . . . and revising their scripts to meet pro standards. They also learn how to launch and sustain a writing career and get a rare look inside the process of creating, selling, and getting a TV show made." (Publisher's note)

"A practical guide to how TV is made, from bright idea to syndication. A raft of instructors from the UCLA Extension Writers' Program (including director Venis) and a pool of professional TV writers whose credits include such series as Mad Men, Frasier and The Simpsons guide aspiring TV writers through the process of joining the ranks of small-screen scribes, from drafting a first script to thriving in a writers' room to pitching an original series. The advice is clear and specific...An engaging and helpful how-to for hopeful TV writers or anyone interested in the nuts and bolts of this ephemeral art."

Now write! screenwriting; exercises by today's best writers and teachers. [by] Sherry Ellis with Laurie Lamson. Jeremy P. Tarcher/Penguin 2011 343p il pa $14.95 **808.2**
1. Motion picture plays -- Technique
ISBN 978-1-58542-851-9

LC 2010-29424

The editors "compile guidelines from successful screenwriters on all of the details of writing a screenplay, from choosing your story to structure to character development. Readers will be interested to hear the opinions of such estimated screenwriters as Linda Seger and Syd Field and their takes on what motivates them to write screenplays and how they cope with writer's block and revisions. . . . This guide stands out from the crowd by incorporating the techniques of a variety of different screenwriters rather than just one professional's approach. Highly recommended for readers interested in writing, screenwriting, film, and storytelling." Libr J

808.3   Rhetoric of fiction

Butler, Robert Olen
From where you dream; the process of writing fiction. edited, with an introduction by Janet Burroway. Grove Press 2005 269p $24; pa $13 **808.3**
1. Authorship 2. Fiction -- Technique
ISBN 0-8021-1795-3; 0-8021-4257-5 pa

LC 2005-40251

This is a collection of lectures the author has given for his creative writing course at Florida State University.

This "is a remarkably candid, clarifying, and profoundly demanding how-to. . . . Incisive and provocative, Butler's tutorials are a must for anyone even thinking about writing fiction, and readers, too, will benefit from his passionate exhortations." Booklist

Cohen, Richard
How to Write like Tolstoy; A Journey into the Minds of Our Greatest Writers. Richard Cohen. Random House 2016 xx, 323 p.p (acid-free paper) $28 **808.3**
1. Authorship 2. Fiction -- Technique 3. Fiction -- Authorship
ISBN 9780812998306

LC 2015018626

This book, by Richard Cohen, "is a thought-provoking journey inside the minds of the world's most accomplished storytellers, from Shakespeare to Stephen King. . . . Cohen has researched the published works and private utterances of our greatest authors to discover the elements that made their prose memorable. The result is a unique exploration of the act and art of writing that enriches our experience of reading both the classics and the best modern fiction." (Publisher's note)

"Even readers with no intentions of writing a novel will relish the opportunity to join their favorite authors at the workbench." Booklist.

Dufresne, John
★ **Flash!** writing the very short story. John Dufresne. W.W. Norton & Company 2018 xiv, 255 p.p $15.95 **808.3**
1. Authorship 2. Creative writing
ISBN 0393352358; 9780393352351

This book, by John Dufresne, "identifies the qualities that make for excellent flash fiction, demystifies the writing process, and guides writers by exercise and example through the world of the very short story. . . . Dufresne's characteristic warmth, wit, and humor remind writers of the joy in the creative process, making this a perfect guide for any writer interested in trying a new form." (Publisher's note)

Eco, Umberto
Confessions of a young novelist. Harvard University Press 2011 231p il (The Richard Ellmann lectures in modern literature) $18.95 **808.3**
1. Authorship
ISBN 9780674058699; 0-674-05869-0

LC 2010-33172

"In the first three essays/lectures here, Eco addresses interesting questions: what is the boundary between fiction and nonfiction? How do novelists put together books? Why do we care about wholly fictional characters like Anna Karenina or Emma Bovary? His answer to the second question—on constructing a novel—is that he builds his novels by scrupulous attention to physical detail. The fourth essay, 'My Lists,' original to this collection, was not a lecture. It seems a throwaway but reflects Eco's pleasure in the detailed, serial listing of names as attempts to exhaust the plenitude of qualities and quiddities potentially attributable to any single object. . . . As always, Eco is diverting to read." Libr J

Includes bibliographical references

Gardner, John
On becoming a novelist; foreword by Raymond Carver. W.W. Norton 1999 xxv, 150p pa $14.95 **808.3**
1. Authorship 2. Fiction -- Technique
ISBN 0-393-32003-0
First published 1983 by Harper & Row
The author "explores the dynamic chemistry at the heart of the writ-

er's creative process. Gardner's book is a superbly written, thoroughly original, eminently useful volume." Choice

Johnson, Charles

The **way** of the writer; reflections on the art and craft of storytelling. Charles Johnson. Simon & Schuster 2016 256 p. (ebook) $16.99; (hardcover) $24.00 **808.3**

1. Storytelling 2. Creative writing

ISBN 9781501147234; 9781501147210; 9781501147227; 1501147218

LC 2016299742

This book, by Charles Johnson, offers an "instructive, inspiring guide to the craft and art of writing. An award-winning novelist, philosopher, essayist, screenwriter, professor, and cartoonist, Charles Johnson has devoted his life to creative pursuit. . . . Organized into six accessible, easy-to-navigate sections, . . . [the book] is both a literary reflection on the creative impulse and a utilitarian guide to the writing process." (Publisher's note)

"All writers will welcome the useful tips and exercises, but the book will also appeal to readers interested in literature and the creative process. Johnson's wonderful prose will engage readers to think more deeply about how to tell a story and consider the truth-telling power of the arts." LJ

Includes bibliographical references.

Koch, Stephen

★ The **modern** library writer's workshop; a guide to the craft of fiction. Modern Library 2003 246p pa $12.95 **808.3**

1. Authorship 2. Fiction -- Technique

ISBN 0-375-75558-6

LC 2002-32593

"Koch's tone is both encouraging and forthright, and his accessible, friendly guide will be essential for aspiring writers." Booklist

Includes bibliographical references

Lukeman, Noah

The **plot** thickens; 8 ways to bring fiction to life. St. Martin's Press 2002 221p $19.95; pa $12.95 **808.3**

1. Fiction -- Technique

ISBN 0-312-28467-5; 0-312-30928-7 pa

LC 2001-58564

"Lukeman focuses on the mechanics of storytelling. He introduces budding writers to the techniques of characterization (ask yourself questions about the people you've created), the various ways of generating suspense (danger, a ticking clock), and the importance of conflict." Booklist

Maass, Donald

Writing the breakout novel; winning advice from a top agent and his bestselling client. foreword by Anne Perry. Writer's Digest Bks. 2001 264p hardcover o.p. pa $16.99 **808.3**

1. Fiction -- Technique

ISBN 1-58297-182-X pa

LC 2001-22036

"Using his own clients as case studies, Maass defines the most crucial elements of a breakout novel—a powerful sense of time and place, larger-than-life characters, a high degree of tension, good subplots, and universal themes—and shows the reader how to use these elements efficiently to write a novel that will generate interest and have the potential to hit the best sellers lists. Each section ends with checklists for review." Libr J

Mattison, Alice

The **kite** and the string; how to write with spontaneity and control - and live to tell the tale. by Alice Mattison. Viking 2016 xx, 234 p.p (hardcover) $25 **808.3**

1. Fiction -- Technique 2. Authorship -- Handbooks, manuals, etc.

ISBN 9780525428541; 9780698189911; 0525428542

LC 2016286057

This book, by Alice Mattison, is "a targeted and insightful guide to the stages of writing fiction and memoir without falling into common traps. . . . [It] urges writers to let playfulness and spontaneity breathe life into the work--letting the kite move with the winds of feeling--while still holding on to the string that will keep it from flying away." (Publisher's note)

"This is a visually unassuming book, but its contents provide a gold mine for writers across a spectrum of experience levels." Booklist

Includes bibliographical references (pages 223-225) and index.

Moore, Dinty W.

The **story** cure; a book doctor's pain-free guide to finishing your novel or memoir. Dinty W. Moore. Ten Speed Press 2017 181 p. illustrations (paperback) $14.99 **808.3**

1. Autobiographies 2. Creative writing 3. Advice literature 4. Fiction -- Technique 5. Fiction -- Authorship 6. Autobiography -- Authorship

ISBN 0399578803; 9780399578809; 9780399578816

LC 2016036789

This book, by Dinty W. Moore, is "a collection of cures for writer's block, plotting and characterization issues, and other ailments writers face when completing a novel or memoir. . . . [This] hard-hitting handbook provides inspiring solutions for diagnoses such as character anemia, flat plot, and silent voice, and is peppered with flashes of Moore's signature wit and unique take on the writing life." (Publisher's note)

"In a field littered with gimmicky advice, this strong, lean title stands out." Booklist

Includes bibliographical references (pages 163-170) and index.

Morrell, Jessica Page

Thanks, but this isn't for us; a (sort of) compassionate guide to why your writing is being rejected. Jeremy P. Tarcher-Penguin 2009 357p pa $16.95 **808.3**

1. Authorship

ISBN 978-1-58542-721-5

LC 2009-23252

The author "explores several mistakes new authors make in their manuscripts among them lack of conflict, unbelievable dialogue, and details that lack specific sensory appeal. Each chapter begins with a lively overview of a common problem, then lists what Morrell calls 'deal breakers'—particular habits such as lack of subplots and one-dimensional bad guys—that deter an editor from accepting a manuscript for publication. She concludes each chapter with exercises designed to improve storytelling, and then lists book resources for those wanting to delve more deeply into studies of character, emotion, tension and plot. . . . Emerging and established writers alike will benefit from Morrell's shrewd observations." Writer

Includes bibliographical references

Nabokov, Vladimir Vladimirovich

Lectures on literature; {by} Vladimir Nabokov; edited by Fredson Bowers; introduction by John Updike. Harcourt Brace Jovanovich 1980 xxviii, 385p il hardcover o.p. pa $18 **808.3**

1. Poets 2. Authors 3. Novelists 4. Dramatists 5. Essayists 6. Travel writers 7. Literary critics 8. Short story writers 9. Fiction

-- History and criticism
ISBN 978-0-15-602775-5; 0-15-602775-5

LC 79-3690

Companion volume to Lectures on Russian literature

In the early 1950s, before Nabokov became a famous writer, he taught literature at Wellesley and Cornell. The editor, with the help of Nabokov's wife and son, has collected seven lectures on "Mansfield Park," "Bleak House," "Madame Bovary," "The Strange Case of Dr. Jekyll and Mr. Hyde," "The Walk by Swann's Place," "The Metamorphosis" and "Ulysses." There are two additional lectures on other topics related to literature. The volume includes a sample examination for the course and pages of original manuscripts with maps and diagrams which the author used to illustrate his lectures

Percy, Benjamin

Thrill me; essays on fiction. Benjamin Percy. Graywolf Press 2016 174 p. (alk. paper) $16 **808.3**
1. Authorship 2. Creative writing 3. Fiction -- History and criticism
ISBN 9781555977597; 9781555979546

LC 2016931536

This book, by Benjamin Percy, presents "essays on how to craft a thrilling read--in any genre. . . . Percy challenges the notion that literary and genre fiction are somehow mutually exclusive. The title essay is an ode to the kinds of books that make many readers fall in love with fiction: science fiction, fantasy, mysteries, horror, from J.R.R. Tolkien to Anne Rice, Ursula K. Le Guin to Stephen King." (Publisher's note)

"Percy's essays skillfully dissect the structure, mechanics, and concrete details of what makes good writing sparkle." Pub Wkly

Piercy, Marge

So you want to write; how to master the craft of writing fiction and memoir. [by] Marge Piercy and Ira Wood. 2nd ed.; Leapfrog Press 2005 324p pa $16.95 **808.3**
1. Biography as a literary form 2. Fiction -- Technique
ISBN 0-9728984-5-X
First published 2001

This book "uses talks, exercises, anecdotes and examples proven in the classroom, to address: How to begin a piece by seducing your reader, How to create characters that embody the infinite contradictions of human behavior, How to master the elements of plotting fiction, How to create a strategy for telling the story of your life, How to learn to read critically, like a professional writer, How to write about painful personal material without coming off as a victim, [and] How to proceed if your work is continually rejected by publishers." Publisher's note

Includes bibliographical references

Scofield, Sandra

The **last** draft; a novelist's guide to revision. Sandra Scofield. Penguin Books 2017 xxviii, 240 p.p (paperback) $17 **808.3**
1. Creative writing 2. Authorship -- Fiction 3. Fiction -- Technique 4. Fiction -- Authorship 5. Manuscripts -- Editing
ISBN 9780143131359; 9781524705084; 0143131354

LC 2017032030

This book, by Sandra Scofield, "shows writers how to turn first-draft manuscripts into the novels of their dreams. . . . Scofield illustrates how to reread a work of fiction with a view of its subject and vision, and how to take it apart and put it back together again, stronger and deeper. . . . The detailed, step-by-step plan laid out in The Last Draft offers invaluable advice to both novice and experienced writers alike." (Publisher's note)

Includes bibliographical references (pages 205-209).

Swain, Dwight V.

Creating characters; how to build story people. Writer's Digest Bks. 1990 195p hardcover o.p. pa $14.99 **808.3**
1. Characters and characteristics in literature 2. Fiction -- Technique
ISBN 0-89879-662-8 pa

LC 90-39640

"Swain talks to his readers in a conversational tone, suggesting techniques, giving examples to illuminate his points, and offering activities for sharpening character development skills. This is a book for those already committed to writing fiction and who want to think about the craft of writing." SLJ

Includes bibliographical references

Wheat, Carolyn

How to write killer fiction; the funhouse of mystery & the roller coaster of suspense. Perseverance Press 2003 191p il pa $13.95 **808.3**
1. Mystery fiction -- Technique 2. Suspense fiction -- Technique
ISBN 1-88028-462-6

LC 2002-15588

Wheat begins with a "discussion of the distinction between mystery and suspense . . . and then devotes a section to each genre. She offers up plenty of useful tips, such as how to dispense vital information in subtle ways and how to plant clues without being too obvious about it." Booklist

Includes bibliographical references

Wood, James

★ **How** fiction works. Farrar, Straus and Giroux 2008 265p $24 **808.3**
1. Fiction
ISBN 0-374-17340-0; 978-0-374-17340-1

LC 2008-10290

The author addresses such questions as "What is character, point of view, the value of metaphor and simile, and detail? Is it all artifice or realism, or could it be labeled imaginative truth? His engaging discussion covers narration in all its forms, the impersonal author, the tension that exists between an author's and a character's style, flat vs. round characters, irony, and more. Wood uses excerpts from works by notable authors, from Miguel Cervantes and Jane Austen to Saul Bellow and John Updike, to illustrate his statements with pinpoint precision. Whether he is commenting on a work's weakness or strength, he supports his opinion with reasoned scholarship." Libr J

Includes bibliographical references

808.5 Rhetoric of speech

Anderson, Chris

TED talks; the official TED guide to public speaking. Chris Anderson. Houghton Mifflin Harcourt 2016 xv, 269 p.p (hardcover) $28 **808.5**
1. Communication 2. Public speaking 3. Public speaking -- Handbooks, manuals, etc
ISBN 9780544634497

LC 2015048798

This book, by Chris Anderson, "explains how the miracle of powerful public speaking is achieved, and equips you to give it your best shot. There is no set formula; no two talks should be the same. The goal is for you to give the talk that only you can give. . . . . Anderson has worked behind the scenes with all the TED speakers who have inspired us the most, and here he shares insights from such favorites as Sir Ken Robinson, Amy Cuddy, Bill Gates, [and] Elizabeth Gilbert." (Publisher's note)

"While, as expected, the examples here come from TED Talks, readers will be able to use the techniques for any manner of public speaking." Booklist

Detz, Joan

How to write & give a speech; a practical guide for anyone who has to make every word count. Joan Detz. 3rd edition St. Martin's Griffin 2014 224 p. pbk $16.99   **808.5**
  1. Public speaking
  ISBN 9781250041074; 1250041074

                 LC 2013032029

"This newly updated how to guide offers sound advice on every aspect of researching, writing, and delivering an effective speech. Filled with anecdotes, tips, examples, and practical advice, this accessible guide makes one of the most daunting tasks manageable-and even fun. . . . Updated to include new examples and the latest technology, as well as a section on social media, this is a must-have for anyone who writes and delivers speeches, whether novices or experienced veterans at the podium." (Publisher's note)

Includes bibliographical references and index

Flaherty, Francis

The **elements** of story; field notes on nonfiction writing. HarperCollins 2009 xxi, 293p $24.99   **808.5**
  1. Rhetoric 2. Storytelling
  ISBN 978-0-06-168914-7; 0-06-168914-9

                 LC 2008-53946

The author offers 50 "tips on the many elements writers can convey in stories. Not a style guide, this is instead a nuts-and-bolts examination of the larger elements of a story. . . . This book can be read in one fell swoop to expose yourself to the full spectrum of story elements—such as theme, motion, artfulness, truth and fairness, leads, and titles—or it can be used as a guide during the process of writing nonfiction. An essential read for both freelance writers and students of journalism." Libr J

Includes bibliographical references

Meyers, Peter

As we speak; how to make your point and have it stick. by Peter Meyers and Shann Nix. Atria Books 2011 viii, 275 p.p ill. $25   **808.5**
  1. Public speaking 2. Business communication 3. Communication in management 4. Interpersonal communication
  ISBN 1439153051; 9781439153055

                 LC 2011015029

In this book, "Peter Meyers and Shann Nix offer a comprehensive approach for tackling the underlying obstacles that almost all of us experience when faced with speaking in public. In 'As We Speak,' you'll learn to master the three building blocks at the core of their approach: Content . . . Delivery . . . [and] State. . . . Meyers and Nix also emphasize that effective communication is impossible without first becoming aware of your own true goals and personal beliefs." (Publisher's note)

Includes bibliographical references (p. 273-275)

Pinsky, Robert

The **sounds** of poetry; a brief guide. Farrar, Straus & Giroux 1998 129p hardcover o.p. pa $13   **808.5**
  1. Poetry
  ISBN 0-374-52617-6

                 LC 98-18873

"By bringing his passion for the sound of language—so evident in his own poems—to his expert interpretations of the work of others,

Pinsky cracks open the glass case that seems to separate poetry from everyday language, allowing the song of each poem to ring bright and clear." Booklist

Includes bibliographical references

808.8   Collections of literary texts from more than two literatures

DiBattista, Maria

At home in the world; women writers and public life, from Austen to the present. Maria DiBattista and Deborah Epstein Nord. Princeton University Press 2017 xiv, 279 p.p (cloth: alk. paper) $29.95   **808.8**
  1. Women authors 2. Women in literature 3. Feminism and literature
  ISBN 9780691138114

                 LC 2016945501

This book, by Deborah Epstein Nord and Maria DiBattista, "explores works by a wide range of writers, including canonical figures such as Jane Austen, Charlotte Brontë, George Eliot, Harriet Jacobs, Edith Wharton, Virginia Woolf, Willa Cather, Gertrude Stein, and Toni Morrison; neglected or marginalized writers like Mary Antin, Tess Slesinger, and Martha Gellhorn; and recent and contemporary figures, including Nadine Gordimer, Anita Desai, Edwidge Danticat, and Jhumpa Lahiri." (Publisher's note)

"Sure to become an important addition to feminist literary theory and cultural studies." LJ.

Includes bibliographical references (pages 253-270) and index.

The **Paris** review book of heartbreak, madness, sex, love, betrayal, outsiders, intoxication, war, whimsy, horrors, God, death, dinner, baseball, travels, the art of writing, and everything else in the world since 1953; by the editors of the Paris review; with an introduction by George Plimpton. Picador 2003 751p $30; pa $19   **808.8**
  1. Literature -- Collections
  ISBN 0-312-42238-5; 0-312-42239-3 pa

                 LC 2003-45971

This anthology includes works by "W.H. Auden, Ernest Hemingway, William Faulkner, Jack Kerouac, Elizabeth Bishop, Truman Capote, William Burroughs, Susan Sontag, Joyce Carol Oates, Toni Morrison, Jonathan Franzen, Ian McEwan and Alice Munro." Publ Wkly

808.81   Collections in specific forms

The **20th** Century in Poetry. W W Norton & Co Inc 2012 860 p. $35.00   **808.81**
  1. Poetry -- Collections 2. Poetry -- History and criticism -- 20th century
  ISBN 1605983640; 9781605983646

This poetry anthology, edited by Michael Hulse and Simon Rae, "presents in chronological order over four hundred poems written during the twentieth century. The authors, both published poets themselves, give an overview of each period of history, while notes to the poems place each one in its historical context and trace the century's poetic development. Concise biographies for each poet complete the anthology." (Publisher's note)

The **Columbia** Granger's Index to poetry in collected and selected works; edited by Keith Newton. 2nd ed, completely rev; Columbia Univ. Press 2004 xxi, 1847p $225 **808.81**
1. Reference books 2. Poetry -- Indexes
ISBN 0-231-12528-3

LC 2003-51469

First published 1996

This "edition includes 315 works, by 266 different poets, locating more than 65,000 poems by title, first line, author, and subject. Included . . . are the works of many of the major American and British poets of the last thirty years, such as Robert Pinsky, Seamus Heaney, and Paul Muldoon; important twentieth-century American poets such as Langston Hughes, Dorothy Parker, and Robert Penn Warren; twentieth-century foreign poets in new translations, such as Eugenio Montale and Paul Celan; and diverse poets from all times and places, collected in new editions, such as Cold Mountain, Jones Very, and Guido Cavalcanti." Publisher's note

Granger, Edith

The **Columbia** Granger's index to poetry in anthologies; edited by Tessa Kale. 13th ed., completely rev., indexing anthologies published through May 31, 2006; Columbia University Press 2007 xxviii, 2376p $295 **808.81**
1. Reference books 2. Poetry -- Indexes
ISBN 0-231-13988-8; 978-0-231-13988-5

LC 2006-14853

First edition, edited by Edith Granger, published 1904 by A. C. McClurg with title: Index to poetry and recitations. Fifth through eighth editions have title Granger's index to poetry

"The 400 total entries are organized alphabetically into three sections: 'Title, First Line, Last Line,' 'Author,' and 'Subject.' The anthologies referenced appear as abbreviations explained in a 14-page introductory list. An essential purchase for literature and poetry collections." Libr J

Includes bibliographical references

★ **Language** for a new century; contemporary poetry from the Middle East, Asia, and beyond. edited by Tina Chang, Nathalie Handal, and Ravi Shankar. W.W. Norton 2008 l, 734p il pa $27.95 **808.81**
1. Poetry -- Collections
ISBN 978-0-393-33238-4; 0-393-33238-1

LC 2007-49424

"Even a diligent reader of contemporary poetry will leave this gathering feeling humbled by ignorance of the immense poetic energy of what used to be called the East." Booklist

Includes bibliographical references

Merwin, W. S. (William Stanley), 1927-

Selected translations 1948-2010; 1948-2011. [compiled by] W.S. Merwin. Copper Canyon Press 2012 407 p. (alk. paper) $40 **808.81**
1. Poetry 2. Translating and interpreting 3. Poetry -- Collections 4. Poetry -- Translations into English
ISBN 1556594097; 9781556594090

LC 2012025545

This poetry collection, translated by W.S. Merwin, "is the lifework from one of America's greatest poets and translators. Dedicated to the art of translation since his undergraduate years at Princeton, Poet Laureate W.S. Merwin achieved an unmatched oeuvre of translated poems from every corner of the earth, from dozens of languages." (Publisher's note)

Music of a distant drum; classical Arabic, Persian, Turkish, and Hebrew poems. translated and introduced by Bernard Lewis. Princeton Univ. Press 2001 222p il hardcover o.p. pa $17.95 **808.81**
1. Arabic poetry -- Collections 2. Hebrew poetry -- Collections 3. Persian poetry -- Collections 4. Turkish poetry -- Collections
ISBN 0-691-15010-9 pa; 0-691-08928-0

LC 2001-19858

"Lewis, one of the foremost scholars of the Middle East, has devoted much of his career to the history of Islam; this volume collects his translations of poems—nearly all appearing in English for the first time—that span eleven centuries and four major Middle Eastern traditions. Many of the most striking works address, in spare, stirring lines, the twin demands of serving the self and serving God." New Yorker

Includes bibliographical references

The **new** Oxford book of war poetry; edited by Jon Stallworthy. Oxford University Press 2014 xl, 406 p.p **808.81**
1. War poetry
ISBN 9780198704485; 9780198704478

LC 2013497520

"There can be no area of human experience that has generated a wider range of powerful feelings than war. Jon Stallworthy's classic and celebrated anthology spans centuries of human experience of war, from Homer's Iliad, through the First and Second World Wars, the Vietnam War, and the wars fought since. This new edition, published to mark the centenary of the outbreak of the First World War, includes a new introduction and additonal poems from David Harsent and Peter Wyton, among others. The new selection provides improved coverage of the two World Wars and the Vietnam War, and new coverage of the wars of the late twentieth and early twenty-first centuries." (Publisher's note)

Includes bibliographic references (pages 381-384) and index

The **Paraclete** poetry anthology, 2005-2016; selected and new poems. edited and introduced by Mark S. Burrows Foreword by Jon M. Sweeney. Paraclete Press Inc. 2016 xxvii, 188 p.p (trade pbk. with french flaps) $20 **808.81**
1. Anthologies 2. Religious poetry 3. American poetry -- Collections 4. Christian poetry, American
ISBN 9781612619064

LC 2016041812

This poetry collection, edited by Mark S. Burrows, features "poems by Phyllis Tickle, Scott Cairns, Paul Mariani, Anna Kamienska, Fr. John-Julian, SAID, Bonnie Thurston, Greg Miller, William Woolfitt, Rami Shapiro, Thomas Lynch, Paul Quenon, and Rainer Maria Rilke, . . . [which] spans the first ten years of the poetry series at Paraclete Press." (Publisher's note)

"The range of poetic expression here encompasses spiritual journaling, prayer, legends and biography, visionary and ordinary mysticism, nature contemplation, and, of course, prayer as well as both formally relaxed and formally precise individual poems." Booklist

Includes bibliographical references (pages xxv-xxvii, 187-188).

Poems to read; a new favorite poem project anthology. edited by Robert Pinsky and Maggie Dietz. Norton 2002 xxv, 352p $27.95 **808.81**
1. Poetry -- Collections
ISBN 0-393-01074-0

LC 2002-321

"A graceful, sometimes jubilant, sometimes lyrical, sometimes brooding, but always welcoming and stirring collection." Booklist

Includes bibliographical references

The **Poetry** of our world; an international anthology of contemporary poetry. edited by Jeffrey Paine. HarperCollins Pubs. 2000 xxviii, 511p hardcover o.p. pa $18.95   **808.81**
1. Poetry -- Collections
ISBN 0-06-055369-3; 0-06-095193-1 pa

LC 99-34921

In this global anthology "each section is preceded by a thoughtful introduction of several pages by the selector in that area. . . . A stunning and highly readable anthology." Libr J

808.86   Collections of letters

Letters of note; an eclectic collection of correspondence deserving of a wider audience. compiled by Shaun Usher. Chronicle Books Llc 2014 xvi, 352 p.p illustrations (hardback) $40   **808.86**
1. Letters
ISBN 1452134251; 9781452134253

LC 2013050330

This collection of more than 125 letters, compiled by Shaun Usher, "offers a never-before-seen glimpse of the events and people of history--the brightest and best, the most notorious, and the endearingly every day. Entries include a transcript of the letter; a short contextual introduction; and, in 100 cases, a captivating facsimile of the letter itself." (Publisher's note)

Mallon, Thomas
Yours ever; people and their letters. Pantheon Books 2009 338p $26.95   **808.86**
1. Letters
ISBN 978-0-679-44426-8; 0-679-44426-2

LC 2009-06315

Companion volume to A book of one's own (1984)

This is "an astute, exhilarating tour of the mailbag. . . . [It] is nuanced, informed, full-blooded, a vigorous literary salute." N Y Times Book Rev

Includes bibliographical references (p. 313-320)

Usher, Shaun
Letters of note; an eclectic collection of correspondence deserving of a wider audience / Volume 2. compiled by Shaun Usher. Chronicle Books Llc 2016 352 p. illustrations (some color) (ebook) $36.39; $40   **808.86**
1. Letters 2. Letter writing
ISBN 9781452140865; 1452153833; 9781452153834

LC 2016043167

This book, compiled by Shaun Ushe, presents "more than 125 captivating letters. Each turn of the page brings delight and discovery in a collection of correspondence that spans centuries and place, written by the famous, the not-so-famous, and the downright infamous. Entries are accompanied by a transcript of the letter, a short contextual introduction, and a spirited illustration—in most cases, a facsimile of the letter itself." (Publisher's note)

"This fantastic collection of over 125 letters is endlessly entertaining." Pub Wkly

808.88   Collections of miscellaneous writings

Lend me your ears; Oxford dictionary of political quotations. edited by Sir Antony Jay. 4th ed; Oxford University Press 2010 xxv, 446p $24.95   **808.88**
1. Reference books 2. Political science -- Quotations
ISBN 978-0-19-957267-0

LC 2010-923325

First published 1996 with title: The Oxford dictionary of political quotations

Entries are organized "by speaker rather than by topic. Don't know the origin of a quotation? Fear not. Turn to the extensive keyword index or the briefer 'selective subject index' in the back of the volume. Helpful also are one-page special category quotes: epitaphs, misquotations, mottoes, slogans, etc. . . . [This is] a great value and an excellent choice for libraries lacking a current work in this area." Libr J

O'Brien, Geoffrey
Bartlett's familiar quotations; a collection of passages, phrases, and proverbs traced to their sources in ancient and modern literature. by John Bartlett; Geoffrey O'Brien, general editor. 18th ed. Little, Brown, and Co. 2012 lxi, 1438 p.p (hardcover) $50.00   **808.88**
1. Quotations 2. Quotations, English
ISBN 0316017590; 9780316017596

LC 2012019870

This book, in its 18th edition, presents a collection of quotations "from the times of ancient Egyptians to the present day." (Publisher's note) It "includes 2500 new quotes and more than 800 newcomers, from Julia Child to David Foster Wallace. Quotes have been culled to bring in more foreigners and women and more material from fiction and poetry." (Library Journal)

The **Oxford** book of aphorisms; chosen by John Gross. Oxford University Press 2003 383p pa $19.95   **808.88**
1. Quotations
ISBN 0-19-280456-1

LC 2003-269712

First published 1983

"Contains a well-chosen collection of aphorisms, maxims, quotations, and pensees from ancient times to the present. Entries, arranged under 58 subject sections, are identified with name of aphorist, source, publication date, or approximate date of original statement. Headings include 'nature,' 'good and evil,' 'illusion and reality,' and 'secrets.' An introduction gives definitions of aphorisms and their use throughout history." Wynar. Guide to Ref Books for Sch Media Cent. 3d edition

Includes bibliographical references

Oxford Dictionary of Humorous Quotations; Gyles Daubeney Brandreth. 5th edition Oxford University Press 2015 496 p. $20.95   **808.88**
1. Quotations 2. Wit and humor 3. Wit and humor -- Dictionaries 4. Quotations, English -- Dictionaries
ISBN 0199681376; 9780199681372

LC 2013474663

In this book, author "Gyles Brandreth has completely revised Ned Sherrin's classic collection of wisecracks, one-liners, and anecdotes. With over 1,000 new quotations from all media, it's easy to find hilarious quotes on subjects ranging from Argument to Diets, from Computers to The Weather. Add sparkle to your speeches and presentations, or just enjoy a good laugh in company with Oscar Wilde, Mark Twain, Joan Rivers, Kathy Lette, Frankie Boyle, and friends." (Publisher's note)

809 History, description, critical appraisal of more than two literatures

Atwood, Margaret, 1939-

In other worlds; SF and the human imagination. Nan A. Talese/Doubleday 2011 255p pa $24.95 **809**

1. Science fiction -- Authorship 2. Science fiction -- History and criticism

ISBN 978-0-385-53396-6

LC 2011013776

"Atwood is well known to sf readers for such novels as The Handmaid's Tale, Oryx and Crake, and The Year of the Flood. In this collection of essays and short fiction, she further explores the genre, beginning with her three previously unpublished Richard Ellman Lectures in Modern Literature, which she delivered at Emory University in 2010. . . . A clever, thoughtful investigation that will appeal to science fiction readers and Atwood's loyal fans." Libr J

Includes bibliographical references

Black literature criticism; classic and emerging authors since 1950. Jelena O. Krstovic, project editor; forward by Howard Dodson. 2nd ed.; Gale Cengage Learning 2008 3v il set $459 **809**

1. Blacks in literature 2. English literature -- Black authors -- History and criticism 3. American literature -- African American authors -- History and criticism

ISBN 978-1-4144-3170-3; 1-4144-3170-8

First published 1992

"This work includes African American, Caribbean, and African writers who produce works in English. Authors range from relative newcomers . . . to classic authors. . . . [This is] a worthwhile purchase." Booklist

Includes bibliographical references

Bloom, Harold

The **Western** canon; the books and school of the ages. Riverhead Bks. 1995 546p pa $18 **809**

1. Blind 2. Poets 3. Judges 4. Authors 5. Diplomats 6. Novelists 7. Dramatists 8. Essayists 9. Translators 10. Lexicographers 11. Poets laureate 12. Psychoanalysts 13. Literary critics 14. Nonfiction writers 15. Writers on science 16. Short story writers 17. Writers on medicine 18. Writers on religion 19. Nobel laureates for peace 20. Nobel laureates for literature 21. Literature -- History and criticism

ISBN 1-57322-514-2; 978-1-57322-514-4

First published 1994 by Harcourt Brace & Co.

The "book succeeds not as a polemic but as a passionate, erudite and highly idiosyncratic series of essays about the literature dearest to one of America's most influential academics." Publ Wkly

Boyd, Brian

On the origin of stories; evolution, cognition, and fiction. Belknap Press of Harvard University Press 2009 540p il $35 **809**

1. Evolution 2. Authorship 3. Fiction -- Authorship 4. Fiction -- History and criticism

ISBN 978-0-674-03357-3; 0-674-03357-4

LC 2009-07642

The author "has created a compelling, erudite, and thoroughly original work about the nature of humanistic expression in art and literature. Beautifully written and wide-ranging, the book delves into social science, evolutionary biology, art, and literature to create a comprehensive account of the evolutionary origins of art and storytelling." Choice

Includes bibliographical references

Calvino, Italo

Why read the classics? translated from the Italian by Martin McLaughlin. Pantheon Bks. 1999 277p hardcover o.p. pa $13 **809**

1. Literature -- History and criticism

ISBN 0-679-74349-9 pa

LC 99-21535

Original Italian edition, 1991

"Calvino celebrates a wide range of great thinkers in these provocative essays. Here are writers from the ancient world, the Renaissance and recent times, and from the old and new worlds. . . . [These essays] are a reminder to us that 'rereading' the classics can amuse as well as reward." New Sci

Includes bibliographical references

Coetzee, J. M., 1940-

Late essays; 2006-2017. J. M. Coetzee. Penguin Group USA 2018 304 p. $28 **809**

1. Essays 2. Literature -- 18th century

ISBN 0735223912; 9780735223912

In this essay collection, author J. M. Coetzee "examines the work of some of the world's greatest writers, from Daniel Defoe in the early eighteenth century to Goethe and Irène Némirovsky to Coetzee's contemporary Philip Roth. Challenging yet accessible, literary master Coetzee writes these essays with great clarity and precision, offering readers an illuminating and wise analysis of a remarkable list of works of international literature that span three centuries." (Publisher's note)

"Continuing in the vein of his earlier essay collections, including Inner Workings (2007), Nobel laureate Coetzee again demonstrates his range and precision as a literary critic and his gift for rendering challenging material accessible. His interest is in probing the Western canon for works that are praiseworthy, but also those that fall short in interesting ways." Booklist

Damrosch, David

The **buried** book; the loss and rediscovery of the great Epic of Gilgamesh. H. Holt 2007 315p il map hardcover o.p. pa $16.99 **809**

1. Gilgamesh

ISBN 978-0-8050-8029-2; 0-8050-8029-5; 978-0-8050-8725-3 pa; 0-8050-8725-7 pa

LC 2006-49523

"Combining acuity about cultural contexts with wide-ranging knowledge, Damrosch's account is a superb and engrossing popular presentation." Booklist

Includes bibliographical references

Danticat, Edwidge, 1969-

Art of death; writing the final story. Edwidge Danticat. Graywolf Press 2017 181 p. (Art of series) (paperback) $14 **809**

1. Death 2. Mother-child relationship 3. Children of cancer patients 4. Authorship 5. Death in literature 6. Mortality in literature 7. Literature -- History and criticism

ISBN 9781555977771; 9781555979690

LC 2016951195

National Book Critics Circle Award Finalist: Criticism (2017)

This book, by Edwidge Danticat, "is at once a personal account of her mother dying from cancer and a deeply considered reckoning with the ways that other writers have approached death in their own work.

. . . The book moves outward from the shock of her mother's diagnosis and sifts through Danticat's writing life and personal history, all the while shifting fluidly from examples that range from Gabriel García Márquez's One Hundred Years of Solitude to Toni Morrison's Sula." (Publisher's note)

"This slim volume wraps literary criticism, philosophy, and memoir into a gracefully circling whole, echoing the nature of grief as 'circles and circles of sorrow.'" Pub Wkly

Includes bibliographical references (pages 177-181).

Donoghue, Emma

Inseparable; desire between women in literature. Emma Donoghue. Alfred A. Knopf 2010 x, 271p ill. (hc: alk. paper) $27.95   **809**

1. Female friendship 2. Women in literature 3. Lesbianism in literature
ISBN 9780307270948; 0307270947

LC 2009048368

Stonewall Book Awards: Israel Fisherman Non-Fiction Award (2011)

This book "explores the little-known literary tradition of love between women in Western literature, from Chaucer and Shakespeare to Charlotte Brontë, Dickens, Agatha Christie, and many more. . . . [It] examine[s] how desire between women in English literature has been portrayed, from schoolgirls and vampires to runaway wives, from cross-dressing knights to contemporary murder stories. [Author Emma] Donoghue looks at the work of those writers who have addressed the 'unspeakable subject,' examining whether such desire between women is freakish or omnipresent, holy or evil, heartwarming or ridiculous as she excavates a long-obscured tradition of (inseparable) friendship between women, one that is . . . central to our cultural history." (Publisher's note)

Includes bibliographical references (p. [207]-260) and index

Ghosh, Amitav, 1956-

The **great** derangement; Climate Change and the Unthinkable. Amitav Ghosh. University of Chicago Press 2016 176 p. (cloth: alk. paper) $22   **809**

1. Climate change 2. Climatic changes in literature
ISBN 9780226323039

LC 2016018232

This book, by Amitav Ghosh, asks "are we deranged? . . . Ghosh argues that future generations may well think so. How else to explain our imaginative failure in the face of global warming? . . . Ghosh ends by suggesting that politics, much like literature, has become a matter of personal moral reckoning rather than an arena of collective action." (Publisher's note)

"A slim but certainly significant contribution to the climate crisis dialogue sure to provoke discussion and increased awareness about our imperiled planet." Kirkus

Includes bibliographical references (pages 165-196).

Handy, Bruce

Wild things; the joy of reading children's literature as an adult. Bruce Handy. Simon & Schuster 2017 xxiii, 307 p.p illustrations (hardback) $26   **809**

1. Children -- Books and reading 2. Children's literature -- History and criticism 3. Books and reading
ISBN 9781501150425; 9781451609950; 9781451609967

LC 2017003959

In this book, author Bruce Handy "revisits the classics of every American childhood, from fairy tales to 'The Very Hungry Caterpillar,' and explores the back stories of their creators, using context and biography to understand how some of the most insightful, creative, and witty

authors and illustrators of their times created their often deeply personal masterpieces." (Publisher's note)

"As well-researched as it is seamlessly composed, this book entertains as it educates." Kirkus

Includes bibliographical references and index

Hollands, Neil

Fellowship in a ring; a guide for science fiction and fantasy book groups. Libraries Unlimited 2010 300p pa $40   **809**

1. Books and reading 2. Book clubs (Discussion groups) 3. Fantasy fiction -- Bibliography 4. Science fiction -- Bibliography 5. Fantasy fiction -- History and criticism 6. Science fiction -- History and criticism
ISBN 978-1-59158-703-3; 1-59158-703-4

LC 2009-46456

This is "is an excellent resource for both novices looking to initiate groups, and veterans seeking to breathe new life into existing factions. The first chapter delineates the practical building blocks necessary to develop a thriving science fiction/fantasy book group, from suggestions of how to ward off potential problems and keep discussions interesting to creative ideas for preventing meetings from becoming stagnant. . . . Included is a list of fifty recommended science fiction and fantasy novels, with helpful information such as author background, plot summaries, a reading guide, and discussion questions. An especially thorough listing of themes for discussion consists of resources, thematic questions, and suggested works." Voice Youth Advocates

Includes bibliographical references

Isherwood, Christopher, 1904-1986

Liberation; Diaries:1970-1983. HarperCollins 2012 928 p. $39.99   **809**

1. Gay men 2. Novelists
ISBN 0062084747; 9780062084743

This book is the "third and final volume of [Christopher] Isherwood's . . . diaries [and] concludes with a 136-page 'glossary' of names . . . . As the 1970's commence, lover Don Bachardy has just had his screenplay for 'Cabaret' . . . rejected. . . . The last diary entry dates to July 4, 1983, exactly two and a half years before Isherwood's death from cancer. In between, he regales readers with accounts of . . . dinners, parties, and foreign travels." (Publishers Weekly)

Iyer, Pico

The **man** within my head; Pico Iyer. Alfred A. Knopf 2012 241 p.   **809**

1. Travel 2. Self-realization 3. Fathers and sons 4. Novelists, English -- 20th century -- Biography
ISBN 030726761X; 9780307267610

LC 2011041285

In this book, author Pico "Iyer describes [writer Graham] Greene as constantly in his mind as a kind of imaginative touchstone. . . . In the second half . . . [Iyer] answers the question he poses in the first half. Why Greene? . . . His answer focuses on the ways that Greene's characters--Pyle and Fowler in 'The Quiet American,' for example - have a kind of father-and-son relationship to each other." (Washington Times)

Jarrell, Randall

No other book; selected essays. edited and introduced by Brad Leithauser. HarperCollins Pubs. 1999 xx, 376p hardcover o.p. pa $15   **809**

1. Poets 2. Authors 3. Lawyers 4. Novelists 5. Physicians 6. Essayists 7. Memoirists 8. Biographers 9. Translators 10. College teachers 11. Children's authors 12. Short story writers 13. Insurance executives 14. Nobel laureates for literature 15.

Literature -- History and criticism 16. American poetry -- History and criticism
ISBN 0-06-095638-0 pa

LC 98-55353

"Jarrell taught his peers to appreciate first the young Robert Lowell and W. H. Auden, then Marianne Moore, William Carlos Williams, Elizabeth Bishop, Walt Whitman and Robert Frost. . . . The later Jarrell divided his prose between appreciations of poets, digressions on idiosyncratic passions, and funny or sad indictments of 1950s-style popular culture. . . . As a convincing, above all personal, guide to modern poets, and as a captivating writer of criticism Jarrell has no obvious 20th century equal." Publ Wkly

Karr, Mary

The **Art** of Memoir; by Mary Knarr. HarperCollins 2015 256 p. $24.99   **809**
1. Autobiographies
ISBN 0062223062; 9780062223067

LC bl2015030986

Author Mary Karr "teaches a selective memoir writing graduate class at Syracuse University, and offers her wisdom in this instructive guide to the genre. . . . For writers in particular, Karr covers such essential topics as the quest for truth . . . finding one's own 'true' voice or 'you-ness,' . . . the crucial process of revision, evoking the five senses, and how to deal with family and others who play major parts in the memoir." (Publishers Weekly)

Kirsch, Adam

★ The **people** and the books; 18 Classics of Jewish Literature. Adam Kirsch. W W Norton & Co Inc 2016 432 p. map (ebook) $50; (hardcover) $28.95   **809**
1. Jewish literature 2. Bible. Old Testament 3. Jewish literature -- History and criticism 4. Bible. Old Testament -- Criticism, interpretation, etc
ISBN 9780393608311; 9780393241761

LC 2016024818

This book, by Adam Kirsch, is an "exploration of a rich literary tradition from the Bible to modern times. . . . [It] shows how central questions and themes of our history and culture are reflected in the Jewish literary canon: the nature of God, the right way to understand the Bible, the relationship of the Jews to their Promised Land, and the challenges of living as a minority in Diaspora." (Publisher's note)

"A fascinating, impeccably written, personal tour of the great books of Judaism." Kirkus

Includes bibliographical references and index

Kundera, Milan

Encounter; translated from the French by Linda Asher. Harper 2010 178p $23.99   **809**
1. Art appreciation 2. Music -- History and criticism 3. Literature -- History and criticism
ISBN 978-0-06-189441-1; 0-06-189441-9

LC 2010-04908

Original French edition, 2009

"Of specific interest are chapters comparing Francis Bacon to Samuel Beckett; Kundera's devilish mixing up of Roland Barthes with the dour theologian Karl Barth in a chance conversation; several discussions on the virtues of Rabelais as well as a restoration to prominence of Anatole France, who had been given the French intellectualist bum's rush; a powerful coupling of the bright birth of film with the sad death of Fellini; a scholar's relishing of Bertolt Brecht's body odor; the music of his fellow Czech Leos Janacek. Like the proverbial meal at the Chinese restaurant, the delicious musings of this book are filling at first. Two

hours later, one craves more." Publ Wkly

The **literature** book; DK; James Canton, consultant editor. DK Publishing 2016 352 p. illustrations (some color) (Big ideas simply explained) (hardcover) $25   **809**
1. Literature -- History and criticism
ISBN 9781465429889; 1465429883; 9781465454553

This book in the Big Ideas Simply Explained series, from DK, "is a fascinating journey through the greatest works of world literature, from the Iliad to Don Quixote to The Great Gatsby. Around 100 crystal-clear articles explore landmark novels, short stories, plays, and poetry that reinvented the art of writing in their time, whether Ancient Greece, post-classical Europe, or modern-day Korea." (Publisher's note)

"The attractive presentation (not to mention price point) makes this suitable for the circulating collections of most libraries, where readers will find it as entertaining as it is informative." Booklist

Includes bibliographical references and index.

Masters, Alexander

A **life** discarded; 148 diaries found in the trash. Alexander Masters. Farrar, Straus & Giroux 2016 272 p. illustrations (hardcover) $26   **809**
1. Diaries 2. Diarists -- Great Britain 3. Women -- Great Britain -- Biography 4. Great Britain -- Social life and customs -- 20th century -- Anecdotes
ISBN 9780374178185; 9780374714536

LC 2016950129

This book, by Alexander Masters, uncovers the identity of the author of a diary contained in "148 tattered and mold-covered notebooks [that] were discovered lying among broken bricks in a bin on a building site in Cambridge, England. Tens of thousands of pages were filled to the edges with urgent handwriting. . . . The anonymous author, known only as 'I,' is revealed as the tragicomic patron saint of everyone who feels their life should have been more successful." (Publisher's note)

"A lovely, elegant book of interest to historians and biographers as much as to general readers." Kirkus

McKee, Robert

Dialogue; The Art of Verbal Action for Page, Stage, and Screen. Robert McKee. Twelve 2016 xviii, 312 p.p (hardcover) $35   **809**
1. Authorship 2. Television plays -- Technique 3. Dialogue 4. Playwriting 5. Fiction -- Technique 6. Motion picture authorship
ISBN 9781455591916

LC 2016001679

This book by Robert McKee "offers the same in-depth analysis for how characters speak on the screen, on the stage, and on the page in believable and engaging ways. From 'Macbeth' to 'Breaking Bad,' McKee deconstructs key scenes to illustrate the strategies and techniques of dialogue. . . . [It] applies a framework of incisive thinking to instruct the prospective writer on how to craft artful, impactful speech." (Publisher's note)

"An exceptionally thorough guide to the difficult art of dialogue from a proven expert in the field." Booklist

Includes bibliographical references and index

Moore, Steven, 1978-

The **novel;** an alternative history: beginnings to 1600. Continuum 2010 698p $39.95   **809**
1. Fiction -- History and criticism
ISBN 9781441177049; 1-4411-7704-3

LC 2010-279268

"Reveling in the most innovative and daring creations, Moore energetically evaluates tales fantastic, chilling, hilarious, erotic, and tragic, comparing centuries-old novels to those of Barth, Gaddis, Pynchon, and Vollmann. Destined for controversy, Moore's erudite, gargantuan, kaleidoscopic, and venturesome alternative history will leave readers feeling as though they've been viewing literature with blinders on." Booklist

Includes bibliographical references

Nevala-Lee, Alec

Astounding; John W. Campbell, Isaac Asimov, Robert A. Heinlein, L. Ron Hubbard, and the golden age of science fiction. Alec Nevala-Lee. HarperCollins 2018 528 p. $28.99 **809**

1. Biography

ISBN 006257194X; 9780062571946

This book, by Alec Nevala-Lee, "is the landmark account of the extraordinary partnership between four controversial writers--John W. Campbell, Isaac Asimov, Robert A. Heinlein, and L. Ron Hubbard--who set off a revolution in science fiction and forever changed our world. This remarkable cultural narrative centers on the figure of John W. Campbell, Jr., whom Asimov called 'the most powerful force in science fiction ever.'" (Publisher's note)

"The golden age of science fiction, spanning the years 1939 to 1950, gets an authoritative examination in this fascinating appraisal of its key players. The primary focus is John W. Campbell, editor of Astounding Science Fiction magazine, and the three very different writers who served him best: Isaac Asimov, Robert A. Heinlein, and L. Ron Hubbard." Pub Wkly

Nissley, Tom

A **reader's** book of days; true tales from the lives and works of writers for every day of the year. Tom Nissley; with illustrations by Joanna Neborsky. W.W. Norton & Co. Inc. 2014 464 p. (hardcover) $24.95 **809**

1. Authors 2. Anecdotes 3. Authorhip 4. Best books 5. Books and reading 6. Literature -- History and criticism

ISBN 0393239624; 9780393239621

LC 2013031250

This book, by Tom Nissley, "features bite- size accounts of events in the lives of great authors for every day of the year. Fictional events that take place within beloved books are also included. {Authors featured include} Martin Amis, Jane Austen, James Baldwin, . . . [and] F.Scott Fitzgerald." (Publisher's note)

"The book itself is guaranteed to occupy plenty of pleasant hours, but Nissley's recommended reading lists are a bibliophilic bonus." Kirkus

Poe, Edgar Allan

Essays and reviews. Library of Am. 1984 1544p $40 **809**

ISBN 0-940450-19-4

LC 83-19923

This volume is divided into six main divisions: Theory of poetry, Reviews of British and Continental authors; Reviews of American authors and American criticism; Magazines and criticism; The literary and social scene; and Articles and marginalia

Includes bibliographical references

Puchner, Martin

The **written** world; the power of stories to shape people, history, civilization. Martin Puchner. Random House 2017 xxiii, 412 p.p illustrations (some color) (hardback) $32 **809**

1. Books and reading 2. Literature -- History and criticism 3. Literature and society

ISBN 9780812998931; 9780812998948

LC 2017002438

This book, by Martin Puchner, explores "the powerful role stories and literature have played in creating the world we have today. Puchner introduces us to numerous visionaries as he explores sixteen foundational texts selected from more than four thousand years of world literature and reveals how writing has inspired the rise and fall of empires and nations, the spark of philosophical and political ideas, and the birth of religious beliefs." (Publisher's note)

"By providing snapshots of key moments in the written word's evolution, Puchner creates a gripping intellectual odyssey." Pub Wkly

Includes bibliographical references (pages 341-388) and index.

Pullman, Philip, 1946-

Daemon voices; on stories and storytelling. Philip Pullman; edited by Simon Mason. Alfred A. Knopf 2018 480 p. (hardcover) $30 **809**

1. Authorship 2. Storytelling 3. Books and reading 4. Literature -- Appreciation 5. Storytelling in literature 6. Authors, English -- Books and reading 7. Books and reading -- Psychological aspects

ISBN 9780525521174

LC 2017049677

In this essay collection, author Philip Pullman "charts the history of his own enchantment with story--from his own books to those of Blake, Milton, Dickens, and the Brothers Grimm, among others--and delves into the role of story in education, religion, and science. At once personal and wide-ranging, 'Daemon Voices' is both a revelation of the writing mind and the methods of a great contemporary master, and a fascinating exploration of storytelling itself." (Publisher's note)

" A collection of pieces infused with abundant wisdom, provocative notions, and illuminating insights." Kirkus

Includes bibliographical references and index

Roth, Philip

Shop talk; a writer and his colleagues and their work. Houghton Mifflin 2001 160p $23 **809**

1. Authors 2. Literature -- History and criticism

ISBN 0-618-15314-4

LC 2001-24523

"In this collection of encounters with distinguished minds—unguarded interviews with Primo Levi and Aharon Appelfeld, among others; an odd exchange of letters with Mary McCarthy; fondly contentious portraits of Bernard Malamud and the painter Philip Guston—Roth manages to tease from his subjects the convictions that fuel their work and the vulnerabilities that make them human." N Y Times Book Rev

Vanity Fair's writers on writers; edited by Graydon Carter with an introduction by David Friend. Penguin Books 2016 viii, 424 p.p (pbk.) $20 **809**

1. Authors -- Biography 2. Literature -- Collections 3. Literature 4. Influence (Literary, artistic, etc.)

ISBN 9780143111764; 9781101993019; 0143111760

LC 2016031514

This book, edited by Graydon Carter, is a "collection of beloved authors on beloved writers, including Martin Amis on Saul Bellow, Truman Capote on Willa Cather, and Salman Rushdie on Christopher Hitchens, as featured in 'Vanity Fair.'. . . Collected here for the first time are forty-one essays exploring how writers influence one another and our culture, from James Baldwin to Joan Didion to James Patterson." (Publisher's note)

Wilson, Jean Moorcroft, 1941-

Robert Graves; from Great War poet to Good-bye to All That (1895-1929) Jean Moorcroft Wilson. St. Martin's Press

2018 480 p. $35   **809**
1. Novelists 2. English poets
ISBN 1472929144; 9781472929143

In this biography, author Jean Moorcroft Wilson "traces how [writer and poet Robert] Graves' compelling life informed the development of his poetry during the First World War, his thinking about the conflict and his shifting attitude towards it. This illuminating look at Graves' life and poetic work reaffirms his place among the important poets of the Great War." (Publisher's note)

Yagoda, Ben

Memoir; a history. Riverhead Books 2009 291p $25.95 **809**
1. Autobiography
ISBN 1-59448-886-X; 978-1-59448-886-3

LC 2009-30859

"Yagoda traces the memoir from its birth in early Christian writings and Roman generals' journals . . . [through the] year of 2007." (Publisher's note) Index.

"With its mixture of literary criticism, cultural history and just enough trivia, Yagoda's survey is sure to appeal to scholars and bibliophiles alike." Publ Wkly

Includes bibliographical references

809.1   Literature in specific forms other than miscellaneous writings

Borges, Jorge Luis

This craft of verse; edited by Calin-Andrei Mihailescu. Harvard Univ. Press 2000 154p il (Charles Eliot Norton lectures) $25; pa $14.95   **809.1**
1. Poetry -- History and criticism
ISBN 0-674-00290-3; 0-674-00820-0 pa

LC 00-33541

This volume is based on the Argentine writer's "Charles Eliot Norton lectures [delivered] at Harvard in 1967-68. . . . [Borges] discusses some of his favorite texts, conducting a literary journey that began in his father's library in Buenos Aires." N Y Times Book Rev

Includes bibliographical references

Brodsky, Joseph

Less than one; selected essays. Farrar, Straus & Giroux 1986 501p hardcover o.p. pa $18   **809.1**
1. Poets 2. Authors 3. Essayists 4. College teachers
ISBN 0-374-52055-0 pa

LC 85-15900

The essays in this volume "begin and end with autobiographical pieces; in between there are alternate homages to favorite poets, both Russian and non-Russian, as well as substantial discussions of such topics as geography and history, political force and ethical choice, and literary tradition." N Y Times Book Rev

Burt, Stephen

Close calls with nonsense; reading new poetry. Graywolf Press 2009 374p bibl f pa $19   **809.1**
1. Poetry -- History and criticism
ISBN 1-55597-521-6; 978-1-55597-521-0

LC 2008-935602

"This collection of 30 essays, many of which began as book reviews, confirms Stephen Burt's reputation as the leading poetry critic of his generation. Informative, matter-of-fact and abounding with an excited spirit more common to film and pop music reviews than to literary criticism, these essays will appeal to the unpracticed reader of contemporary poetry as well as the seasoned reader. . . . Burt comes to the poets he considers—including Rea Armantrout, Juan Felipe Herrera, Paul Muldoon and James Merrill—as both a scholar and a practitioner of the art, but he eschews the specialist's jargon as well as the indulgent lyricality that makes some poets' criticism more dazzling than illuminating." Publ Wkly

Includes bibliographical references

Classic writings on poetry; edited by William Harmon. Columbia University Press 2003 538p $79; pa $27.50   **809.1**
1. Poetry -- History and criticism
ISBN 0-231-12370-1; 0-231-12371-X pa

LC 2003-40917

This anthology contains "writing on poetry by such philosophical royalty as Plato, Aristotle, Milton, Sir Philip Sidney, Wordsworth, and Emily Dickinson. Readers are given a peek through the hole of history's fence into the lives and worlds of our poetic geniuses and reminded of the poem's matchless role in conveying reverence, remembering wars, recording history, entertaining, expressing deep emotion, and above all, allowing the finite mind, for one moment, to contain infinity." Libr J

Includes bibliographical references

Gioia, Dana

Can poetry matter? essays on poetry and American culture. Dana Gioia. 10th Anniversary ed; Graywolf Press 2002 231p pa $16   **809.1**
1. Poets 2. Artists 3. Authors 4. Lawyers 5. Painters 6. Criticism 7. Dramatists 8. Editors 9. Translators 10. Poets laureate 11. College teachers 12. Literary critics 13. Magazine editors 14. Writers on nature 15. Short story writers 16. Insurance executives 17. Poetry -- History and criticism
ISBN 1-55597-370-1

LC 2002-102971

First published 1992

In addition to addressing the business of being a poet and the new formalism, the author offers readings of Robinson Jeffers, Weldon Kees, Robert Bly and others.

"Gioia makes his case with erudition and skill, and the best essays bring attention to underappreciated poets like Ted Kooser." Libr J

Hirsch, Edward

Poet's choice; Edward Hirsch. Harcourt 2006 432p $25   **809.1**
1. Poetry -- History and criticism
ISBN 0-15-101356-X; 978-0-15-101356-2

LC 2005-26890

"Hirsch's aesthetic is unerring, and his interpretations are profound as he considers our 'collective destiny' and takes measure of poetry's encompassing vision." Booklist

Koch, Kenneth

Making your own days; the pleasures of reading and writing poetry. Simon & Schuster 1999 317p pa $15   **809.1**
1. Poetry -- Collections 2. Poetry -- History and criticism
ISBN 0-684-82438-8

LC 98-115810

First published 1998 by Scribner

"This book is divided into two parts: a series of essays on subjects such as meter, rhyme, and personification and an anthology of favorite poems. Most remarkably, non-English poems often appear with several translations, underscoring the flexibility of poetic language. Making Your Own Days will be most useful to writers already familiar with the basics." Libr J

Paglia, Camille

★ **Break,** blow, burn; Camille Paglia. Pantheon Books 2005 247p $20; pa $12.95   **809.1**
1. English poetry -- History and criticism 2. American poetry -- History and criticism
ISBN 0-375-42084-3; 0-375-72539-3 pa

LC 2004-56573

This work "is vintage Paglia: bracing, opinionated, and deliciously enjoyable." Natl Rev

Includes bibliographical references

★ **Poetry** in person; twenty-five years of conversation with America's poets. edited and with an introduction by Alexander Neubauer; postscript by Robert Polito. Alfred A. Knopf 2010 343p il $27.95   **809.1**
1. Poetics 2. Poetry -- Authorship 3. Poetry -- History and criticism
ISBN 978-0-307-26967-6

LC 2009-29277

"For almost 30 years, beginning in 1970, Pearl London taught a course at the New School called Works in Progress, to which she asked famous poets to come with drafts of new poems in hand. This book is a series of transcripts of discussions from those classes, taken from a series of previously unknown recordings found after London's death. . . . Represented in these 23 conversations are such acknowledged masters of late 20th–century poetry as Robert Hass, Lucille Clifton, Amy Clampitt, and Charles Simic." Publ Wkly

809.3   Fiction – Criticism

Ellis, Samantha

How to Be a Heroine; Or, what I've learned from reading too much. by Samantha Ellis. Chatto & Windus 2014 272 p. $14.95   **809.3**
1. Heroes and heroines 2. Characters and characteristics in literature
ISBN 0701187514; 1101872098; 9780701187514; 9781101872093

LC 2014021162

This book, by Samantha Ellis, is "a retrospective look at the literary ladies—the characters and the writers—whom she has loved since childhood. From early obsessions with the March sisters to her later idolization of Sylvia Plath, Ellis evaluates how her heroines stack up today. And, just as she excavates the stories of her favorite characters, Ellis also shares a frank, often humorous account of her own life growing up in a tight-knit Iraqi Jewish community in London." (Publisher's note)

"The book could equally be titled How to Be a Reader; Ellis is passionate and engaged, railing against writers who shortchange their creations and celebrating those whose characters represent their best selves. She is frank about times she has misread works, and she employs a rigorous feminist lens. Primarily, though, this is a rousing call for women to be the heroines in their own lives, and it's good fun, to boot." Booklist

809.7   Humor – Criticism

Dauber, Jeremy

Jewish comedy; a serious history. Jeremy Dauber. W W Norton & Co Inc 2017 xviii, 364 p.p (hardcover) $28.95 **809.7**
1. Jewish wit and humor 2. Wit and humor -- History and criticism
3. Jews -- Humor 4. Jewish wit and humor -- History and criticism

ISBN 9780393247886; 9780393247879

LC 2017017864

In this book, author Jeremy Dauber "traces the origins of Jewish comedy and its development from biblical times to the age of Twitter. Organizing the product of Jews' comic imagination over continents and centuries into what he calls the seven strands of Jewish comedy--including the satirical, the witty, and the vulgar--he traces the ways Jewish comedy has mirrored, and sometimes even shaped, the course of Jewish history." (Publisher's note)

"Dauber takes in a wide swath of intellectual territory—from Kafka to Mad magazine—but he delicately mixes scholarship with comedy in what is an entertaining and even profound book." Booklist

Includes bibliographical references and index

Jennings, Ken

Planet funny; how comedy took over our culture. Ken Jennings. Simon & Schuster 2018 320 p. $26   **809.7**
1. Comedy 2. American wit and humor 3. Wit and humor -- History and criticism
ISBN 1501100580; 9781501100581

In this book, author "Ken Jennings, [offers] a history of humor--from fart jokes on clay Sumerian tablets all the way up to the latest Twitter gags and Facebook memes--that tells the story of how comedy came to rule the modern world. . . . Jennings explains how we built our humor-saturated modern age, where lots of us get our news from comedy shows and a comic figure can even be elected President of the United States purely on showmanship." (Publisher's note)

809.933   Literature dealing with specific themes and subjects

Literary Wonderlands; A Journey Through the Greatest Fictional Worlds Ever Created. by Laura Miller (Editor), Lev Grossman (Contributor), John Sutherland (Contributor) Hachette Books 2016 320 p. illustrations (chiefly color) $29.99   **809.933**
1. Literature -- Settings 2. English fiction -- History and criticism
3. American fiction -- History and criticism
ISBN 0316316385; 9780316316385

This book, edited by Laura Miller, with contributions from Lev Grossman and John Sutherland, "delves deep into the inception, influences, and literary and historical underpinnings of nearly 100 of our most beloved fictional realms. . . . It explores the timeless and captivating features of fiction's imagined worlds including the relevance of the writer's own life to the creation of the story . . . and the meaning that can be extracted from the details of the work." (Publisher's note)

"An encyclopedic look at literary landscapes featuring an encyclopedia's breadth and lack of depth." Kirkus

810   Literatures of specific languages and language families

Acosta-Belen, Edna

The **Norton** anthology of Latino literature; Ilan Stavans, general editor; [editors], Edna Acosta-Belen [et al.] W.W. Norton & Co. 2010 2489p il map $59.95   **810**
1. American literature -- Hispanic American authors -- Collections
ISBN 978-0-393-08007-0; 0-393-08007-2

LC 2010-15108

"With a great array of writers celebrated and too little known, and invaluable supporting materials, this grand and affecting treasury of culturally rich and aesthetically dynamic poems, fiction, drama, letters, diaries, and essays illuminates every aspect of Latino life." Booklist

Includes bibliographical references

★ **Baseball:** a literary anthology; edited by Nicholas Davidoff. Library of Am. 2002 721p $35 **810**

1. Baseball 2. American literature -- Collections

ISBN 1-931082-09-X

LC 2001-38654

"Beginning with Thayer's Casey at the Bat and ending with Buster Olney, there are more than 700 pages of prose and poetry, fiction and sportswriting, writers and players. Scanning the table of contents, it almost seems like everybody wrote about baseball: Damon Runyon, Ring Lardner, James Weldon Johnson, William Carlos Williams, James Thurber. But so did Paul Gallico, Nelson Algren, Tallulah Bankhead, and Jacques Barzun. . . . Ineffable, indispensable, inimitable—just like baseball." Booklist

Black women writers (1950-1980) a critical evaluation. edited by Mari Evans. Anchor Press 1984 xxviii, 543p hardcover o.p. pa $25 **810**

1. Poets 2. Actors 3. Authors 4. Singers 5. Novelists 6. Dramatists 7. Editors 8. Essayists 9. Columnists 10. Memoirists 11. College teachers 12. Literary critics 13. Social activists 14. Children's authors 15. Short story writers 16. Young adult authors 17. Theatrical directors 18. Motion picture directors 19. Nobel laureates for literature 20. American literature -- Women authors 21. American literature -- History and criticism 22. American literature -- African American authors

ISBN 0-385-17125-0 pa

LC 81-43914

Critical essays on Maya Angelou, Alice Childress, Toni Morisson, Lucille Clifton, and 11 other post World War II Afro-American women writers

"This important work, a tribute to the corpus of literature produced by black women, is an indispensable resource for any serious student, scholar or teacher desiring to probe the depths of the Afro-American literary tradition." Freedomways

Includes bibliographical references

Cheever, Susan

American Bloomsbury; Louisa May Alcott, Ralph Waldo Emerson, Margaret Fuller, Nathaniel Hawthorne, and Henry David Thoreau: their lives, their loves, their work. Simon & Schuster 2006 223p il $26 **810**

1. Authors, American 2. American literature -- History and criticism

ISBN 0-7432-6461-4; 978-0-7432-6461-7

LC 2006-45015

This book offers a "glimpse into life in Concord, MA, from about 1840 to the mid-1860s, when such luminaries as Louisa May Alcott, Ralph Waldo Emerson, Margaret Fuller, Nathaniel Hawthorne, and Henry David Thoreau lived, worked, and loved. . . . [This] volume examines the dynamic relationships among these remarkable men and women, who constituted what may be considered the first American literary community. . . . Essential reading for anyone with an interest in American letters." Libr J

Includes bibliographical references

★ The Chronology of American literature; America's literary achievements from the colonial era to modern times. edited by Daniel S. Burt. Houghton Mifflin 2004 805p il $40 **810**

1. American literature -- Collections

ISBN 0-618-16821-4

LC 2003-51142

"This chronology includes more than 8,400 literary works by more than 5,000 writers. Sections for each year are grouped in five chapters by period, from 1582 to 1999. Within each year, entries are grouped by genre, such as diaries and other personal writings, fiction, essays, literary criticism and scholarship, nonfiction, poetry, and drama. Within each genre, authors are listed alphabetically, generally with birth and death dates and short descriptions of named works for the year. . . . The Chronology of American Literature is easy to browse and, for book lovers, difficult to put down." Booklist

Includes bibliographical references

Elie, Paul

The **life** you save may be your own; an American pilgrimage. Farrar, Straus and Giroux 2003 554p il hardcover o.p. pa $16 **810**

1. Monks 2. Poets 3. Authors 4. Novelists 5. Journalists 6. Reference books 7. Essayists 8. Social reformers 9. Newspaper editors 10. Nonfiction writers 11. Short story writers 12. Writers on religion 13. American literature -- Bio-bibliography 14. American literature -- History and criticism

ISBN 0-374-25680-2; 978-0-374-52921-5 pa; 0-374-52921-3 pa

LC 2002-192522

"This thoroughly researched and well-sourced work deserves attention from students of history, literature and religion, but it will be of special significance to Catholic readers interested in the expression of faith in the modern world." Publ Wkly

Encyclopedia of African-American writing; five centuries of contribution: trials & triumphs of writers, poets, publications and organizations. Shari Dorantes Hatch, editor. 2nd ed.; Grey House Pub. 2009 xxii, 863p il $165 **810**

1. Reference books 2. American literature -- African American authors -- Encyclopedias 3. American literature -- African American authors -- Bio-bibliography

ISBN 978-1-59237-291-1

First published 2000 by ABC-CLIO with title: African-American writers: a dictionary

"This voluminous and inclusive collection consists of 738 entries that cover authors and other topics related to African American writing, such as newspapers, magazines, journals, and publishers and figures such as educators, playwrights, journalists, academics, editors, and librarians from the past 500 years. . . . Although unsigned, the entries are highly accessible, very current, and chock-full of information for a range of audiences." Libr J

Includes bibliographical references

Encyclopedia of American Indian literature; [edited by] Jennifer McClinton-Temple, Alan Velie. Facts on File 2007 466p (Encyclopedia of American ethnic literature) $75 **810**

1. Reference books 2. Native American literature -- Encyclopedias 3. Native Americans in literature -- Encyclopedias

ISBN 0-8160-5656-0; 978-0-8160-5656-9

LC 2006-23762

"This book brings together solid information from scattered sources, facilitating research on an esoteric subject." Libr J

Includes bibliographical references

Facts on File, Inc.

★ **Encyclopedia** of American literature; 2nd ed; Facts on File 2008 4v il (Facts on File library of American literature)

set $375 **810**

1. Reference books 2. American literature -- Encyclopedias
ISBN 978-0-8160-6476-2 LC 2007-25662

First published 2002

Entries in this encyclopedia cover works, writers, movements and other American literature-related topics from colonial times to the present. Each volume includes a chronology.

Includes bibliographical references

Jewish American literature; a Norton anthology. [compiled and edited by] Jules Chametzky [et al.] Norton 2000 xxiv, 1221p il $39.95 **810**

1. American literature -- Collections 2. American literature -- Jewish authors
ISBN 0-393-04809-8

LC 00-55393

The editors have attempted "to encompass Jewish literature from 1654 to the present in this collection of poems, cartoons, sermons, diaries, letters, stories, speeches, plays, prayers, novel excerpts, and critical writings either translated from Hebrew or Yiddish or written in English. Major sections group the literature chronologically to help identify large movements. . . . This great anthology is essential for Jewish studies and American literature collections." Libr J

Includes bibliographical references

★ **Latino** and Latina writers; Alan West-Durán, editor. Charles Scribner's Sons 2004 1072p 2v (Scribner writers series) set $265 **810**

1. American literature -- Hispanic American authors
ISBN 0-684-31293-X

LC 2003-15728

This set "begins with five essays of social and historical commentary that focus on key elements of Latino culture in this country. What follows is a series of ten to 20-page biocritical essays on nearly 60 authors (e.g., Gary Soto, Pat Mora, Sandra Cisneros, Victor Villase or, Julia Alvarez, Richard Rodriguez, and Lorna Dee Cervantes). . . . One of the most comprehensive anthologies available of Latino writing in the United States." Libr J

Includes bibliographical references

★ **Magill's** survey of American literature; edited by Steven G. Kellman. Rev. ed; Salem Press 2007 6v il set $499 **810**

1. Reference books 2. Literature -- Bio-bibliography 3. Literature -- History and criticism
ISBN 978-1-58765-285-1; 1-58765-285-4

LC 2006-16503

First published 1992 with two volume supplement published 1996 under the editorship of Frank Northen Magill

"Examining selected works of 339 U.S. and Canadian writers, from Anne Bradstreet and Benjamin Franklin to Edward Bloor and Octavia E. Butler, this clearly written resource provides sturdy support for assignments, and will also be popular with discussion groups and with general readers of literature." SLJ

Includes bibliographical references

Matthiessen, F. O.

★ **American** renaissance; art and expression in the age of Emerson and Whitman. Oxford Univ. Press 1941 xxiv, 678p il hardcover o.p. pa $53 **810**

1. Poets 2. Artists 3. Authors 4. Novelists 5. Sculptors 6. Naturalists 7. Philosophers 8. Essayists 9. Pacifists 10. Writers on nature 11. Nonfiction writers 12. Short story writers 13. American literature -- History and criticism

ISBN 0-19-500759-X pa

A critical study of works by Emerson, Thoreau, Melville, Hawthorne and Whitman and their impact on American intellectual history.

Morgan, Bill

The **typewriter** is holy; the complete, uncensored history of the beat generation. Free Press 2010 291p il $28 **810**

1. Beat generation 2. American literature -- History and criticism 3. American literature -- 20th century -- History and criticism
ISBN 1-4165-9242-3; 978-1-4165-9242-6

LC 2009-42224

In this book, Bill Morgan "employs a wide focus to portray the remarkable group of writers and artists that became known as the Beat Generation. He suggests that Jack Kerouac, Lawrence Ferlinghetti, Gary Snyder, Gregory Corso, William Burroughs, and others had such divergent aims and styles that they cannot properly be considered a literary movement. Instead, he sees them as a circle of friends who loved literature and were united by [Allen] Ginsberg." (Library Journal)

"Morgan clearly loves his subjects, but he doesn't gloss over their erratic lifestyle, which involved amazing amounts of drugs and alcohol, and their consummate selfishness. . . . Morgan's own prose is straightforward, even pedestrian, but his ability to draw together so many events and personalities is astonishing." Providence J

Includes bibliographical references

National Story Project (U.S.)

I thought my father was God and other true tales from the National Story Project; edited and introduced by Paul Auster; Nelly Reifler, assistant editor. Holt & Co. 2001 xxi, 383p il hardcover o.p. pa $15 **810**

1. American literature -- Collections
ISBN 0-8050-6714-0; 0-312-42100-1 pa

LC 00-54397

"These are stop-you-in-your-tracks stories about hair-raising coincidences, miracles, tragedies, redemption, and moments of pure hilarity." Booklist

A **new** literary history of America; edited by Greil Marcus and Werner Sollors. Belknap Press of Harvard University Press 2009 1095p bibl f il (Harvard University Press reference library) $49.95 **810**

1. United States -- Civilization 2. American literature -- History and criticism
ISBN 978-0-674-03594-2; 0-674-03594-1

LC 2009014255

"This is an adventurous, jazzily choral, and kaleidoscopic book of interpretations, illuminations, and revitalized history." Booklist

Includes bibliographical references and index

★ The **Norton** anthology of African American literature; Henry Louis Gates, Jr., general editor, Nellie Y. McKay, general editor. 2nd ed; Norton 2003 2800p 2 computer laser optical discs pa $70.30 **810**

1. American literature -- African American authors -- Collections
ISBN 0-393-97778-1

LC 2003-66176

First published 1996

"The anthology is divided into seven sections, each with a separate introduction giving the sociopolitical factors that impacted on the material included therein. Featured are 120 writers, 52 of whom are women, richly representing African American vernacular literature, poetry, drama, short stories, novels, slave narratives, and autobiographies." Libr J

[review of 1996 edition]
    Includes bibliographical references

★ The **Oxford** encyclopedia of American literature; Jay Parini, editor-in-chief. Oxford University Press 2004 4v il set $495   **810**
    1. Reference books 2. American literature -- Encyclopedias
    ISBN 0-19-515653-6

LC 2002-156325

    This set "provides a wealth of reliable information on standard bearers of American literature in an easy-on-the-eyes format for students and general readers." SLJ

Parini, Jay
    Promised land; thirteen books that changed America. Doubleday 2008 385p il $24.95   **810**
    1. American national characteristics 2. American literature -- History and criticism
    ISBN 978-0-385-52276-2

LC 2008-9990

    This is "a mind-expanding book of books guaranteed to provoke discussion and fuel reading groups." Booklist
    Includes bibliographical references

Pierpont, Claudia Roth
    Passionate minds; women rewriting the world. Knopf 2000 298p il hardcover o.p. pa $13   **810**
    1. Poets 2. Actors 3. Authors 4. Lawyers 5. Novelists 6. Dramatists 7. Philosophers 8. Women authors 9. Diarists 10. Essayists 11. Feminists 12. Memoirists 13. Folklorists 14. Screenwriters 15. College teachers 16. Literary critics 17. Nonfiction writers 18. Short story writers 19. Writers on politics 20. Political scientists 21. Nobel laureates for literature 22. Political and social philosophers 23. English literature -- Women authors -- History and criticism 24. American literature -- Women authors -- History and criticism
    ISBN 0-679-43106-3; 0-679-75113-0 pa

LC 99-33349

    "A scintillating collection of brief lives of women writers, a book that sparkles with intelligence, wit and human interest. . . . Unfolding with the dramatic élan of a novella, each one is exhaustively researched, sharply focused, convincingly opinionated." N Y Times Book Rev

The **Portable** sixties reader; edited by Ann Charters. Penguin Bks. 2003 xli, 628p il pa $16   **810**
    1. American literature -- Collections 2. United States -- History -- 1961-1974
    ISBN 0-14-200194-5

LC 2002-32266

    This reader includes "essays, poetry, and fiction under thematic subjects, such as civil rights; women's rights; the sexual revolution; environmental issues; the antiwar, free-speech, and black-arts movements; and the use of drugs in pursuit of enlightenment. . . . [Includes works by] James Baldwin, Thomas Merton, Susan Sontag, Gary Snyder, Allen Ginsburg, Rachel Carson, Kate Millett, Nikki Giovanni, and many more." Booklist
    Includes bibliographical references

★ The **Pushcart** Prize XLIII; edited by Bill Henderson with the Pushcart Prize editors. Pushcart 2018   **810**
    1. American literature -- Collections
    Annual. First published 1976
    Each volume "consists of short stories, poems and essays; includes

the work of established and beginning writers, and has a faintly subversive character. Its audience would seem to be primarily the young, yet among its contributors are many of the best writers in America. . . . Like all interesting literary journals, 'The Pushcart Prize' is eclectic and uneven. . . . The number and diversity of journals represented and the sheer length of it are impressive." Books of the Times
    Includes bibliographical references

Salem Press Inc.
    ★ **Notable** Latino writers; from the editors of Salem Press. Salem Press 2005 3v il (Magill's choice) set $207   **810**
    1. American literature -- Hispanic American authors -- History and criticism
    ISBN 1-58765-243-9; 978-1-58765-243-1

LC 2005-17567

    These volumes feature "122 essays about Latino novelists, shortstory writers, poets, and playwrights of the Western Hemisphere who write in English, Spanish, or Portuguese. . . . This set may prove to be a useful research tool for students, teachers, and librarians." Libr J
    Includes bibliographical references

Samet, Elizabeth D.
    ★ **Soldier's** heart; reading literature through peace and war at West Point. Farrar, Straus and Giroux 2007 259p $23 **810**
    1. United States Military Academy 2. Soldiers -- United States 3. Literature -- Study and teaching
    ISBN 978-0-374-18063-8; 0-374-18063-6

LC 2007-9159

    "Like the best professors, Samet asks tough questions and offers no easy answers. Her book is filled with lively classroom discussions and poignant e-mails from former students now in Iraq, often writing about the books they're reading there. . . . I know of no other new book that's a better choice for any reading group that loves to debate literature and politics." USA Today

Showalter, Elaine, 1941-
    ★ A **jury** of her peers; American women writers from Anne Bradstreet to Annie Proulx. Alfred A. Knopf 2009 586p $30   **810**
    1. Women in literature 2. Literature -- Women authors 3. American literature -- Women authors 4. Women in literature -- United States 5. Women and literature -- United States -- History 6. American literature -- Women authors -- Bio-bibliography 7. American literature -- Women authors -- History and criticism
    ISBN 978-1-4000-4123-7; 1-4000-4123-6

LC 2008-42312

    "Showalter's writing is clear, lively, and authoritative; her research is impressive." Libr J
    Includes bibliographical references

Taylor, Todd W.
    ★ The **Companion** to southern literature; themes, genres, places, people, movements, and motifs. edited by Joseph M. Flora and Lucinda H. MacKethan; associate editor, Todd Taylor. Louisiana State Univ. Press 2001 xxvi, 1054p $69.95   **810**
    1. Reference books 2. Southern States -- Intellectual life 3. American literature -- Southern States -- Encyclopedias
    ISBN 0-8071-2692-6

LC 2001-29959

    "This unique compilation [is] . . . an excellent addition to libraries that support studies of Southern literature." Libr J
    Includes bibliographical references

Transcendentalism; a reader. [edited by] Joel Myerson. Oxford Univ. Press 2001 xxxvii, 712p hardcover o.p. pa $32 **810**

1. New England -- Intellectual life 2. Transcendentalism -- Collections

ISBN 0-19-512212-7; 0-19-512213-5 pa

LC 00-21484

This reader "draws together in their entirety the essential writings of the Transcendentalist group during its most active period, 1836-1844. It includes the major publications of the Dial, the writings on democratic and social reform, the early poetry, nature writings, and all of Emerson's major essays, as well as an . . . introduction and annotations by Myerson." Publisher's note

Includes bibliographical references

Wall, Cheryl A.

Women of the Harlem Renaissance. Indiana Univ. Press 1995 246p il (Women of letters) hardcover o.p. pa $14.95 **810**

1. Nurses 2. Authors 3. Novelists 4. Dramatists 5. Harlem Renaissance 6. Editors 7. Essayists 8. Memoirists 9. Folklorists 10. Literary critics 11. Short story writers 12. American literature -- African American authors

ISBN 0-253-20980-3 pa

LC 95-3132

This study of women writers of the Harlem Renaissance begins with an overview: On being young—a woman—and colored, followed by critical and biographical studies of Jessie Redmond Fauset, Nella Larsen, and Zora Neale Hurston

"Wall offers strong critiques of these women's work, uncovering certain similarities, including, most importantly, the travel motif as not only a reflection of the mass migrations of the day but also a larger dislocation." Publ Wkly

Includes bibliographical references

Wilson, Edmund

Patriotic gore; studies in the literature of the American Civil War. Norton 1994 816p pa $19.95 **810**

1. Poets 2. Clergy 3. Judges 4. Authors 5. Lawyers 6. Generals 7. Pianists 8. Diplomats 9. Educators 10. Governors 11. Novelists 12. Presidents 13. Journalists 14. Abolitionists 15. Flutists 16. Essayists 17. Memoirists 18. Sociologists 19. Army officers 20. Political leaders 21. State legislators 22. Children's authors 23. Nonfiction writers 24. Secretaries of war 25. White supremacists 26. Members of Congress 27. Novelists, American 28. Short story writers 29. Writers on politics 30. Civil rights activists 31. Supreme Court justices 32. Spouses of prominent persons 33. American literature -- History and criticism 34. United States -- History -- 1861-1865, Civil War 35. United States -- History -- 1861-1865, Civil War -- Poetry 36. United States -- History -- 1861-1865, Civil War -- Biography

ISBN 978-0-393-31256-0; 0-393-31256-9

First published 1962 by Oxford University Press

"A collection of sixteen essays on writing related to the war including the memoirs of Union generals Grant and Sherman and Confederates Mosby and Lee, diaries, political writing, and fiction by writers such as Ambrose Bierce and John De Forest." Benet's Reader's Ency of Am Lit

810.8 American literature (English) -- Collections

Bohemians, bootleggers, flappers, and swells; the best of early Vanity fair. introduction by Graydon Carter; edited by David Friend. The Penguin Press 2014 432 p. $29.95 **810.8**

1. Periodicals 2. World history -- 20th century 3. Literature, Modern -- 20th century 4. American literature -- 20th century 5. United States -- Civilization -- 20th century -- Literary collections

ISBN 1594205981; 9781594205989

LC 2014009783

Edited by Graydon Carter "In honor of the 100th anniversary of Vanity Fair magazine, 'Bohemians, Bootleggers, Flappers, and Swells' celebrates the publication's astonishing early catalogue of writers, with works by Dorothy Parker, Noël Coward, P. G. Wodehouse, Jean Cocteau, Colette, Gertrude Stein, Edna St. Vincent Millay, Sherwood Anderson, Robert Benchley, Langston Hughes--and many others." (Publisher's note)

"These delightful period pieces reflecting the social mores of their time hold up in their innovation, style, and concern about modern life nearly a century later." Booklist

810.9 American literature (English) -- History and criticism

African American literature; a guide to reading interests. edited by Alma Dawson and Connie Van Fleet. Libraries Unlimited 2004 xx, 470 p.p (alk. paper) $65 **810.9**

1. African Americans in literature 2. American literature -- African American authors 3. African Americans in literature -- Bibliography 4. African Americans -- Intellectual life -- Bibliography 5. African Americans in literature -- Handbooks, manuals, etc 6. American literature -- African American authors -- Bibliography 7. African Americans -- Intellectual life -- Handbooks, manuals, etc 8. American literature -- African American authors -- History and criticism -- Handbooks, manuals, etc

ISBN 1563089319; 9781563089312

LC 2004048928

This book, edited by Alma Dawson and Connie Van Fleet, "is the first readers' advisory guide to focus specifically on African American literature. It is designed to help book professionals better serve not only African American readers, but all readers who enjoy works by African American authors. . . . Each chapter is further organized by subgenre and theme. Title-author and subject indexes provide additional access." (Publisher's note)

Includes bibliographical references (p. 419-431) and indexes

Bram, Christopher

Eminent outlaws; the gay writers who changed America. Christopher Bram. Twelve 2012 372 p. **810.9**

1. Social change 2. American authors 3. Gay men's writings 4. Gay men -- Biography 5. Homosexuality -- United States -- History 6. Gay authors -- United States 7. Authors, American -- 20th century 8. Gays' writings, American -- History and criticism

ISBN 9780446563130

LC 2011029910

"This book is a history, literary critique, and collective biography in one. Novelist [Christopher] Bram . . . discusses gay men . . . from Gore Vidal in the early postwar years up through the 1990s and close to the present. His main thesis, that 'good art can lay the groundwork for social change,' is demonstrated and contextualized in dozens of examples of how literature can be not just a reflection of the times but also a catalyst for change." (Library Journal)

Includes bibliographical references (p. 351-354) and index

Ginsberg, Allen, 1926-1997

The **best** minds of my generation; a literary history of the Beats. Allen Ginsberg; with a foreword by Anne Waldman; edited by Bill Morgan. First Grove Atlantic hardcover Grove Press 2017 xxviii, 460 p.p (hardcover) $27 **810.9**

1. Beat generation 2. American literature -- 20th century -- History and criticism

ISBN 9780802126498; 0802126499

LC 2017003026

"In 1977, twenty years after the publication of his landmark poem 'Howl,' and Jack Kerouac's seminal book 'On the Road,' Allen Ginsberg decided it was time to teach a course on the literary history of the Beat Generation. . . . Compiled and edited by renowned Beat scholar Bill Morgan, and with an introduction by Anne Waldman, . . . [this book] presents the lectures in edited form, complete with notes, and paints a portrait of the Beats as Ginsberg knew them." (Publisher's note)

"A rich sourcebook for literary historians and fans of the passionate, iconoclastic Beats." Kirkus

Includes bibliographical references.

Laing, Olivia

The **Trip** to Echo Spring; On Writers and Drinking. Olivia Laing. 1st U.S. ed. Picador 2014 352 p. illustrations, map (hbk.) $26 **810.9**

1. Alcoholism 2. Creation (Literary, artistic, etc.) 3. American literature -- History and criticism 4. Alcoholics in literature 5. Alcoholism in literature 6. Alcoholics -- United States 7. Authorship -- Psychological aspects 8. Creative ability -- Psychological aspects 9. Authors, American -- 20th century -- Alcohol use 10. American literature -- 20th century -- History and criticism

ISBN 1250039568; 9781250039569

LC 2013038323

In this book, "Olivia Laing examines the link between creativity and alcohol through the work and lives of six extraordinary men: F. Scott Fitzgerald, Ernest Hemingway, Tennessee Williams, John Berryman, John Cheever, and Raymond Carver. . . . Olivia Laing grew up in an alcoholic family herself. One spring, wanting to make sense of this ferocious, entangling disease, she took a journey across America that plunged her into the heart of these overlapping lives." (Publisher's note)

"Intently observant, curious, and empathetic, Laing, with shimmering detail and arresting insights, presents a beautifully elucidating and moving group portrait of writers enslaved by drink and redeemed by 'the capacity of literature to somehow . . . make one feel less flinchingly alone.' " Booklist

Includes bibliographical references

Pierpont, Claudia Roth

American rhapsody; writers, musicians, millionaires, movie stars, and one great building. Claudia Roth Pierpont. Farrar, Straus & Giroux 2016 320 p. illustrations (ebook) $60; (hardback) $26 **810.9**

1. Performing arts -- 20th century -- Biography 2. American authors -- 20th century -- Biography 3. Popular culture -- United States -- 20th century 4. Authors, American -- 20th century -- Biography

ISBN 9780374708771; 9780374104405

LC 2015036371

This book, by Claudia Roth Pierpont, "presents a kaleidoscopic story of the creation of a culture. Here is a series of deeply involving portraits of American artists and innovators who have helped to shape the country

in the modern age. . . . Pierpont expertly mixes biography and criticism, history and reportage, to bring these portraits to life and to link them in surprising ways." (Publisher's note)

"As vital and entertaining as the creators and work it celebrates, American Rhapsody is an uncommonly satisfying celebration of the cultural kaleidoscope known as the United States." Kirkus

Roberts, Kim

A **literary** guide to Washington, DC; walking in the footsteps of American writers from Francis Scott Key to Zora Neale Hurston. Kim Roberts. University of Virginia Press 2018 240 p. (pbk.: alk. paper) $27.95 **810.9**

1. American authors 2. American literature 3. Literary landmarks -- United States 4. Washington (D.C.) -- Guidebooks 5. Washington (D.C.) -- Intellectual life 6. Literary landmarks -- Washington (D.C.) -- Guidebooks 7. American literature -- Washington (D.C.) Bio-bibliography 8. Authors, American -- Homes and haunts -- Washington (D.C.) -- Guidebooks

ISBN 9780813941165; 9780813941172

LC 2017059448

"In 'A Literary Guide to Washington, DC,' Kim Roberts offers a guide to the city's rich literary history. Part walking tour, part anthology, [the book] is organized into five sections, each corresponding to a particularly vibrant period in Washington's literary community. . . . Written for tourists, literary enthusiasts, amateur historians, and armchair travelers, [the book] offers a cultural tour of our nation's capital through a literary lens." (Publisher's note)

"The perfect accompaniment for a literature-inspired vacation in the U.S. capital. The compact size, clearly labeled maps, and succinct, informative text make this a handy guide to slip into your suitcase." LJ

Includes bibliographical references and index

A **story** larger than my own; women writers look back on their lives and careers. edited by Janet Burroway. University of Chicago Press 2014 199 p. (cloth: alkaline paper) $55 **810.9**

1. Women poets 2. Women authors 3. Autobiographies 4. Women authors, American -- Literary collections

ISBN 022601407X; 9780226014074; 9780226014104

LC 2013032197

"In this engrossing volume edited by [Janet] Burroway . . ., 19 accomplished female authors reflect on their careers and offer insights on craft and life. The contributors, all of whom are 60 or older, came of professional age during second wave feminism, confronted the prejudice against women writers of the 1950's and 60's, and continue to publish in the digital age. The variety of voices and styles adds up to a mesmerizing tapestry of a generation, made up of both individual experiences and the commonalities between them." Pub Wkly

811 American poetry

180 more; extraordinary poems for every day. selected and with an introduction by Billy Collins. Random House 2005 xxiii, 373p pa $14.95 **811**

1. American poetry -- Collections

ISBN 0-8129-7296-1

LC 2005-42798

Sequel to: Poetry 180

This is a second collection of 180 poems for each day of the school year, designed to expose high school students to poetry.

Ackerman, Diane, 1948-

Origami bridges; poems of psychoanalysis and fire. HarperCollins Pubs. 2002 147p $22.95; pa $11.95   **811**
1. Poetry -- By individual authors
ISBN 0-06-019988-1; 0-06-055529-7 pa

LC 2002-24685

"Sometimes addressed to herself and her personal history, at least as often addressed to 'Dr. B—,' Ackerman's passionate free verse (short, fluent and adorned by irregular rhyme) describes with nearly unmixed awe the relationship she created with her analyst, and the personal transformation she achieved." Publ Wkly

Addonizio, Kim

Mortal trash; poems. Kim Addonizio. W W Norton & Co Inc 2016 107 p. (hardcover) $25.95   **811**
1. American poetry
ISBN 9780393249163

LC 2016008753

This book of poems, by Kim Addonizio, "transports the readers into a world of wit, lament, and desire. In a section called 'Over the Bright and Darkened Lands,' canonical poems are torqued into new shapes. 'Except Thou Ravish Me,' reimagines John Donne's famous 'Batter my heart, Three-person'd God' as told from the perspective of a victim of domestic violence." (Publisher's note)

"The prolific Addonizio . . . maintains her practice of brash and boozy musings where the minor catastrophes of love, lust, and aging mingle with the grander horrors of terrorism and global warming." Pub Wkly

Akbar, Kaveh

Calling a wolf a wolf; Kaveh Akbar. Alice James Books 2017 89 p.   **811**
1. Poetry 2. Alcoholism -- Poetry 3. Alcoholics -- Rehabilitation -- Poetry
ISBN 9781938584725; 9781938584671

LC 2017015979

This debut collection of poems, by Kaveh Akbar, "confronts addiction and courses the strenuous path of recovery, beginning in the wilds of the mind. Poems confront craving, control, the constant battle of alcoholism and sobriety, and the questioning of the self and its instincts within the context of this never-ending fight." (Publisher's note)

"His work stands out among literature on the subject for a refreshingly unshowy honesty; Akbar runs full tilt emotionally but is never self-indulgent." LJ

Alexander, Elizabeth, 1962-

Crave radiance; new and selected poems 1990-2010. Graywolf Press 2010 255p   **811**
1. Poetry -- By individual authors
ISBN 9781555975685

LC 2010-922921

"This potent retrospective collection offers the best of Alexander's five previous books, including selections from her young-adult title, Miss Crandall's School for Young Girls and Little Misses of Color (2007), which hold their own as poems for adults of all ages here. . . . Alexander brings intellectual power, musicality, sensuousness, and vernacular immediacy to her lyrics, which entwine the personal with the social, the tactile with the imaginary, the past with the present." Booklist

Alexie, Sherman

Face. Hanging Loose Press 2009 159p $28; pa $15 **811**
1. Poetry -- By individual authors

ISBN 978-1-931236-71-3; 1-931236-71-2; 978-1-931236-70-6 pa; 1-931236-70-4 pa

LC 2008-46580

The author "has mastered both the metrical dance and fixed forms. A sequence of sonnets finds the Seven Deadly Sins in marriage, for instance; a villanelle begins with Mount Rushmore but eases into a consideration of America's Presidents, complemented by wry and smart footnotes. . . . There are a lot of serious undercurrents in his poetry, and they are always a pleasure to find." Libr J

Alsadir, Nuar

Fourth person singular; Nuar Alsadir. Liverpool University Press 2017 73 p. (paperback) $19.95   **811**
1. Self 2. Poetry 3. Literature -- Collections
ISBN 9781786940193; 1786940191
National Book Critics Circle Award Finalist: Poetry (2017)

This poetry book, in the Pavilion Poetry LUP series, by Nuar Alsadir, "continues to blow open the relationship between self and world in a working through of lyric shame, bending poetic form through fragment, lyric essay, aphorisms mined from the unconscious, and pop-up associations, to explore the complexities, congruities, disturbances - as well as the beauty - involved in self-representation in language." (Publisher's note)

Alvarez, Julia

The woman I kept to myself; poems. Algonquin Books of Chapel Hill 2004 155p hardcover o.p. pa $14.95   **811**
1. Poetry -- By individual authors
ISBN 1-56512-406-5; 1-61620-072-3 pa

LC 2003-70807

This "collection of 75 poems is divided into three sections, and each poem has three stanzas, exactly . . . The poet, who is from the Dominican Republic, writes about being raised with her sisters in New York. The subjects are personal—love, marriage, rejection, divorce, death, religion—but also universal." SLJ

★ **American** poetry, the twentieth century. Library of Am. 2000 2v ea $35   **811**
1. American poetry -- Collections
ISBN 1-88301-177-9 v1; 1-88301-178-7 v2

LC 99-43721

These volumes represent a "remarkable feat of assemblage, with excellent capsule biographies and explanatory notes at the end of each volume—the biographies, especially, are well worth reading." N Y Times Book Rev
Includes bibliographical references

★ **American** poetry: the seventeenth and eighteenth centuries; edited by David Shields. Library of America 2007 xxiii, 952p $40   **811**
1. American poetry -- Collections
ISBN 978-1-931082-90-7; 1-931082-90-1

LC 2007-929763

"Besides hefty helpings of the few figures meagerly represented in general American-lit surveys—Anne Bradstreet, Edward Taylor, John Trumbull, Timothy Dwight, Philip Freneau, Phyllis Wheatley—here are poems short and . . . long by dozens of others, most of them obscure to even thoroughgoing, historically minded poetry lovers. . . . The subject matter isn't all religion and politics. Work, family, leisure, and exceptional events and lives (one man recounts escape from the limited slavery that was indenture) are all written up. And, in regular rhymes and meters, it's all quite readable. Early-American history buffs as much as, if not more than, poetry readers may consider the book a gold mine."

Booklist
Includes bibliographical references

American religious poems; an anthology by Harold Bloom. Harold Bloom and Jesse Zuba, editors. Library of America 2006 685p $40 **811**
  1. Religious poetry 2. American poetry -- Collections
  ISBN 1-931082-74-X

                      LC 2006-41031
An anthology of "verse on Christian, Jewish, Islamic, Buddhist, Native American spiritual, Transcendentalist and even agnostic themes, from 17th-century European colonists (one poet is Roger Williams, who founded Rhode Island) to up-and-comers in contemporary verse. Pious readers will have no trouble finding high-quality poetry that confirms their beliefs—from the monk Thomas Merton, the Anglican T.S. Eliot, the Jewish liturgical poet Esther Schor and the Louisiana-based Christian poet Martha Serpas. Yet from the 19th century to the present, from the decidedly heterodox Emily Dickinson forwards, the anthology often highlights the ways in which American spirituality has challenged all doctrines about who God is and what God does. . . . More than half of the book is taken up by 20th-century poets, who offer varied takes on what religion has come to mean in America." Publ Wkly

★ **American** war poetry; an anthology. edited by Lorrie Goldensohn. Columbia University Press 2006 413p $27.95 **811**
  1. War poetry 2. American poetry -- Collections
  ISBN 0-231-13310-3

                      LC 2005-54762
"Arranged by war, the book begins with the Colonial period and proceeds through Whitman admiring Civil War soldiers crossing a river to end with Brian Turner, who published his first book in 2005, beckoning a bullet in contemporary Iraq. Many voices, by turns elegiac, outraged, rhetorical and ecstatic are represented." Publ Wkly
Includes bibliographical references

American wits; an anthology of light verse. John Hollander, editor. Library of America 2003 xxv, 194p (American poets project) $20 **811**
  1. American poetry -- Collections 2. Humorous poetry -- Collections
  ISBN 978-1-931082-49-5; 1-931082-49-9

                      LC 2003-46636
This anthology "offers some exceptionally clever writing, much of which will be unfamiliar to many readers (and therefore all the more amusing). Hollander sensibly allots the most space to Ogden Nash and Dorothy Parker; the selections from both are solid. But Hollander's good judgment is best demonstrated by the third most represented poet here, the screenwriter Samuel Hoffenstein (1890-1947). . . . The poetry world currently has a surplus of writers who are eager, sometimes even desperate, to be funny, but we're suffering from a shortage of genuine wit." Poetry (Modern Poetry Association)

Ammons, A. R., 1926-2001
  ★ The **complete** poems of A. R. Ammons; Volume 2 1978-2005. edited by Robert M. West; introduction by Helen Vendler. W W Norton & Co Inc 2017 liii, 1031 p.p Vol. 2 (hardcover: v. 2) $49.95 **811**
  1. American poetry 2. American literature 3. American poetry -- 20th century
  ISBN 9780393254891

                      LC 2017047332
This poetry collection "presents the second half of Archie Randolph Ammons's long career, including the complete texts of his two book-length poems from that period: 'Garbage,' for which he won his second

National Book Award, and 'Glare,' which drew special praise from the Academy of American Poets as it bestowed on him its highest honor, the Wallace Stevens Award." (Publisher's note)
  Includes bibliographical references and index

Angelou, Maya
  ★ The **complete** collected poems of Maya Angelou. Random House 1994 273p $24.95 **811**
  1. Poetry -- By individual authors
  ISBN 0-679-42895-X

                      LC 94-14501
This volume contains all of Angelou's published poems including her inaugural poem On the pulse of morning

I shall not be moved. Random House 1997 48p $15; pa $9.95 **811**
  1. Poetry -- By individual authors
  ISBN 0-679-45708-9; 0-553-35458-3 pa
  First published 1990
  "Angelou's themes include loss of love and youth, human oneness in diversity, the strength of blacks in the face of racism and adversity." Publ Wkly

Angles of ascent; a Norton anthology of contemporary African American poetry. edited by Charles Henry Rowell. W.W. Norton & Co. 2012 672 p. (pbk.) $24.95 **811**
  1. American poetry -- African American authors 2. American poetry -- 21st century
  ISBN 0393339408; 9780393339406

                      LC 2011042967
This poetry anthology, edited by Charles Henry Rowell, features "more than seventy [African American] poets. . . . These poets bear witness to the interior landscapes of their own individual selves or examine the private or personal worlds of invented personae and, therefore, of human beings living in our modern and postmodern worlds. The anthology focuses on post-1960s poetry and includes such poets as Rita Dove, . . . Natasha Trethewey, . . . and Yusef Komunyakaa." (Publisher's note)

Armantrout, Rae
  Versed. Wesleyan University Press 2009 121p (Wesleyan poetry) $22.95 **811**
  1. Poetry -- By individual authors
  ISBN 978-0-8195-6879-3; 0-8195-6879-1

                      LC 2008-43809
  National Book Critics Award (2010)
  Pulitzer Prize (2010)
  Pulitzer Prize Finalist (2010)
  National Book Award Finalists (2009)
  This book "book comprises two sequences — 'Versed' and 'Dark Matter'— of loosely interlinked poems dealing with the prolific poet's usual subjects (the body, contemporary society, violence) as well as more personal explorations of illness and mortality, all relayed in Armantrout's concentrated, crystalline voice, with a predilection for skipping some steps along the way to sense." Publ Wkly

Ashbery, John
  Collected poems 1956-1987; [edited by Mark Ford] Library of America 2008 1042p $40 **811**
  1. Poetry -- By individual authors
  ISBN 978-1-59853-028-5
  "This major book, the first collection from Library of America by a living poet, offers a view of Ashbery's artistic development over many

decades. . . . Watching Ashbery's art grow from the slippery romanticism and verbal hijinks of the early poems through the philosophical, if sideways, inquiry of the '70s, to the chattier, colloquial period inaugurated in the early '80s, is arresting. Though Ashbery has confounded and inspired in seemingly equal measure, he is, according to both his admirers and critics, the towering figure in contemporary American poetry." Publ Wkly

Notes from the air; selected later poems. Ecco 2007 364p $34.95 **811**

1. Poetry -- By individual authors
ISBN 978-0-06-136717-5; 0-06-136717-6
LC 2008-270813

This "volume—beginning with poems from April Galleons (1987) and ending with Where Shall I Wander (2005)—presents . . . [a] panoramic view of Ashbery's second phase, in which he explores, celebrates, sends up and revels in the American vernacular. . . . This is an essential book." Publ Wkly

Planisphere; new poems. Ecco 2009 143p $24.99 **811**

1. Poetry -- By individual authors
ISBN 978-0-06-191521-5; 0-06-191521-1

"In his rendering of American speech, slang, cliché, Ashbery has surpassed most of his contemporaries. But his persistent reach into the 'rut' of tradition should not be forgotten. He could say (with the great Nicaraguan poet Rubén Darío) that he is very 18th century and very archaic and very modern, daring and cosmopolitan. When he becomes most serious, it is in the presence of either catastrophe or truth. His onslaughts of tragedy, emotional or physical, are of geological force while not relinquishing the vocabulary of iron." N Y Times Book Rev

★ **Where** shall I wander; new poems. J. Ecco 2005 81p $22.95 **811**

1. Poetry -- By individual authors
ISBN 0-06-076529-1
LC 2004-53267

National Book Award Finalist: Poetry (2005)

This collection of poetry features the poems "Ignorance of the Law Is No Excuse" and "A Visit to the House of Fools."

"Ashbery expresses a sly playfulness, a tender theatricality, a surreal sensibility, and an urbane wit. . . . Mercurial, elegant, funny, and magical, these mind-bending and beautifully haunting poems are the knowing work of a virtuoso." Booklist

★ **A worldly** country; new poems. Ecco Press 2007 76p $23.95 **811**

1. Poetry -- By individual authors
ISBN 0-06-117383-5; 978-0-06-117383-7
LC 2006-50279

This is a volume of poems by the author of Some Trees (1956); The Tennis Court Oath (1957); Rivers and Mountains (1966); Sunrise in Suburbia (1968); The Double Dream of Spring (1970); Self-portrait in a Convex Mirror (1975); Houseboat Days (1977); As We Know (1979); Shadow Trains (1981); Your Name Here (2000); and Where Shall I Wander (2006).

"Ashbery's syncopated lyrics are sheer pleasure in their music, collaged images, stabbing perceptions. Mysterious and truth-bearing poems that inspire us to 'flame on, flame on.'" Booklist

Austin, Derrick

Trouble the water; poems. by Derrick Austin; foreword by Mary Szybist. BOA Editions Ltd. 2016 96 p. (A. Poulin, Jr. New Poets of America Series) (paperback) $16 **811**

1. Poetry -- Collections 2. Poetry
ISBN 1942683049; 9781942683049
LC 2015046377

This book of poetry, by Derrick Austin, "is an intriguing exploration of race, sexuality, and identity, particularly where self-hood is in constant flux. These intimate, sensual poems interweave pop culture and history—moving from the Bible through several artistic eras—to interrogate what it means to be, as Austin says, fully human as a 'queer, black body' in 21st century America." (Publisher's note)

"Whether encountering European catacombs or the Gulf Coast's post-oil-spill devastation, all of Austin's lyrical poems are poignant and empowered." Booklist

Includes bibliographical references (pages 89-90)

Baca, Jimmy Santiago

Spring poems along the Rio Grande. New Directions Pub. 2007 75p pa $12.95 **811**

1. Poetry -- By individual authors
ISBN 978-0-8112-1685-2; 0-8112-1685-3
LC 2006-101678

"The Rio Grande, as both setting and symbol of freedom and life, meanders through the poems, evoking a natural progression of time and the natural ebb and flow of feelings such as love, hope, and connection. The bosque along the river is home to birds both resident and migratory, trees, fish, bushes, insects, and encroaching urban life represented by power lines and interstate traffic noise. Jogging here, Baca evinces a love of his hometown of Albuquerque but, even more, reveals his well of poetic inspiration: Chicano, Catholic religiosity, Native American symbolism, and universal milestones. . . . With its highly accessible language and thoughtful reflections on the natural world, readers will find Baca's poetry extremely inviting." Booklist

Bang, Mary Jo

The **bride** of E; poems. Graywolf Press 2009 90p $22 **811**

1. Poetry -- By individual authors
ISBN 978-1-55597-539-5; 1-55597-539-9
LC 2009-926850

"The book takes the form of an abecedarian in which E stands for existence, with the engine of the alphabet overriding the entropy of emptiness, in which 'all action is in the mind, a cluster of notions/ in depravity's head independent of the dreadful/ invention of the magnetic temporary where/ a partition is positioned between right and wrong.' Many of these poems refer to the precariousness of human future, with Bang's medical background contributing convincing detail, and her sharp wit buoys the description with bleak meaning." Libr J

A **doll** for throwing; poems. Mary Jo Bang. Graywolf Press 2017 76 p. illustrations (paperback) $16 **811**

1. American poetry -- Collections 2. American poetry -- 21st century
ISBN 9781555977818; 9781555979737
LC 2016951417

This poetry collection in the 2017 series, by Mary Jo Bang, "takes its title from the Bauhaus artist Alma Siedhoff-Buscher's Wurfpuppe, a flexible and durable woven doll that, if thrown, would land with grace. . . . Bang's prose poems in this fascinating book create a speaker who had been a part of the Bauhaus school in Germany a century ago and who had also seen the school's collapse when it was shut by the Nazis in 1933." (Publisher's note)

"Bang's impeccable collection reads as a 'circular mirror of the social order,' reflecting the historicity of our current moment with wit, subtlety, and grace." Pub Wkly

Elegy; poems. Graywolf 2007 92p $20   **811**
1. Poetry -- By individual authors
ISBN 978-1-55597-483-1; 1-55597-483-X
         LC 2007-924768

The author "captures the complexity and courage of surviving the death of a child, an adult child, an imperfect child. The grief is multi-layered, palpable. In this rendition of living in pain, in absence, in an altered reality, the reader never questions the authenticity of the work. . . . This is a book of exceptional grace and strength; it belongs in every library." Libr J

Barnett, Catherine

★ The **game** of boxes; poems. Catherine Barnett. Graywolf Press 2012 88 p. (alk. paper) $15.00   **811**
1. American poetry -- Collections
ISBN 1555976204; 9781555976200
         LC 2012936220

This book of poetry by Catherine Barnett "is organized into three . . . sections; the first is called 'endless forms most beautiful.' Scattered amid poems about a mother and her son are pieces written from the first-person plural perspective of an amorphous chorus. . . . Fragmentary poems . . . [about] lust, sex, and sorrow form the book's second section, 'sweet double, talk-talk.' . . . 'The modern period,' the book's last section is . . . the most lucidly personal." (Publishers Weekly)

Beat poets; selected and edited by Carmela Ciuraru. Knopf 2002 250p (Everyman's library pocket poets) $12.50 **811**
1. Beat generation 2. American poetry -- Collections
ISBN 978-0-375-41332-2; 0-375-41332-4
         LC 2002-510236

"The defining work of Allen Ginsberg and Jack Kerouac provides the foundation for this collection, which also features statements on Beat poetics, selections from the alternately ardent, incendiary, and earnest correspondence of Beat Generation writers, and the improvisational verse of such Beat legends as Robert Creeley, Diane Di Prima, Gregory Corso, Denise Levertov, Lawrence Ferlinghetti, Philip Whalen, Bob Kaufman, and Peter Orlovsky, along with the work of other women writers and the lesser-known poets of this school." Publisher's note

Berkson, Bill

★ **Portrait** and dream; new and selected poems. Coffee House Press 2009 314p pa $22   **811**
1. Poetry -- By individual authors
ISBN 978-1-56689-229-2; 1-56689-206-6
         LC 2008-52607

"There was always something of a mythical aura about Berkson, the collaborator of Frank O'Hara and one of the chiefs of the New York School whose friends included painters as well as poets. . . . Berkson's own poetry is subtle and demonstrably abstract in the manner of, let's say, DeKooning: it has an imagistic hardness and lushness that sweeps aside whatever you might have been thinking before." Exquisite Corpse

Bernstein, Charles, 1950-

All the whiskey in heaven; selected poems. Farrar, Straus and Giroux 2010 300p $26   **811**
1. Poetry -- By individual authors
ISBN 0-374-10344-5; 978-0-374-10344-6
         LC 2009-10187

"This gathering of 30 years worth of work by the prominent L=A=N=G=U=A=G=E poet and essayist offers a . . . critique of the art of poetry itself, which means, among other things, a thorough investigation of language and the mind. Varied voices and genres are at play, from a colloquial letter of complaint to the manager of a Manhattan subway station to a fragmentary meditation on the forces that underlie the formation of knowledge." (Publishers Weekly)

"Bernstein takes his place in the mainstream of American poetry, the very 'Official Verse Culture' he's attacked entertainingly for years—a fate awaiting all our best outsiders. . . . Early Bernstein can be opaque, annoying those who see difficulty as elitist and who want poetry to be cuddly and educational. But everyone should love the later Bernstein, a writer who is accessible, enormously witty, often joyful—and even more evilly subversive." N Y Times Book Rev

Berrigan, Ted

★ The **collected** poems of Ted Berrigan; edited by Alice Notley, with Anselm Berrigan and Edmund Berrigan; introduction and notes by Alice Notley. University of California Press 2005 749p $60; pa $24.95   **811**
1. Poetry -- By individual authors
ISBN 978-0-520-23986-9; 0-520-23986-5; 978-0-520-25155-7 pa; 0-520-25155-5 pa
         LC 2005-42259

This volume collects the published and unpublished works of a leading figure of the second-generation New York School. Includes the first presentation of the Easter Monday sequence in the order authorized by Berrigan shortly before his death.

"More than 20 years in preparation, this is a major volume of 20th-century American poetry. . . . Berrigan was a notoriously charismatic reader, teacher and participant in the community that developed around the Poetry Project at St. Mark's Church; his persona has been cited as often as his poems. This book closes the gap once and for all." Publ Wkly

Berry, Wendell

Given; new poems. Shoemaker & Hoard 2005 152p $22   **811**
1. Poetry -- By individual authors
ISBN 1-59376-061-2
         LC 2005-3762

"The latter half, 'Sabbaths 1998-2004,' . . . [contains] the meditational poems Berry conceives on Sundays alone in the woods on his farm. The other half's three parts contain, respectively, short poems of observation, hortatory poems varying in length from epigram to six-page public epistle, and a brief verse play. . . . For those who believe that life and the world are gifts, this is an invaluable book." Booklist

A **timbered** choir; the sabbath poems, 1979-1997. Counterpoint 1998 216p hardcover o.p. pa $14.95   **811**
1. Poetry -- By individual authors
ISBN 978-15823-006-5
         LC 98-4925

"Berry has continued periodically to write poems out-of-doors on days of little other work. This book reprints Sabbaths, a collection of that writing, adding to it about one and a half times as much new work. . . . Few other poets have such chaste and precise diction or manage line and stanza with such unaffected serenity." Booklist

Berry, Wendell, 1934-

New collected poems. Counterpoint 2012 391 p. $30.00   **811**
1. Haiku 2. Fathers -- Poetry 3. Poetry -- Collections
ISBN 1582438153; 9781582438153

This book "makes [poet Wendell] Berry's first Collected [volume] since 1987 and draws on volumes up through 'Leavings.'" It includes "a long elegy for Berry's father and a set of haiku-sized poems. Benedictions and prayers coexist with manifestos and georgic, the ancient genre of poems about rural hard work." (Publishers Weekly)

Berryman, John

Collected poems, 1937-1971; edited and introduced by Charles Thornbury. Farrar, Straus & Giroux 1989 347p hardcover o.p. pa $25 **811**

1. Poetry -- By individual authors

ISBN 978-0-374-52281-0; 0-374-52281-2

LC 89-30944

"Berryman's poetry, sometimes mannered, elliptical, and convoluted, is distinguished by precise technical control and continued experiments with style." Reader's Ency. 4th edition

★ The **dream** songs. Farrar, Straus & Giroux 1969 xx, 427p hardcover o.p. pa $18 **811**

1. Poetry -- By individual authors

ISBN 978-0-374-53066-2; 0-374-53066-1

This book contains the author's 385 'dream songs' that originally appeared in various magazines, the Pulitzer Prize winning 77 dream songs (1964) and His toy, his dream, his rest (1968). The poet also provides a brief note about Henry, the poems' central character

"Berryman makes brilliant use of his speaker's indiscriminately retentive perception—the patter of jukeboxes, of cocktail parties, of the gutter and the cathedral—to drop us dizzily into an original world where life is lived naked and unashamed." Va Q Rev

The **best** American poetry. Scribner **811**

1. American poetry 2. Poetry -- Collections

Annual

Yearly guest-edited collection of the year's best American poetry.

★ **Best** of the Best American Poetry; 25th Anniversary. guest editor, Robert Pinsky; series editor, David Lehman. Simon & Schuster 2013 xxviii, 322 p.p (hardcover) $35 **811**

1. American poetry 2. Poetry -- Collections

ISBN 1451658877; 9781451658873

This poetry anthology, edited by David Lehman, "celebrates twenty-five years of the 'Best American Poetry' series. . . . From its inception in 1988, it has been hotly debated, keenly monitored, ardently advocated (or denounced), and obsessively scrutinized. . . . Out of the 1,875 poems that have appeared in 'The Best American Poetry,' here are 100 that Robert Pinsky, the distinguished poet and man of letters, has chosen for this milestone edition." (Publisher's note)

Bidart, Frank

Star dust. Farrar, Straus and Giroux 2005 84p $20 **811**

1. Poetry -- By individual authors

ISBN 0-374-26973-4

LC 2004-56293

National Book Award Finalist: Poetry (2005)

This is a collection of poetry by the author of Desire.

"The poems in this collection range from terribly lame confections questioning the appellation of 'poem' itself—to gracefully and powerfully moving lyrics. . . . The more formal Bidart gets, the stronger his work, like a living example of Richard Wilbur's dictum that the genie gains his strength from confinement in the bottle." Am Book Rev

Watching the spring festival. Farrar, Straus & Giroux 2008 61p $25 **811**

1. Poetry -- By individual authors

ISBN 978-0-374-28603-3; 0-374-28603-5

LC 2007-40513

National Book Award Finalist: Poetry (2008)

This book is "a collection of masterful, carefully modulated lyrics, glimpses of the millennium's turn and dispatches from an ancient world." Antioch Rev

Bidart, Frank, 1939-

★ **Half**-light; collected poems 1965-2016. Frank Bidart. Farrar, Straus & Giroux 2017 736 p. (hardcover) $40 **811**

1. Poetry -- Collections

ISBN 9780374125950; 0374125953

LC 2015038552

National Book Award: Poetry (2017)

Pulitzer Prize: Poetry (2018)

This book, by Frank Bidart, "encompasses all of Bidart's previous books, and also includes a new collection, 'Thirst,' in which the poet austerely surveys his life, laying it plain for us before venturing into something new and unknown. Here Bidart finds himself a 'Creature coterminous with thirst,' still longing, still searching in himself, one of the 'queers of the universe.'" (Publisher's note)

"Bidart's poems strive, more than anything else, to present particular voices speaking, which accounts for their distinctive punctuation . . . and idiosyncratic interior capitalization, more than to express meaning. But meaning there is, of course, concerning love, death, conflict, ambition, and disappointment, found between lacunae and jump cuts like in a Godard movie or an Eliot poem." Booklist

★ **Metaphysical** dog; Frank Bidart. Farrar, Straus and Giroux 2013 128 p. (hardcover) $24 **811**

1. Metaphysics -- Poetry 2. Poetry -- Collections

ISBN 0374173613; 9780374173616

LC 2012048069

National Book Critics Circle Award (2013)

National Book Award: Poetry Finalist (2013)

In this poetry collection by Frank Bidart, the author explores the themes of "words and sex, art and flesh." The book "reflects what the poet sees as fundamental in human feeling, what psychologists and mystics have called the 'hunger for the Absolute'--a hunger as fundamental as any physical hunger. This hunger must confront the elusiveness of the Absolute, our self-deluding, failed glimpses of it." (Publisher's note)

"There is a quiet, stirring grandeur here as Bidart contemplates the spectrum of existence, life's endless transformations, and our 'hunger for the absolute.'" Booklist

Includes bibliographical references and index

Bishop, Elizabeth

Edgar Allan Poe & the juke-box; uncollected poems, drafts, and fragments. edited and annotated by Alice Quinn. Farrar, Straus, and Giroux 2006 367p $30 **811**

1. Poetry -- By individual authors

ISBN 0-374-14645-4

LC 2005-11511

"The publication of 'Edgar Allan Poe & the Juke-Box,' which gathers for the first time Bishop's unpublished material, isn't just a significant event in our poetry; it's part of a continuing alteration in the scale of American life." N Y Times Book Rev

Includes bibliographical references

★ **Poems;** Elizabeth Bishop; edited by Saskia Hamilton. Farrar, Straus & Giroux 2011 xiv, 352 p.p $16 **811**

1. American literature 2. American poetry -- 20th century 3. Poetry -- Women authors -- Collections 4. Poetry -- By individual authors

ISBN 0374532362; 9780374532369

LC 2010038535

This poetry collection, by Elizabeth Bishop, presents poems that "combine humor and sadness, pain and acceptance, and observe nature and lives in perfect miniaturist close-up. The themes central to . . . [Bishop's] poetry are geography and landscape--from New England, where she grew up, to Brazil and Florida, where she later lived--human connection with the natural world, questions of knowledge and perception, and the ability or inability of form to control chaos." (Publisher's note)

Blues poems; selected and edited by Kevin Young. Knopf 2003 256p (Everyman's library pocket poets) $12.50 **811**
1. Blues music -- Poetry 2. American poetry -- Collections
ISBN 978-0-375-41458-9; 0-375-41458-4

LC 2003-53149

A collection of "blues-influenced and blues-inflected poems from, among others, Gwendolyn Brooks, Allen Ginsberg, June Jordan, Richard Wright, Nikki Giovanni, Charles Wright, Yusef Komunyakaa, and Cornelius Eady. And here, too, are classic song lyrics—poems in their own right—from Bessie Smith, Robert Johnson, Ma Rainey, and Muddy Waters." Publisher's note

Bly, Robert

The **night** Abraham called to the stars; poems. HarperCollins Pubs. 2001 95p hardcover o.p. pa $12.95 **811**
1. Poetry -- By individual authors
ISBN 0-06-093444-1 pa

LC 00-66360

"The book's 48 lyrics are written in a single (here terceted) form, the ghazal, used by such great Islamic poets as Ghalib, and harness high points of Western art and literature to draw general, biblically backed conclusions about the human condition out of the mire." Publ Wkly

Collected poems; Robert Bly. W W Norton & Co. Inc. 2018 576 p. (hardcover) $39.95 **811**
1. American poetry 2. American literature
ISBN 0393652440; 9780393652444

LC 2018028547

This poetry collection presents the full magnitude of . . . [poet Robert Bly's] body of work for the first time. . . . [The book] gathers the fourteen volumes of his impressive oeuvre into one place, including his imagistic debut, 'Silence in the Snowy Fields' (1962); . . . 'The Light Around the Body' (1967); . . . and the fiercely introspective, uniquely American ghazals of his latest collection, 'Talking into the Ear of a Donkey' (2011)." (Publisher's note)

Bonair-Agard, Roger

Bury my clothes; by Roger Bonair-Agard. Haymarket Books 2013 160 p. (pbk.) $16 **811**
1. Art 2. Race 3. Violence
ISBN 1608462692; 9781608462698

LC 2013006344

National Book Award: Poetry Long List (2013)

This book, by Roger Bonair-Agard, "is a meditation on violence, race, and the place in art at which they intersect. Art—specifically in oppressed communities—is about survival, . . . Bonair-Agard asserts, and establishing personhood in a world that says you have none. Through poetry, [he attempts to] transform both the world of art and the world itself." (Publisher's note)

Borland, Bryan

Dig; Bryan Borland. Stillhouse Press 2016 86 p. **811**
1. Poetry 2. LGBT people 3. Self-perception
ISBN 9780990516989; 9780990516996

LC 2016935266

Stonewall Honor Book in Literature (2017)

"Bryan Borland's third poetry collection examines what it means to dig—to undertake the intense labor of unearthing the personal/political/artistic self and embracing the consequences of that knowledge. These poems assert that to dig is to reveal the bedrock on which we may rebuild ourselves; to discover the beauty and reward of life buried deep within us—no matter how many layers of earth we need to overturn." (Publisher's note)

Borzutzky, Daniel

Lake Michigan; Daniel Borzutzky. University of Pittsburgh Press 2018 88 p. $15.95 **811**
1. Race relations -- Poetry 2. American poetry -- Collections 3. American poetry -- 21st century
ISBN 0822965224; 9780822965220

This book in the Pitt Poetry Series, by Daniel Borzutzky, is "a series of 19 lyric poems [which] imagines a prison camp located on the beaches of a Chicago that is privatized, racially segregated, and overrun by a brutal police force. . . . But while the influences in this book . . . are international, the focus here is local as the book takes a hard look at neoliberal urbanism in the historic city of Chicago." (Publisher's note)

"A searing indictment and an immediate, dangerous, and urgent work." Booklist

Boss, Todd

Tough luck; poems. Todd Boss. W W Norton & Co Inc 2017 xii, 100 p.p (hardcover) $26.95 **811**
1. American poetry -- Collections 2. American poetry -- 21st century 3. American poetry -- 21st century
ISBN 9780393608632; 9780393608625

LC 2016058733

Written by Todd Boss "at the center of [the book] is a poem about the ill-fated I-35W Bridge in Minneapolis and its disastrous collapse, which killed 13 people and injured 145. The freighted, swiftly moving poems in 'Tough Luck' crisscross the chasm between peril and safety as if between opposing riverbanks, revealing a frequently heart-stopping view of the muscled waters below. Marriage, family, home--all come crashing down." (Publisher's note)

Brock-Broido, Lucie, 1956-2018

Stay, Illusion; Poems. By Lucie Brock-Broido. Random House Inc 2013 112 p. (Hardcover) $26 **811**
1. Bereavement 2. American poetry 3. Emotions -- Poetry
ISBN 0307962024; 9780307962027

LC 2013023978

National Book Critics Circle Award Finalist: Poetry (2013)
National Book Award: Poetry Finalist (2013)

Author Lucie Brock-Broido presents a poetry collection designed to "spin, drape, and sculpt its virtuosic figures around the ideas and emotions of mourning. Often Brock-Broido commemorates her father, remembering him on his own, in her family, in conjunction with her own past selves." (Publishers Weekly)

Includes bibliographical references

Brooks, Gwendolyn

The **essential** Gwendolyn Brooks; Elizabeth Alexander, editor. Library of America 2005 148p il (American poets project) $20 **811**
1. Poetry -- By individual authors
ISBN 978-1-931082-87-7; 1-931082-87-1

LC 2005-44162

"A book like [this] can't make the statement that needs to be made: Gwendolyn Brooks is as important to twentieth-century American poetry as Robert Lowell. . . . Her best poems offer a curative, not only to the narcissistic gloom that we've inherited from the Confessionals, but to Eliot's overaestheticized visions of social life. That Brooks's purposes were so different from Eliot's only strengthens the connection. It shows the vitality of true poetic inspiration, how it can cut across time, temperament, race, and even the motives of its own practitioners." Poetry (Modern Poetry Association)

In Montgomery, and other poems. Third World Press 2003 146p $22.95 **811**
1. African Americans -- Poetry 2. Poetry -- By individual authors
ISBN 0-88378-232-4

LC 2003-50749

This is a "posthumous collection consisting primarily of dramatic monologues in a stunning variety of voices, from those of urban children to Winnie Mandela's. Reading the title sequence resembles randomly tuning a radio dial to listen to the diverse voices of Montgomery, Alabama, a city of 'leaning and lostness, glazed paralysis.' . . . Especially moving are the children's monologues. . . . Brooks captures the fierce purity of these children's needs and desires. Her loving witness never sounded more clearly than in these late poems." Booklist

Budbill, David
Happy life. Copper Canyon Press 2011 117p pa $16 **811**
1. Poetry -- By individual authors
ISBN 978-1-55659-374-1

LC 2011

The poems evoke "a recognizable immediacy and honesty, accompanied by an endearing wit. . . . Budbill's economical, brush-stroke approach . . . evinces a hard-won clarity, a pure, human tone." Libr J

Bukowski, Charles
★ The **pleasures** of the damned; poems, 1951-1993. edited by John Martin. Ecco 2007 556p $29.95 **811**
1. Poetry -- By individual authors
ISBN 978-0-06-122843-8; 0-06-122843-5

LC 2007-282394

This book is "an insightful walk through the work of a poet by the man who knew him best, and it reveals Bukowski in the many, often conflicting dimensions that make him such a popular, accessible, and, yes, great artist. . . . This extraordinary collection establishes Bukowski as much more than just another West Coast Beat poet." Washington Post

Callow, Philip
From noon to starry night: a life of Walt Whitman. Dee, I.R. 1992 394p il $28.50; pa $14.95 **811**
1. Poets 2. Authors 3. Essayists
ISBN 0-929587-95-2; 1-56663-133-5 pa

LC 92-5311

"Infused with tenderness and respect, this fine biography deciphers the complexity of Whitman's sexuality and passionate creativity while celebrating his abiding compassion and grandeur of spirit." Booklist
Includes bibliographical references

Carruth, Hayden
★ **Toward** the distant islands; new & selected poems. edited and with an introduction by Sam Hamill. Copper Canyon Press 2006 181p pa $17 **811**
1. Poetry -- By individual authors
ISBN 1-55659-236-1 pa

LC 2005-28705

Carruth's "books encompass Frostian tales of farm life with New

England eccentrics, compilations of haiku, long and unguarded poems of erotic devotion, autobiographical laments, and sensitive odes to jazz greats. . . . All sides of Carruth's oeuvre find a place in this welcome volume. . . . The selection here gives just enough of everything Carruth has learned, and he has learned a lot, especially about the ways and landscapes of New England." Publ Wkly

Carson, Anne
Autobiography of red; a novel in verse. Knopf 1998 149p hardcover o.p. pa $12 **811**
1. Poetry -- By individual authors
ISBN 0-375-70129-X pa

LC 97-49472

"Is it poetry? Is it a novel in verse? A fable? A myth? However you define Carson's distinctive and wildly inventive new work, it is riveting reading. . . . Wistful yet whimsical, offhand yet intense, funky yet erudite . . . this is a reading experience like no other." Libr J

The **beauty** of the husband; a fictional essay in 29 tangos. Knopf 2001 147p $24; pa $12 **811**
1. Poetry -- By individual authors
ISBN 0-375-40804-5; 0-375-70757-3 pa

LC 00-62002

This poem is "at once the story of a failed marriage and an exploration of Romantic notions of beauty and truth. But Carson's idiosyncratic voice and her punchy declarative style—'You want a clean life I live a dirty one'—quickly make it clear that hers is a thoroughly modern take on the intimate cruelties of married life. And this is the primary pleasure of her writing: it is both entirely new and strangely familiar, like remembering a private language we thought we'd forgotten." New Yorker

Men in the off hours. Knopf 2000 166p il hardcover o.p. pa $12 **811**
1. Poetry -- By individual authors
ISBN 0-375-70756-5 pa

LC 00-267850

The author "makes bold references to everyone from Oedipus to Akhamatova, but the effect of these astute, gemlike little poems is less a history lesson than a challenging conversation in a sunlit garden." Libr J

Nox. New Directions 2010 un il $29.95 **811**
1. Poetry -- By individual authors
ISBN 978-0-8112-1870-2; 0-8112-1870-8

LC 2009-01330

This "is an epitaph in the form of a book, a facsimile of a handmade book Carson wrote and created after the death of her brother." (N Y Times Book Rev)

The "book comes in a box the color of a rainy day, with a sliver of a family snapshot on the front. Inside is a Xerox-quality reproduction of a notebook, made after the death of her brother, including text and photographs and letters, pasted-in inkjet printouts, handwriting, paintings and collage. 'Nox' has no page numbers, and it's accordion-folded. It carries a whiff of visual art multiple or gift shop souvenir or 'Griffin & Sabine.' But trust me: it's an Anne Carson book. Maybe her best." N Y Times Book Rev

Red doc>; Anne Carson. 1st ed. Alfred A. Knopf 2013 167 p. (hardcover) $24.95; (ebook) $74.85 **811**
1. Epic poetry 2. Monsters -- Poetry 3. Literature -- Adaptations 4. Epic poetry, Greek -- Adaptations
ISBN 0307960587; 9780307960580; 9780307960597

LC 2012032322

This book, by Anne Carson, is a mixed poetry-prose genre story following the author's character Geryon from her 1988 book "Autobiography of Red." The book "finds a way to push Geryon into new territories of dry, vaudevillian Americana. Whether she's talking war vets, flying cows, Latin etymology or Elvis, Carson once again blurs the lines of prose and poetry, and challenging both genres within a single poem." (American Poet)

Clark, Tom

★ **Light** & shade; new and selected poems. introduction by Amy Gerstler. Coffee House Press 2006 338p pa $20 **811**
    1. Poetry -- By individual authors
    ISBN 1-56689-183-3

LC 2005-35810

"Disarmingly casual yet saturated with loss, Clark's body of work revels in simplicities: lovers, friends, cities and landscapes (New York, Southern California, the Southwest), baseball, basketball, modern painters, sad weather, brief visions and ethereal promises. All make repeat appearances in a poetry rooted at once in spontaneity and in High Romantic aspiration." Publ Wkly

Clifton, Lucille, 1936-2010

★ The **collected** poems of Lucille Clifton 1965-2010; edited by Kevin Young and Michael S. Glaser; foreword by Toni Morrison; afterword by Kevin Young. BOA Editions 2012 xxxiv, 769 p.p **811**
    1. Women -- Poetry 2. Feminism -- Poetry 3. African Americans -- Poetry
    ISBN 1934414905; 9781934414903

LC 2012014244

This book, edited by Kevin Young and Michael S. Glaser, "combines all eleven of Lucille Clifton's published collections with more than fifty previously unpublished poems. The unpublished poems feature early poems from 1965-1969 . . . [and] a collection-in-progress titled the book of days (2008). . . . In the last year of her life, she was named the first African American woman to receive the . . . Ruth Lilly Poetry Prize . . . and was posthumously awarded the Robert Frost Medal." (Publisher's note)

Mercy; poems. 1st ed; BOA Editions 2004 79p (American poets continuum series) $22; pa $14.95 **811**
    1. Poetry -- By individual authors
    ISBN 1-929918-54-2; 1-929918-55-0 pa

LC 2004-10396

"These are poems where great restraint mingles with disarming primal imagery to convey poems which hold tremendous emotional weight." Va Q Rev

Cloud, Abigail

Sylph; Poems. Abigail Cloud. Pleiades Press 2014 88 p. (pbk.: alk. paper) $17.95 **811**
    1. Poetry -- Collections
    ISBN 0807156930; 9780807156933

LC 2014931676

In this book of poems, Abigail Cloud "draws inspiration from nineteenth-century European Romantic ballets, which often portrayed scorned females as mystical spirits such as sylphs, shades, and wilis. Some of these creatures seduced men into dancing until they died punishment for inconstancy or lured them into love. For Cloud, the dark gravity that holds these enchanters to the earth is the same as our own and thus these demons are as everyday as air." (Publisher's note)

Cole, Henri

Middle earth; poems. Farrar, Straus & Giroux 2003 55p

$23; pa $11 **811**
    1. Poetry -- By individual authors
    ISBN 0-374-20881-6; 0-374-52928-0 pa

LC 2002-29776

The author "examines the dichotomies between life and death, animal and human, and the lover and the beloved. Many of the poems, including, 'My Tea Ceremony' and 'Self-Portrait at the Red Princess,' show a marked Japanese influence; others record a grown son's grief over the death of his father. . . . Cole writes with clarity and an emotive resonance. These poems succeed as the best poems do: they transport the reader to other worlds, no less beautiful or complicated than our own. Highly recommended." Libr J

Collins, Billy

Nine horses; poems. Random House 2002 120p $21.95; pa $12.95 **811**
    1. Poetry -- By individual authors
    ISBN 1-4000-6177-6; 0-375-75520-9 pa

LC 2002-24868

Collins is "often able to proceed unburdened by many of the tools—assonance, alliteration, wordplay, complex metrics—that hang from the poet's belt; he makes his way in the world by being funny." N Y Times Book Rev

★ **Sailing** alone around the room; new and selected poems. Random House 2001 171p $21.95; pa $13.95 **811**
    1. Poetry -- By individual authors
    ISBN 0-375-50380-3; 0-375-75519-5 pa

LC 99-52861

"Collins will tackle any topic: his subject matter varies from snow days to Aristotle to forgetfulness. The results are accessible but not trite, comical but not laughable, and well crafted but not overly flamboyant. Collins relies heavily on imagery, which becomes the cornerstone of the entire volume." Libr J

The **trouble** with poetry and other poems; Billy Collins. Random House 2005 88p $22.95 **811**
    1. Poetry -- By individual authors
    ISBN 0-375-50382-X

LC 2005-46562

"Skeptical of love and scornful of pretension, Collins is breathtaking in his appreciation of the earth's beauty and the precious daily routines that define life." Booklist

Crane, Hart

★ **Complete** poems and selected letters. Library of America 2006 849p $40 **811**
    1. Poetry -- By individual authors
    ISBN 1-93108-299-5

LC 2006-40922

This volume "gathers all of the author's poetry and collected prose with a large sampling of his letters, some appearing in print for the first time. The correspondents include top writers William Carlos Williams, Marianne Moore, e.e. cummings, and Katherine Anne Porter. A good one-stop resource for Crane." Libr J

Creeley, Robert

The **collected** poems of Robert Creeley. University of California Press 1982 2v v1 o.p.; v1 pa $27.50; v2 $60; v2 pa $24.95 **811**
    1. Poetry -- By individual authors
    ISBN 0-520-04243-3 v1; 978-0-520-24158-9 v1 pa; 978-0-520-

24159-6 v2; 978-0-520-25620-0 v2 pa

Creeley's style is "notably spare and laconic; his primary subject is love and the infinite incongruities that characterize love relationships. There is a distinct dearth of imagery in his poetry; the themes are rendered in a cerebral rather than sensual manner. For Creeley, the intent of the poem is definition, not description." Reader's Ency. 4th edition

Cummings, E. E.

★ **Complete** poems, 1904-1962; containing all the published poetry. edited by George J. Firmage. rev corr & expanded ed; Norton 1994 xxxii, 1102p $50 **811**

1. Poetry -- By individual authors

ISBN 978-0-87140-152-6; 0-87140-152-5

LC 91-29158

Expanded version of Complete poems, 1913-1962 (1972)

"This volume has been prepared directly from the poet's original manuscripts, preserving the original typography and format. It includes all the previously published works, from Tulips (1922) to Etcetera (1983), as well as 36 uncollected poems that originally appeared in little magazines or anthologies." Libr J

Dickinson, Emily, 1830-1886

★ The poems of Emily Dickinson; edited by R.W. Franklin. Reading ed; Belknap Press 1999 692p pa $18.50; $34.50 **811**

1. Poetry -- By individual authors

ISBN 0-674-01824-9 pa; 0-674-67624-6; 978-0-674-01824-2 pa; 978-0-674-67624-4

LC 99-11821

This work "includes a single version of each poem included in the 1998 Variorum. In this one-volume edition, Franklin selects the latest 'manifestation' of a poem in those not uncommon instances when Dickinson herself produced multiple copies." (Am Lit) Index.

"Within the guidelines Franklin has set himself, his choices of versions and of alternatives within versions are extremely sensible-and they are efficiently recorded at the end of the volume, making this the first time any volume of Dickinson's poems aimed at a general audience has offered information about the derivation of its texts." Raritan

Dickman, Michael

The **end** of the west. Copper Canyon Press 2009 89p pa $15 **811**

1. Poetry -- By individual authors

ISBN 978-1-55659-289-8; 1-556-59289-2

LC 2008-39990

"Some form of light—sunlight, moonlight, starlight, streetlight—appears in every one of the 18 poems in [this book.] . . . Slight and spare, the poems' frequent recurring themes accumulate beneficially, linking all the individual poems into one, more substantial, piece. Nothing grand takes place in these poems, but the quietness of the language and the creeping, sinister subject matter (heroin addiction, abusive fathers) make this . . . book captivating and very readable." Publ Wkly

Donovan, Karen

Your enzymes are calling the ancients; poems. Karen Donovan. Persea Books 2016 87 p. (softcover: acid-free paper) $15.95 **811**

1. Women authors 2. American poetry

ISBN 9780892554768

LC 2016022139

This collection of poetry, by Karen Donovan, "continues to mine the language and systems of science and social science as a way of portraying our lineage of experience. Whether through the symbols of an ancient Irish alphabet or the 'lost gospel of ribosome,' Donovan traces the way our inner and outer expressions and gestures combine to form our humanness." (Publisher's note)

"Donovan expertly crafts a cohesive book from so many seemingly different parts of art and nature and weaves them through the loom and perspective of human experience." Booklist

Dorn, Edward

★ **Way** more West; new and selected poems. introduction by Dale Smith; edited by Michael Rothenberg. Penguin Books 2007 321p (Penguin poets) $20 **811**

1. Poetry -- By individual authors

ISBN 978-0-14-303869-6

LC 2006-50727

"Throughout his career, he was the least endearing, domesticated or predictable of poets, always determined to go his own way, no matter what anyone thought. And if he hadn't been that way, American poetry would be a lot less vital and interesting." N Y Times Book Rev

Includes bibliographical references

Doty, Mark

Deep lane; poems. Mark Doty. W W Norton & Co Inc 2015 96 p. (hardcover) $25.95 **811**

1. Nature poetry 2. American poetry -- Collections

ISBN 9780224099837; 9780393070231

LC 2015000660

In this poetry collection, by Mark Doty, "these poems seek repair, finally, through the possibilities that sustain the speaker above ground: gardens and animals; the pleasure of seeing; the world tuned by the word. Time and again, an image of immolation and sacrifice is undercut by the fierce fortitude of nature: nature that is not just a solace but a potent antidote and cure." (Publisher's note)

"A somber, struggling, honest collection for Doty's many fans." LJ

Fire to fire; new and selected poems. Harper 2008 336p $22.95; pa $15.95 **811**

1. Poetry -- By individual authors

ISBN 978-0-06-075247-7; 0-06-075247-5; 978-0-06-075251-4 pa; 0-06-075251-3 pa

LC 2007-44646

National Book Award: Poetry (2008)

The author "combines new poems with the best of his previous volumes. His narrative style is expansive, filled with what has been described as a 'lyric glitter' that creates radiance around the ordinary." Libr J

Includes bibliographical references

Dove, Rita

American smooth; poems. W.W. Norton 2004 143p $22.95; pa $13.95 **811**

1. Poetry -- By individual authors

ISBN 0-393-05987-1; 0-393-32744-2 pa

LC 2004-11793

"In these free-verse poems, Dove speaks from her own perspective—as well as from that of biblical characters, black soldiers from World War I, a ten-year-old girl from Harlem, several musicians, and a pair of dancers. The selections work by lists, line breaks where ideas collide, and a juxtaposition of voices. Then using razor-sharp metaphors, Dove goes for the jugular and usually finds it. Although the book's sense of audience seems inconsistent, with some poems suitable for A Child's Garden of Verses and others for The Kama Sutra, the poems are evocative." Libr J

Collected poems; 1974-2004. Rita Dove. W W Norton & Co Inc 2016 448 p. (hardcover) $39.95; (ebook) $50   **811**
1. American poets 2. American poetry
ISBN 9780393285949; 9780393285956

LC 2016007501

National Book Award Finalist: Poetry (2016)

This book by Rita Dove presents "three decades of powerful lyric poetry. . . . This volume compiles Dove's fresh reflections on adolescence in 'The Yellow House on the Corner,' . . . the multifaceted gems of 'Grace Notes,' the exquisite reinvention of Greek myth in the sonnets of 'Mother Love,' . . . and the homage to America's kaleidoscopic cultural heritage in 'American Smooth," all celebrate Dove's mastery of narrative context with lyrical finesse." (Publisher's note)

"Through her alluring language, Dove has long made the exceedingly difficult seem effortless; each poem here is a testament to her brilliance." Pub Wkly

Includes bibliographical references and index.

On the bus with Rosa Parks; poems. Norton 1999 95p hardcover o.p. pa $12.95   **811**
1. Poetry -- By individual authors
ISBN 0-393-32026-X

LC 98-45057

Dove's "poems effortlessly suggest grand narratives and American myths, yet ground themselves tersely in localities, characters, practicalities and particulars. This seventh collection leads off with a Dove specialty, the historical sequence: her 'Cameos' lend broad, social relevance to an intermittently abandoned Depression-era wife and her family." Publ Wkly

Selected poems. Vintage Bks. 1993 xxvi, 210p pa $13 **811**
1. Poetry -- By individual authors
ISBN 0-679-75080-0

LC 93-26112

"This volume places three previous collections under one cover. . . . The selection begins with The Yellow House on the Corner, Dove's first book, most notable for its poems derived from slave narratives. Museum, her second book, offers a potpourri of work that ranges over several continents and many millenia; Dove's tirelessly exact language illuminates the lives of saints, contemporary lifestyles, and Greek myths." Booklist

Dugan, Alan
★ **Poems** seven; new and complete poetry. Seven Stories Press 2001 422p $35; pa $18.95   **811**
1. Poetry -- By individual authors
ISBN 1-58322-265-0; 1-58322-512-9 pa

LC 2001-41089

National Book Award: Poetry (2001)

This collection documents "Dugan's project of comic, bleak and formally varied commentary on a dirty, terminally frayed and yet attractive America. . . . This carefully constructed, funny and sometimes unvarying volume combines all six of Dugan's previous books with a decade's worth of new verse." Publ Wkly

Duhamel, Denise
Ka-ching! University of Pittsburgh Press 2009 86p il (Pitt poetry series) $14.95   **811**
1. Poetry -- By individual authors
ISBN 978-0-8229-6021-8; 0-8229-6021-4 pa

"What better poetry for the current economic period than Denise Duhamel's hymns to money, ATMs, her IRA accounts, the Treasury,

gambling. . .and Sean Penn? . . . Using prose poems, sonnets, sestinas, and other forms in Ka-Ching!, Duhamel is a wily technician, a touching humanist, a poet deserving stardom." Entertainment Wkly

Dunn, Stephen
Different hours; poems. Norton 2000 121p $22; pa $12.95   **811**
1. Poetry -- By individual authors
ISBN 0-393-04986-8; 0-393-32232-7 pa

LC 00-30556

"Stephen Dunn's poetry is strangely easy to like: philosophical but not arid, lyrical but rarely glib, his storytelling balanced effortlessly between the casual and the vivid. But don't mistake that ease for lack of staying power." N Y Times Book Rev

Local visitations; poems. Norton 2003 96p $21.95 **811**
1. Poetry -- By individual authors
ISBN 0-393-05200-1

LC 2002-14204

"The opening section of poems recasts Dunn's average American as the mythic Sisyphus, imprisoned by repetitive work ('a repetition/which would never mean more/at the end than at the start') and yet bereft without it ('But more often he finds himself dreaming/of his rock, wishing it back, the better/to defend himself against so many hours'). Nearly half the collection transports 19th-century literary figures to contemporary New Jersey towns ('Mary Shelley in Brigantine,' 'Hawthorne in Tuckerton'), a series of poems more attractive in concept than in practice, where the subjects often fail to transcend the contrivance they inhabit." Libr J

New & selected poems, 1974-1994. Norton 1994 296p hardcover o.p. pa $16.95   **811**
1. Poetry -- By individual authors
ISBN 978-0-393-31300-0; 0-393-31300-X

LC 93-33212

"Dunn might be called a Neo-Horatian poet. He is level-headed, witty, conversational in his diction, and willing to see in domestic life his means for attaining and imparting wisdom. Yet Dunn's variations on Horatian odes and epodes are rarely the drab reportorial missives from the daily grind which are found in so much contemporary poetry. He knows that his first duty is to keep the quotidian life interesting, and this is no mean feat. . . . This is to say that Dunn's a gifted talker, a kind of querulous raconteur, and even his less successful poems are highly readable." Poetry (Modern Poetry Association)

Eady, Cornelius
Brutal imagination; poems. Putnam 2001 108p $24; pa $13   **811**
1. Poetry -- By individual authors
ISBN 0-399-14718-7; 0-399-14720-9 pa

LC 00-62674

National Book Award Finalist: Poetry (2001)

In this "collection of poetry, Eady invokes a chorus of fictional black characters, from Uncle Tom to the invented criminal whom Susan Smith blamed for the kidnapping of her children. A white woman's 'stray thought,' this man haunts the best of these spare, stirring poems. If the poet's premise—the personification of a black figment of the white imagination—is complex, his verse is unsettlingly direct." New Yorker

Eliot, T. S.
★ **Collected** poems, 1909-1962. Harcourt Brace Jovanovich 1963 221p $23   **811**
1. Poetry -- By individual authors

ISBN 0-15-118978-1

This volume contains the complete text of 'Collected poems, 1909-1935,' the 'Four quartets,' and several other poems accompanied by brief prefatory notes

★ The **complete** poems and plays, 1909-1950. Harcourt Brace & Co. 1952 392p $35   **811**
1. Poetry -- By individual authors
ISBN 0-15-121185-X

Ellis, Thomas Sayers, 1963-
Skin, Inc. identity repair poems. Graywolf Press 2010 181p il $23.00   **811**
1. Poetry -- By individual authors
ISBN 1555975674; 9781555975678

LC 2010-922920

This is a collection of poetry by the author of The Maverick Room (2005).

This collection of the author's poems "constitutes an impassioned argument for revitalizing America's calcified literary culture ('Flat, fixed and finished'), whose conventional assumptions about the expression of racial identity severely limit the aesthetic choices available to both writers and readers of color. . . . With honesty, eloquence, and precision, Ellis calls for resistance to the outward imposition of social and personal identity while acknowledging the difficulty of the task. . . . Certain to ignite debate on campuses and blogs, this work is the perfectly realized embodiment of its author's intent, likely to inspire poets of all ethnic backgrounds for some time to come." Libr J

Encyclopedia of American poetry, the twentieth century; edited by Eric L. Haralson. Fitzroy Dearborn Pubs. 2001 846p $125   **811**
1. Reference books 2. Poets, American -- Dictionaries 3. American poetry -- Bio-bibliography
ISBN 1-57958-240-0

"The volume features more than 400 entries written by academic contributors on individual poets, landmark poems, and major topics. The poet entries are usually 1,000 to 2,000 words long and offer critical treatment of the poet's career and major achievements along with a capsule biography. . . . Approximately one-third of the poet entries include subentries for one or more landmark poems. The 'major topics' entries are longer (around 3,000 words) and include periods or movements (Black Arts movement, Dada), verse traditions (often ethnic, such as Asian American poetry), and styles and themes (Confessional poetry, War and antiwar poetry)." Booklist

Erdrich, Louise
Original fire; selected and new poems. HarperCollins Pubs. 2003 158p $23.95; pa $13.95   **811**
1. Poetry -- By individual authors
ISBN 0-06-620986-2; 0-06-093534-0 pa

LC 2003-40700

"With this volume, drawn from two previous collections and including 100 pages of new poems, {the author} presents her first collection in over a decade. . . . Poems from the first collection chronicle her Native American childhood and early schooling, while those from the second rework or invent Native American mythology. The new poems are more rooted in Catholicism and life as a middle-class American. . . . Essential reading for fans of Erdrich's fiction, this volume can be expected to draw poetry readers into the fold." Libr J

Fagan, Deirdre
Critical companion to Robert Frost; a literary reference to

his life and work. Facts on File 2007 454p il $75   **811**
1. Poets 2. Authors
ISBN 0-8160-6182-3; 978-0-8160-6182-2

LC 2006-13269

"This encyclopedic guide offers critical entries on each of Frost's published poems, including such classics as 'The Road Not Taken,' 'Stopping By Woods on a Snowy Evening,' and 'The Death of the Hired Man.'" Publisher's note
Includes bibliographical references

Faizullah, Tarfia
Registers of illuminated villages; poems. Tarfia Faizullah. Graywolf Press 2018 96 p. (alk. paper) $16   **811**
1. American poetry -- Collections 2. American poetry -- 21st century
ISBN 9781555978006

LC 2017938024

This poetry collection, by Tarfia Faizullah, "extends and transforms her powerful accounts of violence, war, and loss into poems of many forms and voices--elegies, outcries, self-portraits, and larger-scale confrontations with discrimination, family, and memory. . . . Faizullah is an essential new poet whose work only grows more urgent, beautiful, and--even in its unsparing brutality--full of love." (Publisher's note)

Fearing, Kenneth
Selected poems; Robert Polito, editor. Library of America 2004 xxi, 183p (American poets project) $20   **811**
1. Poetry -- By individual authors
ISBN 978-1-931082-57-0; 1-932082-57-X

LC 2003-60482

"Kenneth Fearing writes noir poetry, which is no surprise, considering that he also wrote several noir novels. . . . His poems flirt with narrative (but rarely commit), and they're written in a jittery free verse that sounds like the byproduct of a paranoid, slightly strung-out Whitman. . . . There are plenty of people currently writing variations on Fearing (possibly without being aware of it), but it's tough to beat the stylish chill of the original. These poems may be leaves the wind blows from one gutter to another, but sometimes the gutter's the only place to be." Poetry (Modern Poetry Association)

Fenton, James
Selected poems. Farrar, Straus & Giroux 2006 196p pa $14   **811**
1. Poetry -- By individual authors
ISBN 978-0-374-26065-1; 0-374-26065-6

LC 2006-2691

This "collection offers an introduction to the work of a leading British poet and former professor of poetry at Oxford. Love and menace are the principal muses for Fenton's dark wit. Whether describing how an ex is safe because she's no longer loved . . . or narrating war's awful arithmetic . . . the control behind these lines is often terrifying." Publ Wkly

Ferry, David
Bewilderment; new poems and translations. David Ferry. University of Chicago Press 2012 xii, 113 p.p (paper: alkaline paper) $18   **811**
1. Death -- Poetry 2. Future life -- Poetry 3. Poetry -- Collections
ISBN 0226244881; 0226244903; 9780226244884; 9780226244907

LC 2011050366

National Book Award Finalist: Poetry (2012)
This is a collection of poems from 88-year-old poet David Ferry. The

poems here "are concerned with personal memories, death, and life beyond corporeality. The translations that dot the book—of Catullus, Virgil, and Horace; Rilke, Montale, and Cavafy; and the Anglo-Saxon Genesis A ("The Offering of Isaac")—touch those themes, too." (Booklist)

Includes bibliographical references

Finney, Nikky

★ **Head** off & split; poems. TriQuarterly Books/Northwestern University 2011 97p pa $15.95 **811**

1. Poetry -- By individual authors

ISBN 978-0-8101-5216-8; 0-8101-5216-9

LC 2010-28888

National Book Award: Poetry (2011)

"Finney picks through the past selectively, and with flicks of the blade that are personal, political, poetic and always musical, gives us back the present moment with an intensity that makes a reader feel as if, until reading her volume, we have been unfed." Cleveland Plain Dealer

Flynn, Nick

The **captain** asks for a show of hands; poems. Graywolf Press 2011 94p $22 **811**

1. Poetry -- By individual authors

ISBN 978-1-55597-574-6

LC 2010-937512

In this poetry collection, the author "considers the quandary of soldiers trained never to question authority and the profound betrayal of trust encoded in orders to commit torture. His masterfully concise poems deploy lulling meter, evocative images, and shocking disclosures. . . . Each word is a lit match, a thrown stone, a howling blast, a choking torrent. Flynn has forged daringly intimate and clarion poems of conscience." Booklist

Forche, Carolyn

Blue hour. HarperCollins Pubs. 2003 73p hardcover o.p. pa $13.95 **811**

1. Poetry -- By individual authors

ISBN 0-06-009912-7; 978-0-06-009913-8 pa; 0-06-009013-5 pa

LC 2002-27270

This "gathering of elegiac meditations calls up ghostly memories both personal and universal as the poet mourns the terrible death of her grandmother, gives thanks for the blessing of her son's birth, and alludes with few words and deep feelings to the anguish of war and exile." Booklist

Ford, Katie

Blood lyrics; poems. Katie Ford. Graywolf Press 2014 80p. (alk. paper) $16 **811**

1. Mothers -- Poetry 2. Poetry -- Collections

ISBN 1555976921; 9781555976927

LC 2014935705

Los Angeles Times Book Prizes Finalist: Poetry (2014)

This collection of poems by Katie Ford "is a mother's song, one seared with the knowledge that her country wages long, aching wars in which not all lives are equal. There is beauty imparted, too, but it arrives at a cost." (Publisher's note)

"Taken together, the poems become a meditation on the concurrence of abundance and peril, where sumptuous language expresses stark suffering and musical phrasing portrays a world of discord. Given these conditions, on the prospect 'That it is even possible to stay alive,' Ford posits, 'we should wake/ to each other and ransack/ this flushed skin of everything/ but praise.'" Pub Wkly

From totems to hip-hop; edited by Ishmael Reed. Thunder's Mouth Press 2003 xxx, 523p $34.95; pa $17.95 **811**

1. American poetry -- Collections

ISBN 1-56025-500-5; 1-56025-458-0 pa

LC 2002-75691

This is "a dynamic and original anthology, an unprecedented amalgam of poets representing many facets of American culture and society." Booklist

Frost, Robert

★ **Collected** poems, prose, & plays. Library of Am. 1995 1036p $35 **811**

1. Poetry -- By individual authors

ISBN 1-883011-06-X

LC 94-43693

This volume contains "all of the plays, a generous selection of prose, all collected poems, and 94 uncollected poems, as well as 17 poems that were previously unpublished." Libr J

Gallagher, Tess

Dear ghosts, poems. Graywolf Press 2006 140p $20 **811**

1. Poetry -- By individual authors

ISBN 1-55597-443-0

LC 2005-938149

"So compelling are Gallagher's graceful poems, they leave the reader feeling 'rearranged from the cells out.'" Booklist

Galvin, Brendan

★ **Habitat**; new and selected poems, 1965-2005. Brendan Galvin. Louisiana State University Press 2005 250p $49.95; pa $26.95 **811**

1. Poetry -- By individual authors

ISBN 0-8071-3046-X; 0-8071-3047-8 pa

LC 2004-22441

National Book Award Finalist: Poetry (2005)

"Galvin's work is not only accessible, it turns the commonplace over into something new. A dory, a cormorant, a pack of dogs, a chickadee—all served up with the eye of someone who can take you on a trip of rediscovery into your own backyard." Cape Cod Voice

Gander, Forrest

Core samples from the world; with photographs by Raymond Meeks, Graciela Iburtide and Lucas Foglia. New Directions 2011 95p il **811**

1. Poetry -- By individual authors

ISBN 0-8112-1887-2; 978-0-8112-1887-0

LC 2011-01154

"Gander is an experimental poet in the most literal sense of the word, in that each of his books attempts things that haven't been tried before, either by him or others. In this eighth collection, four sequences of poems respond to pictures by three photographers—Raymond Meeks, Graciela Iturbide, and Lucas Foglia—making of the images metaphors for people and places that are easy to see but difficult to penetrate. The poems don't describe the pictures so much as work in chorus with them. . . . Concluding each section is a piece of jumpy prose, a kind of lyric essay, narrating one of four journeys-to Xinjiang, Mexico, Bosnia-Herzegovina, and Chile. . . . In these pieces, Gander gets as close as one can to the sensations of being an outsider straining toward empathy." Publ Wkly

★ **Eye** against eye; with ten photographs by Sally Mann. New Directions 2005 80p il pa $14.95 **811**

1. Poetry -- By individual authors

ISBN 0-8112-1635-7

LC 2005-14907

The "opener, 'Burning Towers, Standing Wall,' compares the building of a Mayan wall and its destruction–both from political and natural forces–to the collapse of the Twin Towers. In three long poems, linked with pieces that contrast a couple's relationship with a boy's budding adolescence, the reader is asked to regard the relationships between words and subjects. . . . Owing to the poems' placement and the near absence of punctuation, the reader is propelled through the verse, left with a sense of urgency and awe." Libr J

Torn awake. New Directions 2001 95p pa $13.95 **811**
1. Poetry -- By individual authors
ISBN 0-8112-1486-9

LC 2001-32657

"There is no solid ground in the world Forrest Gander conjures in his new book of poems, yet his tentativeness is one of this book's essential qualities. . . . The voices vary throughout this book's six highly speculative sequences, . . . yet again and again they call from their spectral airiness a single recurring image, an elemental configuration of man, woman and child." N Y Times Book Rev

Gerstler, Amy

Scattered at sea; Amy Gerstler. Penguin Books 2015 96 p. (Penguin poets) (paperback) $20 **811**
1. American poetry -- Collections 2. American poetry -- Women authors -- Collections
ISBN 014312689X; 9780143126898

LC 2015002411

NBA Longlist

This poetry collection by Amy Gerstler, long-listed for the 2015 National Book Award for Poetry, "evokes notions of dispersion, diaspora, sowing one's wild oats, having one's mind expanded or blown, losing one's wits, and mortality. Making use of dramatic monologue, elegy, humor, and collage, these poems explore hedonism, gender, ancestry, reincarnation, bereavement, and the nature of prayer." (Publisher's note)

"Accomplished and involving; for all poetry collections." LJ

Gibbons, Reginald

Creatures of a day; poems. Louisiana State University Press 2008 79p $45; pa $16.95 **811**
1. Poetry -- By individual authors
ISBN 978-0-8071-3317-0; 978-0-8071-3318-7 pa

LC 2007-34185

National Book Award Finalist: Poetry (2008)

The author "presents intense encounters with everyday people amidst the historical and social contexts of everyday life. His poems are meditations on memory, obligation, love, death, celebration, and sorrow." Publisher's note

Includes bibliographical references

It's time: poems. Louisiana State Univ. Press 2002 64p $22.95; pa $15.95 **811**
1. Poetry -- By individual authors
ISBN 0-8071-2814-7; 0-8071-2815-5 pa

LC 2002-73076

"If the thoughtful poems in Gibbons' elegant seventh collection were pieces of music, they would be measured piano sonatas, each note, each word, carefully struck, precisely enunciated." Booklist

Gilbert, Jack

Collected poems; by Jack Gilbert. Alfred A. Knopf 2012 408 p. **811**

1. Love poetry 2. Grief -- Poetry 3. Marriage -- Poetry 4. Poetry -- Collections
ISBN 9780307269683

LC 2011025743

This book is a collection of "poems about the joys and complexities of romantic love, about grief and about the power of experience deeply felt. . . . Here are also many and many kinds of poems about travel or life in farflung places, particularly Greece. Plentiful, too, are poems of marriage--its difficulties ("Eight years/ and her love for me quieted away"), its ecstasies, and its ending: divorce is memorably figured as "looking/ out at the bright moonlight on concrete." Gilbert is perhaps best known, however, for the grief-stricken poems that chart the dying of and then mourning over his wife, Michiko, of whom he writes, "The arches of her feet are like voices/ of children calling in the grove of lemon trees,/ where my heart is as helpless as crushed birds."" (Publishers Weekly)

The **dance** most of all; poems. Alfred A. Knopf 2009 60p $25 **811**
1. Poetry -- By individual authors
ISBN 978-0-307-27076-4; 0-307-27076-9

LC 2008-44670

"These poems are deeply elegiac, looking back over a long life lived in the various modes one comes to associate with Gilbert: desire, love, longing and happiness. In short, Gilbert is as Romantic as ever, but that romance is tinged with a hard grief, a sense of loss, but ultimately one of acceptance. These are the poems of a man who realizes without reserve that his time is coming to an end. Death lingers in the background of these lines, reflected in the landscapes that close readers of Gilbert have come to know: Pittsburgh, Greece, Italy, Paris, the woods of Massachusetts where he now resides." Oregonian

★ **Refusing** heaven; poems. Knopf 2005 92p $25 **811**
1. Poetry -- By individual authors
ISBN 1-4000-4365-4

LC 2004-48844

"Jack Gilbert is a poet of reckless charisma and its aftermaths: a catch-as-catch-can Castiglione, consigned by the waywardness of his imagination to write his canon of manners and gestures in lyric poetry. The poems have the quality of brilliant, searching, addled talk after a wild night out. There's a sort of strung-out sprezzatura to this poet, as he bobs and weaves among the memories of old loves in old, European cities. . . . These poems are the stream-of-consciousness work of a consciousness radically narrowed over time, practically armored against new experience. At their best, shuttling associatively between a few old obsessions, they attain claustrophobic beauty that sounds like nobody else." Poetry (Modern Poetry Association)

Ginsberg, Allen

★ **Collected** poems, 1947-1997. HarperCollins Publishers 2006 xx, 1189p il hardcover o.p. pa $25.99 **811**
1. Poetry -- By individual authors
ISBN 978-0-06-113974-1; 0-06-113974-2; 978-0-06-113975-8 pa; 0-06-113975-0 pa

LC 2006-41191

First published 1984 with title: Collected poems, 1947-1980

This books "reprints the complete text of 1984's Collected Poems 1947-1980, along with the collections that followed: White Shroud, Cosmopolitan Greetings, and Death and Fame, including the original book attributes of each collection. A poet of extremes at times too trusting of his instincts, Ginsberg could be playful, angry, strident, obscene, graceful, and hilarious in the space of a page, and by now his readers know they are likely to encounter as many embarrassing poems as enlightening ones. Still, this compendium provides the most complete edition of Ginsberg available." Libr J

Gioia, Dana

Disappearing ink; poetry at the end of print culture. Graywolf Press 2004 271p pa $16   **811**
1. Poetry -- By individual authors 2. American poetry -- History and criticism
ISBN 1-55597-410-4

LC 2004-104190

In this collection of essays, the author discusses the current relevance of poetry and the ways in which it is evolving with the times.

The author "offers accessible, necessary criticism for lay and academic readers of serious poetry." Am Book Rev

99 Poems; New & Selected. by Dana Gioia. Graywolf Press 2016 194 p. $24   **811**
1. Poetry -- Collections 2. American poetry -- 20th century
ISBN 1555977324; 9781555977320

LC 2015953592

This book of poetry, by Dana Gioia, "gathers for the first time work from across his career, including many remarkable new poems. Gioia has not arranged this selection chronologically but instead has organized it by theme in seven sections: Mystery, Place, Remembrance, Imagination, Stories, Songs, and Love. The result is a book that reveals and renews the pleasures, consolations, and sense of wonder that poetry bestows." (Publisher's note)

"Gioia (Pity the Beautiful) displays his immense talents for structure and for tackling difficult subject matter in this first new and selected volume of his career." Pub Wkly

Giovanni, Nikki

Bicycles; love poems. William Morrow 2009 109p $16.95   **811**
1. Poetry -- By individual authors
ISBN 978-0-06-172645-3

"Disarming, sly, sensual, and knowing, Giovanni's poems scan like the teasing and wise songs favored by Dinah Washington and Etta James." Booklist

Blues; for all the changes: new poems. Morrow 1999 100p $15   **811**
1. Poetry -- By individual authors
ISBN 0-688-15698-3

LC 98-50996

"Giovanni never loses sight of the people in her work. In poems built with broken lines and paragraphs of prose, she spars with the ills that confront us, but every struggle has a human face." Libr J

Chasing Utopia; Nikki Giovanni. William Morrow 2013 160 p. $19.99   **811**
1. Poetry -- Collections
ISBN 0688156975; 9780688156978

LC 2013008776

This collection of poems, by Nikki Giovanni, focuses on "the everyday where family and lovers gather, friends commune, and those no longer with us are remembered. And at every gathering there is food, food as sustenance, food as aphrodisiac, food as memory. A pot of beans are flavored with her mother's sighs, this sigh part cardamom, that one the essence of clove; a lover requests a banquet as an affirmation of ongoing passion; an homage is paid to the most time-honored appetizer, soup." (Publisher's note)

In Giovanni's "accessible, teasing, and poignant collection, she of-

fers straightforward, plain-speaking, sneakily resonant poems, many in prose form." Booklist

Includes bibliographical references

The **collected** poetry of Nikki Giovanni, 1968-1998; chronology and notes by Virginia C. Fowler. William Morrow 2003 xliii, 452p $24.95   **811**
1. Poetry -- By individual authors
ISBN 0-06-054133-4

LC 2004-302269

"Giovanni observes and embraces the world like few other poets; seize on these poems spanning three decades, and listen to her sing." Booklist

Includes bibliographical references

A **good** cry; What We Learn from Tears and Laughter. Nikki Giovanni. HarperCollins 2017 128 p. $19.99   **811**
1. African American authors 2. American poetry -- African American authors
ISBN 0062399454; 9780062399458

LC bl2017044178

In this poetry collection, author Nikki Giovanni, "takes us into her confidence, describing the joy and peril of aging and recalling the violence that permeated her parents' marriage and her early life. She pays homage to the people who have given her life meaning and joy. . . Nikki also celebrates her good friend, Maya Angelou, and the many years of friendship, poetry, and kitchen-table laughter they shared before Angelou's death in 2014." (Publisher's note)

"Her clear-eyed and heartfelt work reflects on how internal and external influences shaped her artistic journey. For Giovanni, poetry is not a self-contained medium. Rather, it's a subtle and nuanced mosaic pieced together from the challenges of choosing to truly live rather than succumb to the stasis of merely existing." (Pub Wkly)

Quilting the black-eyed pea; poems and not quite poems. William Morrow 2002 110p $16.95   **811**
1. Poetry -- By individual authors
ISBN 978-0-06-009952-7; 0-06-009952-6

LC 2002-66025

Giovanni "entwines the political and the personal and celebrates womanhood and black society and culture. Hers is an embracing, uplifting, and sustaining voice, one given to both anger and humor." Booklist

Gluck, Louise

Averno. Farrar, Straus and Giroux 2006 79p $22   **811**
1. Poetry -- By individual authors
ISBN 0-374-10742-4; 978-0-374-10742-0

LC 2005-42658

National Book Award Finalist: Poetry (2006)

"Empathic and unforgiving, the voice that unifies Persephone's despondent homelessness, Demeter's rageful mothering and Hades's smitten jealousy is unique in recent poetry, and reveals the flawed humanity of the divine." Publ Wkly

★ **Faithful** and virtuous night; Louise Gluck. 1st ed. Farrar, Straus & Giroux 2014 80 p. (Hardcover) $23   **811**
1. American poetry
ISBN 0374152012; 9780374152017

LC 2013048984

National Book Award: Poetry (2014)

A poetry collection by Louise Glück, "This is a story of adventure, an encounter with the unknown, a knight's undaunted journey into the kingdom of death; this is a story of the world you've always known, that first primer where 'on page three a dog appeared, on page five a ball' and every familiar facet has been made to shimmer like the contours of a dream, 'the dog float[ing] into the sky to join the ball." (Publisher's note)

"Witty, philosophical, and sensuous, Glück embraces dichotomies . . . while gracefully posing provocative questions about the nexus between nature and art and the churning complexity of consciousness." Booklist

Poems 1962-2012; Louise Glück. Farrar, Straus and Giroux 634 p. (alk. paper) $40   **811**
1. Free verse 2. Poetry -- Collections
ISBN 0374126089; 9780374126087

LC 2011051349

This book, by Louise Gluck, features selections from the American author's poetry published between 1962 and 2012. "With each successive book her drive to leave behind what came before has grown more fierce, . . . she invented a form to accommodate this need, the book-length sequence of poems, like a landscape seen from above, a novel with lacunae opening onto the unspeakable." (Publisher's note)

A **village** life. Farrar, Straus, and Giroux 2009 72p $23 **811**
1. Poetry -- By individual authors
ISBN 978-0-374-28374-2; 0-374-28374-5

LC 2008-49218

"Glück's achievement in this collection is to show, through the exigencies of the place she has chosen, how interpersonal relationships are formed, shaped and broken by the particular landscape in which they unfurl. Though the poems are intimate and deeply sympathetic, there remains the suggestion of a distance between Glück and the village life she writes about. When she declaims, 'No one really understands/ the savagery of this place,' it feels as though she is speaking less about her chosen subjects than about herself." Publ Wkly

Goldbarth, Albert
★ The **kitchen** sink; new and selected poems, 1972-2007. Graywolf Press 2007 345p $26   **811**
1. Poetry -- By individual authors
ISBN 978-1-55597-462-6; 1-55597-462-7

LC 2006-929502

"Albert Goldbarth just may be the American poet of his generation for the ages. Often humorous but always serious, Goldbarth combines erudite research, pop-culture fanaticism, and personal anecdote in ways that make his writings among the most stylistically recognizable in the literary world." Georgia Rev

Good poems; selected and introduced by Garrison Keillor. Viking 2002 xxvi, 476p $25.95; pa $15   **811**
1. English poetry -- Collections 2. American poetry -- Collections
ISBN 0-670-03126-7; 0-14-200344-1 pa

LC 2002-16881

Keillor "has put together a collection of close to 300 poems he has read during . . . [the] PBS broadcast, The Writer's Almanac. . . . Poems are arranged by 19 general themes, such as 'Snow,' 'Failure,' and 'A Good Life.' Authors range from well-known oldies like Emily Dickinson and Robert Frost to unknowns like C.K. Williams. . . . An outstanding feature of this collection is that the selections are all so accessible—even folks who say they don't like poetry can find something here to enjoy." SLJ

Graham, Jorie
The **dream** of the unified field; selected poems, 1974-1994. Ecco Press 1995 199p hardcover o.p. pa $15   **811**
1. Poetry -- By individual authors

ISBN 0-88001-476-8 pa

LC 95-16572

"Combining great vision like Blake's, a Dickinsonian philosophical introspection, and a richly modern sensuality, this selection demonstrates the full range of Graham's poetic gifts." Booklist

Overlord; poems. Ecco 2005 93p $22.95   **811**
1. Poetry -- By individual authors
ISBN 0-06-074565-7

LC 2004-53681

"In a distinctly forthright and empathic collection, Graham has constructed poems of lyrical steeliness and cauterizing beauty." Booklist

Graham, Jorie, 1950-
Fast; Jorie Graham. Ecco, an imprint of HarperCollins Publishers 2017 84 p. (hardcover) $25.99   **811**
1. Philosophy 2. Poetry -- Collections 3. American poetry -- 21st century
ISBN 9780062663481; 0062663488

In this poetry collection Jorie Graham "explores the limits of the human and the uneasy seductions of the post-human. Conjuring an array of voices and perspectives--from bots, to the holy shroud, to the ocean floor, to a medium transmitting from beyond the grave--these poems give urgent form to the ever-increasing pace of transformation of our planet and ourselves." (Publisher's note)

"Each of Graham's poems is a daring voyage from the harbors of facts through the rapids of feelings and thoughts, leaving readers exhilarated and transformed." Booklist

From the New World; Poems 1976-2014. Jorie Graham. HarperCollins 2015 384 p. $29.99   **811**
1. Love 2. Poetry 3. Politics
ISBN 0062315404; 9780062315403
Los Angeles Times Book Prize: Poetry (2015)

This book is a "volume of poems, selected from almost four decades of work, that tracks the evolution of one of our most renowned contemporary poets, Pulitzer Prize-winner Jorie Graham. [Readers] can witness the unfolding of Graham's signature ethical and eco-political concerns, as well as her deft exploration of mythology, history, love and, increasingly, love of the world in a time of crisis." (Publisher's note)

"Although Graham never mentions the word Oversoul here, these difficult language poems are suggestive of transcendentalism in its truest sense. Graham may not visit Walden Pond, but she hangs clothes in her backyard, walks in the woods, and tends her garden (among the subjects of the poems here), using these occasions to mark the place where daily life meets the infinite." LJ

Greenbaum, Jessica
The **two** Yvonnes; poems. Jessica Greenbaum. Princeton University Press 2012 57 p. (pbk.: acid-free paper) $12.95 **811**
1. Motherhood -- Poetry 2. Poetry -- Collections
ISBN 0691156638; 9780691156620; 9780691156637

LC 2012020320

This book is Jessica Greenbaum's second poetry collection. "With fluent free verse broken up by sonnets, an abecedary and a pantoun, in allegories, comic anecdotes, and pivotal, confessional memories, Greenbaum lets us travel along with her as she grows from too-patient girl to agitated student, from the mother of a sick young child to all the sensations of being alive' after the child (to judge by the poems) has moved out." (Publishers Weekly)

Gregg, Linda
All of it singing. Graywolf Press 2008 224p $24   **811**

1. Poetry -- By individual authors
ISBN 978-1-55597-507-4; 1-55597-507-0

LC 2008-928247

This retrospective "selects from all of Gregg's published books—from her 1981 debut Too Bright to See to 2006's In the Middle Distance—including a group of new poems that show her ongoing investigations into the inner intensities of everyday brutality and grace. . . . The poems travel the globe, set in New England, California, Mexico, Greece and beyond, though wherever her poems go, Gregg never forgets that 'if paradise is to be here/ it will have to include her.' Gregg offers up poems of love lost and won, and of an average life lived with extraordinary force. . . . The poems always rejoice, however dark their subjects, in a powerful sense of simply being alive." Publ Wkly

Guest, Barbara

The **collected** poems of Barbara Guest; edited by Hadley Haden Guest. Wesleyan University Press 2008 525p (Wesleyan poetry) $39.95 **811**
1. Poetry -- By individual authors
ISBN 978-0-8195-6860-1; 0-8195-6860-0

LC 2008-20147

"It is impossible for a reader to leave The Collected Poems of Barbara Guest without appreciating the enormous spiritual gift her work has always offered in the form of an aesthetic and philosophical challenge." Boston Rev

Includes index. `Works by Barbara Guest¿: p. xxvii-xxix

Hacker, Marilyn

Squares and courtyards. Norton 2000 107p $21; pa $12 **811**
1. Poetry -- By individual authors
ISBN 0-393-04830-6; 0-393-32095-2 pa

LC 99-39110

"With customary fortitude and intelligence, Hacker confronts such sobering subjects as the trauma of her own chemotherapy and the loss of friends, in poems that are at once clear-sighted and emotionally full." New Yorker

Hacker, Marilyn, 1942-

A **stranger's** mirror; new and selected poems 1994/2014. by Marilyn Hacker. W W Norton & Co Inc 2015 320 p. (hardcover) $29.95 **811**
1. Poetry -- Collections
ISBN 0393244644; 9780393244649

LC 2014037031

This collection of poetry, by Marilyn Hacker, "include[s[work from four previous volumes along with twenty-five new poems. . . . Her poems belong to an urban world of cafés, bookshops, bridges, traffic, demonstrations, conversations, and solitudes. From there, Hacker reaches out to other sites and personas: a refugee camp on the Turkish/Syrian border; contrapuntal monologues of a Palestinian and an Israeli poet; intimate and international exchanges abbreviated on Skype." (Publisher's note)

"Hacker is an empathic, daring, and bracing poet of border-crossings and global conscience." Booklist

Halaby, Laila

My name on his tongue; poems. Laila Halaby. 1st ed. Syracuse University Press 2012 xi, 131 p.p (pbk.: alk. paper) $17.95 **811**
1. Arab Americans 2. Narrative poetry 3. Poetry -- Collections
ISBN 0815632940; 9780815632948

LC 2012006950

In this "poetry collection . . . [Laila] Halaby . . . narrates the need of Arab Americans to navigate new realities while giving voice to old ones. She writes about her personal feelings and daily experiences in a confessional mode. . . . She . . . interweaves insights about peace, war, family, nostalgia, exile, and sociopolitical conflicts, among other subjects, Halaby promotes poetry as both testimony and instrument of change." (Library Journal)

Hall, Donald

The **back** chamber. Houghton Mifflin Harcourt 2011 82p $22 **811**
1. Poetry -- By individual authors
ISBN 978-0-547-64585-8

LC 2011009152

This is "a mix of naughty, funny, sweet, and sad pieces about love, family, death, and the poignancy of things. The old rooms of his grandfather's farmhouse in New Hampshire, where Hall has lived since the 1970s, set the stage for recalled intimacies with his late wife, the poet Jane Kenyon, and recollections of the childhood that first brought him there. . . . Featuring moving, amusing, musical poems about love, aging, and baseball, this work will have broad appeal and is recommended for all collections." Libr J

White apples and the taste of stone; poems, 1946-2006. Houghton Mifflin Co. 2006 431p $30; pa $16.95 **811**
1. Poetry -- By individual authors
ISBN 978-0-618-53721-1; 0-618-53721-X; 978-0-618-91999-4 pa; 0-618-91999-6 pa

LC 2005-20047

"Given to formal short work in the '50s, to lengthy verse essays and verse memoirs later on, Hall shows consistent topics and moods: adult life among New Hampshire's farms and mountains, childhood in the Connecticut suburbs, equanimity and nostalgia, satire and self-satire, middle age and old age, regret and reserve. Most original in his long poems from the '80s and '90s, Hall achieved popular success in recent years, . . . collecting elegies and laments for his late wife, the poet Jane Kenyon." Publ Wkly

Hall, Donald, 1928-2018

A **carnival** of losses; notes nearing ninety. Donald Hall. Houghton Mifflin Harcourt 2018 224 p. (hardback) $25 **811**
1. Aging 2. Old age 3. Poets, American -- 20th century
ISBN 9781328826343

LC 2017049735

"Before his passing in 2018, nearing ninety, [Donald] Hall delivered this new collection of self-knowing, fierce, and funny essays on aging, the pleasures of solitude, and the sometimes astonishing freedoms arising from both. He intersperses memories of exuberant days--as in Paris, 1951, with a French girl memorably inclined to say, 'I couldn't care less'--with writing, visceral and hilarious, on what he has called the 'unknown, unanticipated galaxy' of extreme old age." (Publisher's note)

Harjo, Joy

A **map** to the next world; poetry and tales. Norton 2000 138p hardcover o.p. pa $13.95 **811**
1. Poetry -- By individual authors
ISBN 978-0-393-32096-1; 0-393-32096-0

LC 99-41099

"One of the most significant American Indian poets here expands her poetic practice to include what she calls tales but might as easily be considered prose poems. Harjo's verse has lately taken on a flowing, narrative quality; these tales, by contrast, take an imagistic, stream-of-consciousness form. . . . Written with authority and Harjo's trademark exploratory verve, this is fine, mature work." Booklist

Harris, Francine J.

Play dead; Francine J. Harris. Alice James Books 2016 xii, 85 p.p (softcover: acid-free paper) $15.95 **811**
 1. Poetry -- Collections 2. Poetry
 ISBN 1938584252; 9781938584251

LC 2015036404

This book of poetry, by Francine J. Harris, "challenges us to look at our cultivated selves as products of circumstance and attempts to piece together patterns amidst dissociative chaos. Harris unearths a ruptured world dictated by violence—a place of deadly what ifs, where survival hangs by a thread." (Publisher's note)

"Harris is a keen observer of self and other, writing not as a distant anthropologist, but as an empathetic and silent witness." Pub Wkly

Harrison, Jim

In search of small gods. Copper Canyon Press 2009 120p $22 **811**
 1. Poetry -- By individual authors
 ISBN 978-155659-300-0; 1-55659-300-7

LC 2008-39992

Harrison "writes like a man reconciling the world at large with the natural world he knows well, one that still fascinates and inspires him. Many of his small gods are dogs, and many of them are fish or birds, that is, chickadees and hawks, willow flycatchers and hummingbirds. . . . He looks at them all with awe and ironic amusement. A group of prose poems centers this volume. Whether he imagines an Estonian World War II veteran who is fascinated by light or Vallejo in Paris, collecting empty wine bottles for small change, Harrison is heavily invested in narrative elements that range from the real to the surreal." Libr J

Harrison, Jim, 1937-2016

Songs of unreason. Copper Canyon Press 2011 143p $22 **811**
 1. Poetry -- By individual authors
 ISBN 978-1-55659-389-5

LC 2011025560

"It wouldn't be a Harrison collection without the poet, novelist, and food critic's reverence for rivers, dogs, and women, but that's not to say Harrison has grown stale or uninteresting in his late poems. Often, as in 'A Part of My History,' which finds the poet tracking the ghost of García Lorca through Granada, his poems stun us simply, with the richness of the clarity, detail, and the immediacy of Harrison's voice. . . . Pushing his formal boundaries, Harrison closes the collection with the meditative 'Suite of Unreason,' a piece that boils down his sharp, epigrammatic lines into a sequence of fist-pumping short poems. But it also wouldn't be a Harrison poem without the hard melancholy that has come to define his voice." Publ Wkly

Harrison, Leslie

The **book** of endings; Leslie Harrison. University of Akron Press 2017 88 p. (Akron series in poetry) (paper) $14.95 **811**
 1. Poetry -- Collections 2. American poetry -- 21st century
 ISBN 9781629220659; 1629220639; 9781629220628; 9781629220635

LC 2016026149

National Book Award Finalist: Poetry (2017)

This book of poetry, by Leslie Harrison, "tr[ies] to make sense of, or at least come to some kind of reckoning with absence - the death of the author's mother, the absence of the beloved, the absence of an accountable god, cicadas, the dead stars arriving, the dead moon aglow in the night sky." (Publisher's note)

"Harrison (Displacement) reveals a psyche made strange through grieving in this luminous and musical collection." Pub Wkly Annex

Includes bibliographical references (pages 87-88)

Hass, Robert

The **apple** trees at Olema; new and selected poems. Ecco 2010 352p $34.99 **811**
 1. Poetry -- By individual authors
 ISBN 978-0-06-192382-1; 0-06-192382-6

This "retrospective collection, drawn from five previous books, beginning with Field Guide (1973), opens with a generous selection of new poems redolent of Whitman and the blues. Narrative poems are droll and astringent in their musings over love's paradoxes and history's shifting claims, children's pleasures, poverty, and danger. . . . Hass distills experiences down to their essence as he limns landscapes, portrays friends and loved ones, and imagines the struggles of strangers. The ordinary is cracked open to reveal metaphysical riddles in poems that feel so natural, their formal complexities nearly elude our detection." Booklist

Time and materials; poems, 1997-2005. Ecco 2007 88p $22.95 **811**
 1. Poetry -- By individual authors
 ISBN 978-0-06-134960-7; 0-06-134960-7

LC 2007-30294

National Book Award: Poetry (2007)

This collection of poetry by the former U.S. poet laureate "show a rare internal variety, even as they reflect his constant concerns. One is human impact on the planet at the century's end. . . . Another concern is biography and memory, not so much Hass's own life as the lives of family and friends. . . . Through it all runs a rare skill with long sentences, a light touch, a wish to make claims not just on our ears but on our hearts, and a willingness to wait—few poets wait longer, it seems—for just the right word." Publ Wkly

Includes bibliographical references

Hayden, Robert Earl

Collected poems; edited by Frederick Glaysher. Liveright 1985 205p hardcover o.p. pa $15 **811**
 1. Poetry -- By individual authors
 ISBN 978-0-87140-159-5; 0-87140-159-2

LC 84-28880

"Hayden's poetry is a blend of unrivaled craftsmanship with a sharp, unrestrained vision. His subjects encompass the whole of human experience, from the extremely personal but never obscure ('Approximations') to the historical but never pedantic ('Belsen, Day of Liberation'). His technique is similarly varied. Hayden is as adept with haiku, imitations of Eskimo song-poems, or sonnets as he is with free verse. A particularly important addition to libraries with black literature collections." Booklist

Hayes, Terrance, 1971-

American sonnets for my past and future assassin; Terrance Hayes. Penguin Books 2018 112 p. (paperback) $18 **811**
 1. Sonnets 2. United States -- Poetry 3. American poetry -- 21st century
 ISBN 9780143133186

LC 2017057838

National Book Award Finalist: Poetry (2018)

This book in the Penguin Poets series, by Terrance Hayes, presents "seventy poems bearing the same title . . . [that explore] the meanings of American, of assassin, and of love in the sonnet form. Written during the first two hundred days of the [Donald] Trump presidency, these poems are haunted by the country's past and future eras and errors, its dreams and nightmares." (Publisher's note)

How to be drawn; Terrance Hayes. Penguin Books 2015 112 p. (pbk.) $20 **811**
1. Art -- Poetry 2. American poetry -- Collections
ISBN 9780143126881; 0143126881
LC 2014045785
National Book Award Finalist: Poetry (2015)
NAACP Image Award: Outstanding Literary Work - Poetry (2016)
National Book Critics Circle Award Finalist: Poetry (2015)
This poetry collection, by Terrance Hayes "explores how we see and are seen. While many of these poems bear the clearest imprint yet of Hayes's background as a visual artist, they do not strive to describe art so much as inhabit it. Thus, one poem contemplates the principle of blind contour drawing while others are inspired by maps, graphs, and assorted artists." (Publisher's note)
"Hayes writes far-reaching yet intimate monologues that are simultaneously subtle and hard-hitting; he unearths shards of shameful antebellum history and takes measure of the current state of moral and political paralysis." Booklist

Lighthead. Penguin Books 2010 95p (Penguin poets) pa $18 **811**
1. Poetry -- By individual authors
ISBN 978-0-14-311696-7; 0-14-311696-7
LC 2009-53319
National Book Award: Poetry (2010)
This collection is a "celebration and castigation of American culture, one worthy of the term 'Americanist.' The title references the light of inspiration and the fire that pours from the heads of two teenage lynching victims in one of the opening poems. The fact that the title can do both inspiration and elegy is indicative of how meaning is contested terrain in Hayes' work. . . . [He] deftly quilts together different textures of language. Rants move into love poems and biting humor butts up against meditations. . . . Sound is of primary importance to Mr. Hayes. Throughout the book he borrows from hip-hop, jazz, slang, lists, and T-shirt slogans. Content aside, his poems are full of pure pleasure of sound in his startling and sonically dense images." Pittsburgh Post-Gazette

Hecht, Anthony
Collected later poems. Knopf 2003 255p hardcover o.p. pa $16.95 **811**
1. Poetry -- By individual authors
ISBN 978-0-375-71030-8; 0-375-71030-2
LC 2003-44601
This volume contains: The transparent man (1990), Flight among the tombs (1996), and The darkness and the light (2001)
"From the outset a fastidious craftsman, Hecht developed out of the legacy of modernism a stately, intricate, rigorously formal poetry that slowly expanded in its range of tones and subject matter." Times Lit Suppl

Hicok, Bob, 1960-
Elegy owed; Bob Hicok. Copper Canyon Press 2013 120 p. (hardcover: alk. paper) $22 **811**
1. American poetry -- Collections
ISBN 1556594364; 9781556594366
LC 2012043531
National Book Critics Circle Award Finalist: Poetry (2013)
This collection of poetry by Bob Hicok was a National Book Critics Circle Award finalist and won the Paterson Award for Literary Excellence. "In his seventh collection, Hicok builds startling images out of the everyday and the surreal, the comic and the sorrowful. . . . Intimate lyrics of love, fear, loss, and cosmic perplexity are matched by robust dissections and protests." (Booklist)
"Words have weight in Hicok's poems. They feel nailed in place, and the meter hits like the sure pounding of a hammer. Yet as heft, muscle, and precision draw you forward, Hicok evokes not solidity but, rather, shifting ground, flux, metamorphosis, and, most arrestingly, most unnervingly, death... This trenchant collection's got heart and soul." Booklist

Hirsch, Edward
Gabriel; a poem. by Edward Hirsch. Alfred A. Knopf 2014 78 p. $26.95 **811**
1. American poetry 2. Grief -- Poetry 3. Children -- Death 4. Children -- Death -- Poetry
ISBN 038535357X; 9780385353571; 9780385353731; 9780804172875
LC 2013049301
National Book Award Longlist: Poetry (2014)
"This unabashed sequence speaks directly from [poet Edward] Hirsch's heart to our own, without sentimentality. . . . In propulsive three-line stanzas, he tells the story of how a once unstoppable child, who suffered from various developmental disorders, turned into an irreverent young adult, funny, rebellious, impulsive." (Publisher's note)

The **living** fire; new and selected poems, 1975-2010. Alfred A. Knopf 2010 237p $27 **811**
1. Poetry -- By individual authors
ISBN 978-0-375-41522-7; 0-375-41522-X
LC 2009-24452
In Hirsch's work, things are not always what they seem. Certainly, his poems work to dignify the everyday. But they do more than that. What makes Hirsch so singular in American poetry is the balance he strikes between the quotidian and something completely other an irrational counterforce, the living fire that gives its name to his new selected poems. . . . Literary and allusive, but also domestic and intimate, as it rises toward praise, Hirsch's voice resounds with both force and subtlety. One of the pleasures of reading the new selected poems is the chance to see that voice develop and then range freely and surprisingly. N Y Times Book Rev

Special orders; poems. Alfred A. Knopf 2008 64p $25 **811**
1. Poetry -- By individual authors
ISBN 978-0-307-26681-1; 0-307-26681-8
LC 2007-40336
This collection "brings its demotic, heartfelt, autobiographical pieces together to form a picture of Hirsch's whole life, with sadness always visible, but joy in the foreground. He begins with his immigrant 'grandfather,/ an old man from the Old World'; remembers 'the second-story warehouse' where the young poet 'filled orders for the factory downstairs'; and moves on to his own life as a struggling, and then a successful, writer, teacher and father. Jewish and Yiddish heritage, in memory and on canvas (Chaim Soutine, Marc Chagall) pervades the first half of the volume. . . . The second half follows Hirsch as an adult, to Houston (where he taught for many years) and back to New York City, where he now heads the Guggenheim Foundation." Publ Wkly

Hirshfield, Jane
After; poems. HarperCollins 2006 97p $23.95 **811**
1. Poetry -- By individual authors
ISBN 0-06-077916-0
LC 2005-50260
"These poems' topics range from global warming to insomnia, pas-

sion, cheese making, and sneezing. . . . [The author] engages historical figures from Rembrandt, Poe, and Tu Fu to Linnaeus, Roget, and Darwin. The beauty of these historically engaging poems, though, is that they remain firmly tied to our contemporary world." Va Q Rev

The **beauty**; poems. Jane Hirshfield. Alfred A. Knopf 2015 128 p. (hardback) $26   **811**
1. Poetry -- Collections 2. American poetry -- Collections
ISBN 0385351070; 9780385351072
             LC 2014025831
NBA Longlist
This collection of poems, by Jane Hirshfield, "opens with a series of dappled, ranging 'My' poems--'My Skeleton,' 'My Corkboard,' 'My Species,' 'My Weather'--using materials sometimes familiar, sometimes unexpected, to explore the magnitude, singularity, and permeability of our shared existence." (Publisher's note)
"These open, approachable poems offer insights that ring true for anyone who's lived a little; they will appeal to a wide range of readers." LJ

Hoagland, Tony
Unincorporated persons in the late Honda dynasty; poems. Graywolf Press 2010 90p pa $15   **811**
1. Poetry -- By individual authors
ISBN 978-1-55597-549-4; 1-55597-549-6
             LC 2009-933818
"There are 15 or 20 better poets in America than Tony Hoagland, but few deliver more pure pleasure. His erudite comic poems are back-loaded with heartache and longing, and they function, emotionally, like improvised explosive devices: the pain comes at you from the cruelest angles, on the sunniest of days. . . . On a superficial level Mr. Hoagland's poems — he writes in an alert, caffeinated, lightly accented free verse — resemble those of many writers in what one is tempted to call the Amiable School of American Poets, a group for which Billy Collins serves as both prom king and starting point guard. But Mr. Hoagland's verse is consistently, and crucially, bloodied by a sense of menace and by straight talk." N Y Times (Late N Y Ed)

What narcissism means to me. Graywolf Press 2003 78p pa $14   **811**
1. Poetry -- By individual authors
ISBN 1-55597-386-8 pa
             LC 2003-101172
The author's "speaker devotes considerable energy to unmasking . . . {his} vulnerable self, revealing its ugliness, hatred and social sensitivity. . . . In milder poems, which often revolve around eating dinner, drinking wine and hanging out with friends (typically other creative writing professors), he explores a more social self, slipping into a 'he said, she said' mode, and reporting at great length on friends' witticisms." Publ Wkly

Hollander, John
A **draft** of light; poems. Alfred A. Knopf 2008 109p $26   **811**
1. Poetry -- By individual authors
ISBN 978-0-307-26911-9; 0-307-26911-6
             LC 2008-4751
"As one would expect of a poet whose work has been set to music, Hollander sees poetry as an oral art even though it is first written on paper. What one might not expect from this 78-year-old poet is the word-play, lighthearted tone, and general mischievousness that seems to come trippingly from his pen. . . . This volume's title poem, for example, ends with a paraphrase of T.S. Eliot's 'Little Gidding.' Other poems paraphrase Percy Bysshe Shelley, Wallace Stevens, and Joyce Kilmer, to say

nothing of William Shakespeare. Like Shakespeare, Hollander fuses a somber tone with comic conventions, resulting in the poetic equivalent of the problem play." Libr J
Includes bibliographical references

Hong, Cathy Park, 1976-
Engine empire; Cathy Park Hong. W.W. Norton & Co. 2012 95 p.   **811**
1. Art -- Poetry 2. East Asian poetry 3. Computers -- Poetry 4. Poetry -- Collections 5. Frontier and pioneer life -- West (U.S.) -- Poetry
ISBN 0393082849; 9780393082845
             LC 2012000596
"Engine Empire is a trilogy of lyric and narrative poems that evoke an array of genres and voices. . . . The first sequence, called 'Ballad of Our Jim,' draws inspiration from the Old West and follows a band of outlaw fortune seekers who travel to a California mining town during the 1800s. In the second sequence, 'Shangdu, My Artful Boomtown!' a fictional industrialized boomtown draws its inspiration from present-day Shenzhen, China. The third and last section, 'The World Cloud,' is set in the far future and tracks how individual consciousness breaks up when everything--books, our private memories--becomes immediately accessible data." (Publisher's note)
"The middle and final sections of this triptych are stronger than the first, where sound gets the better of sense, but much of this book is deliciously inventive. . . . A smart, disorienting look at our present-future set out in a rich hybrid language." LJ

Howard, Richard
★ **Inner** voices; selected poems, 1963-2003. Farrar, Straus and Giroux 2004 428p $35   **811**
1. Poetry -- By individual authors
ISBN 0-374-25862-7
             LC 2004-40464
The author "chooses artists and art as the personae and subjects of many of his poems. . . . Besides artists, Howard often chooses writers as personae, including prominent Victorians (Whitman, Ruskin and Browning); correspondents with other writers and artists; and increasingly, himself as traveler, museumgoer, and engaged reader." Booklist

★ The **silent** treatment; new poems. Turtle Point Press 2005 114p pa $16.95   **811**
1. Poetry -- By individual authors
ISBN 1-885586-38-3
             LC 2004-113837
Hannah Arendt, George Eliot, Cosima Wagner, and a boy in a photograph by Arkansas photographer Mike Disfarmer are among the speakers in this collection.
"In characterizing the poems of Richard Howard's latest collection, one is tempted to bypass 'golden' as a description and head straight on to platinum. Now in his eighth decade, Howard has long been--along with the late James Merrill, who jokingly coined the phrase--one of American poetry's 'Great Fancies.'" Wkly Stand

Without saying; new poems. Turtle Point Press 2008 108p pa $16.95   **811**
1. Poetry -- By individual authors
ISBN 978-1-933527-14-7 pa; 1-933527-14-5 pa
             LC 2007-907229
National Book Award Finalist: Poetry (2008)
"In this 14th collection of his own verse, [the author] returns to the kinds of poems that made him famous: elaborate dramatic monologues, impersonations and dialogues that are intricately alert to literary history

and sexual desire. . . . In these thoughtful new poems, Howard offers, and excels in, sophisticated verbal comedy." Publ Wkly

Howe, Fanny, 1940-

Second childhood; Fanny Howe. Graywolf Press 2014 80 p. (alk. paper) $16 **811**

1. Chance 2. Poetry

ISBN 1555976824; 9781555976828

LC 2013958013

National Book Award Shortlist: Poetry (2014)

In this poetry collection by Fanny Howe "the observing poet is an impersonal figure who accompanies Howe in her encounters with chance and mystery. She is not one age or the other, in one time or another. Fanny Howe's poetry is known for its lyricism, fragmentation, experimentation, religious engagement, and commitment to social justice." (Publisher's note)

"Howe may occupy some familiar and traditional poetic spaces, but she populates them beautifully." Pub Wkly

Howe, Susan

That this. New Directions Pub. 2010 109p il pa $15.95 **811**

1. Poetry -- By individual authors

ISBN 978-0-8112-1918-1 pa; 0-8112-1918-6 pa

LC 2010-41791

"Death is one of the preeminent subjects of poetry, and Howe . . . approaches this topic with the gravitas of one who has endured loss. . . . [This] volume deals chiefly with the death of her husband, Peter Hare. The book juxtaposes Howe's personal recollections with excerpts from an assortment of documents, ranging from 18th-century diaries to an array of half-decayed ephemera, such as bits of Poussin prints and fragments of linguistic sculpture. . . . An intelligent and unorthodox treatment of grief, this title will appeal to poetry and visual arts enthusiasts." Libr J

Hughes, Langston

Selected poems of Langston Hughes; drawings by E. McKnight Kauffer. Knopf 1959 297p il hardcover o.p. pa $13.95 **811**

1. Poetry -- By individual authors

ISBN 0-679-72818-X; 978-0-679-72818-4

This collection represents Langston Hughes' own decisions as to which of his poems he wanted to preserve and reprint

The **Hungry** Ear; poems of food & drink. edited by Kevin Young. St Martins Pr 2012 336 p. $25 **811**

1. Food -- Poetry 2. Poetry -- Collections

ISBN 1608195511; 9781608195510

This book, edited by Kevin Young, is a collection of poems related to food. "While some of the poems here are explicitly about the food itself: the blackberries, the butter, the barbecue--all are evocative of the experience of eating. Many of the poems are also about the everything else that accompanies food: the memories, the company, even the politics. . . . Poets include: Elizabeth Alexander, Elizabeth Bishop, Billy Collins, Mark Doty, Robert Frost, [and] Allen Ginsberg." (Publisher's note)

Huntington, Cynthia

Heavenly bodies; Cynthia Huntington. Southern Illinois University Press 2012 vii, 75 p.p (pbk.: alk. paper) $15.95 **811**

1. Nineteen sixties 2. Addiction -- Poetry 3. Sexual liberation -- Poetry

ISBN 0809330636; 0809330644; 9780809330638; 9780809330645

LC 2011022095

National Book Award Finalist: Poetry (2012)

In this "collection of lyric poems, Cynthia Huntington gives an intimate view of the sexual revolution and rebellion in a time before the rise of feminism. 'Heavenly Bodies' is a testament to the duality of sex, the twin seductiveness and horror of drug addiction, and the social, political, and personal dramas of America in the 1960s." (Publisher's note)

Includes bibliographical references (p. 74-75)

Jackson, Major

Holding company. W.W. Norton & Co. 2010 91p $24.95 **811**

1. Poetry -- By individual authors

ISBN 978-0-393-07080-4

LC 2010-17728

"The sonnet sequence has been a staple of love poetry; Major Jackson tries here a sequence of tenline poems, instead of the fourteen of the sonnet, and the form, as always, pressures the poet toward specific meanings. There is greater urgency to get to the point, and it makes the expression of love only more dire, more taut and almost unmanageable. The effect of these poems individually is a certain serenity, a distance toward public turmoil, but cumulatively they amount to a desperate rebellion, a willful declaration of immortality." Huffington Post

Hoops; poems. Norton 2006 125p $23.95 **811**

1. Poetry -- By individual authors

ISBN 0-393-05937-5; 978-0-393-05937-3

LC 2005-33320

The author's "poems are witty, musical, and intelligent; he is equally happy discussing the war on terror . . . or describing early crushes." New Yorker

Jazz poems. Alfred A. Knopf 2006 256p (Everyman's library pocket poets) $12.50 **811**

1. Jazz music -- Poetry 2. American poetry -- Collections

ISBN 978-1-4000-4251-7; 1-4000-4251-8

A collection of poetry inspired by jazz music. Includes poems by Langston Hughes, E. E. Cummings, William Carlos Williams, Frank O'Hara, Gwendolyn Brooks, Yusef Komunyakaa, Charles Simic, Rita Dove, Ntozake Shange, Mark Doty, William Matthews, and C. D. Wright, among others.

Jeffers, Robinson

The **selected** poetry of Robinson Jeffers; edited by Tim Hunt. Stanford Univ. Press 2001 758p pa $34.95 **811**

1. Poetry -- By individual authors

ISBN 978-0-8047-4108-8; 0-8047-4108-5

LC 00-48490

"Hunt's edition strips the punctuation added by contemporary printers (which 'often obscures the rhythm and pacing of what Jeffers actually wrote, and at points even obscures meaning and nuance') and includes a carefully weighed choice of long and short works, as well as unpublished work. . . . This new selection will get readers closer than ever to the poems as Jeffers himself saw them." Publ Wkly

Jess, Tyehimba, 1965-

★ **Olio**; Tyehimba Jess. Wave Books 2016 256 p. illustrations (softcover) $25 **811**

1. Poetry -- Collections 2. American poetry -- African American authors

ISBN 9781940696201; 9781940696225

LC 2015026171

Pulitzer Prize: Poetry (2017)

This book, by Tyehimba Jess, winner of the 2017 Pulitzer Prize for poetry, "weaves sonnet, song, and narrative to examine the lives of mostly unrecorded African American performers directly before and after the Civil War up to World War I. 'Olio' is an effort to understand how they met, resisted, complicated, co-opted, and sometimes defeated attempts to minstrelize them." (Publisher's note)

"Highly recommended; this formally risky collection proves to be a character-rich, historically informed page-turner." LJ

Includes bibliographical references (pages 228-230).

Johnson, James Weldon

Complete poems; edited with an introduction by Sondra Kathryn Wilson. Penguin Bks. 2000 xxxiii, 202p pa $14 **811**
1. Poetry -- By individual authors
ISBN 0-14-118545-7

LC 00-39969

This volume contains Fifty years and other poems (1917), God's trombones (1927), Saint Peter relates an incident of the resurrection day (1935), and a number of previously unpublished poems. The editor's introduction considers Johnson's achievements and influence

Includes bibliographical references

Johnson, Jenny

In full velvet; poems. Jenny Johnson. Sarabande Books 2017 72 p. (hardback) $16.95 **811**
1. Poetry -- Collections
ISBN 9781941411377

LC 2016014117

The poems in this book, by Jenny Johnson, "interrogate the nuances of desire, love, gender, ecology, LGBTQ lineage and community, and the tension between a body's material limits and the forms made possible by the imagination. Characterized by formal poise, vulnerability, and compassion, Johnson's debut collection is one of resounding generosity and grace." (Publisher's note)

"In this stunningly lyrical debut, Johnson probes issues of queer culture and love from an array of existential perspectives, creating a melodic and thought-provoking symphony on queer identity." Pub Wkly.

Includes bibliographical references and index

Johnston, Devin

★ Traveler. Farrar, Straus and Giroux 2011 67p $23 **811**
1. Poetry -- By individual authors
ISBN 978-0-374-27933-2; 0-374-27933-0

LC 2011-08457

This collection brings Johnston's "careful, graceful, almost neo-classical pen to scenes from all over the world—Japan, Shanghai, 'the Mongol steppes,' the Midwest 'when a thunderstorm/ trundles down the Wabash,' and the Scottish holy isle of Iona. . . . Sometimes sublime, more often astringent, Johnston's poems of places and things seen—they make up most of the volume—should please fans of that older world traveler, August Kleinzahler. Yet Johnston may be most original when his subjects turn up close to home: his cool temperament meets its fruitful complement when he writes of family and children, most of all his young daughter, who in the brief, fine triptych entitled 'Appetites' 'lies awake/ talking in confidential tones/ with one she calls/ my friend who eats me.' It would take a hard heart to resist such humor, such warmth, set amid such control as Johnston shows." Publ Wkly

Jones, Saeed

★ Prelude to bruise; Poetry. by Saeed Jones. First edition Coffee House Press 2014 124 p. (pbk.) $16 **811**
1. Poetry 2. American poetry -- 21st century
ISBN 1566893747; 9781566893749

LC 2014008086
National Book Critics Circle Award Finalist: Poetry (2014)
Stonewall Book Award: Literature (2015)

In this poetry collection, by Saeed Jones, the author "has crafted a fever dream, something akin to magic. A dark night of the soul presented as the finest of evening gowns, these poems pulse with an elemental sensuality. . . . Using a personal symbology of femininity, violence, and the history of black America, Jones weaves a coming-of-age tale that is both terrible and revelatory." (Publishers' Weekly)

"In these searing, searching meditations on masculinity, race, and love, poet and Buzzfeed LGBT editor Jones peels back layers of beauty and pain." LJ

Jordan, June

★ Directed by desire; the collected poems of June Jordan. edited by Jan Heller Levi and Sara Miles. Copper Canyon Press 2005 649p $40 **811**
1. Poetry -- By individual authors
ISBN 1-55659-228-0

LC 2005-11701

Jordan's poems "consistently display a loving devotion to black English and pride in her femininity, race, and individuality. Directed by Desire is an important addition to African American or feminist poetry collections." Booklist

Justice, Donald Rodney

★ Collected poems. Knopf 2004 288p $25 **811**
1. Poetry -- By individual authors
ISBN 1-4000-4239-9

LC 2003-65735
National Book Award Finalist: Poetry (2004)

"Though its primary subject is the past, his work as a whole is more extraordinarily present—more thrillingly contemporary—than most of the styles that have advertised their commitment to 'making it new' over the past half-century." N Y Times Book Rev

Kasischke, Laura

Space, in chains. Copper Canyon Press 2011 113p pa $16 **811**
1. Poetry -- By individual authors
ISBN 978-1-55659-333-8; 1-55659-333-3

LC 2010-40037

"Known for her representations of mothers and teenagers in her poems and in her many novels, Kasischke now takes equal interest in illness and old age: rightly celebrated for her irregular, spiky, and intricately rhyming lines, Kasischke has now extended her interest (begun with her last book, Lilies Without) in the prose poem, using its fragments for recollection. . . . For all its length and all its lists, the volume ends up tightly, almost wrenchingly focused on the omnipresence of suffering, the fact of mortality and the persistence of grief. Some readers might call it melodramatic; many more ought to call it symphonic, perceptive, profound." Publ Wkly

Kelly, Robert

Lapis; poems. Godine 2005 221p pa $18.95 **811**
1. Poetry -- By individual authors
ISBN 1-57423-186-3

LC 2004-16724

This collection "offers dream narratives, elegies, prayers, anecdotes, parables, dialogues, and folktales from a land that may not exist. . . . Kelly has done something remarkable. He has given magic back its dignity, finding it in human warmth." Bookforum

Kendall, Tim

The **art** of Robert Frost; Tim Kendall. Yale University Press 2012 xvi, 392 p.p (cloth: alk. paper) $35 **811**
ISBN 0300118139; 9780300118131

LC 2011041416

"This book presents a . . . selection of sixty-five poems from across [Robert] Frost's writing career, beginning in the 1890s and ending with . . . the 1940s. . . . In addition to close readings of the poems, 'The Art of Robert Frost' traces the development of Frost's writing career and relevant aspects of his life. The book also assesses . . . the poet's style, how it changes over time, and how it relates to the works of contemporary poets and movements, including Modernism." (Publisher's note)

Includes bibliographical references (p. 385-388) and index.

Kenner, Hugh

The **Pound** era. University of Calif. Press 1971 606p il hardcover o.p. pa $26.95 **811**
1. Poets 2. Authors 3. Literary critics 4. Poetry -- By individual authors
ISBN 978-0-520-02427-4; 0-520-02427-3

"As a reader of Pound, Kenner is superb. He moves with ease and authority through the most tangled passages of allusion, ideogram and fragments of Greek and Latin." N Y Times Book Rev

Includes bibliographical references

Kenyon, Jane

★ **Collected** poems. Graywolf Press 2005 357p $26 **811**
1. Poetry -- By individual authors
ISBN 1-55597-428-7

"This collected edition reproduces verbatim the four books Kenyon saw through to press; the poems from two posthumous collections, Otherwise and A Hundred White Daffodils; Kenyon's translations of Akhmatova; and four previously uncollected poems. . . . Taken as a whole, Kenyon's poems remain a sustaining record of a life staked out in very difficult terrain." Publ Wkly

Kerouac, Jack

★ **Book** of sketches, 1952-53; introduction by George Condo. Penguin Books 2006 413p (Penguin poets) pa $18 **811**
1. Poetry -- By individual authors
ISBN 978-0-14-200215-5; 0-14-200215-1

LC 2005-44535

"Somewhere between diary, verbal sketchbook and play-by-play account of whatever passed before his eyes, this collection of poems transcribed from notebooks Kerouac kept in his pocket between 1952 and 1954 turns out to rank with his most interesting work. . . . Kerouac hits all the notes for which he and his fellow beats are known. While not everything here is golden, the immediacy and unpretentiousness of this off-the-cuff writing makes it an intimate glimpse into the consciousness of a man who simply couldn't stop observing." Publ Wkly

Kinnell, Galway

★ **Collected** poems; Galway Kinnell; introduction by Edward Hirsch. Houghton Mifflin Harcourt 2017 xliv, 591 p.p (hardback) $35 **811**
1. Nature poetry 2. Grief -- Poetry 3. Family life -- Poetry
ISBN 0544875214; 9780544875210

LC 2017044904

This poetry collection, by Galway Kinnell, "brings together for the first time . . . [his] life's work. . . . From the book-length poem memorializing the grit, beauty, and swarming assertion of immigrant life along a lower Manhattan avenue, to searing poems of human conflict and war, to incandescent reflections on love, family, and the natural world . . . to the unflinchingly introspective poems of his later life, Kinnell's work lastingly shaped the consciousness of his age." (Publisher's note)

"Although the voice in the poems is always his, his power of imaginative recreation and his cognitive scope make him—though, he grants, most limited by sex, race, nationality—seem to speak for everyone. As he proceeds through life and work, he comes to see living itself as the answer to the big questions. His masters, perhaps peers, were Whitman and Frost." Booklist

Includes bibliographical references and index

A **new** selected poems. Houghton Mifflin 2000 173p hardcover o.p. pa $14 **811**
1. Poetry -- By individual authors
ISBN 978-0-618-15445-6; 0-618-15445-0

LC 99-48904

"New England resides in these pages. Kinnell is a native of America's first literary region. Cold snow and clear nights work their way into his poems. The sounds of the woods are everywhere. But these sounds do not echo Emerson. Like any good transcendentalist, Kinnell sees the spiritual in material things." Christ Sci Monit

Strong is your hold. Houghton Mifflin 2006 69p $25; pa $14.95 **811**
1. Poetry -- By individual authors
ISBN 978-0-618-22497-5; 0-618-22497-1; 978-0-547-05366-0 pa; 0-547-05366-5 pa

LC 2006-11292

"To many readers, the most appealing of these poems will be the half dozen in which the aging poet writes about his wife: cuddling with her in sleep, making love with startling ferocity, waking to find they are holding hands, preparing to say goodbye if one dies before the other. Getting old, as we've heard, is not for sissies. The poet who once chased bears may have slowed a step, but here he's still making like Johnny Cash as he walks the line between sex and death, the odd and the normal, domesticity and wildness, this world and the next. . . . 'Strong Is Your Hold' comes with a CD of Kinnell reading his work in a steady, pleasant voice." N Y Times Book Rev

Kirby, David

Talking about movies with Jesus; poems. Louisiana State University Press 2011 70p (Southern messenger poets) $50; pa $17.95 **811**
1. Poetry -- By individual authors
ISBN 978-0-8071-3771-0; 0-8071-3771-5; 978-0-8071-3772-7 pa; 0-8071-3772-3 pa

LC 2010-24229

"David Kirby's poems will put you and your imagination on a jet plane and fly you both around the world. They'll take you to Italy and France or into conversations with Jesus and Elvis. They'll even force all of you serious critics to crack a smile." Flashpoint

Kizer, Carolyn

Cool, calm & collected; poems 1960-2000. Copper Canyon Press 2000 509p $30; pa $20 **811**
1. Poetry -- By individual authors
ISBN 1-55659-146-2; 1-55659-181-0 pa

LC 00-10243

Kizer "covers civil rights, women's rights and almost everything in between, but even when she's writing about more intimate matters, her underlying concern is freedom. . . . Despite her constant railing against the machine, however, Kizer's poetry remains fundamentally optimistic, perhaps because she seems to love existence almost in spite of herself."

N Y Times Book Rev

Kleinzahler, August

Sleeping it off in Rapid City; poems, new and selected. Farrar, Straus and Giroux 2008 234p $26   **811**

1. Poetry -- By individual authors

ISBN 978-0-374-26583-0; 0-374-26583-6

LC 2007-41926

This is a collection of poetry by the author of Earthquake Weather (1989), Red Sauce, Whiskey, and Snow (1996), and Live from the Hong Kong Nile Club (2000).

The author "writes most often in a strongly accented free verse that is among the most articulate and alive sounds American poetry is currently making. He plays effortlessly with forms, voices, registers. And his range of cultural reference—from Catullus to Custer, from Lorca to Eric Dolphy—is wide and artfully deployed. Rarely does high, learned poetic art sound this casual." N Y Times (Late N Y Ed)

Klink, Joanna

Raptus. Penguin Books 2010 60p (Penguin poets) pa $18   **811**

1. Poetry -- By individual authors

ISBN 978-0-14-311772-8; 0-14-311772-6

LC 2010-08246

"What happens when a relationship fails? Klink gets into the nooks and crannies of that question in her third collection. She sinks into every aspect of the life past and present. . . . She has a rhythmic dedication, a sense that every last emotional corner will be examined in its own time and a keen focus aimed as much at herself as at others. As it cycles through need and loss, this book illuminates just how inextricable experiences can be from the people with whom they are shared." Publ Wkly

Includes bibliographical references

Koch, Kenneth

★ The **collected** poems of Kenneth Koch. Knopf 2005 761p $40   **811**

1. Poetry -- By individual authors

ISBN 1-4000-4499-5

LC 2004-63827

"The products of a lifetime of continual inventing are beautifully on display in this awe-inspiring banquet of a book." Publ Wkly

On the edge; collected long poems. Alfred A. Knopf 2007 411p $35   **811**

1. Poetry -- By individual authors

ISBN 978-0-307-26284-4; 0-307-26284-7

LC 2007-24041

"A principal force behind the New York School of poets that flourished at mid-century, Kenneth Koch never quite won the pride of place occupied by the likes of Frank O'Hara and John Ashbery. This volume compiles Koch's long poems, making an eloquent argument for his unique stature." New York

Komunyakaa, Yusef

The **chameleon** couch; poems. Farrar, Straus and Giroux 2011 115p il $24   **811**

1. Poetry -- By individual authors

ISBN 978-0-374-12038-2; 0-374-12038-2

LC 2010-33148

National Book Award Finalist: Poetry (2011)

In this collection, the author "shares unusually personal reflections steeped in his intimacy with ancestors, gods, and monsters. These finely

formed lyrics are timeless in their shadows and wounds, and startlingly fresh in mood, metaphor, image, and such pairings as gargoyles and power lines, sugar and salt." Booklist

Talking dirty to the gods; poems. Farrar, Straus & Giroux 2000 134p hardcover o.p. pa $13   **811**

1. Poetry -- By individual authors

ISBN 0-374-52793-8 pa

LC 00-21277

"Komunyakaa's mournful surrealism seems to have found a perfect mathematical embodiment in this . . . collection, which comprises a hundred and thirty-two poems of four four-line stanzas. These are poems about the uncontrollable human and natural mysteries, and they are made sharper and more mysterious by the eternal recurrence of the stanzaic structure." New Yorker

Thieves of paradise. University Press of New England 1998 128p (Wesleyan poetry) $26; pa $14.95   **811**

1. Poetry -- By individual authors

ISBN 0-8195-6330-7; 0-8195-6422-2 pa

LC 97-40294

"The central subjects of Komunyakaa's poetry—his experiences in the Vietnam War and as an African-American male—have always been made compelling in his hands, and equally compelling has been the moodily energetic, jazz-inspired improvisatory technique that he employs with increasing mastery. But what is most gratifying about Komunyakaa's surrealist riffs, with their almost hallucinatory lushness, is their power to convince us that the individual imagination is more than equal to the most excruciating historical burden." New Yorker

Warhorses; poems. Farrar, Straus and Giroux 2008 86p $24   **811**

1. War poetry 2. Poetry -- By individual authors

ISBN 978-0-3742-8643-9; 0-3742-8643-4

LC 2007-51760

"The poems that comprise [this] new collection provide an astonishingly panoramic view of the totality of war. . . . Strongly recommended." Libr J

Kooser, Ted

Delights & shadows; poems. Copper Canyon Press 2004 87p pa $15   **811**

1. Poetry -- By individual authors

ISBN 1-55659-201-9

LC 2003-18447

These "poems reflect a joy for life through powerful human images and intimate observations of everyday things." Booklist

Flying at night; poems, 1965-1985. University of Pittsburgh Press 2005 142p (Pitt poetry series) $24.95; pa $14.95   **811**

1. Poetry -- By individual authors

ISBN 0-8229-4258-5; 0-8229-5877-5 pa

LC 2004-28397

"There is a simplicity to these poems, a healthy, peaceful spirit. . . . Kooser is a skilled craftsman, with a sharp eye and fine ear." Libr J

Kumin, Maxine

Connecting the dots; poems. Norton 1996 86p $18.95; pa $11.95   **811**

1. Poetry -- By individual authors

ISBN 0-393-03962-5; 0-393-31695-5 pa

LC 95-44441

"Kumin's is a poetry of wide sympathy and tact in which the ecumenical flavor is dominant, starting with the author's description of herself as a 'Jewish agnostic' educated at a convent school. Here both the odd and the even are at home: New Hampshire farm country as well as cosmopolitan Boston, Heidegger and Berlioz interwoven among depictions of spring training, Bosnia, and a New Year's Eve party. This collection is full of generational severance and renewal." New Yorker

Jack and other new poems. W.W. Norton & Co 2005 112p hardcover o.p. pa $13.95 **811**

1. Poetry -- By individual authors

ISBN 978-0-393-32852-3; 0-393-32852-X

LC 2004-21762

This collection of poetry "focuses on three subjects the poet knows well: first, the fauna (wild and domestic) in and around her New Hampshire farm; second, the troubles and lessons of advancing age; third, large-scale political history, 'this century born in blood and bombs' as this Jewish-American poet has known it. . . . Most of her strongest work (the title poem included) concerns elderly or deceased animals, obvious analogues for Kumin's ill, deceased or grieving human beings." Publ Wkly

The **long** marriage; poems. Norton 2001 118p $21; pa $12 **811**

1. Poetry -- By individual authors

ISBN 0-393-04351-7; 0-393-32437-0 pa

LC 2001-34553

"Although several of the poems treat Kumin's 50-plus year marriage, one feels that the book's title may refer to 'marriage' as a kind of covenant between the poet and her environment. . . . Divided into seven sections, this collection also includes poems about sociopolitical situations (capital punishment, extinct wildlife, revolutions), considerations of aging and rehabilitation, and tributes to Hopkins, Wordsworth, Rukeyser, and Rilke." Libr J

Selected poems, 1960-1990. Norton 1997 294p $27.50; pa $17.95 **811**

1. Poetry -- By individual authors

ISBN 0-393-04073-9; 0-393-31836-2 pa

LC 96-42433

"A pastoral poet who was strongly influenced by friend and mentor Anne Sexton, Kumin is quite simply one of the very best poets writing today. The present collection represents a lifetime . . . of Kumin's work and includes selections from all her published volumes." Libr J

Kunitz, Stanley

★ The **collected** poems. Norton 2000 285p $27.95; pa $15.95 **811**

1. Poetry -- By individual authors

ISBN 0-393-05030-0; 0-393-32294-7 pa

LC 00-41130

"What makes this collection of a lifetime's work so valuable is the way it allows us to perceive the interconnectedness of all Kunitz has written. Each poem stands alone, but each also enriches the others." N Y Times Book Rev

Includes bibliographical references

Kyger, Joanne

About now; collected poems. National Poetry Foundation 2007 798p il $49.95; pa $34.95 **811**

1. Poetry -- By individual authors

ISBN 978-0-943373-72-0; 0-943373-72-7; 978-0-943373-71-3 pa; 0-943373-71-9 pa

LC 2006-48192

This volume "begins with poems of the 1950's, written when Kyger first came to San Francisco and joined the circle of poets around Robert Duncan and Jack Spicer, and ends with Night Palace, poems written in 2003 to 2004. . . . What is exciting about Kyger's poetry is the way she highlights moments which might seem mundane, but under her perceptive eye connect the individual with a greater reality, opening readers' awareness in the process. That immersion in the details of everyday life, quail crossing a yard, a phone call from a friend, or a retelling of last night's dream, is plumbed by Kyger to great depth and is epitomized by the collection's title." Jacket

Includes bibliographical references

Larkin, Philip

The **complete** poems; Philip Larkin; edited by Archie Burnett. Farrar, Straus and Giroux 2012 729 p. **811**

1. English poetry 2. Poetry -- Collections 3. English poetry -- History and criticism

ISBN 0374126968; 9780374126964

LC 2011945978

This collection edited by Archie Burnett "brings together all of Philip Larkin's poems. In addition to those that appear in 'Collected Poems' (1988) and 'Early Poems and Juvenilia' (2005), some unpublished pieces from Larkin's typescripts and workbooks are included, as well as verse . . . that had been tucked away in his letters. . . . Larkin's poems are [also] given a comprehensive commentary. This . . . covers closely relevant historical contexts, persons and places, allusions and echoes, and linguistic usage. Prominence is given to the poet's comments on his own poems, which often outline the circumstances that gave rise to a poem or state what he was trying to achieve." (Publisher's note)

Laughlin, James

The **collected** poems of James Laughlin; with an introduction by Hayden Carruth. Moyer Bell 1994 xxxi, 574p il $34.95; pa $19.95 **811**

1. Poetry -- By individual authors

ISBN 978-1-559-21067-6; 1-559-21067-2; 978-1-559-21128-4 pa; 1-559-21128-8 pa

LC 91-32232

"These poems are the work of a man of keen intellectual and moral sophistication, who has read, thought, and lived deeply." Libr J

The **secret** room; poems. New Directions 1997 184p $22.95; pa $14.95 **811**

1. Poetry -- By individual authors

ISBN 0-8112-1343-9; 0-8112-1344-7 pa

LC 96-26188

Laughlin "shares his thoughts with humor and tenderness as he wades in the waters of his golden years. The speaker in many of these poems admires young women and thinks, 'I could see I was entirely out of/my depth.' He realizes he is not as strong as he once was, but he can still 'make old, sick words sound new.'" Libr J

Lauterbach, Ann

Or to begin again. Penguin Books 2009 115p (Penguin poets) pa $18 **811**

1. Poetry -- By individual authors

ISBN 978-0-14-311520-5; 0-14-311520-0

LC 2008-38414

National Book Award Finalist: Poetry (2009)

"Intelligent but no less deeply feeling, this collection confirms Lauterbach's position as one of the most highly principled and tirelessly innovative poets writing today." Publ Wkly

Lax, Robert

Love had a compass; journals and poetry. edited by James J. Uebbing. Grove Press 1996 253p $22   **811**

1. Poetry -- By individual authors

ISBN 978-0-8021-1587-4; 0-8021-1587-X

LC 96-1255

The author has produced "some of the sparest imagist poetry in English with no thought about publishing where the literary high and mighty would read him. Lax dispenses with metaphor and largely with ego . . . to present what he sees with elemental forcefulness, as if in strong Mediterranean sunlight." Booklist

A thing that is; new poems. edited by Paul Spaeth. Overlook Press 1997 77p $25; pa $14.95   **811**

1. Poetry -- By individual authors

ISBN 978-0-87951-699-4; 0-8795-1699-2; 978-0-87951-885-1 pa; 0-87951-885-5 pa

LC 96-29264

"Given to short lines arranged in long columns, Lax's poems link the natural and personal in simple, direct, deadpan narration. The simplicity can be misleading, not in its initially unnoticed depth or metaphor but in its very purity, its almost ascetic singleness of purpose. . . . Lax has been working at the margins for a long time and has found a crisp and comfortable way of ordering and exploring his contemplations. This collection is not for everyone, but it is a essential for that special audience for truly avante-garde work." Libr J

Lazarus, Emma

Emma Lazarus; selected poems. John Hollander, editor. Library of America 2005 151p (American poets project) $20   **811**

1. Poetry -- By individual authors

ISBN 978-1-931082-77-8; 1-931082-77-4

LC 2004-61551

"At the age of eighteen [Lazarus] had written an impressive poem titled 'In the Jewish Synagogue at Newport,' which all readers recognized as a response to Longfellow's dignified and respectful poem about the Jewish cemetery there. . . . Lazarus became perhaps the most accomplished American writer of sonnets between the generations of Longfellow and Robert Frost. . . . [Her] remarkable 'Little Poems in Prose,' the title borrowed from Baudelaire, ranged with visionary power across centuries of Jewish experience." N Y Rev Books

Le Guin, Ursula K., 1929-2018

So far so good; poems, 2014-2018. Ursula K. Le Guin. Copper Canyon Press 2018 100 p. $23   **811**

1. Nature poetry 2. Women authors 3. American authors 4. Poetry

ISBN 9781556595387

LC 2018016185

"Legendary author Ursula K. Le Guin was lauded by millions for her ground-breaking science fiction novels, but she began as a poet, and wrote across genres for her entire career. In this clarifying and sublime collection--completed shortly before her death in 2018--Le Guin is unflinching in the face of mortality, and full of wonder for the mysteries beyond. . . . Rich sounds playfully echoing myth and nursery rhyme, Le Guin bookends a long, daring, and prolific career." (Publisher's note)

Lee, Li-Young

Behind my eyes. W.W. Norton 2008 106p $24.95   **811**

1. Poetry -- By individual authors

ISBN 978-0-393-06542-8; 0-393-06542-1

"In this fourth collection by [the author], timely immigration issues

drive such poems as 'Self-Help for Fellow Refugees,' but Lee swiftly folds them into broader inquiries about inheritance, memory and loss. . . . Lee's ringing clarity and his compelling life story have brought him uncommonly loyal readers: this volume should swell their ranks. A CD of Lee reading many of the poems is included." Publ Wkly

The undressing; poems. Li-Young Lee. W W Norton & Co Inc 2018 96 p. (hardcover) $25.95   **811**

1. American poetry -- 20th century 2. American poetry -- Asian American authors

ISBN 9780393065435

LC 2017051768

This poetry collection, by Li-Young Lee, "is a tonic for spiritual anemia; it attempts to uncover things hidden since the dawn of the world. Short of achieving that end, these mysterious, unassuming poems investigate the human violence and dispossession increasingly prevalent around the world, as well as the horrors the poet grew up with as a child of refugees." (Publisher's note)

Leiter, Sharon

Critical companion to Emily Dickinson; a literary reference to her life and work. Facts on File 2006 448p il $75 **811**

1. Poets 2. Authors

ISBN 0-8160-5448-7; 978-0-8160-5448-0

LC 2005-28123

This book "opens with a foreword by poet and Dickinson scholar Gregory Orr and includes an introduction; an approximately 20-page biography of Dickinson; explications of 150 of her best-known poems (e.g., 'Because I Could Not Stop for Death'); an A-to-Z dictionary of relevant persons, places, and ideas illustrated with black-and-white photos; a chronology; bibliographies; and a comprehensive index." Libr J

Includes bibliographical references

Leonard, Keith

Ramshackle ode; Keith Leonard. Mariner Books 2016 93 p. illustrations (paperback) $17.95   **811**

1. American poetry 2. American poetry -- 21st century

ISBN 9780544649682; 9780544649675

LC 2015046790

This poetry collection, by Keith Leonard, "offers elegies and odes as necessary partners to bring out the greatest power in each. By turns celebratory, meditative, tender, and rebellious, these poems reimagine the divisions and intersections of life and death, the human and the natural world, the brutal and the beautiful. Time and again, they choose hope." (Publisher's note)

"In his lovely first collection, Pushcart Prize nominee Leonard offers poems both tough and tender about becoming a man—effectively so, as these works are not full of false bravado but touching reflection." LJ

Includes bibliographical references (page [92])

Lerner, Ben

Angle of yaw. Copper Canyon Press 2006 127p pa $15   **811**

1. Poetry -- By individual authors

ISBN 1-55659-246-9

LC 2006-14260

National Book Award Finalist: Poetry (2006)

"Employing the language of aphorism, advertising, parable, personal essay, political tirade, journalism and journal, the collage-like poems of Lerner's . . . collection express the ennui of American life in an era when even war feels like a television event." Publ Wkly

Levertov, Denise

Selected poems; with a preface by Robert Creeley; edited and with an afterword by Paul Lacey. New Directions 2002 220p hardcover o.p. pa $14.95 **811**

1. Poetry -- By individual authors

ISBN 978-0-8112-1554-1; 0-8112-1520-2

LC 2002-11891

This volume "endeavors to do what all 'selecteds' do: give readers a chance to see for themselves the development of a poetic sensibility. Editor Paul A. Lacey has brought together poems from nearly every collection of Levertov's oeuvre, producing a catalogue of the wildly diverse subjects that engaged her throughout her long career. Here are poems about love and war, about religion and art, about sorrow and joy, about political resistance and familial intimacy and, perhaps most significantly for Levertov's legacy, numerous poems about the practice of poetry itself." Harvard Rev

Levin, Phillis, 1954-

Mr. memory; & other poems. Phillis Levin. Penguin 2016 80 p. (Penguin Poets) (softcover) $18 **811**

1. American poetry -- 21st century

ISBN 9780143128113

LC 2015042145

This book in the Penguin Poets series, by Phillis Levin, "encompasses a wide array of styles and voices while staying true to a visionary impulse sparked as much by the smallest detail as the most sublime landscape. From expansive meditation to haiku, in ode and epistle, dream sequence and elegy, Levin's new poems explore motifs deeply social and historical, personal and metaphysical." (Publisher's note)

"Pathos and sweetness dominate the careful, information-rich book, which should appeal to readers who admire Robert Pinsky or Gjertrud Schnackenberg." Pub Wkly

Includes bibliographical references (pages 75-77).

Levine, Philip

Breath; poems. Knopf 2004 82 p. $23 **811**

1. Poetry -- By individual authors

ISBN 1400042917

LC 2004040839

This is a collection of poetry by the author of Ashes, What Work Is, and The Simple Truth.

The author writes "free verse about American manliness, physical labor, simple pleasures and profound grief, often set in working-class Detroit (where Levine grew up) or in central California (where he now resides), sometimes tinged with reference to his Jewish heritage or to the Spanish poets of rapt simplicity (Machado, Lorca) who remain his most visible influence. Levine's 18th book will neither disappoint his devotees nor silence the doubters." Publ Wkly

The **mercy**; poems. Knopf 1999 81p hardcover o.p. pa $16 **811**

1. Poetry -- By individual authors

ISBN 978-0-375-70135-1; 0-375-70135-4

LC 98-43353

"Levine's poetry has been steadily moving to the front rank of American poetry for three decades. . . . If Walt Whitman's vision contained multitudes, and if Emerson's vision of nature transcended what it saw with its own eyes, Levine's poetic vision, nearly religious, transcends class, transcends natural boundaries, and transcends time." Atl Mon

New selected poems. Knopf 1991 292p hardcover o.p. pa $20 **811**

1. Poetry -- By individual authors

ISBN 978-0-679-74056-8; 0-679-74056-2

LC 90-53422

This selection contains poems Levine chose for his earlier Selected poems (1984), plus 15 new works

"This is a monumental work that somehow remains wonderfully accessible, largely because Levine has chosen pieces carefully, favoring shorter works and poems that address his staple themes of family (like 'Uncle' and 'My Son and I') and childhood ('Coming Home'). Many of the poems are powerfully imagistic." Libr J

News of the world; poems. Alfred A Knopf 2009 65p $25 **811**

1. Poetry -- By individual authors

ISBN 978-0-307-27223-2

LC 2009-16517

A volume of prose poems and formal verses includes pieces on breakfasting late-shift Detroit auto workers, a woman who sings with the Spanish dawn, and an Andorran communist black-market supplier.

The author's "flirtations with death in both prose poems and formal verse have a weightiness that remains long after you close the book. . . . These poems exude a certain melancholia, but Levine's ability to examine expertly the beauty in this sadness keeps them from veering toward the unnecessarily depressing. He can paint even the strange with simple, natural language in a way that's subtly moving, and the nostalgic glow he applies to his memories makes this work the perfect addition to the oeuvre that has come to define his life." Libr J

The **simple** truth; poems. Knopf 1994 69p hardcover o.p. pa $16 **811**

1. Poetry -- By individual authors

ISBN 978-0-679-76584-4; 0-679-76584-0

LC 94-14508

This "collection of poetry is largely about the past: friends lost, fates assigned, potatoes eaten, decisions made. . . . Levine's mingling of realism and romanticism, involving many near-meetings between them, produces fascinating, emotionally persuasive shifts and tonal modulations that closely approach a lived truth." Publ Wkly

What work is; poems. Knopf 1991 77p hardcover o.p. pa $15 **811**

1. Poetry -- By individual authors

ISBN 978-0-679-74058-2; 0-679-74058-9

LC 90-53421

"This collection amounts to a hymn of praise for all the workers of America. These proletarian heroes, with names like Lonnie, Loo, Sweet Pea, and Packy, work the furnaces, forges, slag heaps, assembly lines, and loading docks at places with unglamorous names like Brass Craft or Feinberg and Breslin's First-Rate Plumbing and Plating. . . . But Levine's characters are also significant for their inner lives, not merely their jobs." Libr J

Levis, Larry, 1946-1996

The **darkening** trapeze; last poems. Larry Levis; edited and with an afterword by David St. John. Graywolf Press 2016 100 p. (paperback) $16 **811**

1. American poetry -- 20th century 2. Poetry

ISBN 9781555977276; 1555977278; 9781555979201

LC 2015952175

This book "collects the last poems by Larry Levis, written during the extraordinary blaze of his final years when his poetry expanded into the ambitious operatic masterpieces he is known for. Edited and with an afterword by David St. John and published twenty years after Levis's death, this collection contains major unpublished works, including final elegies, brief lyrics, and a coda believed to be the last poem Levis wrote, a heart-wrenching poem about his son." (Publisher's note)

"Levis writes quietly yet with grand, persuasive intent about what we stare down at the end—what it all means." LJ

Lewis, Robin Coste

★ **Voyage** of the Sable Venus and other poems; Robin Coste Lewis. Alfred A. Knopf 2016 160 p. (hardcover) $26	**811**

1. Feminism 2. Black women

ISBN 9781101875438; 9781101911204; 1101875437

LC 2014047762

National Book Award: Poetry (2015)

Poet Robin Coste Lewis presents " this meditation on the black female figure throughout time. Lewis's electrifying collection is a triptych that begins and ends with lyric poems considering the roles desire and race play in the construction of the self." (Publisher's note)

"Lacking a coherence across the sections, this title reads like two separate books." LJ

Limón, Ada, 1976-

Bright dead things; Poems. by Ada Limon. Milkweed Editions 2015 128 p. (alk. paper) $16	**811**

1. Poetry -- Collections

ISBN 1571314717; 9781571314710

LC 2015000088

National Book Award Finalist: Poetry (2015)
National Book Critics Circle Award Finalist: Poetry (2015)

This book of poems, by Ada Limón, "examines the chaos that is life, the dangerous thrill of living in a world you know you have to leave one day, and the search to find something that is ultimately 'disorderly, and marvelous, and ours.'" (Publisher's note)

"Recurring instances of anxiety about mortality in Limón's poems complicate experiences so richly written and felt." Pub Wkly.

The **carrying**; poems. Ada Limón. Milkweed Editions 2018 120 p. (hardcover: acid-free paper) $22	**811**

1. Poetry -- Collections 2. American poetry -- 21st century

ISBN 9781571315120

LC 2017061361

"Vulnerable, tender, acute, these are serious poems, brave poems, exploring with honesty the ambiguous moment between the rapture of youth and the grace of acceptance. A daughter tends to aging parents. A woman struggles with infertility--'What if, instead of carrying / a child, I am supposed to carry grief?'--and a body seized by pain and vertigo... . [Ada] Limón shows us, as ever, the persistence of hunger, love, and joy, the dizzying fullness of our too-short lives." (Publisher's note)

"Limón's vision is realistic, at times bleak, yet these poems often brim with optimism, revealing a reverent, extraordinary take on the world." LJ

Includes bibliographical references

Lindsay, Sarah

Twigs & knucklebones. Copper Canyon Press 2008 117p $15	**811**

1. Poetry -- By individual authors

ISBN 9781556591648 pa

LC 2008-19578

This is a book of poems by the author of Primate Behavior (1997) and Mount Clutter (2002).

"Sarah Lindsay uses oddities and 'flukes' as a point of entry to broader questions regarding fate, bygone civilizations, and human nature. Written in finely crafted narrative verse, her poems take place in a diverse set of locales, both ancient and contemporary, and often explore the intersection of the unfamiliar with the everyday. . . . [This] is an enigmatic, evocative, and compelling book." Pedestal

Liu, Xiaobo, 1955-2017

★ **June** fourth elegies; [Nian nian liu si / Liu Xiaobo]; translated from the Chinese by Jeffrey Yang; foreword by Dalai Lama. Liu Xiaobo. Jonathan Cape 2012 xxv, 228 p.p	**811**

1. China -- Poetry 2. Political activists 3. Human rights -- Poetry 4. Chinese poetry -- Collections 5. Tiananmen Square Incident, Beijing (China), 1989 -- Poetry 6. China -- History -- Tiananmen Square Incident, 1989 -- Poetry

ISBN 1555976107; 9780224096812

LC 2012427497

This book is the "first publication of the poetry of 2010 Nobel Peace Prize Winner Liu Xiaobo . . . [who is] the foremost symbol of the struggle for human rights in China. . . . 'June Fourth Elegies' presents Liu's poems written across twenty years in memory of fellow protestors at Tiananmen Square, as well as poems addressed to his wife, Liu Xia. In this bilingual volume, Liu's poetry is . . . published . . . in both English translation and in the Chinese original." (Publisher's Note)

"Xiaobo rebukes his nation, 'used to memorializing tombs as palaces,' and his 'city of near perfect/ shamelessness.' He also casts a harsh eye on himself . . . 'Even if I have the courage/ to be jailed again,' Xiaobo writes, 'it isn't courage enough/ to excavate memories of the dead.'" (Publishers Weekly)

Nian nian liu si

Longenbach, James

★ **Earthling**; poems. James Longenbach. W.W. Norton & Co. 2018 94 p. (pbk.) $16.95	**811**

1. American poetry -- Collections

ISBN 0393353435; 9780393353433

LC 2017015728

National Book Critics Circle Award Finalist: Poetry (2017)

This book of poetry, James Longenbach, "traces the life of a modern-day earthling as he looks squarely at his little patch of earth and at the vast emptiness of interstellar space. Beginning with the death of the earthling's mother and ending with a confrontation with his own mortality, the poems within Earthling resist complaint or agitation." (Publisher's note)

Longenbach's language remains sparse, calm, and graceful even as his poems confront the finiteness of individual human lives. --Publishers Weekly (October 2017)

Includes bibliographical references (pages 93-94).

Longfellow, Henry Wadsworth

★ **Poems** and other writings. Library of Am. 2000 854p $35	**811**

1. Poetry -- By individual authors

ISBN 1-88301-185-X

LC 00-26678

This volume includes "Hiawatha, Evangeline, The Courtship of Miles Standish and 'The Midnight Ride of Paul Revere.' Here, too, are some surprisingly powerful lyric and meditative poems—well made, deeply felt, and not much like the schoolhouse favorites." Publ Wkly

Includes bibliographical references

Lorde, Audre

The **collected** poems of Audre Lorde. Norton 1997 489p $35; pa $17.95	**811**

1. Poetry -- By individual authors

ISBN 0-393-04090-9; 0-393-31972-5 pa

LC 97-10878

"Since her death in 1992, Lorde's reputation has continued to grow. In life a tough, eloquent crusader who demanded that we honor the varieties of human experience, she retained her hold on readers despite the unavailability of much of her work. This edition, then, should be welcomed wherever there is interest in women's, minority, and lesbian literature. It includes Lorde's passionately private early work as well as her later, more obviously political work." Booklist

Lowell, Amy

Selected poems; Honor Moore, editor. Library of America 2004 xxxi, 156p (American poets project) $20   **811**

1. Poetry -- By individual authors
ISBN 978-1-93108-270-9; 1-93108-270-7

LC 2004-48505

This volume contains "the 'cadenced verse' of [Lowell's] Imagist . . . works, her experiments in 'polyphonic prose,' her narrative poetry, and her adaptations from the classical Chinese." Publisher's note

Lowell, Robert

★ **Collected** poems; edited by Frank Bidart and David Gewanter, with the editorial assistance of DeSales Harrison. Farrar, Straus & Giroux 2003 1186p il $45   **811**

1. Poetry -- By individual authors
ISBN 0-374-12617-8

This collection includes "Lowell's first book, Land of Unlikeness (1944); and poems from his 11 ensuing collections, including Life Studies (1959) and The Dolphin (1973). . . . Substantial notes, a chronology, glossary, and critical essays make this an essential title. Readers who think they know Lowell's work will discover new facets, and readers just venturing into Lowell's potently rendered and ceaselessly evocative poetic universe will find much to contemplate." Booklist

Includes bibliographical references

Macdonald, Helen, 1970-

Shaler's fish; poems. Helen Macdonald. Atlantic Monthly Press 2016 viii, 82 p.p (hardcover) $22   **811**

1. Poetry -- Collections 2. Poetry -- Women authors 3. Poetry
ISBN 9780802190703; 9780802124630; 0802124631

The poems in this collection by Helen Macdonald, roam "both the outer and inner landscapes of the poet's universe, seamlessly fusing reflections on language, science, and literature, with the loamy environments of the natural worlds around her. Moving between the epic--war, history, art, myth, philosophy--and the specific--CNN, Ancient Rome, Auden, Merleau-Ponty--Macdonald examines with humor and intellect what it means to be awake and watchful in the world." (Publisher's note)

"Macdonald employs her knowledge of the natural sciences as she deftly works scientific discoveries into poems on such subjects as love, politics, solitude, death, and more." Pub Wkly

MacGowan, Christopher J.

Twentieth-century American poetry; [by] Christopher MacGowan. Blackwell Pub 2004 331p (Blackwell guides to literature) $66.95; pa $27.95   **811**

1. Poetry -- By individual authors 2. American poetry -- History and criticism
ISBN 0-631-22025-9; 0-631-22026-7 pa

LC 2003-12196

This guide explores the historical and cultural contexts within which twentieth-century American poetry was created and includes a biographical dictionary of such key writers as Robert Frost, Ezra Pound, T. S. Eliot, Langston Hughes, James Dickey, Adrienne Rich, and Rita Dove

Includes bibliographical references

Mackey, Nathaniel

Splay anthem. New Directions Book 2006 126p pa $15.95   **811**

1. Poetry -- By individual authors
ISBN 0-8112-1652-7

LC 2005-35051

National Book Award: Poetry (2006)

"Often turning adversity to their advantage, the poems sing not of resurrection but repair, and Splay Anthem is the most delicate and delirious installment of Mackey's epic song of salvage. Its poems speak with a torn voice, a rasp punctuated by gasps of anguish and rumbling with the desire for rejuvenation." Nation

Majmudar, Amit

Dothead; poems. Amit Majmudar. Alfred A. Knopf 2016 ix, 104 p.p (hardcover) $26.95   **811**

1. Poetry -- Collections 2. Poetry 3. East Indian Americans -- Poetry
ISBN 9781101947074; 9781101947098

LC 2015020310

This book of poems, by Amit Majmudar, "is an exploration of selfhood both intense and exhilarating. . . . Majmudar asserts the claims of both the self and the other: the title poem shows us the place of an Indian American teenager in the bland surround of a mostly white peer group, partaking of imagery from the poet's Hindu tradition; the very next poem is a fanciful autobiography, relying for its imagery on the religious tradition of Islam." (Publisher's note)

"Lively with dramatic tension and frankness, this will be a great treat for all poetry lovers." LJ.

Manning, Maurice

The common man. Houghton Mifflin Harcourt 2010 96p $22   **811**

1. Poetry -- By individual authors
ISBN 978-0-547-24961-2; 0-547-24961-6

LC 2009-29080

"The book balances our cynical, back-foot expectations as readers of contemporary poetry with its own unpretentious ambition incredibly well—the natural world becomes strange in Manning's hands, but not unrecognizably so." Sycamore Rev

Martin, Justin

Rebel Souls; Walt Whitman and America's First Bohemians. Justin Martin. Da Capo Press 2014 368 p. 16 plates; illustrations (A Merloyd Lawrence book) (hardback) $27.99 **811**

1. Bohemianism -- New York (N.Y.) 2. New York (N.Y.) -- Intellectual life -- 19th century 3. Bohemianism -- New York (State) -- New York -- History -- 19th century 4. Bars (Drinking establishments) -- New York (State) -- New York -- History -- 19th century
ISBN 0306822261; 9780306822261; 9780306822278

LC 2014008822

This book, by Justin Martin, is "about the colorful group of artists--regulars at Pfaff's Saloon in Manhattan--rightly considered America's original Bohemians. Besides a young [Walt] Whitman, the circle included actor Edwin Booth; trailblazing stand-up comic Artemus Ward; psychedelic drug pioneer and author Fitz Hugh Ludlow; and brazen performer Adah Menken, famous for her Naked Lady routine." (Publisher's note)

"This book is a lively and entertaining read for students of American literature, history, and culture." Choice

Includes bibliographical references and index

Matthews, Airea D.

Simulacra; Airea D. Matthews; foreword by Carl Phillips. Yale University Press 2017 xviii, 80 p.p (Yale series of younger poets) (pbk.: alk. paper) $20   **811**
1. American poetry -- 21st century
ISBN 9780300223965; 9780300223972

LC 2016952569

Winner of the 2016 Yale Series of Younger Poets prize

This book, by Airea D. Matthews, winner of the 2016 Yale Series of Younger Poets prize, "explores the topic of want and desire with power, insight, and intense emotion. Her poems cross historical boundaries and speak emphatically from a racialized America, where the trajectories of joy and exploitation, striving and thwarting, violence and celebration are constrained by differentials of privilege and contemporary modes of communication." (Publisher's note)

"Matthews's deft, shape-shifting debut . . . investigates the parameters of want and rebellion as a host of historical literary figures confront 21st-century life." Pub Wkly

Includes bibliographical references (pages 75-77).

May, Jamaal

Hum; Jamaal May. Alice James Books 2013 80 p. (pbk.) $15.95   **811**
1. Poetry -- Collections
ISBN 1938584023; 9781938584022

LC 2013022185

In this collection of poems, by Jamaal May, "poems buzz and purr like a well-oiled chassis. Grit, trial, and song thrum through tight syntax and deft prosody. From the resilient pulse of an abandoned machine to the sinuous lament of origami animals, here is the ever-changing hum that vibrates through us all, connecting one mind to the next." (Publisher's note)

"May, a teacher, seems acutely aware of the injustices in our current condition, but he seeks to educate rather than preach; his poems, exquisitely balanced by a sharp intelligence mixed with earnestness, makes his debut a marvel." Pub Wkly

Mayer, Bernadette

Scarlet tanager. New Directions 2005 117p pa $14.95 **811**
1. Poetry -- By individual authors
ISBN 0-8112-1582-2

LC 2005-5539

This collection demonstrates Mayer's "ease in many poetic forms, her attraction to New York City and to the Berkshires (where she now lives), her recovery from a recent stroke and her continued enthusiastic enmeshment with writing itself." Publ Wkly

McCrae, Shane

In the language of my captor; Shane McCrae. Wesleyan University Press 2017 86 p. (Wesleyan poetry) (cloth: alk. paper) $24.95   **811**
1. Freedom 2. Poetry -- Collections 3. American poetry -- 21st century
ISBN 9780819577139; 9780819577115

LC 2016035696

This poetry collection, by Shane McCrae, is "about freedom told through stories of captivity. Historical persona poems and a prose memoir at the center of the book address the illusory freedom of both black and white Americans. In the book's three sequences, McCrae explores the role mass entertainment plays in oppression, he confronts the myth that freedom can be based upon the power to dominate others." (Publisher's note)

McGrath, Campbell

XX; poems for the twentieth century. Campbell McGrath. Ecco, an imprint of HarperCollins Publishers 2016 xiv, 222 p.p (hardcover) $25.99   **811**
1. American poetry 2. Historical poetry
ISBN 0062427350; 9780062427359; 9780062427373

LC 2017295008

Pulitzer Prize Finalist: Poetry (2017)

This book "is award-winning poet Campbell McGrath's astonishing sequence of one hundred poems--one per year--written in a vast range of forms, and in the voices of figures as varied as Picasso and Mao, Frida Kahlo and Elvis Presley. Based on years of historical research and cultural investigation, 'XX' turns poetry into an archival inquiry and a choral documentary. . . . Its range of interest encompasses the entire century of art and culture, invention and struggle." (Publisher's note)

McHugh, Heather

★ **Upgraded** to serious. Copper Canyon Press 2009 85p $22   **811**
1. Poetry -- By individual authors
ISBN 978-1-55659-306-2

LC 2009-13347

This collection "offers exactingly ravishing poetry that digs deeply into big themes: free will, consciousness, ideas of language. . . . Thinking poems are often poems with lots of moving parts, and when reading (and rereading) this book one notes the elegance with which everything – perception, reflection, feeling – is held in play. And 'play' is the operative word: McHugh's method always involves some winning blend of precision and momentum." Globe and Mail

McLane, Maureen N., 1967-

My poets; Maureen N. McLane. Farrar, Straus and Giroux 2012 273 p. (hc: alk. paper) $25.00   **811**
1. Poets 2. Poetry -- History and criticism 3. Poetry -- Influence
ISBN 0374217491; 9780374217495

LC 2011041208

In this book, poet and critic Maureen N. McLane "presents an esoteric tour of her personal pantheon, the poets that have shaped her life." The text is a "mixture of prose criticism, memoir, anecdote, and imitative verse written in tribute." The poets discussed include Geoffrey Chaucer, Elizabeth Bishop, H. D., and Gertrude Stein. (Publishers Weekly)

This Blue; Maureen N. McLane. Farrar Straus & Giroux 2014 128 p. (hardcover) $24   **811**
1. Nature 2. Poetry -- Collections
ISBN 0374275939; 9780374275938

LC 2013033882

National Book Award Shortlist: Poetry (2014)

In this poetry collection, author Maureen N. McLane presents "songs for and of a new century, poems both archaic and wholly now. In the middle of life, stationed in our common 'Terran Life,' the poet conjures urban pigeons, Adirondack mountains, Genoa, Andalucía, Belfast, Parma; here is a world sounded out, broken, possibly shareable, newly named." (Publisher's note)

"An exciting collection that celebrates the extraordinary in the ordinary: 'I've left words/ in woods the thrushes/ sing in refusing/ the extinction/ of the day.'" LJ

McMichael, James

Capacity. Farrar, Straus and Giroux 2006 74p $22   **811**

1. Poetry -- By individual authors
ISBN 978-0-374-11890-7; 0-374-11890-6

LC 2005-51628

National Book Award Finalist: Poetry (2006)

"Better known for the infrastructural sweep of his work, McMichael is also a poet of the kind of centripetal force and barely contained emotional heat that we more often associate with the short lyric. What makes him unique in American poetry right now is the strength and subtlety with which he blends conceptual ambition with emotional power. It's very common these days to hear poets talking about their 'projects.' But in James McMichael we actually have a poet whose sustained investigation of a small set of obsessions has produced the most integral and surprising structures." Yale Rev

Melville, Herman

★ The **poems** of Herman Melville; edited by Douglas Robillard. rev ed; Kent State Univ. Press 2000 349p pa $29 **811**
1. Poetry -- By individual authors
ISBN 0-87338-660-4

LC 99-52872

First published 1976 by College and University Press Service

This volume "presents the complete texts of 'Battle-Pieces,' 'John Marr and Other Sailors,' and 'Timoleon,' as well as additional manuscript poems. Also presented are excerpts from the long narrative poem Clarel to give the reader a taste of the style and content of this work. The editor's introduction, as well as his notes at the end of each section, are informative as well as appreciative of Melville's status as a poet." Libr J

Includes bibliographical references

Menashe, Samuel

★ **New** and selected poems; Christopher Ricks, editor. Library of America 2005 191p (American poets project) $20 **811**
1. Poetry -- By individual authors
ISBN 1-931082-85-5

LC 2005-44161

"Menashe is a curious and meticulous writer, whose brief, sparsely punctuated poems depend on difficult rhyme and assonance schemes to relay his observations. A wry but basically optimistic poet, his best writing shows that the stylistic restrictions one selects rapidly cease to be restrictions, even when one identifies them as such." N Y Times Book Rev

Merrill, James

The **changing** light at Sandover; with the stage adaptation Voices from Sandover. edited by J.D. McClatchy and Stephen Yenser. 2nd Knopf hardcover ed.; Knopf 2006 627p il $40 **811**
1. Poetry -- By individual authors
ISBN 978-0-307-26321-6; 0-307-26321-5

LC 2006-273431

First published 1982 by Atheneum; 1992 by Knopf, without Voices from Sandover

This "is an arduous poem, steep and lofty, more than a little difficult to climb, explore, and comprehend, its intricate faceting of the serious and unserious, sacred and profane, vexing to many a reader; but it has, I believe, one controlling stratagem, Merrill's persistent use of doubling or 'entwining.'. . . The trilogy (though it goes on far too long, gets periodically dizzy, has too much felix culpa and not enough mea culpa) is, surely, an astonishing performance." N Y Rev Books

★ The **collected** poems of James Merrill; edited by J.D. McClatchy and Stephen Yenser. Knopf 2001 xx, 885p $40; pa $27.50 **811**

1. Poetry -- By individual authors
ISBN 0-375-41139-9; 0-375-70941-X pa

LC 00-40542

"Excluded are some juvenilia and light verse, as well as Merrill's book-length poem The Changing Light at Sandover, in print as a separate volume. Merrill's sonnets, sapphics, longer sequences and sinuous sentences encompass lyric pathos, ebullient comedy, rapt romance and acrid satire. Their formal sophistication can belie their depth of feeling, which is exactly what some readers love best about Merrill's work." Publ Wkly

Merton, Thomas

In the dark before dawn; new selected poems of Thomas Merton. edited with an introduction and notes by Lynn R. Szabo; preface by Kathleen Norris. New Directions 2005 253p pa $16.95 **811**
1. Poetry -- By individual authors
ISBN 978-0-8112-1613-5; 0-8112-1613-6

LC 2004-30957

"Szabo has drawn widely from the furious poetic writing of Merton's final years. This new spectrum of poems helps us tap into the complexity and mystery of Thomas Merton. Readers of Merton's journals will be aware of his shifting attitude to all sorts of things—being an American, being a monk at Gethsemani, being a writer, in particular a poet. Szabo helps us here by assembling the poems in eight thematic sections, so as to display the multiple Mertons. There was the contemplative, drawn to the silent beauties of Gethsemani Abbey, especially at night. There was the stinging and at times declamatory social critic, the admiring and painstaking translator, the avant garde experimentalist and, toward the end, the lovelorn monk." America

Merwin, W. S.

★ **Migration**; new & selected poems. Copper Canyon Press 2005 545p $40 **811**
1. Poetry -- By individual authors
ISBN 1-55659-218-3

LC 2004-17473

National Book Award Finalist: Poetry (2005)

This volume contains poetry from sixteen of Merwin's collections.

"Complex, spiritual, and evocative, Merwin is a major poet, and this is a sublime measure of his achievements." Booklist

Middlebrook, Diane Wood

Anne Sexton; a biography. Vintage Bks. 1992 xxiii, 498p il pa $14 **811**
1. Poets 2. Authors 3. Dramatists 4. Poets, American
ISBN 0-679-74182-8

LC 92-50093

First published 1991 by Houghton Mifflin

"Ms. Middlebrook has written a wonderful book: just, balanced, insightful, complex in its sympathies and in its judgment of Sexton both as a person and as a writer." NY Times Book Rev

Includes bibliographical references

Millay, Edna St. Vincent

★ **Selected** poems; J.D. McClatchy, editor. Library of Am. 2003 xxxiii, 231p (American poets project) $20 **811**
1. Poetry -- By individual authors
ISBN 1-931082-35-9

LC 2002-32126

This collection draws from all Millay's "verse books to display her career-long adroitness in her favorite form, the sonnet, and her variety by including even excerpts from an opera libretto. . . . Read occasionally and mixed with her saucy lyrics about erotic love, . . . [her sonnets] reveal their strengths—not of imagery, but of surprising attitudes expressed within strictly observed poetic conventions." Booklist

Moore, Marianne

New collected poems; Marianne Moore; edited by Heather Cass White. Farrar, Straus & Giroux 2017 xxvi, 453 p.p illustrations (hardcover) $30   **811**

1. Poetry -- Collections 2. American poetry -- 20th century
ISBN 9780374716059; 0374221049; 9780374221041
LC 2017003857

This collection of poetry, by Marianne Moore, edited by Heather Cass White, "offers an answer to the question of how to represent the work of a poet so skillful and singular, giving a portrait of the range of her voice and of the modernist culture she helped create." (Publisher's note)

★ The **poems** of Marianne Moore; edited by Grace Schulman. Viking 2003 449p hardcover o.p. pa $18   **811**

1. Poetry -- By individual authors
ISBN 0-14-303908-3 pa
LC 2003-50159

"The great modernist poet finally gets her due with this outstanding compliation." Libr J
Includes bibliographical references

Murphy, Russell E.

Critical companion to T.S. Eliot; a literary reference to his life and work. [by] Russell Elliott Murphy. Facts on File 2007 614p il (Facts on File library of American literature) $75 **811**

1. Poets 2. Authors 3. Dramatists 4. Editors 5. Essayists 6. Literary critics 7. Nobel laureates for literature
ISBN 978-0-8160-6183-9; 0-8160-6183-1
LC 2006-34076

"This is an excellent and exhaustive resource and a good buy for most libraries." Booklist
Includes bibliographical references

Nadelberg, Amanda

Bright brave phenomena; poems. Amanda Nadelberg. Coffee House Press 2012 118 p.   **811**

1. Emotions -- Poetry 2. Poetry -- Collections 3. Man-woman relationship -- Poetry
ISBN 1566893038; 9781566893039
LC 2011029251

This collection of poetry "focus[es] on the ways life itself changes, depending on emotional shadings: 'I turned into a blanket and went everywhere. With him there was great purpose.' . . . A longer segmented poem chronicles various unhappinesses: 'And when her boyfriend walks to/ her, she looks like death, the/ face of death, big drapes/ in a tall room in France.' The boyfriend in this poem is just as mutable, taking the form of a blue door and a French vampire. Nadelberg's ebullient language captures the giddiness of love and youth. . . . But love can also deflate like 'two people and/ a broken thing/ as a road somewhere.' Her perspective is always staunchly feminine, unfolding like a present, her 'hysteria as a garden, a house/ the colors are beautiful.'" (Publishers Weekly)

Nemerov, Howard

★ The **selected** poems of Howard Nemerov; edited by Daniel Anderson; foreword by Wyatt Prunty. Swallow Press, Ohio University Press 2003 xxi, 154p $24.95; pa $16.95 **811**

1. Poetry -- By individual authors
ISBN 0-8040-1059-5; 0-8040-1060-9 pa
LC 2003-42380

The selections in this volume span Nemerov's entire poetic output
This volume "represents the broad spectrum of Nemerov's virtues as a poet—his intelligence, his wit, his compassion, and his irreverence. It stands as the retrospective collection of the best of what Nemerov left behind." Publisher's note

Niedecker, Lorine

Collected works; edited by Jenny Penberthy. University of Calif. Press 2002 xxiii, 471p $55; pa $25.95   **811**

1. Poetry -- By individual authors
ISBN 978-0-520-22433-9; 0-520-22433-7; 978-0-520-22434-6 pa; 0-520-22434-5 pa
LC 2001-5376

Niedecker "is often likened to Emily Dickinson. She, too, remained in the backwater where she was born. Large-scale interest in her work came only years after her death. Her characteristic poems are, like Dickinson's, short or in short stanzas, short-lined, and elliptical. But she wasn't reclusive; she connected with the Objectivists, New York poets 'led' by Louis Zukofsky. . . . Whereas Dickinson's poetry is metaphysical, Niedecker's mature work is profoundly physical, sparked by wry, class-conscious humor and usually rooted in her Black Lake Island, Wisconsin, neighborhood." Booklist
Includes bibliographical references

Norris, Kathleen

Journey: new and selected poems, 1969-1999. University of Pa. 2001 131p hardcover o.p. pa $16.95   **811**

1. Poetry -- By individual authors
ISBN 0-8229-5761-2 pa

A collection of Norris' "poetry spanning 30 years. Here are poems, arranged chronologically in four sections each beginning with a verse from the Song of Solomon, that tenderly describe an event or scene, examine it, and conclude with a flash of seemingly unrelated insight, leaving profound questions in the reader's heart. . . . Carrying her readers along on her deeply Christian journey, Norris avoids spiritual certainty and preachiness, remaining ever the seeker. Her poems are lyrical, accessible, and hauntingly touching to read and to reread." Libr J

Notley, Alice

★ **Grave** of light; new and selected poems, 1970-2005. Wesleyan University Press 2006 364p $29.95   **811**

1. Poetry -- By individual authors
ISBN 0-8195-6772-8
LC 2006-15712

"Experimental in every sense of the word, Alice Notley has produced an extensive body of work over 30 years in print. This new collection unites previously unpublished poems as well as those from both small-press chapbooks and more widely distributed volumes. Arranged in chronological order while maintaining poetic sequences, Notley's poems tell the story of her artistic development and bear witness to the multitude of styles and influences that Notley has explored. . . . Diversity is Notley's most consistent quality, and this makes her not only somewhat of an enigma aesthetically but also appealing to varying poetic tastes." Booklist

In the pines. Penguin Books 2007 131p (Penguin poets) pa $18   **811**

1. Poetry -- By individual authors
ISBN 978-0-14-311254-9; 0-14-311254-6
LC 2007-12076

"Notley takes the title of her 30-somethingth collection from a notorious American folk song: a man tries to get his lover to admit she's been unfaithful, asking her where she's slept, and her ambiguous answer—in the pines—only makes things worse. That menacing rhetorical moment informs the whole of this searing collection, which is part autobiography, part riposte to literary culture, and part lyrical reclamation of feminist territory. . . . This master poet continues to inspire and challenge." Publ Wkly

Nye, Naomi Shihab

You & yours: poems. BOA Editions 2005 87p (American poets continuum series) hardcover o.p. pa $15.50   **811**
    1. Poetry -- By individual authors
    ISBN 1-929918-68-2; 1-929918-69-0 pa
               LC 2005-11360
"Tender yet forceful, funny and commonsensical, reflective and empathic, Nye writes radiant poems of nature and piercing poems of war, always touching base with homey details and radiant portraits of family and neighbors." Booklist

Olds, Sharon, 1942-

★ **Stag's** leap; by Sharon Olds. Alfred A. Knopf 2012 x, 89 p.p   **811**
    1. Divorced people -- Poetry
    ISBN 0307959902; 9780307959904; 9780375712258
               LC 2012004426
Pulitzer Prize: Poetry (2013)
This collection of poems by Sharon Olds "tells the story of a divorce, embracing strands of love, sex, sorrow, memory, and new freedom. . . . [Olds] shar[es] the feeling of invisibility that comes when we are no longer standing in love's sight; the surprising physical bond that still exists between a couple during parting; the loss of everything from her husband's smile to the set of his hip." (Publisher's note)

Oliver, Charles M.

Critical companion to Walt Whitman; a literary reference to his life and work. Facts on File 2005 408p il (Facts on File library of American literature) $65   **811**
    1. Poets 2. Authors 3. Essayists
    ISBN 0-8160-5768-0
               LC 2005-4172
The author "begins this work with a biographical essay that includes several illustrations. A large portion of this book addresses Whitman's works, with entries for the individual poems and for the complete volumes. Each entry describes when and where the book was published and includes a brief account of the poem and its context. The third section of the volume covers people, places, publications, and topics related to Whitman's life and work." Choice
Includes bibliographical references

Oliver, Mary

★ **Devotions**; the selected poems of Mary Oliver. Mary Oliver. Penguin Press 2017 xx, 455 p.p (hardcover) $30 **811**
    1. American poetry -- Collections
    ISBN 0399563245; 9780399563249
               LC 2017025254
This book, by Mary Oliver, "presents a personal selection of her best work in this definitive collection spanning more than five decades of her esteemed literary career. . . . Carefully curated, these 200 plus poems feature Oliver's work from her very first book of poetry, No Voyage and Other Poems, published in 1963 at the age of 28, through her most recent collection, Felicity, published in 2015." (Publisher's note)
...An excellent pick for the introspective literature lover. --BookPage

Reviews (December 2017)

★ **New** and selected poems. Beacon Press 2005 2v v1 $28.50; v1 pa $16; v2 $24.95; v2 pa $16   **811**
    1. Poetry -- By individual authors
    ISBN 0-8070-6878-0 v1; 0-8070-6877-2 v1 pa; 0-8070-6886-1 v2; 0-8070-6887-X v2 pa
    Vol. 1 first published 1992; redesigned ed. to accompany the publication of vol. 2
    Volume one contains poems written from 1965 to 1992. Volume two contains poems written from 1994 to 2005.

A **thousand** mornings; poems. Mary Oliver. Penguin Press 2012 82 p. $24.95   **811**
    1. Nature poetry 2. Literature -- 21st century 3. American poetry -- Women authors
    ISBN 1594204772; 9781594204777
               LC 2012027310
In author Mary Oliver's book of poetry, she transports "us to the marshland and coastline of her beloved home, Provincetown, Massachusetts. In these pages, Oliver shares the wonder of dawn, the grace of animals, and the transformative power of attention. Whether studying the leaves of a tree or mourning her adored dog, Percy, she is ever patient in her observations and open to the teachings contained in the smallest of moments." (Publisher's note)

Oppen, George

★ **New** collected poems; edited with an introduction and notes by Michael Davidson; preface by Eliot Weinberger. New Directions 2002 xlv, 433p il $37.95   **811**
    1. Poetry -- By individual authors
    ISBN 0-8112-1488-5
               LC 2001-44048
Replaces The collected poems of George Oppen (1975)
"Oppen, a Communist and an objectivist poet deeply influenced by Pound and Williams, believed that there were no ideas except in things, but he also believed, fiercely, that our relationship to things was inherently moral. . . . In 1934, he published a book of stunning, elliptical lyrics about 'big-Business' and American capitalism; he then fell silent for the next twenty-five years, during which he struggled to reconcile his fealty to social causes with the demands of aesthetic originality. The culmination of this struggle was his Pulitzer Prize-winning collection 'Of Being Numerous,' published in 1968, which, to a degree unmatched by any book of American poetry since, movingly portrays the individual in a collective world." New Yorker
Includes bibliographical references

Ostriker, Alicia

No heaven; [by] Alicia Suskin Ostriker. University of Pittsburgh Press 2005 136p (Pitt poetry series) pa $12.95   **811**
    1. Poetry -- By individual authors
    ISBN 0-8229-5875-9
In this "collection of clarion poems intimate and worldly, Ostriker writes about her life as a wife, mother, and grandmother with tenderness, but she is also edgy, erotic, funny, and ornery." Booklist

★ The **Oxford** anthology of African-American poetry; edited by Arnold Rampersad; associate editor, Hilary Herbold. Oxford University Press 2006 432p $32.50   **811**
    1. American poetry -- African American authors -- Collections
    ISBN 0-19-512563-0; 978-0-19-512563-4
               LC 2005-15242

"Predicated on the fact that there is a vast body of poetry written by gifted black poets, this . . . anthology tells the story of African American culture and explicates its crucial role within the larger literary tradition. . . . There is much to admire about the artistry of the poems, and even more to discover about the African American experience." Booklist

★ The **Oxford** book of American poetry; chosen and edited by David Lehman; associate editor, John Brehm. Oxford University Press 2006 lvii, 1132p $35 **811**
1. American poetry -- Collections
ISBN 0-19-516251-X; 978-0-19-516251-6

LC 2005-36590
First published 1950 with title: The Oxford book of American verse
"The book is not only a sound historical survey, but also gives the reader a powerful taste of poetry's impact upon the wider world." Economist
Includes bibliographical references

Padgett, Ron, 1942-
Collected Poems; Ron Padgett. Coffee House Press 2013 810 p. (Trade Cloth) $44 **811**
1. American poetry -- Collections
ISBN 1566893429; 9781566893428

LC 2013017190
LA Times Book Prize Winner: Poetry (2013)
This collection of poems by Ron Padgett "gather[s] the work of more than fifty years. . . . Padgett's poems reverberate with his reading and friendships, from Andrew Marvell to Woody Guthrie and Kenneth Koch. Wry, insightful, and direct, they offer readers the rewards of his endless curiosity and generous spirit." (Publisher's note)
"That is Padgett at his most joyful. But this exemplar of the gloriously zany, this champion of comic-book characters, turns out also to be a fount of wisdom and good sense: 'It's not embarrassing to be sentimental/When the sentiment equals/ Seeing things just as they are here now.'" David Lehman is the founder and editor of the Best American Poetry series and the author of the just-published New and Selected Poems (Scribner)." Pub Wkly

Pankey, Eric, 1959-
Trace; poems. Eric Pankey. 1st ed. Milkweed Editions 2013 68 p. (paperback) $16 **811**
1. Belief and doubt -- Poetry 2. Depression (Psychology) -- Poetry
ISBN 1571314490; 9781571314499

LC 2012028097
This collection of poems, by Eric Pankey, "locates itself at a threshold between faith and doubt--between the visible and the invisible, the say-able and the ineffable, the physical and the metaphysical. Also a map of the poet's journey into a deep depression, these poems confront one man's struggle to overcome depression's smothering weight and presence." (Publisher's note)

Pardlo, Gregory, 1968-
Air traffic; a memoir of ambition and manhood in America. Gregory Pardlo. Alfred A. Knopf 2018 288 p. (hardback) $26.95 **811**
1. Father-son relationship 2. African American men -- Biography
ISBN 9780525432210; 9781524731762

LC 2017047413
This book "follows Gregory [Pardlo] as he builds a life that honors his history without allowing it to define his future. Slowly, he embraces the challenges of being a poet, a son, and a father as he enters recovery for alcoholism and tends to his family. In this memoir, . . . Gregory tries to free himself from the overwhelming expectations of race and class,

and from the tempting yet ruinous legacy of American masculinity." (Publisher's note)
"Endlessly introspective, wide-ranging, and lucid, Pardlo's fearless inventory stuns with beautifully written, fully saturated snapshots of rich and complicated familial love." Booklist

Digest; Gregory Pardlo. Four Way Books 2014 75 p. (pbk.: alk. paper) $15.95 **811**
1. American poetry -- Collections
ISBN 1935536508; 9781935536505

LC 2014011291
Pulitzer Prize: Poetry (2015)
This collection of poems, by Gregory Pardlo, "draws from the present and the past to form an intellectual, American identity. In poems that forge their own styles and strategies, we experience dialogues between the written word and other art forms. Within this dialogue we hear Ben Jonson, we meet police K-9s, and we find children negotiating a sense of the world through a father's eyes and through their own." (Publisher's note)
Includes bibliographical references

Parini, Jay
Robert Frost; a life. Holt & Co. 1999 514p il $35; pa $16 **811**
1. Poets 2. Authors
ISBN 0-8050-3181-2; 0-8050-6341-2 pa

LC 98-26690
"Rarely has Frost's story been told this dexterously, or with a better understanding of the relation of Frost's personal crises to his accomplishment as a poet." Publ Wkly
Includes bibliographical references

Parker, Morgan
There are more beautiful things than Beyoncé; Morgan Parker. Tin House Books 2017 85 p. (softcover: acid-free paper) $14.95 **811**
1. American poetry -- 21st century 2. American poetry -- African American authors
ISBN 9781941040539; 9781941040546

LC 2016049158
In this book of poems, author "Morgan Parker stands at the intersections of vulnerability and performance, of desire and disgust, of tragedy and excellence. Unrelentingly feminist, tender, ruthless, and sequined, these poems are an altar to the complexities of black American womanhood in an age of non-indictments and deja vu, and a time of wars over bodies and power." (Publisher's note)

★ The **Penguin** anthology of twentieth-century American poetry; edited with an introduction by Rita Dove. Penguin Books 2011 lii, 599 p.p **811**
1. American poetry -- Collections 2. American poetry -- 20th century
ISBN 9780143106432

LC 2011036342
The book provides an anthology of 20th century U.S. poetry. "Selecting from the canon of American poetry throughout the twentieth century, [Rita] Dove has created an anthology that represents the full spectrum of aesthetic sensibilities. . . . Featuring poems both classic and contemporary, this collection reflects both a dynamic and cohesive portrait of modern American poetry and outlines its trajectory over the past century." (Publisher's note)

Perez, Craig Santos

★ **From** unincorporated territory [guma'] Craig Santos Perez. Omnidawn Publishing 2014 81 p. (Trade Paperback: alk. paper) $17.95 **811**

1. Postcolonialism 2. Poetry -- Collections 3. Guam -- Poetry
ISBN 9781890650919

LC 2013045798

"Craig Santos Perez, a native Chamoru from the Pacific Island of Guahan (Guam), has lived for two decades away from his homeland. This new collection maps the emotional and geographic cartographies of his various migrations, departures, and arrivals. Through a variety of poetic forms, the poet highlights the importance of origins and customs amidst new American cultures and terrains." (Publisher's note)

Includes bibliographical references.

Perillo, Lucia Maria

Inseminating the elephant; [by] Lucia Perillo. Copper Canyon Press 2009 93p $22 **811**

1. Poetry -- By individual authors
ISBN 978-1-55659-291-1; 1-55659-291-4

LC 2008-44772

Perillo "writes accessible, often funny poems that border on the profane. The title poem of this collection, her fifth, is about just what it says: zoologists tasked with helping impregnate an elephant (it's not easy). There's also an ode to bad smells, a middle-aged narrator's reluctant acceptance of cell phones and a meditation on a Viagra ad. Perillo has another rare power among versifiers: She is able to make dire, life-or-death concerns go down easy. . . . Physical decline is one of Perillo's major themes, one that she tackles with wry humor." Time Out N Y

Phillips, Patrick

Elegy for a broken machine; poems. by Patrick Phillips. Alfred A. Knopf 2015 80 p. (hardback) $26 **811**

1. Death 2. Poetry -- Collections 3. Father-son relationship
ISBN 0385353758; 9780385353755; 9780385353762

LC 2014026436

National Book Award Finalist: Poetry (2015)

This book of poems, by Patrick Phillips, "is at its core a son's lament for his father. This book of elegies takes us from the luminous world of childhood to the fluorescent glare of operating rooms and recovery wards, and into the twilight lives of those who must go on. . . . Phillips documents the unsung joys of midlife, the betrayals of the human body, and his realization that as the crowd of ghosts grows, we take our places, next in line." (Publisher's note)

"Phillips (Boy) examines masculinity and loss with a surgeon's precision in his elegiac third book... Phillips's careful language consciously breaks down these distinctions, fusing the roles men play throughout their lives, and connecting past to present... And Phillips ponders just what makes a human body different from any other relinquished object, imagining his mattress decaying at the dump 'as it sloughs its guts into the dirt.'" Pub Wkly

On the spectrum of possible deaths; Lucia Perillo. Copper Canyon Press 2012 81 p. **811**

1. Death -- Poetry 2. American poetry -- Collections 3. American poetry -- Women authors -- Collections
ISBN 155659397X; 9781556593970

LC 2011050110

This book is a poetry collection written by the 2009 Pulitzer Prize finalist author Lucia Perillo. "Perillo has long lived with, and written about, her struggle with debilitating multiple sclerosis. Her . . . sixth book of poems, published concurrently with her debut story collection, takes a . . . look at mortality." (Booklist) "with subjects ranging from coyotes and Scotch broom to local elections and family history. . . . the mythic and mundane, of media and daily life, as she faces the treachery of illness." (Publisher's note)

Phillips, Rowan Ricardo

Heaven; poems. Rowan Ricardo Phillips. Farrar, Straus & Giroux 2015 80 p. (hardback) $24 **811**

1. Heaven 2. Spiritual life
ISBN 9780374168520; 0374168520

LC 2014039377

NBA Longlist

In this poetry collection, author Rowan Ricardo Phillips "offers many answers, and none at all. Swerving elegantly from humor to heartbreak, from Colorado to Florida, from Dante's 'Paradise' to Homer's 'Iliad,' from knowledge to ignorance to awe, Phillips turns his gaze upward and outward, probing and upending notions of the beyond." (Publisher's note)

"Consistently smart and clearly talented, Phillips is one to read now and to watch for in the future." Booklist

Pico, Tommy

Junk; Tommy Pico. Tin House Books 2018 80 p. $15.95 **811**

1. Grief -- Poetry 2. Loss (Psychology) -- Poetry 3. American poetry -- Native American authors
ISBN 1941040977; 9781941040973

This book-length poem, by Tommy Pico, "explores the experience of loss and erasure, both personal and cultural. . . . [It] is a breakup poem in couplets: ice floe and hot lava, a tribute to Janet Jackson and nacho cheese. In the static that follows the loss of a job or an apartment or a boyfriend, what can you grab onto for orientation? The narrator wonders what happens to the sense of self when the illusion of security has been stripped away." (Publisher's note)

Piercy, Marge

Colors passing through us; poems. Knopf 2003 157p $23; pa $15 **811**

1. Poetry -- By individual authors
ISBN 0-375-41537-8; 0-375-71005-1 pa

LC 2002-66145

The author "tempers 1960s politics and 1970s feminism with nostalgia for the world of her childhood. . . . Piercy celebrates daily life on Cape Cod, where she and her husband live, with poems about gardening, cats, cooking, canning, and sex after 60. While all of these poems are eminently readable, the best are angry and funny. . . . Piercy fans, of which there are many, will relish this collection." Libr J

Pinsky, Robert

The **figured** wheel; new and collected poems, 1966-1996. Farrar, Straus & Giroux 1996 303p hardcover o.p. pa $17 **811**

1. Poetry -- By individual authors
ISBN 0-374-52506-4

LC 95-47617

"Brought together here are 16 new poems, the work of Pinsky's four original collections and a sampling of his fine translations, including a canto from his well-received version of the Inferno. Taken as a whole, this is the record of a poet who grows from highly competent to near-transcendent." Publ Wkly

Plath, Sylvia, 1932-1963

Ariel; the restored edition. foreword by Frieda Hughes.
HarperCollins Publishers 2004 xxi, 211p $24.95   **811**

1. Poetry -- By individual authors

ISBN 0-06-073259-8

LC 2004-47703

First published 1955 in the United Kingdom

Sylvia Plath's posthumous volume of poetry, Ariel, was first published in the mid-1960s. "This facsimile edition restores, for the first
time, the selection and arrangement of the poems as Sylvia Plath left
them at the point of her death. In addition to the facsimile pages of Sylvia Plath's manuscript, this edition also includes in facsimile the complete working drafts of the title poem, 'Ariel,' in order to offer a sense
of Plath's creative process as well as notes the author made for the BBC
about some of the manuscript poems." (Publisher's note)

"Readers can see Plath's actual manuscript in this handsome facsimile, which provides a missing piece in the Plath annals and proves
that there's nothing like going to the source." Booklist

The **letters** of Sylvia Plath; volume 2: 1956-1963. edited
by Peter K. Steinberg and Karen V. Kukil. HarperCollins 2018
1088 p. $45   **811**

1. American poets 2. American authors

ISBN 006274058X; 9780062740588

This book, edited by Peter K. Steinberg and Karen V. Kukil, is "the
second volume in the definitive, complete collection of the letters of
Pulitzer Prize-winning poet, Sylvia Plath, from the early years of her
marriage to Ted Hughes to the final days leading to her suicide in 1963,
many never before seen." (Publisher's note)

Poe, Edgar Allan

Complete poems; edited by Thomas Ollive Mabbott. University of Ill. Press 2000 xxx, 627p il pa $25   **811**

1. Poetry -- By individual authors

ISBN 0-252-06921-8

LC 00-38639

This book contains 101 poems and their variants. In addition to classic poems such as The raven, The bells, and Annabel Lee, this volume
contains previously uncollected poems, fragments, verses published in
reviews, and poems attributed to Poe

Includes bibliographical references

Poems from the women's movement; edited by Honor Moore.
Library of America 2009 238p (American poets project)
$20   **811**

1. Women's movement 2. American poetry -- Women authors --
Collections

ISBN 978-1-59853-042-1

This is an anthology of poetry written by women during the wom-
en's movement of the late 1960s and 1970s.

"These direct, vibrant, potent, passionate, wild, strong, free, and
freeing poems come less like a breath of fresh air than a strong wind."
Booklist

Poetry 180; a turning back to poetry. selected and with an
introduction by Billy Collins. Random House Trade Paperbacks 2003 xxiv, 323p pa $13.95   **811**

1. American poetry -- Collections

ISBN 0-8129-6887-5

LC 2002-36949

The editor "has collected 180 accessible modern poems: one for
each day of the school year and together signifying a 180° turning back

to poetry. These are poems, he says, you can 'get' the first time around,
and he hopes that high schools will expose students to a poem a day via
public address system or assemblies. A fine gathering of contemporary
poets." Libr J

Includes bibliographical references

The **Poetry** anthology, 1912-2002; ninety years of America's
most distinguished verse magazine. edited by Joseph Parisi & Stephen Young; with an introduction by Joseph Parisi.
Ivan R. Dee 2002 lv, 509p $29.95; pa $16.95   **811**

1. American poetry -- Collections

ISBN 1-56663-468-7; 1-56663-604-3 pa

LC 2002-31178

A collection of 600 poems previously published in Poetry magazine,
written by such poets as W.H. Auden, Elizabeth Bishop, Sylvia Plath,
James Merrill, and Susan Hahn

This is a "comprehensive and thrilling anthology, a veritable history
of twentieth-century poetry in English." Booklist

Poetry speaks expanded; hear poets from Tennyson to Plath
read their own work. Elise Paschen & Rebekah Pres-
son Mosby, editors; Charles Osgood, narrator. [2nd ed.];
Sourcebooks 2007 384p il $49.95   **811**

1. English poetry -- Collections 2. American poetry -- Collections

ISBN 978-1-4022-1062-4; 1-4022-1062-0

LC 2007-37080

First published 2001 with title: Poetry speaks

"Reluctant poetry readers may find themselves drawn to the printed
page by the spoken work, and poetry fans are likely to find much to love
here." Publ Wkly

The **poets** laureate anthology; edited and with introductions by
Elizabeth Hun Schmidt; foreword by Billy Collins. W.W.
Norton & Co. 2010 liii, 762p $39.95   **811**

1. American poetry -- Collections

ISBN 978-0-393-06181-9

LC 2010-21692

Poems by each of the forty-three poets who have been named our
nation's Poet Laureate since the post (originally called Consultant in
Poetry to the Library of Congress) was established in 1937.

"A hefty and worthy read that everyone will want to savor. Essential
for all contemporary poetry collections." Libr J

Poets of the Civil War; J.D. McClatchy, editor. Library of
America 2005 211p il (American poets project) $20 **811**

1. American poetry -- Collections 2. United States -- History --
1861-1865, Civil War -- Poetry

ISBN 978-1-93108-276-1; 1-93208-276-6

LC 2004-61552

"The poems wisely selected represent not only the main kinds of
responses to the war but also the radically conflicting sympathies of the
poets—with the Union cause or with the Confederacy—and the important postwar theme of reconciliation of North and South. McClatchy's
selection has not only breadth of representation but fine choices within
forms, causes, and poets." Sewanee Rev

★ **Poets** of World War II; Harvey Shapiro, editor. Library of
Am. 2003 xxxii, 262p (American poets project) $20 **811**

1. World War, 1939-1945 -- Poetry

ISBN 1-931082-33-2

LC 2002-32125

The editor's "objective is to show that the American poets of the

Second World War were as significant as their English counterparts in the first one, if different in tone. Even at their most biting, Siegfried Sassoon and Wilfred Owen struck a heroic note, penning anthems for 'doomed youth' and the destruction of innocence. . . . But those who survived battles of the second conflict to become important poets avoided the attempt to sound noble, or to celebrate fallen comrades. . . . Shapiro, a B-17 gunner, takes pains to show the spectrum of opinion that actually existed and how it evolved." New Leader

Includes bibliographical references

Postmodern American poetry; a Norton anthology. edited by Paul Hoover. 2nd ed. W W Norton & Co Inc 2013 lvii, 982 p.p (paperback) $39.95 **811**
1. Postmodernism 2. American poetry 3. American poetry -- 20th century 4. American poetry -- 21st century 5. Postmodernism (Literature) -- United States
ISBN 0393341860; 9780393341867

LC 2012039473

This book, edited by Paul Hoover, is a the second edition of an anthology of poems written after 1950, by such authors as "Robert Duncan, Denise Levertov, James Schuyler, Robert Creeley, Allen Ginsberg, Gary Snyder, Ted Berrigan, Clarence Major, Mei-Mei Berssenbrugge, and David Shapiro." (Booklist) It includes "important recent movements such as Newlipo, conceptual poetry, and Flarf." (Publisher's note)

Includes bibliographical references and index.

Pound, Ezra

★ The **cantos** of Ezra Pound. New Directions 1970 802p $42; pa $22.95 **811**
1. Poetry -- By individual authors
ISBN 0-8112-0350-6; 0-8112-1326-9 pa

"The first sections of the 'Cantos' were published in magazine form as early as 1917. Pound's conception of his epic changed several times during different phases of his life. Originally intended as a didactic treatise for 'philistine' Americans, it combined elements from classical myth, ancient Oriental poetry, Provençal ballads, and modern economic theory, to create a vast disjointed panorama of the growth of civilization. A monumental work of poetic enterprise." Reader's Ency. 4th edition

★ **Poems** and translations. Library of America 2003 1363p $45 **811**
1. Poetry -- By individual authors
ISBN 978-1-931082-41-9; 1-931082-41-3

LC 2003-40142

This volume "offers, in addition to the convenience of having Pound's shorter works compacted into a single volume, a useful chronology of his life and some very helpful, if at times overly terse, annotations to the poems' myriad foreign phrases and proper nouns. Richard Sieburth, an award-winning translator and the author of a previous book on Pound, is clearly at home with the material. . . . More important than all of this, however, what emerges from Poems and Translations is a personality, one of the strongest and strangest in modern poetry." Parnassus: Poetry in Review

Powell, D. A., 1963-

Repast; tea, lunch, and cocktails. D. A. Powell. Graywolf Press 2014 224 p. (alk. paper) $20 **811**
1. Gay men -- Poetry 2. AIDS (Disease) -- Poetry
ISBN 1555976964; 9781555976965

LC 2014935838

This collection of poetry by D. A. Powell combines his books "Tea," "Lunch," and "Cocktails," with an introduction by novelist David Leavitt. Many of the poems are concerned with the AIDS epidemic

among U.S. gay men in the late 20th century. "The trilogy's narrative arc, with its focus on survival, subverts the all-too-typical cliché of the gay man suffering and dying." (New Yorker)

Useless landscape; or, a guide for boys. D. A. Powell. Graywolf Press 2012 80 p. (alk. paper) $22 **811**
1. Youth -- Poetry 2. Gay men -- Poetry 3. Diseases -- Poetry 4. Human body -- Poetry 5. Poetry -- Collections
ISBN 9781555976057

LC 2011942041

In this collection of poetry, D. A. Powell "revisits themes of body and illness, sacred space and seductive desecration. The first section is an examination of beauty divorced from utility; the second a . . . portrait of young people in acts of exploration." (Booklist) The poems vary in tone, . . . some based on life stories and others built on puns . . . the impoverished spaces of [Powell's] youth stand out among his backgrounds and metaphors for ecological disaster, for gay sexual awakening, for sex itself, for illness, and for love." (Publishers Weekly)

Raab, Lawrence, 1946-

Mistaking each other for ghosts; poems. Lawrence Raab. Tupelo Press 2015 84 p. (pbk.: alk. paper) $16.95 **811**
1. American poetry
ISBN 1936797658; 9781936797653

LC 2015017797

NBA Longlist

The poems in this collection by Lawrence Raab feature "angels and human monsters, decades and generations, universities turned into ashes, the consolation of philosophy, despair in the middle of the night, a tutorial in lucid dreaming. Only his poetic humor gives away his American citizenship." (Publisher's note)

"With identifiable scenes that Raab has twisted for fresh insight, these are accessible poems most readers will appreciate." LJ

Rankine, Claudia, 1963-

★ **Citizen**; an American lyric. Claudia Rankine. Graywolf Press 2014 160 p. illustrations (some color) $20 **811**
1. American essays 2. Racism -- Poetry 3. United States -- Race relations
ISBN 1555976905; 9781555976903

LC 2014935702

National Book Award Shortlist: Poetry (2014)
National Book Critics Circle Finalist: Criticism (2014)
National Book Critics Circle Finalist: Poetry (2014)

This book, by Claudia Rankine, "recounts mounting racial aggressions in ongoing encounters in twenty-first-century daily life and in the media. Some of these encounters are slights, seeming slips of the tongue, and some are intentional offensives in the classroom, at the supermarket, at home, on the tennis court with Serena Williams and the soccer field with Zinedine Zidane, online, on TV--everywhere, all the time." (Publisher's note)

"Combining poetry, essay, and images from media and contemporary art, Rankine's poetics capture the urgency of her subject matter." Pub Wkly

Rasmussen, Matt

Black aperture; poems. Matt Rasmussen. Louisiana State University Press 2013 64 p. (pbk.: alk. paper) $17.95 **811**
1. Suicide 2. Bereavement 3. Poetry -- Collections
ISBN 080715086X; 9780807150863

LC 2012038045

National Book Award Finalist: Poetry (2013)

In this collection of poems, Matt Rasmussen "faces the tragedy of his brother's suicide, . . . blurring the edge between grief and humor. In Outgoing, the speaker erases his brother's answering machine message. . . . In other poems, once-ordinary objects become dreamlike. . . . Destructive and redemptive, [it] opens to the complicated entanglements of mourning: damage and healing, sorrow and laughter, and torment balanced with moments of relief." (Publisher's note)

Reed, Ishmael

New and collected poems, 1966-2006. Carroll & Graf 2006 xxi, 482p $25.95; pa $17.95   **811**
     1. Poetry -- By individual authors
     ISBN 978-0-7867-1788-0; 978-1-56858-341-9 pa
         LC 2006-299409
     "The mixture of humor and anger is . . . a hallmark of Ishmael Reed, whose strength as an editor, essayist, and novelist (and whose reputation as provocateur) has overshadowed his achievement as a poet. That achievement . . . is based in the vernacular, as well as in his use of folk materials, his fearlessness with form, and his 'irrational' tendency toward the spiritual, which stands as an indictment of the impoverished soul of a bottom-line age." Harvard Review

Reed, Justin Phillip

Indecency; Justin Phillip Reed. Coffee House Press 2018 70 p. (softcover) $16.95   **811**
     1. Prose poetry 2. Concrete poetry 3. American poetry -- Collections
     ISBN 9781566895149
         LC 2017039180
     National Book Award: Poetry (2018)
     "In these poems, Justin Phillip Reed experiments with language to explore inequity and injustice and to critique and lament the culture of white supremacy and the dominant social order. Political and personal, tender, daring, and insightful--the author unpacks his intimacies, weaponizing poetry to take on masculinity, sexuality, exploitation, and the prison industrial complex and unmask all the failures of the structures into which society sorts us." (Publisher's note)
     "Reed's visceral and teasingly cerebral debut probes black identity, sexuality, and violence and is inseparably personal and political." Pub Wkly
     Includes bibliographical references (page 69)

Rekdal, Paisley

Animal eye; Paisley Rekdal. University of Pittsburgh Press 2012 86 p.   **811**
     1. Love poetry 2. Poetry -- Collections 3. Loss (Psychology) -- Poetry 4. American poetry
     ISBN 0822961792; 9780822961796
         LC 2011277541
     This book is a collection of poetry from Paisley Rekdal. "In poems long and short, Rekdal looks at paintings and wax models . . . , a stuffed fox . . . , a front-yard garden, a bouquet of flowers, all of which become harsh mirrors reflecting the painful lessons of lost love. "What's the point of pain if it heals," Rekdal asks, thinking of finding new love after divorce: these poems don't want to be let off easy. Even tango lessons aren't just for fun: "The point is not to give yourself away but to connect/ as closely as you are able to// your partner's will in the embrace, so that intent/ slides seamlessly through two// sets of veins." There's a bit of willful masochism in this dance--in any of life's various dances--when the goal is to join 'two separate hearts.'" (Publishers Weekly)

Revell, Donald

     ★ **Pennyweight** windows; new & selected poems. Alice James 2005 220p $26.95; pa $18.95   **811**

     1. Poetry -- By individual authors
     ISBN 1-882295-51-X; 1-882295-52-8 pa
         LC 2004-26191
     "Using history, mythology, and contemporary events as a backdrop . . . [the author] tries to balance a public, nearly didactic voice with a personal and revealing one. . . . This readable and well-edited collection— mostly culled from eight previous collections, with some new poems added—is a good representation of Revell's work." Libr J

Rexroth, Kenneth

     ★ The **complete** poems of Kenneth Rexroth; edited by Sam Hamill & Bradford Morrow. Copper Canyon Press 2003 xxxvi, 764p hardcover o.p. pa $24   **811**
     1. Poetry -- By individual authors
     ISBN 1-55659-217-5 pa
         LC 2002-1706
     "If you love looking things up and taking reading side-trips, Rexroth is one of the most readable and rewarding twentieth-century American poets." Booklist

Reznikoff, Charles

     ★ The **poems** of Charles Reznikoff; 1918-1975. edited by Seamus Cooney. David R. Godine 2005 445p $45; pa $21.95   **811**
     1. Poetry -- By individual authors
     ISBN 1-57423-204-5; 1-57423-203-7 pa
         LC 2005-21218
     First published 1989 with title: Poems 1918-1975
     This collection "of his poems . . . will be welcomed both by old and new readers of his work." Publ Wkly
     Includes bibliographical references

Rich, Adrienne

     The **school** among the ruins: poems, 2000-2004. W.W. Norton 2004 113p $22.95   **811**
     1. Poetry -- By individual authors
     ISBN 0-393-05983-9
         LC 2004-8370
     "Rich, a clarion poet of conscience, gets the fractured timbre of our times just right in a collection of vigorous lyric poems about cell phones and television, terror and war, commercialization and 'social impotence.'" Booklist

     ★ Selected poems, 1950-2012; Adrienne Rich; edited by Albert Gelpi, Barbara Charlesworth Gelpi, and Brett C. Millier. W W Norton & Co. 2018 496 p. (pbk.) $17.95   **811**
     1. American poetry 2. American literature
     ISBN 039335511X; 9780393355116
         LC 2018016676
     This poetry collection, by Adrienne Rich, edited by Albert Gelpi, Barbara Charlesworth Gelpi, and Brett C. Millier, "encompasses her best-known work--the clear-sighted and passionate feminist poems of the 1970s, including 'Diving into the Wreck,' 'Planetarium,' and 'The Phenomenology of Anger'--and offers the full range of her evolution as a poet." (Publisher's note)

Rich, Adrienne, 1929-2012

     Essential essays; culture, politics, and the art of poetry. Adrienne Rich, edited by Sandra M. Gilbert. W W Norton & Co Inc 2018 352 p. $27.95   **811**
     1. Essays 2. LGBT literature
     ISBN 039365236X; 9780393652369

Edited by Sandra M. Gilbert, this book "gathers twenty-five of . . . [Adrienne Rich's] most renowned essays into one volume, demonstrating the lasting brilliance of her voice, her prophetic vision, and her revolutionary views on social justice. Rich's essays unite the political, personal, and poetical like no other. . . . Emphasizing Rich's lifelong intellectual engagement, the essays selected here range from the 1960s to 2008." (Publisher's note)

Ronk, Martha

Ocular proof; Martha Ronk. Omnidawn 2016 75 p. (paperback: alk. paper) $17.95   **811**
   1. American poetry -- 21st century
   ISBN 9781632430250
                          LC 2016017043

This book of poems, by Martha Ronk, "explores not only what each of us sees, but also how photographs modify sight as they capture, distort, frame, and simultaneously encourage discovery. These poems play off critical insights about the function of photographs and the power of visual imagery in the modern world and yet are decidedly personal. They address the unreality of one's own life, the illegibility of the past and future, and our strong attraction to focused details." (Publisher's note)

Ruefle, Mary

Selected poems. Wave Books 2010 154p $24   **811**
   1. Poetry -- By individual authors
   ISBN 978-1-933517-45-2; 1-933517-45-X
                       LC 2010-05808

"This first retrospective collection from Ruefle, which selects from her nine previous books of poetry, the earliest of which first appeared in 1982, shows her to be a poet of visionary imagination, abiding sensitivity, and melancholy humor." Publ Wkly

Ruhl, Sarah

Letters from Max; a book of friendship. Mark Rivko and Sarah Ruhl. Milkweed Editions 2018 336 p. (hardcover: alk. paper) $26   **811**
   1. Cancer patients   2. American poets -- 20th century -- Correspondence 3. Drama teachers -- Correspondence 4. Cancer -- Patients -- Correspondence 5. Poets, American -- 20th century -- Correspondence 6. Women dramatists, American -- 20th century -- Correspondence
   ISBN 9781571313690
                       LC 2018007328

In this book, by Mark Rivko and Sarah Ruhl, "over the next four years--in which Ritvo's illness returned and his health declined, even as his productivity bloomed--the two exchanged letters that spark with urgency, humor, and the desire for connection. . . . Studded with poems and songs, . . . [this book] is a deeply moving portrait of a friendship, and a shimmering exploration of love, art, mortality, and the afterlife." (Publisher's note)

"This companion volume to The Final Voicemails (2018), a moving compilation of the late Ritvo's incandescent poems, takes readers behind the curtain of his writing to expose his hard-won, well-lived, if sadly brief life, including his painful struggle with cancer, evolving love and marriage, and the tree-bud-to-redwood maturation of an intimate friendship with award-winning playwright Ruhl." Booklist

Rukeyser, Muriel

Selected poems; Adrienne Rich, editor. Library of America 2004 xxv, 180p (American poets project) $20   **811**
   1. Poetry -- By individual authors
   ISBN 978-1-931082-58-7; 1-931082-58-8
                       LC 2003-60484

"Rukeyser was born in 1913, which puts her in the generation of Bishop, Berryman, Lowell, and Jarrell. Her poems range from the sprawling to the epigrammatic; they often have a flat, documentary feel ('The tunnel is part of a huge water power project/begun, latter part of 1929'), and they're formally various (excerpted sections from a single long poem, 'Letter to the Front,' contain both a sonnet and a sestina). . . . At its best, Rukeyser's work can be open, energetic, and well constructed, if a little enamored of its own goody-goodness." Poetry (Modern Poetry Association)

Ryan, Kay

The **best** of it; new and selected poems. Grove Press 2010 288p $24   **811**
   1. Poetry -- By individual authors
   ISBN 978-0-8021-1914-8; 0-8021-1914-X

Ryan's "poems are as slim as runway models, so tiny you could almost tweet them. Their compact refinement, though, does not suggest ease or chic. Her voice is quizzical and impertinent, funny in uncomfortable ways, scuffed by failure and loss. Her mastery, like Emily Dickinson's, has some awkwardness in it, some essential gawkiness that draws you close. . . . [This] is a generous and nearly career-spanning collection of her verse." N Y Times Book Rev

Salah, Trish

Wanting in Arabic; poems. by Trish Salah. Mawenzi House Pub 2002 90 p. $19.95   **811**
   1. Gender identity -- Poetry
   ISBN 9781927494301; 9781894770002
                       LC 2003430842

Lambda Award: Transgender Fiction (2014)

This poetry collection, by Trish Salah, "dwells on the contradictions of a transsexual poetics, in its attendant disfigurations of lyric, ghazal, l'ecriture feminine, and, in particular, her own sexed voice. Without a memory of her father's language, the questions her poems ask are those for a home known through photographs, for a language lost with childhood." (Publisher's note)

Salter, Mary Jo, 1954-

The **surveyors**; poems. Mary Jo Salter. First Edition Alfred A. Knopf 2017 112 p. $27   **811**
   1. Poetry -- Collections
   ISBN 9781524732660
                       LC 2016042321

This book, by Mary Jo Salter, "brings us poems of puzzlement and acceptance in the face of life's surprises. . . . Time is hurtling, but these poems try to slow it down to examine its curious by-products--the prints of Durer, an Afghan carpet, photographs of people we've lost. The title poem, a crown of sonnets, takes up key moments in the poet's past, the quirky advent of poetic inspiration, and the seemingly sci-fi future of the universe." (Publisher's note)

"[T]his, her seventh collection, is an understated register of life lived and the passage of time—recollections of childhood, her own and her children's; memories of a deceased classmate; and gratitude for the blossoming of new love. She is superbly skilled in the old appurtenances of meter and rhyme, deploying coincidences of rhythm and sound that only rereading discloses—but her ease extends to the freer lyric style as well." Library Journal

Includes bibliographical references (page 89).

Sanchez, Erika L.

Lessons on expulsion; poems. Erika L. Sanchez. Graywolf Press 2017 73 p. (alk. paper) $16   **811**
   1. Poetry -- Collections 2. Women -- Poetry 3. Immigrants --

Poetry
ISBN 9781555977788; 9781555979706

LC 2016951419

This book of poetry, by Erika L. Sanchez, "explores what it means to live on both sides of the border—the border between countries, languages, despair and possibility, and the living and the dead. Sánchez tells her own story as the daughter of undocumented Mexican immigrants and as part of a family steeped in faith, work, grief, and expectations." (Publisher's note)

"This compelling debut recounts the experiences of crossing borders, whether by force or choice." Booklist

Schulman, Grace

Days of wonder; new and selected poems. Houghton Mifflin 2002 189p $25; pa $14 **811**

1. Poetry -- By individual authors
ISBN 0-618-08623-4; 0-618-34082-3 pa

LC 2001-39531

"In a characteristic Schulman poem, large, difficult questions resonate in the small, singular moments of appreciation. . . . There are allusions to canonical painters and canonical poems, and a variety of religious references, which engender equal portions of reverence and lament. Many of the poems' small pleasures are found amid sometimes difficult sometimes serene backdrops." Publ Wkly

Schultz, Philip, 1945-

Luxury; poems. Philip Schultz. W W Norton & Co Inc 2018 96 p. (hardcover) $26.95 **811**

1. Emotions -- Poetry 2. American poetry -- Collections
ISBN 9780393634686

LC 2017033688

In this poetry collection, poet "Philip Schultz's wry and incisive poetic voice takes on both the eternal questions of meaning and happiness and essentially modern complexities--the collective power of women's marches, the strangeness of googling oneself, the refugee crisis, the emotions associated with visiting the 9/11 memorial. At once philosophical and droll, Schultz explores life's luxuries and challenges with masterly precision." (Publisher's note)

"Not a perfect collection, but one that will provide revelations with each rereading." LJ

Schuyler, James

Collected poems. Farrar, Straus & Giroux 1993 429p hardcover o.p. pa $32 **811**

1. Poetry -- By individual authors
ISBN 978-0-374-52403-6; 0-374-52403-3

LC 92-40977

"Schuyler's subject is his life, and his poems often read like elegant journal entries. The book presents intimate and conversational accounts of life in the Eastern literary landscape—New York City, New England, Long Island. In urbane free verse, the poet recalls and meditates on music and painting, homosexuality, weekends with friends—John Ashbery and Fairfield Porter among them—deaths, a drive to the Hamptons. . . . Rarely has a poet imparted so much of his experience as honestly and engagingly as Schuyler does here." Publ Wkly

Seidel, Frederick

Poems 1959-2009. Farrar, Straus, and Giroux 2009 509p $40 **811**

1. Poetry -- By individual authors
ISBN 978-0-374-12655-1; 0-374-12655-0

LC 2008-47161

"Long regarded as a kind of elegant cult figure in poetry circles,

Seidel has a reputation that precedes him into every room: decadent, name-dropper, sexual dalliant, Ducati enthusiast, son of privilege. This runs counter to the man himself. He doesn't do poetry readings and has, for the most part, shunned interviews. There is no doubt that Seidel is one of the best poets alive today, and now, with the release of 'Poems: 1959-2009,' his collected works can be taken at their measure: They are haughty, funny and terrifying, with plenty of delicious contention throughout." Los Angeles Times

Sendak, Maurice, 1928-2012

★ **My** brother's book; Maurice Sendak; [edited by] Michael di Capua. HarperCollins 2013 32 p. (hardcover bdg.) $18.95 **811**

1. Poetry 2. Poetry -- Collections
ISBN 0062234897; 9780062234896

LC 2012942549

In this book, "with influences from Shakespeare and William Blake, [Maurice] Sendak pays homage to his late brother, Jack, whom he credited for his passion for writing and drawing. Pairing Sendak's . . . poetry with his . . . artwork, . . . Sendak's tribute to his brother is an expression of both grief and love. . . . Pulitzer Prize--winning literary critic and Shakespearean scholar Stephen Greenblatt contributes a[n] . . . introduction." (Publisher's note)

Seuss, Diane

Still life with two dead peacocks and a girl; poems. Diane Seuss. Graywolf Press 2018 120 p. (alk. paper) $16 **811**

1. American poetry -- 21st century
ISBN 9781555978068

LC 2017953321

This book of poetry, by Diane Seuss, "takes its title from Rembrandt's painting, a dark emblem of femininity, violence, and the viewer's own troubled gaze. In . . . Seuss's new collection, the notion of the still life is shattered and Rembrandt's painting is presented across the book in pieces. . . . With invention and irreverence, these poems escape gilded frames and overturn traditional representations of gender, class, and luxury." (Publisher's note)

Shange, Ntozake

Wild beauty; new and selected poems. Ntozake Shange; translated by Alejandro Álvarez Nieves. 37 Ink/Atria 2017 xxx, 255 p.p **811**

ISBN 9781501169939; 9781501169953

LC 2018286361

In this book, poet Ntozake Shange "draws from her experience as a feminist black woman in American to craft groundbreaking poetry about pain, beauty, and color. In the bestselling tradition of Rupi Kaur's Milk and Honey, Wild Beauty is more than a poetry collection; it is an exquisite call to action for a new generation of women, people of color, feminists, and activists to follow in the author's footsteps in the pursuit of equality and understanding." (Publisher's note)

"Shange's ability to breathe life into myriad characters and voices is on display throughout the collection. And, despite the instances of disappointment, violence, and struggle, the poems all highlight hope, joy, and optimism. This is an exemplary representation of Shange's body of poetic work." Pub Wkly

Shapiro, Alan, 1952-

Reel to reel; Alan Shapiro. University of Chicago Press 2014 77 p. (pbk.: alk. paper) $18 **811**

1. American poetry -- Collections
ISBN 022611063X; 9780226110639

LC 2013016631

Pulitzer Prize Finalist: Poetry (2015)

This book, "Alan Shapiro's twelfth collection of poetry, moves outward from the intimate spaces of family and romantic life to embrace not only the human realm of politics and culture but also the natural world, and even the outer spaces of the cosmos itself. In language richly nuanced yet accessible, these poems inhabit and explore fundamental questions of existence, such as time, mortality, consciousness, and matter." (Publisher's note)

Shapiro, David

New and selected poems (1965-2006) Overlook Press 2007 267p $21.95 **811**
  1. Poetry -- By individual authors
  ISBN 978-1-58567-877-8; 1-58567-877-5
                  LC 2006-52718

"Shapiro is usually thought of as a New York School poet, but from the evidence of this selection it would probably be more accurate to call him a Greater New York School poet. His metropolis radiates outward to comprehend Weequahic Park and the Palisades, and his aleatory, portent-free sophistication seems confident enough to accommodate primitive, endearing, and frankly tender tropes and situations, as when a poet faces an ailing mother or a growing son. A perennial drama in this volume is that of an erudite and restlessly modernizing mind confronting pains and peculiarities that no amount of urbanity can assuage. . . . The effect is of unforeseen intimacy at the heart of abstraction." New Yorker

Shapiro, Karl Jay

  ★ **Selected** poems; [by] Karl Shapiro; John Updike, editor. Library of Am. 2003 xxxi, 197p il (American poets project) $20 **811**
  1. Poetry -- By individual authors
  ISBN 1-931082-34-0
                  LC 2002-32123

"Karl Shapiro, one of the more influential voices of the late 20th century, displayed complex and contrary tendencies in both his life and his poetry. Editor Updike notes that Shapiro's experimentation with voices and forms alienated those who admired the metrical dexterity of his early poems." Libr J

Includes bibliographical references

Shaughnessy, Brenda

Human dark with sugar. Copper Canyon Press 2008 77p pa $15 **811**
  1. Poetry -- By individual authors
  ISBN 978-1-55659-276-8 pa; 1-55659-276-0 pa
                  LC 2007-52225

"The book's three sections contain nine, 11 and 10 poems, respectively, and that off-kilter triangulation . . . proves the right three-cornered lens for looking into the darkest corners of human relationships, including their embodiment. . . . This is a brilliant, beautiful and essential continuation of the metaphysical verse tradition." Publ Wkly

Shaw, Anne

  ★ **Dido** in winter; poems. Anne Shaw. A Karen & Michael Braziller Book/Persea Books 2014 84 p. (original trade paperback: alk. paper) $15.95 **811**
  1. American poetry -- Collections 2. American poetry -- 21st century
  ISBN 9780892554294
                  LC 2013042147

This poetry collection, by Anne Shaw, "is a mapping of the senses, in which rapture and disillusionment shadow each other, reflecting a world 'where sun swirls on the rock-face by the spring/moving its blue and yellow hands/then vanishing.' It is a book searching for truth beyond beauty by a poet who shines increasingly bright." (Publisher's note)

Includes bibliographical references (page 84).

Shockley, Evie

The **new** black; poems. Wesleyan University Press 2011 104p il (Wesleyan poetry) **811**
  1. Poetry -- By individual authors
  ISBN 978-0-81957-140-3
                  LC 2010046345

In this book, the author "tells the reader not of some oversimplified and inaccurate version of 'the African-American experience' but of the plethora of experiences that inform the consciousness of one black woman in contemporary America. Shockley's work incorporates elements of myth without being patently 'mythical' and is personal without being self-indulgent, sentimental without being saccharine." Libr J

Semiautomatic; Evie Shockley. Wesleyan University Press 2017 110 p. illustrations (chiefly color) (Wesleyan poetry) (cloth: alk. paper) $24.95 **811**
  1. Violence -- Poetry 2. American poetry -- Collections 3. American poetry -- 21st century
  ISBN 9780819577450; 9780819577436; 9780819577443
                  LC 2016059299

Pulitzer Prize Finalist: Poetry (2018)

In this book in the Wesleyan Poetry series, by Evie Shockley, "the poems trace a whole web of connections between the kinds of violence that affect people across the racial, ethnic, gender, class, sexual, national, and linguistic boundaries that do and do not divide us. How do we protect our humanity, our ability to feel deeply and think freely, in the face of a seemingly endless onslaught of physical, social, and environmental abuses?" (Publisher's note)

Includes bibliographical references.

Simic, Charles, 1938-

The **Lunatic**; Poems. HarperCollins 2015 96 p. $22.99 **811**
  1. Poetry -- Collections
  ISBN 006236474X; 9780062364746
                  LC 2014450552

This book of poems, by Charles Simic, is "a dazzling collection of poems as original, meditative, and humorous as the legendary poet himself. . . . These seventy luminous poems range in subject from mortality to personal ads, from the simple wonders of nature to his childhood in war-torn Yugoslavia." (Publisher's note)

"Spiked with clues to larger mysteries, Simic's unnerving puzzle poems are works of insomniac witnessing and tempered love for our precious, haunted, rapturous, and dangerous world." Booklist

New and selected poems 1962-2012; Charles Simic. Houghton Mifflin Harcourt 2013 384 p. (hardcover) $30 **811**
  1. Poetry -- Collections
  ISBN 0547928289; 9780547928289
                  LC 2012042188

This poetry collection, by Pulitzer-prize winner and U.S poet laureate Charles Simic, "combin[es] for the first time the best of his early poems with his later works—including nearly three dozen revisions—along with seventeen new, never-before-published poems. Simic's body of work draws inspiration from a range of topics, from the inscrutability of ordinary life to American blues, from folktales to marriage and war." (Publisher's note)

Scribbled in the dark; poems. Charles Simic. Ecco, an imprint of HarperCollins Publishers 2017 xiv, 72 p.p (hardcover) $22.99 **811**

1. American poetry -- 21st century

ISBN 9780062661197; 9780062661173; 0062661175

This collection of poems, by Charles Simic, "brings the poet's signature sardonic sense of humor, piercing social insight, and haunting lyricism to diverse and richly imagined landscapes. Peopled by policemen, presidents, kids in Halloween masks, a fortune-teller, a fly on the wall of the poet's kitchen; on crowded New York streets, on park benches, and under darkened skies: the pages within toy with the end of the world and its infinity." (Publisher's note)

"Image by image, Simic composes miniature masterpieces, offering what appears as a seemingly effortless study in language's cinematic possibilities." Pub Wkly

★ The **voice** at 3:00 a.m; selected late & new poems. Harcourt 2003 177p $25 **811**

1. Poetry -- By individual authors

ISBN 0-15-100842-6

LC 2002-38715

National Book Award Finalist: Poetry (2003)

"An important purchase for all libraries." Libr J

Simpson, Louis Aston Marantz

★ The **owner** of the house; new collected poems, 1940-2001. [by] Louis Simpson. BOA 2003 407p (American poets continuum series) $30.95; pa $19.95 **811**

1. Poetry -- By individual authors

ISBN 1-929918-38-0; 1-929918-39-9 pa

LC 2003-45241

National Book Award Finalist: Poetry (2003)

The author "opens with 42 new poems and continues with selections from his 11 previous books, ending with There You Are. This work is filled with evocations of places like Jamaica, Manhattan, Paris, and Venice and range over time from tsarist Russia to World War II to the 1960s. Simpson's obsessive theme is the stultifying effect of middle-class suburban life. . . . The result is a collection both timely and accessible. . . . Highly recommended for all poetry collections." Libr J

Smith, Danez

Don't call us dead; poems. Danez Smith. Graywolf Press 2017 88 p. (paperback) $16 **811**

1. Gay men 2. African American men 3. Poetry -- Collections 4. Gay men -- Poetry 5. HIV-positive men -- Poetry 6. Transgender people -- Poetry 7. African American men -- Poetry 8. American poetry -- 21st century 9. African American men -- Violence against -- Poetry

ISBN 9781555977856; 9781555979775

LC 2017930111

National Book Award Finalist: Poetry (2017)

This poetry collection, by Danez Smith, "opens with a heartrending sequence that imagines an afterlife for black men shot by police, a place where suspicion, violence, and grief are forgotten and replaced with the safety, love, and longevity they deserved here on earth. Smith turns then to desire, mortality--the dangers experienced in skin and body and blood--and a diagnosis of HIV positive." (Publisher's note)

"Luminous and piercing, this collection reassembles shattering realities into a shimmering and sharp mosaic." Pub Wkly

Smith, Patricia

Shoulda been Jimi Savannah; Patricia Smith. Coffee House Press 2012 115 p. (alk. paper) $16.00 **811**

1. Women poets 2. African American women 3. Chicago (Ill.) -- Poetry

ISBN 1566892996; 9781566892995

LC 2011029282

[Patricia] Smith's mother bestowed on the poet a name fitting for a woman that would 'never idly throat the Lord's name or wear one/ of those thin, sparkled skirts that flirted with her knees./ She'd be a nurse or a third-grade teacher or a postal drone.' . . . But her father, though acquiescing, secretly called her Jimi Savannah, embodying 'the blues-bathed moniker of a ball breaker.' . . . This duality bursts forth in her poems about . . . growing up black and a woman during the 1960s." (Publishers Weekly)

Smith, Tracy K.

The **body's** question. Graywolf Press 2003 **811**

1. Poetry -- By individual authors

ISBN 1-55597-391-4

"Winner of the Cave Canem Poetry Prize for a first collection by an African American poet, this is a rich collection of stories, histories, and moments that glow with the clean, direct language of a charming new voice. Attuned to the music of the streets-and to her heart-Smith is nevertheless attentive to craft, always aware of the integrity of the line. The result is poetry that is seductive yet powerful, subtle yet certain. . . . Though she explores themes of family, race, and loss, her poems exude a sense of joy or prayer." (Library Journal)

Duende; poems. Tracy K. Smith. Graywolf Press 2007 87 p. (pbk.: acid-free paper) $16 **811**

1. American poetry 2. Poetry -- Collections 3. American poetry -- 21st century

ISBN 1555974759; 9781555974756; 9781555978648

LC 2006938264

This second poetry collection, by Tracy K. Smith, "explores history and the intersections of folk traditions, political resistance, and personal survival. Duende gives passionate testament to suppressed cultures, and allows them to sing." (Publisher's note)

"The poet's lyric brilliance and political impulses never falter under the considerable weight of her subject matter." Pub Wkly

Life on Mars. Graywolf Press 2011 75p. pa $15 **811**

1. Poetry -- By individual authors

ISBN 1-55597-584-4; 978-1-55597-584-5

LC 2011920674

Pulitzer Prize: Poetry (2012)

"Smith shows herself to be a poet of extraordinary range and ambition. It's not easy to be so convincing in both the grand gesture and the reverent contemplation of a humble plate of eggs, and the early successes of this collection far outweigh its later missteps. As all the best poetry does, 'Life on Mars' first sends us out into the magnificent chill of the imagination and then returns us to ourselves, both changed and consoled." N Y Times Book Rev

Snodgrass, W. D.

★ **Not** for specialists; new and selected poems. BOA Editions 2006 251p (American poets continuum series) $27.95; pa $21.95 **811**

1. Poetry -- By individual authors

ISBN 1-92991-877-1; 1-92991-876-3 pa

LC 2005-54846

"If you think that writing primarily in rhyme and meter bespeaks equanimity, or sweetness of character, read Snodgrass. Oh, he mellows out in the face of nature, but he's prickly. . . . His many profoundly bemused and persuasive poems of love's tougher moments, his marvelous angry and denunciatory poems, and the chilling Fuehrer Bunker poems in the voices of the major Nazis during the war's last month—all these might have been impossible if Snodgrass was a nice, easygoing guy. He's not that sort, and his best work seems permanent because he isn't." Booklist

Spicer, Jack

★ **My** vocabulary did this to me; the collected poetry of Jack Spicer. edited by Peter Gizzi and Kevin Killian. Wesleyan University Press 2008 496p il $35 **811**

1. Poetry -- By individual authors

ISBN 978-0-8195-6887-8

LC 2008-24997

"Impeccably edited, this collection gathers the remarkable output of a poet whose writing and person were too counter even for the counterculture of the late '50s and '60s. Spicer's work manages to combine heartbreak, hermeticism, and postwar disquiet in a way both completely of its time and still ahead of ours." Village Voice

Stevens, Wallace

Collected poetry and prose. Library of Am. 1997 xxii, 1032p $35 **811**

1. Poetry -- By individual authors

ISBN 1-88301-145-0

LC 97-7023

Having all of Stevens' "poems—especially all the late poems—in one volume is a great thing (previously, one had to seek them out in three different books); the 'Adagia' and his replies to questionnaires are marvelous; and even in the somewhat turgid prose pieces, he sometimes expresses himself with exemplary force and concision." N Y Times Book Rev

Stone, Ruth

What love comes to; new & selected poems. foreword by Sharon Olds. Copper Canyon Press 2008 359p $32 **811**

1. Poetry -- By individual authors

ISBN 978-1-55659-271-3; 1-55659-271-X

LC 2007045832

Pulitzer Prize Finalist (2009)

"In a field in which collections of selected writings are constantly being released, this book stands out because Stone shows that simplicity can be a deceiving doorway into some of the most challenging poems written by an American poet. Stone's poems blend the personal with dimensions of the larger world in a manner reminiscent of the late William Stafford. Few poets have this gift for taking the workings of ordinary life and fusing them with a poetic process that sustains intense emotion, allowing human experience to be felt through the mysteries of language. . . . Ruth Stone belongs to every generation of poets who have taken the responsibility to give back to the world." Bloomsbury Rev

Strand, Mark, 1934-2014

Collected poems; by Mark Strand. Alfred A. Knopf 2014 520 p. (Hardcover) $30 **811**

ISBN 0385352514; 9780385352512

LC 2013049034

National Book Award Longlist: Poetry (2014)

"Gathered here is a half century's magnificent work by the former poet laureate of the United States and Pulitzer Prize winner whose haunting and exemplary style has influenced an entire generation of American poets." Publisher's Note

"For all the streamlined sadness of his dreamlike domain, Strand remains aware of other poets, which is particularly evident in his homages,

translations, and elegies. His recent string of short sardonic prose poems are all quite distinct from one another, but all are instantly, recognizably Strand, 'erasing the world and leaving instead/ The invisible lines of its calling: Out there, out there.'" Pub Wkly

Sze, Arthur

Compass Rose; Arthur Sze. Copper Canyon Press 2014 68 p. $16 **811**

1. Poetry -- Collections

ISBN 1556594674; 9781556594670

LC 2013025678

Pulitzer Prize Finalist: Poetry (2015)

This collection of poems by Arthur Sze features a "child playing a game, tea leaves resting in a bowl, an abandoned dog, a foot sticking out from a funeral pyre, an Afghan farmer pausing as mortars fire at the enemy." (Publisher's note)

"It's easy for readers to become lost in the intricacies, but the beauty of image and symmetry of ideas offer balance and direction." LJ

Includes bibliographical references

Szybist, Mary

★ **Incarnadine**; Mary Szybist. Graywolf Press 2013 72 p. (paperback) $15 **811**

ISBN 1555976352; 9781555976354

LC 2012953979

National Book Award: Poetry Winner

This poetry anthology, by the National Book Critics Circle Award finalist Mary Szybist, is her second published collection. "One poem is presented as a diagrammed sentence. Another is an abecedarium made of lines of dialogue spoken by girls overheard while assembling a puzzle. Several poems arrive as a series of Annunciations, while others purport to give an update on Mary, who must finish the dishes before she will open herself to God." (Publisher's note)

Tarn, Nathaniel

Selected poems; 1950-2000. Wesleyan University Press 2002 335p (Wesleyan poetry) $45; pa $19.95 **811**

1. Poetry -- By individual authors

ISBN 978-0-8195-6541-9; 0-8195-6541-5; 978-0-8195-6542-6 pa; 0-8195-6542-3 pa

LC 2002-1701

"Arranged chronologically, [this volume] has reprints from nineteen of Tarn's thirty-five books. Here the literary reader can find reality hybrids and can experience the camaraderie of whole image systems from the twentieth century. No syllable is lonely or aloof. One is often reminded, by Tarn's references, his subjects, and his dedications, not only of Blake but of Yeats, Vallejo, Charles Olson, and Robert Duncan. Like those writers, his work brings together mythology, Western and Eastern philosophy (including Gnostic thought), political commentary, scientific investigations, naturalist descriptions and very personal love poetry." Jacket

Trinidad, David

Dear Prudence; new and selected poems. Turtle Point 2011 493p pa $19 **811**

1. Poetry -- By individual authors

ISBN 978-1-933527-47-5

A collection of poetry from gay poet Trinidad.

The author's "lucid, amusing, and sad journal poems, memoir poems, prose poems, couplets, elegies, sonnets, and impressive pantoums may seem to valorize trash, but that trash sustains a flawed yet invaluable soul aching for loving acceptance." Booklist

Troupe, Quincy

★ **Transcircularities**; new and selected poems. Coffee House Press 2002 368p $30; pa $17   **811**
1. Poetry -- By individual authors
ISBN 1-56689-137-X; 1-56689-135-3 pa

LC 2002-71277

Troupe's "verse returns continually to swing, bebop and free-jazz giants, imitating, commemorating or praising Coltrane, Duke, Bud Powell and others in a series of musicianly poems culminating in the recent 'Back to the Dream Time: Miles Speaks from the Dead.' Troupe's forms, driven by performability, range from ecstatic odes to overtly political expostulations." Publ Wkly

Twentieth-century American poetry; edited by Dana Gioia, David Mason, Meg Schoerke. McGraw Hill 2004 xlvi, 1143p il pa $79.69   **811**
1. American poetry -- Collections
ISBN 0-07-240019-6

LC 2003-61449

"The text is divided into sections like 'Realism and Naturalism' and 'The Harlem Renaissance,' with each section prefaced by a penetrating overview and each poet introduced by a biographical essay. Included are poets as diverse as Sherman Alexie, Ezra Pound, and Lucille Clifton, along with Nuyorican poets, New Formalists, Beats, imagists, and surrealists. Make room for this affordable, remarkable volume." Libr J
Includes bibliographical references

Twichell, Chase

Horses where the answers should have been; new and selected poems. Copper Canyon Press 2010 255p pa $19   **811**
1. Poetry -- By individual authors
ISBN 978-1-55659-318-5; 1-55659-318-X

LC 2009-48885

"To read a well done 'selected poems' is to follow a life, and we find that here as we watch the poet grow from one in love with thought and language to one who quietly yet intensely contemplates the world by leaning toward the essential. Hers is a world of wounded beauty which she confronts and records for us." N Y Journal of Books
Includes bibliographical references

Valentine, Jean

Door in the mountain; new and collected poems, 1965-2003. Wesleyan University Press 2004 285p (Wesleyan poetry) $29.95   **811**
1. Poetry -- By individual authors
ISBN 0-8195-6712-4

LC 2004-16019

National Book Award: Poetry (2004)
"The defiant, angular, yet propulsively emotional recent poems that occupy the first and last parts of the book should please both fans of Valentine's earliest poetry and fans of her strongly feminist middle period." Publ Wkly
Includes bibliographical references

Van Duyn, Mona

★ **Selected** poems. Knopf 2002 218p $27.50; pa $16 **811**
1. Poetry -- By individual authors
ISBN 0-375-41369-3; 0-375-70980-0 pa

LC 2001-50672

"Characterized by candor and compassion, Van Duyn's poetry depicts the pleasures and drudgeries of middle-class American life, an approach that at its best becomes an exploration of the spiritual and psy-

chological dimensions of that life. . . . The casually formal surfaces of Van Duyn's poems often resemble those of her model, Elizabeth Bishop, and like Bishop she excels at both formal and free verse." N Y Times Book Rev

Vang, Mai Der

Afterland; poems. Mai Der Vang. Graywolf Press 2017 94 p. (alk. paper) $16   **811**
1. Poetry -- Collections 2. Laos -- Politics and government 3. Refugees -- Laos -- Poetry 4. Hmong (Asian people) -- Poetry
ISBN 9781555979645; 9781555977702

LC 2016938843

Walt Whitman Award of the Academy of American Poets (2016)
This book of poetry, by Mai Der Vang, " recounts with devastating detail the Hmong exodus from Laos and the fate of thousands of refugees seeking asylum. Mai Der Vang is telling the story of her own family, and by doing so, she also provides an essential history of the Hmong culture's ongoing resilience in exile." (Publisher's note)
"In this sinewy and unflinching debut . . . Vang shares the story of the Hmong diaspora who were forced out of Laos and into exile as a result of America's secret war of the 1960s and '70s." Pub Wkly

The **Vintage** book of African American poetry; edited and with an introduction by Michael S. Harper and Anthony Walton. Vintage Bks. 2000 xxxiii, 403p pa $14.95   **811**
1. American poetry -- African American authors -- Collections
ISBN 0-375-70300-4

LC 99-39428

"Included in chronological order here are over two centuries of poets, from Jupitor Hammon (1720-1800) to Reginald Shepherd (b.1963). . . . The editors' eloquent, outspoken vision provides a springboard for further examination of what constitutes the mainstream of American poetry." Libr J
Includes bibliographical references

Walcott, Derek, 1930-2017

Omeros. Farrar, Straus & Giroux 1990 325p hardcover o.p. pa $16   **811**
1. Poetry -- By individual authors
ISBN 0-374-52350-9 pa

LC 90-33592

In this epic poem, Helen "is the maid in a household of British colonialists called the Plunketts. . . . Her husband, Achille, the hero of Omeros, is a fisherman. . . . Her lover Hector has traded in his canoe for a taxi. While Achille lives in the older world of natural rhythms—wind, sand, surf, and stars—Hector has embraced the new world of tourism and speed. The quarrel between the two fisherman/warriors is also a quarrel between past and present, tradition and modernity, Africa and Europe." (New Repub)
"No poet rivals Mr. Walcott in humor, emotional depth, lavish inventiveness in language or in the ability to express the thoughts of his characters and compel the reader to follow the swift mutations of ideas and images in their minds. This wonderful story moves in a spiral, replicating human thought." N Y Times Book Rev

The **Poetry** of Derek Walcott 1948-2013; Derek Walcott; [selected by the poet Glyn Maxwell] Farrar, Straus & Giroux 2014 640 p. (hardcover) $40   **811**
1. Poetry 2. Nature poetry 3. Identity (Psychology)
ISBN 0374125619; 9780374125615

LC 2013034997

This book of poetry by Derek Walcott, edited by Glyn Maxwell, "draws from every stage of the poet's storied career. . . . Across sixty-five years, Walcott has grappled with the themes that have defined his work as they have defined his life. . . . This collection, . . . will prove as enduring as the questions, the passions, that have driven Walcott to write for more than half a century." (Publisher's note)

"A doorstop of a book, this collection reaches across Nobel laureate Walcott's career. A defining, definitive postcolonial poet, he writes of St. Lucia, the West, imperialism and identity, and memory and pain." LJ

Waldrop, Keith

Transcendental studies; a trilogy. University of California Press 2009 201p (New California poetry) $50; pa $19.95 **811**
 1. Poetry -- By individual authors
 ISBN 978-0-520-25877-8; 978-0-520-25878-5 pa
 LC 2008-25958

National Book Award: Poetry (2009)

"Comprising three sequences—each almost a book in itself—plus an epilogue, it is an extended philosophical meditation on what are, broadly, the major themes of all poetry: perception, the imagination, the body, and how the human inner life interacts with the larger world. In mostly short, jagged free verse pieces, Waldrop goes at these lofty concepts head-on in accessible, if cerebral, language." Publ Wkly

Walker, Alice, 1944-

Hard times require furious dancing; new poems. foreword and illustrations by Shiloh McCloud. New World Library 2010 165p il $18 **811**
 1. Poetry -- By individual authors
 ISBN 978-1-57731-930-6
 LC 2010-29972

In this poetry collection, the author "writes of loss and disappointment, and the strength that rises from meeting them unflinchingly. . . . These are powerful anthems of womanhood and age, although just as likely to be empowering to men and to the not-yet-old." Booklist

Taking the arrow out of the heart; Alice Walker. Atria / 37 INK 2018 256 p. $25 **811**
 1. Women authors 2. Poetry -- Collections
 ISBN 1501179527; 9781501179525

In this book, author Alice Walker "shares a timely collection of nearly seventy works of passionate and powerful poetry that bears witness to our troubled times, while also chronicling a life well-lived. From poems of painful self-inquiry, to celebrating the simple beauty of baking frittatas, Walker offers us a window into her magical, at times difficult, and liberating world of activism, love, hope and, above all, gratitude." (Publisher's note)

Warren, Robert Penn

★ The **collected** poems of Robert Penn Warren; edited by John Burt; with a foreword by Harold Bloom. Louisiana State Univ. Press 1998 xxvi, 830p $44.95 **811**
 1. Poetry -- By individual authors
 ISBN 0-8071-2333-1
 LC 98-26104

"This immense volume gathers 15 books of poetry—as well as uncollected verse from the beginning and end of his writing life—from a formidable American man of letters and our first poet laureate. . . . Scholars will especially cherish the careful, copious textual and explanatory notes provided by Warren's literary executor Burt . . . and fans of American poetry and literary history alike should welcome this opportunity to explore the prodigious oeuvre of one of the New Criticism's most forceful, convincing proponents." Publ Wkly

Wheatley, Phillis

The **poems** of Phillis Wheatley; edited with an introduction by Julian D. Mason, Jr. rev & enl ed; University of N.C. Press 1989 235p hardcover o.p. pa $22.95 **811**
 1. Poetry -- By individual authors
 ISBN 0-8078-4245-1 pa
 LC 88-23280

First published 1966

This volume contains all of the poems and letters known to have been written by Wheatley, America's first significant black woman writer

Whitman, Walt

★ **Complete** poetry and collected prose. Library of Am. 1982 1380p $35; pa $17.95 **811**
 1. Poetry -- By individual authors
 ISBN 0-940450-02-X; 1-883011-35-3 pa
 LC 81-20768

"Presented here is the great culminating edition of 1891-92, the last supervised by Whitman himself. Whitman's prose, no less extraordinary, includes reminiscences of 19th-century New York City and notes on the Civil War, especially his service in Washington hospitals and glimpses of President Lincoln." Publisher's Note

★ **Leaves** of grass; edited and with a new afterword by David S. Reynolds. 150th anniversary ed.; Oxford University Press 2005 167p $23 **811**
 1. Poetry -- By individual authors
 ISBN 0-19-518342-8
 LC 2004-26509

First published 1855

"The book, radical in form and content, takes its title from the themes of fertility, universality, and cyclical life. . . . As he revised and added to the original edition, Whitman arranged the poems in a significant autobiographical order." Reader's Ency. 4th edition

★ **Selected** poems; Harold Bloom, editor. Library of Am. 2003 xxxi, 221p (American poets project) $20 **811**
 1. Poetry -- By individual authors
 ISBN 1-931082-32-4
 LC 2002-32124

The editor "is concerned with Whitman's construction of his all-encompassing persona, and he selects with that in mind. . . . Bloom connects Whitman's project to the thesis of his The American Religion (1992) that the tendency of religion in America is to replace God with man, and with the fragments, Bloom presents explicit evidence of the attempt." Booklist

Includes bibliographical references

Whittier, John Greenleaf

Selected poems; Brenda Wineapple, editor. Library of America 2004 xxvii, 187p $20 **811**
 1. Poetry -- By individual authors
 ISBN 978-1-931082-59-4; 1-931082-59-6
 LC 2003-60483

"Touching and effective as [many of] these poems are, there is a longer one that ensures Whittier's place in our canon. Of course I have 'SnowBound' in mind. This poem of over nine hundred lines evokes a rural way of life, already past when it was written, in its memories of a family isolated in their farmhouse for a week by a blizzard. . . . This new selection may not restore Whittier to the schoolroom wall, but surely it will help readers reassess the author of one major long poem and a score of attractive lyrics and narratives that deserve their place in our poetic tradition." Sewanee Rev

Wicker, Marcus

Silencer; Marcus Wicker. Mariner Books 2017 73 p. (paperback) $15.99   **811**

1. Grief -- Poetry 2. African Americans -- Poetry 3. American poetry -- 21st century 4. African Americans -- 21st century -- Poetry 5. African American men -- 21st century -- Poetry 6. African American young men -- 21st century -- Poetry

ISBN 9781328715586; 9781328715548

LC 2017014165

This book of poetry, by Marcus Wicker, sings out the dangers for a young black man "of unspoken taboos present on quiet Midwestern cul-de-sacs and in stifling professional settings, the dangers in closing the window on 'a rainbow coalition of cops doing calisthenics around/a six-foot, three-hundred-fifty-pound man, choked back into the earth for what/looked a lot, to me, like sport.'" (Publisher's note)

"In bold, brash, open-hearted poems delivered with satisfying sass, Wicker, author of the National Poetry Series-winning Maybe the Saddest Thing, reflects on simply being while black." LJ

Wilbur, Richard, 1921-2017

Anterooms; new poems and translations. Houghton Mifflin Harcourt 2010 63p $20   **811**

1. Poetry -- By individual authors

ISBN 978-0-547-35811-6; 0-547-35811-3

LC 2010-05772

"The better work in Anterooms, however limited in quantity, is as good as anything Wilbur has ever written, and upholds certain virtues other poets would do well to acknowledge, even if they travel roads different from the relatively straight one Wilbur has followed." N Y Times Book Rev

★ **Collected** poems, 1943-2004. Harcourt 2004 608p il $35   **811**

1. Poetry -- By individual authors

ISBN 0-15-101105-2

LC 2004-9228

A comprehensive collection of works written throughout the course of the poet's more than sixty-year career includes "In Trackless Woods" and several new and previously unpublished pieces

"Technically, Wilbur remains assured and impressive; he is the premier American master of formal verse. His knowledge has expanded with his life, and his wit has grown in humor while mellowing linguistically. . . . He's indispensable." Booklist

Williams, C. K.

★ **Collected** poems. Farrar, Straus and Giroux 2006 682p $40   **811**

1. Poetry -- By individual authors

ISBN 978-0-374-12652-0; 0-374-12652-6

LC 2005-51867

"This weighty, even daunting, tome shows new and old readers the long arc of this Pulitzer Prize and National Book Award winner's career, from the morbid sanguinities of his apprentice work to the careful, moving, stanzaic focus evident in 21 new poems." Publ Wkly

Williams, Jonathan

★ **Jubilant** thicket; new & selected poems. Jonathan Williams. Copper Canyon Press 2005 pa $20   **811**

1. Poetry -- By individual authors

ISBN 1-55659-202-7

LC 2004-20436

"Pared down from 1,450 works over 55 years, this selection features jaunty dances through naughty woods . . . , jokes to and about Ezra Pound, selected listings from the Western Carolina Telephone Company phone book, limericks, 'meta-fours' (poems in which each line has four words), a poem for each Mahler symphony and acrostics using the names of friends like Guy Davenport. . . . By the end of the book, it becomes clear that Williams can make a verse out of whatever's at hand; the result is a kind of commonplace book for a life lived, with wry but inextinguishable enthusiasm, in the company of artists and arts." Publ Wkly

Williams, William Carlos

★ The **collected** poems of William Carlos Williams. New Directions 1986 2v v1 $40; v1 pa $23.95; v2 $38; v2 pa $22.95   **811**

1. Poetry -- By individual authors

ISBN 0-8112-0999-7 v1; 0-8112-1187-8 v1 pa; 0-8112-1063-4 v2; 0-8112-1188-6 v2 pa

"Williams's poetry is firmly rooted in the commonplace detail of everyday American life. He conceived of the poem as an object: a record of direct experience that deals with the local and the particular. He abandoned conventional rhyme and meter in an effort to reduce the barrier between the reader and his consciousness of his immediate surroundings. . . . Williams's original approach to poetry, his insistence on the importance of the ordinary, and his successful attempts at making his verse as 'tactile' as the spoken word had a far-reaching effect on American poetry." Reader's Ency. 4th edition

Paterson; prepared by Christopher MacGowan. rev ed; New Directions 1992 311p hardcover o.p. pa $15.95   **811**

1. Poetry -- By individual authors

ISBN 978-0-8112-1298-4; 0-8112-1298-X

LC 92-22956

First published 1963

"Set in Paterson, N.J., the poem is a statement on contemporary civilization. Williams uses one dominant metaphor throughout: the city is the human mind beside the river of time; the language of contemporary events (the waterfall) gives the only kind of meaning possible in the flux of time. The poem is composed of lyrics, narrative episodes, prose interludes, bits of letters, etc., to comprise an ecstatic statement on human life." Herzberg. Reader's Ency of Am Lit

Winder, Elizabeth

Pain, Parties, Work; Sylvia Plath in New York, Summer 1953. Elizabeth Winder. HarperCollins 2013 288 p. (hardcover) $25.99   **811**

1. New York (N.Y.)

ISBN 0062085492; 9780062085498

This biography, by Elizabeth Winder, follows "a young Sylvia Plath and the life-changing month that would lay the groundwork for her seminal novel, 'The Bell Jar.' In May of 1953, a twenty-one-year-old Plath arrived in New York City. . . . She was supposed to be having the time of her life. But what would follow was, in Plath's words, twenty-six days of pain, parties, and work, that ultimately changed the course of her life." (Publisher's note)

Words for the hour; a new anthology of American Civil War poetry. edited by Faith Barrett and Cristanne Miller. University of Massachusetts Press 2005 xxx, 401p il lib bdg $80; pa $27.95   **811**

1. War poetry 2. American poetry -- Collections 3. United States

-- History -- 1861-1865, Civil War -- Poetry
ISBN 1-55849-510-X lib bdg; 1-55849-509-6 pa

LC 2005-18477

For this collection, the editors "limit their selection to work written between 1834 and 1891 by poets who lived through and often actively participated in antebellum, wartime, and aftermath events. . . . An interpretational, literary, and documentary monument." Booklist

Includes bibliographical references

Wright, C. D.

One with others; [a little book of her days] Copper Canyon Press 2010 168p pa $18 **811**

1. Poetry -- By individual authors 2. African Americans -- Civil rights -- Poetry
ISBN 978-1-55659-324-6; 1-55659-324-4

LC 2010-16789

National Book Award Finalist: Poetry (2010)

"In August, 1969, a Memphis man known as Sweet Willie Wine led a group of black men on a four-day March Against Fear, from West Memphis to Little Rock, passing through the small towns of the Arkansas delta. . . . [This book] tells the story of the march, and of the only outsider to join it, a small-town white woman, Margaret Kaelin McHugh, whom Wright calls V. . . . [It] represents Wright's most audacious experiment yet in loading up lyric with evidentiary fact. . . . An affecting element of this book is the way its elegiac impulses accord with, even as they chafe against, the documentary impulses." New Yorker

★ **Steal** away; selected and new poems. Copper Canyon Press 2002 235p $25; pa $17 **811**

1. Poetry -- By individual authors
ISBN 1-55659-172-1; 1-55659-194-2 pa

LC 2001-7423

Wright's "poems are crazy quilts constructed out of bits of conversation, a to-do list, dreams, a treatment for a harrowing silent film, and a saxophone solo, but Wright also offers sophisticated readings of the routines and cycle of ordinary life, and ponders the amazing persistence of the ever-hungry body and the tricky mind. It's a boon to have such a wealth of her crackling, intelligent, erotic, 'painfully beautiful,' keep-you-on-your-toes poems in one place. New works accompany selections from nine previous, mostly out of print collections, and all are electrifying in their clear-eyed reports on desire, determination, and survival." Booklist

Wright, Charles

★ **Negative** blue; selected later poems. Farrar, Straus & Giroux 2000 206p $23; pa $15 **811**

1. Poetry -- By individual authors
ISBN 0-374-22020-4; 0-374-52773-3 pa

LC 99-36987

The author "collects a decade's worth of striking description and laid-back meditation in this sample of work from his last three books. . . . Wright's power lies less in whole poems than in lines within them: those linear strenghts owe something to Ezra Pound, and something more to the antiphonal balances of the Psalms. Wright ends the volume with seven new short poems." Publ Wkly

Wright, Jay

★ **Transfigurations**; collected poems. Louisiana State Univ. Press 2000 619p $59.95; pa $24.95 **811**

1. Poetry -- By individual authors
ISBN 0-8071-2629-2; 0-8071-2630-6 pa

LC 00-40560

"Lyric poetry is a way of compressing experience into a heightened

moment, but what happens when the experience is one of wanting not to be contained? Wright is an African-American poet who has contended with this dilemma for the last thirty years, and the result is a substantial collection of work. His forcefully musical rhythms drive even poems of everyday experience to a pleasingly contradictory transport. And the later, meditative poems are bound to the world by their attention to the sensual within the spiritual." New Yorker

Xie, Jenny

Eye level; poems. Jenny Xie. Graywolf Press 2018 80 p. (alk. paper) $16 **811**

1. Loneliness 2. Poetry -- Collections 3. American poetry -- 21st century
ISBN 9781555978020

LC 2017938013

National Book Award Finalist: Poetry (2018)

This poetry collection, by Jenny Xie, "takes us far and near, to Phnom Penh, Corfu, Hanoi, New York, and elsewhere, as we travel closer and closer to the acutely felt solitude that centers this searching, moving collection. Animated by a restless inner questioning, these poems meditate on the forces that moor the self and set it in motion, from immigration to travel to estranging losses and departures." (Publisher's note)

Includes bibliographical references (page 79)

Young, Kevin

Ardency; a chronicle of the Amistad rebels. compiled from authentic sources by Kevin Lowell Young. Alfred A. Knopf 2011 249p il map $27.95 **811**

1. Slavery -- Poetry 2. Amistad (Schooner) -- Poetry 3. Poetry -- By individual authors
ISBN 0307267644; 9780307267641

LC 2010-30007

"Young gathers here a chorus of voices that tells the story of the Africans who mutinied onboard the slave ship Amistad." (Publisher's note)

This poetry collection "chronicles the slave mutiny aboard the schooner Amistad in 1839. This three-part book focuses on the 53 Africans who rebelled against their would-be slave owners. Young expertly blends cultural and social history as well as religion to dramatize the lives of the rebels. His evocative use of language—punctuated with stunning metaphors—keeps the historical context clear while moving the gripping true story forward." Libr J

Brown; poems. Kevin Young. Alfred A. Knopf 2018 176 p. (hardcover) $27 **811**

1. Popular culture -- Poetry 2. African Americans -- Poetry
ISBN 9781524732547

LC 2017029270

This book, by Kevin Young, presents "thirty-two taut poems and poetic sequences, including an oratorio based on Mississippi 'barkeep, activist, waiter' Booker Wright that was performed at Carnegie Hall and the vibrant sonnet cycle 'De La Soul Is Dead,' about the days when hip-hop was growing up. . . . [The poems] remind us that blackness and brownness tell an ongoing story." (Publisher's note)

Zapruder, Matthew

Come on all you ghosts; Matthew Zapruder. Copper Canyon Press 2010 xi, 111p (alk. paper) $16 **811**

1. American poetry 2. Poetry -- Collections 3. Heroes and heroines -- Poetry 4. Poetry -- By individual authors
ISBN 1556593228; 9781556593222

LC 2010016787

This book of poetry is written by Matthew Zapruder, the winner of the William Carlos Williams Award. "The title poem is an elegy for heroes and mentors—from David Foster Wallace to Zapruder's father—and demonstrates a[n] . . . expansive range for the poet, highlighting as well a larger body of poetry that . . . wrestles with the desires to live rightly, to make art, and to confront the vast events of the day." (Publisher's note) "Zapruder invokes a variety of second persons: sometimes it's a particular intimate, as in . . . 'Letter to a Lover' or . . . 'Poem for Hannah,' sometimes a recognizable public figure, as in . . . 'Poem for Ferlinghetti.' . . . Greeting and address help the poet to escape the solitary confinement of consciousness." (LA Review of Books)

The poet "speaks 'with a voice that pretends to be shy/ and actually is, always in search of the question/ that might make you ask me one in return.' In his . . . signature, meandering style, he'll often begin with simple, even childlike observations ('Oh this Diet Coke is really good') that set off associative chains in search of subjects that resonate, psychologically or philosophically, with past personal experiences. . . . Seeming to discover themselves as they go, Zapruder's improvisations (or so they appear) enlist the reader as coexplorer, stumbling into candid self-revelations ('I am also/ always balancing/ on the smooth blade of not/ letting other people down') or surreal quips ('I feel like an elk getting a pelvic exam') with wide-eyed grace." Libr J

Zukofsky, Louis

Selected poems; Charles Bernstein, editor. Library of America 2006 xxvii, 172p $20   **811**

1. Poetry -- By individual authors
ISBN 978-1-93108-295-2

LC 2006-40808

"Contemporary poet Charles Bernstein uses these pages skillfully to present a compact but diverse selection of Zukofsky's writing, and he supplies a cogent introduction to both the biography and the poetics." Tikkun

811.008   American poetry – Collections

Black girl magic; edited by Mahogany L. Browne, Idrissa Simmonds, and Jamila Woods; foreword by Patricia Smith. Haymarket Books 2018 264 p. $19.95   **811.008**

1. American poetry -- 21st century 2. American poetry -- African American authors
ISBN 1608468577; 9781608468577

LC 2018055335

This poetry book in the BreakBeat Poets series, focuses "on some of the most exciting Black women writing today. This anthology breaks up the myth of hip-hop as a boys' club, and asserts the truth that the cypher is a feminine form. . . . Poet and vocalist Jamila Woods was raised in Chicago, and graduated from Brown University, where she earned a BA in Africana Studies and Theatre & Performance Studies. . . . Idrissa Simmonds is a fiction writer and poet." (Publisher's note)

811.54   American poetry – 194 -1999

Ashbery, John, 1927-

Commotion of the Birds; New Poems. John Ashbery. HarperCollins 2016 112 p. $22.99   **811.54**

1. American poetry
ISBN 0062565095; 9780062565099

This collection of poems, by John Ashbery, showcases his "mastery of a staggering range of voices and his singular lyric agility: wry, frank, contemplative, resigned, bemused, and ecstatic. The poet in this new collection is at once removed from and immersed in the terrain of his

examination. Disarmingly conversational, he invites the reader to join him in looking out onto the future with humor, curiosity, and insight." (Publisher's note)

"From a much-honored poet whose works are still best for adventurous readers, these pieces are for lovers of modern poetry not based on narrative or landscape." LJ

Boruch, Marianne, 1950-

Eventually one dreams the real thing; Marianne Boruch. Copper Canyon Press 2016 xi, 127 p.p (pb: alk. paper) $15   **811.54**

1. Poetry -- Collections 2. American poetry
ISBN 9781556594915

LC 2015032450

In this book of poems, "Marianne Boruch displays a historical omnipresence, as she converses with Dickinson, envisions Turner painting, and empathizes with Arthur Conan Doyle. She looks unabashedly at the brutality of recent history, from drone warfare to the disaster in New Orleans from Hurricane Katrina. Poems that turn her gaze towards childhood, nature, animals, and her own poetics are patches of light in the collection's chiaroscuro." (Publisher's note)

"Only a poet as accomplished as Boruch (Cadaver, Speak) could make such beautiful verse while leading us through the everyday, of life's subtle, steady shiftings..." LJ.

Collins, Billy, 1941-

★ The **rain** in Portugal; Billy Collins. Random House 2016 128 p. (ebook) $65; (hardcover: acid-free paper) $26   **811.54**

1. Poetry -- Collections
ISBN 9780399588303; 9780679644064

LC 2016008639

This poetry collection "sheds [poet Billy] Collins's ironic light on such subjects as travel and art, cats and dogs, loneliness and love, beauty and death. His tones range from the whimsical . . . to the elegiac in a reaction to the death of Seamus Heaney. A student of the everyday, here Collins contemplates a weather vane, a still life painting, the calendar, and a child lost at a beach." (Publisher's note)

"Another worthwhile collection from two-time Poet Laureate Collins, certain to please his large readership and a good place for readers new to Collins to begin, with at least half a dozen poems as fine as any he has written thus far." LJ

Collins, Martha, 1940-

Admit One; An American Scrapbook. by Martha Collins. University of Pittsburgh Press 2016 89 p. (Pitt poetry series) $15.95   **811.54**

1. Poetry -- Collections 2. Racism -- Poetry 3. Eugenics -- Poetry
ISBN 0822964058; 9780822964056

This book of poems, by Martha Collins, "is poised at the juncture between the lyric and ethics. . . . Collins has addressed some of the most traumatic social issues of the twentieth century . . . in supple and complex poems." (Publisher's note)

"Despite its innocuous-sounding title, Collins' (White Papers, 2012) eighth poetry collection is an unflinching look at the underpinnings of racism in the U.S." Booklist

Includes bibliographical references (pages 86-89)

Gizzi, Peter

★ **Archeophonics**; Peter Gizzi. Wesleyan University Press 2016 108 p. (cloth: alk. paper) $24.95; (ebook) $18.99 **811.54**

1. Poetry -- Collections

ISBN 0819576808; 9780819576804; 9780819576811
LC 2016021168
National Book Award Finalist: Poetry (2016)

This book, by Peter Gizzi, "is a series of discrete poems that are linked by repeated phrases and words, and its themes and nothing less than joy, outrage, loss, transhistorical thought, and day-to-day life. It is a private book of public and civic concerns." (Publisher's note)

"Award-winning poet Gizzi here uses spare, focused language to reflect on language itself: its origins, structure, uses, and music." LJ

Hall, Donald, 1928-2018

★ The **selected** poems of Donald Hall; Donald Hall. Houghton Mifflin Harcourt 2015 160 p. (hardcover) $22; (ebook) $22 **811.54**

1. Poetry -- Collections
ISBN 9780544555600; 9780544555617
LC 2015004341
National Book Award Longlist: Poetry (2016)

In this book, "former poet laureate Donald Hall selects [his] essential work. . . . Instead of creating new poems, he has looked back over his astonishingly rich body of work and hand-picked poems for this final, concise volume that will delight, and endure." (Publisher's note)

"Hall's best work combines these goals with a very dry humor, an almost too-mild regret; much of it stretches out over pages at an unrhymed, close-cut, dignified length." Pub Wkly

Karr, Mary

Tropic of squalor; poems. Mary Karr. HarperCollins 2018 96 p. $22.99 **811.54**

1. Poetry -- Collections 2. American poetry -- Women authors
ISBN 0062699822; 9780062699824

In this poetry collection, author Mary Karr "dares to address the numinous--that mystery some of us hope towards in secret, or maybe dare to pray to. The 'squalor' of meaninglessness that every thoughtful person wrestles with sits at the core of human suffering, and Karr renders it with power--illness, death, love's agonized disappointments." (Publisher's note)

"Karr's poems are thrilling in their vitality, dazzle, nerve, longing, and camouflaged depth." Booklist

Lima, Frank

Incidents of travel in poetry; new and selected poems. Frank Lima; edited by Garrett Caples, Julien Poirier. City Lights Books 2016 316 p. (softcover) $19.95 **811.54**

1. Latinos (U.S.) 2. Poetry -- Collections
ISBN 9780872866676
LC 2015035462

This book, by Frank Lima, edited by Garrett Caples and Julien Poirier, is a "re-introduction to the work of this major Latino poet. . . . [It] includes selections from Lima's previous volumes, tracing his development from his early snapshots of street life to his later surrealist-influenced abstract lyricism. The bulk of the collection comes from his later unpublished manuscripts." (Publisher's note)

"Highly recommended for reasons that go beyond historical completeness." LJ

Marshall, Megan

Elizabeth Bishop; A Miracle for Breakfast. Megan Marshall. Houghton Mifflin Harcourt 2017 384 p. (hardcover) $30 **811.54**

1. Women poets -- Biography 2. American poets -- Biography
ISBN 9780544617308; 0544617304

LC 2016043922

This biography of American poet Elizabeth Bishop by Megan Marshall reveals "a much darker childhood than has been known, a secret affair, and the last chapter of . . . [Bishop's] passionate romance with Brazilian modernist designer Lota de Macedo Soares. These elements of Bishop's life, along with her friendships with fellow poets Marianne Moore and Robert Lowell, both important champions of her work, are brought to life with novelistic intensity." (Publisher's note)

"But even if the poet herself remains elusive in this telling, this book is still a generous, enjoyable piece of work." Pub Wkly

Includes bibliographical references and index.

Mead, Jane

World of made and unmade; Jane Mead. Alice James Books 2016 100 p. (softcover: acid-free paper) $15.95 **811.54**

1. Death 2. Poetry -- Collections
ISBN 9781938584329
LC 2016011688
National Book Awards Longlist: Poetry (2016)

This book of poetry by Jane Mead "candidly and openly explores the long process that is death. These resonant poems discover what it means to live, die, and come home again. We're drawn in by sorrow and grief, but also the joys of celebrating a long life and how simple it is to find laughter and light in the quietest and darkest of moments." (Publisher's note)

"This accessible work will appeal to a wide range of readers." LJ

Myles, Eileen

I Must Be Living Twice; New and Selected Poems 1975-2014. by Eileen Myles. HarperCollins 2015 368 p. $16.99; (ebook) $19.59 **811.54**

1. Poetry -- Collections
ISBN 0062389084; 0062389092; 9780062389084; 9780062389091; 9780062389107
LC 2016297462

This collection of poems, by Eileen Myles, "brings together selections from the poet's previous work with a set of bold new poems that reflect her sardonic, unapologetic, and fiercely intellectual literary voice." (Publisher's note)

"Readers will be thrilled not only that this old work is available again, but that the new work is as impressive as ever." Pub Wkly

Perillo, Lucia, 1958-2016

Time will clean the carcass bones; selected and new poems. Lucia Perillo. Copper Canyon Press 2016 239 p. (hardcover) $23 **811.54**

1. Poetry -- Collections
ISBN 9781556594731
LC 2015034497

This book of poetry, by Lucia Perillo, "confronts the failings and wonder of nature, particularly the frail and resilient human body. This generous collection draws upon five previous volumes, including books selected as a New York Times '100 Notable Books of the Year' and as a finalist for the Pulitzer Prize." (Publisher's note)

"With this volume that spans more than 20 years and six poetry collections, Perillo (On the Spectrum of Possible Deaths), a poet, fiction writer, and MacArthur Fellow, exhibits her range and depth in exquisite yet unfussy poems." Pub Wkly

Phillips, Carl, 1959-

Wild is the wind; Carl Phillips. Farrar, Straus & Giroux 2018 55 p. (hardcover) $23 **811.54**

1. Poetry -- Collections 2. American poetry
ISBN 9780374717100; 0374290261; 9780374290269

LC 2017025629

In this book, "Carl Phillips reflects on love as depicted in the jazz standard for which the book is named—love at once restless, reckless, and yet desired for its potential to bring stability. In the process, he pitches estrangement against communion, examines the past as history versus the past as memory, and reflects on the past's capacity both to teach and to mislead us—also to make us hesitate in the face of love, given the loss and damage that are, often enough, love's fallout." (Publisher's note)

Includes bibliographical references

Plath, Sylvia, 1932-1963

The **letters** of Sylvia Plath; 1940-1956. Sylvia Plath. HarperCollins 2017 1424 p. $45   **811.54**
1. American poets -- 20th century -- Correspondence
ISBN 0062740431; 9780062740434

LC 2017047516

This book presents "the first volume in the definitive, complete collection of the letters of [poet] Sylvia Plath--most never before seen. . . . [It] is the breathtaking compendium of this prolific writer's correspondence with more than 120 people, including family, friends, contemporaries, and colleagues. . . . [It] also includes twenty-seven of Plath's own elegant line drawings . . . as well as twenty-two previously unpublished photographs." (Publisher's note)

Rich, Adrienne, 1929-2012

★ **Collected** poems; 1950-2012. Adrienne Rich. W W Norton & Co Inc 2016 1216 p. (ebook) $50; (hardcover) $50   **811.54**
1. American poetry -- Collections
ISBN 9780393285123; 9780393285116

LC 2016009163

Pulitzer Prize Finalist: Poetry (2017)

This poetry collection, by Adrienne Rich, "traces the evolution of her poetry, from her earliest work, which was formally exact and decorous, to her later work, which became increasingly radical in both its free-verse form and feminist and political content. The entire body of her poetry is on display in this vast volume, including the National Book Award–winning 'Diving Into the Wreck' and her prize-winning 'Atlas of the Difficult World.'" (Publisher's note)

"A collection for the ages showcasing the work of a valiantly forthright, artistically adventurous, compassionate, and immensely influential poet of conscience." Booklist

Includes bibliographical references and index

Rivard, David, 1953-

Standoff; poems. David Rivard. Graywolf Press 2016 81 p. (paperback) $16   **811.54**
1. American poetry -- 21st century
ISBN 9781555977450; 9781555979416; 1555977456

LC 2015953718

In this poetry book author David Rivard "asks an essential question: In a world of noise, of global anxiety and media distraction, how can we speak to each other with honesty? . . . [His] poems scan the shifting horizons of our world. . . . The work of these poems is a counterweight to the work of the world. It wants to deepen the mystery we are to ourselves, stretching toward acceptance and tenderness in ways that are hard-won and true, even if fleeting." (Publisher's note)

"Rivard's tender collection examines death and the inevitability of loss, as well as the desperate, eternal search for self-meaning." Booklist

Rogers, Pattiann, 1940-

Quickening fields; Pattiann Rogers. Penguin Books 2017 ix, 114 p.p (Penguin poets) (softcover) $20   **811.54**
1. Poetry -- Collections
ISBN 9780143131328; 9781524705060

LC 2016053786

This book, by Pattiann Rogers, "gathers fifty-three poems that focus on the wide variety of life forms present on earth and their unceasing zeal to exist, their constant 'push against the beyond' and the human experience among these lives. Whether a glassy filament of flying insect, a spiny spider crab, a swath of switch grass, barking short-eared owls, screeching coyotes, or racing rat-tailed sperm, all are testifying to their complete devotion to being." (Publisher's note)

"With this harmonious and lyrical confluence of science, sex, nature, and myth, poet and essayist Rogers (Holy Heathen Rhapsody) fills a distinctive void in modern writing." Pub Wkly

Shaughnessy, Brenda, 1970-

So much synth; Brenda Shaughnessy. Copper Canyon Press 2016 88 p. (ebook) $14.99; (hardcover) $22   **811.54**
1. American poetry -- 21st century
ISBN 9781619321557; 9781556594878

LC 2015042109

"Subversions of idiom and cliché punctuate [poet Brenda] Shaughnessy's fourth collection as she approaches middle age and revisits the memories, romances, and music of adolescence. 'So Much Synth' is a brave and ferocious collection composed of equal parts femininity, pain, pleasure, and synthesizer. While Shaughnessy tenderly winces at her youthful excesses, we humbly catch glimpses of our own." (Publisher's note)

"Shaughnessy (Our Andromeda) finds ever new ways to rend the heart in this biting and poignant anthropological study of girlhood and adolescence." Pub Wkly

Smith, Patricia

★ **Incendiary** art; poems. Patricia Smith. TriQuarterly Books/Northwestern University Press 2017 144 p. (pbk.: alk. paper) $18.95   **811.54**
1. African Americans -- Poetry 2. Poetry -- Women authors -- Collections
ISBN 9780810134331; 9780810134348

LC 97023613

LA Times Book Prize: Poetry (2017)
Pulitzer Prize Finalist: Poetry (2018)

In this poetry collection, poet "Patricia Smith fearlessly confronts the tyranny against the black male body and the tenacious grief of mothers. . . . She writes an exhaustive lament for mothers of the 'dark magicians,' and revisits the devastating murder of Emmett Till. These dynamic sequences serve as a backdrop for present-day racial calamities and calls for resistance. Smith embraces elaborate and eloquent language." (Publisher's note)

"In searing elegies, laments, and protests, Smith presents the smoldering facts about the killing of black men in America and the anguish of their mothers with autopsy-specific attention to the battle scars of body and soul." Booklist

Stanford, Frank

What about this; the collected poems of Frank Stanford. Frank Stanford; edited by Michael Wiegers; introduction by Dean Young. Copper Canyon Press 2015 640 p. illustrations (hardcover) $40   **811.54**
1. American poetry -- Collections

ISBN 9781556594687

LC 2014045989

National Book Critics Circle Award Finalist: Poetry (2015)

This poetry collection, by Frank Stanford, edited by Michael Wiegers, is a posthumously-edited volume collecting a large selection of the literary works of Frank Stanford. It "includes hundreds of previously unpublished poems, a short story, an interview, and is richly illustrated with draft poems, photographs, and odd ephemera." (Publisher's note)

"Stanford demanded of poetry that it 'mean and sing,' and this is the definitive document of his uncanny ability to do just that." Pub Wkly

Williams, C. K. (Charles Kenneth), 1936-2015

Falling ill; Last Poems. C. K. Williams. Farrar, Straus & Giroux 2017 64 p. (hardcover) $23; (ebook) $60   **811.54**
1. Death -- Poetry 2. Grief -- Poetry 3. Loss (Psychology) -- Poetry 4. Mortality -- Poetry
ISBN 9780374152208; 9780374715465

LC 2016025612

"Over the past half century, the great shape-shifting poet C. K. Williams took upon himself the poet's task: to record with candor and ardor 'the burden of being alive.' In . . . his final volume of poems, he brings this task to its conclusion, bearing witness to a restless mind's encounter with the brute fact of the body's decay, the spirit's erasure." (Publisher's note)

"Williams's masterly use of irony underscores this stirring collection's intimate content. Highly recommended." LJ

Wright, C. D., 1949-2016

★ **Shallcross**; C.D. Wright. Copper Canyon Press 2016 153 p. (hardback) $23   **811.54**
1. Poetry -- Collections
ISBN 1556594968; 9781556594960

LC 2015043519

This book of poetry, by C.D. Wright, "ranges across seven poetic sequences, including a collaborative suite responding to photographic documentation of murder sites in New Orleans." (Publisher's note)

"Wright possessed a gift for mining the rifts and limitations that define and haunt human experience—a power fully displayed here." Pub Wkly

Young, Kevin

Blue laws; selected & uncollected poems, 1995-2015. Kevin Young. Alfred A. Knopf 2016 608 p. (ebook) $65; (hardcover) $30   **811.54**
1. American poetry 2. Poetry -- Collections
ISBN 9781101946947; 9780385351508

LC 2015017451

National Book Awards Longlist: Poetry (2016)

"'Blue Laws' gathers poems written over the past two decades, drawing from all nine of Kevin Young's previously published books of poetry and including a number of uncollected, often unpublished, poems. . . . This collection provides a grand tour of a poet whose personal poems and political poems are equally riveting." (Publisher's note)

"Young is an essential, dynamic, and resonant poet, and this commanding, 20-year retrospective belongs in libraries large and small." Booklist

Includes bibliographical references.

811.6   American poetry – 2000

Asghar, Fatimah

If they come for us; poems. Fatimah Asghar. Random House Inc 2018 128 p. $16   **811.6**
1. Identity (Psychology) 2. Poetry -- Collections 3. Pakistani American women
ISBN 052550978X; 9780525509783

In this book, author Fatimah Asghar's "poems at once bear anguish, joy, vulnerability, and compassion, while also exploring the many facets of violence: how it persists within us, how it is inherited across generations, and how it manifests itself in our relationships. In experimental forms and language both lyrical and raw, Asghar seamlessly braids together marginalized people's histories with her own understanding of identity, place, and belonging." (Publisher's note)

Borzutzky, Daniel

★ The **performance** of becoming human; Daniel Borzutzky. Brooklyn Arts Press 2016 98 p. (pbk) $18   **811.6**
1. Globalization
ISBN 1936767465; 9781936767465

LC 2015028529

National Book Award: Poetry (2016)

In this book of poetry, author Daniel Borzutzky "returns to confront the various ways nation-states and their bureaucracies absorb and destroy communities and economies. . . . To become human is to navigate borders, including the fuzzy borders of institutions, the economies of privatization, overdevelopment, and underdevelopment, under which humans endure state-sanctioned and systemic abuses in cities, villages, deserts." (Publisher's note)

Chai, Eleanor

Standing water; poems. Eleanor Chai. Farrar, Straus & Giroux 2016 112 p. illustrations (ebook) $40; (hardback) $23   **811.6**
1. Poetry -- Collections 2. American poetry -- 21st century
ISBN 9780374714918; 9780374269487

LC 2015035372

This book of poetry, by Eleanor Chai, "is a journey into the past as well as the present--into the narrative hidden from the poet since birth, as well as the strategies that she has adopted to survive. It is a journey about how we learn to cope with, to perceive and describe, the world. It is a story about savage privilege and deprivation." (Publisher's note)

"A brilliantly formed, gracefully devastating poem sequence about the timeless struggle between men and women, the annihilation of innocence, and the alchemy of the self." Booklist

Choi, Don Mee

Hardly war; Don Mee Choi. Wave Books 2016 97 p. (softcover) $18   **811.6**
1. Poetry -- Collections 2. American poetry -- Korean American authors
ISBN 9781940696218; 9781940696232

LC 2015025698

This book, by Don Mee Choi, "defies history, national identity, and militarism. Using artifacts from Choi's father, a professional photographer during the Korean and Vietnam wars, she combines memoir, image, and opera to explore her paternal relationship and heritage. Here poetry and geopolitics are inseparable twin sisters, conjoined to the belly of a warring empire." (Publisher's note)

"Choi's zany take on militarism and the Korean diaspora may seem absurdist, but it is an inventive and daring waltz that upends what is commonly understood as the 'Forgotten War.'" Pub Wkly.

Fitzgerald, Adam

George Washington; poems. Adam Fitzgerald. Liveright Publishing Corp., a division of W W Norton & Co Inc. 2016 112 p. (hardcover) $25.95; (ebook) $50   **811.6**
     1. Poetry -- Collections 2. American poetry -- 21st century
     ISBN 9781631491009; 9781631491016

             LC 2016018129
   The poems in this collection, by Adam Fitzgerald, "channel the proper names and product placement in the suburban New Jersey memescape of the 1990s. Fitzgerald's catalogs—a world of video games and love songs, entertainment franchises and widespread anomie—seek out the proxies by which millions now live their most intimate experiences, examining everything from sexuality and faith to the spectacles of shopping and mass shootings." (Publisher's note)
   "In a bold turn of artistic versatility, Fitzgerald eschews the high modernist roots of his dazzling first collection, The Late Parade (2003), and plunges full-throttle into the queasy stream of contemporary Americana." Booklist

Forsythe, Kelly

Perennial; Kelly Forsythe. Coffee House Press 2018 75 p. (trade pbk.) $16.95   **811.6**
     1. Violence -- Poetry 2. American poetry -- Collections
     ISBN 9781566895170

             LC 2018000107
   "The events of 1999's Columbine shooting preoccupy [Kelly] Forsythe in these poems, refracting her vision to encompass killer, victim, and herself as a girl, suddenly aware of the precarity of her own life and the porousness of her body to others' gaze, demands, violence. Deeply researched and even more deeply felt, Perennial inhabits landscapes of emerging adulthood and explosive cruelty." (Publisher's note)
   "Forsythe's moving catalogue of a horrific event becomes a diagram of senselessness where minutiae take on a stark and eerie resonance when read beside today's headlines." Publishers' Weekly
   Includes bibliographical references

Gay, Ross, 1974-

Catalog of Unabashed Gratitude; by Ross Gay. University of Pittsburgh Press 2015 112 p. $15.95   **811.6**
     1. Poetry -- Collections
     ISBN 0822963310; 9780822963318
   NAACP Image Award Nominee: Outstanding Literary Work - Poetry (2016)
   National Book Critics Circle Award Finalist: Poetry (2015)
   National Book Award Finalist: Poetry (2015)
   This book of poems, by Ross Gay, "is a sustained meditation on that which goes away—loved ones, the seasons, the earth as we know it—that tries to find solace in the processes of the garden and the orchard. That is, this is a book that studies the wisdom of the garden and orchard, those places where all—death, sorrow, loss—is converted into what might, with patience, nourish us." (Publisher's note)
   "Whether by contemplating the extraordinary within everyday acts (sleeping in clothes, drinking water, buttoning and unbuttoning a shirt), or by entwining past and present as he pays homage to parents, friends, even his former love, Gay embraces the natural cycles of life and death as only an introspective gardener and accomplished poet can." Booklist

Girmay, Aracelis

The black Maria; poems. by Aracelis Girmay. BOA Editions Ltd. 2016 104 p. (softcover: acid-free paper) $16 **811.6**
     1. Poetry -- Collections 2. American poetry -- 21st century

ISBN 9781942683025

             LC 2015043256
   This poetry collection, in the American Poets Continuum Series, by Aracelis Girmay, "investigates African diasporic histories, the consequences of racism within American culture, and the question of human identity. Central to this project is a desire to recognize the lives of Eritrean refugees who have been made invisible by years of immigration crisis, refugee status, exile, and resulting statelessness." (Publisher's note)
   "Girmay effortlessly slips between collective history and personal memory, tackling the subject of black pain without victimizing herself or exploiting the voices of the marginalized." Pub Wkly

Hieu Minh Nguyen

Not here; Hieu Minh Nguyen. Coffee House Press 2018 120 p. (softcover: acid-free paper) $16.99   **811.6**
     1. Desire 2. Loneliness 3. Poetry -- Collections
     ISBN 9781566895095

             LC 2017040746
   Written by Hieu Minh Nguyen, "Not Here is a flight plan for escape and a map for navigating home; a queer Vietnamese American body in confrontation with whiteness, trauma, family, and nostalgia; and a big beating heart of a book. Nguyen's poems ache with loneliness and desire and the giddy terrors of allowing yourself to hope for love, and revel in moments of connection achieved."

Hoagland, Tony, 1953-2018

Priest turned therapist treats fear of God; poems. Tony Hoagland. Graywolf Press 2018 88 p. (alk. paper) $16 **811.6**
     1. Poetry -- Collections 2. American poetry -- 20th century
     ISBN 9781555978075

             LC 2017953461
   In this poetry book author Tony Hoagland "interrogate human nature and contemporary culture with an intimate and wild urgency, located somewhere between outrage, stand-up comedy, and grief. His new poems are no less observant of the human and the worldly, no less skeptical, and no less amusing, but they have drifted toward the greater depths of open emotion. Over six collections, Hoagland's poetry has gotten bigger, more tender, and more encompassing." (Publisher's note)

Hopler, Jay

★ **The Abridged** History of Rainfall; by Jay Hopler. McSweeney's 2016 80 p. $22   **811.6**
     1. Poetry -- Collections
     ISBN 1944211268; 9781944211264

             LC 2016050071
   National Book Award Finalist: Poetry (2016)
   This book of poetry, by Jay Hopler, "documents the struggle to live in the face of great loss, a task that sends him ranging through Florida's torrid subtropics, the mountains of the American West, the streets of Rome, and the Umbrian countryside." (Publisher's note)

Hutchinson, Ishion

★ **House** of lords and commons; poems. Ishion Hutchinson. Farrar, Straus & Giroux 2016 96 p. (ebook) $60; (hardcover) $23   **811.6**
     1. Poetry -- Collections 2. American poetry -- 21st century
     ISBN 9780374714543; 9780374173029

             LC 2015045801
   National Book Critics Circle Award: Poetry (2017)
   In this collection of poems, author Ishion Hutchinson "returns to the difficult beauty of the Jamaican landscape with remarkable lyric precision. Here, the poet holds his world in full focus but at an astonishing angle: from the violence of the seventeenth-century English Civil War as

refracted through a mythic sea wanderer, right down to the dark interior of love." (Publisher's note)

"A challenging collection requiring careful reading to pick out the poet's full intent but definitely worth the effort. Highly recommended." LJ

Kaur, Rupi

Milk and honey; Rupi Kaur. Andrews McMeel Pub 2015 204 p. illustrations (paperback) $14.99; (ebook) $9.99 **811.6**
1. Healing 2. Poetry -- Collections
ISBN 9781449474256; 144947425X; 9781449478650
LC 2015946719

This book by Rupi Kaur "is a collection of poetry and prose about survival. About the experience of violence, abuse, love, loss, and femininity. The book is divided into four chapters, and each chapter serves a different purpose. Deals with a different pain. Heals a different heartache.... [It] takes readers through a journey of the most bitter moments in life and finds sweetness in them because there is sweetness everywhere if you are just willing to look." (Publisher's note)

The **sun** and her flowers; Rupi Kaur. Andrews McMeel Pub. 2017 248 p. illustrations (paperback) $16.99 **811.6**
1. Poetry -- Collections 2. Self-actualization (Psychology) -- Poetry
ISBN 9781449486792; 9781449488895; 1449486797
LC 2017948761

This book, by Rupi Kaur, is "her long-awaited second collection of poetry. A vibrant and transcendent journey about growth and healing. Ancestry and honoring one's roots. Expatriation and rising up to find a home within yourself. Divided into five chapters and illustrated by Kaur, [it] is a journey of wilting, falling, rooting, rising, and blooming. A celebration of love in all its forms." (Publisher's note)

Long Soldier, Layli

★ **Whereas**; Layli Long Soldier. Graywolf Press 2017 114 p. (ebook) $20; (alk. paper) $16 **811.6**
1. Native Americans 2. Poetry -- Collections
ISBN 9781555979614; 9781555977672
LC 2016938845

National Book Critics Circle Award: Poetry (2017)
National Book Award Finalist: Poetry (2017)

This book "confronts the coercive language of the United States government in its responses, treaties, and apologies to Native American peoples and tribes, and reflects that language in its officiousness and duplicity back on its perpetrators. Through ... short lyrics, prose poems, longer narrative sequences, resolutions, and disclaimers, Layli Long Soldier has created [an] innovative text to examine histories, landscapes, her own writing, and her predicament inside national affiliations." (Publisher's note)

Ritvo, Max

★ **Four** reincarnations; Poems. Max Ritvo. Milkweed Editions 2016 96 p. (hardcover) $22 **811.6**
1. Death -- Poetry 2. Cancer -- Poetry 3. Poetry -- Collections 4. American poetry -- 21st century
ISBN 9781571314901; 1571314903
LC 2016030740

In this collection of poems by cancer patient Max Ritvo, he "explores the prospect of death with singular sensitivity, but he is also a poet of life and of love--a cool-eyed assessor of mortality and a fervent champion for his body and its pleasures. Ritvo writes to his wife, exlovers, therapists, fathers, and one mother. He finds something to love and something to lose in everything: Listerine PocketPak breath strips, Indian mythology, wool hats." (Publisher's note)

"Slippery and terrifyingly urgent, funny yet despairingly so, Ritvo (1990–2016) hits all the right notes in an accomplished, surprising, and bizarrely erotic debut made more poignant by his death weeks before publication." Pub Wkly

Schiff, Robyn

A **woman** of property; Robyn Schiff. Penguin Books 2016 81 p. (Penguin Poets) (softcover) $20 **811.6**
1. Poetry -- Collections 2. Poetry -- 21st century
ISBN 9780143128274
LC 2015048702

This book of poems, by Robyn Schiff, "stages an urgent and deeply imperiled boundary dispute where haunting, illusion, the presence of the past, and disembodied voices only further unsettle questions of material and spiritual possession. This is a theatrical book of dilapidated houses and overgrown gardens, of passageways and thresholds, edges, prosceniums, unearthings, and root systems." (Publisher's note)

"Few collections this year are likely to match the subtle intelligence in this third outing from Schiff..." Pub Wkly.

Sharif, Solmaz

★ **Look**; Poems. by Solmaz Sharif. Farrar, Straus & Giroux 2016 96 p. (ebook) $20; $16 **811.6**
1. Poetry -- Collections
ISBN 9781555979409; 1555977448; 9781555977443
LC 2015953717

National Book Award Finalist: Poetry (2016)

This book of poetry, by Solmaz Sharif, "asks us to see the ongoing costs of war as the unbearable loss of human lives and also the insidious abuses against our everyday speech. In this virtuosic array of poems, lists, shards, and sequences, Sharif assembles her family's and her own fragmented narratives in the aftermath of warfare." (Publisher's note)

"In form, content, and execution, Sharif's debut is arguably the most noteworthy book of poetry yet about recent U.S.-led wars in Afghanistan, Iraq, and the greater Middle East." Pub Wkly

Sinclair, Safiya

Cannibal; Safiya Sinclair. University of Nebraska Press 2016 126 p. (paperback: alk. paper) $17.95 **811.6**
1. Jamaican poetry 2. Human body -- Poetry 3. Poetry -- Collections 4. Women -- Identity -- Poetry
ISBN 9780803290631; 9780803295384
LC 2016007774

"The poems in Safiya Sinclair's 'Cannibal' explore Jamaican childhood and history, race relations in America, womanhood, otherness, and exile.... Blooming with intense lyricism and fertile imagery, these full-blooded poems are elegant, mythic, and intricately woven. Here the female body is a dark landscape; the female body is cannibal. Sinclair shocks and delights her readers with her willingness to disorient and provoke." (Publisher's note)

"This is a tight, focused collection, and through her visceral language Sinclair paints the institution of white supremacy as not just an individualized phenomenon, but as a ruthless and menacing force." Pub Wkly

Smith, Tracy K., 1972-

★ **Wade** in the water; poems. Tracy K. Smith. Graywolf Press 2018 83 p. (hardback) $24 **811.6**
1. Poetry -- Collections 2. Slavery in literature 3. American poetry -- African American authors 4. American poetry -- 21st century
ISBN 9781555978136; 9781555978631
LC 2017951515

In this poetry collection, "Tracy K. Smith boldly ties America's contemporary moment both to our nation's fraught founding history and to a sense of the spirit, the everlasting. These are poems of sliding scale: some capture a flicker of song or memory; some collage an array of documents and voices; and some push past the known world into the haunted, the holy." (Publisher's note)

"The sacred and the malevolent are astutely juxtaposed in this beautifully formed, deeply delving, and caring volume." Booklist

Includes bibliographical references (pages 77-81).

Vuong, Ocean

★ **Night** sky with exit wounds; Ocean Vuong. Copper Canyon Press 2016 70 p. (ebook) $14.99; (pbk.) $16   **811.6**
1. American poetry -- 21st century
ISBN 9781619321564; 9781556594953; 155659495X
LC 2015038100

The poems in this book, by Ocean Vuong, winner of the 2016 Whiting Award, "possess a tensile precision reminiscent of Emily Dickinson's work, combined with a Gerard Manley Hopkins-like appreciation for the sound and rhythms of words. Mr. Vuong can create startling images (a black piano in a field, a wedding-cake couple preserved under glass, a shepherd stepping out of a Caravaggio painting) and make the silences and elisions in his verse speak as potently as his words." (New York Times)

"By juxtaposing startling observations with more common images, Vuong forges poems that feel familiar, yet honest and original." Pub Wkly

Youn, Monica

Blackacre; Poems. Monica Youn. Graywolf Press 2016 88 p. (ebook) $20; (alk. paper) $16   **811.6**
1. American poetry 2. American literature
ISBN 9781555979461; 9781555977504
LC 2016931136

National Book Awards Longlist: Poetry (2016)

This book, by Monica Youn, "is a centuries-old legal fiction—a placeholder name for a hypothetical estate. Treacherously lush or alluringly bleak, these poems reframe their subjects as landscape, as legacy—a bereavement, an intimacy, a racial identity. . . . With a surveyor's keenest tools, Youn marks the boundaries of the given, what we have been allotted: acreage that has been ruthlessly fenced, previously tenanted, ploughed and harvested, enriched and depleted." (Publisher's note)

"Youn's mesmerizing collection does the diligent work of presenting an aspect of death and loss from an entirely unique perspective." Booklist

Includes bibliographical references (page 83).

Yu, Josephine

Prayer book of the anxious; Josephine Yu. Elixir Press 2016 96 p. (alk. paper) $17   **811.6**
1. American poetry -- 21st century
ISBN 9781932418583
LC 2015048259

This poetry collection, by Josephine Yu, is a "winner of the 15th Annual Elixir Press Poetry Awards. Contest judge, Sarah Kennedy, says: 'These are smart, savvy poems, but they are also humane in the best sense of that word: interested in the human and compassionate to all beings.'" (Publisher's note)

"With a perceptiveness and poise that serve as a curative balm, Yu brilliantly tackles the notion of healing in a society that can make its most aware citizens ill." Pub Wkly

812   American drama in English

Abbotson, Susan C. W.

Critical companion to Arthur Miller; a literary reference to his life and work. Facts on File 2006 518p il (Facts on File library of American literature) $75   **812**
1. Authors 2. Dramatists 3. Screenwriters
ISBN 0-8160-6194-7; 978-0-8160-6194-5
LC 2006-22902

This book "covers Miller's entire canon, including plays, screenplays, fiction, short stories, and poetry, as well as many of his important essays and critical pieces. Also included are . . . entries on literary, theatrical, and personal figures important to Miller; key terms and topics connected to his work; and various theatrical companies and places with which he has been associated." Publisher's note

Includes bibliographical references

Adler, Stella

★ **Stella** Adler on America's master playwrights; Eugene O'Neill, Thornton Wilder, Clifford Odets, William Saroyan, Tennessee Williams, William Inge, Arthur Miller, Edward Albee. edited and with commentary by Barry Paris. Alfred A. Knopf 2012 xi, 385 p.p ill.   **812**
1. American drama 2. Drama -- Technique 3. American dramatists 4. Drama -- Explication 5. American drama -- 20th century -- History and criticism
ISBN 0679424431; 9780679424437
LC 2012018983

This book by Stella Adler, edited by Barry Paris "Brings together [Adler's] most important lectures on America's plays and playwrights, the giants of the twentieth century, men she knew, loved, and worked with. Adler considers, among them, Eugene O'Neill, . . . Tennessee Williams, . . . Clifford Odets, . . . [and] Arthur Miller." (Publisher's note)

Albee, Edward

★ **Who's** afraid of Virginia Woolf? Scribner Classics 2003 243p $24   **812**
1. New England -- Drama 2. Married people -- Drama 3. College teachers -- Drama
ISBN 0-7432-5525-9
LC 2003-54206

A reissue of the title first published 1962 by Atheneum Pubs.

Characters: 2 men, 2 women. 3 acts. First produced at the Billy Rose Theatre, New York City, October 13, 1962

"The play is a virulent unveiling of the relationship between George, a history professor, and his wife, Martha, the college president's daughter. Another couple, Nick and Honey, get caught in the crossfire of George and Martha's verbal and emotional lacerations, and it becomes clear that each character is engaged in an isolated struggle through a personal hell." Reader's Ency. 4th edition

Auburn, David

Proof; a play. Faber & Faber 2001 83p pa $13   **812**
1. Mathematicians -- Drama 2. Fathers -- Death -- Drama 3. Man-woman relationships -- Drama
ISBN 0-571-19997-6
LC 00-50284

Characters: 2 men, 2 women. 2 acts, 9 scenes. First produced by the Manhattan Theatre Club, New York City, May 23, 2000

"Twenty-five-year-old Catherine, who sacrificed college to care for her mentally ill father (once a brilliant, much-admired mathematician), is left in a kind of limbo after his death. Socially awkward and a bit of a shut-in, she is gruff with Hal, a former student who shows up even before the funeral wanting to root through the countless notebooks her father kept in the years of his decline, hoping to find mathematical gold. On the heels of his arrival comes Claire, Catherine's cosmopolitan, blandly successful, and pushy sister, with plans to sell their father's house and take Catherine . . . with her back to New York." SLJ

Includes bibliographical references and index

Baraka, Imamu Amiri

Dutchman, and The slave; two plays. [by] LeRoi Jones. Morrow 1964 88p hardcover o.p. pa $9.95 **812**

ISBN 978-0-688-21084-7; 0-688-21084-8

In Dutchman Baraka "explores the revolutionary potential of the educated black middle-class intellectual, represented by the protagonist, Clay, a would-be poet. When Clay is exposed as dangerous—that is, as a latent killer—by white society, seductively imaged as a beautiful white woman named Lula, he is summarily executed by that society. The Slave (1964), a fable set in a future of war between the races, continues the theme of black revolutionary militancy." Benet's Reader's Ency of Am Lit

The **Best** American short plays; edited by Howard Stein and Glenn Young. Applause Theatre Bk. Pubs. **812**

1. One act plays 2. Drama -- Collections

This series of annual collections was begun in 1937 under the editorship of Margaret Mayorga with title: Best one-act plays, and published by Dodd, Mead through 1955 (starting in 1953 title changed to The best short plays). Beacon Press published the volumes from 1956 through 1961 when publication was suspended. Resumed 1968 under the editorship of Stanley Richards. From 1981 through 1989 edited by Ramon Delgado. Changed to current title and editors with 1990/1991 volume. Volumes prior to 1988 o.p. Apply to publisher for availability and price of retrospective annuals

In addition to the plays each annual contains brief biographical and bibliographical data about dramatists represented

Butler, Isaac

The **world** only spins forward; the ascent of Angels in America. Isaac Butler and Dan Kois. St. Martin's Press 2018 448 p. $30 **812**

1. Musicals 2. Performing arts

ISBN 1635571766; 9781635571769

In this book, authors "Isaac Butler and Dan Kois offer the definitive account of [the Broadway musical] 'Angels in America' in the most fitting way possible: through oral history, the vibrant conversation and debate of actors. . . . Their intimate storytelling reveals the on- and offstage turmoil of the play's birth--a hard-won miracle beset by artistic roadblocks, technical disasters, and disputes both legal and creative." (Publisher's note)

"Highly recommended for anyone interested in performance, cultural history, and theater." LJ

Cruz, Nilo

Anna in the tropics. Theatre Communications Group 2003 84p pa $12.95 **812**

ISBN 1-55936-232-4

LC 2003-15859

Characters: 5 men, 3 women. 2 acts, 10 scenes. First produced at the New Theatre, Coral Gables, Florida, October 12, 2002

"Set in a cigar factory in Tampa, Florida, in 1929, where the Cuban-American employees have just hired a new 'lector' to read novels to them while they work, Anna and the Tropics is written in the lyrical, somewhat formalized parlance of a folktale. The play is both a piece of

cultural history and a warm-spirited tribute to the transformative power of art." Time

Dowling, Robert M.

Critical companion to Eugene O'Neill; a literary reference to his life and work. Facts On File 2009 2v il (Facts on File library of American literature) set $150 **812**

1. Authors 2. Dramatists 3. Nobel laureates for literature

ISBN 978-0-8160-6675-9; 0-8160-6675-2

LC 2008-24135

"These volumes are wonderfully organized and very easy to use. . . . Entries are of a length to provide a good background of O'Neill's works and life." Booklist

Includes bibliographical references

Foote, Horton

Beginnings; a memoir. Scribner 2001 270p il $24; pa $14 **812**

1. Actors 2. Authors 3. Novelists 4. Dramatists 5. Screenwriters 6. Television scriptwriters

ISBN 0-7432-1115-4; 0-7432-1116-2 pa

LC 2001-47088

Foote "chronicled his Wharton, TX, childhood in Farewell. . . . Now he continues his story where he left off, leaving Wharton at 17 to study to become an actor. He travels to theater school in Pasadena but eventually makes it to New York by way of Martha's Vineyard, where he soon discovers his talent for writing and hobnobs with the likes of Martha Graham, Tennessee Williams, and Agnes de Mille." Libr J

Collected plays. v2 Smith & Kraus 1996 216p v2 hardcover o.p. pa $19.95 **812**

ISBN 978-1-57525-019-9; 1-57525-019-5

"Foote's ear for naturalistic dialogue never fails him, and even in the midst of telling an exciting story . . . he never lets the potential for melodrama overwhelm things." Booklist

Gibson, William

★ The **miracle** worker. Scribner 2008 112p pa $12.99 **812**

1. Deaf 2. Blind 3. Authors 4. Memoirists 5. Humanitarians 6. Teachers of the deaf 7. Inspirational writers 8. Teachers of the blind 9. Social welfare leaders

ISBN 978-1-4165-9084-2; 1-4165-9084-6

LC 2008-275273

First published 1957

A text of the television play, intended for reading, of Anne Sullivan Macy's attempts to teach her pupil, Helen Keller, to communicate.

"The present text is meant for reading, and differs from the telecast version in that I have restored some passages that read better than they play and others omitted in performance for simple lack of time." Author's note

Goodrich, Frances

The **diary** of Anne Frank; by Frances Goodrich and Albert Hackett; newly adapted by Wendy Kesselman. Dramatists Play Service 2000 70p il pa $7.50 **812**

1. World War, 1939-1945 -- Jews -- Drama 2. Netherlands -- History -- 1940-1945, German occupation -- Drama

ISBN 0-8222-1718-X

LC 2006-455205

First published 1956 by Random House

Awarded the Pulitzer Prize and the New York Drama Critics Circle Award for 1956

Characters: 5 men, 5 women. 2 acts. First produced at the Cort Theatre, New York City, October 5, 1955.

Gurney, A. R.

Love letters and two other plays: The golden age and What I did last summer; with an introduction by the playwright. Penguin Bks. 1990 209p pa $14   **812**

   1. American drama -- 20th century

   ISBN 978-0-452-26501-1; 0-452-16501-0

        LC 90-34177

   Love letters dramatizes the 30-year epistolary "exchange between an upper-class man and an upper-upper-class woman. . . . The Golden Age is an updated, romantic-comic variation upon Henry James' Aspern Papers in which a young academic locates an old woman who may possess a missing chapter of The Great Gatsby and schemes to get it from her. What I did Last Summer is about 14-year-old Charlie's bohemian season with Anna, the Pig Woman, who fosters his creativity as she once did his mother's." Booklist

Hansberry, Lorraine

   ★ A **raisin** in the sun. Modern Lib. 1995 xxvi, 135p $14.95; pa $6.50   **812**

   ISBN 0-679-60172-4; 0-679-75533-0 pa

        LC 95-16074

   First published 1959

   Awarded the New York Drama Critics Circle Award for the 1958-1959 season

   Characters: 8 men, 3 women. 6 scenes in 3 acts. First produced at the Ethel Barrymore Theatre, New York City, March 11, 1959

   "Hansberry's drama focuses on the Youngers, a 1950s African-American working-class family in Chicago striving to realize their individual dreams of prosperity and education, and their collective dream of a better life. It was the first play by an African-American woman to be produced on Broadway." Reader's Ency. 4th edition

Heintzelman, Greta

   Critical companion to Tennessee Williams; [by] Greta Heintzelman, Alycia Smith Howard. Facts on File 2005 436p il (Facts on File library of American literature) $65; pa $19.95   **812**

   1. Authors 2. Novelists 3. Dramatists 4. Short story writers

   ISBN 0-8160-4888-6; 0-8160-6429-6 pa

        LC 2004-7362

   The authors "offer an excellent resource for those studying Williams's life and extensive body of work." Choice

   Includes bibliographical references

Hughes, Langston

   Five plays; edited with an introduction by Webster Smalley. Indiana Univ. Press 1963 258p hardcover o.p. pa $14.95 **812**

   ISBN 0-253-32230-8; 0-253-20121-7 pa

   Contents: Mulatto.--Soul gone home.--Little Ham.--Simply heavenly.--Tambourines to glory.

Kushner, Tony

   Angels in America; a gay fantasia on national themes. 1st combined pbk. ed.; Theatre Communications Group 2003 289p pa $15.95   **812**

   1. Lawyers 2. Government officials

   ISBN 1-55936-231-6

        LC 2003-17904

   Part one awarded the Pulitzer Prize, 1993

Millennium approaches first presented at the Eureka Theatre Company, San Francisco, May 1991. Perestroika first presented at the Mark Taper Forum, Los Angeles, November 1992.

Lawrence, Jerome

   Inherit the wind; [by] Jerome Lawrence and Robert E. Lee. Ballantine Books trade pbk. ed.; Ballantine Books 2007 129p pa $9.95   **812**

   1. Evolution -- Study and teaching -- Drama

   ISBN 978-0-345-50103-5; 0-345-50103-9

        LC 2007-281039

   Characters: 23 men, 7 women. 3 acts 5 scenes. First produced at the National Theater, New York City, April 21, 1955

Mamet, David

   Speed-the-plow. Grove Press 1988 82p (An Evergreen bk) pa $13   **812**

   ISBN 978-0-8021-3046-4; 0-8021-3046-1

        LC 87-7252

   Characters: 2 men 1 woman. 3 acts. First produced on Broadway at the Royale Theater, May 3, 1988

   "A brilliant black comedy, a dazzling dissection of Hollywood cupidity and another tone poem by our foremost master of the language of moral epilepsy. . . . On its deepest level it belongs with the darker disclosures of movie-biz pathology like Nathanael West's The Day of the Locust and F. Scott Fitzgerald's The Last Tycoon. In a sense Speed-the-Plow distills all of these to a stark quintessence: there's hardly a line in it that isn't somehow insanely funny or scarily insane." Newsweek

Miller, Arthur

   ★ **Collected** plays, 1944-1961. Library of America 2006 774p $35   **812**

   ISBN 978-1-931082-91-4; 1-931082-91-X

        LC 2005-49442

O'Neil, Eugene

   Complete plays; edited by Travis Bogard. Literary Classics of the United States 1988 3v (Library of America) v1 $40; v2 $40; v3 $35   **812**

   ISBN 978-0-940450-48-6 v1; 978-0-940450-49-3 v2; 978-0-940450-50-9 v3

Parks, Suzan-Lori

   Topdog /underdog. Theatre Communications Group 2001 110p pa $12.95   **812**

   ISBN 1-55936-201-4

        LC 2001-27316

   Characters: 2 men. 6 scenes. First produced at The Joseph Papp Public Theater/New York Shakespeare Festival, New York City, July 22, 2001

   This is "the story of Lincoln and Booth, two brothers whose names were given to them as a joke foretelling a lifetime of sibling rivalry and resentment. Haunted by the past, the brothers are forced to confront the shattering reality of their future." Publisher's note

The **play** that changed my life; America's foremost playwrights on the plays that influenced them. edited by Ben Hodges. Applause Theatre & Cinema Books 2009 173p il pa $18.99   **812**

   1. Authorship 2. Drama -- Technique 3. Dramatists, American

   ISBN 978-1-557837-40-0; 1-55783-740-6

        LC 2009-32452

"Edited by Hodges, with a foreword by Paula Vogel, the book assembles 19 of the theater's usual suspects, many of them Pulitzer Prize winners, to explain what lured them into their line of work." Arts J

★ **Playwrights** at work; Paris review. edited by George Plimpton. Modern Lib. 2000 411p il pa $14.95 **812**
1. Poets 2. Actors 3. Authors 4. Novelists 5. Dramatists 6. Essayists 7. Memoirists 8. Screenwriters 9. Short story writers 10. Theatrical directors 11. Motion picture directors 12. Television scriptwriters 13. Nobel laureates for literature
ISBN 0-679-64021-5

LC 99-44064
"This is an excellent gathering of brilliant minds in the theater, and these interviews provide significant insight into the works of the writers." Libr J

Rose, Reginald
Twelve angry men; introduction by David Mamet. Penguin Books 2006 73p (Penguin classics) pa $11 **812**
ISBN 0-14-310440-3; 978-0-14-310440-7

LC 2006-46006
First published 1955 by Dramatic Pub.
Characters: 12 men. 3 acts. Original television broadcast on CBS program Studio One, September 20, 1954.

Shepard, Sam
Fool for love, and other plays; introduction by Ross Wetzsteon. Bantam Bks. 1984 307p pa $15 **812**
ISBN 978-0-553-34590-2; 0-553-34129-4

LC 84-45182
"Sam Shepard fills the role of professional playwright as a good ballet dancer or acrobat fulfills his role in performance. That is, he always delivers, he executes feats of dexterity and technical difficulty that an untrained person could not, and makes them seem easy." Village Voice

The **unseen** hand and other plays. Vintage Bks. 1996 383p pa $14.95 **812**
ISBN 978-0-679-76789-3; 0-679-76789-4

LC 95-47723

Simon, Neil
Brighton Beach memoirs. Plume 1995 130p pa $12 **812**
ISBN 0-452-27528-8

LC 95-21788
First published 1984 by Random House
Awarded the New York Drama Critics Circle Award for best play, 1983
"Sex and baseball are the primary preoccupations of 15-year-old Eugene Jerome, narrator of a seriocomic slice of lower-middle-class Jewish family life in Depression-era New York City. The several adolescent characters in the extended family add to the teenage appeal of Simon's . . . play." Booklist

★ The **collected** plays of Neil Simon; with an introduction by Neil Simon. Random House 1979 4v hardcover o.p. v1-2 each pa $25, v3 o.p., v4 pa $17 **812**
ISBN 978-0-452-25870-9 v1; 978-0-452-26358-1 v2; 978-0-679-40889-5 v3; 978-0-684-84785-6 v4

Lost in Yonkers. Plume 1993 120p (Plume drama) pa $12 **812**
ISBN 0-452-26883-4

LC 92-29111
First published 1991 by Random House
Awarded the Pulitzer Prize, 1991
Characters: 4 men, 3 women. 2 acts. First presented at the Stevens Center for the Performing Arts, Winston-Salem, December 31, 1990.
This play, "set in 1940s New York, is a sad-funny portrait of a dysfunctional family, headed by a woman who provided for her children but never showed them love." Booklist

The **play** goes on; a memoir. Simon & Schuster 1999 348p il hardcover o.p. pa $14 **812**
1. Authors 2. Dramatists 3. Screenwriters 4. Television scriptwriters
ISBN 0-684-86980-2 pa

LC 99-36449
Sequel to Rewrites
This memoir "recounts the second half of Simon's life, starting with the life-shattering impact of the death of his first wife, Joan, of cancer at 40, and proceeding through the ensuing 30 years, during which Simon had periods of incredible fertility and others in which his creativity dried up and he feared he would never write again." Booklist

Rewrites; a memoir. Simon & Schuster 1996 397p hardcover o.p. pa $14 **812**
1. Authors 2. Dramatists 3. Screenwriters 4. Television scriptwriters
ISBN 0-684-83562-2 pa

LC 96-13691
This first volume of the dramatist's memoirs focuses on his career as it evolved from writing high school skits to TV programs to Broadway
"This is a gentleman's autobiography, and Simon never stoops to dishing the dirt on his show biz cronies." Libr J

Wasserstein, Wendy
The **Heidi** chronicles and other plays. Vintage Bks. 1991 249p pa $13.95 **812**
ISBN 0-679-73499-6

LC 90-55681
First published 1990 by Harcourt Brace Jovanovich
This collection traces "three decades of changing styles, mores, life objectives, and intellectual challenges. Wasserstein examines her characters and their times with great good humor, complexity, depth of feeling, and a firm refusal to accept trite and easy images." Libr J

Wilder, Thornton
Collected plays & writings on theater. Library of America 2007 871p $40 **812**
1. Poetry -- By individual authors
ISBN 978-1-59853-003-2; 1-59853-003-8

LC 2006-48620
"Complementing the selection of plays is [a] . . . group of essays that captures Wilder's reflections on his plays and contains a revealing epistolary account of the film adaptation of Our Town, as well as evaluations of dramatists such as Sophocles, George Bernard Shaw, and the Austrian satirist Johann Nestroy (whose farce Einen Jux will er sich machen Wilder . . . transformed into The Matchmaker)." Publisher's note

★ **Our** town; a play in three acts. foreword by Donald Margulies. HarperCollins Pubs. 2003 xx, 181p $19.95; pa $9.95 **812**
ISBN 0-06-053525-3; 0-06-051263-6 pa
A reissue with a new foreword of the title first published 1938 by

Coward-McCann

Large mixed cast. First produced at McCarter's Theatre, Princeton, N.J., January 22, 1938.

"Presented without scenery of any kind, utilizing a narrator and loose episodic form, adventurous and imaginative in style, this unique play . . . is one of the most distinguished in the modern repertoire. It deals with the simplest and most touching aspects of life in a small town." Harper-Collins Reader's Ency of Am Lit

Williams, Tennessee

★ **Plays,** 1937-1955. Library of America 2000 1054p $40   **812**
ISBN 978-1-883011-86-4; 1-883011-86-4

★ **Plays,** 1957-1980. Library of America 2000 999p $40   **812**
ISBN 978-1-883011-87-1; 1-883011-87-6

★ A **streetcar** named desire; with an introduction by Arthur Miller. New Directions 2004 192p pa $9.95   **812**
ISBN 0-8112-1602-0

LC 2004-11654

First published 1947

Characters: 6 women, 7 men. 11 scenes. First produced at the Barrymore Theatre, New York City, December 3, 1947

"A study of sexual frustration, violence, and aberration, set in New Orleans, in which Blanche Dubois' fantasies of refinement and grandeur are brutally destroyed by her brother-in-law, Stanley Kowalski, whose animal nature fascinates and repels her." Oxford Companion to Engl Lit. 5th edition

Wilson, August

Fences; a play. introduction by Lloyd Richards. New Am. Lib. 1986 101p pa $12   **812**
ISBN 978-0-452-26401-4

LC 86-5264

Awarded the Pulitzer Prize, 1987

Characters: 5 men, 1 woman, 1 girl. 2 acts, 9 scenes. First produced at the Yale Repertory Theatre, New Haven, Connecticut, April 30, 1985

Ma Rainey's black bottom; a play in two acts. New Am. Lib. 1985 111p pa $12   **812**
ISBN 978-0-452-26113-6; 0-452-26113-9

LC 84-27156

Characters: 8 men, 2 women. 2 acts. First produced at the Yale Repertory Theatre, New Haven, Connecticut, April 6, 1984

The **piano** lesson. New Am. Lib. 1990 108p hardcover o.p. pa $12   **812**
ISBN 978-0-452-26534-9; 0-452-26534-7

LC 90-38734

Awarded the Pulitzer Prize and the New York Drama Critics Circle Award, 1990

Characters: 5 men, 3 women. 2 acts, 7 scenes. First presented at the Yale Repertory Theatre, New Haven, November 26, 1987

Seven guitars. Dutton 1996 107p hardcover o.p. pa $12   **812**
ISBN 978-0-452-27692-5; 0-452-27692-6 pa

LC 95-50536

Winner of the New York Drama Critics Circle award, 1996

Characters: 4 men, 3 women. 2 acts, 9 scenes. First produced at the

Goodman Theater, Chicago, January 21, 1995

"Pittsburgh, summer 1948. Five of his friends gather after the funeral of Floyd Barton, mysteriously murdered at 35, just as his first blues record had become a hit. The sixth play in Wilson's cycle concerned with twentieth-century African American lives is mostly a flashback. We learn what happened to Floyd, but before that horrifying climax, Wilson steeps us in the pathos that Floyd glimpsed a way to escape. . . . As powerful as modern drama gets." Booklist

Two trains running; foreword by Laurence Fishburne. Theatre Communications Group 2007 99p $25   **812**
1. Nineteen sixties -- Drama. 2. African Americans -- Drama. 3. African American neighborhoods -- Drama. 4. Hill District (Pittsburgh, Pa.) -- Drama.
ISBN 978-1-55936-303-7

LC 2007-22095

First published 1992 by Dutton

Characters: 6 men, 1 woman. 2 acts 8 scenes. First produced at the Yale Repertory Theatre, New Haven, Ct., March 27, 1990

Wilson, August, 1945-2005

Jitney; August Wilson. Overlook Press 2003 96p hardcover o.p. pa $14.95   **812**
ISBN 1585673706; 9781585673704

LC 200133962

Winner of the New York Drama Critics Circle Award, 2000

This play, by August Wilson, is "set in the 1970s in Pittsburgh's Hill District, and . . . [depicts] gypsy cabdrivers who serve black neighborhoods. 'Jitney' is the seventh in Wilson's 10-play cycle (one for each decade) on the black experience in twentieth century America. He writes not about historical events or the pathologies of the black community, but, as he says, about the unique particulars of black culture." (Publisher's note)

Wilson, Lanford

21 short plays. Smith & Kraus 1993 268p pa $19.95 **812**
ISBN 1-880399-31-8

LC 93-34434

"The plays range in form from finely crafted one-act plays to short 'skits' written for various benefits. They are arranged in chronological order and the collection spans the years from 1963 to 1991. Wilson's dramatic style has been characterized by such phrases as 'lyric realism' and 'poetic realism,' but these short plays represent a far greater range of styles." Voice Youth Advocates

The **Talley** trilogy. Smith & Kraus 1999 272p (Collected works) hardcover o.p.   **812**

"Wilson didn't begin what became, ultimately, a tetralogy with the idea of creating a play cycle. He just wanted to write a play set in the late 1970s that reflected in some way the post-Vietnam, post-Watergate letdown much of young America was feeling. . . . The resultant four-play cycle captures the Talley's foibles and follies as thoroughly—and as entertainingly—as J.D. Salinger's set of stories and short novels did the Glass family." Booklist

813 American fiction in English

Alice Walker; edited and with an introduction by Harold Bloom. New edition; Bloom's Literary Criticism; an im-

print of Infobase Publishing 2007 223p (Modern critical views) $45 **813**
1. Poets 2. Authors 3. Novelists 4. Editors 5. Essayists 6. College teachers 7. Short story writers
ISBN 978-0-7910-9611-6
First published 1989
A collection of critical essays discussing the work of The Color Purple author Alice Walker.
Includes bibliographical references

Alice Walker's The color purple; edited and with an introduction by Harold Bloom. New ed.; Bloom's Literary Criticism 2008 191p (Modern critical interpretations) $45 **813**
1. Poets 2. Authors 3. Novelists 4. Editors 5. Essayists 6. College teachers 7. Short story writers
ISBN 978-0-7910-9614-7; 0-7910-9614-9

LC 2008-2775

First published 2000
A collection of ten essays providing international appraisal and interpretation of Walker's novel.
Includes bibliographical references

Anderson, William

The **selected** letters of Laura Ingalls Wilder; Laura Ingalls Wilder; edited by William Anderson. HarperCollins 2016 xxvii, 395 p.p illustrations (hardcover) $26.99 **813**
1. American authors 2. Authors -- Correspondence 3. Authors, American -- 20th century -- Correspondence
ISBN 9780062419682; 0062419684
This book is "a vibrant, deeply personal portrait of . . . American author [Laura Ingalls Wilder]. . . . Biographer William Anderson collected and researched references throughout these letters and the result is an invaluable historical collection, tracing Wilder's life through the final days of covered wagon travel, her life as a farm woman, a country journalist, Depression-era author, and years of fame as the writer of the Little House books." (Publisher's note)

Atlas, James

Bellow; a biography. Random House 2000 686p il hardcover o.p. pa $29 **813**
1. Authors 2. Novelists 3. Dramatists 4. Authors, American 5. Short story writers 6. Nobel laureates for literature
ISBN 0-375-75958-1 pa

LC 00-42529

"Atlas shares his subject's devotion to literature, intimacy with Chicago (the city Bellow immortalized), and Jewishness, and he succeeds brilliantly in chronicling and interpreting Bellow's very full life, difficult personality, and powerful work." Booklist
Includes bibliographical references

Blume, Lesley M. M.

Everybody behaves badly; the true story behind Hemingway's masterpiece The Sun Also Rises. Lesley Blume. Eamon Dolan/Houghton Mifflin Harcourt 2016 352 p. illustrations, portraits (hardback) $27 **813**
ISBN 9780544276000

LC 2015037016

This book, by Lesley Blume, focuses on the "making of Ernest Hemingway's The Sun Also Rises, the outsize personalities who inspired it, and the vast changes it wrought on the literary world. . . . Blume resurrects the explosive, restless landscape of 1920s Paris and Spain and reveals how Hemingway helped create his own legend." (Publisher's note)

"Blume's reimagining of 1920s Paris and its scandalous denizens is vivid, spirited, and absorbing." Kirkus
Includes bibliographical references (pages 245-320) and index.

Boyd, Brian

Vladimir Nabokov: the American years. Princeton Univ. Press 1991 783p il hardcover o.p. pa $49 **813**
1. Poets 2. Authors 3. Novelists 4. Authors, Russian 5. Essayists 6. Memoirists 7. Translators 8. College teachers 9. Literary critics 10. Short story writers
ISBN 0-691-06797-X; 0-691-02471-5 pa

LC 90-26374

This volume, which completes the biography begun with Vladimir Nabokov: The Russian Years (1990), is an account of the writer's life from 1940, when he arrived in the United States.
Includes bibliographical references

Vladimir Nabokov: the Russian years. Princeton Univ. Press 1990 607p il hardcover o.p. pa $49 **813**
1. Poets 2. Authors 3. Novelists 4. Authors, Russian 5. Essayists 6. Memoirists 7. Translators 8. College teachers 9. Literary critics 10. Short story writers
ISBN 0-691-06794-5; 0-691-02470-7 pa

LC 90-8040

The author aims to "describe the liberal milieu of the aristocratic Nabokovs, their escape from Russia [after the Revolution], Nabokov's education at Cambridge, and the murder of his father in Berlin. Boyd then turns to the years that Nabokov spent, impoverished, in Germany and France, until the coming of Hitler forced him to flee, with wife and son, to the United States." Publisher's note
Includes bibliographical references

Burroughs, Augusten

★ **Running** with scissors; a memoir. St. Martin's Press 2002 304p $23.95; pa $14 **813**
1. Authors 2. Novelists 3. Memoirists
ISBN 0-312-28370-9; 0-312-42227-X pa

LC 2001-58857

In this memoir the author recalls his youth with a mentally ill mother, living with his mother's psychiatrist in a chaotic household, and his early homosexual experiences
"Burroughs tempers the pathos with sharp, riotous humor in stories that are self-deprecating, raunchy, sexually explicit." Booklist

Burroughs, William S., 1914-1997

Rub out the words; the letters of William S. Burroughs 1959-1974. edited and with an introduction by Bill Morgan. Ecco 2012 xxxv, 444 p.p (hardcover) $35 **813**
1. Letters 2. Beat generation -- Correspondence 3. American authors -- Correspondence 4. Authors, American -- 20th century -- Correspondence
ISBN 006171142X; 9780061711428

LC 2012371022

This collection of correspondence by author William S. Burroughs "contains over 300 . . . letters written mostly to friends, family, and business associates between the publication of 'Naked Lunch' and Burroughs's return to New York City to teach at City College. While old friends like Allen Ginsberg are among the recipients, more of the letters are addressed to newer companions whom Burroughs met while living abroad, including Brion Gysin, Paul Bowles, and Alex Trocchi. Many letters evidence Burroughs's obsessions with the cut-up method, Scientology, and the effectiveness of apomorphine as a cure for addiction; others reveal a caring father concerned about his son's well-being and financial security.... [Editor Bill] Morgan includes helpful explanatory notes, a chronology, and a list of sources identifying the repositories holding the letters." (Libr J)

Includes bibliographical references and index

Cather, Willa, 1873-1947

The **selected** letters of Willa Cather; edited by Andrew Jewell and Janis Stout. 1st ed. Alfred A. Knopf 2013 752 p. (hardcover) $37.50; (ebook) $85.00 **813**

1. Authors -- Correspondence 2. Novelists, American -- 20th century -- Correspondence

ISBN 0307959309; 9780307959300; 9780307959317

LC 2012036882

This book is a collection of some of author Willa Cather's personal correspondence. "Beginning with a witty missive written in 1888 when she was only 14, the volume continues through her early years as a successful magazine editor for McLure's, into the 1910s and '20s, when she experienced success as a novelist, all the way through to her death in 1947." (Publishers Weekly)

★ The **Columbia** companion to the twentieth-century American short story; Blanche H. Gelfant, editor. Columbia Univ. Press 2000 660p $83.50; pa $24.50 **813**

1. Reference books 2. American fiction -- Bio-bibliography 3. Short stories -- History and criticism 4. American fiction -- History and criticism

ISBN 0-231-11098-7; 0-231-11099-5 pa

LC 00-31610

"The first 100 pages are devoted to thematic essays that focus on the form of the short story, the development of the genre, several distinct subject types (e.g., short stories of the Holocaust or of the working class), and four different ethnic groups (African American, Asian American, Chicano Latino American, and Native American). . . . The remainder of the book is devoted to over 100 individual author essays that focus on reading for pleasure and understanding rather than critical interpretation. Entries discuss the development of each author and the content and meaning of his or her major short stories." Libr J

Includes bibliographical references

Cott, Jonathan

There's a mystery there; the primal vision of Maurice Sendak. Jonathan Cott. Doubleday 2017 242 p. illustrations (chiefly color) (hardback) $30 **813**

1. Children -- Books and reading 2. Children's stories, American -- Illustrations 3. Children's stories, American -- History and criticism 4. Children -- Books and reading -- United States -- History -- 20th century

ISBN 9780385540438; 9780385540445

LC 2016050812

This book, by Jonathan Cott, examines "the inner workings of . . . [Maurice Sendak's] torments and inspirations that ranges over the entirety of his work and his formative life experiences, and uses 'Outside Over There,' . . . as the key to understanding just what made . . . [the] man tick. To gain multiple perspectives on that book, Cott also turns to four 'companion guides': a Freudian analyst, . . . and Sendak's great friend and admirer, the playwright Tony Kushner." (Publisher's note)

"Cott approaches Sendak from virtually every angle, making this a remarkably complete picture of a complex and dynamic oeuvre." Pub Wkly

Facts on File, Inc.

★ The **Facts** on File companion to the American novel;

edited by Abby H.P. Werlock; assistant editor, James P. Werlock. Facts on File 2005 3v (Facts on File library of American literature) set $195 **813**

1. Reference books 2. American fiction -- Encyclopedias 3. American fiction -- Bio-bibliography

ISBN 0-8160-4528-3; 978-0-8160-4528-0

LC 2005-12437

"This A-to-Z reference contains 450 biographical overviews of American and foreign-born authors living in the United States and 500 signed analytical essays on their novels. . . . Libraries will value this compact set for including classics as well as hard-to-find contemporary authors." SLJ

Includes bibliographical references

Fargnoli, A. Nicholas

Critical companion to William Faulkner; a literary reference to his life and work. [by] A. Nicholas Fargnoli, Michael Golay, Robert W. Hamblin. Facts On File 2008 562p il (Facts on File library of American literature) $75 **813**

1. Authors 2. Novelists 3. Screenwriters 4. Short story writers 5. Nobel laureates for literature

ISBN 978-0-8160-6432-8

LC 2007-32361

First published 2001 with title: William Faulkner A to Z

"Coverage includes: Faulkner's major works, including novels, short stories, poetry, and nonfiction; descriptions of characters in Faulkner's fiction, such as Benjy and Quentin from The Sound and the Fury; details about Faulkner's family, friends, colleagues, and critics; real and fictional places important to Faulkner's life and literary development, from Yoknapatawpha County, Mississippi to Hollywood; interviews and speeches given by Faulkner; [and] ideas and events that influenced his life and works, including slavery, the Civil War, World War I, and civil rights." Publisher's note

Includes bibliographical references

Farrell, Susan Elizabeth

Critical companion to Kurt Vonnegut; a literary reference to his life and work. [by] Susan Farrell. Facts On File 2008 532p il (Facts on File library of American literature) $75 **813**

1. Authors 2. Novelists 3. Journalists 4. Biographers 5. Short story writers 6. Science fiction writers

ISBN 978-0-8160-6598-1

LC 2007-37900

This "book covers all his works, including his novels, such as the unforgettable Slaughterhouse-Five; his short stories, such as 'Harrison Bergeron'; and his lectures and essays. . . . Entries on his life, related people, places, and topics are also included." Publisher's note

Includes bibliographical references

Gifford, Justin

Street poison; the life and times of Iceberg Slim. Justin Gifford. Doubleday 2015 288 p. 8 plates; ills.; portraits (hardcovers) $26.95 **813**

1. African American authors -- Biography 2. Pimps -- Illinois -- Chicago -- Biography 3. African Americans -- Illinois -- Chicago -- Biography

ISBN 0385538340; 9780385538343

LC 2014037252

This book, by Justin Gifford, is a "biography of one of America's bestselling, notorious, and influential writers of the twentieth century: Iceberg Slim, né Robert Beck. . . . From a career as a . . . ruthless pimp in the '40s and '50s, Iceberg Slim refashioned himself as the first and still the greatest of 'street lit' masters, whose vivid books have made him an icon . . . and a presiding spirit of 'blaxploitation' culture." (Publisher's note)

"Recommended for readers of popular fiction and African American literature." LJ

Gillespie, Carmen

Critical companion to Alice Walker; a literary reference to her life and work. Facts on File 2011 452p il (Facts on File library of American literature) $75 **813**
1. Poets 2. Authors 3. Novelists 4. Editors 5. Essayists 6. College teachers 7. Short story writers
ISBN 978-0-8160-7530-0; 978-1-4381-3488-8 ebook
LC 2010-18639
This book contains "entries on all of Walker's major works, including such novels as The Color Purple, Meridian, The Third Life of Grange Copeland, and Possessing the Secret of Joy; essay collections and essays, such as 'Beauty: When the Other Dancer Is the Self'; poetry collections and poems; and short stories. Each entry on a major work of fiction contains subentries on the work's main characters." Publisher's note
Includes bibliographical references

Critical companion to Toni Morrison; a literary reference to her life and work. Facts On File 2008 484p il (Facts on File library of American literature) $75 **813**
1. Authors 2. Novelists 3. Dramatists 4. Essayists 5. College teachers 6. Literary critics 7. Nobel laureates for literature
ISBN 978-0-8160-6276-8
LC 2006-38231
This book "examines Morrison's life and writing, featuring critical analyses of her work and themes, as well as . . . entries on related topics and relevant people, places, and influences." Publisher's note
Includes bibliographical references

Haralson, Eric L.

Critical companion to Henry James; a literary reference to his life and work. [by] Eric Haralson and Kendall Johnson. Facts On File 2009 516p il (Facts on File library of American literature) $75 **813**
1. Authors 2. Novelists
ISBN 978-0-8160-6886-9
LC 2008-36451
This book "covers the life and works of Henry James as well as the related people, places, and topics that shaped his writing. Other features in this . . . title include a chronology of James's life, bibliographies of his works and of secondary sources, and black-and-white photographs and illustrations." Publisher's note
Includes bibliographical references

Hardwick, Elizabeth

Herman Melville. Viking 2000 161p (Penguin lives series) $19.95 **813**
1. Authors 2. Novelists 3. Authors, American
ISBN 0-670-89158-4
LC 00-36510
"Interweaving critical readings of his fiction and poetry with events in Melville's life, Hardwick offers glimpses into his tortured writing career, his sometimes difficult family life, and his ambivalent relationship with his friend Nathaniel Hawthorne." Libr J
Includes bibliographical references

Harkness, Deborah E., 1965-

The **world** of all souls; the complete guide to A Discovery of witches, Shadow of night, and The Book of life. Deborah Harkness, illustrated by Colleen Madden. Viking 2018 ix, 484 p.p (hardcover) $40 **813**
1. Magic -- Fiction 2. Fantasy fiction -- History and criticism 3. Fantasy fiction, American -- History and criticism -- Handbooks, manuals, etc
ISBN 0735220743; 9780735220744
LC 2018013211
In this book, illustrated by Colleen Madden, author Deborah Harkness "shares the rich sources of inspiration behind her bewitching novels. She draws together synopses, character bios, maps, recipes, and even the science behind creatures, magic, and alchemy--all with her signature historian's touch. Bursting with fascinating facts and dazzling artwork, this essential handbook is a must-have for longtime fans and eager newcomers alike." (Publisher's note)

Harrison, Kathryn, 1961-

The **kiss**; Kathryn Harrison. Random House 1997 207 p. **813**
1. Authors, American -- Biography 2. Novelists, American -- 20th century -- Biography
ISBN 067944999X; 9780679449997
LC 97153826
In this memoir, Kathryn "Harrison here turns an unflinching eye on the episode in her life that has most influenced those books: a secret, sexual affair with her father that began when she was 20. . . . Abandoned by her father as a child, neglected by an emotionally remote and impetuous mother, Harrison is raised by her grandparents. . . . A minister and amateur cameraman, her father visits Harrison after an absence of 10 years, when she is home from college on spring break. The boundary between flirtation and paternal affection is soon blurred. . . . Gradually consenting to his demands for sex, Harrison drops out of college and moves in with her father's new family, extricating herself from the affair only when her mother is stricken with metastatic breast cancer." (Publishers Weekly)

Herbert, Brian

★ **Dreamer** of Dune; the biography of Frank Herbert. TOR Bks. 2003 576p il $27.95; pa $16.95 **813**
1. Authors 2. Novelists 3. Science fiction writers
ISBN 0-7653-0646-8; 0-7653-0647-6 pa
LC 2002-42951
"This moving, sometimes painfully obsessive biography is an impressive testament to family loyalty and love. A must-read for Herbert fans (both senior and junior), it includes family photos and a bibliography." Publ Wkly

Hillerman, Tony

Seldom disappointed; a memoir. HarperCollins Pubs. 2001 341p il hardcover o.p. pa $13.95 **813**
1. Authors 2. Novelists 3. Journalists 4. Mystery writers 5. Authors, American
ISBN 0-06-050586-9 pa
LC 2001-24160
In this memoir Hillerman "relates his childhood in Oklahoma during the Depression, his service in World War II, his university education, his career in journalism and academia, and his eventual turn to writing mysteries. The entire book will appeal to his fans, but the first half is intensely gripping." Libr J
Includes bibliographical references

Hiney, Tom

Raymond Chandler; a biography. Atlantic Monthly Press 1997 310p il hardcover o.p. pa $14   **813**
1. Authors 2. Novelists 3. Screenwriters 4. Mystery writers
ISBN 0-8021-3637-0 pa

LC 97-264

"Hiney traces the writer's nomadic childhood from pre-Mafia Chicago to pre-telephone Nebraska, from Quaker Ireland and Edwardian England to his education south of London at Dulwich College and his 1913 arrival in the 'mean streets' of Los Angeles, the later setting for his crime fiction.... Living at over 100 addresses, he sustained no long friendships, and was 'variously rich, poor, drunk, teetotal, sacked, married and suicidal.'... No rough edges have been filed off for this revealing, well-written biography." Publ Wkly
Includes bibliographical references

Hood, Ann

Morningstar; Growing Up With Books. Ann Hood. W W Norton & Co Inc 2017 186 p. (hardcover) $22.95   **813**
1. Books and reading 2. Novelists, American -- 20th century -- Biography
ISBN 9780393254815; 9780393254822; 039325481X

LC 2017015737

This book, by Ann Hood, is "a memoir about the magic and inspiration of books.... Growing up in a mill town in Rhode Island, in a household that didn't foster a love of literature, Hood discovered nonetheless the transformative power of books. She learned to channel her imagination, ambitions, and curiosity by devouring ever-growing stacks." (Publisher's note)

"Hood has beautifully crafted a very convincing case for discovering literature and getting lost in the pages." Pub Wkly

Hurston, Zora Neale, 1891-1960

Novels and stories; Zora Neale Hurston. Library of Am. 1995 1041 p. $40   **813**
1. Short stories 2. African Americans 3. African Americans -- Fiction
ISBN 0940450836; 9780940450837

LC 94025757

This book "brings together for the first time all of [Zora Neale] Hurston's best works in one authoritative set. It features the acclaimed 1937 novel 'Their Eyes Were Watching God,' a lyrical masterpiece about a woman's struggle for love and independence.... A selection of short stories further displays Hurston's unique fusion of folk traditions and literary modernism--comic, ironic, and soaringly poetic." (Publisher's note)

"This two-volume set brings together for the first time all of Hurston's best works: four novels, two books of folklore, and the first complete edition of her famous autobiography, Dust Tracks on a Road." LJ

J.D. Salinger; edited with an introduction by Harold Bloom. New ed; Chelsea House 2008 254p (Modern critical views) $45   **813**
1. Authors 2. Novelists 3. Short story writers
ISBN 978-0-7910-9813-4

LC 2007-44662
First published 1987
This collection of nine essays provides a view of Salinger's critical reception. Among the contributors are David Galloway, Anthony Kaufman and Robert Coles.
Includes bibliographical references

John Steinbeck; edited and with an introduction by Harold Bloom. New ed; Bloom's Literary Criticism 2008 176p (Modern critical views) $45   **813**
1. Authors 2. Novelists 3. Screenwriters 4. Nobel laureates for literature
ISBN 978-0-7910-9787-8; 0-7910-9787-0

LC 2007-38676

First published 1987
A selection of criticism, arranged in chronological order of publication, devoted to the fiction of John Steinbeck.
Includes bibliographical references (p. 167-9)

Jones, Sharon L.

Critical companion to Zora Neale Hurston; a literary reference to her life and work. Facts On File 2008 288p il (Facts on File library of American literature) $75   **813**
1. Authors 2. Novelists 3. Dramatists 4. Memoirists 5. Folklorists 6. Short story writers
ISBN 978-0-8160-6885-2; 0-8160-6885-2

LC 2008-10052

This "covers all her writings, including Their Eyes Were Watching God; her landmark works of folklore and anthropology, such as Mules and Men; and shorter works." Publisher's note
Includes bibliographical references

King, Stephen, 1947-

On writing; a memoir of the craft. Scribner 2000 288p hardcover o.p. pa $14.95; pa $17   **813**
1. Authors 2. Novelists 3. Authorship 4. Authors, American 5. Short story writers 6. Science fiction writers
ISBN 0-671-02425-6 pa; 9781439156810

LC 00-30105

The author recounts "his life from early childhood through the aftermath of the 1999 accident that nearly killed him. Along the way, King touts the writing philosophies of William Strunk and Ernest Hemingway, advocates a healthy appetite for reading, expounds upon the subject of grammar, critiques a number of popular writers, and offers the reader a chance to try out his theories.... Recommended for anyone who wants to write and everyone who loves to read." Libr J

Kirk, Connie Ann

Critical companion to Flannery O'Connor. Facts on File 2008 415p il (Facts on File library of American literature) $75   **813**
1. Authors 2. Novelists 3. Short story writers
ISBN 978-0-8160-6417-5

LC 2007-6512

This book examines O'Connor's "life and works, and includes critical analyses of some of the themes in her writing, as well as entries on related topics and relevant people, places, and influences." Publisher's note
Includes bibliographical references

Levy, Andrew

Huck Finn's America; Mark Twain and the Era That Shaped His Masterpiece. Andrew Levy. Simon & Schuster 2014 368 p. $25   **813**
1. American literature -- History and criticism
ISBN 1439186960; 9781439186961

LC 2014040482

This book, by Andrew Levy, "shows how modern readers have been misunderstanding 'Huckleberry Finn' for decades. [Mark] Twain's masterpiece . . . is often discussed either as a carefree adventure story for children or a serious novel about race relations, yet Levy argues . . . it is neither. Instead, Huck Finn was written at a time when Americans were nervous about youth violence . . . and a debate was raging about education, popular culture, and responsible parenting." (Publisher's note)

"Delving deeply into 19th-century sources, generations of readers' responses and a wide range of Twain's writing, Levy complicates the possibilities of what the novel meant for its contemporaries and what it might mean for readers." Kirkus

Meanwhile there are letters; the correspondence of Eudora Welty and Ross Macdonald. edited and with an introduction by Suzanne Marrs and Tom Nolan. Arcade Publishing 2015 568 p. illustrations (some color) (hardback) $35   **813**
1. Authors -- Correspondence 2. Authors, American -- 20th century -- Correspondence
ISBN 1628725273; 9781628725278

LC 2015005957

This book, edited by by Suzanne Marrs and Tom Nolan, presents correspondence between authors Ross Macdonald and Eudora Welty. "They brought their literary talents to bear on a wide range of topics, discussing each others' publications, the process of translating life into fiction, the nature of the writer's block each encountered, books they were reading, and friends and colleagues they cherished." (Publisher's note)

"An intimate, luminous portrait of a friendship." Kirkus

Includes bibliographical references and index

Murphy, Mary McDonagh
Scout, Atticus, and Boo; a celebration of fifty years of To kill a mockingbird. Harper 2010 217p il $24.99   **813**
1. Authors 2. Novelists 3. Essayists 4. Short story writers
ISBN 978-0-06-192407-1; 0-06-192407-5

LC 2010-06739

The author tells the story of how the quiet, publicity-shy Southerner Harper Lee came to write her classic. She also conducts interviews (which will later be included in a documentary) with famous folks whose childhoods were transformed by the novel, such as Oprah, Tom Brokaw, and Scott Turow. Lee, now 84, didn't talkshe never does, God bless herbut you come away from Murphy's book with a renewed amazement at what Lee was able to achieve with a single perfect novel. Entertainment Wkly

Nabokov, Vladimir Vladimirovich
Speak, memory; an autobiography revisited. {by} Vladimir Nabokov; with an introduction by Brian Boyd. Knopf 1999 xxxv, 268p il map $17; pa $14   **813**
1. Poets 2. Authors 3. Novelists 4. Authors, Russian 5. Essayists 6. Memoirists 7. Translators 8. College teachers 9. Literary critics 10. Short story writers
ISBN 0-375-40553-4; 0-679-72339-0 pa

LC 98-49237

A revised version of the memoir first published 1951 in the United States with title: Conclusive evidence

These recollections of the author's youthful years give an account of a vanishing world. They offer a picture of the author's family, their flight from Russia, education in England, and émigré life in Paris and Berlin

Includes bibliographical references

Nadel, Ira Bruce
Critical companion to Philip Roth; a literary companion to his life and work. [by] Ira B. Nadel. Facts On File, Inc. 2011 356p il (Facts on File library of American literature) $75 **813**

1. Authors 2. Novelists 3. Short story writers
ISBN 978-0-8160-7795-3; 978-1-4381-3555-7 ebook

LC 2010022769

"Coverage includes: a . . . biography of Roth; entries on all of Roth's works; . . . entries on related people, places, and topics, such as anti-Semitism, Claire Bloom, Newark, satire, and . . . more; [and] appendixes, including a chronology, a bibliography of Roth's works, and a secondary-source bibliography." Publisher's note

Includes bibliographical references

Oliver, Charles M.
Critical companion to Ernest Hemingway; a literary reference to his life and work. Facts on File 2006 630p il (Facts on File library of American literature) $75   **813**
1. Poets 2. Authors 3. Novelists 4. Short story writers 5. Nobel laureates for literature
ISBN 0-8160-6418-0; 978-0-8160-6418-2

LC 2006-7970

First published 1999 with title: Ernest Hemingway A to Z

"This volume features entries on all of Hemingway's major and minor works, places and events related to his works, major figures in his life, and more. Appendixes include a complete list of Hemingway's works; a chronology; a genealogy; a . . . map for readers of Islands in the Stream; a list of film, stage, and radio adaptations; and a bibliography of secondary sources." Publisher's note

Includes filmography and bibliographical references

Parker, Hershel
Herman Melville; v1 a biography. Johns Hopkins Univ. Press 1996 942p v1 il maps $50; pa $29.95   **813**
1. Authors 2. Novelists 3. Authors, American 4. Biography, Individual
ISBN 0-8018-5428-8; 0-8018-8185-4 pa

LC 96-18984

This, the first volume of a projected two-volume "biography of Melville, ends in 1851, when the author presented to his . . . friend Nathaniel Hawthorne an inscribed pre-publication copy of Moby-Dick." (Atl Mon) Index.

This, the first volume of a two-volume "biography of Melville, ends in 1851, when the author presented to his . . . friend Nathaniel Hawthorne an inscribed pre-publication copy of Moby-Dick." Atl Mon

Includes bibliographical references

Philbrick, Nathaniel
Why read Moby-Dick? Viking 2011 x, 131 p.p (hbk.) $25   **813**
1. Whaling -- Fiction 2. Shipwrecks -- Fiction 3. American literature -- History and criticism 4. Sea stories -- History and criticism
ISBN 0670022993; 9780670022991

LC 2011019766

This book attempts to offer Herman "Melville's [book 'Moby-Dick' a] . . . broad contemporary audience. . . . [Author] Nathaniel Philbrick . . . unpacked the story of the wreck of the whaleship Essex, the real-life incident that inspired Melville to write 'Moby-Dick.' Now, he sets his sights on the fiction itself, offering a . . . tour of . . . [the] novel. . . . Philbrick . . . navigates Melville's world and illuminates the book's humor and . . . characters-finding the thread that binds Ishmael and Ahab to our own time." (Publisher's note)

"In this cogent and passionate polemic for Melville's masterpiece, Philbrick . . . combines a critical eye and a reader's adoration to make a case for Moby-Dick. The plights of the Pequod, Ishmael and Ahab may seem irrelevant (or worse, quaint) compared to today's troubles, but Philbrick opines that within the pages of this American classic lie timeless archetypes whose relevance stretches across human history. . . . Less lit-crit and more readers' guide, this tome will remind fans why they loved the book in the first place, and whet the appetites of trepid potential readers." Publ Wkly

Includes bibliographical references

Phillips, Julie

James Tiptree, Jr. the double life of Alice B. Sheldon. St. Martin's Press 2006 469p il $27.95 **813**

1. Authors 2. Science fiction writers

ISBN 0-312-20385-3; 978-0-312-20385-6

LC 2006-40095

This is a biography of the American science fiction writer.

The author "has achieved a wonder: an evenhanded, scrupulously documented, objective yet sympathetic portrait of a deliberately elusive personality." Publ Wkly

Includes bibliographical references

Pritchard, William H.

Updike. University of Massachusetts Press 2005 350p pa $24.95 **813**

1. Poets 2. Authors 3. Novelists 4. Short story writers

ISBN 978-1-55849-507-4; 1-55849-507-X

First published 2000 by Steerforth Press

"All in all, Pritchard's book is a gentle and intelligent request for a little more thought and a little less cranky let'smoveon speed in judging the work of one of America's pre-eminent writers." N Y Times Book Rev

Includes bibliographical references

Rehak, Melanie

Girl sleuth; Nancy Drew and the women who created her. Harcourt 2005 364p il $25; pa $14 **813**

1. Authors 2. Mystery writers 3. Children's authors 4. Young adult authors 5. Drew, Nancy (Fictitious character)

ISBN 0-15-101041-2; 0-15-603056-X pa

LC 2005-9129

"Packed with revealing anecdotes, Rehak's meticulously researched account of the publishing phenomenon that survived the Depression and WWII . . . will delight fans of the beloved gumshoe whose gumption guaranteed that every reprobate got his due." Booklist

Includes bibliographical references

Reynolds, David S., 1948-

Mightier than the sword; Uncle Tom's cabin and the battle for America. W. W. Norton & Co. 2011 351p il $27.95 **813**

1. Authors 2. Novelists 3. Abolitionists 4. Children's authors 5. Nonfiction writers 6. Short story writers

ISBN 978-0-393-08132-9; 0-393-08132-X

LC 2011-00702

"The powerful antislavery message of 'Uncle Tom's Cabin' fueled the flames leading to the Civil War, making it the most influential novel in American history. . . . Stowe claimed the novel came to her in a vision and God was its true author. Accordingly, her book is weighted with religious symbolism, which Reynolds interprets with typical English professor's zeal. He also examines its impacts not just on public attitudes toward slavery, but on women's rights, temperance, capitalism, minstrel shows, sexual customs and other aspects of mid-19th century American life. Reynolds dissects dozens of imitative novels, plays and minstrel shows — some against, others for slavery or segregation — and traces the influence of Stowe's novel into modern times, including film spin-offs. . . .[This is] not easy reading, but it offers virtually everything you ever wanted to know about 'Uncle Tom's Cabin' — and probably a

lot more." Seattle Times

Rioux, Anne Boyd

Meg, Jo, Beth, Amy; the story of Little Women and why it still matters. Anne Boyd Rioux. W W Norton & Co Inc 2018 352 p. (hardcover) $27.95 **813**

1. American fiction 2. Sisters -- Fiction

ISBN 9780393254730

LC 2018006602

In this book, author Anne Boyd Rioux "recounts how Louisa May Alcott came to write Little Women, drawing inspiration for it from her own life. Rioux also examines why this tale of family and community ties, set while the Civil War tore America apart, has resonated through later wars, the Depression, and times of changing opportunities for women." (Publisher's note)

Includes bibliographical references and index

Roth, Philip

The **facts**; a novelist's autobiography. Vintage Bks. 1997 195p pa $14 **813**

1. Authors 2. Novelists 3. Authors, American 4. Short story writers

ISBN 0-679-74905-5; 978-0-679-74905-9

LC 96-28807

First published 1988 by Farrar, Straus & Giroux

"The Facts is a lively and serious version of a novelist's life, but it seems even more interesting as a new way of formulating the questions about the imagination that Roth has been pursuing with increasing complication in the Zuckerman novels." N Y Rev Books

Rowley, Hazel

Richard Wright; the life and times. Holt & Co. 2001 626p il hardcover o.p. pa $18 **813**

1. Authors 2. Novelists 3. Dramatists 4. Essayists 5. Nonfiction writers 6. Short story writers

ISBN 0-8050-7088-5 pa

LC 00-54249

"The strength of {this book} is {the} painstaking research. Rowley . . . has a daunting dedication to primary sources and her documentation is meticulous." N Y Times Book Rev

Includes bibliographical references

Sallis, James

Chester Himes; a life. Walker & Co. 2000 368p il $28; pa $18.95 **813**

1. Authors 2. Novelists 3. Mystery writers 4. Short story writers

ISBN 0-8027-1362-9; 0-8027-7639-6 pa

LC 00-63328

This is a biography of the African-American crime novelist. "Sentenced to 25 years in prison for armed robbery when he was 19, he turned to writing while behind bars and, when released after serving eight years, published two novels. Their poor reception by the white establishment only confirmed Himes's beliefs about racism in America. He eventually moved to Paris, spending most of the rest of his life abroad. . . . The author succeeds splendidly in fleshing Himes out in this riveting biography." Libr J

Includes bibliographical references

Savigneau, Josyane

Carson McCullers; a life. translated by Joan E. Howard. Houghton Mifflin 2001 370p il $30 **813**

1. Authors 2. Novelists 3. Dramatists 4. Short story writers

ISBN 0-395-87820-9

LC 00-46547

This is a "heartfelt, honest portrait of one of the great novelists of the American South." Libr J

Includes bibliographical references

Schultz, Jeffrey D.

Critical companion to John Steinbeck; a literary reference to his life and work. [by] Jeffrey Schultz, Luchen Li. Facts on File 2005 406p il (Facts on File library of American literature) $65; pa $19.99 **813**

1. Authors 2. Novelists 3. Screenwriters 4. Nobel laureates for literature

ISBN 0-8160-4300-0; 0-8160-4301-9 pa

LC 2004-26100

"Useful, succinct, and reasonably priced, it packs an abundance of information into one compact resource." Libr J

Includes bibliographical references

Scottoline, Lisa

I see life through rosé-colored glasses; true stories and confessions. Lisa Scottoline and Francesca Serritella. St Martin's Press 2018 352 p. $24.99 **813**

1. Everyday life 2. American essays

ISBN 1250163056; 9781250163059

This book, by Lisa Scottoline and Francesca Serritella, presents a "collection of essays about the possibilities and pitfalls of everyday life. The New York Times bestselling mother daughter duo are back with more hilarious, witty, and true tales from their lives. Whether they are attempting to hike the Grand Canyon, . . . or learning what 'adulting' means, Lisa and Francesca are guaranteed to make you laugh, cry, and appreciate the funniest moments in life." (Publisher's note)

Smiley, Jane

Thirteen ways of looking at the novel. Knopf 2005 591p $26.95 **813**

1. Authorship 2. Fiction -- History and criticism

ISBN 1-4000-4059-0

LC 2005-45181

"The book is roughly divided into three sections: the first classifies the novel, beginning with the most simple of definitions (e.g., it's long, in prose, has a protagonist), and adds moral and aesthetic complexity as it moves along. The second section consists of a primer for fledgling novelists. . . . The result is a thorough reflection on the art and craft of the novel from one of its best-known contemporary practitioners." Publ Wkly

Includes bibliographical references

Tate, Mary Jo

Critical companion to F. Scott Fitzgerald; a literary reference to his life and work. foreword by Matthew J. Bruccoli. Facts on File 2006 464p il (Facts on File library of American literature) $75 **813**

1. Authors 2. Novelists 3. Screenwriters 4. Short story writers

ISBN 0-8160-6433-4; 978-0-8160-6433-5

LC 2006-11393

First published 1998 with title: F. Scott Fitzgerald A to Z

This book "studies the legacy of this writer, highlighting significant themes and historical references of his various works." Publisher's note

Includes bibliographical references

Vap, Sarah

Viability; Sarah Vap. Penguin Books 2016 161 p. (National Poetry Series) (paperback) $22 **813**

1. Women authors 2. Poetry -- Collections

ISBN 9780698407350; 9780143128281

LC 2015011853

This book in the National Poetry Series, by Sarah Vap, "is an ambitious and highly imaginative collection of prose poems that braids together several kinds of language strands in an effort to understand and to ask questions about the bodies (and minds, maybe even souls) that are owned by capitalism." (Publisher's note)

"In her sixth collection . . . Vap . . . innovatively mediates language of the body—membranes, tonsils, embryos, and blood—through prose poems in an imaginative structure based on the rhizome." Pub Wkly

Vonnegut, Kurt, 1922-2007

Kurt Vonnegut; letters. edited by Dan Wakefield. Delacorte Press 2012 436 p. $35 **813**

1. American letters 2. Authors -- Correspondence

ISBN 0385343752; 9780345535399; 9780385343756

LC 2012001544

Author Kurt Vonnegut and editor Dan Wakefield present Vonnegut's "collection of personal correspondence." It includes "the letter a twenty-two-year-old Vonnegut wrote home immediately upon being freed from a German POW camp" and "wry dispatches from Vonnegut's years as a struggling writer slowly finding an audience and then dealing with sudden international fame in middle age." (Publisher's note)

Walker, Alice

The **same** river twice; honoring the difficult: a meditation on life, spirit, art, and the making of the film The color purple, ten years later. Scribner 1996 302p il hardcover o.p. pa $14 **813**

1. Poets 2. Authors 3. Novelists 4. Editors 5. Essayists 6. College teachers 7. Short story writers 8. Color purple (Motion picture)

ISBN 0-671-00377-1 pa

LC 95-30056

This "book finds the Pulitzer Prize-winning author still grappling with criticism of the film version of her novel The Color Purple. . . . Walker's memoir pieces together assorted journal entries, magazine clippings, occasional photographs and even her original screenplay to form an intimate scrapbook of the period." Publ Wkly

Includes bibliographical references

Wallace, David Foster, 1962-2008

The **David** Foster Wallace Reader; David Foster Wallace. Little, Brown & Co. 2014 963 p. (hardback) $35 **813**

ISBN 0316182397; 9780316182393

LC 2014032157

This book presents a collection of writings by David Foster Wallace. His "explorations of morality, self-consciousness, addiction, sports, love, and the many other subjects that occupied him are represented here in both fiction and nonfiction. . . . A dozen writers and critics, including Hari Kunzru, Anne Fadiman, and Nam Le, add afterwords to favorite pieces." (Publisher's note)

Walton, Jo, 1964-

What Makes This Book So Great; Re-reading the classics of science fiction and fantasy. Jo Walton. Tor 2014 448 p. (hardback) $26.99 **813**

1. Books and reading 2. Fantasy fiction -- History and criticism

3. Science fiction -- History and criticism 4. Books and reading --
United States 5. Fantasy fiction, American -- History and criticism
6. Science fiction, American -- History and criticism
ISBN 0765331934; 9780765331939

LC 2013028170

"This collection gathers 130 of [novelist Jo] Walton's blog posts
from science fiction site Tor.com about her favorites works of sci-fi and
fantasy. . . . The themes of the essays interweave . . . many are meditations on the genre as a whole more than reviews of specific works, and
Walton often ties her points back to earlier posts." (Publishers Weekly)

"Walton shares not only her deep love for sf and fantasy in general and these novels in particular but the insights of a truly thoughtful
reader." LJ

White, Edmund

★ **My** lives. Ecco 2006 356p il $25.95   **813**
1. Authors 2. Novelists 3. Memoirists 4. Biographers 5. Short
story writers
ISBN 0-06-621397-5; 978-0-06-621397-2

LC 2005-49506

First published 2005 in the United Kingdom

This is an autobiography by "an award-winning author and leader
of the gay liberation movement of the 1960s. . . . The stories of his
mother's egotism and incessant chatter, struggle to master the French
language, obsession with European culture, literary associates, and work
as a novelist, teacher, and essayist are largely overshadowed by graphic
and explicit tales of the men in his life. . . . White's writing is amusing,
descriptive, shocking, and, ultimately, thought-provoking." Libr J

Wideman, John Edgar

Hoop roots. Houghton Mifflin 2001 242p $24; pa $13 **813**
1. Authors 2. Novelists 3. Memoirists 4. College teachers 5.
Nonfiction writers 6. Short story writers
ISBN 0-395-85731-7; 0-618-25775-6 pa

LC 2001-26455

Wideman "examines his lifelong relationship with basketball. He argues that basketball first allowed him to set his own standard in a white
world that often imposes definitions of success on black people. A poignant, thought-provoking memoir." Booklist

Wiesel, Elie

★ **And** the sea is never full; memoirs, 1969- translated
from the French by Marion Wiesel. Knopf 1999 429p hardcover o.p. pa $15   **813**
1. Authors 2. Novelists 3. Journalists 4. Holocaust survivors 5.
Human rights activists 6. Nobel laureates for peace 7. Holocaust,
1933-1945 -- Personal narratives
ISBN 0-8052-1029-6 pa

LC 99-15604

Continues the author's memoirs begun in All the rivers run to the sea
Original French edition, 1996

"This concluding volume begins when the author is age 40. He continues his travels . . . and he continues to write, his books including
Souls on fire, Four Hasidic Masters, Twilight, and more. . . . Wiesel is
the most significant writer to have made the Holocaust the major theme
of his work, just as it has been of major importance to his life. The horror of the Holocaust can be felt in this memoir with an intensity beyond
words." Booklist

William Faulkner; edited and with an introduction by Harold
Bloom. New ed.; Bloom's Literary Criticism 2008 269p
(Modern critical views) $45   **813**
1. Authors 2. Novelists 3. Screenwriters 4. Short story writers 5.

Nobel laureates for literature
ISBN 978-0-7910-9786-1

LC 2007-33754

First published 1986

"This volume of . . . critical essays examines The Sound and the
Fury, Light in August, As I Lay Dying, Absalom, Absalom!, and other
key works by this preeminent writer of the twentieth century." Publisher's note

Includes bibliographical references

Wright, Sarah Bird

Critical companion to Nathaniel Hawthorne; a literary reference to his life and work. Facts on File 2006 392p il (Facts
on File library of American literature) $75   **813**
1. Authors 2. Novelists 3. Short story writers
ISBN 0-8160-5583-1; 978-0-8160-5583-8

LC 2005-34648

This book "offers critical entries on Hawthorne's novels, short stories, travel writing, criticism, and other works, as well as portraits of
characters, including Hester Prynne and Roger Chillingworth. This . .
. reference also provides entries on Hawthorne's family, friends—ranging from Herman Melville to President Franklin Pierce—publishers,
and critics, as well as periodicals that published his work and important
places and events in his life." Publisher's note

Includes bibliographical references

Zora Neale Hurston; edited and with an introduction by Harold
Bloom. New ed; Chelsea House Publishers 2008 238p
(Modern critical views) $45   **813**
1. Authors 2. Novelists 3. Dramatists 4. Memoirists 5. Folklorists
6. Short story writers
ISBN 978-0-7910-9610-9

LC 2007-49161

First published 1986

"Featuring supplemental material such as a chronology, a bibliography, and an index, [this book is a] critical look at Hurston's work and its
influence on contemporary themes, such as race and gender in American
society." Publisher's note

Includes bibliographical references

813.009   American fiction – History and criticism

Nafisi, Azar

★ The **Republic** of Imagination; America in Three Books.
Azar Nafisi; illustrations by Peter Sis. Windmill Books 2015
352 p. illustrations (hardback) $28.95   **813.009**
1. Democracy 2. Imagination 3. Books and reading 4. American
fiction 5. English teachers 6. Iranian American women 7. National
characteristics in literature
ISBN 0670026069; 9780099558934; 0099558939;
9780670026067

LC 2014022287

This book, by Azar Nafisi, is an "original tribute to the vital importance of fiction in a democratic society. . . . [She blends] memoir
and polemic with close readings of her favorite American novels--'The
Adventures of Huckleberry Finn,' 'Babbitt,' and 'The Heart Is a Lonely
Hunter,' among others." (Publisher's note)

"The author's literary exegesis lightly moves through her own experiences as a student,teacher, friend and new citizen. Touching on myriad
literary examples, from L.Frank Baum to James Baldwin, her work is
both poignant and informative." Kirkus

Town, Caren J.

LGBTQ young adult fiction; a critical survey, 1970s-2010s. Caren J. Town. McFarland & Company, Inc., Publishers 2017 vii, 197 p.p (softcover: alk. paper) $39.95   **813.009**

1. Homosexuality in literature 2. American literature -- History and criticism 3. Queer theory 4. Lesbians in literature 5. Adolescence in literature 6. Gender identity in literature 7. Homosexuality and literature -- United States 8. Gays' writings, American -- History and criticism 9. Young adult fiction, American -- History and criticism 10. Sexual minority youth -- Books and reading -- United States

ISBN 0786496940; 9780786496945

LC 2017023518

This book, by Caren J. Town, "explores a selection of recent novels--many of which may be new to readers--and places them in the wider contexts of LGBTQ literature and history. Chapters discuss a range of topics, including the relationship of Queer Theory to literature, LGBTQ families, and recent trends in utopian and dystopian science fiction." (Publisher's note)

"In this important survey, Town . . . deftly balances several elements to serve a variety of readers: librarians, teacher education faculty, middle- and high-school teachers, parents and advocates, and young people of all gender identities." Choice

Includes bibliographical references (pages 187-193) and index

813.54   American fiction – 1945-1999

Bass, Rick, 1958-

The **traveling** feast; on the road and at the table with my heroes. Rick Bass. Little, Brown & Co. 2018 288 p. $28 **813.54**

1. Travel writing 2. American authors -- Biography

ISBN 9780316381239

LC 2018933125

In this memoir, author Rick Bass "takes on the role of a roving wordsmith caterer, traveling the country to visit the writers who have inspired him and thanking them by preparing them home-cooked meals... Conversation inevitably flows through a series of wonderful, sincere encounters...Bass ruminates on what makes good writing and great writers while obsessing over his multicourse gourmet feasts with nearly the same devotion to detail." (Publishers Weekly)

"Bass' reflective, funny, and generous chronicle of culinary adventures and nourishing literary encounters will renew readers' appreciation for stories and storytellers and how literature guides us back 'to some deeper, older place.'" Booklist

Conroy, Pat, 1945-2016

A **lowcountry** heart; Reflections on a Writing Life. Pat Conroy. Nan A. Talese 2016 320 p. illustrations (some color) (ebook) $65; (hardback) $25   **813.54**

1. American essays

ISBN 9780385530873; 9780385530866

LC 2016026695

This book, by Pat Conroy, "brings together some of the most charming interviews, magazine articles, speeches, and letters from his long literary career. . . . Ranging across diverse subjects, such as favorite recent reads, the challenge of staying motivated to exercise, and processing the loss of dear friends, Conroy's eminently memorable pieces offer a unique window into the life of a true titan of Southern writing." (Publisher's note)

"Conroy's style is always accessible, lively, and heartfelt. This book is a worthy memorial—filled with love, humor, and great stories." LJ

813.6   American fiction – 2000-

Galchen, Rivka, 1976-

Little labors; Rivka Galchen. New Directions 2016 96 p. (ebook) $50; (alk. paper) $16.95   **813.6**

1. American essays 2. American literature -- 21st century

ISBN 0811225585; 9780811222976; 9780811225588

LC 2015044623

This book, by Rivka Galchen, "is a slanted, enchanted literary miscellany. Varying in length from just a sentence or paragraph to a several-page story or essay, Galchen's puzzle pieces assemble into a shining, unpredictable, mordant picture of the ordinary-extraordinary nature of babies and literature. Anecdotal or analytic, each part opens up an odd and tender world of wonder." (Publisher's note)

"The book is an endearing compilation of social criticism, variously contentious, commonplace, funny, and incisive." Pub Wkly

Nadler, Daniel

Lacunae; 100 imagined ancient love poems. Daniel Nadler. Farrar, Straus & Giroux 2016 128 p. (ebook) $60; (hardback) $23   **813.6**

1. Love poetry 2. American poetry -- 21st century

ISBN 9780374714819; 9780374182694

LC 2015035422

This poetry collection, by Daniel Nadler, "is a project of constant negotiation, one that bends his poems into new shapes. He attends to an impulse of restoration and conservation, in turns. From this tension arises verse of searing simplicity and clarity of vision, imbued with that trembling quality of new life: 'luminous and half-naked.'" (Publisher's note)

"Intriguing, meditative, and ambitious, this work can go over the top but will remind devotees of that sense of magic that attracted them to poetry in the first place." LJ

814   American essays in English

Als, Hilton, 1960-

★ **White** Girls; Hilton Als. McSweeney's 2013 300 p. $24   **814**

1. Race 2. Culture 3. Gender role

ISBN 1936365812; 9781936365814

National Book Critics Circle Award Finalist: Criticism (2013)

Lambda Literary Awards Winner - LGBT Nonfiction (2014)

This book by Hilton Als presents a collection of essays. "His eponymous 'white girls' include Louise Brooks, Flannery O'Connor, Truman Capote, Richard Pryor, Malcolm X, Michael Jackson, Eminem, and others. Using his subjects as a springboard to analyze literature, photography, films, music, television, performance, race, gender, sexual orientation, and history, Als offers wry insights throughout." (Publishers Weekly)

"Whether his subject is his mother, himself, or seminal artists, Als is a fine, piercing observer and interpreter, a writer of lashing exactitude and veracity." Booklist

Angelou, Maya

Wouldn't take nothing for my journey now. Random House 1993 141p hardcover o.p. pa $6.99   **814**

ISBN 0-679-42743-0; 0-553-56907-4 pa

LC 93-5904

The author "shares her thoughts about humankind: how to respect others of different cultures, opinions, and values as taught by universal philosophies. . . . Angelou's prose is brisk, fluid, and entrancing. This work will provide a taste of wisdom to all who read it." Libr J

Arndt, Rachel Z.

Beyond measure; essays. by Rachel Z. Arndt. Sarabande Books 2018 160 p. (softcover) $15.95   **814**
1. Sexism 2. Narcolepsy 3. Weight loss
ISBN 9781946448132

LC 2017032569

This book, by Rachel Z. Arndt, "is a fascinating exploration of the rituals, routines, metrics and expectations through which we attempt to quantify and ascribe value to our lives. With mordant humor and penetrating intellect, Arndt casts her gaze beyond event-driven narratives to the machinery underlying them: judo competitions measured in weigh-ins and wait times; the significance of the elliptical's stationary churn; . . . the stupefying sameness of the daily commute." (Publisher's note)

Atwood, Margaret, 1939-

Writing with intent; essays, reviews, personal prose, 1983-2005. Carroll & Graf Publishers 2005 427p $26   **814**
ISBN 0-7867-1535-9

LC 2005-42086

Some of the essays in this volume were first published 2004 in Canada with title: Moving targets

In these essays, the author "comments on world events, fellow writers, and her own development. She reviews books by John Updike, Italo Calvino, Antonia Fraser, and Dashiell Hammett, as well as the lesser-known Robert Bringhurst, Hilary Mantel, and H. Rider Haggard. . . . This collection will not disappoint Atwood fans as her analyses both challenge and entertain." Libr J
Includes bibliographical references

Baker, Nicholson, 1957-

The **way** the world works; essays. Nicholson Baker. Simon & Schuster 2012 336 p. (hardcover) $25.00   **814**
1. American essays 2. Electronic books 3. Books and reading
ISBN 1416572473; 9781416572473

LC 2011052741

This book is a "collection of essays," in which "[Nicholson] Baker . . . poses important questions about our era of digital readership. As he notes in his essay on the Kindle 2, there is a distinction between a writer's work and its presentation in book form. Many essays staunchly defend the reading of print books and newspapers. . . . A proud defender of libraries and newspapers, Baker acknowledges the perception of him as 'a weirdo cultist, a ringleader' for books." (Publishers Weekly)

Baldwin, James

★ **Collected** essays. Library of Am. 1998 869p $35 **814**
ISBN 1-883011-52-3

LC 97-23496

The essays in this volume were selected by Toni Morrison. "Morrison has reprinted all of the material contained in Baldwin's previous collected essays, The Price of the Ticket (1985). She has added eleven pieces, the earliest of which dates from 1947—Baldwin's first published review, of a biography of Frederick Douglass, in the Nation—and the latest from 1984." Times Lit Suppl

The **beholder's** eye; a collection of America's finest personal journalism. edited and with an introduction by Walt Harrington. Grove Press 2005 xxii, 256p pa $14   **814**
ISBN 0-8021-4224-5

LC 2005-46242

"Each writer takes a unique approach to the subject, drawing the reader into the experience of pit-bull fighting or hunting with the Inuit. Among the collection: Harrington, who is married to a black woman, explores his evolving attitudes on race through the lens of his relationship with his in-laws, Pete Earley returns to his hometown in search of the meaning of a sister's death in their youth, Ron Rosenbaum explores his own outlook on life in a philosophical discourse with then-New York governor Mario Cuomo, Davis Miller is unabashedly starstruck in a comfortable and closeup look at Muhammad Ali at the home of Ali's mother, and Stephen S. Hall is personally probing in his exploration, via MRI, of his own brain and its functioning. These stories are amusing, insightful, and touching in a way that only something personal can be." Booklist

Berry, Wendell

Imagination in place; essays. Counterpoint 2010 196p $24   **814**
ISBN 978-1-58243-562-6; 1-58243-562-6

LC 2009-38104

"For those who've already come to admire Berry's moral clarity and closely argued critiques of contemporary society, 'Imagination in Place' is a welcome chance to continue the conversation." Christ Sci Monit
Includes bibliographical references

★ The **Best** American essays of the century; Joyce Carol Oates, editor; Robert Atwan, coeditor; with an introduction by Joyce Carol Oates. Houghton Mifflin 2000 596p hardcover o.p. pa $18   **814**
ISBN 0-618-04370-5; 0-618-15587-2 pa

This anthology includes essays "that contemplate diverse worlds, from nature to courtrooms, war and family memories. Race is a pervasive theme, explored with candor and insight by many, including James Baldwin, Zora Neale Hurston, and, in a jolting 1912 condemnation of a Coatesville, Pennsylvania, lynching, John Jay Chapman." Booklist
Includes bibliographical references

Bradbury, Ray

Bradbury speaks; too soon from the cave, too far from the stars. William Morrow 2005 243p hardcover o.p. pa $14.95   **814**
ISBN 0-06-058568-4; 0-06-058569-2 pa

LC 2005-41489

In this collection of essays, the author "weighs in on a medley of topics, including the allure of Paris, his enthusiasm for trains, the genesis of his most popular novels, and his reasons for remaining a diehard optimist. . . . By turns whimsical, insightful, and unabashedly metaphoric, his prose is immediately accessible as well as thought-provoking. Fans and nonfans alike should enjoy." Booklist

Burn this book; PEN writers speak out on the power of the word. edited by Toni Morrison. HarperStudio 2009 118p $16.99   **814**
1. Authorship 2. Censorship 3. Freedom of speech
ISBN 978-0-06-177400-3

"Published in conjunction with the PEN American Center, this slim collection of essays has an amazing list of contributors—Toni Morrison, John Updike, David Grossman, Francine Prose, Pico Iyer, Russell Banks, Paul Auster, Orhan Pamuk, Salman Rushdie, Ed Park, and Nadine Gordimer. . . . [They] discuss the importance of writing from various views, political and social. They illustrate the need for freedom of speech and human rights, and they emphasize the target writers become in a tyranny. . . . This is not an easy read, but it is a profound, absorbing,

and moving collection of work." Libr J
Includes bibliographical references

Capote, Truman

★ **Portraits** and observations; the essays of Truman Capote. Random House 2007 518p $28.95   **814**
ISBN 978-1-4000-6661-2; 1-4000-6661-1

LC 2007-36624

This is a collection of 42 essays written by Capote from 1946 to 1984.

"The featured works cover the artist's interests in travel, celebrities, the arts—both visual and literary—crimes of passion, and himself. . . . This collection offers the highest quality of writing from a genuine American stylist." Libr J

Chabon, Michael

Maps and legends; reading and writing along the borderlands. McSweeney's 2008 222p $24   **814**
1. Authorship
ISBN 978-1-932416-89-3; 1-932416-89-7

"In 16 essays, Chabon maps his enthusiasms. . . . Although in part a fragmentary memoir—we receive revealing glimpses of Chabon's family, boyhood home of Columbia, Md., and personal history—'Maps and Legends' is also a manifesto, a declaration of literary principles that asserts the value, even necessity, of genre. Especially in the book's first half, Chabon makes this argument through example, by closely examining and celebrating Arthur Conan Doyle's Sherlock Holmes tales, Philip Pullman's 'His Dark Materials' series, M.R. James' ghost stories, and the comics of Howard Chaykin, Ben Katchor and Will Eisner. . . . However disparately engaging you find the ruminations on other writers, the book's concluding quintet of pieces on the inspirations behind Chabon's major work will prove an illuminating delight for those of us who have the same fannish devotion to his work as he does to Conan Doyle's." St. Louis Post-Dispatch

Chee, Alexander

★ **How** to write an autobiographical novel; essays. Alexander Chee. Houghton Mifflin Harcourt 2018 288 p. (trade paper) $15.99   **814**
1. Essays 2. American authors -- Biography
ISBN 9781328764522; 1328764524

LC 2017045808

This essay collection, by Alexander Chee, is his "manifesto on the entangling of life, literature, and politics, and how the lessons learned from a life spent reading and writing fiction have changed him. In these essays, he grows from student to teacher, reader to writer, and reckons with his identities as a son, a gay man, a Korean American, an artist, an activist, a lover, and a friend." (Publisher's note)

"His quotable, pristine essays consider Chee's family's struggles, his AIDS activism and related losses, his tarot obsession, the labor of writing, the legacies of trauma, and the essentiality of making and having art. Hand to readers searching for something to follow 2017's incredible parade of writers' memoirs, including Roxane Gay's Hunger and Amy Tan's Where the Past Begins." Booklist

Daum, Meghan

The **unspeakable**; and other subjects of discussion. Meghan Daum. Farrar, Straus & Giroux 2014 256 p. (hardback) $26   **814**
1. Social adjustment 2. Social conditions
ISBN 0374280444; 9780374280444

LC 2014014643

In this collection of essays, by Meghan Daum, "her old encounters with overdrawn bank accounts and oversized ambitions in the big city have given way to a new set of challenges. . . . She skewers the marriage-industrial complex and recounts a harrowing near-death experience following a sudden illness. Throughout, Daum pushes back against the false sentimentality and shrink-wrapped platitudes that surround so much of contemporary American experience." (Publisher's note)

"This book will appeal to memoir enthusiasts seeking an insightful reading experience that will entertain as well as challenge." LJ

Didion, Joan

We tell ourselves stories in order to live; collected nonfiction. with an introduction by John Leonard. Knopf 2006 1122p $30   **814**
ISBN 978-0-307-26487-9; 0-307-26487-4

LC 2006-41043

This volume "contains seven books of journalism—all of [Didion's] nonfiction except her 2005 memoir of new widowhood, 'The Year of Magical Thinking.' Didion's writing was from the beginning startlingly individual. . . . Say what you will about her somewhat self-centered style; America needs more courageous thinkers who will write about life as it is lived—not as elites on all sides seek to manufacture it." Nat Rev
Includes bibliographical references

Du Bois, W. E. B.

★ **Writings**. Library of Am. 1986 1334p $40; pa $15.95   **814**
ISBN 0-940450-33-X; 1-883011-31-0 pa

LC 86-10565

Includes bibliographical references
Contents: The suppression of the African slave-trade; The souls of black folk; Dusk of dawn; Essays; Articles from The crisis

Ellison, Ralph

The **collected** essays of Ralph Ellison; edited with an introduction by John F. Callahan; preface by Saul Bellow. Modern Lib. 1995 xxix, 856p hardcover o.p. pa $18   **814**
1. Artists 2. Authors 3. Pianists 4. Educators 5. Novelists 6. Dramatists 7. Economists 8. Journalists 9. Essayists 10. Screenwriters 11. Music teachers 12. Cabinet members 13. Newspaper editors 14. Nonfiction writers 15. Classical musicians 16. Short story writers 17. Civil rights activists 18. Jazz music -- History and criticism 19. International organization officials 20. Nobel laureates for economic sciences
ISBN 978-0-8129-6826-2 pa; 0-8129-6826-3 pa

LC 95-4719

This book "includes posthumously discovered reviews, criticism, and interviews, as well as the essay collections Shadow and Act (1964) . . . and Going to the Territory (1986), an exploration of literature and folklore, jazz and culture, and the nature and quality of lives that black Americans lead." Publisher's note

Ephron, Nora, 1941-2012

I feel bad about my neck; and other thoughts on being a woman. Nora Ephron. Knopf 2006 137p pa $12.95; (alk. paper) $21.95   **814**
1. Aging 2. Women
ISBN 0307276821; 9780307264558; 9780307276827; 0307264556

LC 2005057780

In this book, author Nora Ephron offers "a candid, hilarious look at women who are getting older and dealing with the tribulations of maintenance, menopause, empty nests, and life itself. . . . Ephron chronicles her life as an obsessed cook, passionate city dweller, and hapless parent. She recounts her anything-but-glamorous days as a White House intern. . . . But mostly she speaks frankly and uproariously about life as a woman of a certain age." (Publisher's note)

"While very little in the book is meant to be taken seriously, it is clever enough to qualify as more than just an assemblage of one-liners. Whether you agree with her observations or not, Ephron's perspective as an admittedly high-maintenance, New York-dwelling, successful screenwriter will keep you entertained." Christ Sci Monit

The **Most** of Nora Ephron; by Nora Ephron. Alfred A. Knopf 2013 576 p. (hardcover) $35   **814**
1. Anthologies 2. Women authors 3. Romance fiction
ISBN 038535083X; 9780385350839
LC 2013016426

This posthumously-published book collects writings by Nora Ephron. Ephron and her editor "decided to structure it around the subject matters she explored and the genres she used to explore them. As a result, the text of her novel Heartburn (1983) is included, as is the screenplay for Ephron's most beloved movie, When Harry Met Sally, and her late-in-life play, Lucky Guy. The remainder of the anthology consists of much briefer entries across a . . . diverse set of topics." (Kirkus Reviews)

"Whether Ephron is writing about politics or purses, sexism or soufflé, her appeal is her intelligent, incisive sense of humor." LJ

Franzen, Jonathan, 1959-
★ The **end** of the end of the earth; essays. Jonathan Franzen. Farrar, Straus & Giroux 2018 240 p. (hbk.) $27   **814**
1. American essays
ISBN 0374147930; 9780374147938

In this essay collection, author "Jonathan Franzen returns with renewed vigor to the themes--both human and literary--that have long preoccupied him. . . . Taken together, these essays trace the progress of a unique and mature mind wrestling with itself, with literature, and with some of the most important issues of our day, made more pressing by the current political milieu." (Publisher's note)

"Whether observing the eerie beauty of Antarctica ('far from having melted,' he reports) or dispensing 'Ten Rules for the Novelist,' Franzen makes for an entertaining, sometimes prickly, but always quotable companion." Pub Wkly

★ **Farther** away; Jonathan Franzen. Farrar, Straus and Giroux 2012 321 p.   **814**
1. American essays 2. Literature -- History and criticism 3. Interpersonal relations in literature
ISBN 0374153574; 9780374153571
LC 2011046067

The author presents "a collection of recent essays, speeches, and reviews, in which he lays out a view of literature in which storytelling and character development trump lyrical acrobatics, and unearths a few forgotten classics. . . . [Jonathan Franzen discusses] books that revel in the frustrations, despairs, and near-blisses of human relationships. . . . This intimate read is packed with provocative questions about technology, love, and the state of the contemporary novel." (Publishers Weekly)

The **Fun** of it; stories from The talk of the town, The New Yorker. edited by Lillian Ross; introduction by David Remnick. Modern Lib. 2001 xxi, 478p pa $16.95   **814**
1. New Yorker (Periodical)
ISBN 0-375-75649-3
LC 00-68237

A "selection of stories from 'Talk' in chronologically arranged sec-

tions that begin with the 1920s and end in 2000. Many of the early contributions were unsigned, but through archival research Ross ferrets out and reveals the authors of many of those initial pieces. Included in this lively collection are pieces by writers—some of whom became New Yorker regulars—such as Robert Benchley, James Thurber, E. B. White, A. J. Liebling, John Updike, Garrison Keillor, Ann Beattie, Bill McKibben, Roger Angell, Steve Martin, and Susan Orlean." Libr J

Gay, Roxane, 1974-
Bad Feminist; essays. Roxane Gay. HarperCollins 2014 336 p. $15.99   **814**
1. Feminism 2. Feminist criticism
ISBN 0062282719; 9780062282712

This book, by Roxane Gay, is a "collection of essays spanning politics, criticism, and feminism. . . . Gay takes us through the journey of her evolution as a woman (Sweet Valley High) of color (The Help) while also taking readers on a ride through culture of the last few years (Girls, Django in Chains) and commenting on the state of feminism today (abortion, Chris Brown)." (Publisher's note)

"Writing about race, politics, gender, feminism, privilege, and popular media, [Gay] highlights how deeply misogyny is embedded in our culture, the careless language used to discuss sexual violence (seen in news reports of sexual assault), Hollywood's tokenistic treatment of race, the trivialization of literature written by women, and the many ways American society fails women and African-Americans." Pub Wkly

Ginsberg, Allen
★ **Deliberate** prose; selected essays, 1952-1995. HarperCollins Pubs. 2000 xxiv, 536p hardcover o.p. pa $17   **814**
ISBN 0-06-093081-0 pa
LC 99-41360

This collection of over 100 prose pieces "organizes the material under several general topics: 'Politics and Prophecies,' 'Drug Culture,' 'Manifestations and Spirituality,' 'Censorship and Sex Laws,' 'Autobiographical Fragments,' 'Literary Techniques and the Beat Generation,' 'Writer,' and 'Further Appreciations,' tributes to artistic collaborators and cultural heroes such as Robert Frank, Philip Glass, Andy Warhol, and the Beatles. . . . Taken together, they provide a rare glimpse into Ginsberg's creative practice, a key to sources and influences, and a good overview of his life and art." Libr J

Includes bibliographical references

Glück, Louise, 1943-
American originality; essays on poetry. Louise Glück. Farrar, Straus & Giroux 2017 189 p. (hardcover) $24   **814**
1. American poetry 2. Creative ability 3. Originality in literature 4. American poetry -- 20th century -- Criticism and interpretation
ISBN 9780374299552; 9781466875685; 0374299552
LC 2016026993

This collection of essays, by Louise Glück, "forces readers to consider contemporary poetry and its demigods in radical, unconsoling, and ultimately very productive ways. Determined to wrest ample, often contradictory meaning from our current literary discourse, Glück comprehends and destabilizes notions of 'narcissism' and 'genius' that are unique to the American literary climate." (Publisher's note)

"A love of poetry—of the poet's life—infuses these essays and brings a glow to the theoretical and a bright flame to the personal." Kirkus

Goldbarth, Albert, 1948-
The **adventures** of form and content; essays. Albert Goldbarth. Graywolf Press 2017 103, 89 p.p (alk. paper) $16 **814**
1. American essays 2. Essays
ISBN 9781555977610

LC 2016938022

This book of essays, by Albert Goldbarth, "is about the mysteries of dualities, the selves we all carry inside, the multiverses that we are. This collection takes its shape from the ACE Doubles format of the 1950s: turn this book one way, and read about the checkered history of those sci-fi and pulp fictions, or about the erotic poetry of Catullus . . .; turn this book the other way, and read about prehistoric cave artists and NASA astronauts, or about illness and health." (Publisher's note)

"A nostalgic, rueful, and sometimes sweetly funny collection." Kirkus

Gottlieb, Robert Adams

★ **Lives** and letters. Farrar, Straus and Giroux 2011 426p $30 **814**

1. Persons 2. Celebrities
ISBN 978-0-374-29882-1; 0-374-29882-3

LC 2010-38530

"Having headed up two formidable cultural institutions, The New Yorker and the Alfred A. Knopf publishing house, Gottlieb is a fairly formidable cultural institution himself. When he passes judgment, we are inclined to listen. Befitting a man of letters, some of the essays meditate on literary figures and questions that attracted Gottlieb's curiosity. In one he examines the unlikely author-editor collaboration between Marjorie Kinnan Rawlings and Maxwell Perkins; in another he ponders how the 'wildly uneven' works of John Steinbeck have all managed to stay in print. The crowd-pleasing portion of the collection is provided by Gottlieb's critical reflections on biographies, many featuring celebrities who soared through life, egos ablaze. Discussing books about prima donnas as diverse as Margot Fonteyn and Judy Garland, Gottlieb is genteelly shocked by salacious revelations he considers an invasion of privacy, though not too shocked to give examples." Boston Globe

Hall, Donald, 1928-2018

Essays After Eighty; Donald Hall. Houghton Mifflin Harcourt 2014 144 p. (hardback) $22 **814**

1. Essays 2. Old age 3. Older men
ISBN 0544287045; 9780544287044

LC 2014016310

This book, by Donald Hall, presents a "collection of essays delivering . . . [an] unexpected view from the vantage point of very old age. . . . In . . . 'No Smoking,' he looks back over his lifetime, and several of his ancestors' lifetimes, of smoking unfiltered cigarettes, packs of them every day. Hall paints his past . . . [and], poignantly, often joyfully, he limns his present." (Publisher's note)

"America's 14th poet laureate and recipient of the National Medal of the Arts, among countless other honors, Hall offers essays that report meditatively from the 'unknown, unanticipated galaxy' of advanced age. He still lives to write, enjoying life at his ancestral Eagle Pond Farm." LJ

Hamid, Mohsin, 1971-

Discontent and its civilizations; dispatches from Lahore, New York, and London. Mohsin Hamid. Penguin Group USA 2015 240 p. (cloth) $27.95 **814**

1. Popular culture 2. Social conditions
ISBN 1594633657; 9781594633652; 9780241146323

LC 2014027668

This essay collection, by Mohsin Hamid, "brings together a wide variety of his work, a number of which appeared in print before, that touch on such subjects as international politics, the East-West divide, President Barack Obama's 2009 speech in Cairo, fundamentalism, and nationalism. Other more lighthearted topics: books and reading, the challenges the author faced moving back to Pakistan at a young age, and fatherhood, are also considered." (Library Journal)

"Hamid is an intelligent and impassioned writer whose work deserves a wide readership. Those interested in memoirs, world politics, and cultural and religious differences will enjoy these essays." LJ

Hardwick, Elizabeth

The **collected** essays of Elizabeth Hardwick; Elizabeth Hardwick, edited and with an introduction by Darryl Pinckney. New York Review Books 2017 640 p. (paperback: acid-free paper) $19.95 **814**

1. Civil rights 2. American essays 3. Literature -- Collections
ISBN 9781681371542

LC 2017014041

This book in the New York Review Books Classics series, by Elizabeth Hardwick, edited by Darryl Pinckney, presents "the first-ever collection of essays from across . . . Hardwick's illustrious writing career, including works not seen in print for decades. . . . Individual lives and the life of New York, the setting or backdrop for most of these stories, are strikingly and memorably depicted in Hardwick's beautiful and razor-sharp prose." (Publisher's note)

"This wonderful volume of essays about place and time is recommended for libraries with large literature and women's studies collections." (LJ)

Hemon, Aleksandar, 1964-

The **book** of my lives; Aleksandar Hemon. Farrar, Straus and Giroux 2013 214 p. (hardcover: alk. paper) $25 **814**

1. Sarajevo (Bosnia and Hercegovina)
ISBN 0374115737; 9780374115739

LC 2012034564

National Book Critics Circle Award Finalist: Autobiography (2013)

This collection of essays by Aleksandar Hemon focuses on "the war in the former Yugoslavia and its transformative effect on the material and metaphysical circumstances of Hemon's life. . . . In 'The Lives of a Flaneur,' in which he meditates on the loss of Sarajevo, he frames the story in geographical terms. . . . In 'Let There Be What Cannot Be,' by contrast, he frames the story of the war in literary terms: as a Serbian epic poem come to life." (The Nation)

Hitchens, Christopher, 1949-2011

Arguably; Essays by Christopher Hitchens. Christopher Hitchens. Twelve 2011 788p $30.00 **814**

1. American essays 2. Literature -- History and criticism 3. Criticism
ISBN 085789255X Atlantic Books; 9780857892553 Atlantic Books; 9781455502776; 9781455506781

LC 2011930917

This collection of essays by Christopher Hitchens "supplies fresh perceptions of such figures as varied as Charles Dickens, Karl Marx, Rebecca West, George Orwell, J.G. Ballard, and Philip Larkin . . . [and] pungent discussions and intrepid observations, gathered from a lifetime of traveling and reporting from such destinations as Iran, China, and Pakistan. . . . [This] volume is an intellectual self-portrait of a writer with . . . [a] vision of the human longing for reason and justice." (Publisher's note)

"Goading, brilliant, funny, and caring, Hitchens is a voice of enlightenment in a wilderness of cant." Booklist

Hustvedt, Siri

Living, thinking, looking; essays. Siri Hustvedt. Picador 2012 xiii, 384 p.p $18.00 **814**

1. Authorship 2. American essays 3. Psychologists -- Research 4. Hallucinations and illusions 5. Human beings

ISBN 1250009529; 9781250009524

LC 2011035714

In this essay collection, "[n]ovelist and essayist [Siri] Hustvedt . . . gathers 32 pieces (most previously published), written over the past six years, that she says are linked by an abiding curiosity about 'what it means to be human.'" Topics include a premigraine hallucination of Paul Bunyan, researching her novel "The Sorrows of an American," and the artist Louise Bourgeois. (Publishers Weekly)

Includes bibliographical references (p. [355]-380)

The **Inevitable;** contemporary writers confront death. edited by David Shields and Bradford Morrow; with an introduction by the editors. W. W. Norton & Co. 2011 332p $17.95 **814**

1. Death

ISBN 9780393339369 pa

LC 2010-43479

"Often poetic and at times funny or gruesome while exposing raw grief, the writers . . . tackle the subject of death with honesty and courage." Publ Wkly

Includes bibliographical references

Irby, Samantha

We are never meeting in real life; essays. Samantha Irby. Vintage Books 2017 xii, 275 p.p (paperback) $15.95   **814**

1. Conduct of life -- Humor 2. Comedians -- United States -- Biography 3. Bloggers -- United States -- Biography

ISBN 9781101912201; 1101912197; 9781101912195

LC 2017002278

In this book, "blogger and comedian Samantha Irby turns the serio-comic essay into an art form. Whether talking about how her difficult childhood has led to a problem in making 'adult' budgets, explaining why she should be the new Bachelorette . . . , or dispensing advice on how to navigate friendships with former drinking buddies . . . --she's as deft at poking fun at the ghosts of her past self as she is at capturing powerful emotional truths." (Publisher's note)

"In her new book of essays, Irby . . . is once again the inimitably candid, über-confessional friend readers will happily spend a few hundred pages with." Booklist

Jamison, Leslie

★ The **empathy** exams; essays. Leslie Jamison. Graywolf Press 2014 256 p. (alk. paper) $15   **814**

1. Pain 2. Essays 3. Empathy

ISBN 1555976719; 9781555976712

LC 2013946927

"Beginning with her experience as a medical actor who was paid to act out symptoms for medical students to diagnose, Leslie Jamison's visceral and revealing essays ask essential questions about our basic understanding of others: How should we care about each other? How can we feel another's pain, especially when pain can be assumed, distorted, or performed? Is empathy a tool by which to test or even grade each other?" (Publisher's note)

"Jamison exhibits at once a journalist's courage to bear witness to acts and conditions that test human limits--incarceration, laboring in a silver mine, ultramarathoning, the loss of a child, devastating heartbreak, suffering from an unacknowledged illness--and a poet's skepticism at her own motives for doing so." Kirkus

Includes bibliographical references

Kreider, Tim

I wrote this book because I love you; essays. Tim Kreider. Simon & Schuster 2018 224 p. $26   **814**

1. Friendship 2. Man-woman relationship 3. Human-animal relationships

ISBN 1476738998; 9781476738994

In this essay collection, author Tim Kreider "focuses his unique perception and wit on his relationships with women--romantic, platonic, and the murky in-between. He talks about his difficulty finding lasting love, and seeks to understand his commitment issues. . . . He talks about his valued female friendships. . . . He [also] talks about his nineteen-year-old cat, wondering if it's the most enduring relationship he'll ever have." (Publisher's note)

"Kreider's clever hand and philosophic—rather than solipsistic—viewpoint place him in a different realm than writers like David Sedaris and David Foster Wallace who share his affection for details, uncommon settings, and nuance." Pub Wkly

Le Guin, Ursula K., 1929-2018

★ **No** time to spare; thinking about what matters. Ursula K. Le Guin; introduction by Karen Joy Fowler. Houghton Mifflin Harcourt 2017 215 p. Hardcover $22   **814**

1. Old age 2. Civilization 3. Aging 4. Literature 5. United States -- Civilization

ISBN 9781328661593

LC 2017019808

This book, by Ursula K. Le Guin, "collects the best of Ursula's blog, presenting perfectly crystallized dispatches on what matters to her now, her concerns with this world, and her wonder at it. On the absurdity of denying your age, she says, 'If I'm ninety and believe I'm forty-five, I-m headed for a very bad time trying to get out of the bathtub.' [And] on cultural perceptions of fantasy: 'The direction of escape is toward freedom. So what is 'escapism' an accusation of?'" (Publisher's note)

"Spirited, wry reflections on aging, literature, and America's moral life."--Kirkus Reviews

Lethem, Jonathan

The **ecstasy** of influence; nonfictions, etc. Doubleday 2011 437p $27.95   **814**

ISBN 978-0-385-53495-6; 9780385534956

LC 2011016248

"Mr. Lethem's crowded pantheon, 'The Ecstasy of Influence' makes clear, includes Marvel comic books and misfit writers like Philip K. Dick, J. G. Ballard, Shirley Jackson and Charles Willeford. It includes improvisational filmmakers like John Cassavetes, little-known bands like the Go-Betweens and rumpled, bohemian critics like Manny Farber. Mr. Lethem is all about the underdogs, and he counts himself snug among their number. 'Most of my heroes,' he declares, 'are partly or entirely out of print.' Mailer gets a hall pass because he is, like Mr. Lethem, from Brooklyn, and because he took a grizzled interest in things like 'graffiti, underground film, marijuana and space travel.' Like almost everything Mr. Lethem has written, 'The Ecstasy of Influence' is a reflection of, and a pixelated homage to, those whose work he fetishizes. If this book has a thesis, it's this: For an artist, influence is everything." N Y Times (Late N Y Ed)

More alive and less lonely; on books and writers. Jonathan Lethem; edited and with an introduction by Christopher Boucher. Melville House 2017 xix, 300 p.p (hardback) $26.99 **814**

1. Authorship 2. Books and reading 3. Literature -- History and criticism 4. Authors and readers 5. Literature -- History and criticism -- Theory, etc

ISBN 9781612196046; 9781612196039

LC 2016036950

This book, by Jonathan Lethem, edited and with an introduction by Christopher Boucher, "collects over a decade of . . . Lethem's finest writing on writing, with new and previously unpublished material, including: impassioned appreciations of forgotten writers and overlooked books, razor-sharp critical essays, and personal accounts of his most extraordinary literary encounters and discoveries." (Publisher's note)

"One of America's most accomplished writers looks back between the pages of other writers' books." Kirkus

Includes bibliographical references.

Morales, Angela

The **girls** in my town; essays. Angela Morales. University of New Mexico Press 2016 ix, 170 p.p (River Teeth Literary Nonfiction Prize) (pbk.: alk. paper) $19.95   **814**
    1. American essays 2. American authors 3. Girls -- California -- Los Angeles
    ISBN 9780826356628
                           LC 2015020149

This book by Angela Morales, winner of the River Teeth Literary Nonfiction Prize, features "autobiographical essays . . . [that] create an unforgettable portrait of a family in Los Angeles. Reaching back to her grandmother's childhood and navigating through her own girlhood and on to the present." (Publisher's note)

"Essays that are as thematically ambitious as they are deeply personal." Kirkus

Oates, Joyce Carol, 1938-

Soul at the white heat; inspiration, obsession, and the writing life. Joyce Carol Oates. Ecco, an imprint of HarperCollins Publishers 2016 x, 390 p.p (hardcover) $27.99   **814**
    1. Criticism 2. Authorship 3. Essays 4. Creation (Literary, artistic, etc.) 5. American literature -- Criticism and interpretation
    ISBN 9780062564504; 9780062564535; 0062564501
                           LC 2017295288

This book, by Joyce Carol Oates, is a "collection of critical and personal essays on writing, obsession, and inspiration. . . . Oates deploys her keenest critical faculties, conjuring contemporary and past voices whose work she deftly and creatively dissects for clues to these elusive questions. Virginia Woolf, John Updike, Emily Dickinson, Henry James, J. M. Coetzee, Margaret Atwood, Joan Didion, Zadie Smith, and many others appear as predecessors and peers." (Publisher's note)

"Another collection of sparkling literary essays from the prolific author of both fiction and nonfiction." Kirkus

Ozick, Cynthia

★ **Quarrel** & quandary; essays. Knopf 2000 247p hardcover o.p. pa $13   **814**
    1. Authors 2. Children 3. Novelists 4. Diarists 5. Holocaust victims 6. Short story writers 7. Literature -- History and criticism
    ISBN 0-375-72445-9 pa
                           LC 99-89889

Among the topics discussed in this collection of personal and literary essays are Henry James, Anne Frank, Kafka, poetry, and public intellectuals.

"All the essays collected here began life elsewhere as reviews and higher journalism. This kind of gathering of literary leftovers is usually not worth reprinting. Ozick's work is an exception. Her pieces have genuine durability. They are great essays." N Y Times Book Rev

Packer, George

Interesting times; writings from a turbulent decade. Farrar, Straus and Giroux 2009 409p $28   **814**
    ISBN 978-0-3741-7572-6; 0-3741-7572-1
                           LC 2009-10186

A collection "essays chronicling global political and cultural tumult between 9/11 and the 2008 presidential election. . . . From Lagos to Myanmar, Tal Afar to Baghdad, the author reports on location and presents on-the-ground particulars that bring robust perspective to issues that are generally broadly reported. . . . In an era marked by the swift decline of well-researched, long-form journalism, these often heart-wrenching essays bring to life social, political and personal elements of far-flung crises in ways that elude more concise mediums." Kirkus

Paterniti, Michael

Love and Other Ways of Dying; Essays. Michael Paterniti. Random House Inc 2015 464 p. $28   **814**
    1. Grief 2. Emotions
    ISBN 0385337027; 9780385337021
                           LC 2014033162

In this essay collection, author "Michael Paterniti turns a keen eye on the full range of human experience, introducing us to an unforgettable cast of everyday people. He brings his full literary powers to bear, pondering happiness and grief, memory and the redemptive power of human connection." (Publisher's note)

"A wide variety of places and people are given Paterniti's trademark scrutiny here, and the resulting essays are illuminating and pleasantly verbose." LJ

Read Harder; edited by Ed Park and Heidi Julavits. McSweeney's 2014 336 p. illustrations $18   **814**
    1. Essays 2. Periodicals
    ISBN 1940450187; 9781940450186

Editors Ed Park and Heidi Julavits present a collection of "essays from the second half of the Believer's decade-long (and counting) run. Featured articles include Nick Hornby on his first job, Rebecca Taylor on her time acting in no-budget horror movies, Francisco Goldman on the failings of memoir in dealing with personal tragedy, Megan Abbott and Sara Gran on V.C. Andrews." (Publisher's note)

"For fans of Eggers and McSweeny's publications, pop culture enthusiasts, and readers of literary magazines." LJ

Reece, Erik

Practice resurrection; and other essays. Erik Reece. Counterpoint Press 2017 214 p. (alk. paper) $25   **814**
    1. American essays 2. Essays 3. Spiritual life 4. Nature -- Religious aspects
    ISBN 9781619026087; 1619026082
                           LC 2017004033

In this book of essays, by Erik Reece, "ideas are the main characters. Written over ten years, and revealing Reece's continued obsession with religion, family and the natural world, in many ways these essays represent a sequel to his stirring memoir." (Publisher's note)

"Reece's insightful, witty, and reflective essays offer up new ways of thinking about spirituality, culture, and the environment." Kirkus

Includes bibliographical references and index.

Remnick, David

Reporting; writings from The New Yorker. Knopf 2006 483p $27.95   **814**
    1. Essays 2. Journalism -- United States
    ISBN 0-307-26358-4; 978-0-307-26358-2
                           LC 2005-44709

The author "is an ideal reporter, combining erudition, curiosity, wit, an eye for the telling anecdote and empathy." Publ Wkly

Robinson, Marilynne, 1943-

When I was a child I read books; Marilynne Robinson. Farrar, Straus & Giroux 2012 xvi, 206 p   **814**

1. Theology 2. Calvinism 3. American essays 4. Political science
5. United States -- Civilization 6. Philosophy, American 7.
Theology -- United States 8. Calvinism -- United States 9. United
States -- Civilization -- Philosophy 10. Political science -- United
States -- Philosophy

ISBN 0374298785; 9780374298784

LC 2011041206

This collection of essays by Marilynne Robinson offers a critique of
U.S. culture and politics. "Her enemies are many and varied -- militant
atheists, scientists, . . . a political system that sees everything in terms
of economic value, a government that commits the arch-crimes of closing libraries and filleting universities. . . . She observes that the idea
of a public sector is now condemned by many Americans as 'socialism,' a stance at odds with the civic principles on which the country was
founded." (New Statesman)

Includes bibliographical references.

Russo, Richard, 1949-

★ The **destiny** thief; essays on writing, writers, and life.
Richard Russo. Alfred A. Knopf 2018 224 p. (hardcover)
$25.95   **814**

1. American novelists 2. American authors -- Biography

ISBN 9781524733513

LC 2017024819

In this essay collection, author Richard Russo "provides insight into
his life as a writer, teacher, friend, and reader. From a commencement
speech he gave at Colby College, to the story of how an oddly placed
toilet made him reevaluate the purpose of humor in art and life, to a
comprehensive analysis of Mark Twain's value, . . . [this book] reflects
the broad interests and experiences of one of America's most beloved
authors." (Publisher's note)

"For aspiring writers, Russo's musings on the art and craft of the
novel are a trove of knowledge and guidance. For adoring readers, they
are a window into the imagination and inspiration for Russo's beloved
novels, screenplays, and short stories." Booklist

Said, Edward W.

Reflections on exile and other essays. Harvard Univ. Press
2000 xxxv, 617p (Convergences) $36.95; pa $19.95   **814**

1. Authors 2. Criticism 3. Novelists 4. Nationalism 5.
Philosophers 6. Psychologists 7. Palestinian Arabs 8. Politics in
literature 9. Literary critics 10. Short story writers 11. Egypt --
Civilization 12. Motion picture directors 13. Literature -- History
and criticism

ISBN 0-674-00302-0; 0-674-00997-5 pa

LC 00-44996

"Written between 1967 and the present by a literary critic and advocate for the Palestinian cause, these pieces often deal with the self-
deceiving fictions of the colonizers about the people they oppress; others
deplore some fashionable critical theories as unengaged with real life
and history." N Y Times Book Rev

Includes bibliographical references

Salter, James, 1925-2015

Don't save anything; uncollected essays, articles, and
profiles. James Salter; with a preface by Kay Eldredge Salter.
Counterpoint Press 2017 xiv, 303 p.p (hardcover) $26   **814**

1. Essays

ISBN 9781619029361; 9781640090019; 1619029367

LC 2017017393

This book, by James Salter, "is a volume of the best of Jim's non-
fiction--articles published but never collected in one place until now.

Though those many boxes were overflowing with papers, in the end it's
not really a matter of quantity. These pieces reveal some of the breadth
and depth of Jim's endless interest in the world and the people in it."
(Publisher's note)

"Crisp and razor sharp, Salter's work peels away illusions to reveal
the matter-of-fact nuances of his and our lives." Pub Wkly

Sedaris, David

Dress your family in corduroy and denim. Little, Brown
2004 257p $24.95   **814**

ISBN 0-316-14346-4

LC 2003-65673

The author "has a unique ability to supply exactly the right details
to bring every funny, awkward, ludicrous, painful, horrible real-life moment into harrowingly crisp focus." Booklist

Let's explore diabetes with owls; by David Sedaris. 1st ed.
Little, Brown, and Co. 2013 ix, 275 p.p (hardcover) $27.00;
(hardcover) $29.00   **814**

1. Swimming 2. Sea turtles 3. American essays

ISBN 0316154695; 9780316154697; 9780316233910 large print

LC 2013930473

This is an essay collection by David Sedaris. He draws on a "well
of appalling childhood memories revolving around his mounting fears
about being unlike other boys." He shares stories about his swimming
competitions where "his irascible father vociferously championed his
son's rival," his "courtship of a shy African American girl," and his "inept handling of captured baby sea turtles." (Booklist)

Me talk pretty one day. Little, Brown 2000 272p $22.95;
pa $14.95   **814**

ISBN 0-316-77772-2; 0-316-77696-3 pa

LC 00-25052

"In this collection of 27 fairly short essays, some of which appeared
in Esquire and The New Yorker, Sedaris gives the impression of ease
and naturalness. Whether he is writing about overcoming a lisp, learning
to play the guitar, trying to master French, or taking an IQ test, whether
the locales are North Carolina, New York, or France, the author is both
amused and amusing." Libr J

★ **Theft** by finding; diaries 1977-2002. David Sedaris.
Little, Brown & Co. 2017 514 p. (hardcover) $28   **814**

1. Comedians 2. Humorists 3. Diaries

ISBN 9780316501293; 9780316154727

LC 2016959026

This book, by David Sedaris, shares "the story of how a drug-abus-
ing dropout with a weakness for the International House of Pancakes
and a chronic inability to hold down a real job became one of the funniest people on the planet. . . . 'Theft By Finding' proves that Sedaris
is one of our great modern observers. It's a potent reminder that when
you're as perceptive and curious as Sedaris, there's no such thing as a
boring day." (Publisher's note)

"A candid, socially incisive, and sharply amusing chronicle of the
evolution of an arresting comedic artist." Booklist

Solnit, Rebecca

The **Faraway** Nearby; Rebecca Solnit. Penguin Group
USA 2013 272 p. $25.95   **814**

1. Iceland 2. Dementia 3. American essays 4. Storytelling
5. Autobiography -- Authorship 6. Narration (Rhetoric) --
Psychological aspects

ISBN 0670025968; 9780670025961

LC 2013001563

National Book Critics Circle Award Finalist: Autobiography (2013)

In this essay collection, National Book Critics Circle Award-winner Rebecca Solnit offers a "study in empathy through these meandering reflections on subjects as diverse as her mother's descent into dementia, Che Guevara, and Solnit's own 'magical rescue' to Iceland for some months as resident at the Library of Water museum." (Publishers Weekly)

Sontag, Susan

★ **At** the same time; essays and speeches. edited by Paolo Dilonardo and Anne Jump; with a foreword by David Rieff. Farrar, Straus & Giroux 2007 235p $23   **814**

ISBN 0-374-10072-1; 978-0-374-10072-8

LC 2006-31179

This is a "collection of 16 essays written toward the end of . . . [Sontag's] life. . . . Every public and academic library should crave to own this." Libr J

Spiegelman, Willard

Senior moments; looking back, looking ahead. Willard Spiegelman. Farrar Straus & Giroux 2016 xiii, 190 p.p (hardback) $24   **814**

1. Happiness 2. Life change events 3. Aging -- Psychological aspects 4. Pleasure 5. Life change events -- Psychological aspects 6. Authors, American -- 20th century -- Biography 7. Authors, American -- 21st century -- Biography 8. College teachers -- United States -- Biography

ISBN 9780374712990; 9780374261221

LC 2015048666

In this essay collection, author Willard Spiegelman "reflects with candid humor and sophistication on growing old. . . . [This book] is a foray into the felicity and follies that age brings; a consideration of how and what one reads or rereads in late adulthood; the eagerness for, and disappointment in, long-awaited reunions, at which the past comes alive in the present." (Publisher's note)

"Readers of a similar age will savor his delight in language and life as he ponders the past and peers into the future." Booklist

Styron, William, 1925-2006

My generation; collected nonfiction. William Styron; edited by James L. W. West III. Random House Inc. 2015 656 p. illustrations (hardback) $35   **814**

1. Essays

ISBN 0812997050; 9780812997057; 9780812997064

LC 2014038029

This book, by William Styron, edited by James L. W. West III, "is the definitive gathering of William Styron's nonfiction. . . . Here are fifty years of Styron's essays, memoirs, reviews, op-eds, articles, eulogies, and speeches, reflecting the same brilliant style and informed thinking that he brought to his towering fiction and to a deeply committed public life." (Publisher's note)

"Elegant and entertaining, the writings in My Generation compose a definitive volume that will appeal to a broad audience. Summing Up: Highly recommended. Lower-division undergraduates through faculty; general readers." Choice

Tan, Amy

The **opposite** of fate; a book of musings. Putnam 2003 398p il $24.95; pa $15   **814**

1. Authors 2. Novelists 3. Essayists 4. Children's authors 5. Short story writers

ISBN 0-399-15074-9; 0-14-200489-8 pa

LC 2003-47190

"No matter how much readers already revere Tan, their appreciation for her will grow tenfold after experiencing these provocative and unforgettable revelations." Booklist

Teicher, Craig Morgan

We begin in gladness; how poets progress. Craig Morgan Teicher. Graywolf Press 2018 176 p. (alk. paper) $16   **814**

1. Poets 2. Poetry -- Authorship 3. Poetry -- History and criticism

ISBN 9781555978211

LC 2018934489

In this book, author Craig Morgan Teicher "considers how poets start out, how they learn to hear themselves, and how some offer us that rare, glittering thing: lasting work. Teicher traces the poetic development of the works of Sylvia Plath, John Ashbery, Louise Glück, and Francine J. Harris, among others, to illuminate the paths they forged--by dramatic breakthroughs or by slow increments, and always by perseverance." (Publisher's note)

Tevis, Joni

The **world** is on fire; scrap, treasure, and songs of apocalypse. Joni Tevis. Milkweed Editions 2015 256 p. (softcover: acid-free paper) $16   **814**

1. American essays 2. End of the world

ISBN 1571313478; 9781571313478

LC 2014038727

In this book, by Joni Tevis, the author "reckons with her childhood fears by exploring the uniquely American fascination with apocalypse. From a haunted widow's wildly expanding mansion, to atomic test sites in the Nevada desert, her settings are often places of destruction and loss. And yet Tevis transforms these eerie destinations into sites of creation as well, uncovering powerful points of connection." (Publisher's note)

"Tevis's essays provide a travelog of her life. Her insights take readers from the steel of scissor blades and the cold waters of Alaska to the fire of atomic bomb testing grounds as seen through a View-Master." LJ

Updike, John

Due considerations; essays and criticism. Alfred A. Knopf 2007 xxii, 703p il $40   **814**

ISBN 978-0-307-26640-8; 0-307-26640-0

LC 2007-18665

"A lush book to be savored over a long period of time." Booklist

Vidal, Gore

The **selected** essays of Gore Vidal; edited by Jay Parini. Doubleday 2008 458p $27.50   **814**

ISBN 978-0-385-52484-1; 0-385-52484-6

LC 2008-13517

"Regardless of what one thinks of Vidal, what Vidal thinks is never in doubt in these 24 essays, divided here into two groups: literary criticism and historical or cultural commentary. His writing is clear, sharp, and disciplined, and his approbation of William Dean Howells and Italo Calvino are as finely tuned as his excoriation of John Updike and Herman Wouk." Libr J

Includes bibliographical references

Vonnegut, Kurt

★ A **man** without a country; edited by Daniel Simon. Seven Stories Press 2005 146p il $23.95   **814**

ISBN 1-58322-713-X

LC 2005-14967

The author discusses politics, human nature, and other topics "in this collection of articles written over the last five years, many from the alternative magazine In These Times." Publ Wkly

Walker, Alice

The **cushion** in the road; meditation and wandering as the whole world awakens to being in harm's way. Alice Walker. The New Press 2013 336 p. (hardcover) $26.95   **814**
    1. Essays 2. Political science
    ISBN 1595588728; 9781595588722
                        LC 2012041852

This book, by Alice Walker, offers a "collection of wide-ranging meditations. . . . [The book] revisits themes the . . . [author] has addressed throughout her career: racism, Africa, solidarity with the Palestinian people, the presidential campaign of Barack Obama, Cuba, healthcare, and the work of Aung San Suu Kyi. In doing so, Walker explores her conflicting impulses to retreat into inner contemplation and to remain deeply engaged with the world." (Publisher's note)

Wallace, David Foster

Consider the lobster; and other essays. Little, Brown 2005 343p il $25.95   **814**
    ISBN 0-316-15611-6
                        LC 2005-10886

"Wallace's complex essays are written, and rightfully so, to be read more than once." Booklist
Includes bibliographical references

Weinberger, Eliot

The **ghosts** of birds; Eliot Weinberger. New Directions Publishing 2016 211 p. (softcover: acid-free paper) $16.95 **814**
    1. American essays 2. Essays
    ISBN 9780811226196; 9780811226189
                        LC 2016021273

This book "offers thirty-five essays by Eliot Weinberger: the first section of the book continues his linked serial-essay, 'An Elemental Thing,' which pulls the reader into 'a vortex for the entire universe.' . . . The second section collects Weinberger's essays on a wide range of subjects--some of which have been published in 'Harper's,' 'New York Review of Books,' and 'London Review of Books'--including his notorious review of George W. Bush's memoir 'Decision Points.'" (Publisher's note)

"A new book of essays proves to be as erudite, compelling, and delightfully strange as we have come to expect from Weinberger (An Elemental Thing, 2007)." Booklist
Includes bibliographical references

White, E. B.

Essays of E.B. White. Perennial Classics 1999 364p il pa $14.95   **814**
    1. Ornithologists 2. Florida -- Description and travel 3. United States -- Politics and government 4. New York (N.Y.) -- Description and travel
    ISBN 0-06-093223-6
                        LC 98-56019

First published 1977
Most of the essays first appeared in The New Yorker. "They range from a 1934 piece on the St. Nicholas Magazine 'League' and the distinguished writers who were members of it as children, to a 1975 report from Allen Cove, Maine, where White had retreated from the bedlam of the city." Publ Wkly

Williams, Terry Tempest

Finding beauty in a broken world. Pantheon Books 2008 419p $26   **814**
    1. Aesthetics
    ISBN 978-0-375-42078-8; 0-375-42078-9
                        LC 2008-7196

The naturalist author of Refuge and An Unspoken Hunger reflects on what it means to be human, the interconnection between the natural and human worlds, and how they combine to produce both tumult and peace, ugliness and beauty.

"Scientific in her exactitude, compassionate in her receptivity, and rhapsodic in expression, Williams has constructed a beautiful mosaic of loss and renewal that affirms, with striking lucidity, the need for reverence for all of life." Booklist
Includes bibliographical references

Wiman, Christian

He held radical light; the art of faith and the faith of art. Christian Wiman. Farrar, Straus & Giroux 2018 128 p. (hardcover) $23   **814**
    1. Faith 2. Religion 3. Spirituality
    ISBN 9780374168469
                        LC 2018003844

This book, by Christian Wiman, "is a love letter to poetry, filled with moving, surprising, and sometimes funny encounters with the poets Wiman has known. Seamus Heaney opens a suddenly intimate conversation about faith; Mary Oliver puts half of a dead pigeon in her pocket; A. R. Ammons stands up in front of an audience and refuses to read." (Publisher's note)

"Readers who allow themselves to be swept along by Wiman's beautiful style and oblique considerations will come away with fresh strategies for unpacking faith in the contemporary world." Pub Wkly

814.4   move back into 814

James, Henry, 1843-1916

Travels With Henry James; Henry James. Nation Books 2016 304 p. illustrations (ebook) $12.99; $19.99   **814.4**
    1. Travel writing
    ISBN 9781568585789; 1568585772; 9781568585772
                        LC 2016030750

"This new collection of travel essays reintroduces Henry James as a formidable travel companion. Whether for a trip to Lake George or an afternoon visit to an art exhibit in Paris, James will delight readers with his insights and make them feel nostalgic for places they've never been." (Publisher's note)

"James devotees will find that his essays are delightful, vivid, and generally uplifting." Pub Wkly
Includes bibliographical references and index.

814.54   American essays – 1945-1999

Dillard, Annie, 1945-

The **abundance**; narrative essays old and new. Annie Dillard. HarperCollins 2016 304 p. (hardcover) $25.99   **814.54**
    1. American essays
    ISBN 9780062432964; 9780062432971; 0062432974
                        LC 2016003136

This book, by Annie Dillard, presents collected essays by the Pulitzer Prize winning author, "including her most beloved pieces and some rarely seen work, rigorously curated by the author herself. . . . [It] reminds us that Dillard's brand of 'novelized nonfiction' pioneered the form long before it came to be widely appreciated. Intense, vivid, and fearless, her work endows the true and seemingly ordinary aspects of life." (Publisher's note)

"This collection is an excellent entry point into Dillard's writing and would especially appeal to new readers, although Dillard devotees will also enjoy this kaleidoscopic retrospective, this new way of 'seeing' her prose." LJ

Frazier, Ian

★ **Hogs** wild; selected reporting pieces. Ian Frazier. Farrar, Straus & Giroux 2016 384 p. (hardback) $26   **814.54**
1. Essays
ISBN 9780374298524; 0374298521

LC 2015036372

This book, by Ian Frazier, "assembles a decade's worth of his finest essays and reportage, and demonstrates the irrepressible passions and artful digressions that distinguish his enduring body of work. Part muckraker, part adventurer, and part raconteur, Frazier beholds, captures, and occasionally reimagines the spirit of the American experience." (Publisher's note)

"His celebrated humor glows rather than erupts in these more expository pieces. Pieces that show Frazier's ranging curiosity, lucent style, and capacious heart." Kirkus

Hustvedt, Siri

A **woman** looking at men looking at women; essays on art, sex, and the mind. Siri Hustvedt. Simon & Schuster 2016 576 p. (ebook) $13.99; (hardcover) $35   **814.54**
1. Art 2. Feminism 3. Neurosciences
ISBN 9781501141119; 9781501141096; 9781501141102

LC 2016022677

This book, by Siri Hustvedt, presents "a collection of essays on art, feminism, neuroscience, psychology, and philosophy. . . . Divided into three parts, the first section . . . investigates the perceptual and gender biases that affect how we judge art, literature, and the world in general. . . . The second part . . . is about the age-old mind/body problem. . . . The final section . . . discusses neurological disorders and the mysteries of hysteria." (Publisher's note)

"A wide-ranging, irreverent, and absorbing meditation on thinking, knowing, and being." Kirkus

Includes bibliographical references.

Jenkins, Jeffrey

★ **David** Sedaris diaries; a visual compendium. introduction and design, Jeffrey Jenkins; foreword, David Sedaris. Little, Brown & Co. 2017 249 p. (hc) $50   **814.54**
ISBN 0316431710; 9780316431712

LC 2016955673

In this book, "readers will for the first time experience the diaries David Sedaris has kept for nearly 40 years in the elaborate, three-dimensional, collaged style of the originals. A celebration of the unexpected in the everyday, the beautiful and the grotesque, this visual compendium offers unique insight into the author's view of the world and stands as a striking and collectible volume in itself." (Publisher's note)

Kinsley, Michael, 1951-

Old age; a beginner's guide. Michael Kinsley. Tim Duggan Books 2016 160 p. (hardback) $18   **814.54**
1. Life 2. Aging 3. Values 4. Parkinson's disease 5. Meaning (Psychology) 6. Aging -- United States 7. Authors, American

-- Biography 8. Baby boom generation -- United States 9. Life change events -- Psychological aspects 10. Parkinson's disease -- Patients -- United States -- Biography
ISBN 9781101903766; 9781101903780

LC 2015038958

In this book, author "Michael Kinsley uses his own battle with Parkinson's disease to unearth answers to questions we are all at some time forced to confront. 'Sometimes,' he writes, 'I feel like a scout from my generation, sent out ahead to experience in my fifties what even the healthiest Boomers are going to experience in their sixties, seventies, or eighties.'" (Publisher's note)

"Kinsley's superb prose and well-judged tone—both frustrated and hopeful for the future—make this a valuable book for anyone interested in exploring ideas around life, death, and legacy." Pub Wkly

Oliver, Mary, 1935-

Upstream; Mary Oliver. Penguin Group USA 2016 192 p. (ebook) $65; $26.00   **814.54**
1. American essays
ISBN 9780698405622; 1594206708; 9781594206702

LC 2016043612

This book is "a collection of essays in which revered poet Mary Oliver reflects on her willingness, as a young child and as an adult, to lose herself within the beauty and mysteries of both the natural world and the world of literature. Emphasizing the significance of her childhood 'friend' Walt Whitman, . . . Oliver meditates on the forces that allowed her to create a life for herself out of work and love." (Publisher's note)

"A lyrical, tender essay collection." Kirkus

Robinson, Marilynne, 1943-

What are we doing here? essays. Marilynne Robinson. Farrar, Straus & Giroux 2018 xiv, 315 p.p (hardcover) $27 **814.54**
1. Theology 2. American essays 3. American essays -- 21st century
ISBN 9780374717780; 0374282218; 9780374282219

LC 2017038302

This book, by Marilynne Robinson, presents "new essays on theological, political, and contemporary themes. . . . Whether she is investigating how the work of great thinkers about America like Emerson and Tocqueville inform our political consciousness or discussing the way that beauty informs and disciplines daily life, Robinson's peerless prose and boundless humanity are on full display." (Publisher's note)

"Robinson's gorgeous, demanding, and enlightening essays, propelled by her intricate vision of unity, radiantly recharge both mind and soul." Booklist

Searcy, David

Shame and wonder; essays. David Searcy. Random House Inc 2016 240 p. illustrations (ebook) $65; (acid-free paper) $26   **814.54**
1. Essays
ISBN 9780812993950; 9780812993943

LC 2014046233

The essays in this book "are born of . . . curiosity that has led [author] David Searcy into some strange and beautiful territory, where old Uncle Scrooge comic books reveal profound truths. . . . Whether ruminating on an old El Camino pickup truck, those magical prizes lurking in the cereal boxes of our youth, or a lurid online ad for 'Sexy Girls Near Dallas,' Searcy brings his unique blend of affection and suspicion to the everyday wonders that surround and seduce us." (Publisher's note)

"While the narrative style may not be for everyone, readers who appreciate it will enjoy this collection." LJ

814.6   American essays – 2000-

Broder, Melissa

So sad today; personal essays. Melissa Broder. Grand Central Publishing 2016 224 p. (ebook) $48; (paperback) $15.99   **814.6**

1. Essays 2. Depression (Psychology)
ISBN 9781455591848; 9781455562725

LC 2015039433

In this book, author Melissa Broder who "began @sosadtoday, an anonymous Twitter feed that allowed her to express her darkest feelings, and which quickly gained a dedicated following . . . , delves deeper into the existential themes she explores on Twitter, grappling with sex, death, love, low self-esteem, addiction, and the drama of waiting for the universe to text you back." (Publisher's note)

"Broder's central insight is clear: it is okay to be sad, and our problems can't be reduced to a single diagnosis. All of the essays are linked together by the art of learning to love oneself, sadness and all." Pub Wkly

Crosley, Sloane

★ Look alive out there; essays. Sloane Crosley. MCD/Farrar, Straus & Giroux 2018 240 p. (hardcover) $26   **814.6**

1. Essays 2. Motherhood 3. Celebrities
ISBN 9780374711801; 9780374279844

LC 2017038323

In this collection of essays, "whether it's scaling active volcanoes, crashing shivas, playing herself on 'Gossip Girl,' befriending swingers, or squinting down the barrel of the fertility gun, [author Sloane] Crosley continues to rise to the occasion with unmatchable nerve and electric one-liners. And as her subjects become more serious, her essays deliver not just laughs but lasting emotional heft and insight." (Publisher's note)

"A smart, droll essay collection that is all over the map but focused by Crosley's consistently sharp eye." Kirkus

Holt, Jim

★ When Einstein walked with Gödel; excursions to the edge of thought. Jim Holt. Farrar, Straus & Giroux 2018 xi, 368 p.p (hardcover) $28   **814.6**

1. Science 2. Philosophy 3. Mathematics
ISBN 9780374717841; 9780374146702

LC 2017038334

In this collection of essays, author Jim Holt "explores the human mind, the cosmos, and the thinkers who've tried to encompass the latter with the former. With his trademark clarity and humor, Holt probes the mysteries of quantum mechanics, the quest for the foundations of mathematics, and the nature of logic and truth. Along the way, he offers intimate biographical sketches of celebrated and neglected thinkers." (Publisher's note)

"A collection of incisive essays that make learning about science fun." Kirkus

Includes bibliographical references and index.

Knapp, Cheston

Up up, down down; essays. Cheston Knapp. Scribner 2018 ix, 310 p.p illustrations (hardcover) $25   **814.6**

1. American essays 2. Conduct of life 3. American wit and humor
ISBN 9781501161025; 9781501161049; 1501161024

In this collection of essays, author Cheston Knapp "tackles the Big Questions through seemingly unlikely avenues. In his dexterous hands, an examination of a local professional wrestling promotion becomes a meditation on pain and his relationship with his father. A profile of UFO enthusiasts ends up probing his history in the church and . . . the

nature and limits of faith itself. Attending an adult skateboarding camp launches him into a virtuosic analysis of nostalgia." (Publisher's note)

"Knapp is a master of collage, both in subject and in tone . . . The essays are hyperarticulate, literary, and occasionally self-conscious, but Knapp uses these tendencies to masterful effect." Booklist

Notaro, Laurie

Housebroken; Admissions of an Untidy Life. Laurie Notaro. Ballantine Books 2016 x, 270 p.p (paperback) $17 **814.6**

1. Home economics 2. Women -- Humor 3. Humorists, American -- 20th century -- Biography
ISBN 9781101886083; 9781101886090

LC 2016008624

This book, by Laurie Notaro, "chronicles her chronic misfortune in the domestic arts, including cooking, cleaning, and putting on Spanx while sweaty. . . . From defying nature in the quest to make her own Twinkies, to begging her new neighbors not to become urban livestock keepers, to teaching her eight-year-old nephew about hoboes, Notaro recounts her best efforts--and hilarious failures--in keeping a household inches away from being condemned." (Publisher's note)

"Notaro, a humorist and novelist (It Looked Different on the Model) recounts her forays into the domestic realm with this latest collection of essays." LJ.

Orner, Peter

Am I alone here? notes on living to read and reading to live. Peter Orner; illustrations by Eric Orner. Catapult 2016 xvii, 316 p.p illustrations (paperback) $16.95   **814.6**

1. Essays 2. Books and reading 3. Creative nonfiction
ISBN 1936787253; 9781936787258

LC 2015955986

This book, by Peter Orner, presents a "collection of essays about reading, writing, and living. Orner reads—and writes—everywhere he finds himself: a hospital cafeteria, a coffee shop in Albania, or a crowded bus in Haiti. The result is 'a book of unlearned meditations that stumbles into memoir.'" (Publisher's note)

"Book lovers will devour these genuine, personal tales about literature and reading." Kirkus.

Passarello, Elena, 1978-

Animals strike curious poses; essays. by Elena Passarello. Sarabande Books 2017 214 p. illustrations (hardcover) $19.95   **814.6**

1. Essays 2. Animals 3. Famous animals
ISBN 9781941411391

LC 2016039498

Each essay, in this collection by Elena Passarello, "investigates a different famous animal named and immortalized by humans. Modeled loosely after a medieval bestiary, these witty, playful, whipsmart essays traverse history, myth, science, and more, bringing each beast vibrantly to life." (Publisher's note)

"The entire collection satisfies through a feast of surprising juxtapositions and gorgeous prose." Pub Wkly.

Includes bibliographical references.

Sedaris, David, 1956-

★ Calypso; David Sedaris. Little, Brown & Co. 2018 viii, 259 p.p (hardcover) $28   **814.6**

1. Aging 2. Mortality 3. Wit and humor
ISBN 9780316392419; 1408707829; 9781408707821; 0316392383; 9780316392389

LC 2017950359

In this book author David Sedaris "sets his formidable powers of observation toward middle age and mortality.... These stories are very, very funny-it's a book that can make you laugh 'til you snort, the way only family can. Sedaris's powers of observation have never been sharper, and his ability to shock readers into laughter unparalleled." (Publisher's note)

"The author's fans and newcomers alike will be richly rewarded by this sidesplitting collection." Pub Wkly

Talese, Gay, 1932-

High notes; selected writings of Gay Talese. Gay Talese; introduction by Lee Gutkind. Bloomsbury USA 2017 288 p. (paperback) $20; (ebook) $48   **814.6**
  1. Journalism 2. Literature -- Collections
  ISBN 9781632867469; 9781632867476
                          LC 2016031081
"Admired by generations of reporters, Gay Talese has for more than six decades enriched American journalism with an unmatched ability to inhabit the worlds of his subjects.... The pieces collected in 'High Notes' are classics of the journalistic style Talese pioneered--'the art of hanging out,' as he called it--and a bold testament to his enduring talent for unparalleled cultural observation and impeccable literary craftsmanship." (Publisher's note)

"A worthy collection that would have benefitted from further effort from the book's editor and publisher." Kirkus

Includes bibliographical references.

815 American speeches in English

★ **American** speeches. Library of America 2006 2v ea $35   **815**
  1. American speeches
  ISBN 1-931082-97-9 v1; 1-931082-98-7 v2
                          LC 2006-40928
This is a collection of over 120 historical speeches delivered between 1761 and 1997.

Includes bibliographical references

817 American humor and satire in English

Andersen, Kurt

You can't spell America without me; the really tremendous inside story of my fantastic first year as President Donald J. Trump (a so-called parody) by Alec Baldwin & Kurt Andersen. Penguin Press 2017 246 p. illustrations (hardcover) $29 **817**
  1. Presidents -- United States 2. Political satire, American 3. Presidents -- United States -- Humor 4. United States -- Politics and government -- 2017- -- Humor
  ISBN 9780525522003; 9780525521990; 0525521992
                          LC 2017031393
This book, by Alec Baldwin and Kurt Andersen, is "Donald Trump's presidential memoir, as recorded by two world-renowned Trump scholars, and experts on greatness generally.... Trump was elected because he was the most frank presidential candidate in history, a man eager to tell the unvarnished truth about others' flaws and tout his own amazing excellence. Now he levels his ... un-PC candor at his landslide election victory as well as his role as commander-in-chief." (Publisher's note)

"A rollicking spoof by classically trained actor Baldwin (Nevertheless, 2017), who has made considerable hay in the past year as the foremost Donald Trump impersonator, and Spy magazine co-founder Andersen ..." Kirkus

Carlin, George

Napalm & silly putty. Hyperion 2001 269p $22.95; pa $12.95   **817**
  ISBN 0-7868-6413-3; 0-7868-8758-3 pa
                          LC 00-54055
The comedian "covers a wide range of issues from rape and religion to the homeless.... And any topic is fair game: abortion, airport security, cars, funerals, language, organ donors, sports, technology, TV and war.... Over 100 scintillating short pieces are interrupted by loony lists and hundreds of clever one-liners." Publ Wkly

Hull, Raymond

The **Peter** principle; why things always go wrong. [by] Laurence J. Peter and Raymond Hull. 1st Collins Business ed.; Collins Business 2009 xxvi, 161p il $19.99   **817**
  1. Management -- Anecdotes
  ISBN 978-0-06-169906-1
                          LC 2008-44122
First published 1969
"In a delightful spoof of administrative inefficiency in both public and private enterprise, the authors expound their theory known as the Peter Principle—'in a hierarchy every employee tends to rise to his level of incompetence.' From this they develop their science of hierarchiology." Cincinnati Public Libr

Includes bibliographical references

Mirth of a nation; the best contemporary humor. edited by Michael J. Rosen. HarperPerennial 2000 619p pa $15.95 **817**
  1. American wit and humor
  ISBN 0-06-095321-7
                          LC 99-44293
An anthology of more than 50 contributors, "most represented by two or three short works. Included are veterans like Dave Barry, Roy Blount Jr., and Fran Lebowitz, and rising stars like David Sedaris, Sandra Tsing Loh, Patricia Marx, and David Rakoff. Though many of the pieces have been published or broadcast previously, some appear in this volume for the first time." Booklist

Trillin, Calvin, 1935-

Quite enough of Calvin Trillin; forty years of funny stuff. Calvin Trillin. Random House 2011 340 p. (hardcover) $27.00   **817**
  1. American wit and humor 2. Politicians -- Humor 3. Civilization -- Humor 4. Authors, American -- 20th century -- Biography
  ISBN 1400069823; 0812982215; 9780812982213; 9781400069828; 9780679604808
                          LC 2011004050
This is "a collection of author-selected excerpts from [Calvin Trillin's] memoirs, satires, and novels includes entries ranging from descriptions of untraditional holiday celebrations to observations about literary pop culture.... He addresses the horrors of witnessing a voodoo economics ceremony and the mystery of how his mother managed for thirty years to feed her family nothing but leftovers.... He even skewers deserving political figures in poetry." (Publisher's note)

The author "entertains with this collection of his song lyrics, comic verse, and more than 130 of the brief essays he originally wrote for the New Yorker, the New York Times, the Nation, and his syndicated King Features column.... Trillin dances around a subject, examines it from different angles, and often finds fun in the commonplace throughout this huge and hilarious comedic compendium." Publ Wkly

Twain, Mark, 1835-1910

Mark Twain's library of humor; illustrated by E.W. Kemble; Steve Martin, series ed.; introduction by Roy Blount. Modern Library 2000 xl, 560p il pa $17 **817**
1. American wit and humor
ISBN 978-0-679-64036-3

LC 00-25971

"Beginning with the piece that made Mark Twain famous—'The Notorious Jumping Frog of Calaveras County'—and ending with his fanciful 'How I Edited an Agricultural Paper,' this . . . anthology, an abridgment of the 1888 original, collects twenty of Twain's own pieces, in addition to tall tales, fables, and satires by forty-three of Twain's contemporaries, including Washington Irving, Harriet Beecher Stowe, Ambrose Bierce, William Dean Howells, Joel Chandler Harris, Artemus Ward, and Bret Harte." Publisher's note

818 American miscellaneous writings in English

Alvarez, Julia, 1950-

A **wedding** in Haiti; Julia Alvarez. Algonquin Books of Chapel Hill 2012 287 p. **818**
1. Weddings 2. Friendship 3. Dominican Americans 4. Haiti Earthquake, Haiti, 2010 5. Haiti -- Description and travel 6. Haitians -- Dominican Republic -- Biography
ISBN 9781616201302

LC 2012000452

This book by Julia Alvarez presents a memoir "about her pre- and post-earthquake travels around the island of Hispaniola and the Haitian boy who inspired them. The author met Piti, . . . in 2001, on a chance visit to a coffee farm [in] . . . the Dominican Republic. . . . In 2009, she received a surprise call from Piti telling her that she was invited to his wedding. . . . Eventually Piti called . . . to help him care for his extended family in the aftermath of the 2010 earthquake." (Kirkus)

Angelou, Maya, 1928-2014

Mom & me & mom; by Maya Angelou. 1st ed. Random House 2012 224 p. (ebook) $66.00; (hardcover) $22.00 **818**
1. Mother-daughter relationship 2. African American authors -- Biography 3. Entertainers -- United States -- Biography 4. Authors, American -- 20th century -- Biography
ISBN 1400066115; 9780679645474; 9781400066117

LC 2012022257

This memoir, by Maya Angelou, "shares . . . her relationship with her mother. . . . Angelou reveals the triumphs and struggles of being the daughter of Vivian Baxter. . . . Vivian famously sent three-year-old Maya and her older brother away from their California home to live with their grandmother in Stamps, Arkansas. The subsequent feelings of abandonment stayed with Angelou for years, but their reunion, a decade later, began a story that has never before been told." (Publisher's note)

A **song** flung up to heaven. Random House 2002 212p $23.95; pa $13 **818**
1. Poets 2. Actors 3. Singers 4. Dramatists 5. Essayists 6. Memoirists 7. Children's authors
ISBN 0-375-50747-7; 0-553-38203-9 pa

LC 2001-34914

"This sixth installment in Angelou's autobiographical works begins in 1964 as Angelou returned to the U.S. from Ghana. . . . She worked in Watts at the time of the riots, and Malcolm X and Martin Luther King Jr. were both assassinated just before she was to begin working with them. . . . She moved to New York, where she rejoined a vibrant group of famous writers, intellectuals, and friends; worried about her young-adult son; and understood the humor and heartache of a painful love affair. . . . Spiced with her mother's aphorisms, her often-poetic prose is best at the end, as she muses on the condition of black women and sitting at her mother's table, begins to write I Know Why the Caged Bird Sings." Booklist

Baraka, Imamu Amiri

The **LeRoi** Jones/Amiri Baraka reader; by Amiri Baraka; edited by William Harris in collaboration with Amiri Baraka. 2nd ed; Thunder's Mouth Press 2000 xxxiii, 586p pa $16.95 **818**
1. Poets 2. Clergy 3. Mayors 4. Authors 5. Dramatists 6. Blues music 7. African American music 8. Television personalities 9. Cuba 10. Essayists 11. Talk show hosts 12. Political leaders 13. Members of Parliament 14. Civil rights activists 15. Presidential candidates
ISBN 1-56025-238-3

LC 99-32364

First published 1991

A collection of Baraka's poems, plays, and other writings. "The selections included are arranged chronologically in four distinct periods: The Beat Period (1957-62), The Transitional Period (1963-65), The Black Nationalist Period (1965-74), and The Third World Marxist Period (1974-present)." Libr J [review of 1991 edition]

Includes bibliographical references

Beam, Alex

The **feud**; Vladimir Nabokov, Edmund Wilson, and the End of a Beautiful Friendship. Alex Beam. Pantheon Books 2016 224 p. illustrations (ebook) $65; (hardback) $26.95 **818**
ISBN 9781101870235; 9781101870228

LC 2016007056

This book, by Alex Beam, narrates "how two literary giants destroyed their friendship in a fit of mutual pique and egomania. In 1940, Edmund Wilson was the undisputed big dog of American letters. Vladimir Nabokov was a near-penniless Russian exile seeking asylum in the States. . . . The feud . . . erupted in full when Nabokov published his hugely footnoted and virtually unreadable literal translation of Pushkin's famously untranslatable verse novel, 'Eugene Onegin.'" (Publisher's note)

"An outstanding and entertaining book that could have surprising appeal beyond its intended literary audience. Readers who give it a chance will soon find themselves unable to put it down." LJ

Includes bibliographical references and index

Berry, Wendell, 1934-

★ The **world**-ending fire; the essential Wendell Berry. Wendell Berry; selected and introduced by Paul Kingsnorth. Allen Lane 2017 352 p. $26 **818**
1. American essays 2. Farm life -- United States 3. Agriculture -- United States
ISBN 0241279208; 1640090282; 9780241279205; 9781640090286

The essays in this collection by Wendell Berry, selected and introduced by Paul Kingsnorth, "are the unique product of a life spent farming the fields of rural Kentucky with mules and horses, and of the rich, intimate knowledge of the land cultivated by this work. These are essays written in defiance of the false call to progress and in defense of local landscapes, essays that celebrate our cultural heritage, our history, and our home." (Publisher's note)

"A great place to start for those who are not familiar with Berry's work; for those who are, it will be a nostalgic stroll down a rural, wooded Memory Lane. In this day and age, his writings are must-reads." Kirkus

Bishop, Elizabeth

Poems, prose, and letters; [selected and edited by Robert Giroux and Lloyd Schwartz] Library of America 2008 979p $40 **818**

1. Criticism 2. Poetry -- By individual authors
ISBN 978-1-59853-017-9; 1-59853-017-8

LC 2007-935885

"From the quietly riveting photograph on the dust jacket through the thorough index, the book is an elegant achievement that one imagines even the scrupulous and discriminating Elizabeth Bishop would approve. . . . This generous new collection lets us make connections across boundaries among many genres: poems, some hitherto uncollected and some mighty rough; translations over many years from ancient Greek, French, Spanish, and Portuguese; 'Personal Essays, Reminiscences, and Reporting'; 'Literary Statements and Reviews'; . . . and letters." Yale Rev

Blount, Roy

Alphabetter juice, or, The joy of text; [by] Roy Blount, Jr. Farrar, Straus and Giroux 2011 283p $26; ebook $12.99 **818**

1. Vocabulary 2. American wit and humor 3. English language -- Dictionaries
ISBN 978-0-374-10370-5; 978-1-4299-2278-4 ebook

LC 2010-39937

This book "is almost a subgenre of its own, a reference book from a leading language expert that's also downright funny. . . . Anybody as eclectic as Blount is worth paying attention to; his passion for the sounds and senses of words makes this book infectiously fun reading for word lovers everywhere." Writer

Bryson, Bill

I'm a stranger here myself; notes on returning to America after 20 years away. Broadway Bks. 1999 288p hardcover o.p. pa $14.95 **818**

1. United States -- Description and travel 2. United States -- Social life and customs
ISBN 0-7679-0382-X pa

LC 99-18074

The author collects "columns on America he wrote weekly, while living in New Hampshire in the mid-to-late 1990s, for a British Sunday newspaper. Although he happily describes himself as dazzled by American ease, friendliness and abundance, Bryson has no trouble finding comic targets, among them fast food, computer efficiency and, ironically, American friendliness and putative convenience." Publ Wkly

Cather, Willa

★ **Stories,** poems, and other writings. Library of Am. 1992 1039p $35 **818**

1. Nebraska -- Literary collections
ISBN 0-940450-71-2

LC 91-62294

This volume contains the novels Alexander's bridge (1912) and My mortal enemy (1926); the poetry collection April twilights, and other poems (1923); the essay collection Not under forty (1936); and the following short story collections: Youth and the bright Medusa (1920); Obscure destinies (1932); The old beauty, and others (1948); and uncollected stories from 1892-1929

Crawford, Alan Pell

★ **How** not to get rich; the financial misadventures of Mark Twain. Alan Pell Crawford. Houghton Mifflin Harcourt 2017 xi, 224 p.p $27 **818**

1. Speculation 2. Personal finance 3. Authors, American
ISBN 0544836464; 9780544836464

This book, by Alan Pell Crawford, presents "an uproarious account of Mark Twain's endless attempts to strike it rich, all of which served only to empty his pockets. . . . Twain's lifetime spans America's era of greatest economic growth. . . . But far from striking it rich, the man who coined the term 'Gilded Age' failed with comical regularity to join the ranks of plutocrats who made this period in America notorious for its wealth and excess." (Publisher's note)

Includes bibliographical references (pages 199-218) and index.

Dick, Philip K.

The **exegesis** of Philip K. Dick; edited by Pamela Jackson and Jonathan Lethem; Erik Davis, annotations editor. Houghton Mifflin Harcourt 2011 944p $40 **818**

1. Technology and civilization 2. Science fiction -- Authorship
ISBN 978-0-547-54925-5; 0-547-54925-3

LC 2011-28561

"'I sure have odd nights,' wrote Philip K. Dick in a July 1974 letter to a young woman writing her thesis on him. It's a tremendous understatement, and its inclusion in the early pages of The Exegesis — the long-awaited compendium of the sci-fi writer's papers — acts as a palate cleanser, a wry little weigh station wherein Dick pulls back from his own dense, circuitous investigation of his visions; laughs a little at himself; and then dives back in, allowing the reader to do the same. . . . Dick wrote more than eight thousand pages in the eight years leading up to his death in 1982, all in his attempts to decipher a series of visionary, multisensory experiences he had in February and March of '74 ('2-3-74') wherein he glimpsed a vast truth of the world." East Bay Express

Didion, Joan, 1934-

South and west; from a notebook. Joan Didion; foreword by Nathaniel Rich. Alfred A. Knopf 2017 xx, 126 p.p (hardcover) $21 **818**

1. American travelers 2. Southern States -- Description and travel 3. Essays
ISBN 9780525434191; 9781524732806; 1524732796; 9781524732790

LC 2016962161

Author "Joan Didion has always kept notebooks: of overheard dialogue, observations, interviews, drafts of essays and articles--and here is one such draft that traces a road trip she took with her husband, John Gregory Dunne, in June 1970, through Louisiana, Mississippi, and Alabama. She interviews prominent local figures, describes motels, diners, a deserted reptile farm, a visit with Walker Percy, a ladies' brunch at the Mississippi Broadcasters' Convention." (Publisher's note)

"Students of social history, fans of Didion, and those seeking a quick, engaging read will appreciate this work: the raw immediacy of unedited prose by a master has an urgency that more polished works often lack." Pub Wkly

Dillard, Annie

The **Annie** Dillard reader. HarperCollins Pubs. 1994 455p hardcover o.p. pa $15.95 **818**
ISBN 0-06-092660-0 pa

LC 94-19482

This reader includes Holy the firm; excerpts from Pilgrim at Tinker Creek, An American childhood, and Teaching a stone to talk; and a reworked version of the 1978 short story The living

"This selection of writings, chosen by Dillard herself, provides a perfect sampling of her incisive, versatile, and impeccable achievements." Booklist

Pilgrim at Tinker Creek. Harper & Row 1974 271p hardcover o.p. pa $14.95   **818**
1. Natural history -- Virginia ISBN 0-06-123332-3 pa; 978-0-06-123332-6 pa

This work is "in an honored tradition of literature, not quite environmentalism and not the philosophy of science, it is rather the refraction of natural philosophy through the prismatic conscience of art. Highly recommended for the general reader—any general reader, anywhere—who wishes to deepen his awareness of his yard of world and to reflect upon it more profoundly." Choice

Ellison, Ralph

★ **Going** to the territory. Random House 1986 338p hardcover o.p. pa $14.95   **818**
1. Artists 2. Authors 3. Composers 4. Novelists 5. Dramatists 6. Jazz musicians 7. Essayists 8. Band leaders 9. Nonfiction writers 10. Short story writers
ISBN 978-0-679-76001-6 pa; 0-679-76001-6 pa

LC 85-28117

"This collection of essays, addresses, and reviews deals with topics in literature, music, and race relations.... Ellison tries to view American culture as a cloth of one piece. His analysis of the growth of the culture, and of the dynamic interaction of the diverse elements within it, is perceptive and convincing." Libr J

Faludi, Susan

★ **In** the Darkroom; by Susan Faludi. Henry Holt & Co. 2016 432 p. $32   **818**
1. Identity (Psychology) 2. Sex reassignment surgery 3. Father-daughter relationship
ISBN 080508908X; 9780805089080

LC 2016013605

Kirkus Prize: Nonfiction (2016)

Pulitzer Prize Finalist: Biography or Autobiography (2017)

This book begins when author Susan Faludi "learned that her 76-year-old father--long estranged and living in Hungary--had undergone sex reassignment surgery . . . The author travels to Hungary to reunite with [him] . . . Faludi's struggle to come to grips with her father's metamorphosis takes her across borders--historical, political, religious, sexual--to bring her face to face with the question of the age: Is identity something you 'choose,' or is it the very thing you can't escape?" (Publisher's note)

"A moving and penetrating inquiry into manifold struggles for identity, community, a nd authenticity." Kirkus

Franklin, Benjamin

★ **Autobiography,** Poor Richard, and later writings; letters from London, 1757-1775, Paris, 1776-1785, Philadelphia, 1785-1790, Poor Richard's almanack, 1733-1758, The autobiography. Library of America 1997 816p $30   **818**
ISBN 1-883011-53-1

LC 97-21611

"This collection of Franklin's works begins with letters sent from London (1757-1775) describing the events and diplomacy preceding the Revolutionary War. The volume also contains political satires, bagatelles, pamphlets, and letters written in Paris (1776-1785), where he represented the revolutionary United States at the court of Louis XVI,

as well as his speeches given in the Constitutional Convention and other works written in Philadelphia (1785-1790), including his last published article, a . . . satire against slavery. Also included are the . . . prefaces to Poor Richard's Almanack (1733-1758). . . . [The] Autobiography, Franklin's last word on his greatest literary creation—his own invented personality—is presented here in a new edition." Publisher's note

Includes bibliographical references

Gibran, Kahlil

The **collected** works; with eighty-four illustrations by the author. Everyman's Library 2007 880p il $27.50   **818**
ISBN 978-0-307-26707-8; 0-307-26707-5

LC 2007-28736

This anthology of writings by the Syrian poet includes The Madman, The Forerunner, The Prophet, Sand and Foam, Jesus the Son of Man, Earth Gods, The Wanderer, The Garden of the Prophet, Prose Poems, Spirits Rebellious, Nymphs of the Valley, and A Tear and a Smile.

Gurwitch, Annabelle

Wherever you go, there they are; stories about my family you might relate to. Annabelle Gurwitch. Blue Rider Press 2017 300 p. (hardcover) $26   **818**
1. Family life 2. Family -- Humor 3. Actors -- United States -- Biography 4. Families -- Humor 5. Television personalities -- United States -- Biography
ISBN 9780399574887; 9780399574900

LC 2016052134

This book is "a hysterically funny and slyly insightful new collection of essays from New York Times bestselling author Annabelle Gurwitch, about her own family of scam artists and hucksters, as well as the sisterhoods, temporary tribes, communities, and cults who have become surrogates along the way." (Publisher's note)

"Gurwitch's breezy writing style, even while mixing in social commentary, keeps the book relatable and readable throughout." Booklist

Hogan, Linda

The **woman** who watches over the world; a native memoir. Norton 2001 224p $24.95; pa $13.95   **818**
1. Poets 2. Authors 3. Novelists 4. Dramatists 5. Native Americans 6. Essayists 7. Short story writers
ISBN 0-393-05018-1; 0-393-32305-6 pa

LC 00-49005

In this memoir the author chronicles "her difficult childhood, alcoholism, the anguish of her two psychologically damaged adopted children, and struggles with a neuromuscular disease. She also expresses a lacerating yet crucial vision of the tragic legacies of the U.S. government's brutal war on Native Americans." Booklist

Hughes, Langston

★ **I** wonder as I wander; an autobiographical journey. introd. by Arnold Rampersad. 2nd Hill and Wang ed; Hill & Wang 1993 xxii, 405p (American century series) pa $16 **818**
1. Poets 2. Authors 3. Novelists 4. Dramatists 5. African American authors 6. Poets, American 7. Short story writers 8. Young adult authors
ISBN 0-8090-1550-1

LC 92-39307

First published 1956 by Rinehart

Continuing the autobiography begun in The big sea (1940), this volume contains an account of Hughes' journeys through Russia, Spain, China, and Japan, as well as some incidents of his poetry readings in this country

Jackson, Shirley, 1916-1965

Let me tell you; new stories, essays, and other writings. Shirley Jackson; edited by Laurence Jackson Hyman and Sarah Hyman DeWitt. Random House Inc. 2015 432 p. (acid-free paper) $30   **818**

    1. Essays 2. American short stories
    ISBN 0812997662; 9780812997668

                               LC 2014036656

This book, edited by Laurence Hyman, Sarah Hyman DeWitt, and Ruth Frankling, "brings together the deliciously eerie short stories [Shirley] Jackson is best known for, along with frank, inspiring lectures on writing; comic essays about her large, boisterous family; and whimsical drawings. Jackson's landscape here is most frequently domestic: dinner parties and bridge, household budgets and homeward-bound commutes, children's games and neighborly gossip." (Publisher's note)

Includes bibliographical references

Jefferson, Thomas, 1743-1826

Writings. Library of Am. 1984 1600p $35   **818**
ISBN 0-940450-16-X

                               LC 83-19917

This is "the largest and most skillfully edited single-volume Jefferson ever published." N Y Times Book Rev

Includes bibliographical references

Johnson, James Weldon

The **essential** writings of James Weldon Johnson; edited and with an introduction by Rudolph P. Byrd; foreword by Charles Johnson. Modern Library 2008 xxx, 321p (Modern library classics) pa $15   **818**

    ISBN 978-0-8129-7532-1; 0-8129-7532-4

"This collection of poetry, fiction, criticism, autobiography, political writing and two unpublished plays by James Weldon Johnson (1871-1938) spans 60 years of pure triumph over adversity. . . . [Johnson's] nobility, his inspiration shine forth from these pages, setting moral and artistic standards." Los Angeles Times Book Rev

Johnson, Joyce, 1935-

★ The **voice** is all; the lonely victory of Jack Kerouac. Joyce Johnson. Viking 2012 xx, 489 p.p $32.95   **818**

    1. American authors -- Biography 2. Beat generation -- Biography 3. Authors, American -- 20th century -- Biography
    ISBN 0670025100; 9780670025107

                               LC 2012000603

In this biography of Jack Kerouac, author Joyce Johnson "peels away layers of the Kerouac legend to show how, caught between two cultures and two languages, he forged a voice to contain his dualities. Looking . . . into how Kerouac's French Canadian background enriched his prose and gave him a unique outsider's vision of America, she tracks his development from boyhood through the phenomenal breakthroughs of 1951." (Publisher's note)

Includes bibliographical references (p 439-471) and index

Kaling, Mindy, 1979-

Is everyone hanging out without me? (and other concerns) Mindy Kaling. Crown Archetype 2011 ix, 222 p.p ill   **818**

    1. Actresses 2. American essays 3. American wit and humor
    ISBN 9780307886262; 9780307886286

                               LC 2011033922

'In this book, author "Mindy Kaling . . . [offers thoughts about what she] thinks makes a great best friend (someone who will fill your prescription in the middle of the night), or what makes a great guy (one who is aware of all elderly people in any room at any time and acts accordingly), or what is the perfect amount of fame (so famous you can never get convicted of murder in a court of law), or how to maintain a trim figure (you will not find that information in these pages). . . . Mindy invites readers on a tour of her life and her unscientific observations on romance, friendship, and Hollywood." (Publisher's note)

Kiernan, Frances

Seeing Mary plain: a life of Mary McCarthy. Norton 2000 845p il $35; pa $25   **818**

    1. Authors 2. Novelists 3. Essayists 4. Memoirists 5. Literary critics 6. Short story writers
    ISBN 0-393-03801-7; 0-393-32307-2 pa

                                 LC 99-41098

Kiernan uses "her interviews with more than 200 sources to provide multiple points of view on McCarthy's life and work. McCarthy knew most of her generation's literary leading lights, from the Partisan Review crowd to anti-Vietnam activists. . . . Each chapter includes commentary by McCarthy, friends, ex-lovers, admirers, and adversaries." Booklist

Includes bibliographical references

Le Guin, Ursula K., 1929-2018

★ **Words** are my matter; writings about life and books, 2000-2016, with a journal of a writer's week. Ursula K. Le Guin. Small Beer Press 2016 iv, 316 p.p (alk. paper) $24 **818**

    1. Speeches 2. Short stories 3. American essays 4. Books -- Reviews
    ISBN 1618731343; 9781618731340; 9781618731210

                               LC 2016029895

This book "collects talks, essays, introductions to beloved books, and book reviews by Ursula K. Le Guin, one of our fore-most public literary intellectuals. . . . It is a manual for investigating the depth and breadth of con- temporary fiction — and, through the lens of deep considerations of contemporary writing, a way of exploring the world we are all living in." (Publisher's note)

"The wide-ranging collection includes essays, lectures, introductions, and reviews, all informed by Le Guin's erudition, offered without academic mystification, and written (or spoken) with an inviting grace." Pub Wkly

Includes bibliographical references.

The moment; edited by Larry Smith. Harper Perennial 2012 344p.   **818**

    1. Autobiographies 2. American authors 3. American literature -- 21st century 4. Authors, American -- 21st century -- Biography
    ISBN 9780061719653; 9780062099211

                                 LC 2011033766

This book contains "stories of life-changing events from a cadre of ready, self-aware authors, each done in a page or two. A short selection of the contributors: A.J. Jacobs, Melissa Etheridge, Gregory Maguire, Dave Eggers, Elizabeth Gilbert, Jennifer Egan and Judy Collins. There are many 'wake-up calls,' some smiles and plenty of tears in these first-person explorations of a few eternal truths. Each of the 125 participants . . . tell of coming out and hiding, of seeking the light, the path, the truth, the way and/or the writers' inner selves. Those goals were achieved by aid of a word, sign, teacher, family road trip, some dope, an inner voice or, more than once, a Eurail pass." (Kirkus)

"Each author's ability to concisely describe such big moments pulls the reader in. Book and writing groups will have a lot to talk about after reading this first-rate collection." (Libr J)

★ The **Oxford** companion to Mark Twain; editor, Gregg Camfield. Oxford Univ. Press 2003 xxi, 767p il $75 **818**
1. Authors 2. Humorists 3. Novelists 4. Essayists 5. Satirists 6. Memoirists 7. Travel writers 8. Short story writers
ISBN 0-19-510710-1

LC 2002-151880

This volume "begins with 300 alphabetically arranged entries of varying lengths devoted to all [Twain's] works, places and people related to his life, and analyses of his views on a variety of topics, from animals to spiritualism. Next come a bibliography of his published works collated from other bibliographies, a chronology, and a general index." Choice
Includes bibliographical references

Plath, Sylvia
The **unabridged** journals of Sylvia Plath, 1950-1962; edited by Karen V. Kukil. Anchor Press 2000 732p il pa $18 **818**
1. Poets 2. Authors 3. Novelists
ISBN 0-385-72025-4

LC 00-42024

First published 2000 in the United Kingdom with title: Journals of Sylvia Plath, 1950-1962
"This is essential for anyone engaged in Plath studies." Libr J
Includes bibliographical references

Poe, Edgar Allan
★ **Poetry** and tales. Library of Am. 1984 1408p $37.50 **818**
1. Fantasy poetry 2. Horror fiction
ISBN 0-940450-18-6

LC 83-19931

This volume contains 70 stories and Poe's poetic work in its entirety
Includes bibliographical references

A **political** companion to James Baldwin; edited by Susan J. McWilliams. University Press of Kentucky 2017 396 p. (hardcover: alk. paper) $80 **818**
1. Literature and politics 2. United States -- Politics and government 3. Politics in literature 4. Politics and literature -- United States -- History -- 20th century
ISBN 0813169917; 9780813169910

LC 2017038157

In this book in the Political Companions to Great American Authors, edited by Susan J. McWilliams, a group of prominent scholars assess . . . [James Baldwin's] relevance to present-day political challenges. . . . [T]hey address Baldwin as a democratic theorist, activist, and citizen, examining his writings on the civil rights movement, religion, homosexuality, and women's rights." (Publisher's note)
Includes bibliographical references and index

Rampersad, Arnold
★ The **life** of Langston Hughes Volume II: 1941-1967; I dream a world. 2nd ed; Oxford Univ. Press 2002 576p il hardcover o.p. pa $33 **818**
1. Poets 2. Authors 3. Novelists 4. Dramatists 5. African American authors 6. Poets, American 7. Short story writers 8. Young adult authors
ISBN 0-19-515161-5; 0-19-514643-3 pa

LC 2001-58766

First published 1988
This second volume of a two-volume biography of the Harlem Renaissance poet and author "finds Hughes rooting himself in Harlem,

receiving stimulation from his rich cultural surroundings. Here he rethought his view of art and radicalism, and cultivated relationships with younger, more militant writers such as Richard Wright, Ralph Ellison, James Baldwin, and Amiri Bakara." Publisher's note
Includes bibliographical references

Rollyson, Carl E.
Susan Sontag; the making of an icon. {by} Carl Rollyson and Lisa Paddock. Norton 2000 370p il $29.95 **818**
1. Authors 2. Novelists 3. Essayists 4. Literary critics 5. Short story writers
ISBN 0-393-04928-0

LC 00-20402

The authors "have unearthed a deluge of information on Sontag's personal life—on her early years and family life, her lesbianism. . . her relationship with son David Rieff and her battles with breast cancer. While the authors provide an intelligent, though not strikingly original, analysis of her work, they are best at detailing how Sontag and her publishers have marketed her image as much as her thought." Publ Wkly
Includes bibliographical references

Scottoline, Lisa
I Need a Lifeguard Everywhere but the Pool; Lisa Scottoline & Francesca Serritella. St. Martin's Press 2017 ix, 323 p.p illustrations (hardcover) $21.99 **818**
1. Women -- Humor 2. Mother-daughter relationship 3. Humor
ISBN 9781250059963; 9781466865266; 1250059968

LC 2017004247

This book, by Lisa Scottoline and Francesca Serritella, presents "a new collection of stories from their real lives, guaranteed to make you laugh out loud. Join Lisa and Francesca as they regret drunk-shopping online, try smell-dating, and explore the freedom of a hiatus from men - a Guyatus. They offer a fresh and funny take on the triumphs and face-palm moments of modern life, showing that when it comes to navigating the crazy world we live in, you're always your own best lifeguard." (Publisher's note)

Silko, Leslie
Storyteller. Arcade Publishing 1989 278p pa $17.95 **818**
ISBN 978-1-55970-005-4; 1-55970-005-X
First published 1981 by Seaver Books
This "consists of short stories, anecdotes, folktales, poems, historical and autobiographical notes, and photographs." N Y Times Book Rev

Sova, Dawn B.
Critical companion to Edgar Allan Poe; a literary reference to his life and work. Facts on File 2007 458p il (Facts on File library of American literature) $75 **818**
1. Poets 2. Authors 3. Essayists 4. Short story writers
ISBN 0-8160-6408-3; 978-0-8160-6408-3

LC 2006-29466

First published 2001 with title: Edgar Allan Poe, A-Z
"Biographical, historical, and critical material on Poe's life and work is presented in alphabetical order in three sections. The entries on Poe's works each provide a synopsis, a publication history, and character descriptions, while major works such as 'The Cask of Amontillado' and 'The Purloined Letter' have . . . [a] commentary and . . . further-reading suggestions." SLJ
Includes bibliographical references

Stein, Gertrude
Writings, 1903-1932. Library of Am. 1998 941p $40 **818**

ISBN 978-1-883011-40-6; 1-883011-40-X

LC 97-28915

In Stein's "early works, she sought a new kind of realism exemplified here by Q.E.D. (written 1903, published posthumously), a novel about lesbian entanglements at college, and the modern classic Three Lives (1909), a set of novellas about the lives of three ordinary women, described in the simplest and most direct of prose. In her . . . abstract 'portraits' Stein uses an extraordinary array of verbal techniques to evoke those friends and collaborators—Matisse, Picasso, Apollinaire, Juan Gris, Satie, Mabel Dodge, Carl Van Vechten, Sherwood Anderson, Virgil Thomson—with whom she shared decades of revolutionary ferment in the arts. Her play Four Saints in Three Acts (1927), which became the basis for an opera by Virgil Thomson, is written for a freewheeling theater of the mind where everything becomes possible. In 'Lifting Belly' and other works she joyously celebrates her lifelong relationship with Alice B. Toklas, one of the most famous domestic partnerships of that century. The Autobiography of Alice B. Toklas (1933), Stein's oblique and playful memoir, became an immediate bestseller and sealed Stein's international celebrity." Publisher's note

★ **Writings,** 1932-1946. Library of Am. 1998 844p $40 **818**

ISBN 1-883011-41-8

LC 97-28916

In addition to theater pieces, fiction, and poetry "memoir, philosophical speculation, literary criticism and theory, all sorts of briefer forms that are hard to account for but easy to marvel at and even to delight in, pack these volumes, and constitute, as the editors surely intended us to discover, the most consistently achieved representation of new ways of responding to life and new possibilities of getting experience into words that American literature has to show." N Y Times Book Rev

Thoreau, Henry David, 1817-1862

★ **Collected** essays and poems. Library of Am. 2001 703p $35 **818**

ISBN 1-883011-95-7

LC 00-46234

Among the 27 essays included are Civil disobedience, Walking, Martyrdom of John Brown, A Yankee in Canada, and Life without principle. Many of the poems were taken from Thoreau's journals and manuscripts
Includes bibliographical references

★ **Walden,** or, Life in the woods; with an introduction by Verlyn Klinkenborg. Knopf 1992 xxxi, 295p $19 **818**

ISBN 0-679-41896-2

LC 92-54444

First published 1854
"Philosophy of life and observations of nature drawn from the author's solitary sojourn of two years in a cabin on Walden Pond near Concord, Massachusetts." Pratt Alcove
Includes bibliographical references

A **week** on the Concord and Merrimack rivers; Walden, or, Life in the woods; The Maine woods; Cape Cod. Library of Am. 1985 1114p il $35 **818**

ISBN 0-940450-27-5

LC 85-5175

"Politically the most conscious of the Transcendentalists, an acute observer of natural and social facts, Thoreau was an outstanding prose stylist." Reader's Ency
Includes bibliographical references

Thursby, Jacqueline S.

Critical companion to Maya Angelou; a literary reference to her life and work. Facts On File 2011 430p il (Facts on File of American literature) $75 **818**

1. Poets 2. Actors 3. Singers 4. Dramatists 5. Essayists 6. Memoirists 7. Children's authors
ISBN 978-0-8160-8093-9; 978-1-4381-3610-3 ebook

LC 2010032716

Coverage includes a "biography of Angelou; entries on all of Angelou's major works, including all six of her book-length autobiographies, her major poems and poetry collections, her major essays and essay collections, her children's books, and more; entries on the autobiographical works contain subentries on the main figures in the work; entries on related people, places, and topics, such as Harlem, Michelle Obama, racism, San Francisco, and more; [and] appendixes, including chronologies, a bibliography of Angelou's works, and a secondary source bibliography." Publisher's note
Includes bibliographical references

Trethewey, Natasha D., 1966-

Beyond Katrina; a meditation on the Mississippi Gulf Coast. University of Georgia Press 2010 127p il **818**

1. Hurricane Katrina, 2005 2. African Americans -- Mississippi
ISBN 0-8203-3381-6; 978-0-8203-3381-6

LC 2010011417

A collection of essays, poems, and letters, chronicling the effects of Hurricane Katrina on the Mississippi Gulf Coast.
"By looking at the vast devastation with sober and poetic eyes, Trethewey has written a hauntingly beautiful book." Publ Wkly

Updike, John, 1932-2009

Higher gossip; essays and criticism. edited by Christopher Carduff. 1st ed. Alfred A. Knopf 2011 528 p. ill. ebook $21.99; (hbk.) $40; (pbk.) $20 **818**

ISBN 9780307957177; 9780307957153; 9780812983685

LC 2011013586

This book is a "collection of miscellaneous prose [that] opens with a self-portrait of the writer in winter. . . . It concludes with a . . . meditation on a modern world robbed of imagination--a world without religion, without art--and on the difficulties of faith in a disbelieving age. In between are previously uncollected stories and poems, a pageant of scenes from seventeenth-century Massachusetts, five late 'golf dreams,' and several of Updike's commentaries on his own work. At the heart of the book are his . . . reviews--of John Cheever, Ann Patchett, Toni Morrison, William Maxwell, John le Carré, and essays on Aimee Semple McPherson, Max Factor, and Albert Einstein, among others. Also included are two decades of art criticism--on Chardin, El Greco, Blake, Turner, Van Gogh, Max Ernest, and more." (Publisher's note)

This is a compilation of "nearly 100 uncollected pieces by 'the preeminent literary journalist of our times.' Predominantly comprising literary and art criticism from a range of magazines, the volume also embraces poetry, fiction, memoir, and Updike's comments on his own work." Publ Wkly

Walsh, John Evangelist

Midnight dreary; the mysterious death of Edgar Allan Poe. St. Martin's Minotaur 2000 199p il pa $14.95 **818**

1. Poets 2. Authors 3. Essayists 4. Short story writers
ISBN 0-312-22732-9; 978-0-312-22732-6

LC 00-25571

First published 1998 by Rutgers Univ. Press
Walsh "has undertaken a superbly informed speculation on the week

proceeding the mysterious death of Edgar Allan Poe 150 years ago." Libr J

Includes bibliographical references

Wayne, Tiffany K.

Critical companion to Ralph Waldo Emerson; a literary reference to his life and work. Facts On File 2010 444p il (Facts on File library of American literature) $75   **818**
1. Poets 2. Authors 3. Philosophers 4. Essayists
ISBN 978-0-8160-7358-0; 978-1-4381-3048-4 ebook
LC 2009-24809

"This reference book examines the life and works of a central thinker in American history. . . . It begins with Emerson's biography for context. Part 2 focuses on 140 significant (in the view of scholars) individual works, including 60 poems (most with one to three pages of synopses, critical commentary, and further reading). Part 3 covers related people, places, and topics. . . . The final appendixes offer a chronology of Emerson's life and times, bibliographies of both his works and relevant secondary sources." Choice

Includes bibliographical references. 'Bibliography of Emerson's works': p. 406-407. (BLCM)

Wilson, Ronaldo V.

Farther traveler; poetry, prose, other. Ronaldo V. Wilson. Counterpath 2014 157 p. (pbk.: alk. paper) $22   **818**
1. Poetry -- Collections 2. American prose literature
ISBN 1933996331; 9781933996332
LC 2014034097

This book, by Ronaldo V. Wilson, "is an expansive, complex hybrid of poetry, prose, and memoir that engages with contemporary culture, race and sexuality." (Publisher's note)

818.602   Jokes – American literature – 2000-

Ajayi, Luvvie

I'm judging you; the do-better manual. Luvvie Ajayi. Henry Holt & Co. 2016 256 p. (paperback) $17; (ebook) $60   **818.602**
1. Conduct of life -- Humor
ISBN 9781627796064; 9781627796071
LC 2016009018

This book, by Luvvie Ajayi, is her debut collection "of humorous essays that dissects our cultural obsessions and calls out bad behavior in our increasingly digital, connected lives. It passes on lessons and side-eyes on life, social media, culture, and fame, from addressing those terrible friends we all have to serious discussions of race and media representation to what to do about your fool cousin sharing casket pictures from Grandma's wake on Facebook." (Publisher's note)

"Be prepared for some laughs, but also be prepared to think and confront tougher issues. Bits of humor help these occasionally hard-hitting essays go down." Kirkus

Jacobson, Abbi, 1984-

Carry This Book; Abbi Jacobson. Penguin Group USA 2016 144 p. $25   **818.602**
1. Wallets -- Miscellanea -- Humor 2. Handbags -- Miscellanea -- Humor 3. Celebrities -- Miscellanea -- Humor
ISBN 0735221596; 9780735221598
LC 2016044009

In this book, author Abbi Jacobson "brings to life actual and imagined items found in the pockets and purses, bags and glove compartments of

real and fantastical people—whether it's the contents of Oprah's favorite purse, Amelia Earhart's pencil case, or Bernie Madoff's suitcase. How many self-tanning lotions are in Donald Trump's weekender? What's inside Martha Stewart's hand-knit fanny pack?" (Publisher's note)

"As an exercise in creativity or as a way of understanding history, this would make good inspiration for workshops for middle schoolers through adults." LJ

Leary, Denis, 1957-

Why we don't suck; and how all of us need to stop being such partisan little bitches. Dr. Denis Leary. Crown Archetype 2017 x, 304 p.p color maps (hardcover) $27   **818.602**
1. Wit and humor 2. Popular culture -- United States 3. United States -- Politics and government -- Humor 4. Popular culture -- United States -- Humor 5. United States -- Politics and government -- 21st century -- Humor 6. United States -- Social life and customs -- 21st century -- Humor
ISBN 9781524762759; 1524762733; 9781524762735
LC 2017299308

In this book Denis Leary "takes a bipartisan look at the topics we all hold so dear to our patriotic hearts—including family, freedom, and the seemingly endless search for fame and diet vodka. Denis will answer important questions like: When will Hillary blame herself? Why does Beyoncé think he's Bryan Adams? And why doesn't he follow the millennial lead and post pictures of his food on social media? (Spoiler alert: He's too busy actually eating it.)" (Publisher's note)

"A fun and thought-provoking romp through politics and popular culture." Kirkus

Scottoline, Lisa

I've got sand in all the wrong places; by Lisa Scottoline & Francesca Serritella. St. Martin's Press 2016 306 p. illustrations (hardcover) $21.99   **818.602**
1. Women -- Humor 2. Mother-daughter relationship 3. Short stories -- Collections 4. Mothers and daughters -- Humor
ISBN 9781250059956
LC 2016003973

Authors Lisa Scottoline and Francesca Serritella "are back with another collection of warm and witty stories that will strike a chord with every woman. . . . This seventh volume will not disappoint as it hits the humorous and poignant note that fans have come to expect from the beloved mother-daughter duo." (Publisher's note)

"More light, bright essays to delight fans of this mother-daughter writing team." Kirkus.

820   English and Old English (Anglo-Saxon) literatures

★ The **Cambridge** guide to literature in English; edited by Dominic Head. 3rd ed; Cambridge University Press 2006 xxiii, 1241p il $50   **820**
1. Reference books 2. English literature -- Dictionaries 3. American literature -- Dictionaries 4. English literature -- Bio-bibliography
ISBN 978-0-521-83179-6; 0-521-83179-2
LC 2006-271458

First published 1988 under the editorship of Ian Ousby

"The scope of material covered . . . extends to the literature of the United Kingdom and well beyond: Africa, Asia, Australia, Canada, the Caribbean, India, New Zealand, and the U.S. are all well represented. . . . Literary terms are explained, literary movements are summarized, and literary magazines are sketched in unsigned entries ranging in length from a few lines to a few paragraphs or more. . . . With its broad coverage, clearly written and accessible text, and relatively modest price, this is a must purchase for most reference collections." Booklist

Coles, Robert

Handing one another along; literature and social reflection. edited by Trevor Hall and Vicki Kennedy. Random House 2010 xxiv, 273p il $27; ebook $27   **820**

1. English literature -- History and criticism 2. American literature -- History and criticism

ISBN 978-1-4000-6203-4; 978-0-679-60403-7 ebook

LC 2009-47337

The author "adapts his undergraduate lectures on literature's contribution to the development of our moral character. . . . While less than comprehensive and eschewing more technical analyses, it delves into a generous handful of writers and artists—perennials like George Orwell, James Agee, Zora Neale Hurston, Tillie Olsen, Ralph Ellison, and Raymond Carver, among others—with uncommon insight and a personal touch, while offering excerpts of poetry and prose that often whet the appetite for more." Publ Wkly

Includes bibliographical references

The **history** of British women's writing; edited by Maroula Joannou. Palgrave Macmillan 2010 340 p. (hbk.) $90 **820**

1. English authors 2. English literature -- 20th century 3. English literature -- Women authors 4. Women and literature -- Great Britain -- History 5. English literature -- Women authors -- History and criticism

ISBN 0230282792; 9780230282797 (v. 8)

LC 2010026127

This book, edited by Maroula Joannou, examines British women authors who "do not fit into a recognized version of the modernist canon. Their complex and often troubled relationship to modernity – as readers, consumers, and travellers at home and abroad – requires new critical frameworks in which to discuss their writing as well as a revision of the territory that has been staked out as the preserve of Modernism by critical theory and practice." (Publisher's note)

Includes bibliographical references and indexes

Lee, Hermione

Virginia Woolf's nose; essays on biography. Princeton University Press 2005 141p $19.95   **820**

1. Poets 2. Authors 3. Novelists 4. Biography as a literary form 5. Diarists 6. Essayists 7. Military officials 8. Short story writers 9. Government officials 10. Members of Parliament

ISBN 0-691-12032-3

LC 2004-58457

"Lee's immensely enjoyable study will energize debate among thoughtful readers and should become essential reading for aficionados of literary biography." Publ Wkly

Includes bibliographical references

The **Norton** anthology of English literature; edited by Stephen Greenblatt. 10th edition W W Norton & Co 2018 6v 6v   **820**

1. English literature -- Collections

ISBN 9780393603071; 9780393603033; 9780393603057; 9780393603064; 9780393603040; 9780393603026

First published 1962. Periodically revised

"The Tenth Edition introduces 6 much-requested contemporary writers, all global in reach--including Chimamanda Ngozi Adichie, Kazuo Ishiguro, and Hilary Mantel. There are also 5 new complete longer works, among them Shakespeare's Othello and Swift's Gulliver's Travels." (Publisher's note)

Includes bibliographical references

★ The **Oxford** companion to English literature; edited by Dinah Birch. 7th ed; Oxford University Press 2009 1164p $150   **820**

1. Reference books 2. English literature -- Dictionaries 3. American literature -- Dictionaries 4. English literature -- Bio-bibliography 5. American literature -- Bio-bibliography

ISBN 978-0-19-280687-1

LC 2009-455948

First published 1932 under the editorship of Sir Paul Harvey

"The subjects of the entries include literary works, authors, themes, archetypes, journals, and forms. . . . This companion is a highly authoritative resource, with clear, concise, and approachable entries on literary topics of high interest to students and scholars of English literature. An essential reference for most public, high school, and academic libraries." Libr J

★ The **Oxford** guide to literature in English translation; edited by Peter France. Oxford Univ. Press 2000 xxii, 656p hardcover o.p. pa $29.95   **820**

1. Translating and interpreting 2. Literature -- History and criticism

ISBN 0-19-924784-6 pa

LC 99-28791

This "guide emphasizes 'high-culture' books in translation that have had the most lasting impact on English-speaking culture since the Middle Ages. . . . The first 116 pages cover translation theory and history, while the heart of this guide is the 17 geographic sections that follow, starting with African languages, moving through Latin, and ending with the West Asian languages. There are excellent bibliographies and an author index." Libr J

Includes bibliographical references

Sanders, Andrew

The **short** Oxford history of English literature; 3rd ed; Oxford University Press 2004 756p pa $45   **820**

1. English literature -- History and criticism

ISBN 978-0-19-926338-7; 0-19-926338-8

LC 2004-49555

First published 1994

"The History provides detailed discussion of Old and Middle English literature, the Renaissance, Shakespeare, the seventeenth and eighteenth centuries, the Romantics, Victorian and Edwardian literature, Modernism, and postwar writing. Discussions of key writers and works are combined with analysis of the impact on literature of contemporary political, social, and intellectual developments. The book includes Scottish, Irish, and Welsh writers, and it asks about the future of the canon in the light of the fragmented condition of British writing in the post-imperial period." Publisher's note

Includes bibliographical references

Vendler, Helen Hennessy

Coming of age as a poet; Milton, Keats, Eliot, Plath. [by] Helen Vendler. Harvard Univ. Press 2003 174p il $22.95 **820**

1. Blind 2. Poets 3. Authors 4. Novelists 5. Dramatists 6. Editors 7. Essayists 8. Literary critics 9. Writers on medicine 10. Nobel laureates for literature 11. English poetry -- History and criticism 12. American poetry -- History and criticism

ISBN 0-674-01024-8

LC 2002-27287

Vendler "succeeds in revealing the aesthetic power and technical beauty of great poetry." N Y Times Book Rev

Includes bibliographical references

820.9　　English literature -- History and criticism

Midorikawa, Emily

A **secret** sisterhood; the literary friendships of Jane Austen, Charlotte Bronte, George Eliot, & Virginia Woolf. by Emily Midorikawa and Emma Claire Sweeney, foreword by Margaret Atwood. Houghton Mifflin Harcourt 2017 331 p. (hardback) $27　　**820.9**

1. Friendship 2. English literature -- Women authors

ISBN 9781328532381; 9780544883734

LC 2017044906

In this book, by Emily Midorikawa and Emma Claire Sweeney, foreword by Margaret Atwood, "the world's best-loved female authors are usually mythologized as solitary eccentrics or isolated geniuses.... Midorikawa and ... Sweeney prove this wrong, thanks to their discovery of a wealth of surprising collaborations: the friendship between Jane Austen and ... playwright Anne Sharp; ... and Virginia Woolf and Katherine Mansfield." (Publisher's note)

"The authors (who are themselves close friends) astutely explain that the friendships they depict became lost to cultural memory due to prevailing stereotypes of female authors as "solitary eccentrics or isolated geniuses." It is a delight to learn about them here, as related by two talented authors." PW.

Includes bibliographical references and index.

Tóibín, Colm, 1955-

Mad, bad, dangerous to know; the fathers of Wilde, Yeats, and Joyce. Colm Tóibín. Scribner 2018 240 p. $26　　**820.9**

1. Father-son relationship 2. Irish authors -- Biography

ISBN 1476785171; 9781476785172

"From Colm Tóibín, ... an illuminating, intimate study of Irish culture, history, and literature told through the lives and work of three men--William Wilde, John Butler Yeats, and John Stanislaus Joyce--and the complicated, influential relationships they had with their complicated sons.... Tóibín recounts the resistance to English cultural domination, the birth of modern Irish cultural identity, and the extraordinary contributions of these ... masterful authors." (Publisher's note)

821　　English poetry

★ 100 essential modern poems; selected and introduced by Joseph Parisi. Ivan R. Dee 2005 305p $24.95　　**821**

1. English poetry -- Collections 2. American poetry -- Collections

ISBN 1-56663-612-4

LC 2005-9897

"Preceded by wonderfully conversational and expertly appreciative biocritical essays about each poet, his choices are superb as he lingers over Yeats and Stevens and includes often-overlooked witty and satirical poets, among them Dorothy Parker, Ogden Nash, Kay Ryan, Frank O'Hara, and Billy Collins." Booklist

★ 100 great poems of the twentieth century; [edited by] Mark Strand. Norton 2005 320p $24.95　　**821**

1. English poetry -- Collections 2. American poetry -- Collections

ISBN 0-393-05894-8

LC 2005-2150

The editor "has selected works by poets of Europe and North and South America, and because there are so many gifted American poets, he restricted himself to those born before 1927. The result is a marvelously graceful, shimmering cosmos of poems by the likes of Anna Akhmatova, A. R. Ammons, Amy Clampit, Robert Desnos, Robert Frost, Nazim Hik-

met, Kenneth Koch, Edna St. Vincent Millay, Gabriela Mistral, Eugenio Montale, Octavio Paz, and Derek Walcott." Booklist

Adamson, Robert

★ The **goldfinches** of Baghdad. Flood Editions 2006 103p pa $13.95　　**821**

1. Poetry -- By individual authors

ISBN 0-9746902-8-7

Adamson "lives on the Hawksbury River in New South Wales.... To give an overview of his poetry is difficult, but it is largely concerned with where he is: the river, the natural environment and creatures, his life and history, his neighbours, love and death. It has little of the 'pastoral' feel about it, being obsessively attached to the present condition, and it never gives any sense of a contented settled existence free from urban cares, quite the reverse. There is indication indeed of a quite fraught personal existence, both past and present, without the poetry ever for a moment becoming 'confessional'. It is to objective for that and too poetic." Shearsman

Adcock, Fleur

★ **Poems** 1960-2000. Bloodaxe Books 2000 287p $54.95; pa $24.95　　**821**

1. Poetry -- By individual authors

ISBN 1-85224-529-8; 1-85224-530-1 pa

Adcock's "imagination thrives on what threatens her peace of mind, and only when she is unguarded can these threats have their full creative effect.... Throughout her writing life, she has made a fine art from holding on to principles of orderliness and good clear sense; but she has made an even finer one from loosening her grip on them." Times Lit Suppl

An **anthology** of modern Irish poetry; edited by Wes Davis. Belknap Press of Harvard University Press 2010 976p $35　　**821**

1. Irish poetry -- Collections 2. Irish poetry -- 20th century 3. English poetry -- Irish authors

ISBN 0-674-04951-9; 9780674049512

LC 2009-37231

Collected here is a "representation of Irish poetic achievement in the twentieth and twenty-first centuries, from poets such as Austin Clarke and Samuel Beckett who were writing while Yeats and Joyce were still living; to those who came of age in the turbulent '60s as sectarian violence escalated, including Seamus Heaney and Michael Longley; to a new generation of Irish writers, represented by such ... voices as David Wheatley (born 1970) and Sinead Morrissey (born 1972). Editor Wes Davis has chosen work by more than fifty leading modern and contemporary Irish poets." (Publisher's note) Index.

This volume, "running to almost a thousand pages, comes from a country with a population roughly equal to that of Tennessee. The book includes upwards of 50 poets— and there's not a dull page in it. Editor Wes Davis's selection is judicious, while his introduction and notes are as informative as they are brief." Wall Street J

Auden, W. H.

★ **Collected** poems; edited by Edward Mendelson. Modern Library 2007 928p $40　　**821**

1. Poetry -- By individual authors

ISBN 978-0-679-64350-0; 0-679-64350-8

LC 2006-47163

Originally published in different form by Random House in 1976

A compilation of all the poems Auden wished to preserve, in his final revisions. Previous collected editions and later shorter poems are included. There is also an absurdist play written 1928: Paid on both sides.

Bentley, G. E.

The **stranger** from paradise: a biography of William Blake. Yale Univ. Press 2001 xxvii, 532p il maps $39.95; pa $24.95 **821**

1. Poets 2. Artists 3. Authors 4. Engravers 5. Illustrators

ISBN 0-300-08939-2; 0-300-10030-2 pa

The author "traces Blake from his natal landscape, youth, marriage, and apprenticeship through to his later years as a working engraver, poet, and radical visionary. Bentley is academic and thorough, and this is more of a straight biography than an analysis." Libr J

Includes bibliographical references

★ The **Best** poems of the English language; from Chaucer through Robert Frost. selected and with commentary by Harold Bloom. HarperCollins Publishers 2004 xxviii, 972p $34.95; pa $19.95 **821**

1. English poetry -- Collections 2. American poetry -- Collections

ISBN 0-06-054041-9; 0-06-054042-7 pa

LC 2003-51104

"Arranged chronologically by author, the poems are preceded by commentaries that extol their specific virtues and place them in historical context. Taken together, they provide an overview of Bloom's own theories of writing, such as his notion that the greatest poems manifest an 'inevitability' of phrasing . . . Bloom rarely bores, and at his best he achieves a cogency . . . worthy of the poets he so deeply admires." Libr J

Includes bibliographical references

Blake, William

The **complete** poetry and prose of William Blake; edited by David V. Erdman; with a new foreword and commentary by Harold Bloom. Newly rev. ed., 1st Calif. ed.; University of California Press 2008 xxvi, 990p il $70 **821**

1. Poetry -- By individual authors

ISBN 978-0-520-04473-9; 9780520256378

First published 1965 with title: Poetry and prose of William Blake

In addition to all of Blake's poetry, this volume also includes miscellaneous prose, marginalia, and letters

"The crucial preliminary problem [in establishing Blake's text] is simply to make out what Blake wrote. . . . Erdman has used modern aids such as infrared photography and microphotography. . . but his real achievement has been to look at Blake's text more closely and intelligently than any previous editor." N Y Rev Books

Boland, Eavan

New collected poems. W.W. Norton 2008 320p $27.95 **821**

1. Poetry -- By individual authors

ISBN 978-0-393-06579-4; 0-393-06579-0

LC 2007-42554

First published 2005 in the United Kingdom

"Boland's resilient braid of outspoken feminism with Irish identity has given her a following on both sides of the Atlantic. Here is the recent Boland whose rapid verse celebrates women's courage and women's work, both public (several poems acknowledge Mary Robinson, the former president of the Irish Republic) and unsung: the poet remembers herself, when young, asking a statue in Dublin to 'Make me a heroine.' Here is the poet who learned from Adrienne Rich, among others, how to tackle big topics of loyalty, rebellion, descent and dissent." Publ Wkly

Boland, Eavan, 1944-

A **woman** without a country; poems. Eavan Boland. W W Norton & Co Inc 2014 96 p. (hardcover) $24.95 **821**

1. Mothers 2. Daughters 3. Nationalism 4. Poetry -- Collections

ISBN 039324444X; 9780393244441

LC 2014030073

This collection of poems, by Eavan Boland, "looks at how we construct one another and how nationhood and history can weave through, reflect, and define the life of an individual. Themes of mother, daughter, and generation echo throughout these . . . poems, as they examine how--even without country or settled identity--a legacy of love can endure." (Publisher's note)

"A superb collection not to be missed, full of exquisite language, music, knowledge and emotion." LJ

Brown, Terence

The **life** of W.B. Yeats; a critical biography. Blackwell 1999 410p il (Blackwell critical biographies) $66.95; pa $29.95 **821**

1. Poets 2. Authors 3. Dramatists 4. Poets, Irish 5. Memoirists 6. Nobel laureates for literature

ISBN 0-631-18298-5; 0-631-22851-9 pa

LC 99-28388

In this biography Brown places "Yeats's work as poet and dramatist in its political and social—as well as personal and erotic—context." N Y Times Book Rev

Includes bibliographical references

Browning, Elizabeth Barrett

★ **Sonnets** from the Portuguese; a celebration of love. St. Martin's Press 1986 [63] il $9.95 **821**

1. Poetry -- By individual authors

ISBN 0-312-74501-X

LC 86-13755

A series of sonnets which "were written during a period of seven years and are considered by some scholars to have been inspired by her love for her husband poet Robert Browning." New Century Handb of Engl Lit

Browning, Robert

Robert Browning; the major works. edited with notes by Adam Roberts; with an introduction by Daniel Karlin. Oxford University Press 2005 xxxii, 828p pa $18.95 **821**

1. Poetry -- By individual authors

ISBN 978-0-19-280626-0; 0-19-280626-2

LC 2006-277696

This "selection includes over eighty of [Browning's] shorter poems, amongst them his most famous and best-loved dramatic monologues, as well as the complete text of many of his longer poems. It contains three books from The Ring and the Book and Browning's critical writing, Essay on Shelley. This edition also selects generously from the love letters between Browning and Elizabeth Barrett." Publisher's note

Includes bibliographical references

★ **Robert** Browning's poetry; authoritative texts, criticism. selected and edited by James F. Loucks and Andrew M. Stauffer. 2nd ed.; W. W. Norton & Co. 2007 689p (A Norton critical edition) pa $14.50 **821**

1. Poetry -- By individual authors

ISBN 978-0-393-92600-2; 0-393-92600-1

LC 2006-47308

First published 1980

This collection of Browning's poetry, which includes Pauline, "reprints the texts of the seventeen-volume 'Fourth and complete edition' (Smith, Elder), of which all but the final volume were approved by Browning before his death. The poems are ordered chronologically according to their first appearance in book form." Publisher's note

Bunting, Basil

Complete poems; associate editor, Richard Caddel. New Directions Books 2003 239p pa $16.95   **821**

1. Poetry -- By individual authors

ISBN 978-0-8112-1563-3; 0-8112-1563-6

LC 2003-15465

This volume "offers adventure, a confident voice, neat takes on history (both recent and archaic), an attractively careworn secular ethics and an even more attractive combination of archaic and vernacular English models. It also offers superb verbal command, chiseling every stanza to the fewest, densest possible words, giving each an aural shape. Those shapes are not always mellifluous—sometimes they are harsh, a mouthful—but each demonstrates Bunting's mastery, proving itself on the page as well as in the ear, where all good poems find their place." Nation

Burns, Robert, 1759-1796

Burns; poems. edited and introduced by Gerard Carruthers. Alfred A. Knopf 2007 255p (Everyman's library pocket poets) $12.50   **821**

1. Poetry -- By individual authors

ISBN 978-0-307-26616-3; 0-307-26616-8

LC 2006-47299

"A pioneer of the Romantic movement, Burns wrote in a light Scots dialect with brio, emotional directness, and wit, drawing on classical and English literary traditions as well as Scottish folklore.... All of his most famous lyrics and poems are here, from 'A Red, Red Rose,' 'To a Mouse,' and 'To a Louse' to Tam o'Shanter, 'Holy Willie's Prayer,' and 'Auld Lang Syne.'" Publisher's note

Byron, George Gordon Byron

Selected poetry of Lord Byron; edited by Leslie A. Marchand; introduction by Thomas Disch; notes by Jeffrey Vail. Modern Library 2001 745p (The Modern Library classics) pa $16   **821**

1. Poetry -- By individual authors

ISBN 978-0-375-75814-0; 0-375-75814-3

LC 2001-42771

"From 'Manfred,' with its evocation of the figure that came to be called the 'Byronic hero,' to the melancholy 'Childe Harold,' to the satirical masterpiece 'Don Juan' (presented here in judiciously selected form), this . . . [selection seeks to include] the essential Byron." Publisher's note

Coleridge, Samuel Taylor

The **complete** poems; edited by William Keach. Penguin 1997 xxx, 626p (Penguin classics) pa $18   **821**

1. Poetry -- By individual authors

ISBN 978-0-14-042353-2

This edition "contains the final texts of all the poems published in the poet's lifetime, together with a substantial selection from the verse still in manuscript on his death. William Keach's notes draw attention to significant variants, and important earlier versions of 'Monody on the Death of Chatterton', 'The Eolian Harp', 'The Rime of the Ancient Mariner' and 'Dejection: An Ode' are included in full. The poems are arranged in chronological order of composition." Publisher's note

Constantine, David

Collected poems. Bloodaxe Books 2005 384p pa $31.95   **821**

1. Poetry -- By individual authors

ISBN 1-85224-667-7

"From the first line on this book's first page ('As our bloods separate the clock resumes') to the first sentence on its last ('When the kingfisher flitted/ Under the hazels I entered again into boyhood') Constantine declares himself a Romantic, in almost all the loaded, unfashionable and daring senses that once-omnipresent term can bear. In his elaborate lines, intelligence and strong emotion are collaborators, not competitors; he knows how to let them spur each other on." Times Lit Suppl

★ **Contemporary** poets; editor, Thomas Riggs; with a preface by Diane Wakoski. 7th ed; St. James Press 2001 xxiii, 1443p (Contemporary writers series) $230   **821**

1. Reference books 2. Poets, English -- Dictionaries 3. Poets, American -- Dictionaries 4. American poetry -- Bio-bibliography

ISBN 1-55862-349-3

LC 00-45882

First published 1970 with title: Contemporary poets of the English language

"A biographical handbook of contemporary poets, arranged alphabetically. Entries consist of a short biography, full bibliography, comments by many of the poets, and a signed critical essay." Ref Sources for Small & Medium-sized Libr. 6th edition

Includes bibliographical references

Davie, Donald

Collected poems; edited by Neil Powell. Carcanet 2002 xxi, 634p (Poetry pléiade) $49.95; pa $24.95   **821**

1. English poetry -- 20th century 2. Poetry -- By individual authors

ISBN 978-1-85754-579-1; 1-85754-579-6; 978-1-85754-406-0 pa; 1-85754-406-4 pa

"Davie's poetic output, which abundantly stretches from Hardyesque lyrics ('Bride of Reason,' 'A Winter Talent,' 'The Battered Wife') to cognitively powerful long poems ('Six Epistles to Eva Hesse,' 'The Forests of Lithuania'), from translations of Pasternak and Mandelstam to lyrically brutal political commentary ('August, 1968'), evinces a kind of wide sweep and committed imagination that doesn't necessarily close itself off to confrontation and experiential risk, nor resign itself to failure as the phenomenological and lyrical refusal of further inquiry. In this sense, Davie has always seemed to be a poet working in the very high art of his eighteenth-century forebears." Jacket

Davis, Dick

Belonging; poems. Swallow Press 2002 54p $24.95; pa $14.95   **821**

1. Poetry -- By individual authors

ISBN 0-8040-1042-0; 0-8040-1043-9 pa

LC 2002-17749

Davis' "poems are full of fine emotion, intelligence, wit, and multinational culture. He lithely celebrates the legendary rake Casanova; poignantly conjures 'Kipling's Kim, Thirty Years On'; economically reports a father's aching futility in comforting his child ('A Bit of Paternity'); deftly valorizes the power of art ('Just So'); and often muses on the shortness of life and the limitations of being human, so cogently that a single quatrain can take one's breath away." Booklist

Day Lewis, C.

The **complete** poems of C. Day Lewis; [edited by] Jill Balcon. Stanford Univ. Press 1992 745p hardcover o.p. pa $32.95   **821**

1. Poetry -- By individual authors

ISBN 978-0-8047-2585-9; 0-8047-2585-3

LC 91-68076

"The still lively fascination of his verse seems to depend on the variety of tones [Day Lewis] could pick up, change, and discard at will. . . . His modesty was genuine and profound, giving his verse texture its winning versatility, its air that 'tenure is not for me.' . . . Nothing that Day Lewis wrote is lacking its own sort of ephemeral though rediscoverable effectiveness. He was well aware of this, and it was a part of his modesty, as Jill Balcon points out in her thoughtful and sensitive introduction. . . . For anyone who likes poetry there is real interest here in [this] complete record." N Y Rev Books

Donne, John

★ The **complete** poetry and selected prose of John Donne; edited by Charles M. Coffin; introduction by Denis Donoghue; notes by W. T. Chmielewski. Modern Lib. 2001 xxxii, 697p pa $14.95   **821**
 1. Poetry -- By individual authors
 ISBN 0-375-75734-1
                                     LC 2001-30077
A reissue of the Modern Library edition published 1994
This volume contains Donne's love poetry, satires, epigrams, verse letters and holy sonnets. Also includes selected prose and a sampling of private letters.

Poems and prose. A.A. Knopf 1995 256p (Everyman's library pocket poets) $12.50   **821**
 1. Poetry -- By individual authors
 ISBN 978-0-679-44467-1; 0-679-44467-X
                                     LC 95-15330
"Contains Songs and Sonnets, Letters to the Countess of Bedford, The First Anniversary, Holy Sonnets, Divine Poems, excerpts from Paradoxes and Problems, Ignatius His Conclave, The Sermons, Essays and Devotions, and an index of first lines." Publisher's note

Dryden, John

John Dryden; the major works. edited with an introduction and notes by Keith Walker. Oxford University Press 2003 xviii, 967p pa $18.95   **821**
 1. Poetry -- By individual authors
 ISBN 978-0-19-284077-6; 0-19-284077-0
                                     LC 2003-270051
This "edition brings together a unique combination of Dryden's poetry and prose—all the major poems in full, literary criticism, and translations—to give the essence of his work and thinking. The collection includes the poems, MacFlecknoe and Absalom and Achitophel as well as Dryden's classical translations; his versions of Homer, Horace, and Ovid are reproduced in full. There are also substantial selections from Dryden's Virgil, Juvenal, and other classical writers. Fables, Ancient and Modern, taken from Chaucer, Ovid, Boccaccio, and Homer, his last and possibly greatest work, also appears in full." Publisher's note
Includes bibliographical references

Dunmore, Helen, 1952-2017

Inside the wave; Helen Dunmore. Bloodaxe Books 2017 63 p. $22   **821**
 1. Mortality 2. English poetry 3. Poetry -- Collections 4. English poetry -- 21st century
 ISBN 1780373589; 9781780373584
                                     LC 2017296582
In this poetry collection, by Helen Dunmore, "to be alive is to be inside the wave, always travelling until it breaks and is gone. These poems are concerned with the borderline between the living and the dead--the underworld and the human living world--and the exquisitely intense being of both. They possess a spare, eloquent lyricism as they explore the bliss and anguish of the voyage." (Goodreads)

Feinstein, Elaine

Ted Hughes; the life of a poet. Norton 2001 273p il $29.95; pa $15.95   **821**
 1. Poets 2. Authors 3. Poets laureate
 ISBN 0-393-04967-1; 0-393-32362-5 pa
                                     LC 2001-44925
This biography of the English poet examines Hughes's relationship with "his first wife, Sylvia Plath, who committed suicide in 1963 during the acrimonious breakup of their marriage, . . . {and with} Assia Wevill, the woman for whom Hughes left Plath, and who later killed herself and their child." Economist
Includes bibliographical references

Fisher, Roy

★ **Selected** poems; edited by August Kleinzahler. Flood Editions 2011 158p pa $15.95   **821**
 1. Poetry -- By individual authors
 ISBN 978-0-9819520-6-2
"Fisher's texts have never been as well served on the page as they are here. The poems are given real space and the movement of Fisher's breath, rhythm and cadence is as clear as it possibly could be." Manchester Rev

Foster, R. F.

W.B. Yeats: a life. v2 Oxford Univ. Press 2003 xxiv, 798p v2 il $47.50   **821**
 1. Poets 2. Authors 3. Dramatists 4. Poets, Irish 5. Memoirists 6. Nobel laureates for literature
 ISBN 0-19-818465-4
This second volume of a two-volume biography covers Yeats's final decades, from his 50th year to his death in 1939.
Includes bibliographical references

Foster, R. F. (Robert Fitzroy), 1949-

W.B. Yeats: a life. v1 Oxford Univ. Press 1997 xxxi, 640p v1 il hardcover o.p. pa $29.95   **821**
 1. Poets 2. Authors 3. Dramatists 4. Poets, Irish 5. Memoirists 6. Biography, Individual 7. Nobel laureates for literature
 ISBN 0-19-211735-1; 0-19-288085-3 pa
                                     LC 96-31671
This is the first installment of a two-volume biography of the Irish poet. Index.

Foulds, Adam

The **broken** word; an epic poem of the British Empire in Kenya, and the Mau Mau uprising against it. Penguin 2011 60p (Penguin poets) pa $16   **821**
 1. Kenya -- Poetry 2. Mau Mau -- Poetry
 ISBN 978-0-14-311809-1
First published 2008 in the United Kingdom
Offers a lyrical poem about Tom, a young man who gets caught up in the violent 1950s Mau Mau Uprising in Kenya protesting the British colonial control of that country.
"A tour de force of a long narrative poem, rare in contemporary English poetry." Libr J

Fuller, John

The **Oxford** book of sonnets; edited by John Fuller. Oxford Univ. Press 2000 xxxiv, 362p $25; pa $15.95   **821**

1. English poetry -- Collections 2. American poetry -- Collections
ISBN 0-19-214267-4; 0-19-280389-1 pa

LC 00-36757

"Indisputable masterpieces appear plentifully, but Fuller's determination to present a large number of distinguished practitioners assures that there are also many superb poems by virtual unknowns. And Fuller's introduction is a sharp-witted miracle of concise comprehensiveness." Booklist

Includes bibliographical references

Geoffrey Chaucer's The Canterbury tales; edited and with an introduction by Harold Bloom. New ed; Chelsea House 2008 286p (Modern critical interpretations) $45 **821**
1. Poets 2. Authors 3. Poetry -- By individual authors
ISBN 978-0-7910-9618-5

LC 2007-49158

First published 1988 in three separate editions focusing on the Prologue, The knight's tale, and The pardoner's tale

A collection of eleven critical essays on Chaucer's well-known work, arranged in chronological order of their original publication.

Includes bibliographical references

Gunn, Thom

Boss Cupid. Farrar, Straus & Giroux 2000 111p hardcover o.p. pa $13 **821**
1. Poetry -- By individual authors
ISBN 0-374-52771-7 pa

LC 99-57739

"Boss Cupid offers a splendid introduction for the uninitiated. Almost all of Gunn's virtues are on display here: his playful, metrical dexterity, his unflinching celebration both of beauty and of transience. . . . Advancing age and the AIDS-related deaths of friends—'my ever-present dead'—figure prominently in these poems, but so does Gunn's humorous touch." Time

Collected poems. Farrar, Straus & Giroux 1994 495p pa $20 **821**
1. Poetry -- By individual authors
ISBN 978-0-374-52433-3; 0-374-52433-5

LC 93-74183

There is a "a unity of purpose that extends throughout the work, from the watchful early metrics through the syllabics, the reach and skill of the free verse and, in much of the latest work, a return to strong form that might be termed triumphant had it not been called into the service of matter so saddening." Times Lit Suppl

Hardy, Thomas

Thomas Hardy; the complete poems. edited by James Gibson. Palgrave 2001 xxxvi, 1003p il pa $33.95 **821**
1. Poetry -- By individual authors
ISBN 978-0-333-94929-0; 0-333-94929-3

LC 2001-32732

First published 1976

This collection "includes Hardy's more than 900 poems, complemented by detailed notes. Collected here are his eight books of verse, all the uncollected poems, Domicilium, and the songs from The Dynasts. This edition contains an additional poem, The Sound of Her." Publisher's note

Includes bibliographical references

Heaney, Seamus

District and circle. Farrar, Straus and Giroux 2006 78p

$20 **821**
1. Poetry -- By individual authors
ISBN 0-374-14092-8; 978-0-374-14092-2

LC 2005-44687

This "collection of robust lyrics celebrates work, memory, and the physicality of existence. Brimming with anvils, hammers, shovels, and pumps, these poems are scored into the page with Heaney's signature accentual and alliterative force." Libr J

Electric light. Farrar, Straus & Giroux 2001 98p hardcover o.p. pa $13 **821**
1. Poetry -- By individual authors
ISBN 0-374-14683-7; 0-374-52841-1 pa

LC 00-67278

Heaney's "book of poems is a compendium of poetic genres set in an array of forms and tuned to many kinds of experience, the work of a mature poet and world citizen, aware of his cultural authority as a public man and of the rights and responsibilities that go with it." N Y Times Book Rev

★ **Finders** keepers; selected prose 1971-2001. Farrar, Straus & Giroux 2002 452p $30; pa $15 **821**
1. Poets 2. Authors 3. Novelists 4. Dramatists 5. Librarians 6. Editors 7. Essayists 8. Memoirists 9. Translators 10. Poets laureate 11. College teachers 12. Literary critics 13. Nobel laureates for literature 14. Poetry -- History and criticism
ISBN 0-374-15496-1; 0-374-52878-0 pa

This collection "gathers Heaney's occasional prose from four decades, much of it meditating upon other poets who have moved him, including familiar members of the canon, such as Eliot and Yeats and Auden, and lesser-known and newer moderns, such as Hugh MacDiarmid, Thomas Kinsella, and Norman MacCaig, whose work draws his interest. Not surprisingly for a poet from a war-wracked land, Heaney comes back again and again to the question of how poetry can matter against human savagery." Booklist

Human chain. Farrar, Straus and Giroux 2010 85p $24 **821**
1. Poetry -- By individual authors
ISBN 978-0-374-17351-7

LC 2010-10274

This is the Irish poet and Nobel laureate's latest collection of verse.

"Nostalgia and memory, numinous visions and the earthy music of compound adjectives together control the short poems and sequences of the Irish Nobel laureate's 14th collection of verse. . . . Old teachers, schoolmates, farmhands, and even the employees of an 'Eelworks' arrive transfigured through Heaney's command of sound. . . . For all the variety of Heaney's framed glimpses, though, the standout poems grow from occasions neither trivial nor topical: Heaney in 2006 had a minor stroke, and the discreet analogies and glimpsed moments in poems such as 'Chanson d'Aventure' (about a ride in an ambulance) and 'In the Attic' ('As I age and blank on names') bring his characteristic warmth and subtlety to mortality, rehabilitation, recent trauma, and old age." Publ Wkly

Opened ground; selected poems, 1966-1996. Farrar, Straus & Giroux 1998 443p hardcover o.p. pa $16 **821**
1. Poetry -- By individual authors
ISBN 0-374-52678-8 pa

LC 98-4331

"The best of nobel laureate Heaney's poems, gathered from 12 previous collections, create a substantial volume that charts the course of one man's thoroughly examined personal life and reflects a volatile era in the life of his troubled country, Northern Ireland, though the particulars

Heaney renders so vibrantly become archetypal and unbounded in their tragedy and bliss." Booklist

Herbert, George

Herbert: poems. Alfred A. Knopf 2004 253p (Everyman's library pocket poets) $12.50   **821**

1. Poetry -- By individual authors 2. Christian poetry, English -- Early modern, 1500-1700.

ISBN 978-1-4000-4329-3; 1-4000-4329-8

LC 2005-273574

Herbert experimented with a variety of forms, "from hymns and sonnets to 'pattern poems,' the shape of which reveal their subjects. Such technical agility never seems ostentatious, however, for precision of language and expression of genuine feeling were the primary concerns of this poet who admonished his readers to 'dare to be true.' An Anglican priest who took his calling with deep seriousness, he brought to his work a religious reverence richly allied with a playful wit and with literary and musical gifts of the highest order." Publisher's note

Hill, Geoffrey

★ The **orchards** of Syon. Counterpoint 2002 72p $24 **821**

1. Poetry -- By individual authors

ISBN 1-58243-166-3

LC 2001-47245

"Cast as a sequence of 72 uniform blank-verse soliloquies compounded out of a dissonant amalgam of demotic jabber and oracular utterance, 'The Orchards of Syon' confirms that Hill, for all his newfound volubility, can be as refractory as ever. . . . But for readers with the patience and stamina to stick with it, Hill's brooding meditations on his ancestral countryside's 'wintry swamp-thickets, brush-heaps of burnt light' or 'the burring air of the fell' carry the haunting force of a last will and testament." N Y Times Book Rev

Selected poems. Yale University Press 2009 276p   **821**

1. Poetry -- By individual authors

ISBN 978-0-300-12156-8

LC 2008-930384

First published 2006 in the United Kingdom

"After four decades with just five books, the past 10 years have seen Hill offer six more, including a trio of long works some liken to Dante and Blake. This first selected since 1994 . . . should get instant critical attention (and sustained academic adoption) even though it contains no new work. Here, entire, is Mercian Hymns, with its gorgeously medievalized evocation of a rural English upbringing. Here, complete, are all three recent long poems, with their erudite mix of elegy and jeremiad. . . . Here, too, are the descriptive beauties that sparkle through even Hill's most rebarbative works." Publ Wkly

Without title. Yale University Press 2007 81p $26; pa $16   **821**

1. Poetry -- By individual authors

ISBN 978-0-300-12176-6; 0-300-12176-8; 0-300-12157-1 pa; 978-0-300-12157-5 pa

LC 2006-926124

First published 2006 in the United Kingdom

"For much of Hill's five-decade career, his forbiddingly allusive and elliptical style, his sometimes peevish tone, his interest in English church history, and his rapt pastoralism have made him an unfashionable figure, but also a highly individual one. His latest collection exhibits typical erudition: who else would name-drop the Jesuit theologian Karl Rahner or describe Jimi Hendrix as an 'exquisite player of neumes' ('neumes' being an archaic form of musical notation)? Though the method is a magpie one, the impression that emerges is of absolute control and sin-

gle-mindedness. And while Hill's outlook can seem willfully bleak . . . there is genuine grace in his descriptions of natural beauty." New Yorker

Hollis, Matthew

Now all roads lead to France; A Life of Edward Thomas. Matthew Hollis. Faber & Faber 2011 416 p. ill., maps   **821**

1. English poets -- Biography 2. World War, 1914-1918 -- Biography 3. Great Britain -- Armed forces -- Recruiting and enlistment -- Biography 4. Poets 5. Authors 6. Essayists 7. Writers on nature 8. Biography, Individual

ISBN 0571245994; 9780571245994

LC 2011505697

Costa Biography Award Winner (2011)

This book presents "a study of [poet Edward] Thomas's life and work from (roughly) the winter of 1913 onwards, with a strong emphasis on his poetic aspirations." (Times Literary Supplement). "[Matthew] Hollis gives a portrait of the artist as a man at work: shaping, revising, making poems. The biography . . . [is] a story of . . . the last four years of his life, during which he developed a close friendship with Robert Frost, decided to enlist in the army and fight in the First World War, and turned himself into a poet." (New Statesman)

Includes bibliographical references and index.

Hopkins, Gerard Manley

Poems and prose. Alfred A. Knopf 1995 256p (Everyman's library pocket poets) $13.50   **821**

1. Poetry -- By individual authors

ISBN 978-0-679-44469-5; 0-679-44469-6

LC 95-15331

This volume "contains a full selection of Hopkins's work, including selected verse, prose, and letters, and an index of first lines." Publisher's note

Hughes, Ted, 1930-1998

Collected poems; edited by Paul Keegan. Farrar, Straus and Giroux 2003 1376p $50; pa $25   **821**

1. Poetry -- By individual authors

ISBN 978-0-374-12538-7; 0-374-12538-4; 978-0-374-52965-9 pa; 0-374-52965-5 pa

LC 2003-59938

"Paul Keegan has taken Hughes's New Selected Poems of 1995 as his model, and intercalated the expected and familiar Faber texts with uncollected or small press works like a Viennese layer cake—in astonishing quantity and quality." Poetry (Modern Poetry Association)

Jonson, Ben

The **complete** poems; edited by George Parfitt. Penguin Books 1988 634p (Penguin classics) pa $17   **821**

1. Poetry -- By individual authors

ISBN 978-0-14-042277-1; 0-14-042277-3

LC 88-196178

"As well as the entire body of Jonson's nondramatic verse, extensively annotated, this edition contains many of the songs from his plays and masques and his translation of 'Horace, of the Art of Poetry'. His 'Conversations with Drummond', which adds much to our sense of the man, appears as an Appendix, as does 'Discoveries'; together they shed valuable light on Jonson's poetic theory and practice." Publisher's note

Kipling, Rudyard, 1865-1936

Complete verse; definitive edition. Doubleday 1989 850p hardcover o.p. pa $20   **821**

1. Poetry -- By individual authors

ISBN 0-385-26089-X pa

LC 88-7364

Replaces Rudyard Kipling's verse: definitive edition, published 1940

This edition includes all of Kipling's published poetry and, in addition, more than 20 poems which have not previously appeared in the inclusive edition of his verse

Langland, William

Piers Plowman; the Donaldson translation, Middle English text, sources and backgrounds, criticism. edited by Elizabeth Robertson and Stephen H.A. Shepherd. Norton 2006 xxviii, 644p pa $15 **821**

1. Poetry -- By individual authors

ISBN 978-0-393-97559-8; 0-393-97559-2

LC 2004-57578

This Middle English poem is "written in 'Alliterative Verse' like Old English poetry and uses a deliberately rustic and archaic dialect. It is an allegorical moral and social satire, written as a 'vision' of the common medieval type." Reader's Ency. 4th edition

Larkin, Philip

★ **Collected** poems; edited and with an introduction by Anthony Thwaite. Farrar, Straus and Giroux 2004 218p pa $15 **821**

1. Poetry -- By individual authors

ISBN 978-0-374-52920-8; 0-374-52920-5

LC 2003-60846

First published 2003 in the United Kingdom

"Thwaite has gathered all the poems Larkin wrote between 1946 and 1985, the year of his death; he also includes a generous selection of work written earlier, before Larkin found his characteristic voice. In all, there are some 240 poems, 83 of them never published before. The unpublished work comes from every period of Larkin's career and increases by half the number of poems in his canon. The poet we now have is considerably more prolific than the one who issued only three small, mature collections in his lifetime. With or without the new poems, Larkin is a major postwar British writer, and this is the best available collection of his poetry." Libr J

Lawrence, D. H.

The **complete** poems; collected and edited with an introduction and notes by Vivian de Sola Pinto and Warren Roberts. Penguin Books 1993 1079p (Penguin twentieth-century classics) pa $24.95 **821**

1. Poetry -- By individual authors

ISBN 978-0-14-018657-4; 0-14-018657-3

First published 1964 by Viking

This "collection of Lawrence's poems, with appendices containing juvenilia, variants, and early drafts, and Lawrence's own critical introductions to his poems, also includes full textual and explanatory notes, glossary, and index." Publisher's note

Lear, Edward

The **complete** verse and other nonsense; compiled and edited with an introduction and notes by Vivien Noakes. Penguin Bks. 2002 566p il pa $18 **821**

1. Nonsense verses 2. Poetry -- By individual authors

ISBN 0-14-200227-5

LC 2002-28998

This volume "presents all of Lear's verse and other nonsense writings, including stories, letters, and illustrated alphabets, as well as previously unpublished material, line drawings, and . . . [an] introduction by scholar Vivien Noakes." Publisher's note

Includes bibliographical references

The **Making** of a poem; a Norton anthology of poetic forms. edited by Mark Strand and Eavan Boland. Norton 2000 xxxi, 366p hardcover o.p. pa $15.95 **821**

1. English poetry -- Collections 2. American poetry -- Collections

ISBN 0-393-32178-9 pa

LC 99-55233

A "collection of villanelles, sestinas, sonnets, elegies, pastorals, ballads, pantoums, odes, and other familiar structures that have shaped English poetry since Beowulf. Each chapter focuses on a single form. . . . . Most useful are the selections themselves, which illustrate how particular forms have been employed over time, from canonical classics by Chaucer, Shelley, and Elizabeth Bishop through newer pieces by Hayden Carruth, Michael Palmer, and Thylias Moss." Libr J

Includes bibliographical references

Marvell, Andrew

Poems; [selected by Peter Washington] A. A. Knopf 2004 256p (Everyman's library pocket poets) $12.50 **821**

1. Poetry -- By individual authors

ISBN 978-1-4000-4252-4; 1-4000-4252-6

The "metaphysical poet Andrew Marvell was one of the chief wits and satirists of his time as well as a passionate defender of individual liberty. Today, however, he is known chiefly for his brilliant lyric poems, including 'The Garden,' 'The Definition of Love,' 'Bermudas,' 'To His Coy Mistress,' and the 'Horatian Ode' to Cromwell." Publisher's note

Maxwell, Glyn, 1962-

One thousand nights and counting; selected poems. Farrar, Straus and Giroux 2011 239p **821**

1. Poetry -- By individual authors

ISBN 9780374226480

LC 2011005176

"The British poet Maxwell's first U.S. selected presents a conversational style that is a constant throughout, as is the setting of England and New England; otherwise, these often surreal and opaque poems range across moods and subjects. The best moments occur when readers can lose themselves in the very long poems, in particular the inventive reimagining of the story of Noah's Ark, 'Out of the Rain,' and the elegiac 'Letters to Edward Thomas,' in which the speaker waits for a friend who never arrives. . . . Maxwell's poetry can be playful and inventive, beautiful and melancholic, but can also be self-aggrandizing . . . and even pretentious. . . . Yet Maxwell is one of stars of poetry across the pond and a rising presence here; this book should win him new fans." Publ Wkly

Morrissey, Sinéad

Parallax; and selected poems. Sinead Morrissey. Farrar, Straus & Giroux 2015 211 p. (hardcover) $26 **821**

1. Empiricism 2. Irish poetry

ISBN 0865478295; 9780865478299

LC 2014043835

National Book Critics Circle Award Finalist: Poetry (2015)

This poetry collection, by Sinead Morrissey, "which won the 2013 T. S. Eliot Prize, . . . explores what is captured, and what is lost, when houses and cityscapes, servants and saboteurs, are arrested in time by photography (or poetry), subjected to the authority of a particular perspective. Assured and disquieting, Morrisey's poems explore the paradoxes that result when we attempt to freeze our passing experience through art." (Publisher's note)

"An impressive collection showcasing an impressive career." Booklist

Motion, Andrew

Keats. University of Chicago Press 1999 636p il pa
$18 **821**

1. Poets 2. Authors 3. Poets, English 4. Writers on medicine
ISBN 0-226-54240-8; 978-0-226-54240-9

LC 98-41014

First published 1997 in the United Kingdom

"Motion emphasizes that Keats was no otherworldly creature of exquisite sensibilities but a man whose liberal politics and commitment to medicine animated his aesthetics and enlightened his poetry." Booklist

Includes bibliographical references

Muldoon, Paul

★ **Horse** latitudes. Farrar, Straus and Giroux 2006 107p
$22 **821**

1. Poetry -- By individual authors
ISBN 978-0-374-17305-0; 0-374-17305-2

LC 2006-306

"Beginning with a sequence of sonnets whose titles start with the letter B, to a series of instant messages formatted as haiku, to an ending that tributes rocker Warren Zevon, readers are in for a lively ride." Libr J

Maggot; poems. Farrar, Straus and Giroux 2010 134p
$24 **821**

1. Poetry -- By individual authors
ISBN 978-0-374-20032-9; 0-374-20032-7

LC 2010-05700

"The play on the word maggot, which can also mean a whim or extravagant notion as well as the larva, tells us all we need to know about Paul Muldoon's poetics. So comfortable is he in both worlds, the debased and the ecstatic, that critics often willfully misunderstand him. . . . Everywhere in 'Maggot,' Mr. Muldoon chafes at the bit, belatedly, against duty and responsibility. He is most susceptible to the charge of triviality in his longer poems, and often in 'Maggot,' he does indeed flirt too closely with absurdity. . . . [He] barely squeaks by on the side of seriousness, but just barely! Credit him with continuing to walk that trapeze, with no net underneath him." Pittsburgh Post-Gazette

★ **Poems,** 1968-1998. Farrar, Straus & Giroux 2001 479p
$35; pa $19 **821**

1. Poetry -- By individual authors
ISBN 0-374-12543-0; 0-374-52844-6 pa

LC 00-45607

"Language is heightened, experimental, and also utterly mundane, even coarse. His subjects match the language, what with trips on mescaline chockablock with bucolic landscapes. The luck of this collection is that it is long and dense enough to show the poet wrestling not only with craft—his intricate and often hidden rhymes show, right from the start, his obsession with form—but also with the reason for poetry in a technological age." Booklist

Murray, Les A.

The **biplane** houses. Farrar, Straus and Giroux 2007 99p
$23 **821**

1. Poetry -- By individual authors
ISBN 978-0-374-11548-7; 0-374-11548-6

LC 2006-31763

First published 2006 in Australia

"Murray's poems, never exactly intimate and often patrolled by details and place-names nearly indecipherable to an outsider, reflect a life lived self-consciously and rather flamboyantly off the beaten track. . . . Pastoral is a sophisticated game pitting poets against earlier poets, like a

chess match played across time. No poet writing about the natural world entirely opts out of the game, but Murray's poetry of elk and emus, bougainvillea and turmeric dust, comes close." New Yorker

★ **Conscious** and verbal; [by] Les Murray. Farrar, Straus & Giroux 2001 94p $23; pa $13 **821**

1. Poetry -- By individual authors
ISBN 0-374-12882-0; 0-374-52860-8 pa

LC 2001-40222

"The poet became a minor celebrity when he awoke from a three-week coma and was pronounced 'conscious and verbal,' but this new volume is more concerned with his familiar Australian topography: dead dogs, the 'Internationale,' oysters, soil, the color yellow. Murray sticks to the cheerfully formal lines that distinguish his work while letting his voice shift between chestnuts of local dialect and a brawny but humble standard English." New Yorker

Poems the size of photographs; [by] Les Murray. Farrar, Straus & Giroux 2003 128p $20 **821**

1. Poetry -- By individual authors
ISBN 0-374-23520-1

LC 2002-192520

First published in 2002 in the United Kingdom

"Murray concentrates his muscular style, passion for landscape, and satirical humor into short and pithy poems. Tightly framed, most can be taken in at a glance, and yet, like developing photographs, they fully disclose their finer details and nuances more slowly. Murray begins with a mischievous tribute to the 'new hieroglyphics,' the international symbols of airports and restaurants, pictographs of the forbidden and the required. The contrasts between words and images intrigue Murray and inform his sly, sometimes startling, always colorful and animated lyrics, yarns, and epigrams." Booklist

Taller when prone; poems. [by] Les Murray. Farrar, Straus and Giroux 2011 82p $24 **821**

1. Poetry -- By individual authors
ISBN 978-0-374-27237-1

LC 2010033150

First published 2010 in Australia

This "is Les Murray's first volume of new poems since The Biplane Houses, published five years ago." (Publisher's note)

The title of Murray's collection "plays with the notion of cutting self down to size. He uses humour to restore perspective (although the punchline to the wonderful and ludicrous 'A Frequent Flyer Proposes a Name', in which he suggests a name for a new London airport, does not qualify as a deflationary joke). There are many more serious and ambitious pieces here, too. There are elegies in the tradition of Gerard Manley Hopkins's 'Felix Randal' – 'Rugby Wheels', about a disabled rugby player, and 'Double Diamond', about a gauche octogenarian soldier at his wife's funeral. It is a collection filled with celebrations of ordinary people, extraordinary Australian birds and open endings. Murray has a gentle way with his poems, letting them go, never forcing a conclusion. One of his great gifts is that he is noninterventionist, never blocks a view – art in apparent artlessness." Guardian (UK)

★ The **New** Oxford book of Irish verse; edited, with translations, by Thomas Kinsella. Oxford Univ. Press 2001 xxx, 423p pa $16.95 **821**

1. Irish poetry -- Collections
ISBN 0-19-280192-9

LC 2001-278442

Replaces The Oxford Book of Irish verse, XVIIth century-XXth century, chosen by Donagh MacDonagh and Lennox Robinson (1958);

this is a reissue of the 1986 edition

"This selection is divided into three parts. Book I opens with the earliest pre-Christian poetry in Old Irish and ends in the fourteenth century with the first Irish poetry in the English language. Book II covers the fourteenth to the eighteenth centuries and Book III the nineteenth and twentieth centuries." Publisher's note

O'Driscoll, Dennis

Stepping stones; interviews with Seamus Heaney. Farrar, Straus, and Giroux 2008 xxx, 552p il map $32 **821**

1. Poets 2. Authors 3. Essayists 4. Translators 5. Nobel laureates for literature

ISBN 978-0-374-26983-8; 0-374-26983-1

LC 2008-41252

"The book is a collection of questions and answers, compiled, largely by correspondence, over a period of some seven years. The compiler, Dennis O'Driscolla poet, senior tax inspector and strict questioner—persuades you that there will be no tolerance of arrears for Heaney here. The replies are tantamount to, while not pre-empting, an autobiography, by someone who says he 'inclines to discretion' but is not a 'self-concealing person'. This is a forthright though not a confessional book, inclined both to 'elevated stuff' and to jokes." Times Lit Suppl

Includes bibliographical references

Ormsby, Frank

The **darkness** of snow; Frank Ormsby. First North American edition Wake Forest University Press 2017 143 p. (pbk.: alk. paper) $14.95 **821**

1. Poetry -- Collections 2. Poetry -- 21st century

ISBN 9781780373676; 1930630824; 9781930630826

LC 2017931446

National Book Critics Circle Award Finalist: Poetry (2017)

This book "is Frank Ormsby's most varied and versatile [poetry] collection to date. It includes three substantial sets of poems whose themes are refreshingly and sometimes painfully new. One is a suite of poems - sombre, good-humoured, flippant - about the early stages of Parkinson's Disease. Ormsby was diagnosed as having the disease in 2011. Another was prompted by the work of Irish painters in Normandy, Brittany and Belgium at the end of the 19th century." (Publisher's note)

★ The **Oxford** book of comic verse; edited by John Gross. Oxford University Press 2009 xxxiv, 512p pa $19.95 **821**

1. English poetry -- Collections 2. American poetry -- Collections 3. Humorous poetry -- Collections

ISBN 978-0-19-956161-2

LC 2009-291577

First published 1994

The editor "defines comic verse as primarily meant to amuse. From this bland definition he delves his principles of inclusion: funny poems that do not exceed the boundaries of good taste. No bawdy lyrics, no skewering satire here. Within these limits, he surveys the field from Chaucer to Glyn Maxwell (1962)." Publ Wkly

Includes bibliographical references

The **Oxford** companion to Chaucer; edited by Douglas Gray. Oxford University Press 2003 xxiii, 526p il map $95 **821**

1. Poets 2. Authors 3. Poetry -- By individual authors

ISBN 0-19-811765-5

LC 2004-270323

This reference includes "more than 2,000 signed entries on various aspects of Chaucer and his works as well as their larger cultural and literary context." Choice

Includes bibliographical references

Paterson, Don

Rain. Farrar, Straus, and Giroux 2010 61p $24; pa $13 **821**

1. Poetry -- By individual authors

ISBN 978-0-374-24629-7; 978-0-374-53268-0 pa

LC 2009-938696

"There's something of the shadow puppeteer in Don Paterson — reading his poems, you don't know what's real and what's illusion; they play with the reader's perceptions and sense of perspective, so that you aren't quite sure whether what you're looking at are the moving figures themselves or the backlit projection screen. At their best, this gives them a curiously disorienting quality, like looking at a photographic negative, in which the world or its representation has been turned inside out." Guardian (London)

The **Penguin** book of the sonnet; 500 years of a classic tradition in English. edited by Phillis Levin. Penguin Bks. 2001 419p pa $18 **821**

1. English poetry -- Collections 2. American poetry -- Collections

ISBN 0-14-058929-5

LC 00-62350

In an introductory essay, Levin "discusses the sonnet's origins, history, traditions, and possibilities. . . . Interwoven with the history are approaches to interpreting and criticizing this poetic form. The bulk of the text is an anthology of over 600 sonnets composed by more than 230 poets. Over 150 of the poets represented wrote during the 20th century." Libr J

Includes bibliographical references

Pickard, Tom

★ **Hole** in the wall; new & selected poems. Flood Editions 2004 139p pa $15 **821**

1. Poetry -- By individual authors

ISBN 0-9710059-3-1

"In the Objectivist tradition, paring words down to broaden their sound and register meaning, Pickard's work here is of compact, dazzling, Bunting-esque musicality. It also bursts with a fluid sensual appeal reminiscent of D.H. Lawrence." Skanky Possum

Pope, Alexander

Selected poetry; edited with an introduction and notes by Pat Rogers. Oxford University Press 1998 xxiii, 226p (Oxford world's classics) pa $12.95 **821**

1. Verse satire, English. 2. Poetry -- By individual authors

ISBN 978-0-19-283494-2; 0-19-283494-0

LC 98-230887

Pope achieved "success with his first published work at the age of twenty-one. A succession of brilliant poems followed, including An Essay on Criticism (1711), Windsor Forest (1715), and his masterpiece, The Rape of the Lock. A second period of great poetry was begun in 1728 with the appearance of the first Dunciad. All these works . . . are included in this selection of his poetry." Publisher's note

Includes bibliographical references

Presley, Frances

Myne; new & selected poems and prose 1976-2005. Shearsman Books 2006 199p $20 **821**

1. Poetry -- By individual authors

ISBN 0-907562-87-6 pa

"Myne is a survey of Frances Presley's career to date, as well as a new collection of her poems. It begins with two recent cycles: the title sequence inspired by the Somerset landscape, and 'Stone Settings' which retraces the enigmatic patterns of prehistoric stones on Exmoor. Also here are the entire Somerset Letters, and Linocut, both originally published by Oasis Books, plus substantial selections from the author's first two books, The Sex of Art and Hula Hoop." Publisher's note

Raine, Kathleen, 1908-2003

The **collected** poems of Kathleen Raine. Counterpoint 2001 368p $30   **821**

1. Imagination -- Poetry 2. Poetry -- By individual authors
ISBN 1-58243-135-3; 978-1-58243-135-2

LC 00-64448

"Raine's poetry asks us to notice the divine in nature and thereby to walk a path of mindfulness. The Collected Poems draws from more than fifty years of published work, including some nineteen previously uncollected poems." (Women's Rev Books)

"Here is a signature collection of [Raine's] work that will delight many and introduce her to many others. She deserves a very wide audience, as she has much to teach us. . . . Her personal religious journey was from a strict Protestant upbringing through conversion to Roman Catholicism to Eastern Vedic belief. From first to last, her poetry is unified by a tone of transcendental belief in visions, presence, angels, and oracles rooted in her Scottish mother's experience of nature." World Lit Today

Ramazani, Jahan

★ The **Norton** anthology of modern and contemporary poetry; edited by Jahan Ramazani, Richard Ellmann, Robert O'Clair. 3rd ed; Norton 2003 2v pa set $75   **821**

1. English poetry -- Collections 2. American poetry -- Collections
ISBN 9780393979787

LC 2002-37990

First published 1973 with title: The Norton anthology of modern poetry

This volume includes "1596 poems by 195 poets. . . . The anthology includes the works of such masters as Walt Whitman, Ezra Pound, Dylan Thomas, Langston Hughes, Gertrude Stein, Lucille Clifton, Louise Erdrich, and Allen Ginsberg. . . . Extensive, and beautifully composed introductions provide insight, observations, and historical context for the selections. . . . This ambitious, highly successful work is a veritable tribute to the enduring power of literature and language." SLJ

Includes bibliographical references

Robinson, Edwin Arlington

Poems; selected and edited by Scott Donaldson. A. A. Knopf 2007 553p (Everyman's library pocket poets) $12.50   **821**

1. Poetry -- By individual authors
ISBN 978-0-307-26576-0; 0-307-26576-5

LC 2006-48269

"Wisely concentrating on poems of short and middling length, Donaldson . . . admits extracts only from Captain Craig and the ending of Lancelot. . . . [He] gives us whole texts of 'Rembrandt to Rembrandt,' 'Isaac and Archibald,' 'Aunt Imogen,' 'John Brown,' and 'Ben Jonson Entertains a Man from Stratford'— major poems all. For texts, he draws entirely from the Collected Poems, save for 'Romance' and four poems given as they appeared in magazines." New Criterion

Ross, David A.

Critical companion to William Butler Yeats; a literary reference to his life and work. Facts On File 2008 652p il (Facts on File library of world literature) $75   **821**

1. Poets 2. Authors 3. Dramatists 4. Memoirists 5. Nobel laureates for literature

ISBN 978-0-8160-5895-2

LC 2008-13642

"Coverage includes: all of Yeats's . . . poems, as well as all his volumes of poetry; all his plays and important drama-related topics, including Dublin's Abbey Theatre, which he helped establish; his critical and other nonfiction writing, including his . . . autobiographies; important themes in his work; [and] friends and literary influences, including Maud Gonne and James Joyce." Publisher's note

Includes bibliographical references

Rossetti, Christina Georgina

Christina Rossetti; the complete poems. text [edited] by R.W. Crump; notes and introduction by Betty S. Flowers. Penguin 2001 lv, 1221p (Penguin Classics) pa $20   **821**

1. Poetry -- By individual authors
ISBN 978-0-14-042366-2; 0-14-042366-4

LC 2002-281810

This "fully annotated collection, based on the definitive texts, brings together fantasy poems such as 'Goblin Market,' terrifyingly vivid verses for children, love lyrics, sonnets, hymns, and ballads, as well as the vast body of her devotional poetry. . . . [This edition] incorporates contextual notes as well as notes on the text and language, an introduction, and a chronology of Rossetti's life and work." Publisher's note

Includes bibliographical references

Rossignol, Rosalyn

Critical companion to Chaucer; a literary reference to his life and work. Facts on File 2006 648p il $85   **821**

1. Poets 2. Authors
ISBN 0-8160-6193-9; 978-0-8160-6193-8

LC 2006-99

First published 1999 with title: Chaucer A to Z

This book on the works of Chaucer includes a biography of Chaucer, synopses and critical commentary on his works (including the Canterbury Tales), and lists of related people, places and topics.

Includes bibliographical references

Satyamurti, Carole

Mahabharata; a modern retelling. by Carole Satyamurti. W W Norton & Co Inc 2015 1200 p. 32 plates; color illustrations (hardcover) $39.95   **821**

1. Indian poetry 2. Sanskrit language 3. India -- History -- To 324 B.C. -- Poetry
ISBN 9780393081756; 0393081753

LC 2014033595

In this book, author "Carole Satyamurti's English retelling covers all eighteen books of the Mahabharata. This new version masterfully captures the beauty, excitement, and profundity of the original Sanskrit poem as well as its magnificent architecture and extraordinary scope." (Publisher's note)

"Satyamurti's exquisitely lucid and involving retelling is bookended with expert commentary by Wendy Doniger (The Hindus: An Alternative History, 2009) and translator and scholar Vinay Dharwadker." Booklist

Includes bibliographical references

Schmidt, Michael

★ **Lives** of the poets. Knopf 1999 975p hardcover o.p. pa $20   **821**

1. Poets, English -- Biography 2. Poetry -- By individual authors 3. English poetry -- History and criticism 4. American poetry -- History and criticism

ISBN 0-375-70604-6 pa

LC 98-51913

First published 1998 in the United Kingdom

In this "survey of poetry in English, Schmidt . . . enthuses about more than 250 poets whose work dates from the 14th century to 1998. More than a critical essay, this friendly and accessible history embodies the life of poetry and conveys its changeable, subjective beauty." Libr J

Includes bibliographical references

Shelley, Percy Bysshe

Poems. Knopf 1993 250p (Everyman's library pocket poets) $12.50   **821**

1. Poetry -- By individual authors

ISBN 978-0-679-42909-8; 0-679-42909-3

LC 93-78335

"Among the English Romantics, [Shelley] has recovered his position as an undoubted major figure: the poet of volcanic hope for a better world, of fiery inspirations shot upward through bitter gloom." Oxford Companion to Engl Lit. 6th edition rev.

Shelley's poetry and prose; authoritative texts, criticism. selected and edited by Donald H. Reiman and Neil Fraistat. 2nd ed; Norton 2002 xxii, 786p il pa $18.75   **821**

1. Poetry -- By individual authors

ISBN 0-393-97752-8

LC 2001-30903

First published 1977

"This edition includes all of Shelley's greatest poetry and other poems frequently taught or discussed . . . as well as three of his most important prose works." Preface

Includes bibliographical references

Sisson, C. H.

Selected poems; foreword by M.L. Rosenthal. New Directions 1996 94p pa $9.95   **821**

1. Poetry -- By individual authors

ISBN 978-0-8112-1327-1; 0-8112-1327-7

LC 95-47599

"C.H. Sisson's Christianity is an austere, rural form that forbids pity for a newborn duckling that will obviously not survive. Yet Sisson, like Frost, sees death and old age as part of a design, not so much insidious as inexorable and thus no occasion for tears. Like Donne, whom he commemorates in 'A Letter to John Donne,' Sisson understands probably better than any contemporary poet the struggle between the call of the flesh and the love of God, and he knows, like Donne, that their reconciliation can only occur in art. . . . The poems [collected here] are sardonic, elegiac, but not despairing." World Lit Today

Spark, Muriel, 1918-2006

All the poems of Muriel Spark. New Directions 2004 130p pa $13.95   **821**

1. Poetry -- By individual authors

ISBN 0-8112-1576-8; 978-0-8112-1576-3

LC 2004-948

This volume collects the poems of the author of Memento Mori (1959) and The Prime of Miss Jean Brodie (1961).

"As one might expect from a novelist who has always made use of the full range of fictional genres and devices, All the Poems does not come in a straightforward, chronological package or arrangement; from the outset, the book, like so much else written by Spark, is amusingly perverse. Beginning with 'A Tour of London' (c1950-51), it then immediately skips, in terms of both time and place, to 'The Dark Music of the Rue du Cherche-Midi' (2000), comes right up to date with 'The Creative

Writing Class' (2003), travels back to 'The Victoria Falls' (c1948) and 'Shipton-under-Wychwood' (c1950), before regressing finally to a series of translations from Latin (c1949). The reader is therefore encouraged to search for the persistent themes and obvious connections. There is clearly a concern and interest in certain technical forms; there is a ballad, an ode, a couple of villanelles. There's the sharp intelligence and wry wit demonstrated in poems that function mainly as conundrums, unanswered questions and, possibly, as skipping rhymes. . . . But the most memorable parts of the book are those that give some clue to Spark's lifelong determination and dedication to her craft." Guardian (UK)

Spencer, Bernard, 1909-1963

Complete poetry: translations & selected prose; edited by Peter Robinson. Bloodaxe Books 2011 351p pa $33.95 **821**

1. Poetry -- By individual authors

ISBN 978-1-85224-891-8 pa; 1-85224-891-2 pa

Spencer "was not a natural self-promoter, publishing sparely and modestly; moreover, his semi-expatriate status and the adventurousness of his reading all but excluded him from narrower and more familiar English traditions. . . . This new edition by Peter Robinson, who has worked extensively with the Spencer archive at Reading University, is the first to appear since Roger Bowen's Collected Poems of 1981, and aims to stir new interest in the work. As well as Spencer's two published collections, Aegean Islands and Other Poems (1946) and With Luck Lasting (1963), and the later poems collected by Bowen, Robinson includes previously uncollected and unpublished drafts, prose drawn from interviews, lectures and notes, and Spencer's pioneering translations of George Seferis, Odysseus Elytis and Eugenio Montale. Reading these alongside his own poems, it becomes clearer than ever how much Spencer drew on Greek and Latin traditions, blending them with the green-grass Englishness of Edward Thomas, and the civilised anguish of MacNeice to make what Robinson's excellent introduction calls 'a European poetry in English'." Guardian (UK)

Spenser, Edmund

★ The **faerie** queene; edited by Thomas P. Roche, Jr., with the assistance of C. Patrick O'Donnell, Jr. Penguin Books 1987 1246p (Penguin classics) pa $20   **821**

1. Poetry -- By individual authors

ISBN 978-0-14-043307-8; 0-14-042207-2

"The greatest work of Spenser, of which the first three books were entrusted to the printer in Nov. 1589, and the second three were published in 1596." Oxford Companion to Engl Lit

Stevenson, Anne

★ **Poems**, 1955-2005. Bloodaxe Books 2005 413p $64.95; pa $29.95   **821**

1. Poetry -- By individual authors

ISBN 1-85224-721-5; 1-85224-699-5 pa

"While Anne Stevenson is most certainly, and rightly, regarded as one of the major poets of our period, it has never been by virtue of this or that much anthologised poem, but by the work or mind as a whole. It is not so much a matter of the odd lightning-struck tree as of an entire landscape, and that landscape is always humane, intelligent and sane, composed of both natural and rational elements, and amply furnished with patches of wit and fury, which only serve to bring out the humanity." London Magazine

Swift, Daniel

Bomber County; the poetry of a lost pilot's war. Farrar, Straus and Giroux 2010 269p il $26   **821**

1. World War, 1939-1945 -- Poetry 2. Great Britain -- Royal Air Force 3. English poetry -- History and criticism 4. War poetry,

English -- History and criticism 5. World War, 1939-1945 --
Literature and the war 6. English poetry -- 20th century -- History
and criticism 7. World War, 1939-1945 -- Great Britain -- Literature
and the war

ISBN 0374273316; 9780374273316

LC 2010-23402

'Bomber County' narrates the story of Daniel Swift's grandfather,
"a pilot with the 83rd Squadron of the Royal Air Force, who on June
12, 1943, climbed aboard a Lancaster bomber, along with six other men
for a raid on Münster, Germany. His plane never returned." (N Y Times
(Late N Y Ed))

"Swift has found an ingeniously oblique way to throw fresh light
on history. His main achievement here is not new facts but what is done
with them, in a subtle exercise in traversing genres." Times Lit Suppl

Includes bibliographical references

Tennyson, Alfred Tennyson

Poems. A. A. Knopf 2004 255p (Everyman's library pocket poets) $12.50   **821**

1. Poetry -- By individual authors

ISBN 978-1-4000-4187-9; 1-4000-4187-2

LC 2003-49505

"This collection includes such famous poems as 'The Lady of Sha-
lott' and 'The Charge of the Light Brigade.' There are extracts from all
the major masterpieces—Idylls of the King, The Princess, In Memoriam—and several complete long poems, such as 'Ulysses' and 'Demeter and Persephone,' that demonstrate his narrative grace. Finally, there
are many of the short lyrical poems, such as 'Come into the Garden,
Maud' and 'Break, Break, Break,' for which he is justly celebrated."
Publisher's note

Thomas, Dylan

The **poems** of Dylan Thomas; edited with an introduction
and notes by Daniel Jones; with a preface by Dylan Thomas. rev
ed; New Directions 2003 xxix, 320p il $34.95   **821**

1. Poetry -- By individual authors

ISBN 978-0-8112-1541-1; 0-8112-1541-5

LC 2002-155790

First published 1971

"To the 90 poems Thomas published in Collected Poems, 1934-1952
Jones has added 102 and placed the total, as far as he could determine,
in the chronological order of their composition. Some of the poems were
still in manuscript form when Thomas died; others had been published in
periodicals and anthologies. In an appendix, Jones offers Thomas' early
poems—including one written when the poet was 12." Libr J [review of
1971 edition]

Includes bibliographical references

Tomlinson, Charles

Selected poems; 1955-1997. New Directions 1997 226p
pa $13.95   **821**

1. Poetry -- By individual authors

ISBN 978-0-8112-1369-1; 0-8112-1369-2

LC 97-25373

"These poems are a fine achievement; they are the work of a consciousness mostly at ease with its dwelling in this world, and unabashed
by a lack of inclination to dwell unduly on shadows rather than light.
The sunniness of disposition, both geographically and psychologically,
combined with Tomlinson's canny ability to metrically heighten what
still sounds to the ear like the language of common day, give a tone
that might be rationally described as Tomlinsonian. This . . . [is] a book
essential to any collection of the best poetry of the postwar years." Am

Book Rev

Skywriting and other poems. Ivan R. Dee 2003 96p
$18.95   **821**

1. Poetry -- By individual authors

ISBN 978-1-566-63541-7; 1-556-63541-1

LC 2003-55504

"Mr Tomlinson is an eloquent poet of place—in this collection he
moves through Mexico, Italy, Japan, and his home county of Glouces-
tershire—whose work combines visual exactitude with an uncommon
gracefulness of expression." Economist

Turnbull, Gael

★ **There** are words; collected poems. Shearsman Books
2006 495p pa $30   **821**

1. Poetry -- By individual authors

ISBN 0-90756-289-2

"Restlessly experimental—but never for its own sake—Turnbull
was constantly doing what Ezra Pound asked of poets at the beginning
of the twentieth century, namely to make it new. His range is very wide.
He employed the long line before C.K. Williams or Ciaran Carson; he
experimented with prose-poems, found-poems; he wrote ballads, poems meant to be read out loud, poems that deftly rhyme and ones that
deftly don't; he shaped poems on the page with varying line-lengths and
indentings; he used the spaces between lines and verses functionally;
the touch is sometimes light, sometimes profoundly earnest. . . . In the
almost 500pp of this superb Collected Poems there isn't one dud piece,
one poem that doesn't have genuine poetic power and resonance." Stride
(UK)

West, Richard

Chaucer, 1340-1400; the life and times of the first English
poet. Carroll & Graf Pubs. 2000 302p il map hardcover o.p.
pa $14   **821**

1. Poets 2. Authors 3. Great Britain -- History -- 1154-1399,
Plantagenets

ISBN 0-7867-0925-1 pa

LC 00-712752

West's biography "combines history and literary criticism. He places
Chaucer within his historical context and examines his life and writings." Libr J

Wordsworth, William

★ **Selected** poetry of William Wordsworth; edited by Mark
Van Doren; introduction by David Bromwich. Modern Lib.
2001 xxii, 687p $24.95; pa $11.95   **821**

1. Poetry -- By individual authors

ISBN 0-679-64224-2; 0-375-75941-7 pa

LC 00-66444

This collection "represents Wordsworth's prolific output, from the
poems first published in Lyrical Ballads in 1798 . . . to the late 'Yarrow
Revisited.' Wordsworth's poetry is celebrated for its deep feeling, its use
of ordinary speech, the love of nature it expresses, and its representation
of commonplace things and events." Publisher's note

Yeats, W. B.

The **collected** poems of W.B. Yeats; edited by Richard J.
Finneran. Rev. 2nd ed.; Scribner Paperback Poetry 1996 xxv,
544p pa $20   **821**

1. Poetry -- By individual authors

ISBN 978-0-684-80731-7; 0-684-80731-9

LC 96-23314

First published 1989 by Collier Books

This volume "includes all of the poems authorized by Yeats for inclusion in his standard canon. . . . Revised and corrected, this edition includes Yeats's own notes on his poetry, complemented by explanatory notes from . . .Yeats scholar Richard J. Finneran." Publisher's note

821.3   English poetry – 1558-1625

Scarry, Elaine

Naming thy name; Cross Talk in Shakespeare's Sonnets. Elaine Scarry. Farrar, Straus & Giroux 2016 304 p. illustrations (hardback) $27; (ebook) $60   **821.3**
1. Sonnets, English -- History and criticism 2. Love poetry, English -- History and criticism
ISBN 9780374279936; 9780374713867

LC 2016016700

This book, by Elaine Scarry, "lays bare William Shakespeare's devotion to a beloved whom he not only names but names repeatedly in the microtexture of the sonnets, in their architecture, and in their deep fabric, immortalizing a love affair. By naming his name, Scarry enables us to hear clearly, for the very first time, a lover's call and the beloved's response." (Publisher's note)

Includes bibliographical references

821.914   English poetry – 1945-1999

Muldoon, Paul, 1951-

Selected poems 1968-2014; Paul Muldoon. Farrar, Straus & Giroux 2016 240 p. (hardback) $27; (ebook) $60 **821.914**
1. Poetry -- Collections
ISBN 9780374260828; 9780374715779

LC 2016033242

This book, by Paul Muldoon, "offers forty-six years of work drawn from twelve individual collections by a poet who 'began as a prodigy and has gone on to become a virtuoso' (Michael Hofmann). Hailed by Seamus Heaney as 'one of the era's true originals,' Paul Muldoon seems determined to escape definition, yet this volume, compiled by the poet himself, serves as an indispensable introduction to his trademark combination of intellectual hijinks and emotional honesty." (Publisher's note)

"Equal parts bar crawl and blessing, formal adventure and shaggy dog, Muldoon's work looks both backward and forward and finds new ways to rhyme them." Pub Wkly

Oswald, Alice, 1966-

Falling awake; Alice Oswald. W W Norton & Co Inc 2016 96 p. (hardcover) $25.95   **821.914**
1. Nature poetry 2. Poetry -- Collections 3. English poetry -- 21st century
ISBN 9780393285284

LC 2016012940

Written by Alice Oswald, the book defines "life as a slowly falling weight, where beings fight against their inevitable end. Oswald reimagines classical figures such as Orpheus and Tithonus alive in an English landscape together with shadows, flies, villagers, dew, crickets—all characterized in tension between the weight of death and their own willpower." (Publisher's note)

"In an era in which most poetry is concerned with personality, prize-winning Oswald takes a different approach in her attention to phenomena." Booklist.

822   English drama

Bennett, Alan, 1934-

The **history** boys; a play. Alan Bennett. Faber and Faber 2006 xxvii, 109p (pbk.) $13   **822**
1. England -- Drama. 2. Education -- Drama. 3. Boarding schools -- Drama. 4. Teacher-student relationships -- Drama.
ISBN 9780571224647; 0571224644

LC 2005936593

First published 2004 in the United Kingdom

In this play playwright "Alan Bennett evokes the special period and place that the sixth form represents in an English boy's life. In doing so, he raises--with gentle wit and pitch-perfect command of character--not only universal questions about the nature of history and how it is taught but also questions about the purpose of education today." (Publisher's note)

"Nothing could diminish the incendiary achievement of this subtle, deep-wrought and immensely funny play about the value and meaning of education. . . . In short, a superb, life-enhancing play." Guardian

Christie, Agatha

The **mousetrap** and other plays. New American Library 2000 742p hardcover o.p. pa $7.99   **822**
1. English drama -- Collections
ISBN 0-451-20118-3; 0-451-20114-0 pa

LC 00-64727

First published 1978 by Dodd, Mead

"The noted mystery writer composed adaptations of seven novels and stories into arresting plays as well as creating one original theater piece ('Verdict'). . . . All are as delightful to read for pleasure as Christie's mystery novels, especially since some that earlier appeared in the latter form have been intriguingly altered." Booklist

Churchill, Caryl

Mad forest; a play from Romania. Theatre Communications Group 1996 87p pa $13.95   **822**
ISBN 1-55936-114-X; 978-1-55936-114-9

LC 96-12875

First published 1991 in the United Kingdom

Large mixed cast. 3 acts. First performed at the New York Theater Workshop, New York, December 4, 1991

This play "explores the reactions of two ordinary families to the confused events of the Romanian revolution: the dreadful damage done to people's lives by years of repression, and the painful difficulties of sudden but lasting change." Publisher's note

Dryden, John

★ **All** for love; edited by David M. Vieth. University of Neb. Press 1972 xxxiv, 146p (Regents Restoration drama series) hardcover o.p. pa $24.95   **822**
1. Queens
ISBN 0-8032-5379-6 pa

An English Restoration tragedy which is an adaptation of Shakespeare's "Antony and Cleopatra" done in blank verse

Everyman, and medieval miracle plays; edited by A. C. Cawley; with a new preface and bibliography by Anne Rooney. Tuttle 1993 256p hardcover o.p. pa $6.95   **822**
1. Mysteries and miracle plays
ISBN 0-460-87280-X pa
First Everyman's library edition published 1909 with title: Everyman, with other interludes including eight miracle plays

In addition to Everyman, this collection includes plays from the Towneley, Coventry, York and Chester cycles.

Includes bibliographical references

Fugard, Athol

Blood knot and other plays. Theatre Communications Group 1991 202p hardcover o.p. pa $15   **822**

ISBN 978-1-55936-019-7; 1-55936-019-4

LC 90-29029

"The brothers of Blood Knot—one dark-skinned, one light—betray their dream of a better future with the impossible wish of passing for white. In Hello and Goodbye, a poor white brother and sister churn through their once-promising past to comprehend their bleak present. Boesman and Lena, black husband and wife, tramp homelessly through a severe and unforgiving landscape, discovering strength and delivering devotion through an encounter with a mysterious old African." Publisher's note

★ **Master** Harold-- and the boys. Vintage Books 2009 60p pa $12.95   **822**

1. South Africa -- Race relations -- Drama

ISBN 978-0-307-47520-6; 0-307-47520-4

LC 2010-292381

First published 1982 by Random House

Characters: 3 men. 1 act. First produced at the Yale Repertory theatre, New Haven, Connecticut, 1982.

Heaney, Seamus

The **burial** at Thebes; a version of Sophocles' Antigone. Farrar, Straus and Giroux 2004 79p $18   **822**

ISBN 0-374-11721-7

LC 2004-43986

"There are many translations of Sophocles' Antigone but few with the understated power and spare beauty of . . . Heaney's version. . . . Written in a muscular but lively style, the translation, like Heaney's best poetry, finds music in the language of the streets and reveals the raw, primal power in the most carefully constructed rhetorical tropes." Booklist

Jonson, Ben

Volpone and other plays; edited by Michael Jamieson. Penguin 2004 496p (Penguin classics) pa $12   **822**

ISBN 978-0-14-144118-4; 0-14-144118-6

LC 2004-275516

First published 1966 in the United Kingdom with title: Three comedies

"Ben Jonson created in Volpone and The Alchemist hilarious portraits of cupidity and chicanery, while in Bartholomew Fair he portrays his fellow Londoners at their most festive—and most bawdy." Publisher's note

Osborne, John

Look back in anger. Penguin 1982 96p (Penguin Plays) pa $12   **822**

ISBN 0-14-048175-3; 978-0-14-048-175-4

LC 82-9144

First published 1957 by Criterion Books

Characters: 3 men, 2 women. First produced at the Royal Court Theatre, London, May 8, 1956.

This play "introduced a new strain of realism to British theatre and set the tone for the generation of anti-Establishment writers who became known as the Angry Young Men. Osborne described his own parents as 'impoverished middle class,' but his play deals with the frustrations,

crude language, and squalid conditions of working-class life." Reader's Ency. 4th edition

Peters, Sally

Bernard Shaw; the ascent of the superman. Yale Univ. Press 1996 328p il hardcover o.p. pa $22   **822**

1. Authors 2. Novelists 3. Dramatists 4. Dramatists, English 5. Essayists 6. Nonfiction writers 7. Nobel laureates for literature

ISBN 0-300-06097-1; 0-300-07500-6 pa

LC 95-37248

An "exploration of the ambiguities and passions that formed this great playwright and thinker. Shaw's sexuality, always a good topic of speculation, is studied here, but one wishes for more insights and indepth analysis. Peters does devote a chapter to Shaw's close relationship with the actor and playwright Harley Granville Barker, mainly from Shaw's point of view. One may not agree with Peter's conclusions, but they will prove to be of interest to anyone studying Shaw." Libr J

Includes bibliographical references

Plays

The **complete** plays; edited by Frank Romany and Robert Lindsey. Penguin Books 2003 xliv, 702p (Penguin classics) pa $15   **822**

ISBN 978-0-14-043633-4; 0-14-043633-2

LC 2004-268858

Includes bibliographical references

Contents: Dido, queen of Carthage; Tamburlaine the Great, part one; Tamburlaine the Great, part two; The Jew of Malta; Doctor Faustus; Edward the Second; The massacre at Paris

Shaffer, Peter, 1926-2016

★ **Equus.** Scribner 2005 112p pa $12   **822**

ISBN 0-7432-8730-4; 978-0-7432-8730-2

LC 2005-51600

First published 1973 in the United Kingdom

Characters: 5 men, 4 women. 1 act, 35 scenes. First produced by the National Theater, London, July 26, 1973

Drama about "a jolting confrontation between a psychiatrist and a 17-year-old boy who has blinded six horses from the stable where he is employed. As the probe into the boy's attitudes and behavior deepens, this criminal act is revealed to have been a result of his notions of a sexual/religious spirit in horses." Booklist

★ **Peter** Shaffer's Amadeus; with an introduction by the director Sir Peter Hall and a wholly new preface by the author. Perennial Bks. 2001 xxxiv, 124 p.p pa $15   **822**

1. Composers

ISBN 0-06-093549-9

LC 2001-278382

First published 1980 in the United Kingdom

Characters: 9 men, 1 woman, extras. 2 acts. First produced at the National Theater of Great Britain, November 1979

Shaw, Bernard

Arms and the man; a pleasant play. [by] Bernard Shaw; introduction by Rodelle Weintraub; definitive text under the editorial supervision of Dan H. Laurence. Penguin Books 2006 xxvi 73 (Penguin classics) pa $9   **822**

ISBN 978-0-14-303976-1; 0-14-303976-8

LC 2005-56724

First produced 1894. Comedy set in Bulgaria satirizing romantic attitudes about war.

Heartbreak House; a fantasia in the Russian manner on English themes. definitive text under the editorial supervision of Dan H. Laurence; with an introduction by David Hare. Penguin Books 2000 160p il (Penguin Classics) pa $10   **822**

  ISBN 978-0-14-043787-4; 0-14-043787-8

                            LC 2001-266517

  Written in 1913, first produced 1920

"A complex allegorical work in which Shaw indicts apathy, confusion, and lack of purpose as the causes of the world's problems. The characters—all larger than life and with symbolic names—are gathered at the home of an eccentric sea captain; they each represent an evil in the modern world. Into their midst comes young Ellie Dunn, whose search for a husband Shaw treats as a new generation searching for a way of life." Benet's Reader's Ency. 4th edition

Includes bibliographical references

Major Barbara; definitive text under the editorial supervision of Dan H. Laurence; with an introduction by Margery Morgan. Penguin Books 2000 156p (Penguin classics) pa $11 **822**

  1. Crime 2. Salvation Army 3. Father-daughter relationship

  ISBN 978-0-14-043790-4; 0-14-043790-8

                            LC 2002-275028

In this "comedy, originally staged in 1905, Andrew Undershaft, a millionaire armaments dealer, loves money and despises poverty. His energetic daughter Barbara, however, is a devout major in the Salvation Army. She sees her father as just another soul to be saved. But when the Salvation Army needs funds to keep going, it is Undershaft who saves the day." Publisher's note

Man and Superman; a comedy and a philosophy. definitive text under the editorial supervision of Dan H. Laurence; introduced by Stanley Weintraub. Penguin 2000 264p (Penguin classics) pa $11   **822**

  ISBN 978-0-14-043788-1; 0-14-043788-6

"In Man and Superman, Shaw combined seriousness with comedy to create a satirical and buoyant exposé of the eternal struggle between the sexes. . . . This volume includes Shaw's Preface of 1903 and his appendix, 'The Revolutionist's Handbook', the cast list from the first production of Man and Superman and a list of his principal works." Publisher's note

★ **Pygmalion** . . . and My fair lady; [Pygmalion] by George Bernard Shaw; and My fair lady/based on Shaw's Pygmalion; adaptation and lyrics by Alan Jay Lerner; music by Frederick Loewe. 50th anniversary ed.; Signet Classic 2006 219p pa $5.95   **822**

  ISBN 0-451-53009-8

My fair lady was awarded the New York Drama Critics Circle Award for 1956

This volume includes the complete texts of Shaw's Pygmalion and Lerner's musical adaptation My fair lady.

Saint Joan; a chronicle play in six scenes and an epilogue. definitive text under the editorial supervision of Dan H. Laurence; with 'On playing Joan' by Imogen Stubbs; and an introduction by Joley Wood. Penguin 2003 xx, 168p (Penguin classics) pa $12   **822**

  1. Saints

  ISBN 978-0-14-043791-6; 0-14-04379-1

First produced 1923

Chronicle play in "which Joan of Arc, the young girl who led France to victory over the English, emerges as an unlettered country girl gifted with masterful will and innate intelligence." McGraw-Hill Ency World Drama

Sheridan, Richard Brinsley

The **school** for scandal and other plays; edited with an introduction by Eric S. Rump. New ed; Penguin 2004 288p (Penguin classics) pa $12   **822**

  1. Great Britain -- Social life and customs

  ISBN 978-0-14-043240-4

  First published 1988

"In The Rivals, Captain Absolute becomes his own rival for the hand of Lydia Languish wooing her under another name, while her aunt, the verbally inept Mrs Malaprop, wishes her to marry the real Captain. The Critic, featuring the pompous Puff and the arrogant Sneer, is a mocking depiction of the theatre, playwrights and, of course, critics. And The School for Scandal continues the theme of imposture when Sir Oliver Surface tests his nephews by appearing before them in disguise, and learns that reputation and the approval of society are of little value. In his introduction, Eric S. Rump places the plays in their historical and dramatic context and examines their enduring popularity." Publisher's note

Synge, J. M.

The **complete** plays. Vintage Bks. 1960 268p pa $10 **822**

  ISBN 0-394-70178-X

Contents: In the shadow of the glen; Riders to the sea; The tinker's wedding; The well of the saints; The playboy of the Western world; Deirdre of the sorrows

Wilde, Oscar

★ The **importance** of being earnest and other plays; introduction by Terrence McNally; notes by Michael F. Davis. Modern Library 2003 257p pa $9.95   **822**

  ISBN 0-8129-6714-3

                            LC 2003-44566

The title play, written in 1895, is a drawing room comedy exposing quirks and foibles of Victorian society with plot revolving around amorous pursuits of two men who face social obstacles when they woo young ladies of quality. The book also features Lady Windermere's fan (1893), a four act comedy about a woman who has an affair when she suspects her husband of adultery, and An ideal husband (1895), a comedy about a blackmail scheme involving a lord's investment in the Suez Canal days before the British government's purchase of it, and his wife's reaction to her husband's past misdeeds.

822.3   Drama of Elizabethan period, 1558-1625

Baker, William

The **facts** on file companion to Shakespeare; William Baker and Kenneth Womack. Facts On File 2011 5 v. (acid-free paper) $375.00   **822.3**

  1. English drama -- History and criticism

  ISBN 0816078203; 9780816078202

                            LC 2010054012

This book focuses on the author William Shakespeare. "Volume 1 is made up of background essays and more on Shakespeare's times and texts. Poems and sonnets are covered in volume 2, offering for each analysis and a bibliography. In volumes 3, 4, and 5, plays are covered in a 'complete works' fashion designed for use as a textbook. . . .

. These are followed by an overview essay and excerpts from 'classic criticism.'"(Booklist)

Includes bibliographical references and index

Bate, Jonathan

Soul of the age; a biography of the mind of William Shakespeare. Random House 2009 471p il map $35   **822.3**

1. Poets 2. Authors 3. Dramatists
ISBN 978-1-4000-6206-5

LC 2008-16561

In this biography of Shakespeare, the author uses "the Bard's own 'Seven Ages of Man' speech from As You Like It to envision him as an infant, a school boy, a lover, a soldier, a justice, a pantaloon, and an old man entering 'oblivion.' The result is a fresh new way to look at Shakespeare and a welcome reminder of what literary biography can still do." Libr J

Includes bibliographical references

Bloom, Harold

Hamlet: poem unlimited. Riverhead Bks. 2003 154p hardcover o.p. pa $13   **822.3**

1. Poets 2. Authors 3. Dramatists
ISBN 1-57322-233-X; 1-57322-377-8 pa

LC 2002-31691

"Far superior to existing theories of performance and worth yards of criticism for each well-wrought page." Libr J

Shakespeare: the invention of the human. Riverhead Bks. 1998 xx, 745p hardcover o.p. pa $18   **822.3**

1. Poets 2. Authors 3. Dramatists
ISBN 1-57322-751-X pa

LC 98-21325

"The passion and obsessiveness of Bloom's approach are its greatest recommendation." N Y Rev Books

Boyce, Charles

Critical companion to William Shakespeare; a literary reference to his life and work. Rev. ed; Facts on File 2005 2v il (Facts on File library of world literature) set $104.50   **822.3**

1. Poets 2. Authors 3. Dramatists
ISBN 0-8160-5373-1

LC 2004-25769

First published 1990 with title: Shakespeare A to Z

"The first two-thirds [of this set] covers the plays. Arranged alphabetically by title, the 3000 entries generally consist of a scene-by-scene summary, a commentary, sources, theatrical history, and character sketches. The last one-third features entries for actors, composers, musicians, places that figured in the plays, and miscellaneous items." Libr J

Includes bibliographical references

Bryson, Bill

Shakespeare; the world as stage. Atlas Books/HarperCollins 2007 199p (Eminent lives) $19.95   **822.3**

1. Poets 2. Authors 3. Dramatists
ISBN 978-0-06-074022-1; 0-06-074022-1

LC 2007-21647

In this biography, the author marshals "the usual little facts that others might overlook—for example, that in Shakespeare's day perhaps 40% of women were pregnant when they got married—to paint a portrait of the world in which the Bard lived and prospered. . . . Bryson is a pleasant and funny guide to a subject at once overexposed and elusive—as Bryson puts it, he is a kind of literary equivalent of an electron—for-

ever there and not there." Publ Wkly

Includes bibliographical references

Butler, Colin

The **practical** Shakespeare; the plays in practice and on the page. Ohio University Press 2005 205p $39.95; pa $19.95   **822.3**

1. Poets 2. Authors 3. Dramatists
ISBN 0-8214-1621-9; 0-8214-1622-7 pa

LC 2004-30580

"Notes on staging, acting behaviors, scenes not shown, entrances, exits, characterizations, prologues, choruses, and staging are each featured in the text. References to specific scenes in the plays are used to illustrate and support the material. Any group preparing a production of one of the plays should find this a useful reference." Univ Press Books for Public and Second Sch Libr, 2006

Includes bibliographical references

Collins, Paul

★ The **book** of William; how Shakespeare's first folio conquered the world. Bloomsbury 2009 246p $25   **822.3**

1. Poets 2. Authors 3. Dramatists 4. Rare books
ISBN 978-1-59691-195-6; 1-59691-195-6

LC 2009-6722

"Witty, detailed, and highly entertaining, . . . [this book] will be appreciated by fans of Shakespeare, history, or human folly." Libr J

Includes bibliographical references

Falk, Dan

The **Science** of Shakespeare; a New Look at the Playwright's Universe. Dan Falk. Thomas Dunne Books/St. Martin's Press 2014 384 p. illustrations (hardback) $27.99 **822.3**

1. Science -- History 2. Literature and science 3. Literature and science -- England -- History -- 17th century
ISBN 1250008778; 9781250008770

LC 2013046842

This book by Dan Falk "explores the connections between the famous playwright and the beginnings of the Scientific Revolution---and how, together, they changed the world forever. We meet a colorful cast of Renaissance thinkers, including Thomas Digges, who . . . lived in the same neighborhood as Shakespeare; Thomas Harriot--'England's Galileo--who aimed a telescope at the night sky months ahead of his Italian counterpart; and Danish astronomer Tycho Brahe." (Publisher's note)

"This eminently readable book should prove fascinating to both lovers of science and bardolators." LJ

Includes bibliographical references and index

Garber, Marjorie

Shakespeare after all. Pantheon Books 2004 989p hardcover o.p. pa $20   **822.3**

1. Poets 2. Authors 3. Dramatists
ISBN 0-375-42190-4; 0-385-72214-1 pa

LC 2004-40063

The author "provides a handbook on Shakespeare's plays. After an introduction supplying standard overviews of the Renaissance theater and Shakespeare's life, she offers a critical essay on each play, complete with bibliographies and filmographies. The strength of this work is that Garber shows how the plays are interrelated by recurring language, characters, and themes, how each era has interpreted Shakespeare for itself, and how Shakespeare continues to shape today's culture." Libr J

Includes bibliographical references

Shakespeare and modern culture. Pantheon Books 2008
326p il $30   **822.3**
1. Poets 2. Authors 3. Dramatists
ISBN 978-0-307-37767-8; 0-307-37767-9
                                        LC 2008-26802
"Writing on ten plays, [Garber] offers examples of their 'uncanny'
anticipation of present-day phenomena and our own appropriations of
them, as in the now fashionable use of 'Henry V' as a blueprint for success in business. (She quotes one manual that calls Bardolph's hanging
the 'ultimate pink slip.') Garber's approach is eclectic, spanning Freud
and evolutionary biology; occasionally, she gets caught up in secondary
concerns, but she is an inspiring reader." New Yorker
Includes bibliographical references

Greenblatt, Stephen J.
Will in the world; how Shakespeare became Shakespeare.
[by] Stephen Greenblatt. Norton 2004 430p il $26.95 **822.3**
1. Poets 2. Authors 3. Dramatists
ISBN 0-393-05057-2
                                        LC 2004-11512
National Book Award Finalist: Nonfiction (2004)
"Greenblatt is at his best when he merges his gifts as a literary critic
and scholar with his instincts as a biographer. He writes with real subtlety and skill about the sonnets. . . . He also writes very well about the
climate of fear and the use of public punishment and torture in Elizabethan and early Jacobean England, and how this enters into the very spirit
of Shakespeare's work." N Y Times Book Rev
Includes bibliographical references

★ The **Greenwood** companion to Shakespeare; a comprehensive guide to students. edited by Joseph Rosenblum. Greenwood Press 2005 4v set $299.95   **822.3**
1. Poets 2. Authors 3. Dramatists
ISBN 0-313-32779-3
                                        LC 2004-28690
"Each of the set's four volumes relates to a specific genre—Overviews and the History Plays (Vol. 1), The Comedies (Vol. 2), The Tragedies (Vol. 3), and The Romances and Poetry (Vol. 4)—and is organized
in 'Cliff Notes' fashion, devoting each entry to a single play, long poem,
sonnet, or sonnet pair. . . . A great introduction to the Bard." Libr J
Includes bibliographical references

Heylin, Clinton
So long as men can breathe; the untold story of Shakespeare's Sonnets. Da Capo Press 2009 280p $24   **822.3**
1. Poets 2. Authors 3. Dramatists
ISBN 978-0-306-81805-9; 0-306-81805-1
                                        LC 2009-08999
An account of the publication of Shakespeare's Sonnets. The author
"introduces us to the 'unholy alliance' involved in this precarious enterprise: Thomas Thorpe, the publisher, a self-described 'well wishing
adventurer;' George Eld, the printer, heavily embroiled in large-scale
pirating; William Aspley, the prestigious bookseller, who mysteriously
ended his association with Thorpe soon after. Leaving the calamitous
world of Elizabethan publishing, Heylin goes on to chart the many editions of the Sonnets through the years and the editorial decisions that led
to their present configuration." Publisher's note
Includes bibliographical references

Kermode, Frank
Shakespeare's language. Farrar, Straus & Giroux 2000
324p hardcover o.p. pa $15   **822.3**

1. Poets 2. Authors 3. Dramatists
ISBN 0-374-52774-1 pa
                                        LC 99-55846
Kermode "devotes particular attention to the four great tragedies
written at the height of Shakespeare's powers: Hamlet, Othello, King
Lear and Macbeth. While Kermode's concern is with the Bard's verse,
he betrays no simplistic notions about literary language operating in a
vacuum. A careful, close analysis of passages in each play is informed
by a breathtaking knowledge of Elizabethan history and culture, as well
as by the entire history of Shakespeare criticism from Coleridge to Eliot
and the new historicists." Publ Wkly
Includes bibliographical references

Lamb, Charles
Tales from Shakespeare; by Charles & Mary Lamb; with
an introduction by Marina Warner. Penguin Books 2007 304p
(Penguin classics) pa $12   **822.3**
1. Poets 2. Authors 3. Dramatists
ISBN 978-0-14-144162-7; 0-14-144162-3
First published 1807
A now classic collection of twenty plays by Shakespeare adapted as prose stories—the comedies by Mary Lamb, the tragedies by
Charles Lamb
"The Tales were the first version of 'Shakespeare' to be published
specifically for children. They are written in a clear, vigorous style, not
often encumbered by the attempt to make the language resemble that
of the original. A lot is left out. . . . But the literary quality of the Tales
makes them outshine almost every other English children's book of
this period, and they proved an immediate and lasting success." Oxford
Companion to Child Lit

★ **Living** with Shakespeare; essays by writers, actors, and directors. Edited by Susannah Carson; Foreword by Harold
Bloom. Vintage Books, A Division of Random House, Inc.
2013 xxviii, 500 p.p ill. (paperback) $16   **822.3**
ISBN 0307742911; 9780307742919
                                        LC 2012039745
This book, edited by Susanna Carson, presents collected essays re-
flecting on the works and influence of playwright William Shakespeare.
"Carson invites forty actors, directors, scholars, and writers to reflect
on why his work is still such a vital part of our culture. We hear from
James Earl Jones on reclaiming Othello as a tragic hero, Julie Taymor
on turning Prospero into Prospera, Camille Paglia on teaching the plays
to actors, . . . [and] Germaine Greer on the playwright's home life."
(Publisher's note)
"Editor Carson's eclecticism aims to break down the usual disciplinary borders and reduce the intimidating distance that often yawns
between Shakespeare experts and general readers... The essays include
much justified reverence, but also some healthy questioning, as well as
limited forays into cross-cultural dialogues... [A] consistently stimulating read..." Pub Wkly

Mays, Andrea E.
The **millionaire** and the bard; Henry Folger's obsessive
hunt for Shakespeare's first folio. by Andrea E. Mays. Simon &
Schuster 2015 368 p. illustrations, portraits (trade paperback)
$16   **822.3**
1. Book collecting 2. Publishers and publishing -- History 3. New
York (N.Y.) -- Intellectual life 4. New York (N.Y.) -- Commerce
-- History 5. London (England) -- Intellectual life -- 17th century
6. Millionaires -- New York (State) -- New York -- Biography 7.
Book collectors -- New York (State) -- New York -- Biography 8.

Publishers and publishing -- England -- London -- History -- 17th century

ISBN 9781439118238; 9781439118252

LC 2015001458

This book, by Andrea E. Mays, "tells the . . . story of the making of the First Folio. . . . When Shakespeare died in 1616 half of his plays died with him. No one—not even their author—believed that his writings would last. . . . Seven years later, in 1623, Shakespeare's business partners, companions, and fellow actors, John Heminges and Henry Condell, gathered copies of the plays and manuscripts, edited and published thirty-six of them." (Publisher's note)

Includes bibliographical references and index

Norwich, John Julius

Shakespeare's kings; the great plays and the history of England in the Middle Ages, 1337-1485. Scribner 2000 401p il hardcover o.p. pa $16   **822.3**

1. Poets 2. Authors 3. Dramatists
ISBN 0-7432-0031-4 pa

LC 99-58271

The author offers "overviews of Edward III; Richard II; Henry IV, parts 1 and 2; Henry V; Henry VI, parts 1, 2, and 3; and Richard III, examining each play through the lens of history. In addition to providing the necessary historical commentary, he also fills in the gaps between the plays, enabling readers to thoroughly comprehend the entire series in the proper historical context." Booklist

Nuttall, A. D.

Shakespeare the thinker. Yale University Press 2007 428p $30   **822.3**

1. England -- Intellectual life -- 16th century 2. England -- Intellectual life -- 17th century
ISBN 978-0-300-11928-2; 0-300-11928-3

LC 2006-35179

The author "traces ideas about motivation, identity, speech, and symbol in Shakespeare's plays. His study is rich in unexpected juxtapositions: Hippolyta, of 'A Midsummer Night's Dream,' finds herself in casual conversation with David Hume, and Titus Andronicus is seen in the context of 'Goodfellas.' The analysis never pulls too far away from the action onstage; indeed, Nuttall painstakingly shows Shakespeare's skill at negotiating abstract ideas through suspense, conflict, and character." New Yorker

Includes bibliographical references

★ The **Oxford** companion to Shakespeare; general editor, Michael Dobson; associate general editor, Stanley Wells. Oxford Univ. Press 2001 xxix, 541p il maps hardcover o.p. pa $39.95   **822.3**

1. Poets 2. Authors 3. Dramatists 4. Reference books
ISBN 0-19-280614-9 pa; 0-19-811735-3

LC 2001-277478

This volume "illuminates not only Shakespeare's life and works but also the many forms that interpretation of Shakespeare has taken in the centuries since his death." Booklist

Includes bibliographical references

Rasmussen, Eric

The **Shakespeare** thefts; in search of the first folios. Palgrave Macmillan 2011 212p il   **822.3**

1. Poets 2. Theft 3. Authors 4. Dramatists 5. Rare books 6. Book collecting
ISBN 9780230109414; 9780230341203 ebook

LC 2011028287

This book discusses "the known surviving copies of the 1623 First Folio, which published 36 of [William] Shakespeare's plays. Of the 232 recorded surviving copies, the majority are in public institutions rather than private hands. [Eric] Rasmussen . . . and his team of researchers were part of the global quest to catalog every extant copy." (Library Journal)

"Part literary history and part detective story, this is an engaging book about the known surviving copies of the 1623 First Folio, which published 36 of Shakespeare's plays. Of the 232 recorded surviving copies, the majority are in public institutions rather than private hands. Rasmussen . . . and his team of researchers were part of the global quest to catalog every extant copy. Rasmussen uses a lively, nonacademic style and engrossing anecdotes to tell us about one of history's most fascinating books." Libr J

Includes bibliographical references

Rosenbaum, Ron

The **Shakespeare** wars; clashing scholars, public fiascoes, palace coups. Random House 2006 601p $35   **822.3**

1. Poets 2. Authors 3. Dramatists
ISBN 0-375-50339-0; 978-0-375-50339-9

LC 2006-42541

The author "conveys the impassioned arguments of leading directors and scholars concerning how Shakespeare should be printed and performed. . . . Balancing academic reportage with his own lively observations, Rosenbaum wrestles with the weightiest issues of Shakespeare studies in a down-to-earth manner that readers will applaud." Publ Wkly

Includes bibliographical references

Shakespeare, William, 1564-1616

★ The **complete** works; general editors, Stanley Wells and Gary Taylor; editors, Stanley Wells . . . [et al.]; with introductions by Stanley Wells. 2nd ed.; Clarendon Press; Oxford University Press 2005 lxxv, 1344p il $40   **822.3**

ISBN 0-19-926717-0

LC 2005-47272

First published 1986

This anthology "features a brief introduction to each work as well as [a] General Introduction. . . . [The volume includes] essay on language, a list of contemporary allusions to Shakespeare, an index of Shakespearean characters, a glossary, a consolidated bibliography, and an index of first lines of the Sonnets." Publisher's note

Shapiro, James

Contested Will; who wrote Shakespeare? James Shapiro. Simon & Schuster 2010 339 p. $26   **822.3**

1. Poets 2. Authors 3. Dramatists
ISBN 978-1-4165-4162-2; 1-4165-4162-4; 1416541624; 9781416541622

LC 2009032710

"A thorough, engaging work whose arguments would prove more persuasive were we not living in an era of such fierce anti-intellectualism and pervasive conspiracy theory." Kirkus

Includes bibliographical references and index

A **year** in the life of William Shakespeare, 1599. HarperCollins Publishers 2005 394p il map $27.95   **822.3**

1. Poets 2. Authors 3. Dramatists 4. Biography, Individual
ISBN 0-571-21448-0

LC 2005-43342

Shapiro discusses the year 1599 in the life of William Shakespeare, the year when he wrote Henry the Fifth, Julius Caesar, As You Like It, and Hamlet, and became involved with the new Globe theatre. Index.

The author "offers a critical examination of four plays Shakespeare wrote in the seminal year of 1599—Henry V, Julius Caesar, As You Like It, and Hamlet—and of the events that influenced the Bard at the time of their writing. . . . This work gives the reader a realistic sense of the multilayered and complex political, social, and literary pressures that influenced Shakespeare as a citizen of England, as a business partner in the Globe Theatre, and as a writer." Libr J

Includes bibliographical references

Wells, Stanley W.

★ **Shakespeare**: for all time; [by] Stanley Wells. Oxford Univ. Press 2003 xxi, 442p il $40   **822.3**
1. Poets 2. Authors 3. Dramatists
ISBN 0-19-516093-2

LC 2002-27412

First published 2002 in the United Kingdom

"Chapters on Shakespeare's life in Stratford and in London offer a . . . view of the development of the writer's career and personality. At the core of the book lies a . . . study of the writings themselves—how Shakespeare set about writing a play, his relationships with the company of actors with whom he worked, his developing mastery of the literary and rhetorical skills that he learned at the Stratford grammar school, the essentially theatrical quality of the structure and language of his plays. Subsequent chapters trace the fluctuating fortunes of his reputation and influence." Publisher's note

Includes bibliographical references

Wills, Garry

Verdi's Shakespeare; man of the theater. Viking 2011 220p $25.95   **822.3**
1. Opera 2. Poets 3. Authors 4. Composers 5. Dramatists 6. Italy -- History -- 19th century
ISBN 978-0-670-02304-2

LC 2011019768

Includes bibliographical references

Yoshino, Kenji

A **thousand** times more fair; what Shakespeare can teach us about justice. Ecco 2011 305p $26.99; ebook $12.99 **822.3**
1. Poets 2. Authors 3. Dramatists 4. Law in literature
ISBN 0-06-176910-X; 0-06-208772-X ebook; 978-0-06-176910-8; 978-0-06-208772-0 ebook

Looks at the roles of justice and law in the lives of modern-day people through the lens of Shakespeare's plays.

"Readers will find Yoshino provocative, often controversial, and Shakespeare, as always, entertaining." Publ Wkly

Includes bibliographical references

822.33   William Shakespeare

Bloom, Harold, 1930-

Lear; the great image of authority. Harold Bloom. Scribner 2018 xi, 160 p.p (Shakespeare's personalities) (hardcover) $24   **822.33**
1. Characters and characteristics in literature 2. Kings and rulers in literature
ISBN 9781501164194; 9781501164217; 1501164198

LC 2017061767

In this book in the Shakespeare's Personalities series, author Harold

Bloom describes "King Lear's" "title characters as one of Shakespeare's 'most challenging personalities' Bloom guides the reader scene by scene through the play, quoting long but well-chosen swaths of text and interjecting commentary that reveals the nuances of Shakespeare's word choices he is also deft at bringing out dramatic contrasts between characters." (Publishers Weekly)

"Bloom's short, superb book has a depth of observation acquired from a lifetime of study, and the author knows when to let Shakespeare and his play speak for themselves." Pub Wkly

Greenblatt, Stephen, 1943-

Tyrant; Shakespeare on politics. Stephen Greenblatt. W W Norton & Co Inc 2018 212 p. (hardcover) $21.95   **822.33**
1. Politics in literature 2. Literature and politics 3. Dictators in literature 4. Power (Social sciences) in literature
ISBN 9780393635768; 9780393635751

LC 2018002449

This book, by Stephen Greenblatt, explores "the psyche (and psychoses) of the likes of Richard III, Macbeth, Lear, . . . and the societies they rule over . . . [to illuminate] the ways in which William Shakespeare delved into the lust for absolute power and the catastrophic consequences of its execution. . . . [The playwright] shone a spotlight on the infantile psychology and unquenchable narcissistic appetites of demagogues. . . and imagined how they might be stopped." (Publisher's note)

"An incisive and instructive study of personality politics and the abuse of power—topical literary criticism with classical virtues." Kirkus

Includes bibliographical references and index

Shapiro, James

The **year** of Lear; Shakespeare in 1606. James Shapiro. Simon & Schuster 2015 xi, 367 p.p illustrations (some color) (hardback) $30   **822.33**
1. English drama -- History and criticism 2. Great Britain -- History -- James I, 1603-1625 3. English drama -- 17th century -- History and criticism 4. Literature and society -- England -- History -- 17th century
ISBN 9781476745794; 1416541640; 9781416541646

LC 2015031731

This book, by James Shapiro, "shows how the tumultuous events in England in 1606 affected [William] Shakespeare and shaped the three great tragedies he wrote that year. . . . Since the death of Queen Elizabeth . . . , Shakespeare's great productivity had ebbed. . . . But that year, at age forty-two, he found his footing again, finishing a play he had begun the previous autumn--'King Lear'--then writing two other great tragedies, 'Macbeth' and 'Antony and Cleopatra.'" (Publisher's note)

"His well-written, scholarly exploration will stand as a n influential work that is a joy to read." Kirkus

Includes bibliographical references (pages 311-354) and index

Smith, Emma

Shakespeare's first folio; four centuries of an iconic book. Emma Smith. Oxford University Press 2016 xiv, 379 p.p illustrations (hardback) $29.95   **822.33**
1. English drama -- History and criticism 2. Early printed books -- 17th century
ISBN 9780198754367

LC 2015945824

This book, by Emma Smith, "is a biography of a book: the first collected edition of [William] Shakespeare's plays printed in 1623 and known as the First Folio. It begins with the story of its first purchaser in London in December 1623, and goes on to explore the ways people have interacted with this iconic book over the four hundred years of its history." (Publisher's note)

"Smith condenses a remarkable amount of scholarship into her study, and her writing is lively and insightful." Pub Wkly

Includes bibliographical references and index.

823 English fiction

Achebe, Chinua

Home and exile. Anchor Bks. 2001 115p pa $11   **823**
1. Africa -- Civilization
ISBN 978-0-385-72133-2; 0-385-72133-1

LC 2001-22599

First published 2000 by Oxford University Press

"This slim volume—told in Achebe's subtle, witty and gracious style—is one of those small gems of literary and historical analysis that readers will treasure and reread over the years." Publ Wkly

Includes bibliographical references

There was a country; a personal history of Biafra. Chinua Achebe. Penguin Press 2012 352 p. $27.95   **823**
1. Autobiographies 2. Nigeria -- History -- Civil War, 1967-1970 3. Authors, Nigerian -- 20th century -- Biography 4. Nigeria -- History -- Civil War, 1967-1970 -- Personal narratives
ISBN 1594204829; 9781594204821

LC 2012005603

This memoir recounts author Chinua Achebe's experience of "the Nigerian civil war, also known as the Biafran War, of 1967–1970. The conflict was infamous for its savage impact on the Biafran people, Chinua Achebe's people, many of whom were starved to death after the Nigerian government blockaded their borders. . . . [Achebe] took the Biafran side in the conflict and served his government as a roving cultural ambassador, from which vantage he absorbed the war's full horror." (Publisher's note)

Includes bibliographical references and index.

Attwell, David

J. M. Coetzee and the Life of Writing; Face-to-Face With Time. Prof David Attwell. Penguin Group USA 2015 272 p. illustrations, map, portraits (hbk.) $27.95; (pbk.) $17.00 **823**
ISBN 9780525429616; 9780143128816; 9780198746331; 0198746334; 0525429611; 0143128817

In this book author "David Attwell explores the extraordinary creative processes behind [J.M.] Coetzee's novels. Using Coetzee's manuscripts, notebooks and research papers--recently deposited at the Harry Ransom Center of the University of Texas at Austin--Attwell produces a fascinating story. He shows convincingly that Coetzee's work is strongly autobiographical, the memoirs being continuous with the fictions, and that his writing proceeds with never-ending self-reflection." (Publisher's note)

"This accessible, nonacademic study doesn't reveal much in the way of deep biography yet provides a valuable examination of the Nobel laureate's fiction that will appeal to students and fans of Coetzee and anyone interested in the process and work of writing." LJ

Baker, William

Critical companion to Jane Austen; a literary reference to her life and work. Facts on File 2008 644p il (Facts on File library of world literature) $75   **823**
1. Authors 2. Novelists
ISBN 978-0-8160-6416-8

LC 2006-102848

This book examines Jane Austen's "life and works, and includes crit-

ical analyses of the themes within her writing, as well as entries on related topics and relevant people, places, and influences." Publisher's note

Includes bibliographical references

Ballard, J. G., 1930-2009

Miracles of life; Shanghai to Shepperton: an autobiography. J.G. Ballard. Liveright Pub. Corporation 2013 272 p. il (hardcover) $25.95   **823**
1. Authorship 2. World War, 1939-1945 -- Influence 3. Novelists, English -- 20th century -- Biography
ISBN 0871404206; 9780871404206

LC 2012033865

This book presents an autobiography by the English novelist and short story writer J. G. Ballard. "the first half of the book portrays Ballard's experiences in the Lunghua internment camp near Shanghai during World War II and sheds light on his relationship with his parents. He also describes the tragic death of his wife, just after he started to establish himself as a writer, and to a lesser degree his unconventional relationship with lifelong partner Claire Walsh." (Kirkus Reviews)

Barnes, Julian, 1946-

Levels of life; by Julian Barnes. Alfred A. Knopf 2013 144 p. (hardcover) $22.95   **823**
1. Grief 2. Bereavement
ISBN 0385350775; 9780345806581; 9780385350778

LC 2013004601

In this book author Julian Barnes presents his thoughts on the subject of grief "beginning in the nineteenth century and leading . . . into an entirely personal account of loss." (Publisher's note) "It is divided into three . . . parts: a . . . discussion of ballooning; a . . . short story about the fictional romance of a real English adventurer named Fred Burnaby and the celebrated actress Sarah Bernhardt; and a . . .consideration of grief." (New York Review of Books)

Bowker, Gordon, 1934-

★ **James** Joyce; a new biography. Gordon Bowker. Farrar, Straus and Giroux 2012 608 p. ill. (hbk.: alk. paper) $35.00   **823**
1. Authors, Irish 2. Authors, Irish -- 20th century -- Biography
ISBN 0374178720; 9780374178727

LC 2011045954

This biography of James Joyce "show[s] the complexities and contradictions of the man. . . . The author charts . . . his struggle to survive in the early days of his adulthood and marriage, the sad madness of his daughter, . . . and his difficulty finding publishers for 'Dubliners' and the more controversial works that followed. . . . We see Joyce, too, as a prodigious worker." (Kirkus Reviews)

Includes bibliographical references and index

Campbell, Hayley

The **art** of Neil Gaiman; by Hayley Campbell. Harper Design Intl 2014 320 p. illustrations (some color) $39.99 **823**
1. English authors
ISBN 0062248561; 9780062248565

In this book, author Hayley Campbell "gives an insider's glimpse into the artistic inspirations and musings of . . . Neil Gaiman. . . . A master of several genres, including, but not limited to, bestselling novels, children's books, groundbreaking comics, and graphic novels, . . . Gaiman has been called a rock star of the literary world. Now, for the first time, Gaiman reveals the inspiration behind his signature artistic motifs." (Publisher's note)

"Campbell has clearly taken great care to construct such a lavish and detailed offering and fans will be hanging on every word and illustration for a deeper insight into Gaiman's eccentric genius. Highly recommended for anyone who has dearly loved any of his many works." LJ

Conradi, Peter

Iris Murdoch; a life. {by} Peter J. Conradi. Norton 2001 xxix, 706p il $35; pa $19.95 **823**
    1. Authors 2. Novelists 3. Philosophers 4. Essayists
    ISBN 0-393-04875-6; 0-393-32401-X pa

                      LC 2001-32972

"Rich footnoting leads the reader to expansions on the narrative as well as to the authority behind the biographer's statements. Scholars need this text, but it will also intrigue lay readers." Libr J
    Includes bibliographical references

Cusk, Rachel, 1967-

    ★ **Aftermath**; on marriage and separation. Rachel Cusk. Farrar, Straus and Giroux 2012 146 p. (alk. paper) $20.00 **823**
    1. Marriage 2. Biography 3. Family life 4. Divorce -- Psychological aspects 5. Marriage -- Psychological aspects 6. Authors, English -- 20th century -- Biography
    ISBN 0374102139; 9780374102135

                      LC 2012003807

Author Rachel Cusk looks at "the breakdown of her domestic life. [The book tells the traditional story of] man meets woman . . . [and] create a family . . . [then the] family falls apart . . . [and the] man, woman and children grieve . . . [S]he weaves in figures from ancient Greek drama (Oedipus, Antigone, Agamemnon, Clytemnestra) . . . The last and most unorthodox chapter is told, by Cusk, from the perspective of her au pair Sonia, a scared, scarred girl whom the author abruptly fired when her husband left." (Kirkus)

Davis, Paul B.

    ★ **Critical** companion to Charles Dickens; a literary reference to his life and work. Rev ed; Facts on File 2007 676p il (Facts on File library of world literature) $75 **823**
    1. Authors 2. Novelists
    ISBN 0-8160-6407-5; 978-0-8160-6407-6

                      LC 2006-3026

First published 1998 with title: Charles Dickens A-Z

This "reference contains entries on this writer's works, including the characters in each work, . . . historical and thematic information, and critical discussion. It also includes entries on related people, places, themes, topics, and influences. Additional features include 116 illustrations, a chronology, a bibliography of primary and secondary sources, and much more." Publisher's note
    Includes bibliographical references

Dirda, Michael

On Conan Doyle; or, The whole art of storytelling. Princeton University Press 2011 210p (Writers on writers) $19.95 **823**
    1. Authors 2. Novelists 3. Mystery writers
    ISBN 978-0-691-15135-9; 0-691-15135-0

                      LC 2011-20674

"Dirda is at his best in his sensitive appreciation of Doyle's style, direct, fluent, and surprisingly flexible as he moves from genre to genre, and in his account of manly civic inspiration as the value Doyle aimed above all to inculcate in his writing . . . . An endearing, well-balanced introduction to a writer the Strand Magazine called 'the greatest natural storyteller of his age.'" Kirkus
    Includes bibliographical references

★ The **Facts** on File companion to the British novel. Facts on File 2005 2v (Facts on File library of world literature) set $140 **823**
    1. English fiction -- History and criticism
    ISBN 0-8160-6377-X; 978-0-8160-6377-2

                      LC 2004-20914

"With more than one thousand entries, each with a selected bibliography and a set of very usable appendixes, this work accomplishes much in a compact set." Ref & User Services Quarterly
    Includes bibliographical references

Fargnoli, A. Nicholas

Critical companion to James Joyce; a literary companion to his life and work. [by] A. Nicholas Fargnoli, Michael Patrick Gillespie. Rev ed; Facts On File 2006 450p il (Facts on File library of world literature) $65; pa $19.95 **823**
    1. Poets 2. Authors 3. Novelists 4. Dramatists 5. Short story writers
    ISBN 0-8160-6232-3; 978-0-8160-6232-4; 0-8160-6689-2 pa; 978-0-8160-6689-6 pa

                      LC 2005-15721

First published 1995 with title: James Joyce A to Z

The authors "divide this reference to the writer's life and work into four parts. Part 1 is a brief biography. Part 2 focuses on individual works (e.g., Dubliners), including its publication date, a brief history, a synopsis, early critical reception, contemporary perspectives, and one or two recommended titles for further reading. The entries in Part 3 cover people (including friends and relatives), places, and ideas related to Joyce. Part 4 contains an appendix, a bibliography of the writer's work, a bibliography of secondary sources, chronologies, family trees, and more. . . . [This is] a great primer for those needing a detailed introduction into Joyce's world." Libr J
    Includes bibliographical references

Ford, Paul F.

Companion to Narnia; a complete guide to the magical world of C.S. Lewis's The chronicles of Narnia. foreword by Madeleine L'Engle; illustrated by Lorinda Bryan Cauley. Rev and expanded; HarperSanFrancisco 2005 xxvi, 530p il map pa $16.95 **823**
    1. Authors 2. Novelists 3. Theologians 4. Essayists 5. Satirists 6. Literary critics 7. Children's authors
    ISBN 0-06-079127-6

First published 1980

C. S. Lewis wrote seven books of fantasy that are collectively called The Chronicles of Narnia. This book "is an encyclopedia of Narnian names and terms and related matters, with . . . footnoted articles, page references to American and British hardcover editions, cross-references, and a running footline for quick location of materials in the alphabet." Choice
    Includes bibliographical references

Frank, Katherine

Crusoe; Daniel Defoe, Robert Knox and the creation of a myth. Katherine Frank. Bodley Head 2011 338 p. **823**
    1. Castaways in literature 2. Crusoe, Robinson (Fictitious character)
    ISBN 0224073095; 9780224073097

                      LC 2011486701

This book "introduces Robert Knox, once a true captive, who survived on his wits and the English practice of making your environment adapt to your needs rather than adjusting to it. . . . As Defoe cherry-picked incidents from different lives, he adapted them to reflect disasters he had suffered. . . . Frank parallels the lives and adventures of Defoe, Knox and Crusoe, illustrating a deep relationship between author and models. This side-by-side biography of the two men shows similarities between their lives and their attitudes toward disaster, although their personalities and moralities were markedly different. Many have said that Crusoe is much more a self-help book than a novel, while Knox's story is a treatise rather than a travel book." (Kirkus)

Includes bibliographical references and index.

French, Paul

City of devils; the two men who ruled the underworld of old Shanghai. Paul French. St. Martins Press 2018 352 p. $28 **823**

1. Criminals 2. Organized crime
ISBN 1250170583; 9781250170583

In this book, by Paul French, "in 1940, Lucky Jack and Dapper Joe bestrode the Shanghai Badlands like kings, while all around the Solitary Island was poverty, starvation, and war. They thought they ruled Shanghai, but the city had other ideas. This is the story of their rise to power, their downfall, and the trail of destruction left in their wake. Shanghai was their playground for a flickering few years." (Publisher's note)

Gordimer, Nadine

Conversations with Nadine Gordimer; edited by Nancy Topping Bazin and Marilyn Dallman Seymour. University Press of Miss. 1990 xxiv, 321p (Literary conversations series) $46 **823**

1. Authors 2. Novelists 3. Dramatists 4. Essayists 5. Short story writers 6. Nobel laureates for literature
ISBN 0-87805-444-8

LC 90-12556

This is a collection of interviews in which Gordimer talks "about her life as a white South African, about her fiction, and about writers she admires." Booklist

Includes bibliographical references

Hardy, Thomas, 1840-1928

The **Collected** Letters of Thomas Hardy; Further Letters 1861-1927. edited by Michael Millgate and Keith Wilson. Oxford University Press 2012 320 p. $160 **823**

1. Letters
ISBN 0199607753; 9780199607754

LC 77030355

This book, edited by Michael Millgate and Keith Wilson, "contains previously unpublished letters from all periods of [poet Thomas] Hardy's career, his earliest known letter among them. It introduces important new correspondents, throws fresh light on existing correspondences, and richly enhances the reader's understanding of both familiar and hitherto unfamiliar aspects of Hardy's life and work and of the times in which he lived." (Publisher's note)

Head, Dominic

★ The **Cambridge** introduction to modern British fiction, 1950-2000. Cambridge Univ. Press 2002 307p $65; pa $22 **823**

1. English fiction -- History and criticism
ISBN 0-521-66014-9; 0-521-66966-9 pa

LC 2001-43261

"Anyone with an interest in the contemporary novel, not just British fiction, will appreciate this outstanding survey and analysis. . . . The quality of discussion is admirably consistent within and between each chapter, the prose as carefully crafted as the judgments are measured. . . . This book should become a standard reference work for its subject."

Choice
Includes bibliographical references

★ **Horror:** another 100 best books; edited by Stephen Jones and Kim Newman; with a foreword by Peter Straub. Carroll & Graf Publishers 2005 456p pa $16.95 **823**

1. Best books 2. Horror fiction -- History and criticism
ISBN 0-7867-1577-4
First published 1988

"Horror fans seeking what to read next will not only find out here; they'll also have their taste and appreciative capacity refined by the intelligent, passionate commentary of the 100 writers who selected these 100 books." Booklist

Hughes, Kathryn

George Eliot; the last Victorian. Cooper Square Press 2001 383p il pa $19.95 **823**

1. Authors 2. Novelists 3. Essayists 4. Authors, English
ISBN 0-8154-1121-9; 978-0-8154-1121-5

LC 2001-28024

First published 1998 in the United Kingdom

In this biography Hughes "shows how George Eliot (nee Mary Anne Evans, 1819-80), in spite of her outwardly anti-Victorian lifestyle, was in fact a true Victorian. . . . A solitary, ascetic child and young woman, she was raised in an upwardly mobile country family. . . . In 1852 she met the married writer and editor George Henry Lewes, with whom she lived until his death in 1878." Libr J

Includes bibliographical references

James, P. D., 1920-2014

Talking about detective fiction. Alfred A. Knopf 2009 198p il $22 **823**

1. Mystery fiction -- History and criticism 2. Detective and mystery stories, English -- History and criticism
ISBN 978-0-307-59282-8

LC 2009-38501

P. D. James offers a "book-length essay on the roots, ethics and methods of the detective story." (N Y Times (Late N Y Ed))

"For crime fiction fans, this master class from one of the leading practitioners of the art will be a real treat." Publ Wkly

Includes bibliographical references

Time to be in earnest; a fragment of autobiography. Knopf 2000 269p hardcover o.p. pa $12.95 **823**

1. Authors 2. Novelists 3. Mystery writers
ISBN 0-345-44212-1 pa

LC 99-57603

"In 1997, on the eve of her 77th birthday noted mystery novelist James . . . decided to keep a diary for the first time ever, recording one year in her life. The result is this 'fragment of autobiography,' a mix of memoir, ruminations on everything from her writing career to Princess Diana's death, and literary criticism." Libr J

Kermode, Frank

Concerning E.M. Forster. Farrar, Straus and Giroux 2009 180p $24 **823**

1. Authors 2. Novelists 3. Essayists 4. Literary critics 5. Short story writers
ISBN 978-0-374-29899-9; 0-374-29899-8

LC 2009-39143

"Overall, Kermode's occasional exasperation with his subject enlivens rather than distorts his eminently fair assessment. Like all good criticism, Concerning EM Forster makes one want to read the books under discussion once more, and it ends on an appropriately affectionate note." Times (London)

Includes bibliographical references

Kiberd, Declan

Ulysses and us; the art of everyday life in Joyce's masterpiece. W.W. Norton & Co. 2009 399p $28.95   **823**

1. Poets 2. Authors 3. Novelists 4. Dramatists 5. Short story writers

ISBN 978-0-393-07099-6; 0-393-07099-9

LC 2009014101

This "is an ideal introduction [to Ulysses] for the uninitiated—accessible, richly argued, funny and, in a kind of devil's advocacy fashion, begging for rebuttal." Publ Wkly

Includes bibliographical references

King, Dean

Patrick O'Brian; a life revealed. Holt & Co. 2000 397p il hardcover o.p. pa $15   **823**

1. Authors 2. Novelists 3. Biographers 4. Writers on the sea 5. Short story writers

ISBN 0-8050-5977-6 pa

LC 99-48495

"This is exactly the sort of literary biography that O'Brian, the author of the celebrated Aubrey/Maturin naval novels, hoped to avoid. Reluctant to provide facts about himself, and often untruthful when he did so, O'Brian . . . had much in his past that he wanted buried. He walked away from his first marriage, changed his name from Russ to O'Brian, and pretended Anglo-Irish ancestry. King's diligent research yields pleasing details." New Yorker

Includes bibliographical references

Le Carré, John, 1931-

★ The **Pigeon** Tunnel; Stories from My Life. by John le Carré. Penguin Group USA 2016 320 p. $30   **823**

1. Authors 2. Espionage 3. Autobiographies 4. Intelligence service

ISBN 0735220778; 9780735220775

In this memoir, author John le Carré is "writing about . . . visiting Rwanda's museums of the unburied dead in the aftermath of the genocide, celebrating New Year's Eve 1982 with Yasser Arafat and his high command, interviewing a German woman terrorist in her desert prison in the Negev, listening to the wisdoms of the great physicist, dissident, and Nobel Prize winner Andrei Sakharov, [and] meeting with two former heads of the KGB." (Publisher's note)

The author's "self-deprecating humor and wit are never far away, and he proves a most elegant and genial host on this tour of his life and work." PW

Maunder, Andrew

The **Facts** on File companion to the British short story. Facts on File 2006 528p (Facts on File library of world literature) $75   **823**

1. Short stories -- History and criticism

ISBN 0-8160-5990-X; 978-0-8160-5990-4

LC 2006-6897

More than 450 alphabetically arranged entries cover authors, characters, and major short stories. Literary terms, themes, and motifs are covered. Winners of prizes and awards are noted.

Includes glossary and bibliographical references

Mead, Rebecca

★ **My** life in Middlemarch; Rebecca Mead. CrownCrown Publishers 2014 304 p. $25   **823**

1. Creation (Literary, artistic, etc.)

ISBN 0307984761; 9780307984760

LC 2013011477

In this "hybrid work of literary criticism, biography, and memoir," author Rebecca Mead discusses her relationship with the book "Middlemarch" by George Eliot. She " identifies strongly with aspects of Eliot's life and that of the characters in Middlemarch, [and] returns to the novel during various stages of her life: as a young Englishwoman finding her way in New York; in relationships with difficult men; as a stepmother and wife; and eventually as the mother of a son." (Publishers Weekly)

"A rare and remarkable fusion of techniques that draws two women together across time and space." Kirkus

Includes bibliographical references

Miller, Laura

The **magician's** book; a skeptic's adventures in Narnia. Little, Brown and Co. 2008 311p $25.99   **823**

1. Authors 2. Novelists 3. Theologians 4. Essayists 5. Satirists 6. Literary critics 7. Children's authors 8. Children's literature -- History and criticism

ISBN 978-0-316-01763-3; 0-316-01763-9

LC 2008-20629

The author explores the meaning and influence of C.S. Lewis' Chronicles of Narnia series while revealing how Lewis's troubled childhood, unconventional love life, and friendship with J. R. R. Tolkien affected his writing.

"Miller's book is itself a welcome bit of magic: part reader's log, part biography, part literary criticism." N Y Times Book Rev

Montillo, Roseanne

★ The **lady** and her monsters; a tale of dissections, attempts to reanimate dead tissue, and the writing of Mary Shelley's Frankenstein. Roseanne Montillo. 1st ed. William Morrow 2013 322 p. ill. (hardcover) $26.99; (ebook) $21.99 **823**

1. Women and literature -- England -- History -- 19th century

ISBN 9780062025814; 9780062025838; 9780062235886

LC 2012021509

This book, by Roseanne Motillo, "brings to life the . . . science, and real-life horrors behind Mary Shelley's gothic masterpiece, 'Frankenstein.' Montillo recounts how--at the intersection of the Romantic Age and the Industrial Revolution--Shelley's Victor Frankenstein was inspired by actual scientists of the period: curious and daring iconoclasts who were obsessed with the inner workings of the human body and how it might be reanimated after death." (Publisher's note)

"Fraught with suicides, superstitions, natural disasters, and love affairs, the life of Mary Shelley shares much emotionally with the harrowing tale of her great protagonist, Victor Frankenstein. A delicious and enticing journey into the origins of a masterpiece." Pub Wkly

Includes bibliographical references (p. 305-310) and index.

Moore, Wendy

★ **How** to create the perfect wife; Britain's most ineligible bachelor and his enlightened quest to train the ideal mate. Wendy Moore. Basic Books 2013 360 p. (hardcover) $27.99 **823**

1. Wives 2. Marriage 3. Authors, English -- 18th century 4. Marriage -- Great Britain -- History -- 18th century

ISBN 0465065740; 9780465065745

LC 2012048149

This book, by Wendy Moore, tells "tale of one man's mission to groom his ideal mate. [18th-century British writer Thomas] Day adopted two young orphans from the Foundling Hospital and, guided by the writings of Jean-Jacques Rousseau and the principles of the Enlightenment, attempted to teach them to be model wives. His peculiar experiment inevitably backfired--though not before he had taken his theories about marriage, education, and femininity to shocking extremes." (Publisher's note)

Includes bibliographical references and index

Naipaul, V. S.

Between father and son; selected correspondence of V.S. Naipaul and his family, 1949-1953. edited by Gillon Aitken. Knopf 2000 297p $26; pa $13 **823**
1. Authors 2. Novelists 3. Journalists 4. Essayists 5. Travel writers 6. Radio reporters 7. Nonfiction writers 8. Short story writers 9. Nobel laureates for literature
ISBN 0-375-40730-8; 0-375-70726-3 pa
LC 99-31089
"In 1950, at the age of 17, famous-writer-in-the-making V. S. Naipaul ventured to Oxford University in England on a scholarship supplied by the government of his native Trinidad. He and his father maintained a rich, full correspondence during his time away, and these letters fortunately have been gathered into book form." Booklist

Include bibliographical references

Ngugi wa Thiong'o, 1938-

In the house of the interpreter; a memoir. Ngugi wa'Thiong'o. Pantheon Books 2012 240 p. (hardback) $25.95 **823**
1. Revolutionaries -- Kenya -- Biography 2. Authors, Kenyan -- 20th century -- Biography
ISBN 0307907694; 9780307907691
LC 2012013986
The book by author Ngugi wa Thiong'o presents a collection of his writings. It focuses on the "author's life and times at boarding school--the first secondary educational institution in British-ruled Kenya--in the 1950s, against the backdrop of the tumultuous Mau Mau Uprising for independence and Kenyan sovereignty." Throughout his journey, "he falls victim to the forces of colonialism in the person of a police officer encountered on a bus journey, and he is thrown into jail for six days." (Publisher's note)

Nokes, David

Jane Austen; a life. University of Calif. Press 1998 577p il pa $24.95 **823**
1. Authors 2. Novelists 3. Women authors 4. Authors, English
ISBN 0-520-21606-7; 978-0-520-21606-8
LC 98-15785
First published 1997 by Farrar, Straus & Giroux
"Eschewing the biographer's usual perspective of omniscient foreknowledge in favor of a novelistic perspective of ambiguous immediacy, Nokes allows us to see Austen's talent as a mystery unfolding, not a fact explained. We thus witness the emergence of a personality sufficiently subtle and complex to produce Sense and Sensibility, Pride and Prejudice, and Emma. Readers of Austen's fiction will rejoice at having a biography so carefully nuanced, so refreshingly candid." Booklist

Includes bibliographical references

O'Brien, Edna

James Joyce. Viking 1999 179p (Penguin lives series) $19.95 **823**
1. Poets 2. Authors 3. Novelists 4. Dramatists 5. Short story

writers
ISBN 0-670-88230-5
LC 99-23214
O'Brien "tells the story of the aspiring young writer and his downwardly mobile family, his escape to Europe, the constant struggle to scrape together enough money to live on, and finally his relative comfort, thanks to patrons, once Ulysses was published. She also provides thoughtful appreciations of Joyce's major works." Booklist

Includes bibliographical references

Olsen, Kirstin

All things Austen; an encyclopedia of Austen's world. Greenwood Press 2005 2v il maps set $157.95 **823**
1. Authors 2. Novelists 3. Reference books
ISBN 0-313-33032-8
LC 2004-28664
"This well-written and meticulously researched work provides a convenient means for general readers, students, and scholars to gain a better understanding of the social, cultural, and political climate of Austen's time." Booklist

Saler, Michael

As if; modern enchantment and the literary pre-history of virtual reality. Michael Saler. Oxford University Press 2012 x, 283 p.p (pbk.: acid-free paper) $27.95 **823**
1. Virtual reality 2. Imaginary places 3. Books and reading 4. Fantastic, The, in literature 5. Marvelous, The, in literature 6. Virtual reality in literature 7. Imaginary societies in literature
ISBN 0195343174; 9780195343168; 9780195343175
LC 2011010276
This book by Michael Saler was "named one of the 'Best Books of 2012' by the editors of 'The Huffington Post.' . . . It explains how, "beginning in the late nineteenth century, when Sherlock Holmes became the world's first 'virtual reality' character, readers began to colonize imaginary worlds. . . . From Lovecraft's Cthulhu Mythos and Tolkien's Middle-earth to the World of Warcraft and Second Life, 'As If' provides a cultural history that reveals how we can remain enchanted but not deluded in an age where fantasy and reality increasingly intertwine." (Publisher's note)

Includes bibliographical references and index.

Sampson, Fiona

In search of Mary Shelley; the girl who wrote Frankenstein. Fiona Sampson. W W Norton & Co Inc 2018 368 p. $28.95 **823**
1. English women authors -- Biography
ISBN 1681777525; 9781681777528
In this book, author Fiona Sampson "delivers a major new biography of Mary Shelley--as she has never been seen before. . . . In this probing narrative, . . . Sampson pursues Mary Shelley through her turbulent life, much as Victor Frankenstein tracked his monster across the arctic wastes. . . . [She] answers the question of how it was that a nineteen-year-old came to write a novel so dark . . . and psychologically astute that it continues to resonate two centuries later." (Publisher's note)

Shakespeare, Nicholas

Bruce Chatwin. Talese 2000 618p il $35; pa $18 **823**
1. Authors 2. Novelists 3. Memoirists 4. Travel writers
ISBN 0-385-49829-2; 0-385-49830-6 pa
LC 99-36474
"This life of the author of 'The Songlines', who died of AIDS in 1989, portrays a man, beset with an almost biological lust for loneliness, whose singular genius was for passionate transitory connection." N Y

Times Book Rev

Includes bibliographical references

Standiford, Les

★ The **man** who invented Christmas; how Charles Dickens's "A Christmas carol" rescued his career and revived our holiday spirits. Les Standiford. Broadway Books 2017 337 p. $17 **823**

1. Christmas -- History

ISBN 1524762466; 9781524762469

This book, by Les Standiford, is "the story of how Charles Dickens revived [Christmas]. . . . Dickens used what little money he had to put out A Christmas Carol himself. He worried it might be the end of his career as a novelist. The book immediately caused a sensation. And it breathed new life into a holiday that had fallen into disfavor." (Publisher's note)

Includes bibliographical references (pages 219-221).

A **truth** universally acknowledged; 33 great writers on why we read Jane Austen. edited by Susannah Carson; foreword by Harold Bloom. Random House 2009 295p $25 **823**

1. Authors 2. Novelists

ISBN 978-1-4000-6805-0; 1-4000-6805-3

LC 2009-12904

"A collection for both newcomers to the charms of Jane Austen and those longtime 'Janeites'. . . . The writers in this volume explain their own relationship with Austen and together are a kind of invitation for us, whether we're Janeites or not, to understand why we are so in her thrall." Chicago Trib

Includes bibliographical references

Wainaina, Binyavanga, 1971-

One day I will write about this place. Graywolf Press 2011 256p **823**

1. Authors 2. Novelists 3. Journalists 4. College teachers 5. Short story writers 6. Biography, Individual

ISBN 1555975917; 9781555975913

LC 2011923190

In this memoir, the Kenyan writer describes "his school days, his mother's religious period, his failed attempt to study in South Africa as a computer programmer, a moving family reunion in Uganda, and his travels around Kenya. The landscape in front of him always claims his main attention, but he also evokes the shifting political scene that unsettles his views on family, tribe, and nationhood. Throughout, reading is his refuge and his solace. And when, in 2002, a writing prize comes through, the door is opened for him to pursue the career that perhaps had been beckoning all along." (Publisher's note)

Weldon, Fay

Auto da Fay. Grove Press 2003 366p il $25; pa $14 **823**

1. Authors 2. Novelists 3. Dramatists 4. Short story writers

ISBN 0-8021-1750-3; 0-8021-4142-0 pa

LC 2002-44685

First published 2002 in the United Kingdom

This "autobiography primarily focuses on her peripatetic childhood and difficult years of single parenthood, concluding in the 1960s with her second marriage and the beginning of her writing career. . . . Filled with warmth, wit, and her trademark irreverence, Weldon's memoir is a vivid and engaging account of a brave and brainy 'lost girl' who found her way." Booklist

Winterson, Jeanette, 1959-

Why be happy when you could be normal? Jeanette Winterson. Jonathan Cape 2011 230 p. $25 **823**

1. Novelists 2. Autobiographies 3. Adopted children 4. Mother-daughter relationship 5. Women authors -- Biography 6. Authors, English -- 20th century -- Biography

ISBN 0224093452; 0802120105; 9780224093453; 9780802120106

LC 2011507186

Guardian Best Book of 2011

In this book, "author [Jeanette Winterson] ponders her youth and examines how those challenging years changed and shaped her as an adult. Frequently locked out on the doorstep by her abusive, Pentecostal, adoptive mother or often told she was 'a fault to heaven, a fault against the dead, and a fault to nature,' Winterson wondered if she had ever been wanted, by her biological or adoptive mother. . . . At age 16, she was kicked out of the house and forced to live in her car. Books and words brought comfort and led Winterson to Oxford and writing, but she descended into a deep depression when her lover left her. The search for her true identity and her birth mother helped bring her back from the darkness." (Kirkus)

823.7 English fiction – 1800 1837

Jones, Wendy

Jane on the brain; exploring the science of social intelligence with Jane Austen. Wendy Jones. Pegasus Books 2017 xix, 392 p.p illustrations (hardcover) $27.95 **823.7**

1. Intellect 2. Women authors 3. Social intelligence

ISBN 9781681775548; 9781681776057; 1681775549

In this book, author Wendy Jones "reveals Jane Austen's intuitive ability to imbue her characters with hallmarks of social intelligence--and how these beloved works of literature can further illuminate the mind-brain connection. . . . Jones explores the many facets of social intelligence and juxtaposes them with the Austen cannon." (Publisher's note)

"In a fascinating mash-up of literary analysis and neuroscience, psychotherapist and former English professor Jones attributes Jane Austen's everlasting appeal to her ability to empathize." Booklist

Includes bibliographical references (pages 359-379) and index.

823.8 English fiction -- 1837-1899

Sims, Michael

Arthur and Sherlock; Conan Doyle and the creation of Holmes. Michael Sims. Bloomsbury USA 2017 256 p. (hardback) $27; (ebook) $63 **823.8**

1. Physicians -- Great Britain -- Biography 2. Spiritualists -- Great Britain -- Biography 3. Authors, Scottish -- 19th century -- Biography 4. Authors, Scottish -- 20th century -- Biography

ISBN 9781632860392; 9781632860408; 9781632860385

LC 2016033351

This book, by Michael Sims, "traces the circuitous development of Conan Doyle as the father of the modern mystery, from his early days in Edinburgh surrounded by poverty and violence, through his escape to University . . . , leading to his own medical practice in 1882. Five hardworking years later--after Doyle's only modest success in both medicine and literature--Sherlock Holmes emerged in 'A Study in Scarlet.'" (Publisher's note)

"Sims's skill and deftness with narrative biography will lead Sherlockians to hope that he continues the story of Conan Doyle's life in a future volume." Pub Wkly

Includes bibliographical references and index

Skal, David J.

★ **Something** in the Blood; The Untold Story of Bram Stoker, the Man Who Wrote Dracula. by David J. Skal. W W Norton & Co Inc 2016 672 p. illustrations (some color) $35 **823.8**

ISBN 1631490109; 9781631490101

LC 2016028093

This book, by David J. Skal, is a biography of writer Bram Stoker. "Skal exhumes the inner world and strange genius of the writer who birthed an undying cultural icon, painting an astonishing portrait of the age in which Stoker was born—a time when death was no metaphor but a constant threat easily imagined as a character existing in flesh and blood." (Publisher's note)

"An engagingly written, well-documented biography of a famous writer we all think we know, even if we really don't." Booklist

Includes bibliographical references and index.

823.91   English fiction – 20th century

Goldstein, Bill

The **world** broke in two; Virginia Woolf, T. S. Eliot, D. H. Lawrence, E. M. Forster and the year that changed literature. Bill Goldstein. Henry Holt & Co. 2017 x, 351 p.p illustrations (hardback) $30 **823.91**

1. Authors 2. Eliot, T. S. (Thomas Stearns), 1888-1965 3. Nineteen twenty-two, A.D 4. Modernism (Literature) -- Great Britain 5. Literature and society -- History -- 20th century 6. English fiction -- 20th century -- History and criticism

ISBN 9781627795296; 9780805094022

LC 2017001569

This book, by Bill Goldstein, "tells the . . . story of the intellectual and personal journeys four legendary writers, Virginia Woolf, T. S. Eliot, E. M. Forster, and D. H. Lawrence, make over the course of one pivotal year. As 1922 begins, . . . [they are] at a loss for words, confronting an uncertain creative future despite success in the past. . . . [The book] captures both the literary breakthroughs and . . . dramas of these beloved writers as they strive for greatness." (Publisher's note)

"Goldstein's ardently detailed, many-faceted story of a pivotal literary year illuminates all that these tormented visionaries had to overcome to 'make the modern happen.'" Booklist

Includes bibliographical references (pages [295]-334) and index.

823.914   English fiction -- 1945-1999

Murdoch, Iris

Living on paper; letters from Iris Murdoch, 1934-1995. Iris Murdoch; [edited by] Avril Horner, Anne Rowe. Princeton University Press 2016 688 p. illustrations, portraits (ebook) $74.95; (cloth) $39.95 **823.914**

1. English letters 2. Women novelists, English -- 20th century -- Correspondence

ISBN 9781400880300; 9780691170565

LC 2015952098

This collection of letters, by novelist Iris Murdoch, edited by Avril Horner and Anne Rowe, gives "a rounded self-portrait of one of the twentieth century's greatest writers and thinkers. With more than 760 letters, fewer than forty of which have been published before, the book

provides a unique chronicle of Murdoch's life from her days as a schoolgirl to her last years." (Publisher's note)

"An impressively edited, sharply revealing life in letters." Kirkus

Includes bibliographical references and index.

824   English essays

Bennett, Alan, 1934-

Keeping on keeping on; Alan Bennett. Farrar, Straus & Giroux 2017 xi, 722 p.p illustrations (hardcover) $40 **824**

1. Essays 2. English authors 3. Authors, English -- 20th century -- Diaries

ISBN 9780374716974; 0374181055; 9780374181055

LC 2017034577

This collection of diaries and essays, by Alan Bennett, "follows in the footsteps of the phenomenally successful 'Writing Home' and 'Untold Stories.' . . . [It] contains Bennett's diaries from 2005 to 2015-- with everything from his much celebrated essays to his irreverent comic pieces and reviews--reflecting on a decade that saw four major theater premieres and the films of 'The History Boys' and 'The Lady in the Van.'" (Publisher's note)

De Quincey, Thomas

The **confessions** of an English opium-eater and other writings. Penguin Books 2003 xliv, 296p pa $14 **824**

1. Drug abuse

ISBN 978-0-14-043901-4; 0-14-043901-3

"Confessions forged a link between artistic self-expression and addiction, paving the way for later generations of literary drug-users from Baudelaire to Burroughs, and anticipating psychoanalysis with its insights into the subconscious. This edition is based on the original serial version of 1821, and reproduces the two 'sequels', 'Suspiria de Profundis' (1845) and 'The English Mail-Coach' (1849). It also includes a critical introduction discussing the romantic figure of the addict and the tradition of confessional literature, and an appendix on opium in the nineteenth century." Publisher's note

Dyer, Geoff

Otherwise known as the human condition; selected essays and reviews, 1989-2010. Geoff Dyer. Graywolf Press 2011 421p il **824**

1. Criticism

ISBN 1555975798; 9781555975791

LC 2010937517

This book of essays by Geoff Dyer covers "a broad territory stretching from photographers such as Richard Avedon and William Gedney . . .; musicians Miles Davis and Def Leppard; writers like D.H. Lawrence, Ian McEwan, and Richard Ford; as well as personal ruminations on, say, reader's block." (Publishers Weekly)

"A grab-bag of critical essays, reportage and personal stories from the irrepressibly curious Dyer. . . . The title of this hefty tome, featuring pieces published in two United Kingdom–only collections, suggests ponderous philosophizing. But though Dyer takes his art seriously, his prose is as relaxed and self-effacing as it is informed. . . . Though the book is wide-ranging, his command is consistent, whether he's writing about Richard Avedon or model airplanes." Kirkus

Includes bibliographical references

White sands; experiences from the outside world. Geoff Dyer. Pantheon Books 2016 x, 233 p.p illustrations (some color) (hardback) $25 **824**

1. Travel 2. Travel writing 3. Self-consciousness 4. Essays
ISBN 9781101870853; 9781101870860

LC 2015030019

This essay collection, by Geoff Dyer, is "about travel, unexpected awareness, and the questions we ask when we step outside ourselves. Geoff Dyer's restless search—for what? is unclear, even to him—continues in this series of fascinating adventures and pilgrimages: with a tour guide who may not be a tour guide in the Forbidden City in Beijing; with friends in New Mexico, . . . [and] with a hitchhiker picked up on the way from White Sands." (Publisher's note)

"A mesmerizing compendium that reflects on time, place, and just what, exactly, we are doing here." Kirkus

Includes bibliographical references.

Gaiman, Neil, 1960-

The **view** from the cheap seats; Selected Nonfiction. Neil Gaiman. William Morrow 2016 544 p. (hardback) $26.99 **824**
1. Essays
ISBN 0062262262; 9780062262264

LC 2015046480

This book, by Neil Gaiman, is a "collection of nonfiction essays. . . . [It] explores a broad range of interests and topics, including (but not limited to): authors past and present; music; storytelling; comics; bookshops; travel; fairy tales; America; inspiration; libraries; ghosts; and the title piece, . . . which recounts the author's experiences at the 2010 Academy Awards in Hollywood." (Publisher's note)

"With this volume, Gaiman has shown that his nonfiction rivals his much-lauded fiction." Pub Wkly

James, Clive

As of this writing; the essential essays, 1968-2002. Norton 2003 619p $35 **824**
1. Literature -- History and criticism
ISBN 0-393-05180-3
"James writes with fluent wit, remarkable warmth, deep knowledge, and an exhilarating sense of mission." Booklist

Kermode, Frank

★ **Pieces** of my mind; essays and criticism, 1958-2002. Farrar, Straus & Giroux 2003 466p $26; pa $16 **824**
ISBN 0-8090-7601-2; 0-374-52936-1 pa

LC 2003-54727

The author "parses complicated, even esoteric aspects of story and text, metaphysics and poetry, and the link between social change and the evolution of the novel, yet he is unfailingly clear and cheerfully engaging, classy, and stimulating." Booklist
Includes bibliographical references

O'Faolain, Nuala

A **radiant** life; Nuala O'Faolain; [introduction by Fintan O'Toole; note by Sheridan Hay]. Abrams Image 2011 302p pa $18.95 **824**
1. Women -- Ireland 2. Catholic Church -- Ireland
ISBN 978-0-8109-9806-3; 0-8109-9806-8

LC 2010-37687

"The collection spans two decades and runs the gamut, from feminism to social justice, from pop culture to the elusive fruits of progress. It makes little difference that they spring from a quintessentially Irish voice; they are universal in their appeal. Read more: Book review: Nuala O'Faolain's Irish prose holds universal appeal." Denver Post

Orwell, George, 1903-1950

Essays; selected and introduced by John Carey. Alfred A. Knopf 2002 xlv, 1369p (Everyman's library) $35 **824**
ISBN 978-0-375-41503-6; 0-375-41503-3
"The real reason we read Orwell is because his own fault-line, his fundamental schism, his hybridity, left him exceptionally sensitive to the fissure—which is everywhere apparent–between what ought to be the case and what actually is the case. He says the unsayable." Financial Times

Pratchett, Terry, 1948-2015

★ A **slip** of the keyboard; collected nonfiction. Terry Pratchett. Doubleday 2014 336 p. (hardback) $26.95 **824**
1. Wit and humor
ISBN 0385538308; 9780385538305; 9780804169226

LC 2014011949

This book, by Terry Pratchett, is a collection of the author's "nonfiction work, and it brings together the finest examples of his extraordinary wit and his persuasive prose. Whether in short opinion pieces (on death and taxes), or in long essays, speeches, and interviews (covering a range of topics from mushrooms to orangutans), this collection is a fascinating look inside an extraordinary writer's mind." (Publisher's note)

"The essays, letters, speeches, and articles feature all the wit and charm of his beloved novels and allow readers a more personal look at Pratchett's life and beliefs. In a mere 336 pages, Pratchett ruminates on the underappreciated role of fantasy fiction and its importance in the literary world; the trick to becoming a successful author (hint: there isn't one); the care and feeding of authors while on book tours; and his work with fellow writer and friend Neil Gaiman." Booklist

Smith, Zadie, 1975-

Changing my mind; occasional essays. Penguin Press 2009 306p $26.95 **824**
ISBN 978-1-59420-237-7; 1-59420-237-0

LC 2009-23419

The author has organized this collection of "essays into sections on reading, being, seeing, feeling, and remembering to create a strong and piquant collection. As the title implies, Smith's thinking evolves before our eyes as she articulates her responses to art and life. . . . Smith is a superb essayist of skill, candor, and caring." Booklist
Includes bibliographical references

Wilde, Oscar

The **artist** as critic; critical writings of Oscar Wilde. edited by Richard Ellmann. University of Chicago Press 1982 xxviii, 446p pa $36.50 **824**
1. Criticism 2. Literature -- History and criticism
ISBN 978-0-226-89764-6; 0-226-89764-8

LC 82-13361

Wilde's "book reviews and occasional pieces prove that while Wilde could be superbly malicious with fatheads, he was a generous and painstaking critic, quick to find merit and delighted to announce the discovery. It is easy to damn a book amusingly. Wilde could praise amusingly, a rare and difficult trick." Atlantic

Young, Ashleigh

Can you tolerate this? essays. Asheigh Young. Penguin Group USA 2018 256 p. (hardcover) $26 **824**
1. Aging 2. Youth 3. Essays
ISBN 9780525534037; 0525534032

LC 2017057498

This essay collection, by Ashleigh Young, "presents a vivid self-portrait of an introspective yet widely curious young woman, the colorful, isolated community in which she comes of age, and the uneasy tensions--between safety and risk, love and solitude, the catharsis of grief and the ecstasy of creation--that define our lives." (Publisher's note)

824.914   English essays – 1945-1999

Amis, Martin, 1949-

★ The **rub** of time; Bellow, Nabokov, Hitchens, Travolta, Trump: essays and reportage, 1986-2017. by Martin Amis. Alfred A. Knopf 2018 416 p.   **824.914**
    1. American essays 2. Reportage literature, American
ISBN 9781400044535
                     LC 2017017321

In this essay collection, author Martin Amis "writes about finally confronting the effects of aging on his athletic prowess. He revisits, time and time again, the worlds of Bellow and Nabokov, his 'twin peaks,' masters who have obsessed and inspired him. Brilliant, incisive, and savagely funny, . . . [this book] is a vital addition to any Amis fan's bookshelf, and the perfect primer for readers discovering his fierce and tremendous journalistic talents for the first time." (Publisher's note)

"Amis writes with buoyant and cutting authority. His vocabulary, cross-pollinated by his trans-Atlantic reading and life, is pinpoint and peppery; his syntax supple and ensnaring. The pleasure Amis takes in observation, cogitation, and composition is palpable, and he is acidly funny." Booklist

824.92   English essays – 2000-

Cole, Teju

★ **Known** and strange things; essays. Teju Cole. Random House 2016 400 p. color illustrations (ebook) $51; (paperback) $17   **824.92**
    1. Essays 2. Literature and politics
ISBN 9780812989793; 9780812989786
                     LC 2015042074

This essay collection, by Teju Cole, offers "more than fifty pieces on politics, photography, travel, history, and literature. . . . On page after page, deploying prose dense with beauty and ideas, he finds fresh and potent ways to interpret art, people, and historical moments, taking in subjects from Virginia Woolf, Shakespeare, and W. G. Sebald to Instagram, Barack Obama, and Boko Haram." (Publisher's note)

"A bold, honest, and controversially necessary read." Kirkus
Includes bibliographical references

Moran, Caitlin

Moranifesto; Caitlin Moran. Harper Perennial 2016 xiv, 329 p.p $15.99   **824.92**
    1. Anecdotes 2. Celebrities 3. Celebrities -- Anecdotes 4. Great Britain -- Social life and customs -- 21st century -- Anecdotes
ISBN 006243375X; 9780062433756
                     LC 2016388280

This book, by Caitlin Moran, "takes a clever, hilarious look at celebrities, society, and the wacky world we live in today. . . . Caitlin combines the best of her recent columns with lots of new writing unique to this book as she offers a characteristically fun and witty look at the news, celebrity culture, and society. Featuring strong and important pieces on poverty, the media, and class, [it] also focuses on how socially engaged we've become as a society." (Publisher's note)

"With her exuberant vocabulary full of Briticisms, Moran's wise,

bracing observations about politics, pop culture, feminism, and nearly everything else are no-holds-barred, and made easy and fun to digest by her crackling humor." Booklist.

Smith, Zadie, 1975-

★ **Feel** free; essays. Zadie Smith. Penguin Press 2018 452 p. illustrations (hardcover) $28   **824.92**
    1. English essays 2. Global warming 3. Social networking
ISBN 9781594206252; 9780698178885; 1594206252
                     LC 2017478938

This collection of essays, by Zadie Smith, "offers a survey of important recent events in culture and politics, as well as Smith's own life. Equally at home in the world of good books and bad politics, Brooklyn-born rappers and the work of Swiss novelists, she is by turns wry, heartfelt, indignant, and incisive--and never any less than perfect company." (Publisher's note)

"In this collection of conversational essays, novelist Smith (Swing Time) brings her precise observations and distinct voice to an expansive range of topics." Pub Wkly
Includes bibliographical references (pages 438-444) and index.

828   English miscellaneous writings

Angel, Katherine

Unmastered; a book on desire, most difficult to tell. by Katherine Angel. Farrar, Straus and Giroux 2013 368 p. (alk. paper) $26   **828**
    1. Sex 2. Women -- Sexual behavior 3. Desire
ISBN 0374280401; 9780374280406
                     LC 2012048072

Author Katherine Angel presents a "personal meditation on sex, power, and female desire. It is also a powerful reckoning with our contradictory and deeply entrenched notions of sexuality. Angel embraces the highly charged oppositions—dominance versus submission, liberation versus dependence—and probes the porousness between masculine and feminine, thought and sensation, self and culture, power and pliancy, always reveling in the elusiveness of easy answers." (Publisher's note)
Includes bibliographical references and index

DeGategno, Paul J.

Critical companion to Jonathan Swift; a literary reference to his life and works. [by] Paul J. DeGategno, R. Jay Stubblefield. Facts on File 2006 474p il (Facts on File library of world literature) $75   **828**
    1. Poets 2. Clergy 3. Authors 4. Satirists 5. Pamphleteers 6. Writers on politics
ISBN 0-8160-5093-7; 978-0-8160-5093-2
                     LC 2005-25470

This "work is divided into five parts. These parts consist of a ten-page biography of satirist Jonathan Swift (1667-1745); a 'Works A-Z' section that includes synopses and commentaries that generally run to several hundred words on virtually all of Swift's poems, essays, and books; a 'Related Entries' section with similar brief articles on persons, topics, and places relevant to Swift studies; appendixes that include a chronology of Swift's life; a . . . bibliography of primary and secondary works; and an index." Libr J
Includes bibliographical references

Huxley, Elspeth

The **flame** trees of Thika; memories of an African childhood. Penguin Bks. 2000 280p pa $15   **828**

1. Authors 2. Novelists 3. Kenya 4. Memoirists
ISBN 0-14-118378-0; 978-0-14-118378-7

LC 99-47965

First published 1959 by Morrow

This is an account of the author's childhood on a coffee plantation in Kenya. She describes the landscape, the Kikuya peoples, the European settlers and the difficulties her parents faced adjusting to life in the bush.

James, Clive, 1939-

Latest readings; Clive James. Yale University Press 2015 192 p. (cloth: alk. paper) $25   **828**
1. Critics 2. Books and reading
ISBN 0300213190; 9780300213195

LC 2014958943

This memoir, by Clive James, "contains his reflections on what may well be his last reading list. A look at some of James's old favorites as well as some of his recent discoveries, this book also offers a revealing look at the author himself, sharing his evocative musings on literature and family, and on living and dying." (Publisher's note)

"James relishes the limited reading time he has and makes no bones about it, providing sparkling commentary on his old favorites and new discoveries." Pub Wkly

Johnson, Samuel

Samuel Johnson; the major works. edited with an introduction and notes by Donald Greene. Oxford University Press 2000 xxvii, 840p (Oxford world's classics) pa $18.95   **828**
ISBN 978-0-19-284042-4; 0-19-284042-8

LC 83-17280

"This volume celebrates Johnson's astonishing talent by selecting widely across the full range of his work. It includes 'London' and 'The Vanity of Human Wishes' among other poems, and many of his essays for the Rambler and Idler. The prefaces to his edition of Shakespeare and his famous Dictionary, together with samples from the texts, are given, as well as selections from A Journey to the Western Islands of Scotland, the Lives of the Poets, and Rasselas in its entirety. There is also a substantial representation of lesser-known prose, and of his poetry, letters, and journals." Publisher's note

Includes bibliographical references

Ker, Ian

G. K. Chesterton; a biography. Ian Ker. Oxford University Press 2011 747 p. ill. $65.00   **828**
1. Intellectuals 2. English authors -- Biography 3. Poets 4. Authors 5. Essayists 6. Novelists 7. Biographers 8. Travel writers 9. Literary critics 10. Short story writers 11. Biography -- Individual
ISBN 0199601283; 9780199601288

LC 2010940318

This book, by Ian Ker, offers a biography of the author G. K. Chesterton. "Remembered as a brilliant creator of nonsense and satirical verse, author of the Father Brown stories, . . . and yet today he is not counted among the major English novelists and poets. However, this . . . biography argues that Chesterton should be seen as the successor of the great Victorian prose writers, Carlyle, Arnold, Ruskin, and above all Newman." (Publisher's note)

Includes bibliographical references and index

Martin, Peter

★ A **life** of James Boswell. Yale Univ. Press 2000 613p $35; pa $18.95   **828**
1. Authors 2. Lawyers 3. Biographers
ISBN 0-300-08489-7; 0-300-09312-8 pa

This is a biography of the diarist and author of The life of Samuel Johnson

"Martin has written the best biography of the greatest biographer in the English language. . . . One of the many virtues of Martin's work is his successful synthesis of Boswell's life story with a keen analysis of Boswell's artistry." Atl Mon

Includes bibliographical references

Mda, Zakes

Sometimes there is a void; memoirs of an outsider. Zakes Mda. Farrar, Straus and Giroux 2012 561 p.   **828**
1. Authors, South African 2. South Africa -- Politics and government 3. Authors, South African -- 20th century -- Biography
ISBN 9780374280949

LC 2011020817

In this book, "South African novelist, playwright and poet [Zakes] Mda . . . pens a memoir setting his experiences against the backdrop of a country in turmoil. . . . Although he spent his early years in Soweto, Mda was forced to escape to Lesotho after his father was exiled because of his activism against apartheid. . . . Mda's . . . journeys of romance, rebellion and his search for an artistic calling often kept him feeling like an outsider, a theme repeated throughout the memoir." (Kirkus Reviews)

Meyers, Jeffrey

Orwell; wintry conscience of a generation. Norton 2000 380p il maps hardcover o.p. pa $16.95   **828**
1. Authors 2. Novelists 3. Essayists
ISBN 0-393-32263-7 pa

LC 00-38020

"With wit and acumen, Meyers portrays a complex, eccentric, intelligent, and unbending man hard on family and friends, a writer of singular gifts, and a 'prophetic moralist' whose vision continues to illuminate society's dark side." Booklist

Includes bibliographical references

★ The **New** Oxford book of literary anecdotes. Oxford University Press 2006 385p il hardcover o.p. pa $16.95   **828**
1. Authors, English -- Anecdotes 2. Authors, American -- Anecdotes 3. English literature -- Anecdotes
ISBN 0-19-280468-5; 978-0-19-280468-6; 0-19-954341-0 pa; 978-0-19-954341-0 pa

LC 2005-33698

First published 1975 under the editorship of James Sutherland with title: The Oxford book of literary anecdotes

The editor "has compiled more than 700 anecdotes about English-language writers, from Geoffrey Chaucer to J.K. Rowling. The brief, chronologically-arranged (by subject's birth date) entries offer a glimpse into the personalities and times of these authors." Libr J

Includes bibliographical references

Orwell, George, 1903-1950

★ **Diaries**; George Orwell; edited by Peter Davison; introduction by Christopher Hitchens. 1st American ed. Liveright 2012 597 p.   **828**
1. Diaries 2. English authors 3. English novelists 4. English literature 5. Authors 6. Essayists 7. Novelists 8. Biography, Individual
ISBN 0871404109; 9780871404107

LC 2012009895

This book, edited by Peter Davison, offers the personal writings of the British author George Orwell. "Written as individual books throughout his career, the eleven surviving diaries collected here record Orwell's youthful travels among miners and itinerant laborers, the fearsome rise of totalitarianism, the horrific drama of World War II, and the fever-ish composition of his great masterpieces 'Animal Farm' and '1984.'" (Publisher's note)

Includes bibliographical references and index.

Quinn, Edward

Critical companion to George Orwell; a literary reference to his life and work. Facts On File 2009 450p il (Facts on File library of world literature) $75   **828**

1. Authors 2. Novelists 3. Essayists

ISBN 978-0-8160-7091-6

LC 2008-26727

This volume provides a "review of Orwell's life and covers all his novels, nonfiction, and other writings. . . . It is a superb resource for those desiring an introduction to George Orwell, the man and the writer." Booklist

Includes bibliographical references

Sisman, Adam

Boswell's presumptuous task; the making of the life of Dr. Johnson. Penguin 2002 351p il pa $15   **828**

1. Authors 2. Lawyers 3. Biographers

ISBN 978-0-14-200175-2; 0-14-200175-9

First published 2000 in the United Kingdom

James Boswell's The Life of Samuel Johnson was published in 1791, six years after the death of its subject. In this book, Sisman chronicles Boswell's motives for writing his biography and the techniques he adopted.

"Mr. Sisman's book is illuminating both of Boswell's character and of all aspects of his authorship." Economist

Includes bibliographical references

Swift, Graham

Making an elephant; writing from within. Alfred A. Knopf 2009 400p il $26.95   **828**

ISBN 978-0-307-27099-3

LC 2009-14052

"Out from behind the scrim of fiction, Swift is highly entertaining, at once welcoming and teasing, clever and probing." Booklist

Includes bibliographical references

Thomas, Dylan

A **child's** Christmas in Wales; with woodcuts by Ellen Raskin. New Directions 2007 51p il pa $9.95   **828**

1. Christmas -- Wales

ISBN 978-0-8112-1731-6; 0-8112-1731-0

LC 2007-24727

First published 1954

The Welsh poet Dylan Thomas recalls the celebration of Christmas with his family and the feelings it evoked in him as a child.

For any season of the year "the language is enchanting and the poetry shines with an unearthly radiance." N Y Times Book Rev

Zaretsky, Robert

Boswell's enlightenment; Robert Zaretsky. Belknap Press of Harvard University Press 2015 288 p. (cloth: alkaline paper) $26.95   **828**

1. Travelers 2. Enlightenment 3. Philosophy and religion 4. Enlightenment -- Scotland 5. Europe -- Description and travel 6. Scots -- Europe -- History -- 18th century 7. Authors, Scottish -- 18th century -- Biography 8. Travelers -- Europe -- History -- 18th century 9. Philosophy and religion -- Scotland -- History -- 18th

century

ISBN 0674368231; 9780674368231

LC 2014037309

This book, by Robert Zaretsky, "examines the conflicting credos of reason and faith, progress and tradition that pulled [James] Boswell, like so many eighteenth-century Europeans, in opposing directions. . . . In his relentless quizzing of Voltaire and Rousseau, Hume and Johnson, Paoli and Wilkes on topics concerning faith, the soul, and death, he was not merely a celebrity-seeker but-- for want of a better term-- a truth-seeker." (Publisher's note)

Includes bibliographical references and index

831   German poetry

Celan, Paul, 1920-1970

Breathturn into timestead; the collected later poetry: a bilingual edition. Paul Celan; translated by Pierre Joris. Farrar Straus & Giroux 2014 736 p. (hardback) $40   **831**

1. German poetry 2. Europe -- History -- 20th century

ISBN 0374125988; 9780374125981

LC 2014020543

Translator Pierre Joris presents the "first appearance in English of the complete late volumes [of poet Paul Celan]. The later poems--six books, three of them posthumous--comprise new compounds, alienated images, hauntingly crystallized phrases that sound like nobody's native tongue." (Publishers Weekly)

"Celan's poetry focuses on a new (and very ancient) kind of light: the light of 'the other's Other,' the dark, invisible light beyond all fictions of the abyssal non-origin of being, time, and space. Poetry suffers from what Celan calls Lichtzwang, "light duress," which has prevented poetry from 'darkening over' to its essence. Summing Up: Highly recommended. Upper-division undergraduates through faculty." Choice

Includes bibliographical references and index

★ **Poems** of Paul Celan; translated by Michael Hamburger. Rev and expanded; Persea Bks. 2002 xxxiv, 366p $35; pa $18.95   **831**

1. Poetry -- By individual authors

ISBN 0-89255-275-1; 0-89255-276-X pa

LC 2001-59341

First published 1980 with title: Paul Celan: poems

"This bilingual German-English selection culled from [the poet's] nine collections reveals that his is a poetry of darkness: anguish over what life offers and denies; the ever-present shadow of death that shades each breath. . . . Yet it also expresses an undefined, perhaps undefinable, joy." Booklist [review of 1989 edition]

Goethe, Johann Wolfgang von

Selected poetry; translated with an introduction and notes by David Luke. Penguin Books 2005 xliv, 283p (Penguin classics) pa $16   **831**

1. Poetry -- By individual authors

ISBN 978-0-14-042456-0; 0-14-042456-3

First published 1999 in the United Kingdom

"The introduction gives a thoughtful summary of Goethe's fascinating and problematic life. . . . What Luke triumphantly does is not only to stay close to the original, but also to create a total structure that gives a convincing sense of the overall movement of the poem. . . . Goethe made no secret of his huge debt to Shakespeare; perhaps the English tradition might celebrate the new millennium by learning something from him in return. David Luke's selection makes an excellent starting point." Times Lit Suppl

Morike, Eduard Friedrich

Mozart's journey to Prague and a selection of poems; [by] Eduard Mörike; translated and with an introduction and notes by David Luke; Scots translations by Gilbert McKay. rev ed; Penguin Books 2003 xl, 216p (Penguin Classics) pa $14 **831**

1. Poetry -- By individual authors

ISBN 978-0-14-044737-8; 0-14-044737-7

LC 2004-298957

First published 1997 in the United Kingdom

A selection of Mörike's most popular romantic and classical folk and fairy-tale poems. Also includes the 1855 novella Mozart's journey to Prague, an imaginary recreation of the journey Mozart made from Vienna to Prague in 1787 to conduct the first performance of Don Giovanni.

Includes bibliographical references

Rilke, Rainer Maria

★ **Duino** elegies; translated by David Young; with an introduction and commentary. W. W. Norton 2006 202p pa $13.95 **831**

1. Poetry -- By individual authors

ISBN 978-0-393-32884-4; 0-393-32884-8

LC 2006-9872

First English translation published 1939; this translation was originally published in Field, Contemporary Poetry and Poetics, issues 5 through 9 and as a Norton paperback edition in 1992

"These elegies, the last great work of the poet, were named for the castle of Duino on the Adriatic, where they were first conceived." New Statesman (1913)

New poems; selected and translated by Edward Snow. rev bilingual ed; North Point Press 2001 329p pa $15 **831**

1. Poetry -- By individual authors

ISBN 0-86547-612-8

LC 2001-42714

In this "translation, Edward Snow renders into believable English the complete text of Rilke's work of early maturity. . . . Maintaining fidelity to Rilke's idiosyncratic and problematic German, Snow does not reproduce his formal structures but does capture the rhythms, tone shifts, and overall feel of the poems to an admirable degree. Bilingual edition." Booklist [review of 1984 edition of New poems (1907)]

★ **Sonnets** to Orpheus; translated by M.D. Herter Norton. W. W. Norton 2006 160p pa $13.95 **831**

1. Poetry -- By individual authors

ISBN 0-393-32885-6

First English translation 1936 in the United Kingdom; this translation first published 1942

"Deeply rooted in the symbolist tradition, the 'Sonnets' collapse the barriers that exist between the inner and the outer world and celebrate the inherently musical quality of language. In his masterful translation of the 'Sonnets', Young captures the fluidity of the original with sensitivity and precision." Libr J

Uncollected poems; selected and translated by Edward Snow. Bilingual ed; North Point Press 1995 265p hardcover o.p. pa $15 **831**

1. Poetry -- By individual authors

ISBN 0-86547-513-X pa

LC 94-24438

"Snow is particularly adept at capturing what one might call the non-Orphic side of Rilke's voice. Even in the most complex and rhetorically charged pieces, however, Snow is careful never to simplify Rilke. . . . Most important of all, these translations . . . let us get beyond the simplifications of the Rilke legend with its cycles of transcendent inspiration and imaginative paralysis." New Repub

Sebald, Winfried Georg, 1944-2001

Across the land and the water; new and selected poems, 1964-2001. W.G. Sebald; [translated from the German by Iain Galbraith] Random House 2012 166 p. **831**

1. Authors, German 2. German poetry -- Collections 3. World War, 1939-1945 -- Germany -- Poetry

ISBN 9781400068906

LC 2011025272

The book "compiles [W. G. Sebald's] . . . poetic output from his student days through to the last years of his life. . . . Sebald's poems engage . . . with the private archives of Germany's memory of the war. . . . Each poem, in its way, reaches towards the irreducible truth of a large number of individuals, Jewish and non-Jewish, brutally transported from home and out of recognition and existence." (New Statesman)

Includes bibliographical references

832 German drama

Durrenmatt, Friedrich

The **visit**; a tragi-comedy. translated from the German by Patrick Bowles. Grove Press 1962 109p pa $12 **832**

ISBN 0-8021-3066-6

Characters: 28 men, 6 women, extras. 3 acts. First produced in the United States at the Lunt-Fontaine Theatre, New York City, May 5, 1958

This play "concerns millionaire Claire Zachanassian's return to her small home town where, in her youth, she was seduced and abandoned by III. She seeks revenge and, to get it, she bribes the entire population: every man, woman and child will be rich for the rest of their lives if they agree to put III to death. After a feeble moral struggle and a travesty of a trial, the people of Güllen condemn and execute the erstwhile lover. In so doing they condemn themselves and Dürrenmatt condemns society as a whole." Cambridge Guide to World Theatre

Goethe, Johann Wolfgang von

★ **Goethe's** Faust; the original German and a new tr. and introduction by Walter Kaufmann; part one and sections from part two. Anchor Books 1962 503p pa $10.95 **832**

ISBN 978-0-385-03114-1; 0-385-03114-9

Part I first published 1808; Part II 1832

In this epic drama "Mephistopheles makes a bargain with the aged Faust. If Faust is granted one moment of complete contentment, he loses his soul. Faust regains his youth and with Mephistopheles he travels about enjoying every form of earthly pleasure." Haydn. Thesaurus of Book Dig

Lessing, Gotthold Ephraim

Nathan the Wise, Minna von Barnhelm, and other plays and writings; edited by Peter Demetz; foreword by Hannah Arendt. Continuum 1991 xxvii, 335p (German library) hardcover o.p. pa $29.95 **832**

ISBN 0-8264-0706-4; 0-8264-0707-2 pa

Contents: Minna von Barnhelm, translated by Kenneth J. Northcott; Emilia Galotti, translated by Anna Johanna Gode von Aesch; The Jews, translated by Ingrid Walsøe-Engel; Nathan the Wise, translated by Bayard Quincy Morgan; Ernst and Falk, translated by William L. Zwiebel; Selections from Lessing's philosophical, theological writings, translated by Henry Chadwick

LC 91-19344

Schiller, Friedrich

Don Carlos and Mary Stuart; translated with notes by Hilary Collier Sy-Quia; adapted in verse drama by Peter Oswald; with an introduction by Lesley Sharpe. Oxford University Press 2008 xxx, 359p il pa $13.95 **832**

1. Queens 2. Princes
ISBN 978-0-19-954074-7

LC 2008-275155

First published 1996

This volume contains Don Carlos and Mary Stuart, two German historical dramas. "Dating from 1787 and 1800 respectively, one play was written immediately before the French Revolution, the other in its aftermath. These new translations into blank verse are accurate, elegant, and playable. The Introduction, Notes, and Chronology set the plays in their cultural and intellectual background, while a family tree explains the historical relationship between Don Carlos and Mary Stuart." Publisher's note

Includes bibliographical references

The **robbers** [and] Wallenstein; translated with an introduction by F. J. Lamport. Penguin Books 1979 472p (Penguin classics) pa $16 **832**

ISBN 978-0-14-044368-4; 0-14-044368-1

In The robbers (1782) a man, cheated out of his inheritance by his brother, forms a band of thieves. The Wallenstein trilogy, based on the fall of the German general Count Albrecht von Wallenstein, is comprised of: Wallenstein's camp (1798), The Piccolominis (1799), and Wallenstein's death (1799).

838 German miscellaneous writings

Grass, Günter, 1927-2015

Of All That Ends; by Günter Grass, translated by Breon Mitchell. Houghton Mifflin Harcourt 2016 176 p. illustrations $28; (ebook) $28 **838**

1. Prose poetry 2. German poetry
ISBN 054478538X; 9780544785380; 9780544787636

This book is "the final work of Nobel Prize winning writer Günter Grass a witty and elegiac series of meditations on writing, growing old, and living in the world. In spite of the trials of old age, and with the end in sight, suddenly everything seems possible again: love letters, soliloquies, scenes of jealousy, swan songs, social satire, and moments of happiness crowd onto the page. . . . A wealth of touching stories is condensed into artful miniatures." (Publisher's note)

"Fractured but elegant musings on dying and, most poignantly, living." Kirkus

Kleist, Heinrich von

Selected writings; edited and translated by David Constantine. Hackett Pub. 2004 xxvii, 442p $44; pa $14.95 **838**

ISBN 978-0-87220-744-8; 0-87220-744-7; 978-0-87220-743-1 pa; 0-87220-743-9 pa

LC 2004-54378

"This volume includes the majority of Kleist's writings in English translation. An outstanding representation of his work, this selection offers three plays, eight short stories, five anecdotes, and three es-

says. Kleist's dramas and stories resonate with complex circumstances and obscure consequences that the characters struggle to sail through. Things are not always what they seem to be; intriguingly, the guilty can look innocent and the innocent guilty. The play The Broken Jug, as well as the stories 'Michael Kohlhaas' and 'The Chilean Earthquake,' depict predicaments of the falsely accused who are denied justice. Constantine . . . does an outstanding job of conveying the beauty of Kleist's literary style while allowing himself some liberties in translation." Libr J

Includes bibliographical references

Sebald, Winfried Georg

★ **On** the natural history of destruction; with essays on Alfred Andersch, Jean Amery, and Peter Weiss. {by} W.G. Sebald; translated by Anthea Bell. Random House 2003 202p $23.95; pa $12.95 **838**

1. Artists 2. Authors 3. Painters 4. Novelists 5. Dramatists 6. Philosophers 7. Essayists 8. Nonfiction writers 9. Short story writers 10. German literature -- History and criticism 11. World War, 1939-1945 -- Literature and the war
ISBN 0-375-50484-2; 0-375-75657-4 pa

LC 2002-75187

Original German edition, 1999

"During World War Two, 131 German cities and towns were targeted by Allied bombs, a good number almost entirely flattened. Six hundred thousand German civilians died—a figure twice that of all American war casualties. Seven and a half million Germans were left homeless. Given the astonishing scope of the devastation, W. G. Sebald asks, why does the subject occupy so little space in Germany's cultural memory?" (Publisher's note)

839   Other Germanic literatures

★ The **Sagas** of Icelanders; a selection. preface by Jane Smiley; introduction by Robert Kellogg. Viking 2000 lxvi, 782p il maps (World of the sagas) hardcover o.p. pa $20 **839**

1. Sagas 2. Old Norse literature
ISBN 0-14-100003-1 pa

LC 99-44111

"The Icelandic Sagas are among the masterpieces of world literature whose composition stretches from about the year 1000 to 1500. Presenting the adventures of Norse and Viking heroes, the sagas are told with ritual simplicity and a realism that anticipate the modern novel." Libr J

Includes bibliographical references

Singer, Isaac Bashevis

More stories from my father's court; translated by Curt Leviant. Farrar, Straus & Giroux 2000 216p hardcover o.p. pa $12 **839**

1. Authors 2. Novelists 3. Journalists 4. Essayists 5. Jews -- Poland 6. Children's authors 7. Short story writers 8. Nobel laureates for literature
ISBN 0-374-52798-9 pa

LC 00-37583

Sequel to In my father's court

These pieces were first published in Yiddish in the Jewish daily Forward from 1955-1960

These autobiographical sketches depict the workings of the beth din, the rabbinical court that met in the Singer's Warsaw home

"This book is a portrait of the artist as a voyeuristic yeshiva boy, someone who assimilated into his soul the weird contradictions of modern Jewish life and, half chronicler and half creator, spun them into lasting stories." N Y Times Book Rev

839.3   Netherlandish literatures

Prose, Francine

    Anne Frank; the book, the life, the afterlife. HarperCollins 2009 322p $24.99   **839.3**

    1. Children 2. Creative writing 3. Diarists 4. Holocaust victims 5. Holocaust, 1933-1945 -- Personal narratives

    ISBN 978-0-06-143079-4; 0-06-143079-X

                        LC 2009-17703

    "In this definitive, deeply moving inquiry into the life of the young, imperiled artist, and masterful literary exegesis of The Diary of a Young Girl, Prose tells the crushing story of the Frank family, performs a revelatory analysis of Anne's exacting revision of her coming-of-age memoir, and assesses her father's editorial decisions as he edited his murdered daughter's manuscript for publication. . . . Extraordinary testimony to the power of literature and compassion." Booklist

    Includes bibliographical references

839.7   Swedish literature

Hammarskjold, Dag

    Markings; translated from the Swedish by Leif Sjöberg & W. H. Auden; with a foreword by W. H. Auden. Knopf 1964 xxiii, 221p hardcover o.p. pa $13.95   **839.7**

    1. Spiritual life

    ISBN 0-394-43532-X; 0-307-27742-9 pa; 978-0-307-27742-8 pa

    Original Swedish edition, 1963

    The author described this account as a sort of white book concerning his negotiations with himself and with God. A record of his inner life, it opens with a poem he wrote around 1925; most of the entries were made during the nineteen forties and fifties—and the book ends with a poem written only a few weeks before his plane crashed.

Prideaux, Sue

    Strindberg; a life. Sue Prideaux. Yale University Press 2012 371 p. (cl: alk. paper) $40.00   **839.7**

    1. Dramatists -- Biography 2. Authors, Swedish -- 19th century -- Biography

    ISBN 0300136935; 9780300136937

                        LC 2011038050

    This book is a biography of the Swedish playwright August Strindberg. "Strindberg (1849-1912) had a miserable childhood and became the devoted father of five children. . . . His plays, murderously claustrophobic scorpion dances of marriage, portray extreme psychological states. He also painted Turneresque pictures, was an expert photographer and gardener, and dabbled fruitlessly in alchemy and the occult." (Booklist)

    Includes bibliographical references and index.

Tranströmer, Tomas, 1931-2015

    The **great** enigma; Tomas Tranströmer; translated from the Swedish by Robin Fulton. New Directions 2006 xxi, 262 p.p (paperback) $16.95   **839.7**

    ISBN 9780811216722; 0811216721

                        LC 2006022551

    Author Tomas Tranströmer won the Nobel Prize in Literature in 2011.

This volume "offers the most generous collection of Tranströmer's poems to date. . . . Lean and uncluttered, Fulton's translations in The Great Enigma neither preach nor moralize. They refuse staged psychology and let interiority take shape as mysterious judgments, made by the selection of detail and the juxtaposition of things and times and experiences." Boston Rev

839.8   Danish and Norwegian literatures

Ibsen, Henrik

    ★ The **complete** major prose plays; translated [from the Norwegian] and introduced by Rolf Fjelde. New American Library 1978 1143p pa $28   **839.8**

    ISBN 978-0-452-26205-8; 0-452-26205-4

                        LC 78-50714

    First published 1978 by Farrar, Straus & Giroux

    Contents: Pillars of society; A doll house; Ghosts; An enemy of the people; The wild duck; Rosmersholm; The lady from the sea; Hedda Gabler; The master builder; Little Eyolf; John Gabriel Borkman; When we dead awaken

    Includes bibliographical references

Jacobsen, Rolf

    The **roads** have come to an end now; selected and last poems of Rolf Jacobsen. translated by Robert Bly, Roger Greenwald, and Robert Hedin. Copper Canyon Press 2001 168p pa $16   **839.8**

    ISBN 1-55659-165-9

                        LC 2001-4488

    "This bilingual (Norwegian-English) edition of 73 poems demonstrates a poet whose vision of the natural world and humanity's place in it is cosmically penetrative. Jacobsen regards the world as filled with an essential energy, animated by what must be God, and reading his work induces a certain calm ecstasy about everyday existence." Booklist

839.82   Norwegian literature

Knausgård, Karl Ove, 1968-

    Home and away; writing the beautiful game. Karl Ove Knausgaard, Fredrik Ekelund; translated by Don Bartlett; translated by Séan Kinsella. Farrar, Straus & Giroux 2017 432 p. (paperback) $16; (ebook) $60   **839.82**

    1. Soccer fans 2. Soccer in literature

    ISBN 9780374279837; 9780374714642

                        LC 2016041352

    This book, by Karl Ove Knausgaard and Fredrik Ekelund, translated by Don Bartlett and Seéan Kinsella, "is an unusual soccer book, in which the two authors use soccer and the World Cup in Brazil as the arena for reflections on life and death, art and politics, class and literature. What does it mean to be at home in a globalized world? This exchange of letters opens up new vistas and gives us stories from the lives of two creative writers." (Publisher's note)

    "The discourse is so open, so productive and thoughtful, that when readers reach the final letter, from Ekelund, sadness takes over; we can't read Knausgaard's reply. Hopefully they'll still be corresponding in 2018." Pub Wkly

839.823   Norwegian fiction

Knausgård, Karl Ove, 1968-

Spring; Karl Ove Knausgaard; with illustrations by Anna Bjerger; translated from the Norwegian by Ingvild Burkey. Penguin Press 2018 192 p. (hardback) $27   **839.823**
   1. Fatherhood 2. Father-daughter relationship
   ISBN 9780399563362; 0399563369

                                          LC 2018006367
   This book, by Karl Ove Knausgaard, with illustrations by Anna Bjerger and translated by Ingvild Burkey, is "the recommencement of Knausgaard's fantastic and spellbinding literary project of assembling a personal encyclopedia of the world addressed directly to his newly born daughter. But here Knausgaard must also tell his daughter the story of what happened during the time when her mother was pregnant, and explain why he now has to attend appointments with child services." (Publisher's note)

840.9   French literature -- History and criticism

Becker, Daniel Levin

Many subtle channels; in praise of potential literature. Daniel Levin Becker. Harvard University Press 2012 x, 338 p.p (alk. paper) $27.95   **840.9**
   1. Authorship 2. Intellectuals 3. Literary style 4. Oulipo (Association) 5. Literary form 6. Authors, American -- 21st century -- Biography
   ISBN 0674065778; 9780674065772

                                          LC 2011044577
   This book centers on the achievements of "Ouvroir de Littérature Potentielle, or Oulipo, a collective of writers and mathematicians. . . . Since the group's formation in 1960, members of the Oulipo . . . have been concocting . . . intricate [literary] challenges . . . 'Many Subtle Channels' is Levin Becker's personal history of this literature and his tribute to the people who helped create it, including [Georges] Perec, Jacques Roubaud, Italo Calvino, and Marcel Duchamp." (Bookforum)

841   French poetry

Baudelaire, Charles

Les fleurs du mal; the complete text of The flowers of evil. in a new translation by Richard Howard; illustrated with nine original monotypes by Michael Mazur. Godine 1982 xxxii, 365p il hardcover o.p. pa $18.95   **841**
   1. Poetry -- By individual authors
   ISBN 978-0-87923-462-1 pa; 0-87923-462-8 pa

                                          LC 81-13283
   Original French edition, 1857
   "Howard puts the original's rhymed alexandrines primarily into iambic pentameter blank verse, which allows him to capture the immediate, concrete, visceral quality of Baudelaire's imagery." Choice

Poems. Knopf 1993 256p (Everyman's library pocket poets) $12.50   **841**
   1. Poetry -- By individual authors
   ISBN 0-679-42910-7

                                          LC 93-14363
   A representative selection of poetry by the French symbolist.

Beckett, Samuel

Collected poems in English and French. Grove Press 1977 147p hardcover o.p. pa $13.95   **841**
   1. Poetry -- By individual authors
   ISBN 978-0-8021-3096-9 pa

                                          LC 77-77855
   This work contains poems written by Beckett in English and French along with his translations and bilingual versions of poems by Eluard, Rimbaud, Apollinaire, and Chamfort

Bloch, R. Howard

One toss of the dice; the incredible story of how a poem made us modern. R. Howard Bloch; translation of "Un coup de dés jamais n'abolira le hasard" by J.D. McClatchy. Liveright Publishing Corporation 2016 320 p. illustrations $27.95 **841**
   1. Modernism in literature -- France 2. Modernism (Literature) -- France 3. Literature and society -- France -- History -- 19th century
   ISBN 9781631490866; 0871406632; 9780871406637

                                          LC 2016023400
   In this book, author R. Howard Bloch "masterfully decodes the poem still considered among the most enigmatic ever written. In Bloch's shimmering portrait of Belle Époque Paris, [Stéphane] Mallarmé stands as the spiritual giant of the era, gathering around him every Tuesday a luminous cast of characters including Émile Zola, Victor Hugo, Claude Monet, André Gide, Claude Debussy, Oscar Wilde, and even the future French prime minister Georges Clemenceau." (Publisher's note)
   "Bloch's analysis of the poem's verbal and syntactical acrobatics and its resonance with later works is enlightening." Pub Wkly
   Includes bibliographical references (pages 295-306) and index.

Chanson de Roland

   ★ The **song** of Roland; translated, with an introduction, by W.S. Merwin. Modern Library 2001 137p pa $11.95   **841**
   1. Roland (Legendary character)
   ISBN 0-375-75711-2

                                          LC 00-48989
   "This heroic poem celebrates the mighty feats of Roland, the great French hero in the time of Charlemagne. The medieval legend has replaced and transformed the actual facts of history to a great extent but the epic poem has continued in popularity." Bookman's Manual
   Includes bibliographical references

French poetry, 1820-1950, with prose translations; selected, translated, and introduced by William Rees. Penguin Books 1994 xli, 854p (Penguin classics) pa $22   **841**
   1. French poetry -- Collections
   ISBN 978-0-14-042385-3; 0-14-042385-0

                                          LC 91-127343
   First published 1990 in the United Kingdom
   "While this anthology contains . . . generous selections from the established giants—Baudelaire, Rimbaud, Mallarmé, Valéry, Apollinaire, Michaux—it also draws attention to interesting 'minor' poets, such as Claudel or Cendrars, whose writing has been vital to the evolution of poetry in France. William Rees gives us an introduction to each poet, his or her life, affinities and aesthetics, and the significant literary movements Romanticism, the Parnassian Movement, Symbolism, Cubism, Surrealism and 'Négritude' are signposted and discussed." Publisher's note

Mallarme, Stephane

Collected poems and other verse; translated with notes by E.H. and A.M. Blackmore; with an introduction by Elizabeth McCombie. Oxford University Press 2006 xxxvii, 282p pa

$15.95   **841**

1. Poetry -- By individual authors

ISBN 978-0-19-280362-7; 0-19-280362-X

This collection presents Mallarme's "Poesies in the last arrangement known to have been approved by the author. Prose poems, uncollected verse, and the unique, unclassifiable Un Coup de des. . . (A Dice Throw. . .) are also present, including over 20 items that have never previously been translated. Original spelling, punctuation, and lineation have been preserved throughout." Publisher's note

Rimbaud, Arthur

Poems; [selected by Peter Washington] Knopf 1994 288p (Everyman's library pocket poets) $12.50   **841**

1. Poetry -- By individual authors

ISBN 978-0-679-43321-7; 0-679-43321-X

LC 94-2496

A collection of work by the French Symbolist known for his daring images and pioneering prose poems

Verlaine, Paul

Selected poems; translated by C. F. MacIntyre. University of Calif. Press 1948 xx, 228p il pa $15.95   **841**

1. Poetry -- By individual authors

ISBN 0-520-01298-4

Eighty poems, chosen from Verlaine's first six books. French originals and translations are on facing pages. Contains a preface by the translator

The translator "has done Verlaine a gracious courtesy, and American readers a great kindness. The charm, verbal fireworks, sympathy and nostalgia of this major French poet are Englished with color and convictions." Chicago Sunday Trib

Includes bibliographical references

842   French drama

Beckett, Samuel

Dramatic works; Paul Auster, series editor; introduction by Edward Albee. Grove Press 2006 509p (Samuel Beckett: the Grove centenary edition) $24.95   **842**

ISBN 0-8021-1819-4

LC 2005-55078

Contents: Waiting for Godot; Endgame; All that fall; Act without words I; Embers; Act without words II; Krapp's last tape; Rough for theatre I; Rough for theatre II; The old tune; Happy days; Rough for radio I; Rough for radio II; Words and music; Cascando; Play; Film; Come and go; Eh Joe; Breath; Not I; That time; Footfalls; Ghost trio; . . . but the clouds . . .; A piece of monologue; Rockaby; Ohio impromptu; Quad; Catastrophe; Nacht und Träume; What where

Camus, Albert

Caligula & three other plays; translated from the French by Stuart Gilbert; with a preface written specially for this edition and translated by Justin O'Brien. Knopf 1958 302p hardcover o.p. pa $13   **842**

ISBN 978-0-394-70207-0 pa; 0-394-70207-7 pa

"Four of the author's best-known plays, written between 1938 and 1950. 'Caligula,' about the infamous emperor's self-destroying rebellion against fate; 'The Misunderstanding,' about the murder of a man by his ghoulish mother and sister,' 'The Just Assassins,' on the self-questionings of terrorists; and 'State of Siege,' an allegory about the refusal of one individual in a plague-stricken city to compromise with evil." Publ Wkly

Genet, Jean

The **maids** [and] Deathwatch; two plays. with an introduction by Jean-Paul Sartre; translated from the French by Bernard Frechtman. Grove Press 1954 166p hardcover o.p. pa $14   **842**

ISBN 978-0-8021-5056-1 pa; 0-8021-5056-X pa

Deathwatch, a one-act play written 1947 and first produced 1949 "deals with an insignificant criminal who tries to assume the highly desirable and prestigious role of murderer. . . . In 'The Maids (Les bonnes),' produced in 1947, . . . two servant girls have created an elaborate ritual in which they impersonate their mistress and finally murder her symbolically." McGraw-Hill Ency of World Drama

Goldsby, Robert W.

Molière on stage; what's so funny? Robert W. Goldsby. Anthem Press 2012 xx, 202 p.p (pbk.: alk. paper) $39.95 **842**

ISBN 0857284428; 0857284444; 9780857284426; 9780857284440

LC 2012001708

This book by Robert W. Goldsby "takes the reader onstage, backstage and into the audience of Molière's plays, analyzing the performance of his works in both his own time and in ours. . . . This text . . . investigates four key topics. . .: Molière's early experiences that lead to his later theater experiences; his central great plays of love and lust; his comedic genius and his passion for the stage; and the final words and performances of his life." (Publisher's note)

Includes bibliographical references (p. [191]-196) and index

Ionesco, Eugene

Rhinoceros, and other plays; translated by Derek Prouse. Grove Press 1960 141p pa $10   **842**

ISBN 0-8021-3098-4

Three satirical comedies by a leading dramatist of the "theater of the absurd." In Rhinoceros, one man resists the pressure to conform as everyone about him accepts their transformation into rhinoceroses and he finds himself socially isolated. In The future is in eggs, a couple must produce eggs destined to become intellectuals. The leader is a satire on the mass adulation of political figures in which the leader turns out to be a headless figure

Moliere

The **misanthrope** and other plays. Signet Classics 2005 524p pa $7.95   **842**

ISBN 0-451-52987-1; 978-0-451-52987-9

LC 2006-276841

"Written during the triumphant final years of Molière's career, these seven works represent the mature flowering of his artistry and the most profound development of his vision of humanity." (Publisher's note)

★ **Tartuffe** and other plays. Signet Classics 2007 xxiv, 408p pa $7.95   **842**

ISBN 978-0-451-53033-2

LC 2007-275593

"Including The Ridiculous Precieuses, The School for Husbands, The School for Wives,Don Juan, The Versailles Impromptu, and The Critique of the School for Wives, this collection showcases the talent of perhaps the greatest and best-loved French playwright." (Publisher's note)

Includes bibliographical references

Samuel Beckett's Waiting for Godot; edited and with an introduction by Harold Bloom. New ed; Chelsea House 2008 172p (Modern critical interpretations) $45 **842**
1. Poets 2. Authors 3. Novelists 4. Dramatists 5. Short story writers 6. Nobel laureates for literature
ISBN 978-0-7910-9793-9

LC 2007-49864

First published 1987

Critical interpretations of Beckett's classic tragicomedy illustrating the apparent meaninglessness of life.

Includes bibliographical references

Sartre, Jean Paul
★ **No** exit, and three other plays. Vintage Bks. 1989 275p pa $12 **842**
ISBN 0-679-72516-4

LC 89-40097

No exit is a modern morality play; The flies is a reworking of the Orestes-Electra story. The third play concerns a young Communist intellectual's attempt to maintain his integrity as party line changes and personal relationships alter perceptions of his murder of a party boss who had fallen out of favor, but whose memory is later rehabilitated. The last play concerns a prostitute's involvement in false charges of rape against a murdered black man and his companion in a town in the American South

843   French fiction

Bellos, David
The **Novel** of the Century; the extraordinary adventure of Les Misérables. David Bellos. Farrar, Straus & Giroux 2017 320 p. illustrations $27 **843**
1. French literature -- History and criticism
ISBN 0374223238; 9780374223236

LC 2016049133

In this book, author David Bellos "brings to life the extraordinary story of how Victor Hugo managed to write his novel of the downtrodden despite a revolution, a coup d'état, and political exile; how he pulled off a pathbreaking deal to get it published; and how his approach to the 'social question' would define his era's moral imagination. . . . [He] also shows that what 'Les Misérables' has to say about poverty, history, and revolution is full of meaning today." (Publisher's note)

"Anyone who loves Hugo, France, and the French language will revel in this delightful book that explains all the intimacies of 19th-century French life." Kirkus

Includes bibliographical references (pages 278-289) and index.

Carrère, Emmanuel, 1957-
Limonov; Emmanuel Carrère; translated by John Lambert. Farrar Straus & Giroux 2014 352 p. (hardback) $30 **843**
1. Russians 2. Dissenters
ISBN 0374192014; 9780374192013; 9780374709211

LC 2014004040

Author Emmanuel Carrere's "pseudobiography isn't a novel, but it reads like one: from [Eduard] Limonov's grim childhood to his desperate, comical, ultimately successful attempts to gain the respect of Russia's literary intellectual elite; to his immigration to New York, then to Paris; to his return to the motherland." (Publisher's note)

Carter, William C.
Marcel Proust; a life. Yale Univ. Press 2000 946p $45; pa $18.95 **843**
1. Authors 2. Novelists 3. Essayists 4. Literary critics
ISBN 0-300-08145-6; 0-300-09400-0 pa

LC 99-53701

"Excavating biographic details out of such material as untranslated memoirs and recently collected letters, Carter . . . accounts for the daily affairs of this social butterfly-turned-hypochondriac and shut-in. Proust's romances and infatuations, his political action during the Dreyfus affair, and his literary runs-ins with Anatole France and André Gide, as well as larger issues such as his homosexuality, all receive lengthy treatment." Publ Wkly

Includes bibliographical references

Shattuck, Roger
Proust's way; a field guide to In search of lost time. Norton 2000 xxiv, 290p hardcover o.p. pa $16.95 **843**
1. Authors 2. Novelists 3. Essayists 4. Literary critics
ISBN 0-393-32180-0 pa

LC 99-58472

Shattuck "explains the major settings of the work, summarizes character and plot, and discusses central themes. Shattuck acknowledges that there is no one right interpretation of In Search of Lost Time but succeeds in providing a framework to help readers get through it. He addresses readers coming to the work for the first time." Libr J

Includes bibliographical references

844   French essays

Camus, Albert
★ The **myth** of Sisyphus, and other essays; translated from the French by Justin O'Brien. Knopf 1955 212p hardcover o.p. pa $12.95 **844**
ISBN 0-679-73373-6 pa

Personal reflections on the meaning of life and the philosophical questions surrounding suicide

Resistance, rebellion, and death; translated from the French and with an introduction by Justin O'Brien. Knopf 1961 271p hardcover o.p. pa $13.95 **844**
ISBN 978-0-679-76401-4 pa; 0679764011 pa

"A selection of forthright essays on contemporary world politics, on capital punishment and the relations of the state and the individual, and on art, chosen from the three volumes of 'Actuelles,' published in France between 1950 and 1958." Publ Wkly

Frampton, Saul
When I am playing with my cat, how do I know she is not playing with me? Montaigne and being in touch with life. Pantheon Books 2011 300p $26; ebook $12.99 **844**
1. Judges 2. Authors 3. Essayists
ISBN 978-0-375-42471-7; 978-0-307-37959-7 ebook

LC 2010-43642

The author "renders a rigorous history of ideas in this engaging account of the life and the work of Michel de Montaigne (1533–1592). . . . Frampton tucks a good deal of biography into his tour of the evolution of the essays and the events that inspired them—but his extraordinary achievement is in conveying—and inviting the reader to commune with—Montaigne's unique sensibility and his take on death, sex, travel, friendship, kidney stones, the human thumb, and above all, 'the power of the ordinary and the unremarkable, the value of the here-and-now.' This scholarly romp through the Renaissance is a jewel." Publ Wkly

Includes bibliographical references

848   French miscellaneous writings

Mabanckou, Alain

The **lights** of Pointe-Noire; a memoir. Alain Mabanckou; translated by Helen Stevenson. The New Press 2016 208 p. illustrations (hardback) $23.95   **848**

1. Authors   2. Congo (Republic)   3. Authors, Congolese (Brazzaville) -- Biography

ISBN 9781620971901

LC 2015032791

In this memoir, "Alain Mabanckou left Congo in 1989, at the age of twenty-two, not to return until a quarter of a century later. When he finally came back to Pointe-Noire, a bustling port town on Congo's southeastern coast, he found a country that in some ways had changed beyond recognition: the cinema where, as a child, Mabanckou gorged on glamorous American culture had become a Pentecostal temple, and his secondary school has been renamed in honor of a previously despised colonial ruler." (Publisher's note)

"Mabanckou blurs past and present further with a subtle writing style that involves a variety of techniques. It's no wonder he has won multiple awards. He is an artist—even of the memoir form." LJ

Rimbaud, Arthur

Rimbaud; complete works, selected letters: a bilingual edition. translated with an introduction and notes by Wallace Fowlie; updated, revised and with a foreword by Seth Whidden. University of Chicago Press 2005 xxxvi, 458p il $50; pa $19   **848**

ISBN 978-0-226-71976-4; 0-226-71976-6; 978-0-226-71977-1 pa; 0226719774 pa

LC 2005-41859

First published 1966

In this bilingual edition of Rimbaud's work the original French texts are accompanied by English prose translations. In addition to the complete poetic works there are two prose fragments, a short story in the form of a seminarian's journal, and a selection of letters chosen to illustrate biographical details and Rimbaud's credo as a poet.

Includes bibliographical references

Sartre, Jean-Paul, 1905-1980

We Have Only This Life to Live; Selected Essays, 1939-1975. by Jean-Paul Sartre; edited by Ronald Aronson and Adrian van den Hoven. Random House Inc 2013 600 p. (paperback) $22.95   **848**

1. Life   2. Literature   3. Modern philosophy

ISBN 1590174933; 9781590174937

LC 2013001043

This collection, by Jean-Paul Sartre, edited by Adrian van den Hoven and Ronald Aronson, presents essays by the author collected between 1939 and 1975. "Here Sartre writes about Faulkner, Bataille, Giacometti, Fanon, the liberation of France, torture in Algeria, existentialism and Marxism, friends lost and found, and much else." (Publisher's note)

Voltaire

The **portable** Voltaire; edited, and with an introduction by Ben Ray Redmen. Viking 1949 569p hardcover o.p. pa $17   **848**

ISBN 0-14-015041-2 pa

The selections from Voltaire's works include: Candide, part one; Three stories: Zadig, Micromegas, and Story of a good Brahmin; Letters, and selections from the Philosophical Dictionary and other works. The editor's introduction gives a biographical sketch of Voltaire.

849   Occitan, Catalan, Franco-Proven?ï¿½al literatures

Pla, Josep

The **Gray** Notebook; Josep Pla; translated from the Catalan by Peter Bush; introduction by Valentí Puig. New York Review Books 2013 656 p. (New York Review Books Classics) (alk. paper) $19.95   **849**

1. Diaries   2. Authors, Spanish   3. Authors, Catalan -- 20th century -- Biography

ISBN 1590176715; 9781590176719

LC 2013028497

This book presents the diary of author Joseph Pla, translated by Peter Bush. "Aspiring to be a writer, not a lawyer, he resolved to hone his style by keeping a journal. In it he wrote about his family, local characters, . . . the quips, quarrels, ambitions, and amours of his friends; writers he liked and writers he didn't; and the long . . . walks he would take in the countryside under magnificent skies." (Publisher's note)

"Pla . . . is considered one of the greatest writers of Catalan language, and this beautiful translation lets English readers glory in the quiet strength of his words." Kirkus

850   Literatures of Italian, Dalmatian, Romanian, Rhaetian, Sardinian, Corsican languages

★ The **Oxford** companion to Italian literature; edited by Peter Hainsworth and David Robey. Oxford Univ. Press 2002 xli, 644p maps $95   **850**

1. Reference books   2. Italian literature -- Dictionaries   3. Italian literature -- Bio-bibliography

ISBN 0-19-818332-1

LC 2001-59301

"A magisterial addition to the Oxford companions to literature, this volume goes far beyond its core subject of Italian literature to cover its substrate and context. . . . An excellent ready-reference companion for readers seeking less an introduction to the summits of the literature . . . but a reminder of relevant details." Choice

Includes bibliographical references

Ruud, Jay

Critical companion to Dante; a literary reference to his life and work. Facts on File 2008 566p il (Facts on File library of world literature) $75   **850**

1. Poets   2. Authors

ISBN 978-0-8160-6521-9

LC 2007-33473

This title covers the works of Dante, including The Divine Comedy, La Vita Nuova, and his philosophical works.

"Ruud has written a useful introductory resource that students and lay readers alike can enjoy." Booklist

Includes bibliographical references

851   Italian poetry

Ariosto, Lodovico

Orlando Furioso/The frenzy of Orlando, part 1; a romantic epic. by Ludovico Ariosto; translated with an introduction by Barbara Reynolds. Penguin Books 1975 827p map (Penguin classics) pa $18   **851**
  1. Poetry -- By individual authors
  ISBN 978-0-14-044311-0; 0-14-044311-8
                                                        LC 75-327748
An English verse translation in the original meter of the epic poem by the sixteenth-century Italian poet, courtier, and statesman, which is based on the adventures of Roland and other knights of Charlemagne in the wars against the Saracens

This translation is "lucid, lively, and eminently readable. . . . The first volume contains one-half (23) of the cantos plus invaluable aids for the reader: a lengthy, informative introduction, a list of characters and devices, maps and genealogical tables, notes for each canto and an index of proper names." Choice

Orlando Furioso/The frenzy of Orlando, part 2; a romantic epic. [by] Ludovico Ariosto; translated with an introduction by Barbara Reynolds. Penguin Books 1977 794p (Penguin Classics) pa $18   **851**
  1. Poetry -- By individual authors
  ISBN 978-0-14-044310-3; 0-14-044310-X
"The value of this faithful translation is primarily that it helps you with the Italian. It lets you make your way painlessly into the poem. . . . It does not . . . draw attention to itself. Modestly, it points across, to the things going on in the original." Times Lit Suppl

Dante Alighieri

The **divine** comedy; translated by Allen Mandelbaum; with an introduction by Eugenio Montale; and notes by Peter Armour. Alfred A. Knopf 1995 798p il (Everyman's library) $25   **851**
  1. Poetry -- By individual authors
  ISBN 978-0-679-43313-2; 0-679-43313-9
                                                        LC 95-75206
An epic poem, completed in 1321, in which the poet describes his visionary spiritual journey through Hell, Purgatory and Paradise—guided first by the classical poet Vergil and then by his beloved Beatrice—which results in a purification of his religious faith.

The **Inferno**; translated by Robert Hollander and Jean Hollander; introduction & notes by Robert Hollander. Doubleday 2000 704p hardcover o.p. pa $16.95   **851**
  1. Poetry -- By individual authors
  ISBN 978-0-385-49698-8 pa; 0-385-49698-2 pa
                                                        LC 00-34531
A translation of Dante's poem, in which the Roman poet Virgil guides Dante through the underworld.

"The heart of the Hollanders' edition is the translation itself, which nicely balances the precision required for a much-interpreted allegory and the poetic qualities that draw most readers to the work. The result is a terse, lean Dante with its own kind of beauty. . . . The Hollanders' lines will satisfy both the poetry lover and scholar; they are at once literary, accessible and possessed of the seeming transparence that often characterizes great translations. The Italian text is included on the facing page for easy reference, along with notes drawing on some 60 Dante scholars, several indexes, a list of works cited and an introduction by Robert Hollander." Publ Wkly

Includes bibliographical references

Paradiso; a verse translation by Robert & Jean Hollander; introduction & notes by Robert Hollander. Doubleday 2007 915p $40; pa $19.95   **851**
  1. Poetry -- By individual authors
  ISBN 978-0-385-50678-6; 0-385-50678-3; 978-1-4000-3115-3 pa; 1-4000-3115-X pa
                                                        LC 2007-18070
This is a verse translation of the third volume of Dante's Divine Comedy with the original Italian text on facing pages and an introduction and notes.

"Dante's terza rima is impossible to recreate satisfactorily in English, but the Hollanders have produced a fine verse substitute. . . . Splendid as this new translation is, the endlessly valuable notes are what make this edition supplant all others. The commentary here has evolved not only from extensive research but also from the famous Dante Seminar Hollander has taught at Princeton for many years." Natl Rev

Purgatorio; a verse translation by Jean and Robert Hollander; introduction and notes by Robert Hollander. Doubleday 2003 xxiv, 742p hardcover o.p. pa $18.95   **851**
  1. Poetry -- By individual authors
  ISBN 978-0-385-49700-8 pa
                                                        LC 2002-67100
"To enter Dante's Purgatorio is to step into a charmed world, balanced by the rhythmic interplay of sleep, dreams, light, shadows, smiles, tears, and the reverberations of both solo and choral song. This is the most aesthetically vibrant of Dante's three realms, the one in which the artisanal gestures of poet, painter, and musician prevail. . . . The Hollanders have rendered both the supple lyricism and the rich imagery of the Purgatorio with an admirably informed expertise, preserving the stately economy of Dante's Italian throughout." Literary Rev (Madison, N. J.)

Includes bibliographical references

Montale, Eugenio

The **collected** poems of Eugenio Montale 1925-1977; translated by William Arrowsmith; edited by Rosanna Warren. W. W. Norton & Co. 2012 793 p.   **851**
  1. Italian poetry 2. Poetry -- Collections 3. Modernism in literature
  ISBN 0393080633; 9780393080636
                                                        LC 2011034993
This poetry collection features works of the 20th-century Nobel Prize-winning writer Eugenio Montale, edited by Rosanna Warren and translated by William Arrowsmith. "Hailed as one of the key poets of the modern era, Eugenio Montale . . . helped to create international Modernism. . . . His poems chart [a] . . . response to the shocks of modernity, fascism, and two world wars." Publisher's note)

Includes bibliographical references and index.

★ **Collected** poems, 1920-1954; translated and annotated by Jonathan Galassi. rev ed; Farrar, Straus & Giroux 2000 625p pa $18   **851**
  1. Poetry -- By individual authors
  ISBN 0-374-52625-7
                                                        LC 00-35456
First published 1997
"It is generally agreed that the core of Montale's work consists of three major collections: Cuttlefish Bones (1925), The Occasions (1939), and The Storm, etc. (1956). Galassi chooses to publish all three together, separating them from a body of work of almost equal length that came

later. He defends this decision in a brilliant afterword that offers the best short account I have yet come across of the nature, import, and elusive content of Montale's work." N Y Rev Books {review of 1997 edition}

Includes bibliographical references

Saba, Umberto

Songbook; the selected poems of Umberto Saba. translated by George Hochfield and Leonard Nathan; introduction, notes, and commentary by George Hochfield. Yale University Press 2009 562p $35   **851**

1. Poetry -- By individual authors
ISBN 978-0-300-13603-6; 0-300-13603-X

LC 2008-17685

"The author of more than fifteen individual books of poetry and a thousand pages of prose, Saba is best known for his Il Canzoniere (The Songbook), a continually revised and augmented collection in poems of his life's work. . . . [This volume] has been handsomely produced by Yale University Press; not among the least of its attractions is how well it fits in the hand. The edition includes, among other work, a generous number of Saba's earliest poems; all fifteen sonnets of his important Autobiografia (1924); several of his experimental works of 1928-29, titled Preludes and Fugues; and a sampling of his late-life poems, including his beautiful sequence Uccelli (Birds) from 1948. . . . Clearly a labor of love, these collaborative versions, presented with the Italian on facing pages, occupied Hochfield and Nathan for more than a decade." Nation

854   Italian essays

Calvino, Italo, 1923-1985

★ **Collection** of Sand; essays. Italo Calvino; translated by Martin McLaughlin. First U.S. Edition Mariner Books 2014 288 p. $13.95   **854**

1. Essays
ISBN 0544146468; 9780544146464

LC 2014001373

This collection of essays, by Italo Calvino, is "the last of his works published during his lifetime. Here he applies his graceful intellect to the delights of the visual world, in essays on subjects ranging from cuneiform and antique maps to Mexican temples and Japanese gardens." (Publisher's note)

"The book offers a delectable array of cognitive insights, ancient history, and Calvino's indispensable voice." Pub Wkly

Eco, Umberto

How to travel with a salmon & other essays; translated from the Italian by William Weaver. Harcourt Brace & Co. 1994 248p il hardcover o.p. pa $15   **854**

ISBN 978-0-15-600125-0 pa; 0-15-600125-X pa

LC 94-10340

"In this collection of parodies, satires and whimsical mini-essays written over the last 30 years, Italian novelist/critic Eco . . . takes readers on a delightful romp through the absurdities of modern life." Publ Wkly

860   Literatures of Spanish, Portuguese, Galician languages

★ The **Cambridge** history of Spanish literature; edited by David T. Gies. Cambridge University Press 2004 863p $160   **860**

1. Spanish literature -- History and criticism
ISBN 0-521-80618-6

LC 2004-45601

"The classics of the canon of eleven centuries of Spanish literature are covered, from Berceo, Cervantes and Calderón to García Lorca and Martín Gaite, but attention is also paid to lesser-known writers and works. . . . The volume concludes with a consideration of the influences of film and new media on modern Spanish literature." Publisher's note

Includes bibliographical references

Concise encyclopedia of Latin American literature; editor, Verity Smith. Fitzroy Dearborn Pubs. 2000 xxi, 678p $75 **860**

1. Reference books 2. Latin American literature -- Encyclopedias 3. Latin American literature -- Bio-bibliography
ISBN 1-57958-252-4

Based on the Encyclopedia of Latin American literature (1997)

Contains entries on 50 leading writers and 50 important works of Latin American and Caribbean literature. Also includes survey articles on the literature of individual countries and topical essays. Bibliographies of primary and secondary sources are listed

Includes bibliographical references

861   Spanish poetry

Aleixandre, Vicente

A **longing** for the light; selected poems of Vicente Aleixandre. edited by Lewis Hyde. 2nd ed; Copper Canyon Press 2007 xxi, 279p pa $18   **861**

1. Poetry -- By individual authors
ISBN 978-1-55659-254-6; 1-55659-254-X

LC 2007-992

First published 1979 by Harper & Row

This "is the only available bilingual Spanish-English translation of the poetry of Nobel Laureate Vicente Aleixandre. The collection spans the entirety of Aleixandre's career—from early surrealist work to his complex and fascinating 'dialogues.' It also contains prose interludes, an introduction by editor Lewis Hyde, and a descriptive bibliography." Publisher's note

Borges, Jorge Luis

★ **Selected** poems; edited by Alexander Coleman. Viking 1999 477p hardcover o.p. pa $20   **861**

1. Poetry -- By individual authors
ISBN 0-14-058721-7 pa

LC 99-10318

"Poetry is the heart of Borges' metaphysical, mythical, and cosmopolitan oeuvre. . . . Editor Coleman commissioned a wealth of new translations for this unprecedented and invaluable collection, and the roster of translators includes such luminaries as Robert S. Fitzgerald, W.S. Merwin, Mark Strand, and John Updike." Booklist

Cardenal, Ernesto

Pluriverse; new and selected poems. edited by Jonathan Cohen; with a foreword by Lawrence Ferlinghetti; translations from the Spanish by Jonathan Cohen [et al.] New Directions

Pub. 2009 249p pa $17.95   **861**
    1. Poetry -- By individual authors
    ISBN 978-0-8112-1809-2 pa; 0-8112-1809-0 pa

LC 2008-40582

"Cardenal, now in his 80s, is a Roman Catholic priest and was a leading light of the Nicaraguan Sandinistas. One of his country's most revered figures, Cardenal is these days being persecuted by President Daniel Ortega, the leader whose legend Cardenal did much to create and who has slid now into authoritarian rule. Such tends to be the fate of the revolutionary writer. Cardenal is political, of course, and much of the work presented here (translated by many illustrious hands, including Jonathan Cohen, Thomas Merton and Kenneth Rexroth) deals with the struggle and history of his country and Latin America at large. But he can sing lyrically too. . . . Beautiful." Los Angeles Times Book Rev

Cid

The **poem** of the Cid; translated by Rita Hamilton and Janet Perry; with an introduction and notes by Ian Michael. Penguin 1984 242p map pa $14   **861**
    1. Poetry -- By individual authors
    ISBN 0-14-044446-7

"The poem is based on the exploits of Rodrigo or Ruy Diaz de Bivar (c.1043-1099), who was known as 'el Cid.' . . . Similar in form to the 'Chanson de Roland,' the poem is notable for its simplicity and directness and for its exact, picturesque detail. Despite the inclusion of much legendary material, the figure of the Cid who is depicted as the model Castilian warrior, is not idealized to an extravagant degree." Reader's Ency. 4th edition

Cortazar, Julio

Save twilight; selected poems. Julio Cortázar; translated by Stephen Kessler. City Lights Publishers 2016 xvii, 257 p.p illustrations (Pocket poets series) (softcover) $16.95   **861**
    1. Poetry -- Collections 2. Spanish poetry -- 20th century
    ISBN 0872867099; 9780872867093

LC 2016008225

"Originally published as Salvo el crepâusculo by Editorial Nueva Imagen, S.A., Mexico City, 1984" -- Title page verso.

This book, by Julio Cortazar, has "nearly one hundred new pages of poems, prose and illustrations. . . . Ranging from the intimate to the political, tenderness to anger, heartbreak to awe, in styles both traditionally formal and free, Cortázar the poet and subverter of genres is revealed as a versatile and passionate virtuoso." (Publisher's note)

"Cortázar is a people's poet, accessible from every angle, and his position as a titan of the Latin American boom is indisputable." Pub Wkly

Garcia Lorca, Federico

Collected poems; edited and with an introduction and notes by Christopher Maurer; translated by Francisco Aragon [et al.] Farrar, Straus & Giroux 1991 893p (Poetical works) hardcover o.p. pa $25   **861**
    1. Poetry -- By individual authors
    ISBN 978-0-374-52691-7; 0-374-52691-5 pa

This bilingual edition of Garcia Lorca's poetry, "which modestly claims not to be 'definitive,' includes every poem written by the acclaimed Spanish poet except Poet in New York. Assembled in the light of recent scholarship, its contents have been rendered into English by newer translators such as Alan S. Trueblood, Catherine Brown, Will Kirkland, and Greg Simon; older translators such as Stephen Spender, Langston Hughes, and Ben Belitt are not represented. Generally, rhyme and assonance are sacrificed to the 'silent counterpoint of poetic mean-

ing,' and old-fashioned diction is avoided." Libr J

Poet in New York; edited and with an introduction and notes by Christopher Maurer; translated by Greg Simon and Steven F. White. Farrar, Straus & Giroux 1988 xxx, 275p il pa $18 **861**
    1. New York (N.Y.) -- Poetry
    ISBN 978-0-374-52540-8; 0-374-52083-4

LC 87-33154

This "is one of the perplexing classics of twentieth-century poetry. It is a difficult, sometimes bewildered, often hermetic work. It is elusive and enigmatic, mysterious, tortured—a book, to borrow one of the poet's own phrases, 'that can baptize in dark water all who look at it.' Reading it in [this] convincing new translation, . . . one feels the anguished authority and the demonic force and impact of the original. For all its strangeness, Lorca's testament may well be one of the greatest books of poems ever written about New York City." New Yorker

Includes bibliographical references

Neruda, Pablo

★ The **poetry** of Pablo Neruda; edited and with an introduction by Ilan Stavans. Farrar, Straus and Giroux 2003 996p hardcover o.p. pa $20   **861**
    1. Poetry -- By individual authors
    ISBN 0-374-29995-1; 0-374-52960-4 pa

LC 2002-32548

"Stavans has assembled the most complete anthology of Neruda yet available in English, drawing evenhandedly from the various stages of the poet's long and complex career. Neruda was, it seems, at least half a dozen poets, many of them in competition with the others. Needless to say, there are wonders in these pages that will delight readers unfamiliar with the tumultuously varied planet known as Neruda." Nation

Includes bibliographical references

Paz, Octavio

★ The **collected** poems of Octavio Paz, 1957-1987; edited & translated by Eliot Weinberger; with additional translations by Elizabeth Bishop [et al.] New Directions 1987 669p il hardcover o.p. pa $26.95   **861**
    1. Poetry -- By individual authors
    ISBN 978-0-8112-1173-4 pa; 0-8112-1173-8 pa

LC 87-23989

"Dense, weighty, and miraculous, this bilingual edition compresses into one volume all the poems published in book form since 1957. Nearly 200 poems, some newly translated, many new to an English-language edition, conclusively demonstrate Paz's power." Libr J

Includes bibliographical references

The **poems** of Octavio Paz; edited and translated by Eliot Weinberger with additional translations by Elizabeth Bishop, Paul Blackburn, Denise Levertov, Muriel Rukeyser, and Charles Tomlinson. New Directions 2012 606 p. (cloth: acid-free paper) $39.95   **861**
    1. Mexican poetry 2. Poetry -- Collections
    ISBN 0811220435; 9780811220439

LC 2012016228

This book edited and translated by Eliot Weinberger is "the first retrospective collection of [Octavio] Paz's poetry to span his entire writing career. . . . This edition includes many poems that have never been translated into English before, new translations based on Paz's final revisions, and a . . . capsule biography of Paz by Weinberger, as well as notes on the poems in Paz's own words, taken from various interviews he gave throughout his life." (Publisher's note)

Includes bibliographical references and index.

The **Penguin** book of Spanish verse; introduced and edited by J.M. Cohen; with plain prose translations of each poem. 3rd ed; Penguin 1988 xliii, 596p pa $18 **861**
1. Spanish poetry -- Collections
ISBN 978-0-14-058570-4; 0-14-058570-2

LC 88-166999

First published 1956
More than 300 works by 100 poets reflect nine centuries of poetry in Spain.

Then come back; the lost Neruda. Pablo Neruda; translated by Forrest Gander. Copper Canyon Press 2016 160 p. color ill., facimilies (hardback) $23 **861**
1. Poetry -- Collections
ISBN 9781556594946

LC 2015048546

This book, translated by Forrest Gander, presents "Pablo Neruda's lost poems. . . . Originally composed on napkins, playbills, receipts, and notebooks, Neruda's lost poems are full of eros and heartache, complex wordplay and deep wonder. Presented with the Spanish text, full-color reproductions of handwritten poems, and dynamic English translations, [it] simultaneously completes and advances the oeuvre of the world's most beloved poet." (Publisher's note)
Includes bibliographical references.

Torre, Monica de la
Reversible monuments; contemporary Mexican poetry. edited by Mónica de la Torre and Michael Wiegers. Copper Canyon Press 2002 675p pa $20 **861**
1. Mexican poetry -- Collections
ISBN 1-55659-159-4

LC 2002-6189

This bilingual anthology includes 31 contributors, "most writing in Spanish but some in indigenous languages. Spacious and accommodating, this work presents a generous number of gracefully translated poems by each poet, a felicitous in-depth approach that makes this much more than a sampler, and a sound decision given the poet's propensity for long, dreamy poems. Sensuality is ever-present, as is an intimate connection with nature. . . . This is without doubt a landmark volume." Booklist

862   Spanish drama

Calderon de la Barca, Pedro
Life's a dream; a prose translation and critical introduction by Michael Kidd. University Press of Colorado 2004 159p hardcover o.p. pa $13,95 **862**
ISBN 978-0-87081-777-9 pa

LC 2004-10260

17th century Spanish verse play in prose translation. King of Poland tests son, imprisoned from birth because of prophecy, to see if he will become tyrant. Savage at first, Prince later shows true nobility, exposing actual meaning of prophecy.
"Michael Kidd advances the work of two often-exclusive camps of comediantes: scholarship and performance. While his introduction provides ample criticism for the scholar, he successfully presents an accessible script for theatre practitioners looking to enact the story of the play." Bulletin of Hispanic Studies
Includes bibliographical references

Vega, Lope de
Three major plays; translated with an introduction and notes by Gwynne Edwards. Oxford University Press 2008 xli, 300p (Oxford world's classics) pa $14.95 **862**
ISBN 978-0-19-954017-4; 0-19-954017-9

LC 98-26991

Reissue of a title first published 1999
"Fuente Ovejuna , based on Spanish history, and revealing how tyranny leads to rebellion, is perhaps [Vega's] best-known play. The Knight from Olmedo is a moving dramatization of impetuous and youthful passion which ends in death. Punishment without Revenge, Lope's most powerful tragedy, centres on the illicit relationship of a young wife with her stepson and the revenge of a dishonoured husband." Publisher's note
Includes bibliographical references

863   Spanish fiction

Allende, Isabel
My invented country; a nostalgic journey through Chile. translated from the Spanish by Margaret Sayers Peden. Harper-Collins Pubs. 2003 199p map $23.95; pa $13.95 **863**
1. Authors 2. Novelists 3. Dramatists 4. Journalists 5. Authors, Chilean 6. Chile 7. Children's authors
ISBN 0-06-054564-X; 0-06-054567-4 pa

LC 2002-191267

"In this memoir-cum-study of her 'home ground,' the author delves into the history, social mores and idiosyncrasies of Chile, where she was raised, showing, in the process, how that land has served as her muse. . . . This is a reflective book, lacking the pull of Allende's fiction but unearthing intriguing elements of the author's captivating history." Publ Wkly

Galeano, Eduardo, 1940-2015
Hunter of stories; Eduardo Galeano; translated by Mark Fried. Nation Books 2017 xviii, 251 p.p illustrations (hardback) $26 **863**
1. Latin America 2. Literature -- Collections 3. Authors, Uruguayan -- 20th century
ISBN 9781568588322; 9781568589909

LC 2017014189

This book, by Eduardo Galeano, translated by Mark Fried "is a deeply considered collection of [the author's] final musings and stories on history, memory, humor, and tragedy. Written in his signature style-vignettes that fluidly combine dialogue, fables, and anecdotes--every page displays the original thinking and compassion that has earned Galeano decades and continents of renown." (Publisher's note)
"A worthy addition to the celebrated oeuvre of a writer who remains a towering figure both as an artist and a voice of conscience across Latin America and the world." Pub Wkly

864   Spanish essays

Borges, Jorge Luis
★ **Selected** non-fictions; edited by Eliot Weinberger; translated by Esther Allen, Suzanne Jill Levine & Eliot Weinberger. Viking 1999 559p hardcover o.p. pa $20 **864**
ISBN 978-0-14-029011-0 pa; 0-14-029011-7 pa

LC 99-12386

"Shifting effortlessly from Homer to Hitler, from Kafka to King

Kong, these hundred and sixty-one essays, appreciations, prologues, and philosophical investigations are dizzying in scope and dazzling in execution. But it is Borges's dogged pursuit of familiar themes—infinity and eternity, reflexivity and recurrence—which gives this collection its unusual unity and depth." New Yorker

Includes bibliographical references

Fuentes, Carlos

Myself with others; selected essays. Farrar, Straus & Giroux 1988 214p $19.95; pa $18   **864**

ISBN 0-374-21750-5; 0-374-52237-5 pa

LC 87-7448

Essays by the Mexican writer on subjects ranging from the cinema of Buñuel to the literary output of Cervantes, Borges and Garcia Marquez

Paz, Octavio

★ The **labyrinth** of solitude; The other Mexico, Return to the labyrinth of solitude, Mexico and the United States, The philanthropic ogre. Grove Press 1985 398p hardcover o.p. pa $14.50   **864**

1. Mexican national characteristics 2. Mexico -- Civilization

ISBN 978-0-8021-5042-4 pa; 0-8021-5042-X pa

LC 82-47999

The labyrinth of solitude and The other Mexico were first published 1961 and 1972 respectively

In this collection of essays and one interview, Paz explorers the cultural and historical influences on the social behavior of his countrymen

Vargas Llosa, Mario

The **language** of passion; translated by Natasha Wimmer. Farrar, Straus & Giroux 2003 292p $24; pa $14   **864**

ISBN 0-374-18326-0; 0-312-42254-7 pa

LC 2002-37909

"This collection focuses on the essays that appeared during the 1990s, most of which are imbued with a wit and an intellect that make them instantly engaging." Libr J

Includes bibliographical references

868   Spanish miscellaneous writings

Abad, Hector

Oblivion; a memoir. Héctor Abad; translated from the Spanish by Anne McLean and Rosalind Harvey. Farrar, Straus and Giroux 2012 263 p.   **868**

1. Biography 2. Political activists 3. Father-son relationship 4. Physicians -- Colombia -- Biography 5. Political activists -- Crimes against 6. Colombia -- Politics and government -- 1974- 7. Political activists -- Colombia -- Biography 8. Authors, Colombian -- 20th century -- Biography

ISBN 0374223971; 9780374223977

LC 2011045885

This memoir by Héctor Abad describes the life and work of the author's father "Héctor Abad Gómez, a professor and doctor devoted to his family . . . and committed to a better Colombia. The latter aspiration cost him his life when he was assassinated in 1987." Topics include "Gómez's public health and human rights projects" such as founding "the Colombian Institute of Family Wellbeing, which built aqueducts and sewer systems in villages, rural districts, and cities." (Publishers Weekly)

Biron, Rebecca E.

Elena Garro and Mexico's modern dreams; Rebecca E.

Biron. Bucknell University Press 2012 294 p. (Buckell studies in Latin American literature and theory) (cloth: alk. paper) $90   **868**

1. Mexico -- Civilization 2. Modernism in literature 3. Modernism (Literature) -- Mexico 4. National characteristics, Mexican, in literature

ISBN 1611484707; 9781611484700

LC 2012042552

Author Rebecca E. Biron's book focuses on Elena Garro. "The famously scandalous first wife of Nobel Prize winner poet Octavio Paz, and an award-winning author in her own right, Garro constructed a mysterious and often contradictory persona through her very public participation in Mexican political conflicts. . . . Garro's public persona and critical perspective expose the anxieties regarding ethnicity, gender, economic class, and professional identity that define Mexican modernity." (Publisher's note)

Includes bibliographical references and index

869   Literatures of Portuguese and Galician languages

Antunes, Antonio Lobo

The **fat** man and infinity; and other writings. translated with an introduction by Margaret Jull Costa. W. W. Norton & Company 2009 396p il $26.95   **869**

ISBN 978-0-393-06198-7; 0-393-06198-1

LC 2008-41551

This volume "collects the short, impressionistic newspaper columns, or 'cronicas,' that [Antunes] has written for various publications, notably the Portuguese newspaper O Público. Mr. Antunes has played down these columns, referring to them as 'divertissments' written to earn pocket money. But as this book's translator, Margaret Jull Costa, points out, in Portugal these collections 'have enjoyed the kind of popular success his novels never have.' (This book also contains a selection of Mr. Antunes's short stories. . .). Mr. Antunes makes for an unusual newspaper columnist. Jimmy Breslin he's not. His bite-size essays contain no political ruminations and almost nothing about sports, or popular culture, or literary criticism or run-ins with the great and good. Instead they are interior diaries of a kind, most of them imbued with a deep nostalgia for the author's youth." N Y Times Book Rev

Camoes, Luis de

★ **Selected** sonnets; edited and translated by William Baer. Bilingual ed; University of Chicago Press 2005 199p il $26   **869**

1. Poetry -- By individual authors

ISBN 0-226-09266-6

LC 2004-58521

Camões "is Portugal's great sonneteer. He published only one sonnet in his lifetime, and many of doubtful authorship crept into the canon during their first century of great popularity. Baer presents 70 in Portuguese and his own English versions, formally faithful to the originals except that in the octaves Baer uses four (abba, cddc) rather than Camoes' two (abba, abba) rhymes. A sketch of Camoes' amazingly adventurous and colorful life, his works, and his reputation precedes the poems." Booklist

871   Latin poetry

Horace

The **epistles** of Horace; [translated by] David Ferry. Farrar, Straus, and Giroux 2001 203p hardcover o.p. pa $19   **871**

1. Poetry -- By individual authors
ISBN 978-0-374-52852-7 pa; 0-374-52852-7 pa

LC 00-52746

"Ferry takes his bearings from the great blank verse poets of the last two hundred years, especially Frost, and while he manages to be faithful to the meaning, substance and shades, of the Latin original, Ferry achieves through his historical, cultural, and linguistic cross-pollination something more important and lasting than mere translation: he brings to life new as well as old possibilities for poetry in America now." Harvard Rev

Includes bibliographical references

Virgil

The **eclogues** of Virgil; a translation by David Ferry. Farrar, Straus & Giroux 1999 101p hardcover o.p. pa $14   **871**
1. Poetry -- By individual authors
ISBN 978-0-374-52696-2 pa; 0-374-52696-6 pa

LC 98-52547

The Eclogues "comprise not much more than 800 lines in total, but they may be the most influential collection of short poems by one author ever written. . . . It is a conspicuous merit of Ferry's translations that they have a kind of transparency; he does not intrude his style or his personality between the reader and himself. His versions are rather plain, unfussy, and usually of a quiet dignity." New Republic

872   Latin dramatic poetry and drama

Plautus, Titus Maccius

The **pot** of gold, and other plays; [by] Plautus; tr. by E. F. Watling. Penguin Books 1965 267p (Penguin Classics) pa $12   **872**
ISBN 978-0-14-044149-9; 0-14-044149-2

LC 65-8577

Plautus "romanized many of the plots and characters of New Greek Comedy. Through his plays, he introduced to the non-Greek world characters which have since become part of traditional western European comedy, among them the braggard soldier (in his Miles Gloriosus) and the sly servant (in his Pseudolus)." Benet's Reader's Ency. 4th edition

The **rope,** and other plays; [by] Plautus; tr. by E. F. Watling. Penguin Books 1964 284p (Penguin Classics) pa $12   **872**
ISBN 978-0-14-044136-9; 0-14-044136-0

LC 63-2117

Contents: The ghost (Mostellaria); The rope (Rudens); A three-dollar day (Trinummus); and Amphitruo

Virgil

The **Georgics** of Virgil; a translation. a translation [translated] by David Ferry. Farrar, Straus and Giroux 2005 xx, 202p hardcover o.p. pa $14   **872**
ISBN 978-0-374-16131-0 pa; 0-374-16131-9 pa

LC 2004-20023

"Ferry shows tremendous skill with his taut yet pliant pentameter. He also employs demotic and high lyrical diction with equal finesse. His version contains all the freshness of American speech and all the classical poise of the original: it comes across neither as a curatorial act of conservation nor as a modish remake. . . . This is the best poetry of Ancient Rome, rendered by the best translator of modern America." Poetry (Modern Poetry Association)

873   Latin epic poetry and fiction

Ovid

★ **Metamorphoses**; [by] Ovid; translated and with notes by Charles Martin; introduction by Bernard Knox. W.W. Norton & Co 2004 xxvi, 597p $57; pa $17.95   **873**
ISBN 0-393-05810-7; 0-393-32642-X pa

LC 2003-14491

"A series of tales in Latin verse. . . . Dealing with mythological, legendary, and historical figures, they are written in hexameters, in fifteen books, beginning with the creation of the world and ending with the deification of Caesar and the reign of Augustus." Reader's Ency. 4th edition

Includes bibliographical references

Virgil

The **Aeneid**; translated by Robert Fitzgerald. Knopf 1992 xxvii,483 (Everyman's library) $20   **873**
1. Poetry -- By individual authors
ISBN 978-0-679-41335-6; 0-679-41335-9

LC 91-58698

This translation first published 1983 by Random House

"Fitzgerald's is so decisively the best modern Aeneid that it is unthinkable anyone will want to use any other version for a long time to come. Latinists, as they read it, will be led to consider their original afresh. Those without Latin are going to find, to their surprise, and I hope their pleasure, that the poem is still as good as anyone ever said it was." N Y Rev Books

874   Latin lyric poetry

Catullus, Gaius Valerius

★ The **poems** of Catullus; a bilingual edition. translated, with commentary by Peter Green. University of California Press 2005 339p (Joan Palevsky imprint in classical literature) $24.95   **874**
1. Poetry -- By individual authors
ISBN 0-520-24264-5

LC 2004-13920

This is "a translation of the complete poems of Catullus, with facing Latin original and extensive notes. . . . Green's translation should encourage readers of all kinds to read or reread Catullus, one of the greatest and most influential of all classical poets." New Repub

Horace

The **odes** of Horace; a translation by David Ferry. Farrar, Straus & Giroux 1997 343p hardcover o.p. pa $28   **874**
1. Poetry -- By individual authors
ISBN 978-0-374-52572-9 pa; 0-374-52572-2 pa

LC 97-9483

Ferry "wisely does not try to reproduce Horace's meters in English. . . . And he often rearranges Horace's material to fit the run of his own verse, sometimes to stunning effect. . . . This is a Horace for our times." N Y Rev Books

875   Latin speeches

Cicero, Marcus Tullius

Political speeches; [by] Cicero; translated with introductions and notes by D.H. Berry. Oxford University Press 2006

xl, 345p map pa $13.95 **875**
1. Speeches 2. Rome -- History
ISBN 978-0-19-283266-5; 0-19-283266-2

LC 2005-20919

"Cicero (106-43 BC) was the greatest orator of the ancient world and a leading politician of the closing era of the Roman republic. This book presents nine speeches which reflect the development, variety, and drama of his political career,among them two speeches from his prosecution of Verres, a corrupt and cruel governor of Sicily; four speeches against the conspirator Catiline; and the Second Philippic , the famous denunciation of Mark Antony which cost Cicero his life. Also included are On the Command of Gnaeus Pompeius , in which he praises the military successes of Pompey, and For Marcellus , a panegyric in praise of the dictator Julius Caesar." Publisher's note

Includes bibliographical references

877 Latin humor and satire

Erasmus, Desiderius
Praise of folly; and, Letter to Maarten Van Dorp, 1515. [by] Erasmus of Rotterdam; translated by Betty Radice; with an introduction and notes by A.H.T. Levi. Penguin Books 1993 lvi, 188p (Penguin classics) pa $13 **877**
ISBN 978-014-044608-1; 0-14-044608-7

LC 94-142502

A "satirical monologue in Latin. . . . Folly praises herself and proclaims her superiority over Wisdom. The author's argument, of course, is 'that it is folly not to see things as they really are; scholars should not abandon ideals just because they cannot be fully realized but should apply their learning and reason as best they can to daily living.'" Reader's Adviser

Juvenal
The **sixteen** satires; translated with an introduction and notes by Peter Green. 3rd ed; Penguin Books 1999 lxviii, 252p (Penguin classics) pa $13 **877**
ISBN 978-0-14-044704-0; 0-14-044704-0

LC 99-987049

First published 1967

"The sixteen 'Satires' of Juvenal, which contain a vivid picture of contemporary Rome under the Empire, have seldom been equalled as biting diatribes. . . . Juvenal's invectives in powerful hexameters, exact and epigrammatic, were aimed at lax and luxurious society, tyranny, criminal excesses, and the immorality of women." Reader's Adviser

878 Latin miscellaneous writings

Cicero, Marcus Tullius
On the good life; translated with an introduction by Michael Grant. Penguin Books 1971 382p map (Penguin classics) pa $16 **878**
1. Ethics
ISBN 978-0-14-044244-1; 0-14-044244-8

LC 77-30399

For "Roman orator and statesman Cicero, 'the good life' was at once a life of contentment and one of moral virtue and the two were inescapably intertwined. This volume brings together a wide range of his reflections upon the importance of moral integrity in the search for happiness. . . . Cicero presents his views upon the significance of friendship and duty to state and family, and outlines a clear system of practical ethics."

Publisher's note

Martial
Epigrams; selected and translated by James Michie; introduction by Shadi Bartsch. Modern Library 2002 xxxiv, 199p (Modern Library classics) pa $14.95 **878**
1. Epigrams
ISBN 978-0-375-76042-6; 0-375-76042-3

LC 2002-22343

First published 1972

Michie "has translated a selection of the epigrams—about one tenth of what Martial wrote. He has the text on the facing page—a great advantage if you can read Latin—an Introduction [and] Notes. . . . [He] uses rhyme, and makes his Martial much more like the English idea of an epigram than like the epigrams in the Greek Anthology. There isn't much pure humor in Latin literature (as opposed to waspishness and scurrility) but Martial is often very funny." Encounter (London, England)

Includes bibliographical references

Suetonius Tranquillus, C.
★ The **twelve** Caesars; {by} Gaius Suetonius Tranquillus; translated by Robert Graves; revised with an introduction by Michael Grant. Penguin Bks. 2003 363p maps pa $14 **878**
1. Emperors 2. Rome -- History 3. Emperors -- Rome
ISBN 0-14-044921-3

LC 2003-267782

A reissue with new Chronology and updated further reading of the translation published 1957

"A detailed account of the life and times of the first twelve emperors from Caesar to Domitian." Reader's Ency. 4th edition

Includes bibliographical references

Tacitus, Cornelius
Complete works of Tacitus; translated from the Latin by Alfred John Church and William Jackson Brodribb; edited and with an introduction by Moses Hadas. McGraw-Hill 1964 773p il pa $14.75 **878**
1. Generals 2. Rome -- History 3. Colonial administrators 4. Germany -- History -- 0-1517
ISBN 0-07-553639-0; 978-0-07-553639-0

First published 1942 by Modern Lib.

Contains: The annals; The history; The life of Cnaeus Julius Agricola; Germany and its tribes; A dialogue on oratory

880 Classical Greek literature and literatures of related Hellenic languages

Jenkyns, Richard
★ **Classical** literature; an epic journey from homer to virgil and beyond. Richard Jenkyns. Basic Books 2015 288 p. (hardcover) $27.99 **880**
1. Epic poetry 2. Romance language literature
ISBN 0465097979; 9780465097975

LC 2015953494

In this book, author "Richard Jenkyns explores a thousand years of classical civilization, carrying readers from the depths of the Greek dark ages through the glittering heights of Rome's empire. Jenkyns begins with Homer and the birth of epic poetry before exploring the hypnotic poetry of Pindar, Sappho, and others from the Greek dark ages." (Publisher's note)

"A rich, witty, perceptive, and brief account of the Greek and Latin classics and their importance, both in themselves and in their enduring influence on the Western world. One of the best introductions available to the general reader." LJ

Includes bibliographical references (pages 247-259) and index.

★   The **Oxford** companion to classical literature; edited by M.C. Howatson. 3rd ed.; Oxford University Press 2011 un map $65   **880**

1. Reference books 2. Classical literature -- Dictionaries
ISBN 978-0-19-954854-5
First published 1937 under the editorship of Sir Paul Harvey

This work "covers classical literature from the appearance of the Greeks, around 2200 B.C., to the close of the Athenian philosophy schools in A.D. 529. It includes articles on authors, major works, historical notables, mythological figures, and topics of literary significance. Short summaries of major works, chronologies, charts, and maps are special features." Nichols. Guide to Ref Books for Sch Media Cent. 4th edition

Thorburn, John E.

The **Facts** on File companion to classical drama. Facts on File 2005 680p map (Facts on File library of world literature) $71.50   **880**

1. Reference books 2. Classical drama -- Encyclopedias
ISBN 0-8160-5202-6

LC 2004-16803

"It is difficult to think of any other resource quite this thorough that combines all of Greek and Roman drama into a convenient single-volume publication." Libr J

Includes bibliographical references

881   Classical Greek poetry

Apollonius

The **voyage** of Argo: the Argonautica; translated with an introd. by E.V. Rieu. 2nd ed; Penguin Books 1971 213p map (Penguin Classics) pa $14   **881**

1. Argonauts (Greek mythology) 2. Poetry -- By individual authors
ISBN 978-0-14-044085-0; 0-14-044085-0
This translation first published 1959

An epic account of Jason's voyage in quest of the Golden Fleece written in the third century B.C.

882   Classical Greek dramatic poetry and drama

Aeschylus

Aeschylus; edited by David Grene and Richmond Lattimore. University of Chicago Press 1992 352p (Complete Greek tragedies) $55   **882**

ISBN 978-0-226-30764-0; 0-226-30764-6
Contents: Agamemnon; Libation bearers; Eumenides; Suppliant maidens; Persians; Seven against Thebes; Prometheus bound

The **Oresteia**; translated by Alan Shapiro and Peter Burian. Oxford University Press 2003 285p (The Greek tragedy in new translations) hardcover o.p. pa $11.95   **882**

ISBN 978-0-19-513592-3 pa; 0-19-513592-X pa

LC 2002-66272

"The collaboration of poet and scholar . . . produces a language that is easy to read and easy to speak." Libr J

Includes bibliographical references

Aristophanes

The **complete** plays; the new translations by Paul Roche. New American Library 2005 715p pa $17   **882**

1. Athens (Greece) -- Drama.
ISBN 978-0-451-21409-6; 0-451-21409-9

LC 2004-56681

Contents: Acharnians; Knights; Clouds; Wasps; Peace; Birds; Lysistrata; Women at Thesmophoria festival; Frogs; A parliament of women; Plutus (Wealth)

Euripides

Euripides; edited by David Grene and Richmond Lattimore. University of Chicago Press 1992 665p (Complete Greek tragedies) $65   **882**

ISBN 978-0-226-30766-4; 0-226-30766-2
First published 1942

Contents: Alcestis; Medea; Heracleidae; Hippolytus; Cyclops; Heracles; Iphigenia in Tauris; Helen; Hecuba; Andromache; The Trojan women

Euripides [2] edited by David Grene and Richmond Lattimore. University of Chicago Press 1992 314p (Complete Greek tragedies) $44   **882**

ISBN 978-0-226-30767-1; 0-226-30767-0
First published 1958

Contents: Ion; Rhesus; The suppliant women; Orestes; Iphigenia in Aulis; Electra; The Phoenician women; The Bacchae

The **Greek** plays; sixteen plays by Aeschylus, Sophocles, and Euripides. edited by Mary Lefkowitz and James Romm. Random House Inc 2017 864 p. $25   **882**

1. Anthologies 2. Stage adaptations 3. Greek drama -- Collections
ISBN 0812983092; 9780812983098

This book, edited by Mary Lefkowitz and James Romm, presents "a landmark anthology of the masterpieces of Greek drama, featuring all-new, highly accessible translations of some of the world's most beloved plays. . . . [It] also offers short biographies of the playwrights, enlightening and clarifying introductions to the plays, and helpful annotations at the bottom of each page." (Publisher's note)

Seneca, Lucius Annaeus

Four tragedies, and Octavia; [by] Seneca; tr. with an introduction by E. F. Watling. Penguin Books 1966 318p (Penguin Classics) pa $14   **882**

ISBN 978-0-14-044174-1; 0-12-044174-3

LC 66-8618

"Although their themes are borrowed from Greek drama, these exuberant and often macabre plays focus on action rather than moral concerns and are strikingly different in style from Seneca's prose writing." Publisher's note

Sophocles

Sophocles; edited by David Grene and Richmond Lattimore. University of Chicago Press 1992 466p (Complete Greek tragedies) $50   **882**

ISBN 978-0-226-30765-7; 0-226-30765-4
Contents: Oedipus the King; Oedipus at Colonus; Antigone; Ajax; The women of Trachis; Electra; Philoctetes

The **Theban** plays of Sophocles; translated by David R. Slavitt. Yale University Press 2007 237p $28   **882**
ISBN 978-0-300-11776-9; 0-300-11776-0
LC 2006-26965

"This version is meant to be an updated one, and the easy currency of its diction is a great virtue. The natural cadences of its free verse slide smoothly and sometimes beautifully into the ear." Claremont Rev Books

Includes bibliographical references

883   Classical Greek epic poetry and fiction

Alexander, Caroline

The **war** that killed Achilles; the true story of Homer's Iliad and the Trojan War. Viking 2009 296p map $26.95   **883**
1. Poets 2. Authors 3. Trojan War 4. War in literature
ISBN 978-0-670-02112-3; 0-670-02112-1
LC 2009-20160

"In its bones and sinews, the book is a nobly bold, even rousing, venture, a read-through of the 'Iliad,' from beginning to end, always with a sharp eye to half a century of revealing scholarship, by great Hellenists like Gregory Nagy, Jasper Griffin, M.L. West and many others. The book's best ideas won't be new to readers versed in this work, but it would be hard to find a faster, livelier, more compact introduction to such a great range of recent Iliadic explorations." N Y Times Book Rev

Includes bibliographical references

Homer

The **Iliad**; translated by Robert Fitzgerald. Knopf 1992 xxi, 594p (Everyman's library) $22   **883**
1. Poetry -- By individual authors
ISBN 978-0-679-41075-1; 0-679-41075-9
LC 91-53222

This translation first published 1974 by Anchor Press/Doubleday
Homer's epic of the Trojan War in blank verse

"Fitzgerald has solved virtually every problem that has plagued translators of Homer. The narrative runs, the dialogue speaks, the military action is clear, and the repetitive epithets become useful text rather than exotic relics. Aside from the ability to write poetry, which is basic to the undertaking, Mr. Fitzgerald's success derives from the use of a predominantly Anglo-Saxon vocabulary, a concentration on specific meanings, and an occasional arbitrary, but highly effective, substitution of implication for literal sense." Atlantic

Iliad; translated by Stanley Lombardo; introduction by Sheila Murnaghan. Hackett 1997 516p $37.95; pa $12.95   **883**
1. Poetry -- By individual authors
ISBN 978-0-87220-353-2; 0-87220-353-0; 978-0-87220-352-5 pa; 0-87220-352-2 pa
LC 96-53368

This is a translation from the Greek of the epic poem on the Trojan War

"Lombardo manages to be respectful of Homer's dire spirit while providing on nearly every page some wonderfully fresh refashioning of his Greek. The result is a vivid and sometimes disarmingly hard-bitten reworking of a great classic. . . . Not all of Lombardo's gambles pay off, and his attention-grabbing colloquialisms sometimes undermine the force of the original. . . . Still, the success of so many of Lombardo's choices more than makes up for the false notes." N Y Times Book Rev

The **Iliad**; translated by Robert Fagles; introduction and

notes by Bernard Knox. Viking 1990 683p $40; pa $15.95 **883**
1. Poetry -- By individual authors
ISBN 978-0-670-83510-2; 978-0-14-027536-0 pa
LC 89-70695

Homer's epic of the Trojan War.

"Fagles gives us a stark and terrible poem, an Iliad about, as its first word announces, rage. He conveys, far better than either Lattimore or Fitzgerald, the psychological experience of combat and war." Classical World

Odyssey; translated by Stanley Lombardo; introduction by Sheila Murnaghan. Hackett 2000 414p il $37.95; pa $12.95   **883**
1. Poetry -- By individual authors
ISBN 978-0-87220-485-0; 0-87220-485-5; 978-0-87220-484-3 pa; 0-87220-484-7 pa
LC 99-54175

A retelling of Homer's epic that describes the wanderings of Odysseus after the fall of Troy.

Lombardo "has brought his laconic wit and love of the ribald, as well as his clever use of idiomatic American slang, to his version of the 'Odyssey.' His carefully honed syntax gives the narrative energy and a whirlwind pace. The lines, rhythmic and clipped, have the tautness and force of Odysseus' bow." N Y Times Book Rev

Includes bibliographical references

The **Odyssey**; translated by Robert Fagles; introduction and notes by Bernard Knox. Viking 1996 541p $35; pa $16 **883**
1. Poetry -- By individual authors
ISBN 978-0-670-82162-4; 978-0-14-026886-7 pa
LC 96-17280

This is a verse translation of Homer's epic poem

"Fagles' Odyssey is the one to put into the hands of younger, first-time readers, not least because of its paucity of notes, which, though sometimes frustrating, is a sign that translation has been used to do the work of explanation. Altogether, an outstanding piece of work." Booklist

Includes bibliographical references

The **Odyssey**; Homer; translated, with an introduction and notes, by Stephen Mitchell. Atria Books 2013 xlv, 375 p.p map (hdbk.) $35   **883**
1. Greek literature
ISBN 1451674171; 9781451674170
LC 2012050572

This version of Homer's work, translated by Stephen Mitchell, "brings Odysseus and his adventures vividly to life. . . . One-eyed maneating giants; irresistibly seductive sirens; shipwrecks and narrow escapes; princesses and monsters; ghosts sipping blood at the Underworld's portal, desperate for a chance to speak to the living; and the final destruction of all Odysseus's enemies in the banquet hall." (Publisher's note)

"Employing the five-beat, minimally iambic line he used for his translation of The Iliad (2011), Mitchell retells the first, still greatest adventure story in Western literature with the same clarity, sweep, and force." Booklist

Includes bibliographical references

Homer's The Iliad and The Odyssey; a biography. Atlantic Monthly Press 2008 285p (Books that changed the world) $19.95   **883**
1. Poets 2. Authors 3. Epic poetry

ISBN 978-0-87113-976-4; 0-87113-976-6

First published 2007 in the United Kingdom

A "study of the influence of The Iliad and The Odyssey on Western literature. First describing the two epics and the Homer question, Manguel then compares various translations in English, Spanish, French, and German, a move that brings out the complexities and richness of Homer's language. Does the poet sing of the rage, wrath, anger, rancor, or mania of Achilles? Then, following a more or less chronological progression, Manguel surveys the various shifting interpretations of the epics from Plato and Virgil to the present, including extended discussions of Derek Walcott, Timothy Findley, and Jorge Luis Borges. Highly recommended for general readers." Libr J

Nicolson, Adam

Why Homer matters; by Adam Nicolson. Henry Holt & Co 2014 320 p. 8 plates; color ills., maps (hardcover) $30   **883**
1. Epic poetry 2. Greek poetry -- History and criticism 3. Landscapes -- Europe 4. Europe -- Description and travel 5. Epic poetry, Greek -- History and criticism
ISBN 1627791795; 9781627791793

LC 2014006763

In this book, author Adam Nicolson, "sees the Iliad and the Odyssey as the foundation myths of Greek-- and our-- consciousness, collapsing the passage of 4,000 years and making the distant past of the Mediterranean world as immediate to us as the events of our own time. . . . [The book] is a magical journey of discovery across wide stretches of the past, sewn together by the poems themselves and their metaphors of life and trouble." (Publisher's note)

"Nicolson writes in a clear, fluid prose with apparently effortless ease; his vivid descriptions of landscapes and archaeological remains and his passionate engagement with history make this book a page-turner. Classicists will no doubt find fault with some of Nicholson's statements, but they will also be grateful to the author for explaining to the larger public in such an appealing fashion why Homer is not only unique but also relevant and necessary today. Summing Up: Highly recommended. General readers." Choice

Includes bibliographical references and index

884   Classical Greek lyric poetry

Pindar

★ The **complete** odes of Pindar; translated by Anthony Verity; with an introduction and notes by Stephen Instone. Oxford University Press 2007 xxvii, 186p (Oxford world's classics) pa $15.95   **884**
1. Poetry -- By individual authors
ISBN 978-0-19-280553-9; 0-19-280553-3

LC 2006-39673

The Odes (Epinicia) celebrated victories in the great national games, and were accompanied by music, which is lost to us. The fragments represent almost every kind of lyric poem.

"Since Pindar's Epinicia are generally concerned with mythical subjects, reserving praise of the mortal victor for the end of the ode, his works are a fine source of legend." Reader's Ency. 4th edition

Sappho

★ **If** not, winter; fragments of Sappho. translated by Anne Carson. Knopf 2002 397p $27.50; pa $14   **884**
1. Poetry -- By individual authors
ISBN 0-375-41067-8; 0-375-72451-6 pa

LC 2001-50247 "Carson's translation follows

Sappho's diction and form . . . closely and includes the Greek original on the facing page. Much of what survives of Sappho are fragments, often just a stray word, phrase, or even a few letters. Like many modern poets, Carson deploys these on the blank page, letting their suggestiveness fill the gaps and create whole lyrics in the imagination of the readers." Libr J

Includes bibliographical references

888   Classical Greek miscellaneous writings

Plato

The **collected** dialogues of Plato, including the letters; edited by Edith Hamilton and Huntington Cairns. With introd. and prefatory notes. Princeton University Press 1961 xxv, 1743p (Bollingen series) $49.50   **888**
ISBN 978-0-691-09718-3; 0-691-09718-6

"This elegant edition contains many of the best and most readable English translations of the Dialogues and Letters. . . . Judiciously edited, beautifully printed." Rev of Metaphysics

The **republic**; edited by G.R.F. Ferrari; translated by Tom Griffith. Cambridge Univ. Press 2000 xlviii, 382p (Cambridge texts in the history of political thought) $38; pa $11   **888**
1. Utopias 2. Political science
ISBN 0-521-48173-2; 0-521-48443-X pa

LC 00-24471

Griffith's "aim was to translate the Greek text as if it were a conversation, and he has succeeded admirably. The text does indeed flow like a conversation, with the entire back-and-forth interaction that such exchanges involve. . . . [He] has also written a very useful introduction that places the work in a historical context and provides a glossary that will help readers identify individuals and places mentioned in the work." Libr J

Includes bibliographical references

889   Modern Greek literature

Cavafy, Constantine P.

★ **Collected** poems; [by] C.P. Cavafy; translated, with introduction and commentary, by Daniel Mendelsohn. Alfred A. Knopf 2009 547p $35   **889**
1. Poetry -- By individual authors
ISBN 978-0-375-40096-4; 0-375-40096-6

LC 2008-34718

"Mendelsohn drew together his interests in ancient history, literature, gay life and culture, and beautiful language to produce the finest, most readable version of the modern Greek poet Cavafy (1863-1933) to come along in decades." Publ Wkly

★ The **unfinished** poems; [by] C.P. Cavafy; the first English translation, with introduction and commentary, by Daniel Mendelsohn. Alfred A. Knopf 2009 121p $30   **889**
1. Poetry -- By individual authors
ISBN 978-0-307-26546-3; 0-307-26546-3

LC 2008-34717

Original Greek edition, 1994

This book "contains the first English versions of 30 poems that Cavafy had not finished entirely to his satisfaction when he died. All are in his most developed manner, in which apprehension of the past is so rich and powerful as to expunge mere nostalgia. They are historical vignettes of the declines of Alexander's Hellenistic hegemony, imperial

Rome, and the Byzantine Empire; and glowing memories, triggered by news items, drink, or moonlight, of decades-old homosexual rapture. . . . One could become well informed about centuries of seldom-taught history just by reading the notes, though yet more so by absorbing the poems, as well." Booklist

Elytes, Odysseus

The **collected** poems of Odysseus Elytis; translated by Jeffrey Carson and Nikos Sarris; introduction and notes by Jeffrey Carson. Rev and expanded ed; Johns Hopkins University Press 2005 $60 **889**

1. Poetry -- By individual authors
ISBN 0-8018-8045-9

LC 2004-13496

First published 1997

"The work of 1979 Nobel Prize winner Elytis (1911-96) has the quality of a cathedral or epic—vast in scope yet richly decorated. This excellent 'complete' collected edition (it omits unpublished poems) testifies to the bountiful, sincere nature of Elytis's voice as patriot and poet. . . . Containing informative annotations, a chronology, an autobiographical essay, and the author's Nobel address, this work is a valuable resource on international poetry." Libr J

Includes bibliographical references

891 East Indo-European and Celtic literatures

Barks, Coleman

Rumi: the big red book; the great masterpiece celebrating mystical love and friendship. the collected translations of Coleman Barks, based on the work of John Moyne ... [et al.] HarperOne 2010 492p $29.95; ebook $14.99 **891**

1. Poetry -- By individual authors
ISBN 978-0-06-190582-7; 978-0-06-202078-9 ebook

LC 2010-7895

This is "a vast collection centering on Shams Tabrizi, a wandering mystic who transformed Rumi's life. Rumi was already renowned when Shams arrived in Konya, in today's Turkey, having wandered for years searching for someone with a soul as profound as his own with whom to share 'sobbet,' a mystical conversation about God and love. Rumi and Shams inspired each other for several years, until Shams mysteriously disappeared. He lives on in Rumi's searching poems. . . . Richly sensual yet never flowery, Barks' language emphasizes Rumi's embodied spirituality in a book to savor." Booklist

Includes bibliographical references

Firdawsi

★ **Shahnameh**; the Persian book of kings. [by] Abolqasem Ferdowsi; translated by Dick Davis; with a foreword by Azar Nafisi. Viking 2006 xxxvii, 886p il $45 **891**

ISBN 0-670-03485-1

LC 2005-42352

"Unlike Western epics that grasp the events of a single generation, whether of men or angels, Persia's Book of Kings encompasses whole ages of the world, chronicling the stratagems of Kings and heroes as real as Alexander the Great and as legendary as Rostam. . . . Action, myth, and history fairly fly off the page, for Davis renders Ferdowsi's 50,000 sesquipedalian lines of poetry as a prose narrative that here and there erupts into sonnet-sized snatches of verse. The scheme works brilliantly. Repeated for pages on end, Ferdowsi's lines, each longer than an heroic couplet, breed longueurs, but Davis's carefully rendered snatches of the best classic Farsi poetry illuminate the English text like so many Persian

miniatures." New Criterion

Hafiz

The **gift**; poems by the great Sufi master. translated by Daniel James Ladinsky. Penguin/Arkana 1999 333p pa $16 **891**

1. Poetry -- By individual authors
ISBN 978-0-14-019581-1; 0-14-019581-5

LC 99-10920

"Less well known in the U.S. than his Sufi predecessor, Rumi, Hafiz (Shams-ud-din Muhammad) is also worthy of attention, and Ladinsky's free translations should help see that he gets it. Hafiz is so beloved in Iran that he outsells the Koran. Many know his verses by heart and recite them with gusto. And gusto is appropriate to this passionate, earthy poet who melds mind, spirit, and body in each of his usually brief pensees. Ladinsky has deliberately chosen a loose and colloquial tone for this collection, which might grate on the nerves of purists but makes Hafiz come vividly alive for the average reader." Booklist

I am the beggar of the world; landays from contemporary Afghanistan. translated and presented by Eliza Griswold; photographs by Seamus Murphy. Farrar Straus & Giroux 2014 160 p. illustrations (hardcover) $24 **891**

1. Afghan literature 2. Poetry -- Collections 3. Poetry -- Women authors -- Collections 4. Folk poetry, Pushto -- Translations into English 5. Pushto poetry -- 20th century -- Translations into English 6. Pushto poetry -- Women authors -- Translations into English
ISBN 0374191875; 9780374191870

LC 2013035179

Translated by Eliza Griswold, with photographs by Seamus Murphy, this book is a "collection of clandestine poems by Afghan women. . . . War, separation, homeland, love--these are the subjects of landays, which are brutal and spare, can be remixed like rap, and are powerful in that they make no attempts to be literary." (Publisher's note)

"Griswold's selections illustrate the rich potential of this poetic form, at once contemporary and timeless. Murphy's stunning photographs complement the text perfectly." Booklist

Jalal al-Din Rumi

The **essential** Rumi; translated by Coleman Barks, with John Moyne, A.A. Arberry, Reynold Nicholson. Harper 1995 302p $23.95; pa $14.95 **891**

1. Poetry -- By individual authors
ISBN 978-0-06-250958-1; 0-06-250958-6; 978-0-06-250959-8 pa; 0-06-250959-4 pa

LC 94-44995

A collection of ecstatic verse by the 13th-century Sufi mystic

Narayan, R. K.

★ The **Ramayana**; a shortened modern prose version of the Indian epic (suggested by the Tamil version of Kamban) introduction by Pankaj Mishra. Penguin Books 2006 157p (Penguin classics) pa $13 **891**

ISBN 0-14-303967-9

LC 2006-45201

First published 1972

A retelling of Prince Rama's courtship of the fourteen-year-old Sita, their exile, Sita's abduction, the search, and the great battle with her abductor Ravana, involving a pantheon of gods, heroes, and evil spirits.

Persian poets; selected and edited by Peter Washington. Knopf 2000 254p (Everyman's library pocket poets) $12.50 **891**

1. Persian poetry -- Collections

ISBN 978-0-375-41126-7

Includes works by Omar, Sanai, Attar, Rumi, Saadi, Hafez, and Jami

Tagore, Rabindranath

Selected poems; translated by William Radice. Penguin Books 2005 202p (Penguin classics) pa $14   **891**

1. Poetry -- By individual authors

ISBN 978-0-14-044988-4

"This collection offers a wide array of Tagore's poems from 1882 to 1941, plus textual notes and other scholarly extras." Libr J

891.6   Celtic literatures

Tain bo Cuailnge

The **Tain**; translated from the Irish epic Tain Bo Cuailnge. [translated] by Thomas Kinsella; with brush drawings by Louis le Brocquy. Oxford University Press 2002 282p il map pa $19.95   **891.6**

ISBN 0-19-280373-5

LC 2002-726950

This translation first published 1969

This Irish epic is the "centerpiece of the eighth-century Ulster cycle of heroic tales. . . . [This] translation is based on the partial texts in two medieval manuscripts, with elements from other versions. This edition includes a group of related stories which prepare for the action of the Tain." Publisher's note

Includes bibliographical references

891.7   Russian literature and related East Slavic literatures

Akhmatova, Anna Andreevna

Poems; [by] Akhmatova; translated by D.M. Thomas. New expanded ed.; Knopf 2006 6p (Everyman's library pocket poets) $12.50   **891.7**

1. Poetry -- By individual authors

ISBN 978-0-307-26424-4; 0-307-26424-6

LC 2006-297217

First published 1985 in the United Kingdom with title: You will hear thunder

A representative selection of material from all her major works—including "Requiem" commemorating the victims of Stalin's terror.

Batuman, Elif

The **possessed**; adventures with Russian books and the people who read them. Farrar, Straus and Giroux 2010 296p pa $15   **891.7**

1. Russian literature -- History and criticism

ISBN 978-0-374-53218-5; 0-374-53218-4

LC 2009-25416

In this book, the author "makes you look at Russian literature from a fresh perspective, using an unusual blend of memoir and travelogue as she delves into the lives and personalities of such Russian literary giants as Isaac Babel, Fyodor Dostoevsky and Leo Tolstoy. Many of the chapters are extensions of pieces Batuman first wrote for The New Yorker and n+1 and range geographically from Palo Alto, Calif., where Batuman managed to lose one of Babel's daughters at the local airport, to Uzbekistan, where Batuman spent a few months studying Uzbek. In a sense, the details of Batuman's essays are less significant than the tone.

She cruises through minor crises with an air of detached amusement, eye focused on the little absurdities that make travel—and people—fun." Cleveland Plain Dealer

Includes bibliographical references

Brodsky, Joseph

★ **Collected** poems in English, 1972-1999; edited by Ann Kjellberg. Farrar, Straus & Giroux 2000 539p $30; pa $18   **891.7**

1. Poetry -- By individual authors

ISBN 0-374-12545-7; 0-374-52838-1 pa

LC 00-21059

This volume "gathers all the poetry in English Brodsky originally saw through to press in books (or had earmarked for eventual publication), including Russian poems he translated or co-translated. Originally Russian verse from the '60s and '70s gives way to the later, sometimes lighter, work of his last two decades, when he found a second home in the speech of his adoptive country." Publ Wkly

Callow, Philip

Chekhov, the hidden ground; a biography. Dee, I.R. 1998 428p il $30; pa $18.95   **891.7**

1. Authors 2. Dramatists 3. Physicians 4. Short story writers

ISBN 1-56663-187-4; 1-56663-395-8 pa

LC 97-46679

"Callow sees Chekhov as distant in virtually all his relationships, with romantic disillusionment and the search for intimacy recurring themes in his writing. He argues persuasively that while Chekhov's art is resplendent with human emotion, his own life was strangely cold and remote. . . . Not strictly a literary biography, this book is particularly effective in discussing Chekhov's work as it relates to his life." Libr J

Includes bibliographical references

Chekhov, Anton Pavlovich

Chekhov; the four major plays. in new translations by Curt Columbus. Ivan R. Dee 2005 294p pa $15.95   **891.7**

ISBN 978-1-56663-626-1; 1-56663-626-4

LC 2004-48612

"Columbus's translation triumphs through its clarity and consistent use of the active voice." Chicago Reader

The **complete** plays; [by] Anton Chekhov; translated, edited, and annotated by Laurence Senelick. W. W. Norton 2006 lx, 1060p pa $22.95   **891.7**

ISBN 978-0-393-04885-8; 0-393-04885-3; 978-0-393-33069-4 pa; 0-393-33069-9 pa

LC 2005-24362

"This volume contains work never previously translated, including the newly discovered farce The Power of Hypnotism, the first version of Ivanov, Chekhov's early humorous dialogues, and a description of lost plays and those Chekhov intended to write but never did." Publisher's note

The **portable** Chekhov; edited and with an introduction by Avrahm Yarmolinsky. Viking 1947 631p hardcover o.p. pa $17   **891.7**

ISBN 0-14-015035-8 pa

This collection contains "two plays, 'The Cherry Orchard' and 'The Boor,' 28 short stories and selections from Chekhov's letters." Publ Wkly

Malcolm, Janet

Reading Chekhov; a critical journey. Random House 2001

209p hardcover o.p. pa $13.95 **891.7**
1. Authors 2. Dramatists 3. Physicians 4. Short story writers
ISBN 0-375-50668-3; 0-375-76106-3 pa

LC 2001-19585

"The author's pilgrimage to Chekhov's Russia—Moscow, St. Petersburg, the gardens of his villa in Yalta—is a reunion with this most reticent of literary fathers. Malcolm analyzes the transformations that Chekhov grants his redeemable roués and guileless heroines, and illuminates the hidden surreality and waywardness of his realism." New Yorker

Includes bibliographical references

Mandelstam, Osip

The **selected** poems of Osip Mandelstam; translated by Clarence Brown and W.S. Merwin. New York Review Books 2004 167p (New York Review Books classics) pa $14.95 **891.7**
1. Poetry -- By individual authors
ISBN 978-1-59017-091-1; 1-59017-091-1

LC 2004-14656

First published 1974 by Atheneum

"The Brown/Merwin versions represent a sensitive and sensible selection of Mandelstam's poetry. The translations do not attempt to imitate Mandelstam's fluid syntax or subtle sound play. But they are honest representations of Mandelstam's themes and recurrent imagery and many of them, particularly certain of the poems in the section 'Poems of the Thirties,' come across as fine English poems." Libr J

Nabokov, Vladimir Vladimirovich

Lectures on Russian literature; edited with an introduction by Fredson Bowers. Harcourt Brace Jovanovich 1981 324p il hardcover o.p. pa $16 **891.7**
1. Authors 2. Novelists 3. Dramatists 4. Physicians 5. Communism and literature 6. Memoirists 7. Short story writers 8. Writers on religion 9. Russian literature -- History and criticism
ISBN 0-15-602776-3 pa
Companion volume Lectures on literature

This book is "derived from notes Nabokov made for his literature classes at Wellesley and Cornell. Included are chapters on Gogol, Turgenev, Dostoevsky, Tolstoy, Chekhov, and Gorki, as well as several miscellaneous essays on censorship and the art of translation." Libr J

Popoff, Alexandra

The **wives**; The Women Behind Russia's Literary Giants. Alexandra Popoff. Pegasus Books 2012 332 p. $27.95 **891.7**
1. Wives 2. Authorship 3. Authors, Russian
ISBN 1605983667; 9781605983660

This book, by Alexandra Popoff, explores the "women behind the greatest works of Russian literature. . . . From Sophia Tolstoy to Vera Nabokov, . . . Anna Dostevsky, and Natalya Solzhenitsyn, these women ranged from stenographers and typists to editors, researchers, translators, and even publishers. Living under restrictive regimes, many of these women battled censorship and preserved the writers' illicit archives, often risking their own lives to do so." (Publisher's note)

Tolstaia, Tat'iana

Pushkin's children; writings on Russia and Russians. [by] Tatyana Tolstaya; translated by Jamey Gambrell. Houghton Mifflin 2003 242p pa $15 **891.7**
1. Poets 2. Authors 3. Novelists 4. Presidents 5. Prime ministers 6. Political prisoners 7. Cabinet members 8. Communist leaders 9. Nonfiction writers 10. Short story writers 11. Writers on politics 12. Nobel laureates for peace 13. Nobel laureates for literature 14. Russia -- Politics and government

ISBN 0-618-12500-0

LC 2002-27610

"Tolstaya's essays in this compact, historically significant volume offer a fascinating, highly intelligent analysis of Russian society and politics." Publ Wkly

Tsvetaeva, Marina Ivanovna

Selected poems; [by] Marina Tsvetayeva; translated and introduced by Elaine Feinstein; with literal versions provided by Angela Livingstone . . . [et al.] Penguin Books 1994 131p (Penguin twentieth-century classics) pa $15 **891.7**
ISBN 978-0-14-018759-5; 0-14-018759-6
First published 1971 by Oxford Univ. Press

"As a poet Tsvetayeva impresses with her psychic energy, she is on fire with poetry, and nothing is put in perspective, everything is immediate, emotional in the best sense." N Y Times Book Rev

Volkov, Solomon

Romanov riches; Russian writers and artists under the tsars. translated from the Russian by Antonina W. Bouis. Alfred A. Knopf 2011 285p il $30 **891.7**
1. Emperors 2. Empresses 3. Russian arts 4. Authors, Russian 5. Arts, Russian 6. Artists -- Russia 7. Russia -- History 8. Composers -- Russia 9. Russia -- Kings and rulers 10. Russia -- Intellectual life 11. Russian literature -- History and criticism
ISBN 0-307-27063-7; 978-0-307-27063-4

LC 2010-45132

This is a "cultural history of Russia from the rise of the house of Romanov in 1613 to its downfall at the hands of the Bolsheviks in 1917." (Publisher's note) Index.

"Volkov revitalizes our understanding of rebellious poet Pushkin and offers fresh insights into Tchaikovsky, Dostoevsky, and Turgenev. A thrillingly anecdotal and incisive look at the paradigmatic and paradoxical Romanov world of politics, patronage, and the quest for artistic freedom." Booklist

Includes bibliographical references

Yevtushenko, Yevgeny Aleksandrovich

Selected poems; [by] Yevgeni Yevtushenko; translated by Robin Milner-Gulland and Peter Levi; with an introduction by Robin Milner-Gulland. Penguin Books 2008 90p il (Penguin Classics) pa $14 **891.7**
1. Poetry -- By individual authors
ISBN 978-0-14-042477-5; 0-14-042477-6
First published 1961

"These poems beat and tumble and thrash with life." Daily Telegraph

891.73 Russian fiction

Finn, Peter

The **Zhivago** affair; the Kremlin, the CIA, and the battle over a forbidden book. Peter Finn and Petra Couvee. Pantheon Books 2013 368 p. (hard cover: alkaline paper) $26.95 **891.73**
1. Cold war 2. Books -- Censorship 3. Dissenters -- Soviet Union -- Biography 4. Prohibited books -- Soviet Union -- History 5. Authors, Russian -- 20th century -- Biography 6. Politics and literature -- Soviet Union -- History 7. Soviet Union -- Foreign relations -- United States 8. United States -- Foreign relations -- Soviet Union 9. Soviet Union -- Politics and government -- 1953-1985 10. United States. Central Intelligence Agency -- History -- 20th century

ISBN 0307908003; 9780307908001

LC 2013033875

National Book Critics Circle Finalist: Nonfiction (2014)

This book, by Peter Finn and Petra Couvele, offers "the dramatic story of how a forbidden book in the Soviet Union became a secret CIA weapon in the ideological battle between East and West. . . . The CIA . . . published a Russian-language edition of 'Doctor Zhivago' and smuggled it into the Soviet Union. Copies were devoured in Moscow and Leningrad, sold on the black market, and passed surreptitiously from friend to friend." (Publisher's note)

"Drawing on recently declassified CIA documents, Finn and Couvée present an engaging thriller, in which bureaucratic obstructions and Cold War politics threaten the publication of a controversial masterpiece of world literature." Booklist

Includes bibliographical references and index

Pitzer, Andrea

★ The **Secret** History of Vladimir Nabokov; Andrea Pitzer. W W Norton & Co Inc 2013 352 p. (hardcover) $29.95 **891.73**

1. Authors, Russian -- 20th century -- Biography. 2. Authors, American -- 20th century -- Biography. 3. Nabokov, Vladimir Vladimirovich, 1899-1977 -- Criticism and interpretation.

ISBN 1605984116; 9781605984117

This book, by Andrea Pitzer, discusses the life and work of the Russian novelist Vladimir Nabokov, who "witnessed the horrors of his century, escaping Revolutionary Russia then Germany under Hitler. . . . He repeatedly faced accusations of turning a blind eye to human suffering to write artful tales of depravity. But does one of the greatest writers in the English language really deserve the label of amoral aesthete bestowed on him by so many critics?" (Publisher's note)

"Drawing on new biographical material and her sharp critical senses, Pitzer reveals the tightly woven subtext of the novels, always keen to shine a light where the deception is not obvious. . . . Though no substitute for Brian Boyd's definitive two-volume biography, this is a brilliant examination that adds to the understanding of an inspiring and enigmatic life." Kirkus

891.8   Slavic (Slavonic) literatures

Dimkovska, Lidija

PH neutral history; Lidija Dimkovska; translated from the Macedonian by Ljubica Arsovska and Peggy Reid. Copper Canyon Press 2012 120 p. (pbk.: alk. paper) $16.00 **891.8**

1. Suicide -- Poetry 2. Nostalgia -- Poetry 3. Macedonia (Republic) -- Folklore -- Poetry

ISBN 1556593759; 9781556593758

LC 2011044017

In this, the "sixth collection of poetry" by "Macedonian poet and novelist Lidija Dimkovska," the author "scrutinizes life's customary and trivial details in a quest for greater meaning." Topics referenced include "religious tenents," "native folklore," and "nostalgia for her youth." Her brother's suicide offers her "reflections on death and its neutralization: life." (Publisher's note)

Havel, Vaclav

The **garden** party and other plays. Grove Press 1993 273p $13.00; pa $14 **891.8**

ISBN 978-0-8021-3307-6; 0-8021-3307-X

LC 93-8656

"Gathered together here for the first time are seven plays that span Havel's career from his early days at the Theater of the Balustrade through the Prague Spring, Charter 77, and the repeated imprisonments that made Havel's name into a rallying cry and propelled him to the leadership of his country." Publisher's note

Herbert, Zbigniew

The **collected** poems, 1956-1998; translated and edited by Alissa Valles; with additional translations by Czes¿aw Mi¿osz and Peter Dale Scott; introduction by Adam Zagajewski. Ecco Press 2007 600p $34.95 **891.8**

1. Poetry -- By individual authors

ISBN 978-0-06-078390-7; 0-06-078390-7

LC 2006-40856

Herbert is a "titan of not only Polish poetry, but of twentieth-century European poetry. His celebrated alter ego, Mr. Cogito, ranks as the one of the most original characters in modern poetry. . . . Herbert lived through the Nazi occupation of 1941 and the Soviet occupations of 1939 and 1944 and was an active member of Poland's underground resistance. Decades later, after marshal law was declared in Poland in 1981, Herbert supported the underground opposition to communism and was an important figure in the Solidarity movement. . . . If Herbert is a political poet, he's political in the way Don Quixote is political. He doesn't make us more aware. He makes us more human." Brooklyn Rail

Milosz, Czeslaw

Legends of modernity; essays and letters from occupied Poland, 1942-1943. translated from the Polish by Madeline G. Levine; introduction by Jaroslaw Anders. Farrar, Straus and Giroux 2005 266p $25 **891.8**

1. Miłosz, Czesław -- Correspondence. 2. Andrzejewski, Jerzy, 1909-1983 -- Correspondence. 3. Authors, Polish -- 20th century -- Correspondence.

ISBN 0-374-18499-2

LC 2005-40950

Original Polish edition, 1996

"Written to the young intellectual Jerzy Andrejewski, the letters reveal Milosz's concern about the political climate of the era and the deterioration of religious influence owing to the chaos all across Europe and the rest of the world. . . . The essays explore the ideas of William James, André Gide, Stendhal (Henri Beyle), Honoré de Balzac, and others as they relate to religious faith, reason and rationalism, contradictions, doubting, and believing in a civilized world and its religious institutions. . . . Reading Milosz is a demanding, rewarding, and ultimately powerful experience for the mind and the soul." Libr J

★ **Milosz's** ABCs; translated from the Polish by Madeline G. Levine. Farrar, Straus & Giroux 2001 313p hardcover o.p. pa $14 **891.8**

ISBN 0-374-52795-4 pa

LC 00-42176

"The short prose entries in this quiet book take note of some of the people and places and ideas that contributed to the making of Milosz. The subjects of his sketches range from Alchemy and Curiosity to Rimbaud and Whitman, from childhood friends to Polish intellectuals little known in the West. But what could have been no more than a light memory work becomes almost a registry of gratitude: a meditation on the obligations of having lived a life and the responsibilities inherent in its particulars." New Yorker

Includes bibliographical references

★ Monologue of a dog; new poems. translated from the Polish by Clare Cavanagh and Stanislaw Baranczak; [foreword by Billy Collins] Harcourt 2005 96p $22 **891.8**

1. Poetry -- By individual authors

ISBN 0-15-101220-2

LC 2005-16084

Original Polish edition, 2002

This is a collection of poems by the author of Miracle Fair (2001).

In this volume, Nobel laureate Szymborska "invites readers to linger over moments small, earthly, and sometimes life-altering. With characteristically simple language and imagery, wit and irony, she shows us how life can change at any moment. Hers are the politics of the everyday, little observations on the value of life." Libr J

★ **New** and collected poems 1931-2001. HarperCollins Pubs. 2001 xxi, 776p $45; pa $19.95 **891.8**

1. Poetry -- By individual authors
ISBN 0-06-019667-X; 0-06-051448-5 pa

LC 2001-50123

"Milosz has stated repeatedly in his poems his belief in the power of language to rescue from the void all he has seen and all the people he has known in a long life. But beneath this belief, it now appears, was the deeper belief that none of this was possible because of the inadequacy of language to capture reality, though he maintains this always has to be the poet's goal. . . . Throughout his career and throughout this vast collection, Milosz argues with himself about his poetics." N Y Times Book Rev

A **roadside** dog. Farrar, Straus & Giroux 1998 208p hardcover o.p. pa $14 **891.8**

ISBN 0-374-52623-0 pa

LC 98-14026

"Milosz makes a wise, wryly humane fin de siècle companion." Publ Wkly

To begin where I am; selected essays. edited and with an introduction by Bogdana Carpenter and Madeline G. Levine. Farrar, Straus & Giroux 2001 462p hardcover o.p. pa $15 **891.8**

1. Poets 2. Authors 3. Novelists 4. Dramatists 5. Philosophers 6. Political prisoners 7. Editors 8. Essayists 9. Translators 10. College teachers 11. Literary critics 12. Short story writers 13. Vilnius (Lithuania) 14. Nobel laureates for literature 15. Political and social philosophers

ISBN 0-374-52859-4 pa

LC 2001-33356

A retrospective of Milosz's "prose works, in which he weaves autobiography and portraits of people, famous and otherwise, who have influenced him into graceful and provocative musings on time, history, religion, science, and art." Booklist

Includes bibliographical references

Ristovic, Ana

Directions for use; Ana Ristović, translated by Steven Teref & Maja Teref. Zephyr Press 2017 111 p. (paperback) $15 **891.8**

1. Poetry 2. Interpersonal relations
ISBN 9781938890147; 1938890140

National Book Critics Circle Award Finalist: Poetry (2017)

This book, by Ana Ristović, translated by Steven Teref and Maja Teref, presents "erotic, wry, feminist poems concern[ing] daily routines (washing laundry, doing crossword puzzles). . . . [Ristović] explores inner and outer worlds, sex, and relationships. This bilingual (Serbian and English) selection unveils a rich embroidery of frank sexuality and lyric images." (Publisher's note)

Sosnowski, Andrzej

Lodgings; selected poems, 1987-2010. translated from the Polish by Benjamin Paloff. Open Letter 2011 163p pa $13.95 **891.8**

1. Poetry -- By individual authors
ISBN 978-1-934824-32-0; 1-934824-32-1

LC 2010-52054

With this volume, "translator Benjamin Paloff has made an important contribution to the body of Polish poetry currently available to readers in English. Complete with a translator's note, a conversation between Sosnowski and Paloff, and poems that span Sosnowski's entire career to date (1987-2010), Lodgings offers an unusual glimpse into a polyphonous, expansive, and chameleonic strain of Polish poetry. The poems included are pulled from nine of Sosnowski's collections . . . , and they are presented, with two exceptions, in their original order." Words without Borders

Szymborska, Wislawa

Map; Collected and Last Poems. Houghton Mifflin Harcourt 2015 464 p. $32 **891.8**

ISBN 0544126025; 9780544126022

LC 2015297265

This collection of poems by Wislawa Szymborska, translated by Clare Cavanaugh and Stanislaw Baranczak, "trace Szymborska's work until her death in 2012. Of the approximately two hundred and fifty poems included here, nearly forty are newly translated; thirteen represent the entirety of the poet's last Polish collection, Enough, never before published in English." (Publisher's note)

"Throughout, Szymborska considers loss and fragility, as when former lovers walk past each other and an aging professor is no longer allowed his vodka and cigarettes. She writes, too, of the imprecision of memory, and in the title poem, the discovery that maps 'give no access to the vicious truth.' This is a brilliant and important collection." Booklist

Poems, new and collected, 1957-1997; translated from the Polish by Stainslaw Baranczak and Clare Cavanagh. Harcourt Brace & Co. 1998 273p $27; pa $17 **891.8**

ISBN 0-15-100353-X; 0-15-601146-8 pa

LC 97-32277

This career-spanning collection by the 1996 Nobel Prize winner includes her Nobel lecture

Szymborska's "work is ultimately wisdom literature, written in a first person that expresses a universal humanity that American poets—lockstep individualists all—haven't dared essay since early in this century." Booklist

Zagajewski, Adam, 1945-

Eternal enemies; translated from the Polish by Clare Cavanagh. Farrar, Straus and Giroux 2008 116p **891.8**

1. Poetry -- By individual authors
ISBN 0-374-21634-7; 978-0-374-21634-4

LC 2007-42855

This is a collection of poetry by the author of Two Cities (1995), Without End (2002), and A Defense of Ardor (2004).

"Cavanagh's supple translations let the verse sing in American English without making this Polish poet sound too American." Publ Wkly

Unseen hand; translated from the Polish by Clare Cavanagh. Farrar, Straus and Giroux 2011 107p $23 **891.8**

1. Poetry -- By individual authors
ISBN 978-0-374-28089-5; 0-374-28089-4

LC 2010-46274

Original Polish edition, 2009

The book "is Adam Zagajewski's sixth book of poetry translated into English. . . . If Szymborska is a poet of imaginary journeys, Zagajewski is a real traveler with a ticket and a suitcase. He even has a poem called 'Self-Portrait in an Airplane.' Many of his poems are about towns and cities in Europe and the United States that he had either lived in or visited. Poetry and travel are allied, Czeslaw Milosz once claimed, since poetry is an expression of wondering at things, landscapes, people, their habits and mores. . . . He compares the impassive river Garonne, flowing in silence, to an Indian brave in plumes of sun; a plane taking off from an airport to a zealous pupil who believes what the old masters told him; the light bulbs hissing in gray hallways at night to the signals of sinking ships." (New York Review of Books)

"The collective calm of these poems creates an odd tension: Within [Zagajewski's] clear, contemplative lines, the indifference of time can always be felt drifting unstoppably by, even as we attempt to scaffold it with history or cage it with memory. . . . [The poems,] translated by the admirably consistent Clare Cavanagh, move through the various locales of Zagajewski's life; from his Polish upbringing in Lvov and the provincial garrison town of Gliwice (to which his family was forced to move shortly after his birth in 1945), to various stints in Krakow, Paris, and Chicago. Markers of place and time are everywhere, but Zagajewski is especially perceptive of the ways the past is channeled through the present — his 'now' tends to carry the authority of an 'always.'" Boston Globe

★ **Without** end; new and selected poems. translations by Clare Cavanagh [et al.] Farrar, Straus & Giroux 2002 285p $30; pa $15 **891.8**

ISBN 0-374-22096-4; 0-374-52861-6 pa

LC 2001-40252

"Zagajewski's poetic evolution is clearly charted in 'Without End,' a new anthology of his work that is made up of his three English-language collections—'Tremor' (1985), 'Canvas' (1991) and 'Mysticism for Beginners' (1997)—as well as his most recent work and new translations of some early poems. . . . Zagajewski's poems pull us from whatever routine threatens to dull our senses, from whatever might lull us into mere existence. This is an astonishing book." N Y Times Book Rev

892   Afro-Asiatic literatures

Amichai, Yehuda

Poems of Jerusalem; and, Love poems; a bilingual edition. Sheep Meadow Press 1992 265p pa $16.95 **892**

1. Poetry -- By individual authors

ISBN 1-87881-819-8

LC 92-31558

Poems of Jerusalem first published 1988 by Perennial Lib.; Love poems first published 1981 by Harper & Row

This work is "actually drawn from eight previous works and boasts an even larger array of translators (including Stephen Mitchell, David Rosenberg, Ted Hughes, and the poet himself). The thematic arrangement deftly emphasizes the Israeli poet's constant preoccupation with both Jerusalem and love." Libr J

The **selected** poetry of Yehuda Amichai; edited and translated from the Hebrew by Chana Bloch and Stephen Mitchell. newly rev & expanded ed; University of Calif. Press 1996 195p pa $16.95 **892**

1. Poetry -- By individual authors

ISBN 0-520-20538-3

LC 96-18580

First published 1986

"Although much of Amichai's poetry focuses on war, he is able to describe its horrors by maintaining a clear distance between himself and his subject. The result is a finely controlled emotional pitch that allows the poet to convey his sense of pain and outrage without pathos or sentimentality. He writes colloquially, in language that is always commensurate with emotional experience." Reader's Ency. 4th edition

Gilgamesh

★ **Gilgamesh**; a new English version [by] Stephen Mitchell. Free Press 2004 290p $25; pa $14 **892**

ISBN 0-7432-6164-X; 0-7432-6169-0 pa

LC 2004-50072

"Relying on existing translations (and in places where there are gaps, on his own imagination), Mitchell seeks language that is as swift and strong as the story itself. . . . This wonderful new version of the story of Gilgamesh shows how the story came to achieve literary immortality— not because it is a rare ancient artifact, but because reading it can make people in the here and now feel more completely alive." Publ Wkly

Includes bibliographical references

892.4   Hebrew literature

Amichai, Yehuda

Open closed open; poems. translated from the Hebrew by Chana Bloch and Chana Kronfeld. Harcourt Brace & Co. 2000 184p $25 **892.4**

1. Poetry -- By individual authors

ISBN 0-15-100378-5

LC 00-23537

Original Hebrew edition, 1998

Amichai "writes with the casual wisdom and generous humor of a master." Booklist

Oz, Amos, 1939-2018

Dear zealots; letters from a divided land. Amos Oz; translated from the Hebrew by Jessica Cohen. Chatto & Windus 2018 127 p. $23 **892.4**

1. Judaism 2. Fanaticism 3. Toleration 4. Judaism and humanism 5. Arab-Israeli conflict 6. Israel -- Foreign relations 7. Democracy -- Religious aspects -- Judaism

ISBN 1328987000; 1784742384; 9781328987006; 9781784742386

LC 2017473483

This book, by Amos Oz, translated by Jessica Cohen, "offers three powerful essays that speak directly to our present age, on the rise of zealotry in Israel and around the world. . . . [The essays address] the universal nature of fanaticism and its possible cures, on the Jewish roots of humanism and the need for a secular pride in Israel, and on the geopolitical standing of Israel in the wider Middle East and internationally." (Publisher's note)

"Oz's book leaves readers with a strong message about the need for a greater societywide openness to doubt and ambiguity." Pub Wkly

Includes bibliographical references (pages 125-127)

Shabtai, Aharon

War & love, love & war; new and selected poems. translated by Peter Cole. New Directions 2010 175p pa $15.95 **892.4**

1. Poetry -- By individual authors
ISBN 978-0-8112-1890-0; 0-8112-1890-2

LC 2010-10440

"Gritty, controversial and intensely lyrical, this is an excellent collection from one of Israel's most important contemporary poets. Spanning more than three-anda-half decades of writing, it exhibits a wealth of experimentation with various styles, and a multitude of yearnings and obsessions. As the title implies, engagement with the Israeli-Palestinian conflict is one of the book's chief subjects. The real gem, though, is the closing cycle of poems, which mourns the passing of Shabtai's wife, Tanya Reinhart." Forward

Includes bibliographical references

892.7 Arabic and Maltese literatures

Darwish, Mahmud

If I were another; translated from the Arabic by Fady Joudah. Farrar, Straus and Giroux 2009 201p $28   **892.7**

1. Poetry -- By individual authors
ISBN 978-0-374-17429-3; 0-374-17429-6

LC 2009-11521

This volume "comprises four nonconsecutive books of longer poems spanning 1990 to 2005. These works follow Darwish's poetic development from a historically focused middle period to the devastatingly personal lyric-epic of his late style. Formally varied—Rubaiyats alternate with sprawling freeform poems, in which prose paragraphs meet both long and short verse lines—Darwish's Sufi-inspired poetry probes, admires, describes, longs for and questions." Publ Wkly

Includes bibliographical references

Night and horses and the desert; an anthology of classical Arabic literature. edited by Robert Irwin. Anchor Books 2001 462p pa $16   **892.7**

1. Arabic literature -- Collections 2. Arabic literature -- History and criticism
ISBN 0-385-72155-2

LC 2001-53721

First published 2000 by Overlook Press

"The chapter on the Qur'an is perhaps the most essential as it examines just how vital the dogma of Islam has been for the Arabic understanding of culture and art. . . . This persuasive work will surely fill in the gap in the study of Arabic literature in this country." Publ Wkly

Includes bibliographical references

The poetry of Arab women; a contemporary anthology. edited by Nathalie Handal. Interlink Bks. 2000 xxi, 355p pa $22   **892.7**

1. Arabic poetry -- Collections
ISBN 978-1-56656-374-1; 1-56656-374-7

LC 00-58054

"Handal deserves high praise for producing an anthology that mirrors faithfully Arab women's creative role throughout the last century." Multicultural Rev

Tales of the Marvellous and News of the Strange; translated by Malcolm C. Lyons; introduced by Robert Irwin. Penguin Group USA 2015 496 p. (hbk.) $30   **892.7**

1. Short stories 2. Arabic literature
ISBN 0141395036; 9780141395036

LC 2014472568

This book, translated by Malcolm C. Lyons and illustrated by Coralie

Bickford-Smith, is "a great cache of ancient, magical stories in the same tradition as 'The Arabian Nights.' . . . Dating from at least a millennium ago, these are the earliest-known Arabic short stories, which survived in a single, ragged manuscript in a library in Istanbul." (Publisher's note)

"Coupled with an informative introduction by Robert Irwin, author of The Arabian Nights: A Companion, this book is a welcome and recommended addition to those who enjoy the Arabian Nights." LJ

Includes bibliographical references

892.71 Arabic poetry

Adonis, 1930-

Concerto al-quds; Adonis; translated by Khaled Mattawa. Yale University Press 2017 85 p. (Margellos world republic of letters book) (hardcover) $25   **892.71**

1. Jerusalem -- Poetry 2. Arabic poetry -- Collections
ISBN 9780300197648

LC 2017941088

In this poetry collection about Jerusalem in The Margellos World Republic of Letters series, "Syrian poet Adonis, who has been hailed as a founding voice in Arabic-language modernism, envisions the poem as a space for dialogue between traditions, nations, and historical milieux. [Khaled] Mattawa's careful English [translation] preserves the integrity of Adonis's cosmopolitan influences, paying homage to the book's various inspirations." (Publishers Weekly)

"In this stunning volume about Jerusalem (al-Quds in Arabic), Syrian poet Adonis, who has been hailed as a founding voice in Arabic-language modernism, envisions the poem as a space for dialogue between traditions, nations, and historical milieux." Pub Wkly

894 Literatures of Altaic, Uralic, Hyperborean, Dravidian languages; literatures of miscellaneous languages of south Asia

Pamuk, Orhan

Other colors; essays and a story. translated from the Turkish by Maureen Freely. Alfred A. Knopf 2007 433p il $27.95   **894**

ISBN 978-0-307-26675-0; 0-307-26675-3

LC 2007-21132

Original Turkish edition, 1999

"Whether he's writing wistfully about Andre Gide as the hero of Turkish intellectuals . . . or recalling how he used to collect Coca-Cola cans as a boy, from the trash cans of expat Americans, Pamuk is taking the world we thought we knew and making it fresh and alive." N Y Times Book Rev

895.1 Chinese literature

The **Columbia** history of Chinese literature; Victor H. Mair, editor. Columbia Univ. Press 2001 xx, 1342p $78 **895.1**

1. Chinese literature -- History and criticism
ISBN 0-231-10984-9

LC 2001-28236

This "history explores a wide range of Chinese literature, from the classics to humor to folk tales to oral traditions, and moves from ancient times to the end of the 20th century. . . . Mair has overseen a host of excellent scholars writing on a vast subject." Libr J

Includes bibliographical references

Mountain home; the wilderness poetry of ancient China. selected and translated by David Hinton. New Directions Pub. 2005 xxi, 295p map pa $17.95   **895.1**
1. Chinese poetry -- Collections
ISBN 978-0-8112-1624-1

LC 2005-869

First published 2002 by Counterpoint

"Translator and scholar Hinton ensures that Western readers will experience this supreme collection of Chinese rivers-and-mountains (shan-shui) poetry at the deepest possible level by succinctly explaining the cosmology inherent in this vital and profoundly influential tradition. The keys to understanding the elegant poetry of such masters as T'ao Ch'ien (365-427), Li Po (701-762), and Lu Yu (1125-1210) are realizing that they perceive no divide between the human and what we call nature, or between being and nonbeing. . . . Oneness with life at its purest is the desired mode for these thoughtful, yet often playful, poets, and dwelling within these meditative pages is the first step on the way there." Booklist

The **New** Directions anthology of classical chinese poetry; edited by Eliot Weinberger; translations by William Carlos Williams . . . [et al.] New Directions 2003 xxvii, 242p $24.95; pa $16.95   **895.1**
1. Chinese poetry -- Collections
ISBN 978-0-8112-1540-4; 0-8112-1540-7; 978-0-8112-1605-0 pa; 0-8112-1605-5 pa

LC 2002-156731

The poems are "translated into English by four of the best-known American poets of the 20th century—Ezra Pound, William Carlos Williams, Kenneth Rexroth and Gary Snyder—and an academic scholar/translator called David Hinton, who deserves to be as well known as the others. It is not often that an anthology really demands attention. . . . This poetry means what it says. It feels companionable, and even sexy. It is not excessively—or confusingly—metaphorical. It is not foggy with abstract philosophising. It lacks the shriek of rhetoric; it seems to move, so often, at an agreeable walking pace. It feels spacious. In fact, there seems to be space between the words themselves. It mixes the high and the low with seeming ease. Its temper suggests that there is no unsuitable subject matter for poetry at all." New Statesman

895.6   Japanese literature

Haiku before haiku; from the Renga masters to Basho. translated, with an introduction, by Steven D. Carter. Columbia University Press 2011 163p (Translations from the Asian classics) $69.50; pa $22.50; ebook $9.99   **895.6**
1. Haiku 2. Renga 3. Japanese poetry
ISBN 978-0-231-15648-6; 978-0-231-15647-9 pa; 978-0-231-52706-4 ebook

LC 2010-37030

"While the rise of the charmingly simple, brilliantly evocative haiku is often associated with the seventeenth-century Japanese poet Matsuo Basho, the form had already flourished for more than four hundred years before Basho even began to write. These early poems, known as hokku, are identical to haiku in syllable count and structure but function differently as a genre. Whereas each haiku is its own constellation of image and meaning, a hokku opens a series of linked, collaborative stanzas in a sequence called renga. . . . [This anthology] presents 320 hokku composed between the thirteenth and early eighteenth centuries, from the poems of the courtier Nijo Yoshimoto to those of the genre's first 'professional' master, Sogi, and his disciples. It features 20 masterpieces by Basho himself." Publisher's note

Includes bibliographical references

Keene, Donald
Five modern Japanese novelists. Columbia Univ. Press 2002 113p $26   **895.6**
1. Japanese literature -- History and criticism
ISBN 0-231-12610-7

LC 2002-73412

The author's essays, "part memoir and part literary evaluation, are ideal introductions to their subjects." Booklist

Includes bibliographical references

Seeds in the heart; Japanese literature from earliest times to the late sixteenth century. with a new preface by the author, Donald Keene. Columbia University Press 1999 1265p (History of Japanese literature) pa $37   **895.6**
1. Japanese literature -- History and criticism
ISBN 0-231-11441-9

LC 99-25990

First published 1993 by Holt & Co.

This volume completes the author's history of Japanese literature begun with: World within walls (1977) and Dawn to the West (1984).

"The first half of 'Seeds in the Heart' encompasses everything from the myths, legends, songs and poems of the eighth-century 'Kojiki' ('Record of Ancient Matters') and 'Manyoshu,' a collection of 4,500 poems, to the 'The Tale of Genji' and later works of fiction. . . . During Japan's middle ages (1185-1600), Buddhism and popular (rather than aristocratic) forms of storytelling and theater generated a repertory of characters and genres that would eventually form the country's first broadly based, national culture. The literature of these centuries has rarely attracted the scholarly attention paid to the earlier 'high' classical tradition. So Mr. Keene's attention to this period makes the second half of 'Seeds in the Heart' especially valuable." N Y Times Book Rev

Includes bibliographical references

Waley, Arthur
The **No** plays of Japan; an anthology. Dover Publications 1998 270p pa $12.95   **895.6**
1. No plays
ISBN 978-0-486-40156-0

LC 97-46053

First published 1921 in the United Kingdom; first United States edition published 1922 by Knopf

Contains translation of 20 No plays and summaries of 16 more. In his introduction Mr. Waley gives a brief history of the No drama, its origin, the text of the plays, and the chief playwrights. He also tells about the stage settings, costumes and properties used in the production of these plays. The greatest representation is given to the works of Seami and Zenchiku Ujinobu

896   African literatures

The **Penguin** book of modern African poetry; edited by Gerald Moore and Ulli Beier. 4th ed.; Penguin Books 2007 xxvi, 448p pa $17   **896**
1. African poetry -- Collections
ISBN 978-0-14-042472-0; 0-14-042472-5

First published 1963 in the United Kingdom with title: Modern poetry from Africa

This anthology includes over 200 poems by 67 poets from 23 countries.

Includes bibliographical references

897 Literatures of North American native languages

The **Cambridge** companion to Native American literature; edited by Joy Porter and Kenneth M. Roemer. Cambridge University Press 2005 343p il map hardcover o.p. pa $26.95 **897**

1. Native American literature -- History and criticism
ISBN 978-0-521-52979-2 pa; 0-521-52979-4 pa

LC 2005-44298

Essays organized "by historical and cultural context, by genre, and according to individual authors. Particularly insightful and informative are the tightly written essays on the eight currently best-known Indian writers. Also included are maps, a time line, suggested readings, and a brief series of 40 biobibliographies of notable Native American writers. . . . Readers of this volume should probably already have a working knowledge of the main figures in this increasingly important and respected segment of American literature." Libr J

900 HISTORY

900 History, geography, and auxiliary disciplines

Báez, Fernando
A **universal** history of the destruction of books; from ancient Sumer to modern-day Iraq. translated by Alfred MacAdam. Atlas & Co. 2008 354p il map $25 **900**

1. Censorship 2. Books -- Censorship 3. Books and reading -- History 4. Libraries -- Destruction and pillage
ISBN 978-1-934633-01-4

LC 2008-932321

Original Spanish edition, 2004

This is a "horrific chronicle of the centuries-long assault on human memory. . . . A sobering reminder of just how deep-seated is the instinct to destroy other people's truths." Kirkus

Includes bibliographical references

901 Philosophy and theory of history

MacMillan, Margaret
Dangerous games; the uses and abuses of history. Modern Library 2009 188p $22 **901**

1. Historiography 2. History -- Philosophy
ISBN 978-0-679-64358-6; 0-679-64358-3

First published 2008 in Canada with title: The uses and abuses of history

Explores the ways in which history has been used to influence people and government, focusing on how reportage of past events has been manipulated to justify religious movements and political campaigns. Based on the Joanne Goodman lecture series of the University of Western Ontario.

"This is a must read for anyone who wants to understand the importance of correctly understanding the past." Publ Wkly

Includes bibliographical references

Ortega, Jose
The **revolt** of the masses; translated, annotated, and with an introduction by Anthony Kerrigan; edited by Kenneth Moore; with a foreword by Saul Bellow. University of Notre Dame Press 1985 xxxi, 192p hardcover o.p. pa $13.95 **901**

1. Proletariat 2. Civilization 3. Europe -- Civilization
ISBN 0-393-31095-7

LC 81-40457

Original Spanish edition, 1930; first English translation, 1932

This work argues for the "leveling out of outstanding qualities in men and culture, as it traces the development of the 'mediocre soul' out of 19th-century bourgeois culture to the advent of the new totalitarian democracy in which none are nor aspire to be superior to others but rather to be 'just like everybody else.' The masses are not the impoverished or politically oppressed proletariat but span the classes marked by a 'qualitative determinant': 'the mass is the average man.'" (Libr J) First published in Spain in 1929. For an earlier English translation see BRD 1932.

902 Miscellany of history

Grun, Bernard
★ The **timetables** of history; a historical linkage of people and events. 4th ed.; Simon & Schuster 2005 835p $25 **902**

1. Historical chronology
ISBN 0-7432-7003-7; 978-0-7432-7003-8

LC 2005-49766

Original German edition, 1946; first published in the United States 1975

This chronology "includes material from 4500 BCE to 2004. . . . The information is listed by year in seven columns labeled 'History, Politics', 'Literature, Theater', 'Religion, Philosophy, Learning', 'Visual Arts', 'Music', 'Science, Technology, Growth', and 'Daily Life.' . . . This work is an excellent chronological tool, and should be found in all libraries." Choice

The **timetables** of American history; Laurence Urdang, editor; with an introduction by Henry Steele Commager and a new foreword by Arthur Schlesinger, Jr. Simon & Schuster 2001 534p il pa $24 **902**

1. Historical chronology
ISBN 0-7432-0261-9

First published 1982

Presents information chronologically in tabular form. Each double-page spread has columns for history and politics, the arts, science and technology, and miscellaneous.

902.02 Chronologies

★ **Timelines** of history; the ultimate visual guide to the events that shaped the world. DK Publishing. DK Publishing 2018 512 p. $27.99 **902.02**

1. World history 2. Historical chronology
ISBN 1465470026; 9781465470027

Produced by DK Publishing, and "beginning with the emergence of our earliest African ancestors and taking readers through the history of cultures and nations around the world to arrive at the present day, . . . [this book] caters to readers who want a broad overview, a good story to read, or the nitty-gritty of historical events." (Publisher's note)

"An excellent overview to history, with a place in all school and public libraries." Library Journal

902.2   Illustrations, models, miniatures

National Geographic Society (U.S.)

National Geographic visual history of the world; [authors, Klaus Berndl . . . et al.]. National Geographic Society 2005 656p il $35   **902.2**
1. World history
ISBN 0-7922-3695-5

LC 2005-541553

"Over 4,000 illustrations and photographs cover individuals and events from prehistory (the beginning to ca. 4000 BCE) to the contemporary world (1945 to the present). . . . This educational and entertaining volume of social, cultural, and military history will appeal to a wide readership." Choice

Terra Maxima; The Records of Humankind. edited by Wolfgang Kunth. Firefly Books Ltd 2013 576 p. color illustrations $49.95   **902.2**
1. World records 2. Technological innovations
ISBN 1770852425; 9781770852426

LC 2013456556

This book, edited by Wolfgang Kunth, "is comprised of more than 3,000 full-color photographs . . . that showcase the biggest and the best religious, cultural, and technological marvels of the world. The work is broken down into 10 sections: 'Countries and Nations,' 'Languages and Scripts,' 'Faith and Religion,' 'Cities and Metropolises,' 'Urban Megastructures,' 'Transportation and Traffic,' 'Aviation and Space Travel,' 'Art and Culture,' 'Science and Research,' and 'Sports and Leisure.'" (Booklist)

"The emphasis is on the visual, with sumptuous color photographs printed on heavy stock, many appearing on full spreads. The text, while minimal, is nevertheless informative, pointing out interesting historical, architectural, and other details about the structures pictured." LJ

904   Collected accounts of events

Davis, Lee Allyn

Man-made catastrophes; [by] Lee Davis. rev ed; Facts on File 2002 402p il $60   **904**
1. Disasters
ISBN 0-8160-4418-X

LC 2001-54324

First published 1993

This describes man-made disasters "from the burning of Babylon in 538B.C. to the 2001 terrorist attack on the World Trade Center in New York City. . . . [The entries] are organized by disaster type: air crashes, civil unrest and terrorism, explosions, maritime disasters, nuclear and industrial accidents, railway disasters, and space disasters." Publisher's note
Includes bibliographical references

907   Education, research, related topics of history

Hamilton, Nigel

Biography; a brief history. Harvard University Press 2007 345p il $21.95   **907**
1. Biography as a literary form

ISBN 978-0-674-02466-3; 0-674-02466-4

LC 2006-51132

"Hamilton has given readers a thoughtprovoking look at biography in its various forms; a fascinating and handy reference book for anyone wishing to know more about the history and art of biography." Libr J
Includes bibliographical references (p. 315-21)

Mills, Elizabeth S.

Evidence explained; citing history sources from artifacts to cyberspace. [by] Elizabeth Shown Mills. 3rd edition Genealogical Pub. Co. 2015   **907**
1. History -- Sources 2. History -- Research
ISBN 9780806320403
First published 2007
This resource is "indispensable for scholars and accessible enough to meet the needs of amateur genealogists and students." Libr J
Includes bibliographical references

Tuchman, Barbara Wertheim

Practicing history; selected essays. by Barbara W. Tuchman. Knopf 1981 306p hardcover o.p. pa $14.95   **907**
1. Diplomats 2. Governors 3. Presidents 4. Historiography 5. Modern history 6. Executive power 7. Vietnam War, 1961-1975 8. Israel 9. Financiers 10. College presidents 11. Nobel laureates for peace 12. World War, 1914-1918 -- United States 13. China -- Foreign relations -- United States 14. United States -- Foreign relations -- China
ISBN 0-345-30363-6 pa

LC 81-47509

A collection of essays on the nature, methodology and writing of history

909   World history

Africana: the encyclopedia of the African and African American experience; editors, Kwame Anthony Appiah, Henry Louis Gates, Jr. 2nd ed; Oxford University Press 2005 5v set $550   **909**
1. Reference books 2. Africa -- Encyclopedias 3. Blacks -- Encyclopedias 4. African diaspora -- Encyclopedias 5. African Americans -- Encyclopedias
ISBN 978-0-19-517055-9; 0-19-517055-5

LC 2004-20222

First published 1999 by Basic Civitas Bks.

This encyclopedia covers "prominent individuals, events, trends, places, political movements, art forms, business and trade, religions, ethnic groups, organizations, and countries on both sides of the ocean. . . There are articles on contemporary nations of sub-Saharan Africa, ethnic groups from various regions of Africa, African American Academy award winners, Caribbean musical styles, African religions in Brazil, and European colonial powers." Booklist [review of 1999 edition]
Includes bibliographical references

Biale, David

★ **Cultures** of the Jews; a new history. edited with an introduction by David Biale. Schocken Bks. 2002 xxxiii, 1196p il $45   **909**
1. Jewish civilization 2. Jews -- History
ISBN 0-8052-4131-0; 9780805241310

LC 2002-23008

"The book is truly one of the most important works on the subject ever published." Booklist

Includes bibliographical references

Boorstin, Daniel J.

The **creators**. Random House 1992 811p il hardcover o.p.
pa $18.95 **909**

1. Arts 2. Civilization 3. Creation (Literary, artistic, etc.)

ISBN 0-394-54395-5; 0-679-74375-8 pa

LC 91-39948

In this volume "Boorstin undertakes an interpretive history of creativity in Western civilization. Packed with shrewd, entertaining profiles of Dante, Goethe, Benjamin Franklin and dozens of others, this stimulating synthesis sets the achievements of individual geniuses into a coherent narrative of humanity's advance from ignorance." Publ Wkly

Includes bibliographical references

Brendon, Piers

★ The **decline** and fall of the British Empire, 1781-1997.
Alfred A. Knopf 2008 xxii, 786p il map $37.50 **909**

1. Great Britain -- History 2. Great Britain -- Colonies 3. Great Britain -- Civilization 4. Commonwealth countries -- History

ISBN 978-0-307-26829-7; 0-307-26829-2

LC 2008-14192

First published 2007 in the United Kingdom

"A richly detailed, lucid account of how the British Empire grew and grew—and then, not quite inexorably, fell apart." Kirkus

Includes bibliographical references

Brown, Cynthia Stokes

A **big** history; from the Big Bang to the present. Distributed by W.W. Norton 2007 288p il map $25.95 **909**

1. Human ecology 2. World history

ISBN 978-1-59558-196-9; 1-59558-196-0

LC 2007-6741

"In a multidisciplinary narrative subtly emphasizing the mutual impact of people and planet, Brown covers Earth's history from the big bang through the development of life and the growth of civilization. . . . This exciting saga crosses space and time to illustrate how humans, born of stardust, were shaped—and how they in turn shaped the world we know today." Publ Wkly

Cahill, Thomas

The **gifts** of the Jews; how a tribe of desert nomads changed the way everyone thinks and feels. Talese 1998 291p (Hinges of history) $23.50; pa $14 **909**

1. Jews -- History 2. Judaism -- History 3. Bible -- O.T. -- History of Biblical events

ISBN 0-385-48248-5; 0-385-48249-3 pa

LC 97-45139

In this colloquial look at the influence of the Hebrew Bible on civilization, the author gives "the Jews credit for revolutionizing the concepts of democracy, universal law, monotheism, linear time, personal vocation, destiny, self-improvement and the belief in the equality of all humans. He stumbles on the odd aside and occasionally is surprisingly insensitive. . . Still, his passion and breadth of knowledge are admirable." N Y Times Book Rev

Includes bibliographical references

Sailing the wine-dark sea; why the Greeks matter. Talese 2003 304p (Hinges of history) $27.50; pa $14.95 **909**

1. Greece -- Civilization

ISBN 0-385-49553-6; 0-385-49554-4 pa

LC 2003-50725

This author "begins with a discussion of Homer's Iliad and Odyssey and how these two epic poems relate to the history of Greece. He then focuses on such themes as the Greek alphabet, literature, and political system, and its playwrights, philosophers, and artists. A final chapter examines the effects that Greco-Roman and Judeo-Christian traditions had on each other." Booklist

Includes bibliographical references

Cliff, Nigel

Holy war. Harper 2011 x, 547 p.p col. ill., maps (chiefly col) **909**

1. Muslims 2. Explorers 3. Christians 4. Trade routes 5. World history -- 15th century

ISBN 978-0-06-173512-7

LC 2011021331

This book presents an historical "interpretation of Vasco da Gama's groundbreaking voyages, seen as a turning point in the struggle between Christianity and Islam." It was the author's intent to demonstrate "that both Vasco da Gama and his archrival, Christopher Columbus, set sail with the clear purpose of launching a Crusade whose objective was to reach the Indies; seize control of its markets in spices, silks, and precious gems from Muslim traders; and claim for Portugal or Spain, respectively, all the territories they discovered. Vasco da Gama triumphed in his mission and drew a dividing line between the Muslim and Christian eras of history -- what we in the West call the medieval and the modern ages." (Publisher's note)

Includes bibliographical references and index.

Cole, Juan

The **New** Arabs; How the Wired and Global Youth of the Middle East Is Transforming It. Juan Cole. Simon & Schuster 2014 384 p. (hardback) $26 **909**

1. Arab Spring, 2010- 2. Youth -- Political activity 3. Arab countries -- Politics and government

ISBN 9781451690392; 1451690398

LC 2014005627

This book, by Juan Cole, "illuminates the role of today's Arab youth-who they are, what they want, and how they will affect world politics. Beginning in January 2011, the revolutionary wave of demonstrations and protests, riots, and civil wars that comprised what many call 'the Arab Spring' shook the world. These upheavals were spearheaded by youth movements, and yet the crucial role they played is relatively unknown." (Publisher's note)

"Cole's deep, nuanced exploration of political and social currents underneath the uprisings shines; he shows Westerners who think the Arab world is divided between corrupt despots and Islamist zealots just how strong and pervasive the tendencies towards liberalism and democracy are." Pub Wkly

Includes bibliographical references and index

Crowley, Roger

Conquerors; how Portugal forged the first global empire. by Roger Crowley. Random House Inc 2015 416 p. illustrations, maps $30 **909**

1. Imperialism 2. Portugal -- History 3. Imperialism -- History 4. Portugal -- Colonies -- History -- 16th century

ISBN 0812994000; 9780812994001

LC 2015008152

This book, by Roger Crowley, focuses on "the history of Portuguese exploration. . . . Drawing on extensive first-hand accounts, it brings to life the exploits of an extraordinary band of conquerors - men such as Afonso de Albuquerque, the first European since Alexander the Great to found an Asian empire - who set in motion five hundred years of European colonisation and unleashed the forces of globalisation." (Publisher's note)

"An impressive history of global clashes, religious zealotry, and economic triumph." Kirkus

Includes bibliographical references and index

Culbertson, Shelly

The **fires** of spring; a post-Arab Spring journey through the turbulent new Middle East. Shelly Culbertson. St. Martin's Press 2016 384 p. map (hardback) $29.99   **909**

1. Arab Spring, 2010- 2. Arab countries -- Politics and government 3. Arab countries -- Politics and government -- 21st century
ISBN 9781250067043; 9781466874954

LC 2015043186

This book, by Shelly Culbertson, "bring[s] the post Arab Spring world to light in a holistic context. . . . Culbertson strives to answer the questions 'what led to the Arab Spring,' 'what is it like there now,' and 'what trends after the Arab Spring are shaping the future of the Middle East?' . . . It delves into what Arab Spring optimism was about, and at the same time sheds light on the pain and dysfunction that continues to plague some parts of the region." (Publisher's note)

"A book rich in invaluable information about both current conditions and possible future trends in Middle Eastern life and politics." Booklist
Includes bibliographical references (pages 315-355) and index.

Daily life through world history in primary documents; Lawrence Morris, general editor. Greenwood Press 2009 3v il set $299.95   **909**

1. Reference books 2. Civilization -- History -- Sources 3. Manners and customs -- History -- Sources
ISBN 978-0-313-33898-4

LC 2008-8925

"Each of the three volumes . . . begins with a chronology of the era covered as well as a clear, concise historical overview that provides readers with core knowledge of the cultures discussed. The more than 530 entries are grouped into seven categories: domestic, economic, intellectual, material, political, recreational, and religious life." Booklist
Includes bibliographical references

Davidson, Peter

Atlas of empires; Peter Davidson. CompanionHouse Books 2018 240 p. (pbk.) $19.99   **909**

1. Historical atlases 2. Imperialism -- History 3. Imperialism -- Maps
ISBN 9781620082874

LC 2017048739

This book, by Peter Davidson, "tells the story of how and why the great empires of history came into being, operated and . . . declined, and discusses the future of the empire in today's globalized world. Featuring 60 beautiful and detailed maps of the empires' territories at different stages of their existence and organized thematically to reflect the different driving forces behind empires throughout history . . . , each section discusses the rise and fall of the empires." (Publisher's note)

"Essentially covering 4,000 years of world history, this new work by History Channel writer Davidson takes a textbook-like approach, using gorgeous and detailed maps and clearly written text to tell the story of the great empires of world history." Booklist

Davis, Jack E.

★ The **Gulf**; the making of an American sea. Jack E. Davis. First edition. W W Norton & Co Inc 2017 608 p. Illustra-

tions, maps paperback $17.95; $29.95   **909**

1. Human ecology 2. Gulf of Mexico 3. Human influence on nature 4. Mexico, Gulf of -- History 5. Human ecology -- Mexico, Gulf of 6. Mexico, Gulf of -- Environmental conditions 7. Environmental degradation -- Mexico, Gulf of 8. Nature -- Effect of human beings on -- Mexico, Gulf of
ISBN 9781631494024; 087140866X; 9780871408662

LC 2016051692

National Book Critics Circle Award Finalist: Nonfiction (2017)
Kirkus Prize: Nonfiction (2017)
Pulitzer Prize: History (2018)

This book about the Gulf of Mexico, by Jack E. Davis, "tells the larger narrative of the American Sea--from the sportfish that brought the earliest tourists to Gulf shores to Hollywood's engagement with the first offshore oil wells--as it inspired and empowered, sometimes to its own detriment, the ethnically diverse groups of a growing nation." (Publisher's note)

"An elegant narrative braced by a fierce, sobering environmental conviction." Kirkus

de Bellaigue, Christopher

The **Islamic** Enlightenment; The Struggle Between Faith and Reason, 1798 to Modern Times. by Christopher de Bellaigue. W W Norton & Co Inc 2017 560 p. $35   **909**

1. Islam -- History
ISBN 0871403730; 9780871403735

This book, by Christopher de Bellaigue, "presents an absorbing account of the political and social reformations that transformed the lands of Islam in the nineteenth and early twentieth centuries. Flying in the face of everything we thought we knew, [it] becomes an astonishing and revelatory history that offers a game-changing assessment of the Middle East since the Napoleonic Wars." (Publisher's note)

"Recommended for historians, religious scholars, or anyone interested in relations between the Middle East and the West." LJ

Encyclopedia of Islam and the Muslim world; Richard C. Martin, editor in chief. 2nd edition Macmillan Reference USA 2016 820 p. illustrations   **909**

1. Islam -- Encyclopedias
ISBN 9780028662695; 9780028662701; 9780028662718

LC 2015015535

Edited by Richard C. Martin, "the second edition of this well-received two-volume study of Islam updates and adds to its predecessor 40 percent new content. It updates and revises most of the original 500+ entries and adds new topics to reflect changes in the Muslim world since 2004, from the emergence/re-emergence of Islamic regimes to challenges to the rule of religious leaders (Iran), to continuing instability across North Africa and the Middle East." (Publisher's note)

Includes bibliographical references and index

Encyclopedia of the developing world; Thomas M. Leonard, editor. Routledge 2005 3v set $625   **909**

1. Reference books 2. Developing countries -- Encyclopedias
ISBN 1-57958-388-1

LC 2005-49976

The entries "detail developments from 1945 forward. In addition to basic statistical and geographical information, country-focused entries detail history, economy, and political situation. Thematic entries cover people (e.g., Jomo Kenyatta), historical topics (e.g., colonialism), economic and government models (e.g., communism), the environment (e.g., water) and organizations (e.g., WTO)." Libr J

Includes bibliographical references

Ferguson, Niall

Empire: the rise and demise of the British world order and the lessons for global power. Basic Books 2003 392p il map hardcover o.p. pa $17.95 **909**

1. Imperialism 2. Commonwealth countries 3. Great Britain -- Colonies 4. Great Britain -- Foreign relations

ISBN 0-465-02329-0 pa

LC 2003-41469

First published 2002 in the United Kingdom

This book "is ambitious, provocative, and entertaining—a rare hat trick in the genre of historical writing—in its meticulous charting of the rise and fall of the world's largest empire. . . . Ferguson makes a subtle, but impressive, argument that free trade, the English language, and superior education helped improve the lot of those under colonial rule." Natl Rev

Includes bibliographical references

Frankopan, Peter

The **Silk** Roads; a new history of the world. by Peter Frankopan. Alfred A. Knopf 2016 656 p. ill. (some col.), maps **909**

1. Imperialism 2. Acculturation 3. East and West 4. World history 5. Culture conflict 6. Silk Road -- History 7. Trade routes -- Central Asia 8. Imperialism -- History 9. Trade routes -- History 10. Acculturation -- History 11. East and West -- History 12. Culture conflict -- History

ISBN 9781101946329

LC 2015013264

In this book, author Peter Frankopan "realigns our understanding of the world, pointing us eastward. He vividly re-creates the emergence of the first cities in Mesopotamia and the birth of empires in Persia, Rome and Constantinople, as well as the depredations by the Mongols, the transmission of the Black Death and the violent struggles over Western imperialism. Throughout the millennia, it was the appetite for foreign goods that brought East and West together." (Publisher's note)

"A timely challenge to conventional thinking about a pivotal part of the globe." Booklist

Includes bibliographical references and index.

Galeano, Eduardo H.

Mirrors; stories of almost everyone. [by] Eduardo Galeano; English translation by Mark Fried. Nation Books 2009 391p il $26.95 **909**

1. History -- Miscellanea

ISBN 978-1-56858-423-2; 1-56858-423-7

LC 2009-004518

This book contains some 600 meditations on events or persons in history.

"Each entry is an avatar of outrage over the depredations of power against its multifarious victims, those rendered helpless by poverty, religion, race, sexual identity or—as in the vignettes about Galileo and Isaac Babel—the simple accident of being right when the truth defined by the prevailing authority was wrong. . . . As in his previous books, [Galeano] succeeds in capturing the bottomless horror of the state's capacity to inflict pain on the individual, offering as effective an act of political dissent as exists anywhere in contemporary literature." N Y Times Book Rev

Great events from history, The 17th century, 1601-1700; editor, Larissa Juliet Taylor. Salem Press 2005 2v il map set $160 **909**

1. Reference books 2. World history -- 17th century

ISBN 1-58765-225-0; 978-1-58765-225-7

LC 2005-17362

Companion volume to Great lives from history, The 17th century, 1601-1700

Some of the essays in this work were originally published in Chronology of European history, 15,000 B.C. to 1997 (1997) and Great events from history: North American series. Rev. ed. (1997)

This set "offers two to three-page essays that detail the major milestones of the century as well as social developments that were reflective of daily life during the period. The perspective here is international and spans a variety of categories, including religion and theology, cultural and intellectual history, expansion and land acquisition, and natural disasters. A list of key figures involved in each event is provided." SLJ

Includes bibliographical references

Great events from history, The Renaissance & early modern era, 1454-1600; editor, Christina J. Moose. Salem Press 2005 2v il map set $160 **909**

1. Renaissance 2. Reference books 3. World history -- 15th century 4. World history -- 16th century

ISBN 1-58765-214-5; 978-1-58765-214-1

LC 2004-28878

Companion volume to Great lives from history, The Renaissance & early modern era, 1454-1600

Some of the essays were previously published in various works

This collection of essays covers events in the scientific, intellectual, literary, sociological, political and military disciplines that happened worldwide during the Renaissance.

Includes bibliographical references

Harari, Yuval Noah

Sapiens; a brief history of humankind. Yuval Noah Harari. HarperCollins 2015 464 p. illustrations, maps $29.99 **909**

1. Evolution 2. Human beings

ISBN 0062316095; 9780062316097

LC 2014028418

This book, by Yuval Noah Harari, offers a "narrative of humanity's creation and evolution . . . that explores the ways in which biology and history have defined us and enhanced our understanding of what it means to be 'human.' . . . Dr. Harari also compels us to look ahead, because over the last few decades humans have begun to bend laws of natural selection that have governed life for the past four billion years." (Publisher's note)

"Although Harari's ideas may be controversial for some readers, those who are interested in history, anthropology, and evolution will find his work a fascinating, hearty read." LJ

A **Historical** atlas of the Jewish people; from the time of the patriarchs to the present. general editor, Eli Barnavi; English edition editor, Miriam Eliav-Feldon; cartography, Michel Opatowski; new edition revised by Denis Charbit. new ed; Schocken Bks. 2002 321p il maps $45 **909**

1. Jews -- History -- Maps

ISBN 0-8052-4226-0

LC 2003-279553

First published 1992 by Knopf

"Covering three millennia of Jewish history and culture through a combination of concise text, accurate and well-drawn maps, and a sumptuous array of photographs, diagrams, and reproductions of paintings, this atlas succeeds in covering all the main themes of the Jewish experience. The material is arranged chronologically and systematically. . . . The result is a reference that will profit both scholars and lay readers." Libr J [review of 1992 edition]

History; the definitive visual guide: from the dawn of civilization to the present day. editorial consultant, Adam Hart-Davis. Dorling Kindersley Limited, a Penguin Random House Company 2015 620 p. ill. (some color), color maps $50 **909**
1. World history 2. Civilization -- History 3. World history -- Pictorial works
ISBN 1465437975; 9781465437976

LC 2015451995

This book, edited by Adam Hart-Davis, "tells the story of mankind from prehistory to the present day using a unique visual approach, filled with timelines, images of artifacts, photography, graphics, and more. Now in its third edition, . . . [it] has been revised and updated to bring today's current events into wider context and includes all new material on the global recession, green technologies, and the Internet and social media." (Publisher's note)

The **history** book; contributors, Reg Grant, consultant editor, Fiona Coward, Thomas Cussans, Joel Levy, Philip Parker, Sally Regan, Philip Wilkinson. DK Publishing 2016 352 p. illustrations (some color) $25 **909**
1. World history-- Juvenile literature 2. World history -- Juvenile literature
ISBN 1465445102; 9781465445100

LC 2016429085

This book "is a fascinating journey through the most significant events in history and the big ideas behind each one, from the dawn of civilization to the lightning-paced culture of today. One hundred crystal-clear articles explore the Law Code of Hammurabi, the Renaissance, the American Revolution, World War II, and much, much more, bringing the events and people of history to life." (Publisher's note)
Includes bibliographical references and index

History of the world in 1,000 objects; DK Publishing Inc. DK Publishing 2014 480 p. illustrations, color maps $50 **909**
1. World history 2. Material culture 3. History -- Sources 4. World history -- Sources 5. Material culture -- History
ISBN 1409354660; 1465422897; 9781409354666; 9781465422897

LC 2014497752

This reference book, published by Dorling Kindersley, overviews world history through the examination of 1,000 objects exhibited through the U.S. Smithsonian Museums. "With objects revealing how our ancestors lived, what they believed and valued, and how these items helped shape civilization, . . . [the book] contains a treasure trove of human creativity from earliest cultures to the present day." (Publisher's note)

Hourani, Albert Habib
A **history** of the Arab peoples; with a new afterword by Malise Ruthven. 2nd ed; Belknap Press 2002 xx, 565p il maps hardcover o.p. pa $18.95 **909**
1. Arab civilization 2. Arab countries -- History
ISBN 0-674-01017-5; 0-674-05819-4 pa

LC 2003-269357

First published 1991
This history of the Arab peoples is divided into five parts: The making of a world (seventh-tenth century); Arab Muslim societies (eleventh-fifteenth century); The Ottoman age (sixteenth-eighteenth century); The age of European empires (1800-1939); The age of nation-states (since 1939). Includes a 2002 afterword, genealogies and dynasties
Includes bibliographical references

Kennedy, Hugh
★ The **great** Arab conquests; how the spread of Islam changed the world we live in. Da Capo 2007 421p (paperback) $21.15; $27.95 **909**
1. Islamic civilization 2. Islam -- History
ISBN 9780753823897; 0-306-81585-0; 978-0-306-81585-0

LC 2008-297360

The author "has produced an extremely readable work chronicling the early Arab conquests to 750 CE. In the flowing narrative style for which he has become known, Kennedy brings together Arab, Byzantine, Armenian, Coptic, and Persian histories, legends, and anecdotes related to Arab expansion into the lands stretching from the Iberian Peninsula to the Sind. . . . Each chapter details the conquest of a given region, intertwining historic reality with legendary tales to provide for very colorful reading." Choice
Includes bibliographical references

Kwarteng, Kwasi
Ghosts of empire; Britain's legacies in the modern world. Kwasi Kwarteng. Perseus Books Group 2012 480 p. (hardcover) $29.99 **909**
1. Colonization 2. Modern history 3. Great Britain -- Colonies 4. Imperialism -- History 5. Decolonization -- History 6. Great Britain -- Colonies -- History
ISBN 1610391209; 9781610391207

LC 2011935845

Author Kwasi Kwarteng presents "a narrative history of the British Empire, one that . . . sees the Empire for what it was: a series of local fiefdoms administered in varying degrees of competence or brutality by a cast of characters as outsized and eccentric as anything conjured by Gilbert and Sullivan. The truth, as Kwarteng reveals, is that there was no such thing as a model for imperial administration . . . The idiosyncracies of viceroys and soldier-diplomats who ran the colonial enterprise continues to impact the world, from Kashmir to Sudan, Baghdad to Hong Kong." (Publisher's note)
Includes bibliographical references (p. [433]-446) and index

Lamb, David
The **Arabs**; journeys beyond the mirage. 2nd Vintage Books ed, rev and updated; Vintage Bks. 2002 348p map pa $15 **909**
1. Arab countries
ISBN 1-4000-3041-2

LC 2002-524048

First published 1987 by Random House
"Intelligent and incisive . . . Mr. Lamb has the first-rate reporter's tools, and he uses them to relate, with compelling detail, who the Arabs are." N Y Times Book Rev
Includes bibliographical references

Morris, Ian
Why the West rules--for now; the patterns of history, and what they reveal about the future. Farrar, Straus and Giroux 2010 750p il map **909**
1. East and West 2. Modern civilization 3. Western civilization 4. Civilization, Modern 5. Civilization, Western 6. Comparative civilization
ISBN 0374290024; 9780374290023

LC 2010005702

Morris argues that Western dominance is largely "the result of geography on the everyday efforts of ordinary people as they deal with crises of resources, disease, migration, and climate." (Publisher's note)

Bibliography. Index.

"It may seem at first sight a little odd to recommend a history book as a guide to the future. But Morris' new book illustrates perfectly why one really scholarly book about the past is worth a hundred fanciful works of futurology." Foreign Affairs

Includes bibliographical references

National Geographic concise history of the world; an illustrated timeline. edited by Neil Kagan. Revised edition National Geographic Society 2013 416 p. ill. (some col.), maps $40   **909**
1. World history 2. Historical chronology
ISBN 1426211783; 9781426211782

LC 2015430064

"For readers of all ages, world history is easily accessible, depicted as never before—so that events occurring simultaneously around the world can be viewed at-a-glance together. . . . The book's innovative time line truly sets it apart, allowing readers to scan across a spread and explore a single area or compare contemporary societies across the globe." (Publisher's note)

Includes bibliographical references (pages 405-406) and index

Pagden, Anthony

Peoples and empires; a short history of European migration, exploration, and conquest from Greece to the present. Modern library ed; Modern Lib. 2001 xxv, 206p hardcover o.p. pa $10.95   **909**
1. Colonies 2. World history 3. Immigration and emigration
ISBN 0-679-64096-7; 0-8129-6761-5 pa

LC 00-66204

This "overview of European empire building and colonization commences with the diffusion of Greek civilization and traces the subsequent evolution of the ensuing Roman, Spanish, French, and British empires. More interesting than how those empires physically expanded is the insightful discussion on what motivated individual men and entire nations to migrate and conquer." Booklist

Includes bibliographical references

Parker, Geoffrey

Global crisis; war, climate change and catastrophe in the seventeenth century. Geoffrey Parker. Yale University Press 2012 871 p. (cloth: alkaline paper) $40   **909**
1. World history -- 17th century 2. Climate change -- History -- 17th century 3. History, Modern -- 17th century 4. Military history -- 17th century 5. Civil war -- History -- 17th century 6. Disasters -- History -- 17th century 7. Revolutions -- History -- 17th century 8. Climatic changes -- Social aspects -- History -- 17th century
ISBN 0300153236; 9780300153231

LC 2012039448

This book "presents a history of the 17th century. . . . Focusing on climate-driven unrest around the world, [Geoffrey] Parker illustrates how events such as drought can drive disease, war, and social change. . . . He traces connections between climate and population and war, factors further influencing attitudes toward education and consumption." (Publishers Weekly)

Includes bibliographical references

Roberts, Callum

The **unnatural** history of the sea. Island Press/Shearwater Books 2007 435p il map $28   **909**
1. Ocean 2. Commercial fishing 3. Human influence on nature
ISBN 978-1-59726-102-9; 1-59726-102-5

LC 2007-1841

"Starting with the eighteenth-century voyages of Vitus Bering, Roberts leads the reader through a wealth of maritime history revealing countless examples of overfishing. . . . Thoughtful, inspiring, devastating, and powerful, Roberts' comprehensive, welcoming, and compelling approach to an urgent subject conveys large problems in a succinct and involving manner. Readers won't be able to put it down." Booklist

Includes bibliographical references

Roberts, J. M.

The **history** of the world; J.M. Roberts and O.A. Westad. 6th edition Oxford University Press 2013 260 p.   **909**
1. World history
ISBN 9780199936762

LC 2012041862

"In this new edition, Bancroft Prize-winning historian Odd Arne Westad has completely revised this landmark work to bring the narrative up to the twenty-first century, including the 9/11 attacks and the wars in the Middle East. Westad utilizes the remarkable gains in scholarship in recent decades to enhance the book's coverage of early human life and vastly improve the treatment of India and China, Central Eurasia, early Islam, and the late Byzantine Empire, as well as the history of science, technology, and economics." (Publisher's note)

Includes bibliographical references and index

Schama, Simon, 1945-

★ The **story** of the Jews; Volume two Belonging 1492-1900. by Simon Schama. Ecco, an imprint of HarperCollins Publishers 2017 790 p. illustrations (some color) (hardcover) $39.99   **909**
1. Jews -- History 2. Judaism -- History 3. Jews -- Civilization 4. Jews -- Social conditions
ISBN 9780062339577; 9780062348746; 0062339575

This book, by Simon Schama, "details the story of the Jewish people from 1492 through the end of nineteenth century. . . . [It] tells the stories of many who seldom figure in Jewish histories: not just the rabbis and the philosophers but a poetess in the ghetto of Venice; a general in Ming China; a boxer in Georgian England, a Bible showman in Amsterdam; a teacher of the deaf in eighteenth-century France, an opera composer in nineteenth-century Germany." (Publisher's note)

"This is a wonderful chronicle spanning centuries in the development of an enduring people." Booklist

Includes bibliographical references and index.

Treuer, Anton

Everything you wanted to know about Indians but were afraid to ask; Anton Treuer. Borealis Books 2012 190 p. (pbk.: alk. paper) $15.95   **909**
1. Native Americans 2. Native Americans -- History 3. Native Americans -- Social life and customs
ISBN 0873518616; 0873518624; 9780873518611; 9780873518628

LC 2011053026

In this book Anton Treuer "endeavors to address misconceptions held by non-natives about the American Indian experience in the United States. He accomplishes his task by posing and answering approximately 125 questions divided into ten categories: 'Terminology,' 'History,' 'Religion, Culture & Identity,' 'Powwow,' 'Tribal Languages,' 'Politics,' 'Economics,' 'Education,' 'Perspectives: Coming to Terms and Future Directions,' and 'Finding Ways to Make a Difference.'" (Library Journal)

Includes bibliographical references and index

Watson, Peter, 1943-

The **great** divide; nature and human nature in the old world and the new. Peter Watson. Harper 2012 610 p. $31.99   **909**

1. World history 2. America -- History 3. America -- Civilization 4. Eastern hemisphere -- History 5. Eastern hemisphere -- Civilization
ISBN 0061672459; 9780061672453

This book by Peter Watson "compares the development of humankind in the Old World and the New between 15,000 BC and AD 1500. Watson identifies three major differences between the two worlds -- climate, domesticable mammals, and hallucinogenic plants -- that combined to produce very different trajectories of civilization in the two hemispheres." The author draws on "knowledge in archaeology, anthropology, geology, meteorology, cosmology, and mythology." (Publisher's note)

Includes bibliographical references and index.

Ideas; a history of thought and invention, from fire to Freud. Peter Watson. HarperCollins 2005 xix, 822 p.p $19.99   **909**

1. Civilization -- History 2. Intellectual life -- History
ISBN 0060935642; 006621064X; 9780060935641

LC 2005050255

This book by Peter Watson presents an "overview of the intellectual development of humans from the discovery of fire up to the beginning of the twentieth century." Topics include "the emergence of language . . . the exploration of the physical world with the Atomists, mathematics, astronomy, literature . . . the rise of Christianity, [and] the rise of the Arabs." (Institute of Public Affairs Review)

Includes bibliographical references (p. [747]-804) and indexes

Winchester, Simon

Pacific; Silicon Chips and Surfboards, Coral Reefs and Atom Bombs, Brutal Dictators, Fading Empires, and the Coming Collision of the World's Superpowers. Simon Winchester. HarperCollins 2015 480 p. illustrations, maps $28.99   **909**

1. Pacific Ocean 2. Pacific region 3. Pacific Coast (North America)
ISBN 0062315412; 9780062315410

LC 2015020468

"Simon Winchester offers an enthralling biography of the Pacific Ocean and its role in the modern world, exploring our relationship with this imposing force of nature. Winchester takes us from the Bering Strait to Cape Horn, the Yangtze River to the Panama Canal, and to the many small islands and archipelagos that lie in between. He observes the fall of a dictator in Manila, visits aboriginals in northern Queensland, and is jailed in Tierra del Fuego, the land at the end of the world. " (Publisher's note)

"Winchester . . . does not do the expected: there is no chapter about the geological history of the ocean, followed by a slow chronology. Instead, realizing the difficulty of his own task, the author focuses on 10 aspects of the ocean and its inhabitants--islanders, those on the shores-- and uses them to illustrate some historical points." Kirkus

Includes bibliographical references and index

Worth, Robert F.

★ A **rage** for order; the Middle East in turmoil, from Tahrir Square to ISIS. Robert F. Worth. Farrar, Straus & Giroux 2016 272 p. (hardback) $26   **909**

1. Arab Spring, 2010- 2. Middle East -- Politics and government 3. Arab countries -- Politics and government -- 21st century
ISBN 9780374252946; 9780374710712; 0374252947

LC 2015041559

This book, by Robert F. Worth, is "the first work of literary journalism to track the tormented legacy of . . . the Arab Spring. We meet a

Libyan rebel who must decide whether to kill the Qaddafi-regime torturer who murdered his brother; a Yemeni farmer who lives in servitude to a poetry-writing, dungeon-operating chieftain; and an Egyptian doctor who is caught between his loyalty to the Muslim Brotherhood and his hopes for a new, tolerant democracy." (Publisher's note)

General readers and policymakers will find this timely volume enlightening." Library Journal

909.07   General historical periods

Asbridge, Thomas

★ The **crusades**; the authoritative history of the war for the Holy Land. [by] Thomas Asbridge. Ecco Press 2010 767p il map   **909.07**

1. Crusades 2. Medieval civilization 3. Christianity and other religions 4. Religion and civilization 5. Church history -- 600-1500, Middle Ages
ISBN 9780060787288

Asbridge sets out to "uncover what drove Muslims and Christians alike to embrace the ideals of 'jihad' and crusade, and considers how these holy wars reshaped the medieval world and why they continue to influence events today." (Publisher's note) Index.

"Covering the 200-year period of the Crusades in a single volume is a monumental task, but Asbridge . . . handles it well, presenting an evenhanded view of the actions of Christian and Muslim forces and paying particular attention to the larger-than-life figures of Richard the Lionheart and Saladin. In addition to relating the facts of the expeditions, he explores both the motivations of the Crusaders . . . and the reasons that Christians eventually failed to retain any hold on conquered territory." Libr J

Includes bibliographical references

Catlos, Brian A.

Infidel kings and unholy warriors; faith, power, and violence in the age of crusade and jihad. Brian A. Catlos. Farrar, Straus and Giroux 2014 416 p. illustrations, maps (hardback) $28   **909.07**

1. Crusades 2. Mediterranean region -- History 3. Crusades -- Influence 4. Mediterranean Region -- History -- 476-1517
ISBN 0809058375; 9780809058372

LC 2013043160

In this history of the Crusades, author Brian A. Catlos "puts us on the ground in the Mediterranean world of 1050-1200. We experience the sights and sounds of the region just as enlightened Islamic empires and primitive Christendom began to contest it. We learn about the siege tactics, theological disputes, and poetry of this enthralling time. And we see that people of different faiths coexisted far more frequently than we are commonly told." (Publisher's note)

Includes bibliographical references and index

Cobb, Paul M.

The **race** for paradise; an Islamic history of the crusades. Paul M. Cobb. Oxford University Press 2014 360 p. illustrations, maps (hardback) $29.95   **909.07**

1. Crusades 2. Muslims -- History 3. Muslims -- Mediterranean Region -- History -- To 15000 4. Islam -- Relations -- Christianity -- History -- To 1500 5. Christianity and other religions -- Islam -- History -- To 1500
ISBN 0199358117; 9780199358113

LC 2013040040

This book, by Paul M. Cobb, "offers a new history of the confrontations between Muslims and Franks we now call the 'Crusades,' one that emphasizes the diversity of Muslim experiences of the European holy war.... Cobb considers the Arab perspective on all shores of the Muslim Mediterranean, from Spain to Syria." (Publisher's note)

"Cobb's multidisciplinary approach illuminates the experience of invaded societies in their chaotic and climactic contacts with the Other." Pub Wkly

Includes bibliographical references and index

The **Middle** Ages in 50 objects; Elina Gertsman, Barbara H. Rosenwein. Cambridge University Press 2018 xvii, 233 p.p $34.95 **909.07**
1. Europe -- Antiquities 2. Medieval civilization 3. Civilization, Medieval -- Miscellanea
ISBN 1107150388; 9781107150386
LC 2017037848
Written by Elina Gertsman and Barbara H. Rosenwein, "the extraordinary array of images included in this volume reveals the full and rich history of the Middle Ages. Exploring material objects from the European, Byzantine and Islamic worlds, the book casts a new light on the cultures that formed them, each culture illuminated by its treasures." (Publisher's note)

Includes bibliographical references (pages 214-221) and index
Middle Ages in fifty objects

909.08   Modern history, 1450/1500-

Aaronovitch, David
Voodoo histories; the role of the conspiracy theory in shaping modern history. Riverhead Books 2010 388p il $26.95 **909.08**
1. Conspiracies
ISBN 978-1-59448-895-5
LC 2009-37018
First published 2009 in the United Kingdom
"The book is an evenhanded, lively, and fascinating look not just at the people who believe these theories but also at the people who promote them: the evidence manipulators, the liars, the con artists, and the almost pathetically gullible and uninformed." Booklist

Includes bibliographical references

Jasanoff, Maya
Edge of empire; lives, culture, and conquest in the East, 1750-1850. Knopf 2005 404p il $27.95 **909.08**
1. Collectors and collecting 2. Great Britain -- Colonies
ISBN 1-4000-4167-8
LC 2004-60221
"In graceful prose and with evocative illustrations, Jasanoff scores her points about conquest, collecting, and cultural crossing, offering a thoughtful and highly subtle study." Libr J

Includes bibliographical references

Tuchman, Barbara Wertheim
The **march** of folly; from Troy to Vietnam. [by] Barbara W. Tuchman. Knopf 1984 447p il hardcover o.p. pa $16.95 **909.08**
1. Popes 2. Trojan War 3. Reformation 4. Modern history 5. Vietnam War, 1961-1975 6. Great Britain -- Colonies -- America 7. United States -- History -- 1600-1775, Colonial period
ISBN 0-345-30823-9 pa
LC 83-22206

The author analyzes examples of governmental bumbling including the Trojan horse, the U.S. involvement in Vietnam, and the British loss of the American colonies.

Includes bibliographical references

909.7   Specific historical periods since 1700

Winik, Jay
★ The **great** upheaval; America and the birth of the modern world, 1788-1800. Harper 2007 xx, 659p il map $29.95; pa $17.95 **909.7**
1. Modern history 2. Modern civilization 3. United States -- History -- 1783-1809
ISBN 0-06-008313-1; 978-0-06-008313-7; 0-06-008314-X pa; 978-0-06-008314-4 pa
"An outstandingly wide-ranging account of this vital era in world history." Booklist

Includes bibliographical references

909.8   World history--1800-

Mishra, Pankaj
Age of Anger; A History of the Present. Pankaj Mishra. Farrar, Straus & Giroux 2017 320 p. $26 **909.8**
1. World history 2. World politics 3. Social conflict 4. International relations
ISBN 0374274789; 9780374274788
This book by Pankaj Mishra shows "that as the world became modern, those who were unable to fulfill its promises--freedom, stability and prosperity--were increasingly susceptible to demagogues. The many who came late to this new world or were left, or pushed, behind, reacted in horrifyingly similar ways: intense hatred of invented enemies, attempts to re-create an imaginary golden age, and self-empowerment through spectacular violence." (Publisher's note)

Includes bibliographical references and index.

909.82   World history--20th century, 1900-1999

Dallek, Robert
The **lost** peace; leadership in a time of horror and hope, 1945-1953. Harper 2010 420p il $28.99; ebook $22.99 **909.82**
1. Cold war 2. World politics -- 1945- 3. World War, 1939-1945 -- Peace
ISBN 978-0-06-162866-5; 978-0-06-201671-3 ebook
LC 2010-05727
The author's "interpretation of the thinking and actions of American, Chinese, European, and Soviet leaders is worth the book's reasonable price. This is solid historical scholarship from a master." Libr J

Includes bibliographical references

Emmerson, Charles
1913; in search of the world before the great war. Charles Emmerson. PublicAffairs 2013 544 p. (hardcover) $30 **909.82**
1. World history -- 19th century 2. World War, 1914-1918 -- Causes 3. Nineteen thirteen, A.D
ISBN 1610392566; 9781610392563; 9781610392570
LC 2013935895
In this book, author Charles Emmerson "surveys a selection of cities around the world as they appeared in 1913. Portraying the Euro-

pean capitals of the next year's belligerent countries, Emmerson strikes a cosmopolitan tone by noting social interconnections linking London to Paris to Berlin to Constantinople. Diarists and travelers populate his narratives, their descriptions lending eyewitness immediacy to his delineation of streetscapes, new architecture, and political issues." (Booklist)

"By staying so tightly focused on this single year, Emmerson is able to reveal causal mechanisms while simultaneously making readers wonder what could have been." Pub Wkly

Includes bibliographical references (p. [495]-501) and index

Gilbert, Martin

History of the twentieth century. Morrow 2001 783p maps hardcover o.p. pa $19.95   **909.82**
    1. World history -- 20th century
    ISBN 0-06-050594-X pa

                         LC 2001-32612
Condensed version of the three-volume work first published 1997-1999

The author "chronicles world events year by year, from the dawn of aviation to the flourishing technology age, taking us through World War I to the inauguration of Franklin Roosevelt as president of the United States and Hitler as chancellor of Germany. He continues on to document wars in South Africa, China, Ethiopia, Spain, Korea, Vietnam, and Bosnia, as well as apartheid, the arms race, the moon landing, and the beginnings of the computer age, while interspersing the influence of art, literature, music, and religion." Publisher's note

Harari, Yuval Noah

   ★ **21** lessons for the 21st century; Yuval Noah Harari. Spiegel & Grau 2018 400 p. $28   **909.82**
    1. Culture 2. World politics 3. Modern civilization 4. Civilization, Modern -- 21st century
    ISBN 9780525512172; 9780525512189; 9781984801494
                         LC 2018013856
This book, by Yuval Noah Harari, "is a probing and visionary investigation into today's most urgent issues as we move into the uncharted territory of the future. As technology advances faster than our understanding of it, hacking becomes a tactic of war, and the world feels more polarized than ever, Harari addresses the challenge of navigating life in the face of constant and disorienting change and raises the important questions we need to ask ourselves in order to survive." (Publisher's note)

"Magnificently combining historical, scientific, political, and philosophical perspectives, Harari (Sapiens and Homo Deus), a Hebrew University of Jerusalem history professor, explores 21 of what he considers to be today's "greatest challenges."" Pub Wkly

Includes bibliographical references and index

Twenty one lessons for the twenty first century

Hillstrom, Kevin

The **Cold** War; foreward by Christian Ostermann. Omnigraphics 2006 xx, 536p il (Primary sourcebook series) $65   **909.82**
    1. Cold war 2. World politics -- 1945-1991
    ISBN 0-7808-0934-3; 978-0-7808-0934-5
                         LC 2006-15330
"The wide-ranging scope of documents compiled in this volume will provide AP history and social studies classes with a wealth of information for research and analysis." Libr Media Connect

Includes glossary and bibliographical references

Hochschild, Adam

Lessons from a dark time and other essays; Adam Hochs-

child. University of California Press 2018 296 p. (cloth: alk. paper) $27.95   **909.82**
    1. Political ethics 2. World politics -- 20th century -- Moral and ethical aspects
    ISBN 9780520297241
                         LC 2018009384
"In this rich collection, bestselling author Adam Hochschild has selected and updated over two dozen essays and pieces of reporting from his long career. Threaded through them all is his concern for social justice and the people who have fought for it. The articles here range from a California gun show to a Finnish prison, from a Congolese center for rape victims to the ruins of gulag camps in the Soviet Arctic." (Publisher's note)

Huntington, Samuel P.

The **clash** of civilizations and the remaking of world order. Simon & Schuster 1996 367p il maps hardcover o.p. pa $17   **909.82**
    1. World politics -- 1965- 2. Modern civilization -- 1950-
    ISBN 0-684-84441-9 pa
                         LC 96-31492
"The Huntington argument that the West should stop intervening in civilizational conflicts it doesn't understand makes a powerful claim that internationalists cannot easily ignore." N Y Times Book Rev

Jeffery, Keith

   1916; A Global History. by Keith Jeffery. St. Martin's Press 2016 448 p. 16 plates; illustrations; maps $30   **909.82**
    1. World War, 1914-1918
    ISBN 1620402696; 9781620402696
In this book, "blood-soaked trenches of the Low Countries and North-Eastern Europe were essential battlegrounds during the First World War, but the war reached many other corners of the globe, and events elsewhere significantly affected its course. Covering the twelve months of 1916, eminent historian Keith Jeffery uses twelve moments from a range of locations and shows how they reverberated around the world." (Publisher's note)

"A brilliant compendium of everything-you-didn't-know-about World War I, which, for many readers, will be a great deal." Kirkus

Judt, Tony

Reappraisals; reflections on the forgotten twentieth century. Penguin Press 2008 448p bibl f $29.95   **909.82**
    1. Modern history 2. World history -- 20th century
    ISBN 978-1-59420-136-3; 1-59420-136-6
                         LC 2007-30297
The author "writes informatively about Manes Sperber, tenderly about Primo Levi, enthusiastically about Hannah Arendt. . . . [Tony Judt is] not only a historian of the first rank but (in a word we need an equivalent for) a politicologue who gives engagement a good name." N Y Times Book Rev

Includes bibliographical references and index

Junger, Sebastian

Fire. Norton 2001 224p $24.95   **909.82**
    1. War 2. Disasters 3. Terrorism 4. World politics -- 1991-
    ISBN 0-393-01046-5
                         LC 2001-45236
The stories are "all told with Junger's unfailing eye for detail, which often lends the pieces a disturbing authenticity." Libr J

Kurlansky, Mark

1968; the year that rocked the world. Ballantine 2004 xx, 441p il $26.95 **909.82**

1. Insurgency 2. Radicalism 3. World history -- 1945-
ISBN 0-345-45581-9

LC 2004-299128

This is an account "of the global, social, and political upheaval, warfare, and assassinations that define one year in a tumultuous decade." Booklist

Includes bibliographical references

Lukacs, John, 1924-

A **short** history of the twentieth century; by John Lukacs. The Belknap Press of Harvard University Press 2013 220 p. (hardcover) $24.95 **909.82**

1. World War, 1939-1945 2. World history -- 20th century 3. History, Modern -- 20th century
ISBN 9780674725362; 0674725360

LC 2013007948

This book, written by historian John Luckacs, offers a concise history of the twentieth century--its two world wars and cold war, its nations and leaders. The great themes woven through this spirited narrative are . . . the fading of liberalism, the rise of populism and nationalism, the achievements and dangers of technology, and the continuing democratization of the globe." (Publisher's note)

Includes bibliographical references and index.

The **Oxford** history of the twentieth century; edited by Michael Howard and Wm. Roger Louis. Oxford Univ. Press 1998 xxii, 458p il hardcover o.p. pa $26.50 **909.82**

1. World history -- 20th century
ISBN 978-0-19-280378-8 pa; 0-19-280378-6 pa

LC 98-12861

"Besides global wars hot and cold, population explosion and urbanization impacted the entire century, as one of 27 articles in Twentieth Century underscores. Embracing nonpolitical topics in areas such as physics, modernism in art, and international economics, this work exposes the interested reader to developments that have affected most people." Booklist

Includes bibliographical references

Sebestyen, Victor

1946; The Making of the Modern World. by Victor Sebestyen. Random House Inc 2015 464 p. 16 plates; illustrations; maps $30 **909.82**

1. World politics -- 1945-1991 2. World history -- 20th century
ISBN 1101870427; 9781101870426

LC 2015014902

This book is "about the year that would signal the beginning of the Cold War, the end of the British Empire, and the beginning of the rivalry between the United States and the USSR. Victor Sebestyen reveals the events of 1946 by chronologically framing what was taking place in Europe, the Middle East, and Asia, with seminal decisions made by heads of state that would profoundly change the old order forever." (Publisher's note)

"Highly recommended for anyone interested in world history or for those seeking to understand why the world is as it is today." LJ

Service, Robert, 1947-

The **End** of the Cold War, 1985-1991; Robert Service. PublicAffairs 2015 xxii, 643 p.p illustrations (HC) $35 **909.82**

1. Cold war 2. United States -- Foreign relations -- Soviet Union

3. Disarmament 4. World politics -- 1945-1989 5. Cold War -- Diplomatic history 6. Germany -- History -- Unification, 1990 7. Soviet Union -- Foreign relations -- 1985-1991 8. United States -- Foreign relations -- 1981-1989 9. Soviet Union -- Foreign relations -- United States
ISBN 9781610394994; 9781610395007

LC 2015942161

Author Robert Service's book is an "investigation of the final years of the Cold War. [It] opens a window onto the dramatic years that would irrevocably alter the world's geopolitical landscape, and the men at their fore. 'The End of the Cold War' captures the astonishing relationship between [Ronald] Reagan and [Mikhail] Gorbachev, two exceptional politicians who cooperated against all odds during extraordinary times." (Publisher's note)

"A wholly satisfying, likely definitive, but not triumphalist account of the end of an era." Kirkus

Includes bibliographical references (pages 501-518) and index

Tuchman, Barbara Wertheim

The **proud** tower; a portrait of the world before the war, 1890-1914. [by] Barbara W. Tuchman. 1st Ballantine Books ed; Ballantine Books 1996 528p il pa $15.95 **909.82**

1. Composers 2. Socialism 3. Anarchism and anarchists 4. Army officers 5. Europe -- Social conditions 6. World history -- 19th century 7. World history -- 20th century 8. United States -- Social conditions
ISBN 0-345-40501-3

LC 96-96511

First published 1966 by Macmillan

The author describes prewar social conditions in the U.S., France, England and Germany.

Includes bibliographical references

Vinen, Richard

1968; radical protest and its enemies. Richard Vinen. HarperCollins 2018 448 p. $29.99 **909.82**

1. Radicalism 2. Protest movements 3. World politics -- 1965-
ISBN 0062458744; 9780062458742

LC 2018079926

In this book, author Richard Vinen recounts the "extraordinary range of protests across much of the western world [that happened in 1968.] Some of these were genuinely revolutionary--around ten million French workers went on strike and the whole state teetered on the brink of collapse. Others were more easily contained, but had profound longer-term implications--terrorist groups, feminist collectives, gay rights activists could all trace important roots to 1968." (Publisher's note)

"Although British historian Richard Vinen's rather academic examination lacks storytelling finesse, it is rich in distinct and acute observations. His subject is not the year per se but rather "the long 68," that is, the "radical movements and rebellion of the late 1960s and early 1970s."" Booklist

909.825 World history, 1950-1959

Chamberlin, Paul Thomas

The **Cold** War's killing fields; rethinking the long peace. Paul Thomas Chamberlin. HarperCollins 2018 629 p. ill., maps, portraits $29.99 **909.825**

1. Cold war 2. Military history
ISBN 006236720X; 9780062367204

In this book Paul Thomas Chamberlin offers a "comprehensive

international military history of the Cold War in which he views the decade-long superpower struggles as one of the three great conflicts of the twentieth century. . . . Chamberlin reframes this era in global history and explores in detail the numerous battles fought to prevent nuclear war, bolster the strategic hegemony of the U.S. and the U.S.S.R., and determine the fate of societies throughout the Third World." (Publisher's note)

Includes bibliographical references (pages 567-605) and index

Westad, Odd Arne

The **Cold** War; A World History. Odd Arne Westad. Basic Books 2017 710 p. (hardcover) $40   **909.825**
    1. Cold war 2. World history -- 20th century 3. Cold War 4. World politics -- 1945-1989
    ISBN 9781541698284; 9780465054930

                 LC 2017939229

In this book, author "Odd Arne Westad argues that the Cold War must be understood as a global ideological confrontation, with early roots in the Industrial Revolution and ongoing repercussions around the world. . . . Westad offers a new perspective on a century when great power rivalry and ideological battle transformed every corner of our globe. . . . This book expands our understanding of the Cold War both geographically and chronologically." (Publisher's note)

"He ably synthesizes contemporary scholarship to produce an accessible narrative that provides a fresh perspective on the conflict's pervasive global influence." Pub Wkly

Includes bibliographical references (pages 637-675) and index.

909.826   World history, 1960-1969

The **60s;** the story of a decade. The New Yorker; edited by Henry Finder; introduction by David Remnick. Random House Inc. 2016 752 p. $35   **909.826**
    1. Nineteen sixties 2. New York (N.Y.) -- History 3. United States -- Civilization -- 1945-
    ISBN 9780679644835

                 LC 2016013617

"The third installment of a fascinating decade-by-decade series, this anthology collects historic New Yorker pieces from the most tumultuous years of the twentieth century—including work by James Baldwin, Pauline Kael, Sylvia Plath, Roger Angell, Muriel Spark, and John Updike—alongside new assessments of the 1960s by some of today's finest writers." (Publisher's note)

"Collectively, the essays provide a keen intellectual view of the 1960s while reintroducing readers to some of the best writers of the decade." LJ

909.83   World history--21st century, 2000-2099

Bergen, Peter L.

The **longest** war; the enduring conflict between America and al-Qaeda. Free Press 2011 xx, 473p il map   **909.83**
    1. Terrorism 2. Iraq War, 2003-2011 3. War on terrorism 4. Al Qaeda (Organization) 5. War on Terrorism, 2001- 6. Terrorism -- United States -- Prevention
    ISBN 0743278933; 1439160597; 9780743278935; 9781439160596

                 LC 2010-15268

"Most histories of the war on terror have been written largely from the American perspective, while this book [aims to] fold into the nar-

rative the perspective of al-Qaeda and allied jihadist groups. . . . This book is first a narrative history of the 'war on terror' based upon a synthesis of . . . available open-source materials, together with my own interviewing and reporting. . . . The book also aspires to provide an analytic net assessment of the 'war on terror' to see what conclusions might now be drawn about what al-Qaeda and its allied groups accomplished in the first decade of the twenty-first century and where the United States and her partners have succeeded and failed." (Author's note) Bibliography. Index.

This is "a broad, almost stereoscopic account that brings an array of sources together into an illuminating synthesis. . . . If you want a solid, readable history of the Long War, this is a great place to start." Washington Monthly

Includes bibliographical references

Harari, Yuval Noah

Homo Deus; A Brief History of Tomorrow. Yuval Noah Harari. HarperCollins 2017 448 p. $35   **909.83**
    1. Forecasting 2. Modern civilization
    ISBN 0062464310; 9780062464316

                 LC 2017000348

In this book, author Yuval Noah Harari addresses questions such as "what . . . will replace famine, plague, and war at the top of the human agenda? As the self-made gods of planet earth, what destinies will we set ourselves, and which quests will we undertake? . . . [This book] explores the projects, dreams and nightmares that will shape the twenty-first century--from overcoming death to creating artificial life. It asks the fundamental question: Where do we go from here?" (Publisher's note)

"A relentlessly fascinating book that is sure to become—and deserves to be—a bestseller." Kirkus

Klosterman, Chuck, 1972-

★ **But** What If We're Wrong? Thinking About the Present As If It Were the Past. Chuck Klosterman. Penguin Group USA 2016 288 p. (ebook) $85.50; (hardback) $26   **909.83**
    1. Forecasting 2. Future life 3. Popular culture -- United States 4. United States -- Civilization -- 1970-
    ISBN 9780451484901; 9780399184123; 0399184120

                 LC 2016023103

This book, by Chuck Klosterman, "visualizes the contemporary world as it will appear to those who'll perceive it as the distant past. Chuck Klosterman asks questions that are profound in their simplicity: How certain are we about our understanding of gravity? How certain are we about our understanding of time? What will be the defining memory of rock music, five hundred years from today? How seriously should we view the content of our dreams?" (Publisher's note)

"Replete with lots of nifty, whimsical footnotes, this clever, speculative book challenges our beliefs with jocularity and perspicacity." Kirkus

Includes bibliographical references and index.

Chuck Klosterman X; a highly specific, defiantly incomplete history of the early 21st century. Chuck Klosterman. Blue Rider Press 2017 xvii, 444 p.p (hardcover) $27   **909.83**
    1. Social conditions 2. World history -- 21st century 3. Popular culture -- United States
    ISBN 9780399184178; 0399184155; 9780399184154

                 LC 2017004695

This book, by Chuck Klosterman, is "a collection of journalistic pieces that remain provocative... [It] offers insight into the relations among artist, art, and audience that goes considerably deeper [and] will leave readers with fresh appreciation for both the subjects and the journalist." (Kirkus Reviews)

"This collection features his best pieces from the last ten years. Although a majority of the articles focus on music or sports, Klosterman also ruminates on literature, pop culture, death, and much more." LJ

910 Geography and travel

Allaby, Michael

The **encyclopedia** of Earth; a complete visual guide. [authors, Michael Allaby ... [et al.]] University of California Press 2008 608p il map $39.95   **910**

1. Reference books 2. Earth sciences -- Encyclopedias
ISBN 978-0-520-25471-8; 0-520-25471-6

LC 2008-6956

This "source includes six main sections. 'Birth' is an overview of Earth's history and evolution; 'Fire' covers its inner workings, structure, and landscape; 'Land' covers rocks, minerals, and habitats; 'Air' covers weather; 'Water' includes information on oceans, rivers, and lakes; and 'Humans' is about humankind's relationship with Earth, including management of its resources. . . . This is a stunning, reasonably priced resource, especially useful for those in need of illustrations or a visual representation of a phenomenon or concept." Choice

The **CIA** World Factbook. Skyhorse Publishing various pagings maps   **910**

1. Almanacs 2. Geopolitics 3. Population -- Statistics
Annual

This book "offers complete and up-to-date information on the world's nations. This comprehensive guide is packed with data on the politics, populations, military expenditures, and economics." (Publisher's note)

Fuller, Gary

The **trivia** lover's guide to the world; geography for the lost and found. Gary Fuller. Rowman & Littlefield Publishers, Inc. 2012 270 p. (pbk.: alk. paper) $16.95   **910**

1. Geography -- Miscellanea
ISBN 1442214031; 9781442214033; 9781442214040

LC 2011051863

In this book on geography for general-interest readers, "using a game-show format and trivia questions, [Gary] Fuller goes beyond short answers to expound on a wide variety of geographic topics. . . . The chapters are arranged around particular themes, which include state capitals, the why and where of various cities, and the links between religion and geography." (Booklist)

Hauserman, Julie

Drawn to the deep; the remarkable underwater explorations of Wes Skiles. Julie Hauserman. University Press of Florida 2018 256 p. (cloth: alk. paper) $24.95   **910**

1. Biography 2. Environmentalists -- Biography
ISBN 9780813056982

LC 2018933358

This book, by Julie Hauserman, "celebrates the life of an extraordinary adventurer [Wes Skiles]. . . . His passion for diving and his innovative camera techniques earned him assignments with 'National Geographic' and 'Outside.' [Hauserman shares the] inspiring story of an explorer and activist who uncovered environmental abuses, advanced the field of underwater photography, and astonished the world with unprecedented views of the secret depths of the planet." (Publisher's note)

910.2 Geography--Miscellany; world travel guides

Foer, Joshua

★ **Atlas** Obscura; An Explorer's Guide to the World's Hidden Wonders. Joshua Foer; Dylan Thuras; Ella Morton. Workman Pub Co 2016 480 p. $35   **910.2**

1. Adventure travel 2. Exploration -- Atlases 3. Curiosities and wonders
ISBN 0761169083; 9780761169086

LC 2016041548

This book by Joshua Foer, Dylan Thuras and Ella Morton "celebrates over 700 of the strangest and most curious places in the world. Talk about a bucket list: here are natural wonders—the dazzling glowworm caves in New Zealand, or a baobob tree in South Africa that's so large it has a pub inside. . . . Architectural marvels, including the M.C. Escher-like stepwells in India, . . . [and] mind-boggling events, like the Baby Jumping Festival in Spain." (Publisher's note)

"Featuring full-color illustrations, this hefty and gorgeously produced tome will be eagerly pored over by readers of many ages and fans of the original website." Booklist

Secret marvels of the world; written by Alex Howard and 51 others; illustrator, Lauren Crow; editors, Samantha Forge, Nick Mee, Christina Webb. Lonely Planet 2017 304 p. illustrations, maps (hardcover) $24.99   **910.2**

1. Travel writing 2. Curiosities and wonders 3. Travel -- Guidebooks 4. Curiosities and wonders -- Guidebooks
ISBN 9781786578655; 9781787010048; 1786578654

This book, by Lonely Planet, "takes its readers on a journey through the world's lesser known marvels. Dive into an underworld of the planet's most surprising, fun, perplexing, kitsch and downright bizarre sights - and explore human stories and mysterious happenings that you won't find inside a regular guidebook." (Publisher's note)

"This is a good resource for browsing at will, referencing specific locations via the handy index, and letting readers' dream-trip imaginations run wild." Booklist

Ultimate travel; our list of the 500 best places to see... ranked. by Lonely Planet (Author) Lonely Planet 2015 328 p. color illustrations $24.99   **910.2**

1. Travel 2. Voyages and travels
ISBN 1760342777; 9781760342777

This travel guide published by Lonely Planet, "is a compilation of the 500 most unmissable sights and attractions in the world. . . . Ranked by Lonely Planet's global community of travel experts, . . . big name mega-sights such as the Eiffel Tower and the Taj Mahal battle it out with lesser-known hidden gems for a prized place in the top 10, making this the only bucket list you'll ever need." (Publisher's note)

"Travelers with a competitive edge will savor this work as they plan their next excursions." LJ

The **world**; a traveller's guide to the planet. second edition Lonely Planet 2017 991 p illustrations $29.99   **910.2**

1. Travel -- Guidebooks
ISBN 9781786576538

"We've taken the highlights from the world's best guidebooks and put them together into one 900+ page whopper to create the ultimate guide to Earth. This user-friendly A-Z gives a flavour of each country in the world, including a map, travel highlights, info on where to go and how to get around, as well as some quirkier details to bring each place to life. In Lonely Planet's trademark bluespine format, this is the ultimate planning resource." (Publisher's note)

World Heritage Sites; a complete guide to 1,073 UNESCO World Heritage Sites. by UNESCO. 8th edition Firefly Books 2018 960 p. illustrations $35   **910.2**
1. Historic sites 2. Historic buildings
ISBN 9780228101352

"This eighth edition contains all 1,073 World Heritage Sites in 168 countries, principalities and island states in Africa, Asia, Australia, Europe, North America, the Arab States, Latin America, the Caribbean and the world's oceans. Forty-two are new to this edition." (Publisher's note)

910.285   Computer applications

Bray, Hiawatha
You are here; from the compass to GPS, the history and future of how we find ourselves. Hiawatha Bray. Basic Books 2014 272 p. (hardback) $27.99   **910.285**
1. Navigation 2. Global Positioning System 3. Technological innovations -- Social aspects 4. Geospatial data 5. Electronics in navigation -- History 6. Geographic information systems -- History
ISBN 0465032850; 9780465032853
LC 2014002731
This book, by Hiawatha Bray, "examines the rise of our technologically aided era of navigational omniscience--or how we came to know exactly where we are at all times. In a sweeping history of the development of location technology in the past century, Bray shows how . . . humankind ingeniously solved one of its oldest and toughest problems--only to herald a new era in which it's impossible to hide." (Publisher's note)
Includes bibliographical references and index

910.3   Geography--Dictionaries, encyclopedias, concordances, gazetteers

The **Columbia** gazetteer of the world; edited by Saul B. Cohen. 2nd ed.; Columbia University Press 2008 3v set $595   **910.3**
1. Gazetteers 2. Reference books
ISBN 978-0-231-14554-1
LC 2008-9181
First published 1952 with title: The Columbia Lippincott gazetteer of the world
"The 170,000-plus entries cover political, physical, and special places, including monuments and historic sites. . . . Historically accurate, this title can be considered a reference standard." Libr J

The **Oxford** companion to world exploration; David Buisseret, editor in chief. Oxford University Press 2007 2v il map set $250   **910.3**
1. Exploration
ISBN 0-19-514922-X; 978-0-19-514922-7
LC 2006-27968
"The entries are presented in alphabetical order and cover not only individual explorers, but also some geographic regions, wars, commercial operations, and religious organizations. . . . This work will become the first stop for students and general readers who seek either basic information or a starting point for further reading." Sci Books Films
Includes bibliographical references

Worldmark encyclopedia of the nations; 14th edition Gale / Cengage Learning 2017 5v $767   **910.3**
1. Reference books 2. Geography -- Encyclopedias 3. World history -- Encyclopedias 4. World politics -- Encyclopedias
ISBN 9781410338983
"Presents easy-to-understand information on more than 200 countries and dependencies from around the world in 5 volumes. The 4 country volumes are arranged by global region--Africa, Americas, Asia & Oceania, and Europe--while a United Nations volume focuses on that organization's purposes, principles, and agencies, including the Security Council and Human Rights Commission. Each country entry breaks the country's information into 49 numbered headings that allow users to compare countries in a variety of ways." (Publisher's note)

910.4   Accounts of travel and facilities for travelers

Baggett, Jennifer
The **lost** girls; three friends, four continents, one unconventional detour around the world. [by] Jennifer Baggett, Holly C. Corbett, Amanda Pressner. HarperCollins 2010 542p map $24.99; ebook $11.99   **910.4**
1. Backpacking 2. Voyages and travels 3. Women -- Travel
ISBN 978-0-06-168906-2; 978-0-06-199347-3 ebook
LC 2009-54294
"Friends Pressner, Baggett, and Corbett were all busy climbing the corporate ladder of Manhattan media when they realized that, in their late twenties, they weren't sure they wanted the golden handcuffs of New York success. Reprioritizing, they decide on a rebellious, extreme course of action: quit their jobs, abandon their boyfriends, and take a yearlong trip around the world. In this group memoir, the three take turns chronicling a journey from Peru to Kenya to Vietnam to Australia, and everywhere in between. . . . [The authors] provide passionate, vivid descriptions of their far-flung travels, bolstered by thoughtful insights and genuine intentions, making this an intensely enjoyable read for fans of travel writing." Publ Wkly

Bellec, Francois
Unknown lands; the log books of the great explorers. translated by Lisa Davidson and Elizabeth Ayre. Overlook Press 2002 213p il map $55   **910.4**
1. Explorers 2. Voyages and travels
ISBN 1-58567-201-7
LC 2001-36800
"Weaving together logs, correspondence, and stories of the 'ordinary and extraordinary men' who explored the oceans and unknown lands over five centuries, Bellec offers a . . . snapshot of the cultural and political circumstances that set the stage for maritime adventures and New World discoveries. Eyewitness accounts retold alongside maps and drawings contribute to an enlightening view of the minds, hearts, and talents of adventurers such as Columbus, Vasco de Gama, and James Cook. . . . This is simply a stunning book." Libr J
Includes bibliographical references

Bergreen, Laurence
Over the edge of the world; Magellan's terrifying circumnavigation of the globe. Morrow 2003 458p il maps hardcover o.p. pa $15.95   **910.4**
1. Explorers 2. Voyages around the world
ISBN 0-06-621173-5; 0-06-093638-X pa; 978-0-06-093638-9 pa
LC 2003-50143
The author "tells a well-rounded story of Magellan, not just that of

the romanticized hero but also that of the explorer's darker side. . . . Fascinating reading for history buffs, and a great story that rivals any seagoing adventure." Booklist

Includes bibliographical references

The Best American Travel Writing 2016; edited by Bill Bryson and Jason Wilson. Houghton Mifflin Harcourt 2016 320 p. (paperback) $14.95; (ebook) $14.95 **910.4**
    1. Travel writing
    ISBN 9780544812093; 9780544812161; 0544812093
                    LC 2016042123

This collection of travel essays, edited by Bill Bryson and Jason Wilson, asks "why do I travel? Why does anyone of us travel? . . . Whether traversing the Arctic by dogsled, attending a surreal film festival in North Korea, or strolling the streets of a fast-changing Havana, their insights into the world and the human condition are illuminating and enthralling, providing an answer." (Publisher's note)

"Featuring a large cross-section of writings and writers of diverse subjects, this title will entertain and educate travel buffs as well as readers of cultural and historical works." LJ

The best American travel writing 2017; edited with an introduction by Lauren Collins; Jason Wilson, series editor. Houghton Mifflin Harcourt 2017 320 p. $15.99 **910.4**
    1. Travel 2. Travel writing
    ISBN 1328745732; 9781328745736

This book on travel writing in the Best American Series, edited by Lauren Collins and Jason Wilson, offers "readers glimpses into places that many will never see or experience except through the eyes and words of these writers." (Kirkus Reviews) "This far-ranging collection of top notch travel writing is, quite simply, the genre's gold standard." (Publisher's note)

Brandt, Anthony
The man who ate his boots; the tragic history of the search for the Northwest Passage. Alfred A. Knopf 2010 441p il map $28.95 **910.4**
    1. Explorers 2. Northwest Passage 3. Arctic regions -- Exploration
    ISBN 978-0-307-26392-6; 0-307-26392-4
                    LC 2009-38835

The author tells the story of the search for the Northwest Passage, from its beginnings early in the age of exploration through its development into a British national obsession to the final sordid, terrible descent into scurvy, starvation, and cannibalism.

"Often witty in his approach, Brandt makes the absurdity of Arctic exploration and the quest for the Northwest Passage entertaining for the general reader. Highly recommended for fans of British or Arctic exploration history." Libr J

Includes bibliographical references

Burgin, Robert
Going places; a reader's guide to travel narratives. Robert Burgin. Libraries Unlimited 2013 xxx, 572 p.p (Real stories series) (hardcopy: alk. paper) $70 **910.4**
    1. Travel writing
    ISBN 1598849727; 9781598849721
                    LC 2012035744

This book, by Robert Burgin, "examines the subgenres of the travel narrative genre in its seven chapters, categorizing and describing approximately 600 titles according to genres and broad reading interests, and identifying hundreds of other fiction and nonfiction titles as readalikes and related reads by shared key topics. The author has also identi-

fied award-winning titles and spotlighted further resources on travel lit." (Publisher's note)

Includes bibliographical references and indexes

Butler, Daniel Allen
"Unsinkable" the full story of the RMS Titanic. Daniel Allen Butler. Revised edition Da Capo Press 2012 310 p $18 **910.4**
    1. Shipwrecks 2. Titanic (Steamship)
    ISBN 9780306820984

Describes the construction and maiden voyage of the "unsinkable" Titanic, which sank after colliding with an iceberg in the North Atlantic in April 1912.

Chaplin, Joyce E.
Round about the earth; circumnavigation from Magellan to orbit. Joyce E. Chaplin. Simon & Schuster 2012 535 p. (hardcover) $35 **910.4**
    1. Travel -- History 2. Transportation -- History 3. Voyages around the world -- History
    ISBN 1416596194; 9781416596196; 9781416596202; 9781439100066
                    LC 2012016459

This book, by Joyce E. Chaplin, offers a "full history of . . . circumnavigation. . . . For almost five hundred years, human beings have been finding ways to circle the Earth. . . . The story begins with the first centuries of circumnavigation, when few survived the attempt. . . . Once continental railroads were built, circumnavigators could traverse sea and land. . . . Finally humans took to the skies to circle the globe in airplanes. Not much later, . . . in orbit." (Publisher's note)

Includes bibliographical references and index.

Cordingly, David
Women sailors and sailors' women; an untold maritime history. Random House 2001 286p il hardcover o.p. pa $14.95 **910.4**
    1. Women 2. Voyages and travels 3. Adventure and adventurers
    ISBN 0-375-75872-0 pa
                    LC 00-62762

A look at "the lives of the intrepid women who went to sea during the great age of sail. Countless females set sail for reasons of adventure, romance, or duty in the seventeenth, eighteenth, and nineteenth centuries. Included among their numbers were the wives or mistresses of ships' officers, prostitutes, female pirates, and women disguised as male sailors. . . . A significant contribution to both women's history and maritime scholarship." Booklist

Includes bibliographical references

Dana, Richard Henry
Two years before the mast; a personal narrative of life at sea. introduction by Gary Kinder; notes by Duncan Hasell. Modern Library 2001 xxiv, 516p il pa $12.95 **910.4**
    1. Seafaring life 2. Voyages and travels
    ISBN 0-375-75794-5
                    LC 2001-31243

First published anonymously in 1840

The author "shipped out of Boston in 1834 on the Pilgrim and sailed around the Horn to California on a hide-trading expedition. The book is based on the journal he kept during the voyage. Horrified by the brutal captain's mistreatment of the sailors, and shocked by their lack of legal redress, Dana wrote with a burning indignation that did much to rouse the public to the mariners' plight." HarperCollins Reader's Ency of Am

Lit. 2d edition

Duncombe, Laura Sook

Pirate women; the princesses, prostitutes, and privateers who ruled the Seven Seas. Laura Sook Duncombe. Chicago Review Press 2017 xiv, 250 p.p (hardcover) $26.99 **910.4**
1. Piracy -- History 2. Women pirates -- Biography 3. Women pirates -- History
ISBN 9781613736012; 9781613736043
LC 2016031175

This book, by Laura Sook Duncombe, focuses on "women, both real and legendary, who through the ages sailed alongside--and sometimes in command of--their male counterparts. . . . Here are their stories, from ancient Norse princess Alfhild and warrior Rusla to Sayyida al-Hurra of the Barbary corsairs; from Grace O'Malley, who terrorized shipping operations . . . during the reign of Queen Elizabeth I; to Cheng I Sao, who commanded a fleet of four hundred ships off China." (Publisher's note)

"Duncombe's well-researched account will appeal to history and women's studies aficionados, lovers of myth and lore, and all interested in viewing the past through a new lens." Booklist

Includes bibliographical references and index

Fagan, Brian

Beyond the blue horizon; how the earliest mariners unlocked the secrets of the oceans. Brian Fagan. New York 2012 313 p. ill., maps $28 **910.4**
1. Exploration 2. Ocean travels -- History 3. Seafaring life -- History 4. Sea peoples -- History 5. Navigation, Prehistoric 6. Ocean travel -- History
ISBN 1608190056; 9781608190058
LC 2011045758

In this book, "historian Brian Fagan tackles . . . the enduring quest to master the oceans, the planet's most mysterious terrain. . . . From the moment when ancient Polynesians first dared to sail beyond the horizon, Fagan . . . explains how our mastery of the oceans changed the course of human history. . . . Fagan reveals how seafaring evolved so that the forbidding realms of the sea gods were transformed from barriers into a nexus of commerce and cultural exchange." (Publisher's note)

Includes bibliographical references and index

Garcia Marquez, Gabriel

The **story** of a shipwrecked sailor; who drifted on a life raft for ten days . . . translated from the Spanish by Randolph Hogan. Knopf 1986 106p hardcover o.p. pa $11 **910.4**
1. Survival after airplane accidents, shipwrecks, etc.
ISBN 0-679-72205-X pa
LC 85-45673

Original Spanish edition, 1970

"In 1955 Garcia Marquez was working as a reporter in Colombia. One of his stories was a serialized account of a sailor who was swept overboard with seven other crew members of a Colombian destroyer and who was the only one to survive. This book presents Garcia Marquez' version of the sailor's first-person narrative." Booklist

Heat-Moon, William Least

Here, there, elsewhere; stories from the road. William Least Heat-Moon. Little, Brown and Co. 2013 402 p. $29.99 **910.4**
1. Travel
ISBN 0316110248; 9780316110242
LC 2012953180

This book is a collection of short writings from travel writer William Least Heat-Moon. "Culled from 30 years of magazine articles,

these pieces roam across terrain both familiar and exotic. Many find magic in mundane patches of America, from improbably delicious fried-fish stands on Minnesota's Lake Superior shore to oddly idyllic Gulf Coast industrial canals and Seattle's rebel micro-breweries." (Publishers Weekly)

Henion, Leigh Ann

Phenomenal; a hesitant adventurer's search for wonder in the natural world. Leigh Ann Henion. Penguin Press 2015 276 p. map (hardcover) $26.95 **910.4**
1. Spiritual life 2. Voyages and travels 3. Spiritual biography 4. Women shamans -- Biography
ISBN 1594204713; 9780143108030; 9781594204715
LC 2014036661

This memoir, by Leigh Ann Henion, "begins in hardship: with Henion deeply shaken by the birth of her beloved son, shocked at the adversity a young mother faces with a newborn. . . . Convinced that the greatest key to happiness—both her own and that of her family—lies in periodically venturing into the wider world beyond home, Henion sets out on a global trek to rekindle her sense of wonder." (Publisher's note)

Heyerdahl, Thor

Kon-Tiki; across the Pacific by raft. translated by F.H. Lyon. Washington Square Press 1984 240p map (Enriched classics series) pa $5.99 **910.4**
1. Pacific Ocean 2. Ethnology -- Polynesia 3. Kon-Tiki Expedition (1947)
ISBN 0-671-72652-8
LC 84-42785

Original Norwegian edition, 1948

The "story of the six men who crossed the Pacific from Peru to the Polynesians on a primitive balsa-log raft such as Peruvian natives of the fifth century used, to prove that it was possible that the legendary race that came to Easter Island and the Polynesians could have come from Peru." Wis Libr Bull

Hoffman, Carl

The **lunatic** express; discovering the world -- via its most dangerous buses, boats, trains, and planes. Broadway Books 2010 286p map $24.99 **910.4**
1. Transportation 2. Voyages and travels
ISBN 0-7679-2980-2; 978-0-7679-2980-6
LC 2009-21477

Hoffman "manages to be both brave and compassionate as he lurches on his near-interminable journey from his home turf in the Adams Morgan neighborhood of Washington to the Gobi Desert and back again. He learns enough about himself en route to satisfy the travel-writing theorists, true, and this can be a little tedious. But—more important—he learns along the way a great deal about the habits of the world's peripatetic poor, and he writes about both the process and the people with verve and charity, making this book both extraordinary and extraordinarily valuable." Wall Street J

An **Innocent** Abroad; Dave Eggers, Richard Ford, Pico Iyer, John Berendt, Alexander McCall Smith and Jane Smiley. Lonely Planet 2014 320 p. $15.99 **910.4**
1. Travel 2. Authors 3. Celebrities
ISBN 1743603606; 9781743603604

In this book "more than 20 well-known writers and celebrities share the travel experiences that shaped their personalities and changed their lives. Contributors include Dave Eggers, Richard Ford, Pico Iyer, John Berendt, Alexander McCall Smith and Jane Smiley." (Publisher's note)

"Most but not all of these vignettes effectively convey the sense of novelty, and sometimes wide-eyed wonder, that youthful travelers are often fortunate to experience." Booklist

Junger, Sebastian

★ The **perfect** storm; a true story of men against the sea. Norton 1997 226p il map $23.95; pa $14.95 **910.4**
  1. Storms 2. Shipwrecks
  ISBN 0-393-04016-X; 0-393-33701-4 pa

  LC 96-42412

"With waves as high as a hundred feet and winds so strong that anemometers were torn from their moorings, the storm of the title struck unsuspecting mariners off the coast of Nova Scotia in October, 1991. Junger traces the last voyage of the Andrea Gail—a commercial swordfishing boat that was lost, with all six hands, in the storm—and his account is relentlessly suspenseful." New Yorker

Lord, Walter

★ A **night** to remember. Holt & Co. 1955 209p il hardcover o.p. pa $14 **910.4**
  1. Shipwrecks 2. Titanic (Steamship)
  ISBN 0-03-027615-2; 0-8050-7764-2 pa
  A detailed account of "the tragic drama of that terrible night—April 4, 1912—when the 'Titanic,' the unsinkable ship, struck an iceberg and went down in the icy waters of the Atlantic." Libr J

Macleod, Alasdair

Explorers; great tales of adventure and endurance. Royal Geographical Society; [written by Alasdair Macleod] DK in association with the Smithsonian Institution 2010 360p il $40 **910.4**
  1. Explorers 2. Exploration
  ISBN 978-0-7566-6737-5
"The book covers the history of exploration from the discovery of the ancient Egyptians in Nubia to the exploration of space by the Soviet Union and the United States in the 20th century. . . . [It] is a wonderful introduction to the various personalities who, over a period of several thousand years, devoted themselves, to studying the world and revealing its fascinatingly diverse landscapes, conditions, and cultures." Sci Books Films

Read, Piers Paul

★ **Alive**; sixteen men, seventy-two days, and insurmountable odds--the classic adventure of survival in the Andes. Harper Perennial 2005 398p il pa $13.95 **910.4**
  1. Survival after airplane accidents, shipwrecks, etc. 2. Andes
  ISBN 0-06-077866-0
  First published 1974 by Lippincott
  The author describes the extraordinary hardships endured by the survivors of a horrific plane crash in the Andes.

Rosenbloom, Stephanie

Alone time; four seasons, four cities, and the pleasures of solitude. Stephanie Rosenbloom. Viking 2018 288 p. (hardback) $27 **910.4**
  1. Travel 2. Solitude 3. Travelers 4. Travelers -- Psychology
  ISBN 9780399562303

  LC 2018011925

"Through on-the-ground reporting and recounting the experiences of artists, writers, and innovators who cherished solitude, Stephanie Rosenbloom considers how being alone as a traveller--and even in one's own city--is conducive to becoming acutely aware of the sensual details of the world--patterns, textures, colors, tastes, sounds--in ways that are difficult to do in the company of others." (Publisher's note)

Sides, Hampton

★ **In** the kingdom of ice; the grand and terrible polar voyage of the U.S.S. Jeannette. Hampton Sides. Doubleday 2014 480 p. illustrations, maps $28.95 **910.4**
  1. Arctic regions -- Exploration 2. United States -- Exploring expeditions 3. Jeannette (Steamer) -- History 4. Shipwrecks -- Arctic Ocean -- History -- 19th century
  ISBN 0385535376; 9780385535373

  LC 2014004367

This book by Hampton Sides recounts how "James Gordon Bennett . . . funded an official U.S. naval expedition to reach the Pole, choosing as its captain a young officer named George Washington De Long, who had gained fame for a rescue operation off the coast of Greenland. . . . De Long led a team of 32 men deep into uncharted Arctic waters. . . . On July 8, 1879, the USS Jeannette set sail from San Francisco to cheering crowds." (Publisher's note)

"Sides . . . tapped amazing archival material, including diaries, letters, and the ship logs, to render a completely thrilling saga of survival in unbelievably harsh conditions." Booklist
  Includes bibliographical references

Turner, Steve

The **band** that played on; the extraordinary story of the 8 musicians who went down with the Titanic. Thomas Nelson 2011 259p $24.99 **910.4**
  1. Titanic (Steamship) 2. Musicians -- Biography
  ISBN 978-1-59555-219-8; 1-59555-219-7

  LC 2010-47182

This is the "first book since the great ship went down to examine the lives of the eight musicians who were employed by the Titanic. What these men did – standing calmly on deck playing throughout the disaster – achieved global recognition. But their individual stories, until now, have been largely unknown. What Turner has uncovered is a narrow but unique slice of history – one more chapter of compelling Titanic lore." Christ Sci Monit
  Includes bibliographical references

Wheeler, Sara

The **magnetic** north; notes from the Arctic circle. Farrar, Straus and Giroux 2011 315p il map $26; ebook $12.99 **910.4**
  1. Arctic regions -- Description and travel
  ISBN 9780374200138; 0374200130; 9781429991940 ebook

  LC 2010-14576

"With wry humor and extensive research, Wheeler captures a swiftly transforming region with which we all have a symbiotic relationship." N Y Times Book Rev
  Includes bibliographical references (p. [297]-302) and index.

Williams, Glyndwr

Arctic labyrinth; the quest for the Northwest Passage. [by] Glyn Williams. University of California Press 2010 439p il map $34.95 **910.4**
  1. Explorers 2. Northwest Passage 3. Arctic regions -- Exploration
  ISBN 978-0-5202-6627-8

  LC 2009-35546

First published 2009 in the United Kingdom
"If you read one book on the history of the mythic Northwest Passage, read this one. . . . Williams deftly weaves together explorers' logbooks and diaries (published and unpublished) with a lifetime of re-

search, and the result is a masterpiece." Libr J

Includes bibliographical references

Wilson, Penny

Lusitania; triumph, tragedy, and the end of the Edwardian age. Greg King and Penny Wilson. St. Martin's Press 2015 370 p. 8 plates; illustrations (hardback) $27.99 **910.4**

1. Shipwreck victims 2. Lusitania (Steamship) 3. Upper class -- United States -- Biography 4. Ocean travel -- North Atlantic Ocean -- Anecdotes 5. Shipwreck victims -- North Atlantic Ocean -- Anecdotes 6. Upper class -- Social life and customs -- 20th century

ISBN 1250052548; 9781250052544

LC 2014040843

In this book on the Lusitania, "the authors tell the grim tale of the titular doomed passenger liner, which was torpedoed by a German U-boat in the early stages of World War I. The ship sank within 18 minutes; sending nearly 1,200 people of all ages, nationalities, and social classes to terrible deaths in the Irish Sea and setting off a political firestorm that would eventually culminate in the United States joining the war." (Library Journal)

"The authors devote inordinate portions of the text to biographies of passengers and still more to the lives of the survivors, but their exploration of the facts surrounding the mystery is the primary pleasure of the book. Those who relish tales of the rich and famous will appreciate this book, but the real joy is in the authors' detective work and attention to detail." Kirkus

World's best travel experiences; 400 extraordinary places with recollections by Bill Bryson, Anna Quindlen, and more. by National Geographic. National Geographic 2012 319 p. col. ill., col. map (hardcover: alk. paper) $40 **910.4**

1. Voyages and travels

ISBN 1426209592; 9781426209598

LC 2012016594

This travel guide offers "400 awe-inspiring destinations chosen by National Geographic's family of globe-trotting contributors; dozens of fun, 'Best of the World' themed lists; illuminating sidebars, several by travel and literary luminaries such as Anna Quindlen, Bill Bryson, Gore Vidal, and Pico Iyer; and hundreds of . . . images to bring to life a wide variety of location categories--from entire countries to mountaintop villages to pristine lakes to ancient wonders." (Publisher's note)

"Readers will dip into this book for inspiration for future travel as well as for fuel for beautiful daydreams." LJ

910.45   Ocean travel and seafaring adventures

Bown, Stephen R.

Island of the blue foxes; disaster and triumph on the world's greatest scientific expedition. Stephen R. Bown. Da Capo Press 2017 xi, 327 p.p illustrations, maps (hardcover) $28 **910.45**

1. Scientific expeditions 2. Discoveries in geography 3. Alaska -- Discovery and exploration -- Russian 4. Scientific expeditions -- History -- 18th century 5. Arctic regions -- Discovery and exploration -- Russian 6. Scientific expeditions -- Arctic regions -- History -- 18th century 7. Northwest Coast of North America -- Discovery and exploration -- Russian

ISBN 9780306903137; 0306825198; 9780306825194

LC 2017951372

This book, in the A Merloyd Lawrence Book series, by Stephen R. Bown, is "the story of the world's largest, longest, and best financed scientific expedition of all time. . . . The immense 18th-century scien-

tific journey, variously known as the Second Kamchatka Expedition or the Great Northern Expedition, from St. Petersburg across Siberia to the coast of North America, involved over 3,000 people and cost Peter the Great over one-sixth of his empire's annual revenue." (Publisher's note)

"Luckily for readers, diaries, letters, and official reports provide Bown ample material for a gripping account of 'the most extensive scientific expedition in history,' whose impressive results were certainly matched by i ts duration and miseries." Kirkus

Includes bibliographical references (pages 275-305) and index.

910.452   Shipwrecks

Mearns, David L.

The **shipwreck** hunter; a lifetime of extraordinary discoveries on the ocean floor. David L. Mearns. Pegasus Books 2018 416 p. $28.95 **910.452**

1. Shipwrecks 2. Marine archaeologists

ISBN 1681777606; 9781681777603

In this memoir, author and marine archaeologist David L. Mearns "chronicles his most intriguing finds. It describes the extraordinary techniques used, the detailed research and mid-ocean stamina (and courage) required to find a wreck thousands of feet beneath the sea, as well as the moving human stories that lie behind each of these oceanic tragedies." (Publisher's note)

910.9   History, geographic treatment, biography

Herbert, Kari

Explorers' sketchbooks; the art of discovery & adventure. [compiled by] Huw Lewis-Jones, Kari Herbert; foreword by Robert Macfarlane. Chronicle Books 2017 320 p. ills.(some color), maps (hardcover: alk. paper) $40 **910.9**

1. Explorers -- Diaries 2. Explorers -- Miscellanea 3. Adventure and adventurers -- Miscellanea

ISBN 9781452158273; 1452158274

LC 2017000417

This book, by Huw Lewis-Jones and Kari Herbert, "showcases 70 such sketchbooks, kept by intrepid men and women as they journeyed perilous and unknown environments--frozen wastelands, high mountains, barren deserts, and dense rainforests--with their senses wide open. Figures such as Charles Darwin and Sir Edmund Hillary are joined here by lesser-known explorers such as Adela Breton, who braved the jungles of Mexico to make a record of Mayan monuments." (Publisher's note)

"This compilation of excerpts and facsimiles of 70 notebooks belonging to explorers throughout history is as educational as it is visually enticing." Pub Wkly

Includes bibliographical references and index

Journey; an illustrated history of travel. foreword, Michael Collins; contributors, Simon Adams, R.G. Grant, Andrew Humphreys. DK Publishing 2017 440 p. illustrations, maps (hardcover) $50 **910.9**

1. Travel -- History 2. Explorers -- History 3. Emigration and immigration -- History

ISBN 9781465464149; 146546414X

LC 2017297217

This book from DK, with foreword by Michael Collins, presents "an illustrated account of human movement, travel, exploration, and scientific discovery--from the first trade networks in ancient Sumer to the epic Voyager missions. . . . [It] traces each through lively accounts, alongside the biographies of conquerors, explorers, and travelers; stories of technological innovation; literary journals; and works of art." (Publisher's note)

"Divided into seven great ages of travel, this lavishly illustrated and well-written volume provides the reader with a sense of the difficulties and the experiences of each voyage." Booklist

Winter, Kathleen

Boundless; tracing land and dream in a new Northwest Passage. Kathleen Winter. Counterpoint Press 2015 272 p. 16 plates; illustrations; map (hardcover) $27 **910.9**
1. Northwest Passage 2. Inuit -- Canada -- Social conditions 3. Northwest Passage -- Description and travel
ISBN 1619025671; 9781619025677

LC 2015022219

This book describes how "author Kathleen Winter took a journey across the legendary Northwest Passage--connecting the Pacific and Atlantic Oceans--alongside marine scientists, historians, archaeologists, anthropologists, and curious passengers. From Greenland to Baffin Island and all along this arctic passage, Winter witnesses the new mathematics of the melting North. . . . Throughout the journey she also learns much from her fellow travellers." (Publisher's note)

"Perceptive and thoughtful, Winter's ruminations on Arctic life and its continuous clashes with modern civilization are compelling and thought-provoking. The north is a place rarely visited and little understood, but it looms ever larger in our collective future, and to ignore it and its people would be an act of global arrogance." Booklist

910.91   Geography of and travel in areas, regions, places in general

Franklin, Jonathan

438 days; an extraordinary true story of survival at sea. Jonathan Franklin. Atria Books 2015 288 p. color illustrations, maps (ebook) $16.99; (hardcover) $26 **910.91**
1. Survival at sea -- Pacific Ocean 2. Chiapas (Mexico) -- Biography 3. Shipwrecks -- Marshall Islands 4. Fishing boats -- Mexico -- Chiapas 5. Illegal aliens -- Mexico -- Biography 6. Fisheries -- Mexico -- Chiapas -- History 7. Fishers -- Mexico -- Chiapas -- Biography 8. Salvadorans -- Mexico -- Chiapas -- Biography 9. Fishing villages -- Mexico -- Chiapas -- Social life and customs
ISBN 9781501116315; 9781501116292

LC 2015030740

This book by Jonathan Franklin tells the story of Salvador Alvarenga, "the fisherman who survived fourteen months in a small boat seven thousand miles across the Pacific Ocean. On November 17, 2012, a pair of fishermen left the coast of Mexico, . . . a violent storm ambushed them as they were fishing eighty miles offshore. . . . On January 30, 2014, Alvarenga, . . . wild-bearded and half-mad castaway, washed ashore on a nearly deserted island on the far side of the Pacific." (Publisher's note)

"Franklin sprinkles the story with expert opinions to give it depth and context, but the most striking details are those offered by Alvarenga himself about the challenges he faced day in and day out. A spectacular triumph of grit over adversity, 438 Days is an intense, immensely absorbing read." Booklist

Kurson, Robert

Pirate hunters; the search for the Golden Fleece. Robert Kurson. Random House Inc 2014 304 p. color illustrations (hardcover) $28 **910.91**

1. Adventure fiction 2. Shipwrecks -- Fiction 3. Buried treasure -- Fiction 4. Deep diving 5. Treasure troves 6. Pirates -- History 7. Golden Fleece (Ship) 8. Shipwrecks -- Dominican Republic
ISBN 9781400063369; 9780804194662; 1400063361

LC 2014020225

In this book by Robert Kurson, "John Chatterton and John Mattera are willing to risk everything to find . . . the ship of the infamous pirate Joseph Bannister. . . . They must travel the globe in search of historic documents and accounts of the great pirate's exploits, face down dangerous rivals, battle the tides of nations and governments and experts. But it's only when they learn to think and act like pirates . . . that they become able to go where no pirate hunters have gone before." (Publisher's note)

"An enjoyable read, especially if you've got a thing for pirates." Kirkus

O'Neill, Zora

All strangers are kin; adventures in Arabic and the Arab world. Zora O'Neill. Houghton Mifflin Harcourt 2016 336 p. (hardcover) $25 **910.91**
1. Arabic language 2. Middle East -- Description and travel 3. Arab countries -- Description and travel 4. O'Neill, Zora -- Travel -- Arab countries 5. Travel writers -- United States -- Biography 6. Women journalists -- United States -- Biography 7. Arabic language -- Study and teaching -- Foreign speakers
ISBN 9780547853185

LC 2015020508

In this book, readers join author Zora O'Neill "for a grand tour through the Middle East. You will laugh with her in Egypt, delight in the stories she passes on from the United Arab Emirates, and find yourself transformed by her experiences in Lebanon and Morocco. She's packed her dictionaries, her unsinkable sense of humor, and her talent for making fast friends of strangers." (Publisher's note)

" What emerges is the idea of language as a connection, passion, and a reflection of the lives and history of diverse Arab peoples, a view which is lacking in the general news coverage of Middle Eastern conflict. Glimpses of daily life, particularly of Arab women, are intriguing and sometimes unexpected, including the rich assortment of Lebanese cursing while driving." LJ

Includes bibliographical references

Seaman, Camille

Melting away; a ten-year journey through our endangered Polar Regions. Camille Seaman. Princeton Architectural Press 2015 156 p. color illustrations (alk. paper) $55 **910.91**
1. Icebergs 2. Polar regions -- Pictorial works 3. Animals -- Polar regions -- Pictorial works 4. Icebergs -- Polar regions -- Pictorial works 5. Natural history -- Polar regions -- Pictorial works 6. Climatic changes -- Environmental aspects -- Polar regions -- Pictorial works
ISBN 9781616892609

LC 2014018830

This book, written and illustrated by Camille Seaman, presents photography of the polar regions, documenting climate change. "As an expedition photographer aboard small ships in the Arctic and Antarctic, she has chronicled the accelerating effects of global warming on the jagged face of nearly fifty thousand icebergs." (Publisher's note)

"In her inimitable way, Seaman writes that she was "recording the voice of these places with my cameras." That voice is quiet and deeply affecting—a relief from the shouted rhetoric that so often accompanies conversation on climate change. A sterling addition to all photography collections." LJ

Slade, Rachel

★ **Into** the raging sea; thirty-three mariners, one mega-storm, and the sinking of El Faro. Rachel Slade. Ecco 2018 xiv, 391 p.p color illustrations (hardcover) $27.99   **910.91**
1. Hurricanes 2. Marine accidents -- History 3. El Faro (Ship) 4. Shipwrecks -- Bahamas 5. Brookline (Mass.) -- Authors
ISBN 9780062699701; 9780062699718; 0062699709

"On October 1, 2015, Hurricane Joaquin barreled into the Bermuda Triangle and swallowed the container ship El Faro whole. . . . No one could fathom how a vessel equipped with satellite communications, a sophisticated navigation system, and cutting-edge weather forecasting could suddenly vanish--until now. Relying on hundreds of exclusive interviews[,] . . . journalist Rachel Slade unravels the mystery of the sinking of El Faro." (Publisher's note)

"A pulse-pounding, Perfect Storm-style tale of a shipping disaster. . . . A taut, chilling, and emotionally charged retelling of a doomed ship's final days." Kirkus

Includes bibliographical references (pages 371-373) and index.

Vallely, Kevin

Rowing the Northwest Passage; Adventure, Fear, and Awe in a Rising Sea. by Kevin Vallely. Greystone Books 2017 226 p. color illustrations (paperback) $18.95   **910.91**
1. Northwest Passage 2. Adventure and adventurers 3. Rowing -- Northwest Passage 4. Northwest Passage -- Description and travel
ISBN 9781771641340; 9781771641357; 1771641347

In this book, by Kevin Vallely, "four seasoned adventurers navigate a sophisticated, high-tech rowboat across the Northwest Passage. One of the 'last firsts' remaining in the adventure world, this journey is only possible because of the dramatic impacts of global warming in the high Arctic, which provide an ironic opportunity to draw attention to the growing urgency of climate change." (Publisher's note)

"A rousing combination of science and adventure in the Arctic." Booklist

910.911   Frigid zones – Travel

Welky, David

★ **A wretched** and precarious situation; in search of the last Arctic frontier. David Welky. W W Norton & Co Inc 2016 512 p. illustrations, map (ebook) $50; (hardcover) $28.95 **910.911**
1. Arctic regions -- Exploration 2. Crocker Land Expedition (1913-1917) 3. MacMillan, Donald Baxter, 1874-1970 -- Travel -- Arctic regions 4. Arctic regions -- Discovery and exploration -- American
ISBN 9780393254426; 9780393254419

LC 2016023022

This book by David Welky tells "a remarkable true story of adventure, betrayal, and survival set in one of the world's most inhospitable places. . . . George Borup and Donald MacMillan, assembled a team of amateur adventurers to investigate Crocker Land. . . . What followed was a sequence of events that none of the explorers could have imagined. . . . The men endured howling blizzards, unearthly cold, food shortages, isolation, . . . disease, dissension and a horrific crime." (Publisher's note)

"Long, leisurely, and vastly entertaining." Kirkus

Includes bibliographical references and index

910.915   Regions by type of vegetation

Atkins, William

The **immeasurable** world; journeys in desert places. Wil-liam Atkins. Doubleday, a division of Penguin Random House LLC 2018 368 p. (hardback) $28.95   **910.915**
1. Deserts 2. Voyages around the world
ISBN 9780385539883

LC 2017053583

In this book, author William Atkins "takes readers on a thoroughly enjoyable tour of the world's deserts. After . . . a week spent with Cistercian monks in southwest England, Atkins . . . became obsessed with deserts. . . . And so began an odyssey that took Atkins to eight deserts across the globe: the Empty Quarter in Oman, the Gobi and Taklamakan in China, . . . the Aral Sea area in Kazakhstan, the Black Rock and Sonoran in the U.S., and Egypt's Eastern Desert." (Publishers Weekly)

"The subject is riveting, the gorgeous prose reminiscent of nature observers from Thoreau to Leopold. Lovers of good descriptive writing will eat up this book." Library Journal

Includes bibliographical references

911   Historical geography

Atlas of exploration; cartography by Philip's; foreword by John Hemming. Oxford University Press 2008 256p il map $50   **911**
1. Reference books 2. Exploration -- Atlases
ISBN 978-0-19-534318-2

LC 2008-626565

First published 1998 with title: Oxford atlas of exploration

"This atlas describes many of the explorations and participants that changed history and enhanced man's knowledge and perception of the world. . . . The volume is a visual delight, festooned with more than 100 specially drawn maps and 300 b&w and color photographs, period paintings, and illustrations on the various explorations." Libr Media Connect

Hayes, Derek

Historical atlas of the American West; with original maps. University of California Press 2009 288p il map   **911**
1. Reference books 2. Historical atlases 3. West (U.S.) -- Historical geography 4. Western states -- Historical geography -- Maps
ISBN 9780520256521

LC 20090279536

"The West, for the purpose of this atlas, is defined as the Dakotas, Nebraska, Kansas, Oklahoma, Texas, and all states west of them, including Alaska, but not Hawai'i. More than 600 maps have been carefully selected and beautifully reproduced in full color. They provide the primary-source documentation for the historical narrative, written for the general reader, tracing the development of the Western United States from its indigenous inhabitants to European exploration, the migration of settlers, and 20th-century events. . . . A high quality publication at an amazingly low price, this atlas is highly recommended for all public and academic libraries, history buffs, and map enthusiasts." Libr J

Includes bibliographical references

Historical atlas of the United States; with original maps. University of California Press 2007 280p il map $45   **911**
1. Atlases 2. Reference books 3. United States -- Historical geography -- Maps
ISBN 978-0-520-25036-9; 0-520-25036-2

LC 2006-42405

"Hayes has produced an excellent visual history of the land that became the US. The work includes 535 maps gathered from a variety of international collections, coupled with more than 60 other illustrations to chronicle the expansion and development of the nation over the last 500 years." Choice

Includes bibliographical references

Hellmann, Paul T.

★ **Historical** gazetteer of the United States. Routledge 2005 865p $150 **911**

1. Reference books 2. United States -- Gazetteers 3. United States -- Local history -- Dictionaries 4. United States -- Historical geography -- Dictionaries

ISBN 0-415-93948-8

LC 2004-11421

This reference provides "historical records of U.S. cities and towns. Arrangement is alphabetical by state, including the District of Columbia. Each state chapter contains a brief description of major cities, date of incorporation into the U.S., the number of counties, and a rough breakdown of how the state categorizes municipalities, towns, townships, and cities. This is followed by alphabetical entries for significant places. Inclusion is determined more by historical importance (national or regional) than by population. All county seats are included. Entries are in paragraph form and typically begin by noting the country and the part of the state in which the place is located as well as its approximate distance from the state's most important city. Events are listed chronologically ." Booklist

Magocsi, Paul R.

Historical atlas of Central Europe; [by] Paul Robert Magocsi. rev and expanded ed; University of Wash. Press 2002 274p maps (History of East Central Europe) hardcover o.p. pa $45 **911**

1. Atlases 2. Reference books 3. Central Europe -- Historical geography -- Maps

ISBN 0-295-98146-6

LC 2001-27907

First published 1993 with title: Historical atlas of East Central Europe

"The volume is arranged chronologically, with coverage beginning about A.D. 400 (roughly the time of the demise of the Roman Empire) and continuing through the end of the 20th century. The maps and tables provide information on military affairs; population and population movements; economy; ethnolinguistic distributions; and religious, cultural, and educational institutions. All are extremely well done." SLJ

912 Graphic representations of surface of earth and of extraterrestrial worlds

Atlas A-Z. DK 2012 432 p. $11.95 **912**

1. Atlases 2. Geography

ISBN 0756689775; 9780756689773

LC 2012587235

This book is the updated fifth edition of Dorling Kindersley Publishing's pocket atlas. Readers can "[c]arry the world in [their] pocket[s] with this . . . global guide combining maps, facts, and statistics" about world geography. (Publisher's note)

The **atlas** of cities; mapping the urban world. Paul Knox. Columbia University Press 2014 256 p. color illustrations, maps (cloth) $49.50 **912**

1. Atlases 2. Cities and towns

ISBN 0691157812; 9780691157818

LC 2013954981

This atlas by Paul Knox focuses on cities. "Each of the 13 chapters addresses a specific type of city, including those that are typically discussed (imperial, industrial, and megacity), as well as other types of cit-

ies (e.g., celebrity, green, and creative). Each chapter focuses on a core city with secondary cities as supporting documentation for the subtopic discussion." (Choice: Current Reviews for Academic Libraries)

"This fascinating survey effectively complemented and enriched by color maps, charts, and illustrations, celebrates the urban landscape's past, present, and potential for the future. Intended for the general reader, Knox's reference is recommended to anyone interested in urban studies and geography." LJ

Atlas of the World; [prepared by National Geographic Maps for the Book Division] Random House Inc 2014 448 p. 1 atlas; color maps; color ils $195 **912**

1. Atlases

ISBN 1426213549; 9781426213540

LC 200445002

This book presents "illustrated maps and informational graphics [that] chart rapidly changing global themes such as population trends, urbanization, health and longevity, human migration, climate change, communications, and the world economy. The core of any atlas is the reference mapping section and the 10th Edition boasts the largest and most comprehensive collection of political maps ever published by National Geographic." (Publisher's note)

Garfield, Simon

On the Map; a mind-expanding exploration of the way the world looks. Simon Garfield. Penguin Group USA 2012 464 p. (hardcover) $27.50 **912**

1. Maps

ISBN 159240779X; 9781592407798

This book by Simon Garfield explores the "relationship between man and map. . . . Follow the history of maps from the early explorers' maps and the awe-inspiring medieval Mappa Mundi to Google Maps and the satellite renderings on our smartphones, Garfield explores the unique way that maps relate and realign our history--and reflect the best and worst of what makes us human." (Publisher's note)

Lavin, Stephen J.

Atlas of the great plains; Stephen J. Lavin, Fred M. Shelley, and J. Clark Archer; foreword by David J. Wishart; introduction by John C. Hudson. University of Nebraska Press 2011 335p il $39.95 **912**

1. Atlases 2. Reference books 3. Great Plains -- History -- Maps

ISBN 978-0-8032-1536-8

Lester, Toby

The **fourth** part of the world; the race to the ends of the Earth, and the epic story of the map that gave America its name. Free Press 2009 462p il map $30 **912**

1. Map drawing 2. World maps 3. Cartographers 4. America -- Maps 5. Cartography -- History 6. Voyages and travels -- History 7. Discoveries in geography -- History

ISBN 1416535314; 9781416535317

LC 2009-1230

This "chronicle of the early 16th-century creation of the Waldseemüller map offers insight into how monks, classicists, merchants and other contributors from earlier periods shaped the map's creation and subsequently informed modern worldviews." (Publisher's note) The book is "history of the centuries-long European fascination with depicting the world in two dimensions." (Reviews in American History).

"In 2003, the Library of Congress paid $10 million for a 1507 map of the world that first used the name 'America' for lands in the New World. It was touted as America's birth certificate. Lester . . . traces the fascinating background to the creation of this map, as Europeans tried to assimilate the discoveries of Columbus, Vespucci, and other explorers into their worldview. . . . Lester provides an engrossing adventure for both general and informed lay readers." Libr J

Includes bibliographical references

A **Map** of the World; According to Illustrators & Storytellers. edited by Antonis Antoniou, Robert Klanten, Sven Ehmann, and Hendrik Hellige. Prestel Pub 2013 224 p. chiefly color illustrations $60 **912**
1. Maps 2. Map drawing 3. Cartography 4. Thematic maps 5. Artists as cartographers
ISBN 3899554698; 9783899554694

LC 2013482415

This book, edited by Antonis Antoniou, R. Klanten, H. Ehmann, H. Hellige, "features the most original and sought-after map illustrators whose work is in line with the zeitgeist. [It] is a compelling collection of their work--from accurate and surprisingly detailed representations to personal, naïve, and modernistic interpretations. The featured projects from around the world range from maps and atlases inspired by classic forms to cartographic experiments and editorial illustrations." (Publisher's note)

National Geographic visual atlas of the world; 2nd edition National Geographic 2017 416 p illustrations, maps $115 **912**
1. Atlases 2. Reference books
ISBN 9781426218385

"Updated for the first time since 2008, National Geographic's visual atlas of the world will delight and inspire history lovers, current event buffs, and cartography fans alike. From spectacular space imagery to UNESCO World Heritage Sites, this stunning book showcases the diverse natural and cultural treasures of the world in glorious color. Featuring more than 200 fascinating maps, 350 new photos, and state-of-the-art cartography and satellite imagery, this is an essential reference for families, travelers, students, librarians, and scholars." (Publisher's note)

The **new** atlas of the Arab world. American University in Cairo Press 2010 144p il map $39.50 **912**
1. Atlases 2. Reference books 3. Arab countries -- Maps
ISBN 978-977-416-419-4

This atlas contains maps of the Arab world "showing physical features, political boundaries, towns, and communication networks. In addition, each of the twenty-two countries is the subject of an illustrated essay, with notes and . . . statistics on the geography, population, history and politics, and economy of the country. The countries covered are: Algeria, Bahrain, Comoros, Djibouti, Egypt, Iraq, Jordan, Kuwait, Lebanon, Libya, Mauritania, Morocco, Oman, Palestine, Qatar, Saudi Arabia, Somalia, Sudan, Syria, Tunisia, United Arab Emirates, Yemen." Publisher's note

★ **Oxford** Atlas of the world. Oxford University Press 448 p. il map **912**
1. Atlases 2. Earth -- Maps 3. Physical geography 4. Reference books

First published 1992. Updated annually. Variant title: Atlas of the world

"The only world atlas updated annually, guaranteeing that users will find the most current geographic information, Oxford's Atlas of the World is the most authoritative atlas on the market. Full of crisp, clear cartography of urban areas and virtually uninhabited landscapes around the globe, the Atlas is filled with maps of cities and regions at carefully selected scales that give a striking view of the Earth's surface." (Publisher's note)

Oxford new concise world atlas; [cartography by Philip's; text, Keith Lye]. 3rd ed; Oxford University Press 2010 1 atlas (224 p.) col. ill., col. maps $39.95 **912**
1. Atlases 2. Reference books
ISBN 0195393295; 9780195393293

LC 2009292676

Containing over 100 pages of the most up-to-date topographic and political maps, the New Concise World Atlas also features a unique overview of the planet's human and natural processes in photographs, accessible text, and thematic maps. (Publisher's note)

"This update of the 2006 edition contains 128 pages of full-color, computer-generated maps by Philip's, a division of Octopus Publishing, with detailed and dramatic terrain modeling... This condensed and abridged version of the premium Oxford Atlas of the World offers all libraries outstanding value in an up-to-date, medium-sized atlas for an amazingly low price.— LJ

Includes index.

Rand McNally Goodes World Atlas; edited by Howard Veregin. 22nd ed. Rand McNally 2009 400 p. $45 **912**
1. Maps 2. Atlases
ISBN 0528877542; 9780528877544

This book, edited by Howard Veregin, "features over 250 pages of maps, from definitive physical and political maps to important thematic maps that illustrate the spatial aspects of many important topics. [It] includes 160 pages of new, digitally produced reference maps, as well as new thematic maps on global climate change, sea level rise, CO_2 emissions, polar ice fluctuations, deforestation, extreme weather events, infectious diseases, water resources, and energy production." (Publisher's note)

The **Times** Comprehensive Atlas of the World; 15th edition Trafalgar Square Books 2018 223 p maps $199.95 **912**
1. Atlases
ISBN 9780008293383

"The 15th edition contains over 200,000 place names, more than any other world atlas, which means even small villages are included in the index and on the maps. It is a benchmark of cartographic excellence, trusted by governments, media and international organisations as well as being a go to reference source for households across the country. It's independent—apolitical and neutral, elegant in an attractive slipcase, and endlessly fascinating." (Publisher's note)

912.09 History and biography of maps and map making

Atlas of Yellowstone; senior editor, W. Andrew Marcus; cartographic editor, James E. Meacham; Yellowstone editor, Ann W. Rodman; production manager, Alethea Y. Steingisser; consulting editor, Stuart Allan; text editor, Ross West. University of California Press/University of Oregon 2012 1 atlas (xxi, 274 p.)p ill. (some col.), chiefly col. (cloth: alk. paper) $65 **912.09**
1. Yellowstone National Park -- Atlases 2. Physical geography -- Yellowstone National Park -- Maps
ISBN 0520271556; 9780520271555

LC 2011037533

This book by W. Andrew Marcus presents an atlas of Yellowstone National Park. "Material ranges from broad overviews to specific details. The 524 maps are presented in five sections: 'Geographic Setting' . . . 'Human Geography' . . . 'Physical Geography' . . . 'Wildlife' . . . and 'Reference Maps.' . . . The atlas also includes 50 color illustrations and more than 260 line illustrations." (Library Journal)

Includes bibliographical references (p. 262-267) and index

Brotton, Jerry

Great maps; Jerry Brotton. DK Publishing 2014 256 p. illustrations (some color) $25 **912.09**

1. Maps 2. Map drawing 3. Cartography 4. Cartography -- History

ISBN 1465424636; 9781465424631

LC 2012278182

In this book, by Jerry Brotton, "[t]he world's finest maps [are] explored and explained, . . . [f]rom Ptolemy's world map to the Hereford's Mappa Mundi, through Mercator's map of the world to the latest maps of the Moon and Google Earth. . . . Revealing the stories behind 55 historical maps by analyzing graphic close-ups, [it] also profiles key cartographers and explorers to look why each map was commissioned, who it was for and how they influenced navigation." (Publisher's note)

"The thematic maps are particularly interesting, including a 'Cholera Map' from 1854, a map depicting the slave population of the Southern states, and Dr. Livingstone's map of Africa." Booklist

Janes, Andrew

Maps; Their Untold Stories. Rose Mitchell and Andrew Janes. St. Martin's Press 2014 256 p. color illustrations; maps $50 **912.09**

1. Maps 2. Map drawing

ISBN 1408189674; 9781408189672

This book by Rose Mitchell and Andrew Janes "drawn from seven centuries of maps held in the National Archives at Kew, looks at a variety of maps, from those found in 14th Century manuscripts, through early estate maps, to sea charts, maps used in military campaigns, and maps from treaties." (Publisher's note)

912.747 New York (State) – Maps

Harmon, Katharine

You are here NYC; Mapping the Soul of the City. Katharine Harmon. Princeton Architectural Press 2016 192 p. color ill., color maps, plans (ebook) $24.95; (alk. paper) $24.95 **912.747**

1. Maps 2. Map drawing 3. New York (N.Y.) 4. New York (N.Y.) -- In art -- Maps 5. New York (N.Y.) -- Pictorial works 6. Cartography -- New York (State) -- New York 7. Imaginary places -- New York (State) -- New York -- Maps

ISBN 9781616895495; 9781616895266

LC 2016004560

In this book, by Katharine Harmon, "New York is rife with mapmaking possibilities, thick with mythology, and glutted with history. . . . [Harmon] assembles some two hundred maps charting every inch and facet of the five boroughs, depicting New Yorks of past and present, and a city that never was." (Publisher's note)

"A wonderful treat for New Yorkers and for lovers of geography- and cartography-inspired looks at life in the past and today." LJ

914 Geography of and travel in Europe

Baxter, John

The **most** beautiful walk in the world; a pedestrian in Paris. Harper Perennial 2011 298p il pa $14.99 **914**

1. Walking 2. Paris (France) -- Description and travel

ISBN 978-0-06-199854-6; 0-06-199854-0

LC 2010-46259

The author "knows Paris, both the modern, cosmopolitan city of today as well as the 1920s cultural mecca of expat American authors like Ernest Hemingway and F. Scott Fitzgerald. Baxter, in fact, lives in the same Paris building that once was a Jazz Age hangout for literary greats like James Joyce, Ezra Pound, Hemingway, and others. It's also the site of Sylvia Beach's famous bookstore, Shakespeare and Company. . . . [He] takes us on a tour of the city's outdoor cafes, amazing restaurants, cabarets, and gorgeous architecture; he tells us about its history and its unique passion for art. Baxter gives us a Paris that is not just a place but an idea." Boston Globe

Bryson, Bill

Notes from a small island. Morrow 1996 324p hardcover o.p. pa $14 **914**

1. Great Britain -- Civilization 2. Great Britain -- Description and travel

ISBN 0-380-72750-1 pa

LC 95-43437

"Before his return to the U.S. after a 20-year residence in England, journalist Bryson . . . embarked on a farewell tour of his adopted homeland. His trenchant, witty and detailed observations of life in a variety of towns and villages will delight Anglophiles." Publ Wkly

The **road** to Little Dribbling; adventures of an American in Britain. by Bill Bryson. Doubleday, an Imprint of Penguin Random House 2016 400 p. illustrations, map (hardcover) $28.95 **914**

1. Great Britain -- Description and travel 2. Great Britain -- Civilization -- 21st century

ISBN 9780385539289

LC 2015027450

In this book travel writer and humorist Bill Bryson revisits England after having lived there as an expatriate 20 years earlier. "Bryson rediscovers the wondrously beautiful, magnificently eccentric, endearingly singular country that he both celebrates and, when called for, twits. . . . He offers acute and perceptive insights into all that is best and worst about Britain today." (Publisher's note)

"Anglophiles will find Bryson's field notes equally entertaining and educational." Kirkus

Caro, Ina

Paris to the past; traveling through French history by train. W.W. Norton & Co. 2011 381p map $27.95 **914**

1. Historic sites 2. Railroads -- France 3. France -- Description and travel 4. Paris (France) -- Description and travel

ISBN 978-0-393-07894-7; 0-393-07894-9

LC 2011-03060

"One single Paris Metro line can take you through a dazzling panoply of history: the Chateau de Vincennes, Charles V's 14th-century fortress; Francis I's Hotel de Ville; the Place de la Concorde, constructed by Louis V in the mid-18th century; the Palais-Royal, fashioned by Philippe Egalite in the late 18th century; and the 21st-century neighborhood of La Defense. Take another Metro line, and Caro discovered gleefully, and you can descend to the period of the Romans, on the Ile-de-la-Cite, then arrive glamorously in the 19th century, at the Opera Garnier. Moreover, you can manage day trips to sites as far away as Tours (90 minutes by TGV) in one day, returning to Paris. In this cheerful, logical, easy-to-follow narrative (which includes favorite restaurants and hotels), Caro builds on previous trips to France and presents her timeline through history chronologically, from the 12th-century Basilica of Saint-Denis, where nearly all of the French kings and queen are buried, to the Gare d'Orsay, now fabulously converted into a museum of 19th-century art."

Kirkus

Includes bibliographical references

Kerkeling, Hape

I'm off then; my journey along the Camino de Santiago. translated from the German by Shelley Frisch. Free Press 2009 333p il pa $15   **914**

1. Spain -- Description and travel
ISBN 978-1-416-55387-8; 1-416-55387-8

LC 2008-51464

Original German edition, 2006

"Hape Kerkeling, a popular TV talk-show host and cabaret star in his native Germany, cuts loose from the comforts of Düsseldorf and sets off on a hike across the Pyrenees to the grave of St. James at the Cathedral of Santiago de Compostela. Searching for spiritual meaning, this self-described 'couch potato' follows a 1,000-year-old pilgrimage route that lures 100,000 trekkers each year, experiencing almost insufferable heat and physical agony in the process. . . . He skips some of the hardest stretches to hitch rides with local farmers or hop aboard trains, and he avoids fetid pilgrims' hostels whenever possible in favor of the best hotel in town (often not much better). Despite such tactics, this gregarious traveler soon gets into the spirit of things, and his encounters with fellow pilgrims, including a Peruvian shaman with a creepy fondness for 'Mein Kampf,' can be both funny and moving." N Y Times Book Rev

Macfarlane, Robert

Landmarks; Robert Macfarlane. Penguin Group USA 2016 448 p. illustrations (paperback) $18   **914**

1. Great Britain 2. English language 3. English literature
ISBN 0241967872; 9780241967874; 9780241146538
Includes additional glossary.

This book, by Robert Macfarlane, shortlisted for the 2015 Samuel Johnson prize for non-fiction, "explores the linguistic and literary terrain of the British archipelago, from the Shetlands to Cornwall and from Cumbria to Suffolk, offering themed glossaries of hundreds of these rare, deeply local, poetical terms, organized by . . . geographical terrains." (Publisher's note)

Includes bibliographical references and index.

The **wild** places. Penguin Books 2008 340p map pa $15   **914**

1. Wilderness areas 2. Ireland -- Description and travel 3. Great Britain -- Description and travel
ISBN 978-0-14-311393-5; 0-14-311393-3

LC 2008-17162

First published 2007 in the United Kingdom

"Evocative and well-written, a delight for nature and travel buffs." Kirkus

Includes bibliographical references

Mayes, Frances

A **year** in the world; journeys of a passionate traveller. Broadway Books 2006 xx, 420p map hardcover o.p. pa $15   **914**

1. Europe -- Description and travel
ISBN 0-7679-1005-2; 978-0-7679-1005-7; 978-0-7679-1006-4 pa; 0-7679-1006-0 pa

LC 2005-50831

"Befitting her gifts as a poet, Mayes' prose shines with evocative imagery, bringing life to every subject she encounters across her peripatetic year." Booklist

Includes bibliographical references

Rumiz, Paolo

The **fault** line; traveling the other Europe, from Finland to Ukraine. Paolo Rumiz. Rizzoli Ex Libris 2015 256 p. map (alk. paper) $27.95   **914**

1. Eastern Europe 2. Europe -- Description and travel
ISBN 0847845427; 9780847845422

LC 2014944522

In this book, author Paolo Rumiz "traces the path that has twice cut Europe in two-- first by the Iron Curtain and then by the artificial scaffolding of the EU-- moving through vibrant cities and abandoned villages, some places still gloomy under the ghost of these imposing borders, some that have sought to erase all memory of it and jump with both feet into the West (if only the West would have them)." (Publisher's note)

"Exploring the border between Russia and the European Union, Rumiz realized that he was traveling "a seismic fault that's only apparently dormant" because Russia, under Putin, is becoming a renewed threat. A richly detailed journey into Europe's dark past and vulnerable present." Kirkus

914.2

Barber, Emily

Blue guide London; Emily Barber. Edit.18 Blue Guides Ltd 2014 592 p. (Blue guide) (paperback) $26.95   **914.2**

1. Travel guidebooks 2. London (England) -- Description and travel 3. London (England) -- Guidebooks
ISBN 1905131631; 9781905131631

This book in the Blue Guide series, by Emily Barber, with its "focus on history, art and architecture combined with excellent museums coverage . . . , [is] the best guide to London since its original release in 1918. Now fully rewritten and updated by the Blue Guides team. With extensive mapping . . . [and an] excellent new format." (Publisher's note)

Macfarlane, Robert, 1976-

The **old** ways; a journey on foot. Robert Macfarlane. Viking 2012 432 p.   **914.2**

1. Trails 2. Walking 3. Landscapes 4. Natural history 5. Voyages and travels 6. England -- Description and travel 7. Scotland -- Description and travel
ISBN 9780670025114

LC 2012005887

This book of nature writing by Robert Macfarlane recounts his travels on "the old ways -- the footpaths and tracks, the sea lanes and ghost roads -- that criss-cross the planet. . . . The central subject matter of 'The Old Ways' . . . is the land immediately around us, a land we too readily take for granted, and so fail to see as holy. Here the author's guides are the spirits of such former saunterers as Edward Thomas and Eric Ravilious, as well as the many nameless others who revered and cherished that land." (New Statesman)

Includes bibliographical references and index

914.304   Germany – Travel

Dk Eyewitness Munich & the Bavarian Alps. DK Pub 2018 336 p. color ill., color maps (paperback) $25   **914.304**

1. Munich (Germany) -- Description and travel 2. Bavaria (Germany) -- Description and travel
ISBN 9781465468239

This book "is your go-to guide to this beautiful region. Discover the best that Munich and the Bavarian Alps have to offer, from local festivals and markets to all the must-see sights. Experience Oktoberfest, ski down the Alps, and tour Neuschwanstein Castle." (Publisher's note)

Fodor's Germany; Fodor's Travel Publications, Inc. Random House Inc 2016 896 p. (paperback) $24.99   **914.304**
    1. Travel 2. Germany -- Description and travel
    ISBN 110187970X; 9781101879702

      LC 2016015119

    This travel guidebook, published by the Fodor's Travel Publications company, "covers the best Germany has to offer. This full-color guide will help travelers plan the perfect trip, from scenic drives through quaint half-timber towns to wine tasting in the country's top wine regions." (Publisher's note)

Germany; Joanna Egert-Romanowska and Malgorzata Omilanowska. DK Pub 2016 584 p. color ill., color map (paperback) $30   **914.304**
    1. Germany -- Description and travel
    ISBN 9781465440181; 1465440186

    This travel guide "takes you by the hand, leading you straight to the best attractions [that Germany] . . . has to offer, from its beautiful castles and cathedrals to its popular beer halls, festivals, and Christmas markets to walks and hikes through the countryside." (Publisher's note)

914.404   France – Travel

Baxter, John, 1939-
    Five nights in Paris; after dark in the City of Light. John Baxter. William Morrow 2015 352 p. illustrations (paperback) $14.99   **914.404**
    1. Autobiographies 2. Paris (France) -- Description and travel 3. Paris (France) -- Tours 4. Paris (France) -- Intellectual life 5. Walking -- France -- Paris -- Guidebooks 6. Paris (France) -- Social life and customs 7. Nightlife -- France -- Paris -- Guidebooks 8. Neighborhoods -- France -- Paris -- Guidebooks
    ISBN 0062296256; 9780062296252

      LC 2015000100

    This memoir by John Baxter "takes [readers] on a nocturnal stroll through five iconic Parisian neighborhoods and his own memories. As he takes you through five of the city's greatest neighborhoods-- Montmartre, Montparnasse, the Marais, and more-- Baxter shares pithy anecdotes about his life in France, as well as fascinating knowledge he has gleaned from leading literary tours of the city by dark." (Publisher's note)

    "In closing, Baxter writes, "each of us must, in our own way, as with a new lover, seduce, or allow ourselves to be seduced by the Paris night." This is not a walking guide to Paris, but it is most certainly a guide to seeing and knowing Paris, one no Francophile should be without." Kirkus

France; edited by Rosemary Bailey. DK Pub 2016 672 p. illustrations (paperback) $30   **914.404**
    1. France -- Description and travel
    ISBN 9781465440174; 1465440178

    This book, printed by Dorling Kindersley, edited by Rosemary Bailey, is part of the publisher's "Eyewitness Travel Guides" series. It presents "the best attractions . . . [that France] has to offer. Discover France region-by-region, from Champagne in the north to the sun-blessed corner of Provence and the Côte d'Azur. Stand in awe of the châteaux of the Loire, lie on the beautiful beaches of Corsica, and climb to the top of the Eiffel Tower." (Publisher's note)

Gray-Durant, Delia
    Blue guide Paris; Delia Gray-Durant. Edit.12 Blue Guides Ltd 2015 592 p. (Blue guide) (paperback) $26.95   **914.404**
    1. Travel guidebooks 2. Paris (France) -- Description and travel
    ISBN 9781905131679; 1905131674

    This new edition of the Blue Guide to Paris, France, by Delia Gray-Durant, "helps you know what you need to see as well as where to stay and what to eat. Perfect for on-street use and armchair reference, this is a mini-encyclopedia of a great European city. [It contains] 16 color maps, 15 2-color maps and plans, [and] 25 B&W Photographs." (Publisher's note)

914.5   Italy – Geography

Parks, Tim
    Italian ways; on and off the rails from Milan to Palermo. Tim Parks. W W Norton & Co Inc 2013 288 p. (hardcover) $25.95   **914.5**
    1. Railroad travel -- Italy 2. Italy -- Description and travel 3. Italy -- Social life and customs
    ISBN 0393239322; 9780393239324

      LC 2013011386

    In this book, author Tim Parks "pokes affectionate fun at his fellow train travelers and surveys a rapidly changing Italian landscape. . . . Here, he chronicles his adventures on the nation's rails. . . . Train travel in Italy is the ultimate leveler, Parks finds, and it provides a microcosm of what is transpiring in the society as a whole since globalization has taken root. His observations mingle travelogue, history and memoir, spanning the years from 2005 to the present." (Kirkus Reviews)

914.504   Italy – Travel

Macadam, Alta
    Blue guide Florence; Alta Macadam. Eleventh edition W W Norton & Co Inc 2017 440 p. illustrations, color maps (Blue guide) (paperback) $24.95   **914.504**
    1. Florence (Italy) 2. Travel guidebooks 3. Cities and towns -- Italy 4. Florence (Italy) -- Guidebooks
    ISBN 1905131755; 9781905131754

    This book on Florence, Italy in the Blue Guide series, by Alta Macadam, edited by Annabel Barber, "contains superb coverage of painting, architecture and sculpture as well as updates on museums including the reorganized Uffizi. Detailed coverage of where to stay and eat. The depth of information and quality of research make this book the best guide for the independent cultural traveller as well as for all students of art history, architecture and Italian culture." (Publisher's note)

    Blue guide Venice; Alta Macadam. Edit.9 Blue Guides Ltd 2014 416 p. (Blue guide) (paperback) $24.95   **914.504**
    1. Travel guidebooks 2. Venice (Italy) -- Guidebooks
    ISBN 1905131607; 9781905131600

    This new edition of a key Blue Guides title, by Alta Macadam, "presents Venice's splendor and history as well as recommending where to stay and where to eat: crucial advice in a city where the best establishments are not necessarily the most obvious. [This book features] 25 maps, 40 illustrations, and 30 photos." (Publisher's note)

The **rough** guide to Italy; edited by Amanda Tomlin and Claire Saunders. Rough Guides 2016 1038 p. (paperback) $26.99   **914.504**

1. Travel 2. Italy -- Description and travel
ISBN 0241216222; 9780241216224

LC 2006204291

This book, edited by Amanda Tomlin and Claire Saunders, part of the publisher's "Rough Guides" series, offers a "travel guide to [Rome, Italy.] . . . From the top draws of Rome and Florence to the hidden corners of Friuli and Liguria, this guide will help you make the most of your trip to Italy. You will find all the detailed information you need, from vaporetto routes in Venice to hole-in-the-wall pizza joints in Naples to the best spot to watch the sunset on the Amalfi Coast." (Publisher's note)

914.58   Sicily

Keahey, John

Sicilian splendors; discovering the secret places that speak to the heart. John Keahey. St Martins Pr 2018 304 p. $28.99   **914.58**

1. Travel writing 2. Sicily (Italy) -- Description and travel
ISBN 1250104696; 9781250104694

This book "explores the history, politics, food, Mafia, and people which [author] John Keahey encounters throughout his travels during his return to Sicily. Through conversing with natives and immersing himself in culture, Keahey illustrates a brand new Sicily no one has ever talked about before. . . . Keahey's never-ending curiosity as a traveler shines light on Sicily's mythical mysteries and portrays the island not only through his eyes but also through Sicily's heart." (Publisher's note)

"This insightful book, with its unique portraits of historically diverse small villages, should be a must-read for everyone interested in Sicily and Mediterranean Europe." Booklist

914.6   Spain – Geography

Dk Eyewitness Back Roads Spain; edited by Anna Ghose. DK Pub 2016 264 p. color ill., color maps (paperback) $25   **914.6**

1. Spain -- Description and travel
ISBN 9781465440433; 1465440437

This book, printed by Dorling Kindersley, edited by Anna Ghose, is part of the publisher's "Eyewitness Travel Back Roads" series. It presents "scenic routes to discover charming villages, local restaurants, and intimate places to stay [in Spain]. Twenty-five themed drives, each lasting one to seven days, reveal breathtaking views, hidden gems, and authentic local experiences that can only be discovered by road." (Publisher's note)

914.7   Russia -- geography

Eichar, Donnie

Dead Mountain; the true story of the Dyatlov Pass incident. by Donnie Eichar. Chronicle Books 2013 288 p. illustrations, map (hardback) $24.95   **914.7**

1. Mountaineering 2. Mysterious deaths 3. Hiking -- Russia (Federation) -- Ural Mountains Region 4. Ural Mountains Region (Russia) -- History -- 20th century 5. Mountaineering accidents -- Russia (Federation) -- Ural Mountains Region -- 20th century

ISBN 1452112746; 9781452112749

LC 2013014843

This book, by Donnie Eichar, focuses on how "in February 1959, a group of nine experienced hikers in the Russian Ural Mountains died mysteriously on an elevation known as Dead Mountain. Eerie aspects of the incident--unexplained violent injuries, signs that they cut open and fled the tent without proper clothing or shoes, a strange final photograph taken by one of the hikers, and elevated levels of radiation found on some of their clothes--have led to decades of speculation over what really happened." (Publisher's note)

"Eichar marries the short story of the students' lives with the procedural tale of the official investigation and then integrates his own amateur investigation. . . . [A] well-told and accurate whodunit." Kirkus

Greene, David

Midnight in Siberia; A Journey into the Heart of Russia. David Greene. W W Norton & Co Inc 2014 320 p. illustrations, map $26.95   **914.7**

1. Russia 2. Social change 3. Railroad travel 4. Russia (Federation) -- Biography 5. Interviews -- Russia (Federation) 6. Social change -- Russia (Federation) 7. Railroad travel -- Russia (Federation) 8. Social problems -- Russia (Federation) 9. Russia (Federation) -- Social conditions 10. Russia (Federation) -- Description and travel 11. Russia (Federation) -- Social life and customs 12. Velikaia Sibirskaia magistral'
ISBN 0393239950; 9780393239959

LC 2014029382

This book "chronicles David Greene's journey on the Trans-Siberian Railway, a 6,000-mile cross-country trip from Moscow to the Pacific port of Vladivostok. In quadruple-bunked cabins and stopover towns sprinkled across the country's snowy landscape, Greene speaks with ordinary Russians about how their lives have changed in the post-Soviet years." (Publisher's note)

"With abundant interpersonal detail, Greene delivers a lively, tangible feeling of meeting modern Russians on one of the world's famous railroads." Booklist

914.94   Switzerland

Bewes, Diccon

Slow Train to Switzerland; One Tour, Two Trips, 150 Years - and a World of Change Apart. by Diccon Bewes. Nicholas Brealey Publishing 2014 320 p. illustrations, map, portraits (hardcover) $29.95   **914.94**

1. Locomotives 2. Switzerland -- Description and travel
ISBN 9781857886092; 9781857886252; 1857886097

LC 2015451055

This book, by Diccon Bewes, describes train travel throughout Europe. It "follows Thomas Cook's groundbreaking tour from England to the Swiss Alps. Bewes uses traveler Jemima Morell's diary from 1863 to retrace the trip and explore the revolutionary affect the journey had on both Britain and Switzerland." (Publisher's note)

"Covering the development of tourism, rail travel, and hospitality, this account informs while providing an entertaining read for lovers of history and travel." LJ

915   Geography of and travel in Asia

Belliveau, Denis

In the footsteps of Marco Polo; [by] Denis Belliveau and

Francis O'Donnell. Rowman & Littlefield Publishers 2008 280p il map $29.95 **915**

1. Travelers 2. Travel writers 3. Asia -- Description and travel
ISBN 978-0-7425-5683-6; 0-7425-5683-2

LC 2008-23411

"The stunning photographs in this elegant book should please even the most casual reader, while the authors' unpretentious observations will satisfy those who want to know more about a still alien world. A travel/adventure book rather than a study of Marco Polo the man or a history of his travels, this volume deserves many readers. Warmly recommended." Libr J

Includes bibliographical references

Elliot, Jason

Mirrors of the unseen; journeys in Iran. St. Martin's Press 2006 415p il $26.95 **915**

1. Iran -- Description and travel
ISBN 978-0-312-30191-0; 0-312-30191-X

LC 2006-42918

The author discusses his travels in Iran.

"With Iran so central in the news, this is a good read for the armchair traveler and amateur geopolitical strategist alike." Publ Wkly

Feiler, Bruce S.

Walking the Bible; a journey by land through the five books of Moses. by Bruce Feiler. Morrow 2001 451p $26; pa $14.95 **915**

1. Middle East -- Description 2. Bible -- O.T. -- Pentateuch -- Geography
ISBN 0-380-97775-3; 0-380-80731-9 pa

LC 00-56076

"Determined to connect more deeply with his religious roots, Feiler joined an archaeologist in a trek through the Middle East, visiting the sites mentioned in the Pentateuch, the first five books of the Hebrew Bible. A book full of wonder and awe and personal enlightenment." Booklist

Includes bibliographical references

Gargan, Edward A.

A **river's** tale; a year on the Mekong. Knopf 2002 332p il maps hardcover o.p. pa $14.95 **915**

1. Southeast Asia -- Description and travel
ISBN 0-375-70559-7 pa

LC 2001-38056

"A chronicle of a year-long journey along the nearly 3,000 miles of the Mekong River as it descends from the Tibetan plateau through southern Asia, Gargan's book is a vivid look at the disparate peoples [that] settled the length of the river's path." Publ Wkly

Includes bibliographical references

Grange, Kevin

Beneath blossom rain; discovering Bhutan on the toughest trek in the world. University of Nebraska Press 2011 336p il map (Outdoor lives) pa $19.95 **915**

1. Mountaineering 2. Bhutan -- Description and travel
ISBN 978-0-8032-3433-8; 0-8032-3433-3

LC 2010-28970

"For the armchair traveler, Grange does a fine job of showing readers the nature, history, and landscape of Bhutan, as well as taking us to remote villages and monasteries. . . He is equally open about what is essentially a personal search for meaning." Seattle Post-Intelligencer

Includes bibliographical references.

Horwitz, Tony

Baghdad without a map, and other misadventures in Arabia. Dutton 1991 276p map hardcover o.p. pa $16 **915**

1. Middle East -- Description and travel
ISBN 0-452-26745-5 pa

LC 90-46653

"Horwitz mixes insight and humor in these observations that illustrate on an everyday level both the contradictions and the idiosyncrasies of the Arab world." Booklist

Jubber, Nicholas

Drinking arak off an ayatollah's beard; a journey through the inside-out worlds of Iran and Afghanistan. Da Capo Press 2010 327p il map pa $15.95 **915**

1. Shahnameh (Epic poem) 2. Iran -- Social conditions 3. Iran -- Description and travel 4. Afghanistan -- Social conditions 5. Afghanistan -- Description and travel
ISBN 978-0-306-81884-4

LC 2009-48191

"Jubber's account offers a full and satisfying panorama of the region with its rich paradoxes and complexities intact." Publ Wkly

Includes bibliographical references

Man, John

Marco Polo; The Journey That Changed the World. John Man. HarperCollins 2014 400 p. 16 plates; ills.; maps; plans $15.99 **915**

1. Exploration
ISBN 0062375075; 9780062375070

Author John Man presents the "story of the world's most famous traveler, retracing his legendary journey from Venice to China, the moment East first met West. Man traveled in Marco Polo's footsteps to Xanadu then on to Beijing and through modern China in search of the history behind the legend. [He] draws on his own journey, new archaeological findings, and deep archival study to paint a vivid picture of Marco Polo and the great court of Kublai Khan." (Publisher's note)

Morris-Suzuki, Tessa

To the Diamond Mountains; a hundred-year journey through China and Korea. Rowman & Littlefield Publishers 2010 201p il map $34.95 **915**

1. Artists 2. Authors 3. Adventurers 4. China -- Description and travel 5. China -- Social life and customs 6. Korea (North) -- Description and travel 7. Korea (South) -- Description and travel 8. Korea (North) -- Social life and customs 9. Korea (South) -- Social life and customs
ISBN 978-1-4422-0503-1; 978-1-4422-0505-5 ebook

LC 2010023685

"Morris-Suzuki, an Australian professor, recently traveled through northeast China and the two Koreas; she was retracing the route of Emily Kemp, an extraordinary writer, artist, and intrepid adventurer who wrote about her experiences a century ago. Morris-Suzuki, like her predecessor, is a keen observer and a fine writer; she has combined the disciplines of history and travel writing in an absorbing analysis of the past, present, and future of this volatile region." Booklist

Includes bibliographical references

Polo, Marco, 1254-ca. 1323

The **travels** of Marco Polo; the illustrated edition. Marco Polo, edited by Morris Rossabi, translated by Henry Yule. Sterling Signature 2012 377 p. $40 **915**

1. Exploration 2. Mongols -- Hsitory 3. Voyages and travels 4.

Asia -- Description and travel -- Early works to 1800
ISBN 1402796307; 9781402796302

LC 2011051047

This book, written by Marco Polo and edited by Morris Rossabi, "offers the complete text of Polo's travelogue, enhanced with more than 200 images--including illuminated manuscripts, paintings, photographs, and maps. Sidebars and dozens of informative footnotes combine to present Polo and his travels." (Publisher's note)

Theroux, Paul
Riding the iron rooster; by train through China. Paul Theroux. 1st Mariner Books ed.; Houghton Mifflin 2006 480p map pa $7.50 **915**
1. Railroads 2. China -- Description and travel
ISBN 978-0-6186-5897-8

LC 2006028745

First published 1988 by Putnam's

This is an account of the author's yearlong rail journey through China. "For Theroux, traveling is both about people—their thoughts, customs, and peculiarities-and a form of autobiography, and here we learn as much about his own quirks and fancies as we do about the intriguing world of contemporary China." Libr J

Thubron, Colin
Shadow of the Silk Road. Harper Collins 2007 363p map $25.95 **915**
1. Asia -- Description and travel
ISBN 978-0-06-123172-8; 0-06-123172-X

LC 2006-52142

First published 2006 in the United Kingdom
"An illuminating account of a breathtaking journey." Booklist

To a mountain in Tibet. Harper 2011 227p map $24.99; ebook $19.99 **915**
1. Tibet (China) -- Description and travel
ISBN 978-0-06-176826-2; 978-0-06-206605-3 ebook

LC 2010-43013

"Emotional subtlety and vivid evocations of the people and places are only part of what makes the book so enjoyable. The present-tense narration allows readers make discoveries alongside Thubron, which adds immeasurably to the intimacy and immediacy of the reading experience. A powerful and hauntingly elegiac hybrid of travelogue and memoir." Kirkus

Winchester, Simon
The **river** at the center of the world; a journey up the Yangtze and back in Chinese time. Holt & Co. 1996 xx, 410p maps hardcover o.p. **915**
1. Yangtze River valley (China)

LC 96-12399

In 1994, the author followed the Yangtze's "course from the East China Sea to Tibet by boat, car, train, plane, bus and foot; but this is more than an ordinary account of a traveler's pilgrimage, although it is a must for any visitor to China. Wryly humorous, gently skeptical, immensely knowledgeable as he wends his way along the 3900 miles of the great river, Winchester provides an irresistible feast of detail about the character of the river itself, the landscape, the cities, villages and people along its banks." Publ Wkly

Includes bibliographical references

915.204 Japan – Travel

Denson, Abby
Cool Tokyo guide; adventures in the city of kawaii fashion, train Sushi and Godzilla. Abby Denson. Tuttle Pub. 2018 128 p. (pbk.) $14.99 **915.204**
1. Travel 2. Tokyo (Japan)
ISBN 9784805314418

LC 2017950583

This book, by Abby Denson, focuses on "Tokyo's exciting streets and a little bit beyond. . . . [It introduces readers to a] restaurant where clowns drive robots and mermaids ride on sharks, fantastic shops for lovers of everything from vintage manga to dollar-store treasures . . . , famous sites both old and new, from Sensoji Temple to Tokyo Tower . . . [and] must-visit spots like Ueno Park and even a few spots outside the city." (Publisher's note)

"The overall result is a love song to a city and an inspiration for prospective visitors." Booklist

915.404 India – Travel

DeRoche, Torre
The **worrier's** guide to the end of the world; love, loss, and other catastrophes through Italy, India, and beyond. Torre DeRoche. Seal Press 2017 xxi, 259 p.p (paperback) $16.99 **915.404**
1. Female friendship 2. India -- Description and travel 3. Italy -- Description and travel 4. Women travelers -- India -- Biography 5. Women travelers -- Italy -- Biography
ISBN 9781580056854

LC 2017025963

In this memoir, author Torre DeRoche "is at rock bottom following a breakup and her father's death when she crosses paths with the goofy and spirited Masha, who is pusuing her dream of walking the world. When Masha invites Torre to join her pilgrimage through Tuscany--drinking wine, foraging wild berries, and twirling on hillsides--Torre straps on a pair of flimsy street shoes and gets rambling." (Publisher's note)

"This page-turning memoir is a thoughtful and entertaining addition to the minigenre of grief-induced travelogues like Cheryl Strayed's Wild (2012) and Shannon Leone Fowler's Traveling with Ghosts (2017)." Booklist

915.6 Middle East – Geography

Taseer, Aatish
★ **Stranger** to history; a son's journey through Islamic lands. by Aatish Taseer. Canongate 2009 323 p. ill., map $16 **915.6**
1. Islam 2. Islamic civilization 3. Middle East -- Description and travel 4. Fathers and sons 5. Islam -- Middle East
ISBN 155597628X; 1847670717; 9781555976286; 9781847670717

LC 2009483559

This book, by Aatish Taseer, "is the story of the journey [which the author] made to try to understand what it means to be Muslim in the twenty-first century. Starting from Istanbul, Islam's once greatest city, he travels to Mecca, its most holy, and then home through Iran and Pakistan. Ending in Lahore, at his estranged father's home, on the night Benazir Bhutto was killed, it is also the story of Taseer's divided family over the past fifty years." (Publisher's note)

915.804   Central Asia – Travel

Harris, Kate

Lands of lost borders; a journey on the Silk Road. Kate Harris. HarperCollins 2018 320 p. $24.99   **915.804**

1. Cycling 2. Travel writing

ISBN 0062839349; 9780062839343

This book, by Kate Harris, presents a "travelogue and memoir of her journey by bicycle along the Silk Road. . . . [It] chronicle[s] . . . Harris's odyssey and . . . [explores] the importance of breaking the boundaries we set ourselves; [is] an examination of the stories borders tell, and the restrictions they place on nature and humanity; and a meditation on the existential need to explore--the essential longing to discover what in the universe we are doing here." (Publisher's note)

915.9   Southeast Asia – Geography

DK Eyewitness Travel Cambodia & Laos.   DK Publishing 2016 288 p. col. ill., col. maps $25   **915.9**

1. Cambodia 2. Laos -- Description and travel

ISBN 1465440062; 9781465440068

LC 2011205904

This travel guide from DK Publishing explains how "whether you want to explore the temples of Angkor Wat, take a boat trip through the famous Tham Kong Lo caves, or sunbathe on stunning white beaches in southern Cambodia, Cambodia and Laos offer exhilarating options for visitors." (Publisher's note)

"For readers who intend to go to Cambodia and/or Laos, this guide provides a nice snapshot of the countries' look, history, and culture with some specifics for planning purposes and a compact size for portability." LJ

Eyewitness Travel Malaysia & Singapore; edited by Aruna Ghose. DK Publishing 2016 356 p. col. ill., col. maps (paperback) $25   **915.9**

1. Malaysia -- Description and travel 2. Singapore -- Description and travel

ISBN 1465440054; 9781465440051

This book, edited by Aruna Ghose and the staff of Dorling Kindersley Eyewitness Travel, presents a travel guide for Malaysia and Singapore. "Whether you want to discover the best places to spot colorful fish and jungle-dwelling animals like orangutans, or are looking to sample the incredible food in the ultra-modern metropolises of Kuala Lumpur and Singapore, this region offers an astounding range of experiences." (Publisher's note)

"This inclusive photographic treat will make even 'stay at home' travelers feel like they are actually there." LJ

Houton, Jody

A **geek** in Thailand; discovering the land of golden buddhas, pad thai and kickboxing. Jody Houton. Tuttle Publishing 2016 160 p. illustrations (chiefly color) (pbk.) $18.95   **915.9**

1. Asia -- Description and travel 2. Thailand -- Social life and customs

ISBN 0804844488; 9780804844482

LC 2015949992

This book, by Jody Houton, "offers a concise but insightful take on Thailand for tourists, expats, would-be expats, and others--anyone, in fact, with an interest in visiting or learning about the Land of Smiles. Subjects range from the touchstones of Thai culture and history, such as its politics and economy, Buddhism and folklore, to chapters on tra-

ditional Thai design and craftsmanship, including its highly acclaimed architecture and fine silk textiles." (Publisher's note)

"Warning: after reading this alluring book, you will have to travel to Thailand." Library Journal

916   Geography of and travel in Africa

Campbell, James T.

Middle passages; African American journeys to Africa, 1787-2005. [by] James Campbell. Penguin Press 2006 513p il (The Penguin history of American life) $29.95   **916**

1. Africa -- Description and travel

ISBN 1-59420-083-1; 978-1-59420-083-0

LC 2005-58672

"From the repatriation of former slaves in the early years of the United States to the recent heritage tourism featuring Goree Island and other slave-trading sites, Campbell provides an artful reconstruction of the often bittersweet experience of return and reunion." N Y Times Book Rev

Grant, Richard

Crazy river; a journey to the source of the Nile. Free Press 2011 336p pa $15; ebook $9.99   **916**

1. Explorers 2. Travel writers 3. Asian studies specialists 4. Tanzania -- Social conditions 5. East Africa -- Social conditions 6. Middle Eastern studies specialists 7. Tanzania -- Description and travel 8. East Africa -- Description and travel

ISBN 978-1-4391-5414-4 pa; 978-1-4391-5764-0 ebook

LC 2011012168

"The Malagarasi River in Tanzania had not been fully traveled by either Westerners or Africans. So, the tradition of 19th-century British explorers, first and foremost Richard Burton, who became his spectral travel companion, Grant set out to do so. But his adventures on the river—disease and disappointment, danger from crocs, hippos and bandits—became but part of his larger story about what Africa is and how to make sense of it. . . . Dyspeptic, disturbing and brilliantly realized, Grant's account of Africa is literally unforgettable." Kirkus

Tayler, Jeffrey

Angry wind; through Muslim Black Africa by truck, bus, boat, and camel. Houghton Mifflin 2005 252p map $25 **916**

1. Sahel -- Description and travel

ISBN 0-618-33467-X

LC 2004-54066

"This substantial and informative work is no mere travel tale—it is a firsthand account of the author's deeply personal quest for knowledge and understanding of a people and a region that continues to struggle with extreme poverty and unrest." Libr J

Theroux, Paul

Dark star safari; overland from Cairo to Cape Town. Houghton Mifflin 2003 472p maps $28   **916**

1. Africa -- Description and travel

ISBN 0-618-13424-7

LC 2002-32710

First published 2002 in the United Kingdom

"Where Theroux sees Africa uncluttered by preconceived notions, his writing can be brilliant. . . . But where Theroux has traveled before—40 years ago, as first a Peace Corps teacher, then a lecturer at Uganda's Makerere University in the golden years just after the country's independence—he sees Africa not for what it is, but for what it might have been." Christ Sci Monit

Last train to Zona Verde; my ultimate African safari. Paul Theroux. Houghton Mifflin Harcourt 2013 368 p. $27 **916**
1. Angola -- Description and travel 2. South Africa -- Description and travel 3. Namibia -- Description and travel
ISBN 061883933X; 9780618839339

LC 2013000388

In this book, by Paul Theroux, the author "sets out on a new journey through the continent he knows and loves best. Theroux first came to Africa as a twenty-two-year-old Peace Corps volunteer. . . . Now he returns, after fifty years on the road, to explore the little-traveled territory of western Africa and to take stock both of the place and of himself." (Publisher's note)

"The acclaimed travel writer and novelist chronicles his journey through Africa as tourist, adventure-seeker, thinker and hopeful critic... Reading this enlightening book won't only open a window into Theroux's mind, it will also impart a deeper understanding of Africa and travel in general." Kirkus

916.2 Egypt – Geography

Wood, Levison
Walking the Nile; by Levison Wood. Atlantic Monthly Press 2016 352 p. color ill., map, portraits $26 **916.2**
1. Nile River -- Description and travel
ISBN 0802124496; 9780802124494

This book, by Levison Wood, "is a captivating account of a remarkable and unparalleled Nile journey. Starting in November 2013 in a forest in Rwanda, . . . Wood set forth on foot, aiming to become the first person to walk the entire length of the fabled river. He followed the Nile for nine months, over 4,000 miles, through six nations—Rwanda, Tanzania, Uganda, South Sudan, the Republic of Sudan, and Egypt—to the Mediterranean coast." (Publisher's note)

Armchair travelers and those looking for a side of Africa not generally seen will find adventure sprinkled with culture and history in this narrative that circumvents the colonial pomp while following in the shadow of the original British explorers of Africa.

Includes index (p. [328] - 338).

917 Geography of and travel in North America

Ambrose, Stephen E., 1936-2002
★ **Undaunted** courage; Meriwether Lewis, Thomas Jefferson, and the opening of the American West. Simon & Schuster 1996 511p il maps $30; pa $17 **917**
1. Explorers 2. Lewis and Clark Expedition (1804-1806) 3. Biography, Individual 4. Territorial governors 5. West (U.S.) -- Exploration
ISBN 0-684-81107-3; 0-684-82697-6 pa

LC 95-37146

This is a "portrait of Meriwether Lewis, the co-leader with William Clark of the . . . {1804-1806} expedition across the North American continent." (America) Bibliography. Index.

This treatment of the Lewis and Clark Expedition "is essentially a biography of Lewis, although the bulk of it is a lively retelling of the journey of the two captains—together with their party of soldiers and frontiersmen, Clark's black slave, York, and the legendary Shoshone Indian woman, Sacagawea, and her infant son—conveyed with passionate enthusiasm by Mr. Ambrose and sprinkled liberally with some of the most famous and vivid passages from the travelers' journals." N Y Times Book Rev
Includes bibliographical references

Bryson, Bill
A **walk** in the woods; rediscovering America on the Appalachian Trail. Broadway Bks. 1998 276p hardcover o.p. pa $14.95 **917**
1. Appalachian region -- Description and travel
ISBN 0-7679-0251-3; 0-7679-0252-1 pa

LC 97-32627

"Bryson's breezy, self-mocking tone may turn off readers who hanker for another 'Into Thin Air' or 'Seven Years in Tibet.' Others, however, may find themselves turning the pages with increasing amusement and anticipation as they discover that they're in the hands of a satirist of the first rank, one who writes (and walks) with Chaucerian brio." N Y Times Book Rev
Includes bibliographical references

Fletcher, Colin
The **man** who walked through time. Vintage Bks. 1989 247p il pa $14.95 **917**
1. Grand Canyon (Ariz.)
ISBN 0-679-72306-4; 978-0-679-72306-6

LC 72-4082

First published 1967 by Knopf
An account of the author's journey on foot through the Grand Canyon National Park.

Gimlette, John
Theatre of fish; travels through Newfoundland and Labrador. Alfred A. Knopf 2005 xxii, 360p il map $25 **917**
1. Atlantic Coast (North America)
ISBN 1-4000-4322-0

LC 2005-44149

"Readers will be fascinated by Newfoundland's and Labrador's bizarre, often tragic pasts and equally strange presents, and they will be glad it was the eloquent Gimlette who made the trip so they don't have to." Publ Wkly
Includes bibliographical references

Heat Moon, William Least
Blue highways; a journey into America. photographs by the author; with a new afterword by the author. Back Bay Bks. 1999 429p il $29.95; pa $14.95 **917**
1. United States -- Description and travel
ISBN 0-316-35391-4; 0-316-35329-9 pa

LC 00-265444

A reissue of the title first published 1982 by Little, Brown
An account of the author's journey across the U.S. in a van taking only secondary roads

Home ground; language for an American landscape. Barry Lopez, editor; Debra Gwartney, managing editor. Trinity University Press 2006 xxiv, 449p il $29.95 **917**
1. Reference books 2. Americanisms -- Encyclopedias 3. Geographic names -- Encyclopedias
ISBN 978-1-59534-024-5; 1-59534-024-6

LC 2006-19942

This is a "collection of geographical terms from every region of the United States. The 45 contributors, among them Jon Krakauer and Barbara Kingsolver, chose words that Americans use to describe landscape features where they live, then enriched their definitions with literary quotes, comments, irony, and humor. The result is a readable A-to-Z geological and geographical dictionary that surpasses other dictionaries in both scope and coverage." Libr J

Includes bibliographical references

Jenkins, Peter

A **walk** across America. Morrow 1979 288p il maps hardcover o.p. pa $6.99   **917**

1. United States -- Description and travel
ISBN 0-06-095955-X pa

LC 78-10320

This book chronicles the author's journey with his dog from New York to the Gulf of Mexico

Krakauer, Jon, 1954-

Into the wild; Jon Krakauer. Villard Bks. 1996 xi, 207 p.p maps hardcover o.p. (pbk.) $12.95; (hbk.) $26   **917**

1. Alaska -- Description and travel 2. Alaska -- Biography 3. Alaska -- Description 4. Biography, Individual 5. West (U.S.) -- Biography
ISBN 0385486804; 067942850X; 9780679428503

LC 95020008

This book, by Jon Krakauer, is the "story of a young man on a quest for knowledge and experience. . . . Chris McCandless loved the road, the unadorned life, the Tolstoyan call to asceticism. After graduating college, he took off on another of his long destinationless journeys, this time cutting all contact with his family and changing his name to Alex Supertramp. . . . Ultimately, in 1992, his terms got him into mortal trouble when he ran up against something--the Alaskan wild." (Kirkus Reviews)

National Geographic Society (U.S.)

★ **National** Geographic guide to the national parks of the United States; [project manger, Caroline Hickey] 8th ed. National Geographic 2016 480p il pa $28   **917**

1. National parks and reserves -- United States
ISBN 9781426216510
Updated periodically

This guide provides information on each of the fifty-eight national parks, including things to do, campgrounds and accommodations, and facilities for the disabled.

"You can't do better than this guide. . . . Highly detailed and beautiful, this one is a must for all collections." Libr J

Wallis, Michael

Route 66: the mother road. St. Martin's Griffin 2001 276p il maps $35; pa $19.95   **917**

1. West (U.S.) -- Description and travel
ISBN 0-312-28167-6; 0-312-28161-7 pa

LC 2001-31944

This is a reissue of the title first published 1990

The author examines the highway's history, roadside diners, towns, motels, and people

Includes bibliographical references

Wright, Carol Von Pressentin

Blue guide New York; Carol von Pressentin Wright. Edit.5 Blue Guides Ltd 2016 608 p. (Blue guides) (paperback) $26.95   **917**

1. Travel guidebooks 2. New York (N.Y.) -- Guidebooks
ISBN 1905131704; 9781905131709

This Blue Guide to New York City, by Carol von Pressentin Wright, "takes you on a meticulous tour of the well-known, lesser-known and almost unknown sights of the city as well as . . . [showing] where to stay and eat. Ideal for on-street use and at-home reference, the depth of coverage is second to none: this is a mini-encyclopedia of a multi-layered city. 'Blue Guide New York' forms the basis for study for accredited NYC tour guides." (Publisher's note)

917.104   Canada – Travel

Canada; edited by Rebecca Miles. DK Pub 2018 440 p. color ill., color maps $25   **917.104**

1. Canada -- Description and travel
ISBN 9781465468246

This book, printed by Dorling Kindersley, edited by Rebecca Miles, is part of the publisher's "Eyewitness Travel Guides" series. It presents "the best attractions . . . [that Canada] has to offer, from the rich historical and cultural treasures of its cities to the stunning scenery of its landscapes and coastlines. Visit the Citadelle of Quebec, eat world-class cuisine in Vancouver, take in the beauty of Niagara Falls, and go whale watching on the coasts." (Publisher's note)

917.28   Central America – Geography

Hely, Steve

The **wonder** trail; true stories from Los Angeles to the end of the world. Steve Hely. Dutton 2016 336 p. illustrations, map (hardcover) $27   **917.28**

1. Travel writing 2. South America -- Description and travel 3. Central America -- Description and travel 4. Curiosities and wonders -- South America 5. South America -- Social life and customs 6. Central America -- Social life and customs 7. Curiosities and wonders -- Central America
ISBN 9780525955016

LC 2015038442

This book, by Steve Hely, "is the story of a trip from Los Angeles to the bottom of South America. . . . From Mexico City to Oaxaca; into ancient Mayan ruins; the jungles, coffee plantations, and remote beaches of Central America; across the Panama Canal; by sea to Colombia; to the wild Easter celebration of Popayán; to the Amazon rainforest; the Inca sites of Cuzco and Machu Picchu; to the Galápagos Islands; the Atacama Desert of Chile; and down to wind-worn Patagonia." (Publisher's note)

"Hely's hilarious descriptions of the stunning sights and quirky people he encounters along the way will delight experienced globetrotters and armchair travelers alike." LJ

Wood, Levison

★ **Walking** the Americas; 1,800 miles, eight countries, and one incredible journey from Mexico to Colombia. Levison Wood. Atlantic Monthly Press 2018 viii, 291 p.p $27 **917.28**

1. Travel writing 2. Central America -- Description and travel
ISBN 0802127495; 9780802127495

In this book, author Levinson Wood chronicles his journey "across the spine of the Americas, . . . from Mexico to Colombia. . . . Wood encounters indigenous tribes in Mexico, revolutionaries in . . . [Nicaragua], fellow explorers, and migrants heading toward the United States. The relationships he forges along the way are at the heart of his travels--and the personal histories, cultures, and popular legends he discovers paint a riveting history of Mexico and Central America." (Publisher's note)

917.3   Geography of and travel in United States

Abroad at home; the best international travel in North America. National Geographic. National Geographic Books 2015 288 p. color illustrations (pbk.: alk. paper) $24.95   **917.3**
1. Travel 2. North America 3. Canada -- Description and travel 4. United States -- Description and travel
ISBN 1426214995; 9781426214998

LC 2014037548

This book from National Geographic "presents a potpourri of international experiences in the United States and Canada. Discover the villages, neighborhoods, and regions that cover the breadth of North America's great global diversity--Chinatowns and Little Italys, of course, but also Polish, German, French, Russian, and Japanese enclaves." (Publisher's note)

"Recommended for those seeking an international flavor in their hometown or nearby cities, or travelers planning a trip with a singular flair to North American regions." LJ

Gill, A. A. (Adrian Anthony), 1954-2016

To America with love; A.A. Gill. Simon & Schuster 2013 256 p. (hardback) $25   **917.3**
1. Cultural critique 2. United States -- Description and travel 3. United States -- Social life and customs
ISBN 1416596216; 9781416596219; 9781439100448

LC 2013019543

This book is Scottish-born A.A. Gill's tribute to America. He "devotes his . . . to defending the country's earnest belief in government by the people, as well as its brashness of character, frank celebration of success, sublime sense of nature, and childish delight in speechifying and hucksterism, among other things." (Publishers Weekly)

National Geographic Guide to the State Parks of the United States; 5th edition National Geographic 2018 479 p illustrations $28   **917.3**
1. Parks -- United States 2. United States -- Guidebooks
ISBN 9781426218859

Provides simple information about state parks in the United States, offers tips from parks staff, and suggests trails for biking, hiking, and flower gazing.

Savoy, Lauret

Trace; a journey through memory, history, and the American land. Lauren Edith Savoy. Counterpoint Press 2015 240 p. (hardback) $25   **917.3**
1. United States -- Race relations 2. United States -- Social conditions
ISBN 1619025736; 9781619025738

LC 2015009588

Author Lauret Savoy "explores how the country's still unfolding history, and ideas of "race," have marked her and the land. From twisted terrain within the San Andreas Fault zone to a South Carolina plantation, from national parks to burial grounds, from 'Indian Territory' and the U.S.-Mexico Border to the U.S. capital, 'Trace' grapples with a searing national history to reveal the often unvoiced presence of the past." (Publisher's note)

"Springing from the literal Earth to metaphor, Savoy demonstrates the power of narrative to erase as easily as it reveals, yielding a provocative, eclectic exposé of the palimpsest historically defining the U.S. as much as any natural or man-made boundary." Kirkus

917.47   Northeastern United States – Geography

Freudenheim, Ellen

The **Brooklyn** experience; the ultimate guide to neighborhoods & noshes, culture & the cutting edge. Ellen Freudenheim. Rutgers University Press 2016 360 p. (paperback: alkaline paper) $23.95   **917.47**
1. Brooklyn (New York, N.Y.) 2. New York (N.Y.) -- Description and travel 3. New York (N.Y.) -- Guidebooks 4. Brooklyn (New York, N.Y.) -- Guidebooks
ISBN 9780813577432

LC 2015035672

This book, by Ellen Freudenheim, is a "comprehensive Brooklyn guidebook. . . . Walk over the Brooklyn Bridge at dawn or sunset, discover thirty-eight unique Brooklyn neighborhoods, and experience the borough like a native. Find out where to go to the beach and to eat great pizza, what to do with the kids, how to enjoy free and cheap activities, and where to savor Brooklyn's famous cuisines." (Publisher's note)

"Even those readers who think they know everything about this New York City borough will probably find a surprising tidbit in these pages." LJ

Includes bibliographical references and index

917.64   Texas – Geography

Wright, Lawrence, 1947-

God save Texas; a journey into the soul of the Lone Star State. Lawrence Wright. Alfred A. Knopf 2018 352 p. (hardback) $27.95   **917.640**
1. Texas -- Description and travel 2. Texas -- Politics and government 3. Texas -- Social conditions -- 21st century 4. Texas -- Economic conditions -- 21st century 5. Texas -- Politics and government -- 21st century
ISBN 9780525520108

LC 2017031324

This book, by Lawrence Wright, "is a journey through the most controversial state in America. It is a red state in the heart of Trumpland that hasn't elected a Democrat to a statewide office in more than twenty years; . . . Texas looks a lot like the America that Donald Trump wants to create. And Wright's profound portrait of the state not only reflects our country back as it is, but as it was and as it might be." (Publisher's note)

"Wright's large-scale portrait, which reveals how Texas is only growing in influence,is comprehensive, insightful, and compulsively entertaining." Pub Wkly

917.91   Arizona – Geography

Owen, David, 1955-

Where the water goes; life and death along the Colorado River. David Owen. Riverhead Books 2017 274 p. map (hardcover) $28   **917.91**
1. Water supply 2. Stream ecology 3. Colorado River (Colo.-Mexico) 4. Water-supply -- West (U.S.) 5. Stream ecology -- Colorado River (Colo.-Mexico) 6. Colorado River (Colo.-Mexico) -- Description and travel 7. Colorado River (Colo.-Mexico) -- Environmental conditions
ISBN 9781594633775; 9780698189904

LC 2016039410

This book, by David Owen, "traces all that water from the Colorado . . . [River's] headwaters to its parched terminus, once a verdant wetland but now a million-acre desert. He takes readers on an adventure down-river, along a labyrinth of waterways, reservoirs, power plants, farms, fracking sites, ghost towns, and RV parks, to the spot near the U.S.-Mexico border where the river runs dry." (Publisher's note)

"With water shortages looming across the globe, Owen's work provides invaluable lessons on the rewards and pitfalls involved in managing an essential natural resource." Booklist

Includes bibliographical references (pages 261-266) and index.

917.94   California – Geography

Anywhere that is wild; John Muir's first walk to Yosemite. [edited by] Peter Thomas, Donna Thomas. Yosemite Conservancy 2018 64 p. (alk. paper) $14.99   **917.94**
1. Travel 2. Natural history -- California
ISBN 9781930238831

LC 2017956271

This book, edited by Peter and Donna Thomas, is about the walk of John Muir from San Francisco, California to the Yosemite in April 1868. "Using Muir's personal correspondence and published articles, Peter and Donna Thomas have reconstructed the real story of Muir's literal ramblings over California hills and through dales, with lofty Sierra Nevada peaks, Englishmen, and bears mixed in for good measure." (Publisher's note)

917.98   Alaska – Geography

Adams, Mark, 1967-
Tip of the iceberg; my 3,000-mile journey around wild Alaska, the last great American frontier. Mark Adams. Dutton, an imprint of Penguin Random House LLC 2017 336 p. (hardcover) $28   **917.98**
1. Travel writing 2. Voyages and travels 3. Alaska -- Description and travel
ISBN 9781101985106; 9781101985120

LC 2017039007

This book, by Mark Adams, describes his "journey into Alaska, America's last frontier, retracing the historic 1899 Harriman Expedition. . . . Using the state's intricate public ferry system, the Alaska Marine Highway System, Adams travels three thousand miles, following the George W. Elder's itinerary north through Wrangell, Juneau, and Glacier Bay, then continuing west into the colder and stranger regions of the Aleutians and the Arctic Circle." (Publisher's note)

"Tourists will certainly enjoy reading about both the past and the present, and the breezy, self-deprecating tone makes for an obvious vacation diversion." Booklist

918   Geography of and travel in South America

Chatwin, Bruce
In Patagonia; introduction by Nicholas Shakespeare. Penguin Books 2003 204p il map (Penguin classics) pa $15 **918**
1. Patagonia (Argentina and Chile) -- Description and travel
ISBN 0-14-243719-0; 978-0-14-243719-3

LC 2002-45038

First published 1977 in the United Kingdom

This travelogue "captures the exotic characters and scenery Chatwin encountered in the southern tip of South America on a search for an important prehistoric artifact." Booklist

Grann, David
The lost city of Z; a tale of deadly obsession in the Amazon. Doubleday 2009 339p il map $27.50   **918**
1. Explorers 2. Amazon River valley
ISBN 978-0-385-51353-1; 0-385-51353-4

LC 2008-17432

Interweaves the story of British explorer Percy Fawcett, who vanished during a 1925 expedition into the Amazon, with the author's own quest to uncover the mysteries surrounding Fawcett's final journey and the secrets of what lies deep in the Amazon jungle.

"A colorful tale of true adventure, marked by satisfyingly unexpected twists, turns and plenty of dark portents." Kirkus

Includes bibliographical references (p. 315-326)

Insight Guide Explore Rio; Insight Guides. Insight Guides 2016 128 p. $12.99   **918**
1. Rio de Janeiro (Brazil) -- Description and travel
ISBN 1780055536; 9781780055534

This travel guide for Rio de Janeiro, Brazil, "is the ideal pocket companion when discovering this exciting city: a full-colour guide containing 14 easy-to-follow routes through the city's many fascinating neighbourhoods, from the Centro Histórico and the charming Santa Teresa district to the fabled beaches of Copacabana to Ipanema and beyond to the Costa Verde." (Publisher's note)

"In time for the Summer Games, this focused and travel-friendly (5.9" x 0.9" x 8.3") guide to Rio is filled with the clear, beautiful photographs for which the 'Insight' series is so well known." LJ

918.1   Brazil – Geography

Brazil; DK Publishing. DK Publishing 2018 448 p. ill. (chiefly col.), col. maps $30   **918.1**
1. Brazil -- Description and travel
ISBN 9781465467966

This book "is your in-depth guide to the very best of [Brazil]. . . . Whether you want to explore the streets of Rio de Janeiro or lounge on its beaches, celebrate the culture of Carnaval and discover the best places to hear the sounds of bossa nova and samba, or explore the vast Amazon rain forest in the north, Brazil proves to be an extraordinarily diverse country of modern cities, verdant landscapes, and rich heritage." (Publisher's note)

"With lots of color photos and easy-to-read descriptions, these guides also serve as a good reference source and aide-mémoire when patrons return home and need to identify locations in photos." LJ

Fitzgerald, Holly
Ruthless river; love and survival by raft on the Amazon's relentless Madre de Dios. Holly FitzGerald. Vintage Books 2017 xii, 316 p.p illustrations, map (Vintage Departures) (trade pbk.) $16   **918.1**
1. Amazon River 2. United States -- Description and travel 3. Amazon River -- Description and travel 4. Amazon River Region -- Description and travel
ISBN 9780525432784; 9780525432777

LC 2016037102

This book in the Vintage Departures series, by Holly Conklin FitzGerald, tells "a true and thrilling adventure of a young married couple who survive a plane crash only to later raft hundreds of miles across Peru and Bolivia, ending up in a channel to nowhere, a dead end so flooded there is literally no land to stand on. Their raft--a mere four logs--separates them from the piranha-and-caiman-infested water until they finally realize that there is no way out but to swim." (Publisher's note)

"Recommended for fans of survival narratives, coming-of-maturity stories, and travelogues from off the beaten path." Booklist

Stafford, Ed

Walking the Amazon; 860 days. one step at a time. Ed Stafford. Plume Books 2012 319 p. $16.00 **918.1**

1. Hiking 2. Amazon River 3. Autobiographies 4. Amazon River valley 5. Hiking -- Amazon River Region 6. Amazon River Region -- Description and travel

ISBN 0452298261; 9780452298262

LC 2012010986

In this "memoir . . . about becoming the first person to perambulate the Amazon's entire length, [Ed] Stafford chronicles the countless obstacles he faced, including canoes of armed indigenous peoples, dehydration, sickness, lack of sleep . . . and overwhelming swarms of insects. In addition . . . the author explores his friendship with the longest lasting of his many walking companions, Gadiel 'Cho' Sanchez Rivera." (Kirkus Reviews)

918.15 Peru – Geography

Dk Eyewitness Top 10 Rio De Janeiro; DK Publishing. DK Publishing 2016 128 p. col. ill., col. maps. $14 **918.15**

1. Rio de Janeiro (Brazil) -- Description and travel

ISBN 1465440925; 9781465440921

This book is a "newly updated pocket travel guide for Rio de Janeiro. [It] will lead you straight to the best attractions the city has to offer, from visiting the iconic Cristo Redentor statue to experiencing the Carnival parade at the Sambodromo to soaking up the atmosphere on the famous Copacabana Beach." (Publisher's note)

"This trim 128-page, 13-ounce handy guide is an impressive package. It essentially lists top-ten sites by category: beaches, Carnival, shopping, tours/excursions, museums and galleries, children's activities, restaurants, bars/nightclubs, sports, and insider tips." LJ

Lonely Planet Rio De Janeiro; by Lonely Planet. Lonely Planet 2016 263 p. color ill., color maps $21.99 **918.15**

1. Rio de Janeiro (Brazil) -- Description and travel

ISBN 1743217676; 9781743217672

This travel guide for Rio de Janeiro, Brazil, "is your passport to all the most relevant and up-to-date advice on what to see, what to skip, and what hidden discoveries await you. Stroll barefoot on Ipanema beach, take in the view from Pao de Acucar (Sugarloaf), or shake your hips at an old-fashioned samba club; all with your trusted travel companion. Get to the heart of Rio de Janeiro and begin your journey now!" (Publisher's note)

Rigby, Claire

Fodor's Rio de Janeiro & Sao Paulo; by Fodor's Travel Guides. 4th edition Random House Inc 2018 264 p. illustrations $19.99 **918.15**

1. Brazil -- Description and travel 2. Rio de Janeiro (Brazil) -- Description and travel

ISBN 9781640971059

"With the FIFA World Cup in 2014 and the Olympic Games in 2016, Rio de Janeiro and São Paulo have experienced rapid change. Rio continues to see an influx of visitors, and this colorful city, along with the equally vibrant metropolis of São Paulo, never disappoint. Whether you want to soak in the sun on Rio's glamorous Copacabana Beach, shop in São Paulo's cutting-edge fashion boutiques, or indulge in Latin American's most innovative cuisine, Fodor's Rio De Janeiro & São Paulo will ensure that you get the most out of these two exciting cities." (Publisher's note)

919 Geography of and travel in Australasia, Pacific Ocean islands, Atlantic Ocean islands, Arctic islands, Antarctica and on extraterrestrial worlds

Bell, Jim, 1965-

The **interstellar** age; inside the forty-year Voyager mission. Jim Bell. Dutton 2015 336 p. 8 plates; color illustrations (hardback) $27.95 **919**

1. Project Voyager 2. Planets -- Exploration 3. Outer space -- Exploration 4. Astronautics -- United States 5. Voyager Project

ISBN 0525954325; 9780525954323

LC 2014031706

This book, by planetary scientist Jim Bell, presents the "story of the men and women who drove the Voyager spacecraft mission. . . . Bell reveals what drove and continues to drive the members of this extraordinary team, including Ed Stone, Voyager's chief scientist and the onetime head of NASA's Jet Propulsion Lab; [and] Charley Kohlhase, an orbital dynamics engineer who helped to design many of the critical slingshot maneuvers around planets that enabled the Voyagers to travel so far." (Publisher's note)

"A highly enjoyable read for anyone with an interest in popular science." LJ

Bryson, Bill

In a sunburned country. Broadway Bks. 2000 307p il maps hardcover o.p. pa $14.95 **919**

1. Australia -- Description and travel

ISBN 0-7679-0386-2 pa

LC 00-25566

In this book, Bryson "chronicles his exploration of Australia, he introduces us to a town that went without electricity until the early 1990s, a former high-ranking politician who hawks his own autobiography to passersby, an assortment of coffee shops and restaurants, . . . a type of giant worm, and the world's most poisonous creature, the box jellyfish." Booklist

Includes bibliographical references

Fleming, Fergus

Ninety degrees North; the quest for the North Pole. Grove Press 2002 xxi, 470p il maps $26; pa $15 **919**

1. North Pole 2. Arctic regions -- Exploration

ISBN 0-8021-1725-2; 0-8021-4036-X pa

LC 2002-21469

Companion volume to Barrow's boys (2000)

First published 2001 in the United Kingdom

"The book is fascinating for how Fleming renders the haughty, post-Enlightenment brio of the principal adventurers and the extreme, often fatal ends toward which it pushed them." Publ Wkly

Includes bibliographical references

Geiger, John

Frozen in time; the fate of the Franklin expedition. Owen Beattie & John Geiger. Greystone Books 1998 xi, 185 p.p ill. (some col.), maps $17.95 **919**

1. Northwest Passage

ISBN 1550546163; 1771640790; 9781771640794

LC 00688217

This book, by Owen Beattie and John Geiger, "tells the dramatic story of how Sir John Franklin's elite naval forces came within sight of the Northwest Passage, only to succumb to unimaginable horrors. . . . It shows how the excavation of three sailors from the 1845-48 Franklin expedition, buried for 138 years on the Arctic headland of Beechey Island, has shed new light on what has been one of the world's great maritime mysteries." (Publisher's note)

"The authors present a richly researched history of the expedition and the following relief expeditions and seamlessly merge the worlds of forensic anthropology and 19th-century history. Reading almost like a whodunit page-turner, Beattie and Geiger capture the thrill of making new scientific discoveries and finding important clues to solve a haunting mystery." Pub Wkly

Includes bibliographical references (p. 169-174) and index

Roberts, David, 1943-

Alone on the ice; the greatest survival story in the history of exploration. David Roberts. W. W. Norton & Company 2013 256 p. (hardcover) $27.95 **919**

1. Wilderness survival 2. Antarctica -- Exploration 3. Antarctica -- Discovery and exploration
ISBN 0393083713; 9780393083712

LC 2012037677

This book by David Roberts presents a "portrait of Aussie explorer Douglas Mawson and his arduous trek through some of the most treacherous icy Antarctic terrain. . . . Roberts parallels the courageous achievements of Mawson's team on the 1911-1913 journey along the previously uncharted regions of the landscape with those of his acclaimed peers . . . battling the bitter cold, starvation, and peril to the limits of human endurance." (Publishers Weekly)

Includes bibliographical references and index

Solomon, Susan

The **coldest** March. Yale Univ. Press 2001 xxii, 383p il maps hardcover o.p. pa $16.95 **919**

1. Explorers 2. South Pole 3. Antarctica -- Exploration 4. British Antarctic ("Terra Nova") Expedition (1910-1913)
ISBN 0-300-08967-8; 0-300-09921-5 pa

LC 00-54996

"In November 1911, Capt. Robert Falcon Scott and his British team set out to be the first to reach the South Pole. Battling the brutal weather of Antarctica, they reached the pole in January 1912 only to discover that a Norwegian team had beat them there by nearly a month. On their return from the Pole, Scott and four of his companions died in harsh conditions. Ever since, history has not known whether to label them heroes or bunglers. Solomon . . . analyzes all the factors present during Scott's expedition in an attempt to explain that his failure was due not to incompetence but to a combination of unpredictable weather, erroneous choices and bad luck." Libr J

Includes bibliographical references

Theroux, Paul

The **happy** isles of Oceania; paddling the Pacific. Houghton Mifflin Co. 2006 528p map pa $15.95 **919**

1. Oceania -- Description and travel
ISBN 978-0-618-65898-5; 0-618-65898-X

LC 2006-28742

First published 1992 by Putnam

The author "spent 18 months in a one-man collapsible kayak exploring such exotic Pacific islands as New Zealand, Australia, the Soloman and Cook Islands, Fiji, Samoa, Tahiti, Easter Island, and Hawaii. . . . A brilliant storyteller with an eye for the absurd, Theroux takes the reader to little-known places where time seems to have stood still and people lead simple lives totally unrelated to 20th-century America." Libr J

919.4   Bolivia – Geography

Winton, Tim, 1960-

Island home; a landscape memoir. Tim Winton. First US edition Milkweed Editions 2017 241 p. illustrations (paperback) $16 **919.4**

1. Nature 2. Australia -- Description and travel 3. Travel writing 4. Landscapes -- Australia 5. Landscapes in literature 6. Authors, Australian -- 20th century -- Biography
ISBN 1571311246; 9781571311245; 9781571319586

LC 2017002185

This book presents "a memoir of Australia's unique landscape, and how that singular place has shaped [author] Tim Winton and his writing. From boyhood, Winton's relationship with the world around him—rock pools, sea caves, scrub, and swamp—has been as vital as any other connection. . . . [He] has felt the place seep into him, and learned to see landscape as a living process. In 'Island Home,' Winton brings this landscape . . . to life through personal accounts and environmental history." (Publisher's note)

"The world's largest island deserves nothing less than Winton's beautifully curated, intimate, environmentally sensitive history." Booklist

Includes bibliographical references (pages 237-239)

919.804   Arctic islands – Travel

Watson, Paul, 1950-

Ice Ghosts; The Epic Hunt for the Lost Franklin Expedition. Paul Watson. W W Norton & Co Inc 2017 384 p. $27.95 **919.804**

1. Arctic regions -- Exploration 2. Northwest Passage -- Exploration
ISBN 0393249387; 9780393249385

LC 2017003644

This book, by Paul Watson, "weaves together the epic story of the Lost Franklin Expedition of 1845—whose two ships and crew of 129 were lost to the Arctic ice—with the modern tale of the scientists, divers, and local Inuit behind the incredible discovery of the flagship's wreck in 2014." (Publisher's note)

"A keen, entertaining chronicle of the various attempts to locate a sensationally doomed expedition." Kirkus

919.89   Antarctica – Geography

Grann, David

★ The **white** darkness; David Grann. Doubleday 2018 144 p. $20 **919.89**

1. Explorers -- Biography 2. Antarctica -- Exploration
ISBN 038554457X; 9780385544573

This book, by David Grann, presents "a powerful true story of adventure and obsession in the Antarctic. . . . Henry Worsley was a devoted husband and father and a decorated British special forces officer who believed in honor and sacrifice. He was also a man obsessed. He spent his life idolizing Ernest Shackleton, the nineteenth-century polar explorer, who tried to become the first person to reach the South Pole, and later sought to cross Antarctica on foot." (Publisher's note)

"Grann chronicles the Antarctic adventures of Henry Worsley." Library Journal

McOrist, Wilson

Shackleton's heroes; the epic story of the men who kept the Endurance expedition alive. Wilson McOrist; foreword by Sir Ranulph Fiennes. Skyhorse Publishing 2016 362 p. ill. (some color), maps (ebook) $24.78; $24.99   **919.89**

1. Antarctica -- Exploration 2. Antarctica -- Discovery and exploration

ISBN 9781849549035; 1510710752; 9781510710757

LC 2014455778

This book, by Wilson McOrist, "is the incredible but often forgotten tale of the Mount Hope Party (also known as the Ross Sea party)—six men who worked in the shadow of [Sir Ernest] Shackleton's greater cause. Sent to the opposite side of the Polar continent, these men dropped life-saving food and fuel depots across the Great Ice Barrier, ensuring that Shackleton had the supplies necessary to complete his mission." (Publisher's note)

"All polar enthusiasts will be impressed anew by not only what the Ross Sea Party endured but also how hard McOrist has worked to share their words with the world." Booklist

Includes bibliographical references 9pages 341-345) and index

Shapiro, Laurie Gwen

The **stowaway**; a young man's extraordinary adventure to Antarctica. Laurie Gwen Shapiro. Simon & Schuster 2018 239 p. illustrations (hardcover: alkaline paper) $26   **919.89**

1. Antarctica -- Description and travel 2. Stowaways -- Antarctica -- Biography 3. Ocean travel -- History -- 20th century 4. Adventure and adventurers -- Antarctica -- Biography 5. Teenage boys -- New York (State) -- New York -- Biography

ISBN 9781476753881; 9781476753867

LC 2017007428

In this book, author Laurie Gwen Shapiro describes "the spectacular, true story of a scrappy teenager from New York's Lower East Side who stowed away on the Roaring Twenties' most remarkable feat of science and daring: an expedition to Antarctica. . . . The night before the expedition's flagship set off, Billy Gawronski--a mischievous, first-generation New York City high schooler . . . jumped into the Hudson River and snuck aboard." (Publisher's note)

"This coming-of-age story about a strong-willed boy with an insatiable appetite for adventure is evocative of the Hardy Boys and will appeal to both adult and young adult readers." Pub Wkly

Includes bibliographical references and index

92   Individual Biography

Aaron, Hank, 1934-

Bryant, Howard. The **last** hero; a life of Henry Aaron. Pantheon Books 2010 600p il $29.95   **92**

1. Baseball players 2. African American athletes 3. Baseball -- Biography

ISBN 978-0-375-42485-4; 0-375-42485-7

LC 2009-40573

This biography of the baseball player "reveals a multifaceted man, a great American, and an accomplished athlete, in that order. . . . Bryant evokes the apparently distant world marked by cruel segregation, racism, and poverty of the soul, as well as reliving some of the greatest moments of baseball. A most welcome book, most highly recommended." Libr J

Includes bibliographical references

Abbott, Alysia

Abbott, Alysia. **Fairyland**; a memoir of my father. by Alysia Abbott. 1st ed. W.W. Norton & Co. Inc. 2013 352 p. (hardcover) $25.95   **92**

1. Gay parents 2. Children of gay parents 3. Gay fathers -- Biography 4. Gay men -- California -- San Francisco -- Biography

ISBN 0393082520; 9780393082524

LC 2013011614

Lambda Literary Awards Finalist (2014)
Stonewall Book Awards: Nonfiction Honor Book (2014)

This book by Alysia Abbot recounts her relationship with her father, Steve Abbot, who "in the early 1970s . . . embraced his homosexuality and moved to San Francisco." The "memoir describes life with her poet-activist father and his openly gay lifestyle. . . . She watches as friends, and then her father, contract AIDS, and at age 21, she returns home to help care for him and is conflicted over feelings of duty and the desire to begin a life of her own." (Library Journal)

Includes bibliographical references.

Abdul-Jabbar, Kareem, 1947-

★ Abdul-Jabbar, Kareem. **On** the shoulders of giants; my journey through the Harlem Renaissance. [by] Kareem Abdul-Jabbar with Raymond Obstfeld. Simon & Schuster 2007 274p il hardcover o.p. pa $18.99   **92**

1. Harlem Renaissance 2. Basketball players 3. Nonfiction writers 4. African Americans -- Biography

ISBN 1-4165-3488-1; 978-1-4165-3488-4; 1-4165-3489-X pa; 978-1-4165-3489-1 pa

LC 2006-51776

"By mixing personal anecdotes with traditional research and reporting, . . . [Abdul-Jabbar] acts as a knowledgeable, passionate tour guide through the artistic and social history of one America's most dynamic creative eras." N Y Times Book Rev

Includes bibliographical references

Abdul-Jabbar, Kareem, 1947- **Coach** Wooden and me; our 50-year friendship on and off the court. Kareem Abdul-Jabbar. Grand Central Pub. 2017 290 p. illustrations (hardcover) $29   **92**

1. Friendship 2. Basketball coaches 3. Coach-athlete relationships -- United States 4. Basketball coaches -- United States -- Biography 5. University of California, Los Angeles -- Basketball -- History 6. African American basketball players -- United States -- Biography

ISBN 9781455542253; 9781455542277; 9781455571246; 9781478914754; 9781478914761

LC 2017933519

In this book author Kareem Abdul-Jabbar "explores his 50-year friendship with Coach John Wooden, one of the most enduring and meaningful relationships in sports history. . . . [He] reveals the inspirational story of how his bond with John Wooden evolved from a history-making coach-player mentorship into a deep and genuine friendship that transcended sports, shaped the course of both men's lives, and lasted for half a century." (Publisher's note)

"Abdul-Jabbar and Wooden shared a priceless friendship, and this sensitive, sharply written account brings it to full, vivid life." Booklist

Abdullahi, Asad

Steinberg, Jonny. A **man** of good hope; by Jonny Steinberg. Alfred A. Knopf 2014 336 p. illustrations, maps (hardcover: alk. paper) $26.95   **92**

1. African Refugees 2. Somalia -- Social conditions 3. Refugees -- Somalia 4. Somalia -- Biography 5. Somalis -- South Africa --

Biography 6. Somalis -- United States -- Biography
ISBN 0385352727; 9780385352727; 9780385352734;
9780804171045

LC 2013046388

"In January 1991, when civil war came to Mogadishu, the capital of Somalia, two-thirds of the city's population fled. Among them was eight-year-old Asad Abdullahi. . . . Serially betrayed by the people who promised to care for him, Asad lived his childhood at a skeptical remove from the adult world, his relation to others wary and tactical. . . . By the time he reached the cusp of adulthood, Asad had honed an array of wily talents." (Publisher's note)

"Steinberg's solid prose is perfect for the task of sharing Asad's history. He probes the darkest moments of his subject's life without ever becoming maudlin, telling the story starkly and bluntly." Kirkus

Abu-Jaber, Diana.

Abu-Jaber, Diana, 1960- **Life** Without a Recipe; A Memoir of Food and Family. Diana Abu-Jaber. W W Norton & Co Inc 2016 256 p. $26.95 **92**
1. Food 2. Family
ISBN 0393249093; 9780393249095

LC 2016000543

This memoir, by Diana Abu-Jaber, is the author's "celebration . . . of escaping family and making family on one's own terms. As Diana discovers, however, building confidence in one's own path sometimes takes a mistaken marriage or two—or in her case, three: to a longhaired boy-poet, to a dashing deconstructionist literary scholar, and finally to her steadfast, outdoors-loving Scott. It also takes a good deal of angst . . . and even when she knew what she wanted . . . the nerve to pursue it." (Publisher's note)

"Abu-Jaber renders her relationships to both food and family in rich, joyful detail." Booklist

Achebe, Chinua, 1930-2013

Achebe, Chinua, 1930-2013. The **education** of a British-protected child; essays. A.A. Knopf 2009 172p $24.95; pa $14.95 **92**
1. Poets 2. Racism 3. Authors 4. Novelists 5. Authors, Nigerian 6. Nigeria 7. Essayists 8. Short story writers 9. Nigeria -- Colonization 10. African literature -- History and criticism
ISBN 978-0-3072-7255-3; 9780307473677

LC 2009017480

This is a collection of essays by the author of Things Fall Apart. In the title piece, Achebe discusses "growing up in colonial Nigeria and inhabiting its 'middle ground,' recalling both his happy memories of reading novels in secondary school and the harsher truths of colonial rule. . . . Politics and history figure in 'What Is Nigeria to Me?,' 'Africa's Tarnished Name,' and 'Politics of the Politicians of Language.' And Achebe's . . . family comes into view in 'My Dad and Me' and 'My Daughters.'" (Publisher's note)

"With African literature emerging as a world force, it's good to have Achebe back after more than 20 years, offering 17 sterling essays." (Library Journal)

Includes bibliographical references

Acheson, Dean, 1893-1971

Chace, James. **Acheson**; the Secretary of State who created the American world. Simon & Schuster 1998 512p hardcover o.p. pa $20 **92**
1. Authors 2. Nonfiction writers 3. Secretaries of state 4. United States -- Foreign relations
ISBN 978-1-416-54865-2; 1-416-54865-3

LC 98-3801

"Dean Acheson was Truman's Secretary of State from 1949 to 1953, and today's world, as Chace shows in this lucid biography, was shaped in no small degree by his efforts." New Yorker

Includes bibliographical references

Adams, Abigail, 1744-1818

Abigail Adams; letters. Edith Gelles, editor. The Library of America 2016 xxxix, 1180 p.p (ebook) $40; (alk. paper) $40 **92**
1. American letters 2. Presidents' spouses -- United States 3. United States -- History -- 1783-1815 -- Sources 4. Presidents' spouses -- United States -- Correspondence 5. United States -- History -- Revolution, 1775-1783 -- Sources
ISBN 9781598535297; 1598534653; 9781598534658

LC 2015935694

This book, by Abigail Adams and edited by Edith Gelles, presents "430 letters—more than a hundred published for the first time—to John Adams, John Quincy Adams, Thomas Jefferson, Mercy Otis Warren, James and Dolley Madison, and Martha Washington, among many others. Including her famous call to 'Remember the Ladies,' letters from the 1760s and 1770s offer an unrivalled portrait of the American Revolution on the home front." (Publisher's note)

Includes bibliographical references and index.

★ Adams, John, 1947- **My** dearest friend; letters of Abigail and John Adams. edited by Margaret A. Hogan and C. James Taylor. Belknap Press of Harvard University Press 2007 508p il map $35 **92**
1. Presidents 2. Vice-presidents 3. Parents of presidents 4. Spouses of presidents 5. Presidents -- United States 6. Presidents' spouses -- United States
ISBN 978-0-674-02606-3; 0-674-02606-3

LC 2007-4380

This collection of correspondence between John and Abigail Adams includes "selection from the entire body of the Adams' correspondence, from their courtship . . . until Abigail left the White House near the end of John's presidential term, reminding him, 'I want to see the list of judges.' . . . This is a treasure, for general readers and scholars alike." Booklist

Holton, Woody. **Abigail** Adams; a life. Free Press 2009 483p il map $30 **92**
1. Presidents 2. Vice-presidents 3. Biography, Individual 4. Parents of presidents 5. Spouses of presidents 6. Presidents' spouses -- United States 7. Women in politics -- United States -- History -- 18th century
ISBN 978-1-4165-4680-1; 1-4165-4680-4

LC 2009016288

This is a "reinterpretation of Adams's life story and of women's roles in the creation of the republic." (Publisher's note) Index.

"Holton's superb biography shows us a three-dimensional Adams as a forward-thinking woman with a mind of her own." Publ Wkly

Includes bibliographical references

Adams, Henry, 1838-1918

Adams, Henry. The **education** of Henry Adams; an autobiography. with a new introduction by Donald Hall. Houghton Mifflin 2000 517p pa $12 **92**
1. Authors 2. Novelists 3. Historians 4. Essayists
ISBN 0-618-05666-1

LC 00-26235

First published 1918

"The book omits any mention of the thirteen years of Adams's marriage and the seven years following his wife's suicide. It does, however, present a vivid picture of the people and places the author knew." Reader's Ency. 4th edition

Adams, John Quincy, 1767-1848

Cooper, William J. The **lost** founding father; John Quincy Adams and the transformation of American politics. William J. Cooper. Liveright Publishing Corporation 2017 xv, 526 p.p illustrations (hardcover) $35   **92**

  1. Founding Fathers of the United States 2. United States -- Politics and government -- 1783-1865 3. Statesmen -- United States -- Biography 4. Presidents -- United States -- Biography 5. United States -- History -- Revolution, 1775-1783 6. Founding Fathers of the United States -- Biography 7. United States. Constitution -- Signers -- Biography 8. United States -- Politics and government -- 1783-1789

  ISBN 9780871404350; 9781631493898; 0871404354

                                   LC 2017036932

This book, by William J. Cooper, profiles "John Quincy Adams (1767-1848), . . . remembered, if at all, as an ineffective president during an especially rancorous time. . . . William J. Cooper has reframed the sixth president's life in an entirely original way, demonstrating that Adams should be considered our lost Founding Father, his morality and political philosophy the final link to the great visionaries who created our nation." (Publisher's note)

"Cooper's balanced, well-sourced, and accessible work focuses on a rarely examined yet pivotal period in American history." Pub Wkly

  Includes bibliographical references and index.

Kaplan, Fred, 1937- **John** Quincy Adams; American visionary. Fred Kaplan. HarperCollins Publishers 2014 672 p. ill. (some col.), col. map $29.99   **92**

  1. Presidents -- United States 2. Presidents -- United States -- Biography

  ISBN 0061915416; 9780061915413

                                   LC 2013035334

This book, by Fred Kaplan, "brings into focus the . . . life of John Quincy Adams--the little known . . . sixth president of the United States and the first son of John and Abigail Adams. . . . Kaplan draws on a trove of unpublished archival material to trace Adams's evolution from his childhood during the Revolutionary War to his brilliant years as Secretary of State to his time in the White House and beyond." (Publisher's note)

"Kaplan sees not an inadequate man in a position he could not manage. He sees instead a "visionary," who stood for a united American republic free of the divisiveness of slavery." Booklist

  Includes bibliographical references and index

Remini, Robert Vincent. **John** Quincy Adams; [by] Robert V. Remini. Times Bks. 2002 172p (American presidents series) $20   **92**

  1. Presidents 2. Senators 3. Members of Congress 4. Secretaries of state 5. Presidents -- United States 6. United States -- Politics and government -- 1783-1865

  ISBN 0-8050-6939-9

                                   LC 2002-24210

The author's "judicious, eloquent survey of the sixth president's life and career intends not to proffer new and explosive ideas but to fashion recent scholarship into a highly readable overview for the general reader." Booklist

  Includes bibliographical references

★ Thomas, Louisa. **Louisa**; The Extraordinary Life of Mrs. Adams. by Louisa Thomas. Penguin Group USA 2016 512 p. portrait $30   **92**

  1. Presidents' spouses -- United States

  ISBN 1594204632; 9781594204630

In this biography, author Louisa Thomas, "unfolds the portrait of Louisa Catherine Adams, the wife of John Quincy Adams who witnessed firsthand the greatest transformations of her time. Born in London to an American father and a British mother . . . Louisa Catherine Johnson was raised in circumstances very different from the New England upbringing of the future president John Quincy Adams. . . . Their often tempestuous but deeply close marriage lasted half a century." (Publisher's note)

"Thomas has written an excellent account of the life of this woman, who certainly merits greater attention and praise." Booklist

Traub, James. **John** Quincy Adams; militant spirit. James Traub. Basic Books, a member of the Perseus Books Group 2016 640 p. (hardcover) $35   **92**

  1. Presidents -- United States -- Biography 2. United States -- Politics and government 3. United States -- History -- 1783-1865 4. United States -- Foreign relations -- 1783-1865 5. United States -- Politics and government -- 1783-1865

  ISBN 9780465028276

                                   LC 2015030745

In this book, by James Traub, "[John Quincy] Adams surfaces as an ambitious intellectual with deeply held convictions striving to hold his family together through illness, tragedy, and financial woes while relentlessly promoting a strong, active federal government as the young but rapidly expanding and diversifying nation grappled with geographic sectionalism and political partisanship." (Library Journal)

"An impassioned biography of 'a coherent and consistent thinker who adhered to his core political convictions across his decades of public service.'" Kirkus

  Includes bibliographical references and index

Unger, Harlow Giles. **John** Quincy Adams; Harlow Giles Unger. Da Capo Press 2012 xv, 364 p.p ill., map (hardcover: alk. paper) $27.50   **92**

  1. Statesmen -- United States -- Biography 2. Presidents -- United States -- Biography 3. United States -- Politics and government -- 1789-1815 4. United States -- Politics and government -- 1825-1829

  ISBN 030682129X; 9780306821295; 9780306821301

                                   LC 2012009399

This book, by Harlow Giles Unger, offers a biography of the U.S. president John Quincy Adams. "He fought for Washington, served with Lincoln, witnessed Bunker Hill, and sounded the clarion against slavery on the eve of the Civil War. He negotiated an end to the War of 1812, . . . and won the Supreme Court decision that freed the African captives of 'The Amistad.' He served his nation as minister to six countries, secretary of state, senator, congressman, and president." (Publisher's note)

  Includes bibliographical references (p. 339-348) and index.

Adams, John, 1735-1826

★ Adams, John, 1947- **My** dearest friend; letters of Abigail and John Adams. edited by Margaret A. Hogan and C. James Taylor. Belknap Press of Harvard University Press 2007 508p il map $35   **92**

  1. Presidents 2. Vice-presidents 3. Parents of presidents 4. Spouses of presidents 5. Presidents -- United States 6. Presidents' spouses -- United States

  ISBN 978-0-674-02606-3; 0-674-02606-3

LC 2007-4380

This collection of correspondence between John and Abigail Adams includes "selection from the entire body of the Adams' correspondence, from their courtship . . . until Abigail left the White House near the end of John's presidential term, reminding him, 'I want to see the list of judges.' . . . This is a treasure, for general readers and scholars alike." Booklist

★ Grant, James. **John** Adams; party of one. [by] James L. Grant. Farrar, Straus and Giroux 2005 530p il $30   **92**
1. Presidents 2. Vice-presidents 3. Presidents -- United States
ISBN 0-374-11314-9

LC 2004-10863

The author "is excellent at developing Adams' devotion to liberty, honed by British policies that affronted him and turned him into a revolutionary. In Grant's fine synthesis, Adams on the page is the pious, ambitious, and loving man he was in life." Booklist

Includes bibliographical references

Holton, Woody. **Abigail** Adams; a life. Free Press 2009 483p il map $30   **92**
1. Presidents 2. Vice-presidents 3. Biography, Individual 4. Parents of presidents 5. Spouses of presidents 6. Presidents' spouses -- United States 7. Women in politics -- United States -- History -- 18th century
ISBN 978-1-4165-4680-1; 1-4165-4680-4

LC 2009016288

This is a "reinterpretation of Adams's life story and of women's roles in the creation of the republic." (Publisher's note) Index.

"Holton's superb biography shows us a three-dimensional Adams as a forward-thinking woman with a mind of her own." Publ Wkly

Includes bibliographical references

McCullough, David G., 1933- **John** Adams; {by} David McCullough. Simon & Schuster 2001 751p il maps $35; pa $18.95   **92**
1. Presidents 2. Vice-presidents 3. Large print books 4. Presidents -- United States 5. United States -- Politics and government -- 1775-1783 6. United States -- Politics and government -- 1783-1809 7. United States -- Politics and government -- 1797-1801 8. United States -- Politics and government -- 1775-1783, Revolution
ISBN 0-684-81363-7; 0-7432-2313-6 pa

LC 2001-27010

This is a biography of the second president of the United States. Index.

"This is a wonderfully stirring biography; to read it is to feel as if you are witnessing the birth of a country firsthand." Booklist

Includes bibliographical references

Adams, John, 1947-

Adams, John, 1947- **Hallelujah** junction; composing an American life. Farrar, Straus and Giroux 2008 340p il $26 **92**
1. Composers
ISBN 978-0-374-28115-1; 0-374-28115-7

LC 2008-17922

An eminent composer shares the story of his life, from his childhood and early studies in classical composition to his minimalist and "docu-opera" achievements, in an account that evaluates his professional relationships and the social movements that inspired his creative process

"Readers will enjoy the candor and completeness of the book, which serves as a gateway to an accomplished body of work. Like the author's music: carefully considered, deliberate and often exciting, gathering together many disparate elements of American life." Kirkus

Adams, Louisa Catherine, 1775-1852

★ Thomas, Louisa. **Louisa**; The Extraordinary Life of Mrs. Adams. by Louisa Thomas. Penguin Group USA 2016 512 p. portrait $30   **92**
1. Presidents' spouses -- United States
ISBN 1594204632; 9781594204630

In this biography, author Louisa Thomas, "unfolds the portrait of Louisa Catherine Adams, the wife of John Quincy Adams who witnessed firsthand the greatest transformations of her time. Born in London to an American father and a British mother . . . Louisa Catherine Johnson was raised in circumstances very different from the New England upbringing of the future president John Quincy Adams. . . . Their often tempestuous but deeply close marriage lasted half a century." (Publisher's note)

"Thomas has written an excellent account of the life of this woman, who certainly merits greater attention and praise." Booklist

Addams, Jane, 1860-1935

Knight, Louise W. **Jane** Addams; spirit in action. W. W. Norton 2010 334p il $28.95   **92**
1. Authors 2. Philanthropists 3. Hull House (Chicago, Ill.) 4. Essayists 5. Pacifists 6. Social welfare leaders 7. Nobel laureates for peace 8. Chicago (Ill.) -- Social conditions
ISBN 978-0-393-07165-8

LC 2010-20648

"Knight, the author of Citizen (2006), provides the first full-length biography of Jane Addams in 35 years. She carefully traces Addams' philosophical progression as she Addams evolvedfrom a passive reformer into an active collaborator, who tirelessly worked with, not for, others to usher in a new era of democracy and social justice." (Booklist)

Includes bibliographical references

Agassi, Andre

Agassi, Andre, 1970- **Open**; an autobiography. A. Knopf 2009 385p il $28.95   **92**
1. Tennis 2. Tennis players 3. Tennis -- Biography 4. Biography, Individual
ISBN 0-307-26819-5; 978-0-307-26819-8

LC 2009-24004

This is a memoir by the eight-time Grand Slam championship winner who founded the Andre Agassi Charitable Foundation and the Andre Agassi College Preparatory Academy for underprivileged children in Las Vegas. Agassi discusses his childhood, his relationship with his father, his tennis matches, his addiction in 1997 to crystal meth and his recovery, his rivalries with other players such as Pete Sampras, his fall out of the top 100 ranked players and his return to become the oldest man ever ranked number one, and the final match of his career at the U.S. Open on September 3, 2006.

"By sharing an unvarnished, at times inspiring story in an arresting, muscular style, Agassi may have just penned one of the best sports autobiographies of all time. Check—it's one of the better memoirs out there, period. . . . Fans will devour Agassi's juicy revelations about both himself and other tennis luminaries." Time

Agassiz, Louis, 1807-1873

Irmscher, Christoph. **Louis** Agassiz; creator of American science. Christoph Irmscher. Houghton Mifflin Harcourt 2013 448 p. $35   **92**
1. Natural history -- United States -- History 2. Naturalists -- United States -- Biography 3. Natural history -- United States -- History -- 19th century
ISBN 0547577672; 9780547577678

LC 2012014225

This book, by Christoph Irmscher, is a biography of the scientist Louis Agassiz, sometimes called the "founding father of American science. . . . The irrepressible Louis Agassiz, . . . focused his prodigious energies on the fauna of the New World. Invited to deliver a series of lectures in Boston, he never left, becoming the most famous scientist of his time." (Publisher's note)

"A masterful portrait illuminating the tangled human dynamics of science." Booklist

Includes bibliographical references and index

Agg, Jen, 1975-

★ Agg, Jen. **I** hear she's a real bitch; Jen Agg. Penguin Books 2017 355 p. (paperback) $17 **92**

1. Restaurateurs 2. Women -- Canada 3. Restaurants -- Canada -- Toronto 4. Women in the hospitality industry 5. Restaurateurs -- Canada -- Biography

ISBN 0143132644; 9780143132646

LC 2017022292

This book, by Jen Agg, "tells the story of how she fought her way through the patriarchal service industry and made it happen, from getting her first job pouring drinks all the way to starting Toronto's culinary revival and running some of Canada's most famous restaurants. And she shares what she discovered through years of hard work and learning from her mistakes: how to run a great restaurant that's also a great business." (Publisher's note)

Aitkenhead, Decca

Aitkenhead, Decca. **All** at sea; A Memoir. Decca Aitkenhead. Nan A. Talese/Doubleday 2016 240 p. (hardback) $25 **92**

1. Bereavement 2. Journalists -- Biography 3. Journalists -- Great Britain -- Biography

ISBN 9780385540650

LC 2016006847

In this memoir, "on a hot, still morning on a beautiful beach in Jamaica, Decca Aitkenhead's life changed forever. Her four-year-old son was paddling peacefully at the water's edge when a wave pulled him out to sea. Her partner, Tony, swam out and saved their son's life—then drowned before her eyes." (Publisher's note)

"While her grief is nearly incapacitating, readers will appreciate the frank manner in which she shares it. Intense and surprising from start to finish." Booklist

Akana, Anna

Akana, Anna. **So** much I want to tell you; letters to my little sister. Anna Akana. Ballantine Books 2017 xviii, 176 p.p illustrations (paperback) $16 **92**

1. YouTube (Electronic resource) 2. Actors -- United States -- Biography 3. Internet personalities -- United States -- Biography

ISBN 9780399594922; 9780399594939

LC 2017009745

In this book, author Anna Akana "opens up about her own struggles with poor self-esteem and reveals both the highs and lows of coming-of-age. She offers fresh, funny, hard-won advice for young women on everything from self-care to money to sex, and she is refreshingly straightforward about the realities of dating, female friendship, and the hustle required to make your dreams come true." (Publisher's note)

"Frank advice on how to live a productive, happy life despite certain odds, written in tribute to a 'fearless, talented, and bold' sister." Kirkus

Akhmatova, Anna Andreevna, 1889-1966

★ Feinstein, Elaine. **Anna** of all the Russias; the life of

Anna Akhmatova. Knopf 2006 331p il $27.50 **92**

1. Poets 2. Authors

ISBN 1-4000-4089-2; 978-1-4000-4089-6

LC 2005-44542

First published 2005 in the United Kingdom

"In her superb and concise biography, Feinstein brings to life the complex interplay between poetic truth and the ordinary truth of experience in the poet's life and work. . . . Feinstein's poetic sensibility gives her book a distinctive quality, setting it apart from previous biographies." N Y Rev Books

Includes bibliographical references

Al Abed, Bana

★ Alabed, Bana. **Dear** world; a Syrian girl's story of war and plea for peace. Bana al Abed. Simon & Schuster 2017 205 p. $22 **92**

1. Refugees -- Syria 2. Syria -- History -- Civil War, 2011- 3. Girls -- Syria -- Biography 4. Refugee children -- Syria -- Biography 5. Syria -- Social life and customs -- 21st century

ISBN 150117844X; 9781501178443; 9781501178450

LC 2017030329

In this book, by Bana Al Abed, "Bana's happy childhood was abruptly upended by civil war when she was only three years old. Over the next four years, she knew nothing but bombing, destruction, and fear. Her harrowing ordeal culminated in a brutal siege where she, her parents, and two younger brothers were trapped in Aleppo, with little access to food, water, medicine, or other necessities." (Publisher's note)

Includes bibliographical references and index

Al Samawi, Mohammed

Al Samawi, Mohammed. The **fox** hunt; a refugee's memoir of coming to America. Mohammed Al Samawi. William Morrow, an imprint of HarperCollins Publishers 2018 viii, 324 p.p illustrations, map (hardcover) $27.99 **92**

1. Refugees 2. Refugees -- Yemen (Republic) -- Biography 3. Yemen (Republic) -- History -- Civil War, 2015- -- Personal narratives

ISBN 9780062678195; 0062678191

This memoir, by Mohammed Al Samawi, presents "a young man's moving story of war, friendship, and hope in which he recounts his harrowing escape from a brutal civil war in Yemen with the help of a daring plan engineered on social media by a small group of interfaith activists in the West." (Publisher's note)

"Gracious and generous, this personal account of a remarkable life is a reminder of how peace comes in small increments as the result of the work of committed individuals." Kirkus

Al-Maria, Sophia

Al-Maria, Sophia. The **Girl** Who Fell to Earth; A Memoir. HarperCollins 2012 288 p. (paperback) $14.99 **92**

1. Arab Americans 2. Culture conflict

ISBN 006199975X; 9780061999758

In this memoir, "when Sophia Al-Maria's mother sends her away from rainy Washington State to stay with her husband's desert-dwelling Bedouin family in Qatar, she intends it to be a sort of teenage cultural boot camp. What her mother doesn't know is that there are some things about growing up that are universal. In Qatar, Sophia is faced with a new world she'd only imagined as a child. She sets out to find her freedom, even in the most unlikely of places." (Publisher's note)

Albee, Edward, 1928-2016

Gussow, Mel. **Edward** Albee; a singular journey: a biogra-

phy. Applause 2001 448p il pa $16.95 **92**
1. Authors 2. Dramatists 3. Dramatists, American
ISBN 978-1-55783-447-8; 1-55783-447-4
First published 1999 by Simon & Schuster
"Albee regained his position as one of America's greatest playwrights with the 1994 production of 'Three Tall Women,' achieving a level of theatrical mastery and critical acclaim that he hadn't seen since 'Who's Afraid of Virginia Woolf' and 'A Delicate Balance,' almost two decades earlier. The years in between were marked by excessive drinking, outrageous behavior, inferior work, and a diminished career, but Gussow, with a light and generous touch, shows us the strengths of an artist whose core of resilience ultimately insured his survival." New Yorker
Includes bibliographical references

Albertine, Viv, 1954-

Albertine, Viv. **Clothes,** Clothes, Clothes. Music, Music, Music. Boys, Boys, Boys; A Memoir. Viv Albertine. St. Martins Press 2014 432 p. illustrations (hbk.) $27.99 **92**
1. Guitarists 2. Punk rock music 3. Women rock musicians 4. Slits (Musical group) 5. Punk rock musicians -- Great Britain -- Biography
ISBN 1250065992; 9781250065995
LC 2014029971
In this memoir, punk rock musician Viv Albertine presents a "look at a traditionally male-dominated scene. . . . The author recalls rebelling from conformity and patriarchal society ever since her days as an adolescent girl in the same London suburb of Muswell Hill where the Kinks formed. With brash honesty . . . Albertine writes of immersing herself into punk culture among the likes of the Sex Pistols." (Publisher's note)
"This pioneer and pivotal punk rocker discusses her relationships/friendships with fellow musicians Joe Strummer, Johnny Rotten, Sid Vicious, and Johnny Thunders in this fascinating insider's look at the punk scene from a female perspective." Booklist

Albright, Madeleine Korbel

Albright, Madeleine Korbel, 1937- **Prague** winter; a personal story of remembrance and war, 1937-1948. Madeleine Albright with Bill Woodward. HarperCollins 2012 x, 467 p.p $29.99 **92**
1. Czechoslovakia -- History -- 1918-1968 2. World War, 1939-1945 -- Personal narratives 3. Prague (Czech Republic) -- Biography 4. Czechoslovakia -- History -- 1938-1945 5. World War, 1939-1945 -- Czechoslovakia 6. World War, 1939-1945 -- Czech Republic -- Prague 7. Prague (Czech Republic) -- History -- 20th century 8. Jewish families -- Czech Republic -- Prague -- Biography
ISBN 0062030310; 9780062030313
LC 2011049416
This book by Madeleine Albright chronicles her personal "experiences, and those of her family . . . [during] the years of 1937 to 1948. . . . The book takes readers from the Bohemian capital . . . to the bomb shelters of London, from the desolate prison ghetto of Terezin to the highest councils of European and American government. Albright reflects on her discovery of her family's Jewish heritage many decades after the war, [and] on her Czech homeland's tangled history." (Publisher's note)
Includes bibliographical references and index.

Alcott, Amos Bronson, 1799-1888

Matteson, John. **Eden's** outcasts; the story of Louisa May Alcott and her father. W.W. Norton 2007 497p il $29.95 **92**
1. Authors 2. Educators 3. Novelists 4. Philosophers 5. Authors, American 6. Nonfiction writers 7. Young adult authors

ISBN 978-0-393-05964-9
LC 2007-13707
"Matteson's lucid, commanding biography casts new light on an unusual father-daughter bond and a new land at war with itself." Booklist
Includes bibliographical references

Alcott, Louisa May, 1832-1888

Matteson, John. **Eden's** outcasts; the story of Louisa May Alcott and her father. W.W. Norton 2007 497p il $29.95 **92**
1. Authors 2. Educators 3. Novelists 4. Philosophers 5. Authors, American 6. Nonfiction writers 7. Young adult authors
ISBN 978-0-393-05964-9
LC 2007-13707
"Matteson's lucid, commanding biography casts new light on an unusual father-daughter bond and a new land at war with itself." Booklist
Includes bibliographical references

Reisen, Harriet. **Louisa** May Alcott; the woman behind Little women. Henry Holt 2009 362p $26 **92**
1. Authors 2. Novelists 3. Authors, American 4. Young adult authors
ISBN 978-0-8050-8299-9; 0-8050-8299-9
LC 2009-10637
In this biography of the American author, "Reisen analyzes Louisa's great pleasure in writing lucrative pulp fiction, her sacrifices, adventures, and brilliant career. Here . . . is Alcott whole, a trailblazing woman grasping freedom in a time of sexual inequality and war, a survivor of cruel tragedies, a quintessential American writer." Booklist
Includes bibliographical references

Alden, Ginger

Alden, Ginger. **Elvis** and Ginger; Ginger Alden. Ace Books 2014 400 p. illustrations (chiefly color) (hardcover) $26.95 92
1. Actresses -- United States -- Biography 2. Rock musicians -- United States -- Biography
ISBN 0425266338; 9780425266335
LC 2014009089
In this memoir Ginger Alden discusses her " whirlwind romance [with Elvis Presley] from first kiss to his stunning proposal of marriage. She details his exploration of Eastern religions, his perception of being a 'legend,' his devotion to family and friends, and her attempt to know the insular group surrounding Elvis. And for the very first time she talks about the devastating end of it all, and the 50,000 mourners and reporters who descended on Graceland in 1977." (Publisher's note)
"It's an outpouring of affection for a man who has stayed in the author's mind all these years, a way for her to show the world the Elvis she knew. The book has a pretty much guaranteed readership, as many Elvis fans will read anything and everything that appears in print about their idol." Booklist

Aldridge, John

Aldridge, John. A **speck** in the sea; a story of survival and rescue. John Aldridge and Anthony Sosinski. Weinstein Books 2017 x, 262 p.p illustrations (chiefly color) (hardcover) $27 **92**
1. Fishing 2. Survival after airplane accidents, shipwrecks, etc. 3. Anna Mary (Ship) 4. Survival at sea -- New York (State) -- Montauk 5. Search and rescue operations -- New York (State) -- Montauk
ISBN 1602863288; 9781602863286; 9781602865310
This book, by John Aldridge and Anthony Sosinksi, tells the search and rescue effort to save Aldridge who "was thrown off the back of the Anna Mary while his fishing partner, . . . Sosinski, slept below. As desperate hours ticked by, Sosinski, the families, the local fishing community, and the U.S. Coast Guard in three states mobilized in an unprec-

edented search effort that culminated in a rare and exhilarating success."
(Publisher's note)

"Told from multiple viewpoints, the book takes readers into the water with Aldridge as he shares first-person accounts of shark encounters and the mind games he played while clinging to his rubber boots to stay afloat." Pub Wkly Annex

Includes bibliographical references and index.

Aldrin, Buzz

Aldrin, Buzz, 1930- **No** dream is too high; life lessons from a man who walked on the Moon. Buzz Aldrin with Ken Abraham. National Geographic 2016 224 p. illustrations (chiefly color) (hardback) $22   **92**

1. Astronauts 2. Scientists 3. Conduct of life 4. Space flight to the moon 5. Conduct of life -- Philosophy 6. Astronauts -- United States -- Biography
ISBN 9781426216497

LC 2015037069

In this book, astronaut Buzz Aldrin "reflects on the wisdom, guiding principles, and irreverent anecdotes he's gathered through his event-filled life—both in outer space and on earth—in this inspiring guide-to-life for the next generation. Everywhere he goes, crowds gather to meet Buzz Aldrin. . . . Best known for a generation of astronauts whose achievements surged in just a few years from the first man in space to first men on the moon." (Publisher's note)

"Aldrin's journey will engage space exploration enthusiasts, and his motivational advice will connect especially well with young adults." LJ

Alexander, Elizabeth, 1962-

Alexander, Elizabeth, 1962- The **light** of the world; a memoir. Elizabeth Alexander. Grand Central Publishing 2015 224 p. (hardback) $26   **92**

1. Marriage 2. Bereavement 3. Loss (Psychology) 4. Women poets, American -- Biography
ISBN 9781455599875

LC 2014020884

NAACP Image Award Nominee: Outstanding Literary Work- Nonfiction (2016)

National Book Critics Circle Award Finalist: Autobiography (2015)
Pulitzer Prize Finalist: Biography (2016).

In this memoir, by Elizabeth Alexander, named Best Book of 2015 by several venues including the "New York Times," "NPR," and "Library Journal," the author "finds herself at an existential crossroads after the sudden death of her husband. . . . She reflects on the beauty of her married life, the trauma resulting from her husband's death, and the solace found in caring for her two teenage sons." (Publisher's note)

"Fashioning her mellifluous narrative around the beauty she found in Ghebreyesus, Alexander is grateful, patient, and willing to pursue a fit of magical thinking that he might just return." Pub Wkly

Alexandra, Empress, consort of Nicholas II, Emperor of Russia, 1872-1918

Massie, Robert K., 1929- **Nicholas** and Alexandra. Ballantine Books 2000 613p il map pa $18.95   **92**

1. Monks 2. Emperors 3. Empresses 4. Courtiers 5. Russia -- History 6. Russia -- Kings and rulers
ISBN 0-345-43831-0; 978-0-345-43831-7

LC 99-91507

First published 1967 by Atheneum

This study provides an intimate account of the Romanov family and the coming of the Russian Revolution. Kerensky, Lenin and Rasputin are among the personalities profiled.

This book, "solid with research, reads as lightly as a novel, as authoritatively as a textbook. Dialogue and lively description lend a sense of immediacy, but his notes, discreetly relegated to the back of the book, show how carefully he has avoided slipping into fiction." Christ Sci Monit

Includes bibliographical references

Alexie, Sherman, 1966-

Alexie, Sherman, 1966- **You** don't have to say you love me; a memoir. Sherman Alexie. Little, Brown & Co. 2017 432 p. hardcover $28; paperback $16.99   **92**

1. Mother-son relationship 2. American authors -- Biography 3. Native Americans -- Biography
ISBN 9780316395649; 9780316270755; 9780316270748

LC 2016958327

In this memoir, Sherman Alexie "remembers his complicated mother, Lillian, [who] had a contentious relationship with her son featuring bitter fights and years-long silent treatments. [It describes a] close-knit but floridly dysfunctional family and a reservation community rife with joblessness, alcoholism and drug abuse, fatal car crashes, violence, rape and child molestation, murder, and a general sense of being excluded from and besieged by white society." (Publishers Weekly)

"Presented as a series of vignettes, some in prose, others in poetry, about Alexie's life and family, the narrative transitions between styles, which feels natural as Alexie searches for the best way to present complex memories and stories." LJ

Ali, Muhammad, 1942-2016

Montville, Leigh. **Sting** like a bee; Muhammad Ali vs. the United States of America, 1966-1971. Leigh Montville. Doubleday 2017 354 p. illustrations (hardcover) $30   **92**

1. African American athletes 2. Boxers (Sports) -- United States -- Biography 3. African American Muslims -- Biography 4. African American boxers -- United States -- Biography 5. Vietnam War, 1961-1975 -- Conscientious objectors -- United States
ISBN 9780385536059; 9780385536066

LC 2016056528

In this biography, by Leigh Montville, "[Muhammad Ali] was a bold young African American. . . . He renounced his name--Cassius Clay--as being his 'slave name,' and joined the Nation of Islam. . . . [I]n 1966, after being drafted, he refused to join the military for religious and conscientious reasons. . . . What followed was a period of legal battles, of cultural obsession, and in some ways of being the very embodiment of the civil rights movement." (Publisher's note)

"A dramatic, pleasing tale of a sports iconoclast fighting for his rights during tumultuous times." Kirkus

Includes bibliographical references (pages 336-339) and index.

Remnick, David. **King** of the world: Muhammad Ali and the rise of an American hero. Random House 1998 326p il hardcover o.p. pa $14   **92**

1. African American athletes 2. Boxers (Persons)
ISBN 0-375-50065-0; 0-375-70229-6 pa

LC 98-24539

"This is the best book ever on Muhammad Ali and one of the best on America in the 1960s." Booklist

Includes bibliographical references

Shanahan, Tim. **Runnng** with the champ; my heavyweight friendship with Muhammad Ali. by Tim Shanahan with Chuck Crisafulli. Simon & Schuster 2016 320 p. (hardcover) $27 **92**

1. Friendship 2. Boxers (Sports) 3. Boxers (Sports) -- United

States -- Biography
ISBN 1501102303; 9781501102301

LC 2015034685

This book, by Tim Shanahan, is a "personal tribute to the remarkable friendship between [himself] and Muhammad Ali, including dozens of never-before-told stories about Ali, his family, his entourage, and various celebrities along the way—as well as never-before-published personal photos." (Publisher's note)

"Ali is the heart of the book, and Shanahan presents a complex but less bombastic person than is popularly associated with the name; generous to a fault, devoted to his religion and (despite four marriages) family, and a champion of the less fortunate." LJ

★ Smith, Johnny. **Blood** brothers; the fatal friendship of Muhammad Ali and Malcolm X. Randy Roberts and Johnny Smith. Basic Books 2016 392 p. illustrations (hardcover: alk. paper) $28.99　　**92**
1. African Americans -- Biography 2. Black Muslims -- Biography
ISBN 9780465079704

LC 2015043982

In this book, historians Randy Roberts and Johnny Smith "reveal how Malcolm [X] molded Cassius Clay into Muhammad Ali, helping him become an international symbol of black pride and black independence. . . . Malcolm's death marked the end of a critical phase of the civil rights movement, but the legacy of his friendship with Ali has endured. We inhabit a new era where the roles of entertainer and activist, of sports and politics, are more entwined than ever before." (Publisher's note)

"A page-turning tale from the 1960s about politics and sports and two proud, extraordinary men whose legacies endure." Kirkus

Includes bibliographical references and index

Ali, Nujood

Ali, Nujood. **I** am Nujood, age 10 and divorced; [by] Nujood Ali, with Delphine Minoui; translated by Linda Coverdale. Three Rivers Press 2010 188p pa $12　　**92**
1. Children 2. Child marriage 3. Yemen 4. Abused persons
ISBN 978-0-307-58967-5; 0-307-58967-6

LC 2009-33063

"One of 16 children living in squalor in Yemen, Nujood was married off at about age 10. Though her husband vowed he'd wait for sex until she reached puberty, he rapes her on their first night together. After months of abuse, Nujood goes to the courthouse, where with heartbreaking naiveté, she tells a judge she wants a divorce. Supported by the legal system, Nujood gets her wish." People

Includes bibliographical references

Ali, Taha Muhammad

★ Hoffman, Adina. **My** happiness bears no relation to happiness; a poet's life in the Palestinian century. Yale University Press 2009 454p il map $27.50　　**92**
1. Poets 2. Authors
ISBN 978-0-300-14150-4

LC 2008-37298

"An exceptional introduction to a literary world that has, until now, been little known to English-language readers, this is highly recommended for all libraries." Libr J

Includes bibliographical references

Alinizhad, Masih, 1976-

Alinejad, Masih. The **wind** in my hair; my fight for freedom in modern Iran. Masih Alinejad. Little, Brown & co. 2018 400 p.　　**92**

ISBN 9780316548915

LC 2017959142

"Alinejad's journey both within and outside of Iran depicts her resilience and determination to lead a full life amid an often repressive society. For all readers interested in women's memoirs and women's rights." LJ

Alkhanshali, Mokhtar

★ Eggers, Dave, 1970- The **monk** of Mokha; by Dave Eggers. Alfred A. Knopf 2018 xiii, 327 p.p map (hardcover) $28.95　　**92**
1. Yemeni Americans 2. Coffee industry -- Yemen 3. Coffee industry -- Yemen (Republic) 4. Coffee industry -- California -- San Francisco 5. Businesspeople -- California -- San Francisco -- Biography 6. Yemeni Americans -- California -- San Francisco -- Biography
ISBN 9781101947326; 9781101947319; 9781101971444

LC 2017032893

In this book, by Dave Eggers, "Mokhtar Alkhanshali is twenty-four and working as a doorman when he discovers the astonishing history of coffee and Yemen's central place in it. He leaves San Francisco and travels deep into his ancestral homeland to tour terraced farms high in the country's rugged mountains and meet beleaguered but determined farmers. But when war engulfs the country and Saudi bombs rain down, Mokhtar has to find a way out of Yemen." (Publisher's note)

"Eggers's book works as both a heartwarming success story with a winning central character and an account of real-life adventures that read with the vividness of fiction." Pub Wkly

Allen, Ray

Arkush, Michael. **From** the outside; my journey through life and the game I love. Ray Allen with Michael Arkush. HarperCollins 2018 288 p. $27.99　　**92**
1. Basketball players -- United States -- Biography
ISBN 0062675478; 9780062675477

In this memoir, National Basketball Association's player Ray Allen with Michael Arkush "reflects on his work ethic, his on-the-court friendships and rivalries, the great teams he's played for, and what it takes to have a long and successful career. . . . Allen talks openly about his fellow players, coaches, owners, and friends. . . . He reveals how, as a kid growing up in a military family, he learned about responsibility and respect." (Publisher's note)

Allen, Richard, 1760-1831

Newman, Richard S. **Freedom's** prophet; Bishop Richard Allen, the AME Church, and the Black founding fathers. New York University Press 2008 359p il $34.95　　**92**
1. Slaves 2. Bishops 3. African Methodist Episcopal Church
ISBN 978-0-8147-5826-7; 0-8147-5826-6

LC 2007-43259

"Newman's beautifully written study is not only a first-rate social history of the early Republic and African-American culture and religion, it provides a detailed sketch of Allen that is sure to become the definitive biography of the leader." Publ Wkly

Includes bibliographical references

Allen, Sandra (Nonfiction writer)

Allen, Sandra. A **kind** of mirraculas paradise; a true story about schizophrenia. Sandra Allen. Scribner 2018 288 p. (hardcover) $26　　**92**
1. Schizophrenia 2. Mentally ill -- Biography 3. Schizophrenia -- Patients -- Biography

ISBN 9781501134036

LC 2017034690

In this book, author "[Sandra] Allen translates her uncle's autobiography, artfully creating a gripping coming-of-age story while sticking faithfully to the facts as he shared them. Lacing [her uncle] Bob's narrative with chapters providing greater contextualization, Allen also shares background information about her family, . . . and the vitally important questions surrounding schizophrenia and mental healthcare in America more broadly." (Publisher's note)

"A page-turning biography and family history along the lines of Bryan Mealer's The Kings of Big Spring. Don't be put off by the subject—although Allen includes bits of medical history, this is a deeply personal story about an enigmatic person living the only way he knows how: by trial and error. In that, many can relate." (LJ)

Allen, Tina Alexis

Allen, Tina Alexis. **Hiding** out; a memoir of drugs, deception, and double lives. by Tina Alexis Allen. Dey St. 2018 x, 278 p.p (hardcover) $26.99   **92**

1. Actresses -- Biography 2. Lesbians -- United States -- Biography 3. Gay fathers -- United States -- Biography 4. Catholic gays -- United States -- Biography 5. Fathers and daughters -- United States -- Biography 6. Children of gay parents -- United States -- Biography
ISBN 9780062565709; 9780062565679; 0062565672

"Actress and playwright Tina Alexis Allen's audacious memoir unravels her privileged suburban Catholic upbringing that was shaped by her formidable father--a man whose strict religious devotion and dedication to his large family hid his true nature and a life defined by deep secrets and dangerous lies." (Publisher's note)

"A writer candidly confronts her personal truth in her quest for transformation, transcendence, and redemption." Kirkus

Allende family

★ Allende, Isabel. **Paula**; translated from the Spanish by Margaret Sayers Peden. HarperPerennial 2008 330, 23p pa $14.99   **92**

1. Authors 2. Novelists 3. Dramatists 4. Journalists 5. Authors, Chilean 6. Children's authors
ISBN 978-0-06-156490-1
First published 1995

Allende "interweaves the story of her own life with the slow dying of her 28-year-old daughter, Paula." Publ Wkly

Allende, Isabel

★ Allende, Isabel. **Paula**; translated from the Spanish by Margaret Sayers Peden. HarperPerennial 2008 330, 23p pa $14.99   **92**

1. Authors 2. Novelists 3. Dramatists 4. Journalists 5. Authors, Chilean 6. Children's authors
ISBN 978-0-06-156490-1
First published 1995

Allende "interweaves the story of her own life with the slow dying of her 28-year-old daughter, Paula." Publ Wkly

Allende, Isabel. The **sum** of our days; translated from the Spanish by Margaret Sayers Peden. HarperCollins 2008 320p $26.95   **92**

1. Authors 2. Novelists 3. Dramatists 4. Journalists 5. Authors, Chilean 6. Children's authors
ISBN 978-0-06-155183-3; 0-06-155183-X

LC 2007-33251

"In this sequel to her memoir Paula (1995), about the yearlong coma suffered by her daughter, Chilean novelist Allende tells of the difficult years following Paula's death. . . . Surprisingly candid, frequently funny, and highly aware of her own failings, Allende is a person fully engaged in life, and readers will find her eloquent memoir inspirational reading." Booklist

Allilueva, Svetlana, 1926-2011

★ Sullivan, Rosemary. **Stalin's** daughter; the extraordinary and tumultuous life of Svetlana Alliluyeva. Rosemary Sullivan. Harper 2015 752 p. illustrations (hardback) $35   **92**

1. Defectors -- United States -- Biography 2. Immigrants -- United States -- Biography 3. Soviet Union -- History -- 1925-1953 -- Biography 4. Children of heads of state -- Soviet Union -- Biography
ISBN 0062206109; 9780062206107; 9780062206121

LC 2014045982

National Book Critics Circle Award Finalist: Biography (2015)

This book, by Rosemary Sullivan, offers a "biography of Svetlana Stalin, a woman fated to live her life in the shadow of one of history's most monstrous dictators--her father, Josef Stalin. . . . Svetlana Stalin spent her youth inside the walls of the Kremlin . . . , but she did not escape tragedy. . . . As she gradually learned about the extent of her father's brutality after his death, Svetlana . . . in 1967 shocked the world by defecting to the United States." (Publisher's note)

"Svetlana's letters and family photographs enhance the portrait of a woman tortured by the secrets, lies, and intrigues at the center of her early life as a Kremlin princess and in later years as the object of fascination and scorn as the daughter of the feared Russian dictator." Booklist

Includes biblliographical references

Altman, Robert, 1925-2006

Zuckoff, Mitchell. **Robert** Altman; the oral biography. Alfred A. Knopf 2009 560p il   **92**

1. Motion picture producers and directors 2. Television directors 3. Biography, Individual 4. Motion picture directors 5. Motion picture producers
ISBN 0-307-26768-7; 978-0-307-26768-9

LC 2009-19847

This is a biography of the director of such films as MASH (1970), Nashville (1975), The Player (1992), and Gosford Park (2001). Filmography. Index.

This "is a smart, amusing, lively book, full of anecdotes and a generous step toward perceiving the glorious and perverse ways of Altman himself." New Repub

Includes filmography

Ames, Robert, 1934-1983

Bird, Kai, 1951- The **Good** Spy; The Life and Death of Robert Ames. by Kai Bird. Random House Inc 2014 448 p. illustrations $26   **92**

1. Intelligence service -- United States 2. United States. Central Intelligence Agency
ISBN 0307889750; 9780307889751

LC 2013049480

This book, by Kai Bird, is a biography "of CIA agent Robert Ames, one of America's most important assets in the [Middle East] until his life was cut short by the bomb that exploded outside the American Embassy in Beirut in April 1983." (Library Journal)

"A low-key, respectful life of a decent American officer whose quietly significant work helped lead to the Oslo Accords." Kirkus

Includes bibliographical references (pages 403-410) and index

Amis, Kingsley, 1922-1995

Amis, Martin. **Experience**. Hyperion 2000 406p il $23.95; pa $14   **92**
1. Poets 2. Authors 3. Humorists 4. Novelists 5. Essayists 6. Literary critics 7. Short story writers
ISBN 0-7868-6652-7; 0-375-72683-7 pa

LC 00-699777

This is a "portmanteau of personal history, ancestor worship and promiscuous opinionizing, and a piñata of literary gossip that Amis beats with a stick, causing many names to drop. . . . And if we stay put till the last 100 pages, it will break our heart." N Y Times Book Rev

Leader, Zachary. The **life** of Kingsley Amis. Pantheon Books 2007 996p $39.95   **92**
1. Poets 2. Authors 3. Humorists 4. Novelists 5. Essayists 6. Literary critics 7. Short story writers
ISBN 978-0-375-42498-4; 0-375-42498-9

LC 2006-35012

First published 2006 in the United Kingdom
The "great virtue of Leader's biography of Amis is that you do not have to share his high opinion of the subject to benefit from the book's prodigious research and wealth of information so well presented." San Francisco Chronicle
Includes bibliographical references

Amis, Martin

Amis, Martin. **Experience**. Hyperion 2000 406p il $23.95; pa $14   **92**
1. Poets 2. Authors 3. Humorists 4. Novelists 5. Essayists 6. Literary critics 7. Short story writers
ISBN 0-7868-6652-7; 0-375-72683-7 pa

LC 00-699777

This is a "portmanteau of personal history, ancestor worship and promiscuous opinionizing, and a piñata of literary gossip that Amis beats with a stick, causing many names to drop. . . . And if we stay put till the last 100 pages, it will break our heart." N Y Times Book Rev

Amundsen, Roald, 1872-1928

Bown, Stephen R. The **last** Viking; the life of Roald Amundsen. Stephen R. Bown. Da Capo Press 2012 xxii, 357 p.p ill., maps (hardcover: alk. paper) $27.50   **92**
1. Explorers -- Norway -- Biography 2. North Pole -- Discovery and exploration -- Norweigian 3. Arctic regions -- Discovery and exploration -- Norweigian
ISBN 0306820676; 9780306820670; 9780306821622

LC 2012012126

This book by Stephen R. Bown is a biography of Roald Amundsen, "a legend of the heroic age of exploration. . . . In 1900, the four great geographical mysteries--the Northwest Passage, the Northeast Passage, the South Pole, and the North Pole--remained blank spots on the globe. Within twenty years Roald Amundsen would claim all four prizes. . . . Féted in his lifetime as an international celebrity, pursued by women and creditors, he died in the Arctic on a rescue mission." (Publisher's note)
Includes bibliographical references and index

Andalibian, Rahimeh

Andalibian, Rahimeh. The **rose** hotel; a memoir of secrets, loss, and love from Iran to America. Rahimeh Andalibian. National Geographic 2015 336 p. (hardback) $26   **92**
1. Iranian Americans 2. Iran -- History -- 1941-1979 3. Iranian American women -- Biography 4. Political refugees -- Iran -- Biography 5. Political refugees -- United States -- Biography 6. Iran -- History -- Revolution, 1979 -- Personal narratives
ISBN 1426214790; 9781426214790

LC 2014037952

"In this . . . memoir, Iranian-born author Rahimeh Andalibian tells the story of her family: how they survived the 1979 revolution; their move to California; and their attempts to adapt in the face of addiction, teenage rebellion, and new traditions. Andalibian struggles to make sense of two brutal crimes: a rape, avenged by her father, and a murder, of which her beloved oldest brother stands accused." (Publisher's note)
"A powerful and uplifting memoir of tragedy and healing." Kirkus

Andersen, Hans Christian, 1805-1875

Andersen, Jens. **Hans** Christian Andersen: a new life; translated from the Danish by Tiina Nunnally. Overlook Press 2005 624p il hardcover o.p. pa $22.95   **92**
1. Authors 2. Novelists 3. Dramatists 4. Authors, Danish 5. Children's authors 6. Short story writers
ISBN 1-58567-642-X; 1-58567-737-X pa

LC 2004-65985

The author examines Andersen's "considerable gifts as an oral storyteller; his eccentric, often annoying public habits; his ambivalent sexuality; his bouts of narcissism; his painfully slow transformation from rough-hewn provincial and awkward melodramatist into brilliant, internationally famous writer-celebrity. The biography is best and most moving when it is frank about formerly suppressed aspects of Andersen's life." Booklist
Includes bibliographical references

Wullschlager, Jackie. **Hans** Christian Andersen; the life of a story teller. University of Chicago Press 2002 489p il map pa $19   **92**
1. Authors 2. Novelists 3. Dramatists 4. Authors, Danish 5. Children's authors 6. Short story writers
ISBN 0-226-91747-9; 978-0-226-91747-4

LC 2002-18010

First published 2000 in the United Kingdom
"Wullschlager succeeds brilliantly at portraying Andersens inner mind and uncovering his hopes and fears and details the historical context that served to produce such a grand body of literature. . . . [This biography] will be a standard study for years to come." Libr J
Includes bibliographical references

Anderson, Alice, 1966-

Anderson, Alice. **Some** bright morning, I'll fly away; a memoir. Alice Anderson. St. Martin's Press 2017 279 p. (hardcover) $25.99   **92**
1. Wife abuse 2. Domestic violence 3. Abused wives -- United States -- Biography 4. Poets, American -- 20th century -- Biography 5. Poets, American -- 20th century -- Family relationships
ISBN 9781250111852; 9781250094964; 1250094968

LC 2017297026

In this memoir, author Alice Anderson narrates how, after Hurricane Katrina, she returned home to assess the damage to her beloved Mississippi coastline and the home she'd "carefully cultivated for her husband, Dr. Liam Rivers. . . . But in the wake of this natural disaster, a more terrifying challenge emerges as Liam's mental health spirals out of control, culminating in a violent attack at knifepoint, from which Alice is saved by their three-year-old son." (Publisher's note)
"Anderson is a gifted writer who vividly describes both settings and emotions. Her powerful story gives voice and hope to women caught in similarly terrible conditions." Booklist

Anderson, Marian, 1897-1993

Keiler, Allan. **Marian** Anderson; a singer's journey. University of Illinois Press 2002 447p hardcover o.p. pa $21.95 **92**

1. African American singers 2. Opera singers 3. African American women -- Biography

ISBN 0-684-80711-4; 0-252-07067-4 pa

LC 99-43319

First published 2000 by Scribner

The author's "clear, succinct prose, initially lacking narrative coherence, gains strength and momentum as his subject matures from a young and struggling artist into one of the enduring voices of our century." Publ Wkly

Includes discography and bibliographical references

Anderson, Terry A., 1949-

Anderson, Sulome. The **Hostage's** Daughter; A Story of Family, Madness, and the Middle East. by Sulome Anderson. HarperCollins 2016 288 p. $25.99 **92**

1. Hostages 2. Lebanese 3. Father-daughter relationship 4. Middle East -- Social conditions

ISBN 0062385496; 9780062385499

In this book, Sulome Anderson, "a journalist and daughter of one of the world's most famous hostages, Terry Anderson, takes an intimate look at her father's captivity during the Lebanese Hostage Crisis and the ensuing political firestorm on both her family and the United States—as well as the far-reaching implications of those events on Middle Eastern politics today." (Publisher's note)

"Through these dual narratives, Anderson creates a compelling depiction of the collateral damage of terrorism and a remarkable piece of investigative journalism with a surprise twist." Pub Wkly

Anderson, Tim, 1972-

Anderson, Tim. **Sweet** Tooth; a memoir. Tim Anderson. Lake Union Pr 2014 334 p. $14.95 **92**

1. Gay teenagers 2. Autobiographies

ISBN 1477818073; 9781477818077

LC 2013919514

"'Sweet Tooth' is Tim Anderson's . . . memoir of life after his hormones and blood sugar both went berserk at the age of fifteen. With Morrissey and The Smiths as the soundtrack, Anderson self-deprecatingly recalls love affairs with vests and donuts, first crushes, coming out, and inaugural trips to gay bars. What emerges is the story of a young man trying to build a future that won't involve crippling loneliness or losing a foot to his disease." (Publisher's note)

"Staying true to his experiences, Anderson evokes the juvenile tendency toward self-destruction in a way that is simultaneously funny and frustrating. The combination gives readers a visceral taste of the rollercoaster ride that was his young adulthood." Pub Wkly

Andrews, Julie

Andrews, Julie. **Home**; a memoir of my early years. Hyperion 2008 339p il $26.95 **92**

1. Actors 2. Singers 3. Children's authors

ISBN 978-0-7868-6565-9; 0-7868-6565-2

LC 2007-48830

"Spanning events from her 1935 birth to the early 1960s, . . . [the author] covers her rise to fame and ends with Walt Disney casting her in Mary Poppins (1963). . . . The heart of her book documents the rehearsals, tryouts and smash 1956 opening of My Fair Lady. Readers will rejoice, since Andrews is an accomplished writer who holds back nothing while adding a patina of poetry to the antics and anecdotes throughout this memoir of bittersweet backstage encounters and theatri-

cal triumphs." Publ Wkly

Angell, Roger

Angell, Roger, 1920- **This** old man; all in pieces. Roger Angell. Doubleday 2015 320 p. illustrations (hardback) $26.95 **92**

1. Criticism 2. Popular culture

ISBN 0385541139; 9780385541138

LC 2015018255

This book, by Roger Angell, offers "a selection of writings that celebrate a view from the tenth decade of an engaged, vibrant life. . . . Angell won the 2015 American Society of Magazine Editors' Best Essay award for 'This Old Man,' which forms a centerpiece for this book. . . . The book gathers essays, letters, light verse, book reviews, Talk of the Town stories, farewells, haikus, Profiles, Christmas greetings, late thoughts on the costs of war." (Publisher's note)

"While essays such as the titular 'This Old Man' and 'Over the Wall' grab and hold tighter than others, fans of The New Yorker (and of baseball, one of Angell's most beloved subjects), will take pleasure in digging into this rich collection culled from an extraordinary career." Library Journal

Angelou, Maya

★ Angelou, Maya. **I** know why the caged bird sings. Random House 2002 281p $21.95 **92**

1. Poets 2. Actors 3. Singers 4. Dramatists 5. Women authors 6. African American authors 7. Essayists 8. Memoirists 9. Children's authors

ISBN 0-375-50789-2

LC 2001-41914

First published 1969

The first volume in the author's autobiographical series covers her childhood and adolescence in rural Arkansas, St. Louis, and San Francisco.

"Angelou is a skillful writer; her language ranges from beautifully lyrical prose to earthy metaphor, and her descriptions have power and sensitivity." Libr J

Followed by Gather together in my name (1974); Singin' and swingin' and gettin' merry like Christmas (1976); The heart of a woman (1981); All God's children need traveling shoes (1986); A song flung up to heaven (2002)

Angelou, Maya, 1928-2014. **Letter** to my daughter. Random House 2008 166p $25 **92**

1. Poets 2. Actors 3. Singers 4. Dramatists 5. Women authors 6. African American authors 7. Essayists 8. Memoirists 9. Children's authors

ISBN 978-1-4000-6612-4

LC 2008-28843

"A slim volume packed with nourishing nuggets of wisdom." Kirkus

Gillespie, Marcia Ann. **Maya** Angelou; a glorious celebration. [by] Marcia Ann Gillespie, Rosa Johnson Butler and Richard A. Long; foreword by Oprah Winfrey. Doubleday 2008 191p il $30 **92**

1. Poets 2. Actors 3. Singers 4. Dramatists 5. Women authors 6. African American authors 7. Essayists 8. Memoirists 9. Children's authors

ISBN 978-0-385-51108-7

LC 2007-31301

This look at Maya Angelou's life as well as her myriad interests and accomplishments by the people who know her best (longtime friends

Marcia Ann Gillespie and Richard Long and niece Rosa Johnson Butler) features over 150 sepia portraits, family photographs, and letters. Includes a bibliography of her works.

"A loving tribute to one of the most renowned authors today, this work is highly recommended." Libr J

Ankiel, Rick

Ankiel, Rick. The **phenomenon**; pressure, the yips, and the pitch that changed my life. Rick Ankiel and Tim Brown. PublicAffairs 2017 292 p. (hardcover) $27   **92**
   1. Baseball pitchers 2. Baseball players -- Biography 3. Performance anxiety 4. Baseball players -- United States -- Biography 5. Pitchers (Baseball) -- United States -- Biography
   ISBN 9781610396868; 9781610399302

       LC 2016050707

In this memoir, baseball player Rick Ankiel, with Tim Brown, shares "how . . . .[he] lost his . . . ability to pitch . . . due to . . . a mysterious anxiety condition widely known as the Yips. . . . For four and a half years, he fought the Yips with . . .: psychotherapy, medication, deep-breathing exercises, self-help books, and, eventually, vodka. And then, . . . [he] made an amazing turnaround: returning to the Major Leagues as a hitter." (Publisher's note)

"A solid sports memoir that explores more than just sports." Kirkus

Anne Boleyn, Queen, consort of Henry VIII, King of England, 1507-1536

Weir, Alison. The **lady** in the tower; the fall of Anne Boleyn. Ballantine Books 2009 434p il $28   **92**
   1. Queens 2. Great Britain -- History -- 1485-1603, Tudors
   ISBN 978-0-345-45321-1; 0-345-45321-2

       LC 2009-42748

Historian Weir is "well equipped to parse the evidence, ferret out the misconceptions and arrive at sturdy hypotheses about what actually befell Anne. Her command of minutiae is impressive, as is her enthusiasm for even the most minor aspects of Anne's frequently distorted story." N Y Times Book Rev

   Includes bibliographical references

Anne, Queen of Great Britain, 1665-1714

Somerset, Anne. **Queen** Anne; the politics of passion. Anne Somerset. Alfred A. Knopf 2013 621 p. illustrations, portraits $35   **92**
   1. Queens -- Great Britain 2. Great Britain -- Kings and rulers 3. Queens -- Great Britain -- Biography 4. Great Britain -- History -- Anne, 1702-1714
   ISBN 0307962881; 9780307962881

       LC 2012035334

This book, by Anne Somerset, is a biography of British Queen Anne. "She ascended the thrones of England, Scotland and Ireland in 1702, at age thirty-seven, . . . and five years later united two of her realms, England and Scotland, as a sovereign state, creating the Kingdom of Great Britain. She had a history of personal misfortune, overcoming ill health . . . and living through seventeen miscarriages, stillbirths, and premature births in seventeen years." (Publisher's note)

"Anne's natural reserve and her instinct for discretion has led historians to believe that she was weak and dominated by women of stronger character. Somerset's impressive scholarship debunks that belief and shows Anne as a masterful, even authoritative, queen who survived the influence of her 'friends.'" Kirkus

   Includes bibliographical references and index

Anselmo, Lisa

Anselmo, Lisa. **My** (part-time) Paris life; How Running Away Brought Me Home. Lisa Anselmo. Thomas Dunne Books/St. Martin's Press 2016 256 p. (hardcover) $25.99; (ebook) $66   **92**
   1. Self-realization 2. Mother-daughter relationship 3. Paris (France) -- Description and travel 4. Paris (France) -- Biography 5. Self-actualization (Psychology) 6. Mothers -- United States -- Death 7. Women -- France -- Paris -- Biography 8. Mothers and daughters -- United States 9. Americans -- France -- Paris -- Biography 10. Paris (France) -- Social life and customs
   ISBN 9781250067470; 9781466875821

       LC 2016007864

This memoir by Lisa Anselmo, "is for anyone who's ever felt lost or hopeless, but still dreams of something more. . . . [It] explores one woman's search for peace and meaning, and how the ups and downs of expat life in Paris taught her to let go of fear, find self-worth, and create real, lasting happiness in the City of Light." (Publisher's note)

"In the end, this is a sweet and inspiring account of one woman's taxing yet rewarding search for peace, happiness, and contentment in the City of Light." Pub Wkly

Antonia, Mother

Jordan, Mary. The **prison** angel; Mother Antonia's journey from Beverly Hills to a life of service in a Mexican jail. [by] Mary Jordan and Kevin Sullivan. Penguin Press 2005 237p il $24.95   **92**
   1. Nuns
   ISBN 1-59420-056-4

       LC 2004-60238

The authors describe the "journey of a woman who, at the age of 50, left the comforts of suburban L.A. to begin a charity mission in Mexico. . . . This is an inspiring story of one woman's compassion and her own journey of spiritual growth." Booklist

Antonius, Marcus, ca. 83-30 B.C.

Goldsworthy, Adrian Keith. **Antony** and Cleopatra; [by] Adrian Goldsworthy. Yale University Press 2010 470p il map $35   **92**
   1. Queens 2. Generals 3. Statesmen 4. Orators 5. Rome -- History 6. Egypt -- History
   ISBN 978-0-300-16534-0

       LC 2010-929122

"Narrating [Antony] and Cleopatra's parts in the tumultuous end of the Roman Republic, Goldsworthy skillfully integrates the partial and partisan source material into an accessible presentation of a classic tale from classical times." Booklist

   Includes bibliographical references

Apana, Chang, 1871-1933

Yunte Huang. **Charlie** Chan; the untold story of the honorable detective and his rendezvous with American history. W.W. Norton 2010 354p il map   **92**
   1. Detectives 2. Biography, Individual 3. Chan, Charlie (Fictional character) 4. Chan, Charlie (Fictitious character)
   ISBN 0393069621; 9780393069624

       LC 2010016653

This is a history of Charlie Chan, the detective feaured in six novels and 47 movies. Huang contends that Charlie Chan is based upon Chang Apana, a real-life Chinese detective on the Honolulu police force. Bibliography. Index.

This "is a terrifically enjoyable and informative book, one that should appeal to both students of racial history and to fans of one of cinema's greatest detectives." Washington Post Book World

Includes bibliographical references

Apess, William, 1798-1839

Gura, Philip F., 1950- The **life** of William Apess, Pequot; Philip F. Gura. University of North Carolina Press 2014 216 p. (cloth: alk. paper) $26　　　　　　　　　**92**

1. Pequot Indians 2. Methodist Church 3. Pequot Indians -- Biography 4. Indians, Treatment of -- New England -- History 5. Methodist Church -- New England -- Clergy -- Biography

ISBN 1469619989; 9781469619989

LC 2014026609

In this book, author Philip F. Gura "offers the first book-length chronicle of [Pequot Indian preacher William] Apess's fascinating and consequential life. After an impoverished childhood marked by abuse, Apess soldiered with American troops during the War of 1812, converted to Methodism, and rose to fame as a lecturer who lifted a powerful voice of protest against the plight of Native Americans in New England and beyond." (Publisher's note)

Includes bibliographical references and index

Appleseed, Johnny, 1774-1845

Means, Howard B. **Johnny** Appleseed; the man, the myth, the American story. [by] Howard Means. Simon & Schuster 2011 320p il map $26; ebook $12.99　　　　　　　**92**

1. Apples 2. Frontier and pioneer life 3. Pioneers 4. Fruit growers

ISBN 978-1-4391-7825-6; 978-1-4391-7827-0 ebook

LC 2011-665

"Delightfully wry and perceptive, Means' quest to understand Chapman/Appleseed is a captivating achievement in Americana." Booklist

Arana, Marie

Arana, Marie. **American** chica; two worlds, one childhood. Dial Press (NY) 2001 309p hardcover o.p. pa $12.95　　**92**

1. Authors 2. Novelists 3. Editors 4. Memoirists 5. Literary critics

ISBN 0-385-31963-0 pa

LC 00-47529

National Book Award Finalist: Nonfiction (2001)

The author, born to a Peruvian father and an American mother, writes of her childhood in Peru

Arana "blends a journalist's dedication to research with a style that sings with humor. Her memoir is an outstanding contribution to the growing shelf of Latina literature." Publ Wkly

Arbus, Diane, 1923-1971

Lubow, Arthur. **Diane** Arbus; Portrait of a Photographer. Arthur Lubow. HarperCollins 2016 752 p. illustrations $35 **92**

1. Photography 2. Women photographers -- Biography

ISBN 0062234323; 9780062234322

LC 2016015617

This book, by Arthur Lubow, is a "biography of . . . Diane Arbus, one of the most influential and important photographers of the twentieth century. He deftly traces Arbus's development from a wealthy, sexually precocious free spirit into first, a successful New York fashion photographer and then, a singular artist who coaxed secrets from her subjects. Lubow reveals that Arbus's profound need not only to see her subjects but to be seen by them drove her to forge unusually close bonds with these people." (Publisher's note)

"Lubow's portrait is the most sharply focused, encompassing, and incisive to date." Booklist

Includes bibliographical references (pages 619-714) and index.

Archimedes, ca. 287-212 B.C.

Hirshfeld, Alan. **Eureka** man; the life and legacy of Archimedes. Walker 2009 242p il map $26　　　　　　　**92**

1. Scientists 2. Mathematicians 3. Writers on science 4. Science -- Greece -- History

ISBN 978-0-8027-1618-7; 0-8027-1618-0

LC 2009-05608

"Thoroughly enjoyable look at the tumultuous life and resounding influence of a genius of antiquity. . . . Hirshfeld writes clearly and with enthusiasm, navigating even the occasional dense mathematical concept with easy-to-understand language and accompanying diagrams." Kirkus

Includes bibliographical references

Arkin, Alan, 1934-

Arkin, Alan. An **improvised** life; a memoir. Da Capo Press 2011 201p $17　　　　　　　　　　　　**92**

1. Actors 2. Theatrical directors

ISBN 978-0-306-81966-7

LC 2010-45034

"Arkin looks back on his career as an actor, but this memoir forgoes the backstage gossip and star-studded anecdotes readers might expect. In fact, the author largely ignores his accomplishments in favor of charting his inner evolution as an artist, focusing on intellectual and spiritual epiphanies that have shaped his approach to acting. . . . Earnest, intelligent and well-observed—less a celebrity memoir than a serious consideration of the principles of acting and improvisation. " Kirkus

Armstrong, Karen

Armstrong, Karen. The **spiral** staircase; my climb out of darkness. Knopf 2004 xxii, 305p hardcover o.p. pa $14 **92**

1. Nuns 2. Religious scholars

ISBN 0-375-41318-9; 0-385-72127-7 pa

LC 2003-47550

This "is the story of Armstrong's personal spiritual quest, which led her at age 17 to join a convent. However, she found that her own skeptical nature and the physical constraints of convent life crippled her intellectually and spiritually. . . . After seven years, Armstrong left the convent." SLJ

Armstrong, Louis, 1900-1971

Armstrong, Louis. **Louis** Armstrong, in his own words; selected writings. edited and with an introduction by Thomas Brothers; annotated index by Charles Kinzer. Oxford Univ. Press 1999 xxvii, 255p il hardcover o.p. pa $14.95　　　**92**

1. Singers 2. Jazz musicians 3. Band leaders 4. Trumpet players

ISBN 0-19-514046-X

LC 99-17040

In this collection Armstrong "recounts episodes from his childhood in New Orleans, pays tribute to other musicians, and extolls the virtues of marijuana, laxatives, and rice and beans while speaking candidly about race relations, the music business, and his extramarital affairs. The joy he took in expressing himself on paper is abundantly evident." New Yorker

Includes bibliographical references

★ Brothers, Thomas. **Louis** Armstrong, master of modernism; by Thomas Brothers. W.W. Norton & Co. Inc. 2014 608 p. illustrations (hardcover) $39.95　　　　　　　**92**

1. Jazz musicians -- Biography

ISBN 0393065820; 9780393065824

LC 2013037726

Pulitzer Prize Finalist: Biography or Autobiography (2015)

Author Thomas Brothers presents an "account of [jazz musician] Louis Armstrong--his life and legacy--during the most creative period of his career . . . in the 1920s and early 1930s, when Armstrong created not one but two modern musical styles. [The book] blends cultural history, musical scholarship, and personal accounts from Armstrong's contemporaries to reveal his enduring contributions to jazz and popular music." (Publisher's note)

A "monumental follow-up to Louis Armstrong's New Orleans (2006). . . . Brothers' work, covering an astonishingly creative decade, is comprehensive and firmly grounded in musicology and in the racial and cultural climate of the 1920s. It is voluminously researched, compellingly written, and supported by a valuable discography and bibliography." Booklist

Includes bibliographical references, discography, and index

Teachout, Terry. **Pops**; a life of Louis Armstrong. Houghton Mifflin Harcourt 2009 475p il $30 **92**

1. Jazz musicians 2. Biography, Individual 3. Jazz -- History and criticism

ISBN 978-0-15-101089-9; 0-15-101089-7

LC 2009-6035

"The author makes an eloquent case for Armstrong's status as a pioneer, not just in jazz but in the broader context of 20th-century art. A rewarding jazz biography and a revealing look at a broad swath of American cultural history." Kirkus

Includes discography and bibliographical references

Armstrong, Neil, 1930-2012

Barbree, Jay. **Neil** Armstrong; A Life of Flight. Jay Barbree. St. Martin's Press 2014 320 p. illustrations $27.99 **92**

1. Astronauts 2. Air pilots -- Biography 3. Project Apollo (U.S.) -- History 4. Space flight to the moon -- History 5. Astronauts -- United States -- Biography

ISBN 125004071X; 9781250040718

LC 2014008696

"Working from 50 years of conversations he had with [astronaut] Neil [Armstrong] . . . , [author Jay] Barbree writes about Neil's three passions--flight, family, and friends. This is the inside story of Neil Armstrong from the time he flew . . . in the Korean War and then flew a rocket plane called the X-15 to the edge of space, to when he saved his Gemini 8 by flying the first emergency return from Earth orbit and then flew Apollo-Eleven to the moon's Sea of Tranquility." (Publisher's note)

"The author paints a detailed and colorful picture of his subject and an unbiased depiction of the period in which he lived, while also demonstrating reverence for Armstrong as a confidant." LJ

Ashbery, John, 1927-

Roffman, Karin. The **songs** we know best; John Ashbery's early life. Karin Roffman. Farrar, Straus & Giroux 2017 xv, 316 p.p illustrations (hardcover) $30 **92**

1. Biography 2. American poets -- Biography 3. American poetry -- 20th century 4. Poets, American -- 20th century -- Biography

ISBN 9780374293840; 9781429949804

LC 2016045038

This book, by Karin Roffman, is "the first comprehensive biography of the early life of John Ashbery . . . [which] reveals the unusual ways he drew on the details of his youth to populate the poems that made him one of the most original and unpredictable forces of the last century in arts and letters. . . . [It] shows how Ashbery's poetry arose from his early lessons both on the family farm and in 1950s New York City. . . ." (Publisher's note)

"This tender, youth-focused biography will be most enjoyed by Ashbery's fans and readers interested in a remarkable gay artist's midcentury coming-of-age story." Booklist

Includes bibliographical references (pages 247-297) and index.

Astaire, Adele

Riley, Kathleen, 1974- The **Astaires**; Fred & Adele. Kathleen Riley. Oxford University Press 2012 xxiii, 241 p.p (alk. paper) $27.95 **92**

1. Actors -- United States -- Biography 2. Dancers -- United States -- Biography 3. Actresses -- United States -- Biography

ISBN 0199738416; 9780199738410

LC 2011018462

This book, by Kathleen Riley, offers a biography of the sibling-entertainers Fred and Adele Astaire. "Kathleen Riley traces the Astaires' rise to fame from . . . child performers on small-time vaudeville stages . . . to their 1917 debut on Broadway to star billings on both sides of the Atlantic. . . . Ultimately, Fred's dancing expertise surpassed his sister's, and their paths diverged: Adele married into British aristocracy, and Fred headed for Hollywood." (Publisher's note)

Includes bibliographical references and index.

Astaire, Fred

Riley, Kathleen, 1974- The **Astaires**; Fred & Adele. Kathleen Riley. Oxford University Press 2012 xxiii, 241 p.p (alk. paper) $27.95 **92**

1. Actors -- United States -- Biography 2. Dancers -- United States -- Biography 3. Actresses -- United States -- Biography

ISBN 0199738416; 9780199738410

LC 2011018462

This book, by Kathleen Riley, offers a biography of the sibling-entertainers Fred and Adele Astaire. "Kathleen Riley traces the Astaires' rise to fame from . . . child performers on small-time vaudeville stages . . . to their 1917 debut on Broadway to star billings on both sides of the Atlantic. . . . Ultimately, Fred's dancing expertise surpassed his sister's, and their paths diverged: Adele married into British aristocracy, and Fred headed for Hollywood." (Publisher's note)

Includes bibliographical references and index.

Atanasoff, John V.

Smiley, Jane. The **man** who invented the computer; the biography of John Atanasoff, digital pioneer. Doubleday 2010 246p il $25.95 **92**

1. Inventors 2. Physicists 3. Mathematicians 4. Computer scientists

ISBN 978-0-385-52713-2; 0-385-52713-6

LC 2010-18887

"Engrossing. Smiley takes science history and injects it with a touch of noir and an exciting clash of vanities." Kirkus

Includes bibliographical references

Athill, Diana

Athill, Diana. **Alive,** alive oh! and other things that matter; and other things that matter. Diana Athill. W W Norton & Co Inc 2016 176 p. (ebook) $40; (hardcover) $24.95 **92**

1. Aging 2. English authors -- Biography 3. Life 4. Old age 5. Memory in old age 6. Editors -- Great Britain -- Biography 7. Women editors -- Great Britain -- Biography 8. Authors, English -- 20th century -- Biography 9. Women authors, English -- 20th century -- Biography

ISBN 9780393253726; 9780393253719

LC 2015042206

In this memoir book editor Diana Athill, "begins to reflect on the things that matter after a lifetime of remarkable experiences, and the memories that have risen to the surface and sustain her in her very old age. . . . [It] sparkles with wise and often very funny reflections on the condition of being old. Athill reminds us of the joy and richness of every stage of life--and what it means to live life fully, without regrets." (Publisher's note)

"Athill has a charming and captivating way with a story, and a graceful, plainspoken manner of revealing the humor, gravity, and momentary beauty of a life fully lived." Pub Wkly

Atkins, Vera, 1908-2000

Helm, Sarah. A **life** in secrets; Vera Atkins and the missing agents of WWII. Nan A. Talese 2006 493p il map hardcover o.p. pa $16 **92**
1. Intelligence service agents 2. World War, 1939-1945 -- Secret service 3. Great Britain -- Special Operations Executive
ISBN 0-385-50845-X; 978-1-4000-3140-5 pa; 1-4000-3140-0 pa
LC 2005-56870

First published 2005 in the United Kingdom

This is a biography of "the highest-ranking female official in the French section of a WWII British intelligence unit that aided the resistance. Atkins sent 400 agents into France, including 39 women she'd personally recruited and supervised. . . . Helm has produced a memorable portrait of a woman who knowingly sent other women to their deaths and a searing history of female courage and suffering during WWII." Publ Wkly

Includes bibliographical references

Atlas, James

Atlas, James. The **shadow** in the garden; a biographer's tale. James Atlas. Pantheon Books 2017 388 p. illustrations (hardcover) $28.95 **92**
1. Intellectuals 2. Authors -- Biography 3. Biography as a literary form 4. Biographers -- United States -- Biography
ISBN 9781101871690; 9781101871706
LC 2016057846

In this book, James Atlas "takes us back to his own childhood in suburban Chicago, where he fell in love with literature and, early on, found in himself the impulse to study writers' lives. . . . We get to know Atlas's first subject, the 'self-doomed' poet Delmore Schwartz. And we are introduced to a bygone cast of intellectuals such as Edmund Wilson and Dwight Macdonald." (Publisher's note)

"Atlas' expert, provocative, and enlightening 'biographer's tale' is a work of both depth and radiance." Booklist

Includes bibliographical references (pages 357-366) and index.

Attenborough, David, 1926-

Attenborough, David, 1926- **Adventures** of a young naturalist; the zoo quest expeditions. David Attenborough. Quercus 2018 400 p. (hardback) $26.99 **92**
1. Zoo animals 2. Zoological specimens -- Collection and preservation 3. Zoology 4. Wild animal collecting
ISBN 9781635060690; 9781635060706
LC 2017048329

"Living legend and presenter of BBC's Planet Earth series Sir David Attenborough tells the story of his early career as a broadcaster and a naturalist in his own words. In 1954, . . . Attenborough, . . . was offered the opportunity of a lifetime--to travel the world finding rare and elusive animals for the London Zoo's collection, and to film the expedition for the BBC for a new show called Zoo Quest. This is the story of those voyages." (Publisher's note)

Attila, King of the Huns, d. 453

Kelly, Christopher. The **end** of empire; Attila the Hun and the fall of Rome. W.W. Norton 2009 350p il map $26.95 **92**
1. Huns 2. Tribal leaders 3. Rome -- History
ISBN 978-0-393-06196-3
LC 2009-009072

First published 2008 in the United Kingdom with title: Attila the Hun: barbarian terror and the fall of the Roman Empire

The author "paints an engaging portrait of Attila the Hun's rise to prominence and places the feared warlord in the context of his own time." Libr J

Includes bibliographical references

Aubrey, John, 1626-1697

Scurr, Ruth. **John** Aubrey; My Own Life. by Ruth Scurr. New York Review Books 2016 544 p. illustrations (alk. paper) $35 **92**
1. Biography as a literary form 2. Antiquarians -- England -- Biography
ISBN 1681370425; 9781681370422
LC 2016009388

This book is a biography of biographer John Aubrey. "This intimate diary of Aubrey's days is composed of his own words, collected, collated, and enlarged upon by Ruth Scurr. . . . Scurr's biography honors and echoes Aubrey's own innovations in the art of biography." (Publisher's note)

Includes bibliographical references and index

Audibert-Boulloche, Christiane

Kaiser, Charles. The **cost** of courage; by Charles Kaiser. Other Press 2015 288 p. illustrations (hardcover) $26.95 **92**
1. World War, 1939-1945 -- Biography 2. World War, 1939-1945 -- Underground movements -- France 3. Guerrillas -- France -- Biography 4. France -- History -- German occupation, 1940-1945 -- Biography 5. World War, 1939-1945 -- Underground movements -- France -- Biography
ISBN 1590516141; 9781590516140
LC 2015008560

This book, by Charles Kaiser, tells the "heroic true story of the three youngest children of a . . . family who worked together in the French Resistance. . . . In the autumn of 1943, André Boulloche . . . coordinat[ed] all the Resistance movements in the nine northern regions of France only to be betrayed by one of his associates . . . and taken prisoner. His sisters carried on the fight without him until the end of the war." (Publisher's note)

"Kaiser's account of a family's devotion and resilience in the face of horrific tyranny tells a highly recommended story of resolve and bravery that can't help but feel romantic in its selfless and profound obligation, but this is not gloss nor ungrounded canonization." LJ

Audubon, John James, 1785-1851

Rhodes, Richard. **John** James Audubon; the making of an American. Knopf 2004 528p il $30; pa $16 **92**
1. Artists 2. Painters 3. Naturalists 4. Ornithologists 5. Writers on science 6. Biography, Individual 7. Artists -- United States
ISBN 0-375-41412-6; 0-375-71393-X pa
LC 2003-69489

This is a biography of the American ornithologist and painter.

The author "chronicles Audubon's ineluctable sense of mission, phenomenal skills, and triumph over adversity. . . . Rhodes sets Audubon's engrossing tale within the context of the War of 1812, the Louisiana Purchase, the wars against Native Americans (whom Audubon profoundly admired), and the rapid decimation of the American wilderness. . . . Full of passion and discovery, hardship and transcendence, Audubon's story is at once intimate and mythic, and Rhodes' fresh, comprehensive biography will capture the imagination of readers everywhere." Booklist

Includes bibliographical references

Augustine, Saint, Bishop of Hippo

Williams, Rowan, 1950- **On** Augustine; Rowan Williams. Bloomsbury USA Academic 2016 240 p. (ebook) $80; $42 **92**

1. Theology -- History 2. Church history -- 30-600, Early church
ISBN 9781472925282; 1472925270; 9781472925275

In this book, retired Archbishop of Canterbury Rowan Williams "turns his attention to St Augustine. St Augustine not only shaped the development of Western theology, he also made a major contribution to political theory ('City of God') and through his 'Confessions' to the understanding of human psychology. Rowan Williams has an entirely fresh perspective on these matters and the chapter titles in this new book demonstrate this." (Publisher's note)

Includes bibliographical references and index.

Augustus, Emperor of Rome, 63 B.C.-14 A.D.

★ Everitt, Anthony. **Augustus**; the life of Rome's first emperor. Random House 2006 377p il map $26.95 **92**

1. Emperors 2. Rome -- History
ISBN 1-4000-6128-8; 978-1-4000-6128-0

LC 2006-41735

The author's "writing is so crisp and so lively he brings both Rome and Augustus to life in this magnificent work, a must-read for anyone interested in classical times." Booklist

Includes bibliographical references

Aung San Suu Kyi

Wintle, Justin. **Perfect** hostage; a life of Aung San Suu Kyi, Burma's prisoner of conscience. Skyhorse Pub. 2008 464p il map $27.95 **92**

1. Political prisoners 2. Women political activists 3. Dissenters 4. Political leaders 5. Nonfiction writers 6. Human rights activists 7. Nobel laureates for peace 8. Myanmar -- Politics and government 9. National League for Democracy (Burma)
ISBN 978-1-60239-266-3; 1-60239-266-8

LC 2007-51031

This is a biography of the Burmese human rights activist.

The author "writes with a snarling wit, firm grasp of Burma's horrors, and penetrating respect for this tenacious and composed prisoner of conscience, detailing her genius for connecting with people, the threats against her life, and her devotion to peace." Booklist

Includes bibliographical references (p. 432-9)

Austen, Jane, 1775-1817

Harman, Claire. **Jane's** fame; how Jane Austen conquered the world. Henry Holt and Co. 2010 277p il $26 **92**

1. Authors 2. Novelists 3. Women authors 4. Authors, English
ISBN 978-0-8050-8258-6; 0-8050-8258-1

LC 2009-22291

First published 2009 in the United Kingdom

"Engagingly written and full of fascinating bits of information as well as valuable insights, this is a must for any serious Austen reader." Booklist

Includes bibliographical references

Kelly, Helena. **Jane** Austen, the secret radical; Helena Kelly. First American edition Alfred A. Knopf 2017 318 p. illustrations (hardcover) $27.95 **92**

1. Social problems in literature
ISBN 9781524732110; 9781524732103

LC 2016042656

In this book, author Helena "Kelly illuminates the radical subjects--slavery, poverty, feminism, the Church, evolution, among them--considered treasonous at the time, that Austen deftly explored in the six novels that have come to embody an age.... We see a writer who understood that the novel--until then seen as mindless 'trash'--could be a great art form and who, perhaps more than any other writer up to that time, imbued it with its particular greatness." (Publisher's note)

"A fine-grained study that shows us how to read between the lines to discover the remarkable woman who helped transform the novel from trash to an absolute art form." Kirkus

Includes bibliographical references and index

Shields, Carol. **Jane** Austen. Viking 2001 185p (Penguin lives series) hardcover o.p. pa $13 **92**

1. Authors 2. Novelists 3. Women authors 4. Authors, English
ISBN 0-670-89488-5; 0-14-303516-9 pa

LC 00-43807

"In chronicling her subject's life and personality, Shields emphasizes Austen's keen ability to listen, observe, and capture clearly the social mores of her time and explore human nature in her writing. Shields contends that historical references are behind many of the scenes and characters in Austen's novels, and as a way of more clearly personalizing Austen's experiences or feelings, she interjects commentary regarding writing and publishing that is presumably based on personal experience." Libr J

Worsley, Lucy. **Jane** Austen at home; a biography. Lucy Worsley. St. Martin's Press 2017 387 p. illustrations (hardcover) $29.99 **92**

1. Literary landmarks 2. England -- In literature 3. Literary landmarks 4. Novelists, English -- 19th century -- Biography 5. Novelists, English -- Homes and haunts -- England
ISBN 9781250131607; 9781473632240; 9781250131614; 125013160X

LC 2017009308

In this biography, by Lucy Worsley, "take a trip back to Jane Austen's world and the many places she lived as historian Lucy Worsley visits Austen's childhood home, her schools, her holiday accommodations, the houses--both grand and small--of the relations upon whom she was dependent, and the home she shared with her mother and sister towards the end of her life." (Publisher's note)

"Worsley (If Walls Could Talk) writes with a historian's acumen and a Janeite's passion, using these skills to unlock the doors of the many houses of Jane Austen (1775–1817)." LJ

Includes bibliographical references (pages 333-340) and index.

Auster, Paul, 1947-

Auster, Paul, 1947- **Report** from the interior; Paul Auster. Henry Holt and Company 2013 352 p. (hardback) $27 **92**

1. Letters 2. Adolescence 3. Authors, American -- 20th century -- Biography
ISBN 0805098577; 9780805098570

LC 2013002417

Author Paul Auster has divided this book into four parts. The "first is a childhood psychobiography, to the age of 12, recognizing the distortions and holes in memory while discovering the magic of literature... . The second consists of exhaustively detailed synopses of two movies that he saw in his midteens, The Incredible Shrinking Man (1957) and was a Fugitive from a Chain Gang (1932)." The third and fourth parts include letters to his wife and a scrapbook. (Kirkus Reviews)

Austin, Paul, 1955-

Austin, Paul. **Beautiful** eyes; a father transformed. Paul Austin. W.W. Norton & Company 2014 288 p. (hardcover) $25.95 **92**

1. Father and child 2. Down syndrome -- Patients -- Biography 3. Parents of children with disabilities -- Biography 4. Children with mental disabilities -- United States -- Biography
ISBN 039308244X; 9780393082449

LC 2014025600

This book, by Paul Austin, "is the story of a father's journey toward acceptance of a child who is different.... [The author] chronicles his life with his daughter [with Down syndrome]: watching her learn to walk and talk and form her own opinions, making decisions about her future, and navigating cultural assumptions and prejudices—all the while confronting, with poignancy and moving candor, his own limitations as her father." (Publisher's note)

"This tender, bright and flawed child showed how being different enhanced her humanity rather than detracted from it. A poignant and candid father's memoir." Kirkus

Autry, Gene, 1907-1998

George-Warren, Holly. **Public** cowboy no. 1; the life and times of Gene Autry. Oxford University Press 2007 406p il $28 **92**

1. Actors 2. Singers 3. Country musicians 4. Cowboys 5. Baseball executives 6. Broadcasting executives
ISBN 978-0-19-517746-6; 0-19-517746-0

LC 2006-36369

This is a biography of the radio performer, singer and actor who performed in rodeos and appeared in such movies as Public Cowboy No.1 (1937) and The Phantom Empire (1935).

"This colorful study is much more than a biography of Autry; it also tells the story of country-western music, singing cowboys, radio and early television, and celebrity." Choice

Includes filmography, discography, and bibliographical references

Auvinen, Karen

★ Auvinen, Karen. **Rough** beauty; forty seasons of mountain living. Karen Auvinen. Scribner 2018 x, 303 p.p illustrations (hardcover) $27 **92**

1. Mountain life 2. Rocky Mountains 3. American authors 4. Solitude 5. Mountain life -- Rocky Mountains 6. Authors, American -- 21st century -- Biography
ISBN 9781501152283; 9781501152306; 1501152289

LC 2017061755

This book, by Karen Auvinen, is "a stunning, inspirational memoir from an award-winning poet who ventures into the wilderness to seek answers to life's big questions and finds her way back after losing everything she thought she needed.... [The book] is a luminous, lyric exploration of and homage to her forty seasons in the mountains, embracing the unpredictability and grace of living intimately with the forces of nature while making peace with her own wildness." (Publisher's note)

"This breathtaking memoir honors the wildness of the Rockies and shows readers how they might come to rely on their animal companions." Pub Wkly

Avedon, Richard

Stevens, Norma. **Avedon**; something personal. Norma Stevens & Steven M.L. Aronson. Spiegel & Grau 2017 x, 699 p.p illustrations (hardcover) $40 **92**

1. Biography 2. Photographers -- United States -- Biography
ISBN 9780812994438; 9780812994445; 0812994434

In this biography, author "Norma Stevens and co-author Steven M. L. Aronson masterfully trace [Richard] Avedon's life from his birth to his death, in 2004, at the age of eighty-one, while at work in Texas for 'The New Yorker.'... 'Avedon: Something Personal' is the confiding, compelling full story of a man who for half a century was an enormous influence on both high and popular culture, on both fashion and art." (Publisher's note)

Avery, Sean

McKinley, Michael. **Ice** capades; a memoir of fast living and tough hockey. Sean Avery with Michael McKinley. Blue Rider Press 2017 xi, 316 p.p illustrations (chiefly color) (hardcover) $28 **92**

1. Hockey players 2. Hockey players -- Canada -- Biography
ISBN 9780399575761; 9780399575754; 0399575758

LC 2017289448

This book, by Sean Avery with Michael McKinley, presents a "no-holds-barred memoir of high living and bad behavior in the NHL--coupled with the behind-the-scenes glitter of celebrity and media nightlife in New York and LA.... Avery goes deep inside the sport to reveal every aspect of an athlete's life, from what they do with their money and nights off to how they stay sharp and competitive in the league." (Publisher's note)

Axelrod, David, 1955-

Axelrod, David, 1955- **Believer**; My Forty Years in Politics. David Axelrod. Penguin Group USA 2015 416 p. illustrations $35 **92**

1. United States -- Politics and government -- 1989-
ISBN 1594205876; 9781594205873

LC 2015302608

This memoir, by David Axelrod, focuses on his "twenty-year friendship with Barack Obama, a warm partnership that inspired both men even as it propelled each to great heights. Taking a chance on an unlikely candidate for the U.S. Senate, Axelrod ultimately collaborated closely with Obama on his political campaigns, and served as the invaluable strategist who contributed to the tremendous victories of 2008 and 2012." (Publisher's note)

"Axelrod's careful connection of the dots provides an illuminating study in how political power moves from generation to generation. The book-closing call to remake politics would sound like so much cheerleading in other hands, but Axelrod's connecting of Obama to JFK makes it work. Obama has been profiled many times but seldom with so practical an outlook. An excellent view of politics from the inside." Kirkus

Axelrod, Howard, 1973-

Axelrod, Howard. The **point** of vanishing; a memoir of two years in solitude. Howard Axelrod. Beacon Press 2015 224 p. (hardback: acid-free paper) $16 **92**

1. Solitude 2. Vision disorders 3. Self-perception 4. Visual perception 5. Vermont -- Biography 6. Solitude -- Psychological aspects 7. Young men -- United States -- Biography 8. Vision, Monocular -- Psychological aspects 9. People with visual disabilities -- United States -- Biography 10. Eye -- Wounds and injuries -- Patients -- United States -- Biography
ISBN 9780807075463

LC 2015004216

This memoir, by Howard Axelrod, named a Best Book by several journals including "Slate," "Chicago Tribune," and "Entropy Magazine," follows the author's life after an accident which blinded his right eye. "Desperate for a sense of orientation he could trust, he retreated to a jerry-rigged house in the Vermont woods, where he lived without a computer or television, and largely without human contact, for two years." (Publisher's note)

"This memoir is a keeper, touching and eloquent, full of hard lessons learned. Readers will hope for more from first-time-author Axelrod." Booklist

Ayers, Nathaniel Anthony

★ Lopez, Steve. The **soloist**; a lost dream, an unlikely friendship, and the redemptive power of music. G. P. Putnam's Sons 2008 273p hardcover o.p. pa $15 **92**

1. Violinists 2. Homeless persons 3. Homeless 4. Schizophrenics 5. Street entertainers

ISBN 978-0-399-15506-2; 0-399-15506-6; 978-0-425-23836-3 pa; 0-425-23836-9 pa

LC 2007-46314

The true story of Nathaniel Ayers, a musician who becomes schizophrenic and homeless, and his friendship with Steve Lopez, the Los Angeles columnist who discovers and writes about him in the newspaper.

"With self-effacing humor, fast-paced yet elegant prose and unsparing honesty, Lopez tells an inspiring story of heartbreak and hope." Publ Wkly

Baartman, Saartjie

Crais, Clifton C. **Sara** Baartman and the Hottentot Venus; a ghost story and a biography. [by] Clifton Crais and Pamela Scully. Princeton University Press 2009 232p il map $29.95 **92**

1. Biography, Individual 2. Racism in museum exhibits 3. Museum exhibits -- Moral and ethical aspects

ISBN 9780691135809; 0-691-13580-0

LC 2008-14918

"A member of a small indigenous tribe of herdsmen dubbed the Hottentots by Dutch colonists (but known today by their name Khoikhoi), Baartman was captured in the course of ongoing colonial warfare that effected a genocidal destruction of this peaceful people. Having been enslaved, she was taken to Europe by a member of the family that 'owned' and exhibited her much as an exotic animal might be. . . . [The authors] have done an excellent job not only of telling this rebarbative story but of putting it into the context of its time. This enables them to explain what permitted such an exhibition while at the same time viewing it through our (thankfully) more humane and enlightened lens." Los Angeles Times Book Rev

Includes bibliographical references

★ Holmes, Rachel. **African** queen; the real life of the Hottentot Venus. Random House 2007 161p il $23.95 **92**

1. Entertainers

ISBN 978-1-4000-6136-5; 1-4000-6136-9

LC 2006-45166

"This is a probing look at historical racism and sexual exploitation presented through the life of an extraordinary woman." Booklist

Includes bibliographical references

Babbage, Charles, 1791-1871

Essinger, James. **Ada's** algorithm; how Lord Byron's daughter Ada Lovelace launched the digital age. James Essinger. Melville House 2014 272 p. illustrations (hardback) $25.95 **92**

1. Computers -- History 2. Women mathematicians 3. Mathematicians -- Biography 4. Computers -- History -- 19th century 5. Mathematicians -- Great Britain -- Biography 6. Women mathematicians -- Great Britain -- Biography

ISBN 1612194087; 9781612194080

LC 2014021837

In this book, author James Essinger "makes the case that the computer age could have started two centuries ago if [Ada] Lovelace's contemporaries had recognized her research and fully grasped its implications. . . . [S]tarting with the outrageous behavior of her father [Lord Byron], which made Ada instantly famous upon birth. Ada would go on to overcome numerous obstacles to obtain a level of education typically forbidden to women of her day." (Publisher's note)

"Essinger (Spellbound: The Surprising Origins and Astonishing Secrets of English Spelling, 2007, etc.) presents Ada's story with great enthusiasm and rich detail, painting her life as one that was rich with opportunity and access but stifled by sexism. Ada continues to inspire, and by using her own voice via letters and research, the author brings her to life for a new generation of intrepid female innovators. A robust, engaging and exciting biography." Kirkus

Includes bibliographical references and index

Bacall, Lauren, 1924-2014

Bacall, Lauren. **By** myself and then some. HarperEntertainment 2005 506p il $26.95 **92**

1. Actors

ISBN 0-06-075535-0

LC 2005-40256

First published 1979 by Knopf with title: Lauren Bacall by myself

In this memoir, the actress describes how she got her start in acting and her relationships with other actors, including Humphrey Bogart.

"Certainly more intelligently written than your average celebrity autobiography, this memoir tells a fascinating story of one woman's journey through life with an intimacy that's sure to engage legions of readers." Booklist

Bach, Johann Sebastian, 1685-1750

Gardiner, John Eliot. **Bach**; music in the castle of heaven. by John Eliot Gardiner. Alfred A. Knopf 2013 672 p. il. (chiefly col.), map, music (hardback) $35 **92**

1. Composers, German 2. Composers -- Biography 3. Composers -- Germany -- Biography

ISBN 0375415297; 9780375415296

LC 2013030398

"Originally published in Great Britain as Music in the castle of heaven, by Allen Lane"--Title page verso

National Book Critics Circle Award Finalist: Biography (2013)

In this book, author John Eliot Gardiner, "takes us . . . into [German composer Johann Sebastian] Bach's works and mind . . . explaining in . . . detail the ideas on which Bach drew, how he worked, how his music is constructed, how it achieves its effects--and what it can tell us about Bach the man." (Publisher's note)

"Although Gardiner celebrates Bach's accomplishments through this dense, demanding but rewarding work, he reminds readers continually that the composer was no saint. . . . [T]he author's focus is not so much on the man but on the music." Kirkus

Includes bibliographical references and index

★ Geck, Martin. **Johann** Sebastian Bach; life and work. translated from the German by John Hargraves. Harcourt 2006 738p il $40 **92**

1. Composers

ISBN 978-0-15-100648-9; 0-15-100648-2

LC 2006-12390

This book "adds original scholarship to an exhaustive study of other studies of Bach. And although it is often dense with information, it is just as often entertaining: rich in anecdotes and scintillating in its conjectures." N Y Times (Late N Y Ed)

Includes bibliographical references

Wolff, Christoph. **Johann** Sebastian Bach; the learned musician. Norton 2000 599p il hardcover o.p. $21.95   **92**

1. Composers

ISBN 9780393322569; 0393322564

LC 99-54364

This work "is likely to be the standard one-volume Bach biography for some time to come. It is a solid, richly informative treatment, presenting the copious details of Bach's life in a coherent, readable narrative." N Y Rev Books

Includes bibliographical references

Baer, Max, 1909-1959

Schaap, Jeremy. **Cinderella** Man; James J. Braddock, Max Baer, and the greatest upset in boxing history. Houghton Mifflin 2005 324p il hardcover o.p. pa $13.95   **92**

1. Boxers (Persons) 2. Boxing -- Biography

ISBN 0-618-55117-4; 0-618-71190-2 pa

LC 2004-66085

The author goes into "detail on the brawny, reserved Braddock, who, at his lowest moments, was reduced to living off government relief and doing grueling work on the Hoboken, N.J., docks. But the story is as much about Max Baer, the lovably clownish and handsome heavyweight Braddock defeated as a 10-to-one underdog. . . . Boxing enthusiasts will be more than satisfied by Schaap's meticulous account, which includes round-by-round details of the fight, as well as profiles of other fighters of the era." Publ Wkly

Includes bibliographical references

Bailey, Blake, 1963-

Bailey, Blake. The **Splendid** Things We Planned; A Family Portrait. by Blake Bailey. W.W. Norton & Co. Inc 2014 288 p. illustrations $25.95   **92**

1. Alcoholism 2. Drug abuse 3. Family life 4. Mental illness 5. Authors, American -- Biography 6. Biographers -- United States -- Biography

ISBN 0393239578; 9780393239577

LC 2013039720

National Book Critics Circle Finalist: Autobiography (2014)

In this book, "biographer [Blake] Bailey tells the story of his own life by chronicling his brother Scott's alcoholism and drug addiction, which causes him to descend into violence and madness. Told in chronological order, starting with the marriage of his straight-laced lawyer father to his bohemian, German-immigrant mother, Bailey's story captures the contradictions and tensions that simmer just below the surface of the family, as they try to live a normal suburban life in Oklahoma." (Publishers Weekly)

A "haunting portrait of more than one tortured soul and a heartfelt probing of the limits of brotherly love." Booklist

Bailey, Elisabeth Tova

Bailey, Elisabeth Tova. The **sound** of a wild snail eating. Algonquin Books of Chapel Hill 2010 190p il $18.95   **92**

1. Snails 2. Authors 3. Essayists 4. Short story writers 5. Biography, Individual

ISBN 978-1-56512-606-0

LC 2010-18603

"A small, short book filled with an enormous amount of natural history and science about snails; also, an acknowledgment of an individ-

ual's determination to recover and regain life with humor and insight. Highly recommended." Libr J

Includes bibliographical references

Baker, Russell, 1925-

Baker, Russell, 1925- **Growing** up. New American Library 1983 278p pa $15   **92**

1. Authors 2. Humorists 3. Journalists 4. Essayists 5. Satirists 6. Memoirists

ISBN 0-452-25550-3

First published 1982 by Congdon & Weed

This book "recounts the first 24 years of [Baker's] life as the son of an independent and deep-rooted Virginian family." Natl Rev

Balanchine, George, 1904-1983

Gottlieb, Robert Adams. **George** Balanchine: the ballet maker. HarperCollins\Atlas Books 2004 224p (Eminent lives) $19.95; pa. $13.99   **92**

1. Ballet 2. Dancers 3. Choreographers

ISBN 0-06-075070-7; 9780060750718

LC 2004-48856

"This loving tribute captures Balanchine's legacy: his energy, confidence, lack of pretension and, most important, his joy in creation." Publ Wkly

Includes bibliographical references

★ Teachout, Terry. **All** in the dances: a brief life of George Balanchine. Harcourt 2004 208p $22   **92**

1. Ballet 2. Dancers 3. Choreographers

ISBN 0-15-101088-9

LC 2004-9226

"Balanchine's ballets are modern masterpieces, and Teachout, moving chronologically from work to work, uses them as stepping stones to tell Balanchine's own story. This is highly recommended as a first book on the life and art of George Balanchine for students and the general reader." Publ Wkly

Includes bibliographical references

Baldwin, Alec, 1958-

Baldwin, Alec, 1958- **Nevertheless**; A Memoir. Alec Baldwin. HarperCollins 2017 288 p. $28.99   **92**

1. Actors -- United States -- Biography

ISBN 0062409700; 9780062409706

LC 2017006406

This memoir, by Alec Baldwin, "chronicles the highs and lows of his life. . . . Baldwin transcends his public persona, making public facets of his life he has long kept private. . . . He introduces us to the Long Island child who felt burdened; . . . the Washington, DC, college student; . . . the young soap actor; . . . the addict drawn to drugs and alcohol; . . . the husband and father who acknowledges his failings; . . . and the consummate professional." (Publisher's note)

Ball, Lucille, 1911-1989

Ball, Lucille. **Love,** Lucy; {by} Lucille Ball with Betty Hannah Hoffman; foreword by Lucie Arnaz. Putnam 1996 286p il pors $24.95   **92**

1. Entertainers -- United States -- Biography

ISBN 0-399-14205-3

LC 96-20751

Lucille Ball's autobiography is "the story of the ingenue from Jamestown, New York, determined to go to Broadway, destined to make a big splash, bound to marry her Valentino, Desi Arnaz. It tells of their life together - both storybook and turbulent: intimate stories of their children and friends; wonderful backstage anecdotes; the creation of the most popular show on TV; the production empire they founded; the dissolution of their marriage. And, with a heartfelt happy ending, her enduring marriage to Gary Morton." (Publisher's note)

Balzac, Honoré de, 1799-1850

Robb, Graham. **Balzac**; a life. Norton 1994 521p il hardcover o.p. pa $15   **92**

1. Authors 2. Novelists 3. Short story writers
ISBN 0-393-31387-5 pa

LC 94-18614

"Balzac's life was more cause for incredulity than anything he wrote, and Robb compellingly sets out the documentable facts against and within the world Balzac created from them. . . . The result is nearly a novel, although Robb does not fictionalize with re-created dialogs and hypothetical events. He has in fact produced an extensive traditional biography . . . not a critical reassessment." Libr J

Includes bibliographical references

Bamberger, Louis, 1855-1944

Forgosh, Linda B. **Louis** Bamberger; Department Store Innovator and Philanthropist. Linda B. Forgosh. Brandeis University Press 2016 296 p. (cloth: alk. paper) $29.95   **92**

1. Department stores 2. Philanthropists -- United States 3. Jews -- United States -- Biography 4. Newark (N.J.) -- History 5. Jews -- New Jersey -- Newark -- Biography 6. Department stores -- New Jersey -- Newark -- History 7. Philanthropists -- New Jersey -- Newark -- Biography 8. Jewish businesspeople -- New Jersey -- Newark -- Biography
ISBN 9781611689815

LC 2016004971

This biography, by Linda B. Forgosh, focuses on "Louis Bamberger (1855–1944). . . . Born in Baltimore, this son of German immigrants built his business—the great, glamorous L. Bamberger & Co. department store in Newark, N.J.—into the sixth-largest department store in the country. A multimillionaire by middle age, he joined the elite circle of German Jews who owned Macy's, Bloomingdale's, and Filene's." (Publisher's note)

"This biography is the first comprehensive examination of Bamberger's life, and it is long overdue." LJ

Includes bibliographical references and index

Banier, François-Marie

Sancton, Tom. The **Bettencourt** affair; the world's richest woman and the scandal that rocked Paris. Tom Sancton. Dutton 2017 xv, 396 p.p illustrations, map (hardcover) $28   **92**

1. Swindlers and swindling 2. Businesswomen -- Biography 3. L'Oréal (Firm) -- History 4. Older women -- France -- Biography 5. Billionaires -- France -- Biography 6. Businesswomen -- France -- Biography 7. Scandals -- France -- Paris -- History -- 21st century 8. Swindlers and swindling -- France -- Paris -- History -- 21st century
ISBN 1101984473; 9781101984475; 9781101984499; 9781101984482

LC 2016058788

This book, by Tom Sancton, uncovers "L'Oréal's . . . corporate history and buried World War II secrets. From the Right Bank mansions to the Left Bank artist havens; and from the Bettencourts' servant quarters to the office of President Nicolas Sarkozy. . . . It all began when Liliane met François-Marie Banier, an artist and photographer. . . . Over the next two decades, Banier was given hundreds of millions of dollars . . . . by Liliane. What, exactly, was their relationship?" (Publisher's note)

"A well-researched, crisply written, and entertaining story of family,

greed, wealth, and the complex relations among them." Kirkus
Includes bibliographical references (pages 339-396).

Banville, John

★ Banville, John, 1945- **Time** pieces; a Dublin memoir. John Banville; photographs by Paul Joyce. Alfred A. Knopf 2018 212 p. $26.95   **92**

1. Irish dramatists 2. Dublin (Ireland) -- History 3. Dublin (Ireland) -- Social life and customs -- 20th century 4. Dublin (Ireland) -- Description and travel 5. Dublin (Ireland) -- Social life and customs
ISBN 1524732834; 9781524732837

LC 2017950648

"Alternating between vignettes of [John] Banville's own past, and present-day historical explorations of the city, Time Pieces is a vivid evocation of childhood and memory--that 'bright abyss' in which 'time's alchemy works'--and a tender and powerful ode to a formative time and place for the artist as a young man." (Publisher's note)

". Featuring excellent photographs by Paul Joyce, the short tome resembles a whimsical, funnier version of W. G. Sebald's meditative style. A richly rewarding and personal work of Irish history and culture." Booklist

Includes bibliographical references (pages 209-210)

Bard, Elizabeth

Bard, Elizabeth. **Lunch** in Paris; a love story, with recipes. Little, Brown and Co. 2010 324p $23.99   **92**

1. Journalists 2. French cooking 3. Art historians 4. Americans -- France 5. Paris (France) -- Description and travel
ISBN 978-0-316-04279-6; 0-316-04279-X

LC 2009-22064

"Falling in love with a Frenchman was not in Elizabeth Bard's master plan, but then he took her to a local canteen: 'Not to minimize Gwendal's many charms, but he was half way to home base as soon as I cut into that marvelous steak,' she writes. Culture shock set in as she learned to shop and cook in Paris, standing in line here for the best green beans, going there for the best walnuts. I thought the recipes were a cutesy touch until I made a few of them: chicken tagine with two kinds of lemon, spiced apricots, chouquettes. Forget the narrative — you could just buy this as a cookbook." Entertainment Wkly

Baret, Jeanne, 1740-1807

Ridley, Glynis. The **discovery** of Jeanne Baret; a story of science, the high seas, and the first woman to circumnavigate the globe. Crown Publishers 2010 288p il $25; ebook $25   **92**

1. Botanists 2. Explorers 3. Women scientists 4. Voyages around the world
ISBN 978-0-307-46352-4; 978-0-307-46354-8 ebook

LC 2010-16778

This is a biography "of Jeanne Baret. Born in 1740 in France's Loire valley, Baret became an expert 'herb woman' who proved to be indispensable to the ambitious botanist Philibert Commerson, accompanying him as his assistant when Commerson was appointed naturalist for France's first expedition to circumnavigate the globe. But women were forbidden, so Baret dressed as a man. . . . Woven throughout this gripping story are Ridley's piquant insights into eighteenth-century exploration, botany, taxonomy, biopiracy, and sexism. Baret could not have asked for a more exacting and expressive champion. Ridley is incandescent in her passion for the truth." Booklist

Includes bibliographical references

Barlow, John P. (John Perry)

Greenfield, Robert. **Mother** American night; my life and

crazy times. John Perry Barlow with Robert Greenfield. Crown Archetype 2018 288 p. (hardcover) $27   **92**

1. Grateful Dead (Musical group) 2. Lyricists -- United States -- Biography

ISBN 9781524760182; 9781524760199

LC 2017050430

This memoir "is the wild, funny, heartbreaking, and often unbelievable (yet completely true) story of an American icon. Born into a powerful Wyoming political family, John Perry Barlow wrote the lyrics for thirty Grateful Dead songs while also running his family's cattle ranch. . . . And after befriending a legendary early group of computer hackers known as the Legion of Doom, Barlow became a renowned internet guru who then cofounded . . . Electronic Frontier Foundation." (Publisher's note)

Barnard, Anne Lindsay, Lady, 1750-1825

Taylor, Stephen. **Defiance**; The Extraordinary Life of Lady Anne Barnard. by Stephen Taylor. First American edition W W Norton & Co Inc 2017 x, 388 p.p illustrations (some color) (hardcover) $28.95   **92**

1. Nobility -- Great Britain -- Biography 2. Artists -- Great Britain -- Biography 3. Socialites -- Great Britain -- Biography 4. Travel writers -- Great Britain -- Biography 5. Authors, English -- 18th century -- Biography 6. Cape of Good Hope (South Africa) -- Description and travel

ISBN 9780393248173; 9780393248180; 0393248178

LC 2017011470

This book, by Stephen Taylor, is "the first major biography of eighteenth-century writer and socialite Lady Anne Barnard. Born in Scotland in 1772, Lady Anne Barnard lived at the heart of Georgian society. She wrote one of the most popular ballads of her day, captivated Sir Walter Scott with her poetry, rubbed shoulders with the Prince of Wales, and dazzled Samuel Johnson with her repartee." (Publisher's note)

"This is a page-turning introduction to a fascinating life." Pub Wkly

Includes bibliographical references (pages 345-373) and index.

Barr, Nevada

Barr, Nevada. **Seeking** enlightenment--hat by hat; a skeptic's path to religion. Putnam 2003 222p $21.95; pa $13 **92**

1. Authors 2. Park rangers 3. Mystery writers

ISBN 0-399-15057-9; 0-425-19603-8 pa

LC 2003-43101

The author "charts the course of her spiritual evolution, how she sought to understand the many aspects of spiritual life, from forgiveness ('a sigh of relief on which the memory of evil is breathed out') to pain ('it is a duty to relieve our own pain') to commitment ('not a contract with the world but with the self'). Barr's account of her transformation from nonbeliever to committed churchgoer—but one who maintains a healthy sense of doubt even as she prays and attends Bible studies—is moving but never saccharine." Booklist

Barringer, James A.

Maynard, Joyce. The **best** of us; a memoir. Joyce Maynard. Bloomsbury USA 2017 viii, 437 p.p (hardcover) $27 **92**

1. Women authors -- United States -- Biography 2. Authors, American -- 20th century -- Biography 3. Pancreas -- Cancer -- Patients -- United States -- Biography

ISBN 9781635570366; 9781635570342

LC 2016058363

This book, by Joyce Maynard, is "a memoir about discovering strength in the midst of great loss. . . . Maynard met the first true partner she had ever known. Jim wore a rakish hat over a good head of hair; he

asked real questions and gave real answers; he loved to see Joyce shine, both in and out of the spotlight; and he didn't mind the mess she made in the kitchen. He was not the husband Joyce imagined, but he quickly became the partner she had always dreamed of." (Publisher's note)

"This haunting story, penned by a master wordsmith, is a reminder to savor every loved one and every day." Booklist

Barthelme, Donald

Daugherty, Tracy. **Hiding** man; a biography of Donald Barthelme. St. Martin's Press 2008 581p il $35   **92**

1. Authors 2. Novelists 3. Authors, American 4. Short story writers

ISBN 978-0-312-37868-4; 0-312-37868-8

LC 2008-29881

"Not dwelling on Barthelme's dark soul or his uneven work, Daugherty has created a convincing narrative from a life that was engaged, passionate and maybe even fulfilled." N Y Times Book Rev

Includes bibliographical references (p. 549-556)

Bartholomew, Geoffrey R.

Bartholomew, Rafe. **Two** and two; McSorley's, my dad, and me. Rafe Bartholomew. Little, Brown & Co. 2017 276 p. illustrations (chiefly color) (hardcover) $27   **92**

1. Bars 2. Bartenders 3. Father-son relationship 4. Fathers and sons 5. New York (N.Y.) -- History 6. Bartenders -- United States -- Biography 7. Historic sites -- New York (State) -- New York 8. McSorley's Old Ale House (New York, N.Y.) -- Anecdotes 9. Bars (Drinking establishments) -- New York (State) -- New York -- History

ISBN 9780316231596; 9780316365840

LC 2016959023

This book, by Rafe Bartholomew, is "a deeply stirring memoir of fathers, sons, and the oldest bar in New York City. Since it opened in 1854, McSorley's Old Ale House has been a New York institution. . . . But in addition to the bar's rich history, McSorley's is home to a deeply personal story about . . . Rafe Bartholomew, the writer who grew up in the . . . pub, and his father, Geoffrey "Bart" Bartholomew, a career bartender who has been working the taps for forty-five years." (Publisher's note)

"Bartholomew does both his father and McSorley's proud with this touching, redolent memoir." Kirkus

Bartholomew, Rafe

Bartholomew, Rafe. **Two** and two; McSorley's, my dad, and me. Rafe Bartholomew. Little, Brown & Co. 2017 276 p. illustrations (chiefly color) (hardcover) $27   **92**

1. Bars 2. Bartenders 3. Father-son relationship 4. Fathers and sons 5. New York (N.Y.) -- History 6. Bartenders -- United States -- Biography 7. Historic sites -- New York (State) -- New York 8. McSorley's Old Ale House (New York, N.Y.) -- Anecdotes 9. Bars (Drinking establishments) -- New York (State) -- New York -- History

ISBN 9780316231596; 9780316365840

LC 2016959023

This book, by Rafe Bartholomew, is "a deeply stirring memoir of fathers, sons, and the oldest bar in New York City. Since it opened in 1854, McSorley's Old Ale House has been a New York institution. . . . But in addition to the bar's rich history, McSorley's is home to a deeply personal story about . . . Rafe Bartholomew, the writer who grew up in the . . . pub, and his father, Geoffrey "Bart" Bartholomew, a career bartender who has been working the taps for forty-five years." (Publisher's note)

"Bartholomew does both his father and McSorley's proud with this touching, redolent memoir." Kirkus

Bartolo, Pietro, 1956-

Bartolo, Pietro. **Tears** of salt; a doctor's story. Pietro Bartolo and Lidia Tilotta; with the collaboration of Giacomo Bartolo; translated from the Italian by Chenxin Jiang. W W Norton & Co Inc 2018 205 p. map (hardcover) $25.95 **92**

1. Refugees 2. Physicians -- Biography 3. Immigrants -- Italy -- Lampedusa 4. Physicians -- Italy -- Lampedusa -- Biography 5. Immigrants -- Services for -- Italy -- Lampedusa

ISBN 9780393651294; 0393651282; 9780393651287

LC 2017051956

This autobiography, by Pietro Bartolo, with Lidia Tilotta, is a "moving account of his life and work . . . [for refugees]. With quiet dignity and an unshakable moral center, he tells unforgettable tales of pain and hope, stories of those who didn't make it and those who did. 'Tears of Salt' is a lasting work of literature and an intimate portrait of a remarkable man whose inspiring message rings clear: "We can't and we won't be governed by our fears." (Publisher's note)

"In this moving account of attending to victims of war, Italian physician Bartolo makes an impassioned plea for more public awareness of and effective humanitarian solutions for refugees from Africa and the Middle East." Pub Wkly

Basie, Count, 1904-1984

Basie, Count. **Good** morning blues: the autobiography of Count Basie; as told to Albert Murray. Da Capo Press 1995 399p il pa $17.95 **92**

1. Pianists 2. Jazz musicians 3. African American musicians 4. Band leaders

ISBN 0-306-81107-3

LC 94-44697

"Basie pays tribute to his colleagues and managers (and to John Hammond for 'discovering' him), but does not hesitate to discuss their weaknesses and short-comings; his language is direct and earthy. Although some of the book reads more like a catalogue or itinerary than an autobiography, it will have strong appeal for jazz buffs and fans of the late bandleader." Publ Wkly

Bass, Rick, 1958-

Bass, Rick. **Why** I came West. Houghton Mifflin Co. 2008 238p $24; pa $14.95 **92**

1. Authors 2. Novelists 3. Geologists 4. Conservationists 5. Literary landmarks 6. Essayists 7. West (U.S.) 8. Authors, American 9. Writers on nature 10. Short story writers

ISBN 978-0-618-59675-1; 0-618-59675-5; 978-0-5472-3771-8 pa; 0-5472-3771-5 pa

LC 2007-30660

Bass "tells the tale of his apprenticeship to literature and the place that has defined his life for the past two decades, Montana's Yaak Valley. Bass looks back to his Houston childhood, Utah college years, and work as an oil geologist in Mississippi, searching for clues to his love-at-first sight response to the Yaak. As he describes his deep immersion in this bountiful land as a hunter, hiker, artist, and environmentalist, he . . . shares his anguish over the clear-cutting of woods, and chronicles the hard work of wilderness advocacy and the virulent hatred it arouses. Versed in paradox, Bass is bracing in his candor about how difficult it will be to change our destructive ways, and incandescent in his reasoned call to preserve the few remaining unspoiled places." Booklist

Bastianich, Lidia Matticchio

Bastianich, Lidia Matticchio. **My** American dream; a life of love, family, and food. Lidia Matticchio Bastianich. Alfred A. Knopf 2018 viii, 339 p.p illustrations (hardcover) $28.95 **92**

1. Italian cooking 2. Cooks -- United States -- Biography 3. Cooking, Italian 4. Restaurateurs -- United States -- Biography 5. World War, 1939-1945 -- Refugees -- Istria (Croatia and Slovenia) -- Biography

ISBN 9781524731618; 9781524731625

LC 2017045478

This memoir, by Lidia Matticchio Bastianich, "begins with her upbringing in Pula, a formerly Italian city turned Yugoslavian under Tito's communist regime. . . . When the communist regime begins investigating the family, they flee to Trieste, Italy, where they spend two years in a refugee camp waiting for visas to enter the United States--an experience that will shape Lidia for the rest of her life." (Publisher's note)

"A warm story of a life buoyed by resilience, determination, love of family, and food." Kirkus

Bauman, Jeff

Witter, Bret. **Stronger**; Jeff Bauman, with Bret Witter. Grand Central Publishing 2014 244 p. illustrations (hardcover) $26 **92**

1. Terrorism victims 2. Amputees -- Rehabilitation 3. Boston Marathon Bombing, Boston, Mass., 2013

ISBN 1455584371; 9781455584376

LC 2013050788

Jeff Bauman was next to the bomb when it exploded at the Boston Marathon on April 15, 2013. Pictures of him flooded the media as he became the iconic image of the tragedy: Bauman in a wheel chair, legs missing from the knees down. The following weeks of speculation and the eventual police shootout with the Tsarnaev brothers is well documented. Bauman and co-author Bret Witter are telling a different story, a personal story. . . . Bauman does not sugar coat the heroism of his situation. He's upfront about the difficulties of amputation, of his family adjusting to new realities, [and] of being a sudden media personality." (Publishers Weekly)

"Only a misanthrope would fail to be moved by Bauman's guileless narration of the horrors of rehabilitation or his frustration with learning to live with his new prosthetic legs. This is the simple story of one decent guy who fights hard to stay strong in the face of adversity." LJ

Baylor, Elgin

Baylor, Elgin. **Hang** time; my life in basketball. Elgin Baylor with Alan Eisenstock. Houghton Mifflin Harcourt 2018 320 p. (hardback) $27 **92**

1. Basketball 2. African Americans -- Biography 3. Basketball players -- United States -- Biography 4. African American basketball players -- Biography

ISBN 9780544617056

LC 2017045607

In this memoir, written with Alan Eisenstock, Elgin Baylor describes his "epic all-star career in the NBA--during which he transformed basketball from a horizontal game to a vertical one--and his fights against racism during his career as a player and as general manager of the LA Clippers under the infamous Donald Sterling. . . . He's played with the legends, lived with them, and knows more about the NBA than anyone living, and is finally ready to set the record straight." (Publisher's note)

Beach, Sylvia

The **letters** of Sylvia Beach; edited by Keri Walsh; with a foreword by Noël Riley Fitch. Columbia University Press 2010 347p il $29.95 **92**

1. Booksellers and bookselling 2. Memoirists 3. Booksellers 4. Shakespeare and Company 5. Booksellers and bookselling -- France -- Paris 6. Paris (France) -- Intellectual life -- 20th century

ISBN 978-0-231-14536-7; 0-231-14535-5

LC 2009-45434

"Beach's story has been told before. . . . [But these letters] have an unvarnished charm all their own. Written to friends, writers, customers and family members, they depict a witty and resourceful woman struggling to keep her business, her writers and her precarious existence afloat." N Y Times Book Rev

Includes bibliographical references

Beah, Ishmael

★ Beah, Ishmael, 1980- A **long** way gone; memoirs of a boy soldier. Farrar, Straus & Giroux 2007 229p map pa $12; $22   **92**

1. Refugees 2. Soldiers 3. Children and war 4. Memoirists 5. Social activists 6. Sierra Leone -- History -- Civil War, 1991- 7. Sierra Leone -- History -- Civil War, 1991-2002

ISBN 0-374-53126-9 pa; 0-374-95191-8; 978-0-374-10523-5; 978-0-374-53126-3 pa

LC 2006-17101

Alex Awards (2008)

The author writes about his experiences as a recruit in the Sierra Leone Army.

"In 1993, when the author was twelve, rebel forces attacked his home town, in Sierra Leone, and he was separated from his parents. For months, he straggled through the war-torn countryside, starving and terrified, until he was taken under the wing of a Shakespeare-spouting lieutenant in the government army. Soon, he was being fed amphetamines and trained to shoot an AK-47. . . . Beah's memoir documents his transformation from a child into a hardened, brutally efficient soldier who high-fived his fellow-recruits after they slaughtered their enemies—often boys their own age—and who 'felt no pity for anyone.'" New Yorker

Beasley, Sandra

Beasley, Sandra. **Don't** kill the birthday girl; tales from an allergic life. Crown Publishers 2011 229p il $23; ebook $11.99   **92**

1. Poets 2. Authors 3. Food allergy

ISBN 978-0-307-58811-1; 978-0-307-58813-5 ebook

LC 2010043724

"If you didn't have sympathy for this relatively new generation of sufferers, you will after Beasley's book. . . . The emotional stuff is the best—from worrying about kissing boys who may have eaten forbidden foods, to considering the implications of having kids who'll have to wash their hands before hugging their mother." Maclean's

Beatty, Warren, 1937-

Biskind, Peter. **Star**; how Warren Beatty seduced America. Simon & Schuster 2010 627p il $30   **92**

1. Actors 2. Motion picture directors 3. Motion picture producers

ISBN 978-0-7432-4658-3; 0-7432-4658-6

LC 2009-22225

"Biskind brings his historian's acumen to bear on the production of era-defining triumphs like Bonnie and Clyde (1967), Shampoo (1975) and Reds (1981), as well as notorious flops like Ishtar (1987), Love Affair (1994) and Town & Country (2001), and his accounts are full of juicy gossip and intriguing insights into the actor's psychology. . . . A gripping portrait of a difficult talent." Kirkus

Includes bibliographical references

Beauvoir, Simone de, 1908-1986

Bair, Deirdre. **Simone** de Beauvoir; a biography. Summit Bks. 1990 718p il hardcover o.p. pa $31.95   **92**

1. Authors 2. Novelists 3. Dramatists 4. Philosophers 5. Essayists

6. Feminists 7. Biographers 8. Nonfiction writers 9. Short story writers 10. Nobel laureates for literature

ISBN 0-671-74180-2 pa

LC 89-22029

"Bair's biography of the French author, philosopher, and feminist aims to restore the balance between interest in de Beauvoir's personal life—as the lifelong companion of Jean-Paul Sartre and sometime lover of Nelson Algren—and the question of her achievements as a writer and thinker." Booklist

Includes bibliographical references

Becker, Suzy

Becker, Suzy. **I** had brain surgery, what's your excuse? an illustrated memoir. Workman Pub 2003 282p il $19.95   **92**

1. Authors 2. Humorists 3. Cartoonists 4. Illustrators 5. Memoirists 6. AIDS activists 7. Social activists 8. Nonfiction writers

ISBN 0-7611-2478-0

LC 2003-60039

Becker "was suffering seizures but didn't tell anyone until a friend witnessed an incident. Eventually, she was scheduled for brain surgery to remove a tumor. Writing with the dry sense of humor that some of us rely on to make it through situations, Becker recalls her reactions to her medical problems, from liking the first doctor who gave her no bad news ('just stress') to the terror of the eventual diagnosis. Her descriptions of the surgery and its dreadful, but temporary, effects on her ability to speak, read, write, and draw make for especially compelling reading. . . . Becker has turned one person's experience into a universal story of family, healing, and the return to creativity." Libr J

Beckett, Samuel, 1906-1989

Gordon, Lois G. The **world** of Samuel Beckett, 1906-1946; {by} Lois Gordon. Yale Univ. Press 1996 250p il $50; pa $16.95   **92**

1. Poets 2. Authors 3. Novelists 4. Dramatists 5. Short story writers 6. Nobel laureates for literature

ISBN 0-300-06409-8; 0-300-07495-6 pa

LC 95-22851

Gordon "examines the first 40 years of the playwright/novelist's 83-year life, which includes periods in Ireland, where he was born; in Paris, where he spent much of his life; and in London, Germany, and other parts of France. . . . Gordon has been thorough in her research and careful in her presentation." Choice

Includes bibliographical references

Rosset, Barney. **Dear** Mr. Beckett; the Samuel Beckett file. Barney Rosset; foreword by Edward Beckett, preface by Paul Auster, edited by Lois Oppenheim, curated by Astrid Myers Rosset. Opus Books 2016 473 p. illustrations (Author file series) $32.95   **92**

1. Authors, Irish 2. Literature, Modern -- History and criticism

ISBN 1623160707; 9781623160708

This book, with a preface by Paul Auster, a foreword by Edward Beckett, edited by Lois Oppenheim, and curated by Astrid Myers Rosset, presents "letters, contracts, photos, interviews, speeches, reviews and memorabilia most of which has never before been made public [and] a rare personal and professional friendship unfolds between [Samuel Beckett and Barney Roset]; through their embrace, they shifted and turned the tide of literature in America." (Publisher's note)

Includes bibliographical references and index.

Beecher, Henry Ward, 1813-1887

★ Applegate, Debby. The **most** famous man in America; the biography of Henry Ward Beecher. Doubleday 2006 529p il map $27.95 **92**

1. Clergy 2. Nonfiction writers
ISBN 0-385-51396-8; 978-0-385-51396-8

LC 2005-54842

This is a biography of the American clergyman.

"By illuminating Beecher's position in history, Applegate has produced a biography worthy of its subject." N Y Times Book Rev

Includes bibliographical references

Beethoven, Ludwig van, 1770-1827

Morris, Edmund, 1940- **Beethoven**: the universal composer. HarperCollins Publishers 2005 243p (Eminent lives) $21.95; pa $13.99 **92**

1. Composers
ISBN 0-06-075974-7; 978-0-06-075974-2; 9780060759759

LC 2006-274925

This is a biography of the German composer.

The author "clearly admires his subject not only for the work but also for his constant fight against the odds, and he has written an ideal biography for the general reader." Publ Wkly

Includes bibliographical references

Suchet, John. **Beethoven**; the man revealed. John Suchet. Grove Press 2013 xiii, 273 p.p illustrations (chiefly color) (hbk.) $30 **92**

1. Composers, German 2. Composers -- Biography 3. Composers -- Germany -- Biography
ISBN 080212206X; 9780802122063

LC 2012518710

This book, by John Suchet, is a biography of composer Ludwig von Beethoven. "Suchet illuminates the composer's difficult childhood, his struggle to maintain friendships and romances, his ungovernable temper, his obsessive efforts to control his nephew's life, and the excruciating decline of his hearing." It also discusses "the landmark events in Beethoven's career--from his competitive encounters with Mozart to the circumstances surrounding the creation of the well-known 'Fur Elise' and 'Moonlight Sonata.'" (Publisher's note)

"For the many readers lacking the proper background in musical theory, British broadcaster and Beethoven authority Suchet's explanations of Beethoven's music sing to us almost as if we could hear it." Kirkus

Includes bibliographical references and index

★ Swafford, Jan. **Beethoven**; anguish and triumph: a biography. Jan Swafford. Houghton Mifflin Harcourt 2014 1104 p. illustrations $40 **92**

1. Composers, German 2. Composers -- Biography 3. Composers -- Germany -- Biography
ISBN 061805474X; 9780618054749

LC 2014011681

In this book, music historian Jan Swafford "mines sources never before used in English-language biographies to reanimate the revolutionary ferment of Enlightenment-era Bonn, where Beethoven grew up and imbibed the ideas that would shape all of his future work. Swafford then tracks his subject to Vienna, capital of European music, where Beethoven built his career in the face of critical incomprehension, crippling ill health, romantic rejection, and . . . his ever-encroaching deafness." (Publisher's note)

"Rich in biographical detail, the volume contains revealing excerpts from many of Beethoven's letters and from the written observations of

his visitors and family; it also contains detailed analyses of many of his most notable works." Kirkus

Includes bibliographical references and index

Belafonte, Harry

Belafonte, Harry. **My** song; a memoir. with Michael Shnayerson. Alfred A. Knopf 2011 469p il **92**

1. Actors 2. Singers 3. African American singers 4. Social activists
ISBN 9780307272263; 9780307700483

LC 2011014602

The popular singer and former UNICEF Goodwill Ambassador shares the story of his life and career, from his impoverished childhood in Harlem and Jamaica and his racial barrier-breaking career to his commitment to numerous civil causes.

The author "covers his public career as an American entertainment icon (which solidified with his 1956 album, Calypso) and his interactions with many politicians and celebrities, e.g., Paul Robeson, Poitier, Marlon Brando, and Robert Kennedy, among many others. How these different strands interweave—the anger generated by the poverty and racial discrimination of his early years, the socially conscious reformer, and the well-respected entertainer—make for a potent memoir of our times." Libr J

Smith, Judith E. **Becoming** Belafonte; black artist, public radical. by Judith E. Smith. University of Texas Press 2014 368 p. (Discovering America) (cloth: alkaline paper) $35 **92**

1. Black musicians 2. Actors, Black -- United States -- Biography 3. Musicians, Black -- United States -- Biography 4. African American civil rights workers -- Biography
ISBN 0292729146; 9780292729148

LC 2014006424

This book, by Judith E. Smith, part of the "Discovering America" series, is a biography of the African American musician Henry Belafonte. The author "sets Belafonte's compelling story within a history of American race relations, black theater and film history, McCarthy-era hysteria, and the challenges of introducing multifaceted black culture in a moment of expanding media possibilities and constrained political expression." (Publisher's note)

Includes bibliographical references and index

Bell, Alexander Graham, 1847-1922

★ Gray, Charlotte. **Reluctant** genius; Alexander Graham Bell and the passion for invention. Arcade Pub. 2006 466p il map $29.95 **92**

1. Inventors 2. Teachers of the deaf 3. Telecommunications executives
ISBN 1-55970-809-3; 978-1-55970-809-8

LC 2005-29609

The author "recounts both the inventor of the telephone's creation of the device and the projects he pursued once his future was secured. . . . Combining the household history of the Bells with that of Alexander's successive enthusiasms (Helen Keller, kites, airplanes, hydrocraft), Gray fairly portrays the attractions and exasperations of Bell's life." Booklist

Includes bibliographical references

Bell, Gertrude Margaret Lowthian, 1868-1926

Howell, Georgina. **Gertrude** Bell; queen of the desert, shaper of nations. Farrar, Straus and Giroux 2007 481p il map hardcover o.p. pa $16 **92**

1. Explorers 2. Travelers 3. Archeologists 4. Archaeologists 5. Women -- Travel 6. Biography, Individual 7. Middle East -- History

-- 20th century 8. Great Britain -- Colonies -- Administration -- History -- 20th century
ISBN 0-374-16162-3; 0-374-53135-8 pa; 978-0-374-16162-0; 978-0-374-53135-5 pa

LC 2006-29994

First published 2006 in the United Kingdom with title: Daughter of the desert

This is a biography of the British archaeologist and author of Desert and the Sown (1907) and Persian Pictures (1928). Bell "advised the Viceroy of India; then, as an army major, she traveled to the front lines in Mesopotamia. There she supported the creation of an autonomous Arab nation for Iraq, promoting and manipulating the election of King Faisal to the throne and helping to draw the borders of the fledgling state." (Publisher's note) Index.

"Bell's role in the creation of Iraq and the placement of Faisal upon the throne, is fully detailed. . . . But the strength and delight of Howell's superb biography is in the fullness with which Bell's character is drawn." Publ Wkly

Includes bibliographical references

Bellamy, Richard

Stein, Judith E., 1943- **Eye** of the sixties; Richard Bellamy and the Transformation of Modern Art. Judith E. Stein. Farrar, Straus & Giroux 2016 384 p. (hardback) $27   92
1. Art dealers 2. Art -- 20th century 3. Art dealers -- United States -- Biography 4. Art and society -- United States -- History -- 20th century
ISBN 9780374151324; 9780374715205

LC 2015036468

This book, by Judith E. Stein, focuses on "Richard Bellamy . . . one of the first advocates of pop art, minimalism, and conceptual art. Based on decades of research and hundreds of interviews with artists, friends, dealers, and lovers, . . . 'Eye of the Sixties' recovers the elusive Bellamy and tells the story of a counterculture that became the mainstream." (Publisher's note)

"This is an endearing and illuminating work of biography. A shadowy figure of the 1960s art world is gloriously revealed." Kirkus

Includes bibliographical references and index

Belle, Dido Elizabeth, 1761-1804

Byrne, Paula. **Belle**; the slave daughter and the Lord Chief Justice. Paula Byrne. Harper Perennial 2014 304 p. illustrations (paperback) $14.99   92
1. Racially mixed people 2. Great Britain -- Race relations 3. Great Britain -- History -- 18th century 4. Slaves -- England -- Biography 5. Nobility -- England -- Biography
ISBN 0062310771; 9780062310774

LC 2014007447

"From . . . biographer Paula Byrne, the . . . tale that inspired the major motion picture 'Belle' (May 2014) starring Tom Wilkinson, Miranda Richardson, Emily Watson, Penelope Wilton, and Matthew Goode--a stunning story of the first mixed-race girl introduced to high society England and raised as a lady. . . . Growing up in his lavish estate, Dido was raised as a sister and companion to her white cousin, Elizabeth." (Publisher's note)

"Byrne brings to this brief history an eye for telling details of daily life, slaveholders' unthinkable cruelty, and the fervent work of a few good men and women who changed their world." Kirkus

Includes bibliographical references

Bellow, Saul, 1915-2005

Bellow, Saul, 1915-2005. **Saul** Bellow; letters. edited by Benjamin Taylor. Viking 2010 571p il $35   92

1. Authors 2. Novelists 3. Dramatists 4. Authors, American 5. Short story writers 6. Biography, Individual 7. Nobel laureates for literature
ISBN 978-0-670-02221-2; 0-670-02221-7

LC 2010-22395

"Collected for the first time, Bellow's letters offer an alluring backstory to the Chicago-bred imagination that created The Adventures of Augie March, Herzog, Humboldt's Gift and won the Nobel Prize. Like the fiction, the missives can be brilliant, glistening, scathing, boring, funny, generous, probing and always genuinely human. . . . The correspondents throughout are friends, lovers, wives, agents and publishers. Among the dozens of major literary figures with whom Bellow corresponded were William Faulkner, Bernard Malamud, Edmund Wilson, John Berryman, Ralph Ellison, Robert Penn Warren, Philip Roth and Martin Amis. While nothing can substitute for a Bellow novel, Letters offers a strong salve to those who miss his familiar voice. The range of interests, battles fought and art created reflected here is Olympian. Yet the cauldron for much of it was the everyday streets of Chicago." Chicago Sun-Times

Leader, Zachary. The **Life** of Saul Bellow; to fame and fortune, 1915-1964. by Zachary Leader. Alfred A. Knopf 2015 832 p. 24 plates; illustrations (hardback) $40   92
1. American authors -- Biography 2. Novelists, American -- 20th century -- Biography
ISBN 0307268837; 9780307268839; 9780307388933

LC 2014020092

This book, by Zachary Leader, is the first of a two-volume biography of the writer Saul Bellow. This volume "traces Bellow's Russian roots; his birth and early childhood in Quebec; his years in Chicago; his travels in Mexico, Europe, and Israel; the first three of his five marriages; and the novels from 'Dangling Man' and 'The Adventures of Augie March' to the best-selling 'Herzog.'" (Publisher's note)

"To be sure, offended friends and former wives have interpreted Bellow's literary treatment of their life facts as mean-spirited and vindictive. But millions of appreciative readers recognize in Bellow's work the grit of a James T. Farrell and the exuberance of a Charles Dickens. A must-read for students of American literature." Booklist

Includes bibliographical references and index

Leader, Zachary. The **life** of Saul Bellow; love and strife, 1965-2005. Zachary Leader. Alfred A. Knopf 2018 784 p. (hardcover) $40   92
1. American novelists 2. Novelists, American -- 20th century -- Biography
ISBN 9781101875162

LC 2017053381

"This masterful account of the second half of [Saul] Bellow's life from [author Zachary] Leader . . . is impressive in both content and accessibility. The biography opens at an exciting point: Bellow, with the publication of the bestselling and critically acclaimed Herzog, catapults to the highest echelons of literary success. Leader combines Bellow's life story with close readings of his major . . . texts, highlighting the autobiographical content of Bellow's fiction." (Publishers Weekly)

"This is biography at its best and will appeal widely." Library Journal
Includes bibliographical references and index

Benga, Ota

Newkirk, Pamela. **Spectacle**; the astonishing life of Ota Benga. Pamela Newkirk. HarperCollins 2015 320 p. illustrations (hardcover) $25.99   92
1. Pygmies -- United States -- Biography 2. Human zoos -- United States -- History -- 20th century

ISBN 006220100X; 9780062201003

NAACP Image Award: Outstanding Literary Work- Nonfiction (2016)

In this book, by Pamela Newkirk, "an award-winning journalist reveals a little-known and shameful episode in American history, when an African man was used as a human zoo exhibit--a shocking story of racial prejudice, science, and tragedy in the early years of the twentieth century." (Publisher's note)

"Newkirk gives us more than the tragic story of one Congolese man. She offers a look into the history of American eugenics and the concepts of racial anthropology that have served as the foundation for racial intolerance for generations. Benga's story is one part of a bigger problem--a problem that continues to exist--and Newkirk doesn't allow us to forget him. Nor should she." LJ

Bergen, Candice, 1946-

Bergen, Candice, 1946- A **fine** romance; Candice Bergen. Simon & Schuster 2015 368 p. 16 plates; illustrations (hardcover) $28   **92**

1. Marriage 2. Actresses 3. Actors -- United States -- Biography
ISBN 1476746095; 9780684808277; 9781476746098
LC 2014029293

In this memoir, actress Candice Bergen "describes her first marriage at age thirty-four to famous French director Louis Malle; her overpowering love for her daughter, Chloe; the unleashing of her inner comic with 'Murphy Brown'; her trauma over Malle's death; her joy at finding new love; and her pride at watching Chloe blossom." (Publisher's note)

"Witty and poignant and touching upon the many phases and challenges of daily existence, this book will appeal to a wide audience, especially those who are familiar with Bergen's work. For circulating libraries and entertainment collections." Library Journal

Bergman, Ingrid, 1915-1982

Spoto, Donald. **Notorious**; the life of Ingrid Bergman. Da Capo Press 2001 474p il pa $22   **92**

1. Actors
ISBN 978-0-306-81030-5; 0-306-81030-1
First published 1997 by HarperCollins

The author's "perceptions about Bergman personally and professionally are keen, and the narrative reads like a full-bodied story, not just a listing of professional credits and personal landmarks." Booklist

Includes bibliographical references

Berlin, Lucia

★ Berlin, Lucia, 1936-2004. **Welcome** home; a memoir with selected photographs and letters. Lucia Berlin. Farrar, Straus & Giroux 2018 160 p. $24   **92**

1. Diaries 2. Women authors -- United States -- Biography
ISBN 0374287597; 9780374287597

This book, by Lucia Berlin, is an essential nonfiction companion to . . . [her] stories. . . . From Alaska to Argentina, Kentucky to Mexico, New York City to Chile, Berlin's world was wide. And the writing here is, as we've come to expect, dazzling. She describes the places she lived and the people she knew with all the style and wit and heart and humor that readers fell in love with in her stories." (Publisher's note)

"An excellent start to understanding a writer and her work." Kirkus Reviews

Bernanke, Ben

Bernanke, Ben, 1953- The **Courage** to Act; A Memoir of a Crisis and Its Aftermath. by Ben S. Bernanke. W W Norton & Co Inc. 2015 448 p. 32 plates; ills; portraits $35   **92**

1. Global Financial Crisis, 2008-2009 2. United States -- Economic conditions
ISBN 039324721X; 9780393247213

This memoir, by former chair of the Federal Reserve Ben S. Bernanke, is an "unrivaled look at the fight to save the American economy. . . . Working with two U.S. presidents, and under fire from a fractious Congress and a public incensed by behavior on Wall Street, the Fed—alongside colleagues in the Treasury Department—successfully stabilized a teetering financial system." (Publisher's note)

"One of the finest memoirs on the financial crisis to date, this title belongs in all libraries with holdings in economic and social history. Readers desiring further readings on the economic crisis might consult Alan S. Blinder's After the Music Stopped." LJ

Bernard, Pierre, 1875-1955

Love, Robert. The **Great** Oom; the improbable birth of yoga in America. Viking 2010 402p il   **92**

1. Yoga 2. Yogis 3. United States -- Religion
ISBN 067002175X; 9780670021758
LC 2009044784

This book focuses on Pierre Bernard's involvement in the popularization of Yoga in the United States. Bibliography. Index.

A "history of yoga's early days in America. The spiritual discipline that has colonized America's gyms and trendy loft spaces was once a fringe practice, its advocates treated as charlatans and, occasionally, criminals. Yoga's cultural rise is a story of scandal, financial shenanigans, bodily discipline, oversize egos and bizarre love triangles, with a few performing elephants thrown in for good measure. Mr. Love tells his story through the life of one of yoga's earliest promoters, Pierre Bernard—known as the 'Great Oom'—a zany man whose talent for self-invention rivaled that of P.T. Barnum." Wall Street J

Includes bibliographical references

Bernini, Gian Lorenzo, 1598-1680

Mormando, Franco. **Bernini**; his life and his Rome. University of Chicago Press 2011 429p il map pa $35   **92**

1. Artists 2. Sculptors 3. Architects 4. Artists, Italian
ISBN 978-0-226-53852-5; 0-226-53852-4
LC 2011023774

In this biography "of Baroque sculptor Gian Lorenzo Bernini since his death in 1680, . . . Mormando constructs a comprehensive, extraordinarily vivid portrait of the sculptor known as 'the Michelangelo of his age.' . . . Of great interest to general readers seeking a well-researched, highly readable portrait of the sculptor and those interested in the cultural history of baroque Rome." Publ Wkly

Includes bibliographical references

Bernstein, Leonard, 1918-1990

★ Bernstein, Burton. **Leonard** Bernstein; American original; how a modern renaissance man transformed music and the world during his New York Philharmonic years, 1943-1976. [by] Burton Bernstein and Barbara B. Haws. HarperCollins 2008 223p il $29.95   **92**

1. Composers 2. Musicians 3. Conductors (Music) 4. New York Philharmonic 5. Composers -- United States
ISBN 978-0-06-153786-8; 0-06-153786-1
LC 2008-13702

"A flat-out wonderful book." Booklist

Harmon, Charlie. **On** the road & off the record with Leonard Bernstein; my years with the exasperating genius. by Charlie Harmon; foreword by Harold Prince. Charlesbridge 2018

272 p. (reinforced for library use) $24.99   **92**
1. Musicians -- United States -- Biography
ISBN 9781623545277; 9781632892195

LC 2017059790

This book, by Charlie Harmon, foreword by Harold Prince, presents a biography of musician Leonard Bernstein. "Harmon was hired to manage the day-to-day parts of Bernstein's life. There was one additional responsibility: make sure Bernstein met the deadline for an opera commission. But things kept getting in the way." (Publisher's note)
On the road and off the record with Leonard Bernstein

Shawn, Allen. **Leonard** Bernstein; An American Musician. Allen Shawn. Yale University Press 2014 360 p. (Jewish lives) (cloth: alk. paper) $25   **92**
1. Composers -- United States 2. Musicians -- United States
ISBN 0300144288; 9780300144284

LC 2014941713

This book, by Allen Shawn, is a biography on musician Leonard Bernstein. "[T]he breadth of Bernstein's musical composition is explored, through the spectacular range of music he composed-from 'West Side Story' to 'Kaddish' to 'A Quiet Place' and beyond-and through his intensely public role as an internationally celebrated conductor." Publisher's note
"Shawn gives some space to Bernstein's critics, as well, and he does not neglect the composer's final sad slide. A nearly impossible task, recording this lush life, but Shawn helps us comprehend the magic." Kirkus

Berra, Yogi, 1925-2015

★ Barra, Allen. **Yogi** Berra; eternal Yankee. W. W. Norton & Co. 2009 451p il $27.95   **92**
1. Baseball players 2. Baseball coaches 3. Baseball managers 4. Baseball -- Biography 5. New York Yankees (Baseball team)
ISBN 978-0-393-06233-5; 0-393-06233-3

LC 2008-45799

"Barra brings to his sporting version of the Everyman story an encyclopedic knowledge and warm understanding of the game of baseball; meticulous research into business, sociology, and history; and a fluid writing style. . . . Baseball biography taken to a higher level." Booklist
Includes bibliographical references

Bettencourt, Liliane

Sancton, Tom. The **Bettencourt** affair; the world's richest woman and the scandal that rocked Paris. Tom Sancton. Dutton 2017 xv, 396 p.p illustrations, map (hardcover) $28   **92**
1. Swindlers and swindling 2. Businesswomen -- Biography 3. L'Oréal (Firm) -- History 4. Older women -- France -- Biography 5. Billionaires -- France -- Biography 6. Businesswomen -- France -- Biography 7. Scandals -- France -- Paris -- History -- 21st century 8. Swindlers and swindling -- France -- Paris -- History -- 21st century
ISBN 1101984473; 9781101984475; 9781101984499; 9781101984482

LC 2016058788

This book, by Tom Sancton, uncovers "L'Oréal's . . . corporate history and buried World War II secrets. From the Right Bank mansions to the Left Bank artist havens; and from the Bettencourts' servant quarters to the office of President Nicolas Sarkozy. . . . It all began when Liliane met François-Marie Banier, an artist and photographer. . . . Over the next two decades, Banier was given hundreds of millions of dollars . . . . by Liliane. What, exactly, was their relationship?" (Publisher's note)
"A well-researched, crisply written, and entertaining story of family, greed, wealth, and the complex relations among them." Kirkus
Includes bibliographical references (pages 339-396).

Bewick, Thomas, 1753-1828

Uglow, Jennifer S. **Nature's** engraver; a life of Thomas Bewick. Farrar, Straus and Giroux 2007 458p il map $30 **92**
1. Artists 2. Woodcuts 3. Illustrators 4. Woodcut artists
ISBN 978-0-374-11236-3; 0-374-11236-3

LC 2006-31878

First published 2006 in the United Kingdom
"Biographies rarely afford a glimpse behind the office door, and it is the image of Bewick at work that is so valuable here. . . . It is hard to imagine a better biographer for this subject than Uglow, with her background in publishing and her knowledge of the North of England and the eighteenth century. It is also hard to imagine a more beautifully produced and illustrated book: scores of Bewick's frameless vignettes float frame-free and captionless throughout, appearing as they would have done in his own time, tale pieces every one." Times Lit Suppl
Includes bibliographical references

Bezos, Jeffrey

Davenport, Christian. The **space** barons; Jeff Bezos, Elon Musk, and the quest to colonize the cosmos. Christian Davenport. PublicAffairs 2018 320 p. (hardcover) $28   **92**
1. Space industrialization 2. SpaceX (Firm) 3. Blue Origen (Firm) 4. Outer space -- Civilian use 5. Aerospace industries -- United States 6. Space industrialization -- United States 7. Industrialists -- United States -- Biography 8. Aerospace engineers -- United States -- Biography
ISBN 9781610398299

LC 2017053089

This book, by Christian Davenport, "is the story of a group of billionaire entrepreneurs who are pouring their fortunes into the epic resurrection of the American space program. . . . These Space Barons--most notably Elon Musk and Jeff Bezos, along with Richard Branson and Paul Allen--are using Silicon Valley-style innovation to dramatically lower the cost of space travel, and send humans even further than NASA has gone." (Publisher's note)
Includes bibliographical references and index

Bhutto, Benazir

★ Bhutto, Benazir. **Reconciliation**; Islam, democracy, and the West. HarperCollins 2008 328p $27.95   **92**
1. Prime ministers 2. Islam and politics 3. Political leaders 4. Prime ministers -- Pakistan 5. Pakistan -- Politics and government
ISBN 978-0-06-156758-2; 0-06-156758-2
This "is a book of enormous intelligence, courage and clarity. . . . Washington should arrange to have the portions of the book about Islam republished as a separate volume and translated into several languages. It would do more to win the battle of ideas within Islam than anything an American president could ever say." N Y Times Book Rev
Includes bibliographical references

Bialosky, Jill

Bialosky, Jill. **Poetry** will save your life; a memoir. by Jill Bialosky. Atria Books 2017 xvi, 222 p.p (hardcover) $24 **92**
1. Poetry 2. Bildungsromans 3. American poetry -- 21st century 4. Poets, American -- 20th century -- Biography
ISBN 9781451693218; 9781451693201; 1451693206

LC 2016056306

This book, by Jill Bialosky, is a "coming-of-age memoir organized around forty-three remarkable poems by poets such as Robert Frost, Emily Dickinson, Wallace Stevens and Sylvia Plath. . . . While Bialosky's personal stories animate each poem, they touch on many universal experiences, from the awkwardness of girlhood, to crises of faith and identity, from braving a new life in a foreign city to enduring the loss of a loved one, from becoming a parent to growing creatively as a poet and artist." (Publisher's note)

"With brief poet biographies, this is a resplendent and invaluable anthology and an involving, richly illuminating narrative." Booklist

Biden, Beau, 1969-2015

Biden, Joe. **Promise** me, Dad; a year of hope, hardship, and purpose. Joe Biden. Flatiron Books 2017 260 p. (hardcover) $27 **92**

    1. Father-son relationship 2. Vice-presidents -- United States 3. Vice-Presidents -- United States -- Biography 4. Fathers and sons -- United States -- Biography 5. Presidents -- United States -- Election -- 2016 6. Cancer -- Patients -- United States -- Biography 7. United States -- Politics and government -- 2009-2017

ISBN 9781250171672; 9781250171689; 1250171679

                        LC 2017041080

This book, by Joe Biden, is a "memoir about the year that would forever change both a family and a country. In November 2014, . . . the Biden family gathered on Nantucket for Thanksgiving. . . . But this year felt different. . . . Joe and Jill Biden's eldest son, Beau, had been diagnosed with a malignant brain tumor . . . and his survival was uncertain. . . . The year that followed . . . would be the most momentous and challenging in Joe Biden's extraordinary life and career." (Publisher's note)

"Written without an ounce of self-pity, it serves instead as an homage to a man Biden admired above all others and offers a passionate ray of hope to those who have suffered the loss of a loved one with the reassuring message that there is, indeed, a way through their grief." Booklist

Biden, Joseph R.

Biden, Joe. **Promise** me, Dad; a year of hope, hardship, and purpose. Joe Biden. Flatiron Books 2017 260 p. (hardcover) $27 **92**

    1. Father-son relationship 2. Vice-presidents -- United States 3. Vice-Presidents -- United States -- Biography 4. Fathers and sons -- United States -- Biography 5. Presidents -- United States -- Election -- 2016 6. Cancer -- Patients -- United States -- Biography 7. United States -- Politics and government -- 2009-2017

ISBN 9781250171672; 9781250171689; 1250171679

                        LC 2017041080

This book, by Joe Biden, is a "memoir about the year that would forever change both a family and a country. In November 2014, . . . the Biden family gathered on Nantucket for Thanksgiving. . . . But this year felt different. . . . Joe and Jill Biden's eldest son, Beau, had been diagnosed with a malignant brain tumor . . . and his survival was uncertain. . . . The year that followed . . . would be the most momentous and challenging in Joe Biden's extraordinary life and career." (Publisher's note)

"Written without an ounce of self-pity, it serves instead as an homage to a man Biden admired above all others and offers a passionate ray of hope to those who have suffered the loss of a loved one with the reassuring message that there is, indeed, a way through their grief." Booklist

Bierce, Ambrose, 1842-1914?

Morris, Roy. **Ambrose** Bierce; alone in bad company. Oxford University Press 1998 306p pa $19.95 **92**

    1. Authors 2. Journalists 3. Essayists 4. Authors, American 5. Short story writers

ISBN 0-19-512628-9

                        LC 98-33467

First published 1995 by Crown

"Mr. Morris's disturbing, vividly realized biography brings to life a haunted writer whose private torments mirrored a turbulent era." NY Times Book Rev

Includes bibliographical references

Bilal, Wafaa, 1966-

Bilal, Wafaa. **Shoot** an Iraqi; art, life and resistance under the gun. by Wafaa Bilal and Kari Lydersen. City Lights 2008 177p il pa $16.95 **92**

    1. Artists 2. Video artists 3. Performance artists 4. Iraq War, 2003-2011 -- Art and the war

ISBN 978-0-8728-6491-7; 0-8728-6491-X

                        LC 2008-20487

The creator of 'Domestic Tension,' an unsettling interactive performance piece that speaks to the horrors of life in a conflict zone, reveals his experiences growing up under Saddam Hussein's rule.

"A powerful and demanding read, that is, frankly, a literary punch to the gut." Booklist

Billy, the Kid

Gardner, Mark L. **To** hell on a fast horse; Billy the Kid, Pat Garrett, and the epic chase to justice in the Old West. William Morrow 2010 325p il $26.99 **92**

    1. Outlaws 2. Sheriffs

ISBN 978-0-06-136827-1; 0-06-136827-X

                        LC 2009025467

A "double biography of the iconic western outlaw Billy the Kid and Sheriff Pat Garrett. Maintaining an objective perspective on both men in a narrative closely tied to historic source materials, Gardner's quick-moving story follows events of the civil war in Lincoln County, New Mexico Territory in 1877–78, and the Kid's death-by-shooting at the hands of Garrett in 1881. . . . The final chapters describing Garrett as an old-style lawman in a postfrontier society, with interactions with President Theodore Roosevelt, serve to distinguish this book from other recent Kid biographies." Libr J

Includes bibligraphical references

  ★ Wallis, Michael. **Billy** the Kid; the endless ride. W.W. Norton & Co. 2007 328p il map $25.95 **92**

    1. Outlaws

ISBN 978-0-393-06068-3; 0-393-06068-3

                        LC 2006-101364

"Drawing on archival sources and interviews as well as documents and secondary works, Wallis digs beneath the surface, clearly identifying what is known or probable and presenting the reasonable alternatives for what is conjecture." Libr J

Includes bibliographical references

Bin Laden, Osama, 1957-2011

O'Neill, Robert. The **operator**; firing the shots that killed Osama bin Laden and my years as a SEAL Team warrior. Robert O'Neill. Scribner 2017 ix, 358 p.p illustrations (hardcover) $28 **92**

    1. Autobiographies 2. Terrorism -- Prevention 3. Afghan War, 2001- --- Personal narratives 4. Butte (Mont.) -- Biography 5. United States. Navy. SEALs -- Biography 6. Special operations (Military science) -- Pakistan 7. Afghan War, 2001- -- Personal narratives, American 8. United States. Navy. SEALs -- History -- 21st century 9. Afghan War, 2001- -- Commando operations -- United States 10. War on Terrorism, 2001-2009 -- Personal narratives, American 11. Special operations (Military science) -- United States -- History -- 21st century

ISBN 9781501145056; 9781501145032; 9781501145049

                        LC 2017007867

This autobiography "ranges across SEAL Team Operator Robert

O'Neill's awe-inspiring four-hundred-mission career, which included his involvement in attempts to rescue "Lone Survivor" Marcus Luttrell and abducted-by-Somali-pirates Captain Richard Phillips and which culminated in those famous three shots that dispatched the world's most wanted terrorist, Osama bin Laden." (Publisher's note)

Bingham, Hiram, 1875-1956

Heaney, Christopher. **Cradle** of gold; the story of Hiram Bingham, a real-life Indiana Jones, and the search for Machu Picchu. Palgrave Macmillan 2010 285p il $27   92

1. Incas 2. Explorers 3. Governors 4. Historians 5. Senators 6. Machu Picchu (Peru) 7. Peru -- Antiquities

ISBN 0-230-61169-9; 978-0-230-61169-6

LC 2009-38535

"On an archaeological trip to Peru on July 24, 1911, Hiram Bingham, an American explorer and history professor at Yale, happened upon the ruins of the Inca city of Machu Picchu. Although the site was already known to the local native people, Bingham made the Machu Picchu ruins famous and received acclaim as their 'discoverer.' Heaney presents a well-researched and very readable biography of Bingham from his childhood in Hawaii as the son of missionaries, through his education and careers as historian, educator, explorer, and finally politician. He probes the depths of Bingham's work and character, examining setbacks, scandals, and achievements and skillfully unraveling Bingham's role in the controversy that still exists today between the government of Peru and Yale University over the ownership of the Machu Picchu burials and artifacts." Libr J

Includes bibliographical references

Bingham, Millicent Todd, 1880-1968.

Dobrow, Julie. **After** Emily; two remarkable women and the legacy of America's greatest poet. Julie Dobrow. W W Norton & Co Inc 2018 384 p. $29.95   92

1. Friendship 2. Mother-daughter relationship 3. Dickinson, Emily, 1830-1886 -- Friends and associates 4. Dickinson, Emily, 1830-1886

ISBN 0393249263; 9780393249262

LC 2018016671

"Despite Emily Dickinson's world renown, the story of the two women most responsible for her initial posthumous publication--Mabel Loomis Todd and her daughter, Millicent Todd Bingham--has remained in the shadows of the archives. A rich and compelling portrait of women who refused to be confined by the social mores of their era, [Julie Dobrow's] 'After Emily' explores Mabel and Millicent's complex bond, as well as the powerful literary legacy they shared." (Publisher's note)

"Dobrow's intimate portrait of these artistically talented and intelligent women, based largely on their extensive, detailed diaries and correspondence, reveals fallible women who painstakingly attempted to share an extraordinary poet's vision." Booklist

Bismarck, Otto, Furst von, 1815-1898

Steinberg, Jonathan. **Bismarck**; Jonathan Steinberg. Oxford University Press 2011 x, 577 p., [16] p. of platesp $34.95   92

1. Statesmen -- Germany -- Biography 2. Germany -- Politics and government -- 1866-1918

ISBN 978-0-19-978252-9; 0-19-978252-0; 9780199782529

LC 2010045387

The author of this biography of German Chancellor Otto von Bismarck argues that his subject "remains 'the most remarkable and complex political leader of the nineteenth century' . . . [Jonathan] Steinberg sets out to understand how the man with 'an extraordinary, gigantic self' did it. He reminds readers that Bismarck succeeded only as long as he was indispensable to his royal master and ultimately he fell when

Wilhelm II had had enough. Prof. Steinberg also uses his knowledge of nineteenth-century European history . . . to describe the stage on which Bismarck acted. In addition he pays great attention to original sources and Bismarck's collected works." (Contemporary Review) Index.

"This is a beautifully written book that provides a stimulating and enjoyable introduction to the history of modern Europe." New Statesman

Includes bibliographical references (p. [528]-537) and index

Black Elk, 1863-1950

Black Elk. **Black** Elk speaks; being the life story of a holy man of the Oglala Sioux. [as told through] John G. Neihardt; foreword by Vine Deloria, Jr.; with illustrations by Standing Bear; essays by Alexis N. Petri and Lori Utecht. University of Nebraska Press 2004 xxix, 270p il map pa $19.95; pa $14.95   92

1. Shamans 2. Oglala Indians 3. Native Americans -- Biography

ISBN 9780803283916; 0-8032-8385-7

LC 2004-12692

A reprint of the title first published 1932 by Morrow

The Indian whose life story this is, was born in 1863. He was a famous warrior and hunter in his youth, and became a practicing medicine man among his people. Of him Neihardt says, "As an indubitable seer, he seemed to represent the consciousness of the Plains Indian more fully than any other I had ever known."

This "is about as near as you can get to seeing life and death, war and religion, through an Indian's eyes." Outlook

Black, Derek

Saslow, Eli. **Rising** out of hatred; the awakening of a former white nationalist. Eli Saslow. Doubleday, a division of Penguin Random House LLC 2018 304 p. (hardback) $26.95   92

1. Racism 2. Nationalism 3. White supremacy movements 4. Attitude change 5. Hate groups -- United States 6. Men, White -- United States -- Biography 7. Whites -- Race identity -- United States 8. United States -- Race relations -- 21st century 9. Intercultural communication -- United States -- Case studies 10. White nationalism -- United States -- History -- 21st century 11. New College of Florida (Sarasota, Fla.) -- Students -- Biography 12. White supremacy movements -- United States -- History -- 21st century

ISBN 9780385542869; 9780525434955

LC 2017061173

This book, by Eli Saslow, "tells the story of how white-supremacist ideas migrated from the far-right fringe to the White House through the intensely personal saga of one man who eventually disavowed everything he was taught to believe. . . . With great empathy, . . . Saslow asks what Derek [Black's] story can tell us about America's increasingly divided nature. This is a book to help us understand the American moment and to help us better understand one another." (Publisher's note)

"The heart of this book is the impact we do and can have on one another through meaningful, respectful interaction. Anyone looking to learn more about the history of white nationalism, and gain clarity of the arguments against it, will appreciate this compelling biography." Library Journal

Blackburn, Lucie, d. 1895

Smardz Frost, Karolyn. **I've** got a home in glory land; a lost tale of the Underground Railroad. Farrar, Straus & Giroux 2006 450p il map $30   92

1. Slaves 2. Underground railroad 3. Coach drivers

ISBN 978-0-374-16481-2; 0-374-16481-9

LC 2006-64

The author's "fascination with her subject and love of detailed historical documentation are evident in this engrossing look at a couple who defied slavery with their escape and their assistance to other fugitive slaves." Booklist

Includes bibliographical references

Blackburn, Thornton, 1813 or 14-1890

Smardz Frost, Karolyn. **I've** got a home in glory land; a lost tale of the Underground Railroad. Farrar, Straus & Giroux 2006 450p il map $30   **92**
  1. Slaves 2. Underground railroad 3. Coach drivers
  ISBN 978-0-374-16481-2; 0-374-16481-9

LC 2006-64

The author's "fascination with her subject and love of detailed historical documentation are evident in this engrossing look at a couple who defied slavery with their escape and their assistance to other fugitive slaves." Booklist

Includes bibliographical references

Blackjack, Ada, 1898-1983

Niven, Jennifer. **Ada** Blackjack; a true story of survival in the Arctic. Hyperion 2003 431p il map $24.95   **92**
  1. Explorers 2. Arctic regions -- Exploration 3. Wrangel Island (Russia) -- Exploration
  ISBN 0-7868-6863-5

LC 2003-50826

The book "is exhilarating reading." Booklist
Includes bibliographical references

Blair, Tony

Blair, Tony. A **journey**; my political life. Alfred A. Knopf 2010 699p il $35; ebook $35   **92**
  1. Prime ministers 2. Political leaders 3. Members of Parliament 4. Prime ministers -- Great Britain
  ISBN 978-0-307-26983-6; 978-0-307-59487-7 ebook

LC 2010-28262

These are the memoirs of the British Labour Party politician who served as the prime minister of the United Kingdom from 1997 to 2007.

"Without delving too deeply into his personal life, . . . [Blair] gives the reader a good sense of his role not just as a public figure but also as a son, husband, and father. . . . Particulars of British party politics might elude some American readers, but the narrative keeps flowing. Essential for readers of current British politics." Libr J

Includes bibliographical references

Blanco, Richard, 1968-

Blanco, Richard, 1968- The **Prince** of Los Cocuyos; A Miami Childhood. Richard Blanco. HarperCollins 2014 272 p. $25.99   **92**
  1. Poets 2. Gay men 3. Cuban Americans
  ISBN 0062313762; 9780062313768

LC 2014501685

Author Richard Blaco offers his "inspiring memoir from the first Latino and openly gay inaugural poet, which explores his coming-of-age as the child of Cuban immigrants and his attempts to understand his place in America while grappling with his burgeoning artistic and sexual identities. (Publisher's note)

"Filled with colorful characters, often poignant and sometimes melancholy, Blanco's episodic memoir is a meditation on belonging, on self-acceptance, and on his family's almost mystical connection to Cuba." Booklist

Bogart, Humphrey, 1899-1957

Thomson, David, 1941- **Humphrey** Bogart; photo research by Lucy Gray. Faber and Faber, Inc. 2010 127p il (Great stars) pa $14   **92**
  1. Actors
  ISBN 978-0-86547-933-3

LC 2009-41758

First published 2009 in the United Kingdom

In this biography, the author "focuses on how long it took the well-bred and educated Bogart to develop his trademark style as the rough-hewn, disillusioned, world-weary, wisecracking, fallen romantic of Casablanca and The Maltese Falcon. He charts Bogart's progress from New York stage performer to featured player in 1930s Hollywood, where he was often cast as a certain kind of feral street rat, to star." Booklist

Bolick, Kate

Bolick, Kate. **Spinster**; a life of one's own. Kate Bolick. Crown 2015 336 p. illustrations, portraits (hardback) $26 **92**
  1. Single women 2. Single women -- History
  ISBN 0385347138; 9780385347136

LC 2014037871

This book examines "the pleasures and possibilities of remaining single. Using her own experiences as a starting point, journalist and cultural critic Kate Bolick invites us into her carefully considered, passionately lived life, weaving together the past and present to examine why she--along with over 100 million American women, whose ranks keep growing--remains unmarried." (Publisher's note)

"Smartly written, intimate, and heartfelt, Spinster challenges readers to reconsider what a successful life feels like for women and gifts them with a wondrous group of historic figures to immerse themselves in. A brilliant and timely narrative for twenty-first-century bluestockings, and book groups shall rejoice from all the wonders it has to offer." Booklist

Bolivar, Simon, 1783-1830

Arana, Marie. **Bolivar**; American liberator. Marie Arana. Simon & Schuster 2013 603 p. ill. (chiefly col.), maps (hardcover) $35   **92**
  1. Venezuela -- History -- 1810-1830 2. Heads of state -- South America -- Biography 3. South America -- History -- Wars of Independence, 1806-1830
  ISBN 1439110190; 9781439110195; 9781439124956

LC 2012034661

In this book, "Peruvian journalist [Marie] Arana . . . chronicles Gen. Simón Bolívar's struggle against the Spanish Empire in the 1810s and '20s through several dizzying cycles of battlefield victory, triumphal procession, demoralizing reversal, and squalid exile, before he finally drove imperial forces out of Venezuela, Colombia, Ecuador, and Peru." (Publishers Weekly)

"Drawing on Bolívar's voluminous correspondence and political writings, Arana assembles a chronological narrative that does justice to both Bolívar's august achievements and his human imperfections. This well-rounded work reveals not just an accomplished military tactician but also an able statesman." LJ

Includes bibliographical references and index

Bonaparte, Paolina, 1780-1825

Fraser, Flora. **Pauline** Bonaparte; Venus of Empire. Alfred A. Knopf 2009 287p il $28.95   **92**
  1. Princesses 2. Patrons of the arts
  ISBN 978-0-307-26544-9; 0-307-26544-7

LC 2008-28639

This "narrative by British biographer Fraser . . . fleshes out the privileged and politically unstable world of Pauline, who both commissioned and modeled nearly nude for Canova's symbolic marble statue Venus Victorious as a testament to herself. Pauline's raison d'être was the joyful pursuit of astonishing variety in her love affairs, which Fraser asserts may have been a source of her invalidism throughout her adult life. But her life showcased the dangers in Napoleonic France as well as its pleasures: she faced death from yellow fever and insurrection in French colonial Haiti. Fraser's narrative provides insight into the permissive culture of the French Empire and glimpses into Napoleon as a protective and exasperated older brother while simultaneously engaged in politics, invasions and his eventual fall from power." Publ Wkly

Includes bibliographical references

Bonhoeffer, Dietrich, 1906-1945

Marsh, Charles. **Strange** glory; a life of Dietrich Bonhoeffer. by Charles Marsh. Alfred A. Knopf 2014 528 p. illustrations (hardcover) $35   **92**
1. Clergy 2. Theologians 3. Germany -- History -- 1933-1945
ISBN 0307269817; 9780307269812; 9780307390387
LC 2013045873
This book, by Charles Marsh, offers a biography of "Dietrich Bonhoeffer, the German pastor, theologian, and anti-Hitler conspirator. . . . [I]t was the Nuremberg laws that set Bonhoeffer's earthly life on an ineluctable path toward destruction. His denunciation of the race statutes as heresy and his insistence on the church's moral obligation to defend all victims of state violence, regardless of race or religion, alienated him from what would become the Reich church." (Publisher's note)

"Marsh's portrait is of a spoiled, materialistic, and selfish young man who develops, over time, into a German hero. The writing is clear and concise, the endnotes extensive, and the index generous." LJ

Includes bibliographical references and index

Metaxas, Eric. **Bonhoeffer**; pastor, martyr, prophet, spy: a Righteous Gentile vs. the Third Reich. Thomas Nelson 2010 591p il   **92**
1. Spies 2. Clergy 3. Theologians 4. Dissenters 5. Writers on religion 6. Biography, Individual 7. Germany -- History -- 1933-1945
ISBN 1595551387; 1595552464; 9781595551382; 9781595552464 pa
LC 2009013944
This is a biography of the German Lutheran pastor and theologian executed by the Nazis for plotting to overthrow Hitler.

"Insightful and illuminating, this tome makes a powerful contribution to biography, history and theology." Publ Wkly

Includes bibliographical references

Boogaard, Derek, 1982-2011

Branch, John. **Boy** on ice; the life and death of Derek Boogaard. John Branch. W.W. Norton & Co. Inc 2014 352 p. illustrations (hardcover) $26.95   **92**
1. Hockey players 2. Violence in sports 3. Brain -- Concussion 4. Hockey players -- Canada -- Biography
ISBN 039323939X; 9780393239393
LC 2014015731
"The tragic death of hockey star Derek Boogaard at twenty-eight was front-page news across the country in 2011 and helped shatter the silence about violence and concussions in professional sports. . . . 'Boy on Ice' is the richly told story of a mountain of a man who made it to the absolute pinnacle of his sport. Widely regarded as the toughest man in the NHL, Boogaard was a gentle man off the ice but a merciless fighter on it." (Publisher's note)

Includes bibliographical references and index

Boone, Daniel, 1734-1820

Morgan, Robert. **Boone**; a biography. Algonquin Books of Chapel Hill 2007 538p il map $29.95   **92**
1. Frontier and pioneer life 2. Scouts 3. Pioneers 4. Biography, Individual 5. Frontier and pioneer life -- Kentucky
ISBN 1-56512-455-3; 978-1-56512-455-4
LC 2007-14204
This is a biography of the frontiersman. Index.
This is an "absorbing and stirring chronicle of the great frontiersman." Booklist

Includes bibliographical references

Booth, John Wilkes, 1838-1865

Alford, Terry. **Fortune's** Fool; The Life of John Wilkes Booth. Terry Alford. Oxford University Press 2015 416 p. illustrations $29.95   **92**
1. Actors -- United States -- Biography 2. United States -- History -- 1861-1865, Civil War
ISBN 0195054121; 9780195054125
LC 2014040917
National Book Critics Circle Award Finalist: Biography (2015)
In this biography of John Wilkes Booth, author "Terry Alford provides the first comprehensive look at the life of an enigmatic figure whose life has been overshadowed by his final, infamous act. Tracing Booth's story from his uncertain childhood in Maryland, characterized by a difficult relationship with his famous actor father, to his successful acting career on stages across the country, Alford offers a nuanced picture of Booth as a public figure, performer, and deeply troubled man." (Publisher's note)

Borges, Jorge Luis, 1899-1986

Williamson, Edwin. **Borges,** a life. Viking 2004 416p $34.95   **92**
1. Poets 2. Authors 3. Novelists 4. Essayists 5. Translators 6. Literary critics 7. Short story writers
ISBN 0-670-88579-7
LC 2004-41290
This "is a richly psychological, dynamically intellectual, and deeply affecting portrait of an often anguished and inhibited man who, through heroic perserverance and spiritual conviction, found salvation in writing and transformed literature for all time." Booklist

Includes bibliographical references

Borgia, Lucrezia, 1480-1519

Bradford, Sarah. **Lucrezia** Borgia; life, love, and death in Renaissance Italy. Viking 2004 xxiv, 421p il map $27.95; pa $16   **92**
1. Patrons of the arts
ISBN 0-670-03353-7; 0-14-303595-9 pa
LC 2004-54881
The author "presents Lucrezia as an intelligent noblewoman, powerless to defy her family's patriarchal order, yet an enlightened ruler in her own right as Duchess of Ferrara. . . . As a project designed to distinguish the historical Lucrezia Borgia from the legend, Bradford's readable biography resoundingly succeeds." Publ Wkly

Includes bibliographical references

Born, Max, 1882-1970

Greenspan, Nancy Thorndike. The **end** of the certain world; the Nobel physicist who ignited the quantum revolution. Basic Books 2005 374p il $26.95   **92**
1. Physicists 2. Nobel laureates for physics

ISBN 0-7382-0693-8

LC 2004-21809

"This empathetic work . . . lifts a deserving figure out of semi-obscurity and adds a valuable perspective on the origin of modern physics." Publ Wkly

Includes bibliographical references

Bosworth, Patricia

Bosworth, Patricia. The **Men** in My Life; a memoir of love and art in 1950s Manhattan. Patricia Bosworth. HarperCollins 2017 384 p. illustrations (ebook) $26.99; $27.99 **92**
1. Actresses -- Biography 2. Journalists -- Biography
ISBN 9780062287922; 0062287907; 9780062287908

LC 2017003351

In this book, journalist Patricia Bosworth "chronicles how she repressed her grief and guilt, recklessly threw herself into harrowing situations, and embraced exhilarating opportunities. . . . Lush with tales of Lee Strasberg, Marilyn Monroe, Gore Vidal, Elaine Stritch, Audrey Hepburn, and many more, and spiked with arresting observations about glamour and about toxic sexism and homophobia, Bosworth's riveting memoir brings the covertly wild 1950s into startlingly close focus." (Booklist)

"A forthright memoir of pain and aspirations enlivened by sharp portraits of a host of colorful celebrities." Kirkus

Boulloche, André

Kaiser, Charles. The **cost** of courage; by Charles Kaiser. Other Press 2015 288 p. illustrations (hardcover) $26.95 **92**
1. World War, 1939-1945 -- Biography 2. World War, 1939-1945 -- Underground movements -- France 3. Guerrillas -- France -- Biography 4. France -- History -- German occupation, 1940-1945 -- Biography 5. World War, 1939-1945 -- Underground movements -- France -- Biography
ISBN 1590516141; 9781590516140

LC 2015008560

This book, by Charles Kaiser, tells the "heroic true story of the three youngest children of a . . . family who worked together in the French Resistance. . . . In the autumn of 1943, André Boulloche . . . coordinat[ed] all the Resistance movements in the nine northern regions of France only to be betrayed by one of his associates . . . and taken prisoner. His sisters carried on the fight without him until the end of the war." (Publisher's note)

"Kaiser's account of a family's devotion and resilience in the face of horrific tyranny tells a highly recommended story of resolve and bravery that can't help but feel romantic in its selfless and profound obligation, but this is not gloss nor ungrounded canonization." LJ

Bourdain, Anthony

Bourdain, Anthony. **Kitchen** confidential; adventures in the culinary underbelly. Updated ed; Harper Perennial 2007 312, 22p pa $15.99 **92**
1. Cooks 2. Authors 3. Novelists 4. Television personalities 5. Memoirists
ISBN 978-0-06-089922-6; 0-06-089922-0

LC 2007-280057

First published 2000

"This is one bitter, nasty, searing, hard-to-swallow piece of work. But if you can choke the thing down, you'll probably wake up grinning in the middle of the night. . . . In a style partaking of Hunter S. Thompson, Iggy Pop and a little Jonathan Swift, Bourdain gleefully rips through the scenery to reveal private backstage horrors little dreamed of by the trusting public. . . . To a world infested with synthesized romance, candlelit illusions and sentimental piety, 'Kitchen Confidential' offers a nice palate-clearing taste of poison." N Y Times Book Rev

Bourdain, Anthony. **Medium** raw; a bloody valentine to the world of food and the people who cook. Ecco Press 2010 281p $26.99 **92**
1. Cooks 2. Authors 3. Novelists 4. Television personalities 5. Memoirists
ISBN 978-0-06-171894-6; 0-06-171894-7

This book mixes personal memoir with travelogues and ruminations on such matters as the degradation of the American hamburger, the dumbing down of the Food Network, the tedium of multicourse tasting menus and the rise of food gurus such as David Chang. . . . Mr. Bourdain is a vivid, bawdy and often foul-mouthed writer. He thrills in the attack, but he is also an enthusiast who writes well about things he holds dear. His detailed reporting on the backroom lives of restaurant employees is terrific. Wall Street J

Bowie, David

Morley, Paul. The **age** of Bowie; how David Bowie made a world of difference. by Paul Morley. Simon & Schuster 2016 483 p. illustrations (some color) $30 **92**
1. Rock musicians -- England -- Biography
ISBN 1501151150; 9781501151156

In this book, author Paul Morley "constructs a definitive story of Bowie that explores how he worked, played, aged, structured his ideas, influenced others, invented the future, and entered history as someone who could and would never be forgotten. Morley captures the greatest moments from across Bowie's life and career." (Publisher's note)

"There is a great deal of cultural history to enjoy in this personal, engaged and slyly scholarly biography. Morley's triumph is to know there is no such thing as the definitive story: new generations of fans will continue to make it up as they go along." New Statesman

Bowie, David, 1947-2016. **Bowie** on Bowie; interviews and encounters with David Bowie. edited by Sean Egan. Chicago Review Press 2015 432 p. (hardback) $28.95 **92**
1. Rock musicians -- England 2. Rock musicians -- England -- Interviews
ISBN 9781569769775

LC 2014042080

This book, edited by Sean Egan, "presents some of the best interviews [rock musician David] Bowie has granted in his near five-decade career. Each interview traces a new step in his unique journey, successively freezing him in time as young novelty hit-maker, hairy hippie, Ziggy Stardust, Aladdin Sane, the Thin White Duke, . . . and, finally, . . . beloved elder statesman of challenging popular music. In all of these iterations he is remarkably articulate." (Publisher's note)

" Egan's curation places each interview in context, though the editorial language is choppy, giving helpful social reference points and highlighting the musician's notable remarks. Documented identities include Bowie as the brassy, bright-eyed newcomer, the rakish bisexual glam star, the evocative ambient artist using music as rehab, well into his later years as the reserved family man who has little use for the press. . . . this is a fascinating journey through the mind of a musician many people claim to "know" but who proves time and again that his own essence is often foreign to himself. An asset for Bowie fans." LJ

Includes bibliographical references and index

Bown, Mike Spencer

Bown, Mike Spencer. The **world's** most travelled man; a twenty-three-year odyssey to and through every country on the planet. Mike Spencer Bown. Douglas & McIntyre 2018 352

p. $29.95   **92**
1. Travel 2. Voyages and travels 3. Voyages around the world
ISBN 1771621427; 9781771621427

This book, by Mike Spencer Bown, "is an eye-opening account of the universal human experience as seen from each corner of the changing world. Blending a romantic connection to nature through solitude and the social examination of culture, Bown fully immerses himself in each experience, however diverse, dangerous or dirty, veering way, way off the backpacker circuit to see the world through an unparalleled perspective." (Publisher's note)

Boylan, Jennifer Finney, 1958-

Boylan, Jennifer Finney. **I'm** looking through you; growing up haunted. Broadway Books 2008 270p il $23.95   **92**
1. Ghosts 2. Authors 3. Novelists 4. Transsexualism 5. Transsexuals 6. Authors, American 7. Short story writers 8. Young adult authors
ISBN 978-0-7679-2174-9; 0-7679-2174-7

LC 2007-19199

The author, a male-to-female transgendered person, "uses the metaphor of 'being haunted' throughout to illustrate not only her boyhood experiences but also the memories that have shaped her as a person as she struggled with her gender identity throughout most of her life. . . . Her writing style is witty, self-deprecating, entertaining, and often poignant, especially when describing family and friends who have passed away. An adventure to read, this is highly recommended for all libraries." Libr J

Brackett, Charles, 1892-1969

It's the pictures that got small; Charles Brackett on Billy Wilder and Hollywood's golden age. edited by Anthony Slide. Columbia University Press 2014 448 p. 16 unnumbered pages of plates (cloth: alk. paper) $34.95   **92**
1. Motion pictures -- Production and direction 2. Screenwriters -- United States -- Diaries 3. Motion picture producers and directors -- United States -- Diaries 4. Motion pictures -- Production and direction -- United States -- History -- 20th century
ISBN 9780231167086

LC 2014015801

This book, edited by Anthony Slide, offers an "annotated collection of writings taken from dozens of [screenwriter Charles] Brackett's unpublished diaries . . . [and] clarifies Brackett's critical contribution to [director Billy] Wilder's films and Hollywood history while enriching our knowledge of Wilder's achievements in writing, direction, and style." (Publisher's note)

"Though the diary format is not for all readers, anyone interested in the golden age of film should enjoy this very entertaining and illustrative look at the film industry of the 1930s and 1940s." LJ

Includes bibliographical references and index

Bradbury, Ray

Eller, Jonathan R. **Becoming** Ray Bradbury. University of Illinois Press 2011 324p il $34.95   **92**
1. Authors 2. Novelists 3. Screenwriters 4. Authors, American 5. Children's authors 6. Short story writers 7. Science fiction writers
ISBN 978-0-252-03629-3

LC 2011008562

The author "provides a detailed account of the experiences that shaped Ray Bradbury's life and writing career from his childhood until he embarked on the screenplay for John Huston's Moby Dick in late 1953. . . . Eller's work is thorough and enlightening on the subject of one of science fiction's greatest minds. Highly recommended not just for Bradbury fans but for all students of science fiction." Libr J

Includes bibliographical references

Weller, Sam. The **Bradbury** chronicles; the life of Ray Bradbury. William Morrow 2005 384p il $26.95; pa $15.95   **92**
1. Authors 2. Novelists 3. Screenwriters 4. Authors, American 5. Children's authors 6. Short story writers 7. Science fiction writers
ISBN 0-06-054581-X; 0-06-054584-4 pa

LC 2004-59491

"Weller's research—based on interviews with Bradbury as well as family members and colleagues—is almost exhaustive in its detail, and he does a fine job of presenting the facts of his subject's unique life. The lively, conversational prose brings out the writer's winning personality and turns his struggles and successes into a highly readable story." SLJ

Includes bibliographical references

Braddock, James J., 1906-1974

Schaap, Jeremy. **Cinderella** Man; James J. Braddock, Max Baer, and the greatest upset in boxing history. Houghton Mifflin 2005 324p il hardcover o.p. pa $13.95   **92**
1. Boxers (Persons) 2. Boxing -- Biography
ISBN 0-618-55117-4; 0-618-71190-2 pa

LC 2004-66085

The author goes into "detail on the brawny, reserved Braddock, who, at his lowest moments, was reduced to living off government relief and doing grueling work on the Hoboken, N.J., docks. But the story is as much about Max Baer, the lovably clownish and handsome heavyweight Braddock defeated as a 10-to-one underdog. . . . Boxing enthusiasts will be more than satisfied by Schaap's meticulous account, which includes round-by-round details of the fight, as well as profiles of other fighters of the era." Publ Wkly

Includes bibliographical references

Brady, Tom, 1977-

Myers, Gary. **Brady** vs Manning; the untold story of the rivalry that transformed the NFL. Gary Myers. Crown Archtype 2015 264 p. 8 unnumbered pages of plates (hbk.) $26   **92**
1. National Football League 2. Sports rivalries -- United States 3. Football -- United States -- History 4. Football players -- United States -- Biography 5. Quarterbacks (Football) -- United States -- Biography
ISBN 0804139377; 9780804139373

LC 2015027579

Author Gary Meyer presents this "inside account of the greatest rivalry in NFL history. Myers tackles this subject from every angle and with unprecedented access and insight, drawing on a huge number of never-before-heard interviews with [Tom] Brady and [Peyton] Manning, their coaches, their families, and those who have played with them and against them." (Publisher's note)

"Myers is a thorough professional with impeccable contacts to successfully tell this account, which will be of interest to all football fans." Library Journal

Includes bibliographical references and index

Bragg, Rick

Bragg, Rick. **All** over but the shoutin' Pantheon Bks. 1997 xxii, 329p hardcover o.p. pa $14   **92**
1. Authors 2. Journalists 3. Memoirists
ISBN 0-679-44258-8; 0-679-77402-5 pa

LC 97-9918

"Honest, unsentimental, and so elegantly spare it nearly hurts to read, this memoir by Pulitzer Prize-winning journalist Bragg recounts a dirt-poor childhood in Alabama and the debt he owes his mother." Libr J

★ Bragg, Rick. The **best** cook in the world; tales from my momma's table. Rick Bragg. Alfred A. Knopf 2018 512 p. (hardcover) $28.95 **92**

1. Cookbooks 2. Southern cooking 3. Cooking, American -- Southern style

ISBN 9781400040414

LC 2017024979

This book, by Rick Bragg, presents a "food memoir, cookbook, and loving tribute to a region, a vanishing history, a family, and, especially, to his mother. . . . [It includes] seventy-four mouthwatering Bragg family recipes for classic southern dishes passed down through generations. . . . [Bragg tells] the stories that framed his mother's cooking and education, from childhood into old age." (Publisher's note)

"For readers who crave soul with their recipes (some 75 here), this is a fitting tribute to foodways that are fast slipping away." LJ

Bragg, Rick. The **prince** of Frogtown. Alfred A. Knopf 2008 255p $24 **92**

1. Authors 2. Journalists 3. Stepfathers 4. Father-son relationship 5. Memoirists

ISBN 978-1-4000-4040-7; 1-4000-4040-X

LC 2007-38884

The author "merges his father's history of severe hardships and simple joys with a tale from the present: his own relationship with his 10-year-old stepson. . . . [This book] is lush with narratives about manhood, fathers and sons, families and the changing face of the rural South." Publ Wkly

Brand, Cristo

Jones, Barbara. **Mandela**; My Prisoner, My Friend. Christo Brand, with Barbara Jones. Thomas Dunne Books/St. Martin's Press 2014 288 p. 16 plates; ills; portraits $26.99 **92**

1. Political prisoners 2. African National Congress -- Biography 3. Robben Island (South Africa) -- Anecdotes 4. South Africa -- Race relations -- Anecdotes 5. Pollsmoor Prison (South Africa) -- Anecdotes 6. Political prisoners -- South Africa -- Biography 7. Correctional personnel -- South Africa -- Biography 8. South Africa -- Politics and government -- Anecdotes

ISBN 1250055261; 9781250055262

LC 2014026586

In this book by Christo Brand and Barbara Jones, Nelson Mandela's "life's sacrifices [are] recounted in vivid detail by the prison guard with whom he became lifelong friends. For 12 years Brand watched Mandela scrub floors, empty his toilet bucket, grieve over the deaths of family and friends yet remain as strong as any freedom fighter in history. Won over by Madiba's charm and authentic concern for the well-being of others, Brand became Mandela's confidant and at times accomplice." (Publisher's note)

"The author quickly recounts Mandela's general biography, including the Rivonia trial for sabotage that landed him in prison, but this is really a tale of two men and their shared humanity in an inhumane place. A worthy addition to the canon of Mandela literature that details a relationship that many knew about but few truly understood." Kirkus

Brandeis, Gayle

Brandeis, Gayle. The **art** of misdiagnosis; surviving my mother's suicide. Gayle Brandeis. Beacon Press 2017 240 p. (hardback) $26.95 **92**

1. Suicide 2. Mother-child relationship 3. Suicide victims -- Biography 4. Mother and child -- Biography 5. Schizophrenics

-- Family relationships -- Biography

ISBN 9780807044865

LC 2017002002

"Gayle Brandeis's mother disappeared just after Gayle gave birth to her youngest child. Several days later, her body was found: she had hanged herself in the utility closet of a Pasadena parking garage. In this searing, formally inventive memoir, Gayle describes the dissonance between being a new mother, a sweet-smelling infant at her chest, and a grieving daughter trying to piece together what happened, who her mother was, and all she had and hadn't understood about her." (Publisher's note)

Brandeis, Louis Dembitz, 1856-1941

Urofsky, Melvin I. **Louis** D. Brandeis; a life. Pantheon Books 2009 955p il **92**

1. Judges 2. Lawyers 3. Biography, Individual 4. Supreme Court justices 5. United States -- Supreme Court 6. Law -- United States -- History

ISBN 9780375423666

LC 200903992

This is a biography of the American lawyer who was nominated to the Supreme Court in 1916 and served as a justice until his retirement in 1939. Index.

This is a "monumental, authoritative and appreciative biography of the man Franklin D. Roosevelt called 'Isaiah.'" N Y Times Book Rev

Includes bibliographical references

Braun, Eva

Gortemaker, Heike B. **Eva** Braun; life with Hitler. by Heike B. Görtemaker; translated from the German by Damion Searls. Alfred A. Knopf 2011 324 p. $27.95; ebook $13.99 **92**

1. Women -- Germany -- Biography 2. Mistresses -- Germany -- Biography 3. Germany -- History -- 1933-1945 -- Biography 4. Spouses of heads of state -- Germany -- Biography

ISBN 978-0-307-59582-9; 978-0-307-70139-8 ebook; 9780307595829

LC 2011009551

Originally published 2010 in Germany

This book offers a biography of Adolf Hilter's mistress Eva Braun. "Although by the early-to-mid-Thirties Eva Braun thought that her relationship with Hitler was now on a more established footing, she was soon disillusioned by even longer absences. . . . Görtemaker writes of Eva Braun's 'practically unassailable position at Hitler's side,' even if in the dangerous and byzantine world of the Nazi hierarchy nothing was guaranteed. . . . Hitler . . . appreciate[d] her unquestioning loyalty. . . . Eva Braun . . . probably knew little of the sadism, the squalor, and the horror of the camps. As an impressionable young woman, she had been molded in her opinions during her time in Hitler's presence." (New York Review of Books)

The author "coaxes from history's shadows the woman who for 14 years was the companion, lover and, near the end, wife of Adolf Hitler." Kirkus

Includes bibliographical references

Braverman, Blair

Braverman, Blair. **Welcome** to the Goddamn Ice Cube; Chasing Fear and Finding Home in the Great White North. by Blair Braverman. HarperCollins 2016 288 p. $25.99 **92**

1. Young women 2. Arctic regions

ISBN 0062311565; 9780062311566

This book, by Blair Braverman, is a "memoir of a young woman reclaiming her courage in the stark landscapes of the north. By the time Blair Braverman was eighteen, she had left her home in California, moved to arctic Norway to learn to drive sled dogs, and found work as a tour guide on a glacier in Alaska. Determined to carve out a life as a 'tough girl' . . . she slowly developed the strength and resilience the landscape demanded of her." (Publisher's note)

"Her external experiences are extraordinary in the frigid north that so few have experienced, but it's what happens internally that both sets this memoir apart and gives it universal resonance. Indelible characters, adventurous spirit, and acute psychological insight combine in this multilayered debut." Kirkus

Brennan, Thomas J. (Thomas James)

Brennan, Thomas J. **Shooting** ghosts; a U.S. Marine, a combat photographer, and their journey back from war. Thomas J. Brennan, USMC (Ret.), and Finbarr O'Reilly. Viking 2017 x, 340 p.p illustrations (chiefly color) (hardcover) $27   **92**

1. Photographers -- Biography 2. United States. Marine Corps -- Biography 3. War -- Psychological aspects 4. War photographers -- Africa -- Biography 5. War photographers -- Afghanistan -- Biography 6. Afghan War, 2001- -- Personal narratives, American 7. United States. Marine Corps -- Officers -- Biography
ISBN 9780399562563; 9780399562549; 0399562540

LC 2017019760

This book is "a unique joint memoir by a U.S. Marine and a conflict photographer whose unlikely friendship helped both heal their warwounded bodies and souls. . . . Their story, told in alternating first-person narratives, is about the things they saw and did, the ways they have been affected, and how they have navigated the psychological aftershocks of war and wrestled with reforming their own identities and moral centers." (Publisher's note)

"A courageous breaking of the code of silence to seek mental health for veterans and the war-scarred." Kirkus

Includes bibliographical references (pages [317]-325) and index.

Brennan-Jobs, Lisa

Brennan-Jobs, Lisa. **Small** fry; Lisa Brennan-Jobs. Grove Press 2018 304 p. illustrations $26   **92**

1. Children of single parents 2. Father-daughter relationship
ISBN 0802128238; 9780802128232

This book "is a captivating memoir by [Lisa Brennan-Jobs,] the daughter of Apple founder Steve Jobs. . . . Scrappy, wise, and funny, young Lisa is an unforgettable guide, marveling at the particular magic of growing up in this family, . . . while grappling with her feelings of illegitimacy and shame. Part portrait of a complex family, part love letter to California in the seventies and eighties, . . . [this book] is an enthralling story by an insightful new literary voice." (Publisher's note)

"Brennan-Jobs skillfully relays her past without judgement, staying true to her younger self. It is a testament to her fine writing and journalistic approach that her memoir never turns maudlin or gossipy. Rather than a celebrity biography, this is Brennan-Jobs' authentic story of growing up in two very different environments, neither of which felt quite like home." Booklist

Brenner, Carl

Brenner, Marie. **Apples** and oranges; my brother and me, lost and found. Farrar, Straus & Giroux 2008 268p il $24; pa $15   **92**

1. Cancer 2. Lawyers 3. Journalists 4. Fruit growers
ISBN 978-0-374-17352-4; 0-374-17352-4; 978-0-312-42880-8 pa; 0-312-42880-4 pa

LC 2008-08929

"In this elegiac memoir, the author, a reporter, applies the same investigative skills that led to her exposé of the tobacco industry and Enron to a more intimate subject: her contentious relationship with her late brother. From an eccentric Jewish Texan family of compulsive record keepers—their father maintained a four-page list of his life's achievements—Marie became a New York liberal, Carl a diehard conservative who abandoned a legal career to farm apples. As a teenager, he smashed his sister's Joan Baez records; as an adult, given a diagnosis of terminal cancer, he informed her via FedEx. Her attempts to smooth over their differences by mastering the language of fruit (Carl often started conversations, 'I am going to give you a quiz') are at once comic and tinged with regret." New Yorker

Brenner, Marie

Brenner, Marie. **Apples** and oranges; my brother and me, lost and found. Farrar, Straus & Giroux 2008 268p il $24; pa $15   **92**

1. Cancer 2. Lawyers 3. Journalists 4. Fruit growers
ISBN 978-0-374-17352-4; 0-374-17352-4; 978-0-312-42880-8 pa; 0-312-42880-4 pa

LC 2008-08929

"In this elegiac memoir, the author, a reporter, applies the same investigative skills that led to her exposé of the tobacco industry and Enron to a more intimate subject: her contentious relationship with her late brother. From an eccentric Jewish Texan family of compulsive record keepers—their father maintained a four-page list of his life's achievements—Marie became a New York liberal, Carl a diehard conservative who abandoned a legal career to farm apples. As a teenager, he smashed his sister's Joan Baez records; as an adult, given a diagnosis of terminal cancer, he informed her via FedEx. Her attempts to smooth over their differences by mastering the language of fruit (Carl often started conversations, 'I am going to give you a quiz') are at once comic and tinged with regret." New Yorker

Brierley, Saroo

Brierley, Saroo. A **long** way home; a memoir. Saroo Brierley with Larry Buttrose. G.P. Putnam's Sons 2014 272 p. illustrations, maps (paperback) $16   **92**

1. Adopted children 2. Missing children 3. International adoption 4. Hobart (Tas.) -- Biography 5. Kolkata (India) -- Biography 6. Intercountry adoption -- India 7. East Indians -- Australia -- Biography 8. Birthparents -- India -- Identification 9. Intercountry adoption -- Australia -- Tasmania 10. Adopted children -- Australia -- Tasmania -- Biography
ISBN 0425276198; 9780399169281; 9780425276198

LC 2014003745

This memoir by Saroo Brierley with Larry Buttrose narrates how Brierley, as a child, "got lost on a train in India. . . . He survived alone for weeks on the rough streets of Calcutta before ultimately being transferred to an agency and adopted by a couple in Australia. . . . With the advent of Google Earth, he had the opportunity to look for the needle in a haystack he once called home. . . . After years of searching, he . . . set off to find his family." (Publisher's note)

Briggs, Kate (Teacher)

Briggs, Kate. **This** little art; Kate Briggs. Fitzcarraldo Editions 2017 365 p. $20   **92**

1. Women authors 2. Translating and interpreting 3. Translators
ISBN 1910695459; 9781910695456

LC 2017434790

"An essay with the reach and momentum of a novel, Kate Briggs's . . . [book] is a genre-bending song for the practice of literary translation, offering fresh, fierce and timely thinking on reading, writing and living with the works of others. Taking her own experience of translating Roland Barthes's lecture notes as a starting point, the author threads various stories together to give us this portrait of translation as a compelling, complex and intensely relational activity." (Publisher's note)

"Lucid and engaging, Briggs's book is essential, not just for translators, but anyone who has felt the magic of reading." Pub Wkly

Includes bibliographical references

Brinkley, John Richard, 1885-1942

Brock, Pope. **Charlatan**; America's most dangerous huckster, the man who pursued him, and the age of flimflam. Crown Publishers 2008 324p il   92

1. Physicians 2. Quacks and quackery 3. Swindlers 4. Broadcasters 5. Biography, Individual 6. Quacks and quackery -- United States

ISBN 0307339882; 9780307339881

LC 2007-10074

This is a biography of John Richard Brinkley. In 1917, Brinkley arrived in "Milford, Kansas. He set up a medical practice and introduced . . . [a] surgical method of using goat glands to restore the fading virility of local farmers. . . . Thousands of paying customers quickly turned 'Dr.' Brinkley into America's richest and most famous surgeon." (Publisher's note)

"Presentation is everything in telling this elaborate, many-faceted story. And Mr. Brock's has three outstanding virtues. First of all, he has a terrific ear for singling out quotations. . . . Second, he is selective. This fast-moving, light-stepping book takes care not to throw in extraneous detail. Third, his own voice is wry enough to compete with the actual Brinkley material, which is saying a great deal." N Y Times (Late N Y Ed)

Includes bibliographical references

Britten, Benjamin, 1913-1976

Powell, Neil, 1948- **Benjamin** Britten; a life for music. by Neil Powell. Henry Holt and Company 2013 528 p. $37   92

1. Composers -- Biography 2. Composers -- England -- Biography

ISBN 0805097740; 9780805097740

LC 2012051536

In this biography of "Benjamin Britten, the celebrated British composer . . . [Neil] Powell . . . traces the development of Britten's musical gifts from his childhood and youth in England to his travels to America, his meetings and lifelong friendship with W.H. Auden, and his crucial role in helping to establish the Alderburgh Festival. . . . He probes the genius of Britten's compositions from Sinfonietta . . . to the triptych of Peter Grimes . . . Billy Budd, and Death in Venice." (Publishers Weekly)

Includes bibliographical references and index

Brodak, Molly

Brodak, Molly. **Bandit**; a daughter's memoir. Molly Brodak. Black Cat 2016 240 p. (ebook) $16; (paperback) $16 92

1. American poets -- Biography 2. Father-daughter relationship 3. Poets, American -- 20th century -- Biography 4. Fathers and daughters -- United States -- Biography

ISBN 9780802189615; 9780802125637

LC 2016017971

In this memoir, author Molly Brodak "recounts her childhood and attempts to make sense of her complicated relationship with her father, a man she only half knew. At some angles he was a normal father: there was a job at the GM factory, a house with a yard, birthday treats for Molly and her sister. But there were darker glimmers, too. . . . She unearths and reckons with her childhood memories and the fracturing impact her father had on their family." (Publisher's note)

"An intelligent, disturbing, and profoundly honest memoir." Kirkus

Brokaw, Tom

Brokaw, Tom, 1940- A **Lucky** Life Interrupted; A Memoir of Hope. Tom Brokaw. Random House Inc. 2015 240 p.

$27   92

1. Journalists 2. Cancer patients 3. Physician and patient 4. Multiple myeloma -- Treatment 5. Multiple myeloma -- Patients -- United States -- Biography

ISBN 1400069696; 9781400069699

LC 2015008653

In this memoir, journalist Tom Brokaw reflects on his diagnosis with "multiple myeloma, a treatable but incurable blood cancer. Brokaw takes us through all the seasons and stages of this surprising year, the emotions, discoveries, setbacks, and struggles--times of denial, acceptance, turning points, and courage. After his diagnosis, Brokaw began to keep a journal, approaching this new stage of his life in a familiar role: as a journalist." (Publisher's note)

"Brokaw's account lacks the depth and fire of Christopher Hitchens' Mortality (2013), but it belongs on the same shelf as a wise and oddly comforting look at the toughest news of all." Kirkus

Brontë, Charlotte, 1816-1855

Harman, Claire. **Charlotte** Bronte; a fiery heart. Claire Harman. Alfred A. Knopf 2016 480 p. illustrations (some color) (ebook) $60; (hardcover: acid-free paper) $30   92

1. English novelists -- Biography 2. English women authors -- Biography 3. Novelists, English -- 19th century -- Biography 4. Women authors, English -- 19th century -- Biography

ISBN 9780307962096; 9780307962089

LC 2015028359

"Drawing on letters unavailable to previous biographers, [author Claire] Harman depicts Charlotte's inner life with absorbing, almost novelistic intensity. She seizes upon a moment in Charlotte's adolescence that ignited her determination to reject poverty and obscurity: While working at a girls' school in Brussels, Charlotte fell in love with her married professor, Constantin Heger, a man who treated her as 'nothing special to him at all.'" (Publisher's note)

"A delightfully engaging biography of a highly talented but deeply troubled prodigy of English literature." Kirkus

Includes bibliographical references (pages 441-444) and index.

Gaskell, Elizabeth Cleghorn. The **life** of Charlotte Bronte; [by] Elizabeth Gaskell; edited with an introduction and notes by Angus Eason. Oxford University Press 2001 xxxvi, 587p (Oxford world's classics) pa $13.95   92

1. Poets 2. Authors 3. Novelists 4. Women authors 5. Authors, English

ISBN 0-19-283805-9

First published 1857

"Mrs. Gaskell was herself a popular novelist, who commanded a very wide audience. She brought to bear upon the biography of Charlotte Bronte all those literary gifts which had made the charm of her seven volumes of romance. . . . It is quite certain that Charlotte Bronte would not stand on so splendid a pedestal today but for the single-minded devotion of her accomplished biographer." Clement K. Shorter

Includes bibliographical references

Gordon, Lyndall. **Charlotte** Bronte; a passionate life. Norton 1995 418p il hardcover o.p. pa $17   92

1. Poets 2. Authors 3. Novelists 4. Women authors 5. Authors, English

ISBN 0-393-31448-0 pa

First published 1994 in the United Kingdom

The author "dismantles once and for all the image of Charlotte Brontë as a figure of pathos and presents, instead, a courageous survivor, a determined writer, and a woman of volcanic emotion. . . . Gordon, as skilled at literary analysis as at chronicling a life, approaches Brontë's tragic and enduringly relevant story from several angles, carefully identifying all the autobiographical elements of her novels and contrasting her commitment to writing and her independent spirit to her era's strict and pitiless code of behavior for women." Booklist

Includes bibliographical references

Brookhiser, Richard

Brookhiser, Richard. **Right** time, right place; coming of age with William F. Buckley, Jr. and the conservative movement. Basic Books 2009 262p $27.50 **92**

1. Authors 2. Novelists 3. Historians 4. Journalists 5. Conservatism 6. Columnists 7. Biographers 8. National review 9. Magazine editors

ISBN 978-0-465-01355-5; 0-465-01355-4

LC 2009-03073

"Think of a cause you care about deeply. Who's the figure you most admire in that movement? Now picture that person taking you to lunch, when you're 23, and declaring that you – you! – will be his successor. Such was the fantasy that Richard Brookhiser lived as a protégé of National Review editor William F. Buckley Jr., conservatism's standard-bearer for a half-century. Brookhiser was, to put it mildly, a prodigy. He wrote his first magazine cover story at 14. Steep falls often follow such precocious rises. But when Buckley changed his mind and sought a different heir, Brookhiser didn't self-destruct; he just rejiggered his career. Such equanimity means Right Time, Right Place is refreshingly free of spicy score settling and juicy revelations. Instead, readers get tasty morsels of candor caramelized in the searing heat of self-reflection. The result is a psychologically rich personal narrative." Christ Sci Monit

Brookins, Cara

Brookins, Cara. **Rise**; How a House Built a Family. by Cara Brookins. SDC Publications 2017 320 p. color illustrations $25.99 **92**

1. Mothers 2. Divorced people 3. House construction

ISBN 1250095662; 9781250095664

LC 2016036419

This book, by Cara Brookins, is the "true story of a woman taking the greatest risk of her life in order to heal from the unthinkable. After escaping an abusive marriage, Cara Brookins had four children to provide for and no one to turn to but herself. In desperate need of a home but without the means to buy one, she did something incredible. Equipped only with YouTube instructional videos, a small bank loan and a mile-wide stubborn streak, Cara built her own house from the foundation up." (Publisher's note)

"Brookings deftly narrates the extreme learning curve the family experienced during the construction process, while putting a family back together again." Pub Wkly

Brooks, Gwendolyn, 1917-2000

Jackson, Angela. A **surprised** queenhood in the new black sun; the life & legacy of Gwendolyn Brooks. Angela Jackson. Beacon Press 2017 204 p. (hardcover: alk. paper) $24.95 **92**

1. American poets -- Biography 2. African American poets -- Biography 3. Poets, American -- 20th century -- Biography

ISBN 9780807025055; 9780807025048

LC 2017001533

This biography, by Angela Jackson, focuses on "Pulitzer-Prize winning poet Gwendolyn Brooks. . . . Jackson delves deep into the rich fabric of Brooks's work and world. Granted unprecedented access to Brooks's family, personal papers, and writing community, Jackson traces the literary arc of this artist's long career and gives context for the world in which Brooks wrote and published her work." (Publisher's note)

"Jackson presents an incisive portrait of poet Gwendolyn Brooks

(1917–2000), sharing with her subject the experiences of an African American woman poet in Chicago." Booklist

Includes bibliographical references

Brosh, Allie

Brosh, Allie. **Hyperbole** and a half; unfortunate situations, flawed coping mechanisms, mayhem, and other things that happened. Allie Brosh. Simon & Schuster 2013 384 p. $28 **92**

1. Blogs 2. American wit and humor 3. Conduct of life -- Humor 4. Comedians -- United States -- Biography

ISBN 1451666179; 147676459X; 9781451666175; 9781476764597

LC 2013025527

This book, by blogger Allie Brosh, is a "humorous memoir/collection of illustrated essays. . . . She tells personal stories that name things we can all relate to, including fear, love, depression and hope . . . [and] she approaches her subject matter from a vulnerable, childlike place, complete with Paintbrush caricatures." (Kirkus Reviews)

Brown, Carolyn

Brown, Carolyn. **Chance** and circumstance; twenty years with Cage and Cunningham. Alfred A. Knopf 2007 645p il $37.50 **92**

1. Poets 2. Authors 3. Dancers 4. Composers 5. Choreographers 6. Essayists

ISBN 978-0-394-40191-1; 0-394-40191-3

LC 2006-48799

The author "traces the trajectory of her modern dance career with that organization during its crawling stages in the 1950s and 1960s, when composer John Cage was musical director and artist Robert Rauschenberg was set and costume designer. Brown documents the company's early struggles for acceptance (it was considered avant-garde), various tours, and eventual world recognition. . . . This book will appeal to modern dance buffs and memoir readers." Libr J

Brown, Helen Gurley

Hirshey, Gerri. **Not** pretty enough; The Unlikely Triumph of Helen Gurley Brown. Gerri Hirshey. Sarah Crichton Books; Farrar, Straus & Giroux 2016 528 p. illustrations (Hardback) $27 **92**

1. Women authors 2. Periodicals -- United States 3. Editors -- United States -- Biography 4. Periodical editors -- United States -- Biography

ISBN 9780374169176; 9780374712235

LC 2016007143

This book, by Gerri Hirshey, is a biography of Helen Gurley Brown. "Her life story is astonishing, from her roots in the Ozark Mountains of Arkansas, to her single-girl decade as a Mad Men–era copywriter in Los Angeles, which informed her first bestseller, to her years at the helm of Cosmopolitan. Helen Gurley Brown told her own story many times, but coyly, with plenty of camouflage." (Publisher's note)

"This account sheds light on a complex woman whose controversial personality helped form both second-wave feminism and the magazine industry." LJ

Includes bibliographical references and index

Scanlon, Jennifer. **Bad** girls go everywhere: the life of Helen Gurley Brown. Oxford University Press 2009 270p il $27.95 **92**

1. Columnists 2. Magazine editors 3. Nonfiction writers

ISBN 978-0-19-534205-5; 0-19-534205-4

LC 2008-30466

This is a biography of Helen Gurley Brown, former editor of Cosmopolitan magazine and author of Sex and the Single Girl (1962), Sex and the Office (1964), and Single Girl's Cookbook (1969).

"Jennifer Scanlon delivers Helen Gurley Brown's 'delightfully knotty life story' in a neat and satisfying package. . . . This is not chick lit but cultural history, the first serious biography of the woman who, in Scanlon's view, 'ushered in and has long continued to define the feminist mainstream.'" Natl Rev

Includes bibliographical references

Brown, James

Brown, James. **James** Brown, the godfather of soul; by James Brown with Bruce Tucker; new introduction by Bruce Tucker; epilogue by Dave Marsh. Thunder's Mouth Press 1997 352p il pa $14.95   **92**
   1. Singers 2. African American singers 3. Soul musicians
   ISBN 978-1-56025-115-6; 1-56025-115-8
LC 90-31961

First published 1986 by Macmillan

This "is a solid, informative autobiography, and fans will welcome its vast discography." N Y Times Book Rev

Includes discography

★ McBride, James, 1957- **Kill** 'em and leave; searching for the real James Brown. James McBride. Spiegel & Grau 2016 256 p. $28   **92**
   1. Musicians -- United States 2. Soul musicians -- United States -- Biography
   ISBN 9780679645627; 9780812993509
LC 2015026358

Carnegie Medal Longlist: Nonfiction (2017)

This book, by James McBride, "is more than a book about James Brown. Brown's rough-and-tumble life, through McBride's lens, is an unsettling metaphor for American life: the tension between North and South, black and white, rich and poor. McBride's travels take him to forgotten corners of Brown's never-before-revealed history." (Publisher's note)

"An unconventional and fascinating portrait of Soul Brother No. 1 and the significance of his rise and fall i n American culture." Kirkus

Smith, R. J. The **one**; the life and music of James Brown. RJ Smith. Gotham Books 2012 455 p. $18   **92**
   1. Funk (Music) 2. Soul musicians -- United States -- Biography
   ISBN 1592406572; 1592407420; 9781592406579; 9781592407422
LC 2011028536

This is R.J. Smith's "look at the life and times of the late, great James Brown, self-proclaimed Soul Brother Number One and Hardest Working Man in Show Business and leading inspiration to a generation of singers like [Mitch] Ryder. . . . Smith considers Brown's life and career story, right down to brushes with the law, including his incarcerations at both and early age and later in life, when age and substance abuse overcame Brown's legendary control of his image and lifestyle." (Booklist)

Includes bibliographical references and index

Brown, James, 1957-

Brown, James. The **Los** Angeles diaries; a memoir. Morrow 2003 200p $21.95; pa $12.95   **92**
   1. Authors 2. Novelists 3. Short story writers
   ISBN 0-06-052151-1; 0-06-052152-X pa
LC 2003-48779

"Brown's revelations have no smugness or self-congratulation; they reek of remorse and desire, passion and futility. . . . The result is a grimly exquisite memoir that reads like a noir novel but grips unrelentingly like the hand of a homeless drunk begging for help." Publ Wkly

Brown, Jim, 1936-

Zirin, Dave. **Jim** Brown; last man standing. Dave Zirin. Blue Rider Press 2018 336 p. (hardcover) $27   **92**
   1. Brown, Jim, 1936- 2. Football players -- United States -- Biography
   ISBN 9780399173448
LC 2017035828

This biography, by Dave Zirin, tells the story of "Jim Brown--football legend, Hollywood star, and controversial activist. . . . Zirin's book redefines an American icon, and not always in a flattering light. At eighty-one years old, Brown continues to speak out and look for fights. His recent public support of Donald Trump and criticism of Colin Kaepernick are just the latest examples of someone who seems restless if he is not in conflict." (Publisher's note)

Brown, John, 1800-1859

★ Horwitz, Tony. **Midnight** rising; John Brown and raid that sparked the Civil War. Henry Holt and Co. 2011 365p il map $29; ebook $12.99   **92**
   1. Abolitionists 2. Pioneers 3. Harpers Ferry (W. Va.) -- History -- John Brown's Raid, 1859
   ISBN 978-0-8050-9153-3; 0-8050-9153-X; 978-1-4299-9698-3 ebook; 1-4299-9698-6 ebook
LC 2011015659

The author presents a "narrative of Brown and the raid on Harpers Ferry that in many ways set the stage for Southern secession and civil war. . . . Horwitz's Brown did not die in vain. By recalling the drama that fired the imagination and fears of Brown's time, Midnight Rising calls readers to account for complacency about social injustices today. This is a book for our time." Libr J

Includes bibliographical references

Reynolds, David S. **John** Brown, abolitionist; the man who killed slavery, sparked the Civil War, and seeded civil rights. Alfred A. Knopf 2005 578p il $35   **92**
   1. Abolitionists
   ISBN 0-375-41188-7
LC 2004-48864

"Almost every page forces you to think hard, and in new ways, about American violence, American history, and what used to be called the American character." New Yorker

Includes bibliographical references

Brown, Tina

Brown, Tina. The **Vanity** Fair diaries; 1983-1992. Tina Brown. Henry Holt & Co. 2017 x, 436 p.p (hardcover) $32 **92**
   1. Women periodical editors -- Biography 2. Vanity fair (New York, N.Y.) 3. Women periodical editors -- United States -- Biography
   ISBN 9781627791366
LC 2017028578

In this book, author Tina Brown shares the "daily diaries [that she kept] throughout her eight spectacular years as editor-in-chief of 'Vanity Fair.' . . . Here are the inside stories of 'Vanity Fair' scoops and covers that sold millions--the Reagan kiss, . . . the sensational Annie Leibovitz cover of a gloriously pregnant, naked Demi Moore. In the diary's cinematic pages, the drama, the comedy, and the struggle of running an 'it' magazine come to life." (Publisher's note)

"High and low, perceptive and prescient (in 1987, she speculated that the American public won't be able to resist the crassness of Donald Trump), this is a wildly entertaining, essential look at print journalism before the fall. Let us all pray that Brown also kept diaries of her years in the 1990s as editor of the New Yorker." Booklist

Brownstein, Carrie, 1974-

Brownstein, Carrie, 1974- **Hunger** Makes Me a Modern Girl; A Memoir. Carrie Brownstein. Riverhead Books 2015 244 p. illustrations $27.95 **92**

1. Women -- Biography 2. Riot grrrl movement 3. Singers -- Biography 4. Women rock musicians 5. Rock musicians -- United States -- Biography 6. Singers -- United States -- Biography 7. Women singers -- United States -- Biography 8. Women rock musicians -- United States -- Biography
ISBN 1594486638; 9781594486630

LC 2015024629

This memoir, by Carrie Brownstein, is "a narrative of her escape from a turbulent family life into a world where music was the means toward self-invention, community, and rescue. . . . Brownstein chronicles the excitement and contradictions within the era's flourishing and fiercely independent music subculture, including experiences that sowed the seeds for the observational satire of the popular television series Portlandia years later." (Publisher's note)

"A strong, engaging pop culture memoir: personal detail, a little dish, and a well-written look at what made the music, and the culture that spawned it, matter." LJ

Bruni, Frank, 1964-

Bruni, Frank. **Born** round; the secret history of a full-time eater. Penguin Press 2009 354p il $25.95; pa $16 **92**

1. Obesity 2. Food critics
ISBN 978-1-59420-231-5; 1-59420-231-1; 978-0-14-311767-4 pa; 0-14-311767-X pa

LC 2009-09532

"The book does not contain paeans to the glories of locavorism. It's not a tale of bawdy kitchen exploits, or of finding your true self over a bowl of pasta in Rome . . . His memoir tells a story of food addiction, eating disorders, and a lifelong struggle with his voracious appetite . . . Born Round makes for a breezy read. Even at its darkest, it goes down easy." Village Voice

Bryan, William Jennings, 1860-1925

Kazin, Michael. A **godly** hero; the life of William Jennings Bryan. Knopf 2006 374p il hardcover o.p. pa $16.95 **92**

1. Authors 2. Lawyers 3. Political leaders 4. Secretaries of state 5. Presidential candidates
ISBN 0-375-41135-6; 978-0-385-72056-4 pa; 0-385-72056-4 pa

LC 2005-44105

"Kazin is not the first biographer to tackle the Great Commoner, but he is definitely the best writer among them. 'A Godly Hero' is a richly textured narrative with an excellent pace." Christ Sci Monit

Includes bibliographical references

Bryant, Kobe, 1978-

Lazenby, Roland. **Showboat**; The Life of Kobe Bryant. Roland Lazenby. Little, Brown & Co. 2016 640 p. illustrations (some color) (ebook) $96; (hardback) $32 **92**

1. Basketball players -- United States -- Biography
ISBN 9780316387156; 9780316387248

LC 2016016821

This book, by Roland Lazenby, is a biography of Kobe Bryant. "Eighteen-time all-star; scorer of 81 points in a game; MVP and a shoot-

ing guard second only to Jordan in league history: Kobe Bryant is one of basketball's absolute greatest players, a fascinating and complicated character who knew when he was a mere boy that he would be better than Jordan on the court." (Publisher's note)

"As always, Lazenby does fine work bringing together the star's on- and off-court lives into an entertaining narrative that will draw NBA fans young and old." Booklist

Includes bibliographical references and index

Bryson, Bill

Bryson, Bill, 1951- The **life** and times of the thunderbolt kid; a memoir. Broadway Books 2006 270p il $25 **92**

1. Authors 2. Journalists 3. Essayists 4. Linguists 5. Lexicographers 6. Travel writers 7. Nonfiction writers 8. Biography, Individual
ISBN 0-7679-1936-X; 978-0-7679-1936-4

LC 2006-43859

In this book, Bill Bryson "recounts his childhood and teen years. When he was very young, he ran about his town with a towel for a cape, declaring himself the superhero, Thunderbolt Kid. His father wrote for the local paper, his mother worked there as well, leaving their home rather free from 'the domestic arts' (i.e. rather dirty). As he grew up, some of his friends were demonically destructive, while others were skilled at liberating boxcar loads of beer." (Voice of Youth Advocates)

The author "recounts the world of his younger self, buried in comic books in the Kiddie Corral at the local supermarket, resisting civil defense drills at school, and fruitlessly trying to unravel the mysteries of sex. . . . The larger world of 1950s America emerges through the lens of 'Billy's' world, including the dark underbelly of racism, the fight against communism, and the advent of the nuclear age." Libr J

Includes bibliographical references

Buck, Joan Juliet

Buck, Joan Juliet. The **price** of illusion; a memoir. Joan Juliet Buck. Atria Books 2017 416 p. illustrations (some color) (ebook) $20.99; (hardback) $30 **92**

1. Women authors -- Biography 2. Women periodical editors -- Biography 3. Vogue 4. Celebrities -- Biography 5. Rich people -- Biography 6. Fashion editors -- Biography 7. Americans -- Europe -- Biography 8. Women authors, American -- 21st century -- Biography
ISBN 9781476762968; 9781476762944; 9781476762951

LC 2016032072

This memoir, by Joan Juliet Buck, presents "a fabulous account of four decades spent in the creative heart of London, New York, Los Angeles, and Paris. . . . She chronicles this journey in beautiful and at times heartbreaking prose, taking the reader through the wild parties and the fashion, the celebrities and creative geniuses as well as love, loss, and the loneliness of getting everything you thought you wanted and finding it's not what you'd imagined." (Publisher's note)

"Buck includes a brilliant amount of detail in this memoir." Pub Wkly

Buck, Pearl S. (Pearl Sydenstricker), 1892-1973

Spurling, Hilary. **Pearl** Buck in China; journey to The Good Earth. Simon & Schuster 2010 304p il map $27; ebook $12.99 **92**

1. Authors 2. Novelists 3. Short 4. Essayists 5. Memoirists 6. Biographers 7. Authors, American 8. Biography, Individual 9. Nobel laureates for literature
ISBN 978-1-4165-4042-7; 1-4165-4042-3; 978-1-4391-8044-0 ebook; 1-4391-8044-X ebook

LC 2010-07712

Published in the United Kingdom with title: Burying the bones
This is a biography of the American author of The Good Earth

(1931).

The author's "account of Buck's 'rootless and fractured existence' provides a fascinating dissection of the tortured relationships between a man of God, the hapless wife sucked into supporting his mission and their increasingly sceptical daughter, Pearl, who, in 1933, publicly turned her back on her late father's church. It is also just as revealing about the no less tortured relationship between the West and China in the early part of the last century." Economist

Includes bibliographical references

Buckingham, George Villiers, Duke of, 1592-1628

Woolley, Benjamin. The **king's** assassin; the secret plot to murder King James I. Benjamin Woolley. St. Martin's Press 2018 342 p. $29.99   **92**

    1. Assassination 2. Great Britain -- History 3. Great Britain -- History -- James I, 1603-1625 -- Biography

    ISBN 1250125030; 9781250125033

                      LC 2018006541

This book, by Benjamin Woolley, is "an absorbing account of the conspiracy to kill King James I by his handsome lover, the Duke of Buckingham, an historical crime that has remained hidden for 400 years. . . . Combining vivid characterization and a strong narrative with historical scholarship and forensic investigation, Woolley tells the story of King James's death, and of the captivating figure at its center." (Publisher's note)

"Woolley presents an engrossing portrait of an ambitious man trusted by two kings that both casual readers and Stuart history fans can enjoy." Publishers' Weekly

Includes bibliographical references and index

Buckley, Bryan

Sielski, Mike. **Fading** echoes; a true story of rivalry and brotherhood from the football field to the fields of honor. Berkley Books 2009 342p il $24.95   **92**

    1. School sports 2. Iraq War, 2003-2011 3. Marines 4. Army officers 5. Football -- Biography 6. Soldiers -- United States

    ISBN 978-0-425-22974-3

                      LC 2009-17001

"Bryan Buckley was the captain of Central Bucks West and [Colby] Umbrell was one of the leaders of Central Bucks East when their teams clashed in their senior year of 1998. Eight years later, both were officers leading men in combat in Iraq, Buckley as a marine and Umbrell as an army ranger. Both were proudly fighting for ideals in which they believed, and only one would come home alive. Sielski . . . chronicles the lives of these two athletes and illustrates how their personalities and values were formed from interactions with family, friends, coaches, and community. In the process, he writes of much broader topics in contemporary American life: dreams, competition, resolve, war, honor, sacrifice, and true heartbreak." Libr J

Includes bibliographical references

Buckley, Christopher Taylor, 1952-

Buckley, Christopher Taylor. **Losing** Mum and Pup; a memoir. [by] Christopher Buckley. Twelve 2009 251p il $24.99; pa $13.99   **92**

    1. Authors 2. Humorists 3. Novelists 4. Philanthropists 5. Columnists 6. Socialites 7. Speechwriters 8. Magazine editors 9. Authors, American 10. Spouses of prominent persons

    ISBN 978-0-446-54094-0; 0-446-54094-3; 978-0-446-54095-7 pa; 0-446-54095-1 pa

                      LC 2008-43532

"Christopher Buckley has not written a 'Mommie Dearest' for the Evelyn Waugh set. 'Losing Mum and Pup' is a subtle, fond and, above

all, honest chronicle of his celebrated parents. . . . Buckley has pulled off what eludes many writers: he has written candidly but not unkindly about people whose vices and virtues he sees clearly." Newsweek

Buckley, Gail Lumet, 1937-

★ Buckley, Gail Lumet, 1937- The **Black** Calhouns; From Civil War to Civil Rights With One African American Family. by Gail Lumet Buckley. Atlantic Monthly Press 2016 336 p. 8 plts; ills; gen tbls; ports $26   **92**

    1. African Americans -- Biography

    ISBN 0802124542; 9780802124548

In this book, author "Gail Lumet Buckley—daughter of actress Lena Horne—delves deep into her family history, detailing the experiences of an extraordinary African-American family from Civil War to Civil Rights. Beginning with her great-great grandfather Moses Calhoun, a house slave who used the rare advantage of his education to become a successful businessman in post-war Atlanta, Buckley follows her family's two branches: one that stayed in the South, and the other that settled in Brooklyn." (Publisher's note)

Buckley, Pat

Buckley, Christopher Taylor. **Losing** Mum and Pup; a memoir. [by] Christopher Buckley. Twelve 2009 251p il $24.99; pa $13.99   **92**

    1. Authors 2. Humorists 3. Novelists 4. Philanthropists 5. Columnists 6. Socialites 7. Speechwriters 8. Magazine editors 9. Authors, American 10. Spouses of prominent persons

    ISBN 978-0-446-54094-0; 0-446-54094-3; 978-0-446-54095-7 pa; 0-446-54095-1 pa

                      LC 2008-43532

"Christopher Buckley has not written a 'Mommie Dearest' for the Evelyn Waugh set. 'Losing Mum and Pup' is a subtle, fond and, above all, honest chronicle of his celebrated parents. . . . Buckley has pulled off what eludes many writers: he has written candidly but not unkindly about people whose vices and virtues he sees clearly." Newsweek

Buckley, William F. (William Frank), 1925-2008

★ Bogus, Carl T. **Buckley**; William F. Buckley Jr. and the rise of American Conservatism. Carl T. Bogus. Bloomsbury 2011 416 p. $30.00   **92**

    1. Conservatism -- United States -- History 2. United States -- Politics and government 3. Journalists -- United States -- Biography 4. Conservatism -- United States -- Biography

    ISBN 1596915803; 9781596915800

                      LC 2011012734

This book is not only a biography of publisher William F. Buckley; it also looks at "the story of the conservative movement's origins" in the U.S. during the 20th century. Author Carl T. Bogus "explains the competing philosophies of different conservative sects—Burkean conservatism, libertarianism, Ayn Rand's objectivism." (Library Journal)

Includes bibliographical references and index.

Brookhiser, Richard. **Right** time, right place; coming of age with William F. Buckley, Jr. and the conservative movement. Basic Books 2009 262p $27.50   **92**

    1. Authors 2. Novelists 3. Historians 4. Journalists 5. Conservatism 6. Columnists 7. Biographers 8. National review 9. Magazine editors

    ISBN 978-0-465-01355-5; 0-465-01355-4

                      LC 2009-03073

"Think of a cause you care about deeply. Who's the figure you most admire in that movement? Now picture that person taking you to lunch, when you're 23, and declaring that you – you! – will be his successor. Such was the fantasy that Richard Brookhiser lived as a protégé of National Review editor William F. Buckley Jr., conservatism's standard-bearer for a half-century. Brookhiser was, to put it mildly, a prodigy. He wrote his first magazine cover story at 14. Steep falls often follow such precocious rises. But when Buckley changed his mind and sought a different heir, Brookhiser didn't self-destruct; he just rejiggered his career. Such equanimity means Right Time, Right Place is refreshingly free of spicy score settling and juicy revelations. Instead, readers get tasty morsels of candor caramelized in the searing heat of self-reflection. The result is a psychologically rich personal narrative." Christ Sci Monit

Buckley, Christopher Taylor. **Losing** Mum and Pup; a memoir. [by] Christopher Buckley. Twelve 2009 251p il $24.99; pa $13.99 **92**
1. Authors 2. Humorists 3. Novelists 4. Philanthropists 5. Columnists 6. Socialites 7. Speechwriters 8. Magazine editors 9. Authors, American 10. Spouses of prominent persons
ISBN 978-0-446-54094-0; 0-446-54094-3; 978-0-446-54095-7 pa; 0-446-54095-1 pa

LC 2008-43532

"Christopher Buckley has not written a 'Mommie Dearest' for the Evelyn Waugh set. 'Losing Mum and Pup' is a subtle, fond and, above all, honest chronicle of his celebrated parents. . . . Buckley has pulled off what eludes many writers: he has written candidly but not unkindly about people whose vices and virtues he sees clearly." Newsweek

Hendershot, Heather. **Open** to debate; How William F. Buckley Put Liberal America on the Firing Line. Heather Hendershot. Broadside 2016 432 p. illustrations (ebook) $27.99; (hardback: alkaline paper) $28.99 **92**
1. Political culture -- United States 2. Television personalities -- Biography 3. Journalists -- United States -- Biography 4. Firing line (Television program) -- History 5. United States -- Intellectual life -- 20th century 6. United States -- Politics and government -- 1945-1989 7. Television personalities -- United States -- Biography 8. Conservatism -- United States -- History -- 20th century 9. Political culture -- United States -- History -- 20th century
ISBN 9780062430472; 9780062430458; 9780062430465

LC 2016015903

This book, by Heather Hendershot, is a "unique and compelling portrait of William F. Buckley as the champion of conservative ideas in an age of liberal dominance, taking on the smartest adversaries he could find while singlehandedly reinventing the role of public intellectual in the network television era." (Publisher's note)

"Using interviews and transcripts, Hendershot does more than tell the history of a uniquely influential show and personality; her thorough, compelling, and very readable book provides a three-decade journey through the center of the nation's intellectual life." Pub Wkly

Includes bibliographical references and index.

Buffalo Bill, 1846-1917

Warren, Louis S. **Buffalo** Bill's America; William Cody and the Wild West Show. Alfred A. Knopf 2005 652p il $30 **92**
1. Entertainers 2. Frontier and pioneer life 3. Scouts 4. Hunters 5. Circus executives 6. Circus performers
ISBN 0-375-41216-6

LC 2004-63280

This is a biography of the American showman.

This book "is well written and exhaustively researched, the weightiest and surely the most ambitious book ever published about Cody and his times." N Y Times Book Rev

Includes bibliographical references

Buffett, Warren E.

Schroeder, Alice D. The **snowball**: Warren Buffett and the business of life; [by] Alice Schroeder. Bantam Books 2008 960p il $35 **92**
1. Capitalists and financiers 2. Financiers
ISBN 978-0-553-80509-3; 0-553-80509-6

LC 2008-17338

A portrait of the life and career of investment guru Warren Buffett

"In a book that is dominated by unstinting descriptions of Buffett's appetites—for profit, women (particularly nurturing maternal types), food (Buffett maintained his and his family's weight by 'dangling money')—it is refreshing that Schroeder keeps her tone free of judgment or awe; Buffett's plain-speaking suffuses the book and renders his public and private successes and failures wonderfully human and universal. . . . Inspiring managerial advice abounds and competes with gossipy tidbits . . . in this rich, surprisingly affecting biography." Publ Wkly

Includes bibliographical references

Bui, Thi

★ Thi Bui. The **best** we could do; an illustrated memoir. Thi Bui. Abrams ComicArts 2017 327 p. chiefly color illustrations (hardcover) $24.95 **92**
1. Vietnamese Americans -- Biography 2. Vietnam War, 1961-1975 -- Personal narratives, Vietnamese 3. Graphic novels 4. Autobiographical comics 5. Vietnamese Americans -- Biography -- Comic books, strips, etc 6. Refugees -- United States -- Biography -- Comic books, strips, etc. 7. Vietnam War, 1961-1975 -- Personal narratives, Vietnamese -- Comic books, strips, etc.
ISBN 9781613129302; 9781419718779

LC 2016940170

National Book Critics Circle Award Finalist: Autobiography (2017)

In this memoir, author Thi Bui "documents the story of her family's daring escape after the fall of South Vietnam in the 1970s, and the difficulties they faced building new lives for themselves. At the heart of Bui's story is a universal struggle: While adjusting to life as a first-time mother, she ultimately discovers what it means to be a parent--the endless sacrifices, the unnoticed gestures, and the depths of unspoken love." (Publisher's note)

"In creatively telling a complicated story with the kind of feeling words alone rarely relay, The Best We Could Do does the very best that comics can do." Booklist

Bullock-Prado, Gesine, 1970-

Bullock-Prado, Gesine. **Confections** of a closet master baker; one woman's sweet journey from unhappy Hollywood executive to contented country baker. illustrations by Raymond G. Prado. Broadway Books 2009 226p il $24 **92**
1. Baking 2. Bakers 3. Motion picture executives
ISBN 978-0-7679-3268-4

LC 2009-945

The author "chronicles her career change from schmoozing Hollywood production company executive to running a bakery in Montpelier, VT. . . . Memoir lovers will find this a lighthearted, entertaining read filled with humor and acerbic wit; foodies will enjoy the insider's view of running a bakery." Libr J

Bunch, Robert, 1820-

Dickey, Christopher. **Our** Man in Charleston; Britain's Secret Agent in the Civil War South. Christopher Dickey. Crown 2015 368 p. illustrations, map (hardback) $27 **92**
1. Diplomats -- Great Britain -- Biography 2. United States -- History -- 1861-1865, Civil War 3. Spies -- Great Britain -- History

-- 19th century 4. Great Britain -- Foreign relations -- United States 5. United States -- Foreign relations -- Great Britain 6. Espionage -- Great Britain -- History -- 19th century 7. Confederate States of America -- Foreign relations -- Great Britain 8. Great Britain -- Foreign relations -- Confederate States of America 9. Diplomatic and consular service, British -- Confederate States of America 10. Diplomatic and consular service, British -- United States -- History -- 19th century

ISBN 9780307887276; 0307887278

LC 2015016637

This book, by Christopher Dickey, profiles the career of Robert Bunch, the British consul officer assigned to Charleston, South Carolina in 1853, who acted as an influential figure regarding the British official position on the U.S. Civil War. "Between the Confederacy and recognition by Great Britain stood one unlikely Englishman who hated the slave trade. His actions helped determine the fate of a nation." (Publisher's note)

"A great book explaining the workings of what Dickey calls an erratic, cobbled-together coalition of ferociously independent states. It should be in the library of any student of diplomacy, as well as Civil War buffs." Kirkus

Bundy, Ted

Rule, Ann. The **stranger** beside me; Updated 20th anniversary ed; Signet 2001 548p il pa $7.99   **92**

1. Criminals 2. Murderers

ISBN 0-451-20326-7; 978-0-451-20326-7

First published 1980 by Norton

This is a biography of Ted Bundy, written by someone who "worked a suicide hotline in Seattle with Ted Bundy, not knowing he was a serial killer." Libr J

Bunker, Chang, 1811-1874

Yunte Huang. **Inseparable**; the original Siamese twins and their rendezvous with American history. Yunte Huang. Liveright Publishing Corporation, a Division of W.W. Norton & Company 2018 xxvi, 388 p.p (hardcover) $28.95   **92**

1. Twins 2. Conjoined twins 3. Conjoined twins -- United States -- Biography 4. Conjoined twins -- United States -- History -- 19th century

ISBN 9781631493850; 9780871404473

LC 2017055799

In this book, author Yunte Huang provide a "portrait of Chang and Eng Bunker . . . , twins conjoined at the sternum by a band of cartilage and a fused liver, who were 'discovered' in Siam by a British merchant in 1824. . . . Huang depicts the twins, arriving in Boston in 1829, first as museum exhibits but later as financially savvy showmen who gained their freedom and traveled the backroads of rural America to bring 'entertainment' to the Jacksonian mobs." (Publisher's note)

"Huang offers a vivid portrait of two men who did the best they could to live ordinary lives, and a revealing look at a somewhat scandalous side of the prim-and-proper Victorian Era." Booklist

Includes bibliographical references and index

Bunker, Eng, 1811-1874

Yunte Huang. **Inseparable**; the original Siamese twins and their rendezvous with American history. Yunte Huang. Liveright Publishing Corporation, a Division of W.W. Norton & Company 2018 xxvi, 388 p.p (hardcover) $28.95   **92**

1. Twins 2. Conjoined twins 3. Conjoined twins -- United States -- Biography 4. Conjoined twins -- United States -- History -- 19th century

ISBN 9781631493850; 9780871404473

LC 2017055799

In this book, author Yunte Huang provide a "portrait of Chang and Eng Bunker . . . , twins conjoined at the sternum by a band of cartilage and a fused liver, who were 'discovered' in Siam by a British merchant in 1824. . . . Huang depicts the twins, arriving in Boston in 1829, first as museum exhibits but later as financially savvy showmen who gained their freedom and traveled the backroads of rural America to bring 'entertainment' to the Jacksonian mobs." (Publisher's note)

"Huang offers a vivid portrait of two men who did the best they could to live ordinary lives, and a revealing look at a somewhat scandalous side of the prim-and-proper Victorian Era." Booklist

Includes bibliographical references and index

Burbank, Luther, 1849-1926

Smith, Jane S. The **garden** of invention; Luther Burbank and the business of breeding plants. Penguin Press 2009 354p il $25.95   **92**

1. Plant breeding 2. Horticulturists

ISBN 978-1-59420-209-4

LC 2009-1822

"An accessible introduction to an agricultural innovator that gives equal weight to his life of experimentation and what it has meant for society." Kirkus

Includes bibliographical references

Burgess, Guy, 1911-1963

Lownie, Andrew. **Stalin's** Englishman. St. Martin's Press 2016 448 p. illustrations (ebook) $60; $29.99   **92**

1. Spies 2. Cold war

ISBN 9781250101013; 1250100992; 9781250100993

LC 2016028503

This book, by Andrew Lownie, provides a biography of British spy Guy Burgess. "An engaging and charming companion to many, an unappealing, utterly ruthless manipulator to others, . . . gaining access to thousands of highly sensitive secret documents which he passed to his Russian handlers. . . . Lownie shows us how even Burgess's chaotic personal life of drunken philandering did nothing to stop his penetration and betrayal of the British Intelligence Service." (Publisher's note)

"A crack biography of a man who was a preposterous enigma." Kirkus

Includes bibliographical references and index.

Burke, Edmund, 1729-1797

Norman, Jesse. **Edmund** Burke; the first conservative. by Jesse Norman. Basic Books, A Member of the Perseus Books Group 2013 325 p. ill. ports, maps (hardcover) $27.99   **92**

1. Political philosophy 2. Orators -- Great Britain -- Biography 3. Statesmen -- Great Britain -- Biography 4. Political scientists -- Great Britain -- Biography 5. Great Britain -- Politics and government -- 1760-1820

ISBN 0465058973; 9780465058976

LC 2013935334

This book, written by Jesse Norman, presents a biography of Edmund Burke "an 18th-century Irish philosopher and statesman [and] champion of human rights and the Anglo-American constitutional tradition, and a lifelong campaigner against arbitrary power. As Norman reveals, Burke was often ahead of his time, anticipating the abolition of slavery and arguing for free markets, equality for Catholics in Ireland, and responsible government in India." (Publisher's note)

Includes bibliographical references (p. [299]-305) and index.

Burns, Robert, 1759-1796

Crawford, Robert. The **bard**; Robert Burns, a biography. Princeton University Press 2009 465p $35　　　**92**

　1. Poets 2. Authors

　ISBN 978-0-691-14171-8; 0-691-14171-1

LC 2008-937561

"Crawford's Burns, merrily mixing high and low culture, seems eerily contemporary. He shares with great hip-hop artists a genius for catchy, sexy, and memorable rhymes gloriously liberated from the hegemony of standard English." New Yorker

Includes bibliographical references

Burroughs, Augusten

Burroughs, Augusten. **Lust** and Wonder; Augusten Burroughs. St. Martin's Press 2016 298 p. $26.99　　　**92**

　1. Love 2. Dating (Social customs) 3. Interpersonal relations

　ISBN 0312342039; 9780312342036

LC 2015041615

In this memoir "chronicling the development and demise of the different relationships he's had while living in New York, [author] Augusten Burroughs examines what it means to be in love, what it means to be in lust, and what it means to be figuring it all out." (Publisher's note)

"His brutal honesty about himself—and others—is as sharp and surprising as ever, and how Burroughs manages to effortlessly convey so much of his complicated histories, such as a lifelong need to bury his fears in the purchase of jewelry, is a lesson in the elegant use of narrative as a vehicle for truth." Booklist

Burroughs, William S., 1914-1997

Miles, Barry. **Call** Me Burroughs; A Life. Barry Miles. Twelve 2014 736 p. illustrations (hardback) $32　　　**92**

　1. Beat generation 2. American authors 3. Novelists, American -- 20th century -- Biography

　ISBN 1455511951; 9781455511952

LC 2013032565

Writer William "Burroughs was the original cult figure of the Beat Movement, and with the publication of his novel 'Naked Lunch,' which was originally banned for obscenity, he became a guru to the 60s youth counterculture. In 'Call Me Burroughs,' biographer and Beat historian Barry Miles presents the first full-length biography of Burroughs to be published in a quarter century." (Publisher's note)

A "dense, detailed, yet wonderfully readable and entertaining narrative that illuminates, without sensationalizing, Burroughs's manifold peculiarities." Pub Wkly

Includes bibliographical references and index

Burton, Richard, 1925-1984

Kashner, Sam. **Furious** love; Elizabeth Taylor, Richard Burton, and the marriage of the century. [by] Sam Kashner and Nancy Schoenberger. Harper 2010 500p il $27.99　　　**92**

　1. Actors

　ISBN 978-0-06-156284-6; 0-06-156284-X

LC 2010-06732

"In this dual biography of the two legendary film stars, the authors draw upon new information, including interviews with Elizabeth Taylor and with the Burton family, to capture the famously passionate and tumultuous relationship between the legendary couple. . . . It's a mesmerizing tale, but it's also sad, and sometimes ugly, as the two stars engaged in vicious fights, nursed their jealousies and insecurities, and descended into alcoholism while outwardly living a life of glamour and sophistication." Booklist

Includes bibliographical references

Bush, Barbara, 1981-

Bush, Jenna, 1981- **Sisters** first; stories from our wild and wonderful life. Jenna Bush Hager; Barbara Pierce Bush; foreword by Laura Bush. Grand Central Publishing 2017 256 p. $28　　　**92**

　1. Presidents -- United States -- Children

　ISBN 1538711419; 9781538711415

In this memoir, by Jenna Bush Hager and Barbara Pierce Bush, with foreword by Laura Bush, "former first daughters and #1 bestselling authors Jenna . . . and Barbara . . . share intimate stories and reflections from the Texas countryside to the storied halls of the White House and beyond. . . . [The sisters] spent their college years watched over by Secret Service agents and became fodder for the tabloids, with teenage mistakes making national headlines." (Publisher's note)

"The two first daughters emerge as surprisingly well-adjusted, intelligent young women with strong family bonds in this insightful look at life inside the White House." (Booklist)

Bush, George W.

Bush, George W. (George Walker), 1946- **Decision** points. Crown Publishers 2010 497p il $35; ebook $14.99　　　**92**

　1. Governors 2. Presidents 3. Biography, Individual 4. Children of presidents 5. Presidents -- United States

　ISBN 978-0-307-59061-9; 0-307-59061-5; 978-0-307-59062-6 ebook

"Critics on both the left and right are challenged to walk in his shoes, and may come away with a new view of the former president—or at least an appreciation of the hard and often ambiguous choices he was forced to make. . . . Honest, of course, but also surprisingly approachable and engaging." Kirkus

Bush, George, 1924-2018

Bush, George W. (George Walker), 1946- **41**; a portrait of my father. by George W. Bush. Random House Inc 2014 304 p. portraits (chiefly color) $28　　　**92**

　1. Presidents -- United States -- Biography

　ISBN 0553447785; 9780553447781

LC 2014469972

In this book, by George W. Bush, "the 43rd President of the United States [offers] . . . a personal biography of his father, George H. W. Bush, the 41st President. . . . The book covers the entire scope of . . . [his father's] life and career, including his service in the Pacific during World War II, his pioneering work in the Texas oil business, and his political rise as a Congressman, U.S. Representative to China and the United Nations, CIA Director, Vice President, and President." (Publisher's note)

★ Meacham, Jon. **Destiny** and Power; The American Odyssey of George Herbert Walker Bush. by Jon Meacham. Random House Inc. 2015 848 p. color illustrations, map $35　**92**

　1. Presidents -- United States -- Biography

　ISBN 1400067650; 9781400067657

LC 2015016550

This biography, by Jon Meacham, "chronicles the life of George Herbert Walker Bush. Drawing on President Bush's candid personal diaries; on the diaries of his wife, Barbara; and on extraordinary access to the forty-first president and to his family, Meacham paints an intimate and surprising portrait of an intensely private man who led the nation through tumultuous times." (Publisher's note)

"In Zelig-like fashion, George H. W. Bush was present at many of the most important events of the last 65-plus years, and the remarkable story of his life and times comes vividly alive in the words of this highly skilled writer." Booklist

Byron, Anne Isabella Noel, Baroness, 1792-1860

Markus, Julia. **Lady** Byron and Her Daughters; Julia Markus. W W Norton & Co Inc 2015 384 p. illustrations $28.95
92

1. Single parents 2. Mother-daughter relationship
ISBN 0393082687; 9780393082685

LC 2015022540

This biography by Julia Markus is a "reevaluation of Lady Byron's marriage and the untold story of her complex life as single mother and progressive force. The center of public attention after her tumultuous marriage to Lord Byron, Annabella Milbanke transformed herself from a neglected wife into a figure of incredible resilience and social vision." (Publisher's note)

Caesar, Julius, 100-44 B.C.

★ Goldsworthy, Adrian Keith. **Caesar**; life of a colossus. [by] Adrian Goldsworthy. Yale University Press 2006 583p il map $35
92

1. Statesmen 2. Historians 3. Rome -- History
ISBN 978-0-300-12048-6; 0-300-12048-6

LC 2006-922060

This biography draws "together Julius Caesar's personal, political, and military history into a single volume. . . . This is an engaging and well-drawn resource for those who wish to be introduced to the man who was Caesar." Libr J

Includes bibliographical references

Cage, John

Brown, Carolyn. **Chance** and circumstance; twenty years with Cage and Cunningham. Alfred A. Knopf 2007 645p il $37.50
92

1. Poets 2. Authors 3. Dancers 4. Composers 5. Choreographers 6. Essayists
ISBN 978-0-394-40191-1; 0-394-40191-3

LC 2006-48799

The author "traces the trajectory of her modern dance career with that organization during its crawling stages in the 1950s and 1960s, when composer John Cage was musical director and artist Robert Rauschenberg was set and costume designer. Brown documents the company's early struggles for acceptance (it was considered avant-garde), various tours, and eventual world recognition. . . . This book will appeal to modern dance buffs and memoir readers." Libr J

Silverman, Kenneth, 1936-2017. **Begin** again; a biography of John Cage. Alfred A. Knopf 2010 483p il $40
92

1. Poets 2. Authors 3. Composers 4. Essayists 5. Biography, Individual
ISBN 1-4000-4437-5; 978-1-4000-4437-5

LC 2010-09525

This is a biography of the American "musician, inventor, composer, poet." (Publisher's note) Index.

In this biography of "one of the most influential composers of the 20th century . . . [the author traces Cage's] innovations chronologically—his breakthrough years as a composer of experimental dance and percussion music, his definitive decade inventing chance-derived music as a member of the New York School of artists and musicians in the '50s, and his later development of indeterminate music, the content of which could be created by the performer. . . . Not just an exemplary biography, but a significant contribution to the cultural history of American music." Kirkus

Includes bibliographical references

Cagney, James, 1899-1986

McCabe, John. **Cagney**. Carroll & Graf Pub. 1999 439p il pa $18.95
92

1. Actors
ISBN 978-0-7867-0580-1; 0-7867-0580-9

First published 1997 by Knopf

This work "exceeds the typical standards of celebrity biography because McCabe is fully attentive to the many dimensions of his subject's artistry." Commonweal

Includes filmography and bibliographical references

Cahun, Claude, 1894-1954

Shaw, Jennifer L. **Exist** otherwise; the life and works of Claude Cahun. Jennifer L. Shaw. Reaktion Books 2017 326 p. illustrations (hardcover) $45
92

1. Women artists -- Biography 2. Artists, French -- Biography 3. Artists -- France -- Biography 4. Photographers -- France -- Biography
ISBN 9781780237282; 1780237286

This book, by Jennifer L. Shaw, "is the first work in English to the tell the full story of Claude Cahun's art and life, . . . [The book also] examines her relationship with Marcel Moore--Cahun's stepsister, lover, and life partner. . . . Offering some of Cahun's writings . . . alongside a wide array of her artworks . . . this book is a must-have for any fan of this iconic artist or anyone interested in this crucial period in artistic and cultural history." (Publisher's note)

"Shaw . . . provides the first English-language biography of Cahun that will leave readers enthralled by this artist who lived life on her own terms despite numerous challenges, including Nazi imprisonment for resistance activities." LJ

Calder, Alexander, 1898-1976

★ Perl, Jed. **Calder**; the conquest of time: the early years, 1898-1940. Jed Perl. Alfred A. Knopf 2017 viii, 687 p.p illustrations (some color) (hardcover) $55
92

1. Sculptors -- United States -- Biography 2. Artists -- United States -- Biography
ISBN 9780451494214; 9780307272720

LC 2016054731

This book, by Jed Perl, is "the first biography of America's greatest twentieth-century sculptor, Alexander Calder: an authoritative and revelatory achievement, based on a wealth of letters and papers never before available, and written by one of our most renowned art critics. . . . More than 350 illustrations in color and black-and-white--including little-known works and many archival photographs that have never before been seen--further enrich the story." (Publisher's note)

"Not only an essential record of the first 40 years of Calder's life, but an exceptional chronicle of the genesis of modernism." Kirkus

Includes bibliographical references (pages 607-649) and index.

Caldwell, Gail, 1951-

★ Caldwell, Gail. **Let's** take the long way home; a memoir of friendship. Random House 2010 190p $23
92

1. Friendship 2. Journalists 3. Columnists 4. Memoirists 5. Literary critics
ISBN 978-1-4000-6738-1; 1-4000-6738-3

LC 2009-29384

"This is a book you'll want to share with your own 'necessary pillars of life,' as Caldwell refers to her nearest and dearest. . . . Her memoir, a tribute to the enduring power of friendship, is a lovely gift to readers." Washington Post

Caldwell, Gail. **New** life, no instructions; a memoir. by Gail Caldwell. Random House 2014 176 p. (alk. paper) $23   **92**
1. Journalists -- United States -- Biography 2. Critics -- United States -- Biography 3. Total hip replacement -- Patients -- Biography
ISBN 1400069548; 9781400069545

LC 2013015486

In this memoir, author Gail Caldwell "confronts . . . the hurdles that life throws her way—in this case, hip surgery while tending to a new pet Samoyed. . . . After the death of her beloved Clementine, in 2008, she tracked down a Samoyed breeder . . . and procured a new puppy, Tula. However, at age 57 and with a 'bum leg,' . . . Caldwell wondered at the wisdom of getting a very muscular, high-octane dog when her leg strength seemed to be diminishing." (Publishers Weekly)

"Readers will enjoy Caldwell's thoughtful, wide-eyed view of the world around her and her musings on how we get our bearings in midlife." Kirkus

Includes bibliographical references and index

Camilla, Duchess of Cornwall, 1947-

Junor, Penny. The **Duchess**; Camilla Parker Bowles and the love affair that rocked the crown. Penny Junor. HarperCollins 2018 320 p. $28.99   **92**
1. Biography 2. Great Britain -- Kings and rulers
ISBN 0062471104; 9780062471109

In this book, "royal biographer Penny Junor tells the unlikely and extraordinary story of [Camilla Parker Bowles,] the woman reviled as a pariah who, thanks to numerous twists of fate, became the popular princess consort. . . [Junor] casts her insightful, sensitive eye on the intriguing, once widely despised, and little-known Camilla Parker Bowles, revealing in full, for the first time, the remarkable rise of a woman who was the most notorious mistress in the world." (Publisher's note)

Campbell, William, 1730?-1778

Harris, J. William. The **hanging** of Thomas Jeremiah; a free Black man's encounter with liberty. Yale University Press 2009 223p il map $27.50   **92**
1. Diplomats 2. Merchants 3. Ship captains 4. Colonial leaders 5. Plantation owners 6. Government officials 7. Colonial administrators 8. Slavery -- United States 9. South Carolina -- Race relations 10. African Americans -- Social conditions
ISBN 978-0-300-15214-2; 0-300-15214-0

LC 2009-15233

This is an "account of nebulous historical figure Thomas Jeremiah. . . . Owner of a fishing company and worth $200,000 in 2009 dollars, . . . [Jeremiah] was probably the richest black man in North America; he was also a slaveowner. That didn't stop him from becoming a scapegoat, accused by patriot leader Henry Laurens—a wealthy plantation owner with hundreds of slaves—of secretly leading a British-sponsored slave insurrection. Though Governor William Campbell, aggrieved by the unlawfulness of Jeremiah's trial, interceded, it didn't stop those determined to hang Jeremiah. . . . Readers will learn much about the darker side of American institutions; students of American history and civil rights will appreciate Harris's impassive approach and thorough standards." Publ Wkly

Includes bibliographical references

Camus, Albert, 1913-1960

Todd, Olivier. **Albert** Camus; a life. translated by Benjamin Ivry. abr & ed English version; Knopf 1997 434p il $30   **92**
1. Authors 2. Novelists 3. Dramatists 4. Authors, French 5. Essayists 6. Nobel laureates for literature

ISBN 0-679-42855-0

LC 97-2991

Original French edition, 1996

This is a biography of the French novelist, playwright, literary editor, and philosopher.

"Todd's exhaustive biography, which aims—and succeeds—in presenting 'the man' and not just the writer, has been shortened for its English translation, which refers readers to the French edition for notes, sources and bibliography." Publ Wkly

Cantú, Francisco (Essayist)

Cantú, Francisco. The **line** becomes a river; dispatches from the border. Francisco Cantú. Riverhead Books 2018 256 p.   **92**
1. United States -- Boundaries 2. Illegal aliens -- Mexican-American Border Region 3. U.S. Border Patrol -- Officials and employees -- Biography 4. Mexican-American Border Region -- Emigration and immigration 5. Border security -- Social aspects -- Mexican-American Border Region
ISBN 9780735217713

LC 2017014247

In this book, author Francisco Cantú describes his time in the U.S. Border Patrol as a field agent. "He and his partners are posted to remote regions crisscrossed by drug routes and smuggling corridors, where they learn to track other humans under blistering sun and through frigid nights. They haul in the dead and deliver to detention those they find alive. Cantú tries not to think where the stories go from there." (Publisher's note)

'An ex–Border Patrol agent finds himself on both sides of the battle over illegal immigration in this fraught memoir of his time patrolling the Arizona, New Mexico, and Texas borders from 2008 to 2012, an experience that roiled his emotions and shook his sense of his own part-Mexican identity." Publishers Weekly

Capone, Al, 1899-1947

Bair, Deirdre. **Al** Capone; His life, legacy, and legend. Deirdre Bair. Nan A. Talese/Doubleday 2016 416 p. illustrations (hardback) $30   **92**
1. Criminals -- United States -- Biography 2. Gangsters -- United States -- Biography 3. Organized crime -- United States -- History -- 20th century
ISBN 9780345804518; 9780385537155

LC 2016009367

This book, by Deirdre Bair, looks at the "life of legendary gangster Al Capone. . . . From his heyday to the present moment, . . . Capone-Public Enemy Number One--has gripped popular imagination. Rising from humble Brooklyn roots, Capone went on to become the most infamous gangster in American history. . . . [This book] provides new answers to the enduring questions about [Capone], who was equal parts charismatic gangster, devoted patriarch, and calculating monster." (Publisher's note)

"Bair has written perhaps the last word on Capone. Highly recommended." LJ

Includes bibliographical references and index

Balsamo, William. **Young** Al Capone; the untold story of Scarface in New York, 1899-1925. [by] William Balsamo and John Balsamo. Skyhorse Pub. 2010 270p il $24.95   **92**
1. Mafia 2. Criminals 3. Mobsters 4. Bootleggers
ISBN 978-1-616-08085-3

LC 2010-34682

"Before he became the mythical untouchable 'Scarface,' Alphonse Capone (1899-1947) was a young, cunningly brutal thug schooled by hardboiled criminal minds in pre-Depression Brooklyn, N.Y. . . . [The authors] revisit Capone's apprenticeship years in the violent Brooklyn Navy Yard street gangs and his transformation from a wayward youth to polished, cold-blooded gangster under the tutelage of two master mobsters, Johnny Torrio and 'Frankie Yale' Ioele. . . . With insider facts and spare narrative, the authors show us not only how Capone got his scarred face; they deliver a scathing portrait of a power-mad predator coming up through the criminal ranks." Publ Wkly

Eig, Jonathan. **Get** Capone; the real story of America's legendary gangster. Simon & Schuster 2010 468p il $28 **92**
1. Criminals 2. Organized crime 3. Mobsters 4. Bootleggers
ISBN 978-1-4165-8059-1; 1-4165-8059-X
LC 2009-33949
The author "rescues the narrative of Al Capone from the realm of pop melodrama, offering vibrant historical storytelling and a nuanced, enigmatic portrait of Capone and his Chicago milieu. . . . An impressive, accessible history of a troubled time." Kirkus
Includes bibliographical references

Capote, Truman, 1924-1984

★ Capote, Truman. **Too** brief a treat; the letters of Truman Capote. edited by Gerald Clarke. Random House 2004 487p il $27.95; pa $16 **92**
1. Authors 2. Novelists 3. Nonfiction writers 4. Short story writers
ISBN 0-375-50133-9; 0-375-70241-5 pa
LC 2004-50313
"Capote's untrammeled personality fairly falls off the pages of these letters, and rather than being irritating, his disregard of reticence is especially poignant in this day of sterile e-mailing. Ideal for devotees to dip into here and there instead of reading from start to finish." Booklist
Includes bibliographical references

Caravaggio, Michelangelo Merisi da, 1573-1610

Ebert-Schifferer, Sybille. **Caravaggio**; the artist and his work. Sybille Ebert-Schifferer. J. Paul Getty Museum 2012 319 p. (hardback) $59.95 **92**
1. Painters 2. Art -- History
ISBN 1606060953; 9781606060957
LC 2011045619
This book is a biography of painter Michelangelo Merisi da Caravaggio. "Rather than accept the stories of the artist as merely an uneducated troublemaker (albeit a wildly talented one), . . . [Sybille] Ebert-Schifferer instead strictly focuses her attention on historical documents and technical research. Beholden to incontrovertible evidence, and taking advantage of X-ray examinations of the paintings, the author finds her way to frequent insight." (Publishers Weekly)
Includes bibliographical references and index.

Prose, Francine. **Caravaggio**; painter of miracles. Atlas Books/HarperCollins 2005 149p il (Eminent lives) $21.95 **92**
1. Artists 2. Painters 3. Artists, Italian
ISBN 0-06-057560-3
LC 2005-40203
"A contemporary of Shakespeare, Caravaggio was 'belligerent, contemptuous, and competitive,' a revered artist and a notorious street fighter wanted for murder who died at 39 under tragic circumstances. Much has been written about Caravaggio and his dramatic paintings, especially his daringly earthy depictions of biblical scenes, but somehow Prose's concentrated interpretation has a stronger impact. Not only does she cover all the biographical essentials but she also more clearly and descriptively explicates the pioneering painter's unique perception

of the miraculous in everyday life. Prose also reveals, with both subtlety and flourish, how Caravaggio's frank interpretations of violence and pain, fear and grief, dignity and transcendence are matched with a brilliant subversion of our sense of reality." Booklist

Carew, Tom (Thomas Arthur)

Carew, Keggie, 1957- **Dadland**; Keggie Carew. Atlantic Monthly Press 2017 432 p. illustrations, maps $26 **92**
1. World War, 1939-1945 -- Biography 2. World War, 1939-1945 -- Secret service
ISBN 080212514X; 9780802125149
LC 2016058365
In this book, by Keggie Carew, winner of the Costa Book Award for Biography, Keggie has been "kept at arm's length from her father's personal history, but when she is invited to join him for the sixtieth anniversary of the Jedburghs—an elite special operations unit . . . [of] American and British Secret Services during World War II—a new door opens in their relationship. As dementia stakes a claim over his memory, Keggie embarks on a quest to unravel her father's story." (Publisher's note)
"Carew is as vicious in her portrayal of this possessive, controlling stepmother as she is empathetic to her father's loss of his adventuresome past and, more tragically, sense of identity. A tender evocation of an extraordinary life." Kirkus
Includes bibliographical references (pages 399-407).

Carhart, Thaddeus

Carhart, Thad. **Finding** Fontainebleau; an American boy in France. Thad Carhart. Viking 2016 304 p. map (hardback) $27 **92**
1. Americans -- France 2. France -- Description and travel 3. Fontainebleau (France) -- Biography 4. Boys -- France -- Fontainebleau -- Biography 5. Americans -- France -- Fontainebleau -- Biography 6. Fontainebleau (France) -- Buildings, structures, etc 7. Château de Fontainebleau (Fontainebleau, France) 8. Fontainebleau (France) -- Social life and customs -- 20th century
ISBN 9780525428800; 0525428801
LC 2016008395
This book, by Thad Carhart, is a "memoir of a childhood in 1950s Fontainebleau. Each trip to Fontainebleau introduces him to entirely new aspects of the château's history, enriching his memories and leading him to Patrick Ponsot, the head of the château's restoration, who becomes Carhart's guide to the hidden Fontainebleau." (Publisher's note)
"Carhart's meandering, warmly evocative anecdotes register both the quirkiness of France's traditions and the civilizing, humanizing influence they exert." Pub Wkly

Carlin, Kelly, 1963-

Carlin, Kelly. A **Carlin** Home Companion; Growing Up With George. Kelly Carlin. St. Martin's Press 2015 336 p. $26.99 **92**
1. Comedians -- Family relationships
ISBN 1250058252; 9781250058256
LC 2015017795
This book by Kelly Carlin offers a glimpse of the inner life of her father, comedian George Carlin. Kelly was "born at the very beginning of his decades-long career in comedy. . . . She witnessed his transformation in the '70s, as he fought back against---and talked back to---the establishment. . . . Kelly not only watched her father constantly reinvent himself and his comedy, but also had a front row seat to the roller coaster turmoil of her family's inner life." (Publisher's note)
"A funny, honest, and compassionate account of growing up with a master of comedy." Kirkus

Carlyle, Jane Welsh, 1801-1866

Chamberlain, Kathy. **Jane** Welsh Carlyle and Her Victorian World; A Story of Love, Work, Marriage, and Friendship. Kathy Chamberlain. Overlook Duckworth 2017 398 p. color illustrations (hardcover) $37.50   **92**

     1. Women authors -- Biography 2. Great Britain -- History -- Victoria, 1837-1901 3. Intellectuals -- Great Britain -- Biography 4. Women intellectuals -- Great Britain -- Biography

     ISBN 9781468314205; 1468314203

This book, by Kathy Chamberlain, is "the untold story of Jane Welsh Carlyle, the wife of the renowned Thomas Carlyle. . . . Caught between her own literary aspirations and Victorian society's oppression of women, Jane Welsh Carlyle hoped to move beyond domestic life and become a respected published writer." (Publisher's note)

"This humane, well-documented book provides a solid and readable lay introduction to a fascinating literary figure and her world." Pub Wkly

Includes bibliographical references and index.

Carlyle, Thomas, 1795-1881

Chamberlain, Kathy. **Jane** Welsh Carlyle and Her Victorian World; A Story of Love, Work, Marriage, and Friendship. Kathy Chamberlain. Overlook Duckworth 2017 398 p. color illustrations (hardcover) $37.50   **92**

     1. Women authors -- Biography 2. Great Britain -- History -- Victoria, 1837-1901 3. Intellectuals -- Great Britain -- Biography 4. Women intellectuals -- Great Britain -- Biography

     ISBN 9781468314205; 1468314203

This book, by Kathy Chamberlain, is "the untold story of Jane Welsh Carlyle, the wife of the renowned Thomas Carlyle. . . . Caught between her own literary aspirations and Victorian society's oppression of women, Jane Welsh Carlyle hoped to move beyond domestic life and become a respected published writer." (Publisher's note)

"This humane, well-documented book provides a solid and readable lay introduction to a fascinating literary figure and her world." Pub Wkly

Includes bibliographical references and index.

Carnegie, Andrew, 1835-1919

Nasaw, David. **Andrew** Carnegie. Penguin Press 2006 878p il $35; pa $20   **92**

     1. Philanthropists 2. Metal industry executives

     ISBN 1-59420-104-8; 0-14-311244-9 pa

                 LC 2006-44840

This is a biography of the Scottish-born businessman and philanthropist. Carnegie was the founder of the Carnegie Steel Company which later became U.S. Steel.

"Highly readable despite it's length, 'Andrew Carnegie' shows signs of prodigious original research on almost every page." N Y Times (Late N Y Ed)

Includes bibliographical references

Wall, Joseph Frazier. **Andrew** Carnegie. University of Pittsburgh Press 1989 1137p il hardcover o.p. pa $22.50 **92**

     1. Philanthropists 2. Metal industry executives

     ISBN 0-8229-5904-6 pa

                 LC 88-38160

A reissue of the title first published 1970 by Oxford University Press

This biography follows Carnegie from his boyhood in Scotland through his emigration to America, his rise in the business world, and his early ventures in oil, railroads, telegraphy, and the iron and steel industries

Includes bibliographical references

Carnegie, Dale, 1888-1955

Watts, Steven. **Self**-help Messiah; Dale Carnegie and success in modern America. by Steven Watts. Other Press 2013 32 p. $29.95   **92**

     1. Self-help techniques 2. Success 3. Conduct of life 4. Orators -- United States -- Biography 5. Teachers -- United States -- Biography 6. Authors, American -- 20th century -- Biography

     ISBN 1590515021; 9781590515020

                 LC 2013003227

This book, by Steven Watts, "tells the story of [Dale] Carnegie's personal journey and how it gave rise to the movement of self-help and personal reinvention. His book, 'How to Win Friends and Influence People,' became a best seller worldwide. Carnegie conceived his book to help people learn to relate to one another and enrich their lives through effective communication. His success was extraordinary, so hungry was 1920s America for a little psychological insight." (Publisher's note)

"A fascinating portrait of the father of self-help and incisive analysis of the mercurial era that produced him." Kirkus

Caro, Helga Gerda

★ Seth, Vikram, 1952- **Two** lives; Vikram Seth. HarperCollins 2005 503p ill. (pbk.) $15.95; o.p.   **92**

     1. Poets 2. Authors 3. Dentists 4. Novelists 5. London (England) -- Biography" 6. East Indians -- England -- London 7. Interracial marriage -- England -- London 8. Authors, English -- 20th century -- Biography 9. Authors, Indic -- Homes and haunts -- England -- London 10. London (England) -- Social life and customs -- 20th century

     ISBN 9780060599676; 0060599669

                 LC 2005052694

In this book, the author presents biographies of "his Shanti Uncle and Aunty Henny. . . . Shanti was Seth's grandfather's brother, a dentist who studied in Berlin, lodging with Fau Caro, whose daughter, Henny was in love with someone else. He left for Britain in 1936. . . . [I]n 1940, as war broke out, he enlisted, served throughout and lost his right arm in combat. . . . Meanwhile, Henny, a German Jew, arrived in Britain weeks before war was declared, leaving her beloved mother and sister behind to death camp murder. . . . Part two of his narrative focuses on Shanti. Part three, Henny's story . . . is based on a trove of remarkable letters she received and wrote. . . . Part four examines their marriage (they didn't marry until seven years after the war), and part five details a family mystery about Shanti's will and Seth's . . . research into these lives." (Publishers Weekly)

"In clear and elegant writing, Seth explores the macrocosm through the microcosm, resulting in a most unusual, worthwhile book." Publ Wkly

Carr, David

Carr, David. The **night** of the gun; a reporter investigates the darkest story of his life, his own. Simon & Schuster 2008 389p il $26; pa $15   **92**

     1. Journalists 2. Drug addicts 3. Columnists 4. Memoirists

     ISBN 978-1-4165-4152-3; 1-4165-4152-7; 978-1-4165-4153-0 pa; 1-4165-4153-5 pa

                 LC 2008-12178

Carr "takes a detailed inventory of his years of drug addiction, chronicling the slide from drinking and marijuana use during his teen years in Minneapolis to shooting cocaine and smoking crack while trying to maintain his life as a reporter and the father of twin girls. Carr is meticulous in the investigation of his past, reconstructing events with the aid of police reports, magazine rejection letters, and more than sixty interviews with friends, former dealers, and fellow-addicts. His journalistic skills are on full display as he works to excavate the truth from his often hazy memories. He evinces genuine remorse for his frequently reprehensible behavior and succeeds in creating something more than merely another entry in what he terms the 'growing pile of junkie memoirs.'" New Yorker

Carson, Rachel, 1907-1964

Lytle, Mark Hamilton. The **gentle** subversive; Rachel Carson, Silent spring, and the rise of the environmental movement. Oxford University Press 2007 277p il $23; $12.95   **92**
1. Authors 2. Conservationists 3. Environmental movement 4. College teachers 5. Marine biologists 6. Writers on nature 7. Writers on science 8. Biography, Individual 9. Environmentalism -- History
ISBN 0-19-517246-9; 0-19-517247-7 pa; 978-0-19-517246-1; 978-0-19-517247-8 pa

LC 2006-49350

This book, by Mark Hamilton Lytle, presents a biography of Rachel Carson, an "accomplished marine biologist who worked for many years for the US Fish and Wildlife Service. In mid-career she gained wide fame as a lyrical popular science writer specializing in studies of the ocean and seashore life. 'Silent Spring' (1962), her final work, won acclaim as a breakthrough book that transformed people's conceptions of the place of science in the natural world." (Choice: Current Reviews for Academic Libraries)

The author "examines the life of Rachel Carson, founder of today's environmental movement and antithesis of the stereotypical 1950s woman. Carson was educated in the sciences, worked full time, and was her family's primary provider and caregiver. Genteel in appearance, she was firmly committed to her goal of preserving nature. Using a lyrical, narrative style, Lytle probes Carson's interests and her purposes in writing a series of wellknown books that include The Sea Around Usand her most famous, Silent Spring." Libr J

Includes bibliographical references

Souder, William. **On** a farther shore; the life and legacy of Rachel Carson. William Souder. 1st ed. Crown Publishing Group 2012 496 p. ill. (hardcover) $30.00; (ebook) $85.00   **92**
1. Biology 2. Women authors 3. Carson, Rachel, 1907-1964 4. Naturalists -- United States -- Biography 5. Environmentalism -- United States -- History 6. Science writers -- United States -- Biography 7. Environmentalists -- United States -- Biography 8. Marine biologists -- United States -- Biography 9. Environmental ethics -- United States -- History 10. Pesticides -- Environmental aspects -- United States -- History
ISBN 030746220X; 9780307462206; 9780307462213; 9780307462220

LC 2012003077

In "this . . . biography, [William] Souder . . . portrays [Rachel] Carson as a woman passionate in friendship, poetic and innovative in her books about the sea, gentle but ambitious, assiduously keeping tabs on her publisher's promotion of her work. A writer since childhood, Carson, inspired by a college professor, developed a love for biology and combined her two passions in a career that included three bestselling books." (Publishers Weekly)

Includes bibliographical references (p. 477-486) and index.

Carter, Angela, 1940-1992

Gordon, Edmund. The **invention** of Angela Carter; a biography. Edmund Gordon. Oxford University Press 2017 xvii, 525 p.p illustrations, portraits (hardcover) $35   **92**
1. Women authors -- Biography 2. Authors, English -- 20th century -- Biography

ISBN 0190626844; 9780190626846

LC 2016042329

National Book Critics Circle Award Finalist: Biography (2017)

This biography, by Edmund Gordon, "followed in Angela Carter's footsteps - travelling to the places she lived in Britain, Japan, and the USA - to uncover a life rich in adventure and incident. With unrestricted access to her manuscripts, letters, and journals, and informed by interviews with Carter's friends and family, Gordon offers an unrivalled portrait of one of the twentieth century's most dazzlingly original writers." (Publisher's note)

"Written with grace and assurance, this volume will long stand as the definitive biography of Carter." Choice

Includes bibliographical references and index

Carter, Jimmy, 1924-

Carter, Jimmy. **Everything** to gain; making the most of the rest of your life. [by] Jimmy and Rosalynn Carter. University of Arkansas Press 1995 176p pa $21.95   **92**
1. Governors 2. Presidents 3. Nobel laureates for peace 4. Presidents -- United States
ISBN 978-1-55728-388-7; 1-55728-388-5
First published 1987 by Random House

"The former president and First Lady alternate first-person reminiscences with sections written jointly to tell the story of their lives after leaving the White House in 1980. Frankly acknowledging the trauma of the lost election, the Carters record their efforts to overcome the difficulties of making a fresh start while deeply in debt, adjusting to life in a small house in Plains, Ga., and other challenges." Publ Wkly

Carter, Jimmy. An **hour** before daylight; memories of my rural boyhood. Simon & Schuster 2001 284p il hardcover o.p. pa $15   **92**
1. Governors 2. Presidents 3. Nobel laureates for peace 4. Presidents -- United States 5. Georgia -- Social life and customs
ISBN 0-7432-1193-6; 0-7432-1199-5 pa

LC 00-48248

In this memoir, the thirty-ninth president of the United States remembers his childhood in rural Georgia.

This "is social and agricultural history as plain and honest as one of the tables the author makes in his workshop—an American classic." New Yorker

Carter, Jimmy. **Keeping** faith: memoirs of a president. University of Ark. Press 1995 633p il pa $34.95   **92**
1. Governors 2. Presidents 3. Nobel laureates for peace 4. Presidents -- United States
ISBN 1-55728-330-3

LC 95-9691

A reissue of the title first published 1982 by Bantam Bks.

These memoirs treat such matters as "improving relations with China; enacting energy legislation; negotiating the second Strategic Arms Limitation treaty (SALT II); concluding the Panama Canal treaties; and convincing Menachem Begin and Anwar Sadat to reach agreement at Camp David. Carter also devotes more than a quarter of the book to the frustrations arising from the capture of hostages in Tehran." N Y Rev Books

Carter, Jimmy. **Sharing** good times. Simon & Schuster 2004 174p $21; pa $13   **92**
1. Governors 2. Presidents 3. Nobel laureates for peace 4. Presidents -- United States
ISBN 0-7432-7033-9; 0-7432-7068-1 pa

LC 2004-51351

The author "recalls various occasions in his life that became 'lasting sources of pleasure.' . . . [These remembrances] include his personal reasons for seeing his father as a hero, watching minor and major-league baseball games growing up, his days in the navy, road trips with his wife and children, his entry into politics, taking vacations while in the White House, his famous volunteer work, and even his hobbies." Booklist

Carter, Jimmy, 1924- A **full** life; reflections at ninety. Jimmy Carter. Simon & Schuster 2015 272 p. illustrations (chiefly color) (hardcover: alk. paper) $28   92

1. Presidents -- United States -- Biography 2. United States -- Politics and government -- 1977-1981

ISBN 1501115634; 9781501115639; 9781501115646

LC 2015007489

In this memoir, by Jimmy Carter, "Jimmy Carter, thirty-ninth President, Nobel Peace Prize winner, international humanitarian, fisherman, reflects on his full and happy life with pride, humor, and a few second thoughts. . . . Carter tells what he is proud of and what he might do differently. He discusses his regret at losing his re-election, but how he and Rosalynn pushed on and made a new life and second and third rewarding careers." (Publisher's note)

"The drawings and poems by the author add even more of a personal touch, though crises in his marriage and his "estrangement" from the Obama presidency offer the most noteworthy revelations. A memoir that reads like an epilogue to a life of accomplishment." Kirkus

Carter, Jimmy, 1924- **White** House diary. Farrar, Straus and Giroux 2010 570p il $30; ebook $14.99   92

1. Biography, Individual 2. Presidents -- United States 3. United States -- Politics and government -- 1974-1989 4. United States -- Politics and government -- 1977-1981

ISBN 978-0-374-28099-4; 978-1-4299-9065-3 ebook

LC 2010-15544

Jimmy Carter, the 39th president of the United States, presents an edited and annotated version of a diary he kept during his term in office.

"That the language is blunt and occasionally a little un-Christian may come as a surprise. . . . But the writings here reflect the Mr. Carter we know: boastful and painfully confessional, sanctimonious and callous, insightful and un-self-aware. These are the thoughts of a secular preacher and calculating politician, surrounded by friends and yet often alone." N Y Times (Late N Y Ed)

Carter, Robert, 1728-1804

Levy, Andrew. The **first** emancipator; the forgotten story of Robert Carter, the founding father who freed his slaves. Random House 2005 310p hardcover o.p. pa $15.95   92

1. Plantation owners 2. Biography, Individual 3. Slavery -- United States

ISBN 0-375-50865-1; 0-375-76104-7 pa

LC 2004-54054

"In 1791, [Robert] Carter began a manumission process that would eventually free some 450 people on his northern Virginia plantations and beyond. . . . [Levy focuses] on Carter's psychic and religious struggles as he progressed haltingly toward the act of manumission." (N Y Times Book Rev) Index.

"This well-written and thoroughly engaging book will certainly appeal to readers interested in the history of 18th- and 19th-century Virginia, but also to those interested in the history of slavery and racism in America and in historical biography." Publ Wkly

Includes bibliographical references

Carver, Raymond

Sklenicka, Carol. **Raymond** Carver; a writer's life. Scrib-

ner 2009 578p il $35   92

1. Poets 2. Authors 3. Authors, American 4. Short story writers

ISBN 978-0-7432-6245-3; 0-7432-6245-X

LC 2009-27291

This is a biography of the American short-story writer and poet.

The author "spoke with nearly everyone in Carver's orbit, making the book a kind of history of American fiction in the '70s and '80s, capturing the crucial writers (Richard Ford, Tobias Wolff, John Cheever) and sea changes in the publishing industry that made Carver such a powerful influence on writers today. The epic biography that Carver deserves." Kirkus

Includes bibliographical references

Cash, Johnny

Hilburn, Robert. **Johnny** Cash; the life. by Robert Hilburn. Little, Brown and Co. 2013 608 p. $32   92

1. Musicians -- United States

ISBN 0316194751; 9780316194754

LC 2013941828

In this biography, "drawing upon his personal experience with [musician Johnny] Cash and a trove of never-before-seen material from the singer's inner circle, [author Robert] Hilburn creates [a] . . . deeply human portrait of one of the most iconic figures in modern popular culture - not only a towering figure in country music, but also a seminal influence in rock, whose personal life was far more troubled, and whose musical and lyrical artistry much more profound." (Publisher's note)

"The personal knowledge aided by extensive archival research and always compelling, accessible writing make this an instant-classic music biography with something to offer all generations of listeners." Kirkus

Kleist, Reinhard. **Johnny** Cash; I see a darkness: a graphic novel. [translated from the German edition by Michael Waaler] Abrams ComicArts 2009 221p il pa $17.95   92

1. Singers 2. Graphic novels 3. Country musicians 4. Biographical graphic novels 5. Songwriters 6. Country musicians -- Graphic novels

ISBN 978-0-8109-8463-9

LC 2010-279149

Original German edition, 2006

The author "presents a biography (with seemingly invented dialog that stays true to the facts) focusing on Cash's turning points: from his poor family's 1935 relocation to a New Deal-created cotton farming community, through his troubled first marriage, endless touring, the amphetamine abuse of his early musical career, and climaxing with a famous, highly charged 1968 concert at California's Folsom Prison. Kleist also dramatizes several of Cash's songs and relates the tragic story of Glen Sherley, a Folsom inmate who sent Cash a song he had written hoping Cash would play it in the show. The ruggedness of Kleist's black-and-white illustrations suits their subject, as the stark portrayal of Cash's withdrawal from drugs is inventive and harrowing. . . . This thoughtful and compelling portrait of a towering talent with a tortured soul is recommended for all teen and adult music fans." Libr J

The author "presents a biography (with seemingly invented dialog that stays true to the facts) focusing on Cash's turning points: from his poor family's 1935 relocation to a New Deal-created cotton farming community, through his troubled first marriage, endless touring, the amphetamine abuse of his early musical career, and climaxing with a famous, highly charged 1968 concert at California's Folsom Prison. Kleist also dramatizes several of Cash's songs and relates the tragic story of Glen Sherley, a Folsom inmate who sent Cash a song he had written hoping Cash would play it in the show. The ruggedness of Kleist's black-and-white illustrations suits their subject, as the stark portrayal of Cash's withdrawal from drugs is inventive and harrowing. . . . This thoughtful and compelling portrait of a towering talent with a tortured soul is recommended for all teen and adult music fans." Libr J

Light, Alan. **Johnny** Cash; the life and legacy of the Man in Black. Alan Light. Smithsonian Books 2018 216 p. illustrations (hardcover) $40 **92**

1. Country musicians -- United States -- Biography
ISBN 9781588346391

LC 2018011525

This biography of country musician Johnny Cash, by Alan Light, "reveals Cash's personal and professional life through largely unpublished material from the Cash family, including his handwritten notes and set lists; personal photographs of Cash with his family, traveling, and performing onstage; and beloved objects from his home and private recording studio." (Publisher's note)

"The author draws on Cash's autobiographies, music history and criticism, interviews, and writings by Cash's family to produce an intimate and engaging portrait. By far the greatest strength of the book, though, are the illustrations: memorabilia from family archives and abundant photographs that capture Cash's undeniable charisma." Kirkus

Streissguth, Michael. **Johnny** Cash; the biography. Da Capo Press 2006 334p il hardcover o.p. pa $15.95 **92**

1. Singers 2. Country musicians 3. Songwriters
ISBN 0-306-81368-8; 0-306-81565-6 pa

LC 2006-101191

This is a biography of the country singer and songwriter.

The author "leaves us mightily impressed with the volume of Cash's work and the convictions that animate it, and perhaps even more impressed by Cash's endurance of his own self-destructiveness. . . . Streissguth gives everyone interested in Cash a very satisfying book about him." Booklist

Includes bibliographical references

Cash, Rosanne, 1955-
★ Cash, Rosanne. **Composed**; a memoir. Viking 2010 343p $26.95 **92**

1. Singers 2. Country musicians 3. Songwriters
ISBN 978-0-670-02196-3

LC 2010-10327

"The moving chapters about Roseanne Cash's glorious career—and the moments of great tenderness and tension with her legendary family—are like exquisite album tracks: Individually they are great reads, but together they add up to something cohesive and powerful. Composed provides no bombshell confessions about her failed marriage to Rodney Crowell or her wonderfully complicated relationship with her dad, Johnny. (Though she does dismiss the biopic Walk the Line as 'an egregious oversimplification of our family's private pain.') Instead, Cash delivers writerly meditations on what it means to be an artist and a public person and, yes, a daughter. Rare is the celebrity memoir that is so full of self-awareness and dignity." Entertainment Wkly

Casso, Gaspipe, 1942-
Carlo, Philip. **Gaspipe**; confessions of a Mafia boss. William Morrow 2008 346p il $25.95 **92**

1. Mafia 2. Criminals 3. Organized crime 4. Mobsters 5. Informers
ISBN 978-0-06-142984-2

LC 2008-2683

"This powerful story is required reading for anyone with a yen for the Mafia, the criminal underworld and a law enforcement system struggling to keep up." Publ Wkly

Castelli, Leo, 1907-1999
Cohen-Solal, Annie. **Leo** & his circle; the life of Leo Castelli. Alfred A. Knopf 2010 540p il $35 **92**

1. Art dealers
ISBN 978-1-4000-4427-6; 1-4000-4427-8

LC 2009-34454

First published 2009 in France

This is a biography of the art dealer from Trieste who came to New York in 1941 and opened his first New York gallery in 1957. Castelli displayed early work by Andy Warhol, Jasper Johns, Roy Lichtenstein, and Cy Twombly.

This "biography fleshes out not only a fascinating portrait of Castelli but also the excitement of the developing American art world to which he was so central." Publ Wkly

Includes bibliographical references

Castro, Fidel, 1926-2016
★ Castro, Fidel. **Fidel** Castro: my life; a spoken autobiography. [by] Fidel Castro and Ignacio Ramonet; translated by Andrew Hurley. Scribner 2008 723p il map $40 **92**

1. Presidents 2. Communist leaders 3. Cuba -- Politics and government
ISBN 978-1-4165-5328-1; 1-4165-5328-2

Original Spanish edition, 2006

Ramonet "sat down with Castro over the course of many hours, engaging him in long, involved discussions about his revolutionary life (and little about his personal life). The result is, in the words of the interviewer, Castro's 'political testament, an oral summoning-up of Fidel Castro's life by Fidel himself at almost eighty.' That rather simple description does not begin to cover the magnitude and significance of this major document. . . . By itself an incomplete history of the Cuban Revolution, to be sure, but an important—the ultimate insider view—contribution to the complete picture." Booklist

Includes bibliographical references

Coltman, Leycester. The **real** Fidel Castro; with a foreword by Julia E. Sweig. Yale Univ. Press 2003 335p il map $30; pa $20 **92**

1. Presidents 2. Communist leaders 3. Cuba -- Politics and government
ISBN 0-300-10188-0; 0-300-10760-9 pa

LC 2003-12942

This biography "offers a fresh assessment of the revolutionary leader. . . . It chronicles the events of Castro's extraordinary life and explores the contradiction between the private character and the public reputation." Univ Press Books for Public and Second Sch Libr, 2004

Includes bibliographical references

Szulc, Tad. **Fidel**; a critical portrait. Post Road Press 2000 703p map pa $18.95 **92**

1. Presidents 2. Communist leaders 3. Cuba -- Politics and government
ISBN 978-0-380-80888-5; 0-380-80888-9

First published 1986 by Morrow

The author "devotes the greater part of this book to Castro's early, formative years and the forging and triumph of his revolutionary movement. The years of Castro's rule after the Bay of Pigs invasion receive briefer treatment. Well written and very readable." Choice

Includes bibliographical references

Catharine Parr, Queen, consort of Henry VIII, King of Eng-

land, 1512-1548

Porter, Linda. **Katherine** the queen; the remarkable life of Katherine Parr, the last wife of Henry VIII. St. Martin's Press 2010 383p il $27.99   **92**

1. Queens 2. Biography, Individual 3. Great Britain -- History -- 1485-1603, Tudors 4. Great Britain -- History -- Henry VIII, 1509-1547

ISBN 9780312384388

LC 2010035251

In this biography of Katherine Parr, Porter argues that "Henry VIII's last queen was a more human, complex and modern figure than has hitherto been realized." (Publisher's note) Index.

"Although often depicted by the Victorians as a matronly nurse to an elderly king, Katherine Parr (1512–1548), according to Porter, was a stylish trendsetter of 30, sensual, confident, dynamic, exceptionally educated and cultured, and able to perform with aplomb on both an English and international stage. . . . Rich, perceptive, nuanced and creative, this first full-scale biography gives one of Britain's best but least-known queens her due." Publ Wkly

Includes bibliographical references

Catherine II, the Great, Empress of Russia, 1729-1796

★ Catherine. The **memoirs** of Catherine the Great; a new translation by Mark Cruse and Hilde Hoogenboom. Modern Library 2005 xc, 247p il map $26.95   **92**

1. Empresses 2. Russia -- History 3. Russia -- Kings and rulers

ISBN 0-679-64299-4

LC 2004-61107

Original French edition, 1859

This is "a source of major importance and every serious library should own it." Choice

Jaques, Susan. The **Empress** of Art; Catherine the Great and the Transformation of Russia. by Susan Jaques. W W Norton & Co Inc 2016 384 p. color illustrations $35   **92**

1. Russia -- History

ISBN 160598972X; 9781605989723

This book, by Susan Jaques, is an "art-oriented biography of . . . Catherine the Great. . . . A German princess who married a decadent and lazy Russian prince, Catherine mobilized support amongst the Russian nobles, playing off of her husband's increasing corruption and abuse of power. She then staged a coup that ended with him being strangled with his own scarf in the halls of the palace, and she being crowned the Empress of Russia." (Publisher's note)

"An absorbing account of a fascinating figure and her legacy." Booklist

Includes bibliographical references (pages 407-447) and index.

Rounding, Virginia. **Catherine** the Great; love, sex and power. St. Martin's Press 2007 566p il $29.95   **92**

1. Empresses 2. Russia -- History 3. Russia -- Kings and rulers

ISBN 978-0-312-32887-0; 0-312-32887-7

LC 2006-47084

First published 2006 in the United Kingdom

The author "relies on memoirs, private letters and previous monographs as she details how, after dissolution of the unhappy marriage that brought Catherine (1729-1798) to Russia from Germany, the empress juggled her relationships with men as she attempted to thrust Russia into the modern era and make it a European power. . . . [This] work will appeal to Catherine-philes and those interested in women's history." Publ Wkly

Includes bibliographical references

Catherine, Duchess of Cambridge, 1982-

Nicholl, Katie. **Kate**; the future queen. Katie Nicholl. Weinstein Books 2013 354 p. x, illustrations (hardcover) $26   **92**

1. Princesses -- Great Britain -- Biography

ISBN 1602862265; 9781602862265

LC 2013387679

This book, by Katie Nicholl, "gives an inside look into the life of the future Queen of England, Kate Middleton. Since becoming Duchess Catherine of Cambridge in 2011, Middleton has captivated royals fans around the world and now, Nicholl delivers the story of her early life, first romances, and love with Prince William. Nicholl will reveal new details on Middleton's initiation into royal life and, of course, her first pregnancy." (Publisher's note)

Includes bibliographical references (page 317) and index.

Caveney, Graham.

Caveney, Graham. The **boy** with the perpetual nervousness; a memoir. Graham Caveney. Simon & Schuster 2018 272 p. $26   **92**

1. Adult child abuse victims

ISBN 1501165968; 9781501165962

In this memoir, Graham Caveney "recounts the ups and downs of coming-of-age, set against the music and literature of the 1970s. Raised in a small town in the north of England, . . . Caveney armed himself against the confusing nature of adolescence with a thick accent, a copy of Kafka, and a record collection. . . . All three provided him the opportunity to escape, even if just in mind. . . . But, when those passions are noticed and preyed upon by a mentor, everything changes." (Publisher's note)

Dery, Mark. **Born** to be posthumous; the eccentric life and mysterious genius of Edward Gorey. Mark Dery. Little, Brown & Co. 2018 496 p. $35   **92**

1. Biography 2. Gorey, Edward 3. American authors -- Biography

ISBN 9780316188548

LC 2018941034

This book, by Mark Dery, presents the biography of American writer and artist Edward Gorey. "He published over a hundred books and illustrated works by Samuel Beckett, T.S. Eliot, Edward Lear, John Updike, Charles Dickens, Hilaire Belloc, Muriel Spark, Bram Stoker, Gilbert & Sullivan, and others. At the same time, he was a deeply complicated and conflicted individual, a man whose art reflected his obsessions with the disquieting and the darkly hilarious." (Publisher's note)

"Fans will like the immersion in Gorey-ana, but others may feel that this colorful protagonist lacks a compelling plot." Pub Wkly

Cayce, Edgar, 1877-1945

Kirkpatrick, Sidney. **Edgar** Cayce; an American prophet. Riverhead Bks. 2000 564p il hardcover o.p. pa $16   **92**

1. Psychics

ISBN 1-57322-896-6 pa

LC 00-27975

This is a "fair, fascinating, and well-researched biography of one of 20th-century America's most famous psychics." Libr J

Cayton-Holland, Adam

Cayton-Holland, Adam. **Tragedy** plus time; a tragi-comic memoir. by Adam Cayton-Holland. Touchstone 2018 256 p. (hardcover) $26   **92**

1. Siblings 2. Comedians -- United States -- Biography 3. Brothers and sisters -- United States -- Biography 4. Suicide victims --

Family relationships -- United States
ISBN 9781501170164; 9781501170171

LC 2017049067

In this memoir, author Adam Cayton-Holland's "wry and wiry voice . . . elegantly transitions from half-cynical stand-up pose to thoughtful interpretation of the contradictions of grief ('I like to remember her constantly; I try not to think of her at all') without losing a beat. This is a vivid and heartbreaking account of two bright lives, one blessed with hard-fought success and one cut painfully short." (Publishers Weekly)

"This is Cayton-Holland's heartbreaking work of genius: his story of Lydia, his best friend and closest confidant, and her tragic suicide at 28. He writes with candor and care of Lydia's bright light and his own darkest hour, making for an unforgettable read." Booklist

Chabon, Michael

Chabon, Michael. **Manhood** for amateurs; the pleasures and regrets of a husband, father, and son. Harper 2009 306p $25.99   **92**
    1. Authors 2. Fathers 3. Novelists 4. Men -- Psychology 5. Short story writers
    ISBN 978-0-06-149018-7; 0-06-149018-0

LC 2009-4749

"For the most part in these pages [Chabon] manages to write about himself, his family and his generation with humor and introspective wisdom. As in his novels, he shifts gears easily between the comic and the melancholy, the whimsical and the serious, demonstrating once again his ability to write about the big subjects of love and memory and regret without falling prey to the Scylla and Charybdis of cynicism and sentimentality." N Y Times (Late N Y Ed)

Chagall, Marc, 1887-1985

★ Wullschlager, Jackie. **Chagall**; a biography. Alfred A. Knopf 2008 582p il $40   **92**
    1. Artists 2. Painters 3. Artists, Russian
    ISBN 978-0-375-41455-8; 0-375-41455-X

LC 2008-6162

This is a biography of the Russian artist and author of Lithographs (1960), My Life (1960), and The Jerusalem Windows (1962).

"This biography presents Chagall's moving portraits of a vanished age in colors as glowing and haunting as his own canvases." Washington Post Book World

Includes bibliographical references

Chaloner, William, d. 1699

Levenson, Thomas. **Newton** and the counterfeiter; the unknown detective career of the world's greatest scientist. Houghton Mifflin Harcourt 2009 318p $25; pa $14.95   **92**
    1. Physicists 2. Mathematicians 3. Counterfeits and counterfeiting 4. Counterfeiters 5. Writers on science
    ISBN 978-0-15-101278-7; 0-15-101278-4; 978-0-547-33604-6 pa; 0-547-33604-7 pa

LC 2008-53511

"Levenson demonstrates a surpassing felicity in his brisk treatment of this late-17th-century true-crime adventure. . . . Swift, agile treatment of a little known but highly entertaining episode in a legendary life." Kirkus

Includes bibliographical references

Chambers, Julius L. (Julius LeVonne), 1936-2013

Mosnier, Joseph. **Julius** Chambers; A Life in the Legal Struggle for Civil Rights. Richard A. Rosen and Joseph Mosnier. University of North Carolina Press 2016 408 p. illustra-

tions (cloth: alk. paper) $35   **92**
    1. African Americans -- Civil rights 2. Civil rights lawyers -- North Carolina -- Biography 3. African American lawyers -- North Carolina -- Biography 4. Civil rights movements -- Southern States -- History -- 20th century 5. African Americans -- Civil rights -- North Carolina -- History -- 20th century
    ISBN 9781469628547

LC 2016020980

In this book, by Richard A. Rosen and Joseph Mosnier, "Julius Chambers (1936–2013) escaped the fetters of the Jim Crow South to emerge in the 1960s and 1970s as the nation's leading African American civil rights attorney. Following passage of the Civil Rights Act of 1964, Chambers worked to advance the NAACP Legal Defense Fund's strategic litigation campaign for civil rights, ultimately winning landmark school and employment desegregation cases at the U.S. Supreme Court." (Publisher's note)

"Essential reading for those interested in African American history; the civil rights movement; and legal history, especially relating to North Carolina." LJ

Includes bibliographical references and index

Champlain, Samuel de, 1567-1635

★ Fischer, David Hackett. **Champlain's** dream. Simon & Schuster 2008 834p il map $40   **92**
    1. Explorers 2. America -- Exploration
    ISBN 978-1-4165-9332-4; 1-4165-9332-2

LC 2008-16286

The author "offers the definitive biography of an extraordinary and flawed man: Samuel de Champlain (1567-1635): spy, explorer, courtier, soldier and founder and governor of New France (today's Quebec)." Publ Wkly

Includes bibliographical references

Chanel, Coco, 1883-1971

Garelick, Rhonda K. **Mademoiselle**; Coco Chanel and the pulse of history. Rhonda Garelick. Random House 2014 608 p. illustrations (hardback) $35   **92**
    1. Fashion design 2. Fashion designers 3. Fashion designers -- France -- Biography 4. Fashion design -- History -- 20th century
    ISBN 1400069521; 9781400069521

LC 2014006844

This book, by Rhonda Garelick, is a biography of fashion designer Coco Chanel. "Raised in rural poverty and orphaned early, the young Chanel supported herself as best she could. Then, as an uneducated nineteen-year-old café singer, she attracted the attention of a wealthy and powerful admirer and parlayed his support into her own hat design business. For the rest of Chanel's life, the professional, personal, and political were interwoven." (Publisher's note)

"Garelick pursues the catalog of Chanel's subsequent ill-fated lovers, her work with the Ballets Russes, her vast earnings from Chanel No. 5 and her fraught partnership with the Wertheimer brothers while frankly discussing her relentless, social-climbing attraction to right-wing, reactionary and racist elements.Certainly a definitive portrait, especially considering Garelick's intriguing venture into modern 'branding.'" Kirkus

Includes bibliographical references and index

Vaughan, Hal. **Sleeping** with the enemy; Coco Chanel's secret war. Knopf 2011 279p il $27.95; ebook $13.99   **92**
    1. Fashion designers 2. Perfumers 3. German espionage 4. Biography, Individual 5. Cosmetics industry executives 6. World War, 1939-1945 -- Secret service
    ISBN 978-0-307-59263-7; 978-0-307-95703-0 ebook; 0-7011-

8500-7 Chatto & Windus; 978-0-7011-8500-8 Chatto & Windus

LC 2011020430

The author argues "that there were two sides to the elegant Coco Chanel. Using information from French counterintelligence sources as well as other documents hidden for years in French, German, Italian, Soviet, and U.S. archives, he unmasks her activities during the war years; she embarked on a romance with a senior German officer in occupied Paris and cooperated with German military intelligence agents. . . . Engrossing and accessible, this is recommended for general readers interested in fashion celebrity, espionage, or World War II." Libr J

Includes bibliographical references and index

Chaplin, Charlie, 1889-1977

Ackroyd, Peter, 1949- **Charlie** Chaplin; Peter Ackroyd. Nan A. Talese/Doubleday 2014 272 p. illustrations (Ackroyd's brief lives) (alk. paper) $25.95   **92**

1. Comedians -- Biography 2. Actors -- United States 3. Comedians -- United States -- Biography 4. Motion picture actors and actresses -- United States -- Biography

ISBN 0385537379; 9780385537377

LC 2014013009

This book, by Peter Ackroyd, is a biography of silent film actor Charlie Chaplin. It "turns the spotlight on Chaplin's life as well as his work, from his humble theatrical beginnings in music halls to winning an honorary Academy Award. Everything is here, from the glamor of his golden age to the murky scandals of the 1940s and eventual exile to Switzerland." (Publisher's note)

"Readers are left with an understanding of Chaplin's background, the biographical details of his long and troubled life, and some idea of the hellish conditions on the exacting filmmaker's sets, but conclusions about his significance as an artist, his work's relationship to the culture at large, and the internal forces that engendered such personal misery and creative transcendence fail to cohere. A comprehensive look at Chaplin the man but lacking as a portrait of the artist and his legacy." Kirkus

Includes bibliographical references and index

The **essential** Chaplin; perspectives on the life and art of the great comedian. edited with an introduction by Richard Schickel. I.R. Dee 2006 315p $27.50; pa $16.95   **92**

1. Actors 2. Motion picture directors 3. Motion picture producers 4. Motion picture producers and directors -- Biography

ISBN 978-1-56663-682-7; 1-56663-682-5; 978-1-56663-701-5 pa; 1-56663-701-5 pa

LC 2005-37250

"The book's best feature is its organized cacophony, its trace of this astonishingly long and rich body of work and personal travail . . . in some several dozen voices of fading or lasting memory, and with countless aesthetic and ideological grudges beyond the narrow province of the movies. There is much to savor in these essays; and the book might also serve as a worthy companion to a reader's return to Chaplin's films themselves." Va Q Rev

Chapman, Eddie, 1914-1997

Macintyre, Ben, 1963- **Agent** Zigzag; a true story of Nazi espionage, love, and betrayal. Harmony Books 2007 364p il $25.95   **92**

1. Thieves 2. Intelligence service agents 3. World War, 1939-1945 -- Secret service

ISBN 978-0-307-35340-5

LC 2006-101603

This is a biography of Eddie Chapman, a British double agent during World War II.

"Meticulously researched—relying extensively on recently released wartime files of Britain's Secret Intelligence Service—Macintyre's biography often reads like a spy thriller." Publ Wkly

Includes bibliographical references

Charles I, King of England, 1600-1649

★ De Lisle, Leanda. The **White** King; Charles I, traitor, murderer, martyr. Leanda de Lisle. PublicAffairs, an imprint of Perseus Books, a subsidiary of Hachette Book Group 2017 xxxiii, 401 p.p (hardcover) $30   **92**

1. Great Britain -- History 2. Regicides 3. Great Britain -- History -- Charles I, 1625-1649 4. Great Britain -- History -- Civil War, 1642-1649

ISBN 9781610395601

LC 2017953678

This book, by Leanda de Lisle, tells "the tragic story of Charles I, his warrior queen, Britain's civil wars and the trial for his life. . . . In this vivid portrait--informed by previously unseen manuscripts, including royal correspondence between the king and his queen--Leanda de Lisle depicts a man who was principled and brave, but fatally blinkered." (Publisher's note)

Includes bibliographical references and index.

Charles II, King of England, 1630-1685

Uglow, Jennifer S. A **gambling** man; Charles II's Restoration game. [by] Jenny Uglow. Farrar, Straus and Giroux 2009 580p il map $35   **92**

1. Kings 2. Great Britain -- History -- 1660-1688, Restoration

ISBN 978-0-374-28137-3; 0-374-28137-8

LC 2009-25469

"When Charles II became King of England, in 1660, his task was daunting: to restore the authority of the monarchy while courting a fractious parliament. Uglow's vivid history of the first decade of his reign shows how boldly Charles embraced the openness and experimentation of the Age of Reason." New Yorker

Includes bibliographical references

Charles, Prince of Wales, 1948-

Mayer, Catherine. **Born** to be king; Prince Charles on planet Windsor. Catherine Mayer. Henry Holt & Co. 2015 258 p. 8 plates; color illustrations (hardcover) $28   **92**

1. Princes 2. Princes -- Great Britain -- Biography

ISBN 1627794387; 9781627794381

LC 2014042418

This book, by Catherine Mayer, offers a "portrait of Charles, Prince of Wales. . . . Now sixty-six, Prince Charles has spent his entire life preparing to be king while insisting on being his own man. In this brilliant portrait, he emerges as a complex character driven by a painful past, a questing intellect, and a powerful impulse not only to reshape the monarchy but to use the long wait for the throne to work toward high ideals." (Publisher's note)

"Though far from comprehensive, Mayer's intriguing snapshot of Prince Charles reveals the often overlooked intricacies of his personality." Kirkus

Includes bibliographical references and index

Smith, Sally Bedell, 1948- **Prince** Charles; the passions and paradoxes of an improbable life. Sally Bedell Smith. Random House 2017 xxii, 596 p.p ills.(chiefly color), map (hardcover) $32   **92**

1. Princes -- Great Britain -- Biography

ISBN 9780812988437; 9781400067909

LC 2016031117

In this book, author Sally Bedell Smith gives "us a new look at Prince Charles, the oldest heir to the throne in more than three hundred years. This vivid . . . biography—the product of four years of research and hundreds of interviews with palace officials, former girlfriends, spiritual gurus, and more, . . . is the first authoritative treatment of Charles's life that sheds light on the death of Diana, his marriage to Camilla, and his preparations to take the throne one day." (Publisher's note)

"In this biography, historian and frequent biographer Smith . . . presents a multidimensional portrait of a complex, sensitive, and often visionary man . . . who has carved out a dynamic public role as he waits his turn to govern." LJ

Includes bibliographical references (pages [515]-569) and index.

Charlotte Augusta, Princess of Great Britain, 1796-1817

Williams, Kate. **Becoming** Queen Victoria; the tragic death of Princess Charlotte and the unexpected rise of Britain's greatest monarch. Ballantine Books 2010 448p il $30; ebook $30
92

1. Queens 2. Princesses 3. Great Britain -- Kings and rulers
ISBN 978-0-345-46195-7; 978-0-345-52193-4 ebook
LC 2010-13227

First published 2008 in the United Kingdom with title: Becoming queen

"A lively, juicy read, full of the sordid details of the debauched rule of kings and princes that led to the moralistic rule of a queen focused on creating a royal family that embodied the ideals of a nation. Perfect for fans of royal histories and historical television shows or armchair historians interested in a swift and enjoyable read." Libr J

Includes bibliographical references

Chatwin, Bruce

Under the sun; the letters of Bruce Chatwin. selected and edited by Elizabeth Chatwin and Nicholas Shakespeare. Viking 2011 554p il $35
92

1. Authors 2. Novelists 3. Memoirists 4. Travel writers 5. Authors, English 6. Biography, Individual
ISBN 0670022462; 9780670022465
LC 2010-33591

First published 2010 in the United Kingdom

This is a collection of letters by the author of In Patagonia (1977) and The Songlines (1987). "'Under the Sun' contains letters written across four decades, from the time Chatwin was a boy in an English boarding school to letters dictated from his deathbed." (N Y Times (Late N Y Ed)) Index.

"Chatwin's many appreciators will see the compilation in its overall significance as a personal visit with one of their literary heroes, as much as that is possible now." Booklist

Chaucer, Geoffrey, d. 1400

Ackroyd, Peter. **Chaucer;** Peter Ackroyd. 1st ed in the U.S.A; Nan A. Talese/Doubleday 2005 188p il (Ackroyd's brief lives) $19.95
92

1. Poets 2. Authors
ISBN 0-385-50797-6
LC 2004-49796

This "account of the life of Geoffrey Chaucer (1343?-1400) [is also] a consideration of his role in shaping England's national identity. The poet is hailed as the 'progenitor of a national style,' and deft literary analysis explicates Chaucer's innovations while acknowledging the influence of other poets. . . . Much is made of Chaucer's position in the royal court, which provided the financial means to live comfortably while writing his verse." Publ Wkly

Includes bibliographical references

Chavez, Cesar, 1927-1993.

Pawel, Miriam. The **Crusades** of Cesar Chavez; a biography. Miriam Pawel. St. Martin's Press 2014 560 p. ill (some col), map $35
92

1. Hispanic Americans -- History 2. Hispanic Americans -- Biography 3. Labor movement -- United States
ISBN 1608197107; 9781608197101
National Book Critics Circle Finalist: Biography (2014)

This book by Miriam Pawel presents a "biography of the innovative, daring, and persevering activist" Cesar Chavez. "Chavez (1927-93) dropped out of school to work in the fields to support his destitute, homeless family, joining the ranks of California's exploited Mexican American migrant workers. Driven by his social conscience, pragmatic genius, and motivational ardor . . . Chavez created a scrappy and revolutionary labor union for 'the poorest, most powerless workers in the country.'" (Booklist)

"Pawel's clear, accessible prose befits a subject famous for his plain rhetoric, ensuring a broad readership can appreciate this valuable exploration of Chavez's unique legacy." Pub Wkly

Includes bibliographical references and index.

Cheever, John, 1912-1982

Bailey, Blake. **Cheever;** a life. Alfred A. Knopf 2009 770p il $35
92

1. Authors 2. Novelists 3. Authors, American 4. Short story writers
ISBN 978-1-4000-4394-1; 1-4000-4394-8
LC 2008-42277

The author "plunges deeply into the murky, sometimes fetid stew of John Cheever's life (1912-82). Beginning with his 1982 appearance at Carnegie Hall to receive the National Medal for Literature (more details appear some 650 pages later), the author proceeds in chronological fashion to tell the story of a deeply needy, difficult man. . . . [This is a] superb work that shows Cheever wrestling with dark angels, but wresting from those encounters some celestial prose." Kirkus

Includes bibliographical references

Chekhov, Anton Pavlovich, 1860-1904

Chekhov, Anton Pavlovich. **Anton** Chekhov's life and thought; selected letters and commentary. translated from the Russian by Michael Henry Heim, in collaboration with Simon Karlinsky; selection, introduction, and commentary by Simon Karlinsky. Northwestern Univ. Press 1997 494p pa $39.95 **92**

1. Authors 2. Dramatists 3. Physicians 4. Short story writers
ISBN 978-0-8101-1460-9; 0-8101-1460-7
LC 96-41240

First published 1973 by Harper & Row with title: Letters of Anton Chekhov

"Karlinsky's extended commentary and detailed notes amount to a first-rate critical biography, with much unfamiliar information and arrows pointing us toward further investigation." Newsweek

Chen, Pauline W.

★ Chen, Pauline W. **Final** exam; a surgeon's reflections on mortality. Alfred A. Knopf 2007 267p $23.95
92

1. Surgeons 2. Terminal care -- Ethical aspects
ISBN 978-0-307-26353-7; 0-307-26353-3
LC 2006-49361

"A graceful, precise, and empathetic writer enthralled by her work, Chen imparts much about medical schooling and surgery, too." Booklist

Includes bibliographical references

Chevigné, Laure de, 1859-1936

Chiang, Kai-shek, 1887-1975

Taylor, Jay. The **generalissimo**; Chiang Kai-shek and the struggle for modern China. Belknap Press of Harvard University Press 2009 722p il map $35   **92**

1. Generals 2. Presidents 3. Presidents -- China 4. Presidents -- Taiwan 5. China -- History -- 1912-1949

ISBN 978-0-674-03338-2

LC 2008-40492

This is a biography of the Chinese president who was forced into exile in Taiwan in 1949.

"Taylor's fact-based chronological presentation of Chiang should temper the preexisting opinions of him that history readers may take into reading the book. . . . An important biography, essential to the Chinese history shelves." Booklist

Includes bibliographical references

Chiang, Mei-ling, 1898-2003

Li, Laura Tyson. **Madame** Chiang Kai-Shek; China's eternal first lady. Atlantic Monthly 2006 557p il map $30   **92**

1. Spouses of presidents

ISBN 0-87113-933-2; 978-0-87113-933-7

LC 2005-58858

This is a biography of the wife of former Chinese president Chiang Kai-Shek.

"With access to newly opened files, fluent insights into China's convulsive transformation, and a phenomenal gift for elucidating intricate politics and complicated psyches, Li brilliantly analyzes a fearless and profoundly conflicted woman of extraordinary force." Booklist

Includes bibliographical references

Pakula, Hannah. The **last** empress; Madame Chiang Kai-Shek and the birth of modern China. Simon & Schuster 2009 787p il map $35   **92**

1. Spouses of presidents 2. China -- History -- 1912-1949

ISBN 978-1-4391-4893-8; 1-4391-4893-7

LC 2009-17576

This is a biography of Soong Mei-ling, who became the wife of the Chinese Nationalist leader Chiang Kai-shek.

"A winning combination of measured, balanced research and critical evaluation—the definitive account of an important figure in 20th-century Chinese politics." Kirkus

Includes bibliographical references

Child, Julia

As always, Julia; the letters of Julia Child and Avis DeVoto: food, friendship, and the making of a masterpiece. selected and edited by Joan Reardon. Houghton Mifflin Harcourt Pub. Co. 2010 416p il $26   **92**

1. Cooks 2. Television personalities 3. Editors 4. Cookbook writers 5. Literary critics 6. Biography, Individual

ISBN 9780547417714

LC 2010-25840

This volume presents "the previously unpublished correspondence between the American chef and her unofficial literary agent from 1952 to 1965, offering insight into such events as Julia's early experiences as a new bride in Paris, her support of her diplomat husband and her views on period politics." (Publisher's note) Index.

"Their letters span a wide range of topics, from cookbooks, menus, recipes, and restaurants to Balzac, sex, goose stuffing, gardening, learning languages, the political climate, Sunday afternoon cocktail parties, and proofreading. Witty, enlightening and entertaining." Publ Wkly

★ Child, Julia. **My** life in France; [by] Julia Child with Alex Prud'homme. Knopf 2006 317p il $25.95   **92**

1. Cooks 2. Television personalities 3. Cookbook writers

ISBN 1-4000-4346-8; 978-1-4000-4346-0

LC 2005-44727

This is a "memoir of the famous chef's first, formative sojourn in France with her new husband, Paul Child, in 1949. . . . This is a valuable record of gorgeous meals in bygone Parisian restaurants, and the secret arts of a culinary genius." Publ Wkly

Prud'homme, Alex. **France** is a feast; the photographic journey of Paul and Julia Child. Alex Prud'Homme & Katie Pratt. Thames & Hudson 2017 207 p. illustrations, portraits (hardcover) $35   **92**

1. French cooking 2. Cooks -- Biography 3. Photographers -- Biography 4. Cooking, French 5. France -- Pictorial works 6. Cooks -- France -- Biography 7. Cooks -- United States -- Biography

ISBN 9780500519073

LC 2016932144

This book, by Katherine Pratt and Alex Prud'homme, "documents how Julia Child first discovered French cooking and the French way of life. Paul and Julia moved to Paris in 1948. . . . Their wanderings through the French capital and countryside . . . help lead . . . Julia's brilliant and celebrated career in books and on television. . . . [The book] . . . also brings to light Paul Child's own remarkable photographic achievement." (Publisher's note)

"This thoroughly delicious book illustrates how two creative minds can impact public taste." Pub Wkly

★ Spitz, Bob. **Dearie**; the remarkable life of Julia Child. Bob Spitz. A.A. Knopf 2012 viii, 557 p.p ill.   **92**

1. French cooking 2. Cooks -- Biography 3. Cooking, French 4. Cooks -- France -- Biography 5. Cooks -- United States -- Biography

ISBN 0307272222; 9780307272225

LC 2012019632

This book, by Bob Spitz, offers a biography of the television cooking personality Julia Child. "At its heart, [the book] is a story about a woman's search for her own unique expression. . . . Julia Child was a directionless . . . woman who ran off halfway around the world to join a spy agency during World War II. She eventually settled in Paris, where she learned to cook and collaborated on . . . a book that changed the food culture of America." (Publisher's note)

"An engrossing biography of a woman worthy of iconic status." Kirkus

Includes index.

Child, Paul

Prud'homme, Alex. **France** is a feast; the photographic journey of Paul and Julia Child. Alex Prud'Homme & Katie Pratt. Thames & Hudson 2017 207 p. illustrations, portraits (hardcover) $35   **92**

1. French cooking 2. Cooks -- Biography 3. Photographers -- Biography 4. Cooking, French 5. France -- Pictorial works 6. Cooks -- France -- Biography 7. Cooks -- United States -- Biography

ISBN 9780500519073

LC 2016932144

This book, by Katherine Pratt and Alex Prud'homme, "documents how Julia Child first discovered French cooking and the French way of life. Paul and Julia moved to Paris in 1948.... Their wanderings through the French capital and countryside . . . help lead . . . Julia's brilliant and celebrated career in books and on television. . . . [The book] . . . also brings to light Paul Child's own remarkable photographic achievement." (Publisher's note)

"This thoroughly delicious book illustrates how two creative minds can impact public taste." Pub Wkly

Chopin, Frédéric, 1810-1849

Kildea, Paul. **Chopin's** piano; in search of the instrument that transformed music. Paul Kildea. W. W. Norton & Company 2018 288 p. (hardcover) $27.95   **92**
    1. Pianos 2. Pianists -- Biography
    ISBN 9780393652222
                  LC 2018027829
This book, by Paul Kildea, presents the "captivating story of Fré-déric Chopin and the fate of both his Mallorquin piano and musical Ro-manticism from the early nineteenth to the mid-twentieth century. . . . [It] traces the history of Chopin's twenty-four Preludes through the in-struments on which they were played, the pianists who interpreted them, and the traditions they came to represent." (Publisher's note)

"Densely written and packed with details, this title will appeal not only to readers who enjoy Chopin but also those interested in piano his-tory." LJ

    Includes bibliographical references and index

Walker, Alan. **Fryderyk** Chopin; a life and times. Alan Walker. Farrar, Straus & Giroux 2018 768 p. (hardcover) $40   **92**
    1. Composers -- Biography
    ISBN 9780374159061
                  LC 2017046936
This book, by Alan Walker, "is the most comprehensive biography of . . . Polish composer [Fryderyk Chopin that] appear in English in more than a century. Walker's work is a corrective biography, intended to dispel the many myths and legends that continue to surround Chopin. 'Fryderyk Chopin' is an intimate look into a dramatic life; of particular focus are Chopin's childhood and youth in Poland . . . and Chopin's romantic life with George Sand." (Publisher's note)

"General readers should find this accessible as well as engrossing, despite the abundant scholarly apparatus—annotated contents, list of works, illustrations, musical notations, and genealogical charts. Heartily recommended to everyone with an interest in the subject." LJ

    Includes bibliographical references and index

Eisler, Benita. **Chopin's** funeral. Knopf 2003 230p il $23; pa $13.95   **92**
    1. Pianists 2. Composers 3. Classical musicians
    ISBN 0-375-40945-9; 0-375-70868-5 pa
                  LC 2002-73097
"Eisler is a compelling storyteller, sweeping the reader into the ex-hilarating milieu of Paris in the 1820s and 1830s." Libr J

    Includes bibliographical references

Christensen, Kate, 1962-

Christensen, Kate. **Blue** plate special; an autobiography of my appetites. Kate Christensen. Doubleday 2013 368 p. (hardcover: alkaline paper) $26.95   **92**
    1. Food -- Psychological aspects 2. Appetite -- Psychological aspects 3. Mothers and daughters -- United States 4. Authors, American -- 21st century -- Biography 5. Women authors, American -- 21st century -- Biography

ISBN 0385536267; 9780385536264
                  LC 2012048556
In this memoir, "food--eating it, cooking it, reflecting on it--becomes the vehicle for unpacking a life. [Kate] Christensen explores her history of hunger--not just for food but for love and confidence and a sense of belonging . . . starting with her unorthodox childhood in 1960s Berkeley. . . . After a whirlwind adolescent awakening, Christensen strikes out to chart her own destiny within the literary world and the world of men, both equally alluring and dangerous." (Publisher's note)

Christgau, Robert

Christgau, Robert. **Going** Into the City; Portrait of a Critic As a Young Man. Robert Christgau. HarperCollins 2015 384 p. $27.99   **92**
    1. New York (N.Y.) 2. Popular culture
    ISBN 0062238795; 9780062238795
This memoir by Robert Christgau "is a look back at the upbring-ing that grounded him, the history that transformed him, and the music, books, and films that showed him the way. It is a loving portrait of a lost New York. It's an homage to the city of Christgau's youth from Queens to the Lower East Side--a city that exists mostly in memory today. And it's a love story about the Greenwich Village girl who roamed this realm of possibility with him." (Publisher's note)

"Christgau is a critic's critic and a music aficionado. This one is a must-have for those interested in music, journalism, pop culture, and U.S. history." LJ

Christie, Agatha, 1890-1976

Thompson, Laura. **Agatha** Christie; A Mysterious Life. W W Norton & Co Inc 2018 544 p. $35   **92**
    1. Women authors -- Biography
    ISBN 1681776537; 9781681776538
"A tour-de-force, this thorough and eminently readable book will delight current Christie fans while also engaging new ones. Ideal for all collections." (LJ)

Churchill, Clementine, 1885-1977

Purnell, Sonia. **Clementine**; The Life of Mrs. Winston Churchill. by Sonia Purnell. Penguin Group USA 2015 448 p. 16 plates; ills; portraits $30   **92**
    ISBN 0525429778; 9780525429777
                  LC 2015373202
This book, by Sonia Purnell, presents an overview of the wife of British Prime Minister Winston Churchill. "Born into impecunious ar-istocracy, the young Clementine was the target of cruel snobbery. Many wondered why Winston married her, but their marriage proved to be an exceptional partnership. Beautiful and intelligent, but driven by her own insecurities, she made his career her mission." (Publisher's note)

Churchill, Winston Sir, 1874-1965

D'Este, Carlo. **Warlord**; a life of Winston Churchill at war, 1874-1945. Harper 2008 845p il map $39.95   **92**
    1. Statesmen 2. Historians 3. Prime ministers 4. Memoirists 5. Cabinet members 6. Members of Parliament 7. Nobel laureates for literature 8. Prime ministers -- Great Britain
    ISBN 978-0-06-057573-1; 0-06-057573-5
                  LC 2008-9272
A biography of Winston Churchill's military career from his youth through World War II.

"D'Este has produced an outstanding work that should take its right-ful place alongside the dozens of other studies of this most remarkable statesman." Libr J

Includes bibliographical references

Johnson, Paul. **Churchill**. Viking 2009 181p il $24.95 **92**
1. Statesmen 2. Historians 3. Prime ministers 4. Memoirists 5.
Cabinet members 6. Members of Parliament 7. Nobel laureates
for literature 8. Prime ministers -- Great Britain 9. Great Britain
-- Politics and government -- 20th century
ISBN 978-0-670-02105-5; 0-670-02105-9

LC 2009-08326

"From his beginnings as a youthful war correspondent, to his mature
political career, to his hobbies of landscape painting and bricklaying,
no aspect of Churchill's life is ignored. . . . An overview of Churchill's
life that instructs rather than awes is Johnson's great achievement."
New Criterion
Includes bibliographical references

Manchester, William. The **last** lion, Winston Spencer
Churchill; visions of glory, 1874-1932. Little, Brown 1983
973p il maps $50   **92**
1. Statesmen 2. Historians 3. Prime ministers 4. Memoirists
5. Cabinet members 6. Biography, Individual 7. Members of
Parliament 8. Nobel laureates for literature 9. Prime ministers
-- Great Britain 10. Great Britain -- Politics and government -- 20th
century
ISBN 0-316-54503-1

LC 82-24972

This first volume of a projected three-volume biography of Churchill
covers the life of the British statesman from his birth up to his split with
the Conservative party over its policy regarding Indian self-rule.
Includes bibliographical references

Manchester, William. The **last** lion, Winston Spencer
Churchill; alone, 1932-1940. Little, Brown 1988 xxvi, 756p
il map $50   **92**
1. Statesmen 2. Historians 3. Prime ministers 4. Memoirists
5. Cabinet members 6. Biography, Individual 7. Members of
Parliament 8. Nobel laureates for literature 9. Prime ministers
-- Great Britain 10. Great Britain -- Foreign relations 11. Great
Britain -- Politics and government -- 20th century
ISBN 0-316-54512-0

LC 82-24972

This second volume of a projected three-volume biography of the
British statesman "covers the years leading up to the outbreak of World
War II." (Time) For volume one see BRD 1983.
This second volume of a projected three-volume biography of the
British statesman "covers the years leading up to the outbreak of World
War II." Time
Includes bibliographical references

★ Manchester, William. The **last** lion, Winston Spencer
Churchill; defender of the realm, 1940-1965. by William Manchester. Little, Brown 2012 1183 p. ill., [32] p. of plates, maps
$40   **92**
1. Great Britain -- History 2. World War, 1939-1945 -- Great Britain
3. Great Britain -- Foreign relations -- 20th century 4. Great Britain
-- Politics and government -- 20th century
ISBN 9780316547703 (v. 3)

LC 82024972

This book, by William Manchester and Paul Reid, "picks up shortly
after Winston Churchill became Prime Minister. . . . Churchill organized
his nation's military response and defense; compelled [Franklin Delano
Roosevelt] into supporting America's beleaguered cousins, and personified the . . . ethos that helped the Allies win the war, while at the same

time adapting . . . his country to the . . . shift of world power from the
British Empire to the United States." (Publisher's note)
Includes bibliographies and indexes

Roberts, Andrew, 1963- **Churchill**; walking with destiny.
Andrew Roberts. Viking 2018 1088 p. $40   **92**
1. Biography 2. Prime ministers -- Great Britain
ISBN 1101980990; 9781101980996

In this biography, "Andrew Roberts gives readers the full and definitive Winston Churchill, from birth to lasting legacy, as personally
revealing as it is compulsively readable. Roberts gained exclusive access to extensive new material. . . . The Royal Family permitted Roberts
. . . to read the detailed notes taken by King George VI in his diary
after his weekly meetings with Churchill during World War II." (Publisher's note)

"This biography is exhaustively researched, beautifully written and
paced, deeply admiring but not hagiographic, and empathic and balanced in its judgments—a magnificent achievement." Pub Wkly

Toye, Richard. **Churchill's** empire; the world that made
him and the world he made. Henry Holt 2010 xx, 423p il
$32   **92**
1. Statesmen 2. Historians 3. Prime ministers 4. Memoirists
5. Cabinet members 6. Members of Parliament 7. Great Britain
-- Colonies 8. Nobel laureates for literature 9. Prime ministers
-- Great Britain
ISBN 978-0-8050-8795-6

LC 2010-1427

In this biography, the author "stresses that Churchill (1874-1965), a
Victorian aristocrat, assumed white superiority but regularly proclaimed
that nonwhites deserved equal rights and, eventually, independence once
they discarded their primitive ways and achieved European levels of
culture. . . . This work is a valuable contribution to greater understanding
of a historical icon." Booklist
Includes bibliographical reference

Cicero, Marcus Tullius, 106-43 B.C.

Everitt, Anthony. **Cicero**; the life and times of Rome's
greatest politician. Random House 2002 359p il maps hardcover o.p. pa $14.95   **92**
1. Statesmen 2. Philosophers 3. Orators 4. Rome -- History
ISBN 0-375-75895-X pa

LC 2001-48531

This "masterful biography draws on Cicero's letters to his friend Atticus to give a clear picture of the famous Roman orator, noting both his
brilliance and his faults." Booklist
Includes bibliographical references

Ciezadlo, Annia

Ciezadlo, Annia. **Day** of honey; a memoir of food, love,
and war. Free Press 2011 382p $26; pa $12.99   **92**
1. Journalists 2. Women journalists 3. Memoirists 4. Food --
Social aspects 5. Lebanon -- Social life and customs 6. Baghdad
(Iraq) -- Social life and customs
ISBN 978-1-4165-8393-6; 1-4165-8393-9; 978-1-4165-8422-3
pa; 1-4165-8422-6 pa

LC 2010-19739

"There are many good reasons to read 'Day of Honey.' It's a carefully researched tour through the history of Middle Eastern food. It's
filled with adrenalized scenes from war zones, scenes of narrow escapes
and clandestine phone calls and frightening cultural misunderstandings.
. . . These things wouldn't matter much, though, if her sentences didn't
make such a sensual, smart, wired-up sound on the page." N Y Times

Book Rev
Includes bibliographical references

Cixi, Empress dowager of China, 1835-1908

Jung Chang, 1952- **Empress** Dowager Cixi; the concubine who launched modern China. by Jung Chang. Alfred A. Knopf 2013 480 p. ill (some color), map (hardcover) $30   **92**
    1. Empresses 2. China -- History -- 19th century 3. China -- History -- 1861-1912 4. Empresses -- China -- Biography 5. China -- Politics and government -- 19th century
    ISBN 0307271609; 9780307271600; 9780307456700
                    LC 2013020766

Author Jung Chang "provides a revisionist biography of a controversial concubine who rose through the ranks to become a long-reigning, power- wielding dowager empress during the delicate era when China emerged from its isolationist cocoon to become a legitimate player on the international stage. [He shows how] as Cixi's power and influence grew . . . she radically shifted official attitudes toward Western thoughts, ideas, trade, and technology." (Booklist)

Chang "uses the work of revisionist scholars to paint a largely plausible portrait of a ruthless, farsighted politician who welcomed change and restructured the state." LJ

Includes bibliographical references and index

Clapper, James R. (James Robert), 1941-

Clapper, James R. (James Robert), 1941- **Facts** and fears; hard truths from a life in intelligence. James R. Clapper with Trey Brown. Viking 2018 424 p. (hardback) $30   **92**
    1. WikiLeaks (Organization) 2. Cyberterrorism -- United States 3. Intelligence service -- United States 4. United States. Office of the Director of National Intelligence -- Officials and employees -- Biography
    ISBN 9780525558644
                    LC 2018023679

In this book, James R. Clapper, former director of U.S. National Intelligence, with Trey Brown, "traces his career through the growing threat of cyberattacks, his relationships with presidents and Congress, and the truth about Russia's role in the presidential election. He describes, in the wake of Snowden and WikiLeaks, his efforts to make intelligence more transparent and to push back against the suspicion that Americans' private lives are subject to surveillance." (Publisher's note)

"If Clapper's revelations undermine the support of an irrational Trump among voters, he will consider the book a success, however limited. However, if the book fails to contribute to the halting of Trump's widespread corruption, Clapper makes clear he will do whatever he can from his retirement to protect what is left of American democracy." Kirkus

Clapton, Eric

Clapton, Eric, 1945- **Clapton**; the autobiography. Broadway Books 2007 343p il $26   **92**
    1. Singers 2. Guitarists 3. Rock musicians 4. Biography, Individual
    ISBN 978-0-385-51851-2; 0-385-51851-X
                    LC 2007-15482

"As he retraces every step of his career, from the early stints with the Yardbirds and Cream to his solo successes, Clapton also devotes copious detail to his drug and alcohol addictions, particularly how they intersected with his romantic obsession with Pattie Boyd. . . . Both the youthful excesses and the current calm state are narrated with an engaging tone that nudges Clapton's story ahead of other rock 'n' roll memoirs." Publ Wkly

★ Norman, Philip, 1943- **Slowhand**; the life and music of Eric Clapton. Philip Norman. Little, Brown & Co. 2018 352 p. $30   **92**
    1. Musicians 2. Rock music
    ISBN 031656043X; 9780316560436

This book, by Philip Norman, presents a "definitive biography of Eric Clapton, a Rock legend whose life story is as remarkable as his music, which transformed the sound of a generation. . . . [Norman] follows Clapton through his distinctive and scandalous childhood, early life of reckless rock 'n' roll excess, and twisting [and] turning struggle with addiction in the 60s and 70s. . . . With new information . . . [this] reveals the complex character behind a living legend." (Publisher's note)

Schumacher, Michael. **Crossroads**; the life and music of Eric Clapton. Citadel Press 2003 420p il pa $15.95   **92**
    1. Singers 2. Guitarists 3. Rock musicians
    ISBN 978-0-8065-2466-5; 0-8065-2466-9
    First published 1995 by Hyperion

The author "chronicles the life and career of the reclusive British blues performer. . . . Schumacher covers a tale of unhappy personal relationships, a failed marriage, drug and alcohol addiction and the tragic death of the performer's infant son, while giving full account of Clapton's significant accomplishments as guitarist and vocalist, his forays into rock and his performances and recordings." Publ Wkly

Clare, John, 1793-1864

Bate, Jonathan. **John** Clare: a biography. Farrar, Straus & Giroux 2003 648p il map $40   **92**
    1. Poets 2. Authors
    ISBN 0-374-17990-5
                    LC 2003-44063

This biography "succeeds splendidly . . . not only making generous use of Clare's own wonderful prose and verse but adding historical perspective and a constant, intelligent probing which amount almost to a dialogue with Clare's view of himself." Times Lit Suppl

Includes bibliographical references

Clark, Huguette, 1906-2011

Dedman, Bill, 1960- **Empty** mansions; the mysterious life of Huguette Clark and the spending of a great American fortune. Bill Dedman and Paul Clark Newell, Jr. Ballantine Books 2013 496 p. illustrations (some color) (hardback: acid-free paper) $28   **92**
    1. Wealth 2. Housing 3. Mansions -- United States -- History 4. Recluses -- United States -- Biography 5. Heiresses -- United States -- Biography 6. Eccentrics -- United States -- Biography 7. Collectors and collecting -- United States -- Biography
    ISBN 0345534522; 9780345534521
                    LC 2013023933

This book by Bill Dedman and Paul Clark Newell, Jr. is about "wealth and loss, connecting the Gilded Age opulence of the nineteenth century with a twenty-first-century battle over a $300 million inheritance. At its heart is a reclusive heiress named Huguette Clark, a woman so secretive that, at the time of her death at age 104, no new photograph of her had been seen in decades." (Publisher's note)

"Although William Mangam's The Clarks: An American Phenomenon (1941) examined Huguette's father, Gilded Age millionaire W.A. Clark, and C.B. Glasscock's The War of the Copper Kings includes him, this is the first book on Huguette. An enlightening read for those interested in the opulent lifestyles afforded the offspring of the Gilded Age magnates and the mysterious ways of wealth." LJ

Includes bibliographical references and index

Clark, Kenneth, 1903-1983

Stourton, James. **Kenneth** Clark; Life, Art and Civilisation. James Stourton. Alfred A. Knopf 2016 496 p. illustrations (hardcover) $35   **92**

1. Art historians -- Great Britain -- Biography
ISBN 9780385351164; 9780385351171

       LC 2016940293

This biography of arts patron and television pioneer Kenneth Clark, by James Stourton, "reveals the formidable intellect and the private man behind the figure who effortlessly dominated the art world for more than half a century: his privileged upbringing, his interest in art history beginning at Oxford, his remarkable early successes. At 27 he was keeper of Western Art at the Ashmolean in Oxford and at 29, the youngest director of The National Gallery." (Publisher's note)

"A sparkling, thoroughly entertaining portrait of a brilliant popularizer who brought art to the masses." Kirkus

Includes bibliographical references (pages 417-459) and index.

Clay, Henry, 1777-1852

Heidler, David Stephen. **Henry** Clay; the essential American. [by] David S. Heidler and Jeanne T. Heidler. Random House 2010 595p il $30   **92**

1. Statesmen 2. Senators 3. Members of Congress 4. Secretaries of state 5. Speakers of the House 6. United States -- Congress 7. Statesmen -- United States 8. United States -- Politics and government -- 1815-1861
ISBN 978-1-4000-6726-8; 1-4000-6726-X

       LC 2009-27872

"Anyone wanting to understand political, economic, and social life in the early republic will appreciate the Heidlers' command of sources and balanced treatment of a man too long in the shadow of Andrew Jackson and very much a metaphor for his era." Libr J

Includes bibliographical references

Cleage, Pearl

Cleage, Pearl. **Things** I Should Have Told My Daughter; Lies, Lessons & Love Affairs. Pearl Cleage. Atria Books 2014 320 p. (hardback) $23.99   **92**

1. Motherhood 2. Women authors 3. Self-realization 4. Self-realization in women 5. Women authors, American -- Biography
ISBN 1451664699; 9781451664690; 9781451664706

       LC 2013034164

This book, by Pearl Cleage, "reprints journal entries chronicling her tumultuous life in the 1970s and '80s . . . the decades in which she discovered her vocation as a playwright, poet and novelist while remaining deeply engaged in political activism, as a speechwriter for the first black mayor of Atlanta, and as a feminist grappling with marriage, motherhood, divorce and subsequent sexual freedom." (Kirkus Reviews)

Includes bibliographical references and index

Cleese, John

Cleese, John, 1939- **So,** anyway... John Cleese. Crown Archetype 2014 392 p. 24 plates; illustrations (cloth) $28 **92**

1. Comedians -- Biography 2. Actors -- Great Britain -- Biography 3. Comedians -- Great Britain -- Biography 4. Motion picture actors and actresses -- Great Britain -- Biography
ISBN 038534824X; 9780385348249

       LC 2014037869

In this book, actor and comedian John Cleese "takes readers on a Grand Tour of his ascent in the entertainment world, from his humble beginnings in a sleepy English town and his early comedic days at Cambridge University (with future Python partner Graham Chapman), to the founding of the landmark comedy troupe that would propel him to worldwide renown." (Publisher's note)

Cleland, Max, 1942-

Cleland, Max. **Heart** of a patriot; how I found the courage to survive Vietnam, Walter Reed and Karl Rove. [by] Max Cleland, with Ben Raines. Simon & Schuster 2009 259p il $26 **92**

1. Amputees 2. Veterans 3. Senators 4. Government officials 5. Veterans -- United States 6. State government officials 7. United States -- Congress -- Senate
ISBN 978-1-4391-2605-9

       LC 2009-11620

"This heartrending memoir is aimed at former soldiers who have struggled with the trauma of war and at those of us who haven't served in the military but need to understand the personal cost to those who have." Booklist

Includes bibliographical references

Clemente, Roberto, 1934-1972

Maraniss, David. **Clemente**; the passion and grace of baseball's last hero. Simon & Schuster 2006 401p il maps hardcover o.p. pa $15   **92**

1. Baseball players 2. Baseball -- Biography
ISBN 0-7432-1781-0; 978-0-7432-1781-1; 0-7432-9999-X; 978-0-7432-9999-2 pa

       LC 2006-42235

The author "has produced a baseball-savvy book sensitive to the social context that made Clemente, a black Puerto Rican, a leading indicator of baseball's future." N Y Times Book Rev

Includes bibliographical references

Santiago, Wilfred. **21**; the story of Roberto Clemente: a graphic novel. Wilfred Santiago. Fantagraphics 2011 148p. chiefly ill. $22.99   **92**

1. Graphic novels 2. Baseball players -- Graphic novels 3. Baseball -- Graphic novels
ISBN 978-1-56097-892-3

Presents the story of baseball star Roberto Clemente and his journey from an impoverished childhood to fame and fortune, as he strives to go the distance for respect.

"Santiago opens his dazzlingly drawn comics biography of the pioneering Puerto Rican ballplayer on the final game of the 1972 season, with Clemente just one hit shy of joining the 3,000-hit club. Fans will know, of course, that 3,000 would also be his final tally, as he would die in a plane crash delivering relief supplies to the earthquake-rocked Nicaragua that winter. Santiago skitters around formative scenes from Clemente's childhood—striking a complex chord of family, homeland, and a driving passion for baseball—before tracing significant moments from his professional career: staring down racism with the same resolute demeanor with which he faced a high heater, snagging batting championships and fans' hearts many times over, and always looking for ways to honor his heritage." Booklist

Includes bibliographic references.

Cleopatra, Queen of Egypt, d. 30 B.C.

Fletcher, Joann. **Cleopatra** the great; the woman behind the legend. Harpercollins 2011 454p map $27.99   **92**

1. Queens 2. Egypt -- History
ISBN 978-0-06-058558-7

First published 2008 in the United Kingdom

In this biography, the author "argues that Cleopatra's genius as a strategist, which allowed her to restore a fading Egypt to its former glory, is what makes her the 'true heir' to her ancestor Alexander the Great. . . . Those interested in Cleopatra, ancient history, or a well-written and academically sound biography will enjoy this authentic look at a queen of Egypt who managed to be all things to all people—mother, queen, goddess, and whore." Libr J

Includes bibliographical references

Goldsworthy, Adrian Keith. **Antony** and Cleopatra; [by] Adrian Goldsworthy. Yale University Press 2010 470p il map $35 **92**
1. Queens 2. Generals 3. Statesmen 4. Orators 5. Rome -- History 6. Egypt -- History
ISBN 978-0-300-16534-0

LC 2010-929122

"Narrating [Antony] and Cleopatra's parts in the tumultuous end of the Roman Republic, Goldsworthy skillfully integrates the partial and partisan source material into an accessible presentation of a classic tale from classical times." Booklist

Includes bibliographical references

★ Schiff, Stacy, 1961- **Cleopatra**; a life. Little, Brown and Co. 2010 368p il map $29.99; ebook $14.99 **92**
1. Queens 2. Egypt -- History 3. Biography, Individual
ISBN 978-0-316-00192-2; 0-316-00192-9; 978-0-316-12180-4 ebook

LC 2010-06988

"It's dizzying to contemplate the thicket of prejudices, personalities and propaganda Schiff penetrated to reconstruct a woman whose style, ambition and audacity make her a subject worthy of her latest biographer. After all, Stacy Schiff's writing is distinguished by those very same virtues." N Y Times Book Rev

Includes bibliographical references

Cleveland, Grover, 1837-1908

Graff, Henry F. **Grover** Cleveland. Times Bks. 2002 154p il (American presidents series) $20 **92**
1. Mayors 2. Governors 3. Presidents 4. District attorneys 5. Presidents -- United States
ISBN 0-8050-6923-2

LC 2002-20315

A biography of the only American president to serve two nonconsecutive terms

This "volume is a valuable addition to the literature on the Presidency and is a compelling argument for taking Cleveland seriously as a President." Libr J

Includes bibliographical references

Cleveland, Pat

Cleveland, Pat. **Walking** with the muses; A Memoir. by Pat Cleveland (with Lorraine Glennon) 37 INK 2016 352 p. illustrations (some color) (hardcover: alk. paper) $26.99; (ebook) $18.99 **92**
1. Fashion models 2. African American women -- Biography 3. Fashion -- United States 4. Fashion designers -- United States 5. African American models -- Biography
ISBN 9781501108228; 9781501108235; 9781501108242

LC 2015041692

This memoir is an "account of the international adventures of fashion model Pat Cleveland—one of the first black supermodels during the wild sixties and seventies. . . . Ranging from the streets of New York to the jet-set beaches of Mexico, from the designer retailers of Paris to the offices of Diana Vreeland, here is Cleveland's larger-than-life story." (Publisher's note)

"Some readers will be particularly interested in her discussion of Bill Cosby, but Cleveland is the real star of her own story of passion, strength, and elegance above all." Pub Wkly

Includes bibliographical references and index

Clinton, Bill, 1946-

Clinton, Bill. **My** life. Knopf 2004 957p il $35 **92**
1. Governors 2. Presidents 3. Presidents -- United States 4. United States -- Politics and government -- 1989-
ISBN 0-375-41457-6

LC 2004-107564

In this memoir the former president traces his life from his childhood in Arkansas through his time as governor of Arkansas and then focuses on his White House years

"Clinton's memoir has the raw material for a blockbuster book." Publ Wkly

Clinton, Hillary Rodham

Bernstein, Carl. A **woman** in charge; the life of Hillary Rodham Clinton. Alfred A. Knopf 2007 628p il $27.95 **92**
1. Lawyers 2. Senators 3. Secretaries of state 4. Spouses of presidents 5. Presidential candidates
ISBN 978-0-375-40766-6; 0-375-40766-9

LC 2007-17472

The author "offers a three-dimensional portrait of a person with enduring strengths (discipline, tenacity, a sustaining religious faith) and weaknesses (excessive secrecy, a tendency to self-righteousness and a habit of nursing grudges). . . . Bernstein almost always finds new facts and telling details. [His] account benefits enormously from remarkably candid on-the-record assessments of both Clintons by intimates such as close friend Jim Blair and Betsey Wright, Clinton's gubernatorial chief of staff in Arkansas." Los Angeles Times Book Rev

Includes bibliographical references

Clinton, Hillary Rodham, 1947- **Hard** choices; Hillary Rodham Clinton. Simon & Schuster 2014 656 p. ill. (chiefly color), maps $35 **92**
1. Autobiographies 2. Women politicians 3. United States -- Foreign relations
ISBN 1476751447; 9781476751443

LC 2014407811

This book by Hillary Rodham Clinton discusses how "to her surprise, her former rival for the Democratic Party nomination, newly elected President Barack Obama, asked her to serve in his administration as Secretary of State. This memoir is the story of the four . . . years that followed, and the hard choices that she and her colleagues confronted." (Publisher's note)

"Hillary Clinton follows the well-trod path of possible presidential candidates: a few years out, write a book. Unlike the authors of a lot of these tomes, Clinton actually has an interesting story to tell, beginning with the loss of the 2008 presidential election and how she was convinced to become part of Barack Obama's team of rivals when she took the job as Secretary of State. . . . Clinton goes into deep detail about her work in Asia, Iraq and Afghanistan, Latin America, and other hot spots around the globe. She details her vision for U.S. foreign policy and the role of diplomacy. Along the way, she introduces readers to a who's who of world leaders and gives insight into the way they think and do business. Written engagingly (and some will say with calculation), the book also offers Clinton the opportunity to get certain issues out of the way (not that her apologies about her Iraq vote and Benghazi will placate her critics)." Booklist

Clinton, Hillary Rodham. **Living** history. Simon & Schuster 2003 562p il $28; pa $16 **92**

1. Lawyers 2. Senators 3. Secretaries of state 4. Spouses of presidents 5. Presidential candidates

ISBN 0-7432-2224-5; 0-7432-2225-3 pa

LC 2003-276264

"This book is important not because of the history Senator Clinton records, but because of the history she doesn't record, and what that airbrushing tells us about the history she aspires to shape." N Y Times Book Rev

Cobain, Kurt, 1967-1994

Cross, Charles R. **Heavier** than heaven: a biography of Kurt Cobain. Hyperion 2001 381p il $24.95; pa $14.95 **92**

1. Singers 2. Guitarists 3. Rock musicians 4. Nirvana (Musical group)

ISBN 0-7868-6505-9; 0-7868-8402-9 pa

LC 2001-24187

This is a biography of Kurt Cobain, the lead singer of the rock group Nirvana, who committed suicide in 1994 at the age of 27

"Cross followed the Nirvana juggernaut from the beginning, and though he nearly bludgeons the reader with tales of Cobain's debauched excesses, one is still drawn to the artist's forceful personality." Libr J

Cross, Charles R. **Here** we are now; the lasting impact of Kurt Cobain. Charles R. Cross. It Books 2014 192 p. illustration (hardcover) $22.99 **92**

1. Popular culture -- United States 2. Rock musicians -- United States -- Biography 3. Nirvana (Musical group) 4. Rock music -- 1991-2000 -- History and criticism

ISBN 0062308211; 9780062308214; 9780062308221

LC 2013045769

"In 'Here We Are Now: The Lasting Impact of Kurt Cobain,' [author] Charles R. Cross . . . examines the legacy of the Nirvana front man and takes on the question: why does Kurt Cobain still matter so much, 20 years after his death? Kurt Cobain is the icon born of the 90s, a man whose legacy continues to influence pop culture and music. Cross explores the impact Cobain has had on music, fashion, film, and culture, and attempts to explain his lasting and looming legacy." (Publisher's note)

"This short but intriguing book explores the troubled musician as a kind of muse for seemingly unrelated fields (modern hip-hop, medical studies, high-end fashion) as well as a champion for gay and women's rights and racial equality." LJ

Cobb, Ty, 1886-1961

Leerhsen, Charles. **Ty** Cobb; a terrible beauty. Charles Leerhsen. Simon & Schuster 2015 352 p. 8 plates; illustrations (hardback) $27.50 **92**

1. Baseball players -- Biography 2. Baseball players -- United States -- Biography

ISBN 1451645767; 9781451645767

LC 2014041478

This book, by Charles Leerhsen, is an "authoritative biography of [baseball player] Ty Cobb. . . . [W]hen he retired in 1928, after twenty-one years with the Detroit Tigers and two with the Philadelphia Athletics, he held more than ninety records. . . . But Cobb was also one of the game's most controversial characters. He got in a lot of fights, on and off the field, and was often accused of being overly aggressive." (Publisher's note)

"This is an important work for baseball and American historians as Cobb was one of the country's first true superstars. How he dealt with fame, a new byproduct of the modern age, serves as a useful social history." LJ

Includes bibliographical references and index

Cockburn, Henry, 1982-

Cockburn, Henry. **Henry's** demons; living with schizophrenia: a father and son's story. [by] Patrick Cockburn and Henry Cockburn. Scribner 2011 238p il $25; ebook $11.99 **92**

1. Artists 2. Painters 3. Schizophrenia 4. Father-son relationship 5. Schizophrenics

ISBN 978-1-4391-5470-0; 1-4391-5470-8; 978-1-4391-6035-0 ebook; 1-4391-6035-X ebook

LC 2010-17760

"This straightforward, unsentimental book, is a bold plea for more research and cutting-edge therapies to combat mental illness." Publ Wkly

Cohen, Leonard, 1934-2016

Leonard Cohen on Leonard Cohen; interviews and encounters. edited by Jeff Burger. Chicago Review Press 2014 624 p. illustrations (Musicians in Their Own Words) (cloth) $29.95 **92**

1. Singers 2. Composers 3. Singers -- Canada -- Interviews 4. Composers -- Canada -- Interviews 5. Poets, Canadian -- 20th century -- Interviews

ISBN 1613747586; 9781613747582

LC 2013034568

This book, edited by Jeff Burger, "collects interviews from various sources to present the singular Leonard Cohen in his own voice. The earliest piece is an interview on Canadian television in 1966; the most recent is an article in the Guardian from January of [2014]. Editor Burger divides the book into four parts: the 1960s and 1970s . . . the 1980s . . . the 1990s . . . and the new millennium." (Booklist)

"Burger's discerning editorial hand selects those conversations with Cohen that offer insights into his music." Pub Wkly

★ Simmons, Sylvie. **I'm** your man; the life of Leonard Cohen. Sylvie Simmons. Ecco 2012 570 p. **92**

ISBN 0061994987; 9780061994982

Author Sylvie Simmons' biography of Leonard Cohen, "[t]he legend behind such songs as 'Suzanne,' 'Bird on the Wire' and 'Hallelujah' and the poet and novelist behind such groundbreaking literary works as 'Beautiful Losers' and 'Book of Mercy,' . . . traces the arc of his prodigious achievements to his remarkable retreat in the mid-nineties -- when . . . he entered a monastery on a rocky mountaintop above Los Angeles -- and finally to his reemergence for a sold-out world tour." (Publisher's note)

Cohn, Billy

Swartz, Mimi. **Ticker**; the quest to create an artificial heart. Mimi Swartz. Crown 2018 320 p. (hardback) $27 **92**

1. Surgeons 2. Artificial heart 3. United States 4. Heart, Artificial

ISBN 9780804138000

LC 2017058910

This book on the quest to build an artificial heart, by Mimi Swartz, is "part investigative journalism, part medical mystery. . . . [It] is a dazzling story of modern innovation, recounting fifty years of false starts, abysmal failures and miraculous triumphs, as experienced by one the world's foremost heart surgeons, O.H. 'Bud' Frazier, who has given his life to saving the un-savable." (Publisher's note)

"Told in an appropriately over-the-top style, this is a quintessentially Texas story: sprawling, unpredictable, and teeming with risk and opportunity." Publishers' Weekly

Includes bibliographical references and index

Colby, William Egan, 1920-1996

★ Woods, Randall B. **Shadow** warrior; William Egan Colby and the CIA. Randall B. Woods. Basic Books 2013 576 p. (hbk.: alk. paper) $29.99 **92**

1. United States. Central Intelligence Agency 2. Intelligence officers -- United States -- Biography 3. United States. Central Intelligence Agency -- Biography 4. World War, 1939-1945 -- Secret service -- United States 5. Vietnam War, 1961-1975 -- Secret service -- United States

ISBN 0465021948; 9780465021949; 9780465037889

LC 2012040332

This book by Randall B. Woods presents a biography of "World War II commando, Cold War spy, and CIA director under presidents [Richard] Nixon and [Gerald] Ford, William Egan Colby. Drawing on multiple new sources, including interviews with members of Colby's family, Woods has crafted a . . . biography of one of the most fascinating and controversial figures of the twentieth century." (Publisher's note)

Includes bibliographical references and index

Cole, Nat King, 1919?-1965

Epstein, Daniel Mark. **Nat** King Cole. Northeastern University Press 2000 437p il pa $20 **92**

1. Singers 2. Pianists 3. Jazz musicians 4. African American singers

ISBN 1-555-53469-4; 978-1-555-53469-1

LC 00-42727

First published 1999 by Farrar, Straus & Giroux

"The biographer sometimes digs too deep into esoterica, spending pages analyzing the lyrics of Straighten Up and Fly Right, for example. But when he recounts the singer's personal struggles, including a shocking 1956 onstage kidnapping attempt by Alabama racists, the human drama is, well unforgettable." Time

Includes bibliographical references

Cole, Natalie

Cole, Natalie. **Angel** on my shoulder; an autobiography. written with Digby Diehl. Warner Bks. 2000 353p il $38 **92**

1. Singers 2. Pop musicians

ISBN 978-0-446-52746-0; 0-446-52746-7

LC 00-61455

In this memoir by the daughter of the late Nat King Cole, the Grammy Award-winning songstress recalls her childhood, her personal battle and victory over drugs and alcohol, and the legal battles with her mother and siblings over her father's estate

"Although she concentrates mostly on the good times, Cole isn't shy about the bad times, which makes this intriguing, engaging, and inspirational life story worthy of attention." Booklist

Colette, 1873-1954

Thurman, Judith. **Secrets** of the flesh: a life of Colette. Knopf 1999 592p il hardcover o.p. pa $18.95 **92**

1. Authors 2. Novelists 3. Biographers

ISBN 0-345-37103-8 pa

LC 99-18959

Thurman focuses on the "morally subversive Colette in the social milieu of early-20th-century Paris. . . . {She} does not hesitate to expose the dishonest, selfish, exploitive facets of the feminist icon who wrote articles for Occupation newspapers and sometimes behaved heartlessly toward lovers. Nevertheless, her Colette comes off as an appealing, even heroic, figure." Publ Wkly

Includes bibliographical references

Collins, Lauren

Collins, Lauren. **When** in French; Love in a Second Language. Lauren Collins. Penguin Press 2016 256 p. (hardback) $27; (ebook) $65 **92**

1. Love 2. Man-woman relationship 3. French as a second language

ISBN 9781594206443; 9780698191075

LC 2016017611

In this book, by Lauren Collins, "a language barrier is no match for love. . . . Collins discovered this firsthand when, in her early thirties, she moved to London and fell for a Frenchman named Olivier. . . . In learning French, Collins must wrestle with the very nature of French identity and society—which, it turns out, is a far cry from life back home in North Carolina." (Publisher's note)

"Throughout, the author ably weaves together the personal and the historical. A memoir filled with pleasing passages in every chapter." Kirkus

Colonna, Vittoria, 1492-1547

Targoff, Ramie. **Renaissance** woman; the life of Vittoria Colonna. Ramie Targoff. Farrar, Straus & Giroux 2018 352 p. (hardcover) $30 **92**

1. Women poets -- Biography 2. Poets, Italian -- Early modern, 1500-1700 -- Biography

ISBN 9780374140946; 9780374713843

LC 2017036978

This book, by Ramie Targoff, offers "a biography of Vittoria Colonna, confidante of Michelangelo, scion of one of the most powerful families of her era, and a pivotal figure in the Italian Renaissance. . . . Marchesa of Pescara. Vittoria has long been celebrated by scholars of Michelangelo as the artist's best friend. . . . [She] was not only a critical political actor and negotiator but also the first woman to publish a book of poems in Italy." (Publisher's note)

"Targoff's well-researched, thoughtful biography reveals Colonna as a complex woman who turned grief and a spiritual quest into a renowned literary reputation." Pub Wkly

Includes bibliographical references and index

Coltrane, John, 1926-1967

Ratliff, Ben. **Coltrane**; the story of a sound. Farrar, Straus & Giroux 2007 xxi, 250p il hardcover o.p. pa $16 **92**

1. Jazz musicians 2. African American musicians 3. Saxophonists

ISBN 978-0-374-12606-3; 0-374-12606-2; 978-0-312-42778-8 pa; 0-312-42778-6 pa

LC 2007-4362

This is a biography of the jazz musician.

This is an "engaging study of the jazz saxophonist's artistic influence. . . . Ratliff patiently explicates Coltrane's legend, writing in short, aphoristic bursts, often as elliptically as his subject played tenor saxophone, but never less than lucidly." N Y Times Book Rev

Includes bibliographical references

Columbus, Christopher

Morison, Samuel Eliot. **Admiral** of the ocean sea: a life of Christopher Columbus; maps by Erwin Raisz; drawings by Bertram Greene. Little, Brown 1942 xx, 680p il maps hardcover o.p. pa $28.99 **92**

1. Explorers

ISBN 0-316-58478-9 pa

A condensation of the author's two-volume work with same title also published in 1942 but now o.p.

"An authoritative . . . biography of Columbus which is also decidedly original in its emphasis on the ability of Columbus as seaman and navigator and in the amount of space given to tracing the routes of the voyages and landings." Libr J

Commerson, Philibert, 1727-1773

Ridley, Glynis. The **discovery** of Jeanne Baret; a story of science, the high seas, and the first woman to circumnavigate the globe. Crown Publishers 2010 288p il $25; ebook $25 **92**

1. Botanists 2. Explorers 3. Women scientists 4. Voyages around the world

ISBN 978-0-307-46352-4; 978-0-307-46354-8 ebook

LC 2010-16778

This is a biography "of Jeanne Baret. Born in 1740 in France's Loire valley, Baret became an expert 'herb woman' who proved to be indispensable to the ambitious botanist Philibert Commerson, accompanying him as his assistant when Commerson was appointed naturalist for France's first expedition to circumnavigate the globe. But women were forbidden, so Baret dressed as a man. . . . Woven throughout this gripping story are Ridley's piquant insights into eighteenth-century exploration, botany, taxonomy, biopiracy, and sexism. Baret could not have asked for a more exacting and expressive champion. Ridley is incandescent in her passion for the truth." Booklist

Includes bibliographical references

Common (Musician)

Common. **One** day it'll all make sense; a memoir. by Common with Adam Bradley. 1st Atria Books hardcover ed.; Atria Books 2011 305 p. ill. (chiefly col.) $25 **92**

1. Fame 2. Gangs 3. Rap music 4. African Americans -- Chicago (Ill.) 5. African American entertainers -- Biography 6. Rap musicians -- United States -- Biography

ISBN 9781451625875; 9781451625882 pa; 9781451625905

LC 2011021691

Street Lit Book Award Medal: Adult Non-Fiction (2012)

The author of the book, the hip-hop musician Common, "discusses fame and the deeper meanings of his life. . . . He portrays himself as an openhearted, curious kid, trying to understand the tumult of Chicago's African-American South Side. . . . Common writes frankly about his youthful involvement with gang culture, portrayed as an inevitable rite of passage that became increasingly violent. . . . By 1989, his early demos as Common Sense were drawing industry attention, and he dropped out of college to pursue this calling, over his mother's objections. Much of what follows is a . . . showbiz narrative, moving from hip-hop to film acting." (Kirkus)

Includes bibliographical references and index

Conant, James Bryant, 1893-1978

Conant, Jennet. **Man** of the hour; James B. Conant, warrior scientist. Jennet Conant. Simon & Schuster 2017 x, 587 p.p illustrations (hardcover) $30 **92**

1. Chemists 2. Manhattan Project (U.S.) -- History 3. Chemists -- United States -- Biography 4. Cold War -- Decision making -- History 5. Atomic bomb -- United States -- History 6. Educators -- United States -- Biography

ISBN 9781476730882; 9781476730929; 1476730881

LC 2017033241

This biography, by Jennet Conant, focuses on the "remarkable life of one of the most influential men of the greatest generation, James B. Conant. . . . Conant was a towering figure. He was at the center of the mammoth threats and challenges of the twentieth century. As a young eminent chemist, he supervised the production of poison gas in WWI. As a controversial president of Harvard University, he was a champion of meritocracy and open admissions." (Publisher's note)

"Including frank portrayals of family situations and problems, Jennet Conant's capable, informative portrait should be included in collections about the history of American science." Booklist

Includes bibliographical references (pages [501]-561) and index.

Connolly, Kevin Michael, 1985-

Connolly, Kevin Michael. **Double** take; a memoir. HarperStudio 2009 227p il $19.99; pa $14.99 **92**

1. Skiing 2. Athletes 3. Photographers 4. Skateboarding 5. People with disabilities 6. Skiers 7. Athletes with disabilities

ISBN 978-0-06-179153-6; 978-0-06-179152-9 pa

LC 2009-30496

"An X Games competitive skier and photographer recounts an extraordinary life spent overcoming immense physical limitations. Connolly was born without legs in the summer of 1985, in Helena, Mont. . . . A courageous, immensely rewarding chronicle expressed in arresting words and pictures." Kirkus

Connors, Philip

Connors, Philip. A **song** for the river; by Philip Connors. Cinco Puntos Press 2018 246 p. (cloth: alk. paper) $22.95 **92**

1. Biography 2. Gila National Forest (N.M.) 3. Environmentalists -- Biography 4. Fire lookouts -- New Mexico -- Gila National Forest -- Biography

ISBN 9781941026908; 9781941026915

LC 2017057947

In this book, Phillip Connors recalls the "blaze he had always feared: a megafire that forced him off . . . [the Gila National Forest of New Mexico], and forever changed the forest and watershed he loved. It was one of many transformations that arrived in quick succession, not just fire and flood, but the death of a fellow lookout in a freak accident and a tragic plane crash that rocked the community he called home." (Publisher's note)

"This slim but potent volume of essays from Connors (Fire Season) beautifully examines themes of fire and water, life and death, and wonder and grief in the Gila Wilderness of New Mexico." Pub Wkly

Cook, James, 1728-1779

Blainey, Geoffrey. **Sea** of dangers; Captain Cook and his rivals in the South Pacific. Ivan R. Dee 2009 322p il map $27.50 **92**

1. Explorers 2. Voyages around the world 3. Ship captains 4. Naval officers 5. Travel writers 6. Oceania -- Exploration

ISBN 978-1-56663-825-8; 1-56663-825-9

LC 2008-52623

"An excellent work of popular history that recounts the exploits of men who dramatically expanded our knowledge of the globe." Booklist

Includes bibliographical references

Cooke, Sam

★ Guralnick, Peter. **Dream** boogie; the triumph of Sam Cooke. Little, Brown 2005 750p il $27.95 **92**

1. Singers 2. Soul musicians

ISBN 0-316-37794-5

LC 2005-77

This is a biography of the American singer.

"For those who only know the singer through his pop hits—'You Send Me'; 'Twistin' the Night Away'—the extensive account of his childhood background in gospel music will prove fascinating, and the evocation of the harsh realities faced by African-American musicians touring the South a powerful reminder of just how explosive this music could be." Publ Wkly

Includes discography and bibliographical references

Coolidge, Calvin, 1872-1933

Shlaes, Amity. **Coolidge**; Amity Shlaes. Harper 2013 viii, 565 p., [14] p. of platesp ill. $35   **92**

1. United States -- History -- 1919-1933 2. United States -- Economic conditions -- 1919-1933 3. Presidents -- United States -- Biography 4. United States -- Politics and government -- 1923-1929
ISBN 0061967556; 9780061967559

LC 2012032098

In this biography of U.S. President Calvin Coolidge, "[Amity] Shlaes shows that the mid-1920s was . . . a triumphant period that established our modern way of life. . . . Coolidge's discipline and composure, Shlaes reveals, represented not weakness but strength. . . . Coolidge proved unafraid to take on the divisive issues of this crucial period: reining in public-sector unions, unrelentingly curtailing spending, and rejecting funding for new interest groups." (Publisher's note)

Includes bibliographical references and index

Cooper, Alex, 1994-

Cooper, Alex. **Saving** Alex; when I was fifteen I told my Mormon parents I was gay, and that's when my nightmare began. Alex Cooper and Joanna Brooks. HarperOne 2016 256 p. (hardcover) $24.99   **92**

1. Mormons 2. Lesbians 3. LGBT youth 4. United States -- Biography 5. Mormon gays -- United States -- Biography
ISBN 9780062374608; 9780062374622; 9780062455291

LC 2015031520

In this memoir, author Alex Cooper "told her parents that she was gay, and the nightmare began. She was driven from her home in Southern California to Utah, where, against her will, her parents handed her over to fellow Mormons who promised to save Alex from her homosexuality. For eight harrowing months, Alex was held captive in an unlicensed 'residential treatment program' modeled on the many 'therapeutic' boot camps scattered across Utah." (Publisher's note)

"Alex's horrifying story is one that needs to be heard, and her book is an eloquent testament to that. It is encouraging proof that, as Alex is told, things do get better." Booklist

Cooper, Anderson

Cooper, Anderson, 1967- The **rainbow** comes and goes; a mother and son talk about life, love, and loss. Anderson Cooper and Gloria Vanderbilt. HarperCollins 2016 290 p. illustrations (hardback) $27.99   **92**

1. Mother-son relationship 2. Celebrities -- Biography 3. Journalists -- Biography 4. Celebrities -- United States -- Biography 5. Mothers and sons -- United States -- Correspondence 6. Television journalists -- United States -- Biography
ISBN 0062454943; 9780062454942; 9780062454966; 9780062466730

LC 2016000369

This book, by Anderson Cooper and Gloria Vanderbilt, "offers a rare window into their close relationship and fascinating life stories, including their tragedies and triumphs. In these often humorous and moving exchanges, they share their most private thoughts and the hard-earned truths they've learned along the way. In their words their distinctive personalities shine through—Anderson's journalistic outlook on the world is a sharp contrast to his mother's idealism and unwavering optimism." (Publisher's note)

"Vanderbilt and her son, Cooper, relate the touching story of how an epistolary exchange created new emotional intimacy between them." Pub Wkly

Cooper, Anderson, 1967- The **rainbow** comes and goes; a

mother and son talk about life, love, and loss. Anderson Cooper and Gloria Vanderbilt. HarperCollins 2016 290 p. illustrations (hardback) $27.99   **92**

1. Mother-son relationship 2. Celebrities -- Biography 3. Journalists -- Biography 4. Celebrities -- United States -- Biography 5. Mothers and sons -- United States -- Correspondence 6. Television journalists -- United States -- Biography
ISBN 0062454943; 9780062454942; 9780062454966; 9780062466730

LC 2016000369

This book, by Anderson Cooper and Gloria Vanderbilt, "offers a rare window into their close relationship and fascinating life stories, including their tragedies and triumphs. In these often humorous and moving exchanges, they share their most private thoughts and the hard-earned truths they've learned along the way. In their words their distinctive personalities shine through—Anderson's journalistic outlook on the world is a sharp contrast to his mother's idealism and unwavering optimism." (Publisher's note)

"Vanderbilt and her son, Cooper, relate the touching story of how an epistolary exchange created new emotional intimacy between them." Pub Wkly

Cooper, Elisha

Cooper, Elisha. **Falling**; a daughter, a father, and a journey back. Elisha Cooper. Pantheon 2016 viii, 146 p.p (hardback) $23.95   **92**

1. Cancer patients 2. American authors 3. Father-daughter relationship 4. Cancer -- Patients -- Biography 5. Illustrators -- United States -- Biography 6. Authors, American -- 20th century -- Biography 7. Fathers and daughters -- United States -- Biography
ISBN 9781101871232

LC 2015042319

In this novel, author Elisha Cooper "captures his family's journey through a perilous time and, in the process, shows how we are all transformed by the fear and hope we feel for those we love. When he discovers a lump in five-year-old Zoë's midsection as she sits on his lap at a Chicago Cubs game, everything changes. Elisha and his wife strive to help their daughters maintain a sense of stability and joy in their family life." (Publisher's note)

"The children's book author shows masterful control in this memoir of a life careening beyond his control." Kirkus.

Cooper, Helene

Cooper, Helene. The **house** at Sugar Beach; in search of a lost African childhood. Simon & Schuster 2008 354p il map $25   **92**

1. Journalists 2. Liberia
ISBN 0-7432-6624-2; 978-0-7432-6624-6

The author traces her childhood in wartorn Liberia and her reunion with a foster sister who had been left behind when her family fled the region.

"A coming-of-age story told with unremitting honesty. With her pedigree and her freedom from internalized racism, Cooper is liberated to enjoy a social universe that is a fluid mix of all things American and African. . . . While Cooper's memoir is mesmerizing in its portrayal of a Liberia rarely witnessed, its description of the psychological devastation—and coping mechanisms—brought on by profound loss is equally captivating." N Y Times Book Rev

Cooper, James Fenimore, 1789-1851

Franklin, Wayne. **James** Fenimore Cooper; the early years. Yale University Press 2007 708p il map $40   **92**

1. Authors 2. Novelists 3. Authors, American
ISBN 978-0-300-10805-7; 0-300-10805-2

LC 2006-31247

"This volume profoundly enriches our understanding of how the young writer helped forge our national mythology in works such as The Last of The Mohicans and The Pioneers." Booklist

Includes bibliographical references

Copeland, Misty

Copeland, Misty, 1982- **Life** in motion; an unlikely ballerina. Misty Copeland with Charisse Jones. Touchstone Books 2014 186 p. (hardcover) $17.99   **92**
1. Ballet 2. Ballet dancers 3. African American dancers -- Biography 4. Ballerinas -- United States -- Biography 5. Ballet dancers -- United States -- Biography
ISBN 9781476737980; 9781476737997; 1476737991; 1476737983; 9781476738000

LC 2016036841

This book presents a memoir by Misty Copeland, an African American soloist for the American Ballet Theatre. "When a teacher encouraged I 3-year-old Misty to take ballet at the Boys and Girls Club of Los Angeles, she discovered a hidden talent. Her natural flexibility and grace had her on pointe within two months, something other ballerinas work years to achieve. She was offered lead roles before finishing high school." (Booklist)

"Her story is an inspiration to anyone--man or woman, black or white--who has ever chased a dream against the odds, and the grace with which she triumphs is an example for us all." Booklist

Includes bibliographical references and index

Coronado, Rodney A., 1966-

Kuipers, Dean. **Operation** Bite Back; Rod Coronado's war to save American wilderness. Bloomsbury 2009 309p il $25   **92**
1. Environmentalists 2. Animal rights movement 3. Animal rights activists
ISBN 1-59691-458-0; 978-1-59691-458-2

LC 2009-6600

This "account of animal rights activist Rod Coronado follows the charismatic Coronado from his introduction to animal protection in the 1980s to his campaign of sabotage against the fur industry, his life in the underground and on reservations among fellow Native Americans, and ultimately his arrests and incarcerations. . . . An important book that will appeal to readers interested in environmental and social issues." Libr J

Corrigan, Kelly, 1967-

Corrigan, Kelly. **Glitter** and Glue; A Memoir. by Kelly Corrigan. Random House Inc 2014 240 p. ill. $26   **92**
1. Travel 2. Nannies 3. Mother-daughter relationship 4. Motherhood 5. Mothers and daughters 6. Sydney (N.S.W.) -- Biography 7. Americans -- Australia -- Sydney (N.S.W.) -- Biography
ISBN 034553283X; 9780345532831

LC 2013041936

This memoir, by Kelly Corrigan, "examines the bond . . . between mothers and daughters. . . . After college, . . . [Corrigan] took off for Australia to see things and do things. . . . In a matter of months, her savings shot, she had a choice: get a job or go home. That's how Kelly met John Tanner, a newly widowed father of two looking for a live-in nanny. . . . Every day she spent with the Tanner kids was a day spent reconsidering her relationship with her mother." (Publisher's note)

"Written in a breezy style with humor and heart, the book reminds us how rewarding it can be to see a parent outside the context of our own needs." Kirkus

Corrigan, Kelly. The **middle** place. Voice/Hyperion 2008 266p il $23.95; pa $14.95   **92**
1. Breast cancer 2. Columnists 3. Cancer patients
ISBN 978-1-4013-0336-5; 978-1-4013-4093-3 pa

LC 2007-15316

The author "was a happily married mother of two young daughters when she discovered a cancerous lump in her breast. She was still undergoing treatment when she learned that her beloved father, who'd already survived prostate cancer, now had bladder cancer. Corrigan's story could have been unbearably depressing had she not made it clear from the start that she came from sturdy stock. . . . Those learning to accept their own adulthood might find strength—and humor—in Corrigan's feisty memoir." Publ Wkly

Costello, Elvis

Costello, Elvis, 1954- **Unfaithful** Music & Disappearing Ink; by Elvis Costello. Penguin Group USA 2015 352 p. illustrations, portraits (ebook) $32.50; $30   **92**
1. Musicians -- Biography
ISBN 9780698140653; 0399167250; 9780399167256

LC 2015032865

This memoir, by Elvis Costello, "offers his unique view of his unlikely and sometimes comical rise to international success, with diversions through the previously undocumented emotional foundations of some of his best-known songs and the hits of tomorrow. It features many stories and observations about his renowned cowriters and co-conspirators, though Costello also pauses along the way for considerations of the less appealing side of fame." (Publisher's note)

"Costello comes across as the perennial outsider, as someone who is surprised that he has been invited to the party. A must for Costello fans everywhere." Booklist

Cox, Lynne

Cox, Lynne. **Swimming** to Antarctica; tales of a long-distance swimmer. Knopf 2004 323p $24.95   **92**
1. Women athletes 2. Swimmers
ISBN 0-375-41507-6

LC 2003-47577

"Cox is a pleasure. . . . Many passages are grip-the-page exciting, whether she's dodging Antarctic icebergs or Nile River sewage." Booklist

Crabapple, Molly

Crabapple, Molly. **Drawing** Blood; by Molly Crabapple. HarperCollins 2015 336 p. color illustrations $29.99   **92**
1. Artists 2. Young women 3. Culture conflict
ISBN 0062323644; 9780062323644

In this memoir, "Molly Crabapple had the eye of an artist and the spirit of a radical. After a restless childhood on New York's Long Island, she left America to see Europe and the Near East, a young artist plunging into unfamiliar cultures. . . . Returning to New York City after 9/11 to study art, she posed nude for sketch artists and sketchy photographers, danced burlesque, and modeled for the world famous Suicide Girls." (Publisher's note)

"Lavishly illustrated, the book offers a candid portrayal of an artist's journey to self-knowledge and fulfillment." Kirkus

Craddock, Ida C., 1857-1902

Schmidt, Leigh Eric. **Heaven's** bride; the unprintable life of Ida C. Craddock, American mystic, scholar, sexologist, mar-

tyr, and madwoman. Basic Books 2010 335p il   **92**
1. Mysticism 2. Occultists 3. Sex researchers 4. Biography, Individual
ISBN 9780465002986

LC 2010-929343

This is a biography of the American freethinker. Index.

The author "delineates the life of Philadelphia-born self-styled religion scholar and sexologist Ida Craddock (1857–1902), who navigated two important currents in late-19th-century America: the campaign for 'moral purity' waged by a righteous Protestant majority, and a spirit of liberalism and spiritualism as advocated by women's-rights activists, intellectuals and free-thinkers. . . . A colorful contextual study of Craddock and her teeming era." Kirkus

Includes bibliographical references

Crais, Clifton C.

Crais, Clifton. **History** lessons; a memoir of madness, memory, and the brain. Clifton Crais. The Overlook Press 2014 272 p. (alk. paper) $26.95   **92**
1. Amnesia 2. Autobiographies 3. Collective memory 4. Autobiographical memory 5. New Orleans (La.) -- Biography 6. Historians -- United States -- Biography
ISBN 1468303686; 9781468303681

LC 2014002373

"Born in Louisiana to a soon-to-be absent father and an alcoholic mother--who tried to drown him in a bathtub when he was three-- [author] Clifton Crais spent his childhood . . . living with relatives too old or infirmed to care for him, or rambling on his own through New Orleans. . . . Crais examines the science of memory and forgetting, from the ways in which experience shapes the developing brain to . . . chronic childhood amnesia . . . from which he suffers." (Publisher's note)

"The ambiguities of a life only half recalled are fully illuminated in this chronicle of trying to understand what has been forgotten.—" LJ

Crazy Horse, Sioux Chief, ca. 1842-1877

McMurtry, Larry. **Crazy** Horse. Viking 1999 148p (Penguin lives series) hardcover o.p. pa $14   **92**
1. Oglala Indians 2. Indian chiefs 3. Native Americans -- Biography
ISBN 0-670-88234-8; 0-14-303480-4 pa

LC 98-26644

"Though essentially a loner and devoid of political ambition, Crazy Horse was a respected military tactician, equally feared and admired for the strength and the intensity of his convictions. Rather than merely attempting to sort out fact from fiction, McMurtry incorporates conjecture and legend into this philosophical portrait of both the man and the myth." Booklist

Powers, Thomas. The **killing** of Crazy Horse. Alfred A. Knopf 2010 568p il map $30   **92**
1. Oglala Indians 2. Indian chiefs 3. Biography, Individual 4. Dakota Indians -- Wars
ISBN 978-0-375-41446-6; 0-375-41446-0

LC 2010-16842

"With the Great Sioux War as background and context, . . . Powers recounts the final months and days of Crazy Horse's life." (Publisher's note) Bibliography. Index.

"Despite the title, this beautifully written and absorbing work is less about the death of Crazy Horse and more about the personality and life of the Native American icon. It is also an insightful and scrupulously fair examination of the culture of Plains Indian bands and their interaction with advancing white civilization in the nineteenth century." Booklist

Includes bibliographical references

Cregar, Laird, 1913-1944

Mank, Gregory William. **Laird** Cregar; a Hollywood tragedy. Gregory William Mank. McFarland & Company, Inc., Publishers 2017 329 p. (softcover: illustrated case bound) $49.95   **92**
1. Weight loss 2. Motion picture actors and actresses -- United States -- Biography 3. Actors -- United States -- Biography
ISBN 9780786449569

LC 2017048598

This biography, by Gregory William Mank, tells the tragic story of Hollywood actor Laird Cregar. "In 1944, . . . Cregar played Jack the Ripper in The Lodger. . . . It was the climax of a strange celebrity that saw the young American actor--who stood 6' 3" and weighed more than 300 pounds--earn distinction as a portrayer of psychopaths and villains. Determined to break free of this typecasting, he desperately . . . [embarked] on an extreme diet that killed him at 31." (Publisher's note)

"Like the actors and actresses who died from too much alcohol or too many drugs, Cregar's obsession with becoming a success wound up killing him, and yet Mank finds joy as well as tragedy in Cregar's attempt to live his dream. Many showbiz biographies reduce the lives of stars to formula; this one gives rich life to an unknown Hollywood story." Booklist

Includes bibliographical references and index

Crews, Harry, 1935-2012

Geltner, Ted. **Blood,** bone, and marrow; a biography of Harry Crews. Ted Geltner. University of Georgia Press 2016 456 p. (hardcover: alk. paper) $32.95   **92**
1. American novelists -- Biography 2. Novelists, American -- 20th century -- Biography
ISBN 9780820349237

LC 2015032701

This biography of Harry Crews, by Ted Geltner, tells the story of "a writer who emerged from a dirt-poor South Georgia tenant farm and went on to create a singularly unique voice of fiction. With books such as 'Scar Lover,' 'Body,' and 'Naked in Garden Hills,' Crews opened a new window into southern life, focusing his lens on the poor and disenfranchised, . . . the 'grits,' as Crews affectionately called his characters and himself." (Publisher's note)

"An absorbing but sad chronicle of a tormented writer." Kirkus

Includes bibliographical references

Cromwell, Thomas, 1485?-1540

Borman, Tracy. **Thomas** Cromwell; The Untold Story of Henry Viii's Most Faithful Servant. Tracy Borman. Atlantic Monthly Press 2015 336 p. 16 plates; illustrations; maps $30   **92**
1. Great Britain -- History -- 1485-1603, Tudors
ISBN 0802123171; 9780802123176

This biography by Tracy Borman profiles Thomas Cromwell. "As Henry VIII's right-hand man, Cromwell was the architect of the English Reformation, secured Henry's divorce from Catherine of Aragon and plotted the downfall of Anne Boleyn. Borman reveals a different side of one of the most notorious figures in history: that of a caring husband and father, a fiercely loyal servant and friend, and a revolutionary who helped make medieval England into a modern state." (Publisher's note)

"Neglecting neither the public persona nor the private man, Borman provides an insightful biography of a much-maligned historical figure." Booklist

MacCulloch, Diarmaid. **Thomas** Cromwell; a revolutionary life. Diarmaid MacCulloch. Penguin Group USA 2018

640 p. $35   **92**
1. Great Britain -- History -- 1485-1603, Tudors
ISBN 0670025577; 9780670025572

In this book, author "Diarmaid MacCulloch has emerged with a tantalizing new understanding of Henry's mercurial chief minister, the inscrutable and utterly compelling Thomas Cromwell. . . . MacCulloch sifted through letters and court records . . . and found Cromwell's fingerprints on some of the most transformative decisions of Henry's turbulent reign. But he also found Cromwell the man, an administrative genius, rescuing him from myth and slander." (Publisher's note)

"A must-read biography of a man whose role in shaping English and Protestant history has long been misunderstood." Library Journal

Cronkite, Walter

★ Brinkley, Douglas. **Cronkite**; Douglas Brinkley. Harper, an imprint of HarperCollins Publishers 2012 xi, 819 p.p illustrations (hardback) $34.99   **92**
1. Television broadcasting of news 2. Journalists -- United States -- Biography 3. Television journalists -- United States -- Biography
ISBN 0061374261; 9780061374265

LC 2011051467

This book, by Douglas Brinkley, is a biography of Walter Cronkite. "For decades, Walter Cronkite was known as 'the most trusted man in America'. . . . Brinkley traces Cronkite's story from his roots in Missouri and Texas through the Great Depression, . . . to World War II [and later]. . . . [H]e covered presidential elections, the space program, Vietnam, and the first televised broadcasts of the Olympic Games, as both a reporter and later as an anchor for the evening news." (Publisher's note)

Crosby, Bing, 1903-1977

★ Giddins, Gary. **Bing** Crosby; swinging on a star: the war years, 1940-1946. Gary Giddins. Little, Brown & Co. 2018 736 p. $40   **92**
1. Biography 2. Singers -- United States -- Biography
ISBN 0316887927; 9780316887922

In this biography, "cultural critic Gary Giddins . . . focuses on [singer and actor Bing] Crosby's most memorable period, the war years and the . . . story of 'White Christmas.' . . . [T]his groundbreaking work traces Crosby's skyrocketing career as he fully inhabits a new era of American entertainment and culture. . . . Crosby's legacy would be forever intertwined with his impact on the home front, a unifying voice for a nation at war." (Publisher's note)

"For a twenty-first-century audience, the idea of Bing Crosby as both a swoonworthy movie idol and an inspiration to battle-hardened soldiers may seem difficult to comprehend, but that is the brilliance of Giddins' work: he makes us see how, in a very different time, Crosby's easygoing, waggish style was just what the country craved, on records and radio, at the movies, and in person." Booklist

Crowell, Rodney, 1950-

★ Crowell, Rodney. **Chinaberry** sidewalks. Alfred A. Knopf 2011 259p il $24.95   **92**
1. Singers 2. Country musicians 3. Songwriters
ISBN 978-0-307-59420-4

LC 2010-35996

"Crowell is among the best storytellers to emerge from Nashville. Up to now, he told his stories in song, but with this heartfelt memoir, he can now be called a writer of the first order. Houston, where Crowell grew up in the 1950s and early 1960s, was a city full of characters found in stereotypical country songs: hard-drinking fathers and longsuffering mothers singing along to the beer-soaked ballads of Hank Williams. But this is not fiction; Crowell actually lived the life, soaking up its exhilarating and disturbing atmosphere. Crowell is unsparingly honest, yet

there is an admirable restraint here, too." Booklist

Crystal, Billy

Crystal, Billy, 1948- **Still** foolin' 'em; where i've been, where i'm going, and where the hell are my keys? by Billy Crystal. Henry Holt and Company 2013 288 p. (hardback) $28   **92**
1. Aging 2. American wit and humor 3. Comedians -- United States -- Biography
ISBN 0805098208; 9780805098204

LC 2013012238

Author and comedian Billy Crystal "outlines the absurdities and challenges that come with growing old, from insomnia to memory loss to leaving dinners with half your meal on your shirt. Crystal not only catalogues his physical gripes, but offers a road map to his 77 million fellow baby boomers who are arriving at this milestone age with him. He also looks back at the most powerful and memorable moments of his long and storied life." (Publisher's note)

"Avoiding the trappings—-excess schmaltz, laundry list of famous friends, boozy party log—-of so many celebrity memoirs, Crystal delivers a funny and genuinely moving chronicle of his life inside and outside Hollywood." Pub Wkly

Culkin, Jennifer

Culkin, Jennifer. A **final** arc of sky; a memoir of critical care. Beacon Press 2009 237p $24.95   **92**
1. Nurses 2. Authors 3. Nursing 4. Essayists
ISBN 978-0-8070-7285-1

LC 2008-46810

"It's clear that Culkin has little use for cheap sentiment. However, this memoir time and again shares with us her efforts to make meaning of the pain and fear and loss that is intrinsic to her line of work. . . . The author gets even more personal when she shares stories from her own family. With unflinching honesty, she talks about how she coped with the decline of her father's health; what she did at the deathbed of her mother; and how she came to terms with her own MS diagnosis. 'A Final Arc of Sky' tackles that toughest of subjects—our own mortality—with grit, compassion, and humor." Bellingham Herald

Includes bibliographical references

Cummings, E. E. (Edward Estlin), 1894-1962

★ Sawyer-Laucanno, Christopher. **E.E.** Cummings; a biography. Sourcebooks 2004 606p il $29.95; pa $16.95   **92**
1. Poets 2. Authors
ISBN 1-570-71775-3; 1-4022-0594-5 pa

LC 2004-12234

This biography of poet and artist e.e. cummings draws parallels between cummings' private life and his work.

This "is a responsible, adept, and necessary contribution to the body of secondary work about one of America's greatest poets." Christ Sci Monit

Cunningham, Merce

Brown, Carolyn. **Chance** and circumstance; twenty years with Cage and Cunningham. Alfred A. Knopf 2007 645p il $37.50   **92**
1. Poets 2. Authors 3. Dancers 4. Composers 5. Choreographers 6. Essayists
ISBN 978-0-394-40191-1; 0-394-40191-3

LC 2006-48799

The author "traces the trajectory of her modern dance career with that organization during its crawling stages in the 1950s and 1960s, when composer John Cage was musical director and artist Robert Rauschenberg was set and costume designer. Brown documents the company's early struggles for acceptance (it was considered avant-garde), various tours, and eventual world recognition. . . . This book will appeal to modern dance buffs and memoir readers." Libr J

Cunningham, William J

★ Cunningham, Bill, 1929-2016. **Fashion** climbing; a memoir with photographs. Bill Cunningham; preface by Hilton Als. Penguin Press 2018 256 p. (hardcover) $27   **92**
    1. Fashion -- New York (State) -- New York 2. Photographers -- United States -- Biography 3. Millinery -- United States -- History 4. Fashion designers -- United States -- Biography 5. Portrait photographers -- United States -- Biography
    ISBN 9780525558705
                            LC 2018024955

In this memoir, author Bill Cunningham recalls his efforts to become the most recognized fashion photographer in New York City. "When he arrived in New York, he reveled in people-watching. He spent his nights at opera openings and gate-crashing extravagant balls, where he would take note of the styles. . . . This was his education, and the birth of the democratic and exuberant taste that he came to be famous for as a photographer for The New York Times." (Publisher's note)

"It documents his unparalleled eye and appreciation for fashion's magic, mystery, and illusions; style's potential to invent and transform. As both the very personal autobiography of an icon and a valuable social history, this wins." Booklist

Curie, Marie, 1867-1934

Brian, Denis. The **Curies**; a biography of the most controversial family in science. Wiley 2005 438p il $30   **92**
    1. Chemists 2. Physicists 3. Nobel laureates for physics
    ISBN 0-471-27391-0
                            LC 2005-7001

This book "follows five generations of the Sklodowska-Curie-Joliot family. Beginning before Marie Sklodowska and Pierre Curie meet, Brian details their courtship and 11-year marriage, bringing the reader to the Curie dinner table and into the converted garden shed (replete with a leaking roof) where the Curies' work on polonium and radium transformed physics and won them two Nobel prizes. . . . Extremely well-done and highly recommended." Publ Wkly
    Includes bibliographical references

Dry, Sarah. **Curie**; with an essay by Sabine Seifert. Haus 2003 170p il (Life & times) pa $15.95   **92**
    1. Chemists 2. Physicists 3. Women scientists 4. Chemists -- France 5. Chemists -- Poland 6. Women chemists -- France 7. Women chemists -- Poland 8. Nobel laureates for physics
    ISBN 1-904341-29-2

This is a biography of the first woman to win two Nobel Prizes, one for physics and the other for chemistry

"Concise and engaging, this amply illustrated history of Madame Curie . . . makes an excellent introduction to the feminist icon and scientific pioneer. Dry does an excellent job of delineating the major events of Curie's life, including her early education in the underground schools of the 19th-century Polish resistance movement, her heady intellectual courtship with Pierre Curie in France, and later their discovery of radioactivity in 1898. Sidebars on topics such as the invention of the laboratory, and the inclusion of Seifert's essay on Irène Joliot-Curie, Marie Curie's less famous daughter and co-worker, make this pocket sized book especially comprehensive, and a wonderful introduction to a fascinating and inspiring career." Publ Wkly
    Includes bibliographical references

Curie, Pierre, 1859-1906

Brian, Denis. The **Curies**; a biography of the most controversial family in science. Wiley 2005 438p il $30   **92**
    1. Chemists 2. Physicists 3. Nobel laureates for physics
    ISBN 0-471-27391-0
                            LC 2005-7001

This book "follows five generations of the Sklodowska-Curie-Joliot family. Beginning before Marie Sklodowska and Pierre Curie meet, Brian details their courtship and 11-year marriage, bringing the reader to the Curie dinner table and into the converted garden shed (replete with a leaking roof) where the Curies' work on polonium and radium transformed physics and won them two Nobel prizes. . . . Extremely well-done and highly recommended." Publ Wkly
    Includes bibliographical references

Custer, George A. (George Armstrong), 1839-1876

McMurtry, Larry, 1936- **Custer**; Larry McMurtry. Simon & Schuster 2012 178 p. (hardcover) $35   **92**
    1. Little Bighorn, Battle of the, 1876 2. Native Americans -- Wars 3. United States. Army -- Biography 4. Generals -- United States -- Biography 5. Little Bighorn, Battle of the, Mont., 1876 6. United States -- History -- Civil War, 1861-1865
    ISBN 9781451626209; 1451626207
                            LC 2012012374

Author Larry McMurtry presents a biography of George Armstrong Custer. "On June 25, 1876, General George Armstrong Custer and his 7th Cavalry attacked a large Lakota Cheyenne village on the Little Bighorn River in Montana Territory. He lost not only the battle but his life--and the lives of his entire cavalry. 'Custer's Last Stand' was a spectacular defeat that shocked the country and grew quickly into a legend that has reverberated in our national consciousness to this day." (Publisher's note)
    Includes bibliographical references.

Stiles, T. J. **Custer's** trials; a life on the frontier of a new America. T. J. Stiles. Alfred A. Knopf 2015 592 p. illustrations (hardcover) $30   **92**
    1. Native Americans -- Wars 2. United States. Army -- Biography 3. Generals -- United States -- Biography 4. Little Bighorn, Battle of the, Mont., 1876 5. United States -- History -- Civil War, 1861-1865
    ISBN 0307592642; 9780307592644
                            LC 2015002070

National Book Critics Circle Award Finalist: Biography (2015)
Pulitzer Prize Finalist: Biography (2016)

This biography of George Armstrong Custer, by T. J. Stiles, "paints a portrait of Custer both deeply personal and sweeping in scope, proving how much of Custer's legacy has been ignored. . . . The key to understanding Custer, Stiles writes, is keeping in mind that he lived on a frontier in time. In the Civil War, the West, and many areas overlooked in previous biographies, Custer helped to create modern America, but he could never adapt to it." (Publisher's note)

"Stiles ably points out [Custer's] many defining flaws: his heroic style didn't work in an era of tact and skill, and there is no doubt that he was self-serving, generally assuming that rules weren't made for him and never showing remorse. In addition to examining Custer's life, the author also introduces his cook, the fascinating Eliza Brown, an escaped slave who deserves a biography of her own." Kirkus
    Includes bibliographical references and index

D'Amato, Cus

Tyson, Mike, 1966- **Iron** ambition; my life with Cus D'Amato. Mike Tyson; with Larry "Ratso" Sloman. Blue Rider Press 2017 465 p. illustrations (some color) (hardcover) $28 **92**

1. Boxers (Sports) 2. Boxing -- Biography 3. African American boxers -- Biography 4. Boxers (Sports) -- United States -- Biography 5. Boxing trainers -- United States -- Biography
ISBN 0399177035; 9780399177033; 9780698413092

LC 2017007907

In this book, boxer Mike Tyson "elaborates on the life lessons that [Cus] D'Amato passed down to him, and reflects on how the trainer's words of wisdom continue to resonate with him outside the ring. The book also chronicles Cus's courageous fight against the mobsters who controlled boxing, revealing more than we've ever known about this singular cultural figure." (Publisher's note)

"A belated but welcome homage to a boxing legend who died shortly before Tyson's career took off." Kirkus

D'Annunzio, Gabriele, 1863-1938

Hughes-Hallett, Lucy. **Gabriele** d'Annunzio; poet, seducer and preacher of war. by Lucy Hughes-Hallett. Alfred A. Knopf 2013 608 p. $35 **92**

1. Nationalists -- Italy -- Biography 2. Fascism -- Italy -- History -- 20th century 3. Poets, Italian -- 20th century -- Biography 4. Rijeka (Croatia) -- History -- 20th century 5. Italy -- Politics and government -- 1914-1945 6. Militarism -- Italy -- History -- 20th century 7. Politics and literature -- Italy -- History -- 20th century 8. World War, 1914-1918 -- Territorial questions -- Croatia -- Rijeka
ISBN 0307263932; 9780307263933

LC 2012033943

This book by Lucy Hughes Hallett presents a biography of "the Italian modernist writer and demagogue" Gabriele d'Annunzio. "He was a brilliant, scandalous literary celebrity . . . a ruthless seducer of women; an avowed Nietzschean superman and an effeminate voluptuary who loved fashion, furnishings, and flowers; and a blood-thirsty militarist who helped propel Italy into World War I with his pro-war oratory and reveled in the carnage he witnessed at the front." (Publishers Weekly)

Includes bibliographical references and index

Dahl, Roald

Sturrock, Donald. **Storyteller**; the authorized biography of Roald Dahl. Simon & Schuster 2010 655p il $30 **92**

1. Authors 2. Authors, English 3. Children's authors 4. Short story writers
ISBN 978-1-4165-5082-2; 1-4165-5082-8

LC 2010-07175

"In this authorized biography of Dahl, Sturrock, the artistic director of the Roald Dahl Foundation, reveals a life marked by tragedy: the early deaths of Dahl's father and sister, his son's tragic accident, the death of a daughter at seven, and the debilitating stroke of his wife, Patricia Neal, at age 39...This carefully researched and unflinching portrait of an immensely complicated and talented writer will appeal to Dahl's fans and other serious readers of biography." (Library Journal)

Includes bibliographical references

Dalai Lama II, 1476-1542

Mullin, Glenn H. The **second** Dalai Lama; his life and teachings. translated, edited, introduced, and annotated by Glenn H. Mullin. Snow Lion Publications 2005 270p pa $16.95 **92**

ISBN 1-55939-233-9

LC 2005-281580

Dalai Lama XIV, 1935-

★ Bstan-'dzin-rgya-mtsho, Dalai Lama XIV, 1935- **Freedom** in exile; the autobiography of the Dalai Lama. HarperCollins Pubs. 1990 288p il maps hardcover o.p. pa $15 **92**

1. Buddhism 2. Tibet (China) 3. Buddhist leaders 4. Political leaders 5. Nobel laureates for peace
ISBN 0-06-098701-4

LC 89-46523

"The Dalai Lama's story is, in part, a chapter in the 2,500-year history of Buddhism as well as a testament to the 'mendacity and barbarity' of Communist China. He shares the details of his amazing life, a glimpse at some of the mysteries of Tibetan Buddhism, and his unshakable belief in the basic good of humanity." Booklist

★ Iyer, Pico. The **open** road; the global journey of the fourteenth Dalai Lama. Bloomsbury 2008 288p $24 **92**

1. Buddhist leaders 2. Political leaders 3. Nobel laureates for peace
ISBN 978-0-307-26760-3; 0-307-26760-1

LC 2007-43991

"The combination of Iyer's exacting observations, incisive analysis, and frank respect for the unknowable results in a uniquely internalized, even empathic portrait of one of the world's most embraced and least understood guiding lights." Booklist

Includes bibliographical references

Danticat, Edwidge, 1969-

★ Danticat, Edwidge, 1969- **Brother,** I'm dying. Alfred A. Knopf 2007 272p hardcover o.p. pa $15 **92**

1. Authors 2. Novelists 3. Dramatists 4. Women authors 5. Editors 6. Essayists 7. Children's authors 8. Short story writers 9. Biography, Individual
ISBN 1-4000-3430-2 pa; 1-4000-4115-5; 978-1-4000-3430-7 pa; 978-1-4000-4115-2

LC 2007-06887

National Book Award Finalist: Nonfiction (2007)

This family memoir by the author of The Dew Breaker (2004) centers on the experiences of "her father, Mira, and his older brother, Joseph." (Publisher's note)

The author "has written a fierce, haunting book about exile and loss and family love, and how that love can survive distance and separation, loss and abandonment and somehow endure, undented and robust." N Y Times (Late NY Ed)

Danticat, Edwidge, 1969- **Create** dangerously; the immigrant artist at work. Princeton University Press 2010 189p (Toni Morrison lecture series) $19.95 **92**

1. Authors 2. Novelists 3. Dramatists 4. Women authors 5. Editors 6. Essayists 7. Children's authors 8. Short story writers 9. Biography, Individual 10. Haiti -- Social conditions
ISBN 0-691-14018-9; 978-0-691-14018-6

LC 2010-10302

This is Danticat's "new collection of essays, adapted and updated from the Toni Morrison Lecture she gave in 2008 at Princeton University, and expanded with her writing for The New Yorker, The Progressive and other publications." (N Y Times Book Rev) Index.

This "tender . . . book about loss and the unquenchable passion for homeland makes us remember the powerful material from which most fiction is wrought: it comes from childhood, and place. No matter her geographic and temporal distance from these, Danticat writes about them with the immediacy of love." N Y Times Book Rev

Includes bibliographical references

Danton, Georges Jacques, 1759-1794

Lawday, David. The **giant** of the French Revolution; Danton, a life. Grove Press 2010 294p il map $27.50　　**92**

1. Revolutionaries 2. France -- History -- 1789-1799, Revolution
ISBN 978-0-8021-1933-9

"This is the best biography of Danton to be written since Hilaire Belloc's over 100 years ago. Both the scholar and the general reader will find this biography an informative and lively read." Libr J

Includes bibliographical references

Darling, Ron, 1960-

Darling, Ron. The **complete** game; reflections on baseball, pitching, and life on the mound. by Ron Darling, with Daniel Paisner. Alfred A. Knopf 2009 272p $24.95　　**92**

1. Baseball players 2. Baseball -- Biography
ISBN 978-0-307-26984-3; 0-307-26984-1

LC 2008-55706

Darling, "the stalwart ex-Mets starter and incumbent Mets broadcaster . . . offers pitches and outcomes (but no box scores) from ten selected games in his career, including a successful World Series start against the Red Sox at Fenway Park in 1986, a gruesome windy-day thumping suffered at Wrigley Field, and his celebrated extra-inning near-no-hitter back when he was pitching for Yale. Among them are enough oddities and thrilling turns of baseball to make a reader glad to be here and—well, not out there." New Yorker

Darnley, Henry Stewart, Lord, 1545-1567

Weir, Alison. **Mary,** Queen of Scots, and the murder of Lord Darnley. Ballantine Bks. 2003 670p il map $27.95; pa $16.95　　**92**

1. Queens 2. Princes 3. Scotland -- History -- 16th century
ISBN 0-345-43658-X; 0-8129-7151-5 pa

LC 2002-34467

"No stone is left unturned in {Weir's} investigation, and despite its detail, her book is as dramatic as witnessing firsthand the most riveting court case." Booklist

Darrow, Clarence, 1857-1938

Farrell, John A. **Clarence** Darrow; attorney for the damned. Doubleday 2011 561p il $32.50; ebook $15.99　　**92**

1. Lawyers 2. Memoirists 3. Writers on law 4. State legislators
ISBN 978-0-385-52258-8; 0-385-52258-4; 978-0-385-53451-2 ebook

LC 2010-46273

This is a biography of the American lawyer who defended John Scopes, Nathan Leopold and Richard Loeb.

"Farrell gleans from previously undisclosed material to offer a completely engaging portrait of a flawed man of noble ideals." Booklist

Includes bibliographical references

Darwin, Charles, 1758-1778

★ Wilson, A. N., 1950- **Charles** Darwin; Victorian mythmaker. A.N. Wilson. HarperCollins 2017 438 p. $32.50　**92**

1. Biography 2. Naturalists -- Great Britain -- Biography 3. Naturalists -- England -- Biography
ISBN 0062433490; 9780062433497

In this biography, author A. N. Wilson "argues that [Charles] Darwin was not an original scientific thinker, but a ruthless and determined self-promoter who did not credit the many great sages whose ideas he advanced in his book. Furthermore, Wilson contends that religion and Darwinism have much more in common than it would seem, for the acceptance of Darwin's theory involves a pretty significant leap of faith."

(Publisher's note)

Includes bibliographical references (pages 401-422) and index.

Darwin, Charles, 1809-1882

Browne, Janet. **Charles** Darwin. v2 Knopf 2002 591p v2 il $37.50　　**92**

1. Naturalists 2. Travel writers 3. Writers on science
ISBN 0-679-42932-8

This second volume of Browne's biography of Darwin begins "a year before the publication of On the Origin of Species, with the arrival of a package from Alfred Russel Wallace, whose own ideas on natural selection virtually mirrored Darwin's, forcing him to go public. . . . Browne's subject is monumental, but her writing style is never overburdened by the weight. Rather, her prose is elegant in its clarity of thought, her craftsmanship impeccable in the way it weaves a coherent whole from the innumerable threads of thought, experience and persona that comprised this colossal life." Publ Wkly

Includes bibliographical references

Byrne, Eugene. **Darwin**; a graphic biography. by Eugene Byrne; illustrated by Simon Gurr. Smithsonian Books 2013 96 p. ill. (paperback) $9.95　　**92**

1. Evolution 2. Graphic novels 3. Natural selection -- Comic books, strips, etc 4. Evolution (Biology) -- Comic books, strips, etc
ISBN 1588343529; 9781588343529

LC 2012951786

This work of graphic nonfiction by Eugene Byrne and Simon Gurr presents a "summary of [Charles] Darwin's life and achievement. . . . Darwin was an indifferent student . . .until he received an invitation to take a voyage that 'would change the course of history.' . . .The animals he encountered seemed so different . . . that he theorized that if it weren't a matter of different conditions that resulted in such 'transmutation,' they might well have had a different creator." (Kirkus Reviews)

Includes bibliographical references.

David, King of Israel

Pinsky, Robert. The **life** of David. Schocken 2005 209p (Jewish encounters) $19.95　　**92**

1. Kings
ISBN 0-8052-4203-1

LC 2005-41696

The author "considers the peculiarities, paradoxes, and timeless significance of David's often baffling story from his golden days as a handsome upstart confronting King Saul in 'gangsterish' encounters to David's wild years as a desert Robin Hood and ascension to the throne. . . . Witty, frank, skeptical, and clearly moved by mercurial David's chutzpah and losses, Pinsky brings remarkable lucidity, depth, and creativity to his dynamic and poetic reading of a legendary figure who has become emblematic of both destructive and heroic aspects of human nature." Booklist

Davidman, Joy

Santamaria, Abigail. **Joy**; poet, seeker, and the woman who captivated C. S. Lewis. Abigail Santamaria. Houghton Mifflin Harcourt 2015 416 p. 16 plates; illustrations (hardback) $28　　**92**

1. Women poets 2. Women poets, American -- Biography 3. Authors' spouses -- Great Britain -- Biography 4. Christian converts from Judaism -- United States -- Biography
ISBN 0151013713; 9780151013715

LC 2014034506

This book, by Abigail Santamaria, offers a "biography of Joy Davidman [that] brings her out from C. S. Lewis's shadow. . . . A poet and radical, Davidman was a frequent contributor to the communist vehicle New Masses and an active member of New York literary circles in the 1930s and 40s. . . . A mother, a novelist, a vibrant and difficult and intelligent woman, she set off for England in 1952, determined to captivate the man whose work had changed her life." (Publisher's note)

"With access to unpublished documents and family papers, Santamaria has fashioned a compelling narrative, remaining cleareyed about her subject's many personal failings." Kirkus

Includes bibliographical references and index

Davies, Dawn (Dawn S.)

Mothers of Sparta; a memoir in pieces. Dawn Davies. Flatiron Books 2018 272 p. (hardcover) $24.99   92
1. Mothers 2. Sjogren's syndrome 3. American literature -- Women authors 4. Sjogren's syndrome -- Patients -- Biography 5. Women authors, American -- 21st century -- Biography 6. Mothers of autistic children -- United States -- Biography
ISBN 9781250133700

LC 2017041747

This book, by Dawn Davies, is "about a young girl who moves to a new town every couple of years; a misfit teenager who finds solace in a local music scene; an adrift twenty-something who drops out of college to pursue her dream of making cheesecake on a stick a successful business franchise (ah, the ideals of youth). . . . In stories that cut to the quick, Davies explores passion, loss, illness, pain, and joy, told from her singular, gimlet-eyed, hilarious perspective." (Publisher's note)

"Davies' first book is magnetic attraction in memoir form: it will pull readers in with stories that are funny, insightful, and bordering on farce while also pushing them away with darker pieces about loss, mental illness, and an immense amount of physical pain. Davies uses her oodles of talent to remind readers that human beings are never just one thing, and in her essays, we see a whole life revealed." Booklist

Memoir in pieces

Davis, Bette, 1908-1989

Thomson, David, 1941- **Bette** Davis; photo research by Lucy Gray. Faber and Faber 2010 128p il (Great stars) pa $14   92
1. Actors
ISBN 978-0-86547-931-9

LC 2009-41760

First published 2009 in the United Kingdom

"Chronicling Davis' life and evolution in Hollywood, Thomson illustrates how changes in her often-disappointing private life (she had a habit of marrying the wrong men) influenced and often deepened her onscreen persona. Reading of how Davis bounced from one bad movie to the next in the early years of her career, it's hard not to share Thomson's enthusiasm for her talent, drive, and will. And it is hard not to feel Thomson's disappointment when Davis' major, artistic breakthroughs (The Little Foxes, All About Eve) are followed by lapses into forgettable mediocrity (The Man Who Came to Dinner, Payment on Demand)." Booklist

Includes filmography and bibliographical references

Davis, Jennifer Pharr

Davis, Jennifer Pharr. **Called** again; a story of love and triumph. by Jennifer Pharr Davis. Beaufort Books 2013 298 p. (ebook) $15.95; pbk $15.95   92
1. Hikers -- United States -- Biography
ISBN 9780825306532; 0825307457; 9780825306938; 9780825307454

LC 2014036228

"In 2011, Jennifer Pharr Davis became the overall record holder on the Appalachian Trail. By hiking 2,181 miles in 46 days - an average of 47 miles per day - she became the first female to ever set that mark. . . . This is Jennifer's story, in her own words, about how she started this journey with a love for hiking and more significantly a love for her husband Brew." (Publisher's note)

"A serviceably written yet inspired exploration of the meaning of commitment." Kirkus

Davis, Miles

Cook, Richard. **It's** about that time; Miles Davis on and off record. Oxford University Press 2007 373p il $27   92
1. Jazz musicians 2. African American musicians 3. Band leaders 4. Flugelhornists 5. Trumpet players
ISBN 978-0-19-532266-8; 0-19-532266-5

LC 2006-50694

"Cook's thoughtful, illuminating criticism and boundless knowledge of his subject make this a rich and satisfying read for jazz aficionados and novices alike." Publ Wkly

Includes discography and bibliographical references

Davis, Miles. **Miles,** the autobiography; {by} Miles Davis with Quincy Troupe. Simon & Schuster 1989 431p il hardcover o.p. pa $15   92
1. Jazz musicians 2. African American musicians 3. Band leaders 4. Flugelhornists 5. Trumpet players
ISBN 0-671-72582-3 pa

LC 89-19652

"The legendary jazz musician Miles Davis . . . takes us on a historical journey that begins with his growing up in the mid-1920s in East St. Louis, then moves on to New York City in the 1940s, where he was a student at the Julliard School of Music, and to his encounters with other jazz greats like Charlie Parker, Dizzy Gillespie, Billie Holiday, Herbie Hancock, and George Duke." Libr J

Dawkins, Richard, 1941-

Dawkins, Richard, 1941- An **Appetite** for Wonder; The Making of a Scientist. HarperCollins 2013 304 p. $27.99 92
1. Atheism 2. Scientists -- Biography
ISBN 0062225790; 9780062225795

"In the first volume of a projected two-volume memoir, evolutionary biologist and ethologist [Richard] Dawkins . . . looks back on his life from childhood through the publication of his first and most famous book, 'The Selfish Gene,' in 1976. . . . Ultimately, this is a self-portrait of a . . . man whose radical positions are the logical outgrowth of his skeptical, science-based approach. . . . . His memoir is more about science than atheism, although both topics crop up." (Library Journal)

Day, Dorothy, 1897-1980

Hennessy, Kate. **Dorothy** Day; the world will be saved by beauty: an intimate portrait of my grandmother. Kate Hennessy. Simon & Schuster 2017 384 p. illustrations (ebook) $20.99; $27.99   92
1. Catholics -- United States -- Biography 2. Social reformers -- United States -- Biography
ISBN 9781501133985; 1501133969; 9781501133961

LC 2016052573

This book, by Kate Hennessy, talks about "the life and work of Dorothy Day--the iconic, celebrated, and controversial Catholic whom Pope Francis called a 'great American.' . . . Day is an unusual candidate for sainthood. Before her conversion, she lived what she called a 'disorderly life,' during which she had an abortion and then gave birth to a child out of wedlock. After her conversion, she was both an obedient servant and a rigorous challenger of the Church." (Publisher's note)

"Hennessy has created an amazing tapestry of Day's life and the memories she left with her loved ones." Pub Wkly

De Cadenet, Amanda

De Cadenet, Amanda. **It's** messy; on boys, boobs, and badass women. Amanda de Cadenet. Harper Wave 2017 210 p. (hardcover) $26.99   **92**
1. Essays 2. Motion picture actors and actresses -- United States -- Biography 3. Actors -- United States -- Biography 4. Photographers -- United States -- Biography 5. Television personalities -- United States -- Biography
ISBN 9780062412478; 9780062412461; 9780062412454; 0062412450
LC 2017020860
This book, by Amanda de Cadenet, is a "deeply personal collection of essays. . . . From childhood fame to a high-profile marriage (and divorce) to teen motherhood to the sexism that threatened to end her career before it started, Amanda shares the good, the bad, and the messy of her life, synthesizing lessons she's learned along the way." (Publisher's note)

"De Cadenet boasts a triumphant and storied past, and her essays are a treat to devour." Booklist

De Mille, Cecil B., 1881-1959

★ Eyman, Scott. **Empire** of dreams; the epic life of Cecil B. DeMille. Simon & Schuster 2010 579p il $35; ebook $16.99   **92**
1. Motion picture producers and directors 2. Motion picture directors 3. Motion picture producers
ISBN 978-0-7432-8955-9; 0-7432-8955-2; 978-1-4391-8041-9 ebook; 1-4391-8041-5 ebook
LC 2010-27710
This is a biography of the film director and producer Cecil B. DeMille, whose movies include King of Kings and The Ten Commandments.

"Eyman's evocative prose and exhaustive research makes this an engaging and authoritative biography." Publ Wkly
Includes bibliographical references

De Quincey, Thomas, 1785-1859

Wilson, Frances. **Guilty** thing; a life of Thomas De Quincey. Frances Wilson. Farrar, Straus & Giroux 2016 416 p. illustrations, maps (hardcover) $30; (ebook) $60   **92**
1. English authors -- Biography 2. Authors, English -- 19th century -- Biography
ISBN 9780374167301; 9780374710415
LC 2015048947
This biography of English essayist Thomas De Quincey, by Frances Wilson, reveals that De Quincey "was obsessed with Wordsworth and Coleridge, whose 'Lyrical Ballads' provided the script to his life. . . . Running away from school to pursue the two poets, De Quincey insinuated himself into their world. Basing his sensibility on Wordsworth's and his character on Coleridge's, he forged a triangle of unusual psychological complexity." (Publisher's note)

"A new, but not revisionist, portrait of a troubled artist." Kirkus
Includes bibliographical references and index

De Voto, Avis, 1904-1989

As always, Julia; the letters of Julia Child and Avis DeVoto: food, friendship, and the making of a masterpiece. selected and edited by Joan Reardon. Houghton Mifflin Harcourt Pub. Co.

2010 416p il $26   **92**
1. Cooks 2. Television personalities 3. Editors 4. Cookbook writers 5. Literary critics 6. Biography, Individual
ISBN 9780547417714
LC 2010-25840
This volume presents "the previously unpublished correspondence between the American chef and her unofficial literary agent from 1952 to 1965, offering insight into such events as Julia's early experiences as a new bride in Paris, her support of her diplomat husband and her views on period politics." (Publisher's note) Index.

"Their letters span a wide range of topics, from cookbooks, menus, recipes, and restaurants to Balzac, sex, goose stuffing, gardening, learning languages, the political climate, Sunday afternoon cocktail parties, and proofreading. Witty, enlightening and entertaining." Publ Wkly

DeVita, Vincent T., Jr., 1935-

★ DeVita-Raeburn, Elizabeth, 1966- The **death** of cancer; after fifty years on the front lines of medicine, a pioneering oncologist reveals why the war on cancer is winnable--and how we can get there. Vincent T. DeVita, Jr., M.D., Elizabeth DeVita-Raeburn. Sarah Crichton Books/Farrar, Straus & Giroux 2015 336 p. 16 plates; illustrations (hardback) $28   **92**
1. Cancer 2. Cancer -- History 3. Cancer -- Chemotherapy 4. Oncologists -- United States -- Biography
ISBN 0374135606; 9780374135607
LC 2015011104
This book on cancer, by Vincent T. DeVita and Elizabeth DeVita-Raeburn, is an "illuminating and deeply personal look at the science and the history of one of the world's most formidable diseases. . . . DeVita believes that we're well on our way to curing cancer but that there are things we need to change in order to get there." (Publisher's note)

"Highly recommended for all readers interested in cancer or medical research. Those seeking a more comprehensive and a less intimate chronicle should check out Siddhartha Mukherjee's The Emperor of All Maladies." Library Journal

Dean, James, 1931-1955

★ Gehring, Wes D. **James** Dean: rebel with a cause. Indiana Historical Society Press 2005 303p il (Indiana biography series) $19.95   **92**
1. Actors
ISBN 0-87195-181-9
LC 2005-41440
This is a "study of Dean's entire life and an appreciation of his rightful place in film history. Gehring makes the point that audiences have confused the actor with his troubled-teenager roles, and he counters that misimpression with a fuller portrait." Booklist
Includes filmography and bibliographical references

Dederer, Claire, 1967-

Dederer, Claire. **Love** and trouble; a midlife reckoning. Claire Dederer. Alfred A. Knopf 2017 237 p. (hardcover) $25.95   **92**
1. Motherhood 2. Midlife crisis 3. Middle aged persons 4. Middle-aged persons -- United States -- Biography
ISBN 9781101946503; 9781101946510
LC 2016035870
This book, by Claire Dederer, is "a ferocious, sexy, hilarious memoir about going off the rails at midlife and trying to reconcile the girl she was with the woman she has become. . . . Dederer is a happily married mother of two, ages nine and twelve, when she suddenly finds herself totally despondent and, simultaneously, suffering through a kind of erotic

reawakening." (Publisher's note)

"In her frank and frankly hilarious new memoir, Dederer (Poser, 2011) explores the female midlife crisis in all its glorious, tear-streaked, and hormone-crazed inconvenience." Booklist

Deford, Frank, 1938-2017

Deford, Frank, 1938-2017. **Over** time; my life as a sportswriter. Frank Deford. Atlantic Monthly Press 2012 354 p. $25   **92**

1. Autobiographies 2. Sports journalism

ISBN 0802120156; 9780802120151

In this autobiography sportswriter Frank Deford describes how he "joined 'Sports Illustrated' in 1962. . . . In 1990, he was Editor-in-Chief of 'The National Sports Daily,' one of the most ambitious--and ill-fated--projects in the history of American print journalism. But then, he's endured: writing ten novels, winning an Emmy . . . , [and reading] commentary on NPR's 'Morning Edition.'" (Publisher's note)

Delany, Mary Granville Pendarves, 1700-1788

Peacock, Molly, 1947- The **paper** garden; an artist begins her life's work at 72. Bloomsbury USA 2010 397p il $30 **92**

1. Artists 2. Collage 3. Women artists 4. Flowers in art 5. Artists, British 6. Creation (Literary, artistic, etc.) 7. Biography, Individual 8. Creative ability in old age

ISBN 978-1-60819-523-7; 1-60819-523-6

"The author entwines the story of Delany with private reflections on her own life as an artist and a woman. As Peacock undertook her eccentric quest to discover the life of the woman who created the beautiful paper mosaics that she so admired, she discovered resonant parallels. . . . A lyrical, meditative rumination on art and the blossoming beauty of self that can be the gift of age and love." Kirkus

Includes bibliographical references

Descartes, René, 1596-1650

★ Watson, Richard A. **Cogito** ergo sum: the life of Rene Descartes; {by} Richard Watson. Godine 2002 375p $35 **92**

1. Authors 2. Philosophers 3. Mathematicians

ISBN 1-56792-184-1

LC 2001-40858

"For all of his puckish delight in a juicy anecdote, Watson recognizes and carefully explicates the cultural centrality of Descartes' intellectual legacy. That legacy ensures numerous readers sure to praise a biographer who delivers both the philosopher's cerebral doctrines and his unmistakably human conduct." Booklist

Includes bibliographical references

Devonshire, Deborah Vivien Freeman-Mitford Cavendish, Duchess of, 1920-2014

Thompson, Laura. The **six**; the lives of the Mitford sisters. Laura Thompson. St. Martin's Press 2016 400 p. ill., genealogical table (hardcover) $29.99 **92**

1. Sisters 2. Women authors 3. Great Britain -- Biography 4. Sisters -- Great Britain -- Biography 5. Authors, English -- 20th century -- Biography 6. Women authors, English -- 20th century -- Biography

ISBN 9781250099532

LC 2016024061

This book, by Laura Thompson, focuses on "the Mitford sisters: Nancy, Pamela, Diana, Unity, Jessica, and Deborah. Born into country-house privilege in the early years of the 20th century, they became prominent as "bright young things" in the high society of interwar London. Then, as the shadows crept over 1930s Europe, the stark—and very

public—differences in their outlooks came to symbolize the political polarities of a dangerous decade." (Publisher's note)

"Appreciators of biography and social history will find much to engage their interest here." Booklist

Includes bibliographical references and index

DiMaggio, Joe

Kennedy, Kostya. **56**; Joe DiMaggio and the last magic number in sports. Sports Illustrated Books 2011 367p il por $26.95 **92**

1. Baseball players 2. Baseball -- Biography 3. New York Yankees (Baseball team)

ISBN 9781603201773; 1603201777

Recounts Joe DiMaggio's streak during the summer of 1941 and how it found its way into countless lives.

"From the private world inhabited only by DiMaggio and his new bride to Newark barbershops, the playgrounds of Queens, and the streets of DiMaggio's hometown, San Francisco, Kennedy humanizes an immortal accomplishment." Publ Wkly

Includes bibliographical references (p. 351-357) and index.

Positano, Rock. **Dinner** with Dimaggio; Memories of an American Hero. Dr. Rock Positano and John Positano; With a foreword by Francis Ford Coppola and an introduction by Fay T. Vincent. Simon & Schuster 2017 xiii, 350 p.p illustrations (hardback) $26 **92**

1. Baseball players 2. Baseball players -- United States -- Biography

ISBN 9781501156861; 1501156845; 9781501156847

LC 2016051476

Author Rock Postiano presents this "memoir of a decade-long friendship [that] reveals the very private DiMaggio as he really was--sometimes demanding, sometimes big-hearted, always impeccable, loyal, and a true stand-up guy--while serving up illuminating stories and rare insights about the people in his life, including his teammates, Muhammad Ali, Sandy Koufax, Woody Allen, and more." (Publisher's note)

"Positano, helped by his brother John, renders a wholly human portrait of an American icon navigating his way through an adoring yet relentlessly demanding public." Booklist

Diaghilev, Serge, 1872-1929

Scheijen, Sjeng. **Diaghilev**; a life. translated by Jane Hedley-Prôle and S.J. Leinbach. Oxford University Press 2010 552p il **92**

1. Ballet dancers 2. Theatrical producers 3. Biography, Individual

ISBN 0199751498; 9780199751495

LC 2010-02205

Original Dutch edition, 2009; first English translation published 2009 in the United Kingdom

This is a "biography of Serge Diaghilev, founder and impresario of the Ballets Russes." (Publisher's note) Bibliography. Index.

"The parade of great dancers, composers, and artists through Diaghilev's life give this book the sweep of a Russian novel with a fascinating, brilliant, and complex protagonist who, according to the author, lived a very public life, but kept his most intimate feelings hidden." Publ Wkly

Includes bibliographical references

Diana, Princess of Wales, 1961-1997

Bradford, Sarah, 1938- **Diana**; Sarah Bradford. Penguin Books 2007 443 p. (paperback) $25 **92**

1. Princesses -- Great Britain -- Biography

ISBN 9780143112464; 9781101533246; 0143112465

"An icon remembered in death as vividly as she appeared in life,

Diana, Princess of Wales, is one of the most enduring personalities of the twentieth century-and one of the most enigmatic. With exclusive access to all those closest to Diana, Sarah Bradford now casts aside the gossip and lies and takes us to the very heart of the royal family to separate the myth from the truth of the Diana years." (Publisher's note)

Brown, Tina. The **Diana** chronicles. Doubleday 2007 542p $27.50 **92**
1. Princesses
ISBN 978-0-385-51708-9; 0-385-51708-4
This is a biography of Diana, Princess of Wales.

"Like scraping barnacles off an old hulk, Tina Brown has taken the story of Princess Diana, hosed off layers of hearsay and myth, sifted through tons of accumulated legend, and presented us with a fresh and vividly perceptive portrait." Times Lit Suppl

Includes bibliographical references

★ Morton, Andrew. **Diana**; Her True Story - In Her Own Words. Andrew Morton. Revised 25th anniversary ed. Simon & Schuster Paperbacks 2017 448 p. illustrations (chiefly color) (paperback) $17 **92**
1. Princesses -- Great Britain -- Biography
ISBN 9781782431053; 9781501169731; 1501169734
LC 2017302299

This book, by Andrew Morton, is a "biography of Princess Diana, written with her cooperation. . . . Never before had a senior royal spoken in such a raw, unfiltered way about her unhappy marriage, her relationship with the Queen, her extraordinary life inside the House of Windsor, her hopes, her fears, and her dreams. Now, twenty-five years on, biographer Andrew Morton has revisited the secret tapes he and the late princess made to reveal startling new insights into her life and mind." (Publisher's note)

Remembering Diana; a life in photographs. foreword by Tina Brown. National Geographic 2017 199 p. illustrations (chiefly color) (hardcover: alk. paper) $30 **92**
1. Princesses -- Great Britain -- Biography 2. Princesses -- Great Britain -- Biography -- Pictorial works
ISBN 1426218532; 9781426218538
LC 2017006355

"For the millions who adored the People's Princess, this lavish book presents Diana Spencer's life in glorious color. Page after page of inside photos document the royal's most memorable moments in the spotlight; a luminous, personal remembrance by friend and biographer Tina Brown adds context and nuance to a poignant life twenty years after her tragic death." (Publisher's note)

Includes bibliographical references.

Dickens, Charles, 1812-1870

★ Slater, Michael. **Charles** Dickens. Yale University Press 2009 696p il $35 **92**
1. Authors 2. Novelists 3. Authors, English
ISBN 978-0-300-11207-8; 0-300-11207-6
LC 2009-26834

This "biography actually feels somewhat austere: Slater sticks to the known Gradgrindian facts, emphasizes the writing and public performances, seldom goes in for much scene-painting or gratuitous anecdote, and refuses to speculate unduly without evidence. . . . For anybody who wants to know more about this dynamo of Victorian letters, Michael Slater's superb biography is the one to read." Washington Post Book World

Includes bibliographical references (p. 624-626)

Tomalin, Claire. **Charles** Dickens; a life. Claire Tomalin. Penguin Press 2011 527 p. ill., maps $35 **92**
ISBN 978-1-59420-309-1; 1-59420-309-1
LC 2011031466

The book presents a biography of author Charles Dickens, with topics including "the familiar story of the idyllic childhood years in Kent . . . the terrible experience of being forced to work in a blacking factory rather than go to school . . . a rapid, improbable journey from obscure clerk to diligent reporter and sketch-writer . . . [and] Dickens' moral and physical decline as he abandoned his wife . . . to pursue and ultimately seduce [actress Nelly Ternan]." (History Today)

The author "tells a story. Clear-eyed, sympathetic and scholarly, she spreads the whole canvas, alive with incident and detail, with places and people. She writes of publishers, illustrators, collaborators and all Dickens's intersecting circles of friends and family. It is wonderfully done." Economist

Dickinson, Amy

Dickinson, Amy. The **mighty** queens of Freeville; a mother, a daughter, and the town that raised them. Hyperion Books 2009 225p $22.99 **92**
1. Authors 2. Journalists 3. Advice columnists
ISBN 978-1-4013-2285-4; 1-4013-2285-9
LC 2008-26525

"In the summertime of 2002, after spending months living off of her credit cards between freelance writing jobs, Dickinson sent in an audition column to the Chicago Tribune and became the paper's replacement for the late Ann Landers. Here, Dickinson traces her own personal history, as well as the history of her mother's family whose members make up the Mighty Queens of Freeville, N.Y., the small town where Dickinson was raised, and where she raised her own daughter between stints in London; New York City; Washington, D.C.; and Chicago. Dickinson writes with an honesty that is at once folksy and intelligent, and brings to life all of the struggles of raising a child (Dickinson was a single mother) and the challenges and rewards of having a supportive extended family." Publ Wkly

Dickinson, Amy. **Strangers** tend to tell me things; a memoir of love, loss, and coming home. Amy Dickinson. Hachette Books 2017 xi, 223 p.p illustrations (hardcover) $27 **92**
1. Journalists 2. Advice columnists -- United States -- Biography
ISBN 9780316352574; 9780316352642
LC 2016027999

In this book author Amy Dickinson "shares her journey of family, second chances, and finding love. . . . [This book] speaks to all who have faced challenges in the wake of life's twists and turns. From finding love in middle-age to her storied experience with stepparenting to overcoming disordered eating to her final moments spent with her late mother, Dickinson's trademark humorous tone delivers punch and wit that will empower, entertain, and heal." (Publisher's note)

"In this extension of her debut memoir, Dickinson remains an engagingly chatty, witty, and relatable writer with sage insights." Kirkus

Dickinson, Bruce, 1958-

Dickinson, Bruce. **What** does this button do? an autobiography. Bruce Dickinson. Dey St., an imprint of William Morrow 2017 x, 371 p.p illustrations (chiefly color) (hardcover) $28.99 **92**
1. Autobiographies 2. Rock music -- History and criticism 3. Rock musicians -- England -- Biography 4. Heavy metal (Music) 5. Iron Maiden (Musical group)
ISBN 9780062468130; 9780062468154; 0062468138

This book, Bruce Dickinson, is "a long-awaited memoir from the larger-than-life, multifaceted lead vocalist of Iron Maiden, one of the most successful, influential and enduring rock bands ever. . . . Dickinson turns his unbridled creativity, passion, and anarchic humour to reveal some fascinating stories from his life, including his thirty years with Maiden, his solo career, . . . fatherhood and family, and his recent battle with cancer." (Publisher's note)

Dickinson, Emily, 1830-1886

★ Gordon, Lyndall. **Lives** like loaded guns; Emily Dickinson and her family's feuds. Viking 2010 491p il $32.95 **92**

1. Poets 2. Authors 3. Poets, American
ISBN 978-0-670-02193-2; 0-670-02193-8

LC 2009-46311

The author argues that "it wasn't heartbreak that kept the poet sequestered, . . . it was epilepsy, a then-uncontrollable and shameful malady. With one stroke, Gordon recasts Dickinson's entire oeuvre. She then reveals the outrageous treachery of the poet's esteemed brother, Austin, who held his unmarried sisters, wife Susan, and their children hostage to his passion for his ambitious mistress, Mabel Loomis Todd, whose scheming husband encouraged the affair. . . . A jolting and utterly intriguing watershed achievement." Booklist

Includes bibliographical references

Didion, Joan, 1934-

Daugherty, Tracy. The **Last** Love Song; A Biography of Joan Didion. by Tracy Daugherty. St. Martin's Press 2015 672 p. 8 plates; ills.; portraits (hardcover) $35 **92**

1. American authors
ISBN 9781250010025; 1250010020

LC 2015017162

This book, by Tracy Daugherty, "delves deep into the life of distinguished American author and journalist Joan Didion. . . . Daugherty takes readers on a journey back through time, following a young Didion in Sacramento, through to her adult life as a writer interviewing those who know and knew her personally, while maintaining a respectful distance from the reclusive literary great." (Publisher's note)

"A strong biography. Who won't want to read this "hot" book?" LJ

Diski, Jenny

Diski, Jenny, 1947-2016. **In** gratitude; Jenny Diski. St. Martin's Press 2016 256 p. (hardcover) $26; (ebook) $60 **92**

1. English women authors -- Biography
ISBN 9781632866868; 9781632866882; 1632866862

This book, by Jenny Diski, describes how "in July 2014, Jenny Diski was diagnosed with inoperable lung cancer and given 'two or three years' to live. She didn't know how to react. . . . To find the response that felt wholly her own, she had to face the cliches and try to write about it. And there was another story to write, one she had not yet told: that of being taken in at age fifteen by the author Doris Lessing, and the subsequent fifty years of their complex relationship." (Publisher's note)

"Both heavy and light, Diski's beautifully written memoir is worth any reader's time." Pub Wkly

Disney, Walt, 1901-1966

Gabler, Neal. **Walt** Disney; the triumph of the American imagination. Neal Gabler. Alfred A. Knopf 2006 xx, 851 p.p 32 plates: illustrations $23 **92**

1. Walt Disney Company 2. Animators -- United States -- Biography
ISBN 067943822X; 0679757473; 9780679438229; 9780679757474

LC 2006045257

This book, by Neal Gabler, presents a biography of the American entertainer Walt Disney. "Gabler shows us the young Walt Disney breaking free of a heartland childhood of discipline and deprivation and making his way to Hollywood. We see the visionary, whose desire for escape . . . led him to the reinvention of animation. . . . Gabler also reveals a wounded, lonely, and often disappointed man, who, despite worldwide success, was plagued with financial problems much of his life." (Publisher's note)

"Although Gabler focuses on corporate matters at the expense of critical treatment of the films, he presents a balanced treatment of the man and his achievements, realistically assessing Disney's considerable impact and offering insight into the hidden, restless soul who constantly challenged himself, risking the financial stability of his empire more than once in his unceasing pursuit of his dreams." Booklist

Includes bibliographical references (p. [805]-815) and index

Dixon, Willie

Inaba, Mitsutoshi, 1964- **Willie** Dixon; preacher of the blues. Scarecrow Press 2011 xxxi, 445p il (African American cultural theory and heritage) $55; ebook $57.99 **92**

1. Singers 2. Blues musicians 3. African American musicians 4. Blues music -- History and criticism
ISBN 978-0-8108-6993-6; 978-0-8108-6994-3 ebook

LC 2009033237

"This exhaustive biography and analysis of Dixon's music, the most comprehensive study of Dixon's life and work available, features extensive references, many details drawn from interviews, an analysis of Dixon's composition and studio methods, and a complete discography. Inaba . . . tells the story of Dixon's life, from his 1915 birth in Vicksburg, Mississippi, through his childhood in an impoverished area blemished further by racism, to his adulthood in Chicago as a boxer and musician. . . . From the Big Three Trio to Dixon's highly productive years with Chess Records to finally, his own Blues Factory studio, Inaba traces and comments on the significance of Dixon's lasting imprint on music." Publ Wkly

Includes discography and bibliographical references

Dolan, Timothy Michael

Boyle, Christina. An **American** Cardinal; the biography of Cardinal Timothy Dolan. Christina Boyle. St. Martin's Press 2014 304 p. illustrations (hardcover) $27.99 **92**

1. Cardinals 2. Cardinals -- United States -- Biography
ISBN 1250032873; 9781250032874

LC 2014028470

Author Christina Boyle presents "a book about power and the Roman Catholic church today framed by the life of a man who might someday become the first American pope. Timothy Michael Dolan was born in Maplewood, Missouri in 1950. In 2009, he was made Archbishop of New York. Several months later he was elevated to cardinal. There were clear signs that the ailing Pope Benedict XVI saw him as a bright hope for the future." (Publisher's note)

"All readers, not just Roman Catholics, will be inspired by this story of a Midwestern boy-turned-prominent figure and leaders can learn a lot from his handling of opposition, conflict, and the press." LJ

Dolby, Thomas

Dolby, Thomas. The **speed** of sound; Breaking the Barriers Between Music and Technology: A Memoir. Thomas Dolby. Flatiron Books 2016 288 p. (hardcover) $27.99 **92**

1. Composers -- Biography 2. Music and technology 3. Composers -- England -- Biography
ISBN 9781250071842; 9781250071910

LC 2016021708

This memoir, by Thomas Dolby, is the "story of rising to the top of the music charts, a second act as a tech pioneer, and the sustaining power of creativity and art. . . . Starting out in a rat-infested London bedsit, a teenage . . . Dolby stacks boxes by day at the grocery and tinkers with a homemade synthesizer at night. . . . London on the eve of the 1980s is a hotbed for music and culture, and a new sound is beginning to take shape, merging technology with the musical energy of punk rock." (Publisher's note)

"This stellar book will appeal to students, scholars, and general readers interested in modern technology's startling effects on music and popular culture." Kirkus

Domino, Fats, 1928-2017

Coleman, Rick. **Blue** Monday; Fats Domino and the lost dawn of rock 'n' roll. Da Capo 2006 364p il map hardcover o.p. pa $15.95 **92**

1. Singers 2. Pianists 3. Rock musicians 4. African American musicians

ISBN 0-306-81491-9; 978-0-306-81531-7 pa; 0-306-81531-1 pa

Coleman has crafted a "biography of Fats Domino, drawing on new interviews with the pianist himself. From his childhood in New Orleans through the early days of rock'n'roll, when he endured travel difficulties in the segregated South and frequent riots at his concerts, Fats remained a shy but demanding performer and personality. A homesick father who seemed to cherish his family, Fats was also a hard-drinking womanizer, and Coleman tells his story with compassion and honesty up to Fats's survival of Hurricane Katrina in his Ninth Ward home. His argument that rock'n'roll sprung from Fats and the New Orleans sound is hard to dispute, as Fats was playing long before others now credited with starting the revolution. Despite the occasional slips into fandom, this is an essential purchase for any library collecting the history of rock'n'roll." Libr J

Includes bibliographical references

Donlan, Christian

Donlan, Christian. The **inward** empire; mapping the wilds of mortality and fatherhood. Christian Donlan. Little, Brown & Co. 2018 336 p. $27 **92**

1. Fatherhood 2. Father-daughter relationship

ISBN 9780316509367

LC 2017955471

In this memoir, Christian Donlan describes how, "soon after his daughter Leontine is born, . . . [his] world shifted an inch to the left. He started to miss door handles and light switches when reaching for them. He was suddenly unable to fasten the tiny buttons on his new daughter's clothes. These experiences were the early symptoms of multiple sclerosis, an incurable and degenerative neurological illness." (Publisher's note)

"n this earnest memoir, journalist and first-time author Donlan chronicles his efforts to "navigate the world" as his life changes in his 30s after two almost simultaneous events: the birth of his daughter and his diagnosis of multiple sclerosis." Pub Wkly

Dorey-Stein, Beck

Dorey-Stein, Beck. **From** the corner of the oval; a memoir. Beck Dorey-Stein. Random House Inc 2018 352 p. $28 **92**

1. Biography 2. Presidents -- United States -- Staff -- Biography

ISBN 0525509127; 9780525509127

LC 2017053262

In this memoir, Beck Dorey-Stein recalls her life "as one of Barack Obama's stenographers. . . . [S]he joins the elite team who accompany the president wherever he goes, recorder and mic in hand. . . . As she learns to navigate White House protocols and more than once runs afoul of the hierarchy, Beck becomes romantically entangled with a consummate D.C. insider, and suddenly the political becomes all too personal." (Publisher's note)

"Dorey-Stein relates the highs and lows of the Obama presidency intermixed with those from her personal life in a compulsively readable style—think history lesson meets soap opera. In this poignant, brutally honest, and often-funny work of self-reflection, Dorey-Stein pulls no punches and tells all she learned from and about the president who "taught me to look up." " Booklist

Dostoyevsky, Fyodor, 1821-1881

★ Frank, Joseph. **Dostoevsky**; a writer in his time. edited by Mary Petrusewicz. Princeton University Press 2009 959p il $35 **92**

1. Authors 2. Novelists 3. Authors, Russian 4. Short story writers

ISBN 978-0-691-12819-1

LC 2009-1418

An abridged edition of the author's five volume work published 1976-2002

"Frank displays a brilliant command of Dostoyevsky's heroic endeavors, and his biography reads readily, especially for such a scholarly work." Libr J

Includes bibliographical references and index

Doty, James R.

Doty, James R. **Into** the Magic Shop; A Neurosurgeon's Quest to Discover the Mysteries of the Brain and the Secrets of the Heart. by James R. Doty MD (Author) Penguin Group USA 2016 288 p. illustrations $26 **92**

1. Altruism 2. Surgeons 3. Compassion 4. Mind and body 5. Nervous system

ISBN 1594632987; 9781594632983

In this memoir, by James R. Doty, "Growing up in the high desert of California, Jim Doty was poor, with an alcoholic father and a mother chronically depressed. . . . Today he is the director of the . . . (CCARE) at Stanford University. But back then his life was at a dead end until at twelve he wandered into a magic shop looking for a plastic thumb. Instead, he met Ruth, a woman who taught him a series of exercises to ease his own suffering and manifest his greatest desires." (Publisher's note)

"An optimistic and engagingly well-told life story that incorporates scientific investigation into its altruistic message." Kirkus

Doty, Mark

Doty, Mark, 1953- **Dog** years; a memoir. HarperCollins Publishers 2007 215p $23.95 **92**

1. Poets 2. Authors 3. Dogs 4. Essayists

ISBN 0-06-117100-X; 978-0-06-117100-0

LC 2006-46491

"In a memoir, the poet Mark Doty meditates on grief and the death of his dogs." (N Y Times Book Rev)

The author "celebrates the 16 lovely years his two beloved 70-pound Labs, Beau and Arden, gave him. . . . Against a backdrop of devastating human loss, both personal (the death of his partner) and public (9/11), Doty bears witness to the inexorable decline of his beloved retrievers. . . . Poignant, intelligent, and quite simply superb." Libr J

Doughty, Caitlin

Doughty, Caitlin. **Smoke** gets in your eyes; and other lessons from the crematory. Caitlin Doughty. W W Norton & Co Inc. 2014 272 p. (hardcover) $24.95 **92**

1. Cremation 2. Autobiographies 3. Undertakers and undertaking 4. Undertakers and undertaking -- Anecdotes 5. Undertakers and

undertaking -- United States -- Biography
ISBN 0393240231; 9780393240238

LC 2014017294

This book describes how author Caitlin Doughty "took a job at a crematory, turning morbid curiosity into her life's work. Thrown into a profession of gallows humor and vivid characters (both living and very dead), Caitlin learned to navigate the secretive culture of those who care for the deceased. 'Smoke Gets in Your Eyes' tells an unusual coming-of-age story full of bizarre encounters and unforgettable scenes." (Publisher's note)

"Not shying away from candid descriptions of corpses, cremation, and putrefaction, Doughty— . . . details postmortem proceedings not to repulse but to reveal our modern society's 'death denial.'" Booklist
Includes bibliographical references

Douglas, Marjory Stoneman

Davis, Jack E. An **Everglades** providence; Marjory Stoneman Douglas and the American environmental century. University of Georgia Press 2009 758p il map $34.95   **92**
1. Authors 2. Novelists 3. Conservationists 4. Nature conservation 5. Centenarians 6. Everglades (Fla.) 7. Writers on nature 8. Short story writers 9. Biography, Individual 10. Everglades (Fla.) -- Environmental conditions
ISBN 0-8203-3071-X; 978-0-8203-3071-6

LC 2008-49073

This book presents a biography of Marjory Stoneman Douglas, "a suffragist, a lifetime feminist and supporter of the ERA, a champion of social justice, and an author of diverse literary talent. She came of age literally and professionally during the American environmental century, the century in which Americans mobilized an unprecedented popular movement to counter the equally unprecedented liberties they had taken in exploiting, polluting, and destroying the natural world." (Publisher's note)

This is "both a portrait of one of the 20th century's most important environmental figures and a history of Florida's Everglades. The long-lived Douglas (1890-1998) is best known for the classic The Everglades: River of Grass and her tireless efforts to preserve that region. But she was also a lifelong feminist and social activist who worked to advance human rights. . . . In addition to the rich detail and documentation of Douglas's life, Davis offers an impressive look at America during Douglas's lifetime and the growth of America's environmental movement." Libr J
Includes bibliographical references

Douglass, Frederick, 1818-1895

★ Blight, David W. **Frederick** Douglass; prophet of freedom. David W. Blight. Simon & Schuster 2018 896 p. (hardback) $37.50   **92**
1. Slaves -- United States -- Biography 2. African American abolitionists -- Biography 3. Abolitionists -- United States -- Biography 4. African American abolitionists -- United States -- Biography 5. Antislavery movements -- United States -- History -- 19th century
ISBN 1416590315; 9781416590316

LC 2018007511

This book, by David W. Blight, presents "the definitive, dramatic biography of the most important African-American of the nineteenth century: Frederick Douglass, the escaped slave who became the greatest orator of his day and one of the leading abolitionists and writers of the era. . . . Initially mentored by William Lloyd Garrison, Douglass spoke widely, often to large crowds, using his own story to condemn slavery." (Publisher's note)

"A masterful, comprehensive biography, particularly of Douglass'

Civil War, Reconstruction, and Gilded Age years and occupations."
Includes bibliographical references and index

★ Douglass, Frederick, 1818-1895. **Autobiographies**. Library of Am. 1994 1126p $35; pa $13.95   **92**
1. Slaves 2. Authors 3. Abolitionists 4. Memoirists 5. African Americans -- Biography
ISBN 0-940450-79-8; 1-883011-30-2 pa

LC 93-24168

"This one volume containing Douglass's seminal works is highly recommended for black history collections." Libr J
Includes bibliographical references

Dilbeck, D. H. **Frederick** Douglass; America's prophet. D. H. Dilbeck. University of North Carolina Press 2018 208 p. (cloth: alk. paper) $28   **92**
1. Biography 2. African American abolitionists -- Biography 3. African American orators -- United States -- Biography
ISBN 9781469636184

LC 2017026932

This book, by D. H. Dilbeck, "offers a provocative interpretation of [Frederick] Douglass's life through the lens of his faith. In an era when the role of religion in public life is as contentious as ever, Dilbeck provides essential new perspective on Douglass's place in American history." (Publisher's note)

"Dilbeck investigates Douglass' legacy as America's moral voice and conscience, from his teenage conversion to Christianity to his search for a church that strongly opposed slavery as stridently as he did. The result is a biography that offers an insightful new understanding of an extraordinary man." Booklist
Includes bibliographical references and index

Douglass, Frederick, 1818-1895. **My** bondage and my freedom; edited with an introduction and notes by John David Smith. Penguin Bks. 2003 lx, 366p (Penguin Classics) pa $12   **92**
1. Slaves 2. Authors 3. Abolitionists 4. Memoirists 5. African Americans -- Biography
ISBN 0-14-043918-8

LC 2002-28992

First published 1855 by Orton & Mulligan
In this autobiography Douglass tells of his life as a slave and his early years in the abolitionist movement.
Includes bibliographical references

Douglass, Frederick, 1818-1895. **Narrative** of the life of Frederick Douglass, an American slave; written by himself; edited with an introduction by Houston A. Baker, Jr. Penguin Bks 1982 159p il pa $10   **92**
1. Slaves 2. Authors 3. Abolitionists 4. Memoirists 5. African Americans -- Biography
ISBN 0-14-039012-X

LC 82-5371

Originally published 1845 by the Boston Anti-slavery office
"Frederick Douglass became famous as a slave who escaped to the North and spent his lifetime in the abolitionist movement. His 'Narrative,' one of three autobiographical works written by the self-taught slave, is the story of his life up to his escape to freedom." Libr J
Includes bibliographical references

Stauffer, John. **Picturing** Frederick Douglass; An Illustrated Biography of the Nineteenth Century's Most Photographed

American. John Stauffer, Zoe Trodd, and Celeste-Marie Bernier. W W Norton & Co Inc 2015 320 p. illustrations (some color) $49.95   **92**

1. Abolitionists -- Biography 2. Abolitionists -- United States -- Biography 3. African American abolitionists -- Biography
ISBN 0871404680; 9780871404688

LC 2015020546

This biography, by John Stauffer, Zoe Trodd, and Celeste-Marie Bernier, focuses on "Frederick Douglass (1818–1895), the ex-slave turned leading abolitionist, eloquent orator, and seminal writer whose fiery speeches transformed him into one of the most renowned and popular agitators of his age. Now, . . . Douglass emerges as a leading pioneer in photography, both as a stately subject and as a prescient theorist." (Publisher's note)

"The authors have pieced together an illuminating life portrait without extraneous biographical material, focusing intensely on their subject's belief in the strength of photographs." Kirkus

Includes bibliographical references and index

Doyle, Arthur Conan Sir, 1859-1930

★ Doyle, Arthur Conan. **Arthur** Conan Doyle; his life in letters. edited by Jon Lellenberg, Daniel Stashower & Charles Foley. Harper Press 2007 706p il $37.95   **92**

1. Authors 2. Novelists 3. Authors, Scottish 4. Mystery writers
ISBN 978-1-59420-135-6; 1-59420-135-8

LC 2007-14692

This volume presents the selected correspondence of the British author at various points during his life.

"This will be essential reading for all fans of Conan Doyle and his sleuth." Publ Wkly

Doyle, Arthur Conan, 1859-1930

Jaher, David. The **witch** of lime street; séance, seduction, and Houdini in the spirit world. David Jaher. Crown Publishers 2015 448 p. illustrations (alk. paper) $28   **92**

1. Spiritualism 2. Spiritualists -- United States -- Biography 3. Women mediums -- United States -- Biography 4. Spiritualism -- United States -- History -- 20th century
ISBN 0307451062; 9780307451064

LC 2015009392

In this book, by David Jaher, "in 1924, the pretty wife of a distinguished Boston surgeon came to embody the raging national debate over Spiritualism. . . . Reporters dubbed her the blonde Witch of Lime Street, but she was known to her followers simply as Margery. . . . Margery was the best hope for the psychic practice to be empirically verified. Her supernatural gifts beguiled four of the judges. There was only one left to convince...the acclaimed escape artist, Harry Houdini." (Publisher's note)

"Through a combination of feminine seduction and illusionist skill that even Houdini admired, Crandon became the one psychic to almost win the respect of the scientific community and outshine Houdini as an entertainer. Jaher's narrative style is as engaging as his character portraits are colorful. Together, they bring a bygone age and its defining spiritual obsessions roaring to life. Fascinating, sometimes thrilling, reading." Kirkus

Includes bibliographical references and index

Dresner, Amy

Dresner, Amy. **My** fair junkie; a memoir of getting dirty and staying clean. Amy Dresner. Hachette Books 2017 242 p. (hardcover) $27   **92**

1. Drug abuse 2. Drug addicts -- Rehabilitation 3. Substance abuse -- United States 4. Addicts -- United States -- Biography 5. Addicts -- Rehabilitation -- United States 6. Drug addicts -- United States -- Biography
ISBN 9780316430968; 9780316430951

LC 2017016499

This book, by Amy Dresner, is "a darkly funny and revealing debut memoir of one woman's twenty-year battle with sex, drugs, and alcohol addiction, and what happens when she finally emerges on the other side. Growing up in Beverly Hills, Amy Dresner had it all. . . . Smart and charming, with Daddy's money to fall back on, she sort of managed to keep it all together. But on Christmas Eve 2011 all of that changed." (Publisher's note)

"Dresner brings humility, wit, and sensitivity to a topic many readers are unfamiliar with, and those that are will recognize her truths." Booklist

Druckerman, Pamela

Druckerman, Pamela. **There** are no grown-ups; a midlife coming-of-age story. Pamela Druckerman. Penguin Group USA 2018 288 p. $27   **92**

1. Self-acceptance 2. Middle aged women -- Biography 3. Middle aged persons -- Biography
ISBN 1594206376; 9781594206375

LC 2018006194

In this memoir, Pamela Druckerman "investigates life in her forties, and wonders whether her mind will ever catch up with her face. . . . [She] leads us on a quest for wisdom, self-knowledge and the right pair of pants. A witty dispatch from the front lines of the forties, 'There Are No Grown-ups' is a (midlife) coming-of-age story, and a book for anyone trying to find their place in the world." (Publisher's note)

"Half memoir and half ironic how-to guide, Druckerman's book is not only a humorous meditation on the gains and pains of a time in life 'when you become who you are'; it is also a thought-provoking meditation on 'what it means to be a grown-up." Kirkus

Du Bois, W. E. B. (William Edward Burghardt), 1868-1963

★ Lewis, David Levering. **W.E.B.** Du Bois; a biography. Henry Holt and Co. 2009 893p hardcover o.p. pa $25   **92**

1. Authors 2. Novelists 3. Historians 4. Editors 5. Essayists 6. Sociologists 7. Nonfiction writers 8. Civil rights activists 9. African Americans -- Biography 10. African Americans -- Civil rights
ISBN 978-0-8050-8769-7; 0-8050-8769-9; 978-0-8050-8805-2 pa; 0-8050-8805-9 pa

LC 2008-696

Condensed and updated edition of a 2 volume set, first published 1993-2000

This is a biography of the African American scholar who helped bring forth the civil rights movement.

Includes bibliographical references

Du Maurier, Daphne, 1907-1989

De Rosnay, Tatiana. **Manderley** forever; a biography of Daphne Du Maurier. Tatiana de Rosnay; translated from the French by Sam Taylor. St. Martin's Press 2017 x, 340 p.p ills. (some color), maps $27.99   **92**

1. English novelists -- Biography
ISBN 1250099137; 9781250099136

LC 2016049032

In this biography, by Tatiana de Rosnay, translated by Sam Taylor, the author "pays homage to the writer who influenced her so deeply, following [Daphne] Du Maurier from a shy seven-year-old, a rebellious sixteen-year-old, . . . and finally a cantankerous old lady. With a rhythm and intimacy to its prose characteristic of all de Rosnay's works, 'Manderley Forever' is a vividly compelling portrait and celebration of . . . [a] critically underrated writer." (Publisher's note)

"Through De Rosnay's novel-like narrative, exhaustive research, and unbridled admiration, du Maurier's spirit comes alive on the page, endearing her to a new generation of fans." Pub Wkly.

Includes bibliographical references (pages 313-327) and index.

Dubus, Andre, 1959-

Dubus, Andre, 1959- **Townie**; a memoir. [by] Andre Dubus III. W. W. Norton & Co. 2011 387p $25.95   **92**
1. Authors 2. Novelists 3. Authors, American 4. Short story writers 5. Biography, Individual
ISBN 978-0-393-06466-7; 0-393-06466-2

LC 2010038029

This is a memoir by the author of Bluesman (1993) and The Garden of Last Days (2008). "Young Andre and his siblings, two sisters and a brother, grew up in a series of Massachusetts mill towns after their father left their mother for one of his . . . young students." (N Y Times (Late N Y Ed))

"The author grew up poor in Massachusetts mill towns, the oldest of four children of the celebrated short-story writer Andre Dubus (1936–1999), who abandoned the family in 1968 to pursue a young student. Beautifully written and bursting with life, the book tells the story of a boy struggling to express his 'hurt and rage,' first through violence aimed at school and barroom bullies and ultimately through the power of words." Kirkus

Dulles, Allen Welsh, 1893-1969

Grose, Peter. **Gentleman** spy; the life of Allen Dulles. University of Mass. Press 1996 641p il pa $19.95   **92**
1. Lawyers 2. Diplomats 3. Government officials 4. Intelligence service officials 5. United States -- Central Intelligence Agency
ISBN 1-55849-044-2; 978-1-55849-044-4

LC 96-19010

First published 1994 by Houghton Mifflin

This biography of the CIA director under Eisenhower and Kennedy "renders the interplay of person and public event and allows readers to enter the dark world of US-sponsored terror and covert paramilitary operations. . . . Grose sets forth in fascinating and often unfamiliar detail the spectacular CIA covert operations: in Iran, Guatemala, Indonesia; the U2 incident; the Bay of Pigs." Choice

Talbot, David. The **Devil's** Chessboard; Allen Dulles and the Rise of America's Secret Government. by David Talbot. HarperCollins 2015 704 p. illustrations $29.99   **92**
1. United States. Central Intelligence Agency
ISBN 0062276166; 9780062276162

LC 2015487367

This book, by David Talbot, is a "portrait of Allen Dulles, the man who transformed the CIA into the most powerful--and secretive--colossus in Washington. . . . Drawing on . . . U.S. government documents, U.S. and European intelligence sources, the personal correspondence and journals of Allen Dulles's wife and mistress, and exclusive interviews with the children of prominent CIA officials . . . Talbot reveals the underside of one of America's most powerful and influential figures." (Publisher's note)

Includes bibliographical references and index

Duncan, Isadora, 1877-1927

Duncan, Isadora, 1877-1927. **My** life; Isadora Duncan; introduction by Joan Acocella; with a prefatory essay by Doree

Duncan. Liveright paperback ed. Liveright Publishing Corporation, a division of W. W. Norton & Company 2013 368 p. (paperback) $17.95   **92**
1. Dance 2. Women dancers -- Biography
ISBN 0871403188; 9780871403186

LC 2012049575

This book, by Isadora Duncan, presents the autobiography of "the choreographer and dancer . . . [who] not only revolutionized dance in the twentieth century but blazed a path for other visionaries who would follow in her wake. . . . From her early enchantment with classical music and poetry to her great successes abroad, to her sensational love affairs and headline-grabbing personal tragedies, Duncan's story is a dramatic one." (Publisher's note)

Dykeman, Wilma

Dykeman, Wilma. **Family** of earth; a Southern mountain childhood. Wilma Dykeman; foreword by Robert Morgan. The University of North Carolina Press 2016 xxiii, 177 p.p illustrations (pbk: alk. paper) $18   **92**
1. North Carolina 2. American authors 3. Authors, American -- North Carolina -- Biography
ISBN 9781469629148; 9781469630540

LC 2015049261

This book "allows us to see into the young mind of author and Appalachian native Wilma Dykeman (1920–2006), who would become one of the American South's most prolific and storied writers. Focusing on her childhood in Buncombe County, Dykeman reveals a perceptive and sophisticated understanding of human nature, the environment, and social justice." (Publisher's note)

"A captivating, poetic, difficult-to-categorize book that abundantly showcases the author's talent for making words dance." Kirkus.

Dylan, Bob, 1941-

Bell, Ian. **Once** upon a time; the lives of Bob Dylan. Ian Bell. Pegasus 2013 590 p. $35; $17.95   **92**
1. Musicians -- United States 2. Singers -- United States -- Biography
ISBN 1605984817; 1605986275; 1780574568; 1780575734; 9781605984810; 9781605986272; 9781780574561; 9781780575735

LC 2012545195

"In Once upon a time, award-winning writer Ian Bell draws together the tangled strands of the many lives of Bob Dylan in all their contradictory brilliance. For the first time, the laureate of modern America is set in his entire context: musical, historical, literary, political and personal." (Publisher description)

"This is best described as a fully formed emotional biography, a fascinating read about an artist who, to this day, defends his right of "artistic autonomy," refusing to be anyone but himself, whoever that may be." Booklist

Lives of Bob Dylan

Dylan, Bob, 1941- **Chronicles**. v1 Simon & Schuster 2004 293p v1 il $24   **92**
1. Singers 2. Folk musicians 3. Rock musicians 4. Songwriters 5. Biography, Individual
ISBN 0-7432-2815-4

LC 2004-564

This is the first installment of a projected three-volume autobiography by the American singer and songwriter.

"This book will stand as a record of a young man's self-education, as contagious in its frank excitement as the letters of John Keats and as sincere in its ramble as Jack Kerouac's On the Road, to which Dylan frequently refers. A person of Dylan's stature could have gotten away with far less; that he has been so thoughtful in the creation of this book is a measure of his talents, and a gift to his fans." Publ Wkly

Brown, Donald. **Bob** Dylan; American troubadour. Donald Brown. Rowman & Littlefield Publishers, Inc. 2014 308 p. (Tempo: a Rowman & Littlefield music series on rock, pop, and culture) (cloth: alk. paper) $40   **92**
  1. Musicians -- United States
  ISBN 0810884208; 9780810884205; 9780810884212
                      LC 2013044394
This biography, by Daniel Brown, "follows [Bob] Dylan chronologically through his career, from young troubadour in Greenwich Village who unwittingly became the spokesman of a generation through his controversial electric transformation to the 'rural glory' of the Basement Tapes to his richly creative Blood on the Tracks period to his born-again phase to his current renaissance as a rock elder and cultural force." (Booklist)
"While it covers familiar territory, the book's strength is a thorough assessment of Dylan's career, album by album, song by song." LJ
Includes bibliographical references, discography, and index

Dyson, Freeman J.

Dyson, Freeman J., 1923- **Maker** of patterns; an autobiography through letters. Freeman Dyson. W W Norton & Co Inc 2018 320 p. $27.95   **92**
  1. Letters 2. Physicists -- Biography
  ISBN 0871403862; 9780871403865
In this autobiography, "Freeman Dyson, the 94-year-old theoretical physicist, has . . . chronicled the stories of those who were engaged in solving some of the most challenging quandaries of twentieth-century physics. Written between 1940 and the early 1980s, these letters to relatives form an historic account of modern science and its greatest players. . . . Dyson offers a firsthand account of one of the greatest periods of scientific discovery of our modern age." (Publisher's note)
"Who but Dyson formulates revolutionary physics while riding on a Greyhound bus through Iowa cornfields? In other episodes in this remarkable epistolary autobiography, readers join Dyson as he assesses with Godel equations for a rotating version of Einstein's universe, as he defends Feynman's quantum theorems against Oppenheimer's doubts, and as he explores with Bohr the prospects for a nuclear spaceship." Booklist

Schewe, Phillip F. **Maverick** Genius; The Pioneering Odyssey of Freeman Dyson. Phillip F. Schewe. St Martins Pr 2013 352 p. $27.99   **92**
  1. Physicists -- Biography 2. Mathematicians -- Biography
  ISBN 0312642350; 9780312642358
Author Phillip F. Schewe presents a biography of Freeman J. Dyson. "Schewe examines the life of a man whose accomplishments have shaped our world in many ways," focusing on theoretical physics "from quantum physics to national defense, from space to biotechnology . . . Many of his [Dyson's] colleagues, including Nobelists Steven Weinberg and Frank Wilczek, as well as his wives and his children, Esther and George Dyson, have been interviewed for this book." (Publisher's note)

Earhart, Amelia, 1898-1937

Winters, Kathleen C. **Amelia** Earhart; the turbulent life of an American icon. Palgrave Macmillan 2010 242p il map $25   **92**
  1. Air pilots 2. Missing persons 3. Women air pilots 4. Memoirists

ISBN 978-0-230-61669-1
                    LC 2010-20026
"With erudite analysis of everything from Earhart's flying to her marriage and longtime financial support of her parents and sister, Winters proves there is still much to learn about this American icon." Booklist
Includes bibliographical references

Earhardt, Ainsley, 1976-

Earhardt, Ainsley, 1976- The **light** within me; an inspirational memoir. Ainsley Earhardt; with Mark Tabb. HarperCollins 2018 240 p. $27.99   **92**
  1. Christian life 2. Women -- Religious life 3. Television personalities -- Biography
  ISBN 0062697471; 9780062697479
                    LC 2018003716
In this memoir, author Ainsley Earhardt, with Mark Tabb, "offers a powerful, uplifting look at her life and her spiritual journey, reflecting on her family, her faith, and her successful career. . . . Filled with inspirational quotes taken from Scripture and illustrated with sixteen pages of never-before-seen photos, her memoir is infused with her spiritual beliefs and will touch the hearts of all her fans, reminding them to count the blessings God has given them." (Publisher's note)

Earp, Wyatt, 1848-1929

Barra, Allen. **Inventing** Wyatt Earp; his life and many legends. Carroll & Graf Pubs. 1998 432p hardcover o.p. pa $15.95   **92**
  1. Sheriffs
  ISBN 0-7867-0685-6 pa
"Barra is at his best in describing the efforts of assorted Hollywood icons, including John Ford, John Sturges, and Kevin Costner, to depict the 'real' Earp." Booklist

Tefertiller, Casey. **Wyatt** Earp; the life behind the legend. Wiley 1997 403p $45; pa $19.95   **92**
  1. Sheriffs
  ISBN 0-471-18967-7; 0-471-28362-2 pa
                    LC 97-2932
"An engrossing, satisfying inspection of a quintessential figure in American popular culture." Booklist
Includes bibliographical references

Ebert, Roger

Ebert, Roger, 1942-2013. **Life** itself; a memoir. Grand Central Pub. 2011 436p il $27.99; ebook $12.99   **92**
  1. Autobiographies 2. Motion picture industry 3. Motion pictures -- History and criticism 4. Writers on film 5. Motion picture critics
  ISBN 978-0-446-58497-5; 978-0-446-58498-2 ebook
                    LC 2011022442
The book presents an autobiography by newspaper film reviewer Roger Ebert. It is "an episodic tour of Ebert's memory cabinet, one three-or-four page jot at a time, from his upbringing and his college opportunities to his days as a cub reporter in Chicago, his decision to quit drinking and join AA in 1979, [and] his screenwriting with Russ Meyer. . . . [Ebert] spends many chapters recalling the dinners and interviews he had with Martin Scorsese, Werner Horzog, Robert Mitchum, Woody Allen etc. Naturally, he also ruminates at length about his testy relationship with TV co-host Gene Siskel." (Sight & Sound)
"Ebert illuminates and assesses his life with the same insight and clarity that mark his acclaimed movie reviews." Booklist

Eckford, Elizabeth, 1942-

Margolick, David. **Elizabeth** and Hazel; two women of Little Rock. Yale University Press 2011 310p il $26 **92**

1. School integration 2. Arkansas -- Race relations 3. Little Rock (Ark.) -- Race relations 4. Central High School (Little Rock, Ark.) 5. School integration -- Arkansas -- Little Rock -- History -- 20th century

ISBN 978-0-300-14193-1; 0-300-14193-9

LC 2011-14101

"When Elizabeth Eckford braved the gauntlet of white hecklers leading to the newly desegregated Central High School in Little Rock, Arkansas, in 1957, photographers captured her image and that of the angry young white woman behind her. Elizabeth, the stoic, and Hazel Bryan, the tormentor, were frozen as icons. Elizabeth was part of the Little Rock Nine, the black teens who became the targets of race hatred as well as national and international inspirations. . . . Margolick draws on interviews and press reports of the time to present a very nuanced analysis of how Elizabeth and Hazel were affected by the scene that made them famous. . . . A complex look at two women at the center of a historic moment." Booklist

Includes bibliographical references

Edelman, Marian Wright, 1939-

Edelman, Marian Wright. **Lanterns**; a memoir of mentors. HarperPerennial 2000 xxi, 208p il pa $14 **92**

1. Mentoring 2. Social welfare leaders 3. Children's rights advocates

ISBN 0-06-095859-6

LC 00-33430

First published 1999 by Beacon Press

"Throughout this absorbing memoir, Edelman's voice resounds with spirituality, a reliance on her faith, and a belief in equality." Booklist

Includes bibliographical references

Edge, Rosalie

Furmansky, Dyana Z. **Rosalie** Edge, hawk of mercy; the activist who saved nature from the conservationists. [by] Dyana Z. Furmansky; with a foreword by Bill McKibben & an afterword by Roland C. Clement. University of Georgia Press 2009 312p il $28.95 **92**

1. Suffragists 2. Conservationists 3. Feminists

ISBN 978-0-8203-3341-0; 0-8203-3341-7

LC 2009-8551

The book discusses "Mabel Rosalie Barrow Edge (1877–1962) [who was] . . . a conservation activist . . . [and t]he founder of the Emergency Conservation Committee (ECC). . . . Using previously unavailable primary sources, Dyana Z. Furmansky offers an engaging portrait of Edge as activist while piecing together the story of Edge as a daughter, wife, mother, friend, and colleague. . . . Furmansky notes that Edge's writings, public testimony, and sometimes-assertive personal style inspired others to see and care about nature as she did. Furmansky looks for clues to Edge's commitment to nature in her privileged New York childhood, in her experiences abroad, and in her engagement with the suffrage movement. Edge's activism began after she read a 1929 pamphlet called 'Crisis in Conservation,' written in part by Willard Van Name, who would become Edge's mentor and financial backer. This pamphlet inspired Edge to found the ECC." (Journal of American History)

A biography of the conservationist and suffragette who "founded the Hawk Mountain Sanctuary and fought hard for the Olympic National Park. Clearly relishing every moment of Edge's remarkable life, Furmansky vividly enriches environmental history with her inspiring portrait of this indomitable champion of the wild." Booklist

Includes bibliographical references

Edison, Thomas A. (Thomas Alva), 1847-1931

Degraaf, Leonard. **Edison** and the rise of innovation; Leonard DeGraaf; foreword by Bill Gates. Sterling Signature 2013 xxvii, 244 p.p color illustrations; map $29.95 **92**

1. Inventions -- History 2. Inventors -- United States -- Biography

ISBN 1402767366; 9781402767364

LC 2013443854

This book, by Leonard DeGraaf, "presents, in intimate detail, the man who helped engineer the modern world. One of history's most prolific inventors, and perhaps America's first celebrity, Thomas Alva Edison did more than bring incandescent light into every household and industry; he created a world-renowned brand, raised capital to support research and business, and pursued patents for his 1,000+ inventions." (Publisher's note)

"A worthy and visually pleasing mid-length biography recommended for those who prefer Edison the businessman and social phenomenon to the scientist. With a foreword by Bill Gates." LJ

Includes bibliographical references and index

★ Israel, Paul. **Edison**; a life of invention. Wiley 1998 552p il $50; pa $18.95 **92**

1. Inventors

ISBN 0-471-52942-7; 0-471-36270-0 pa

LC 98-10105

This biography focuses on Edison's technical work, experiments, and business dealings

"Dozens of facsimiles of his original drawings are reproduced, which fortify the impression of Edison's meticulousness, as do Israel's accounts of his business ventures." Booklist

Includes bibliographical references

Edmundson, Mark, 1952-

Edmundson, Mark. **Why** football matters; my education in the game. Mark Edmundson. The Penguin Press 2014 240 p. $26.95 **92**

1. Football players 2. Father-son relationship 3. Fathers and sons 4. Football players -- United States -- Biography

ISBN 1594205752; 9781594205750

LC 2014009726

"When Mark Edmundson's son began to play organized football, and proved to be very good at it, Edmundson had to come to terms with just what he thought about the game. Doing so took him back to his own childhood, when as a shy, soft boy growing up in a blue-collar Boston suburb in the sixties, he went out for the high school football team. 'Why Football Matters' is the story of what happened to Edmundson when he tried to make himself into a football player." (Publisher's note)

"Beautifully written and impressively thought out, this smart memoir should appeal to a wide audience." LJ

Edward I

Morris, Marc. A **Great** & Terrible King; Edward I and the Forging of Britain. by Marc Morris. W W Norton & Co Inc 2015 480 p. 8 plates; color ills., maps $29.95 **92**

1. Great Britain -- Kings and rulers 2. Great Britain -- History -- 0-1066 3. Biography, Individual 4. Great Britain -- History -- Edward I, 1272-1307

ISBN 1605986844; 9781605986845

This biography, by Marc Morris, depicts the life of the English king known as "Longshanks." Edward I "defeated and killed the famous Simon de Montfort in battle; travelled across Europe to the Holy Land on crusade; conquered Wales, extinguishing forever its native rulers, and constructed [castles] at Conwy, Harlech, Beaumaris and Caernarfon."

(Publisher's note)

"Highly recommended for scholars and generalists alike interested in the Middle Ages." LJ

Edward III, King of England, 1312-1377

Ormrod, W. Mark. **Edward** III; W. Mark Ormrod. Yale University Press 2012 xx, 721 p.p (cl: alk. paper) $45.00 **92**

    1. Great Britain -- Kings and rulers -- Biography 2. Great Britain -- History -- Edward III, 1327-1377 3. Great Britain -- Politics and government -- 1327-1377

    ISBN 0300119100; 9780300119107

LC 2011013536

In this biography of Edward III of England, it was the author's intent to demonstrate "that Edward's personality and ambitions remained absolutely at the heart of English royal policy for at least forty years, and that his skills as a politician shaped a unique political culture that brought about a long period of domestic stability within England." (Times Literary Supplement)

Includes bibliographical references and index.

Edward VII, King of Great Britain, 1841-1910

Hibbert, Christopher. **Edward** VII; The Last Victorian King. by Christopher Hibbert. St. Martin's Press 2007 xiii, 348 p.p illustrations (paperback) $20 **92**

    1. Great Britain -- Kings and rulers 2. Great Britain -- Kings and rulers -- Biography 3. Great Britain -- History -- Edward VII, 1901-1910

    ISBN 9780230610750; 9781403983770; 1403983771

This book, by Christopher Hibbert, is a "biography that vividly captures the life and times of the last Victorian king. To his mother, Queen Victoria, he was 'poor Bertie,' to his wife he was 'my dear little man,' while the President of France called him 'a great English king,' and the German Kaiser condemned him as 'an old peacock.' King Edward VII was all these things and more." (Publisher's note)

Includes bibliographical references (p. 320-325) and index.

★ Ridley, Jane. The **heir** apparent; a life of Edward VII, the playboy prince. Jane Ridley. Random House Inc 2013 752 p. (alk. paper) $35 **92**

    1. Great Britain -- Kings and rulers 2. Great Britain -- Kings and rulers -- Biography 3. Great Britain -- History -- Edward VII, 1901-1910

    ISBN 1400062551; 9780812994759; 9781400062553

LC 2013002597

This biography, by Jane Ridley, "chronicles the . . . life of Queen Victoria's firstborn son. . . . Born Prince Albert Edward . . . the future King Edward VII had a . . . reputation for debauchery. . . . Yet by the time he died . . . he had proven himself a deft diplomat, hardworking head of state, and the architect of Britain's modern constitutional monarchy." (Publisher's note)

Includes bibliographical references and index

Edward, Prince of Wales, 1330-1376

Jones, Michael. The **Black** Prince; England's greatest medieval warrior. Michael Jones. W W Norton & Co Inc 2018 488 p. $29.95 **92**

    1. Great Britain -- History

    ISBN 168177741X; 9781681777412

LC 2018056219

This book, by Michael Jones, tells the "inspiring story of one of the greatest warrior-princes of the Middle Ages--and an unforgettably vivid portrait of warfare and chivalry in the fourteenth century. . . . He was

Edward of Woodstock, eldest son of Edward III, and better known to posterity as 'the Black Prince.' His military achievements captured the imagination of Europe: heralds and chroniclers called him 'the flower of all chivalry' and 'the embodiment of all valor.'" (Publisher's note)

Includes bibliographical references and index.

Eger, Edith Eva

Eger, Edith Eva. The **choice**; embrace the possible. Dr. Edith Eva Eger with Esmé Schwall Weigand. Scribner 2017 xiii, 288 p.p (hardcover) $27 **92**

    1. Forgiveness 2. Autobiographies 3. Holocaust survivors 4. Psychologists -- United States -- Biography 5. Holocaust survivors -- United States -- Biography 6. Holocaust, Jewish (1939-1945) -- Personal narratives

    ISBN 1501130781; 9781501130816; 9781501130786

This book is a "moving memoir—and a practical guide to healing—written by Dr. Edith Eva Eger, an eminent psychologist whose own experiences as a Holocaust survivor help her treat patients and allow them to escape the prisons of their own minds. . . . Edie has chosen to forgive her captors and find joy in her life every day. . . . She combines her clinical knowledge and her own experiences with trauma to help others who have experienced painful events large and small." (Publisher's note)

"A searing, astute study of intensive healing and self-acceptance through the absolution of suffering and atrocity." Kirkus

Eichenwald, Kurt

Eichenwald, Kurt. A **mind** unraveled; a memoir. Kurt Eichenwald. Random House Inc 2018 416 p. $28 **92**

    1. Epilepsy 2. Biography 3. Nervous system -- Diseases

    ISBN 0399593624; 9780399593628

LC 2018018965

In this book, author Kurt Eichenwald describes his "ongoing struggle with epilepsy. . . . From his early experiences of fear and denial to his exasperating search for treatment, Eichenwald provides a deeply candid account of his years facing this misunderstood and often stigmatized condition. . . . [The book] chronicles how Eichenwald, faced often with his own mortality, transformed trauma into a guide for reaching the future he desired." (Publisher's note)

"Eichenwald has created a universal tale of resilience wrapped in a primal scream against the far-too-savage world. Book clubs will clamor for this tale of survival and call for compassion." Booklist

Eichmann, Adolf, 1906-1962

Stangneth, Bettina. **Eichmann** before Jerusalem; the unexamined life of a mass murderer. by Bettina Stangneth; translated from the German by Ruth Martin. Alfred A. Knopf 2014 608 p. (hardback) $35 **92**

    1. War criminals 2. Holocaust, Jewish (1939-1945) 3. War criminals -- Germany -- Biography

    ISBN 0307959678; 9780307959676

LC 2014001031

National Jewish Book Award Finalist: Holocaust (2014)

This book, by Bettina Stangneth, translated by Ruth Martin, offers a "reassessment of the life of Adolf Eichmann--a . . . work . . . that reveals his activities and notoriety among a global network of National Socialists following the collapse of the Third Reich and that permanently challenges Hannah Arendt's notion of the 'banality of evil.'" (Publisher's note)

"Stangneth masterfully sifts through the information from these lively social gatherings conducted at journalist Sassen's home three years before Eichmann's kidnapping by Israeli agents. A rigorously documented, essential work not only about Eichmann's masterly masquerade, but also about how we come to accept appearances as truth." Kirkus

Includes bibliographical references (pages 535-555) and index

Einstein, Albert, 1879-1955

Einstein, Albert. **Einstein** on politics; his private thoughts and public stands on nationalism, Zionism, war, peace, and the bomb. edited by David E. Rowe and Robert Schulmann. Princeton University Press 2007 xxxiv, 523p il $29.95 **92**
1. Politics 2. Physicists 3. Nobel laureates for physics
ISBN 978-0-691-12094-2; 0-691-12094-3

LC 2006-100303

This is a collection of excerpts from Albert Einstein's writings on politics and other social topics.

"Powerful in its personal and political disclosures, this is an essential primary source." Booklist

Includes bibliographical references

★ Isaacson, Walter. **Einstein**: his life and universe. Simon & Schuster 2007 xxii, 675p il hardcover o.p. pa $17.95 **92**
1. Physicists 2. Nobel laureates for physics
ISBN 0-7432-6473-8; 0-7432-6474-6 pa; 978-0-7432-6473-0; 978-0-7432-6474-7 pa

LC 2006-51264

This book tells the story of the German-American physicist's life.

"This is a warm, insightful, affectionate portrait with a human and immensely charming Einstein at its core." N Y Times (Late N Y Ed)

Includes bibliographical references

Eire, Carlos M. N.

Eire, Carlos M. N., 1951- **Learning** to die in Miami; confessions of a refugee boy. [by] Carlos Eire. Free Press 2010 307p $26 **92**
1. Cuban refugees 2. Cuban Americans 3. Memoirists 4. Miami (Fla.) 5. College teachers 6. Religious scholars 7. Writers on religion 8. Biography, Individual
ISBN 978-1-4391-8190-4; 1-4391-8190-X

LC 2009052286

Continues Waiting for snow in Havana (2003)

The author, a professor of history and religious studies at Yale, continues the memoir begun with Waiting for Snow in Havana (2003). In the present volume he writes about his introduction to America in 1962, when he was eleven.

The author "takes readers on his personal journey, beginning in 1962 when he and his brother arrived in Florida as part of Operation Peter Pan—an evacuation of 14,000 Cuban children whose parents arranged for their relocation to the United States, away from Castro. Eire's prose engages us throughout as we learn of the challenges he faced as he assimilated to his new world. . . . Readers of memoir and immigrant stories will appreciate Eire's journey and celebrate his accomplishments." Libr J

Eire, Carlos M. N., 1951- **Waiting** for snow in Havana; confessions of a Cuban boy. {by} Carlos Eire. Free Press 2003 383p il hardcover o.p. pa $15 **92**
1. Memoirists 2. Havana (Cuba) 3. College teachers 4. Religious scholars 5. Operation Peter Pan 6. Writers on religion 7. Havana (Cuba) -- Biography 8. Chicago (Ill.) -- Biography 9. Cuban Americans -- Biography 10. Refugee children -- United States -- Biography
ISBN 0-7432-1965-1; 0-7432-4641-1 pa; 978-0-7432-4641-5

LC 2002-73875

National Book Award: Nonfiction (2003)

"From 1960 through 1962, some fourteen thousand Cuban children were airlifted—unaccompanied—to the United States by Operation Pedro (Peter) Pan. Once here, they were farmed out to CIA-funded refugee camps, then to foster homes. Many never saw their island parents again. Carlos Eire, now a Yale professor of history and religious studies, was a Peter Pan. {This memoir} tells mostly of Eire's privileged boyhood during the pre-Castro 1950s." Commonweal

Eisenhower, Dwight D. (Dwight David), 1890-1969

Ambrose, Stephen E. **Eisenhower**; soldier and president. Simon & Schuster 1990 635p il hardcover o.p. pa $18 **92**
1. Generals 2. Presidents 3. College presidents 4. Presidents -- United States
ISBN 0-671-74758-4 pa

LC 90-9701

Condensed version of a two volume work published 1983-1984

"Tracing Eisenhower's family background, education, military and political careers, and influence as elder statesman, the author chronicles Eisenhower's triumphs and failures and at the same time provides a vivid picture of the off-duty Ike. . . . This is the definitive one-volume biography of Eisenhower." Publ Wkly

Includes bibliographical references

Johnson, Paul, 1928- **Eisenhower**; a life. Paul Johnson. Viking 2014 144 p. $25.95 **92**
1. Presidents -- United States 2. Generals -- United States -- Biography 3. Presidents -- United States -- Biography
ISBN 0670016829; 9780670016822

LC 2014005313

In this biography, author Paul "Johnson chronicles President Eisenhower's modest childhood in Kansas, his college years at West Point, and his rapid ascent through the military ranks, culminating in his appointment as Supreme Commander of the Allied Forces in Europe during World War II. . . . Johnson notes that when Eisenhower left the White House at age 70 . . . he feared for the country's future and prophetically warned of the looming military-industrial complex." (Publisher's note)

"Johnson views Eisenhower positively and asserts that Eisenhower not being a combat general but a staff officer for most of his career contributed to his success as president. Johnson's contribution will serve as a great introduction to 'Ike' the man, but anyone interested in the details of WWII generalship or the politics of the Eisenhower administration will have to look elsewhere."

Includes bibliographical references and index

Whitney, Catherine. **Three** days in January; Dwight Eisenhower's final mission. Bret Baier; with Catherine Whitney. HarperCollins 2017 320 p. illustrations $28.99; (ebook) $27.99 **92**
1. Presidents -- United States
ISBN 0062569031; 9780062569035; 9780062569066

LC 2016051650

This book, by Bret Baier, with Catherine Whitney, focuses on President Dwight Eisenhower's last days in power. "Baier masterfully casts the period between Eisenhower's now-prophetic farewell address on the evening of January 17, 1961, and Kennedy's inauguration on the afternoon of January 20 as the closing act of one of modern America's greatest leaders — during which Eisenhower urgently sought to prepare both the country and the next president for the challenges ahead." (Publisher's note)

"A focused and timely study of Eisenhower's significant speech and the sticky transition to JFK's inherited new world." Kirkus

Includes bibliographical references (pages 305-328) and index.

Eisner, Will, 1917-2005

Schumacher, Michael. **Will** Eisner; a dreamer's life in comics. Bloomsbury 2010 359p il $28   **92**

1. Authors 2. Cartoonists 3. Comic book writers 4. Publishing executives
ISBN 978-1-60819-013-3

LC 2010-11283

"Born in 1917, Will Eisner, now known as the father of the graphic novel, grew up in the Bronx poor but resourceful. . . . [The author] zeroes in on the essence of Eisner's success: his rare ability to unite art (he inherited his phenomenal gift for drawing from his immigrant artist father) with practicality (his mother's specialty). . . . Propelled by Eisner's geyserlike energy and output, Schumacher keenly chronicles Eisner's brilliant career within a lively history of American comics and creates an inspiring portrait of a perpetually diligent and innovative artist whose belief in comics as fine art fueled a new and fertile creative universe." Booklist

Includes bibliographical references

Eleanor, of Aquitaine, Queen, consort of Henry II, King of England, 1122?-1204

Weir, Alison. **Eleanor** of Aquitaine; a life. Ballantine Bks. 2000 xxi, 441p il maps $28; pa $15.95   **92**

1. Queens
ISBN 0-345-40540-4; 0-345-43487-0 pa

LC 99-54785

First published 1999 in the United Kingdom with title Eleanor of Aquitaine: by the wrath of God, Queen of England

A biography of the twelfth-century queen, first of France, then of England, the consort of Henry II and mother of Richard the Lionhearted

"In approaching as complex a subject as feudalism, Weir wears her learning lightly and has a pleasant habit of anticipating all the questions of a curious reader." Publ Wkly

Includes bibliographical references

Eliot, T. S. (Thomas Stearns), 1888-1965

Crawford, Robert, 1959- **Young** Eliot; from St. Louis to The Waste Land. Robert Crawford. Farrar, Straus & Giroux 2015 512 p. 16 plates; illustrations (hardback) $35   **92**

1. Poets 2. Eliot, T. S. (Thomas Stearns), 1888-1965 3. Poets, American -- 20th century -- Biography
ISBN 0374279446; 9780374279448

LC 2014047118

In this book on poet T.S. Eliot, "biographer Robert Crawford presents us with the first volume of a comprehensive account of this poetic genius. 'Young Eliot' traces the life of the twentieth century's most important poet from his childhood in St. Louis to the publication of his revolutionary poem 'The Waste Land.'" (Publisher's note)

"It's hard to imagine a literary biography of greater merit being published this year." Booklist

Includes bibliographical references and index

★ Gordon, Lyndall. **T.S.** Eliot; an imperfect life. Norton 1999 721p $35; pa $18.95   **92**

1. Poets 2. Authors 3. Dramatists 4. Editors 5. Essayists 6. Literary critics 7. Nobel laureates for literature
ISBN 0-393-04728-8; 0-393-32093-6 pa

LC 98-46864

First published 1998 in the United Kingdom

"Gordon's book is the most authoritative life of Eliot thus far, and is certain to spark new controversies." Publ Wkly

Includes bibliographical references

Elizabeth I, Queen of England, 1533-1603

Hilton, Lisa. **Elizabeth**; Renaissance Prince. Lisa Hilton. Houghton Mifflin Harcourt 2015 384 p. 16 unnumbered pages of plates $27   **92**

1. Great Britain -- History -- 1558-1603, Elizabeth
ISBN 0544577841; 9780544577848

LC 2015004340

This biography of Queen Elizabeth I of England, by Lisa Hilton, is a "fresh interpretation . . . of a queen who saw herself primarily as a Renaissance prince and used Machiavellian statecraft to secure that position. A decade since the last major biography, this 'Elizabeth' breaks new ground and depicts a queen who was much less constrained by her femininity than most treatments claim." (Publisher's note)

"Those who enjoyed Hilton's previous books will most likely want to read this one, as will die-hard fans of Elizabeth. Readers seeking a more nuanced look at the queen and Tudor politics should turn instead to works by Antonia Fraser or Alison Weir." LJ

Guy, John. **Elizabeth**; The Forgotten Years. John Guy. Penguin Group USA 2016 512 p. ill., facimiles, map, portrait (hardcover) $35   **92**

1. Great Britain -- History -- 1558-1603, Elizabeth
ISBN 9780670786022; 0670786020

This book, by John Guy, offers a biography of Queen Elizabeth I of England, focusing on her struggles in establishing her power. "For twenty-five years she had struggled to assert her authority over advisers who pressed her to marry and settle the succession; now, she was determined not only to reign but also to rule. . . . John Guy introduces us to a woman who is refreshingly unfamiliar: at once powerful and vulnerable, willful and afraid." (Publisher's note)

"Near the end, Guy's comparisons to Richard II, the usurped king, the usurper Bolingbroke, and Shakespeare's play take your breath away. One of the best biographies of Elizabeth ever." Kirkus

Includes bibliographical references and index.

Norton, Elizabeth. The **Temptation** of Elizabeth Tudor; Elizabeth I, Thomas Seymour, and the Making of a Virgin Queen. by Elizabeth Norton. W W Norton & Co Inc 2016 416 p. $28.95   **92**

1. Queens -- Great Britain 2. Great Britain -- History -- 1485-1603, Tudors
ISBN 1605989487; 9781605989488

In this book, by Elizabeth Norton, the "Tudor court in the wake of Henry VIII's death had never been more perilous for the young Elizabeth. . . . Elizabeth is living with the king's widow, Catherine Parr, and her new husband, Thomas Seymour. . . . Ambitious and dangerous, Seymour begins an overt flirtation with Elizabeth that ends with Catherine sending her away. When Catherine dies a year later and Seymour is arrested for treason soon after, a scandal explodes." (Publisher's note)

"Highly recommended for readers interested in British history and the Tudor dynasty. Fans of historical fiction such as Philippa Gregory's 'Tudor Court' series will also find themselves invested in the real-life scandal that befell one of England's most famous queens" LJ

Includes bibliographical references and index.

Elizabeth II, 1926- (Queen of Great Britain)

Queen Elizabeth II and the Royal Family; edited by Constance Novis and Helen Fewster. DK Publishing 2015 320 p. illustrations (hardcover) $40   **92**

1. Queens -- Great Britain 2. Great Britain -- History -- 1952- 3. Great Britain -- History 4. Monarchy -- Great Britain -- History 5. Great Britain -- Kings and rulers -- History

ISBN 9781465438003; 9781465449122; 1465438009

LC 2015487921

This book is a "tribute to the life and reign of Queen Elizabeth II and a celebration of the British royal family. . . . Highly illustrated with photographs and timelines throughout, [it] tells the story of the House of Windsor, and includes events such as the royal wedding of Prince William and Kate Middleton and profiles on key people such as Princess Diana and Prince Harry." (Publisher's note)

Smith, Sally Bedell, 1948- **Elizabeth** the Queen; the life of a modern monarch. Sally Bedell Smith. Random House Trade Paperbacks 2012 xxii, 685 p.p illustrations (some color) (paperback) $20   **92**
1. Queens -- Great Britain 2. Queens -- Great Britain -- Biography 3. Great Britain -- History -- Elizabeth II, 1952-
ISBN 9780679643937; 9780812979794; 0812979796

LC 2012532373

This book, by Sally Bedell Smith, is a "biography of Queen Elizabeth II. . . . We meet the thirteen-year-old Lilibet as she falls in love with a young navy cadet named Philip and becomes determined to marry him. . . . We see the teenage Lilibet repairing army trucks during World War II and standing with Winston Churchill on the balcony of Buckingham Palace on V-E Day. We see the young Queen struggling to balance the demands of her job with her role as the mother of two young children." (Publisher's note)

"A microscopically detailed portrait of the reigning Queen of England." Kirkus

Includes bibliographical references (pages 649-657) and index

Williams, Kate. **Young** Elizabeth; The Making of the Queen. Kate Wililams. Pegasus Books 2015 326 p. illustrations (hardcover) $28.95   **92**
1. Great Britain -- Kings and rulers 2. Queens -- Great Britain -- Biography 3. Great Britain -- Kings and rulers -- Biography
ISBN 160598891X; 9781681772530; 9781605988924; 9781605988917

LC 2015452055

This book, by Kate Wililams, is a biography of Queen Elizabeth II in her early reign. "Elizabeth's determination to share in the struggles of her people marked her out from a young age. . . . Kate Williams reveals how the 25-year-old young queen carved out a lasting role for herself amid the changes of the 20th century. Her monarchy . . . and its continuing popularity in the 21st century owes much to the intelligence and elusive personality of this remarkable woman." (Publisher's note)

"Offering a gracious yet honest viewpoint of the strengths and weaknesses of the longest-reigning monarch, Williams tours Elizabeth's beginning years and illuminates the often overlooked humanity of her personal life." LJ

Includes bibliographical references (page 307-316) and index.

Elizabeth, Queen, consort of George VI, King of Great Britain, 1900-2002

Shawcross, William. The **Queen** Mother; the official biography. Alfred A. Knopf 2009 1096p il $40   **92**
1. Queens 2. Monarchy 3. Centenarians 4. Great Britain -- Kings and rulers
ISBN 978-1-4000-4304-0; 1-4000-4304-2

LC 2009-934986

Includes bibliographical references

Ellington, Duke, 1899-1974

Teachout, Terry. **Duke**; a life of Duke Ellington. Terry Teachout. Gotham Books 2013 496 p. $30   **92**
1. Jazz musicians -- United States -- Biography
ISBN 1592407498; 9781592407491

LC 2013011138

National Book Awards: Nonfiction Long List (2013)

This book presents a biography of musician Duke Ellington. "The grandson of a slave, he dropped out of high school to become one of the world's most famous musicians, a showman of incomparable suavity who was as comfortable in Carnegie Hall as in the nightclubs where he honed his style. He wrote some fifteen hundred compositions, many of which . . . remain beloved standards, and he sought inspiration in an endless string of transient lovers." (Publisher's note)

Ellis, William Henry, 1864-1923

Jacoby, Karl. The **strange** career of William Ellis; the Texas slave who became a Mexican millionaire. Karl Jacoby. W W Norton & Co Inc 2016 336 p. illustrations, map (hardcover) $27.95   **92**
1. Slaves -- Emancipation 2. Businessmen -- Biograpy 3. Reconstruction (1865-1876) 4. African Americans -- Biography 5. Slaves -- Texas -- Biography 6. Businessmen -- Mexico -- Biography 7. Millionaires -- Mexico -- Biography 8. United States -- Race relations -- History 9. Mexican-American Border Region -- Biography 10. Passing (Identity) -- United States -- History 11. African Americans -- Texas -- Politics and government 12. Reconstruction (U.S. history, 1865-1877) -- Biography
ISBN 9780393239256

LC 2016007019

In this book, by Karl Jacoby, "Guillermo Eliseo was a fantastically wealthy Mexican. . . . But for all his obvious riches and his elegant appearance, Eliseo was also the possessor of a devastating secret: he was not, in fact, from Mexico at all. Rather, he had begun life as a slave named William Ellis, born on a cotton plantation in southern Texas during the waning years of King Cotton." (Publisher's note)

"Jacoby's masterly writing places race and its meaning at the center of this essential work. Readers will gain fresh insight into life during Reconstruction as well as the riddle of racial identities." LJ

Includes bibliographical references and index

Ellison, Ralph

★ Rampersad, Arnold. **Ralph** Ellison; a biography. Alfred A. Knopf 2007 657p il $35   **92**
1. Authors 2. Novelists 3. Essayists 4. Literary critics 5. Short story writers
ISBN 978-0-375-40827-4; 0-375-40827-4

LC 2006-26464

National Book Award Finalist: Nonfiction (2007)

"As the first scholar granted complete access to the Ellison papers, Rampersad introduces us to people and places that reveal the total range of Ellison's sensibilities. . . . Through elegant and lively prose, Rampersad reveals sides of Ellison that are disturbing and instructive." Charlotte Observer

Includes bibliographical references

Emwazi, Mohammed, -2015

★ Mekhennet, Souad. **I** was told to come alone; my journey behind the lines of jihad. Souad Mekhennet. Henry Holt & Co. 2017 354 p. (hardback) $30   **92**
1. Jihad 2. Terrorism -- Middle East 3. IS (Organization)
ISBN 9781627798969; 9781627798976

LC 2016054740

In this memoir, "we accompany [Souad] Mekhennet as she journeys behind the lines of jihad, starting in the German neighborhoods where the 9/11 plotters were radicalized and the Iraqi neighborhoods where Sunnis and Shia turned against one another, and culminating on the Turkish/Syrian border region where ISIS is a daily presence. In her travels across the Middle East and North Africa, she documents her chilling run-ins with various intelligence services." (Publisher's note)

"A riveting memoir and a literary bombshell that effectively eviscerates every preconception, misconception, and prejudice readers have about the Arab world, I Was Told to Come Alone reinforces the singular significance of journalism, especially foreign journalism, at a time when it is facing its greatest challenges." Booklist

Includes bibliographical references and index.

Engels, Friedrich, 1820-1895

Hunt, Tristram. **Marx's** general; the revolutionary life of Friedrich Engels. Metropolitan Books 2009 430p il $32   **92**

1. Political and social philosophers
ISBN 978-0-8050-8025-4; 0-8050-8025-2

LC 2009-03845

"A useful and well-done study of Engels and the radical epoch he helped create." Booklist

Includes bibliographical references

English, Paul M., 1963-

Kidder, Tracy. A **truck** full of money; one man's quest to recover from great success. Tracy Kidder. Random House Inc 2016 288 p. (ebook) $65; (hardback) $28   **92**

1. Internet industry -- United States 2. Businesspeople -- United States -- Biography 3. Wealth -- United States 4. Venture capital -- United States 5. Entrepreneurship -- United States 6. Information technology -- United States
ISBN 9780812995251; 9780812995244

LC 2015050454

This book, by Tracy Kidder, "tells the story of Paul English, a kinetic and unconventional inventor and entrepreneur, who as a boy rebelled against authority. Growing up in working-class Boston, English discovers a medium for his talents the first time he sees a computer. As a young man, despite suffering from what would eventually be diagnosed as bipolar disorder, he begins his pilgrim's journey through the ups and downs in the brave new world of computers." (Publisher's note)

"While eminently readable as a biography, Kidder's book is also a trenchant study of the new American economy and the technological world that built it. More engrossing work from a gifted practitioner of narrative nonfiction." Kirkus

Includes bibliographical references (pages 255-259).

Ephron, Nora

Carlson, Erin. **I'll** have what she's having; how Nora Ephron's three iconic films saved the romantic comedy. Erin Carlson. Hachette Books 2017 341 p. illustrations (some color) (hardcover) $27   **92**

1. Comedy films 2. Comedy films -- Authorship 3. Romantic comedy films -- United States -- History and criticism
ISBN 9780316353885; 9780316473675

LC 2017014826

This book, by Erin Carlson, "tells the story of the real Nora Ephron and how she reinvented the romcom through her trio of instant classics. With a cast of famous faces including Rob Reiner, Tom Hanks, Meg Ryan, and Billy Crystal, Carlson takes readers on a . . . trip to Ephron's New York City, where reality took a backseat to romance and Ephron--who always knew what she wanted and how she wanted it--ruled the set with an attention to detail that made her actors feel safe." (Publisher's note)

"Hollywood Reporter journalist Carlson's first book pays affectionate and clear-eyed tribute to the three most popular movies associated with screenwriter and director Nora Ephron." Booklist

Includes bibliographical references and index

Equiano, Olaudah, 1745-1797

★ Carretta, Vincent. **Equiano,** the African; biography of a self-made man. University of Georgia Press 2005 xxiv, 436p il map $29.95   **92**

1. Slaves 2. Abolitionists 3. Memoirists
ISBN 0-8203-2571-6

LC 2005-11898

"This is a thoroughly rich, engrossing, and well-researched portrait of an exceptional man and the cause he championed." Booklist

Includes bibliographical references

Erdrich, Louise

Erdrich, Louise. **Books** and islands in Ojibwe country. National Geographic Soc. 2003 143p il map (National Geographic directions) $20   **92**

1. Poets 2. Authors 3. Novelists 4. Ojibwa Indians 5. Essayists 6. Children's authors 7. Short story writers
ISBN 0-7922-5719-7

LC 2003-45906

"Fans of Erdrich's bestselling fiction will recognize her signature combination of the sacred and the ordinary in this lively traveler's memoir, and many will enjoy the rare glimpse of her personal life as well as the physical facts of her journey from her home in Minneapolis to the lakes and islands of her Ojibwe ancestors in Ontario and Minnesota." Booklist

Escoffier, A. (Auguste), 1846-1935

Barr, Luke. **Ritz** & Escoffier; the hotelier, the chef, and the rise of the leisure class. Luke Barr. Clarkson Potter/Publishers 2018 320 p. (hardcover) $26   **92**

1. Hospitality industry -- History 2. Leisure class 3. Savoy Hotel (London, England) -- History 4. Hospitality industry -- Social aspects -- History -- 19th century 5. Hospitality industry -- Social aspects -- History -- 20th century
ISBN 9780804186292

LC 2017015344

In this book, author Luke Barr, "transports readers to turn-of-the-century London and Paris to discover how celebrated hotelier César Ritz and famed chef Auguste Escoffier joined forces at the Savoy Hotel to spawn the modern luxury hotel and restaurant, where women and American Jews mingled with British high society, signaling a new social order and the rise of the middle class." (Publisher's note)

" A well-researched, glitzy, and flawed history of conspicuous consumption." Kirkus

Includes bibliographical references and index

Esfandiari, Haleh, 1940-

Esfandiari, Haleh. **My** prison, my home; one woman's story of captivity in Iran. Ecco/HarperCollins 2009 230p il $25.99   **92**

1. Political prisoners 2. Middle Eastern studies specialists 3. Iran -- Foreign relations -- United States 4. United States -- Foreign relations -- Iran
ISBN 978-0-06-158327-8; 0-06-158327-8

"Esfandiari, born in Tehran in 1940, had been living in the U.S. with her Jewish husband since 1980 when she returned to Tehran in December 2006 to visit her aging mother. On the eve of her departure for the

U.S. she was picked up for interrogation—and ended up spending four months in solitary confinement in the dreaded Evin Prison, drawing worldwide attention. In her remarkable memoir, Esfandiari tells the story of her education, her evolution from an apolitical student to an ardent feminist and staunch supporter for the rights of Iranian women, and her many accomplishments, including serving as director of the Woodrow Wilson Center's Middle East Program." Booklist

Eteraz, Ali

Eteraz, Ali. **Children** of dust; a memoir of Pakistan. HarperOne 2009 337p $25.99   **92**

1. Muslims 2. Radicalism 3. Journalists 4. Islamic fundamentalism 5. Bloggers 6. Memoirists 7. Writers on politics 8. Writers on religion
ISBN 978-0-06-156708-7

LC 2009-9666

The author "opens his memoir with a vivid description of his father promising Allah that if God bestowed him with a son, that boy 'will become a great leader and servant of Islam.' The rest of the book finds Eteraz, whose given name is Abir ul Islam (which translates as 'Perfume of Islam') trying to come to terms with his father's mannat, or covenant, and understand the role that Islam will play in his life as well as the role he will play for Islam. . . . A gifted writer and scholar, Eteraz is able to create a true-life Islamic bildungsroman as he effortlessly conveys his coming-of-age tale while educating the reader. When his religious awakening finally occurs, his catharsis transcends the page." Publ Wkly

Evers, Medgar Wiley, 1925-1963

Evers, Medgar Wiley. The **autobiography** of Medgar Evers: a hero's life and legacy revealed through his writings, letters, and speeches; edited by Myrlie Evers-Williams and Manning Marable. Basic Civitas Books 2005 xxiv, 352p il $26; pa $14   **92**

1. Civil rights activists
ISBN 0-465-02177-8; 0-465-02178-6 pa

LC 2006-296327

This is a collection of "Evers's unpublished papers and personal collections as well as [his widow] Evers-Williams's recollections. The resulting text resurrects the life, intellectual output, and creative legacy of the slain civil rights hero." Libr J
Includes bibliographical references

Evert, Chris

Howard, Johnette. The **rivals**; Chris Evert vs. Martina Navratilova: their epic duels and extraordinary friendship. Broadway Books 2005 296p il $24.95   **92**

1. Tennis players 2. Tennis -- Biography
ISBN 0-7679-1884-3

LC 2004-61918

"This work makes a fine contribution to the history of women in sports." Publ Wkly

Exmouth, Edward Pellew, Viscount, 1757-1833

Taylor, Stephen. **Commander**; the life and exploits of Britain's greatest frigate captain. Stephen Taylor. W.W. Norton 2012 320 p.   **92**

1. War 2. Biography 3. Military personnel 4. Great Britain -- History, Naval -- 18th century 5. Great Britain -- History, Naval -- 19th century 6. Great Britain. Royal Navy. Officers -- Biography 7. Frigates -- Great Britain -- History -- 18th century 8. Frigates -- Great Britain -- History -- 19th century
ISBN 9780393071641

LC 2012027783

This book by Stephen Taylor presents a biography of British naval commander Edward Pellew. He discusses "Pellew's meteoric rise to midshipman within four years and his first command by age 25. Rare in a seaman, he could swim and more than once dove into the sea to save a crewmember, and his physical prowess . . . was the stuff of legend." In addition, Taylor describes "life at sea during wars in America, the English Channel, the Indian Ocean and the Mediterranean." (Kirkus Reviews)
Includes bibliographical references and index

Fairbanks, Douglas, 1883-1939

Goessel, Tracey. The **first** king of Hollywood; the life of Douglas Fairbanks. Tracey Goessel. Chicago Review Press 2015 560 p. 24 plates; illustrations (hardback) $34.95   **92**

1. Actors -- United States -- Biography 2. Motion picture producer and directors -- United States -- Biography
ISBN 9781613734049

LC 2015018526

This book, by Tracey Goessel, presents a biography of the film actor Douglas Fairbanks. "Irrepressibly vivacious, he spent his life leaping over and into things, from his early Broadway successes to his marriage to the great screen actress Mary Pickford to the way he made Hollywood his very own town. . . . And in founding United Artists with Pickford, Charlie Chaplin, and D. W. Griffith, he challenged the studio system." (Publisher's note)

"The author draws on the actor's voluminous speeches and public statements, as well as a cache of love letters between Doug and Mary. Sadly, many Fairbanks films have been lost, but this highly recommended book illuminates a vanished era of American film." LJ
Includes bibliographical references and index

Fairchild, David, 1869-1954

Stone, Daniel. The **food** explorer; the true adventures of the globe-trotting botanist who transformed the American dinner table. Daniel Stone. Dutton 2018 xvi, 397 p.p illustrations (some color) (hardcover) $28   **92**

1. Eating customs 2. Botanists -- United States -- Biography
ISBN 9781101990605; 9781101990582

LC 2017030324

This book, by Daniel Stone, is "the true adventures of David Fairchild, a late-nineteenth-century food explorer who traveled the globe and introduced diverse crops like avocados, mangoes, seedless grapes-- and thousands more--to the American plate. . . . Fairchild's finds weren't just limited to food: From Egypt he sent back a variety of cotton that revolutionized an industry, and via Japan he introduced the cherry blossom tree, forever brightening America's capital." (Publisher's note)

"An erudite and entertaining historical biography of a food pioneer with particular interest for gastronomes and agriculture enthusiasts." Kirkus
Includes bibliographical references and index

Falcone, Ben, 1973-

Falcone, Ben, 1973- **Being** a dad is weird; lessons in fatherhood from my family to yours. Ben Falcone; [foreword by Melissa McCarthy] Dey St., an imprint of William Morrow 2017 xxi, 216 p.p illustrations (hardcover) $25.99   **92**

1. Parenting 2. Fatherhood 3. Fatherhood -- Anecdotes
ISBN 006247362X; 9780062473622; 9780062473608

"In this winning collection of stories, Ben [Falcone] shares his funny and poignant adventures as the husband of Melissa McCarthy, and the father of their two young daughters. He also shares tales from his own childhood in Southern Illinois, and life with his father--an outspoken, brilliant, but unconventional man with a big heart and a somewhat casual approach to employment named Steve Falcone." (Publisher's note)

Fanon, Frantz, 1925-1961

Macey, David. **Frantz** Fanon; a biography. Picador 2001 640p maps $40; pa $20   **92**

1. Diplomats 2. Psychiatrists 3. Revolutionaries 4. Algeria -- History 5. Writers on medicine 6. Algeria -- Biography 7. Political and social philosophers 8. Intellectuals -- Algeria -- Biography 9. Psychiatrists -- Algeria -- Biography 10. Revolutionaries -- Algeria -- Biography

ISBN 0-312-27550-1; 0-312-30042-5 pa

LC 2001-21807

"Based on extensive research and original research, an objective look at the author of one of the most unsettling books of the 1960s, The Wretched of the Earth, reveals Frantz Fanon to be a complex figure--writer, psychiatrist, propagandist, and ambassador." (Publisher's note)

"Macey's writing and research is rich with historical context and personal information that both Fanon loyalists and general readers will appreciate." Libr J

Includes bibliographical references

Faraday, Michael, 1791-1867

Hirshfeld, Alan. The **electric** life of Michael Faraday. Walker & Co. 2006 258p il $24   **92**

1. Chemists 2. Physicists 3. Writers on science

ISBN 0-8027-1470-6

LC 2005-25533

In this biography of the English scientist, the author "explains Faraday's status as one of the most inspirational and significant figures of science. . . . A vibrant portrayal that emphasizes Faraday's qualities of wonder, acuity, and diligence, which propelled him to greatness." Booklist

Includes bibliographical references

Faulkner, William, 1897-1962

★ Parini, Jay. **One** matchless time; a life of William Faulkner. HarperCollins Publishers 2004 492p il $29.95; pa $14.95   **92**

1. Authors 2. Novelists 3. Screenwriters 4. Short story writers 5. Nobel laureates for literature

ISBN 0-06-621072-0; 0-06-093555-3 pa

LC 2004-42891

The author "offers a portrait of a man always trying to invent a new mask for himself as well as the portrait of an artist consumed by a desire to tell about the South and its class struggles, its depravity, and its captivity to the double bonds of land and history. Parini examines each of Faulkner's novels, from Soldier's Pay to The Reivers, and connects the Snopses, Sutpens, and Compsons of Faulkner's mythic Yoknapatawpha County foibles, his insecurities, and his inestimable literary achievement." Libr J

Includes bibliographical references

Favre, Brett

Pearlman, Jeff. **Gunslinger**; The Remarkable, Improbable, Iconic Life of Brett Favre. Jeff Pearlman. Houghton Mifflin Harcourt 2016 448 p. illustrations (hardcover) $28   **92**

1. Football players -- United States -- Biography

ISBN 9780544454378; 0544454375

This biography of quarterback Brett Favre by Jeff Pearlman describes Favre's "journey from his rough rural childhood and lackluster high school football career to landing the last scholarship at Southern Mississippi to a car accident that nearly took his life. Favre clawed back, getting drafted into the NFL by the Atlanta Falcons, then finding his way to Green Bay, where he restored the Packers to greatness." (Publisher's note)

"Pearlman's book is a complete, satisfying biography of a gunslinger who, for both better and worse, was far more complex than most fans have understood." Kirkus

Includes bibliographical references (pages 384-415) and index.

Feiffer, Jules

Feiffer, Jules. **Backing** into forward; a memoir. Nan A. Talese-Doubleday 2010 440p il $30   **92**

1. Artists 2. Authors 3. Novelists 4. Dramatists 5. Cartoonists 6. Illustrators 7. Satirists 8. Authors, American 9. Children's authors

ISBN 978-0-385-53158-0

LC 2009-21933

This is an autobiography by the American syndicated cartoonist.

"Feiffer is masterful at self-analyzing the skinny Jewish kid from the Bronx who grew up during the Depression, whose sister was a Communist, and whose distant cousin Roy Cohn was a Red-baiter, while he himself was full of insecurities but fortunate enough to 'luck into the zeitgeist.' . . . He offers social commentary and memorable moments from career and family life as he moved from cartooning to screen and playwriting, to authoring children's books, all the while maintaining a wry perspective that shows in the cartoons interspersed throughout this wonderful memoir." Booklist

Feinstein, Michael

Feinstein, Michael, 1956- The **Gershwins** and me; a personal history in twelve songs. by Michael Feinstein with Ian Jackman. Simon & Schuster 2012 351 p. illustrations (some color) (hc: alk. paper) $45   **92**

1. Popular music -- Writing and publishing -- United States

ISBN 1451645309; 9781451645309; 9781451645316; 9781451645323; 9781451645330

LC 2012006833

Here, author Michael Feinstein "begins with a swift account of how he met Ira Gershwin, the lyricist of the celebrated duo, and how he subsequently went to work for him for six years. . . . Although he tells the Gershwins' stories, childhood to grave, he also . . . discusses the Gershwins' love lives, the significant performers of their work (from Fred Astaire to Ethel Merman), their successes and flops, their experiences in Hollywood and the devastation of George's shocking death at 38 (brain tumor)." (Kirkus)

Includes bibliographical references and index

Feldman, Deborah, 1986-

Feldman, Deborah. **Exodus**; a memoir. by Deborah Feldman. Blue Rider Press 2014 304 p.   **92**

1. Hasidism 2. Jews -- New York (N.Y.) 3. New York (N.Y.) -- Biography 4. Jews -- New York (State) -- New York -- Identity 5. Jews -- New York (State) -- New York -- Biography

ISBN 9780399162770

LC 2013046263

"In 2009, at the age of twenty-three, Deborah Feldman packed up her young son and their few possessions and walked away from her insular Hasidic roots. She was determined to forge a better life for herself, away from the rampant oppression, abuse, and isolation of her Satmar upbringing in Williamsburg, Brooklyn. Out of her experience came the incendiary, bestselling memoir Unorthodox, and now, just a few years later, Feldman has embarked on a triumphant journey of self-discovery—a journey in which she begins life anew as a single mother, an independent woman, and a religious refugee." Publisher's Note

"The overall effect is captivating, entertaining and informative, providing readers with an honest assessment of the strength of one's convictions and the effect a strict religious background can have on a person. An enthralling account of how one Orthodox Jewish woman turned her back on her religion and found genuineness and validity in her new life." Kirkus

Feldman, Deborah. **Unorthodox**; the scandalous rejection of my Hasidic roots. Deborah Feldman. Simon & Schuster 2012 p. cm. illustrations   **92**
1. Hasidim 2. Jews -- New York (N.Y.) 3. Jews -- New York (State) -- New York -- Biography 4. Hasidim -- New York (State) -- New York -- Biography 5. Hasidim -- New York (State) -- New York -- Social conditions
ISBN 9781439187005; 9781439187012; 9781439187029
LC 2011001386
"In her bestselling memoir, . . . Deborah Feldman recounts the story of her apostasy from the Satmar community of Hasidic Jews in which she was raised. . . . As often happens for those who eventually leave the ultra-Orthodox fold, secular books become the portal through which one comes to see a larger world. The teenage Feldman revels in the freedom of the public library. . . . She provides a litany of abuse stories to explain her growing disillusionment with the Satmar." (Commentary)
"Born into the insular and exclusionary Hasidic community of Satmar in Brooklyn to a mentally disabled father and a mother who fled the sect, Feldman, as she recounts in this nicely written memoir, seemed doomed to be an outsider from the start. Raised by devout grandparents who forbade her to read in English, the ever-curious child craved books outside the synagogue teaching. Feldman's spark of rebellion started with sneaking off to the library and hiding paperback novels under her bed. . . . She starts to experience panic attacks and the stirrings of her final break with being Hasidic. It's when she finally does get pregnant and wants something more for her child that the full force of her uprising takes hold and she plots her escape. Feldman, who now attends Sarah Lawrence College, offers this engaging and at times gripping insight into Brooklyn's Hasidic community." Pub Wkly

Fennelly, Beth Ann, 1971-

Fennelly, Beth Ann, 1971- **Heating** & cooling; 52 micromemoirs. Beth Ann Fennelly. W W Norton & Co Inc 2017 111 p. (hardcover) $22.95   **92**
1. American poetry 2. Autobiographies
ISBN 9780393609486; 0393609472; 9780393609479
LC 2017026664
"The 52 micro-memoirs in . . . [this book, by Beth Ann Fennelly], offer bright glimpses into a richly lived life, combining the compression of poetry with the truth-telling of nonfiction into one heartfelt, celebratory book. Ranging from childhood recollections to quirky cultural observations, these micro-memoirs build on one another to arrive at a portrait of . . . Fennelly as a wife, mother, writer, and deeply original observer of life's challenges and joys." (Publisher's note)
"A sleek, delightful collection." Kirkus
Includes bibliographical references

Ferlinghetti, Lawrence

Ferlinghetti, Lawrence, 1919- **Writing** Across the Landscape; Travel Journals 1950-2013. by Lawrence Ferlinghetti; edited by Giada Diana and Matthew Gleeson. W W Norton & Co Inc 2015 496 p. illustrations $35   **92**
1. Travel writing
ISBN 163149001X; 9781631490019
LC 2015026292
This book, edited by Giada Diana and Matthew Gleeson, "present[s]

a Lawrence Ferlinghetti never before encountered, an elegant prose stylist and tireless political activist who was warning against the pernicious sins of our ever-expansive corporate culture long before such thoughts ever seeped into mainstream consciousness. . . . Evoking each journey with a mixture of travelogue and poetry as well as his own hand-drawn sketches, Ferlinghetti adopts the role of an American bard." (Publisher's note)
"Avid readers of Ferlinghetti's work will welcome this collection as the 100th anniversary of his birth in 2019 draws ever nearer. It may also provide grist for future biographers." LJ

Fermi, Enrico, 1901-1954

★ Schwartz, David N. The **last** man who knew everything; the life and times of Enrico Fermi, father of the nuclear age. David N. Schwartz. Basic Books, an imprint of Perseus Books, a subsidiary of Hachette Book Group 2017 480 p. $35   **92**
1. Nuclear physicists -- Biography 2. Physicists -- Italy -- Biography 3. Nuclear physicists -- Italy -- Biography 4. Physicists -- United States -- Biography 5. Nuclear physicists -- United States -- Biography
ISBN 0465072925; 9780465072927
LC 2017020558
This book, by David N. Schwartz, presents "the definitive biography of the brilliant, charismatic, and very human physicist and innovator Enrico Fermi. In 1942, a team at the University of Chicago achieved what no one had before: a nuclear chain reaction. At the forefront of this breakthrough stood . . . Fermi. Straddling the ages of classical physics and quantum mechanics, . . . Fermi truly was the last man who knew everything--at least about physics." (Publisher's note)
"Though comparable to Segrè and Hoerlin's The Pope of Physics (2016) as an account of Fermi's groundbreaking science, Schwartz's biography delivers a much fuller personal portrait, illuminating how this generous friend to scientific colleagues, this inspiring mentor to students, often proved a difficult husband and negligent father. A sophisticated portrayal of a complex man." (Booklist)
Includes bibliographical references and index

★ Segrè, Gino. The **Pope** of Physics; Enrico Fermi and the birth of the atomic age. Gino Segrè and Bettina Hoerlin. Henry Holt & Co. 2016 368 p. illustrations, portraits (hardcover) $30.00   **92**
1. Physics -- History 2. Physicists -- Biography 3. Physicists -- Italy -- Biography 4. Physicists -- United States -- Biography
ISBN 9781627790055; 1627790055; 1627790063; 9781627790062
LC 2016013398
This book, by Gino Segrè and Bettina Hoerlin, presents a biography of "Enrico Fermi . . . , unquestionably among the greats of the world's physicists, the most famous Italian scientist since Galileo. Called the Pope by his peers, he was regarded as infallible in his instincts and research. His discoveries changed our world; they led to weapons of mass destruction and conversely to life-saving medical interventions." (Publisher's note)
"A vivid retelling of events that still shape our lives today." Kirkus
Includes bibliographical references and index

Fey, Tina, 1970-

Fey, Tina, 1970- **Bossypants**. Little, Brown and Co. 2011 277p il $26.99   **92**
1. Actors 2. Comedians 3. Autobiographies 4. American wit and humor 5. Screenwriters 6. Biography, Individual 7. Television scriptwriters
ISBN 978-0-316-05686-1

LC 2011002415

In this book, comedian "Tina Fey's story can be told. From her youthful days as a vicious nerd to her tour of duty on 'Saturday Night Live'; from her passionately halfhearted pursuit of physical beauty to her life as a mother eating things off the floor; from her one-sided college romance to her nearly fatal honeymoon -- from the beginning of this paragraph to this final sentence. Tina Fey reveals all, and proves what we've all suspected: you're no one until someone calls you bossy." (Publisher's note)

"Perhaps best known to mass audiences for her writing and performances on Saturday Night Live, Fey's most inventive work is likely her writing for the critically acclaimed TV show 30 Rock, in which she stars alongside Alec Baldwin and fellow SNL alum Tracy Morgan. In typical self-deprecating style, the author traces her awkward childhood and adolescence, rise within the improv ranks of Second City and career on the sets of SNL and 30 Rock." Kirkus

Feynman, Richard Phillips, 1918-1988

Krauss, Lawrence Maxwell. **Quantum** man; Richard Feynman's life in science. [by] Lawrence M. Krauss. W.W. Norton 2011 350p il (Great discoveries) $24.95   **92**
1. Authors 2. Physicists 3. Writers on science 4. Nobel laureates for physics
ISBN 978-0-393-06471-1; 0-393-06471-9

LC 2010-45512

"This book is highly recommended for readers who want to get to know one of the preeminent scientists of the 20th century." Publ Wkly
Includes bibliographical references

Ottaviani, Jim. **Feynman**; written by Jim Ottaviani; art by Leland Myrick; coloring by Hilary Sycamore. 1st ed. First Second 2011 262 p. chiefly ill. (some col.) (hardcover) $29.99; (paperback) $19.99; (prebind) $33.99   **92**
1. Atomic bomb 2. Nobel Prizes 3. Musicians -- Biography 4. Biography, Individual 5. Physicists -- Graphic novels
ISBN 1596432594; 9781596432598; 9781596438279; 9781451722406

LC 2010036260

Author Jim Ottaviani presents a "graphic novel biography . . . [of] Nobel-winning quantum physicist, adventurer, musician, world-class raconteur, and one of the greatest minds of the twentieth century: Richard Feynman . . . [The book] tells the story of the great man's life from his childhood in Long Island to his work on the Manhattan Project and the Challenger disaster." (Publisher's note)

"This is a fascinating look at the life of an eccentric genius, a man who worked on the Manhattan Project, won a Nobel Prize, was the first great physicist to teach freshmen classes, and was the investigator into the cause of the Challenger explosion who discovered the problem was the 0-rings. This work was so entertaining it was difficult to put down." Voice Youth Advocates

Fillmore, Millard, 1800-1874

Finkelman, Paul. **Millard** Fillmore. Times Books 2011 171p (American presidents series) $23; ebook $10.99   **92**
1. Presidents 2. Vice-presidents 3. Members of Congress 4. Presidents -- United States 5. United States -- Politics and government -- 1815-1861
ISBN 978-0-8050-8715-4; 978-1-4299-2301-9 ebook

LC 2010-47174

The author "describes Millard Fillmore's nearly forgotten presidency by rigidly contrasting him with Abraham Lincoln, another self-made man who wrestled with racial and regional tensions as president. . . . This book is an enlightening view into the often overlooked beginnings

of the Civil War, which history buffs and students alike will find enjoyable." Publ Wkly
Includes bibliographical references

Finnegan, William

Finnegan, William. **Barbarian** Days; A Surfing Life. by William Finnegan. Penguin Group USA 2015 464 p. illustrations (hardcover) $27.95   **92**
1. Surfing
ISBN 1594203474; 9781594203473
Pulitzer Prize: Biography (2016)

This memoir, by William Finnegan, is a "self-portrait of a lifelong surfer. . . . Raised in California and Hawaii, Finnegan started surfing as a child. He has chased waves all over the world, wandering for years through the South Pacific, Australia, Asia, Africa. A bookish boy, and then an excessively adventurous young man, he went on to become a distinguished writer and war reporter." (Publisher's note)

"The constants flowing through this part coming-of-age story and part travelog are the ocean and the waves that the author tries to better understand. The result is an up-close and personal homage to the surfing lifestyle through the author's journey as a lifelong surfer." LJ

Fischer, Bobby, 1943-2008

Brady, Frank. **Endgame**; Bobby Fischer's remarkable rise and fall--from America's brightest prodigy to the edge of madness. Crown 2010 402p il $25.99   **92**
1. Chess 2. Chess players
ISBN 978-0-307-46390-6; 0-307-46390-7

LC 2010-33840

"Brady's insightful biography of the legendary chess player focuses more on Fischer's life as a chess champion than on his much-publicized legal troubles and alleged psychological breakdowns. Brady first became friends with Fischer at a chess tournament when they were both children, and he combines a traditional biography with a personal memoir. . . . Brady is uniquely qualified to write this book. Not only is he a seasoned biographer and someone who knew Fischer on a personal level; he's also an accomplished chess player himself, able to convey the game's intricacies to the reader in a clear, uncomplicated manner." Booklist

Fisher, Carrie

Fisher, Carrie, 1956-2016. The **Princess** Diarist; by Carrie Fisher. Blue Rider Press 2016 272 p. illustrations (pbk.) $16; (hbk.) $26; (ebook) $65   **92**
1. Actors -- United States -- Biography
ISBN 0399185798; 9780399185793; 0399173595; 9780399173592; 9780698188365

LC 2016054189

This book is actress Carrie Fisher's "intimate and revealing recollection of what happened on one of the most famous film sets of all time—and what developed behind the scenes. Fisher also ponders the joys and insanity of celebrity, and the absurdity of a life spawned by Hollywood royalty, only to be surpassed by her own outer-space royalty." (Publisher's note)

"Outspoken, honest commentary of what it's like to be Princess Leia on and off the screen." Kirkus

Fisher, Todd

Fisher, Todd. **My** girls; a lifetime with Carrie and Debbie. Todd Fisher. HarperCollins 2018 352 p. $27.99   **92**
1. Actors -- United States
ISBN 0062792318; 9780062792310

This book, by Todd Fisher, is "a revelatory and touching tribute to the lives of Carrie Fisher and Debbie Reynolds. . . . Todd shares his heart and his memories of Debbie and Carrie with deeply personal stories from his earliest years to those last unfathomable days. His book, part memoir, part homage, celebrates their legacies through a more intimate, poignant, and often hilarious portrait of these two remarkable women than has ever been revealed before." (Publisher's note)

Fisk, Carlton, 1947-

Wilson, Doug. **Pudge**; the biography of Carlton Fisk. Doug Wilson. Thomas Dunne Books 2015 368 p. 8 plates; illustrations (hardcover: alk. paper) $26.99   **92**

    1. Baseball players 2. Catchers (Baseball) -- United States -- Biography
ISBN 1250065437; 9781250065438

                                     LC 2015027529

In this biography of baseball player Carlton Risk, author Doug Wilson "uses his own extensive research and interviews with childhood friends and major league teammates to examine the life and career of a leader who followed a strict code and played with fierce determination. Fisk retired having played in more games and hit more home runs than any other catcher before him. A baseball superstar in the 1970s and 80s, Fisk was known not just for his dedication to the sport and tremendous plays but for the respect with which he treated the game." (Publisher's note)

"A well-researched account of a legendary ball player." LJ

Includes bibliographical references and index

Fitzgerald, F. Scott (Francis Scott), 1896-1940

Brown, David S., 1966- **Paradise** lost; a life of F. Scott Fitzgerald. David S. Brown. The Belknap Press of Harvard University Press 2017 397 p. illustrations (hardcover: alk. paper) $29.95   **92**

    1. American authors -- Biography 2. Nostalgia in literature 3. Authors, American -- Biography 4. American literature -- 20th century -- History and criticism
ISBN 9780674504820; 9780674978263

                                     LC 2016048811

In this book, author "David Brown contends that [F. Scott] Fitzgerald's deepest allegiances were to a fading antebellum world he associated with his father's Chesapeake Bay roots. Yet as a midwesterner, an Irish Catholic, and a perpetually in-debt author, he felt like an outsider in the haute bourgeoisie haunts of Lake Forest, Princeton, and Hollywood--places that left an indelible mark on his worldview." (Publisher's note)

"Carefully researched and a pleasure to read, Brown's persuasive, original account will entice Fitzgerald fans and cultural historians alike." Pub Wkly

Includes bibliographical references and index

Fitzgerald, Zelda, 1900-1948

Brown, David S., 1966- **Paradise** lost; a life of F. Scott Fitzgerald. David S. Brown. The Belknap Press of Harvard University Press 2017 397 p. illustrations (hardcover: alk. paper) $29.95   **92**

    1. American authors -- Biography 2. Nostalgia in literature 3. Authors, American -- Biography 4. American literature -- 20th century -- History and criticism
ISBN 9780674504820; 9780674978263

                                     LC 2016048811

In this book, author "David Brown contends that [F. Scott] Fitzgerald's deepest allegiances were to a fading antebellum world he associated with his father's Chesapeake Bay roots. Yet as a midwesterner, an

Irish Catholic, and a perpetually in-debt author, he felt like an outsider in the haute bourgeoisie haunts of Lake Forest, Princeton, and Hollywood--places that left an indelible mark on his worldview." (Publisher's note)

"Carefully researched and a pleasure to read, Brown's persuasive, original account will entice Fitzgerald fans and cultural historians alike." Pub Wkly

Includes bibliographical references and index

Fitzmaurice, Simon

Fitzmaurice, Simon, ca. 1974-2017. **It's** not yet dark; a memoir. Simon Fitzmaurice. Houghton Mifflin Harcourt 2017 165 p. (hardback) $23   **92**

    1. Amyotrophic lateral sclerosis
ISBN 9781328916716; 9781328918581

                                     LC 2017016109

This memoir, by Simon Fitzmaurice, is "a story of courage, of heart, of coming back for more, of love and struggle and the power of both. . . . Fitzmaurice was diagnosed with ALS, or Lou Gehrig's disease. He was given four years to live. In 2010, in a state of lung-function collapse, Simon knew with crystal clarity that now was not his time to die. Against all prevailing medical opinion, he chose to ventilate in order to stay alive." (Publisher's note)

"Fitzmaurice communicates well, making his own case and advocating for the right of the afflicted to make their own choices in how they will live and die. A fine and heartfelt memoir from an author hopeful in his determination to endure against the odds." Kirkus

Flaherty, Meghan

Flaherty, Meghan. **Tango** lessons; a memoir. Meghan Flaherty. Houghton Mifflin Harcourt 2018 320 p. $26   **92**

    1. Dancers 2. Ballroom dancing
ISBN 0544980700; 9780544980709

In this memoir, author Meghan Flaherty recounts how she learned to dance tango, became more comfortable in her own skin and in the arms of others. "As Meghan moved from beginner classes to the late-night dance halls of New York's vibrant tango underground, she discovered that more than any footwork, the hardest and most essential lesson of the dance was to follow with strength and agency; to find her balance, regardless of the lead." (Publisher's note)

Flaubert, Gustave, 1821-1880

Brown, Frederick. **Flaubert**; a biography. Little, Brown 2006 628p il $35   **92**

    1. Authors 2. Novelists 3. Short story writers
ISBN 0-316-11878-8

                                     LC 2005-17036

This is a biography of the nineteenth-century French novelist.

The author "has put together a judicious work that sticks to the record and relies on expertly chosen passages from Flaubert's brilliant letters and the works of his contemporaries to develop a convincing portrait, brushstroke by brushstroke." N Y Times (Late N Y Ed)

Includes bibliographical references

Fleming, Victor, 1883-1949

Sragow, Michael. **Victor** Fleming; an American movie master. Pantheon 2008 645p il $40   **92**

    1. Motion picture directors 2. Motion picture producers and directors -- Biography
ISBN 978-0-375-40748-2; 0-375-40748-0

                                     LC 2008-15255

Fleming "was the director MGM tapped to take over two thorny, unwieldy and expensive projects—'The Wizard of Oz' and 'Gone With the Wind'—and make them into enormous successes. Had he never completed those two epics, Fleming's other cinematic triumphs had already sealed his reputation. They included 'The Virginian,' 'Red Dust,' 'Mantrap,' 'Bombshell' and 'Captains Courageous.' . . . Mr. Sragow deftly takes us through the twists and turns of Fleming's life, with a vital sense of time and place. We learn much not only about Fleming, but also about his contemporaries and the Hollywood they lived in." Washington Times

Includes bibliographical references and filmography

Flynn, Nick, 1960-

Flynn, Nick. **Another** bullsh #t night in Suck City; a memoir. W.W. Norton & Co 2004 347p il $23.95   **92**

1. Poets 2. Authors
ISBN 0-393-05139-0

LC 2004-11796

This "memoir describes the years poet Flynn . . . spent, in his late 20s, working at one of the city's homeless shelters, where his path crisscrossed with his down-and-out father's. . . . Although it's depressing, the book never seems hopeless, because readers know the author has succeeded at doing what his father only pretended to do: write, and write well." Publ Wkly

Flynt, Wayne, 1940-

Flynt, Wayne. **Mockingbird** songs; my friendship with Harper Lee. Wayne Flynt. HarperCollins Publishers 2017 xv, 215 p.p illustrations (chiefly color) (hardcover: alk. paper) $25.99   **92**

1. Women authors -- Biography 2. Personal correspondence 3. Women authors -- United States
ISBN 9780062660107; 9780062660084; 9780062660091

LC 2016044095

This book, by Wayne Flynt, is "an indelible portrait of one of the most famous and beloved authors in the canon of American literature--a collection of letters between Harper Lee and one of her closest friends that reveals the famously private writer as never before, in her own words." (Publisher's note)

"Southern historian Flynt (Keeping the Faith) shares his relationship with Harper Lee in a series of affectionate, playful, and mutually admiring letters." Pub Wkly

Fogerty, John, 1945-

Fogerty, John. **Fortunate** son; my life, my music. John Fogerty. Little, Brown & Co. 2015 416 p. 16 plates; illustrations (hc) $30   **92**

1. Musicians 2. Bands (Music)
ISBN 0316244570; 9780316244572

LC 2015943212

This book is the "memoir from John Fogerty, the legendary singer-songwriter and creative force behind Creedence Clearwater Revival. He reveals how he brought CCR to number one in the world, eclipsing even the Beatles in 1969. By the next year, though, Creedence was falling apart; their amazing, enduring success exploded and faded in just a few short years." (Publisher's note)

"This isn't just an account of one musician's ups and downs with art and life; Fogerty has created a solid study of popular music over the past 50 years." Pub Wkly

Foles, Nick

Foles, Nick, 1989- **Believe** it; my journey of success, failure, and overcoming the odds. Nick Foles, with Joshua Cooley. Tyndale Momentum, the nonfiction imprint of Tyndale House Publishers, Inc. 2018 xvi, 236 p.p (hardcover) $26.99   **92**

1. Biography 2. Quarterbacks (Football) 3. Football players --

United States -- Biography 4. Football players -- Religious life -- United States 5. Quarterbacks (Football) -- United States -- Biography
ISBN 1496436490; 9781496436498

LC 2018021881

In this book, Nick Foles, with Joshua Cooley, offers a behind-the-scenes look at . . . [his] unlikely path to the Super Bowl, the obstacles that threatened to hold him back, his rediscovery of his love for the game, and the faith that grounded him through it all. Learn from the way Nick handled the trials and tribulations that made him into the man he is today--and discover a path to your own success." (Publisher's note)

Foner, Moe, 1915-2002

Foner, Moe. **Not** for bread alone; a memoir. by Moe Foner with Dan North; foreword by Ossie Davis. Cornell Univ. Press 2002 142p $25   **92**

1. Labor leaders 2. Health care personnel
ISBN 0-8014-4061-0

LC 2002-5100

Foner's "memoir is a unique window into the evolution of 1199 SEIU from its origins as a tiny conglomeration of drugstore employees into the country's largest healthcare union." Libr J

Includes bibliographical references and index

Foner, Moe. **Not** for bread alone; a memoir. by Moe Foner with Dan North; foreword by Ossie Davis. Cornell Univ. Press 2002 142p $25   **92**

1. Labor leaders 2. Health care personnel
ISBN 0-8014-4061-0

LC 2002-5100

Foner's "memoir is a unique window into the evolution of 1199 SEIU from its origins as a tiny conglomeration of drugstore employees into the country's largest healthcare union." Libr J

Includes bibliographical references

Fontaine, Tessa

Fontaine, Tessa. The **electric** woman; a memoir in death-defying acts. Tessa Fontaine. Farrar, Straus & Giroux 2018 384 p. (cloth) $27   **92**

1. Mothers and daughters -- United States 2. Women circus performers -- United States 3. Sideshows -- United States 4. World of Wonders (Sideshow) 5. Circus performers -- United States -- Biography 6. Mothers and daughers -- United States -- Biography 7. Women circus performers -- United States -- Biography
ISBN 9780374158378

LC 2017038360

This book, "follows [author Tessa Fontaine] on a life-affirming journey of loss and self-discovery--through her time on the road with the last traveling American sideshow and her relationship with an adventurous, spirited mother. . . . A story for anyone who has ever imagined running away with the circus, wanted to be someone else, or wanted a loved one to live forever." (Publisher's note)

"This remarkable, beautifully written memoir explores the depth of mother-daughter love and the courageous acts of overcoming fear and accepting change." Pub Wkly

Ford, Betty, 1918-2011

★ McCubbin, Lisa. **Betty** Ford; first lady, women's advocate, survivor, trailblazer. Lisa McCubbin; foreword by Susan Ford Bales. Gallery Books, an imprint of Simon & Schuster, Inc. 2018 400 p. (hardback) $28   **92**

1. Biography 2. Presidents' spouses -- United States -- Biography

ISBN 9781501164682

LC 2018009239

This book, by Lisa McCubbin, with foreword by Susan Ford Bales relates "the inspiring story of an ordinary Midwestern girl thrust onto the world stage and into the White House under extraordinary circumstances. Setting a precedent as First Lady, Betty Ford refused to be silenced by her critics as she publicly championed equal rights for women, and spoke out about issues that had previously been taboo--breast cancer, depression, abortion, and sexuality." (Publisher's note)

"This timely biography of Betty Ford will introduce her to millennials and remind others of her importance in championing equal rights for women and speaking out on breast cancer, abortion, depression, and addiction at a time when women, especially a first lady, did not discuss these issues in public." Booklist

Includes bibliography and index.

Ford, Edna Akin, 1910-1981

★ Ford, Richard, 1944- **Between** them; remembering my parents. Richard Ford. Ecco, an imprint of HarperCollinsPublishers 2017 179 p. illustrations (hardcover) $25.99 **92**

1. Parents 2. Parent and child -- United States 3. Authors, American -- 20th century -- Biography

ISBN 0062661884; 9780062661906; 9780062661883

This book, by Richard Ford, is a "narrative of memory and parental love. For Ford, the questions of what his parents dreamed of, how they loved each other and loved him become a striking portrait of American life in the mid-century. . . . [The book] is his vivid image of where his life began and where his parents' lives found their greatest satisfaction." (Publisher's note)

"Illustrated with family photographs, Ford's remembrance of his parents is a masterful distillation of sensuous description, psychological intricacy, social insights, and a keen sense of place." Booklist

Ford, Henry, 1863-1947

Watts, Steven. The **people's** tycoon; Henry Ford and the American century. Knopf 2005 614p il $30 **92**

1. Antisemitism 2. Philanthropists 3. Automobile executives

ISBN 0-375-40735-9

LC 2004-48594

"Steven Watts is intelligent, thorough and engaging . . . in telling the story of an American who not only was influential but remains unavoidable to this day." N Y Times Book Rev

Includes bibliographical references

Ford, Parker

★ Ford, Richard, 1944- **Between** them; remembering my parents. Richard Ford. Ecco, an imprint of HarperCollinsPublishers 2017 179 p. illustrations (hardcover) $25.99 **92**

1. Parents 2. Parent and child -- United States 3. Authors, American -- 20th century -- Biography

ISBN 0062661884; 9780062661906; 9780062661883

This book, by Richard Ford, is a "narrative of memory and parental love. For Ford, the questions of what his parents dreamed of, how they loved each other and loved him become a striking portrait of American life in the mid-century. . . . [The book] is his vivid image of where his life began and where his parents' lives found their greatest satisfaction." (Publisher's note)

"Illustrated with family photographs, Ford's remembrance of his parents is a masterful distillation of sensuous description, psychological intricacy, social insights, and a keen sense of place." Booklist

Ford, Richard, 1944-

★ Ford, Richard, 1944- **Between** them; remembering my

parents. Richard Ford. Ecco, an imprint of HarperCollinsPublishers 2017 179 p. illustrations (hardcover) $25.99 **92**

1. Parents 2. Parent and child -- United States 3. Authors, American -- 20th century -- Biography

ISBN 0062661884; 9780062661906; 9780062661883

This book, by Richard Ford, is a "narrative of memory and parental love. For Ford, the questions of what his parents dreamed of, how they loved each other and loved him become a striking portrait of American life in the mid-century. . . . [The book] is his vivid image of where his life began and where his parents' lives found their greatest satisfaction." (Publisher's note)

"Illustrated with family photographs, Ford's remembrance of his parents is a masterful distillation of sensuous description, psychological intricacy, social insights, and a keen sense of place." Booklist

Foreman, Tom

Foreman, Tom. **My** year of running dangerously; a dad, a daughter, and a ridiculous plan. Tom Foreman. Blue Rider Press, an imprint of Penguin Random House 2015 288 p. illustrations (hardback) $25.95 **92**

1. Father-daughter relationship 2. Marathon running -- Training 3. Aging -- Psychological aspects 4. Marathon running -- United States 5. Fathers and daughters -- United States 6. Journalists -- United States -- Biography 7. Marathon running -- Psychological aspects 8. Middle-aged men -- United States -- Biography 9. Long-distance runners -- United States -- Biography

ISBN 0399175474; 9780399175473

LC 2015017237

This memoir is author Tom Foreman's "journey through four half-marathons, three marathons, and one 55-mile race. What started as an innocent request from his daughter quickly turned into a rekindled passion for long-distance running--for the training, the camaraderie, the defeats, and the victories. Told with honesty and humor, Foreman's account captures the universal fears of aging and failure alongside the hard-won moments of triumph." (Publisher's note)

"Even the author's long-suffering family had to admit at the end of the season that he was happier, and readers will enjoy running alongside him." Kirkus

Forhan, Chris, 1959-

Forhan, Chris. **My** father before me; a memoir. Chris Forhan. Scribner 2016 320 p. illustrations (ebook) $5.99; (hardcover: alkaline paper) $26 **92**

1. Dysfunctional families 2. American poets -- Biography 3. Suicide -- United States 4. Irish Americans -- Biography 5. Poets, American -- Biography 6. Silence -- Psychological aspects 7. Fathers -- United States -- Death 8. Fathers and sons -- United States 9. Catholics -- United States -- Biography 10. Dysfunctional families -- United States

ISBN 9781501131325; 9781501131264; 9781501131318

LC 2015034743

In this memoir, by Chris Forhan, Forhan reveals how "he and his siblings learned, without being told, that certain thoughts and feelings were not to be shared. On the evenings his father didn't come home, the rest of the family would eat dinner without him, his whereabouts unknown, his absence pronounced but not mentioned. And on a cold night in 1973, just before Christmas, Forhan's father killed himself in the carport." (Publisher's note)

"Forhan describes his family's healing and acceptance with warmth, humor, and an admirable lack of bitterness." Kirkus

Forster, E. M. (Edward Morgan), 1879-1970

Moffat, Wendy. A **great** unrecorded history; a new life of E.M. Forster. Farrar, Straus and Giroux 2010 480p il $32.50 **92**

    1. Authors 2. Novelists 3. Essayists 4. Authors, English 5. Literary critics 6. Short story writers

    ISBN 978-0-374-16678-6; 0-374-16678-1

                        LC 2009-29504

In this "well-written, intelligent and perceptive biography of Forster . . . [the author attemps] to draw a picture of a figure who was sensitive, sensuous and kind, an artist who possessed a keen, plain sort of wisdom and lightness of touch that make him, to this day, an immensely influential novelist, almost a prophet. She uses the sources for our knowledge of Forster's sexuality, including letters and diaries, without reducing the mystery and sheer individuality of Forster, without making his sexuality explain everything." N Y Times Book Rev

Includes bibliographical references

Fort, Charles, 1874-1932

Steinmeyer, Jim. **Charles** Fort; the man who invented the supernatural. J. P. Tarcher/Penguin 2008 332p il $24.95 **92**

    1. Supernatural 2. Parapsychology 3. Curiosities and wonders 4. Parapsychologists 5. Writers on science

    ISBN 978-1-58542-640-9; 1-58542-640-7

                        LC 2008-5961

"Steinmeyer is an elegant and unobtrusive author who shows us an entirely fascinating, shy, and witty man. . . . This book is not to be missed." Libr J

Includes bibliographical references

Fosdick, Sarah Graves, 1825-1871

Brown, Daniel. The **indifferent** stars above; the harrowing saga of a Donner Party bride. [by] Daniel James Brown. William Morrow 2009 337p il $25.99 **92**

    1. Donner party 2. Overland journeys to the Pacific 3. Pioneers 4. Frontier and pioneer life -- California

    ISBN 978-0-06-134810-5; 0-06-134810-4

                        LC 2008-40646

"In April 1846, as young newlywed Sarah Graves departed her Illinois home on a journey to California, she could not foresee the misery and horror that awaited her. After numerous delays on their difficult westward path, she and her family found themselves dangerously behind schedule as winter loomed, and they decided to join an ill-fated wagon train under the leadership of George Donner. Ending up snowbound and starving in the Sierra Nevada range, the Donner party descended into cannibalism. . . . Never melodramatic or maudlin, Brown's work gracefully balances graphic depictions of extreme privation with humanizing glimpses of the emigrants' everyday hopes and fears." Libr J

Includes bibliographical references

Fosse, Bob, 1927-1987

★ Wasson, Sam. **Fosse**; by Sam Wasson. Houghton Mifflin Harcourt 2013 672 p. $32 **92**

    1. Choreographers 2. Choreographers -- United States -- Biography

    ISBN 0547553293; 9780547553290

                        LC 2013026082

This book, by Sam Wasson, presents a biography of choreographer and director Bob Fosse. "Fosse revolutionized nearly every facet of American entertainment, forever marking Broadway and Hollywood with his iconic style--hat tilted, fingers splayed--that would influence generations of performing artists. Yet in spite of Fosse's innumerable achievements, no accomplishment ever seemed to satisfy him, and off-stage his life was shadowed in turmoil and anxiety." (Publisher's note)

Fowler, Shannon Leone

Fowler, Shannon Leone. **Traveling** with ghosts; a memoir. Shannon Leone Fowler. Simon & Schuster 2017 304 p. (ebook) $19.99; (Hardcover) $26 **92**

    1. Women marine biologists -- Biography 2. Marine biology 3. Marine biologists -- Great Britain -- Biography 4. Women marine biologists -- Great Britain -- Biography

    ISBN 9781501107870; 9781501107795; 9781501107863

                        LC 2016022676

In this memoir marine biologist Shannon Leone Fowler "shares the solo journey she took--through war-ravaged Eastern Europe, Israel, and beyond--to find peace after her fiancé suffered a fatal attack by a box jellyfish in Thailand. . . . Shattered and untethered, Shannon's life paused indefinitely so that she could travel around the world to find healing." (Publisher's note)

"This is nicely written and informative journey on the path to healing." Pub Wkly

Fox Starr, Rebecca, 1985-

Fox Starr, Rebecca. **Beyond** the baby blues; anxiety and depression during and after pregnancy. Rebecca Fox Starr. Rowman & Littlefield 2018 154 p. (cloth: alk. paper) $32 **92**

    1. Anxiety 2. Postpartum depression 3. Depression (Psychology) 4. Postpartum depression -- Treatment

    ISBN 9781442273900

                        LC 2017023086

In this book, "Rebecca Fox Starr shares her personal story of marriage, motherhood, prenatal anxiety and depression, severe postpartum anxiety and depression, recovery process and hope for the future. Woven throughout the narrative, Dr. Amy Wenzel, a specialist in the field of Perinatal Mood Disorders, provides readers with clinical information and advice, addressing risk factors, warning signs, definitions and recovery options." (Publisher's note)

"This work promises to be a valuable refuge for expectant mothers and their families confronting the specter of prenatal and postpartum depression." Pub Wkly

Includes bibliographical references and index

Fox, Michael J.

Fox, Michael J. **Always** looking up; the adventures of an incurable optimist. Hyperion 2009 279p il $25.99 **92**

    1. Actors 2. Parkinson's disease -- Personal narratives

    ISBN 978-1-4013-0338-9

                        LC 2008-55129

An autobiography of the actor and Parkinson's disease sufferer.

Fox, Michael J. **Lucky** man; a memoir. Hyperion 2002 304p $22.95; pa $12.95 **92**

    1. Actors 2. Parkinson's disease -- Personal narratives

    ISBN 0-7868-6764-7; 0-7868-8874-1 pa

In this autobiography the actor discusses his professional career in feature films and television. He also "writes of the last 10 years, during which--with the unswerving support of his wife, family, and friends--he has dealt with his illness. He talks about what Parkinson's has given him: the chance to appreciate a wonderful life and career, and the opportunity to help search for a cure and spread public awareness of the disease." Publisher's note

Francis, Pope, 1936-

Cool, Michel. **Francis,** a new world pope; Michel Cool;

translated by Regan Kramer. William B. Eerdmans Publishing Company 2013 viii, 120 p.p illustrations (pbk.: alk. paper) $14 **92**

ISBN 0802871003; 9780802871008

LC 2013020717

Author Michel Cool "surveys Pope Francis's journey to the papacy, his convictions, his personality, his writings, and the challenges he faces in his new office--governance of the church, new evangelization in secularized societies, and poverty, among many others." (Publisher's note)

"An intelligent and prudent guide to the new pope, Cool's book urges a modest optimism about Francis's leadership." LJ

Includes bibliographical references and index

Shriver, Mark. **Pilgrimage**; My Search for the Real Pope Francis. by Mark K. Shriver. Random House Inc 2016 304 p. $28 **92**

1. Popes -- Biography 2. Catholic Church -- Clergy -- Biography
ISBN 0812998022; 9780812998023

LC 2016022799

This book by Mark K. Shriver "retraces [Pope] Francis's personal journey, revealing the origins of his open, unpretentious style and explaining how it revitalized Shriver's own faith and renewed his commitment to the Church. To help us understand how Jorge Mario Bergoglio became Pope Francis, Shriver travels to Bergoglio's native Argentina to meet with the people who knew him as a child, as a young Jesuit priest, and as a reformist bishop." (Publisher's note)

"In this excellent book, Shriver takes readers on a pilgrimage to numerous significant people and places in the life of Pope Francis." Pub Wkly

Includes bibliographical references.

Vallely, Paul. **Pope** Francis; the struggle for the soul of Catholicism. Paul Vallely. St. Martin's Press 2015 496 p. 8 plates; illustrations $30 **92**

1. Catholic Church
ISBN 1632861151; 9781632861153

In this book author "Paul Vallely reexamines the complex past of Jorge Mario Bertoglio and adds nine new chapters, revealing many untold, behind-the-scenes stories from his first years in office that explain this Pope of paradoxes. Vallely lays bare the intrigue and in-fighting surrounding Francis's attempt to cleanse the scandal-ridden Vatican Bank. He unveils the ambition and arrogance of top bureaucrats resisting the Pope's reform of the Roman Curia." (Publisher's note)

"A well-written, balanced portrait of a man leading the church in a new direction. This title will appeal to anyone who seeks a well-rounded study of the current Pope." LJ

Francis, of Assisi, Saint, 1182-1226

Martin, Valerie. **Salvation**: scenes from the life of St. Francis. Knopf 2001 268p hardcover o.p. pa $13 **92**

1. Saints 2. Writers on religion
ISBN 0-375-70883-9 pa

LC 00-44361

"This portrait will be most interesting to readers who are already familiar with the basic facts of Francis's life and remain open to exploring a new, gritty interpretation of them." Publ Wkly

Includes bibliographical references

Frank family

Gies, Miep. **Anne** Frank remembered; the story of the woman who helped to hide the Frank family. [by] Miep Gies and Alison Leslie Gold. Simon & Schuster trade pbk. ed.; Si-

mon and Schuster Paperbacks 2009 264p il pa $15 **92**

1. Holocaust, 1933-1945 2. Amsterdam (Netherlands) 3. Netherlands -- History -- 1940-1945, German occupation
ISBN 978-1-4165-9885-5; 1-4165-9885-5

LC 2009294295

First published 1987

"A memoir by the courageous Dutch woman who helped hide the Frank family, this book augments the Anne Frank story. Perceptive characterizations, with insight into life in Amsterdam during the Nazi occupation." SLJ

Frank, Anne, 1929-1945

Barnouw, David. The **diary** of Anne Frank: the critical edition; rev Critical ed; Doubleday 2003 851p il $75 **92**

1. Children 2. Diarists 3. Holocaust victims 4. Jews -- Netherlands 5. Holocaust, 1933-1945 6. World War, 1939-1945 -- Jews 7. Netherlands -- History -- 1940-1945, German occupation
ISBN 0-385-50847-6

LC 2003-269527

First published 1989

This volume brings together "the three known versions of Frank's diary—the original, a self-edited version . . . {and} another edited by her father. It also contains . . . handwriting and paper analyses, new documentation regarding the Frank family's arrest, and . . . information about the diary's troubled publication history." Libr J {review of 1989 edition}

Includes bibliographical references

★ Frank, Anne. The **diary** of a young girl: the definitive edition; edited by Otto H. Frank and Mirjam Pressler; translated by Susan Massotty. Bantam 1997 340p $29.95; pa $7.99 **92**

1. Children 2. Diarists 3. Holocaust victims 4. Jews -- Netherlands 5. Holocaust, 1933-1945 6. World War, 1939-1945 -- Jews 7. Netherlands -- History -- 1940-1945, German occupation
ISBN 0-385-47378-8; 9780553577129

LC 94-41379

"This new translation of Frank's famous diary includes material about her emerging sexuality and her relationship with her mother that was originally excised by Frank's father, the only family member to survive the Holocaust." Libr J

Jacobson, Sidney. **Anne** Frank; the Anne Frank House authorized graphic biography. [by] Sid Jacobson and Ernie Colón. Hill and Wang 2010 152p il $30; pa $16.95 **92**

1. Children 2. Graphic novels 3. Biographical graphic novels 4. Jews -- Netherlands -- Graphic novels 5. Holocaust, 1933-1945 -- Graphic novels 6. World War, 1939-1945 -- Jews -- Graphic novels
ISBN 978-0-8090-2684-5; 978-0-8090-2685-2 pa

LC 2010-5776

Draws on the archives of the Anne Frank House to relate the short but inspiring life of the Jewish teen memoirist, from the lives of her parents to Anne's years keeping her private diary while hidden from the Nazis to her untimely death in a concentration camp.

"Panel arrangements effectively show simultaneous events happening in the life of the family and in the world, while brief 'snapshots' provide enough historical information to make motives, fears, and expectations sensible to anyone unfamiliar with the Holocaust's machinery. More than simply poignant, this biography elucidates the complex emotional aspects of living a sequestered adolescence as a brilliant, budding writer." Booklist

Includes bibliographical references

Müller, Melissa, 1967- **Anne** Frank; the biography. by

Melissa Muller; translated by Rita and Robert Kimber. 2nd U.S. ed. Metropolitan Books/Henry Holt and Company 2013 480 p. hardcover o.p. (hardcover) $35 **92**

1. Children 2. Amsterdam (Netherlands) -- Biography 3. Jewish children in the Holocaust -- Biography 4. Jews -- Netherlands -- Amsterdam -- Biography 5. Holocaust, Jewish (1939-1945) -- Netherlands -- Amsterdam -- Biography
ISBN 0805087311; 9780805087314

LC 2013000297

This biography of Anne Frank "was originally published in 1998, but this expanded edition takes into account diary entries that had previously been redacted by Anne's father [Otto], as well as recently discovered letters from Otto to relatives in the United States and unpublished documents provided to [Melissa] Müller during interviews with those who knew Anne and her family." (Publishers Weekly)

"Müller includes a family tree; a family history; and considerable insight into the character, personality, and quality of life of Anne's parents, relatives, and friends. Interviews with many of these surviving people give a clearer idea of the situation and Anne's reactions to it." SLJ

Frank, Barney, 1940-

★ Frank, Barney, 1940- **Frank**; A Life in Politics from the Great Society to Same-Sex Marriage. by Barney Frank. Farrar, Straus & Giroux 2015 400 p. 16 plates; illustrations (hardback) $28 **92**

1. Politicians -- United States 2. United States. Congress. House 3. Legislators -- United States -- Biography 4. United States -- Politics and government -- 20th century 5. United States -- Politics and government -- 21st century 6. Politicians -- Massachusetts -- Biography 7. United States. Congress. House -- Biography 8. Gay legislators -- United States -- Biography 9. United States -- Politics and government -- 1989- 10. United States -- Politics and government -- 1945-1989
ISBN 9780374280307

LC 2014040383

In this memoir, politician Barney Frank "discusses the satisfactions, fears, and grudges that come with elected office. He recalls the emotional toll of living in the closet and how his public crusade against homophobia conflicted with his private accommodation of it. He discusses his painful quarrels with allies; his friendships with public figures; . . . and how he found love with his husband, Jim Ready, becoming the first sitting member of Congress to enter a same-sex marriage." (Publisher's note)

"Anyone interested in contemporary history or politics will definitely want to read this highly accessible memoir." LJ

Frank, Michael, 1959 June 2-

Frank, Michael. The **mighty** Franks; a memoir. Michael Frank. Farrar, Straus & Giroux 2017 304 p. (hardback) $26 **92**

1. Aunts 2. Family life 3. Domestic relations
ISBN 9780374210120; 9780374715960

LC 2016041346

This book, by Michael Frank, offers "a psychologically acute memoir about an unusual Hollywood family. . . . Strangest of all is the way Auntie Hankie . . . talented, mercurial, and lavish with her love, . . . divides Michael from his parents and his two younger brothers as she takes charge of his education, guiding him to the right books to read (Proust, not Zola), the right painters to admire (Matisse, not Pollock), the right architectural styles to embrace." (Publisher's note)

"In this complex and fascinating memoir, journalist Frank describes the spell cast over his childhood by his screenwriter aunt and her fury at his attempts to break away from her." Pub Wkly

Frank, Robert, 1924-

Smith, R. J. **American** witness; the art and life of Robert Frank. RJ Smith. Da Capo Press 2017 352 p. (hardcover) $35 **92**

1. Photographers -- United States -- Biography
ISBN 9780306823367; 9780306823374

LC 2017953589

This biography, by R. J. Smith, "is the first comprehensive look at the life of [renowned photographer and filmmaker Robert Frank] . . . who's as mysterious and evasive as he is prolific and gifted. Leaving his rigid Switzerland for the more fluid United States in 1947, Frank found himself at the red-hot social center of bohemian New York in the '50s and '60s, becoming friends with everyone [including,] Jack Kerouac, Allen Ginsberg, and Peter Orlovsky." (Publisher's note)

"Smith compellingly tells the story of one of the most iconic and notoriously aloof artists of the 20th century in a way that is neither dry nor contrived; he helps us to know a seemingly unknowable artist." (Kirkus)

Frankl, Viktor E.

★ Frankl, Viktor E. (Viktor Emil), 1905-1997. **Man's** search for meaning; part one translated by Ilse Lasch; foreword by Harold S. Kushner; afterword by William J. Winslade. Beacon Press 2006 165p pa $13 **92**

1. Psychologists 2. Holocaust, 1933-1945 -- Personal narratives
ISBN 0-8070-1427-3; 978-0-8070-1427-1

LC 2006-287144

Original German edition, 1946

"Between 1942 and 1945 Frankl labored in four different camps, including Auschwitz, while his parents, brother, and pregnant wife perished. Based on his own experience and the experiences of others he treated later in his practice, Frankl argues that we cannot avoid suffering but we can choose how to cope with it, find meaning in it, and move forward with renewed purpose. Frankl's theory—known as logotherapy, from the Greek word logos ('meaning')—holds that our primary drive in life is not pleasure, as Freud maintained, but the discovery and pursuit of what we personally find meaningful." Publisher's note

Franklin, Aretha

★ Ritz, David. **Respect**; the life of Aretha Franklin. David Ritz. 1st edition Little, Brown & Co. 2014 528 p. illustrations (hardcover) $30 **92**

1. African American singers -- Biography 2. Singers 3. Soul musicians
ISBN 0316196835; 9780316196833

LC 2014018985

This biography by David Ritz describes how "it was not until 1967, when a white Jewish producer insisted [singer Aretha Franklin] return to her gospel-soul roots, that fame and fortune finally came via 'Respect' and a rapidfire string of hits. She has evolved ever since, amidst personal tragedy, surprise Grammy performances, and career reinventions." (Publisher's note)

"[C]ommendable for its depth, much of which comes from interviews with key figures and family members, as well as Ritz's highly readable, captivating style. It's a compelling record of the life of a musical titan and a fascinating picture of the process of recording some of the seminal popular music of our time." LJ

Includes bibliographical references, discography, filmography and index

Franklin, Benjamin, 1706-1790

Bunker, Nick. **Young** Benjamin Franklin; the birth of ingenuity. by Nick Bunker. Alfred A. Knopf 2018 464 p. (hard-

cover) $30 **92**
1. Biography 2. Statesmen 3. Statesmen -- United States -- Biography
ISBN 9781101874417

LC 2017057711

In this biography of Benjamin Franklin, author Nick Bunker "portrays him as a complex, driven young man who elbows his way to success. From his early career as a printer and journalist, to his scientific work and his role as a founder of a new republic, . . . Franklin has always seemed the inevitable embodiment of American ingenuity. But in his youth he had to make his way through a harsh colonial world where he fought many battles." (Publisher's note)

"This thoroughly researched examination of the development of America's earliest preeminent scientist and statesman will appeal to academics and popular history readers." Library Journal

Epstein, Daniel Mark. The **loyal** son; the war in Ben Franklin's house. Daniel Mark Epstein. Ballantine Books 2017 xx, 438 p.p illustrations, maps (hardcover) $30 **92**
1. Statesmen -- United States -- Biography 2. American loyalists -- Biography 3. Governors -- New Jersey -- Biography 4. Statesmen's children -- United States -- Biography 5. United States -- Politics and government -- 1775-1783
ISBN 0345544218; 9780345544223; 9780345544216

LC 2017013553

This book, by Daniel Mark Epstein, tells the "complex and confounding relationship [of Benjamin Franklin] with his illegitimate son William. . . . He adopted the boy, raised him, and educated him to be his aide. Ben and William became inseparable. . . . The outbreak of the American Revolution caused a devastating split between father and son. By then, William was royal governor of New Jersey, while Ben was one of the foremost champions of American independence." (Publisher's note)

"A perceptive, gritty portrayal of the frenzy of war and a father and son caught at its tumultuous center." Kirkus

Includes bibliographical references and index.

★ Franklin, Benjamin. The **autobiography** of Benjamin Franklin; introduction by Lewis Leary. Simon & Schuster 2004 143p pa $10.95 **92**
1. Authors 2. Diplomats 3. Inventors 4. Statesmen 5. Scientists 6. Writers on science 7. Members of Congress 8. Statesmen -- United States
ISBN 0-7432-5506-2

LC 2003-54477

Written between 1771 and 1788

"Franklin's account of his life, written for his son William. . . . During the Revolutionary War, the manuscript was put aside. . . . Franklin later more than doubled the length . . . but still took the story only to 1757-1759, ending before the period of his greatest public service. Still, the book remains the first undisputed classic of American literature and one of the most interesting autobiographies in English." Benet's Reader's Ency of Am Lit

Isaacson, Walter. **Benjamin** Franklin; an American life. Simon & Schuster 2003 590p il $30; pa $16.95 **92**
1. Authors 2. Diplomats 3. Inventors 4. Statesmen 5. Scientists 6. Writers on science 7. Members of Congress 8. Statesmen -- United States
ISBN 0-684-80761-0; 0-7432-5807-X pa

LC 2003-50463

This "is a thoroughly researched, crisply written, convincingly argued chronicle that is also studded with little nuggets of fresh informa-

tion." N Y Times Book Rev
Includes bibliographical references

★ Lepore, Jill. **Book** of ages; the life and opinions of Jane Franklin. Jill Lepore. Alfred A. Knopf 2013 464 p. $27.95 **92**
1. Boston (Mass.) -- Biography 2. Women -- United States -- Social conditions -- 18th century
ISBN 0307958345; 9780307958341

LC 2013001012

National Book Awards: Nonfiction Finalist (2013)

This book on Jane Franklin Mecom by Jill Lepore tells "the story of Benjamin Franklin's youngest sister . . . using only a few of her letters and a small archive of births and deaths." (Kirkus Reviews) "Jane's surviving letters are . . . the correspondence of a smart, witty, hardworking woman who 'loved best books about ideas,' reveled in gossip, expressed 'impolite' opinions on religion and politics, and shared piquant observations of the struggle for American independence." (Booklist)

Includes bibliographical references

Franklin, Missy, 1995-

Paisner, Daniel. **Relentless** spirit; the unconventional raising of a champion. Missy Franklin and D.A. and Dick Franklin; with Daniel Paisner. Penguin Group USA 2016 320 p. illustrations (chiefly color) (ebook) $65; $27 **92**
1. Swimmers -- United States -- Biography 2. Women swimmers -- United States -- Biography
ISBN 9781101984932; 1101984929; 9781101984925

LC 2016046031

This book, by Missy Franklin and D.A. and Dick Franklin, with Daniel Paisner, tells "the story of how Missy became the athlete she is today, a six-time Olympic medalist, five of them gold. Since her Olympic debut in London's 2012 games—when Missy was just seventeen—people who have met the Franklins or seen them on TV have wondered what it was like to raise such a champion. What was the training like? How did Missy handle school?" (Publisher's note)

"A consistently sunny, family-oriented story of persistence and achievement." Kirkus

Franklin, Rosalind, 1920-1958

Maddox, Brenda. **Rosalind** Franklin: the dark lady of DNA. HarperCollins Pubs. 2002 380p il $29.95; pa $15.95 **92**
1. DNA 2. Chemists 3. Biologists 4. Geochemists
ISBN 0-06-018407-8; 0-06-098508-9 pa

LC 2002-68898

The author "does an excellent job of revisiting Franklin's scientific contributions . . . while revealing Franklin's complicated personality." Libr J

Includes bibliographical references

Franklin, William, 1731-1813

Epstein, Daniel Mark. The **loyal** son; the war in Ben Franklin's house. Daniel Mark Epstein. Ballantine Books 2017 xx, 438 p.p illustrations, maps (hardcover) $30 **92**
1. Statesmen -- United States -- Biography 2. American loyalists -- Biography 3. Governors -- New Jersey -- Biography 4. Statesmen's children -- United States -- Biography 5. United States -- Politics and government -- 1775-1783
ISBN 0345544218; 9780345544223; 9780345544216

LC 2017013553

This book, by Daniel Mark Epstein, tells the "complex and confounding relationship [of Benjamin Franklin] with his illegitimate son William. . . . He adopted the boy, raised him, and educated him to be his aide. Ben and William became inseparable. . . . The outbreak of the American Revolution caused a devastating split between father and son. By then, William was royal governor of New Jersey, while Ben was one of the foremost champions of American independence." (Publisher's note)

"A perceptive, gritty portrayal of the frenzy of war and a father and son caught at its tumultuous center." Kirkus

Includes bibliographical references and index.

Franzen, Jonathan

Franzen, Jonathan. The **discomfort** zone; a personal history. Farrar, Straus & Giroux 2006 195p $22   92
1. Authors 2. Novelists
ISBN 978-0-374-29919-4; 0-374-29919-6
                                                    LC 2006-2700

This is a memoir by the author of The Corrections.

"For those who admire the razor-sharp jabs Franzen makes at himself and anyone else standing too close, 'The Discomfort Zone' is both a delicious read and a clever showcase for Franzen's talents." Christ Sci Monit

Frazier, O. Howard

Swartz, Mimi. **Ticker**; the quest to create an artificial heart. Mimi Swartz. Crown 2018 320 p. (hardback) $27   92
1. Surgeons 2. Artificial heart 3. United States 4. Heart, Artificial
ISBN 9780804138000
                                                    LC 2017058910

This book on the quest to build an artificial heart, by Mimi Swartz, is "part investigative journalism, part medical mystery. . . . [It] is a dazzling story of modern innovation, recounting fifty years of false starts, abysmal failures and miraculous triumphs, as experienced by one of the world's foremost heart surgeons, O.H. 'Bud' Frazier, who has given his life to saving the un-savable." (Publisher's note)

"Told in an appropriately over-the-top style, this is a quintessentially Texas story: sprawling, unpredictable, and teeming with risk and opportunity." Publishers' Weekly

Includes bibliographical references and index

Frederick II, King of Prussia, 1712-1786

Blanning, Tim. **Frederick** the Great; king of Prussia. Tim Blanning. Random House Inc 2016 688 p. chiefly ill. (some col.), maps (acid-free paper) $35   92
1. Prussia -- Kings and rulers 2. Seven Years' War, 1756-1763 3. Enlightenment -- Germany -- Prussia 4. Prussia (Germany) -- Kings and rulers -- Biography 5. Prussia (Germany) -- Intellectual life -- 18th century 6. Prussia (Germany) -- History -- Frederick II, 1740-1786 7. Social change -- Germany -- Prussia -- History -- 18th century
ISBN 1400068126; 9781400068128
                                                    LC 2015030616

Author Tim Blanning presents this biography of Frederick the Great, "the legendary autocrat whose enlightened rule transformed the map of Europe and changed the course of history. In examining Frederick's private life, Blanning also carefully considers the long-debated question of Frederick's sexuality, finding evidence that Frederick lavished gifts on his male friends and maintained homosexual relationships throughout his life, while limiting contact with his estranged, unloved queen to visits that were few and far between." (Publisher's note)

"Readers both casual and scholarly will enjoy this profile for the in-depth examination of its subject, his placement in the historical events of the time, and his future in German history." LJ

Includes bibliographical references and index

Freeman, Judith, 1946-

Freeman, Judith. The **latter** days; a memoir. Judith Freeman. Pantheon 2016 336 p. illustrations (ebook) $65; (hardback) $28.95   92
1. Women authors 2. Church of Jesus Christ of Latter-day Saints 3. Ex-church members -- Mormon Church -- Biography 4. Women authors, American -- 20th century -- Biography
ISBN 9780307908629; 9780307908612
                                                    LC 2015042317

This memoir, by Judith Freeman, is "about the path the author took—sometimes unwittingly—out of her Mormon upbringing and through a thicket of profound difficulties to become a writer. At twenty-two, Judith Freeman was working in the Mormon church–owned department store in the Utah town where she'd grown up. In the process of divorcing the man she had married at seventeen, she was living in her parents' house with her four-year-old son, who had already endured two heart surgeries." (Publisher's note)

"This look at family and the choices we make, and how those choices present the opportunity for self-examination, emphasizes that it's never too late to alter the course of our lives. Recommended for anyone contemplating a big life change." LJ

Freud, Sigmund, 1856-1939

Gay, Peter. **Freud**; a life for our time. with a new foreword. Norton 2006 810p il pa $21.95   92
1. Psychoanalysts 2. Writers on medicine
ISBN 0-393-32861-9
                                                    LC 2006-283026
First published 1988

"The book is beautifully written. Gay's approach is to try to understand Freud and his alliances and environment rather than to worship or challenge him." Choice

Includes bibliographical references

★ Roudinesco, Élisabeth. **Freud**; In His Time and Ours. Élisabeth Roudinesco; translated by Catherine Porter. Harvard University Press 2016 592 p. (ebook) $43.97; $35   92
1. Psychoanalysis -- History 2. Psychoanalysts -- Austria -- Biography 3. Austria -- History -- 19th century 4. Austria -- History -- 20th century
ISBN 9780674974517; 9780674659568
                                                    LC 2016013065

This book, by Élisabeth Roudinesco, translated by Catherine Porter, "offers a bold and modern reinterpretation of the iconic founder of psychoanalysis. Based on new archival sources, this is [Sigmund] Freud's biography for the twenty-first century—a critical appraisal, at once sympathetic and impartial, of a genius greatly admired and yet greatly misunderstood in his own time and in ours." (Publisher's note)

"Though Roudinesco credits Freud with insights into individual psyches, she exposes his tardiness in recognizing the collective threat of fascism. A revealing portrait of a cultural revolutionary." Booklist

Includes bibliographical references and index

Friedan, Betty, 1921-2006

Friedan, Betty. **Life** so far. Simon & Schuster 2000 399p il hardcover o.p. pa $17   92
1. Authors 2. Feminism 3. Feminists 4. Nonfiction writers 5. Organization officials
ISBN 0-684-80789-0; 978-0-7432-9986-2 pa; 0-7432-9986-8 pa
                                                    LC 00-23920

In this memoir, "Friedan reminisces over a life of social activism that has included helping to found the National Organization for Women, the National Abortion and Reproductive Rights Action League, and the National Women's Political Caucus, as well as writing the pivotal The Feminine Mystique." Libr J

Friedman, Elizebeth, 1892-1980

Fagone, Jason. The **woman** who smashed codes; a true story of love, spies, and the unlikely heroine who outwitted America's enemies. Jason Fagone. HarperCollins 2017 xvi, 444 p.p (hardcover) $27.99   **92**

1. Ciphers 2. Women spies 3. Cryptography -- United States -- History 4. Cryptographers -- United States -- Biography
ISBN 9780062430502; 0062430483; 9780062430489

This book, by Jason Fagone, "chronicles the life of [Elizebeth Smith] . . . , who played an integral role in our nation's history. . . . After World War I, Smith used her talents to catch gangsters and smugglers during Prohibition, then accepted a . . . mission to discover and expose Nazi spy rings that were spreading . . . [in] South America, advancing . . . to the United States. As World War II raged, Elizebeth fought a . . . classified battle of wits against Hitler's Reich." (Publisher's note)

"Riveting, inspiring, and rich in colorful characters, Fagone's extensively researched and utterly dazzling title is popular history at its very best and a book club natural." Booklist

Fu, Ping, 1958-

Ping Fu. **Bend,** not break; a life in two worlds. Ping Fu with MeiMei Fox. Portfolio/Penguin 2013 288 p. $27.95 **92**

1. Resilience (Personality trait) 2. Geomagic (Firm) 3. Young women -- China -- Biography 4. Chinese American women -- Biography 5. Businesswomen -- United States -- Biography 6. Entrepreneurship -- United States -- Biography 7. Nanjing hang kong hang tian da xue -- Biography 8. Political refugees -- United States -- Biography 9. Women computer scientists -- United States -- Biography 10. China -- History -- Cultural Revolution, 1966-1976 -- Personal narratives
ISBN 1591845521; 9781591845522

LC 2012035389

This book, by Ping Fu with MeiMei Fox, is the autobiography of a Chinese immigrant. "Born on the eve of China's Cultural Revolution, Ping . . . grew up fighting hunger . . . and shielding her younger sister from the teenagers in Mao's Red Guard. At twenty-five, she found her way to the United States." This book "depicts a journey from . . . the dogmatic anticapitalism of Mao's China to the high-stakes, take-no-prisoners world of technology start-ups in the United States." (Publisher's note)

Fuller, Alexandra, 1969-

★ Fuller, Alexandra. **Don't** let's go to the dogs tonight; an African childhood. Random House 2002 301p il hardcover o.p. pa $13.95   **92**

1. Authors 2. Zimbabwe 3. Memoirists
ISBN 0-375-50750-7; 0-375-75899-2 pa

LC 2001-41752

"Fuller grew up in Rhodesia (now Zimbabwe) during the civil war, and she watched her parents fight against the local Africans to keep their farm. In a memoir powerful in its frank straightforwardness, she neither apologizes for nor champions her family's views and actions. Instead she gives us an honest, moving portrait of one family struggling to survive tumultuous times." Booklist

Followed by Cocktail hour under the tree of forgetfulness (2011)

Fuller, Alexandra, 1969- **Leaving** Before the Rains Come; Alexandra Fuller. Penguin Press 2015 258 p. map (hardcover)

$26.95   **92**

1. Divorced women 2. Africans -- United States 3. Women -- Biography 4. Zambia -- Biography 5. Wyoming -- Biography 6. Intercountry marriage 7. Zimbabwe -- Biography 8. Divorced women -- Biography
ISBN 1594205868; 9781594205866

LC 2014036654

This memoir tells how, "a child of the Rhodesian wars and daughter of two deeply complicated parents, [author] Alexandra Fuller is no stranger to pain. But the disintegration of Fuller's own marriage leaves her shattered. Looking to pick up the pieces of her life, she finally confronts the tough questions about her past, about the American man she married, and about the family she left behind in Africa." (Publisher's note)

"Although her batty and unhinged relatives emerge more vividly than her taciturn husband, Fuller's talent as a storyteller makes this memoir sing." Kirkus

Fuller, Margaret, 1810-1850

★ Marshall, Megan. **Margaret** Fuller; a new American life. Megan Marshall. Houghton Mifflin Harcourt 2013 496 p. illustrations (hardback) $30   **92**

1. Feminism 2. Women authors 3. Feminists -- United States -- Biography 4. Authors, American -- 19th century -- Biography
ISBN 0547195605; 9780547195605

LC 2012042179

Pulitzer Prize: Biography (2014)

This book, by Megan Marshall, presents a biography of American writer and intellectual Margaret Fuller. "Though organized around places Fuller lived, the book's real driving force is her relationships, from the perfectionist father who gave her a thirst for education early on to the circle of academics and radicals over whom Fuller exerted her influence, among them Ralph Waldo Emerson." (Publishers Weekly)

"A magnificent biography of a revolutionary thinker, witness, and writer." Booklist

Includes bibliographical references and index.

Matteson, John. The **lives** of Margaret Fuller; John Matteson. W. W. Norton & Co. 2012 384p.   **92**

1. Feminism 2. Women authors 3. Feminists -- United States -- Biography 4. Women authors, American -- 19th century -- Biography
ISBN 9780393068054

LC 2011040432

This book offers a biography of "writer and a fiery social critic, Margaret Fuller (1810–1850). . . . She became the leading female figure in the transcendentalist movement, wrote a celebrated column of literary and social commentary for Horace Greeley's newspaper, and served as the first foreign correspondent for an American newspaper. . . , In 1848 she joined the fight for Italian independence and, the following year, reported on the struggle." (Publisher's note)

Includes bibliographical references and index.

Galilei, Galileo, 1564-1642

Heilbron, J. L. **Galileo.** Oxford University Press 2010 508p il $34.95   **92**

1. Astronomers 2. Writers on science 3. Astronomy -- History 4. Biography, Individual 5. Italy -- Intellectual life 6. Science -- Italy -- History
ISBN 978-0-19-958352-2; 0-19-958352-8

This "will no doubt become the standard, comprehensive biography. . . . In one of his most inventive sections, [Heilbron] creates a Galilean dialogue on issues of algebra and geometry. Though not easy to read, it brilliantly expresses the ambiguities and blind alleys as Galileo wrestled with the conceptual difficulty of introducing a nongeometrical quantity—time itself— into the proportions." N Y Times Book Rev

Includes bibliographical references

Gandhi, Mahatma, 1869-1948

Gandhi, Mahatma. An **autobiography**; the story of my experiments with truth. translated from the original in Gujarati by Mahadev Desai; with a foreword by Sissela Bok. Beacon Press 1993 528p $10.95 **92**

ISBN 0-8070-5909-9

LC 93-19758

"In [Gandhi's] classic autobiography he recounts the story of his life and how he developed his concept of active nonviolent resistance, which propelled the Indian struggle for independence and countless other nonviolent struggles of the twentieth century." (Publisher's note)

Guha, Ramachandra, 1958- **Gandhi**; The Years That Changed the World. Ramachandra Guha. Random House Inc 2018 688 p. $40 **92**

1. Statesmen -- India -- Biography 2. Political activists -- Biography
ISBN 0385532318; 9780385532310

"The second and concluding volume of the magisterial biography . . . [by Ramachandra Guha] opens with Mohandas Gandhi's arrival in Bombay in January 1915 and takes us through his epic struggles over the next three decades: to deliver India from British rule, to forge harmonious relations between India's Hindu and Muslim populations, to end the pernicious Hindu practice of untouchability, and to develop India's economic and moral self-reliance." (Publisher's note)

★ Guha, Ramachandra, 1958- **Gandhi** before India; Ramachandra Guha. Alfred A. Knopf 2014 672 p. illustrations, maps $35 **92**

1. India -- History -- 20th century 2. Statesmen -- India -- Biography 3. South Africa -- Politics and government -- 1836-1909 4. East Indians -- South Africa -- Politics and government
ISBN 0385532296; 9780385532297

LC 2013025014

This biography "takes us from Mohandas Gandhi's birth in 1869 through his upbringing in Gujarat, his two years as a student in London, and his two decades as a lawyer and community organizer in South Africa." Author Ramachandra Guha "makes clear that Gandhi's work in South Africa--far from being a mere prelude to his accomplishments in India--was profoundly influential on his evolution as a political thinker, social reformer, and beloved leader." (Publisher's note)

"This first volume in a two-part biography of Gandhi from Guha . . . proves itself an essential work for its bold purpose, extensive research, and engaging prose." Pub Wkly

Includes bibliographical references and index

Lelyveld, Joseph. **Great** soul; Mahatma Gandhi and his struggle with India. Alfred A. Knopf 2011 425p il map $28.95; ebook $14.99 **92**

1. Authors 2. Journalists 3. Essayists 4. Pacifists 5. Memoirists 6. Political leaders 7. Statesmen -- India 8. Writers on politics 9. Biography, Individual 10. India -- Politics and government 11. India -- Politics and government -- 1919-1947
ISBN 978-0-307-26958-4; 978-0-307-59536-2 ebook

LC 2010-34252

"Mr. Lelyveld has restored human depth to the Mahatma, the plaster saint, allowing his flawed human readers to feel a little closer to his lofty ideals of nonviolence and universal brotherhood." N Y Times (Late N Y Ed)

Includes bibliographical references

Mohandas. **Gandhi**; the man, his people, and the empire. University of California Press 2008 xv, 738p il map $34.95 **92**

1. Authors 2. Journalists 3. Essayists 4. Pacifists 5. Memoirists 6. Political leaders 7. Writers on politics 8. India -- Politics and government
ISBN 978-0-520-25570-8; 0-520-25570-4

LC 2007-40986

First published 2006 in India with title: Mohandas: a true story of a man, his people, and an empire

The author exhibits a deep "understanding of the social and political landscape of India, of the cleavages of caste and religion, and of the dynamics of the dominant Congress Party (to which Gandhi had a lifelong allegiance). Rajmohan takes us at a leisurely pace through the broad sweep of Gandhi's personal and public life." Times Lit Suppl

Includes bibliographical references (p. 703-708)

García Márquez, Gabriel, 1928-

Garcia Marquez, Gabriel. **Living** to tell the tale; translated by Edith Grossman. Knopf 2003 483p maps $26.95; pa $14.95 **92**

1. Authors 2. Novelists 3. Journalists 4. Short story writers 5. Nobel laureates for literature
ISBN 1-4000-4134-1; 1-4000-3454-X pa

LC 2003-58924

"Garcia Márquez tells the entrancing story of his remarkable family, chronicles the turbulence of his troubled country, Colombia, and offers a piquant portrait of himself as a struggling young writer. A resplendent memoir written with compassion and artistry." Booklist

★ Martin, Gerald. **Gabriel** Garcia Marquez; a life. Alfred A. Knopf 2009 642p il map **92**

1. Authors 2. Novelists 3. Journalists 4. Authors, Colombian 5. Short story writers 6. Nobel laureates for literature
ISBN 978-0-307-27177-8

LC 200903806

First published 2008 in the United Kingdom

This is a biography of the Colombian novelist and author of One Hundred Years of Solitude (1967) and Love in the Time of Cholera (1985).

"This superbly researched biography is nothing short of a tour de force. . . . This work not only details the life of a great writer but also provides considerable insight into life in Latin America." Libr J

Includes bibliographical references

Garcia, Jerry

Jackson, Blair. **Garcia**; an American life. Viking 1999 497p hardcover o.p. $18 **92**

1. Singers 2. Guitarists 3. Rock musicians 4. Grateful Dead (Musical group)
ISBN 978-0-14-029199-5; 0-14-029199-7

LC 99-28775

"Jackson has written a wonderful account of the beginnings of the band . . . in the mid-1960's, their relationship with Ken Kesey and his Merry Pranksters, their embrace of psychedelic drugs and the adoration and obsession of Deadheads throughout the country." N Y Times Book Rev

Includes bibliographical references

Garcia, Mayte, 1973-

Garcia, Mayte. The **most** beautiful; my life with Prince. Mayte Garcia. Hachette Books 2017 294 p. illustrations (chiefly color) (hardcover) $27 **92**

1. Rock musicians -- United States -- Biography 2. Dancers -- United States -- Biography

ISBN 9780316468978; 9780316468992; 9780316468985

LC 2016054437

In this book, Mayte Garcia shares her love story with musician Prince. "[She] shares the deeply personal story of their relationship and offers a singular perspective on the music icon and their world together: from their unconventional meeting backstage at a concert . . . , to their fairy-tale wedding (and their groundbreaking artistic partnership), to the devastating losses that ultimately dissolved their romantic relationship for good." (Publisher's note)

"A genial, candid portrait of Prince's ill-fated turn as a family man." Kirkus

García Lorca, Federico, 1898-1936

Gibson, Ian. **Federico** Garcia Lorca: a life. Pantheon Bks. 1989 xxii, 551p il hardcover o.p. pa $18 **92**

1. Poets 2. Authors 3. Dramatists 4. Theatrical directors

ISBN 0-679-77401-7 pa

LC 88-28871

Loosely based on the two-volume Spanish work published 1985-1987

This is a biography of the Spanish writer who was assassinated during the Spanish Civil War

"Gibson's sense of place is equalled by his sense of person. His recreation of the teeming artistic talent and the café life of Spain in the 1930s is superb. So effective is Gibson's account of Lorca's vitality and fecundity that along with admiration for the poet's opulent talent, he provokes a fierce outrage at his ultimate fate." Times Lit Suppl

Includes bibliographical references

Gardner, Chris

Gardner, Chris. The **pursuit** of happyness; [by] Chris Gardner with Quincy Troupe and Mim Eichler Rivas. Amistad 2006 302p il map $25.95 **92**

1. Securities brokers

ISBN 978-0-06-074486-1; 0-06-074486-3

LC 2005-57203

The author "recounts his 'long walk to Wall Street,' a journey that took him from a childhood in the ghettos of Milwaukee to an enormously successful career as a stockbroker in New York city." Libr J

Garfunkel, Art

Garfunkel, Art, 1941- **What** is it all but luminous; notes from an underground man. Art Garfunkel. Alfred A. Knopf 2017 241 p. illustrations (chiefly color) (hardcover) $27.95 **92**

1. Singers -- United States -- Biography

ISBN 9780385352468; 9780385352475

LC 2016037296

In this memoir, author "Art Garfunkel writes about his life before, during, and after Simon & Garfunkel . . . about their folk-rock music in the roiling age that embraced and was defined by their pathbreaking sound. He writes about growing up in the 1940s and '50s. . . . [and] about their becoming Simon & Garfunkel, . . . ruling the pop charts from the time he was sixteen. . . . He writes of being an actor. . . .[,] about being a husband, a father and much more." (Publisher's note)

"Sensitive, soulful, sharp-tongued, and serious, Garfunkel vies for a place in the pantheon of singers." Booklist

Garner, Helen, 1942-

Garner, Helen. **Everywhere** I look; by Helen Garner. The Text Publishing Company 2016 229 p. (paperback) $16.95 **92**

1. Life 2. Authorship

ISBN 9781922253644; 9781925355369

LC 2015463935

This book, by Helen Garner, "is a book full of intuition, insight and humor. It takes us from backstage at the ballet to the trial of a woman for the murder of her newborn baby. It moves effortlessly from the significance of moving house to the pleasure of re-reading Pride and Prejudice." (Publisher's note)

"Garner, one of Australia's most acclaimed writers (This House of Grief), gives her fans a captivating collection of personal essays and diary entries." Pub Wkly

Garnett, Edward, 1868-1937

Smith, Helen. The **uncommon** reader; a life of Edward Garnett, mentor and editor of literary genius. Helen Smith. Farrar, Straus & Giroux 2017 440 p. illustrations (hardcover) $35 **92**

1. Critics 2. Editors 3. Authors -- Great Britain -- Biography 4. Critics -- Great Britain -- Biography 5. Book editors -- Great Britain -- Biography

ISBN 9780374717414; 9780374281120

LC 2017025507

This book, by Helen Smith, "brings to life . . . [the] intimate and at times stormy relationships [of English-language editor Edward Garnett] with . . . writers. . . . All turned to Garnett for advice and guidance at critical moments in their careers, and their letters and diaries--in which Garnett often features as a feared but deeply admired protagonist--tell us not only about their creative processes, but also about their hopes and fears." (Publisher's note)

"With Smith's fine sense of pacing and a fascinating subject, her book both delights and informs." Pub Wkly

Includes bibliographical references and index

Garrett, Pat F. (Pat Floyd), 1850-1908

Gardner, Mark L. **To** hell on a fast horse; Billy the Kid, Pat Garrett, and the epic chase to justice in the Old West. William Morrow 2010 325p il $26.99 **92**

1. Outlaws 2. Sheriffs

ISBN 978-0-06-136827-1; 0-06-136827-X

LC 2009025467

A "double biography of the iconic western outlaw Billy the Kid and Sheriff Pat Garrett. Maintaining an objective perspective on both men in a narrative closely tied to historic source materials, Gardner's quick-moving story follows events of the civil war in Lincoln County, New Mexico Territory in 1877–78, and the Kid's death-by-shooting at the hands of Garrett in 1881. . . . The final chapters describing Garrett as an old-style lawman in a postfrontier society, with interactions with President Theodore Roosevelt, serve to distinguish this book from other recent Kid biographies." Libr J

Includes bibligraphical references

Gates, Henry Louis

Gates, Henry Louis. **Colored** people; a memoir. [by] Henry Louis Gates, Jr. Knopf 1994 216p hardcover o.p. pa $13 **92**

1. Authors 2. Philologists 3. College teachers 4. Literary critics 5. Social scientists 6. Nonfiction writers

ISBN 0-679-73919-X pa

LC 93-12256

"As Gates traces his evolution from 'Negro' to Afro-wearing 'black,' he also traces the evolution of Piedmont (and, by extension, of much of America) at a time when the relationship between the races was being redefined." Newsweek

Gates, Robert Michael, 1943-

Gates, Robert Michael, 1943- A **passion** for leadership; lessons on change and reform from fifty years of public service. Robert M. Gates. Alfred A. Knopf 2016 256 p. $27.95 **92**

1. Leadership 2. Civil service 3. Leadership -- United States 4. Organizational change -- United States 5. United States -- Politics and government 6. Texas A & M University System -- Biography 7. Cabinet officers -- United States -- Biography 8. Public administration -- United States -- Anecdotes 9. Administrative agencies -- United States -- Reorganization 10. United States. Department of Defense -- Officials and employees -- Biography 11. United States. Central Intelligence Agency -- Officials and employees -- Biography

ISBN 030795949X; 9780307959492

LC 2015010209

Author Robert Gates presents this "assessment of why big institutions are failing us and how smart, committed leadership can effect real improvement regardless of scale. He offers us the ultimate insider's look at how major bureaus, organizations, and companies can be transformed, which is by turns heartening and inspiring and always instructive." (Publisher's note)

"Solid advice that should be passed on to leaders at any season of life and particularly helpful to those new to such responsibility." Library Journal

Gaulle, Charles de, 1890-1970

Jackson, Julian. **De** Gaulle; Julian Jackson. The Belknap Press of Harvard University Press 2018 928 p. $39.95 **92**

1. Generals 2. France -- Politics and government 3. Generals -- France -- Biography 4. Presidents -- France -- Biography 5. France -- Politics and government -- 20th century

ISBN 0674987217; 9780674987210

LC 2018015618

In this biography of French general and statesman Charles de Gaulle, author Julian Jackson, "reveals the conservative roots of de Gaulle's intellectual formation, sheds new light on his relationship with [Winston] Churchill, and shows how he confronted riots at home and violent independence movements from the Middle East to Vietnam." (Publisher's note)

"A long but excellent, highly useful addition to the library of modern European history as well as the political history of World War II and the Cold War." Kirkus

Includes bibliographical references and index

Gay, Roxane

★ Gay, Roxane, 1974- **Hunger**; a memoir of (my) body. Roxane Gay. HarperCollins 2017 320 p. hardcover $25.99; paperback $16.99 **92**

1. Body image 2. Eating disorders

ISBN 9780062362599; 9780062420718; 9780062362605; 0062362593

National Book Critics Circle Award Finalist: Autobiography (2017)

This book, by Roxane Gay, offers "a searingly honest memoir of food, weight, self-image, and learning how to feed your hunger while taking care of yourself. . . . She casts an insightful and critical eye on her childhood, teens, and twenties--including the devastating act of violence that acted as a turning point in her young life--and brings readers into the present and the realities, pains, and joys of her daily life." (Publisher's note)

"In 88 short, lucid chapters, Gay powerfully takes readers through realities that pain her, vex her, guide her, and inform her work." Booklist

Geddes, Norman Bel, 1893-1958

Szerlip, B. Alexandra. The **man** who designed the future; Norman Bel Geddes and the invention of twentieth-century America. B. Alexandra Szerlip. Melville House 2017 xvii, 396 p.p illustrations (hardcover) $28.99 **92**

1. Industrial design 2. Designers -- United States -- Biography 3. Design -- United States -- History -- 20th century

ISBN 9781612195551; 9781612195629

LC 2016050576

This book, by B. Alexandra Szerlip, "reveals precisely how central Bel Geddes was to the history of American innovation. He presided over a moment in which theater became immersive, function merged with form, and people became consumers. A polymath with humble Midwestern origins, Bel Geddes' visionary career would launch him into social circles with the Algonquin roundtable members, stars of stage and screen, and titans of industry." (Publisher's note)

"In this fascinating and minutely researched biography, Szerlip brings the brilliant, indefatigable industrial designer's imagination to life so we can marvel once more." Booklist

Includes bibliographical references (pages 386-387) and index.

Gehrig, Lou, 1903-1941

Robinson, Ray. **Iron** horse: Lou Gehrig in his time. Norton 1990 300p il pa $14.95 **92**

1. Baseball players 2. Baseball -- Biography

ISBN 978-0-393-32882-0 pa; 0-393-32882-1 pa

LC 89-29272

"Playing in the considerable shadow of Babe Ruth, Lou Gehrig's accomplishments as baseball's 'Iron Horse' include a legendary record of 2,130 consecutive games played. . . . Robinson's narrative not only traces Gehrig's life and career but also provides an insightful look at baseball in the 1920s and the Depression years." Libr J

Gehry, Frank O., 1929-

Goldberger, Paul. **Building** art; the life and work of Frank Gehry. by Paul Goldberger. Alfred A. Knopf 2015 528 p. 8 plates; illustrations (hardback) $35 **92**

1. Architecture -- United States 2. Architects -- United States -- Biography

ISBN 0307701530; 9780307701534

LC 2015026562

This book, by Paul Goldberger, is "an engaging, nuanced exploration of the life and work of Frank Gehry, undoubtedly the most famous architect of our time. This . . . critical biography presents and evaluates the work of a man who has almost single-handedly transformed contemporary architecture in his innovative use of materials, design, and form, and who is among the very few architects in history to be both respected by critics . . . and embraced by the general public." (Publisher's note)

"With avid precision and invaluable insight, Goldberger charts the complicated, punishing battles Gehry waged to construct his ambitious, dreamworld buildings, from private homes to Guggenheim Bilbao, the Walt Disney Concert Hall, Facebook headquarters, and beyond. The result is an involving work of significant architectural history and a discerning and affecting portrait of a daring and original master builder." Booklist

Isenberg, Barbara. **Conversations** with Frank Gehry. Alfred A. Knopf 2009 290p il map $40 **92**

1. Architects
ISBN 978-0-307-26800-6; 0-307-26800-4

LC 2008-47616

This book "brings together in one book a series of candid interviews that the accomplished Isenberg recorded between 2004 and 2008, embracing Gehry's entire life and career, comprising a kind of verbal autobiography. . . . This very accessible, readable volume will be a gold mine for scholars and the general public for generations." Libr J

Gelb, Arthur, 1924-

Gelb, Arthur. **City** room. Putnam 2003 664p $29.95; pa $17.95   **92**

1. Newspaper editors 2. New York Times Company
ISBN 0-399-15075-7; 0-425-19831-6 pa

LC 2003-43154

This is a "memoir of life at The New York Times by one who spent nearly 50 years there, rising from copy boy to managing editor; {the author} has the power to evoke whole generations of change in the news business, reaching back to the glorious postwar years of manual typewriters, chain smokers, and all-nighters." N Y Times Book Rev

Genghis Khan, 1162-1227

Weatherford, J. McIver. **Genghis** Khan and the making of the modern world; [by] Jack Weatherford. Crown 2004 320p   **92**

ISBN 0-609-61062-7

LC 2003-20659

"When the Mongols, led by Genghis Khan, exploded out of the central Asian steppes in the early thirteenth century, they began the acquisition of the largest land empire in history. Eventually, the Mongol Empire extended from the Pacific to the Mediterranean and from northern Siberia to Southeast Asia. Yet the West focuses primarily on Mongol savagery. In his revisionist history of the empire, anthropology professor Weatherford uses the so-called Secret History, a long-suppressed Mongol text, to balance the scales." (Booklist)

George III, King of Great Britain, 1738-1820

Hadlow, Janice. A **royal** experiment; the private life of King George III. Janice Hadlow. Henry Holt & Co 2014 704 p. 16 plates; ills.; gen. table (hardback) $40   **92**

1. Great Britain -- Kings and rulers 2. Great Britain -- Kings and rulers -- Biography 3. Great Britain -- History -- George III, 1760-1820
ISBN 0805096566; 9780805096569; 9780805096576

LC 2014024707

In this book, author Janice Hadlow examines the "story of King George III's radical pursuit of happiness in his private life with Queen Charlotte and their 15 children. Against his irresistibly awful family background--of brutal royal intrigue, infidelity, and betrayal--George fervently pursued a radical domestic dream: he would have a faithful marriage and raise loving, educated, and resilient children." (Publisher's note)

"Extended forays into the king's periods of madness, which began in 1788 and finally incapacitated him for good in 1811, also diffuse the narrative focus. Unconvincing as revisionist history but enjoyable for its vivid depiction of several varieties of royal lifestyles - and plenty of royal gossip." Kirkus

Includes bibliographical references and index

Georges, Nicole J.

Georges, Nicole J. **Calling** Dr. Laura; a graphic memoir. Nicole J. Georges. Houghton Mifflin Harcourt 2013 260 p. illustrations pbk $16.95   **92**

1. Lesbians' writings 2. Autobiographical graphic novels 3. Family secrets -- Comic books, strips, etc 4. Identity (Psychology) -- Comic books, strips, etc
ISBN 0547615590; 9780547615592

LC 2012022389

Lambda Award: Graphic Novel (2014)

This graphic novel by Nicole J. Georges tells how when she "was two years old, her family told her that her father was dead. When she was twenty-three, a psychic told her he was alive. Her sister, saddled with guilt, admits that the psychic is right and that the whole family has conspired to keep him a secret. Sent into a tailspin about her identity, Nicole turns to radio talk-show host Dr. Laura Schlessinger for advice." (Publisher's note)

"Georges' quirky, big-faced, and evocative drawings, tempered by a variety of panel sizes, show the bespectacled author as she comes to terms with her mother's lies to her as a child about her father being dead. . . . An excellent graphic memoir offering engaging insights for those who share--or don't share00any of Georges' worries and traits." Booklist

Gerald, Casey

Gerald, Casey. **There** will be no miracles here; a memoir. Casey Gerald. Riverhead Books 2018 400 p. $27   **92**

1. American dream 2. Race discrimination
ISBN 0735214204; 9780735214200

In this memoir, Casey Gerald "pulls no punches in telling his extraordinary story, which he relates with unsparing truth, no small amount of feeling, and a complete lack of sentimentality. Painful lessons dart in and pummel his unsuspecting self, and scenes of startling intensity are often pierced--and pieced back together--by light and humor Richly layered writing on poverty, progress, race, belief, and the actual American Dream." (Booklist)

"Hardly a by-the-numbers memoir, this is a powerful book marked by the author's refreshingly complicated and insightful storytelling." Kirkus Reviews

Geronimo, 1829-1909

★ Utley, Robert Marshall, 1929- **Geronimo**; Robert M. Utley. Yale University Press 2012 348 p. (clothbound: alk. paper) $30   **92**

1. Apache Indians -- History 2. Apache Indians -- Wars, 1883-1886 3. Apache Indians -- Kings and rulers -- Biography
ISBN 9780300126389; 0300126387

LC 2012019521

This book by Robert M. Utley is a biography of "the Apache fighter Geronimo. . . . Utley unfolds the story through the alternating perspectives of whites and Apaches. . . . What it was like to be an Apache fighter-in-training, why Indians as well as whites feared Geronimo, how Geronimo maintained his freedom, and why he finally surrendered--the answers to these questions and many more fill the pages of this . . . volume." (Publisher's note)

Includes bibliographical references and index

Gershwin, George, 1898-1937

Feinstein, Michael, 1956- The **Gershwins** and me; a personal history in twelve songs. by Michael Feinstein with Ian Jackman. Simon & Schuster 2012 351 p. illustrations (some color) (hc: alk. paper) $45   **92**

1. Popular music -- Writing and publishing -- United States
ISBN 1451645309; 9781451645309; 9781451645316; 9781451645323; 9781451645330

LC 2012006833

Here, author Michael Feinstein "begins with a swift account of how he met Ira Gershwin, the lyricist of the celebrated duo, and how he subsequently went to work for him for six years. . . . Although he tells the Gershwins' stories, childhood to grave, he also . . . discusses the Gershwins' love lives, the significant performers of their work (from Fred Astaire to Ethel Merman), their successes and flops, their experiences in Hollywood and the devastation of George's shocking death at 38 (brain tumor)." (Kirkus)

Includes bibliographical references and index

Hyland, William G. **George** Gershwin; a new biography. Praeger Pubs. 2003 312p il $39.95   **92**

1. Composers
ISBN 0-275-98111-8

LC 2003-46303

"This fresh and well-researched biography of one of America's great composers is highly recommended for all libraries." Libr J

Includes bibliographical references

★ Pollack, Howard. **George** Gershwin; his life and work. University of California Press 2006 884p il $39.95   **92**

1. Composers
ISBN 978-0-520-24864-9; 0-520-24864-3

LC 2006-17926

"This engaging biography is also a tour de force of scholarship." Booklist

Includes bibliographical references

Gershwin, Ira, 1896-1983

Feinstein, Michael, 1956- The **Gershwins** and me; a personal history in twelve songs. by Michael Feinstein with Ian Jackman. Simon & Schuster 2012 351 p. illustrations (some color) (hc: alk. paper) $45   **92**

1. Popular music -- Writing and publishing -- United States
ISBN 1451645309; 9781451645309; 9781451645316; 9781451645323; 9781451645330

LC 2012006833

Here, author Michael Feinstein "begins with a swift account of how he met Ira Gershwin, the lyricist of the celebrated duo, and how he subsequently went to work for him for six years. . . . Although he tells the Gershwins' stories, childhood to grave, he also . . . discusses the Gershwins' love lives, the significant performers of their work (from Fred Astaire to Ethel Merman), their successes and flops, their experiences in Hollywood and the devastation of George's shocking death at 38 (brain tumor)." (Kirkus)

Includes bibliographical references and index

Gessner, David, 1961-

Gessner, David. **Ultimate** glory; Frisbee, obsession, and my wild youth. David Gessner. Riverhead Books 2017 xii, 338 p.p illustrations (paperback) $16   **92**

1. Autobiographies 2. Sports -- Biography 3. Athletes -- Biography 4. Ultimate (Game)
ISBN 9780735210561; 9780735210578

LC 2016048991

In this memoir, author David Gessner describes how he "devoted his twenties to a cultish sport called Ultimate Frisbee. . . . His only goal: to win Nationals and go down in Ultimate history as one of the greatest athletes no one has ever heard of. With humor and raw honesty, Gessner explores what it means to devote one's life to something that many consider ridiculous." (Publisher's note)

"An anecdotal tour of a sport that has only been around for a few decades but that claims legions of adherents." Kirkus

Gettleman, Jeffrey, 1971-

Gettleman, Jeffrey. **Love,** Africa; A Memoir of Romance, War, and Survival. Jeffrey Gettleman. HarperCollins 2017 325 p. (hardcover) $27.99   **92**

1. Love 2. Journalists -- Biography 3. Africa -- Description and travel 4. War correspondents -- United States -- Biography
ISBN 9780062284112; 9780062284099; 0062284096

This book, by Jeffrey Gettleman, is a "story about finding love and finding a calling, set against one of the most turbulent regions in the world. . . . At nineteen, Gettleman fell in love, twice. On a do-it-yourself community service trip in college, he went to East Africa—a terrifying, exciting, dreamlike part of the world in the throes of change that imprinted itself on his imagination and on his heart. But around that same time he also fell in love with a fellow Cornell student." (Publisher's note)

"A stark, eye-opening, and sometimes-horrifying portrait by a reporter enthralled by the 'power and magic' of Africa." Kirkus

Gevisser, Mark

Gevisser, Mark. **Lost** and Found in Johannesburg, a memoir; Lost and Found in Johannesburg, a memoir. Mark Gevisser. Farrar, Straus & Giroux 2014 328 p. illustrations, maps (hardback) $27   **92**

1. Africa -- Social conditions 2. South Africa -- Race relations 3. Johannesburg (South Africa) -- Biography 4. Authors, South African -- 20th century -- Biography
ISBN 0374176760; 9780374176761

LC 2013033018

In this memoir Mark Gevisser "remembers his privileged childhood in a walled white world. Then, in the mid-1990s, visiting Johannesburg . . . Gevisser is held hostage at gunpoint, bound and gagged with two women friends when three brutal robbers break into their home. Is his assailant a prisoner from the apartheid war? The honest blend of sympathy and fury drives the story: his guilt now about his privilege, but also relief and sadness." (Booklist)

"With lots of photos that show the people and places, including the mountains of yellow mine dumps from Jo'burg's gold, this is a must for those who want to experience the personal reality of apartheid and its aftermath." Booklist

Includes bibliographical references

Gidla, Sujatha, 1963-

Gidla, Sujatha. **Ants** among elephants; an untouchable family and the making of modern India. Sujatha Gidla. Farrar, Straus & Giroux 2017 306 p. (hardcover) $28   **92**

1. Caste 2. India 3. Poets -- India -- Biography 4. Dalits -- India -- Biography 5. Kakinada (India) -- Biography 6. Families -- India -- Biography 7. Teachers -- India -- Biography 8. India -- Social conditions -- 1947- 9. Revolutionaries -- India -- Biography 10. Caste -- India -- History -- 20th century
ISBN 9780374711382; 9780865478114

LC 2016052857

This book, by Sujatha Gidla, is the "true story of an untouchable family. . . . Like one in six people in India, Sujatha Gidla was born an untouchable. While most untouchables are illiterate, her family was educated by Canadian missionaries in the 1930s, making it possible for Gidla to attend elite schools and move to America at the age of twenty-six. It was only then that she saw how extraordinary—and yet how typical—her family history truly was." (Publisher's note)

"Gidla writes about the heavy topics of poverty, caste and gender inequality, and political corruption with grace and wit . . . an essential contribution to contemporary Indian literature." Pub Wkly

Gilbert, Elizabeth, 1969-

Gilbert, Elizabeth, 1969- **Eat,** pray, love; one woman's search for everything across Italy, India and Indonesia. Viking 2006 334p $24.95   **92**
 1. Authors 2. Novelists 3. Journalists 4. Short story writers 5. Biography, Individual
 ISBN 0-670-03471-1

LC 2005-42435

"In order to give herself the time and space to find out who she really was and what she really wanted, [the author] got rid of her belongings, quit her job, and undertook a yearlong journey around the world—all alone. Eat, Pray, Love is the . . . chronicle of that year." (Publisher's note)

"A probing, thoughtful title with a free and easy style, this work seamlessly blends history and travel for a very enjoyable read." Libr J

Gill, A. A., 1954-2016

Gill, A. A. (Adrian Anthony), 1954-2016. **Pour** me a life; A.A. Gill. Blue Rider Press 2016 268 p. (hardback) $26 **92**
 1. Alcoholics -- Great Britain -- Biography 2. Journalists -- Great Britain -- Biography
 ISBN 9780399574931; 9780399574917

LC 2016026427

This book, by A.A. Gill, "is a riveting memoir of the author's alcoholism, seen through the lens of the memories that remain, and the transformative moments in art, food, religion, and family that saved him from a lifelong addiction and early death. . . . When Gill was confronted at age thirty by a doctor who questioned his drinking, he answered honestly for the first time, not because he was ready to stop, but because his body was too damaged to live much longer." (Publisher's note)

"A wry and frank report on overcoming addiction." Booklist

Ginsberg, Allen, 1926-1997

Ginsberg, Allen. The **letters** of Allen Ginsberg; edited by Bill Morgan. DaCapo Press 2008 468p $30   **92**
 1. Poets 2. Authors 3. Poets, American
 ISBN 978-0-30681-463-1; 0-30681-463-3

LC 2008-11054

"Morgan, Ginsberg's biographer (I Celebrate Myself) and archivist, studied 3700 letters left behind by the poet, selecting 165 of the most significant for this edition; over 125 appear here for the first time. Always intelligent, sometimes gossipy, and occasionally cranky and impatient, Ginsberg is accurately reflected in these letters taken together. Correspondents include Ginsberg's father, Louis, and brother, Eugene; the poet's longtime companion, Peter Orlovsky; fellow Beat writers Jack Kerouac, William Burroughs, and Gregory Corso; and a host of friends and acquaintances." Libr J

Includes bibliographical references

Morgan, Bill. **I** celebrate myself; the somewhat private life of Allen Ginsberg. Viking 2006 702p il $29.95   **92**
 1. Poets 2. Authors 3. Beat generation
 ISBN 0-670-03796-6

LC 2006-50045

"Relying heavily on Ginsberg's journals and letters, as well as interviews with close friends, [Morgan] creates here a detailed, revealing portrait of Ginsberg as a gifted poet and flawed human being driven by a fierce hunger for love and an insatiable thirst for fame. This most exhaustive biography to date chronicles Ginsberg's life from cradle to grave, but a major theme is Ginsberg's love life especially his relationship with Peter Orlovsky. Although he became an icon for gay libera-

tion, Ginsberg tended to fall in love with straight men like Jack Kerouac, Neal Cassady, and Orlovsky, which, of course, led to a good deal of rejection and frustration. Morgan's is the first life of Ginsberg to explore this curious paradox in any depth. Cleverly designed, his book includes marginal references to the poems Ginsberg was working on at the time. A monumental work." Libr J

Ginsburg, Ruth Bader

Carmon, Irin. **Notorious** RBG; the life and times of Ruth Bader Ginsburg. Irin Carmon and Shana Knizhnik. Dey Street Books, An Imprint of William Morrow Publishers 2015 227 p. illustrations (some color) (ebook) $21.99; $22.99   **92**
 1. Judges -- Biography 2. Judges -- United States -- Biography
 ISBN 9780062415820; 0062415824; 0062415832; 0062425714; 0062425730; 9780062415837

LC 2015027547

Amelia Bloomer Project 2016

Written by Irin Carmon and Shana Knizhnik, "'Notorious RBG,' inspired by the Tumblr that amused the Justice herself and brought to you by its founder and an award-winning feminist journalist, is more than just a love letter. It draws on intimate access to Ginsburg's family members, close friends, colleagues, and clerks, as well an interview with the Justice herself." (Publisher's note)

"The brief, cogent excerpts from her court opinions are annotated in plain language by prominent legal academics. Moreover, the authors successfully situate RBG's work within a larger historical context, thereby illustrating her central role in advancing equal rights for all." LJ

Includes bibliographical references and index

★ De Hart, Jane Sherron. **Ruth** Bader Ginsburg; a life. Jane Sherron de Hart. Knopf 2018 768 p. (hardback) $35 **92**
 1. Women judges -- United States 2. United States. Supreme Court -- Officials and employees 3. Judges -- United States -- Biography 4. Women judges -- United States -- Biography
 ISBN 9781400040483

LC 2018004415

This book, by Jane Sherron De Hart, is "the first full life--private, public, legal, philosophical--of the 107th Supreme Court Justice, one of the most profound and profoundly transformative legal minds of our time; a book fifteen years in work, written with the cooperation of Ruth Bader Ginsburg herself and based on many interviews with the justice, her husband, her children, her friends, and her associates." (Publisher's note)

"This extensively documented account, incorporating more than 100 pages of chapter notes and a bibliography that cites hundreds of resources, is also quite engaging and very easy to read." Booklist

Includes bibliographical references and index

★ Ginsburg, Ruth Bader, 1933- **My** own words; Ruth Bader Ginsburg with Mary Hartnett with Wendy W. Williams. Simon & Schuster 2016 400 p. illustrations (hardback) $30; (ebook) $20.99   **92**
 1. Women judges 2. Women lawyers 3. United States. Supreme Court. -- Biography 4. Women judges -- United States -- Biography 5. Women lawyers -- United States -- Biography
 ISBN 9781501145247; 9781501145254; 9781501145261

LC 2016031635

This book, by Ruth Bader Ginsburg, with Mary Hartnett and Wendy Williams, presents a "collection of writings and speeches from the woman who has had a powerful and enduring influence on law, women's rights, and popular culture. . . . offers Justice Ginsburg on wide-ranging topics, including gender equality, the workways of the Supreme Court, being Jewish, law and lawyers in opera, and the value of looking beyond

US shores when interpreting the US Constitution." (Publisher's Note)

"The variety of subjects is impressive, and Ginsburg's gift for concision enables her to discuss them in enough detail to engage interest while leaving the reader wanting more." Pub Wkly

Includes bibliographical references and index

Gionfriddo, Tim

Gionfriddo, Paul. **Losing** Tim; How our health and education systems failed my son with schizophrenia. Paul Gionfriddo. Columbia University Press 2014 264 p. (cloth: alk. paper) $24.95 **92**

1. Schizophrenia 2. Education -- United States 3. Mental health services -- United States 4. Mental health policy -- United States 5. Schizophrenia in children -- Patients -- United States -- Biography
ISBN 9780231168281

LC 2014008507

This book, by Paul Gionfriddo, "describes how [the author's son] Tim and others like him come to live on the street. Gionfriddo takes stock of the numerous injustices that kept his son from realizing his potential from the time Tim first began to show symptoms of schizophrenia to the inadequate educational supports he received growing up, . . . and his frequent encounters with the . . . criminal-justice system and its substandard mental health care." (Publisher's note)

Includes bibliographical references

Giraldi, William

Giraldi, William. The **Hero's** Body; A Memoir. by William Giraldi. Liveright Pub Corp 2016 288 p. illustrations, portraits $25.95 **92**

1. Death 2. Masculinity 3. Father-son relationship
ISBN 0871406667; 9780871406668

This book, by William Giraldi, is a "memoir of motorcycles and muscles, of obsession and grief, and of a young man who learned how to stay alive through literature. At just forty-seven years old, William Giraldi's father was killed in a horrific motorcycle crash while racing on a country road. . . . Giraldi writes . . . about the fragility and might of the American male." (Publisher's note)

"A hearty, bittersweet familial chronicle of masculinity drawing on the underappreciated bond between fathers and sons." Kirkus

Gisleson, Anne

Gisleson, Anne. The **futilitarians**; our year of thinking, drinking, grieving, and reading. Anne Gisleson. Little, Brown & Co. 2017 260 p. (hardcover) $27 **92**

1. Books and reading 2. Book clubs (Discussion groups) 3. Grief -- Biography 4. Loss (Psychology) -- Biography 5. New Orleans (La.) -- Biography 6. Books and reading -- Social aspects 7. Books and reading -- Psychological aspects 8. Book clubs (Discussion groups) -- Louisiana -- New Orleans
ISBN 9780316501279; 9780316393904

LC 2017932689

This memoir, by Anne Gisleson, is about "friendship and literature chronicling a search for meaning and comfort in great books, and a beautiful path out of grief. . . . Anne and Brad, in the midst of forging their happiness, found that their friends had been suffering their own losses and crises as well. . . . Together these resilient New Orleanians formed what they called the Existential Crisis Reading Group, jokingly dubbed 'The Futilitarians.'" (Publisher's note)

"A graceful narrative that seamlessly interweaves philosophical reflections and intimate revelations." Kirkus

Includes bibliographical references (pages 257-260).

Giuliani, Rudolph W.

Siegel, Frederick F. The **prince** of the city; Giuliani, New York, and the genius of American life. [by] Fred Siegel, with Harry Siegel. Encounter Books 2005 386p $26.95 **92**

1. Mayors 2. Lawyers 3. District attorneys 4. Presidential candidates 5. New York (N.Y.) -- Politics and government
ISBN 1-594-03084-7

LC 2005-40127

This is a "narrative of Giuliani's eight years (1994-2001) as New York's chief elected executive. The account engagingly portrays how Giuliani made things happen, ranging from Giuliani the man to Giuliani the politician to Giuliani the policy innovator." Choice

Includes bibliographical references

Glass, Philip

Glass, Philip, 1937- **Words** Without Music; A Memoir. W W Norton & Co Inc 2015 288 p. illustrations $29.95 **92**

1. Composers -- Biography 2. Musicians -- Biography
ISBN 0871404389; 9780871404381

LC 2015000421

"In this episodic narrative of intellectual and artistic development, famed American composer [Philip] Glass describes his involvement in the avant-garde music and art scenes in New York in the 1950s through the 1980s. . . . He recounts touring the Indian subcontinent in search of a guru and eventually winning fame for repetitive compositions like 'Einstein on the Beach' and 'Koyaanisqatsi,' which delighted some listeners and enraged others." (Publishers Weekly)

"Aspiring musicians and artists will learn much from Glass, as will general readers, musical or not, who will discover an artistic life exceptionally well lived." Booklist

Goddard, Robert Hutchings, 1882-1945

★ Clary, David A. **Rocket** man; Robert H. Goddard and the birth of the space age. Hyperion 2003 324p il $24.95 **92**

1. Rocketry 2. Physicists 3. Aerospace engineers 4. Aeronautical engineers
ISBN 0-7868-6817-1

LC 2002-27321

In this biography Goddard emerges "as a paradoxical man who relentlessly promoted his work, winning hundreds of thousands of dollars in Guggenheim grants, while shunning offers to collaborate with other scientists. Clary presents a clear and relatively straightforward narrative of his subject's life. . . . Readers who come to this generally well-written biography with some knowledge of Goddard's significance will find much of interest to fill out their knowledge of this complex and fascinating scientist for whom NASA's Goddard Space Center is named." Publ Wkly

Includes bibliographical references

Gödel, Kurt

Goldstein, Rebecca. **Incompleteness**; the proof and paradox of Kurt Godel. Rebecca Goldstein. W.W. Norton 2005 296p il (Great discoveries) $22.95 **92**

1. Mathematicians
ISBN 0-393-05169-2

LC 2004-23052

This "is a stimulating exploration of both the power and the limitations of the human intellect." Publ Wkly

Includes bibliographical references

Goebbels, Joseph, 1897-1945

Longerich, Peter. **Goebbels**; a biography. Peter Longerich;

translated by Alan Bance, Jeremy Noakes and Lesley Sharpe. Random House 2014 1024 p. illustrations (hardback) $40 **92**
1. National socialism -- History 2. Germany -- History -- 1933-1945 3. World War, 1939-1945 -- Germany 4. National socialism 5. Nazis -- Biography 6. Germany -- History -- 1918-1933
ISBN 1400067510; 9781400067510

LC 2014004828

This biography, by historian Peter Longerich, focuses on "Joseph Goebbels . . . one of Adolf Hitler's most loyal acolytes. . . . [It] documents Goebbels's ascent through the ranks of the Nazi Party, where he became a member of the Führer's inner circle and launched a brutal campaign of anti-Semitic propaganda. Though endowed with near-dictatorial control of the media . . . Goebbels is a man dogged by insecurities and beset by bureaucratic infighting." (Publisher's note)

"As Longerich acknowledges, his reliance on Goebbels' diaries as a primary source is problematic, since Goebbels' accounts of events and personalities seem designed to impress himself. Still Longerich's efforts to glean the truth from exaggerations and distortions are credible, and this is an outstanding contribution to our understanding of the Nazi regime." Booklist

Includes bibliographical references and index

Goethe, Johann Wolfgang von, 1749-1832

Armstrong, John. **Love,** life, Goethe; lessons of the imagination from the great German poet. 1st American ed.; Farrar, Straus and Giroux 2007 482p il $30   **92**
1. Poets 2. Authors 3. Novelists 4. Dramatists 5. Essayists 6. Nonfiction writers 7. Writers on science
ISBN 978-0-374-29968-2; 0-374-29968-4

LC 2006-34072

First published 2006 in the United Kingdom

"Armstrong's thoughtful analysis of Goethe's life and works enables readers to fully appreciate the great German poet as an eminently human genius striving for growth and wholeness." Booklist

Includes bibliographical references

Safranski, Rudiger, 1945- **Goethe**; life as a work of art. Rüdiger Safranski; translated by David Dollenmayer. Liveright Publishing Corporation 2017 xxvi, 651 p.p (hardcover) $35   **92**
1. Authors, German
ISBN 9780871404916; 9780871404909; 0871404907

LC 2017008798

This book, by Rüdiger Safranski, translated by David Dollenmayer, is a "biography of . . . Johann Wolfgang von Goethe. . . . No other writer . . . [has] captivated the intellectual life of late eighteenth- and early nineteenth-century Europe. . . . Drawing upon the trove of letters, diaries, and notebooks Goethe left behind, . . . Safranski weaves a rich tale of Europe in the throes of revolution and of the man whose ideas heralded a new era." (Publisher's note)

"Scholars will welcome this intellectual biography, richly embellished by primary sources and aided by the strong Dollenmayer translation." Pub Wkly

Includes bibliographical references and index.

Gogh, Vincent van, 1853-1890

Naifeh, Steven. **Van** Gogh; [by] Steven Naifeh and Gregory White Smith. Random House 2011 xiii, 953 p.p some colored ill, maps   **92**
1. Painters 2. Mental illness 3. Biography, Individual
ISBN 9781588360472; 9780375507489; 0375507485

LC 2010053005

This book offers a biography of Vincent van Gogh. The book explores "his early struggles to find his place in the world; his intense relationship with his brother Theo; his impetus for turning to brush and canvas; and his move to Provence, where in a brief burst of . . . productivity he painted some of the best-loved works in Western art. The authors also shed . . . light on . . . Van Gogh's inner world: his deep immersion in literature and art; his erratic and tumultuous romantic life; and his bouts of depression and mental illness." (Publisher's note)

Includes bibliographical references and index.

Gold, Glen David, 1964-

Gold, Glen David. **I** will be complete; a memoir. Glen David Gold. Alfred A. Knopf 2018 496 p. (hardback) $29.95 **92**
1. Autobiographies 2. Mother-son relationship 3. American authors -- Biography 4. Parents -- United States 5. Authors -- United States -- Biography
ISBN 9781101946398

LC 2017049131

In this memoir, author Glen David Gold recalls that he "was raised rich, briefly, in southern California at the end of the go-go 1960s. But his father's fortune disappears, his parents divorce, and Glen falls out of his well-curated life and into San Francisco . . . Gold grows up with his mother, among con men and get-rich schemes. Then, one afternoon when he's twelve, she moves to New York without telling him, leaving him to fend for himself." (Publisher's note)

Goldstein, Meredith

Goldstein, Meredith. **Can't** help myself; lessons & confessions from a modern advice columnist. Meredith Goldstein. Grand Central Pub 2018 272 p. $26   **92**
1. Life change events 2. Interpersonal relations
ISBN 1455543772; 9781455543779

This memoir, by advice columnist Meredith Goldstein, is "about giving advice when you're not sure what you're doing yourself. Every day, . . . Goldstein takes on the relationship problems of thousands of dedicated readers. They look to her for wisdom on all matters of the heart. . . . Meredith finds herself looking for insight, just like her readers. As she searches for responses to their concerns, she's surprised to discover answers to her own." (Publisher's note)

"The book will appeal to loyal readers of advice columns—particularly Goldstein's—but be forewarned, this book is a tearjerker." Pub Wkly

Gooch, Brad, 1952-

Gooch, Brad. **Smash** Cut; Brad Gooch. HarperCollins 2015 256 p. illustrations $27.99   **92**
1. New York (N.Y.) 2. Art -- 20th century
ISBN 0062354957; 9780062354952

LC 2015460361

Written by Brad Gooch, this book is a "memoir of life in 1980s New York City--a colorful and atmospheric tale of wild bohemians, glamorous celebrity, and complicated passions--with cameo appearances by Madonna, Robert Mapplethorpe, William Burroughs, and a host of other legendary artists. . . . At its center is his love affair with film director Howard Brookner, pieced together from fragments of memory and fueled by a panoply of emotions." (Publisher's note)

"This candid memoir lovingly evokes a life, and a world, lost." Kirkus

Goodall, Jane, 1934-

★ Goodall, Jane. **Beyond** innocence; an autobiography in letters: the later years. edited by Dale Peterson. Houghton Mif-

flin 2001 418p il $28; pa $15 **92**
1. Women scientists 2. Primatologists 3. Writers on nature 4. Nonfiction writers
ISBN 0-618-12520-5; 0-618-25734-9 pa

LC 00-54124

In this "volume of Goodall's letters, a lively portrait is formed through her missives as the young woman rose to the height of her scientific contributions and fame. She became a mother, divorced her first husband, married her second, and lost him to cancer. She was also the first to observe cannibalism in chimps, lost many of her study troop during a polio epidemic, and weathered the kidnapping of a group of her students. . . . This illuminating glimpse into the mind, emotions, and philosophy of an important scientist who also happens to be a celebrated figure will be requested in all libraries." Booklist

Peterson, Dale. **Jane** Goodall: the woman who redefined man. Houghton Mifflin 2006 740p il $24.95; pa $17.95 **92**
1. Women scientists 2. Primatologists 3. Writers on nature 4. Nonfiction writers
ISBN 978-0-395-85405-1; 0-395-85405-9; 978-0-547-05356-1 pa; 0-547-05356-8 pa

LC 2006-6050

Peterson "vividly and significantly enriches our understanding of Goodall as a scientist, spiritual thinker, and humanist." Booklist
Includes bibliographical references

Gorbachev, Mikhail Sergeevich, 1931-

★ Taubman, William, 1940- **Gorbachev**; his life and times. William Taubman. W W Norton & Co Inc 2017 xxv, 852 p.p illustrations (hardcover) $39.95 **92**
1. Heads of state -- Soviet Union -- Biography 2. Soviet Union -- Politics and government -- 1985-1991
ISBN 9780393245684; 9780393647013; 0393647013

LC 2017015009

National Book Critics Circle Award Finalist: Biography (2017)
In this book author William Taubman presents a biography of Soviet leader Mikhail Gorbachev and "shows how a peasant boy . . . clambered to the top of a system designed to keep people like him down. . . . Drawing on interviews with Gorbachev himself, . . . and interviews with Kremlin aides and adversaries, . . . Taubman's intensely personal portrait extends to Gorbachev's remarkable marriage to a woman he deeply loved, and to the family that they raised together." (Publisher's note)
"Taubman (political science, Amherst College) has written a monumental, groundbreaking study of Soviet President Mikhail Sergeyevich Gorbachev." Choice
Includes bibliographical references (pages 785-804) and index.

Gorey, Edward, 1925-2000

Dery, Mark. **Born** to be posthumous; the eccentric life and mysterious genius of Edward Gorey. Mark Dery. Little, Brown & Co. 2018 496 p. $35 **92**
1. Biography 2. Gorey, Edward 3. American authors -- Biography
ISBN 9780316188548

LC 2018941034

This book, by Mark Dery, presents the biography of American writer and artist Edward Gorey. "He published over a hundred books and illustrated works by Samuel Beckett, T.S. Eliot, Edward Lear, John Updike, Charles Dickens, Hilaire Belloc, Muriel Spark, Bram Stoker, Gilbert & Sullivan, and others. At the same time, he was a deeply complicated and conflicted individual, a man whose art reflected his obsessions with the disquieting and the darkly hilarious." (Publisher's note)
"Fans will like the immersion in Gorey-ana, but others may feel that this colorful protagonist lacks a compelling plot." Pub Wkly

Gottlieb, Robert, 1931-

Gottlieb, Robert, 1931- **Avid** reader; a life. Robert Gottlieb. Farrar, Straus & Giroux 2016 352 p. illustrations (some color) (ebook) $60; (hardcover) $28 **92**
1. Book editors -- United States -- Biography 2. Periodical editors -- United States -- Biography 3. Publishers and publishing -- United States -- Biography 4. Publishers and publishing -- United States -- History -- 20th century
ISBN 9780374713904; 9780374279929

LC 2015048673

A memoir by Robert Gottlieb, "this account of a life founded upon reading is about more than the arc of a singular career--one that also includes a lifelong involvement with the world of dance. It's about transcendent friendships and collaborations, 'elective affinities' and family, psychoanalysis and Bakelite purses, the alchemical relationship between writer and editor, the glory days of publishing, and--always--the sheer exhilaration of work." (Publisher's note)
"While book lovers will revel in Gottlieb's intimate publishing revelations, his memoir is also a vital, generous, and captivating story of a life lived to the fullest." Booklist

Gould, Florence, 1895-1983

Ronald, Susan. A **dangerous** woman; American beauty, noted philanthropist, Nazi collaborator: the life of Florence Gould. Susan Ronald. St. Martin's Press 2018 400 p. $27.99 **92**
1. Socialites -- Biography 2. World War, 1939-1945 -- Collaborationists
ISBN 1250092213; 9781250092212

This biography, by Susan Ronald, tells the story of "Florence Gould, fabulously wealthy socialite and patron of the arts, who hid a dark past as a Nazi collaborator in 1940's Paris. . . . During the Occupation, Florence took several German lovers and hosted a controversial salon. As the Allies closed in, the unscrupulous Florence became embroiled in a notorious money laundering operation for fleeing high-ranking Nazis." (Publisher's note)
"Although Florence's letters and photographs were inaccessible to the author, Ronald compensates with layers of research into the period and surrounding players. While the dense historical detail may deter lay readers, history lovers will welcome this impressive book about a captivating, flawed woman." (Pub Wkly)

Gould, Glenn, 1932-1982

Hafner, Katie. A **romance** on three legs; Glenn Gould's obsessive quest for the perfect piano. Bloomsbury 2008 259p il $24.99; pa $16 **92**
1. Pianos 2. Pianists 3. Composers 4. Steinway & Sons
ISBN 978-1-59691-524-4; 1-59691-524-2; 978-1-59691-525-1 pa; 1-59691-525-0 pa

LC 2007-48808

"When Gould was paired with the right composer, Bach especially, he could make you wonder if he was altogether human. And reading Hafner on Gould is sometimes as much fun as listening to him play. And that's saying a lot." Newsweek
Includes bibliographical references

Grace, Princess of Monaco, 1929-1982

Bowman, Manoah. **Grace** Kelly; Hollywood dream girl. Jay Jorgensen and Manoah Bowman. Dey St., an imprint of William Morrow 2017 287 p. illustrations (hardcover) $45 **92**
1. Princesses -- Biography 2. Motion picture actors and actresses -- United States -- Biography 3. Motion picture actors and actresses

-- United States -- Pictorial works
ISBN 9780062643339; 0062643339

This book, by Jay Jorgensen and Manoah Bowman, is "the definitive visual biography of Grace Kelly's unforgettable Hollywood career, chronicled in 400 extraordinary black-and white and color photographs, including many never-before-seen. . . . This breathtaking compendium traces every step of her artistic journey . . . [It] is a fresh, celebratory look at her remarkable career and her enduring cultural influence." (Publisher's note)

Graham, Ashley, 1987-

Graham, Ashley. A **new** model; what confidence, beauty, and power really look like. Ashley Graham with Rebecca Paley. Dey St., an imprint of William Morrow Publishers 2017 xxiii, 198 p.p color illustrations (hardcover) $26.99   **92**
1. Body image 2. Fashion models 3. Self-acceptance 4. Body size -- Psychological aspects 5. Models (Persons) -- United States -- Biography
ISBN 9780062667946; 9780062667960; 0062667947

"Ashley Graham has been modeling professionally since the age of thirteen. Discovered at a shopping mall in Nebraska, her stunning face and sexy curves have graced the covers of top magazines. . . . In this collection of insightful, provocative essays illustrated with a dozen photos, Ashley shares her perspective on how ideas around body image are evolving—and how we still have work to do; the fun—and stress—of a career in the fashion world." (Publisher's note)

"Positive, understanding, and uplifting." Booklist

Graham, Billy, 1918-2018

Wacker, Grant. **America's** pastor; Billy Graham and the shaping of a nation. Grant Wacker. The Belknap Press of Harvard University Press 2014 448 p. illustrations (alk. paper) $27.95   **92**
1. Christianity -- United States 2. Christianity and culture -- United States -- History -- 20th century
ISBN 0674052188; 9780674052185

LC 2014014155

This book, by Grant Wacker, "is an appraisal of the roles [Billy] Graham, the great evangelist, played during a career spanning from the late 1930s to his last crusade in 2005. Wacker examines not so much what Graham did as how he did it--a matter of manners and management as much as of vision and talent." (Booklist)

"Wacker doesn't shrink, however, from showing how Graham's fascination with presidential politics led him astray repeatedly while allowing that he was a genuine spiritual counselor to the presidents—Lyndon Johnson, in particular. If a great subject deserves a great book, Billy Graham has one." Booklist

Includes bibliographical references and index

Graham, Mark (Mark A.)

Dreazen, Yochi. The **invisible** front; a story of loss and love. Yochi Dreazen. Crown 2014 320 p. 8 plates; illustrations (hardback) $26   **92**
1. Suicide -- United States 2. War -- Psychological aspects 3. Sons -- United States -- Death 4. United States. Army -- Biography 5. Sociology, Military -- United States 6. Generals -- United States -- Biography 7. Soldiers -- Mental health -- United States 8. Posttraumatic stress disorder -- United States
ISBN 0385347839; 9780385347839

LC 2014007360

This book by Yochi Dreazen is "is the story of how one family tries to set aside their grief and find purpose in almost unimaginable loss. The

Grahams work to change how the Army treats those with PTSD and to erase the stigma that prevents suicidal troops from getting the help they need before making the darkest of choices." (Publisher's note)

"Mental health care workers, sociologists, and military historians will find this book a useful first step in a much larger conversation. Readers dealing with mental health issues can take comfort in knowing they are not alone, and others may find motivation in the stories Dreazen relates to help generate change." LJ

Grande, Lance

Grande, Lance. **Curators**; behind the scenes of natural history museums. Lance Grande. University of Chicago Press 2017 xvi, 412 p.p ills., maps, portraits (cloth: alk. paper) $35   **92**
1. Museums 2. Curatorship 3. Natural history museums 4. Natural history museum curators 5. Field Museum of Natural History -- Biography 6. Biologists -- Illinois -- Chicago -- Biography 7. Paleontologists -- Illinois -- Chicago -- Biography 8. Natural history museum curators -- Illinois -- Chicago -- Biography
ISBN 9780226192758

LC 2016032596

This book, by Lance Grande, "offers a portrait of curators and their research. . . . Grande uses the personal story of his own career—most of it spent at Chicago's storied Field Museum—to structure his account as he explores the value of research and collections, the importance of public engagement, changing ecological and ethical considerations, and the impact of rapidly improving technology." (Publisher's note)

"Grande's illumination of the evolving role of the natural history museum and of collection curators completes this passionate memoir and celebration of an essential public resource." Booklist

Includes bibliographical references and index

Grande, Reyna

Grande, Reyna. The **distance** between us; a memoir. Reyna Grande. Atria Books 2012 336 p. (hardcover) $25.00   **92**
1. Poor 2. Novelists 3. Immigrants -- United States 4. Mexican Americans -- Biography 5. Los Angeles (Calif.) -- Biography 6. Immigrants -- United States -- Biography 7. Mexican American women authors -- Biography 8. Abused children -- United States -- Biography 9. Mexico -- Emigration and immigration -- Social aspects 10. United States -- Emigration and immigration -- Social aspects
ISBN 1451661770; 9781451661774; 9781451661781; 9781451661804

LC 2012001634

This book presents a memoir by "award-winning novelist . . . [Reyna] Grande. . . . Four-year-old Grande and her two siblings lived with their cruel grandmother after both parents departed for the U.S. in search of work. . . . Eight years later her father returned and reluctantly agreed to take his children to the States. . . . Surrounded by family turmoil, Grande discovered a love of writing . . . and went on to become the first person in her family to graduate from college." (Publishers Weekly)

Grandmaster Flash, 1958-

Grandmaster Flash. The **adventures** of Grandmaster Flash; my life, my beats. by Grandmaster Flash with David Ritz. Broadway Books 2008 258p il $22.95   **92**
1. Hip-hop 2. Musicians 3. Rap musicians 4. Disc jockeys (Club)
ISBN 978-0-7679-2475-7; 0-7679-2475-4

LC 2007-48224

"Grandmaster Flash is best known in conjunction with the Furious Five, the first hip-hop artists inducted into the Rock and Roll Hall of Fame. But before the fame, Joseph Robert Saddler was born into an abusive family in the Bronx. His evolution from a kid spinning records in the streets to hip-hop stardom is an inspiring story filled with heartbreak, determination, and perseverance." Libr J

Includes discography and bibliographical references

Grant, Ulysses S. (Ulysses Simpson), 1822-1885

Bunting, Josiah. **Ulysses** S. Grant; [by] Josiah Bunting III. Times Books 2004 xx, 180p (American presidents series) $20   **92**

   1. Generals 2. Presidents 3. United States -- History -- 1861-1865, Civil War

   ISBN 0-8050-6949-6

                 LC 2004-47889

"This superb book should support those who are gradually moving Grant from the lower to the upper half of rankings of chief executives." Publ Wkly

Includes bibliographical references

★ Chernow, Ron. **Grant**; Ron Chernow. Penguin Press 2017 xxiii, 1074 p.p illustrations, maps (hardback) $40   **92**

   1. Presidents -- United States 2. Generals -- United States -- Biography 3. United States. Army -- Biography 4. Presidents -- United States -- Biography

   ISBN 9780525521952; 159420487X; 9781594204876

                 LC 2017025263

In this book, author Ron Chernow presents "a sweeping and dramatic portrait of one of our most compelling generals and presidents, Ulysses S. Grant. . . . Grant's military fame translated into a two-term presidency, but one plagued by corruption scandals involving his closest staff members. . . . Chernow's probing portrait of Grant's lifelong struggle with alcoholism transforms our understanding of the man at the deepest level." (Publisher's note)

"In this sympathetic biography, the author continues the revival of Grant's reputation. At nearly 1,000 pages, Chernow delivers a deeply researched, everything-you-ever-wanted-to-know biography, but few readers will regret the experience." Kirkus

Includes bibliographical references (pages 1021-1031) and index.

Korda, Michael. **Ulysses** S. Grant: the unlikely hero. Atlas Books\HarperCollins 2004 161p (Eminent lives) $19.95 **92**

   1. Generals 2. Presidents 3. United States -- History -- 1861-1865, Civil War

   ISBN 0-06-059015-7

                 LC 2004-46125

The author "freshly characterizes his man without psychologizing an unpromising subject. . . . This is a highly readable, accurate study of the man." Publ Wkly

Includes bibliographical references

Smith, Jean Edward. **Grant**. Simon & Schuster 2001 781p il $35; pa $20   **92**

   1. Generals 2. Presidents 3. United States -- History -- 1861-1865, Civil War

   ISBN 0-684-84926-7; 0-684-84927-5 pa

                 LC 00-53794

This biography surveys the career and achievements of the 18th U.S. president, from his days at West Point to the Civil War campaigns and his subsequent elevation to the presidency

"While he acknowledges Grant's failure to rein in his 'friends' and cabinet members as president, Smith convincingly illustrates how Grant's backbone and political skills were used to advance the cause of former slaves in the South. This is an outstanding and long overdue reevaluation of the life and career of a great American." Booklist

Includes bibliographical references

★ White, Ronald C. (Ronald Cedric), 1939- **American** Ulysses; A Life of Ulysses S. Grant. Ronald C. White. Random House 2016 880 p. illustrations, maps (hardcover) $35   **92**

   1. Generals -- United States -- Biography 2. Presidents -- United States -- Biography 3. United States -- Politics and government -- 1869-1877 4. United States -- History -- Civil War, 1861-1865 -- Biography

   ISBN 9781400069026

                 LC 2015044513

This biography of Ulysses S. Grant by Ronald C. White "shows Grant to be a generous, curious, introspective man and leader. . . . Grant was not only a brilliant general but also a passionate defender of equal rights in post-Civil War America. . . . He used the power of the federal government to battle the Ku Klux Klan. He was the first president to state that the government's policy toward American Indians was immoral, and the first ex-president to embark on a world tour." (Publisher's note)

"The author portrays a humble, gentle, independent soul—a writer, in the end, who found his voice writing his extraordinary memoirs just before his death in 1885. An engaging resurrection of Grant featuring excellent maps and character sketches." Kirkus

Includes bibliographical references and index

Gray, Hanna Holborn

Gray, Hanna Holborn, 1930- An **academic** life; a memoir. Hanna Holborn Gray. Princeton University Press 2018 352 p. (hardback) $29.95   **92**

   1. Women historians -- Biography 2. Women college teachers -- Biography 3. Women in higher education -- United States 4. Women historians -- United States -- Biography 5. University of Chicago -- Presidents -- Biography 6. Women college teachers -- United States -- Biography

   ISBN 9780691179186

                 LC 2017036151

This book "is a candid self-portrait by [Hanna Holborn Gray,] one of academia's most respected trailblazers. Gray describes what it was like to grow up as a child of refugee parents, and reflects on the changing status of women in the academic world. She discusses the migration of intellectuals from Nazi-held Europe and the transformative role these exiles played in American higher education--and how the émigré experience in America transformed their own lives and work." (Publisher's note)

Includes bibliographical references and index

Graziano, Rocky, 1922-1990

Sussman, Jeffrey. **Rocky** Graziano; fists, fame, and fortune. Jeffrey Sussman. Rowman & Littlefield 2018 226 p. (hardback: alk. paper) $36   **92**

   1. Boxing 2. Boxers (Sports) -- United States -- Biography

   ISBN 1538102617; 9781538102619

                 LC 2017035354

In this book, "Jeffrey Sussman tells the . . . story of Tommy Rocco Barbella, . . . known as Rocky Graziano. Raised by an abusive father, Graziano took to the streets and soon found himself in reformatories and prison cells. Drafted into the U.S. Army, Graziano went AWOL but was eventually caught, tried, and sent to prison for a year. After his release, Rocky went on to have one successful boxing match after another and quickly ascended up the pyramid of professional boxing." (Publisher's note)

Includes bibliographical references and index

Grealy, Lucy, 1963-2002

Patchett, Ann. **Truth** & beauty; a friendship. HarperCollins Publishers 2004 257p hardcover o.p. pa $13.95   **92**
1. Poets 2. Authors 3. Novelists 4. Women authors 5. Memoirists
ISBN 0-06-057214-0; 0-06-057215-9 pa

LC 2003-67586

"As young writers. Patchett and Lucy Grealy began an intense friendship that lasted until Grealy's tragic death. With intimacy, gracy, and humor, Patchett's memoir captures Lucy's exuberance and her roller-coaster struggles with disfigurement and depression." Booklist

Green, Robin

Green, Robin. The **only** girl; my life and times on the masthead of Rolling Stone. Robin Green. Little, Brown & Co. 2018 304 p. $28   **92**
1. Women journalists -- United States -- Biography
ISBN 0316440027; 9780316440028

LC 2018935533

This book, by Robin Green, is "a raucous and vividly dishy memoir by the only woman writer on the masthead of Rolling Stone Magazine in the early Seventies. . . . With irreverent humor and remarkable nerve, Green spills stories of sparring with Dennis Hopper on a film junket in the desert, scandalizing fans of David Cassidy and spending a legendary evening on a water bed in Robert F. Kennedy Jr.'s dorm room." (Publisher's note)

"Reading like a real-life road novel, Green's memoir is a must for aspiring writers." Library Journal

Greene, Graham, 1904-1991

Greene, Graham, 1904-1991. **Graham** Greene; a life in letters. edited by Richard Greene. W. W. Norton & Company 2008 446p il $35   **92**
1. Authors 2. Novelists 3. Essayists 4. Travel writers 5. Short story writers 6. Motion picture critics
ISBN 978-0-393-06642-5; 0-393-06642-8

LC 2008-40452

First published 2007 in the United Kingdom

"Greene is presented in these letters through the five main preoccupations of his life: Roman Catholicism, politics, love, travel and . . . the processes of writing and publishing. . . . This well-thought-out collection newly reveals a remarkable activist-writer." Publ Wkly

Includes bibliographical references

Greenspan, Alan

Greenspan, Alan, 1926- The **age** of turbulence; adventures in a new world. Penguin Press 2007 531p il $35   **92**
1. Economists 2. Bankers 3. Government officials 4. Biography, Individual 5. Presidential advisers 6. Regulatory agency officials 7. United States -- Economic conditions -- 1945-
ISBN 978-1-59420-131-8

LC 2007-13169

This is a memoir by the American economist who served as "Chairman of the Federal Reserve Board, from 1987 to 2006." (Publisher's note) Index.

"The former U. S. Federal Reserve Board chair relates his life story, focusing on lessons learned in government service, particularly post-9/11. He also includes political anecdotes, asserts his faith in market capitalism, and shares his predictions for the world of 2030." Libr J

Includes bibliographical references

Mallaby, Sebastian. The **Man** Who Knew; The Life and Times of Alan Greenspan. Sebastian Mallaby. Penguin Group USA 2016 800 p. illustrations (ebook) $65; $40   **92**
1. Economists -- Biography 2. Monetary policy -- United States
ISBN 9780698170018; 1594204845; 9781594204845

LC 2016017300

In this book, author Sebastian Mallaby presents a "biography of the most important economic statesman of our time. . . . To understand [Alan] Greenspan's story is to see the economic and political landscape of the last 30 years . . . in a whole new light. . . . Greenspan spent a lifetime grappling with a momentous shift: the transformation of finance from the fixed and regulated system of the post-war era to the free-for-all of the past quarter century." (Publisher's note)

"He has written a masterful, detailed portrait of one of the leading economic figures of our time." Pub Wkly

Includes bibliographical references (pages 695-755) and index.

Greffulhe, Elisabeth, comtesse, 1860-1952

Proust's duchess; how three celebrated women captured the imagination of fin de siècle Paris. Caroline Weber. Alfred A. Knopf 2018 736 p. (hardcover) $35   **92**
1. Biography 2. Women -- Biography 3. Women -- France -- Paris -- Biography 4. Paris (France) -- Intellectual life -- 19th century 5. Paris (France) -- Social life and customs -- 19th century 6. Aristocracy (Social class) -- France -- Paris -- Biography
ISBN 9780307961785; 9780345803122

LC 2017038855

This book, by Caroline Weber, presents "the first in-depth study of the three women [Marcel] Proust used to create his supreme fictional character, the Duchesse de Guermantes. Geneviève Halévy Bizet Straus; Laure de Sade, Comtesse de Adhéaume de Chevigné; and Élisabeth de Riquet de Caraman-Chimay, the Comtesse Greffulhe--these were the three superstars of fin-de-siècle Parisian high society." (Publisher's note)

Includes bibliographical references

Gregorian, Vartan

Gregorian, Vartan. The **road** to home; my life and times. Simon & Schuster 2003 354p il hardcover o.p. pa $15   **92**
1. Library directors 2. College presidents 3. Foundation officials
ISBN 0-684-80834-X; 978-0-7432-5565-3; 0-7432-5565-8 pa

LC 2003-45566

In this "memoir, Gregorian explains how he went from a childhood in a poor section of Tabriz, Iran, to become president of the New York Public Library and, later, the president of Brown University." Publ Wkly

Gregory, Rebekah

Flacco, Anthony. **Taking** my life back; my story of faith, determination, and surviving the Boston Marathon bombing. Rebekah Gregory with Anthony Flacco. Revell, a division of Baker Publishing Group 2017 230 p. color illustrations (hardcover) $19.99   **92**
1. Amputees 2. Bombings 3. Victims of terrorism 4. Christian biography -- United States 5. Boston Marathon Bombing, Boston, Mass., 2013 6. Amputees -- Rehabilitation -- Massachusetts -- Boston
ISBN 9780800728212

LC 2016048311

This memoir of Boston Marathon bombing victim Rebekah Gregory, with Anthony Flacco, "tells the story of her recovery, including her triumphant return to Boston two years later to run part of the race, and explores the peace we experience when we learn to trust God with every part of our lives--the good, the bad, and even the terrifying." (Publisher's note)

"This is a truly feel-good book that doesn't stint on the challenges that life throws at us." Pub Wkly

Grey, Jane, Lady, 1537-1554

Tallis, Nicola. **Crown** of Blood; The Deadly Inheritance of Lady Jane Grey. Nicola Tallis. W W Norton & Co Inc 2016 400 p. color illustrations $27.95; (ebook) $50 **92**

    1. Queens -- Great Britain -- Biography 2. Great Britain -- History -- 1485-1603, Tudors
ISBN 1681772442; 9781681772448; 9781681772875

LC 2016047401

This book, by Nicola Tallis, is "a significant retelling of the often-misunderstood tale of Lady Jane Grey's journey through her trial and execution. . . . Jane is known to history as 'the Nine Days Queen,' but her reign lasted, in fact, for thirteen days. The human and emotional aspects of her story have often been ignored, although she is remembered as one of the Tudor Era's most tragic victims." (Publisher's note)

"Readers will share Tallis' sympathy with the devout, passive Jane but also approve of her emphasis on the more powerful, ambitious, and unpleasant men and women that surrounded her." Kirkus

Includes bibliographical references (pages 352-362) and index.

Grey, Joel, 1932-

Grey, Joel. **Master** of ceremonies; a memoir. Joel Grey. Flatiron Books 2016 256 p. illustrations (hardback) $27.99; (ebook) $40 **92**

    1. Actors -- United States -- Biography 2. Photographers -- United States -- Biography
ISBN 9781250057235; 9781250057242

LC 2015040157

"Joel Grey, the Tony and Academy Award-winning Master of Ceremonies in Cabaret finally tells his remarkable life story. Born Joel David Katz to a wild and wooly Jewish American family in Cleveland, Ohio in 1932, Joel began his life in the theater at the age of 9, starting in children's theater and then moving to the main stage. He was hooked, and his seven decades long career charts the evolution of American entertainment." (Publisher's note)

"The diminutive, unforgettable creator of the emcee in Cabaret both on stage and on screen writes frankly of his diverse career, exacting mother, and public embrace of his homosexuality." Kirkus

Grey, Zane, 1872-1939

Pauly, Thomas H. **Zane** Grey; his life, his adventures, his women. University of Illinois Press 2005 385p il map $34.95 **92**

    1. Authors 2. Novelists 3. Western writers 4. Biography, Individual
ISBN 0-252-03044-3; 978-0-252-03044-4

LC 2005-9413

This is a biography of the "author of westerns like 'Riders of the Purple Sage,' 'The Light of Western Stars' and 'Code of the West.'" (N Y Times Book Rev) Index.

The author "offers an honest exploration of the complex author. . . . A solid, entertaining read." Choice

Includes bibliographical references

Groberg, Florent, 1983-

Sileo, Tom. **8** seconds of courage; a soldier's story, from immigrant to the Medal of Honor. Flo Groberg and Tom Sileo. Simon & Schuster 2017 ix, 191 p.p illustrations, map (hardcover) $25 **92**

    1. Courage 2. Military personnel -- United States 3. Medal of Honor -- Biography 4. French Americans -- Biography 5. Afghan War, 2001- -- Biography 6. Immigrants -- United States -- Biography 7. United States. Army -- Officers -- Biography 8. Afghan War, 2001- -- Casualties -- United States 9. Afghan War, 2001- -- Campaigns -- Afghanistan -- Asadābād
ISBN 9781501165894; 9781501165887; 1501165887

LC 2017036187

This memoir, by Flo Groberg, looks at "his childhood in France to his decision to enlist and the grueling training he underwent at US Army Ranger School. Through trial and error, he learned to be a field commander and on the front lines in Afghanistan formed close and lasting bonds with his fellow soldiers. It was this powerful sense of responsibility that compelled him to take his brave action to save lives, even at the risk of his own." (Publisher's note)

"In this short, candid book, Groberg . . . offers insight into the profound sense of duty that drives members of the military while celebrating one man's extraordinary courage." Kirkus

Grove, Andrew S., 1936-2018

Tedlow, Richard S. **Andy** Grove; the life and times of an American. Portfolio 2006 512p $29.95 **92**

    1. Intel Corp. 2. College teachers 3. Electronics industry executives
ISBN 978-1-591-84139-5; 1-591-84139-9

LC 2006-49829

The author "presents the story of Andy Grove, a penniless Hungarian immigrant who became an icon of twentieth-century corporate America. Grove joined Intel in 1968 at its founding, and while he was CEO from 1987 to 1998, 'market capitalization increased from $4.3 billion to $197.6 billion, a compound annual growth rate of 42% and a total increase of almost 4,500%.' Grove led the company with Intel's 386 microprocessor, which became the industry standard. Tedlow describes Grove, Time magazine's 1997 man of the year, as an extraordinary manager, author, and significant player in the fights against prostate cancer and Parkinson's disease. With unique access to Grove and Intel's internal resources and documents, Tedlow claims objectivity, telling the truth as he sees it in this laudatory narrative, although he also confirms his close ties to the subject." Booklist

Gucci Mane, 1980-

Martinez-Belkin, Neil. The **autobiography** of Gucci Mane; by Gucci Mane with Neil Martinez-Belkin. Simon & Schuster 2017 xv, 286 p.p illustrations (chiefly color) (hardcover: alk. paper) $27 **92**

    1. Rap musicians 2. Rap musicians -- United States -- Biography
ISBN 9781501165337; 1501165321; 9781501165320; 9781501165344

LC 2017019427

In this book, author Gucci Mane, with Neil Martinez-Belkin, "tells his story in his own words. It is the captivating life of an artist who forged an unlikely path to stardom and personal rebirth. Gucci Mane began writing his memoir in a maximum-security federal prison. Released in 2016, he emerged radically transformed. He was sober, smiling, focused, and positive--a far cry from the Gucci Mane of years past." (Publisher's note)

"Atlanta has always played a significant role in shaping the sound and culture of rap and hip-hop, and the influence of Gucci Mane (né Radric Davis) can't be overstated. . . .This autobiography, written while he was serving time in a federal prison for possession of a firearm, paints a rich portrait." SLJ

Guevara, Che, 1928-1967

Guervara, Ernesto Che. **Diary** of a combatant; from the Sierra Maestra to Santa Clara, Cuba, 1956-58. Ernesto Che Guevara; edited by María del Carmen Ariet. Ocean Press 2011 368

p. ill., map, facsim. $23.95   **92**
1. Diaries 2. Cuba -- History -- 1958-1959, Revolution
ISBN 0987077945; 9780987077943

LC 2011943989

This book is a translation of the diary "Ernesto Che Guevara kept during the guerrilla war in Cuba when he joined the struggle to overthrow the Batista dictatorship that led to the 1959 revolution.... [It was] meticulously transcribed by his widow, Aleida March.... Other features of this new book are fifty-eight unpublished photos from Che's personal archive and unpublished letters (including correspondence between Che and Fidel)." (Publisher's note)

"Editor Ariet has included a useful chronology and a most helpful biographical glossary, detailing many of the names Che introduces in these diaries." LJ

Includes bibliographical references

Guggenheim, Peggy, 1898-1979

★ Gill, Anton. **Art** lover; a biography of Peggy Guggenheim. HarperCollins Pubs. 2002 480p il $29.95; pa $15.95   **92**
1. Art collectors 2. Patrons of the arts
ISBN 0-06-019697-1; 0-06-095681-X pa

LC 2001-51731

Guggenheim "was known as much for her sexual exploits as for her championing of modern art, a fact Gill ... examines with candor, sensitivity, and mellifluous grace." Booklist

Includes bibliographical references

Guidry, Ron, 1950-

Guidry, Ron, 1950- **Gator**; my life in pinstripes. by Ron Guidry, with Andrew Beaton. Crown Archetype 2017 240 p. (hardback) $26   **92**
1. Baseball pitchers 2. New York Yankees (Baseball team) 3. Baseball players -- United States -- Biography 4. Pitchers (Baseball) -- United States -- Biography 5. New York Yankees (Baseball team) -- History -- 20th century
ISBN 9780451499301

LC 2017040975

In this book, "legendary New York Yankees pitcher Ron Guidry, [with Andrew Beaton,] recounts his years playing for ... the world champion New York Yankees during their heyday in the Bronx Zoo years, with manic manager Billy Martin, headline loving owner George Steinbrenner, and an ego-driven all-star cast that included everyone from slugger Reggie Jackson and All star catcher Thurman Munson to Cy Young Award winners Sparky Lyle and Catfish Hunter." (Publisher's note)

Gunn, Paul Irvin, 1899-1957

Bruning, John R. **Indestructible**; One Man's Rescue Mission That Changed the Course of WWII. John R. Bruning. Hachette Books 2016 544 p. illustrations, maps (ebook) $84; (hardcover) $28   **92**
1. Air pilots -- United States -- Biography 2. World War, 1939-1945 -- Aerial operations -- United States 3. Americans -- Philippines -- Biography 4. Prisoners of war -- Philippines -- Biography 5. Rescues -- Philippines -- History -- 20th century 6. World War, 1939-1945 -- Aerial operations, American 7. World War, 1939-1945 -- Prisoners and prisons, Japanese 8. Philippine Airlines -- Officials and employees -- Biography 9. Aeronautics, Military -- Technological innovations -- History -- 20th century
ISBN 9780316312226; 9780316339407; 9780316464307

LC 2016021715

This book, by John R. Bruning, tells "the story of how one man's struggle to free his family after the fall of the Philippines in World War II inspired him to create new weapons systems that hastened the Allied victory.... [Naval aviator] Paul Irvin 'Pappy' Gunn (1899-1957) [was] ... living in Manila with his wife and children, ... [enjoying] the good life.... When Manila fell, he was on a long-distance mission, too far away to save his family, who went into a prison camp." (Kirkus)

"Verdict Fans of World War II history, aviation and military technological leaps, and stories of the human spirit conquering terrible odds will enjoy this tome." LJ

Includes bibliographical references and index

Gunness, Belle, 1859-1908

Schechter, Harold. **Hell's** princess; the mystery of Belle Gunness, Butcher of Men. Harold Schechter. Amazon Pub 2018 334 p. $24.95   **92**
1. Serial killers 2. Women criminals
ISBN 1477808957; 9781477808955

In this book, by Harold Schechter, "in the pantheon of serial killers, Belle Gunness stands alone. She was the rarest of female psychopaths, a woman who engaged in wholesale slaughter, partly out of greed but mostly for the sheer joy of it.... 'Hell's Princess' is a riveting account of one of the most sensational killing sprees in the annals of American crime: the shocking series of murders committed by the woman who came to be known as Lady Bluebeard." (Publisher's note)

"This biography of a prolific and brutal serial killer will be of interest to Midwestern regional history buffs as well as true crime fans." LJ

Guo, Xiaolu, 1973-

Guo, Xiaolu, 1973- **Nine** continents; a memoir in and out of China. Xiaolu Guo. Grove Press 2017 366 p. illustrations (hbk.) $26   **92**
1. Authors, Chinese 2. China -- Social conditions 3. China -- History
ISBN 9780802189325; 0802127134; 9780802127136

LC 2017032639

National Book Critics Circle Award Finalist: Autobiography (2017)

This memoir, by Xiaolu Guo, "presents a fascinating portrait of China in the eighties and nineties, how the Cultural Revolution shaped families, and how the country's economic ambitions gave rise to great change. It is also a moving testament to the birth of a creative spirit, and of a new generation being raised to become citizens of the world. It confirms Xiaolu Guo as one of world literature's most urgent voices." (Publisher's note)

"A rich and insightful coming-of-age story of not only a woman, but an artist and the country in which she was born." Kirkus

Guppy, Joe

Guppy, Joe. **My** fluorescent God; a psychotherapist confronts his most challenging case--his own. by Joe Guppy. Booktrope Editions 2014 197 p. illustrations $14.95   **92**
1. Paranoia 2. Mental health 3. Mentally ill -- Washington (State) -- Seattle -- Biography 4. Psychotherapists -- Washington (State) -- Seattle -- Biography 5. Paranoia -- Patients -- Washington (State) -- Seattle -- Biography 6. Psychoses -- Patients -- Washington (State) -- Seattle -- Biography
ISBN 1620154412; 9781620154410

LC 2014912378

This book by Joe Guppy, "recreated from journal entries and the notes of mental-health professionals, [is] the story of the author's struggle to rebuild his sanity. Joe Guppy's life derailed in 1979. The 23-year-old was dealing with a bad breakup and existential angst, but it was a few stomach pills he took in Mexico that pushed him over the edge into paranoid psychosis." (Publisher's note)

"Beautifully written, honest, enlightening, hope-giving and valuable - essential for anyone interested in or struggling with mental health issues." Kirkus

Includes bibliographical references (page [200])

Guthrie, Woody, 1912-1967

Klein, Joe. **Woody** Guthrie; a life. Knopf 1980 475p il pa $17 **92**

1. Singers 2. Folk musicians 3. Memoirists 4. Songwriters 5. Musicians -- United States

ISBN 0-385-33385-4 pa

LC 80-7634

"The author incorporates into his text a great deal of information sifted from Guthrie's voluminous unpublished writings. . . . He also uses information from historical sources, published works, and hundreds of interviews to place Guthrie in a social and historical perspective. The result of all this research is . . . a very interesting and personal biography." Libr J

Haddish, Tiffany

Haddish, Tiffany. The **last** black unicorn; Tiffany Haddish. Simon & Schuster 2017 288 p. $26 **92**

1. African American actors 2. Comedians -- United States -- Biography

ISBN 1501181823; 9781501181825

In this book, comedian Tiffany Haddish "recounts with heart and humor how she came from nothing and nowhere to achieve her dreams by owning, sharing, and using her pain to heal others. By turns hilarious, filthy, and brutally honest, 'The Last Black Unicorn' shows the world who Tiffany Haddish really is--humble, grateful, down-to-earth, and funny as hell. And now, she's ready to inspire others through the power of laughter." (Publisher's note)

Hadfield, Chris, 1959-

Hadfield, Chris, 1959- An **astronaut's** guide to life on earth; what going to space taught me about ingenuity, determination, and being prepared for anything. Col. Chris Hadfield. Little, Brown and Co. 2013 304 p. ill. (some col.) $28 **92**

1. Astronauts 2. Outer space -- Exploration

ISBN 0316253014; 9780316253017

LC 2013943519

Author and astronaut Chris Hadfield "takes readers deep into his years of training and space exploration to show how to make the impossible possible. Through eye-opening, entertaining stories filled with the adrenaline of launch, the mesmerizing wonder of spacewalks, and the measured, calm responses mandated by crises, he explains how conventional wisdom can get in the way of achievement-and happiness." (Publisher's note)

"The author emphasizes that becoming an astronaut involved developing physical capabilities and technical skills through tireless practice and a fanatic attention to detail. . . . A page-turning memoir of life as a decorated astronaut." Kirkus

Hadrian, Emperor of Rome, 76-138

Everitt, Anthony. **Hadrian** and the triumph of Rome. Random House 2009 xxix, 392p il map $30 **92**

1. Emperors 2. Rome -- History 3. Emperors -- Rome

ISBN 978-1-4000-6662-9; 1-4000-6662-X

LC 2009-05683

"Emperor from 117 to 138 A.D., Hadrian styled himself princeps, or first among equals, and his reversal of his predecessors' expansionist

policies contributed to an era of prosperity and relative calm. He was unapologetically Hellenic, a poet and a dabbler in magic, and he kept in his retinue a young male lover whom he later deified. If Hadrian is indeed an enigma, it's because so few accounts of his life have survived, and this is where Everitt—whose books rely heavily on primary sources—runs into difficulty. One gets a clear and compelling sense of Hadrian's times, but the Emperor himself remains tantalizingly unknowable." New Yorker

Includes bibliographical references

Hagel, Chuck, 1946-

Bolger, Daniel P. **Our** year of war; two brothers, Vietnam, and a nation divided. Daniel P. Bolger. Da Capo Press 2017 xii, 336 p.p illustrations, maps (hardcover) $28 **92**

1. Vietnam War, 1961-1975 2. Nineteen sixty-eight, A.D. 3. Vietnam War, 1961-1975 -- Biography 4. Brothers -- United States -- Biography 5. Vietnam War, 1961-1975 -- United States 6. Cabinet officers -- United States -- Biography

ISBN 9780306903243; 9780306903267

LC 2017953360

In this book, by Daniel P. Bolger, "two brothers--Chuck and Tom Hagel--who went to war in Vietnam, fought in the same unit, and saved each other's life. . . . Together they fought in the Mekong Delta, battled snipers in Saigon, chased the enemy through the jungle, and each saved the other's life under fire. But when their one-year tour was over, these two brothers came home side-by-side but no longer in step--one supporting the war, the other hating it." (Publisher's note)

"A crisp account of a messy war, focusing on two Nebraska brothers, one of whom would later become a senator and Secretary of Defense." Kirkus

Includes bibliographical references (pages 271-317) and index.

Hagel, Tom

Bolger, Daniel P. **Our** year of war; two brothers, Vietnam, and a nation divided. Daniel P. Bolger. Da Capo Press 2017 xii, 336 p.p illustrations, maps (hardcover) $28 **92**

1. Vietnam War, 1961-1975 2. Nineteen sixty-eight, A.D. 3. Vietnam War, 1961-1975 -- Biography 4. Brothers -- United States -- Biography 5. Vietnam War, 1961-1975 -- United States 6. Cabinet officers -- United States -- Biography

ISBN 9780306903243; 9780306903267

LC 2017953360

In this book, by Daniel P. Bolger, "two brothers--Chuck and Tom Hagel--who went to war in Vietnam, fought in the same unit, and saved each other's life. . . . Together they fought in the Mekong Delta, battled snipers in Saigon, chased the enemy through the jungle, and each saved the other's life under fire. But when their one-year tour was over, these two brothers came home side-by-side but no longer in step--one supporting the war, the other hating it." (Publisher's note)

"A crisp account of a messy war, focusing on two Nebraska brothers, one of whom would later become a senator and Secretary of Defense." Kirkus

Includes bibliographical references (pages 271-317) and index.

Hager, Jenna Bush, 1981-

Bush, Jenna, 1981- **Sisters** first; stories from our wild and wonderful life. Jenna Bush Hager; Barbara Pierce Bush; foreword by Laura Bush. Grand Central Publishing 2017 256 p. $28 **92**

1. Presidents -- United States -- Children

ISBN 1538711419; 9781538711415

In this memoir, by Jenna Bush Hager and Barbara Pierce Bush, with foreword by Laura Bush, "former first daughters and #1 bestselling authors Jenna . . . and Barbara . . . share intimate stories and reflections from the Texas countryside to the storied halls of the White House and beyond. . . . [The sisters] spent their college years watched over by Secret Service agents and became fodder for the tabloids, with teenage mistakes making national headlines." (Publisher's note)

"The two first daughters emerge as surprisingly well-adjusted, intelligent young women with strong family bonds in this insightful look at life inside the White House." (Booklist)

Hahn, Emily, 1905-1997

Grescoe, Taras. **Shanghai** grand; forbidden love and international intrigue in a doomed world. Taras Grescoe. St. Martin's Press 2016 480 p. illustrations, map (hardcover) $28.99   **92**

1. Shanghai (China) -- History 2. Shanghai (China) -- Biography 3. Aliens -- China -- Shanhai -- Biography 4. Cathay Hotel (Shanghai, China) -- History 5. Americans -- China -- Shanhai -- Biography 6. Adventure and adventurers -- China -- Shanhai -- Biography 7. Shanghai (China) -- Social life and customs -- 20th century 8. Sino-Japanese War, 1937-1945 -- Social aspects -- China -- Shangahi
ISBN 9781250049711; 9781466850675

     LC 2016001124

This book, by Taras Grescoe, offers a biography of American journalist Emily Hahn "in free-wheeling 1930s Shanghai. . . . New Yorker writer Emily Hahn arrived there in 1935, intending to stay for two weeks. She fled, along with other expatriates, in 1943. Those eight years were filled with adventure, danger, love, and sex." (Kirkus Reviews)

"Grescoe (Straphanger, 2012) interweaves a cast of intriguing international characters into this seductive biography of a time, a place, a poet, and a girl." Booklist

Includes bibliographical references and index.

Halbreich, Betty, 1927-

Halbreich, Betty. **I'll** drink to that; a life in fashion, straight, no chaser. Betty Halbreich. The Penguin Press 2014 304 p. $27.95   **92**

1. Fashion 2. Clothing and dress 3. Personal appearance 4. Beauty, Personal 5. Image consultants -- United States -- Biography
ISBN 1594205701; 9781594205705

     LC 2014009695

This memoir is by "Betty Halbreich, [who] has spent nearly forty years as the legendary personal shopper at Bergdorf Goodman. . . . She has helped many find their true selves through clothes, frank advice, and her own brand of wisdom. She is trusted by the most discriminating persons--including Hollywood's top stylists--to tell them what looks best. But Halbreich's personal transformation from a cosseted young girl to a fearless truth teller is the greatest makeover of her career." (Publisher's note)

"Names are dropped and stories are told in Halbreich's distinctive voice. Fashion mavens will enjoy the industry gossip while mere mortals may benefit from the closet organization tips." LJ

Hale, Robert (Robert Allen), 1941-2008

Kizzia, Tom. **Pilgrim's** wilderness; a true story of faith and madness on the Alaska Frontier. by Tom Kizzia; edited by Kevin Doughten. Crown 2013 336 p. illustrations, map $25   **92**

1. Alaska 2. Dysfunctional families 3. Cults -- Alaska -- McCarthy 4. Incest -- Alaska -- McCarthy 5. McCarthy (Alaska) -- Biography 6. Pioneers -- Alaska -- McCarthy -- Biography 7. Criminals -- Alaska -- McCarthy -- Biography 8. Dysfunctional families -- Alaska -- McCarthy 9. Abusive men -- Alaska -- McCarthy -- Biography 10. Fundamentalists -- Alaska -- McCarthy -- Biography

ISBN 0307587827; 9780307587824; 9780307587848

     LC 2012016502

This book, by Tom Kizzia, edited by Kevin Doughten, presents the "true story of a modern-day homesteading family in the deepest reaches of the Alaskan wilderness--and of the chilling secrets of its maniacal, spellbinding patriarch. . . . [The book] unfolds the . . . story of a charismatic spinner of American myths who was not what he seemed, the townspeople caught in his thrall, and the family he brought to the brink of ruin." (Publisher's note)

"The horror at the heart of this story about religious extremism on the fringes of the last American frontier is slow to reveal itself, but when that horror fully emerges, it will swallow most readers. Provocative and disturbing." Kirkus

Includes bibliographical references

Haley, Alex

Norrell, Robert J. **Alex** Haley and the books that changed a nation; by Robert J. Norrell. Palgrave Macmillan 2015 272 p. 8 plates; illustrations (hardback) $26.99   **92**

1. African American authors 2. African American journalists -- Biography 3. Authors, American -- 20th century -- Biography
ISBN 1137279605; 9781137279606

     LC 2015016043

This biography on Alex Haley, by Robert J. Norrell, "follows him from his childhood in relative privilege in deeply segregated small town Tennessee to fame and fortune in high powered New York City. It was in the Navy, that Haley discovered himself as a writer, which eventually led his rise as a star journalist in the heyday of magazine personality profiles." (Publisher's note)

"With such a strong focus on the writing of Haley's two major works, this book will appeal primarily to readers who enjoyed or were inspired by The Autobiography of Malcolm X and Roots and wish to learn their backstories." LJ

Hall, Kevin A., 1969-

Pilon, Mary. The **Kevin** show; an olympic athlete's battle with mental illness. Mary Pilon. Bloomsbury USA 2018 336 p. (HB: alk. paper) $28   **92**

1. Schizophrenia 2. Olympic athletes -- BIography 3. Sailors -- Biography 4. Schizophrenia -- Patients -- Biography
ISBN 9781632866820

     LC 2017018771

In this book, author Mary Pilon "reveals the many-sided struggle of [Olympian] Kevin [Hall], his family, and the medical profession--to understand and treat a psychiatric disorder whose euphoric highs and creative ties to pop culture have become inextricable from Kevin's experience of himself. Kevin suffers from what doctors are beginning to call Truman Show delusion, a form of bipolar disorder named for the 1998 movie 'The Truman Show.'" (Publisher's note)

"Pilon's compelling portrait of a remarkable young man and the challenges he faces as a cancer survivor, Olympic athlete, and bipolar patient underscores all the difficulties involved, especially in treating mental illness, and offers insights into the effects it has on patients and their families." Booklist

Includes bibliographical references

Hall, Sands

★ Hall, Sands. **Flunk.** start. reclaiming my decade lost in Scientology. Sands Hall. Counterpoint Press 2018 416 p. $26   **92**

1. Scientology 2. Spiritual life 3. Autobiographies 4. Scientologists -- United States -- Biography 5. Ex-church members -- United States -- Biography

ISBN 9781619021785

LC 2017038728

In this memoir, author Sands Hall "chronicles her slow yet willing absorption into the Church of Scientology. Her time in the Church, the 1980s, includes the secretive illness and death of its founder, L. Ron Hubbard, and the ascension of David Miscavige. Hall compellingly reveals what drew her into the religion--what she found intriguing and useful--and how she came to confront its darker sides." (Publisher's note)

"An early candidate for memoir of the year, this is a thrilling story of one woman's search for truth and her place in the world." LJ

Hallberg, David

Hallberg, David. A **body** of work; dancing to the edge and back. David Hallberg. Touchstone 2017 424 p. illustrations (hardback) $28   92

1. Ballet dancers 2. Ballet dancers -- United States -- Biography
ISBN 9781476771175; 1476771154; 9781476771151; 9781476771168

LC 2017031000

This book, by David Hallberg, "presents an intimate journey through his artistic life. . . . Beginning with his real-life Billy Elliot childhood—an all-American story marred by intense bullying—and culminating in his hard-won come-back, Hallberg's brave memoir dives deep into life as an artist as he wrestles with ego, pushes the limits of his body, and searches for ecstatic perfection and fulfillment as one of the world's most acclaimed ballet dancers." (Publisher's note)

"Balletomanes and anyone interested in the creative process will appreciate this thoughtful account of the life of an accomplished artist." Booklist

Hamer, Frank, 1884-1955

Boessenecker, John, 1953- **Texas** Ranger; the epic life of Frank Hamer, the man who killed Bonnie and Clyde. John Boessenecker. Thomas Dunne Books 2016 528 p. illustrations (ebook) $60; (hardcover) $29.99   92

1. Police -- West (U.S.) 2. Law enforcement -- History 3. Texas Rangers -- Biography 4. Police -- Texas -- Biography 5. Law enforcement -- Texas -- History
ISBN 9781466879867; 9781250069986

LC 2015048659

In this book, "historian John Boessenecker sets out to restore [Frank] Hamer's good name and prove that he was, in fact, a classic American hero. From the horseback days of the Old West through the gangster days of the 1930s, Hamer stood on the frontlines of some of the most important and exciting periods in American history. . . . When at last his career came to an end, it was only when he ran up against another legendary Texan: Lyndon B. Johnson." (Publisher's note)

"Through the extraordinary experiences of this straight-shooting, honor-bound lawman, Boessenecker sets forth a critically needed look at the history of Texas lynchings and race riots while presenting evidence for the murderous nature of Bonnie and Clyde that foreordained their violent deaths." LJ

Includes bibliographical references

Hamilton, Alexander, 1757-1804

★ Chernow, Ron. **Alexander** Hamilton. Penguin Press 2004 818p il $35   92

1. Statesmen 2. Secretaries of the treasury 3. United States -- Politics and government -- 1783-1809
ISBN 1-594-20009-2

LC 2003-65641

"Chernow makes fresh contributions to Hamiltoniana: no one has discovered so much about Hamilton's illegitimate origins and harrowed

youth; few have been so taken by Hamilton's long-suffering, loving wife, Eliza. . . . This is a fine work that captures Hamilton's life with judiciousness and verve." Publ Wkly

Includes bibliographical references

Hamilton, Alexander, 1762-1824

★ Mazzeo, Tilar J. **Eliza** Hamilton; the extraordinary life and times of the wife of Alexander Hamilton. Tilar J. Mazzeo. Gallery Books 2018 352 p. (hardcover) $27   92

1. United States -- History -- 1775-1783, Revolution 2. Politicians' spouses -- United States -- Biography
ISBN 9781501166327; 9781501166303; 1501166301

LC 2018008245

This biography, by Tilar J. Mazzeo, "follows Eliza [Hamilton] through her early years in New York, into the ups and downs of her married life with Alexander [Hamilton], beyond the aftermath of his tragic murder, and finally to her involvement in many projects that cemented her legacy as one of the unsung heroes of our nation's early days. . . . 'Eliza Hamilton' is the captivating account of the woman behind the famous man." (Publisher's note)

"Mazzeo (Irena's Children) centers love and devotion in this satisfying cradle-to-grave biography, the first written about the wife of the first U.S. secretary of the treasury." Pub Wkly

Hamilton, Elizabeth Schuyler, 1757-1854

★ Mazzeo, Tilar J. **Eliza** Hamilton; the extraordinary life and times of the wife of Alexander Hamilton. Tilar J. Mazzeo. Gallery Books 2018 352 p. (hardcover) $27   92

1. United States -- History -- 1775-1783, Revolution 2. Politicians' spouses -- United States -- Biography
ISBN 9781501166327; 9781501166303; 1501166301

LC 2018008245

This biography, by Tilar J. Mazzeo, "follows Eliza [Hamilton] through her early years in New York, into the ups and downs of her married life with Alexander [Hamilton], beyond the aftermath of his tragic murder, and finally to her involvement in many projects that cemented her legacy as one of the unsung heroes of our nation's early days. . . . 'Eliza Hamilton' is the captivating account of the woman behind the famous man." (Publisher's note)

"Mazzeo (Irena's Children) centers love and devotion in this satisfying cradle-to-grave biography, the first written about the wife of the first U.S. secretary of the treasury." Pub Wkly

Hamilton, Gabrielle, 1965-

Hamilton, Gabrielle. **Blood,** bones & butter; the inadvertent education of a reluctant chef. Random House 2011 291p $26   92

1. Cooks 2. Restaurateurs 3. Biography, Individual
ISBN 978-1-4000-6872-2; 1-4000-6872-X; 978-1-58836-931-4 ebook; 1-58836-931-5 ebook

LC 2010-17518

This book recounts how "when [Gabrielle] Hamilton was growing up, her parents would throw enormous parties for their friends and neighbors. Cooking for more than one hundred people was a common event in her family life. As she grew up, she sought to recreate the challenge and joy of feeding all those people and, unsurprisingly, she became a world-class chef. Her journey to owning her own New York City restaurant was not smooth, and took her all over the world." (Voice of Youth Advocates)

Though this book "is rhapsodic about food—in every variety, from the humble egg-on-a-roll sandwich served by Greek delis in New York to more esoteric things like 'fried zucchini agrodolce with fresh mint and hot chili flakes'—the book is hardly just for foodies. Ms. Hamilton

. . . is as evocative writing about people and places as she is at writing about cooking." N Y Times (Late N Y Ed)

Hamilton, Jeremiah G., -1875

White, Shane. **Prince** of darkness; the untold story of Jeremiah G. Hamilton, Wall Street's first black millionaire. Shane White. Palgrave Macmillan 2015 360 p. $27.99   **92**

1. Finance -- United States 2. African Americans -- Biography 3. African American businesspeople 4. United States -- Social conditions 5. United States -- Race relations -- History 6. Millionaires -- United States -- Biography 7. United States -- Social conditions -- 19th century 8. Finance -- United States -- History -- 19th century 9. African Americans -- Social conditions -- 19th century 10. African American capitalists and financiers -- Biography 11. United States -- Race relations -- History -- 19th century

ISBN 9781250070562

LC 2015011416

In this book, author Shane White "reveals the larger than life story of [Jeremiah G. Hamilton] who defied every convention of his time. He wheeled and dealt in the lily white business world, he married a white woman, he bought a mansion in rural New Jersey, he owned railroad stock on trains he was not legally allowed to ride, and generally set his white contemporaries' teeth on edge when he wasn't just plain outsmarting them." (Publisher's note)

"Superb scholarship and a sprightly style recover an unaccountably overlooked life in our history." Kirkus

Includes bibliographical references (pages 325-354) and index.

Hampl, Patricia, 1946-

Hampl, Patricia. The **art** of the wasted day; Patricia Hampl. Viking 2018 288 p. (hardcover) $26   **92**

1. Leisure 2. Travel writing

ISBN 9780525429647; 0525429646

LC 2017032689

This memoir, by Patricia Hampl, "is a picaresque travelogue of leisure written from a lifelong enchantment with solitude. . . . Hampl visits the homes of historic exemplars of ease who made repose a goal, even an art form. She begins with two celebrated eighteenth-century Irish ladies who ran off to live a life of 'retirement' in rural Wales. Her search then leads to Moravia to consider the monk-geneticist, Gregor Mendel, and finally to Bordeaux for Michel Montaigne." (Publisher's note)

"For all the vital, sensuous, enrapturing descriptions that engender a powerful sense of presence, this is also a contemplation of absence and solitude as Hampl tenderly contends with the sudden death of her husband. An exquisite anatomy of mind and an incandescent reflection on nature, being, and rapture." Booklist

Hanagarne, Joshua, 1977-

Hanagarne, Josh. The **world's** strongest librarian; a memoir of Tourette's, faith, strength, and the power of family. Joshua Hanagarne. Gotham Books 2013 288 p. (hardcover) $26   **92**

1. Tourette syndrome 2. Public libraries -- Utah -- Salt Lake City 3. Librarians -- Utah -- Salt Lake City -- Biography

ISBN 1592407870; 9781592407873

LC 2012037713

This memoir, by Josh Hanagarne, is the story of a Mormon with Tourette Syndrome. "By the time [Josh Hanagarne] was twenty, . . . his Tourette's tics escalated to nightmarish levels. Determined to conquer his affliction, Josh underwent everything from quack remedies to lethargy-inducing drug regimes. . . . At last, an eccentric, autistic strongman . . . taught Josh how to 'throttle' his tics into submission through strength-training." (Publisher's note)

Hanchett, Jannelle

Hanchett, Janelle. **I'm** just happy to be here; a memoir of recklessness, rehab, and renegade mothering. Janelle Hanchett. Hachette Books 2018 320 p. (hardcover) $26   **92**

1. Motherhood 2. Substance abuse

ISBN 9780316503778; 9780316549431; 9781478969808

LC 2017952977

In this book, Janelle Hanchett chronicles "her tumultuous journey from young motherhood to abysmal addiction and a recovery she never imagined possible. . . . Hers is a story we rarely hear--of the addict mother not redeemed by her children; who longs for normalcy but cannot maintain it; and who, having traveled to seemingly irreversible depths, makes it back, only to discover she is still an outsider." (Publisher's note)

"Hanchett illuminates how addiction can take over a person's life. She thoughtfully writes about returning to motherhood after periods of absence when her children were young. At times witty, heartbreaking, and enlightening, Hanchett's memoir will resonate with parents and nonparents alike." Booklist

Handel, George Frideric, 1685-1759

Harris, Ellen T. **George** Frideric Handel; a life with friends. Ellen T. Harris. W. W. Norton & Company 2014 496 p. illustrations (hardcover) $37.95   **92**

1. Composers -- Biography

ISBN 0393088952; 9780393088953

LC 2014008148

This book, by Ellen T. Harris, is "[a]n intimate portrait of [George Frideric] Handel's life and inner circle. . . . Harris has spent years tracking down the letters, diaries, personal accounts, legal cases, and other documents connected to these bequests. The result is a tightly woven tapestry of London in the first half of the eighteenth century, one that interlaces vibrant descriptions of Handel's music with stories of loyalty, cunning, and betrayal." (Publisher's note)

A "readable tale of one of the world's most enigmatic musicians and composers." Pub Wkly

Includes bibliographical references, discography, and index

Handwerker, Nathan, 1892-1974

Handwerker, Lloyd. **Famous** Nathan; a family saga of Coney Island, the American dream, and the search for the perfect hot dog. Lloyd Handwerker and Gil Reavill. Flatiron Books 2016 320 p. illustrations (hardback) $26.99   **92**

1. Hot dogs 2. Coney Island (New York, N.Y.) 3. Family-owned business enterprises 4. Nathan's Famous 5. Coney Island (New York, N.Y.) -- History 6. Frankfurters -- New York (State) -- History 7. Hot dog stands -- New York (State) -- History 8. Fast food restaurants -- New York (State) -- History

ISBN 9781250074546; 1250074541

LC 2016001605

In this book, written with Gil Reavill, author Lloyd Handwerker "relates every knowable detail about Nathan's Famous: employee tensions, how the potatoes were sourced, even who painted the signed. He also nestles his grandfather's story in the greater context of family struggles, Coney Island, the history of hot dogs, and the evolving American landscape." (Publishers Weekly)

"It's an American Dream tale with a captivating central character, served with the same delicious snap as an authentic Nathan's hot dog." Booklist

Includes bibliographical references.

Hanna-Attisha, Mona

Hanna-Attisha, Mona. **What** the eyes don't see; a story of crisis, resistance, and hope in an American city. Mona Hanna-Attisha. One World 2018 384 p. (hardback) $28   **92**
1. Physicians 2. Lead poisoning 3. Drinking water -- Contamination 4. Lead poisoning -- Michigan -- Flint 5. Flint (Mich.) -- Environmental conditions 6. Physicians -- Michigan -- Flint -- Biography 7. Water quality management -- Michigan -- Flint 8. Drinking water -- Lead content -- Michigan -- Flint
ISBN 9780399590832

LC 2018002721

This book, by Mona Hanna-Attisha, "is the inspiring story of how . . . [the author] proved that Flint's kids were exposed to lead and then fought her own government and a brutal backlash to expose that truth to the world. . . . [It] shows how misguided austerity policies, the withdrawal of democratic government, and callous bureaucratic indifference placed an entire city at risk." (Publisher's note)

"Essential for all readers who care about children, health, and the environment. This should be required reading for public servants as an incisive cautionary tale, and for pediatricians and youth advocates as a story of heroism in the ranks of people who have the capacity to make a difference." Library Journal

Includes bibliographical references

Hannibal, 247 B.C.-182 B.C

Hunt, Patrick N. **Hannibal**; Patrick N. Hunt. Simon & Schuster 2017 xv, 362 p.p maps (hardcover) $28   **92**
1. Military history 2. Carthage (Extinct city) 3. Punic Wars, 264 B.C.-146 B.C. 4. Carthage (Extinct city) -- Biography 5. Punic War, 2nd, 218-201 B.C. -- Campaigns 6. Generals -- Tunisia -- Carthage (Extinct city) -- Biography
ISBN 1439102171; 9781439109779; 9781439102176

LC 2016051474

This book, by Patrick M. Hunt, tells the story of "one of the greatest commanders of the ancient world, . . . Hannibal [Barca of Carthage], the brilliant general who successfully crossed the Alps with his war elephants and brought Rome to its knees. . . . Hunt has led archeological expeditions in the Alps and elsewhere to study Hannibal's achievements. Now he brings Hannibal's incredible story to life in this riveting and dramatic book." (Publisher's note)

"This easily digestible and engrossing biography is ideal for general readers with an interest in ancient history." Booklist

Includes bibliographical references and index

Hansberry, Lorraine, 1930-1965

Hansberry, Lorraine. **To** be young, gifted, and Black; Lorraine Hansberry in her own words. adapted by Robert Nemiroff; with drawings and art by Lorraine Hansberry; introduction by James Baldwin; and a new preface by Jewell Handy Gresham Nemiroff. 1st Vintage Books ed; Vintage Books 1995 xxx, 261p il pa $8.95; pa $13.95   **92**
1. Authors 2. Dramatists 3. Essayists 4. Newspaper editors 5. Nonfiction writers 6. Dramatists, American 7. African American women -- Biography
ISBN 9780451531780; 0-679-76415-1

LC 96-119999

First published 1969 by Prentice-Hall

Work on this book and on the script for the play of the same title, which was presented at New York's Cherry Lane Theatre in 1969, "proceeded concurrently, each drawing upon the experiences and creative discoveries of the other, but ultimately diverging quite drastically." Postscript

Hansen, Suzy, 1977-

Hansen, Suzy. **Notes** on a foreign country; an American abroad in a post-American world. Suzy Hansen. Farrar, Straus & Giroux 2017 276 p. (hardcover) $26   **92**
1. Turkey 2. United States -- Foreign opinion 3. Turkey -- Relations -- United States 4. United States -- Relations -- Turkey 5. United States -- Foreign public opinion, Turkish 6. Foreign correspondents -- United States -- Biography
ISBN 9780374712440; 9780374280048

LC 2016059415

Pulitzer Prize Finalist: General Nonfiction (2018)

In this memoir, Suzy Hansen, describes how she move from New Jersey to Istanbul "in the wake of the September 11 attacks and the U.S.-led invasion of Iraq. . . . Blending memoir, journalism, and history, and deeply attuned to the voices of those she met on her travels, . . . [this] is a moving reflection on America's place in the world." (Publisher's note)

"A mostly illuminating literary debut that shows how Americans' ignorance about the world has made turmoil and terrorism possible." Kirkus

Includes bibliographical references (pages [249]-259) and index.

Harden, Marcia Gay

Harden, Marcia Gay, 1959- The **seasons** of my mother; a memoir of love, family, and flowers. Marcia Gay Harden. Atria Books 2018 325 p $27   **92**
1. Alzheimer's disease 2. Mother-daughter relationship
ISBN 1501135708; 9781501135705

In this memoir, actress Marcia Gay Harden "uses the imagery of flowers and the art of Ikebana to depict the unique creative bond that she has had with her mother throughout the years and how, together, they are facing her mother s struggle with Alzheimer s disease." (Publisher's note)

"Praise, love, and honor all play roles in this respectful, highly affectionate memoir about a spirited mother-daughter relationship." Kirkus

Harding, Ian, 1986-

Harding, Ian. **Odd** birds; Ian Harding. St. Martin's Press 2017 viii, 254 p.p illustrations (hardcover) $25.99   **92**
1. Bird watching 2. Actors -- United States -- Biography 3. Bird watching -- Anecdotes
ISBN 9781250117083; 9781250117076

LC 2017001939

This book, by Ian Harding, "is more than just a Hollywood memoir or tell-all. At its heart, this book is a coming-of-age story in which Ian wrestles with an ever evolving question— how can he still be himself, while also being a celebrity. Each humorous and heartfelt story features a particular bird—sometimes literal, at other times figurative. Using this framework, Ian explores a variety of topics." (Publisher's note)

"Harding recounts with charm and enthusiasm his road to success as an actor (including the semester he had to spend portraying a jellyfish) and his rediscovery of the joys of birding." Booklist

Hardy, Thomas, 1840-1928

Tomalin, Claire. **Thomas** Hardy. Penguin Group 2006 xxv, 486p il map $35   **92**
1. Poets 2. Authors 3. Novelists 4. Short story writers
ISBN 1-59420-118-8; 978-1-59420-118-9

LC 2007-295886

"A priceless resource for the general reader and the Victorian scholar." Booklist

Includes bibliographical references

Hari, Daoud

Hari, Daoud. The **translator**; a tribesman's memoir of Darfur. Random House 2008 204p hardcover o.p. pa $13   **92**

1. Refugees 2. Memoirists 3. Guides (Persons) 4. Sudan -- History -- Darfur conflict, 2003-

ISBN 978-1-4000-6744-2; 1-4000-6744-8; 978-0-8129-7917-6 pa; 0-8129-7917-6 pa

LC 2007-42308

In this memoir, the author recounts his life in Darfur, Sudan before and after the conflict in 2003.

"Those with the courage to join Hari's odyssey may find this a life-changing read." Publ Wkly

Harpham, Heather Elise, 1967-

Harpham, Heather. **Happiness**; the crooked little road to semi-ever after. Heather Harpham. Henry Holt & Co. 2017 305 p. (hardcover) $27   **92**

1. Blood -- Diseases 2. Parent-child relationship 3. Newborn infants -- Hospital care 4. Blood -- Transfusion 5. Parent and child -- Biography 6. Blood diseases in pregnancy -- United States 7. Newborn Infants -- Diseases -- United States -- Biography

ISBN 9781250131577; 9781250131560

LC 2016040488

This memoir, by Heather Harpham, "begins with a charming courtship between hopelessly attracted opposites: Heather, a world-roaming California girl, and Brian, an intellectual, homebody writer, kind and slyly funny, but loath to leave his Upper West Side studio. Their magical interlude ends, full stop, when Heather becomes pregnant. . . . Heather returns to California to deliver their daughter alone, buoyed by family and friends." (Publisher's note)

"Harpham has written a heartfelt exploration of familial bonds and the sometimes incredibly bumpy journey one must take to get to contentment." Pub Wkly

Harris, Jessica B.

Harris, Jessica B. **My** soul looks back; a memoir. Jessica B. Harris. Scribner 2017 xi, 257 p.p (hardcover) $25   **92**

1. Women authors 2. American cooking 3. African American cooking 4. Cooking, American 5. African American cooks -- Biography 6. African American college teachers -- Biography 7. Women food writers -- United States -- Biography

ISBN 9781501127007; 9781501125904; 9781501125928

LC 2017012143

In this memoir, "award-winning writer Jessica B. Harris recalls a lost era—the vibrant New York City of her youth, where her social circle included Maya Angelou, James Baldwin, and other members of the Black intelligentsia. . . . The book is framed by Harris's relationship with Sam Floyd, a fellow professor at Queens College, who introduced her to Baldwin." (Publisher's note)

"This is a lively, entertaining, and informative recounting of a time and place that shaped and greatly enriched American culture." Pub Wkly

Harris, Neil Patrick, 1973-

Harris, Neil Patrick, 1973- **Neil** Patrick Harris; choose your own autobiography. by Neil Patrick Harris; as unshredded and pasted back together by David Javerbaum. Crown Archetype 2014 ix, 294 p.p 8 plates; color illustrations (hardcover) $26   **92**

1. Plot-your-own stories 2. Actors -- United States -- Biography

ISBN 0385346999; 9780385346993

LC 2014016637

In this book, by Neil Patrick Harris, edited by David Javerbaum, a "Joycean experiment in light celebrity narrative, actor/personality/ carbon-based-life-form Neil Patrick Harris lets you, the reader, live his life. You will be born to New Mexico. You will get your big break at an acting camp. You will get into a bizarre confrontation outside a nightclub with actor Scott Caan. Even better, at each critical juncture of your life you will choose how to proceed." (Publisher's note)

Harrington, Shawn

Bradbud, Rus. **All** the dreams we've dreamed; a story of hoops and handguns on Chicago's West Side. Rus Bradbur. Independent Pub Group 2018 272 p. $26.99   **92**

1. Violence 2. Basketball 3. Basketball coaches

ISBN 1613739311; 9781613739310

This book, by Rus Bradbur, presents "a true story of courage, endurance, and friendship in one of America's most violent neighborhoods. . . . Bradbur, who has an intimate forty-year relationship to Chicago basketball, tells . . . [Shawn Harrington's] story with empathy and care, exploring the intertwined tragedies of gun violence, health care failure, racial assumptions, struggling educational systems, corruption in athletics--and the hope that can survive them all." (Publisher's note)

Harrison, George, 1943-2001

Thomson, Graeme. **George** Harrison; Behind the Locked Door. Graeme Thomson. Overlook Books 2015 464 p. 8 plates; ills.; portraits $29.95   **92**

1. Beatles 2. Musicians

ISBN 1468310658; 9781468310658

In this biography, author Graeme Thompson "challenges the image of George Harrison as 'the quiet Beatle,' portraying the guitarist as a complex person trying to navigate a middle course between materiality and spirituality, and fame and reclusivity. . . . Thomson chronicles Harrison's life from his rather run-of-the mill childhood and his early days of making music with The Quarrymen to the beginnings of The Beatles, their rapid ascent to fame and their just as speedy descent." (Publishers Weekly)

"Thomson is especially compelling in his illumination of Harrison's inner life, his robust spirituality, and his deep love of Indian culture." Booklist

Harrison, William Henry, 1773-1841

Collins, Gail. **William** Henry Harrison; Gail Collins. Times Books/Henry Holt and Co. 2012 xviii, 153 p.p   **92**

1. War of 1812 2. Presidents -- United States -- Biography 3. Governors -- Indiana -- Biography 4. United States -- History -- 1783-1865 5. Presidents -- United States -- Election -- 1840 6. United States -- Politics and government -- 1841-1845

ISBN 9780805091182

LC 2011018976

This book offers a biography of U.S. former president William Henry Harrison. "Despite the legendary 1840 campaign featuring a 'log cabin, hard cider' frontiersman with humble origins, Harrison was born on a Virginia plantation, built himself a mansion as governor of the rough Indiana frontier territory, and avoided alcohol. His fame rested on two victories: the 1811 battle of Tippecanoe against the Shawnee Indians, and the 1813 Battle of the Thames during the War of 1812, in which the Indian leader Tecumseh was killed. For decades afterward, he struggled as a farmer and Ohio politician; he lost the 1836 presidential election but won four years later." (Publishers Weekly)

Includes bibliographical references and index

Harry, Prince, Duke of Sussex, 1984-

Levin, Angela. **Harry**; a biography of a prince. Angela

Levin. W W Norton & Co Inc 2018 295 p. $26.95 **92**

1. Biography 2. Princes -- Great Britain -- Biography
ISBN 1681779102; 9781681779102

This biography of Prince Harry of Sussex, by Angela Levin, "is a three-dimensional look at what Harry is really like as a person, both on and off royal duty. . . . [It] unwraps the real man behind the camera, and his own perceptive insights. It delves into his troubled childhood and the lasting effect of losing his adored mother, Diana, Princess of Wales, so young. It explores his rebellious teenage years and the key defining moments that have enabled him to face his demons." (Publisher's note)

"Journalist Levin (Diana's Babies), who interviewed England's Prince Harry for a Newsweek cover story in 2017, provides an admiring, if not all that revealing, look at the popular royal's life from the tragic death of his mother to his romance with actress Meghan Markle." Pub Wkly

Hart, Hannah

Hart, Hannah. **Buffering**; Unshared Tales of a Life Fully Loaded. by Hannah Hart. HarperCollins 2016 240 p. illustrations $23.99 **92**

1. Essays 2. Biography 3. Autobiographies
ISBN 0062457519; 9780062457516
Alex Award (2017)

In this book, author Hannah Hart is "stirring up memories and tales from her past. By combing through the journals that Hannah has kept for much of her life, this collection of narrative essays deliver a fuller picture of her life, her experiences, and the things she's figured out about family, faith, love, sexuality, self-worth, friendship and fame." (Publisher's note)

"Although she is currently living the life of a public figure, a fact that she teasingly points out throughout the piece, Hart focuses on her past; its complexities, juxtapositions, and contradictions make up the bulk of her entertaining and honest story." Pub Wkly

Hart, Kevin, 1979-

Hart, Kevin. **I** can't make this up; life lessons. Kevin Hart with Neil Strauss. 37 Ink/Atria 2017 378 p. illustrations (hardcover) $26.99 **92**

1. Autobiographies 2. Comedians -- United States -- Biography 3. Motion picture actors and actresses -- United States -- Biography 4. African American comedians -- Biography 5. North Philadelphia (Philadelphia, Pa.) -- Biography
ISBN 9781501155581; 9781501155574; 9781501155567; 1501155563

LC 2016478508

In this memoir, Kevin Hart "turns his immense talent to the written word by writing some words. Some of those words include: the, a, for, above, and even even. Put them together and you have the funniest, most heartfelt, and most inspirational memoir on survival, success, and the importance of believing in yourself since Old Yeller." (Publisher's note)

"A truthful, self-deprecating, and funny look at the hard work behind Hart's success." Booklist

Hatshepsut, Queen of Egypt

Cooney, Kara, 1972- The **woman** who would be king; Hatshepsut's Rise to Power in Ancient Egypt. Kara Cooney. Crown Publishers 2014 384 p. 8 plates; ills; plans; maps $28 **92**

1. Queens 2. Egypt -- Kings and rulers 3. Pharaohs -- Biography 4. Queens -- Egypt -- Biography 5. Egypt -- Kings and rulers -- Biography 6. Egypt -- History -- Eighteenth dynasty, ca. 1570-1320 B.C

ISBN 0307956768; 9780307956767

LC 2014000243

This book, by Kara Cooney, is a "biography of the longest-reigning female pharaoh in Ancient Egypt. . . . Hatshepsut--the daughter of a general who usurped Egypt's throne and a mother with ties to the previous dynasty--was born into a privileged position in the royal household. . . . Her failure to produce a male heir was ultimately the twist of fate that paved the way for her improbable rule as a cross-dressing king." (Publisher's note)

"By examining her subject within the context of the stringent gender restrictions of her time and place, [Cooney] attempts to explain the motivations and the thought processes of one of the most successful female leaders of the ancient world." Booklist

Ryan, Donald P. **Beneath** the sands of Egypt; adventures of an unconventional archaeologist. William Morrow 2010 286p il $26.99; ebook $12.99 **92**

1. Queens 2. Archeologists 3. Archaeologists 4. College teachers 5. Egypt -- Antiquities 6. Excavations (Archeology) -- Egypt
ISBN 978-0-06-173282-9; 0-06-173282-6; 978-0-06-200280-8 ebook; 0-06-200280-5 ebook

LC 2010-20355

"Ryan, the archaeologist who rediscovered tomb KV 60 in the Valley of the Kings (later identified as the final resting place of the pharoah Hatshepsut), takes us through his life, career, and numerous expeditions. It's a thrilling book, not because it's full of Indiana Jones heroics but because Ryan's enthusiasm for what he does (more dirt-sifting than bull-whip-wielding) is manifested on every page; and . . . he catches us up in his excitement, makes us wish we weren't just reading about this stuff but were actually doing it. . . . This wonderful adventure story should be must reading for anyone aspiring to become an archaeologist, but even those of us who harbor no such dreams will be aching to get a little dirt under our fingernails." Booklist

Havel, Václav

Zantovsky, Michael. **Havel**; A Life. Michael Zantovsky. Grove Press 2014 512 p. illustrations $30 **92**

1. Czech authors
ISBN 0802123155; 9780802123152

LC 2015430681

This book by Michael Zantovsky is a biography of "Václav Havel . . . one of the most prominent figures of the twentieth century: iconoclast and intellectual, renowned playwright turned political dissident, president of a united then divided nation, and dedicated human rights activist. Written by Michael Zantovsky--Havel's former press secretary, advisor, and longtime friend--[it] presents a revelatory portrait of this giant among men." (Publisher's note)

"Zantovský lends a more impartial eye to Havel's subsequent 10-year term as president of the newly formed Czech Republic, when he was no longer at Havel's side, and to the travails of his last years. This moving, perceptive chronicle succeeds in showing the many dimensions of a towering 20th-century figure." Pub Wkly

Hawa Abdi, 1947-

Abdi, Hawa. **Keeping** hope alive; one woman, 90,000 lives changed. Hawa Abdi with Sarah J. Robbins. Grand Central Pub. 2013 272 p. (hardcover) $26.99 **92**

1. Refugees -- Somalia 2. Somalia -- Biography 3. Gynecologists -- Somalia -- Biography 4. Women gynecologists -- Somalia -- Biography 5. Human rights workers -- Somalia -- Biography 6. Women human rights workers -- Somalia -- Biography
ISBN 1455503762; 9781455503766; 9781619696389

LC 2012041781

This book presents a memoir by physician Haw Abdi, "who, along with her daughters, has kept 90,000 of her fellow citizens safe, healthy, and educated for over 20 years in Somalia." The author "is the founder of a massive camp for internally displaced people located a few miles from war-torn Mogadishu, Somalia. Since 1991, when the Somali government collapsed . . . she has dedicated herself to providing help for people whose lives have been shattered by violence and poverty." (Publisher's note)

Hawking, Stephen, 1942-2018

Hawking, Stephen, 1942-2018. **My** brief history; Stephen Hawking. Bantam Books 2013 144 p. illustrations $22   **92**
1. Cosmology 2. Black holes (Astronomy) 3. Physicists -- Biography
ISBN 0345535286; 9780345535283

LC 2013027938

In this autobiography, Stephen Hawking "opens up about the challenges that confronted him following his diagnosis of ALS at age twenty-one. Tracing his development as a thinker, he explains how the prospect of an early death urged him onward through numerous intellectual breakthroughs, and talks about the genesis of his masterpiece 'A Brief History of Time'". (Publisher's note)

"Hawking says it all with charm, intermingling his personal life with abstruse theoretical physics in nontechnical language. Revealing the power of mind over body, this is an enjoyable, entertaining, and inspiring work." Choice

Hawthorne, Nathaniel, 1804-1864

★ Wineapple, Brenda. **Hawthorne**: a life. Alfred A. Knopf 2003 xii, 509 p.p il $30   **92**
1. Authors 2. Novelists 3. Short story writers
ISBN 0-375-40044-3; 9780812972917

LC 2002-192485

In this biography Wineapple discusses the "public controversies that shaped [Hawthorne's] world: the Whig triumphs that cost him his customhouse job and forced him into writing; the critical exchanges that heartened him with praise for his work . . . and wounded him with disparagement; and the Civil War battles that drove him to despair—and into political disrepute as a copperhead." Booklist

Includes bibliographical references (p. 473-486) and index.

Haydn; edited by David Wyn Jones; consultant editor Otto Biba. Oxford Univ. Press 2002 xxi, 515p il map (Oxford composer companions) $75   **92**
1. Composers
ISBN 0-19-866216-5

LC 2002-510033

"This volume will be useful to persons who need quick, specific information about Haydn, his works, and 18th-century style." Choice

Hayes, Bill, 1961-

Hayes, Bill. **Insomniac** city; New York, Oliver, and me. Bill Hayes. St. Martin's Press 2017 304 p. (HC) $27   **92**
1. New York (N.Y.) -- Description and travel
ISBN 9781620404935; 1620404931

LC 2017017262

This memoir is "a moving celebration of what [author] Bill Hayes calls 'the evanescent, the eavesdropped, the unexpected' of life in New York City, and an intimate glimpse of his relationship with the late Oliver Sacks. . . . [It] is both a meditation on grief and a celebration of life. Filled with Hayes's distinctive street photos of everyday New Yorkers, the book is a love song to the city and to all who have felt the particular magic and solace it offers." (Publisher's note)

"A unique and exuberant celebration of life and love." Kirkus

Hazan, Marcella

Hazan, Marcella. **Amarcord,** Marcella remembers; the remarkable life story of the woman who started out teaching science in a small town in Italy, but ended up teaching America how to cook Italian. Gotham Books 2008 307p il $27.50 **92**
1. Cooks 2. Italian cooking 3. Cookbook writers 4. Cooking teachers
ISBN 978-1-59240-388-2; 1-59240-388-3

LC 2007-46197

This is a memoir by the author of The Classic Italian Cook Book (1973) and More Classic Italian Cooking (1978).

"Hazan has selected the best stories from her own life to present Amarcord with all the warmth and humor of a long meal in famiglia made from the choicest ingredients. . . . If you've never been [to] Italy, the time spent with Hazan will have you planning your next vacation faster than you can say manicotti." Christ Sci Monit

Hearst family

Nickliss, Alexandra M. **Phoebe** Apperson Hearst; a life of power and politics. Alexandra M. Nickliss. University of Nebraska Press 2017 664 p. (cloth: alk. paper) $39.95   **92**
1. Women philanthropists -- Biography 2. San Francisco (Calif.) -- Biography 3. Philanthropists -- California -- Biography 4. Upper class women -- United States -- Biography 5. Women philanthropists -- California -- Biography 6. California -- Politics and government -- 1850-1950 7. University of California (System). Regents -- Biography
ISBN 9781496202277

LC 2017026677

Author "Alexandra M. Nickliss offers the first biography of one of the Gilded Age's most prominent and powerful women. A financial manager, businesswoman, and reformer, Phoebe Apperson Hearst was one of the wealthiest and most influential women of the era and a philanthropist, almost without rival, in the San Francisco Bay Area." (Publisher's note)

Includes bibliographical references and index

Hearst, Phoebe Apperson, 1842-1919

Nickliss, Alexandra M. **Phoebe** Apperson Hearst; a life of power and politics. Alexandra M. Nickliss. University of Nebraska Press 2017 664 p. (cloth: alk. paper) $39.95   **92**
1. Women philanthropists -- Biography 2. San Francisco (Calif.) -- Biography 3. Philanthropists -- California -- Biography 4. Upper class women -- United States -- Biography 5. Women philanthropists -- California -- Biography 6. California -- Politics and government -- 1850-1950 7. University of California (System). Regents -- Biography
ISBN 9781496202277

LC 2017026677

Author "Alexandra M. Nickliss offers the first biography of one of the Gilded Age's most prominent and powerful women. A financial manager, businesswoman, and reformer, Phoebe Apperson Hearst was one of the wealthiest and most influential women of the era and a philanthropist, almost without rival, in the San Francisco Bay Area." (Publisher's note)

Includes bibliographical references and index

Hearst, William Randolph, 1863-1951

Nasaw, David. The **chief**: the life of William Randolph Hearst. Houghton Mifflin 2000 687p il $35; pa $16   **92**

1. Newspaper editors 2. Newspaper executives
ISBN 0-395-82759-0; 0-618-15446-9 pa

LC 99-462122

"Few publishers have loomed as large in their lifetimes, or cast as long a shadow after death, as William Randolph Hearst. . . . Nasaw's judicious and comprehensive biography sensibly seeks to understand its subject, not to judge him." New Yorker

Includes bibliographical references

Whyte, Kenneth. The **uncrowned** king; the sensational rise of William Randolph Hearst. Counterpoint 2009 546p il $30   **92**

1. Publishers and publishing 2. Newspaper editors 3. Newspaper executives
ISBN 978-1-58243-467-4; 1-58243-467-0

LC 2008-47442

"A very worthwhile reexamination of the rise of a flawed but accomplished man." Booklist

Includes bibliographical references (p. 505-511)

Heath, Robert G. (Robert Galbraith), 1915-1999

Frank, Lone. The **pleasure** shock; the rise of deep brain stimulation and its forgotten inventor. Lone Frank. Dutton 2018 320 p. (hardcover) $28   **92**

1. Brain stimulation 2. Mental illness -- Treatment 3. Louisiana 4. History, 20th Century 5. Physicians -- history 6. Mental Disorders -- therapy 7. Deep Brain Stimulation -- history
ISBN 9781101986530

LC 2017029957

This book, by Lone Frank, tells the "history of Robert Heath's brain pacemaker, investigating the origins and ethics of one of today's most promising medical breakthroughs: deep brain stimulation. . . . Frank has uncovered lost documents and accounts of Heath's pioneering efforts. She has tracked down surviving colleagues and patients. And she has delved into the current embrace of deep brain stimulation by scientists and patients alike." (Publisher's note)

"Frank has written an excellent, balanced portrait of an inventive psychiatrist with a complicated legacy." Pub Wkly

Includes bibliographical references

Hegar, Mary Jennings

Hegar, Mary Jennings. **Shoot** like a girl; one woman's dramatic fight in Afghanistan and on the home front. Mary Jennings Hegar. New American Library 2017 viii, 292 p.p illustrations (hardcover) $26   **92**

1. Women soldiers -- Biography 2. United States -- National Guard 3. Afghan War, 2001- -- Personal narratives 4. United States. Air Force -- Women -- Biography 5. United States -- Air National Guard -- Biography 6. Sexual harassment in the military -- United States 7. Afghan War, 2001- -- Search and rescue operations -- United States 8. Sex discrimination against women -- United States -- History -- 21st century
ISBN 9781101988459; 9781101988435

LC 2015047084

In this book, author Mary Jennings Hegar "takes the reader on a dramatic journey through her military career: an inspiring, humorous, and thrilling true story of a brave, high-spirited, and unforgettable woman who has spent much of her life ready to sacrifice everything for her country, her fellow man, and her sense of justice." (Publisher's note)

"Hegar's inspirational memoir reflects the strength and grace with which she approached her service to her country, whether she was venturing behind enemy lines to rescue wounded soldiers or standing up for women's right to be on the front line." Booklist

Heisenberg, Werner, 1901-1976

Cassidy, David C., 1945- **Beyond** uncertainty; Heisenberg, quantum physics, and the bomb. David C. Cassidy. Bellevue Literary Press 2009 480 p. $27   **92**

1. Physicists 2. Biography, Individual 3. Nobel laureates for physics 4. Physicists -- Germany -- Biography 5. World War, 1939-1945 -- Science -- Germany 6. Atomic bomb -- Germany -- History -- 20th century
ISBN 978-1-934137-13-0; 1-934137-13-8; 1934137138; 9781934137130

LC 2008039885

This is a biography "of the German wunderkind Werner Heisenberg (1901–1976), who won the 1932 Nobel Prize in physics for revolutionizing the nascent field of quantum physics, first with his matrix interpretation of quantum mechanics, then with his famous uncertainty principle. . . . Exhaustively detailed yet eminently readable, this is an important book." Publ Wkly

Includes bibliographical references (p. [411]-456) and index

Heller, Joseph

Daugherty, Tracy. **Just** one catch; a biography of Joseph Heller. St. Martin's Press 2011 548p il $35   **92**

1. Authors 2. Novelists 3. Authors, American 4. Short story writers 5. Biography, Individual
ISBN 978-0-312-59685-9; 0-312-59685-5

LC 2011-20749

This biography offers "countless insightful, amusing anecdotes from Heller's childhood, military service and postpublication notoriety as a celebrated literary figure. But the writing, publishing and ensuing aftermath of Catch-22 is the clear focal point of Daugherty's book. Lacking the self-assured swagger of Norman Mailer and the countercultural sway of the Beats, Heller was a long-frustrated and surprising emergent on the literary scene. A reluctant participant in the burgeoning Madison Avenue advertising world of the 1950s, Heller seemed a figure unlikely to publish a work of such unimpeachable influence. Published when Heller was 39, Catch-22 represents the high-water mark of his career and to some extent his personal life—it is as if everything prepublication was prologue and everything that followed was postscript. Heller wrote copiously throughout the remainder of his life but never attained those heights again, critically or commercially. Nonetheless, Daugherty persuasively endorses the view of Heller as a pivotal figure in American letters." Time Out N Y

Includes bibliographical references

Hellman, Lillian, 1906-1984

Martinson, Deborah. **Lillian** Hellman; a life with foxes and scoundrels. Counterpoint 2005 448p il $27.95   **92**

1. Authors 2. Dramatists 3. Memoirists 4. Dramatists, American
ISBN 1-58243-315-1

LC 2005-16616

This is "a richly thorough, sometimes somber, and fairly objective portrait of an enigmatic individual." Libr J

Includes bibliographical references

Hemingway, Ernest, 1899-1961

★ Dearborn, Mary V. **Ernest** Hemingway; a biography. Mary V. Dearborn. Alfred A. Knopf 2017 752 p. (hardcover) $35   **92**

1. American authors -- 20th century -- Biography 2. Authors, American -- 20th century -- Biography
ISBN 9780307594679

LC 2016015837

This book, by Mary V. Dearborn, looks "into the life and work of Ernest Hemingway, considered in his time to be the greatest living American novelist and short-story writer, winner of the 1953 Pulitzer Prize for Fiction and the Nobel Prize in Literature in 1954. . . . And whose seven novels and six-short story collections informed--and are still informing--fiction writing generations after his death." (Publisher's note)

"Dearborn's account shines from beginning to end, helped by Hemingway's dramatic life and charismatic personality." Pub Wkly

Includes bibliographical references

Di Robilant, Andrea. **Autumn** in Venice; Ernest Hemingway and his last muse. Andrea Di Robilant. Alfred A. Knopf 2018 368 p. (hardback) $26.95   **92**
   1. American authors -- Biography 2. Venice (Italy) -- In literature 3. Americans -- Italy -- Venice -- Biography 4. Authors, American -- 20th century -- Biography
   ISBN 9781101946657
                     LC 2017044036

This book, by Andrea Di Robilant, "gives us the remarkable story of [Ernest] Hemingway's love affair with both the city of Venice and the muse he found there--[Adriana Ivancich,] a vivacious eighteen-year-old who inspired the man thirty years her senior to complete his great final work. . . . [The book] . . . is an intimate look at the fractured heart and changing art of Hemingway in his fifties." (Publisher's note)

Mort, Terry. **Hemingway** at war; Ernest Hemingway's Adventures as a World War II Correspondent. Terry Mort. W W Norton & Co. Inc. 2016 336 p. illustrations (hardcover) $27.95; (ebook) $50   **92**
   1. World War, 1939-1945 -- Journalists 2. American authors -- 20th century -- Biography 3. War correspondents -- United States -- Biography
   ISBN 9781681772479; 9781681772905; 1681772477

This book, by Terry Mort, narrates "Ernest Hemingway's adventures in journalism during World War II. In the spring of 1944, Hemingway traveled to London and then to France to cover World War II for 'Colliers Magazine.' . . . He flew missions with the RAF . . .; he went on a landing craft on Omaha Beach on D-Day; he went on to involve himself in the French Resistance forces in France and famously rode into the still dangerous streets of liberated Paris." (Publisher's note)

Includes bibliographical references (pages 277-279) and index.

Reynolds, Nicholas. **Writer,** sailor, soldier, spy; Ernest Hemingway's secret adventures, 1935-1961. by Nicholas Reynolds. HarperCollins 2017 336 p. illustrations $27.99   **92**
   ISBN 0062440136; 9780062440136
                     LC 2017002589

This book, by Nicholas Reynolds, "illuminates Hemingway's immersion in the life-and-death world of the revolutionary left, from his passionate commitment to the Spanish Republic; his successful pursuit by Soviet NKVD agents, who valued Hemingway's influence, access, and mobility; his wartime meeting in East Asia with communist leader Chou En-Lai, the future premier of the People's Republic of China; and finally to his undercover involvement with Cuban rebels in the late 1950s and his sympathy for Fidel Castro." (Publisher's note)

"Although Reynolds is forced to guess about much of Hemi n gway's secret life as a spy, his conclusions seem consistent with the well-known portrait of the novelist striving to prove his manliness and power." Kirkus

Includes bibliographical references (pages 269-279, [289]-346) and index.

Hendrix, Jimi

   ★ Cross, Charles R. **Room** full of mirrors; a biography of Jimi Hendrix. Hyperion 2005 384p il $24.95; pa $15.99 **92**
   1. Singers 2. Guitarists 3. Rock musicians
   ISBN 1-401-30028-6; 0-7868-8841-5 pa
                     LC 2005-46362

"Admirably comprehensive and well referenced, this is the Hendrix biography to acquire if you can acquire only one." Booklist

Includes bibliographical references

Henry Frederick, Prince of Wales, 1594-1612

Fraser, Sarah. The **prince** who would be king; the life and death of Henry Stuart. Sarah Fraser. HarperCollins 2018 352 p. (hbk.) $27.99   **92**
   1. Princes -- Great Britain -- Biography 2. Great Britain -- Kings and rulers -- Biography
   ISBN 0007548087; 9780007548088; 9780007548095

This book, by Sarah Fraser, presents a biography of "Henry Stuart, Prince of Wales, [who] was once the hope of Britain. . . . Henry was the epitome of heroic Renaissance princely virtue, his life set against a period about as rich and momentous as any. . . . Henry's life is the last great forgotten Jacobean tale: . . . a man who, had he lived, might have saved Britain from King Charles I, his spaniels and the Civil War with its appalling loss of life his misrule engendered." (Publisher's note)

"Fraser fills a gap in the Stuart story while making the family legacy of regicides, religious wars, and licentiousness even more tragic in context of the story of the king who never was." Pub Wkly

Henry VIII, King of England, 1491-1547

Lipscomb, Suzannah. The **King** Is Dead; The Last Will and Testament of Henry VIII. Suzannah Lipscomb. W W Norton & Co Inc 2016 208 p. ill. (chiefly color), col. map (ebook) $50; $26.95   **92**
   1. Great Britain -- Kings and rulers 2. Wills -- England -- History -- 16th century
   ISBN 9781681772943; 168177254X; 9781681772547
                     LC 2016047426

"On 28 January 1547, . . . King Henry VIII died at Whitehall. Just hours before his passing, his last will and testament had been read, stamped, and sealed. . . . Henry's will is one of the most intriguing and contested documents in British history. . . . As well as examining the background to the drafting of the will and describing Henry's last days, Suzannah Lipscomb offers her . . . interpretation of one of the most significant constitutional documents of the Tudor period." (Publisher's note)

"A delightful story of intrigue and manipulation that shows how Henry really couldn't control his kingdom." Kirkus

Includes bibliographical references (pages 179-185) and index.

Weir, Alison. The **lost** Tudor princess; the life of Margaret Douglas of Scotland. Alison Weir. Ballantine Books 2016 576 p. illustrations, maps (hardcover: alk. paper) $30   **92**
   1. Great Britain -- History -- 1485-1603, Tudors 2. Nobility -- Great Britain -- Biography 3. Nobility -- Great Britain -- History -- 16th century 4. Great Britain -- History -- Tudors, 1485-1603 -- Biography
   ISBN 9780345521392
                     LC 2015037958

This book, by Alison Weir, offers a "biography of Margaret Douglas, the beautiful, cunning niece of Henry VIII of England who used her sharp intelligence and covert power to influence the succession after the death of Elizabeth I. . . . Lady Margaret Douglas, Countess of Lennox, was an important figure in Tudor England, yet today, while her contemporaries—Anne Boleyn, Mary, Queen of Scots, Elizabeth I—have achieved celebrity status, she is largely forgotten." (Publisher's note)

"An abundantly detailed history from an author steeped in England's past." Kirkus

Includes bibliographical references and index

Henry, Patrick, 1736-1799

Kukla, Jon. **Patrick** Henry; champion of liberty. Jon Kukla. Simon & Schuster 2017 xiv, 541 p.p illustrations, maps (hardcover) $35   **92**

   1. Governors -- Biography 2. Legislators -- United States -- Biography 3. Governors -- Virginia -- Biography 4. Legislators -- Virginia -- Biography 5. Virginia -- History -- Revolution, 1775-1783

   ISBN 9781439190814; 9781439190838; 143919081X

LC 2016027735

In this book, author "Jon Kukla has thoroughly researched [Patrick] Henry's life, even living on one of Henry's estates. He brings both newly discovered documents and new insights to the story of the patriot who played a central role in the movement to independence, the Revolution, the Constitutional era, and the early Republic. This book is an important contribution to our understanding of the nation's founding." (Publisher's note)

"Kukla's fluid prose and careful attention to detail ensure that this biography will appeal to both general readers interested in the founding fathers and scholars interested in learning more about the development of the early republic." Pub Wkly

Includes bibliographical references (pages 397-522) and index

Hensley, William L., 1941-

Hensley, William L. **Fifty** miles from tomorrow; a memoir of Alaska and the real people. [by] William L. Iggiagruk Hensley. Farrar, Straus and Giroux 2008 256p il map $24   **92**

   1. Inupiat 2. Eskimo leaders 3. State legislators

   ISBN 978-0-374-15484-4; 0-374-15484-8

LC 2008-31409

The author "manages to make fresh an old narrative of people who arise just as their culture is being erased—be they 'Braveheart' Scotsmen or outback Aborigines. His book is also bright and detailed, moving along at a clip most sled dogs would have trouble keeping up with." N Y Times Book Rev

Henson, Jim

Jones, Brian Jay. **Jim** Henson; the biography. Brian Jay Jones. Ballantine Books 2013 608 p. (hbk.) $35; (pbk.) $20   **92**

   1. Muppet show (Television program) 2. Sesame Street (Television program) 3. Puppeteers -- United States -- Biography 4. Television producers and directors -- United States -- Biography

   ISBN 0345526112; 9780345526113; 9780345526120; 0345526112

LC 2013024039

This book explores "the life of Muppets creator Jim Henson (1936-1990) . . . explaining how Henson grew up to become a daring puppeteer and scriptwriter, how he managed to attract so much remarkable talent to his side, and how his stressful business relationship with the Disney Company might have aggravated the bacterial infection that weakened the normally healthy Henson, who died at age 53 while trying to negotiate the planned Disney purchase of the franchise." (Kirkus Reviews)

Includes bibliographical references and index

Henson, Matthew Alexander, 1866-1955

Larson, Edward J. (Edward John), 1953- **To** the edges of the earth; 1909, the race for the three poles, and the climax of the age of exploration. Edward J. Larson. HarperCollins 2018 352 p. $29.99   **92**

   1. Mountaineering 2. Sports records 3. Sports -- History

   ISBN 0062564471; 9780062564474

LC 2018000736

In this book historian Edward J. Larson looks at "the most adventurous year of all time, when three expeditions simultaneously raced to the top, bottom, and heights of the world. . . . In the course of one extraordinary year, Americans Robert Peary and Matthew Henson were hailed worldwide at the discovers of the North Pole; Britain's Ernest Shackleton had set a new geographic 'Furthest South' record, while . . . Australian Douglas Mawson, had reached the Magnetic South Pole." (Publisher's note)

" A fascinating look at the adventures of remarkably resilient men, so well-related as to make you feel the chill." Kirkus

Henson, Taraji P

Henson, Taraji P., 1970- **Around** the way girl; Taraji P. Henson with Denene Millner. 37 Ink 2016 256 p. illustrations (chiefly color) (ebook) $13.99; (hardcover: alk. paper) $26 **92**

   1. African American actors 2. Actors -- United States -- Biography

   ISBN 9781501126017; 9781501125997; 9781501126000

LC 2016028253

This book, by Taraji P. Henson, is "a classic actor's memoir in which Taraji reflects on the world-class instruction she received at Howard University and the pitfalls that come with being a black actress. With laugh-out-loud humor and candor, she shares the challenges and disappointments of the actor's journey and shows us that behind the red carpet moments, she is ever authentic. She is at heart just a girl in pursuit of her dreams." (Publisher's note)

"Recommended for fans and aspiring actors alike." LJ

Hepburn, Katharine, 1907-2003

Berg, A. Scott. **Kate** remembered. Putnam 2003 370p il $25.95; pa $15   **92**

   1. Actors

   ISBN 0-399-15164-8; 0-425-19909-6 pa

LC 2003-545232

In this posthumous biography, the author reveals "details about such pivotal events as the death of her brother by hanging, her relationships with powerful men like Howard Hughes and John Ford, and her slow, sad decline. . . . Berg's writing is so intimate that readers may feel they are hiding behind a curtain as they listen to the stories he elicits from his subject. Kate herself comes across pretty much the way she did on screen: bossy, courageous, and self-involved." Booklist

Mann, William J. **Kate**: the woman who was Hepburn. H. Holt 2006 xxviii, 621p il $30   **92**

   1. Actors

   ISBN 978-0-8050-7625-7; 0-8050-7625-5

This is a biography of the American actress.

"This will surely be the definitive version of Hepburn's life for decades to come, as it is an outstanding example of painstaking research matched with splendid writing." Publ Wkly

Includes bibliographical references

Hernandez, Keith

Hernandez, Keith. **I'm** Keith Hernandez; Keith Hernandez. Little, Brown & Co. 2018 352 p. $30   **92**

1. Baseball players -- United States
ISBN 0316552437; 9780316395731; 9780316552431

LC 2017963935

In this memoir Keith Hernandez "takes us along on his journey to baseball immortality. There are the hellacious bus rides and south-of-the-border escapades of his minor league years. His major league benchings . . . and role in one of the most exciting batting races in history against Pete Rose. Indeed, from the Little League fields of Northern California . . . to the grand stages of Busch Stadium and beyond." (Publisher's note)

"Often candid and even self-deprecating memories by an athlete who once stood at the summit o f his profession." Kirkus

Herriman, George, 1880-1944

Tisserand, Michael. **Krazy**; George Herriman, a Life in Black and White. Michael Tisserand. HarperCollins 2016 560 p. illustrations (ebook) $32.99; $35   92
1. African American cartoonists -- Biography 2. Cartoonists -- United States -- Biography
ISBN 9780062098054; 0061732990; 9780061732997

LC 2016052808

This biography of Krazy Kat creator George Herriman, by Michael Tisserand, "lays bare the truth about his art, his heritage, and his life on America's color line. . . . Herriman used his work to explore the human condition, creating a modernist fantasia that was inspired by the landscapes he discovered in his travels—from chaotic urban life to the Beckett-like desert vistas of the Southwest." (Publisher's note)

"Essential reading for comics fans and history buffs, Krazy is a roaring success, providing an indispensable new perspective on turn-of-the-century America." Kirkus

Includes bibliographical references (pages 499-517) and index.

Hersch, Fred

Hersch, Fred. **Good** things happen slowly; a life in and out of jazz. Fred Hersch. Crown Archetype 2017 x, 307 p.p illustrations (some color) (hardcover) $28   92
1. Biography 2. Pianists -- United States -- Biography 3. Jazz musicians -- United States -- Biography 4. Composers -- United States -- Biography 5. Gay musicians -- United States -- Biography 6. AIDS (Disease) -- Patients -- United States -- Biography
ISBN 9781101904343; 9781101904367; 9781101904350

LC 2017028036

This memoir, by Fred Hersch, is "the story of the first openly gay, HIV-positive jazz player; a deep look into the cloistered jazz culture that made such a status both transgressive and groundbreaking; and a profound exploration of how Hersch's two-month-long coma in 2007 led to his creating some of the finest, most direct, and most emotionally compelling music of his career." (Publisher's note)

"Like much of his music, his memoir is deceptively simple, thoroughly humble, and extraordinarily honest." Booklist

Hersh, Seymour M.

★ Hersh, Seymour, 1937- **Reporter**; a memoir. Seymour M. Hersh. Alfred A. Knopf 2018 355 p. illustrations (hardback) $27.95   92
1. Biography 2. Journalists -- United States -- Biography
ISBN 9780525521587; 9780307263957

LC 2017051856

In this memoir, reporter Seymour Hersh "describes what drove him and how he worked as an independent outsider, even at the nation's most prestigious publications. . . . Hersh divulges previously unreported information about some of his biggest scoops, including the My Lai massacre and the horrors at Abu Ghraib." (Publisher's note)

"Rarely has a journalist's memoir come together so well, with ad-mirable measures of self-deprecation, transparent pride, readable prose style, and honesty." Kirkus

Miraldi, Robert. **Seymour** Hersh; scoop artist. Robert Miraldi. Potomac Books, An Imprint of the University of Nebraska Press 2013 415 p. (cloth: alk. paper) $34.95   92
1. Journalism -- United States 2. Journalists -- United States -- Biography 3. United States -- Foreign relations -- 1989- 4. United States -- Foreign relations -- 1945-1989 5. United States -- Politics and government -- 1989- 6. United States -- Politics and government -- 1945-1989
ISBN 1612344755; 9781612344751

LC 2013023619

This book, by Robert Miraldi, offers a biography of the investigative reporter Seymour Hersh. "From his exposé of the My Lai massacre in 1969 to his revelations about torture at Abu Ghraib prison in 2004, Hersh has consistently captured the public imagination, spurred policy-makers to reform, and drawn the ire of presidents. . . . This . . . biography captures a . . . successful career of important exposés and outstanding accomplishments." (Publisher's note)

"A deep biographical treatment of the Pulitzer Prize–winning journalist who is the scourge of those in power. . . . Hersh comes across as a good guy of limited patience when approached by fellow journalists and as a bulldog with sharp teeth when in his reporter mode." Kirkus

Includes bibliographical references and index

Heuze, Marcel, 1912-1992

Porter, Carolyn. **Marcel's** letters; a font and the search for one man's fate. Carolyn Porter. Skyhorse Publishing 2017 344 p. illustrations (hardcover: alkaline paper) $24.99   92
1. Typography 2. World War, 1939-1945 -- Biography 3. Graphic artists -- Minnesota -- Biography 4. Daimler-Benz Aktiengesellschaft -- Biography 5. French -- Germany -- Berlin -- Correspondence 6. World War, 1939-1945 -- Personal narratives, French 7. Berlin (Germany) -- History, Military -- 20th century 8. Prisoners of war -- Germany -- Berlin -- Correspondence 9. World War, 1939-1945 -- Conscript labor -- Germany -- Berlin 10. Penmanship, French -- Germany -- Berlin -- History -- 20th century
ISBN 9781510719347; 9781510719330

LC 2017001221

This book, by Carolyn Porter, describes how, "seeking inspiration for a new font design in an antique store in small-town Stillwater, Minnesota, [a] graphic designer . . . stumbled across a bundle of letters and . . . their beautifully expressive pen-and-ink handwriting. . . . Reading [them] opened a portal to a different time, and what began as mere curiosity quickly became an obsession with . . . the letter writer, Marcel Heuzé." (Publisher's note)

"Porter's captivating memoir describes her journey to find answers, noting how her fascination with Marcel proved infectious as she faces obstacle after obstacle and enlists the help of experts to discover the fate that awaited him." Booklist

Includes bibliographical references and index.

Higashida, Naoki, 1992-

Naoki Higashida. The **reason** I jump; the inner voice of a thirteen-year-old boy with autism. by Naoki Higashida; translated by KA Yoshida and David Mitchell. Random House 2013 176 p. illustrations (acid-free paper) $22   92
1. Autism 2. Autistic children 3. Autistic people -- Psychology 4. Autistic people -- Japan -- Biography
ISBN 0812994868; 9780812994865

LC 2012045703

In this book, "a 13-year-old Japanese author illuminates his autism from within. . . . The book takes the form of a series of straightforward questions followed by answers. . . . He describes the difficulty of expressing through words what the brain wants to say, the challenge of focusing and ordering experience, the obsessiveness of repetition, the comfort found in actions that others might find odd, and the frustration of being the source of others' frustration." (Kirkus Reviews)

A "a mixture of invaluable anecdotal information, practical advice and whimsical self-expression." Pub Wkly

Highsmith, Patricia, 1921-1995

Schenkar, Joan. The **talented** Miss Highsmith; the secret life and serious art of Patricia Highsmith. St. Martin's Press 2009 684p il $40   **92**

1. Authors 2. Novelists 3. Mystery writers 4. Authors, American
ISBN 978-0-312-30375-4

LC 2009-18363

"It is hard to imagine a more thoroughly fact-filled or energetic biography than 'The Talented Miss Highsmith' or one more determined to examine the deepest recesses of its complicated subject. Ms. Schenkar's presentation is cubist, off-putting at first, featuring separated essays that isolate various topics. The dislocation can be confusing, yet one soon comes to accept the method as a way of mining the many veins of a very strange life." Wall Street J

Includes bibliographical references

Hilfiger, Tommy

Hilfiger, Tommy, 1951- **American** dreamer; My Life in Fashion & Business. Tommy Hilfiger with Peter Knobler; foreword by Quincy Jones. Ballantine Books 2016 352 p. (hardcover: alk. paper) $30   **92**

1. Fashion designers 2. Fashion designers -- United States -- Biography
ISBN 9781101886212

LC 2016023113

In this memoir, fashion designer "Tommy Hilfiger shares his . . . life story for the first time. . . . [It] brims with anecdotes that cover Tommy's years as a club kid and scrappy entrepreneur in 1970s New York as well as unique insights into the exclusive A-list personalities with whom he's collaborated and interacted. . . . Tommy takes us behind the scenes of every decision—and every mistake—he's ever made, offering advice on leadership, business, team-building, and creativity." (Publisher's note)

"An honest, straightforward, mostly entertaining autobiography of the man who created a classic yet hip line of clothing." Kirkus

Hill, Joe, 1879-1915

Adler, William M. The **man** who never died; the life, times, and legacy of Joe Hill, American labor icon. Bloomsbury 2011 435p il $30   **92**

1. Poets 2. Authors 3. Folk musicians 4. Songwriters 5. Revolutionaries 6. Biography, Individual 7. Industrial Workers of the World
ISBN 978-1-59691-696-8; 1-59691-696-6

LC 2011009821

This is a biography of the poet, songwriter and labor activist who was executed in 1915. Index.

"Presenting Hill as man and symbol, Adler contributes vitally to labor history." Booklist

Includes bibliographical references

Hilleman, Maurice R., 1919-2005

Offit, Paul A. **Vaccinated**; one man's quest to defeat the world's deadliest diseases. Smithsonian Books/Collins 2007

254p $26.95   **92**

1. Biologists 2. Vaccination 3. Microbiologists
ISBN 978-0-06-122795-0; 0-06-122795-1

LC 2006-53054

"This book leaves one with a great appreciation for the work of the Salks and Sabins of the world, and it makes one want to lead a movement to enshrine Maurice Hilleman in the pantheon of American pop heroes." Choice

Includes bibliographical references

Himmler, Heinrich, 1900-1945

Breitman, Richard. The **architect** of genocide; Himmler and the final solution. University Press of New England 1992 335p (The Tauber Institute for the Study of European Jewry) pa $30   **92**

1. Heads of state 2. National socialism 3. Nazi leaders 4. Germany -- Politics and government -- 1933-1945
ISBN 0-87451-596-3; 978-0-87451-596-1

LC 92-53857

First published 1991 by Knopf

"This engrossing, detailed study constitutes a powerful refutation of revisionist scholars who claim that Hitler did not plan the Final Solution in advance but instead improvised it out of either military or political frustration." Publ Wkly

Includes bibliographical references

Hines, Richard, 1945-

Hines, Richard. **No** Way but Gentlenesse; A Memoir of How Kes, My Kestrel, Changed My Life. Richard Hines. St. Martin's Press 2016 288 p. (hardcover) $26   **92**

1. Falconry
ISBN 9781632865021; 1632865025

This memoir, by Richard Hines, describes "how catching and training a kestrel changed the life of a young British boy. . . . Always a naturalist at heart, Hines soon was reading all he could find regarding falconry. It was near Tankersley Old Hall that he took his first kestrel, called Kes, and began training her." (Kirkus Reviews)

"A delightful story of a boy, his birds, and his pursuit of knowledge in spite of society's dictates." Kirkus

Hinton, Anthony Ray

Hinton, Anthony Ray. The **sun** does shine; how I found life and freedom on death row. Anthony Ray Hinton; Lara Love Hardin; foreword by Bryan Stevenson. St. Martin's Press 2018 272 p. (hardcover) $26.99   **92**

1. Mistaken identity 2. Death row -- Alabama -- Bessemer 3. Death row inmates -- United States 4. Mistaken identity -- United States 5. Capital punishment -- United States 6. Trials (Murder) -- Alabama -- Bessemer 7. Compensation for judicial error -- United States
ISBN 9781250124715; 9781250124722

LC 2017044467

This book, by Anthony Ray Hinton with Lara Love Hardin, "is an extraordinary testament to the power of hope sustained through the darkest times. Destined to be a classic memoir of wrongful imprisonment and freedom won, Hinton's memoir tells his dramatic thirty-year journey and shows how you can take away a man's freedom, but you can't take away his imagination, humor, or joy." (Publisher's note)

Hirohito, Emperor of Japan, 1901-1989

★ Bix, Herbert P. **Hirohito** and the making of modern Japan. HarperCollins Pubs. 2000 800p il maps hardcover o.p.

pa $18 **92**

1. Emperors 2. Japan -- Politics and government
ISBN 0-06-093130-2 pa

LC 99-89427

"In 1945, fearing that the Japanese would resist American occupation unless the Emperor ordered them to obey, General MacArthur colluded with Hirohito in maintaining that the sovereign had been powerless to control Japan's military leaders. . . . {Bix}, uses newly available sources to argue that Hirohito was a war criminal. An imperialist whose policies reflected his belief in the racial superiority of the Japanese, Hirohito governed by manipulation for almost two decades, and used the threat of Soviet Communism to justify domestic repression and soaring military budgets. The author's virtuoso scholarship and accessible narrative invite us into Hirohito's world." New Yorker

Includes bibliographical references

Hirsi Ali, Ayaan, 1969-

Hirsi Ali, Ayaan. **Infidel**. Free Press 2007 353p il $26; pa $15 **92**

1. Refugees 2. Muslim women 3. Feminists 4. Memoirists 5. Members of Parliament
ISBN 0-7432-8968-4; 978-0-7432-8968-9; 0-7432-8969-2 pa; 978-0-7432-8969-6 pa

LC 2006-49762

"A Somali by birth and a recently elected member of the Dutch Parliament, Ms. Hirsi Ali had waged a personal crusade to improve the lot of Muslim women. Her warnings about the dangers posed to the Netherlands by unassimilated Muslims made her Public Enemy No. 1 for Muslim extremists, a feminist counterpart to Salman Rushdie. The circuitous, violence-filled path that led Ms. Hirsi Ali from Somalia to the Netherlands is the subject of 'Infidel,' her brave, inspiring and beautifully written memoir." N Y Times (Late N Y Ed)

Hirsi Ali, Ayaan, 1969- **Nomad**; from Islam to America: a personal journey through the clash of civilizations. Ayaan Hirsi Ali. Atria Books 2011 xxv, 277 p.p (pbk.) $16 **92**

1. Islam 2. Refugees 3. Muslim women 4. Islam -- Social aspects 5. Muslim women -- Civil rights 6. Somalis -- Netherlands -- Biography 7. Women social reformers -- Biography 8. Somalis -- United States -- Biography 9. Muslim women -- Civil rights -- Europe 10. Netherlands. Staten-Generaal -- Biography 11. Muslim women -- United States -- Biography 12. Women refugees -- Netherlands -- Biography
ISBN 9781439171820; 9781439157312; 1439157316; 1439157324; 9781439157329

LC 2010001481

In this book, author Ayaan "Hirsi Ali tells of coming to America to build a new life, an ocean away from the death threats made to her by European Islamists, the strife she witnessed, and the inner conflict she suffered. It is the story of her physical journey to freedom and, more crucially, her emotional journey to freedom—her transition from a tribal mind-set that restricts women's every thought and action to a life as a free and equal citizen in an open society." (Publisher's note)

"A thought-provoking book sure to stir as much debate and controversy as Infidel." Booklist

Hitchcock, Alfred, 1899-1980

Chandler, Charlotte. **It's** only a movie; Alfred Hitchcock, a personal biography. Simon & Schuster 2005 349p il $26 **92**

1. Motion picture directors
ISBN 0-7432-4508-3

LC 2004-52559

The author reveals "several insights into Hitchcock's technical ge-

nius, creative worldview and personality. . . . Chandler allows her sources to reminisce at great length, and they tend to tell fascinating stories." Publ Wkly

Includes filmography

Hitchens, Christopher, 1949-2011

Hitchens, Christopher, 1949-2011. **Hitch**-22; a memoir. Twelve 2010 435p il $26.99 **92**

1. Authors 2. Journalists 3. Essayists 4. Writers on politics 5. Biography, Individual
ISBN 978-0-446-54033-9

LC 2009051959

This is an autobiography by the British journalist. Christopher Hitchens is the author of For the Sake of Argument: Essays and Minority Reports (1993); Blood, Class, and Nostalgia (1990); Blood, Class, and Empire (2004), and God is Not Great (2007). Index.

Few authors can rile as easily as Hitchens does, but even his detractors might find it difficult to put down a book so witty, so piercing, so spoiling for a fight. He makes you want to be as good a reader as he is a writer. Booklist

Hitler, Adolf, 1889-1945

Breitman, Richard. The **architect** of genocide; Himmler and the final solution. University Press of New England 1992 335p (The Tauber Institute for the Study of European Jewry) pa $30 **92**

1. Heads of state 2. National socialism 3. Nazi leaders 4. Germany -- Politics and government -- 1933-1945
ISBN 0-87451-596-3; 978-0-87451-596-1

LC 92-53857

First published 1991 by Knopf

"This engrossing, detailed study constitutes a powerful refutation of revisionist scholars who claim that Hitler did not plan the Final Solution in advance but instead improvised it out of either military or political frustration." Publ Wkly

Includes bibliographical references

Cornwell, John. **Hitler's** pope: the secret history of Pius XII. Viking 1999 430p il hardcover o.p. pa $15 **92**

1. Popes 2. Heads of state 3. Nazi leaders
ISBN 0-14-029627-1 pa

LC 99-28311

"Relying on exclusive access to Vatican and Jesuit archives, . . . {the author} argues that through a 1933 Concordat with Hitler, Pope Pius XII facilitated the dictator's rise—and, ultimately, the Holocaust." Libr J

Includes bibliographical references

Kershaw, Ian. **Hitler**; a biography. W.W. Norton 2008 1029p il map $39.95 **92**

1. Heads of state 2. Nazi leaders
ISBN 978-0-393-06757-6; 0-393-06757-2

LC 2008-37294

This abridgment of the author's two-volume biography on Hitler "retains two themes of Kershaw's full-scale original: analyzing the political support the demagogue mustered from the populace and key institutional centers of Germany on his ascent to and exercise of power; and the decisive personal role of Hitler in instigating World War II and genocide. The narrative Kershaw constructs on this foundation is a superb organization and expression of Hitler's chronological arc that plummeted the world into catastrophe and moral trauma, a trajectory informed by Kershaw's attention to rationalizations by which people in and outside Germany, whether leaders or led, buried doubts about Hitler until his power was unrestrained, impossible to stop but by war or assassination.

Manifestly, Kershaw constitutes core-collection material." Booklist
Includes bibliographical references

Weber, Thomas. **Becoming** Hitler; the making of a Nazi. Thomas Weber. Basic Books 2017 xxiii, 422 p.p illustrations, maps (hardcover) $35 **92**
1. National socialists 2. National socialism -- History 3. Nazis -- Germany -- Biography 4. Heads of state -- Germany -- Biography 5. Right-wing extremists -- Germany -- Biography 6. Germany -- Politics and government -- 1918-1933
ISBN 9781541697669; 9780465032686
LC 2017022799
This book, by Thomas Weber, "charts [Adolf] Hitler's radical transformation after World War I from a directionless loner into a powerful National Socialist leader. . . . Weber examines Adolf Hitler's time in Munich between 1918 and 1926, the years when Hitler shed his awkward, feckless persona and transformed himself into a savvy opportunistic political operator who saw himself as Germany's messiah." (Publisher's note)
"Compelling research and original insights bring a fuller understanding to the mind and motives of the demagogue." Kirkus
Includes bibliographical references and index

Ullrich, Volker. **Hitler**; ascent, 1889-1939. Volker Ullrich; translated from the German by Jefferson Chase. Alfred A. Knopf 2016 1008 p. (hardcover) $40 **92**
1. Dictators 2. National socialism 3. Personality -- Case studies 4. Germany -- History -- 1933-1945 5. Dictators -- Germany -- Biography 6. Heads of state -- Germany -- Biography 7. Germany -- Politics and government -- 1933-1945
ISBN 038535438X; 9780385354387
LC 2015047202
This biography of Adolf Hitler, by Volker Ullrich, "reveals the man behind the public persona, from Hitler's childhood to his failures as a young man in Vienna to his experiences during the First World War to his rise as a far-right party leader. Ullrich deftly captures Hitler's intelligence, instinctive grasp of politics, and gift for oratory as well as his megalomania, deep insecurity, and repulsive worldview." (Publisher's note)
"Above all, in this long but skillfully narrated study, Ullrich reveals Hitler to have been an eminently practical politician—and frighteningly so... one of the best works on Hitler and the origins of the Third Reich to appear in recent years." Kirkus

Hockney, David

Sykes, Chrisopher Simon. **David** Hockney; the biography, 1937-1975. Christopher Simon Sykes. Doubleday 2012 384 p. $35 **92**
1. Artists -- Great Britain -- Biography
ISBN 9780385531443; 0385531443
LC 2011041629
This book is the first volume of "the ever-evolving English artist. . . . A friend of the artist, photographer Sykes . . . provides [a] . . . sense of what has fed the artist's fertile, restless imagination. . . . His attendance at the Royal College of Art in London in 1959 drew out the tremendous talents of this awkward provincial kid, exposing him to modern art for the first time . . . and shaping his sense as a gay artist. . . . His work attracted the attention of hot young London dealer John Kasmin, and he visited New York City and resolved to go blonde after watching a TV commercial. . . . Considered bright, witty and inventive, Hockney spent the transformative years of 1963-5 in Los Angeles, creating his early iconic work." (Kirkus)

Includes bibliographical references and index

Sykes, Christopher Simon. **David** Hockney; The Biography, 1975-2012. Christopher Simon Sykes. Random House Inc 2014 448 p. 16 plates; illustrations $40 **92**
1. British art 2. Artists, British
ISBN 0385535902; 9780385535908
LC 2011041629
In this biography, Christopher Simon Sykes "explores the life and work of . . . [British artist] David Hockney. . . . His career has spanned and epitomized the art movements of the past five decades. Picking up Hockney's story in 1975, this book finds him flitting between Notting Hill and California, where he took inspiration for the swimming pool series of paintings; creating acclaimed set designs for operas around the world; and embracing emerging technologies." (Publisher's note)
"Recommended for anyone interested in the remarkable life of this highly regarded painter. Rich with archival detail and the insight of family, friends, and the artist himself, the book is an engaging read." LJ

Hodgman, George

Hodgman, George. **Bettyville**; a memoir. George Hodgman. Viking Adult 2015 288 p. (hardback) $27.95 **92**
1. Gay men 2. Aging parents 3. Parent-adult child relationship 4. Mothers and sons -- United States 5. Aging parents -- Care -- United States 6. Caregivers -- United States -- Biography 7. Sons -- Family relationships -- United States 8. Gay men -- Family relationships -- United States 9. Adult children of aging parents -- United States -- Biography
ISBN 9780525427209; 0525427201
LC 2014038536
National Book Critics Circle Award Finalist: Autobiography (2015)
In this memoir, by George Hodgman, the author "leaves Manhattan for his hometown of Paris, Missouri, he finds himself . . . in a head-on collision with his aging mother, Betty, a woman of wit and will. . . . He can't bring himself to force her from the home both treasure . . . , and, behind the dusty antiques, a rarely acknowledged conflict: Betty, who speaks her mind but cannot quite reveal her heart, has never really accepted the fact that her son is gay." (Publisher's note)
"A tender, resolute look at a place, literal and figurative, baby boomers might find themselves." Booklist

Hodgman, John

Hodgman, John. **Vacationland**; true stories from painful beaches. John Hodgman. Viking 2017 257 p. (hardcover) $25 **92**
1. Travel 2. Travelers 3. Humorists -- 21st century -- Biography 4. Authors, American -- 21st century -- Biography
ISBN 9780735224810; 9780735224803; 0735224803
LC 2017031760
In this book, John Hodgman presents his "real life wanderings, and through them you learn of the horror of freshwater clams, the evolutionary purpose of the mustache, and which animals to keep as pets and which to kill with traps and poison. There is also some advice on how to react when the people of coastal Maine try to sacrifice you to their strange god." (Publisher's note)
"Hodgman is a disarmingly witty storyteller, at once waggish and incisive, droll and tender. Indeed, deep feelings flow beneath the mirth." Booklist

Hoffa, Jimmy, b. 1913

Russell, Thaddeus. **Out** of the jungle; Jimmy Hoffa and the remaking of the American working class. Temple University

Press 2003 272p il (Labor in crisis) pa $21.95 **92**
1. Missing persons 2. Labor leaders 3. Trucking executives 4. International Brotherhood of Teamsters, Chauffeurs, Warehousemen and Helpers of America
ISBN 1-592-13027-5; 978-1-592-13027-6

LC 2002-43556

First published 2001 by Knopf
"Russell makes good use of a range of primary-source materials plus period newspaper accounts and other materials to highlight this story." Libr J

Includes bibliographical references

Hoffman, Claire

Hoffman, Claire. **Greetings** from Utopia Park; Claire Hoffman. HarperCollins 2016 288 p. illustrations $25.99 **92**
1. Iowa 2. Women journalists 3. Transcendental meditation
ISBN 0062338846; 9780062338846

In this memoir, Claire Hoffman "reflects on her childhood in the heartland, growing up in an increasingly isolated meditation community in the 1980s and '90s. When Claire Hoffman's alcoholic father abandons his family, his desperate wife, Liz, tells five-year-old Claire and her seven-year-old brother, Stacey, that they are going to heaven--Iowa--to live in Maharishi's national headquarters for Heaven on Earth." (Publisher's note)

"With honesty and sincerity, this account of coming of age within the ostensible confines of an alternative lifestyle delivers valuable knowledge of another phenomenon of cultural divergence." LJ

Holiday, Billie, 1915-1959

★ Holiday, Billie. **Lady** sings the blues; [Billie Holiday with William Dufty] 50th anniversary ed.; Harlem Moon 2006 231p il pa $15.95 **92**
1. Singers 2. Blues musicians 3. African American singers
ISBN 978-0-7679-2386-6; 0-7679-2386-3

LC 2007-271682

First published 1956 by Doubleday
"A hard, bitter and unsentimental book, written with brutal honesty and having much to say not only about Billie Holiday, the person, but about what it means to be poor and black in America." N Y Her Trib Books

Includes discography

Holman, James, 1786-1857

Roberts, Jason. A **sense** of the world; how a blind man became history's greatest traveler. HarperCollins Publishers 2006 382p il $26.95; pa $14.95 **92**
1. Blind 2. Naval officers 3. Travel writers
ISBN 0-00-716106-9; 978-0-00-716106-5; 0-00-716126-3 pa; 978-0-00-716126-3 pa

LC 2005-58166

The author "narrates the life of a 19th-century British naval officer who was mysteriously blinded at 25, but nevertheless became the greatest traveler of his time. . . . Roberts does Holman justice, evoking with grace and wit the tale of this man once lionized as 'The Blind Traveler.'" Publ Wkly

Includes bibliographical references

Holmes, Dave, 1971-

Holmes, Dave. **Party** of one; a memoir in 21 songs. Dave Holmes. Crown Archetype 2016 288 p. (ebook) $65; (hardback) $26 **92**
1. Gay men -- Biography 2. Comedians -- United States --

Biography 3. Authors, American -- Biography 4. Coming of age -- United States 5. Self-acceptance -- United States 6. Gay men -- United States -- Biography 7. Popular music -- United States -- Miscellanea 8. Radio personalities -- United States -- Biography 9. Television personalities -- United States -- Biography
ISBN 9780804188005; 9780804187985

LC 2015047486

This memoir, by Dave Holmes, features "the music of the '80s, '90s, and today as his soundtrack. . . . [It] tells the hilariously painful and painfully hilarious tales--in the vein of Rob Sheffield, Andy Cohen, and Paul Feig--of an outsider desperate to get in, of a misfit constantly changing shape, of a music geek who finally learns to accept himself." (Publisher's note)

"A hilarious and touching coming-of-age story that will strike a particular nerve among Generation Y." Kirkus

Holmes, Richard, 1945-

Holmes, Richard, 1945- **This** long pursuit; reflections of a romantic biographer. Richard Holmes. Pantheon Books 2017 viii, 360 p.p illustrations (some color) (hardcover) $30 **92**
1. Romanticism 2. Authors -- Biography 3. Romanticism in literature 4. Biography as a literary form
ISBN 030737968X; 9780307379689; 9781101871768

LC 2016040528

This book, by Richard Holmes, "is a luminous meditation on the art of biography that fuses the author's own experiences with a history of the genre and explores the fascinating and surprising relationship between fact and fiction. . . . [Here,] Holmes confesses to a lifetime's obsession with his Romantic subjects. . . . [The book] gives us a unique insider's account of a biographer at work: traveling, teaching, researching, fantasizing, forgetting, and even ballooning." (Publisher's note)

Hooks, Bell

Hooks, Bell. **Belonging**; a culture of place. Routledge 2008 230p $95; pa $19.95 **92**
1. Home 2. Poets 3. Authors 4. Dramatists 5. Women authors 6. African American authors 7. Kentucky 8. Essayists 9. Feminists 10. Memoirists 11. Social critics 12. College teachers 13. Children's authors 14. Nonfiction writers
ISBN 978-0-415-96815-7; 978-0-415-96816-4 pa

LC 2008-21846

The author "writes about the solace she found as a girl in the hills of Kentucky, her long years away, and her return, which has inspired a fresh look at the self-reliant communities of black Appalachians and their nurturing connection to the land." Booklist

Includes bibliographical references

Hooks, Bell. **Wounds** of passion; a writing life. Holt & Co. 1997 xxiii, 260p hardcover o.p. pa $13 **92**
1. Poets 2. Authors 3. Dramatists 4. Essayists 5. Feminists 6. Memoirists 7. Social critics 8. College teachers 9. Children's authors 10. Nonfiction writers
ISBN 0-8050-5722-6 pa

LC 97-23506

In this continuation of the author's autobiography, Hooks chronicles "her rigorous education, both in a long, complicated relationship with a fellow writer and as a college and graduate student, experiences that led her away from poetry (her first literary love) to groundbreaking prose that expressed her feminist convictions and views on the status of black women in America." Booklist

Hoover, Herbert, 1874-1964

Rappleye, Charles. **Herbert** Hoover in the White House;

the ordeal of the presidency. Charles Rappleye. Simon & Schuster 2016 576 p. illustrations (hardcover) $32.50   **92**
    1. United States -- Politics and government -- 1929-1933 2. Presidents -- United States -- Biography
    ISBN 9781451648676; 9781451648683

                        LC 2015027333
    This book, by Charles Rappleye, offers an alternative "portrait of [the] Depression-era president Herbert Hoover [that] reveals a very different figure than the usual Hoover, engaged and active but loathe to experiment and conscious of his inability to convey hope to the country. . . . The Hoover we see here—bright, well meaning, energetic—lacked the single critical element to succeed as president. He had a first-class mind and a second-class temperament." (Publisher's note)
    "A fair, fresh, and fantastic reappraisal of a forgotten figure." LJ
    Includes bibliographical references and index

    Whyte, Kenneth. **Hoover**; an extraordinary life in extraordinary times. Kenneth Whyte. Alfred A. Knopf 2017 736 p. (hardback) $35   **92**
    1. Biography 2. Presidents -- United States -- Biography 3. United States -- Politics and government -- 1919-1933 4. United States -- Politics and government -- 1929-1933
    ISBN 9780307597960; 9780307743879; 9781524732462

                        LC 2017015685
    National Book Critics Circle Award for Biography finalist, 2017.
    This book, by Kenneth Whyte, is "the definitive biography of Herbert Hoover, one of the most remarkable Americans of the twentieth century--a revisionist account that will forever change the way Americans understand the man, his presidency, and his battle against the Great Depression. . . . Whyte brings to life Hoover's complexity and contradictions--his modesty and ambition, ruthlessness and extreme generosity--as well as his political legacy." (Publisher's note)
    "With adept explanations of the Depression's complexities and a refreshing sense of objectivity regarding Hoover's approach to combatting it, Whyte portrays a figure to be neither pitied nor reviled, but better understood." PW.
    Includes bibliographical references and index.

Hope, Bob, 1903-2003

    Quirk, Lawrence J. **Bob** Hope: the road well-traveled. Applause Theatre Bk. Pubs. 1998 327p il hardcover o.p. pa $14.95   **92**
    1. Actors 2. Comedians
    ISBN 1-55783-353-2; 1-55783-450-4 pa

                        LC 98-87957
    "Quirk recaps Hope's life and surveys his relationships with myriad entertainment personalities. . . . This is a good, solid Hollywood bio by a veteran Tinseltown observer." Booklist
    Includes filmography and bibliographical references

    Zoglin, Richard. **Hope**; entertainer of the century. Richard Zoglin. Simon & Schuster 2014 576 p. 16 plates; illustrations (hardcover) $30   **92**
    1. Comedians -- United States -- Biography
    ISBN 1439140278; 9781439140277; 9781439140284

                        LC 2014014371
    This book, by Richard Zoglin, presents a biography of Bob Hope, "born in 1903, and until his death in 2003, . . . [he was] the only entertainer to achieve top-rated success in every major mass-entertainment medium, from vaudeville to television and everything in between. . . . [This book] is both a celebration of an entertainer whose vast contribution has never been properly appreciated, and a complex portrait of a

gifted but flawed man." (Publisher's note)
    "Not just for Hope fans, Zoglin's work will also appeal to readers interested in the colorful history of American entertainment, in which Hope played a prominent role." Booklist
    Includes bibliographical references and index

Hopkins, Lightnin', 1912-1982

    Govenar, Alan B. **Lightnin'** Hopkins; his life and blues. Chicago Review Press 2010 334p il $28.95   **92**
    1. Singers 2. Guitarists 3. Blues music 4. Blues musicians 5. African American musicians 6. Songwriters
    ISBN 978-1-55652-962-7

                        LC 2009-48798
    In this "biography of the prolific and influential blues icon Sam 'Lightnin' Hopkins, . . . [the author] presents important new research and employs neglected primary sources to offer an accessible critical analysis of Hopkins's artistic achievement buttressed by generous quotations from his lyrics. . . . [This] biography of an important figure in blues history is an essential purchase for anyone interested in American popular music or African American culture." Libr J
    Includes discography and bibliographical references

Hopper, Grace, 1906-1992

    ★ Beyer, Kurt W. **Grace** Hopper and the invention of the information age. MIT Press 2009 398p il (Lemelson Center studies in invention and innovation) $27.95   **92**
    1. Admirals 2. Computer scientists 3. Computer programming 4. Biography, Individual 5. COBOL (Computer program language)
    ISBN 978-0-262-01310-9

                        LC 2008-44229
    This is a biography of the computer programmer who "abandoned academia to serve her country in the Navy after Pearl Harbor. . . . Hopper made herself 'one of the boys' in Howard Aiken's wartime Computation Laboratory at Harvard, then moved on to the Eckert and Mauchly Computer Corporation. . . . . Hopper's greatest technical achievement was to create the tools that would allow humans to communicate with computers in terms other than ones and zeroes." (Publisher's note) Index.
    "In Beyer's fascinating mix of biography and technological history, Grace Hopper comes vividly to life as a navy admiral who launched the art of computer programming." Booklist
    Includes bibliographical references

Hopps, Walter

    Hopps, Walter, 1933-2005. The **dream** colony; a life in art. Walter Hopps; edited by Deborah Treisman, from interviews with Anne Doran; introduction by Ed Ruscha. Bloomsbury USA 2017 xix, 312 p.p illustrations (some color) (hardback) $30   **92**
    1. Biography 2. Art -- Exhibitions 3. Art museums -- United States 4. Art museum curators -- Biography 5. Art museum curators -- United States -- Biography
    ISBN 9781632865311; 9781632865298

                        LC 2016055073
    This biography, by Walter Hopps, edited by Deborah Treisman, from interviews with Anne Doran and introduced by Ed Ruscha, is "a panoramic look at art in America in the second half of the twentieth century. . . . Hopps founded his first gallery . . . at the age of twenty-one. . . . When Hopps became the director of Washington's Corcoran Gallery of Art at age thirty-four, the New York Times hailed him as "the most gifted museum man on the West Coast. . . ." (Publisher's note)
    "Readers interested in 20th-century art will enjoy this memoir by influential gallery owner and curator Walter Hopps (1932–2005)." LJ

Hopwood, Shon

Burke, Dennis. **Law** man; Shon Hopwood with Dennis Burke. Crown Publishers 2012 308 p. col. ill. $25.00   **92**
1. Lawyers -- Biography 2. Prisoners -- Biography 3. Jailhouse lawyers -- Nebraska -- Biography
ISBN 0307887839; 9780307887832; 9780307887856
LC 2011035313

This book, by Shon Hopwood with Dennis Burke, offers a memoir of a man who reformed after being imprisoned for bank robbery into a successful jailhouse lawyer. "By the time Shon walked out of Pekin Prison he'd pulled off a series of legal miracles, earned the undying gratitude of numerous inmates, won the woman of his dreams, and built a new life for himself far greater than anything he could have imagined." (Publisher's note)

"Hopwood's prison memoir and long journey back into society are told with brutal and riveting honesty." LJ

Horace, Matthew

★ Horrace, Matthew. The **black** and the blue; a cop reveals the crimes, racism, and injustice in America's law enforcement. Matthew Horace and Ron Harris. Hachette Books 2018 256 p. (hardcover) $27   **92**
1. Discrimination 2. Law enforcement 3. Police brutality -- United States
ISBN 9780316440073; 9780316440080; 9781549194498
LC 2018938061

This book, by Matthew Horace and Ron Harris "presents an insider's examination of police tactics, which . . . [Horace] concludes is an 'archaic system' built on 'toxic brotherhood.' . . . Horace provides fresh analysis on communities experiencing the high killing and imprisonment rates due to racist policing such as Ferguson, New Orleans, Baltimore, and Chicago from a law enforcement point of view and uncovers what has sown the seeds of violence." (Publisher's note)

"An astute, unvarnished account that should stand out from the crowd of pro- and anti-law enforcement books." Kirkus

Horne, Lena

Gavin, James. **Stormy** weather; the life of Lena Horne. Atria 2009 598p il $27; pa $16   **92**
1. Actors 2. Singers 3. African American women 4. African American singers
ISBN 978-0-7432-7143-1; 0-7432-7143-2; 978-0-7432-7144-8 pa; 0-7432-7144-0 pa
LC 2009-08170

This is a biography of the American singer who has appeared in the films Stormy Weather and Cabin in the Sky (both 1943) and on Broadway in Jamaica (1957) and The Lady and Her Music (1981).

Horne "has had a life so rich in ups and downs as to make page after page eventful and suspenseful. This all the more so since the book is also two books in one: a thorough and fluent biography and a history of the slow social rise of black people despite crippling discrimination and stinging humiliations—a history in which Horne's story is embedded." N Y Times Book Rev

Includes discography, filmography, and bibliographic references

Horner, Sally

Weinman, Sarah. The **real** Lolita; the kidnapping of Sally Horner and the novel that scandalized the world. Sarah Weinman. HarperCollins Publishers 2018 320 p. $27.99   **92**
1. Child abuse 2. Kidnapping victims 3. Captivity -- United States -- Case studies 4. Kidnapping -- United States -- Case studies 5. Child abuse -- United States -- Case studies

ISBN 9780062661920; 9780062661937; 9780062661951; 9780062861184
LC 2018006366

This book "tells Sally Horner's full story for the very first time. Drawing upon extensive investigations, legal documents, public records, and interviews with remaining relatives, [author] Sarah Weinman uncovers how much [novelist Vladimir] Nabokov knew of the Sally Horner [abduction] case and the efforts he took to disguise that knowledge during the process of writing and publishing 'Lolita.'" (Publisher's note)

"This intricate balance of journalism and cultural critique is perfect for historical crime readers, feminist scholars, victims' rights advocates, and literature lovers. Recommended as a squirm-inducing read-along with Nabokov's novel." Library Journal

Includes bibliographical references and index

Houdini, Harry, 1874-1926

Jaher, David. The **witch** of lime street; séance, seduction, and Houdini in the spirit world. David Jaher. Crown Publishers 2015 448 p. illustrations (alk. paper) $28   **92**
1. Spiritualism 2. Spiritualists -- United States -- Biography 3. Women mediums -- United States -- Biography 4. Spiritualism -- United States -- History -- 20th century
ISBN 0307451062; 9780307451064
LC 2015009392

In this book, by David Jaher, "in 1924, the pretty wife of a distinguished Boston surgeon came to embody the raging national debate over Spiritualism. . . . Reporters dubbed her the blonde Witch of Lime Street, but she was known to her followers simply as Margery. . . . Margery was the best hope for the psychic practice to be empirically verified. Her supernatural gifts beguiled four of the judges. There was only one left to convince...the acclaimed escape artist, Harry Houdini." (Publisher's note)

"Through a combination of feminine seduction and illusionist skill that even Houdini admired, Crandon became the one psychic to almost win the respect of the scientific community and outshine Houdini as an entertainer. Jaher's narrative style is as engaging as his character portraits are colorful. Together, they bring a bygone age and its defining spiritual obsessions roaring to life. Fascinating, sometimes thrilling, reading." Kirkus

Includes bibliographical references and index

House, Callie, 1861-1928

Berry, Mary Frances. **My** face is black is true; Callie House and the struggle for ex-slave reparations. Knopf 2006 314p il pa $14.95; $26.95   **92**
1. Needleworkers 2. Laundry workers 3. Social activists 4. Biography, Individual 5. African Americans -- Reparations 6. African American women -- Biography
ISBN 0-307-27705-4 pa, Vintage; 1-4000-4003-5 Knopf; 978-0-307-27705-3 pa, Vintage
LC 2004-51330

This is a biography of Carrie House, an African American washerwoman and former slave. House was a leader of the National Ex-Slave Mutual Relief, Bounty, and Pension Association (ESMRBPA). Index.

The author "unearths the intriguing story of Callie House (1861–1928), a Tennessee washerwoman and seamstress become activist, and the organization she led, the National Ex-Slave Mutual Relief, Bounty and Pension Association. . . . Students and scholars of African-American history, as well as those engaged in the current reparations debates, will be deeply informed by the rise and fall of the Ex-Slave Association." Publ Wkly

Includes bibliographical references

House, Edward Mandell, 1858-1938

Neu, Charles E. **Colonel** House; a biography of Woodrow Wilson's silent partner. Charles E. Neu. Oxford University Press 2015 720 p. 16 plates $34.95 **92**
1. American diplomatic and consular service 2. Treaty of Versailles (1919) 3. World War, 1914-1918 -- Peace 4. Statesmen -- United States -- Biography 5. United States -- Foreign relations -- 1913-1921 6. United States -- Politics and government -- 1913-1921
ISBN 0195045505; 9780195045505

LC 2014015227

Author Charles E. Neu presents a biography of Edward M. House "who rose to become one of the century's greatest political operators. Ambitious and persuasive, House worked largely behind the scenes, developing ties of loyalty and using patronage to rally party workers behind his candidates. In 1911 he met Woodrow Wilson, and almost immediately the two formed what would become one of the most famous friendships in American political history." (Publisher's note)

"Neu deems House a 'patient, crafty, and sometimes cynical' infighter and 'a shrewd observer of human foibles,' widely admired but faulted by some at the height of his fame for developing an exaggerated sense of his own importance. A significant, brightly written American story." Kirkus

Includes bibliographical references and index

Howe, Ben Ryder

Howe, Ben Ryder. **My** Korean deli; risking it all for a convenience store. Henry Holt and Co. 2010 304p $25 **92**
1. Korean Americans 2. Convenience stores 3. Editors 4. Small business owners
ISBN 978-0-8050-9343-8; 0-8050-9343-5

LC 2010-24962

The author's "wife Gab bought (with the money the couple had saved for a down payment on their first house) her hardworking Korean parents a deli in Brooklyn as a gesture of thanks for all their self-sacrifice. What follows is a series of both comic and tragic vignettes that will leave the reader as surprised as the author about how emotionally invested you can get in a deli. . . . [Howe] delivers a smartly written narrative about love, literature, and the lengths one goes to for family, which turns out to be epically far." Maclean's

Howe, Gordie, 1928-2016

Howe, Gordie, 1928-2016. **Mr.** Hockey; My Story. Gordie Howe. Penguin Group USA 2014 320 p. 16 plates; color illustrations $27.95 **92**
1. Hockey players 2. Autobiographies
ISBN 0399172912; 9780399172915

LC 2015410204

In this autobiography, former hockey player Gordie Howe "takes us through it all, from his Depression-era childhood and early obstacles through the ups and downs of his spectacular career, to his enduring marriage and close relationship with his children, to his thoughts on the game of hockey today." (Publisher's note)

"The author intersperses portions of personal letters he sent to and received from family members. Lots of action, a bit of rumination and few regrets in this unremarkable work by a most remarkable athlete." Kirkus

Howe, Julia Ward, 1819-1910

Showalter, Elaine, 1941- The **civil** wars of Julia Ward Howe; a biography. Elaine Showalter. Simon & Schuster 2016 xiv, 303 p.p illustrations (hardcover) $28 **92**
1. Feminists -- United States -- Biography 2. United States --

History -- 1861-1865, Civil War -- Women 3. Authors, American -- 19th century -- Biography 4. United States -- History -- Civil War, 1861-1865 -- Women
ISBN 9781451645927; 9781451645903; 9781451645910

LC 2015027331

This book, by Elaine Showalter, is "the first biography to reveal Julia Ward Howe--the author of 'The Battle Hymn of the Republic'--as a feminist pioneer who fought her own battle for creative freedom and independence. Julia Ward (1819-1910) was an heiress and aspiring poet when she married Dr. Samuel Gridley Howe, an internationally-acclaimed pioneer in the education of the blind." (Publisher's note)

"A robust and enlightening feminist portrait of a national icon." Booklist

Includes bibliographical references and index

Hughes, Langston, 1902-1967

Rampersad, Arnold. The **life** of Langston Hughes Volume I: 1902-1941; I, too, sing America. 2nd ed; Oxford University Press 2002 478p il hardcover o.p. pa $33 **92**
1. Poets 2. Authors 3. Novelists 4. Dramatists 5. African American authors 6. Poets, American 7. Short story writers 8. Young adult authors
ISBN 0-19-515160-7; 0-19-514642-5 pa
First published 1986
This is the first volume of a two-volume set chronicling the life of the Harlem Renaissance poet and author.
Includes bibliographical references

Humbert, Agnès, 1894-1963

Humbert, Agnes. **Resistance**; a woman's journal of struggle and defiance in occupied France. Bloomsbury 2008 370p il $26 **92**
1. Art historians 2. Underground leaders 3. World War, 1939-1945 -- Personal narratives 4. World War, 1939-1945 -- Prisoners and prisons 5. World War, 1939-1945 -- Underground movements 6. France -- History -- 1940-1945, German occupation
ISBN 978-1-59691-559-6; 1-59691-559-5

LC 2008-16603

Original French edition, 1946

"Humbert's firsthand account of her work for the resistance in occupied Paris and her subsequent arrest and deportation to a forced-labor camp in Germany is an invaluable addition to works highlighting the role of women during wartime." Publ Wkly

Includes bibliographical references

Humboldt, Alexander von, 1769-1859

★ Wulf, Andrea. The **invention** of nature; Alexander von Humboldt's new world. by Andrea Wulf. Alfred A. Knopf 2015 496 p. ill. (some col.), maps (hardcover) $30 **92**
1. Scientists -- Biography 2. Naturalists -- Biography 3. Scientists -- Germany -- Biography 4. Naturalists -- Germany -- Biography
ISBN 038535066X; 9780385350662

LC 2015017505

Carnegie Medal Shortlist: Nonfiction (2016)
Los Angeles Times Book Prize: Science & Technology (2015)
This book, by Andrea Wulf, "reveals the forgotten life of Alexander von Humboldt, the visionary German naturalist whose ideas changed the way we see the natural world--and in the process created modern environmentalism. . . . She . . . discusses his prediction of human-induced climate change, his remarkable ability to fashion poetic narrative out of scientific observation, and his relationships with iconic figures such as Simón Bolívar and Thomas Jefferson." (Publisher's note)
Wulf "presents with zest and eloquence the full story of Humboldt's

adventurous life and extraordinary achievements, from making science 'accessible and popular' to his early warnings about how deforestation, monoculture agriculture, and industrialization would engender disastrous climate change." Booklist

Includes bibliographical references and index

Humiston, Grace (Mary Grace), 1869-1948

Ricca, Brad. **Mrs.** Sherlock Holmes; The True Story of New York City's Greatest Female Detective and the 1917 Missing Girl Case That Captivated a Nation. Brad Ricca. St. Martin's Press 2017 448 p. $27.99; (ebook) $60 **92**

1. Women lawyers -- New York (State) -- New York -- Case studies 2. Private investigators -- New York (State) -- New York -- Case studies
ISBN 1250072247; 9781250072245; 9781466883659

LC 2016036711

This book, by Brad Ricca, tells the "story of Mrs. Grace Humiston, the detective and lawyer who turned her back on New York society life to become one of the nation's greatest crime fighters during an era when women weren't even allowed to vote. After graduating from N.Y.U. law school, Grace opened a legal clinic in the city for low-income immigrant clients, and quickly established a reputation as a fierce, but fair lawyer who was always on the side of the disenfranchised." (Publisher's note)

"Rapid, compelling storytelling informed by rigorous research and enlivened by fecund imagination." Kirkus

Includes bibliographical references (pages 371-418) and index.

Hurston, Zora Neale, 1891-1960

Boyd, Valerie. **Wrapped** in rainbows; the life of Zora Neale Hurston. Scribner 2003 527p il $30 **92**

1. Authors 2. Novelists 3. Dramatists 4. African American authors 5. Memoirists 6. Folklorists 7. Short story writers 8. African American women -- Biography
ISBN 0-684-84230-0

LC 2002-17011

This is a biography of the folklorist and author of Their Eyes Were Watching God (1937), Tell My Horse (1938), Dust Tracks on a Road (1942) and Seraph on the Suwanee (1948)

"As the author adeptly and passionately analyzes Hurston's revolutionary books, intense spirituality, and myriad adventures, Hurston emerges in all her splendor—not only smarter, tougher, and more dazzlingly alive than most people but also freer." Booklist

Includes bibliographical references

★ Hurston, Zora Neale. **Dust** tracks on a road; an autobiography. with a foreword by Maya Angelou. 1st Harper Perennial Modern Classic ed; Harper Perennial Modern Classics 2006 308p il pa $13.95 **92**

1. Authors 2. Novelists 3. Dramatists 4. African American authors 5. Memoirists 6. Folklorists 7. Short story writers 8. African American women -- Biography
ISBN 0-06-085408-1; 978-0-06-085408-9

LC 2005-52616

First published 1942 by Lippincott

The author describes her wanderings in and out of schools and jobs as a young girl, finishing her course work at Barnard, and beginning her life's work.

Includes bibliographical references

Hurston, Zora Neale. **Zora** Neale Hurston: a life in letters; collected and edited by Carla Kaplan. Doubleday 2002 880p il $40; pa $19.95 **92**

1. Authors 2. Novelists 3. Dramatists 4. African American authors 5. Memoirists 6. Folklorists 7. Short story writers 8. African American women -- Biography
ISBN 0-385-49035-6; 0-385-49036-4 pa

LC 00-65671

A collection of over 500 letters by the Harlem Renaissance author

These letters reveal "a gifted yet complex personality at once humorous, cynical, and analytical." Libr J

Includes bibliographical references

Hussein, King of Jordan, 1935-1999

Ashton, Nigel. **King** Hussein of Jordan; a political life. [by] Nigel Ashton. Yale University Press 2008 431p il map $35 **92**

1. Kings 2. Jordan -- History 3. Biography, Individual 4. Jordan -- Kings and rulers 5. Jordan -- Politics and government 6. Jordan -- Politics and government -- 1952-1999
ISBN 0-300-09167-2; 978-0-300-09167-0

LC 2008-10803

This is a biography of King Hussein of Jordan, who "reigned for nearly half a century, from his grandfather's assassination in 1953 to his own death in 1999." (Publisher's note) Bibliography. Index.

With "unprecedented access to the late king's entire correspondence and more than two dozen interviews . . . Ashton reveals Hussein's long-standing covert contact with Israel and his clandestine communications with Israelis in the immediate aftermath of the 1967 war to suggest the possibilities and missed opportunities (including by the U.S.) for a peaceful settlement in the Palestinian-Israeli conflict." Publ Wkly

Includes bibliographical references (p. 371-378)

Huston, Anjelica

Huston, Anjelica, 1951- **Watch** me; a memoir. by Anjelica Huston. Scribner 2014 400 p. illustrations (some color) (hardback) $27.99 **92**

1. Actresses -- Biography 2. Motion picture actors and actresses -- United States -- Biography
ISBN 1476760349; 9781476760346; 9781476760360

LC 2014029235

This memoir, by actress Anjelica Huston, is an "account of her seventeen-year love affair with Jack Nicholson, her rise to stardom, and her mastery of the craft of acting. . . . She writes about . . . her Academy Award-winning portrayal of Maerose Prizzi in Prizzi's Honor; about her collaborations with many of the greatest directors in Hollywood. . . . She movingly and beautifully describes the death of her father John Huston and her marriage to sculptor Robert Graham." (Publisher's note)

"This memoir with both substance and flair is a must-read for Huston fans, those who enjoy film, and anyone who wishes to be inspired by a richly textured life well presented. For all entertainment collections." LJ

Includes bibliographical references and index

Huston, John, 1906-1987

Meyers, Jeffrey. **John** Huston; courage and art. Crown Archetype 2011 475p il $30; ebook $14.99 **92**

1. Motion picture producers and directors 2. Screenwriters 3. Motion picture directors
ISBN 978-0-307-59067-1; 978-0-307-59069-5 ebook

LC 2010047642

"By balancing the flamboyant life with the landmark works of legendary movie director John Huston, . . . Meyers reveals how a flawed man produced nearly flawless and indelible films." Booklist

Includes filmography and bibliographical references

Hylton, Donna

Hylton, Donna. A **little** piece of light; a memoir of hope, prison, and a life unbound. Donna Hylton, with Kristine Gasbarre. Hachette Books 2018 272 p. (hardcover) $28   **92**

1. Corrections 2. Women prisoners 3. Administration of criminal justice -- United States 4. Corrections -- United States 5. Women prisoners -- United States -- Biography 6. Prison reformers -- United States -- Biography 7. Criminal justice, Administration of -- United States 8. Female offenders -- Rehabilitation -- United States -- Biography

ISBN 9780316559256

LC 2017055248

This memoir, by Donna Hylton, "tells the heartfelt, often harrowing tale of . . . [her] journey back to life as she faced the truth about the crime that locked her away for 27 years . . . and celebrated the family she found inside prison that ultimately saved her. Behind the bars of Bedford Hills Correctional Facility, alongside this generation's most infamous criminals, Donna learned to fight, then thrive." (Publisher's note)

Hynde, Chrissie.

Hynde, Chrissie, 1951- **Reckless**; My Life as a Pretender. by Chrissie Hynde. Random House Inc 2015 352 p. 32 plates; color illustrations $26.95   **92**

1. Rock musicians -- United States -- Biography

ISBN 0385540612; 9780385540612

LC 2015027449

This memoir, by musician Chrissie Hynde, "tells her life story in full and utterly fascinating detail, from her all-American Ohio fifties childhood to her classic baby-boomer seduction by the rock of the sixties to her sojourn in the crucible of punk that was seventies London to her instant emergence with her band, The Pretenders, in 1980 into stardom as a frontwoman and songwriter." (Publisher's note)

Ian, Janis, 1951-

Ian, Janis. **Society's** child; my autobiography. Jeremy P. Tarcher/Penguin 2008 xxii, 361p il $26.95   **92**

1. Singers

ISBN 9781585426751

LC 2008-17130

This is a memoir by the American folk singer.

"Fans will love the book, of course, but many nonfans, too, should find this painfully candid memoir hard to put down." Booklist

Includes bibliographical references

Ibadi, Shirin.

Ebadi, Shirin, 1947- **Until** We Are Free; My Fight for Human Rights in Iran. by Shirin Ebadi. Random House Inc 2016 304 p. $27   **92**

1. Human rights 2. Women -- Iran 3. Women lawyers 4. Human rights advocacy 5. Iran -- Social conditions

ISBN 0812998871; 9780812998870

LC 2015027147

In this book, Iranian human rights lawyer Shirin Ebadi "tells her story of courage and defiance in the face of a government out to destroy her, her family, and her mission: to bring justice to the people and the country she loves. For years the Islamic Republic tried to intimidate Ebadi. . . . Despite finding herself living under circumstances reminiscent of a spy novel, nothing could keep Ebadi from speaking out and standing up for human dignity." (Publisher's note)

"The captivating and candid story of a woman who took on the Iranian government and survived, despite every attempt to make her fail." Kirkus

Ice-T

Ice-T. **Ice**; a memoir of gangster life and redemption--from South Central to Hollywood. [by] Ice-T and Douglas Century. One World Books 2011 251p il $25; ebook $12.99   **92**

1. Actors 2. Rap music 3. African American musicians 4. Rap musicians

ISBN 978-0-345-52328-0; 978-0-345-52330-3 ebook

LC 2010-41069

"A fascinating and inspiring story about an African American orphan who beat the odds to become successful, this memoir will appeal to fans of hip-hop and popular culture." Booklist

Irving, Apricot Anderson

Irving, Apricot. The **gospel** of trees; a memoir. Apricot Irving. Simon & Schuster 2018 384 p. $26   **92**

1. Biography 2. Family life 3. Christian missionaries

ISBN 1451690452; 9781451690453

In this memoir, author "Apricot Irving recounts her childhood as a missionary's daughter in Haiti during a time of upheaval--both in the country and in her home. . . . [The book] is the story of a family crushed by ideals, and restored to kindness by honesty. Told against the backdrop of Haiti's long history of intervention--often unwelcome--it grapples with the complicated legacy of those who wish to improve the world." (Publisher's note)

"With insight and admirable even-handedness, Irving shows the complex forces at play in both the story of Haiti's cycle of poverty and the more personal dynamics at play in her family as they struggle mightily to do God's work." Booklist

Isabella I, Queen of Spain, 1451-1504

Downey, Kirstin. **Isabella**; the warrior queen. Kirstin Downey. Nan A. Talese/Doubleday 2014 544 p. 16 plates; illustrations; maps (alk. paper) $35   **92**

1. Spain -- History 2. Queens -- Spain -- Biography 3. Spain -- History -- Ferdinand and Isabella, 1479-1516

ISBN 0385534116; 9780385534116

LC 2014003895

Los Angeles Times Book Prize Finalist: Biography (2014)

Author Kirstin Downey presents a "biography of Isabella of Castile, the controversial Queen of Spain who sponsored Christopher Columbus's journey to the New World, established the Spanish Inquisition, and became one of the most influential female rulers in history." (Publisher's note)

"As one of the most influential political players of the transitional era bridging the Middle Ages and the Renaissance, Isabella has earned her place in the spotlight." Booklist

Includes bibliographical references and index

Ishi

★ Kroeber, Theodora. **Ishi** in two worlds; a biography of the last wild Indian in North America. University of Calif. Press 1976 262p il $50; pa $16.95   **92**

1. Yana Indians 2. Linguistic informants

ISBN 0-520-00674-7; 0-520-22940-1 pa

First published 1961

An account "of the life of the sole survivor of a California Indian tribe. The author, wife of the famed anthropologist, reconstructs the decimation of Ishi's {Yana} people and his reluctant entry in 1911 into the world of his conquerors." Booklist

Ishikawa, Masaji

Ishikawa, Masaji. A **river** in darkness; one man's escape

from North Korea. Masaji Ishikawa. Amazon Pub 2018 172 p.
$19.95 **92**

    1. Biography 2. Activists -- Biography
    ISBN 1503936902; 9781503936904

    In this memoir, Masaji "Ishikawa candidly recounts his tumultuous
upbringing and the brutal thirty-six years he spent living under a crushing totalitarian regime, as well as the challenges he faced repatriating
to Japan after barely escaping North Korea with his life. 'A River in
Darkness' is not only a shocking portrait of life inside the country but a
testament to the dignity--and indomitable nature--of the human spirit."
(Publisher's note)

    "Ishikawa relates his painful story with sardonic humor and unwav-
ering familial love even in the depths of despair, making human the
often impersonal news coverage of mysterious and threatening North
Korea." (Booklist)

Ivan IV, the Terrible, Czar of Russia, 1530-1584

    De Madariaga, Isabel. **Ivan** the Terrible; first tsar of Russia.
Yale University Press 2005 xxi, 484p il map $35 **92**

    1. Emperors
    ISBN 0-300-09757-3

                  LC 2004-29807

    This is a biography of the Russian tsar.

    This "is a persuasively argued, widely researched and impressively
authoritative work that casts new light on the Tsar, his reign, and Russia
in the sixteenth century." Times Lit Suppl

    Includes bibliographical references

Ives, Charles Edward, 1874-1954

    Swafford, Jan. **Charles** Ives; a life with music. Norton
1996 525p il hardcover o.p. $18.95 **92**

    1. Composers
    ISBN 978-0-393-31719-0; 0-393-31719-6

                  LC 95-22549

    "Ives was a professional organist, a successful insurance executive,
a political idealist, and an immensely prolific composer. The author believes that Ives's transcendentalism was central to his identity, ceaselessly inspiring him while also spurring him on to an inevitable physical
collapse. Swafford—a composer himself—intersperses his biography
with valuable 'entr'actes' of approachable musical analysis, and ends
with a ringing endorsement of Ives as an ideal composer for a democratic society." New Yorker

    Includes bibliographical references

Izzard, Eddie

    Izzard, Eddie, 1962- **Believe** me; a memoir of love, death,
and jazz chickens. Eddie Izzard, with Laura Zigman. Blue Rider Press 2017 348 p. illustrations (some color) (hardcover)
$28 **92**

    1. Entertainers 2. Comedians -- Great Britain -- Biography 3.
    Entertainers -- Great Britain -- Biography
    ISBN 9780399175831; 9780698405660

                  LC 2017008493

    In this memoir, author Eddie Izzard "reflects on a childhood marked
by the loss of his mother, boarding school, and alternative sexuality, as
well as a life in comedy, film, politics, running and philanthropy. With
his brand of keenly intelligent humor that ranges from world history to
historical politics, sexual politics, mad ancient kings, and chickens with
guns, Eddie Izzard has built an extraordinary fan base that transcends
age, gender, and race." (Publisher's note)

    "In this witty and honest memoir, performer Izzard (Dress To Kill)
chronicles his life and career thus far." LJ

Jackson, Andrew, 1767-1845

    ★ Brands, H. W. **Andrew** Jackson; his life and times.
Doubleday 2005 620p il map $35 **92**

    1. Generals 2. Presidents 3. Presidents -- United States
    ISBN 0-385-50738-0; 978-0-385-50738-7

                  LC 2005-42178

    This is a biography of the seventh president of the United States.

    This book "is a bracing, human portrait of both a remarkable man
and of American democracy as it was transformed from a 'government
of the people' into a 'government by the people.'" Publ Wkly

    Includes bibliographical references

    Meacham, Jon. **American** lion; Andrew Jackson in the
White House. Random House 2008 483p il $30 **92**

    1. Generals 2. Presidents 3. Presidents -- United States
    ISBN 978-1-4000-6325-3; 1-4000-6325-6

                  LC 2008-23466

    The author "looks past the theatrics and posturing to the essential el-
ements of Jackson's many showdowns. Mr. Meacham . . . dispenses with
the usual view of Jackson as a Tennessee hothead and instead sees a can-
nily ambitious figure determined to reshape the power of the presidency
during his time in office (1829 to 1837). Case by case, Mr. Meacham
dissects Jackson's battles and reinterprets them in a revealing new light."
N Y Times (Late N Y Ed)

    Includes bibliographical references

    Remini, Robert Vincent. **Andrew** Jackson; [by] Robert V.
Remini; foreword by General Wesley K. Clark. Palgrave Macmillan 2008 204p il map (Great generals series) $21.95 **92**

    1. Generals 2. Presidents 3. Presidents -- United States
    ISBN 0-230-60015-8; 978-0-230-60015-7

                  LC 2008-394

    This is a "study of Jackson from a military perspective. Remini
maintains a birth-to-death narrative while keeping the focus on Jackson's fundamental existence as a soldier. The result is a fine introduction based on years of advanced knowledge on the subject, distilled by
Remini into a very good read." Libr J

    Includes bibliographical references

    Wilentz, Sean. **Andrew** Jackson. Times Books 2005 195p
(American presidents series) $20 **92**

    1. Generals 2. Presidents 3. Presidents -- United States
    ISBN 0-8050-6925-9

                  LC 2005-52857

    The author "shows that our complicated seventh president was a
central figure in the development of American democracy. . . . It is rare
that historians manage both Wilentz's deep interpretation and lively narrative." Publ Wkly

    Includes bibliographical references

Jackson, Michael, 1958-2009

    ★ Greenburg, Zack O'Malley, 1985- **Michael** Jackson,
Inc; the rise, fall and rebirth of a billion-dollar empire. Zack
O'Malley Greenburg. Atria Books 2014 293 p. $26 **92**

    1. Music industry 2. Musicians -- United States 3. Popular music
    -- Economic aspects -- United States
    ISBN 1476705968; 9781476705965

                  LC 2013045449

    "'Michael Jackson, Inc.' reveals the incredible rise, fall, and rise
again of Michael Jackson's fortune--driven by the unmatched perfectionism of the King of Pop. 'Forbes' senior editor Zack O'Malley Greenburg uncovers never-before-told stories from interviews with more than

100 people, including music industry veterans Berry Gordy, John Branca, and Walter Yetnikoff; artists 50 Cent, Sheryl Crow, and Jon Bon Jovi; and members of the Jackson family." (Publisher's note)

"A quick-moving yet comprehensive narrative of the singer's career, downfall and unlikely post-mortem second act." Kirkus

Includes bibliographical references and index

Jackson, Shirley, 1916-1965

★ Franklin, Ruth. **Shirley** Jackson; A Rather Haunted Life. by Ruth Franklin. W W Norton & Co Inc 2016 656 p. (ebook) $50; $35   **92**

1. Women authors -- Biography
ISBN 9781631492129; 0871403137; 9780871403131
     LC 2016014711
National Book Critics Circle Award: Biography (2017)

This biography, by Ruth Franklin, "establishes Shirley Jackson as a towering figure in American literature. . . . Placing Jackson within an American Gothic tradition that stretches back to Hawthorne and Poe, Franklin demonstrates how her unique contribution to this genre came from her focus on 'domestic horror.'" (Publisher's note)

"A consistently interesting biography that deftly captures the many selves and multiple struggles of a true American original." Kirkus

Includes bibliographical references (pages 503-580) and index.

Jackson, Stonewall, 1824-1863

Gwynne, S. C. **Rebel** Yell; The Violence, Passion, and Redemption of Stonewall Jackson. S. C. Gwynne. Simon & Schuster 2014 688 p. illustrations, maps, portraits $35   **92**

1. Confederate States of America -- History 2. United States -- History -- 1861-1865, Civil War
ISBN 1451673280; 9781451673289
     LC 2014010046
National Book Critics Circle Finalist: Biography (2014)

This book, by S. C. Gwynne, is an "account of how Civil War general Thomas 'Stonewall' Jackson became a great and tragic American hero. . . . In April 1862 Jackson was merely another Confederate general in an army fighting what seemed to be a losing cause. By June he had engineered perhaps the greatest military campaign in American history and was one of the most famous men in the Western world. He had, moreover, given the Confederate cause what it had recently lacked--hope." (Publisher's note)

"Gwynne presents Jackson's eccentric personality in biographical episodes that he injects into the arc of Jackson's Civil War campaigns and battles. . . . [The] technique succeeds, thanks to his spry prose and cogent insight, in revealing Jackson's character." Booklist

Includes bibliographical references (pages 577-634) and index

Jacobs, Harriet A., 1813-1897

Yellin, Jean Fagan. **Harriet** Jacobs: a life. Basic Civitas Books 2004 394p il map $27.50; pa $16.95   **92**

1. Slaves 2. Authors 3. Domestics 4. Memoirists
ISBN 0-465-09288-8; 0-465-09289-6 pa
     LC 2003-17256
"This scholarly account, woven in a reader friendly fashion, restores 'an heroic woman who lived in an heroic time' to history and to us." Publ Wkly

Includes bibliographical references

Robertson, James I. **Stonewall** Jackson; James I. Robertson, Jr. Macmillan 1997 xxiii, 950 p.p illustrations, maps $63   **92**

1. Confederate States of America -- History 2. United States -- History -- 1861-1865, Civil War 3. Biography, Individual 4. Confederate States of America -- Army
ISBN 9780028646855; 0028646851
     LC 96017042
In this biography of Stonewall Jackson, author James Robertson "traces his life from his humble beginnings, through his military career, to his untimely death in 1863, discussing his military campaigns and strategies, religious beliefs, personal eccentricities, and more." (Publisher's note)

"Robertson's bibliography, which runs to 25 pages of fine print, reveals the solid bedrock on which this work is built; his documentation is a model of thoroughness. The book is illustrated with rare photographs. A highly readable, remarkably interesting study of Jackson as both man and military leader." Choice

Includes bibliographical references (p. 793-787) and index

Jacobs, Jane, 1916-2006

★ Kanigel, Robert. **Eyes** on the street; The Life of Jane Jacobs. by Robert Kanigel. Alfred A. Knopf 2016 512 p. illustrations, map (hardcover) $35   **92**

1. City planning 2. Urban renewal 3. Women authors -- Biography 4. Sociology, Urban -- Philosophy 5. City planners -- Canada -- Biography 6. City planners -- United States -- Biography 7. City planning -- Canada -- History -- 20th century 8. Urban renewal -- Canada -- History -- 20th century 9. City planning -- United States -- History -- 20th century 10. Urban renewal -- United States -- History -- 20th century
ISBN 9780307961907
     LC 2015050758
Carnegie Medal Longlist: Nonfiction (2017)

This biography of Jane Jacobs by Robert Kanigel tells the story of the "woman who raised three children, wrote seven groundbreaking books, saved neighborhoods, stopped expressways, was arrested twice, and engaged at home and on the streets in thousands of debates--all of which she won." (Publisher's note)

Includes bibliographical references and index

Jaffrey, Madhur

Jaffrey, Madhur. **Climbing** the mango trees; a memoir of a childhood in India. Knopf 2006 297p il $25   **92**

1. Actors 2. Cookbook writers
ISBN 1-4000-4295-X; 978-1-4000-4295-1
     LC 2006-45255
First published 2005 in the United Kingdom

This is the memoir by the Indian actress and cookbook author.

The author's "taste memories sparkle with enthusiasm, and her talent for conveying them makes the book relentlessly appetizing." N Y Times Book Rev

Jahren, Hope

★ Jahren, Hope, 1969- **Lab** girl; Hope Jahren. Alfred A. Knopf 2016 304 p. (hardcover) $26.95   **92**

1. Biologists 2. Friendship 3. Geobiology -- Research -- Anecdotes 4. Biologists -- United States -- Biography
ISBN 9781101874936; 1101874937
     LC 2015024305
National Book Critics Circle Award: Autobiography (2017)
Carnegie Medal Longlist: Nonfiction (2017)

This memoir, by Hope Jahren, is "about work, love, and the mountains that can be moved when those two things come together. It is told through Jahren's remarkable stories: about her childhood in rural Minnesota with an uncompromising mother and a father who encouraged hours of play in his classroom's labs; about how she found a sanctuary in science, and learned to perform lab work done ... and about the inevitable disappointments, but also the triumphs and exhilarating discoveries, of scientific work." (Publisher's note)

"Jahren's forthright, beautifully expressed, and galvanizing chronicle deserves the widest possible readership." Booklist

Includes bibliographical references

James, Charles, 1906-1978

Klein, Michèle Gerber. **Charles** James; portrait of an unreasonable man: fame, fashion, art. Michèle Gerber Klein, foreword by Harold Koda. Rizzoli Ex Libris 2018 256 p. (hardcover) $37.50   **92**

1. Fashion design 2. Fashion designers -- Biography
ISBN 9780847861453

LC 2017958943

This book, by Michele Gerber Klein and Harold Koda, "is the first biography of the visionary fashion designer Charles James. ... [It] follows his career through his complex and turbulent relationships with exceptional women such as Elsa Schiaparelli and Eleanor Lambert, ending with his penurious death in New York's fabled Chelsea Hotel." (Publisher's note)

"Determined to tell his side of the story, James spent his last years writing letters to his former friends and associates—a handful of which are excerpted here. The result is a juicy account of the influence of an often-overlooked figure in the history of fashion." Pub Wkly

James, Eloisa

★ James, Eloisa. **Paris** in love; a memoir. Eloisa James. Random House 2012 x, 260 p.p   **92**

1. Autobiographies 2. Women -- Biography 3. Americans -- France 4. Paris (France) -- Description and travel 5. Life change events 6. Authors, American -- Biography 7. Cancer -- Patients -- Biography 8. Self-actualization (Psychology) 9. Quality of life -- France -- Paris 10. Women authors, American -- Biography 11. Americans -- France -- Paris -- Biography
ISBN 9780679604440; 9781400069569; 0679604448; 1400069564

LC 2011040662

This expatriate memoir by Eloisa James tells how "in 2009, [the] . . . author ... sold her house, took a sabbatical from her job as a Shakespeare professor, and moved her family to Paris. [The story} chronicles her joyful year ... [w]ith no classes to teach, no committee meetings to attend, no lawn to mow or cars to park, Eloisa revels in the ordinary pleasures of life ... She copes with her Italian husband's notions of quality time; her two hilarious children, ages eleven and fifteen, as they navigate schools—not to mention puberty—in a foreign language; and her mother-in-law Marina's raised eyebrow in the kitchen (even as Marina overfeeds Milo, the family dog)." (Publisher's note)

James, Etta, 1938-2012

James, Etta. **Rage** to survive; the Etta James story. [by] Etta James with David Ritz. Da Capo Press 2003 288p il pa $18   **92**

1. Singers 2. Blues musicians 3. Songwriters 4. Soul musicians 5. Singers -- United States
ISBN 0-306-81262-2; 978-0-306-81262-0

First published 1995 by Villard Books

"With a supporting cast resembling the roster of the Rock Hall of Fame, this autobiography reads as its author sings-rough, gritty, and brutally honest." Libr J

Discography

James, William, 1842-1910

Richardson, Robert D. **William** James; in the maelstrom of American modernism: a biography. Houghton Mifflin 2006 622p il $30   **92**

1. Philosophers 2. Psychologists 3. Writers on science
ISBN 978-0-618-43325-4; 0-618-43325-2

LC 2005-37776

This is a biography of the psychologist and philosopher.

The author's "enthusiasm for what he calls 'the matchless incandescent spirit' of William James is contagious." Publ Wkly

Includes bibliographical references (p. 586-9)

Jamison, Kay R.

Jamison, Kay R. **Nothing** was the same; a memoir. by Kay Redfield Jamison. Alfred A. Knopf 2009 208p $25   **92**

1. Bereavement 2. Psychiatrists 3. Psychologists 4. Hodgkin's disease 5. Manic-depressive illness 6. College teachers
ISBN 978-0-307-26537-1; 0-307-26537-4

LC 2009-11096

"The great gift Jamison offers here, beyond her honesty and the beauty of her writing, is perspective: a clear-eyed view of illness and death, sanity and insanity, love and grief. ... Jamison seems to be telling the truth, no matter how difficult it may be, in a way that avoids self-pity and inspires courage." Washington Post Book World

Jang, Jin-sung

Jang Jin-sung. **Dear** Leader; poet, spy, escapee?: a look inside North Korea. Jang Jin-sung; translated by Shirley Lee. 37 Ink/Atria Books 2014 368 p. (hardback) $27.99   **92**

1. Poets 2. Korea (North) 3. Autobiographies 4. Korea (North) -- Biography 5. Propaganda -- Korea (North) 6. Poets -- Korea (North) -- Biography 7. Political refugees -- Korea (North) -- Biography 8. Korea (North) -- Politics and government -- 1994-2011
ISBN 147676655X; 9781476766553

LC 2014010236

This memoir tells how "[a]s North Korea's State Poet Laureate, Jang Jin-sung led a charmed life. With food provisions . . . , a travel pass, access to strictly censored information, and audiences with Kim Jong-il himself, his life in Pyongyang seemed safe and secure. But this privileged existence was about to be shattered. When a strictly forbidden magazine he lent to a friend goes missing, Jang Jin-sung must flee for his life." (Publisher's note)

"A defector of Kim Jong-il's rarefied inner circle reveals the desperate, despicable machinations of North Korea's police state." Kirkus

Jang, Lucia

McClelland, Susan. **Stars** Between the Sun and Moon; One Woman's Life in North Korea and Escape to Freedom. Lucia Jang and Susan McClelland. Douglas & McIntyre 2014 288 p. $26.95   **92**

1. Refugees 2. Korea (North) -- Politics and government
ISBN 0393249220; 1771620358; 9780393249224; 9781771620352

LC 2015019384

This book by Lucia Jang and Susan McClelland is Jang's "memoir by a North Korean woman who defied the government to keep her family alive. Happy to serve her country, Jang worked in a factory as a young woman. There, a man she thought was courting her raped her. Forced to marry him when she found herself pregnant, she continued to be abused by him. She knew that, to keep the child, she had to leave North Korea. In a dramatic escape, she was smuggled with her newborn to China, fled to Mongolia . . . before eventually settling in Canada." (Publisher's note)

"An emotional and engrossing work that sheds light on daily life in this opaque country. Highly recommended for readers interested in North Korea as well as those who enjoy inspirational stories. Fans of Barbara Demick's Nothing To Envy will especially appreciate this work." LJ

Janowitz, Tama.

Janowitz, Tama. **Scream**; A Memoir of Glamour and Dysfunction. Tama Janowitz. HarperCollins 2016 304 p. illustrations hardcover $25.99   **92**

1. Women authors

ISBN 9780062391322; 0062391321

This memoir by Tama Janowitz "recalls the quirky literary world of young downtown New York in the go-go 1980s and reflects on her life today far away from the city indelible to her work. . . . Janowitz . . . [recounts] the vagaries of fame and fortune as a writer devoted to her art. Here, too, is Tama as daughter, wife, and mother, wrestling with aging, loss, and angst, both adolescent (her daughter) and middle aged (her own)." (Publisher's note)

"Sniping, scathing, grim, and hilarious, Janowitz's primal scream exposes the poisoned wellspring that gave rise to the gritty and canny ludicrousness of her novels, the highs and lows of her writing life, and the boons and traumas of fame and love." Booklist

Jauhar, Sandeep, 1968-

Jauhar, Sandeep. **Doctored**; the disillusionment of an American physician. Sandeep Jauhar. Farrar, Straus and Giroux 2014 288 p. (hardback) $26   **92**

1. Physicians 2. Medical care -- United States 3. Physicians -- United States -- Autobiography 4. Delivery of Health Care -- trends -- United States

ISBN 0374141398; 9780374141394

LC 2013041344

This memoir, by Sandeep Jauhar, "observes the crisis of American medicine through the eyes of an attending cardiologist. . . . With a decade's worth of elite medical training behind him, he is eager to settle down and reap the rewards of countless sleepless nights. Instead, he is confronted with sobering truths. . . . Provoked by his unsettling experiences, [the author] . . . has written an introspective memoir that is also an impassioned plea for reform." (Publisher's note)

"At times whiny, Jauhar's narrative provides a grim picture of modern medicine and the plight of contemporary physicians. And do not forget the domino effect: 'Unhappy doctors make for unhappy patients.' " Booklist

Jefferson, Margo, 1947-

★ Jefferson, Margo. **Negroland**; A Memoir. Margo Jefferson. Random House Inc 2015 240 p. illustrations $25 **92**

1. Aristocracy 2. African Americans 3. United States -- Social conditions 4. African Americans -- Race identity 5. Chicago Region (Ill.) -- Biography 6. Elite (Social sciences) -- Illinois -- Chicago Region 7. African American women -- Illinois -- Chicago -- Biography 8. Chicago (Ill.) -- Race relations -- History -- 20th century -- Anecdotes 9. Chicago Region (Ill.) -- Social life and customs -- 20th century -- Anecdotes 10. African Americans -- Illinois -- Chicago -- Social life and customs -- 20th century 11. African American girls -- Illinois -- Chicago Region -- Social conditions -- 20th century

ISBN 0307378454; 9780307378453

LC 2015006843

National Book Critics Circle Award Finalist: Autobiography (2015)

This memoir by Margo Jefferson is a "meditation on race, sex, and

American culture through the prism of the author's rarefied upbringing and education among a black elite concerned with distancing itself from whites and the black generality. Jefferson has spent most of her life among (call them what you will) the colored aristocracy, . . . inhabitants of Negroland, 'a small region of Negro America where residents were sheltered by a certain amount of privilege.'" (Publisher's note)

"Jefferson swings the narrative back and forth through her life, exploring the tides of racism, opportunity, and dignity while also provocatively exploring the inherent contradictions for Jefferson and her family members in working so tirelessly to differentiate themselves." Kirkus

Includes bibliographical references (pages [243]-248)

Jefferson, Thomas, 1743-1826

Bernstein, Richard B. **Thomas** Jefferson; [by] R.B. Bernstein. Oxford University Press 2003 253p il hardcover o.p. pa $15.95   **92**

1. Architects 2. Presidents 3. Vice-presidents 4. Essayists 5. Presidents -- United States

ISBN 0-19-516911-5; 978-0-19-518130-2 pa; 0-19-518130-1 pa

LC 2003-5556

The author "provides a . . . view not of Jefferson the politician, but of the man whose ideas changed the world and provided the US with a sense of purpose. This short biography provides a judicious synthesis of the prevailing scholarship on the third president and explores more deeply his views on government and union, slavery (revealing what is known about the Sally Hemings affair and what cannot yet be determined), and debt. . . . Its concise form, limited notes, and evenhanded style will appeal to general readers seeking insight into an incredibly complex historical figure." Choice

Includes bibliographical references

Boles, John B. **Jefferson**; architect of American liberty. John B. Boles. Basic Books 2017 xi, 626 p.p illustrations (hardcover) $35   **92**

1. Presidents -- United States -- Biography 2. United States -- Politics and government -- 1775-1783 3. United States -- Politics and government -- 1783-1809

ISBN 9780465094684; 9781541697966

LC 2017934233

This biography, by John B. Boles, "does not ignore the aspects of Jefferson that trouble us today, but strives to see him in full, and to understand him amid the sweeping upheaval of his times. We follow Jefferson from his early success as an abnormally precocious student and lawyer in colonial Virginia through his drafting of the Declaration of Independence at age 33, his travels in Europe on the eve of the French Revolution, his acidic personal battles with Hamilton, his triumphant ascent to the presidency in 1801, his prodigious efforts to found the University of Virginia, and beyond." (Publisher's note)

"A fully fleshed biography of Thomas Jefferson (1743-1826) that emphasizes his creative paradoxes and accomplishments." Kirkus

Includes bibliographical references and index.

Ellis, Joseph J. **American** sphinx: the character of Thomas Jefferson. Knopf 1997 365p $29.95; pa $15 **92**

1. Architects 2. Presidents 3. Vice-presidents 4. Essayists

ISBN 0-679-44490-4; 0-679-76441-0 pa

LC 96-26171

"Penetrating Jefferson's placid, elegant facade, this extraordinary biography brings the sage of Monticello down to earth without either condemning or idolizing him." Publ Wkly

★ Gordon-Reed, Annette. **Most** Blessed of the Patriarchs; Thomas Jefferson and the Empire of the Imagination. Annette

Gordon-Reed and Peter S. Onuf. Liveright 2016 320 p. illustrations, maps $27.95   **92**

1. Christianity 2. United States -- History -- 1775-1783, Revolution
ISBN 0871404427; 9780871404428

LC 2016000927

This biography of Thomas Jefferson, by Annette Gordon-Reed and Peter S. Onuf, "present[s] an absorbing and revealing character study that dispels the many clichés that have accrued over the years about our third president. Tracing Jefferson's philosophical development from youth to old age, the authors explore what they call the 'empire' of Jefferson's imagination—an expansive state of mind born of his origins in a slave society, his intellectual influences, and the vaulting ambition that propelled him into public life." (Publisher's note)

"An elegant, astute study that is both readable and thematically rich." Kirkus

Includes bibliographical references and index.

Hitchens, Christopher. **Thomas** Jefferson: author of America. HarperCollins Publishers 2005 188p (Eminent lives) $19.95   **92**

1. Architects 2. Presidents 3. Vice-presidents 4. Essayists 5. Presidents -- United States
ISBN 0-06-059896-4

LC 2005-296593

"Beginning with his aristocratic upbringing, . . . this biography explores both the private and public aspects of Jefferson's life, from his political philosophies to his affair with his slave Sally Hemings. . . . This opinionated, lively narrative sheds light not only on Jefferson's complex personality but on the politics of his time, making it both a fascinating character study and an excellent review of early American history." Publ Wkly

★ Meacham, Jon. **Thomas** Jefferson; the art of power. Jon Meacham. 1st ed. Random House 2012 448 p. (acid-free paper) $35   **92**

1. Presidents -- United States -- Biography 2. United States -- Politics and government -- 1783-1809
ISBN 1400067669; 9780679645368; 9781400067664

LC 2012013700

In this book, author Jon Meacham "claims that previous . . . scholars have not grasped the authentic [Thomas] Jefferson . . . a power-hungry, masterful, pragmatic leader who was not above being manipulative to achieve his goal: an enduring, democratic republic defined by him. A brilliant philosopher whose lofty principles were sometimes sidelined for more realistic goals, Meacham's Jefferson, neither idol nor rogue, is a complex mortal with serious flaws and contradictions." (Library Journal)

Includes bibliographical references and index.

Jenner, Caitlyn, 1949-

Jenner, Caitlyn, 1949- The **secrets** of my life; Caitlyn Jenner; with Buzz Bissinger. Grand Central Publishing 2017 x, 320 p.p illustrations (some color) (hardcover) $30   **92**

1. Transgender people 2. Transgender people -- United States -- Biography 3. Transgender athletes -- United States -- Biography 4. Track and field athletes -- United States -- Biography
ISBN 9781455596751; 9781455596768

LC 2017000493

This book, by Caitlyn Jenner, with Buzz Bissinger, "reflects on the inner conflict . . . experienced [by Caitlyn] growing up in an era of rigidly defined gender identities. . . . She recounts her Olympic triumph, [and] her rise to fame. . . . She also talks . . . about her life in the public eye . . . , her decision to become Caitlyn, and how she, her family, the transgender community, and the rest of the world has since embraced her new life." (Publisher's note)

"Painting a life both shallow and deep, painstakingly choreographed and unscripted, Jenner's candid portrait of a self in the remaking is a marvel to behold." Kirkus

Jeremiah, Thomas, d. 1775

Harris, J. William. The **hanging** of Thomas Jeremiah; a free Black man's encounter with liberty. Yale University Press 2009 223p il map $27.50   **92**

1. Diplomats 2. Merchants 3. Ship captains 4. Colonial leaders 5. Plantation owners 6. Government officials 7. Colonial administrators 8. Slavery -- United States 9. South Carolina -- Race relations 10. African Americans -- Social conditions
ISBN 978-0-300-15214-2; 0-300-15214-0

LC 2009-15233

This is an "account of nebulous historical figure Thomas Jeremiah. . . . Owner of a fishing company and worth $200,000 in 2009 dollars, . . . [Jeremiah] was probably the richest black man in North America; he was also a slaveowner. That didn't stop him from becoming a scapegoat, accused by patriot leader Henry Laurens—a wealthy plantation owner with hundreds of slaves—of secretly leading a British-sponsored slave insurrection. Though Governor William Campbell, aggrieved by the unlawfulness of Jeremiah's trial, interceded, it didn't stop those determined to hang Jeremiah. . . . Readers will learn much about the darker side of American institutions; students of American history and civil rights will appreciate Harris's impassive approach and thorough standards." Publ Wkly

Includes bibliographical references

Jesus Christ

Schiavone, Aldo. **Pontius** Pilate; deciphering a memory. Aldo Schiavone; translated by Jeremy Carden. Liveright Publishing Corp. 2017 240 p. (ebook) $50; (hardcover) $24.95 **92**

1. Palestine -- History 2. Palestine -- History -- To 70 A.D 3. Governors -- Palestine -- Biography
ISBN 9781631492365; 1631492357; 9781631492358

LC 2016056360

In this biography, by Aldo Schiavone, translated by Jeremy Carden, "the Roman prefect Pontius Pilate has been cloaked in rumor and myth since the first century, but what do we actually know of the man who condemned Jesus of Nazareth to the Cross? . . . Schiavone explains what might have happened in that brief meeting between the governor and Jesus, and why the Gospels—and history itself—have made Pilate a figure of immense ambiguity." (Publisher's note)

"A levelheaded, engaging reading of the Gospels and historical account that forms a solid sense of this pivotal personage and his role on the epic stage." Kirkus

Includes bibliographical references and index

Jewel, 1974-

Jewel, 1974- **Never** broken; songs are only half the story. Jewel. Blue Rider Press 2015 384 p. illustrations (some color) (ebook) $48; $27.50   **92**

1. Singers -- Biography 2. Singers -- United States -- Biography
ISBN 9780698192102; 9780399174339

LC 2015024911

This book, by musician Jewel, "tells the story of her life, and the lessons learned from her experience and her music. Living on a homestead in Alaska, Jewel learned to yodel at age five, and joined her parents' entertainment act, working in hotels, honky-tonks, and biker bars. Behind a strong-willed family life with an emphasis on music and artistic talent, however, there was also instability, abuse, and trauma." (Publisher's note)

"Jewel's lyrics, generously included throughout, reflect her authenticity and generosity. This is a solidly good read." Pub Wkly

Joan, of Arc, Saint, 1412-1431

Castor, Helen. **Joan** of Arc; a history. by Helen Castor. Harper 2015 352 p. color illustrations; map (hardcover) $27.99 **92**
1. Medieval civilization 2. Hundred Years' War, 1339-1453 3. Soldiers -- France -- Biography 4. Women heroes -- France -- Biography 5. Women soldiers -- France -- Biography 6. France -- History -- Charles VII, 1422-1461 7. Christian women saints -- France -- Biography
ISBN 0062384392; 9780062384393; 9780062384409
LC 2014029053

In this biography of Joan of Arc, author "Helen Castor tells afresh the gripping story of the peasant girl from Domremy who hears voices from God, leads the French army to victory, is burned at the stake for heresy, and eventually becomes a saint. Instead of an icon, she gives us a living, breathing woman confronting the challenges of faith and doubt, a roaring girl who, in fighting the English, was also taking sides in a bloody civil war." (Publisher's note)

"Castor carefully combs the record of her interrogation then and rehabilitation 25 years later. An unorthodox yet erudite and elegant biography of this 'massive star.'" Kirkus

Includes bibliographical references and index

Pernoud, Regine. **Joan** of Arc: her story; Régine Pernoud, Marie-Véronique Clin; translated and revised by Jeremy duQuesnay Adams; edited by Bonnie Wheeler. St. Martin's Griffin 1999 xxii, 304p il map hardcover o.p. pa $16.95 **92**
1. Saints 2. Christian saints 3. France -- History -- 1328-1589, House of Valois
ISBN 0-312-21442-1; 0-312-22730-2 pa
LC 98-45059

Original French edition, 1986

This work "traces the appearance of Joan as a documented historical character rather than adhering to a standard chronological sequence. Informing the narrative is a novel interpretation of Joan as a political prisoner. Moving beyond the narrative, the American translator . . . has added a series of appendixes containing valuable contextual material. . . . These materials discuss key historical events, provide biographical information on Joan's contemporaries, and discuss Joan's afterlife in history, literature, folklore, art, and iconography." Libr J

Includes bibliographical references

Jobrani, Maziyar, 1972-

Jobrani, Maz, 1972- **I'm** not a terrorist, but I've played one on tv; memoirs of a Middle Eastern funny man. Maz Jobrani. Simon & Schuster 2014 240 p. (hardcover) $24 **92**
1. Actors 2. Iranian Americans 3. Stereotype (Social psychology) 4. Iranian Americans -- Biography 5. Actors -- United States -- Biography 6. Comedians -- United States -- Biography 7. Stereotypes (Social psychology) -- United States
ISBN 9781476749983; 1476749981
LC 2014015012

Author Maz Jobrani presents this "memoir of growing up Iranian in America, and the quest to make it in Hollywood. Maz shares his struggle to build an acting career in post-9/11 Hollywood. But finally, through patience, determination, and only the occasional unequivocal compromising of his principles, he found a path to stardom." (Publisher's note)

"A funny and occasionally insightful memoir of an Iranian-American comedian finding a voice in showbiz." Kirkus

Jobs, Steve, 1955-2011

★ Isaacson, Walter. **Steve** Jobs. Simon & Schuster 2011 656p il por **92**
1. Executives 2. Biography, Individual 3. Apple Computer, Inc. -- History 4. Businesspeople -- United States -- Biography 5. Computer engineers -- United States -- Biography
ISBN 9781451648546; 1451648537; 9781451648539; 9781451648553; 1451648553 ebook
LC 2011045006

This is a biography of the former CEO of Apple, Inc.

This book discusses the "basic outlines of [Steve] Jobs' career. . . . He was the co-creator of the personal computer. . . . [A]gainst the backdrop of [Jobs's] abrasive personality, [Walter] Isaacson's book offers an overriding message . . . he was a creative genius whose profound understanding of consumer appetites allowed him to create technology that no one else imagined or even thought feasible." (Commentary)

This "is an encyclopedic survey of all that Mr. Jobs accomplished, replete with the passion and excitement that it deserves." N Y Times Book Rev

Includes bibliographical references and index

Tetzeli, Rick. **Becoming** Steve Jobs; the evolution of a reckless upstart into a visionary leader. Brent Schlender and Rick Tetzeli. Crown Business 2015 447 p. 16 plates; color illustrations (hardback) $30 **92**
1. Apple Inc. 2. Leadership 3. Apple Computer, Inc. -- Management 4. Businesspeople -- United States -- Biography 5. Computer engineers -- United States -- Biography
ISBN 0385347405; 9780385347402; 9780804138369
LC 2014031660

In this book, authors Brent Schlender and Rick Tezeli "focus on the years after Jobs's 1985 ouster from Apple and then on his 1997 return to guide the company's resurgence with a string of hit iProducts. They depict a spiritual journey . . . where he learned the art of not interfering with talented subordinates; he emerged a more patient man with a tempered strategic outlook and an ability to listen to underlings when they screamed back at him." (Publishers Weekly)

"Schlender and Tetzeli's account is unusually intimate thanks to voluminous interviews and Schlender's many personal encounters with Jobs over decades of covering him, and a reverential tone sometimes surfaces—as when Jobs's lieutenant Tim Cook offered Jobs his own liver for a transplant—in this corrective to Walter Isaacson's more jaundiced biography. But the authors are clear-eyed about Jobs's flaws and give lucid, detailed analyses of his maneuverings and product initiatives; theirs is one of the most nuanced and revealing assessments of Jobs's controversial career." Pub Wkly

John Paul II, Pope, 1920-2005

Flynn, Raymond. **John** Paul II; a personal portrait of the pope and the man. St. Martin's Press 2001 204p il hardcover o.p. pa $14.95 **92**
1. Popes
ISBN 0-312-28328-8 pa
LC 00-45965

Flynn, the "former mayor of Boston and ex-ambassador to the Vatican, tells us . . . what his book is not: It is not a biography, or an analysis. . . . Flynn views it, rather, as a profile based on his own experiences with Pope John Paul II, dating back to a 1969 visit to Boston of then-Cardinal Karol Wojtyla." Natl Rev

O'Connor, Garry. **Universal** Father: a life of John Paul II.

Bloomsbury 2005 436p il map $24.95 **92**

1. Popes

ISBN 1-59691-096-8

"The text is divided into four distinct phases of Pope John Paul II's life: '1920-1946,' '1946-1978,' '1978-1990,' and '1990-2005.' Each phase balances fact with anecdotal evidence, which lends the biography both credibility and charm. . . . This timely and remarkable biography will be sought after by serious readers." Libr J

John, King of England, 1167-1216

Morris, Marc. **King** John; Treachery and Tyranny in Medieval England: the Road to Magna Carta. Marc Morris. W.W. Norton & Co. Inc. 2015 400 p. 8 plates; color ills., maps $29.95 **92**

1. Middle Ages 2. Great Britain -- Kings and rulers

ISBN 1605988855; 9781605988856

LC 2015452049

This book on England's King John by Marc Morris "offers a compelling portrait of an extraordinary man, whose reign marked a momentous turning point in the history of Britain and Europe. Morris draws on contemporary chronicles and the king's own letters to bring the real King John vividly to life." (Publisher's note)

"Describing the king's exactions, Morris shows how they provoked opposition from England's magnates. Despite Magna Carta's subsequent renown as the foundation of constitutional law, at the time it was a truce surrounded by civil war. That the war ended quickly after John died in 1216 points, suggests Morris, to his personal shortcomings as significant causes of the disasters of his reign. Balanced and dramatic, Morris' riveting account will effortlessly attract history readers." Booklist

Johnson, Andrew, 1808-1875

Gordon-Reed, Annette. **Andrew** Johnson. Times Books/ Henry Holt and Company 2011 166p il (American presidents series) $23 **92**

1. Governors 2. Presidents 3. Vice-presidents 4. Members of Congress 5. Presidents -- United States 6. United States -- Politics and government -- 1865-1898

ISBN 978-0-8050-6948-8

LC 2010-32595

"Andrew Johnson rose from humble beginnings in the South to serve as Lincoln's second vice president, thus becoming President just as the Civil War was ending. He showed none of his predecessor's political finesse and is often viewed as among the worst to hold the office. . . . [The author] argues that the nation went from the best President to the worst during this most crucial period of its history. This slim study does cover Johnson from birth to death (1808–75), but the focus is assuredly on his presidency." Libr J

Includes bibliographical references

Johnson, Harriet McBryde

Johnson, Harriet McBryde. **Too** late to die young; nearly true tales from a life. Henry Holt and Co. 2005 261p $23; pa $14 **92**

1. Lawyers 2. Human rights activists

ISBN 0-8050-7594-1; 0-312-42571-6 pa

LC 2004-54007

In this memoir, the wheelchair-bound lawyer and activist describes her battles for disability rights.

"From her first demonstration against the MDA telethon to her celebrated debate with Peter Singer of Harvard, who has stated that killing a disabled infant is not morally equivalent to killing a person, this lady pulls no punches. An entertaining look at an activist who insists on living life her way, disability or no." Libr J

Johnson, Jack, 1878-1946

★ Ward, Geoffrey C. **Unforgivable** blackness; the rise and fall of Jack Johnson. Knopf 2004 492p il $26.95 **92**

1. Boxers (Persons)

ISBN 0-375-41532-7

LC 2004-48524

The author "brings us back into Johnson's life and times with exquisitely rendered details, and the fight scenes themselves are gripping: fights so bloody that referees have to change shirts midbout, for instance, and a manager who pulls a gun on his fighter to keep him from quitting. The authoritative biography of Johnson for sure, but also one of the best boxing books in recent memory." Booklist

Includes bibliographical references

Johnson, Lacy M., 1978-

Johnson, Lacy M. The **other** side; a memoir. Lacy M. Johnson. Tin House Books 2014 232 p. (paperback) $15.95 **92**

1. Kidnapping 2. Rape victims 3. Autobiographies 4. Rape victims -- United States -- Biography 5. Kidnapping victims -- United States -- Biography

ISBN 1935639838; 9781935639831

LC 2014006794

National Book Critics Circle Award Finalist: Autobiography (2014)

A memoir by Lacy Johnson, "'The Other Side' is the haunting account of a first passionate and then abusive relationship; the events leading to Johnson's kidnapping, rape, and imprisonment; her dramatic escape; and her hard-fought struggle to recover. . . . In language both stark and poetic, Johnson weaves together a . . . personal narrative with police and FBI reports, psychological records, and neurological experiments, delivering a . . . story of trauma and transformation." (Publisher's note)

Johnson, Lady Bird, 1912-2007

Caroli, Betty Boyd. **Lady** Bird and Lyndon; the hidden story of a marriage that made a president. Betty Boyd Caroli. Simon & Schuster 2015 464 p. 16 plates; illustrations (hardcover) $29.99 **92**

1. Presidents -- United States -- Biography 2. Married people -- United States -- Biography 3. Presidents' spouses -- United States -- Biography

ISBN 1439191220; 9781439191224; 9781439191231

LC 2015011027

This biography of the marriage of U.S. President Lyndon B. Johnson, by Betty Boyd Caroli, offers "a fresh look at Lady Bird Johnson that upends her image as a plain Jane who was married for her money and mistreated by Lyndon. This Lady Bird worked quietly behind the scenes through every campaign, every illness, and a trying presidency as a key strategist, fundraiser, barnstormer, peacemaker, and indispensable therapist." (Publisher's note)

"Caroli's suggestion and amplification of a virtual pact teased out of Lyndon and Bird's correspondence during a very brief courtship frames the story of this alliance. Recommended for history buffs and devotees of human behavior." LJ

Includes bibliographical references and index

Gillette, Michael L. **Lady** Bird Johnson; an oral history. Michael L. Gillette. Oxford University Press 2012 400 p. illustrations (hardback: alk. paper) $29.95 **92**

1. United States -- History 2. Presidents' spouses -- United States -- Biography 3. United States -- Politics and government -- 1945-1989

ISBN 0199908087; 9780199908080

LC 2012011580

For this book, Michael L. Gillette, "former director of the LBJ Library's oral history program, has selected and edited these interviews" with former U.S. First Lady Lady Bird Johnson. The histories "cover the first lady's life from her birth in 1912 through [Lyndon B.] Johnson's presidency, thus throwing light on a more than half a century of American history." (Publishers Weekly)

Includes bibliographical references and index

Johnson, Lyndon B. (Lyndon Baines), 1908-1973

★ Caro, Robert A., 1935- The **passage** of power; Robert A. Caro. Alfred A. Knopf 2012 xix, 712 p.p **92**
1. Biography 2. Presidents -- United States -- Biography 3. United States -- Politics and government -- 1945- 4. United States -- Politics and government -- 1963-1969
ISBN 0679405070; 9780679405078

LC 2012010752

National Book Award Finalist: Nonfiction (2012)

This fourth book of Robert A. Caro's series on Lyndon Baines Johnson (LBJ) "chronicles LBJ's life from 1958 to the passage of the Civil Rights Act, in July 1964. It follows Johnson as he . . . seeks the Democratic presidential nomination in 1960; as he is outmaneuvered by John F. Kennedy; as he" cultivates himself to be the "most powerful Senate majority leader in American history" and finally "as he has the presidency thrust upon him following Kennedy's murder." (Atlantic Monthly)

Includes bibliographical references and index.

Gillette, Michael L. **Lady** Bird Johnson; an oral history. Michael L. Gillette. Oxford University Press 2012 400 p. illustrations (hardback: alk. paper) $29.95 **92**
1. United States -- History 2. Presidents' spouses -- United States -- Biography 3. United States -- Politics and government -- 1945-1989
ISBN 0199908087; 9780199908080

LC 2012011580

For this book, Michael L. Gillette, "former director of the LBJ Library's oral history program, has selected and edited these interviews" with former U.S. First Lady Lady Bird Johnson. The histories "cover the first lady's life from her birth in 1912 through [Lyndon B.] Johnson's presidency, thus throwing light on a more than half a century of American history." (Publishers Weekly)

Includes bibliographical references and index

Peters, Charles. **Lyndon** B. Johnson. Times Books 2010 199p (American presidents series) $23 **92**
1. Presidents 2. Vice-presidents 3. Senators 4. Members of Congress 5. Presidents -- United States 6. United States -- Politics and government -- 1945-
ISBN 978-0-8050-8239-5

LC 2009-45612

"Peters describes Johnson's Texas childhood, his years in Congress, his frustrating years as Kennedy's vice president, and the triumphs and failures of his presidency (1963-68). . . . This book is aimed at general readers who want a brief account of this controversial President. . . . Its intended audience will not be disappointed with this fast-moving story." Libr J

Includes bibliographical references

Johnson, Philip

Lamster, Mark. The **man** in the glass house; Philip Johnson, architect of the modern century. Mark Lamster. Little, Brown & Co. 2018 528 p. $35 **92**
1. Architects
ISBN 0316126438; 9780316126434

In this book, architectural critic and biographer Mark Lamster "lifts the veil on [architect Philip] Johnson's controversial and endlessly contradictory life to tell the story of a charming yet deeply flawed man. A rollercoaster tale of the perils of wealth, privilege, and ambition, this book probes the dynamics of American culture that made him so powerful, and tells the story of the built environment in modern America." (Publisher's note)

"Award-winning architectural critic/historian Lamster details Johnson's life and aesthetics." Library Journal

Johnson, Robert, 1911-1938

★ Wald, Elijah. **Escaping** the delta; Robert Johnson and the invention of the blues. Amistad 2004 342p $24.95; pa $14.95 **92**
1. Singers 2. Guitarists 3. Blues music 4. Blues musicians 5. African American musicians 6. Songwriters
ISBN 0-06-052423-5; 0-06-052427-8 pa

LC 2003-52287

The author "writes better than anyone else ever has about the blues. If you read only one book about blues—maybe ever—read this one." Booklist

Includes bibliographical references

Johnson, Samuel, 1709-1784

Boswell, James. The **life** of Samuel Johnson; with an introduction by Claude Rawson. Random House 1992 liii, 127p il (Everyman's library) $30 **92**
1. Lexicographers 2. Literary critics
ISBN 0-679-41717-6

LC 92-52915

First published 1791

"The most famous biography in the English language. It is an intimate and minute delineation of the great lexicographer's life, character and person, enlivened with small-talk, gossip and bits of familiar correspondence. It is also an admirable portrayal of the society of which Johnson was the outstanding figure." Pratt Alcove

Includes bibliographical references

Martin, Peter. **Samuel** Johnson; a biography. Harvard University Press 2008 608p il $35 **92**
1. Lexicographers 2. Literary critics
ISBN 978-0-674-03160-9; 0-674-03160-1

LC 2008-11327

This "biography of the English essayist, lexicographer, and literary personality . . . emphasizes aspects of Johnson not covered by any previously published biographies . . . notably Johnson's deep depressions; his liberal views on women writers, slavery, and poverty (he was not the complete Tory that others have painted him); and Johnson as a writer whose works deserve to be better known by the general public. Martin covers all the well-known facts and accomplishments of Johnson's life, and he emphasizes the turbulent times in which Johnson lived and the intriguing people he knew. Scholarly but written in an engaging manner and featuring many quotations from Johnson and his friends and acquaintances, this [is a] new portrait of a complex, multifaceted writer and thinker." Libr J

Includes bibliographical references (p. 565-572)

Meyers, Jeffrey. **Samuel** Johnson; the struggle. Basic Books 2008 528p il $35 **92**
1. Lexicographers 2. Authors, English 3. Literary critics
ISBN 978-0-465-04571-6; 0-465-04571-5

LC 2008-12302

This biography "departs from a strict chronology to narrate significant events and their meaning for Johnson. A central concern involves one of Johnson's darkest secrets, which Meyers says other biographers have evaded: his masochistic sexuality at the hands of his confidante Mrs. Hester Thrale. The biography also speculates on other aspects of Johnson's sex life, both during his marriage to a much older woman and after her death. But Meyers's book is balanced and accomplishes much else." Publ Wkly

Includes bibliographical references

Johnson-Sirleaf, Ellen, 1938-

Cooper, Helene. **Madame** President; the extraordinary journey of Ellen Johnson Sirleaf. Helene Cooper. Simon & Schuster 2017 336 p. illustrations (some color) (ebook) $18.99; (hardcover) $27   **92**

1. Women presidents -- Liberia -- Biography 2. Liberia -- Politics and government -- 1980- 3. Liberia -- Biography 4. Presidents -- Liberia -- Biography

ISBN 9781451697377; 9781451697353; 9781451697360

LC 2016042087

This biography, by Helene Cooper, presents "the inspiring, often heartbreaking story of [Ellen Johnson] Sirleaf's evolution from an ordinary Liberian mother of four boys to international banking executive, from a victim of domestic violence to a political icon, from a post-war president to a Nobel Peace Prize winner." (Publisher's note)

"A brisk chronicle of a strong-willed, tireless, and determined leader." Kirkus

Includes bibliographical references (pages 295-308) and index.

Jones, Chipper, 1972-

Jones, Chipper, 1972- **Ballplayer**; Chipper Jones, with Carroll R. Walton. Dutton, an imprint of Penguin Random House LLC 2017 384 p. (hc) $27   **92**

1. Baseball players -- Biography 2. Sports journalism 3. Athletes -- United States 4. Atlanta Braves (Baseball team) 5. Baseball players -- United States -- Biography

ISBN 1101984406; 9781101984406; 9781101984420

LC 2016031331

In this book, "Chipper Jones tells the story of his rise to the MLB ranks and what it took to stay with one organization his entire career in an era of booming free agency. His journey begins with learning the art of switch-hitting and takes off after the Braves made him the number one overall pick in the 1990 draft, setting him on course to become the linchpin of their lineup at the height of their fourteen-straight division-title run." (Publisher's note)

"There will be little readership for the book outside of baseball fans, especially in the Atlanta area, but those fans will find a clear, readable old-school account of a player who almost certainly will be voted into the Hall of Fame, possibly as early as 2018, his first year of eligibility." Kirkus

Jones, John Paul, 1747-1792

★ Thomas, Evan. **John** Paul Jones; sailor, hero, father of the American Navy. Simon & Schuster 2003 383p il hardcover o.p. pa $16   **92**

1. Naval officers 2. United States -- Naval history

ISBN 0-7432-0583-9; 978-0-7432-5804-3; 0-7432-5804-5 pa

LC 2003-42411

"The complex portrait is rendered with nautical precision—the author knows his topsail from his topgallant—and a lively eye for such details as the Enlightenment virtues espoused by Freemasonry or the proper way to kiss a French lady in the eighteenth century." Publ Wkly

Includes bibliographical references

Jones, Malcolm, 1952-

Jones, Malcolm. **Little** boy blues; a crash course in growing up. Pantheon Books 2010 228p il map $24.95   **92**

1. Journalists 2. Magazine editors

ISBN 978-0-307-37772-2; 0-307-37772-5

LC 2009-17838

"In the background of this memoir, the South also complicates the child's horizon, with its own coded vocabulary, reprimanding glances and generations clinging to a crumbling way of life. . . . With all the hype, marketing and lying that the genre's been subjected to in recent years, I had forgotten that it is also the most vulnerable, intimate form a writer can employ. Often, this gets covered over in support-speak: the way a writer's memories turn into a way to help alleviate the pain of others suffering from similar memories. Jones is far too good a writer to indulge in messianic messages." PopMatters

Jones, Mother, 1830-1930

Gorn, Elliott J. **Mother** Jones; the most dangerous woman in America. Hill & Wang 2001 408p il hardcover o.p. pa $14   **92**

1. Centenarians 2. Labor leaders

ISBN 0-8090-7094-4 pa

LC 00-44997

This is a biography of union organizer and labor leader Mary Harris Jones, known more popularly as Mother Jones

Gorn "has successfully separated fact from myth . . . situating Jones's story within a wider cultural frame." Publ Wkly

Includes bibliographical references

Jones, Nathaniel R., 1926-

Jones, Nathaniel R. **Answering** the call; a memoir of the modern struggle to end racial discrimination in America. Judge Nathaniel R. Jones; foreword by Evelyn Brooks Higginbotham. The New Press 2016 416 p. (hardback) $35; (ebook) $35 **92**

1. Judges -- United States -- Biography 2. Civil rights -- United States -- History

ISBN 9781620970751; 9781620970713

LC 2015043150

This memoir, by Judge Nathaniel R. Jones, "is an extraordinary eyewitness account from an unsung hero of the battle for racial equality in America. . . . Jones's pathbreaking career was forged in the 1960s: as the first African American assistant U.S. attorney in Ohio; as assistant general counsel of the Kerner Commission; and, beginning in 1969, as general counsel of the NAACP. . . . He also led the national response to the attacks against affirmative action." (Publisher's note)

"A forthright testimony by a witness to history." Kirkus

Includes bibliographical references and index

Jones, Quincy, 1933-

Jones, Quincy. **Q**: the autobiography of Quincy Jones. Doubleday 2001 412p il $26; pa $15.95   **92**

1. Composers 2. Conductors (Music) 3. Music arrangers 4. Recording producers

ISBN 0-385-48896-3; 0-7679-0510-5 pa

LC 2001-28151

"With some chapters written by Jones, and others by his family and friends . . . this (auto)biography full of behind-the-scenes anecdotes has an improvisational feel that suits its subject: a jazz musician and superstar composer. . . . Jones has composed a life story that gives much more than the typical celebrity memoir." Publ Wkly

Includes discography and filmography

Joplin, Janis

Cooke, John Byrne, 1940-2017. **On** the road with Janis Joplin; John Byrne Cooke. Berkley Books 2014 432 p. 8 plates; illustrations (hardcover) $27.95 **92**

1. Rock music -- United States 2. Rock musicians -- United States -- Biography

ISBN 9780425274118

LC 2014034647

This book, by John Byrne Cooke, is the memoir of the road manager of the Rock musician Janis Joplin. "In 1967, as the new sound of rock and roll was taking over popular music, John Byrne Cooke was at the center of it all. . . . He witnessed the astonishing breakout performances of Janis Joplin and Jimi Hendrix at the Monterey Pop Festival that June. Less than six months later, he was on a plane to San Francisco, taking a job as road manager for Janis and her band." (Publisher's note)

"Rock music fans will love reading this up-close view of Joplin. The end of the book feels like losing her all over again." LJ

Jordan, Michael, 1963-

Lazenby, Roland. **Michael** Jordan; the life. Roland Lazenby. Little Brown & Co 2014 720 p. ill. (some col.) $30 **92**

1. African American baseball players 2. Basketball players -- United States -- Biography

ISBN 0316194778; 9780316194778

LC 2014932746

In this biography about basketball player Michael Jordan, "basketball journalist Roland Lazenby . . . draws on his personal relationships with Jordan's coaches; countless interviews with Jordan's friends, teammates, and family members; and interviews with Jordan himself to provide the first truly definitive study of Michael Jordan: the player, the icon, and the man." (Publisher's note)

"Lazenby's thoroughly enjoyable biography is an impressive portrait of a man consumed by his competitive ambitions." LJ

Includes bibliographical references and index

Josephine, Empress, consort of Napoleon I, Emperor of the French, 1763-1814

Williams, Kate. **Ambition** and desire; the dangerous life of Josephine Bonaparte. Kate Williams. Ballantine Books 2015 400 p. 16 plates; color illustrations (hardback: alkaline paper) $30 **92**

1. Empresses 2. Empresses -- France -- Biography

ISBN 0345522834; 9780345522832

LC 2014030438

This book, by Kate Williams, focuses on "Napoleon Bonaparte['s] wife, Josephine. . . . Born Marie-Josèphe-Rose de Tascher de La Pagerie on the Caribbean island of Martinique, the woman Napoleon would later call Josephine was the ultimate survivor. She endured a loveless marriage to a French aristocrat-- executed during the Reign of Terror-- then barely escaped the guillotine blade herself. Her near-death experience only fueled [her] ambition. . . . In 1795, she met Napoleon." (Publisher's note)

"Meeting her match in Napoléon Bonaparte, Josephine and he embarked on a doomed marital odyssey characterized by personal jealousies and political obsessions. An in-depth portrait of the substantive woman behind the throne." Booklist

Includes bibliographical references and index

Joyce, James, 1882-1941

Ellmann, Richard. **James** Joyce; new and rev ed; Oxford Univ. Press 1982 887p il hardcover o.p. pa $27.50 **92**

1. Poets 2. Authors 3. Novelists 4. Dramatists 5. Short story writers

ISBN 0-19-503381-7 pa

LC 81-22455

First published 1959

This "is a vast undertaking and continuing achievement—massive, masterly, and definitive, rich in anecdote and detail. It is also extremely readable; the easy, often sympathetic style communicates gracefully not only facts but analysis." Choice

Includes bibliographical references

Judas Iscariot

★ Gubar, Susan. **Judas**; a biography. W. W. Norton & Co. 2009 453p il $27.95 **92**

1. Apostles

ISBN 978-0-393-06483-4; 0-393-06483-2

LC 2008-42967

An account of the story of the New Testament's archvillain and his history over the past 2000 years in which Gubar links Christian anti-Semitism with Christianity's attempt to grapple with transcendent evil.

"An exhaustive, beautifully written cultural history of our favorite wrongdoer, Gubar's work is an immensely rewarding and crucially important book." Libr J

Includes bibliographical references

Julien, Maude

Julien, Maude. The **only** girl in the world; a memoir. Maude Julien, with Ursula Gauthier, translated by Adriana Hunter. Little, Brown & Co. 2017 288 p. $27 **92**

1. Post-traumatic stress disorder 2. Adult child abuse victims -- Biography

ISBN 9780316466622

LC 2017934593

This book, by Maude Julien, with Ursula Gauthier, translated by Adriana Hunter, is a "memoir of one woman rising above an unimaginable childhood. . . . Julien's parents were fanatics who believed it was their sacred duty to turn her into the ultimate survivor--raising her in isolation, tyrannizing her childhood and subjecting her to endless drills designed to 'eliminate weakness.' . . . She endured a life without heat, hot water, adequate food, friendship, or any kind of affectionate treatment." (Publisher's note)

"Julien's frank descriptions of each atrocity underline the stark reality that she lived in—a reality where emotions were forbidden and no one was to be trusted. It is Julien's relationships with animals that keep her alive, teaching her love and empathy and bringing a compelling warmth and hope into an often-devastating memoir." Booklist

Kael, Pauline, 1919-2001

Kellow, Brian. **Pauline** Kael; a life in the dark. Viking 2011 417p il $27.95 **92**

1. Motion pictures 2. Writers on film 3. Motion picture critics

ISBN 978-0-670-02312-7; 0-670-02312-4

LC 2011-21798

This book by Brian Kellow presents a biography of film critic Pauline Kael. "She first came to some prominence as a movie maven in San Francisco, where she selected programs for an art house and opined on films for listener-supported radio. She was already 50 when she began writing for the New Yorker, but those two decades of her life take up roughly 75 percent of Kellow's book," which "tell[s] her story mostly through her most famous (and notorious) reviews." (Kirkus Reviews)

"During her glory years at The New Yorker from 1968 to 1991, Pauline Kael enlivened the quiet art of analyzing movies with a lusty noise that echoes in certain movie-festival hallways a decade after her death. . . . [Kellow] brings two unassailable strengths to a bio that's bound to be catnip for both Kael's fans and her naysayers. First, he is impressively thorough in his research. He ferrets out illuminating information about Kael's childhood as the daughter of Polish Jewish chicken farmers in California, her never-quite-satisfactory romantic relationships with men, her dependence on the daughter she raised as a single mother, her financial struggles, and (most juicily) her oil-and-water clashes with The New Yorker's painfully genteel editor William Shawn. As for Kellow's second strength, it's an elegantly simple one: He's a movie lover but not a professional critic. Kael had many axes to grind, but Kellow appears to have none." Entertainment Wkly

Kafka, Franz, 1883-1924

★ Kafka, die Jahre der Entscheidungen/English. **Kafka, the decisive years; the decisive years.** translated from the German by Shelley Frisch. 1st U.S. ed.; Harcourt 2005 581p il $35   92

1. Poets 2. Authors 3. Novelists 4. Short story writers
ISBN 0-15-100752-7

LC 2005-14554

Original German edition, 2002

This first of a projected three-volume biography focuses on Kafka's life from 1910 to 1915, during which he wrote "The Metamorphosis" and The Trial.

"Essential reading for all Kafka devotees." Booklist

Includes bibliographical references

Murray, Nicholas. **Kafka.** Yale University Press 2004 440p il $30   92

1. Poets 2. Authors 3. Novelists 4. Short story writers
ISBN 0-300-10631-9

LC 2004-107048

This biography "relates Kafka's brief life, trying valiantly to depict a more normal Kafka, a man who lived in society with good friends, enjoyed sex, had wide-ranging intellectual interests and became enamored of Judaism. In Murray's account, Kafka's employer valued him highly, and under the imprint of no less a figure than Kurt Wolff, he experienced some literary success. Despite Murray's best efforts to contain Kafka's idiosyncrasies, though, the writer remains the tormented soul who created out of his personal anxieties and agonies some of the most acclaimed works of the 20th century." Publ Wkly

Includes bibliographical references

Stach, Reiner. **Kafka;** the decisive years. Reiner Stach; translated from the German by Shelley Frisch. Princeton University Press 2013 vi, 581 p.p illustrations (pbk.: acid-free paper) $27.95   92

1. Austrian authors -- 20th century -- Biography 2. Authors, Austrian -- 20th century -- Biography
ISBN 0691147418; 9780691147413

LC 2013930936

This book is the second volume of Reiner Stach's three-part biography of Franz Kafka. "He picks up Kafka's life not in childhood, but in 1910, the fitful beginning of his literary career, and follows it only until 1915. But these were the years when Kafka produced some of his greatest works, including 'The Metamorphosis' and The Trial. We see the writer in all his torments, but also his moments of triumph, however fleeting." (Publishers Weekly)

Includes bibliographical references (p. [551]-562) and index

Stach, Reiner. **Kafka;** The Early Years. Reiner Stach; translated by Shelley Frisch. Princeton University Press 2016 584 p. illustrations (hardback) $35   92

1. Austrian authors -- 20th century -- Biography 2. Authors, Austrian -- 20th century -- Biography
ISBN 9780691151984

LC 2016021490

This book, by Reiner Stach, translated by Shelley Frisch, is the final volume in a "definitive biography of the writer [Franz Kafka] . . . , describing the complex personal, political, and cultural circumstances that shaped the young . . . [Kafka]. It tells the story of the years from his birth in Prague to the beginning of his professional and literary career in 1910, taking the reader up to just before the breakthrough that resulted in his first masterpieces." (Publisher's note)

"Brod's detailed reflections, which dominate much of this final volume, will chiefly interest Kafka scholars, but all Kafka devotees will find this biography's insights deeply fulfilling." Pub Wkly

Includes bibliographical references and index

Stach, Reiner. **Kafka,** the years of insight; Reiner Stach; translated by Shelley Frisch. Princeton University Press 2015 682 p. (hardcover) $35; $24.95   92

1. Tuberculosis 2. Authors, Austrian -- 20th century -- Biography
ISBN 0691147515; 069116584X; 9780691147512; 9780691165844

LC 2012042048

This book is part of Reiner Stach's three-part biography of author Franz Kafka. This volume "covers the period from 1916 to 1924, his terminal years." Topics include "his father's disapprobation, his job at the Worker's Accident Insurance Institute, his turbulent courtships with Felice Bauer, Milena Jesenská, and Dora Diamant, and finally his encounter with malignant and fatal tuberculosis." (Library Journal)

"This well-researched new biography details the last nine years of Franz Kafka's life and explores the personal, social, and political events that shaped his writing." Pub Wkly

Includes bibliographical references and index.

Kaganovich family

Laskin, David. The **Family;** Three Journeys into the Heart of the Twentieth Century. David Laskin. Viking Adult 2013 400 p. $32   92

1. Jews 2. Genealogy 3. World history -- 20th century 4. Jews -- Belarus -- Biography 5. Valozhyn (Belarus) -- Biography 6. Jews, Belarusian -- Palestine -- Biography 7. Jews, Belarusian -- United States -- Biography
ISBN 067002547X; 9780670025473

LC 2013017047

Author David Laskin presents a "work of twentieth century history through the riveting story of one extraordinary Jewish family. In tracing the roots of . . . his own family . . . Laskin honors the traditions, the lives, and the choices of his ancestors: revolutionaries and entrepreneurs, scholars and farmers, tycoons and truck drivers." (Publisher's note)

Includes bibliographical references (pages 341-371) and index

Kahlo, Frida, 1907-1954

Kahlo, Frida. The **diary** of Frida Kahlo; an intimate self-portrait. introduction by Carlos Fuentes; essay and commentaries by Sarah M. Lowe; [project director, Claudia Madrazo; editor, Phyllis Freeman; translators, Barbara Crow de Toledo and Ricardo Pohlenz] 2005 ed.; Harry N. Abrams 2005 295p il $24.95   92

1. Artists 2. Painters 3. Artists, Mexican
ISBN 0-8109-5954-2

LC 2006-284768

First published 1995

"Sprinkled with irony, black humor, even gaiety . . . this volume is a testament to Kahlo's resilience and courage." Publ Wkly

Includes bibliographical references

Kalibbala, Gladys

Yu, Jessica. **Garden** of the lost and abandoned; the extraordinary story of one ordinary woman and the children she saves. Jessica Yu. Houghton Mifflin Harcourt 2017 384 p.   **92**

   1. Abandoned children 2. Children -- Uganda 3. Child welfare -- Uganda 4. Orphans -- Care -- Uganda 5. Abandoned children -- Care -- Uganda

   ISBN 9780544617063

                   LC 2017044919

In this book, by Jessica Yu, "at least 5,000 children live on the streets of Uganda's capital city of Kampala. . . . Gladys Kalibbala—part journalist, part detective, part Good Samaritan—does not hesitate to dive into difficult or even dangerous situations to aid a child. Author of a newspaper column called 'Lost and Abandoned,' she is a resource that police and others turn to when they stumble across a stranded kid with a hidden history." (Publisher's note)

"This is a powerful and inspiring tale of how one woman can make a tremendous difference in her community." Booklist

Kaling, Mindy

Kaling, Mindy, 1979- **Why** not me? Mindy Kaling. Crown Archetype 2015 228 p. illustrations (hardcover) $25   **92**

   1. Actresses 2. Adulthood 3. Adulthood -- Humor 4. Conduct of life -- Humor 5. Actors -- Unted States -- Biography

   ISBN 9780804138147; 0804138141

                   LC 2015020444

In this collection of essays, author Mindy Kaling "shares her ongoing journey to find contentment and excitement in her adult life, whether it's falling in love at work, seeking new friendships in lonely places, attempting to be the first person in history to lose weight without any behavior modification whatsoever, or most important, believing that you have a place in Hollywood when you're constantly reminded that no one looks like you." (Publisher's note)

"Photos and subheadings divide chapters for zippy reading. There are thoughtful lessons, too: entitlement can be good, if it comes from confidence and hard work--hence the book's title. And having confidence, for that matter, if you're not a certain color, size, or gender is a wonderful kind of subversion." Booklist

Kambalu, Samson, 1975-

Kambalu, Samson. The **jive** talker; an artist's genesis: a memoir. Free Press 2008 320p $24   **92**

   1. Artists

   ISBN 978-1-4165-5931-3; 1-4165-5931-0

                   LC 2008-26784

"Artist Kambalu recounts his long journey from poverty in Malawi to fame in the London art world. The 'jive talker' was his father, a hospital administrator whose career ups and downs set the mood for the entire family even as they endured the political fortunes of Malawi under Life President Hastings Banda. Kambalu senior died of AIDS in 1995, bequeathing his family memories of his odd assortment of books and love of words." Booklist

Kamkwamba, William, 1987-

Kamkwamba, William. The **boy** who harnessed the wind; William Kamkwamba and Bryan Mealer. William Morrow 2009 273 p. (hbk.) $25.99; pa $14.99   **92**

   1. Windmills -- Malawi 2. Malawi -- Rural conditions 3. Water-

supply, Rural -- Malawi 4. Rural electrification -- Malawi 5. Electric power production -- Malawi 6. Mechanical engineers -- Malawi -- Biography

   ISBN 0-06-173032-7; 0-06-173033-5 pa; 0061730327; 978-0-06-173032-0; 978-0-06-173033-7 pa; 9780061730320

                   LC 2010275963

Autobiography of a teenager in Malawi who builds a windmill and brings electricity to his village.

"This exquisite tale strips life down to its barest essentials, and once there finds reason for hopes and dreams, and is especially resonant for Americans given the economy and increasingly heated debates over health care and energy policy." Publ Wkly

Kane, Elisha Kent, 1820-1857

McGoogan, Kenneth. **Race** to the Polar Sea; the heroic adventures of Elisha Kent Kane. [by] Ken McGoogan. Counterpoint 2008 380p il map $28   **92**

   1. Explorers 2. Physicians 3. Travel writers 4. Arctic regions -- Exploration

   ISBN 978-1-58243-440-7; 1-58243-440-9

                   LC 2008-12045

This is a biography of the American explorer who discovered the Humboldt Glacier.

"With his access to previously unknown Kane logbooks, McGoogan makes an impressive case for the bravery and importance of the explorer who first identified the Greenland ice sheet." Publ Wkly

Includes bibliographical references

Karajan, Herbert von

Osborne, Richard. **Herbert** von Karajan; a life in music. Northeastern Univ. Press 2000 851p il $37.50   **92**

   1. Conductors (Music)

   ISBN 1-55553-425-2

                   LC 99-59108

First published 1998 in the United Kingdom

"Because Karajan's career developed in Nazi Germany, Osborne dwells at length . . . on Karajan's involvement with the regime and his postwar exoneration. Drawing on a vast variety of source materials and quoting him in full, Osborne takes us on the enthralling musical journey that was the life of one of the greatest of conductors." Booklist

Includes bibliographical references

Karp, Brianna, 1985-

Karp, Brianna. The **girl's** guide to homelessness; a memoir. Harlequin 2011 344p pa $16.95   **92**

   1. Office workers 2. Homeless persons 3. Homeless

   ISBN 978-0-373-89235-8

                   LC 2010044201

"Sexually and emotionally abused by her parents, Karp left home ASAP. Self-sufficiency delighted her; she adored her job and beach cottage. She lost both to the recession and moved into a trailer she parked in a Walmart lot while using free Starbucks wi-fi and her laptop to apply for jobs. She began blogging about her situation, documenting her struggles with homelessness and trying to regain stability. Candidly humorous, Karp's memoir is sharp and insightful, reminding readers just how perilous the security of a permanent address can be and offering tips on what to do if it is lost." Libr J

Karr, Mary

Karr, Mary. **Lit**; a memoir. Harper 2009 386p $25.99; pa $14.95   **92**

   1. Poets 2. Authors 3. Alcoholics 4. Essayists 5. Memoirists 6. Poets, American 7. College teachers

ISBN 978-0-06-059698-9; 0-06-059698-8; 978-0-06-059699-6
pa; 0-06-059699-6 pa

LC 2009-24810

The author reveals how, shortly after giving birth to a child she adored, she drank herself into the same numbness that nearly devoured her charismatic but troubled mother, reaching the brink of suicide before a spiritual awakening led her to sobriety.

Karr "has written a book that lassos you, hogties your emotions and won't let you go. It's a memoir that . . . explores the subjectivity of memory even as it chronicles with searching intelligence, humor and grace the author's slow, sometimes exhilarating, sometimes painful discovery of her vocation." N Y Times (Late N Y Ed)

Katkin, Elizabeth L

Katkin, Elizabeth L. **Conceivability**; what I learned exploring the frontiers of fertility. Elizabeth L. Katkin. Simon & Schuster 2018 320 p. (hardback) $26   **92**
1. Pregnancy 2. Childbirth 3. Infertility 4. Conception 5. Infertility -- Treatment 6. Polycystic ovary syndrome -- Treatment
ISBN 9781501142369; 9781501142376

LC 2017053978

"Part memoir, part guide, [by Elizabeth L. Katkin], this [is a] personal and . . . informative account of [her] gripping journey through the global fertility industry in search of the solution to her own 'unexplained infertility' [that] exposes . . . information about the medical, financial, legal, scientific, emotional and ethical issues at stake. . . . Katkin . . . offers a look inside one of the most difficult, painful, rewarding, and loving journeys a woman can take." (Publisher's note)

Includes bibliographical references and index

Katlama, Jacqueline Boulloche, 1918-1994

Kaiser, Charles. The **cost** of courage; by Charles Kaiser. Other Press 2015 288 p. illustrations (hardcover) $26.95 92
1. World War, 1939-1945 -- Biography 2. World War, 1939-1945 -- Underground movements -- France 3. Guerrillas -- France -- Biography 4. France -- History -- German occupation, 1940-1945 -- Biography 5. World War, 1939-1945 -- Underground movements -- France -- Biography
ISBN 1590516141; 9781590516140

LC 2015008560

This book, by Charles Kaiser, tells the "heroic true story of the three youngest children of a . . . family who worked together in the French Resistance. . . . In the autumn of 1943, André Boulloche . . . coordinat[ed] all the Resistance movements in the nine northern regions of France only to be betrayed by one of his associates . . . and taken prisoner. His sisters carried on the fight without him until the end of the war." (Publisher's note)

"Kaiser's account of a family's devotion and resilience in the face of horrific tyranny tells a highly recommended story of resolve and bravery that can't help but feel romantic in its selfless and profound obligation, but this is not gloss nor ungrounded canonization." LJ

Kaukonen, Jorma

Kaukonen, Jorma. **Been** so long; my life and music. Jorma Kaukonen. St. Martin's Press 2018 368 p. (hardcover) $29.99   **92**
1. Biography 2. Folk musicians -- United States -- Biography 3. Rock musicians -- United States -- Biography 4. Blues musicians -- United States -- Biography
ISBN 9781250125484

LC 2018010693

"From [Jorma Kaukonen], the man who made a name for himself as a founding member and lead guitarist of Jefferson Airplane comes

a memoir that offers a rare glimpse into the heart and soul of a musical genius--and a vivid journey through the psychedelic era in America. . . . [It] charts not only Jorma's association with the bands that made him famous but goes into . . . details about his addiction and recovery, his troubled first marriage and still-thriving second, and more." (Publisher's note)

"Entertaining and emotional, alternately exhilarating and depressing, this is a special musician's memoir, and it will strike a resounding chord with fans of classic rock." Booklist

Kazin, Alfred, 1915-1998

Cook, Richard M., 1941- **Alfred** Kazin's journals; selected and edited by Richard M. Cook. Yale University Press 2011 598p $45   **92**
1. Biography, Individual
ISBN 978-0-300-14203-7; 0-300-14203-X

LC 2010-45254

The literary critic's "passions — for sex, for novels, for ideas, for talk, for city life — spill from 'Alfred Kazin's Journals,' edited by his biographer, Richard M. Cook. This is a remarkable book, easily one of the great diaries and moral documents of the past American century. What it lacks in cohesiveness it makes up in its frankness, its quick-pivoting angularities. Kazin dismisses his journal at one point as a 'disorderly pile of shavings.' That disorder only adds to its amplitude." N Y Times Book Rev

Includes bibliographical references

Keeling, Ida, 1915-

Keeling, Ida, 1915- **Can't** nothing bring me down; chasing myself in the race against time. Ida Keeling with Anita Diggs. Zondervan 2018 208 p. (hardcover) $22.99   **92**
1. African American women -- Biography 2. Women runners -- United States -- Biography 3. Runners (Sports) -- United States -- Biography
ISBN 0310349893; 9780310349891

LC 2017041065

This book presents "the memoir of 101-year-old, world-record-holding runner Ida Keeling. . . . Her fierce independence helped her through the Depression and the Civil Rights movement. . . . Keeling shares her inspirational story about growing up as a child of immigrants during the Depression and later raising four children as a single mother. She offers time-tested truths gathered from a lifetime of watching a nation change and from a life-long faith in Jesus." (Publisher's note)

Keenan, George F. (George Frost), 1904-2005

Gaddis, John Lewis, 1941- **George** F. Kennan; An American Life. John Lewis Gaddis. Penguin Press 2011 xi, 784p.p 16 p. of plates $39.95   **92**
1. Cold war 2. Diplomats 3. Historians 4. World Politics -- 1945-1989 5. Cold War -- Diplomatic history 6. United States -- Foreign Relations 7. Ambassadors -- United States -- Biography
ISBN 1594203121; 9781594203121

LC 2011021786

Pulitzer Prize: Biography or Autobiography (2012)
National Book Critics Circle Award: Biography (2011)

The book presents a biography of U.S. statesman George F. Kennan, which the author composed using "Kennan's . . . diary, . . . the 300-plus boxes of other papers by Kennan now open for research at Princeton, . . . interviews with the former diplomat and his associates, . . . [and] family papers still in the possession of Kennan's daughter." The author "sides largely with Kennan's critics . . . . in the heated debate over Kennan's advocacy in 1957-1958 for US 'disengagement' from the cold war in Europe." (New York Review of Books)

Includes bibliographical references and index.

Keller, Helen, 1880-1968

Herrmann, Dorothy. **Helen** Keller; a life. University of Chicago Press 1999 394p il pa $22   **92**

1. Deaf 2. Blind 3. Authors 4. Memoirists 5. Humanitarians 6. Inspirational writers 7. Social welfare leaders

ISBN 0-226-32763-9; 978-0-226-32763-1

LC 99-23242

First published 1998 by Knopf

The author "takes us beyond the image of Helen Keller portrayed in The Miracle Worker to unearth a passionate, politically radical woman whose inspiration and teacher, Annie Sullivan, is equally fiery and brilliant. Herrmann brings us into the every day lives of the famous pair, but the story is hardly mundane. . . . Herrmann gives us fascinating details via archives and unpublished memoirs to show how society's view of disabled people was greatly shaped by Keller and Sullivan." Libr J

Includes bibliographical references

Keller, Helen. **Helen** Keller: selected writings; edited by Kim E. Nielsen; consulting editor, Harvey J. Kaye. New York University Press 2005 317p il (History of disability series) $35   **92**

1. Deaf 2. Blind 3. Authors 4. Memoirists 5. Humanitarians 6. Inspirational writers 7. Social welfare leaders

ISBN 0-8147-5829-0

LC 2004-28974

This is a collection "of Keller's personal letters, political writings, speeches, and excerpts of her published materials from 1887 to 1968." Univ Press Books for Public and Second Sch Libr, 2006

Includes bibliographical references

★ Keller, Helen. The **story** of my life; edited and with a preface by James Berger. The restored ed.; Modern Library 2003 xlvi, 343p il hardcover o.p. pa $9.95   **92**

1. Deaf 2. Blind 3. Authors 4. Memoirists 5. Humanitarians 6. Inspirational writers 7. Social welfare leaders

ISBN 0-679-64287-0; 0-8129-6886-7 pa

LC 2002-40971

First published 1903

This biography of the inspirational Keller contains accounts of her home life and her relationship with her devoted teacher Anne Sullivan.

Includes bibliographical references

Kellogg, John Harvey, 1852-1943

Markel, Howard. The **Kelloggs**; the battling brothers of Battle Creek. Howard Markel. Pantheon Books 2017 xxix, 506 p.p illustrations (hard cover: alk. paper) $35   **92**

1. Health 2. Kellogg Company -- History 3. Battle Creek (Mich.) -- Biography 4. Physicians -- Michigan -- Biography 5. Industrialists -- Michigan -- Biography 6. Kellogg Toasted Corn Flake Company -- History 7. Battle Creek Sanitarium (Battle Creek, Mich.) -- History

ISBN 9780307907271; 9780307907288

LC 2016053946

National Book Critics Circle Award Finalist: Biography (2017)

This book, by Howard Markel, "tells the sweeping saga of [John Harvey and Will Kellogg] . . . , whose lifelong competition and enmity toward one another changed America's notion of health and wellness from the mid-nineteenth to the mid-twentieth centuries, and who helped change the course of American medicine, nutrition, wellness, and diet. The brothers Kellogg . . . came up with a ready-to-eat, easily digested cereal they called Corn Flakes." (Publisher's note)

"A superb warts-and-all account of two men whose lives help illuminate the rise of health promotion and the modern food industry." Kirkus

Includes bibliographical references (pages [393]-480) and index.

Kellogg, W. K. (Will Keith), 1860-1951

Markel, Howard. The **Kelloggs**; the battling brothers of Battle Creek. Howard Markel. Pantheon Books 2017 xxix, 506 p.p illustrations (hard cover: alk. paper) $35   **92**

1. Health 2. Kellogg Company -- History 3. Battle Creek (Mich.) -- Biography 4. Physicians -- Michigan -- Biography 5. Industrialists -- Michigan -- Biography 6. Kellogg Toasted Corn Flake Company -- History 7. Battle Creek Sanitarium (Battle Creek, Mich.) -- History

ISBN 9780307907271; 9780307907288

LC 2016053946

National Book Critics Circle Award Finalist: Biography (2017)

This book, by Howard Markel, "tells the sweeping saga of [John Harvey and Will Kellogg] . . . , whose lifelong competition and enmity toward one another changed America's notion of health and wellness from the mid-nineteenth to the mid-twentieth centuries, and who helped change the course of American medicine, nutrition, wellness, and diet. The brothers Kellogg . . . came up with a ready-to-eat, easily digested cereal they called Corn Flakes." (Publisher's note)

"A superb warts-and-all account of two men whose lives help illuminate the rise of health promotion and the modern food industry." Kirkus

Includes bibliographical references (pages [393]-480) and index.

Kelly, Scott, 1964-

Kelly, Scott, 1964- **Endurance**; a year in space, a lifetime of discovery. Scott Kelly with Margaret Lazarus Dean. First edition. Alfred A. Knopf 2017 400 p. (hardcover) $29.95 **92**

1. Biography 2. Space flight 3. Astronauts -- Biography 4. Astronauts -- United States -- Biography

ISBN 9781524731595

LC 2017024799

This memoir, by Scott Kelly with Margaret Lazarus Dean, is "a[n] . . . account of his . . . voyage, of the journeys that preceded it, and of his colorful and inspirational formative years. . . . He describes navigating the extreme challenge of long-term spaceflight, both life-threatening and mundane: the devastating effects on the body; the isolation from everyone he loves and the comforts of Earth; [and] the catastrophic risks of colliding with space junk." (Publisher's note)

"It's fascinating stuff, a tale of aches and pains, of boredom punctuated by terror and worries about what's happening in the dark and back down on Earth." Kirkus.

Kennan, George Frost, 1904-2005

Kennan, George Frost. **Sketches** from a life. W. W. Norton 2000 365p pa $14.95   **92**

1. Authors 2. Diplomats 3. Historians 4. Centenarians 5. Nonfiction writers 6. United States -- Foreign relations

ISBN 978-0-393-32139-5; 0-393-32139-8

First published 1989 by Pantheon

"This is a collection of very private reflections spanning some 60 years of foreign service in Nazi Germany, the Baltic states, the Low Countries, the Soviet Union, as well as nonofficial travels covering the entire globe. Kennan has marvelous insight into his ever-changing surroundings—an insight that is always sharp, sometimes melancholy, and punctuated frequently by dry, Midwestern wit." Libr J

Includes bibliographical references

Thompson, Nicholas. The **hawk** and the dove; Paul Nitze,

George Kennan, and the history of the Cold War. Henry Holt 2009 403p il $27.50   **92**

1. Authors 2. Cold war 3. Diplomats 4. Statesmen 5. Historians 6. Centenarians 7. Nonfiction writers 8. Government officials 9. Biography, Individual 10. Secretaries of the navy 11. United States -- Officials and employees 12. United States -- Foreign relations -- 1945-1989 13. National security -- United States -- History -- 20th century 14. Anti-communist movements -- United States -- History -- 20th century

ISBN 0805081429; 9780805081428

LC 2009-09225

This biography of Nitze and Kennan focuses on their "careers as statesmen, policy makers and public intellectuals." (N Y Times Book Rev) Index.

This book "does an inspired job of telling the story of the Cold War through the careers of two of its most interesting and important figures." Washington Monthly

Includes bibliographical references

Kennedy family

McKeon, Kathy. **Jackie's** girl; my life with the Kennedy family. Kathy McKeon. Gallery Books 2017 309 p. illustrations (chiefly color) (hardcover: alk. paper) $26   **92**

1. Women household employees -- Biography 2. Household employees -- United States -- Biography 3. Irish American women -- United States -- Biography 4. Women household employees -- United States -- Biography

ISBN 9781501158964; 9781501158940; 9781501158957

LC 2017003981

This book, by Kathy McKeon, is a "coming-of-age memoir by a young woman who spent thirteen years as Jackie Kennedy's personal assistant. . . . In 1964, Kathy McKeon was . . . hired as the personal assistant to former first lady Jackie Kennedy. The next thirteen years of her life were spent in Jackie's service, during which Kathy . . . played a crucial role in raising young Caroline and John Jr., . . . [and] had a front-row seat to some of the twentieth century's most significant events." (Publisher's note)

"Celebrity watchers who covet an insider's role will find McKeon's frank yet benevolent memoir to be both a sobering reality check and an engaging foray into the ever-fascinating world of the Kennedy dynasty." Booklist

Kennedy, Edward Moore, 1932-2009

English, Bella. **Last** lion; the fall and rise of Ted Kennedy. Simon & Schuster 2009 464p il $28   **92**

1. Senators 2. Siblings of presidents 3. Presidential candidates 4. United States -- Congress -- Senate

ISBN 978-1-4391-3817-5; 1-4391-3817-6

LC 2008-50491

"A respectful but not stuffy . . . [biography] of Edward Kennedy, the playboy of legendary appetites turned senior statesman. . . . A balanced, nuanced, warts-and-all portrait." Kirkus

Includes bibliographical references

★ Kennedy, Edward Moore. **True** compass; a memoir. [by] Edward M. Kennedy. Twelve 2009 532p il $35   **92**

1. Senators 2. Siblings of presidents 3. Presidential candidates 4. United States -- Congress -- Senate

ISBN 978-0-446-53925-8; 0-446-53925-2

This autobiography by the former senator from Massachusetts was published posthumously.

"Mr. Kennedy's conversational gifts as a storyteller and his sense of humor . . . shine through here, as does his old-school sense of public service and his hard-won knowledge, in his son Teddy Jr.'s words, that 'even our most profound losses are survivable.'" N Y Times (Late N Y Ed)

Includes bibliographical references

Kennedy, John F. (John Fitzgerald), 1917-1963

Brinkley, Alan. **John** F. Kennedy; Alan Brinkley. 1st ed. Times Books 2012 xviii, 202 p.p $23   **92**

1. Biography 2. Kennedy family 3. United States -- Politics and government 4. Presidents -- United States -- Biography 5. United States -- Politics and government -- 1961-1963

ISBN 0805083499; 9780805083491

LC 2011043747

Author Alan Brinkley discusses John F. Kennedy, suggesting that "he left an enormous legacy as a charismatic leader and a glamorous symbol of hope and purpose long after his death." Brinkley describes Kennedy as "the handsome, unscholarly, self-indulgent son of Joseph Kennedy, whose enormous wealth and ambition cleared his path through Massachusetts and then national politics." The book features Kennedy's experiences "as a [president,] congressman and senator, [describing his views on] . . . military spending . . . [and] civil rights." (Kirkus Reviews)

Includes bibliographical references and index

Clarke, Thurston. **JFK's** last hundred days; the transformation of a man and the emergence of a great president. Thurston Clarke. The Penguin Press 2013 448 p. (hardcover) $29.95 **92**

1. United States -- Politics and government -- 1961-1974 2. Change (Psychology) -- Case studies 3. Presidents -- United States -- Biography 4. Political leadership -- United States -- Case studies 5. United States -- Politics and government -- 1961-1963

ISBN 159420425X; 9781594204258

LC 2012047456

"This . . . look at J.F.K.'s last 100 days makes the case that had he survived that fateful November afternoon, his political star would've only continued to rise in a seemingly assured second term. [Thurston] Clarke . . . contends that Kennedy's successful resolution of the Cuban Missile Crisis, as well as his popular stances on civil rights, lunar exploration, arms reduction, and tax cuts would've overshadowed his romantic scandals, [and] tensions relating to Vietnam." (Publishers Weekly)

Includes bibliographical references and index

Dallek, Robert. **Let** every nation know; John F. Kennedy in his own words. [by] Robert Dallek and Terry Golway. Sourcebooks MediaFusion 2006 289p il $29.95; pa $19.95   **92**

1. Presidents 2. Senators 3. Members of Congress 4. Presidents -- United States 5. United States -- Politics and government -- 1961-1974

ISBN 1-4022-0647-X; 978-1-4022-0647-4; 1-4022-0922-3 pa; 978-1-4022-0922-2 pa

LC 2005-37973

"The voice of John F. Kennedy is burned into the brains of people of a certain age. But younger citizens may not be familiar with his ideas and the distinctive way in which he expressed himself. There have been past recordings of JFK's presidential speeches, but this unique package pairs a CD of the speeches with a collection of essays on them by historians Golway and Dallek (the latter wrote his own JFK book, An Unfinished Life, 2003). The result is nothing short of terrific..." (Booklist)

Includes bibliographical references

Dallek, Robert. An **unfinished** life; John F. Kennedy, 1917-1963. Little, Brown 2003 838p il $30; pa $17.95   **92**

1. Presidents 2. Senators 3. Members of Congress 4. Presidents -- United States 5. United States -- Politics and government -- 1961-

1974
ISBN 0-316-17238-3; 0-316-90792-8 pa

LC 2002-116388

This is a biography of the thirty-fifth president of the United States

The author "has written the most accessible, balanced, and scholarly biography yet of JFK. . . . It is the Kennedy biography against which others will be measured." Libr J

Includes bibliographical references

Mahoney, Richard D. **Sons** and brothers: the days of Jack and Bobby Kennedy. Arcade Pub. 1999 441p il $27.95; pa $14.95 **92**

1. Diplomats 2. Presidents 3. Senators 4. Financiers 5. Attorneys general 6. Members of Congress 7. Parents of presidents 8. Siblings of presidents 9. Presidential candidates 10. Regulatory agency officials 11. United States -- Politics and government -- 1961-1974

ISBN 1-55970-480-2; 1-55970-534-5 pa

LC 99-25681

"Writing in a steady, almost relentlessly elegiac tone, Mahoney proves that the lives and deaths of John F. and Robert F. Kennedy remain as compelling now as they were throughout the turbulent 1960s." Publ Wkly

Includes bibliographical references

Sorensen, Theodore C., 1928-2010. **Counselor**; a life at the edge of history. [by] Ted Sorensen. HarperCollins 2008 556p il $27.95 **92**

1. Lawyers 2. Presidents 3. Senators 4. Members of Congress 5. Government officials 6. Biography, Individual 7. Presidential advisers 8. United States -- Politics and government -- 20th century

ISBN 0-06-079871-8; 978-0-06-079871-0

LC 2007-47328

This is a memoir by President Kennedy's advisor and speechwriter. Index.

"This book is instantly essential for any student of the period. It fills gaps in the historical record; it vividly conveys life inside the administration; and it generously dishes anecdotes." Washington Post Book World

Kennedy, Joseph P., 1888-1969

Mahoney, Richard D. **Sons** and brothers: the days of Jack and Bobby Kennedy. Arcade Pub. 1999 441p il $27.95; pa $14.95 **92**

1. Diplomats 2. Presidents 3. Senators 4. Financiers 5. Attorneys general 6. Members of Congress 7. Parents of presidents 8. Siblings of presidents 9. Presidential candidates 10. Regulatory agency officials 11. United States -- Politics and government -- 1961-1974

ISBN 1-55970-480-2; 1-55970-534-5 pa

LC 99-25681

"Writing in a steady, almost relentlessly elegiac tone, Mahoney proves that the lives and deaths of John F. and Robert F. Kennedy remain as compelling now as they were throughout the turbulent 1960s." Publ Wkly

Includes bibliographical references

★ Nasaw, David. The **patriarch**; the remarkable life and turbulent times of Joseph P. Kennedy. David Nasaw. Penguin Press 2012 xxiv, 868 p.p ill. $40 **92**

1. Presidents -- United States -- Family 2. Ambassadors -- United States -- Biography 3. Politicians -- United States -- Biography 4. Businesspeople -- United States -- Biography

ISBN 1594203768; 9781594203763

LC 2012027315

In this biography, "[David] Nasaw takes on Joseph P. Kennedy, businessman, Hollywood mogul, founding chair of the Securities and Exchange Commission, U.S. ambassador to Britain, and, of course, father to our 35th President. He had exclusive access to Kennedy's papers and addresses some longstanding questions." (Library Journal)

Includes bibliographical references (p. [793]-834) and index

Kennedy, Kathleen, 1920-1948

Byrne, Paula. **Kick**; The True Story of JFK's Sister and the Heir to Chatsworth. Paula Byrne. Harper 2016 352 p. illustrations (hardcover) $29.99 **92**

1. Kennedy family 2. Aristocracy -- Great Britain 3. Americans -- England -- Biography 4. Young women -- England -- Biography 5. Socialites -- United States -- Biography 6. Young women -- United States -- Biography 7. Aristocracy (Social class) -- Great Britain -- Biography 8. Great Britain -- Social life and customs -- 20th century 9. United States -- Social life and customs -- 20th century 10. Presidents -- United States -- Brothers and sisters -- Biography

ISBN 9780062296276

LC 2016008270

This book, by Paula Byrne, is a "biography of the . . . young Kennedy sister who charmed American society and the English aristocracy, and would break with her family for love. . . . The fourth Kennedy child, the irrepressible Kathleen, stood out. . . . [She] shock[ed] and alienate[d] her devout family by falling in love and marrying the scion of a virulently anti-Catholic family— William Cavendish, the heir apparent of the Duke of Devonshire and Chatsworth." (Publisher's note)

"At first, the book is less a biography and more a society report of England's upper class, but it evolves into an exciting, heartbreakingly tense love story." Kirkus

Includes bibliographical references and index

True story of Kick Kennedy, JFK's forgotten sister and the heir to Chatsworth

Leaming, Barbara. **Kick** Kennedy; the charmed life and tragic death of the favorite Kennedy daughter. Barbara Leaming. Thomas Dunne Books, an imprint of St. Martin's 2016 304 p. illustrations (hardcover) $27.99 **92**

1. Kennedy family 2. Aristocracy -- Great Britain 3. Catholics -- England -- Biography 4. Socialites -- United States -- Biography 5. Young women -- United States -- Biography 6. Americans -- England -- London -- Biography 7. Young women -- England -- London -- Biography 8. Aristocracy (Social class) -- Great Britain -- Biography 9. Great Britain -- Social life and customs -- 20th century 10. Presidents -- United States -- Brothers and sisters -- Biography

ISBN 9781250071316

LC 2016007364

This book, by Barbara Leaming, is a biography of "Kathleen 'Kick' Kennedy. . . . The daughter of the American ambassador to the Court of St James's, Kick swept into Britain's aristocracy like a fresh wind on a sweltering summer day. In a decaying world where everything was based on stultifying sameness and similarity, she was gloriously, exhilaratingly different. Kick was the girl whom all the boys fell in love with, the girl who remained painfully out of reach for most of them." (Publisher's note)

"Leaming candidly demystifies the life of one of the least-known Kennedys and vividly illuminates the complex world of British aristocracy." Booklist

Includes bibliographical references and index.

Kennedy, Robert F., 1925-1968

Allen, C. Richard. **RFK**; his words for our times. Robert F. Kennedy, C. Richard Allen, and Edwin O Guthman. HarperCollins 2018 480 p. $29.99 **92**

1. United States -- Politics and government -- 1953-1961
ISBN 006283410X; 9780062834102

This book, by Robert F. Kennedy, C. Richard Allen and Edwin O. Guthman, is "a celebration of [Robert Francis] Kennedy's life and legacy, [and] was published to enormous acclaim. Now, a quarter century later, this . . . volume has been thoroughly edited and updated. Through his own words we get a direct and intimate perspective on Kennedy's views on civil rights, social justice, the war in Vietnam, . . . the need to eliminate poverty, and the role of hope in American politics." (Publisher's note)

"Rich background information on policy and historical context introduces each chapter and frames each speech, which reveal Kennedy's appeal to Democrats and Republicans, minorities and the middle class." Library Journal

Clarke, Thurston. The **last** campaign; Robert F. Kennedy and 82 days that inspired America. Thurston Clarke. Henry Holt 2008 321p il $25; pa $15 **92**

1. Senators 2. Attorneys general 3. Siblings of presidents 4. Presidential candidates 5. United States -- Politics and government -- 20th century
ISBN 978-0-8050-7792-6; 0-8050-7792-8; 978-0-8050-9022-2 pa; 0-8050-9022-3 pa

LC 2007-45880

In this account of Robert F. Kennedy's run for president, Clarke "follows on Bobby's heels as he plunged headlong into his campaign, from Kansas and Indiana to Oregon and California, throwing off his brother's mantle and becoming at last his own man. He spoke passionately, almost recklessly, inciting crowds to frenzy with his idealistic speeches about the moral shame of Vietnam, the needs of the poor and minorities and the responsibility of each American. Incorporating accounts by a gamut of reporters, politicians, family and 'Honorary Kennedys,' as well as extracts from Bobby's own stunning stump speeches, Clarke compellingly recreates this 'huge, joyous adenture.'" Kirkus

Includes bibliographical references

Mahoney, Richard D. **Sons** and brothers: the days of Jack and Bobby Kennedy. Arcade Pub. 1999 441p il $27.95; pa $14.95 **92**

1. Diplomats 2. Presidents 3. Senators 4. Financiers 5. Attorneys general 6. Members of Congress 7. Parents of presidents 8. Siblings of presidents 9. Presidential candidates 10. Regulatory agency officials 11. United States -- Politics and government -- 1961-1974
ISBN 1-55970-480-2; 1-55970-534-5 pa

LC 99-25681

"Writing in a steady, almost relentlessly elegiac tone, Mahoney proves that the lives and deaths of John F. and Robert F. Kennedy remain as compelling now as they were throughout the turbulent 1960s." Publ Wkly

Includes bibliographical references

Matthews, Chris. **Bobby** Kennedy; a raging spirit. Chris Matthews. Simon & Schuster 2017 396 p. illustrations (hardcover) $28 **92**

1. Politicians -- United States 2. Legislators -- United States -- Biography 3. United States. Congress. Senate -- Biography 4. Cabinet officers -- United States -- Biography 5. Presidential candidates -- United States -- Biography 6. United States -- Politics and government -- 1945-1989
ISBN 9781501111860; 9781501111884; 1501111868

LC 2017302462

This biography, by Chris Matthews, looks at "the public and private worlds of Robert Francis Kennedy. He shines a light on all the important moments of his life, from his early years and his start in politics to his crucial role as attorney general in his brother's administration and his tragic run for president. This definitive book brings Bobby Kennedy to life like never before and is destined to become a political classic." (Publisher's note)

"A child of that era himself, best-selling Matthews, host of MSNBC's Hardball, regards RFK's legacy through personal recollections and cogently illustrates leadership qualities Kennedy possessed that are sorely lacking in today's divisive culture." Booklist

Includes bibliographical references (pages 347-382) and index.

Schlesinger, Arthur M. (Arthur Meier), 1917-2007. **Robert** Kennedy and his times; {by} Arthur M. Schlesinger, Jr. Houghton Mifflin 1978 1066p il hardcover o.p. pa $17.95 **92**

1. Senators 2. Attorneys general 3. Siblings of presidents 4. Presidential candidates 5. United States -- Politics and government -- 20th century
ISBN 978-0-618-21928-5 pa; 0-618-21928-5 pa

LC 78-8469

"A highly sympathetic and readable political biography covering in depth Robert Kennedy's tenure in public life. At times extremely partisan, at times dispassionate, Schlesinger's study effectively captures Kennedy's impact on national politics and the main currents of American politics during the 1950s and 1960s." Choice

Includes bibliographical references

★ Thomas, Evan. **Robert** Kennedy; his life. Simon & Schuster 2000 509p il hardcover o.p. pa $15 **92**

1. Senators 2. Attorneys general 3. Siblings of presidents 4. Presidential candidates 5. United States -- Politics and government -- 20th century
ISBN 0-7432-0329-1 pa

LC 00-41995

"A solid, judicious life of a politician whose tragic death inspired a generation of what-if history." Booklist

Includes bibliographical references

★ Tye, Larry. **Bobby** Kennedy; the making of a liberal icon. Larry Tye. Random House Inc 2016 608 p. $32 **92**

1. Legislators -- United States -- Biography 2. United States. Congress. Senate -- Biography 3. United States -- Politics and government -- 1945-1989
ISBN 0812993349; 9780812993349

LC 2016004991

This biography of Robert F. Kennedy by Larry Tye "draws on unpublished memoirs, unreleased government files, and fifty-eight boxes of papers that had been under lock and key for the past forty years. He conducted hundreds of interviews with RFK intimates--including Bobby's widow, Ethel, his sister Jean, and his aide John Siegenthaler--many of whom have never spoken to another biographer." (Publisher's note)

"The author chides RFK for such things as slanting his account of the Bay of Pigs, his perhaps excessive pursuit of Jimmy Hoffa, and his early hawkishness on Vietnam. But the contrary image is clear: a good, if not great man; an unspeakable loss." Kirkus

Includes bibliographical references and index

Kennedy, Rosemary, 1918-2005

Larson, Kate Clifford. **Rosemary**; The Hidden Kennedy Daughter. Kate Clifford Larson. Houghton Mifflin Harcourt 2015 320 p. 16 plates; illustrations $27 **92**
1. Kennedy family
ISBN 0547250258; 9780547250250

LC 2015028793

In this biography by Kate Clifford Larson "major new sources -- Rose Kennedy's diaries and correspondence, school and doctors' letters, and exclusive family interviews -- bring Rosemary alive as a girl adored but left far behind by her competitive siblings. Larson reveals both the sensitive care Rose and Joe gave to Rosemary and then . . . the often desperate and duplicitous arrangements the Kennedys made to keep her away from home as she became increasingly intractable." (Publisher's note)

"This expertly researched work offers a candid examination of a once-forgotten member of one of America's most famous families. It will appeal to Kennedy devotees and readers interested in society's evolving understanding of the intellectually and physically disabled."

Kenney, David Ngaruri, 1973-

Kenney, David Ngaruri. **Asylum** denied; a refugee's struggle for safety in America. [by] David Ngaruri Kenney and Philip G. Schrag. University of California Press 2008 352p il map $40; pa $17.95 **92**
1. Refugees 2. Political refugees 3. Kenya 4. Immigrants -- United States
ISBN 978-0-520-25510-4; 0-520-25510-0; 978-0-520-26159-4 pa; 0-520-26159-3 pa

LC 2007-48703

"One cannot read this book without experiencing rage, disbelief, and an overwhelming sense of sadness over the inhumanity Kenney suffered, both in Kenya and in this country. Still, it is also an inspiring story of human courage, heartfelt friendships, and unrelenting devotion to fighting the good fight. . . . This account should be required reading for anyone who has contact with immigrants in America. It should also be on the reading list of anyone who cares about the preservation of human rights and human dignity in our world." Calif Lawyer

Includes bibliographical references

Kerstetter, Jon

Kerstetter, Jon. **Crossings**; a doctor-soldier's story. Jon Kerstetter. Crown 2017 viii, 342 p.p (hardcover) $27 **92**
1. Autobiographies 2. SURGEONS -- United States -- Biography 3. Iraq War, 2003-2011 -- Personal narratives, American 4. Iraq War, 2003-2011 -- Medical care 5. Physicians -- United States -- Biography 6. Disabled veterans -- United States -- Biography 7. United States. Army -- Flight surgeons -- Biography 8. Brain damage -- Patients -- United States -- Biography 9. Cerebrovascular disease -- Patients -- United States -- Biography 10. Post-traumatic stress disorder -- Patients -- United States -- Biography
ISBN 9781101904374; 9781101904381; 1101904372

LC 2017024442

This memoir, by Jon Kerstetter, looks at his life as a U.S. military surgeon. "Trained as an emergency physician, Kerstetter's thirst for intensity led him to volunteer in war-torn Rwanda, Kosovo, and Bosnia, and to join the Army National Guard. His three tours in the Iraq War marked the height of the American struggle there. The story of his work in theater . . . is a bracing, unprecedented evocation of a doctor's life at war." (Publisher's note)

"The author's medical perspective on his own condition and critical therapeutic moments adds depth to an already solid story. An inspiring memoir that will be highly useful to readers struggling with PTSD and other wartime injuries." Kirkus

Keynes, John Maynard, 1883-1946

Davenport-Hines, R. P. T. (Richard Peter Treadwell), 1953- **Universal** Man; The Lives of John Maynard Keynes. Richard Davenport-Hines. Basic Books 2015 432 p. illustration $29.99 **92**
1. Economists -- Biography
ISBN 0465060676; 9780465060672

LC 2015934354

In this book author "Richard Davenport-Hines revives our understanding of John Maynard Keynes (1883-1946), the twentieth century's most charismatic and revolutionary economist. Keynes helped FDR launch the New Deal, saved Britain from financial crisis twice over the course of two World Wars, and instructed Western nations on how to protect themselves from revolutionary unrest, economic instability, high unemployment, and social dissolution." (Publisher's note)

"Although this approach necessitates recovering some chronological ground—obviously he was a pundit and lover most of his life—the author is quite successful in avoiding redundancy. The result is that the intellectual, social, professional, and personal aspects of Keynes are described and analyzed both independently and as they interrelated to create a complex and brilliant thinker. This is a splendid biography that will fascinate the general reader and give new insight to the scholar. Summing Up: Highly recommended. Undergraduates through faculty; two-year technical students; general readers." Choice

Khakpour, Porochista

★ Khakpour, Porochista. **Sick**; a memoir. Porochista Khakpour. Harper Perennial 2018 272 p. (paperback) $15.99 **92**
1. Chronically ill 2. Lyme disease -- Patients 3. Chronically ill -- Biography 4. Lyme disease -- Patients -- Biography
ISBN 9780062428738

LC 2017059572

"Sick is [Porochista] Khakpour's grueling, emotional journey--as a woman, an Iranian-American, a writer, and a lifelong sufferer of undiagnosed health problems--in which she examines her subsequent struggles with mental illness and her addiction to doctor prescribed benzodiazepines, that both aided and eroded her ever-deteriorating physical health. Divided by settings, Khakpour guides the reader through her illness by way of the locations that changed her course." (Publisher's note)

"Lyme disease is difficult to diagnose, and Khakpour's frank memoir will give hope to others who are struggling with this devastating illness." Booklist

Khan, Khizr, 1950-

Khan, Khizr. An **American** family; a memoir of hope and sacrifice. Khizr Khan. Random House 2017 xiii, 271 p.p illustrations (some color) (hardcover) $27 **92**
1. Immigration and emigration 2. Biography as a literary form 3. Pakistani Americans -- Biography 4. Iraq War, 2003-2011 -- Veterans 5. Muslims -- United States -- Biography
ISBN 9780399592508; 9780399592492

LC 2017031372

In this memoir, Khizr Khan tells his "family's pursuit of the American dream. . . . [Khizr] was the oldest of ten children born to farmers in Pakistan. . . . He was a university student who read the Declaration of Independence and was awestruck by what might be possible in life. . . . He was and is a patriot, and a fierce advocate for the rights, dignities, and values enshrined in the American system." (Publisher's note)

"Khan's aspirational memoir reminds us all why Americans should welcome newcomers from all lands." Kirkus

Khan-Cullors, Patrisse, 1984-

★ Bandele, Asha. **When** they call you a terrorist; a Black Lives Matter memoir. Patrisse Khan-Cullors and Asha Bandele; foreword by Angela Davis. St. Martin's Press 2018 xiv, 257 p.p (hardcover) $24.99   **92**

1. Social movements -- United States 2. African American women -- Biography 3. Black lives matter movement 4. African American women political activists -- Biography

ISBN 9781250171092; 9781250171085; 1250171083

LC 2017036191

This book, by Patrisse Khan-Cullors and Asha Bandele, is "a poetic and powerful memoir about what it means to be a Black woman in America--and the co-founding of a movement that demands justice for all in the land of the free. Raised by a single mother . . . , Patrisse Khan-Cullors experienced firsthand the prejudice and persecution Black Americans endure at the hands of law enforcement. For Patrisse, the most vulnerable people in the country are Black people." (Publisher's note)

"With great candor about her complex personal life, Khan-Cullors has created a memoir as compelling as a page-turning novel." Booklist

Khrushchev, Nikita Sergeevich, 1894-1971

Nikita Khrushchev; edited by William Taubman, Sergei Khrushchev, and Abbott Gleason; translated by David Gehrenbeck, Eileen Kane, and Alla Bashenko. Yale Univ. Press 2000 391p $45   **92**

1. Heads of state 2. Communist leaders 3. Political leaders 4. Soviet Union -- Politics and government

ISBN 0-300-07635-6

LC 99-51323

A collection of essays re-evaluating aspects of Khrushchev's political career. Topics include his rise to power and his domestic, foreign, and military policy. Two essays compare Khrushchev and Gorbachev

Includes bibliographical references and index

Taubman, William. **Khrushchev**; the man and his era. Norton 2003 p. cm   **92**

1. Heads of state 2. Communist leaders 3. Political leaders 4. Heads of state -- Soviet Union -- Biography

ISBN 0-393-05144-7

LC 2002-26404

Includes bibliographical references and index

Kiki, 1901-1953

Bocquet, José-Louis. **Kiki** de Montparnasse; illustrated by Catel; written by José-Louis Bocquet; translated from the Belgian edition by Nora Mahony. SelfMadeHero 2011 416 p. chiefly ill. (pbk.) $24.95   **92**

1. Painters 2. Artists' models 3. Women -- France -- History 4. Artists' models -- France -- Biography -- Comic books, strips, etc

ISBN 9781906838256

LC 2011431146

This book offers a graphic biography of artist model and actress Alice Prin, better known as Kiki de Montparnasse. In "bohemian Montparnasse [in Paris, France] of the 1920s, Kiki escaped poverty to become one of the most charismatic figures of the avant-garde years between the wars. Partner to [artist] Man Ray, and one of the first emancipated women of the 20th century, Kiki made her mark with her freedom of style, word, and thought that could be learned from only one school— the school of life." (Publisher's note)

Includes bibliographical references (p. 413-415)

Kilgore, Bernard, 1908-1967

Tofel, Richard J. **Restless** genius; Barney Kilgore, The Wall Street journal, and the invention of modern journalism. St. Martin's Press 2009 271p il $25.95   **92**

1. Journalists 2. Wall Street journal 3. Newspaper executives

ISBN 978-0-312-53674-9; 0-312-53674-7

LC 2008-29880

"What makes this work especially appealing is the incorporation of the many letters Kilgore wrote to his father, giving the reader a glimpse into this esteemed newsman's way of thinking about his newspaper and the news of the day." Libr J

Includes bibliographical references

Kim, Eunsun

Kim, Eunsun, 1986- A **Thousand** Miles to Freedom; My Escape from North Korea. by Eunsun Kim, Sébastien Falletti, translated by David Tian. St. Martin's Press 2015 240 p. (hardcover) $24.99   **92**

1. Refugees 2. Korea (North)

ISBN 1250064643; 9781250064646

LC 2015015581

In this book, by Eunsun Kim, Sébastien Falletti, and translated by David Tian, the author describes how "her mother decided to escape North Korea with [her] and her sister, not knowing that they were embarking on a journey that would take them nine long years to complete. Before finally reaching South Korea and freedom, Eunsun and her family would live homeless, fall into the hands of Chinese human traffickers, survive a North Korean labor camp, and cross the deserts of Mongolia on foot." (Publisher's note)

"An urgent cry for compassion for the author's fellow North Koreans, trapped and strangled of liberty and life." Kirkus

Kim, Jong-il, 1942-2011

Jang Jin-sung. **Dear** Leader; poet, spy, escapee?: a look inside North Korea. Jang Jin-sung; translated by Shirley Lee. 37 Ink/Atria Books 2014 368 p. (hardback) $27.99   **92**

1. Poets 2. Korea (North) 3. Autobiographies 4. Korea (North) -- Biography 5. Propaganda -- Korea (North) 6. Poets -- Korea (North) -- Biography 7. Political refugees -- Korea (North) -- Biography 8. Korea (North) -- Politics and government -- 1994-2011

ISBN 147676655X; 9781476766553

LC 2014010236

This memoir tells how "[a]s North Korea's State Poet Laureate, Jang Jin-sung led a charmed life. With food provisions . . . , a travel pass, access to strictly censored information, and audiences with Kim Jong-il himself, his life in Pyongyang seemed safe and secure. But this privileged existence was about to be shattered. When a strictly forbidden magazine he lent to a friend goes missing, Jang Jin-sung must flee for his life." (Publisher's note)

"A defector of Kim Jong-il's rarefied inner circle reveals the desperate, despicable machinations of North Korea's police state." Kirkus

Kim, Joseph, 1990-

Kim, Joseph. **Under** the same sky; from starvation in North Korea to salvation in America. by Joseph Kim; contributions by Stephan Talty. Houghton Mifflin Harcourt 2015 288 p. (hardback) $28   **92**

1. Famines 2. Refugees 3. Human rights 4. Christian ethics 5. Immigrants -- United States 6. Rescue work -- China 7. Christian ethics -- China 8. Human rights -- Korea (North) 9. Victims of famine -- Korea (North) 10. Refugees -- Korea (North) -- Biography

11. Immigrants -- United States -- Biography
ISBN 0544373170; 9780544373174

LC 2014039686

This book, by Joseph Kim, is a "searing story of starvation and survival in North Korea, followed by a dramatic escape, rescue by activists and Christian missionaries, and success in the United States thanks to newfound faith and courage." (Publisher's note)

"Both volumes put a human face to an often misunderstood country and will appeal to a wide range of readers." LJ

Kim, Suki, 1970-

★ Kim, Suki, 1970- **Without** you, there is no us; my time with the sons of North Korea's elite. Suki Kim. Crown Publishers 2014 291 p. illustrations, maps (pbk.) $15   **92**
1. Teachers 2. Korea (North) -- Social conditions 3. English language -- Study and teaching 4. Elite (Social sciences) -- Korea (North) 5. English teachers -- Korea (North) -- Biography 6. Education -- Government policy -- Korea (North) 7. Korea (North) -- Politics and government -- 2011- 8. Korea (North) -- Social conditions -- 21st century
ISBN 9780307720672; 9780307720658; 9780307720665

LC 2014012730

This memoir describes the lives of "the 270 students at the all-male Pyongyang University of Science and Technology (PUST), a walled compound where portraits of Kim Il-sung and Kim Jong-il look on impassively from the walls of every room, and where [author] Suki [Kim] has accepted a job teaching English." (Publisher's note)

"The result is a touching portrayal of the student experience in North Korea, which provides readers with a rare glimpse of life in the enigmatic country." LJ

Kimball, Kristin

Kimball, Kristin. The **dirty** life; on farming, food, and love. Scribner 2010 276p $25; ebook $11.99   **92**
1. Authors 2. Farmers 3. Journalists 4. Organic farming 5. Farm life -- New York (State)
ISBN 978-1-4165-5160-7; 978-1-4391-8714-2 ebook

"A hearty, chromatic account of a meaningful accomplishment in farming, 'that dirty concupiscent art.'" Kirkus

King, Clarence, 1842-1901

Sandweiss, Martha A. **Passing** strange; a Gilded Age tale of love and deception across the color line. Penguin Press 2009 370p il $27.95   **92**
1. Geologists 2. Travel writers 3. Passing (Identity) 4. Writers on science 5. Government officials 6. Biography, Individual 7. United States -- Race relations 8. African Americans -- Race identity 9. Racially mixed people -- Race identity
ISBN 978-1-59420-200-1

LC 2008-34886

The book tells the story of "Clarence King (1842–1901), the eminent nineteenth-century geologist . . . [and] mapper of the American West . . . [who] successfully avoided military service in the Civil War and chose instead to cultivate his manliness in the rugged life of a western explorer." In particular the book looks at his travels across the color line in the U.S. and how "for the last thirteen years of his life he led a double life in Brooklyn as James Todd, a light-skinned African American Pullman porter." (Journal of American History)

Sandweiss's "great accomplishment is to have explored not only how the 19th-century explorer and scientist Clarence King reinvented himself but also why that reinvention was so singularly American. Best of all are Ms. Sandweiss's insights into what King's deception and its consequences really mean." N Y Times (Late N Y Ed)

Includes bibliographical references

King, Coretta Scott, 1927-2006

★ Reynolds, Barbara. **My** Life, My Love, My Legacy; Coretta Scott King; as told to the Rev. Dr. Barbara Reynolds. Henry Holt & Co 2017 368 p. illustrations $30; (ebook) $60   **92**
1. African American women -- Biography
ISBN 1627795987; 9781627795982; 9781627795999

LC 2016039557

This book is "the life story of Coretta Scott King—wife of Martin Luther King Jr., founder of the Martin Luther King Jr. Center for Nonviolent Social Change (The King Center), and singular twentieth-century American civil and human rights activist—as told fully for the first time, toward the end of her life, to Rev. Dr. Barbara Reynolds." (Publisher's note)

"King was undoubtedly a singular woman, and readers will be struck by just how strongly her exceedingly compelling story resonates today. She was much more than just the woman behind the man, and now, in the most eloquent of language, she proves that truth once and for all to generations of readers who will embrace her all over again." Booklist

King, Martin Luther, Jr., 1929-1968

Burns, Rebecca. **Burial** for a King; Martin Luther King Jr.'s funeral and the week that transformed Atlanta and rocked the nation. Scribner 2011 244p il $25; ebook $11.99   **92**
1. Clergy 2. Nonfiction writers 3. Civil rights activists 4. Nobel laureates for peace 5. Atlanta (Ga.) -- Race relations 6. United States -- Race relations
ISBN 978-1-4391-3054-4; 978-1-4391-4309-4 ebook

LC 2010-29980

This is a "recreation of the aftermath of Martin Luther King Jr.'s assassination. . . . [The author] provides a snapshot of a still-segregated nation poised between uneasy reconciliation and violent chaos. Using terse language and precise, straightforward descriptions . . . she views the crisis and aftermath of King's death in Memphis through multiple points of view, beginning with the traumatic center of his family and closest associates in Atlanta. . . . A pertinent, you-are-there historical page-turner with a strong moral message." Kirkus

Flowers, Arthur. **I** see the promised land; a life of Martin Luther King Jr. [text by] Arthur Flowers, [illustrations by] Manu Chitrakar, [design by] Guglielmo Rossi. Groundwood Books/House of Anansi Press 2013 154 p. il $16.95   **92**
1. Clergy 2. Graphic novels 3. Biographical graphic novels 4. Nonfiction writers 5. Civil rights activists 6. Nobel laureates for peace 7. African Americans -- Civil rights -- Graphic novels
ISBN 1554983282; 9781554983285

This book is an illustrated biography of civil rights activist Martin Luther King Jr. by African American novelist and performance poet Arthur Flowers. "He weaves the entire history of the enslavement of black Americans into King's story, refers to unspecified gods taking an interest in affairs, and comments on King's speeches." (School Library Journal)

"A myth-making take on King's life that has both emotional and intellectual impact, the Flowers/Chitrakar collaboration supplies fresh color and richness to the oft-told history of this game-changer." Libr J

Jackson, Troy. **Becoming** King; Martin Luther King, Jr. and the making of a national leader. introduction by Clayborne Carson. University Press of Kentucky 2008 248p (Civil rights and the struggle for Black equality in the twentieth century) $35   **92**

1. Clergy 2. Nonfiction writers 3. Civil rights activists 4. Nobel laureates for peace 5. African Americans -- Civil rights
ISBN 978-0-8131-2520-6; 0-8131-2520-0

LC 2008-25041

"The author's comprehensive analysis of King's sermons before, during and after the boycott artfully depicts a man in transition, from naive do-gooder to world-changer. Jackson's treatment of Montgomery in the post-boycott era offers new insight into the void in leadership and the fractious infighting among the movement's luminaries after King departed the scene. An informed investigation of the struggles that defined a time and place-and the man who gave them a voice." Kirkus

Includes bibliographical references (p. 229-239) and index.

★ Reynolds, Barbara. **My** Life, My Love, My Legacy; Coretta Scott King; as told to the Rev. Dr. Barbara Reynolds. Henry Holt & Co 2017 368 p. illustrations $30; (ebook) $60   **92**
  1. African American women -- Biography
  ISBN 1627795987; 9781627795982; 9781627795999

LC 2016039557

This book is "the life story of Coretta Scott King—wife of Martin Luther King Jr., founder of the Martin Luther King Jr. Center for Nonviolent Social Change (The King Center), and singular twentieth-century American civil and human rights activist—as told fully for the first time, toward the end of her life, to Rev. Dr. Barbara Reynolds." (Publisher's note)

"King was undoubtedly a singular woman, and readers will be struck by just how strongly her exceedingly compelling story resonates today. She was much more than just the woman behind the man, and now, in the most eloquent of language, she proves that truth once and for all to generations of readers who will embrace her all over again." Booklist

Rosenbloom, Joseph. **Redemption**; Martin Luther King Jr.'s last 31 hours. Joseph Rosenbloom. Beacon Press 2018 289 p. (hardcover; alk. paper) $24.95   **92**
  1. Civil rights demonstrations -- United States 2. African American civil rights workers -- Biography 3. African Americans -- Biography 4. Baptists -- United States -- Clergy -- Biography 5. Civil rights workers -- United States -- Biography 6. African Americans -- Civil rights -- History -- 20th century 7. Civil rights movements -- United States -- History -- 20th century
  ISBN 9780807083383

LC 2017024226

This book, by Joseph Rosenbloom, "is an intimate look at the last thirty-one hours and twenty-eight minutes of [Dr. Martin Luther] King [Jr.'s] life. . . . On the stormy night of April 3rd, King gathered the strength to speak at a rally on behalf of sanitation workers. . . . [The book] draws on dozens of interviews by the author with people who were immersed in the Memphis events, features recently released documents from Atlanta archives, and includes compelling photos." (Publisher's note)

Includes bibliographical references and index

Young, Andrew. An **easy** burden; the civil rights movement and the transformation of America. foreword by Quincy Jones. Baylor University Press 2008 550p il pa $29.95   **92**
  1. Clergy 2. Mayors 3. Nonfiction writers 4. Members of Congress 5. Civil rights activists 6. United Nations officials 7. Nobel laureates for peace 8. United States -- Race relations 9. African Americans -- Civil rights
  ISBN 978-1-602580-73-2

LC 2007-49679

First published 1996 by HarperCollins Pubs.

This memoir focuses on Young's early life as a middle-class African American growing up in segregated New Orleans, his call to the ministry, and his years working with Dr. King and the Southern Christian Leadership Conference.

Kingston, Maxine Hong

Kingston, Maxine Hong, 1940- The **woman** warrior; China men. Maxine Hong Kingston; with an introduction by Mary Gordon. Everyman's Library 2005 xxix, 541 p.p $25   **92**
  1. Chinese Americans -- History 2. California -- Biography 3. Chinese Americans -- California -- Biography 4. Authors, American -- 20th century -- Biography 5. Chinese Americans -- California -- Social life and customs
  ISBN 1400043840; 9781400043842

LC 2004061143

National Book Critics Circle Award for General Nonfiction (1976)

This volume, by Maxine Hong Kingston, reprints of her award winning books "The Woman Warrior" and "China Men." The first work "is Kingston's disturbing and fiercely beautiful account of growing up Chinese-American in California." The second is "Kingston's unforgettable imaginative journey into the hearts and minds of generations of Chinese men in America, from those who worked on the transcontinental railroad in the 1840s to those who fought in Vietnam." (Publisher's note)

Kipling, Rudyard, 1865-1936

Gilmour, David. The **long** recessional: the imperial life of Rudyard Kipling. Farrar, Straus & Giroux 2002 351p il maps $26; pa $15   **92**
  1. Poets 2. Authors 3. Novelists 4. Memoirists 5. Children's authors 6. Short story writers 7. Nobel laureates for literature
  ISBN 0-374-18702-9; 0-374-52896-9 pa

LC 2002-100585

This biography focuses on Kipling's social and political views in relation to the British Empire, especially as expressed in his fiction and poetry

The author "offers a brief, sympathetic, well-informed, and highly readable account of Kipling." Libr J

Includes bibliographical references

Ricketts, Harry. **Rudyard** Kipling; a life. Carroll & Graf Pubs. 2000 434p il hardcover o.p. pa $16   **92**
  1. Poets 2. Authors 3. Novelists 4. Memoirists 5. Children's authors 6. Short story writers 7. Nobel laureates for literature
  ISBN 0-7867-0830-1 pa

First published 1999 in the United Kingdom with title: The unforgiving minute: a life of Rudyard Kipling

This work "succeeds in disentangling some of the political muddle of Kipling's life. Ricketts' literary analysis is competent, if unsophisticated. Most valuably, he traces the debt to Browning and the many other resonant literary allusions in Kipling's work, thus undermining the charges of philistinism . . . levelled against it." New Statesman (Engl)

Kirshenblatt, Mayer, 1916-2009

Kirshenblatt, Mayer. **They** called me Mayer July; painted memories of a Jewish childhood in Poland before the Holocaust. [by] Mayer Kirshenblatt, Barbara Kirshenblatt-Gimblett. University of California Press 2007 411p il (S. Mark Taper Foundation imprint in Jewish studies) $39.95   **92**
  1. Artists 2. Painters 3. Holocaust survivors 4. Memoirists 5. Jews -- Poland
  ISBN 978-0-520-24961-5

LC 2006-36182

"Kirshenblatt's illustrated memoir of growing up as a Jew in pre-World War II Poland reads like an episodic novel as he introduces the reader to village life and the myriad of unusual and interesting characters." Univ Press Books for Public and Second Sch Libr, 2008

Includes bibliographical references

Kissinger, Henry, 1923-

Dallek, Robert. **Nixon** and Kissinger; partners in power. HarperCollins Publishers 2007 740p il $32.50   **92**

1. Presidents 2. Vice-presidents 3. Senators 4. College teachers 5. Nonfiction writers 6. Members of Congress 7. Writers on politics 8. Secretaries of state 9. Presidential advisers 10. Nobel laureates for peace 11. United States -- Foreign relations 12. International relations specialists

ISBN 978-0-06-072230-2; 0-06-072230-4

LC 2006-52100

A look "behind the scenes at this quintessential pair of power brokers and their lasting influence, for good and ill, on the political stage." Bookmarks Magazine

Includes bibliographical references

Ferguson, Niall, 1964- **Kissinger**; The Idealist, 1923-1968. Penguin Group USA 2015 656 p. 32 plates: illustrations $36   **92**

1. Diplomacy

ISBN 1594206538; 9781594206535

Author "Niall Ferguson shows in this magisterial two-volume biography, drawing not only on [Henry] Kissinger's hitherto closed private papers but also on documents from more than a hundred archives around the world, the idea of Kissinger as the ruthless arch-realist is based on a profound misunderstanding." (Publisher's note)

"It will surprise many readers how quickly Kissinger finds his principles incompatible with the Kennedy-Johnson policy in Vietnam, and how reluctant he is to serve under the devious Nixon. A sophisticated portrait, certain to stir debate--and to heighten expectations for the sequel." Booklist

Klarsfeld, Beate, 1939-

Klarsfeld, Beate. **Hunting** the truth; memoirs of Beate and Serge Klarsfeld. Beate and Serge Klarsfeld; translated from the French by Sam Taylor. Farrar, Straus & Giroux 2018 464 p. illustrations (hardcover) $30   **92**

1. Holocaust, 1939-1945 2. Holocaust, Jewish (1939-1945) -- Personal narratives

ISBN 9780374279820; 9780374714703; 0374279829

LC 2017035981

"For the past half century, Beate and Serge Klarsfeld have hunted, confronted, prosecuted, and exposed Nazi war criminals all over the world, tracking down the notorious torturer Klaus Barbie in Bolivia and attempting to kidnap the former Gestapo chief Kurt Lischka on the streets of Cologne. . . . They have fought relentlessly not only for the memory of all those who died in the Holocaust but also for modern-day victims of genocide and discrimination across the world. " (Publisher's note)

"A masterful work of historical importance." Booklist

Klarsfeld, Serge, 1935-

Klarsfeld, Beate. **Hunting** the truth; memoirs of Beate and Serge Klarsfeld. Beate and Serge Klarsfeld; translated from the French by Sam Taylor. Farrar, Straus & Giroux 2018 464 p. illustrations (hardcover) $30   **92**

1. Holocaust, 1939-1945 2. Holocaust, Jewish (1939-1945) --

Personal narratives

ISBN 9780374279820; 9780374714703; 0374279829

LC 2017035981

"For the past half century, Beate and Serge Klarsfeld have hunted, confronted, prosecuted, and exposed Nazi war criminals all over the world, tracking down the notorious torturer Klaus Barbie in Bolivia and attempting to kidnap the former Gestapo chief Kurt Lischka on the streets of Cologne. . . . They have fought relentlessly not only for the memory of all those who died in the Holocaust but also for modern-day victims of genocide and discrimination across the world. " (Publisher's note)

"A masterful work of historical importance." Booklist

Klein, Jessi, 1975-

★ Klein, Jessi, 1975- **You'll** grow out of it; Jessi Klein. Grand Central Publishing 2016 256 p. (ebook) $78; (hardback) $26   **92**

1. Short stories -- Collections

ISBN 9781455540518; 1455531189; 9781455531189

LC 2016009270

In this memoir, Jessi Klein "offers-through an incisive collection of real-life stories-a relentlessly funny yet poignant take on a variety of topics she has experienced along her strange journey to womanhood and beyond. These include her 'transformation from Pippi Longstocking-esque tomboy to are-you-a-lesbian-or-what tom man,' attempting to find watchable porn, and identifying the difference between being called 'ma'am' and 'miss' ('Miss sounds like you weigh ninety-nine pounds')." (Publisher's note)

"This uplifting and uproarious collection of personal essays will be repeatedly shared among friends." Pub Wkly

Knapp, Caroline

★ Caldwell, Gail. **Let's** take the long way home; a memoir of friendship. Random House 2010 190p $23   **92**

1. Friendship 2. Journalists 3. Columnists 4. Memoirists 5. Literary critics

ISBN 978-1-4000-6738-1; 1-4000-6738-3

LC 2009-29384

"This is a book you'll want to share with your own 'necessary pillars of life,' as Caldwell refers to her nearest and dearest. . . . Her memoir, a tribute to the enduring power of friendship, is a lovely gift to readers." Washington Post

Knausgaard, Karl Ove, 1968-

Knausgård, Karl Ove, 1968- **Autumn**; Karl Ove Knausgaard; with illustrations by Vanessa Baird; translated from the Norwegian by Ingvild Burkey. Penguin Press 2017 224 p. (hardcover) $27   **92**

1. Autumn 2. Seasons 3. Nature writing 4. Authors, Norwegian -- 21st century -- Biography

ISBN 039956330X; 9780399563300; 9780399563317

LC 2017031387

This book "begins with a letter Karl Ove Knausgaard writes to his unborn daughter, showing her what to expect of the world. He writes one short piece per day, describing the material and natural world with the precision and mesmerising intensity that have become his trademark. He describes with acute sensitivity daily life with his wife and children in rural Sweden, drawing upon memories of his own childhood." (Publisher's note)

"An engagingly wide-ranging set of meditations." Kirkus

Knausgård, Karl Ove, 1968- **Summer**; Karl Ove Knausgaard; with illustrations by Anselm Kiefer; translated from the Norwegian by Ingvild Burkey. Penguin Press 2018 416 p. (hardback) $30.00 **92**

1. Essays

ISBN 9780399563393; 0399563393

LC 2018025191

This book, by Karl Ove Knausgaard, illustrated by Anselm Kiefer and translated by Ingvild Burkey, "intersperses short vividly descriptive essays with emotionally-raw diary entries addressed directly to Knausgaard's newborn daughter. . . . Knausgaard writes for his daughter, striving to make ready and give meaning to a world at once indifferent and achingly beautiful." (Publisher's note)

Knausgård, Karl Ove, 1968- **Winter**; Karl Ove Knausgaard; with illustrations by Lars Lerin; translated from the Norwegian by Ingvild Burkey. Penguin Press 2018 254 p. color illustrations (hardcover) $27 **92**

1. Nature writing 2. Natural history 3. Authors, Norwegian -- 21st century -- Biography

ISBN 0399563334; 9780399563331; 9780399563348

In this book, "we rejoin the great Karl Ove Knausgaard as he waits for the birth of his daughter. In preparation for her arrival, he takes stock of the world, seeing it as if for the first time. . . . [H]e writes about the moon, water, messiness, owls, birthdays--to name just a handful of his subjects. . . . New life is on the horizon, but the earth is also in hibernation, waiting for the warmer weather to return, and so a contradictory melancholy inflects his gaze." (Publisher's note)

"A winningly interior journey into the most interior of seasons." Kirkus

Companion to:

Autumn (2017)

Spring (2018)

Summer (2018)

Knight, Philip H., 1938-

Knight, Philip H., 1938- **Shoe** dog; Phil Knight. Scribner, an imprint of Simon & Schuster, Inc. 2016 386 p. (hardback) $29 **92**

1. Nike (Firm) 2. Businesspeople -- United States -- Biography 3. Sporting goods industry -- United States -- History

ISBN 1501135910; 9781501135910; 9781501150111

LC 2016010080

In this memoir, "Nike founder and board chairman Phil Knight shares the inside story of the company's early days as an intrepid start-up and its evolution into one of the world's most iconic, game-changing, and profitable brands. . . . In this age of start-ups, Knight's Nike is the gold standard, and its swoosh is more than a logo. A symbol of grace and greatness, it's one of the few icons instantly recognized in every corner of the world." (Publisher's note)

"Has anyone else ever written as evocatively about selling shoes? Well, George Pelecanos wrote a crime novel called Shoedog, and there's a character in it who sells shoes with a definite flair, but that's really something very different. And, yet, maybe not. Pelecanos brings his street characters to vivid life and makes us care about them. Remarkably, Knight does the same thing for a giant corporation—certainly an even more formidable task." Booklist

Koenigswarter, Pannonica de, Baroness, 1913-1988

Kastin, David. **Nica's** dream; the life and legend of the jazz baroness. W. W. Norton 2011 336p il $26.95 **92**

1. Patrons of the arts 2. Jazz music -- History and criticism

ISBN 978-0-393-06940-2

LC 2011013213

"Kastin succeeds in bringing the surprisingly selfeffacing Nica to blazing life while also capturing the transcendent synergy among now-iconic jazz musicians, beat writers, and abstract painters, a creative cosmos profoundly enriched by the passion, largesse, and daring of the incomparable baroness." Booklist

Includes discography and bibliographical references

Koestler, Arthur, 1905-1983

Scammell, Michael. **Koestler**; the literary and political odyssey of a twentieth-century skeptic. Random House 2009 xxi, 689p il **92**

1. Authors 2. Novelists 3. Journalists 4. Essayists 5. Authors, English

ISBN 0-394-57630-6; 978-0-394-57630-5

LC 2008-51108

"Although he wrote more than 30 books, Koestler is today known primarily, perhaps exclusively, as the author of 'Darkness at Noon,' his gripping short novel of Stalinist coercion. The biographer Michael Scammell wants to put Koestler's multifaceted intelligence back on display and to show that something more than frivolity or opportunism lay behind his ever-shifting preoccupations and allegiances. As a source of information, 'Koestler,' the work of two decades, will never be surpassed. As an argument for the man's importance, however, it must contend with the eccentricity of Koestler's preoccupations and—although Scammell does not always seem to realize it—his vices." N Y Times Book Rev

Includes bibliographical references

Kohler, Sheila

Kohler, Sheila. **Once** we were sisters; A Memoir. Sheila Kohler. Penguin Books 2016 256 p. illustrations (paperback) $16; (ebook) $48 **92**

1. Women -- South Africa -- Biography 2. South African women authors -- Biography 3. Sisters -- South Africa -- Death 4. Authors, South African -- Biography 5. Sisters -- South Africa -- Biography 6. Women authors, South African -- Biography 7. South Africa -- History -- 1961-1994 -- Biography

ISBN 9780143129295; 9781101993170

LC 2016005921

In this book, "Sheila Kohler recounts the lives she and her sister led. . . . Kohler tells of the death of her father when she and Maxine were girls, which led to the family abandoning their house and the girls being raised by their mother, at turns distant and suffocating. . . . They plan grand lives for themselves—lives that are interrupted when both marry young. . . . Kohler evokes the bond between sisters and shows how that bond changes but never breaks, even after death." (Publisher's note)

"In spare, delicate prose, Kohler brings a seasoned novelist's skills to this deeply moving, compelling memoir." Kirkus

Koppel, Ted, 1940-

Koppel, Ted. **Off** camera; private thoughts made public. Knopf 2000 320p hardcover o.p. pa $14 **92**

1. Television moderators 2. Television news anchors

ISBN 0-375-72708-6 pa

LC 00-34919

The television journalist of Nightline presents a daily diary for 1999 chronicling "the controversial events from the century's last year, such as the Clinton impeachment trial and the Columbine High School shootings. . . . The subtitle of the book may lead some readers to expect a bit of muckraking, but they will be disappointed. . . . Yet one does not get the sense that Koppel is restraining himself or hiding anything, merely that this is a person who lives his life with integrity so that his private thoughts are full of the same." Libr J

Koretz, Leo, 1879-1925

Jobb, Dean. **Empire** of deception; the incredible story of a master swindler who seduced a city and captivated the nation. by Dean Jobb. Algonquin Books of Chapel Hill 2015 352 p. illustrations (paperback) $16.95   **92**
1. Swindlers and swindling -- United States -- History 2. Chicago (Ill.) -- Biography 3. Lawyers -- Illinois -- Chicago -- Biography 4. Chicago (Ill.) -- Social conditions -- 20th century 5. Chicago (Ill.) -- Economic conditions -- 20th century 6. Swindlers and swindling -- Illinois -- Chicago -- Biography 7. Fugitives from justice -- Nova Scotia -- Halifax -- Biography 8. Capitalists and financiers -- Illinois -- Chicago -- Biography 9. Ponzi schemes -- Illinois -- Chicago -- History -- 20th century 10. Commercial crimes -- Illinois -- Chicago -- History -- 20th century
ISBN 1616205350; 9781616205355; 9781616201753
LC 2014042711
This book, by Dean Jobb, describes how in 1920s Chicago, Illinois, "a slick, smooth-talking, charismatic lawyer named Leo Koretz [sought] to entice hundreds of people to invest as much as $30 million--upwards of $400 million today--in phantom timberland and nonexistent oil wells in Panama." (Publisher's note)
"The author keeps readers on edge following the scam's collapse and the worldwide manhunt, as they wait to see if Koretz might just get away with it. A highly readable, entertaining story offering a solid education for anyone lacking scruples and wanting to make money. Surely Bernie Madoff studied Koretz's methods." Kirkus
Includes bibliographical references and index

Kramer, Clara, 1927-

Kramer, Clara. **Clara's** war; one girl's story of survival. [by] Clara Kramer with Stephen Glantz. Ecco 2009 339p il $25.99   **92**
1. Holocaust survivors 2. Memoirists 3. Jews -- Poland 4. Holocaust, 1933-1945 -- Personal narratives
ISBN 978-0-06-172860-0; 0-06-172860-8
First published 2008 in the United Kingdom
ALA RUSA Sophie Brody Award Honor Book (2010)
"Based on her wartime diary, which she kept while hiding in a basement in Poland, Kramer's book vividly recalls the tensions within her hidden community after the Nazis overtook the town of Zolkiew in 1942. Of particular interest are revelations about the family who hid the Kramers, particularly how an anti-Semitic Polish householder demonstrated great courage in shielding Jews in his basement." Libr J

Krasner, Lee, 1908-1984

Levin, Gail, 1948- **Lee** Krasner; a biography. William Morrow 2011 546p il $30; ebook $23.99   **92**
1. Artists 2. Painters 3. Women artists 4. Biography, Individual 5. Artists -- United States
ISBN 978-0-06-184525-3; 0-06-184525-6; 978-0-06-207462-1 ebook; 0-06-207462-8 ebook
LC 2010-46347
This is a "full-length treatment of the talented and tenacious painter. . . . Levin piles up adequate evidence to assure Krasner's place in the American abstract expressionist pantheon. Detailed and meticulously researched, this is essential reading for those who want to know more about protofeminist artist Krasner, New York-based action/abstract expressionist painting, and the postwar NYC art scene." Libr J

Kreuger, Ivar, 1880-1932

Partnoy, Frank. The **match** king; Ivar Kreuger, the financial genius behind a century of Wall Street scandals. PublicAffairs 2009 272p $26.95; pa $15.95   **92**
1. Swindlers and swindling 2. Capitalists and financiers 3. Financiers 4. Kreuger & Toll, Inc. 5. Manufacturing executives
ISBN 978-1-58648-743-0; 1-58648-743-4; 978-1-58648-812-3 pa; 1-58648-812-0 pa
The author "delivers a thrilling account of the grandfather of all Ponzi and Madoff schemes—Ivar Kreuger (1880-1932), who made his fortune in the 1920s by raising money from American investors to lend to European governments in exchange for match monopolies. . . . A fascinating depiction of a man and his era." Publ Wkly
Includes bibliographical references (p. 230-235)

Kroc, Joan B

Napoli, Lisa. **Ray** and Joan; the man who made the McDonald's fortune and the woman who gave it all away. Lisa Napoli. Penguin Random House LLC 2016 368 p. (ebook) $65; (hardcover) $27   **92**
1. Businesspeople 2. Antinuclear movement 3. Fast food restaurants 4. Women and peace -- Biography 5. San Diego (Calif.) -- Biography 6. McDonald's Corporation -- Biography 7. Restaurateurs -- United States -- Biography 8. Businesspeople -- United States -- Biography 9. Women -- California -- San Diego -- Biography 10. Women philanthropists -- United States -- Biography 11. Antinuclear movement -- United States -- History -- 20th century -- Biography
ISBN 9781101984963; 9781101984956
LC 2016023340
This book, by Lisa Napoli, "is a quintessentially American tale of corporate intrigue and private passion: a struggling Mad Men-era salesman with a vision for a fast-food franchise that would become one of the world's most enduring brands, and a beautiful woman willing to risk her marriage and her reputation to promote controversial causes that touched her deeply." (Publisher's Note)
"Napoli's energetic, slightly tabloidesque narrative style make this a must-read for anyone who loves a good love story behind a business success." Pub Wkly
Includes bibliographical references
Man who made the McDonald's fortune and the woman who gave it all away

Kroc, Ray, 1902-1984

Napoli, Lisa. **Ray** and Joan; the man who made the McDonald's fortune and the woman who gave it all away. Lisa Napoli. Penguin Random House LLC 2016 368 p. (ebook) $65; (hardcover) $27   **92**
1. Businesspeople 2. Antinuclear movement 3. Fast food restaurants 4. Women and peace -- Biography 5. San Diego (Calif.) -- Biography 6. McDonald's Corporation -- Biography 7. Restaurateurs -- United States -- Biography 8. Businesspeople -- United States -- Biography 9. Women -- California -- San Diego -- Biography 10. Women philanthropists -- United States -- Biography 11. Antinuclear movement -- United States -- History -- 20th century -- Biography
ISBN 9781101984963; 9781101984956
LC 2016023340
This book, by Lisa Napoli, "is a quintessentially American tale of corporate intrigue and private passion: a struggling Mad Men-era salesman with a vision for a fast-food franchise that would become one of the world's most enduring brands, and a beautiful woman willing to risk

her marriage and her reputation to promote controversial causes that touched her deeply." (Publisher's Note)

"Napoli's energetic, slightly tabloidesque narrative style make this a must-read for anyone who loves a good love story behind a business success." Pub Wkly

Includes bibliographical references

Man who made the McDonald's fortune and the woman who gave it all away

Kumar, Pradyumna

Andersson, Per J. The **amazing** story of the man who cycled from India to Europe for love; Per J. Andersson; translated by Anna Holmwood. Oneworld Publications 2017 281 p. illustrations (hardcover) $19.99   **92**

1. Artists -- Biography 2. Man-woman relationship 3. International travel 4. East Indians -- Biography

ISBN 9781786070333; 1786070332

This book, by Per J. Andersson, translated by Anna Holmwood, tells "the remarkable true story of [Pradyumna Kumar and] how [he,] . . . armed with nothing more than a handful of paintbrushes and a second-hand Raleigh bicycle[,] made his way across Asia and Europe in search of the woman he loves." (Publisher's note)

"A beautiful, epic tale of love and perseverance." Booklist

Kumin, Maxine, 1925-2014

Kumin, Maxine, 1925-2014. The **Pawnbroker's** Daughter; A Memoir. W W Norton & Co Inc. 2015 160 p. illustrations $25.95   **92**

1. Poets 2. Women authors

ISBN 0393246337; 9780393246339

LC 2015009312

This memoir by Maxine Kumin "charts her journey from a childhood in a Jewish community in Depression-era Philadelphia, where [her] father was a pawnbroker, to Radcliffe College, where she comes into her own as an intellectual and meets the soldier-turned-Los Alamos scientist who would become her husband; to her metamorphosis from a poet of 'light verse' to a 'poet of witness'; to her farm in rural New England, the subject and setting of much of her later work." (Publisher's note)

"The real joy of this book is the author's love of all things country and New England. Kumin and her husband experienced an idyllic life on their 200-acre horse farm in New Hampshire, 'living a wide-open lifestyle.' Happily, she shared that life with the rest of us through her writing." Kirkus

Kupperman, Michael

Kupperman, Michael. **All** the answers; Michael Kupperman. Simon & Schuster 2018 224 p. illustrations $25   **92**

1. Radio broadcasting 2. Gifted children -- United States -- Biography -- Comic books, strips, etc. 3. Fathers and sons -- United States -- Biography -- Comic books, strips, etc. 4. Radio personalities -- United States-- Biography -- Comic books, strips, etc.

ISBN 1501166433; 9781501166433

LC 2018080304

"In this moving graphic memoir, . . . [author] Michael Kupperman traces the life of his reclusive father--the once-world-famous Joel Kupperman, 'Quiz Kid.' . . . Following a childhood spent in the public eye, . . . Joel deliberately spent the remainder of his life removed from the world at large. . . . Kupperman presents a fascinating account of mid-century radio and early television history . . . and the early age of modern celebrity culture." (Publisher's note)

"Kupperman's solid, line-heavy drawings, which impart credibility to the preposterous concepts of his humorous strips, are equally effec-

tive at conveying this real-life drama. His clear-eyed yet touching portrait of his father serves as a a powerful indictment of celebrity culture." Booklist

Kurson, Robert, 1963-

Kurson, Robert. **Crashing** through; a story of risk, adventure, and the man who dared to see. Random House 2007 306p il $25.95   **92**

1. Authors 2. Journalists 3. Nonfiction writers

ISBN 978-1-4000-6335-2; 1-4000-6335-3

LC 2007-3092

The book "becomes most interesting when the flaws in Mr. May's new eyesight become apparent. He makes wondrous discoveries of things blind people never hear about—shadows, freckles, the movement and transparency of running water—but has more difficulty with the cognitive aspects of pattern recognition. He can see facial features but cannot decipher facial expressions. . . . Eventually the joy of sight fades for him and the investigatory challenges begin." N Y Times (Late N Y Ed)

Kurzweil, Allen

Kurzweil, Allen. **Whipping** Boy; The Forty-year Search for My Twelve-year-old Bully. HarperCollins 2015 384 p. 16 plates; illustrations; maps $27.99   **92**

1. Bullies

ISBN 0062269488; 9780062269485

LC 2014027555

This book "chronicles Allen Kurzweil's search for his twelve-year-old nemesis, a bully named Cesar Augustus. The obsessive inquiry, which spans some forty years, takes Kurzweil all over the world, from a Swiss boarding school (where he endures horrifying cruelty) to the slums of Manila, from the Park Avenue boardroom of the world's largest law firm to a federal prison camp in Southern California." (Publisher's note)

"More important than even the scam and the man Cesar became, however, is the poignant way that Kurzweil strives to get an explanation for the bully's bad behavior in order to heal the wounds he's carried since school. The story will resonate with anyone who had a Cesar growing up, as so many did." Booklist

Kym, Min

Kym, Min. **Gone**; a girl, a violin, a life unstrung. Min Kym. Crown 2017 227 p. (hardcover) $25   **92**

1. Violinists 2. Loss (Psychology) 3. Violinists -- Biography

ISBN 9780451496072; 9780451496089; 9780451496096

LC 2016054104

This book, by Min Kym, is "the spellbinding memoir of a violin virtuoso who loses the instrument that had defined her both on stage and off -- and who discovers, beyond the violin, the music of her own voice. . . . Kym reckons with the space left by her violin's absence. She sees with new eyes her past as a child prodigy, with its isolation and crushing expectations; her combustible relationships with teachers and with a domineering boyfriend; and her navigation of two very different worlds." (Publisher's note)

"A pellucid memoir of letting go and coming to terms." Kirkus

La Rochefoucauld, Robert de, 1923-2012

Kix, Paul. The **Saboteur**; the aristocrat who became France's most daring anti-Nazi commando. Paul Kix. HarperCollins 2017 viii, 286 p.p (hardcover) $27.99   **92**

1. France -- History -- 1940-1945, German occupation 2. World War, 1939-1945 -- Underground movements -- France 3. Guerrillas

-- France -- Biography 4. France -- History -- German occupation, 1940-1945

ISBN 9780062322524; 9780062322548; 0062322524

LC 2017276823

This book, by Paul Kix, tells the story of "an unsung hero of the French Resistance during World War II--Robert de La Rochefoucauld, an aristocrat turned anti-Nazi saboteur--and his daring exploits as a résistant trained by Britain's Special Operations Executive. . . . [Kix] recounts La Rochefoucauld's enthralling adventures . . . [and] whatever the mission, . . . La Rochefoucauld acquitted himself nobly, with the straight-back aplomb of a man of aristocratic breeding." (Publisher's note)

"This thoroughly sourced account is highly readable and effectively showcases the life of a fascinating, complex man whose too-little-known role in the Resistance will be of great interest to followers of WWII history." Booklist

Includes bibliographical references and index.

La Tour du Pin Gouvernet, Henriette Lucie Dillon, marquise de, 1770-1853

Moorehead, Caroline. **Dancing** to the precipice: Lucie de la Tour du Pin and the French Revolution. HarperCollins 2009 480p il $27.99 **92**

1. Memoirists 2. France -- Social life and customs 3. United States -- Social life and customs

ISBN 978-0-7011-7904-5; 0-7011-7904-X

"In 1820, at the age of forty-nine, Lucie Dillon, the Marquise de la Tour du Pin, started writing her memoirs, an endeavor that went on for thirty years and produced one of the great monuments of French history. Lucie began life as an aristocrat, débuting at Versailles at the age of eleven; at the beginning of the Terror, as friends and relatives fell to the guillotine, she fled France with her husband and children. Resilient and resourceful, the family thrived on a farm in upstate New York, where Lucie churned butter, traded with Indians, and played hostess to Talleyrand. A return to France brought Lucie and her husband into Napoleon's inner circle; in later years, following an exile in London, they found favor with the restored Bourbon monarchy. Moorehead's biography, drawing on a trove of previously unpublished correspondence, captures the rhythm of the radical contrasts in her subject's life." New Yorker

Includes bibliographical references

LaMarche, Una

Lamarche, Una. **Unabrow**; misadventures of a late bloomer. Una LaMarche. Plume 2015 272 p. illustrations (paperback) $16 **92**

1. Mothers 2. Young women 3. Bildungsromans 4. Conduct of life 5. Popular culture -- United States 6. Coming of age -- United States 7. Mothers -- United States -- Biography 8. Young women -- United States -- Biography 9. Popular culture -- United States -- Miscellanea

ISBN 9780142181447

LC 2014021212

In this memoir, author Una LaMarche "shares the cringe-inducing lessons she's learned from a life as a late bloomer, including the seven deadly sins of DIY bangs, how not to make your own jorts, and how to handle pregnancy, plucking, and the rites of passage during which your own body is your worst frenemy." (Publisher's note)

"LaMarche is entertaining and fresh; readers will want to savor this sassy, offbeat commentary." Pub Wkly

Lacks, Henrietta

★ Skloot, Rebecca, 1972- The **immortal** life of Henrietta Lacks. Crown Publishers 2010 369p il $26 **92**

1. Cancer 2. Homemakers 3. Human experimentation in medicine 4. Cancer patients 5. African American women -- Biography

ISBN 978-1-4000-5217-2

LC 2009-31785

"A thorny and provocative book about cancer, racism, scientific ethics and crippling poverty, 'The Immortal Life of Henrietta Lacks' also floods over you like a narrative dam break, as if someone had managed to distill and purify the more addictive qualities of 'Erin Brockovich,' 'Midnight in the Garden of Good and Evil' and 'The Andromeda Strain.' More than 10 years in the making, it feels like the book Ms. Skloot was born to write." N Y Times Book Rev

Includes bibliographical references

Lafayette, Marie Joseph Paul Yves Roch Gilbert Du Motier, marquis de, 1757-1834

Auricchio, Laura. The **marquis**; Lafayette reconsidered. Laura Auricchio. Alfred A. Knopf 2014 416 p. illustrations, maps (harcover: alk. paper) $30 **92**

1. Generals -- France -- Biography 2. France. Armée -- Biography 3. Statesmen -- France -- Biography 4. Generals -- United States -- Biography 5. United States -- History -- Revolution, 1775-1783 -- Biography 6. United States -- History -- Revolution, 1775-1783 -- Participation, French

ISBN 0307267555; 9780307267559; 9780307387455

LC 2013046386

This book, by Laura Auricchio, offers "a major biography of the Marquis de Lafayette, French hero of the American Revolution, who, at age nineteen, volunteered to fight under George Washington; a biography that looks past the storybook hero and selfless champion of righteous causes who cast aside family and fortune to advance the transcendent aims of liberty and justice commemorated in America." (Publishera's note)

"A first-rate work that should appeal to history readers of all kinds." LJ

Includes bibliographical references

Gaines, James R. **For** liberty and glory; Washington, Lafayette, and their revolutions. W.W. Norton & Co. 2007 533p il map $29.95 **92**

1. Generals 2. Statesmen 3. Presidents 4. France -- History -- 1789-1799, Revolution 5. United States -- History -- 1775-1783, Revolution

ISBN 0-393-06138-8; 978-0-393-06138-3

LC 2007-22449

Gaines examines the relationship between George Washington and the Marquis de Lafayette.

This is a "fresh and engaging new look at the pair. . . . Gaines has a dry sense of humor and an appreciation for human foibles. . . . The American founding fathers, in particular, come across as extraordinary men with ordinary obsessions and—surprise!—senses of humor." Christ Sci Monit

Includes bibliographical references

Lahidji, Changiz, 1950-

Pezzullo, Ralph. **Full** battle rattle; my story as the longest-serving special forces A-Team soldier in American history. Changiz Lahidji and Ralph Pezzullo. St. Martin's Press 2018 viii, 290 p.p illustrations (some color) (hardcover) $26.99 **92**

1. Afghan War, 2001- 2. Persian Gulf War, 1991 3. Iranian Americans -- Biography 4. United States. Army. Special Forces -- History 5. Afghan War, 2001- -- Personal narratives, American 6. Special operations (Military science) -- United States 7. Persian

Gulf War, 1991 -- Personal narratives, American 8. United States. Army. Special Forces -- Officers -- Biography

ISBN 9781250121165; 1250121159; 9781250121158

LC 2017037543

This book, by Changiz Lahidji and Ralph Pezzullo, "tells the legend of a soldier who served America in every war since Vietnam. Master Sergeant Changiz Lahidji served on Special Forces A teams longer than anyone in history, completing over a hundred combat missions in Afghanistan. Changiz is a Special Forces legend. He also happens to be the first Muslim Green Beret." (Publisher's note)

Lahiri, Jhumpa

Lahiri, Jhumpa, 1967- **In** other words; Jhumpa Lahiri; translated from the Italian by Ann Goldstein. Alfred A. Knopf 2016 256 p. (ebook) $48; (hardback) $26.95 **92**

1. Italian language 2. Language and languages -- Study and teaching 3. Interlanguage (Language learning) -- Biography

ISBN 9781101875568; 9781101875551

LC 2015020998

This book, by Jhumpa Lahiri, translated by Ann Goldstein, is "an autobiographical work written in Italian, investigates the process of learning to express oneself in another language, and describes the journey of a writer seeking a new voice. Presented in a dual-language format, this is a wholly original book about exile, linguistic and otherwise." (Publisher's note)

"Lahiri's unexpected metamorphosis provides a captivating and insightful lesson in the power of language to transform." Pub Wkly

Lahti, Christine

Lahti, Christine. **True** stories from an unreliable eyewitness; a feminist coming of age. Christine Lahti. Harper Wave 2018 xviii, 200 p.p (hardcover) $25.99 **92**

1. Biography 2. Actors -- Biography 3. Women political activists -- Biography 4. Actors -- United States -- Biography

ISBN 9780062663696; 9780062663672; 0062663674

In this essay collection, Christine Lahti, "focuses on three major periods of her life: her childhood, her early journey as an actress and activist, and the realities of her life as a middle-aged woman in Hollywood today. . . . Taken together, the collection illuminates watershed moments in Lahti's life, revealing her struggle to maintain integrity, fight her need for perfection, and remain true to her feminist inclinations." (Publisher's note)

"Her style is irreverent, bawdy, and laugh-out-loud funny, but she doesn't shirk from painful subjects, including family mental illness. Lahti is one of those rare celebrities who not only has a fascinating life but who can also tell a relatable story with humility and humor." Booklist

Lake, Dianne, 1953-

Herman, Deborah. **Member** of the family; my story of Charles Manson, life inside his cult, and the darkness that ended the sixties. by Dianne Lake and Deborah Herman. HarperCollins 2017 384 p. **92**

ISBN 0062695576; 9780062695574

LC 2017277072

In this book, "Dianne Lake chronicles her years with Charles Manson, revealing for the first time how she became the youngest member of his Family and offering new insights into one of the twentieth century's most notorious criminals. . . . Though she never participated in any of the group's gruesome crimes and was purposely insulated from them, Dianne was arrested with the rest of the Manson Family, and eventually learned enough to join the prosecution's case against them." (Publisher's note)

Lakshmi, Padma.

Lakshmi, Padma, 1970- **Love,** loss, and what we ate; Padma Lakshmi. HarperCollins 2016 325 p. (hardcover) $26.99 **92**

1. Cooking

ISBN 0062202618; 9780062202611

This book, by Padma Lakshmi, is a "memoir of food and family, survival and triumph . . . [that] traces the arc of Padma Lakshmi's unlikely path from an immigrant childhood to a complicated life in front of the camera. . . . [It shares] Lakshmi's extraordinary account of her journey from that humble kitchen, ruled by ferocious and unforgettable women, to the judges' table of Top Chef and beyond." (Publisher's note)

Lamarr, Hedy, 1913-2000

Rhodes, Richard. **Hedy's** folly; the life and breakthrough inventions of Hedy Lamarr, the most beautiful woman in the world. Doubleday 2011 261p il $26.95; ebook $13.99 **92**

1. Actors

ISBN 978-0-385-53438-3; 978-0-385-53439-0 ebook

LC 2011021746

"Here's a recipe that might surprise you: take a silver-screen sex goddess (Hedy Lamarr), an avant-garde composer (George Antheil), a Hollywood friendship, and mutual technological curiosity, and mix well. What results is a patent for spread-spectrum radio, which has impacted the development of everything from torpedoes to cell phones and GPS technologies. This surprising and long-forgotten story is brought to life . . . [by Rhodes,] who deftly moves between Nazi secrets, scandalous films, engineering breakthroughs, and musical flops to weave a taut story that straddles two very different worlds—the entertainment industry and wartime weaponry—and yet somehow manages to remain a delectable read." Libr J

Includes bibliographical references

Shearer, Stephen Michael. **Beautiful**; the life of Hedy Lamarr. Thomas Dunne Books 2010 464p il $29.99 **92**

1. Actors

ISBN 978-0-312-55098-1; 0-312-55098-7

LC 2010-13058

This biography chronicles "the life of Hollywood legend Hedy Lamarr, from her cosseted childhood in an assimilated Jewish family in Austria to her early breaks in Max Reinhardt's internationally famous theater company; her scandalous, career-launching nude scene in the Czech film Ecstasy; her tortured first marriage to Jewish Nazi arms manufacturer Friedrich Mandl (dubbed an 'honorary Aryan' by the Third Reich); and her daring escape from the sadistic Mandl and Nazi Germany to Los Angeles and MGM. . . . One finishes the book feeling that one has read a complete portrait of Hedy Lamarr, actor and inventor, a biography that reveals, with drama and wit, how much more there was to this complex, brilliant woman than her ethereal natural beauty." Booklist

Includes bibliographical references

Lancaster, Burt, 1913-1994

Buford, Kate. **Burt** Lancaster; an American life. Da Capo Press 2001 447p il pa $20 **92**

1. Actors 2. Motion picture producers

ISBN 978-0-306-81019-0; 0-306-81019-0

First published 2000 by Knopf

"Lancaster's decades-long political involvement with liberal causes (and his constant run-ins with the House Un-American Activities Committee in the 1950s) are a central theme in this well-researched and engaging biography, which also details the artist's acting career, his turns as a producer and his personal life." Publ Wkly

Includes filmography and bibliographical references

Landowska, Wanda

Kildea, Paul. **Chopin's** piano; in search of the instrument that transformed music. Paul Kildea. W. W. Norton & Company 2018 288 p. (hardcover) $27.95 **92**

1. Pianos 2. Pianists -- Biography
ISBN 9780393652222

LC 2018027829

This book, by Paul Kildea, presents the "captivating story of Frédéric Chopin and the fate of both his Mallorquin piano and musical Romanticism from the early nineteenth to the mid-twentieth century. . . . [It] traces the history of Chopin's twenty-four Preludes through the instruments on which they were played, the pianists who interpreted them, and the traditions they came to represent." (Publisher's note)

"Densely written and packed with details, this title will appeal not only to readers who enjoy Chopin but also those interested in piano history." LJ

Includes bibliographical references and index

Landry, Tom

Ribowsky, Mark. The **last** cowboy; a life of Tom Landry. Mark Ribowsky. Liveright Publishing Corporation 2014 720 p. (hardcover) $29.95 **92**

1. Football coaches 2. Dallas Cowboys (Football team) 3. Dallas Cowboys (Football team) -- History 4. Football coaches -- United States -- Biography
ISBN 9780871403339

LC 2013034731

Author Mark Ribowsky presents a biography of professional football coach Tom Landry. He "begins amid the dusty roads of Mission, Texas, where Tom Landry's childhood played out like a homespun American fable. It then takes us to the war-torn skies over western Europe, where the straight-A student and high school football star piloted a B-17 through thirty harrowing, at times near-fatal, missions. And finally back to a booming Texas, where he continued his faithful march toward gridiron immortality." (Publisher's note)

Includes bibliographical references and index

Lane, Rose Wilder, 1886-1968

★ Fraser, Caroline. **Prairie** fires; the American dreams of Laura Ingalls Wilder. by Caroline Fraser. Metropolitan Books 2017 xii, 625 p.p illustrations, map (hardcover) $35 **92**

1. Women authors -- United States -- Biography 2. Frontier and pioneer life -- United States 3. Women pioneers -- United States -- Biography 4. Authors, American -- 20th century -- Biography
ISBN 9781627792776; 9781627792769; 1627792767

LC 2017028870

Pulitzer Prize: Biography (2018)

National Book Critics Circle Award: Biography (2017)

This book, by Caroline Fraser, is "the first comprehensive historical biography of Laura Ingalls Wilder, the beloved author of the Little House on the Prairie books. . . . Revealing the grown-up story behind the most influential childhood epic of pioneer life, . . . [Fraser] chronicles Wilder's tumultuous relationship with her journalist daughter, Rose Wilder Lane, setting the record straight regarding charges of ghostwriting that have swirled around the books." (Publisher's note)

"A vivid portrait of frontier life and one of its most ardent celebrants." Kirkus

Includes bibliographical references (pages [517]-602) and index

Lange, Dorothea, 1895-1965

Gordon, Linda. **Dorothea** Lange; a life beyond limits. W.W. Norton 2009 xxiii, 536p il $35 **92**

1. Women photographers 2. Biography, Individual 3. Photography -- History -- United States
ISBN 978-0-393-05730-0; 0-393-05730-5

LC 2009-19639

This is a biography of the American photographer who worked for the Historical Section of the Farm Security Administration (FSA) during the Depression.

"Gordon's elegant biography is testament to Lange's gift for challenging her country to open its eyes." N Y Times Book Rev

Includes bibliographical references

Lanier, Jaron

Lanier, Jaron. **Dawn** of the new everything; encounters with reality and virtual reality. Jaron Lanier. Henry Holt & Co. 2017 xv, 351 p.p illustrations (hardcover) $30 **92**

1. Biography 2. Virtual reality 3. Computer scientists -- United States -- Biography 4. Virtual reality -- Philosophy 5. Virtual reality -- Social aspects
ISBN 9781627794107; 9781627794091

LC 2017010792

In this book, author Jaron Lanier "explains . . . [virtual reality's] dazzling possibilities by reflecting on his own lifelong relationship with technology. Bridging the gap between tech mania and the experience of being inside the human body, Dawn of the New Everything is a look at what it means to be human at a moment of unprecedented technological possibility." (Publisher's note)

"This culturally significant title with its compelling personal narrative proves yet again that Lanier is a thinker whose work should be read and contemplated." Booklist

Includes bibliographical references and index

Larsen, Nella

Hutchinson, George. **In** search of Nella Larsen; a biography of the color line. Belknap Press of Harvard University Press 2006 611p il $39.95 **92**

1. Nurses 2. Authors 3. Novelists 4. Short story writers
ISBN 0-674-02180-0; 978-0-674-02180-8

LC 2005-58129

This is a biography of the author of Quicksand (1928) and Passing (1929).

The author "has produced what must be the definitive biography of Larsen. It's hard to think of a stone he hasn't looked under in his quest to establish the facts, correct mistakes and trace her private life. But Hutchinson's biography also manages to be an insightful reconsideration of a much-studied period in American literature and black cultural history." Nation

Includes bibliographical references

Laskin, David, 1953-

Laskin, David. The **Family**; Three Journeys into the Heart of the Twentieth Century. David Laskin. Viking Adult 2013 400 p. $32 **92**

1. Jews 2. Genealogy 3. World history -- 20th century 4. Jews -- Belarus -- Biography 5. Valozhyn (Belarus) -- Biography 6. Jews, Belarusian -- Palestine -- Biography 7. Jews, Belarusian -- United States -- Biography
ISBN 067002547X; 9780670025473

LC 2013017047

Author David Laskin presents a "work of twentieth century history through the riveting story of one extraordinary Jewish family. In tracing the roots of . . . his own family . . . Laskin honors the traditions, the lives, and the choices of his ancestors: revolutionaries and entrepreneurs, scholars and farmers, tycoons and truck drivers." (Publisher's note)

Includes bibliographical references (pages 341-371) and index

Latus, Amy, 1965-2002

Latus, Janine. **If** I am missing or dead. Simon & Schuster 2007 309p il $25   **92**
1. Journalists 2. Abused women 3. Memoirists 4. Abused persons 5. Murder victims 6. Social activists
ISBN 978-0-7432-9653-3; 0-7432-9653-2

LC 2006-52313

"When journalist Latus's younger sister Amy vanishes at age 37 in 2002, authorities find a chiller of a note in Amy's desk: 'If I am missing or dead . . . question Ron.' Ron Ball is Amy's ex-con boyfriend, and when Amy's body is found, something shatters in Latus. A victim of abuse herself, Latus tunnels back to her difficult suburban childhood to decode why two smart, talented sisters might be so starving for love that they would risk their lives to get it. Latus's book unfolds like a gripping novel, getting at the brutal heart of darkness that underscores domestic violence." People

Latus, Janine, 1959-

Latus, Janine. **If** I am missing or dead. Simon & Schuster 2007 309p il $25   **92**
1. Journalists 2. Abused women 3. Memoirists 4. Abused persons 5. Murder victims 6. Social activists
ISBN 978-0-7432-9653-3; 0-7432-9653-2

LC 2006-52313

"When journalist Latus's younger sister Amy vanishes at age 37 in 2002, authorities find a chiller of a note in Amy's desk: 'If I am missing or dead . . . question Ron.' Ron Ball is Amy's ex-con boyfriend, and when Amy's body is found, something shatters in Latus. A victim of abuse herself, Latus tunnels back to her difficult suburban childhood to decode why two smart, talented sisters might be so starving for love that they would risk their lives to get it. Latus's book unfolds like a gripping novel, getting at the brutal heart of darkness that underscores domestic violence." People

Lauper, Cyndi, 1953-

Lauper, Cyndi, 1953- **Cyndi** Lauper; a memoir. Cyndi Lauper with Jancee Dunn. Atria Books 2012 338 p. 16 unnumbered pages of plates $26   **92**
1. Women rock musicians 2. Singers -- United States -- Biography
ISBN 143914785X; 9781439147856

LC 2013560375

Author Cyndi Lauper "left her home in Ozone Park, Queens, at age 17 to escape a sexually abusive stepfather and the limitations on life—especially for women—imposed by a hardscrabble working-class neighborhood and male-dominated family culture. . . . Her life changed in 1983, however, with the release of She's So Unusual, which . . . made Lauper an instant star. . . . Inevitably, her superstar aura faded, but her eclectic musical output did not." (Kirkus)

Laurens, Henry, 1724-1792

Harris, J. William. The **hanging** of Thomas Jeremiah; a free Black man's encounter with liberty. Yale University Press 2009 223p il map $27.50   **92**
1. Diplomats 2. Merchants 3. Ship captains 4. Colonial leaders 5. Plantation owners 6. Government officials 7. Colonial administrators 8. Slavery -- United States 9. South Carolina -- Race relations 10. African Americans -- Social conditions
ISBN 978-0-300-15214-2; 0-300-15214-0

LC 2009-15233

This is an "account of nebulous historical figure Thomas Jeremiah.

. . . Owner of a fishing company and worth $200,000 in 2009 dollars, . . . [Jeremiah] was probably the richest black man in North America; he was also a slaveowner. That didn't stop him from becoming a scapegoat, accused by patriot leader Henry Laurens—a wealthy plantation owner with hundreds of slaves—of secretly leading a British-sponsored slave insurrection. Though Governor William Campbell, aggrieved by the unlawfulness of Jeremiah's trial, interceded, it didn't stop those determined to hang Jeremiah. . . . Readers will learn much about the darker side of American institutions; students of American history and civil rights will appreciate Harris's impassive approach and thorough standards." Publ Wkly

Includes bibliographical references

Laveau, Marie, 1794-1881

Ward, Martha Coonfield. **Voodoo** queen; the spirited lives of Marie Laveau. by Martha Ward. University Press of Mississippi 2004 246p il map $26   **92**
1. Witches 2. Voodooism
ISBN 1-578-06629-8

LC 2003-18292

"Spiritual leaders Marie Laveau, mother and daughter, reigned in New Orleans between the 1820s and 1880s. Through their story, Ward offers fresh perspective on Creole culture and voodoo." Booklist

Including bibliographical references

Lawrence, D. H. (David Herbert), 1885-1930

Worthen, John. **D.H.** Lawrence; the life of an outsider. Counterpoint 2005 xxvi, 518p il $29.95   **92**
1. Poets 2. Authors 3. Novelists 4. Dramatists 5. Essayists 6. Short story writers
ISBN 1-58243-341-0

"Using as a unifying theme Lawrence's perpetual status as an outsider, both in working-class Nottinghamshire and in the English literary world, Worthen gives us the full sweep of this groundbreaking writer's utterly unconventional, often torturous, and occasionally rhapsodic life." Booklist

Includes bibliographical references

Lawrence, Sarahlee

Lawrence, Sarahlee. **River** house; a memoir. Tin House Books 2010 272p pa $16.95   **92**
1. Farmers 2. Rafting (Sports) 3. Adventure and adventurers
ISBN 978-0-9825691-3-9

LC 2010-7702

"Handy with tools and rafts, a good neighbor, and a mighty fine horsewoman, Lawrence is also adept with language, writing with arresting lucidity and a driving need to understand her father, her legacy, the land, community, work, and herself. A true adventure story of rare dimension." Booklist

Lawrence, T. E. (Thomas Edward), 1888-1935

★ Brown, Malcolm. **T.E.** Lawrence. New York University Press 2003 160p il map (Historic lives) $21.95   **92**
1. Authors 2. Soldiers 3. Archaeologists 4. Travel writers
ISBN 0-8147-9920-5

LC 2003-51387

"The book is a major literary work." Publ Wkly
Includes bibliographical references

Korda, Michael, 1933- **Hero**; the life and legend of Lawrence of Arabia. Harper 2010 762p il map $34.99   **92**
1. Authors 2. Soldiers 3. Archaeologists 4. Travel writers 5.

Biography, Individual 6. Soldiers -- Great Britain 7. World War, 1914-1918 -- Middle East 8. World War, 1914-1918 -- Campaigns -- Turkey 9. World War, 1914-1918 -- Campaigns -- Middle East
ISBN 978-0-06-171261-6

LC 2010-33189

This is a biography of T. E. Lawrence, the "British scholar, adventurer, soldier, and hero who became a myth in his lifetime." (Publisher's note) Index.

"This magisterial biography of British soldier and adventurer T.E. Lawrence celebrates a life spent subverting authority in the most glamorous—and bizarre—ways. . . . [The author] gives a rousing, lucid account of Lawrence's leadership of the Arab revolt against the Ottoman Empire during WWI and his diplomatic championing of Arab nationalism. But it's Lawrence's artistic bent . . . and his magnetic but tortured soul that take center stage." Publ Wkly

Includes bibliographical references

Sattin, Anthony. The **Young** T. E. Lawrence; Anthony Sattin. W W Norton & Co Inc 2015 352 p. illustrations, maps $28.95 **92**
1. Middle East -- History 2. Soldiers -- Great Britain -- Biography 3. Archaeologists -- Great Britain -- Biography 4. World War, 1914-1918 -- Campaigns -- Arab countries
ISBN 0393242668; 9780393242669

LC 2014032063

This book, by Anthony Sattin, profiles "the years that turned T. E. Lawrence into Lawrence of Arabia. . . . This intimate biography is the first to focus on Lawrence in his twenties, the untold story of the awkward archaeologist from Oxford who, on first visiting 'The East,' fell in love with Arab culture and found his life's mission." (Publisher's note)

"Recommended as an insightful, gracefully written, and sensitive account that explains how a shy, private young man developed into a widely known and revered 'hero' who was never comfortable with his fame." LJ

Includes bibliographical references and index

Lawson, Jenny, 1979-

Lawson, Jenny. **Furiously** happy; a funny book about horrible things. Jenny Lawson. Flatiron Books 2015 352 p. illustrations (hardback) $26.99 **92**
1. Mental illness -- Humor 2. Journalists -- United States -- Biography 3. Humorists, American -- 21st century -- Biography
ISBN 1250077001; 9781250077004

LC 2015022196

In this book, by Jenny Lawson, the author "pokes fun at herself as she addresses the serious nature of her mental and physical illnesses. . . . Rather than hiding the facts, she openly divulges, in a darkly humorous way, how she copes with rheumatoid arthritis, depression, panic attacks, anxiety, and the days when she is driven to pull her hair out or cut herself." (Kirkus Reviews)

"Lawson's goal is not to offend, although that might happen to some readers, but to lay bare the truth about her struggles in life so that others can benefit. She does a solid job exposing the hidden nature of mental illness by putting a direct spotlight on her own issues, thereby illuminating an often taboo subject. Her amusing essays open up a not-so-funny topic: mental illness in its many guises. Kudos to Lawson for being a flagrant and witty spokesperson for this dark subject matter." Kirkus

Laymon, Kiese

★ Laymon, Kiese. **Heavy**; an American memoir. by Kiese Laymon. Scribner 2018 256 p. (hbk.) $26 **92**
1. Eating disorders 2. Compulsive eating 3. African Americans -- Biography 4. Mother and child -- United States 5. Compulsive

gamblers -- United States -- Biography 6. Eating disorders -- Patients -- United States -- Biography
ISBN 9781501125652; 9781501125669

LC 2018002915

Kirkus Prize Finalist: Nonfiction (2018)

In this memoir, author Kiese Laymon "writes eloquently and honestly about growing up a hard-headed black son to a complicated and brilliant black mother in Jackson, Mississippi. From his early experiences of sexual violence, to his suspension from college, to his trek to New York as a young college professor, Laymon charts his complex relationship with his mother, grandmother, anorexia, obesity, sex, writing, and ultimately gambling." (Publisher's note)

"Laymon applies his book's title to his body and his memories; to his inheritance as a student, a teacher, a writer, an activist, a black man, and his mother's son—but also to the weight of truth, and writing it." Booklist

Le Guin, Ursula K., 1929-2018

Naimon, David. **Ursula** K. Le Guin; conversations on writing. Ursula K. Le Guin and David Naimon. Tin House Books 2018 150 p. (hardcover) $14.95 **92**
1. Authorship 2. Science fiction -- Authorship 3. American fiction -- Women authors 4. Literature 5. Fantasy fiction -- Authorship 6. United States -- Civilization 7. Authors, American -- 20th century -- Interviews 8. Women authors, American -- 20th century -- Biography
ISBN 9781941040997

LC 2018003429

In this book, Ursula K. Le Guin with David Naimon, "discusses craft, aesthetics, and philosophy in her fiction, poetry, and nonfiction respectively. The discussions provide ample advice and guidance for writers of every level, but also give Le Guin a chance to to sound off on some of her favorite subjects: the genre wars, the patriarchy, the natural world, and what, in her opinion, makes for great writing." (Publisher's note)

"Readers and writers who have enjoyed Le Guin in her many forms throughout the years will likely relish the intimate insights the novelist shares. That said, the interviews are freely available online for those interested in listening to Le Guin's words in her own voice." LJ

LeFavour, Cree

Lefavour, Cree. **Lights** on, rats out; a memoir. Cree LeFavour. Grove Press 2017 312 p. (hardcover) $25 **92**
1. Psychotherapy 2. Self-mutilation 3. Self-mutilation -- Treatment 4. Psychotherapy patients -- Biography 5. Self-injurious behavior -- Treatment
ISBN 9780802189158; 9780802125965

LC 2016048377

In this memoir, author Cree LeFavour "began to organize her days around the cruel, compulsive logic of self-harm. . . . [This book] describes a fiercely smart and independent woman's charged attachment to a mental health professional and the dangerous compulsion to keep him in her life at all costs." (Publisher's note)

"A searing, brilliant memoir revealing the therapeutic process and its ability 'to turn our ghosts into ancestors.'" Booklist

LeMieux, Richard

LeMieux, Richard. **Breakfast** at Sally's; one homeless man's inspirational journey. Skyhorse 2008 433p il $24.95 **92**
1. Homeless persons 2. Homeless 3. Memoirists
ISBN 978-1-60239-293-9; 1-60239-293-5

LC 2008-24420

"Former successful businessman Richard LeMieux has lived better than the average American, but descended, through economic and personal failures, to homelessness for almost two years. Writing of life on the streets with his dog, Willow, he introduces a cast of characters from his experiences. . . . This inspirational political and social memoir can offer readers hope for a renewal of faith—in God and humanity. All public libraries will want this book for their collections." Libr J

LeMond, Greg

De Vise, Daniel. The **comeback**; Greg Lemond, thirty-odd shotgun pellets, and the world's greatest bicycle race. Daniel de Visé. Atlantic Monthly Press 2018 432 p. (hardcover) $27 **92**
    1. Cycling 2. Athletes -- United States 3. Cyclists -- United States -- Biography
    ISBN 9780802127945

LC 2017061342
This book, by Daniel de Visé, "chronicles the life of [Greg LeMond,] one of America's greatest athletes, from his roots in Nevada and California to the heights of global fame, to a falling out with his own family and a calamitous confrontation with Lance Armstrong over allegations the latter was doping--a campaign LeMond would wage on principle for more than a decade before Armstrong was finally stripped of his own Tour titles." (Publisher's note)
    Includes bibliographical references

Leadbelly, 1885-1949

Wolfe, Charles K. The **life** and legend of Leadbelly; [by] Charles Wolfe and Kip Lornell. Da Capo Press 1999 333p il pa $16.95   **92**
    1. Singers 2. Guitarists 3. Blues music 4. African American musicians 5. Songwriters 6. Accordionists
    ISBN 978-0-306-80896-8; 0-306-80896-X
    First published 1992 by HarperCollins
"Drawing on a variety of primary and secondary sources, including numerous interviews, Wolfe and Lornell attempt to separate fact from fiction. . . . Photographs, informative notes, and a full discography are valuable additions." Choice
    Includes discography and bibliographical references

Lear, Norman

Lear, Norman, 1922- **Even** This I Get to Experience; Norman Lear. Penguin Group USA 2014 448 p. illustrations, portraits $32.95   **92**
    1. Autobiographies 2. Comedy television programs
    ISBN 1594205728; 9781594205729

LC 2014032903
This memoir by Norman Lear describes how "Lear led a charmed life throughout postwar Hollywood's golden years, befriending the likes of Carl Reiner and Mel Brooks; writing and directing Frank Sinatra, Robert Redford, Dick Van Dyke, and Martha Raye; becoming the highest paid comic writer in the country while working for Jerry Lewis and Dean Martin. Not to mention, Lear flew some fifty bombing missions over Germany with the Fifteenth Air Force." (Publisher's note)
    "A big-hearted, richly detailed chronicle of comedy, commitment and a long life lived fully." Kirkus

Leary, Timothy, 1920-1996

Greenfield, Robert. **Timothy** Leary; a biography. Harcourt, Inc. 2006 689p il $28   **92**
    1. Psychologists 2. College teachers 3. Social reformers
    ISBN 0-15-100500-1; 978-0-15-100500-0

LC 2005-30154
This is a biography of LSD guru and counterculture icon Timothy Leary.

"A veritable who's who of the age of Aquarius and a real page-turner, Greenfield's cornerstone portrait of the acidhead who would be king brilliantly illuminates the paradoxes of the psychedelic age." Booklist

Minutaglio, Bill. The **most** dangerous man in America; Timothy Leary, Richard Nixon and the hunt for the fugitive king of LSD. Bill Minutaglio and Steven L. Davis. Twelve 2018 x, 384 p.p illustrations (hardcover) $30   **92**
    1. Counterculture 2. Fugitives from justice 3. LSD (Drug) -- History -- 20th century 4. Counterculture -- History -- 20th century 5. Psychologists -- United States -- Biography 6. Escapes -- California -- San Luis Obispo County 7. Fugitives from justice -- United States -- Biography 8. United States -- Politics and government -- 1969-1974 9. Radicalism -- United States -- History -- 20th century
    ISBN 9781478974215; 9781455563586; 9781478923664

LC 2017032575
This book, by Bill Minutaglio and Steven L. Davis, narrates "President Nixon's careening, global manhunt for Dr. Timothy Leary [as it] winds its way among homegrown radicals, European aristocrats, a Black Panther outpost in Algeria, an international arms dealer, hash-smuggling hippies from the Brotherhood of Eternal Love, and secret agents on four continents, culminating in one of the trippiest journeys through the American counterculture." (Publisher's note)
    "Minutaglio and Davis are superb storytellers, and throughout the narrative, they nimbly move between their two converging subjects. Their account is expertly detailed and blessedly fat-free." Kirkus
    Includes bibliographical references and index.

Leavitt, Henrietta Swan, 1868-1921

Johnson, George. **Miss** Leavitt's stars; the untold story of the woman who discovered how to measure the universe. W. W. Norton 2005 162p il (Great discoveries) $22.95   **92**
    1. Astronomers 2. Photometrists
    ISBN 0-393-05128-5

LC 2005-02823
This is a biography of the American astronomer whose research concerned the measuring of distance in space.
    This book is "a fine tribute to a remarkable woman of science." Publ Wkly
    Includes bibliographical references

Lebovitz, David

Lebovitz, David. **L'appart**; the delights and disasters of making my Paris home. David Lebovitz. Crown 2017 354 p. illustrations (hardback) $27   **92**
    1. Apartments 2. French cooking 3. Americans -- France 4. Paris (France) -- Social life and customs 5. Cooking, French 6. Cooking -- France -- Paris 7. Paris (France) -- Biography 8. Cooks -- France -- Paris -- Biography 9. Americans -- France -- Paris -- Biography 10. Apartments -- Remodeling -- France -- Paris
    ISBN 9780804188395; 0804188386; 9780804188388

LC 2017009159
In this book, "bestselling author and world-renowned chef David Lebovitz continues to mine the rich subject of his evolving ex-Pat life in Paris, using his perplexing experiences in apartment renovation as a launching point for stories about French culture, food, and what it means to revamp one's life. Includes dozens of new recipes." (Publisher's note)
    "Lebovitz peels off the plaster to reveal a Paris beyond tourism. Lebovitz's stories shimmer with despair, distress, and regret, but he nevertheless embraces life with all its flaws in the city he loves." Pub Wkly

Ledyard, John, 1751-1789

Gifford, Bill. **Ledyard**; in search of the first American explorer. Harcourt 2007 331p il map $25   92

1. Explorers 2. Travel writers

ISBN 978-0-15-101218-3; 0-15-101218-0

LC 2006-17064

This book "makes an important contribution to the existing literature through its personal approach to Ledyard's life. Few of Ledyard's letters and journals remain . . . but, by using most of what's available and tracking down details through his own travels, the author paints a fascinating portrait of the man he calls the 'archetype of the restless American wanderer.'" N Y Times Book Rev

Lee, Bruce, 1940-1973

★ Polly, Matthew. **Bruce** Lee; a life. Matthew Polly. Simon & Schuster 2018 656 p. (hardback) $35   92

1. Biography 2. Actors -- United States -- Biography 3. Martial artists -- United States -- Biography

ISBN 9781501187629; 9781501187636

LC 2018013592

In this biography, author Matthew Polly "explores [Bruce] Lee's early years as a child star in Hong Kong cinema; . . . his beginnings as a martial arts teacher, . . .; his struggles as an Asian-American actor in Hollywood and frustration seeing role after role he auditioned for go to . . . white actors . . .; his challenges juggling a sky-rocketing career with his duties as a father and husband; and his shocking end that to this day is still shrouded in mystery." (Publisher's note)

"A fascinating story of a remarkable figure in popular culture, this is the biography Bruce Lee's legion of fans have been waiting for." Booklist

Lee, Gypsy Rose, 1914-1970

Abbott, Karen. **American** rose; a nation laid bare: the life and times of Gypsy Rose Lee. Random House 2010 422p il $26; ebook $12.99   92

1. Actors 2. Novelists 3. Striptease 4. Stripteasers

ISBN 978-1-4000-6691-9; 978-0-679-60456-3 ebook

LC 2010-15081

"Imaginative and engaging, Abbott's biography of the celebrated stripper, who died in 1970 at age 59, also proves a well-informed look at the evolution of musical theater in the early 20th century." Publ Wkly

Includes bibliographical references

Lee, Harper

Atticus Finch; the biography: Harper Lee, her father, and the making of an American icon. Joseph Crespino. Basic Books 2018 272 p. (hardback) $28   92

1. American authors -- 20th century -- Biography 2. Authors, American -- 20th century -- Biography

ISBN 9781541644946

LC 2017056457

In this book, "historian Joseph Crespino draws on exclusive sources to reveal how Harper Lee's father provided the central inspiration for each of her books. . . . Lee created the Atticus of 'Go Set a Watchman' out of the ambivalence she felt toward white southerners like him. But when a militant segregationist movement arose that mocked his values, she revised the character in 'To Kill a Mockingbird' to defend her father and to remind the South of its best traditions." (Publisher's note)

Includes bibliographical references and index

Flynt, Wayne. **Mockingbird** songs; my friendship with Harper Lee. Wayne Flynt. HarperCollins Publishers 2017 xv,

215 p.p illustrations (chiefly color) (hardcover: alk. paper) $25.99   92

1. Women authors -- Biography 2. Personal correspondence 3. Women authors -- United States

ISBN 9780062660107; 9780062660084; 9780062660091

LC 2016044095

This book, by Wayne Flynt, is "an indelible portrait of one of the most famous and beloved authors in the canon of American literature--a collection of letters between Harper Lee and one of her closest friends that reveals the famously private writer as never before, in her own words." (Publisher's note)

"Southern historian Flynt (Keeping the Faith) shares his relationship with Harper Lee in a series of affectionate, playful, and mutually admiring letters." Pub Wkly

Mills, Marja. The **Mockingbird** Next Door; Life with Harper Lee. Marja Mills. The Penguin Press 2014 288 p. illustrations (hardback) $27.95   92

1. Alabama 2. American authors 3. Alabama -- Biography 4. Authors, American -- 20th century -- Biography

ISBN 1594205191; 9781594205194

LC 2013039938

This book, by Marja Mills, is a memoir recounting her friendship with "To Kill a Mockingbird" author Harper Lee. "Journalists have trekked to her hometown of Monroeville, Alabama, where . . . Lee, known to her friends as Nelle, has lived with her sister, Alice, for decades, trying and failing to get an interview with the author. But in 2001, the Lee sisters opened their door to Chicago Tribune journalist Marja Mills. It was the beginning of a long conversation--and a great friendship." (Publisher's note)

Lee, Hyeonseo

Lee, Hyeonseo. The **Girl** With Seven Names; A North Korean Defector's Story. Hyeonseo Lee with David John. HarperCollins 2015 304 p. illustrations (chiefly color) (hardcover) $26.99   92

1. Refugees 2. Korea (North) 3. Communism -- Korea (North) -- History 4. Defectors -- Korea (North) -- Biography 5. Defectors -- Korea (South) -- Biography

ISBN 9780007554836; 9780007554850; 9780007554867; 0007554834

In this memoir, "as a child growing up in North Korea, Hyeonseo Lee was one of millions trapped by a secretive and brutal communist regime. Her home on the border with China gave her some exposure to the world beyond the confines of the Hermit Kingdom and, as the famine of the 1990s struck, she began to wonder, question and to realise that she had been brainwashed her entire life." (Publisher's note)

"Remarkable bravery fluently recounted." Kirkus

Lee, Richard Henry, 1732-1794

Unger, Harlow Giles. **First** founding father; Richard Henry Lee and the call to independence. Harlow Giles Unger. Da Capo Press 2017 xiii, 306 p.p illustrations, maps (hardcover: alk. paper) $28   92

1. Founding Fathers of the United States 2. Revolutionaries -- United States -- Biography 3. United States -- History -- 1775-1783, Revolution 4. Virginia -- Biography 5. Politicians -- United States -- Biography 6. United States -- History -- Revolution, 1775-1783 -- Biography 7. United States. Declaration of Independence -- Signers -- Biography

ISBN 9780306902598; 0306825619; 9780306825613

LC 2017040744

This book, by Harlow Giles Unger, "will startle most Americans with the revelation that many historians have ignored for more than two centuries: Richard Henry Lee, not Thomas Jefferson, was the author of America's original Declaration of Independence." (Publisher's note)

"Unger's thorough research, smooth narrative, and placement of Lee in the context of 18th-century America will inform both general readers and historians." Choice

Includes bibliographical references and index

Lee, Robert E. (Robert Edward), 1807-1870

★ Blount, Roy. **Robert** E. Lee; a Penguin life. [by] Roy Blount, Jr. Lipper/Viking Bk. 2003 210p (Penguin lives series) $19.95; pa $13   **92**
1. Generals 2. College presidents 3. Confederate States of America -- Army 4. United States -- History -- 1861-1865, Civil War
ISBN 0-670-03220-4; 0-14-303866-4 pa
LC 2002-32423

This is a biography of "the famous Southern general admired for his military leadership but also scorned for defending the Confederacy. Blount's concise writing keeps his biography trim and succinct, and his admiration for the subject allows for enjoyable reading." Booklist
Includes bibliographical references

Fellman, Michael. The **making** of Robert E. Lee. Johns Hopkins Univ. Press 2003 360p il pa $19.95   **92**
1. Generals 2. College presidents 3. United States -- History -- 1861-1865, Civil War
ISBN 0-8018-7411-4
LC 2002-43290

First published 2000 by Random House

"Struggling to subdue his ambitions and passions in a peacetime military career whose monotony was only momentarily breached by the Mexican American War and at Harpers Ferry, Lee found in the Civil War a chance to express himself fully. In a study rich with discussions of Lee's religious beliefs and political opinions, the author skewers previous efforts to detach Lee from slavery, racism, and the mentality of the Lost Cause. Sure to arouse debate, this book challenges and delights." Libr J
Includes bibliographical references

Freeman, Douglas Southall, 1886-1953. **Lee**; an abridgment in one volume, by Richard Harwell, of the four-volume R. E. Lee. with a new foreword by James M. McPherson. Scribner 1991 xxiii, 601p il maps hardcover o.p. pa $18   **92**
1. Generals 2. College presidents 3. United States -- History -- 1861-1865, Civil War
ISBN 0-684-82953-3 pa
LC 91-20088

First published 1961

"Students of history will continue to want and to use the original four-volume work but most general readers will find this abridgment more convenient and adequate to their interest. All footnotes and all of the appendix have been omitted as well as details of Civil War action that are not necessary to show the main course of Lee's life and action." Booklist

Horn, Jonathan. The **Man** Who Would Not Be Washington; Robert E. Lee's Civil War and His Decision That Changed American History. Jonathan Horn. Simon & Schuster 2015 384 p. illustrations, maps $28   **92**
1. United States -- History -- 1861-1865, Civil War -- Biography
ISBN 147674856X; 9781476748566

LC 2014029702

This book, by Jonathan Horn, offers the "true story of Robert E. Lee, the brilliant soldier bound by marriage to George Washington's family but turned by war against Washington's crowning achievement, the Union. . . . This . . . biography follows Lee through married life, military glory, and misfortune. The story that emerges is more complicated, more tragic, and more illuminating than the familiar tale." (Publisher's note)

"In tracing Lee's biography, Horn establishes the powerful connection that both Lee and Washington had to slavery and the complex meaning of both states' rights and the Founding Fathers to white Southerners of Lee's generation. Historians will find little that is new, but undergraduates will consider it informative. Summing Up: Recommended. Public and undergraduate libraries." Choice

Korda, Michael, 1933- **Clouds** of Glory; The Life and Legend of Robert E. Lee. Michael Korda. HarperCollins 2014 640 p. illustrations, maps $40   **92**
1. Command of troops 2. United States -- History -- 1861-1865, Civil War
ISBN 0062116290; 9780062116291

LC 2014415636

This book, by Michael Korda, is a "historical biography of General Robert E. Lee. . . . [It] analyzes Lee's command during the Civil War and explores his responsibility for the fatal stalemate at Antietam, his defeat at Gettysburg . . . and ultimately, his failed strategy for winning the war. As Korda shows, Lee's dignity, courage, leadership, and modesty made him a hero on both sides of the Mason-Dixon Line." (Publisher's note)

Korda "examines the life of Robert E. Lee from start to finish, illuminating not just the man, but his extended family and the society which produced him." Pub Wkly
Includes bibliographical references and index

Thomas, Emory M. **Robert** E. Lee; a biography. Norton 1995 472p il maps pa $17.95   **92**
1. Generals 2. College presidents 3. United States -- History -- 1861-1865, Civil War
ISBN 0-393-31631-9 pa

LC 95-10522

"Civil War historian Thomas presents Lee as neither an icon nor a flawed figure, but rather as a man who made the best of his lot, whose comic vision of life ultimately shaped him into an individual who was both more and less than his legend." Publ Wkly
Includes bibliographical references

Legler, Casey

★ Legler, Casey. **Godspeed**; a memoir. Casey Legler. Atria Books, an imprint of Simon & Schuster, Inc. 2018 176 p. (hardcover) $25   **92**
1. Alcoholism 2. Drug addicts 3. Women swimmers -- United States -- Biography 4. Conduct of life 5. Olympics -- History -- 20th century
ISBN 9781501135750

LC 2018022193

In this memoir, by Casey Legler, "at fifteen, . . . Legler is already one of the fastest swimmers in the world. She is also an alcoholic, isolated from her family, and incapable of forming lasting connections with those around her. . . . In searing, evocative, visceral prose, Casey gives language to loneliness in this startling story of survival, defiance, and of the embers that still burn when everything else in us goes dark." (Publisher's note)

"A coming-of-age drama captured through poetic prose and convincing honesty." Kirkus

Leiber, Jerry, 1933-2011

Leiber, Jerry. **Hound** dog; the Leiber & Stoller autobiography. [by] Jerry Leiber and Mike Stoller with David Ritz. Simon & Schuster 2009 322p il $25 **92**

1. Composers 2. Lyricists 3. Songwriters 4. Rock music -- History and criticism

ISBN 978-1-4165-5938-2; 1-4165-5938-8

LC 2008-47821

"Collaboration is a messy business. So is autobiography. But it shouldn't be forgotten that Leiber and Stoller were among the pioneers who helped bring black and white musical forms together. It has been a historically fraught process, but the collision of cultures is probably what has given such energy and tension to American music. Hound Dog is an important part of that story." N Y Times Book Rev

Includes bibliographical references

Leiris, Antoine

Leiris, Antoine. **You** Will Not Have My Hate; Antoine Leiris. Penguin Group USA 2016 144 p. photograph (ebook) $65; $23 **92**

1. Widowers 2. Terrorism 3. Death in literature 4. Motherless families 5. Fathers in literature 6. Terrorism in literature 7. Paris Terrorist Attacks, Paris, France, 2015

ISBN 9780735222144; 0735222118; 9780735222113

LC 2016035301

This memoir, by Antoine Leiris, "is the rare and unforgettable testimony of a survivor, and a universal message of hope and resilience. Leiris confronts an incomprehensible pain with a humbling generosity and grandeur of spirit. He is a guiding star for us all in these perilous times. His message--hate will be vanquished by love--is eternal." (Publisher's note)

"Courageous and inspirational, without a wasted word." Kirkus

Lenin, Vladimir Il'ich, 1870-1924

Pomper, Philip. **Lenin's** brother; the origins of the October Revolution. W.W. Norton & Co. 2010 276p il $24.95 **92**

1. Heads of state 2. Revolutionaries 3. Communist leaders 4. Political leaders 5. Soviet Union -- History -- 1917-1921, Revolution

ISBN 978-0-393-07079-8

LC 2009-27390

"In 1887, the future leader of the Russian revolution, Vladimir Ulyanov (later Lenin), was 17 when his 21-year-old brother was hanged for his role in a bungled attempt to assassinate Czar Alexander III. Historians consider this the seminal event that launched Lenin's career as a revolutionary. . . . [The author] delivers an absorbing and surprisingly detailed account of Alexander Ulyanov's short life and even shorter career (four months) as a terrorist." Publ Wkly

Includes bibliographical references

Sebestyen, Victor. **Lenin**; the man, the dictator, and the master of terror. Victor Sebestyen. Pantheon 2017 xix, 569 p.p illustrations, maps (hardcover: alkaline paper) $35 **92**

1. Dictators -- Soviet Union -- Biography 2. Revolutionaries -- Soviet Union -- Biography 3. Soviet Union -- Politics and government -- 1917-1936 4. State-sponsored terrorism -- Soviet Union -- History

ISBN 9781101871645; 9781101871638

LC 2017008076

This biography of Vladimir Ilyich Lenin, by Victor Sebestyen, "is not only a political examination of one of the most important historical figures of the twentieth century but also a fascinating portrait of Lenin the man. . . . With Lenin's personal papers and those of other leading

political figures now available, Sebestyen gives us new details that bring to life the dramatic and gripping story of how Lenin seized power in a coup and ran his revolutionary state." (Publisher's note)

"Sebestyen is to be commended for bringing the true Lenin to life for historians to consider. His study will rank with those of Richard Pipes and Robert Service in modern historiography." Choice

Includes bibliographical references (pages 519-547) and index.

Lennon, John, 1940-1980

Greenberg, Keith Elliot. **December** 8, 1980; the day John Lennon died. Backbeat Books 2010 240p il $24.99 **92**

1. Singers 2. Rock musicians 3. Songwriters

ISBN 978-0-87930-963-3

LC 2010-31425

"Greenberg's definitive and unforgettable inquiry into John Lennon's death illuminates the cruel mysteries of madness, and, more resonantly, all the qualities that made Lennon such an exceptional and compelling artist." Booklist

Includes bibliographical references

Norman, Philip. **John** Lennon; the life. Ecco HarperCollins 2008 851p il $34.95; pa $19.99 **92**

1. Singers 2. Rock musicians 3. Songwriters

ISBN 978-0-06-075401-3; 0-06-075401-X; 978-0-06-075402-0 pa; 0-06-075402-8 pa

LC 2008-4684

This is a biography of the singer-songwriter and author of In His Own Write (1964), A Spaniard in the Works (1965), and Lennon Remembers (1971).

This work's "ambitious range proves to be its strength, enveloping you in ways that a quicker read could not. . . . [This] is a gift of a book, heartfelt and heart-rending." Christ Sci Monit

Riley, Tim. **Lennon**; the man, the myth, the music--the definitive life. Hyperion 2011 765p il $35 **92**

1. Singers 2. Rock musicians 3. Songwriters 4. Biography, Individual

ISBN 978-1-4013-2452-0; 1-4013-2452-5

LC 2011-15657

"Here is Lennon in the fullness of his diffracted personality, across the spectrum of his phases and faces. Leather John, mugging sailors in Hamburg — 'A Lennon punch felled him to his knees' — is superseded by Beatle John, mugging for the world's press. . . . Beatle John contains both 'Ed Sullivan' John, yodeling harmonies and bending his knees in awkward demi-pliés, and 'Revolver' John, acidhead, sleepyhead, drug dormouse, singing in that cold little cocoon voice (Riley calls it 'time-frozen') about floating downstream and not wanting to be woken up. Then there's 'Imagine' John, the drooping sage. And finally, of course, John the martyr." N Y Times Book Rev

Includes bibliographical references and discography

Lennox, Margaret Douglas, Countess of, 1515-1578

Weir, Alison. The **lost** Tudor princess; the life of Margaret Douglas of Scotland. Alison Weir. Ballantine Books 2016 576 p. illustrations, maps (hardcover: alk. paper) $30 **92**

1. Great Britain -- History -- 1485-1603, Tudors 2. Nobility -- Great Britain -- Biography 3. Nobility -- Great Britain -- History -- 16th century 4. Great Britain -- History -- Tudors, 1485-1603 -- Biography

ISBN 9780345521392

LC 2015037958

This book, by Alison Weir, offers a "biography of Margaret Douglas, the beautiful, cunning niece of Henry VIII of England who used her sharp intelligence and covert power to influence the succession after the death of Elizabeth I. . . . Lady Margaret Douglas, Countess of Lennox, was an important figure in Tudor England, yet today, while her contemporaries—Anne Boleyn, Mary, Queen of Scots, Elizabeth I—have achieved celebrity status, she is largely forgotten." (Publisher's note)

"An abundantly detailed history from an author steeped in England's past." Kirkus

Includes bibliographical references and index

Lenz, Frank, d. 1894

Herlihy, David V. The **lost** cyclist; the epic tale of an American adventurer and his mysterious disappearance. [by] David V. Herlihy. Houghton Mifflin Harcourt 2010 326p il map **92**
1. Cycling 2. Photographers 3. Cyclists 4. Murder victims 5. Retail personnel 6. Biography, Individual
ISBN 0-547-19557-5; 0-547-52198-7 pa; 978-0-547-19557-5; 978-0-547-52198-5 pa

LC 2009-28857

This is a biography of "Frank Lenz, a 24-year-old wheelman [who] departed New York in 1892 to round the globe. . . . [Lenz disappeared in] eastern Turkey, in the midst of a Turkish and Kurdish campaign that would kill some 10,000 Armenian civilians." (N Y Times Book Rev) Index.

"This well-researched and stylishly written book puts Lenz back in the public eye as well as offering readers a look at the very early days of modern cycling." Booklist

Leonardo, da Vinci, 1452-1519

Aquino, Lucia. **Leonardo** Da Vinci; preface by Mario Pomilio; [translation, Miriam Hurley] Rizzoli 2005 173p il (Art classics) pa $9.95 **92**
1. Artists 2. Painters 3. Scientists 4. Artists, Italian 5. Writers on science
ISBN 978-0-8478-2677-3; 0-8478-2677-5

LC 2004-099908

This book "features a literary introduction and . . . description of a selection of the artist's masterpieces. . . . [It also includes] a visual chart with captions as to the whereabouts of each painting and a . . . bibliography." Publisher's note

Includes bibliographical references

★ Isaacson, Walter. **Leonardo** da Vinci; Walter Isaacson. Simon & Schuster 2017 599 p. (hardback) $35 **92**
1. Artists, Italian 2. Artists -- Italy -- Biography 3. Scientists -- Italy -- Biography 4. Gifted persons -- Italy -- Biography
ISBN 9781501139161; 9781501139178; 9781501139154

LC 2017020817

This book, by Walter Isaacson, "brings Leonardo da Vinci to life in this exciting new biography. Based on thousands of pages from Leonardo's astonishing notebooks and new discoveries about his life and work, Walter Isaacson weaves a narrative that connects his art to his science. He shows how Leonardo's genius was based on skills we can improve in ourselves, such as passionate curiosity, careful observation, and an imagination so playful that it flirted with fantasy." (Publisher's note)

"Encompassing in its coverage, robust in its artistic explanations, yet written in a smart, conversational tone, this is both a solid introduction to the man and a sweeping saga of his genius." Booklist.

Includes bibliographical references and index.

White, Michael. **Leonardo**; the first scientist. St. Martin's Press 2000 370p il $27.95; pa $16.95 **92**
1. Artists 2. Painters 3. Scientists 4. Artists, Italian 5. Writers on science

ISBN 0-312-20333-0; 0-312-27026-7 pa

The author "focuses on the scientific creations of da Vinci, emphasizing his notebooks, which had been lost for 200 years and only portions of which have been recovered. White describes how da Vinci's personal life affected his scientific discoveries and predictions, and vice versa." Booklist

Lerner, Betsy

Lerner, Betsy. The **bridge** ladies; a memoir. Betsy Lerner. Harper Wave 2016 320 p. (hardback) $25.99 **92**
1. Bridge (Game) 2. Female friendship 3. Intergenerational relations 4. Mother-daughter relationship 5. Female friendship -- United States 6. Women bridge players -- United States 7. Mothers and daughters -- United States 8. Intergenerational relations -- United States 9. Literary agents -- United States -- Biography 10. Bridge clubs -- Social aspects -- United States 11. Older women -- United States -- Social life and customs
ISBN 9780062354464; 9780062467164

LC 2015043022

In this memoir, by Betsy Lerner, "a fifty-year-old Bridge game provides an unexpected way to cross the generational divide between a daughter and her mother. . . . Lerner finds herself back in her childhood home, not five miles from the mother she spent decades avoiding. When Roz needs help after surgery, it falls to Betsy to take care of her. She expected a week of tense civility; what she got instead were the Bridge Ladies." (Publisher's note)

"This beautifully written, bittersweet story of ladies of a certain age and era will have wide appeal." Pub Wkly

Lessing, Doris May, 1919-2013

★ Lessing, Doris May. **Under** my skin; volume one of my autobiography, to 1949. {by} Doris Lessing. HarperCollins Pubs. 1994 419p il hardcover o.p. pa $15 **92**
1. Authors 2. Novelists 3. Dramatists 4. Essayists 5. Short story writers 6. Nobel laureates for literature
ISBN 0-06-092664-3 pa

LC 94-20051

"In this immediate, vivid, beautifully paced memoir, Doris Lessing sets the individual against history, the personal against the general, and shows, by the example of her own life set down honestly, how biography and fiction mesh, how fiction transmutes the personal to the general, how the particular experience illuminates the universe." London Rev Books

Levi, Primo, 1919-1987

Angier, Carole. The **double** bond: Primo Levi, a biography. Farrar, Straus & Giroux 2002 xxvi, 898p il $40; pa $20 **92**
1. Poets 2. Authors 3. Chemists 4. Novelists 5. Holocaust survivors 6. Essayists 7. Memoirists 8. Short story writers
ISBN 0-374-11315-7; 0-374-52898-5 pa

This is a biography of the Italian Jewish chemist and writer. Levi was the author of The Periodic Table, Survival in Auschwitz, The Drowned and the Saved and Other People's Trades

"Angier's long, gripping narrative of Levi's time in Auschwitz synthesizes the best of his memoirs, poetry, fiction, essays, and scientific writing. . . . A compelling biography and a must for all Holocaust collections." Booklist

Includes bibliographical references

Levy, Ariel

Levy, Ariel. The **rules** do not apply; a memoir. Ariel Levy. Random House 2017 xi, 207 p.p (hardback: acid-free paper) $27 **92**

1. Women journalists -- Biography 2. Lesbians -- United States -- Biography 3. Sex role -- United States 4. Miscarriage -- United States 5. Life change events -- United States 6. Young women -- United States -- Biography 7. Women journalists -- United States -- Biography
ISBN 9780812996937; 9780812996944

LC 2016043502

In this memoir, "when thirty-eight-year-old New Yorker writer Ariel Levy left for a reporting trip to Mongolia in 2012, she was pregnant, married, financially secure, and successful on her own terms. A month later, none of that was true. Levy picks you up and hurls you through the story of how she built an unconventional life and then watched it fall apart with astonishing speed." (Publisher's note)

"Levy's generous portrait of modern feminism—at turns bleak, heartrending, inspired, and hopeful—speaks strongly and directly to readers." Booklist

Levy, Deborah

Levy, Deborah, 1959- The **cost** of living; a working autobiography. Deborah Levy. St. Martin's Press 2018 144 p. $20
92
1. Autobiography 2. American poets -- Biography
ISBN 163557191X; 9781635571912

LC 2018125825

"In this 'living autobiography' infused with warmth and humor, Deborah Levy critiques the roles that society assigns to us, and reflects on the politics of breaking with the usual gendered rituals. What does it cost a woman to unsettle old boundaries and collapse the social hierarchies that make her a minor character in a world not arranged to her advantage? Levy draws on her own experience of attempting to live with pleasure, value, and meaning." (Publisher's note)

"This timely look at how women are viewed (and often dismissed) by society will resonate with many readers, but particularly with those who have felt marginalized or undervalued." Pub Wkly

Lewin, W. H. G. (Walter H. G.)

★ Goldstein, Warren. **For** the love of physics; from the end of the rainbow to the edge of time--a journey through the wonders of physics. [by] Walter Lewin and Warren Goldstein. Free Press 2011 302p il $26; ebook $12.99
92
1. Physicists 2. Physics -- Study and teaching 3. Colleges and universities -- Faculty
ISBN 978-1-4391-0827-7; 978-1-4391-2354-6 ebook

LC 2010-47737

"MIT's Lewin is deservedly popular for his memorable physics lectures . . . and this quick-paced autobiography-cum-physics intro fully captures his candor and lively teaching style. . . . [This text] glows with energy and should please a wide range of readers." Publ Wkly

Lewis, C. S. (Clive Staples), 1898-1963

McGrath, Alister E., 1953- **C.** S. Lewis; a life: eccentric genius, reluctant prophet. Alister McGrath. Tyndale House Publishers 2013 350 p. (hc) $24.99
92
1. Authors -- Biography 2. Christian literature 3. Authors, English -- 20th century -- Biography
ISBN 9781414339351; 1414339356

LC 2012033140

This book, by Alister McGrath, is a biography of the 20th century Christian author and apologist Clive Staples Lewis. "After thoroughly examining recently published Lewis correspondence, Alister challenges some of the previously held beliefs about the exact timing of Lewis's shift from atheism to theism and then to Christianity. [The author] paints a portrait of an eccentric thinker who became an inspiring, though reluctant, prophet for our times." (Publisher's note)

Includes bibliographical references and index

Lewis, Jerry, 1926-2017

Lewis, Jerry. **Dean** & me; a love story. Doubleday 2005 340p il $26.95
92
1. Actors 2. Singers 3. Comedians 4. Television personalities 5. Motion picture directors
ISBN 0-7679-2086-4

LC 2005-49682

"This is a wild, joyous book, but also a heartbreaking one." N Y Times Book Rev

Lewis, John, 1940-

★ Lewis, John. **March**; Book Two. by John Lewis and Andrew Aydin; illustrated by Nate Powell. Top Shelf Productions 2015 192 p. chiefly ill. (pbk) $19.95
92
1. African Americans -- Civil rights -- Graphic novels 2. Civil rights movements 3. African American legislators 4. Legislators -- United States 5. African Americans -- Civil rights 6. African American civil rights workers 7. Civil rights workers -- United States 8. Autobiographical comic books, strips, etc.
ISBN 9781603094009; 1603094008

LC 2015004150

Eisner Award: Best Reality-Based Work (2016)
Eisner Nominee: Best Publication for Teens (2016)
Ignatz Nominee: Outstanding Series (2015)
This graphic novel, by John Lewis and Andrew Aydin, illustrated by Nate Powell, "takes us behind the scenes of some of the most pivotal moments of the Civil Rights Movement. . . . After the success of the Nashville sit-in campaign, John Lewis is more committed than ever to changing the world through nonviolence -- but as he and his fellow Freedom Riders board a bus into the vicious heart of the deep south, they will be tested like never before." (Publisher's note)

"Heroism and steadiness of purpose continue to light up Lewis' frank, harrowing account of the civil rights movement's climactic days. . . . The contrast between the dignified marchers and the vicious, hate-filled actions and expressions of their tormentors will leave a deep impression on readers." Kirkus

★ Lewis, John R., 1940- **March**; Book One. John Lewis; [co-written by] Andrew Aydin; [art by] Nate Powell. Top Shelf Productions 2013 121 p. chiefly ill. (acid-free paper) $14.95
92
1. African Americans -- Civil rights -- Graphic novels 2. Civil rights movements -- United States -- Comic books, strips, etc
ISBN 9781603093002

LC 2013218903

Coretta Scott King (Author) Honor Book (2014)
This graphic novel, by U.S. congressman John Lewis, "in collaboration with co-writer Andrew Aydin and New York Times best-selling artist Nate Powell . . . spans John Lewis' youth in rural Alabama, his life-changing meeting with Martin Luther King, Jr., the birth of the Nashville Student Movement, and their battle to tear down segregation through nonviolent lunch counter sit-ins, building to a . . . climax on the steps of City Hall." (Publisher's note)

"This is superb visual storytelling that establishes a convincing, definitive record of a key eyewitness to significant social change." SLJ

★ Lewis, John R., 1940- **March**; Book Three. by John Lewis and Andrew Aydin; illustrated by Nate Powell. Top Shelf

Productions 2016 256 p. chiefly illustrations pbk $19.99 **92**

1. Civil rights -- United States
ISBN 9781603094023; 1603094024
YALSA Award for Excellence in Nonfiction for Young Adults (2017)
Eisner Award: Best Reality-Based Work (2017)
Printz Award (2017)
National Book Award: Young People's Literature (2016)
Sibert Informational Book Award (2017)
Coretta Scott King (Author) Book Award (2017)

This book is the "conclusion of the award-winning and best-selling March trilogy. Congressman John Lewis, an American icon and one of the key figures of the civil rights movement, joins co-writer Andrew Aydin and artist Nate Powell to bring the lessons of history to vivid life for a new generation, urgently relevant for today's world." (Publisher's note)

"Though Lewis and Aydin throw a lot at readers in this volume, their message, helped along seamlessly and splendidly by Powell's fantastic, cinematic artwork, is abundantly clear: the victories of the civil rights movement, symbolized in particular by Barack Obama's inauguration, are hard-won and only succeeded through the dogged dedication of a wide variety of people." Booklist

Li, Charles N., 1940-

Li, Charles N. The **bitter** sea; coming of age in a China before Mao. HarperCollins Publishers 2008 283p il hardcover o.p. pa $14.99 **92**

1. Anthropologists 2. Linguists 3. College teachers 4. China -- History -- 1949-
ISBN 978-0-06-134664-4; 0-06-134664-0; 978-0-06-170954-8 pa; 0-06-170954-9 pa

LC 2007-25697

The author, "who had an extraordinary life growing up in pre-Communist China, shares his story of betrayal, loss, hope, and triumph in this lyrical account. . . . This brilliant memoir is as much about modern Chinese history as it is about familial relationships." Libr J

Li, Leslie, 1945-

Li, Leslie. **Daughter** of heaven; a memoir with earthly recipes. Arcade Pub. 2005 274p $25; pa $13.95 **92**

1. Chinese cooking
ISBN 1-55970-768-2; 1-55970-800-X pa

LC 2004-23452

The book centers on the author's "relationship with both her father and Nai-nai, her grandmother, who lands in New York City for an extended visit. . . . In stories and in the nearly 20 recipes (including Drunken Chicken and Cantonese Fried Rice), Li reveals the tale of an Asian woman caught between many different worlds and times and places." Booklist

Li, Yiyun, 1972-

Yiyun Li. **Dear** friend, from my life I write to you in your life; Yiyun Li. Random House Inc 2017 224 p. (hardback) $27 **92**

1. Depression (Psychology) 2. American authors -- Biography 3. Authors, American -- 21st century -- Biography 4. Depressed persons -- United States -- Biography
ISBN 9780399589096

LC 2016017675

This autobiography describes how "Yiyun Li grew up in China and has spent her adult life as an immigrant. . . . She has been a scientist, an author, a mother, a daughter--and through it all she has been sustained by a profound connection with the writers and books she loves. . . . Interweaving personal experiences with a wide-ranging homage to her most cherished literary influences, Yiyun Li confronts the two most essential questions of her identity: Why write? And why live?" (Publisher's note)

Liddell, Eric, 1902-1945.

Hamilton, Duncan. **For** the Glory; Eric Liddell's Journey from Olympic Champion to Modern Martyr. Duncan Hamilton. Penguin Group USA 2016 400 p. illustrations (hardcover) $28 **92**

1. Christian biography
ISBN 9781594206207; 1594206201

This book, by Duncan Hamilton, offers the "inspiring story of Eric Liddell, hero of [The film] 'Chariots of Fire,' from his Olympic medal to his missionary work in China to his last, brave years in a Japanese work camp during WWII. . . . Liddell ran--and lived--for the glory of his God. After winning gold, he dedicated himself to missionary work. He travelled to China to work in a local school and as a missionary." (Publisher's note)

"Poignant and tragic yet stimulating, Liddell's personality leaps off the pages and will draw in all readers, from history and sports enthusiasts to casual fans of nonfiction." LJ

Includes bibliographical references (pages 359-376) and index.

Lightman, Alan P., 1948-

Lightman, Alan P., 1948- **Screening** room; a memoir. Alan Lightman. Pantheon Books 2014 272 p. illustrations (hard cover: alk. paper) $25.95 **92**

1. Family life 2. Memphis (Tenn.) -- History
ISBN 9780307379399; 0307379396

LC 2013049341

In this memoir, by Alan P. Lightman, describes life in "Memphis[, Tennessee] from the 1930s through the 1960s that includes the early days of the movies and a powerful grandfather whose ghost remains an ever-present force in the lives of his descendants. . . . At the heart of it all is a family haunted by the memory of its domineering patriarch and the author's struggle to understand his conflicted loyalties." (Publisher's note)

"The cumulative effect of Lightman's memories is wrenching: Loss and illness and death wander freely in his pages, reminding us of the evanescence of youth and promise. The author shows us many small moments, igniting each with sparks of passion, memory and intelligence." Kirkus

Lincoln, Abraham, 1809-1865

Blumenthal, Sidney, 1948- A **self**-made man; the political life of Abraham Lincoln, 1809-1849. Sidney Blumenthal. Simon & Schuster 2016 576 p. illustrations (The Political Life of Abraham Lincoln) (hardback) $35 **92**

1. Politicians -- United States 2. Presidents -- United States -- Biography 3. United States -- Politics and government -- 1815-1861
ISBN 147677725X; 9781476777252; 9781476777269

LC 2015027339

This biography of Abraham Lincoln by Sideny Blumenthanl "describes a socially awkward suitor. His marriage to the upper class Mary Todd was crucial to his social aspirations and his political career. Blumenthal's robust portrayal is based on prodigious research of Lincoln's record and of the period and its main players. It reflects both Lincoln's time and the struggle that consumes our own political debate." (Publisher's note)

"In this engrossing life-and-times study of the formative years of Abraham Lincoln (1809–65), before he became a national figure, political journalist and historian Blumenthal (The Strange Death of Republican America) takes the reader deep into Illinois and national politics to locate the character and content of Lincoln's ideas, interests, and identity, and to understand his driving ambition to succeed in law and politics. In doing so, the author makes the important point that Lincoln gained empathy and understanding of "the people" from his own self-awareness and need to escape his own origins of relative poverty and hard struggle. . . . If Blumenthal sometimes loses Lincoln in his detailed accounting of patronage, politicking, and personalities, great and small, he effectively shows that the president's Illinois was a proving ground for the politics of expansion, economic development, nativism, anti-Mormonism, and slavery that both reflected and affected national concerns. Lincoln, the self-made man, is revealed as tried-and-true, ready for the troubled times that came in the years leading up to the Civil War." LJ

Includes bibliographical references and index

Blumenthal, Sidney, 1948- **Wrestling** with his angel; 1849-1856. Sidney Blumenthal. Simon & Schuster 2017 xx, 581 p.p Vol. 2 illustrations (The Political Life of Abraham Lincoln) (hardcover) $35   **92**
1. Presidents -- United States 2. Presidents -- United States -- Biography 3. Illinois -- Politics and government -- To 1865 4. Lawyers -- Illinois -- Springfield -- Biography 5. United States -- Politics and government -- 1815-1861
ISBN 9781501153785; 9781501153808; 1501153781
LC 2015027339
In this book author Sidney Blumenthal, "explains how [Abraham] Lincoln and his friends operate behind the scenes to destroy the anti-immigrant party in Illinois to clear the way for a new Republican Party. Lincoln takes command and writes its first platform and vaults onto the national stage as the leader of a party that will launch him to the presidency." (Publisher's note)

"A painstakingly researched portrait of the political landscape as the country inched toward civil war." Kirkus

Includes bibliographical references and index.

Brookhiser, Richard. **Founders'** son; a life of Abraham Lincoln. Richard Brookhiser. Basic Books 2014 376 p. 8 plates; color illustrations (hardcover) $27.99   **92**
1. Presidents -- United States 2. United States -- Politics and government -- 1861-1865 3. Presidents -- United States -- Biography
ISBN 046503294X; 9780465032945
LC 2014021173
In this book, "historian Richard Brookhiser presents a compelling new biography of Abraham Lincoln that highlights his lifelong struggle to carry on the work of the Founding Fathers. Following Lincoln from his humble origins in Kentucky to his assassination in Washington, D.C., Brookhiser shows us every side of the man: laborer, lawyer, congressman, president; storyteller, wit, lover of ribald jokes; depressive, poet, friend, visionary." (Publisher's note)

"This highly accessible read will appeal most to readers who desire to learn more about Lincoln and especially the ideas, dogmas, and dreams that moved him to his public career and life in the White House." LJ

Includes bibliographical references and index

Burlingame, Michael. **Abraham** Lincoln; a life. Johns Hopkins University Press 2008 2v il set $125   **92**
1. Lawyers 2. Presidents 3. State legislators 4. Members of Congress 5. Biography, Individual 6. Presidents -- United States
ISBN 0-8018-8993-6; 978-0-8018-8993-6
LC 2007-52919
In this 2-volume set on U.S. President Abraham Lincoln, "volume 1 covers Lincoln's early childhood, his experiences as a farm boy in Indiana and Illinois, his legal training, and the political ambition that led

to a term in Congress in the 1840s. In volume 2, [Michael] Burlingame examines Lincoln's life during his presidency and the Civil War, narrating . . . the crisis over Fort Sumter and Lincoln's own battles with relentless office seekers, hostile newspaper editors, and incompetent field commanders." (Publisher's note)

The author "has produced the finest Lincoln biography in more than 60 years. . . . Future Lincoln books cannot be written without it, and from no other book can a general reader learn so much about Abraham Lincoln." Publ Wkly

Includes bibliographical references

Carwardine, Richard. **Lincoln**: a life of purpose and power. Knopf 2006 394p il map $27.50   **92**
1. Lawyers 2. Presidents 3. State legislators 4. Members of Congress 5. Presidents -- United States 6. United States -- History -- 1861-1865, Civil War
ISBN 1-4000-4456-1
LC 2005047230
First published 2003 in the United Kingdom
This book "is not only analytical and smart, it's also delightfully readable—and it will surely emerge as one of the most important Lincoln books to be published this decade." Publ Wkly

Includes bibliographical references

Donald, David Herbert. **Lincoln**. Simon & Schuster 1995 714p il maps hardcover o.p. pa $20   **92**
1. Lawyers 2. Presidents 3. State legislators 4. Members of Congress 5. Presidents -- United States
ISBN 0-684-80846-3; 0-684-82535-X pa
LC 95-4782
This biography examines: "Lincoln's relationship with his father; his romance with Ann Rutledge; his bouts of 'hypo,' which amounted at times almost to clinical depression; his marriage; his political ambition; his attitudes toward slavery and black people; his relations with radical Republicans during the Civil War; the mistakes and successes of his wartime leadership." Atl Mon

Includes bibliographical references

Freehling, William W., 1935- **Becoming** Lincoln; William W. Freehling. University of Virginia Press 2018 384 p. (cloth: alk. paper) $29.95   **92**
1. Presidents -- United States -- Biography
ISBN 9780813941561
LC 2017061669
In this book, historian William Freehling "emphasizes the prewar years [of Abraham Lincoln], revealing how Lincoln came to be the extraordinary leader who would guide the nation through its most bitter chapter. . . . [It] traces Lincoln from his tough childhood . . . , a superb lawyer, a canny two-party politician, a great orator, a failed state legislator, and a losing senatorial candidate, to a winning presidential contender and a besieged six weeks as a pre-war president." (Publisher's note)

"Built on Freehling's vast knowledge of the time period, this commendable biography shows the geographical division of opinions leading up to war and the life events that made the man who saved the union." Kirkus

Includes bibliographical references and index

★ Goodwin, Doris Kearns, 1943- **Team** of rivals; the political genius of Abraham Lincoln. Simon & Schuster 2005 916p il map $35   **92**
1. Lawyers 2. Governors 3. Presidents 4. Senators 5. Attorneys general 6. State legislators 7. Members of Congress 8. Secretaries of state 9. Biography, Individual 10. Supreme Court justices

11. Presidential candidates 12. Presidents -- United States 13. Secretaries of the treasury 14. United States -- Politics and government -- 1861-1865
ISBN 0-684-82490-6

LC 2005-44615

"The knowledge gained here about these three significant figures who well attended Lincoln gain for the reader an even keener appreciation of the rare individual that he was." Booklist

Includes bibliographical references

Holzer, Harold. **Lincoln** president-elect; Abraham Lincoln and the great secession winter 1860-1861. Simon & Schuster 2008 623p il $30 **92**
1. Lawyers 2. Presidents 3. State legislators 4. Members of Congress 5. Presidents -- United States
ISBN 978-0-7432-8947-4; 0-7432-8947-1

LC 2008-21520

"This excellent study fills a gap about which not much has been written in Lincoln's presidential career." Choice

Includes bibliographical references

Keneally, Thomas. **Abraham** Lincoln. Viking 2003 183p (Penguin lives series) hardcover o.p. pa $14 **92**
1. Lawyers 2. Presidents 3. State legislators 4. Members of Congress 5. Presidents -- United States 6. United States -- History -- 1861-1865, Civil War
ISBN 0-670-03175-5; 0-14-311475-1 pa

LC 2003-268078

"Keneally's Lincoln is a self-actuated farm boy made good by self-discipline, savvy instincts, wit, the wisdom acquired from courtrooms, friendships, and political huckstering—and luck . . . [The author] recounts Lincoln's early missteps in romance, business, and politics and his self-doubts and depression as his star dimmed several times, and he concedes Lincoln's erratic course toward emancipation and a successful strategy for Union victory during the Civil War . . . This is an epic compressed into a tightly written biography that all Americans might read with profit. Keneally's occasional tendency to let folklore stand as fact notwithstanding, there is no better brief introduction to Lincoln and his American dream." Libr J

Kunhardt, Philip B. **Looking** for Lincoln; the making of an American icon. [by] Philip B. Kunhardt III, Peter W. Kunhardt and Peter W. Kunhardt, Jr.; foreword by David Herbert Donald; introduction by Doris Kearns Goodwin. Alfred A. Knopf 2008 494p il $50 **92**
1. Lawyers 2. Presidents 3. State legislators 4. Members of Congress 5. Presidents -- United States
ISBN 978-0-307-26713-9; 0-307-26713-X

LC 2008-14193

Sequel to: Lincoln: an illustrated biography
"The Kunhardts' book represents a visual and literary feast for all devotees of the sacred national idol that is Lincoln." Publ Wkly

Includes bibliographical references

The **Lincoln** anthology; great writers on his life and legacy from 1860 to now. edited by Harold Holzer. Library of America 2009 964p il $40 **92**
1. Lawyers 2. Presidents 3. State legislators 4. Members of Congress 5. Presidents -- United States
ISBN 978-1-59853-033-9; 1-59853-033-X

LC 2008-934337

This "is a solid compilation of work on Abraham Lincoln from a diverse selection of writers in various genres, celebrating his extensive legacy and providing insight from a number of angles and time periods." Publ Wkly

Includes bibliographical references

Lind, Michael. **What** Lincoln believed; the values and convictions of America's greatest president. Doubleday 2005 358p $27.95 **92**
1. Lawyers 2. Presidents 3. State legislators 4. Members of Congress 5. Presidents -- United States
ISBN 0-385-50739-9

LC 2004-41333

"Some readers may not recognize their own cherished Lincoln in Lind's well-researched and reasoned book. Yet it adds a valuable perspective to the vast arena of Lincoln scholarship." Christ Sci Monit

Includes bibliographical references

Marvel, William (Author) **Lincoln's** autocrat; the life of Edwin Stanton. William Marvel. University of North Carolina Press 2015 632 p. illustrations (Civil War America) (cloth: alk. paper) $35 **92**
1. Reconstruction (1865-1876) 2. Statesmen -- United States -- Biography 3. United States -- Politics and government -- 19th century 4. United States -- History -- 1861-1865, Civil War -- Biography 5. United States. War Department -- Biography 6. Cabinet officers -- United States -- Biography 7. Reconstruction (U.S. history, 1865-1877) -- Biography 8. United States -- Politics and government -- 1861-1865 9. United States -- Politics and government -- 1865-1869 10. United States -- History -- Civil War, 1861-1865 -- Biography
ISBN 1469622491; 9781469622491

LC 2014032690

This biography, by William Marvel, focuses on "Edwin M. Stanton, . . . Lincoln's Secretary of War during most of the Civil War and under Johnson during the early years of Reconstruction. . . . Climbing from a difficult youth to the pinnacle of power, Stanton used his authority--and the public coffers--to pursue political vendettas, and he exercised sweeping wartime powers with a cavalier disregard for civil liberties." (Publisher's note)

"A complex work that will appeal to Civil War scholars and general readers who want a deeper treatment of Stanton than found in Doris Kearns Goodwin's Team of Rivals." LJ

Includes bibliographical references and index

★ McPherson, James M. **Abraham** Lincoln. Oxford University Press 2009 79p $12.95 **92**
1. Lawyers 2. Presidents 3. State legislators 4. Members of Congress 5. Presidents -- United States
ISBN 978-0-19-537452-0; 0-19-537452-5

LC 2008-35623

"McPherson, America's leading authority on Lincoln and his times, demonstrates his complete command of his subject in this concise but remarkably rich and perceptive biography. . . . This little book is bigger than its pages and should be in every library, schoolhouse, and home." Libr J

Includes bibliographical references

★ McPherson, James M., 1936- **Tried** by war; Abraham Lincoln as commander in chief. Penguin Press 2008 329p il map hardcover o.p. pa $17 **92**
1. Lawyers 2. Presidents 3. State legislators 4. Members of Congress 5. Presidents -- United States 6. Executive power --

United States -- History 7. United States -- History -- 1861-1865, Civil War 8. United States -- History -- Civil War, 1861-1865 9. United States -- Politics and government -- 1861-1865
ISBN 0-14-311614-2 pa; 1-594-20191-9; 978-0-14-311614-1 pa; 978-1-594-20191-2

LC 2008-25229

This is an account of the ways in which Lincoln "worked with, or against, his senior commanders to defeat the Confederacy and reshape the presidential role." (Publisher's note) Index.

This book "is a perfect primer, not just for Civil War buffs or fans of Abraham Lincoln, but for anyone who wishes to understand the evolution of the president's role as commander in chief." N Y Times Book Rev
Includes bibliographical references

★ **Our** Lincoln; new perspectives on Lincoln and his world. edited by Eric Foner. W.W. Norton 2008 336p il   **92**
1. Lawyers 2. Presidents 3. State legislators 4. Members of Congress 5. Presidents -- United States 6. United States -- History -- 19th century 7. United States -- History -- Civil War, 1861-1865 8. United States -- Politics and government -- 1861-1865
ISBN 0-393-06756-4; 9780393067569

LC 2008-17096

"Twelve essays present the ideas of recent historians on Lincoln's evolving views on race, religion, and civil liberties, his military leadership, his family, photographs and portraits of Lincoln, and the use of his memory in the 21st century." (Publisher's note) Index.

Historians "collectively situate Lincoln's ideas, interests, and policies and the meanings various people from abolitionists to neo-Confederates have found in Lincoln, from the microscopic to a wider historical context of politics, culture, and memory. Essays explore such topics as presidential leadership, civil liberties, citizenship and rights, democratic politics, mass-produced imagery, African colonization, antislavery, race, religion, family life, writing sensibilities and style, and the need to claim Lincoln for one's own cause. The eloquent and compelling results show how and why Lincoln was both a man of his time and a man for all time." Libr J
Includes bibliographical references

Pinsker, Matthew. **Lincoln's** sanctuary; Abraham Lincoln and the Soldiers' Home. Oxford University Press 2003 256p il maps hardcover o.p. pa $17.95   **92**
1. Lawyers 2. Presidents 3. State legislators 4. Members of Congress 5. Presidents -- United States 6. United States Soldiers' and Airmen's Home (Washington, D.C.)
ISBN 0-19-516206-4; 978-0-19-517985-9 pa; 0-19-517985-4 pa

LC 2003-1215

The author "follows the War President to his 'retreat' at the Soldiers' Home away from the daily noise, posturing, and politicking of the capital and finds there a serenity that allowed Lincoln to relax with his family, think through issues, conduct secret meetings with allies and enemies, and reinvigorate his resolve. . . . Through Pinsker's probing inquiry into sources heretofore surprisingly underused, the ever elusive private Lincoln comes into new light. A book for our time and for all libraries." Libr J

Sandburg, Carl. **Abraham** Lincoln: The prairie years and The war years; illustrated ed; Harcourt Brace Jovanovich 1970 640p il maps hardcover o.p. pa $26   **92**
1. Lawyers 2. Presidents 3. Frontier and pioneer life 4. State legislators 5. Members of Congress 6. Presidents -- United States 7. United States -- History -- 1861-1865, Civil War
ISBN 0-15-602752-6 pa
First published 1954

A condensation of the two volumes of "The prairie years" (1926) and the four volumes of "The war years" (1939). The author has taken advantage of material made available since the original volumes were published to include in this edition of his lifetime study of Lincoln

"A biography that as a whole is superior to the longer life. This one volume has a form which the six lacked. It is a tighter and tidier book. It retains the superb qualities of the original work without the faults of the latter." Saturday Rev
Includes bibliographical references

Shenk, Joshua Wolf. **Lincoln's** melancholy; how depression challenged a president and fueled his greatness. Houghton Mifflin 2005 350p $25   **92**
1. Lawyers 2. Presidents 3. State legislators 4. Members of Congress 5. Presidents -- United States
ISBN 0-618-55116-6

LC 2005-9653

"An estimable contribution to the Lincoln literature." Booklist
Includes bibliographical references

★ Stahr, Walter. **Stanton**; Lincoln's war secretary. Walter Stahr. Simon & Schuster 2017 xix, 743 p.p illustrations (hardback) $35   **92**
1. Reconstruction (1865-1876) 2. United States -- History -- 1861-1865, Civil War 3. Statesmen -- United States -- Biography 4. United States. War Department -- Biography 5. Cabinet officers -- United States -- Biography 6. Reconstruction (U.S. history, 1865-1877) -- Biography 7. United States -- Politics and government -- 1861-1865 8. United States -- Politics and government -- 1865-1869 9. United States -- History -- Civil War, 1861-1865 -- Biography
ISBN 9781476739328; 9781476739304; 9781476739311

LC 2017022628

This book, by Walter Stahr, "tells the story of Abraham Lincoln's indispensable Secretary of War, Edwin Stanton, the man the president entrusted with raising the army that preserved the Union. . . . Stanton raised, armed, and supervised the army of a million men who won the Civil War. . . . . He directed military movements from his telegraph office. . . . He arrested and imprisoned thousands for 'war crimes.'" (Publisher's note)

"A lively, lucid, and opinionated history, and his research supports his skepticism on some historical claims. The book should be Stanton's definitive biography for some time to come." Kirkus
Includes bibliographical references and index

Symonds, Craig L. **Lincoln** and his admirals; Abraham Lincoln, the U.S. Navy, and the Civil War. Oxford University Press 2008 430p il $27.95   **92**
1. Lawyers 2. Presidents 3. State legislators 4. Military officials 5. Members of Congress 6. Government officials 7. Newspaper executives 8. United States -- Navy 9. Secretaries of the navy 10. State government officials 11. Presidents -- United States 12. United States -- History -- 1861-1865, Civil War -- Naval operations
ISBN 978-0-19-531022-1; 0-19-531022-5

LC 2008-4251

"For scholars and the general reader alike, an insightful and highly readable treatment of a neglected dimension of Lincoln's wartime leadership." Kirkus
Includes bibliographical references (p. 407-416)

Van Sciver, Noah. The **Hypo**; The Melancholic Young Lincoln. Noah Van Sciver. Fantagraphics 2012 192 p. chiefly ill. $24.99   **92**

1. Depression (Psychology) 2. Biographical graphic novels
ISBN 1606996193; 9781606996195

This graphic novel, by Noah Van Sciver, "is based on [Abraham] Lincoln's battle with depression. . . . [It] follows the twenty-something Abraham Lincoln as . . . a rising Whig in the state's legislature as he arrives in Springfield, IL to practice law. . . . But, as time passes and uncertainty creeps in, young Lincoln is forced to battle a dark cloud of depression brought on by a chain of defeats and failures culminating into a nervous breakdown that threatens his life and sanity." (Publisher's note)

"A thoroughly engaging graphic novel that seamlessly balances investigation and imagination." Pub Wkly

White, Ronald C. **A.** Lincoln; a biography. Random House Pub. Group 2009 796p il map $35   **92**
1. Lawyers 2. Presidents 3. State legislators 4. Members of Congress 5. Presidents -- United States 6. United States -- Politics and government -- 1861-1865
ISBN 978-1-4000-6499-1

LC 2008-28840

In this biography, the author "follows the familiar trajectory of the 16th President's life; what's unique is his insight into the moral and intellectual framework of Lincoln's thinking. . . . An exceptional work that belongs in every public and academic library." Libr J

Includes bibliographical references (p. [745]-764) and index.

White, Ronald C. The **eloquent** president: a portrait of Lincoln through his words; [by] Ronald C. White, Jr. Random House 2005 xxiii, 448p il $26.95; pa $15.95   **92**
1. Lawyers 2. Presidents 3. State legislators 4. Members of Congress 5. Presidents -- United States
ISBN 1-400-06119-9; 0-8129-7046-2 pa

LC 2004-50766

The author "traces Lincoln's evolving rhetoric over the course of his presidency in a series of highly detailed critical essays. He follows Lincoln from the cautious, lawyerly text of the First Inaugural to the soaring, triumphant poetics of the Gettysburg Address." Publ Wkly

Includes bibliographical references

Lincoln, Mary Todd, 1818-1882

Clinton, Catherine. **Mrs.** Lincoln; a life. HarperCollins 2009 415p il $26.99   **92**
1. Spouses of presidents 2. Presidents' spouses -- United States
ISBN 978-0-06-076040-3; 0-06-076040-0

The author "sifts through the many criticisms of Mary Lincoln to offer a sensitive reassessment that debunks unjust attacks and reveals Mrs. Lincoln's many strengths—charitableness, devotion to family and nation, unwavering love and encouragement for her beleaguered husband—alongside the mental illness and flaws of temperament for which she is better known. . . . Written in a style that will appeal to the general reader, Clinton's book features sufficient nuance to satisfy scholars looking for a greater interpretation of the life of this controversial historical figure." Libr J

Includes bibliographical references

Lindbergh, Anne Morrow, 1906-2001

Hertog, Susan. **Anne** Morrow Lindbergh; a biography. Talese 1999 561p il hardcover o.p. pa $17   **92**
1. Poets 2. Authors 3. Novelists 4. Diarists 5. Essayists 6. Memoirists 7. Spouses of prominent persons
ISBN 0-385-72007-6 pa

LC 99-28759

After her marriage to Charles Lindbergh, Anne Morrow "soon recognized the difficulty of reconciling her literary ambitions with ac-

companying her husband as copilot, navigator and radio operator. After the tragic kidnapping and death of their first child, which they blamed in part on dogged press coverage of their personal life, the Lindberghs moved abroad. They became embroiled with the leaders of Nazi Germany, according to Hertog, because Charles believed that the democratic system was weak and ineffectual. . . . This sympathetic portrayal of Anne as a wife, mother, poet and feminist may well find a readership more interested in a talented woman's creative struggle than in the oft-told Lindbergh story." Publ Wkly

Includes bibliographical references

Lindbergh, Reeve. **Under** a wing; a memoir. Delta Trade Paperbacks 1999 223p il pa $15   **92**
1. Poets 2. Authors 3. Generals 4. Novelists 5. Air pilots 6. Diarists 7. Essayists 8. Memoirists 9. Air force officers 10. Children's authors 11. Spouses of prominent persons 12. Children of prominent persons
ISBN 978-0-385-33444-0; 0-385-33444-3

First published 1998 by Simon & Schuster

"A rare memoir whose goal is not to expose but finally to understand." Libr J

Winters, Kathleen C. **Anne** Morrow Lindbergh; first lady of the air. Palgrave Macmillan 2006 241p il map $24.95 **92**
1. Poets 2. Authors 3. Novelists 4. Diarists 5. Essayists 6. Memoirists 7. Spouses of prominent persons
ISBN 978-1-4039-6932-3; 1-4039-6932-9

LC 2006-43290

This book focuses on Anne Morrow Lindbergh's career as an aviator. "She was one of the earliest female pilots, as well as the first American female glider pilot, and a radio operator. . . . Winters shows in great detail that Lindbergh accomplished this under the glare of an unremitting spotlight, and in the company of an often-demanding spouse. That the author is able to bring something new to the Lindbergh story is impressive, and she does it through both technical explanations of Lindbergh's accomplishments and Anne's own words about her flying exploits, marriage, and writing." Booklist

Includes bibliographical references

Lindbergh, Charles, 1902-1974

Kessner, Thomas. The **flight** of the century; Charles Lindbergh & the rise of American aviation. Oxford University Press 2010 313p il map (Pivotal moments in American history) **92**
1. Generals 2. Air pilots 3. Memoirists 4. Air force officers 5. Biography, Individual 6. Aeronautics -- United States -- History
ISBN 0-19-532019-0; 978-0-19-532019-0

LC 2010-06082

Thomas Kessner's book examines "how and why Lindbergh elicited so much popular excitement and what his status as an international hero meant for the development of aviation." (J Am Hist) Index.

"In May 1927 at the age of 25, the 'Lone Eagle' flew from New York to Paris, a startling accomplishment that made the awkward, reticent aviator the world's best-known person. But Lindbergh lived until 1974, and two elements were added to his legacy — he was the father whose tiny son was kidnapped and slain by Bruno Hauptmann, and, much worse for his reputation, he was the fascist-tinged advocate of U.S. neutrality before World War II. . . . [Kessner's book] aims to balance the equation. His book recaps Lindbergh's epochal flight and carries it forward, discussing his subsequent role in the aviation boom that followed. While there is nothing particularly earth-shattering about what he has written, Kessner's fresh perspective breathes new life into Lindbergh's tale." Philadelphia Inquirer

Includes bibliographical references and index

Lindbergh, Reeve. **Under** a wing; a memoir. Delta Trade Paperbacks 1999 223p il pa $15   **92**
1. Poets 2. Authors 3. Generals 4. Novelists 5. Air pilots 6. Diarists 7. Essayists 8. Memoirists 9. Air force officers 10. Children's authors 11. Spouses of prominent persons 12. Children of prominent persons
ISBN 978-0-385-33444-0; 0-385-33444-3
First published 1998 by Simon & Schuster
"A rare memoir whose goal is not to expose but finally to understand." Libr J

Lindbergh, Reeve

Lindbergh, Reeve. **Under** a wing; a memoir. Delta Trade Paperbacks 1999 223p il pa $15   **92**
1. Poets 2. Authors 3. Generals 4. Novelists 5. Air pilots 6. Diarists 7. Essayists 8. Memoirists 9. Air force officers 10. Children's authors 11. Spouses of prominent persons 12. Children of prominent persons
ISBN 978-0-385-33444-0; 0-385-33444-3
First published 1998 by Simon & Schuster
"A rare memoir whose goal is not to expose but finally to understand." Libr J

Linder, Joselin

Linder, Joselin, 1975- The **family** gene; a mission to turn my deadly inheritance into a hopeful future. Joselin Linder. Ecco Press 2017 261 p. ills., genealogical table (hardcover) $28.99   **92**
1. Medical genetics 2. Genetic disorders 3. Disease susceptibility -- Genetic aspects
ISBN 0062378899; 9780062378897; 9780062378927
In this book, author Joselin Linder tells the story of her family's deadly gene: "the lives it claimed and the future of genomic medicine with the potential to save those that remain. Digging into family records and medical history, conducting interviews with relatives and friends, and reflecting on her own experiences . . . , Joselin pieces together the lineage of this deadly gene to write a gripping and unforgettable exploration of family, history, and love." (Publisher's note)
"Linder's narrative is a combination of a fascinating medical detective story and an absorbing, powerfully written family chronicle." Kirkus
Includes bibliographical references (pages 251-257).

Lindgren, Astrid, 1907-2002

Astrid Lindgren; the woman behind Pippi Longstocking. Jens Andersen, translated by Caroline Waight. Yale University Press 2018 360 p. $30   **92**
1. Women authors -- Biography
ISBN 0300226101; 9780300226102
This biography of Astrid Lindgren, by Jens Andersen, translated by Caroline Waight, "provides a moving and revealing portrait of the beloved Scandinavian literary icon whose adventures of Pippi Longstocking have influenced generations of young readers all over the world. Lindgren's sometimes turbulent life as an unwed teenage mother, outspoken advocate for the rights of women and children, and celebrated editor and author is chronicled in fascinating detail." (Publisher's note)
"Andersen incisively and resonantly chronicles the evolution of Lindgren's progressive work and its impact, along with her influence as a children's-book editor and environmental activist, bringing to new light a writer as empowered and exhilarating as her most cherished cre-

ation." Booklist

Lindhout, Amanda

★ Corbett, Sara. A **house** in the sky; a memoir. Amanda Lindhout, Sara Corbett. Scribner 2013 373 p. (paperback) $16   **92**
1. Somalia 2. Hostages 3. Somalia -- History -- 1991- 4. Hostages -- Somalia -- Biography 5. Journalists -- Canada -- Biography
ISBN 1451645619; 9781451645606; 9781451645613
LC 2013016015
In this book, "Canadian journalist [Amanda] Lindhout gives . . . [an] account of her 459-day captivity at the hands of Somali Islamist rebels. . . . Convinced war-torn Somalia would be the 'hurricane' to make her career, in August 2008, at age 25, she . . . set off to view a displaced-persons' camp but was instead carjacked by a group of kidnappers. . . . Her captors moved her frequently from hideout to hideout, and she . . . was raped and tortured." (Publishers Weekly)
Includes bibliographical references and index

Link, Mardi

Link, Mardi. **Bootstrapper**; from broke to badass on a northern Michigan farm. Mardi Jo Link. Alfred A. Knopf 2013 272 p. (hardback) $24.95   **92**
1. Farmers 2. Divorced women 3. Autobiographies
ISBN 0307596915; 9780307596918; 9780307743589
LC 2012042425
In this memoir, author Mardi Jo Link details how following her divorce, "more broke than ever, [she] makes a seemingly impossible resolution: to hang on to her century-old farmhouse in northern Michigan and continue to raise her three boys on well water and wood chopping and dirt. Armed with an unfailing sense of humor and three resolute accomplices, Link . . . withstands any blow to her pride in order to preserve the life she wants." (Publisher's note)
"Link's pride in her sons and the life they have made shines throughout the book and is obviously well deserved. Neither sugarcoated nor wallowing in self-pity, Link's storytelling is as tough, honest, and unyielding as one would expect from a Michigan farmer. Her account, told with humor and panache, of pulling oneself up after disappointment and loss will appeal to the bootstrapper in all of us." Booklist

Link, Mardi Jo. The **Drummond** Girls; A Story of Fierce Friendship Beyond Time and Chance. Mardi Link. Grand Central Publishing 2015 272 p. illustrations, map (hardcover) $26   **92**
1. Women 2. Female friendship
ISBN 145555474X; 9781455554744
LC 2015010926
This book, by Mardi Jo Link, is a "memoir about the friendship between eight women forged over two decades. The eight Drummond Girls first met in 1991. . . . At the time, they were all waitresses, bartenders, or regular customers. When one of them got engaged, they celebrated with a trip to Drummond Island. . . . They've made this voyage every year since then as a way to retain a piece of their wild youth, despite the taming influence of marriage, motherhood, and management." (Publisher's note)
"Link ably portrays her initial sense of isolation and need for friendship, providing descriptions of the wilderness she has found on the island and her increasing allegiance to these women as they all gradually grow older and experience life events that change them forever. A moving, honest, and laughter-filled account of eight women who gather one weekend every year and enjoy themselves to the fullest." Kirkus

Linné, Carl von, 1707-1778

Blunt, Wilfrid. **Linnaeus,** the compleat naturalist; with an introduction by William T. Stearn. Princeton Univ. Press 2002 264p il maps $35   **92**

1. Botanists 2. Writers on science

ISBN 0-691-09636-8

First published 1971 by Viking with title: The compleat naturalist: a life of Linnaeus

This biography traces the Swedish scientist's life from his days as a poor student at Lund University through his scientific achievements and academic career at Uppsala

Includes bibliographical references

Lipska, Barbara K.

McArdle, Elaine. The **neuroscientist** who lost her mind; my tale of madness and recovery. Barbara K. Lipska with Elaine McArdle. Houghton Mifflin Harcourt 2018 208p. (hardcover) $25

1. Cancer 2. Mental illness 3. Brain -- Cancer 4. Neuroscientists -- Biography 5. Melanoma -- Patients -- Biography 6. Brain metastasis -- Patients -- Biography

ISBN 9781328787309

LC 2017046211

In this book, author Barbara K. "Lipska describes her extraordinary ordeal and its lessons about the mind and brain. She explains how mental illness, brain injury, and age can change our behavior, personality, cognition, and memory. She tells what it is like to experience these changes firsthand. And she reveals what parts of us remain, even when so much else is gone." (Publisher's note)

Includes bibliographical references and index

Liptrot, Amy

Liptrot, Amy. The **outrun;** Amy Liptrot. W W Norton & Co. 2017 xiv, 280 p.p maps (hardcover) $25.95   **92**

1. Alcoholics 2. Orkney (Scotland) -- History 3. Women alcoholics -- Rehabilitation 4. Orkney (Scotland) -- Social life and customs

ISBN 9780393609004; 0393608964; 9780393608960

LC 2016039760

In this memoir, "when Amy Liptrot returns to Orkney after more than a decade away, she is drawn back to the Outrun on the sheep farm where she grew up. Approaching the land that was once home, memories of her childhood merge with the recent events that have set her on this journey. . . . She moved to London and found herself in a hedonistic cycle. Unable to control her drinking, alcohol gradually took over." (Publisher's note)

"Whether she writes of walking along the wind-scoured coasts or taking polar-bear dips in the icy waters, her prose is spare, lean, and beautiful, much like the country about which she writes." Booklist

Lispector, Clarice, 1925-1977

Moser, Benjamin. **Why** this world; a biography of Clarice Lispector. Oxford University Press 2009 479p il $29.95 **92**

1. Authors 2. Novelists 3. Journalists 4. Women authors 5. Short story writers 6. Biography, Individual

ISBN 0-19-538556-X; 978-0-19-538556-4

LC 2008-55639

This is a biography of the Brazilian novelist.

"Lispector makes a difficult, often lurid subject, and Moser's account of her life is riveting—he draws extensively on previously untranslated letters and criticism (he does the translations himself, from Yiddish, German, French and Portuguese); at times the book reads like a gothic horror story." Nation

Includes bibliographical references

Lithgow, John, 1945-

Lithgow, John, 1945- **Drama;** an actor's education. John Lithgow. Harper 2011 $26.99; $12.99   **92**

1. Actors -- United States -- Biography

ISBN 978-0-06-173497-7; 978-0-06-209773-6 ebook; 9780061734977

LC 2011008172

"More than the run-of-the-mill 'And then I met . . . And then I was in . . .' actor's autobiography, this is both a memoir full of emotion and a cautionary tale." Libr J

Little Richard

White, Charles. The **life** and times of Little Richard; the quasar of rock. Updated ed; Da Capo Press 1994 282p il pa $16   **92**

1. Singers 2. Rock musicians 3. African American musicians

ISBN 0-306-80552-9; 978-0-306-80552-3

LC 93-48054

First published 1984 by Harmony Bks.

This biography of the American singer discusses "his flamboyant stage antics; his blatant flaunting of racial taboos; his sexual experiences; his bewildering career that careened between show business and the church; and exactly how he created the music that would become a symbol of rebellion for kids all over the world." Publisher's note

Includes discography and filmography

Lively, Penelope, 1933-

Lively, Penelope. A **house** unlocked. Grove Press 2002 225p il $23; pa $13   **92**

1. Authors 2. Novelists 3. Children's authors 4. Short story writers

ISBN 0-8021-1712-0; 0-8021-4007-6 pa

LC 2001-55745

First published 2001 in the United Kingdom

"The British novelist Penelope Lively spent her early childhood in Egypt, but it was her school holidays at Golsoncott—a manor house that her grandparents bought in the wilds of Somerset, in 1923—that shaped her life. In this slim, beguiling book, Lively describes the contents and customs of the house. . . . By meticulously tracing the provenance of these objects, she re-creates the life they once furnished." New Yorker

Includes bibliographical references

Lively, Penelope, 1933-

Life in the garden; Penelope Lively. Viking 2018 208 p. (hardback) $25   **92**

1. Gardening 2. English novelists 3. Gardens in literature 4. Novelists, English -- 20th century -- Biography

ISBN 9780525558378

LC 2018013220

"Penelope Lively takes up her key themes of time and memory, and her lifelong passions for art, literature, and gardening in this philosophical and poetic memoir. From the courtyards of her childhood home in Cairo to a family cottage in Somerset, to her own gardens in Oxford and London, Lively conducts an expert tour, taking us from Eden to Sissinghurst and into her own backyard, . . . while imparting her own sly and spare wisdom." (Publisher's note)

Lloyd Webber, Andrew, 1948-

Lloyd Webber, Andrew, 1948- **Unmasked;** Andrew Lloyd

Weber. HarperCollins 2018 viii, 517 p.p illustrations (some color) (hardcover) $28.99 **92**

    1. Musicals 2. Performing arts 3. Composers -- Biography 4. Composers -- England -- Biography

    ISBN 9780062424204; 9781540027665; 0062424203

                      LC 2017568260

    In this memoir, composer Andrew Lloyd Webber, "takes stock of his achievements, the twists of fate and circumstance which brought him both success and disappointment, and the passions that inspire and sustain him. . . . Lloyd Webber looks back at the development of some of his most famous works and illuminates his collaborations with luminaries such as Tim Rice, Robert Stigwood, . . . and Trevor Nunn." (Publisher's note)

Lobdell, William

    Lobdell, William. **Losing** my religion; how I lost my faith reporting on religion in America--and found unexpected peace. Collins 2009 291p $25.99 **92**

    1. Journalists 2. Bloggers

    ISBN 978-0-06-162681-4; 0-06-162681-3

                      LC 2008-24010

    "Lobdell's spiritual journey fascinates, not least on account of the irony of his trajectory from agnosticism to belief to atheism while covering religion. It's a story that may raise eyebrows among believers and nonbelievers alike." Booklist

    Includes bibliographical references

Lobo, Julio, 1898-1983

    Rathbone, John Paul. The **sugar** king of Havana; the rise and fall of Julio Lobo, Cuba's last tycoon. Penguin Press 2010 304p il map $27.95 **92**

    1. Sugar 2. Businessmen 3. Cuba -- History 4. Agribusiness executives

    ISBN 978-1-59420-258-2; 1594202583

                      LC 2010-13790

    "An exceptionally rich portrait not only of an empire and its progenitor but Cuba itself, and the economic legacy of Castro's revolution, the loss of capital, and the end of Cuba's 'great age of sugar.'" Publ Wkly

    Includes bibliographical references

Locke, Alain, 1885-1954

    ★ Stewart, Jeffrey C. The **new** Negro; the life of Alain Locke. Jeffrey C. Stewart. Oxford University Press 2018 xii, 932 p.p (hardcover: acid-free paper) $39.95 **92**

    1. Harlem Renaissance 2. African Americans -- Intellectual life 3. African American arts -- History 4. African American philosophers -- Biography 5. African American intellectuals -- Biography 6. African American college teachers -- Biography

    ISBN 9780195089578

                      LC 2017026626

    National Book Award: Nonfiction (2018)

    In this book author Jeffrey C. Stewart "offers the definitive biography of the father of the Harlem Renaissance, based on the extant primary sources of his life and on interviews with those who knew him personally. He narrates the education of [Alain] Locke. . . . Stewart's thought-provoking biography recreates the worlds of this illustrious, enigmatic man who, in promoting the cultural heritage of Black people, became--in the process--a New Negro himself." (Publisher's note)

    Includes bibliographical references (pages 879-914) and index.

Lockwood, Belva Ann, 1830-1917

    Norgren, Jill. **Belva** Lockwood; the woman who would be president. New York University Press 2007 311p il $40; pa $22 **92**

    1. Lawyers 2. Suffragists 3. Lecturers 4. Biography, Individual 5. Presidential candidates 6. Women in politics -- United States

    ISBN 0-8147-5834-7; 0-8147-5851-7 pa; 978-0-8147-5834-2; 978-0-8147-5851-9 pa

                      LC 2006-34486

    This is a biography of Belva Lockwood, a lawyer and suffragist who twice ran for president. Index.

    "Those with interests in women's, political, social, and cultural history will enjoy Lockwood." Choice

    Includes bibliographical references

Lockwood, Patricia

    Lockwood, Patricia, 1982- **Priestdaddy**; a memoir. Patricia Lockwood. Riverhead Books 2017 352 p. hardcover $27 **92**

    1. American poets -- Biography 2. Poets, American -- 21st century -- Biography 3. Authors, American -- 21st century -- Biography

    ISBN 1594633738; 9781594633737

                      LC 2016029241

    Kirkus Prize Finalist: Nonfiction (2017)

    In this book author Patricia Lockwood "interweaves emblematic moments from her childhood and adolescence--from an ill-fated family hunting trip and an abortion clinic sit-in where her father was arrested to her involvement in a cultlike Catholic youth group-with scenes that chronicle the eight-month adventure she and her husband had in her parents' household after a decade of living on their own. Lockwood details her education of a seminarian who is also living at the rectory." (Publisher's note)

    "Lockwood magically combines laugh-aloud moments with frank discussions of social issues and shows off her poet's skills with lovely, metaphor-filled descriptions that make this memoir shine." Booklist

Lomax, Alan, 1915-2002

    Szwed, John F. **Alan** Lomax; the man who recorded the world. Viking 2010 438p $29.95 **92**

    1. Authors 2. Folk music 3. Folklorists 4. Musicologists 5. Writers on music 6. Biography, Individual

    ISBN 978-0-670-02199-4

                      LC 2010-15332

    This is a biography of the American folklorist and ethnomusicologist. This "biography is a worthy testament to Lomax's passions and ideals, which gifted the world some of the most important American recordings ever made." New Statesman

    Includes bibliographical references

Lombardi, Vince

    Maraniss, David. **When** pride still mattered: a life of Vince Lombardi. Simon & Schuster 1999 541p il hardcover o.p. pa $16 **92**

    1. Football coaches 2. Green Bay Packers (Football team)

    ISBN 0-684-77018-5 pa

                      LC 99-37859

    "From Lombardi's formative years as a player and coach at Fordham University through assistantships with West Point and the Giants and, finally, to his tenure as head coach of the Packers, Maraniss presents a portrait of a complicated human being who was a great teacher but a mediocre listener, an effective psychologist despite being rife with flaws." Publ Wkly

    Includes bibliographical references

London, Jack, 1876-1916

Adam, Philip. **Jack** London, photographer; [by] Jeanne Campbell Reesman, Sara S. Hodson, & Philip Adam. University of Georgia Press 2010 271p il $49.95　　**92**

1. Authors 2. Novelists 3. Photographers 4. Authors, American 5. Short story writers

ISBN 978-0-8203-2967-3

LC 2010005973

"This book will be of great appeal to a broad range of audiences interested in history, American literature, and photography." Libr J

Includes bibliographical references

Labor, Earle. **Jack** London; an American life. Earle Labor. Farrar Straus & Giroux 2013 480 p. (hardback) $30　　**92**

1. American authors -- Biography 2. Authors, American -- 19th century -- Biography 3. Authors, American -- 20th century -- Biography

ISBN 0374178488; 9780374178482

LC 2012050948

This book presents a biography of writer Jack London. "Born in San Francisco in 1876 to an impoverished single mother, London . . . took up factory work to support his household while still a child, and by age 18 had worked as an oyster pirate, sailor, and rail-riding hobo. Omnivorous reading and sporadic education fueled his desire to write, and a year spent surviving the Yukon Gold Rush (1897-1898) provided him with inspiration for his earliest nonfiction and fiction." (Publishers Weekly)

Includes bibliographical references and index

Longworth, Alice Roosevelt, 1884-1980

Cordery, Stacy A. **Alice**; Alice Roosevelt Longworth, from White House princess to Washington power broker. Viking 2007 590p il $32.95　　**92**

1. Socialites 2. Children of presidents

ISBN 978-0-670-01833-8

LC 2006-103087

This is a biography of Alice Roosevelt Longworth, the Washington hostess and author of Crowded Hours (1933).

The author "pens an authoritative, intriguing portrait of a first daughter who broke the mold." Publ Wkly

Includes bibliographical references (p. [555]-572) and index.

Louis XIV, King of France, 1638-1715

Fraser, Antonia. **Love** and Louis XIV; the women in the life of the Sun King. Nan A. Talese/Doubleday 2006 xxviii, 388p il $32.50　　**92**

1. Kings

ISBN 978-0-38550984-8; 0-385-50984-7

LC 2006-44674

This is an account of Louis XIV's relationships with his wife and his mistresses.

"One of the most enveloping popular histories of the current publishing season." Booklist

Includes bibliographical references

Louis, Joe, 1914-1981

Roberts, Randy. **Joe** Louis; hard times man. Yale University Press 2010 308p il $27.50　　**92**

1. African American athletes 2. Boxing -- History 3. Boxing -- Biography 4. Biography, Individual

ISBN 978-0-300-12222-0

LC 2010-15422

In this biography of the American boxer, "Roberts handles the box-ing action with professional aplomb, and he knows when to cut away to tell us something of consequence and when to return to the ring. The author ably chronicles Louis's rise from Alabama cotton fields to the cavernous Yankee Stadium, where celebrities glittered in the ringside seats for his big fights; the development of the mass media (boxing was enormously popular on radio); Louis's career in the U.S. Army; and his sad decline, amid unpayable debts and mental illness. All legendary athletes should hope for treatment by such capable, compassionate hands." Kirkus

Includes bibliographical references and index

Lovelace, Ada King, Countess of, 1815-1852

Essinger, James. **Ada's** algorithm; how Lord Byron's daughter Ada Lovelace launched the digital age. James Essinger. Melville House 2014 272 p. illustrations (hardback) $25.95　　**92**

1. Computers -- History 2. Women mathematicians 3. Mathematicians -- Biography 4. Computers -- History -- 19th century 5. Mathematicians -- Great Britain -- Biography 6. Women mathematicians -- Great Britain -- Biography

ISBN 1612194087; 9781612194080

LC 2014021837

In this book, author James Essinger "makes the case that the computer age could have started two centuries ago if [Ada] Lovelace's contemporaries had recognized her research and fully grasped its implications. . . . [S]tarting with the outrageous behavior of her father [Lord Byron], which made Ada instantly famous upon birth. Ada would go on to overcome numerous obstacles to obtain a level of education typically forbidden to women of her day." (Publisher's note)

"Essinger (Spellbound: The Surprising Origins and Astonishing Secrets of English Spelling, 2007, etc.) presents Ada's story with great enthusiasm and rich detail, painting her life as one that was rich with opportunity and access but stifled by sexism. Ada continues to inspire, and by using her own voice via letters and research, the author brings her to life for a new generation of intrepid female innovators. A robust, engaging and exciting biography." Kirkus

Includes bibliographical references and index

Loy, Myrna

Leider, Emily W. **Myrna** Loy; the only good girl in Hollywood. [by] Emily W. Leider. University of California Press 2011 411p il $34.95　　**92**

1. Actors

ISBN 978-0-520-25320-9; 0-520-25320-5

LC 2011-11571

"Loy's gifts are easy to enjoy, hard to describe. She's been lucky in attracting an even-tempered sympathetic biographer like Ms. Leider, whose book, like the best of its genre, sends you back to the films." Wall Street J

Includes bibliographical references

Lucarelli, Leonardo, 1977-

Lucarelli, Leonardo. **Mincemeat**; Leonardo Lucarelli; translated from the Italian by Lorena Rossi Gori and Danielle Rossi. Other Press 2016 320 p. (hardcover) $25.95　　**92**

1. Cooks -- Italy -- Biography 2. Restaurateurs -- Italy -- Biography

ISBN 9781590517918

LC 2016017657

This book, by Leonardo Lucarelli, translated by Lorena Rossi Gori and Danielle Rossi, takes readers "through the underbelly of Italy's restaurant world. Lucarelli is a professional chef who for almost two decades has been roaming Italy opening restaurants, training underpaid, sometimes hopelessly incompetent sous-chefs, courting waitresses, working long hours, riding high on drugs, and cursing a culinary passion he inherited as a teenager from his hippie father." (Publisher's note)

"Wise and often very funny, the book offers sumptuous glimpses into human foibles and provides readers an unforgettable taste of the unabashedly sordid realities that underlie the high-gloss world of Italian cuisine. A wickedly candid memoir." Kirkus

Lucas, George, 1944-

★ Jones, Brian Jay. **George** Lucas; a life. Brian Jay Jones. Little, Brown & Co. 2016 560 p. illustrations (chiefly color) (ebook) $96; (hc) $32 **92**

1. Motion picture producers and directors -- Biography
ISBN 9780316257435; 9780316257442

LC 2016941644

This biography of filmmaker George Lucas, by Brian Jay Jones, presents "a long-awaited, revelatory look into the life and times of the man who created Luke Skywalker, Han Solo, and Indiana Jones. . . . Lucas's colleagues and competitors offer tantalizing glimpses into his life. His entire career has been stimulated by innovators including Steven Spielberg and Francis Ford Coppola, actors such as Harrison Ford, and the very technologies that enabled the creation of his films." (Publisher's note)

"Masterful and essential for film and pop culture enthusiasts." Booklist

Includes bibliographical references (pages 479-529), filmography (pages 529-530), and index.

Luce, Henry Robinson, 1898-1967

★ Brinkley, Alan. The **publisher**; Henry Luce and his American century. Alfred A. Knopf 2010 531p il $35 **92**

1. Journalists 2. Publishers and publishing 3. Magazine editors 4. Magazine executives
ISBN 978-0-679-41444-5; 0-679-41444-4

LC 2009-38834

"In this superb biography Alan Brinkley . . . has told the curiously depressing story of a brilliant man who got everything wrong, including so many of the things that mattered most to him. Mr Brinkley has an eye for both the telling detail and the broad sweep of Luce's role as the man who saw the need for a national news magazine and foresaw the American century." Economist

Includes bibliographical references

Luther, Martin, 1483-1546

Hendrix, Scott H. **Martin** Luther; visionary reformer. Scott H. Hendrix. Yale University Press 2015 368 p. illustrations, maps (cl: alk. paper) $35 **92**

1. Reformation 2. Reformation -- Germany -- Biography
ISBN 9780300166699; 0300166699

LC 2015017636

This book, by Scott H. Hendrix, is an "account of the life of Martin Luther [that] provides a new perspective on one of the most important religious figures in history, focusing on Luther's entire life, his personal relationships and political motivations, rather than on his theology alone. Relying on the latest research and quoting extensively from Luther's correspondence, Hendrix paints a richly detailed portrait of an extraordinary man who, while devout and courageous, had a dark side as well." (Publisher's note)

"This carefully documented, fast-paced telling will delight readers of biography, history, and fiction; historians, theologians, and psychologists may gain deeper insights into how flaws in personality and the zeitgeist itself often prejudice the pursuit of truth." LJ

Includes bibliographical references and index.

Metaxas, Eric. **Martin** Luther; the man who rediscovered God and changed the world. Eric Metaxas. Viking 2017 xiii, 480 p.p illustrations (some color) (hardcover) $30 **92**

1. Protestantism 2. Monks -- Biography 3. Luther, Martin, 1483-1546 -- Juvenile literature
ISBN 9781101980033; 9781101980019

LC 2017025388

This book, by Eric Metaxas, tells the story of Martin Luther, "whose adamantine faith cracked the edifice of Western Christendom and dragged medieval Europe into the future. . . . Luther's monumental faith and courage gave birth to the ideals of liberty, equality, and individualism that today lie at the heart of all modern life." (Publisher's note)

"A masterful portrait of a seminal figure." Booklist

Includes bibliographical references (pages 453-464) and index.

Roper, Lyndal. **Martin** Luther; renegade and prophet. Lyndal Roper. Random House Inc 2017 608 p. $40.00 **92**

1. Reformation -- Germany -- Biography 2. Lutheran Church -- Germany -- Clergy -- Biography
ISBN 9780812996197

LC 2016027660

This biography of Martin Luther, by Lyndal Roper, "goes beyond Luther's theology to investigate the inner life of the religious reformer who has been called 'the last medieval man and the first modern one.' . . . Luther was a brilliant writer whose biblical translations had a lasting impact on the German language. Yet he was also a strident fundamentalist whose scathing rhetorical attacks threatened to alienate those he might persuade." (Publisher's note)

"This volume will be of great appeal to scholars, but it is also extremely readable and will find a welcome audience among history enthusiasts." Pub Wkly

Includes bibliographical references and index

Schilling, Heinz. **Martin** Luther; rebel in an age of upheaval. Heinz Schilling, translated by Rona Johnston. Oxford University Press 2017 576 p. (hardback) $39.95 **92**

1. Protestantism -- History 2. Reformation -- Germany -- Biography
ISBN 9780198722816

LC 2016958734

In this biography, by Heinz Schilling, translated by Rona Johnston, "we see [Martin] Luther as a rebel, but not as a lone hero; as a soldier in a mighty struggle for the universal reform of Christianity and its role in the world. The foundation of Protestantism changed the religious landscape of Europe, and subsequently the world, but the author chooses to show Luther not simply as a reformer, but as an individual." (Publisher's note)

Wilson, Derek A. **Out** of the storm; the life and legacy of Martin Luther. [by] Derek Wilson. St. Martin's Press 2008 399p il $29.95 **92**

1. Reformation 2. Theologians 3. Social reformers 4. Religious leaders 5. Writers on religion 6. Europe -- Church history
ISBN 978-0-312-37588-1; 0-312-37588-3

LC 2007-39331

"A nuanced portrait of a perplexing titan." Booklist

Includes bibliographical references

Luxenberg, Steve

Luxenberg, Steve. **Annie's** ghosts; a journey into a family secret. Hyperion Books 2009 401p il $24.99 **92**

1. Newspaper editors
ISBN 978-1-4013-2247-2; 1-4013-2247-6

LC 2008-55661

"Part memoir, part mystery, part history of the mental-health movement, . . . [this] is a fascinating account of a life lived in the shadows." Booklist

Includes bibliographical references

Lynch, David, 1946-

Lynch, David, 1946- **Room** to dream; by David Lynch and Kristine McKenna. Random House 2018 xii, 577 p.p illustrations (hardcover) $32   **92**

1. Actors -- United States -- Biography 2. Motion picture producers and directors -- United States -- Biography
ISBN 9780399589195; 9780399589201; 0399589198

LC 2017058580

"In this unique hybrid of biography and memoir, [filmmaker] David Lynch opens up for the first time about a life lived in pursuit of his singular vision, and the many heartaches and struggles he's faced to bring his unorthodox projects to fruition. Lynch's lyrical, intimate, and unfiltered personal reflections riff off biographical sections written by close collaborator Kristine McKenna." (Publisher's note)

"An incandescently detailed and complexly enlightening chronicle of a fervent, uncompromising life devoted to 'pure creativity.'" Booklist

Includes bibliographical references, filmography, and index.

Lynn, Loretta

Lynn, Loretta. **Still** woman enough; a memoir. {by} Loretta Lynn with Patsi Bale Cox. Hyperion 2002 244p il $24.95; pa $7.99   **92**

1. Singers 2. Country musicians 3. Songwriters
ISBN 0-7868-6650-0; 0-7868-8987-X pa

In this sequel to Coal miner's daughter, "Lynn mostly focuses on her marriage and the trials and pleasures of Nashville stardom, including fond recollections of friends like Conway Twitty and Tammy Wynette. . . Though her grammar may make purists flinch . . . Lynn's literary voice is as natural and endearing as her songs." Publ Wkly

Lythcott-Haims, Julie

Lythcott-Haims, Julie. **Real** American; a memoir. Julie Lythcott-Haims. Henry Holt & Co. 2017 288 p. (hardcover) $27   **92**

1. United States -- Race relations 2. Racially mixed people -- United States -- Biography 3. Reston (Va.) -- Biography 4. New York (N.Y.) -- Biography 5. Palo Alto (Ca.) -- Biography 6. Standford (Ca.) -- Biography 7. Race -- Social aspects -- United States 8. Racially mixed people -- Race identity -- United States 9. Racially mixed people -- United States -- Social conditions
ISBN 9781250137746

LC 2017009272

In this memoir, author Julie Lythcott-Haims describes "her personal battle with the low self-esteem that American racism routinely inflicts on people of color. The only child of a marriage between an African-American father and a white British mother, she shows indelibly how so-called 'micro' aggressions in addition to blunt force insults can puncture a person's inner life with a thousand sharp cuts." (Publisher's note)

"A compelling and important addition to any collection of personal narratives by women of color." (LJ)

Maathai, Wangari, 1940-2001

Maathai, Wangari. **Unbowed**; a memoir. [by] Wangari Muta Maathai. Knopf 2006 314p il hardcover o.p. pa $15 **92**

1. Biologists 2. Conservationists 3. Environmentalists 4. Kenya 5. Nobel laureates for peace 6. Green Belt Movement (Kenya)
ISBN 0-307-26348-7; 978-0-307-26348-3; 0-307-27520-5 pa; 978-0-307-27520-2 pa

LC 2006-44729

"Nobel Peace Prize winner Maathai tells the unforgettable story of her Kenya girlhood, struggles as a biologist and professor, and founding of the Green Belt Movement to restore Kenya's decimated forests and provide women with work." Booklist

MacArthur, Douglas, 1880-1964

Borneman, Walter R., 1952- **Macarthur** at war; world war II in the Pacific. Walter R. Borneman. Little, Brown & Co. 2016 608 p. illustrations, maps (hc) $30   **92**

1. World War, 1939-1945
ISBN 0316405329; 9780316405324

LC 2016931808

This book, by Walter R. Borneman, is the "definitive account of General Douglas MacArthur's rise during World War II. . . . Architect of stunning triumphs and inexplicable defeats, General MacArthur is the most intriguing military leader of the twentieth century. There was never any middle ground with MacArthur. This in-depth study of the most critical period of his career shows how MacArthur's influence spread far beyond the war-torn Pacific." (Publisher's note)

"An able researcher and fluent writer, Borneman holds solid appeal for the military history audience." Booklist

Includes bibliographical references (pages 561-577) and index.

Frank, Richard B. **MacArthur**; foreword by Wesley K. Clark. Palgrave Macmillan 2007 224p (Great generals series) hardcover o.p. pa $12.95   **92**

1. Generals
ISBN 1-4039-7658-9; 978-1-4039-7658-1; 0-230-61397-7 pa; 978-0-230-61397-3 pa

This biography of the World War II general is an "assessment of both the man and the soldier, covering the failures and triumphs in an assured and dispassionate tone. . . . A good starting point for generalists." Libr J

★ Herman, Arthur. **Douglas** MacArthur; American warrior. Arthur Herman. Random House 2016 912 p. illustrations, maps (ebook) $65; $40   **92**

1. Generals -- United States -- Biography 2. United States. Army -- Biography 3. United States -- History, Military -- 20th century
ISBN 9780812994896; 9780812994889

LC 2015039817

This book, by Arthur Herman, is a biography of Douglas MacArthur. "MacArthur's life spans the emergence of the United States Army as a global fighting force. Its history is to a great degree his story. The son of a Civil War hero, he led American troops in three monumental conflicts—World War I, World War II, and the Korean War. Born four years after Little Bighorn, he died just as American forces began deploying in Vietnam." (Publisher's note)

"Herman presents a superb reexamination of MacArthur and his role in American history." Booklist

Includes bibliographical references and index

Maclean, Donald

Philipps, Roland. A **spy** named Orphan; the enigma of Donald Maclean. Roland Philipps. W W Norton & Co Inc 2018 448 p. $28.95   **92**

1. Cold war 2. Spies -- Biography
ISBN 0393608573; 9780393608571

Author Roland Philipps presents "the first full biography of one of the twentieth century's most notorious spies. Donald Maclean was one of the most treacherous spies of the Cold War era and a key member of the infamous 'Cambridge Five' spy ring, yet the full extent of this shrewd, secretive man's betrayal has never been explored--until now. Drawing on a wealth of previously classified files and unseen family papers, [the book] meticulously documents his extraordinary story." (Publisher's note)

MacLeod, Janice

Macleod, Janice. A **Paris** year; my day-to-day adventures in the most romantic city in the world. Janice MacLeod. St. Martin's Griffin 2017 266 p. (hardcover) $24.99 **92**
    1. Paris (France) -- Description and travel 2. Travel writing 3. Artists -- Canada -- Biography 4. Paris (France) -- Pictorial works 5. Expatriate artists -- France -- Paris -- Biography
ISBN 1250130123; 9781250130129; 9781250134516
                              LC 2017004257
   This nonfiction book by Janice MacLeod "chronicles, day by day, one woman's French sojourn in [Paris]. The end result is more than a diary: it's a detailed and colorful love letter to one of the most romantic and historically rich cities on earth. Combining personal observations and anecdotes with stories and facts about famous figures in Parisian history, this visual tale of discovery, through the eyes of an artist, is sure to delight, inspire, and charm." (Publisher's note)
   "MacLeod's (Paris Letters) outsider view of Paris is a lovely portrayal of the romantic city, as she shares her experiences living there as an expat." LJ

Machiavelli, Niccolò, 1469-1527

Benner, Erica. **Be** like the fox; Machiavelli's lifelong quest for freedom. Erica Benner. First American edition W W Norton & Co Inc 2017 xxii, 360 p.p maps (hardcover) $27.95 **92**
    1. Diplomacy 2. Florence (Italy) -- History
ISBN 9780393609721; 9780393609738
                              LC 2017000694
   This biography by Erica Benner "interweaves Machiavelli's words with those of his friends and enemies, giving us a biography with all the energy of fiction. Through dialogues and diaries, we witness dramatic episodes, including Savonarola's fiery sermons against the elite in Florence's piazza, Machiavelli's secret negotiations with Caterina Sforza at the court of Forlì, and the Florentines' frantic preparations to resist Pope Julius's plan to over-throw their Republic." (Publisher's note)
   "Ideal as a companion to The Prince in university courses, Benner's work places readers in Machiavelli's daily life and recreates his world for academic and casual readers alike." Pub Wkly
   Includes bibliographical references and index

Unger, Miles J. **Machiavelli**; a biography. Miles J. Unger. 1st Simon & Schuster hc. ed. Simon & Schuster 2011 x, 400 p.p ill. (some col.) , map (hardcover) $28 **92**
    1. Authors 2. Statesmen 3. Dramatists 4. Philosophers 5. Authors, Italian -- Biography 6. Statesmen -- Italy -- Biography 7. Intellectuals -- Italy -- Biography 8. Italy -- History -- 1492-1559 -- Biography 9. Political scientists -- Italy -- Biography 10. Florence (Italy) -- History -- 1421-1737 -- Biography
ISBN 1416556281; 9781416556282
                              LC 2010054130
   This book is Miles J. Unger's biography of Machiavelli. "Unger utilizes Machiavelli's correspondence to present a complex portrait, showing his subject in the varied public roles he played: civil servant, diplomat, political philosopher, and playwright. All of Machiavelli's writings are discussed and analyzed here." (Library Journal)

Includes bibliographical references (p. [353]-386) and index.

Viroli, Maurizio. **Niccolo's** smile: a biography of Machiavelli; translated from the Italian by Antony Shugaar. Farrar, Straus & Giroux 2000 271p maps hardcover o.p. pa $13 **92**
    1. Authors 2. Statesmen 3. Dramatists 4. Writers on politics 5. Political and social philosophers
ISBN 0-374-52800-4 pa
                              LC 00-29380
   This biography of the Italian political philosopher traces his life "from respected secretary of the Florentine republic, dispatched on crucial diplomatic missions to Europe's most illustrious courts, to forgotten commoner.... Viroli provides a detailed, historical background for Machiavelli's personal triumphs and woes. But the strength of this work lies in his ceaseless concentration on Machiavelli the man, who comes alive on each page." Publ Wkly
   Includes bibliographical references

Madison, Dolley, 1768-1849

Allgor, Catherine. A **perfect** union; Dolley Madison and the creation of the American nation. Henry Holt & Co. 2006 493p il $30 **92**
    1. Biography, Individual 2. Spouses of presidents
ISBN 0-8050-7327-2; 978-0-8050-7327-0
                              LC 2005-55127
   This is a biography of the First Lady. Allgor argues that while Dolley Madison's "gender prevented her from openly playing politics, those very constraints of womanhood allowed her to construct an American democratic ruling style, and to achieve her husband [James's] political goals." (Publisher's note) Index.
   "In this evocative study a remarkable woman, creator of the 'first lady' role, comes vividly to life. " N Y Times Book Rev
   Includes bibliographical references

Madison, James, 1751-1836

Broadwater, Jeff. **James** Madison; a son of Virginia & a founder of the nation. Jeff Broadwater. University of North Carolina Press 2012 xvi, 266 p.p **92**
    1. Presidents -- United States 2. Founding Fathers of the United States 3. Statesmen -- United States -- Biography 4. Presidents -- United States -- Biography 5. United States -- Politics and government -- 1789-1815 6. United States -- Politics and government -- 1809-1817
ISBN 9780807835302
                              LC 2011035946
   In this biography of U.S. President James Madison, professor "[Jeff] Broadwater specifically provides readers with a detailed account of Madison's attempts to secure religious freedom in his native Virginia, his relationship with his charismatic wife Dolley Madison (sometimes referred to as 'Lady Presidentess'), and his ongoing struggle with his ideas about slavery." (Publishers Weekly)
   Includes bibliographical references and index.

Cheney, Lynne V., 1941- **James** Madison; a life reconsidered. Lynne Cheney. Viking Adult 2014 576 p. illustrations (hardback) $36 **92**
    1. Presidents -- United States 2. Statesmen -- United States -- Biography 3. United States -- Politics and government -- 1783-1865
ISBN 0670025194; 9780670025190
                              LC 2013047837
   This biography of U.S. president James Madison, by Lynne Cheney, "explores the astonishing story of a man of vaunted modesty.... Among

the Founding Fathers, Madison was a true genius of the early republic. Outwardly reserved, Madison was the intellectual driving force behind the Constitution and crucial to its ratification. His visionary political philosophy and rationale for the union of states--so eloquently presented in The Federalist papers--helped shape . . . America." (Publisher's note)

"Cheney conclusively demonstrates through the historical record that Madison, in word and deed, was a primary figure in shaping early American development." Pub Wkly

Includes bibliographical references and index

Feldman, Noah. The **three** lives of James Madison; genius, partisan, president. Noah Feldman. Random House 2017 xviii, 773 p.p illustrations (some color) (hardcover) $35   **92**
1. Presidents -- United States -- Biography 2. Founding Fathers of the United States -- Biography
ISBN 9780679643845; 9780812992755

LC 2017000125

This book, by Noah Feldman, "offers an intriguing portrait of [James Madison] . . . and the constitutional republic he created--and how both evolved to meet unforeseen challenges. Madison hoped to eradicate partisanship yet found himself giving voice to, and institutionalizing, the political divide. Madison's lifelong loyalty to Thomas Jefferson led to an irrevocable break with George Washington, hero of the American Revolution." (Publisher's note)

"With its lively prose and political acumen, this biography will be of interest to general-history readers and scholars alike." Pub Wkly

Includes bibliographical references and index

Signer, Michael. **Becoming** Madison; the extraordinary origins of the least likely founding father. Michael Signer. Public Affairs 2015 384 p. (hardcover: alk. paper) $28.99   **92**
1. Founding Fathers of the United States 2. Presidents -- United States -- Biography 3. United States -- Politics and government -- 1783-1809
ISBN 1610392957; 9781610392952

LC 2014038885

This book offers the "story of James Madison's coming of age, providing . . . insight into the Founding Father. Michael Signer takes a fresh look at the life of our fourth president. His focus is on Madison before he turned thirty-six, the years in which he did his most enduring work: battling with Patrick Henry . . . over religious freedom; introducing his framework for a strong central government; becoming the intellectual godfather of the Constitution." (Publisher's note)

"A perfect introduction to a deeply private and immensely important man." Kirkus

Includes bibliographical references and index

Wills, Garry. **James** Madison. Times Bks. 2002 xx, 184p (American presidents series) $20   **92**
1. Presidents 2. Members of Congress 3. Secretaries of state 4. Presidents -- United States
ISBN 0-8050-6905-4

LC 2002-19692

The author "maintains that Madison possessed qualities that served him well early in his career but proved to be a handicap during his Presidency. . . . Written with flair, this clear and balanced account is based on a sure handling of the material." Libr J

Includes bibliographical references

Mahler, Gustav, 1860-1911

Lebrecht, Norman. **Why** Mahler? how one man and ten symphonies changed our world. Pantheon Books 2010 326p

$27.95   **92**
1. Composers 2. Conductors (Music)
ISBN 978-0-375-42381-9; 0-375-42381-8

LC 2010-06034

"This is music history, criticism, and biography at its best. A treasure trove for Mahler fans, this is also likely to convert even the most obstinate detractor. Highly recommended for all music lovers." Libr J

Includes bibliographical references

Maier, Vivian, 1926-2009

Bannos, Pamela. **Vivian** Maier; a photographer's life and afterlife. Pamela Bannos. University of Chicago Press 2017 362 p. illustrations (cloth: alk. paper) $35   **92**
1. Women photographers -- Biography 2. Street photography -- United States 3. Women photographers -- United States -- Biography
ISBN 022647075X; 9780226470757

LC 2017022051

This biography, by Pamela Bannos, "contrasts [Vivian] Maier's life with the mythology that strangers—mostly the men who have profited from her work—have created around her absence. Bannos shows that Maier was extremely conscientious about how her work was developed, printed, and cropped, even though she also made a clear choice never to display it." (Publisher's note)

"Bannos's biography is a vital contribution to understanding the historical relevance of Maier's work and an important challenge to the way in which Maier's work and legacy have been represented thus far." Pub Wkly

Includes bibliographical references and index

Mailer, Norman

Lennon, J. Michael. **Norman** Mailer; a double life. J. Michael Lennon. Simon & Schuster 2013 928 p. $40   **92**
1. American novelists 2. Journalists -- United States -- Biography 3. Authors, American -- 20th century -- Biography
ISBN 1439150192; 9781439150191

LC 2013005097

In this biography of Norman Mailer, author J. Michael Lennon depicts his subject "as a dual-natured personality: a passive observer and an activist, a family man and a philanderer,. . . . While Lennon treats readers to accounts of Mailer's celebrity and his relations with stars such as Muhammad Ali . . . he also explores the writer's seamier side, including his stabbing of Adele Morales, his second wife, and his support of Jack Abbott, who committed murder after being paroled." (Library Journal)

"Detailed and anecdotal without being gossipy . . . and a must-read for students and admirers of Mailer's work." Kirkus

Includes bibliographical references and index

Mailhot, Terese-Marie

Mailhot, Terese-Marie. **Heart** berries; a memoir. Terese Marie Mailhot. Counterpoint Press 2018 160 p. $23   **92**
1. Manic-depressive illness 2. Post-traumatic stress disorder 3. Native American women -- Biography 4. Indian women -- Northwest, Pacific -- Biography 5. Manic-depressive illness -- Patients -- Northwest, Pacific -- Biography 6. Post-traumatic stress disorder -- Patients -- Northwest, Pacific -- Biography
ISBN 9781619023345

LC 2017051069

In this memoir, Terese Marie Mailhot recalls her life "on the Seabird Island Band in the Pacific Northwest. . . . [The book is] a memorial for Mailhot's mother, a social worker and activist who had a thing for prisoners; a story of reconciliation with her father--an abusive drunk and a brilliant artist--who was murdered under mysterious circumstances; and an elegy on how difficult it is to love someone while dragging the long shadows of shame." (Publisher's note)

Majorana, Ettore

Magueijo, Joao. A **brilliant** darkness; the extraordinary life and disappearance of Ettore Majorana, the troubled genius of the nuclear age. Basic Books 2009 280p il $27.50   **92**

  1. Physicists 2. Nuclear physics

  ISBN 978-0-465-00903-9; 0-465-00903-4

                     LC 2009-37678

The author "paints the life of a twenty something math prodigy who joined Enrico Fermi, Emilio Segre, and the other 'Via Panisperna Boys' who in 1934 discovered nuclear fusion. The author could have easily fallen into the jargon of his profession to describe the work of a fellow scientist, but he does not. His clear explanation of Majorana's insight into nuclear physics, often accompanied with drawings and illustrations, will appeal to a wide audience." Libr J

Includes bibliographical references

Malek, Alia, 1974-

Malek, Alia. The **home** that was our country; A Memoir of Syria. Alia Malek. Nation Books 2017 304 p. illustrations, map $27.99   **92**

  1. Damascus (Syria) 2. Syria -- History -- Civil War, 2011- 3. Syria -- History 4. Damascus (Syria) -- History 5. Damascus (Syria) -- Biography

  ISBN 9781568585321

                   LC 2016037114

This memoir, by Alia Malek, "is a deeply researched, personal journey that shines a delicate but piercing light on Syrian history, society, and politics. Teeming with insights, the narrative weaves acute political analysis with a century of intimate family history, ultimately delivering an unforgettable portrait of the Syria that is being erased." (Publisher's note)

"Moving and insightful, Malek's memoir combines sharp-eyed observations of Syrian politics, only occasionally overdone, with elegiac commentary on home, exile, and a bygone era. Provocative, richly detailed reading." Kirkus

Includes bibliographical references (pages 329-334).

Mandela, Nelson

Mandela, Nelson. **Long** walk to freedom: the autobiography of Nelson Mandela. Little, Brown 1994 558p il hardcover o.p. pa $16.95   **92**

  1. Presidents 2. Political prisoners 3. Political leaders 4. Human rights activists 5. Nobel laureates for peace 6. South Africa -- Race relations 7. South Africa -- Politics and government

  ISBN 0-316-54818-9 pa

                     LC 94-79980

This book "provides important new evidence to the forty-year story of apartheid, as seen by its most formidable opponent. And there is enough candour to provide insights into the nature of leadership." Times Lit Suppl

Mandela, Nelson, 1918-2013. **Conversations** with myself. Farrar Straus & Giroux 2010 454p il map $28   **92**

  1. Presidents 2. Political prisoners 3. Political leaders 4. Biography, Individual 5. Human rights activists 6. Apartheid -- South Africa 7. Nobel laureates for peace 8. Presidents -- South Africa 9. South Africa -- Race relations 10. South Africa -- Politics and government 11. South Africa -- Politics and government -- 20th century

  ISBN 978-0-374-12895-1; 0-374-12895-2

                   LC 2010-933174

This "is a moving account of Mandela's struggle and a testament to his triumph." Publ Wkly

Includes bibliographical references

Mandela, Nelson, 1918-2013. **In** his own words; edited by Kader Asmal, David Chidester, [and] Wilmot James. Little, Brown 2003 558p il $28.95   **92**

  1. Presidents 2. Political prisoners 3. Political leaders 4. Human rights activists 5. Nobel laureates for peace 6. South Africa -- Race relations 7. South Africa -- Politics and government

  ISBN 0-316-11019-1

                   LC 2004-107807

"This collection of Mandela's speeches shows why he remains a universal hero. . . . This volume will be in great demand for the personal drama, the history, and, yes, for the inspiring moral values." Booklist

Jones, Barbara. **Mandela**; My Prisoner, My Friend. Christo Brand, with Barbara Jones. Thomas Dunne Books/St. Martin's Press 2014 288 p. 16 plates; ills; portraits $26.99   **92**

  1. Political prisoners 2. African National Congress -- Biography 3. Robben Island (South Africa) -- Anecdotes 4. South Africa -- Race relations -- Anecdotes 5. Pollsmoor Prison (South Africa) -- Anecdotes 6. Political prisoners -- South Africa -- Biography 7. Correctional personnel -- South Africa -- Biography 8. South Africa -- Politics and government -- Anecdotes

  ISBN 1250055261; 9781250055262

                   LC 2014026586

In this book by Christo Brand and Barbara Jones, Nelson Mandela's "life's sacrifices [are] recounted in vivid detail by the prison guard with whom he became lifelong friends. For 12 years Brand watched Mandela scrub floors, empty his toilet bucket, grieve over the deaths of family and friends yet remain as strong as any freedom fighter in history. Won over by Madiba's charm and authentic concern for the well-being of others, Brand became Mandela's confidant and at times accomplice." (Publisher's note)

"The author quickly recounts Mandela's general biography, including the Rivonia trial for sabotage that landed him in prison, but this is really a tale of two men and their shared humanity in an inhumane place. A worthy addition to the canon of Mandela literature that details a relationship that many knew about but few truly understood." Kirkus

Sampson, Anthony. **Nelson** Mandela; the authorized biography. Knopf 1999 xxvi, 672p hardcover o.p. pa $19   **92**

  1. Presidents 2. Political prisoners 3. Political leaders 4. Human rights activists 5. Nobel laureates for peace 6. South Africa -- Race relations 7. South Africa -- Politics and government

  ISBN 0-679-78178-1 pa

                   LC 99-18498

"While not neglecting the personality of the man, Mr. Sampson has concentrated on the politics, and, for an authorised life, it can be treated as definitive." Economist

Includes bibliographical references

★ Mandela, Nelson, 1918-2013. **Dare** not linger; the presidential years. Nelson Mandela and Mandla Langa; with a prologue by Graça Machel. Farrar, Straus & Giroux 2017 xix, 358 p.p illustrations (chiefly color) (hardcover) $28   **92**

  1. Presidents -- South Africa 2. Presidents -- South Africa -- Biography 3. South Africa -- Politics and government -- 1994-

  ISBN 9780374717735; 9780374134716; 0374134715

                   LC 2017036979

This book, by Nelson Mandela, Mandla Langa and Graca Machel, "is the story of Mandela's presidency, drawing heavily on the memoir he began to write as he prepared to finish his term as president, but was unable to finish. . . . South African writer Mandla Langa has completed the task using Mandela's unfinished draft, detailed notes that Mandela made as events were unfolding, and a wealth of previously unseen archival material." (Publisher's note)

"Essential to students of Mandela's political career as well as of modern African history." Kirkus

Includes bibliographical references and index.

Mandelstam, Nadezhda, 1899-1980

Mandel'shtam, Nadezhda, 1899-1980. **Hope** against hope; a memoir. translated from the Russian by Max Hayward; with an introduction by Clarence Brown and: Nadezhda Mandelstaum (1899-1980): an obituary, by Joseph Brodsky. Modern Lib. 1999 442p pa $23   **92**
1. Authors 2. Poets 3. Memoirists 4. Translators 5. Poets, Russian -- 20th century -- Biography 6. Soviet Union -- Intellectual life -- 1917-1970 7. Soviet Union -- Politics and government -- 1917-1936 8. Soviet Union -- Politics and government -- 1936-1953
ISBN 0-375-75316-8; 978-0-375-75316-9

                   LC 98-47833

"Mandelstam tells the story of her family's experiences of hardship in Soviet Russia under Stalin. What is remarkable about the book is not just its content but also its authorial voice, which, in Max Hayward's deft translation, is so unique and consistent that the reader can get a sense of it by opening the book at random and reading almost any paragraph. Although Hope Against Hope is a painful book to read, one of the things that makes it bearable, apart from its sheer beauty, is a kind of unquenchable spirit and optimism that keeps rising to the surface, compounding the more mysterious consolations of art." Harper's

Mankell, Henning, 1948-2015

Mankell, Henning, 1948-2015. **Quicksand**; What It Means to Be a Human Being. by Henning Mankell. Random House Inc 2017 320 p. (ebook) $50.85; $16.95   **92**
1. Authors, Swedish 2. Authors -- Biography
ISBN 9780525432166; 0525432159; 9780525432159

                   LC 2016057757

This book, by Henning Mankell, is an "autobiographical look at the myriad experiences that shape a meaningful life. . . . In a series of intimate vignettes, Mankell ranges over rich and varied reflections: of growing up in a small Swedish town, where he experiences a startling revelation on a winter morning as a young boy; of living hand-to-mouth during a summer in Paris as an ambitious young writer; of his work at a theater in Mozambique, where Lysistrata is staged in the midst of civil war." (Publisher's note)

"This book is a compelling attempt to leave behind something for future civilizations to stumble upon, to piece together what it meant to be a human in the 21st century." LJ

Mankiller, Wilma

Mankiller, Wilma. **Mankiller**: a chief and her people; {by} Wilma Mankiller and Michael Wallis. St. Martin's Press 1993 xxiv, 292p il hardcover o.p. pa $14.95   **92**
1. Cherokee Indians 2. Indian chiefs
ISBN 0-312-20662-3 pa

                   LC 93-25698

"A must-read for everyone interested in, specifically, the history of Native Americans and women and, in general, tales of exceptional people." Booklist

Mann, Sally, 1951-

★ Mann, Sally, 1951- **Hold** Still; A Memoir With Photographs. by Sally Mann. Little, Brown & Co. 2015 496 p. illustrations (some color) $32   **92**
1. Genealogy 2. Southern States
ISBN 0316247766; 9780316247764

                   LC 2014959584

National Book Award Finalist: Nonfiction (2015)
Carnegie Medal: Nonfiction (2016)

This book, by Sally Mann, is a "revealing . . . memoir and family history. . . . Mann's preoccupation with family, race, mortality, and the storied landscape of the American South are revealed as almost genetically predetermined, written into her DNA by the family history that precedes her. Sorting through boxes of family papers and yellowed photographs she finds more than she bargained for." (Publisher's note)

"Here photographer Mann chronicles her rich and eccentric family history, told through the exploration of old documents and images stored away in her attic. . . . Raw and darkly humorous, Mann's writing is consistently honest and poignant as she depicts her beloved Virginia farm, her childhood, her parents, and her children." LJ

Includes bibliographical references (page 478)

Manning, Peyton

Myers, Gary. **Brady** vs Manning; the untold story of the rivalry that transformed the NFL. Gary Myers. Crown Archtype 2015 264 p. 8 unnumbered pages of plates (hbk.) $26   **92**
1. National Football League 2. Sports rivalries -- United States 3. Football -- United States -- History 4. Football players -- United States -- Biography 5. Quarterbacks (Football) -- United States -- Biography
ISBN 0804139377; 9780804139373

                   LC 2015027579

Author Gary Meyer presents this "inside account of the greatest rivalry in NFL history. Myers tackles this subject from every angle and with unprecedented access and insight, drawing on a huge number of never-before-heard interviews with [Tom] Brady and [Peyton] Manning, their coaches, their families, and those who have played with them and against them." (Publisher's note)

"Myers is a thorough professional with impeccable contacts to successfully tell this account, which will be of interest to all football fans." Library Journal

Includes bibliographical references and index

Mansfield, William Murray, Earl of, 1705-1793

Byrne, Paula. **Belle**; the slave daughter and the Lord Chief Justice. Paula Byrne. Harper Perennial 2014 304 p. illustrations (paperback) $14.99   **92**
1. Racially mixed people 2. Great Britain -- Race relations 3. Great Britain -- History -- 18th century 4. Slaves -- England -- Biography 5. Nobility -- England -- Biography
ISBN 0062310771; 9780062310774

                   LC 2014007447

"From . . . biographer Paula Byrne, the . . . tale that inspired the major motion picture 'Belle' (May 2014) starring Tom Wilkinson, Miranda Richardson, Emily Watson, Penelope Wilton, and Matthew Goode--a stunning story of the first mixed-race girl introduced to high society England and raised as a lady. . . . Growing up in his lavish estate, Dido was raised as a sister and companion to her white cousin, Elizabeth." (Publisher's note)

"Byrne brings to this brief history an eye for telling details of daily life, slaveholders' unthinkable cruelty, and the fervent work of a few good men and women who changed their world." Kirkus

Includes bibliographical references

Manson, Charles, 1934-2017

Herman, Deborah. **Member** of the family; my story of Charles Manson, life inside his cult, and the darkness that ended the sixties. by Dianne Lake and Deborah Herman. HarperCollins 2017 384 p.   **92**

ISBN 0062695576; 9780062695574

LC 2017277072

In this book, "Dianne Lake chronicles her years with Charles Manson, revealing for the first time how she became the youngest member of his Family and offering new insights into one of the twentieth century's most notorious criminals. . . . Though she never participated in any of the group's gruesome crimes and was purposely insulated from them, Dianne was arrested with the rest of the Manson Family, and eventually learned enough to join the prosecution's case against them." (Publisher's note)

Mantle, Mickey, 1931-1995

★ Leavy, Jane. The **last** boy; Mickey Mantle and the end of America's childhood. HarperCollins Publishers 2010 456p il $27.99   **92**

1. Baseball players 2. Baseball -- History 3. Baseball -- Biography 4. Biography, Individual 5. New York Yankees (Baseball team)
ISBN 978-0-06-088352-2; 0-06-088352-9

This is a biography of the New York Yankees center fielder. Bibliography. Index.

"This is unlike any biography on the sports shelf. Leavy, in exploring her own ambivalent feelings toward Mantle, permits readers to experience the same confusing emotions that many of those around him felt: proud to bask in his reflected glory but too intimidated to confront him. . . . A masterpiece of sports biography." Booklist

Smith, Johnny. A **season** in the sun; the rise of Mickey Mantle. Randy Roberts; Johnny Smith. Basic Books 2018 304 p. (hardcover) $28   **92**

1. Baseball -- United States 2. Baseball players -- United States -- Biography 3. New York Yankees (Baseball team) -- History
ISBN 9780465094424

LC 2017038834

In this book, "acclaimed historians Randy Roberts and Johnny Smith recount the defining moment of [Mickey] Mantle's legendary career: 1956, when he overcame a host of injuries and critics to become the most celebrated athlete of his time. . . . [They] depict Mantle not as an ideal role model or a bitter alcoholic, but a complex man whose faults were smoothed over by sportswriters eager to keep the truth about sports heroes at bay. An incisive portrait of an American icon." (Publisher's note)

"Highly recommended for fans of sports, Americana, and those seeking an informative historical read." LJ

Includes bibliographical references and index

Mao Zedong, 1893-1976

Chang, Jung. **Mao**: the unknown story; [by] Jung Chang, Jon Halliday. Knopf 2005 814p il $35   **92**

1. Heads of state 2. Communist leaders 3. Political leaders 4. China -- Politics and government
ISBN 0-679-42271-4

LC 2004-63826

"This is a magisterial work. . . . This biography supplies substantial . . . information and presents it all in a stylish way that will put it on bedside tables around the world." N Y Times Book Rev

Includes bibliographical references

Mapplethorpe, Robert

★ Smith, Patti, 1946- **Just** kids; Patti Smith. Ecco 2010 278p il $27; pa $16   **92**

1. Rock musicians 2. Poets, American 3. Biography, Individual
ISBN 978-0-06-621131-2; 0-06-621131-X; 978-0-06-093622-8 pa; 0-06-093622-3 pa
National Book Award: Nonfiction (2010)

"In 'Just Kids,' Patti Smith's first book of prose, the legendary American artist offers a never-before-seen glimpse of her remarkable relationship with photographer Robert Mapplethorpe in the epochal days of New York City . . . in the late sixties and seventies. An honest and moving story of youth and friendship, Smith brings the same unique, lyrical quality to 'Just Kids' as she has to the rest of her formidable body of work." (Publisher's note)

This "is one of the best books ever written on becoming an artist— not the race for online celebrity and corporate sponsorship that often passes for artistic success these days, but the far more powerful, often difficult journey toward the ecstatic experience of capturing radiance of imagination on a page or stage or photographic paper." Washington Post

Maraniss, David

Maraniss, David. **Into** the story; a writer's journey through life, politics, sports and loss. Simon & Schuster 2010 283p il $26   **92**

1. Journalists 2. Biographers
ISBN 978-1-4391-6002-2; 1-4391-6002-3

LC 2009-42338

"In this collection of previously published articles and excerpts from his books, . . . [the author] ranges over topics from the death of his sister and the deaths of strangers on September 11 to the political fortunes of Barack Obama, Bill Clinton, and Al Gore and the timeless contributions to sports of legendary figures like Vince Lombardi, Muhammad Ali, and Roberto Clemente. . . . Maraniss's lively sketches illuminate the lives of significant cultural and political figures and intimately capture various moments that define modern American cultural history." Publ Wkly

Maravich, Pete, 1947-1988

★ Kriegel, Mark. **Pistol**; the life of Pete Maravich. Free Press 2007 381p il $27; pa $15   **92**

1. Basketball players
ISBN 978-0-7432-8497-4; 0-7432-8497-6; 978-0-7432-8498-1 pa; 0-7432-8498-4 pa

LC 2006-51526

This is a biography of the basketball player who played at Louisiana State University before joining the N.B.A.

The author "skillfully pulls off the balancing act required of good sports biography. It plays large historical forces (segregation, the rise of televised sports) against the individual magic of its subject." New York

Includes bibliographical references

Marciano, Rocky, 1923-1969

Stanton, Mike, 1957- **Unbeaten**; Rocky Marciano's fight for perfection in a crooked world. Mike Stanton. Henry Holt & Co. 2018 400 p. (hardcover) $32   **92**

1. Boxers (Sports) -- United States -- Biography
ISBN 9781627799195

LC 2017057871

In this biography, author Mike Stanton describes how boxer "Rocky Marciano accomplished a feat that eluded legendary heavyweight champions like Joe Louis, Jack Dempsey, Muhammad Ali, and Mike Tyson: He never lost a professional fight. His record was a perfect 49-0. 'Unbeaten' is the story of this remarkable champion who overcame injury, doubt, and the schemes of corrupt promoters to win the title in a bloody and epic battle with Jersey Joe Walcott in 1952." (Publisher's note)

"This meticulously documented and well-written work should stand for both fans and scholars as Marciano's definitive biography." Library Journal

Includes bibliographical references and index

Marconi, Guglielmo, 1874-1937

Raboy, Marc. **Marconi**; The Man Who Networked the World. Marc Raboy. Oxford University Press 2016 872 p. illustrations, map $39.95   **92**

1. Inventors -- Biography 2. Telecommunication -- History 3. Radio -- Italy -- History 4. Telegraph, Wireless -- History 5. Inventors -- Italy -- Biography 6. Telegraph, Wireless -- Marconi system 7. Electrical engineers -- Italy -- Biography

ISBN 9780199313587

LC 2015042075

This biography of Guglielmo Marconi by Marc Raboy narrates how "Marconi popularized-and, more critically, patented-the use of radio waves. . . . [After] a demonstration of his wireless apparatus in London at the age of 22 in 1896, he established his Wireless Telegraph & Signal Company and seemed unstoppable. He was decorated by the Czar of Russia, named an Italian Senator, knighted by King George V of England, and awarded the Nobel Prize for Physics-all before the age of 40." (Publisher's note)

"A comprehensive portrait of a complicated man, Raboy's meticulous, judicious work merits anchorage on science-history shelves." Booklist

Includes bibliographical references and index

Mardini, Yusra

Mardini, Yusra. **Butterfly**; from refugee to Olympian, my story of rescue, hope, and triumph. Yusra Mardini. St. Martin's Press 2018 288 p. (hardcover) $26.99   **92**

1. Olympic games 2. Refugees -- Biography 3. Women swimmers -- Biography 4. Women swimmers -- Syria -- Biography

ISBN 9781250184405

LC 2017061098

In this memoir, Yusra Mardini, "tells her story, from Syria to the Olympics to her current work with the UN as a Goodwill Ambassador. Mardini is eager to tell her story in the hopes that readers will remember that refugees are ordinary people in extraordinary circumstances, chased from their homes by a devastating war. In today's political climate, this story is guaranteed to inspire and educate readers from every background." (Publisher's note)

Margery, 1888-1941

Jaher, David. The **witch** of lime street; séance, seduction, and Houdini in the spirit world. David Jaher. Crown Publishers 2015 448 p. illustrations (alk. paper) $28   **92**

1. Spiritualism 2. Spiritualists -- United States -- Biography 3. Women mediums -- United States -- Biography 4. Spiritualism -- United States -- History -- 20th century

ISBN 0307451062; 9780307451064

LC 2015009392

In this book, by David Jaher, "in 1924, the pretty wife of a distinguished Boston surgeon came to embody the raging national debate over Spiritualism. . . . Reporters dubbed her the blonde Witch of Lime Street, but she was known to her followers simply as Margery. . . . Margery was the best hope for the psychic practice to be empirically verified. Her supernatural gifts beguiled four of the judges. There was only one left to convince...the acclaimed escape artist, Harry Houdini." (Publisher's note)

"Through a combination of feminine seduction and illusionist skill that even Houdini admired, Crandon became the one psychic to almost win the respect of the scientific community and outshine Houdini as an entertainer. Jaher's narrative style is as engaging as his character portraits are colorful. Together, they bring a bygone age and its defining spiritual obsessions roaring to life. Fascinating, sometimes thrilling, reading." Kirkus

Includes bibliographical references and index

Marie Antoinette, Queen, consort of Louis XVI, King of France, 1755-1793

Lever, Evelyne. **Marie** Antoinette; the last queen of France. translated from the French by Catherine Temerson. Farrar, Straus & Giroux 2000 357p il hardcover o.p. pa $16.95   **92**

1. Queens 2. France -- History -- 1589-1789, Bourbons

ISBN 0-312-28333-4 pa

LC 00-28763

The author examines "the opulent Versailles subculture and the queen whose royal excesses served as a major catalyst for the revolutionary upheaval of 1789. Through the skillful use of memoirs and other primary documents, Lever creates an empathic picture of Louis XVI's headstrong wife." Libr J

Includes bibliographical references

Marion, Robert

Marion, Robert. **Genetic** rounds; a doctor's encounters in the field that has revolutionized medicine. Kaplan Pub. 2009 275p $24.95   **92**

1. Physicians 2. Medical genetics 3. Pediatricians

ISBN 978-1-60714-460-1

LC 2009-19110

This is "a straightforward, and often poignant, collection of true stories. Particularly compelling are several stories that describe the pain and pathos of life for some individuals with genetic disorders." Am J Human Genetics

Maris, Roger, 1934-1985

Clavin, Thomas. **Roger** Maris; baseball's reluctant hero. [by] Tom Clavin and Danny Peary. Simon & Schuster 2010 422p il $26.99   **92**

1. Baseball players 2. Baseball -- Biography 3. New York Yankees (Baseball team)

ISBN 978-1-4165-8928-0; 1-4165-8928-7

LC 2009-39722

The authors "trace the dramatic arc of Maris's life, from his boyhood in Fargo through his early pro career in the Cleveland Indians farm program, to his World Series championship years in New York and beyond. At the center is the exciting story of the 1961 season and the ordeal Maris endured as an outsider in Yankee pinstripes, unloved by fans who compared him unfavorably to their heroes Ruth and Mantle, relentlessly attacked by an aggressive press corps who found him cold and inaccessible, and treated miserably by the organization." Publisher's note

Includes bibliographical references

Markham, Beryl

Markham, Beryl, 1902-1986. **West** with the night; Beryl Markham; illustrated by Alan Phillips. Easton Press 1989 261 p. illustrations $16   **92**

1. Autobiographies 2. Women air pilots 3. Women air pilots -- Africa -- Biography 4. Women air pilots -- Great Britain -- Biography

ISBN 0865477639; 9780865477636

LC 91228442

In this memoir, author Beryl Markham discusses how "she and her father moved to Kenya when she was a girl, and she grew up with a zebra for a pet; horses for friends; baboons, lions, and gazelles for neighbors. She made money by scouting elephants from a tiny plane. And she would spend most of the rest of her life in East Africa as an adventurer, a racehorse trainer, and an aviatrix--she became the first person to fly nonstop from Europe to America." (Publisher's note)

Marlowe, Christopher, 1564-1593

★ Honan, Park. **Christopher** Marlowe; poet & spy. Oxford University Press 2005 421p il $32.50   **92**
1. Authors 2. Dramatists 3. Dramatists, English 4. Great Britain -- History -- 1485-1603, Tudors
ISBN 0-19-818695-9

LC 2005-19761

This is a biography of the sixteenth-century English dramatist.

The author "sheds light on the much-speculated (and previously erroneously reported) aspects of Marlowe's life without neglecting its more ordinary features (his stable two-parent upbringing, his diligent scholarship at Cambridge) or destroying the poet's aura of intrigue." Publ Wkly

Includes bibliographical references

Nicholl, Charles. The **reckoning**; the murder of Christopher Marlowe. University of Chicago Press 1995 413p il pa $33   **92**
1. Authors 2. Dramatists 3. Dramatists, English 4. Great Britain -- History -- 1485-1603, Tudors
ISBN 0-226-58024-5; 978-0-226-58024-1
First published 1992 in the United Kingdom

The author argues that the Elizabethan playwright, who is believed to have been stabbed in a dispute over the bill ('recknynge') at Eleanor Bull's victualling house in 1593, was in fact murdered with government complicity as part of a plot against Sir Walter Raleigh.

"A remarkable piece of scholarship, this work carefully reconstructs the events leading up to the murder with all the excitement and suspense of a modern mystery novel; at the same time it vividly conveys the energy and color of Elizabethan England." Libr J

Includes bibliographical references

Marsh, Henry, 1950-

Marsh, Henry. **Admissions**; life as a brain surgeon. Henry Marsh. Thomas Dunne Books 2017 xvi, 271 p.p (hardcover) $26.99   **92**
1. Medicine 2. Surgeons 3. Neurosurgeons -- Great Britain -- Biography
ISBN 9781250127273; 9781250127266; 1250127262

LC 2017023778

National Book Critics Circle Award Finalist: Autobiography (2017)

In this memoir, by Henry Marsh, the author, "retired from his full-time job in England to work pro bono in Ukraine and Nepal . . . , describes the difficulties of working in these troubled, impoverished countries and the further insights it has given him into the practice of medicine. Marsh also faces up to the burden of responsibility that can come with trying to reduce human suffering." (Publisher's note)

"Another thoughtful, painful, utterly fascinating mixture of nut-and-bolts brain surgery with a compassionate, workaholic surgeon's view of medicine around the world and his own limitations." Kirkus

Marshal, William

Asbridge, Thomas. The **Greatest** Knight; the remarkable life of William Marshal, the power behind five English thrones. Thomas Asbridge. HarperCollins 2014 256 p. illustrations (color), maps $27.99   **92**
1. Knights and knighthood
ISBN 006226205X; 9780062262059

LC 2015431306

This book, by Thomas Asbridge, presents a "portrait of one of history's most illustrious knights--William Marshal. . . . Historian Thomas Asbridge draws upon the thirteenth-century biography and an array of other contemporary evidence to present a compelling account of William Marshal's life and times. Asbridge follows Marshal on his journey from rural England onto the battlefields of France, to the desert castles of the Holy Land and the verdant shores of Ireland." (Publisher's note)

"Matters did not improve after Henry's death, so Marshal's career comes across as a relentless series of intrigues, battles, atrocities, truces quickly broken, internal revolts and treason that often included Marshal for reasons the author must guess because historical evidence is lacking. A valuable biography of an important figure in a distant, violent, barely comprehensible era." Kirkus

Marshall, Dan

Marshall, Dan. **Home** is burning; a memoir. Dan Marshall. Flatiron Books 2015 320 p. (hardback) $27.99   **92**
1. Family life 2. Children of cancer patients 3. Fathers and sons -- United States 4. Mothers and sons -- United States 5. Fathers and daughters -- United States 6. Mothers and daughters -- United States 7. Cancer -- Patients -- Family relationships 8. Cancer -- Patients -- United States -- Biography
ISBN 9781250068828

LC 2015022200

This memoir, by Dan Marshall, named best book of the year for 2015 by "Entertainment Weekly," follows "Dan Marshall. 25, good job, great girlfriend, and living the dream life in sunny Los Angeles without a care in the world. Until his mother calls. . . . It turns out his mom's cancer . . . is back. And to add insult to injury, his loving father has been diagnosed with ALS. Sayonara L.A., Dan is headed home to Salt Lake City, Utah." (Publisher's note)

"Home Is Burning packs a wallop. Marshall doesn't hold back in his descriptions of how a horrific illness wreaks havoc on his dad's body, and he takes an unflinching look at how real families fall apart—and pull together—in their own ways."

Marshall, John, 1755-1835

★ Paul, Joel Richard. **Without** precedent; chief justice John Marshall and his times. Joel Richard Paul. Riverhead Books 2017 512 p. (hardcover) $30   **92**
1. Judges -- United States -- Biography 2. United States. Supreme Court -- Biography
ISBN 9781594488238

LC 2017016049

This biography, by Joel Richard Paul, "is the remarkable story of John Marshall who, as chief justice, statesman, and diplomat, played a pivotal role in the founding of the United States. . . . [The book] is the engrossing account of the life and times of this exceptional man, who with cunning, imagination, and grace shaped America's future as he held together the Supreme Court, the Constitution, and the country itself." (Publisher's note)

"This masterly work elucidates the indelible imprint that Marshall made on the U.S. Constitution and its subsequent interpretation. Perfect for readers of Jean Edward Smith's John Marshall: Definer of a Nation." LJ

Includes bibliographical references and index

Unger, Harlow Giles. **John** Marshall; the chief justice who saved the nation. Harlow Giles Unger. Da Capo Press 2014 384 p. illustrations (hardback) $27.99 **92**

1. Judges -- Biography 2. Judges -- United States -- Biography 3. United States. Supreme Court -- Biography

ISBN 0306822202; 9780306822209; 9780306822216

LC 2014008405

This biography, by Harlow Giles Unger, "reveals how Virginia-born John Marshall emerged from the Revolutionary War's bloodiest battlefields to become one of the nation's most important Founding Fathers: America's greatest Chief Justice. Marshall served his country as an officer, Congressman, diplomat, and Secretary of State before President John Adams named him the nation's fourth Chief Justice, the longest-serving in American history." (Publisher's note)

Includes bibliographical references and index

Marshall, Thurgood, 1908-1993

Williams, Juan. **Thurgood** Marshall; American revolutionary. Times Bks. 1998 459p il hardcover o.p. pa $16 **92**

1. Lawyers 2. Solicitors general 3. Civil rights activists 4. Supreme Court justices 5. African Americans -- Biography 6. United States -- Supreme Court 7. African Americans -- Civil rights

ISBN 0-8129-3299-4 pa

LC 98-9735

"Williams presents Marshall as a revolutionary 'of grand vision,' but this well-rounded portrait of the man also addresses his vanities and warts, from his ascension to his deflation and subsequent redemption. This is a must read for all Americans concerned with the struggle for civil and individual rights." Booklist

Includes bibliographical references

Martin, Billy, 1928-1989

Pennington, Bill. **Billy** Martin; baseball's flawed genius. Bill Pennington. Houghton Mifflin Harcourt 2015 604 p. illustratioins (hardback) $30 **92**

1. Baseball -- Coaching 2. New York Yankees (Baseball team) 3. New York Yankees (Baseball team) -- History 4. Baseball players -- New York (State) -- New York -- Biography 5. Baseball managers -- New York (State) -- New York -- Biography

ISBN 0544022092; 9780544022096; 9780544022942

LC 2014039677

Author Bill Pennignton presents this biography of former New York Yankees baseball player and manager Billy Martin. "Drawing on exhaustive interviews with friends, family, teammates, and countless adversaries, Pennington paints an indelible portrait of a man who never backed down for the game he loved. From his shantytown upbringing in a broken home; to his days playing for the Yankees when he almost always helped his team find a way to win; through sixteen years of managing" (Publisher's note)

"Pennington analyzes the ongoing conflict that was Billy Martin--including his relationships with equally complex individuals such as George Steinbrenner and Reggie Jackson--from all sides (Billy's varied career is covered chronologically, but it's the Yankee years, however sporadic, that matter) and with balance and impressive depth." Booklist

Martin, Dean

Lewis, Jerry. **Dean** & me; a love story. Doubleday 2005 340p il $26.95 **92**

1. Actors 2. Singers 3. Comedians 4. Television personalities 5. Motion picture directors

ISBN 0-7679-2086-4

LC 2005-49682

"This is a wild, joyous book, but also a heartbreaking one." N Y Times Book Rev

Martin, Luther, 1744-1826

Kauffman, Bill. **Forgotten** founder, drunken prophet; the life of Luther Martin. ISI Books 2008 202p $25 **92**

1. Lawyers 2. Members of Congress 3. Law enforcement officials 4. State government officials 5. United States -- Constitutional Convention (1787) 6. United States -- Politics and government -- 1783-1809

ISBN 978-1-933859-73-6; 1-933859-73-3

LC 2008-928223

Kauffman "tells the story of Luther Martin, one of America's less-remembered founding fathers. A livid Anti-Federalist, Martin has gone down in the annals of 18th century America as little more than a footnote. He was accused of being an absolute boor, drinking to excess, rambling in speech with incessant monotony, and having an altogether prickly disposition. Kauffman takes up the cross of giving Martin a fair shake, not by defending the man but just by telling his story. . . . Never the explicit apologist, Kauffman delicately and humorously weaves a more complete portrait of Martin. Furthermore, Kauffman's writing is well-founded upon a towering bibliography that Kauffman adroitly parses." PopMatters

Includes bibliographical references

Martin, Mary, 1913-1990

Kaufman, David. **Some** enchanted evenings; The Glittering Life and Times of Mary Martin. David Kaufman. St. Martin's Press 2016 432 p. illustrations (hardcover) $29.99 **92**

1. Singers -- Biography 2. Singers -- United States -- Biography

ISBN 9781250031754; 9781250031761

LC 2015047863

This biography, by David Kaufman, "is the delectable story of the one and only Mary Martin, a woman who described herself as a chicken farmer from Texas only to become Peter Pan and capture America's heart." (Publisher's note)

"A warm and well-researched... appreciation of one of the stage's most beloved performers and, on the evidence here, least interesting legends." Kirkus

Includes bibliographical references

Martin, Roger H., 1943-

Martin, Roger H. **Racing** Odysseus; a college president becomes a freshman again. University of California Press 2008 262p $24.95 **92**

1. Higher education 2. Biography, Individual 3. Education, Higher -- United States 4. St. John's College (Annapolis, Md.)

ISBN 978-0-520-25541-8; 0-520-25541-0

LC 2007-51017

Martin "examines a number of experiences uncommon to 61-year-old college presidents. On a sabbatical after horrific treatments for cancer, he enrolled as a freshman at St. John's College in Maryland, studied classics, joined the crew team, prepared for a major race, and learned to connect with his 18-year-old classmates. He notes the follies of the students, as well as his own, and offers perceptive and affectionate insights into the challenges of growing up in today's complicated world. Education is his profession, and as he carefully observes the impact of the Great Books curriculum at St. John's, he sees the relevance of the Greek classics to our own time." Libr J

Includes bibliographical references

Martin, Steve, 1945-

Martin, Steve. **Born** standing up; a comic's life. Scribner

2007 209p il $25   **92**
1. Actors 2. Comedians 3. Novelists 4. Dramatists 5. Memoirists 6. Screenwriters
ISBN 978-1-4165-5364-9; 1-4165-5364-9

LC 2007-27143

This is an autobiography by the comedian and author of Shopgirl (2000).

This book "does a sharp-witted job of breaking down the step-by-step process that brought [the author] from Disneyland, where he spent his version of a Dickensian childhood as a schoolboy employee, to both the pinnacle of stardom and the brink of disaster.... Even for readers already familiar with Mr. Martin's solemn side, [this] is a surprising book: smart, serious, heartfelt and confessional without being maudlin." N Y Times (Late NY Ed)

Martin, Trayvon, 1995-2012

Martin, Tracy. **Rest** in power; the enduring life of Trayvon Martin. by Sybrina Fulton and Tracy Martin. Random House Inc 2017 368 p. (ebook) $65; $26   **92**
1. Trials (Homicide) 2. African American youth 3. African Americans -- Civil rights
ISBN 9780812997248; 0812997239; 9780812997231

LC 2017002840

This book, by Sybrina Fulton and Tracy Martin, talks about the murder of African American teenager Trayvor Martin by a gun-wielding neighborhood watchman in Florida. "[Martin] has become a symbol of social justice activism.... But who was ... Martin, before he became, in death, an icon? And how did one black child's death ... become the match that lit a civil rights crusade?" (Publisher's note)

"Given the unconscionable shooting deaths of young black men, many by police, that followed Trayvon's, this galvanizing testimony from parents who channeled their sorrow into action offers a deeply humanizing perspective on the crisis propelling a national movement." Booklist

Marton, Endre, 1910-2005

Marton, Kati. **Enemies** of the people; my family's journey to America. Simon & Schuster 2009 272p il $26   **92**
1. Authors 2. Journalists 3. Political prisoners 4. Hungary -- History 5. Nonfiction writers
ISBN 978-1-4165-8612-8; 1-4165-8612-1

LC 2009-14480

"An American journalist trolls the archives of the Hungarian secret police (AVO) to piece together her parents' imprisonment in and flight from Hungary in the mid-1950s.... The author's probing work effectively renders an enormously unsettled, painful time of shifting allegiances and political treachery.... A dark, compelling narrative of secrecy and betrayal." Kirkus

Includes bibliographical references

Marton, Ilona, 1912-2004

Marton, Kati. **Enemies** of the people; my family's journey to America. Simon & Schuster 2009 272p il $26   **92**
1. Authors 2. Journalists 3. Political prisoners 4. Hungary -- History 5. Nonfiction writers
ISBN 978-1-4165-8612-8; 1-4165-8612-1

LC 2009-14480

"An American journalist trolls the archives of the Hungarian secret police (AVO) to piece together her parents' imprisonment in and flight from Hungary in the mid-1950s.... The author's probing work effectively renders an enormously unsettled, painful time of shifting allegiances and political treachery.... A dark, compelling narrative of secrecy and betrayal." Kirkus

Includes bibliographical references

Marton, Kati

Marton, Kati. **Enemies** of the people; my family's journey to America. Simon & Schuster 2009 272p il $26   **92**
1. Authors 2. Journalists 3. Political prisoners 4. Hungary -- History 5. Nonfiction writers
ISBN 978-1-4165-8612-8; 1-4165-8612-1

LC 2009-14480

"An American journalist trolls the archives of the Hungarian secret police (AVO) to piece together her parents' imprisonment in and flight from Hungary in the mid-1950s.... The author's probing work effectively renders an enormously unsettled, painful time of shifting allegiances and political treachery.... A dark, compelling narrative of secrecy and betrayal." Kirkus

Includes bibliographical references

Marx, Groucho, 1891-1977

Kanfer, Stefan. **Groucho**: the life and times of Julius Henry Marx. Knopf 2000 465p il hardcover o.p. pa $15   **92**
1. Comedians 2. Television personalities 3. Game show hosts
ISBN 0-375-70207-5 pa

LC 99-54002

"Plagued by nagging financial insecurities, partly realized literary ambitions, and difficult, unsatisfying relations with his wives, lovers, and daughters, Groucho was a 'depressive clown,' notes Kanter.... The book also details Groucho's ambivalent relations with his son, Arthur; his brothers; New Deal liberals; intellectuals and collaborators like S. J. Perelman; and his custodian, Erin Fleming." Libr J

Includes bibliographical references

Marx, Jenny

Gabriel, Mary. **Love** and capital; Karl and Jennie Marx and the birth of a revolution. Little, Brown and Company 2011 lviii, 707p il   **92**
1. Marxism 2. Writers on politics 3. Spouses of prominent persons 4. Political and social philosophers
ISBN 0-316-06611-7; 978-0-316-06611-2

LC 2010-44021

National Book Award Finalist: Nonfiction (2011)

An "account of the lives of Karl Marx and his wife, Jenny von Westphalen.... Tracing their tumultuous lives from Prussia, via Paris to Brussels and finally London, Gabriel tells the story of a woman who forswore the comforts of her noble upbringing to raise a family in often very straitened circumstances with a man committed in both his life and letters to social justice and the emancipation of the working class. Equally at home with the details of Marxist theory and revolutionary Europe as she is with the private lives of Karl and Jenny, the author dazzles most with her fascinating accounts of the lives of the Marx children." Publ Wkly

Includes bibliographical references

Marx, Karl, 1818-1883

Gabriel, Mary. **Love** and capital; Karl and Jennie Marx and the birth of a revolution. Little, Brown and Company 2011 lviii, 707p il   **92**
1. Marxism 2. Writers on politics 3. Spouses of prominent persons 4. Political and social philosophers
ISBN 0-316-06611-7; 978-0-316-06611-2

LC 2010-44021

National Book Award Finalist: Nonfiction (2011)

An "account of the lives of Karl Marx and his wife, Jenny von Westphalen. . . . Tracing their tumultuous lives from Prussia, via Paris to Brussels and finally London, Gabriel tells the story of a woman who forswore the comforts of her noble upbringing to raise a family in often very straitened circumstances with a man committed in both his life and letters to social justice and the emancipation of the working class. Equally at home with the details of Marxist theory and revolutionary Europe as she is with the private lives of Karl and Jenny, the author dazzles most with her fascinating accounts of the lives of the Marx children." Publ Wkly

Includes bibliographical references

Liedman, Sven-Eric. A **world** to win; the life and works of Karl Marx. by Sven-Eric Liedman. Verso 2018 768 p. $35 **92**
1. Communism -- History 2. Communists -- Biography 3. Communism -- History -- 19th century
ISBN 9781786635044; 9781786635068

LC 2018003399

This biography of Karl Marx, by Sven-Eric Liedman, give[s] equal weight to both the work and life of . . . Marx. . . . Liedman expertly navigates the imposing, complex personality of his subject through the turbulent passages of global history. . . . [The book] follows Marx through childhood and student days, a difficult and sometimes tragic family life, his far-sighted journalism, and his enduring friendship and intellectual partnership with Friedrich Engels." (Publisher's note)

Sperber, Jonathan. **Karl** Marx; a nineteenth-century life. Jonathan Sperber. W W Norton & Co Inc 2013 512 p. (hardcover) $35 **92**
1. Communists -- Germany -- Biography 2. Philosophers -- Germany -- Biography
ISBN 0871404672; 9780871404671

LC 2012044951

Pulitzer Prize Finalist: Biography or Autobiography (2014)

This book by Jonathan Sperber is a biography of "Karl Marx, the German philosopher and political firebrand turned London émigré journalist. . . . Sperber demonstrates that Marx had more in common with Robespierre than with twentieth-century Communists. Using the complete Marx and Engels database . . . Sperber juxtaposes the private man against the public agitator who helped foment the 1848-49 Revolution and whose incendiary books inflamed the dissident world of Europe." (Publisher's note)

Includes bibliographical references (p.   ) and index

Mary, Blessed Virgin, Saint

Hazleton, Lesley. **Mary**: a flesh-and-blood biography of the Virgin Mother. Bloomsbury 2004 246p $24.95 **92**
1. Saints
ISBN 1-582-34236-9

LC 2003-17403

Hazleton "takes readers through an impressive array of historical, cultural, literary, and spiritual topics. . . . This book is an easy read, and Hazleton's stream-of-consciousness style is intriguing." Libr J
Includes bibliographical references

Mary, Queen of Scots, 1542-1587

Weir, Alison. **Mary,** Queen of Scots, and the murder of Lord Darnley. Ballantine Bks. 2003 670p il map $27.95; pa $16.95 **92**
1. Queens 2. Princes 3. Scotland -- History -- 16th century
ISBN 0-345-43658-X; 0-8129-7151-5 pa

LC 2002-34467

"No stone is left unturned in {Weir's} investigation, and despite its detail, her book is as dramatic as witnessing firsthand the most riveting court case." Booklist

Mary, Queen, consort of George V, King of Great Britain, 1867-1953

Edwards, Anne, 1927- **Matriarch**; Queen Mary and the House of Windsor. by Anne Edwards. Rowman & Littlefield 2014 527 p. (paperback) $19.95 **92**
1. Queens -- Great Britain
ISBN 9781442236561; 9781442236554; 1442236558

This book, by Anne Edwards, is a biography of Queen Mary. "The life of Princess May of Teck is one of the great Cinderella stories in history. From a family of impoverished nobility, she was chosen by Queen Victoria as the bride for her eldest grandson, the scandalous Duke of Clarence, heir to the throne, who died mysteriously before their marriage. Despite this setback, she became queen, mother of two kings, grandmother of the current queen, and a lasting symbol of the majesty of the British throne." (Publisher's note)

Maryam Jameelah, 1934-2012

Baker, Deborah. The **convert**; a tale of exile and extremism. Graywolf Press 2011 246p il $23 **92**
1. Converts 2. Muslim women 3. Biography, Individual
ISBN 1-55597-582-8; 978-1-55597-582-1

National Book Award Finalist: Nonfiction (2011)

This is a biography of the Islamic polemicist Maryam Jameelah. Jameelah was "born as Margaret Marcus in 1934 in New Rochelle, N.Y." (N Y Times Book Rev)

This "is a cogent, thought-provoking look at a radical life and its rippling consequences." Publ Wkly

Includes bibliographical references

Mason, George, 1725-1792

★ Broadwater, Jeff. **George** Mason, forgotten founder. University of North Carolina Press 2006 329p il $34.95 **92**
1. Statesmen 2. Essayists 3. Colonial leaders 4. Plantation owners
ISBN 978-0-8078-3053-6; 0-8078-3053-4

LC 2006-10729

"Because Mason left little evidence of his private life, there are blurred edges in the portrait that Broadwater paints, but overall this is an exemplary biography: sympathetic but dispassionate, thorough but not cluttered, convincing in its interpretations and arguments. It leaves no doubt that Mason deserves to be returned to the esteem and reputation he enjoyed during his lifetime, but in no way is it hagiography." Washington Post Book World
Includes bibliographical references

Massery, Hazel Bryan, 1942-

Margolick, David. **Elizabeth** and Hazel; two women of Little Rock. Yale University Press 2011 310p il $26 **92**
1. School integration 2. Arkansas -- Race relations 3. Little Rock (Ark.) -- Race relations 4. Central High School (Little Rock, Ark.) 5. School integration -- Arkansas -- Little Rock -- History -- 20th century
ISBN 978-0-300-14193-1; 0-300-14193-9

LC 2011-14101

"When Elizabeth Eckford braved the gauntlet of white hecklers leading to the newly desegregated Central High School in Little Rock, Arkansas, in 1957, photographers captured her image and that of the angry young white woman behind her. Elizabeth, the stoic, and Hazel Bryan, the tormentor, were frozen as icons. Elizabeth was part of the Little Rock Nine, the black teens who became the targets of race hatred as well as national and international inspirations. . . . Margolick draws on interviews and press reports of the time to present a very nuanced analysis of how Elizabeth and Hazel were affected by the scene that made them famous. . . . A complex look at two women at the center of a historic moment." Booklist

Includes bibliographical references

Massimino, Mike, 1962-

Massimino, Mike. **Spaceman**; An Astronaut's Unlikely Journey to Unlock the Secrets of the Universe. Mike Massimino. Crown 2016 336 p. color illustrations (hardcover) $28 **92**

1. Astronauts 2. Space flight 3. Astronauts -- United States -- Biography 4. Space flights -- United States -- History 5. Hubble Space Telescope (Spacecraft) -- Maintenance and repair -- History
ISBN 9781101903544

LC 2016011667

In this book, astronaut Mike Massimino "puts you inside the suit, with all the zip and buoyancy of life in microgravity. . . . Taking us through the surreal wonder and beauty of his first spacewalk, the tragedy of losing friends in the Columbia shuttle accident, and the development of his enduring love for the Hubble Telescope . . . Massimino has written an ode to never giving up and the power of teamwork to make anything possible." (Publisher's note)

"This is an engaging and uplifting memoir that's sure to give readers a deeper appreciation for the U.S. space program and inspire some future astronauts." Pub Wkly

Mastromonaco, Alyssa, 1976-

Mastromonaco, Alyssa. **Who** thought this was a good idea? and other questions you should have answers to when you work in the White House. Alyssa Mastromonaco with Lauren Oyler. Twelve 2017 viii, 248 p.p illustrations (chiefly color) (hardback) $27 **92**

1. United States -- Politics and government 2. Government executives -- United States -- Biography 3. United States -- Politics and government -- 2009-2017 4. Women government executives -- United States -- Biography
ISBN 9781455588213; 9781455588220; 9781478961017

LC 2016050683

This book, by Alyssa Mastromonaco with Lauren Oyler, "is an intimate portrait of a president, a book about how to get stuff done, and the story of how one woman challenged, again and again, what a 'White House official' is supposed to look like. Here Alyssa shares the strategies that made her successful in politics and beyond, including the importance of confidence, the value of not being a jerk, and why ultimately everything comes down to hard work." (Publisher's note)

"The memoir abounds with intimate glimpses of Washington, D.C., celebrities . . . and cheerfully dispensed survival strategies." Kirkus

Matar, Hisham, 1970-

★ Matar, Hisham, 1970- The **return**; fathers, sons, and the land in between. Hisham Matar. Random House 2016 288 p. map (hardback) $26 **92**

1. Father-son relationship 2. Fathers & sons
ISBN 9780812994827; 9780812994834

LC 2015047925

Pulitzer Prize: Biography or Autobiography (2017)

Author Hisham Matar presents this "memoir of his journey home to his native Libya in search of the truth behind his father's disappearance. When Hisham Matar was a nineteen-year-old university student in England, his father was kidnapped. One of the Qaddafi regime's most prominent opponents in exile, he was held in a secret prison in Libya. Hisham returns with his mother and wife to the homeland he never thought he'd

go back to again. 'The Return' is the story of what he found there." (Publisher's note)

"A beautifully written, harrowing story of a son's search for his father and how the impact of inexplicable loss can be unrelenting while the strength of family and cultural ties can ultimately sustain." Kirkus

Matisse, Henri

Spurling, Hilary. **Matisse** the master; a life of Henri Matisse, the conquest of colour, 1909-1954. Knopf 2005 xxi, 511p il $40 **92**

1. Artists 2. Painters
ISBN 0-679-43429-1

LC 2004-51074

Companion volume to The unknown Matisse

"Spurling's rich, flexible style is well attuned to the rigors and flights of Matisse's creative life." Publ Wkly

Includes bibliographical references

Matsuhisa, Nobuyuki

Matsuhisa, Nobu. **Nobu**; a memoir. by Nobuyuki Matsuhisa. Emily Bestler Books/Atria 2017 xvii, 206 p.p illustrations (hardcover) $25 **92**

1. Restaurateurs 2. Cooks -- Biography 3. Restaurateurs -- Japan -- Biography 4. Restaurateurs -- United States -- Biography
ISBN 9781501122811; 9781501122798; 9781501122804

LC 2017024524

This memoir, by Nobuyuki Matsuhisa, "divulges both his dramatic life story and reflects on the philosophy and passion that has made him one of the world's most widely respected Japanese fusion culinary artists. Nobu needs no introduction. . . . But now, we are finally introduced to the private Nobu: the man who failed three times before starting the restaurant that would grow into an empire." (Publisher's note)

"A passionate chef with an open mind and a big heart, Matsuhisa shares lessons in humility, gratitude, and empathy that will stick with readers long after they've finished the final chapter." Pub Wkly

Maugham, W. Somerset (William Somerset), 1874-1965

Hastings, Selina. The **secret** lives of Somerset Maugham; a biography. Random House 2010 626p il **92**

1. Authors 2. Novelists 3. Dramatists 4. Travel writers 5. Authors, English 6. Short story writers 7. Biography, Individual
ISBN 978-1-4000-6141-9

LC 2009-35797

This is a biography of the English novelist and playwright.

"This steady-eyed biography of an extraordinary, extravagant, generous and bitter artist will not only fascinate its readers but encourage some to go to his work for the first time." Times Lit Suppl

Includes bibliographical references (p. 599-602)

Maupin, Armistead

★ Maupin, Armistead, 1944- **Logical** family; a memoir. Armistead Maupin. HarperCollins 2017 292 p. illustrations (hardcover) $27.99 **92**

1. Autobiographies 2. Gay men -- Biography 3. Gay authors -- Biography 4. Gay authors -- United States -- Biography 5. Authors, American -- 20th century -- Biography
ISBN 9780062391223; 9780062391230; 0062391224

In this memoir, author Armistead Maupin "chronicles his odyssey from the old South to freewheeling San Francisco, and his evolution from curious youth to ground-breaking writer and gay rights pioneer. . . . Reflecting on the profound impact those closest to him have had on his life, Maupin shares his candid search for his 'logical family,' the people he could call his own." (Publisher's note)

"Engaging reminiscences from an ebullient storyteller." Kirkus

Maxwell, William, 1908-2000

What there is to say we have said; the correspondence of Eudora Welty and William Maxwell. edited by Suzanne Marrs. Houghton Mifflin Harcourt 2011 499p il $35   **92**

1. Authors 2. Novelists 3. Magazine editors 4. Short story writers

ISBN 0547376499; 9780547376493; 978-0-547-37649-3; 0-547-37649-9

LC 2010-42105

"Letters between writers often have a lot of shop talk of interest to other writers and literary cultists, but this collection yields broader pleasures, too. In addition to being stellar writers, Welty and Maxwell were also accomplished critics, and one of the joys of the book is eavesdropping on their assessments of authors as varied as John Updike and Virginia Woolf, Anton Chekhov and Charles Dickens, William Faulkner and E. M. Forster. Welty and Maxwell also shared an intense love of gardening – so much so that Marrs was forced, in the book's index, to include an extensive listing of various varieties of roses. . . . As these letters show, Welty and Maxwell regarded domestic life not as a tedious distraction from the writing desk, but as a crucial source of insight. . . . The title of the collection comes from Maxwell's conclusion, as he and Welty faced their mortality, that 'what there is to say we have said, in one way or the other. You know how much we love you.' That love, a source of sustenance and strength between two great writers, is also a bright tonic for the readers of this volume." Christ Sci Monit

Includes bibliographical references

Mayakovsky, Vladimir, 1893-1930

Night wraps the sky; writings by and about Mayakovsky. edited by Michael Almereyda. Farrar, Straus and Giroux 2008 xxvii, 272p il $27   **92**

1. Poets 2. Authors 3. Dramatists

ISBN 978-0-374-28135-9; 0-374-28135-1

LC 2007-46662

"The book further explores Mayakovsky's relationships with Lili Brik and Tatiana Yakovleva, explains his propaganda work, and addresses his mixture of the surreal, the lyric, and the sarcastic; the text is generously illustrated with photographs of Mayakovsky's friends and contemporaries and artworks of the times." Libr J

Mayer, Louis B. (Louis Burt), 1885-1957

★ Eyman, Scott. **Lion** of Hollywood; the life and legend of Louis B. Mayer. Simon & Schuster 2005 596p il $35   **92**

1. Motion picture executives

ISBN 0-7432-0481-6

LC 2005-42472

"Eyman's extensive knowledge of old Hollywood, his scrupulous research and his refusal to indict the often-pilloried Mayer make this biography an often revelatory delight." Publ Wkly

Includes bibliographical references

Mayes, Frances

Mayes, Frances. **Under** magnolia; a Southern memoir. Frances Mayes. Crown Publishers 2014 336 p. illustrations (hardback) $26   **92**

1. Bildungsromans 2. Autobiographies 3. Southern States 4. Authors, American -- 20th century -- Biography

ISBN 0307885917; 9780307885913

LC 2013042448

"'Under Magnolia' is a . . . moving ode to family and place, and a . . .

meditation on the ways they define us. . . . With acute sensory language, [author Frances] Mayes relishes the sweetness of the South, the smells and tastes at her family table, the fragrance of her hometown trees, and writes an unforgettable story of a girl whose perspicacity and dawning self-knowledge lead her out of the South and into the rest of the world, and then to a profound return home." (Publisher's note)

"With her trademark skill for capturing the essence of place and time, Mayes candidly reveals a youth riddled with psychological abuse and parental neglect that, nevertheless, ignited a fiery passion for adventure and self-discovery." Booklist

Includes bibliographical references

Mayfield, Katherine, 1958-

Mayfield, Kate. The **undertaker's** daughter; Kate Mayfield. Gallery Books 2015 368 p. (hardback) $24.99   **92**

1. Undertakers and undertaking 2. Authors -- United States -- Biography

ISBN 1476757283; 9781476757285; 9781476757292

LC 2014006727

In this memoir, by Kate Mayfield, the author "explores what it meant to be the daughter of a small-town undertaker. . . . After Kate Mayfield was born, she was taken directly to a funeral home. Her father was an undertaker, and for thirteen years the family resided in a place nearly synonymous with death. . . . In a memoir that reads like a Harper Lee novel, Mayfield draws the reader into a world of Southern mystique and ghosts." (Publisher's note)

"Mayfield's "secret life" forced her to lie and sneak around, and her teenage angst was only compounded by the brutal revelation from her sister Evelyn, a thoroughly unpleasant bully, that her father was a serial philanderer and a drunk. Mayfield fashions a poignant send-off to Jubilee in this thoughtfully rendered work." Pub Wkly

Maynard, Joyce, 1953-

Maynard, Joyce. The **best** of us; a memoir. Joyce Maynard. Bloomsbury USA 2017 viii, 437 p.p (hardcover) $27 **92**

1. Women authors -- United States -- Biography 2. Authors, American -- 20th century -- Biography 3. Pancreas -- Cancer -- Patients -- United States -- Biography

ISBN 9781635570366; 9781635570342

LC 2016058363

This book, by Joyce Maynard, is "a memoir about discovering strength in the midst of great loss. . . . Maynard met the first true partner she had ever known. Jim wore a rakish hat over a good head of hair; he asked real questions and gave real answers; he loved to see Joyce shine, both in and out of the spotlight; and he didn't mind the mess she made in the kitchen. He was not the husband Joyce imagined, but he quickly became the partner she had always dreamed of." (Publisher's note)

"This haunting story, penned by a master wordsmith, is a reminder to savor every loved one and every day." Booklist

Mays, Willie, 1931-

Hirsch, James S. **Willie** Mays; the life, the legend. authorized by Willie Mays. Scribner 2010 628p il $30   **92**

1. Baseball players 2. Baseball -- History 3. Baseball -- Biography 4. Biography, Individual 5. New York Giants (Baseball team)

ISBN 978-1-4165-4790-7; 1-4165-4790-8

LC 2009-49214

"This is a superb baseball book, but it's also a riveting narrative of Mays' life and times, ranging from his penchant for fancy suits to urban development in New York City to the giddy cult of celebrity. In the mid-1950s, Willie Mays was as famous as anyone in the country, gracing the cover of Time and other magazines and appearing on numerous television shows. More impressive — and what distinguishes this book from the run-of-the-mill sports biography — is Hirsch's extensive and cogent take on race relations and the civil-rights movement both within and outside of baseball." Seattle Times

Includes bibliographical references

Mbeki, Thabo, 1942-

Gevisser, Mark. A **legacy** of liberation; Thabo Mbeki and the future of the South African dream. Palgrave Macmillan 2009 376p il $29.95   **92**

1. Presidents 2. Political leaders 3. Government officials 4. South Africa -- Politics and government

ISBN 978-0-230-61100-9; 0-230-61100-1

LC 2008-50763

Abridged version of a book first published 2007 in South Africa with title: Thabo Mbeki: the dream deferred

This is a biography of South Africa's second president. Gevisser "traces Mbeki's family back several generations, from colonial dispossession through the struggle for liberation. . . . Mbeki's life story has the makings of a gripping tale. . . . Gevisser writes well, particularly when he is witness to an event, when his narrative leaps off the page." N Y Times Book Rev

Includes bibliographical references (p. [346]-365) and index

McBee, Thomas Page

McBee, Thomas Page. **Man** alive; a true story of violence, forgiveness and becoming a man. Thomas Page McBee. City Lights Publishers 2014 172 p. (City lights/sister spit) (paperback) $15.95   **92**

1. Violence 2. Masculinity 3. Gender identity -- United States 4. Transgender people -- United States -- Biography

ISBN 0872866246; 9780872866249

LC 2014022173

Author "Thomas Page McBee attempts to answer [What does it really mean to be a man?] by focusing on two of the men who most impacted his life; one, his otherwise ordinary father who abused him as a child, and the other, a mugger who almost killed him. Standing at the brink of the life-changing decision to transition from female to male, McBee seeks to understand these examples of flawed manhood." (Publisher's note)

"Full of bravery and clear, far-sighted compassion and devoid of sentiment, victimization, and cliché, McBee's meditations bring him a hard-won sense of self—one that is bound to inspire any reader who has struggled with internal dissonance." Pub Wkly

McBride, James

McBride, James. The **color** of water; a black man's tribute to his white mother. Riverhead Bks. 1996 228p il pa $14; $23.95   **92**

1. Authors 2. Novelists 3. Journalists 4. Memoirists 5. Parents of prominent persons

ISBN 1-57322-578-9 pa; 1-57322-022-1

LC 95-37243

"Told with humor and clear-eyed grace, McBride's memoir is not only a terrific story, it's a subtle contribution to the current debates on race and identity. . . . The sheer strength of spirit, pain and humor of McBride and his mother as they wrestled with different aspects of race and identity is vividly told." Nation

McBride, Sarah, 1990-

★ McBride, Sarah. **Tomorrow** will be different; love, loss, and the fight for trans equality. Sarah McBride. Crown Archetype 2018 288 p. (hardcover) $26   **92**

1. LGBT people -- Civil rights 2. Transgender people -- Biography 3. Transgender people -- Identity 4. Transgender people -- United States -- Biography 5. Transgender people -- Civil rights -- United States

ISBN 9781524761479; 9781524761486

LC 2017040046

This memoir, is author "[Sarah] McBride's story of love and loss and a powerful entry point into the LGBTQ community's battle for equal rights and what it means to be openly transgender. From issues like bathroom access to health care to gender in America, McBride weaves the important political and cultural milestones into a personal journey that will open hearts and change minds." (Publisher's note)

"All readers will find this book enlightening. Those struggling with gender identity, and their families and friends, will find hope in McBride's words." Library Journal

McBride-Jordan, Ruth, 1921-2010

McBride, James. The **color** of water; a black man's tribute to his white mother. Riverhead Bks. 1996 228p il pa $14; $23.95   **92**

1. Authors 2. Novelists 3. Journalists 4. Memoirists 5. Parents of prominent persons

ISBN 1-57322-578-9 pa; 1-57322-022-1

LC 95-37243

"Told with humor and clear-eyed grace, McBride's memoir is not only a terrific story, it's a subtle contribution to the current debates on race and identity. . . . The sheer strength of spirit, pain and humor of McBride and his mother as they wrestled with different aspects of race and identity is vividly told." Nation

McCartney, Paul

Sounes, Howard. **Fab**; an intimate life of Paul McCartney. Da Capo Press 2010 634p il $29.95   **92**

1. Singers 2. Rock musicians 3. Beatles 4. Songwriters

ISBN 978-0-306-81783-0

LC 2010-936124

"Divided into two equally large sections—'With the Beatles' and 'After the Beatles'—Fab covers all the highlights of McCartney's life and long career: his early days in Liverpool; his meeting with John Lennon; the craziness of Beatlemania; his solo albums; the creation and collapse of his post-Beatles band, Wings; his marriage to Linda Eastman; his last meetings with Lennon; his drug bust in Japan; his forays into classical music; his disastrous second marriage to Heather Mills. . . . Sounes is often brutally honest, offering a full portrait—warts and all— of one of the most famous men of the modern era. A must for Beatles and McCartney fans." Booklist

Includes bibliographical references

McClellan, George Brinton, 1826-1885

Sears, Stephen W. **George** B. McClellan; the young Napoleon. Da Capo Press 1999 482p il map pa $16.95   **92**

1. Generals 2. Governors 3. Presidential candidates 4. United States -- History -- 1861-1865, Civil War

ISBN 0-306-80913-3

LC 98-33277

First published 1988 by Ticknor & Fields

This biography of the Civil War general "covers both the awkward character traits that led to McClellan's incompetence and the battlefield actions that he regularly bungled. In addition to its merit as Civil War history, the book is of great interest as the portrait of an intelligent man working at what he failed to realize was the wrong profession." Atlantic

Includes bibliographical references

McClelland, Mac

McClelland, Mac. **Irritable** hearts; a PTSD love story. Mac McClelland. Flatiron Books 2015 320 p. (hardback) $27.99   **92**

1. Journalists 2. Haiti Earthquake, Haiti, 2010 3. Post-traumatic stress disorder 4. Man-woman relationships 5. Earthquakes -- Psychological aspects 6. Journalists -- United States -- Biography 7. Post-traumatic stress disorder -- Patients -- United States -- Biography
ISBN 1250052890; 9781250052896

LC 2014034163

Author Mac McClelland presents her memoir "investigating the damage in her own mind and repairing her broken psyche. She begins to probe the depths of her illness, exploring our culture's history with PTSD, delving into the latest research. When . . . McClelland left Haiti after reporting on the devastating earthquake of 2010, she never imagined how the assignment would irrevocably affect her own life." (Publisher's note)

McCourt, Alphie

McCourt, Alphie. A **long** stone's throw. Sterling & Ross Publishers 2008 267p $24.95   **92**

1. Irish Americans 2. Memoirists 3. Restaurateurs 4. Business managers 5. Immigrants -- United States
ISBN 978-0-9814535-5-2; 0-9814535-5-4

LC 2008-32672

"Alphie is the youngest of the four McCourt brothers and the third—after Frank and Malachy—to pen a memoir about his life in Ireland and the U.S. . . . McCourt always finds irony in life and his tales of the bar and restaurant business and its clientele are laugh-out-loud funny. Sensitive, lyrical, funny, stubborn, impetuous, McCourt writes with a steady hand, a joyful heart, and an Irishman's sense of life's absurdities." Publ WKly

McCourt, Frank

McCourt, Frank. **Teacher** man; a memoir. Scribner 2005 258p $26   **92**

1. Authors 2. Irish Americans 3. Memoirists 4. High school teachers
ISBN 0-7432-4377-3

LC 2005-54113

"Full of gritty specifics, never preachy, often hilarious, McCourt's . . . book thrusts you right into the hormones-and-catcalls chaos of the classroom—where learning is not just a mystery but a flat-out miracle." Newsweek

McCourt, Malachy, 1931-

McDonald, Brian. **Death** need not be fatal; Malachy McCourt with Brian McDonald. Center Street 2017 259 p. illustrations, portraits (hardback) $27   **92**

1. Aging 2. Death 3. Quality of life 4. Quality of life -- Philosophy 5. Aging -- Psychological aspects 6. Death -- Psychological aspects 7. Older men -- New York (State) -- New York -- Biography 8. Irish Americans -- New York (State) -- New York -- Biography
ISBN 9781478974116; 9781478917069; 1478917067

LC 2017001094

In this memoir author Malachy McCourt "shares his views on death - sometimes hilarious and often poignant - and on what will or won't happen after his last breath is drawn. McCourt also trains a sober eye on the tragedies that have shaped his life: the deaths of his sister and twin brothers; the real story behind Angela's famous ashes; and a poignant account of the death of the man who left his mother, brothers, and him to

nearly die in squalor." (Publisher's note)

"Veering at times into philosophical inquiry, addiction narrative, celebrity tell-all, and a tender appraisal of brotherly rivalry, McCourt continually returns to themes of acceptance, gratitude, and love." Booklist

McCracken, Elizabeth

McCracken, Elizabeth. An **exact** replica of a figment of my imagination; a memoir. Little, Brown and Co. 2008 184p $19.99   **92**

1. Authors 2. Novelists 3. Librarians 4. Bereavement 5. Miscarriage 6. Essayists 7. Short story writers 8. Biography, Individual
ISBN 978-0-316-02767-0; 0-316-02767-7

LC 2008-5032

This is a memoir by the American novelist. "Two years ago [Elizabeth McCracken] was living in a remote part of France, working on her novel, and waiting for the birth of her first child. This book is about what happened next. In her ninth month of pregnancy, she learned that her baby boy had died. How do you deal with and recover from this kind of loss? . . . McCracken considers the nature of love and grief [here]." (Publisher's note)

"McCracken has succeeded in writing a beautiful, precise and heartbreaking account without sentimentality or pity." Publ Wkly

McDaniel, Hattie, 1895-1952

Watts, Jill. **Hattie** McDaniel; black ambition, white Hollywood. Amistad 2005 352p il hardcover o.p. pa $14.95 **92**

1. Actors
ISBN 0-06-051490-6; 0-06-051491-4 pa

LC 2005-42126

"Watts is both sympathetic and honest: we pity McDaniel and her unenviable position, but at the same time, see how her intense careerism drove her often to accommodate rather than challenge film industry racism. . . . Watts' research is extensive, her writing clear and accessible, and her book a thorough, engaging, intelligent piece of historical scholarship." Women's Rev of Books

McDermott, Zack

McDermott, Zack. **Gorilla** and the bird; a memoir of madness and a mother's love. Zack McDermott. Little, Brown & Co. 2017 278 p. (hardcover) $27   **92**

1. Mother-son relationship 2. Manic-depressive illness 3. Mothers and sons -- United States -- Biography 4. Manic-depressive persons -- United States -- Biography
ISBN 9780316315142; 9780316315135

LC 2017936279

This book, by Zack McDermott, tells "the story of a young man fighting to recover from a devastating psychotic break and the mother who refuses to give up on him. Zack McDermott, a 26-year-old Brooklyn public defender, woke up one morning convinced he was being filmed, Truman Show-style, as part of an audition for a TV pilot. . . . After a manic spree around Manhattan, Zack, who is bipolar, was arrested on a subway platform and admitted to Bellevue Hospital." (Publisher's note)

McGowan, Rose, 1973-

McGowan, Rose, 1973- **Brave**; cult member, runaway, captive, starlet, victim, sex symbol, justice seeker. Rose McGowan. HarperOne 2018 xiv, 251 p.p (hardback) $27.99   **92**

1. Actors -- United States -- Biography
ISBN 0062655981; 9780062655981

LC 2017058622

This book "is . . . [actress Rose McGowan's] raw, honest, and poignant memoir/manifesto--a no-holds-barred, pull-no-punches account of the rise of a millennial icon, fearless activist, and unstoppable force for change who is determined to expose the truth about the entertainment industry, dismantle the concept of fame, shine a light on a multi-billion-dollar business built on systemic misogyny, and empower people everywhere to wake up and be BRAVE." (Publisher's note)

"Frank and bold, this memoir is a resounding wakeup call to the entertainment industry and to society as a whole." Pub Wkly

McKeon, Kathy

McKeon, Kathy. **Jackie's** girl; my life with the Kennedy family. Kathy McKeon. Gallery Books 2017 309 p. illustrations (chiefly color) (hardcover: alk. paper) $26   **92**

1. Women household employees -- Biography 2. Household employees -- United States -- Biography 3. Irish American women -- United States -- Biography 4. Women household employees -- United States -- Biography
ISBN 9781501158964; 9781501158940; 9781501158957
LC 2017003981

This book, by Kathy McKeon, is a "coming-of-age memoir by a young woman who spent thirteen years as Jackie Kennedy's personal assistant. . . . In 1964, Kathy McKeon was . . . hired as the personal assistant to former first lady Jackie Kennedy. The next thirteen years of her life were spent in Jackie's service, during which Kathy . . . played a crucial role in raising young Caroline and John Jr., . . . [and] had a front-row seat to some of the twentieth century's most significant events." (Publisher's note)

"Celebrity watchers who covet an insider's role will find McKeon's frank yet benevolent memoir to be both a sobering reality check and an engaging foray into the ever-fascinating world of the Kennedy dynasty." Booklist

McKinley, William, 1843-1901

Merry, Robert W., 1946- **President** McKinley; architect of the American century. Robert W. Merry. Simon & Schuster 2017 x, 608 p.p illustrations (hardback) $35   **92**

1. Presidents -- United States -- Biography
ISBN 9781451625448; 9781451625455; 9781451625462
LC 2016050943

In this book, historian Robert Merry "resurrects the presidential reputation of William McKinley, which loses out to the brilliant and flamboyant Theodore Roosevelt who succeeded him after his assassination. He portrays McKinley as a chief executive of consequence whose low place in the presidential rankings does not reflect his enduring accomplishments and the stamp he put on the country's future role in the world." (Publisher's note)

"Critics or admirers of McKinley's presidency will agree it was a momentous one and that Merry's is a fair-minded profile of its central actor." Booklist

Includes bibliographical references (pages 491-500) and index.

McLuhan, Marshall, 1911-1980

Coupland, Douglas. **Marshall** McLuhan; you know nothing of my work! Atlas & Co. 2010 216p $24   **92**

1. Authors 2. Mass media 3. Sociologists 4. Literary critics 5. Nonfiction writers 6. Television critics
ISBN 978-1-935633-16-7

This is a biography of the Canadian mass media specialist.

"The book rewards by refusing to slip into the numbing vortex of academic discourse, taking a fizzy, pop-culture approach to explaining a deep thinker, one who ended up popularized almost in spite of himself." N Y Times Book Rev

McMurtry, Larry

McMurtry, Larry. **Books**; a memoir. Simon & Schuster 2008 259p $24   **92**

1. Authors 2. Novelists 3. Booksellers and bookselling 4. Essayists 5. Authors, American 6. Short story writers
ISBN 978-1-416-58334-9; 1-416-58334-3
LC 2008-10565

"A pleasant amble in Bookland and a treat for the bookishly inclined." Kirkus

McPartland, Marian

De Barros, Paul. **Shall** we play that one together? the life and art of jazz piano legend Marian McPartland. Paul de Barros. St. Martin's Press 2012 496 p. (hardcover) $35.00   **92**

1. Pianists -- United States -- Biography 2. Jazz musicians -- United States -- Biography
ISBN 0312558031; 9780312558031; 9781250019011
LC 2012028242

This biography of Marian McPartland, by Paul de Barros, is "[t]he story of the distinguished female jazz pianist who devoted herself to her art and won popularity, the respect of her colleagues and just about every honor the profession bestows. . . . De Barros tells us about her albums . . . [and] McPartland's versatility and success with Piano Jazz, her NPR show that began in 1978. . . . The author also charts her fierce devotion to jazz education and, sadly, her physical decline." (Kirkus)

Includes bibliographical references

McTell, Blind Willie, 1898?-1959

Gray, Michael. **Hand** me my travelin' shoes; in search of Blind Willie McTell. Chicago Review Press 2009 432p il $26.95   **92**

1. Blind 2. Singers 3. Guitarists 4. Blues music 5. Blues musicians 6. Songwriters
ISBN 978-1-55652-975-7
LC 2009-22329

First published 2007 in the United Kingdom

"Less a conventional biography than a mixture of history, travelogue and detective story, Gray paints an evocative portrait of an artist who defied blues stereotypes." Kirkus

Includes bibliographical references

Meagher, Thomas Francis, 1823-1867

★ Egan, Timothy. The **immortal** Irishman; the Irish revolutionary who became an American hero. Timothy Egan. Houghton Mifflin Harcourt 2016 384 p. (hardcover) $28; (ebook) $28   **92**

1. Revolutionaries 2. Irish -- United States 3. Ireland -- History -- Famine, 1845-1852 4. Irish Americans -- Biography 5. Governors -- Montana -- Biography 6. Prisoners -- Tasmania -- Biography 7. Heroes -- United States -- Biography 8. Generals -- United States -- Biography 9. Revolutionaries -- Ireland -- Biography 10. United States. Army -- Officers -- Biography 11. United States. Army of the Potomac. Irish Brigade 12. United States -- History -- Civil War, 1861-1865 -- Biography
ISBN 9780544272880; 9780544272477
LC 2015037256

In this book, by Timothy Egan, the "Irish-American story, with all its twists and triumphs, is told through the improbable life of one man. A dashing young orator during the Great Famine of the 1840s, . . . Thomas Francis Meagher led a failed uprising against British rule, for which he was banished to a Tasmanian prison colony. He escaped and six months later was heralded in the streets of New York — the revolutionary hero, back from the dead." (Publisher's note)

"A fascinating, well-told story by an author fully committed to his subject. Egan's impeccable research, uncomplicated readability, and flowing narrative reflect his deep knowledge of a difficult and complex man." Kirkus

Includes bib and index

Mealer, Bryan

Mealer, Bryan. The **kings** of Big Spring; God, oil, and one family's search for the American dream. Bryan Mealer. St. Martin's Press 2018 384 p. $27.99   **92**
    1. Millionaires -- Texas 2. Petroleum industry -- Texas -- History
    ISBN 1250058910; 9781250058911

This book, by Bryan Mealer, presents "a saga of family, fortune, faith in Texas, where blood is bond and oil is king In 1892, . . . Mealer's great-grandfather leaves the Georgia mountains and heads west into Texas, looking for wealth and adventure in the raw and open country. But his luck soon runs out. Beset by drought, the family loses their farm just as the dead pastures around them give way to one of the biggest oil booms in American history." (Publisher's note)

"As tribute to the grit of the rural poor, as social history of dirt-and-oil Texas, and as rambunctious family saga, this work triumphs." (LJ)

Mecom, Jane, 1712-1794

★ Lepore, Jill. **Book** of ages; the life and opinions of Jane Franklin. Jill Lepore. Alfred A. Knopf 2013 464 p. $27.95 **92**
    1. Boston (Mass.) -- Biography 2. Women -- United States -- Social conditions -- 18th century
    ISBN 0307958345; 9780307958341

                                                          LC 2013001012
National Book Awards: Nonfiction Finalist (2013)

This book on Jane Franklin Mecom by Jill Lepore tells "the story of Benjamin Franklin's youngest sister . . . using only a few of her letters and a small archive of births and deaths." (Kirkus Reviews) "Jane's surviving letters are . . . the correspondence of a smart, witty, hardworking woman who 'loved best books about ideas,' reveled in gossip, expressed 'impolite' opinions on religion and politics, and shared piquant observations of the struggle for American independence." (Booklist)

Includes bibliographical references

Meeink, Frank, 1975-

Meeink, Frank. **Autobiography** of a recovering skinhead; Frank Meeink's story. as told to Jody M. Roy. Hawthorne Books 2010 350p pa $10   **92**
    1. White supremacy movements 2. Memoirists 3. Gang members 4. Social activists 5. White supremacists 6. Motivational speakers
    ISBN 978-0-9790188-2-4

                                                          LC 2009-27527
"Before he was out of his teens, Meeink, a member of a group of white supremacists, was behind prison bars. But by the time he was released on parole, he was a changed man, having cast off his hatred; he became a public speaker, sharing his experiences, helping others to understand the nature of hatred and to find ways to combat it. . . . Stories of personal redemption don't get much more interesting than this one, and the gritty first-person narrative . . . draws the reader into Meeink's story, giving it an immediacy and a visceral intensity that makes us feel as though we've lived a bit of his life. Readers should be warned that the book is unflinchingly straightforward: some of the language is quite raw, and some of the imagery quite graphic." Booklist

Meghan, Duchess of Sussex, 1981-

Morton, Andrew. **Meghan**; a Hollywood princess. Andrew Morton. Grand Central Publishing 2018 272 p. $27   **92**
    1. Actresses -- Biography 2. Princesses -- Great Britain -- Biography
    ISBN 1538747359; 9781538747353

This book, by Andrew Morton, offers an "inspiring look at Meghan Markle, the confident and charismatic duchess-to-be whose warm and affectionate engagement interview won the hearts of the world. . . . Drawing on exclusive interviews with her family members and closest friends, . . . Morton introduces us to the real Meghan as he reflects on the impact that she has already had on the rigid traditions of the House of Windsor, as well as what the future might hold." (Publisher's note)

Meir, Golda, 1898-1978

Klagsbrun, Francine. **Lioness**; Golda Meir and the nation of Israel. Francine Klagsbrun. Schocken Books 2017 xix, 824 p.p illustrations (hardcover) $40   **92**
    1. Biography 2. Women prime ministers -- Israel -- Biography
    ISBN 9780805242379; 9780805243505

                                                          LC 2017004908
This book, by Francine Klagsbrun, presents a "biography of . . . [Golda Meir,] the fourth prime minister of Israel. . . . As prime minister, Golda negotiated arms agreements with Richard Nixon and Henry Kissinger and had . . . meetings with Jordan's King Hussein in the unsuccessful pursuit of a land-for-peace agreement with Israel's neighbors. But her time in office ended in tragedy, when Israel was caught off guard by Egypt and Syria's surprise attack on Yom Kippur in 1973." (Publisher's note)

"With hundreds of books on Meir available, this one stands out with its depth of resources and research, building a convincing case that Meir's achievements are still relevant." LJ

Includes bibliographical references and index.

Mekhennet, Souad

★ Mekhennet, Souad. **I** was told to come alone; my journey behind the lines of jihad. Souad Mekhennet. Henry Holt & Co. 2017 354 p. (hardback) $30   **92**
    1. Jihad 2. Terrorism -- Middle East 3. IS (Organization)
    ISBN 9781627798969; 9781627798976

                                                          LC 2016054740
In this memoir, "we accompany [Souad] Mekhennet as she journeys behind the lines of jihad, starting in the German neighborhoods where the 9/11 plotters were radicalized and the Iraqi neighborhoods where Sunnis and Shia turned against one another, and culminating on the Turkish/Syrian border region where ISIS is a daily presence. In her travels across the Middle East and North Africa, she documents her chilling run-ins with various intelligence services." (Publisher's note)

"A riveting memoir and a literary bombshell that effectively eviscerates every preconception, misconception, and prejudice readers have about the Arab world, I Was Told to Come Alone reinforces the singular significance of journalism, especially foreign journalism, at a time when it is facing its greatest challenges." Booklist

Includes bibliographical references and index.

Melendez, Benjy

Voloj, Julian. **Ghetto** Brother; Warrior to Peacemaker. Julian Voloj; illustrated by Claudia Ahlering. NBM Publishing 2015 128 p. chiefly b&w ill. $12.99   **92**
    1. Peace movements 2. Gangs -- Graphic novels 3. Puerto Ricans -- New York (N.Y.)
    ISBN 1561639486; 9781561639489

This graphic novel by Julian Voloj, illustrated by Claudia Ahlering, "tells the true story of Benjy Melendez, a Bronx legend, son of Puerto-Rican immigrants, who founded, at the end of the 1960s, the notorious

Ghetto Brothers gang. From the seemingly bombed-out ravages of his neighborhood, wracked by drugs, poverty, and violence, he managed to extract an incredibly positive energy from this riot ridden era: his multiracial gang promoted peace rather than violence." (Publisher's note)

"Using Melendez as narrator-protagonist, Voloj places the seminal events of November and December 1971 in the contexts of post–WWII Puerto Rican immigration and difficult assimilation to New York, and of Melendez's personal development as he learned of and adopted his Jewish heritage. Ahlering bases her artwork partly on news and documentary photography, although she doesn't incorporate or copy photos but draws on them for detail, composition, and tonal variety." Booklist

Mellon, Andrew William, 1855-1937

★ Cannadine, David. **Mellon**; an American life. A.A. Knopf 2006 779p il $35   **92**
1. Philanthropists 2. Financiers 3. Art collectors 4. Secretaries of the treasury
ISBN 0-679-45032-7; 978-0-679-45032-0

LC 2006-45116

This is a "biography of Andrew Mellon, the powerful American financier, secretary of the treasury, and art collector. . . . Cannadine's recounting of Mellon's public career make this a worthy contribution to our understanding of the man and his era." Booklist
Includes bibliographical references

Mellon, Paul, Mrs

★ Gordon, Meryl. **Bunny** Mellon; the life of an American style legend. Meryl Gordon. Grand Central Publishing 2017 532 p. (hardback) $28   **92**
1. Gardeners -- Biography 2. Women philanthropists -- Biography 3. Gardeners -- United States -- Biography 4. Philanthropists -- United States -- Biography 5. Women gardeners -- United States -- Biography 6. Upper class women -- United States -- Biography 7. Women philanthropists -- United States -- Biography
ISBN 9781455588732; 9781455588725; 9781455588749

LC 2017016493

This biography, by Meryl Gordon, looks at the life of "Bunny Mellon, the style icon and American aristocrat who designed the White House Rose Garden for her friend JFK and served as a living witness to 20th Century American history, operating in the high-level arenas of politics, diplomacy, art and fashion." (Publisher's note)

"Readers interested in gardening, art, and interior design will drool over Bunny's fine tastes, and her ease at fulfilling every one of them, but all lovers of biographies will marvel at Gordon's portrayal of Bunny's long life, and the significant figures who buzzed in and out of it." Booklist.
Includes bibliographical references and index

Melton, Glennon Doyle, 1976-

Melton, Glennon Doyle. **Love** warrior; A Memoir. Glennon Doyle Melton. Flatiron Books 2016 272 p. (hardcover) $25.99; (ebook) $60   **92**
1. Women authors 2. Divorced women 3. American authors 4. Divorced women -- United States -- Biography
ISBN 9781250075727; 9781250110152; 9781250075741

LC 2016016415

In this memoir, "just when Glennon Doyle Melton was beginning to feel she had it all figured out—three happy children, a doting spouse, and a writing career so successful . . . —her husband revealed his infidelity and she was forced to realize that nothing was as it seemed. . . . [This book] is the story of one marriage, . . . [and] the healing that is possible for any of us when we refuse to settle for good enough and begin to face pain and love head-on." (Publisher's note)

"Though the memoir sometimes reads like a self-help book rather than a narrative, it nevertheless tells a compelling story about self-discovery and the nature of mature love. Candid, brave, and generous." Kirkus

Melville, Herman, 1819-1891

Delbanco, Andrew. **Melville**; his world and work. Knopf 2005 xxiii, 415p il map $30   **92**
1. Authors 2. Novelists 3. Authors, American
ISBN 0-375-40314-0

LC 2005-40919

"This is sure to elicit new appreciation for Melville's work and could well be the best one-volume biography for some time to come." Libr J
Includes bibliographical references

Melvin, Leland, 1964-

Melvin, Leland. **Chasing** space; an astronaut's story of grit, grace, and second chances. Leland Melvin. Amistad 2017 vii, 241 p.p chiefly color illustrations (hardcover) $25.99   **92**
1. National Football League 2. African American astronauts 3. United States. National Aeronautics and Space Administration 4. Astronauts -- United States -- Biography 5. Football players -- United States -- Biography
ISBN 0062496727; 9780062496775; 9780062496720

In this memoir, by Leland Melvin, "a former NASA astronaut and NFL wide receiver shares his personal journey from the gridiron to the stars, examining the intersecting roles of community, perseverance and grace that align to create the opportunities for success." (Publisher's note)

"The author makes his seemingly larger-than-life experiences relatable to readers, emphasizing how his hard work and confidence were crucial to his success." SLJ

Mencken, H. L. (Henry Louis), 1880-1956

Rodgers, Marion Elizabeth. **Mencken**; the American iconoclast. Oxford University Press 2005 662p il $35   **92**
1. Authors 2. Essayists 3. Philologists 4. Social critics 5. Literary critics 6. Newspaper editors
ISBN 0-19-507238-3

LC 2005-47786

"This is a meticulous portrait of one of the most original and complicated men in American letters." Publ Wkly
Includes bibliographical references

Teachout, Terry. The **skeptic**: the life of H.L. Mencken. HarperCollins Pubs. 2002 410p il $29.95; pa $15.95   **92**
1. Authors 2. Essayists 3. Philologists 4. Social critics 5. Literary critics 6. Newspaper editors
ISBN 0-06-050528-1; 0-06-050529-X pa

LC 2002-24953

This is "an engrossing, sympathetic biography." Booklist
Includes bibliograpical references

Mendeleev, Dmitri I.

Gordin, Michael D. A **well**-ordered thing: Dmitrii Mendeleev and the shadow of the periodic table. Basic Books 2004 364p il $30   **92**
1. Chemists 2. Periodic law
ISBN 0-465-02775-X

LC 2003-25533

"This is not a chronological biography of the man; rather, it is a work that shows Mendeleev as an important part of the changes that occurred in Russia during the days between the freeing of the serfs in 1861 and the crumbling of tsarist power in 1905." Sci Books & Films

Includes bibliographical references

Mendelsohn, Daniel Adam, 1960-

Mendelsohn, Daniel. An **odyssey**; a father, a son, and an epic. Daniel Mendelsohn. Alfred A. Knopf 2017 306 p. (hardcover) $26.95 **92**

1. Father-son relationship

ISBN 9780385350594; 0385350597; 9780385350600

LC 2017011844

This memoir, by Daniel Mendelsohn, is "a deeply moving tale of a father and son's transformative journey in reading--and reliving--Homer's epic masterpiece. When eighty-one-year-old Jay Mendelsohn decides to enroll in the undergraduate 'Odyssey' seminar his son teaches at Bard College, the two find themselves on an adventure as profoundly emotional as it is intellectual." (Publisher's note)

"Mendelsohn weaves family history and trenchant literary analysis into a luminous whole." Pub Wkly

Mendelsohn, Daniel, 1960-

Mendelsohn, Daniel. The **lost**; a search for six of six million. photographs by Matt Mendelsohn. HarperCollins Publishers 2006 512p il $27.95 **92**

1. Journalists 2. Classicists 3. College teachers 4. Literary critics 5. Holocaust, 1933-1945

ISBN 0-06-054297-7

LC 2006-41096

The author describes his efforts to find out what happened to his uncle Shmiel Jager, his wife and four daughters, who lived in the Polish town of Bolechow, and perished during the Holocaust.

"Mr. Mendelsohn, an evocative, ruminative writer, brings to life the vanished world not just of prewar Poland but also of his childhood and his extended family." N Y Times (Late N Y Ed)

Mendelsohn, Jay, 1929-2012

Mendelsohn, Daniel. An **odyssey**; a father, a son, and an epic. Daniel Mendelsohn. Alfred A. Knopf 2017 306 p. (hardcover) $26.95 **92**

1. Father-son relationship

ISBN 9780385350594; 0385350597; 9780385350600

LC 2017011844

This memoir, by Daniel Mendelsohn, is "a deeply moving tale of a father and son's transformative journey in reading--and reliving--Homer's epic masterpiece. When eighty-one-year-old Jay Mendelsohn decides to enroll in the undergraduate 'Odyssey' seminar his son teaches at Bard College, the two find themselves on an adventure as profoundly emotional as it is intellectual." (Publisher's note)

"Mendelsohn weaves family history and trenchant literary analysis into a luminous whole." Pub Wkly

Menil, Dominique de

Middleton, William. **Double** vision; the unerring eye of art world avatars Dominique and John de Menil. William Middleton. Alfred A. Knopf 2018 800 p. (hardcover) $40 **92**

1. Biography 2. Art -- Exhibitions 3. Art -- Collectors and collecting 4. Art -- Collectors and collecting -- United States -- Biography

ISBN 9780375415432

LC 2017027976

This book, by William Middleton, is the "first and definitive biography of the celebrated collectors Dominique and John de Menil, who

became one of the greatest cultural forces of the twentieth century through groundbreaking exhibits of art, artistic scholarship, the creation of innovative galleries and museums, and work with civil rights." (Publisher's note)

"This exhaustively researched, satisfying slab of a book offers a thorough look into the lives and influence of an extraordinary couple." Pub Wkly

Includes bibliographical references and index

Menil, John de

Middleton, William. **Double** vision; the unerring eye of art world avatars Dominique and John de Menil. William Middleton. Alfred A. Knopf 2018 800 p. (hardcover) $40 **92**

1. Biography 2. Art -- Exhibitions 3. Art -- Collectors and collecting 4. Art -- Collectors and collecting -- United States -- Biography

ISBN 9780375415432

LC 2017027976

This book, by William Middleton, is the "first and definitive biography of the celebrated collectors Dominique and John de Menil, who became one of the greatest cultural forces of the twentieth century through groundbreaking exhibits of art, artistic scholarship, the creation of innovative galleries and museums, and work with civil rights." (Publisher's note)

"This exhaustively researched, satisfying slab of a book offers a thorough look into the lives and influence of an extraordinary couple." Pub Wkly

Includes bibliographical references and index

Merkin, Daphne

Merkin, Daphne. **This** close to happy; a reckoning with depression. Daphne Merkin. Farrar, Straus & Giroux 2017 288 p. (hardback) $26 **92**

1. Mental health 2. Postpartum depression 3. Depression (Psychology) 4. Psychotherapist and patient 5. Women -- Health and hygiene 6. Depressed persons -- Biography 7. Postpartum depression -- Treatment 8. Depression in women -- United States -- Biography 9. Postpartum depression -- United States -- Biography 10. Depression in children -- United States -- Biography

ISBN 9780374140366; 9780374711917

LC 2016025616

In this memoir, Daphne Merkin "describes not only the harrowing sorrow that she has known all her life, but also her early, redemptive love of reading and gradual emergence as a writer. Written with an acute understanding of the ways in which her condition has evolved as well as affected those around her, . . . [the book] is an utterly candid coming-to-terms with an illness that many share but few talk about, one that remains shrouded in stigma." (Publisher's note)

"This book is a wonderful addition to literature about the unrelenting battle against depression." Pub Wkly

Merrill, James, 1926-1995

Hammer, Langdon. **James** Merrill; life and art. Langdon Hammer. Alfred A. Knopf 2015 912 p. 32 plates; illustrations (hardback) $40 **92**

1. American poets 2. Gay men -- United States -- Biography 3. Gay authors -- United States -- Biography 4. Poets, American -- 20th century -- Biography

ISBN 0375413332; 9780375413339

LC 2014029325

Lambda Literary Awards: Gay Memoir/Biography (2016)

This book by Langdon Hammer is a biography of poet James Merrill. "The objective seems to look at the line between art and life in Merrill's poetry--not the least of which is seen in the intersection between Merrill's obsession with the Ouija board as literary starter and some of his experimental long poems . . . and the influence of poets Oscar Wilde and Rainer Maria Rilke. Hammer points to Merrill's need to define his own masculinity as a gay man." (Library Journal)

"While certainly organized for readers who adore biographies and life dramas, this will strongly appeal to those who love to discover where art springs from life." Library Journal

Micheaux, Oscar, 1884-1951

McGilligan, Patrick. **Oscar** Micheaux; the great and only; the life of America's first great Black filmmaker. HarperCollins Publishers 2007 402p il $29.95 **92**
1. Authors 2. Novelists 3. Screenwriters 4. Motion picture directors
ISBN 978-0-06-073139-7; 0-06-073130-7

LC 2007-60735

"One of the fascinating side streets in American film is the history of 'race pictures,' celluloid productions by black artists for black audiences during those decades when Jim Crow laws enforced segregation. The mainstay of race pictures was Oscar Micheaux (18841951), an intrepid filmmaker-novelist-entrepreneur whose career spanned four decades and who made more than 40 movies. . . . McGilligan's prose style may be pedestrian, but he organizes his biographical materials into a lively, readable tale." N Y Times Book Rev

Michelangelo Buonarroti, 1475-1564

★ Unger, Miles J. **Michelangelo**; a life in six masterpieces. Miles J. Unger. Simon & Schuster 2014 416 p. illustrations, map (hardback) $29.95 **92**
1. Artists, Italian 2. Artists -- Biography
ISBN 9781451678741; 1451678746

LC 2013045778

In this biography of the artist Michelangelo, author "Miles Unger narrates the astonishing life of this driven and difficult man through six of his greatest masterpieces. Each work expanded the expressive range of the medium, from the Pietà Michelangelo carved as a brash young man, to the apocalyptic Last Judgment, the work of an old man tested by personal trials." (Publisher's note)

"Unger highlights Michelangelo's singular achievement without glossing over the defects in his mercurial character—or obscuring the corruption and violence pervading his Renaissance world. A masterful portrait of a dauntingly complex figure." Booklist
Includes bibliographical references and index

Mike D, 1965-

Horovitz, Adam. **Beastie** Boys book; Michael Diamond and Adam Horovitz. Spiegel & Grau 2018 592 p. $50 **92**
1. Hip-hop 2. Rap musicians -- Biography 3. Beastie Boys 4. Rap musicians -- United States -- Biography
ISBN 9780812995541

LC 2018004935

In this book, Beastie Boys band members Michael Diamond and Adam Horovitz "offer revealing and very funny accounts of their transition from teenage punks to budding rappers; their early collaboration with Russell Simmons and Rick Rubin; the debut album that became the first hip hop record ever to hit #1, 'Licensed to Ill'--and the album's messy fallout as the band broke with Def Jam; . . . their evolution as musicians and social activists . . . and more." (Publisher's note)

Miletich, Patrick Jay, 1968-

Wertheim, L. Jon. **Blood** in the cage; mixed martial arts, Pat Miletich, and the furious rise of the UFC. Houghton Mifflin Harcourt 2009 251p il $25 **92**
1. Martial arts 2. Sportswriters 3. Ultimate Fighting Championship (Organization)
ISBN 978-0-618-98261-5; 0-618-98261-2

LC 2008-36764

"MMA has yet to find its great scribe, its Liebling, Pierce Egan or Norman Mailer, but it is young. Until that new bard of bloodshed comes along, 'Blood in the Cage' will stand as a worthy introduction to the birth of something both awful and beautiful." Salon

Mill, John Stuart, 1806-1873

Mill, John Stuart. **Autobiography**; edited with an introduction by John M. Robson. Penguin Bks. 1989 234p pa $8.95 **92**
1. Economists 2. Philosophers 3. Essayists 4. Writers on politics
ISBN 0-14-043316-3

LC 91-103446

Written 1873

"A human document of unusual interest. Mill, a noble spirit educated by a narrow-minded pedant, shut off from all normal contact, developed an egotism that makes this book so completely an autobiography that besides his father and [his] wife he seems to exist alone in a world of which he has both center and circumference." Pratt Alcove
Includes bibliographical references

Millay, Edna St. Vincent, 1892-1950

Milford, Nancy. **Savage** beauty: the life of Edna St. Vincent Millay. Random House 2001 550p il $29.95; pa $14.95 **92**
1. Poets 2. Authors 3. Dramatists
ISBN 0-394-57589-X; 0-375-76081-4 pa

LC 2001-18598

"In 1923, Edna St. Vincent Millay became the first woman to win the Pulitzer Prize for poetry. To write her biography, Milford . . . persuaded Millay's younger sister and sole heir, Norma, to give her access to hundreds of Millay's personal papers, letters, and notebooks. Selecting from 'this extraordinary collection,' Milford meticulously integrates Millay's major poems, letters received and sent, reactions of friends, and comments from extensive interviews with Norma into an orderly and affecting narrative." Libr J
Includes bibliographical references

Miller, Arthur, 1915-2005

Bigsby, Christopher. **Arthur** Miller; 1915-1962. [by] Christopher Bigsby. Harvard University Press 2009 739p il $35 **92**
1. Authors 2. Dramatists 3. Screenwriters 4. Dramatists, American
ISBN 978-0-674-03505-8; 0-674-03505-4

LC 2009-2489

First published 2008 in the United Kingdom
This is a biography of the American playwright.
"A richly detailed, revealing look at the making of a playwright and a man." Kirkus
Includes bibliographical references

Miller, Lee, 1907-1977

★ Burke, Carolyn. **Lee** Miller; a life. Knopf 2005 426p il $35 **92**
1. Photographers 2. Models (Persons) 3. Biography, Individual
ISBN 0-375-40147-4

LC 2004-43844

This is a biography of the model and photographer. Index.
This "sympathetic tribute sheds further light on the lives of this high-

ly original, often misunderstood woman." Economist

Includes bibliographical references

Miller, Sue

Miller, Sue. The **story** of my father; a memoir. Knopf 2003 173p il $22.50; pa $12.95 **92**

1. Authors 2. Novelists 3. Memoirists 4. Short story writers
ISBN 0-375-41479-7; 0-345-45544-4 pa

LC 2002-69460

"A familiar but still touching story of a parent's descent into Alzheimer's disease; the deeper Miller's father sinks into confusion, the more powerfully candid her writing becomes." N Y Times Book Rev

Mills, Marja

Mills, Marja. The **Mockingbird** Next Door; Life with Harper Lee. Marja Mills. The Penguin Press 2014 288 p. illustrations (hardback) $27.95 **92**

1. Alabama 2. American authors 3. Alabama -- Biography 4. Authors, American -- 20th century -- Biography
ISBN 1594205191; 9781594205194

LC 2013039938

This book, by Marja Mills, is a memoir recounting her friendship with "To Kill a Mockingbird" author Harper Lee. "Journalists have trekked to her hometown of Monroeville, Alabama, where . . . Lee, known to her friends as Nelle, has lived with her sister, Alice, for decades, trying and failing to get an interview with the author. But in 2001, the Lee sisters opened their door to Chicago Tribune journalist Marja Mills. It was the beginning of a long conversation--and a great friendship." (Publisher's note)

Milne, A. A.

Thwaite, Ann. **Goodbye** Christopher Robin; A.A. Milne and the making of Winnie-the-Pooh. by Ann Thwaite. St. Martin's Press 2017 254 p. $16.99 **92**

1. English authors -- Biography
ISBN 1250190908; 9781250190901

LC 2017040980

This book "is drawn from Ann Thwaite's Whitbread Award-winning biography of A. A. Milne, one of England's most successful writers. After serving in the First World War, Milne wrote a number of well-received plays, but his greatest triumph came when he created Winnie-the-Pooh, Piglet, Tigger, Eeyore and, of course, Christopher Robin, the adventurous little boy based on his own son." (Publisher's note)

Min, Anchee, 1957-

★ Min, Anchee, 1957- The **Cooked** Seed; A Memoir. Anchee Min. St. Martin's Press 2013 368 p. $26 **92**

1. Immigrants -- United States 2. China -- History -- 1949-1976 3. Chinese -- United States -- Biography 4. Chinese American authors -- Biography 5. Immigrants -- United States -- Biography
ISBN 1596916982; 9781596916982

LC 2013015953

This book is an "examination of the legacy of Mao Zedong's Cultural Revolution," in which author Anchee Min offers a "contrast between American and Chinese attitudes about human worth and dignity. Raised in Shanghai in a hardscrabble family of four children and educated parents who were denounced as 'bourgeois,' Min was plucked as a teenager from a labor camp in 1974" to appear in propaganda films. At 27, she came to the U.S. (Publishers Weekly)

Includes bibliographical references and index

Min, Anchee. **Red** Azalea. Anchor Books 2006 306p pa

$13 **92**

1. Actors 2. Artists 3. Authors 4. Novelists 5. Photographers 6. Memoirists 7. China -- History -- 1949-
ISBN 978-1-4000-9698-5; 1-4000-9698-7

LC 2006-271433

First published 1994 by Pantheon Bks.

"In this memoir of growing up in China during the Cultural Revolution, sexual freedom becomes a powerful political as well as literary statement." N Y Times Book Rev

Mingus, Charles, 1922-1979

Gabbard, Krin. **Better** git it in your soul; an interpretive biography of Charles Mingus. Krin Gabbard. University of California Press 2016 336 p. illustrations (cloth: alk. paper) $34.95; (ebook) $34.95 **92**

1. Jazz musicians -- Biography 2. Double bassists -- Biography 3. Jazz musicians -- United States -- Biography 4. Double bassists -- United States -- Biography
ISBN 0520260376; 9780520260375; 9780520963740

LC 2015031907

In this biography, author Krin Gabbard "takes a careful look at [Charles] Mingus as a writer as well as a composer and musician. He digs into how and why Mingus chose to do so much self-analysis, how he worked to craft his racial identity in a world that saw him simply as 'black,' and how his mental and physical health problems shaped his career. Gabbard sets aside the myth-making and . . . argues that . . . Mingus created a unique language of emotions—and not just in music." (Publisher's note)

"A solid addition to the literature of jazz." Booklist

Includes bibliographical references and index

Mirvis, Tova

Mirvis, Tova. The **book** of separation; a memoir. Tova Mirvis. Houghton Mifflin Harcourt 2017 302 p. (hardcover) $26 **92**

1. Faith 2. Jewish women 3. Autobiographies 4. Authors, American -- 20th century -- Biography
ISBN 9780544520523; 9780544520547

LC 2017015328

In this memoir, author Tova Mirvis, "leaves her faith and her marriage and sets out to navigate the terrifying, liberating terrain of a newly mapless world. Born and raised in a tight-knit Orthodox Jewish family, Tova Mirvis committed herself to observing the rules and rituals prescribed by this way of life. . . . But over the years, her doubts became noisier than her faith . . . [and] decides to leave her husband and her faith." (Publisher's note)

"The author's sensitive thematic treatment of belonging and individuality and her candor about the terror she experienced leaving the only community she had ever known makes for moving, inspiring reading. A thoughtful, courageous memoir of family, religion, and self-discovery." Kirkus

Miskjian, Stepan, 1886-1974

MacKeen, Dawn Anahid. The **hundred**-year walk; an Armenian odyssey. Dawn Anahid MacKeen. Houghton Mifflin Harcourt 2016 352 p. illustrations, map (hardcover) $24 **92**

1. Genocide -- Armenia 2. Armenian massacres, 1915-1923 3. World War, 1914-1918 -- Armenia 4. Armenian massacres survivors -- Biography 5. Young men -- Armenia -- History -- Biography 6. Escapes -- Armenia -- History -- 20th century 7. Desert survival -- Syria -- History -- 20th century
ISBN 9780618982660

LC 2015016713

In this book, by Dawn Anahid MacKeen, "in the heart of the Otto-man Empire as World War I rages, Stepan Miskjian's world becomes undone. He is separated from his family as they are swept up in the government's mass deportation of Armenians into internment camps. . . . [The book] alternates between Stepan's saga and another journey that takes place a century later, after his family discovers his long-lost journals." (Publisher's note)

"Powerful, terrible stories about what people are willing to do to other people—but leavened with hope and, ultimately, forgiveness." Kirkus

Includes bibliographical references

Mitchell, Joan

Albers, Patricia. **Joan** Mitchell; lady painter: a life. Alfred A. Knopf 2011 xxi, 514p il ebook $21.99; $40   **92**
1. Artists 2. Painters 3. Women artists 4. Abstract expressionism 5. Biography, Individual 6. Artists -- United States
ISBN 978-0-307-59598-0 ebook; 978-0-375-41437-4

LC 2011-00457

This is a "biography of the abstract expressionist painter who came of age in the 1950s, '60s, and '70s." (Publisher's note) Index.

This is a "biography of Joan Mitchell (1925–92), a major 20th-century American artist. . . . This significant biography covers all aspects of Mitchell's life, including her synesthesia, eidetic memory, alcoholism, troubled relationships, and art. Filled with intimate details of her complex personality and unconventional lifestyle, this is a conscientiously objective yet sympathetic portrait of the 'lady painter' and the social and cultural contexts in which she became a successful artist in the male-dominated Parisian and New York art worlds." Libr J

Includes bibliographical references

Mitchell, Joni

Hoskyns, Barney. **Joni**; the anthology. edited by Barney Hoskyns. Picador 2017 310 p. (hardcover) $26   **92**
1. Anthologies 2. Popular music -- History and criticism
ISBN 9781250148629; 9781250148643; 1250148626

LC 2017027146

This book, by Barney Hoskyns, "is an essential collection of writings on Joni Mitchell that charts every major moment of the famed troubadour's extraordinary career, as it happened. . . . [It] illuminates the evolution of modern rock journalism while providing an invaluable and accessible guide to appreciating the highs--and the lows--of a twentieth century legend." (Publisher's note)

"This intriguing anthology captures the essence of award-winning songwriter/performer Joni Mitchell as both individual and artist. . . . The book's concept is singular, and the selection and structuring of the material well done." LJ

Includes bibliographical references and index.

Yaffe, David. **Reckless** daughter; a portrait of Joni Mitchell. David Yaffe. Sarah Crichton Books, Farrar, Straus & Giroux 2017 448 p. (hardcover) $28   **92**
1. Women singers -- Canada -- Biography 2. Women composers -- Canada -- Biography 3. Singers -- Canada -- Biography 4. Composers -- Canada -- Biography
ISBN 9780374248130

LC 2017024370

In this biography of Joni Mitchell, "music critic David Yaffe tells the remarkable, heart-wrenching story of how the blond girl with the guitar became a superstar of folk music in the 1960s, a key figure in the Laurel Canyon music scene of the 1970s, and the songwriter who spoke resonantly to, and for, audiences across the country." (Publisher's note)

"A shimmering portrait of one artist's life, illusions and all." (Book-list)

Includes bibliographical references and index

Mitford family

Thompson, Laura. The **six**; the lives of the Mitford sisters. Laura Thompson. St. Martin's Press 2016 400 p. ill., genealogical table (hardcover) $29.99   **92**
1. Sisters 2. Women authors 3. Great Britain -- Biography 4. Sisters -- Great Britain -- Biography 5. Authors, English -- 20th century -- Biography 6. Women authors, English -- 20th century -- Biography
ISBN 9781250099532

LC 2016024061

This book, by Laura Thompson, focuses on "the Mitford sisters: Nancy, Pamela, Diana, Unity, Jessica, and Deborah. Born into country-house privilege in the early years of the 20th century, they became prominent as "bright young things" in the high society of interwar London. Then, as the shadows crept over 1930s Europe, the stark—and very public—differences in their outlooks came to symbolize the political polarities of a dangerous decade." (Publisher's note)

"Appreciators of biography and social history will find much to engage their interest here." Booklist

Includes bibliographical references and index

Mitford, Jessica, 1917-1996

Thompson, Laura. The **six**; the lives of the Mitford sisters. Laura Thompson. St. Martin's Press 2016 400 p. ill., genealogical table (hardcover) $29.99   **92**
1. Sisters 2. Women authors 3. Great Britain -- Biography 4. Sisters -- Great Britain -- Biography 5. Authors, English -- 20th century -- Biography 6. Women authors, English -- 20th century -- Biography
ISBN 9781250099532

LC 2016024061

This book, by Laura Thompson, focuses on "the Mitford sisters: Nancy, Pamela, Diana, Unity, Jessica, and Deborah. Born into country-house privilege in the early years of the 20th century, they became prominent as "bright young things" in the high society of interwar London. Then, as the shadows crept over 1930s Europe, the stark—and very public—differences in their outlooks came to symbolize the political polarities of a dangerous decade." (Publisher's note)

"Appreciators of biography and social history will find much to engage their interest here." Booklist

Includes bibliographical references and index

Mitford, Nancy, 1904-1973

Thompson, Laura. The **six**; the lives of the Mitford sisters. Laura Thompson. St. Martin's Press 2016 400 p. ill., genealogical table (hardcover) $29.99   **92**
1. Sisters 2. Women authors 3. Great Britain -- Biography 4. Sisters -- Great Britain -- Biography 5. Authors, English -- 20th century -- Biography 6. Women authors, English -- 20th century -- Biography
ISBN 9781250099532

LC 2016024061

This book, by Laura Thompson, focuses on "the Mitford sisters: Nancy, Pamela, Diana, Unity, Jessica, and Deborah. Born into country-house privilege in the early years of the 20th century, they became prominent as "bright young things" in the high society of interwar London. Then, as the shadows crept over 1930s Europe, the stark—and very public—differences in their outlooks came to symbolize the political polarities of a dangerous decade." (Publisher's note)

"Appreciators of biography and social history will find much to engage their interest here." Booklist

Includes bibliographical references and index

Mitford, Pamela, 1907-1994

Thompson, Laura. The **six**; the lives of the Mitford sisters. Laura Thompson. St. Martin's Press 2016 400 p. ill., genealogical table (hardcover) $29.99 **92**

1. Sisters 2. Women authors 3. Great Britain -- Biography 4. Sisters -- Great Britain -- Biography 5. Authors, English -- 20th century -- Biography 6. Women authors, English -- 20th century -- Biography

ISBN 9781250099532

LC 2016024061

This book, by Laura Thompson, focuses on "the Mitford sisters: Nancy, Pamela, Diana, Unity, Jessica, and Deborah. Born into country-house privilege in the early years of the 20th century, they became prominent as "bright young things" in the high society of interwar London. Then, as the shadows crept over 1930s Europe, the stark—and very public—differences in their outlooks came to symbolize the political polarities of a dangerous decade." (Publisher's note)

"Appreciators of biography and social history will find much to engage their interest here." Booklist

Includes bibliographical references and index

Mitford, Unity, 1914-1948

Thompson, Laura. The **six**; the lives of the Mitford sisters. Laura Thompson. St. Martin's Press 2016 400 p. ill., genealogical table (hardcover) $29.99 **92**

1. Sisters 2. Women authors 3. Great Britain -- Biography 4. Sisters -- Great Britain -- Biography 5. Authors, English -- 20th century -- Biography 6. Women authors, English -- 20th century -- Biography

ISBN 9781250099532

LC 2016024061

This book, by Laura Thompson, focuses on "the Mitford sisters: Nancy, Pamela, Diana, Unity, Jessica, and Deborah. Born into country-house privilege in the early years of the 20th century, they became prominent as "bright young things" in the high society of interwar London. Then, as the shadows crept over 1930s Europe, the stark—and very public—differences in their outlooks came to symbolize the political polarities of a dangerous decade." (Publisher's note)

"Appreciators of biography and social history will find much to engage their interest here." Booklist

Includes bibliographical references and index

Mithridates VI Eupator, King of Pontus, ca. 132-63 B.C.

Mayor, Adrienne. The **Poison** King; the life and legend of Mithridates, Rome's deadliest enemy. Princeton University Press 2009 448p il map $29.95 **92**

1. Kings and rulers 2. Kings 3. Rome -- History 4. Black Sea region -- History 5. Mediterranean region -- History

ISBN 9780691126838

LC 2009-15050

National Book Award Finalist: Nonfiction (2009)

This is "a reappraisal of Mithradates's character and a detailed account of his scientific pursuits, notably his in-depth studies of poison. . . . [The author places] him in his proper context as a Greco-Persian ruler following in the footsteps of his purported ancestor Alexander the Great. The most compelling aspect of this book is Mayor's engaging style. A true storyteller, she makes Mithradates's world come alive." Libr J

Includes bibliographical references

Moaveni, Azadeh, 1976-

Moaveni, Azadeh. **Honeymoon** in Tehran; two years of love and danger in Iran. Random House 2009 340p $26 **92**

1. Authors 2. Journalists 3. Iranian Americans 4. Women journalists 5. Memoirists

ISBN 978-1-4000-6645-2; 1-4000-6645-X

The Iranian-American author describes her return to Iran as a reporter for 'Time' magazine, her marriage to an Iranian man, the repressive Iranian society and its impact, and her family's decision to leave Iran.

"This perfect blend of political commentary and social observation is an excellent choice for readers interested in going beyond the headlines to gain an in-depth understanding of twenty-first-century Iran." Booklist

Includes bibliographical references

Moaveni, Azadeh. **Lipstick** jihad; a memoir of growing up Iranian in America and American in Iran. Public Affairs 2005 249p $25; pa $13 **92**

1. Authors 2. Journalists 3. Iran 4. Memoirists

ISBN 1-58648-193-2; 1-58648-378-1 pa

LC 2004-43184

"Moaveni, an Iranian-American who grew up in California, decided to embark on a journey in spring 2000 to rediscover her Iranian heritage. In this account, she . . . conveys the tensions she observed between the fundamentalist mullahs and younger Iranians, who are pushing for a more Westernized, modern Iran. . . . A charming and informative memoir." Libr J

Moghul, Haroon

Moghul, Haroon. **How** to be a Muslim; an American story. Haroon Moghul. Beacon Press 2017 231 p. (pbk.: alk. paper) $17 **92**

1. Islam 2. Muslims -- United States 3. Islam -- Essence, genius, nature 4. Muslims -- United States -- Biography

ISBN 9780807020753; 9780807020746

LC 2016041078

This book, by Haroon Moghul, is a "memoir of his struggles to forge an American Muslim identity. . . . After 9/11, . . . Moghul was becoming a prominent voice for American Muslims even as he struggled with his relationship to Islam. . . . To be true to himself, he needed to forge a unique American Muslim identity that reflected his beliefs and personality." (Publisher's note)

"Highly recommended for its candor and relatability, this book will invite readers to fathom what it means to grasp Islam—and religion and spirituality in general." Pub Wkly

Includes bibliographical references.

Molina, Bengie, 1974-

Molina, Bengie. **Molina**; the story of the father who raised an unlikely baseball dynasty. Bengie Molina with Joan Ryan. Simon & Schuster 2015 272 p. color illustrations (hardback) $25 **92**

1. Baseball 2. Father-son relationship 3. Fathers and sons 4. Fathers -- Puerto Rico 5. Baseball -- Puerto Rico

ISBN 1451641044; 9781451641042; 9781451641059

LC 2014043223

This book, by Bengie Molina with Joan Ryan, is a "memoir about his father, who through baseball taught his three sons about loyalty, humility, courage, and the true meaning of success. Bengie and his two brothers--Jose and six-time All-Star Yadier--became famous catchers in the Major Leagues and have six World Series championships among them." (Publisher's note)

"This memoir will appeal to any baseball fan as well as patrons from

Puerto Rican communities." LJ

Molina, Benjamin

Molina, Bengie. **Molina**; the story of the father who raised an unlikely baseball dynasty. Bengie Molina with Joan Ryan. Simon & Schuster 2015 272 p. color illustrations (hardback) $25   **92**

1. Baseball 2. Father-son relationship 3. Fathers and sons 4. Fathers -- Puerto Rico 5. Baseball -- Puerto Rico
ISBN 1451641044; 9781451641042; 9781451641059

LC 2014043223

This book, by Bengie Molina with Joan Ryan, is a "memoir about his father, who through baseball taught his three sons about loyalty, humility, courage, and the true meaning of success. Bengie and his two brothers--Jose and six-time All-Star Yadier--became famous catchers in the Major Leagues and have six World Series championships among them." (Publisher's note)

"This memoir will appeal to any baseball fan as well as patrons from Puerto Rican communities." LJ

Monet, Claude, 1840-1926

Rubio, Salva. **Monet**; itinerant of light. Salva Rubio, writer; Efa, art; lettering by Ortho; translation by Montana Kane. NBM Graphic Novels 2017 112 p. chiefly color illustrations (hardcover) $24.99   **92**

1. Impressionism (Art) 2. Painters -- France -- Biography
ISBN 9781681121390

LC 2017910452

This book, by Salva Rubio, illustrated by Efa, narrates "the life of . . . French painter, [Claude Monet], one of the founders of Impressionism. . . . From the Salon des Refuses ('Salon of the Rejected') and many struggling years without recognition, money, and yet a family to raise, all the way to great success, critically and financially, Monet pursued insistently one vision: catching the light in painting, refusing to compromise on this ethereal pursuit." (Publisher's note)

"Monet himself narrates, and most of the text focuses on that narration, which allows the imagery to open and explore much of the same visual landscape that occupies his paintings. Efa's illustrations are stunning; full of strong, lush color and bold impressionistic brush strokes that call forth Monet's style but never imitate." LJ

Monk, Thelonious, 1917-1982

★ Kelley, Robin D. G., 1962- **Thelonious** Monk; the life and times of an American original. Free Press 2009 588p il $30   **92**

1. Pianists 2. Jazz musicians 3. African American musicians 4. Jazz 5. Biography, Individual
ISBN 0-684-83190-2; 978-0-684-83190-9

LC 2009-08526

This is a biography of the jazz musician and composer. Discography. Videography. Index.

The author "knows music, especially Monk's music, and his descriptions of assorted studio and live dates, along with what Monk is up to musically throughout, are handled expertly. . . . Likewise, the characters in Monk's life and career are well served. . . . The 'genius of modern music' has gotten the passionate, and compassionate, advocate he deserves." N Y Times Book Rev

Includes discography, videography, and bibliographical references

Monroe, James, 1758-1831

Unger, Harlow G. The **last** founding father; James Monroe and a nation's call to greatness. [by] Harlow Giles Unger. Da

Capo Press 2009 388p il map $26   **92**

1. Presidents 2. Secretaries of state 3. Presidents -- United States 4. United States -- Politics and government -- 1783-1865
ISBN 978-0-306-81808-0

LC 2009-26195

"A worthy attempt to rescue Monroe from obscurity for a mainstream audience." Kirkus

Includes bibliographical references (p. 371-376)

Monroe, Marilyn, 1926-1962

Casillo, Charles. **Marilyn** Monroe; the private life of a public icon. Charles Casillo. St. Martin's Press 2018 368 p. (hardcover) $27.99   **92**

1. Celebrities 2. Actors -- United States 3. Motion picture actors and actresses -- United States -- Biography
ISBN 9781250096869

LC 2018004352

In this book, author "Charles Casillo studies [Marilyn] Monroe's life through the context of her times--in the days before feminism. Before there was adequate treatment for Marilyn's struggle with bipolar disorder. Starting with her abusive childhood, this biography exposes how--in spite of her fractured psyche--Marilyn's extreme ambition inspired her to transform each celebrated love affair and each tragedy into another step in her journey towards immortality." (Publisher's note)

"Beginning with Monroe's illegitimate birth and impoverished childhood in and out of foster homes and orphanages, Casillo traces the deep roots of Monroe's essential feelings of inadequacy and longing for acceptance." Booklist

Includes bibliography and index.

Montaigne, Michel de, 1533-1592

Bakewell, Sarah. **How** to live, or, A life of Montaigne in one question and twenty attempts at an answer. Other Press 2010 389p il map $25; ebook $19.99   **92**

1. Judges 2. Authors 3. Authors, French 4. Essayists
ISBN 978-1-59051-425-2; 978-1-59051-426-9 ebook

LC 2010-26896

"In a wide-ranging intellectual career, Michel de Montaigne found no knowledge so hard to acquire as the knowledge of how to live this life well. By casting her biography of the writer as 20 chapters, each focused on a different answer to the question How to live? Bakewell limns Montaigne's ceaseless pursuit of this most elusive knowledge. Embedded in the 20 life-knowledge responses, readers will find essential facts—when and where Montaigne was born, how and whom he married, how he became mayor of Bordeaux, how he managed a public life in a time of lethal religious and political passions. . . . Because Montaigne's capacious mirror still captivates many, this insightful life study will win high praise from both scholars and general readers." Booklist

Includes bibliographical references

Perry, Michael. **Montaigne** in barn boots; an amateur ambles through philosophy. Michael Perry. HarperCollins 2017 xi, 223 p.p (hardcover) $25.99   **92**

1. Farmers 2. Farm life 3. Farm life -- Wisconsin 4. Farmers -- Wisconsin -- Biography
ISBN 9780062230584; 9780062230560; 0062230565

In this memoir, author Michael Perry "reflects on the lessons he's learned from his unlikely alter ego, French Renaissance philosopher Michel de Montaigne. 'The journey began on a gurney,' writes . . . Perry, describing the debilitating kidney stone that led him to discover the essays of Michel de Montaigne. Reading the philosopher in a manner he equates to chickens pecking at scraps . . . , Perry attempts to learn what he can . . . about himself." (Publisher's note)

Includes bibliographical references (pages 219-222).

Montalván, Luis Carlos

Henican, Ellis. **Tuesday's** promise; one veteran, one dog, and their bold quest to change lives. former U.S. Army Captain Luis Carlos Montalván and Ellis Henican. Hachette Books 2017 x, 294 p.p illustrations (hardcover) $27   **92**

1. Service dogs 2. Human-animal relationships 3. Post-traumatic stress disorder 4. Service dogs -- United States 5. Golden retriever -- United States 6. Human-animal relationships -- United States 7. Disabled veterans -- United States -- Biography 8. People with disabilities -- Services for -- United States 9. Iraq War, 2003-2011 -- Veterans -- United States -- Biography 10. Post-traumatic stress disorder -- Patients -- United States -- Biography

ISBN 0316314412; 9780316314411; 9780316314442

LC 2016057510

Sequel to: Until Tuesday (2011)

In this memoir, by Iraq War veteran Luis Carlos Montalvan and Ellis Henican, Montalvan "took to the road with his beloved Golden Retriever service dog, Tuesday, to advocate for America's wounded warriors and for each other. . . . [Here], he and Tuesday brought their healing mission to the next level, showing how these beautifully trained animals can assist soldiers, veterans, and many others with disabilities." (Publisher's note)

"Speaking to both animal welfare and the well-being of wounded warriors, Montalván's memoir is a testimonial to the 'quest for wholeness' and the healing power of companionship." Kirkus

Montana, Joe, 1956-

Dunnavant, Keith. **Montana**; the biography of football's Joe Cool. Keith Dunnavant. Thomas Dunne Books 2015 336 p. illustrations (chiefly color) (hardcover) $26.99   **92**

1. Football players 2. Football players -- United States -- Biography 3. Quarterbacks (Football) -- United States -- Biography

ISBN 9781250017840; 125001784X

LC 2015019171

Author Keith Dunnavant "builds his portrait through research and dozens of personal interviews with those who have known [Joe] Montana. This . . . volume also tells the less familiar story of Montana's early career and his battles with his high-school and college coaches, both of whom were slow to recognize Montana's talent. That changed in San Francisco, where Montana and coach Bill Walsh were the perfect match." (Booklist)

"Well written and researched, this title will be of interest to a wide range of sports fans." LJ

Mooney, Jonathan

Mooney, Jonathan. The **short** bus; a journey beyond normal. H. Holt 2007 272p hardcover o.p. pa $14.99   **92**

1. Students with disabilities 2. Memoirists 3. Social activists 4. Motivational speakers

ISBN 978-0-8050-7427-7; 0-8050-7427-9; 978-0-8050-8804-5 pa; 0-8050-8804-0 pa

LC 2006-52588

The author's "target audience is not policy makers but his fellow misfits, and his boundless empathy will surely console those who also face the worst that cruel schoolchildren and the educational bureaucracy have to offer." N Y Times Book Rev

Mooney, Paul

Mooney, Paul. **Black** is the new white; a memoir. Simon Spotlight Entertainment 2009 264p il $24.99   **92**

1. Actors 2. Comedians 3. Screenwriters 4. Television scriptwriters 5. United States -- Race relations

ISBN 978-1-4165-8795-8; 1-4165-8795-0

LC 2009-19572

"Paul Mooney recalls the day he became Richard Pryor's shadow partner. It was 1968, and the two young comics were sitting in a Hollywood greasy spoon, with Pryor nursing another hangover, so Mooney lightened the mood with an off-the-cuff, X-rated one-liner that made his buddy convulse. . . . [This book] is Mooney's unvarnished memoir of that friendship. At a time when comedians—even African American icons such as Bill Cosby—never talked about race, Pryor (aided and abetted by Mooney) dared to confront the elephant in the room. Mooney, who has also written for 'In Living Color' and 'Chappelle's Show,' also traces his own path from humble Deep South roots to a comedy elder statesman known for his incisive riffs on racism." Los Angeles Times book Rev

Moore, Darnell

Moore, Darnell L. **No** ashes in the fire; coming of age black and free in America. Darnell L. Moore. Nation Books 2018 256 p. $26   **92**

1. Bildungsromans 2. African American gay men -- Biography

ISBN 1568589484; 9781568589480

In this memoir, author Darnell L. Moore "shares the journey [he has] taken . . . [as a] scared, bullied teenager who not only survived, but found his calling. . . . Moore reminds us that liberation is possible if we commit ourselves to fighting for it, and if we dream and create futures where those who survive on society's edges can thrive." (Publisher's note)

Moore, Marianne, 1887-1972

Leavell, Linda. **Holding** on upside down; the life and work of Marianne Moore. Linda Leavell. Farrar Straus & Giroux 2013 480 p. 16 plates; illustrations (hardcover) $30   **92**

1. Women poets 2. Mother-daughter relationship

ISBN 0374107297; 9780374107291

LC 2013006521

National Book Critics Circle Award Finalist: Biography (2013)

In this book, author Linda Leavell "draws from the archive and private estate of American poet Marianne Moore (1887-1972) to illustrate how the modernist poet evolved from writing carefully crafted, cutting-edge poetry to producing the more prolific poems of her later years. Correspondence reveals that Moore's mother, Mary, used emotional manipulation, money, and a secret family vernacular to control both her son, Warner (John), and Marianne." (Library Journal)

Includes bibliographical references and index

Moore, Mary Tyler

Moore, Mary Tyler. **Growing** up again; life, love, and oh yeah, diabetes. St. Martin's Press 2009 216p il $24.95   **92**

1. Actors 2. Diabetes

ISBN 978-0-312-37631-4; 0-312-37631-6

LC 2008-37579

"While working on The Dick Van Dyke Show, . . . [the author] was diagnosed with juvenile (Type 1) diabetes and quickly discovered that managing the disease is a full-time job. . . . Moore details the daily challenges she faces to maintain healthy blood sugar levels. . . . Moore's humor, authoritative information, and honest evaluation of her own experiences with diabetes make this work essential for diabetes and consumer health collections." Libr J

Moore, Wes, 1975-

Moore, Wes, 1978- The **other** Wes Moore; the story of

one name and two fates. [by] Wes Moore; afterword by Tavis Smiley. Spiegel & Grau 2010 233p il $25   **92**

    1. Prisoners 2. Murderers 3. Memoirists 4. Army officers 5. Baltimore (Md.) 6. African Americans -- Biography

ISBN 978-0-385-52819-1

LC 2009-41663

"In 2000, Wes Moore had recently been named a Rhodes Scholar in his final year of college at Johns Hopkins University when he read a newspaper article about another Wes Moore who was on his way to prison. It turned out that the two of them had much in common, both young black men raised in inner-city neighborhoods by single mothers. Stunned by the similarities in their names and backgrounds and the differences in their ultimate fates, the author eventually contacted the other Wes Moore and began a long relationship. . . . The author examines eight years in the lives of both Wes Moores to explore the factors and choices that led one to a Rhodes scholarship, military service, and a White House fellowship, and the other to drug dealing, prison, and eventual conversion to the Muslim faith, with both sharing a gritty sense of realism about their pasts." Booklist

Moore, Westley W.

Moore, Wes, 1978- The **other** Wes Moore; the story of one name and two fates. [by] Wes Moore; afterword by Tavis Smiley. Spiegel & Grau 2010 233p il $25   **92**

    1. Prisoners 2. Murderers 3. Memoirists 4. Army officers 5. Baltimore (Md.) 6. African Americans -- Biography

ISBN 978-0-385-52819-1

LC 2009-41663

"In 2000, Wes Moore had recently been named a Rhodes Scholar in his final year of college at Johns Hopkins University when he read a newspaper article about another Wes Moore who was on his way to prison. It turned out that the two of them had much in common, both young black men raised in inner-city neighborhoods by single mothers. Stunned by the similarities in their names and backgrounds and the differences in their ultimate fates, the author eventually contacted the other Wes Moore and began a long relationship. . . . The author examines eight years in the lives of both Wes Moores to explore the factors and choices that led one to a Rhodes scholarship, military service, and a White House fellowship, and the other to drug dealing, prison, and eventual conversion to the Muslim faith, with both sharing a gritty sense of realism about their pasts." Booklist

Moore, Wes, 1978- The **work**; creating success in new and meaningful ways. Wes Moore. Spiegel & Grau 2014 272 p. (hardback) $25   **92**

    1. African Americans -- Biography 2. Military personnel -- United States 3. Baltimore (Md.) -- Biography 4. African American men -- Biography

ISBN 9780679646013; 9780812993578

LC 2013038679

This book by Wes Moore is "the story of how one young man traced a path through the world to find his life's purpose. Moore graduated from a difficult childhood in the Bronx and Baltimore to an adult life that would find him at some of the most critical moments in our recent history: as a combat officer in Afghanistan; a White House fellow in a time of wars abroad and disasters at home; and a Wall Street banker during the financial crisis." (Publisher's note)

"This is a beautifully philosophical look at the expectation that work should bring meaning to our lives through service to others." Booklist

Moran, Caitlin, 1975-

   ★ Moran, Caitlin. **How** to be a woman; Caitlin Moran.

Harper Perennial 2011 305 p. (pbk.) $15.99   **92**

    1. Feminism 2. Women -- Great Britain 3. Journalists -- England -- Biography 4. Women journalists -- England -- Biography 5. Women -- Great Britain -- Social conditions -- Humor

ISBN 0062124293; 9780062124296

LC 2012372347

Originally published: London: Ebury Press, 2011.

This book is "part memoir, part postmodern feminist rant" from British TV critic Caitlin Moran. "Moran's journey into womanhood begins on her 13th birthday when boys throw rocks at her 182-pound body, and her only friend, her sister Caz, hands her a homemade card reminding her to please turn 18 or die soon so Caz can inherit her bedroom." Moran "embarrasses herself often enough to become an authority on how to masturbate; name one's breasts; and forgo a Brazilian bikini wax." (Publishers Weekly)

Morante, Elsa, d. 1985

Tuck, Lily. **Woman** of Rome: a life of Elsa Morante. HarperCollins 2008 263p il $25.95   **92**

    1. Poets 2. Authors 3. Novelists 4. Women authors 5. Italian authors 6. Authors, Italian 7. Short story writers

ISBN 978-0-06-147256-5; 0-06-147256-5

LC 2007-44647

"Written with a charming personal touch . . . that warms the narrative to a fine glow, this is a vital biography bringing to American audiences a writer most will have previously known little about." Booklist

Includes bibliographical references (p. 245-246)

Morgan, Jason (paratrooper)

Morgan, Jason. A **dog** called hope; A wounded warrior and the service dog who saved him. Jason Morgan & Damien Lewis. Atria Books 2017 viii, 324 p.p color illustrations (Atria non fiction reprint hardcover) (hardcover: alk. paper) $26   **92**

    1. Service dogs 2. Special forces (Military science) -- United States 3. Service dogs -- United States 4. Paraplegics -- United States -- Biography 5. Parachute troops -- United States -- Biography 6. Disabled veterans -- United States -- Biography 7. Disabled veterans -- Rehabilitation -- United States 8. Animals as aids for people with disabilities -- United States 9. Special forces (Military science) -- United States -- Biography 10. United States. Army. Special Operations Aviation Regiment (Airborne), 160th -- Biography

ISBN 9781476797038; 9781476797007; 9781476797014

LC 2016046725

This book by Jason Morgan and Damien Lewis is a "memoir of an extraordinary service dog whose enduring love brought a wounded soldier back to life. After multiple surgeries, unbearable chronic pain, and numerous setbacks, Morgan was finally making progress when his wife left him and their three young sons. He was a single father confined to a wheelchair and tortured by his pain. At this very dark, very low point, Morgan found light: Napal, the black Labrador who would change his life forever." (Publisher's note)

"Along with military and medical details, this is a story . . . of mental courage and overcoming the odds. It is also a touching love letter to the best friend this man could have." Booklist

Includes bibliographical references and index

Morgan, William, 1928-1961

Weiss, Mitch. The **Yankee** comandante; the untold story of courage, passion, and one American's fight to liberate Cuba. Michael Sallah and Mitch Weiss. Lyons Press 2015 288 p. illustrations, map (hardcover: alk. paper) $26.95   **92**

    1. Cuba -- History -- 1958-1959, Revolution 2. Revolutionaries --

Cuba -- History -- 20th century 3. Revolutionaries -- United States -- History -- 20th century 4. Cuba -- History -- Revolution, 1959 -- Participation, American

ISBN 0762792876; 9780762792870

LC 2014033720

This book by Michael Sallah and Mitch Weiss is the story of "William Morgan, a tough-talking ex-paratrooper, [who[stunned family and friends when in 1957 he left Ohio to join freedom fighters in the mountains of Cuba. He led one band of guerrillas, and Che Guevara another, and together they swept through the country, ultimately forcing corrupt dictator Fulgencio Batista from power." (Publisher's note)

"Olga lives today in the U.S., and Sallah and Weiss interviewed her extensively. They also make clear Morgan's flaws: he had at least three wives and several children by them; was court martialed by the U.S. Army, serving time in prison; and was employed by and associated with known mobsters. Though the tale does not end happily, it's a romantic and entertaining read." Pub Wkly

Includes bibliographical references and index

Morris, Tom, 1821-1908

Cook, Kevin. **Tommy's** honor; the story of old Tom Morris and young Tom Morris, golf's founding father and son. Gotham Books 2007 327p il $27.50   **92**

1. Golf 2. Golfers

ISBN 978-1-59240-297-7; 1-59240-297-6

LC 2007-8165

"In Cook's telling, the story of Tom Morris, winner of golf's first Open Championship in 1860, and his son, Tommy, who won the Open three years in a row, becomes a compelling saga of near-Homeric proportions." Booklist

Includes bibliographical references

Morris, Tom, 1851-1875

Cook, Kevin. **Tommy's** honor; the story of old Tom Morris and young Tom Morris, golf's founding father and son. Gotham Books 2007 327p il $27.50   **92**

1. Golf 2. Golfers

ISBN 978-1-59240-297-7; 1-59240-297-6

LC 2007-8165

"In Cook's telling, the story of Tom Morris, winner of golf's first Open Championship in 1860, and his son, Tommy, who won the Open three years in a row, becomes a compelling saga of near-Homeric proportions." Booklist

Includes bibliographical references

Morrison, Jim, 1943-1971

Hopkins, Jerry. **No** one here gets out alive; by Jerry Hopkins and Daniel Sugerman. Warner Bks. 1980 387p il hardcover o.p. pa $7.99   **92**

1. Singers 2. Rock musicians 3. Songwriters 4. Doors (Musical group)

ISBN 0-446-60228-0 pa

LC 79-26611

This biography of rock musician Jim Morrison gives "an idea of how profoundly Morrison, as lyricist and lead singer of the Doors, affected the youth of America in the late 1960s. . . . The book includes a list of the Doors' records, books, and films." Booklist

Moses, Robert, 1888-1981

Caro, Robert A. The **power** broker: Robert Moses and the fall of New York. Knopf 1974 1246, xxxivp il $50; pa $21.95   **92**

1. Urban planners 2. Local government officials 3. State government officials

ISBN 0-394-48076-7; 0-394-72024-5 pa

This is a biographical critique of the man who in four decades as a public official "built most of the parks, bridges and highways in and around New York City." Newsweek

Includes bibliographical references

Mosley, Diana, 1910-2003

Thompson, Laura. The **six**; the lives of the Mitford sisters. Laura Thompson. St. Martin's Press 2016 400 p. ill., genealogical table (hardcover) $29.99   **92**

1. Sisters 2. Women authors 3. Great Britain -- Biography 4. Sisters -- Great Britain -- Biography 5. Authors, English -- 20th century -- Biography 6. Women authors, English -- 20th century -- Biography

ISBN 9781250099532

LC 2016024061

This book, by Laura Thompson, focuses on "the Mitford sisters: Nancy, Pamela, Diana, Unity, Jessica, and Deborah. Born into country-house privilege in the early years of the 20th century, they became prominent as "bright young things" in the high society of interwar London. Then, as the shadows crept over 1930s Europe, the stark—and very public—differences in their outlooks came to symbolize the political polarities of a dangerous decade." (Publisher's note)

"Appreciators of biography and social history will find much to engage their interest here." Booklist

Includes bibliographical references and index

Motley, Eric L. (Eric Lamar), 1972-

Motley, Eric L. **Madison** Park; a place of hope. Eric L. Motley; foreword by Walter Isaacson. Zondervan 2017 304 p. illustrations (hardcover) $24.99   **92**

1. African Americans -- Biography 2. Montgomery (Ala.) -- Biography 3. Presidents -- United States -- Staff -- Biography 4. African Americans -- Alabama -- Montgomery -- Biography 5. African Americans -- Alabama -- Montgomery -- Social conditions

ISBN 9780310349631; 9780310349648; 031034963X

In this memoir Eric L. Motley "writes with charming flair about the dedicated individuals who shaped him throughout his life. . . . Motley was raised in Madison Park, Ala., an African-American community established by freed slaves. . . . With the strength of his community supporting him, Motley accomplished much, earning his Ph.D. in international relations and later working in the White House as special assistant to George W. Bush." (Publishers Weekly)

Mowat, Farley

King, James. **Farley**: the life of Farley Mowat. Steerforth Press 2002 397p il $27.95   **92**

1. Authors 2. Historians 3. Ethnologists 4. Children's authors 5. Nonfiction writers

ISBN 1-58642-055-0

LC 2002-151149

The author "recounts Mowat's life from his experience in college to his service in World War II and his work in the Northwest Territories as a student biologist. The emerging portrait is of a man whose evolution as both an environmentalist and an artist was profound, an activist who has never backed away from a controversy. The exploration of Mowat's life is detailed but never boring." Libr J

Includes bibliographical references

Moyers, William C.

Moyers, William C. **Broken**: my story of addiction and redemption; [by] William Cope Moyers with Katherine Ketcham. Viking 2006 372p il $25.95 **92**

1. Journalists

ISBN 0-670-03789-3; 978-0-670-03789-6

LC 2006-41378

The author's "gripping account of his struggles with alcohol and crack addiction will have readers rooting for him from the very beginning." Libr J

Mozart, Wolfgang Amadeus, 1756-1791

Suchet, John. **Mozart**; the man revealed. John Suchet. Pegasus Books 2017 xii, 274 p.p illustrations (chiefly color) (hardcover) $27.95 **92**

1. Composers -- Austria -- Biography

ISBN 1681775093; 9781681775760; 9781681775098

In this book, John Suchet, "shows us the real [Wolfgang Amadeus] Mozart--blessed with an abundance of talent yet sometimes struggling to earn a living. His mischievous nature and earthy sense of humor, his ease and confidence in his own incredible abilities; these were traits that never left him. His music has brought comfort to countless generations; his life, though brief, is no less fascinating." (Publisher's note)

"Rich with wit and warmth, this compact biography is thoroughly enchanting." Kirkus

Includes bibliographical references (pages 265-266) and index.

Muir, John, 1838-1914

★ Heacox, Kim. **John** Muir and the ice that started a fire; how a visionary and the glaciers of Alaska changed America. Kim Heacox. Lyons Press 2014 264 p. illustrations, map (hardback) $25.95 **92**

1. Alaska 2. Glaciers 3. Nature conservation 4. Glaciers -- Alaska 5. Climatic changes -- Alaska 6. Nature conservation -- Alaska

ISBN 0762792426; 9780762792429

LC 2013050235

This book, by Kim Heacox, "takes two of the most compelling elements in the narrative of wild America, John Muir and Alaska, and combines them into a brisk and engaging biography. . . . The book also offers an environmental caveat on global climate change and the glaciers' retreat alongside a beacon of hope: Muir shows us how one person changed America, helped it embrace its wilderness, and in turn, gave us a better world." (Publisher's note)

"The book is an engaging and informative look at Muir and his life's work, as well as a timely call to action that poses difficult questions to the reader and the philosophies that underpin modern life." Pub Wkly

Includes bibliographical references and index

Muir, John. The **story** of my boyhood and youth; with a foreword by Vernon Carstensen. University of Wisconsin Press 1965 227p hardcover o.p. pa $17.95 **92**

1. Authors 2. Naturalists 3. Writers on nature

ISBN 0-299-03654-5 pa

LC 65-14539

First published 1913 by Houghton Mifflin

"The naturalist's childhood in a strict Presbyterian home in Scotland, his boyhood experiences of the privations and out-of-door delights of pioneer life on a Wisconsin farm, and his shifts and contrivances while earning his way through the state university." Cleveland Public Libr

Worster, Donald. A **passion** for nature; the life of John Muir. Oxford University Press 2008 535p il map $34.95 **92**

1. Authors 2. Naturalists 3. Writers on nature

ISBN 978-0-19-516682-8; 0-19-516682-5

LC 2008-1441

The author "draws on John Muir's (1838-1914) correspondence and writings to offer an enlightening biography of the influential naturalist. . . . Competently documented, this all-inclusive biography explains the life and times of a figure known to all who love nature and will appeal to general readers and anyone interested in the early roots of today's green movement and its founding fathers." Libr J

Includes bibliographical references (p. 494-508)

Mumler, William H

Manseau, Peter. The **apparitionists**; a tale of phantoms, fraud, photography, and the man who captured Lincoln's ghost. Peter Manseau. Houghton Mifflin Harcourt 2017 xi, 335 p.p illustrations (hardcover) $27 **92**

1. Photographers -- Biography 2. Psychics -- United States -- Biography 3. Photographers -- United States -- Biography 4. Spirit photography -- United States -- History -- 19th century

ISBN 9780544745971; 9780544745988

LC 2017018074

In this book, author Peter Manseau "captures a nation wracked with grief and hungry for proof of the existence of ghosts and for contact with their dead husbands and sons. It took a circus-like trial of [William] Mumler on fraud charges . . . to expose a fault line of doubt and manipulation. And even then, the judge sided with the defense--nobody ever solved the mystery of his spirit photography." (Publisher's note)

"An absorbing read that thoroughly captures the energy and ingenuity of the period." Booklist

Includes bibliographical references (pages [313]-335).

Munch, Edvard, 1863-1944

Prideaux, Sue. **Edvard** Munch; behind the Scream. Yale University Press 2005 391p il map $35 **92**

1. Artists 2. Painters

ISBN 0-300-11024-3

LC 2005-12040

Prideaux's "treatment is very effective and her writing, cohesive, clear, and often compelling." Libr J

Includes bibliographical references

Murad, Nadia

Murad, Nadia, 1993- The **last** girl; my story of captivity, and my fight against the Islamic State. Nadia Murad and Jenna Krajeski; foreword by Amal Clooney. Tim Duggan Books 2017 320 p. (hardback) $27 **92**

1. IS (Organization) 2. Women -- Crimes against -- Iraq -- Mosul 3. Yezidis -- Biography 4. Women and war -- Iraq 5. Human rights workers -- Biography 6. Detention of persons -- Iraq -- Mosul 7. Prisoners -- Abulse of -- Iraq -- Mosul

ISBN 9781524760434; 9781524760441; 9781524762445

LC 2017028775

In this book, author Nadia Murad, "a former captive of the Islamic State[,] tells her harrowing and ultimately inspiring story. . . . On August 15th, 2014, . . . Islamic State militants massacred the people of her village, executing men who refused to convert to Islam and women too old to become sex slaves. . . . Nadia was taken to Mosul and forced, along with thousands of other Yazidi girls, into the ISIS slave trade." (Publisher's note)

" Murad provides a rare glimpse into the rich culture of the Yazidi. Her memoir is powerful and heart-breaking and will inspire the world to action." (LJ)

Murakami, Haruki, 1949-

Murakami, Haruki, 1949- **What** I talk about when I talk about running; a memoir. translated from the Japanese by Philip Gabriel. Alfred A. Knopf 2008 179p $21   **92**

1. Authors 2. Novelists 3. Marathon running 4. Nonfiction writers 5. Short story writers 6. Biography, Individual
ISBN 0-307-26919-1; 978-0-307-26919-5

LC 2008-17774

First published 2007 in Japan

This memoir covers Murakami's "four-month preparation for the 2005 New York City Marathon." (Publisher's note)

Murdoch, Rupert

Wolff, Michael. The **man** who owns the news; inside the secret world of Rupert Murdoch. Broadway Books 2008 446p $29.95   **92**

1. Mass media 2. Businessmen 3. Newspaper executives 4. Publishing executives 5. Broadcasting executives 6. Motion picture executives
ISBN 978-0-385-52612-8; 0-385-52612-1

LC 2008-37414

This biography of the Australian media entrepreneur describes how Rupert Murdoch came to own various companies, including The Wall Street Journal as well as its parent company, Dow Jones.

"There's lots of good material. . . . Perhaps most instructive, Wolff has melded interview and observation into what might be called a plausible theory of Murdoch." LA Times

Includes bibliographical references (p. 430-434)

Murray, Liz

Murray, Liz. **Breaking** night; a memoir of forgiveness, survival, and my journey from homeless to Harvard. Hyperion 2010 334p il $24.99   **92**

1. Students 2. Homeless persons 3. Children of drug addicts 4. Homeless 5. Motivational speakers
ISBN 978-0-7868-6891-9; 0-7868-6891-0

LC 2010-13679

"Neither sensationalizing nor soliciting pity, Murray's generous account of and caring attitude toward her past are not only uplifting, but also a fascinating lesson in the value of dedication." Booklist

Murray, Pauli, 1910-1985

★ Bell-Scott, Patricia. The **firebrand** and the First Lady; portrait of a friendship: Pauli Murray, Eleanor Roosevelt, and the struggle for social justice. Patricia Bell-Scott. Alfred A. Knopf 2016 480 p. illustrations hbk $30   **92**

1. Female friendship -- United States 2. African American feminists -- Biography 3. Episcopal Church -- Clergy -- Biography 4. African American intellectuals -- Biography 5. Presidents' spouses -- United States -- Biography 6. Women social reformers -- United States -- Biography 7. African American women civil rights workers -- Biography
ISBN 0679446524; 9780679446521

LC 2015014872

Carnegie Medal Shortlist: Nonfiction (2017); National Book Awards Longlist: Nonfiction (2016)

This book, by Patricia Bell-Scott, profiles the figures of Pauli Murray and Eleanor Roosevelt. It "tells the story of how a brilliant writer-turned-activist, granddaughter of a mulatto slave, and the first lady of the United States, whose ancestry gave her membership in the Daughters of the American Revolution, forged an enduring friendship that changed each of their lives and helped to alter the course of race and racism in America." (Publisher's note)

"Bell-Scott's groundbreaking portrait of these two tireless and innovative champions of human dignity adds an essential and edifying facet to American history." Booklist

Includes bibliographical references and index

Murrow, Edward R.

Edwards, Bob. **Edward** R. Murrow and the birth of broadcast journalism; {by} Robert A. Edwards. Wiley 2004 174p (Turning points) $19.95   **92**

1. Journalists 2. Radio reporters 3. Government officials 4. Television reporters 5. Television news anchors
ISBN 0-471-47753-2

LC 2003-21223

"The author chronicles Murrow's innovations in radio and television broadcasting, including live radio reports of the war in progress in Europe in 1940; exposure of the despotism of Senator Joseph McCarthy on CBS in 1953; the powerful television documentary Harvest of Shame on the deplorable conditions of migrant workers in the U.S.; and the first in-depth television news program, See It Now. . . . Edwards brings to life the early days of radio and television and the innovations that Murrow sparked. . . . Readers interested in journalism will enjoy this slim book." Booklist

Includes bibliographical references

Sperber, Ann M. **Murrow,** his life and times; {by} A. M. Sperber; with a preface by Neil Hickey. Fordham Univ. Press 1998 xxvi, 795p il $35; pa $25   **92**

1. Journalists 2. Radio reporters 3. Government officials 4. Television reporters 5. Television news anchors
ISBN 0-8232-1881-3; 0-8232-1882-1 pa

LC 98-52507

A reissue of the title first published 1986 by Freundlich Bks.

This "ambitious exploration of Murrow's life places his story in the foreground of what is, as well, a panorama of the years 1935-65." N Y Times Book Rev

Includes bibliographical references

Musk, Elon

Davenport, Christian. The **space** barons; Jeff Bezos, Elon Musk, and the quest to colonize the cosmos. Christian Davenport. PublicAffairs 2018 320 p. (hardcover) $28   **92**

1. Space industrialization 2. SpaceX (Firm) 3. Blue Origen (Firm) 4. Outer space -- Civilian use 5. Aerospace industries -- United States 6. Space industrialization -- United States 7. Industrialists -- United States -- Biography 8. Aerospace engineers -- United States -- Biography
ISBN 9781610398299

LC 2017053089

This book, by Christian Davenport, "is the story of a group of billionaire entrepreneurs who are pouring their fortunes into the epic resurrection of the American space program. . . . These Space Barons--most notably Elon Musk and Jeff Bezos, along with Richard Branson and Paul Allen--are using Silicon Valley-style innovation to dramatically lower the cost of space travel, and send humans even further than NASA has gone." (Publisher's note)

Includes bibliographical references and index

Mutter, Thomas D. (Thomas Dent), 1811-1859

★ Aptowicz, Cristin O'Keefe. **Dr.** Mütter's Marvels; A True Tale of Intrigue and Innovation at the Dawn of Modern Medicine. by Cristin O'Keefe Aptowicz. Gotham Books 2014

384 p. ill (hardcover) $27.50 **92**
1. Surgery -- History 2. Physicians -- Biography 3. Mutter Museum 4. Museums -- History -- Pennsylvania 5. Pathology -- History -- Pennsylvania 6. History, 19th Century -- Pennsylvania 7. Physicians -- Pennsylvania -- Biography 8. General Surgery -- History -- Pennsylvania 9. General Surgery -- Pennsylvania -- Biography
ISBN 1592408702; 9781592408702
LC 2014014747
This book, by Cristin O'Keefe Aptowicz, is a biography of surgeon Thomas Dent Mütter. "Mütter was . . . [a] medical innovator who pioneered the use of ether as anesthesia, the sterilization of surgical tools, and a compassion-based vision for helping the severely deformed, which clashed spectacularly with the sentiments of his time.... He ... amassed an immense collection of medical oddities that would later form the basis of Philadelphia's Mütter Museum." (Publisher's note)
"In her deftly crafted narrative, the author provides an absorbing account of the charismatic surgeon's life and career as well as a vivid look at the medical practices and prejudices of his time." Kirkus
Includes bibliographical references and index

Nadar, Félix, 1820-1910
Begley, Adam. The **great** Nadar; the man behind the camera. Adam Begley. Tim Duggan Books 2017 248 p. illustrations (hardcover) $28 **92**
1. Adventure and adventurers 2. Photographers -- France -- Biography
ISBN 9781101902608; 9781101902622; 9781101902615
LC 2016045382
This book, by Adam Begley, is a biography of Parisian photographer, adventurer, and pioneer Nadar. "The first great portrait photographer, a pioneering balloonist, the first person to take an aerial photograph, and the prime mover behind the first airmail service, Nadar was one of the original celebrity artist-entrepreneurs." (Publisher's note)
"Told in a pleasant, conversational style, this title is not only filled with curious, whimsical details about a lively figure, it is also is a very readable narrative." LJ

Nafisi, Azar
★ Nafisi, Azar. **Reading** Lolita in Tehran; a memoir in books. Azar Nafisi. Random House 2003 347 p. $23.95; pa $11.16 **92**
1. Books and reading 2. Memoirists 3. Women -- Iran 4. College teachers 5. Literary critics
ISBN 0-375-50490-7; 0-8129-7106-X pa
LC 2002-36724
"A spirited tribute both to the classics of world literature and to resistance against oppression." Kirkus.

★ Nafisi, Azar. **Things** I've been silent about; memories. Random House 2008 336p il $27 **92**
1. Memoirists 2. Women -- Iran 3. College teachers 4. Literary critics
ISBN 978-1-4000-6361-1; 1-4000-6361-2
LC 2008-482096
This is the author's "account of growing up under a chilly, tyrannical parent in a changing Iran. . . . An immensely rewarding and beautifully written act of courage, by turns amusing, tender and obsessively dogged." Kirkus

Naipaul, V. S. (Vidiadhar Surajprasad), 1932-2018
French, Patrick. The **world** is what it is; the authorized

biography of V.S. Naipaul. Knopf 2008 554p il $30 **92**
1. Authors 2. Novelists 3. Journalists 4. Essayists 5. Travel writers 6. Radio reporters 7. Nonfiction writers 8. Short story writers 9. Nobel laureates for literature
ISBN 978-1-4000-4405-4; 1-4000-4405-7
LC 2008-6988
This authorized study of Nobel laureate V.S. Naipaul examines his difficult early life as a child of Indian parents in colonial Trinidad, his Oxford education, the depression that marked his life in England, his complex personal life and romantic relationships, and his pursuit of becoming a great writer.
This book "is a prodigious achievement, a wonderful biography, a justification for the art of biography itself." Times Lit Suppl
Includes bibliographical references

Naipaul, V. S. **Reading** & writing; a personal account. New York Review of Bks. 2000 64p $16.95 **92**
1. Authors 2. Novelists 3. Journalists 4. Essayists 5. Travel writers 6. Radio reporters 7. Nonfiction writers 8. Short story writers 9. Nobel laureates for literature
ISBN 0-940322-38-2
LC 99-49615
Naipaul writes about his experiences growing up as an Indian living in Trinidad, his travels in India, his education at Oxford, and his struggles as a young writer in London
The author "elegantly expresses hard-earned wisdom about literature and culture, the political stakes of history and the relationship between the writer and the world." N Y Times Book Rev

Nansen, Odd, 1901-1973
From day to day; One Man's Diary of Survival in Nazi Concentration Camps. Odd Nansen; edited and annotated by Timothy J. Boyce; preface by Thomas Buergenthal; translated by Katherine John. Vanderbilt University Press 2016 616 p. illustrations (hardcover: acid-free paper) $39.95 **92**
1. Nansen, Odd, 1901-1973 -- Diaries 2. Concentration camp inmates -- Germany -- Diaries 3. World War, 1939-1945 -- Norwegian personal narratives 4. World War, 1939-1945 -- Prisoners and prisons, German 5. Veidal Prison Camp 6. Grini (Concentration camp) 7. Sachsenhausen (Concentration camp) 8. Concentration camp inmates -- Norway -- Diaries 9. World War, 1939-1945 -- Personal narratives, Norwegian
ISBN 9780826521002
LC 2015042213
This book, by Odd Nansen, edited and annotated by Timothy J. Boyce, with preface by Thomas Buergenthal and translated by Katherine John, records the author's struggle as victim of the Nazi regime. "[It] contains extensive annotations and new diary selections never before translated into English. Forty sketches of camp life and death by Nansen, an architect and talented draftsman, provide a sense of immediacy and acute observation matched by the diary entries." (Publisher's note)
Includes bibliographical references and index

Napoleon I, Emperor of the French, 1769-1821
Broers, Michael. **Napoleon**; the spirit of the age: 1805-1810. Michael Broers. W W Norton & Co Inc 2018 544 p. $29.95 **92**
1. France -- History -- 1799-1815 2. France -- Kings and rulers -- Biography
ISBN 1681776693; 9781681776699
LC 2018052247
This book is "the second volume of Michael Broers' three volume life of Napoleon, covering the tumultuous years 1805 to 1810, a period which marks the zenith of Napoleon's power and military success. Like

volume one, it is based on the new version of Napoleon's correspondence, made available by the Fondation Napoléon in Paris. It is the story of Napoleon's conquest of Europe--and that of his magnificent Grande Armée-- as they sweep through the length and breadth of Europe." (Publisher's note)

Includes bibliography and index.

Broers, Michael. **Napoleon**; Soldier of Destiny. Michael Broers. W W Norton & Co Inc 2015 608 p. 8 plates; ills.; ports.; maps (hardcover) $35 **92**

ISBN 1605988723; 9781605988726

This biography, by Michael Broers, "is the first life of Napoleon, in any language, that makes full use of his newly released personal correspondence compiled by the Napoléon Foundation in Paris. All previous lives of Napoleon have relied more on the memoirs of others than on his own uncensored words." (Publisher's note)

"Highly recommended for general readers and scholars alike." LJ

Gueniffey, Patrice. **Bonaparte**; 1769-1802. Patrice Gueniffey; translated by Steven Rendall. The Belknap Press of-Harvard University Press 2015 1024 p. (alk. paper) $39.95 **92**

1. France -- History -- 1799-1815 2. Emperors -- France -- Biography 3. Heads of state -- France -- Biography 4. France -- History -- Consulate and First Empire, 1799-1815

ISBN 0674368355; 9780674368354

LC 2014034162

This book, by Patrice Gueniffey, translated by Steven Rendall, "takes up the epic narrative . . . of Napoleon himself. . . . Gueniffey follows Bonaparte from his obscure boyhood in Corsica, to his meteoric rise during the Italian and Egyptian campaigns of the Revolutionary wars, to his proclamation as Consul for Life in 1802. Bonaparte is the story of how Napoleon became Napoleon." (Publisher's note)

Includes bibliographical references and index

★ Roberts, Andrew, 1963- **Napoleon**; a life. Andrew Roberts. Viking 2014 926 p. ill. (chiefly col.), maps hbk $45 **92**

1. Napoleonic Wars, 1800-1815

ISBN 0670025321; 9780670025329

LC 2013497791

Los Angeles Times Book Prizes Winner: Biography (2014)

Author Andrew Roberts presents "the first one-volume biography to take advantage of the recent publication of Napoleon's thirty-three thousand letters, which radically transform our understanding of his character and motivation. Roberts traveled to fifty-three of Napoleon's sixty battle sites, discovered crucial new documents in archives, and even made the long trip by boat to St. Helena. " (Publisher's note)

"Other opinionated observers . . . consider Napoleon a self-absorbed opportunist plagued by his incompetent economics, pugnacious foreign policy, totalitarian government and massive propaganda, but Roberts offers a solid reconsideration." Kirkus

Includes bibliographical references and index

Napoleon III, Emperor of the French, 1808-1873

Strauss-Schom, Alan. The **shadow** emperor; a biography of Napoleon III. Alan Strauss-Schom. St. Martin's Press 2018 512 p. (hardcover) $32.50 **92**

1. Emperors 2. France -- Kings and rulers -- Biography 3. France -- History -- 1848-1870 4. Emperors -- France -- Biography 5. France -- History -- Second Empire, 1852-1870

ISBN 9781250057785

LC 2017060757

In this biography of Napoleon III, author Alan Strauss-Schom "uses his years of primary source research to explore the major cultural, sociological, economical, financial, international, and militaristic long-lasting effects of France's most polarizing emperor. Louis-Napoleon's achievements have been mixed and confusing, even to historians. He completely revolutionized the infrastructure of the state and the economy, but at the price of financial scandals." (Publisher's note)

"Highly recommended for readers of European history and historical biography." Library Journal

Includes bibliographical references and index

Biography of Napoleon III

Nash, Ogden, 1902-1971

Parker, Douglas M. **Ogden** Nash; the life and work of America's laureate of light verse. with a foreword by Dana Gioia. Ivan R. Dee 2005 316p il $27.50 **92**

1. Poets 2. Authors 3. Humorists 4. Children's authors

ISBN 1-566-63637-X

LC 2004-59912

"Parker's is a useful, highly readable biography of one of America's best-loved poets." Publ Wkly

Includes bibliographical references

Navratilova, Martina, 1956-

Howard, Johnette. The **rivals**; Chris Evert vs. Martina Navratilova: their epic duels and extraordinary friendship. Broadway Books 2005 296p il $24.95 **92**

1. Tennis players 2. Tennis -- Biography

ISBN 0-7679-1884-3

LC 2004-61918

"This work makes a fine contribution to the history of women in sports." Publ Wkly

Nawaz, Zarqa.

Nawaz, Zarqa. **Laughing** All the Way to the Mosque; The Misadventures of a Muslim Woman. Zarqa Nawaz. Little, Brown & Co. 2016 240 p. (paperback) $18.99 **92**

1. Wit and humor 2. Islam -- Customs and practices

ISBN 0349005931; 9780349005935

In this book, Muslim writer and humorist Zarqa Nawaz describes how "being a practicing Muslim in the West is sometimes challenging, sometimes rewarding and sometimes downright absurd. How do you explain why Eid never falls on the same date each year; why it is that Halal butchers also sell teapots and alarm clocks; how do you make clear to the plumber that it's essential the toilet is installed within sitting-arm's reach of the tap?" (Publisher's note)

"Nawaz's self-deprecating wit is endearing, and her simple, factual tone provides education without ever being boring. This memoir provides an important glimpse into the everyday life of a Western Muslim family, but, even better, it is a laugh-out-loud story that everyone can enjoy." Pub Wkly

Needham, Joseph, 1900-1995

Winchester, Simon. The **man** who loved China; the fantastic story of the eccentric scientist who unlocked the mysteries of the Middle Kingdom. HarperCollins Publishers 2008 316p il map $27.95 **92**

1. Scientists 2. Biochemists 3. Science historians 4. Writers on science 5. Biography, Individual 6. Science -- China -- History

ISBN 978-0-06-088459-8; 0-06-088459-2

LC 2007-40516

The author "explores Needham's fascinating and sometimes controversial personal life, his travels to China, and especially the significance and topicality of his scholarship on the early accomplishments of Chinese science and technology. . . . Essential for all libraries." Libr J

Includes bibliographical references

Neel, Alice, 1900-1984

Hoban, Phoebe. **Alice** Neel; the art of not sitting pretty. St. Martin's Press 2010 500p il $35 **92**

1. Artists 2. Painters 3. Women artists

ISBN 978-0-312-60748-7; 0-312-60748-7

LC 2010-35781

"Judicious and ardent, Hoban has created a galvanizing portrait of a 'rebel artist' who remained true to her humanist convictions." Booklist

Includes bibliographical references

Nehru, Jawaharlal, 1889-1964

Brown, Judith M. **Nehru**: a political life. Yale University Press 2003 407p il $35 **92**

1. Prime ministers 2. Nonfiction writers 3. Prime ministers -- India

ISBN 0-300-09279-2

LC 2003-5807

"This compelling biography, the most complete and penetrating account of Nehru yet written, casts new light on both the public and private man. It also offers insights into the history of India's nationalist movement and the complexities of constructing a new nation state in the aftermath of imperial rule." Univ Press Books for Public and Second Sch Libr, 2004

Includes bibliographical references

Nelson, Willie

★ Patoski, Joe Nick. **Willie** Nelson; an epic life. Little, Brown 2008 567p il $27.99; pa $16.99 **92**

1. Singers 2. Country musicians 3. Songwriters

ISBN 978-0-316-01778-7; 0-316-01778-7; 978-0-316-01779-4 pa; 0-316-01779-5 pa

LC 2007-44984

A biography of the country music singer and songwriter.

"This impressive, entertaining chronicle of Willie Nelson's life is replete with exactly what you'd expect—honky-tonk, long nights on the open road, whiskey, womanizing and weed—but . . . [the author] looks beyond country music trappings to find the funny, talented, determined man who became an unlikely icon." Publ Wkly

Includes discography and bibliographical references

Nemat, Marina

Nemat, Marina. **Prisoner** of Tehran; a memoir. Free Press 2007 306p $26 **92**

1. Political prisoners 2. Memoirists 3. Iran -- History -- 1979-

ISBN 1-4165-3742-2; 978-1-4165-3742-7

LC 2006-50191

Nemat was sixteen when she was arrested in Iran in early 1982 for political protests against the new fundamentalist regime. This is an account of her prison experiences.

The author's "story is not so much a political history lesson than it is a memoir of faith and love, a protest against violence that cannot be silenced. . . . Her persistence in standing for goodness is a lesson for us all." Christ Sci Monit

Neruda, Pablo, 1904-1973

★ Feinstein, Adam. **Pablo** Neruda; a passion for life. Bloomsbury 2004 497p il $32.50; pa $18.95 **92**

1. Poets 2. Authors 3. Diplomats 4. Novelists 5. Nobel laureates for peace 6. Nobel laureates for literature

ISBN 1-582-34410-8; 1-582-34594-5 pa

LC 2004-715

"Feinstein undoubtedly researched every existent source and found new ones, and the result is a detailed and accurate biography. . . . This is a necessary book, with many beautiful photos." Publ Wkly

Includes bibliographical references

Urrutia, Matilde. **My** life with Pablo Neruda; {translated by} Alexandria Giardino. Stanford University Press 2004 318p $27.95 **92**

1. Poets 2. Authors 3. Diplomats 4. Novelists 5. Nobel laureates for peace 6. Nobel laureates for literature

ISBN 0-8047-5009-2

LC 2004-8535

Original Spanish edition, 1986

"Urrutia, Neruda's third wife, provides a . . . biography from her particular vantage. Her purpose is twofold: to present her Pablo as the exuberant, warm, and loving individual he was and to inform readers of the menace imposed by Chilean dictator Pinochet, who was responsible for the assassination of elected president Allende, Neruda's close friend. Urrutia's account is highly selective but well worth reading for another perspective on this great man." Libr J

Nesmith, Michael

Nesmith, Michael, 1942- **Infinite** Tuesday; An Autobiographical Riff. Michael Nesmith. Crown Archetype 2017 306 p. illustrations (hardcover) $28 **92**

1. Rock musicians -- United States -- Biography

ISBN 9781101907504; 9781101907511; 9781101907528

LC 2016058926

In this book, "Michael Nesmith's eclectic, electric life spans his star-making role on The Monkees, his invention of the music video, and his critical contributions to movies, comedy, and the world of virtual reality. Above all, his is a seeker's story, a pilgrimage in search of a set of principles to live by." (Publisher's note)

"This selectively revealing, insightful memoir casts the cerebral Monkee as a spiritual seeker and self-deprecating visionary." Kirkus

Netanyahu, Binyamin

Caspit, Ben. The **Netanyahu** years; Ben Caspit; translated by Ora Cummings. Thomas Dunne Book 2017 506 p. (hardcover) $29.99 **92**

1. Prime ministers -- Israel 2. Israel -- Politics and government 3. Prime ministers -- Israel -- Biography 4. Israel -- Politics and government -- 1993-

ISBN 9781250087065; 9781250087058

LC 2017010999

This book, by Ben Caspit, translated by Ora Cummings, looks at the life of Benjamin Netanyahu as prime minister of Israel. "Caspit covers a wide swath of topics, including Netanyahu's policies, his political struggles, and his fight against the Iranian nuclear program, and zeroes in on Netanyahu's love/hate relationship with the American administration, America's Jews, and his alliances with American business magnates." (Publisher's note)

"As captured in Cummings's remarkably fluid translation, Caspit's detailed, clear account covers Israel's domestic-policy disputes and Netanyahu's impact as a world leader." Pub Wkly

Nevins, Sheila

Nevins, Sheila. **You** don't look your age . . . and other fairy tales. Sheila Nevins. Flatiron Books 2017 ix, 255 p.p (hardcover) $24.99 **92**

1. Working mothers 2. Television personalities -- Biography 3. Women television producers and directors -- United States -- Biography
ISBN 9781250111302; 1250111307

LC 2017003050

This book, by Sheila Nevins, is "about the real life challenges of being a woman in a man's world, what it means to be a working mother, what it's like to be an older woman in a youth-obsessed culture, the sometimes changing, often sweet truth about marriages, what being a feminist really means, and that you are in good company if your adult children don't return your phone calls." (Publisher's note)

"A miscellany of musings about aging, love, work, and wisdom." Kirkus

Newman, Kurt, M.D.

Newman, Kurt. **Healing** children; a surgeon's stories from the frontiers of pediatric medicine. Kurt Newman M.D. Viking 2017 viii, 262 p.p (hardcover) $27　　　　**92**
1. Physicians -- Biography 2. Children -- Health and hygiene 3. Pediatricians -- Biography 4. Pediatrics -- Popular works
ISBN 9780525428831; 9780698191648; 0525428836

LC 2017025373

In this memoir, "Dr. Kurt Newman draws from his long experience as a pediatric surgeon working at one of our nation's top children's hospitals to make the case that children are more than miniature adults. Through the story of his own career and of the brave kids he has treated over the years--and their equally brave and tenacious parents--he reveals the revolution that is taking place in pediatric medicine." (Publisher's note)

"Written primarily as a guide for parents navigating the unpredictable health of their children, the book also addresses the future of pediatric care, as Newman delves into the most innovative therapies and initiatives in development." Kirkus

Newman, Paul, 1925-2008

Levy, Shawn. **Paul** Newman; a life. Harmony Books 2009 490p il $29.99; pa $16　　　　**92**
1. Actors 2. Motion picture directors 3. Automobile racing drivers
ISBN 978-0-307-35375-7; 0-307-35375-3; 978-0-307-35376-4 pa; 0-307-35376-1 pa

LC 2009-11220

This is a behind-the-scenes examination of the actor's life, from his merry pranks on the set to his lasting romance with Joanne Woodward to the devastating impact of his son's death from a drug overdose

"An illuminating look at one of the true greats, full of humor and intelligent analysis—highly recommended." Kirkus

Includes bibliographical references

Newton, Isaac Sir, 1642-1727

Gleick, James. **Isaac** Newton. Pantheon Bks. 2003 272p il hardcover o.p. pa $13　　　　**92**
1. Physicists 2. Scientists 3. Mathematicians 4. Writers on science
ISBN 0-375-42233-1; 1-4000-3295-4 pa

LC 2002-192696

This "is now the biography of choice for the interested layman. Gleick copes with the complex tapestry of Newton's interests by teasing them apart into individual chapters, assembled into a smooth chronological flow. . . . Newton the man emerges from the shadows." N Y Times Book Rev

Includes bibliographical references

Levenson, Thomas. **Newton** and the counterfeiter; the unknown detective career of the world's greatest scientist. Hough-

ton Mifflin Harcourt 2009 318p $25; pa $14.95　　　　**92**
1. Physicists 2. Mathematicians 3. Counterfeits and counterfeiting 4. Counterfeiters 5. Writers on science
ISBN 978-0-15-101278-7; 0-15-101278-4; 978-0-547-33604-6 pa; 0-547-33604-7 pa

LC 2008-53511

"Levenson demonstrates a surpassing felicity in his brisk treatment of this late-17th-century true-crime adventure. . . . Swift, agile treatment of a little known but highly entertaining episode in a legendary life." Kirkus

Includes bibliographical references

Ngũgĩ wa Thiong'o, 1938-

Ngugi wa Thiong'o, 1938- **Wrestling** with the devil; a prison memoir. Ngugi wa Thiong'o. The New Press 2018 248 p. (hardcover) $25.99　　　　**92**
1. Prisons 2. Biography 3. Prisoners -- Biography 4. Political prisoners' writings, Kenyan 5. Political prisoners -- Kenya -- Biography 6. Authors, Kenyan -- 20th century -- Biography
ISBN 9781620973349; 9781620973332; 1620973332

LC 2017030135

This prison memoir, by Ngugi wa Thiong'o, "begins literally half an hour before his release on December 12, 1978. In one extended flashback he recalls the night, a year earlier, when armed police pulled him from his home and jailed him in Kenya's Maximum Security Prison, one of the largest in Africa. There, he lives in a prison block with eighteen other political prisoners, quarantined from the general prison population." (Publisher's note)

"At once exhilarating and defiant, wa Thiong'o's memoir is a thought provoking document of a grim time in Kenyan history." Pub Wkly

Nicholas II, Emperor of Russia, 1868-1918

Massie, Robert K., 1929- **Nicholas** and Alexandra. Ballantine Books 2000 613p il map pa $18.95　　　　**92**
1. Monks 2. Emperors 3. Empresses 4. Courtiers 5. Russia -- History 6. Russia -- Kings and rulers
ISBN 0-345-43831-0; 978-0-345-43831-7

LC 99-91507

First published 1967 by Atheneum

This study provides an intimate account of the Romanov family and the coming of the Russian Revolution. Kerensky, Lenin and Rasputin are among the personalities profiled.

This book, "solid with research, reads as lightly as a novel, as authoritatively as a textbook. Dialogue and lively description lend a sense of immediacy, but his notes, discreetly relegated to the back of the book, show how carefully he has avoided slipping into fiction." Christ Sci Monit

Includes bibliographical references

Nietzsche, Friedrich Wilhelm, 1844-1900

Prideaux, Sue. **I** am dynamite! a life of Nietzsche. Sue Prideaux. Tim Duggan Books 2018 464 p. $30　　　　**92**
1. Philosophers -- Germany 2. Philosophers -- Biography 3. Philosophers -- Germany -- Biography
ISBN 9781524760823; 9781524760830

LC 2018023928

In this biography, author Sue Prideaux brings readers into the world of . . . [German philosopher Friedrich Nietzsche], illuminating the events and people that shaped his life and work. From his placid, devoutly Christian upbringing--overshadowed by the mysterious death of his father--through his teaching career, lonely philosophizing on high mountains, and heart-breaking descent into madness, Prideaux documents Nietzsche's intellectual and emotional life." (Publisher's note)

Includes bibliographical references and index

Nitze, Paul H.

Thompson, Nicholas. The **hawk** and the dove; Paul Nitze, George Kennan, and the history of the Cold War. Henry Holt 2009 403p il $27.50   **92**

1. Authors 2. Cold war 3. Diplomats 4. Statesmen 5. Historians 6. Centenarians 7. Nonfiction writers 8. Government officials 9. Biography, Individual 10. Secretaries of the navy 11. United States -- Officials and employees 12. United States -- Foreign relations -- 1945-1989 13. National security -- United States -- History -- 20th century 14. Anti-communist movements -- United States -- History -- 20th century

ISBN 0805081429; 9780805081428

LC 2009-09225

This biography of Nitze and Kennan focuses on their "careers as statesmen, policy makers and public intellectuals." (N Y Times Book Rev) Index.

This book "does an inspired job of telling the story of the Cold War through the careers of two of its most interesting and important figures." Washington Monthly

Includes bibliographical references

Nixon, Richard M. (Richard Milhous), 1913-1994

Dallek, Robert. **Nixon** and Kissinger; partners in power. HarperCollins Publishers 2007 740p il $32.50   **92**

1. Presidents 2. Vice-presidents 3. Senators 4. College teachers 5. Nonfiction writers 6. Members of Congress 7. Writers on politics 8. Secretaries of state 9. Presidential advisers 10. Nobel laureates for peace 11. United States -- Foreign relations 12. International relations specialists

ISBN 978-0-06-072230-2; 0-06-072230-4

LC 2006-52100

A look "behind the scenes at this quintessential pair of power brokers and their lasting influence, for good and ill, on the political stage." Bookmarks Magazine

Includes bibliographical references

Denevi, Timothy. **Freak** kingdom; Hunter S. Thompson's manic ten-year crusade against American fascism. Timothy Denevi. Public Affairs 2018 416 p. (hardcover) $28   **92**

1. Politicians -- United States -- Biography 2. United States -- Politics and government -- 1945- 3. Politicians -- United States 4. United States -- Politics and government -- 1945-1989 5. Political campaigns -- United States -- History -- 20th century 6. Presidents -- United States -- Election -- History -- 20th century

ISBN 9781541767942

LC 2018015549

This biography, by Timothy Denevi, presents "the story of Hunter S. Thompson's crusade against Richard Nixon and the threat of fascism in America--and the devastating price he paid for it. [The book shows Thompson as] a fearless opponent of corruption and fascism, one who sacrificed his future well-being to fight against it, rewriting the rules of journalism and political satire in the process." (Publisher's note)

Includes bibliographical references and index

★ Farrell, John A. **Richard** Nixon; the life. John A. Farrell. Doubleday 2017 752 p. illustrations (hardback) $35 **92**

1. Presidents -- United States -- Biography 2. Nixon, Richard M. (Richard Milhous), 1913-1994 3. United States -- Politics and government -- 1961-1974 4. United States -- Politics and government -- 1969-1974

ISBN 9780385537353; 9780385537360

LC 2016049856

Pulitzer Prize Finalist: Biography (2018)

This biography of Richard Nixon, by John A. Farrell, presents "the defining portrait of a man who led America in a time of turmoil and left us a darker age. . . . [E]lected president in 1969, Nixon packed his staff with bright young men who devised forward-thinking reforms addressing health care, welfare, civil rights, and protection of the environment. It was a fine legacy, but Nixon cared little for it." (Publisher's note)

"Full of fresh, endlessly revealing insights into Nixon's political career, less on the matter of his character, refreshingly, than on the events that accompanied and resulted from it." Kirkus

Includes bibliographical references (pages [689]-699) and index.

Thomas, Evan. **Being** Nixon; the fears and hopes of an American president. Evan Thomas. Random House Inc. 2015 656 p. illustrations $35   **92**

1. Presidents -- United States 2. Nixon, Richard M. (Richard Milhous), 1913-1994 3. Presidents -- United States -- Biography 4. United States -- Politics and government -- 1969-1974

ISBN 0812995368; 9780812995367

LC 2015009669

Author Evan Thomas presents this "biography of Richard Nixon, . . . a complicated figure who was both determinedly optimistic and tragically flawed. Thomas reveals the contradictions of a leader whose vision and foresight led him to achieve détente with the Soviet Union and re-establish relations with communist China, but whose underhanded political tactics tainted his reputation long before the Watergate scandal." (Publisher's note)

"Thomas doesn't shy away from showing Nixon at his worst, acknowledging Nixon's penchant for the "maudlin," his "self-pity," his fear of confrontation, and his often poisonous rivalry with Henry Kissinger. Thomas is generous to his subject, contextualizing Nixon and often teasing out his well-concealed desire to do the right thing." Pub Wkly

Includes bibliographical references and index

Niyizonkiza, Deogratias, 1970-

Kidder, Tracy. **Strength** in what remains. Random House 2009 277p $26; pa $16   **92**

1. Genocide 2. Refugees 3. Students 4. Burundi

ISBN 978-1-4000-6621-6; 1-4000-6621-2; 978-0-8129-7761-5 pa; 0-8121-7761-0 pa

LC 2008-44865

"This profoundly gripping, hopeful and crucial testament is a work of the utmost skill, sympathy and moral clarity." Publ Wkly

Includes bibliographical references

Noah, Trevor, 1984-

★ Noah, Trevor, 1984- **Born** a crime; stories from a South African childhood. by Trevor Noah. Spiegel & Grau 2016 304 p. (ebook) $65; $28   **92**

1. Comedians -- Biography 2. Television personalities -- Biography 3. Comedians -- South Africa -- Biography 4. Comedians -- United States -- Biography 5. Television personalities -- United States -- Biography

ISBN 9780399588181; 9780399588174; 9780399590443

LC 2016031399

This memoir, by Trevor Noah, "is the story of a mischievous young boy who grows into a restless young man as he struggles to find himself in a world where he was never supposed to exist. It is also the story of that young man's relationship with his fearless, rebellious, and fervently religious mother—his teammate, a woman determined to save her son from the cycle of poverty, violence, and abuse that would ultimately threaten her own life." (Publisher's note)

"Incisive, funny, and vivid, these true tales are anchored to his portrait of his courageous, rebellious, and religious mother, who defied racially restrictive laws to secure an education and a career for herself—and to have a child with a white Swiss German even though sex between whites and blacks was illegal; neither parent could be seen in public with their son." Booklist

Noguchi, Isamu, 1904-1988

Herrera, Hayden. **Listening** to stone; the art and life of Isamu Noguchi. Hayden Herrera. Farrar Straus & Giroux 2015 592 p. illustrations (hardback) $40   **92**

    1. Sculptors -- United States -- Biography 2. Japanese American sculptors -- Biography

    ISBN 0374281165; 9780374281168

LC 2014031274

Los Angeles Times Book Prize: Biography (2015)

This book, by Hayden Herrera, is a biography of the American artist Isamu Noguchi. "Combining the personal correspondence of and interviews with Noguchi and those closest to him--from artists, patrons, assistants, and lovers--[Hayden] Herrera has created an authoritative biography of one of the twentieth century's most important sculptors." (Publisher's note)

"Herrera adroitly shows that Noguchi was more than just a sculptor--he was a skilled craftsman, a heartbreaker, and a philosopher of design." Pub Wkly

Includes bibliographical references and index

Nolte, Nick

Nolte, Nick, 1941- **Rebel**; my life outside the lines. Nick Nolte. William Morrow 2018 272 p. (hbk.) $28.99   **92**

    1. Acting 2. Motion picture actors and actresses -- United States -- Biography

    ISBN 9780062219572; 006221957X

"Legendary actor Nick Nolte delivers his most revealing performance yet. This intimate memoir is a tale of art, passion, commitment, addiction, and the quest for personal enlightenment. . . . In a career spanning five decades and hundreds of roles, . . . Nolte has become a true Hollywood icon. . . . Nick's untold story, with never-before-seen photos, offers a candid, unvarnished close-up look at the man, the career, the loves, and the life." (Publisher's note)

"Long since on the wagon and an obviously thoughtful man, Nolte seems to share the reader's surprise that he lived long enough to take that role. Better than the usual run of actor memoirs and plenty of fun to boot." Kirkus

Norris, Gloria

Norris, Gloria. **Kookooland**; Gloria Norris. Regan Arts 2015 355 p. illustrations $27   **92**

    1. Family life 2. Autobiographies

    ISBN 1941393608; 9781941393604

LC 2015930624

This memoir by Gloria Norris is a "profound portrait of how violence echoes through a family, and through a community. From the tragedy, Gloria finds a way to carve out a future on her own terms and ends up just where she wants to be. " (Publisher's note)

"A tumble through a tumultuous time, in which the heroine inexplicably, beautifully lands on her feet." Booklist

Norris, Kathleen, 1947-

Norris, Kathleen. **Acedia** & me; a marriage, monks, and a writer's life. Riverhead Books 2008 334p $25.95   **92**

    1. Poets 2. Apathy 3. Authors 4. Melancholy 5. Monasticism and religious orders 6. Inspirational writers

ISBN 978-1-59448-996-9

LC 2008-10150

"The result of Norris's decades-long meditation on acedia is peaceful, graceful prose, amplified by word histories and gentle humor." Christ Today

Includes bibliographical references

Northup, Solomon, 1808-1863?

★ Northup, Solomon. **Twelve** years a slave; Solomon Northup; introduction by Ira Berlin; general editor Henry Louis Gates, Jr. Penguin Books 2012 xxxvi, 240 p.p ill., music (Penguin Classics) (pbk.) $16   **92**

    1. Slaves -- United States -- 19th century 2. Slaves' writings, American 3. African Americans -- Biography 4. Slaves -- United States -- Biography 5. Slavery -- Louisiana -- History -- 19th century 6. Plantation life -- Louisiana -- History -- 19th century

    ISBN 0143106708; 9780143106708

LC 2012012550

This autobiographical book "recounts how Solomon Northup, born a free man in New York, was lured to Washington, D.C., in 1841 with the promise of fast money, then drugged and beaten and sold into slavery. He spent the next twelve years of his life in captivity on a Louisiana cotton plantation. After his rescue, Northup published this . . . detailed account of slave life." (Publisher's note)

Includes bibliographical references and index

Notaro, Tig

Notaro, Tig, 1971- **I'm** just a person; Tig Notaro. Ecco, an imprint of HarperCollinsPublishers 2016 xi, 240 p.p illustrations (some color) $26.99   **92**

    1. Comedians 2. Cancer patients 3. Cancer -- Patients -- Biography 4. Comedians -- United States -- Biography

    ISBN 0062266632; 9780062266637

LC 2016303427

This memoir, by Tig Notaro, is a "raw account of her year of death, cancer, and epiphany. In the span of four months in 2012, Tig Notaro was hospitalized for a debilitating intestinal disease called C. diff, her mother unexpectedly died, she went through a breakup, and then she was diagnosed with bilateral breast cancer. Hit with this devastating barrage, Tig took her grief onstage." (Publisher's note)

"Forthright and private moments are revealed as a stand-up comedian uses her gift of creating laughter to overcome personal and physical disasters." Kirkus.

Novacek, Michael J.

Novacek, Michael J. **Time** traveler; in search of dinosaurs and ancient mammals from Montana to Mongolia. {by} Michael Novacek. Farrar, Straus & Giroux 2002 368p il $26; pa $15   **92**

    1. Curators 2. Paleontologists

    ISBN 0-374-27880-6; 0-374-52876-4 pa

LC 2001-40438

"The author first describes the youthful experiences that inspired him to become a paleontologist. . . . Then Novacek launches into his various expeditions. . . . Interweaving his adventures with explanations of where his finds fit into the geologic past, Novacek has combined the comedic with the informative in this entertaining survey of his career." Booklist

Includes bibliographical references

Nudelman, Meyer

Nuland, Sherwin B. **Lost** in America; a journey with my

father. Knopf 2003 209p $24; pa $12 **92**
1. Authors 2. Surgeons 3. Factory workers 4. Writers on medicine
ISBN 0-375-41294-8; 0-375-75722-1 pa

LC 2002-40795

"Written with enormous empathy, yet without a hint of sentimentality, Nuland's memoir is both heartbreaking and breathtaking." Publ Wkly

Nuland, Sherwin B.

Nuland, Sherwin B. **Lost** in America; a journey with my father. Knopf 2003 209p $24; pa $12 **92**
1. Authors 2. Surgeons 3. Factory workers 4. Writers on medicine
ISBN 0-375-41294-8; 0-375-75722-1 pa

LC 2002-40795

"Written with enormous empathy, yet without a hint of sentimentality, Nuland's memoir is both heartbreaking and breathtaking." Publ Wkly

Nur Jahān, Empress, consort of Jahangir, Emperor of Hindustan, -1645

★ Lal, Ruby. **Empress**; the astonishing reign of Nur Jahan. Ruby Lal. W W Norton & Co Inc 2018 xiii, 308 p.p illustrations (chiefly color) (hardcover) $27.95 **92**
1. Empresses 2. Mogul Empire 3. Empresses -- Mogul Empire -- Biography
ISBN 9780393635409; 9780393239348

LC 2018003419

In this book, author "Ruby Lal uncovers the rich life and world of Nur Jahan. . . . In 1611, . . . Nur . . . became the twentieth and most cherished wife of the Emperor Jahangir. . . . Nur ruled the vast Mughal Empire alongside her husband, and governed in his stead as his health failed and his attentions wandered from matters of state. An astute politician and devoted partner, Nur led troops into battle to free Jahangir when he was imprisoned by one of his own officers." (Publisher's note)

"A page-turning, eye-opening biography that shatters our impressions of India as established by the British Raj." Kirkus

Includes bibliographical references (pages 251-290) and index.

Nureyev, Rudolf, 1938-1993

★ Kavanagh, Julie. **Nureyev**; the life. Pantheon Books 2007 782p il $37.50 **92**
1. Ballet dancers
ISBN 978-0-375-40513-6; 0-375-40513-5

LC 2006-38137

In this biography of the Russian ballet dancer, the author "chronicles Nureyev's many tempestuous relationships, including his legendary work with Margot Fonteyn and his formative affair with the outstanding Danish dancer Erik Bruhn. . . . Kavanagh's consummate biography will stand as a pillar in dance history." Booklist

Includes bibliographical references

Nusseibeh, Sari

David, Anthony. **Once** upon a country; a Palestinian life. [by] Sari Nusseibeh, with Anthony David. Farrar, Straus and Giroux 2007 542p il $27.50 **92**
1. Philosophers 2. Palestinian Arabs 3. Israel-Arab conflicts 4. Political leaders 5. College presidents 6. Biography, Individual
ISBN 0-374-29950-1; 978-0-374-29950-7

LC 2006-13272

This is an autobiography by "Sari Nusseibeh, a Palestinian intellectual and public figure." (N Y Times (Late N Y Ed))

"This is a rare book, one written by a partisan in the struggle over Palestine who nevertheless recognizes—and bravely records—the moral and political failures of his own people." Los Angeles Times

Includes bibliographical references

Nutter, Tommy, 1943-1992

Richardson, Lance. **House** of Nutter; the rebel tailor of Savile Row. Lance Richardson. Crown Archetype 2018 400 p. (hardcover) $28 **92**
1. Gay men -- Biography 2. Fashion designers -- Biography 3. Fashion designers -- Great Britain -- Biography
ISBN 9780451496461; 9780451496478

LC 2017045881

This book, by Lance Richardson, tells the "true story of Tommy Nutter, the Savile Row tailor who changed the silhouette of men's fashion--and his rock photographer brother, David, who captured it all on film. . . . Richardson presents a dual portrait of brothers improvising their way through five decades of extraordinary events, their personal struggles playing out against vivid backdrops of the Blitz, an obscenity trial, . . . and the devastation of the AIDS crisis." (Publisher's note)

Includes bibliographical references

Nyad, Diana

Nyad, Diana, 1949- **Find** a way; one wild and precious life. Diana Nyad. Alfred A. Knopf 2015 304 p. 16 plates; illustrations; map (hardback) $26.95 **92**
1. Success 2. Swimmers -- United States -- Biography
ISBN 0385353618; 9780385353618

LC 2015009932

"At 64, celebrated long-distance swimmer Nyad accomplished a feat that had eluded her at 28--making the first solo swim from Cuba to Florida without a shark cage. While Cuba to the Keys is 94 miles for the proverbial crow, Nyad lacked wings and ultimately covered 110 miles through the powerful Gulf current, navigating hazards that included toxic jellyfish and peckish sharks, as well as severe nausea and dehydration. As Nyad narrates the financial and physical demands of her odyssey, which she undertook after a three-decade break from swimming, she also reviews her career as a television journalist and talk show host." (Publishers Weekly)

"Particularly effective in its ability to portray the complex psychology of an extreme endurance athlete, Nyad's moving account is well suited for readers interested in open-water swimming, endurance sports, athletes' memoirs, or age-defying adventures." LJ

O'Brien, Edna

O'Brien, Edna, 1930- **Country** Girl; A Memoir. by Edna O'Brien. Little, Brown and Co. 2013 x, 357 p.p ill. (hardcover) $27.99 **92**
1. Authors 2. Women authors -- Biography 3. Women authors, Irish -- 20th century -- Biography
ISBN 031612270X; 9780316122702

LC 2012047510

LA Times Book Prize Finalist: Biography (2013)

This memoir, written by Edna O'Brien, starts "with [her] birth in a grand but deteriorating house in Ireland, [and] moves through convent school to elopement, divorce, single-motherhood, the wild parties of the [1960s] in London, and encounters with Hollywood giants, pop stars, and literary titans. There is love and unrequited love, and the glamour of trips to America as an acclaimed writer hosted by Jackie Onassis and Hillary Clinton." (Publisher's note)

"While O'Brien overly devotes her time to cataloguing the notable actors, writers, and politicians of her acquaintance, the accounts of her childhood and her descriptions of Ireland soar with a lyricism reminiscent of Joyce." LJ

O'Brien, Jack, 1939-

O'Brien, Jack. **Jack** be nimble; the accidental education of an unintentional director. Jack O'Brien. Farrar, Straus & Giroux 2013 368 p. (hardback) $35   **92**

    1. Theatrical producers and directors 2. Television producers and directors -- United States -- Biography 3. Theatrical producers and directors -- United States -- Biography

    ISBN 0865478988; 9780865478985

                LC 2012048077

  This book presents a memoir by director Jack O'Brien. "Following a fairly normal Midwestern childhood, O'Brien hoped to make his mark by writing lyrics for Broadway but was instead pulled into the growing American regional theater movement by the likes of John Houseman, Helen Hayes, Ellis Rabb, and Eva Le Gallienne. He didn¿t intend to become a director, or to direct some of the most brilliant . . . personalities of the age, but . . . that's what happened." (Publisher's note)

  "Highly recommended for lovers of the theater and those interested in acting and directing." LJ

  Includes bibliographical references and index

O'Connor, Flannery

  ★ Gooch, Brad. **Flannery**; a life of Flannery O'Connor. Little, Brown and Co. 2009 448p il $30   **92**

    1. Authors 2. Novelists 3. Women authors 4. Authors, American 5. Short story writers 6. Biography, Individual

    ISBN 978-0-316-00066-6; 0-316-00066-3

                LC 2008-28504

  This biography of writer Flannery O'Connor, by Brad Gooch, focuses on "O'Connor's significant friendships--with Robert Lowell, Elizabeth Hardwick, Walker Percy, and James Dickey among others--and her deeply felt convictions, as expressed in her communications with Thomas Merton, Elizabeth Bishop, and Betty Hester. . . . O'Connor's capacity to live fully--despite the chronic disease that eventually confined her to her mother's farm in Georgia" is also discussed. (Publisher's note)

  "Gooch comfortably traces her fiction to its real-life roots in a meticulous yet seemingly effortless writing style, resulting in the definitive biography as well as providing the impetus for general readers to return to O'Connor's timeless fiction." Booklist

  Includes bibliographical references

O'Connor, Sandra Day

  Biskupic, Joan. **Sandra** Day O'Connor; how the first woman on the Supreme Court became its most influential justice. Ecco 2005 419p il $26.95   **92**

    1. Supreme Court justices

    ISBN 0-06-059018-1

                LC 2005-52103

  The author "offers an insightful biography of perhaps the most influential associate justice in recent history." Libr J

  Includes bibliographical references

O'Farrell, Maggie, 1972-

  O'Farrell, Maggie. **I** am, I am, I am; seventeen brushes with death. Maggie O'Farrell. Alfred A. Knopf 2018 288 p. illustrations (hardcover) $25.95   **92**

    1. Authors, Irish 2. Novelists, Irish -- 20th century -- Biography

    ISBN 9780525520238; 0525520228; 9780525520221

                LC 2017028597

  This book "is Maggie O'Farrell's astonishing memoir of the near-death experiences that have punctuated and defined her life. The childhood illness that left her bedridden for a year. . . . A teenage yearning to escape that nearly ended in disaster. An encounter with a disturbed man

on a remote path. And, most terrifying of all, an ongoing, daily struggle to protect her daughter . . . from a condition that leaves her unimaginably vulnerable to life's myriad dangers." (Publisher's note)

  "O'Farrell's intrepidness and determination are awe-inspiring, her experiences overwhelming, and her writing impeccable. This is a memoiristic tour de force." Booklist

O'Keeffe, Georgia, 1887-1986

  Drohojowska-Philp, Hunter. **Full** bloom; the art and life of Georgia O'Keeffe. W.W. Norton 2004 630p hardcover o.p. pa $21.95   **92**

    1. Artists 2. Painters 3. Biography, Individual

    ISBN 0-393-05853-0; 0-393-32741-8 pa

                LC 2003-26071

  This is a biography of the American painter.

  "O'Keeffe lived a long, adventurous, and profoundly productive life, and Drohojowska-Philp charts her triumphs over adversity in an involving, revelatory biography that attains the grand scope and depth her subject deserves." Booklist

  Includes bibliographical references

O'Neill, Eugene, 1888-1953

  Dowling, Robert M. **Eugene** O'Neill; a life in four acts. Robert M. Dowling. Yale University Press 2014 584 p. illustrations (hardback) $35   **92**

    1. American dramatists 2. Dramatists, American -- 20th century -- Biography

    ISBN 0300170335; 9780300170337

                LC 2014014634

  Los Angeles Times Book Prize Finalist: Biography (2014)

  This biography, by Robert M. Dowling, focuses on playwright Eugene O'Neill. "Dowling traces the trajectory of O'Neill's career: his two semesters in George Baker's noted playwriting seminar at Harvard; his professional growth with the Provincetown Players; the production of his first full-length play, Beyond the Horizon (1920), which won a Pulitzer Prize; and his prolific output for the next two decades." (Kirkus Reviews)

  "A well-rounded portrait of the playwright that can serve as a comprehensive introduction while also considering previously unknown facets of O'Neill's life and work." LJ

  Includes bibliographical references and index

  Gelb, Barbara, 1926-2017. **By** women possessed; A Life of Eugene O'Neill. Arthur Gelb and Barbara Gelb. G.P. Putnam's Sons, an imprint of Penguin Random House 2016 896 p. illustrations, portraits (hardback) $50; (ebook) $65   **92**

    1. American dramatists 2. Dramatists, American -- 20th century -- Biography

    ISBN 9780399159114; 9780698170681

                LC 2016008421

  This biography of American playwright Eugene O'Neill, by Arthur Gelb and Barbara Gelb, "follows O'Neill through his great successes, the failures he was able to shrug off, and the long eclipse, a twelve-year period in which, despite the Nobel [Prize], nothing he wrote was produced. But ahead lay his greatest achievements: The Iceman Cometh and Long Day's Journey into Night. Both were ahead of their time and both received lukewarm receptions." (Publisher's note)

  "This is a compelling examination of one of the 20th century's most passionate and troubled minds, and a prime example of expert, diligent, and wryly editorial biographical research." Pub Wkly

  Includes bibliographical references and index

O'Neill, Robert, 1976-

O'Neill, Robert. The **operator**; firing the shots that killed Osama bin Laden and my years as a SEAL Team warrior. Robert O'Neill. Scribner 2017 ix, 358 p.p illustrations (hardcover) $28 **92**

1. Autobiographies 2. Terrorism -- Prevention 3. Afghan War, 2001- -- Personal narratives 4. Butte (Mont.) -- Biography 5. United States. Navy. SEALs -- Biography 6. Special operations (Military science) -- Pakistan 7. Afghan War, 2001- -- Personal narratives, American 8. United States. Navy. SEALs -- History -- 21st century 9. Afghan War, 2001- -- Commando operations -- United States 10. War on Terrorism, 2001-2009 -- Personal narratives, American 11. Special operations (Military science) -- United States -- History -- 21st century

ISBN 9781501145056; 9781501145032; 9781501145049

LC 2017007867

This autobiography "ranges across SEAL Team Operator Robert O'Neill's awe-inspiring four-hundred-mission career, which included his involvement in attempts to rescue "Lone Survivor" Marcus Luttrell and abducted-by-Somali-pirates Captain Richard Phillips and which culminated in those famous three shots that dispatched the world's most wanted terrorist, Osama bin Laden." (Publisher's note)

O'Reilly, Finbarr, 1971-

Brennan, Thomas J. **Shooting** ghosts; a U.S. Marine, a combat photographer, and their journey back from war. Thomas J. Brennan, USMC (Ret.), and Finbarr O'Reilly. Viking 2017 x, 340 p.p illustrations (chiefly color) (hardcover) $27 **92**

1. Photographers -- Biography 2. United States. Marine Corps -- Biography 3. War -- Psychological aspects 4. War photographers -- Africa -- Biography 5. War photographers -- Afghanistan -- Biography 6. Afghan War, 2001- -- Personal narratives, American 7. United States. Marine Corps -- Officers -- Biography

ISBN 9780399562563; 9780399562549; 0399562540

LC 2017019760

This book is "a unique joint memoir by a U.S. Marine and a conflict photographer whose unlikely friendship helped both heal their war-wounded bodies and souls. . . . Their story, told in alternating first-person narratives, is about the things they saw and did, the ways they have been affected, and how they have navigated the psychological aftershocks of war and wrestled with reforming their own identities and moral centers." (Publisher's note)

"A courageous breaking of the code of silence to seek mental health for veterans and the war-scarred." Kirkus

Includes bibliographical references (pages [317]-325) and index.

O'Rourke, Barbara Kelly, d. 2008

O'Rourke, Meghan. The **long** goodbye; a memoir. Riverhead Books 2011 306p $25.95 **92**

1. Poets 2. Authors 3. Bereavement 4. Mother-daughter relationship 5. Essayists 6. Cancer patients 7. Poets, American 8. Magazine editors 9. Biography, Individual 10. Mothers and daughters

ISBN 978-1-59448-798-9

LC 2010047948

"The raw feelings, the inevitable self-pity over each person's own loss, and their futile wishes to somehow make Mother's last days not be her last days will likely feel all too close to home for many who have suffered similarly. . . . Every tear-stained page is not a road map, but rather a lovely gift from a fellow traveler." Booklist

Includes bibliographical references

O'Rourke, Meghan

O'Rourke, Meghan. The **long** goodbye; a memoir. Riverhead Books 2011 306p $25.95 **92**

1. Poets 2. Authors 3. Bereavement 4. Mother-daughter relationship 5. Essayists 6. Cancer patients 7. Poets, American 8. Magazine editors 9. Biography, Individual 10. Mothers and daughters

ISBN 978-1-59448-798-9

LC 2010047948

"The raw feelings, the inevitable self-pity over each person's own loss, and their futile wishes to somehow make Mother's last days not be her last days will likely feel all too close to home for many who have suffered similarly. . . . Every tear-stained page is not a road map, but rather a lovely gift from a fellow traveler." Booklist

Includes bibliographical references

Oates, Joyce Carol, 1938-

Oates, Joyce Carol, 1938- A **widow's** story; a memoir. Ecco 2011 415p il $27.99 **92**

1. Poets 2. Widows 3. Authors 4. Novelists 5. Bereavement 6. Loss (Psychology) 7. Essayists 8. Biographers 9. Magazine editors 10. Authors, American 11. Children's authors 12. Short story writers 13. Biography, Individual 14. Spouses of prominent persons

ISBN 9780062015532

This is an account of the novelist's loss of her "husband of 47 years, Raymond J. Smith. . . . He collaborated with his wife in founding The Ontario Review as well as Ontario Review Books." (N Y Times (Late N Y Ed))

"In a narrative as searing as the best of her fiction, Oates describes the aftermath of her husband Ray's unexpected death from pneumonia. Scattershot moments stand out — the day she cancels their 30-year subscription to The New York Times, unable to bear the sight of his favorite paper; her fury at the tulips, harbingers of spring, pushing through the snow ('Too soon! This is too soon!'); the night she weans herself from Lorazepam. A Widow's Story is the painful, scorchingly angry journey of a woman struggling to live in a house 'from which meaning has departed, like air leaking from a balloon.'" Entertainment Wkly

Obama, Barack, 1961

★ Maraniss, David. **Barack** Obama; the story. David Maraniss. Simon & Schuster 2012 xxiii, 641 p.p $32.50 **92**

1. Children -- Travel 2. Presidents -- United States 3. Hawaii -- Biography 4. Presidents -- United States -- Biography

ISBN 1439160406; 9781439160404; 9781439160411; 9781439167533

LC 2011052983

This book offers a biography of Barack Obama, "the 44th president [of the United States,] through the age of 27." Topics include the "confluence of Kenya and Kansas in Obama's veins," "the legacy of his father's keen intellect, his mother's self-possession, social conscience, and anthropologist's neutrality, and Obama's cosmopolitan childhood spent bouncing between Hawaii and Indonesia." (Publishers Weekly)

Includes bibliographical references (p. 607-609) and index

★ Remnick, David, 1958- The **bridge**; the life and rise of Barack Obama. Alfred A. Knopf 2010 656p il $29.95 **92**

1. Lawyers 2. Presidents 3. Racially mixed people 4. Senators 5. State legislators 6. Biography, Individual 7. Nobel laureates for peace 8. Presidents -- United States 9. African Americans -- Biography 10. United States -- Politics and government -- 2001-2009

ISBN 978-1-4000-4360-6; 1-4000-4360-3

LC 2010-922697

This is a biography of the 44th president of the United States.

Writing with emotional precision and a sure knowledge of politics, Mr. Remnick situates Mr. Obama's career firmily within a historical context. He puts Mr. Obama's life and political philosophy in perspective with the civil rights movement that shaped his imagination, as well as the power politics of Chicago, and the politics of race as it has been played out, often nastily, on the state and national stages. N Y Times (Late N Y Ed)

Includes bibliographical references (p. [617]-623) and index

★ Obama, Barack. **Dreams** from my father; a story of race and inheritance. Crown Publishers 2007 442p $25.95 **92**
1. Lawyers 2. Presidents 3. Racially mixed people 4. Senators 5. State legislators 6. Nobel laureates for peace 7. Presidents -- United States 8. African Americans -- Biography
ISBN 978-0-307-38341-9

LC 2007-271892

First published 1995 by Times Books

This is the autobiography of the Illinois senator who would later become the 44th president of the United States.

The author "offers an account of his life's journey that reflects brilliantly on the power of race consciousness in America. . . . Obama writes well; his account is sensitive, probing, and compelling." Choice [review of 1995 edition]

Alter, Jonathan. The **promise**; President Obama, year one. Simon & Schuster 2010 458p il $28; ebook $12.99 **92**
1. Lawyers 2. Presidents 3. Senators 4. State legislators 5. Nobel laureates for peace 6. Presidents -- United States 7. United States -- Politics and government -- 2001- 8. United States -- Politics and government -- 2009-
ISBN 978-1-4391-0119-3; 978-1-4391-5408-3 ebook

LC 2010-20438

"Alter's writing is sharp. His tone is breezy and engaging but appropriate to the subject matter. No deep, dark secrets are revealed, but readers will come away from this book with a good idea of how the Obama administration understands itself." Commonweal

Includes bibliographical references

Garrow, David. **Rising** star; the making of Barack Obama. David J. Garrow. William Morrow 2017 1472 p. (hardcover) $45 **92**
1. Presidents -- United States -- Biography 2. United States -- Politics and government
ISBN 9780062641830; 0062641832; 9780062641847

LC 2017033946

In this book author David J. Garrow "delivers an epic work about the life of Barack Obama, creating a rich tapestry of a life little understood, until now. . . . Garrow has created a vivid portrait that reveals not only the people and forces that shaped the future president but also the ways in which he used those influences to serve his larger aspirations." (Publisher's note)

"An exhaustive epic of Barack Obama's trajectory to the presidency." Kirkus

Includes bibliographical references and index.

Mastromonaco, Alyssa. **Who** thought this was a good idea? and other questions you should have answers to when you work in the White House. Alyssa Mastromonaco with Lauren Oyler. Twelve 2017 viii, 248 p.p illustrations (chiefly color) (hardback) $27

1. United States -- Politics and government 2. Government executives -- United States -- Biography 3. United States -- Politics and government -- 2009-2017 4. Women government executives -- United States -- Biography
ISBN 9781455588213; 9781455588220; 9781478961017

LC 2016050683

This book, by Alyssa Mastromonaco with Lauren Oyler, "is an intimate portrait of a president, a book about how to get stuff done, and the story of how one woman challenged, again and again, what a 'White House official' is supposed to look like. Here Alyssa shares the strategies that made her successful in politics and beyond, including the importance of confidence, the value of not being a jerk, and why ultimately everything comes down to hard work." (Publisher's note)

"The memoir abounds with intimate glimpses of Washington, D.C., celebrities . . . and cheerfully dispensed survival strategies." Kirkus

Obama, Michelle, 1964-

Slevin, Peter. **Michelle** Obama; a life. Peter B. Slevin. Alfred A. Knopf 2015 432 p. 16 plates; illustrations $27.95 **92**
1. Women lawyers 2. Presidents' spouses -- United States 3. African American lawyers -- Biography 4. African American women lawyers -- Biography 5. Presidents' spouses -- United States -- Biography
ISBN 9780307958822; 0307958825

LC 2014041100

This book, by Peter Slevin, is an "account of the life and times of Michelle Obama. Slevin follows Michelle to the White House from her working-class childhood on Chicago's largely segregated South Side. He illuminates her tribulations at Princeton University and Harvard Law School during the racially charged 1980s and the dilemmas she faced in Chicago while building a high-powered career, raising a family and helping . . . Barack Obama become president of the United States." (Publisher's note)

"She is one of his greatest assets in public office and an important foil to criticism that he is not "black enough." Slevin delivers a somewhat fawning portrait, but when necessary, he is willing to criticize and reveal his subject's missteps." Kirkus

Oher, Michael, 1986-

★ Lewis, Michael. The **blind** side; evolution of a game. W.W. Norton 2006 299p $24.95 **92**
1. College sports 2. Football players 3. Biography, Individual 4. Football -- Biography 5. College sports -- United States
ISBN 0-393-06123-X; 978-0-393-06123-9

LC 2006-23509

Michael Oher, the young man at the center of this story, "will one day be among the most highly paid athletes in the National Football League. When we first meet him, he is one of thirteen children by a mother addicted to crack; he does not know his real name, his father, his birthday, or any of the things a child might learn in school—such as, say, how to read or write. Nor has he ever touched a football. What changes? He takes up football, and school, after a rich, Evangelical, Republican family plucks him from the . . . streets. Their love is the first great force that alters the world's perception of the boy, whom they adopt. The second force is the evolution of professional football itself into a game where the quarterback must be protected at any cost. Our protagonist turns out to be the priceless combination of size, speed, and agility necessary to guard the quarterback's greatest vulnerability: his blind side." (Publisher's note)

The author "describes the NFL's ever-growing obsession with left tackles as a means to counter defenders who seem to grow bigger, stronger, and more vicious each season. He juxtaposes that narrative with the unlikely story of [football player] Michael Oher. . . . The book works on three levels. First as a shrewd analysis of the NFL; second, as an expose of the insanity of big-time college football recruiting; and, third, as a moving portrait of the positive effect that love, family, and education can have in reversing the path of a life that was destined to be lived unhappily and, most likely, end badly." Booklist

Ol' Dirty Bastard, 1969-2004

Lowe, Jaime. **Digging** for dirt; the life and death of ODB. Faber and Faber 2008 273p $25   **92**

1. Rap music 2. African American musicians 3. Rap musicians
ISBN 978-0-8654-7969-2; 0-8654-7969-0

LC 2008-29144

"As one of Wu Tang Clan, Russell Jones became known for his off-kilter raps and odd stage mannerisms. Like bandmates Method Man and Ghostface Killah, he also had a solo career as Ol' Dirty Bastard (ODB) that placed two number-one albums on the rap charts, and his duet with Mariah Carey, 'Fantasy,' brought mainstream success. Simply put, life was good. As time went by, though, he devolved into a more and more disturbed state, and some of his entertaining traits came to suggest mental-health issues. . . . Seemingly unable to avoid incarceration for a variety of offenses, he died of 'heart failure after cerebral hemorrhaging,' arguably caused by years of drug and other abuse. Lowe tells ODB's tale admirably thoroughly, making this a must-have profile of a singular personality and another sad casualty in rap history." Booklist

Ollestad, Norman, 1968-

Ollestad, Norman. **Crazy** for the storm; a memoir of survival. Ecco 2009 272p il $25.99   **92**

1. Aircraft accidents 2. Father-son relationship 3. Memoirists
ISBN 978-0-06-176672-5; 0-061-76672-0

LC 2008-53675

"In the winter of 1979, the 11-year-old Ollestad survived a plane crash in which his father and his father's girlfriend were killed. Alternating with young Norman's nine-hour trek to safety are scenes from the year preceding the crash, when the boy took a surfing trip with his father through the jungle along Mexico's Pacific coast. The flashbacks sections are the most fascinating parts of the book, and Ollestad ably captures the contrast between his charismatically cool father, Norman Sr., and his bullying stepfather-to-be, Nick. . . . [He] presents a captivating account of high-altitude disaster that nicely dovetails with his coming-of-age story in '70s California. Deep and resonant." Kirkus

Olson, Loren A.

Olson, Loren A. **Finally** Out; Letting Go of Living Straight. Loren A. Olson; Foreword by Jack Drescher, M.D. Oak Lane Press 2017 xiii, 286 p.p (paperback) $15.95   **92**

1. Sex 2. LGBT people 3. Coming out (Sexual orientation) 4. Middle-aged gay men -- United States -- Biography
ISBN 0997961430; 9780997961447; 9780997961430

This book by Loren A. Olson is an "exploration of human sexuality, particularly the sexuality of mature men who, like Dr. Olson, lived a large part of their lives as straight men—sometimes long after becoming aware of their same-sex attractions. Olson has frequently been asked two questions: How could you not know that you were gay until the age of forty? Olson answers these questions by telling the inspiring story of his evolving sexuality." (Publisher's note)

"Olson's in-depth yet accessible, candid and useful guidance should prove popular with LGBTQ readers as well as those interested in psychiatry." Booklist

Onassis, Jacqueline Kennedy, 1929-1994

Bowles, Hamish. **Jacqueline** Kennedy; the White House

Years: selections from the John F. Kennedy Library and Museum. {compiled and edited by} Hamish Bowles; with essays by Arthur Schlesinger, Jr., Hamish Bowles, and James Wagner. Bulfinch Press 2001 198p il $50   **92**

1. Editors 2. Socialites 3. Spouses of presidents
ISBN 0-8212-2745-9

LC 00-66237

The selections "examine in detail different aspects of Jackie's life, including the inauguration, her White House style, her travels, and her hats, as well as other topics. . . . Viewers can expect a sense of nostalgia, a swelling of pride, and a tightening of the throat. A time line of Jackie's life is appended." Booklist

Kashner, Sam. The **fabulous** Bouvier sisters; the tragic and glamorous lives of Jackie and Lee. Sam Kashner, Nancy Schoenberger. HarperCollins 2018 336 p. $28.99   **92**

1. Celebrities -- United States 2. Presidents' spouses -- United States
ISBN 0062364987; 9780062364982

In this book, authors Sam Kashner and Nancy Schoenberger "tells the complete story of . . . Jackie Kennedy Onassis and Lee Radziwill. Drawing on new information and extensive interviews with Lee, now eighty-four, this dual biography sheds light on the public and private lives of two extraordinary women who lived through immense tragedy in enormous glamour." (Publisher's note)

Leaming, Barbara. **Jacqueline** Bouvier Kennedy Onassis; the untold story. by Barbara Leaming. Thomas Dunne Books/ St. Martin's Press 2014 368 p. 8 plates; color illustrations (hardcover) $27.99   **92**

1. Widows 2. Presidents' spouses -- United States 3. Celebrities -- United States -- Biography 4. Presidents' spouses -- United States -- Biography 5. Post-traumatic stress disorder -- Patients -- Biography
ISBN 1250017645; 9781250017642

LC 2014026768

This book, by Barbara Leaming, "document[s] Jacqueline Kennedy Onassis' brutal, lonely and valiant thirty-one year struggle with post-traumatic stress disorder (PTSD) that followed JFK's assassination. We see how a spirited young woman's rejection of a predictable life led her to John F. Kennedy and the White House, how she sought to reconcile the conflicts of her marriage . . . and how the trauma of her husband's murder . . . led her to seek a very different kind of life." (Publisher's note)

"Leaming tells a heart-wrenching story of a woman who not only endured a horrific event but also struggled to recover and was often misunderstood as she eventually carved out a life of her own making." Booklist

Includes bibliographical references and index

McKeon, Kathy. **Jackie's** girl; my life with the Kennedy family. Kathy McKeon. Gallery Books 2017 309 p. illustrations (chiefly color) (hardcover: alk. paper) $26   **92**

1. Women household employees -- Biography 2. Household employees -- United States -- Biography 3. Irish American women -- United States -- Biography 4. Women household employees -- United States -- Biography
ISBN 9781501158964; 9781501158940; 9781501158957

LC 2017003981

This book, by Kathy McKeon, is a "coming-of-age memoir by a young woman who spent thirteen years as Jackie Kennedy's personal assistant. . . . In 1964, Kathy McKeon was . . . hired as the personal assistant to former first lady Jackie Kennedy. The next thirteen years of her life were spent in Jackie's service, during which Kathy . . . played a crucial role in raising young Caroline and John Jr., . . . [and] had a front-row seat to some of the twentieth century's most significant events." (Publisher's note)

"Celebrity watchers who covet an insider's role will find McKeon's frank yet benevolent memoir to be both a sobering reality check and an engaging foray into the ever-fascinating world of the Kennedy dynasty." Booklist

Oppenheimer, Frank, 1912-1985

Cole, K. C. **Something** incredibly wonderful happens; Frank Oppenheimer and the world he made up. Houghton Mifflin Harcourt 2009 396p il $27   **92**

1. Physicists 2. College teachers 3. Biography, Individual 4. Museum administrators

ISBN 978-0-15-100822-3; 0-15-100822-1

LC 2008052954

This is a biography of the physicist and young brother of J. Robert Oppenheimer.

"In a thought-provoking and pleasant manner, Cole's much-welcomed book shines a new light on a remarkable man and scientist. Readers interested in good popular science biographies will enjoy this." Libr J

Includes bibliographical references

Oppenheimer, J. Robert, 1904-1967

Bernstein, Jeremy. **Oppenheimer**; portrait of an enigma. Dee, I.R. 2004 223p il $25   **92**

1. Physicists 2. College teachers 3. Government officials

ISBN 1-566-63569-1

LC 2003-66652

The author "recounts Oppenheimer's eclectic life as it evolved in the US through his education and service at several prestigious institutions. . . . The book is not a review of Oppenheimer's contributions to physics or the development of the atomic bomb; rather, it provides insight into the human side of a brilliant individual, all things considered. Of course, his leadership of the Manhattan Project, and his persecution by Congress for alleged communist sympathies, defined Oppenheimer's career. Bernstein provides personalized insights into both." Choice

Includes bibliographical references

★ Bird, Kai. **American** Prometheus; the triumph and tragedy of J. Robert Oppenheimer. [by] Kai Bird and Martin J. Sherwin. Knopf 2005 721p il hardcover o.p. pa $18.95   **92**

1. Physicists 2. College teachers 3. Government officials

ISBN 0-375-41202-6; 0-375-72626-8 pa

LC 2004-61535

The authors explore Oppenheimer's life "from his youth as a child prodigy through his radical political activities in the 1930s, and on to the Manhattan Project and its political fallout. The humanity of the troubled man behind the porkpie hat emerges on every page of this unquestionably definitive account." Booklist

Includes bibliographical references

★ Monk, Ray. **Robert** Oppenheimer; a life inside the center. Ray Monk. 1st American ed. Doubleday 2013 xvi, 825 p.p (hardback) $37.50   **92**

1. Atomic bomb -- History 2. Physicists -- Biography 3. Physicists -- United States -- Biography 4. Atomic bomb -- United States -- History -- 20th century 5. Physicists -- United States -- Intellectual life -- 20th century

ISBN 0385504071; 9780385504072

LC 2012046045

This book by Ray Monk is a biography of physicist Robert Oppen-

heimer. "As a young professor at Berkeley, the wealthy, cultured Oppenheimer finally came into his own as a physicist and also began a period of support for Communist activities. . . . He was chosen to lead the Manhattan Project and develop . . . the atomic bomb. Upon its creation, Oppenheimer . . . refused to help create the far more powerful hydrogen bomb, bringing the wrath of McCarthyite suspicion upon him." (Publisher's note)

Includes bibliographical references and index

Osama bin Laden

Randal, Jonathan C. **Osama**: the making of a terrorist; {by} Jonathan Randal. Knopf 2004 339p $26.95   **92**

1. Terrorism 2. Terrorists

ISBN 0-375-40901-7

LC 2004-46522

The author's "meticulous account of the emergence and spread of the terror virus is less a biography of the strange, desiccated Saudi Arabian terrorist who heads Al Qaeda than a map of the world that produced him and his fellow Islamists. This is the biography of a hatred: deep, detailed, and depressing." N Y Times Book Rev

Includes bibliographical references

Scheuer, Michael. **Osama** bin Laden; [by] Michael Scheuer. Oxford University Press 2011 278p $19.95   **92**

1. Terrorists 2. Biography, Individual

ISBN 978-0-19-973866-3; 0-19-973866-1

LC 2010-21715

The author "offers a serious and nonideological treatment and analysis of bin Laden's thinking. Unlike many Western analysts who dismiss bin Laden as simplistic, uncouth, and incompetent, Scheuer portrays him as a patient, devout, and talented, albeit ruthless, leader who remains a formidable enemy of the West. . . . This informative book is one of the most detailed biographical sketches of bin Laden available in the West and is useful for both the general public and specialists." Libr J

Includes bibliographical references

Osborne, John, 1929-1994

Heilpern, John. **John** Osborne; the many lives of the angry young man. Alfred A. Knopf 2007 527p il $35   **92**

1. Authors 2. Dramatists

ISBN 978-0-375-40315-6; 0-375-40315-9

LC 2006-46575

First published 2006 in the United Kingdom

"Heilpern draws on Osborne's bleak private notebooks to generate acute readings of his often autobiographical plays. Sympathy for the man and admiration for the work don't blind Heilpern to his subject's outsized flaws. Osborne had a talent for invective and could be cruelly intolerant in matters large and small. He threatened theatre critics with physical violence by way of anonymous seaside postcards. Stung by his teenage daughter's indifference to high culture, he damned her as 'criminally commonplace' and never spoke to her again. Without excusing such 'breathtaking abuse,' Heilpern makes a compelling case for Osborne as a necessary 'truthteller' and 'unyielding advocate of individualism in conformist times.'" New Yorker

Includes bibliographical references

Osborne, Steve (Stephen T), 1960-

Osborne, Steve. The **job**; true tales from the life of a New York City cop. by Steve Osborne. Doubleday 2015 272 p. (hardcover) $25.95   **92**

1. Police -- New York (State) -- New York 2. Police -- New York (State) -- New York -- Biography 3. New York (N.Y.). Police Department -- Officials and employees -- Biography

ISBN 0385539622; 9780385539623

LC 2014032375

In this memoir, author and police officer Steve Osborne "has seen a thing or two in his twenty years in the NYPD--some harmless things, some definitely not. . . . From his days as a rookie cop to the time spent patrolling in the Anti-Crime Unit--and his visceral, harrowing recollections of working during 9/11--Steve Osborne's stories capture both the absurdity of police work and the bravery of those who do it." (Publisher's note)

"Osborne's personal life is described only obliquely in the book, including his reasons for leaving the NYPD (although the chapter on 9/11 provides clues), but this is a solid insider's account of what life is like on the force." Pub Wkly

Osbourne, Ozzy

Osbourne, Ozzy. **I** am Ozzy; [by] Ozzy Osbourne with Chris Ayres. Grand Central Publishing 2010 391p $26.99 **92**
1. Singers 2. Rock musicians 3. Black Sabbath (Musical group)
ISBN 978-0-446-56989-7

LC 2009-937230

"Osbourne offers the most detail about growing up and the Black Sabbath years – no surprise as you'd expect decades of drug use have nearly wiped clean those later years. He discusses his youth in England, his brief stint in jail, how a flier posted in a music store – 'Ozzy Zig Needs a Gig' – led to the eventual formation of Black Sabbath, his relationship with his wives and children, his own health scares, and The Osbournes television show. The book is written with Osbourne's wit and sense of humor as he shares laugh-out-loud tales of practical jokes while touring around the world and recording inside a castle. There's even a look at the sensitive side when he discusses the death of guitarist Randy Rhodes and his wife's (Sharon's) battle with cancer." Creative Loafing

Owens, Jesse, 1913-1980

Schaap, Jeremy. **Triumph**; the untold story of Jesse Owens and Hitler's Olympics. Houghton Mifflin 2007 272p il $24; pa $14.95 **92**
1. African American athletes 2. Olympic games, 1936 (Berlin, Ger.) 3. Olympic athletes 4. Runners (Athletes)
ISBN 978-0-618-68822-7; 0-618-68822-6; 978-0-618-91910-9 pa; 0-618-91910-4 pa

LC 2006-26926

"Schaap's chronicle of Jesse Owens's journey to and glorious triumph at the 1936 Berlin Olympics is snappy and dramatic, with an eye for the rousing climax." Publ Wkly

Includes bibliographical references

Oz, Amos

Oz, Amos. A **tale** of love and darkness; translated from the Hebrew by Nicholas de Lange. Harcourt 2004 538p $26 **92**
1. Authors 2. Novelists 3. Essayists 4. Short story writers
ISBN 0-15-100878-7; 9780156032520

LC 2004-7302

"A powerful story of the making of a writer . . . Oz's panoramic memoir enhances the history of literature and of Israel, and the literature of examined lives." Booklist

Ozawa, Seiji, 1935-

Murakami, Haruki, 1949- **Absolutely** on music; conversations. Haruki Murakami with Seiji Ozawa; translated from the Japanese by Jay Rubin. Alfred A. Knopf 2016 xix, 325 p.p (hardcover: alk. paper) $27.95 **92**
1. Conductors (Music) 2. Music -- History and criticism 3. Conductors (Music) -- Interviews
ISBN 9780385354349; 9780804173728

LC 2016008866

This book, by Haruki Murakami with Seiji Ozawa, translated by Jay Rubin, is "a deeply personal, intimate conversation about music and writing between the internationally acclaimed, best-selling author and the former conductor of the Boston Symphony Orchestra. . . . Over the course of two years, Murakami and Ozawa discuss everything from Brahms to Beethoven, from Leonard Bernstein to Glenn Gould, from Bartók to Mahler, and from pop-up orchestras to opera." (Publisher's note)

"A work that general readers will enjoy and the musical cognoscenti will devour." Kirkus.

Padilla Peralta, Dan-el

Padilla Peralta, Dan-el. **Undocumented**; A Dominican Boy's Odyssey from a Homeless Shelter to the Ivy League. by Dan-el Padilla Peralta. Penguin Group USA 2015 320 p. illustrations $27.95 **92**
1. Homeless persons 2. Dominican Americans 3. Unauthorized immigrants 4. United States -- Immigration and emigration
ISBN 159420652X; 9781594206528
Alex Award (2016)

This book, by Dan-el Padilla Peralta, is an "undocumented immigrant's journey from a New York City homeless shelter to the top of his Princeton class. . . . As a boy, he came here legally with his family. Together they left Santo Domingo behind, but life in New York City was harder than they imagined. Their visas lapsed. . . . Without papers, [they] faced tremendous obstacles." (Publisher's note)

Padilla Peralta "writes candidly about hard times including a period spent in a dangerous homeless shelter, breaking through the harsh immigrant clichés to a pure humanistic level that any reader can embrace." Pub Wkly

Paige, Satchel, 1906-1982

Tye, Larry. **Satchel**; the life and times of an American legend. Random House 2009 392p il **92**
1. Baseball players 2. African American athletes 3. Baseball -- Biography 4. Biography, Individual 5. Negro leagues -- History
ISBN 0812977971; 1400066514; 9780812977974; 9781400066513

LC 2008-44858

A biography of the Negro League pitcher Satchel Paige "evaluates the role of discrimination in limiting his career, covering such topics as his near-defeat of a young Joe DiMaggio, the Jim Crow biases that prevented his signing with the big leagues until he was in his forties, and his [legacy]." (Publisher's note)

This is a "discerning, empathetic and hype-free [biography]. . . . While Paige's life has become the stuff of legend, its particulars are not easily verified. . . . Yet 'Satchel' makes a cool, clear, tenacious effort to find the real Paige behind all [the] hyperbole." N Y Times (Late N Y Ed)

Includes bibliographical references

Painter, Nell Irvin

Painter, Nell Irvin, 1942- **Old** in art school; a memoir of starting over. Nell Painter. Counterpoint Press 2018 352 p. $26 **92**
1. Women artists -- Biography 2. African American women artists -- Biography 3. Artists -- United States -- Biography 4. Older artists -- United States -- Biography 5. Adult college students -- United States -- Biography
ISBN 9781640090613

LC 2017055407

"Following her retirement from Princeton University, celebrated historian Dr. Nell Irvin Painter surprised everyone in her life by returning to school--in her sixties--to earn a BFA and MFA in painting. . . . [In this memoir], Painter weaves a frank, funny, and often surprising tale of her move from academia to art." (Publisher's note)

Palm, Angela

★ Palm, Angela. **Riverine**; a memoir from anywhere but here. Angela Palm. Farrar, Straus & Giroux 2016 224 p. (ebook) $20; $16   **92**

1. Friendship in children 2. Prisoners -- Indiana -- Biography
ISBN 9781555979423; 1555977464; 9781555977467

LC 2015953721

In this memoir, author Angela Palm reveals how she "finds herself drawn back, like the [Kankakee] River, to her origins. But this means more than just recalling vibrant, complicated memories of the place that shaped her, or trying to understand the family that raised her. It means visiting the prison where the boy that she loved is serving a life sentence for a brutal murder." (Publisher's note)

"All in all, this is a memoir to linger over, savor and study." Pub Wkly

Palmer, Arnold, 1929-2016

Callahan, Tom. **Arnie**; the life of Arnold Palmer. Tom Callahan. Harper 2017 xiv, 333 p.p illustrations (some color) (hardcover) $27.99   **92**

1. Golfers -- United States -- Biography 2. Branding (Marketing) 3. Golfers -- United States -- Anecdotes
ISBN 9780062439741; 9780062439727; 9780062439765

LC 2017002983

In this biography, "veteran sportswriter Tom Callahan shines a spotlight on one of the greatest golfers ever to play the game, Arnold Palmer. The winner of more than ninety championships, including four Masters Tournaments, Arnold Palmer was a legend in twentieth century sports: a supremely gifted competitor beloved for his powerful hitting, his nerve on the greens, and his great rapport with fans." (Publisher's note)

"Sportswriter Callahan . . . breezily floats from story to story across the life of legendary golfer Arnold Palmer, describing dashing Palmer's enduring appeal from the moment he burst onto the new television screens of the 1950s." Pub Wkly

Palmer, Arnold. A **golfer's** life; {by} Arnold Palmer with James Dodson. Ballantine Bks. 1999 420p il hardcover o.p. pa $15   **92**

1. Golfers
ISBN 0-345-41482-9 pa

LC 98-51681

Palmer's "immense popularity is widely credited with rescuing professional golf in the late 1950s and 1960s. Written with humor and candor, the book recounts Palmer's friendships and rivalries with the greats of the game, his enduring marriage to Winnie Palmer, his legendary triumphs and disasters, and his battle against cancer." Libr J

Palmer, Arnold, 1929-2016. A **life** well played; My Stories. Arnold Palmer. St. Martin's Press 2016 272 p. (hardcover) $22.99; (ebook) $60   **92**

1. Conduct of life 2. Golfers -- United States -- Biography
ISBN 9781250085948; 9781250085955

LC 2016013252

In this book, golfer Arnold Palmer "takes stock of the many experiences of his life, bringing new details and insights to some familiar stories and sharing new ones. . . . Gracious, fair, and a true gentleman, 'Arnie' was the gold standard of how to conduct yourself in your career,

life, and relationships. . . . [His] book offers advice . . . , sharing personal stories of his career on the course, success in business, and . . . relationships that gave meaning to his life." (Publisher's note)

"A heartfelt, sincere, mini-self-portrait by a man who epitomizes class." Kirkus

Palmer, Hannah, 1978-

Palmer, Hannah. **Flight** path; a search for roots beneath the world's busiest airport. by Hannah Palmer. First American edition Hub City Press 2017 211 p. (paperback) $16.95   **92**

1. Airports 2. Atlanta (Ga.) 3. Fulton County (Ga.) -- History, Local 4. Clayton County (Ga.) -- History, Local 5. Atlanta Metropolitan Area (Ga.) -- History 6. Atlanta Metropolitan Area (Ga.) -- Biography 7. Atlanta Metropolitan Area (Ga.) -- Economic conditions 8. Atlanta Metropolitan Area (Ga.) -- Social life and customs 9. William B. Hartsfield-Atlanta International Airport -- Influence
ISBN 9781938235283

LC 2016037303

In this book, author Hannah Palmer "discovers that all three of her childhood houses have been wiped out by the expansion of Atlanta's Hartsfield-Jackson International Airport. Having uprooted herself from a promising career in publishing in her adopted Brooklyn, Palmer embarks on a quest to determine the fate of her lost homes--and of a community that has been erased by unchecked Southern progress." (Publisher's note)

"This thoroughly engaging memoir takes a deeply personal look at the neighborhoods around Atlanta's Hartsfield-Jackson International Airport." Booklist

Papp, Joseph

★ Turan, Kenneth. **Free** for all; Joe Papp, the Public, and the greatest theater story ever told. [by] Kenneth Turan and Joseph Papp; with the assistance of Gail Merrifield Papp. Doubleday 2009 592p il $39.95   **92**

1. Theatrical producers and directors 2. Theatrical directors 3. Theatrical producers 4. Joseph Papp Public Theater (New York, N.Y.)
ISBN 978-0-7679-3168-7

LC 2008-50887

"A wonderful book that clearly and powerfully shows that Papp's own story was the most enduring drama he ever produced." Kirkus

Paracelsus, 1493-1541

Webster, Charles. **Paracelsus**; medicine, magic and mission at the end of time. Yale University Press 2008 326p il $40 **92**

1. Alchemy 2. Physicians 3. Alchemists 4. Writers on science
ISBN 978-0-300-13911-2; 0-300-13911-X

LC 2008-27973

In this consideration of the "Renaissance doctor, alchemist, and theologian, Webster draws on nonscientific writings by Paracelsus that have been made widely available only in the past few decades. . . . [Paracelsus] orbited a wealthy and powerful class of physicians, but his unorthodox views made him a virtual 'vagrant' among his peers. He broke from the millennia-old theory of the humors, developing new medical theories based upon a mystical vision of man as a microcosm of the universe, and an alchemically informed notion of the intrinsic properties of certain metals. Webster paints Paracelsus as a 'religious and social controversialist,' and argues that the diverse strands of his thought were unified by his belief that the end of time was near, when, he imagined, the demise of physical suffering would obviate the need for medical intervention." New Yorker

Includes bibliographical references and index.

Parazynski, Scott

Parazynski, Scott. The **sky** below; Scott Parazynski with Susy Flory. Little A 2017 xiv, 252 p.p illustrations (chiefly color) (hbk.) $24.95   **92**

    1. Biography 2. Astronauts -- Biography 3. Astronauts -- United States -- Biography 4. Physicians -- United States -- Biography
ISBN 9781503936690; 9781503936706; 1503936708

This memoir, by Scott Parazynski with Susy Flory, "re-creates some of the most unforgettable adventures of our time. From dramatic, high-risk spacewalks to author Scott Parazynski's death-defying quest to summit Mount Everest--his body ravaged by a career in space--readers will experience the life of an elite athlete, physician, and explorer." (Publisher's note)

"A genial, readable account of mountain climbing, spaceship travel, and other adventures." Kirkus

    Includes bibliographical references (pages 249-250).

Park, Yeonmi, 1993-

Park, Yeonmi. **In** order to live; a North Korean girl's journey to freedom. Penguin Group USA 2015 288 p. illustrations (ebook) $32.50; $27.95   **92**

    1. Human rights 2. Human trafficking 3. Korea (North) -- Social conditions
ISBN 9780698409361; 1594206791; 9781594206795

                     LC 2015029915

In this book, "author Yeonmi Park shines a light not just into the darkest corners of life in North Korea, describing the deprivation and deception she endured and which millions of North Korean people continue to endure to this day, but also onto her own most painful and difficult memories." (Publisher's note)

Parker, Charlie, 1920-1955

Crouch, Stanley, 1945- **Kansas** City lightning; the rise and times of Charlie Parker. by Stanley Crouch. Harper 2013 384 p. $27.99   **92**

    1. Jazz musicians 2. Jazz musicians -- United States -- Biography
ISBN 0062005596; 9780062005595

                     LC 2013015773

This book, by Stanley Crouch, "is the first installment in . . . [a] portrait of one of the most talented and influential musicians of the twentieth century, from Stanley Crouch, one of the foremost authorities on jazz and culture in America. Drawing on interviews with peers, collaborators, and family members, 'Kansas City Lightning' recreates Parker's Depression-era childhood; his early days navigating the Kansas City nightlife." (Publisher's note)

Parker, Dorothy, 1893-1967

Meade, Marion. **Dorothy** Parker; what fresh hell is this? Penguin 1989 459p il pa $20   **92**

    1. Poets 2. Authors 3. Humorists 4. Dramatists 5. Essayists 6. Screenwriters 7. Authors, American 8. Short story writers
ISBN 0-14-011616-8; 978-0-14-011616-8

                     LC 88-23782

    First published 1988 by Villard Books

"The author has written a disturbing story of a writer whose life was marked by endless disturbances and self-depreciation, and who left behind no correspondence, manuscripts, or private papers. Under the circumstances, Ms. Meade has brilliantly reconstructed her subject's life. . . . The book is a tribute to a woman who left her mark on the literary history of her times and whose coruscating wit is still remembered." West Coast Rev Books

    Includes bibliographical references

Parker, Quanah, Comanche Chief, 1845?-1911

Gwynne, S. C. **Empire** of the summer moon; Quanah Parker and the rise and fall of the Comanches, the most powerful Indian tribe in American history. Scribner 2010 371p il map $27.50   **92**

    1. Comanche Indians 2. Indian chiefs 3. West (U.S.) -- History 4. Comanche Indians -- Wars 5. Western States -- History 6. Comanche Indians -- History 7. Frontier and pioneer life -- West (U.S.) 8. Frontier and pioneer life -- Western States
ISBN 978-1-4165-9105-4; 1-4165-9105-2

                     LC 2009049747

"A welcome contribution to the history of Texas, Westward expansion and Native America." Kirkus

    Includes bibliographical references

Parkinson, James, 1755-1824

Lewis, Cherry. The **enlightened** Mr. Parkinson; the pioneering life of a forgotten surgeon and the mysterious disease that bears his name. Cherry Lewis. Pegasus Books 2017 xii, 306 p.p illustrations (some color) (hardcover) $27.95   **92**

    1. Parkinson's disease 2. Neurologists -- Great Britain -- Biography
ISBN 9781681774541; 9781681774954; 1681774542

This book, by Cherry Lewis, is "a colorful and absorbing portrait of James Parkinson and the turbulent, intellectually vibrant world of Georgian London. . . . In 1817 . . . James Parkinson (1755–1824) defined . . . [Parkinson's disease] so precisely that we still diagnose . . . [it] today by recognizing the symptoms he identified. The story of . . . [his] contributions to the Age of the Enlightenment is told through his . . . passions [for] medicine, politics and fossils." (Publisher's note)

"Lewis's lively, captivating biography illuminates the life and work of a pioneer who may have largely faded from medical history, but whose curiosity and passion are as relevant today as they were 200 years ago." Pub Wkly

    Includes bibliographical references (pages 261-298) and index.

Parks, Rosa, 1913-2005

Brinkley, Douglas. **Rosa** Parks. Viking 2000 246p (Penguin lives series) hardcover o.p. pa $13   **92**

    1. Civil rights activists 2. African Americans -- Civil rights 3. African American women -- Biography
ISBN 0-670-89160-6; 0-14-303600-9 pa

                     LC 00-35916

"Rosa Parks' story takes readers from rural Alabama to the Montgomery Industrial School for Girls, marriage to barber Raymond Parks, quiet activism in the '30s and '40s, a first experience of integration at the Highlander Folk School, arrest in 1955 and the bus boycott, a move to Detroit, and more than 20 years on the staff of Rep. John Conyers (D-Mich.)." Booklist

    Includes bibliographical references

Theoharis, Jeanne. The **rebellious** life of Mrs. Rosa Parks; Jeanne Theoharis. Beacon Press 2012 360 p. (hardcover: alk. paper) $27.95   **92**

    1. Montgomery (Ala.) -- Biography 2. Montgomery (Ala.) -- Race relations 3. Civil rights workers -- Alabama -- Montgomery -- Biography 4. African American women civil rights workers -- Alabama -- Montgomery -- Biography 5. Segregation in transportation -- Alabama -- Montgomery -- History -- 20th century 6. African Americans -- Civil rights -- Alabama -- Montgomery -- History -- 20th century
ISBN 0807050474; 9780807050477; 9780807050484

                     LC 2012031992

This book by Jeanne Theoharis is a "political biography of Rosa Parks [that] examines her six decades of activism, challenging perceptions of her as an accidental actor in the civil rights movement. . . . [Theoharis] shows readers how this civil rights movement radical sought--for more than a half a century--to expose and eradicate the American racial-caste system in jobs, schools, public services, and criminal justice." (Publisher's note)

Includes bibliographical references and index

Parravani, Cara

Parravani, Christa, 1978- **Her**; a memoir. Christa Parravani. Henry Holt & Co 2013 320 p. $26   92

1. Twins 2. Sisters 3. Rape victims 4. Loss (Psychology) 5. Twins -- United States -- Biography 6. Sisters -- United States -- Biography
ISBN 0805096531; 9780805096538

LC 2012029499

In this memoir, author Christa Parravani "deconstructs the intense bonds between identical twins, the trauma of her sister's death and her battle against similar self-destruction. . . . Plagued by unstable and abusive father figures and poverty, [Christa and Cara] still managed to attend prestigious colleges, begin careers as artists and embark on marriages. But following a rape while out walking her dog, [Cara] began a terrifying descent into drugs and self-destruction." (Kirkus Reviews)

A "finely wrought achievement of grace, emotional honesty, and self-possession." Pub Wkly

Parravani, Christa

Parravani, Christa, 1978- **Her**; a memoir. Christa Parravani. Henry Holt & Co 2013 320 p. $26   92

1. Twins 2. Sisters 3. Rape victims 4. Loss (Psychology) 5. Twins -- United States -- Biography 6. Sisters -- United States -- Biography
ISBN 0805096531; 9780805096538

LC 2012029499

In this memoir, author Christa Parravani "deconstructs the intense bonds between identical twins, the trauma of her sister's death and her battle against similar self-destruction. . . . Plagued by unstable and abusive father figures and poverty, [Christa and Cara] still managed to attend prestigious colleges, begin careers as artists and embark on marriages. But following a rape while out walking her dog, [Cara] began a terrifying descent into drugs and self-destruction." (Kirkus Reviews)

A "finely wrought achievement of grace, emotional honesty, and self-possession." Pub Wkly

Parsons, Jack, 1914-1952

Pendle, George. **Strange** angel; the otherworldly life of rocket scientist John Whiteside Parsons. Harcourt 2005 350p il $25; pa $15   92

1. Scientists
ISBN 0-15-100997-X; 0-15-603179-5 pa

LC 2004-10666

"Marshaling a cast of characters ranging from Robert Millikan to L. Ron Hubbard, Pendle offers a fascinating glimpse into a world long past, a story that would make a compelling work of fiction if it weren't so astonishingly true." Publ Wkly

Includes bibliographical references

Pataki, Allison

Pataki, Allison. **Beauty** in the broken places; a memoir of love, faith, and resilience. by Allison Pataki; with foreword by Lee Woodruff. Random House Inc 2018 272 p. (hardback)

$26   92

1. Stroke 2. Biography 3. Married people 4. Cerebral ischemia 5. Caregivers -- Biography 6. Husband and wife -- Biography 7. Young adults -- Diseases -- Biography 8. Cerebrovascular disease -- Patients -- Biography 9. Cerebrovascular disease -- Patients -- Family relationships
ISBN 9780399591655

LC 2017058576

This memoir, by Allison Pataki, with foreword by Lee Woodruff, "is a manifesto for living, an ultimately uplifting story about the transformative power of faith and resilience. It's a tale of a man's turbulent road to recovery, the shifting nature of marriage, and the struggle of loving through pain and finding joy in the broken places." (Publisher's note)

"In this powerful and immersive memoir, Pataki relives the harrowing year that followed her husband's stroke in June 2015." Pub Wkly

Patchett, Ann

Patchett, Ann, 1963- **This** is the story of a happy marriage; Ann Patchett. HarperCollins 2013 320 p. (hardcover) $27.99   92

1. Opera 2. Divorce 3. Human-animal relationships
ISBN 0062236679; 9780062320384; 9780062236678; 9780062292469

LC 2013474298

This is an essay collection from award-winning author Ann Patchett. She explores "some of the milestones of her life, such as her deep love for her dog, Rose (not to be confused with the desire for a baby), learning from scratch how to love opera in order to write her bestseller 'Bel Canto,' preparing with her ex-cop father's guidance for the grueling L.A. Police Academy exams ('The Wall'), . . . and her painful but merciful segue from divorce to remarriage." (Publishers Weekly)

Patel, Eboo, 1975-

Patel, Eboo. **Acts** of faith; the story of an American Muslim, the struggle for the soul of a generation. Beacon Press 2010 195p pa $14   92

1. Multiculturalism 2. Sociologists 3. Youth leaders 4. Religious leaders 5. Writers on religion 6. Organization officials 7. Muslims -- United States
ISBN 978-0-8070-0622-1; 0-8070-0622-X

LC 2010-537438

First published 2007

The author, "a founder of the Interfaith Youth Core, traces the personal journey that led to the group's formation and introduces readers to its philosophy." Kirkus

Includes bibliographical references

Paterson, Katherine

Paterson, Katherine. **Stories** of my life; by Katherine Paterson. Dial Books for Young Readers 2014 320 p. illustrations (hardcover) $17.99   92

1. Autobiographies 2. Women authors -- Biography 3. Children's stories -- Authorship 4. Authors, American -- 20th century -- Biography
ISBN 0803740433; 9780803740433

LC 2013042628

Author Katherine "Paterson's tales reveal details about her life from her childhood with missionary parents, to living as a single woman in Japan, to raising four children in suburban Maryland with her minister husband. . . . Filled with personal photos and letters, this . . . history from a legendary writer lets fans in on the making of literary classics." (Publisher's note)

"Written in a conversational style, these 'kitchen sink stories' will perhaps be received best by professional adults and readers who grew up with her books; much of what she recounts is about the distant past, courtship, and motherhood. What absolutely shines through is Paterson's warm, self-effacing humor, and the extraordinary humility of a writer who has won two National Book Awards, two Newbery Medals, and the Hans Christian Andersen Medal." Pub Wkly

Patterson, Floyd

Levy, Alan Howard. **Floyd** Patterson; a boxer and a gentleman. [by] Alan H. Levy. McFarland & Co. 2008 289p il pa $35   **92**

1. African American athletes 2. Boxers (Persons) 3. Boxing -- Biography
ISBN 978-0-7864-3950-8; 0-7864-3950-5

LC 2008-32250

This is a "biography of the man who was the youngest world heavyweight champion in boxing history as well as the first boxer to regain the championship after losing it. . . . This book is not only an excellent study of Patterson but a superior source on professional boxing from the mid-1950s through the mid-1970s." Libr J

Includes bibliographical references

★ Stratton, W. K. **Floyd** Patterson; the fighting life of boxing's invisible champion. W. K. Stratton. Houghton Mifflin Harcourt 2012 xiv, 269 p.p ill. (hardback) $25.00   **92**

1. Boxers (Sports) 2. African Americans -- Civil rights 3. African American boxers -- Biography 4. Boxers (Sports) -- United States -- Biography
ISBN 0151014302; 9780151014309

LC 2012017319

This biography "examines one of the most complex fighters ever to wear the heavyweight crown," boxer Floyd Patterson. "Patterson started boxing [in high school] and . . . caught the eye of trainer Cus D'Amato . . . . By focusing on historical context, Stratton clarifies how Patterson could be trumpeted as a hero of the civil rights movement, then labeled an 'Uncle Tom' a few years later." (Publishers Weekly)

Includes bibliographical references and index.

Patterson, Pat, 1941-

Patterson, Pat. **Accepted**; by Pat Patterson. ECW Press 2016 320 p. illustrations (some color) $25.95   **92**

1. Wrestling
ISBN 177041293X; 9781770412934

In this memoir, professional wrestler Pat Patterson "recalls the trials and tribulations of climbing to the upper ranks of sports-entertainment — as a performer and, later, as a backstage creative force." (Publisher's note)

"Patterson is a very good storyteller, and his tales from the road about well-known personalities such as the fun-seeking Andre the Giant and the forever-young-at-heart Ray Stevens are wonderfully told, and many of the wrestlers' time-killing pranks are laugh-out-loud funny." Pub Wkly

Paul, Pamela

Paul, Pamela. **My** life with Bob; flawed heroine keeps book of books, plot ensues. Pamela Paul. Henry Holt & Co. 2017 x, 242 p.p (hardback) $27   **92**

1. Authorship 2. Books and reading -- Psychological aspects
ISBN 1627796312; 9781627796323; 9781627796316

LC 2016046990

This book, by Pamela Paul, is "about the deep and powerful relation-

ship between book and reader. It's about the way books provide each of us the perspective, courage, companionship, and imperfect self-knowledge to forge our own path. It's about why we read what we read and how those choices make us who we are. It's about how we make our own stories." (Publisher's note)

"Paul is inspired to question why we read, how we read, what we read, and how reading helps us create our own narratives. Readers will be drawn to this witty and authentic tribute to the extraordinary power of books." Pub Wkly

Payne, Ethel, 1911-1991

Morris, James McGrath. **Eye** on the Struggle; Ethel Payne, the First Lady of the Black Press. James McGrath Morris. HarperCollins 2015 480 p. 16 plates; illustrations $27.99 **92**

1. Journalists 2. African Americans -- Civil rights
ISBN 0062198858; 9780062198853

LC 2015296496

This book examines the life of "Ethel Payne (1911-91), a pioneering journalist, [who] covered the civil rights movement for The Chicago Defender, a premier black newspaper. Biographer [James McGrath] Morris . . . details Payne's work, preserving her legacy and filling in part of the missing history of the fight for equality." (Library Journal)

"Morris' straight-ahead chronicle of Payne's extraordinary frontline life reveals how invincible and incisive she was as she forthrightly "combined journalism with advocacy" and made the most of the "box seat on history" she fought so ardently and courageously to occupy." Booklist

Peace, Robert, 1980-2010

★ Hobbs, Jeff. The **short** and tragic life of Robert Peace; a brilliant young man who left Newark for the Ivy League but did not survive. Jeff Hobbs. Scribner 2014 416 p. illustrations (hardcover) $27   **92**

1. African Americans -- Social conditions 2. Drug dealers 3. Working class African Americans 4. African American college graduates 5. Yale University -- Alumni and alumnae
ISBN 147673190X; 9781476731919; 9781476731902

LC 2014001213

Los Angeles Times Book Prize: Current Interest (2014)

This book, by Jeff Hobbs, is a "biography of the short life of a talented young African-American man who escapes the slums of Newark for Yale University only to succumb to the dangers of the streets--and of one's own nature--when he returns home. . . . [The book] encompasses the most enduring conflicts in America: race, class, drugs, community, imprisonment, education, family, friendship, and love." (Publisher's note)

"Writing with novelistic detail and deep insight, Hobbs, who was Peace's roommate at Yale, registers the disadvantages his friend faced while avoiding hackneyed fatalism and sociology. Hobbs reveals a man whose singular experience and charisma made him simultaneously an outsider and a leader in both New Haven and Newark." Pub Wkly

Includes bibliographical references

Peary, Robert E. (Robert Edwin), 1856-1920

Larson, Edward J. (Edward John), 1953- **To** the edges of the earth; 1909, the race for the three poles, and the climax of the age of exploration. Edward J. Larson. HarperCollins 2018 352 p. $29.99   **92**

1. Mountaineering 2. Sports records 3. Sports -- History
ISBN 0062564471; 9780062564474

LC 2018000736

In this book historian Edward J. Larson looks at "the most adventurous year of all time, when three expeditions simultaneously raced to the top, bottom, and heights of the world. . . . In the course of one extraordinary year, Americans Robert Peary and Matthew Henson were hailed worldwide at the discovers of the North Pole; Britain's Ernest Shackleton had set a new geographic 'Furthest South' record, while . . . Australian Douglas Mawson, had reached the Magnetic South Pole." (Publisher's note)

"A fascinating look at the adventures of remarkably resilient men, so well-related as to make you feel the chill." Kirkus

Peck, Annie S. (Annie Smith), 1850-1935

Kimberley, Hannah. A **woman's** place is at the top; a biography of Annie Smith Peck, queen of the climbers. Hannah Kimberley. St. Martin's Press 2017 xvii, 347 p.p illustrations (hardcover) $26.99 **92**
  1. Mountaineers -- Biography 2. Mountaineering -- History 3. Women mountaineers -- United States -- Biography
  ISBN 9781250105813; 9781250084002
LC 2017010843

This book, by Hannah Kimberley, looks at the life of Annie Smith Peck, "who single-handedly carved her place on the map of mountain climbing and international relations. Peck marched in suffrage parades and became a political speaker and writer before women had the right to vote. She was a propagandist, an expert on North-South American relations, and an author and lecturer contracted to speak as an authority on multinational industry and commerce." (Publisher's note)

"Peck was a dynamic and compelling woman, and her story will be hard to resist for armchair travelers and fans of hidden history." Booklist
Includes bibliographical references (pages [329]-347)

Pelosi, Nancy, 1940-

Pelosi, Nancy. **Know** your power; a message to America's daughters. with Amy Hill Hearth. Doubleday 2008 180p $23.95; pa $14.95 **92**
  1. Women politicians 2. Members of Congress 3. Speakers of the House 4. Politicians -- United States
  ISBN 978-0-385-52586-2; 0-385-52586-9; 978-0-7679-2944-8 pa; 0-7679-2944-6 pa
LC 2008-20607

"In this graceful personal and political history, Pelosi describes growing up as the daughter of a congressman in an Italian-American Catholic world . . . and her burgeoning political interest. . . . Pelosi's book is a simply crafted acknowledgment of the support of her family, mentors and helpful colleagues without rhetorical flourishes, insider scandal or intimate revelations—a gentle account from a tough politician." Publ Wkly

Pepys, Samuel, 1633-1703

Pepys, Samuel. The **diary** of Samuel Pepys. University of Calif. Press 1970 11v il maps **92**
  1. Diarists 2. Military officials 3. Government officials 4. Members of Parliament 5. Great Britain -- Social life and customs 6. Great Britain -- History -- 1603-1714, Stuarts

"Written in shorthand between 1660 and 1669 and not deciphered until 1825, when it was published in part, the Diary was never intended for the public eye. It not only presents a vivid picture of an age, but is also a uniquely uninhibited and spontaneous revelation of its author's life and character." Reader's Ency. 4th edition

Peres, Shimon, 1923-2016

★ Peres, Shimon, 1923-2016. **No** Room for Small Dreams; Courage, Imagination, and the Making of Modern Israel. Shi-

mon Peres. Custom House 2017 xii, 227 p.p illustrations (hardcover) $27.99 **92**
  1. Israel 2. Statesmen -- Israel -- Biography 3. Israel -- Politics and government
  ISBN 9780062561442; 9780062561466; 0062561448
LC 2017042669

This book, by Shimon Peres, "explores what makes for a great leader, how to make hard choices in a climate of uncertainty and distress, the challenges of balancing principles with policies, and the liberating nature of imagination and unpredicted innovation. In doing so, he not only charts a better path forward for his beloved country but provides deep and universal wisdom for younger generations who seek to lead—be it in politics, business, or the broader service of making our planet a safer, more peaceful, and just place." (Publisher's note)

"A look back at Israeli history and forward to what it will take to establish peace in the Middle East." LJ

Perkins, Frances, 1882-1965

Downey, Kirstin. The **woman** behind the New Deal; the life of Frances Perkins, FDR's Secretary of Labor and his moral conscience. Nan A. Talese 2009 458p il $35 **92**
  1. Cabinet officers 2. College teachers 3. Secretaries of labor 4. State government officials 5. United States -- Dept. of Labor
  ISBN 978-0-385-51365-4; 0-385-51365-8
LC 2008-23208

A biography of "one of FDR's confidants and the first female secretary of labor in U.S. history. . . . Like many biographers, Downey . . . is enamored of her subject. But her fascination serves her well, allowing her to construct an intriguing catalog of Perkins's achievements and explore the influences that held sway in her life, a psychological approach lacking in previous Perkins biographies. Here Perkins's triumphs and tragedies are compiled into a compelling narrative that never loses its scholarly touch." Libr J
Includes bibliographical references

Perry, Crystal

Perry, Sarah, 1979- **After** the eclipse; a mother's murder, a daughter's search. Sarah Perry. Houghton Mifflin Harcourt 2017 xv, 350 p.p (hardcover) $27 **92**
  1. Children of murder victims 2. Mother-daughter relationship 3. Murder -- Maine -- Case studies 4. Mothers and daughters -- Maine -- Biography 5. Children of murder victims -- Maine -- Biography
  ISBN 9780544302211; 9780544302655
LC 2017003442

In this memoir, author Sarah Perry attempts to understand the life of her mother who was murdered when she was young. "The killer escaped unseen; it would take the police twelve years to find him. . . . But after the trial, Sarah's questions only grew. She wanted to understand her mother's life, not just her final hours, and so she began a personal investigation, one that drew her back to Maine, taking her deep into the abiding darkness of a small American town." (Publisher's note)

"Deft pacing and vivid portraits result in an absorbing mystery and a forthright memoir of abiding grief." Kirkus

Perry, Michael, 1964-

Perry, Michael. **Montaigne** in barn boots; an amateur ambles through philosophy. Michael Perry. HarperCollins 2017 xi, 223 p.p (hardcover) $25.99 **92**
  1. Farmers 2. Farm life 3. Farm life -- Wisconsin 4. Farmers -- Wisconsin -- Biography
  ISBN 9780062230584; 9780062230560; 0062230565

In this memoir, author Michael Perry "reflects on the lessons he's learned from his unlikely alter ego, French Renaissance philosopher Michel de Montaigne. 'The journey began on a gurney,' writes . . . Perry, describing the debilitating kidney stone that led him to discover the essays of Michel de Montaigne. Reading the philosopher in a manner he equates to chickens pecking at scraps . . . , Perry attempts to learn what he can . . . about himself." (Publisher's note)

Includes bibliographical references (pages 219-222).

Perry, Sarah, 1981-

Perry, Sarah, 1979- **After** the eclipse; a mother's murder, a daughter's search. Sarah Perry. Houghton Mifflin Harcourt 2017 xv, 350 p.p (hardcover) $27 **92**
1. Children of murder victims 2. Mother-daughter relationship 3. Murder -- Maine -- Case studies 4. Mothers and daughters -- Maine -- Biography 5. Children of murder victims -- Maine -- Biography
ISBN 9780544302211; 9780544302655

LC 2017003442

In this memoir, author Sarah Perry attempts to understand the life of her mother who was murdered when she was young. "The killer escaped unseen; it would take the police twelve years to find him. . . . But after the trial, Sarah's questions only grew. She wanted to understand her mother's life, not just her final hours, and so she began a personal investigation, one that drew her back to Maine, taking her deep into the abiding darkness of a small American town." (Publisher's note)

"Deft pacing and vivid portraits result in an absorbing mystery and a forthright memoir of abiding grief." Kirkus

Perry, Tyler

Perry, Tyler, 1969- **Higher** is waiting; Tyler Perry. Spiegel & Grau 2017 xvii, 201 p.p (hardcover) $26 **92**
1. Christian biography 2. African Americans -- Biography 3. New Orleans (La.) -- Biography 4. African American actors -- Biography 5. Christian biography -- United States
ISBN 9780812989366; 9780812989342; 0812989341

LC 2017034266

This spiritual guidebook, by Tyler Perry, presents "a collection of teachings culled from the experiences of a lifetime, meant to inspire readers to climb higher in their own lives and pull themselves up to a better, more fulfilling place. In this intimate book, . . . Perry writes of how his faith has sustained him in hard times, centered him in good times, and enriched his life." (Publisher's note)

Peter, Jason, 1974-

Peter, Jason. **Hero** of the underground; a memoir. [by] Jason Peter with Tony O'Neill. St. Martin's Press 2008 289p $24.95; pa $14.95 **92**
1. Heroin 2. Drug abuse 3. Football players 4. Football -- Biography
ISBN 978-0-312-37576-8; 0-312-37576-X; 978-0-312-56103-1 pa; 0-312-56103-2 pa

LC 2008-12364

A former NFL player traces his journey from professional athlete to drug addict after injuries ended his career, describing the range of physical, psychological, and legal dilemmas that affected his perception of reality and nearly ended his life.

"Avoiding self-help urgings and self-congratulations, Peter (who is now clean) and O'Neill have crafted an unflinching look at the dark side of a life devoted to pleasure." Publ Wkly

Petrushevskaya, Ludmilla

Petrushevskaya, Ludmilla. The **girl** from the Metropol Hotel; Growing Up in Communist Russia. Ludmilla Petrushevska-

ya; translated with an introduction by Anna Summers. Penguin Books 2017 176 p. illustrations (ebook) $48; (paperback) $16 **92**
1. Bildungsromans 2. Autobiographies 3. Authors, Russian 4. Russia -- History -- 1917-1991, Soviet Union 5. Moscow (Russia) -- Biography 6. Coming of age -- Soviet Union 7. Authors, Russian -- 20th century -- Biography 8. Soviet Union -- History -- 1925-1953 -- Biography 9. Communism -- Social aspects -- Soviet Union -- History 10. Hotel Metropol (Moscow, Russia) -- History -- 20th century 11. Moscow (Russia) -- Social life and customs -- 20th century
ISBN 9781101993514; 9780143129974

LC 2016031256

National Book Critics Circle Award Finalist: Autobiography (2017)

This memoir, by Ludmilla Petrushevskaya, is "about coming of age as an enemy of the people and finding her voice in Stalinist Russia. . . . She recounts her childhood of extreme deprivation—of wandering the streets like a young Edith Piaf, singing for alms, and living by her wits like Oliver Twist, a diminutive figure far removed from the heights she would attain as an internationally celebrated writer." (Publisher's note)

"With spunk and defiance, she survived, and transcended, the privations of her youth. A terse, spirited memoir that reads like a picaresque novel." Kirkus

Pham, Thong Van

★ Pham, Andrew X. The **eaves** of heaven; a life in three wars. by Andrew X. Pham, on behalf of my father, Thong Van Pham. Harmony Books 2008 301p $24.95 **92**
1. Refugees 2. Vietnamese Americans 3. Vietnam -- History
ISBN 978-0-307-38120-0; 0-307-38120-X

LC 2007-33894

"In a narrative set between the years of 1940 and 1976, Pham . . . recounts the story of his once wealthy father, Thong Van Pham, who lived through the French occupation of Indochina, the Japanese invasion during WWII, and the Vietnam War. . . . For those not familiar with Vietnamese history, Pham does an admirable job of recounting the complex cast of characters and the political machinations of the various groups vying for power over the years. In the end, he also gracefully delivers a heartfelt family history." Publ Wkly

Includes bibliographical references

Phillips, Sam, 1923-2003

★ Guralnick, Peter. **Sam** Phillips; the man who invented rock 'n' roll. Peter Guralnick. Little, Brown & Co. 2015 752 p. illustrations (hc) $32 **92**
1. Record producers 2. Rock music -- History and criticism 3. Sound recording executives and producers -- United States -- Biography
ISBN 9780316042741

LC 2015024690

In this book, author Peter Guralnick "brings us the life of Sam Phillips, the visionary genius who singlehandedly steered the revolutionary path of Sun Records. The music that he shaped in his tiny Memphis studio with artists as diverse as Elvis Presley, Ike Turner, Howlin' Wolf, Jerry Lee Lewis, and Johnny Cash, introduced a sound that had never been heard before. " (Publisher's note)

"The author emphasizes Phillips's contributions to rock and roll's 1950s emergence in the racially charged South and his personal and professional relationships with not only the many famous singers and musicians who benefited commercially and artistically from his vision, encouragement, and technical skills but also the obscure rockabilly, blues, country, and pop artists who were given an opportunity to express themselves on vinyl. . . . This long but consistently engaging book offers a more detailed and intimate account than Kevin and Tanja Crouch's Sun King and is recommended to fans of early American popular music." LJ

Includes bibliographical references and index

Piazza, Jo

Piazza, Jo. **How** to be married; what I learned from real women on five continents about surviving my first (really hard) year of marriage. Jo Piazza. Harmony Books 2017 xiv, 284 p.p (hardcover) $26 **92**

1. Marriage 2. Newlyweds -- Biography 3. Marriage -- Cross-cultural studies 4. Authors, American -- 21st century -- Biography
ISBN 9780451495556; 9780451495563

LC 2016036609

This book, by Jo Piazza, "offers an honest portrait of an utterly charming couple. When life throws more at them than they ever expected--a terrifying health diagnosis, sick parents to care for, unemployment--they ultimately create a fresh understanding of what it means to be equal partners during the good and bad times. Through their journey, they reveal a framework that will help the rest of us keep our marriages strong, from engagement into the newlywed years and beyond." (Publisher's note)

"Through keenly questioning people from vastly different cultures, Piazza seeks and finds marriage advice from men and women throughout the world." Booklist

Includes bibliographical references (pages 277-281).

Picasso, Pablo, 1881-1973

Unger, Miles J. **Picasso** and the painting that shocked the world; Miles J. Unger. Simon & Schuster 2018 470 p. illustrations (some color) (hardcover) $32.50 **92**

1. Cubism 2. Painting
ISBN 9781476794235; 9781476794211; 1476794219

LC 2017022812

This book, by Miles J. Unger, focuses on Pablo Picasso's painting known as 'Les Demoiselles d'Avignon.' "In 1906, . . . Picasso created a work that captured and defined the disorienting experience of modernity itself. . . . [H]is friends assumed he'd gone mad. Only his colleague George Braque understood what Picasso was trying to do. Over the next few years they teamed up to create Cubism, the most revolutionary and influential movement in twentieth-century art." (Publisher's note)

"This engrossing book chronicles with precision and enthusiasm a painting with lasting impact in today's art world." Pub Wkly

Includes bibliographical references (pages 437-451) and index.

Pilate, Pontius, active 1st century

Schiavone, Aldo. **Pontius** Pilate; deciphering a memory. Aldo Schiavone; translated by Jeremy Carden. Liveright Publishing Corp. 2017 240 p. (ebook) $50; (hardcover) $24.95 **92**

1. Palestine -- History 2. Palestine -- History -- To 70 A.D 3. Governors -- Palestine -- Biography
ISBN 9781631492365; 1631492357; 9781631492358

LC 2016056360

In this biography, by Aldo Schiavone, translated by Jeremy Carden, "the Roman prefect Pontius Pilate has been cloaked in rumor and myth since the first century, but what do we actually know of the man who condemned Jesus of Nazareth to the Cross? . . . Schiavone explains what might have happened in that brief meeting between the governor and Jesus, and why the Gospels—and history itself—have made Pilate a figure of immense ambiguity." (Publisher's note)

"A levelheaded, engaging reading of the Gospels and historical account that forms a solid sense of this pivotal personage and his role on the epic stage." Kirkus

Includes bibliographical references and index

Piniella, Lou, 1943-

Piniella, Lou, 1943- **Lou**; 50 years of kicking dirt, playing hard, and winning big in the sweet spot of baseball. Lou Piniella with Bill Madden. HarperCollins 2017 342 p. illustrations (some color) (hardcover) $27.99 **92**

1. Baseball players -- Biography 2. New York Yankees (Baseball team) 3. Baseball players -- United States -- Biography 4. Baseball managers -- United States -- Biography
ISBN 0062660799; 9780062660817; 9780062660794; 9780062670960

LC 2017302410

In this memoir, by Lou Piniella with Bill Madden, "the beloved New York Yankee legend looks back over his nearly fifty-year career as a player and a manager, sharing insights and stories about some of his most memorable moments and some of the biggest names in Major League Baseball. . . . With respected veteran sportswriter Bill Madden, Piniella now reflects on his storied career, offering fans a glimpse of life on the field, in the dugout, and inside the clubhouse." (Publisher's note)

Pinter, Harold, 1930-2008

Fraser, Antonia. **Must** you go? my life with Harold Pinter. Nan A. Talese/Doubleday 2010 328p il $28.95; ebook $28.95 **92**

1. Authors 2. Dramatists 3. Dramatists, English 4. Screenwriters 5. Authors, English 6. Nobel laureates for literature
ISBN 978-0-385-53250-1; 978-0-385-53251-8 ebook

LC 2010-7374

Harold Pinter's widow, the biographer, historian and novelist Antonia Fraser, recalls their years together from 1975 until the playwright's death of cancer on Christmas Eve in 2008.

The author "simultaneously creates a tender portrait of an exciting marriage, and a deliciously detailed account of living in the thick of creativity and fame." Entertainment Wkly

Piper, Karen.

Piper, Karen. A **girl's** guide to missiles; growing up in America's secret desert. Karen Piper. Penguin Group USA 2018 336 p. (hardcover) $27 **92**

1. Biography 2. Guided missiles 3. Young women -- Biography
ISBN 9780399564543; 0399564543

LC 2018025068

This book, by Karen Piper, presents "a surreal and poignant coming of age on a secretive missile facility, and 'an incredible view of...life in a town built for war.' The China Lake missile range is located in a huge stretch of the Mojave Desert. . . . It was created during the Second World War, and has always been shrouded in secrecy. But people who make missiles and other weapons are regular working people, . . . [including] Piper's parents, her sister, and . . . herself." (Publisher's note)

"A little-known corner of the Atomic Age comes into focus through Piper's skilled storytelling." Kirkus

Pius IX, Pope, 1792-1878

Kertzer, David I., 1948- The **pope** who would be king; the exile of Pius IX and the emergence of modern Europe. David I. Kertzer. Random House 2018 xxx, 474 p.p illustrations, maps (hardcover) $35 **92**

1. Europe -- Church history 2. Europe -- Politics and government -- 1789-1900 3. Europe -- Church history -- 19th century 4. Europe -- Politics and government -- 1848-1871
ISBN 9780812989922; 9780812989915

LC 2017038825

This book, by David I. Kertzer, tells the story of "the bloody revolution that stripped the pope of political power and signaled the birth of modern Europe. Days after his prime minister was assassinated in the middle of Rome in November 1848, Pope Pius IX found himself a virtual prisoner in his own palace. The wave of revolution that had swept through Europe now seemed poised to end the popes' thousand-year reign over the Papal States, if not to the papacy itself." (Publisher's note)

"A consummate storyteller, Kertzer blends academic rigor with fluid, energetic prose, and the result will satisfy specialists while entertaining those who might otherwise expect to be bored stiff by a volume of church history." Pub Wkly

Includes bibliographical references (pages [355]-443) and index.

Pius XII, Pope, 1876-1958

Cornwell, John. **Hitler's** pope: the secret history of Pius XII. Viking 1999 430p il hardcover o.p. pa $15   **92**
1. Popes 2. Heads of state 3. Nazi leaders
ISBN 0-14-029627-1 pa

LC 99-28311

"Relying on exclusive access to Vatican and Jesuit archives, . . . {the author} argues that through a 1933 Concordat with Hitler, Pope Pius XII facilitated the dictator's rise—and, ultimately, the Holocaust." Libr J

Includes bibliographical references

Plummer, Christopher

Plummer, Christopher. **In** spite of myself; a memoir. Knopf 2009 648p il $29.95   **92**
1. Actors
ISBN 978-0-679-42162-7; 0-679-42162-9

LC 2008-31229

The author is "an enchanting observer of the showbiz cavalcade, drawing vivid thumbnails of everyone from Laurence Olivier to Lenny Bruce and tossing off witty anecdotes . . . like the most effortless ad libs. The result is a sparkling star turn from a born raconteur for whom all the world is indeed a stage." Publ Wkly

Poe, Edgar Allan, 1809-1849

Ackroyd, Peter. **Poe**; a life cut short. Nan A. Talese/Doubleday 2008 205p il (Ackroyd's brief lives) $21.95   **92**
1. Poets 2. Authors 3. Essayists 4. Authors, American 5. Short story writers
ISBN 978-0-385-50800-1; 0-385-50800-X

LC 2008-18244

Explores Poe's literary accomplishments and legacy against the background of his erratic, dramatic, and sometimes sordid life, including his marriage to his thirteen-year-old cousin and his much-written-about problems with gambling and alcohol.

This "readable account should appeal to Poe devotees and newcomers alike." Publ Wkly

Includes bibliographical references

Collins, Paul. **Edgar** Allan Poe; the fever called living. Paul Collins. New Harvest/Houghton Mifflin Harcourt 2014 144 p. $20   **92**
1. Authors -- Biography 2. Authors, American -- 19th century -- Biography
ISBN 0544261879; 9780544261877

LC 2013024777

This biography of Edgar Allan Poe by Paul Collins "illuminates Poe's huge successes and greatest flop (a 143-page prose poem titled Eureka), and even tracks down what may be Poe's first published fiction." (Publisher's note)

"Although Collins doesn't provide much new information, the clean, crisp narrative presents the puzzling Poe as a deeply troubled and toweringly talented artist." Kirkus

Includes bibliographical references and index

Poehler, Amy, 1971-

Poehler, Amy, 1971- **Yes** please. HarperCollins 2014 352 p. illustrations (chiefly color) $28.99   **92**
1. Wit and humor 2. Autobiographies
ISBN 0062268341; 9780062268341

LC 2014469870

"A collection of stories, thoughts, ideas, lists, and haikus from the mind of one of our most beloved entertainers, 'Yes Please' offers Amy's thoughts on everything from her 'too safe' childhood outside of Boston to her early days in New York City, her ideas about Hollywood and 'the biz,' the demon that looks back at all of us in the mirror, and her joy at being told she has a 'face for wigs.'" (Publisher's note)

"These quibbles aside, the book is well worth reading for Poehler's fans and anyone who enjoyed Tina Fey's Bossypants or Mindy Kaling's Is Everyone Hanging Out Without Me?" LJ

Poitier, Sidney

★ Poitier, Sidney. The **measure** of a man; a spiritual autobiography. HarperSanFrancisco 2007 299p il $25.95; pa $14.95   **92**
1. Actors 2. Motion picture directors 3. Actors -- United States -- Biography
ISBN 978-0-06-135791-6; 0-06-135791-X; 978-0-06-135790-9 pa; 0-06-135790-1 pa
A reissue of the title first published 2000

"Poitier attempts to unravel for himself his own remarkable life story, looking at early life experiences, his family, and various themes that he believes have contributed to his success. Measure is not a chronological autobiography; the book emphasizes themes that have shaped his life. . . . Poitier's tale is an affirmation of the value of morality and personal integrity in leading a successful, fulfilling life." Booklist

Polk, James K. (James Knox), 1795-1849

Borneman, Walter R. **Polk**; the man who transformed the presidency and America. Random House 2008 422p il map $30   **92**
1. Governors 2. Presidents 3. Members of Congress 4. Speakers of the House 5. Presidents -- United States
ISBN 978-1-4000-6560-8

LC 2007-14040

The author "presents a birth-death biography of Polk. . . . Borneman has a pleasing style and makes fine use of primary sources that all demonstrate why Polk is habitually ranked as one of the ten best presidents by historians." Libr J

Includes bibliographical references

Merry, Robert W., 1946- A **country** of vast designs; James K. Polk, the Mexican War, and the conquest of the American continent. Simon & Schuster 2009 576p il map   **92**
1. Governors 2. Presidents 3. Members of Congress 4. Biography, Individual 5. Speakers of the House 6. Presidents -- United States 7. United States -- Territorial expansion 8. United States -- Territorial expansion -- History 9. United States -- Politics and government -- 1815-1861 10. United States -- Politics and government -- 1841-1845 11. United States -- Politics and government -- 1845-1849 12. United States -- Politics and government -- 1845-1861
ISBN 0743297431; 9780743297431

LC 2009024131

This is a biography of the eleventh president of the United States. Bibliography. Index.

"Merry's chronicle is filled with excellent insights into the critical events and fine portrayals of a cast of statesmen, warriors, and scheming rogues. . . . [This is] an outstanding addition to American history collections." Booklist

Includes bibliographical references (p. 543-550)

Pollard, Robert, 1957-

Cutter, Matthew. **Closer** you are; the story of Robert Pollard and Guided by Voices. by Matthew Cutter. Da Capo Press 2018 368 p. (hardcover) $27 **92**

1. Rock musicians -- United States -- Biography 2. Guided by Voices (Musical group)

ISBN 0306825767; 9780306825767

LC 2017060942

This book, by Matthew Cutter, tells the story of "Robert Pollard, indie rock icon and founder of the music group Guided By Voices. [The book takes] an in-depth look at the man behind it all, with interviews conducted by the author with Pollard's friends, family, and bandmates, along with unfettered access to Pollard himself and his extensive archives." (Publisher's note)

"Though Cutter's attention to detail (especially with regard to gigs and recordings) drags the narrative in spots, he has captured the raucous and squalling voice of a powerful American songwriter." Pub Wkly

Includes bibliographical references

Polo, Marco, 1254-1323?

Bergreen, Laurence. **Marco** Polo; from Venice to Xanadu. Knopf 2007 415p il map $28.95; pa $16.95 **92**

1. Explorers 2. Travelers 3. Voyages and travels 4. Travel writers 5. China -- Description and travel

ISBN 978-1-4000-4345-3; 1-4000-4345-3; 978-1-4000-7880-6 pa; 1-4000-7880-6 pa

LC 2007-21860

This is a biography of the Venetian explorer.

The author "gives a full-blooded rendition of Polo's astonishing journey. It is richly researched and vividly conveyed." Washington Post Book World

Includes bibliographical references (p. 383-391)

Pop, Iggy, 1947-

Trynka, Paul. **Iggy** Pop; open up and bleed. Broadway Books 2007 371p il $23.95; pa $14.95 **92**

1. Singers 2. Rock musicians 3. Punk rock music 4. Songwriters

ISBN 978-0-7679-2319-4; 978-0-7679-2320-0 pa

LC 2006-30216

"Drawing from original interviews with Iggy (né James Newell Osterberg Jr.) and his countless accomplices over the years, Trynka . . . has constructed a comprehensive portrait of the seemingly indestructible rock provocateur, one that touches all the familiar bases in recounting Iggy's riotous ascent from suburban Michigan schoolboy to frontman of the Stooges to solo artist with an intermittently transcendent career to composer of a drug-inspired hit song that became the jingle for a luxury cruise line." N Y Times Book Rev

Includes bibliographical references

Porter, Carolyn

Porter, Carolyn. **Marcel's** letters; a font and the search for one man's fate. Carolyn Porter. Skyhorse Publishing 2017 344 p. illustrations (hardcover: alkaline paper) $24.99 **92**

1. Typography 2. World War, 1939-1945 -- Biography 3. Graphic artists -- Minnesota -- Biography 4. Daimler-Benz Aktiengesellschaft -- Biography 5. French -- Germany -- Berlin -- Correspondence 6. World War, 1939-1945 -- Personal narratives, French 7. Berlin (Germany) -- History, Military -- 20th century 8. Prisoners of war -- Germany -- Berlin -- Correspondence 9. World War, 1939-1945 -- Conscript labor -- Germany -- Berlin 10. Penmanship, French -- Germany -- Berlin -- History -- 20th century

ISBN 9781510719347; 9781510719330

LC 2017001221

This book, by Carolyn Porter, describes how, "seeking inspiration for a new font design in an antique store in small-town Stillwater, Minnesota, [a] graphic designer . . . stumbled across a bundle of letters and . . . their beautifully expressive pen-and-ink handwriting. . . . Reading [them] opened a portal to a different time, and what began as mere curiosity quickly became an obsession with . . . the letter writer, Marcel Heuzé." (Publisher's note)

"Porter's captivating memoir describes her journey to find answers, noting how her fascination with Marcel proved infectious as she faces obstacle after obstacle and enlists the help of experts to discover the fate that awaited him." Booklist

Includes bibliographical references and index.

Posey, Parker, 1968-

Posey, Parker, 1968- **You're** on an airplane; a self-mythologizing memoir. Parker Posey. Blue Rider Press 2018 256 p. (hardcover) $30 **92**

1. Acting 2. Actresses 3. Autobiographies

ISBN 9780735218215; 9780735218192; 0735218196

"In her first book, actress . . . [Parker] Posey opens up about the art of acting, life on the set, and the realities of its accompanying fame. . . . Parker takes us into her childhood home, behind the scenes of the indie film revolution in the 1990s, the delightful absurdity of the big-budget genre thrillers she's turned into art in a whole new way, and the creativity that will always be part of both her acting and her personal life." (Publisher's note)

"Resilient and fiercely observant, Posey is an unflinchingly honest and entertaining interpreter of her many stories." Kirkus

Potter, Beatrix, 1866-1943

★ Lear, Linda J. **Beatrix** Potter; a life in nature. [by] Linda Lear. Allen Lane/Penguin 2007 583p il $30 **92**

1. Artists 2. Authors 3. Illustrators 4. Children's authors

ISBN 9780312369347; 0-312-36934-4

LC 2006-51245

This is a biography of the children's author.

This "is a meticulously researched and brilliantly recreated life that . . . is endlessly fascinating and often illuminating. It is altogether a remarkable achievement." Booklist

Includes bibliographical references (p. 541-544)

Potter, Vanessa

Potter, Vanessa. **Patient** H69; the story of my second sight. Vanessa Potter. Bloomsbury Sigma 2017 288 p. illustrations (some color) (Bloomsbury sigma) (hardcover) $27 **92**

1. Blind 2. Blindness 3. Blindness -- Case studies 4. Optic neuritis -- Case studies 5. Optic neuritis -- Patients -- Great Britain -- Biography

ISBN 1472936108; 9781472936134; 9781472936103

In this book, author Vanessa Potter, "reveals the terror and torment of her blindness. Supported by neuroscientists and Britain's National Health Service, Potter became a science sleuth, uncovering some of the innermost functions of the brain and our complex visual system, while learning meditation and self-hypnosis to help herself endure the ordeal and make a miraculous recovery." (Publisher's note)

"It is a journey toward understanding the brain told through the harrowing story of an intensely curious woman with the foresight to track her progress, and the compassion to use her experience to help others." Booklist

Includes bibliographical references (pages 277-279) and index.

Poulter, Ian

No Limits; My Autobiography. Trafalgar Square Books 2014 320 p. $32.95 **92**
  1. Golfers
  ISBN 1782066888; 9781782066880

This book by golf player Ian Poulter details his career "from his early rejection as a Spurs youth player, right through to his match-winning contributions to successive European Ryder Cup Triumphs. Poulter went from an assistant professional staffing the club shop to a global superstar, turning pro when he still had a handicap of 4 but the drive and self-belief to make it to the top." (Publisher's note)

Powell, Colin L

De Young, Karen. **Soldier**: the life of Colin Powell. Knopf 2006 610p il $28.95 **92**
  1. Generals 2. Secretaries of state 3. Statesmen -- United States
  ISBN 1-400-04170-8

LC 2006-45288

This is a "diligent, sympathetic, but not uncritical full-scale biography." N Y Rev Books
Includes bibliographical references

★ Powell, Colin L., 1937- **It** worked for me; in life and leadership. Colin Powell with Tony Koltz. 1st ed. Harper 2012 xii, 283 p.p (hardcover) $27.99; (paperback) $27.99; (ebook) $21.99 **92**
  1. Leadership 2. Iraq War, 2003-2011 3. African American generals -- Biography 4. Leadership -- United States 5. United States -- Politics and government -- 1993-2001 -- Quotations, maxims, etc
  ISBN 0062135120; 9780062135124; 9780062184061; 9780062135148

LC 2012002970

This autobiography continues the life story of Colin Powell. "The author rose in the military to become 'the first black Army officer to have a four-star troop command.' . . . He describes how . . . his military training also prepared him for his role in government. . . . Powell reviews his profound disagreements with Defense Secretary Donald Rumsfeld and Vice President Dick Cheney on the handling of the war in Iraq, while taking full responsibility for mistakes made on his watch." (Kirkus Reviews)

Powell, John Wesley, 1834-1902

Ross, John F., 1958- The **promise** of the Grand Canyon; John Wesley Powell's perilous journey and his vision for the American West. John F. Ross. Penguin Group USA 2018 400 p. $30 **92**
  1. Scientists -- United States -- Biography 2. Naturalists -- United States -- Biography
  ISBN 0525429875; 9780525429876

"[John F.] Ross's new biography describes [John Wesley] Powell's talents in ethnography, geology, surveying, and mapping, along with his political acuity that helped shape America's federal science and Western land stewardship....In masterly use of primary and secondary sources, Ross makes Powell's wrangling with senators as fascinating as his river expeditions...If you've ever used a topographic map, thank Powell." (Library Journal)

"If you've ever used a topographic map, thank Powell. His legacy deserves more attention, and Ross's biography stands to correct this. For all readers, especially lovers of science, history, and adventure." Library Journal

Powers, J. F. (James Farl), 1917-1999

Suitable accommodations; an autobiographical story of family life: the letters of J. F. Powers, 1942-1963. edited by Katherine A. Powers. Fararr, Straus & Giroux 2013 480 p. illustrations (hardcover) $35 **92**
  1. Letters 2. American authors 3. Authors, American -- 20th century -- Correspondence
  ISBN 0374268061; 9780374268060

LC 2013010997

This book, edited by Katherine A. Powers, presents a "collection of letters from the late J. F. Powers. . . . Beginning in prison, where Powers spent more than a year as a conscientious objector, the letters move on to his courtship, marriage, comically unsuccessful attempt to live in the woods, life in the Midwest and in Ireland, an unorthodox view of the Catholic Church, and an increasingly bizarre search for 'suitable accommodations,' which included three full-scale emigrations to Ireland." (Publisher's note)

Prater, Loretta P.

Prater, Loretta P. **Excessive** use of force; one mother's continuing struggle against police brutality and misconduct. Loretta P. Prater. Rowman & Littlefield Pub Inc 2018 308 p. (cloth: alk. paper) $34 **92**
  1. African American men 2. Mother-son relationship 3. Police brutality -- United States 4. Wrongful death -- United States 5. Mothers and sons -- United States 6. African American men -- Family relationships 7. Discrimination in law enforcement -- United States
  ISBN 9781538108000

LC 2017031630

This book, by Loretta P. Prater, "is the account of an African American family's personal experience with police brutality and misconduct, the behind the scene dynamics, as well as the personal emotional trauma experienced by victims' families. . . . Prater brings a good balance of personal and outside information." (Publisher's note)

"Gathering research and others' experiences nationwide, this book packs a timely, powerful, and thought-provoking punch to the gut of anyone who believes police killings are the actions of a couple of bad apples and not a result of years of individual and systemic racism." Booklist

Presley, Elvis, 1935-1977

Alden, Ginger. **Elvis** and Ginger; Ginger Alden. Ace Books 2014 400 p. illustrations (chiefly color) (hardcover) $26.95 **92**
  1. Actresses -- United States -- Biography 2. Rock musicians -- United States -- Biography
  ISBN 0425266338; 9780425266335

LC 2014009089

In this memoir Ginger Alden discusses her " whirlwind romance [with Elvis Presley] from first kiss to his stunning proposal of marriage. She details his exploration of Eastern religions, his perception of being a 'legend,' his devotion to family and friends, and her attempt to know the insular group surrounding Elvis. And for the very first time she talks about the devastating end of it all, and the 50,000 mourners and reporters who descended on Graceland in 1977." (Publisher's note)

"It's an outpouring of affection for a man who has stayed in the author's mind all these years, a way for her to show the world the Elvis she knew. The book has a pretty much guaranteed readership, as many Elvis fans will read anything and everything that appears in print about their idol." Booklist

Connolly, Ray. **Being** Elvis; a lonely life. Ray Connolly. Liveright Publishing Corporation 2017 xxi, 362 p.p illustrations, portraits (hardcover) $27.95   **92**
    1. Musicians -- United States 2. Rock musicians -- United States -- Biography
    ISBN 9781631492808; 1631492802; 9781631492815
            LC 2016054735

In this biography of Elvis Presley, author "Ray Connolly takes a fresh look at the career of the world's most loved singer, placing him, forty years after his death, not exhaustively in the garish neon lights of Las Vegas but back in his mid-twentieth-century, distinctly southern world. For new and seasoned fans alike, Connolly, who interviewed Elvis in 1969, re-creates a man who sprang from poverty in Tupelo, Mississippi, to unprecedented overnight fame, eclipsing Frank Sinatra and then inspiring the Beatles along the way." (Publisher's note)

"Connolly carefully and sympathetically paints the many faces of Presley, faces eventually shrouded in despair." Kirkus

Includes bibliographical references (pages 343-346) and index.

Mason, Bobbie Ann. **Elvis** Presley. Viking 2002 178p (Penguin lives series) hardcover o.p. pa $13   **92**
    1. Actors 2. Singers 3. Rock musicians
    ISBN 0-670-03174-7; 0-14-303889-3 pa
            LC 2002-28873

The author "chronicles Elvis' sad story: humble origins, 1954 breakthrough, adoption by 'the Colonel' (manager Tom Parker), early TV appearances, army hitch, the death of his mother, marriage to Priscilla, Hollywood, 1968 'comeback', Las Vegas headliner, prescription drug abuse, meeting with Nixon, and death at 42 in 1977." Booklist

Includes discography, filmography and bibliographical references

Preston, Katherine, 1984-

Preston, Katherine. **Out** with it; how stuttering helped me find my voice. Katherine Preston. Atria Books 2013 244 p. (hardback) $24   **92**
    1. Stutterers 2. Speech disorders 3. Stutterers -- Biography
    ISBN 1451676581; 9781451676587; 9781451676594
            LC 2012048984

This book is a memoir by Katherine Preston about her "struggle to come to terms with her stuttering." She began stuttering around the age of 7, and the book starts there, . . . capturing the mix of abject terror and curious observation that childhood stuttering can create. . . . She chronicles her many interviews with fellow stutterers--people bullied, people strengthened, and people driven from those they care about." (Kirkus Reviews)

Priestley, Joseph, 1733-1804

Johnson, Steven, 1968- The **invention** of air; a story of science, faith, revolution, and the birth of America. Riverhead Books 2008 254p il $25.95   **92**
    1. Clergy 2. Chemists 3. Scientists 4. Writers on science 5. Biography, Individual
    ISBN 1-59448-852-5; 978-1-59448-852-8
            LC 2008-46101

This "portrait of scientist and theologian Joseph Priestley evaluates his friendships with such Founding Fathers as Benjamin Franklin and Thomas Jefferson while citing his role in the nation's intellectual development and the founding of the Unitarian Church." (Publisher's note) Bibliography. Index.

"What enlivens the book is that Johnson does not simply describe the system within which Priestley and his contemporaries hashed out the features of classical science; he sets it against other, later systems for comprehending physical reality, showing laymen how far we have come from the classical age of science." N Y Times Book Rev

Includes bibliographical references

Prince

Garcia, Mayte. The **most** beautiful; my life with Prince. Mayte Garcia. Hachette Books 2017 294 p. illustrations (chiefly color) (hardcover) $27   **92**
    1. Rock musicians -- United States -- Biography 2. Dancers -- United States -- Biography
    ISBN 9780316468978; 9780316468992; 9780316468985
            LC 2016054437

In this book, Mayte Garcia shares her love story with musician Prince. "[She] shares the deeply personal story of their relationship and offers a singular perspective on the music icon and their world together: from their unconventional meeting backstage at a concert . . . , to their fairy-tale wedding (and their groundbreaking artistic partnership), to the devastating losses that ultimately dissolved their romantic relationship for good." (Publisher's note)

"A genial, candid portrait of Prince's ill-fated turn as a family man." Kirkus

Greenman, Ben. **Dig** if you will the picture; funk, sex, God and genius in the music of Prince. Ben Greenman. Henry Holt & Co. 2017 xiii, 286 p.p (hardcover) $28   **92**
    1. Musicians 2. Rock musicians -- United States -- Biography
    ISBN 9781250128379; 1250128374; 9781250128362
            LC 2016054759

In this book author Ben Greenman "mines his encyclopedic knowledge of Prince's music to tell both his story and the story of the paradigm-shifting ideas that he communicated to his millions of fans around the world. Greenman's take on Prince is the autobiography of a generation and its ideas. Asking a series of questions--not only 'Who was Prince?' but 'Who wasn't he?' and 'Who are we?'" (Publisher's note)

"As much a fan boy as an authority, rock journalist Greenman . . . investigates Prince's development as an artist, his career trajectory, his massive creative output, and his numerous side projects." Booklist

Includes bibliographical references. Discography: pages [263]-280.

Shahidi, Afshin. **Prince**; a private view. Afshin Shahidi; foreword by Beyoncé Knowles-Carter. St. Martin's Press 2017 xvi, 235 p.p color illustrations   **92**
    1. Illustrated books 2. Photographers -- United States -- Catalogs 3. Rock musicians -- United States -- Portraits 4. Rock musicians -- United States -- Biography -- Portraits
    ISBN 9781250134431
            LC 2017032068

"Prince: A Private View compiles photographer Afshin Shahidi's work into a journey through Prince's extraordinary life. With never-before-seen photos, it is the ultimate collection of shots of Prince. Brief, but complete and rich, stories about Shahidi and Prince's collaboration and time together are alternately incisive, personal, and even funny." (Publisher's note)

Proulx, Annie

Proulx, Annie, 1935- **Bird** cloud; a memoir. Scribner 2011

234p il map $26; ebook $12.99 **92**
1. Authors 2. Novelists 3. Journalists 4. Women authors 5. Editors 6. Nonfiction writers 7. Short story writers 8. Biography, Individual 9. Natural history -- Wyoming 10. Wyoming -- Description and travel
ISBN 978-0-7432-8880-4; 978-1-4391-7171-4 ebook

"'Bird Cloud' is the name Annie Proulx gave to 640 acres of Wyoming wetlands and prairie and four-hundred-foot cliffs plunging down to the North Platte River. On the day she first visited, a cloud in the shape of a bird hung in the evening sky. Proulx also saw pelicans, bald eagles, golden eagles, great blue herons, ravens, scores of bluebirds, harriers, kestrels, elk, deer and a dozen antelope. She fell in love with the land, then owned by the Nature Conservancy, and she knew what she wanted to build on it—a house in harmony with her work, her appetites and her character, a library surrounded by bedrooms and a kitchen.... Bird Cloud is the story of designing and constructing that house—with its solar panels, Japanese soak tub, concrete floor and elk horn handles on kitchen cabinets. It is also a ... natural history and archaeology of the region—inhabited for millennia by Ute, Arapaho and Shoshone Indians—and a family history, going back to nineteenth-century Mississippi riverboat captains and Canadian settlers." (Publisher's note)

"Proulx bought a 640-acre nature preserve by the North Platte River in Wyoming and started building her dream house, a project that took years and went hundreds of thousands of dollars over budget. In her bustling account, Proulx salivates over the prospect of a Japanese soak tub, polished concrete floor, solar panels, and luxe furnishings that often turn into pricey engineering fiascoes.... [This] is a fine evocation of place that becomes a meditation on the importance of a home, however harsh and evanescent." Publ Wkly

Includes bibliographical references

Proust, Marcel, 1871-1922

Weber, Caroline. **Proust's** duchess; how three celebrated women captured the imagination of fin de siècle Paris. Caroline Weber. Alfred A. Knopf 2018 736 p. (hardcover) $35 **92**
1. Biography 2. Women -- Biography 3. Women -- France -- Biography 4. Paris (France) -- Intellectual life -- 19th century 5. Paris (France) -- Social life and customs -- 19th century 6. Aristocracy (Social class) -- France -- Paris -- Biography
ISBN 9780307961785; 9780345803122

LC 2017038855

This book, by Caroline Weber, presents "the first in-depth study of the three women [Marcel] Proust used to create his supreme fictional character, the Duchesse de Guermantes. Geneviève Halévy Bizet Straus; Laure de Sade, Comtesse de Adhéaume de Chevigné; and Élisabeth de Riquet de Caraman-Chimay, the Comtesse Greffulhe--these were the three superstars of fin-de-siècle Parisian high society." (Publisher's note)

Includes bibliographical references

Pryor, Richard, 1940-2005

Henry, David. **Furious** cool; Richard Pryor and the world that made him. by David Henry and Joe Henry. Algonquin Books 2013 400 p. $25.95 **92**
1. Comedians -- Biography 2. Comedians -- United States -- Biography 3. Motion picture actors and actresses -- United States -- Biography
ISBN 1616200782; 9781616200787

LC 2013019665

In this biography of Richard Pryor, authors David Henry and Joe Henry "bring him to life both as a man and as an artist, providing an in-depth appreciation of his talent and his lasting influence, as well as an ... examination of the world he lived in and the influences that shaped both his persona and his art." (Publisher's note)

"A beautifully written account of the troubled life of a manic genius." Booklist

Includes bibliographical references

Mooney, Paul. **Black** is the new white; a memoir. Simon Spotlight Entertainment 2009 264p il $24.99 **92**
1. Actors 2. Comedians 3. Screenwriters 4. Television scriptwriters 5. United States -- Race relations
ISBN 978-1-4165-8795-8; 1-4165-8795-0

LC 2009-19572

"Paul Mooney recalls the day he became Richard Pryor's shadow partner. It was 1968, and the two young comics were sitting in a Hollywood greasy spoon, with Pryor nursing another hangover, so Mooney lightened the mood with an off-the-cuff, X-rated one-liner that made his buddy convulse.... [This book] is Mooney's unvarnished memoir of that friendship. At a time when comedians—even African American icons such as Bill Cosby—never talked about race, Pryor (aided and abetted by Mooney) dared to confront the elephant in the room. Mooney, who has also written for 'In Living Color' and 'Chappelle's Show,' also traces his own path from humble Deep South roots to a comedy elder statesman known for his incisive riffs on racism." Los Angeles Times book Rev

Ptacin, Mira

Ptacin, Mira. **Poor** your soul; Mira Ptacin. Soho Press 2016 320 p. (hardback) $26; (ebook) $15 **92**
1. Loss (Psychology) 2. Women authors -- Biography 3. First pregnancy 4. Women authors, American -- Biography 5. Children -- Death -- Psychological aspects
ISBN 9781616956349; 9781616956356

LC 2015028123

This memoir, by Mira Ptacin, "is a beautiful reflection on sexuality, free will, and the fierce bonds of family. At twenty-eight, Mira Ptacin discovered she was pregnant.... [But] an ultrasound revealed that her child would be born with a constellation of birth defects and no chance of survival outside the womb.... Mira's story is paired with that of her mother, ... who also experienced grievous loss when her only son was killed by a drunk driver." (Publisher's note)

"Ptacin's memoir is a raw and absorbing story of family fortitude and a young woman's struggle to confront and accept the unexpected." Pub Wkly

Puccini, Giacomo, 1858-1924

Berger, William. **Puccini** without excuses; a refreshing reassessment of the world's most popular composer. Vintage Books 2005 471p pa $16 **92**
1. Opera 2. Composers
ISBN 978-1-4000-7778-6; 1-4000-7778-8

LC 2005-46157

The author "sets Puccini within his times before discussing the circumstances of each opera's premiere and famous interpreters of the roles, providing character lists and synopses and fleshing all this out with musical commentary. Chapters on opera production and the genre's relation to film are useful.. . Berger's lucid yet hardly dispassionate views are designed to elicit strong reactions, so this is not the first place one should go for an unbiased introduction to the composer's oeuvre. But the author's grounding information is helpful for the novice, and he refers to some of the current authoritative sources." Libr J

Purkayastha, Ian, 1992-

Purkayastha, Ian. **Truffle** Boy; my unexpected journey through the exotic food underground. Ian Purkayastha with

Kevin West. Hachette Books 2016 304 p. (ebook) $88; (hardcover) $27 **92**

1. Truffles 2. Businessmen -- United States -- Biography 3. Gourmet food industry -- United States -- Biography 4. Restaurants -- New York (State) -- New York -- Equipment and supplies

ISBN 9780316383943; 9780316383950

LC 2016008650

This book, by Ian Purkayastha with Kevin West, "chronicles Ian's high stakes dealings with a truffle kingpin in Serbia, . . . crooked businessmen and maniacal chefs in Manhattan, gypsy truffle hunters in the forests of Hungary, and a supreme adventure to find 'Gucci mushrooms' in the Himalayan foothills. . . . He endures harsh failures along the way but rebuilds with tremendous success by selling not just truffles but . . . other nearly unobtainable ingredients." (Publisher's note)

"This quirky coming-of-age narrative set in the world of high-end food purveyors will teach readers a thing or two about truffles and how the rarest ingredients arrive on the plates of the world's fanciest restaurants." LJ

Pushkin, Aleksandr Sergeevich, 1799-1837

★ Binyon, T. J. **Pushkin**: a biography. Knopf 2003 xxix, 727p il maps $35; pa $20 **92**

1. Poets 2. Authors 3. Novelists 4. Short story writers

ISBN 1-4000-4110-4; 1-4000-7652-8 pa

LC 2003-112113

The author argues that Pushkin's "political views and rebellious temper were a continual source of trouble, inviting criticism and condemnation his entire life and eventually ending it in 1837 when he was fatally wounded in a duel with George D'Anthes. . . . A stunning achievement, this thorough biography is sure to become the definitive account of Pushkin's life for years to come and will appeal to the scholar and general reader alike." Libr J

Includes bibliographical references

Putin, Vladimir

Fitzpatrick, Catherine A. **First** person: an astonishingly frank self-portrait; by Russia's president Vladimir Putin with Nataliya Gevorkyan, Natalya Timakova, and Andrei Kolesnikov; translated by Catherine A. Fitzpatrick. PublicAffairs 2000 206p il pa $15 **92**

1. Presidents 2. Prime ministers

ISBN 1-58648-018-9

LC 00-132549

This volume is "the product of some 24 hours of interviews with Putin conducted by three Russian journalists, with brief comments from other sources, including Putin's family, friends, teachers, and some associates. . . . The approach is chronological , describing Putin as son, schoolboy, university student, young intelligence specialist, spy, democrat, bureaucrat, family man, and politician." Booklist

Lourie, Richard. **Putin**; his downfall and Russia's coming crash. Richard Lourie. St. Martin's Press/Thomas Dunne Books 2017 288 p. (hardcover) $26.99 **92**

1. Russia (Federation) -- Foreign relations 2. Presidents -- Russia (Federation) -- Biography 3. Russia (Federation) -- Politics and government -- 1991- 4. Political culture -- Russia (Federation) -- History -- 21st century 5. Political corruption -- Russia (Federation) -- History -- 21st century

ISBN 9780312538088

LC 2017006939

This book, by Richard Lourie, asserts that "[Vladimir] Putin's Russia will collapse just as Imperial Russia did in 1917 and as Soviet Russia did in 1991. The only questions are when, how violently, and with how much peril for the world. The U.S. election complicates everything. . . . [This book] is an essential read for everybody bewildered and dismayed by the new world order." (Publisher's note)

Includes bibliographical references and index

Myers, Steven Lee. The **new** tsar; the rise and reign of Vladimir Putin. by Steven Lee Myers. Alfred A. Knopf 2015 576 p. illustrations, maps (hardback) $32.50 **92**

1. Presidents 2. Power (Social sciences) 3. Russia -- History -- 1991- 4. Russia -- History -- 1917-1991, Soviet Union 5. Political leadership -- Russia (Federation) 6. Power (Social sciences) -- Russia (Federation) 7. Presidents -- Russia (Federation) -- Biography 8. Russia (Federation) -- Politics and government -- 1991- 9. Soviet Union. Komitet gosudarstvennoĭ bezopasnosti -- Biography

ISBN 9780307961617

LC 2015010720

This book on Russian president Vladmir Putin, by Steven Lee Myers, "recounts Putin's origins—from his childhood of abject poverty in Leningrad, to his ascension through the ranks of the KGB, and his eventual consolidation of rule. Along the way, world events familiar to readers, such as September 11th and Russia's war in Georgia in 2008, as well as the 2014 annexation of Crimea and the ongoing conflict in Ukraine, are presented from never-before-seen perspectives." (Publisher's note)

Includes bibliographical references

Queller, Jessica, 1969-

Queller, Jessica. **Pretty** is what changes; impossible choices, the breast cancer gene, and how I defied my destiny. Spiegel & Grau 2008 247p $24.95 **92**

1. Breast cancer 2. Surgical patients 3. Television scriptwriters 4. Cancer -- Genetic aspects

ISBN 978-0-385-52040-9; 0-385-52040-9

LC 2008-4303

The author tells her story—from her mother's death from ovarian cancer and her positive testing for the breast cancer gene BRCA-1 to her decision to have a double mastectomy and remove her ovaries.

This "story is seamless and gripping; readers will be rooting for Queller and her heroic decision to confront her genetic destiny." Publ Wkly

Questlove

Greenman, Ben. **Mo'** meta blues; the world according to Questlove. by Ahmir "Questlove" Thompson and Ben Greenman. Grand Central Pub. 2013 288 p. (hardcover) $26 **92**

1. Musicians

ISBN 1455501352; 9781455501359

LC 2013932326

This book is a memoir by "Questlove" Thompson, the cofounder and drummer of the band the Roots. Here, he "tells of his work as a DJ and producer with some of the biggest names in the music business, such as Jay-Z and Common, and Dave Chappelle," His "recollections touch on everything from drumming at age five in his father's professional doo-wop and soul band to roller-skating as an adult with Eddie Murphy at a bizarre party hosted by Prince." (Publishers Weekly)

Quiñones-Hinojosa, Alfredo

Quiñones-Hinojosa, Alfredo. **Becoming** Dr. Q; my journey from migrant farm worker to brain surgeon. with Mim Eichler Rivas. University of California Press 2011 317p il $27.50 **92**

1. Surgeons 2. Migrant labor 3. Mexican Americans 4. Neurologists 5. Neurosurgeons

ISBN 978-0-520-27118-0; 0-520-27118-1

LC 2011011531

"When the callow Quiñones-Hinojosa, or Dr. Q, made up his mind to pursue a better life and, especially, an education in the U.S., no border or barrier could have kept him from his destiny: a fate that led eventually to his becoming a Johns Hopkins University neurosurgeon, professor, and brain-cancer research scientist. Indeed, the brash teenager left all that was familiar in his native Mexico and, with less than $70 in his pocket, climbed the fence. In fact, he scaled it twice because he was caught the first time and sent back. . . . Quiñones-Hinojosa's story is gripping, inspiring, and just plain awesome." Booklist

Ramos, Jason A.

Ramos, Jason A. **Smokejumper**; A Memoir by One of America's Most Select Airborne Firefighters. James A. Ramos, Julian Smith. HarperCollins 2015 336 p. illustrations (color), map $27.99 **92**
1. Wildfires 2. Fire fighters
ISBN 0062319620; 9780062319623

LC 2015007015

This memoir, written by Jason A. Ramos with Julian Smith, presents an "inside look at the thrilling world of smokejumpers, the airborne firefighters who parachute into the most remote and rugged areas of the United States, confronting the growing threat of nature's blazes. Ramos takes readers into his exhilarating and dangerous world, explores smokejumping's remarkable history, and explains why their services are more essential than ever before." (Publisher's note)

"Most of us avoid jumping from the frying pan into the fire, but as an elite smokejumper with the Department of the Interior Ramos does it regularly, often alone or with just one partner." LJ

Ramsey, Franchesca, 1983-

Ramsey, Franchesca. **Well,** that escalated quickly; memoirs and mistakes of an accidental activist. Franchesca Ramsey. Grand Central Publishing 2018 256 p. (hardback) $27 **92**
1. YouTube (Electronic resource) 2. Television personalities -- Biography 3. Bloggers -- United States -- Biography 4. YouTube (Electronic resource) -- Biography 5. Television personalities -- United States -- Biography
ISBN 9781478999911; 9781538761038; 9781538761045

LC 2017055221

In this book, author Franchesca Ramsey "explores race, identity, online activism, and the downfall of real communication in the age of social media rants, trolls, and call-out wars. . . . [The book also] includes Ramsey's advice on dealing with internet trolls and low-key racists, . . . and her personal hits and misses in activist debates with everyone from bigoted Facebook friends and misguided relatives to mainstream celebrities and YouTube influencers." (Publisher's note)

Rand, Ayn, 1905-1982

Heller, Anne Conover. **Ayn** Rand and the world she made; [by] Anne C. Heller. Nan A. Talese/Doubleday 2008 567p il $35 **92**
1. Authors 2. Novelists 3. Philosophers 4. Women authors 5. Authors, American 6. Nonfiction writers 7. Objectivism (Philosophy)
ISBN 978-0-385-51399-9

LC 2008-27638

This is a biography of the author of Atlas Shrugged and The Fountainhead.

The author "has delivered a thoughtful, flesh-and-blood portrait of an extremely complicated and self-contradictory woman, coupling this character study with literary analysis and plumbing the quirkier depths

of Rand's prodigious imagination." N Y Times (Late N Y Ed)
Includes bibliographical references

Rankin, Lissa, 1969-

Rankin, Lissa. The **anatomy** of a calling; a road map for awakening to your life's purpose. Lissa Rankin. Rodale 2015 288 p. (trade hardcover) $24.99 **92**
1. Vocation 2. Conduct of life 3. Holistic medicine -- United States 4. Physicians -- United States -- Biography
ISBN 9781623365745

LC 2015040863

In this book, physician Lissa Rankin "shares her story [through the lens of Joseph Campbell's "Hero's Journey" paradigm.] She encourages you to find out where you are on your own journey, offering inspiring guideposts and practices along the way. With compelling lessons on trusting intuition, surrendering to love, and learning to see adversity as an opportunity for soul growth . . . [she] invites you to make a powerful shift in consciousness and reach your highest destiny." (Publisher's note)

"Readers who seek more information and methodology regarding mind/body healing and health through diverse spiritual practices will find Rankin's story fascinating." Pub Wkly

Rasputin, Grigori Efimovich, 1869-1916

Massie, Robert K., 1929- **Nicholas** and Alexandra. Ballantine Books 2000 613p il map pa $18.95 **92**
1. Monks 2. Emperors 3. Empresses 4. Courtiers 5. Russia -- History 6. Russia -- Kings and rulers
ISBN 0-345-43831-0; 978-0-345-43831-7

LC 99-91507

First published 1967 by Atheneum

This study provides an intimate account of the Romanov family and the coming of the Russian Revolution. Kerensky, Lenin and Rasputin are among the personalities profiled.

This book, "solid with research, reads as lightly as a novel, as authoritatively as a textbook. Dialogue and lively description lend a sense of immediacy, but his notes, discreetly relegated to the back of the book, show how carefully he has avoided slipping into fiction." Christ Sci Monit

Includes bibliographical references

★ Smith, Douglas. **Rasputin**; Faith, Power, and the Twilight of the Romanovs. by Douglas Smith. Farrar, Straus & Giroux 2016 848 p. illustrations, maps $35 **92**
ISBN 9780374711238; 0374240841; 9780374240844

LC 2016027558

This book, by Douglas Smith, is a biography of Rasputin. "A hundred years after his murder, Rasputin continues to excite the popular imagination as the personification of evil. Numerous biographies, novels, and films recount his mysterious rise to power as Nicholas and Alexandra's confidant and the guardian of the sickly heir to the Russian throne. His debauchery and sinister political influence are the stuff of legend, and the downfall of the Romanov dynasty was laid at his feet." (Publisher's note)

Includes bibliographical references and index.

Rather, Dan

Diehl, Digby. **Rather** outspoken; my life in the news. Dan Rather with Digby Diehl. Grand Central Pub. 2012 vi, 309 p.p (regular edition) $27.99 **92**
1. CBS Inc. 2. Television broadcasting of news 3. Television journalists -- United States -- Biography
ISBN 1455502413; 9781455502417; 9781455513468

LC 2011052227

This book by Dan Rather presents an "investigation of how the news media has become dangerously intertwined with politics and corporate interests." It focuses on "the circumstances behind his firing from CBS News, where he had worked as a reporter since 1962. . . . In between, he provides . . . portraits of the presidents he has interviewed . . . and expresses concern for the future of independent media in an industry that is increasingly kowtowing to the almighty bottom line." (Kirkus Reviews)

Rausing, Sigrid

Rausing, Sigrid. **Mayhem**; Sigrid Rausing. Alfred A. Knopf 2017 199 p. (hardcover: alk. paper) $25   **92**
1. Drug abuse 2. Drug addicts 3. Families -- Biography 4. Drug abuse -- Biography 5. Drug addicts -- Biography
ISBN 9780451493132; 9780451493125

LC 2016052496

This book is a "memoir about the impact of addiction on a family. In the summer of 2012 a woman named Eva was found dead in the London townhouse she shared with her husband, Hans K. Rausing. The couple had struggled with drug addiction for years, often under the glare of tabloid headlines. Now, writing with singular clarity and restraint, Hans' sister, the editor and publisher Sigrid Rausing, tries to make sense of what happened." (Publisher's note)

"A stylish and devastatingly lucid memoir." Kirkus

Radziwill, Lee Bouvier, 1933-

Kashner, Sam. The **fabulous** Bouvier sisters; the tragic and glamorous lives of Jackie and Lee. Sam Kashner, Nancy Schoenberger. HarperCollins 2018 336 p. $28.99   **92**
1. Celebrities -- United States 2. Presidents' spouses -- United States
ISBN 0062364987; 9780062364982

In this book, authors Sam Kashner and Nancy Schoenberger "tells the complete story of . . . Jackie Kennedy Onassis and Lee Radziwill. Drawing on new information and extensive interviews with Lee, now eighty-four, this dual biography sheds light on the public and private lives of two extraordinary women who lived through immense tragedy in enormous glamour." (Publisher's note)

Reagan, Ronald

★ Brands, H. W. **Reagan**; the life. H.W. Brands. Doubleday 2015 816 p. 16 plates; color illustrations (hardback) $35   **92**
1. Presidents -- United States -- Biography 2. United States -- Politics and government -- 1981-1989
ISBN 0385536399; 9780385536394

LC 2014038054

This biography by H.W. Brands "establishes Ronald Reagan as one of the two great presidents of the twentieth century, a true peer to Franklin Roosevelt. 'Reagan' conveys . . . how the confident force of Reagan's personality and the unwavering nature of his beliefs enabled him to engineer a conservative revolution in American politics and play a crucial role in ending communism in the Soviet Union." (Publishers' note)

"This is a detailed look at a president who sparked much controversy and affection and it belongs in most collections of presidential biography." Booklist

Reagan, Ronald, 1911-2004. The **Reagan** diaries; edited by Douglas Brinkley. HarperCollins 2007 767p il $35; pa $19.99   **92**
1. Biography, Individual 2. Presidents -- United States 3. United States -- Politics and government -- 1974-1989 4. United States

-- Politics and government -- 1981-1989
ISBN 978-0-06-087600-5; 0-06-087600-X; 978-0-06-155833-7 pa; 0-06-155833-8 pa

"There is a kind of touching banality to many of the entries, as though Reagan were just another CEO writing about corporate life at the top, albeit corporate life that revolved around nuclear and hostage negotiations. Edited by Douglas Brinkley . . ., the book shows a Reagan almost sweetly amazed by small trappings of office. . . . Reading these diaries, Americans will find it easier to understand how Reagan did what he did for so long: by steady work, and a steadfast commitment to the job at hand." Newsweek

★ Spitz, Bob. **Reagan**; an American journey. Bob Spitz. Penguin Press, an imprint of Penguin Random House LLC 2018 880 p. $35   **92**
1. Presidents -- United States -- Biography 2. Motion picture actors and actresses -- United States -- Biography
ISBN 1594205310; 9781594205316

This book, by Bob Spitz, "is an absorbing, richly detailed, even revelatory chronicle of the full arc of Ronald Reagan's epic life - giving full weight to the Hollywood years, his transition to politics and rocky but ultimately successful run as California governor, and, ultimately, of course, his iconic presidency, filled with storm and stress but climaxing with his peace talks with the Soviet Union that would serve as his greatest legacy." (Publisher's note)

"In visiting his final years, readers share the pathos of Reagan's descent into dementia and feel the intense sorrow of the millions who mourn his passing. Candid, complete, compelling." Booklist

Rebanks, James

Rebanks, James. The **shepherd's** life; modern dispatches from an ancient landscape. James Rebanks. Flatiron Books 2015 293 p. illustrations (hardcover) $25.99   **92**
1. Shepherds 2. Country life 3. Livestock industry 4. Sheep -- England -- Lake District 5. Farm life -- England -- Lake District 6. Farmers -- England -- Lake District -- Biography 7. Shepherds -- England -- Lake District -- Biography
ISBN 1250060249; 9781250060242

LC 2015011233

This book, by James Rebanks, "takes us through a shepherd's year, offering a unique account of rural life and a fundamental connection with the land that most of us have lost. It is a story of working lives, the people around him, his childhood, his parents and grandparents, a people who exist and endure even as the culture--of the Lake District, and of farming--changes around them." (Publisher's note)

Red Cloud, Sioux Chief, 1822-1909

Drury, Bob. The **heart** of everything that is; the untold story of Red Cloud, an American legend. Bob Drury and Tom Clavin. Simon & Schuster 2013 400 p. illustrations, maps (hardcover) $30   **92**
1. Oglala Indians 2. Red Cloud's War, 1866-1867
ISBN 1451654669; 9781451654660; 9781451654684

LC 2013003200

"Drawing on a wealth of evidence, including Red Cloud's biography, which was lost for nearly a hundred years, this never-before-told story of the great Oglala Sioux chief - the only Plains Indian to defeat the United States Army in a war - places readers at the center of the conflict over western expansion." (Publisher's note)

The authors "offer a battle-and-skirmish account of Sioux leader Red Cloud's war on the whites who invaded the Great Plains, though their narrative is strong on ethnohistorical matters as well. . . . A well-researched and -written account of an often overlooked figure in the his-

tory of the Indian Wars." Kirkus
  Includes bibliographical references and index

Redding, Otis, 1941-1967

Gould, Jonathan. **Otis** Redding; an unfinished life. Jonathan Gould. Crown Archetype 2017 viii, 533 p.p illustrations (hardcover) $30   **92**
  1. African American singers -- Biography 2. Soul musicians -- United States -- Biography
  ISBN 0307453944; 9780307453969; 9780307453945
                                        LC 2016043388

In this book, author "Jonathan Gould finally does justice to [Otis] Redding's incomparable musical artistry, drawing on exhaustive research, the cooperation of the Redding family, and previously unavailable sources of information to present the first comprehensive portrait of the singer's background, his upbringing, and his professional career." (Publisher's note)

"Better late than never, the soul master receives his considerable due in this superbly researched and written biography." Kirkus
  Includes bibliographical references (pages [503]-516) and index.

Ribowsky, Mark. **Dreams** to remember; Otis Redding, Stax Records, and the transformation of Southern soul. Mark Ribowsky. Liveright Publishing Corp., A Division of W.W. Norton & Co. 2015 336 p. 8 plates; illustrations (hardcover) $27.95   **92**
  1. Soul music 2. Soul music -- History and criticism 3. Soul musicians -- United States -- Biography
  ISBN 0871408732; 9780871408730
                                        LC 2015009097

This biography, by Mark Ribowsky, describes how, "when he died in one of rock's string of tragic plane crashes, Otis Redding was only twenty-six, yet already the avatar of a new kind of soul music. The beating heart of Memphis-based Stax Records, he had risen to fame belting out gospel-flecked blues in stage performances that seemed to ignite not only a room but an entire generation." (Publisher's note)

"Unlike other performers who died far too young, Redding's death did not come out of abuse, and though he suffered, it was a universal human suffering--a pain in the heart that, partnered with unerring musical instinct, personal strength, and a little tenderness, he transformed into art. Ribowsky goes into the seamy side of the record business but also the sheer beauty and magic of the sixties soul music that Redding epitomized." Booklist
  Includes bibliographical references and index

Reed, Lou

DeCurtis, Anthony. **Lou** Reed; a life. Anthony DeCurtis. Little, Brown & Co. 2017 viii, 519 p.p illustrations (some color) (hardcover) $32   **92**
  1. Biography 2. Rock musicians -- United States -- Biography
  ISBN 9780316376556; 9780316376525
                                        LC 2017008817

This book, by Anthony DeCurtis, is "the essential biography of one of music's most influential icons: Lou Reed. As lead singer and songwriter for the Velvet Underground and a renowned solo artist, Lou Reed invented alternative rock. His music, at once a source of transcendent beauty and coruscating noise, violated all definitions of genre while speaking to millions of fans and inspiring generations of musicians." (Publisher's note)

"This is a rough-edged, straight-talking biography of a man who became a legend as much for his offstage life as for his musical skills." Booklist

Includes bibliographical references and index

Rehm, Diane

Rehm, Diane, 1936- **On** my own; Diane Rehm. Alfred A. Knopf 2016 176 p. (ebook) $48; (hardback) $23.95   **92**
  1. Widows 2. Bereavement 3. Right to die 4. Loss (Psychology) 5. Parkinson's disease 6. Adjustment (Psychology) 7. Bereavement -- United States 8. Widows -- United States -- Biography 9. Radio broadcasters -- United States -- Biography 10. Parkinson's disease -- Patients -- Family relationships
  ISBN 9781101875292; 9781101875285
                                        LC 2015023006

In this book, by Diane Rehm, "the beloved NPR radio host speaks out about the long drawn-out death (from Parkinson's) of her husband of fifty-four years, and of her struggle to reconstruct her life without him. . . . John's unnecessarily extended death—he begged to be helped to die—culminated in his taking matters into his own hands, simply refusing to take water, food, and medication. His heroic actions spurred Diane into becoming a kind of poster person for the 'right to die' movement." (Publisher's note)

"Rehm's forthright memoir, which probes the process of loss, grief, and renewal, will find a wide audience with fans of her show as well as many others facing this profound passage." Pub Wkly

Rehm, John B.

Rehm, Diane, 1936- **On** my own; Diane Rehm. Alfred A. Knopf 2016 176 p. (ebook) $48; (hardback) $23.95   **92**
  1. Widows 2. Bereavement 3. Right to die 4. Loss (Psychology) 5. Parkinson's disease 6. Adjustment (Psychology) 7. Bereavement -- United States 8. Widows -- United States -- Biography 9. Radio broadcasters -- United States -- Biography 10. Parkinson's disease -- Patients -- Family relationships
  ISBN 9781101875292; 9781101875285
                                        LC 2015023006

In this book, by Diane Rehm, "the beloved NPR radio host speaks out about the long drawn-out death (from Parkinson's) of her husband of fifty-four years, and of her struggle to reconstruct her life without him. . . . John's unnecessarily extended death—he begged to be helped to die—culminated in his taking matters into his own hands, simply refusing to take water, food, and medication. His heroic actions spurred Diane into becoming a kind of poster person for the 'right to die' movement." (Publisher's note)

"Rehm's forthright memoir, which probes the process of loss, grief, and renewal, will find a wide audience with fans of her show as well as many others facing this profound passage." Pub Wkly

Reichl, Ruth

Reichl, Ruth. **Comfort** me with apples; more adventures at the table. Random House 2001 302p $24.95; pa $13.95 **92**
  1. Memoirists 2. Food critics 3. Magazine editors
  ISBN 0-375-50195-9; 0-375-75873-9 pa
                                        LC 00-53355

Sequel to Tender at the bone (1998)

"In this second installment of her memoirs, {Reichl} retraces her route from married life on a commune in late-seventies Berkeley to her first job as a food critic, dining at expensive restaurants in Los Angeles with her glamorous editor. . . . Reichl writes with gusto, and her story has all the ingredients of a modern fairy tale: hard work, weird food, and endless curiosity." New Yorker

Reichl, Ruth. **Garlic** and sapphires. Penguin Press 2005 333p $24.95   **92**
  1. Memoirists 2. Food critics 3. Magazine editors

ISBN 1-594-20031-9

LC 2004-51362

"Reichl's ability to experience meals in such a dramatic way brings an infectious passion to her memoir. Reading this work . . . ensures that the next time readers sit down in a restaurant, they'll notice things they've never noticed before." Publ Wkly

Reinhardt, Django, 1910-1953

Dregni, Michael. **Django**: the life and music of a Gypsy legend. Oxford University Press 2004 326p il $35; pa $16.95 **92**

1. Guitarists 2. Jazz musicians

ISBN 0-19-516752-X; 0-19-530448-9 pa

LC 2004-6214

This "biography does its complex subject justice. And even when Dregni dallies overlong on some byways, his immersion in the period's history enriches his storytelling and our understanding. The panoramic results present Django Reinhardt as he has never been seen." N Y Times Book Rev

Includes bibliographical references

Rembrandt Harmenszoon van Rijn, 1606-1669

Schama, Simon. **Rembrandt's** eyes. Knopf 1999 640p il $50; pa $35   **92**

1. Artists 2. Etchers 3. Painters 4. Drafters

ISBN 0-679-40256-X; 0-375-70981-9 pa

LC 99-19971

Schama's prose unfurls the life of Rembrandt in all its pathos. From prodigy to pauper, the troubled genius of 17th century Dutch painting is intricately conceived as he rises and falls in a world of war, plague and stolid bourgeois comfort. . . . Schama's book is a marvel of storytelling: sometimes heart pounding, always sympathetic and coolly reasoned. Seamlessly joining social history and art, what a triumph of scholarship and imagination." Time

Renoir, Auguste, 1841-1919

White, Barbara Ehrlich. **Renoir**; an intimate biography. Barbara Ehrlich White. Thames & Hudson 2017 432 p. illustrations (some color) (hardcover) $39.95   **92**

1. Artists, French 2. Impressionism (Art) 3. Painters -- France -- Biography

ISBN 9780500774038; 0500239576; 9780500239575

LC 2017931859

This biography of Pierre-Auguste Renoir, by Barbara Ehrlich White, "fully reveals this most intriguing of Impressionist artists. The narrative is interspersed with more than 1,100 extracts from letters by, to, and about Renoir, 452 of which come from unpublished letters. . . . White's lifetime of research informs this fascinating biography that challenges common misconceptions surrounding Renoir's reputation." (Publisher's note)

"Studded with stirring quotations from unpublished letters and embellished with reproductions of many of Renoir's most-beloved works, this is a jewel of a biography, and it will be treasured by anyone interested in art." Booklist

Includes bibliographical references (pages 411-419) and index.

Retta

Retta (Performer) **So** close to being the sh*t, y'all don't even know; Retta. St. Martin's Press 2018 272 p. (hardcover) $26.99   **92**

1. Actors -- United States 2. Comedians -- United States 3. Conduct of life -- Humor 4. Actors -- United States -- Biography 5. Comedians -- United States -- Biography

ISBN 9781250109347; 9781250109354; 9781250199683

LC 2017056742

In this book of essays, "'Parks and Recreation' star Retta takes us on her not-so-meteoric rise from roaches to riches. . . . After winning Comedy Central's stand-up competition, she should be ready for prime time--but a fear of success derails her biggest dream. Whether reminiscing about her days as a contract chemist . . . or expertly stalking the cast of 'Hamilton,' Retta's unique voice and refreshing honesty will make you laugh, cry, and laugh so hard you'll cry." (Publisher's note)

Rhodes, William Reginald

Rhodes, William R. **Banker** to the world; leadership lessons from the front lines of global finance. [by] William R. Rhodes. McGraw-Hill 2011 xxxiii, 249p $25; ebook $25 **92**

1. Leadership 2. Decision making 3. Banks and banking 4. International finance 5. Bankers 6. Biography, Individual 7. Banks and banking, International

ISBN 978-0-07-170425-0; 0-07-170425-6; 978-0-07-170424-3 ebook; 0-07-170424-8 ebook

LC 2010032040

This book "should be required reading not only for other bankers, but also for Washington's would-be reformers of Wall Street, and most of all for the ordinary lay citizen dismayed by the persisting panic that has gripped us since 2007." Am Spectator

Includes bibliographical references

Rice, Anne, 1941-

Rice, Anne. **Called** out of darkness; a spiritual confession. Alfred A. Knopf 2008 245p $24   **92**

1. Authors 2. Novelists 3. Women authors 4. Spiritual life 5. Catholic Church 6. Authors, American

ISBN 0-307-26827-6; 978-0-307-26827-3

LC 2008-20192

This memoir by the author of Interview With the Vampire (1976) focuses on Rice's return to Catholicism.

"As plainly written as a Quaker spiritual journal, Rice's confession of faith will impress many who wouldn't think of reading vampire romances—and possibly many who read little else." Booklist

Includes bibliographical references

Richard III, King of England, 1452-1485

★ Horspool, David. **Richard** III; a ruler and his reputation. David Horspool. Bloomsbury USA, an imprint of Bloomsbury Publishing 2015 viii, 321 p.p $30   **92**

1. Great Britain -- Kings and rulers -- Biography 2. Kings and rulers -- Biography 3. Great Britain -- History -- Richard III, 1483-1485

ISBN 1620405091; 9781620405093

This book, by David Horspool, "dispassionately examines the legend as well as the man to uncover both what we know of the life of Richard, and the way that his reputation has been formed and re-formed over centuries. But beyond simply his reputation, there is no dispute that the last Plantagenet is a pivotal figure in English history." (Publisher's note)

Includes bibliographical references (pages 274-311) and index.

Skidmore, Chris. **Richard** III; England's most controversial king. Chris Skidmore. St. Martin's Press 2018 448 p. $29.99   **92**

1. Great Britain -- Kings and rulers -- Biography

ISBN 1250045487; 9781250045485

This book, by Chris Skidmore, presents "the authoritative biography of Richard III, England's most controversial king, a man alternately praised as a saint and cursed as a villain. . . . Skidmore draws on new manuscript evidence to reassess Richard's life and times. . . . [He] examines in intense detail Richard's inner nature and his complex relations with those around him to unravel the mystery of the last English monarch to die on the battlefield." (Publisher's note)

Richards, Cecile

Richards, Cecile. **Make** trouble; standing up, speaking out, and finding the courage to lead--my life story. Cecile Richards with Lauren Peterson. Touchstone 2018 304 p. (hardback) $27   **92**

1. Women's rights -- United States 2. Leadership in women -- United States 3. Women political activists -- Biography 4. Social justice -- United States -- History 5. Women's rights -- United States -- History 6. Leadership in women -- United States -- History
ISBN 9781501187599; 9781501187605

LC 2017061243

"From Cecile Richards--president of Planned Parenthood Federation of America . . . .--comes a story about learning to lead and make change, based on a lifetime of fighting for women's rights and social justice. . . . She shines a light on the people and lessons that have gotten her through good times and bad, and encourages readers to take risks, make mistakes, and make trouble along the way." (Publisher's note)

Richards, Keith

★ Richards, Keith. **Life**; [by] Keith Richards with James Fox. Little, Brown 2010 564p il $29.99; ebook $14.99 **92**

1. Guitarists 2. Rock musicians 3. Rolling Stones
ISBN 978-0-316-03438-8; 978-0-316-12856-8 ebook

This autobiography of the Rolling Stones guitarist "is way more than a revealing showbiz memoir. It is also a high-def, high-velocity portrait of the era when rock 'n' roll came of age, a raw report from deep inside the counterculture maelstrom of how that music swept like a tsunami over Britain and the United States. It's an eye-opening all-nighter in the studio with a master craftsman disclosing the alchemical secrets of his art. And it's the intimate and moving story of one man's long strange trip over the decades, told in dead-on, visceral prose without any of the pretense, caution or self-consciousness that usually attend great artists sitting for their self-portraits." N Y Times Book Rev

Richardson, Micheal Ray

Rosen, Charles, 1941- **Sugar**; Micheal Ray Richardson, eighties excess, and the NBA. Charley Rosen. University of Nebraska Press 2018 192 p. (hardback: alk. paper) $24.95 **92**

1. National Basketball Association -- History 2. Basketball -- United States -- History 3. Basketball players -- United States -- Biography
ISBN 9781496202161; 9781496206138; 9781496206145

LC 2017038778

In this book author Charley Rosen "describes the life defining pitfalls [Michael Ray] Richardson and other [NBA] players faced and considers key themes such as off court and on court racism, anti-Semitism, womanizing, . . . and drug and alcohol abuse by star players. . . . Rosen illuminates some of the more unseemly aspects of the NBA during this period, going behind the scenes to provide an account of what the league's darker side was like during its celebrated golden age." (Publisher's note)

Richter, Charles F., 1900-1985

Hough, Susan Elizabeth. **Richter's** scale; measure of an earthquake, measure of a man. Princeton University Press 2007 335p il $27.95 **92**

1. Scientists 2. Seismologists 3. College teachers
ISBN 978-0-691-12807-8; 0-691-12807-3

LC 2006-16480

"The discussions of the effects of earthquakes on land, structures, and people and the intense search for an understanding of the complex, underlying science will be of interest to many. Readers with substantially different levels of scientific knowledge will find the book comprehensible and interesting." Sci Books Films

Includes bibliographical references (p. 231-240)

Rickey, Branch, 1881-1965

Breslin, Jimmy, 1928-2017. **Branch** Rickey. Viking 2010 147p (Penguin lives series) $19.95 **92**

1. Baseball managers 2. Baseball executives 3. Baseball -- Biography 4. Biography, Individual 5. Brooklyn Dodgers (Baseball team)
ISBN 0-670-02249-7; 978-0-670-02249-6

LC 2010-35008

This is a biography of Branch Rickey, the president and general manager of the Brooklyn Dodgers, who, in 1947, brought Jackie Robinson to the team.

"Breslin reveals much about the development of baseball, the Dodgers' last years in Brooklyn, and the struggle to overcome the national pastime's racism while tracing the life, deeds, and some (but not all) of Branch Rickey's warts. A breezy read, this 'Penguin Life' is nonetheless insightful, humorous, and biting at times as it traces how the man dubbed 'the Mahatma' by sportswriters emerged from obscurity as an Idaho lawyer to develop the baseball farm system, multiple MLB winners, Vero Beach spring training, the scientific teaching of skills, and the MLB expansion that brought New York the Mets." Libr J

Includes bibliographical references

Ride, Sally

Sherr, Lynn. **Sally** Ride; America's first woman in space. Lynn Sherr. Simon & Schuster 2014 400 p. illustrations (hardcover) $28 **92**

1. Women astronauts 2. Women -- Biography 3. Astronauts -- United States -- Biography
ISBN 1476725764; 9781476725765; 9781476725772

LC 2013039647

This book is "The definitive biography of Sally Ride, America's first woman in space, with exclusive insights from Ride's family and partner, by [journalist Lynn Sherr] who covered NASA during its transformation from a test-pilot boys' club to a more inclusive elite. . . . Sally Ride made history as the first American woman in space." (Publisher's note)

"This is an intimate and enormously appealing biography of a fascinating woman, a triumph of research and sensitivity that lives up to its subject." Booklist

Includes bibliographical references and index

Rideau, Wilbert

Rideau, Wilbert. **In** the place of justice; a story of punishment and deliverance. Alfred A. Knopf 2010 366p il map $26.95 **92**

1. Thieves 2. Prisoners 3. Journalists 4. Murderers 5. Louisiana State Penitentiary
ISBN 978-0-307-26481-7; 0-307-26481-5

LC 2009038526

"In 1961, after a bungled bank robbery, Rideau was convicted of murder at the age of 19 and received a death sentence that was later commuted to life in prison at Louisiana's Angola penitentiary, then the most violent in the nation. Against all expectations, his own included, he turned his up-to-then cursed life around, becoming editor of the prison newsmagazine, the Angolite, and an NPR correspondent who published nationally acclaimed articles on prison violence, rape and sexual slavery, and the cruelty of the electric chair. Rideau frames his 44-year fight to get his conviction reduced to manslaughter and win parole (he succeeded in 2005) as a black man's struggle against a racist criminal justice establishment. . . . Rideau's story is a compelling reminder that rehabilitation should be the focus of a penal system." Publ Wkly

Riefenstahl, Leni, 1902-2003

Bach, Steven. **Leni**: the life and work of Leni Riefenstahl. A.A. Knopf 2007 368p il $30   **92**

1. Actors 2. Centenarians 3. Motion picture directors 4. Motion picture producers

ISBN 978-0-375-40400-9; 0-375-40400-7

LC 2006-49323

This is a biography of the filmmaker.

This "is a lively, incisive look at a compelling and somewhat appalling figure who demonstrated that beauty isn't always truth." Publ Wkly

Includes bibliographical references

Trimborn, Jurgen. **Leni** Riefenstahl; translated from the German by Edna McCown. Faber & Faber 2007 351p il $30   **92**

1. Actors 2. Centenarians 3. Motion picture directors 4. Motion picture producers

ISBN 978-0-374-18493-3; 0-374-18493-3

LC 2006-13263

Original German edition, 2002

This is a biography of the German filmmaker whose work includes Triumph of the Will, a propaganda film for Hitler, and Ölympia, a documentary of the 1936 Olympics in Berlin

Trimborn "interviewed Riefenstahl in 1997, when he was twenty-five, having already spent six years of 'intensive labor' on the project, and he briefly entertained the quixotic hope of writing a definitive book with her blessing and collaboration. Unwilling to misrepresent himself as a hagiographer, he was doomed to fail, though his disappointment does not seem to have warped his fair-mindedness. . . . [The author's] aim was to correct the murky published record and the 'attitudes' of his compatriots. One has to admire the sniperlike precision with which he takes out fugitive falsehoods that have lived under cover for a century." New Yorker

Riggs, Nina

★ Riggs, Nina. The **bright** hour; a memoir of living and dying. Nina Riggs. Simon & Schuster 2017 310 p. (hardback) $25   **92**

1. Autobiographies 2. Terminally ill -- Biography 3. Cancer patients -- Biography 4. Life 5. Death 6. Death -- Psychological aspects 7. Women poets, American -- Biography 8. Mothers -- United States -- Biography 9. Terminally ill -- United States -- Biography 10. Breast -- Cancer -- Patients -- United States -- Biography

ISBN 9781501169366; 9781501169359; 9781501169373

LC 2017007161

This book, by Nina Riggs, offers "an exquisite memoir about how to live--and love--every day with 'death in the room'. . . . [The author] was just thirty-seven years old when initially diagnosed with breast cancer. . . . Within a year, . . . [she] received the devastating news that her cancer was terminal. . . . Exploring motherhood, marriage, friendship, and memory, . . . Riggs's breathtaking memoir . . . . asks, what makes a meaningful life when one has limited time?" (Publisher's note)

"In this tender memoir Riggs displays a keen awareness of and reverence for all the moments of life—both the light, and the dark, 'the cruel, and the beautiful.'" Pub Wkly

Ripert, Eric

Chambers, Veronica. **32** yolks; from my mother's table to working the line. Eric Ripert, with Veronica Chambers. Random House 2016 256 p. (hardback: acid-free paper) $28   **92**

1. Cooks 2. Restaurants 3. Cooking, French 4. Coming of age -- France -- Paris 5. Cooks -- France -- Paris -- Biography 6. Restaurateurs -- France -- Paris -- Biography

ISBN 9780812992984

LC 2015050280

This memoir, by Eric Ripert, is a "coming-of-age story about the making of a French chef, from the culinary icon behind the renowned New York City restaurant Le Bernardin. Taking us from Eric Ripert's childhood in the south of France and the mountains of Andorra into the demanding kitchens of such legendary Parisian chefs as Joël Robuchon and Dominique Bouchet, . . .'32 Yolks' is the . . . story of how one of our greatest living chefs found himself . . . in the kitchen." (Publisher's note)

"Readers may know Ripert as the meditative host of the PBS series Avec Eric; a fan-favorite judge on Bravo's Top Chef; and the owner of Le Bernardin, a French seafood restaurant in New York. His roots, however, are far from that calm and thoughtful adult. This memoir tells of Ripert's tumultuous childhood in France where a love of excellent food was instilled in him early on. . . . Although the loving descriptions of flavors and cooking techniques will make some long for recipes, this narrative sheds light on the carefully controlled chaos behind the scenes at several top restaurants in the 1970s and 1980s. It will appeal to fans of Anthony Bourdain's Kitchen Confidential and Joe Bastianich and Mario Batali's Restaurant Man." LJ

Ripken, Cal, Jr.

Ripken, Cal. The **only** way I know; [by] Cal Ripken, Jr., and Mike Bryan. Viking 1997 326p il hardcover o.p. pa $12.95   **92**

1. Baseball players 2. Baseball -- Biography 3. Baltimore Orioles (Baseball team)

ISBN 0-670-87193-1; 0-14-026626-7 pa

LC 97-9159

"Cal Junior chronicles his moves through the minor leagues and into the majors in great detail, always pointing out what he learned at each step of the journey and who taught it to him. There are some great baseball anecdotes—especially involving fiery Oriole skipper Earl Weaver—and plenty of the behind-the-scenes detail." Booklist

Ritz, César, 1850-1918

Barr, Luke. **Ritz** & Escoffier; the hotelier, the chef, and the rise of the leisure class. Luke Barr. Clarkson Potter/Publishers 2018 320 p. (hardcover) $26   **92**

1. Hospitality industry -- History 2. Leisure class 3. Savoy Hotel (London, England) -- History 4. Hospitality industry -- Social aspects -- History -- 19th century 5. Hospitality industry -- Social aspects -- History -- 20th century

ISBN 9780804186292

LC 2017015344

In this book, author Luke Barr, "transports readers to turn-of-the-century London and Paris to discover how celebrated hotelier César Ritz and famed chef Auguste Escoffier joined forces at the Savoy Hotel to spawn the modern luxury hotel and restaurant, where women and American Jews mingled with British high society, signaling a new social order and the rise of the middle class." (Publisher's note)

" A well-researched, glitzy, and flawed history of conspicuous consumption." Kirkus

Includes bibliographical references and index

Rivera, Diego, 1886-1957

Marnham, Patrick. **Dreaming** with his eyes open; a life of Diego Rivera. University of California Press 2000 350p il pa $29.95 **92**

1. Artists 2. Painters 3. Artists, Mexican
ISBN 0-520-22408-6; 978-0-520-22408-7

LC 99-44964

First published 1998 by Knopf

"For the browsing public as well as specialists in European, Latin American, and American modern art, this book is not to be overlooked." Libr J

Includes bibliographical references

Rivera, Mariano, 1969-

Rivera, Mariano, 1969- The **closer**; Mariano Rivera, Wayne Coffey. Little, Brown & Co. 2014 280 p. ill. (some col.) (hardcover) $28 **92**

1. Baseball pitchers
ISBN 0316400734; 9780316400732; 9780316405621; 9780316277617

LC 2014934754

In this memoir, relief pitcher Mariano Rivera "his extraordinary story of survival, love, and baseball. . . . The thirteen-time All-Star discusses his drive to win; the secrets behind his legendary composure; the story of how he discovered his cut fastball; the untold, pitch-by-pitch account of the ninth inning of Game 7 in the 2001 World Series; and why the lowest moment of his career became one of his greatest blessings." (Publisher's note)

"[I]n this entertaining, admirably subdued autobiography, the glory is God's: Rivera's story brims with examples of his faith." Pub Wkly

Robbins, Jerome

★ Vaill, Amanda. **Somewhere**; the life of Jerome Robbins. Broadway Books 2006 675p il $40 **92**

1. Dancers 2. Choreographers 3. Theatrical directors
ISBN 0-7679-0420-6; 978-0-7679-0420-9

LC 2006-48960

This is a biography of the choreographer of such works as Afternoon of a Faun, On the Town, Gypsy, West Side Story, and Fiddler on the Roof.

"The book is essential reading for lovers of theater and dance." Publ Wkly

Includes bibliographical references

Robbins, Tom, 1932-

Robbins, Tom, 1932- **Tibetan** Peach Pie; A True Account of an Imaginative Life. Tom Robbins. HarperCollins 2014 28 p. $27.99 **92**

1. Autobiographies 2. American authors
ISBN 006226740X; 9780062267405

In this memoir by Tom Robbins, "we travel with Tommy Rotten--his mother's pet name for him--from his birth in Statesville, N.C., through his youth in Virginia--including a stint at Hargrave Military Academy--his meteorological training in the military, and his peripatetic pursuit of language and wonder. . . . Along the way, Robbins offers flashes of enlightenment into the writing of each of his novels." (Publishers Weekly)

"Each piece stands on its own, but when read side by side they develop into a powerful argument about magic and the necessity of imaginative, interior worlds." LJ

Robert I, King of Scots, 1274-1329

Penman, Michael. **Robert** the Bruce; King of Scots. Michael Penman. Yale University Press 2014 456 p. 16 unnumbered pages of plates (cl: alk. paper) $45 **92**

1. Kings and rulers 2. Scotland -- History 3. Scotland -- Kings and rulers -- Biography 4. Scotland -- History -- Robert I, 1306-1329
ISBN 0300148720; 9780300148725

LC 2014007172

This biography, by Michael Penman, is about "Robert the Bruce (1274–1329) [who] famously defeated the English at Bannockburn and became the hero king responsible for Scottish independence. . . . Penman investigates Robert's resettlement of lands and offices, the development of Scotland's parliaments, his handling of plots to overthrow him, his relations with his family and allies, his piety and court ethos, and his conscious development of an image of kingship." (Publisher's note)

"Penman details the social forces Robert faced at the time, from the reconfiguring of aristocratic and ecclesiastical interests to the development of a parliament, from the establishment of a national identity to creation of the symbols and ceremonies of the monarchy. Dense with research, Penman's look at Scotland's King Robert the Bruce fascinates." Booklist

Includes bibliographical references and index

Roberts, Deborah, 1960-

Roberts, Deborah. **Been** there, done that; family wisdom for modern times. Al Roker, Deborah Roberts with Laura Morton. New American Library 2016 288 p. (hardback) $27 **92**

1. Parenting 2. Family life 3. Parenting -- Anecdotes 4. Family life -- Anecdotes 5. African American television journalists -- United States -- Anecdotes
ISBN 0451466365; 9780451466365

LC 2015031342

Authors Al Roker and Deborah Roberts presents this "collection of life lessons, hard-won wisdom, and instructive family anecdotes from [their] lives, from their parents and grandparents, and from dear friends, famous and not. Here, Al and Deborah candidly share childhood obstacles like obesity and growing up in the segregated south; the challenges and blessings that come from raising very different kids; hard-won truths about marriage and career." (Publisher's note)

"Despite Roker's tendency toward hackneyed 'dad jokes' and sometimes trite observations (e.g., technology can get in the way of genuine interactions), this is an entertaining, encouraging read and a sweet testament to the couple's devotion to their marriage and family." Publisher's Weekly

Robertson, Robbie

Robertson, Robbie. **Testimony**; Robbie Robertson. Crown Archetype 2016 512 p. ill. (some color), portraits (hardcover) $30.00 **92**

1. Rock musicians -- Canada -- Biography
ISBN 9780307889782; 9780307889799; 9780307889805

LC 2016031782

In this memoir, guitarist and songwriter Robbie Robertson narrates "the journey that led him to some of the most pivotal events in music history. He recounts the adventures of his half-Jewish, half-Mohawk upbringing on the Six Nations Indian Reserve and on the gritty streets of Toronto; . . . the wild early years on the road with rockabilly legend Ronnie Hawkins and The Hawks; . . . [and] the formation of the Band and the forging of their unique sound," (Publisher's note)

"This book will enrich and delight any rock fan." LJ

Robeson, Eslanda Goode, 1896-1965

Ransby, Barbara. **Eslanda**; the large and unconventional life of Mrs. Paul Robeson. Barbara Ransby. Yale University

Press 2013 424 p. (cloth: alk. paper) $35   **92**
1. Harlem Renaissance 2. African American anthropologists -- Biography 3. Women anthropologists -- United States -- Biography
ISBN 0300124341; 9780300124347

                    LC 2012022359

In this book, Barbara Ransby "details the accomplishments, struggles and impact of Eslanda Cardozo Goode Robeson. . . . Ransby outlines Essie's early life and family history, delves into the high points of her married life in Harlem, and recounts her growing awareness and tenacious engagement in the numerous political causes she supported." (Kirkus)

Includes bibliographical references and index

Robeson, Paul, 1898-1976

Ransby, Barbara. **Eslanda**; the large and unconventional life of Mrs. Paul Robeson. Barbara Ransby. Yale University Press 2013 424 p. (cloth: alk. paper) $35   **92**
1. Harlem Renaissance 2. African American anthropologists -- Biography 3. Women anthropologists -- United States -- Biography
ISBN 0300124341; 9780300124347

                    LC 2012022359

In this book, Barbara Ransby "details the accomplishments, struggles and impact of Eslanda Cardozo Goode Robeson. . . . Ransby outlines Essie's early life and family history, delves into the high points of her married life in Harlem, and recounts her growing awareness and tenacious engagement in the numerous political causes she supported." (Kirkus)

Includes bibliographical references and index

Robeson, Paul. **Here** I stand; with a preface by Lloyd L. Brown and a new introduction by Sterling Stuckey. Beacon Press 1988 xxxvi, 121p hardcover o.p. pa $14   **92**
1. Actors 2. Singers 3. Football players 4. Civil rights activists 5. African Americans -- Civil rights
ISBN 0-8070-6445-9 pa

                    LC 87-47882

First published 1958 by Othello Associates

"Combining a narrative of his life and travels with commentary on history and the events of his time, [the author] relates the fight against segregation to social progress for all Americans, white and black, claiming that 'white supremacy' disenfranchises and impoverishes white workers and white farmers as well as black." Libr J

Robeson, Paul. The **undiscovered** Paul Robeson; the early years (1898-1939) Wiley 2001 383p il $30   **92**
1. Actors 2. Singers 3. Football players 4. Civil rights activists 5. African Americans -- Biography
ISBN 0-471-24265-9

                    LC 2001-17656

This is the first volume of a biography of the African American actor, singer and political activist by his son. It covers the years from Robeson's birth in Princeton, N.J., through the 1930s

"Extensively illustrated with personal photographs, this is a unique account of a brilliant but troubled man." Libr J

Includes bibliographical references

Robespierre, Maximilien, 1758-1794

McPhee, Peter. **Robespierre**; a revolutionary life. Peter McPhee. Yale University Press 2012 299 p. (cloth: alk. paper) $40   **92**
1. Statesmen -- France -- Biography 2. Revolutionaries -- France -- Biography 3. France -- History -- Revolution, 1789-1799 4.

France -- Politics and government -- 1789-1799 5. France -- History -- Reign of Terror, 1793-1794
ISBN 0300118112; 9780300118117

                    LC 2011027640

This book provides a "treatise on the life of one of France's most notorious revolutionaries. Maximilien Robespierre (1758-1794) . . . [became] a leader of the leftist Jacobins in the revolutionary National Convention. . . . Robespierre began his career as an opponent of capital punishment but ended it obsessed with omnipresent treasonous conspiracies and meting out death without trial to perceived enemies of the state . . . . [Author Peter] McPhee . . . strives to rehabilitate Robespierre somewhat, arguing that the sanguinary excesses of the period were necessary to sustain the revolution against attacks from without and within, and that Robespierre's role in them was later exaggerated by other deputies seeking to minimize their own culpability." (Kirkus)

Includes bibliographical references

Robinson, Betty, 1911-1999

Montillo, Roseanne. **Fire** on the track; Betty Robinson and the triumph of the early Olympic women. Roseanne Montillo. Crown Publishers 2017 285 p. illustrations (hardback) $27 **92**
1. Biography 2. Women runners -- United States -- Biography 3. Women Olympic athletes -- United States -- Biography 4. Runners (Sports) -- United States -- Biography
ISBN 9781101906170; 9781101906156

                    LC 2017008783

In this biography, by Roseanne Montillo, "when Betty Robinson assumed the starting position at the 1928 Olympic Games in Amsterdam, she was participating in what was only her fourth-ever organized track meet. She crossed the finish line as a gold medalist and the fastest woman in the world. This improbable athletic phenom was an ordinary high school student, discovered running for a train in rural Illinois mere months before her Olympic debut. Amsterdam made her a star." (Publsher's note)

"Robinson's life story and important role in breaking down barriers for women has already been optioned for film; this well-balanced biography and history of a groundbreaking female track star recalls a time and an athlete worth celebrating." LJ

Includes bibliographical references (pages [253]-273) and index.

Robinson, Jackie, 1919-1972

Robinson, Jackie. **I** never had it made; an autobiography. by Jackie Robinson as told to Alfred Duckett; foreword by Cornel West; introduction by Hank Aaron. Ecco Press 1995 xxii, 275p il hardcover o.p. pa $13.95   **92**
1. Baseball players 2. African American athletes 3. Army officers 4. Baseball -- Biography
ISBN 0-06-055597-1

                    LC 94-45279

This book "focuses on Robinson's political involvements after his career ended in 1956 and his friendships with such diverse characters as Martin Luther King, Malcolm X, William Buckley and Nelson Rockefeller." Publ Wkly

Robinson, Sugar Ray, 1921-1989

★ Haygood, Wil. **Sweet** thunder; the life and times of Sugar Ray Robinson. Alfred A. Knopf 2009 461p il $27.95 **92**
1. Boxers (Persons) 2. Boxing -- Biography
ISBN 978-1-4000-4497-9

                    LC 2009-5534

This "book is certainly one of the best biographies of a boxer ever written . . . [and] an important contribution to both sports literature and African American studies." Washington Post Book World

Includes bibliographical references

Robison, John Elder, 1957-

Robison, John Elder. **Look** me in the eye; my life with Asperger's. Crown Publishers 2007 288p $25.95   **92**

  1. Photographers 2. Asperger's syndrome 3. Mechanics (Persons) 4. Restorers 5. Memoirists

  ISBN 978-0-307-39598-6; 0-307-39598-7

          LC 2007-13139

In this memoir, the author describes growing up with Asperger's syndrome (which went undiagnosed until he was 40 years old), dealing with an alcoholic father and a mentally unstable mother, and developing an affinity for machines that would eventually lead him to a career restoring classic cars.

"Robison's memoir is must reading for its unblinking (as only an Aspergian can) glimpse into the life of a person who had to wait decades for the medical community to catch up with him." Booklist

Includes bibliographical references

Rockefeller, Nelson A. (Nelson Aldrich), 1908-1979

Smith, Richard Norton, 1953- **On** His Own Terms; A Life of Nelson Rockefeller. Richard Norton Smith. Random House Inc 2014 640 p. illustrations, portraits $38   **92**

  1. Politicians -- United States 2. Vice-presidents -- United States

  ISBN 0375505806; 9780375505805

This biography by Richard Norton Smith tells how, "Nelson [Rockefeller] coveted the White House from childhood. . . . Before he was thirty he had helped his father develop Rockefeller Center and his mother establish the Museum of Modern Art. At thirty-two he was Franklin Roosevelt's wartime coordinator for Latin America. As New York's four-term governor he set national standards in education, the environment, and urban policy." (Publisher's note)

Rockwell, Norman, 1894-1978

Solomon, Deborah, 1957- **American** mirror; the life and art of Norman Rockwell. Deborah Solomon. Farrar Straus & Giroux 2013 512 p. illustrations (some color) (hardback) $28   **92**

  1. Illustrators -- United States 2. Painters -- United States -- Biography 3. Illustrators -- United States -- Biography

  ISBN 0374113092; 9780374113094

          LC 2013021682

LA Times Book Prize Finalist: Biography (2013)

This biography of Norman Rockwell "reveals an enormously complicated man whose wholesome vision of America was not merely commercial kitsch, but art that sprung from an emotional life fraught with anxiety, depression, and self-doubt. This sympathetic portrait depicts a repressed and humble Rockwell. . . . Thrice married and an apathetic husband, he clearly preferred the companionship of male friends and was likely a closeted homosexual." (Publishers Weekly)

"Praised for her biographies of Jackson Pollock and Joseph Cornell, noted art critic Solomon makes a surprise leap to rock-solid Americana artist Norman Rockwell. But as she says, Rockwell painted "a history of the American people that had never happened," and she goes on to detail his not-so-apple-pie personality." LJ

Includes bibliographical references (pages 443-468) and index

Rodriguez, Daniel, 1988-

Rodriguez, Daniel. **Rise**; a soldier, a dream, and a promise kept. Daniel Rodriguez; contributions by Joe Layden. Houghton Mifflin Harcourt 2014 256 p. 8 plates; illustrations (hardback) $26   **92**

  1. College football 2. Afghan War, 2001- 3. Military personnel -- United States 4. Layden, Joseph, 1959- 5. Clemson Tigers (Football team) 6. United States. Army -- Biography 7. Soldiers -- United States -- Biography 8. Afghan War, 2001- -- Personal narratives, American 9. Iraq War, 2003-2011 -- Personal narratives, American

  ISBN 0544365607; 9780544365605

          LC 2014016742

Author Daniel Rodriguez presents this memoir, a "narrative of a young soldier, his unlikely dream, and how he found his way out of darkness. He fought in the infamous Battle of Kamdesh and for his bravery he was awarded a Purple Heart and the Bronze Star. Daniel returned home . . . in the clutches of PTSD, He embarked on a grueling training regimen and . . . earned a spot on the Clemson University football team." (Publisher's note)

"This is an uncommonly solid memoir. Recommended for all readers, particularly those interested in sports and military books." LJ

Rodriguez, Richard, 1944-

Rodriguez, Richard. **Hunger** of memory; the education of Richard Rodriguez: an autobiography. Bantam trade pbk. ed.; Bantam Books 2004 212p pa $15   **92**

  1. Poets 2. Authors 3. Television personalities 4. Essayists 5. Memoirists 6. Mexican Americans -- Biography

  ISBN 0-553-38251-9

          LC 2004-269979

First published 1982 by Godine

An account "of the coming of age of a person of Mexican descent and culture in American society and the inevitable transition in the private life of his family. Rodriguez focuses on his educational experiences, from his parochial elementary school . . . to his university years and subsequent experience as an educator." Libr J

Rogers, Fred

★ King, Maxwell. **The good** neighbor; the life and work of Fred Rogers. Maxwell King. Abrams Press 2018 416 p. $30   **92**

  1. Television personalities -- United States

  ISBN 9781419727726

          LC 2017956802

This book, by Maxwell King is "the first full-length biography of Fred Rogers. . . . Drawing on original interviews, oral histories, and archival documents, King traces Rogers's personal, professional, and artistic life through decades of work, including a surprising decision to walk away from the show to make television for adults, only to return to the neighborhood with increasingly sophisticated episodes, written in collaboration with experts on childhood development." (Publisher's note)

"Grown-up fans, pop culture enthusiasts, and anyone interested in the history of educational television and child development will be inspired. An excellent and timely addition to most collections." Library Journal

Rogers, Jimmy

Goins, Wayne Everett. **Blues** all day long; the Jimmy Rogers story. Wayne Everett Goins; foreword by Kim Wilson. University of Illinois Press 2014 416 p. 16 plates (Music in American life) (pbk.: alk. paper) $29   **92**

  1. Guitarists 2. Blues musicians 3. Guitarists -- United States -- Biography 4. Jazz musicians -- United States -- Biography

  ISBN 0252080173; 9780252038570; 9780252080173; 9780252096495

          LC 2014007477

In this biography of musician Jimmy Rogers author "Wayne Everett

Goins mines seventy-five hours of interviews with Rogers' family, collaborators, and peers to follow a life spent in the blues. Goins' account takes Rogers from recording Chess classics and barnstorming across the South to a late-in-life renaissance that included new music, entry into the Blues Hall of Fame, and high profile tours with Eric Clapton and the Rolling Stones." (Publisher's note)

"Goins enthusiastically tracks Rogers' early years playing in the juke-joint South and his arrival in Chicago in 1945, where he began his dynamic, downright telepathic collaboration with Muddy Waters. Fluent in the blues vernacular, Goins gleans fresh facts and vivid memories from dozens of lively interviews to capture the energy and struggles of the Chicago blues scene, from Maxwell Street to the Chess Records studios, as he tracks the ups and downs of devoted family man Rogers' career with Waters, Little Walter, Howlin' Wolf, and many others. Rogers' story, including his retreat from music during the 1960s, triumphant return, and international stardom, is engrossing, and Goins' zeal and nimble expressiveness are thrilling as he praises Rogers' "special brand of lyrics," his "irresistible, buttery-smooth vocal quality," and his "highly sophisticated melodic, harmonic, and rhythmic style" while celebrating Rogers' "timeless passion and conviction." Booklist

Includes bibliographical references, discography, and index

Rogers, Robbie

Marcus, Eric. **Coming** out to play; Robbie Rogers with Eric Marcus. Penguin Books 2014 240 p. color illustrations $17 **92**

1. Gay men 2. Soccer players 3. Gay athletes -- United States -- Biography 4. Soccer players -- United States -- Biography
ISBN 014312661X; 9780143126614

LC 2014011229

In this book, professional soccer player Robbie Rogers " takes readers on his incredible journey from terrified teenager to a trailblazing out and proud professional soccer player for the L.A. Galaxy, who has embraced his new identity as a role model and champion for those still struggling with the secrets that keep them from living their dreams." (Publisher's note)

"Rogers's debut is great inspiration for people of all ages struggling with shame and grappling with identity issues with regard to sexuality or otherwise. Those who enjoy memoir and stories of people who overcome difficulty will embrace this account." LJ

Roiphe, Anne Richardson, 1935-

Roiphe, Anne Richardson. **Art** and madness; a memoir of lust without reason. [by] Anne Roiphe. Nan A. Talese/Doubleday 2011 220p il $24.95 **92**

1. Authors 2. Novelists 3. Women authors 4. Essayists 5. Authors, American 6. Biography, Individual
ISBN 9780385531641

LC 2010-28051

This book recounts the lost years of Anne Roiphe's twenties, when the author put her dreams of becoming a writer on hold to devote herself to the magnetic but coercive male artists of the period.

"Roiphe's narrative moves in punchy, spare episodes, nonchronologically and erratically, veering from past to present tense, and requiring effort on the part of the reader. Yet she is a masterly writer: her work presents vivid, priceless snapshots of the roiling era of Communist hysteria, faddish homosexuality, male privilege, and the heartbreaking fragility of talented men and their dreams of fame." Publ Wkly

Roiphe, Anne Richardson. **Epilogue**; a memoir. [by] Anne Roiphe. Harper 2008 214p il $24.95 **92**

1. Widows 2. Authors 3. Novelists 4. Bereavement 5. Women authors 6. Essayists 7. Authors, American

ISBN 978-0-06-125462-8; 0-06-125462-2

LC 2008-34530

The author "tells an unflinching and unsentimental story of widowhood's stupefying disquiet, of surviving love and living on." Publ Wkly

Roker, Al, 1954-

Roberts, Deborah. **Been** there, done that; family wisdom for modern times. Al Roker, Deborah Roberts with Laura Morton. New American Library 2016 288 p. (hardback) $27 **92**

1. Parenting 2. Family life 3. Parenting -- Anecdotes 4. Family life -- Anecdotes 5. African American television journalists -- United States -- Anecdotes
ISBN 0451466365; 9780451466365

LC 2015031342

Authors Al Roker and Deborah Roberts presents this "collection of life lessons, hard-won wisdom, and instructive family anecdotes from [their] lives, from their parents and grandparents, and from dear friends, famous and not. Here, Al and Deborah candidly share childhood obstacles like obesity and growing up in the segregated south; the challenges and blessings that come from raising very different kids; hard-won truths about marriage and career." (Publisher's note)

"Despite Roker's tendency toward hackneyed 'dad jokes' and sometimes trite observations (e.g., technology can get in the way of genuine interactions), this is an entertaining, encouraging read and a sweet testament to the couple's devotion to their marriage and family." Publisher's Weekly

Roosevelt family

Mann, William J. The **wars** of the Roosevelts; the ruthless rise of America's greatest political family. William J. Mann. HarperCollins 2016 640 p. illustrations, portraits (ebook) $32.99; $35 **92**

ISBN 9780062383358; 0062383337; 9780062383334

LC 2016046398

This book, by William J. Mann, "presents a provocative, thoroughly modern revisionist biographical history of one of America's greatest and most influential families—the Roosevelts—exposing heretofore unknown family secrets and detailing complex family rivalries with his signature cinematic flair. . . . Mann argues that the Roosevelts' rise to power and prestige was actually driven by a series of intense personal contest that at times devolved into blood sport." (Publisher's note)

"Perhaps best known for his popular film biographies and histories, and thus no stranger to tales of scandal and coverup, feuds and intrigue, Mann writes sympathetically about all the Roosevelts but particularly the black sheep, the nonconformists whose births into this powerful family imposed special burdens." Kirkus

Includes bibliographical references (pages 535-590) and index.

McCullough, David G. **Mornings** on horseback; {by} David McCullough. Simon & Schuster 1981 445p il hardcover o.p. pa $16 **92**

1. Governors 2. Presidents 3. Vice-presidents 4. Nobel laureates for peace 5. Presidents -- United States
ISBN 0-671-44754-8 pa

LC 81-1697

This biography follows Theodore Roosevelt from his childhood to his defeat for mayor of New York and marriage to Edith Carow in 1886.

"Based on diligent and thorough research, with emphasis on family, physical ailments, and friends, and written with verve and color, this is a stimulating book that will appeal to the general reader." Libr J

Includes bibliographical references

Peyser, Marc. **Hissing** cousins; the untold story of Eleanor Roosevelt and Alice Roosevelt Longworth. Marc Peyser and Timothy Dwyer. Nan A. Talese/Doubleday 2015 352 p. 8 plates; illustrations (alk. paper) $28.95 **92**
1. Cousins 2. Presidents' spouses -- United States 3. Cousins -- United States -- Biography 4. Presidents' spouses -- United States -- Biography
ISBN 0385536011; 9780385536011

LC 2014026766

This book, by Marc Peyser and Timothy Dwyer, is a "double biography of first cousins Eleanor Roosevelt and Alice Roosevelt Longworth. . . . Do-gooder Eleanor was committed to social justice but hated the limelight; acid-tongued Alice, who became the wife of philandering Republican congressman Nicholas Longworth, was an opponent of big government who gained notoriety for her cutting remarks." (Publisher's note)

"Peyser and Dwyer's detailed and witty double biography is hard to put down, a fascinating look at an era and two exceptionally strong, intelligent women." Booklist

Includes bibliographical references and index

Untold story of Eleanor Roosevelt and Alice Roosevelt Longworth

Roosevelt, Eleanor, 1884-1962

★ Bell-Scott, Patricia. The **firebrand** and the First Lady; portrait of a friendship: Pauli Murray, Eleanor Roosevelt, and the struggle for social justice. Patricia Bell-Scott. Alfred A. Knopf 2016 480 p. illustrations hbk $30 **92**
1. Female friendship -- United States 2. African American feminists -- Biography 3. Episcopal Church -- Clergy -- Biography 4. African American intellectuals -- Biography 5. Presidents' spouses -- United States -- Biography 6. Women social reformers -- United States -- Biography 7. African American women civil rights workers -- Biography
ISBN 0679446524; 9780679446521

LC 2015014872

Carnegie Medal Shortlist: Nonfiction (2017); National Book Awards Longlist: Nonfiction (2016)

This book, by Patricia Bell-Scott, profiles the figures of Pauli Murray and Eleanor Roosevelt. It "tells the story of how a brilliant writer-turned-activist, granddaughter of a mulatto slave, and the first lady of the United States, whose ancestry gave her membership in the Daughters of the American Revolution, forged an enduring friendship that changed each of their lives and helped to alter the course of race and racism in America." (Publisher's note)

"Bell-Scott's groundbreaking portrait of these two tireless and innovative champions of human dignity adds an essential and edifying facet to American history." Booklist

Includes bibliographical references and index

Cook, Blanche Wiesen. **Eleanor** Roosevelt. v2 Viking 1999 686p v2 hardcover o.p. pa $20 **92**
1. Diplomats 2. Columnists 3. Humanitarians 4. Social activists 5. Biography, Individual 6. Spouses of presidents 7. United Nations officials 8. Presidents' spouses -- United States
ISBN 0-14-017894-5 pa

This is the second volume of Cook's projected three-volume biography of Eleanor Roosevelt. Her first book encompassed the years 1884 to 1933. The present volume "covers the Depression years of 1933 to 1938, from F.D.R.'s first Inauguration to the eve of World War II." (Time) Bibliography. Index.

"Cook is unafraid to take on difficult issues . . . thus rendering the biography not simply a riveting read but also a profoundly moving and wise account of how history has been shaped by the intricacies of the human heart, mind and spirit." Publ Wkly

Includes bibliographical references

Goodwin, Doris Kearns. **No** ordinary time; Franklin and Eleanor Roosevelt: the home front in World War II. Simon & Schuster 1994 759p il hardcover o.p. pa $18 **92**
1. Diplomats 2. Governors 3. Presidents 4. People with disabilities 5. Columnists 6. Philatelists 7. Humanitarians 8. Social activists 9. Spouses of presidents 10. United Nations officials 11. United States -- History -- 1933-1945 12. World War, 1939-1945 -- United States
ISBN 0-684-80448-4 pa

LC 94-28565

"This is a nearly day-by-day account of the doings of Franklin and Eleanor Roosevelt during the Second World War. While Eleanor was championing the rights of female munitions workers and of Negroes in segregated Army barracks, her husband was making and breaking policy." New Yorker

Includes bibliographical references

★ Quinn, Susan. **Eleanor** and Hick; The Love Affair That Shaped a First Lady. Susan Quinn. Penguin Group USA 2016 416 p. illustrations, portraits (hardcover) $30; (ebook) $95 **92**
1. Female friendship 2. Presidents' spouses -- United States
ISBN 9781594205408; 9780735289413; 159420540X

LC 2016303873

This book by Susan Quinn offers an "intimate account of the love between Eleanor Roosevelt and reporter Lorena Hickok—a relationship that, over more than three decades, transformed both women's lives and empowered them to play significant roles in one of the most tumultuous periods in American history. . . . The bond these women shared was grounded in their determination to better their troubled world." (Publisher's note)

"A relentlessly captivating study of two remarkable individuals who helped extend the roles of American women in the public policy realm." Kirkus

Includes bibliographical references (pages 363-389) and index.

Roosevelt, Franklin D. (Franklin Delano), 1882-1945

Brands, H. W. **Traitor** to his class; the privileged life and radical presidency of Franklin Delano Roosevelt. Doubleday 2008 888p il $35 **92**
1. Governors 2. Presidents 3. People with disabilities 4. Philatelists 5. Presidents -- United States
ISBN 978-0-385-51958-8; 0-385-51958-3

LC 2008-15164

This is a study of Franklin D. Roosevelt's life and career.

"A thoroughly readable, scrupulously fair assessment of the one president who could inspire a Mt. Rushmore makeover." Kirkus

Includes bibliographical references

Brinkley, Douglas. **Rightful** heritage; Franklin D. Roosevelt and the land of America. Douglas Brinkley. HarperCollins 2016 768 p. charts, illustrations, maps (hardcover) $35 **92**
1. Environmental protection -- United States
ISBN 9780062089236; 0062089234

This book, by Douglas Brinkley, is a political profile of "Franklin Delano Roosevelt, chronicling his essential yet under-sung legacy as the founder of the Civilian Conservation Corps (CCC) and premier protector of America's public lands. FDR built from scratch dozens of State Park systems and scenic roadways." (Publisher's note)

"Brinkley vividly tracks Roosevelt's 'political know-how, legislative muscle, and fearlessness' from a unique and important perspective in this engrossing and richly illuminating portrait of one of the American environment's most ardent and effective champions." Booklist

Includes bibliographical references and index.

★ Dallek, Robert. **Franklin** D. Roosevelt; a political life. Robert Dallek. Viking 2017 x, 692 p.p illustrations (hardcover) $40 **92**

1. Biography 2. Presidents -- United States -- Biography 3. United States -- Politics and government -- 1933-1945 4. United States -- Politics and government -- 1919-1933

ISBN 9780698181724; 9780525427902

LC 2017032686

This biography of former U.S. President Franklin D. Roosevelt, by Robert Dallek, "takes a fresh look at the many compelling questions that have attracted all his biographers: how did a man who came from so privileged a background become the greatest presidential champion of the country's needy? How did someone who never won recognition for his intellect foster revolutionary changes in the country's economic and social institutions?" (Publisher's note)

"The result is a comprehensive retelling of a major American life that will rank among the standard biographies of its subject." Pub Wkly

Includes bibliographical references (pages 665-671) and index.

Goodwin, Doris Kearns. **No** ordinary time; Franklin and Eleanor Roosevelt: the home front in World War II. Simon & Schuster 1994 759p il hardcover o.p. pa $18 **92**

1. Diplomats 2. Governors 3. Presidents 4. People with disabilities 5. Columnists 6. Philatelists 7. Humanitarians 8. Social activists 9. Spouses of presidents 10. United Nations officials 11. United States -- History -- 1933-1945 12. World War, 1939-1945 -- United States

ISBN 0-684-80448-4 pa

LC 94-28565

"This is a nearly day-by-day account of the doings of Franklin and Eleanor Roosevelt during the Second World War. While Eleanor was championing the rights of female munitions workers and of Negroes in segregated Army barracks, her husband was making and breaking policy." New Yorker

Includes bibliographical references

Lelyveld, Joseph. **His** final battle; Franklin Roosevelt in the last months. Joseph Lelyveld. Alfred A. Knopf 2016 416 p. (hardcover) $30 **92**

1. Presidents -- United States -- Health 2. Presidents -- United States -- Biography 3. United States -- Foreign relations -- 1933-1945 4. United States -- Politics and government -- 1933-1945

ISBN 0385350791; 9780385350792

LC 2015050730

This book, by Joseph Lelyveld, examines the "narrative threads of [Franklin] Roosevelt's final months, showing how he juggled the strategic, political, and personal choices he faced as the war, his presidency, and his life raced in tandem to their climax. Lelyveld examines the choices Roosevelt faced, shining new light on his state of mind, preoccupations, and motives, both as leader of the wartime alliance and in his personal life." (Publisher's note)

"An elegant, affecting work that offers fresh insights on a much-mythologized president." Kirkus

Includes bibliographical references and index

Smith, Jean Edward. **FDR**. Random House 2007 858p il $35 **92**

1. Governors 2. Presidents 3. People with disabilities 4. Philatelists 5. Presidents -- United States

ISBN 978-1-4000-6121-1; 1-4000-6121-0

LC 2006-43087

Smith's "FDR is at once a careful, intelligent synopsis of the existing Roosevelt scholarship (the sheer bulk of which is huge) and a meticulous reinterpretation of the man and his record. Smith pays more attention to Roosevelt's personal life than have most previous biographers. He is openly sympathetic yet ready to criticize when that is warranted, and to do so in sharp terms; he conveys the full flavor and import of Roosevelt's career without ever bogging down in detail." Washington Post Book World

Includes bibliographical references

Roosevelt, Quentin, 1897-1918.

Burns, Eric. The **Golden** Lad; The Haunting Story of Quentin and Theodore Roosevelt. by Eric Burns. W W Norton & Co Inc 2016 300 p. illustrations $26.95 **92**

1. Father-son relationship 2. Presidents -- United States -- Children

ISBN 1605989517; 9781605989518

This book, by Eric Burns, is a biography of Theodore Roosevelt and his youngest son Quentin. "How does looking at Theodore's relationship with his son, and understanding him as a father, tell us something new about this larger-than-life-man? Does it reveal a more human side? A more hypocritical side? Or simply, if tragically, a nature so surprisingly sensitive, despite the bluster, that he would die of a broken heart?" (Publisher's note)

"Burns's unique, stirring account of America's most colorful president allows Teddy Roosevelt, the man and father, to step off the page." Pub Wkly

Includes bibliographical references (pages 181-184) and index.

Roosevelt, Theodore, 1858-1919

Brinkley, Douglas. The **wilderness** warrior; Theodore Roosevelt and the crusade for America. Harper 2009 940p il map $34.99 **92**

1. Nature conservation 2. Conservation of natural resources 3. Biography, Individual 4. Presidents -- United States 5. Wilderness areas -- United States 6. Conservation of natural resources -- United States -- History -- 20th century

ISBN 978-0-06-056528-2; 0-06-056528-4

This biography of the 26th president of the United States focuses on his interests and activities on behalf of conservation and nature.

The author "has absorbed a huge amount of research, but encyclopedic inclusiveness and repetition occasionally mar narrative movement. . . . But this book has Rooseveltian energy. It is largehearted, full of the vitality of its subject and a palpable love for the landscape it describes." N Y Times Book Rev

Includes bibliographical references

Burns, Eric. The **Golden** Lad; The Haunting Story of Quentin and Theodore Roosevelt. by Eric Burns. W W Norton & Co Inc 2016 300 p. illustrations $26.95 **92**

1. Father-son relationship 2. Presidents -- United States -- Children

ISBN 1605989517; 9781605989518

This book, by Eric Burns, is a biography of Theodore Roosevelt and his youngest son Quentin. "How does looking at Theodore's relationship with his son, and understanding him as a father, tell us something new about this larger-than-life-man? Does it reveal a more human side? A more hypocritical side? Or simply, if tragically, a nature so surprisingly sensitive, despite the bluster, that he would die of a broken heart?" (Publisher's note)

"Burns's unique, stirring account of America's most colorful president allows Teddy Roosevelt, the man and father, to step off the page." Pub Wkly

Includes bibliographical references (pages 181-184) and index.

Cooper, John Milton. The **warrior** and the priest: Woodrow Wilson and Theodore Roosevelt; [by] John Milton Cooper, Jr. Belknap Press 1983 442p il hardcover o.p. pa $20.95 **92**
1. Governors 2. Presidents 3. Vice-presidents 4. College presidents 5. Nobel laureates for peace 6. Presidents -- United States 7. United States -- Politics and government -- 1898-1919
ISBN 0-674-94751-7 pa

LC 83-6021
The author's "distinctions are sharp, his insights original, his judgments balanced and his narrative unfailingly graceful." N Y Times Book Rev
Includes bibliographical references

McCullough, David G. **Mornings** on horseback; {by} David McCullough. Simon & Schuster 1981 445p il hardcover o.p. pa $16 **92**
1. Governors 2. Presidents 3. Vice-presidents 4. Nobel laureates for peace 5. Presidents -- United States
ISBN 0-671-44754-8 pa

LC 81-1697
This biography follows Theodore Roosevelt from his childhood to his defeat for mayor of New York and marriage to Edith Carow in 1886.
"Based on diligent and thorough research, with emphasis on family, physical ailments, and friends, and written with verve and color, this is a stimulating book that will appeal to the general reader." Libr J
Includes bibliographical references

★ Morris, Edmund. The **rise** of Theodore Roosevelt; Modern Library pa. ed; Modern Lib. 2001 xxxiv, 920p il pa $17.95 **92**
1. Governors 2. Presidents 3. Vice-presidents 4. Nobel laureates for peace 5. Presidents -- United States
ISBN 0-375-75678-7

LC 2001-30520
A reissue of the title first published 1979 by Coward, McCann & Geoghegan
This first volume of a three volume study of the life and times of Theodore Roosevelt "covers Roosevelt's life up to the age of 42, when an assassin's bullet elected him the youngest president in the nation's history." Booklist
Includes bibliographical references
Followed by Theodore Rex (2001) and Colonel Roosevelt (2010)

★ Morris, Edmund. **Theodore** Rex. Random House 2001 772p il map $35; pa $16.95 **92**
1. Governors 2. Presidents 3. Vice-presidents 4. Nobel laureates for peace 5. Presidents -- United States
ISBN 0-394-55509-0; 0-8129-6600-7 pa

LC 2001-19366
"The second entry in Morris's . . . three-volume life of Theodore Roosevelt focuses on the presidential years 1901 through early 1909." Publ Wkly
Includes bibliographical references
Followed by Colonel Roosevelt (2010)

★ Morris, Edmund, 1940- **Colonel** Roosevelt. Random House 2010 766p il map $35; ebook $35 **92**
1. Biography, Individual 2. Presidents -- United States 3. United States -- Politics and government -- 1909-1913 4. United States -- Politics and government -- 1913-1921

ISBN 978-0-375-50487-7; 0-375-50487-7; 978-0-679-60415-0 ebook; 0-679-60415-4 ebook

LC 2010-5890
Sequel to Theodore Rex (2001)
"Mr. Morris has addressed the toughest and most frustrating part of Roosevelt's life with the same care and precision that he brought to the two earlier installments. And if this story of a lifetime is his own life's work, he has reason to be immensely proud." N Y Times (Late N Y Ed)
Includes bibliographical references

Rose, Pete, 1941-
Kennedy, Kostya. **Pete** Rose; An American Dilemma. Kostya Kennedy. Time Home Entertainment Inc. 2014 352 p. illustrations $26.95 **92**
1. Sports betting 2. Rose, Pete, 1941- 3. Major League Baseball 4. Baseball players -- Biography
ISBN 1618930966; 9781618930965

LC 2013949234
This book on former professional baseball player Pete Rose presents a "consideration of Rose's place in baseball history 25 years after his ban from Major League Baseball (MLB) and from Hall of Fame consideration because he bet on baseball games. The narrative shifts between Rose's past--with anecdotes from family, friends, and former teammates--to his present life working the autograph circuit and filming a reality show with his young fiancée." (Library Journal)
"This is a wonderful biography as well as a thoughtful examination of a moral quandary." Booklist
Includes bibliographical references and index

Rosenblatt, Roger
Rosenblatt, Roger. **Making** toast; a family story. Ecco 2010 166p $21.99 **92**
1. Authors 2. Bereavement 3. Journalists 4. Grandparent-grandchild relationship 5. Essayists 6. Authors, American 7. Nonfiction writers 8. Political commentators
ISBN 978-0-06-182593-4; 0-06-182593-X
"A 38-year-old pediatrician named Amy Solomon collapsed on her treadmill at home. She died of what was discovered to be a rare, undiagnosed heart defect. The day she died, Amy's parents—Roger and Ginny Rosenblatt—drove from their house on Long Island to their daughter's home in Bethesda, Md. The Rosenblatts have been there ever since, helping their son-in-law take care of three children, who were 6, 4, and 1 when their mother died. Now, Roger Rosenblatt has written about this reconfigured family in an exquisite, restrained little memoir filled with both hurt and humor." NPR

Ross, Barney, 1909-1967
Century, Douglas. **Barney** Ross. Schocken Books 2006 215p il (Jewish encounters) $19.95 **92**
1. Boxers (Persons)
ISBN 0-8052-4223-6; 978-0-8052-4223-2

LC 2005-49939
This is a biography of the American boxer.
"This is an excellent story of a man and his times. And proof positive that time does not relinquish its hold over men or monuments." N Y Times Book Rev
Includes bibliographical references

Ross, Betsy, 1752-1836
Miller, Marla R. **Betsy** Ross and the making of America. Henry Holt 2010 467p il map $30 **92**
1. Dressmakers 2. Needleworkers 3. Biography, Individual 4. Flags -- United States 5. Philadelphia (Pa.) -- History -- 18th

century 6. Philadelphia (Pa.) -- History -- 19th century 7. United States -- History -- 1775-1783, Revolution
ISBN 0-8050-8297-2; 978-0-8050-8297-5

LC 2009-35385

This is a biography of the flag-maker Betsy Ross and a portrait of Revolutionary War-era Philadelphia. Index.

"This first-rate biography of Ross (1752–1836) is authoritative and engrossing and goes a long way toward recovering the history of early American women and work." Publ Wkly

Includes bibliographical references

Ross, Marion, 1928-

Ross, Marion. **My** days; happy and otherwise. Marion Ross. Kensington Pub Corp 2018 336 p. $26   **92**
1. Television programs 2. Actors -- United States -- Biography
ISBN 1496715152; 9781496715159

LC Laurell, David

"In this warm and candid memoir, . . . [Marion] Ross shares what it was like to be a starry-eyed young girl with dreams in poor, rural Minnesota, and the resilience, sacrifices, and determination it took to make them come true. She recalls her early years in the business, being in the company of such luminaries as Humphrey Bogart, Lauren Bacall, and Noel Coward, yet always feeling the Hollywood outsider." (Publisher's note)

"Happy Days fans will enjoy the anecdotes about the show, but Ross's perseverance also serves as a primer for aspiring actors." LJ

Ross, Steve

Ross, Steve. **From** broken glass; My Story of Finding Hope in Hitler's Death Camps to Inspire a New Generation. Steve Ross with Glenn Frank and Brian Wallace. Hachette Books 2018 288 p. $26   **92**
1. Biography 2. Holocaust survivors -- Biography 3. School psychologists -- Biography
ISBN 0316513040; 9780316513043

This inspiring memoir of Steve Ross, a "survivor of ten Nazi concentration camps who went on to create the New England Holocaust Memorial, . . . is about finding strength in the face of despair. . . . Ross was eight years old when the Nazis invaded his Polish village, forcing his family to flee. He spent his next six years in a day-to-day struggle to survive the notorious camps in which he was imprisoned." (Publisher's note)

Roth, Joseph, 1894-1939

Roth, Joseph, 1894-1939. **Joseph** Roth; Joseph Roth; translated and edited by Michael Hofmann. W. W. Norton 2012 xvii, 551p $39.95   **92**
1. Authors 2. Novelists 3. Journalists 4. Authors, Austrian 5. Short story writers
ISBN 978-0-393-06064-5

LC 2011032677

This book "contains 457 letters [by writer Joseph Roth], only a small number of which are to family or close friends or comment on his novels as he was writing them. Most are to fellow writers . . . or to translators and colleagues at The Frankfurter Zeitung and other newspapers for which Roth wrote essays, reviews, and sketches." He discusses "his personal affairs, . . . and, most of all, his unending financial woes." Other topics include "Nazism, . . . Jewishness, . . . [and] the Soviet Union." (New York Times)

Includes bibliographical references

Rousey, Ronda, 1987-

Rousey, Ronda, 1987- **My** fight / your fight; Ronda Rousey. Regan Arts 2015 301 p. illustrations $27.95   **92**
1. Mixed martial arts 2. Women athletes -- Biography
ISBN 1941393268; 9781941393260

LC 2015930623

In this memoir, by Ronda Rousey, with Maria Burns Ortiz, "marked by her signature charm, barbed wit, and undeniable power, . . . [mixed martial artist Ronda Rousey describes] the toughest fights of her life-- in and outside the Octagon--reveals the painful loss of her father when she was eight years old, the intensity of her judo training, her battles with love, her meteoric rise to fame, the secret behind her undefeated UFC record, and what it takes to become the toughest woman on Earth." (Publisher's note)

"The book is just too long; it could have been more than 50 pages shorter, and Rousey would still have inspired her readers. But her warrior mentality is always evident, and one of her more helpful pieces of advice is to feel angry, not sad, after a loss. She urges would-be elite athletes—and really, anyone—to set goals, then become obsessed with elevating them. Plainspoken, often repetitive, and always fiery. Rousey is a fierce yet endearing role model—and a woman possessed." Kirkus

Rousseau, Jean-Jacques, 1712-1778

★ Damrosch, Leo. **Jean**-Jacques Rousseau; restless genius. Leo Damrosch. Houghton Mifflin Co. 2005 x, 566 p.p ill., map o.p.; (pbk.) $12.00; o.p.   **92**
1. Philosophers 2. Authors 3. Novelists 4. Memoirists 5. Political and social philosophers
ISBN 9780618446964; 9780618872022; 0618446966

LC 2005013579

L.L. Winship/PEN New England Award: Nonfiction (2006)

This book "is [a] . . . single-volume biography of [Jean-Jacques] Rousseau, . . . published in English for the general reader. It . . . illuminate[s] the last decade of his life, a time when his psychological complexity and strangeness came to the fore yet his intellect and creative powers triumphed over his difficult, paranoid temperament. During those ten years, he finished the 'Confessions,' wrote the 'Dialogues,' or 'Rousseau Judge of Jean-Jacques,' which he tried in vain to place in the Notre-Dame cathedral for safekeeping, and began writing 'Reveries of the Solitary Walker.'" (Publisher's note)

"A delight to read, Damrosch comes as close to Rousseau's authentic self as we are likely to get." N Y Times Book Rev

Includes bibliographical references (p. [499]-549) and index.

Rousseau, Jean-Jacques. **Confessions**; edited and introduced by P. N. Furbank. Knopf 1992 2v in 1 $20   **92**
1. Authors 2. Novelists 3. Memoirists 4. Political and social philosophers
ISBN 0-679-40998-X

LC 91-53194

First Everyman's library edition, 1931

"An autobiography by Jean-Jacques Rousseau. The twelve volumes, written between 1766 and 1770, were published posthumously (I-VI, 1781; VII-XII, 1788). In this work, Rousseau 'frankly and sincerely' reveals the details of his erratic and rebellious life. Scholars find, however, that his unconscious motivation was to justify himself in the eyes of his supposedly numerous persecutors." Reader's Ency. 4th edition

Routledge, Katherine, 1866-1935

Van Tilburg, JoAnne. **Among** stone giants; the life of Katherine Routledge and her remarkable expedition to Easter Island. foreword by Andrew Tatham. Scribner 2003 351p il $26   **92**

1. Easter Island 2. Archaeologists
ISBN 0-7432-4480-X

LC 2002-42751

This is a "biography of Katherine Routledge, an Englishwoman who was the first to attempt a methodical archaeological study of Easter Island." N Y Times Book Rev

Includes bibliographical references

Rowbottom, Allie

Rowbottom, Allie. **Jell**-O girls; a family history. Allie Rowbottom. Little, Brown & Co. 2018 288 p. $28 **92**
1. Women 2. Motherhood 3. Family-owned business enterprises
ISBN 0316510610; 9780316510615

This memoir, by Allie Rowbottom, "braids the evolution of one of America's most iconic branding campaigns with the stirring tales of the women who lived behind its façade.... [It] is a family history, a feminist history, and a story of motherhood, love and loss. In crystalline prose, Rowbottom considers the roots of trauma not only in her own family, but in the American psyche as well." (Publisher's note)

" In this compassionate, feminist-flavored memoir, Rowbottom both distances and broadens the family story by setting it in the context of the changes in the lives of American women over the past century, as reflected in the marketing and sales of Jell-O. First viewed as a sweet treat and later as a dietary aid, the dessert serves as an oddly apt reflection of women's concurrent, ambivalent relationships to their appetites and bodies." Booklist

Rudd, Mark, 1947-

Rudd, Mark. **Underground**; my life with SDS and the Weathermen. William Morrow 2009 324p il map $25.99 **92**
1. Teachers 2. Radicalism 3. Youth leaders 4. Revolutionaries 5. Weathermen (Organization) 6. Students for a Democratic Society
ISBN 978-0-06-147275-6; 0-06-147275-1

"Even those who condemn Rudd's work in history can be grateful for Rudd's work of history. 'Underground' is honest and funny, passionate and contrite, meticulously researched and deeply philosophical: an essential document on the '60s." Washington Post Book World

Rufus, Rob

Rufus, Robert. **Die** young with me; by Rob Rufus. Touchstone Books 2016 400 p. (hardcover) $25 **92**
1. Cancer patients 2. Cancer -- Patients -- Biography 3. Punk rock musicians -- United States -- Biography
ISBN 1501142615; 9781501142611; 9781501142628

LC 2016005363

Alex Award (2017)

This memoir, by Rob Rufus, tells "true story of a teenager diagnosed with cancer and how music was the one thing that helped him get through his darkest days.... [Punk rock] blares constantly from the basement of Rob and Nat Rufus—identical twin brothers.... When Rob is diagnosed with a rare form of cancer that has already progressed to Stage Four, not only are his dreams of punk rock stardom completely shredded, there is a very real threat that this is one battle that can't be won." (Publisher's note)

"By refusing to abandon hope, easy though it would have been to do so, Rufus' memoir makes a valuable contribution to the literature of healing and recovery." Kirkus

Rumsfeld, Donald, 1932-

Rumsfeld, Donald, 1932- **When** the center held; Gerald Ford and the rescue of the American presidency. Donald Rumsfeld. Simon & Schuster 2018 352 p. $28 **92**
1. Presidents -- United States -- Biography 2. United States --

Politics and government -- 1974-1989
ISBN 150117293X; 9781501172939

In this political memoir, former U.S. President Gerald Ford's "Secretary of Defense Donald Rumsfeld candidly shares his personal observations of the man himself, and provides a sweeping examination of his crucial years in office. It is a rare and fascinating look behind the closed doors of the Oval Office, including never-before-seen photos, memos, and anecdotes, from a unique insider's perspective--essential reading for any fan of presidential history." (Publisher's note)

"A few flaws aside, this is an engrossing and informative tribute to a man whom Jimmy Carter rightfully thanked in his inaugural address "for all he has done to heal our land."" Kirkus Reviews

Rupert, Prince, Count Palatine, 1619-1682

Spencer, Charles Edward Maurice Spencer. **Prince** Rupert; the last cavalier. [by] Charles Spencer. Weidenfeld and Nicolson 2007 430p il $37.95; pa $19.95 **92**
1. Princes 2. Admirals 3. Generals 4. Great Britain -- History -- 1642-1660, Civil War and Commonwealth
ISBN 978-0-297-84610-9; 0-297-84610-8; 978-0-7538-2401-6 pa; 0-7538-2401-9 pa

"This delightful book could change the nonspecialist reader's perception of the English Civil War era as tedious while impressing those already familiar with it.... highly recommended for any college, high school, or public library." Libr J

Includes bibliographical references

Rushdie, Salman

★ Rushdie, Salman, 1947- **Joseph** Anton; a memoir. Salman Rushdie. Random House 2012 xii, 636 p.p (acid-free paper) $30 **92**
1. Protective custody 2. Freedom of the press 3. Islam and literature 4. Fatwas -- Personal narratives 5. Authors, Indic -- Great Britain -- Biography 6. Blasphemy (Islam) -- History -- 20th century
ISBN 0812992784; 9780679643883; 9780812992786

LC 2012372283

This memoir describes author Salman Rushdie's time under police protection after Iranian leader Ayatollah Khomeini issued a death sentence against the author following the publication of his novel "The Satanic Verses." The book answers questions like "How do a writer and his family live with the threat of murder for more than nine years? How does he go on working? . . . How does despair shape his thoughts and actions, . . . how does he learn to fight back?" (Publisher's note)

Rushin, Steve

Rushin, Steve. **Sting**-ray afternoons; a memoir. Steve Rushin. Little, Brown & Co. 2017 viii, 328 p.p illustrations (some color) (hardcover) $27 **92**
1. Nineteen seventies 2. Journalists -- Biography 3. Journalists -- United States -- Biography 4. Sportswriters -- United States -- Biography
ISBN 9780316392242; 9780316392235

LC 2016958350

This book is author "Steve Rushin's story: of growing up within a '70s landscape populated with Bic pens, . . . lightsabers and those oh-so-coveted Schwinn Sting-Ray bikes. 'Sting-Ray Afternoons' paints an utterly fond, psychedelically vibrant, laugh-out-loud-funny portrait of an exuberant decade. With sidesplitting commentary, Rushin creates a vivid picture of a decade of wild youth, cultural rebirth, and the meaning of parental, brotherly, sisterly, whole lotta love." (Publisher's note)

"Rushin's everykid upbringing and the touchstones of childhood he recounts make Sting-Ray Afternoons a fun-filled and charming trip." Booklist

Includes bibliographical references.

Russo, Richard, 1949-

Russo, Richard, 1949- **Elsewhere**; Richard Russo. Alfred A. Knopf 2012 246 p. $25.95   **92**
1. Biography 2. Authors -- Family life 3. Parent-child relationship 4. Gloversville (N.Y.) -- Biography 5. Novelists, American -- Biography
ISBN 0307959538; 9780307959539

LC 2012016354

Author Richard Russo presents a book that chronicles his life. When he went to college, "his mother joined him as they drove to Arizona, and she'd rarely be far from him in the decades that followed. Russo describes how his life decisions were often limited by the need to accommodate his mother's particular needs and, later, debilitating illness . . . He explores how her options were limited as a single mother in the '60s, as a product of a manufacturing culture that collapsed before her eyes, and as a woman who needed to define herself through other men." (Kirkus Reviews)

Ruth, Babe, 1895-1948

★ Leavy, Jane. The **big** fella; Babe Ruth and the world he created. Jane Leavy. HarperCollins 2018 560 p. illustrations $32.50   **92**
1. Baseball players 2. Baseball -- United States
ISBN 0062380222; 9780062380227

This book, by Jane Leavy, is a "definitive biography of Babe Ruth--the man Roger Angell dubbed 'the model for modern celebrity.' . . . Drawing from more than 250 interviews, a trove of previously untapped documents, and Ruth family records, Leavy breaks through the mythology that has obscured the legend and delivers the man." (Publisher's note)

"A skilled strategist and nearly peerless player, Ruth proves himself worthy of, yes, yet another biography, this one warts-and-all but still admiring. Sparkling, exemplary sports biography, shedding new light on a storied figure in baseball history." Kirkus

Rutherford, Ernest, 1871-1937

Reeves, Richard. A **force** of nature; the frontier genius of Ernest Rutherford. W. W. Norton & Co. 2008 207p il (Great discoveries) $23.95   **92**
1. Physicists 2. Nobel laureates for chemistry
ISBN 978-0-393-05750-8; 0-393-05750-X

LC 2007-33184

The author "re-introduces Ernest Rutherford, one of the founding geniuses of nuclear physics. . . . This biography does an outstanding job of capturing the excitement and almost breathless pace of physics research in the 20th century's first four decades." Publ Wkly
Includes bibliographical references

Ryan, Donald P., 1957-

Ryan, Donald P. **Beneath** the sands of Egypt; adventures of an unconventional archaeologist. William Morrow 2010 286p il $26.99; ebook $12.99   **92**
1. Queens 2. Archeologists 3. Archaeologists 4. College teachers 5. Egypt -- Antiquities 6. Excavations (Archeology) -- Egypt
ISBN 978-0-06-173282-9; 0-06-173282-6; 978-0-06-200280-8 ebook; 0-06-200280-5 ebook

LC 2010-20355

"Ryan, the archaeologist who rediscovered tomb KV 60 in the Valley of the Kings (later identified as the final resting place of the pharoah Hatshepsut), takes us through his life, career, and numerous expeditions. It's a thrilling book, not because it's full of Indiana Jones heroics but because Ryan's enthusiasm for what he does (more dirt-sifting than bull-whip-wielding) is manifested on every page; and . . . he catches us up in his excitement, makes us wish we weren't just reading about this stuff but were actually doing it. . . . This wonderful adventure story should be must reading for anyone aspiring to become an archaeologist, but even those of us who harbor no such dreams will be aching to get a little dirt under our fingernails." Booklist

Sabbag, Robert

Sabbag, Robert. **Down** around midnight; a memoir of crash and survival. Viking 2009 214p $25.95   **92**
1. Journalists 2. Aircraft accidents 3. Survival after airplane accidents, shipwrecks, etc. 4. Authors, American
ISBN 978-0-670-02102-4

LC 2008-46688

"A remarkably powerful, human story not merely of a plane crash but of the impact that one brief moment can have on an entire life." Booklist

Sacagawea, b. 1786

★ Clark, Ella Elizabeth. **Sacagawea** of the Lewis and Clark expedition; {by} Ella E. Clark and Margot Edmonds. University of Calif. Press 1979 171p il hardcover o.p. pa $16.95 **92**
1. Lewis and Clark Expedition (1804-1806) 2. Interpreters 3. Guides (Persons)
ISBN 0-520-05060-6 pa

LC 78-65466

"Sacagawea, the Shoshone Indian woman who accompanied the Lewis and Clark expedition, has been a regional heroine and a feminist celebrity for most of this century. But, as these writers show, her role as 'the guide' was more fictive than actual. . . . Based on careful interpretation of the explorer's journals, this revisionist study does a good job of redefining her actual contributions." Booklist
Includes bibliographical references

Sacks, Oliver W, 1933-2015

Sacks, Oliver, 1933-2015. **On** the move; a memoir. by Oliver Sacks. Alfred A. Knopf 2015 416 p. 32 plates: illustrations (hardcover: alk. paper) $27.95   **92**
1. Drug addicts 2. Scientists -- Biography 3. Neurologists -- England -- Biography 4. Neurologists -- United States -- Biography
ISBN 0385352549; 9780385352543

LC 2015001870

In this autobiography by Oliver Sacks, "as he recounts his experiences as a young neurologist in the early 1960s, first in California, where he struggled with drug addiction, and then in New York, where he discovered a long-forgotten illness in the back wards of a chronic hospital, we see how his engagement with patients comes to define his life." (Publisher's note)

An "engaging and candid introduction to a man who transcended the life of a clinical practitioner to become a medical storyteller and humanitarian." Choice

Sacks, Oliver, 1933-2015

Hayes, Bill. **Insomniac** city; New York, Oliver, and me. Bill Hayes. St. Martin's Press 2017 304 p. (HC) $27   **92**
1. New York (N.Y.) -- Description and travel
ISBN 9781620404935; 1620404931

LC 2017017262

This memoir is "a moving celebration of what [author] Bill Hayes calls 'the evanescent, the eavesdropped, the unexpected' of life in New York City, and an intimate glimpse of his relationship with the late Oliver Sacks. . . . [It] is both a meditation on grief and a celebration of life. Filled with Hayes's distinctive street photos of everyday New Yorkers, the book is a love song to the city and to all who have felt the particular magic and solace it offers." (Publisher's note)

"A unique and exuberant celebration of life and love." Kirkus

Sackville-West, Vita, 1892-1962

Dennison, Matthew. **Behind** the Mask; The Life of Vita Sackville-West. Matthew Dennison. St. Martin's Press 2015 416 p. 16 plates; color illustrations $29.99   **92**

1. Women -- Great Britain 2. Celebrities -- Biography
ISBN 1250033942; 9781250033949

LC 2015002466

Author Matthew Dennison presents this "biography of Vita Sackville-West, the 20th century aristocrat, literary celebrity, devoted wife, famous lover of Virginia Woolf, recluse, and iconoclast who defied categorization. His narrative charts a fascinating course from Vita's lonely childhood at Knole, through her affectionate but 'open' marriage to Harold Nicolson, . . . and through Vita's literary successes and disappointments." (Publisher's note)

"Dennison downplays Vita's relationship with Woolf as a smoldering and significant writerly friendship. His narrative is utterly absorbing in its attention to the minutiae of property, inheritance, houses, clothing, and letters. All the while, the author extracts from Vita's writing rich autobiographical detail. A lively, vigorously written biography of a singular character that beckons readers urgently back to Sackville-West's writing." Kirkus

Sagan, Carl, 1934-1996

Poundstone, William. **Carl** Sagan; a life in the cosmos. Holt & Co. 1999 473p il $30   **92**

1. Authors 2. Novelists 3. Astronomers 4. Essayists 5. Astrophysicists 6. Writers on science 7. Science fiction writers
ISBN 0-8050-5766-8; 9780805057676

LC 99-14615

This is an "exhaustive and detailed account, especially when discussing Sagan's original scientific work and influences." Libr J

Includes bibliographical references

Said, Kurban, 1905-1942

Reiss, Tom. The **Orientalist**; solving the mystery of a strange and a dangerous life. Random House 2005 xxvii, 433p il $25.95; pa $14.95   **92**

1. Authors 2. Novelists 3. Historians 4. Biographers
ISBN 1-4000-6265-9; 0-8129-7276-7 pa

LC 2004-50928

This is a biography of Lev Nussimbaum, a Jew from Baku who wrote in Germany under the pseudonyms Essad Bey and Kurban Said.

The author "takes the reader through his own search for the truth; through the twists of 20th-century history in Russia and Germany, and hence though the life-story itself. This would be hard work if the interweaving of biography, investigation and geopolitics were not so elegant." Economist

Includes bibliographical references

Saks, Elyn R.

Saks, Elyn R. The **center** cannot hold; my journey through madness. Hyperion 2008 351 p. $16   **92**

1. Autobiographies 2. Schizophrenia
ISBN 1401309445; 9781401309442

This book "is the . . . story of [author] Elyn [R. Saks]'s life, from the first time that she heard voices speaking to her as a young teenager, to

attempted suicides in college, through learning to live on her own as an adult in an often terrifying world. Saks discusses frankly the paranoia . . ., the voices in her head telling her to kill herself . . .; as well the . . . obstacles she overcame to become a highly respected professional." (Publisher's note)

Saldana, Stephanie

Saldana, Stephanie. The **bread** of angels; a journey to love and faith. Doubleday 2010 309p $24.95; pa $15   **92**

1. Christianity and other religions 2. Spiritual biography 3. Biography, Individual 4. Islam -- Relations -- Christianity 5. Christianity and other religions -- Islam 6. Damascus (Syria) -- Description and travel
ISBN 978-0-385-52200-7; 0-385-52200-2; 978-0-307-28046-6 pa; 0-307-28046-2 pa

LC 2009-16852

This book "operates on several levels: as a spiritual testament and journey of faith; as a Western woman's positive encounter with Islam; as a writer's successful quest to find poetry and beauty even in the midst of war; and as a love story, told with novelistic suspense and a refreshing humor that keeps the romanticism of her story as grounded in reality as possible. . . . This is the type of memoir, recounting a journey to the depths of the soul, that makes the personal universal." America

Salinger, J. D. (Jerome David), 1919-2010

Beller, Thomas. **J.D.** Salinger; the escape artist. Thomas Beller. New Harvest 2014 160 p. (Icons) (hardback) $20 **92**

1. American authors -- Biography 2. Authors, American -- 20th century -- Biography
ISBN 0544261992; 9780544261990

LC 2013045583

In this book, author Thomas Beller "gives us a sense of life at 'The New Yorker' . . . and a portrait of editor Gus Lobrano, whose relationship with [writer J. D.] Salinger has rarely been written about. He visits Salinger's summer camp and the apartment buildings where the author lived. He reads the famous works with obsessive attention, finding in them an image of his own life experience." (Publisher's note)

"Beller's prose is conversational and intimate, and his admiration for his subject is evident." LJ

Includes bibliographical references

★ Slawenski, Kenneth. **J.D.** Salinger; a life. Random House 2011 450p il $27; ebook $27   **92**

1. Authors 2. Novelists 3. Authors, American 4. Short story writers
ISBN 978-1-4000-6951-4; 978-0-679-60479-2 ebook

LC 201008926

First published 2010 in the United Kingdom

This biography is "a highly informative effort to assess the arc of Salinger's career, the themes of his fiction, and his influence on 20th-century American literature. . . . Slawenski describes Salinger's three marriages, records his contentious relationships with his publishers, his special relationship with the New Yorker, and Slawenski's assiduous research allows him to identify and assess many obscure and unpublished stories. In total, an invaluable work that sheds fascinating light on the willfully elusive author." Publ Wkly

Includes bibliographical references

Salk, Jonas, 1914-1995

Jacobs, Charlotte DeCroes. **Jonas** Salk; a life. Charlotte DeCroes Jacobs. Oxford University Press 2015 576 p. 16 plates; illustrations (hardback) $34.95   **92**

1. Poliomyelitis vaccine 2. AIDS vaccines 3. Influenza vaccines -- History 4. Poliomyelitis vaccine -- History 5. Poliomyelitis -- United States -- History 6. Virologists -- United States -- Biography 7. Poliomyelitis -- Vaccination -- United States -- History
ISBN 0199334412; 9780199334414

LC 2014040267

This book, by Charlotte DeCroes Jacobs, is a "complete biography of Jonas Salk, . . . [which] unravels Salk's story to reveal an unconventional scientist and a misunderstood and vulnerable man. Despite his incredible success in developing the polio vaccine, Salk was ostracized by his fellow scientists, who accused him of failing to give proper credit to other researchers and scorned his taste for media attention." (Publisher's note)

"Throughout, the author demonstrates a deep understanding of the character and the nature of science in the latter half of the 20th century. Jacobs makes a convincing case that Salk was a shy man who never succeeded in making the scientific or personal connections that could bring happiness, but his idealism proved a boon to mankind." Kirkus

Includes bibliographical references and index

Kluger, Jeffrey. **Splendid** solution: Jonas Salk and the conquest of polio. G.P. Putnam's Sons 2004 373p il hardcover o.p. pa $15   **92**
1. Physicians 2. Poliomyelitis 3. Microbiologists 4. Writers on medicine
ISBN 0-399-15216-4; 0-425-20570-3 pa

LC 2004-50527

"Can't-put-it-down medical-science history." Booklist

Includes bibliographical references

Samaras, Tim

Hargrove, Brantley. The **man** who caught the storm; the life of legendary tornado chaser Tim Samaras. Brantley Hargrove. Simon & Schuster 2018 304 p. $26   **92**
1. Tornadoes 2. Storm chasers
ISBN 1476796092; 9781476796093

This book, by Brantley Hargrove, "delivers a masterful tale, chronicling the life of [tornado chaser] Tim Samaras in all its triumph and tragedy. He takes readers inside the thrill of the chase, the captivating science of tornadoes, and the remarkable character of a man who walked the line between life and death in pursuit of knowledge. . . . Hargrove's debut offers an unforgettable exploration of obsession and the extremes of the natural world." (Publisher's note)

"An exemplar of narrative nonfiction; readers from all across the spectrum will enjoy this title." LJ

Sampson, Deborah, 1760-1827

★ Young, Alfred Fabian. **Masquerade**: the life and times of Deborah Sampson, Continental soldier; [by] Alfred F. Young. Knopf 2004 417p il map $26.95; pa $16   **92**
1. Soldiers 2. Women soldiers 3. Memoirists 4. United States -- History -- 1775-1783, Revolution
ISBN 0-679-44165-4; 0-679-76185-3 pa

LC 2003-47549

This book "makes a valuable contribution to American women's history. It offers nuggets of insight about an array of historical topics. . . . What's more, it tells a terrific story." Rev Am Hist

Includes bibliographical references

Samuelsson, Marcus

Chambers, Veronica. **Yes,** chef; a memoir. Marcus Samuelsson. Random House Inc 2012 319 p. ill. (pbk) $16   **92**

1. Cooks 2. Family life 3. Swedish Americans -- Biography 4. Cooks -- United States -- Biography 5. African American cooks -- United States -- Biography
ISBN 9780385342612; 0385342616; 9780385342605; 9780440338819

LC 2011042220

James Beard Foundation Award: Writing and Literature (2013)

In this memoir, the author Marcus Samuelsson, was "born in Ethiopia, . . . placed in an orphanage after his mother died from tuberculosis, and the Samuelsson family adopted him and his sister. After becoming a famous chef, the author sought out his roots in multiple visits to his birth country. During one of those visits, he reconnected with his father, and he has kept in touch with his birth family since then. In rich detail, the author tracks his rise as a chef." (Kirkus Reviews)

"This distinctive and compelling memoir has all the elements of a good story: humor, travel, and a young individual overcoming obstacles via a passionate calling." LJ

Sand, George, 1804-1876

Eisler, Benita. **Naked** in the marketplace; the lives of George Sand. Counterpoint 2006 308p $26.95   **92**
1. Authors 2. Novelists 3. Dramatists
ISBN 978-1-58243-349-3; 1-58243-349-6

LC 2006-21684

This is a biography of the French writer.

"Eisler's portrait of this woman of many firsts brings Sand and her boldly improvised life forward more vividly than ever before." Booklist

Includes bibliographical references

Harlan, Elizabeth. **George** Sand. Yale University Press 2004 376p il $35   **92**
1. Authors 2. Novelists 3. Dramatists
ISBN 0-300-10417-0

LC 2004-10315

"Sand, née, Aurore Dupin, left her husband and two children in provincial France and successfully launched herself as a self-supporting writer in Paris, donning men's clothing to ease passage into the professional world and taking a pseudonym to protect her aristocratic family's name. Sand took on many lovers, among them poet Alfred de Musset and composer Frédéric Chopin. Yet despite Sand's outward daring, as Harlan shows, she obsessed over her identity, as both a woman and an aristocrat. . . . Harlan sensitively analyzes the gaps and idiosyncrasies in her subject's heavily self-edited correspondence, autobiography and novels to uncover a fresh portrait of this volatile, imaginative woman of letters." Publ Wkly

Includes bibliographical references

Jack, Belinda Elizabeth. **George** Sand; a woman's life writ large. {by} Belinda Jack. Knopf 2000 395p il hardcover o.p. pa $16   **92**
1. Authors 2. Novelists 3. Dramatists
ISBN 0-679-77918-3 pa

LC 99-40857

"Prodigious author, cross-dresser, lover of Chopin and Alfred de Musset, intimate of (among others) Liszt, Balzac, Dumas (père and fils), Turgenev, and Flaubert (who cried twice at her funeral), Sand was both before her time and quintessentially of it. Jack's nuanced, moving assessment of the writer's early years . . . is the strongest section of this packed life. When Sand moves onto a larger stage, Jack's style becomes breathless, as if she could barely keep up with her flamboyant subject." New Yorker

Sanders, Bernard

Rall, Ted. **Bernie**; by Ted Rall. Random House Inc 2016 192 p. color illustrations (paperback) $16.95   **92**

1. Biographical graphic novels

ISBN 9781609806989; 1609806980

LC 2015046626

This graphic novel, by Ted Rall, presents a profile of U.S. politician Bernie Sanders and "offers a clear and condensed assessment of the rightward-drifting evolution of the Democratic Party. . . . Most political biographies depict the evolution of a politician. Bernie Sanders, on the other hand, has been politically consistent for half a century. What happened is that the country caught up with him." (Publisher's note)

Sanders, Bernard, 1941- **Outsider** in the White House; Bernie Sanders with Huck Gutman; afterword by John Nichols. Verso Books 2015 368 p. illustrations $16.95   **92**

1. Politicians -- United States 2. United States. Congress. Senate 3. Presidential candidates -- United States -- Biography 4. Legislators -- United States -- Biography 5. United States. Congress. House -- Biography 6. United States -- Politics and government -- 1989-

ISBN 9781784784188; 9781784784195; 9781784784201

LC 2015031867

In this biography, written with Huck Gutman, Bernie Sanders "tells the story of a passionate and principled political life. He describes how, after cutting his teeth in the Civil Rights movement, he helped build a grassroots political movement in Vermont, making it possible for him to become the first independent elected to the US House of Representatives in forty years. The story continues into the US Senate and through the dramatic launch of his presidential campaign." (Publisher's note)

Sanders, Scott R. (Scott Russell), 1945-

Sanders, Scott R. A **private** history of awe; [by] Scott Russell Sanders. North Point Press 2006 322p hardcover o.p. pa $15   **92**

1. Authors 2. Novelists 3. Essayists 4. College teachers 5. Children's authors 6. Short story writers

ISBN 0-86547-693-4; 978-0-86547-693-6; 978-0-86547-734-6 pa; 0-86547-734-5 pa

LC 2005-14236

The author "uses autobiography as a vehicle for far-reaching reflections on nature and humankind. . . . Sanders' thoughtful reflections on the cycles of life, the flashpoints of awe, and our quest for meaning are quietly revelatory." Booklist

Includes bibliographical references

Sanger, Margaret, 1879-1966

Baker, Jean H. **Margaret** Sanger. Hill and Wang 2011 349p il $35   **92**

1. Nurses 2. Birth control 3. Women's rights 4. Essayists 5. Feminists 6. Memoirists 7. Social activists 8. Family planning advocates

ISBN 978-0-8090-9498-1

LC 2011008439

This biography of Margaret Sanger "seeks to clear the noted birth-control pioneer's name of the charges of elitism and racism, which have darkened her reputation in recent years. . . . It was the death of a young woman from a self-induced abortion that impelled her to take up the cause of women's rights to contraception. . . . [The author] acknowledges Sanger's support of eugenics but asserts that Sanger was being pragmatic, requiring allies and finding many in the then-popular eugenics movement." (Kirkus Reviews)

"Baker relates Sanger's crusade with unfailing precision as she recounts Sanger's years as a nurse, when she mended the damage caused by self-induced abortions and listened to the pitiful plights of young women enchained by the relentless cycle of childbirth. Sanger distributed pamphlets on contraception, risking imprisonment on account of their legally designated obscenity; opened the first legal family planning clinic in 1940; and at the culmination of her career, in the 1960s, promoted use of the birth control pill. Connecting the details of each battle Sanger won and lost, Baker recreates the train of events in an arduous, iconic, and controversial journey. A moving biography chronicling the hard-fought struggle for women to gain control of their reproductive destiny." Booklist

Santana, Carlos

Santana, Carlos, 1986- The **universal** tone; my life. Carlos Santana. Little, Brown & Co. 2014 544 p. 32 plates; color illustrations (hardcover) $30   **92**

ISBN 0316244929; 9780316244923

LC 2014940685

This memoir, by Carlos Santana with Ashley Kahn and Hal Miller, "offers a page-turning tale of musical self-determination and inner self-discovery, with personal stories filled with colorful detail and life-affirming lessons. The . . . [book] traces his journey from his earliest days playing the strip bars in Tijuana . . . and brings to light the establishment of his signature guitar sound; his roles as husband, father, recording legend, and rock guitar star." (Publisher's note)

"An appreciative and unpretentious chronicle, this is required reading for Santana fans and devotees of classic rock legends." Kirkus

Saperstein, Jesse A.

Saperstein, Jesse A. **Getting** a life with Asperger's; lessons learned on the bumpy road to adulthood. Jesse A. Saperstein. Penguin Group 2014 220 p. (paperback) $15   **92**

1. Asperger's syndrome 2. Saperstein, Jesse A. -- Mental health 3. Asperger's syndrome -- Patients -- Life skills guides 4. Asperger's syndrome -- Patients -- United States -- Biography

ISBN 0399166688; 9780399166686

LC 2014011613

This book, by Jesse A. Saperstein, is a memoir of growing up with Asperger's syndrome. The author, "diagnosed at the age of 14, . . . has struggled, triumphed, flubbed, soared, educated, and inspired. Along the road to adulthood, he has learned many lessons the hard way. In this honest and engaging book, he offers a guided tour of what he's learned about getting along with others, managing emotions, succeeding in school and work, building relationships, and more." (Publisher's note)

Sargent, John Singer, 1856-1925

★ Herdrich, Stephanie L. **Sargent**; the masterworks. Stephanie L. Herdrich. Rizzoli Electa 2018 224 p. $50   **92**

1. Painters -- United States

ISBN 9780847862399

LC 2017964411

In this book, author Stephanie L. Herdrich "draws on a wealth of new research to provide both an essential overview and a more nuanced understanding of the great American painter [John Singer Sargent.] Richly illustrated, the book's three chapters cover the artist's career from his childhood and early years in Paris, to his mid-career portraits made in England and United States, and his later years painting out of doors." (Publisher's note)

"This visual feast of Sargent's most acclaimed creations is time well spent for art students and curious general readers." Library Journal

Sarkozy, Nicolas, 1955-

Sancton, Tom. The **Bettencourt** affair; the world's richest woman and the scandal that rocked Paris. Tom Sancton. Dutton 2017 xv, 396 p.p illustrations, map (hardcover) $28 **92**

1. Swindlers and swindling 2. Businesswomen -- Biography 3. L'Oréal (Firm) -- History 4. Older women -- France -- Biography 5. Billionaires -- France -- Biography 6. Businesswomen -- France -- Biography 7. Scandals -- France -- Paris -- History -- 21st century 8. Swindlers and swindling -- France -- Paris -- History -- 21st century ISBN 1101984473; 9781101984475; 9781101984499; 9781101984482

LC 2016058788

This book, by Tom Sancton, uncovers "L'Oréal's . . . corporate history and buried World War II secrets. From the Right Bank mansions to the Left Bank artist havens; and from the Bettencourts' servant quarters to the office of President Nicolas Sarkozy. . . . It all began when Liliane met François-Marie Banier, an artist and photographer. . . . Over the next two decades, Banier was given hundreds of millions of dollars . . . . by Liliane. What, exactly, was their relationship?" (Publisher's note)

"A well-researched, crisply written, and entertaining story of family, greed, wealth, and the complex relations among them." Kirkus

Includes bibliographical references (pages 339-396).

Sartre, Jean Paul, 1905-1980

Bair, Deirdre. **Simone** de Beauvoir; a biography. Summit Bks. 1990 718p il hardcover o.p. pa $31.95 **92**

1. Authors 2. Novelists 3. Dramatists 4. Philosophers 5. Essayists 6. Feminists 7. Biographers 8. Nonfiction writers 9. Short story writers 10. Nobel laureates for literature ISBN 0-671-74180-2 pa

LC 89-22029

"Bair's biography of the French author, philosopher, and feminist aims to restore the balance between interest in de Beauvoir's personal life—as the lifelong companion of Jean-Paul Sartre and sometime lover of Nelson Algren—and the question of her achievements as a writer and thinker." Booklist

Includes bibliographical references

Sartre, Jean Paul. The **words**; translated from the French by Bernard Frechtman. Vintage 1981 255p pa $11.95 **92**

1. Authors 2. Novelists 3. Dramatists 4. Philosophers 5. Authors, French 6. Essayists 7. Nonfiction writers 8. Short story writers 9. Nobel laureates for literature ISBN 0-394-74709-7; 978-0-394-74709-5

First published 1964 by Braziller

The French existentialist writer "examines the formation of his character during his childhood years, which were passed in a completely adult world between his widowed mother and her parents. The central event of his childhood was the discovery of the world of words, of language." Libr J

Sattouf, Riad

Sattouf, Riad, 1978- The **Arab** of the Future; A Graphic Memoir. by Riad Sattouf. Metropolitan Books 2015 160 p. chiefly ill. $26 **92**

1. Arabs 2. Nomads ISBN 1627793445; 9781627793445

LC 2014041152

Eisner Nominee: Best Reality-Based Work (2016)
LA Times Book Prize: Graphic Novel/Comics (2015)

In this graphic memoir, author Riad Sattouf "recounts his nomadic childhood growing up in rural France, [Muammar] Gaddafi's Libya, and [Hafez] Assad's Syria--but always under the roof of his father, a Syrian Pan-Arabist who drags his family along in his pursuit of grandiose dreams for the Arab nation." (Publisher's note)

"Caught between his parents, Sattouf makes the best of his situation by becoming a master observer and interpreter, his clean, cartoonish art making a social and personal document of wit and understanding." Pub Wkly

Sattouf, Riad, 1978- The **Arab** of the Future 2; A Childhood in the Middle East, 1984-1985: a Graphic Memoir. Riad Sattouf; translated by Sam Taylor. Metropolitan Books 2016 160 p. chiefly illustrations $26 **92**

1. Autobiographies 2. Middle East -- Social conditions ISBN 1627793518; 9781627793513

The second volume of Riad Sattouf's graphic memoir "takes in the sweep of politics, religion, and poverty, but is steered by acutely observed small moments: the daily sadism of his schoolteacher, the lure of the black market, with its menu of shame and subsistence, and the obsequiousness of his father in the company of those close to the regime." (Publisher's note)

"Rather than being incongruous with the oppressive society and grim events he depicts, Sattouf's broadly cartoonish drawing style imparts a level of attachment that makes his story bearable." Booklist

Saunders, Gerda

Saunders, Gerda. **Memory's** last breath; field notes on my dementia. Gerda Saunders. Hachette Books 2017 xi, 272 p.p illustrations, portraits (hardcover) $27 **92**

1. Dementia 2. Alzheimer's disease 3. Dementia -- Patients -- Biography 4. Alzheimer's disease -- Patients -- Biography ISBN 9780316502627; 9780316502573

LC 2017003005

This book is author Gerda Saunders' "astonishing window into a life distorted by dementia. She writes about shopping trips cut short by unintentional shoplifting, car journeys derailed when she loses her bearings, and the embarrassment of forgetting what she has just said to a room of colleagues. Coping with the complications of losing short-term memory, Saunders, a former university professor, nonetheless embarks on a personal investigation of the brain and its mysteries." (Publisher's note)

"Saunders (Blessings on the Sheep Dog) writes bravely about her early-onset dementia diagnosis, and nicely bridges the intensely personal experience of her failing mind with examinations of neurological science." Pub Wkly

Includes bibliographical references.

Saunders, John, 1955-2016

Bacon, John U. **Playing** Hurt; My Journey from Despair to Hope. John Saunders with John U. Bacon; foreword by Mitch Albom. Da Capo Press 2017 xxv, 293 p.p illustrations (hardcover) $27 **92**

1. Depression (Psychology) 2. Sportscasters -- United States -- Biography ISBN 0306824736; 9780306902369; 9780306824739

LC 2017285301

This book, by John Saunders, with John U. Bacon, "is not an autobiography of a sports celebrity but a memoir of a man facing his own mental illness, and emerging better off for the effort. I will take you into the heart of my struggle with depression, including insights into some of its causes, its consequences, and its treatments." (Publisher's note)

"A story that merits both sympathy and attention." Kirkus

Scalia, Antonin

Murphy, Bruce Allen. **Scalia**; a court of one. Bruce Allen Murphy. Simon & Schuster 2014 736 p. illustrations $35 **92**

1. Constitutional law -- United States 2. Judges -- United States

-- Biography 3. United States. Supreme Court -- Biography
ISBN 0743296494; 9780743296496

LC 2013042971

This biography by Bruce Allen Murphy describes how "Antonin Scalia knew only success in the first fifty years of his life. . . . Scalia's evident legal brilliance . . . led everyone to predict he would unite a new conservative majority. . . . Instead he became a Court of One. Rather than bringing the conservatives together, Scalia drove them apart. . . . 'Scalia: A Court of One' is the . . . story of one of the most polarizing figures ever . . . on the nation's highest court." (Publisher's note)

"Murphy details Scalia's behind-the-scenes angling to push himself as the leading advocate for originalism and to get on the Supreme Court. But his scathing critiques set him at odds with conservatives, most notably Sandra Day O'Connor, pushing many to the center. Murphy offers a highly engaged, well-researched analysis of a brash justice whose single-mindedness may ultimately reduce his legacy." Booklist

Includes bibliographical references and index

Schön, Jan Hendrik

Reich, Eugenie Samuel. **Plastic** fantastic; how the biggest fraud in physics shook the scientific world. Palgrave Macmillan 2009 266p $26.95   **92**
1. Physicists 2. Fraud in science 3. Biography, Individual
ISBN 0230224679; 9780230224674; 0-230-22467-9; 978-0-230-22467-4

LC 2008-51801

This is the story of Bell Laboratories "physicist Jan Hdnrik Schön who faked the discovery of a new superconductor made from plastic." (Publisher's note) Index.

"A compelling look inside big science at one of its least admirable moments." Kirkus

Includes bibliographical references

Schedvin, Charlotte von

Andersson, Per J. The **amazing** story of the man who cycled from India to Europe for love; Per J. Andersson; translated by Anna Holmwood. Oneworld Publications 2017 281 p. illustrations (hardcover) $19.99   **92**
1. Artists -- Biography 2. Man-woman relationship 3. International travel 4. East Indians -- Biography
ISBN 9781786070333; 1786070332

This book, by Per J. Andersson, translated by Anna Holmwood, tells "the remarkable true story of [Pradyumna Kumar and] how [he,] . . . armed with nothing more than a handful of paintbrushes and a second-hand Raleigh bicycle[,] made his way across Asia and Europe in search of the woman he loves." (Publisher's note)

"A beautiful, epic tale of love and perseverance." Booklist

Scheinman, Ted, 1985-

Scheinman, Ted. **Camp** Austen; my life as an accidental Jane Austen superfan. Ted Scheinman. Farrar, Straus & Giroux 2018 176 p. (cloth) $15   **92**
1. Women authors
ISBN 9780865478213

LC 2017038310

This book, by Ted Scheinman, "delivers a hilarious and poignant survey of one of the most enduring and passionate literary coteries in history. Combining clandestine journalism with frank memoir, academic savvy with insider knowledge, 'Camp Austen' is perhaps the most comprehensive study of Austen that can also be read in a single sitting. Brimming with stockings, culinary etiquette, and scandalous dance partners, this is summer camp like you've never seen it before." (Publisher's note)

"While Scheinman is clearly an astute reader of Austen—he includes numerous analyses of Austen's life and work that are insightful and often quite funny—this is also a fascinating window into a man's experience in a largely female realm. Scheinman is a wonderful guide to the world of Austen, and this honest and thoughtful discussion of the role Austen's works have played in his family will delight any Janeite." Booklist

Schemel, Patty, 1967-

Schemel, Patty. **Hit** so hard; a memoir. Patty Schemel with Erin Hosier. Da Capo Press 2017 viii, 280 p.p illustrations (hardcover) $27   **92**
1. Women rock musicians -- United States -- Biography 2. Hole (Musical group) 3. Drummers (Musicians) -- Biography 4. Rock musicians -- United States -- Biography
ISBN 9780306902628; 9780306825071; 0306825074

LC 2017569141

In this memoir, Patty Schemel with Erin Hosier, "intimately documents the events surrounding her dramatic exit from the band [Hole] in 1998 that led to a dark descent into a life of homelessness and crime on the streets of Los Angeles, and the difficult but rewarding path to lasting sobriety after more than twenty serious attempts to get clean." (Publisher's note)

Schiaparelli, Elsa, 1890-1973

Secrest, Meryle. **Elsa** Schiaparelli; A Biography. by Meryle Secrest. Random House Inc 2014 400 p. illustrations $35   **92**
1. Fashion designers
ISBN 030770159X; 9780307701596

LC 2014025820

This biography, by Meryle Secrest, focuses on French fashion designer Elsa Schiaparelli. "She was known as the Queen of Fashion; a headline attraction in the international glitter-glamour show of the late twenties and thirties. . . . Secrest writes of Schiaparelli's keen instincts-- an astute businesswoman, she launched herself into hats, hose, soaps, shoes, handbags, in the space of a few years. By 1930, her company was grossing millions of francs a year." (Publisher's note)

"Richly illustrated and endlessly intriguing, Secrest's biography illuminates the 'daredevil swagger' of Schiaparelli's clothes and the oft-besieged couturier's inexhaustible tenacity and dazzling creativity." Booklist

Volk, Patricia. **Shocked**; my mother, Schiaparelli, and me. Patricia Volk. Alfred A. Knopf 2013 304 p. ill. (some col.) (hardcover) $26.95   **92**
1. Femininity 2. Beauty, Personal 3. Mothers and daughters -- United States 4. Fashion designers -- France -- Paris -- Biography
ISBN 9780307962102; 0307962105

LC 2012034922

This book by Patricia Volk presents a "study of two very different but very glamorous women--her mother, Audrey, an upper-class New York domestic goddess with the looks and manners of Grace Kelly, and genius haute couture European artist Elsa Schiaparelli, whose book, art, and (yes) perfume forever change the course of young Volk's life." (Library Journal)

"[T]he narrative that emerges from Volk's deft interweaving of lives is as sharp-eyed as it is wickedly funny." Kirkus

Includes bibliographical references

Schiff, Dorothy, 1903-1989

Nissenson, Marilyn. The **lady** upstairs; Dorothy Schiff and

the New York Post. St. Martin's Press 2007 500p il $29.95 **92**
1. New York post 2. Newspaper executives
ISBN 978-0-312-31310-4; 0-312-31310-1

LC 2006-53087

This "is Marilyn Nissenson's carefully documented and revealing account of Schiff's nearly four decades of ownership. It's an admiring but not uncritical story of a woman who at her best 'was feisty rather than cowed, personally diffident but professionally forceful,' and who, although married four times, ended up wedded mainly to the paper itself." Columbia J Rev
Includes bibliographical references

Schindler, Oskar, 1908-1974

Crowe, David. **Oskar** Schindler; the untold account of his life, wartime activities, and the true story behind the list. [by] David M. Crowe. Westview Press 2004 766p il $30 **92**
1. Humanitarians 2. Manufacturing executives
ISBN 0-8133-3375-X

LC 2004-13879

This book "is essential in understanding one of the most extraordinary figures from the Holocaust." Booklist
Includes bibliographical references

Schlesinger, Arthur M., 1917-2007

Schlesinger, Arthur M. (Arthur Meier), 1917-2007. **Journals**: 1952-2000; edited by Andrew Schlesinger and Stephen Schlesinger. Penguin Press 2007 894p $40 **92**
1. Authors 2. Historians 3. Biographers 4. Nonfiction writers 5. Government officials 6. Historians -- United States 7. United States -- History -- 1945-
ISBN 978-1-594-20142-4

The distinguished political historian's journals provide an intimate history of postwar America, the writer's contributions to multiple presidential administrations, and his relationships with numerous cultural and intellectual figures.

This book "contains juicy morsels on every one of its [pages]. . . . The book contains not just his witty apercus, but those of hundreds of A-list friends, some of whom are still alive and will blanch at seeing private lunches in print. The presidential scuttlebutt is prime. . . . The private score-settling is fun reading." Newsweek

Schlesinger, Arthur M. (Arthur Meier), 1917-2007. A **life** in the twentieth century; innocent beginnings, 1917-1950. [by] Arthur M. Schlesinger, Jr. Houghton Mifflin 2000 557p il $28.95; pa $15 **92**
1. Authors 2. Historians 3. Biographers 4. Nonfiction writers 5. Government officials 6. Historians -- United States
ISBN 0-395-70752-8; 0-618-21925-0 pa

LC 00-61322

This first volume of Schlesinger's autobiography covers the author's life through the publication of The Age of Jackson and The Vital Center.

Schlesinger's "autobiography, skillfully interweaving the personal and the historical, is elegantly simple and marvellously clear. Complex thoughts are set forth with a lucidity that conceals the depth of the intellectual analysis. Wit, humour and the resources of a natural storyteller sweep the reader along." Economist

★ Aldous, Richard. **Schlesinger**; the imperial historian. Richard Aldous. First edition W.W. Norton & Company 2017 486 p. illustrations (hardcover) $29.95 **92**
1. Historians -- Biography 2. Historians -- United States -- Biography

ISBN 9780393244700

LC 2017019909

This book, by Richard Aldous, is "the first major biography of preeminent historian and intellectual Arthur Schlesinger Jr. . . . Known today as the architect of John F. Kennedy's presidential legacy, [Schlesinger] blazed an extraordinary path from Harvard University to wartime London to the West Wing. The son of a pioneering historian--and a two-time Pulitzer Prize and National Book Award winner in his own right--Schlesinger redefined the art of presidential biography." (Publisher's note)

"Aldous correctly links 'The Vital Center' to Schlesinger's growing discomfort with the treacherous conventional political cant of 'left' and 'right.' Amid the global struggle against totalitarianism, Schlesinger charged, liberals everywhere had to disown communism just as sharply as conservatives had to disown fascism. In defense of democracy, the book also presented a critique of political perfectionism."--New York Review of Books
Includes bibliographical references and index

Schneerson, Menachem Mendel, 1902-1994

Telushkin, Joseph, 1948- **Rebbe**; The Life and Teachings of Menachem M. Schneerson, the Most Influential Rabbi in Modern History. Joseph Telushkin. HarperCollins 2014 640 p. illustrations, portraits $29.99 **92**
1. Rabbis 2. Biography 3. Chabad-Lubavitch
ISBN 0062318985; 9780062318985

National Jewish Book Award Finalist: Biography, Autobiography, Memoir (2014)

"In this . . . biography, Joseph Telushkin offers a . . . portrait of the late Rabbi Menachem Mendel Schneerson, a towering figure who saw beyond conventional boundaries to turn his movement, Chabad-Lubavitch, into one of the most dynamic and widespread organizations ever seen in the Jewish world." (Publisher's note)

"The book is rich with accounts of encounters with the Rebbe, including, besides his own followers, Jews of many denominations, secular Israeli leaders, American politicians, students of philosophy, and non-Jews. What stands out is Schneerson's engagement with the principles by which he managed to wield a considerable and controversial influence upon the American cultural scene and the Jewish world." Pub Wkly

Schriever, Bernard A., 1910-2005

Sheehan, Neil. A **fiery** peace in a cold war; Bernard Schriever and the ultimate weapon. Random House 2009 534p il $32 **92**
1. Cold war 2. Generals 3. Nuclear weapons 4. Ballistic missiles 5. Air force officers
ISBN 978-0-679-42284-6

LC 2009-02247

The author "has written the best kind of biography, one that tells history through a central character. . . . The real story is of the bureaucratic hand-to-hand combat that let to . . . [the ICBM] finally taking flight. . . . Crafting an engrossing five-hundred-page account of a bureaucratic tussle is no easy task. Yet Sheehan makes it work." Columbia J Rev
Includes bibliographical references (p. [501]-509) and index

Schultz, Philip, 1945-

Schultz, Philip. **My** dyslexia. W. W. Norton & Co. 2011 120p $21.95 **92**
1. Poets 2. Authors 3. Dyslexia 4. Poets, American 5. College teachers
ISBN 978-0-393-07964-7

LC 2011015859

The author "tackles his struggle with dyslexia—a condition he only learned he had when his son was diagnosed. Schultz paints a precise and compelling picture of how his brain works, how he sees himself, and how he thinks others have seen him throughout his life. . . . His affecting prose will inspire compassion and leave readers with an understanding not only of dyslexia, but of the lifelong challenges that someone with disabilities may face." Publ Wkly

Schulz, Charles M.

★ Michaelis, David. **Schulz** and Peanuts; a biography. Harper 2007 655p il $34.95   **92**
1. Cartoonists 2. Peanuts (Comic strip)
ISBN 978-0-06-621393-4; 0-06-621393-2

This is a biography of the cartoonist and author of Happiness is a Warm Puppy (1962), The Charlie Brown Dictionary (1973), Peanuts Jubilee (1975), Snoopy's Tennis Book (1979), and Things I Learned After It Was Too Late (1981).

"It is Mr. Michaelis's achievement in these pages that he leaves us with both a shrewd appreciation of Schulz's minimalist art and a sympathetic understanding of Schulz the man." N Y Times (Late N Y Ed)

Includes bibliographical references

Schuman, Rebecca

Schuman, Rebecca. **Schadenfreude,** a love story; Me, the Germans, and 20 Years of Attempted Transformations, Unfortunate Miscommunications, and Humiliating Situations That Only They Have Words For. Rebecca Schuman. Flatiron Books 2017 288 p. (hardcover) $26.99   **92**
1. Journalists -- United States -- Biography 2. Women college students -- United States -- Biography 3. Germany -- Description and travel
ISBN 9781250077578

LC 2016038531

This book, by Rebecca Schuman, "is the story of a teenage Jewish intellectual who falls in love — in love with a boy (who breaks her heart), a language (that's nearly impossible to master), a culture (that's nihilistic, but punctual), and a landscape (that's breathtaking when there's not a wall in the way). . . . Dylan Gellner . . . and Franz Kafka . . . are the axe to the frozen sea that is Rebecca's spirit, and what flows forth is a passion for all things German." (Publisher's note)

"Schuman's engrossing book is a feast of honesty, humility and humor, all the hallmarks of great confessional literature." Pub Wkly

Schumann, Robert, 1810-1856

Chernaik, Judith. **Schumann**; the faces and the masks. Judith Chernaik. Alfred A. Knopf 2018 368 p. $30   **92**
1. Composers 2. Composers -- Germany -- Biography
ISBN 9780451494467

LC 2017060796

This book, by Judith Chernaik, "reveals how [Robert] Schumann (1810-1856) embodied all the contrasting themes of Romanticism--he was intensely original and imaginative but also worshiped the past; he believed in political, personal, and artistic freedom but insisted on the need for artistic form based on the masters. . . . It details his deep involvement with other composers of his time . . . as well as the literary lights of the age." (Publisher's note)

Includes bibliographical references and index

Geck, Martin. **Robert** Schumann; the life and work of a romantic composer. Martin Geck; translated by Stewart Spencer. The University of Chicago Press 2012 320 p. $35   **92**
1. Composers -- Germany -- Biography

ISBN 9780226284699; 0226284697

LC 2012007981

This book by Martin Geck is a biography of Robert Schumann, "one of the most important and representative composers of the Romantic era. . . . Geck shows Schumann to be not only a major composer and music critic . . . but also a political activist, the father of eight children, and an addict of mind-altering drugs. . . . Schumann was able to control his demons and channel the tensions that seethed within him into music that mixes the popular and esoteric." (Publisher's note)

Includes bibliographical references and index

Schumer, Amy

Schumer, Amy, 1981- The **Girl** With the Lower Back Tattoo; Amy Schumer. Simon & Schuster 2016 320 p. illustrations (some color) (ebook) $20.99; $28   **92**
1. Women comedians
ISBN 9781501139901; 1501139886; 9781501139888

LC PN2287

"The Emmy Award-winning comedian, actress, writer, and star of Inside Amy Schumer and the acclaimed film Trainwreck has taken the entertainment world by storm with her winning blend of smart, satirical humor. Now, Amy Schumer has written a refreshingly candid and uproariously funny collection of (extremely) personal and observational essays." (Publisher's note)

"A hilarious and effective memoir from a woman with zero inhibitions." Kirkus

Schwenke, Chloe

★ Schwenke, Chloe. **Self**-ish; a transgender journey toward wholeness. by Chloe Schwenke. Red Hen Press 2018 260 p. $17.95   **92**
1. Transgender people -- Identity 2. Transgender people -- United States -- Biography
ISBN 1597096083; 9781597096089

LC 2017054802

"'SELF-ish' is a narrative drawn from an international life, beginning with some early glimpses out at the world by a girl in a boy's body. Chloe Schwenke was raised as Stephen in a Marine Corps family, and was sent off at age fourteen to 'man-up' at a military academy. . . . Her far-flung global journey was matched in intensity by an inner identity and spiritual struggle and the associated ravages of depression, before she came to the revelation of being a transgender woman." (Publisher's note)

" It is a fascinating, illuminating story of an exemplary life and an essential book in helping people understand the condition of being a transgender person." Booklist

Scott, Dred, ca. 1795-1858

VanderVelde, Lea. **Mrs.** Dred Scott; a life on slavery's frontier. Oxford University Press 2009 480p il map $34.95 **92**
1. Slaves 2. Biography, Individual 3. Slavery -- United States 4. Spouses of prominent persons 5. United States -- Supreme Court 6. Slaves -- Legal status, laws, etc. 7. Slaves -- United States -- Biography
ISBN 0-19-536656-5; 978-0-19-536656-3

LC 2008-27920

This is a "biography of Harriet Scott, wife of Dred Scott, and the story of the family's flight for freedom." (Publisher's note) Bibliography. Index.

"Through Harriet Scott's life, the author is able to create a valuable portrait of the development of slavery on the U.S. frontier during an era in which that scourge was leading the country toward civil war. Despite the wealth of historical knowledge presented, the heart of this well-researched work is the tragic tale of how a loving family's effort to gain their freedom was brutally rejected by Supreme Court justices bent on maintaining the institution of slavery at all costs." Libr J

Includes bibliographical references (p. 443-466)

Scott, Harriet Robinson

VanderVelde, Lea. **Mrs.** Dred Scott; a life on slavery's frontier. Oxford University Press 2009 480p il map $34.95 **92**

1. Slaves 2. Biography, Individual 3. Slavery -- United States 4. Spouses of prominent persons 5. United States -- Supreme Court 6. Slaves -- Legal status, laws, etc. 7. Slaves -- United States -- Biography

ISBN 0-19-536656-5; 978-0-19-536656-3

LC 2008-27920

This is a "biography of Harriet Scott, wife of Dred Scott, and the story of the family's flight for freedom." (Publisher's note) Bibliography. Index.

"Through Harriet Scott's life, the author is able to create a valuable portrait of the development of slavery on the U.S. frontier during an era in which that scourge was leading the country toward civil war. Despite the wealth of historical knowledge presented, the heart of this well-researched work is the tragic tale of how a loving family's effort to gain their freedom was brutally rejected by Supreme Court justices bent on maintaining the institution of slavery at all costs." Libr J

Includes bibliographical references (p. 443-466)

Scott, Wendell, 1921-1990

Donovan, Brian. **Hard** driving: the Wendell Scott story; the odyssey of NASCAR'S first Black driver. Steerfort Press 2008 311p il hardcover o.p. pa $16.99 **92**

1. Automobile racing 2. African American athletes 3. Automobile racing drivers

ISBN 978-1-58642-144-1; 978-1-58642-160-1 pa

LC 2008-24287

For this biography, the author "interviewed Scott extensively over the last 14 months of his life. He also interviewed more than 200 other individuals, including Scott's widow and children. The result is the gripping story of a fascinating, brave man who deserves serious recognition for his solitary accomplishment. . . . A must-read for NASCAR fans." Booklist

Includes bibliographical references

Seattle, Chief, 1790-1866

★ Buerge, David M. **Chief** Seattle and the town that took his name; the change of worlds for the native people and settlers on Puget Sound. David M. Buerge. Sasquatch Books 2017 xxv, 325 p.p (alk. paper) $25.95 **92**

1. Biography 2. Native Americans -- Biography 3. Suquamish Indians -- Biography 4. Seattle Region (Wash.) -- Biography 5. Puget Sound Region (Wash.) -- Biography

ISBN 9781632171351

LC 2017004912

This biography, by David M. Buerge, "is the first thorough historical account of Chief Seattle and his times--the story of a half-century of tremendous flux, turmoil, and violence, during which a native American war leader became an advocate for peace and strove to create a successful hybrid racial community. . . . Buerge has threaded together disparate accounts of the time from the 1780s to the 1860s--including native oral histories, . . .and historic newspaper reporting." (Publisher's note)

Includes bibliographical references (pages 307-316) and index.

Sediqi, Kamela, 1977-

Lemmon, Gayle Tzemach. The **dressmaker** of Khair Khana; five sisters, one remarkable family, and the woman who risked everything to keep them safe. Harper 2011 256p **92**

1. Dressmaking 2. Businesswomen 3. Taliban 4. Afghanistan 5. Dressmakers

ISBN 978-0-06-173237-9

LC 2010-20774

This book "is a fascinating window on Afghan life under the Taliban and a celebration of women the world over who support their loved ones with tenacity, inventiveness and sheer guts." People

Includes bibliographical references

Seeger, Pete

★ Dunaway, David King. **How** can I keep from singing? the ballad of Pete Seeger. Trade paperback ed.; Villard 2008 xxx, 512p il pa $18 **92**

1. Singers 2. Folk musicians 3. Songwriters

ISBN 978-0-345-50608-5

LC 2007-41814

A reprint of the title first published 1981 by McGraw-Hill

"The focus of Seeger's life has been on using music as a force for social change. . . . But he is perhaps best known as the major banjo-playing folksinger who pioneered the folk music revival that flowered in the 1960s. This excellent book provides a well-written and extensively researched account, not only of Seeger's life, but also of the social and political movements of the times in which he lived. An extensive bibliography and discography add to the book's usefulness." Libr J

Includes discography and bibliographical references

Wilkinson, Alec. The **protest** singer; an intimate portrait of Pete Seeger. Alfred A. Knopf 2009 151p il $22.95; pa $14 **92**

1. Singers 2. Folk musicians 3. Songwriters

ISBN 978-0-307-26995-9; 978-0-307-39098-1 pa

LC 2008-54387

The author "draws on interviews with Seeger and others to present a seamless chronicle of his life and music, vivifying his passion for humanity, love of the environment, and deep curiosity about music." Libr J

Seek, Amy, 1977-

Seek, Amy. **God** and Jetfire; confessions of a birth mother. Amy Seek. Farrar, Straus & Giroux 2015 352 p. (hardback) $27 **92**

1. Adoption 2. Motherhood 3. Families 4. Open adoption

ISBN 0374164452; 9780374164454; 9780374713829

LC 2014044643

This book, by Amy Seek, "is a mother's account of her decision to surrender her son in an open adoption and of their relationship over the twelve years that follow. Facing an unplanned pregnancy at twenty-two, Amy Seek and her ex-boyfriend begin an exhaustive search for a family to raise their child. . . . For decades, closed adoptions were commonplace. Now, new laws are guaranteeing adoptees' access to birth records, and open adoption is on the rise." (Publisher's note)

"Seek's prose is lyrical, at times heart-wrenching, as she deeply explores her pain, regret, and longing. The author provides an informative view of open adoption (its advantages as well as its drawbacks). There is nothing prescriptive or commonplace about this true story of a mother who has to learn—as all parents must—both how to embrace, and how to let go." Pub Wkly

Selgin, Peter

Selgin, Peter. The **inventors**; a memoir. by Peter Selgin. Hawthorne Books 2016 416 p. illustrations (paperback) $18.95 **92**

1. American authors 2. Teacher-student relationship 3. Teacher-student relationships -- Biography 4. Authors, American -- 21st century -- Biography

ISBN 9780989360470

LC 2015030856

In this memoir, "at the start of eighth grade, Peter Selgin fell in love with the young teacher who'd arrived from Oxford in Frye boots, with long hair, and a passion for his students that was intense and unorthodox. . . . Over the next decade they met occasionally and corresponded constantly, their last meeting a disaster. Only after he died did Peter learn that the teacher had completely fabricated his past." (Publisher's note)

"A reflective investigation of the self, memory, and invention." Kirkus

Semmelweis, Ignác Fülöp, 1818-1865

Nuland, Sherwin B., 1930-2014. The **doctors'** plague; germs, childbed fever, and the strange story of Ignac Semmelweis. Norton 2003 191p il (Great discoveries) $21.95; pa $13.95 **92**

1. Physicians 2. Writers on medicine 3. Puerperal septicemia

ISBN 0-393-05299-0; 0-393-32625-X pa

LC 2003-11412

This is an account of the work of the 19th-century obstetrician Ignas Semmelweis. "Semmelweis is remembered for the now-commonplace notion that doctors must wash their hands before examining patients. . . . With deaths from childbed fever exploding, Semmelweis discovered that doctors themselves were spreading the disease. While his simple reforms worked immediately, they also threatened the medical establishment." (Publisher's note)

Includes bibliographical references

Seth, Shanti Behari

★ Seth, Vikram, 1952- **Two** lives; Vikram Seth. HarperCollins 2005 503p ill. (pbk.) $15.95; o.p. **92**

1. Poets 2. Authors 3. Dentists 4. Novelists 5. London (England) -- Biography" 6. East Indians -- England -- London 7. Interracial marriage -- England -- London 8. Authors, English -- 20th century -- Biography 9. Authors, Indic -- Homes and haunts -- England -- London 10. London (England) -- Social life and customs -- 20th century

ISBN 9780060599676; 0060599669

LC 2005052694

In this book, the author presents biographies of "his Shanti Uncle and Aunty Henny. . . . Shanti was Seth's grandfather's brother, a dentist who studied in Berlin, lodging with Fau Caro, whose daughter, Henny was in love with someone else. He left for Britain in 1936. . . . [I]n 1940, as war broke out, he enlisted, served throughout and lost his right arm in combat. . . . Meanwhile, Henny, a German Jew, arrived in Britain weeks before war was declared, leaving her beloved mother and sister behind to death camp murder. . . . Part two of his narrative focuses on Shanti. Part three, Henny's story . . . is based on a trove of remarkable letters she received and wrote. . . . Part four examines their marriage (they didn't marry until seven years after the war), and part five details a family mystery about Shanti's will and Seth's . . . research into these lives." (Publishers Weekly)

"In clear and elegant writing, Seth explores the macrocosm through the microcosm, resulting in a most unusual, worthwhile book." Publ Wkly

Seth, Vikram, 1952-

★ Seth, Vikram, 1952- **Two** lives; Vikram Seth. HarperCollins 2005 503p ill. (pbk.) $15.95; o.p. **92**

1. Poets 2. Authors 3. Dentists 4. Novelists 5. London (England) -- Biography" 6. East Indians -- England -- London 7. Interracial marriage -- England -- London 8. Authors, English -- 20th century -- Biography 9. Authors, Indic -- Homes and haunts -- England -- London 10. London (England) -- Social life and customs -- 20th century

ISBN 9780060599676; 0060599669

LC 2005052694

In this book, the author presents biographies of "his Shanti Uncle and Aunty Henny. . . . Shanti was Seth's grandfather's brother, a dentist who studied in Berlin, lodging with Frau Caro, whose daughter, Henny was in love with someone else. He left for Britain in 1936. . . . [I]n 1940, as war broke out, he enlisted, served throughout and lost his right arm in combat. . . . Meanwhile, Henny, a German Jew, arrived in Britain weeks before war was declared, leaving her beloved mother and sister behind to death camp murder. . . . Part two of his narrative focuses on Shanti. Part three, Henny's story . . . is based on a trove of remarkable letters she received and wrote. . . . Part four examines their marriage (they didn't marry until seven years after the war), and part five details a family mystery about Shanti's will and Seth's . . . research into these lives." (Publishers Weekly)

"In clear and elegant writing, Seth explores the macrocosm through the microcosm, resulting in a most unusual, worthwhile book." Publ Wkly

Seton, Elizabeth Ann, Saint, 1774-1821

Barthel, Joan. **American** saint; the life of Elizabeth Seton. Joan Barthel. Thomas Dunne Books 2014 304 p. illustrations (hardback) $26.99 **92**

1. Religious biography 2. Christian saints -- Biography 3. Christian saints -- United States -- Biography

ISBN 0312571623; 9780312571627

LC 2013030995

In this biography of Elizabeth Seton, author Joan Barthel "tells the . . . story of a woman whose life featured wealth and poverty, passion and sorrow, love and loss. Elizabeth was born into a prominent New York City family in 1774. . . . When Elizabeth and her wealthy husband Will sailed to Italy in a doomed attempt to cure his tuberculosis, she and her family were quarantined. . . . And when Elizabeth later became a Catholic, she was so scorned that people talked of burning down her house." (Publisher's note)

"A biography of the first American saint. . . offering a rounded portrait of an ambitious woman who struggled mightily to fulfill the tenets of her faith: to be obedient, merciful and good." Kirkus

Includes bibliographical references and index

Seuss, Dr.

Morgan, Judith. **Dr.** Seuss & Mr. Geisel; a biography. [by] Judith & Neil Morgan. Da Capo Press 1996 345p il pa $18.50 **92**

1. Artists 2. Authors 3. Humorists 4. Illustrators 5. Authors, American 6. Children's authors

ISBN 0-306-80736-X; 978-0-306-80736-7

LC 96-19313

First published 1995 by Random House

"Fans of The Cat in the Hat, The Grinch Who Stole Christmas and other classics may be surprised to learn that Dr. Seuss was terrified of children and had none of his own, and that writing verse was a supreme effort for him. While children's literature is Ted Geisel's principal claim to fame, his creative life was multifarious, including an apprenticeship with film director and army major Frank Capra during WWII and stints in advertising. The authors deftly evoke the settings where Geisel lived and worked." Publ Wkly

Sewall, Samuel, 1652-1730

LaPlante, Eve. **Salem** witch judge; the life and repentance of Samuel Sewall. HarperSanFrancisco 2007 352p il map $25.95   **92**

1. Judges 2. Diarists 3. Colonial leaders 4. Massachusetts -- History -- 1600-1775, Colonial period
ISBN 978-0-06-078661-8; 0-06-078661-2

LC 2007-18392

"In 1692, Salem magistrate Samuel Sewall (1652-1730), along with several others, presided over the conviction and execution of 20 people accused of witchcraft. Five years and much soul-searching later, Sewall publicly repented of his part in the witch trials. . . . [The author] richly narrates his life in its cultural and religious setting." Publ Wkly

Includes bibliographical references

Seward, William Henry, 1801-1872

Stahr, Walter. **Seward**; Lincoln's indispensable man. by Walter Stahr. Simon & Schuster 2012 720 p. $32.50; (hardcover) $32.50   **92**

1. Legislators 2. Statesmen -- United States 3. Statesmen -- United States -- Biography 4. United States. Dept. of State -- Biography 5. Cabinet officers -- United States -- Biography 6. United States -- Foreign relations -- 1861-1865 7. United States -- Politics and government -- 1861-1865
ISBN 9781439127940; 1439121168; 9781439121160; 9781439121184

LC 2011052984

This book presents a biography of William Henry Seward, U.S. Secretary of State under President Abraham Lincoln. "Seward was New York governor and senator, then a rival for Lincoln's place on the 1860 presidential ticket, finally senior cabinet officer. . . . Among other things, he kept Britain out of the Civil War, then negotiated the acquisition of Alaska for the U.S." (Publishers Weekly)

Includes bibliographical references and index

Shabazz, Betty

Rickford, Russell John. **Betty** Shabazz: a remarkable story of survival and faith before and after Malcolm X; foreword by Myrlie Evers-Williams. Sourcebooks 2003 xxii, 633p il $35   **92**

1. Civil rights activists 2. Spouses of prominent persons 3. African Americans -- Civil rights
ISBN 1-4022-0171-0

LC 2002-003447

"Just as the achievements of her husband, Malcolm X, were overshadowed by those of Martin Luther King Jr., Betty Shabazz's accomplishments have been overshadowed by those of King's widow. {The author} corrects that imbalance with this penetrating biography." Booklist

Includes bibliographical references

Shackleton, Ernest Henry, Sir, 1874-1922

Larson, Edward J. (Edward John), 1953- **To** the edges of the earth; 1909, the race for the three poles, and the climax of the age of exploration. Edward J. Larson. HarperCollins 2018 352 p. $29.99   **92**

1. Mountaineering 2. Sports records 3. Sports -- History
ISBN 0062564471; 9780062564474

LC 2018000736

In this book historian Edward J. Larson looks at "the most adventur-ous year of all time, when three expeditions simultaneously raced to the top, bottom, and heights of the world. . . . In the course of one extraordinary year, Americans Robert Peary and Matthew Henson were hailed worldwide at the discovers of the North Pole; Britain's Ernest Shackleton had set a new geographic 'Furthest South' record, while . . . . Australian Douglas Mawson, had reached the Magnetic South Pole." (Publisher's note)

" A fascinating look at the adventures of remarkably resilient men, so well-related as to make you feel the chill." Kirkus

Smith, Michael. **Shackleton**; By Endurance We Conquer. Michael Smith. Oneworld Publications 2014 464 p. illustrations; maps; portraits $30   **92**

1. Antarctica -- Exploration
ISBN 1780745729; 9781780745725

Author Michael Smith offers "a fresh perspective to the Heroic Age of Polar Exploration that was dominated by [Ernest] Shackleton's enduringly fascinating story. His incredible adventures on four expeditions to the Antarctic have captivated generations. But Shackleton was a flawed character whose chaotic private life, marked by romantic affairs, unfulfilled ambitions, and failed business ventures, contrasted with his celebrity status as the leading explorer." (Publisher's note)

"Shackleton is admired for his leadership skills while his repeated off-ice failures are overlooked or unknown. Smith offers a fascinating assessment of his subject, one that will be enjoyed by readers of biographies, polar literature, and adventure stories." LJ

Shakur, Tupac

Dyson, Michael Eric. **Holler** if you hear me: searching for Tupac Shakur. Basic Bks. 2001 292p il hardcover o.p. pa $15   **92**

1. Poets 2. Actors 3. Hip-hop 4. Rap music 5. African American musicians 6. Rap musicians
ISBN 0-465-01755-X; 0-465-01728-2 pa

LC 2001-36564

"Dyson's discussion goes beyond slogans and poses to the actualities of 'thug life' and the consequences of Shakur's passions and allegiances. Piquant and analytical." Booklist

Includes bibliographical references

Shannon, Claude Elwood, 1916-2001

Goodman, Rob. A **mind** at play; how Claude Shannon invented the information age. by Jimmy Soni and Rob Goodman. Simon & Schuster 2017 xv, 366 p.p illustrations (hardcover: alk. paper) $27   **92**

1. Information theory 2. Mathematicians -- United States -- Biography 3. Electrical engineers -- United States -- Biography
ISBN 9781476766706; 9781476766683; 9781476766690

LC 2016050944

This book, by Jimmy Soni and Rob Goodman, "reveal[s] Claude Shannon's full story for the first time. . . . [A] small-town Michigan boy whose career stretched from the era of room-sized computers powered by gears and string to the age of Apple. It's the story of the origins of our digital world in the tunnels of MIT and the 'idea factory' of Bell Labs, in the 'scientists' war' with Nazi Germany, and in the work of Shannon's collaborators and rivals." (Publisher's note)

"A welcome and inspiring account of a largely unsung hero—unsung because, the authors suggest, he accomplished something so fundamental that it's difficult to imagine a world without it." Kirkus

Includes bibliographical references and index

Shapiro, Dani

Shapiro, Dani. **Hourglass**; Time, Memory, Marriage. Dani Shapiro. Alfred A. Knopf 2017 160 p. (hardback) $22.95 **92**

1. Marriage 2. Jewish women 3. Women authors 4. Marriage -- Social aspects 5. Women novelists, American -- Biography 6. Jewish women -- United States -- Biography 7. Novelists, American -- 20th century -- Biography

ISBN 0451494482; 9780451494481

LC 2016029345

This book, by Dani Shapiro, "is an inquiry into how marriage is transformed by time--abraded, strengthened, shaped in miraculous and sometimes terrifying ways by accident and experience. . . . Shapiro opens the door to her house, her marriage, and her heart, and invites us to witness her own marital reckoning--a reckoning in which she confronts both the life she dreamed of and the life she made, and struggles to reconcile the girl she was with the woman she has become." (Publisher's note)

"A sharply observed and frequently moving memoir of a marriage." Kirkus

Sharapova, Maria, 1987-

Sharapova, Maria, 1987- **Unstoppable**; my life so far. Maria Sharapova with Rich Cohen. Sarah Crichton Books, Farrar, Straus & Giroux 2017 292 p. illustrations (chiefly color) (hbk.) $28 **92**

1. Tennis players -- Biography 2. Tennis players -- Russia (Federation) -- Biography 3. Women tennis players -- Russia (Federation) -- Biography

ISBN 9780374715311; 0374279799; 9780374279790

LC 2017017149

In this memoir, by Maria Sharapova, "her story doesn't begin with the 2004 Wimbledon championship, but years before, in a small Russian town, where as a five-year-old she played on drab neighborhood courts with precocious concentration. It begins when her father, convinced his daughter could be a star, risked everything to get them to Florida, that sacred land of tennis academies. It begins when the two arrived with only seven hundred dollars and knowing only a few words of English." (Publisher's note)

"Unstoppable is an inspiring memoir about coming-of-age within the elite tennis community and a tribute to the unconditional support from families and coaches who make success possible." Booklist

Sharon, Ariel

Landau, David. **Arik**; the life of Ariel Sharon. by David Landau. Alfred A. Knopf 2014 656 p. illustrations, map hbk $35 **92**

1. Israel -- History 2. Israel -- Politics and government 3. Generals -- Israel 4. Arab-Israeli conflict 5. Prime ministers -- Israel

ISBN 1400042410; 9781400042418

LC 2012049631

Author David Landau presents a biography of Ariel Sharon, a "man who is considered by many to be Israel's greatest military leader and political statesman, illustrating how Sharon's leadership transformed Israel, and how his views were shaped by the changing nature of Israeli society." (Publisher's note)

"Splendid reporting, comprehensive research and probing analysis inform this unblinking view of a complicated man and a sanguinary geography." Kirkus

Includes bibliographical references and index

Shaw, Artie, 1910-2004

Nolan, Tom. **Three** chords for beauty's sake: the life of Artie Shaw. W.W. Norton 2010 430p il $29.95 **92**

1. Jazz musicians 2. Band leaders 3. Clarinetists

ISBN 978-0-393-06201-4; 0-393-06201-5

LC 2010-06301

In this biography of the swing clarinetist-bandleader Nolan, "who interviewed Shaw and many of his band mates and intimates, appraises his difficult subject with a cool eye. His briskly written work lauds the musician's instrumental virtuosity and ambitious conceptions, but the author cuts Shaw no slack about his many personal failings—his arrogance, anger, selfishness, egocentricity and his horrific relationships with parents, wives and children. It's a multidimensional portrait of a brilliant yet self-absorbed autodidact who could never find happiness or satisfaction, even when his greatest fantasies of fame and success were realized. An exemplary work of jazz biography." Kirkus

Includes bibliographical references

Shawn, Allen

Shawn, Allen. **Wish** I could be there; notes from a phobic life. Viking 2007 267p $24.95 **92**

1. Composers 2. Agoraphobia

ISBN 0-670-03842-3; 978-0-670-03842-8

LC 2006-41368

The author "probes the causes of his long struggle with agoraphobia—a fear of certain spaces which makes it difficult to 'move forward in the world without knowing already what lies ahead'—in this vividly written combination of memoir and scientific inquiry." New Yorker

Includes bibliographical references

Shears, Jake

Shears, Jake. **Boys** keep swinging; Jake Shears. Atria Books 2018 336 p. (hardcover) $26 **92**

1. Singers -- United States -- Biography 2. Rock musicians -- United States -- Biography

ISBN 9781501140129; 9781501140136

LC 2017038858

In this memoir, Jake Shears "transforms the vividness of his musical world into an unforgettable literary account of overcoming odds and finding his true voice. . . . Candid and courageous, Shears's writing sings with the same powerful, spirited presence that he brings to his live performances. . . . 'Boys Keep Swinging' is a raucously entertaining memoir that will be an inspiration to anyone with determination and a dream." (Publisher's note)

Sheehan, Jason

★ Sheehan, Jason. **Cooking** dirty; a story of life, sex, love and death in the kitchen. Farrar, Straus and Giroux 2009 355p $26; pa $15 **92**

1. Cooks 2. Food critics

ISBN 978-0-374-28921-8; 0-374-28921-2; 978-0-374-53227-7 pa; 0-374-53227-3 pa

LC 2008-47158

"Sheehan's memoir is emphatically not about 'the glam end of cooking' or celebrity chefs, but about 'a straight blue-collar gig,' where the kitchens are staffed by the kind of guys who get off on the fact that the work is insanely grueling. . . . The war stories are as profane and outrageous as you'd expect, and Sheehan finds just the right balance between bravado and humility." Publ Wkly

Sheehy, Gail

Sheehy, Gail, 1937- **Daring**; My Passages: a Memoir. Gail Sheehy. William Morrow 2014 416 p. illustrations (some color) $29.99 **92**

1. Women journalists 2. Journalism -- United States -- History 3. Journalists -- United States -- Biography
ISBN 0062291696; 9780062291691

LC 2014034090

This memoir, by Gail Sheehy, is "a chronicle of her trials and triumphs as a groundbreaking 'girl' journalist in the 1960s. . . . [It] is the story of the unconventional life of a writer who dared . . . to walk New York City streets with hookers and pimps to expose violent prostitution; to march with civil rights protesters in Northern Ireland as British paratroopers opened fire; to seek out Egypt's president Anwar Sadat when he was targeted for death after making peace with Israel." (Publisher's note)

"Sheehy gives readers a distinct glimpse into some of the most important events of the last 40 years. . . . Her perspective on the women's movement and the decline of print journalism is especially compelling." LJ

Shelley, Mary Wollstonecraft, 1797-1851

Gordon, Charlotte. **Romantic** outlaws; the extraordinary lives of Mary Wollstonecraft and her daughter Mary Shelley. Charlotte Gordon. Random House Inc 2015 672 p. illustrations (hardback) $30; (paperback) $18.00 **92**
   ISBN 9781400068425; 1400068428; 9780812980479; 0812980476

LC 2014014841

National Book Critics Circle Award Finalist: Biography (2015)

In this biography of Mary Wollstonecraft and Mary Shelley author Charlotte Gordon "reunites the trailblazing author who wrote 'A Vindication of the Rights of Woman' and the Romantic visionary who gave the world 'Frankenstein'--two courageous women who should have shared their lives, but instead shared a powerful literary and feminist legacy." (Publisher's note)

"Gordon's prose is compelling and her scholarship meticulous; her contention that both women led 'lives as memorable as the words they left behind' is brilliantly supported." LJ
   Includes bibliographical references and index

Seymour, Miranda. **Mary** Shelley. Grove Press 2001 655p il $35; pa $20 **92**
   1. Authors 2. Novelists 3. Women authors 4. Authors, English
   ISBN 0-8021-1702-3; 0-8021-3948-5 pa

LC 2001-35094

First published 2000 in the United Kingdom
"A convincing and memorable portrait." Booklist
Includes bibliographical references

Shen, Aisling Juanjuan, 1974-

Shen, Aisling Juanjuan. A **tiger's** heart; the story of a modern Chinese woman. Soho Press 2009 309p $24 **92**
   1. Memoirists 2. Financial analysts 3. Immigrants -- United States 4. Yangtze River valley (China) 5. Chinese Americans -- Biography
   ISBN 978-1-56947-586-7; 1-56947-586-5

LC 2009-5426

"Like a suspense novel, this book is impossible to put down. All readers interested in China, as well as memoir fans (especially of success stories), must read this astonishing title." Libr J

Shepard, Sadia

Shepard, Sadia. The **girl** from foreign; a search for shipwrecked ancestors, forgotten histories, and a sense of home. Penguin Press 2008 364p il map $25.95; pa $16 **92**
   1. Memoirists 2. Jews -- India 3. Motion picture directors
   ISBN 978-1-59420-151-6; 978-0-14-311577-9 pa

LC 2008-3912

A young Muslim-Christian woman travels to an insular Jewish community in India to unlock her family's secret history.

"A readable account that gives a vivid taste of life in present-day India as well as a poignant glimpse of complicated family relations." Kirkus
   Includes bibliographical references

Sherman, William T. (William Tecumseh), 1820-1891

Fellman, Michael. **Citizen** Sherman; a life of William Tecumseh Sherman. University Press of Kansas 1997 486p il pa $19.95 **92**
   1. Generals 2. Memoirists 3. Secretaries of war 4. United States -- History -- 1861-1865, Civil War
   ISBN 978-0-7006-0840-9; 0-7006-0840-0
   First published 1995 by Random House

"This superb biography gives as full a portrait of nineteenth-century family dynamics as of the dynamics of the battlefield. Fellman's Sherman is not a lovable man, but he is a complete one." New Yorker
   Includes bibliographical references

Kennett, Lee B. **Sherman**; a soldier's life. [by] Lee Kennett. HarperCollins Pubs. 2001 426p il maps hardcover o.p. pa $14.95 **92**
   1. Generals 2. Memoirists 3. Secretaries of war 4. United States -- History -- 1861-1865, Civil War
   ISBN 0-06-093074-8 pa

LC 2001-16687

This is a "well-balanced analytical biography." Publ Wkly
   Includes bibliographical references

McDonough, James Lee. **William** Tecumseh Sherman; in the service of my country; a life. James Lee McDonough. W W Norton & Co Inc 2016 832 p. ill., maps, portraits (ebook) $80; (hardcover) $39.95 **92**
   1. Generals -- United States -- Biography 2. United States -- History -- 1861-1865, Civil War 3. United States. Army -- Biography 4. United States -- History -- Civil War, 1861-1865 -- Biography 5. United States -- History -- Civil War, 1861-1865 -- Campaigns
   ISBN 9780393242126; 9780393241570

LC 2016007023

In this biography of General William Tecumseh Sherman, author James Lee McDonough "offers fresh insight into a man tormented by the fear that history would pass him by, who was plagued by personal debts, and who lived much of his life separated from his family. As a soldier, Sherman evolved from a spirited student at West Point into a general who steered the Civil War's most decisive campaigns, rendered here in graphic detail." (Publisher's note)

"McDonough has produced an exhaustive biography told with considerable narrative skill." Pub Wkly
   Includes bibliographical references and index

Woodworth, Steven E. **Sherman**; [foreword by Wesley K. Clark] Palgrave Macmillan 2009 198p il map (Great generals series) $21.95 **92**
   1. Generals 2. Memoirists 3. Secretaries of war 4. United States -- History -- 1861-1865, Civil War
   ISBN 0-230-61024-2; 978-0-230-61024-8

LC 2008-22060

This is a biography of the Civil War general.
"An excellent brief life of a major and controversial figure." Booklist
Includes bibliographical references

Shopsin, Tamara

Shopsin, Tamara, 1980- **Arbitrary** stupid goal; Tamara Shopsin. MCD/Farrar, Straus & Giroux 2017 324 p. illustrations (hardcover) $27   **92**
   1. Bohemianism -- New York (N.Y.) 2. Restaurants -- New York (State) -- New York 3. New York (N.Y.) -- Biography 4. New York (N.Y.) -- Social life and customs 5. Bohemianism -- New York (State) -- New York 6. Greenwich Village (New York, N.Y.) -- Biography 7. Greenwich Village (New York, N.Y.) -- Social life and customs 8. Family-owned business enterprises -- New York (State) -- New York
   ISBN 9780374715809; 9780374105860

LC 2016059399

"Deeply nostalgic but not at all mawkish, Shopsin's supremely charming and affecting memoir of growing up in a pre-gentrified Greenwich Village will enchant fans of restaurant lore and postwar New York history alike." Booklist

Includes bibliographical references.

Short, Martin, 1950-

Short, Martin, 1950- **I** must say; my life as a humble comedy legend. Martin Short; with David Kamp. Harper 2014 336 p. 16 plates; illustrations $26.99   **92**
   1. Comedians 2. Television actors and actresses -- Canada -- Biography
   ISBN 0062309528; 9780062309525

LC 2014028617

In this memoir author "Martin Short takes you on a rich, hilarious, and occasionally heartbreaking ride through his life and times, from his early years in Toronto as a member of the fabled improvisational troupe Second City to the all-American comic big time of Saturday Night Live and memorable roles in movies." (Publisher's note)

"A true vaudevillian, Short is always on as he delivers funny anecdotes from a diffuse and storied career." Kirkus

Shorter, Frank, 1947-

Shorter, Frank. **My** marathon; reflections on a Gold Medal life. Frank Shorter, with John Brant; foreword by Kenny Moore. Rodale 2016 254 p. illustrations (ebook) $21.50; (trade hardcover) $26.99   **92**
   1. Marathon running 2. Long-distance runners 3. Marathon running -- History 4. Runners (Sports) -- United States -- Biography
   ISBN 9781623367251; 1623367247; 9781623367244

LC 2016028782

This book "is a revealing memoir by Frank Shorter, the father of American distance running. After winning the 1969 NCAA title in the 10,000-meters title during his senior year at Yale, Shorter went on to win a staggering 24 national titles on track, road, and cross country courses, but it was in the marathon that Shorter achieved his greatest fame and recognition." (Publisher's note)

Shriver, Eunice Kennedy

★ McNamara, Eileen. **Eunice**; the Kennedy who changed the world. Eileen McNamara. Simon & Schuster 2018 416 p. (hardcover: alk. paper) $28   **92**
   1. Women philanthropists -- Biography 2. Special Olympics, Inc 3. Philanthropists -- United States -- Biography 4. Women philanthropists -- United States -- Biography 5. Presidents -- United States -- Brothers and sisters -- Biography 6. Eunice Kennedy Shriver National Institute of Child Health and Human Development (U.S.)
   ISBN 9781451642261

LC 2017046517

This book, by Eileen McNamara, "examines the life and times of Eunice Kennedy Shriver. . . . McNamara finally brings . . . Shriver out from her brothers' shadow to show an officious, cigar-smoking, indefatigable woman of unladylike determination and deep compassion born of rage: at the medical establishment that had no answers for her sister Rosemary; at the revered but dismissive father . . . and at the government that failed to deliver on America's promise of equality." (Publisher's note)

"Along with providing insights into Eunice's roles as wife, mother, sister, and daughter, McNamara uses her journalistic prowess to produce a complete and detailed portrait of this spirited and magnetic activist." Booklist

Includes bibliographical references and index

Shteyngart, Gary, 1972-

★ Shteyngart, Gary. **Little** failure; a memoir. Gary Shteyngart. Random House Inc 2014 368 p. illustrations hbk $27   **92**
   1. Autobiographies 2. Russian Americans 3. Children of immigrants
   ISBN 0679643753; 9780679643753

LC 2013013217

National Jewish Book Award Finalist: Biography, Autobiography, Memoir (2014)

National Book Critics Circle Award Finalist: Autobiography (2014)

"After three acclaimed novels, Gary Shteyngart turns to memoir in a candid, witty, deeply poignant account of his life so far. Shteyngart shares his American immigrant experience, . . . with self-deprecating humor, moving insights, and literary bravado. . . . Swinging between a Soviet home life and American aspirations, Shteyngart found himself living in two contradictory worlds, all the while wishing that he could find a real home in one." (Publisher's note)

"An immigrant's memoir like few others, with as sharp an edge and as much stylistic audacity as the author's well-received novels." Kirkus

Shulman, Alix Kates

Shulman, Alix Kates. **To** love what is; a marriage transformed. Farrar, Straus and Giroux 2008 160p $22   **92**
   1. Love 2. Authors 3. Marriage 4. Novelists 5. Feminists
   ISBN 978-0-374-27815-1; 0-374-27815-6

LC 2008-21504

"A fall from a loft bed left author Shulman's 75-year-old husband with traumatic brain injury and utterly dependent on his wife, as she recounts in this deeply affecting memoir of their ordeal together. . . . Carving out time for herself and her writing kept her from having a nervous breakdown, and while her hope at times flagged, Shulman's devotion never faltered, as demonstrated by her candid account." Publ Wkly

Sickles, Daniel E., 1825-1914

★ Keneally, Thomas. **American** scoundrel: the life of the notorious Civil War General Dan Sickles. Talese 2002 397p $27.50; pa $15   **92**
   1. Generals 2. Diplomats 3. Members of Congress
   ISBN 0-385-50139-0; 0-385-72225-7 pa

LC 2001-43078

"A frequently spellbinding recitation of the career of a totally awful politician, crook, adulterer and murderer who was no good as a general either." N Y Times Book Rev

Silver, Elizabeth L., 1978-

Silver, Elizabeth L. The **tincture** of time; a memoir of (medical) uncertainty. Elizabeth L. Silver. Penguin Press 2017 x, 258 p.p (hardcover) $27   **92**

1. Parenthood 2. Infants -- Diseases

ISBN 9781101981443; 9781101981467

LC 2016043492

This book is author Elizabeth Silver's "gorgeous and haunting chronicle of [her daughter] Abby's first year. It's a year of unending tests, doctors' opinions, sleepless nights, promising signs and steps backward, and above all, uncertainty: The mysterious circumstances of Abby's hospitalization attract dozens of specialists, none of whom can offer a conclusive answer about what went wrong or what the future holds." (Publisher's note)

"The attempt to balance personal trauma with wider cultural reference is a tricky challenge, but this will resonate with anyone who has experienced diagnostic difficulties." Kirkus

Includes bibliographical references.

Simon, Carly

Simon, Carly, 1945- **Boys** in the trees; a memoir. Carly Simon. Flatiron Books 2015 384 p. illustrations (hardcover) $28.99   **92**

1. Youth 2. Singers 3. Singers -- United States -- Biography

ISBN 1250095891; 9781250095893; 9781250095909

LC 2015038193

This memoir by Carly Simon "reveals her remarkable life, beginning with her storied childhood as the third daughter of Richard L. Simon, the co-founder of publishing giant Simon & Schuster, her musical debut as half of The Simon Sisters performing folk songs with her sister Lucy in Greenwich Village, to a meteoric solo career that would result in 13 top 40 hits, including the #1 song 'You're So Vain.' The memoir recalls a childhood enriched by music and culture, but also one shrouded in secrets that would eventually tear her family apart." (Publisher's note)

"Memoirs by rock icons of the 1960s and '70s are flying fast and furious these days. This is one of the best, lively and memorable. Check the new album that accompanies the book, too." Kirkus

Simon, Paul, 1941-

Hilburn, Robert. **Paul** Simon; the life. Robert Hilburn. Simon & Schuster 2018 448 p. (hardcover) $30   **92**

1. Rock musicians -- United States -- Biography

ISBN 9781501112126; 9781501112133

LC 2018015535

This book, by Robert Hilburn, presents "an intimate, candid, and definitive biography written with [Paul] Simon's full participation. . . . Over the past three years, Hilburn has conducted in-depth interviews with scores of . . . Simon's friends, family, colleagues, and others. . . . The result is a deeply human account of the challenges and sacrifices of a life in music at the highest level." (Publisher's note)

Includes bibliographical references and index

Simon, Scott

Simon, Scott. **Unforgettable**; a son, a mother, and the lessons of a lifetime. Scott Simon. Flatiron Books 2015 256 p. (hardback) $24.99   **92**

1. Death 2. Twitter (Website) 3. Mother-son relationship 4. Journalists -- United States -- Biography

ISBN 125006113X; 9781250061133

LC 2015002582

This book " is a son's spirited, affecting, and inspiring tribute to his remarkable mother and the love between parent and child. When NPR's Scott Simon began tweeting from his mother's hospital room in July 2013, he didn't know that his missives would soon spread well beyond his 1.2 million Twitter followers. . . . Over the course of a few days, Simon chronicled his mother's death and reminisced about her

life, revealing her humor and strength, and celebrating familial love." (Publisher's note)

"Simon appreciates how generously Patti is treated by the staff at the hospital, which brings up memories of the 'lovely' men who courted her. He takes his quirky, devoted, gracious mother on her own terms, and his work shimmers as a touching tribute." Pub Wkly

Simone, Nina

Cohodas, Nadine. **Princess** Noire; the tumultuous reign of Nina Simone. Pantheon Books 2010 449p il $30   **92**

1. Singers 2. Pianists 3. Jazz musicians 4. African American singers 5. African American musicians 6. Songwriters 7. Soul musicians 8. Biography, Individual

ISBN 0-307-37899-3 ebook; 0-375-42401-6; 978-0-307-37899-6 ebook; 978-0-375-42401-4

LC 2009-22252

This is a biography of the singer. Discography. Bibliography. Index.

"Looking at every aspect of Simone's work, from stage decorum to audience interaction, the author offers many rich insights into her subject's conflicted emotional world. Throughout, she nurtures the reader's empathy for the artist but takes care to avoid unfounded speculation on racism or gender bias. In fact, this is a 360-degree profile of Simone, offering solid critical insights at every turn." Choice

Includes discography and bibliographical references

Sin, Tong-hyŏk, 1982-

Harden, Blaine. **Escape** from Camp 14; one man's remarkable odyssey from North Korea to freedom in the West. Blaine Harden. Viking 2012 xvi, 205 p.p illustrations, maps (hardcover) $26.95   **92**

1. Forced labor -- Korea (North) 2. Korea (North) -- Social conditions 3. Concentration camps -- Korea (North) 4. Political prisoners -- Korea (North) -- Biography

ISBN 9781101561263; 9780670023325; 9780143122913; 0670023329

LC 2011037555

In this book, "acclaimed journalist Blaine Harden tells the story of Shin Dong-hyuk and through the lens of Shin's life unlocks the secrets of the world's most repressive totalitarian state. Shin knew nothing of civilized existence--he saw his mother as a competitor for food, guards raised him to be a snitch, and he witnessed the execution of his own family. Through Harden's harrowing narrative of Shin's life and remarkable escape, he offers an unequaled inside account of one of the world's darkest nations and a riveting tale of endurance, courage, and survival." (Publisher's note)

Includes bibliographical references

Sinatra, Frank, 1915-1998

Kaplan, James, 1951- **Frank**; the voice. Doubleday 2010 786p il $35; ebook $35   **92**

1. Actors 2. Singers 3. Biography, Individual

ISBN 0-385-51804-8; 0-385-53364-0 ebook; 978-0-385-51804-8; 978-0-385-53364-5 ebook

LC 2009-31046

This biography covers the life of the American singer and actor from his birth in 1915 to his comeback in 1954 in the film From Here to Eternity. Index.

"Kaplan's enthralling tale of an American icon serves as an introduction of 'old blue eyes' to a new generation of listeners while winning the hearts of Sinatra's diehard fans." Publ Wkly

Includes bibliographical references

★ Kaplan, James, 1951- **Sinatra**; the chairman. by James

Kaplan. Doubleday 2015 992 p. illustrations (hardcover) $35 **92**

1. Singers -- United States -- Biography
ISBN 9780307946935; 9780385535397; 9780385535403

LC 2015008973

"Just in time for the Chairman's centennial, the . . . sequel to James Kaplan's bestselling 'Frank: The Voice.' . . . Like Peter Guralnick on Elvis, Kaplan goes behind the legend to give us the man in full, in his many guises and aspects: peerless singer, (sometimes) accomplished actor, business mogul, tireless lover, and associate of the powerful and infamous." (Publisher's note)

"An appropriately big book for an oversized artistic presence." Kirkus

Includes bibliographical references (pages 936-940) and index.

Santopietro, Tom. **Sinatra** in Hollywood. Thomas Dunne Books 2008 530p il $29.95 **92**

1. Actors 2. Singers
ISBN 978-0-312-36226-3; 0-312-36226-9

LC 2008-24941

"Striving for honest critiques and a witty, encyclopedic coverage, Santopietro begins with Sinatra's 1935 short subjects; dances through the grandiose 1940s MGM musicals; documents Sinatra's professional and personal despair and decline in such giant turkey disasters as The Kissing Bandit (1948); and analyzes his Oscar-winning comeback in From Here to Eternity (1953). . . . This mammoth movie compendium, filled with forgotten facts, 53 b&w photos and a detailed filmography, is certain to satisfy Sinatra's legions of fans." Publ Wkly

Includes bibliographical references

Singh, Sophia Duleep, 1876-1948

Anand, Anita. **Sophia**; Princess, Suffragette, Revolutionary. Anita Anand. St. Martin's Press 2015 432 p. 24 plates; illustrations $30 **92**

1. Suffragists
ISBN 1632860813; 9781632860811

Author Anita Anand present a biography of "Sophia Duleep Singh, [who] was born into Indian royalty. Sophia, god-daughter of Queen Victoria, was raised a genteel aristocratic Englishwoman. But when, in secret defiance of the British government, she travelled to India, she returned a revolutionary. Her causes were the struggle for Indian Independence, the fate of the lascars, the welfare of Indian soldiers in the First World War -- and, above all, the fight for female suffrage." (Publisher's note)

"Anand writes with a journalist's sense for a solid story and a historian's eye for fascinating anecdotes. Filled with rich detail and walks through little-known avenues of the past, this work is bound to enchant history lovers, those interested in women's studies, Anglophiles, and anyone who enjoys biographies." LJ

Sirhan, Kamilah, d. 2001

Hikayati sharhun yatul./English. The **locust** and the bird; my mother's story. translated from the Arabic by Roger Allen. Pantheon Books 2009 302p il $24.95 **92**

1. Muslim women 2. Parents of prominent persons
ISBN 978-0-307-37820-0; 0-307-37820-9

LC 2008-54683

"Al-Shaykh's poignant family history, narrated in the voice of her mother, Kamila, transports us to Beirut in the nineteen-thirties. At eleven, the beautiful and strong-willed Kamila is illiterate, her family penniless. She falls in love with the handsome Muhammad, but at fourteen is married off to an older man. . . . Later, Kamila runs away with Muhammad, abandoning her daughters. Al-Shaykh writes in the prologue that this book is largely an attempt to come to terms with that decision. Through telling her mother's story, she learns to appreciate the sacrifices demanded of so many Arab women in their bid for freedom." New Yorker

Sitting Bull, Dakota Chief, 1831-1890

Utley, Robert Marshall. **Sitting** Bull: the life and times of an American patriot; by Robert M. Utley. Henry Holt 2008 464p il pa $18 **92**

1. Indian chiefs
ISBN 978-0-8050-8830-4; 0-8050-8830-X

A reissue with a new preface by the author of the title first published 1993

"This book is well written, strongly documented, and fairly reasoned to satisfy even specialists within the field. It surpasses all previous biographies of Sitting Bull." Choice

Includes bibliographical references

Yenne, Bill. **Sitting** Bull. Westholme 2008 379p il map $29.95 **92**

1. Dakota Indians 2. Indian chiefs
ISBN 978-1-59416-060-8; 1-59416-060-0

In this biography, the author "captures the extraordinary life of Plains Indian leader Sitting Bull while providing new insight into the nomadic culture of the Lakota." Publ Wkly

Includes bibliographical references

Slouka, Mark

★ Slouka, Mark. **Nobody's** son; a memoir. Mark Slouka. W W Norton & Co Inc 2016 274 p. illustrations (ebook) $50; (hardcover) $26.95 **92**

1. Family secrets 2. Czech Americans -- Biography 3. Mothers and sons -- New York (State) -- Biography 4. New York (State) -- Biography 5. Authors, American -- Biography 6. Family secrets -- New York (State)
ISBN 9780393292312; 9780393292305

LC 2016018257

In this memoir, Mark Slouka "pieces together a remarkable story of refugees and war, displacement and denial--admitting into evidence memories, dreams, stories, the lies we inherit, and the lies we tell--in an attempt to reach his mother, the enigmatic figure at the center of the labyrinth. Her story, the revelation of her life-long burden and the forty-year love affair that might have saved her, shows the way out of the maze." (Publisher's note)

"Slouka's raw candor, narrative skill, and meticulous attention to the traps of his own memory make for powerful reading. However, it is his ability to confront the darkness in his past and acknowledge it as a shaping life force that makes this book especially engrossing. A moving and intense memoir from a gifted author." Kirkus

Slowinski, Joseph, 1962-2001

James, Jamie. The **snake** charmer; a life and death in pursuit of knowledge. Hyperion 2008 260p il $24.95 **92**

1. Snakes 2. Curators 3. Herpetologists
ISBN 978-1-4013-0213-9; 1-4013-0213-0

LC 2007-48987

James recounts "the gritty and sad story of Joe Slowinski, a flamboyant and well-known herpetologist who died in Burma in 2001, aged 38, from the poisonous bite of a krait snake. . . . This book is both a tribute to Slowinski's spirit and scientific accomplishments, and a cautionary tale about the dangers of an overly passionate ambition." Publ Wkly

Smalls, Robert, 1839-1915

Lineberry, Cate. **Be** free or die; the amazing story of Robert Smalls' escape from slavery to Union hero. Cate Lineberry. St. Martin's Press 2017 xiii, 272 p.p illustrations, map (hardcover) $25.99   **92**

1. Fugitive slaves 2. United States -- History -- 1861-1865, Civil War 3. Planter (Steamship) 4. Beaufort (S.C.) -- Biography 5. African Americans -- Biography 6. African American legislators -- Biography 7. Ship captains -- United States -- Biography 8. United States. Congress. House -- Biography 9. Fugitive slaves -- South Carolina -- Beaufort -- Biography 10. United States -- History -- Civil War, 1861-1865 -- Participation, African American
ISBN 9781250101860; 9781250101877

LC 2017004245

This biography, by Cate Lineberry, " illuminates Robert Smalls' amazing journey from slave to Union hero and ultimately United States Congressman. This captivating tale of a valuable figure in American history gives fascinating insight into the country's first efforts to help newly freed slaves while also illustrating the many struggles and achievements of African Americans during the Civil War." (Publisher's note)

"This is unquestionably a remarkable story, and journalist Lineberry . . . ably tells it as a microcosm of the war." Kirkus

Includes bibliographical references (pages 237-263) and index.

Smarsh, Sarah

★ Smarsh, Sarah. **Heartland**; a memoir of working hard and being broke in the richest country on Earth. Sarah Smarsh. Scribner 2018 304 p. $26   **92**

1. Biography 2. Poverty -- United States 3. Working class -- United States
ISBN 1501133098; 9781501133091
Kirkus Prize Finalist: Nonfiction (2018)
National Book Award Finalist: Nonfiction (2018)

This book, by Sarah Smarsh, "is an eye-opening memoir of working-class poverty . . . in Kansas in the 1980s and 1990s. . . . By telling the story of her life and the lives of the people she loves, Smarsh challenges us to look more closely at the class divide in our country and examine the myths about people thought to be less because they earn less." (Publisher's note)

"Will appeal to readers who enjoy memoirs and to sociologists. While Smarsh ends on a hopeful note, she offers a searing indictment of how the poor are viewed and treated in this country." LJ

Smith Rakoff, Joanna, 1972-

Smith Rakoff, Joanna, 1972- **My** Salinger year; by Joanna Smith Rakoff. Alfred A. Knopf 2014 272 p. (hardcover) $25.95   **92**

1. Publishers and publishing -- History -- 20th century 2. Authors, American -- 21st century -- Biography 3. Literature publishing -- United States -- History -- 21st century
ISBN 0307958000; 9780307947987; 9780307958006

LC 2013026931

This book, by Joanna Smith Rakoff, is a "memoir about literary New York in the late nineties, a pre-digital world on the cusp of vanishing, where a young woman finds herself entangled with one of the last great figures of the century. At twenty-three, after leaving graduate school to pursue her dreams of becoming a poet, Joanna Rakoff moves to New York City and takes a job as assistant to the storied literary agent for J. D. Salinger." (Publisher's note)

"As Rakoff recounts her funny and wrenching personal predicaments, she also charts the quiet battle of attrition between the values of the old publishing world, personal and impassioned, and the aggres-

sively invasive corporate imperative. An intriguing look at the ever-fascinating Salinger and a gracefully incisive tale of love and literature, creativity and survival." Booklist

Smith, Adam, 1723-1790

Norman, Jesse. **Adam** Smith; father of economics. Jesse Norman. Basic Books 2018 432 p. (hardcover) $32   **92**

1. Economics -- Philosophy 2. Economists -- Great Britain 3. Capitalism -- Moral and ethical aspects
ISBN 9780465061976

LC 2018015933

In this book, author "Jesse Norman dispels the myths and caricatures, and provides a far more complex portrait of . . . [economist Adam Smith]. Offering a highly engaging account of Smith's life and times, Norman explores his work as a whole and traces his influence over two centuries to the present day. Finally, he shows how a proper understanding of Smith can help us address the problems of modern capitalism." (Publisher's note)

"It's hard to imagine an American politician writing with the same depth and grasp of an inordinately complex subject, but Norman pulls it off quite capably. A worthy addition to the literature surrounding Smith and that of modern conservative thought." Kirkus

Includes bibliographical references and index

Smith, Alfred Emanuel, 1873-1944

Finan, Christopher M. **Alfred** E. Smith, the happy warrior. Hill & Wang 2002 396p il $26; pa $16   **92**

1. Governors 2. Political leaders 3. State legislators 4. Presidential candidates 5. United States -- Politics and government
ISBN 0-8090-3033-0; 0-8090-1632-X pa

LC 2002-19476

"Finan writes well, but for an occasional lapse into anachronism." NY Times Book Rev

Includes bibliographical references

Smith, Joseph, 1805-1844

Bushman, Richard L. **Joseph** Smith; rough stone rolling. [by] Richard Lyman Bushman, with the assistance of Jed Woodworth. Knopf 2005 740p il map $35; pa $18.95   **92**

1. Mormons 2. Mormon leaders
ISBN 1-4000-4270-4; 1-4000-7753-2 pa

LC 2004-61613

In this biography of the founder of the Mormon church, the author "stresses the boy seer's thoroughly ordinary origins—born to a hard-pressed New England farm family and denied all but the rudiments of a formal education—to emphasize the marvel of the religious revolution he brought about. . . . A deft portrait of a deeply controversial figure." Booklist

Includes bibliographical references

Remini, Robert Vincent. **Joseph** Smith. Viking 2002 190p (Penguin lives series) $19.95   **92**

1. Mormons 2. Mormon leaders
ISBN 0-670-03083-X

LC 2001-56762

"A masterful evenhanded précis that will engross history and religion readers alike." Booklist

Includes bibliographical references

Smith, Lee, 1944-

★ Smith, Lee. **Dimestore**; a writer's life. Lee Smith. Algonquin Books 2016 224 p. $24.95   **92**

1. Women authors 2. Appalachian Region 3. Grundy (Va.) -- Biography 4. Grundy (Va.) -- Social life and customs
ISBN 1616205024; 9781616205027

LC 2015023739

This memoir describes how, "set deep in the mountains of Virginia, the Grundy of [author] Lee Smith's youth was a place of coal miners, tent revivals, mountain music, drive-in theaters, and her daddy's dimestore. It was in that dimestore . . . that she became a storyteller. Even when she was sent off to college to earn some 'culture,' she understood that perhaps the richest culture she might ever know was the one she was driving away from." (Publisher's note)

"In this candid, wistful, appreciative, and beguiling memoir, Smith offers a distinctive and intimate look at one writer's beginnings." Booklist

Smith, Patti

★ Smith, Patti, 1946- **Just** kids; Patti Smith. Ecco 2010 278p il $27; pa $16   **92**
1. Rock musicians 2. Poets, American 3. Biography, Individual
ISBN 978-0-06-621131-2; 0-06-621131-X; 978-0-06-093622-8 pa; 0-06-093622-3 pa
National Book Award: Nonfiction (2010)

"In 'Just Kids,' Patti Smith's first book of prose, the legendary American artist offers a never-before-seen glimpse of her remarkable relationship with photographer Robert Mapplethorpe in the epochal days of New York City . . . in the late sixties and seventies. An honest and moving story of youth and friendship, Smith brings the same unique, lyrical quality to 'Just Kids' as she has to the rest of her formidable body of work." (Publisher's note)

This "is one of the best books ever written on becoming an artist— not the race for online celebrity and corporate sponsorship that often passes for artistic success these days, but the far more powerful, often difficult journey toward the ecstatic experience of capturing radiance of imagination on a page or stage or photographic paper." Washington Post

Smith, Patti, 1946- **M** train; Patti Smith. Alfred A. Knopf 2015 272 p. illustrations (hardcover: alk. paper) $25   **92**
1. Women authors 2. Autobiographies 3. Rock musicians -- United States -- Biography 4. Women rock musicians -- United States -- Biography
ISBN 1101875100; 9781101875100; 9781101875117

LC 2015012904

This memoir by Patti Smith is "a meditation on travel, detective shows, literature, and coffee. Through prose that shifts fluidly between dreams and reality, past and present, and across a landscape of creative aspirations and inspirations, we travel to Frida Kahlo's Casa Azul in Mexico; to a meeting of an Arctic explorer¿s society in Berlin; to a ramshackle seaside bungalow in New York's Far Rockaway that Smith acquires just before Hurricane Sandy hits; and to the graves of Genet, Plath, Rimbaud, and Mishima." (Publisher's note)

"In many ways, this book defies categorizing, and that is one of its many charms. It is absorbing and lingers long after its end. Fans of Smith will enjoy this as will writers, artists, and all those inspired by a creative mind." LJ

Smith, Raymond J.

Oates, Joyce Carol, 1938- A **widow's** story; a memoir. Ecco 2011 415p il $27.99   **92**
1. Poets 2. Widows 3. Authors 4. Novelists 5. Bereavement 6. Loss (Psychology) 7. Essayists 8. Biographers 9. Magazine editors 10. Authors, American 11. Children's authors 12. Short story writers 13. Biography, Individual 14. Spouses of prominent persons

ISBN 9780062015532

This is an account of the novelist's loss of her "husband of 47 years, Raymond J. Smith. . . . He collaborated with his wife in founding The Ontario Review as well as Ontario Review Books." (N Y Times (Late N Y Ed))

"In a narrative as searing as the best of her fiction, Oates describes the aftermath of her husband Ray's unexpected death from pneumonia. Scattershot moments stand out — the day she cancels their 30-year subscription to The New York Times, unable to bear the sight of his favorite paper; her fury at the tulips, harbingers of spring, pushing through the snow ('Too soon! This is too soon!'); the night she weans herself from Lorazepam. A Widow's Story is the painful, scorchingly angry journey of a woman struggling to live in a house 'from which meaning has departed, like air leaking from a balloon.'" Entertainment Wkly

Smith, Tracy K.

Smith, Tracy K., 1972- **Ordinary** light; a memoir. Tracy K. Smith. Alfred A. Knopf 2015 368 p. (hardback) $25.95 **92**
1. Authors 2. Poets -- Psychology 3. Home -- Psychological aspects 4. Coming of age -- United States 5. Mothers -- United States -- Death 6. African Americans -- Race identity 7. Identity (Psychology) -- United States 8. Mothers and daughters -- United States 9. African American women authors -- Biography
ISBN 0307962660; 9780307962669

LC 2014026185

National Book Award Finalist: Nonfiction (2015)

Tracy K. Smith "interrogates her childhood in suburban California, her first collision with independence at Harvard, and her Alabama-born parents' recollections of their own youth in the Civil Rights era. These dizzying juxtapositions . . . will in due course compel Tracy to act on her passions for love and 'ecstatic possibility,' and her desire to become a writer." (Publisher's note)

"Smith holds our intellectual and emotional attention ever so tightly as she charts her evolving thoughts on the divides between races, generations, economic classes, and religion and science and celebrates her lifesaving discovery of poetry as 'soul language.'" Booklist

Smithson, James, 1765-1829

Ewing, Heather P. The **lost** world of James Smithson; science, revolution, and the birth of the Smithsonian. [by] Heather Ewing. Bloomsbury 2007 432p il map $29.95   **92**
1. Chemists 2. Geologists 3. Scientists 4. Philanthropists 5. Smithsonian Institution -- History
ISBN 978-1-59691-029-4; 1-59691-029-1

This is a biography of the British chemist who founded the Smithsonian Institution in Washington, DC.

The author "provides a readable and informative perspective on late Enlightenment chemistry, backing it up with extensive archival research and forays into secondary literature on science." Times Lit Suppl

Includes bibliographical references

Snetsinger, Phoebe, 1931-1999

★ Gentile, Olivia. **Life** list; a woman's quest for the world's most amazing birds. Bloomsbury USA 2008 345p il $26   **92**
1. Bird watching 2. Bird watchers 3. Biography, Individual
ISBN 1-59691-169-7; 978-1-59691-169-7

LC 2008-27036

This is a biography of birder Phoebe Snetsinger. Index.

Gentile describes Phoebe Snetsinger as a "frustrated stay-at-home wife and mother during the 1950s and 1960s who began birding to escape the boredom of suburban life. When she was diagnosed with terminal cancer at age 49, she decided to travel the world in search of birds while her health allowed. Each trip became a short-term goal for Phoebe and let her focus on birds instead of the cancer. She did this for 18 years, traveling between two and ten months a year, despite two cancer recurrences, injuries, assaults, kidnapping, and other difficulties. Phoebe eventually amassed a life list of 8,674 species, or 85 percent of living birds then known." Libr J

Includes bibliographical references

Sneum, Thomas, 1917-2007

Ryan, Mark. **Hornet's** sting; the amazing untold story of World War II spy Thomas Sneum. Skyhorse Pub. 2009 386p il map $24.95   **92**

1. Spies 2. World War, 1939-1945 -- Secret service
ISBN 978-1-6023-9710-1

LC 2009-6210

Sneum's "real-life exploits include all the key elements of any good spy story: sex, danger, and intrigue. . . . Readers will find the book hard to put down." Libr J

Includes bibliographical references

Snyder, John

★ Snyder, John. **Hill** of Beans; coming of age in the last days of the Old South. John Snyder. Natl Book Network 2011 256 p. $24.00   **92**

1. Family life 2. Southern States -- History 3. Great Depression, 1929-1939
ISBN 098306220X; 9780983062202

In this memoir, "[John] Snyder documents growing up in the Carolinas during the Great Depression . . . . Presenting remembrances from three geographic locations that shaped his young life, Snyder explores Cedar Mountain, N.C. . . .; Greenville, S.C. . . .; and the Snyder family farm in Walhalla, S.C. . . . Snyder also . . . profiles a wide range of family and friends—most notably his father, a hard man given to arcane phrases . . . and his Aunt Bess." (Publishers Weekly)

Includes bibliographical references and index.

Socrates

★ Hughes, Bettany. The **hemlock** cup; Socrates, Athens, and the search for the good life. Alfred A. Knopf 2011 484p il map $35   **92**

1. Philosophers 2. Athens (Greece) -- History
ISBN 978-1-4000-4179-4; 1-4000-4179-1

LC 2010-45486

"For decades, while his city underwent war and hardship and defeat and civil war and political restructuring, Socrates settled himself in the agora and talked of inner things, the essence of things. Some of his words were taken down by acolytes such as Plato and Xenophon; some of his mannerisms were mocked by playwrights such as Aristophanes; the master himself, a man Hughes claims 'we can all benefit from getting to know a little better,' wrote nothing, but his recorded dialogues, his 'Socratic method' of relentless questioning, have become indispensable pieces of our Western mental furniture. Hughes revisits all of this with the panache of a born explainer, enthusiastically filling out the world of ancient Athens. . . . She takes readers through the torturous birth and early crises of Athenian democracy, and she's refreshingly evenhanded about the resentment such a democracy might feel toward somebody like Socrates." Washington Post

Includes bibliographical (p. 438-472) references

Johnson, Paul, 1928- **Socrates**; a man for our times. Viking 2011 208p $25.95   **92**

1. Philosophers

ISBN 978-0-670-02303-5

LC 2011019767

"A succinct, useful exploration of life in ancient Athens and of the great philosopher's essential beliefs." Kirkus

Includes bibliographical references

Soloway, Jill, 1965-

Soloway, Jill, 1965- **She** wants it; desire, power, and toppling the patriarchy. Jill Soloway. Random House Inc 2018 256 p. $27   **92**

1. Motion picture producers and directors -- United States
ISBN 1101904747; 9781101904749

"In this poignant memoir of personal transformation, Jill Soloway takes us on a patriarchy-toppling emotional and professional journey. . . . [It] chart Jill's evolution from straight, married mother of two to identifying as queer and nonbinary. This intense and revelatory metamorphosis challenges the status quo and reflects the shifting power dynamics that continue to shape our collective worldview." (Publisher's note)

"This is an honest look at Soloway's mind-opening journey, which allowed for deeper understanding of Hollywood's patriarchy as well as of the author's own gender, art, and self." Booklist

Sonnenberg, Susanna

Sonnenberg, Susanna. **Her** last death; a memoir. Scribner 2008 273p $24   **92**

1. Authors 2. Journalists 3. Columnists
ISBN 978-0-7432-9108-8; 0-7432-9108-5

LC 2007-3515

Sonnenberg's memoir illuminates her resolve to forge her independence, to become a woman capable of trust and to be a good mother to her own children after being raised by a mother who was a compulsive liar and a drug user.

"A heartbreaking yet wickedly entertaining portrait of a magically seductive, immensely flawed mother who fails dramatically as a parent and of a daughter who learns to trust and love others despite an orphan-like upbringing marked by disillusion." Libr J

Sontag, Susan, 1933-2004

Sontag, Susan. **Reborn**; journals and notebooks, 1947-1963. edited by David Rieff. Farrar, Straus and Giroux 2008 318p $24   **92**

1. Authors 2. Novelists 3. Women authors 4. Essayists 5. Literary critics 6. Authors, American 7. Short story writers
ISBN 978-0-374-10074-2; 0-374-10074-8

LC 2008-34247

"As a psychic collage, Reborn is far more fascinating than the sum of its parts: lists of errands, scraps of dialogue, notes on the breakup of a marriage. An essential tension animates almost every page. Sontag's theoretical mind always wants to be totalizing—to sum up, distill, command. But journal entries are, like the lives they document, provisional, incomplete, ragged. The resulting clash—with its canceled insights, non sequiturs, and self-critical marginalia—often reads like a brilliant pomo bildungsroman: A Portrait of the Theorist As a Young Woman," New York

Sorensen, Theodore C., 1928-2010

Sorensen, Theodore C., 1928-2010. **Counselor**; a life at the edge of history. [by] Ted Sorensen. HarperCollins 2008 556p il $27.95   **92**

1. Lawyers 2. Presidents 3. Senators 4. Members of Congress 5. Government officials 6. Biography, Individual 7. Presidential advisers 8. United States -- Politics and government -- 20th century

ISBN 0-06-079871-8; 978-0-06-079871-0

LC 2007-47328

This is a memoir by President Kennedy's advisor and speechwriter. Index.

"This book is instantly essential for any student of the period. It fills gaps in the historical record; it vividly conveys life inside the administration; and it generously dishes anecdotes." Washington Post Book World

Sosinski, Anthony

Aldridge, John. A **speck** in the sea; a story of survival and rescue. John Aldridge and Anthony Sosinski. Weinstein Books 2017 x, 262 p.p illustrations (chiefly color) (hardcover) $27 **92**
1. Fishing 2. Survival after airplane accidents, shipwrecks, etc. 3. Anna Mary (Ship) 4. Survival at sea -- New York (State) -- Montauk 5. Search and rescue operations -- New York (State) -- Montauk
ISBN 1602863288; 9781602863286; 9781602865310

This book, by John Aldridge and Anthony Sosinksi, tells the search and rescue effort to save Aldridge who "was thrown off the back of the Anna Mary while his fishing partner, . . . Sosinski, slept below. As desperate hours ticked by, Sosinski, the families, the local fishing community, and the U.S. Coast Guard in three states mobilized in an unprecedented search effort that culminated in a rare and exhilarating success." (Publisher's note)

"Told from multiple viewpoints, the book takes readers into the water with Aldridge as he shares first-person accounts of shark encounters and the mind games he played while clinging to his rubber boots to stay afloat." Pub Wkly Annex

Includes bibliographical references and index.

Soto, Jock

Marshall, Leslie. **Every** step you take; a memoir. with Leslie Marshall. Harper 2011 271p il $24.99; ebook $11.99 **92**
1. Ballet dancers
ISBN 978-0-06-173238-6; 978-0-06-209798-9 ebook

LC 2011012725

"Acclaimed dancer Soto—a principal for the New York City Ballet for 20 years (1985–2005)—writes about his career, his Native American heritage, his homosexuality, his passion for cooking, his struggles to find a family and his discovery of love. . . . A powerful story, affectionately told, about the demands and dimensions of personal and professional success." Kirkus

Sotomayor, Sonia, 1954-

★ Sotomayor, Sonia, 1954- **My** beloved world; Sonia Sotomayor. Knopf 2013 ix, 315 p., [16] p. of platesp ill. (hardback) $27.95 **92**
1. Hispanic American women 2. Hispanic American women -- Biography 3. Judges -- United States -- Biography 4. Hispanic American judges -- Biography 5. United States. Supreme Court -- Officials and employees -- Biography
ISBN 0307594882; 9780307594884

LC 2012031797

Author Sonia Sotomayor presents an autobiography as "the first Hispanic and third woman appointed to the United States Supreme Court . . . She determined to become a lawyer, . . . from valedictorian of her high school class to the highest honors at Princeton, Yale Law School, the New York County District Attorney's office, private practice, and appointment to the Federal District Court before the age of forty." (Publisher's note)

"Graceful, authoritative memoir from the country's first Hispanic Supreme Court justice. . . . The author vividly narrates her scholarly adventures at Princeton, where she advocated for Latino faculty, and Yale Law School, where she dealt with smaller cases in preparation

for the complexities of work in the district attorney's office. In 1992, she received an appointment to the U.S. District Court for the Southern District of New York. The author's text forms a cultural patchwork of memories and reflections as she mines the nuances of her parents' tumultuous relationship, fondly recalls family visits in Puerto Rico and offers insight on a judicial career that's just beginning when the memoir ends. . . . Mature, life-affirmative musings from a venerable life shaped by tenacity and pride." Kirkus

Soyinka, Wole

★ Soyinka, Wole. **You** must set forth at dawn; a memoir. Random House 2006 499p map $26.95 **92**
1. Poets 2. Authors 3. Novelists 4. Dramatists 5. Essayists 6. Memoirists 7. Nobel laureates for literature
ISBN 0-375-50365-X; 978-0-375-50365-8

"By turns panoramic and intimate, ruminative and politically resolute, Soyinka's memoir is a dense but intriguing conversation between a writer and his times." Publ Wkly

Spaak, Suzanne

Nelson, Anne. **Suzanne's** children; a daring rescue in Nazi Paris. Anne Nelson. Simon & Schuster 2017 336 p. (hardcover: alk. paper) $26 **92**
1. Holocaust, 1939-1945 2. Biography as a literary form 3. Righteous Gentiles in the Holocaust -- France -- Paris -- Biography
ISBN 9781501105326; 9781501105333

LC 2017008567

In this biography, auhtor by Anne Nelson tells the story of "Suzanne Spaak, who risked and gave her life to save hundreds of Jewish children from deportation from Nazi Paris to Auschwitz. This is one of the untold stories of the Holocaust.. . . In the final year of the Occupation Suzanne was caught in the Gestapo dragnet that was pursuing a Soviet agent she had aided. She was executed shortly before the liberation of Paris." (Publisher's note)

"This heartfelt story is almost a model for how popular history should be written; it will satisfy lovers of history, Jewish history in particular." (LJ)

Includes bibliographical references and index

Spark, Muriel

Stannard, Martin. **Muriel** Spark; the biography. W.W. Norton & Co. 2010 xxvi, 627p il $35 **92**
1. Authors 2. Novelists 3. Women authors 4. Authors, Scottish 5. Biographers 6. Short story writers
ISBN 978-0-393-05174-2

LC 2009-47982

First published 2009 in the United Kingdom

This is "among the richest and most satisfying literary biographies of our time: not only a portrait of the artist herself but also a rendering of her literary and social context and a judicious examination of her works." Wall Street J

Includes bibliographical references

Speaker, Tris, 1888-1958

Gay, Timothy M. **Tris** Speaker; the rough-and-tumble life of a baseball legend. University of Nebraska Press 2005 314p il $27.95 **92**
1. Baseball players 2. Baseball managers
ISBN 0-8032-2206-8

LC 2005-16975

This is a "look at the Hall of Fame center fielder, whose colorful personality and remarkable talent were overshadowed by contemporaries like Ty Cobb and Cy Young. . . . Gay has insured the righting of history with this biography. A worthwhile read for any sports fan." Publ Wkly

Spector, Phil

★ Brown, Mick. **Tearing** down the wall of sound; the rise and fall of Phil Spector. Knopf 2007 452p il $26.95; pa $16.95   **92**

1. Record producers 2. Songwriters 3. Music arrangers 4. Recording producers

ISBN 978-1-4000-4219-7; 1-400-04219-4; 978-1-4000-7661-1 pa; 1-4000-7661-7 pa

LC 2007-4819

This is a biography of the record producer and songwriter.

"Stacked with incredible anecdotes, Brown's entertaining and nuanced portrait lifts the fog of myth and outright falsehood (including Spector's own) that have obscured the celebrity producer (like an enormous, gravity-defying wig) through the years." Publ Wkly

Includes bibliographical references

Speer, Albert, 1905-1981

Fest, Joachim C. **Speer**: the final verdict; {by} Joachim Fest; translated from the German by Ewald Osers and Alexandra Dring. Harcourt 2002 419p il $30; pa $15   **92**

1. Architects 2. War criminals 3. National socialism 4. Memoirists 5. Nazi leaders 6. Germany -- Politics and government -- 1933-1945

ISBN 0-15-100556-7; 0-15-602874-3 pa

LC 2002-6074

"This is a valuable, important biography, but perhaps it is an effort to explain the unexplainable." Booklist

Includes bibliographical references

Spender, Stephen, 1909-1995

Sutherland, John. **Stephen** Spender; a literary life. Oxford University Press 2005 627p il $40   **92**

1. Poets 2. Authors 3. Novelists 4. Essayists 5. Memoirists 6. Biographers 7. Literary critics 8. Short story writers

ISBN 0-19517-816-5

LC 2004-09727

"Stephen Spender was one of a generation of Oxford-educated English writers, including W. H. Auden and Christopher Isherwood, who sought to revolutionize literature in the 1930s. In this official account of his life . . . emphasis is appropriately placed on the 1930s, when Spender came to prominence writing prose, short stories, criticism, and journalism in addition to his politically charged poetry. He was as experimental in life as in art, as evidenced by his bisexuality and his loyalty to left-wing Socialist causes." Libr J

Spiker, Ted

Spiker, Ted. **Down** size; 12 truths for turning pants-splitting frustration into pants-fitting success. Ted Spiker; foreword by Mehmet C. Oz, MD. Hudson Street Press 2014 288 p. (hardback) $25.95   **92**

1. Weight loss 2. Overweight persons -- United States -- Biography

ISBN 1594631913; 9781594631917

LC 2014015115

In this book, author Ted Spiker "takes readers on an inspiring, candid, and comical journey, exploring the art and science of weight loss through his own struggles as a pear-shaped man in a not-so-pear-shaped world, with research about food, exercise, and the psychology of losing weight. He reveals twelve truths about successful weight loss, in areas such as temptation, frustration, nutrition, and inspiration." (Publisher's note)

"Most importantly, Spiker advocates personalized diets over a one-size-fits-all approach. Throughout the book, he gently nudges and encourages readers, winning their trust by sharing personal moments from his own weight-loss story." Pub Wkly

Sprague, Kate Chase, 1840-1899

Oller, John. **American** queen; the rise and fall of Kate Chase Sprague, Civil War "Belle of the North" and gilded age woman of scandal. John Oller. Da Capo Press, A Member of the Perseus Books Group 2014 416 p. illustrations (hardcover) $25.99   **92**

1. Chase, Salmon P. (Salmon Portland), 1808-1873 2. United States -- Politics and government -- 19th century 3. Socialites -- United States -- Biography

ISBN 0306822806; 9780306822803; 9780306822810

LC 2014012054

This book, by John Oller, focuses on the "daughter of Salmon P. Chase, Lincoln's treasury secretary, Kate Chase. As her widowed father's hostess, she . . . [had] hopes of making her father president and herself his First Lady. To facilitate that goal, she married one of the richest men in the country, the . . . governor of Rhode Island. . . . But when William Sprague turned out to be less of a prince as a husband, Kate found comfort in the arms of a powerful married senator." (Publisher's note)

"Oller's work is less the story of a woman's political rise and fall and more one that reveals how the social limitations of the past created tragic outcomes for talented females. A well-researched, thoughtful biography of a woman who 'became entirely her own person, a rare feat for women of her day.'" Kirkus

Includes bibliographical references and index

Springsteen, Bruce

Carlin, Peter Ames. **Bruce**; Peter Ames Carlin. Simon & Schuster 2012 xi, 494 p.p ill.   **92**

1. Rock musicians -- Biography 2. Rock musicians -- United States -- Biography

ISBN 9781439191828; 9781439191835; 9781439191842

LC 2012020890

This book describes how, "For more than four decades, Bruce Springsteen has reflected the heart and soul of America with a career that includes twenty Grammy Awards, more than 120 million albums sold, two Golden Globes, and an Academy Award. [Author] Peter Ames Carlin . . . encompasses the breadth of Springsteen's astonishing career and explores the inner workings of a man who managed to redefine generations of music." (Publisher's note)

"The author presents his subject as a supremely gifted musician and truly heroic figure, albeit one with a lot on his troubled mind." Kirkus

Includes bibliographical references and index.

★ Springsteen, Bruce, 1949- **Born** to run; Bruce Springsteen. Simon & Schuster 2016 528 p. illustrations (some color) (ebook) $20.99; (hardcover) $32.5   **92**

1. Rock musicians -- United States -- Biography

ISBN 9781501141539; 9781471157790; 9781501141515

LC 2016016742

In this autobiography, singer Bruce Springsteen "describes growing up Catholic in Freehold, New Jersey, amid the poetry, danger, and darkness that fueled his imagination . . . . He vividly recounts his relentless drive to become a musician, his early days as a bar band king in Asbury Park, and the rise of the E Street Band. . . . He also tells for the first time the story of the personal struggles that inspired his best work." (Publisher's note)

"A superb memoir by any standard, but one of the best to have been written by a rock star." Kirkus

Spurrier, Steve, 1945-

Finebaum, Paul. **Head** ball coach; My Life in Football, Doing It Differently--and Winning. Steve Spurrier with Buddy Martin; foreword by Paul Finebaum. Blue Rider Press 2016 320 p. illustrations (hardback) $28; (ebook) $65 **92**

1. Football coaches -- United States -- Biography
ISBN 9780399574665; 9780399574689

LC 2016029233

In this memoir by football coach Steve Spurrier with Buddy Martin and foreword by Paul Finebaum, "Spurrier, shares his story of a life in football--from growing up in Tennessee to winning the Heisman Trophy to playing and coaching in the pros to leading the Florida Gators to six SEC Championships and a National Championship to elevating the South Carolina program to new heights--and coaching like nobody else." (Publisher's note)

"An easy, straightforward read with plenty to chew on for fans of college football, especially the SEC." Kirkus

St. Germain, Jim

St. Germain, Jim. A **stone** of hope; a memoir. Jim St. Germain, with Jon Sternfeld. HarperCollins 2017 x, 292 p.p illustrations (hardcover) $27.99 **92**

1. Social action 2. African Americans 3. Social advocacy -- United States 4. Problem youth -- United States -- Biography 5. African American social reformers -- United States -- Biography
ISBN 9780062458810; 9780062458797; 0062458795

This book, by Jim St. Germain and Jon Sternfeld, is "a searing memoir and clarion call to save our at-risk youth by a young black man who himself was a lost cause--until he landed in a rehabilitation program that saved his life and gave him purpose. . . . 'A Stone of Hope' is more than an incredible coming-of-age story; told with a degree of candor that requires the deepest courage, it is also a rallying cry." (Publisher's note)

"An affecting and earnest testimonial to the power of a humane criminal system built on rehabilitation more than punishment." Kirkus
Includes bibliographical references (pages 291-292).

Stachler, Susan

Stachler, Susan. The **cookie** cure; a mother/daughter memoir of cookies and cancer. Susan Stachler with Laura Stachler. Sourcebooks 2018 xvii, 297 p.p (paperback) $15.99 **92**

1. Businesswomen -- Biography 2. Cancer patients -- Biography 3. Cookie industry -- United States 4. Mothers and daughters -- United States 5. Businesswomen -- United States -- Biography 6. Cancer -- Patients -- United States -- Biography
ISBN 9781492637851; 9781492637837

LC 2017030949

In this memoir, authors Susan and Laura Stachler relate the establishment of their cookie business after battling cancer. "When . . . Susan Stachler was diagnosed with cancer, her mother, Laura, . . .pledged to help Susan through the worst of her treatments. When they discovered that Laura's homemade ginger cookies soothed the side effects of Susan's chemo, the mother-daughter duo soon found themselves opening Susansnaps and sharing their gourmet gingersnaps with the world." (Publisher's note)

"A sweet story of a strong-willed mother-daughter combo team who stood up to cancer and created a thriving business in the process." Kirkus

Stalin, Joseph, 1879-1953

Khlevniuk, Oleg V. **Stalin**; new biography of a dictator. Oleg V. Khlevniuk; translated by Nora S. Favorov. Yale University Press 2015 408 p. 16 plates; illustrations (cloth: alk. paper) $35 **92**

1. Russia -- History -- 1917-1991, Soviet Union 2. Dictators -- Soviet Union -- Biography 3. Heads of state -- Soviet Union -- Biography 4. Soviet Union -- Politics and government -- 1936-1953
ISBN 0300163886; 9780300163889

LC 2014039237

This book, by Oleg V. Khlevniuk, translated by Nora S. Favorov, "offers an unprecedented, fine-grained portrait of [Joseph] Stalin the man and dictator. Without mythologizing Stalin as either benevolent or an evil genius, Khlevniuk resolves numerous controversies about specific events in the dictator's life while assembling many hundreds of previously unknown letters, memos, reports, and diaries into a . . . narrative of a life that altered the course of world history." (Publisher's note)

"Readers with an interest in Soviet history, and those who can't wait for the next two volumes of Kotkin's Stalin, will appreciate this well-documented portrayal of a man whose despotic rule reverberates in Russia to this day." LJ
Includes bibliographical references and index

★ Kotkin, Stephen. **Stalin**; Volume 1 Paradoxes of Power, 1878-1928. Stephen Kotkin. Penguin Group USA 2014 912 p. illustrations, maps hbk $40 **92**

1. Russia -- History -- 1917-1991, Soviet Union 2. Soviet Union -- History -- 1925-1953 3. Dictators -- Soviet Union -- Biography 4. Heads of state -- Soviet Union -- Biography 5. Political culture -- Soviet Union -- History 6. Soviet Union -- Politics and government -- 1917-1936 7. Soviet Union -- Politics and government -- 1936-1953
ISBN 9781594203794; 1594203792

LC 2014032906

Pulitzer Prize Finalist: Biography or Autobiography (2015)
Los Angeles Times Book Prizes Finalist: Biography (2014)

In this biography on Joseph Stalin, author Stephen Kotkin "gives an intimate view of the Bolshevik regime's inner geography of power. . . . Kotkin rejects the inherited wisdom about Stalin's psychological makeup, showing us instead how Stalin's near paranoia was fundamentally political, and closely tracks the Bolshevik revolution's structural paranoia, the predicament of a Communist regime in an overwhelmingly capitalist world, surrounded and penetrated by enemies." (Publisher's note)

"In this first volume of a planned three-volume biography, Kotkin . . . begins unraveling Stalin's strange, monstrous life. This is an epic, thoroughly researched account that presents a broad vision of Stalin, from his birth to his rise to absolute power." Pub Wkly
Includes bibliographical references and index

★ Kotkin, Stephen. **Stalin**; waiting for Hitler, 1929-1941. Stephen Kotkin. Penguin Group USA 2017 976 p. $40 **92**

1. Russia -- History -- 1925-1953
ISBN 1594203806; 9781594203800

This book, by Stephen Kotkin, presents "the definitive biography of Joseph Stalin, from collectivization and the Great Terror to the conflict with Hitler's Germany that is the signal event of modern world history. . . . [The book] is the story of how a political system forged an unparalleled personality and vice versa. . . . [It is also] a history of the world during the build-up to its most fateful hour, from the vantage point of Stalin's seat of power." (Publisher's note)

"The John P. Birkelund Professor in History and International Affairs at Princeton University, Kotkin offers his second in a magisterial three-volume biography of Soviet leader Joseph Stalin, following Pulitzer Prize finalist Stalin. Vol. 1: Paradoxes of Power, 1878–1928." (LJ)

★ Montefiore, Sebag. **Stalin**: the court of the red tsar; by Simon Sebag Montefiore. Knopf 2004 xxvii, 785p il map $30   **92**
1. Dictators 2. Heads of state 3. Communist leaders 4. Political leaders 5. Soviet Union -- History
ISBN 1-400-04230-5
LC 2003-27390
First published 2003 in the United Kingdom
"In the relentless detail, the mood-setting descriptions of the leader's surroundings, the sketches of the people around him and in Stalin's own words, pranks and tempers, Montefiore gives us not only the most intimate view of the general secretary that we have to date but a rounded and complex portrait of a man who could go from charming to lethal in the space of a few seconds." Nation
Includes bibliographical references

★ Montefiore, Sebag. **Young** Stalin; [by] Simon Sebag Montefiore. Knopf 2007 xxxii, 460p il map $30   **92**
1. Dictators 2. Heads of state 3. Communist leaders 4. Political leaders 5. Soviet Union -- History
ISBN 1-4000-4465-0; 978-1-4000-4465-8
LC 2007-29220
Stalin "is brilliantly brought to life in this superb biography." Hist Today
Includes bibliographical references

Pringle, Peter. The **murder** of Nikolai Vavilov; the story of Stalin's persecution of one of the great scientists of the twentieth century. Simon & Schuster 2008 370p il $26   **92**
1. Botanists 2. Heads of state 3. Communist leaders 4. Plant geneticists 5. Political leaders
ISBN 978-0-7432-6498-3; 0-7432-6498-3
LC 2008-03510
This is a biography of the Russian botanist and geneticist who was starved to death in a Soviet prison in 1943.
This "is a must-read to grasp the ultimate, disasterous effect of politics trumping science." Sci Books Films
Includes bibliographical references

Service, Robert. **Stalin**; a biography. Belknap Press of Harvard University Press 2005 715p il map $29.95   **92**
1. Dictators 2. Heads of state 3. Communist leaders 4. Political leaders 5. Soviet Union -- History
ISBN 0-674-01697-1
LC 2004-61115
This book covers Stalin's life "from his early, troubled years in a small town in Georgia to the pinnacle of power in the Kremlin. . . . By providing such a rich and complex portrait of the dictator and the Soviet system, Service humanizes Stalin without ever diminishing the extent of the atrocities he unleashed upon the Soviet population." Publ Wkly
Includes bibliographical references

Stallworth, Ron

Stallworth, Ron. **Black** klansman; a memoir. Ron Stallworth. Flatiron Books 2018 191 p. (hardcover) $25.99   **92**
1. Ku Klux Klan 2. Undercover operations 3. White supremacy movements 4. Ku Klux Klan (1915-) 5. African American police 6. Hate crimes -- United States 7. United States -- Race relations 8. Undercover operations -- United States 9. White supremacy movements -- United States

ISBN 1250299047; 9781250299048
LC 2018003659
In this book, author Ron Stallworth, recounts how he conducted the undercover investigation of the Ku Klux Klan (KKK) in 1978. "Ron recruits his partner Chuck to play the 'white' Ron Stallworth, while Stallworth himself conducts all subsequent phone conversations. During the months-long investigation, Stallworth sabotages cross burnings, exposes white supremacists in the military, and even befriends David Duke, [grand wizard of the KKK.]" Publisher's note)

Staniforth, Nate

Staniforth, Nate. **Here** is real magic; a magician's search for wonder in the modern world. Nate Staniforth. Bloomsbury 2018 x, 245 p.p (hardcover: acid-free paper) $28   **92**
1. Autobiographies 2. Magicians -- United States 3. Magicians -- United States -- Biography
ISBN 9781632864260; 9781632864246
LC 2017016409
This autobiography "follows Nate Staniforth's evolution from an obsessed young magician to a broken wanderer and back again. It tells the story of his rediscovery of astonishment--and the importance of wonder in everyday life--during his trip to the slums of India, where he infiltrated a three-thousand-year-old clan of street magicians." (Publisher's note)
"The result is a personal story that conjures up the wonder and magic of life without any trickery or deceit." Pub Wkly

Stanley, Henry M. (Henry Morton), 1841-1904

Jeal, Tim. **Stanley**; the impossible life of Africa's greatest explorer. Yale University Press 2007 570p il map $38   **92**
1. Explorers 2. Journalists 3. Travel writers
ISBN 978-0-300-12625-9; 0-300-12625-5
LC 2007-923548
This is a biography of the explorer.
"There have been many biographies of Stanley, but Jeal's is the most felicitous, the best informed, the most complete and readable and exhaustive." N Y Times Book Rev
Includes bibliographical references

Stanley, Ralph, 1927-2016

Stanley, Ralph. **Man** of constant sorrow; my life and times. [by] Ralph Stanley with Eddie Dean. Gotham Books 2009 452p $27.50   **92**
1. Bluegrass music 2. Banjo players 3. Bluegrass musicians
ISBN 978-1-592-40425-4
LC 2009-21920
A memoir by the bluegrass singer and banjo player.
"Unashamedly old-fashioned, opinionated and prickly, . . . [the author is] at his best recalling his backwoods upbringing, the vicissitudes of the bluegrass road, the murder of one of his lead singers, regional Democratic politics, the power of gospel music and old-time religion and the fast-vanishing South of his boyhood. An often tart yet affecting music memoir." Kirkus

Stanton, Elizabeth Cady, 1815-1902

Ginzberg, Lori D. **Elizabeth** Cady Stanton; an American life. Hill and Wang 2009 254p il $25   **92**
1. Feminism 2. Suffragists 3. Women -- Suffrage 4. Biography, Individual 5. Women -- Suffrage -- History
ISBN 0-8090-9493-2; 978-0-8090-9493-6
LC 2008-54395
This is a biography of the women's rights activist and author of Eighty Years and More (1898). Bibliography. Index.

The author "makes a convincing case for Stanton as the founding philosopher of the American women's rights movement in a lively voice that enhances her eccentric subject. . . . Ginzberg has created a vibrant portrait of a key, often misrepresented figure in American history." Am Hist

Includes bibliographical references

Stanton, Tom

Stanton, Tom. **Road** to Cooperstown; a father, two sons, and the journey of a lifetime. Thomas Dunne Bks. 2003 260p il $24.95; pa $13.95 **92**
1. Artists 2. Painters 3. Baseball -- Biography 4. National Baseball Hall of Fame and Museum
ISBN 0-312-30350-5; 0-312-33118-5 pa

LC 2003-40862

Companion volume to The final season

The author "examines family, fatherhood, life and, of course, baseball while on a road trip that was a lifetime in the making." Publ Wkly

Staples, Mavis

Kot, Greg. **I'll** take you there; Mavis Staples, the Staple Singers, and the march up freedom's highway. Greg Kot. Scribner 2014 320 p. illustrations (hardback) $26 **92**
1. Staple Singers 2. Gospel musicians -- United States -- Biography
ISBN 1451647859; 9781451647853; 9781451647860

LC 2013032633

This book, by Greg Kot, is a biography of "Mavis Staples--lead singer of the Staple Singers and a major figure in the music that shaped the civil rights era. From her love affair with Bob Dylan, to her creative collaborations with Prince, to her recent revival alongside Wilco's Jeff Tweedy, this . . . account shows Mavis as you've never seen her before. . . Readers will also hear from Prince, Bonnie Raitt, David Byrne, Marty Stuart, Ry Cooder, Steve Cropper, and many other individuals." (Publisher's note)

"Kot's effort remains clear and respectful and takes us deep into the golden age of Mavis and her marvelously talented group." Pub Wkly

Includes bibliographical references, discography, and index

Stapp, John P. (John Paul), 1910-1999

Ryan, Craig. **Sonic** wind; the story of John Paul Stapp and how a renegade doctor became the fastest man on Earth. by Craig Ryan. Liveright Publishing Corp., A Division of W.W. Norton & Co. 2015 384 p. illustrations (hardcover) $27.95 **92**
1. Aeronautics 2. Biophysicists -- United States -- Biography 3. United States. Air Force -- Officers -- Biography 4. Aeronautics -- Safety measures -- Research -- United States -- History -- 20th century 5. Motor vehicles -- Safety appliances -- Research -- United States -- History -- 20th century
ISBN 0871406772; 9780871406774

LC 2015013245

This book, by Craig Ryan, is the "untold story of an eccentric, scientific visionary whose death-defying research has saved millions of lives. . . . The exploits of John Paul Stapp (1910–1999) come to thrilling life in this biography of a Renaissance man who was once blasted . . . across the desert in his Sonic Wind rocket sled, only to be slammed to a stop in barely a second. The experiment . . . revolutionize[d] automobile and aircraft design." (Publisher's note)

"A fine, groundbreaking biography of one of aeromedical sciences' more legendary figures." LJ

Includes bibliographical references and index

Stefanovic, Sofija

Stefanovic, Sofija. **Miss** ex-Yugoslavia; a memoir. Sofija Stefanovic. Pocket Books 2018 272 p. $26 **92**
1. Biography 2. Immigrants -- Biography
ISBN 1501165747; 9781501165740

In this memoir, Sofija Stefanovic tells her "immigrant experience and life as a perpetual fish-out-of-water. . . . [She was born in] 1982 . . . in Belgrade, . . . Yugoslavia. . . . Stefanovic's early life is filled with Yugo rock, inadvisable crushes, and the quirky ups and downs of life in a socialist state. . . . [This] memoir is a window to a complicated culture that she both cherishes and resents." (Publisher's note)

Steffens, Lincoln, 1866-1936

Steffens, Lincoln. The **autobiography** of Lincoln Steffens; foreword by Thomas C. Leonard. Heyday Books 2005 882p il (California legacy book) pa $21.95 **92**
1. Authors 2. Journalists 3. Essayists 4. Biographers 5. Social reformers 6. Writers on politics
ISBN 1-59714-016-3

LC 2005-27009

First published 1931 by Harcourt Brace & Co.

The life of an American reporter, journalist, student of ethics and politics.

"Here is a textbook on journalism; a treasure house for the historian of that wave of social idealism that shook the United States from 1900 to 1917; a casebook for the psychologist of political types. Above all it is the vivid diary of a bold and humane pilgrim." Survey

Stein, Gertrude, 1874-1946

Malcolm, Janet. **Two** lives; Gertrude and Alice. Yale University Press 2007 229p il $25 **92**
1. Poets 2. Authors 3. Novelists 4. Essayists 5. Memoirists 6. Literary critics 7. Authors, American 8. Private secretaries
ISBN 978-0-300-12551-1; 0-300-12551-8

LC 2007-12085

"This is a vital addition to Stein criticism as well as an important work that critiques the political responsibility of the artist (even a genius) to the larger world." Publ Wkly

Includes bibliographical references

Steinberg, Neil

Steinberg, Neil. **Drunkard**; a hard-drinking life. Dutton 2008 270p $24.95; pa $15 **92**
1. Journalists 2. Nonfiction writers 3. Alcoholics -- Rehabilitation
ISBN 978-0-5259-5065-3; 0-5259-5065-6; 978-0-4522-9543-8 pa

LC 2007-51603

"Forced by the court into rehab, Steinberg chronicles his journey to sobriety, following a circuitous route that included plenty of stops in local watering holes along the way. . . . Frank, funny, and insightful, Steinberg writes the book of his life." Booklist

Steinberg, Saul

Bair, Deirdre. **Saul** Steinberg; a biography. Deirdre Bair. Nan A. Talese/Doubleday 2012 732 p. illustrations (some color) (alk. paper) $40 **92**
1. Artists -- United States -- Biography
ISBN 038552448X; 9780385524483

LC 2011050601

This book by Deirdre Bair is a "biography of Saul Steinberg, one of The New Yorker's most iconic artists. . . . Born in Romania, Steinberg was educated in Milan and was already famous for his satirical drawings when World War II forced him to immigrate to the United States. .

. . His wife was the artist Hedda Sterne, . . . but his truly great love was the United States, where he traveled extensively by bus, train, and car, drawing, observing, and writing." (Publisher's note)

Includes bibliographical references and index

Steinem, Gloria

Heilbrun, Carolyn G. The **education** of a woman; the life of Gloria Steinem. Ballantine Books 1996 450p il pa $23 **92**

1. Authors 2. Feminism 3. Journalists 4. Feminists 5. Memoirists 6. Magazine editors

ISBN 0-345-40621-4; 978-0-345-40621-7

First published 1995 by Dial Press

"The portrait that results is nuanced and thoughtful. . . . Heilbrun's goal is at once to understand how Steinem became the woman she is, and what her life can teach us about childhood and family, self and society. Slow at the start, but Heilbrun soon captures readers' interest and imagination." Booklist

Includes bibliographical references

Steinem, Gloria, 1934- **My** life on the road; Gloria Steinem. Random House Inc 2015 304 p. illustrations (hardback) $28 **92**

1. Feminism 2. Women's rights 3. Feminism -- United States 4. Feminists -- United States -- Biography

ISBN 0679456201; 9780679456209

LC 2015010718

This memoir by Gloria Steinem is "the moving, funny, and profound story of Gloria's growth and also the growth of a revolutionary movement for equality-- and the story of how surprising encounters on the road shaped both. From her first experience of social activism among women in India to her work as a journalist in the 1960s; from the whirlwind of political campaigns to the founding of Ms. magazine." (Publisher's note)

"Illuminating and inspiring, this book presents a distinguished woman's exhilarating vision of what it means to live with openness, honesty, and a willingness to grow beyond the apparent confinement of seemingly irreconcilable polarities. An invigoratingly candid memoir from a giant of women's rights." Kirkus

Stengel, Casey

Appel, Marty. **Casey** Stengel; baseball's greatest character. Marty Appel. Doubleday 2017 416 p. (ebook) $65; (hard cover) $27.95 **92**

1. Baseball managers -- United States -- Biography

ISBN 9780385540483; 9780385540476

LC 2016027618

This book, by Marty Appel, presents "the definitive biography of baseball's greatest character. There was nobody like Casey before him, and no one like him since. For more than fifty years, Casey Stengel lived baseball, first as a player . . . , and then as a manager. . . . He made his biggest mark on the game, revolutionizing the role of manager while winning an astounding ten pennants and seven World Series Championships . . . with the Yankees." (Publisher's note)

"Stengel is unquestionably one of baseball's most significant characters, and Appel is the perfect fit to chronicle his life. One of the more skilled biographies baseball fans could hope to find."

Stern, Jessica, 1958-

Stern, Jessica. **Denial**; a memoir of terror. Ecco Press 2010 300p $24.99; ebook $11.99 **92**

ISBN 978-0-06-162665-4; 978-0-06-200011-8 ebook

A scientist and expert on terrorism and post-traumatic stress disor-

der describes her own journey through trauma and its lingering effects after repressing and disassociating her own ordeal as the victim of an unsolved sexual assault as a teenager.

"Though the narrative continually threatens to spiral into stream-of-consciousness ramblings, Stern always manages to hold it together, thus lending a sense of the floating dissociation she often feels while still holding the narrative together as a cohesive whole. She successfully unearths difficult emotional terrain without sinking into utter subjectivity and maintains an orderly progression without becoming clinical. A disturbing, captivating memoir." Kirkus

Includes bibliographical references

Steward, Samuel M., 1909-1993

Spring, Justin. **Secret** historian; the life and times of Samuel Steward, professor, tattoo artist, and sexual renegade. Farrar, Straus and Giroux 2010 478p il $32.50; ebook $16.99 **92**

1. Authors 2. Novelists 3. Tattoo artists 4. College teachers 5. Authors, American 6. Short story writers 7. Biography, Individual

ISBN 0-374-28134-3; 1-4299-3294-5 ebook; 978-0-374-28134-2; 978-1-4299-3294-3 ebook

LC 2009-43086

National Book Award Finalist: Nonfiction (2010)

This book is "drawn from the secret diaries and journals of novelist, poet, and university professor Samuel M. Steward." (Publisher's note) Index.

"This is a rich and exuberant biography of a man who deserves to be better known, as well as a rare window on gay life in an era known mostly for its furtiveness and repression." Economist

Includes bibliographical references

Stoller, Mike, 1933-

Leiber, Jerry. **Hound** dog; the Leiber & Stoller autobiography. [by] Jerry Leiber and Mike Stoller with David Ritz. Simon & Schuster 2009 322p il $25 **92**

1. Composers 2. Lyricists 3. Songwriters 4. Rock music -- History and criticism

ISBN 978-1-4165-5938-2; 1-4165-5938-8

LC 2008-47821

"Collaboration is a messy business. So is autobiography. But it shouldn't be forgotten that Leiber and Stoller were among the pioneers who helped bring black and white musical forms together. It has been a historically fraught process, but the collision of cultures is probably what has given such energy and tension to American music. Hound Dog is an important part of that story." N Y Times Book Rev

Includes bibliographical references

Stone, I. F. (Isidor Feinstein), 1907-1989

Guttenplan, D. D. **American** radical; the life and times of I. F. Stone. Farrar, Straus and Giroux 2009 570p il $35 **92**

1. Authors 2. Journalists 3. Magazine editors

ISBN 978-0-374-18393-6; 0-374-18393-7

LC 2009-09667

This is a biography of the American journalist who published I.F. Stone's Weekly from 1953 until 1971.

"Guttenplan's lively biography brings back to life a man whose work has often been forgotten but whose writing and life provide a model for the kind of freethinking journalism missing in society today." Publ Wkly

Includes bibliographical references (p. [483]-538) and index. (BLCM)

★ MacPherson, Myra. **All** governments lie; the life and times of rebel journalist I.F. Stone. Scribner 2006 564p il

hardcover o.p. pa $20 **92**
1. Authors 2. Journalists 3. Magazine editors
ISBN 978-0-684-80713-3; 0-684-80713-0; 978-1-4165-5679-4
pa; 1-4165-5679-6 pa

LC 2006-42389
"This biography interweaves his life and journalism within the context of the social and political era, providing an engaging overview of a complex man who challenged his contemporaries. Many of the political issues Stone confronted will resonate with today's readers." Libr J
Includes bibliographical references

Stone, Robert, 1937-
Stone, Robert. **Prime** green; remembering the sixties. Ecco 2007 229p il $25.95 **92**
1. Authors 2. Novelists 3. Screenwriters 4. United States -- History -- 1961-1974 ISBN 0-06-019816-8; 978-0-06-019816-9
LC 2006-46351
The author "is a born storyteller, with a wonderful feel for place and character that vividly evokes the cultural gulf America crossed in that decade." Publ Wkly

Straus, Geneviève, 1849-1926
Weber, Caroline. **Proust's** duchess; how three celebrated women captured the imagination of fin de siècle Paris. Caroline Weber. Alfred A. Knopf 2018 736 p. (hardcover) $35 **92**
1. Biography 2. Women -- Biography 3. Women -- France -- Paris -- Biography 4. Paris (France) -- Intellectual life -- 19th century 5. Paris (France) -- Social life and customs -- 19th century 6. Aristocracy (Social class) -- France -- Paris -- Biography
ISBN 9780307961785; 9780345803122
LC 2017038855
This book, by Caroline Weber, presents "the first in-depth study of the three women [Marcel] Proust used to create his supreme fictional character, the Duchesse de Guermantes. Geneviève Halévy Bizet Straus; Laure de Sade, Comtesse de Adhéaume de Chevigné; and Élisabeth de Riquet de Caraman-Chimay, the Comtesse Greffulhe--these were the three superstars of fin-de-siècle Parisian high society." (Publisher's note)
Includes bibliographical references

Stravinsky, Igor, 1882-1971
Joseph, Charles M. **Stravinsky** inside out. Yale Univ. Press 2001 xx, 320p il $29.95 **92**
1. Composers
ISBN 0-300-07537-5
LC 2001-913
This study "reveals a . . . flawed and fragile human being, who craved approval, dealt ungenerously with colleagues, loved James Bond movies, and tried hard to further his son's musical career. Although the aged Stravinsky's eagerness to play the role of celebrity composer for the golden age of television . . . was an embarrassment, most of these episodes testify to the protean survival skills of an artist whose sense of identity was always in flux and whose cunning was commensurate with his talent." New Yorker
Includes bibliographical references

Joseph, Charles M. **Stravinsky** inside out. Yale Univ. Press 2001 xx, 320p il $29.95 **92**
1. Composers
ISBN 0-300-07537-5
LC 2001-913
This study "reveals a . . . flawed and fragile human being, who craved approval, dealt ungenerously with colleagues, loved James Bond

movies, and tried hard to further his son's musical career. Although the aged Stravinsky's eagerness to play the role of celebrity composer for the golden age of television . . . was an embarrassment, most of these episodes testify to the protean survival skills of an artist whose sense of identity was always in flux and whose cunning was commensurate with his talent." New Yorker
Includes bibliographical references and index

Walsh, Stephen. **Stravinsky**: a creative spring; Russia and France, 1882-1934. University of California Press 2002 698p il pa $25.95 **92**
1. Composers
ISBN 978-0-520-22749-1; 0-520-22749-2
LC 2002-23256
First published 1999 by Knopf
"In this reference-oriented biography, Walsh uses diaries, press clippings, and other materials to probe in detail the life of a man kept very busy with effectively dividing his time between performance, composition, family, and mistress." Booklist
Includes bibliographical references

Walsh, Stephen. **Stravinsky**: the second exile; France and America, 1934-1971. Stephen Walsh. Alfred A. Knopf 2006 709p il $40 **92**
1. Composers
ISBN 0-375-40752-9
LC 2005-47231
Sequel to Stravinsky: a creative spring
"This is essential reading for musicologists and other music enthusiasts who wish to delve into the life and mind of perhaps the greatest composer of the 20th century." Libr J
Includes bibliographical references

Strayed, Cheryl, 1968-
Strayed, Cheryl. **Wild**; from lost to found on the Pacific Crest Trail. Cheryl Strayed. Alfred A. Knopf 2012 315 p. map **92**
1. Hiking 2. Bereavement 3. Pacific Crest Trail 4. Mountains -- North America 5. Women authors -- Biography 6. Pacific Crest Trail -- Description and travel 7. Authors, American -- 21st century -- Biography
ISBN 9780307592736; 0307592731
LC 2011033752
The author "recounts her experience hiking the Pacific Crest Trail (PCT) in 1995 after her mother's death and her own subsequent divorce. Designated a National Scenic Trail in 1968 but not completed until 1993, the PCT runs from Mexico to Canada, and [Cheryl] Strayed hiked sections of it two summers after it was officially declared finished. She takes readers with her on the trail, and the transformation she experiences on its course is significant: she goes from feeling out of her element with a too-big backpack and too-small boots to finding a sense of home in the wilderness and with the allies she meets along the way. . . . [She includes] descriptions of the natural wonders near the PCT, particularly Mount Hood, Crater Lake, and the Sierras--what John Muir proclaimed the 'Range of Light.'" (Libr J)

Strayhorn, Billy
Strayhorn; an illustrated life. edited by A. Alyce Claerbaut and David Schlesinger. Bolden 2015 208 p. illustrations (some color) (hardback) $35 **92**
1. Composers -- Biography 2. Jazz musicians -- Biography 3. Composers -- United States -- Biography 4. Jazz musicians -- United

States -- Biography 5. Composers -- United States -- Biography -- Pictorial works 6. Jazz musicians -- United States -- Biography -- Pictorial works

ISBN 1932841989; 9781932841985

LC 2015021651

This book, edited by A. Alyce Claerbaut and David Schlesinger, "is a stunning collection of essays, photographs, and ephemera celebrating Billy Strayhorn, one of the most significant yet under-appreciated contributors to 20th century American music. Released in commemoration of Strayhorn's centennial, this luxurious coffee-table book offers intimate details of the composer's life from musicians, scholars, and Strayhorn's closest relatives." (Publisher's note)

"Readers with even the slightest interest in jazz will be delighted with the endlessly fascinating array of visual treats and star-studded reminiscences that tenderly pay tribute to an often overlooked yet extremely important figure in jazz history." LJ

Includes bibliographical references and index

Streb, Elizabeth

Streb, Elizabeth. **Streb**; how to become an extreme action hero. foreword by Anna Deavere Smith & introduction by Peggy Phelan. Feminist Press 2010 201p il pa $18.95   **92**

1. Dance 2. Dancers 3. Choreographers 4. Human locomotion 5. Biography, Individual 6. Movement, Psychology of 7. Human beings -- Attitude and movement

ISBN 978-1-55861-656-1

LC 2009-52614

"Elizabeth Streb has been testing the potential of the human body since childhood. Can she fly? Can she run up walls? Can she break through glass? How fast can she go? Combining memoir and theory, Streb [aims to] convey how she became an extreme action choreographer, developing a form of movement that's more NASCAR than modern dance, more boxing than ballet." (Publisher's note) Index.

"In this dizzying, inspirational self-help memoir, choreographer and performer Streb details her lifelong exploration of movement, the body, and time while providing brief lessons in math and practical philosophy. . . . In her explanations and experiments, including an unprotected and unrehearsed dive through glass, Streb gives readers news ways to consider the body and its movement, from 'the mechanical measurement of the legs, arms, torso, neck, hips, feet, shoulders, ankles, and knees' to 'the alchemetic processes of the neurological systems.' Accompanied by full-color and black-and-white photographs, Streb's riveting prose should provoke and inspire philosophy students, dancers, and athletes of all kinds." Publ Wkly

Includes bibliographical references

Streisand, Barbra

Mann, William J. **Hello,** gorgeous; becoming Barbra Streisand. William J. Mann. Houghton Mifflin Harcourt 2012 576 p. (hardback) $30.00   **92**

1. Fame 2. Singers 3. Singers -- United States -- Biography

ISBN 0547368925; 9780547368924

LC 2012016364

In this book, "[b]estselling biographer [William J.] Mann . . . chronicles the . . . series of events as [Barbra] Streisand 'gate-crashed her way to fame.' Mann tightens the focus in this . . . volume to just the early, formative years of her career, choosing 1964 as his cutoff point. . . . The marketing of Streisand and the men in her life are key themes throughout." (Publishers Weekly)

Includes bibliographical references and index.

Strouse, Charles

Strouse, Charles. **Put** on a happy face; a Broadway memoir.

Union Square Press 2008 326p il $19.95   **92**

1. Composers 2. Musicians 3. Composers -- United States

ISBN 978-1-4027-5889-8; 1-4027-5889-8

LC 2008-300247

"Three-time Tony Award–winning composer Strouse is best known for the musical Annie and his All in the Family theme, 'Those Were the Days.' While wary of the ghosts that appear, he summons up memories of a career that spans decades, beginning with his Manhattan boyhood, study at Rochester's Eastman School of Music, touring the South with Butterfly McQueen and early collaborations with lyricist Lee Adams. . . . Although he covers his film scores and music for TV commercials, the book's best chapters center on the staging struggles of Annie and Applause, plus breaking racial barriers with Sammy Davis Jr. in Golden Boy. . . . Detailing desperate rewrites, insecurities of theater people, footlight failures and humiliations, as well as theatrical triumphs, Strouse's superb backstage memoir deserves a standing ovation." Publ Wkly

Stuart, Granville, 1834-1918

Milner, Clyde A. **As** big as the West; the pioneer life of Granville Stuart. [by] Clyde A. Milner II and Carol A. O'Connor. Oxford University Press 2009 430p il map $34.95   **92**

1. Miners 2. Diplomats 3. Merchants 4. Frontier and pioneer life 5. Montana 6. Pioneers 7. Ranchers

ISBN 978-0-19-512709-6; 0-19-512709-9

"In fully revealing Stuart's fascinating and complex life, Milner and O'Connor illuminate the conflicting realities of the frontier." Libr J

Includes bibliographical references and index

Stuart, Jeb, 1833-1864

Wert, Jeffry D. **Cavalryman** of the lost cause; a biography of J.E.B. Stuart. Simon & Schuster 2008 496p il map $32; pa $18   **92**

1. Generals 2. Confederate States of America -- Army 3. United States -- History -- 1861-1865, Civil War

ISBN 978-0-7432-7819-5; 0-7432-7819-4; 978-0-7432-7824-9 pa; 0-7432-7824-0 pa

LC 2007-51552

This is a chronicle of the life of "the controversial cavalry leader of the Army of Northern Virginia until his death in combat in 1864. Wert's thoughtful account of Stuart's role at Gettysburg eventuates in a balanced analysis of a well-conceived reconnaissance-in-force. . . . This is a portrait of a Stuart more complex and, indeed, more attractive than either his friends or his enemies have painted in at least a generation." Booklist

Includes bibliographical references

Stuart, Sarah Payne

Stuart, Sarah Payne. **Perfectly** miserable; guilt, God and real estate in a small town. Sarah Payne Stuart. Riverhead Hardcover 2014 320 p. illustrations (hardback) $27.95   **92**

1. Autobiographies 2. Mother-daughter relationship 3. American literature -- New England 4. Authors, American -- 20th century -- Biography 5. Authors, American -- 21st century -- Biography

ISBN 1594631816; 9781594631818

LC 2013048095

"At eighteen, Sarah Payne Stuart fled her mother and all the other disapproving mothers of her too perfect hometown of Concord, Massachusetts, only to return years later when she had children of her own. Whether to defy the previous generation or finally earn their approval and enter their ranks, she hurled herself into upper-crust domesticity. . . . When Stuart's own mother dies, she realizes that there is no one left to approve or disapprove." (Publisher's note)

Sullivan, Ed, 1902-1974

Maguire, James. **Impresario**; the life and times of Ed Sullivan. Billboard Books 2006 344p il $24.95   **92**

1. Television personalities 2. Columnists

ISBN 0-8230-7962-7; 978-0-8230-7962-9 ISBN-13

The author "has written a fascinating biography and meticulously recorded the birth of TV, the heyday of newspaper columnists and the glamour of New York." Publ Wkly

Summitt, Pat Head, 1952-2016

Cornelius, Maria M. The **final** season; the perseverance of Pat Summitt. Maria M. Cornelius. University of Tennessee Press 2016 311 p. illustrations (hardcover: alk. paper) $29.95   **92**

1. Basketball coaches 2. Alzheimer's disease 3. Lady Volunteers (Basketball team) 4. Alzheimer's disease -- Patients -- Biography 5. Basketball coaches -- United States -- Biography

ISBN 1621902722; 9781621902720

LC 2016009421

This book, by Maria M. Cornelius, focuses on "Lady Vol Coach Pat Summitt. . . . Since the beginning of her career as Lady Vol head coach at twenty-two years old, Pat Head Summitt effectively established the University of Tennessee Lady Vols as the top women's athletics program in the nation. The winningest coach in the history of NCAA basketball, Summitt overcame one obstacle after another on the road to every victory." (Publisher's note)

Surville, Jean Francois de, 1717-1770

Blainey, Geoffrey. **Sea** of dangers; Captain Cook and his rivals in the South Pacific. Ivan R. Dee 2009 322p il map $27.50   **92**

1. Explorers 2. Voyages around the world 3. Ship captains 4. Naval officers 5. Travel writers 6. Oceania -- Exploration

ISBN 978-1-56663-825-8; 1-56663-825-9

LC 2008-52623

"An excellent work of popular history that recounts the exploits of men who dramatically expanded our knowledge of the globe." Booklist

Includes bibliographical references

Swift, Jonathan, 1667-1745

★ Damrosch, Leo. **Jonathan** Swift; his life and his world. Leo Damrosch. Yale University Press 2013 573 p. illustrations, maps (The Lewis Walpole Series in Eighteenth-Century Culture and History) (clothbound: alk. paper) $35   **92**

1. Authors, Irish 2. Authors, Irish -- 18th century -- Biography

ISBN 0300164998; 9780300164992

LC 2013013063

Kirkus Prize Finalist: Nonfiction (2014)

Pulitzer Prize Finalist: Biography or Autobiography (2014)

"In this . . . biography, Leo Damrosch draws on discoveries made over the past thirty years to tell the story of [Jonathan] Swift's life anew. Probing holes in the existing evidence, he takes seriously some daring speculations about Swift's parentage, love life, and various personal relationships and shows how Swift's public version of his life--the one accepted until recently--was deliberately misleading." (Publisher's note)

"A rich and rewarding portrait of an irreplaceable genius." Kirkus

Includes bibliographical references and index

Stubbs, John, 1977- **Jonathan** Swift; The Reluctant Rebel. John Stubbs. W W Norton & Co Inc 2017 752 p. illustrations (some color) (ebook) $80; $39.95   **92**

1. Irish authors -- 18th century -- Biography

ISBN 9780393634150; 039323942X; 9780393239423

LC 2016038238

This biography, by John Stubbs, captures the "world that [Jonathan] Swift both scorned and sought to amend. It follows Swift through his many battles, for and against authority, and in his many contradictions, as a priest who sought to uphold the dogma of his church; as a man who was quite prepared to defy convention, not least in his unshakable attachment to an unmarried woman, his 'Stella'; and as a writer whose vision showed that no single creed holds all the answers." (Publisher's note)

"Though his last years were sad, his trajectory as a literary artist had been steadily upward, as Stubbs' ever more engrossing, superlatively literate exposition demonstrates." Booklist

Includes bibliographical references and index.

Sylvester II, Pope, ca. 945-1003

Brown, Nancy Marie. The **abacus** and the cross; the story of the pope who brought the light of science to the Dark Ages. Basic Books 2010 310p il map $27.95   **92**

1. Popes 2. Religion and science 3. Biography, Individual

ISBN 9780465009503; 0465009506

LC 2010-36361

"As readably knowledgeable about Gerbert's political fortunes as about his intellectual influence, Brown is a lively narrator and interesting interpreter of Gerbert's life and world. This portrait gives both the science and the history audiences something to talk about." Booklist

Includes bibliographical references and index.

Taft, Helen Herron, 1861-1943

Anthony, Carl Sferrazza. **Nellie** Taft; the unconventional first lady of the ragtime era. 1st ed; William Morrow 2005 534p il $29.95; pa $15.95   **92**

1. Spouses of presidents

ISBN 0-06-051382-9; 0-06-051383-7 pa

LC 2004-52553

"This lively biography provides an illuminating glimpse into the life of an until-now underappreciated First Lady." Booklist

Includes bibliographical references

Tallchief, Maria

Tallchief, Maria. **Maria** Tallchief; America's prima ballerina. [by] Maria Tallchief with Larry Kaplan. University Press of Florida 2005 368p pa $19.95   **92**

1. Ballet dancers 2. Dance teachers 3. Ballerinas -- United States -- Biography. 4. Osage Indians -- United States -- Biography. 5. Indian ballerinas -- United States -- Biography.

ISBN 0-8130-2846-9; 978-0-8130-2846-0

LC 2005-42211

First published 1997 by Henry Holt

In this memoir Tallchief focuses "on her remembrances of her years with choreographer George Balanchine. . . . She met Balanchine at the start of her career, when she was with the Ballet Russe de Monte Carlo and Balanchine was about to form a company that would become a precursor to the New York City Ballet. Tallchief subsequently became Balanchine's wife, muse, and prima ballerina, and, though the marriage was short-lived, their artistic partnership endures in Balanchine's works created for Tallchief. She also writes about other stars, but the memoir sparkles when she recalls the subtlety and detail of a movement or the beauty of a musical phrase." Libr J

Tambor, Jeffrey, 1944-

Tambor, Jeffrey, 1944- **Are** you anybody? a memoir. Jeffrey Tambor; illustrations by Ben Barnes. Crown Archetype

2017 xviii, 274 p.p illustrations (hardcover) $27   **92**
   1. Actors -- United States -- Biography 2. Television actors and
actresses -- United States -- Biography
   ISBN 9780451496355; 9780451496379; 0451496353
                    LC 2017288987
   In this book, author Jeffrey Tambor "looks back at the key moments
in his life that taught him about creativity and play and pain and fear.
Tambor grew up in San Francisco a husy kid with a lisp, who suffered in
his 'otherness' and found salvation in the theater. . . . Tambor shares the
triumph of landing his first Broadway role. . . He invites you behind the
scenes of his wildly successful television shows, but he doesn't leave out
the pit stops he made at addiction." (Publisher's note)
   "Entertainment enthusiasts, readers interested in the history of TV,
and, naturally, the many fans of Tambor's work will find much to delight
in here." Booklist

Tammet, Daniel, 1979-

   Tammet, Daniel. **Born** on a blue day; inside the extraordinary mind of an autistic savant: a memoir. Free Press 2007
226p il $24; pa $14   **92**
   1. Autism 2. Asperger's syndrome 3. Savants (Savant syndrome)
4. Mental calculators
   ISBN 1-4165-3507-1; 978-1-4165-3507-2; 1-4165-4901-3 pa;
978-1-4165-4901-7 pa
                    LC 2006-41331
   First published 2006 in the United Kingdom
   This "autobiography is as fascinating as Benjamin Franklin's and
John Stuart Mill's, both of which are, like his, about the growth of a
mind." Booklist

Tan, Amy

   ★ Tan, Amy, 1952- **Where** the past begins; a writer's
memoir. Amy Tan. Ecco, an imprint of HarperCollins Publishers 2017 x, 357 p.p illustrations (hardcover) $28.99   **92**
   1. Autobiographies 2. Authors -- Biography 3. Creation (Literary,
artistic, etc.) 4. Novelists, American -- 20th century -- Biography
   ISBN 9780062319302; 9780062319296; 0062319299
                    LC 2017036982
   In this memoir, Amy Tan reveals "the truths and inspirations that
underlie her extraordinary fiction. By delving into vivid memories of her
traumatic childhood . . . and heartbreaking letters to and from her mother, she gives evidence to all that made it both unlikely and inevitable
that she would become a writer. . . . She shows how a fluid fictional state
of mind unleashed near-forgotten memories that became the emotional
nucleus of her novels." (Publisher's note)
   "In her ambushing and revealing memoir, beloved novelist Tan . . .
chronicles with striking candor, sharp wit, and storytelling magic stranger-than-fiction traumas." Booklist

Taylor, Barbara Brown

   Taylor, Barbara Brown. An **altar** in the world; a geography
of faith. HarperOne 2008 216p $24.99   **92**
   1. Clergy 2. Spiritual life 3. Religious scholars 4. Writers on
religion
   ISBN 978-0-06-137046-5
                    LC 2008-18303
   "Taylor is one of those rare people who truly can see the holy in
everything. Since everyone should know such a person, those who don't
can—no, must—read this book, with its friendly reminders of everyday
sacred." Publ Wkly

Taylor, Benjamin, 1952-

   Taylor, Benjamin. The **hue** and cry at our house; a year
remembered. Benjamin Taylor. Penguin books 2017 xx, 182
p.p illustrations (paperback) $16   **92**
   1. Friendship 2. American authors -- 20th century -- Biography 3.
Authors, American -- 20th century -- Biography
   ISBN 9781524705299; 9780143131649
                    LC 2016049441
   In this book, author Benjamin Taylor traces his life after the assassination of U.S. President John F. Kennedy. He recalls "the tumult as
he saw everything he had once considered stable begin to grow more
complex. Looking back on the love and tension within his family, the
childhood friendships that lasted and those that didn't, his memories of
summer camp and family trips, he reflects upon the outsized impact our
larger American story had on his own." (Publisher's note)
   "In this skillful blend of dialogue between youth and maturity, Taylor sums up the value and quality of the years of his treasured past and
unforgettable present, while stressing the sanctity of life." Pub Wkly

Taylor, Cory, 1955-2016

   Taylor, Cory. **Dying**; a memoir. Cory Taylor. First US edition Tin House Books 2017 141 p. (hardcover) $18.95   **92**
   1. Death 2. Cancer patients 3. Death -- Psychological aspects 4.
Terminally ill -- Australia -- Biography
   ISBN 9781941040706; 9781941040713; 1941040705
   This memoir, by Cory Taylor, is a "meditation on dying and a wise
tribute to life. . . . Taylor is dying of melanoma-related brain cancer. Her
illness is no longer treatable: she now weighs less than her neighbor's
retriever. As her body weakens, she describes the experience—the vulnerability and strength, the courage and humility, the anger and acceptance—of knowing she will soon die." (Publisher's note)
   "This slender volume brings a fresh point of view to end-of-life care,
the concept of having a sense of control over the unknown, and the role
of chance in life." Pub Wkly

Taylor, Elizabeth, 1932-2011

   Kashner, Sam. **Furious** love; Elizabeth Taylor, Richard
Burton, and the marriage of the century. [by] Sam Kashner and
Nancy Schoenberger. Harper 2010 500p il $27.99   **92**
   1. Actors
   ISBN 978-0-06-156284-6; 0-06-156284-X
                    LC 2010-06732
   "In this dual biography of the two legendary film stars, the authors
draw upon new information, including interviews with Elizabeth Taylor
and with the Burton family, to capture the famously passionate and tumultuous relationship between the legendary couple. . . . It's a mesmerizing tale, but it's also sad, and sometimes ugly, as the two stars engaged
in vicious fights, nursed their jealousies and insecurities, and descended
into alcoholism while outwardly living a life of glamour and sophistication." Booklist
   Includes bibliographical references

Taylor, Major, 1878-1932

   Balf, Todd. **Major**; a Black athlete, a White era, and the
fight to be the world's fastest human being. Crown Publishers
2008 306p il $24; pa $13.95   **92**
   1. Bicycle racing 2. African American athletes 3. Cyclists
   ISBN 978-0-307-23658-6; 0-307-23658-7; 978-0-307-23659-3
pa; 0-307-23659-5 pa
                    LC 2007-20747
   The author "chronicles the life of the unlikeliest of stars in the early
years of cycling: Marshall 'Major' Taylor. Taylor was an incomparable

athlete, poet and celebrity, but he was also a black man living during a time when the scars of the Civil War and slavery were still fresh in the minds of Americans. Balf . . . does great work presenting the complex nature of Taylor's life, including his upbringing in poverty in Indianapolis, the years he was treated as a son by a rich white family, the fans who both worshipped and vilified him and his close relationships with his white trainer and promoter." Publ Wkly

Includes bibliographical references

Tèffi, N. A. (Nadezhda Aleksandrovna), 1872-1952

Tèffi, N. A. (Nadezhda Aleksandrovna), 1872-1952. **Memories**; from Moscow to the Black Sea. by Teffi; translated by Robert and Elizabeth Chandler, Anne-Marie Jackson and Irina Steinberg; introduction by Edythe Haber. New York Review Books 2016 240 p. illustration (alk. paper) $16.95   **92**

1. Women authors 2. Russia -- History -- 1917-1921, Revolution 3. Women authors, Russian -- 20th century -- Biography 4. Soviet Union -- History -- Revolution, 1917-1921 -- Personal narratives
ISBN 9781590179512

LC 2015043142

This book, by Teffi, is a "personal account of the author's last months in Russia and Ukraine. . . . In 1918, in the immediate aftermath of the Russian Revolution, Teffi, who stories and journalism had made her a celebrity in Moscow, was invited to read from her work in Ukraine. She accepted the invitation eagerly, though she had every intention of returning home. As it happened, her trip ended four years later in Paris, where she would spend the rest of her life in exile." (Publisher's note)

Tea, Michelle

★ Tea, Michelle. **Against** memoir; complaints confessions + criticism. Michelle Tea. The Feminist Press at the City University of New York 2018 300 p. (trade pbk.) $18.95   **92**

1. Lesbians -- United States -- Biography 2. American authors -- 20th century -- Biography 3. Lesbian authors -- United States -- Biography 4. Authors, American -- 20th century -- Biography
ISBN 9781936932184

LC 2017049287

This book, by Michelle Tea, "is a genre- and reality-bending story of quiet triumph for the perennial screw-up and unabashed outsider. A biting, sagacious, and delightfully dark metaliterary novel about finding your way in a world on fire." (Kirkus) "In Tea's skillfully loose, lusty prose, Michelle is both vulnerable and brash, blitzing through lovers and bags of heroin, terrified but also convinced of her own invincibility... [A]n important portrait of the late '90s." (Publishers Weekly)

"Author and poet Tea (Without a Net) covers the gamut of her experience in this unputdownable antimemoir, which consists of previously published articles, talks, essays, and reviews but mostly recollections of her experience as a queer activist." LJ

Teller, Edward, 1908-2003

★ Goodchild, Peter. **Edward** Teller, the real Dr Strangelove. Harvard University Press 2004 xxv, 469p il $29.95 **92**

1. Physicists 2. Writers on science
ISBN 0-674-01669-6

LC 2004-54257

This is a biography of "the 'father of the hydrogen bomb,' a witness against J. Robert Oppenheimer in the latter's security hearing, and, finally, an ardent promoter of the Cold War arms race. . . . {The author} studied a wide range of primary and secondary sources and interviewed many people on both sides of the controversies that swirled around Teller. The result is a remarkably well-balanced study of a notoriously prickly and opinionated person." Libr J

Includes bibliographical references

Teller, Edward. **Memoirs**; a twentieth-century journey in science and politics. {by} Edward Teller with Judith Shoolery. Perseus Bks. 2001 628p il hardcover o.p. pa $18.95   **92**

1. Physicists 2. Writers on science
ISBN 0-7382-0778-0 pa

This memoir, by the nuclear physicist who worked to develop the hydrogen bomb, recounts his origins in the scientific community in Germany prior to the Nazi takeover and describes his "work on safe proliferation of nuclear energy, the so-called Stars Wars defense system and the early detection of earth-crossing objects. . . . Readers can enjoy these panoramic and beautifully written recollections of one of the great scientific, if controversial, figures of all time." Publ Wkly

Includes bibliographical references

Teresa, Mother, 1910-1997

Spink, Kathryn. **Mother** Teresa; a complete authorized biography. by Kathryn Spink. HarperOne 2011 336 p. ill. $15.99   **92**

1. Nuns 2. Nobel Prizes 3. Missions -- India 4. Christian missionaries 5. Biography, Individual 6. Missionaries of Charity
ISBN 0062026143; 9780062026149

LC 2011001621

"Spink's biography benefits from her own 18-year involvement with the work of the Missionaries of Charity Order as well as from the intimate relationship she developed over the years with Mother Teresa. . . . A final chapter in the book provides glimpses of Mother Teresa's affection for Princess Diana, a brief description of Mother Teresa's funeral and a short account of the election of Sister Nirmal as her successor." (Publ Wkly)

Terkel, Studs, 1912-2008

Terkel, Studs, 1912-2008. **Touch** and go; a memoir. [by] Studs Terkel, with Sydney Lewis. New Press 2007 269p il $24.95   **92**

1. Authors 2. Historians 3. Talk show hosts 4. Authors, American 5. Television moderators
ISBN 978-1-59558-043-6; 1-59558-043-3

LC 2007-18673

"Terkel's memoir is . . . a medley of all the extraordinary characters he's encountered through his career, from the adult loners of his youth in Chicago's Wells-Grand Hotel, to New Deal politicians. Terkel details his long journey through law school, the air force, theater, radio, early television, sports commentary, jazz criticism and oral history. . . . Americans might get to know their collective past a lot better if all history lessons were as absorbing and entertaining as this one." Publ Wkly

Tesla, Nikola, 1856-1943

Carlson, W. Bernard. **Tesla**; inventor of the electrical age. W. Bernard Carlson. Princeton University Press 2013 xiii, 500 p.p ill. (hardcover) $29.95   **92**

1. Electricity -- History 2. Inventors -- United States -- Biography 3. Electrical engineers -- United States -- Biography
ISBN 0691057761; 9780691057767

LC 2012049608

This book, by W. Bernard Carlson, presents a biography of the inventor Nikola Tesla, "a major contributor to the electrical revolution . . . at the turn of the twentieth century. His inventions, patents, and theoretical work formed the basis of modern AC electricity, and contributed to the development of radio and television. . . . An astute self-promoter and gifted showman, he cultivated a public image of the eccentric genius."

(Publisher's note)

"Carlson provides not only a more detailed explanation of Tesla's science but also a . . . focused psychological account of Tesla's inventive process." Booklist

Includes bibliographical references and index

Munson, Richard. **Tesla**; inventor of the modern. Richard Munson. W W Norton & Co Inc 2018 320 p. (hardcover) $26.95   **92**

1. Inventors -- United States -- Biography 2. Electrical engineering -- History 3. Electrical engineers -- United States -- Biography
ISBN 9780393635447

LC 2017055596

In this book, author Richard Munson, "pieces together the magnificently bizarre personal life and mental habits of the enigmatic inventor [Nikola Tesla]. . . . He was an acute germaphobe who never shook hands and required nine napkins when he sat down to dinner. Strikingly handsome and impeccably dressed, he spoke eight languages and could recite entire books from memory. . . . He conceived the induction motor while walking through a park and reciting Goethe's Faust." (Publisher's note)

"A lucid, expertly researched biography of the brilliant Nikola Tesla (1856-1943), a contemporary and competitor of Thomas Edison who was equally celebrated during his life." Kirkus

Includes bibliographical references and index

Tey, Josephine, 1896 or 1897-1952.

Henderson, Jennifer Morag. **Josephine** Tey; A Life. by Jennifer Morag Henderson. Dufour Editions 2016 420 p. illustrations, portraits $18   **92**

1. Women authors -- Biography
ISBN 1910124702; 1910985376; 9781910124703; 9781910985373

This book, by Jennifer Morag Henderson, is a biography of Josephine Tey. "Josephine Tey was the pen-name of Elizabeth MacKintosh (1896-1952). Born in Inverness, MacKintosh lived several 'lives': best known as Golden Age of Crime Fiction writer 'Josephine Tey', she was also successful novelist and playwright 'Gordon Daviot'. At one point, she had plays performed simultaneously in the West End in London and on Broadway, and even wrote for Hollywood - all from her home in the north of Scotland." (Publisher's note)

"Henderson ably chronicles her subject's life and provides not just facts but context for her work through thorough research into the stories of family, friends, and the social and political milieu of the times. Photographs, extensive notes, and an index round out the work." LJ

Includes bibliographical references and index.

Thatcher, Margaret

Moore, Charles. **Margaret** Thatcher; At Her Zenith: In London, Washington and Moscow. Charles Moore. Alfred A. Knopf 2013 821 p. illustrations (v. 2: hardcover) $35   **92**

1. Prime ministers -- Great Britain 2. Great Britain -- Politics and government 3. Prime ministers -- Great Britain -- Biography 4. Conservative Party (Great Britain) -- Biography 5. Women prime ministers -- Great Britain -- Biography 6. Great Britain -- Politics and government -- 1979-1997
ISBN 9780307958969; 0307958965

LC 2013020670

In this biographical book, author Charles Moore, "reveals as never before how Mrs. [Margaret] Thatcher transformed relations with Europe, privatized the commanding heights of British industry. . . . It describes her role on the world stage with dramatic immediacy, identifying Mikhail Gorbachev as 'a man to do business with' before he became a leader of the Soviet Union . . . and Ronald Reagan, her great ideo-

logical soul mate, to order world affairs according to her vision." (Publisher's note)

"A chronology of world events, copious notes, and an extensive bibliography enhance an exhaustive narrative that will fascinate students of contemporary British history and politics." Booklist

Includes bibliographical references and index

★ Moore, Charles. **Margaret** Thatcher; The Authorized Biography: From Grantham to the Falklands. Charles Moore. Knopf 2013 896 p. (v. 1: hardcover) $35   **92**

1. Prime ministers -- Great Britain -- Biography 2. Conservative Party (Great Britain) -- Biography 3. Women prime ministers -- Great Britain -- Biography 4. Great Britain -- Politics and government -- 1979-1997
ISBN 9780307958945; 0307958949

LC 2013020670

This "authorized biography of Margaret Thatcher reveals . . . the early life, rise to power, and first years as prime minister of the woman who transformed Britain and the world in the late twentieth century. [Author Charles] Moore has had unique access to all of Thatcher's private and governmental papers, and interviewed her and her family extensively for this book." (Publisher's note)

Includes bibliographical references and index

Theroux, Paul

Theroux, Paul, 1941- **Figures** in a landscape; people and places. Paul Theroux. Houghton Mifflin Harcourt 2018 400 p. (hardback) $28   **92**

1. Essays 2. Biography 3. American authors -- 20th century -- Biography 4. Authors, American -- 20th century -- Biography
ISBN 9780544870307

LC 2017045486

This essay collection, by Paul Theroux, "leads the reader through a dazzling array of sights, characters, and experiences, as Theroux applies his signature searching curiosity to a life lived as much in reading as on the road. This writerly tour-de-force features a satisfyingly varied selection of topics that showcase Theroux's sheer versatility as a writer." (Publisher's note)

Thomas, Abigail, 1941-

Thomas, Abigail. A **three** dog life. Harcourt 2006 182p $22   **92**

1. Authors 2. Novelists 3. Short story writers
ISBN 978-0-15-101211-4; 0-15-101211-3

LC 2005-33782

"Thomas has elevated what could be, at best, an overemotional sermon or, at worst, a grim romp in self-pity to a high plain of true inspiration." Booklist

Thomas, Abigail, 1941- **What** Comes Next and How to Like It; A Memoir. Abigail Thomas. Simon & Schuster 2015 240 p. $24   **92**

1. Widows 2. Adjustment (Psychology)
ISBN 1476785058; 9781476785059

LC 2015295750

This book is a "memoir about many things, but at the center is a steadfast friendship between [author] Abigail Thomas and a man she met thirty-five years ago. Through marriages, child-raising, the vicissitudes and tragedies of life, it is this deep, rich bond that has sustained her." (Publisher's note)

"This episodic memoir is full of love and life. Readers will identify with the feelings and the people even as they realize how different they are, how wondrous." Booklist

Thomas, Dylan, 1914-1953

Lycett, Andrew. **Dylan** Thomas: a new life. Overlook Press 2004 434p il $35　**92**

1. Poets 2. Authors

ISBN 1-58567-541-5

First published 2003 in the United Kingdom

"Other biographies . . . have ably recounted the essential details of Thomas's life, but Lycett here provides a wealth of useful detail, bringing the Welsh poet's life story up to date." Libr J

Includes bibliographical references

Thomas, a Becket, Saint, 1118?-1170

Guy, John. **Thomas** Becket; warrior, priest, rebel: a nine-hundred-year-old story retold. John Guy. Random House 2011 424 p.　**92**

1. Biography 2. Christian saints 3. Christianity and politics 4. Great Britain -- History -- 1066-1154, Norman period 5. Statesmen -- Great Britain -- Biography 6. Christian saints -- England -- Biography 7. Christian martyrs -- England -- Biography 8. Great Britain -- History -- Henry II, 1154-1189 -- Biography

ISBN 1400069076; 9780679603412; 9781400069071

LC 2011042794

This book by John Guy presents a biography "of Thomas Becket (1118–1170), the man who refused to subordinate the power of the church to the power of the state, and was martyred for it. . . . Distilling and disputing materials from several previous Becket biographies, Guy traces his subject's development from a handsome, superficial, and socially ambitious youth to a mature man who rose intellectually, morally, and politically to become lord chancellor to Henry II. In 1162, he was named archbishop of Canterbury, a position he accepted reluctantly, knowing that his honest exercise of the office as a defender of liberty and as one who would assert the church's power to cancel unjust state laws would bring him into conflict with Henry." (Publishers Weekly)

Includes bibliographical references and index.

Thompson, Hunter S

Denevi, Timothy. **Freak** kingdom; Hunter S. Thompson's manic ten-year crusade against American fascism. Timothy Denevi. Public Affairs 2018 416 p. (hardcover) $28　**92**

1. Politicians -- United States -- Biography 2. United States -- Politics and government -- 1945- 3. Politicians -- United States 4. United States -- Politics and government -- 1945-1989 5. Political campaigns -- United States -- History -- 20th century 6. Presidents -- United States -- Election -- History -- 20th century

ISBN 9781541767942

LC 2018015549

This biography, by Timothy Denevi, presents "the story of Hunter S. Thompson's crusade against Richard Nixon and the threat of fascism in America--and the devastating price he paid for it. [The book shows Thompson as] a fearless opponent of corruption and fascism, one who sacrificed his future well-being to fight against it, rewriting the rules of journalism and political satire in the process." (Publisher's note)

Includes bibliographical references and index

McKeen, William. **Outlaw** journalist; the life and times of Hunter S. Thompson. W. W. Norton 2008 428p il $27.95; pa $16.95　**92**

1. Authors 2. Novelists 3. Journalists 4. Satirists 5. Columnists 6. Nonfiction writers

ISBN 978-0-393-06192-5; 0-393-06192-2; 978-0-393-33545-3

pa; 0-393-33545-3 pa

LC 2008-13214

This is a biography of the journalist and author of Hell's Angels (1967), Fear and Loathing in Las Vegas (1972), The Great Shark Hunt (1979) and Generation of Swine (1988).

"The book does justice to the legend that was Thompson. The thorough reporting lends insight to a writer who was as much a personality as a scribe." Am Journalism

Includes bibliographical references

Thompson, Hunter S. The **kingdom** of fear; loathsome secrets of a star-crossed child in the final days of the American century. Simon & Schuster 2003 xx, 354p il hardcover o.p. pa $16　**92**

1. Authors 2. Novelists 3. Journalists 4. Satirists 5. Columnists 6. Nonfiction writers

ISBN 0-684-87323-0; 978-0-684-87324-4; 0-684-87324-9 pa

LC 2002-191228

In this book the American journalist writes about his life and career experiences

"Just as Thompson paved his own way in writing about politics, sports, news and culture throughout the 1960s and '70s, he now offers an autobiography that is typically unorthodox in style but still revealing previously unknown facts about its subject. Wavering between the uproarious and the lunatic, it's vintage Thompson through and through." Publ Wkly

Thompson, Juan F., 1964- **Stories** I tell myself; growing up with Hunter S. Thompson. Juan F. Thompson. Alfred A. Knopf 2016 xii, 274 p.p illustrations (hardback) $26.95　**92**

1. American authors -- Biography 2. Authors, American -- 20th century -- Biography

ISBN 9781101875865; 9780307265357

LC 2015006934

"From the outset [journalist Hunter S. Thompson] was the Wild Man of American journalism with a journalistic appetite that touched on subjects that drove his sense of justice and intrigue. . . . Now Juan Thompson tells the story of his father and of their getting to know each other during their forty-one fraught years together. He writes of the many dark times, of how far they ricocheted away from each other, and of how they found their way back before it was too late." (Publisher's note)

"The son of the legendary gonzo journalist recalls his turbulent but exciting years swimming in the wake of a most mercurial creature." Kirkus

★ Wenner, Jann S. **Gonzo**; the life of Hunter S. Thompson. by Jann S. Wenner & Corey Seymour; introduction by Johnny Depp. Little, Brown 2007 467p il $28.99　**92**

1. Authors 2. Novelists 3. Journalists 4. Satirists 5. Columnists 6. Nonfiction writers

ISBN 978-0-316-00527-2; 0-316-00527-4

LC 2007-11693

This oral biography is a "look at the turbulent life of Gonzo journalism pioneer Hunter S. Thompson (1937-2005). . . . This fine, fond biography amuses, inspires, outrages and haunts at all the right moments—and sometimes all at once." Publ Wkly

Thompson, Juan F.

Thompson, Juan F., 1964- **Stories** I tell myself; growing up with Hunter S. Thompson. Juan F. Thompson. Alfred A. Knopf 2016 xii, 274 p.p illustrations (hardback) $26.95　**92**

1. American authors -- Biography 2. Authors, American -- 20th

century -- Biography
ISBN 9781101875865; 9780307265357

LC 2015006934

"From the outset [journalist Hunter S. Thompson] was the Wild Man of American journalism with a journalistic appetite that touched on subjects that drove his sense of justice and intrigue. . . . Now Juan Thompson tells the story of his father and of their getting to know each other during their forty-one fraught years together. He writes of the many dark times, of how far they ricocheted away from each other, and of how they found their way back before it was too late." (Publisher's note)

"The son of the legendary gonzo journalist recalls his turbulent but exciting years swimming in the wake of a most mercurial creature." Kirkus

Thomson, David, 1941-

Thomson, David, 1941- **Try** to tell the story; a memoir. Alfred A. Knopf 2009 214p $23.95   **92**

1. Authors 2. Novelists 3. Father-son relationship 4. Biographers 5. Film historians 6. World War, 1939-1945 -- Personal narratives
ISBN 978-0-375-41213-4; 0-375-41213-1

LC 2008-19605

"In the heart of this haunting, eloquent memoir, as might be expected, [Thomson] gets rhapsodic when recalling the films that left an indelible impression on him: Red River, Meet Me in St. Louis, Citizen Kane, East of Eden. While following a film critic in the making, we also see the changing cultural landscape of the 1940s and 1950s through his eyes." Publ Wkly

Thoreau, Henry David, 1817-1862

Dann, Kevin. **Expect** great things; the life and search of Henry David Thoreau. by Kevin Dann. TarcherPerigee 2017 387 p. (hardback) $30   **92**

1. Naturalists 2. American authors 3. Transcendentalism 4. Mysticism and literature 5. Spirituality in literature 6. Naturalists -- United States -- Biography 7. Transcendentalists (New England) -- Biography 8. Authors, American -- 19th century -- Biography
ISBN 9780399184666

LC 2016023294

This book, by Kevin Dann, is an "epic biography of Henry David Thoreau. [It] sees Thoreau's world as the mystic himself saw it: filled with wonder and mystery; Native American myths and lore; wood sylphs, nature spirits, and fairies; battles between good and evil; and heroic struggles to live as a natural being in an increasingly synthetic world." (Publisher's note)

"For all Thoreau devotees, who will welcome the sympathetic overview of the author's full life and enthusiasms." LJ.

Includes bibliographical references (pages 353-370) and index.

Sullivan, Robert. The **Thoreau** you don't know; what the prophet of environmentalism really meant. Collins 2009 354p $25.99   **92**

1. Authors 2. Naturalists 3. Essayists 4. Pacifists 5. Authors, American 6. Writers on nature 7. Nonfiction writers
ISBN 978-0-06-171031-5; 0-06-171031-8

LC 2008-34495

The author "endeavors to free Henry David Thoreau from his calcified reputation as a cantankerous hermit and nature worshipper. Sounding like your favorite teacher who manages to make history fun and relevant, Sullivan vibrantly portrays the sage of Walden as a geeky, curious, compassionate fellow of high intelligence and deep feelings who loved company, music, and long walks." Booklist

★ Walls, Laura Dassow. **Henry** David Thoreau; a life.

Laura Dassow Walls. University of Chicago Press 2017 xx, 615 p.p illustrations, maps (cloth: alk. paper) $35   **92**

1. American authors 2. Naturalists -- Biography 3. Naturalists -- United States -- Biography 4. Authors, American -- 19th century -- Biography
ISBN 022634469X; 9780226344690

LC 2016053416

Kirkus Prize Finalist: Nonfiction (2017)
LA Times Book Prize: Biography (2017)

In this biography, Laura Dassow Walls "presents a [Henry David] Thoreau vigorously alive in all his quirks and contradictions: the young man shattered by the sudden death of his brother; the ambitious Harvard College student; the ecstatic visionary who closed 'Walden' with an account of the regenerative power of the Cosmos. [Readers] meet the . . . the solitary walker who found society in nature, but also found his own nature in . . . society." (Publisher's note)

"A superbly researched and written literary portrait that broadens our understanding of the great American writer and pre-eminent naturalist who has too long been regarded as a self-righteous scold." Kirkus

Includes bibliographical references and index

Thorndike, Joseph Jacobs, 1913-2005

Thorndike, John. The **last** of his mind; a year in the shadow of Alzheimer's. Swallow Press 2009 243p il $24.95   **92**

1. Alzheimer's disease 2. Magazine editors
ISBN 978-0-8040-1122-8; 0-8040-1122-2

LC 2009-26118

"A brave, moving story of a son's devotion to his dying father. . . . Thorndike's prose is serenely beautiful and his patience in caring for an Alzheimer's patient is extremely admirable. An affecting work of emotional honesty and forgiveness." Kirkus

Thorp, Edward O

Thorp, Edward O., 1932- A **man** for all markets; From Las Vegas to Wall Street, How I Beat the Dealer and the Market. Edward O. Thorp. Random House 2017 416 p. illustrations $30   **92**

1. Gambling systems 2. Mathematicians -- United States -- Biography 3. Investment advisors -- United States -- Biography 4. Investments 5. Finance -- Mathematical models
ISBN 9781400067961

LC 2016026545

This book, by Edward O. Thorp, tells how he "invented card counting, proving the seemingly impossible: that you could beat the dealer at the blackjack table. As a result he launched a gambling renaissance. . . . Thereafter, Thorp shifted his sights to 'the biggest casino in the world': Wall Street. Devising and then deploying mathematical formulas to beat the market, Thorp ushered in the era of quantitative finance we live in today." (Publisher's note)

"Readers who like to read the life stories of ambitious, creative, and successful people with fascinating stories to tell should be steered in this book's direction." Booklist

Includes bibliographical references and index.

Thorpe, Jim, 1888-1953

Buford, Kate. **Native** American son; the life and sporting legend of Jim Thorpe. Alfred A. Knopf 2010 479p il $35 **92**

1. Athletes 2. Biography, Individual 3. Native Americans -- Biography
ISBN 978-0-375-41324-7; 0-375-41324-3

LC 2010012815

This biography of the Native American athlete covers topics ranging "from the disastrous divvying up of Native American land that young Jim witnessed in 1890s Oklahoma; to Thorpe's stellar performances in football, baseball, and track and field; to the stripping of his 1912 Olympics medals because he was paid to play baseball for two summers; and, finally, to the makeshift life he cobbled together after his playing days ended. Buford imparts a sense of the incandescent skills Thorpe applied to his sports, and the discrimination and self-destruction that shadowed him throughout his life." Booklist

Includes bibliographical references

★ Crawford, Bill. **All** American; the rise and fall of Jim Thorpe. John Wiley & Sons, Inc 2004 284p il $24.95   **92**
1. Athletes 2. Decathletes 3. Pentathletes 4. Olympic athletes 5. Native Americans -- Biography
ISBN 0-471-55732-3

LC 2004-14376

This "terse, punchy biography of sports legend Thorpe (1888–1953) illuminates the current debate over the exploitation of unpaid college athletes by moneymaking, headline-grabbing educational institutions." Publ Wkly

Includes bibliographical references

Timerman, Jacobo, 1923-1999
Timerman, Jacobo. **Prisoner** without a name, cell without a number; translated from the Spanish by Toby Talbot. University of Wisconsin Press 2002 164p (The Americas) pa $17.95   **92**
1. Journalists 2. Political prisoners 3. Newspaper executives
ISBN 978-0-299-18244-1; 0-299-18244-4
First published 1981 by Knopf
The author, "an outspoken Zionist and formerly a newspaper publisher in Buenos Aires, relates his 30-month political incarceration—torture and isolation in a clandestine prison, then detention in an official penal institution—which preceded his expulsion from Argentina in 1979." Publ Wkly

Tirone Smith, Mary-Ann, 1944-
★ Tirone Smith, Mary-Ann. **Girls** of tender age; a memoir. Free Press 2006 285p il map $24   **92**
1. Authors 2. Novelists 3. Memoirists 4. Young adult authors
ISBN 0-7432-7977-8

LC 2005-51376

This memoir, an "unsentimental view of life in a post-World War II working-class family, is interspersed with the story of Bob Malm, a serial pedophile who brutally murdered a fifth-grade classmate of hers in December 1953. . . . This poignant memoir belongs in all collections." Libr J

Includes bibliographical references

Titian, approximately 1488-1576
Hale, Sheila. **Titian**; His Life. Sheila Hale. HarperCollins 2012   **92**
1. Painters -- Biography 2. Venice (Italy) -- History
ISBN 006059876X; 9780060598761
This book by Sheila Hale presents a "biography of [painter] Tiziano Vecellio (c.1480-1576), better known as Titian. . . . Hale examines Titian's life and career within the cultural, economic, political, and social contexts of 16th-century Venice and Italy. As she details his ambitious rise through Venetian society, she also tells the broader story of the artist's stylistic evolution and the world he lived in." (Library Journal)

Hudson, Mark. **Titian**; the last days. Walker 2009 304p il

$27   **92**
1. Artists 2. Painters 3. Artists, French
ISBN 978-0-8027-1076-5; 0-8027-1076-X
"At the time of his death—from plague, in Venice in 1576—Titian had been one of the most celebrated artists in Europe for most of the century, the revered portrait painter of popes, emperors, and kings. But in his final works, as plague swept Venice, Titian, then in his mid-eighties, began confronting darker themes, including his own mortality. Hudson focusses his book on this group of paintings, now largely lost, and discusses Titian's career with humor, enlivening a potentially staid subject." New Yorker

Tocqueville, Alexis de
Epstein, Joseph. **Alexis** De Tocqueville; democracy's guide. Atlas Books 2006 208p (Eminent lives) $21.95   **92**
1. Statesmen 2. Writers on politics 3. Political scientists
ISBN 0-06-059898-0; 978-0-06-059898-3

LC 2006-47175

The author provides an "examination of the man, his works, his influence, his times and what we can learn from Democracy in America. . . . As an introduction to the man and a primer for his works, Epstein's book is admirable." Publ Wkly

Todd, Mabel Loomis, 1856-1932
Dobrow, Julie. **After** Emily; two remarkable women and the legacy of America's greatest poet. Julie Dobrow. W W Norton & Co Inc 2018 384 p. $29.95   **92**
1. Friendship 2. Mother-daughter relationship 3. Dickinson, Emily, 1830-1886 -- Friends and associates 4. Dickinson, Emily, 1830-1886
ISBN 0393249263; 9780393249262

LC 2018016671

"Despite Emily Dickinson's world renown, the story of the two women most responsible for her initial posthumous publication--Mabel Loomis Todd and her daughter, Millicent Todd Bingham--has remained in the shadows of the archives. A rich and compelling portrait of women who refused to be confined by the social mores of their era, [Julie Dobrow's] 'After Emily' explores Mabel and Millicent's complex bond, as well as the powerful literary legacy they shared." (Publisher's note)

"Dobrow's intimate portrait of these artistically talented and intelligent women, based largely on their extensive, detailed diaries and correspondence, reveals fallible women who painstakingly attempted to share an extraordinary poet's vision." Booklist

Toklas, Alice B.
Malcolm, Janet. **Two** lives; Gertrude and Alice. Yale University Press 2007 229p il $25   **92**
1. Poets 2. Authors 3. Novelists 4. Essayists 5. Memoirists 6. Literary critics 7. Authors, American 8. Private secretaries
ISBN 978-0-300-12551-1; 0-300-12551-8

LC 2007-12085

"This is a vital addition to Stein criticism as well as an important work that critiques the political responsibility of the artist (even a genius) to the larger world." Publ Wkly

Includes bibliographical references

Tolstoy, Leo, 1828-1910
★ Bartlett, Rosamund. **Tolstoy**; 1st U.S. ed. Houghton Mifflin Harcourt 2011 544 p.   **92**
1. Biography 2. Novelists 3. Dramatists 4. Authors, Russian 5. Authors 6. Short story writers 7. Writers on religion
ISBN 9781846681387 Profile Books; 1846681383 Profile Books;

9780151014385

LC 2010050015

This book presents a biography of writer Leo Tolstoy which draws primarily upon Russian scholarship, as well as Tolstoy's "memoirs and correspondences," to narrate his life. "As a cultural historian, Bartlett strives to place the man within his time and milieu. Her Tolstoy in his incarnations as aristocrat, muzhik, czar and other roles is thoroughly Russian, and she uses him to introduce her anglophone readers to sometimes exotic details of Russian life and history. . . . She offers, for instance, a brief history of the family of Tolstoy's wife, the Behrses, who came from a different order of Russian society than the counts and princes from whom Tolstoy descended. . . . There are similar . . . digressions about the Caucasus, Russian Orthodoxy, peasant life, Tolstoyans and other matters." (The Globe and Mail)

Toorpakai, Maria, 1990-

Holstein, Katharine. A **Different** Kind of Daughter; The Girl Who Hid from the Taliban in Plain Sight. Maria Toorpakai with Katharine Holstein. Twelve 2016 368 p. 8 plates; illustrations; map $27   **92**

1. Taliban 2. Sports for women 3. Women -- Pakistan
ISBN 1455591416; 9781455591411

This memoir, by Maria Toorpaki with Katharine Holstein, "tells of Maria's harrowing journey to play the sport she knew was her destiny, first living as a boy and roaming the violent back alleys of the frontier city of Peshawar, rising to become the number one female squash player in Pakistan. But it was also a death sentence, thrusting her into the national spotlight and the crosshairs of the Taliban, who wanted Maria and her family dead.Maria knew her only chance of survival was to flee the country." (Publisher's note)

"This astonishing and inspirational memoir chronicles more than Maria's life; it also relates the story of her parents, an incredible couple, who, despite the odds, fought for the betterment and education of themselves, their children, and the Pakistani people." Library Journal

Torre, Joe, 1940-

Torre, Joe. The **Yankee** years; [by] Joe Torre and Tom Verducci. Doubleday 2009 502p il $26.95   **92**

1. Baseball players 2. Baseball managers 3. Baseball -- Biography 4. New York Yankees (Baseball team)
ISBN 978-0-385-52740-8; 0-385-52740-3

LC 2008-52628

Joe Torre, who was manager of the New York Yankees from 1996 to 2007, focuses on the team's circumstances beginning with their loss of the seventh game of the 2001 World Series.

"This is an interesting and fast read and, for those who are not aficionados of baseball, the clash of powerful personalities and drama are more than sufficient to merit attention. Baseball enthusiasts, while undoubtedly familiar with the characters and events, will find the quick review of 12 years of Yankee history enjoyable for its details, particularly as the men's words flesh out the drama behind the sports pages." USA Today

Toulouse-Lautrec, Henri de, 1864-1901

Frey, Julia. **Toulouse**-Lautrec; a life. Phoenix 1995 597p il pa $27.50   **92**

1. Artists 2. Painters 3. Lithographers 4. Artists, French
ISBN 1-85799-363-2; 978-1-85799-363-9

First published 1994 by Viking

"The author chronicles Toulouse-Lautrec's transformation from a pampered invalid into one of the most radical of the fin de siecle artists. . . . Her sensitive, eloquent, and richly illustrated biography has brought the real Toulouse-Lautrec out from behind the scrim of myth." Booklist

Includes bibliographical references

Toussaint Louverture, 1743-1803

★ Bell, Madison Smartt. **Toussaint** Louverture; a biography. Pantheon Books 2007 333p map $27   **92**

1. Generals 2. Revolutionaries
ISBN 978-0-375-42337-6; 0-375-42337-0

LC 2006-45848

This is a biography of the Haitian leader.

"This is the best biography of Toussaint yet, in large part because Bell does not shy away from the man's contradictions." N Y Times Book Rev

Includes bibliographical references

★ Girard, Philippe. **Toussaint** Louverture; A Revolutionary Life. Philippe Girard. Basic Books 2016 352 p. illustrations, maps (ebook) $20.99; (hardcover) $29.99   **92**

1. Revolutionaries 2. Haiti -- History 3. Generals -- Haiti -- Biography 4. Revolutionaries -- Haiti -- Biography 5. Haiti -- History -- Revolution, 1791-1804 -- Biography
ISBN 9780465094141; 9780465094134

LC 2016018088

This book, by Philippe Girard, "reveals the dramatic story of how Louverture transformed himself from lowly freedman to revolutionary hero. In 1791, the unassuming Louverture masterminded the only successful slave revolt in history. By 1801, he was general and governor of Saint-Domingue, and an international statesman who forged treaties with Britain, France, Spain, and the United States-empires that feared the effect his example would have on their slave regimes." (Publisher's note)

"A groundbreaking biography that underscores the difficulties of leading slaves to freedom and avoiding violent extremes." Kirkus

Includes bibliographical references and index

Tracy, Spencer, 1900-1967

Curtis, James. **Spencer** Tracy; a biography. Alfred A. Knopf 2011 1001p il $39.95; ebook $19.99   **92**

1. Actors 2. Biography, Individual
ISBN 978-0-307-26289-9; 978-0-307-59522-5 ebook

LC 2011014719

This is a biography of the actor. Bibliography. Index.

The author "presents an exhaustive and exhausting biography of the legendary Hollywood star, famed for his uncanny naturalism and authority on camera and best remembered for the series of films he made with longtime companion Katharine Hepburn. . . . A monumental, definitive biography of one the finest film actors in the history of the medium." Kirkus

Includes bibliographical references and index

Trebincevic, Kenan, 1980-

Shapiro, Susan. The **Bosnia** list; a memoir of war, exile, and return. Kenan Trebincevic and Susan Shapiro. Penguin Books 2014 336 p. illustrations, map (paperback) $16   **92**

1. Muslims 2. Bosnia and Hercegovina 3. Yugoslav War, 1991-1995 4. Bosnian Americans -- Biography 5. Brčko (Bosnia and Hercegovina) -- Biography 6. Escapes -- Bosnia and Hercegovina -- History -- 20th century 7. Bosnia and Hercegovina -- Ethnic relations -- History -- 20th century 8. Yugoslav War, 1991-1995 -- Bosnia and Hercegovina -- Personal narratives
ISBN 0143124579; 9780143124573

LC 2013035345

In this memoir, author Kenan Trebincevic "blends his childhood experience of Bosnia's tragedy with a return to his original home in Brcko after nearly 20 years in the United States. The titular list is of goals the author intends to accomplish. They include seeking out surviving friends and relatives as well as confronting Serbs guilty of crimes against Trebincevi's defenceless Muslim family." (Library Journal)

"An engaging memoir of war trauma and the redemption to be found in confronting it." Kirkus

Includes bibliographical references and index

Trebing, Katie, 2002-

Whitehouse, Beth. The **match**; savior siblings and one family's battle to heal their daughter. Beacon Press 2010 255p $24.95; pa $16   **92**

1. Sick 2. Fertilization in vitro 3. Procurement of organs, tissues, etc. 4. Bone marrow -- Transplantation

ISBN 978-0-8070-7286-8; 0-8070-7286-9; 978-0-8070-0121-9 pa; 0-8070-0121-X pa

LC 2009035949

The author "tracks Stacy and Steve Trebing and their decision to create a baby boy selected as an embryo as a genetic match for a sister suffering from Diamond-Blackfan anemia, a rare and fatal disease." Publ Wkly

Trillin, Alice, 1938-2001

Trillin, Calvin. **About** Alice. Random House 2007 78p $14.95   **92**

1. Television producers

ISBN 1-4000-6615-8; 978-1-4000-6615-5

LC 2006-45573

"This succinct account of Alice's upbringing, their meeting, their romance, their family, and her career beyond that of Trillin's helpmeet, offers glimpses into a multifaceted character." Booklist

Trotsky, Leon, 1879-1940

★ Service, Robert, 1947- **Trotsky**; a biography. Belknap Press of Harvard University Press 2009 600p il map $35   **92**

1. Revolutionaries 2. Communist leaders 3. Political leaders 4. Nonfiction writers 5. Biography, Individual 6. Soviet Union -- History 7. Communism -- Soviet Union 8. Soviet Union -- Foreign relations

ISBN 0-674-03615-8; 978-0-674-03615-4

LC 2009-25417

This biography discusses Trotsky's "relations with the leaders he was trying to unify; his attempt to disguise his political closeness to Stalin; and his role in the early 1920s as the progenitor of political and cultural Stalinism." (Publisher's note) Index.

"Thick and intensely researched but a pleasure to read, . . . [this] should remain the definitive work for some time. . . . This is a thoughtful, rewarding and essential contribution to 20th-century history." Publ Wkly

Includes bibliographical references

Truman, Harry S., 1884-1972

Dallek, Robert. **Harry** S. Truman; Robert Dallek. Times Books 2008 xviii, 183p.p (American presidents series) $22 **92**

1. Presidents 2. Vice-presidents 3. Senators 4. Presidents -- United States

ISBN 978-0-8050-6938-9

LC 2008-10193

This is a biography of the 33rd president.

This book is "the best starting point for knowledge of Truman's life and for an astute assessment of his career." Publ Wkly

Includes bibliographical references

Donald, Aida D. **Citizen** soldier; a life of Harry S. Truman. Aida D. Donald. Basic Books 2012 xvi, 265 p.p (hardcover: alk. paper) $26.99   **92**

1. Soldiers -- United States -- Biography 2. Presidents -- United States -- Biography 3. United States -- Politics and government -- 1945-1953

ISBN 046503120X; 9780465031207

LC 2012025583

This book by Aida D. Donald is a biography of former U.S. President Harry S. Truman. "When Franklin Roosevelt passed away in April 1945, Truman unexpectedly found himself at the helm of the American war effort--and in command of the atomic bomb, the most lethal weapon humanity had ever seen. Truman's decisive leadership during the remainder of World War II and the period that followed reshaped American politics, economics, and foreign relations." (Publisher's note)

Includes bibliographical references and index

McCullough, David G., 1933- **Truman**; {by} David McCullough. Simon & Schuster 1992 1117p il $40; pa $22 **92**

1. Senators 2. Presidents 3. Vice-presidents

ISBN 0-671-45654-7; 0-671-86920-5 pa

LC 92-5245

This is a biography of the thirty-third president of the United States. Bibliography. Index.

This biography of the 33rd president "not only conveys in rich detail Truman's accomplishments as a politician and statesman, but also reveals the character and personality of this constantly-surprising man— as schoolboy, farmer, soldier, merchant, county judge, senator, vice president and chief executive. The book relates how Truman overcame the stigma of business failure and debt . . . and acquired a reputation for honesty, reliability and common sense." Publ Wkly

Includes bibliographical references

Trump, Donald, 1946-

Barrett, Wayne. **Trump**; the greatest show on earth, the deals, the downfall, the reinvention. Wayne Barrett. Regan Arts 2016 xvii, 476 p.p (pbk) $17.99   **92**

1. Businessmen -- United States -- Biography 2. Businesspeople -- United States -- Biography

ISBN 1682450791; 9781682450796

LC 2016950514

This book, by Wayne Barrett, is the "essential book to understanding Donald Trump as a businessman and leader—and how the biggest deal of his life went down. . . . After decades covering him, few reporters know Trump as Barrett does. Instead of the canny businessman that Trump claims in his own books, Barrett explores how Trump exploited his father's banking and political connections to finance and grease his first major deals." (Publisher's note)

D'Antonio, Michael. The **truth** about Trump; by Michael D'Antonio. St. Martin's Press 2016 389 p. illustrations (ebook) $40; $16.99   **92**

ISBN 9781250116963; 1250105285; 9781250105288

LC 2015916088

This book, by Michael D'Antonio, "presents Trump's full story, from his beginnings as a businessman to his juggernaut presidential campaign. Along the way, D'Antonio charts the successes and failures, scandals and triumphs, and relentless pursuit of money and fame that have made Trump who he is today. D'Antonio also details the origins of the Trump family fortune, Trump's history of using politics to get ahead, and how he has mastered the media to turn publicity into power." (Publisher's note)

Includes bibliographical references (pages 349-371) and index.

Fisher, Marc. **Trump** revealed; An American Journey of Ambition, Ego, Money, and Power. Michael Kranish and Marc Fisher, The Washington Post. Scribner 2016 x, 431 p.p illustrations (some color) (ebook) $19.99; $28.00   **92**
  1. Republican Party (U.S.) 2. Presidents -- United States 3. United States -- Politics and government -- 2001- 4. Republican Party (U.S.: 1854-) 5. Presidents -- United States -- Election -- 2016 6. United States -- Politics and government -- 2009- 7. Presidential candidates -- United States -- Biography
ISBN 9781501155789; 9781501155772
        LC 2016032645
This book, by Michael Kranish and Marc Fisher, is a "deeply researched biography of Donald Trump. . . . The authors examine Trump's wealth, the evolution of his political beliefs, and his peculiar identity as a billionaire businessman, celebrity, global brand, television star, and now candidate for the most powerful office in the world. Few individuals have ever roamed so widely through such diverse realms as real estate, sports, entertainment, and national politics." (Publisher's note)
  "The most definitive book about Trump to date." Booklist
  Includes bibliographical references and index

O'Brien, Timothy L. **TrumpNation**; the art of being The Donald. by Timothy L. O'Brien. Grand Central Publishing 2016 xix, 276 p.p illustrations (softcover) $14.99; (ebook) $19.99   **92**
  1. Businessmen -- United States -- Biography 2. Real estate developers -- United States -- Biography
ISBN 044669617X; 9780446696173; 9781504027496
        LC 2016296345
This book, by Timothy L. O'Brien, is an "entertaining look inside the world of Donald Trump. . . . O'Brien traveled across the country and up and down the East Coast with Trump on his private jet, wheeled around Palm Beach with him in his Ferrari, and spent hours interviewing him in his home, in his office, and on the golf course. He met with the entrepreneur's closest friends and most aggressive rivals, while compiling a treasure trove of Trumpisms from the Donald himself." (Publisher's note)
  "A bemused, entertaining portrait of a gold-toned incarnation of the American dream, plus some believable financials for anyone who wants to know the real fiscal story." Kirkus
  Includes bibliographical references (pages 245-247) and index

Slater, Robert. **No** such thing as over-exposure; inside the life and celebrity of Donald Trump. Prentice Hall 2005 xxiv, 247p $24.95   **92**
  1. Hotel executives 2. Airline executives 3. Real estate developers 4. Construction industry executives
ISBN 0-13-149734-0
        LC 2004-116294
Donald Trump "is not so easily understood, but this book goes a long way toward defining him." Booklist
  Includes bibliographical references

Trussoni, Danielle

Trussoni, Danielle. The **fortress**; a love story. Danielle Trussoni. Dey St., an imprint of William Morrow Publishers 2016 324 p. (hardcover) $27.99   **92**
  1. Dysfunctional families 2. Marriage -- Case studies 3. Dysfunctional families -- Biography
ISBN 9780062458995; 9780062459008; 0062459007

In this memoir, author Danielle Trussoni shares how she "and her husband moved to the south of France, to a picturesque medieval village in the Languedoc. It is here, in a haunted stone fortress . . . , that she comes to understand the dark, subterranean forces that have been following her all along. While Danielle and her husband eventually part, Danielle's time in the fortress brings precious wisdom about life and love that she could not have learned otherwise." (Publisher's note)
  "Told over a 10-year period in Iowa, Bulgaria, Providence, and southern France, The Fortress is an immersive and honest portrayal of human nature bound by commitment." Booklist

Tubman, Harriet, 1820?-1913

Clinton, Catherine. **Harriet** Tubman: the road to freedom. Little, Brown 2004 272p hardcover o.p. pa $14.95   **92**
  1. Abolitionists 2. Underground railroad 3. African American women -- Biography
ISBN 0-316-14492-4; 0-316-15594-2 pa
        LC 2003-56185
  "Clinton turns sobriquets into meaningful descriptors of a unique person. In her hands, a familiar legend acquires human dimension with no diminution of its majesty and power." Publ Wkly
  Includes bibliographical references

Humez, Jean McMahon. **Harriet** Tubman; the life and the life stories. [by] Jean M. Humez. University of Wisconsin Press 2004 471p il (Wisconsin studies in autobiography) hardcover o.p. pa $21.95   **92**
  1. Abolitionists 2. Underground railroad 3. African American women -- Biography
ISBN 0-299-19120-6; 0-299-19124-9 pa
        LC 2003-5676
In this volume the author "includes a collection of Tubman's autobiographical stories culled from rare early publications and manuscript sources. This book will become an important resource for scholars, historians, and general readers interested in slavery, the Underground Railroad, the Civil War, and African American women." Univ Press Books for Public and Second Sch Libr, 2004
  Includes bibliographical references

Larson, Kate Clifford. **Bound** for the promised land; Harriet Tubman, portrait of an American hero. Ballantine Bks. 2003 xxi, 402p il map $26.95; pa $14.95   **92**
  1. Abolitionists 2. Underground railroad 3. African American women -- Biography
ISBN 0-345-45627-0; 0-345-45628-9 pa
        LC 2004-297886
  "Using a clear writing style, Larson does an excellent job of placing Tubman in the context of her times." SLJ
  Includes bibliographical references

Turing, Alan Mathison, 1912-1954

Copeland, B. Jack. **Turing**; Pioneer of the Information Age. by Jack Copeland. Oxford Univ Press 2013 224 p. $21.95 **92**
  1. Mathematicians -- Biography 2. Turing, Alan Mathison, 1912-1954 3. Mathematicians -- Great Britain -- Biography
ISBN 0199639795; 9780199639793
        LC 2012289154
Author Jack Copeland presents an "introduction to . . . scientist [Alan Turing] and his work. Copeland describes Alan Turing's revolutionary ideas about Artificial Intelligence and his pioneering work on Artificial Life, his all-important code-breaking work during World War II, and his contributions to mathematics, philosophy, and the founda-

tions of computer science." (Publisher's note)

Includes bibliographical references and index

Leavitt, David. The **man** who knew too much; Alan Turing and the invention of the computer. W. W. Norton 2006 319p il (Great discoveries) $22.95   **92**

1. Mathematicians

ISBN 0-393-05236-2

LC 2005-18034

This is a biography of the British mathematician.

The author "succeeds in drawing a wonderfully vivid picture of his shy, dry, brilliant hero." Natl Rev

Includes bibliographical references

Turner, J. M. W. (Joseph Mallord William), 1775-1851

★ Moyle, Franny. **Turner**; the extraordinary life & momentous times of J.M.W. Turner. Franny Moyle. Penguin Press 2016 528 p. illustrations (some color) (ebook) $65.00; (hardback) $35.00   **92**

1. Painters -- Biography 2. Painters -- Great Britain -- Biography

ISBN 9780735220935; 9780735220928

LC 2016043479

This book, by Franny Moyle, is a biography of painter J.M.W. Turner. "Turner was very much a man of his changing era. In his lifetime, he saw Britain ravaged by Napoleonic wars, revived by the Industrial Revolution, and embarked upon a new moment of Imperial glory with the ascendancy of Queen Victoria. His own life embodied astonishing transformation." (Publisher's note)

"This excellent biography shows the benefits, and the pitfalls, of such single-minded obsession." Kirkus

Includes bibliographical references and (pages [447]-449) and index.

Turner, Ted, 1938-

Auletta, Ken. **Media** man; Ted Turner's improbable empire. Norton 2004 205p il $22.95   **92**

1. Philanthropists 2. Boat racers 3. Baseball executives 4. Broadcasting executives

ISBN 0-393-05168-4

LC 2004-12215

The author "describes how Turner's upbringing by a domineering father and his marriage to and later divorce from actress and radical Jane Fonda influenced his life and career. He also shows how Turner revolutionized TV by turning a tiny Atlanta station into a national cable powerhouse." Libr J

Includes bibliographical references

Twain, Mark, 1835-1910

Loving, Jerome. **Mark** Twain; the adventures of Samuel L. Clemens. University of California Press 2010 491p il $34.95   **92**

1. Authors 2. Humorists 3. Novelists 4. Essayists 5. Satirists 6. Memoirists 7. Travel writers 8. Authors, American 9. Short story writers 10. Biography, Individual

ISBN 978-0-520-25257-8

LC 2009-15366

The author "serves up a balanced literary biography of a crowded life—'to renew our acquaintance with this familiar stranger in our literature and culture.' Many of the best chapters include sensitive appraisals of The Adventures of Huckleberry Finn, The Tragedy of Pudd'nhead Wilson, and the anonymously published Personal Recollections of Joan of Arc, with The Adventures of Tom Sawyer put in a different context as possibly the most overrated work of American fiction when considered

as adult literature. . . . [This] is a solid contribution to literary interpretation of the man who infused American literature with what has been called 'tragic laughter.'" Publ Wkly

Includes bibliographical references

Powers, Ron. **Mark** Twain; a life. Free Press 2005 722p il $35   **92**

1. Authors 2. Humorists 3. Novelists 4. Essayists 5. Satirists 6. Memoirists 7. Travel writers 8. Short story writers

ISBN 0-7432-4899-6

LC 2005-48816

"A masterful biography of interest to both general readers and academics." Booklist

Includes bibliographical references

Scharnhorst, Gary. The **life** of Mark Twain; the early years, 1835-1871. by Gary Scharnhorst. University of Missouri Press 2018 720 p. (hardcover: alk. paper) $36.95   **92**

1. American authors -- Biography 2. Authors, American -- 19th century -- Biography 3. Humorists, American -- 19th century -- Biography

ISBN 9780826221445

LC 2017044383

In this book in the Mark Twain and His Circle series, author "Gary Scharnhorst has chosen to write a complete biography [of Samuel Clemens] plotted from beginning to end, from a single point of view, on an expansive canvas. . . . Scharnhorst has located documents relevant to Clemens's life in Missouri, along the Mississippi River, and in the West, including some which have been presumed lost." (Publisher's note)

"Besides ferreting out truths Clemens himself concealed, Scharnhorst announces his intention to challenge the misleading perspectives of previous biographers—including those academic specialists whose single-volume tomes deliver skeletal portraits of a robust figure. The signal achievement manifested in this volume will leave readers eagerly awaiting its sequels." Booklist

Includes bibliographical references and index

Shelden, Michael. **Mark** Twain; man in white: the grand adventure of his final years. Random House 2010 xxxix, 484p il $30   **92**

1. Authors 2. Humorists 3. Novelists 4. Essayists 5. Satirists 6. Memoirists 7. Travel writers 8. Authors, American 9. Short story writers

ISBN 978-0-679-44800-6; 0-679-44800-4

LC 2009-19719

The author "tells the story of Twain's last 40 months, richly detailing fresh facts new to most readers and fleshing out the conventional Twain biography to make the man's life complete. . . . This superb biography, told in a nonacademic tone, is saturated with sadness, but every reader will be grateful that, finally, Mark Twain appears before us, warts and all." Libr J

Includes bibliographical references

★ Twain, Mark, 1835-1910. **Autobiography** of Mark Twain; Volume 1 The Complete and Authoritative Edition. Harriet Elinor Smith, editor; associate editors: Benjamin Griffin, Victor Fischer, Michael B. Frank, Sharon K. Goetz, Leslie Myrick. University of California Press 2010 736 p. Volume 1 ill. (The Mark Twain papers) (hbk.) $45.00   **92**

1. Autobiographies 2. Authors, American -- 19th century -- Biography

ISBN 0520267192; 9780520267190 (alk. paper)

LC 2009047700

This is "the first of a projected three-volume edition of the complete, uncensored autobiography. The book became an immediate bestseller and was hailed as the capstone of the life's work of America's favorite author." It includes text that was not to be published until the 100th anniversary of Twain's death. (Publisher's note)

"Laced with Twain's unique blend of humor and vitriol, the haphazard narrative is engrossing, hugely funny, and deeply revealing of its author's mind." Pub Wkly

Includes bibliographical references (p. 681-712) and index

Zacks, Richard. **Chasing** the last laugh; Mark Twain's raucous and redemptive round-the-world comedy tour. Richard Zacks. Doubleday 2016 x, 450 p.p illustrations (hardback) $30   **92**

1. American authors 2. Authors, American -- 19th century -- Biography

ISBN 9780385536448

LC 2015036843

This book, by Richard Zacks, "captures some of Twain's cleverest and funniest moments—many newly discovered in unpublished notebooks and letters—as he rode elephants in India, sorted diamonds in South Africa, and talked his way out of hell ninety minutes at a time. This untold chapter in the author's life began with ridiculously bad choices and ended in hard-won triumph." (Publisher's note)

"Zacks's narrative is well-researched with rich detail...and it will strike ardent Twain fans and history lovers as fresh and inspiring." Pub Wkly.

Includes bibliographical references and index

Tweedy, Damon

Tweedy, Damon. **Black** Man in a White Coat; A Doctor's Reflections on Race and Medicine. Damon Tweedy. St. Martin's Press 2015 304 p. $26   **92**

1. Physicians 2. Medicine -- United States 3. African Americans -- Health and hygiene

ISBN 1250044634; 9781250044631

LC 2015018599

Author Damon Tweedy presents this "memoir of his experience grappling with race, bias, and the unique health problems of black Americans. [It] examines the complex ways in which both black doctors and patients must navigate the difficult and often contradictory terrain of race and medicine. As Tweedy transforms from student to practicing physician, he discovers how often race influences his encounters with patients." (Publisher's note)

"Clearly at odds with the racial and class-stratified machinations of the medical industry, the author writes with dignified authority on the imbalances in opportunities and available social and medical service platforms to the many African-American patients seeking clinical care and of his pivotal role in making a difference." Kirkus

Tye, Laurene, 1931-1989

Tye, Diane. **Baking** as biography; a life story in recipes. McGill-Queen's University Press 2010 268p il   **92**

1. Baking 2. Homemakers 3. Eating customs 4. Women -- Canada 5. Biography, Individual 6. Food -- Social aspects 7. Canada -- Social life and customs

ISBN 978-0-7735-3724-8; 978-0-7735-3725-5 pa

Diane Tye uses her mother's recipe collection as a focus for this memoir and study of Maritime culture. Index

"Using her mother's recipes as a framework, Tye . . . explores Canadian women's roles from 1930 to 1980. She recalls her mother as a minister's wife who didn't care for baking yet consistently produced

an abundance of sweets for her family, church, and community. Her succinct recipes range from simple (biscuits and oatcakes) to 'exotic' (anything involving JELL-O, Dream Whip, or canned pie filling). . . . Because this book blends memoir, biography, culinary history, and research, it should appeal to both scholars and readers who enjoy historical or intellectual food writing." Libr J

Includes bibliographical references

Tyler, John, 1790-1862

★ Crapol, Edward P. **John** Tyler; the accidental president. University of North Carolina Press 2006 332p il map $37.50   **92**

1. Governors 2. Presidents 3. Vice-presidents 4. Senators 5. Members of Congress

ISBN 978-0-8078-3041-3; 0-8078-3041-0

LC 2005-37963

In this biography of the former U.S. president, the author "argues that Tyler was in fact a terrifically strong president who helped strengthen the executive branch. . . . This balanced, fascinating volume will introduce a new generation of readers to an oft-ignored president." Publ Wkly

Includes bibliographical references

May, Gary. **John** Tyler. Times Books/Henry Holt and Co. 2008 183p (American presidents series) $22   **92**

1. Governors 2. Presidents 3. Vice-presidents 4. Senators 5. Members of Congress 6. Presidents -- United States

ISBN 978-0-8050-8238-8; 0-8050-8238-7

LC 2008-18131

This biography of the American president focuses on "Tyler's controversial presidency, which saw him set aside his dedication to the Constitution to gain his two great ambitions: Texas and a place in history." Publisher's note

Includes bibliographical references

Tynan, Tracy

Tynan, Tracy. **Wear** and tear; The Threads of My Life. Tracy Tynan. Scribner 2016 320 p. illustrations (hardcover: alk. paper) $26   **92**

1. Fashion designers 2. Fashion designers -- United States -- Biography 3. Women fashion designers -- United States -- Biography

ISBN 9781501123689; 9781501123696

LC 2015031108

This book, by Tracy Tynan, is a "candid . . . memoir told through clothes. . . . When Tracy started writing about her life she found that clothing was the focus of many of her stories. She recalls her father's dandy attire and her mother's Pucci dresses, as well as her parents' rancorous marriage and divorce, her father's prodigious talents and celebrity lifestyle, and her mother's lifelong struggle with addiction. She tackles issues big and small using clothes as an entrée." (Publisher's note)

"Each of the three-dozen gemlike chapters cover an episode built around a specific piece of clothing, from a designer crepe de chine gown to a maroon plaid dress to a tiny pink knitted cap, a gift of love for Tynan's premature baby. The sum total is an absorbing memoir well-told from a singular perspective." LJ

Tyson, Mike, 1966-

Tyson, Mike, 1966- **Iron** ambition; my life with Cus D'Amato. Mike Tyson; with Larry "Ratso" Sloman. Blue Rider Press 2017 465 p. illustrations (some color) (hardcover) $28   **92**

1. Boxers (Sports) 2. Boxing -- Biography 3. African American

boxers -- Biography 4. Boxers (Sports) -- United States -- Biography 5. Boxing trainers -- United States -- Biography
ISBN 0399177035; 9780399177033; 9780698413092

LC 2017007907

In this book, boxer Mike Tyson "elaborates on the life lessons that [Cus] D'Amato passed down to him, and reflects on how the trainer's words of wisdom continue to resonate with him outside the ring. The book also chronicles Cus's courageous fight against the mobsters who controlled boxing, revealing more than we've ever known about this singular cultural figure." (Publisher's note)

"A belated but welcome homage to a boxing legend who died shortly before Tyson's career took off." Kirkus

U-God, 1970-

Hawkins, Lamont. **Raw**; my journey into the Wu-Tang. Lamont "U-God" Hawkins. Picador 2018 304 p. (hardcover) $27   92
1. Rap musicians -- Biography 2. AFRICAN American musicians -- Biography 3. Wu-Tang Clan (Musical group) 4. Rap musicians -- United States -- Biography
ISBN 9781250191168

LC 2017047146

This memoir, by Lamont 'U-God' Hawkins, is an "explosive, never-before-told story behind the historic rise of the Wu-Tang Clan, as told by one of its founding members. . . . U-God's unforgettable first-person account of his journey, from the streets of Brooklyn to some of the biggest stages around the world, is not only thoroughly affecting, unfiltered, and explosive but also captures, in vivid detail, the making of one of the greatest acts in American music history." (Publisher's note)

"Hawkins is a wonderful storyteller who spares no detail (he writes of using plastic wrap as a prophylactic), and his willingness to share his wisdom in nonsaccharine terms yields an inspirational coming-of-age story." Pub Wkly

Uhlberg, Myron

Uhlberg, Myron. **Hands** of my father; a hearing boy, his deaf parents, and the language of love. Bantam Books 2009 232p il $23   92
1. Deaf 2. Authors 3. Children's authors
ISBN 978-0-553-80688-5; 0-553-80688-2

LC 2008-25628

A memoir about growing up the son of deaf parents in 1940s Brooklyn

"Uhlberg's emotions toward his family, and especially his father, run the gamut from embarrassment to anger to a deep and abiding love. Sections titled 'Memorabilia' pepper the narrative, and many black-and-white photographs are scattered throughout this rich, textured portrait of the deaf community on Coney Island at a turbulent time in U.S. history." SLJ

Ulianov, Aleksandr, 1886-1887

Pomper, Philip. **Lenin's** brother; the origins of the October Revolution. W.W. Norton & Co. 2010 276p il $24.95   92
1. Heads of state 2. Revolutionaries 3. Communist leaders 4. Political leaders 5. Soviet Union -- History -- 1917-1921, Revolution
ISBN 978-0-393-07079-8

LC 2009-27390

"In 1887, the future leader of the Russian revolution, Vladimir Ulyanov (later Lenin), was 17 when his 21-year-old brother was hanged for his role in a bungled attempt to assassinate Czar Alexander III. Historians consider this the seminal event that launched Lenin's career as a revolutionary. . . . [The author] delivers an absorbing and surprisingly detailed account of Alexander Ulyanov's short life and even shorter career (four months) as a terrorist." Publ Wkly

Includes bibliographical references

Ullman, Ellen

Ullman, Ellen. **Life** in code; a personal history of technology. Ellen Ullman. MCD/Farrar, Straus & Giroux 2017 viii, 306 p.p illustrations (hardcover) $27   92
1. Autobiographies 2. Computer programming 3. Computer programmers -- United States -- Biography 4. Internet -- History 5. Computer programming -- History
ISBN 9780374711412; 9780374534516

LC 2017012764

In this book, by Ellen Ullman, "the last twenty years have brought us the rise of the internet, the development of artificial intelligence, the ubiquity of once unimaginably powerful computers, and the thorough transformation of our economy and society. Through it all, . . . Ullman lived and worked inside that rising culture of technology, and in 'Life in Code' she tells the continuing story of the changes it wrought with a unique, expert perspective." (Publisher's note)

"Neither technophilic nor technophobic, this collection creates a time-lapse view of the rapid development of technology in recent years and provides general readers with much-needed grounding for the sweeping changes of the revolution underway." Pub Wkly

Umbrell, Colby, 1981-2007

Sielski, Mike. **Fading** echoes; a true story of rivalry and brotherhood from the football field to the fields of honor. Berkley Books 2009 342p il $24.95   92
1. School sports 2. Iraq War, 2003-2011 3. Marines 4. Army officers 5. Football -- Biography 6. Soldiers -- United States
ISBN 978-0-425-22974-3

LC 2009-17001

"Bryan Buckley was the captain of Central Bucks West and [Colby] Umbrell was one of the leaders of Central Bucks East when their teams clashed in their senior year of 1998. Eight years later, both were officers leading men in combat in Iraq, Buckley as a marine and Umbrell as an army ranger. Both were proudly fighting for ideals in which they believed, and only one would come home alive. Sielski . . . chronicles the lives of these two athletes and illustrates how their personalities and values were formed from interactions with family, friends, coaches, and community. In the process, he writes of much broader topics in contemporary American life: dreams, competition, resolve, war, honor, sacrifice, and true heartbreak." Libr J

Includes bibliographical references

Ung, Chou

★ Ung, Loung. **Lucky** child; a daughter of Cambodia reunites with the sister she left behind. HarperCollins Publishers 2005 268p il $24.95; pa $13.95   92
1. Homemakers 2. Cambodian Americans 3. Memoirists 4. Social activists 5. Cambodia -- History -- 1975-
ISBN 0-06-073394-2; 0-06-073395-0 pa

LC 2004-54346

Sequel to First they killed my father

In this "memoir, Ung picks up where her first . . . left off, with the author escaping a devastated Cambodia in 1980 at age 10 and flying to her new home in Vermont. . . . She and her eldest brother, with whom she escaped, left behind their three other siblings. This book is alternately heart-wrenching and heartwarming, as it follows the parallel lives of Loung Ung and her closest sister, Chou, during the 15 years it took for them to reunite." Publ Wkly

Includes bibliographical references

Ung, Loung, 1970-

★ Ung, Loung. **Lucky** child; a daughter of Cambodia reunites with the sister she left behind. HarperCollins Publishers 2005 268p il $24.95; pa $13.95   **92**

1. Homemakers 2. Cambodian Americans 3. Memoirists 4. Social activists 5. Cambodia -- History -- 1975-

ISBN 0-06-073394-2; 0-06-073395-0 pa

LC 2004-54346

Sequel to First they killed my father

In this "memoir, Ung picks up where her first . . . left off, with the author escaping a devastated Cambodia in 1980 at age 10 and flying to her new home in Vermont. . . . She and her eldest brother, with whom she escaped, left behind their three other siblings. This book is alternately heart-wrenching and heartwarming, as it follows the parallel lives of Loung Ung and her closest sister, Chou, during the 15 years it took for them to reunite." Publ Wkly

Includes bibliographical references

Ungern-Sternberg, Roman, 1885-1921

Palmer, James. The **bloody** white baron; the extraordinary story of the Russian nobleman who became the last khan of Mongolia. Basic Books 2009 274p $26.95   **92**

1. Generals 2. Soviet Union -- History -- 1917-1921, Revolution

ISBN 978-0-465-01448-4; 0-465-01448-8

LC 2008-937254

First published 2008 in the United Kingdom

"What makes 'The Bloody White Baron' so exceptional is Palmer's lucid scholarship, his ability to make perfect sense of the maelstrom of a forgotten war. This is a brilliant book." N Y Times Book Rev

Includes bibliographical references

Union, Gabrielle

Union, Gabrielle, 1972- **We're** going to need more wine; stories that are funny, complicated, and true. Gabrielle Union. HarperCollins 2017 288 p. $26.99   **92**

1. Rape 2. Women 3. Essays

ISBN 0062693980; 9780062693983

This book, by Gabrielle Union, presents "a powerful collection of essays about gender, sexuality, race, beauty, Hollywood, and what it means to be a modern woman. . . . Union tackles a range of experiences, including bullying, beauty standards, . . . puberty, and the divorce of her parents. . . . Throughout, she compels us to be ethical and empathetic, and reminds us of the importance of confidence, self-awareness, and the power of sharing truth, laughter, and support." (Publisher's note)

"This sparkling book collects amusing and heartbreaking stories from the life of actress Union (Being Mary Jane)." Pub Wkly

Updike, John

★ Begley, Adam. **Updike**; Adam Begley. Harper 2014 576 p. illustrations (hardback) $29.99   **92**

1. American authors 2. American literature -- History and criticism 3. Authors, American -- 20th century -- Biography

ISBN 0061896454; 9780061896453

LC 2013039246

Los Angeles Times Book Prize Finalist: Biography (2014)

This biography of John Updike "explores the stages of the writer's pilgrim's progress: his beloved home turf of Berks County, Pennsylvania; his escape to Harvard; his brief, busy working life as the golden boy at The New Yorker; his family years in suburban Ipswich, Massachusetts; his extensive travel abroad; and his retreat to another Massachusetts town, Beverly Farms, where he remained until his death in 2009." (Publisher's note)

"Begley draws on deep research and interviews with the author and his circle to chart his early influences—in particular his ambitious mother, Linda—and rigorously explore the heavily autobiographical dimensions of his fiction and poetry." Pub Wkly

Includes bibliographical references and index

Valadon, Suzanne, 1865-1938

Hewitt, Catherine. **Renoir's** dancer; the secret life of Suzanne Valadon. Catherine Hewitt. St. Martin's Press 2018 viii, 470 p.p illustrations (some color) (hardcover) $27.99   **92**

1. Women artists -- Biography 2. Painters -- France -- Biography 3. Women painters -- France -- Biography

ISBN 9781250157645; 9781250157652

LC 2017041095

This biography, by Catherine Hewitt, tells the story of "Suzanne Valadon, the illegitimate daughter of a provincial linen maid who became famous as a model for the Impressionists and later as a painter in her own right. . . . Some found her vibrant still lifes and frank portraits as shocking as her bohemian lifestyle." (Publisher's note)

"A well-researched tribute to and resurrection of a master of fin de siècle art." Kirkus

Includes bibliographical references and index

Valenti, Jessica.

★ Valenti, Jessica, 1978- **Sex** object; a memoir. Jessica Valenti. HarperCollins 2016 288 p. (hardback) $25.99   **92**

1. Feminism

ISBN 9780062435088; 9780062435095; 0062435086

LC 2016017749

In this memoir, Jessica Valenti "explores the toll that sexism takes on women's lives, from the everyday to the existential. From subway gropings and imposter syndrome to sexual awakenings and motherhood, . . . [it] reveals the painful, embarrassing, and sometimes illegal moments that shaped Valenti's adolescence and young adulthood in New York City." (Publisher's note)

"An entertaining and shocking memoir from a leading feminist writer." Booklist

Vampira, 1921-2008

Poole, W. Scott. **Vampira**; dark goddess of horror. W. Scott Poole. Soft Skull Press 2014 320 p. illustrations (paperback) $16.95   **92**

1. Actresses -- Biography 2. Popular culture -- United States 3. Actresses -- United States -- Biography 4. Entertainers -- United States -- Biography

ISBN 1593765436; 9781593765439

LC 2014014147

This book, by W. Scott Poole, "detail[s] the story of cult horror figure Vampira that actually tells the much wider story of 1950s America and its treatment of women and sex, as well as capturing a fascinating swath of Los Angeles history. . . . Poole gives us the eclectic life of the dancer, stripper, actress, and artist Maila Nurmi, who would reinvent herself as Vampira during the backdrop of 1950s America." (Publisher's note)

"Before there was Dr. Morgus, Svengoolie, and Elvira, there was the titular Vampira. This stone-cold winner belongs in every American studies collection." LJ

Van Buren, Martin, 1782-1862

Widmer, Edward L. **Martin** Van Buren; [by] Ted Widmer. Times Bks. 2005 189p (American presidents series) $20   **92**

1. Presidents 2. Vice-presidents 3. Secretaries of state 4. Presidents -- United States

ISBN 0-8050-6922-4

LC 2004-53652

The author "keenly evokes the environment that enabled Van Buren to thrive. . . . Widmer also lends a certain dignity to Van Buren's post-presidential attempts to resolve the sectional crisis." N Y Times Book Rev

Includes bibliographical references

Van Gogh, Vincent, 1853-1890

Bell, Julian. **Van** Gogh; A Power Seething. Julian Bell. New Harvest 2015 176 p. 8 plates; color illustrations $20 **92**

1. Painters

ISBN 0544343735; 9780544343733

Author Julian Bell presents this book on painter Vincent Van Gogh. "He was a great writer as well. In his six hundred-plus letters to [his brother] Theo he chronicled with heartbreaking urgency his mental breakdowns, acrimonious family relations, and struggles with art dealers. Shading this dark story is the artist's acquaintance with prostitutes and penury, stormy scenes with his friend Paul Gauguin, and dissipated Parisian nights with Henri de Toulouse-Lautrec." (Publisher's note)

"Bell describes with glorious acuity the rapid artistic evolution of this self-taught genius propelled by a 'peculiar inner seething,' celebrating with unique fluency Van Gogh's 'rapturous vision' and the 'visual electricity' of his masterpieces. A vividly illuminating portrait both for readers versed in Van Gogh and those who are newly curious." Booklist

Van Vechten, Carl, 1880-1964

★ White, Edward. The **Tastemaker**; Carl Van Vechten and the Birth of Modern America. Edward White. Farrar, Straus & Giroux 2014 400 p. illustrations (hardback) $30 **92**

1. Photographers -- Biography 2. American authors -- Biography 3. Photographers -- United States -- Biography 4. Authors, American -- 20th century -- Biography

ISBN 0374201579; 9780374201579

LC 2013034003

A biography by Edward White, "'The Tastemaker' explores the many lives of Carl Van Vechten, the most influential cultural impresario of the early twentieth century: a patron and dealmaker of the Harlem Renaissance, a photographer who captured the era's icons, and a novelist who created some of the Jazz Age's most salacious stories." (Publisher's note)

"In orderly chapters, White tackles this complicated, multifaceted, tremendously fascinating and contradictory subject. . . . A vigorous, fully fleshed biography of an important contributor to American culture." Kirkus

Includes bibliographical references and index

Van Zandt, Townes, 1944-1997

Kruth, John. **To** live's to fly; the ballad of the late, great Townes Van Zandt. Da Capo 2007 326p il $26 **92**

1. Singers 2. Guitarists 3. Folk musicians 4. Country musicians 5. Songwriters

ISBN 978-0-306-81553-9; 0-306-81553-2

This is "the first biography of legendary Texas singer/songwriter Townes Van Zandt (1944-97). In his struggle for recognition among a wider public, Van Zandt wrestled for years with depression and alcoholism while writing songs—e.g., 'Pancho and Lefty' and 'Be Here To Love Me'—that today are revered by the elite of Texas and Nashville songwriters as well as by a cult group of fans. Through access to Van Zandt's friends, family members, and fellow musicians, Kruth provides an intimate and unflinching look at the singer's life." Libr J

Vance, J. D.

★ Vance, J. D., 1984- **Hillbilly** elegy; A Memoir of a Family and Culture in Crisis. J. D. Vance. HarperCollins 2016 272 p. $27.99 **92**

1. Family life 2. Working class 3. Social mobility 4. Lawyers -- Biography

ISBN 0062300547; 9780062300546

LC 2016017254

Kirkus Prize Finalist: Nonfiction (2016)

This book by J. D. Vance is a "personal analysis of a culture in crisis--that of white working-class Americans. . . . The Vance family story begins . . . in postwar America. J. D.'s grandparents were 'dirt poor and in love,' and moved north from Kentucky's Appalachia region to Ohio. . . . They raised a middle-class family, and eventually their grandchild (the author) would graduate from Yale Law School, a . . . marker of their success in achieving generational upward mobility." (Publisher's note)

"Both heartbreaking and heartwarming, this memoir is akin to investigative journalism." LJ

Includes bibliographical references (pages 263-264).

Vanderbilt, Cornelius, 1794-1877

Renehan, Edward J. **Commodore**; the life of Cornelius Vanderbilt. [by] Edward J. Renehan Jr. Basic Books 2007 xx, 364p il $27.50 **92**

1. Businessmen 2. Financiers 3. Railroad executives 4. Shipping executives

ISBN 978-0-465-00255-9; 0-465-00255-2

LC 2007-22392

"A warts and more warts portrait of a brilliantly successful, genuinely despicable man." Kirkus

Includes bibliographical references

★ Stiles, T. J. The **first** tycoon; the epic life of Cornelius Vanderbilt. Alfred A. Knopf 2009 719p $37.50 **92**

1. Businessmen 2. Railroads -- History 3. Biography, Individual 4. Steamboats -- History

ISBN 978-0-375-41542-5; 0-375-41542-4

LC 2008-47879

National Book Award: Nonfiction (2009)

This is a biography of the American steamship and railroad magnate. "This is a mighty—and mighty confident—work, one that moves with force and conviction and imperious wit through Vanderbilt's noisy life and times. . . . This is state-of-the-art biography, crisper and more piquant than a 600-page book has any right to be." N Y Times (Late N Y Ed)

Includes bibliographical references

Vanderbilt, Gloria, 1924-

Cooper, Anderson, 1967- The **rainbow** comes and goes; a mother and son talk about life, love, and loss. Anderson Cooper and Gloria Vanderbilt. HarperCollins 2016 290 p. illustrations (hardback) $27.99 **92**

1. Mother-son relationship 2. Celebrities -- Biography 3. Journalists -- Biography 4. Celebrities -- United States -- Biography 5. Mothers and sons -- United States -- Correspondence 6. Television journalists -- United States -- Biography

ISBN 0062454943; 9780062454942; 9780062454966; 9780062466730

LC 2016000369

This book, by Anderson Cooper and Gloria Vanderbilt, "offers a rare window into their close relationship and fascinating life stories, including their tragedies and triumphs. In these often humorous and moving exchanges, they share their most private thoughts and the hard-earned truths they've learned along the way. In their words their distinctive personalities shine through—Anderson's journalistic outlook on the world is a sharp contrast to his mother's idealism and unwavering optimism." (Publisher's note)

"Vanderbilt and her son, Cooper, relate the touching story of how an epistolary exchange created new emotional intimacy between them." Pub Wkly

Varmus, Harold

Varmus, Harold. The **art** and politics of science. W.W. Norton 2009 315p il $24.95   **92**

1. Scientists 2. Nobel Prizes 3. Microbiologists 4. College teachers 5. Government officials 6. Public health officials 7. National Institutes of Health (U.S.) 8. Nobel laureates for physiology or medicine

ISBN 978-0-393-06128-4; 0-393-06128-0

LC 2008-42963

"Varmus offers a plain-spoken and fascinating story of his path from graduate student in English literature to the forefront of biomedical research. His journey to the highest echelons of the scientific establishment is as interesting for its incidental details as for its glimpse into the process of modern biomedical science." Washington Post

Includes bibliographical references

Vaughan, Sarah, 1924-1990

Hayes, Elaine M. **Queen** of bebop; the musical lives of Sarah Vaughan. Elaine M. Hayes. Ecco, an imprint of Harper-Collins Publishers 2017 x, 419 p.p illustrations (hardcover) $27.99   **92**

1. Jazz musicians -- Biography 2. African American women -- Biography 3. Jazz singers -- United States -- Biography

ISBN 9780062364708; 9780062364685; 0062364685

LC 2017562620

This biography, by Elaine M. Hayes, "chronicles the life of jazz singer Sarah Vaughan, one of the most influential and innovative musicians of the twentieth century and a pioneer of women's and civil rights. . . . Drawing . . . on exclusive interviews with Vaughan's friends and former colleagues, 'Queen of Bebop' unravels the many myths and misunderstandings that have surrounded Vaughan while offering insights into this notoriously private woman. . . ." (Publisher's note)

"A deeply illuminating and unforgettable biography of a true American master." Booklist

Includes bibliographical references (pages 371-401) and index.

Vavilov, N. I. (Nikola¿¿ Ivanovich), 1887-1943

Pringle, Peter. The **murder** of Nikolai Vavilov; the story of Stalin's persecution of one of the great scientists of the twentieth century. Simon & Schuster 2008 370p il $26   **92**

1. Botanists 2. Heads of state 3. Communist leaders 4. Plant geneticists 5. Political leaders

ISBN 978-0-7432-6498-3; 0-7432-6498-3

LC 2008-03510

This is a biography of the Russian botanist and geneticist who was starved to death in a Soviet prison in 1943.

This "is a must-read to grasp the ultimate, disasterous effect of politics trumping science." Sci Books Films

Includes bibliographical references

Verdi, Giuseppe, 1813-1901

Suchet, John. **Verdi**; the man revealed. John Suchet. W W Norton & Co Inc 2018 288 p. $27.95   **92**

1. Biography 2. Composers -- Biography

ISBN 1681777681; 9781681777689

In this biography of Italian composer Giuseppe Verdi, author "John Suchet attempts to get under the skin of perhaps the most private composer who ever lived. Unraveling his protestations, his deliberate embellishments and disavowals, Suchet reveals the true character of this great artist--and the art for which he will be forever known." (Publisher's note)

"Obviously, music lovers will want this volume, but the subject is so lively and the presentation so attractive that it will appeal to all who value a solid biography." Library Journal

Vespucci, Amerigo, 1451-1512

★ Fernandez-Armesto, Felipe. **Amerigo**; the man who gave his name to America. Random House 2007 231p il map $24.95; pa $15   **92**

1. Explorers 2. America -- Exploration

ISBN 978-1-4000-6281-2; 1-4000-6281-0; 978-0-8129-7298-6 pa; 0-8129-7298-8 pa

LC 2006-51739

First published 2006 in the United Kingdom

The author chronicles the life and times of the explorer and navigator Amerigo Vespucci

"A well-connected Florentine wheeler-dealer who settled in Seville, Vespucci began by outfitting Columbus's ships and later made voyages of his own. . . . Fernandez-Armesto accepts that Amerigo Vespucci made two voyages to north eastern South America, one in 1499 and another in 1501-02. But the evidence is maddeningly vague on exactly where he went, what he did, and even in what capacity he served (he is unlikely to have been the commander, as he claimed). Faced by such unreliable sources, Fernandez-Armesto sticks to what can be said of Vespucci with confidence, and wisely opts to paint a rich portrait of the times rather than speculate about details that may never be known." Times Lit Suppl

Includes bibliographical references

Victoria, Queen of Great Britain, 1819-1901

★ Baird, Julia. **Victoria**; The Queen: An Intimate Biography of the Woman Who Ruled an Empire. Julia Baird. Random House 2016 720 p.   **92**

1. Queens -- Great Britain -- Biography 2. Great Britain -- History -- Victoria, 1837-1901

ISBN 9781400069880

LC 2015025297

In this biography of Queen Victoria, historian Julia Baird "reveals the real woman behind the myth: a bold, glamorous, unbreakable queen—a Victoria for our times. Drawing on previously unpublished papers, this . . . is a story of love and heartbreak, of devotion and grief. . . . Baird brings . . . to life the fascinating story of a woman who struggled with . . . balancing work and family, raising children, . . . finding an identity, searching for meaning." (Publisher's note)

"Baird does not turn a blind eye on Victoria's darker sides, including her willfulness, selfishness, and self-pity. But that simply adds dimensions to a significant character." Booklist

Includes bibliographical references and index

Erickson, Carolly. **Her** little majesty: the life of Queen Victoria. Simon & Schuster 1997 304p il hardcover o.p. pa $19.95   **92**

1. Queens 2. Great Britain -- History -- 19th century

ISBN 0-7432-3657-2 pa

LC 96-35041

This is a biography of the British monarch

"Erickson has a knack for plucking pithy quotes, and the essentials of the queen's life are often deftly set out." Publ Wkly

Includes bibliographical references

Hibbert, Christopher. **Queen** Victoria; a personal history. Basic Bks. 2000 557p il hardcover o.p. pa $21 **92**

1. Queens 2. Great Britain -- History -- 19th century

ISBN 0-306-81085-9 pa

LC 2001-269136

Hibbert explores the life and reign of the British monarch based on "primary sources, particularly the 60 million words of Victoria's letters and journals. As a result, he renders Victoria and her familial and political relationships with deliciously gossipy and often touching intimacy." N Y Times Book Rev

Includes bibliographical references

Williams, Kate. **Becoming** Queen Victoria; the tragic death of Princess Charlotte and the unexpected rise of Britain's greatest monarch. Ballantine Books 2010 448p il $30; ebook $30 **92**

1. Queens 2. Princesses 3. Great Britain -- Kings and rulers

ISBN 978-0-345-46195-7; 978-0-345-52193-4 ebook

LC 2010-13227

First published 2008 in the United Kingdom with title: Becoming queen

"A lively, juicy read, full of the sordid details of the debauched rule of kings and princes that led to the moralistic rule of a queen focused on creating a royal family that embodied the ideals of a nation. Perfect for fans of royal histories and historical television shows or armchair historians interested in a swift and enjoyable read." Libr J

Includes bibliographical references

★ Wilson, A. N., 1950- **Victoria**; a life. A. N. Wilson. Penguin Group USA 2015 642 p. ill, port, genealogical table (paperback) $20 **92**

1. Queens -- Great Britain 2. Great Britain -- Kings and rulers 3. Great Britain -- History -- Victoria, 1837-1901

ISBN 014312787X; 9780698170056; 9780143127871

LC 2014013973

This biography, by A. N. Wilson, "includes a wealth of new material from previously unseen sources to show us Queen Victoria as she's never been seen before. Wilson explores the curious set of circumstances that led to Victoria's coronation, her strange and isolated childhood, her passionate marriage to Prince Albert and his pivotal influence even after death and her widowhood and subsequent intimate friendship with her Highland servant John Brown." (Publisher's note)

"[F]ew if any previous biographers have viewed her as incisively and absorbingly as Wilson does in his lengthy but smoothly flowing treatment of the queen's long life. . . . [He] sees Victoria as a woman who battled demons and emerged from her various darknesses victorious as a functioning woman and monarch." Booklist

Includes bibliographical references and index

Vidal, Gore, 1925-2012

Parini, Jay. **Empire** of self; a life of Gore Vidal. by Jay Parini. Doubleday 2015 480 p. 32 plates: illustrations (hardback) $35 **92**

1. American authors 2. Authors, American -- 20th century -- Biography

ISBN 0385537565; 9780385537568

LC 2015004719

This book, by Jay Parini, is an "authorized yet frank biography of Gore Vidal. . . . Parini crafts Vidal's life into an accessible, entertaining story that puts the experience of one of the great American figures of the postwar era into context; introduces the author and his works to a generation who may not know him; and looks behind the scenes at the man and his work in ways never possible before his death." (Publisher's note)

"It's difficult to paint an appealing picture of a narcissist, but Parini has produced a balanced account of a man of immense talent who sometimes used it wisely and other times didn't. Lively and insightful, this book should find favor among lovers of literature and biography. It's got heart." LJ

Vidal, Gore. **Point** to point navigation; a memoir, 1964 to 2006. Doubleday 2006 277p il $26 **92**

1. Authors 2. Novelists 3. Dramatists 4. Essayists 5. Screenwriters

ISBN 0-385-51721-1; 978-0-385-51721-8

LC 2006-11644

"The memoir is a perfect encapsulation of Vidal's outsized personality—and readers' reactions will be determined by how they already feel about him." Publ Wkly

Villani, Cedric, 1973-

Villani, Cédric. **Birth** of a theorem; a mathematical adventure. Cédric Villani; illustrations by Claude Gondard. Faber & Faber, Inc. an affiliate of Farrar, Straus & Giroux 2015 272 p. illustrations (hardback) $26 **92**

1. Mathematicians -- Biography 2. Mathematicians -- France -- Biography

ISBN 0865477671; 9780865477674

LC 2014031268

"In 2010, French mathematician Cédric Villani received the Fields Medal, the most coveted prize in mathematics, in recognition of a proof which he devised with his close collaborator Clément Mouhot to explain one of the most surprising theories in classical physics. 'Birth of a Theorem' is Villani's own account of the years leading up to the award. It invites readers inside the mind of a great mathematician as he wrestles with the most important work of his career." (Publisher's note)

"And though readers will marvel at his remarkable genius, they will also recognize how much Villani depends on loving family ties, congenial friendships, and supportive institutions to nurture that genius. A rare portal into stratospheric mathematics." Booklist

Volk, Audrey Morgen

Volk, Patricia. **Shocked**; my mother, Schiaparelli, and me. Patricia Volk. Alfred A. Knopf 2013 304 p. ill. (some col.) (hardcover) $26.95 **92**

1. Femininity 2. Beauty, Personal 3. Mothers and daughters -- United States 4. Fashion designers -- France -- Paris -- Biography

ISBN 9780307962102; 0307962105

LC 2012034922

This book by Patricia Volk presents a "study of two very different but very glamorous women--her mother, Audrey, an upper-class New York domestic goddess with the looks and manners of Grace Kelly, and genius haute couture European artist Elsa Schiaparelli, whose book, art, and (yes) perfume forever change the course of young Volk's life." (Library Journal)

"[T]he narrative that emerges from Volk's deft interweaving of lives is as sharp-eyed as it is wickedly funny." Kirkus

Includes bibliographical references

Volk, Patricia

Volk, Patricia. **Shocked**; my mother, Schiaparelli, and me. Patricia Volk. Alfred A. Knopf 2013 304 p. ill. (some col.) (hardcover) $26.95 **92**

1. Femininity 2. Beauty, Personal 3. Mothers and daughters --

United States 4. Fashion designers -- France -- Paris -- Biography
ISBN 9780307962102; 0307962105

LC 2012034922

This book by Patricia Volk presents a "study of two very different but very glamorous women--her mother, Audrey, an upper-class New York domestic goddess with the looks and manners of Grace Kelly, and genius haute couture European artist Elsa Schiaparelli, whose book, art, and (yes) perfume forever change the course of young Volk's life." (Library Journal)

"[T]he narrative that emerges from Volk's deft interweaving of lives is as sharp-eyed as it is wickedly funny." Kirkus

Includes bibliographical references

Volpe, Joseph

Volpe, Joseph. The **toughest** show on earth; my rise and reign at the Metropolitan Opera. [by] Joseph Volpe with Charles Michener. Knopf 2006 304p il $25.95   **92**
1. Music administrators 2. Metropolitan Opera (New York, N.Y.)
ISBN 0-307-26285-5; 978-0-307-26285-1

LC 2005-57932

This is a memoir by the "general manager of New York's Metropolitan Opera since 1990. . . . This enthralling book provides an insider's view of a complex and fascinating institution." Libr J

Includes bibliographical references

Volpe, Lou

Sokolove, Michael. **Drama** high; the incredible true story of a brilliant teacher, a struggling town, and the magic of theater. by Michael Sokolove. Riverhead Hardcover 2013 352 p. ill (hardback) $27.95   **92**
1. College and school drama 2. Performing arts -- Study and teaching 3. English teachers -- Pennsylvania -- Levittown -- Biography 4. High school teachers -- Pennsylvania -- Levittown -- Biography 5. Theater -- Producers and directors -- Pennsylvania -- Levittown -- Biography
ISBN 1594488223; 9781594488221

LC 2013019393

In this book, author Michael Sokolove "chronicles the [Harry S Truman High School] drama director [Lou Volpe's] last school years and follows a group of student actors as they work through riveting dramas both on and off the stage. This is a story of an economically depressed but proud town finding hope in a gifted teacher and the magic of theater." (Publisher's note)

"During the season Sokolove spends at Truman, Volpe and his kids put on the play Good Boys and True and the musical Spring Awakening—both of which address teen sexuality, angst, and reckless behavior. Volpe pushes his student actors hard, but for most of them, being in one of his productions is transformative. Many alums go on to pursue careers in theater or the arts. A powerful look at the way a dynamic and dedicated teacher can change lives." (Booklist)

Voltaire, 1694-1778

★ Pearson, Roger. **Voltaire** almighty; a life in pursuit of freedom. Bloomsbury 2005 xxxii, 447p il $35   **92**
1. Poets 2. Authors 3. Novelists 4. Dramatists 5. Philosophers 6. Essayists
ISBN 978-1-58234-630-4; 1-58234-630-5

LC 2005-53027

This is a biography of the French philosopher.

The author "has composed a lively and thorough account of the illustrious philosophe's chaotic life." Choice

Includes bibliographical references

Von Braun, Wernher, 1912-1977

Biddle, Wayne. **Dark** side of the moon; Wernher von Braun, the Third Reich, and the space race. W.W. Norton 2009 220p il map $25.95   **92**
1. Rocketry 2. Scientists 3. Aerospace engineers 4. NASA officials
ISBN 978-0-393-05910-6; 0-393-05910-3

LC 2009-15572

"A stern, prosecutorial portrait of the famous German American rocketeer." Booklist

Includes bibliographical references

★ Neufeld, Michael J. **Von** Braun; dreamer of space, engineer of war. A.A. Knopf 2007 587p il $35; pa $19.95 **92**
1. Rocketry 2. Scientists 3. Aerospace engineers 4. NASA officials
ISBN 978-0-307-26292-9; 0-307-26292-8; 978-0-307-38937-4 pa; 0-307-38937-5 pa

LC 2007-5711

This "is a meticulously researched and technically accurate biography of von Braun." N Y Rev Books

Includes bibliographical references

Von Furstenberg, Diane

Von Furstenberg, Diane, 1946- The **woman** I wanted to be; Diane von Furstenberg. Simon & Schuster 2014 256 p. 24 plates; color illustrations (hardback) $26   **92**
1. Cancer patients 2. Fashion designers 3. Women -- Identity 4. Women philanthropists -- Biography 5. Fashion designers -- United States -- Biography 6. Cancer -- Patients -- United States -- Biography 7. Women philanthropists -- United States -- Biography 8. Women fashion designers -- United States -- Biography
ISBN 1451651546; 9781451651546; 9781451651553

LC 2014033232

In this book, fashion designer Diane von Furstenberg "reflects on her extraordinary life-- from childhood in Brussels to her days as a young, jet-set princess, to creating the dress that came to symbolize independence and power for an entire generation of women. . . . She opens up about her family and career, overcoming cancer, building a global brand, and devoting herself to empowering other women." (Publisher's note)

"This is a fascinating glimpse into the life of one of the fashion world's most enduring stars that will fascinate fashionistas and fans of strong, creative women." Pub Wkly

Vonnegut, Kurt, 1922-2007

Shields, Charles J. **And** so it goes: Kurt Vonnegut: a life. Henry Holt and Co. 2011 513p il $30   **92**
1. Authors 2. Novelists 3. Journalists 4. Biographers 5. Authors, American 6. Short story writers 7. Science fiction writers
ISBN 978-0-8050-8693-5

LC 2010-45173

"Kurt Vonnegut had a chip on his shoulder when it came to the critics. Despite being one of the most popular writers of his generation, he routinely complained that his work was overlooked, or miscast as high-concept, middle-brow fiction. The publication of Charles J. Shields's fascinating new biography . . . probably won't put this beef to rest, at least among his loyalists. But it does provide a definitive and disturbing account of the late author, whose ambition and talent transformed him from an obscure science fiction writer to a countercultural icon." Boston Globe

Includes bibliographical references

Vreeland, Diana

Stuart, Amanda Mackenzie. **Empress** of Fashion; A Life of Diana Vreeland. Amanda Mackenzie Stuart. HarperCollins 2012 419 p. ill. (some col.) $35   **92**

1. Fashion

ISBN 0061691747; 9780061691744

This book is a biography of fashion editor Diana Vreeland by Amanda Mackenzie Stuart. Mackenzie describes how Vreeland's "creation of an idealized image she called the Girl, coupled with a creative flair 'and the development of an idiosyncratic way with words,' propelled Vreeland into becoming one of the most influential tastemakers in American fashion." (Publishers Weekly)

Wagner, Alex

Wagner, Alex. **Futureface**; a family mystery, an epic quest, and the secret to belonging. Alex Wagner. Random House Inc 2018 352 p. $28   **92**

1. Irish 2. Genealogy 3. Racially mixed people

ISBN 0812997948; 9780812997941

In this book, journalist Alex Wagner "travels the globe to solve the mystery of her ancestry, confronting the question at the heart of the American experience of immigration, race, and identity: Who are my people? . . . The journey takes Wagner from Burma to Luxembourg, from ruined colonial capitals with records written on banana leaves to Mormon databases and high-tech genetic labs." (Publisher's note)

Wainwright, Loudon, III, 1946-

Wainwright, Loudon, 1946- **Liner** notes; on parents & children, exes & excess, death & decay & a few of my other favorite things. Loudon Wainwright III. Blue Rider Press 2017 306 p. illustrations (hardcover) $27   **92**

1. Autobiographies 2. Actors -- United States -- Biography 3. Singers -- United States -- Biography

ISBN 9780399177026; 9780698413085; 0399177027

LC 2017020391

In this memoir, singer-songwriter Loudon Wainwright III "details the family history his lyrics have referenced and the fractured relationships among generations: the alcoholism, the infidelities, the competitiveness--as well as the closeness, the successes, and the joy. Wainwright reflects on the experiences that have influenced his work, including boarding school, the music business, swimming, . . . sex, incarceration, and something he calls Sir Walter Raleigh Syndrome." (Publisher's note)

"A very funny and candid memoir, in an occasionally cringeworthy sort of way." Kirkus

Waite, Jen

Waite, Jen. A **beautiful,** terrible thing; a memoir of marriage and betrayal. Jen Waite. Penguin Group USA 2017 272 p. $25   **92**

1. Married people 2. Dysfunctional families

ISBN 0735216460; 9780735216464

LC 2017289237

In this memoir, author Jen Waite "recounts each heartbreaking discovery, every life-destroying lie, and reveals what happens once the dust finally settles on her demolished marriage. After a disturbing email sparks Waite's suspicion that her husband is having an affair, she tries to uncover the truth and rebuild trust in her marriage. Instead, she finds more lies, infidelity, and betrayal." (Publisher's note)

"Waite's is a well-written and at times gripping story of deceit." Pub Wkly

Waits, Tom, 1949-

Hoskyns, Barney. **Lowside** of the road; a life of Tom Waits. Broadway Books 2009 xxix, 609p il $29.95   **92**

1. Actors 2. Singers 3. Rock musicians 4. Blues musicians 5. Songwriters

ISBN 978-0-7679-2708-6; 0-7679-2708-7

This "book lights up and whirls like one of the greasy carnival rides in Mr. Waits's own sprawling oeuvre . . . Mr. Hoskyns rummaged through Mr. Waits's interviews, pored through the historical record and talked to those who were willing to speak. Thus his unauthorized biography mirrors, in some ways, Mr. Waits's own junkyard aesthetic. Mr. Hoskyns picks up what shards of Mr. Waits's life he can find and holds them to the light, turning them eagerly in his hands." N Y Times Book Rev

Wallace, Alfred Russel, 1823-1913

Slotten, Ross A. The **heretic** in Darwin's court; the life of Alfred Russel Wallace. Columbia University Press 2004 602p il maps $77.50; pa $25   **92**

1. Naturalists 2. Writers on science

ISBN 0-231-13010-4; 0-231-13011-2 pa

LC 2003-68833

"With a narrative of almost 500 pages, the biography was clearly a labor of love for the author, who is a medical doctor and a Wallace enthusiast. Although some readers may find the amount of material overwhelming, it is quite accessible to general audiences." Sci Books Films

Includes bibliographical references

Wallace, David Foster

Max, D. T., ca. 1962- **Every** love story is a ghost story; a life of David Foster Wallace. D.T. Max. Viking 2012 356 p. $27.95   **92**

1. Suicide 2. Literary style 3. Depression (Psychology) 4. Novelists, American -- 20th century -- Biography

ISBN 0670025925; 9780670025923

LC 2012008488

Author D. T. Max's "book begins with [author David Foster] Wallace's childhood and ends with his suicide, detailing both the highs (his marriage to Karen Green) and lows (his string of breakdowns that began in college). There is the mutating public and critical opinion of his work, his troubled history with women, and his tendency to roam for much of his life while he struggled to balance writing and relationships, and writing and well-being." (Publishers Weekly)

Includes bibliographical references and index.

Wallace, Perry (Law professor)

Maraniss, Andrew. **Strong** inside; Perry Wallace and the collision of race and sports in the South. Andrew Maraniss. Vanderbilt University Press 2014 472 p. illustrations (hardback) $35   **92**

1. African American baseball players 2. Southern States -- Race relations 3. Vanderbilt University -- Basketball -- History 4. Basketball players -- United States -- Biography 5. Vanderbilt Commodores (Basketball team) -- History 6. Civil rights -- History -- Southern States -- 20th century 7. Racism in sports -- Southern States -- History -- 20 century

ISBN 0826520235; 9780826520234; 9780826520241

LC 2014015257

This book, by Andrew Maraniss, offers a "detailed biography of Perry Wallace, the first African American basketball player in the SEC. . . . [It] digs deep beneath the surface to reveal a more complicated and profound story of sports pioneering than we've come to expect from the genre. Perry Wallace's unusually insightful and honest introspection reveals his inner thoughts throughout his journey." (Publisher's note)

"Nuanced and complex, Strong Inside is an invaluable resource for studying the state of race relations in the US, both past and present." Choice

Includes bibliographical references and index

Wallach, Eli, 1915-2014

Wallach, Eli. The **good,** the bad, and me; in my anecdotage. Harcourt 2005 312p il $25; pa $16   92

1. Actors

ISBN 0-15-101189-3; 0-15-603169-8 pa

LC 2004-23121

The author "tells his story, from a Brooklyn childhood as the only Jew in an Italian neighborhood, through Actors Studio days with Brando and others, and on to his long and illustrious career on both stage and screen.... This compelling memoir shows the full range of a remarkable actor's life." Booklist

Walls, Jeannette

★ Walls, Jeannette. The **glass** castle; a memoir. Scribner 2005 288p $25; pa $14   92

1. Authors 2. Novelists 3. Memoirists 4. Gossip columnists

ISBN 0-7432-4753-1; 0-7432-4754-X pa

LC 2004-58907

"Shocking, sad, and occasionally bitter, this gracefully written account speaks candidly, yet with surprising affection, about parents and about the strength of family ties—for both good and ill." Booklist

Walsh, Bill, 1931-2007

Harris, David. The **genius**; how Bill Walsh reinvented football and created an NFL dynasty. Random House 2008 385p il $26   92

1. Football coaches 2. Football -- Biography 3. San Francisco 49ers (Football team)

ISBN 978-1-4000-6665-0; 1-4000-6665-4

LC 2008-16566

"Walsh was one of the NFL's greatest coaches, and Harris' book does him justice." Booklist

Includes bibliographical references

Walsh, Mikey

Walsh, Mikey. **Gypsy** boy; my life in the secret world of the Romany Gypsies. Mikey Walsh. Thomas Dunne Books/St. Martin's Press 2012 278 p.   92

1. Gay men -- Biography 2. England -- Ethnic relations 3. Romanies -- England -- Biography 4. England -- Social life and customs 5. Romanies -- England 6. Young gay men -- England -- Biography

ISBN 9780312622084; 9781250011978

LC 2011038168

This memoir, a "number-one best-seller in the UK following its 2009 release," was written "under a pseudonym to protect . . . [author Mikey] Walsh [who] has ongoing concerns for his safety after leaving the highly secretive Romany Gypsy community 15 years ago. . . . He claims his ultraviolent father once put a contract out on his life. He was born into a roving caravan of outsiders, brutally abused as a child (both physically by his father and sexually by an uncle), and never received any formal education growing up. He is also gay." (Booklist)

Walters, Barbara, 1931-

Walters, Barbara. **Audition**; a memoir. Alfred A. Knopf

2008 612p il $29.95   92

1. Women journalists 2. Talk show hosts 3. Television news anchors

ISBN 978-0-307-26646-0; 0-307-26646-X

LC 2008-05843

This is a memoir by the television newscaster.

"Alternating between tales of her personal struggles, professional achievements and insider anecdotes about the celebrities and world leaders she's interviewed, this mammoth memoir's energy never flags." Publ Wkly

Walton, Bill, 1952-

Walton, Bill, 1952- **Back** from the dead; Bill Walton. Simon & Schuster 2016 336 p. 24 plates; illustrations (hardcover) $27   92

1. Broadcasting 2. Wounds and injuries 3. Basketball players -- United States -- Biography 4. Sportscasters -- United States -- Biography

ISBN 1476716862; 9781476716862

LC 2015031712

This "memoir from sports and cultural icon Bill Walton recounts his devastating injuries and amazing recoveries, set in the context of his UCLA triumphs under John Wooden, his storied NBA career, and his affinity for music and the Grateful Dead. In his own words, 'Back from the Dead' shares this dramatic story, including his basketball and broadcasting careers, his many setbacks and rebounds, and his ultimate triumph as the toughest of champions." (Publisher's note)

"This memoir is defined by trials as much as successes and will appeal to readers who appreciated Walton as player and commentator." Library Journal

Walton, Sam

Walton, Sam. **Sam** Walton, made in America; my story. by Sam Walton with John Huey. Bantam Books 1992 346p il pa $7.99   92

1. Businessmen 2. Retail executives 3. Wal-Mart Stores, Inc.

ISBN 0-553-56283-5; 978-0-553-56283-5

First published 1992 by Doubleday

The founder of Wal-Mart Stores, the largest retail chain in the world, recounts how he made his fortune.

"Readers will enjoy the folksy narrative of the small-town millionaire who revolutionized retail distribution. . . . Coauthor Huey does a fine job of incorporating candid testimonials from family members and associates." Libr J

Wamariya, Clemantine

Weil, Elizabeth. The **girl** who smiled beads; a story of war and what comes after. Clemantine Wamariya; Elizabeth Weil. Random House Inc 2018 288 p. $26   92

1. Refugees 2. Rwanda -- History -- Civil War, 1994

ISBN 0451495322; 9780451495327

In this book, by Clemantine Wamariya and Elizabeth Weil, "[Rwandan refugee] Clemantine provokes us to look beyond the label of 'victim' and recognize the power of the imagination to transcend even the most profound injuries and aftershocks. Devastating yet beautiful, and bracingly original, it is a powerful testament to her commitment to constructing a life on her own terms." (Publisher's note)

Wambach, Abby, 1980-

Wambach, Abby, 1980- **Forward**; a memoir. Abby Wambach. Dey Street Books 2016 230 p. (hardback) $26.99   92

1. Soccer players 2. Women athletes 3. Soccer players -- United

States -- Biography 4. Women soccer players -- United States -- Biography
ISBN 0062466984; 9780062466983; 9780062467003

LC 2016037369

In this memoir, professional soccer player Abby Wambach "shares her inspiring and often brutal journey from girl in Rochester, New York, to world-class athlete. Far more than a sports memoir, [it is a] tale of resilience and redemption—and a reminder that heroism is, above all, about embracing life's challenges with fearlessness and heart." (Publisher's note)

"A cut above the standard sports memoir." Booklist

Warburg, Siegmund George Sir, 1902-1982

Ferguson, Niall, 1964- **High** financier; the lives and time of Siegmund Warburg. Penguin Press 2010 548p il pa $22; $35 **92**

1. Banks and banking 2. Bankers 3. SBC Warburg (Firm) 4. Biography, Individual 5. Banks and banking -- Great Britain -- History -- 20th century
ISBN 978-0-14-311940-1 pa; 978-1-59420-246-9

LC 2010-18353

This is a biography of the founder of the investment bank S. G. Warburg and Company. Index.

"Ferguson draws a richly vivid portrait of this unusual banker, an intellectual who read the Latin and Greek classics in the original and preferred Nietzsche to newspapers." N Y Times Book Rev

Includes bibliographical references

Ward, Jesmyn

★ Ward, Jesmyn. **Men** We Reaped; A Memoir. by Jesmyn Ward. Bloomsbury USA 2013 272 p. $26 **92**

1. Death 2. Grief 3. Poverty -- United States 4. African American men -- Mississippi 5. Rural poor -- Mississippi -- Biography 6. African American women authors -- Biography
ISBN 160819521X; 9781608195213

LC 2013013600

National Book Critics Circle Award Finalist: Autobiography (2013)

In this memoir, author Jesmyn Ward tells how she "grew up in poverty in rural Mississippi. She writes powerfully about the pressures this brings, on the men who can do no right and the women who stand in for family in a society where the men are often absent. She bravely tells her story, revisiting the agonizing losses of her only brother and her friends." (Publisher's note)

Includes bibliographical references and index

Ward, Samuel, 1814-1884

Jacob, Kathryn Allamong. **King** of the lobby; the life and times of Sam Ward, man-about-Washington in the Gilded Age. Johns Hopkins University Press 2010 212p il $40 **92**

1. Lobbying 2. Lobbyists 3. United States -- Politics and government -- 1861-1865 4. United States -- Politics and government -- 1865-1898
ISBN 978-0-8018-9397-1; 0-8018-9397-6

LC 2009-9807

The author's "trim and surprising biography of Sam Ward . . . will not change most people's view of what is essentially a hustler's profession. But she brilliantly shows how, in the hands of a master, lobbying can be lifted to the level of art." Wall Street J

Includes bibliographical references

Wareham, Dean

Wareham, Dean. **Black** postcards; a rock & roll romance.

Penguin Press 2008 324p il $25.95 **92**

1. Singers 2. Guitarists 3. Rock musicians 4. Luna (Musical group) 5. Galaxie 500 (Musical group)
ISBN 978-1-59420-155-4; 1-59420-155-2

LC 2007-35280

"In this collection of over 50 sequential autobiographical essays, . . . [the author] takes us from his childhood in New Zealand, through his formative years exploring New York City's punk scene, to his adult life in Cambridge, MA, where he becomes a notable figure in the alternative music scene. Wareham documents in great detail the history of his two bands, Galaxy 500 and Luna. . . . Fans of Wareham's bands and such bands as Bongwater, Cocteau Twins, R.E.M., and the Velvet Underground, as well as anyone with an interest in American and European alternative music, will find this to be an insightful and entertaining read." Libr J

Warhol, Andy, 1928?-1987

★ Scherman, Tony. **Pop**; the genius of Andy Warhol. [by] Tony Scherman and David Dalton. HarperCollins 2009 509p il $40 **92**

1. Artists 2. Pop art 3. Artists -- United States 4. Motion picture directors
ISBN 978-0-06-621243-2; 0-06-621243-X

LC 2009-24815

This biography covers the artist's career and personal life through 1968.

"Not only is . . . [this book] well written and researched, it manages to unearth details that reframe the debate about Warhol's real importance as an artist." Bookforum

Includes bibliographical references

Wariner, Ruth.

Wariner, Ruth. The **sound** of gravel; a memoir. Ruth Wariner. Flatiron Books 2016 352 p. illustrations (hardcover) $27.99 **92**

1. Mormons 2. Polygamy 3. Wariner, Ruth
ISBN 9781250077691

LC 2015037663

This book, by Ruth Wariner, is "the true story of one girl's coming-of-age in a polygamist family. . . . Growing up on a farm in rural Mexico, where authorities turn a blind eye to the practices of her community, Ruth lives in a ramshackle house. . . . At church, preachers teach that God will punish the wicked by destroying the world. . . . As she begins to doubt her family's beliefs and question her mother's choices, she struggles to . . . forge a better life for herself. " (Publisher's note)

"With power and insight, Wariner's tale shows a road to escape from the most confining circumstances." Booklist

Warren, Elizabeth

Felix, Antonia. **Elizabeth** Warren; her fight, her work, her life. Antonia Felix. Sourcebooks 2018 384 p. (hardcover: alk. paper) $25.99 **92**

1. Women politicians -- United States 2. Legislators -- United States -- Biography 3. United States. Congress. Senate -- Biography 4. Women legislators -- United States -- Biography
ISBN 1492665282; 9781492665281

LC 2018010616

In this biography of United States Senator Elizabeth Warren, "author Antonia Felix carries readers from Warren's hardscrabble roots in Norman, Oklahoma, to her career as one of the nation's most distinguished legal scholars and experts on the economics of working Americans. Felix reveals how Warren brought her expertise to Washington to become an icon of progressive politics in a deeply divided nation." (Publisher's note)

"A complementary portrayal of a compelling political personality. Recommended for readers interested in Senator Warren, politics, and the lives of inspirational women." LJ

Includes bibliographical references and index

Warren, Elizabeth, 1949- A **fighting** chance; Elizabeth Warren. Metropolitan, Henry Holt & Co. 2014 384 p. illustrations (chiefly color) (hardcover) $28   **92**
1. Autobiographies 2. Politicians' writings 3. Middle class -- United States 4. Legislators -- United States -- Biography 5. United States. Congress. Senate -- Biography 6. Women legislators -- United States -- Biography 7. United States -- Politics and government -- 2009-
ISBN 1627790527; 9781627790529
                                              LC 2014000776

This book by Elizabeth Warren tells the "story of the two-decade journey that taught her how Washington really works--and really doesn't. . . . She fought for better bankruptcy laws for ten years and lost. She tried to hold the federal government accountable during the financial crisis but became a target of the big banks. . . . Finally, at age 62, she decided to run for elective office and won the most competitive--and watched--Senate race in the country." (Publisher's note)

"Warren emerges as a committed advocate with real world sensibility, who tasted tough economic times at an early age and did not forget its bitterness." Pub Wkly

Includes bibliographical references and index

Washington, Booker T., 1856-1915
Harlan, Louis R. **Booker** T. Washington: the making of a black leader, 1856-1901. Oxford Univ. Press 1972 379p il hardcover o.p. pa $21.50   **92**
1. Slaves 2. Authors 3. Educators 4. African American educators 5. Memoirists 6. Nonfiction writers 7. Tuskegee Institute 8. Civil rights activists 9. African Americans -- Biography
ISBN 0-19-501915-6 pa

This book "covers Washington's life from his birth as a slave in western Virginia up to [the year 1901, when he dined] with Theodore Roosevelt at the White House, an event signifying white recognition of Washington as the chief spokesman for black interests in the period before World War I." Libr J

Harlan, Louis R. **Booker** T. Washington: the wizard of Tuskegee, 1901-1915. Oxford Univ. Press 1983 548p il hardcover o.p. pa $24.95   **92**
1. Slaves 2. Authors 3. Educators 4. African American educators 5. Memoirists 6. Nonfiction writers 7. Tuskegee Institute 8. Civil rights activists 9. African Americans -- Biography
ISBN 0-19-504229-8 pa
                                              LC 82-14547

This is the second and concluding volume of a life of the black educator and founder of Tuskegee Institute.

"Having avoided the pitfalls of white guilt and black rage and the temptation to judge the past by standards of the present, Mr. Harlan deserves honors for his remarkable achievement." N Y Times Book Rev

Includes bibliographical references

Norrell, Robert J. **Up** from history; the life of Booker T. Washington. Belknap Press of Harvard University Press 2009 508p il $35   **92**
1. Slaves 2. Authors 3. Educators 4. African American educators

5. Memoirists 6. Nonfiction writers 7. Tuskegee Institute 8. Biography, Individual 9. Civil rights activists 10. African Americans -- Biography 11. Race discrimination -- History
ISBN 067403211X; 9780674032118; 978-0-674-03211-8; 0-674-03211-X
                                              LC 2008-32599

This is a biography of the educator who founded the Tuskegee Institute and wrote the memoir Up From Slavery (1901). Index.

This "is in all respects an exemplary book, scrupulously fair to its subject and thus to the reader as well." Washington Post Book World

Includes bibliographical references

Smock, Raymond W. **Booker** T. Washington; black leadership in the age of Jim Crow. [by] Raymond W. Smock. Ivan R. Dee 2009 223p il (Library of African-American biography) $26   **92**
1. Slaves 2. Authors 3. Educators 4. African American educators 5. Memoirists 6. Nonfiction writers 7. Tuskegee Institute 8. Civil rights activists 9. African Americans -- Biography
ISBN 978-1-56663-725-1; 1-56663-725-2
                                              LC 2009-3277

The author "examines Washington's legacy and how he came to be alternately lauded and lambasted for his practical approach to racism following Reconstruction: to build a school to prepare blacks to occupy the unchallenged place set aside for them in the Jim Crow South. . . . This is a nuanced portrait of an enigmatic man of enduring contribution to black leadership." Booklist

Includes bibliographical references

★ Washington, Booker T. **Up** from slavery; edited with an introduction and notes by William L. Andrews. Oxford University Press 2008 xxvii, 196p (Oxford world's classics) pa $9.95   **92**
1. Slaves 2. Authors 3. Educators 4. African American educators 5. Memoirists 6. Nonfiction writers 7. Tuskegee Institute 8. Civil rights activists 9. African Americans -- Biography
ISBN 978-0-19-955239-9
                                              LC 2008-279129

First published 1901

"The classic autobiography of the man who, though born in slavery, educated himself and went on to found Tuskegee Institute." N Y Public Libr

Includes bibliographical references

Washington, George, 1732-1799
Breen, T. H. **George** Washington's journey; the president forges a new nation. T.H. Breen. Simon & Schuster 2015 320 p. illustrations, maps (hardcover) $28   **92**
1. Presidents -- United States -- Travel 2. United States -- Politics and government -- 1789-1797 3. Presidents -- Travel -- United States -- History -- 18th century
ISBN 9781451675429; 9781451675436
                                              LC 2015007283

This book, by T. H. Breen, "introduces us to a George Washington we rarely meet. By nature shy and reserved, the brand new president decided that he would must visit the new citizens in their own states, that only by showing himself could he make them feel part of a new nation. He displayed himself as victorious general . . . and as President. . . . Washington drew on his immense popularity, even hero worship, to send a powerful and lasting message—that America was now a nation." (Publisher's note)

"Breen's superb chronicle offers glimpses into Washington's love of his country and its people, and his willingness to meet them on their own terms to secure the unity of the new republic." Pub Wkly

Includes bibliographical references and index

Chernow, Ron. **Washington**; a life. Penguin Press 2010 xxi, 904p il $40   **92**

1. Biography, Individual 2. Presidents -- United States 3. United States -- Politics and government -- 1775-1783 4. United States -- Politics and government -- 1783-1809

ISBN 978-1-59420-266-7

LC 2010-19154

Chernow "has done justice to the solid flesh, the human frailty and the dental miseries of his subject—and also to his immense historical importance. . . . This is a magnificently fair, full-scale biography. Its judgments are lapidary." Economist

Includes bibliographical references

★ Ellis, Joseph J. **His** Excellency; George Washington. Knopf 2004 320p il hardcover o.p. pa $15   **92**

1. Generals 2. Presidents 3. Presidents -- United States

ISBN 1-4000-4031-0; 1-4000-3253-9 pa

LC 2004-46576

The author "offers a magisterial account of the life and times of George Washington, celebrating the heroic image of the president whom peers like Jefferson and Madison recognized as 'their unquestioned superior' while acknowledging his all-too-human qualities." Publ Wkly

Includes bibliographical references

Flexner, James Thomas. **George** Washington and the new nation, 1783-1793. Little, Brown 1969 466p il map (His George Washington) $42   **92**

1. Generals 2. Presidents 3. Presidents -- United States

ISBN 0-316-28600-1

LC 78-117042

This third volume of a four-volume biography of Washington focuses on the period between the end of the Revolutionary War through his first term as president.

Includes bibliographical references

Flexner, James Thomas. **George** Washington: anguish and farewell 1793-1799. Little, Brown 1972 554p il (His George Washington) $45   **92**

1. Generals 2. Presidents 3. Presidents -- United States

ISBN 0-316-28602-8

LC 72-6875

This final volume of a four-volume biography of Washington covers his second term as president, his retirement, and death.

Includes bibliographical references

Flexner, James Thomas. **George** Washington: the forge of experience, 1732-1775. Little 1965 390p il map (His George Washington) $40   **92**

1. Generals 2. Presidents 3. Presidents -- United States

ISBN 0-316-28597-8

LC 65-21361

The author "covers forty-three years of Washington's life in this volume, the first in a series of four . . . [that carries] Washington through the Revolutionary War and on to the end of his life." Publisher's note

Includes bibliographical references

Fraser, Flora. The **Washingtons**; join'd by friendship, crown'd by love. Flora Fraser. Alfred A. Knopf 2015 448 p.

24 plates; color illustrations (hardcover: alk. paper) $30 **92**

1. United States -- Biography 2. Generals -- United States -- Biography 3. Presidents -- United States -- Biography 4. Generals' spouses -- United States -- Biography 5. Presidents' spouses -- United States -- Biography 6. United States -- History -- Revolution, 1775-1783 -- Biography

ISBN 0307272788; 9780307272782; 9780307474438

LC 2014045521

This book, by Flora Fraser, presents a portrait of the lives and marriage of George and Martha Washington, the first family of the U.S. It "begins in colonial Virginia in 1759, when George Washington woos and weds Martha Dandridge Parke Custis. . . . [The book describes] the public Washington and of the war he waged, and gives us, as well, the domestic Washingtons, whether at Mount Vernon before and during the war or in New York and Philadelphia during his presidency." (Publisher's note)

"Fraser's prose flows well with the voices of her 18th-century subjects. However, the impression that emerges from the copious details of plantation management, children's tutoring, and relatives born and dying is of two busy lives on parallel courses; their devotion to each other is clearly evident, but so are several potential sources of sharp conflict between them. Fraser provides no sense of how these shoals were negotiated or how these formidable individuals actually got on with each other when they could be together. A difficult task crowned with mixed success." Kirkus

Includes bibliographical references and index

Gaines, James R. **For** liberty and glory; Washington, Lafayette, and their revolutions. W.W. Norton & Co. 2007 533p il map $29.95   **92**

1. Generals 2. Statesmen 3. Presidents 4. France -- History -- 1789-1799, Revolution 5. United States -- History -- 1775-1783, Revolution

ISBN 0-393-06138-8; 978-0-393-06138-3

LC 2007-22449

Gaines examines the relationship between George Washington and the Marquis de Lafayette.

This is a "fresh and engaging new look at the pair. . . . Gaines has a dry sense of humor and an appreciation for human foibles. . . . The American founding fathers, in particular, come across as extraordinary men with ordinary obsessions and—surprise!—senses of humor." Christ Sci Monit

Includes bibliographical references

Johnson, Paul. **George** Washington: the Founding Father. HarperCollins Publishers 2005 126p (Eminent lives) $19.95   **92**

1. Generals 2. Presidents 3. Presidents -- United States

ISBN 0-06-075365-X

LC 2004-52907

This is a biography of the first president of the United States.

The author "submits a beautifully cogent, enthrallingly perceptive, and . . . startlingly fresh take on the ultimate American icon." Booklist

Includes bibliographical references

Larson, Edward. The **Return** of George Washington; 1783-1789. Edward J. Larson. Willam Morrow, an imprint of HarperCollins Publishers 2014 xv, 366 p.p 8 plates; color illustrations (hbk.) $29.99   **92**

1. United States -- Politics and government -- 1783-1865 2. Constitutional history -- United States 3. Presidents -- United States -- Biography 4. United States. Constitutional Convention (1787) 5. United States -- Politics and government -- 1783-1789 6. Political

leadership -- United States -- History -- 18th century
ISBN 0062248677; 9780062248671

LC 2013497765

In this book, historian Edward Larson "[reveals] how [George] Washington saved the United States by coming out of retirement to lead the Constitutional Convention and serve as our first president. After leading the Continental Army to victory in the Revolutionary War, George Washington shocked the world: he retired. . . . Yet as Washington contentedly grew his estate, the fledgling American experiment floundered." (Publisher's note)

"Larson identifies Washington's three goals—'respect abroad, prosperity at home, and development westward'—and includes an account of an inaugural dish that makes turducken seem unambitious. Profound, even affectionate, scholarship infuses every graceful sentence." Kirkus

Includes bibliographical references (pages 305-354) and index.

Stark, Peter. **Young** Washington; how wilderness and war forged America's founding father. Peter Stark. Ecco 2018 528 p. (hardcover) $35 **92**

1. Biography 2. Presidents -- United States -- Biography 3. United States -- History -- French and Indian War, 1754-1763 -- Biography
ISBN 9780062416063; 9780062416070; 9780062845993

LC 2017052000

This book, by Peter Stark, "recounts the wilderness trials, controversial battles, and emotional entanglements that transformed [George] Washington from a temperamental striver into a mature leader. . . . Leading the Virginia troops into battle taught him to set aside his own relentless ambitions and stand in solidarity with those who looked to him for leadership. . . . [The book] offers new insights into the dramatic years that shaped the man who shaped a nation." (Publisher's note)

Includes bibliographical references and index

Washington, Martha, 1731-1802

Brady, Patricia. **Martha** Washington; an American life. Viking 2005 276p il $24.95; pa $15 **92**

1. Spouses of presidents 2. Presidents' spouses -- United States
ISBN 0-670-03430-4; 0-14-303713-7 pa

LC 2004-61242

"Brady's splendid biography offers a compelling new portrait of this passionate, committed founding mother who has unjustly been obscured by others, such as Abigail Adams." Publ Wkly

Includes bibliographical references

Fraser, Flora. The **Washingtons**; join'd by friendship, crown'd by love. Flora Fraser. Alfred A. Knopf 2015 448 p. 24 plates; color illustrations (hardcover: alk. paper) $30 **92**

1. United States -- Biography 2. Generals -- United States -- Biography 3. Presidents -- United States -- Biography 4. Generals' spouses -- United States -- Biography 5. Presidents' spouses -- United States -- Biography 6. United States -- History -- Revolution, 1775-1783 -- Biography
ISBN 0307272788; 9780307272782; 9780307474438

LC 2014045521

This book, by Flora Fraser, presents a portrait of the lives and marriage of George and Martha Washington, the first family of the U.S. It "begins in colonial Virginia in 1759, when George Washington woos and weds Martha Dandridge Parke Custis. . . . [The book describes] the public Washington and of the war he waged, and gives us, as well, the domestic Washingtons, whether at Mount Vernon before and during the war or in New York and Philadelphia during his presidency." (Publisher's note)

"Fraser's prose flows well with the voices of her 18th-century subjects. However, the impression that emerges from the copious details of

plantation management, children's tutoring, and relatives born and dying is of two busy lives on parallel courses; their devotion to each other is clearly evident, but so are several potential sources of sharp conflict between them. Fraser provides no sense of how these shoals were negotiated or how these formidable individuals actually got on with each other when they could be together. A difficult task crowned with mixed success." Kirkus

Includes bibliographical references and index

Waters, Alice

Waters, Alice, 1944- **Coming** to my senses; the making of a counterculture cook. Alice Waters, with Cristina Mueller & Bob Carrau. Clarkson Potter/Publishers 2017 xi, 306 p.p illustrations (hardcover) $27 **92**

1. Women cooks 2. Restaurants -- United States -- History 3. Chez Panisse 4. Women cooks -- United States -- Biography 5. Restaurateurs -- United States -- Biography
ISBN 9780307718280; 030771828X; 9781101906651

In this memoir "Alice [Waters] retraces the events that led her to 1517 Shattuck Avenue and the tumultuous times that emboldened her to find her own voice as a cook. Moving from a repressive suburban upbringing to Berkeley in 1964 at the height of the Free Speech Movement and campus unrest, she was drawn into a bohemian circle of charismatic figures whose views on design, politics, film, and food would ultimately inform the unique culture on which Chez Panisse was founded." (Publisher's note)

"Chef, restaurateur, activist, and author Waters writes about her childhood and formative years leading up to the opening of her iconic Berkeley, CA, restaurant Chez Panisse." LJ

Waters, Ethel, 1896-1977

Bogle, Donald. **Heat** wave; the life and career of Ethel Waters. HarperCollins 2011 624p il $26.99 **92**

1. Actors 2. Singers 3. African American singers 4. Biography, Individual
ISBN 0-06-124173-3; 978-0-06-124173-4

LC 2010-29230

This is a biography of the actress and singer Ethel Waters, who starred in the film Cabin in the Sky (1943). Bibliography. Index.

"In this powerful biography, Bogle recovers the rich fullness of singer Ethel Waters's life (1896–1977). In vivid though often exhausting detail, Bogle traces Waters's rise from the poverty of her surroundings in Chester, Pa., through her early musical successes in Harlem in the 1920s and 1930s to her film and Broadway career and her later religious conversion as her health declined." Publ Wkly

Includes bibliographical references

Waters, John, 1946-

Waters, John. **Carsick**; John Waters. Farrar Straus & Giroux 2014 336 p. illustrations (hardcover) $26 **92**

1. Hitchhiking 2. Autobiographies 3. Hitchhiking -- United States 4. United States -- Description and travel 5. United States -- Social life and customs -- 21st century -- Humor 6. Motion picture producers and directors -- United States -- Biography
ISBN 0374298637; 9780374298630

LC 2013034093

In this book, author "John Waters is putting his life on the line. Armed with wit, a pencil-thin mustache, and a cardboard sign that reads 'I'm Not Psycho,' he hitchhikes across America from Baltimore to San Francisco, braving lonely roads and treacherous drivers. But who should we be more worried about, the delicate film director with genteel manners or the unsuspecting travelers transporting the Pope of Trash?" (Publisher's note)

"For more than half of this account of his 2012 cross-country journey . . . [Waters] imagines what lies in store, with dueling full-length novellas that spin best and worst case scenarios. . . . [A] sweet and funny ride." Kirkus

Waters, John. **Role** models. Farrar, Straus and Giroux 2010 304p il $25   **92**
1. Motion picture producers and directors 2. Screenwriters 3. Motion picture directors
ISBN 978-0-374-25147-5; 0-374-25147-9
                                                    LC 2009-42211
"The famed cult-film director recalls the famous—and not-so-famous—people he has idolized over the years. . . . In this consistently charming and witty collection of essays, he fondly remembers the many artists he has admired throughout his life, from stars, such as Little Richard, to such near-unknown figures as the 1960s Baltimore stripper Lady Zorro. . . . An impressive, heartfelt collection by a true American iconoclast." Kirkus
Includes bibliographical references

Watson, James D., 1928-
Watson, James D. **Avoid** boring people; lessons from a life in science. Alfred A. Knopf 2007 347p il $26.95   **92**
1. Scientists 2. College teachers 3. Molecular biologists 4. Nobel laureates for physiology or medicine
ISBN 978-0-375-41284-4; 0-375-41284-0
                                                    LC 2007-15675
"In this memoir, Watson shows by example how to get to the top and stay there. Spanning his boyhood interest in birds to his resignation from Harvard University in 1976 to his leadership of Cold Spring Harbor Laboratory, Watson's reminiscences encompass his claim to fame—cocredit for deducing DNA's structure in 1953—but focus on his ambition and his conduct of academic politics. . . . In angular and opinionated prose, Watson proves as engaging as ever." Booklist
Includes bibliographical references

Watson, James D. **Genes,** girls, and Gamow; after the double helix. Knopf 2002 xxix, 259p il $26; pa $14   **92**
1. College teachers 2. Molecular biologists 3. Nobel laureates for physiology or medicine
ISBN 0-375-41283-2; 0-375-72715-9 pa
                                                    LC 2001-38543
"In 1953, Watson, then 25, and colleague Francis Crick discovered the structure of DNA. . . . Here Watson . . . gives a detailed, journal-writer's account of the aftermath, recalling . . . his younger self's professional and—equally pressing—amorous ambitions. . . . Reading Watson is a delight, an opportunity to breathe the rarefied air of his generation's greatest scientists and to crash a faculty cocktail party or two along the way." Publ Wkly

Watt, Lauren Fern
Watt, Lauren Fern. **Gizelle's** bucket list; my life with a very large dog. Lauren Fern Watt. Simon & Schuster 2017 vii, 244 p.p color illustrations (hardcover) $24.99   **92**
1. Human-animal relationships 2. Mastiff -- New York (State) -- New York
ISBN 9781501123658; 9781501123665
                                                    LC 2016033521
In this memoir, author Lauren Watt narrates how she "took her 160-pound English Mastiff to college . . . [and then] to her first, tiny apartment in New York. Because Gizelle wasn't just a dog; she was a roommate, sister, confidante, dining companion, and everything in between. Together, Gizelle and Lauren went through boyfriends, first jobs,

a mother's struggle with addiction, and the ups and downs of becoming an adult in the big city." (Publisher's note)

"As much a story about growing up as about letting go of things that cannot be changed, Watt's book is also a reminder of the profound healing connection that can exist between humans and the pets they love. A tender, heartfelt story." Kirkus.

Waugh, Evelyn, 1903-1966
Eade, Philip. **Evelyn** Waugh; A Life Revisited. Philip Eade. Henry Holt & Co. 2016 432 p. illustrations (ebook) $60; (hardback) $32   **92**
1. English authors -- Biography 2. English novelists -- Biography
ISBN 9780805097610; 9780805097603; 0805097600
                                                    LC 2016019839
This biography of novelist Evelyn Waugh by Philip Eade "illuminates Waugh's strained relationship with his sentimental father and blatantly favoured elder brother; his love affairs with male classmates at Oxford and female bright young things thereafter; his disastrous first marriage and subsequent conversion to Roman Catholicism; his insane wartime bravery; his drug-induced madness; [and] his singular approach to marriage and fatherhood." (Publisher's note)
"Eade offers up a softer portrait of Waugh that might help bring him some new readers, which he deserves." Kirkus
Includes bibliographical references and index.

Wayne, John, 1907-1979
Eliot, Marc. **American** titan; searching for John Wayne. Marc Eliot. Dey Street Books 2014 432 p. 16 plates; illustrations (hardcover) $28.99   **92**
1. Actors 2. Motion picture actors and actresses -- United States -- Biography
ISBN 0062269003; 9780062269003; 9780062269027
                                                    LC 2014014183
In this book on actor John Wayne, "Marc Eliot digs deep beneath the myth in this revealing look at the most legendary Western film hero of all time; the man with the distinctive voice, walk, and demeanor who was an inspiration to many and a symbol of American masculinity, power, and patriotism. Eliot pays tribute to the man and the myth, identifying and analyzing the many interesting contradictions that made John Wayne who he was." (Publisher's note)
"But given that it tells the same story without any unique insights, the book can't help coming across as a bit been there, done that. Still, it's a solidly written account of Wayne's life and does a credible job with the question of how the legend affected Wayne, the person. Libraries with room on the shelves for two new Wayne biographies should slide this one in beside Eyman's work." Booklist
Includes bibliographical references and index

Eyman, Scott. **John** Wayne: the life and legend; the life and legend. Scott Eyman. Simon & Schuster 2014 672 p. illustrations (hardback) $32.50   **92**
1. Actors -- United States -- Biography 2. Motion picture actors and actresses -- United States -- Biography
ISBN 1439199582; 9781439199589
                                                    LC 2013032604
Author Scott Eyman "interviewed [John] Wayne, as well as many family members, and he has drawn on previously unpublished reminiscences from friends and associates of the Duke in this biography, as well as documents from his production company that shed light on Wayne's business affairs. He traces Wayne from his childhood to his stardom in Stagecoach and dozens of films after that." (Publisher's note)
"Insightful, exhaustive and engrossing—a definitive portrait of the man and the legend." Kirkus

Includes bibliographical references and index

Webb, Jimmy

Webb, Jimmy. The **cake** and the rain; Jimmy Webb. St. Martin's Press 2017 346 p. illustrations (hardcover) $26.99 **92**

1. Autobiographies 2. Composers -- United States -- Biography 3. Country musicians -- United States -- Biography

ISBN 9781466862579; 9781250058416

LC 2017000908

This memoir, by Jimmy Webb, "delivers a snapshot of . . . [the author's] life from 1955 to 1970, from simple and sere Oklahoma to fast and fantastical Los Angeles, from the crucible of his family to the top of his longed-for profession. . . . The sixties were a supernova, and Webb was at their center, whipsawed from the proverbial humble beginnings into a moneyed and manic international world of beautiful women, drugs, cars and planes." (Publisher's note)

"Webb writes in a comfortable, conversational way, as though he's telling a few close friends some stories from his fascinating life, and the book makes a great way for a music fan to pass a few hours." Booklist

Weiner, Jennifer

Weiner, Jennifer, 1970- **Hungry** heart; Adventures in Life, Love, and Writing. Jennifer Weiner. Atria Books 2016 432 p. (ebook) $13.99; (hardback) $27 **92**

1. American authors -- Biography 2. Authors, American -- 20th century -- Biography

ISBN 9781476723440; 9781476723402

LC 2016022112

In this collection of stories, by Jennifer Weiner, "no subject is off-limits: . . . sex, weight, envy, money, her mother's coming out of the closet, her estranged father's death. From lonely adolescence to modern childbirth to hearing her six-year-old daughter say the f-word-fat-for the first time, Jen dives deep into the heart of female experience." (Publisher's note)

"Like her enormously popular commercial fiction, from its very first page this memoir will enthusiastically reach out to female readers and swiftly draw them close." Pub Wkly

Weiss, Piper, 1978-

Weiss, Piper. **You** all grow up and leave me; a memoir of teenage obsession. Piper Weiss. William Morrow, an imprint of HarperCollins Publishers 2018 338 p. (hardcover) $25.99 **92**

1. Sex offenders 2. Child sexual abuse 3. Preppies -- New York (State) -- New York -- Biography 4. Teenage girls -- New York (State) -- New York -- Biography 5. Preparatory school students -- New York (State) -- New York -- Biography

ISBN 9780062456571; 9780062456595; 0062456571

LC 2017025491

In this book, author Piper Weiss recounts the time she spent training with Gary Wilensky, a private tennis coach to Upper East Side prep school students during the 1990s and a child molester. The book "explores the psychological manipulation by child predators--their ability to charm their way into seemingly protected worlds--and the far-reaching effects their actions have on those who trust them most." (Publisher's note)

"Weiss has crafted a dark and brooding yet brisk and eloquently written memoir, and her vivid coming-of-age narration shines a spotlight on the precarious relationship between teenagers and adults and everything that can go awry in between. A bristling, harrowing journey into the life of a stalker and his unsuspecting victims." Kirkus

Weisskopf, Michael

Weisskopf, Michael. **Blood** brothers; among the soldiers of

Ward 57. H. Holt 2006 301p il hardcover o.p. pa $15 **92**

1. Journalists 2. Iraq War, 2003-2011 -- Personal narratives

ISBN 978-0-8050-7860-2; 0-8050-7860-6; 978-0-8050-8660-7 pa; 0-8050-8660-9 pa

LC 2006-43382

"Weisskopf recognizes his own experience in that of the soldiers, making for a wonderful story of tragedy and recovery." Libr J

Includes bibliographical references

Welles, Orson, 1915-1985

Callow, Simon. **Orson** Welles; the road to Xanadu. Simon Callow. Penguin Bks. 1997 640p illustrations pa $14.95; $20 **92**

1. Motion picture producers and directors -- Biography

ISBN 0-14-025456-0; 0140254560; 9780140254563

LC 95037138

This biography, by Simon Callow, covers actor and director Orson Welles's "prodigious childhood; his youth in New York, with its fraught partnership with John Houseman and the groundbreaking triumph of his all-black Macbeth; the pioneering radio work that culminated in the notorious 1938 broadcast of War of the Worlds; and finally, his work in Hollywood, including an authoritative account of the making of Citizen Kane." (Publisher's note)

"His research is effortlessly vast, and Callow corrects many of the myths and dissemblings surrounding Welles, some of them put out by Welles himself." Kirkus

Includes filmography. Includes bibliographical references and index.

Callow, Simon. **Orson** Welles; Volume 2 hello Americans. Simon Callow. Penguin Books 2007 513 p. illustrations, portraits $20 **92**

1. Motion picture producers and directors

ISBN 0140275177; 9780140275179

This biography, by Simon Callow, on actor and director Orson Welles "examines the years following Citizen Kane up to the time of Macbeth, in which Welles's Hollywood film career unraveled. In close and colorful detail, Callow offers a scrupulous analysis of the factors involved, revealing the immense and sometimes self-defeating complexities of Welles's temperament as well as some of the monstrous personalities with whom he had to contend." (Publisher's note)

"Destined to be the definitive word. Highly recommended." LJ

Includes lists of stage productions, radio broadcasts, films, writings, and sound recordings (pages 445-463).

Includes bibliographical references (pages 465-493) and index.

★ Callow, Simon. **Orson** Welles; One-man Band. Simon Callow. Penguin Group USA 2016 624 p. $40 **92**

1. Motion picture producers and directors

ISBN 0670024910; 9780670024919

This biography of Orson Welles, by Simon Callow, "begins with Welles's self-exile from America, and his realization that he could function only to his own satisfaction as an independent film maker, a one-man band, in fact, which committed him to a perpetual cycle of money raising. The book reveals what it was like to be around Welles, and . . ., what it was like to be him, answering the riddle that has long fascinated film scholars and lovers alike: Whatever happened to Orson Welles?" (Publisher's note)

"Welles rightly imagined that people would never stop writing about him after he died. Callow continues to set the standard in this increasingly crowded field." Kirkus

McGilligan, Patrick. **Young** Orson; The Years of Luck

and Genius on the Path to Citizen Kane. by Patrick McGilligan. HarperCollins 2015 832 p. illustrations $40; (ebook) $37.99 **92**

1. Actors -- United States -- Biography 2. Authors -- United States -- Biography

ISBN 0062112481; 9780062112484; 9780062112507

LC 2016297780

In this biography, author Patrick McGilligan "brings young Orson [Welles] into focus as never before. He chronicles Welles's early life growing up in Wisconsin and Illinois as the son of an alcoholic industrialist and a radical suffragist and classical musician, and the magical early years of his career, including his marriage and affairs, his influential friendships, and his artistic collaborations." (Publisher's note)

"Exhaustively researched but well-paced and stuffed with beguiling detail, this is a vivid, sympathetic portrait of Welles's youthful promise and achievement, before the misfires and compromises of his later years." Pub Wkly

Includes bibliographical references and index.

Wellington, Arthur Wellesley, Duke of, 1769-1852

Hibbert, Christopher. **Wellington**; a personal history. Perseus Books 1999 460p il map pa $22 **92**

1. Generals 2. Statesmen 3. Prime ministers 4. Great Britain -- History -- 19th century

ISBN 0-7382-0148-0; 978-0-7382-0148-1

First published 1997 in the United Kingdom by HarperCollins

"Altogether, Wellington does not quite pass the 'niceness' test. . . . He was a difficult man, a major military figure, a minor Prime Minister and in sum a historically important legend. Hibbert skillfully brings out all these characteristics." N Y Times Book Rev

Includes bibliographical references

Wells-Barnett, Ida B., 1862-1931

★ Giddings, Paula J. **Ida**: a sword among lions; Ida B. Wells and the campaign against lynching. Amistad 2008 800p il $35 **92**

1. Authors 2. Lynching 3. Journalists 4. Women political activists 5. Essayists 6. Nonfiction writers 7. Newspaper executives 8. Biography, Individual 9. Civil rights activists 10. African Americans -- Civil rights 11. African American women -- Biography

ISBN 0-06-051921-5; 978-0-06-051921-6

This is a biography of the African American female activist, Ida B. Wells.

"An iconic figure in American history, Wells was not always celebrated by her contemporaries for her groundbreaking activism because of her assertive politics and difficult personality. . . . Giddings offers a look at how Wells' own self-assertion affected her relationships with family, friends, colleagues, and the broader American public as she evolved as a woman and an activist. . . . With meticulous research, including Wells' own diary, Giddings brings to life one of the most fascinating women in American history, giving readers a real feel for the texture and context of Wells' life." Booklist

Includes bibliographical references

Welty, Eudora, 1909-2001

Marrs, Suzanne. **Eudora** Welty: a biography. Harcourt 2005 652p il $28 **92**

1. Authors 2. Novelists 3. Authors, American 4. Short story writers

ISBN 0-15-100914-7

LC 2004-30490

This book "belongs on the shelf beside its subject's own work. Neither hagiography nor pathography, it is, you feel, the thoroughly respectful and straightforward biography its honest, modest, intensely private subject would have wanted." N Y Times Book Rev

Includes bibliographical references

What there is to say we have said; the correspondence of Eudora Welty and William Maxwell. edited by Suzanne Marrs. Houghton Mifflin Harcourt 2011 499p il $35 **92**

1. Authors 2. Novelists 3. Magazine editors 4. Short story writers

ISBN 0547376499; 9780547376493; 978-0-547-37649-3; 0-547-37649-9

LC 2010-42105

"Letters between writers often have a lot of shop talk of interest to other writers and literary cultists, but this collection yields broader pleasures, too. In addition to being stellar writers, Welty and Maxwell were also accomplished critics, and one of the joys of the book is eavesdropping on their assessments of authors as varied as John Updike and Virginia Woolf, Anton Chekhov and Charles Dickens, William Faulkner and E. M. Forster. Welty and Maxwell also shared an intense love of gardening – so much so that Marrs was forced, in the book's index, to include an extensive listing of various varieties of roses. . . . As these letters show, Welty and Maxwell regarded domestic life not as a tedious distraction from the writing desk, but as a crucial source of insight. . . . The title of the collection comes from Maxwell's conclusion, as he and Welty faced their mortality, that 'what there is to say we have said, in one way or the other. You know how much we love you.' That love, a source of sustenance and strength between two great writers, is also a bright tonic for the readers of this volume." Christ Sci Monit

Includes bibliographical references

Wenner, Jann

Hagan, Joe. **Sticky** fingers; the life and times of Jann Wenner and Rolling Stone magazine. Joe Hagan. Alfred A. Knopf 2017 560 p. (hardcover) $29.95 **92**

1. Periodical editors -- United States -- Biography 2. Publishers & publishing -- United States -- Biography 3. Editors -- United States -- Biography 4. Rolling stone (San Francisco, Calif.) 5. Publishers and publishing -- United States -- Biography

ISBN 9781101874370

LC 2017018102

In this biography, author Joe Hagan, "[tells] the story of Jann Wenner, Rolling Stone's founder, editor, and publisher, and the pioneering era he helped curate. . . . [The book] depicts an ambitious, mercurial, wide-eyed rock and roll fan of who exalts in youth and beauty and learns how to package it, marketing late sixties counterculture as a testament to the power of American youth." (Publisher's note)

"This biographical chronicle of the cultural evolution from the 1960s to the present is a must-read for counterculture enthusiasts and historians." (LJ)

West, Jerry, 1938-

Lazenby, Roland. **Jerry** West; the life and legend of a basketball icon. ESPN Books; Ballantine Books 2010 xxi, 422p il $28 **92**

1. Basketball players 2. Basketball executives 3. Basketball -- Biography 4. Los Angeles Lakers (Basketball team)

ISBN 978-0-345-51083-9; 0-345-51083-6

LC 2009-43777

The life of the basketball great from his hardscrabble West Virginia youth to his pro career with the Los Angeles Lakers from 1960 to 1974

"Sports biographies tend to career between breathless hagiography and the slyly salacious. Lazenby . . . has produced something of a different order — a first-rate piece of narrative nonfiction whose subject happens to be a star athlete. His biography of West is, by turns, smart, beautifully reported, well-written and psychologically shrewd. It also manages to put both the NBA and individual players in a telling social and historical context without straying into didacticism." PopMatters

Includes bibliographical references

West, Lindy

West, Lindy. **Shrill**; notes from a loud woman. Lindy West. Hachette Books 2016 272 p. (ebook) $81; (hardcover) $26 **92**
1. Feminists 2. Women journalists -- Biography 3. Women -- Humor 4. Conduct of life -- Humor 5. Feminists -- United States -- Biography 6. Women journalists -- United States -- Biography
ISBN 9780316348478; 9780316348409

           LC 2016001577

This memoir, by Lindy West, is "a feminist rallying cry in a world that thinks gender politics are tedious and that women, especially feminists, can't be funny. Coming of age in a culture that demands women be as small, quiet, and compliant as possible--like a porcelain dove that will also have sex with you--writer and humorist Lindy West quickly discovered that she was anything but." (Publisher's note)

"Sure to be a boon for anyone who has struggled with body image, Shrill is a triumphant, exacting, absorbing memoir that will lay new groundwork for the way we talk about the taboo of being too large." Booklist

Westover, Tara

Westover, Tara. **Educated**; a memoir. Tara Westover. Random House 2018 xv, 334 p.p (hardcover) $28   **92**
1. Idaho 2. Counterculture 3. Home schooling 4. Women college students 5. Idaho -- Biography 6. Christian biography 7. Subculture -- Idaho 8. Women -- Idaho -- Biography 9. Survivalism -- Idaho -- Biography 10. Home schooling -- Idaho -- Anecdotes 11. Idaho -- Rural conditions -- Anecdotes 12. Victims of family violence -- Idaho -- Biography 13. Women college students -- United States -- Biography
ISBN 9780399590504; 9780399590511; 0399590501

           LC 2017037645

This book, by Tara Westover, "is an account of the struggle for self-invention. It is a tale of fierce family loyalty, and of the grief that comes from severing ties with those closest to you. With the acute insight that distinguishes all great writers, Westover has crafted a universal coming-of-age story that gets to the heart of what an education is and what it offers: the perspective to see one's life through new eyes, and the will to change it." (Publisher's note)

" In its keen exploration of family, history, and the narratives we create for ourselves, Educated becomes more than just a success story." Booklist

Wetherall, Tyler, 1983-

Wetherall, Tyler. **No** way home; a memoir of life on the run. Tyler Wetherall. St. Martin's Press 2018 320 p. (hardcover) $26.99   **92**
1. Fugitives from justice 2. Father-daughter relationship 3. American literature -- Women authors -- Biography 4. Women authors, American -- Biography 5. Children of criminals -- United States -- Biography 6. Fathers and daughters -- United States -- Biography 7. Fugitives from justice -- Family relationships -- United States
ISBN 9781250112194

           LC 2017049579

"In this emotionally compelling and gripping memoir, Tyler Wetherall brings to life her fugitive childhood, following the threads that tie a family together through hardship, from her parents' first meeting in 1960s New York to her present life as a restless writer unpacking the secrets of her past. 'No Way Home' is about love, loss, and learning to tell the story of our lives." (Publisher's note)

Wharton, Edith, 1862-1937

Lee, Hermione. **Edith** Wharton. Alfred A. Knopf 2007 869p il $35   **92**
1. Authors 2. Novelists 3. Nonfiction writers 4. Short story writers
ISBN 978-0-375-40004-9; 0-375-40004-4

           LC 2006-48795

"Marked by an elegant literary style that does justice to its subject and a clear, compassionate eye for detail, [this] is not only the best book on its subject, but one of the finest literary biographies to appear in recent years." Atlanta Journal-Constitution

Includes bibliographical references

White, Bill

White, Bill. **Uppity**; my untold story about the games people play. [by] Bill White with Gordon Dillow; foreword by Willie Mays. Grand Central Pub. 2011 303p il $26.99   **92**
1. Baseball players 2. African American athletes 3. Sportscasters 4. Baseball executives 5. Baseball -- Biography 6. Sport association executives 7. United States -- Race relations
ISBN 9780446555258; 0446555258

           LC 2010-38025

"During his 13 years as a player, [Bill White] won All-Star recognition and frequent Gold Gloves as a slick-fielding, power-hitting first baseman, though he was never the flamboyant type who would call attention to himself. Then he embarked on an 18-year career as a broadcaster, memorably providing a balance to the more unpredictable Phil Rizzuto as announcers for the New York Yankees. He capped his career by serving five years as president of the National League. . . . Whatever his level of involvement, White approached baseball as a career through which he made his living rather than a sport he loved, an attitude that is likely to ruffle sentimentalists. . . . He describes the abuse he took from redneck fans during minor league days when he was one of the few black players on a team, through his battles with the white tycoons who exerted increasing control over the industry before he resigned as league president. Yet his account is otherwise color blind as it separates the heroes of White's life (Willie Mays, Bing Devine, Johnny Keane and others in addition to Rizzuto) from the villains." Kirkus

White, E. B. (Elwyn Brooks), 1899-1985

Elledge, Scott. **E.** B. White; a biography. Norton 1984 400p il hardcover o.p. pa $21.95   **92**
1. Poets 2. Authors 3. Humorists 4. Novelists 5. Essayists 6. Satirists 7. Authors, American 8. Children's authors
ISBN 0-393-30305-5 pa

           LC 83-4032

The author is "fair, respectful, thorough, entertaining, skillful and unpedantic. He has performed a splendid exercise in scholarship and literary analysis, and the result is fun." N Y Times Book Rev

Includes bibliographical references

White, E. B. **Letters** of E.B. White; originally collected and edited by Dorothy Lobrano Guth. Rev. ed.; Harper Collins 2006 713p il $35   **92**
1. Poets 2. Authors 3. Humorists 4. Novelists 5. Essayists 6. Satirists 7. Authors, American 8. Children's authors
ISBN 978-0-06-075708-3; 0-06-075708-6

LC 2006-43490
First published 1976

This collection of letters by the essayist, poet, novelist and author of several classic children's books is chronologically arranged. Written between the years 1908 when White was nine and 1985 when he died, they concern his relationships with his wife, Katherine White and his family and friends, which include Harold Ross, James Thurber, Robert Benchley, Alexander Woollcott and others.

White, Edmund, 1940-

White, Edmund. **City** boy; my life in New York during the 1960s and 70s. Bloomsbury USA 2009 297p $26   **92**
    1. Authors 2. Gay men 3. Novelists 4. Memoirists 5. Biographers 6. Authors, American 7. Short story writers 8. New York (N.Y.) -- Intellectual life
    ISBN 978-1-596-91402-5; 1-596-91402-5
LC 2009-12493

The author "weaves erotic encounters and long-ago literati into a vast tapestry of Manhattan memories. . . . This is a brilliant recreation of an era, rich in revels, revolutions and 'leather boys leading the human tidal wave.'" Publ Wkly

White, Michael, 1956-

White, Michael. **Travels** in Vermeer; a memoir. Michael White. Persea Books 2015 178 p. (alk. paper) $17.95   **92**
    1. Divorce 2. Art appreciation
    ISBN 0892554371; 9780892554379
LC 2014016180

This memoir by Michael White is his "account of how a poet, in the midst of a bad divorce, finds consolation and grace through viewing the paintings of Vermeer, in six world cities. Through these travels and his encounters with Vermeer's radiant vision, White finds grace and personal transformation." (Publisher's note)

"An enchanting book about the transformative power of art." Kirkus

Wiesel, Elie, 1928-2016

★ Wiesel, Elie. **Night**; translated from the French by Marion Wiesel; [with a new preface by the author; foreword by Francoise Mauriac] Hill and Wang 2006 xxi, 120p $19.95; pa $9   **92**
    1. Authors 2. Novelists 3. Journalists 4. Holocaust survivors 5. Human rights activists 6. Nobel laureates for peace 7. Holocaust, 1933-1945 -- Personal narratives
    ISBN 0-374-39997-2; 978-0-374-39997-9; 0-374-50001-0 pa; 978-0-374-50001-6 pa; 9780374221997
LC 2005-936797

This is "the autobiographical account of an adolescent boy and his father in Auschwitz. Wiesel writes of their battle for survival, and of his battle with God for a way to understand the wanton cruelty he witnesses each day." Publisher's note

Wiesenthal, Simon

Segev, Tom. **Simon** Wiesenthal; the life and legends. Doubleday 2010 482p il $35; ebook $35   **92**
    1. Authors 2. Architects 3. Holocaust survivors 4. Nazi 5. Essayists 6. Memoirists 7. Nazi hunters 8. Jewish leaders 9. Jews -- Austria 10. Biography, Individual
    ISBN 978-0-385-51946-5; 978-0-385-53371-3 ebook
LC 2009-53480

The book is a biography about "Simon Wiesenthal, . . . the survivor of a succession of concentration camps, . . . [and] the Nazi hunter who tracked down Adolf Eichmann and brought to justice such [war criminals] . . . as Franz Stangl, the commandant of Treblinka, . . . and Hermine Braunsteiner." The author recounts how Wiesenthal "talked his way into jobs with the American military—an army war crimes unit and the local bureau of the counterintelligence corps—and became the head of local refugee groups, . . . as well as a representative of the Joint Distribution Committee, a Jewish relief organization working with DPs. The American connection, which involved identifying and apprehending war criminals, led directly to his life's work: creating a database of Nazi criminals, tracking them down, and bringing them to justice." (New York Review of Books)

"The man who emerges from this text is ultimately more complex, and indeed likable, than the mythologized figure. Segev's study should be the standard for many years." Libr J

Includes bibliographical references

Wilberforce, William, 1759-1833

Hague, William Jefferson. **William** Wilberforce; the life of the great anti-slave trade campaigner. HarperCollins 2008 582p il $35   **92**
    1. Abolitionists 2. Philanthropists 3. Essayists 4. Writers on religion 5. Members of Parliament
    ISBN 978-0-15-101267-1; 0-15-101267-9
LC 2007-45981

First published 2007 in the United Kingdom

Hague describes how Wilberforce, "dedicating his political life to moral causes . . . decided on two: 'the reformation of manners,' as he confided to his diary, and the abolition of African slavery. Wilberforce's campaign against vice had scant historical effect, but that against slavery in British realms arguably prodded the Western world toward abolition. Why Wilberforce's effort (trade in slaves was banned in 1807; abolition occurred in 1834) followed a tortuous path becomes understandable as Hague explains the parliamentary practicalities that Wilberforce faced. Incorporating Wilberforce's domestic life, Hague's effort is a well-rounded portrait of the pioneering British abolitionist." Booklist

Wilde, Oscar, 1854-1900

Ellmann, Richard. **Oscar** Wilde. Knopf 1988 680p il hardcover o.p. pa $19.95   **92**
    1. Poets 2. Authors 3. Novelists 4. Dramatists 5. Lecturers
    ISBN 0-394-75984-2 pa
LC 87-45354

First published 1987 in the United Kingdom

"Wilde's life epitomizes the classic formula for a tragic history, the man who, by hubris, falls from greatness. In Mr. Ellmann's hands, the story becomes as compelling as fiction while never deviating from the facts. Humour and elegance illuminate the accounts of Wilde's family, his friends and the enemies he earned." Economist

Includes bibliographical references

O'Sullivan, Emer, 1957- The **fall** of the house of Wilde; Oscar Wilde and his family. Emer O'Sullivan. Bloomsbury Press 2016 xii, 495 p.p illustrations (hardcover) $35   **92**
    1. Irish authors -- Biography 2. Authors, Irish -- 19th century -- Biography
    ISBN 1608199878; 9781608199877; 9781608199884

This book, by Emer O'Sullivan, is "the first biography of Oscar Wilde that places him within the context of his family and social and historical milieu--a compelling volume that finally tells the whole story. . . . Oscar's mother, Lady Jane Wilde, rose to prominence as a political journalist, advocating a rebellion against colonialism in 1848. . . . His father, Sir William Wilde, was acutely conscious of injustices of the social order." (Publisher's note)

"O'Sullivan's impressively comprehensive biography is equal

parts political history, literary criticism, and Shakespearean tragedy." Pub Wkly

Includes bibliographical references (pages 445-476) and index.

Wilder, Billy, 1906-2002

It's the pictures that got small; Charles Brackett on Billy Wilder and Hollywood's golden age. edited by Anthony Slide. Columbia University Press 2014 448 p. 16 unnumbered pages of plates (cloth: alk. paper) $34.95 **92**
1. Motion pictures -- Production and direction 2. Screenwriters -- United States -- Diaries 3. Motion picture producers and directors -- United States -- Diaries 4. Motion pictures -- Production and direction -- United States -- History -- 20th century
ISBN 9780231167086

LC 2014015801

This book, edited by Anthony Slide, offers an "annotated collection of writings taken from dozens of [screenwriter Charles] Brackett's unpublished diaries . . . [and] clarifies Brackett's critical contribution to [director Billy] Wilder's films and Hollywood history while enriching our knowledge of Wilder's achievements in writing, direction, and style." (Publisher's note)

"Though the diary format is not for all readers, anyone interested in the golden age of film should enjoy this very entertaining and illustrative look at the film industry of the 1930s and 1940s." LJ

Includes bibliographical references and index

Wilder, Laura Ingalls, 1867-1957

★ Fraser, Caroline. **Prairie** fires; the American dreams of Laura Ingalls Wilder. by Caroline Fraser. Metropolitan Books 2017 xii, 625 p.p illustrations, map (hardcover) $35 **92**
1. Women authors -- United States -- Biography 2. Frontier and pioneer life -- United States 3. Women pioneers -- United States -- Biography 4. Authors, American -- 20th century -- Biography
ISBN 9781627792776; 9781627792769; 1627792767

LC 2017028870

Pulitzer Prize: Biography (2018)
National Book Critics Circle Award: Biography (2017)

This book, by Caroline Fraser, is "the first comprehensive historical biography of Laura Ingalls Wilder, the beloved author of the Little House on the Prairie books. . . . Revealing the grown-up story behind the most influential childhood epic of pioneer life, . . . [Fraser] chronicles Wilder's tumultuous relationship with her journalist daughter, Rose Wilder Lane, setting the record straight regarding charges of ghostwriting that have swirled around the books." (Publisher's note)

"A vivid portrait of frontier life and one of its most ardent celebrants." Kirkus

Includes bibliographical references (pages [517]-602) and index.

McDowell, Marta. The **world** of Laura Ingalls Wilder; the frontier landscapes that inspired the Little House books. by Marta McDowell. Timber Press 2017 396 p. illustrations, maps (hardcover) $27.95 **92**
1. Frontier and pioneer life -- United States 2. Nature in literature 3. Gardens in literature 4. Gardening -- United States 5. Family farms -- United States 6. Women pioneers -- United States -- Biography 7. Authors, American -- 20th century -- Biography
ISBN 9781604698336; 9781604697278

LC 2016057864

This book, by Marta McDowell, "explores [Laura Ingalls] Wilder's deep relationship with the landscape. Follow the Wilder's wagon trail starting in the Wisconsin setting of Little House in the Big Woods, through the Dakotas, and finally to Missouri. You'll learn details about

Wilder's life and inspirations, discover how to visit the real places today, and even learn to grow the plants and vegetables featured in the series." (Publisher's note)

"McDowell's warm descriptions of the author, her times, and the plants she loved provide a wonderful companion to Wilder's books, while instructions on growing a Little House-inspired garden add an interactive component." Pub Wkly

Includes bibliographical references (pages 353-375) and index.

Wilder, Laura Ingalls, 1867-1957. **Pioneer** girl; the annotated autobiography. Laura Ingalls Wilder; Pamela Smith Hill, editor. South Dakota Historical Society Press 2014 365 p. illustrations, maps (alk. paper) $39.95 **92**
1. Frontier and pioneer life 2. Frontier and pioneer life -- United States 3. Women pioneers -- United States -- Biography 4. Women authors, American -- 20th century -- Biography
ISBN 0984504176; 9780984504176

LC 2014027174

This autobiography, by Laura Ingalls Wilder, edited by Pamela Smith Hill, "hidden away since the 1930s, . . . reveals the true stories of her pioneering life. Some of her experiences will be familiar; some will be a surprise. . . . [This text] re-introduces readers to the woman who defined the pioneer experience for millions of people around the world." (Publisher's note)

"Lengthy footnotes make the manuscript somewhat tricky to navigate, but Hill's comments are cogent and her arguments strong, and this will be welcomed wherever there are Wilder fans. Illustrated with maps, photos, and artwork, and appended with additional manuscripts and an extensive bibliography." Booklist

Includes bibliographical references and index

Wilder, Thornton, 1897-1975

★ Niven, Penelope, 1939-2014. **Thornton** Wilder; A Life. by Penelope Niven; forward by Edward Albee. HarperCollins 2012 xvi, 832 p.p (hardcover) $39.99; (ebook) $31.99 **92**
1. American authors -- Biography
ISBN 0060831367; 9780060831363; 9780062097774

This book by Penelope Niven presents a biography of "Pulitzer Prize-winning playwright and novelist Thornton Wilder. . . . Niven . . . combed through the author's many published and unpublished personal writings. . . . Through Wilder's own words, the reader is privy to his arrogant thrills and frequent bouts of self-doubt. Chronicling Wilder's successes and failures in various literary forms . . . Niven includes brief criticism and reviews with each of his major works." (Publishers Weekly)

Wilkinson, James, 1757-1825

Linklater, Andro. An **artist** in treason; the extraordinary double life of General James Wilkinson. Walker 2009 392p il map $27 **92**
1. Spies 2. Generals 3. Territorial governors 4. United States -- Politics and government -- 1783-1865
ISBN 978-0-8027-1720-7

LC 2009-19184

A profile of the Continental Army general explores his career with the Spanish secret service, his protection by four presidents in spite of his treasonous acts, and his role in foiling Aaron Burr's conspiracy to break up the Union.

The author "lucidly details the general's often tangled affairs, but he also uses his story to illuminate the personal feuds, political struggles, and international entanglements that helped shape the young United States. He manages to tell this story of skullduggery and self-interest without wagging his finger in high moral dudgeon at Wilkinson's betrayals. In fact, at times the wily double-crosser almost comes across as

sympathetic—but never as someone to trust." Am Heritage
Includes bibliographical references and index.

Willan, Anne

Friedman, Amy. **One** souffle at a time; a memoir of food and France. Anne Willan; with Amy Friedman. St. Martin's Press 2013 320 p. ill. (hardcover) $27.99   **92**
   1. Cooks 2. French cooking 3. Cooking, French
   ISBN 0312642172; 9780312642174; 9781466837027
                          LC 2013004043
IACP Cookbook Award (2014)
In this book, chef Anne Willan "tells her story and the story of the food-world greats--including Julia Child, James Beard, Simone Beck, Craig Claiborne, Richard Olney, and others--who changed how the world eats and who made cooking fun. She writes about how a sturdy English girl from Yorkshire made it not only to the stove, but to France, and how she overcame the exceptionally closed male world of French cuisine to found and run her school." (Publisher's note)
"A charming, if not revelatory, portrait of a woman determined to bring French cuisine to a wider audience, with emphasis on traditional, accessible recipes that respect the intellectual side of cookery." Kirkus

William, Prince, Duke of Cambridge, 1982-

Nicholl, Katie. **Kate**; the future queen. Katie Nicholl. Weinstein Books 2013 354 p. x, illustrations (hardcover) $26   **92**
   1. Princesses -- Great Britain -- Biography
   ISBN 1602862265; 9781602862265
                          LC 2013387679
This book, by Katie Nicholl, "gives an inside look into the life of the future Queen of England, Kate Middleton. Since becoming Duchess Catherine of Cambridge in 2011, Middleton has captivated royals fans around the world and now, Nicholl delivers the story of her early life, first romances, and love with Prince William. Nicholl will reveal new details on Middleton's initiation into royal life and, of course, her first pregnancy." (Publisher's note)
Includes bibliographical references (page 317) and index.

Williams, Art, Jr.

Kersten, Jason. The **art** of making money; the story of a master counterfeiter. Gotham Books 2009 292p $26   **92**
   1. Criminals 2. Counterfeits and counterfeiting 3. Counterfeiters
   ISBN 978-1-59240-446-9
                          LC 2009-9407
This "absorbing account reads like crime fiction, offering an understanding of modern counterfeiting that will appeal to readers of that genre as well as those who like true crime." Libr J

Williams, Hank, 1923-1953

★ Hemphill, Paul. **Lovesick** blues; the life of Hank Williams. Viking 2005 207p $23.95   **92**
   1. Singers 2. Country musicians 3. Songwriters
   ISBN 0-670-03414-2
                          LC 2004-65113
This is a biography of the country singer.
"This is the finest work of literature about Williams yet written." Booklist

Ribowsky, Mark. **Hank**; the short life and long country road of Hank Williams. Mark Ribowsky. Liveright Publishing Corp. 2016 496 p.   **92**
   1. Country musicians -- United States -- Biography

   ISBN 9781631491573
                          LC 2016026928
"Presenting the first fully realized biography of Hiram King Williams in a generation, [author] Mark Ribowsky vividly returns us to the world of country's origins, . . . where Williams was born into the most trying of circumstances, which included a dictatorial mother, a henpecked father, and an agonizing spinal condition. . . . Ribowsky also explores all those cautionary tales that have, until now, remained secreted beneath the grooves of his records." (Publisher's note)
Includes bibliographical references and index

Williams, Jay, 1981-

Williams, Jay. **Life** is not an accident; a memoir of reinvention. Jay Williams. Harper 2015 272 p. color illustrations (hardcover) $26.99   **92**
   1. National Basketball Association 2. Television broadcasting of sports 3. Basketball players -- United States -- Biography 4. Sportscasters -- United States -- Biography
   ISBN 9780062327987
                          LC 2015050965
In this memoir, author Jay Williams, "details his rise to NBA stardom, the terrible accident that ended his career and plunged him into a life-altering depression, and how he ultimately found his way out of the darkness. . . . Williams talks about the accident that transformed him. . . . He tells it straight about the scandalous recruiting process and his decision to return to Duke and Coach K. . . . He also speaks out about corruption . . . and about his time in the NBA." (Publisher's note)
"Recommended for anyone interested in a behind-the-scenes look at the lives of college basketball and NBA players." LJ

Williams, Mary Elizabeth

Williams, Mary Elizabeth. A **series** of catastrophes and miracles; a true story of love, science, and cancer. Mary Elizabeth Williams. National Geographic 2016 304 p. (ebook) $35.90; (hardback) $26   **92**
   1. Immunotherapy 2. Cancer patients 3. Cancer -- Treatment 4. Metastasis 5. Women -- Health and hygiene 6. Cancer -- Patients -- Biography 7. Cancer in women -- Patients -- Biography
   ISBN 9781426216343; 9781426216336
                          LC 2015033584
In this memoir, by Mary Elizabeth Williams, "after being diagnosed in her early 40s with metastatic melanoma . . . , Williams finds herself in a race against the clock. She takes a once-in-a-lifetime chance and joins a clinical trial for immunotherapy, a revolutionary drug regimen that trains the body to vanquish malignant cells. Astonishingly, her cancer disappears entirely in just a few weeks." (Publisher's note)
"This highly recommended account demonstrates the value of cutting-edge cancer research, but it is also beautifully crafted, and many readers will find it entertaining and—though the author might not like this term—inspiring" LJ
Includes bibliographical references (pages 295-299).

Williams, Patricia

Williams, Patricia. **Rabbit**; The Autobiography of Ms. Pat. by Patricia Williams with Jeannine Amber. Dey St., an imprint of William Morrow 2017 viii, 227 p.p (hardcover) $25.99 **92**
   1. Teenage pregnancy 2. African American women 3. Dysfunctional families 4. Atlanta (Ga.) -- Biography 5. African American women comedians -- Biography 6. African American women -- Georgia -- Atlanta -- Biography
   ISBN 9780062407320; 9780062407306; 0062407309
In his book, by Patricia Williams and Jeannine Amber, "Pat watched

as her mother struggled to get by on charity, cons, and petty crimes. At age seven, Pat was taught to roll drunks for money. At twelve, she was targeted for sex by a man eight years her senior. By thirteen, she was pregnant. By fifteen, Pat was a mother of two. Alone at sixteen, Pat was determined to make a better life for her children." (Publisher's note)

"Both savagely honest and often genuinely funny, this is the story of how a resilient woman survived a harrowing early life and found unexpected salvation through humor. Sassy, inspiring, and uplifting." Kirkus

Williams, Patricia (Dental hygienist)

★ Williams, Patricia. **While** they're still here; a memoir. Patricia Williams. She Writes Press 2017 324 p. $16.95   **92**
1. Caregivers 2. Aging parents 3. Parent-adult child relationship 4. Aging parents -- Care 5. Parent and adult child
ISBN 9781631522406

LC 2017943955

In this memoir, by Patricia Williams, "amazing stories with captivating details surface, from the deeds both heroic and horrific her father witnessed in the Navy to her mother's days as a singer, nightclub dancer, and model, along with the poverty both faced growing up in the Depression. The end result is an intimate oral history of a blue-collar, postwar American family revealed by the author in the same touching and heartbreaking manner it was disclosed to her." (Kirkus Reviews)

Williams, Robin, 1951-2014

★ **Robin;** Dave Itzkoff. Henry Holt & Co. 2018 544 p. (hardcover) $30   **92**
1. Biography 2. Comedians -- United States -- Biography 3. Actors -- United States -- Biography
ISBN 9781627794244

LC 2017050678

This book, by author "Dave Itzkoff, [offers] the definitive biography of Robin Williams--a compelling portrait of one of America's most beloved and misunderstood entertainers. . . . Itzkoff shows in this revelatory biography, Williams's comic brilliance masked a deep well of conflicting emotions and self-doubt, which he drew upon in his comedy and in celebrated films like 'Dead Poets Society'; . . . [It] is a fresh and original look at a man whose work touched so many lives." (Publisher's note)

"The book has some nifty trivia (first choices to play Mork from Ork were John Byner and Dom DeLuise), but this isn't one of those skimming-the-surface Hollywood bios. It's a meaty, well-researched, moving story of a man who could never quite come to terms with his own brilliance." Booklist

Includes bibliographical references and index

Williams, Roger, 1604?-1683

Gaustad, Edwin Scott. **Roger** Williams; [by] Edwin S. Gaustad. Oxford University Press 2005 150p il (Lives and legacies) $17.95   **92**
1. Clergy 2. Puritans 3. Colonial leaders 4. Writers on religion 5. United States -- History -- 1600-1775, Colonial period
ISBN 0-19-518369-X

LC 2004-25246

The author "provides not just an excellent introduction to the man but a deep analysis of his largely unacknowledged influence on our political and cultural life." Reason

Williams, Ted, 1918-2002

Bradlee, Benjamin C., 1921-2014. The **kid;** the immortal life of Ted Williams. Ben Bradlee, Jr. Little Brown & Co 2013 864 p. illustrations $35   **92**
1. Baseball -- United States 2. Baseball players -- United States

-- Biography
ISBN 0316614351; 9780316614351

LC 2013028253

This book, by Ben Bradlee, Jr., offers a biography of the baseball player Ted Williams. "Born in 1918 in San Diego, Ted would spend most of his life disguising his Mexican heritage. During his 22 years with the Boston Red Sox, Williams electrified crowds across America--and shocked them, too: His notorious clashes with the press and fans threatened his reputation. Yet while he was a God in the batter's box, he was profoundly human once he stepped away from the plate." (Publisher's note)

"Sprawling, entertaining life of the baseball great, renowned as a sports hero while leading a life as checkered as Babe Ruth's or Ty Cobb's." Kirkus

Includes bibliographical references and index

Williams, Tennessee, 1911-1983

★ Lahr, John. **Tennessee** Williams; Mad Pilgrimage of the Flesh. John Lahr. W W Norton & Co Inc 2014 736 p. illustrations hc $39.95   **92**
1. American dramatists
ISBN 9780393021240; 0393021246

LC 2014022281

National Book Award Shortlist: Nonfiction (2014)
National Book Critics Circle Award: Biography (2014)

Written by John Lahr, "'Tennessee Williams: Mad Pilgrimage of the Flesh' gives intimate access to the mind of one of the most brilliant dramatists of his century, whose plays reshaped the American theater and the nation's sense of itself. This . . . biography sheds a light on Tennessee Williams's warring family, his guilt, his creative triumphs and failures, his sexuality and numerous affairs, his misreported death, even the shenanigans surrounding his estate." (Publisher's note)

"Drawing on vast archival sources and unpublished manuscripts, as well as interviews, memoirs and theater history, he fashions a sweeping, riveting narrative.There is only one word for this biography: superb." Kirkus

Includes bibliographical references (pages 725-730) and index

Leverich, Lyle. **Tom;** the unknown Tennessee Williams. Norton 2007 644p il pa $35   **92**
1. Authors 2. Novelists 3. Dramatists 4. Short story writers 5. Dramatists, American
ISBN 978-0-393-31663-6; 0-393-31663-7

First published 1995 by Crown

This is the first installment of a projected two-volume biography of the American dramatist. Coverage begins with Williams' birth in 1911 and extends to the opening of The Glass Menagerie in 1945.

"The book is a tremendous accomplishment, and Leverich is an appealing biographer: modest, thorough, balanced, and passionate. In prose that is clear—if not scintillating—he bushwhacks a path through a morass of gossip and myth, and prepares the way for a more subtle interpretation of the man and his plays." New Yorker

The **luck** of friendship; the letters of Tennessee Williams and James Laughlin. edited by Peggy L. Fox and Thomas Keith. W W Norton & Co Inc 2018 352 p. (hardcover) $39.95 **92**
1. Authors -- Correspondence 2. Dramatists, American -- 20th century -- Correspondence 3. Publishers and publishing -- United States -- Correspondence 4. Authors and publishers -- United States -- History -- 20th century
ISBN 9780393246209

LC 2018000448

This book, edited by Peggy L. Fox and Thomas Keith, chronicles

"Tennessee Williams and James Laughlin's unlikely yet enduring literary and personal relationship. . . . A little more than a week after . . . [their] first encounter, Tennessee sent a letter to Jay--as he always addressed Laughlin in writing--expressing a desire to get together for an informal discussion of some of Tennessee's poetry. . . . So began a deep friendship that would last for forty-one years." (Publisher's note)

"The rivers of mutual affection, admiration, and artistry form a powerful confluence in these deeply affecting exchanges." Kirkus

Includes bibliographical references and index

Williams, William Carlos, 1883-1963

Leibowitz, Herbert A. **Something** urgent I have to say to you: the life and works of William Carlos Williams; [by] Herbert Leibowitz. Farrar, Straus and Giroux 2011 496p il $40 **92**

1. Poets 2. Authors 3. Physicians 4. Essayists 5. Short story writers

ISBN 978-0-374-11329-2; 0-374-11329-7

LC 2010-46548

"In the 50s when Williams first became popular, convention said critics did not cross boundaries to conjecture on psychological motivations. This book is very much a product of a new century where all is transparent; and if Williams broke taboos in writing, Leibowitz does in reporting. . . . Leibowitz is quick to attribute Williams's writing to his tortured sexuality. The poet's pull between duty and a libidinous fantasy world is well known but never before used so relentlessly as capital. This also makes the book as readable as fiction, something bound to get it off the shelf and into the reader's hands. Leibowitz tackles the poetry through the man, not the other way around. . . . In the second half of the book, Leibowitz's comparison of Williams's book Spring and All to T.S. Eliot's The Waste Land is a brilliant analysis. Also, the careful reasoning behind Williams's In the American Grain is a contribution to literary thought. Another real bonus is that this biography tracks the Little Magazine movement in America nicely." Washington Independent Rev of Books

Includes bibliographical references

Wills, Garry, 1934-

Wills, Garry. **Outside** looking in; adventures of an observer. Viking 2010 195p $25.95 **92**

1. Authors 2. Historians 3. Journalists 4. Essayists 5. Social critics 6. College teachers

ISBN 978-0-670-02214-4

LC 2010-05323

"Wills's curiosity and personal integrity shine through this intellectual memoir that is both intimate and journalistic. Readers who have followed Wills's writing career will welcome these reflections on his life and the world around him." Libr J

Includes bibliographical references

Willughby, Francis, 1635-1672

Birkhead, Tim. The **wonderful** Mr. Willughby; the first true ornithologist. Tim Birkhead. Bloomsbury Publishing, an imprint of Bloomsbury Publishing Plc 2018 368 p. (hardback) $27 **92**

1. Naturalists -- Biography 2. Ornithologists -- Biography 3. Naturalists -- England -- Biography 4. Ornithologists -- England -- Biography

ISBN 9781408878484; 9781408878491

LC 2018018017

This book, by Tim Birkhead, presents "a biography of Francis Willughby, the man who pulled the study of birds out of the dark ages and formed the foundations of modern ornithology. . . . In his too-short life, Francis Willughby helped found the Royal Society, differentiated birds through identification of their distinguishing features, and asked questions that were, in some cases, centuries ahead of their time." (Publisher's note)

"In spite of Willughby's short life, Birkhead ably constructs a full time line of his influence on modern science. For readers, especially ornithologists, with deep interests in natural history and the history of science." Library Journal

Includes bibliographical references and index

Wilson, Brian, 1942-

Wilson, Brian, 1942- **I** am Brian Wilson; A Memoir. Brian Wilson. Da Capo Press 2016 336 p. illustrations (hardcover: alk. paper) $26.99 **92**

1. Rock musicians -- United States -- Biography

ISBN 9780306823060; 9780306823077

LC 2016030071

This memoir, by Brian Wilson, "reveals as never before the man who fought his way back to stability and creative relevance, who became a mesmerizing live artist, who forced himself to reckon with his own complex legacy, and who finally completed Smile, the legendary unfinished Beach Boys record that had become synonymous with both his genius and its destabilization. Today Brian Wilson is older, calmer, and filled with perspective and forgiveness." (Publisher's note)

"Wilson's emotional authenticity is beguiling as he takes readers deeply into his mind, voices and all, to describe his unique manifestation of musical genius." Pub Wkly

Includes bibliographical references and index

Wilson, Diane

Wilson, Diane. An **unreasonable** woman; a true story of shrimpers, politicos, polluters and the fight for Seadrift, Texas. foreword by Kenny Ausubel. Chelsea Green 2005 400p map $27.50; pa $18 **92**

1. Conservationists 2. Environmental protection 3. Fishermen

ISBN 1-931498-88-1; 978-1-931498-88-3; 1-933392-27-4 pa; 978-1-933392-27-1 pa

LC 2005-9894

"With the discovery that her 'piddlin' little county on the Gulf Coast' led the nation in toxic emissions, shrimper Wilson, a mother of five, found herself embarking on a voyage of discovery and activism that would strain her marriage and stretch her horizons. A David up against big-time chemical Goliaths, Wilson is a gifted storyteller, rendering dialogue and pacing plot turns as a novelist might." Publ Wkly

Wilson, Mara

Wilson, Mara, 1987- **Where** am I now? true stories of girlhood and accidental fame. Mara Wilson. Penguin Group USA 2016 272 p. illustrations (paperback) $16 **92**

1. Actors -- United States -- Biography

ISBN 0143128221; 9780143128229

LC 2016019573

In this book former child star actress Mara Wilson presents autobiographical essays that "chart her journey from accidental fame to relative (but happy) obscurity. They also illuminate universal struggles, like navigating love and loss, and figuring out who you are and where you belong." (Publisher's note)

"Wilson is a warm narrator, and the challenges she describes facing and working through will likely resonate with those battling mental illness." Pub Wkly

Wilson, Woodrow, 1856-1924

★ Berg, A. Scott. **Wilson**; A. Scott Berg. G.P. Putnam's

Sons 2013 832 p. $40 **92**

1. Presidents -- United States 2. Presidents -- United States -- Biography 3. United States -- Politics and government -- 1913-1921
ISBN 0399159215; 9780399159213

LC 2013009339

This book is a biography of the United States' 28th president, Woodrow Wilson. Author A. Scott Berg "is generally sympathetic to the man (he puts much emphasis on Wilson's love for his two wives and characterizes him as a passionate lover as well as a determined leader), while taking a more critical stand against his racial views and policies, his handling of the League of Nations, and of the secrecy that surrounded his late-presidency illness." (Publishers Weekly)

★ Brands, H. W. **Woodrow** Wilson. Times Books 2003 169p il (American presidents series) $20 **92**

1. Governors 2. Presidents 3. College presidents 4. Nobel laureates for peace 5. Presidents -- United States
ISBN 0-8050-6955-0

LC 2002-41393

The author "presents Wilson as a moralistic, idealistic intellectual who came to the presidency well versed in domestic policy but sadly lacking in knowledge and experience of international affairs, a leader who ultimately sacrificed his health and his presidential legacy in a doomed battle with Sen. Henry Cabot Lodge to have the League of Nations ratified. . . . Brands's brief, skillful life of the President is recommended for all public libraries." Libr J

Includes bibliographical references

Cooper, John Milton. The **warrior** and the priest: Woodrow Wilson and Theodore Roosevelt; [by] John Milton Cooper, Jr. Belknap Press 1983 442p il hardcover o.p. pa $20.95 **92**

1. Governors 2. Presidents 3. Vice-presidents 4. College presidents 5. Nobel laureates for peace 6. Presidents -- United States 7. United States -- Politics and government -- 1898-1919
ISBN 0-674-94751-7 pa

LC 83-6021

The author's "distinctions are sharp, his insights original, his judgments balanced and his narrative unfailingly graceful." N Y Times Book Rev

Includes bibliographical references

Cooper, John Milton. **Woodrow** Wilson; a biography. Alfred A. Knopf 2009 702p il $35 **92**

1. Governors 2. Presidents 3. College presidents 4. Biography, Individual 5. Nobel laureates for peace 6. Presidents -- United States 7. United States -- Politics and government -- 1898-1919 8. United States -- Politics and government -- 1913-1921 9. United States -- Politics and government -- 1919-1933
ISBN 978-0-307-26541-8

LC 2009-19097

This is a biography of the twenty-eighth president of the United States. Index.

"Cooper exhibits complete command of his materials, a sure knowledge of the man and a nuanced understanding of a presidency almost Shakespearean in its dimensions." Kirkus

Includes bibliographical references (p. [601]-668) and index.

The **moralist**; Woodrow Wilson and the world he made. by Patricia O'Toole. Simon & Schuster 2018 656 p. (hardcover: alk. paper) $35

1. Presidents -- United States -- Biography 2. United States -- Politics and government 3. United States -- Politics and government -- 1913-1921 4. United States -- Foreign relations -- Moral and ethical aspects

ISBN 9780743298094; 9780743298100

LC 2018006628

This book, by Patricia O'Toole, "is a cautionary tale about the perils of moral vanity and American overreach in foreign affairs. In domestic affairs, [Woodrow] Wilson was a progressive who enjoyed unprecedented success in leveling the economic playing field, but he was behind the times on racial equality and women's suffrage. . . . After the war Wilson became the world's most ardent champion of liberal internationalism." (Publisher's note)

Includes bibliographical references and index

Windsor, Edward, Duke of, 1894-1972

Morton, Andrew. **Wallis** in love; the untold life of the Duchess of Windsor, the woman who changed the monarchy. Andrew Morton. Grand Central Publishing 2018 xi, 386 p.p illustrations (hardcover) $28 **92**

1. Nobility -- Great Britain -- Biography 2. Marriages of royalty and nobility -- Great Britain -- History -- 20th century
ISBN 9781538747032; 9781455566976

LC 2017034572

This book, by Andrew Morton, "is a captivating biography of Wallis Simpson, the notorious woman for whom Edward VIII gave up the throne. . . . Using diary entries, letters, and other never-before-seen records, Morton takes us through Wallis's romantic adventures in Washington, China, and her entrance into the strange wonderland that is London society." (Publisher's note)

Includes bibliographical references (page [343]-376) and index.

Sebba, Anne. **That** woman; the life of Wallis Simpson, Duchess of Windsor. Anne Sebba. Griffin 2013 xvi, 344 p.p illustrations (paperback) $19.99 **92**

1. Nobility -- Great Britain -- Biography 2. Marriages of royalty and nobility -- Great Britain -- History -- 20th century
ISBN 9781429962452; 9781250022189; 0297858963; 0297858971; 1250022185; 9780297858966; 9780297858973

LC 2011507458

This book, by Anne Sebba, is a "biography of Wallis Simpson. . . . Sebba offers an eye-opening account of one of the most talked about women of her generation. It explores the obsessive nature of Simpson's relationship with Prince Edward, the suggestion that she may have had a Disorder of Sexual Development, and new evidence showing she may never have wanted to marry Edward at all." (Publisher's note)

"Salacious and consuming, this well-researched biography will appeal to readers interested in British political and women's history." Kirkus

Includes bibliographical references and index

★ Ziegler, Philip. **King** Edward VIII; a life. by Philip Ziegler. Ballantine Books 1992 552 p. (paperback) $27 **92**

1. Great Britain -- Kings and rulers 2. Great Britain -- History -- Edward VIII, 1936
ISBN 9780345375636; 0345375637

This book, by Philip Ziegler, is a biography of Edward VIII. "He was the twentieth century's Prince Charming. Handsome, elegant, quick-witted, charismatic, and an intimate friend of the most powerful and brilliant people of his day, he had everything youth and beauty could hope for—including fabulous wealth and claim to the English throne. Then, a mere eleven months after becoming King, Edward VIII threw everything away to marry the woman he loved—Wallis Simpson, an American divorcee." (Publisher's note)

Windsor, Wallis Warfield, Duchess of, 1896-1986

Morton, Andrew. **Wallis** in love; the untold life of the

Duchess of Windsor, the woman who changed the monarchy. Andrew Morton. Grand Central Publishing 2018 xi, 386 p.p illustrations (hardcover) $28 **92**

    1. Nobility -- Great Britain -- Biography 2. Marriages of royalty and nobility -- Great Britain -- History -- 20th century
ISBN 9781538747032; 9781455566976

        LC 2017034572

This book, by Andrew Morton, "is a captivating biography of Wallis Simpson, the notorious woman for whom Edward VIII gave up the throne. . . . Using diary entries, letters, and other never-before-seen records, Morton takes us through Wallis's romantic adventures in Washington, China, and her entrance into the strange wonderland that is London society." (Publisher's note)

Includes bibliographical references (page [343]-376) and index.

    Sebba, Anne. **That** woman; the life of Wallis Simpson, Duchess of Windsor. Anne Sebba. Griffin 2013 xvi, 344 p.p illustrations (paperback) $19.99 **92**

    1. Nobility -- Great Britain -- Biography 2. Marriages of royalty and nobility -- Great Britain -- History -- 20th century
ISBN 9781429962452; 9781250022189; 0297858963; 0297858971; 1250022185; 9780297858966; 9780297858973

        LC 2011507458

This book, by Anne Sebba, is a "biography of Wallis Simpson. . . . Sebba offers an eye-opening account of one of the most talked about women of her generation. It explores the obsessive nature of Simpson's relationship with Prince Edward, the suggestion that she may have had a Disorder of Sexual Development, and new evidence showing she may never have wanted to marry Edward at all." (Publisher's note)

"Salacious and consuming, this well-researched biography will appeal to readers interested in British political and women's history." Kirkus

Includes bibliographical references and index

Winkfield, Jimmy, 1882-1974

    Drape, Joe. **Black** maestro; the epic life of an American legend. Morrow 2006 280p il $24.95 **92**

    1. Jockeys
ISBN 0-06-053729-9; 978-0-06-053759-6

        LC 2006-41939

This is a biography of "Jimmy Winkfield, the last black jockey to win the Kentucky Derby. . . . This well-researched biography of Jimmy Winkfield and the larger chapter of America his life highlights is a valuable and entertaining read." Publ Wkly

Winters, Richard

    Alexander, Larry. **Biggest** brother; the life of Major D. Winters, the man who led the Band of Brothers. NAL Caliber 2005 287p il $24.95 **92**

    1. Veterans 2. World War, 1939-1945 3. Army officers
ISBN 0-451-21510-9

        LC 2004-27330

This is "the story of what distinguished Easy Company from other first-class field units: its leadership, in the person of Major Richard Winters, its commander. . . . Alexander is especially good at showing how Winters' sense of responsibility developed as a student, an enlistee, in OCS, and as an officer. He also gives a detailed picture of the army of 60-plus years ago, and the process that turned thousands of young civilians into the men who beat the Germans." Booklist

Wittels Wachs, Stephanie

    Wachs, Stephanie Wittels. **Everything** is horrible and wonderful; a tragicomic memoir of genius, heroin, love, and loss. Stephanie Wittels Wachs. Sourcebooks 2018 288 p. (hardcover: alk. paper) $25.99 **92**

    1. Siblings 2. Drug abuse 3. Heroin abuse 4. Heroin abuse -- United States 5. Drug addicts -- Family relationships -- United States
ISBN 9781492664109

        LC 2017046007

In this memoir, author "Stephanie Wittels Wachs alternates between her brother's struggle with addiction, which she learned about three days before her wedding, and the first year after his death, in all its emotional devastation. This compelling portrait of a comedic genius and a profound exploration of the love between siblings is A Year of Magical Thinking for a new generation of readers." (Publisher's note)

" Exploring her brother's untimely death while continuing his legacy, Wachs writes with immense love, humor, and humanity. The title references a famous Harris Wittels witticism, one that fits the excruciating reality of loving an addict. Everything about this book is horrible, wonderful, timely, and not to be missed." Booklist

Wittels, Harris

    Wachs, Stephanie Wittels. **Everything** is horrible and wonderful; a tragicomic memoir of genius, heroin, love, and loss. Stephanie Wittels Wachs. Sourcebooks 2018 288 p. (hardcover: alk. paper) $25.99 **92**

    1. Siblings 2. Drug abuse 3. Heroin abuse 4. Heroin abuse -- United States 5. Drug addicts -- Family relationships -- United States
ISBN 9781492664109

        LC 2017046007

In this memoir, author "Stephanie Wittels Wachs alternates between her brother's struggle with addiction, which she learned about three days before her wedding, and the first year after his death, in all its emotional devastation. This compelling portrait of a comedic genius and a profound exploration of the love between siblings is A Year of Magical Thinking for a new generation of readers." (Publisher's note)

" Exploring her brother's untimely death while continuing his legacy, Wachs writes with immense love, humor, and humanity. The title references a famous Harris Wittels witticism, one that fits the excruciating reality of loving an addict. Everything about this book is horrible, wonderful, timely, and not to be missed." Booklist

Wizenberg, Molly

    Wizenberg, Molly. A **homemade** life; stories and recipes from my kitchen table. illustrations by Camilla Engman. Simon & Schuster 2009 320p il $25 **92**

    1. Cooking 2. Women authors 3. Cookery 4. Bloggers 5. Food critics
ISBN 1-4165-5105-0; 978-1-4165-5105-8

        LC 2008-36430

"When Molly Wizenberg's father died of cancer, everyone told her to go easy on herself, to hold off on making any major decisions for a while. But when she tried going back to her apartment in Seattle and returning to graduate school, she knew it wasn't possible to resume life as though nothing had happened. So she went to Paris, a city that held vivid memories of a childhood trip with her father. . . . She was supposed to be doing research for her dissertation, but more often, she found herself peering through the windows of chocolate shops. . . . Molly's blog Orangette started out merely as a pleasant pastime. But it wasn't long before her writing and recipes developed [a following]. . . . In A Homemade Life: Stories and Recipes from My Kitchen Table, Molly Wizenberg recounts a life with the kitchen at its center." (Publisher's note) Recipe index.

This "delightful . . . book will undoubtedly be gobbled up like a tin of Christmas cookies." Libr J

Wodehouse, P. G. (Pelham Grenville), 1881-1975

McCrum, Robert. **Wodehouse**; a life. Norton 2004 530p il $27.95   **92**

1. Authors 2. Humorists 3. Novelists 4. Dramatists 5. Short story writers

ISBN 0-393-05159-5

LC 2004-18562

The author "takes the reader from Wodehouse's school days at Dulwich to his successful work as a Broadway lyricist and a master storyteller of Edwardian times who gave us Bertie Wooster and Jeeves to his darkest hour during World War II and final years of semi-exile in America. He offers his most spirited and convincing analysis in countering accusations that Wodehouse knowingly collaborated with the Nazis. . . . This work is thoroughly researched and well written; it will please Wodehouse aficionados and general readers alike." Libr J

Includes bibliographical references

Wollstonecraft, Mary, 1759-1797

Gordon, Charlotte. **Romantic** outlaws; the extraordinary lives of Mary Wollstonecraft and her daughter Mary Shelley. Charlotte Gordon. Random House Inc 2015 672 p. illustrations (hardback) $30; (paperback) $18.00   **92**

ISBN 9781400068425; 1400068428; 9780812980479; 0812980476

LC 2014014841

National Book Critics Circle Award Finalist: Biography (2015)

In this biography of Mary Wollstonecraft and Mary Shelley author Charlotte Gordon "reunites the trailblazing author who wrote 'A Vindication of the Rights of Woman' and the Romantic visionary who gave the world 'Frankenstein'--two courageous women who should have shared their lives, but instead shared a powerful literary and feminist legacy." (Publisher's note)

"Gordon's prose is compelling and her scholarship meticulous; her contention that both women led 'lives as memorable as the words they left behind' is brilliantly supported." LJ

Includes bibliographical references and index

Gordon, Lyndall. **Vindication**; a life of Mary Wollstonecraft. HarperCollins 2005 562p il $29.95   **92**

1. Authors 2. Novelists 3. Essayists 4. Feminists 5. Writers on politics

ISBN 0-06-019802-8

LC 2005-40237

The author "tackles this formidable woman with grace, clarity and much new research. . . . Gordon relates Wollstonecraft's story with the same potent mixture of passion and reason her subject personified." N Y Times Book Rev

Includes bibliographical references

Wood, Grant, 1891-1942

Evans, R. Tripp. **Grant** Wood; a life. Alfred A. Knopf 2010 402p il $37.50; ebook $37.50   **92**

1. Artists 2. Painters 3. Artists -- United States

ISBN 978-0-307-26629-3; 978-0-307-59433-4 ebook

LC 2010-18019

"Evans transforms our view of painter Grant Wood and his all-American paintings, including American Gothic, in a revelatory and heartrending biography of an artist forced to conceal his homosexuality." Booklist

Includes bibliographical references

Wooden, John, 1910-2010

Abdul-Jabbar, Kareem, 1947- **Coach** Wooden and me; our 50-year friendship on and off the court. Kareem Abdul-Jabbar. Grand Central Pub. 2017 290 p. illustrations (hardcover) $29   **92**

1. Friendship 2. Basketball coaches 3. Coach-athlete relationships -- United States 4. Basketball coaches -- United States -- Biography 5. University of California, Los Angeles -- Basketball -- History 6. African American basketball players -- United States -- Biography

ISBN 9781455542253; 9781455542277; 9781455571246; 9781478914754; 9781478914761

LC 2017933519

In this book author Kareem Abdul-Jabbar "explores his 50-year friendship with Coach John Wooden, one of the most enduring and meaningful relationships in sports history. . . . [He] reveals the inspirational story of how his bond with John Wooden evolved from a history-making coach-player mentorship into a deep and genuine friendship that transcended sports, shaped the course of both men's lives, and lasted for half a century." (Publisher's note)

"Abdul-Jabbar and Wooden shared a priceless friendship, and this sensitive, sharply written account brings it to full, vivid life." Booklist

Davis, Seth. **Wooden**; a coach's life. Seth Davis. Times Books 2014 608 p. illustrations (hardback) $35   **92**

1. College basketball 2. Basketball coaches -- United States -- Biography

ISBN 0805092803; 9780805092806

LC 2013020209

This book, by Seth Davis, offers a biography of the University of California, Los Angeles basketball coach John Wooden. "His UCLA teams reached unprecedented heights in the 1960s and '70s capped by a run of ten NCAA championships in twelve seasons and an eighty-eight-game winning streak. . . . Davis shows how hard Wooden strove for success, . . . only to discover that reaching new heights brought new burdens and frustrations." (Publisher's note)

"Davis has avoided stultifying, game-by-game detail (but does offer genuinely exciting accounts of several key games) and has provided a multidimensional, nearly cradle-to-grave portrait of a highly successful and revered coach and teacher, in the process delivering a history of the evolution of college basketball and profiles of many of its stars." Booklist

Includes bibliographical references (pages 327-565) index

Woodhull, Victoria C., 1838-1927

Goldsmith, Barbara. **Other** powers; the age of suffrage, spiritualism, and the scandalous Victoria Woodhull. HarperPerennial 1999 531p il pa $16   **92**

1. Feminism 2. Suffragists 3. Spiritualism 4. Feminists 5. Women -- Suffrage 6. Presidential candidates

ISBN 0-06-095332-2

LC 98-33315

First published 1998 by Knopf

"Victoria Woodhull was a charismatic and notorious figure in the struggle for women's rights in the years following the Civil War. She was the first woman to address Congress and the first woman to run for president. Goldsmith . . . has successfully woven together a history of Woodhull's life with the lives of the powerful she touched." Libr J

Includes bibliographical references

Woods, Tiger

Callahan, Tom. **In** search of Tiger; a journey through golf with Tiger Woods. Crown 2003 245p il $23.95; pa $14 **92**
1. Golfers
ISBN 0-609-60943-2; 1-4000-5140-1 pa

LC 2002-11350

The author "examines Tiger's early years, how he got to the top of his game and his vision for the future. Anecdotes and insider insights highlight portraits of major Tiger victories. . . . This is a comprehensive examination of the man, his talent, his competition and the world of professional golf, a must-read for fans and players alike." Publ Wkly

★ Keteyian, Armen. **Tiger** Woods; Jeff Benedict and Armen Keteyian. Simon & Schuster 2018 512 p. $30 **92**
1. Golf 2. Golfers -- United States -- Biography
ISBN 1501126423; 9781501126420

LC 2018038015

This book, by Jeff Benedict and Armen Keteyian, is "a sweeping, revelatory, and defining biography of . . . [American golfer Tiger Woods. Benedict and Keteyian] look deep behind the headlines to produce a richly reported answer . . . [who really is Tiger Woods. T]hey conducted hundreds of interviews with people from every facet of Woods's life-- friends, family members, . . . coaches, business associates, physicians, Tour pros, and members of Woods's inner circle." (Publisher's note)

"Journalists and coauthors Benedict and Keteyian (both, The System) have deconstructed the carefully crafted movie script that has been Tiger Woods's life." Library Journal

Woods, Tiger, 1975- The **1997** Masters; my story. Tiger Woods; with Lorne Rubenstein. Grand Central Publishing 2017 244 p. color illustrations (hardcover) $30 **92**
1. Golf -- United States 2. Golfers -- United States -- Biography
ISBN 1455543586; 9781455543588; 9781455571512
Includes index.

This book, by golfer Tiger Woods with Lorne Rubenstein, marks "the twentieth anniversary of his historic win at the 1997 Masters. . . . Woods, then only 21, won the Masters by a historic 12 shots, which remains the widest margin of victory in the tournament's history, making it an iconic moment for him and sports. Now, 20 years later, Woods is ready to explore his history with the game, how it has changed over the years, and what it was like winning such an important event." (Publisher's note)

"An in-depth, inside look at the legendary golfer's historic 1997 Masters win." Kirkus

Woolf, Leonard, 1880-1969

★ Glendinning, Victoria. **Leonard** Woolf; a biography. Simon & Schuster 2006 498p il $30 **92**
1. Authors 2. Editors 3. Essayists 4. Memoirists 5. Writers on politics 6. Publishing executives
ISBN 978-0-7432-4653-8; 0-7432-4653-5

LC 2006-49784

This is a biography of the publisher and author of Empire and Commerce in Africa (1920), Village in the Jungle (1926), After the Deluge (1931), Quack, Quack! (1935), Barbarians Within and Without (1939), Sowing (1960), Growing (1961), Beginning Again (1964), Downhill All the Way (1967), and The Journey Not the Arrival Matters (1969).

"Glendinning's generous biography does not ignore that Woolf could be grumpy and was too often cheeseparing, but her account does justice to his range of passions, his literary and political contributions and, above all, his human goodness—he was a man who knew how to live." New Statesman

Includes bibliographical references

Woolf, Virginia, 1882-1941

Briggs, Julia. **Virginia** Woolf: an inner life. Harcourt 2005 527p il $30 **92**
1. Authors 2. Novelists 3. Women authors 4. Essayists 5. Authors, English 6. Short story writers
ISBN 0-15-101143-5

LC 2005-16048

"That this book is a must for Woolf fans goes without saying, but it is also a must for anyone interested in the nature of female consciousness at its most self-aware and the workings of artistic sensibility at their most illuminating." Publ Wkly

Includes bibliographical references

Woolman, John, 1720-1772

Slaughter, Thomas P. The **beautiful** soul of John Woolman, apostle of abolition. Hill and Wang 2008 464p il map **92**
1. Clergy 2. Authors 3. Abolitionists 4. Diarists 5. Essayists 6. Quaker leaders 7. Biography, Individual 8. Slavery and the church -- Society of Friends
ISBN 0-8090-9514-9; 978-0-8090-9514-8

LC 2008-22765

This is a biography of the New Jersey Quaker abolitionist. Index.

"Any understanding of the history of social reform in America begins with Woolman, and understanding Woolman begins here." Kirkus

Includes bibliographical references and index

Worden, Alfred M., 1932-

Worden, Al, 1932- **Falling** to Earth; an Apollo 15 astronaut's journey. [by] Al Worden with Francis French. Smithsonian Books 2011 300p il **92**
1. Astronauts 2. Apollo project 3. Space flight to the moon 4. Air force officers 5. Biography, Individual 6. Apollo 15 (Spacecraft)
ISBN 1-58834-309-X; 978-1-58834-309-3

LC 2011003440

"Worden is eloquent, witty, and brutally honest, still in awe of the company he kept and the history he belongs to. A solid addition to space-literature collections."

"Worden is eloquent, witty, and brutally honest, still in awe of the company he kept and the history he belongs to. A solid addition to space-literature collections." Booklist

Includes bibliographical references

Wordsworth, Dorothy, 1771-1855

Wilson, Frances. The **ballad** of Dorothy Wordsworth; a life. Farrar, Straus and Giroux 2009 316p il map $30 **92**
1. Poets 2. Authors 3. Diarists 4. Poets laureate 5. Travel writers 6. Authors, English
ISBN 978-0-374-10867-0; 0-374-10867-6

LC 2008-41263

First published 2008 in the United Kingdom

"Ms. Wilson focuses primarily on the years 1800-3, when Dorothy, then in her late 20s and early 30s, lived with her brother in the Lake District of England and kept her famous Grasmere Journals, which were not published in full until 1958. They were crucial years, not just for her but also for her brother, who was still writing some of his most important poems, and for Samuel Coleridge, who moves in and out of this book like the third magpie in a bustling nest. Ms. Wilson's decision to limit her scope was a small bit of genius. She's written a succinct yet roomy book, one that moves along with novelistic buoyancy and grace." N Y Times Book Rev

Includes bibliographical references

Wordsworth, William, 1770-1850

Wilson, Frances. The **ballad** of Dorothy Wordsworth; a life. Farrar, Straus and Giroux 2009 316p il map $30   **92**
1. Poets 2. Authors 3. Diarists 4. Poets laureate 5. Travel writers 6. Authors, English
ISBN 978-0-374-10867-0; 0-374-10867-6

LC 2008-41263

First published 2008 in the United Kingdom

"Ms. Wilson focuses primarily on the years 1800-3, when Dorothy, then in her late 20s and early 30s, lived with her brother in the Lake District of England and kept her famous Grasmere Journals, which were not published in full until 1958. They were crucial years, not just for her but also for her brother, who was still writing some of his most important poems, and for Samuel Coleridge, who moves in and out of this book like the third magpie in a bustling nest. Ms. Wilson's decision to limit her scope was a small bit of genius. She's written a succinct yet roomy book, one that moves along with novelistic buoyancy and grace." N Y Times Book Rev

Includes bibliographical references

Wouk, Herman, 1915-

Wouk, Herman. **Sailor** and fiddler; reflections of a 100-year-old author. Herman Wouk. Simon & Schuster 2016 xv, 137 p.p (hardback) $20   **92**
1. American authors -- 20th century -- Biography 2. Authors, American -- 20th century -- Biography
ISBN 9781501128561; 9781501128547; 9781501128554

LC 2015037994

In this memoir, author Herman Wouk "reflects on the life experiences that inspired his most beloved novels. Among those experiences are his days writing for comedian Fred Allen's radio show . . .; enlisting in the US Navy during World War II; falling in love with Betty Sarah Brown, the woman who would become his wife (and literary agent) for sixty-six years; [and] writing his Pulitzer Prize-winning novel, 'The Caine Mutiny.'" (Publisher's note)

"Wouk is jaunty and wise in this sparkling memoir of a well-lived life of literature, fame, and love." Booklist

Includes bibliographical references.

Wright, Frank Lloyd, 1867-1959

★ Huxtable, Ada Louise. **Frank** Lloyd Wright. Lipper\ Viking 2004 251p il (Penguin lives series) $19.95   **92**
1. Architects 2. Nonfiction writers
ISBN 0-670-03342-1

LC 2004-46477

"The eventfulness of the extraordinary life and the refreshing intelligence and craft of the author make this book a pleasure to read. That I found myself on occasion arguing with the text only proves the provocative quality of Huxtable's exploration." N Y Times Book Rev

Secrest, Meryle. **Frank** Lloyd Wright; a biography. University of Chicago Press 1998 634p il pa $20   **92**
1. Architects 2. Nonfiction writers
ISBN 0-226-74414-0

LC 97-51590

First published 1992 in the United Kingdom; first United States edition published 1993 by Knopf

A portrait of a "complex, often contradictory architect. . . . Secrest writes with authority and compassion about Wright's long and turbulent career. Her exhaustive scholarship provides fresh insights into Wright's personality." Libr J

Includes bibliographical references

Wright, James, 1927-1980

Blunk, Jonathan. **James** Wright; a life in poetry. Jonathan Blunk. Farrar, Straus & Giroux 2017 xiii, 496 p.p illustrations (hardcover) $35   **92**
1. Biography 2. American poets -- Biography 3. Poets, American -- 20th century -- Biography
ISBN 9780374717377; 9780374178598

LC 2017003852

This book, by Jonathan Blunk, "explores the . . . life and work [of poet James Wright] with exceptional candor, making full use of Wright's extensive unpublished work--letters, poems, translations, and personal journals. Focusing on the tensions that forced Wright's poetic breakthroughs and the relationships that plunged him to emotional depths, Blunk provides a spirited portrait, and a fascinating depiction of this turbulent period in American letters." (Publisher's note)

"A much-needed, engaging, and discerning biography that should help Wright find a new generation of readers." Kirkus

Includes bibliographical references and index

Wright, Orville, 1871-1948

★ McCullough, David. The **Wright** brothers; by David McCullough. Simon & Schuster 2015 320 p. illustrations, maps $30   **92**
1. Aeronautics 2. Aeronautics -- United States -- Biography 3. Aeronautics -- United States -- History -- 20th century
ISBN 1476728747; 9781476728742

LC 2014046049

In this book, author David McCullough "tells the dramatic story-behind-the-story about the courageous brothers who taught the world how to fly: Wilbur and Orville Wright. On a winter day in 1903, in the Outer Banks of North Carolina, two unknown brothers from Ohio changed history. But it would take the world some time to believe what had happened: the age of flight had begun, with the first heavier-than-air, powered machine carrying a pilot." (Publisher's note)

"McCullough's usual warm, evocative prose makes for an absorbing narrative; he conveys both the drama of the birth of flight and the homespun genius of America's golden age of innovation." Pub Wkly

Includes bibliographical references and index

Wright, Orville. **How** we invented the airplane; an illustrated history. edited with an introduction and commentary by Fred C. Kelly; additional text by Alan Weissman. Dover Publs. 1988 87p il pa $9.95   **92**
1. Inventors 2. Aeronautics -- History 3. Aircraft industry executives
ISBN 0-486-25662-6

LC 87-33037

First published 1953 by D. McKay

This "account by the two inventors . . . covers experiments, discovery of aeronautical principles, construction of planes and motors, first flights, and much more. Also included is a later account written by both brothers." Publisher's note

Includes bibliographical references

Wright, Richard, 1908-1960

★ Wright, Richard. **Black** boy; (American hunger): a record of childhood and youth. foreword by Edward P. Jones. 60th anniversary ed., 1st ed.; HarperCollinsPublishers 2005 419p $24.95; pa $14.95   **92**
1. Authors 2. Novelists 3. Dramatists 4. African American authors 5. Essayists 6. Nonfiction writers 7. Short story writers 8. African Americans -- Social conditions

ISBN 0-06-083400-5; 978-0-06-083400-5; 0-06-113024-9 pa; 978-0-06-113024-3 pa

LC 2005-52698

First published 1945 by World Publishing Company

This autobiographical work concludes with Wright "newly arrived in Chicago in 1927 as a fugitive from the white South that never knew him. [It] relates his nomadic life in Tennessee, Arkansas, and Mississippi, abandoned by his father and with his mother working at menial jobs or incapacitated by illness." Benet's Reader's Ency of Am Lit

Includes bibliographical references

Wright, Wilbur, 1867-1912

★ McCullough, David. The **Wright** brothers; by David McCullough. Simon & Schuster 2015 320 p. illustrations, maps $30 **92**

1. Aeronautics 2. Aeronautics -- United States -- Biography 3. Aeronautics -- United States -- History -- 20th century

ISBN 1476728747; 9781476728742

LC 2014046049

In this book, author David McCullough "tells the dramatic story-behind-the-story about the courageous brothers who taught the world how to fly: Wilbur and Orville Wright. On a winter day in 1903, in the Outer Banks of North Carolina, two unknown brothers from Ohio changed history. But it would take the world some time to believe what had happened: the age of flight had begun, with the first heavier-than-air, powered machine carrying a pilot." (Publisher's note)

"McCullough's usual warm, evocative prose makes for an absorbing narrative; he conveys both the drama of the birth of flight and the home-spun genius of America's golden age of innovation." Pub Wkly

Includes bibliographical references and index

Wright, Orville. **How** we invented the airplane; an illustrated history. edited with an introduction and commentary by Fred C. Kelly; additional text by Alan Weissman. Dover Publs. 1988 87p il pa $9.95 **92**

1. Inventors 2. Aeronautics -- History 3. Aircraft industry executives

ISBN 0-486-25662-6

LC 87-33037

First published 1953 by D. McKay

This "account by the two inventors . . . covers experiments, discovery of aeronautical principles, construction of planes and motors, first flights, and much more. Also included is a later account written by both brothers." Publisher's note

Includes bibliographical references

Wright, iO Tillett

Wright, IO Tillett, 1985- **Darling** days; A Memoir. iO Tillett Wright. HarperCollins 2016 400 p. $26.99 **92**

1. Culture 2. Identity (Psychology)

ISBN 0062368206; 9780062368201

This memoir, by iO Tillett Wright, is an "examination of culture and identity, of the instincts that shape us and the norms that deform us, and of the courage and resilience of a child listening closely to her deepest self. When a group of boys refuse to let six-year-old iO play ball, she instantly adopts a new persona, becoming a boy named Ricky, a choice her parents support and celebrate. It is the start of a profound exploration of gender and identity." (Publisher's note)

" It's unclear how this engagingly reckless soul found the poise to launch a publishing, acting, and writing career; she just seemed to be doing it by her late teens. If Wright can pull it off, there's hope for just about everybody. An earnest and heartfelt memoir cloaked under a battle-toughened exterior." Kirkus

Wyatt, Richard Jed, 1939-2002

Jamison, Kay R. **Nothing** was the same; a memoir. by Kay Redfield Jamison. Alfred A. Knopf 2009 208p $25 **92**

1. Bereavement 2. Psychiatrists 3. Psychologists 4. Hodgkin's disease 5. Manic-depressive illness 6. College teachers

ISBN 978-0-307-26537-1; 0-307-26537-4

LC 2009-11096

"The great gift Jamison offers here, beyond her honesty and the beauty of her writing, is perspective: a clear-eyed view of illness and death, sanity and insanity, love and grief. . . . Jamison seems to be telling the truth, no matter how difficult it may be, in a way that avoids self-pity and inspires courage." Washington Post Book World

Wyeth, Andrew, 1917-2009

Wyeth, Andrew. **Andrew** Wyeth; autobiography. [by] Andrew Wyeth and Thomas Hoving. Bulfinch Press 1999 168p il $29.99 **92**

1. Artists 2. Painters 3. Artists -- United States

ISBN 978-0-8212-2569-1; 0-8212-2569-3

First published 1995

"Each painting is accompanied by commentary from the artist that lends insight into his life and character. Several nude studies are included." Booklist [review of 1995 edition]

Includes bibliographical references

Wyeth, N. C. (Newell Convers), 1882-1945

Michaelis, David. **N.C.** Wyeth; a biography. Perennial 2003 555p il pa $27.95 **92**

1. Artists 2. Painters 3. Illustrators 4. Artists -- United States

ISBN 0-06-008926-1; 978-0-06-008926-9

LC 2003-42876

First published 1998 by Knopf

"Michaelis's work is an outstanding example of the biographer's art. Integrating Wyeth's complex personal and psychological life with his artistic oeuvre, Michaelis creates a portrait of both the artist and the man." Libr J

Includes bibliographical references

Wynette, Tammy, 1942-1998

McDonough, Jimmy. **Tammy** Wynette; tragic country queen. Viking 2010 432p il $27.95 **92**

1. Singers 2. Country musicians

ISBN 978-0-670-02153-6; 0-670-02153-9

LC 2009-42565

"Mr. McDonough is crazy about Wynette but also detached enough to see her clearly, writing with obvious respect for both her life and art. . . . You 'bookish types,' as Mr. McDonough describes his readers, will surely want to listen to her sing on the basis of this book's recommendations. With an emphatic sense of her place in country music—at the top of the heap, casting a shadow big enough to obscure today's woefully synthetic assembly-line singers—he combines a love of her overlooked and minor classics with a compelling big-picture life story. His opinions are often corroborated by the colorfully authentic voices of those who knew her well and marveled at her moxie." N Y Times (Late N Y Ed)

Includes bibliographical references

X, Malcolm, 1925-1965

★ Marable, Manning. **Malcolm** X; a life of reinvention. Manning Marable. Viking 2011 594 p., [16] p. of platesp ill. $30 **92**

1. Black Muslims 2. Black Muslim leaders 3. Civil rights activists 4. African Americans -- Biography 5. African Americans -- Civil

rights
ISBN 978-0-670-02220-5; 0-670-02220-9

LC 2010025768

Pulitzer Prize: History (2012)

This "biography of Malcolm X draws on new research to trace his life from his troubled youth through his involvement in the Nation of Islam, his activism in the world of Black Nationalism, and his assassination." (Publisher's note) Glossary. Bibliography. Index.

This is an "account of the 'lives' of Malcolm X (1925–65), including his years as a street hustler in Boston and Harlem, his time in prison where voracious reading led to his transformation into a the devout follower of Elijah Muhammad's Nation of Islam (NOI), his rise as the NOI's chief minister, and, finally, his split from Elijah Muhammad and his acceptance of all people who would work for African American human and economic rights." Libr J

★ Smith, Johnny. **Blood** brothers; the fatal friendship of Muhammad Ali and Malcolm X. Randy Roberts and Johnny Smith. Basic Books 2016 392 p. illustrations (hardcover: alk. paper) $28.99   **92**
    1. African Americans -- Biography 2. Black Muslims -- Biography
    ISBN 9780465079704

LC 2015043982

In this book, historians Randy Roberts and Johnny Smith "reveal how Malcolm [X] molded Cassius Clay into Muhammad Ali, helping him become an international symbol of black pride and black independence.... Malcolm's death marked the end of a critical phase of the civil rights movement, but the legacy of his friendship with Ali has endured. We inhabit a new era where the roles of entertainer and activist, of sports and politics, are more entwined than ever before." (Publisher's note)

"A page-turning tale from the 1960s about politics and sports and two proud, extraordinary men whose legacies endure." Kirkus

Includes bibliographical references and index

Yang, Bee, 1958-

Yang, Kao Kalia, 1980- The **song** poet; a memoir of my father. Kao Kalia Yang. Metropolitan Books 2016 288 p. (ebook) $60; (hardback) $27   **92**
    1. Hmong poetry 2. Hmong Americans -- Biography 3. Hmong poetry -- Minnesota 4. Songs, Hmong -- Minnesota 5. Singers -- Minnesota -- Biography 6. Fathers and daughters -- Minnesota 7. Refugees -- Minnesota -- Biography 8. Hmong (Asian people) -- Laos -- Biography 9. Hmong Americans -- Minnesota -- Biography 10. Hmong (Asian people) -- Social life and customs
    ISBN 9781627794954; 9781627794947

LC 2015032156

In this book, author Kao Kalia Yang "retells the life of her father, Bee Yang, the song poet—a Hmong refugee in Minnesota, driven from the mountains of Laos by America's Secret War. Bee sings the life of his people through the war-torn jungle and a Thai refugee camp. The songs fall away in the cold, bitter world of a St. Paul housing project and on the factory floor, until, with the death of Bee's mother, they leave him for good." (Publisher's note)

"Yang powerfully demonstrates that much of what society doesn't hold valuable—gifts and talents that don't translate into monetary or educational success—still carry immense value, if only we choose to see it." LJ

Yang, Kao Kalia, 1980-

Yang, Kao Kalia, 1980- The **song** poet; a memoir of my father. Kao Kalia Yang. Metropolitan Books 2016 288 p. (ebook) $60; (hardback) $27   **92**

1. Hmong poetry 2. Hmong Americans -- Biography 3. Hmong poetry -- Minnesota 4. Songs, Hmong -- Minnesota 5. Singers -- Minnesota -- Biography 6. Fathers and daughters -- Minnesota 7. Refugees -- Minnesota -- Biography 8. Hmong (Asian people) -- Laos -- Biography 9. Hmong Americans -- Minnesota -- Biography 10. Hmong (Asian people) -- Social life and customs
ISBN 9781627794954; 9781627794947

LC 2015032156

In this book, author Kao Kalia Yang "retells the life of her father, Bee Yang, the song poet—a Hmong refugee in Minnesota, driven from the mountains of Laos by America's Secret War. Bee sings the life of his people through the war-torn jungle and a Thai refugee camp. The songs fall away in the cold, bitter world of a St. Paul housing project and on the factory floor, until, with the death of Bee's mother, they leave him for good." (Publisher's note)

"Yang powerfully demonstrates that much of what society doesn't hold valuable—gifts and talents that don't translate into monetary or educational success—still carry immense value, if only we choose to see it." LJ

Yazbik, Samar

Yazbek, Samar, 1970- The **crossing**; my journey to the shattered heart of Syria. by Samar Yazbek, translated by Nashwa Gowanlock and Ruth Ahmedzai Kemp, foreword by Christina Lamb. Rider & Co 2016 288 p. (paperback) $16.95 **92**
    1. Syria -- History -- Civil War, 2011- 2. Syria -- Social conditions -- 21st century
    ISBN 9781846044885; 9781846044861; 184604488X

This book tells how author Samar Yazbek "revisited her homeland by squeezing through a hole in the fence on the Turkish border. Here she testifies to the appalling reality that is Syria today. From the first innocent demonstrations for democracy, through the beginnings of the Free Syrian Army, to the arrival of ISIS, she offers remarkable snapshots of soldiers, children, ordinary men and women simply trying to stay alive." (Publisher's note)

Young, Andrew, 1932-

Young, Andrew. An **easy** burden; the civil rights movement and the transformation of America. foreword by Quincy Jones. Baylor University Press 2008 550p il pa $29.95 **92**
    1. Clergy 2. Mayors 3. Nonfiction writers 4. Members of Congress 5. Civil rights activists 6. United Nations officials 7. Nobel laureates for peace 8. United States -- Race relations 9. African Americans -- Civil rights
    ISBN 978-1-602580-73-2

LC 2007-49679

First published 1996 by HarperCollins Pubs.

This memoir focuses on Young's early life as a middle-class African American growing up in segregated New Orleans, his call to the ministry, and his years working with Dr. King and the Southern Christian Leadership Conference.

Young, Matt, 1986-

★ Young, Matt. **Eat** the apple; a memoir. Matt Young. Bloomsbury USA, an imprint of Bloomsbury Publishing 2018 251 p. (hardcover) $26   **92**
    1. Autobiographies 2. United States. Marine Corps -- Biography 3. Iraq War, 2003-2011 -- Personal narratives, American 4. California, Southern -- Biography 5. Marines -- United States -- Biography 6. United States. Marine Corps -- Military life
    ISBN 9781632869500

LC 2017011843

This memoir, by Matt Young, "is a daring, twisted, and darkly hilarious story of American youth and masculinity in an age of continuous war. . . . Young joined the Marine Corps at age eighteen. . . . [He] survived the training and then not one, not two, but three deployments to Iraq, where the testosterone, danger, and stakes for him and his fellow grunts were dialed up a dozen decibels." (Publisher's note)

Young's visceral prose, honed in college and writing programs after his tours of duty, confronts shame, guilt, and pain without flinching yet is beyond sympathetic to its subject; it is another act of service. --Booklist (December 1, 2017)

Young, Steve, 1961-
Benedict, Jeff. **QB**; My Life Behind the Spiral. Steve Young with Jeff Benedict. Houghton Mifflin Harcourt 2016 384 p. (hardcover) $30 **92**
1. Football players 2. San Francisco 49ers (Football team) 3. Football players -- United States -- Biography
ISBN 9780544845763

LC 2016024863

In this sports memoir, "former San Francisco 49er, Super Bowl champion, NFL MVP, and Hall of Famer Steve Young gives readers an unprecedented . . . inside look at what it takes to become a super-elite professional quarterback." (Publisher's note)

Yousafzai, Malala, 1997-
★ Lamb, Christina. **I** am Malala; The Girl Who Stood Up for Education and Was Shot by the Taliban. Malala Yousafzai. Little, Brown and Co. 2013 viii, 327 p.p (hardcover) $26.00 **92**
1. Terrorism 2. Women -- Pakistan 3. Girls -- Education
ISBN 0316322407; 9780316322409

LC 2013941811

Amelia Bloomer Project (2014)

This memoir, by Malala Yousafzai, "is the . . . tale of a family uprooted by global terrorism, of the fight for girls' education, of a father who, himself a school owner, championed and encouraged his daughter to write and attend school, and of . . . parents who have a . . . love for their daughter in a society that prizes sons." (Publisher's note)

"On October 9, 2012, the teenaged Yousafzai was very nearly assassinated by members of the Taliban who objected to her education and women's rights activism in Pakistan. Currently, she lives in England, under threat of execution by the Taliban if she returns home. Lamb, who has been reporting from Pakistan for 26 years and was named Foreign Correspondent of the Year five times, helps Yousafzai tell her hugely significant story." (Library Journal)

Yousafzai, Ziauddin. **Let** her fly; a father's journey. Ziauddin Yousafzai. Little, Brown & Co. 2018 144 p. $25 **92**
1. Parenting 2. Fatherhood
ISBN 0316450502; 9780316450508

In this book, Ziauddin Yousafzai traces his "journey, from an unconfident stammering little boy living in a mud hut in the mountainous region of Shangla to a man who has broken with tradition and proven there are many faces of feminism. . . . Yousafzai describes his life before the Talibanization of Mingora, . . . his progressive partnership with his wife Toor Pekai, and the challenge of raising children in an unfamiliar country." (Publisher's note)

"Yousafzai isn't just a Pakistani diplomat, educator, educational activist, and human rights campaigner; he's also the father of Nobel laureate Malala Yousafzai. Here he explains what he has learned from his daughter" Library Journal

Yousafzai, Ziauddin.
Yousafzai, Ziauddin. **Let** her fly; a father's journey. Ziauddin Yousafzai. Little, Brown & Co. 2018 144 p. $25 **92**
1. Parenting 2. Fatherhood
ISBN 0316450502; 9780316450508

In this book, Ziauddin Yousafzai traces his "journey, from an unconfident stammering little boy living in a mud hut in the mountainous region of Shangla to a man who has broken with tradition and proven there are many faces of feminism. . . . Yousafzai describes his life before the Talibanization of Mingora, . . . his progressive partnership with his wife Toor Pekai, and the challenge of raising children in an unfamiliar country." (Publisher's note)

"Yousafzai isn't just a Pakistani diplomat, educator, educational activist, and human rights campaigner; he's also the father of Nobel laureate Malala Yousafzai. Here he explains what he has learned from his daughter" Library Journal

Yurchyshyn, Anya
Yurchyshyn, Anya. **My** dead parents; a memoir. Anya Yurchyshyn. Random House Inc 2018 336 p. $27 **92**
1. Family 2. Daughters 3. Family secrets
ISBN 0553447041; 9780553447040

In this memoir, author Anya Yurchyshyn, "interrogates her memories of her family and examines what it means to be our parents' children. What do we inherit, and what can we choose to leave behind? How do we escape the ghosts of someone else's past? And can we learn to love our parents not as our parents, but simply as people? Universal and personal; heartbreaking and redemptive, [the book] helps us to see why sometimes those who love us best hurt us most." (Publisher's note)

"An inviting debut that is highly recommended to readers with an interest in memoir, narrative nonfiction, and family history." LJ

Zeitoun, Abdulrahman
Eggers, Dave, 1970- **Zeitoun**. McSweeney's 2009 351p il $24 **92**
1. Hurricane Katrina, 2005 2. Contractors 3. House painters 4. New Orleans (La.) 5. Muslims -- United States 6. New Orleans (La.) -- History 7. Arab Americans -- Social conditions 8. Hurricane Katrina, 2005 -- Social aspects
ISBN 978-1-934781-63-0; 1-934781-63-0

This book is a more powerful indictment of America's dystopia in the Bush era than any number of well-written polemics. N Y Times Book Rev

Includes bibliographical references

Zellner, Robert, 1939-
Zellner, Robert. The **wrong** side of Murder Creek; a White southerner in the freedom movement. [by] Bob Zellner, with Constance Curry; foreword by Julian Bond. NewSouth Books 2008 351p il $27.95 **92**
1. Historians 2. Civil rights demonstrations 3. College teachers 4. Civil rights activists 5. Southern States -- Race relations 6. Student Nonviolent Coordinating Committee
ISBN 978-1-58838-222-1; 1-58838-222-2

LC 2008-25962

"Zellner's memoir focuses on his experiences as a civil rights activist from 1960 to 1967. He tells a story that is sometimes horrific, always interesting, and ultimately inspirational about a white Southerner's commitment to racial justice. . . . This powerful portrait of a courageous man is highly recommended." Libr J

Zevon, Warren
Zevon, Crystal. **I'll** sleep when I'm dead; the dirty life and times of Warren Zevon. foreword by Carl Hiassen. Ecco Press

2007 452p il $26.95; pa $15.95 **92**

1. Singers 2. Rock musicians 3. Songwriters

ISBN 978-0-06-076345-9; 0-06-076345-0; 978-0-06-076349-7 pa; 0-06-076349-3 pa

LC 2006-52138

"Interweaving the remembrances of Zevon's many friends with entries from his own journals, Crystal, his widow, presents an intimate look at Zevon's wild life of drugs, women, and music. Among others, Jackson Browne, Linda Ronstadt, Bruce Springsteen, Carl Hiaasen, Stephen King, and the Everly Brothers, with whom Zevon got his start, share reminiscences. . . . All pop music collections need this book." Libr J

Zhao Ziyang, 1919-2005

Prisoner of the state; the secret journal of premier Zhao Ziyang. translated and edited by Bao Pu, Renee Chiang and Adi Ignatius; foreword by Roderick MacFarquhar. Simon and Schuster 2009 306p il $26 **92**

1. Prime ministers 2. Cabinet members 3. Communist leaders 4. Biography, Individual 5. China -- Politics and government 6. China -- Politics and government -- 1976-2002 7. China -- History -- Tiananmen Square Incident, 1989

ISBN 1-4391-4938-0; 978-1-4391-4938-6

This "memoir produced from tapes the former Chinese premier recorded in secrecy during his sixteen years of house arrest discusses his efforts to stop the Tiananmen Square massacre and the need for China to adopt democratic reforms." (Publisher's note)

"Until the appearance of this posthumous work, not a single voice of dissent had ever emerged from the [Chinese Communist] party's inner circle . . . . Fascinating." Economist

Ziegesar, Peter von

Von Ziegesar, Peter. The **looking** glass brother; Peter von Ziegesar. St. Martin's Press 2013 336 p. (hardback) $25.99 **92**

1. Brothers 2. Mentally ill 3. Authors -- United States -- Biography

ISBN 0312592981; 9780312592981

LC 2013004049

In this memoir, Peter von Ziegesar describes his relationship with his mentally ill stepbrother, also named [Little] Peter. They had been out of touch for decades "when Little Peter surfaced in New York City just before Big Peter's first child was born. As Big Peter tried to figure out how to help recalcitrant and homeless Little Peter, he began facing his own fraught past." (Booklist)

Ziegfeld, Florenz, 1869-1932

Mordden, Ethan. **Ziegfeld**; the man who invented show business. St. Martin's Press 2008 335p il **92**

1. Theatrical producers and directors 2. Theatrical producers 3. Biography, Individual

ISBN 0312375433; 9780312375430

LC 2008028746

This is a biography of the impresario whose Ziegfeld Follies showcased such performers as Fanny Brice, Will Rogers, Eddie Cantor, W.C. Fields, and Marilyn Miller. Index.

"In his witty, well-researched biography of the great producer Florenz Ziegfeld, Mordden discusses Ziegfeld's extraordinary eye for talent and transforming approach to staging musicals." Booklist

Includes bibliographical references

Zierman, Addie

Zierman, Addie. **When** we were on fire; a memoir of obsessive faith. Addie Zierman. Convergent Books 2013 256 p. $14.99 **92**

1. Christians 2. Christian life 3. Autobiographies 4. Christian biography -- United States

ISBN 1601425457; 9781601425454

LC 2013022552

In this memoir, author Addie Zierman "grows up in an average, Bible-studying, Christian family but as a teenager, her zeal for being the perfect, evangelical Christian girl reaches a new level, one that disturbs even her parents. Falling in love with a rigid, similarly zealous, boy named Chris who is bound for mission work doesn't hurt these faith pursuits, and is in fact the reason behind her newfound obsessions with purity and perfect devotion to Jesus." (Publishers Weekly)

Zine, Edward E.

Murphy, Terry Weible. **Life** in rewind; the story of a young courageous man who persevered over OCD and the Harvard doctor who broke all the rules to help him. with Michael A. Jenike and Edward E. Zine. HarperCollins 2009 242p il $24.99 **92**

1. Mentally ill 2. Obsessive-compulsive disorder

ISBN 978-0-06-156153-5; 0-06-156153-3

LC 2008-51240

"Murphy, mother of an OCD patient, recounts the . . . tale of Ed Zine, a man so mired in obsessive-compulsive behavior that he was trapped for six years in his squalid basement, compelled to perform an endless series of rituals meant to stop time and the inevitability of death. . . . Murphy traces Zine's illness from its roots in childhood trauma (his mother's death from cancer) through its full flower, shortly after high school graduation, when it began to take over his life. Unable to get Zine out of his house, leading OCD expert Jenike made the three-hour trip from his Boston office to Zine's Cape Cod home once a week. The bond between them developed slowly and with difficulty, but ultimately proved deeper than either suspected. . . . A passionate, faithful narrative from a reporter who understands the stakes and the people behind them, this is a fascinating, hopeful read." Publ Wkly

Zinn, Howard, 1922-2010

Duberman, Martin. **Howard** Zinn; a life on the left. Martin Duberman. New Press 2012 **92**

1. Historians -- United States -- Biography

ISBN 9781595586780

LC 2012017592

This biography of historian Howard Zinn by Martin Duberman, a "bestselling author . . . political activist . . . lecturer, and one of America's most recognizable and admired progressive voices," details Zinn's life "from the battlefields of World War II to the McCarthy era, the civil rights and the antiwar movements, and beyond." (Publisher's note)

Includes bibliographical references and index

Zombory-Moldovan, Bela, 1885-1967

Zombory-Moldován, Béla. The **burning** of the world; a memoir of 1914. by Béla Zombory-Moldován; translated from the Hungarian by Peter Zombory-Moldovan. New York Review Books 2014 184 p. illustrations, maps (New York Review Books classics) (paperback) $16.95 **92**

1. Hungary -- History 2. World War, 1914-1918 -- Personal narratives 3. Artists -- Hungary -- Biography 4. Soldiers -- Hungary -- Biography 5. Veterans -- Hungary -- Biography 6. Hungary -- History -- 1867-1918 -- Biography 7. World War, 1914-1918 -- Social aspects -- Hungary 8. World War, 1914-1918 -- Personal narratives, Hungarian

ISBN 1590178092; 9781590178096

LC 2014013207

In this memoir, "Hungarian artist Béla Zombory-Moldován was on holiday when the First World War broke out in July 1914. Called up by the army, he soon found himself hundreds of miles away, advancing on Russian lines and facing relentless rifle and artillery fire. Badly wounded, he returned to normal life, which now struck him as unspeakably strange. He had witnessed, he realized, the end of a way of life, of a whole world." (Publisher's note)

"This book is recommended for anyone interested in World War I, war memoirs, and the history of eastern Europe." LJ

Zweig, Stefan, 1881-1942

Prochnik, George. The **Impossible** Exile; Stefan Zweig at the end of the world. George Prochnik. Other Press 2014 408 p. illustrations (hardcover) $27.95 **92**

1. Jewish authors -- 20th century -- Biography 2. Authors, Austrian -- 20th century -- Biography 3. Europe -- History -- 20th century -- Biography

ISBN 1590516125; 9781590516126

LC 2013025383

National Jewish Book Award: Biography, Autobiography, Memoir (2014)

In this book, George Prochnik "examines the life of exiled Austrian writer Stefan Zweig (1881–1942) to shed light on the affliction of exile that redefined the lives and works of many intellectuals during WWII. Perhaps best known for his novellas, Zweig, who was Jewish, fled from his native Vienna and spent time abroad (New York, Rio de Janeiro), but was never able to adjust." (Publishers Weekly)

"Intelligent, reflective and deeply sad portrait of a man tragically cut adrift by history." Kirkus

Includes bibliographical references

920 Biography, genealogy, insignia

Abdul-Jabbar, Kareem

Black profiles in courage; a legacy of African American achievement. [by] Kareem Abdul-Jabbar and Alan Steinberg; foreword by Henry Louis Gates, Jr. Morrow 1996 xxiv, 232p il hardcover o.p. pa $13 **920**

1. Slaves 2. Authors 3. Children 4. Explorers 5. Inventors 6. Abolitionists 7. Sheriffs 8. Colonists 9. Dissenters 10. Memoirists 11. Murder victims 12. Revolutionaries 13. Writers on science 14. Civil rights activists 15. African Americans -- Biography

ISBN 0-688-13097-6; 0-380-81341-6 pa

LC 96-26245

The authors have provided "interesting and nuanced accounts of heroic African Americans whose accomplishments changed U.S. history. . . . Although Abdul-Jabbar is highly critical of past and present racism in the U.S., he gives credit to the abolitionist movement and leaders such as William Lloyd Garrison for their efforts toward ending slavery." Publ Wkly

Includes bibliographical references

Acocella, Joan Ross

Twenty-eight artists and two saints; essays. [by] Joan Acocella. Pantheon Books 2007 524p il $30 **920**

1. Artists 2. Art -- 20th century

ISBN 978-0-375-42416-8; 0-375-42416-4

LC 2006-47266

"Like every great critic, Acocella is subjective, uncompromising. She has a distinct point of view, a refreshingly not-fashionable one—she salutes Sunday-school virtues!—and writes from her conviction that

beneath its hectic, irresponsible, even intoxicated surface, art makes singularly unglamorous demands: integrity, sacrifice, discipline." N Y Times Book Rev

Adams, Maureen B.

Shaggy muses; the dogs who inspired Virginia Woolf, Emily Dickinson, Edith Wharton, Elizabeth Barrett Browning, and Emily Bronte. Ballantine Books 2007 299p il $24.95 **920**

1. Dogs 2. Poets 3. Authors 4. Novelists 5. Essayists 6. Nonfiction writers 7. Short story writers

ISBN 978-0-345-48406-2; 0-345-48406-1

LC 2006-101291

"Despite their different personalities and backgrounds, these writers all had in common dogs that provided stability and consistency in their lives. Each chapter is a minibiography of an author emphasizing and offering anecdotes about the deep bond she shared with her dog. By using diaries, letters, illustrations, and sometimes passages from these women's writings, Adams provides a unique perspective of her subjects as pet owners. A recurrent theme is the comfort the dogs provided. . . . From this unusual vantage point, Adams succeeds in linking these writers' lives in various ways." Libr J

Includes bibliographical references

African American lives; edited by Henry Louis Gates, Jr. and Evelyn Brooks Higginbotham. Oxford University Press 2004 xxvi, 1025p $55 **920**

1. African Americans -- Biography

ISBN 0-19-516024-X

LC 2003-23640

"This work opens multiple fresh vistas on proper African American history. . . . Essential for any serious African American collection." Libr J

Includes bibliographical references

Almanac of Famous People; A Comprehensive Reference Guide to More Than 40,000 Famous and Infamous Newsmakers from Biblical Times to the Present. edited by Kristin Mallegg. 10th ed. Gale / Cengage Learning 2011 2887 p. (hardcover) $280 **920**

1. Celebrities -- Encyclopedias

ISBN 1414445482; 9781414445489

This reference book offers "biographical information on more than 30,000 famous individuals and groups." Entries provide the "subject's best-known name, complete name, nickname, [and] name of group," "dates and places of birth and death," and "nationality and occupation. Most entries include citations to sources that provide additional biographical information." (Publisher's note)

Angelo, Bonnie

★ **First** families; the impact of the White House on their lives. Morrow 2005 336p il hardcover o.p. pa $15.95 **920**

1. White House (Washington, D.C.) 2. Presidents -- United States -- Family

ISBN 0-06-056356-7; 0-06-056358-3 pa

LC 2005-41474

"Relying heavily on the recollections and memoirs of presidential family members, White House staff, and D.C. journalists, this chatty slice of Americana is chock-full of fun First Family facts." Booklist

Includes bibliographical references

Baker, John F.

The **Washingtons** of Wessyngton Plantation; stories of my

family's generational journey to freedom. Atria 2009 419p il $26; (pa) $16 **920**

1. Slavery 2. Plantation life

ISBN 978-1-4165-6740-0; 1-4165-6740-2; 9781416567417

LC 2008-18742

"When Baker was in a seventh-grade social studies class, he saw a photograph of four African Americans in a textbook. Baker later learned from his grandmother that the three men and one woman were ancestors, former slaves of the Washington family of Tennessee. . . . Based on the papers of the Washington family, U.S. census records, period newspaper accounts, interviews with 11 family members, and DNA evidence, Baker's book traces his family from its origin in West Africa through enslavement in Virginia and Tennessee, the Civil War, emancipation and sharecropping, and departure from the rural South for the urban North. He also provides a detailed account of life on the Wessyngton Plantation, once the largest tobacco plantation in the United States. Historians will find this book useful for its examination of rural life in the 19th-century South, and general readers will find a moving story of a family achieving freedom." Libr J

Includes bibliographical references

Ball, Edward

The **sweet** hell inside; the rise of an elite Black family in the segregated South. Perennial 2002 384p il pa $13.95 **920**

1. African Americans -- Biography

ISBN 978-0-06-050590-5; 0-06-050590-7

First published 2001 by Morrow

"The Harlestons of South Carolina were descended from a slave woman and her master, the start of a line of fair-skinned blacks who rose to prominence in the state through commerce, social service, and the arts. . . . [The author] was approached by Edwina Harleston Whitlock, a distant black relative (a sixth cousin, twice removed), to take a storehouse of genealogical material she had about her family and to write its history. The result is a stunning look at a fascinating family and the history of blacks in the U.S. from the 1800s to the 1960s." Booklist

Includes bibliographical references

Barrett, Paul M.

American Islam; the struggle for the soul of a religion. Farrar, Straus & Giroux 2006 304p $25 **920**

1. Islam 2. Biography, Collective 3. Muslims -- United States 4. United States -- Ethnic relations

ISBN 0-374-10423-9; 978-0-374-10423-8

LC 2006-11404

The author presents profiles of seven American Muslims. They include Khaled Abou El Fadi, an Egyptian-born law professor and Islamic scholar at UCLA; Osama Siblani, a secular Lebanese Shiite who publishes a weekly newspaper in Dearborn, Mich.; Siraj Wahhaj, an African American prayer leader, formerly a member of the Nation of Islam, now a Sunni; and "Asra Nomani, a colleague of Mr. Barrett's from The Wall Street Journal, who . . . [criticized] the way American mosques demean women." (N Y Times (Late N Y Ed)) Bibliography. Index.

"In the post-9/11 world Muslims have frequently been stereotyped as monolithically murderous. . . . The heated debates among Muslims themselves about violence committed under the banner of Islam are often drowned out in the fray. Paul M. Barrett's timely and engaging new book brings some of those voices in the United States to life." N Y Times (Late N Y Ed)

Includes bibliographical references

Bates, Stephen

Royalty Inc; Britain's best-known brand. by Stephen Bates. Aurum Press 2015 358 p. illustrations (some color)

(hardcover) $29.99 **920**

1. Monarchy 2. Queens -- Great Britain 3. Great Britain -- Kings and rulers 4. Monarchy -- Great Britain -- History 5. Queens -- Great Britain -- Biography 6. Great Britain -- History -- Elizabeth II, 1952-

ISBN 9781781313565; 9781781314791; 1781313563

LC 2015463235

This book, by Stephen Bates, "will combine a history of the British Crown's evolution thorugh the modern age with a journalistic peek behind the curtain at the machinery that sustains the Windsors today. Written by the Guardian's former Royal correspondent, its line will be neither royalist nor republican." (Publisher's note)

Includes bibliographical references (pages 338-344) and index

Bauerschmidt, Tim

Driving Miss Norma; One Family's Journey Saying "Yes" to Living. Tim Bauerschmidt; Ramie Liddle. Harperone, an imprint of HarperCollinsPublishers 2017 239 p. color illustrations (hardcover) $26.99 **920**

1. Travel 2. Older people 3. Parent-child relationship 4. Terminally ill -- Biography 5. Quality of life -- Philosophy 6. Families -- Travel -- United States 7. Cancer -- Patients -- United States -- Biography

ISBN 9780062664327; 9780062664402; 0062664328

LC 2017019317

"A traveler/retiree's account of the lessons he learned about living well from touring the country with his dying nonagenarian mother. . . . [When author Tim Bauerschmidt] learned that his mother, Norma, was dying of cancer . . ., he accepted the challenge of caring for [her] on the open road. In chapters that alternate between Bauerschmidt's and [his wife Ramie] Liddle's voices, the book follows the trio along a route that took them from Norma's home in Michigan all across America." (Kirkus Reviews)

"Depicting the ageless human capacity to learn and grow, the author celebrates life and offers a heartfelt vision of what dying a good death really means." Kirkus

Bell, Eric Temple

★ **Men** of mathematics; [by] E. T. Bell. Simon & Schuster 1937 xxi, 592p il hardcover o.p. pa $18 **920**

1. Authors 2. Physicists 3. Astronomers 4. Theologians 5. Philosophers 6. Mathematicians 7. Essayists 8. Logicians 9. Memoirists 10. College teachers 11. Writers on science 12. Writers on religion

ISBN 0-671-62818-6 pa

This volume looks at the lives and contributions of 35 pioneers of modern mathematics.

Benfey, Christopher E. G.

A **summer** of hummingbirds; love, art, and scandal in the intersecting worlds of Emily Dickinson, Mark Twain, Harriet Beecher Stowe, and Martin Johnson Heade. [by] Christopher Benfey. Penguin Press 2008 287p il $25.95 **920**

1. Poets 2. Artists 3. Authors 4. Painters 5. Humorists 6. Novelists 7. Abolitionists 8. Women in literature 9. Essayists 10. Satirists 11. Memoirists 12. Travel writers 13. Children's authors 14. Nonfiction writers 15. Short story writers 16. United States -- History -- 1865-1898 17. American literature -- History and criticism

ISBN 978-1-594-20160-8; 1-594-20160-9

LC 2007-36512

"Benfey's subtitle neatly conveys the fascinating and sometimes tortuous complexities of this literary/historical snapshot of post–Civil War America. . . . Benfey finds a common connection among these diverse characters through, improbably, hummingbirds, an intense interest in which seems to have taken hold of artists and writers throughout the late nineteenth century. Benfey's eclectic and original approach brings this period and these personalities vividly to life. He presents sensitive critiques of literature and art alongside tales of illicit love and broken, bent, or triumphant lives, all of which makes for compelling reading for specialist and nonspecialist alike." Booklist

Berkin, Carol

Civil War wives; the lives and times of Angelina Grimke Weld, Varina Howell Davis, and Julia Dent Grant. Alfred A. Knopf 2009 361p il $28.95   **920**
1. Authors 2. Abolitionists 3. Feminists 4. Nonfiction writers 5. Spouses of presidents 6. Spouses of prominent persons 7. Women -- United States -- Biography 8. Married women -- United States -- History 9. United States -- History -- 1861-1865, Civil War -- Women 10. United States -- History -- Civil War, 1861-1865 -- Women 11. Women -- United States -- Social conditions -- 19th century
ISBN 978-1-4000-4446-7
LC 2009-19476
This joint biography of First Lady Julia Dent Grant, Varena Davis, the wife of Confederate President Jefferson Davis, and Angelina Grimké, the abolitionist and feminist who married fellow abolitionist Theodore Weld, contends that "their personal beliefs were overshadowed by the supporting roles they played to their high-profile husbands before unique wartime and personal challenges brought their characters to the foreground." (Publisher's note) Bibliography. Index.
"This finely nuanced, absorbing account makes an important contribution to both Civil War literature and the history of American women." Booklist
Includes bibliographical references (p. 317-345)

Black firsts; 4,000 ground-breaking and pioneering events. [edited by] Jessie Carney Smith. 3rd edition Visible Ink Press 2013 700 p. hardcover $33.95   **920**
1. Blacks -- History -- Encyclopedias 2. African Americans -- History -- Encyclopedias 3. Blacks -- History -- Miscellanea 4. African Americans -- History -- Miscellanea 5. World records -- United States -- Miscellanea
ISBN 1480621153; 9781578593699; 9781480621152
LC 2012034407
This book, edited by Jessie Carney Smith, "collects and celebrates the thousands of world-moving people and hard-to-find facts and accomplishments [by people of African descent] that have helped shape society and culture. It recognizes and honors both renowned and lesser-known barrier-breaking trailblazers in all fields--arts, entertainment, business, civil rights, education, government, invention, journalism, religion, science, sports, music, and more." (Publisher's note)
"This is an excellent resource for starting research on black history, but its sheer volume may be overwhelming to casual researchers. The lesser-known figures, however, make the title worth digging into." LJ
Includes bibliographical references and index

Bond, Jenny

Who the hell is Pansy O'Hara? the fascinating stories behind 50 of the world's best-loved books. [by] Jenny Bond & Chris Sheedy. Penguin Books 2008 318p pa $13   **920**
1. Authorship 2. Authors, English 3. Authors, American
ISBN 978-0-14-311364-5; 0-14-311364-X
LC 2007-39840

"From Stephen King's childhood fascination with gruesome comics to the famous family name behind Peter Benchley, . . . Bond and Sheedy light up some intriguing angles on many popular authors. Journalists in Australia, the authors deliver their 50 profiles with reportorial vigor, moving quickly through each profile while highlighting the salient and salacious details of, for example, the role played by Mary Shelley's literary legacy (daughter of two leading British writers) and her free-love husband (poet Percy Shelley) in the genesis of Frankenstein. . . . Between the engaging information and the range of popular texts (Pride and Prejudice, The Origin of Species, The War of the Worlds, In Cold Blood, Lolita, Roots, The Cat in the Hat, The Da Vinci Code), this affectionate literary history should appeal to many readers." Publ Wkly
Includes bibliographical references

Borneman, Walter R., 1952-

The **admirals**; Nimitz, Halsey, Leahy, and King--the five-star admirals who won the war at sea. Walter R. Borneman. Little, Brown and Co. 2012 559 p. ill., maps $29.99   **920**
1. World War, 1939-1945 -- Naval operations 2. United States. Navy -- Biography 3. World War, 1939-1945 -- Biography 4. Admirals -- United States -- Biography 5. United States. Navy -- History -- 20th century 6. Naval art and science -- History -- 20th century 7. World War, 1939-1945 -- Naval operations, American
ISBN 0316097845; 9780316097840
LC 2011032394
This book, by historian Walter R. Borneman, tells the story of the "[o]nly four men in American history [who] have been promoted to the five-star rank of Admiral of the Fleet: William Leahy, Ernest King, Chester Nimitz, and William Halsey. . . . Drawing upon journals, ship logs, and other primary sources, he brings an incredible historical moment to life, showing us how the four admirals revolutionized naval warfare forever with submarines and aircraft carriers." (Publisher's note)
"Borneman deftly manipulates multiple narrative strands and a wealth of detail. He vividly fleshes out the numerous vain, ambitious men vying for power at the top and examines their important decisions and lasting ramifications." Kirkus
Includes bibliographical references and index

Brighton, Terry

Patton, Montgomery, Rommel; masters of war. Crown Forum 2009 426p il map $30   **920**
1. Generals 2. Marshals 3. Army officers 4. World War, 1939-1945 -- Biography
ISBN 978-0-307-46154-4
First published 2008 in the United Kingdom with title: Masters of battle
"Brighton shows how during the period between the wars, each refined his skills, which included reading one another's published treatises on the subject of mobile warfare. The author pulls no punches in revealing their flaws as well. Very highly recommended." Libr J
Includes bibliographical references

Brower, Kate Andersen

First women; the grace and power of America's modern first ladies. Kate Andersen Brower. HarperCollins 2016 380 p. illustrations (chiefly color) (hardcover) $28.99   **920**
1. Women -- United States -- Biography 2. Presidents' spouses -- United States
ISBN 0062439650; 9780062439666; 9780062439659
This book, by Kate Andersen Brower, presents "an intimate, news-making look at the true modern power brokers at 1600 Pennsylvania Avenue: the First Ladies, from Jackie Kennedy to Michelle Obama. One of the most underestimated—and challenging—positions in the world, the

First Lady of the United States must be many things." (Publisher's note)

"Brower writes with grace and ease and finely outlines the lives of these influential figures, providing deep insights into the experiences of each." LJ

Includes bibliographical references (pages [337]-363) and index.

Browne, David

So many roads; the life and times of the Grateful Dead. David Browne. Da Capo Press 2015 520 p. (paperback) 19.99; (hardcover 30.00   **920**

1. Rock musicians 2. Rock music -- History and criticism 3. Grateful Dead (Musical group) 4. Rock musicians -- United States -- Biography

ISBN 0306824477; 9780306824470; 9780306821707

LC 2016561182

In this book, author David Browne presents the history of the San Francisco-based band the Grateful Dead. "Drawing on new interviews with surviving members and those in their inner circle--along with access to the group's extensive archives and his own research from years of covering the group-- . . . Browne does more than merely delve into the Dead's saga. . . . [E]ach chapter centered on a significant or pivotal day in their story." (Publisher's note)

"This very well-told history of the San Francisco-based band the Grateful Dead, which formed 50 years ago, contains new interviews, including with the living members of the group and some of their earliest fans and associates. This adds a freshness to the narrative." LJ

Burns, Ken, 1953-

★ The **Roosevelts**; An Intimate History. by Geoffrey C. Ward and Ken Burns. Random House Inc 2014 576 p. illustrations $60   **920**

ISBN 0307700232; 9780307700230

LC 2014019251

In this companion book to the PBS series, authors Geoffrey C. Ward and Ken Burns "present an intimate history of three extraordinary individuals from the same extraordinary family--Theodore, Eleanor, and Franklin Delano Roosevelt. . . . All the history the Roosevelts made is here, but this is primarily an intimate account, the story of three people who overcame obstacles that would have undone less forceful personalities." (Publisher's note)

"Starting with Teddy's asthma-plagued youth and ending with Eleanor's death in 1962, every aspect of their lives and legacies is touched upon. Hundreds of photos, newspaper clippings, and accompanying captions flesh out the story, which expands to cover their friends and family, enemies, and (alleged) lovers." Pub Wkly

Includes bibliographical references and index

Cannon, John

The **kings** & queens of Britain; [by] John Cannon and Anne Hargreaves. 2nd ed., rev; Oxford University Press 2009 404p il map (Oxford paperback reference) pa $19.99   **920**

1. Reference books 2. Great Britain -- History 3. Great Britain -- Kings and rulers

ISBN 978-0-19-955922-0; 0-19-955922-8

LC 2009-278738

First published 2001

This book "details the pedigree, birth order, and political legacies of 600 English, Irish, and Welsh regents. . . . Studded with informative black-and-white artifact illustrations, maps, portraits, and family trees, this [is an] extensive quick-reference " Libr J

Includes bibliographical references

Carey, Charles W.

American inventors, entrepreneurs & business visionaries; [by] Charles W. Carey, Jr. Rev. ed; Facts On File 2010 xxi, 455p il (Facts on File library of American history) $95   **920**

1. Inventors 2. Businesspeople 3. Reference books 4. United States -- Biography

ISBN 978-0-8160-8146-2; 978-1-4381-3336-2 ebook

LC 2009-54269

First published 2002

"This biographical dictionary includes profiles of more than 300 individuals who have made significant and lasting contributions to American industry dating from the Colonial era to the present. Each entry addresses the subject chronologically through his or her life, focusing on major professional achievements as well as personal triumphs and tragedies. . . . The book paints a fascinating portrait of American ingenuity. A well-written biographical dictionary that will appeal to anyone interested in the history of American invention and entrepreneurialism." Libr J

Includes bibliographical references

Caroli, Betty Boyd

First ladies; from Martha Washington to Michelle Obama. Rev. and updated ed.; Oxford University Press 2010 xxii, 437p il pa $17.95   **920**

1. Presidents' spouses -- United States

ISBN 978-0-19-539285-2; 0-19-539285-X

LC 2010-14673

First published 1987

In addition to profiling each woman who has served as First Lady the author examines the ways the role has evolved over the years.

Includes bibliographical references

Carr, Jonathan

The **Wagner** clan; the saga of Germany's most illustrious and infamous family. Grove Atlantic 2007 409p $27.50; pa $16.95   **920**

ISBN 978-0-87113-975-7; 0-87113-975-8; 978-0-8021-4399-0 pa; 0-8021-4399-7 pa

"Carr's sprightly, fluent narrative places the family in its historical and intellectual context without reducing it to the symbolic effigy it has often become." Publ Wkly

Includes bibliographical references

Carroll, Sean B.

★ **Brave** genius; two remarkable friends and their unlikely journey from the French resistance to the Nobel prize. Sean B. Carroll. Crown Publishers 2013 576 p. $28   **920**

1. World War, 1939-1945 -- France 2. Nobel Prize winners -- France -- Biography 3. France -- Intellectual life -- 20th century 4. Molecular biologists -- France -- Biography 5. Authors, French -- 20th century -- Biography 6. Authors, Algerian -- 20th century -- Biography 7. World War, 1939-1945 -- Underground movements -- France 8. Politics and culture -- France -- History -- 20th century

ISBN 0307952339; 9780307952332; 9780307952349

LC 2012050707

Author Sean B. Carroll tells how "writer Albert Camus and budding scientist Jacques Monod were quietly pursuing ordinary, separate lives in Paris. After the German invasion and occupation of France, each joined the Resistance to help liberate the country [and] after the war . . . they became friends. [He] tells the story of how each man endured the most terrible episode of the twentieth century and then blossomed into extraordinarily creative and engaged individuals." (Publisher's note)

"A rare chronicle of valiant thinkers fighting political oppression and transcending professional boundaries." Booklist

Includes bibliographical references

Castor, Helen

She-wolves; the women who ruled England before Elizabeth. Harper/Collins 2011 480p il map $27.99; ebook $19.99 **920**
1. Queens 2. Great Britain -- Kings and rulers 3. Monarchy -- Great Britain -- History 4. Great Britain -- History -- Elizabeth, 1558-1603
ISBN 978-0-06-143076-3; 978-0-06-206578-0 ebook
LC 2010013263

The author "recounts the lives of six women who exercised—or tried to exercise—political power in England prior to Elizabeth I: Matilda, granddaughter of William the Conqueror; Eleanor of Aquitaine; Isabella of France; Margaret of Anjou; Jane Grey; and Mary Tudor. . . . Readers of popular history of British royals will enjoy their immensely human stories and applaud the indomitable will of these strong protofeminists." Libr J

Includes bibliographical references

Clay, Catrine

King, Kaiser, Tsar; three royal cousins who led the world to war. Walker & Company 2007 416p il $26.95; pa $16.99 **920**
1. Emperors 2. Kings and rulers 3. World War, 1914-1918 4. Kings
ISBN 0-8027-1623-7; 978-0-8027-1623-1; 0-8027-1677-6 pa; 978-0-8027-1677-4 pa

This is a "biography of not one but three significant men. King George V of England, Kaiser Wilhelm II of Germany, and Tsar Nicholas II of Russia (familiarly known as Georgie, Willy, and Nicky) were more than just the leaders of three of the most powerful countries in the world in the early 20th century—they were cousins who had grown up together, played together, and attended family functions together. . . . [The author] provides an intimate look inside the lives of these boys as they grew into manhood and became king, kaiser, and tsar, bringing new pleasures and details to a well-known subject." Libr J

Includes bibliographical references

Cohen, Rich

Sweet and low; a family story. Farrar, Straus and Giroux 2006 272p il $25 **920**
1. Food industry executives 2. Cumberland Packing Corporation
ISBN 0-374-27229-8; 978-0-374-27229-6
LC 2005-15730

This "is a story peopled with eccentrics and naifs and scoundrels, and a story recounted with uncommon acuity and wit." N Y Times (Late N Y Ed)

Coll, Steve

The **Bin** Ladens; an Arabian family in the American century. Penguin Press 2008 671p il $35 **920**
1. Saudi Arabia -- History
ISBN 978-1-59420-164-6
LC 2007-42748

This "book not only gives us the most psychologically detailed portrait of the brutal 9/11 mastermind yet, but in telling the epic story of Osama bin Laden's extended family, it also reveals the crucial role that his relatives and their relationship with the royal house of Saud played in shaping his thinking, his ambitions, his technological expertise and his tactics." N Y Times (Late N Y Ed)

Includes bibliographical references

Collins, Max Allan, 1948-

Scarface and the untouchable; Al Capone, Eliot Ness, and the Battle for Chicago. Max Allan Collins and A. Brad Schwartz. HarperCollins 2018 704 p. $27.99 **920**
1. Gangs
ISBN 0062441949; 9780062441942
LC 2018024767

In this book, authors Max Allan Collins and A. Brad Schwartz offers a "dual portrait of Al Capone, America's most notorious gangster, and Eliot Ness, the legendary Prohibition agent whose extraordinary investigative work crippled his organization. . . . [The book] delivers . . . the definitive account of the 'Battle for Chicago,' the iconic struggle between the mythic yet real combatants who have captivated the world for 90 years." (Publisher's note)

"The authors' intent is to take two men who have been mythologized over decades, strip away the fictions that have been piled on them, and leave us with a clearer sense of the true Ness and Capone. And they succeed admirably." Booklist

Includes bibliography and index.

Contemporary black biography, v68; profiles from the international black community. Gale Res. 2008 275p il $124 **920**
1. African Americans -- Biography
ISBN 978-1-4144-3275-5; 1-4144-3275-5
Started publication 1992. Editors vary

"Included in each volume are biographies of innovators in the black global community who are currently living and/or who have had a lasting impact on society. Every field of endeavor imaginable is represented, from science, politics, and creative arts to sports. . . . This . . . title will be useful for its coverage of current people in the news who are not as easy to find elsewhere." Booklist

Crush; Writers Reflect on Love, Longing and the Lasting Power of Their First Celebrity Crush. [edited by] Cathy Alter and Dave Singleton. HarperCollins 2016 xv, 253 p.p illustrations $19.99 **920**
1. Essays 2. Celebrities -- United States -- Anecdotes
ISBN 0062399551; 9780062399557
LC 2016016410

This book, edited by Cathy Alter and Dave Singleton, presents "a star-studded collection of essays from acclaimed and bestselling authors and celebrities that illuminates the lasting power of desire and longing, and celebrates our initiation into the euphoria, pain, and mystery that is our first celebrity crush." (Publisher's note)

"The seemingly lightweight premise of an anthology built around celebrity crushes yields an outstanding selection of poignant and thought-provoking stories." Kirkus.

Dance, Stanley

The **world** of Count Basie. Da Capo Press 1985 xxi, 399p il pa $18 **920**
1. Singers 2. Pianists 3. Guitarists 4. Jazz musicians 5. Drummers 6. Flutists 7. Trombonists 8. Band leaders 9. Clarinetists 10. Saxophonists 11. Trumpet players
ISBN 0-306-80245-7
LC 85-12901

A reprint of the title first published 1980 by Scribner

This book "consists of numerous tape-recorded and edited interviews with musicians and vocalists associated with Basie, and each gets to tell his own story. Many overlap and there are interesting confirmations and disputes over details. The language has been polished (and no doubt in some cases cleaned up), but Dance does not noticeably impose

his own views on others. There are good photographs." Choice
Includes discography and bibliographical references

Davis, William C.

Crucible of commmand; Ulysses S. Grant and Rober E. Lee -- the war they fought, the peace they forged. William C. Davis. Da Capo Press, a Member of the Perseus Books Group 2014 xxi, 629 p.p 16 plates; illustrations; maps (hardcover) $32.50   **920**
1. United States -- History -- 1861-1865, Civil War 2. United States. Army -- Biography 3. Generals -- United States -- Biography 4. Confederate States of America. Army -- Biography 5. Generals -- Confederate States of America -- Biography 6. United States -- History -- Civil War, 1861-1865 -- Biography
ISBN 0306822458; 9780306822452
LC 2013497767
This book by William C. Davis examines the lives of Ulysses S. Grant and Robert E. Lee. Exploring their personalities, their characters, their ethical and moral compasses, and their political and military worlds, . . . Davis, one of America's preeminent historians, uses substantial, newly discovered evidence on both men to find surprising similarities between them, as well as new insights and unique interpretations on how their lives prepared them for the war." (Publisher's note)
Includes bibliographical references (pages 593-607) and index

De Lisle, Leanda

The sisters who would be queen; Mary, Katherine, and Lady Jane Grey: a Tudor tragedy. Ballantine Books 2009 xxx, 350p il $30   **920**
1. Queens 2. Courtiers 3. Great Britain -- Kings and rulers 4. Great Britain -- History -- 1485-1603, Tudors
ISBN 978-0-345-49135-0
LC 2009-31074
First published 2008 in the United Kingdom
This is a biography of the Grey sisters, "who were victimized in the notoriously vicious Tudor power struggle and whose heirs would otherwise probably be ruling England today." Publisher's note
Includes bibliographical references

De Waal, Edmund

The hare with amber eyes; a family's century of art and loss. Farrar, Straus and Giroux 2010 354p il map $26   **920**
1. Art collections 2. Bankers 3. Art collectors 4. Magazine executives 5. Patrons of the arts
ISBN 978-0-374-10597-6
LC 2010-25539
"From a hard and vast archival mass of journals, memoirs, newspaper clippings and art-history books, Mr de Waal has fashioned, stroke by minuscule stroke, a book as fresh with detail as if it had been written from life, and as full of beauty and whimsy as a netsuke from the hands of a master carver." Economist

Denlinger, Elizabeth Campbell

Before Victoria; extraordinary women of the British Romantic era. by Elizabeth Campbell Denlinger; foreword by Lyndall Gordon. Columbia University Press 2005 188p il $41.50   **920**
1. Women -- Great Britain 2. Great Britain -- History -- 19th century
ISBN 0-231-13630-7
LC 2004-59267
This book "offers portraits of a group of women who were scientists, artists, writers, poets, philanthropists and reformers during the Romantic

Era and details how their accomplishments changed the social and economic landscape for women." Univ Press Books for Public and Second Sch Libr, 2006
Includes bibliographical references

DeWees, Shelley

Not just Jane; rediscovering seven amazing women writers who transformed British literature. Shelley DeWees. Harper Perennial 2016 320 p. (paperback) $15.99   **920**
1. English women authors -- Biography 2. English fiction -- History and criticism 3. Women authors, English -- Biography 4. Women and literature -- Great Britain -- History 5. English literature -- Women authors -- History and criticism
ISBN 9780062394620
LC 2016001019
In this book on seven British female writers, author Shelley DeWees "weaves history, biography, and critical analysis into a rip-roaring narrative of . . . [Britain's] fabulous, yet mostly forgotten, female literary heritage. . . . Rediscover Charlotte Turner Smith, Helen Maria Williams, Mary Robinson, Catherine Crowe, Sara Coleridge, Dinah Mulock Craik, and Mary Elizabeth Braddon." (Publisher's note)
"In addition to being a lively read, this group biography is an important contribution to the scholarship of women's literature." Booklist
Includes bibliographical references (pages [285]-289)

Dinnage, Rosemary

★ Alone! alone!: lives of some outsider women. New York Review Books 2004 296p $24.95   **920**
1. Women authors 2. Women -- Biography
ISBN 1-590-17069-5
LC 2003-27805
The subjects of this volume of biographical essays include: Gwen John, Stevie Smith, Barbara Pym, Simone Weil, Clementine Churchill, Ottoline Morrell, Dora Russell, Giuseppina Verdi, Olive Schreiner, Helena Blavatsky and Annie Besant; Marie Stopes, Enid Blyton, Angela Brazil, Isak Dinesen, Rebecca West, Margaret Oliphant, Alice James and Katherine Mansfield
"The book is dutifully footnoted and academically solid yet is also beautifully written, marked with great feeling and vivid flashes of insight. It cannot fail to enrich a collection." Libr J

Dray, Philip

Capitol men; the epic story of Reconstruction through the lives of the first Black congressmen. Houghton Mifflin Co. 2008 463p il $30   **920**
1. Reconstruction (1865-1876) 2. African Americans -- Biography 3. United States -- Congress -- House 4. United States -- Politics and government -- 1865-1898
ISBN 978-0-618-56370-8; 0-618-56370-9
LC 2008-11292
"A welcome addition to the literature of the Civil War and Reconstruction Era, and important for students of the civil-rights movement and its origins." Kirkus
Includes bibliographical references

Duberman, Martin B., 1930-

★ Hold tight gently; Michael Callen, Essex Hemphill, and the Battlefield of AIDS. Martin Duberman. New Press, The 2014 368 p. illustrations (hardback) $27.95   **920**
1. Gay men 2. AIDS (Disease) 3. Gay artists -- United States -- Biography 4. Gay singers -- United States -- Biography 5. HIV-positive persons -- United States -- Biography 6. AIDS (Disease)

-- Patients -- United States -- Biography
ISBN 1595589457; 9781595589453

LC 2013039158

Stonewall Honor Book - Nonfiction (2015)

In this book, historian Martin Duberman "attempts to revive AIDS awareness by detailing the early years of the epidemic, particularly the period of 1981-1995. He sets the details within a framework constructed around the experiences of two men: white singer/activist Michael Callen and black poet/cultural worker Essex Hemphill, both of whom lived with AIDS for years and died at age 38." (Publishers Weekly)

"This combination of cautionary tale, history, and dual biography of compelling, if obscure, artist-activists is fluidly written." LJ

Includes bibliographical references and index

Emling, Shelley

Marie Curie and her daughters; the private lives of science's first family. Shelley Emling. 1st ed. Palgrave Macmillan 2012 xx, 219 p.p ill. (hardback) $26.00 **920**

1. Mothers and daughters 2. Women chemists -- Biography 3. Women journalists -- Biography 4. Women philanthropists -- Biography 5. Women scientists -- Family relationships
ISBN 0230115713; 9780230115712

LC 2012005625

In this book, Shelley Emling "tells the story of science icon Marie Sklodowska Curie . . . . Emling writes here of Curie's later years and of her relationships with her daughters . . . . Curie's trips to the United States and her relationship with magazine editor and socialite Missy Meloney, who started a fund to buy radium for Curie, are covered here in both personal and professional terms." (Library Journal)

Includes bibliographical references and index.

Englehart, Murray

AC /DC; maximum rock and roll. [by] Murray Engleheart with Arnaud Durieux. Morrow 2007 488p il $25.95 **920**

1. Rock musicians 2. AC\DC (Musical group)
ISBN 0-06-113391-4; 978-0-06-113391-6

LC 2007-295661

This is a "biography of the wildly successful Australian rockers. Covering everything from guitarist Angus Young's first record purchase (Club A Go-Go by the Yardbirds) to the band's induction into the Rock and Roll Hall of Fame and all points in between, this book is a godsend for fans." Publ Wkly

Includes discography

Evans, Claire L.

Broad band; the untold story of the women who made the internet. Claire L. Evans. Portfolio 2018 288 p. (hardback) $27 **920**

1. Internet -- History 2. Women scientists -- Biography 3. Computer scientists -- Biography 4. Women computer scientists -- Biography
ISBN 9780735211759

LC 2017054620

This book, by Claire L. Evans, features "the women who made the internet what it is today. . . . Seek inspiration from Grace Hopper, the tenacious mathematician who democratized computing by leading the charge for machine-independent programming languages after World War II. Meet Elizabeth 'Jake' Feinler, the one-woman Google who kept the earliest version of the Internet online, and Stacy Horn, who ran one of the first-ever social networks on a shoestring . . . in the 1980s." (Publisher's note)

"From COBOL and ARPANET to Silicon Valley and cyberfeminism, women have always played a major role in developing computer technology. Now their collective stories are finally being shared in Evans' fascinating and inspiring work of women's history." Booklist

Evans, Harold

They made America; [by] Harold Evans, with Gail Buckland and David Lefer. Little, Brown 2004 496p $40; pa $18.95 **920**

1. Inventors 2. Inventions
ISBN 0-316-27766-5; 0-316-01385-4 pa

LC 2003-65954

The author "profiles 70 of America's leading inventors, entrepreneurs and innovators, some better known than others. Along with such obvious choices as Henry Ford, Thomas Edison and the Wright brothers, Evans profiles Lewis Tappan (an abolitionist who dreamed up the idea of credit ratings), Gen. Georges Doriot (pioneer of venture capital) and Joan Ganz Cooney, of the Children's Television Workshop." Publ Wkly

Eyman, Scott

★ **Hank** and Jim; the fifty-year friendship of Henry Fonda and James Stewart. by Scott Eyman. Simon & Schuster 2017 367 p. illustrations (hardcover) $29 **920**

1. Actors -- United States -- Biography 2. Motion picture actors and actresses -- United States -- Biography
ISBN 9781501102172; 9781501102196; 1501102176

LC 2017011527

This book, by Scott Eyman, "tells the story of the remarkable friendship of two Hollywood legends who, though different in many ways, maintained a close friendship that endured all of life's twists and turns. Henry Fonda and James Stewart were two of the biggest stars in Hollywood for forty years. . . . This is not another Hollywood story, but a fascinating portrait of an extraordinary friendship that lasted through war, marriages, children, careers, and everything else." (Publisher's note)

"An entertaining, richly documented biography that will be appreciated by film and theater scholars as well as fans of these memorable actors." Kirkus

Includes bibliographical references (pages 325-348) and index.

Farris, Scott

Almost president; the men who lost the race but changed the nation. Lyons Press 2012 339p il $24.95 **920**

1. Presidents -- United States -- Election 2. United States -- Politics and government
ISBN 978-0-7627-6378-8

LC 2011033001

When the author "lost a 1998 race for Wyoming's at-large congressional district, he was prompted to examine the role losers play in democracy. Farris notes that some unsuccessful White House aspirants have had a far greater impact on American history than many who became president. . . . Moving chronologically through 184 years, he finds past/present linkages as he profiles Henry Clay, Stephen Douglas, William Jennings Bryan, Al Smith, Thomas E. Dewey, Barry Goldwater, George McGovern, Ross Perot, Al Gore, John Kerry, and John McCain. . . . Documenting changes in the face of America and the impact of such issues as race, religion, and workplace reform on elections, Farris writes with a lively flair, skillfully illustrating his solid historical research with revelatory anecdotes and facts." Publ Wkly

Includes bibliographical references

Feather, Leonard

From Satchmo to Miles; new foreword by the author. Da Capo Press 1984 258p il (Roots of jazz) hardcover o.p. pa $16 **920**

1. Blind 2. Singers 3. Pianists 4. Composers 5. Jazz musicians 6. Blues musicians 7. African American musicians 8. Band leaders 9. Saxophonists 10. Pop musicians 11. Flugelhornists 12. Trumpet players 13. Recording producers
ISBN 0-306-80302-X pa

LC 83-15223

First published 1972 by Stein & Day

A collection of profiles of jazz musicians including Count Basie, Lester Young, Oscar Peterson, Ray Charles, Don Ellis, Duke Ellington, Billie Holiday, Ella Fitzgerald, Louis Armstrong, Dizzy Gillespie, Norman Granz, Miles Davis and Charlie Parker.

Feldman, Burton

112 Mercer Street; Einstein, Russell, Godel, Pauli, and the end of innocence in science. edited and completed by Katherine Williams. Arcade Pub. 2007 243p $26 **920**
1. Physicists 2. Scientists 3. Philosophers 4. Mathematicians 5. Essayists 6. Logicians 7. Nonfiction writers 8. Nobel laureates for physics 9. Nobel laureates for literature
ISBN 978-1-55970-704-6; 1-55970-704-6

LC 2007-1194

"During the winter of 1943–1944, Albert Einstein met weekly with three other aging geniuses—philosopher Bertrand Russell, mathematician Kurt Gödel and physicist Wolfgang Pauli—in the study of his home at 112 Mercer Street in Princeton, N.J. . . . What the authors present are illuminating biographical sketches of these men and their earlier, groundbreaking work." Publ Wkly

Includes bibliographical references

Feldman, Noah

Scorpions; the battles and triumphs of FDR's great Supreme Court justices. Twelve 2010 513p il $30 **920**
1. Judges 2. Lawyers 3. Governors 4. Presidents 5. People with disabilities 6. Senators 7. Philatelists 8. Attorneys general 9. Government officials 10. Biography, Collective 11. Presidential advisers 12. Supreme Court justice 13. Supreme Court justices 14. Judges -- United States 15. Regulatory agency officials 16. United States -- Supreme Court
ISBN 978-0-446-58057-1; 0-446-58057-0

LC 2010-07788

The book discusses the period of U.S. Supreme Court history in which "FDR had promised the next Supreme Court seat to Joe Robinson, the Senate majority leader who led the fight for the court-packing bill in Congress. As the plan was collapsing in the Senate, the exhausted Robinson died of a heart attack. Roosevelt nominated Senator Hugo Black for the seat. He was able to appoint eight more justices, including Felix Frankfurter, William O. Douglas, and Robert Jackson, who with Black are generally recognized to be among the Court's greatest judges. These four are the subjects of Noah Feldman's 'Scorpions.' . . . Feldman's . . . book is . . . focused on the members of the Court and their decisions; . . . but also takes more time to explain each judge's distinctive theories of the Constitution and the role of judges in interpreting it." (New York Review of Books)

The author argues "that the 'distinctive constitutional theories' of Roosevelt's four greatest justices, all of whom began as New Deal liberals—Hugo Black, William O. Douglas, Felix Frankfurter, and Robert Jackson—have continued to 'cover the whole field of constitutional thought' up to the present day. . . . This is a first-rate work of narrative history that succeeds in bringing the intellectual and political battles of the post-Roosevelt Court vividly to life." Publ Wkly

Includes bibliographical references

Fenn, Lisa

Carry on; A Story of Resilience, Redemption, and an Unlikely Family. Lisa Fenn. HarperCollins 2016 256 p. $25.99 **920**
1. Journalists 2. At risk students 3. People with disabilities
ISBN 0062427830; 9780062427830

This memoir, by Lisa Fenn, is "about [the] ESPN producer's unexpected relationship with two disabled wrestlers from inner city Cleveland, and how these bonds--blossoming, ultimately, into a most unorthodox family--would transform their lives. Dartanyon Crockett was legally blind as a result of Leber's disease; Leroy Sutton lost both his legs at eleven, when he was run over by a train. Fenn dedicated herself to ensuring their success long after the reporting was finished." (Publisher's note)

"When she filmed the story of two talented high school wrestlers in her hometown, Cleveland, multi-award-winning ESPN producer Fenn didn't just end up with a proclaimed feature (also called Carry On). She also became, in effect, family to the two closely bonded young men, both disabled: Leroy Sutton lost his legs at 11 when he was run over by a train and Dartanyon Crockett, who eventually became a member of the U.S. Judo team at the London Olympics and is gearing up for Brazil, is legally blind." LJ

Firsts; women who are changing the world: interviews, photographs, breakthroughs. portraits by Luisa Dörr. Liberty Street 2017 188 p. illustrations (chiefly color) (hardcover) $22 **920**
1. Women 2. Leadership in women 3. Women -- Interviews
ISBN 1683300688; 9781683300687; 9781547840519

LC 2017941458

This book, by the editors of 'TIME,' "profiles nearly 50 women across a range of endeavors: business, politics, science, technology, sports, entertainment and more. A companion to 'TIME's' multi-platform documentary, the book includes 15 first person deep-dives into the lives of influential women such as General Lori Robinson, the first woman to lead troops into combat . . . and Aretha Franklin, the first woman inducted into the Rock and Roll Hall of Fame." (Publisher's note)

Fraser, Flora

Princesses; the six daughters of George III. Knopf 2005 478p il hardcover o.p. pa $16.95 **920**
1. Queens 2. Princesses 3. Kings 4. Great Britain -- Kings and rulers
ISBN 0-679-45118-8; 1-4000-9669-5 pa

First published 2002 in the United Kingdom

This "is a rich and richly hued Regency tale. . . . Fraser is splendidly at home in the 18th century, adroit at teasing history out from between guarded lines." N Y Times Book Rev

Includes bibliographical references

Gigante, Denise

The **Keats** brothers; Denise Gigante. Belknap Press of Harvard University Press 2011 ix, 499p.p ill., maps **920**
1. Brothers 2. Poets, English
ISBN 9780674048560

LC 2011014487

This book examines the impact of "George [Keats]'s 1818 move to the western frontier of the United States," which "created in John [Keats] an abysm of alienation and loneliness that would inspire the poet's most plangent and sublime poetry. [Author] Denise Gigante's account of this emigration places John's life and work in a transatlantic context . . . while revealing the emotional turmoil at the heart of some of the most lasting verse in English." (Publisher's note)

Gordon-Reed, Annette

★ The **Hemingses** of Monticello; an American family. W.W. Norton & Co. 2008 798p il map $35 **920**
1. Slaves 2. Architects 3. Presidents 4. Vice-presidents 5. Essayists 6. Mistresses 7. African Americans -- Biography
ISBN 978-0-393-06477-3

LC 2008-14642

National Book Award: Nonfiction (2008)

The author tells the story of the Hemingses, an American slave family and their close blood ties to Thomas Jefferson.

"This is a masterpiece brimming with decades of dedicated research and dexterous writing." Libr J

Includes bibliographical references

Gould, Jonathan

Can't buy me love; the Beatles, Britain, and America. Harmony Books 2007 661p il $27.50 **920**
1. Rock musicians 2. Beatles
ISBN 978-0-307-35337-5; 0-307-35337-0

LC 2007-13240

"Gould's combination group biography, cultural history, and musical criticism artfully places the Beatles in their time and social context while examining with great skill how they became an international phenomenon comparable only to themselves." Booklist

Includes bibliographical references

Grant, Colin

The **natural** mystics; Marley, Tosh, and Wailer. W. W. Norton 2011 305p il $26.95 **920**
1. Singers 2. Reggae music 3. Songwriters 4. Percussionists 5. Reggae musicians 6. Wailers (Musical group)
ISBN 0-393-08117-6; 9780393081176

LC 2011-12323

This is a history of the Jamaican reggae group, the Wailers. Bibliography. Index.

"This history of the Wailers, among the first acts to bring reggae to a worldwide audience in the 1970s, doesn't function like most music biographies. Grant . . . resists assembling detailed family trees for the band's prime movers, Bob Marley, Peter Tosh and Bunny Wailer. Nor does he obsess over discography or even dwell much on the musical shifts the trio made as it evolved from playful, syncopated ska to emotionally intense Rastafarian reggae. Instead of writing from a critical remove, Grant freely injects the story with first-person asides about his experiences with interviewees. All these tactics are assets, because they help the author avoid stock band-history patter and instead drill into the broader cultural life of 20th-century Jamaica." Kirkus

Includes bibliographical references

Grant, Gail Milissa

At the elbows of my elders; one family's journey toward civil rights. Missouri History Museum 2008 251p il $24.95 **920**
1. Undertakers 2. African Americans -- Biography 3. United States -- Race relations 4. African Americans -- Civil rights
ISBN 978-1-8839-8266-9; 1-8839-8266-9

LC 2008-24219

"Grant's father, a lawyer and civil rights activist in St. Louis in the 1950s, was among the less well known resisters of segregation, eventually working with more prominent figures, from Thurgood Marshall to Ralph Bunche and A. Phillip Randolph, to fight racial inequities in St. Louis. Grant recalls a long line of family resisters, middle-class business owners who were always on the forefront of the racial divide, challenging Jim Crow laws and practices while sustaining the social and economic underpinnings of the segregated black community. . . . This is a fascinating look at the struggles of one black family that mirrored the national struggle for civil rights." Booklist

Includes bibliographical references

Greenburg, Zack O'Malley, 1985-

3 kings; Diddy, Dr. Dre, Jay Z and hip-hop's multibillion-dollar rise. Zack O'Malley Greenburg. Little, Brown & Co. 2018 320 p. $28 **920**
1. Rap musicians 2. Rap music -- History and criticism 3. Rap (Music) -- Economic aspects 4. Rap (Music) -- History and criticism
ISBN 9780316316538

LC 2017021046

This book, by Zack O'Malley Greenburg, "examines the entrepreneurial genius of the first musician tycoons: Diddy, Dr. Dre, and Jay-Z. . . . Based on a decade of reporting, and interviews with more than 100 sources including hip-hop pioneers Russell Simmons and Fab 5 Freddy; new-breed executives like former Def Jam chief Kevin Liles and venture capitalist Troy Carter . . . '3 Kings' tells the . . . story of the rise and rise of the three most influential musicians in America." (Publisher's note)

"Greenburg details the thinking of these three tastemakers throughout their musical careers and into their corporate identities as they focus on shaping the way people enjoy their lives. Each approached rap music through a different outlet. Each carved out a different lasting mark. And all slowly but intentionally made decisions that impacted the business world on a grand scale. Greenburg offers a refreshing perspective on three immensely talented and popular personalities." (Booklist)

Includes bibliographical references and index

Groom, Winston

The **aviators**; Eddie Rickenbacker, Jimmy Doolittle, Charles Lindbergh, and the epic age of flight. Winston Groom. National Geographic 2013 464 p. (hardback: alkaline paper) $30 **920**
1. Air pilots -- Biography 2. World War, 1939-1945 -- Aerial operations 3. Heroes -- United States -- Biography 4. Air pilots -- United States -- Biography 5. Air pilots, Military -- United States -- Biography 6. United States -- History, Military -- 20th century 7. Adventure and adventurers -- United States -- Biography 8. Aeronautics -- United States -- History -- 20th century 9. Aeronautics, Military -- United States -- History -- 20th century
ISBN 1426211562; 9781426211560

LC 2013015171

This book, by Winston Groom, "tells the saga of three . . . aviators--Charles Lindbergh, Eddie Rickenbacker, and Jimmy Doolittle. . . . [Their] adventures take us from . . . World War I through . . . World War II and beyond, including . . . military raids and survival-at-sea. . . . Groom's . . . narrative tells their intertwined stories--from broken homes to Medals of Honor." (Publisher's note)

"A gripping document of a brilliant era in our history and a few of the men who helped make it so." Kirkus

Includes bibliographical references and index

Gross, Michael

Rogues' gallery; the secret history of the moguls and the money that made the Metropolitan Museum. Broadway Books 2009 545p $29.95 **920**
1. Art -- Collectors and collecting 2. Metropolitan Museum of Art (New York, N.Y.) -- History
ISBN 978-0-7679-2488-7; 0-76792488-6

LC 2008-41480

"A deft rendering of the down-and-dirty politics of the art world."
Kirkus

Includes bibliographical references

The **Grove** book of opera singers; edited by Laura Macy. Oxford University Press 2008 626p il $39.95 **920**

1. Opera 2. Singers

ISBN 978-0-19-533765-5; 0-19-533765-4

LC 2008-17065

"A useful and comprehensive tool for novice and experienced opera researchers alike." Libr J

Haley, Alex

★ **Roots**; the saga of an American family: the 30th anniversary edition. Vanguard Books 2007 899p pa $15.95 **920**

1. African American families. 2. African Americans -- Biography.

ISBN 978-1-59315-449-3; 1-59315-449-6

LC 2007-8822

First published 1976 by Doubleday

This book details Haley's "search for the genealogical history of his family. He describes his trip to Gambia, the African homeland of his ancestors, and recounts the lives of his forebears." Benet's Reader's Ency of Am Lit

Hardesty, Von

Black wings; courageous stories of African Americans in aviation and space history. HarperCollins Publishers 2007 180p il $21.95 **920**

1. African American pilots 2. African American astronauts

ISBN 978-0-06-126138-1

LC 2007-21270

"This book companion to the Smithsonian National Air and Space Museum exhibit of the same name offers a look at the little-known and long-neglected history of black pioneers in aviation. . . . [Along with] the Tuskegee Airmen, Hardesty profiles barnstormers, including the Blackbirds; William J. Powell, founder of an aviation club; military flyers, including Benjamin O. Davis Jr.; and astronauts Guy Bluford, Ronald McNair, and Mae Jemison. This is an inspiring look at the adventurous individuals who pushed against the limits of racial discrimination to realize their passion for flying." Booklist

Includes bibliographical references

Hargittai, Istvan

The **Martians** of science; five physicists who changed the twentieth century. Oxford University Press 2006 xxiv, 313p il map $34.50 **920**

1. Physicists 2. Mathematicians 3. College teachers 4. Writers on science 5. Mathematics teachers 6. Aeronautical engineers 7. Nobel laureates for physics

ISBN 978-0-19-517845-6; 0-19-517845-9

LC 2005-29427

This is a "presentation of the lives of five scientists (physicists and engineers) from Hungary who went to Germany and then to the United States. They . . . [are] Theodore von Karman, Leo Szilard, Eugene P. Wigner, John von Neumann, and Edward Teller. . . . [This book is an] extremely valuable account of the lives of these five brilliant and interesting Hungarian physicists." Sci Books Films

Includes bibliographical references

Haskins, James

African American religious leaders; [by] Jim Haskins and

Kathleen Benson. Wiley 2008 162p il (Black stars) lib bdg $24.95 **920**

1. African Americans -- Religion 2. African Americans -- Biography

ISBN 978-0-471-73632-5; 0-471-73632-5

LC 2007-27347

"It's great to have all these figures between two covers, and even a sampling of the entries captures the importance of religion, and its leaders, in African American life." Booklist

Includes bibliographical references

Heller, Nancy

Women artists; an illustrated history. 4th ed.; Abbeville Press 2003 312p il $39.95 **920**

1. Women artists

ISBN 978-0-7892-0768-5; 0-7892-0768-0

LC 2004-269241

First published 1987

"Organized in six chapters by century, the survey provides brief biographical information, some critical analysis and context, and at least one color plate of the work of 125 women artists who lived and worked in Europe or North America. . . . An excellent resource." SLJ

Includes bibliographical references

Herman, Eleanor

The **royal** art of poison; fatal cosmetics, deadly medicine, filthy palaces, and murder most foul. Eleanor Herman. St. Martin's Press 2018 304 p. (hardcover: alk. paper) $27.99 **920**

1. Murder victims 2. Kings and rulers 3. Poisons and poisoning 4. Poisoning -- Europe -- History 5. Poisoning -- Europe -- Biography 6. Murder victims -- Europe -- Biography

ISBN 9781250140869

LC 2017060759

In this book, author Eleanor Herman "combines her unique access to royal archives with cutting-edge forensic discoveries to tell the true story of Europe's glittering palaces: one of medical bafflement, poisonous cosmetics, ever-present excrement, festering natural illness, and, sometimes, murder." (Publisher's note)

"Murder and scandal always sell, and Herman applies this philosophy to her examination—and frequent exhumation—of history's dubiously dispatched royalty." Booklist

Includes bibliographical references and index

Hutchison, Kay Bailey

American heroines; the spirited women who shaped our country. 1st ed; William Morrow 2004 384p il $24.95; pa $14.95 **920**

1. Women -- United States -- Biography

ISBN 0-06-056635-3; 0-06-056636-1 pa

LC 2004-56677

"Hutchinson's lively, personal writing makes this an accessible and important volume." Booklist

James, Clive

Cultural amnesia; necessary memories from history and the arts. W.W. Norton & Co. 2007 xxxii, 876p il $35 **920**

1. Artists 2. Musicians 3. Philosophers 4. Intellectuals 5. Intellectual life 6. Western civilization

ISBN 978-0-393-06116-1; 0-393-06116-7

LC 2006-36398

The author "not only preserves culture and nurtures humanism but also revitalizes the beauty and power of the English language." Booklist

Kane, Joseph Nathan

★ **Facts** about the presidents; a compilation of biographical and historical information. Joseph Nathan Kane, Janet Podell [editors] 8th ed; Wilson, H.W. 2009 720p $150 **920**
1. Reference books 2. Presidents -- United States
ISBN 9780824210878

LC 2008056016
First published 1959

The main part of this work provides an individual chapter on each President, from Washington through Barack Obama, presenting such information as family, education, election, Vice President, main events and accomplishments of his administration, and First Lady. Part two contains tables and lists presenting comparative data on all the Presidents

Kennedy, John F.

★ **Profiles** in courage. HarperCollins Pubs. 2003 xxii, 245p $19.95; pa $13.95 **920**
1. Judges 2. Courage 3. Lawyers 4. Governors 5. Statesmen 6. Presidents 7. Senators 8. Army officers 9. Political leaders 10. State legislators 11. Members of Congress 12. Newspaper executives 13. Secretaries of state 14. Territorial governors 15. Supreme Court justices 16. Presidential candidates 17. Secretaries of the interior 18. Politicians -- United States
ISBN 0-06-053062-6; 0-06-085493-6 pa

LC 2003-40676
A reissue of the title first published 1956

This series of profiles of Americans who took courageous stands at crucial moments in public life includes John Quincy Adams, Daniel Webster, Thomas Hart Benton, Sam Houston, Edmund G. Ross, Lucius Q. C. Lamar, George Norris, Robert A. Taft and others.

Includes bibliographical references

Kerrison, Catherine

Jefferson's daughters; three sisters, white and black, in a young America. Catherine Kerrison. Ballantine Books 2018 xi, 425 p.p illustrations, map (hardcover: alk. paper) $28 **920**
1. Women -- United States -- History 2. Presidents -- United States -- Family 3. Jefferson, Thomas, -- 1743-1826 -- Family 4. Women -- United States -- History -- 18th century 5. Women -- United States -- History -- 19th century 6. Presidents -- Family -- United States -- Biography
ISBN 9781101886250; 9781101886243

LC 2017043540
This book, by Catherine Kerrison, presents "the remarkable untold story of Thomas Jefferson's three daughters--two white and free, one black and enslaved--and the divergent paths they forged in a newly independent America. . . . [Kerrison] recounts the remarkable journey of these three women--and how their struggle to define themselves reflects both the possibilities and the limitations that resulted from the American Revolution." (Publisher's note)

"Incisive and elegant, Kerrison's book is at once a fabulous family story and a stellar work of historical scholarship." Pub Wkly

Includes bibliographical references and index

Kimball, George

Four kings; Leonard, Hagler, Hearns, Duran, and the last great era of boxing. [foreword by Pete Hamill] McBooks Press 2008 339p il $22.95; pa $16.95 **920**
1. Boxers (Persons) 2. Olympic athletes 3. Boxing -- Biography
ISBN 978-1-59013-162-6; 1-59013-162-2; 978-1-59013-238-8 pa; 1-59013-238-6 pa

LC 2008-13825

The author "resurrects Sugar Ray Leonard, Marvin Hagler, Thomas Hearns, and Roberto Duran from the mists of memory, re-creating the nine bouts the middleweights fought against one another in the 1980s. A great boxing book." Booklist

Includes bibliographical references

Kreisler, Harry

Political awakenings; conversations with history. New Press; distributed by Perseus Distribution 2010 286p pa $17.95 **920**
1. Political activists 2. World history -- 1945- 3. World politics -- 1945-
ISBN 978-1-59558-340-6

LC 2009-36808
"As the director of the Institute of International Studies at the University of California at Berkeley, Kreisler has spent 25 years interviewing hundreds of well-regarded economists, politicians, activists, and artists. In this fascinating collection, he offers 20 of those interviews, focusing on the common theme of how their ideas and perspectives were formulated. . . . Interviews are organized under topical headings, including protest and change, environmental issues, imperialism, resistance through the arts, and human rights." Booklist

Laskin, David

The **long** way home; an American journey from Ellis Island to the Great War. Harper 2010 xxiv, 386p il $26.99 **920**
1. Soldiers -- United States 2. Immigrants -- United States 3. World War, 1914-1918 -- Biography
ISBN 978-0-06-123333-3

LC 2009-28191
The author follows "the lives of 12 American doughboys who had been born in Europe and who then returned there to fight for their adopted country in World War I. It's an imaginative concept, and Laskin mines family legends and official documents to tell the stories of these ordinary foot soldiers from Italy and Ireland, Poland and Russia, Slovakia and Norway." Washington Post

Includes bibliographical references

Lattin, Don

The **Harvard** Psychedelic Club; how Timothy Leary, Ram Dass, Huston Smith, and Andrew Weil killed the fifties and ushered in a new age for America. HarperCollins Publishers 2010 256p il $24.99 **920**
1. Physicians 2. Hallucinogens 3. Psychologists 4. Counterculture 5. Yogis 6. Counter culture 7. College teachers 8. Social reformers 9. Harvard University 10. Nonfiction writers 11. Religious scholars 12. Writers on medicine 13. Writers on religion 14. Alternative medicine practitioners
ISBN 978-0-06-165593-7; 0-06-165593-7

LC 2009-26323
"Mr. Lattin does a lovely, gently humorous job of setting the scene and bringing these men together. . . . This groovy story unfurls . . . like a ready-made treatment for a sprawling, elegiac and crisply comic movie, let's say Robert Altman by way of Wes Anderson." N Y Times (Late N Y Ed)

Includes bibliographical references

Leamer, Laurence

The **Kennedy** men; 1901-1963: the laws of the father. Perennial 2002 882p il pa $19.95 **920**
1. Diplomats 2. Presidents 3. Senators 4. Financiers 5. Political leaders 6. Members of Congress 7. Parents of presidents 8.

Regulatory agency officials

ISBN 978-0-06-050288-1; 0-06-050288-6

First published 2001 by Morrow

This is a biography of Joseph P. Kennedy and his sons from the beginning of the last century through the assassination of John F. Kennedy.

"Leamer's writing is impressive throughout, regularly catching the reader up with a felicitous phrase or a surprising insight." Booklist

Includes bibliographical references

Levingston, Steven

Kennedy and King; the president, the pastor, and the battle over civil rights. Steven Levingston. Hachette Books 2017 xi, 511 p.p illustrations (hardcover) $28   **920**

1. Civil rights -- United States -- History 2. Presidents -- United States -- Biography 3. African American civil rights workers -- Biography 4. United States -- Politics and government -- 1961-1963 5. African Americans -- Civil rights -- History -- 20th century 6. Civil rights movements -- United States -- History -- 20th century

ISBN 0316267392; 9780316267373; 9780316267397

LC 2017302125

This book, by Steven Levingston, "traces the emergence of two of the twentieth century's greatest leaders, their powerful impact on each other and on the shape of the civil rights battle between 1960 and 1963. These two men from starkly different worlds profoundly influenced each other's personal development. Kennedy's hesitation on civil rights spurred King to greater acts of courage, and King inspired Kennedy to finally make a moral commitment to equality." (Publisher's note)

"A dual biography chronicles three years of upheaval in the civil rights movement." Kirkus

Includes bibliographical references (pages 483-489) and index.

Life stories; profiles from The New Yorker. edited by David Remnick. Random House 2000 480p hardcover o.p. pa $15.95   **920**

1. Poets 2. Actors 3. Authors 4. Dancers 5. Comedians 6. Novelists 7. Homemakers 8. Journalists 9. Ballet dancers 10. Choreographers 11. Mathematicians 12. Baseball players 13. Television personalities 14. Essayists 15. Memoirists 16. Screenwriters 17. Sportscasters 18. Game show hosts 19. Mystery writers 20. Talk show hosts 21. Boxers (Persons) 22. College teachers 23. Literary critics 24. Magazine editors 25. Writers on crime 26. Advice columnists 27. Children's authors 28. Magazine executives 29. Short story writers 30. Television producers 31. Television scriptwriters 32. United States -- Biography 33. Spouses of prominent persons 34. Nobel laureates for literature

ISBN 0-375-50355-2; 0-375-75751-1 pa

LC 99-53712

An assemblage of 25 biographical profiles spanning the years 1927 to 1999 "with subjects ranging from Ernest Hemingway and Marlon Brando to a fake prince, a pair of eccentric mathematicians, and Biff the show dog." Booklist

Louvin, Charlie, 1927-2011

Satan is real; the ballad of the Louvin Brothers. Charlie Louvin and Benjamin Whitmer. itBooks 2012 297 p. $22.99   **920**

1. Brothers 2. Musicians

ISBN 0062069039; 9780062069030

This book tells "[t]he tempestuous history of country music's Louvin Brothers, recalled by the younger musical sibling [Charlie]. . . . Here, Charlie . . . recounts the twosome's rise from hardscrabble beginnings in Alabama's cotton country to national fame. Basically self-taught, the brothers were reared on church singing before they launched an uphill

professional career in the '40s. Louvin maps the pair's arduous journey through small-town radio gigs and endless regional touring." (Kirkus)

Louvish, Simon

Monkey business; the lives and legends of the Marx brothers: Groucho, Chico, Harpo, Zeppo with added Gummo. St. Martin's Press 2000 471p il hardcover o.p. pa $13.95   **920**

1. Comedians

ISBN 0-312-28382-2 pa

LC 00-302623

First published 1999 in the United Kingdom

In addition to Groucho, the author "expands the canvas to appraise the contributions of the other brothers, plus Margaret Dumont, a regular target of the brothers' mayhem. . . . Louvish does a solid job of separating fact from fiction and includes a family tree and a discussion of the FBI's file on the group." Libr J

Lucey, Donna M., 1951-

Sargent's women; four lives behind the canvas. Donna M. Lucey. W W Norton & Co Inc 2017 xx, 311 p.p illustrations (some color) (hardcover) $29.95   **920**

1. Women -- United States -- Biography 2. United States -- Biography 3. United States -- History -- 1865-1921 4. Upper class women -- United States -- Biography

ISBN 9780393634785; 9780393079036

LC 2017013987

This biography, by Donna M. Lucey, "based on original letters and diaries, . . . illuminates four extraordinary women painted by the iconic high-society portraitist John Singer Sargent. With uncanny intuition, Sargent hinted at the mysteries and passions that unfolded in his subjects' lives. . . . Like characters in an Edith Wharton novel, these women challenged society's restrictions, risking public shame and ostracism." (Publisher's note)

"Perceptive biographies of a quartet of Gilded Age women." Kirkus

Includes bibliographical references and index

Mackrell, Judith

Flappers; Six Women of a Dangerous Generation. Judith Mackrell. Sarah Crichton Books 2014 480 p. illustrations $28   **920**

1. Women's movement 2. Nineteen twenties 3. Women -- United States -- Biography 4. Sex role -- United States -- History -- 20th century 5. Sex customs -- United States -- History -- 20th century 6. Popular culture -- United States -- History -- 20th century

ISBN 0374156085; 9780374156084

LC 2013035397

Originally published: Great Britain: Macmillan, 2013

This book by Judith Mackrell profiles "six women, Zelda Fitzgerald, Diana Cooper, Nancy Cunard, Tallulah Bankhead, Josephine Baker and Tamara de Lempicka, whose careers as drinking, smoking, jazzing party creatures reached their critical mass in 1925. . . . Mackrell draws an analogy between the experimental freedoms of the Roaring Twenties and those of the Swinging Sixties." (Times Literary Supplement)

"Avidly researched and deeply inquisitive, Mackrell's prodigious group portrait is spectacularly dramatic and thought-provoking." Booklist

Includes bibliographical references and index

MacMillan, Margaret

History's People; Personalities and the Past. Margaret MacMillan. House of Anansi Press 2015 304 p. $24.95   **920**

1. Historians 2. Modern history

ISBN 1487000057; 9781487000059

In this book, author and "historian Margaret MacMillan gives her own personal selection of figures of the past, women and men, some famous and some little-known, who stand out for her. Some have changed the course of history and even directed the currents of their times. Others are memorable for being risk-takers, adventurers, or observers." (Publisher's note)

"Although some of the people MacMillan has chosen are not well-known, their accomplishments are no less important than those well-recognized by first or last name. Her prose is succinct and informative, and even when her transitions from one person to another are not the smoothest, the information imparted is solid. A concise, educational overview of some of the men and women who have carved out spots in the annals of history and why they should be remembered. Fans of the author are in for another treat." Kirkus

Malone, John Williams

It doesn't take a rocket scientist; great amateurs of science. {by} John Malone. Wiley 2002 232p $24.95   **920**
1. Clergy 2. Authors 3. Chemists 4. Novelists 5. Architects 6. Physicists 7. Presidents 8. Scientists 9. Astronomers 10. Vice-presidents 11. Essayists 12. Geneticists 13. Photometrists 14. Microbiologists 15. Writers on science 16. Short story writers 17. Science fiction writers
ISBN 0-471-41431-X

LC 2003-269159

This examines the lives and work of ten amateur scientists, including Gregor Mendel, David H. Levy, Henrietta Swan Leavitt, Joseph Priestley, Michael Faraday, Grote Reber, Arthur C. Clarke, Thomas Jefferson, Susan Hendrickson, and Felix d'Herelle
Includes bibliographical references

Martin, James

My life with the saints. Loyola Press 2006 411p $22.95 **920**
1. Christian saints 2. Priests 3. Spiritual life 4. Biography, Individual
ISBN 0-8294-2001-0

LC 2005-28466

James Martin, SJ, presents his reflections on various saints and also on Dorothy Day and Thomas Merton.

The author "relates how he discovered various 'saints' and how each has affected his life. . . . Despite a theme built on a particular facet of Catholic belief, Martin's animated style and wide-ranging experiences make this a book readers of diverse backgrounds will enjoy." Publ Wkly
Includes bibliographical references

Marton, Kati

The **great** escape; nine Jews who fled Hitler and changed the world. Simon & Schuster 2006 271p il $27   **920**
1. Authors 2. Novelists 3. Physicists 4. Journalists 5. Photographers 6. Mathematicians 7. Jewish refugees 8. Essayists 9. Jews -- Hungary 10. College teachers 11. Photojournalists 12. Writers on science 13. Mathematics teachers 14. Motion picture directors 15. Motion picture producers 16. Nobel laureates for physics
ISBN 978-0-7432-6115-9; 0-7432-6115-1

LC 2006-49162

"By looking at these nine lives—salvaged, and crucial—Marton provides a moving measure of how much was lost." New Yorker
Includes bibliographical references

Hidden power; presidential marriages that shaped our recent history. Pantheon Bks. 2001 414p il hardcover o.p. pa

$14   **920**
1. Presidents -- United States 2. Presidents' spouses -- United States
ISBN 0-385-72188-9 pa

This book provides a "survey of a dozen First Couples, from Edith and Woodrow Wilson to Laura and George Bush. Marton mixes some good history with a lot of pop marriage psychology to show the part that patience, tolerance, insight, determination, sex and occasionally even love have played in the pursuit and exercise of presidential power." Time
Includes bibliographical references

Matuz, Roger

Reconstruction era: biographies; Lawrence W. Baker, project editor. UXL 2004 xxiv, 246p il (Reconstruction Era reference library) $60   **920**
1. Reconstruction (1865-1876)
ISBN 0-7876-9218-2

LC 2004-17300

This "volume covers political and military leaders as well as activists, artists, writers, and more. Among them are Louisa May Alcott, Frederick Douglass, Ulysses S. Grant, and Zebulon Vance. Within each biographical entry are cross-references to other individuals covered in this volume." Booklist
Includes bibliographical references

McBrien, Richard P.

Lives of the popes; the pontiffs from St. Peter to John Paul II. HarperOne 2006 522p il pa $19.95   **920**
1. Popes 2. Papacy
ISBN 978-0-06-087807-8; 0-06-087807-X
A reissue of the title first published 1997
McBrien offers "plenty of historical facts and sobering, valuable judgments." N Y Times Book Rev
Includes bibliographical references

The **Mitfords**; letters between six sisters. edited by Charlotte Mosley. Harper 2007 xxi, 834p il $39.95   **920**
1. Eccentrics
ISBN 978-0-06-137364-0; 0-06-137364-8
"The lost art of letter writing is splendidly portrayed in this massive volume of correspondence among the six Mitford sisters: Nancy, Pamela, Diana, Unity, Jessica, and Deborah. . . . Arranged chronologically covering the years 1925-2002, they include footnotes identifying people, places, and activities. In introductions to each of the nine sections of letters, Mosley provides a synopsis of the major events in each sister's life as well as thoughtful commentary and analysis." Libr J
Includes bibliographical references

Mordden, Ethan

Love song; the lives of Kurt Weill and Lotte Lenya. Ethan Mordden. St. Martin's Press 2012 x, 334 p.p (hardcover) $29.99   **920**
1. Singers -- Biography 2. Composers -- Biography
ISBN 0312676573; 9780312676575; 9781250017574

LC 2012028287

This book by Ethan Mordden is "a dual biography [of composer Kurt Weill and actress Lotte Lenya] that unfolds against the background of the tumultuous twentieth century. . . . The romance of Weill, the Jewish cantor's son, and Lenya, the Viennese coachman's daughter, changed the history of Western music. With Bertolt Brecht, they created one of the definitive works of the twentieth century, The Threepenny Opera, a smash that would live on in musical theatre history." (Publisher's note)

Morgan, Edmund Sears

★ **American** heroes; profiles of men and women who shaped early America. [by] Edmund S. Morgan. W.W. Norton & Co. 2009 278p il $27.95 **920**

1. Heroes and heroines 2. United States -- History -- 1783-1809 3. United States -- History -- 1775-1783, Revolution 4. United States -- History -- 1600-1775, Colonial period

ISBN 978-0-393-07010-1; 0-393-07010-7

LC 2009-714

"This book is a perfect gem. . . . Both specialists and general readers will find this book both authoritative and fun to read." Libr J

Morgan, Robert, 1944-

Lions of the West; heroes and villains of the westward expansion. Algonquin Books of Chapel Hill 2011 xxiii, 497p il map $29.95; ebook $28.95 **920**

1. West (U.S.) -- History 2. West (U.S.) -- Biography 3. United States -- Territorial expansion

ISBN 978-1-56512-626-8; 978-1-61620-119-7 ebook

LC 2011023832

This is a "collection of biographical sketches of 10 men largely limited to the pivotal roles each played in America's westward expansion. Included are four U.S. presidents, Thomas Jefferson, Andrew Jackson, James K. Polk, and John Quincy Adams; orchardist and naturalist John 'Johnny Appleseed' Chapman; frontier legends Davy Crockett and Kit Carson; statesmen Sam Houston and Nicholas Trist; and General Winfield Scott. . . . This collective biography provides a digestible introduction to American expansion, Manifest Destiny, and the larger-than-life men who led the inexorable charge westward." Booklist

Includes bibliographical references

Morrow, Lance

The **best** year of their lives; Kennedy, Johnson, and Nixon in 1948: learning the secrets of power. Basic Books 2005 xl, 312p $26 **920**

1. Presidents 2. Vice-presidents 3. Senators 4. Nonfiction writers 5. Members of Congress 6. United States -- Politics and government -- 1945-1953

ISBN 0-465-04723-8

LC 2005-1836

"The book succeeds in drawing together three fascinating characters into an illuminating historical intersection. You don't have to agree with all of Morrow's interpretations to be entertained by his lively treatment of three crucial figures during an important time in American history." N Y Times Book Rev

Includes bibliographical references

Mortimer, Gavin

The **great** swim. Walker & Company 2008 325p il map $24.95 **920**

1. Women athletes 2. Marathon swimming 3. United States -- History -- 1919-1933

ISBN 978-0-8027-1595-1; 0-8027-1595-8

LC 2008-256

Draws on primary sources, diaries, and family interviews to document the story of four American athletes who in 1926 became the first women to swim the English Channel, in an account that also cites the media frenzy that surrounded their achievement.

"The book can be read as the story of a sporting competition or as an exploration of our timeless fascination with celebrity. Either way, it's an absorbing and inspirational saga in the Seabiscuit mold." Booklist

Includes bibliographical references

Nelson, James Carl

The **remains** of Company D; a story of the Great War. St. Martin's Press 2009 363p il map $25.99 **920**

1. Soldiers 2. Veterans 3. Centenarians 4. Soldiers -- United States 5. World War, 1914-1918 -- Personal narratives 6. United States -- Army -- Infantry Regiment, 28th

ISBN 978-0-312-55100-1; 0-312-55100-2

LC 2009-16931

"This outstanding book paints the portrait of a small military unit, in this case, Company D of the Twenty-eighth Infantry Regiment in World War I. . . . Nelson orients the narrative around his grandfather, who lived to 101 despite serious wounds and awakened Nelson's interest in WWI by what he did not say about his experiences. Nelson set out to tell the Company D story from official records and the documents and reminiscences left behind by dozens of other veterans. . . . [The author] writes so clearly about the background, especially trench warfare, that even readers with minimal WWI knowledge will feel educated as well as fascinated." Booklist

Includes bibliographical references

Nine Irish lives; the fighters, thinkers and artists who helped build America. edited by Mark Bailey; illustrated by Edward Hemingway. Algonquin Books of Chapel Hill 2018 272 p. (trade pbk. original: alk. paper) $16.95 **920**

1. Irish Americans -- Biography 2. Irish -- United States -- Biography 3. Immigrants -- United States -- Biography 4. Ireland -- Biography 5. Heroes -- Ireland -- Biography

ISBN 9781616205171

LC 2017042933

"In this . . . anthology, [edited by Mark Bailey,] nine contemporary Irish Americans present the stories of nine inspiring Irish immigrants whose compassion, creativity, and indefatigable spirit helped shape America. The authors here bring to bear their own life experiences as they reflect on their subjects, in each essay telling a unique and surprisingly intimate story." (Publisher's note)

"Readers interested in getting their Irish on will delight in this collection of essays detailing a variety of significant contributions by Irish immigrants to the history of the U.S." Booklist

Includes bibliographical references and index

9 Irish lives

O'Brien, Keith

★ **Fly** girls; how five daring women defied all odds and made aviation history. Keith O'Brien. Houghton Mifflin Harcourt 2018 368 p. $28 **920**

1. Biography 2. Air pilots -- Biography 3. Women air pilots -- Biography

ISBN 1328876640; 9781328876645

This book, by Keith O'Brien, "recounts how a cadre of women banded together to break the original glass ceiling: the entrenched prejudice that conspired to keep them out of the sky. O'Brien weaves together the stories of five remarkable women. . . . Together, they fought for the chance to race against the men--and in 1936 one of them would triumph in the toughest race of all." (Publisher's note)

"Highly recommended for readers with an interest in aviation history, women's history, cultural history, and 20th-century history." LJ

Oppenheimer, Jerry

The **Kardashians**; an American drama. Jerry Oppenheimer. St. Martin's Press 2017 xxii, 313 p.p illustrations (some color) (hardcover) $27.99 **920**

1. Rich 2. Celebrities -- Biography 3. Reality television programs

-- United States 4. Television personalities -- United States -- Biography

ISBN 9781250087140; 9781250087164; 1250087147

LC 2017017721

This book, by Jerry Oppenheimer, "reveals the untold, definitive story [of the Kardashian family] based on two years of investigative reporting and scores of candid, on-the-record interviews, ranging from childhood friends to powerful business associates, who break their silence for the first time. . . . [T]he [book] . . . will make headlines and shock even the most loyal fans." (Publisher's note)

Includes bibliographical references and index.

Pappu, Sridhar

The **Year** of the Pitcher; Bob Gibson, Denny McLain, and the End of Baseball's Golden Age. Sridhar Pappu. Houghton Mifflin Harcourt 2017 xv, 381 p.p (hardback) $28 **920**

1. Baseball pitchers 2. Baseball -- History 3. Pitchers (Baseball) -- United States -- Biography 4. Baseball -- United States -- History -- 20th century

ISBN 0547719272; 9780547719276

LC 2017044909

This book, by Sridhar Pappu, "is the story of the remarkable 1968 baseball season, which culminated in one of the greatest World Series contests ever, with the Detroit Tigers coming back from a 3-1 deficit to beat the Cardinals in Game Seven of the World Series." (Publisher's note)

"The author effectively interweaves the stories of McLain and Gibson in an engaging fashion, engrossing readers with the rivalry of Detroit and St. Louis." Library Journal

Includes bibliographical references and index

Paul, Richard

We could not fail; the first African Americans in the Space Program. by Richard Paul and Steven Moss. University of Texas Press 2015 274 p. illustrations (cloth: alk. paper) $30 **920**

1. African American astronauts 2. United States. National Aeronautics and Space Administration 3. African American engineers -- Biography 4. African American astronauts -- Biography 5. African American professional employees -- Biography 6. Race discrimination -- United States -- History -- 20th century 7. Discrimination in employment -- United States -- History -- 20th century 8. United States. National Aeronautics and Space Administration -- Rules and practice -- History 9. United States. National Aeronautics and Space Administration -- Officials and employees -- History 10. United States. National Aeronautics and Space Administration -- Officials and employees -- Biography

ISBN 0292772491; 9780292772496

LC 2014030513

In this book, authors Richard Paul and Steven Moss "profile ten pioneer African American space workers whose stories illustrate the role NASA and the space program played in promoting civil rights. They recount how these technicians, mathematicians, engineers, and an astronaut candidate surmounted barriers to move, in some cases literally, from the cotton fields to the launching pad." (Publisher's note)

"Vital and of interest to all Americans, from history and space buffs to students, researchers, and casual readers." LJ

Includes bibliographical references and index

First African Americans in the Space Program

Persico, Joseph E.

Franklin and Lucy; President Roosevelt, Mrs. Rutherfurd, and the other remarkable women in his life. Random House 2008 443p il $28; pa $18 **920**

1. Diplomats 2. Governors 3. Presidents 4. People with disabilities 5. Archivists 6. Columnists 7. Philatelists 8. Humanitarians 9. Social activists 10. Private secretaries 11. Parents of presidents 12. Spouses of presidents 13. United Nations officials 14. Presidents -- United States 15. Spouses of prominent persons 16. Presidents' spouses -- United States

ISBN 978-1-4000-6442-7; 1-4000-6442-2; 978-0-8129-7496-6 pa; 0-8129-7496-4 pa

LC 2007-36851

The author "engagingly and eloquently narrates the tangled relationships between Franklin and the various women to whom he became close. . . . Persico offers what will prove an important, lasting addition to the literature of the Roosevelts." Publ Wkly

Includes bibliographical references

Plutarch

Plutarch: the lives of the noble Grecians and Romans; the Dryden translation; edited and revised by Arthur Hugh Clough. Modern Lib. 1992 2v ea $23.95 **920**

1. Rome -- Biography 2. Greece -- Biography

ISBN 0-679-60008-6 v1; 0-679-60009-4 v2

LC 92-50223

First Modern Library edition published 1932

This work is "arranged mainly in pairs in which a Greek and a Roman are contrasted. His subjects, who include Demosthenes and Cicero, were statesmen or generals. In the process of writing about them, he invents dialogue and describes the emotions of the personages involved." Reader's Ency. 4th edition

Povey, Glenn

Echoes: the complete history of Pink Floyd. Chicago Review Press 2010 388p il $39.95 **920**

1. Rock musicians 2. Pink Floyd (Musical group)

ISBN 978-1-56976-313-1; 1-56976-313-5

First published 2007 in the United Kingdom

"Long time fans will find Echoes a pleasure to read as well as to look at. For the most part, the book has the knowing and reverential feeling of liner notes. But occasionally some mordant humor comes through. . . . A congenital defect of tribute volumes is that they tend to recite band lore that you already know about. For the most part, Povey avoids this tendency and digs up some of the strange bypaths of the band's long history." PopMatters

Includes discography and bibliographical references

Quinn, Bridget

Broad strokes; 15 women who made art and made history (in that order) Bridget Quinn; with illustrations by Lisa Congdon. Chronicle Books 2017 189 p. illustrations (chiefly color) (hardcover) $29.95 **920**

1. Women artists 2. Art and society 3. Art -- History 4. Women artists -- History 5. Women artists -- Biography

ISBN 9781452152363; 1452152365; 9781452152837

LC 2016023856

Author "Bridget Quinn delves into the lives and careers of 15 brilliant female artists in text that's smart, feisty, educational, and an enjoyable read. Replete with beautiful reproductions of the artists' works and contemporary portraits of each artist by renowned illustrator Lisa Congdon, this is art history from 1600 to the present day for the modern art lover, reader, and feminist." (Publisher's note)

"Quinn skillfully examines the lives of an eclectic group of artists and the treatment of their work over time, mixing in comments from art historians and her own personal anecdotes." Pub Wkly Annex

Includes bibliographical references and index.

Rader, Peter

Playing to the gods; Sarah Bernhardt, Eleonora Duse, and the rivalry that changed acting forever. Peter Rader. Simon & Schuster 2018 288 p. $26   **920**

1. Acting 2. Theater 3. Actresses -- Biography

ISBN 1476738378; 9781476738376

This book, by Peter Rader, is "the riveting story of the rivalry between the two most renowned actresses of the nineteenth century: legendary Sarah Bernhardt, whose eccentricity on and off the stage made her the original diva, and mystical Eleonora Duse, who broke all the rules to popularize the natural style of acting we celebrate today." (Publisher's note)

"This entertaining chronicle illustrates how both women captivated audiences and made a lasting impact on the theater." Publishers' Weekly

Rappaport, Helen

The **Romanov** sisters; the lost lives of the daughters of Nicholas and Alexandra. Helen Rappaport. St. Martin's Press 2014 448 p. illustrations (hardback) $27.99   **920**

1. Princesses -- Russia -- Biography -- Sources 2. Sisters

ISBN 1250020204; 9781250020208

LC 2014003159

This book, by Helen Rappaport, presents biographical material on "the four captivating Russian Grand Duchesses--Olga, Tatiana, Maria and Anastasia Romanov. . . . [The book] sets out to capture the joy as well as the insecurities and poignancy of those young lives against the backdrop of the dying days of late Imperial Russia, World War I and the Russian Revolution." (Publisher's note)

"A gossipy, revealing story of the doomed Russian family's fairy tale life told by an expert in the field." Kirkus

Includes bibliographical references and index

Ricks, Thomas E.

Churchill and Orwell; the fight for freedom. Thomas E. Ricks. Penguin Press 2017 339 p. illustrations (hardcover) $28   **920**

1. World politics -- 1933-1945 2. Fascism -- History -- 20th century 3. Communism -- History -- 20th century 4. Authors, English -- 20th century -- Biography 5. Prime ministers -- Great Britain -- Biography 6. Great Britain -- Politics and government -- 1936-1945

ISBN 9781594206139; 9780698164543

LC 2016056757

This book, by Thomas E. Ricks, is "a dual biography of Winston Churchill and George Orwell, who preserved democracy from the threats of authoritarianism, from the left and right alike. . . . No one would have predicted that by the end of the 20th century they would be considered two of the most important people in British history for having the vision and courage to campaign tirelessly, in words and in deeds, against the totalitarian threat from both the left and the right." (Publisher's note)

"In vivid prose, Ricks entwines the biographies of two figures who fought in strikingly different ways to achieve similar goals." Pub Wkly

Includes bibliographical references (pages 275-326) and index.

Roberts, Cokie

★ **Founding** mothers; the women who raised our nation. William Morrow 2004 xx, 359p il $24.95; pa $14.95   **920**

1. Women -- United States -- History

ISBN 0-06-009025-1; 0-06-009026-X pa

LC 2004-042873

"In addition to telling wonderful stories, Roberts also presents a very readable, serviceable account of politics—male and female—in early America. If only our standard history textbooks were written with such flair!" Publ Wkly

Ladies of liberty; the women who shaped our nation. William Morrow 2008 481p il $26.95; pa $15.99   **920**

1. Women -- United States -- History 2. Women -- United States -- Biography 3. United States -- History -- 1783-1865

ISBN 978-0-06-078234-4; 0-06-078234-X; 978-0-06-078235-1 pa; 0-06-078235-8 pa

"While Roberts' aim is to see the period from her subjects' point of view, she is not uncritical; for instance, Roberts casts blame on Mrs. Adams's uncompromising partisanship 'in the undoing of her husband.' With a little-seen perspective and fascinating insight into the culture of the day, this is popular history done right." Publ Wkly

Roiphe, Katie

Uncommon arrangements; seven portraits of married life in London literary circles, 1910-1939. Dial Press 2007 343p il $26   **920**

1. Marriage 2. Women authors 3. Authors, English

ISBN 978-0-385-33937-7; 0-385-33937-2

LC 2007-11798

"Roiphe is at her most insightful—and funniest—in showing us where the declared credo of her characters collides with reality. . . . Often these unorthodox unions endured only because someone was willing to knuckle under." N Y Times Book Rev

Rubin, Louis Decimus

My father's people; a family of Southern Jews. {by} Louis D. Rubin Jr. Louisiana State Univ. Press 2002 139p il $22.50   **920**

ISBN 0-8071-2808-2

LC 2002-454

The author "tells the stories of Hyman and Fannie Rubin, his grandparents, and their seven children. . . . Rubin's descriptions are affectionate, yet he doesn't gloss over their flaws, and as a result, those he knows best come alive for readers." Publ Wkly

Salley, Columbus

The **black** 100; a ranking of the most influential African-Americans, past and present. Columbus Salley. rev ed; Kensington Publishing Corp. 1999 384p il pa $18.95   **920**

1. African Americans -- Biography

ISBN 978-0-8065-1550-2; 0-8065-1550-3

LC 98-47713

A reprint of the title first published 1993 by Carol Publishing Group

The author profiles 100 black men and women and ranks them, based upon his subjective evaluation of their contributions to black American society. They include Dr. Martin Luther King, Jr., Malcolm X, Zora Neale Hurston, Paul Robeson, Muhammad Ali, Arthur Ashe, Toni Morrison, Oprah Winfrey, and August Wilson

Includes bibliographical references

Schiff, Karenna Gore

Lighting the way; nine women who changed modern America. Miramax Books/Hyperion 2006 528p il $25.95; pa $17.95   **920**

1. Women -- United States -- Biography

ISBN 1-4013-5218-9; 1-4013-6015-7 pa

LC 2005-56247

"This is an inspirational collection of biographies of women of various social, ethnic, and racial backgrounds fighting for social justice."

Booklist
Includes bibliographical references

Schonberg, Harold C.

The **great** pianists; rev and updated; Simon & Schuster 1987 525p il hardcover o.p. pa $18   **920**
  1. Pianists 2. Composers 3. Musicians 4. Statesmen 5. Prime ministers 6. Conductors (Music) 7. Classical musicians
  ISBN 0-671-63837-8 pa

LC 87-341

First published 1963
Beginning with the Bach family, the author describes the personal lives and careers of outstanding pianists from the eighteenth century to the present

Scott-Heron, Gil, 1949-2011

The **last** holiday; Gil Scott Heron. Grove Press 2012 384p.   **920**
  1. Music industry 2. Autobiographies 3. African American musicians

LC 97808802129017

"This [book, a posthumously published memoir,] is a . . . testament to the career and achievements of [African-American musician and writer] Gil Scott-Heron. But it is also a . . . personal account of his growing up in the South, a . . . portrait of Stevie Wonder, and a . . . narrative vehicle for Scott-Heron's . . . insights into the music industry, the civil rights movement, modern America, governmental hypocrisy, and our wider place in the world." (Publisher's note)

Sebag Montefiore, Simon, 1965-

★ The **Romanovs**; 1613-1918. by Simon Sebag Montefiore. Alfred A. Knopf 2016 784 p. illustrations $35   **920**
  1. Russia -- Kings and rulers 2. Russia -- History -- 0-1917 3. Russia -- History -- 1613-1917 4. Russia -- Kings and rulers -- Biography
  ISBN 9780307266521

LC 2015046026

This book, by Simon Sebag Montefiore, "is the intimate story of twenty tsars and tsarinas, some touched by genius, some by madness, but all inspired by holy autocracy and imperial ambition. . . . Montefiore's . . . chronicle reveals their secret world of unlimited power and ruthless empire-building, overshadowed by palace conspiracy, family rivalries, sexual decadence and wild extravagance, with a global cast of adventurers, courtesans, revolutionaries and poets." (Publisher's note)

"Montefiore's compassionate and incisive portraits of the Romanov rulers and their retinues, his liberal usage of contemporary diaries and correspondence, and his flair for the dramatic produce a narrative that effortlessly holds the reader's interest and attention despite its imposing length." Pub Wkly
Includes bibliographical references

Shapiro, Laura

What she ate; six remarkable women and the food that tells their stories. Laura Shapiro. Viking 2017 307 p. illustrations (hardback) $27   **920**
  1. Food 2. Dinners 3. Celebrities -- Biography 4. Dinners and dining -- History
  ISBN 9780525427643; 9780698178946

LC 2016057055

This book, by Laura Shapiro, presents "short takes on six famous women through the lens of food and cooking--what they ate and how their attitudes toward food offer surprising new insights into their lives. . . . It's a lively and unpredictable array of women . . . [that] include[s]

Dorothy Wordsworth, . . . Rosa Lewis, . . . Eleanor Roosevelt, . . . Eva Braun, . . . Barbara Pym, . . . and Helen Gurley Brown." (Publisher's note)

"A unique and delectable work that sheds new light on the lives of women, food, and men." Kirkus
Includes bibliographical references (pages 271-298) and index.

Sifters: Native American women's lives; edited by Theda Perdue. Oxford Univ. Press 2001 260p (Viewpoints on American culture) $55; pa $19.95   **920**
  1. Native American women
  ISBN 0-19-513080-4; 0-19-513081-2 pa

LC 00-39950

"From Pocahontas, a Powhatan woman of the seventeenth century, to Ada Deer, the Menominee woman who headed the Bureau of Indian Affairs in the 1990s, the essays span four centuries. Each one recounts the experiences of women from vastly different cultural traditions. . . . Contributors focus on the ways in which different women have fashioned lives that remain firmly rooted in their identity as Native women." Publisher's note
Includes bibliographical references

Singer, Mark

Character studies; encounters with the curiously obsessed. Houghton Mifflin 2005 256p hardcover o.p. pa $13.95   **920**
  1. Actors 2. Educators 3. Magicians 4. Eccentrics and eccentricities 5. Collectors 6. Book collectors 7. Hotel executives 8. Airline executives 9. Purchasing managers 10. Real estate developers 11. Motion picture directors 12. Construction industry executives
  ISBN 0-618-77363-0 pa

LC 2004-62757

This is a "mix of . . . [the author's] portraits from The New Yorker, gathered in book form for the first time. In the essays he trains his skills on the likes of Martin Scorsese and Donald Trump; The Wednesday Group, the self-selected intelligentsia of El Paso; well-known bibliophile Michael Zinman; high-powered women who decide to quit the fast track; and Richard Seiverling, a Tom Mix fan determined to preserve the memory of the movie cowboy. It's quite a cast of characters, and Singer lavishly gives them all their due." Libr J

Smith, Andrew

Moondust; in search of the men who fell to earth. Fourth Estate 2005 372p il $24.95; pa $14.95   **920**
  1. Astronauts 2. Apollo project
  ISBN 0-00-71554-17; 978-0-00-715541-5; 0-00-715542-5 pa; 978-0-00-715542-2 pa

LC 2005-40081

This book describes the lives of nine astronauts after they walked on the moon.
"In an artful blend of memoir and popular history, Smith makes flesh-and-blood people out of icons and reveals the tenderness of his own heart." Publ Wkly
Includes bibliographical references

Soud, David

★ **Kings** & queens of Great Britain; every question answered. David Soud. Thunder Bay Press 2014 400 p. illustrations (chiefly color) (hardcover: alk. paper) $24.95   **920**
  1. Monarchy 2. Queens -- Great Britain 3. Great Britain -- Kings and rulers 4. Queens -- Great Britain -- Biography 5. Great Britain -- Kings and rulers -- Biography
  ISBN 9781626862715; 1626862354; 9781626862357

LC 2014003719

This book, by David Soud, presents "biographies of the British monarchs from the time of Roman Britannia to the present day. . . . Details of the kings' and queens' personalities are the focus, with a timeline across the bottom relating the major events of their reigns. Also included is a section devoted to royal edicts." (Publisher's note)

Includes bibliographical references and index

Spera, Keith

Groove interrupted; loss, renewal, and the music of New Orleans. St. Martin's Press 2011 260p $26.99   **920**

1. Musicians 2. Hurricane Katrina, 2005 3. Music -- New Orleans (La.)

ISBN 978-0-312-55225-1; 0-312-55225-4

LC 2011-10122

This look at the music community "of New Orleans is a collection of profiles of individual musicians who all had their ability to make music threatened after Hurricane Katrina in 2005. . . . many of the stories presented here had their origin in Spera's articles written before and after Katrina. All of them show how artists as varied as blues guitarist Clarence 'Gatemouth' Brown, jazz trumpeter Terence Blanchard, heavy metal singer Phil Anselmo of Pantera, and New Orleans legends Fats Domino and Allen Toussaint tried 'to make sense of the storm through music, comforting themselves and uplifting those around them.' Some of the finest profiles—and there is no weak one in the book—detail a combination of sadness and joy, such as Aaron Neville's triumphant return to the city after the death of his wife to close out the 2008 New Orleans Jazz & Heritage Festival." Publ Wkly

Spitz, Bob

★ The **Beatles**: the biography. Little, Brown 2005 983p il hardcover o.p. pa $17.99   **920**

1. Rock musicians 2. Beatles

ISBN 0-316-80352-9; 0-316-01331-5 pa

LC 2005-3838

This "beautifully written chronicle breathes new life into the familiar story of the Liverpool boys who conquered the world and became . . . the most influential entertainers of the past century. The author's passion for his subject, and for every nuance of every scene, electrifies even the most familiar moments in the legend." N Y Times Book Rev

Includes discography and bibliographical references

Stark, Steven D.

Meet the Beatles; a cultural history of the band that shook youth, gender, and the world. HarperEntertainment 2005 344p il $26.95; pa $14.95   **920**

1. Rock musicians 2. Beatles

ISBN 0-06-000892-X; 0-06-000893-8 pa

LC 2004-59794

In this biography of the Beatles, the author focuses "as much on the cultural trends that produced the Beatles—and the trends they created—as on the Fab Four themselves. . . . Throughout, Stark is sharp and insightful, even when he wades into the psychoanalytic waters of the John/Yoko and Paul/Linda relationships." Publ Wkly

Stolen voices; young people's war diaries from World War I to Iraq. edited with commentaries by Zlata Filipovic and Melanie Challenger; foreword by Olara A. Otunnu. Penguin 2007 xxiii, 293p il pa $14   **920**

1. Children and war

ISBN 978-0-14-303871-9; 0-14-303871-0

The editors have "compiled 14 diaries that were kept by children during wartime, from World War I to Iraq. Their poignant voices will break your heart." Libr J

Strathern, Paul

The **artist,** the philosopher, and the warrior; the intersecting lives of da Vinci, Machiavelli, and Borgia and the world they shaped. Bantam Books 2009 xxiii, 456p il map $30   **920**

1. Artists 2. Authors 3. Painters 4. Statesmen 5. Dramatists 6. Scientists 7. Renaissance 8. Heads of state 9. Writers on science 10. Writers on politics 11. Italy -- History -- 0-1559 12. Political and social philosophers

ISBN 978-0-553-80752-3

LC 2009-6950

Strathern "does for Machiavelli and da Vinci what he does for Borgia: creates a flesh-and-blood portrait for each that defies historical stereotype. Using his novelist's eye and a historian's sweep, Strathern conveys the emotional subtleties that animated their lives. It's no small feat that he makes you care deeply for these complex figures who lived half a millennium ago." Washington Post

Includes bibliographical references

Strauss, Neil

Everyone loves you when you're dead; journeys into fame and madness. It Books 2011 507p il pa $16.99   **920**

1. Celebrities 2. Rock musicians

ISBN 978-0-06-154367-8

LC 2010-52255

"By his own count, the author has conducted some 3,000 interviews with the famous, not-so-famous, used-to-be-famous and ought-to-be-famous denizens of popular culture. Here he brings together the best of these interviews in loosely and at times bizarrely connected chapters. All the well-knowns are here, including Madonna, Lady Gaga, David Bowie, The Who, Kenny G, Led Zeppelin, Puffy Combs and Bo Diddley. . . . Gonzo interviewing at its best." Kirkus

Szegedy-Maszák, Marianne

I kiss your hands many times; hearts, souls, and wars in Hungary. Marianne Szegedy-Maszak. Spiegel & Grau, an imprint of The Random House Publishing Group 2013 400 p. $27   **920**

1. Holocaust, 1939-1945 2. World War, 1939-1945 -- Hungary 3. Hungary -- Biography 4. Jews -- Hungary -- Biography 5. Holocaust, Jewish (1939-1945) -- Hungary 6. Hungarians -- United States -- Biography

ISBN 0385524854; 9780385524858; 9780679645221

LC 2012043179

"This . . . family history weaves together the lives of journalist [Marianne] Szegedy-Maszák's parents . . . with the fate of their native Hungary during and after WWII. The author's father, Aladár, was a Gentile civil servant in the Hungarian Foreign Ministry, whereas her mother, Hanna, came from a family of Jewish industrialists who converted to Christianity. Aladár and Hanna's romance . . . continues to grow even after Aladár is shipped off to the Dachau concentration camp." (Publishers Weekly)

Includes bibliographical references

Taraborrelli, J. Randy

After Camelot; an intimate history of the Kennedy family, 1968 to the present. J. Randy Taraborrelli. Grand Central Pub. 2012 602 p.   **920**

1. Kennedy family 2. Presidents' spouses -- United States 3. Presidents -- United States -- Family

ISBN 9780446553902

LC 2011029518

For this book, which "document[s] America's "royal family,"" . . . [J. Randy Taraborrelli] conducted interviews with [Kennedy] family members and their intimates, such people as Eunice Kennedy Shriver, Oleg Cassini, Robert McNamara, Pierre Salinger, Arthur Schlesinger Jr., and numerous confidential sources. He also relied heavily on the 40 years of personal correspondence between Jackie Kennedy and Lady Bird Johnson. . . . [The book offers] a . . . view of family dynamics in crises both public and private: financial negotiations before Jackie's marriage to Onassis; family interference in Pat Kennedy and Peter Lawford's troubled marriage; Ted Kennedy's bad behavior at Chappaquiddick, and his support of Caroline's abortive Senate run to carry on the 'family dynasty.'" (Publishers Weekly)

Includes bibliographical references and index

Jackie, Janet & Lee; the secret lives of Janet Auchincloss and her daughters, Jacqueline Kennedy Onassis and Lee Radziwill. J. Randy Taraborrelli. St. Martin's Press 2018 514 p. illustrations (some color) (hardcover) $29.99   **920**
  1. Mothers and daughters -- United States 2. Presidents' spouses -- United States -- Biography 3. Celebrities -- United States -- Biography
  ISBN 9781250128034; 9781250128010
                             LC 2017036190

This book, by J. Randy Taraborrelli, presents a "biography of three of the most glamorous women of the 20th Century: Jacqueline Bouvier Kennedy Onassis, her mother Janet Lee Auchincloss, and her sister, Princess Lee Radziwill. . . . Based on hundreds of new interviews with friends and family of the Bouviers, . . . Taraborrelli paints an extraordinary psychological portrait of two famous sisters and their ferociously ambitious mother." (Publisher's note)

Includes bibliographical references (pages [461]-494) and index.

Thomas, Robert McG.
  52 McGs; the best obituaries from legendary New York Times writer Robert McG. Thomas Jr. edited by Chris Calhoun; foreword by Thomas Mallon. Scribner 2001 192p il hardcover o.p. pa $14.95   **920**
  1. Obituaries
  ISBN 1-4165-9827-8 pa
                             LC 2001-42952

"This highly browsable collection of 52 obits shows Thomas at his deadline best." Publ Wkly

Tillyard, Stella K.
  A **royal** affair; George III and his scandalous siblings. [by] Stella Tillyard. Random House 2006 xxiv, 352p il $26.95 **920**
  1. Kings 2. Great Britain -- Kings and rulers
  ISBN 978-1-4000-6371-0; 1-4000-6371-X
                             LC 2006-45130

This biography examines the life of King George III of Great Britain and his siblings.

"This riveting account reminds us that in the past, the misdemeanors of royals had serious, not simply gossip-rag, implications." Booklist

Includes bibliographical references

Tinniswood, Adrian
  The **Verneys;** a true story of love, war, and madness in seventeenth-century England. Riverhead Books 2007 569p il map $35   **920**
  1. Great Britain -- History -- 1603-1714, Stuarts
  ISBN 978-1-59448-948-8; 1-59448-948-3
                             LC 2007-911

"The letters of the Verney family survive as the largest and most continuous collection of personal correspondence from seventeenth-century Britain, and Tinniswood draws on them to produce a lively, almost novelistic account of an aristocratic family. . . Their stories range from the outrageous—Sir Francis Verney, who 'turned Turk' and became a pirate along the Barbary Coast; 'Mad' Mary Verney, whose husband's philandering drove her to zelotypia, or morbid jealousy—to the more familiar and heartrending: a father and son separated by political allegiances during civil war; a patriarch who worries about his children's financial security. Tinniswood's portraits are intimate, compelling, and deftly situated within the broader historical period, so that the turbulence of the seventeenth century is rendered as a human drama." New Yorker

Includes bibliographical references

Titchmarsh, Alan
  The **Queen's** Houses; Royal Britain at Home. by Alan Titchmarsh. Trafalgar Square 2015 255 p. (hardcover) $46.95   **920**
  1. Houses 2. Palaces
  ISBN 9781849902175; 1849902178

This book, by Alan Titchmarsh, is a "visual guide and an affectionate look at the personal family stories behind the formal grandeur of the royal residences. The Queen's life is dedicated to her public—every move is scrutinized, every word noted. But her homes are havens where peace can be found, away from watchful eyes; sanctuaries of private calm in a whirlwind life of public duty." (Publisher's note)

Tomkins, Calvin
  Lives of the artists. Henry Holt 2008 254p $26   **920**
  1. Art -- 20th century 2. Artists -- Biography
  ISBN 978-0-8050-8872-4; 0-8050-8872-5
                             LC 2008-13121

"Tomkins is a ruthless observer. . . . Books that trade on content that originally appeared in the New Yorker have become a small industry, but not all are as intimate as this one." Publ Wkly

Unferth, Deb Olin
  Revolution; Deb Olin Unferth. Henry Holt 2011 208p. **920**
  1. Authors 2. Novelists 3. Revolutions 4. Autobiographies 5. Nicaragua -- Politics and government 6. College teachers 7. Short story writers 8. Biography, Individual
  ISBN 978-0-8050-9323-0; 0-8050-9323-0
                             LC 201023471

The author writes about "the year she ran away from college with her . . . boyfriend and followed him to Nicaragua to join the Sandinistas." (Publisher's note)

Updegrove, Mark K.
  The **Last** Republicans; inside the extraordinary relationship between George H.W. Bush and George W. Bush. Mark K. Updegrove. Harperone, an imprint of HarperCollinsPublishers 2017 ix, 479 p.p illustrations (chiefly color) (hardcover) $27.99   **920**
  1. Presidents -- United States -- Biography 2. Fathers and sons -- United States -- Biography 3. United States -- Politics and government -- 1989-
  ISBN 9780062654120; 9780062654144; 0062654128
                             LC 2017034575

This book, by Mark K. Updegrove, "tracks the two Bush presidents from their formative years through their post-presidencies and the failed presidential candidacy of Jeb Bush, derailing the Bush presidential dynasty. . . . Updegrove reveals . . . their influences and perspectives on each other's presidencies; their views on family, public service, and America's role in the world; and their unvarnished thoughts on Donald Trump." (Publisher's note)

"A thoughtful political biography of two dynasts of a now-receding generation of politicians." Kirkus

Includes bibliographical references (pages 411-453) and index.

Waller, Maureen

Sovereign ladies; the six reigning queens of England. St. Martin's Press 2007 554p il $29.95; pa $19.95 **920**

1. Queens 2. Great Britain -- Kings and rulers

ISBN 978-0-312-33801-5; 0-312-33801-5; 978-0-312-38608-5 pa; 0-312-38608-7 pa

LC 2007-16181

First published 2006 in the United Kingdom

This is a "glossy, deeply detailed . . . comparative examination of the six queens who have ruled England in their own right." Kirkus

Includes bibliographical references

Walsh, Jim

The **Replacements**: all over but the shouting; an oral history. MBI Pub. Co. and Voyageur Press 2007 304 p. ill. $21.95 **920**

1. Rock musicians 2. Replacements (Musical group)

ISBN 9780760330623; 076033062X

LC 2007-22576

"In this loving, appropriately ramshackle tribute to one of the most beloved rock-and-roll bands of the 1980s, Walsh gives his subjects the oral history treatment, assembling a wide range of associates, friends and famous fans to put their memories on the record." Publ Wkly

Includes bibliographical references

Waugh, Alexander

Fathers and sons; the autobiography of a family. Nan A. Talese 2007 472p il $27.50 **920**

1. Authors 2. Authors, English

ISBN 978-0-385-52150-5; 0-385-52150-2

LC 2007-5239

First published 2004 in the United Kingdom

"The scion of an illustrious—and fabulously eccentric—English literary dynasty referees four generations of father-son antagonisms in this scintillating family memoir. Waugh . . . focuses on the fraught relationship between his great-grandfather, prominent critic and publisher Arthur Waugh, and Arthur's son, the famous novelist Evelyn. . . . If this tome were merely an excuse to reprint some of Evelyn's hilarious jottings, it would be well worth the price, but it's also an absorbing study of how writers process their most painfully formative experiences." Publ Wkly

Includes bibliographical references

The **House** of Wittgenstein; a family at war. Doubleday 2009 333p il $28.95 **920**

1. Metal industry executives

ISBN 978-0-385-52060-7; 0-385-52060-3

LC 2008-33312

Waugh "tells the story of the downfall of the wealthy Wittgenstein family. He follows the intellectually and musically gifted Wittgenstein children as history conspires to rob them of one of Europe's largest fortunes. Waugh weaves the family's story around that of the fourth son, Paul: losing his arm in the Great War, Paul gained international acclaim as a left-handed concert pianist; at that time, his brother Ludwig's notoriety was limited to a small circle at Cambridge. With the rise of the Nazis, the Wittgenstein siblings were declared racially Jewish and held

hostage for their wealth—a peril that ratchets up the book's tension and contributes to the already tragic atmosphere haunting the family. Waugh sifted through letters and journals held in archives and private collections for this masterfully researched work that brings the characters of this previously untold story to life. He moves seamlessly among historical circumstance, personal relations, and the world of classical composition and performance." Libr J

Includes bibliographical references (p. 315-21)

Waxman, Sharon

Rebels on the backlot; six maverick directors and how they conquered the Hollywood studio system. 1st ed; W. Morrow 2005 386p il $25.95; pa $14.95 **920**

1. Actors 2. Screenwriters 3. Video directors 4. Motion picture directors 5. Motion pictures -- Production and direction

ISBN 0-06-054017-6; 0-06-054018-4 pa

LC 2004-59269

This is the author's "study of six boundary-breaking young directors who revolutionized 1990s filmmaking and still represent a refreshing alternative to 'cookie cutter scripts and cheap MTV imagery.' Her full-blooded profiles introduce Quentin Tarantino (Pulp Fiction), Paul Thomas Anderson (Boogie Nights), David Fincher (Fight Club), Steven Soderbergh (Traffic), David O. Russell (Three Kings) and Spike Jonze (Being John Malkovich). . . . Their stories make for compelling reading." Publ Wkly

Includes bibliographical references

Weber, Nicholas Fox, 1947-

The **Bauhaus** group; six masters of modernism. Alfred A. Knopf 2009 521p il $40 **920**

1. Artists 2. Painters 3. Architects 4. Artists, German 5. Avant-garde (Aesthetics) 6. Bauhaus 7. Weavers 8. Printmakers 9. Art teachers 10. Textile artists 11. Furniture designers 12. Biography, Collective 13. Avant-garde (Aesthetics) -- Germany -- History -- 20th century

ISBN 978-0-307-26836-5; 0-307-26836-5

LC 2009-28729

"A rigorously researched and often fascinating history that morphs into memoir." Kirkus

Includes bibliographical references

Weintraub, Stanley

15 stars; Eisenhower, MacArthur, Marshall: three generals who saved the American century. Free Press 2007 541p il $30 **920**

1. Generals 2. Statesmen 3. Presidents 4. College presidents 5. Secretaries of state 6. Secretaries of defense 7. Nobel laureates for peace

ISBN 978-0-7432-7527-9; 0-7432-7527-6

LC 2007-16018

The author "provides a detailed and absorbing gloss on the relationships among three extraordinary leaders." Libr J

Includes bibliographical references

Weller, Sheila

Girls like us; Carole King, Joni Mitchell, and Carly Simon--and the journey of a generation. Atria Books 2008 584p il $27.95; pa $17 **920**

1. Singers 2. Folk musicians 3. Rock musicians 4. Women musicians 5. Songwriters

ISBN 978-0-743-49147-1; 0-743-49147-5; 978-0-743-49148-8 pa; 0-743-49148-3 pa

LC 2007-43445

This is a biography of the singer-songwriters Carole King, Joni Mitchell, and Carly Simon.

"A must-read for any fan of these artists, this bio will prove an absorbing, eye-opening tour of rock (and American) history for anyone who's appreciated a female musician in the past thirty years." Publ Wkly

West, Cornel, 1953-

Cornel West on Black prophetic fire; in dialogue with and edited by Christa Buschendorf. Beacon Press 2014 248 p. illustrations (hardback: acid-free paper) $25.95 **920**
1. African Americans -- Biography 2. Prophets -- United States -- Biography 3. Revolutionaries -- United States -- Biography
ISBN 0807003522; 9780807003527

LC 2014010359

This book, by Cornel West and edited by Christa Buschendorf, is a "look at nineteenth- and twentieth-century African American leaders and their visionary legacies. . . . [It] provides a fresh perspective on six revolutionary African American leaders: Frederick Douglass, W. E. B. Du Bois, Martin Luther King Jr., Ella Baker, Malcolm X, and Ida B. Wells." (Publisher's note)

Includes bibliographical references and index

Wiencek, Henry

The **Hairstons**; an American family in black and white. St. Martin's Press 1999 xx, 361p il map hardcover o.p. pa $14.95 **920**
1. Slavery -- United States 2. United States -- Race relations 3. African Americans -- Southern States
ISBN 0-312-25393-1 pa

LC 98-44014

Wiencek tells the "story of the Hairston family, the largest slaveholders in the South and one of the wealthiest families in the U.S. Wiencek details the race mixing that occured between master and slave and the family's efforts to keep its dark-skinned members enslaved and to maintain wealth only for its white members. A fascinating book that explores the complexity of family and racial relationships in the U.S." Booklist

Includes bibliographical references

Wolff, Daniel

Grown-up anger; the connected mysteries of Bob Dylan, Woody Guthrie, and the Calumet massacre of 1913. Daniel Wolff. Harper 2017 354 p. (hardcover) $26.99 **920**
1. Music -- Political aspects 2. Italian Hall Disaster, Calumet, Mich., 1913 3. Folk music -- Political aspects -- United States -- History -- 20th century 4. Popular music -- Political aspects -- United States -- History -- 20th century
ISBN 9780062451712; 9780062451705; 9780062451699

LC 2017003018

This book, by Daniel Wolff, is "a dual biography of two of the greatest songwriters, Bob Dylan and Woody Guthrie, that is also a murder mystery and a history of labor relations and socialism, big business and greed in twentieth-century America—woven together in one epic saga that holds meaning for all working Americans today." (Publisher's note)

"Wolff has crafted a fascinating and relevant whirlwind examination of music, economic injustice, and two American icons." Booklist

Includes bibliographical references (pages [261]-331) and index.

★ **How** Lincoln learned to read; twelve great Americans and the educations that made them. Bloomsbury 2009 345p $26 **920**
1. United States -- Biography 2. Education -- United States --

History
ISBN 978-1-59691-290-8; 1-59691-290-1

LC 2008-24695

"This provocative book is not only an important addition to the history of education in America, but also a valuable contribution to the history and understanding of the country's ideas and culture." SLJ

Includes bibliographical references

Wood, Damon

Working for the man, playing in the band; my years with James Brown. Damon Wood. ECW Press 2018 280 p. $26.95 **920**
1. Soul music 2. Soul musicians 3. Guitarists -- United States -- Biography
ISBN 1770413855; 9781770413856

In this book, author "Damon Wood details his six years spent playing guitar for James Brown's Soul Generals. In a memoir certain to fascinate Mr. Dynamite's millions of fans, as well as musicians and industry insiders, Wood recalls how a chance encounter with . . . Brown led him to embrace soul and funk music under the tutelage of its greatest progenitor." (Publisher's note)

"An insider's account that will delight both Brown fans and those interested in what it's like working for such a dedicated showman. Kudos to Wood for delivering the inside scoop on a demanding performer with exacting standards who brought it, every night." Library Journal

Xinran

China witness; voices from a silent generation. translated from Chinese by Nicky Harman, Julia Lovell and Esther Tyldesley. Pantheon Books 2009 434p il map $28.95 **920**
1. China -- Biography
ISBN 978-0-375-42547-9; 0-375-42547-0

LC 2008-35840

First published 2008 in the United Kingdom

The author, "traveling across the expanse of the Chinese Republic over the years, sought out those who had witnessed the rise of communism more than half a century ago. The result is this stirring, startlingly honest account of life under Chairman Mao and the current reformers revamping the socialist state." Publ Wkly

920.003 Dictionaries, encyclopedias, concordances of biography as a discipline

★ **African** American national biography; Henry Louis Gates Jr. and Evelyn Brooks Higginbotham, editors. 2nd edition Oxford University Press 2013 12v $1295 **920.003**
1. Reference books 2. African Americans -- Biography -- Dictionaries
ISBN 9780199920778

"In addition to Frederick Douglass, Booker T. Washington, W. E. B. Du Bois and Martin Luther King Jr., the AANB includes a wide range of African Americans from all time periods and all walks of life. Lives profiled include those already recognized as giants of black history, figures whose stories have never been told and that readers will be discovering for the first time, and living people who are shaping the era in which we now live." (Publisher's note)

American statesmen; secretaries of state from John Jay to Colin Powell. edited by Edward S. Mihalkanin. Greenwood Press 2004 xxxv, 571p $99.95 **920.003**
1. Reference books 2. Statesmen -- United States -- Dictionaries

ISBN 0-313-30828-4

LC 2004-10871

For a fuller review, see: Booklist, Feb. 15, 2005

This biographical dictionary features "65 biographical essays on each of the secretaries of state plus two important interim secretaries. . . . Each essay blends biographical information, early life, education, and influences; career information, appointment, and relations with the president and Congress; and a review of the major issues and accomplishments during the secretary's tenure in office." Am Ref Books Annu, 2005

Includes bibliographical references

Bader, Philip

★ **African**-American writers; revised by Catherine Reef. Rev. ed; Facts On File 2010 340p il (A to Z of African Americans) $49.50   **920.003**
1. Reference books 2. African American authors -- Dictionaries 3. American literature -- African American authors -- Bio-bibliography
ISBN 978-0-8160-8141-7

LC 2010-05463

First published 2004

This book "profiles popular and prominent African-American writers across many genres of literature. Each entry in this . . . resource provides a biographical profile, concentrating on the major literary works and accomplishments of each author as well as an outline of his or her contributions to American literature." Publisher's note

Includes bibliographical references

★ **Biographical** encyclopedia of artists; Sir Lawrence Gowing, general editor. Facts on File 2005 4v il set $260 **920.003**
1. Reference books 2. Artists -- Biography -- Encyclopedias
ISBN 0-8160-5803-2

LC 2005-40500

First published 1983 by Prentice-Hall as volume two of Encyclopedia of visual art

"The artists covered include Laurie Anderson, Frank Gehry, Anselm Kiefer, Jan Vermeer, and Andy Warhol. . . . A visual chronology of artists by country and era functions as an index to artists, and an alphabetical artist/subject index concludes the work." Libr J

Includes bibliographical references

★ **Black** women in America; Darlene Clark Hine, editor in chief. 2nd ed; Oxford University Press 2005 3v il set $325   **920.003**
1. Reference books 2. African American women -- Dictionaries
ISBN 0-19-515677-3

LC 2005-1532

First published 1993 by Carlson Pub.

"The essays offer fascinating glimpses into black women's economic, social, and political contributions, even at the grassroots level, and explore issues such as spirituality, domestic servitude, and mixed-race identity in terms of how they have shaped history." SLJ

Includes bibliographical references

Drew, Bernard A.

100 most popular nonfiction authors; biographical sketches and bibliographies. Libraries Unlimited 2007 438p il (Popular authors series) $65   **920.003**
1. Reference books 2. Authors -- Dictionaries 3. Literature -- Bio-bibliography
ISBN 978-1-59158-487-2

LC 2007-19949

"The authors, chosen by means of consultations with librarians, are

those whose impact has been seen mostly in the last half century, among them Diane Ackerman, John Krakauer, David McCullough, and Cornel West. Entries are headed by author's birth year and birthplace, and, if applicable, date of death, and by signature work and primary genres." Booklist

Includes bibliographical references

Encyclopedia of women's autobiography; edited by Victoria Boynton and Jo Malin; Emmanuel S. Nelson, advisory editor. Greenwood Press 2005 2v set $249.95   **920.003**
1. Autobiography 2. Reference books 3. Women -- Biography -- Encyclopedias
ISBN 0-313-32737-8

LC 2005-8526

This set's "encyclopedic and culturally diverse nature should appeal to a wide audience and provide a valuable starting point for further research." Libr J

Includes bibliographical references

Farmer, David Hugh

The **Oxford** dictionary of saints; 5th ed; Oxford University Press 2004 xxiv, 579p map pa $16.95   **920.003**
1. Reference books 2. Christian saints -- Dictionaries
ISBN 978-0-19-860949-0; 0-19-860949-3 pa

LC 2005-272790

A reissue of the title first published 1978

This biographical dictionary profiles the lives, cults, and artistic associations of over 1,000 saints, from the famous to the obscure. An appendix on pilgrimage sights in Europe is also included

"Even those who do not believe in the saints . . . will be able to enjoy and to profit from this splendid book." Economist

Includes bibliographical references

Friedman, Ian C.

Latino athletes. Facts on File 2007 278p il (A to Z of Latino Americans) $44   **920.003**
1. Reference books 2. Athletes -- Dictionaries 3. Hispanic Americans -- Dictionaries
ISBN 978-0-8160-6384-0; 0-8160-6384-2

LC 2006-16901

"Gymnast Trent Dimas, mountain biker Juli Furtado, and speed skater Derek Parra are among the 176 athletes profiled in this volume. . . . Following the entries, athletes are listed by sport, year of birth, and ethnicity or country of origin." Booklist

Includes bibliographical references

Friedwald, Will

A **biographical** guide to the great jazz and pop singers. Pantheon Books 2010 811p $45   **920.003**
1. Reference books 2. Singers -- Dictionaries 3. Jazz music -- Dictionaries 4. Popular music -- Dictionaries 5. Jazz music -- Bio-bibliography 6. Popular music -- Bio-bibliography
ISBN 978-0-375-42149-5; 0-375-42149-1

LC 2009-44405

The author "celebrates 200-odd performers of jazz and pop standards, from the mid-20th-century titans—Louis Armstrong, Bing Crosby, Ella Fitzgerald, Frank Sinatra—to latter-day acolytes like Diana Krall and Harry Connick Jr., with a raft of unjustly obscure singers in between. . . . Friedwald is all about the music; he primly shies away from his subjects' scandal-prone personal lives, but accords each a substantial career retrospective, selected discography and wonderfully pithy interpretive essay. . . . Friedwald's exuberant medley is that rarest of things: music criticism that actually makes you sit up and listen." Publ Wkly

Gates, Alexander E.

A to Z of earth scientists. Facts on File 2002 336p il (Notable scientists) $45 **920.003**

1. Earth sciences 2. Reference books 3. Scientists -- Dictionaries

ISBN 0-8160-4580-1

LC 2002-14616

This "profiles the lives of 192 people who devoted their careers to the disciplines and subdisciplines of the earth sciences during the 18th century to the present. . . . Entries appear in alphabetic order under the name by which the scientist is most commonly known. Also included are birth date, date of death (if applicable), nationality, and earth science specialty. An essay containing more personal data, including an emphasis on the scientist's main work and contributions to the field follows this information." Am Ref Books Annu, 2003

Includes bibliographical references

Great lives from history, The 17th century, 1601-1700; editor, Larissa Juliet Taylor. Salem Press 2005 2v il set $160 **920.003**

1. Reference books 2. Biography -- Dictionaries 3. World history -- 17th century

ISBN 1-58765-222-6; 978-1-58765-222-6

LC 2005-17804

Companion volume to Great events from history, The 17th century, 1601-1700

First published as part of the Great lives from history series, published 1987-1995 under the editorship of Frank N. Magill; previously published as half of volume 4 of Dictionary of world biography, published 1998-1999

This "is a collection of biographical essays, ranging from three to five pages in length and documenting the lives of those individuals who helped to shape the history of the 17th century. The coverage is also global and includes both well-known and lesser-known figures." SLJ

Includes bibliographical references

Great lives from history, The 19th century, 1801-1900; editor, John Powell. Salem Press 2006 4v il map set $360 **920.003**

1. Reference books 2. Biography -- Dictionaries 3. World history -- 19th century

ISBN 978-1-58765-292-9; 1-58765-292-7

LC 2006-20187

Companion volume to Great events from history, The 19th century, 1801-1900

First published as part of the Great lives from history series, published 1987-1995 under the editorship of Frank N. Magill; previously published as volumes 5 and 6 of Dictionary of world biography, published 1998-1999

"A total of 737 essays covering 757 major figures including 123 on women make up the set. . . . Major world leaders appear here, as well as the giants of religious faith who dominated the century: monarchs, presidents, popes, philosophers, writers, social reformers, educators, and military leaders who left their imprint on political as well as spiritual institutions." Publisher's note

Includes bibliographical references

Great lives from history, The ancient world, prehistory-476 C.E; editor, Christina A. Salowey. Salem Press 2004 2v il, maps set $160 **920.003**

1. Ancient history 2. Reference books 3. Biography -- Dictionaries

ISBN 1-587-65152-1; 978-1-58765-164-9

LC 2004-705

Companion volume to Great events from history, The ancient world, prehistory-476 C.E

First published as part of the Great lives from history series, published 1987-1995 under the editorship of Frank N. Magill; previously published as volume 1 of Dictionary of world biography, published 1998-1999

This "set provides three-to-six-page biographies on major personages from the ancient world. Arranged alphabetically, each article gives basic information such as when and where the individual was born and also where and when he or she died, a description of his or her early life and life's work, the significance of the individual, an annotated bibliography, and related entries in both this set and in the . . . [Great events from history] set." Ref & User Services Quarterly

Includes bibliographical references

Great lives from history, the Middle Ages, 477-1453; editor, Shelley Wolbrink. Salem Press 2005 2v il map set $160 **920.003**

1. Reference books 2. Middle ages -- Biography 3. Biography -- Dictionaries

ISBN 1-58765-164-5; 978-1-58765-164-9

LC 2004-16696

Companion volume to Great events from history, the Middle Ages, 477-1453

First published as part of the Great lives from history series, published 1987-1995 under the editorship of Frank N. Magill; previously published as volume 2 of Dictionary of world biography, published 1998-1999

These "volumes focus on the people throughout the world from after the Fall of Rome, in 476 C.E., to 1453. Coverage is worldwide. . . . Each entry begins with ready-reference information, followed by a summary of the person's life, a paragraph or two on 'Significance,' a list of further readings, and cross-references to entries both within the set and within the [Great events in history] companion set." Booklist

Includes bibliographical references

Great lives from history, the Renaissance & early modern era, 1454-1600; editor, Christina J. Moose. Salem Press 2005 2v il map set $160 **920.003**

1. Renaissance 2. Reference books 3. Biography -- Dictionaries

ISBN 1-58765-211-0; 978-1-58765-211-0

LC 2004-28875

Companion volume to Great events from history, the Renaissance & early modern era, 1454-1600

First published as part of the Great lives from history series, published 1987-1995 under the editorship of Frank N. Magill; previously published as volume 3 of Dictionary of world biography, published 1998-1999

"This two-volume work offers biographies of 338 historical figures in entries that range from two to five pages in length. A publisher's note in volume 1 explains the set's format and use. All the biographies include name, nationality or ethnicity, historical role, dates, and area(s) of achievement; description of early life, work, and significance; an annotated bibliography; and cross-references." Choice

Includes bibliographical references

Great lives from history: Notorious lives; editor, Carl L. Bankston III. Salem Press 2007 3v il set $252 **920.003**

1. Criminals 2. Dictators 3. Terrorists 4. War criminals 5. Reference books 6. Political corruption 7. Biography -- Dictionaries

ISBN 978-1-58765-320-9

LC 2006-32935

"The scope and depth of coverage make it a valuable resource for not just biographies but for criminal justice and popular culture as well." Booklist

Includes bibliographical references

Great lives from history: the 20th century, 1901-2000; editor, Robert F. Gorman. Salem Press 2008 10v il set $795   **920.003**
1. Reference books 2. Biography -- Dictionaries 3. World history -- 20th century
ISBN 978-1-58765-345-2

LC 2008-17125
First published as part of the Great lives from history series, published 1987-1995 under the editorship of Frank N. Magill; previously published as volumes 7-9 of Dictionary of world biography, published 1998-1999
"This ten-volume set offers 1,330 . . . biographies of major personages in world history (many still living) from 1901-2000. . . . The personages covered are identified with one or more of the following regions: Africa, Asia, Australia, Caribbean, Europe, Latin America, Middle East, North America, South America, and Southeast Asia." Publisher's note
Includes bibliographical references

Hamilton, Neil A.
Presidents; a biographical dictionary. Ian C. Friedman, reviser. 3rd ed; Facts on File 2010 496p il (Facts on File library of American history) $85; pa $19.95   **920.003**
1. Reference books 2. Presidents -- United States -- Dictionaries
ISBN 978-0-8160-7708-3; 978-0-8160-8247-6 pa
LC 2009-10191
First published 2001
This book "contains biographies and portraits of all presidents, a . . . chronology of the life of each president, and suggested further reading about each president." Publisher's note
Includes bibliographical references

★ **Holy** people of the world; a cross-cultural encyclopedia. Phyllis G. Jestice, editor. ABC-CLIO 2004 3v il set $285   **920.003**
1. Reference books 2. Religious biography -- Encyclopedias
ISBN 1-576-07355-6
LC 2004-22606
"This edition deserves to become well-worn by the time a second appears." Libr J
Includes bibliographical references

Jaques Cattell Press
Who's who in American politics 2007-2008; [prepared by Marquis Who's Who] 21st ed.; Marquis Who's Who 2007 xxxvi, 1960p $314.10   **920.003**
1. Reference books 2. Politicians -- United States -- Dictionaries
ISBN 978-0-8379-6918-3
Biennial. First published 1967 by Bowker
"Biographical directory of political leaders in the Congress, the executive branch of the federal government, state legislatures, state executive branches, mayors of cities with populations over 50,000, national and state party chairs, national party committee members, county chairs, and state supreme court justices. Entries are arranged by state, then alphabetically by name. Indexed by name." Ref Sources for Small & Medium-sized Libr. 6th edition

Kelly, J. N. D.
The **Oxford** dictionary of Popes; with new material by Michael Walsh. Updated [ed]; Oxford University Press 2006 349p pa $21.43   **920.003**

1. Reference books 2. Popes -- Dictionaries
ISBN 978-0-19-861433-3; 0-19-861433-0
LC 2006-277841
First published 1986
"An excellent source of information, arranged chronologically with an alphabetical index. Includes popes, antipopes, and an appendix on Pope Joan." Ref Sources for Small & Medium-sized Libr. 6th edition
Includes bibliographical references

Krismann, Carol
★ **Encyclopedia** of American women in business; from colonial times to the present. [by] Carol H. Krisman. Greenwood Press 2004 692p 2v set $175   **920.003**
1. Reference books 2. Businesswomen -- Encyclopedias 3. Women executives -- Encyclopedias
ISBN 0-313-32757-2
LC 2004-56065
The author "presents the stories of 327 businesswomen who have succeeded as entrepreneurs, executives, or business owners in profit-making enterprises from Colonial times to this day. . . . In addition to the biographies, the book contains entries for work-related issues like old-boys network, office romance, and diversity as well as profiles of agencies related to women. . . . This excellent reference book is wonderfully readable and should encourage readers to conduct further research of the women profiled." Libr J
Includes bibliographical references

Kuhlman, Erika A.
A to Z of women in world history; [by] Erika Kuhlman. Facts on File 2002 452p il (Facts on File library of world history) $49.50   **920.003**
1. Reference books 2. Women -- Biography -- Dictionaries
ISBN 0-8160-4334-5
LC 2001-54327
"The 260 women who are profiled here have not only made a mark on their own cultures but have also 'influenced other women from diverse cultures and different historical periods pursuing the same goals.'. . . Entries are organized first under 14 areas of accomplishment, from 'Adventurers and Athletes' to 'Writers.'. . . Entries are generally around two pages in length, and each offers suggestions for further reading. . . . A to Z of Women in World History is a good place to start for researchers who are taking a sphere-of-activity approach to women's history. This highly readable volume is recommended." Booklist
Includes bibliographical references

Mandel, David
Who's who in the Jewish Bible. Jewish Publication Society 2007 xx, 422p pa $30   **920.003**
1. Reference books 2. Bible -- O.T. -- Biography -- Dictionaries
ISBN 978-0-8276-0863-4; 0-8276-0863-2
LC 2007-27288
"Using only the Bible as its basis, this encyclopedia catalogues 3,000 characters from A to Z. General readers and students interested in past Jewish life will find this work most useful as a quick reference for information and a starting point for research." Booklist
Includes bibliographical references

Martinez Wood, Jamie
Latino writers and journalists. Facts on File 2007 294p il (A to Z of Latino Americans) $44   **920.003**
1. Reference books 2. Hispanic Americans -- Dictionaries 3. American literature -- Hispanic American authors -- Bio-

bibliography
ISBN 0-8160-6422-9; 978-0-8160-6422-9

LC 2006-17394

This book "brings together 150 writers identified as Latino Americans. Approximately one-third of the profiles are accompanied by photographs." Booklist
Includes bibliographical references

Millar, David

★ The **Cambridge** dictionary of scientists; [by] David Millar [et al.] 2nd ed; Cambridge Univ. Press 2002 464p il hardcover o.p. $99; pa $34.99   **920.003**
1. Reference books 2. Scientists -- Dictionaries
ISBN 0-521-80602-X; 0-521-00062-9 pa

LC 2002-512240

First published 1996 as a revision of: Chambers concise dictionary of scientists

"The alphabetically organized, illustrated biographical dictionary . . . [covers] over 1,500 key scientists . . . from 40 countries. Physics, chemistry, biology, geology, astronomy, mathematics, medicine, meteorology and technology are all represented and special attention is paid to pioneer women." Publisher's note

Monush, Barry

★ **Screen** world presents the encyclopedia of Hollywood film actors; v1 edited by Barry Monush. Applause Theatre and Cinema Bks. 2003 1200p v1 il $35   **920.003**
1. Reference books 2. Actors -- Dictionaries 3. Motion pictures -- Biography -- Dictionaries
ISBN 1-557-83551-9

LC 2002-152728

"The first of a projected two-volume set, this encyclopedia provides biographical profiles of actors who worked in Hollywood between 1915 and 1965 . . . . [The author] includes all Oscar-winning actors as well as performers who became prominent in film before the late 1960s. . . . Entries are arranged in alphabetical order (Bud Abbott and Lou Costello to George Zucco), include vital statistics, and note any higher-education institution the actor attended. . . . This is an item that academic libraries and specialized film libraries will want to add. It would also no doubt find an audience in public libraries." Booklist

Musicians & composers of the 20th century; editor Alfred W. Cramer. Salem Press 2009 5v il set $399   **920.003**
1. Reference books 2. Music -- Bio-bibliography 3. Musicians -- Dictionaries
ISBN 978-1-58765-512-8

LC 2009-2980

"The work covers 614 composers, performers, and teachers, chosen for musical influence as well as fame. All major genres are covered, from classical to rap, along with many subgenres, such as rockabilly, atonal, and funk. . . . This work provides valuable, basic information on the topic as well as multiple, easy-access routes to it. Highly recommended." Libr J
Includes bibliographical references

New dictionary of scientific biography; Noretta Koertge, editor in chief. Scribner's 2008 8v il set $995   **920.003**
1. Reference books 2. Scientists -- Dictionaries
ISBN 978-0-684-31320-7

LC 2007-31384

First published 1970-1980 in 16 volumes with title: Dictionary of scientific biography
This biographical dictionary "contains thousands of biographies of mathematicians and natural scientists from all countries and from all historical periods." Publisher's note
Includes bibliographical references

Newton, David E.

Latinos in science, math, and professions. Facts on File 2007 274p il (A to Z of Latino Americans) $44   **920.003**
1. Reference books 2. Scientists -- Dictionaries 3. Mathematicians -- Dictionaries 4. Hispanic Americans -- Dictionaries
ISBN 978-0-8160-6385-7; 0-8160-6385-0

LC 2006-16769

Among the figures profiled in this biographical dictionary "are sociology expert Maxine Baca Zinn; Ellen Ochoa, the first Latina in space; and research entomologist Fernando E. Vega." Libr J
Includes bibliographical references

Notable American women: the modern period; a biographical dictionary. edited by Barbara Sicherman {et al.} Harvard Univ. Press 1980 xxii, 773p hardcover o.p. pa $41.50   **920.003**
1. Reference books 2. Women -- United States -- Biography 3. United States -- Biography -- Dictionaries
ISBN 0-674-62733-4 pa

LC 80-18402

This set provides "1 1/2- to 2-page biographies and references for 442 American women. Women were chosen from science, business, and engineering as well as from such traditional fields as education, entertainment, and social work, with a wide variety of @career patterns, philosophical outlooks and personal styles' represented. . . . Entries describe the life and personality of the individual, evaluate her career, and place it in an historical context. Special emphasis is given to the conflicting demands of her public and personal lives." Choice

Notable black American men, book II; Jessie Carney Smith, editor. Thomson Gale 2007 xxiv, 827p il $193   **920.003**
1. Reference books 2. United States -- Biography -- Dictionaries 3. African Americans -- Biography -- Dictionaries
ISBN 0-7876-6493-6; 978-0-7876-6493-0

LC 2006-21193

Covering "prominent newsmakers as well as lesser-known individuals, . . . [this second volume of a two-volume work] offers full biographical entries, portraits, addresses for living listees and recommended sources for further study." Publisher's note
Includes bibliographical references

Notable black American women, book I; Jessie Carney Smith, editor. Gale Res. 1992 xlvii, 1334p il $203   **920.003**
1. Reference books 2. African American women -- Dictionaries 3. United States -- Biography -- Dictionaries
ISBN 0-8103-4749-0

LC 91-35074

This first volume of a three-volume biographical encyclopedia "documents the achievements of 500 African-American women who have made significant contributions to American culture from the colonial era to the present. . . . Subjects include women active in all fields of endeavor, from education, science, and the arts, to business, law and politics. . . . Authoritative and entertaining at the same time." Am Libr

Notable black American women, Book III; Jessie Carney Smith, editor. Gale 2003 lxxviii, 881p il $165   **920.003**
1. Reference books 2. African American women -- Dictionaries 3. United States -- Biography -- Dictionaries
ISBN 0-7876-6494-4

In this third volume of a three-volume biographical dictionary, "narrative biographical essays . . . discuss each woman's significant achievements and the public response to those achievements. . . . [This book] features 300 contemporary and historical women, including Sarah Allen, Alicia Keys, Ruth Simmons and . . . more." Publisher's note

Includes bibliographical references

Notable native Americans; Sharon Malinowski, editor; George H.J. Abrams, consulting editor and author of foreword. Gale Res. 1995 xliv, 492p il $105   **920.003**
   1. Reference books 2. Native Americans -- Dictionaries
   ISBN 0-8103-9638-6

                                     LC 94-36202

This is a "compilation of biographical and bibliographical information on more than two hundred and sixty-five notable Native North American men and women throughout history, from all fields of endeavor. . . . Approximately thirty percent of the entries focus on historical figures and seventy percent on contemporary or twentieth-century individuals. Signed narrative essays, ranging from one to three pages in length, include Indian names and their English translations as well as name variants." Preface

Oakes, Elizabeth H.
   ★ **A to Z of chemists**. Facts on File 2002 276p il $45   **920.003**
   1. Chemists 2. Reference books 3. Scientists -- Dictionaries
   ISBN 0-8160-4579-8

                                       LC 2002-68685

"This title includes 152 biographies of chemists, including 23 women. . . . The entries run between 750 and 1200 words (one to one and one-half pages apiece). They all begin with a summary of the subject's major contribution, followed by a chronological biography of their personal and professional life. Appendixes list the birthplace and country of activity of the chemists as well as a chart of their life spans." Libr J

   Includes bibliographical references

   American writers. Facts on File 2004 430p il (American biographies) $65   **920.003**
   1. Reference books 2. Authors, American -- Dictionaries 3. American literature -- Bio-bibliography
   ISBN 0-8160-5158-5

                                       LC 2003-15743

"The volume has alphabetically arranged entries for approximately 260 authors from a variety of genres—poetry, fiction, drama, essay, and autobiography. Each . . . entry contains a short biography, critical analysis, and a bibliography of works about the author in both printed and Web formats. . . . [This book] offers a convenient introduction and is a worthwhile purchase." Booklist

   Includes bibliographical references

Otfinoski, Steven
   Latinos in the arts. Facts on File 2007 277p il (A to Z of Latino Americans) $44   **920.003**
   1. Reference books 2. Actors -- Dictionaries 3. Artists -- Dictionaries 4. Musicians -- Dictionaries 5. Hispanic Americans -- Dictionaries
   ISBN 978-0-8160-6394-9; 0-8160-6394-X

                                     LC 2006-16900

"This volume profiles more than 178 individuals in the performing and visual arts 'who were born in the United States or who settled here permanently,' among them Marc Anthony, Cameron Diaz, Carmen Miranda, Tito Punete, and Shakira. Each entry concludes with a list of 'Further Reading' . . . and, in many cases, 'Further Listening' and 'Further Viewing.'" Booklist

   Includes bibliographical references

Powell, John
   Great lives from history, The 18th century, 1701-1800; editor, John Powell; editor, first edition, Frank N. Magill. Salem Press 2006 2v il map set $160   **920.003**
   1. Reference books 2. Biography -- Dictionaries 3. World history -- 18th century
   ISBN 978-1-58765-276-9; 1-58765-276-5

                                       LC 2006-5336

Companion volume to Great events from history, The 18th century, 1701-1800

First published as part of the Great lives from history series, published 1987-1995 under the editorship of Frank N. Magill; previously published as half of volume 4 of Dictionary of world biography, published 1998-1999

"The alphabetically listed subjects encompass 36 areas of expertise and include John Newbery, Pontiac, Qianlong, Hannah More, Pius IV, Paul Revere, and Shah Wali Allah, among others. Each article is approximately three pages long and lists the subject's major accomplishments, important dates, and areas of achievement. . . . A well-written, useful set." SLJ

   Includes bibliographical references

Rich, Mari
   ★ **World** authors, 2000-2005; editors, Jennifer Curry, David Ramm, Mari Rich, Albert Rolls. Wilson, H. W. 2007 800p il (Authors series) $170   **920.003**
   1. Reference books 2. Authors -- Dictionaries 3. Literature -- Bio-bibliography
   ISBN 978-0-8242-1077-9

This book "covers some 300 novelists, poets, dramatists, essayists, scientists, biographers, and other authors whose books [were] published 2000 through 2005." Publisher's note

Schneider, Dorothy
   ★ **First** ladies; a biographical dictionary. [by] Dorothy Schneider, Carl J. Schneider. 3rd ed; Facts on File 2010 436p il (Facts on File library of American history) $85   **920.003**
   1. Reference books 2. Presidents' spouses -- United States -- Dictionaries
   ISBN 978-0-8160-7724-3

                                       LC 2009-9047

First published 2001

This book "covers all the women who have held this esteemed 'office' since the founding of the United States. . . . Arranged chronologically by term of presidency, each biographical entry includes a . . . biography emphasizing each first lady's life during the presidency, as well as a chronology, appendixes, and suggestions for further reading." Publisher's note

   Includes bibliographical references

The **Scribner** encyclopedia of American lives, The 1960s; William L. O'Neill, volume editor. Scribner 2003 2v il set $250   **920.003**
   1. Reference books 2. United States -- Biography -- Dictionaries
   ISBN 0-684-80666-5

                                       LC 2002-12581

"The two alphabetically arranged volumes in SEAL 1960s contain biographical sketches, usually between 1,000 and 2,000 words, of 647 figures who 'defined the decade, or who were influential at the time.'

Americans from different races, socioeconomic groups, classes, and regions of the U.S. are included, along with the occasional person of another nationality who had long periods of residence in the U.S. and was an influence on American culture. The signed entries, written by scholars, begin with a brief summary of the person's chronology and important accomplishments. This is followed by a narrative of the subject's life.... In many cases, a black-and-white photograph accompanies the narrative, which concludes with an assessment of the subject's overall contribution and a brief bibliography listing a few key sources.... Recommended for all high-school, public, and academic libraries wanting complete SEAL coverage or libraries wanting to supplement their collection of 1960s resources with a purely biographical approach." Booklist

Includes bibliographical references

Shipp, Steve

Latin American and Caribbean artists of the modern era; a biographical dictionary of more than 12,700 persons. McFarland & Co 2002 864p il $115　　　**920.003**
　　1. Reference books 2. Latin American art 3. Artists -- Dictionaries
　　ISBN 0-7864-1057-4
　　　　　　　　　　　　　　　　　　LC 2002-13828
　　"All entries include expected information such as birth date and place and artist's medium, and longer entries also feature biographical sketches, including education and influences, as well as lists of collections, exhibits, and titles.... A good starting point for further research." Libr J
　　Includes bibliographical references

St. **James** guide to Hispanic artists; profiles of Latino and Latin American artists. editor, Thomas Riggs. St. James Press 2002 xx, 682p il $195　　　**920.003**
　　1. Hispanic American art 2. Artists -- United States
　　ISBN 1-55862-470-8
　　　　　　　　　　　　　　　　　　LC 2001-41935
　　This "guide profiles some 375 of the most prominent Hispanic artists of the past century. The entries include basic biographical information, critical commentary, and lists of exhibitions, publications, and collections holding their works." Libr J
　　Includes bibliographical references and indexes

Wakeman, John

World authors, 1970-1975; editor, John Wakeman; editorial consultant, Stanley J. Kunitz. Wilson, H.W. 1980 894p il (Authors series) $140　　　**920.003**
　　1. Reference books 2. Authors -- Dictionaries 3. Literature -- Biobibliography
　　ISBN 0-8242-0641-X
　　　　　　　　　　　　　　　　　　LC 79-21874
　　This volume provides biographical or autobiographical sketches for 348 of the most influential and popular men and women of letters who have come into prominence between 1970 and 1975

Waldrup, Carole Chandler

The **vice** presidents; biographies of the 45 men who have held the second highest office in the United States. McFarland & Co. 1996 271p il hardcover o.p. pa $39.95　　　**920.003**
　　1. Vice-presidents -- United States
　　ISBN 0-7864-0179-6; 978-0-7864-2611-9 pa; 0-7864-2611-X pa
　　　　　　　　　　　　　　　　　　LC 96-30538
　　"Well-written with clear, precise language and vocabulary, this informative book will be useful in either the reference section or with the

collective biographies." Book Rep
　　Includes bibliographical references

Ware, Susan

Notable American women; a biographical dictionary completing the twentieth century. Susan Ware, editor; Stacy Braukman, assistant editor. Belknap Press 2004 xxx, 729p $45　　　**920.003**
　　1. Reference books 2. Women -- United States -- Biography 3. United States -- Biography -- Dictionaries
　　ISBN 0-674-01488-X
　　　　　　　　　　　　　　　　　　LC 2004-48859
　　This volume includes "stars of the golden ages of radio, film, dance, and television; scientists and scholars; politicians and entrepreneurs; authors and aviators; civil rights activists and religious leaders; Native American craftspeople and world-renowned artists. Women from a broad spectrum of ethnic , class, political, religious, and sexual identities are all acknowledged." Publisher's note
　　Includes bibliographical references

★ **Who's** who 2008; an annual biographical dictionary. 160th ed.; A. & C. Black 2007 2574p $325　　　**920.003**
　　1. Reference books 2. Great Britain -- Biography -- Dictionaries
　　ISBN 978-0-7136-8555-8; 0-7136-8555-7
　　Annual. First published 1849
　　"The pioneer work of the who's who type and still one of the most important. Until 1897, it was the handbook of titled and official classes and included lists of names rather than biographical sketches. . . . It is principally British, but a few prominent names of other nationalities are included. Biographies are reliable and fairly detailed; they give main facts, addresses, often telephone numbers and in case of authors, lists of works." Guide to Ref Books. 11th edition

Who's who among African Americans; 21st ed.; Gale Res. 2008 1477p $275　　　**920.003**
　　1. Reference books 2. African Americans -- Biography -- Dictionaries
　　ISBN 978-1-4144-0020-4; 1-4144-0020-9
　　First published 1976 by Educational Communications with title: Who's who among black Americans. Biennial schedule after 5th edition
　　"Short entries focusing on career achievements and positions. Indexes list entries by place of birth and profession." N Y Public Libr Book of How & Where to Look It Up

Who's who in America. Marquis Who's Who　　　**920.003**
　　1. Reference books 2. United States -- Biography -- Dictionaries
　　Annual. First published 1899
　　"The standard dictionary of contemporary biography, containing concise biographical data, prepared according to established practices, with addresses and, in the case of authors, lists of works. . . . Each edition is thoroughly revised, new biographies added, and others dropped. For names of persons dropped because of death, see 'Who was who in America'." Guide to Ref Books. 11th edition

★ **Who's** who in American art, 2008; 28th ed.; Marquis Who's Who 2007 1550p $267.30　　　**920.003**
　　1. Reference books 2. Artists -- United States -- Dictionaries
　　ISBN 978-0-8379-6307-5; 0-8379-6307-9
　　Companion volume to American art directory
　　Biennial. First published 1936 by American Federation of Arts as part of American art annual
　　"Profiles representatives of all segments of the art world including artists, administrators, and librarians. Entries give vital statistics, profes-

sional education and training, commissions and exhibitions, and membership in art societies. Includes geographic and professional classification indexes and cumulative necrology." N Y Public Libr Book of How & Where to Look It Up

★ **Who's** who in finance and business 2008-2009; 36th ed; Marquis Who's Who 2007 1,100 $349   **920.003**
1. Reference books 2. Business -- Biography -- Dictionaries
ISBN 978-0-8379-0356-9
Biennial. First published 1936 with title: Who's who in commerce and industry. Continues Who's who in finance and industry
"Gives international coverage of businessmen. Includes index of firms with references to personnel for whom sketches are included." Guide to Ref Books. 11th edition

★ **Who's** who of American women 2007; 26th ed; Marquis Who's Who 2006 1,700 $305   **920.003**
1. Reference books 2. Women -- United States -- Biography 3. United States -- Biography -- Dictionaries
ISBN 0-8379-0434-X
Biennial. First published for 1958/1959
"This title provides information on women who are successful in a variety of professions, including business, government, education, art and culture, and those who have received prestigious honors or have been selected for honorary institutions. The biographical data are provided by the women themselves so the quality varies. In general it includes name, occupation, birth date, education, career history, publications, professional activities, awards, and home and office addresses. This has long been a standard source in many public and academic libraries." Am Ref Books Annu, 2003

Women in world history; a biographical encyclopedia. Anne Commire, editor, Deborah Klezmer, associate editor. Gale Res. 1999 17v set $1,495   **920.003**
1. Reference books 2. Women -- Biography 3. Women -- History -- Encyclopedias
ISBN 0-7876-3736-X
                                        LC 99-24692
ALA RUSA Dartmouth Medal (2001)
"The editors researched wives, daughters, mothers, and other women who were not documented in traditional, male-oriented sources, especially history books.... Some entries are only a sentence or two because of lack of information, but the majority include most or all of the following: dates, if known, or time of flourishing; an identifying summary of life and achievements; a personal profile with vital statistics and names of family members; events in the life of the biographee; vitae listing such things as works for authors or winning records for athletes; a quotation by or about the individual; and bibliographical references." Booklist
Includes bibliographical references

920.009   Ethnic and national groups

Great lives from history; editors, Carmen Tafolla and Martha P. Cotera. Salem Press 2012 3 v., xxvi, 1058 p.p ill. (set) $395   **920.009**
1. Latinos (U.S.) 2. Hispanic Americans -- Biography -- Encyclopedias
ISBN 9781587658112; 9781587658129; 9781587658136; 1587658100; 9781587658105
                                        LC 2011043168
The authors "[Carmen] Tafolla, an award-winning author of Chicana literature for children and adults, ... and librarian and activist [Martha

P.] Cotera, ... provide brief biographical essays covering 518 figures from Latino history." Among those profiled are actor Desi Arnaz, football player Tony Romo, and actress Rita Hayworth. (Library Journal)
Includes bibliographical references and indexes

Hernández, Daisy
A **cup** of water under my bed; a memoir. by Daisy Hernández. Beacon Press 2014 200 p. (hardback: alkaline paper) $24.95   **920.009**
1. Family 2. Women journalists 3. Women -- Social conditions 4. Cuban Americans -- Biography 5. Colombian Americans -- Biography 6. Women -- New Jersey -- Biography 7. Identity (Psychology) -- United States 8. United States -- Social conditions -- 1980- 9. Bisexual women -- United States -- Biography 10. Young women -- Family relationships -- United States 11. Women journalists -- New York (State) -- New York -- Biography
ISBN 9780807014486; 0807014486
                                        LC 2014000820
In this memoir author "Daisy Hernández chronicles what the women in her Cuban-Colombian family taught her about love, money, and race. In prose that is both memoir and commentary, Daisy reflects on reporting for the New York Times as the paper is rocked by the biggest plagiarism scandal in its history and plunged into debates about the role of race in the newsroom." (Publisher's note)
"She maintains a lively pace by flashing back-and-forth between childhood and adulthood, personal and professional lives, with an emphasis on her ascent from New York Times intern to regular columnist at Ms. An accessible, honest look at the often heart-wrenching effects of intergenerational tension on family ties." Booklist

McCullough, David G., 1933-
★ The **greater** journey; [by] David McCollough. Simon & Schuster 2011 558p. ill. (some col.), maps $37.50; ebook $19.99   **920.009**
1. Artists 2. Paris (France) -- History 3. Intellectuals -- United States 4. Paris (France) -- Intellectual life 5. Authors, American 6. Americans -- France 7. Biography, Collective 8. Paris (France) -- Intellectual life -- 19th century 9. Americans -- France -- Paris -- History -- 19th century
ISBN 978-1-4165-7176-6; 1-4165-7176-0; 978-1-4165-7689-1 ebook; 9781416571766; 9781416576891; 1416576894
                                        LC 2010053001
In this book, "award-winning historian [David] McCullough ... [tells the story of] a cluster of aspiring young people such as portraitist George Healy and lawyer Charles Sumner, eager to expand their horizons [in Paris] in the 1830s.... [The book] include[s] numerous other visitors over an entire eventful century.... [N]ovelist James Fenimore Cooper, widowed schoolteacher Emma Hart Willard and young medical student Oliver Wendell Holmes Sr. all knew their education was not complete without a stint in the medieval capital. For many of these American rubes, exposure to the fine arts, old-world architecture, fashion, fine dining, museums and teaching hospitals proved transformative, and the knowledge they gained would define their professional lives back in America." (Kirkus)
An "account of young Americans, driven by wanderlust, setting out in search of greener Parisian pastures. Well-known figures such as James Fenimore Cooper, Oliver Wendell Holmes Sr., and Mary Cassat, and long-forgotten entities like Elizabeth Blackwell and William Wells Brown, all walked along the Avenue des Champs-Élysées, went to the Musée du Louvre, ate wonderful meals, and became inspired. Their life-changing adventures played a vital role in transforming the course of US history." Christ Sci Monit
Includes bibliographical references (p. 519-537) and index.

920.073   Biography -- United States

Isay, Dave

Callings; A Celebration of Lives of Purpose and Passion. Dave Isay. Penguin Group USA 2016 288 p. illustrations $26   **920.073**

1. Vocational guidance 2. Meaning (Philosophy) 3. Creation (Literary, artistic, etc.)

ISBN 1594205183; 9781594205187

This book, by Dave Isay, "presents unforgettable stories from people doing what they love. Some found their paths at a very young age, others later in life; some overcame great odds or upturned their lives in order to pursue what matters to them. Many of their stories have never been broadcast or published by StoryCorps until now." (Publisher's note)

"These wonderful stories reveal that work becomes meaningful to those who choose—or are in some cases chosen by—the calling that motivates, energizes, and inspires them." Pub Wkly

920.71   Men

Gates, Henry Louis

Thirteen ways of looking at a black man. Random House 1997 xxvii, 226p hardcover o.p. pa $12   **920.71**

1. Actors 2. Authors 3. Dancers 4. Singers 5. Generals 6. Novelists 7. Dramatists 8. Choreographers 9. Football players 10. Essayists 11. Memoirists 12. Screenwriters 13. Sportscasters 14. Literary critics 15. Music historians 16. Social activists 17. Short story writers 18. Young adult authors 19. Black Muslim leaders 20. Secretaries of state 21. African Americans -- Biography
ISBN 0-679-77666-4 pa

LC 96-33138

"Mr. Gates's strong suit is finding the common man in uncommon figures, without losing sight of the ways in which race, class and personal experience have shaped each life." N Y Times Book Rev

920.72   Women

Cohen, Lisa

All we know; three lives. Lisa Cohen. Farrar, Straus and Giroux 2012 429 p. ill. (alk. paper) $30.00   **920.72**

1. Women -- Biography 2. Biography -- 20th century 3. Women intellectuals -- Biography 4. Socialites -- United States -- Biography 5. Women fashion designers -- England -- Biography 6. Modernism (Aesthetics) -- History -- 20th century 7. Women authors, American -- 19th century -- Biography
ISBN 0374176493; 9780374176495

LC 2011041055

This collective biography examines the lives of "Esther Murphy (1897-1962)... Mercedes de Acosta (1893-1968)... and feminist Madge Garland (1898-1990).... They knew each other well from social circles, and none of them had simple lives. [Lisa] Cohen . . . delineates the . . . biographical matters of ancestry, parents, schooling, marriages, affairs, friendships, breakups, work, and death. . . . [A] three-part inquiry into the meaning of failure, style, and sexual identity." (Publishers Weekly)

Includes bibliographical references (p. [359]-406) and index

Livingston, Sonja

Ladies night at the Dreamland; Sonja Livingston. University of Georgia Press 2016 216 p. (hardcover: alk. paper) $24.95   **920.72**

1. Women -- United States -- History 2. Women -- United States -- Biography 3. Women -- United States -- Social conditions
ISBN 9780820349138

LC 2015032665

This essay collection in the Crux series, by Sonja Livingston, "weaves together strands of research and imagination to conjure figures from history, literature, legend, and personal memory. The result is a series of essays that highlight lives as varied, troubled, and spirited as America itself." (Publisher's note)

"Wise, fresh, captivating essays." Kirkus

Includes bibliographical references

Nimura, Janice P.

Daughters of the Samurai; A Journey from East to West and Back. by Janice P. Nimura. W W Norton & Co Inc 2015 352 p. illustrations, map, portraits $26.95   **920.72**

1. Japanese 2. Japanese American women 3. Japan -- Foreign relations -- United States 4. United States -- Foreign relations -- Japan
ISBN 0393077993; 9780393077995

LC 2014046933

This book, by Janice P. Nimura, focuses on "five young girls [who] were sent by the Japanese government to the United States. Their mission: learn Western ways and return to help nurture a new generation of enlightened men to lead Japan. Raised in traditional samurai households during the turmoil of civil war, three of these unusual ambassadors—Sutematsu Yamakawa, Shige Nagai, and Ume Tsuda—grew up as typical American schoolgirls." (Publisher's note)

Schatz, Kate

Rad women worldwide; Artists and Athletes, Pirates and Punks, and Other Revolutionaries Who Shaped History. by Kate Schatz; illustrated by Miriam Klein Stahl. Ten Speed Press 2016 112 p. illustrations (ebook) $47.97; (hardback) $15.99   **920.72**

1. Women -- History 2. Women -- Biography 3. Women -- History -- Juvenile literature 4. Women -- Biography -- Juvenile literature
ISBN 9780399578878; 9780399578861

LC 2016012179

This book by Kate Schatz, illustrated by Miriam Klein Stahl, offers "tales of perseverance and radical success by pairing well researched . . . biographies with . . . cut-paper portraits. From 430 BCE to 2016, . . . the book features an array of diverse figures, including Hatshepsut (. . . who ruled Egypt peacefully for two decades) and Malala Yousafzi (the youngest person to win the Nobel Peace Prize) to Poly Styrene (legendary teenage punk and lead singer of X-Ray Spex)." (Publisher's note)

"Readers of either gender could well find a role model in the India-born U.S. astronaut Kalpana Chawla, or in Wangari Maathai, whose Green Belt Movement in Africa resulted in the planting of more than 30 million environment-reviving trees." Booklist

Includes bibliographical references and index

Ware, Susan

Letter to the world; seven women who shaped the American century. Norton 1998 xxiv, 344p il $25.95   **920.72**

1. Actors 2. Dancers 3. Diplomats 4. Journalists 5. Choreographers 6. Anthropologists 7. Golfers 8. Curators 9. Hurdlers 10. Columnists 11. High jumpers 12. Humanitarians 13. Opera singers 14. Dance teachers 15. Javelin throwers 16. Olympic athletes 17. Social activists 18. Women -- Biography 19. Writers on science 20. Spouses of presidents 21. United Nations officials

ISBN 0-393-04652-4

LC 97-45923

The author "considers the lives of seven women who had an exceptional impact on 20th-century American culture and society's perception of the role of women: Eleanor Roosevelt, Dorothy Thompson, Margaret Mead, Katharine Hepburn, Babe Didrikson Zaharias, Martha Graham, and Marian Anderson. In addition to focusing on outstanding achievements in their chosen fields, Ware looks at their often unconventional private lives." Libr J

Includes bibliographical references

929   Genealogy, names, insignia

Baxter, Angus

In search of your European roots; a complete guide to tracing your ancestors in every country in Europe. 3rd ed; Genealogical 2001 315p pa $18.95   **929**

1. Genealogy

ISBN 0-8063-1657-8

LC 00-136383

First published 1985

This work covers the various types of genealogical records available in approximately 30 European countries. Archival resources from the national to local level are described. Also included are telephone numbers, e-mail addresses, fax numbers, and URL's for various European archives and organizations

Includes bibliographical references (p. {303}-312) and index

Bentley, Elizabeth Petty

Directory of family associations; {by} Elizabeth Petty Bentley, & Deborah Ann Carl. 4th ed; Genealogical 2001 320p $34.95   **929**

1. Genealogy

ISBN 0-8063-1679-9

LC 2001-131456

First published 1991

Contains information on approximately 6,000 family name associations in the United States; lists addresses, phone numbers, contact persons, and publications (if any)

★ The **genealogist's** address book; state and local resources: with special resources including ethnic and religious organizations. 6th ed.; Genealogical Pub. Co. 2009 799p $69.95 **929**

1. Genealogy

ISBN 978-0-8063-1796-0

First published 1991. Periodically revised

This is a source for "fax, phone, web addresses, and contact names for genealogical, historical, and religious societies across the United States. Bentley . . . judiciously divides contact information into three subject segments. The first organizes genealogical and historical associations alphabetically, initially by state, then county, and finally by society name. Essential for genealogists and regional historians." Libr J

Croom, Emily Anne

The **genealogist's** companion and sourcebook; 2nd ed; Betterway Bks. 2003 454p il map pa $19.99   **929**

1. Genealogy

ISBN 1-55870-651-8

LC 2003-50017

First published 1994

This how-to genealogy handbook seeks to explore "collections and

libraries within the U.S. and the records that may be found within them. . . . In addition to covering government records, cemetery records, newspapers, city directories, and other sources, there are chapters of African American and Native American genealogy. . . . Because the volume is easy reading and instructive at the same time, it will be a very popular choice for public libraries." Booklist {review of 1994 edition}

Includes bibliographical references

Franklin, John Hope

★ **In** search of the promised land; a Black family and the Old South. [by] John Hope Franklin, Loren Schweninger. Oxford University Press 2005 286p il map (New narratives in American history) $23; pa $13.95   **929**

1. Slavery -- United States 2. United States -- Race relations 3. African Americans -- Southern States

ISBN 0-19-516087-8; 0-19-516088-6 pa

LC 2004-61666

The authors trace "the history of the Thomas-Rapier family during the antebellum and Civil War eras. Starting with matriarch Sally Thomas, born a slave in 1787, the book enables readers to distinguish the various complex modes within which slavery operated. The resulting family history also traces the evolution of race relations in diverse locations from New Orleans to New York City, Canada, Minnesota, and the Caribbean." Libr J

Includes bibliographical references

Greenwood, Val D.

The **researcher's** guide to American genealogy; 3rd ed; Genealogical 2000 662p il $29.95   **929**

1. Genealogy 2. Archives -- United States

ISBN 0-8063-1621-7

LC 99-73349

First published 1973

"This classic textbook for the more experienced researcher gives detailed answers to questions about primary records, including vital, census, probate, land, court (including adoption), church, military, cemetery, and wills. Completely updated, it remains the outstanding text and reference book in American genealogy and the benchmark against which others must be judged." Libr J {review of 1990 edition}

Includes bibliographical references

Kemp, Thomas Jay

International vital records handbook; 5th ed.; Genealogical Publishing Co. 2009 587p pa $49.95   **929**

1. Registers of births, etc.

ISBN 978-0-8063-1793-9

LC 2008-940022

First published 1988 with title: Vital records handbook

"The book is divided into these three major segments. The first offers approved-form facsimiles for the request of U.S. state-issued documents. The second segment covers request forms issued in U.S. Territories. The third details various procedures and forms necessary to attain official documents in foreign countries. . . . A crucial, time-saving resource." Libr J

Includes bibliographical references

Virtual roots 2.0; a guide to genealogy and local history on the World Wide Web. rev and updated; Scholarly Resources 2003 311p $75; pa $29.95   **929**

1. Genealogy 2. World Wide Web

ISBN 0-8420-2922-2; 0-8420-2923-0 pa

LC 2002-154366

First published 1997

The more than 1,000 "Web sites in this directory are arranged into four primary categories—general subjects, U.S., international, and family associations—each of which is further subdivided by topic, state, country, or family name. Web site entries include organization name, address, telephone number(s), Internet and e-mail addresses, and, where appropriate, other Web links that open even more doorways." Booklist {review of 1997 edition}

Includes bibliographical references

Simpson, Jack

★ **Basics** of genealogy reference; a librarian's guide. Jack Simpson. Libraries Unlimited 2008 xiii, 176 p.p illustrations, maps (paperback) $45 **929**

1. Genealogy 2. Library science 3. United States -- Genealogy 4. Reference services (Libraries) -- United States

ISBN 1591585147; 9780313363634; 9781591585145

LC 2008010596

This book, by Jack Simpson, "offers novice and experienced reference librarians an introduction to tried-and-true genealogy techniques and resources. With the help of four case studies, Simpson outlines a basic starting strategy for conducting genealogy research. Later chapters deal specifically with genealogical librarianship: how to conduct a reference interview, continuing and professional development, and basic resources every collection should have." (Publisher's note)

"This handy manual works well for librarians for group training and self-directed study, and motivated library patrons can also learn from it." Booklist

Includes bibliographical references and index.

929.1 Genealogy

Jacobs, A. J.

It's all relative; adventures up and down the world's family tree. A. J. Jacobs. Simon & Schuster 2017 xiv, 336 p.p illustrations (hardcover) $27 **929.1**

1. Genealogy 2. Reference books 3. Genealogy -- Humor 4. Genetic genealogy -- United States

ISBN 9781476734514; 9781476734491; 1476734496

LC 2017470400

This book, by A. J. Jacobs, chronicles the author's "three-year adventure to help build the biggest family tree in history. Jacobs's journey would take him to all seven continents. He drank beer with a US president, found himself singing with the Mormon Tabernacle Choir, and unearthed genetic links to Hollywood actresses and real-life scoundrels. After all, we can choose our friends, but not our family." (Publisher's note)

"A delightful, easy-to-read, informative book." Kirkus

Includes bibliographical references (pages 303-305) and index.

McCarthy, Andrew

Journeys home; inspiring stories, plus tips and strategies to find your family history. Andrew McCarthy, Joyce Maynard, Pico Iyer, Diane Johnson & the National Geographic travel team; foreword by Dr. Spencer Wells, National Geographic explorer-in-residence. National Geographic 2015 288 p. color illustrations (hardcover: alkaline paper) $26 **929.1**

1. Genealogy 2. Voyages and travels 3. Genealogy -- Anecdotes 4. Voyages and travels -- Anecdotes 5. Celebrities -- Travel -- Anecdotes 6. United States -- Genealogy -- Anecdotes 7. United States -- Genealogy -- Handbooks, manuals, etc 8. Celebrities --

United States -- Genealogy -- Anecdotes

ISBN 1426213816; 9781426213816

LC 2014033593

This book, by Andrew McCarthy, Joyce Maynard, Pico Iyer, Diane Johnson and the National Geographic travel team, "combines intriguing tales of discovery with tips on how to begin your own explorations. Actor and award-winning travel writer Andrew McCarthy's featured story recounts his recent quest to uncover his family's Irish history, while twenty-five other prominent writers tell their own heartfelt stories of connection." (Publisher's note)

"This poignant and information-filled travelog and genealogy primer is ideal for public libraries." LJ

Includes bibliographical references and index

Pennavaria, Katherine

Genealogy; a practical guide for librarians. Katherine Pennavaria. Rowman & Littlefield 2015 xxii, 167 p.p (Practical guides for librarians) (pbk.: alk. paper) $65 **929.1**

1. Genealogy 2. Library science

ISBN 0810891506; 9780810891500; 9780810893252; 9780810891517

LC 2014032466

This book on genealogy for librarians, by Katherine Pennavaria, "offers help on several levels: First, librarians can use this book to learn what resources, both print and online, their library should offer their patron base. . . . Second, both librarians and researchers can find here an in-depth discussion of the research process itself. . . . And third, anyone can use this book to become better informed about the phenomenon of genealogy." (Publisher's note)

Includes bibliographical references and index

929.2 Family histories

Teege, Jennifer

My grandfather would have shot me; a Black woman discovers her family's Nazi past. Jennifer Teege, Nikola Sellmair. The Experiment 2015 240 p. illustrations (cloth) $24.95 **929.2**

1. Grandfathers 2. War criminals 3. National socialists 4. Racially mixed people 5. Nazis -- Family relationships 6. Płaszów (Concentration camp) 7. Racially mixed people -- Germany -- Biography 8. Concentration camp commandants -- Family relationships 9. Grandchildren of war criminals -- Germany -- Biography

ISBN 1615192530; 9781615192533

LC 2014046242

This book, by Jennifer Teege, with Nikola Sellmair, is the "memoir of a German-Nigerian woman who learns that her grandfather was the brutal Nazi commandant depicted in Schindler's List, Amon Goeth." (Publisher's note)

"Originally published in German as Amon: mein Grossvater hätte mich erschossen, Teege's account is an important addition to narratives written by descendants of war criminals. A gripping read, highly recommended for anyone interested in history, memoirs, and biography." LJ

Includes bibliographical references

Well, François

Family trees; a history of genealogy in America. François Weil. Harvard University Press 2013 320 p. (hardcover) $27.95 **929.2**

1. Genealogy 2. United States -- Social conditions 3. National characteristics, American 4. Genealogy -- United States -- History

5. Genealogy -- Social aspects -- United States
ISBN 0674045831; 9780674045835

LC 2012044769

This book is a survey of genealogy in America, which has become easier with the advent of the Internet. "The author enumerates four growth stages in the endeavor," looking at colonial America, the late 18th-century, after the Civil War and modern day. François Weil "explains how the proliferation of genealogy-focused Web sites and DNA testing has transformed the pursuit into a lucrative commercial venture." (Publishers Weekly)

Includes bibliographical references and index

929.4   Personal names

Ciuraru, Carmela

Nom de plume; a (secret) history of pseudonyms. Harper 2011 xxiv, 343p $24.99   **929.4**
1. Authors 2. Pseudonyms
ISBN 978-0-06-173526-4

LC 2010-53603

The author "tells the stories of some of literature's most famous pen names by weaving in details about these secretive, often eccentric writers' lives and works to examine their decision to use pen names. From Lewis Carroll (born Charles Dodgson) to Mark Twain (Samuel Clemens) and Victoria Lucas (Sylvia Plath), one chapter is devoted to each with so much detail that the authors under discussion seem to become characters in Ciuraru's book. . . . For anyone who creates — writers, artists and performers — the book will enthrall. It's as much a meditation on the creative process as it is a tell-all about their names and the intrigue, branding or mind games that created them." Associated Press

Includes bibliographical references

Delahunty, Andrew

Oxford dictionary of nicknames. Oxford University Press 2003 229p $29.95; pa $24   **929.4**
1. Nicknames
ISBN 0-19-860539-0; 0-19-860948-5 pa

LC 2004-273526

"This volume is a treasure trove of popular linguistic creativity. From the Hanging Judge to Hanoi Jane, and from Queen Dick to the Queen of Hearts, it makes for delightful bathroom browsing with just a dab of history and culture." Publ Wkly

★ **Dictionary** of American family names; Patrick Hanks, editor. Oxford Univ. Press 2003 3v set $295   **929.4**
1. Personal names -- United States
ISBN 0-19-508137-4

LC 2003-3844

"This set will be useful for genealogists, historians, and others curious about their family roots." SLJ

Includes bibliographical references

Shane, Neala

Inspired baby names from around the world; 6,000 favorite worldwide names and the meanings behind them. Neala Shane. New World Library 2015 712 p. (paperback: alkaline paper) $21.95   **929.4**
1. Personal names 2. Names, Personal -- Dictionaries
ISBN 1608683206; 9781608683208

LC 2014042449

This book of baby names, by Neala Shane, "includes 6,000-plus names from all corners of the globe, and each entry illuminates the name's distinctive spiritual, historical, and cultural background. . . . Pronunciation guide, origin, alternate spellings, and meaning are enhanced by the affirmation carefully chosen for each name. Lists of names by meaning, names by ethnicity, and most popular names by decade provide easy reference." (Publisher's note)

"While readers can browse this book, it's intended for those putting extensive time and investigation into naming their child. Names can sometimes be tough to live up to. But from Aaron (Hebrew) to Zuri (Swahili), there will be plenty of conversation, controversy, and debate inspired by these pages." LJ

929.5   Cemetery records

Neighbors, Joy

The **family** tree cemetery field guide; how to find, record, & preserve your ancestors' graves. Joy Neighbors. Family Tree Books 2017 239 p. illustrations (hardcover) $24.99   **929.5**
1. Genealogy 2. Registers of births, etc. 3. Cemeteries -- United States 4. United States -- Genealogy -- Handbooks, manuals, etc.
ISBN 9781440352126; 9781440352140; 1440352127

LC 2017276788

This book, by Joy Neighbors, shows "you how to search for and analyze your ancestors' graves. Discover tools for locating tombstones, tips for traipsing through cemeteries, an at-a-glance guide to frequently used gravestone icons, and practical strategies for on-the-ground research. And . . . learn how to incorporate gravestone information into your research, as well as how to upload grave locations to BillionGraves and record your findings in memorial pages on Find A Grave." (Publisher's note)

"Cemeteries are crucial for genealogy research, and this solid, compact, one-stop book shows how to search for and analyze ancestors' graves." Booklist

Includes bibliographical references (pages 226-231) and index.

929.9   Forms of insignia and identification

Leepson, Marc

Flag: an American biography. Thomas Dunne Books/St. Martin's Press 2005 334p il $24.95; pa $14.95   **929.9**
1. Flags -- United States
ISBN 978-0-312-32308-0; 0-312-32308-5; 978-0-312-32309-7 pa; 0-312-32309-3 pa

LC 2004-65920

"From reverence to kitsch, Americans' attitudes to their flag and its mythology have changed over the years, and Leepson does a creditable job of recounting those changes." Publ Wkly

Includes bibliographical references

Minahan, James

The **complete** guide to national symbols and emblems. Greenwood Press 2010 2v il set $180   **929.9**
1. Reference books 2. Signs and symbols 3. National emblems -- Encyclopedias 4. National characteristics -- Encyclopedias
ISBN 978-0-313-34496-1; 978-0-313-34497-8 ebook

LC 2009-36963

"This set is an impressive compilation of material that should be quite useful for anyone looking for current information about flags, anthems, athletic teams, cuisines, and such. The 200-plus entries cover independent nations of the world and some dependent states and territories that seek greater visibility, such as Wallonia (an autonomous region within Belgium) and Puerto Rico. Volume 1 covers Asia and Oceania, Central and South America, and Europe. Volume 2 covers the Middle East and North Africa, North America and the Caribbean, and sub-Saharan Africa. National flags and coats of arms are shown in color." Booklist

Includes bibliographical references

Shearer, Benjamin F.

State names, seals, flags, and symbols; a historical guide. [by] Benjamin F. Shearer and Barbara S. Shearer. 3rd ed, rev and expanded; Greenwood Press 2001 495p il $73.95 **929.9**
  1. Reference books 2. Seals (Numismatics) 3. Flags -- United States 4. Geographic names -- United States
  ISBN 0-313-31534-5

LC 2001-23525

First published 1987

"Chapters on mottoes, flowers, trees, birds, songs, holidays, and license plates are just a sampling of what is covered, and the format is such that the concisely written material can be found as expeditiously as possible. Even though the book is touted predominantly as a reference tool, the information provided makes fascinating and enlightening reading." Libr J [review of 1994 edition]

Includes bibliographical references

Testi, Arnaldo

Capture the flag; the Stars and Stripes in American history. translated by Noor Giovanni Mazhar. New York University Press 2010 165p il $22.95 **929.9**
  1. Patriotism 2. American national characteristics 3. Flags -- United States
  ISBN 978-0-8147-83221; 0-8147-8322-8

LC 2009-39278

Original Italian edition, 2003

"From our July 4th celebrations to the iconic images from 9/11, the American flag is an all-pervasive, definitive symbol of American national identity. . . . [Testi] provides readers with an engaging and fresh perspective that can only be provided by an outsider standing above the fray. Whether discussing the evolution of flag etiquette or its relationship to the U.S. Constitution, Testi deftly explores the shifting cultural meanings of the American symbol, from 1776 through the growth of the American empire to the contentious debates occurring today." Libr J

Includes bibliographical references

Znamierowski, Alfred, 1940-

The **World** Encyclopedia of Flags; The definitive guide to international, flags, banners, standards and ensigns, with over 1400 illustration. by Alfred Znamierowski. Lorenz Books 2013 256 p. $16.99 **929.9**
  1. Flags
  ISBN 0754826295; 9780754826293

This book, by Alred Znamierowski, presents "a directory of flags and a fascinating history of their development and usage, featuring over 600 flags including military signs, royal standards, civic flags, ensigns and national flags, expertly illustrated throughout." (Publisher's note)

930 History of ancient world (to ca. 499)

Beard, Mary, 1955-

Confronting the classics; traditions, adventures, and innovations. Mary Beard. Liveright Publishing Corporation, a Division of W. W. Norton & Company 2013 320 p. (hardcover) $28.95 **930**
  1. Classical education 2. Classical civilization 3. Classical antiquities 4. Civilization, Classical
  ISBN 0871407167; 9780871407160

LC 2013016133

National Book Critics Circle Award Finalist: Criticism (2013)

"This collection comprises a decade's worth of [Mary] Beard's . . . book reviews, mostly from the 'Times Literary Supplement' and the 'New York Review of Books,' plus one lecture not previously published. . . . The work follows a chronological arrangement, with the first section on ancient Greece, the next on early Rome, the third on Imperial Rome, and so forth, with later pieces focusing on the classicists themselves across the subsequent centuries." (Library Journal)

Includes bibliographical references and index

★ **Egypt,** Greece, and Rome; civilizations of the ancient Mediterranean. Charles Freeman. 3rd edition Oxford University Press 2014 759 p illustrations $65 **930**
  1. Mediterranean civilization
  ISBN 9780199651924

"Beginning with the early Middle Eastern civilizations of Sumer, and continuing right through to the Islmic invasions and the birth of modern Europe after the collapse of the Roman empire, the book ranges beyond political history to cover art and architecture, philosophy, literature, society, and economy. A wide range of maps, illustrations, and photographs complements the text. This third edition has been extensively revised to appeal to the general reader with several chapters completely rewritten and a great deal of new material added, including a new selection of images." (Publisher's note)

Frammolino, Ralph

Chasing Aphrodite; the hunt for looted antiquities at the world's richest museum. [by] Jason Felch and Ralph Frammolino. Houghton Mifflin Harcourt 2011 375p il $28.00 **930**
  1. Cultural property 2. Classical antiquities 3. J. Paul Getty Museum 4. Archaeological thefts 5. Classical antiquities -- Italy 6. Cultural property -- Repatriation -- Italy 7. Classical antiquities -- Destruction and pillage
  ISBN 0151015015; 9780151015016

LC 2010-25835

In 1976 "oil billionaire J. Paul Getty left his estate to the museum that bears his name, which was suddenly the wealthiest collecting institution in the world—one whose problem was how to spend rather than raise money. The founder's narrow interests had determined the museum's collecting areas, one of which was Greek and Roman art. The stage was set for trouble, and the trouble is described in fascinating detail in 'Chasing Aphrodite,' an account of the Getty's travails in collection-building by Los Angeles Times reporters Jason Felch and Ralph Frammolino. In 2005, longtime Getty curator Marion True would be indicted by authorities in Rome for traffic in illicit antiquities; not long after, in a related controversy, she was forced to resign. The reporters covered these events, as well as the museum's agreements to repatriate works acquired before and during Ms. True's tenure. They were given access by unidentified sources to the museum's archives, and in this book they document a museum administration often motivated by ambition but eventually also by stirrings of conscience." Wall Street J

Includes bibliographical references and index

Kapuscinski, Ryszard, 1932-2007

Travels with Herodotus; translated from the Polish by Klara Glowczewska. Alfred A. Knopf 2007 275p $25 **930**
  1. Historians 2. Voyages and travels 3. Authors 4. Biographers

5. Journalists 6. Nonfiction writers
ISBN 1-400-04338-5; 9781400043385

LC 2006-39565

Original Polish edition, 2004

Kapuscinski describes his travels "to India, to Afghanistan, to China, to Cambodia, to Rangoon." (Publisher's note)

"A work of art: so eloquent, so simple, that you find yourself marveling at its prose, its gentle observation and the rhythm of the words. And you find yourself applauding such good translation as well." Washington Post Book World

Kemp, Barry

The **city** of Akhenaten and Nefertiti; Amarna and its people. Barry Kemp. Thames & Hudson 2012 320 p. (hardcover) $45   **930**
1. Egypt -- History 2. Egypt -- Antiquities 3. Tell el-Amarna (Egypt)
ISBN 0500051739; 9780500051733

LC 2011945993

This book by Barry Kemp describes the history of "the ancient site of Tell el-Amarna in Middle Egypt, [which] was the capital city of the heretic pharaoh Akhenaten and his chief consort, Nefertiti. Occupied for just sixteen or so years in the fourteenth century BC, the city lay largely abandoned and forgotten until excavations over the last hundred years brought it back into prominence." (Publisher's note)

930.1 Archaeology

Archaeology; the essential guide to our human past. edited by Paul Bahn, with foreword by Brian Fagan. Smithsonian Books 2017 576 p. (hardback) $45   **930.1**
1. Archeology 2. Antiquities 3. Archaeology
ISBN 9781588345912

LC 2017025534

This book, edited by Paul Bahn, "provides a tour of every site of key archaeological importance. From the prehistoric cave paintings of Lascaux to Tutankhamun's tomb, from the buried city of Pompeii to China's Terracotta Army, all of the world's most iconic sites and discoveries are here. So too are the lesser-known yet equally important finds, such as the recent discoveries of our oldest known human ancestors and of the world's oldest-known temple, Göbekli Tepe in Turkey." (Publisher's note)

"An excellent resource for high-school and college students with considerable appeal for the general reader." (Booklist)

Beneath the seven seas; adventures with the Intitute of Nautical Archaeology. edited by George F. Bass. Thames & Hudson 2005 256p il maps $39.95   **930.1**
1. Archeology 2. Shipwrecks 3. Underwater exploration
ISBN 978-0-500-05136-8; 0-500-05136-4

LC 2005-900862

This book features "accounts by many distinguished archaeologists associated with the INA [Institute of Nautical Archaeology]. They tell of the discovery, excavation, and preservation of more than 40 shipwrecks—and one sunken city—the world over, from ancient times through the Byzantine, medieval, and Renaissance eras and on through World War II. . . . This book will appeal to general readers and specialists alike in nautical archaeology." Libr J

Includes bibliographical references

Ceram, C. W.

Gods, graves, and scholars; the story of archaeology. translated from the German by E. B. Garside and Sophie Wilkins. 2nd rev and substantially enl ed; Knopf 1967 441p il maps hardcover o.p. pa $11.16   **930.1**
1. Mayas 2. Aztecs 3. Archeology 4. Hieroglyphics 5. Babel, Tower of 6. Cuneiform inscriptions 7. Rosetta stone inscription 8. Kings 9. Crete (Greece) 10. Egypt -- Antiquities
ISBN 0-394-74319-9 pa

Original German edition, 1949; first English language edition, 1951

"The story of Champollion and the reading of the Rosetta Stone, the decipherment of the inscriptions on the monument of Darius the Great, Leonard Woolley's famous excavations at Ur, and John Lloyd Stephens' discovery of the ruins of a great Mayan city are . . . told in this book." Doors to More Mature Read

Includes bibliographical references

Childs, Craig Leland

Finders keepers; a tale of archaeological plunder and obsession. Little, Brown and Co. 2010 274p $24.99   **930.1**
1. Archeologists -- Ethics
ISBN 978-0-316-06642-6; 0-316-06642-7

LC 2009-51921

"Childs treks the canyon-incised Colorado Plateau in search of pre-Columbian artifacts. Their legal regulation collides with collectors' obsessions to possess them. Childs, though, does not remove what he finds, an ethic that vies with other precepts for the proper preservation of antiquities. For every stand he takes on archaeological morality in this narrative mix of his backcountry experiences and conversations with collectors, curators, dealers, and an occasional looter, Childs engages their justifications for taking custody of ancient objects. . . . Alternating romantic and practical moods, Childs hunts virtue as much as baskets in this engaging discourse." Booklist

Includes bibliographical references

Hunt, Patrick

Ten discoveries that rewrote history. Plume 2007 226p pa $27.95   **930.1**
1. Antiquities 2. Ancient civilization 3. Archeology -- History
ISBN 978-0-452-28877-5; 0-452-28877-0

LC 2007-19808

The author "has produced a wonderful volume of of archaeological history. In doing so, he has provided a seldom seen look at some of the most important scientific developments in the field." Sci Books Films

Includes bibliographical references

Johnson, Marilyn

Lives in ruins; archaeologists and the seductive lure of human rubble. Marilyn Johnson. Harper 2014 288 p. $25.99   **930.1**
1. Archeology 2. Archeologists 3. Archaeology -- Anecdotes 4. Archaeologists -- Anecdotes
ISBN 0062127187; 9780062127181

LC 2014028450

In this book the author, Marilyn Johnson, "turns her . . . eye and . . . wit to the real-life avatars of Indiana Jones--the archaeologists who sort through the muck and mire of swamps, ancient landfills, volcanic islands, and other dirty places to reclaim history for us all. . . . [She] digs and drinks alongside archaeologists, chases them through the Mediterranean, the Caribbean, and even Machu Picchu, and excavates their lives." (Publisher's note)

"Without glitz, the author has created a very enjoyable work that will be appreciated by experts in the field and casual readers alike. Well suited to anyone contemplating archaeology as a career, those curious about what the profession is like, lovers of history and science, and readers who enjoy and are grateful for the lure of prehistory and discovery as a mental process." LJ

Includes bibliographical references

MacGregor, Neil, 1946-

A **history** of the world in 100 objects; Neil MacGregor. Viking 2011 xxvi, 707 p. p col. ill., maps $45   **930.1**

1. Antiques 2. Art objects 3. World history 4. Material culture 5. Ceremonial objects 6. Archaeology, Medieval 7. Classical antiquities 8. Antiquities, Prehistoric

ISBN 0670022705; 1846144132; 9780670022700; 9781846144134

LC 2011021769

The book by Neil MacGregor is the result of "a joint project between the [British M]useum and the British Broadcasting Corporation's Radio Four. . . . In this project, . . . one hundred objects from the museum's enormous holdings [were be chosen]. . . . The book . . . is . . . a compilation of the one hundred objects, arranged more or less chronologically, . . . each with essay and commentary as edited for final broadcast format." (New York Review of Books)

Includes bibliographical references (p. 671-678) and index

The **Oxford** Companion to Archaeology; Edited by Neil Asher Silberman. 2nd edition Oxford University Press 2012 3 vol. illustrations $595   **930.1**

1. Archeology

ISBN 0199735786; 9780199735785

LC 2011051893

"Much has changed in the field [of archaeology] since 1996. Recent developments in methods and analytical techniques (e.g., laser-based mapping and survey systems, new applications of the scanning electron microscope) have revolutionized the ways excavations are performed. Cultural tourism, cultural resource management, heritage, and conservation have been redefined as areas within archaeology, and have been newly emphasized by scholars and administrators. Major site discoveries have expanded our understanding of prehistory and human developments through time. The second edition explores each of these advances in the field, adding approximately 150 entries." (Publisher's note)

932   Egypt to 640

Brier, Bob

The **murder** of Tutankhamen; a true story. Berkley Books 2005 xx, 264p il pa $14   **932**

1. Kings 2. Egypt -- History

ISBN 0-425-20690-4; 978-0-425-20690-4

LC 2005-41085

First published 1998 by Putnam

"Brier obviously knows his subject and is impassioned by it. Readers who enjoy history or true-crime stories will be intrigued by this work." SLJ

Includes bibliographical references

Bunson, Margaret R.

Encyclopedia of ancient Egypt; Margaret R. Bunson. 3rd edition Facts On File 2012 xxviii, 516 p.p ill., maps (alk. paper) $95   **932**

1. Egypt -- History 2. Egypt -- Antiquities -- Encyclopedias 3. Egypt -- Civilization -- Encyclopedias 4. Egypt -- Antiquities -- Dictionaries 5. Egypt -- Civilization -- To 332 B.C. -- Dictionaries

ISBN 0816082162; 9780816082162

LC 2011026433

"Entries are detailed and concise; some have bibliographies, and many summarize why a subject is notable, with references to related entries. The volume explores every aspect of Egyptian culture, from warfare to burial rites. Interesting entries include the ones on Akhenaten, the heretical pharaoh who introduced monotheism; his famous wife Nefertiti; and son Tutankhamun. Alexander the Great's conquest of Egypt and its historical impact are covered extensively in a detailed entry. Deities are discussed for many of the historical periods, and the information concerning Hatshepsut, the female pharaoh, is detailed and enlightening. This volume features a list of illustrations and maps, brief introduction, historical/geographical overview, chronology, and glossary." (Choice)

"This is a useful one-stop, ready-reference resource for general readers interested in ancient Egyptian civilization." LJ

Includes bibliographical references and index

Fletcher, Joann

The **Story** of Egypt; The Civilization that Shaped the World. by Joann Fletcher. Hachette Books 2016 496 p. color illustrations, maps $29.95   **932**

1. Egypt -- History

ISBN 1444785184; 1681771349; 9781444785180; 9781681771342

In this book, "Professor Joann Fletcher pulls together the complete story of Egypt—charting the rise and fall of the ancient Egyptians while putting their whole world into a context to which we can all relate. Fletcher uncovers some . . . revelations: new evidence shows that women became pharaohs on at least ten occasions; that the ancient Egyptians built the first Suez Canal and then circumnavigated Africa." (Publisher's note)

"The authoritative author imparts her vast knowledge in an orderly chronology and lively, intimate history. A perfect choice for budding Egyptologists." Kirkus

Includes bibliographical references (pages 381-460) and index.

Handbook to life in ancient Egypt; Rosalie David. Revised edition Oxford University Press 2007 417 p paperback $25   **932**

1. Egypt -- History -- To 640 A.D.

ISBN 9780195366716

"The Nile Valley civilization, which spanned a period from c. 5000 B.C. to the early centuries A.D., was one of the earliest created by humankind. This handy reference provides a comprehensive overview of more than five millennia of Egyptian history and archeology, from predynastic times to the Old and New Kingdoms to the Ptolemaic and Roman periods. Accessible, authoritative, and clearly organized, the Handbook to Life in Ancient Egypt offers an engaging look at a culture whose art and architecture, religion, and medicine would come to form the basis of Western Civilization." (Publisher's note)

Includes bibliographical references (p. 385-395) and index

Hawass, Zahi A.

Hidden treasures of ancient Egypt; unearthing the masterpieces of Egyptian history. [by] Zahi Hawass; photographs by Kenneth Garrett. National Geographic Society 2004 256p il $35   **932**

1. Egyptian art 2. Egypt -- Antiquities 3. Excavations (Archeology) -- Egypt

ISBN 0-7922-6319-7

LC 2004-44845

The author "narrates the past 150 years of excavation, from the colonial period—when Westerners overwhelmed the ranks of those recovering the nation's treasures—through Egypt's independence and the present era of international cooperation. . . . This breathtaking glimpse at the country's archeological wealth should excite curious and adventurous minds worldwide." Publ Wkly

Tutankhamun and the golden age of the pharaohs; [by] Zahi Hawass; photographs by Kenneth Garrett. National Geographic Books 2005 285p il map $35　　932
1. Kings 2. Egypt -- Antiquities
ISBN 0-7922-3873-7
LC 2005-41678
This companion to an exhibition displaying about 130 items found in the tombs of Tutankhamun and other kings from the same dynasty "describes the physical and symbolic attributes of each object and explains its purpose in the afterlife. . . . An arrestingly visual album destined for high demand." Booklist
Includes bibliographical references

Mertz, Barbara
Temples, tombs, & hieroglyphs; a popular history of ancient Egypt. 2nd ed., 1st William Morrow ed.; William Morrow 2007 xxvi, 324p il map $26.95　　932
1. Queens 2. Hieroglyphics 3. Egyptian language 4. Kings 5. Syria 6. Egypt -- Antiquities 7. Egypt -- Civilization 8. Thebes (Egypt: Extinct city)
ISBN 978-0-06-125276-1; 0-06-125276-X
LC 2007-29118
First published 1964 by Coward-McCann
This is an "introduction to the history of ancient Egypt and Egyptology. . . . Mertz gives special attention to such topics as the kingship (yes) of Queen Hatshepsut, the exploits of Thutmose III, and the Amarna Period with its intriguing players Akhenaten, Nefertiti, and Tutankhamen. Presenting both pros and cons of current theories, Mertz also explains in simple language archaeological techniques such as carbon 14 dating and historical chronology. . . . [This is] an excellent introduction for patrons interested in the land of the pharaohs." Libr J

The Oxford encyclopedia of ancient Egypt; Donald B. Redford, editor in chief. Oxford Univ. Press 2001 3v set $450　932
1. Reference books 2. Egypt -- Antiquities -- Encyclopedias 3. Egypt -- Civilization -- Encyclopedias
ISBN 0-19-510234-7
LC 99-54801
ALA RUSA Dartmouth Medal (2002)
This reference work covers "archaeology, biography, history, language, social history, and more. . . . [It features] essays from more than 250 contributors from various countries and scholarly pursuits, all with solid academic credentials. . . . One is not likely to encounter another work of this magnitude on a subject of such universal interest for some time." Booklist
Includes bibliographical references

Romer, John
A **history** of ancient Egypt; from the Great Pyramid to the fall of the Middle Kingdom. John Romer. St. Martin's Press 2017 592 p. $29.99; (ebook) $40　　932
1. Egypt -- History
ISBN 1250030137; 9781250030139; 9781250030108
In this book in the History of Ancient Egypt series, author "John Romer chronicles the history of Ancient Egypt from the building of

the Great Pyramid through the rise and fall of the Middle Kingdom: a peak of Pharaonic culture and the period when writing first flourished. Through extensive research over many decades of work, [he] reveals how the grand narratives of 19th and 20th century Egyptologists have misled us by portraying a culture of cruel monarchs and chronic war." (Publisher's note)
"This is an essential re-envisioning of ancient Egypt." Pub Wkly

Wilkinson, Richard H.
The **complete** temples of ancient Egypt; Richard H. Wilkinson. Thames & Hudson 2000 256 p. illustrations, maps (hbk.) $39.95　　932
1. Temples 2. Egypt -- Religion 3. Egypt -- Antiquities 4. Temples -- Egypt -- History 5. Architecture, Ancient -- Egypt 6. Egypt -- Religion -- 332 B.C.-640 A.D. 7. Temples -- Egypt -- Design and construction
ISBN 0500051003; 9780500051009; 9780500283967
LC 99066106
This book in the Complete series, by Richard H. Wilkinson, is "a comprehensive survey of all Egypt's temples, from Luxor and Karnak to those in the delta, oases and Nubia. It traces the processes of building and decorating, how they functioned, and what happened when they were robbed and desecrated. It also discusses the Egyptian pantheon, rites and festivals." (Publisher's note)
"An indispensable work for a student of Egyptian life or architecture." LJ

Wilkinson, Toby
★ The **rise** and fall of ancient Egypt; [by] Toby Wilkinson. Random House 2011 611p il map $35　　932
1. Egypt -- History 2. Egypt -- History -- 332-30 B.C. 3. Egypt -- History -- To 332 B.C.
ISBN 978-0-553-80553-6; 0-553-80553-3
LC 2009-47322
The author "offers a revisionist view of the ugly life hidden by the splendors and dazzling treasures of pharaonic Egypt. He shows in rich detail that it was a brutal society where life was cheap, royal power absolute and established through fear and coercion. . . . This is a penetrating and authoritative overview of a violent ancient civilization often revered by contemporary scholars and enthusiasts." Publ Wkly
Includes bibliographical references

933　Palestine to 70

Korb, Scott
Life in year one; what the world was like in first-century Palestine. Riverhead Books 2010 241p $25.95　　933
1. Palestine 2. Jews -- History 3. Bible -- History
ISBN 978-1-59448-899-3
LC 2010-146
The author "calls his retrospective 'a lively romp through the land of Palestine,' circa 5 B.C.E.–70 C.E., but the picture he draws from archeology, ancient historical accounts, and religious texts is anything but lighthearted. . . . Korb's vivid, breezy prose makes accessible a mountain of scholarship that illuminates the past." Publ Wkly
Includes bibliographical references

935 Mesopotamia to 637 and Iranian Plateau to 637

Kriwaczek, Paul

Babylon; Mesopotamia and the birth of civilization. Paul Kriwaczek. Thomas Dunne Books/St. Martin's Press 2012 310 p. **935**

1. Tigris River 2. Euphrates River 3. Iraq -- History 4. Ancient civilization 5. Babylon (Extinct city) 6. Iraq -- History -- To 634 7. Iraq -- Civilization -- To 634 8. Iraq -- Politics and government 9. Babylon (Extinct city) -- History 10. Babylon (Extinct city) -- Civilization 11. Babylon (Extinct city) -- Politics and government

ISBN 9781250000071; 9781429941068

LC 2012003104

This book is an "overview of the rich, ancient civilizations that flourished in the land between the two rivers. . . . The ancient simmering conflict of the Fertile Crescent boils down to the question: "Should the Tigris-Euphrates Valley be mastered from the west or the east"? . . . . The need to organize systems of irrigation in Eridu . . . spawned an "urban revolution," with the invention of cities and all that came with them: division of labor, social classes, engineering, the arts, education, numbers and law, to mention a few. . . . The author keeps close to biblical readings for comparative accounts of the Flood and the succession of kings of the city-states to the founder of the first true empire, Sargon." (Kirkus)

Includes bibliographical references and index

936 Europe north and west of Italian Peninsula to ca. 499

Higgins, Charlotte

Under another sky; journeys in Roman Britain. Charlotte Higgins. The Overlook Press 2015 282 p. illustrations, maps (hardback) $27.95 **936**

1. Rome -- Antiquities 2. Great Britain -- Antiquities 3. Great Britain -- History -- 0-1066 4. Monuments -- Great Britain 5. Landscapes -- Great Britain 6. Great Britain -- History, Local 7. Romans -- Great Britain -- History 8. Great Britain -- Antiquities, Roman 9. Cultural landscapes -- Great Britain

ISBN 1468310895; 9781468310894

LC 2015011873

In this book, by Charlotte Higgins, shortlisted for the Samuel Johnson Prize, the author "sets out to explore the ancient monuments of Roman Britain. She explores the land that was once Rome's northernmost territory and how it has changed since the years after the empire fell. Under Another Sky invites us to see the British landscape, and British history, . . . as indelibly marked by how the Romans first imagined and wrote, these strange and exotic islands." (Publisher's note)

"A thoroughly researched, elegantly written history." Kirkus

Includes bibliographical references and index

936.2 England to 410 and Wales to 410

Hill, Rosemary

Stonehenge. Harvard University Press 2008 242p il map (Wonders of the world) $19.95 **936.2**

1. Stonehenge (England) 2. Megalithic monuments -- Great Britain

ISBN 9780674031326; 0674031326

LC 2008-12024

Hill's "book is a treasure: stylish, thoughtful, miraculously condensed, and as full of knowledge as a megalith is full of megalith." Sunday Times (London)

Includes bibliographical references (p. 211-222)

Pearson, Mike Parker

Stonehenge; a new understanding: solving the mysteries of the greatest stone age monument. by Mike Parker Pearson. The Experiment 2013 432 p. (hardcover) $27.50 **936.2**

1. Stonehenge (England) 2. Excavations (Archeology) 3. England -- Antiquities 4. Megalithic monuments -- England 5. Stonehenge (England) -- History 6. Stonehenge World Heritage Site (England)

ISBN 1615190791; 9781615190799

LC 2012047688

This book, by Mike Parker Pearson, "changes the way we think about [Stonehenge] correcting previously erroneous dating, filling gaps in our knowledge about its builders and how they lived, clarifying the monument's significance both celestially and as a burial ground, and contextualizing Stonehenge . . . within the broader landscape of the Neolithic Age." (Publisher's note)

"Renowned archaeologist Pearson . . . presents the findings of the most ambitious and scientifically informed investigation of Stonehenge thus far. . . . Filled with maps, drawings, photographs and diagrams, the book details the group's findings in a well-organized, absorbing manner." Kirkus

Includes bibliographical references and index

Pryor, Francis

★ **Stonehenge**; the story of a sacred landscape. Francis Pryor. Pegasus Books 2018 207 p. illustrations (chiefly color) (hardcover) $26.95 **936.2**

1. Stonehenge (England) 2. Megalithic monuments -- Great Britain 3. Engineering 4. History, Ancient 5. Wiltshire (England) -- Antiquities 6. Megalithic monuments -- England -- Wiltshire

ISBN 9781681777030; 9781681776408; 1681776405

This book, by Francis Pryor, presents "an illustrated, evocative narrative of the nature and history of Stonehenge that places the enigmatic stone megaliths in a wider cultural context. Perched on the chalk uplands of Salisbury Plain, the megaliths of Stonehenge offer one of the most recognizable outlines of any ancient structure. Its purpose . . . is unknown, but its story is one of the most extraordinary of any of the world's prehistoric monuments." (Publisher's note)

"A renowned archaeologist chronicles the remarkable changes in our knowledge of the builders of Stonehenge and other, equally important and connected henges throughout Britain." Kirkus

Includes bibliographical references (pages 202-205) and index.

936.4 Celtic regions to 486

Omrani, Bijan

★ **Caesar's** footprints; a cultural excursion to ancient France: journeys through Roman Gaul. Bijan Omrani. Pegasus Books 2017 xiii, 386 p.p 28.95 **936.4**

1. Gaul -- Geography

ISBN 1681775662; 9781681775661

This book, by Bijan Omrani, is "an intellectual adventure through ancient France revealing how [Julius] Caesar's conquest of Gaul changed the course of French culture, forever transforming modern Europe. Julius Caesar's conquests in Gaul in the 50s BC were bloody, but the cultural revolution they brought in their wake forever transformed the ancient Celtic culture of that country." (Publisher's note)

Includes bibliographical references (pages 357-370) and index.

937   Italian Peninsula to 476 and adjacent territories to 476

Beard, Mary 1955-

The **fires** of Vesuvius; Pompeii lost and found. Belknap Press of Harvard University Press 2008 360p il map $26.95; pa $17.95   **937**

1. Pompeii (Extinct city)

ISBN 978-0-674-02976-7; 0-674-02976-3; 978-0-674-04586-6 pa; 0-674-04586-6 pa

LC 2008-27513

"The eruption of Mt. Vesuvius in 79 A.D. preserved a uniquely rich sample of Roman life. Buried among the ruins of Pompeii are frescoes, graffiti ('Atimetus got me pregnant'), campaign ads, and housewares; the victims themselves left hollows in the lava that, when cast in plaster, yield details as fine as the imprint of one man's eyebrows. In this lively survey, Beard, a classicist at Cambridge, tempers erudition with a skepticism toward interpretive overreach. " New Yorker

Includes bibliographical references

★ **SPQR**; a history of ancient Rome. Mary Beard. Liveright Publishing Corp. 2015 608 p. ill. (some col.), maps (hardcover) $35   **937**

1. Rome -- History 2. Ancient civilization 3. Rome -- History -- Kings, 753-510 B.C 4. Rome -- History -- Republic, 510-30 B.C 5. Rome -- History -- Empire, 30 B.C.-476 A.D

ISBN 0871404230; 9780871404237

LC 2015036060

National Book Critics Circle Award Finalist: Nonfiction (2015)

Author Mary Beard presents this book "exploring how the Romans themselves challenged the idea of imperial rule, how they responded to terrorism and revolution, and how they invented a new idea of citizenship and nation, while also keeping her eye open for those overlooked in traditional histories: women, slaves and ex-slaves, conspirators, and losers. Beard separates fact from fiction, myth and propaganda from historical record." (Publisher's note)

"Since the author is a well-known popularizer of classical studies, it is no surprise that this is a humorous and accessible work, but it is also extremely rigorous in its questioning of standard conclusions and methods. . . . At all points, her approaches are easy to follow." LJ

Includes bibliographical references and index

Berry, Joanne

The **complete** Pompeii. Thames & Hudson 2007 256p il map $40   **937**

1. Pompeii (Extinct city)

ISBN 978-0-500-05150-4; 0-500-05150-X

LC 2007-922095

This book "covers the origins and evolution of the city, the daily life of its residents, the geography of the region, and the eruption of Mt. Vesuvius, as well as a history of the excavation of the site. Easy to read and with full color pictures of the excavation, along with maps, time lines, diagrams, and vivid art reproductions, this book gives a broad and comprehensive introduction to the Pompeian world. . . . High school libraries should be advised that there is a section on eroticism that contains visually and verbally explicit sexual material." Libr J

Includes bibliographical references

Bunson, Matthew

Encyclopedia of ancient Rome; Matthew Bunson. 3rd ed. Facts On File 2012 xxxvii, 788 p.p ill., maps (acid-free paper) $95.00   **937**

1. Rome -- Antiquities 2. Rome -- Civilization 3. Rome -- History -- Encyclopedias 4. Rome -- History -- Empire, 30 B.C.-476 A.D. -- Encyclopedias

ISBN 0816082170; 9780816082179

LC 2011038366

This encyclopedia, by Matthew Bunson, "provides . . . coverage of the people, places, events, and ideas of ancient Rome. Each entry . . . reflect[s] recent advances in archaeology, historical and literary criticism, and social analysis. In addition, the scope . . . include[s] the entire history of ancient Rome, from the first founding of the city . . . to the final collapse of Roman power in the fifth century CE." (Publisher's note)

"A superb source of detailed, engaging information on the ever fascinating and often perplexing ancient Roman civilization, Bunson's work is a handy reference for classics students and enthusiasts alike." LJ

Includes bibliographical references (p. 757-760) and index

Everitt, Anthony

The **rise** of Rome; the making of the world's greatest empire. Anthony Everitt. 1st ed. Random House 2012 xxxii, 478 p., [8] p. of platesp col. ill., maps (ebook) $85.00; (hardcover: alk. paper) $30.00   **937**

1. Rome -- History 2. Rome -- Politics and government 3. Rome -- History -- Empire, 284-476 4. Rome -- History -- Empire, 30 B.C.-284 A.D

ISBN 1400066638; 9780679645160; 9781400066636; 0679645160

LC 2011048318

This book by Anthony Everitt examines the history of "Rome and its . . . ascent from an obscure agrarian backwater. . . . He chronicles the clash between patricians and plebeians that defined the politics of the Republic. He shows how Rome's . . . strategy of offering citizenship to her defeated subjects was instrumental in expanding the reach of her burgeoning empire. And he outlines the corrosion of constitutional norms that accompanied Rome's . . . expansion." (Publisher's note)

Includes bibliographical references (p. [423]-426) and index.

Freisenbruch, Annelise

Caesars' wives; sex, power, and politics in the Roman Empire. Free Press 2010 xxvi, 337p il $28; ebook $14.99   **937**

1. Empresses 2. Women -- Rome 3. Rome -- History

ISBN 978-1-4165-8303-5; 1-4165-8303-3; 978-1-4165-8357-8 ebook; 1-4165-8357-2 ebook

LC 2010-19368

"Providing well-chosen, scintillating details—e.g., enemies being boiled alive, familial bonds savagely snapped in an instant—alongside careful historical analysis, the author breathes new life into these overlooked subjects. . . . A captivating look at imperial Rome's roots in the making of the modern stateswoman " Kirkus

Includes bibliographical references

Gibbon, Edward

★ The **decline** and fall of the Roman empire; Edward Gibbon; edited, abridged, and with a critical introduction by Hans-Friedrich Mueller; introduction by Daniel J. Boorstin; illustrations by Giovanni Battista Piranesi. Modern Library paperback ed.; Modern Library 2003 xxxvii, 1258p il map pa $15.95   **937**

1. Rome -- History 2. Byzantine Empire

ISBN 0-375-75811-9

LC 2002-32585

First published 1776-1788 in the United Kingdom with title: The history of the decline and fall of the Roman Empire

"In this substantial history of the Roman Empire, Gibbon bridges the abyss between the ancient and the modern world. It is the one historical work of the eighteenth century that is still accepted as authoritative. It covers thirteen centuries of history, during which time paganism was breaking down and Christianity was taking its place." Reader's Adviser

Includes bibliographical references

Goldsworthy, Adrian

Pax romana; War, Peace and Conquest in the Roman World. Adrian Goldsworthy. Yale University Press 2016 528 p. illustrations, maps $32.50 **937**

1. Rome 2. Peace
ISBN 9780300178821

LC 2016941493

This book, by Adrian Goldsworthy, is a "comprehensive history of the Roman Peace. . . . Goldsworthy turns his attention to the Pax Romana, the famous peace and prosperity brought by the Roman Empire at its height in the first and second centuries AD. Yet the Romans were conquerors, imperialists who took by force a vast empire stretching from the Euphrates to the Atlantic coast." (Publisher's note)

"An engrossing account of how the Roman Empire grew and operated." Kirkus

Includes bibliographical references and index.

Harper, Kyle

The **fate** of Rome; climate, disease, and the end of an empire. Kyle Harper. Princeton University Press 2017 440 p. (hardback) $35 **937**

1. Rome -- Civilization 2. Rome -- History -- Empire, 30 B.C.-476 A.D.
ISBN 9780691166834

LC 2017952241

This book in The Princeton History of the Ancient World series, by Kyle Harper, "examine[s] the catastrophic role that climate change and infectious diseases played in the collapse of Rome's power--a story of nature's triumph over human ambition. . . . Harper traces how the fate of Rome was decided not just by emperors, soldiers, and barbarians but also by volcanic eruptions, solar cycles, climate instability, and devastating viruses and bacteria." (Publisher's note)

"There is much to absorb in this significant scholarly achievement, which effectively integrates natural, social, and humanistic sciences to show how the fall of the empire caused the decline of Rome." (Kirkus)

O'Connell, Robert L.

The **ghosts** of Cannae; Hannibal and the darkest hour of the Roman republic. Random House 2010 310p map $27 **937**

1. Generals 2. Punic Wars, 264 B.C.-146 B.C. 3. Rome -- History 4. Punic Wars, 264-146 B.C.
ISBN 978-1-4000-6702-2; 1-4000-6702-2

LC 2009-40006

"The distinctive edge of The Ghosts of Cannae is Robert L. O'Connell's consistently professional instinct for the behavior of men and units on the battlefield. He is able to put himself and his reader on the ground at Cannae, gagging in the heat of a southern Italian midsummer, assailed by an overload from every one of the five senses." N Y Times Book Rev

Includes bibliographical references

Plutarch, ca. 46-120

The **Age** of Caesar; Five Roman Lives. by Plutarch, edited by James Romm, translated by Pamela Mensch. W W Norton & Co Inc 2017 416 p. illustrations, maps $35; (ebook) $50 **937**

1. Rome -- Civilization
ISBN 0393292827; 9780393292824; 9780393292831

LC 2016035735

This book, by Plutarch, edited by James Romm, and translated by Pamela Mensch, is a "new translation of five of history's greatest lives. . . . Pompey, Caesar, Cicero, Brutus, Antony: the names resonate across thousands of years. Major figures in the civil wars that brutally ended the Roman republic, their lives still haunt us as examples of how the hunger for personal power can overwhelm collective politics." (Publisher's note)

"For those with a serious interest in Roman history. As this is an ancient primary source, it is helpful if readers come at this work with a general understanding of the events and people of the first century BCE Roman world" LJ

Includes bibliographical references and index.

Strauss, Barry

The **death** of Caesar; the story of history's most famous assassination. Barry Strauss. Simon & Schuster 2015 352 p. 8 plates; illustrations $27 **937**

1. Assassination
ISBN 1451668791; 9781451668797

LC 2014032045

This book, by Barry Strauss, presents the "dramatic story of one of history's most famous events--the death of Julius Caesar. . . . [William] Shakespeare shows Caesar's assassination to be an amateur and idealistic affair. The real killing, however, was a carefully planned paramilitary operation, a generals' plot, put together by Caesar's disaffected officers and designed with precision." (Publisher's note)

"The author explains how Caesar's funeral was even more dramatic than Shakespeare's version—especially Mark Antony's eulogy. Once again, Strauss takes us deep into the psyche of ancient history in an exciting, twisted tale that is sure to please." Kirkus

Includes bibliographical references and index

938 Greece to 323

Cartledge, Paul

Ancient Greece; a history in eleven cities. Oxford University Press 2009 261p il map $19.95 **938**

1. Greece -- Civilization 2. Greece -- History -- 0-323
ISBN 978-0-19-923338-0

LC 2009-26999

"Aiming for a general audience, Cartledge achieves a fast-paced, highly engaging romp through ancient Greece. An excellent choice for anyone seeking an introduction to the topic; for all its readability, this book doesn't skimp on the research." Libr J

Includes bibliographical references

Garland, Robert

Athens burning; the Persian invasion of Greece and the evacuation of Attica. Robert Garland. Johns Hopkins University Press 2017 viii, 170 p.p illustrations, maps (Witness to ancient history) (pbk.: alk. paper) $19.95 **938**

1. Greece -- History 2. Athens (Greece) -- History 3. Athens (Greece) -- History -- Siege, 480 B.C 4. Civilians in war -- Greece -- Athens -- History -- To 1500 5. Greece -- History -- Persian Wars, 500-449 B.C. -- Campaigns 6. Greece -- History -- Persian Wars, 500-449 B.C. -- Social aspects
ISBN 142142195X; 1421421968; 9781421421957; 9781421421964

LC 2016022026

This book in the Witness to Ancient History series, by Robert Garland, "explores the reasons behind the decision to abandon Attica, the peninsular region of Greece that includes Athens, while analyzing the consequences, both material and psychological, of the resulting invasion. Garland introduces readers to the contextual background of the Greco-Persian wars, which include the famous Battle of Marathon." (Publisher's note)

"This book is by far the best basic introduction to its subject now available in English." Choice

Includes bibliographical references (pages 157-160) and index

Great moments in Greek archaeology; academic coordinator, Panos Valavanis; translated by David Hardy; foreword by Angelos Delivorrias; essays by George F. Bass . . . [et al.] The J. Paul Getty Museum 2007 379p il $75   **938**
1. Greece -- Antiquities 2. Excavations (Archeology) -- Greece
ISBN 978-0-89236-910-2; 0-89236-910-8

LC 2007-16609

"This magnificently illustrated book with essays by leading scholars—frequently the excavators themselves—tells the story of Greek archaeological discoveries, capturing the excitement and rendering details accessible to a wide audience." Libr J

Includes bibliographical references

Green, Peter

The **Hellenistic** age; a history. Modern Library 2007 xxxiii, 199p map (Modern Library chronicles) hardcover o.p. pa $14   **938**
1. Hellenism 2. Greece -- History 3. Mediterranean region -- History
ISBN 978-0-679-64279-4; 0-679-64279-X; 978-0-8129-6740-1 pa; 0-8129-6740-2 pa

LC 2006-46657

Tis study "traces the unfolding of Hellenistic civilization in a linear fashion, while at the same time drawing connections between successive alterations in the political, economic and social landscape of the Hellenistic East and the appearance of new cultural and intellectual perspectives. . . . [The book] provides an interesting and well-written overview of a historical period that Green aptly describes as covering 'some of the most crucial and transformational history of the ancient world. . . . The changes are lasting and fundamental.' If only for this, students of world history are in Green's debt." Philadelphia Inquirer

Includes bibliographical references

Herodotus, ca. 484 B.C.-425 B.C.

The **Histories**; Herodotus; translated by Tom Holland; introduction and notes by Paul Cartledge. Viking Adult 2014 880 p. maps (hbk.) $40   **938**
1. Ancient history 2. Greece -- History -- 0-323 3. History, Ancient 4. Greece -- History -- To 146 B.C
ISBN 0670024899; 9780670024896

LC 2012474647

This book by Herodotus, translated by Tom Holland, "is the earliest surviving work of nonfiction and a thrilling narrative account of (among other things) the war between the Persian Empire and the Greek city-states in the fifth century BC." This edition includes "an introduction and notes by Professor Paul Cartledge, a translator's preface, an index of significant persons and places, maps, and a supplementary index." (Publisher's note)

"This ancient Greek historian could easily be called the father of humor. . .; he irreverently describes events, players and their countless harebrained schemes." Kirkus

Includes bibliographical references (pages 745-746) and indexes

★ The **landmark** Herodotus; the Histories: a new translation. a new translation by Andrea L. Purvis with maps, annotations, appendices, and encyclopedic index; edited by Robert B. Strassler; with an introduction by Rosalind Thomas. Pantheon Books 2007 lxiv, 953p $45   **938**
1. History, Ancient 2. Greece -- History 3. Greece -- History -- To 146 B.C.
ISBN 978-0-375-42109-9; 0-375-42109-2; 0375421092; 9780375421099

LC 2007024149

This is a new translation of Herodotus' Histories. Indexes.

"A major theme of the Histories is the way in which time can effect surprising changes in the fortunes and reputations of empires, cities, and men; all the more appropriate, then, that Herodotus' reputation has once again been riding very high. In the academy, his technique, once derided as haphazard, has earned newfound respect, while his popularity among ordinary readers will likely get a boost from the publication of perhaps the most densely annotated, richly illustrated, and user-friendly edition of his Histories ever to appear: 'The Landmark Herodotus,' edited by Robert B. Strassler and bristling with appendices, by a phalanx of experts, on everything from the design of Athenian warships to ancient units of liquid measure." New Yorker

Includes bibliographical references

Kagan, Donald

The **Peloponnesian** War. Viking 2003 xxvii, 511p il map $29.95; pa $15   **938**
1. Greece -- History -- 431-404 B.C., Peloponnesian War
ISBN 0-670-03211-5; 0-14-200437-5 pa

LC 2002-193377

This is a study of "the conflict between Athens and Sparta in the fifth century B.C.E. . . . {Kagan's} primary source is, of course, Thucydides' epic history, but {he} draws on Aristotle, Xenophon, and others to provide an objective, nuanced perspective on the military drama. And it's quite a drama: the clash of democracy and oligarchy, the testing of great leaders, the innovative military tactics, and the unprecedented human cost." Booklist

Includes bibliographical references

Thucydides; the reinvention of history. Viking 2009 257p map $26.95   **938**
1. Historians 2. Historiography 3. Greece -- Historiography 4. Greece -- Intellectual life -- To 146 B.C. 5. Greece -- History -- 431-404 B.C., Peloponnesian War 6. Greece -- History -- Peloponnesian War, 431-404 B.C.
ISBN 0670921296; 9780670021291

LC 2009-08368

Kagan argues that "The Peloponnesian War differs significantly from other accounts offered by Thucydides' contemporaries and stands as the first modern work of political history." (Publisher's note) Index.

"Kagan's utter mastery is on display in this vigorous, elegantly written, provocative book." PopMatters

Includes bibliographical references

★ The **Landmark** Xenophon's Hellenika; a new translation. translation by John Marincola; with maps, annotations, appendices, and encyclopedic index edited by Robert B. Strassler; with an introduction by David Thomas. Pantheon Books 2009 lxxxii, 579p il map $40   **938**
1. Greece -- History -- To 146 B.C. 2. Greece -- History -- 431-404

B.C., Peloponnesian War 3. Greece -- History -- Peloponnesian War, 431-404 B.C.
ISBN 9780375422553

LC 2009-20970

"The Hellenika is often messy: Athens and Sparta are the primary players, but Corinth and Thebes constantly jump into the fray, and Persia, Sparta's sometime ally, is always lurking at the periphery. All this can be confusing, and one of the more impressive things about the Landmark edition is how much it tries—and succeeds—in making the texts of ancient Greece accessible to contemporary audiences. The extensive footnotes are both informative and readable. . . . Side notes, meanwhile, offer a running plot summary, in case the casual reader neglects to follow, say, the hostilities between Agesilaos and Phleious. The maps generously sprinkled across these pages are uniformly clear, showing both battle maneuvers and shifting geopolitical alliances. And the appendix is a veritable treasure trove of secondary material." New Criterion

Includes bibliographical references and index

Lane Fox, Robin

The **classical** world; an epic history from Homer to Hadrian. Basic Books 2006 656p il map $35   **938**
1. Classical civilization 2. Rome -- Civilization 3. Greece -- Civilization
ISBN 978-0-465-02496-4; 0-465-02496-3

LC 2006-20247

First published 2005 in the United Kingdom

A "portrait of Greek and Roman culture over a period of roughly 900 years. Although he utilizes a broadly chronological approach, Fox goes well beyond the usual, dreary narrative of battles, dynastic changes, and political conflicts that often characterize surveys of the period. Instead, Fox focuses on the gradual development and transformation of various cultural aspects of Greek and Roman societies, and he discusses in often fascinating detail topics that are normally given short shrift in general histories." Booklist

Thucydides

The **landmark** Thucydides; a comprehensive guide to the Peloponnesian War. edited by Robert B. Strassler; introduction by Victor Davis Hanson. A newly revised edition of the Richard Crawley translation with maps, annotations, appendices, and e Free Press 1996 xxxiii,713 $45; pa $25   **938**
1. Greece -- History -- 431-404 B.C., Peloponnesian War
ISBN 978-1-416-59087-3; 0-684-82790-5

LC 96-24555

"Strassler, an unaffiliated scholar of classical studies, has remedied many of the flaws of Richard Crawley's 1874 translation of The Peloponnesian War. He has added descriptive paragraph-by-paragraph synopses, topic headers on every page, numerous maps keyed to the adjoining text, explanatory footnotes, an extensive index, an excellent introduction by Victor Davis Hanson . . . , and 11 appendixes (by various scholars) on politics, warfare, and society in the Greece of the fifth century B.C.E." Libr J

938.03   Persian Wars, 500-479 B.C.

Karnazes, Dean

The **legend** of Marathon; Reliving the Ancient Battle and Epic Run That Inspired the World's Greatest Footrace. by Dean Karnazes. St. Martin's Press 2016 304 p. $25.99   **938.03**
1. Marathon running 2. Democracy -- History 3. Sparta (Extinct city) 4. Marathon, Battle of, 490 B.C.

ISBN 1609614747; 9781609614744

This book, by Dean Karnazes, "is the story of the 153-mile run from Athens to Sparta that inspired the marathon and saved democracy. . . . In 490 BCE, Pheidippides ran for 36 hours straight from Athens to Sparta to seek help in defending Athens from a Persian invasion in the Battle of Marathon. In doing so, he saved the development of Western civilization and inspired the birth of the marathon as we know it." (Publisher's note)

"This is a remarkable and inspiring memoir that will have casual and serious runners cheering." Pub Wkly

938.05   Period of Peloponnesian War, 431-404 B.C.

Roberts, Jennifer T.

The **plague** of war; Athens, Sparta, and the struggle for ancient Greece. Jennifer T. Roberts. Oxford University Press 2017 448 p. illustrations, maps $34.95   **938.05**
1. Greece -- Military history 2. Greece -- History -- 431 B.C.-404 B.C., Peloponnesian War 3. Greece -- History -- 404-362 B.C., Spartan and Theban Supremacies 4. City-states -- Greece -- History 5. Athens (Greece) -- History, Military 6. Greece -- History, Military -- To 146 B.C. 7. Sparta (Extinct city) -- History, Military 8. Greece -- History -- Peloponnesian War, 431-404 B.C. 9. Greece -- History -- Spartan and Theban Supremacies, 404-362 B.C. 10. Greece -- History -- Peloponnesian War, 431-404 B.C. -- Influence
ISBN 9780199996643

LC 2016012098

This book in the Ancient Warfare and Civilization series, by Jennifer T. Roberts, focuses on how "the long simmering rivalry between the city-states of Athens and Sparta erupted into open warfare, and for more than a generation the two were locked in a life-and-death struggle. The war embroiled the entire Greek world, provoking years of butchery previously unparalleled in ancient Greece. Whole cities were exterminated, their men killed, their women and children enslaved." (Publisher's note)

"Literate and lucid—a fine complement and corrective to the ancient sources." Kirkus

Includes bibliographical references and index

938.5   Attica (Greece) – Ancient

Everitt, Anthony

The **rise** of Athens; the story of the world's greatest civilization. Anthony Everitt. Random House Inc 2016 576 p. color illustrations, maps (ebook) $65; (hardcover) $35.00   **938.5**
1. Ancient history 2. Classical civilization 3. Athens (Greece) -- History
ISBN 9780812994599; 9780812994582

LC 2016014843

This book, by Anthony Everitt, "celebrates [ancient Athens, Greece,] the city-state that transformed the world—from the democratic revolution that marked its beginning, through the city's political and cultural golden age, to its decline into the ancient equivalent of a modern-day university town." (Publisher's note)

"Everitt has a gift for making ancient history accessible. Highly recommended to anyone with an interest in world history, Western civilization, philosophy, or political science." LJ

Includes bibliographical references and index

939   Other parts of ancient world

★ **Civilizations** of the Ancient Near East; Jack M. Sasson, editor in chief; John Baines, Gary Beckman, Karen S. Rubinson, associate editors. Hendrickson Publishers 2000 4v in 2 il map set $169.95   **939**
1. Middle East -- Civilization
ISBN 1-56563-607-4

LC 00-63144

First published 1995 by Scribner
This "work concentrates on the Near East, broadly defined to include a region from Northeast Africa to India, Pakistan, and Burma, with principal focus on the core areas of Egypt, Syro-Palestine, Mesopotamia, and Anatolia. The time span ranges from the third millennium B.C.E., when writing was invented, to 330 B.C.E., when Alexander triumphed over the Persian Empire. The 189 contributors from five continents and 16 countries include some of the world's finest scholars." Libr J [review of 1995 edition]
Includes bibliographical references

940   History of Europe

Rydell, Anders
The **Book** Thieves; The Nazi Looting of Europe's Libraries and the Race to Return a Literary Inheritance. by Anders Rydell. Penguin Group USA 2017 384 p. $28   **940**
1. Theft 2. Books and reading 3. National socialism 4. World War, 1939-1945 -- Underground movements
ISBN 0735221227; 9780735221222
This book presents "the story of the Nazis' systematic pillaging of Europe's libraries, and the small team of heroic librarians now working to return the stolen books to their rightful owners.... Through extensive new research that included records saved by the Monuments Men themselves—Anders Rydell tells the untold story of Nazi book theft, as he himself joins the effort to return the stolen books." (Publisher's note)
"An engrossing, haunting journey for bibliophiles and World War II historians." Kirkus

940.1   Europe--Early history to 1453

English, Edward D.
Encyclopedia of the medieval world. Facts on File 2004 2v il map (Facts on File library of world history) set $150   **940.1**
1. Reference books 2. Middle Ages -- Encyclopedias
ISBN 0-8160-4690-5

LC 2003-27825

This encyclopedia "covers the time period from the late antique world to about 1500 C.E. and includes events, people, institutions, and culture in western and eastern Europe, Scandinavia, North Africa, Byzantium, and the Near East. The 2,000 entries discuss significant people, art, politics, literature, religion, economics, law, science, and warfare in an A-Z format." Booklist
Includes bibliographical references

Freeman, Charles
The **closing** of the Western mind; the rise of faith and the fall of reason. Knopf 2003 xxiii, 432p il map $32.50; pa $16.95   **940.1**
1. Hellenism 2. Western civilization 3. Europe -- Intellectual life 4. Europe -- History -- 476-1492 5. Church history -- 30-600,

Early church
ISBN 1-400-04085-X; 1-400-03380-2 pa

LC 2002-44821

"This is one of the best books to date on the development of Christianity..... Beautifully written and impressively annotated, this is an indispensable read for anyone interested in the roots of Christianity and its implications for our modern worldview." Choice
Includes bibliographical references

Gies, Frances
Life in a medieval village; [by] Frances and Joseph Gies. Harper & Row 1990 257p il maps hardcover o.p. pa $14.95   **940.1**
1. Middle Ages 2. Medieval civilization
ISBN 0-06-016215-5; 0-06-092046-7 pa

LC 89-33759

"Elton, England, is the focal point of the authors' efforts to portray the everyday life and social structure of the High Middle Ages. After giving a brief summary of Elton's origins and development in the Roman and Anglo-Saxon periods, the book examines just how the residents lived and worked within the feudal structure at the beginning of the fourteenth century." Booklist
Includes bibliographical references

Gies, Joseph
Life in a medieval castle; [by] Joseph and Frances Gies. Harper & Row 1979 272p il pa $14.95   **940.1**
1. Castles 2. Feudalism 3. Middle Ages 4. Knights and knighthood 5. Hunting -- Great Britain
ISBN 0-06-090674-X

LC 79-103901

First published 1974 by Crowell
Using Chepstow Castle on the Welsh border as a model, the authors provide "descriptions of the medieval world where the castle was household, feudal center, and military target, and by concentrating on Anglo-Norman examples illustrate what existence was like as the dark ages began to brighten." Booklist
Includes glossary and bibliographical references

Gies, Joseph
Life in a medieval city; [by] Joseph and Frances Gies. HarperPerennial 1981 274p il map pa $13.95   **940.1**
1. Middle Ages 2. Medieval civilization
ISBN 0-06-090880-7
First published 1969 by Crowell
"A portrait of a medieval city [Troyes], a flourishing settlement of a type not known in Europe before the Middle Ages." Cincinnati Public Libr
Includes bibliographical references

Knights; in history and in legend. chief consultant Constance Brittain Bouchard. Firefly Books 2009 304p il map $40   **940.1**
1. Knights and knighthood 2. Military art and science -- History
ISBN 978-1-55407-480-8
The history of knights, from their everyday lives to their clothing, training, heraldry and orders, as well as their role in literature and film, and the decline of traditional knighthood.
"Aimed at history and art history lovers, this work would be excellent reading for medieval history enthusiasts and should be welcomed as a library reference resource." Libr J
Includes bibliographical references

Pye, Michael

The **Edge** of the World; a cultural history of the North Sea and the transformation of Europe. by Michael Pye. W W Norton & Co Inc 2015 360 p. 8 plates; color ills., maps (hardcover) $27.95 **940.1**

1. North Sea 2. Europe -- History -- 476-1492

ISBN 1605986992; 9781605986999

This book, by Michael Pye, offers a history of Medieval cultural history "ranging from the terror of the Vikings to the golden age of cities. . . . Saints and spies, pirates and philosophers, artists and intellectuals: they all criss-crossed the grey North Sea in the so-called 'dark ages.' . . . Now the critically acclaimed Michael Pye reveals the cultural transformation sparked by those men and women." (Publisher's note)

"This said, for beginners desirous of a well-written and eclectic glimpse of the medieval period, this is a good book. Those more advanced in their studies will find the thesis and generalizations a bit overdone." Choice

Wickham, Chris

★ The **inheritance** of Rome; a history of Europe from 400 to 1000. Viking 2009 650p il map (The Penguin history of Europe) $35 **940.1**

1. Middle Ages 2. Medieval civilization 3. Rome -- Civilization

ISBN 978-0-670-02098-0

LC 2009-15169

"Wickham's achievement contributes richly to our picture of this often narrowly understood period." Publ Wkly

Includes bibliographical references

940.2   Europe--1453-

Adkin, Mark

The **Trafalgar** companion; a guide to history's most famous sea battle and the life of Admiral Lord Nelson. Aurum Press 2005 560p il map $75 **940.2**

1. Admirals 2. Trafalgar (Spain), Battle of, 1805

ISBN 1-84513-018-9

"Beginning with a prologue that describes the wounding and death of Vice-Admiral Horatio Nelson, the book introduces readers to the history of the campaign from 1802 to 1805 and to . . . information about the men and ships of the Royal Navy, in alternate chapters. . . . It will long stand as the definitive one-volume study of Great Britain's foremost naval hero and his times." Choice

Includes bibliographical references

Barbero, Alessandro

The **Battle**; a new history of Waterloo. Walker & Company 2005 340p il map $28; pa $16 **940.2**

1. Waterloo, Battle of, 1815

ISBN 0-8027-1453-6; 978-0-8027-1453-4; 0-8027-1500-1 pa; 978-0-8027-1500-5 pa

Original Italian edition, 2003

The author's "narrative flows smoothly, making readers feel part of the battle's events. The chapters are short—never more than a few pages—and they pull the reader along with the action." Choice

Includes bibliographical references (p. 318-324)

Barzun, Jacques

From dawn to decadence; 500 years of Western cultural life, 1500 to the present. HarperCollins Pubs. 2000 877p hardcover o.p. pa $20 **940.2**

1. Western civilization 2. Europe -- Civilization 3. Europe -- Intellectual life

ISBN 0-06-092883-2 pa

LC 99-16194

National Book Award Finalist: Nonfiction (2000)

"Encyclopedic without being discontinuous, the book hardly seems as long, as carefully constructed or as densely packed as it is. Though the ideas it explains are often complicated, the explanations it offers are limpidly clear, sparkling with biographical anecdote and counter-canonical observations." N Y Times Book Rev

Includes bibliographical references

Blanning, T. C. W.

★ The **pursuit** of glory; Europe, 1648-1815. [by] Tim Blanning. Viking 2007 xxvii, 707p il map (The Penguin history of Europe) $39.95 **940.2**

1. Europe -- Civilization 2. Europe -- History -- 1492-1789 3. Europe -- History -- 1789-1815

ISBN 978-0-670-06320-8; 0-670-06320-7

LC 2006-37324

The author "thoroughly covers the politics and endless wars of the period. . . . 'The Pursuit of Glory' is history writing at its glorious best." N Y Times (Late N Y Ed)

Includes bibliographical references

Blom, Philipp, 1970-

The **vertigo** years; Europe 1900-1914. Basic Books 2008 466p il $29.95 **940.2**

1. Europe -- History -- 1871-1918 2. Europe -- History -- 20th century 3. Europe -- Civilization -- 20th century

ISBN 0-465-01116-0; 978-0-465-01116-2

LC 2008-935053

Blom examines the period between 1900 and the outbreak of the First World War, as cities grew, "education changed the outlook of millions; mass-produced items transformed daily life; industrial laborers demanded a share of political power; and women sought to change their place in society." (Publisher's note) Bibliography. Index.

"Blom's engrossing history begins with an invitation: 'Imagine yourself looking at the years 1900 to 1914 without the long shadows of the future darkening their historical present.' His imaginative recreation of this period argues that speed—both literal and figurative—came to typify and, ultimately, define modern life. This was the age that gave rise not only to Futurism and Vorticism but also to car racing and the electric chair. Precipitate change also ushered in an age of uncertainty and attraction to the seeming stability of the past. The book's strength is also its charm—a multifaceted, panoramic approach animated by vivacious narration of individual stories." New Yorker

Includes bibliographical references

Coote, Stephen

Napoleon and the Hundred Days. DaCapo Press 2005 308p il $27.50 **940.2**

1. Emperors 2. France -- History -- 1799-1815

ISBN 0-306-81408-0

LC 2004-65505

First published 2004 in the United Kingdom

This history "of the 100 days between Napoleon's escape from Elba and his capitulation after Waterloo uses the period as a lens through which to examine his character in general. . . . This accessible work is reminiscent of the finest classical Roman histories and biographies." Publ Wkly

Includes bibliographical references

Cornwell, Bernard, 1944-

Waterloo; The History of Four Days, Three Armies, and Three Battles. Bernard Cornwell. HarperCollins 2015 352 p. illustrations, maps, portraits $35   **940.2**
  1. Waterloo, Battle of, 1815
  ISBN 0062312057; 9780062312051

                     LC 2015487235

"In his first work of nonfiction, [author] Bernard Cornwell combines his storytelling skills with a meticulously researched history to give a . . . chronicle of every dramatic moment, from Napoleon's daring escape from Elba to the smoke and gore of the three battlefields and their aftermath." (Publisher's note)

Corrigan, Gordon

Waterloo; A New History. Gordon Corrigan. W W Norton & Co Inc 2014 341 p. 16 plates; color ills; map $28.95 **940.2**
  1. Waterloo, Battle of, 1815   2. Waterloo, Battle of, Waterloo, Belgium, 1815
  ISBN 1605986526; 9781605986524

                     LC 2014407633

This book, by historian Gordon Corrigan, focuses on the Battle of Waterloo. "Fought on Sunday, June 18th, 1815, by some 220,000 men over rain-sodden ground in what is now Belgium, [it] brought an end to twenty-three years of almost continual war between imperial France and her enemies. A decisive defeat for Napoleon and a hard-won victory for the Allied armies of the Duke of Wellington and the Prussians, led by the stalwart Marshal Blucher, it brought about the French emperor's final exile." (Publisher's note)

"Those interested in military history, particularly that of England or France, will love the detail in this volume. Corrigan keeps things exciting by blending his own brand of wit with historical fact." LJ

Includes bibliographical references (pages 327-329) and index

Crane, David, 1942-

★ **Went** the day well? witnessing Waterloo. by David Crane. Alfred A. Knopf 2015 384 p. 24 plates; illustrations; maps (hardback) $30   **940.2**
  1. War and civilization   2. Waterloo, Battle of, 1815   3. England -- History, Military -- 19th century -- Sources   4. England -- Social conditions -- 19th century -- Sources   5. War and society -- England -- History -- 19th century -- Sources   6. Waterloo, Battle of, Waterloo, Belgium, 1815 -- Personal narratives, British   7. Waterloo, Battle of, Waterloo, Belgium, 1815 -- Social aspects -- England -- Sources
  ISBN 0307594920; 9780307594921

                     LC 2014044143

This book, by by David Crane, offers an "hour-by-hour chronicle that starts the day before the battle [of Waterloo] that reset the course of world history and continues to its aftermath. Switching perspectives between Britain and Belgium, prison and palace, poet and pauper, lover and betrothed, husband and wife, David Crane paints a picture of Britain as it was that summer when everything changed." (Publisher's note)

"History buffs will relish both of these works. Readers should also consider Brendan Simms's The Longest Afternoon." LJ

Includes bibliographical references and index

Esdaile, Charles J.

Napoleon's wars; an international history, 1803-1815. [by] Charles Esdaile. Viking 2008 621p il map $35   **940.2**
  1. Emperors   2. Europe -- History -- 1789-1815   3. France -- History -- 1799-1815
  ISBN 978-0-670-02030-0; 0-670-02030-3
  First published 2007 in the United Kingdom

"Recapturing the flux of international diplomacy and Napoléon's congenital rejection of compromise, Esdaile persuasively places the diplomatic foundation to popular military histories about the Napoleonic wars." Booklist

Includes bibliographical references (p. 567-602)

Europe 1789 to 1914; encyclopedia of the age of industry and empire. Merriman and Jay Winter, editors in chief. Charles Scribner's Sons 2006 5v il map (Scribner library of modern Europe) set $595   **940.2**
  1. Reference books   2. Europe -- Civilization -- Encyclopedias   3. Europe -- History -- 1789-1900 -- Encyclopedias   4. Europe -- History -- 1871-1918 -- Encyclopedias
  ISBN 0-684-31359-6; 978-0-684-31359-7

                     LC 2006-7335

This encyclopedia covers "the time period between the onset of the French Revolution to the outbreak of World War I." Publisher's note Includes bibliographical references

Grayling, A. C.

★ The **Age** of Genius; The Seventeenth Century and the Birth of the Modern Mind. by A. C. Grayling. St. Martin's Press 2016 368 p. illustrations, map, portraits $30   **940.2**
  1. Europe -- Intellectual life   2. Europe -- History -- 17th century
  ISBN 1620403447; 9781620403440

This book, by A. C. Grayling, "explores . . . the story of the 17th century in Europe. . . . Grayling vividly reconstructs this unprecedented era and breathes new life into the major figures of the seventeenth century intelligentsia who span literature, music, science, art, and philosophy-Shakespeare, Monteverdi, Galileo, Rembrandt, Locke, Newton, Descartes, Vermeer, Hobbes, Milton, and Cervantes, among many more." (Publisher's note)

"Grayling does a fantastic job of proving his assertion that the 17th century saw a dramatic shift in Western thought. Readers with an interest in the history of philosophy and scientific discovery will enjoy this highly engaging book." LJ

Greenblatt, Stephen

★ The **swerve**; [by] Stephen Greenblatt. W.W. Norton 2011 356p il $26.95   **940.2**
  1. Poets   2. Renaissance   3. Philosophers   4. Modern civilization   5. Civilization, Modern   6. Science, Renaissance   7. Philosophy, Renaissance
  ISBN 0393064476; 9780393064476

                     LC 2011019765

Pulitzer Prize: General Nonfiction (2012)
National Book Award: Nonfiction (2011)

The book presents a history of the "ancient Roman philosophical epic, On the Nature of Things, by Lucretius - a beautiful poem of the most dangerous ideas: that the universe functioned without the aid of gods, that religious fear was damaging to human life, and that matter was made up of very small particles in eternal motion, colliding and swerving in new directions." According to the author, "the copying and translation of this ancient book- the greatest discovery of the greatest book-hunter of his age - fueled the Renaissance, inspiring artists such as Botticelli and thinkers such as Giordano Bruno; shaped the thought of Galileo and Freud, Darwin and Einstein; and had a revolutionary influence on writers such as Montaigne and Shakespeare and even Thomas Jefferson." (Publisher's note)

"A fascinating, intelligent look at what may well be the most historically resonant book-hunt of all time." Booklist

Includes bibliographical references (p. [309]-335) and index.

Hobsbawm, E. J.

The **age** of revolution 1789-1848. Vintage Books 1996 356p il map pa $15.95 **940.2**

    1. Industries -- History 2. Europe -- History -- 1789-1900

    ISBN 978-0-679-77253-8; 0-679-77253-7

    First published 1962 by World Pub. Co.

"This book traces the transformation of the world between 1789 and 1848 insofar as it was due to what is here called the 'dual revolution'— the French Revolution of 1789 and the contemporaneous (British) Industrial Revolution." Preface

    Includes bibliographical references

King, David

Vienna, 1814; how the conquerors of Napoleon made love, war, and peace at the Congress of Vienna. Harmony Books 2008 434p il $27.50 **940.2**

    1. Congress of Vienna (1814-1815) 2. Europe -- History -- 1789-1815 3. Europe -- Politics and government

    ISBN 978-0-307-33716-0; 0-307-33716-2

    LC 2007-24680

"The conquerors of Napoleon were in a festive mood when they met in Vienna in the fall of 1814 to decide the fate of Europe. . . . [The author] does a superb job of evoking the bedazzling social scene that served as the backdrop to the Congress of Vienna. His characterizations of such luminaries as Czar Alexander, Metternich, Talleyrand, and Castlereagh are lucid and thoroughly grounded in primary sources. . . . This is a worthy contribution to the study of a critical historical event long neglected by historians." Libr J

    Includes bibliographical references

Lieven, D. C. B.

Russia against Napoleon; the true story of the campaigns of War and Peace. [by] Dominic Lieven. Viking 2010 617p il map $35.95 **940.2**

    1. Emperors 2. Russia -- History 3. Europe -- History -- 1789-1815 4. Napoleonic Wars, 1800-1815 -- Campaigns -- Russia

    ISBN 978-0-670-02157-4

    LC 2009-42564

    First published 2009 in the United Kingdom

"Lieven's book is lucid, engaging and reflects his deep love for Russia. This is a fascinating, exhaustively researched work, an elegant handling of a welter of confusing sources and a vital account of Russia from 1807 to 1814 that is unlikely to be bettered." Hist Today

    Includes bibliographical references

Maclennan, Julio Crespo

Europa; how Europe shaped the modern world. Julio Crespo MacLennan. W W Norton & Co Inc 2018 336 p. $27.95 **940.2**

    1. Europe -- History 2. Imperialism -- History 3. Western civilization -- History

    ISBN 1681777568; 9781681777566

This book, by Julio Crespo MacLennan, presents "an original and innovative examination of . . . [Europe]--and its culture--that was the epicenter of the world for almost five centuries. . . . [The book] reveals the origins of Europe's rapid expansion, which was then expanded upon further by millions of European migrants, who spread their culture and values. . . . Even into the twentieth century, . . . Europe has once again become a global trendsetter." (Publisher's note)

"Why, as the U.S. wrestles with China for global advantage, do both rely heavily on ideas originally forged in Europe? MacLennan answers this question in an epic narrative exceptional in interpretive breadth." Booklist

Mostert, Noel

The **line** upon a wind; the great war at sea, 1793-1815. W.W. Norton & Co. 2008 xxv, 774p il map $35 **940.2**

    1. Naval history 2. Seafaring life 3. Europe -- History -- 1789-1900 4. France -- History -- 1799-1815

    ISBN 978-0-393-06653-1; 0-393-06653-3

    LC 2007-39313

    First published 2007 in the United Kingdom

"This is a vast, fast-moving chronicle that ranges across great distances while examining a host of characters, both well known and relatively obscure. Mostert does justifiably place great emphasis on Admiral Nelson and the critical battle at Trafalgar. He also offers useful and interesting descriptions of less-prominent aspects of the wars, including conflicts with the Barbary pirates and the British struggles against the rise of American naval power. This is an outstanding survey of a prolonged struggle that helped shape world history." Booklist

    Includes bibliographical references (p. 748-752)

O'Brien, Michael

Mrs. Adams in winter; a journey in the last days of Napoleon. Farrar, Straus and Giroux 2010 364p il map $27 **940.2**

    1. Presidents 2. Senators 3. Members of Congress 4. Secretaries of state 5. Spouses of presidents 6. Europe -- History -- 1789-1815 7. Europe -- Description and travel

    ISBN 978-0-374-21581-1; 0-374-21581-2

    LC 2009-25437

The author "pursues Louisa Adams's 40-day trek through a Europe in the process of transformation. The Mrs. Adams in question is not to be confused with Abigail Adams, the Colonial matriarch and wife of the second president. Rather, Louisa Catherine Adams was her London-born daughter-in-law, the wife to Abigail's son John Quincy Adams. . . . O'Brien's narrative is richly contextual, encompassing not only the great personalities of the age, whom Mrs. Adams met, but penetrating the secrets of a complicated marriage. A wide-sweeping historical survey and original intellectual journey." Kirkus

    Includes bibliographical references

O'Keeffe, Paul

Waterloo; The Aftermath. by Paul O'Keeffe. Penguin Group USA 2014 400 p. $37.50 **940.2**

    1. Waterloo, Battle of, 1815

    ISBN 1468311301; 9781468311303

    LC 2015010800

This book moves "from the horrors of the battlefield [at Waterloo] to the drawing rooms of London and Paris, from Napoleon's retreat and surrender to British triumph and celebration. . . . [Author] Paul O'Keeffe employs a multiplicity of contemporary sources and viewpoints to create a reading experience that brings the sights, sounds and smells of the battlefield, of conquest and defeat, of celebration and riot, into focus as never before." (Publisher's note)

Pagden, Anthony

The **Enlightenment**; and why it still matters. Anthony Pagden. 1st ed. Random House 2013 xx, 501 p.p ill. (ebook) $85.00; (hardcover) $30.00 **940.2**

    1. Enlightenment

    ISBN 1400060680; 9780679645313; 9781400060689

    LC 2012043848

This book, by Anthony Pagden, "takes a fresh look at the revolutionary intellectual movement that laid the foundation for the modern world. Liberty and equality. Human rights. Freedom of thought and expression. Belief in reason and progress. The value of scientific inquiry. These are just some of the ideas that were conceived and developed during the Enlightenment, and which changed forever the intellectual landscape of the Western world." (Publisher's note)

Includes bibliographical references (pages 417-480) and index

Pocock, Tom

The **terror** before Trafalgar; Nelson, Napoleon and the secret war. Naval Institute Press 2005 255p il map pa $16.95	**940.2**

1. Admirals 2. Emperors 3. Europe -- History -- 1789-1815

ISBN 978-1-5911-4681-0; 1-5911-4681-X

LC 2004-58185

First published 2003 by Norton

The author "retells the story of the four years in which the French confidently prepared to invade Britain, overrun its army, take out its armaments and replace the government with something easier to control. . . . Pocock's little book . . . gives a chilling insight into ineffectual undercover operations and groundbreaking weaponry: rockets, torpedos, submarines, airships and the construction of an undersea tunnel, all so far ahead of their time that none turned out in the end to be much use in practical terms to either side." N Y Times Book Rev

Includes bibliographical references

Reston, James

Defenders of the faith; Charles V, Suleyman the Magnificent, and the battle for Europe, 1520-1536. Penguin Press 2009 xxi, 407p il map $29.95	**940.2**

1. Emperors 2. Holy Roman Empire 3. Sultans 4. Turkey -- History -- Ottoman Empire, 1288-1918

ISBN 978-1-59420-225-4

LC 2008-54655

"Fast-paced and engaging, this is excellent reading for popular audiences." Libr J

Includes bibliographical references

Roberts, Andrew

Waterloo: June 18, 1815; the battle for modern Europe. HarperCollins 2005 143p il maps (Making history) $21.95; pa $12.95	**940.2**

1. Waterloo, Battle of, 1815

ISBN 0-06-008866-4; 0-06-076215-2 pa

LC 2005-282517

This is a study of the defeat of Napoleon's army at the Battle of Waterloo in June, 1815.

The author "instills an appreciation for Waterloo as a horrific experience saturated with alternative possible outcomes. A must for the military shelf." Booklist

Includes bibliographical references (p. 135-136)

Simms, Brendan

The **longest** afternoon; the 400 men who decided the Battle of Waterloo. Basic Books 2015 186 p. maps $24.99	**940.2**

1. Waterloo, Battle of, 1815

ISBN 0465064825; 9780465064823

LC 2015451024

This book on the Battle of Waterloo by Brendan Simms presents an "account of the bloody, heroic defense of La Haye Sainte, a farmhouse that Napoleon had to capture to reach the Duke of Wellington's army. The massive stone building survives intact; not so its defenders, a battle-

tested unit of the British army." (Kirkus Reviews)

"This thoroughly engrossing account will thrill all history lovers." LJ

Talty, Stephan

The **illustrious** dead; the terrifying story of how typhus killed Napoleon's greatest army. Crown Publishers 2009 315p map $27	**940.2**

1. Typhus 2. Emperors 3. Europe -- History -- 1789-1815 4. France -- History -- 1799-1815

ISBN 978-0-307-39404-0

LC 2008-50646

"Talty delivers a breezy, popular account of a gruesome campaign, emphasizing the equally gruesome epidemic that accompanied it." Publ Wkly

Includes bibliographical references

Wells, C. M.

Sailing from Byzantium; how a lost empire shaped the world. Colin Wells. Delacorte Press 2006 xxx, 335p map $22	**940.2**

1. Byzantine Empire

ISBN 0-553-80381-6

LC 2006-42665

The author "considers how Byzantium, the Eastern, Greek-language Roman Empire of the Middle Ages, influenced three successor civilizations Western Europe, Islam, and the eastern Slavic world of the Balkans and Russia. . . . This history is a needed reminder of the debt that three of our major civilizations owe to Byzantium." Libr J

Includes bibliographical references

Wilson, Ellen Judy

★ **Encyclopedia** of the Enlightenment; Peter Hanns Reill, consulting editor; Ellen Judy Wilson, principal author. rev ed; Facts on File 2004 670p $75	**940.2**

1. Reference books 2. Europe -- Intellectual life 3. Philosophy -- Encyclopedias 4. Enlightenment -- Encyclopedias

ISBN 0-8160-5335-9

LC 2003-22973

First published 1996

This reference provides a "review of the important ideas, people, and events that shaped the world during the Enlightenment. [It] covers the major changes in science, education, philosophy, art and architecture, and politics which took place during the 17th and 18th centuries and led to the birth of the modern era. . . . The biographical entries cover such notables as Robespierre, Schiller, Fielding, Kant, and Voltaire. . . . Larger public, school, and academic libraries looking for a comprehensive overview of the subject for the student or interested reader will find this a valuable and accessible resource." Libr J

Includes bibliographical references

Wilson, Peter H.

The **Thirty** Years War; Europe's tragedy. Belknap Press of Harvard University Press 2009 xxii, 996p il map $35	**940.2**

1. Thirty Years' War, 1618-1648

ISBN 978-0-674-03634-5

LC 2009-11266

This "is a history of prodigious erudition that manages to corral the byzantine complexity of the Thirty Years War into a coherent narrative." Wall Street J

Includes bibliographical references

Zamoyski, Adam

Rites of peace; the fall of Napoleon and the Congress of Vienna. HarperColins 2007 634p il map $29.95 **940.2**
1. Congress of Vienna (1814-1815) 2. Europe -- History -- 1789-1815
ISBN 0-06-077518-1; 978-0-06-077518-6
This "book is old-fashioned, impressively detailed diplomatic history." Economist
Includes bibliographical references

940.28 History of Europe, 1815-1914

Evans, Richard J., 1947-

The **Pursuit** of Power; Europe 1815-1914. Richard J. Evans. Penguin Group USA 2016 848 p. illustrations (chiefly color) (ebook) $65; (hardcover: alk. paper) $40 **940.28**
1. Europe -- History -- 1815-1871 2. Europe -- History -- 1871-1918 3. Europe -- Politics and government -- 1815-1871 4. Europe -- Politics and government -- 1871-1918
ISBN 9780735221215; 0670024570; 9780670024575
LC 2016044050
Contents: The legacies of revolution -- The paradoxes of freedom -- The European spring -- The social revolution -- The conquest of nature -- The age of emotion -- The challenge of democracy -- The wages of empire.
This book in The Penguin History of Europe series, by Richard J. Evans, examines "the period from the fall of Napoleon to the outbreak of World War I. Evans's gripping narrative ranges across a century of social and national conflicts, from the revolutions of 1830 and 1848 to the unification of both Germany and Italy, from the Russo-Turkish wars to the Balkan upheavals that brought this era of relative peace and growing prosperity to an end." (Publisher's note)
"An immensely readable work that considers incremental continental developments up to the outbreak of war in 1914." Kirkus
Includes bibliographical references and index

940.3 World War I, 1914-1918

Audoin-Rouzeau, Stephane

14-18, understanding the Great War; {by} Stéphane Audoin-Rouzeau and Annette Becker; translated from the French by Catherine Temerson. Hill & Wang 2002 280p $24; pa $14 **940.3**
1. World War, 1914-1918
ISBN 0-8090-4642-3; 0-8090-4643-1 pa
LC 2002-111422
Original French edition, 2000
"The authors take an anthropological approach to the cataclysm that engulfed Europe in 1914 and examine three significant aspects of the war: violence, crusade, and mourning. . . . Supported by contemporary documentation, this unique work will become a classic study." Libr J
Includes bibliographical references

Burg, David F.

Almanac of World War I; [by] David F. Burg and L. Edward Purcell; introduction by William Manchester. University Press of Ky. 1998 320p il maps hardcover o.p. pa $22 **940.3**
1. World War, 1914-1918
ISBN 0-8131-2072-1; 0-8131-9087-8 pa; 9780813190877

LC 98-26625
"The bulk of the text is arranged chronologically by year and date, listing almost daily occurrences from 1914 through 1918. . . . The work is international in scope, covering political and military happenings from around the world. . . . There is really nothing comparable to this volume." Booklist
Includes bibliographical references

Carter, Miranda

George, Nicholas, and Wilhelm; three royal cousins and the road to World War I. Alfred A. Knopf 2010 498p il map $30 **940.3**
1. Emperors 2. Kings 3. Biography, Individual 4. World War, 1914-1918 -- Causes 5. Europe -- Politics and government -- 1871-1918
ISBN 978-1-4000-4363-7; 1-4000-4363-8
LC 2009-37690
First published 2009 in the United Kingdom with title: The three emperors
In the years before World War I, the great European powers were ruled by three first cousins: King George V, Kaiser Wilhelm II, and Tsar Nicholas II. Carter uses the cousins' correspondence and a host of historical sources to tell their tragicomic stories.
The author "writes with lusty humour at times, has a fresh clarifying intelligence when unravelling knotty problems of ancien régime life and a sharp eye for telling details about people's gestures, temper, appearance and attitudes. . . . This is traditional narrative history with a 21st-century zing—a real corker of a book." Hist Today
Includes bibliographical references

Clark, Christopher

★ The **sleepwalkers**; how Europe went to war in 1914. Christopher Clark. Harper 2013 697 p. $29.99 **940.3**
1. Europe -- History -- 1871-1918 2. World War, 1914-1918 -- Causes 3. World War, 1914-1918 -- Diplomatic history 4. Europe -- Politics and government -- 1871-1918
ISBN 006114665X; 9780061146657
LC 2012038473
LA Times Book Prize Winner: History (2013)
In this book on the origins of World War I, author Christopher Clark "posits a bad brew of diplomatic contingencies and individual agency as the cause. . . . Clark . . . begins by describing the interactions of Serbia and Austria-Hungary, which sparked the conflict. He presents the former as a 'raw and fragile democracy' whose 'turbulent' politics challenged a neighboring empire held together by habit. Indeed, the instability across Europe further polarized alliance networks." (Publishers Weekly)
Includes bibliographical references and index

The **Encyclopedia** of World War I; a political, social, and military history. ABC-CLIO 2005 5v il map set $485 **940.3**
1. Reference books 2. World War, 1914-1918 -- Encyclopedias
ISBN 1-85109-420-2
LC 2005-22937
This set opens with "four essays discussing the origins, outbreak, overview, and legacy of the war. They are followed by alphabetical entries on virtually every aspect of the conflict, including battles, people, military equipment and strategies, and social and political changes associated with it." SLJ
Includes bibliographical references

Englund, Peter

★ The **beauty** and the sorrow; an intimate history of the First World War. translated by Peter Graves. Alfred A. Knopf

2011 540p il $35　　　　　　　　　　　　940.3
1. World War, 1914-1918 -- Personal narratives
ISBN 978-0-307-59386-3; 0-307-59386-X
　　　　　　　　　　　　　　　　　　LC 2011-20828
Original Swedish edition, 2009

This work "threads together the wartime experiences of 20 more or less unremarkable men and women, on both sides of the war, from schoolgirls and botanists to mountain climbers, doctors, ambulance drivers and clerks. A few of these people will become heroes. A few will become prisoners of war, or lose limbs, go mad or die. . . . Mr. Englund's book is a deviation from standard history books. It is a corrective too to the notion that World War I was only about the dire trench warfare on the Western Front. . . . [It] expertly pans across other theaters of war: the Alps, the Balkans, the Eastern Front, Mesopotamia, East Africa." N Y Times Book Rev

Includes bibliographical references

Gilbert, Martin

The **First** World War; a complete history. Holt & Co. 1994 xxiv, 615p il maps hardcover o.p. pa $25　　　　940.3
1. World War, 1914-1918
ISBN 0-8050-1540-X; 0-8050-7617-4 pa
　　　　　　　　　　　　　　　　　　LC 94-27268

"What Mr. Gilbert seeks to do, and frequently succeeds in doing, is to humanize, indeed to personalize, World War I. His effort and accomplishment make this a rewarding and significant book." N Y Times Book Rev

Includes bibliographical references

Grant, R. G.

World War I; the definitive visual history: from Sarajevo to Versailles. R.G. Grant. 2nd edition DK Publishing 2018 372 p. illustrations, maps $40　　　　　　　940.3
1. Weapons -- History 2. World War, 1914-1918 3. World history -- 20th century 4. World War, 1914-1918 -- Pictorial works
ISBN 1465470018; 9781465470010
　　　　　　　　　　　　　　　　　　LC 2018302543

This book, by R.G. Grant, narrates "how the Great War devastated Europe. Here is an original and exciting guide to the grim challenge of life or death on the Western Front. Devastating first-hand reports and contemporary photographs of the battles that slaughtered millions, together with a clear account of how nation upon nation sent their men to join the carnage, combine to present a dramatic 'eyewitness' view of this most terrible war." (Publisher's note)

"This is a broad, moving, informative account of the war that's perfect for both the young, budding historian and the well-versed WWI reader." Pub Wkly

Hastings, Max

Catastrophe 1914; Europe goes to war. by Max Hastings. Alfred A. Knopf 2013 672 p. (hardback) $35　　　940.3
1. Europe -- History -- 1871-1918 2. World War, 1914-1918 -- Causes 3. Europe -- History -- July Crisis, 1914
ISBN 0307597059; 9780307597052; 9780307743831
　　　　　　　　　　　　　　　　　　LC 2013027865

Author Max Hastings "traces the path to [World War I] making clear why Germany and Austria-Hungary were primarily to blame, and describes the gripping first clashes in the West, where the French army marched into action. Hastings gives us frank assessments of generals and political leaders. He argues passionately against the contention that the war was not worth the cost, maintaining that Germany's defeat was vital to the freedom of Europe." (Publisher's note)

"Readers accustomed to Hastings' vivid battle descriptions, incisive anecdotes from all participants, and shrewd, often unsettling opinions will not be disappointed. Among the plethora of brilliant accounts of this period, this is one of the best." Kirkus

Includes bibliographical references (pages 595-603) and index

Herman, Arthur

1917; Lenin, Wilson, and the birth of the new world disorder. Arthur Herman. Harper 2017 xii, 480 p.p (hardcover) $29.99　　　　　　　　　　　　　　940.3
1. United States -- Foreign relations 2. Nineteen seventeen, A.D. 3. World War, 1914-1918 -- Influence 4. United States -- Foreign relations -- 1913-1921 5. Soviet Union -- History -- Revolution, 1917-1921 -- Influence
ISBN 9780062570925; 9780062570888; 0062570889
　　　　　　　　　　　　　　　　　　LC 2017021669

This book, by Arthur Herman, "reveals how [Vladimir] Lenin and [Woodrow] Wilson rewrote the rules of modern geopolitics. . . . Together Lenin and Wilson unleashed the disruptive ideologies that would sweep the world, from nationalism and globalism to Communism and terrorism, and that continue to shape our world today. Our New World Disorder is the legacy left by Wilson and Lenin, and their visions of the perfectibility of man." (Publisher's note)

"Mixing both real events and a few moments of speculation, a fine account of a climacteric year." Kirkus

Includes bibliographical references (pages 433-450) and index.

Hochschild, Adam

To end all wars; a story of loyalty and rebellion, 1914-1918. Houghton Mifflin Harcourt 2011 xx, 448p map $28; ebook $28　　　　　　　　　　　　　　　　　940.3
1. Pacifism 2. Soldiers -- Great Britain 3. World War, 1914-1918 -- Great Britain 4. World War, 1914-1918 -- Social aspects 5. World War, 1914-1918 -- Psychological aspects 6. World War, 1914-1918 -- Conscientious objectors
ISBN 978-0-618-75828-9; 0-618-75828-3; 978-0-54754-921-7 ebook; 0-54754-921-0 ebook
　　　　　　　　　　　　　　　　　　LC 2010-25836

"An ambitious narrative that presents a teeming worldview through intimate, human portraits." Kirkus

Includes bibliographical references=

Hughes-Wilson, John

The **First** World War in 100 objects; by John Hughes-Wilson. Firefly Books Ltd 2014 448 p. color illustrations; maps $39.95　　　　　　　　　　　　　　　940.3
1. World War, 1914-1918
ISBN 1770854134; 9781770854130

This book, by John Hughes-Wilson, "draws on the most interesting 100 items that describe the causes, progress and outcome of the First World War. From weapons that created carnage to affectionate letters home, these 100 objects are as extraordinary in their diversity and storytelling power as they are devastating in their poignancy. This is the stuff of war at its most horrible." (Publisher's note)

"The text packs in an impressive amount of detail, making it seem fussy at times, but the explanations of facts and events are always clear. Altogether, this is a stunning read that is exciting in its depth, scope and personal feel. After seeing and reading about objects touched, used, cherished and hated by those who experienced the war, it will be impossible not to gain a greater understanding and appreciation of the struggle that 'truly... still shapes the world in which we live.'" Pub Wkly

MacMillan, Margaret

Paris 1919; six months that changed the world. Random House 2002 560p $35; pa $16.95 **940.3**

1. Governors 2. Presidents 3. College presidents 4. Treaty of Versailles 5. Nobel laureates for peace 6. World War, 1914-1918 -- Peace 7. Germany -- History -- 1918-1933 8. Paris Peace Conference (1919-1920)

ISBN 0-375-50826-0; 0-375-76052-0 pa

LC 2002-23707

First published 2001 in the United Kingdom with title: Peacemakers

The author examines the Paris Peace Conference of 1919. Economist John Maynard Keynes blamed "the failure of the conference on the vindictiveness of the French in general and of Clemenceau in particular. Margaret MacMillan . . . argues that the conference has been blamed for many disasters that were, in fact, determined either by events that took place before it began or by later troubles." (Economist) Index.

"MacMillan's lucid prose brings her participants to colorful and quotable life, and the grand sweep of her narrative encompasses all the continents the peacemakers vainly carved up." Publ Wkly

Includes bibliographical references

McMeekin, Sean

★ The **Berlin**-Baghdad express; the Ottoman Empire and Germany's bid for world power. The Belknap Press of Harvard University Press 2010 460p il map **940.3**

1. Jihad 2. Railroads 3. Geopolitics 4. World War, 1914-1918 5. Germany -- Foreign relations -- Turkey 6. Turkey -- Foreign relations -- Germany

ISBN 0-0674-05739-2; 978-0-674-05739-5

LC 2010019199

"Germany saw the ambitious Berlin-to-Baghdad railway as a powerful tool to win World War I. But the doomed project wasn't completed until 1940. The railway debacle provides a colorful backdrop for historian McMeekin's look at the Great War from the German-Turk perspective; as a cast of ruthless characters illustrate Germany's attempt to topple what was then the largest Middle East power: the British Empire." N Y Post

Includes bibliographical references

★ **July** 1914; countdown to war. Sean McMeekin. Basic Books, a member of the Perseus Books Group 2013 xviii, 461 p.p ill. (hardcover) $29.99 **940.3**

1. Austria -- History 2. World War, 1914-1918 -- Causes 3. Europe -- History -- July Crisis, 1914

ISBN 0465031455; 9780465031450

LC 2012049777

This book is a "political history of the weeks between the assassination of Austria's Archduke Franz Ferdinand and the beginning of World War I. . . . Relying on extensive research in numerous archives, as well as diaries and correspondence from key national leaders, [Sean] McMeekin examines the intricacies of Austrian politics and diplomacy." (Publishers Weekly)

Includes bibliographical references and index.

Rogan, Eugene

The **Fall** of the Ottomans; the Great War in the Middle East. Eugene Rogan. Basic Books, a member of the Perseus Books Group 2015 xxvi, 485 p.p $32.00 **940.3**

1. World War, 1914-1918 -- Middle East 2. Turkey -- History -- Ottoman Empire, 1288-1918 3. World War, 1914-1918 -- Turkey 4. World War, 1914-1918 -- Campaigns -- Middle East 5. World War, 1914-1918 -- Campaigns -- Turkey -- Gallipoli Peninsula

ISBN 046502307X; 9780465023073

LC 2015300788

Includes bibliographical references (pages 409-458) and index

Slotkin, Richard, 1942-

Lost battalions; the Great War and the crisis of American nationality. Richard Slotkin. H. Holt 2005 639p il maps **940.3**

1. African American soldiers 2. Minorities -- United States 3. United States -- Ethnic relations 4. African American soldiers -- History 5. World War, 1914-1918 -- United States 6. World War, 1914-1918 -- Regimental histories 7. United States -- Army -- Infantry Regiment, 369th 8. World War, 1914-1918 -- Participation, African American 9. World War, 1914-1918 -- Regimental histories -- United States 10. United States -- Army -- Infantry Division, 77th -- Joint Assault Signal Company, 292nd

ISBN 0-8050-4124-9

LC 2005-46312

Slotkin "follows the Negro soldiers of the 369th and the Jewish, Italian, and other immigrants of the 77th into conflict." (Publisher's note) Index.

This is a "history of the African-American 369th Infantry, known as the 'Harlem Hellfighters,' and the 77th Division, dubbed the 'Melting Pot' for its ranks of Italians, Jews and other eastern Europeans. . . . Slotkin smoothly telescopes from the trenches to the political and social implications for decades to come in this insightful, valuable account." Publ Wkly

Stone, Norman

★ **World** War One. Basic Books 2009 226p il map $25 **940.3**

1. World War, 1914-1918

ISBN 978-0-465-01368-5; 0-465-01368-6

First published 2007 in the United Kingdom

The author presents a narrative history of the First World War.

"Stone is as unconventional as he is brilliant, and this provocative interpretation of the Great War combines impressive command of the literature with a telling eye for relevant facts and a sensitive ear for telling epigrams." Publ Wkly

Includes bibliographical references

Strachan, Hew

The **First** World War. Viking 2004 364p il maps hardcover o.p. pa $16 **940.3**

1. World War, 1914-1918

ISBN 0-14-303518-5 pa; 0-670-03295-6

LC 2003-62191

This book examines "the causes, the major campaigns, and the consequences of the First World War." (Publisher's note) Index.

"Readers already familiar with the sequence of events in strict order will benefit most. But all readers will eventually be gripped, and even the most seasoned ones will praise the insights and the original choice of illustrations." Publ Wkly

Includes bibliographical references

Tooze, Adam

★ The **deluge**; the Great War and the remaking of global order, 1916-1931. Adam Tooze. Viking Adult 2014 672 p. illustrations, maps (hardback) $40 **940.3**

1. World politics 2. Economic conditions 3. World War, 1914-1918 -- Influence 4. Balance of power 5. World politics -- 1919-1932 6. International relations -- History -- 20th century

ISBN 0670024929; 9780670024926

LC 2014005314

Los Angeles Times Book Prize: History (2014)

This book, by Adam Tooze, is an "analysis of the First World War and its anguished aftermath. . . . [The author] revisits this seismic moment in history, challenging the existing narrative of the war, its peace, and its aftereffects. From the day the United States enters the war in 1917 to the precipice of global financial ruin, Tooze delineates the world remade by American economic and military power." (Publisher's note)

"Tooze's grand economic history is stimulating, persuasive, and surprisingly accessible." Pub Wkly

Includes bibliographical references and index

Tuchman, Barbara Wertheim

★ The **guns** of August; [by] Barbara W. Tuchman; [with a new foreword by Robert K. Massie] 1st Ballantine Books ed; Ballantine 1994 xxiv, 511p il, maps pa $14   **940.3**
1. World War, 1914-1918
ISBN 0-345-38623-X

LC 93-90461

First published 1962 by Macmillan

A history of the negotiations that preceded World War I and the course of the war's first month.

Includes bibliographical references

The **Zimmermann** telegram. Ballantine Books 1985 244p il pa $14   **940.3**
1. World War, 1914-1918 -- Causes
ISBN 0-345-32425-0

LC 84-91737

First published 1958 by Macmillan

The author discusses the German plan to induce Mexico to attack the U.S. during World War I.

Includes bibliographical references

The **United** States in the First World War; an encyclopedia. editor, Anne Cipriano Venzon; consulting editor, Paul L. Miles. Garland 1995 xx, 830p maps (Garland reference library of the humanities) $155; pa $45   **940.3**
1. Reference books 2. World War, 1914-1918 -- Encyclopedias
ISBN 0-8240-7055-0; 0-8153-3353-6 pa

LC 95-1782

"Biography, economics, civil rights, women's issues, foreign relations, battles, armaments, and conferences are among the topics included. Arrangement is alphabetical, and most articles are brief—between one column and a page. . . . Most articles include brief bibliographies. There are six maps, but no other illustrations." Libr J

Woodward, David R.

World War I almanac. Facts On File 2009 554p il map (Almanacs of American wars) $95   **940.3**
1. Almanacs 2. Reference books 3. World War, 1914-1918
ISBN 978-0-8160-7134-0; 978-1-4381-1896-3 ebook

LC 2008-41575

This book "would be a welcome addition to public, school, and academic libraries where a student needs to find basic information quickly." Booklist

Includes glossary and bibliographical references

940.303   World War I, 1914-1918 – Dictionaries, encyclopedias, concordances

World War I; the essential reference guide. Spencer C. Tucker, editor. ABC-CLIO 2016 397 p. illustrations, maps (ebook) $89; (alk. paper) $89   **940.303**
1. World War, 1914-1918 2. World War, 1914-1918 -- Sources 3. World War, 1914-1918 -- Encyclopedias
ISBN 9781440841224; 9781440841217

LC 2015043398

This book, edited by Spencer C. Tucker, "provides all the key information readers need to understand this monumental conflict. [It] includes perspective essays on such widely debated topics as what was the primary cause of World War I and whether the conflict made World War II inevitable [and] supplies important primary source documents—such as the Balfour Declaration and the Zimmermann Telegram—that serve to put historical events into clearer context for students." (Publisher's note)

"A quality reference work that condenses a monumental amount of information in an accessible, concise, and instructive manner." LJ

Includes bibliographical references and index

940.311   Causes of war – World War I

Clarke, Peter

The **locomotive** of war; money, empire, power and guilt. Peter Clarke. Bloomsbury Press 2017 ix, 418 p.p illustrations, map (hardcover) $30   **940.311**
1. World politics 2. World history -- 20th century 3. World War, 1914-1918 -- Causes 4. History, Modern -- 20th century 5. World War, 1914-1918 -- Influence 6. Liberalism -- Philosophy -- History -- 20th century
ISBN 9781620406601; 9781620406625; 1620406608

LC 2017027577

This book, by Peter Clarke, "illuminates many crucial issues of the . . . [20th century]: not only leadership and the projection of authority, but also military strategy, war finance and the mobilization of the economy in democratic regimes. . . . 'The Locomotive of War is a fascinating examination of the interplay between key figures in the context of unprecedented all-out warfare, with new insight on the dynamics of history in an extraordinary period." (Publisher's note)

Includes bibliographical references (pages 359-404) and index.

940.312   Peace – World War I

Kazin, Michael, 1948-

War against war; The American Fight for Peace, 1914-1918. Michael Kazin. Simon & Schuster 2017 400 p. illustrations (ebook) $20.99; (hardback) $28.00   **940.312**
1. Peace movements 2. World War, 1914-1918 -- United States 3. Progressivism (United States politics) 4. World War, 1939-1945 -- Women -- United States 5. United States -- Politics and government -- 1913-1921 6. Neutrality -- United States -- History -- 20th century 7. World War, 1914-1918 -- Protest movements -- United States 8. Peace movements -- United States -- History -- 20th century
ISBN 9781476705927; 9781476705903; 9781476705910

LC 2016005355

This book, by Michael Kazin, "is about the Americans who tried to stop their nation from fighting in one of history's most destructive wars and then were hounded by the government when they refused to back down. . . . Soon after the end of the Great War, most Americans believed it had not been worth fighting. And when its bitter legacy led to the next world war, the warnings of these peace activists turned into a tragic prophecy." (Publisher's note)

"A valuable history suitable for all audiences and an important addition to American history and World War I literature." LJ

Includes bibliographical references and index

940.373　World War I, 1914-1918 – United States

Meyer, G. J.

The **world** remade; America in World War I. G.J. Meyer. Bantam, an imprint of Random House, a division of Penguin Random House　2017　688 p.　illustrations (hardback) $30　　　　　　　　　　　　　　　　　　　**940.373**

1. World War, 1914-1918 -- United States
ISBN 9780553393323

LC 2016036502

In this book, author "G. J. Meyer takes readers from the heated deliberations over U.S. involvement, through the provocations and manipulations that drew us into the fight, to the battlefield itself and the shattering aftermath of the struggle. America's entry into the Great War helped make possible the defeat of Germany that had eluded Britain, France, Russia, and Italy in three and a half years of horrendous carnage." (Publisher's note)

"A refreshing look at this still-much-debated world debacle." Kirkus
Includes bibliographical references and index

940.4　Military history of World War I

Anderson, Scott, 1959-

Lawrence in Arabia; war, deceit, imperial folly and the making of the modern Middle East. Scott Anderson. Doubleday　2013　592 p. $28.95　　　　　　　　　　　　**940.4**

1. Middle East -- History 2. Great Britain. Army -- Biography 3. Middle East -- History -- 1914-1923 4. Soldiers -- Great Britain -- Biography 5. World War, 1914-1918 -- Campaigns -- Turkey 6. World War, 1914-1918 -- Campaigns -- Middle East
ISBN 038553292X; 9780385532921

LC 2012049719

National Book Critics Circle Award Finalist: Biography (2013)

In this biography of Lawrence of Arabia, Scott Anderson "reasons that 'Lawrence was both eyewitness to and participant in some of the most pivotal events leading to the creation of the modern Middle East . . . a corner of the earth where even the simplest assertion is dissected and parsed and argued over.' Too many biographers of Lawrence, he suggests, have let political biases and academic hobbyhorses overshadow their work." (Publishers Weekly)

Includes bibliographical references

Bascomb, Neal

The **escape** artists; a band of daredevil pilots and the grandest escape of the Great War. Neal Bascomb. Houghton Mifflin Harcourt　2018　336 p. (hardcover) $28　　　　　**940.4**

1. Prisoners of war 2. World War, 1914-1918 3. Airmen -- Great Britain -- Biography 4. World War, 1914-1918 -- Prisoners and prisons 5. Prisoner-of-war camps -- Germany -- 20th century 6. Prisoner-of-war escapes -- Germany -- 20th century 7. Escaped prisoners of war -- Great Britain -- Biography
ISBN 9780544937116

LC 2017058527

In this book, author "Neal Bascomb . . . delivers the spellbinding story of the downed Allied airmen who masterminded the remarkably courageous--and ingenious--breakout from Germany's most devilish POW camp. . . . A group of Allied prisoners led by ace pilot (and former Army sapper) David Gray hatch an elaborate escape plan. Their plot demands a risky feat of engineering as well as a bevy of disguises, forged documents, fake walls, and steely resolve." (Publisher's note)

Includes bibliographical references and index

Carroll, Andrew

My Fellow Soldiers; General John Pershing and the Americans Who Helped Win the Great War. Andrew Carroll. Penguin Press　2017　xxx, 383 p.p illustrations, maps (hardcover) $30　　　　　　　　　　　　　　　　　　　　　**940.4**

1. World War, 1914-1918 -- United States 2. Generals -- United States -- Biography 3. World War, 1914-1918 -- Biography 4. United States. Army. American Expeditionary Forces
ISBN 9781594206481; 9780698192669; 1594206481

LC 2016056754

This book, by Andrew Carroll, is an "intimate portrait of General Pershing, who led all of the American troops in Europe during World War I. . . . The general surmounted enormous obstacles to build an army and ultimately command millions of U.S. soldiers. But Pershing himself—often perceived as a harsh, humorless, and wooden leader—concealed inner agony from those around him." (Publisher's note)

"Carroll uses the personal correspondence of Gen. Pershing . . . as a means of establishing the war timeline. Varied American perspectives of the war are included, and the letters of African-Americans and women figure prominently in the work." Pub Wkly

Includes bibliographical references (pages [361]-372) and index.

Davenport, Matthew J.

First over there; the attack on Cantigny, America's first battle of World War I. Matthew J. Davenport. Thomas Dunne Books/St. Martin's Press　2015　384 p.　illustrations, maps (hardcover) $28.99　　　　　　　　　　　　　　　**940.4**

1. World War, 1914-1918 -- United States 2. World War, 1914-1918 -- Campaigns -- France 3. Cantigny, Battle of, Cantigny, France, 1918 4. United States. Army. Infantry Division, 1st
ISBN 1250056446; 9781250056443

LC 2015012154

This book, by Matthew J. Davenport, tells the "true story of America's first modern military battle, its first military victory during World War One, and its first steps onto the world stage. At first light on Tuesday, May 28th, 1918, waves of American riflemen from the U.S. Army's 1st Division climbed from their trenches, charged across the shell-scarred French dirt of no-man's-land, and captured the hilltop village of Cantigny from the grip of the German Army." (Publisher's note)

"From the 'creeping barrage' of artillery to the eventual American victory, the reader will hear every explosion, feel each bullet whiz past, and sometimes cry at the loss of a comrade." LJ

Includes bibliographical references and index

Downing, Taylor

Secret Warriors; The Spies, Scientists and Code Breakers of World War I. Taylor Downing. W W Norton & Co Inc　2015　464 p.　16 plates; illustrations $28.95　　　　　　**940.4**

1. Espionage 2. World War, 1914-1918
ISBN 1605986941; 9781605986944

Author Taylor Downing presents this "account of World War I that uncovers how wartime code-breaking, aeronautics, and scientific research that laid the foundation for much of the innovations of the twentieth century. [It] provides an invaluable and fresh history of the World War I, profiling a number of the key incidents and figures which lead to great leaps forward for the twentieth century." (Publisher's note)

"This volume should be of interest to most readers, especially those interested in military history." LJ

Dyer, Geoff

The **missing** of the Somme; Geoff Dyer. Vintage Books 2011 176p.   **940.4**

1. Memory 2. Veterans 3. World War, 1914-1918

ISBN 9780307742971; 9780307743237

LC 2002327412

This book offers an "exploration of the meaning and formal remembrance of British participation in World War I. . . . [Author Geoff] Dyer argues that our perceptions of the WWI are shaped by impressions of the war presented through the literature and public statuary (and, to a lesser degree, photography) produced within 15 years of the Armistice. The dominant theme of these cultural works is . . . sacrifice as a virtue in itself and its formal remembrance, and he believes this was evident even in works produced at the very beginning of the war. . . . Dyer intertwines the story of his travels with two friends to visit monuments and military cemeteries of the Western Front with . . . observations on statuary by Charles Sargeant Jagger, the poetry of Wilfred Owen and the literary criticism of Paul Fussell, among others." (Kirkus)

Eisenhower, John S. D.

Yanks: the epic story of the American Army in World War I; {by} John S. D. Eisenhower with Joanne Thompson Eisenhower. Free Press 2001 353p il maps hardcover o.p. pa $16 **940.4**

1. United States -- Army 2. World War, 1914-1918 -- Campaigns

ISBN 0-684-86304-9; 0-7432-2385-3 pa

LC 2001-23124

"This is an important work that should help alter the historical picture of the American role in the conflict." Booklist

Includes bibliographical references

Farwell, Byron

Over there; the United States in the Great War, 1917-1918. Norton 1999 336p $27.95; pa $15.95   **940.4**

1. World War, 1914-1918 -- United States

ISBN 0-393-04698-2; 0-393-32028-6 pa

LC 98-35705

This history of American intervention in World War I focuses primarily on the military aspects of the war but also discusses its social and economic impact

"This title does provide good coverage on the intervention in Russia and the role of women in the war, notably the 'Hello Girls.' " Libr J

Includes bibliographical references

Harries, Meirion

The **last** days of innocence; America at war, 1917-1918. {by} Meirion and Susie Harries. Random House 1997 573p il hardcover o.p. pa $16   **940.4**

1. World War, 1914-1918 -- United States

ISBN 0-679-74376-6 pa

LC 96-21756

"This is an excellent study of US participation in WWI. The research is in far greater depth than the usual 'popular history,' the analysis is sharp and informative, and the writing is clear and a pleasure to read. The authors strike an even balance between necessity for condensation and the accuracy that comes from detailed treatment." Choice

Includes bibliographical references

Hart, Peter

The **Somme**; the darkest hour on the Western Front. Pegasus Books 2008 589p il map $35; pa $17.95   **940.4**

1. World War, 1914-1918 -- Campaigns -- France

ISBN 978-1-60598-016-4; 1-60598-016-1; 978-1-60598-081-2 pa; 1-60598-081-1 pa

First published 2005 in the United Kingdom

This is an "account of the Somme offensive. . . . [The author evokes] the horrors of combat on the western front, skillfully blending these personal accounts with strategic considerations of a battle that slaughtered nearly a million French, German, and British soldiers. . . . Military history at its best." Libr J

Includes bibliographical references

Herwig, Holger H.

The **Marne,** 1914; the opening of World War I and the battle that changed the world. Random House 2009 391p il map $28   **940.4**

1. World War, 1914-1918 -- Campaigns -- France

ISBN 9781400066711; 1-4000-6671-9

LC 2009-5687

This fine history of World War I's opening battle argues persuasively that it was decisive in setting the pattern for the war, a pattern that made World War II inevitable. . . . Herwig's research has been exhaustive, including of archives long since thought destroyed that help him fill in a great many details about the German side. . . . As fine an addition to scholarly World War I literature as has been seen in some time. Booklist

Includes bibliographical references

Hynes, Samuel

The **unsubstantial** air; American fliers in the First World War. Samuel Hynes. Farrar, Straus & Giroux 2014 336 p. illustrations (cloth: alkaline paper) $26   **940.4**

1. Air pilots 2. World War, 1914-1918 -- Aerial operations 3. Fighter pilots -- United States -- Biography 4. World War, 1914-1918 -- Aerial operations, American 5. World War, 1914-1918 -- Personal narratives, American 6. Fighter pilots -- United States -- History -- 20th century

ISBN 0374278008; 9780374278007

LC 2014008673

This book, by Samuel Hynes, is the "story of the Americans who fought and died in the aerial battles of World War I. Much more than a traditional military history, it is an account of the excitement of becoming a pilot and flying in combat over the Western Front, told through the words and voices of the aviators themselves." (Publisher's note)

"The reader quickly becomes aware of the acute danger pilots faced—the narratives Haynes utilizes to tell the story often end abruptly with a terse account of a death due to a training accident, mechanical failure, or combat. It is a must read for anyone interested in aviation history, military history, and the American experience in the Great War." Pub Wkly

Includes bibliographical references and index

Larson, Erik

★ **Dead** wake; the last voyage of the Lusitania. by Erik Larson. Crown Publishers 2015 464 p. maps (hardcover) $28   **940.4**

1. Lusitania (Steamship) 2. World War, 1914-1918 -- Naval operations

ISBN 0307408868; 9780307408860; 9780307408877

LC 2014034182

This book by Erik Larson describes the history and events surrounding the sinking of the British passenger vessel Lusitania during World War I. "For months, German U-boats had brought terror to the North Atlantic. But the Lusitania . . . and her captain . . . placed tremendous faith in the gentlemanly strictures of warfare that for a century had kept civilian ships safe from attack. Germany, however, was determined to change the rules of the game." (Publisher's note)

"Reader engrossment is tightly sustained as we move back and forth between the Lusitania on its return from New York City to its home port of Liverpool under a black cloud of warnings that the imperial German government considered the waters around Britain to be a war zone, and the rapacious German submarine U-20, stalking the seas for prey like a lion on the Serengeti. Factual and personal to a high degree, the narrative reads like a grade-A thriller." Booklist

Includes bibliographical references and index

Lawrence, T. E.

Seven pillars of wisdom; a triumph. Doubleday 1935 672p il maps hardcover o.p. pa $19.95   **940.4**
1. Arabs 2. Bedouins 3. Wahhabis 4. World War, 1914-1918 -- Middle East
ISBN 0-385-41895-7 pa

"Not only a history of the Arab revolt during the {First} World War, but a commentary on the national characteristics, and political policies of Arabs, Turks and British." Cleveland Public Libr

Lussu, Emilio, 1890-1975

A **soldier** on the southern front; the classic Italian memoir of World War I. Emilio Lussu. Rizzoli Ex Libris 2014 278 p. (alk. paper) $26.95   **940.4**
1. Autobiographies 2. World War, 1914-1918 -- Campaigns -- Italy 3. World War, 1914-1918 -- Personal narratives
ISBN 0847842789; 9780847842780

LC 2013943440

Written by Emilio Lussu, translated by Gregory Conti, this memoir is "a rediscovered Italian masterpiece chronicling the author's experience as an infantryman, newly translated and reissued to commemorate the centennial of World War I. . . . A classic in Italy but virtually unknown in the English-speaking world, it reveals . . . the almost farcical side of the war as seen by a Sardinian officer fighting the Austrian army on the Asiago plateau in northeastern Italy." (Publisher's note)

A "compelling read that enters the mind of a man at the front, exposed daily to terrible scenes and decisions that change who he is." LJ

Massie, Robert K.

Castles of steel; Britain, Germany, and the winning of the Great War at sea. Random House 2003 865p il map pa $17.95; $35   **940.4**
1. Germany -- Kriegsmarine 2. Great Britain -- Royal Navy 3. World War, 1914-1918 -- Naval operations 4. World War, 1914-1918 -- Naval operations, German 5. World War, 1914-1918 -- Naval operations, British
ISBN 0-345-40878-0 pa; 0-679-45671-6

LC 2003-41373

Focusing on Britain's Grand Fleet and Germany's High Seas Fleet, Massie examines the role of sea power in determining the outcome of the First World War. Index.

The author "makes a coherent if long narrative out of a sequence of events familiar to students of naval history but probably not to many other potential readers." Publ Wkly

Millman, Chad

The **detonators**; the secret plot to destroy America and an epic hunt for justice. Little, Brown 2006 330p il map $24.99   **940.4**
1. Sabotage 2. World War, 1914-1918 -- United States
ISBN 978-0-316-73496-7; 0-316-73496-9

LC 2005-24401

"With its obvious contemporary resonance, Millman's able account of an earlier foreign attack on America should draw the espionage audience and more." Booklist

Includes bibliographical references

Mosier, John

The **myth** of the Great War; a new military history of World War I. HarperCollins Pubs. 2001 381p il hardcover o.p. pa $14.95   **940.4**
1. World War, 1914-1918 -- Campaigns
ISBN 0-06-019676-9; 0-06-008433-2 pa

LC 00-46103

"After dissecting the major campaigns on the western front, Mosier concludes that Germany's ultimate defeat was the direct result of the influx of American soldiers into France in 1917 and 1918. . . . This is revisionist history that convincingly smashes the myths that Allied governments, leaders, and propagandists worked so hard to promulgate. Mosier's masterful account is a welcome addition." Booklist

Includes bibliographical references

Neiberg, Michael

★ **Fighting** the Great War; a global history. [by] Michael S. Neiberg. Harvard University Press 2005 xx, 395p il map $27.95   **940.4**
1. World War, 1914-1918
ISBN 0-674-01696-3

LC 2004-54330

"Readers interested in a general overview of WW I can do no better than Neiberg's excellent account." Choice

Includes bibliographical references

Ousby, Ian

The **road** to Verdun; World War I's most momentous battle and the folly of nationalism. Doubleday 2002 393p il maps $30; pa $16   **940.4**
1. World War, 1914-1918 -- Campaigns
ISBN 0-385-50393-8; 0-385-72173-0 pa

LC 2002-19475

This is a study of the Battle of Verdun which "killed 700,000 French and German soldiers, 10% of all those killed in the war. Yet a sense of glory was maintained, however inappropriately, amid the gore: the road leading to the battlefield was called the Sacred Way, and the French General Neville gained immortality by his brave statement, 'They {the Germans} shall not pass.'" Publ Wkly

Paice, Edward

★ **World** War I: the African Front. Pegasus 2008 xxxix, 488p il map $35   **940.4**
1. World War, 1914-1918 -- Campaigns -- East Africa
ISBN 978-1-933648-90-3

"An authoritative summing-up of a grim, complex and little-known part of World War I." Kirkus

Includes bibliographical references

Philpott, William

Three armies on the Somme; the first battle of the twentieth century. [by] William Philpott. Alfred A. Knopf 2010 631p il map $35; ebook $35   **940.4**

1. Germany -- Heer 2. France -- Armée 3. Great Britain -- Army 4. World War, 1914-1918 -- Campaigns -- France

ISBN 978-0-307-26585-2; 978-0-307-59372-6 ebook

LC 2010-4070

First published 2009 in the United Kingdom with title: Bloody victory

"The Battle of the Somme is branded in British memory as the exemplar of WWI: a months-long cataclysm that, at the cost of monumental casualties, repelled the Germans from a few square miles of shell-blasted French countryside. This account by a descendant of an artillerist in the battle has two aims: to narrate the battle from its initial strategic concept to its sputtering-out in late 1916 and to refute historical and popular opinion about the battle. . . . Comprehensive research and convention-bucking argument qualify Philpott for the WWI shelf." Booklist

Includes bibliographical references

Preston, Diana

A **higher** form of killing; six weeks in spring 1915 that changed the nature of warfare forever. Diana Preston. Bloomsbury 2015 352 p. 16 plates; ills.; maps; ports (hardback) $28   **940.4**

1. Strategy 2. World War, 1914-1918 3. Lusitania (Steamship) 4. World War, 1914-1918 -- Chemical warfare 5. Ypres, 2nd Battle of, Ieper, Belgium, 1915 6. War (Philosophy) -- History -- 20th century 7. Just war doctrine -- History -- 20th century 8. Airships -- Germany -- History -- 20th century 9. World War, 1914-1918 -- Naval operations -- Submarine 10. Bombing, Aerial -- England -- London -- History -- 20th century 11. Weapons of mass destruction -- Germany -- History -- 20th century 12. Germany -- Armed Forces -- Weapons systems -- History -- 20th century

ISBN 1620402122; 9781620402122

LC 2014019999

This book by Diana Preston "places the creation of poison gas, the torpedo, and the zeppelin into the context of warfare and the human toll exacted. . . . She explains the scorched-earth policy of Germany under Kaiser Wilhelm II, which mandated a complete triumph for the Fatherland at all cost during the infamous six-week period in 1915 where this trio of deadly weapons was introduced to untold suffering for soldiers and civilians alike." (Publishers Weekly)

"In what is often difficult but necessary reading, Preston provides haunting descriptions of the effects of poison gas. A harrowing—and, in this era of drones, absolutely pertinent—look at the rapacious reaches of man's murderous imagination." Kirkus

Includes bibliographical references and index

Sacco, Joe

The **Great** War; July 1, 1916: the first day of the Battle of the Somme: an illustrated panorama. Joe Sacco. W.W. Norton & Co. Inc. 2013 54 p. chiefly ill. $35   **940.4**

1. World War, 1914-1918 2. Great Britain -- Military history 3. World War, 1939-1945 -- Campaigns -- France 4. Somme, 1st Battle of the, France, 1916 5. Somme, 1st Battle of the, France, 1916 -- Comic books, strips, etc

ISBN 0393088804; 9780393088809

LC 2013010710

This art book by Joe Sacco presents "a single continuous panorama, eight inches tall and twenty-four feet long," which "illustrates, in minutely detailed black-and-white drawings, events just before and during a summer day when the British army suffered more than fifty-seven

thousand dead and wounded, its greatest single-day loss. . . . An accompanying booklet" presents a "brief account of the day by Adam Hoschchild." (Bookforum)

Scott, R. Neil

★ **Many** were held by the sea; the tragic sinking of HMS Otranto. R. Neil Scott. Rowman & Littlefield 2012 249 p. (cloth: alk. paper) $35.00   **940.4**

1. Shipwrecks 2. World War, 1914-1918 -- Naval operations 3. Kashmir (Troopship) 4. Otranto (Troopship) 5. Shipwrecks -- Scotland -- Islay 6. World War, 1914-1918 -- Naval operations, British 7. World War, 1914-1918 -- Casualties -- Great Britain 8. Transports -- Great Britain -- History -- 20th century 9. World War, 1914-1918 -- Transportation -- Great Britain 10. Marine accidents -- Great Britain -- History -- 20th century

ISBN 1442213426; 9781442213425; 9781442213449

LC 2012003033

This book by R. Neil Scott tells the story of a 1918 disaster in which the "HMS Kashmir rammed HMS Otranto off Islay, Scotland. . . . On board were 372 British officers and sailors and 701 American soldiers. . . . The Kashmir managed to back away and follow the harsh wartime order . . . to continue on her prescribed course rather than stop and take on survivors. Thus it was that . . . the severely damaged Otranto was left dead in the water with more than a thousand souls aboard." (Publisher's note)

Includes bibliographical references and index

Sebag-Montefiore, Hugh

Somme; into the breach. Hugh Sebag-Montefiore. The Belknap Press of Harvard University Press 2016 xlviii, 607 p.p illustrations, maps (hardcover) $35; (ebook) $43.95   **940.4**

1. Somme, 1st Battle of the, France, 1916 2. World War, 1914-1918 -- Campaigns -- France 3. World War, 1914-1918 -- France -- Personal narratives 4. World War, 1914-1918 -- Campaigns -- France -- Somme

ISBN 9780674545199; 0674545192; 9780674970038

LC 2016025276

This book on the Battle of the Somme during World War I by Hugh Sebag-Montefiore presents eyewitness accounts that "relive scenes of extraordinary courage and sacrifice, as soldiers ordered 'over the top' ventured into No Man's Land and enemy trenches, where they met a hail of machine-gun fire, thickets of barbed wire, and exploding shells." (Publisher's note)

"A beautifully crafted, blow-by-blow account with deep insight into the lives of these diverse young men." Kirkus

Includes bibliographical references (pages [581]-586) and index

Thompson, Mark

The **white** war; life and death on the Italian front, 1915-1919. Basic Books 2009 454p il map $30   **940.4**

1. World War, 1914-1918 -- Campaigns -- Italy

ISBN 978-0-465-01329-6; 0-465-01329-5

First published 2008 in the United Kingdom

"Penetrating study of one of the forgotten fronts of the Great War. . . . A much-needed addition to the literature of World War I." Kirkus

Includes bibliographical references

Walker, William T.

Betrayal at Little Gibraltar; a German fortress, a treacherous American general, and the battle to end World War I. William T. Walker. Scribner 2016 464 p. $28   **940.4**

1. World War, 1914-1918 2. Military art and science 3. Argonne,

Battle of the, France, 1918 4. World War, 1914-1918 -- Campaigns -- Meuse River Valley 5. Montfaucon (Meuse, France) -- History, Military -- 20th century 6. United States. Army. Infantry Division, 79th -- History -- World War, 1914-1918

ISBN 9781501117893; 9781501117916; 1501117890

LC 2015044665

This book, by William Walker, "tells vivid human stories of the soldiers who fought to capture the giant fortress [Montfaucon] and push the American advance. Using unpublished first-person accounts—and featuring photographs, documents, and maps that place you in the action—Walker describes the horrors of World War I combat, the sacrifices of the doughboys, and the determined efforts of two participants to pierce the cover-up and to solve the mystery of Montfaucon." (Publisher's note)

"He creates a convincing argument for a postwar cover-up of Bullard's actions. A military history for all libraries" LJ

Includes bibliographical references and index

Wawro, Geoffrey

A **mad** catastrophe; the outbreak of World War I and the collapse of the Habsburg Empire. Geoffrey Wawro. Basic Books 2014 472 p. illustrations, maps (hardback) $29.99   **940.4**

1. Austria -- History 2. Hungary -- History 3. World War, 1914-1918 4. World War, 1914-1918 -- Causes 5. Austria -- History -- Franz Joseph I, 1848-1916 6. World War, 1914-1918 -- Campaigns -- Balkan Peninsula 7. World War, 1914-1918 -- Campaigns -- Galicia (Poland and Ukraine)

ISBN 0465028357; 9780465028351

LC 2013039393

"The Austro-Hungarian army that marched east and south to confront the Russians and Serbs in the opening campaigns of World War I had a glorious past but a pitiful present. . . . As prizewinning historian Geoffrey Wawro explains in 'A Mad Catastrophe,' the doomed Austrian conscripts were an unfortunate microcosm of the Austro-Hungarian Empire itself--both equally ripe for destruction." (Publisher's note)

"Wawro's authoritative account is a damning analysis of an empire and a people unready for war." Pub Wkly

Includes bibliographical references and index

Weber, Thomas

Hitler's first war; Adolf Hitler, the men of the List Regiment, and the First World War. Oxford University Press 2010 450p il $34.95   **940.4**

1. Heads of state 2. Nazi leaders 3. Soldiers -- Germany 4. World War, 1914-1918 5. Biography, Individual 6. World War, 1914-1918 -- Germany 7. World War, 1914-1918 -- Campaigns 8. Germany -- Heer -- Bayerisches Reserve-Infanterie-Regiment 16

ISBN 0199233209; 9780199233205

"Hitler claimed that his years as a soldier in the First World War were the most formative years of his life. However, for the six decades since his death in the ruins of Berlin, Hitler's time as a soldier on the Western Front has remained a blank spot. . . . [Weber's book] looks at what really happened to Private Hitler and the men of the Bavarian List Regiment of which he was a member." (Publisher's note) Index.

"A triumph of original research in a very stony field. The conclusion that might be drawn is that Hitler was far more of the opportunist than is generally supposed. He made things up as he went along, including his own past." Wall Street J

Includes bibliographical references

Yockelson, Mitchell A., 1962-

Forty-seven days; how Pershing's warriors came of age to defeat the German Army in World War I. Mitchell Yockelson. New American Library 2016 400 p. illustrations (hardcover)

$28   **940.4**

1. United States -- Military history 2. World War, 1914-1918 -- United States 3. United States. Army. American Expeditionary Forces 4. World War, 1914-1918 -- Campaigns -- Western Front

ISBN 9780451466952

LC 2015039121

This book, by Mitchell Yockelson, offers "the gripping account of the U.S. First Army's . . . triumph over the Germans in America's bloodiest battle of the First World War—the Battle of the Meuse-Argonne. . . . Historian Mitchell Yockelson tells how General John J. 'Black Jack' Pershing's exemplary leadership led to the unlikeliest of victories." (Publisher's note)

"An accessible, elucidating study by a knowledgeable expert." Kirkus

Includes bibliographical references (pages 339-379) and index.

940.44   Air operations

Hamilton-Paterson, James

Marked for death; The First War in the Air. James Hamilton-Paterson. Head of Zeus 2015 356 p. illustrations (some color) (hbk.) $27.95   **940.44**

1. World War, 1914-1918 -- Aerial operations 2. World War, 1914-1918 -- Casualties

ISBN 9781681771588; 1681771586; 1784970395; 9781784970390

LC 2014495526

This book, by James Hamilton-Paterson, is an "account of aerial combat during World War I, revealing the terrible risks taken by the men who fought and died in the world's first war in the air. . . . [It] debunks popular myth to explore the brutal truths of wartime aviation: of flimsy planes and unprotected pilots; of burning nineteen-year-olds falling screaming to their deaths; of pilots blinded by the entrails of their observers." (Publisher's note)

"Best of all, the author—who has a solid body of fiction to his credit—is a consummate storyteller; not only does the book tell a fascinating story, it is nearly impossible to put down." Kirkus

Includes bibliographical references (pages 331-334) and index

940.45   Naval operations

Hernon, Peter

The **great** rescue; American heroes, an iconic ship, and the race to save Europe in WWI. Peter Hernon. HarperCollins Publishers 2017 x, 350 p.p illustrations (hardcover) $27.99   **940.45**

1. Warships -- United States -- History 2. World War, 1914-1918 -- Naval operations 3. Leviathan (Steamship) 4. World War, 1914-1918 -- Transportation 5. World War, 1914-1918 -- Naval operations, American

ISBN 9780062433862; 9780062433879; 9780062433886

LC 2017012596

This book, by Peter Hernon, looks at the story of the "USS Leviathan, the legendary liner turned warship that ferried U.S. soldiers to Europe [during World War I]. . . . Hernon tells the ship's . . . multiple voyages and through the experiences of a diverse cast of participants, including the ship's captain, Henry Bryan; General John Pershing, commander of the American Expeditionary Force; [and] . . . Elizabeth Weaver, an army nurse who saw the war's horrors firsthand." (Publisher's note)

"An intriguing work of World War I research resurrects the little-known history of a massive German luxury liner that was confiscated and retooled for the American war effort." Kirkus

Includes bibliographical references and index.

940.465   Cemeteries – World War I

O'Donnell, Patrick K.

The **unknowns**; the untold story of America's unknown soldier and WWI's most decorated heroes who brought him home. Patrick K. O'Donnell. Atlantic Monthly Press 2018 288 p. $27   **940.465**

1. Soldiers -- United States 2. Arlington National Cemetery (Va.) 3. United States -- Military history
ISBN 0802128335; 9780802128331

In this book, author Patrick O'Donnell "illuminates the saga behind the creation of the Tomb [of the Unknown Soldier] . . . and recreates the moving ceremony during which it was consecrated and the eight Body Bearers, and the sergeant who had chosen the one body to be interred, solemnly united." (Publisher's note)

940.5   Europe--1918-

Hathaway, Oona Anne

The **internationalists**; how a radical plan to outlaw war remade the world. Oona A. Hathaway and Scott J. Shapiro. Simon & Schuster 2017 xxii, 581 p.p illustrations (some color) (hardcover) $30   **940.5**

1. Treaties 2. International relations 3. World history -- 20th century 4. Peace treaties -- 20th century 5. Kellogg-Briand Pact (1928 August 27) 6. International relations -- History -- 20th century
ISBN 1501109863; 9781501109881; 9781501109867

This book, by Oona A. Hathaway and Scott J. Shapiro, "tells the story of the [1928] Peace Pact by placing it in the long history of international law from the seventeenth century through the present, tracing this rich history through a fascinating and diverse array of lawyers, politicians and intellectuals. . . . It details the brutal world of conflict the Peace Pact helped extinguish, and the subsequent era where tariffs and sanctions take the place of tanks and gunships." (Publisher's note)

"Rich in implication, particularly in a bellicose time, and of much interest to students of modern history and international relations." Kirkus

Includes bibliographical references (pages 431-552) and index.

Jarausch, Konrad H.

Out of ashes; a new history of Europe in the twentieth century. Konrad H. Jarausch. Princeton University Press 2015 880 p. illustrations, maps (hardback: acid-free paper) $39.50 **940.5**

1. Europe -- History -- 20th century 2. Europe -- Social conditions -- 20th century 3. Europe -- Politics and government -- 20th century 4. Social change -- Europe -- History -- 20th century
ISBN 0691152799; 9780691152790

LC 2014031328

This book, by Konrad H. Jarausch, offers a "history of twentieth-century Europe. . . [It] tells the story of an era of unparalleled violence and barbarity yet also of humanity, prosperity, and promise. . . . [It also] explores the paradox of the European encounter with modernity in the twentieth century, shedding new light on why it led to cataclysm, inhumanity, and self-destruction, but also social justice, democracy, and peace." (Publisher's note)

"The work isn't designed to be encyclopedic, yet it should be on the shelf of everyone seeking a panoramic, narrative guide to history's

most violent century. This comprehensive history of 20th-century Europe is bound to become the standard work on its subject: a bold, major achievement." Pub Wkly

Includes bibliographical references and index

Kershaw, Ian

To Hell and Back; Europe 1914-1949. Ian Kershaw. Penguin Group USA 2015 592 p. illustrations, maps $35 **940.5**

1. World War, 1914-1918 2. World War, 1939-1945 3. Europe -- History -- 1918-1945
ISBN 0670024589; 9780670024582

LC 2015040523

This book, by Ian Kershaw, part of the "Penguin History of Europe" series, offers an "analysis of the pivotal years of World War I and World War II. The European catastrophe, the long continuous period from 1914 to 1949, was unprecedented in human history. . . . This new volume . . . offers comprehensive coverage of this tumultuous era." (Publisher's note)

"Kershaw concludes with a somewhat less successful appraisal of the vastly altered geopolitical landscape following WWII, the social and economic disruptions, the physical ruin of the continent, and the responses to the devastation offered by the Christian churches, leading intellectuals, and popular entertainments. An ambitious, dense , sometimes-difficult treatment of a vast topic." Kirkus

Mak, Geert

★ In Europe; travels through the twentieth century. translated from the Dutch by Sam Garrett. Pantheon 2007 876p map $35   **940.5**

1. Europe -- Description and travel 2. Europe -- History -- 20th century
ISBN 0-375-42495-4; 978-0-375-42495-3

LC 2007-9260

Original Dutch edition, 2004

This book recounts the author's travels through Europe and examines the history of European countries, particularly focusing on the the effects of the Treaty of Rome.

"Mak's brilliant compendium is difficult to define—is it a history book, a travelogue, a memoir?—but stands out as a remarkable, insightful, exhilarating exposition on that peculiar continent across the Atlantic." Publ Wkly

Sachar, Howard Morley

Dreamland; Europeans and Jews in the aftermath of the Great War. {by} Howard M. Sachar. Knopf 2002 385p map hardcover o.p. pa $15   **940.5**

1. Jews -- Europe 2. Europe -- History -- 1918-1945
ISBN 0-375-70829-4 pa

LC 2001-38471

An overview of Jewish life in Europe during the three decades before the Holocaust

"This scholarly analysis provides a completely original slant on the much-studied interwar period." Booklist

Includes bibliographical references

Talty, Stephan

Agent Garbo; the brilliant, eccentric secret agent who tricked Hitler and saved D-Day. Stephan Talty. Houghton Mifflin Harcourt 2012 301 p.   **940.5**

1. Spies 2. Normandy (France), Attack on, 1944 3. World War, 1939-1945 -- Secret service 4. Spies -- Great Britain -- Biography 5. World War, 1939-1945 -- Secret service -- Great Britain

ISBN 0547614810; 9780547614816

LC 2012005470

This book by Stephan Talty tells the story of "Juan Pujol, the Spanish hotel manager who, in January 1941, waltzed into the British Embassy in Madrid and announced that he wanted to help the Allied war effort. . . . Turned down by the British, Pujol came up with a stunningly audacious plan: he would approach the Germans, offer his services as a spy, gather intelligence, and then go back to the British, operating as a double agent. And here's the thing: it worked." (Booklist)

Includes bibliographical references (pages [281]-283) and index

940.53 World War II, 1939-1945

Ackerman, Diane, 1948-
★ The **zookeeper's** wife. W.W. Norton 2007 368p il $24.95 **940.53**
1. Zoos 2. Jews -- Poland 3. Holocaust, 1933-1945 4. World War, 1939-1945 -- Jews -- Rescue
ISBN 978-0-393-06172-7; 0-393-06172-8

LC 2007-12635

This is an account of how the director of the Warsaw Zoo and his wife, Jan and Antonina Zabinski, respectively, saved 300 Jews during World War II.

"An exemplary work of scholarship and an 'ecstasy of imagining,' Ackerman's affecting telling of the heroic Zabinskis' dramatic story illuminates the profound connection between humankind and nature, and celebrates life's beauty, mystery, and tenacity." Booklist

Includes bibliographical references

Aleksievich, Svetlana, 1948-
The **unwomanly** face of war; an oral history of women in World War II. Svetlana Alexievich; translated by Richard Pevear and Larissa Volokhonsky. Revised edition Random House 2017 384 p. $30 **940.53**
1. World War, 1939-1945 -- Women 2. World War, 1939-1945 -- Soviet Union 3. Women and war -- Soviet Union 4. World War, 1939-1945 -- Participation, Female 5. World War, 1939-1945 -- Women -- Soviet Union 6. World War, 1939-1945 -- Personal narratives, Russian
ISBN 9780399588723; 0399588728

LC 2016036099

Originally published 1985 in Russian
Revised edition
Author Svetlana Alexievich won the Nobel Prize in Literature in 2015.

This book, by Svetlana Alexievich, "chronicles the experiences of the Soviet women who fought on the front lines, on the home front, and in the occupied territories. These women--more than a million in total--were nurses and doctors, pilots, tank drivers, machine-gunners, and snipers. They battled alongside men, and yet, after the victory, their efforts and sacrifices were forgotten." (Publisher's note)

"A worldwide best seller when it was originally published in Russian in 1985, this work by Nobel Prize winner Alexievich . . . combines hundreds of oral history accounts with the author's own reflections. Alexievich conducted these interviews between 1978 and 1985, intending to capture 'women's history of war.'" LJ

Arrington, Leonard J.
Japanese Americans, from relocation to redress; edited by Roger Daniels, Sandra C. Taylor, Harry H.L. Kitano; contributions by Leonard J. Arrington {et al.} rev & updated ed; University of Wash. Press 1991 xxi, 242p il pa $25 **940.53**
1. World War, 1939-1945 -- Reparations 2. Japanese Americans -- Evacuation and relocation, 1942-1945
ISBN 0-295-97117-7

LC 91-2892

First published 1986 by University of Utah Press
A collection of essays on Japanese Americans focusing on their wartime relocation and their efforts to seek reparations.

Includes bibliographical references

Barr, Niall
Eisenhower's Armies; The American-British Alliance During World War II. Niall Barr. W W Norton & Co Inc 2015 544 p. 16 plates; illustrations; maps $35 **940.53**
1. World War, 1939-1945 2. United States -- Foreign relations -- Great Britain
ISBN 1605988162; 9781605988160

This book by Niall Bar "is the story of two very different armies learning to live, work, and fight together even in the face of serious strategic disagreements. The book is also a very human story about the efforts of many individuals . . . who worked and argued together to defeat Hitler's Germany. In highlighting the cooperation, tensions, and disagreements inherent in this military alliance, this work shows that Allied victory was far from pre-ordained and proves that the business of making this alliance work was vital for eventual success." (Publisher's note)

"This dramatic work isn't just for military historians or World War II scholars. It is also highly recommended for students of World War II and of the Atlantic Alliance of the mid-20th century and is a great read for anyone interested in leadership, decision making, international relations and diplomacy, and 20th-century history." LJ

Barrett, Duncan
GI brides; the wartime girls who crossed the Atlantic for love. Duncan Barrett & Nuala Calvi. William Morrow Paperbacks 2014 592 p. 16 plates; illustrations (paperback) $14.99 **940.53**
1. Military spouses 2. World War, 1939-1945 3. British -- United States 4. British Americans -- Biography 5. War brides -- Great Britain -- Biography 6. Women immigrants -- United States -- Biography 7. World War, 1939-1945 -- Women -- Great Britain
ISBN 0062328050; 9780062328052

LC 2014010526

Authors Duncan Barrett and Nuala Calvi present the " tale of romance and resilience--the true story of four British women who crossed the Atlantic for love, coming to America at the end of World War II to make a new life with the American servicemen they married." (Publisher's note)

"Alternating among the women, the authors bring to light the joys and sorrows of each woman, but readers may find it easier to read each story in its entirety before switching to another one. Entertaining stories about four women who embraced life with American soldiers after the end of World War II." Kirkus

Includes bibliographical references and index

Berenbaum, Michael
The **world** must know; the history of the Holocaust as told in the United States Holocaust Memorial Museum. Arnold Kramer, editor of photographs. 2nd ed; United States Holocaust Memorial Museum 2006 xxi, 250p il pa $29.95 **940.53**
1. Holocaust, 1933-1945 2. United States Holocaust Memorial Museum
ISBN 0-8018-8358-X

First published 1993 by Little, Brown

"Visually evocative and unsettling, the book, supplemented with a useful bibliography, is an excellent choice for those with little acquaintance of the subject or those needing a concise synopsis." Libr J [review of 1993 edition]

Includes bibliographical references

Berthon, Simon

Warlords; an extraordinary recreation of World War II through the eyes and minds of Hitler, Roosevelt, Churchill, and Stalin. [by] Simon Berthon and Joanna Potts. Da Capo Press 2006 358p il $24.95   **940.53**

1. Governors 2. Statesmen 3. Historians 4. Presidents 5. Heads of state 6. Prime ministers 7. People with disabilities 8. Memoirists 9. Nazi leaders 10. Philatelists 11. Cabinet members 12. Communist leaders 13. Political leaders 14. Members of Parliament 15. Nobel laureates for literature 16. World War, 1939-1945 -- Diplomatic history

ISBN 0-306-81467-6

LC 2005-432583

First published 2005 in the United Kingdom

This book focuses "on the day-to-day actions of Hitler, Stalin, Churchill, and Roosevelt as they grapple with the war's events and plot strategy. . . . For anyone interested in how these four leaders engaged in the war, here is a great place to start." Libr J

Includes bibliographical references

Beschloss, Michael R.

★ **The conquerors**: Roosevelt, Truman, and the destruction of Hitler's Germany, 1941-1945; {by} Michael Beschloss. Simon & Schuster 2002 377p il maps $26.95; pa $15 **940.53**

1. Governors 2. Presidents 3. Vice-presidents 4. People with disabilities 5. Reconstruction (1939-1951) 6. Senators 7. Philatelists 8. World War, 1939-1945 -- Germany 9. Germany -- Foreign relations -- United States 10. United States -- Foreign relations -- Germany

ISBN 0-684-81027-1; 0-7432-4454-0 pa

LC 2002-30331

"As German forces were driven back in 1943-45, American leaders were anxious that in 20 years, just as it had done after its defeat in 1918, a vengeful Germany would start another world war. To prevent this, two schools of thought flowed through DC's salons of power: punishment or rehabilitation. . . . Beschloss covers the meeting-by-meeting, memo-by-memo political battle between the two approaches. . . . Beschloss' comprehensive research and narration into every nuance opens a significant perspective on bureaucratic politics' effect on the Germany that eventually formed in the early cold war." Booklist

Includes bibliographical references

Beyond Rosie; a documentary History of Women and World War II. edited by Julia Brock, Jennifer W. Dickey, Richard J. W. Harker. University of Arkansas Press 2015 245 p. (pbk.: alk. paper) $22.95   **940.53**

1. World War, 1939-1945 -- Women 2. World War, 1939-1945 -- United States

ISBN 9781557286697; 9781557286703; 9781610755573

LC 2014949011

This book, edited by Julia Brock, Jennifer W. Dickey, Richard Harker, and Catherine Lewis, "offers readers an opportunity to see the numerous contributions [women] made to the fight against the Axis powers and how American women's roles changed during the war. The primary documents (newspapers, propaganda posters, cartoons, excerpts from oral histories and memoirs, speeches, photographs, and editorials) collected here represent cultural, political, economic, and social perspectives on the diverse roles women played during World War II." (Publisher's note)

Bowman, Constance

Slacks and calluses; our summer in a bomber factory. Constance Bowman; illustrated by Clara Marie Allen; introduction by Sandra M. Gilbert. Smithsonian Institution Press 1999 xiv, 181p illustrations   **940.53**

1. World War, 1939-1945 -- Women 2. World War, 1939-1945 -- United States

ISBN 1-560-98368-X; 9781560983682; 1-560-98387-6

LC 99031365

This book, by Constance Bowman and illustrated by Clara Marie Allen, describes how "in 1943 two spirited young teachers decided to do their part for the war effort by spending their summer vacation working the swing shift on a B-24 production line at a San Diego bomber plant. Entering a male-dominated realm . . . , they learned to use tools that they had never seen before, live with aluminum shavings in their hair, and get along with . . . coworkers from all walks of life." (Publisher's note)

Buruma, Ian

★ **Year** zero; 1945 and the aftermath of war. Ian Buruma. Penguin Press 2013 384 p. $29.95   **940.53**

1. World history -- 1945- 2. World politics -- 1945- 3. World War, 1939-1945 -- Influence 4. History, Modern -- 1945-1989 5. World War, 1939-1945 -- Peace

ISBN 1594204365; 9781594204364

LC 2013007702

This book by Ian Buruma "explores the nascent social and political forces that later influenced the Cold War and post-colonial movements. . . . Starting with a world ruined by war, Buruma moves . . . from describing the elation of victory and the desire for revenge to the Allies' attempts to reform societies by eliminating all traces of militarism or fascism and establishing a European welfare state, as destroyed cities are rebuilt and fallen nations reimagined." (Publishers Weekly)

Includes bibliographical references and index

Cahan, Richard

Un-American; the incarceration of Japanese Americans during World War II. Richard Cahan and Michael Williams; images by Dorothea Lange, Ansel Adams, and other government photographers. CityFiles Press 2016 240 p. illustrations, map $39.95   **940.53**

1. Concentration camps -- United States 2. Japanese Americans -- Evacuation and relocation, 1942-1945

ISBN 0991541863; 9780991541867

LC 2016055107

This book reveals how "the United States rounded up 120,000 residents of Japanese ancestry living along the West Coast, . . . sent them to internment camps for the duration of World War II, . . . [and] hired famed photographers Dorothea Lange, Ansel Adams, and others to document the expulsion. . . . Authors Richard Cahan and Michael Williams . . . took a slow, careful look at each of these images as they put together a powerful history of one of America's defining moments." (Publisher's note)

"The result is an intensely revelatory and profoundly resonant book of beauty and strength, history and caution." Booklist

Includes bibliographical references (pages 233-238) and index.

Churchill, Winston

Closing the ring. Houghton Mifflin 1951 749p maps (Sec-

ond World War) hardcover o.p. pa $18   **940.53**
1. World War, 1939-1945 2. World War, 1939-1945 -- Great Britain
ISBN 0-395-41059-2 pa

"'Closing the Ring' sets forth the year of conflict from June 1943 to June 1944. Aided by the command of the oceans, the mastery of the U-boats, and our ever growing superiority in the air, the Western Allies were able to conquer Sicily and invade Italy, with the result that Mussolini was overthrown and the Italian nation came over to our side." Preface

The **gathering** storm. Houghton Mifflin 1948 784p maps (Second World War) hardcover o.p. pa $19   **940.53**
1. World War, 1939-1945 2. World War, 1939-1945 -- Great Britain
ISBN 0-395-41055-X pa

The first volume of Churchill's monumental history of the Second World War describes the days between the false peace and Hitler's near-victory just before Dunkirk

The **grand** alliance. Houghton Mifflin 1950 903p maps (Second World War) hardcover o.p. pa $18   **940.53**
1. World War, 1939-1945 2. World War, 1939-1945 -- Great Britain
ISBN 0-395-41057-6 pa

This volume begins with the German drive in the East, covers the War in Africa and describes the entrance into the war of Russia and, after Pearl Harbor, the United States

The **hinge** of fate. Houghton Mifflin 1950 1000p maps (Second World War) hardcover o.p. pa $18   **940.53**
1. World War, 1939-1945 2. World War, 1939-1945 -- Great Britain
ISBN 0-395-41058-4 pa

Describing events leading to the invasion of Sicily, warfare in Africa, the discouragingly slow job of reconquest in Europe, meetings with Roosevelt, and efforts at collaboration with Stalin, this volume covers the period from January 1942 to May 1943

Their finest hour. Houghton Mifflin 1949 751p maps (Second World War) hardcover o.p. pa $19   **940.53**
1. World War, 1939-1945 2. World War, 1939-1945 -- Great Britain
ISBN 0-395-41056-8 pa

This volume starts with the problems confronting Churchill as he assumed the office of Prime Minister in 1940 and continues with accounts of the Battle of Britain, the Battle of France and Dunkirk

Triumph and tragedy. Houghton Mifflin 1953 800p maps (Second World War) hardcover o.p. pa $18   **940.53**
1. World War, 1939-1945 2. World War, 1939-1945 -- Great Britain
ISBN 0-395-41060-6 pa

The concluding volume of Churchill's history of World War II begins with D-Day and covers campaigns leading to the defeat of Germany and Japan

Clendinnen, Inga
Reading the Holocaust. Cambridge Univ. Press 1999 227p il map $69; pa $19.99   **940.53**
1. Holocaust, 1933-1945 -- Historiography
ISBN 0-521-64174-8; 0-521-01269-4 pa

LC 98-53636

In this reexamination of the Holocaust Clendinnen "first considers the problematic nature of eyewitness accounts, then turns to an unflinching inquiry into the Nazi mentality and finally takes on the tough question of artistic representation. . . . This slim, powerful book forces a reader to re-examine almost all the assumptions we've accepted since

the Holocaust occurred." N Y Times Book Rev
Includes bibliographical references

Cohen, Rich
The **avengers**. Knopf 2000 261p il hardcover o.p. pa $13   **940.53**
1. Poets 2. Authors 3. Underground leaders 4. Holocaust, 1933-1945 5. World War, 1939-1945 -- Underground movements
ISBN 0-375-70529-5 pa

LC 00-21062

Cohen chronicles the resistance efforts of a small group of European Jews during the Second World War. Attention is focused primarily on the activities of three individuals: Rozka Korczak, Vitka Kempner, and Abba Kovner

"Cohen is a skilled writer. His language is spare and muscular, his descriptions evocative, his technique suspenseful." N Y Times Book Rev

Collingham, Lizzie
The **taste** of war; World War II and the battle for food. Lizzie Collingham. Penguin Press 2012 xv, 634 p.p il map $36   **940.53**
1. Strategy 2. World War, 1939-1945 -- Food supply 3. Starvation -- History -- 20th century 4. Food habits -- History -- 20th century 5. Food supply -- History -- 20th century 6. Food security -- History -- 20th century 7. War and society -- History -- 20th century 8. Nutrition policy -- History -- 20th century
ISBN 1594203296; 9781594203299

LC 2011043783

This book examines "the fundamental role that food played in the planning, conduct, and course of the Second World War." Author Lizzie Collingham "explicates how Italy's plans for colonizing Ethiopia and further infiltrating Libya, Japan's expansion into Manchuria and China, and Germany's drive into Russia and the Ukraine were in essence 'battle[s] for Food.'" (Atlantic Monthly)
Includes bibliographical references (p. 581-620) and index

★ **Colors** of confinement; rare Kodachrome photographs of Japanese American incarceration in World War II. edited by Eric L. Muller; with photographs by Bill Manbo. Univ. of North Carolina Pr./Ctr. for Documentary Studies at Duke Univ. 2012 122 p. ill. (some col.) (Documentary arts and culture) (cloth: alk. paper) $35   **940.53**
1. World War, 1939-1945 -- Pictorial works 2. World War, 1939-1945 -- Prisoners and prisons, American 3. Japanese Americans -- Evacuation and relocation, 1942-1945 4. Heart Mountain Relocation Center (Wyo.) -- Pictorial works 5. World War, 1939-1945 -- Concentration camps -- Wyoming -- Pictorial works 6. Japanese Americans -- Evacuation and relocation, 1942-1945 -- Pictorial works
ISBN 0807835730; 9780807835739

LC 2011052817

This book, edited by Eric L. Muller, as part of the "Documentary Arts and Culture" series, with photographs by Bill Manbo, presents images of the Japanese American internments of World War II. "In 1942, Bill Manbo . . . and his family were forced . . . into the Japanese American internment camp at Heart Mountain in Wyoming. While there, Manbo documented . . . his family's struggle to maintain a normal life under the harsh conditions of racial imprisonment." (Publisher's note)
Includes bibliographical references and index

Cooke, Alistair
American home front, 1941-1942. Atlantic Monthly 2006

xx, 327p il $24　　　　　　　　　　**940.53**
1. United States -- Social conditions 2. World War, 1939-1945 --
United States 3. United States -- Description and travel 4. United
States -- Social life and customs
ISBN 978-0-87113-939-9; 0-87113-939-1

LC 2005-58860
"Crisscrossing the American continent from east to west and north
to south, stopping in diners and bus stations and newly humming industrial plants, Mr. Cooke brings to life an America stepping into the
unknown, committing its muscle and blood to an enterprise that most
citizens could barely articulate, in places most of them had never heard
of." N Y Times (Late N Y Ed)

Costigliola, Frank
　　Roosevelt's lost alliances; how personal politics helped
start the Cold War. Frank Costigliola. Princeton University
Press 2012 533 p. $35.00　　　　**940.53**
1. World politics -- 1945-1991 2. Cold war 3. Governors 4.
Statesmen 5. Historians 6. Memoirists 7. Presidents 8. Philatelists
9. Heads of state 10. Cabinet members 11. Prime ministers
12. Communist leaders 13. Political leaders 14. Members of
Parliament 15. Nobel laureates for literature 16. United States
-- Foreign relations 17. World War, 1939-1945 -- Diplomatic
history 18. Soviet Union -- Foreign relations -- United States 19.
United States -- Foreign relations -- Soviet Union 20. Great Britain
-- Foreign relations -- United States 21. United States -- Foreign
relations -- Great Britain
ISBN 069112129X; 9780691121291

LC 2011025271
Author Frank Costigliola "describes the functional alliance among
the big three--Roosevelt, Churchill, and Stalin--during World War II
and how, after Roosevelt's death, it was undermined. . . . Churchill is
presented as an unchanging warrior and colonialist, whereas Stalin is
portrayed" as "a 'realist' who, despite his brutality, sought secure borders, internal order, modernization, and respect. . . . FDR is pictured
as being in reasonable health at Yalta and not bamboozled by Stalin."
(Library Journal)
Includes bibliographical references.

Daniels, Roger
　　Prisoners without trial; Japanese Americans in World War
II. Rev. ed.; Hill and Wang 2004 162p il (Critical issue series)
pa $12　　　　　　　　　　　**940.53**
1. World War, 1939-1945 -- United States 2. Japanese Americans
-- Evacuation and relocation, 1942-1945
ISBN 0-8090-7896-1

LC 2004-47328
First published 1993
An account of "the relocation of Japanese Americans during World
War II, an injustice prompted not by military necessity but by political
and racial motivations. The purpose of this volume is to tell the story in
light of the redress legislation enacted in 1988." Libr J [review of 1993
edition]
Includes bibliographical references

Dawidowicz, Lucy S.
　　The **war** against the Jews, 1933-1945; 10th anniversary ed;
Bantam Books 1986 xxxx, 466p il pa $19　　　　**940.53**
1. Jews -- Europe 2. Holocaust, 1933-1945
ISBN 978-0-553-34532-2; 0-553-34532-X

LC 85-48051
A reissue with new introduction and supplementary bibliography of
the title first published 1975 by Holt, Rinehart & Winston

"One of the best histories of the mass murder of Jews in World War
II. Argues for the centrality of anti-Semitism in Hitler's program." Read-
er's Adviser
Includes bibliographical references

Dobbs, Michael
　　Six months in 1945; FDR, Stalin, Churchill, Truman, and
the birth of the modern world. by Michael Dobbs. 1st ed. Alfred A. Knopf 2012 418 p. (hardcover) $28.95　　　**940.53**
1. Cold war 2. World War, 1939-1945 -- Peace 3. World War,
1939-1945 -- Diplomatic history 4. World politics -- 1945-1955 5.
Cold War -- Diplomatic history 6. Soviet Union -- Foreign relations
-- United States 7. United States -- Foreign relations -- Soviet Union
ISBN 030727165X; 9780307271655

LC 2012021747
This book, by Michael Dobbs, provides an "account of the pivotal
six-month period spanning the end of World War II, the dawn of the
nuclear age, and the beginning of the Cold War. When Roosevelt, Stalin,
and Churchill met in Yalta in February 1945, . . . victory was imminent. The Big Three wanted to draft a blueprint for a lasting peace--but
instead set the stage for a forty-four-year division of Europe into Soviet
and western spheres of influence." (Publisher's note)
Includes bibliographical references and index

Dower, John W., 1938-
　　★ **Ways** of forgetting, ways of remembering; Japan in the
modern world. John W. Dower. New Press 2012 336 p. (hardcover: alk. paper) $26.95　　　　　　　**940.53**
1. Propaganda 2. American essays 3. Japan -- History 4. Japan
-- History -- 1945- 5. World War, 1939-1945 -- Japan 6. World
War, 1939-1945 -- Influence 7. Japan -- Social conditions -- 1945
8. Japan -- Politics and government -- 1945 9. Japan -- History
-- 1945- -- Historiography 10. World War, 1939-1945 -- Japan --
Historiography 11. World War, 1939-1945 -- Social aspects -- Japan
12. Social change -- Japan -- History -- 20th century 13. Collective
memory -- Japan -- History -- 20th century
ISBN 1595586180; 9781595586186

LC 2011033861
This book "brings together a number of [John W. Dower's] essays
written between 1993 and 2007. . . . Most deal with Japan since WWII,
although Dower . . . invokes much earlier history." Particular focus is
given to "national hypocrisy and the misuses of history and memory,
American as well as Japanese. His topics include Japanese racism along
with the enthusiasm with which Japan went to war. . . . Essays on Hiroshima round out the volume." (Publishers Weekly)
Includes bibliographical references and index

Dwork, Deborah
　　★ **Holocaust**: a history; {by} Deborah Dwork, Robert Jan
Van Pelt. Norton 2002 xx, 444p il $27.95; pa $15.95 **940.53**
1. Jews -- Germany 2. Holocaust, 1933-1945 3. Germany --
Politics and government -- 1933-1945
ISBN 0-393-05188-9; 0-393-32524-5 pa

LC 2002-23565
"The authors examine such issues as the historic relationship between Jews, gentiles, and Germans; World War I and its consequences;
National Socialism in the Weimar Republic; the Third Reich and its anti-
Semitic measures; worldwide refugee policies that became a disaster for
the Jews; and Jewish and gentile life under German occupation. They
also examine the efforts by Allied nations to help the Jews. . . . This is a
monumental work of impeccable scholarship." Booklist
Includes bibliographical references

Edsel, Robert M.

The **monuments** men; Allied heros, Nazi thieves, and the greatest treasure hunt in history. Robert M. Edsel with Bret Witter. Center Street 2009 p. cm. **940.53**
1. Art thefts 2. World War, 1939-1945 3. Europe -- History
ISBN 9781599951492

LC 2009012255
Includes bibliographical references.
"At the same time Adolf Hitler was attempting to take over the western world, his armies were methodically seeking and hoarding the finest art treasures in Europe. The Fuehrer had begun cataloguing the art he planned to collect as well as the art he would destroy: "degenerate" works he despised. In a race against time, behind enemy lines, often unarmed, a special force of American and British museum directors, curators, art historians, and others, called the Momuments Men, risked their lives scouring Europe to prevent the destruction of thousands of years of culture." (Publisher's note)

Eisner, Peter

The **Pope's** Last Crusade; How an American Jesuit Helped Pope Pius XI's Campaign to Stop Hitler. HarperCollins 2013 352 p. $27.99 **940.53**
1. Holocaust, 1939-1945 2. Catholic Church -- Relations -- Judaism
ISBN 0062049143; 9780062049148
This book by Peter Eisner offers an account of the "efforts by the Vatican to counter the Nazis before WWII. . . . According to Eisner, the Vatican's track record [regarding the Holocaust] might have been different if Pius XI had lived to deliver a speech in 1939 condemning the German regime" that was "based on the thinking of the Rev. John LaFarge, an American . . . whom Pius XI had commissioned to write a papal encyclical on" church action against racism. (Publishers Weekly)

Encyclopedia of Jewish life before and during the Holocaust; edited by Shmuel Spector and Geoffrey Wigoder. New York Univ. Press 2001 3v il maps set $99 **940.53**
1. Reference books 2. Jews -- Europe 3. Holocaust, 1933-1945 -- Encyclopedias
ISBN 0-8147-9356-8
"Each entry provides vital information on the town's Jewish inhabitants on the eve of German occupation, gives the dates of Jewish roundups and mass executions and estimates how many Jews from that community survived the war." Publ Wkly

★ **Encyclopedia** of World War II; a political, social and military history. Spencer C. Tucker, editor, Priscilla Mary Roberts, editor volume 5. ABC-CLIO 2004 5v il map set $485 **940.53**
1. Reference books 2. World War, 1939-1945 -- Encyclopedias
ISBN 1-576-07999-6

LC 2004-23745
"The 1,465 alphabetically arranged articles provide an international perspective on people; key battles, campaigns, and events; military equipment and strategy; countries; and other relevant topics. . . . Country entries not only cover the main Allied and Axis powers but also such countries as Afghanistan, Brazil, Estonia, Iraq, Mexico, New Zealand, and Somalia as well as world regions. . . . An excellent resource for high-school, public, and academic libraries." Booklist
Includes bibliographical references

Englund, Will, 1953-

March 1917; On the Brink of War and Revolution. Will Englund. W W Norton & Co Inc 2017 416 p. $27.95 **940.53**

1. World War, 1914-1918 2. World history -- 20th century 3. Russia -- History -- 1917-1921, Revolution
ISBN 0393292088; 9780393292084

LC 2016046272
This book, by Will Englund, presents "a riveting history of the month that transformed the world's greatest nations as Russia faced revolution and America entered World War I. . . . Englund creates a highly detailed and textured account of the month that transformed the world's greatest nations, . . . [considering] the dreams of that year's warriors, pacifists, activists, revolutionaries, and reactionaries." (Publisher's note)
"Recommended for those eager to learn about watershed moments in history and all readers interested in World War I." LJ

Evans, Richard J.

★ The **Third** Reich at war. Penguin Press 2009 926p il map $40 **940.53**
1. Germany -- History -- 1933-1945 2. World War, 1939-1945 -- Germany
ISBN 978-1-59420-206-3

LC 2008-44765
First published 2008 in the United Kingdom
This is a "very readable, well-paced account that is fully familiar with the huge amount of specialist scholarship in this field but never gets bogged down by excessive detail." Hist Today
Includes bibliographical references

Faber, David

Munich, 1938; appeasement and World War II. Simon & Schuster 2009 520p il $30 **940.53**
1. World War, 1939-1945 -- Causes 2. Munich Four-Power Agreement (1938) 3. World War, 1939-1945 -- Diplomatic history 4. Europe -- Politics and government -- 1918-1945
ISBN 978-1-4391-3233-3

LC 2008-44896
"The 1938 Munich Conference has been referred to as the Great Betrayal, virtually guaranteeing the start of war in Europe the following year. In return for Hitler's empty promises of peace, the British and French governments acquiesced to his demand to annex the Sudetenland, a largely German-speaking region of Czechoslovakia. The appeasement emboldened Hitler and led directly to the German-Soviet nonaggression pact and their joint invasion of Poland. Faber's account of the preparation for and actual unfolding of the conference is comprehensive, engrossing, and depressing, like viewing a slow-motion train wreck. . . . He does a masterful job of recounting the political maneuvers and infighting within both the British and German camps." Booklist
Includes bibliographical references

Feuchtwanger, Edgar

Hitler, my neighbor; memories of a Jewish childhood,1929-1939. Edgar Feuchtwanger with Bertil Scali; translated by Adriana Hunter. Other Press 2017 209 p. illustrations (hardcover: alkaline paper) $25.95 **940.53**
1. Jewish children -- Germany -- Munich -- Biography 2. Holocaust, Jewish (1939-1945) -- Personal narratives 3. Munich (Germany) -- Biography 4. Jews -- Persecutions -- Germany -- History -- 20th century
ISBN 9781590518656; 1590518640; 9781590518649

LC 2017004211
In this book, Edgar Feuchtwanger with Bertil Scali, "recounts the Nazi rise to power from his unique perspective as a young Jewish boy in Munich, living with Adolf Hitler as his neighbor. . . . In 1933 . . . , Hitler had been named Chancellor. Edgar's parents, stripped of their rights as citizens, tried to protect him from increasingly degrading realities. In

class, his teacher had him draw swastikas, and his schoolmates joined the Hitler Youth." (Publisher's note)

"An intimate look at the horror wrought by Hitler." Kirkus

Friedlander, Saul

The **years** of extermination; Nazi Germany and the Jews, 1939-1945. HarperCollins Publishers 2007 xxvi, 870p $39.95   **940.53**
1. Jews -- Germany 2. Holocaust, 1933-1945 3. Jews -- Persecutions 4. Germany -- History -- 1933-1945
ISBN 0-06-019043-4; 978-0-06-019043-9
LC 2006-48982

The second part of a two-part series starting with Nazi Germany and the Jews: vl: The years of persecution, 1933-1939 (1997)

"This is a masterful synthesis that draws on a lifetime of learning and research." Publ Wkly

Includes bibliographic references

Friedman, Anita

Rywka's Diary; The Writings of a Jewish Girl from the Lodz Ghetto. Anita Friedman. HarperCollins 2015 288 p. 8 plates; color ills., map (hardcover) $35   **940.53**
1. Jewish children in the Holocaust 2. Holocaust, 1939-1945 -- Personal narratives
ISBN 9780062389688; 0062389688

This book, by Anita Friedman, "is the diary of a girl named Rywka Lipszyc who detailed the brutal conditions that Jews in the Lodz ghetto, the second largest in Poland, endured under the Nazis: poverty, hunger and malnutrition, religious oppression, and, in Rywka's case, the death of her parents and siblings. Handwritten in a school notebook between October 1943 and April 1944, the diary ends literally in mid-sentence. What became of Rywka is a mystery." (Publisher's note)

"An incredible addition to Holocaust literature. The historical essays are informative and absorbing to a general audience." LJ

Gilbert, Martin

Kristallnacht; prelude to destruction. HarperCollins Publishers 2006 314p il map (Making history) hardcover o.p. pa $14.99   **940.53**
1. Jews -- Persecutions 2. Germany -- History -- 1933-1945
ISBN 0-06-057083-0; 978-0-06-057083-5; 0-06-112135-5 pa; 978-0-06-112135-7 pa
LC 2005-58169

This is "an account of the Night of Broken Glass, which was unleashed against the Jewish communities across Germany on November 10, 1938. . . . A powerful account of the helplessness of the Jews." Booklist

Includes bibliographical references

The **Routledge** atlas of the Holocaust; 4th ed.; Routledge 2009 286p map $120; pa $30.95   **940.53**
1. Atlases 2. Reference books 3. Holocaust, 1933-1945 -- Maps
ISBN 978-0-415-48481-7; 0-415-48481-2; 978-0-415-48486-2 pa; 0-415-48486-3 pa
LC 2008-43844

First published 1982 in the United Kingdom with title: The Dent atlas of the Holocaust

The author uses "maps, text, and photographs to document Hitler's attempt to destroy Europe's Jews. . . . Commentary offers statistical information, historical background, and something about the people of the area. Archival photographs bring the events to life. . . . This small but effective work demonstrates the magnitude of the Nazi terror by bring-

ing it down to a personal level." Am Ref Books Annu, 2003 [review of 2002 edition]

Includes bibliographical references

Goldhagen, Daniel

Hitler's willing executioners; ordinary Germans and the Holocaust. [by] Daniel Jonah Goldhagen. Knopf 1996 622p il maps hardcover o.p. pa $16   **940.53**
1. Antisemitism 2. National socialism 3. Holocaust, 1933-1945 4. Germany -- History -- 1933-1945
ISBN 0-679-44695-8; 0-679-77268-5 pa
LC 95-38591

The author "endeavors to show that the common apologia for the Germans—that Hitler 'brainwashed' them—is nonsense and that most Germans gave their active assent to genocide. An ordinary German commander, for example, might feel himself bound by a strict code of conduct yet not be at all averse to murdering Jews. The book ends with a detailed notes section and an appendix that explains the correct methodology for studying the Nazi period." Libr J

Goldsmith, Martin

The **inextinguishable** symphony; a true story of music and love in Nazi Germany. Wiley 2000 346p il hardcover o.p. pa $15.95   **940.53**
1. Drummers 2. Jews -- Germany 3. Holocaust, 1933-1945
ISBN 0-471-35097-4; 0-471-07864-6 pa
LC 00-25955

Goldsmith's "weaving together of cultural and personal history constitutes a gripping tale of persecution, intrigue, and love and an insider's—or two insiders'—view of a dark time." Booklist

Includes bibliographical references

Goodman, Simon, 1948-

The **Orpheus** Clock; the search for my family's art treasures stolen by the Nazis. Simon Goodman. Scribner 2015 368 p. 8 pages of color plates; ills. (hardback) $28   **940.53**
1. Art thefts 2. Jews -- Germany 3. World War, 1939-1945 -- Reparations 4. Art thefts -- Investigation 5. Jewish bankers -- Germany -- Biography 6. Holocaust, Jewish (1939-1945) -- Germany 7. Art thefts -- Germany -- History -- 20th century
ISBN 1451697635; 9781451697636; 9781451697643
LC 2015017171

This book, by Simon Goodman, presents the "true story of one man's single-minded quest to reclaim what the Nazis stole from his family, their beloved art collection, and to restore their legacy. Simon Goodman's grandparents . . . , the Gutmanns, as they were known then, . . . amassed a magnificent, world-class art collection. . . . But the Nazi regime snatched from them everything they had worked to build." (Publisher's note)

Groom, Winston

★ **1942**; the year that tried men's souls. Atlantic Monthly Press 2005 459p il maps $27.50   **940.53**
1. World War, 1939-1945
ISBN 0-8711-3889-1
LC 2004-62779

In this military history of one year during World War II, the author "delivers the traditional worshipful portrait of General MacArthur while admitting he made several key blunders that doomed the Philippines in the year's early months. . . . He adds that brains and luck win more battles than courage, providing a perfect illustration in Midway, fought in June 1942. . . . Groom has written a page-turner; readers needing an

introduction will love it." Publ Wkly
Includes bibliographical references

Gross, Jan Tomasz

Neighbors; the destruction of the Jewish community in Jedwabne, Poland. Jan T. Gross. Penguin Books 2002 xxii, 214 p.p illustrations, maps $17   **940.53**
1. Jews -- Poland 2. Holocaust, 1939-1945 3. Jedwabne (Poland) -- Ethnic relations 4. Jews -- Poland -- Jedwabne -- History 5. Holocaust, Jewish (1939-1945) -- Poland -- Jedwabne 6. World War, 1939-1945 -- Collaborationists -- Poland -- Jedwabne
ISBN 9781400843251; 0142002402; 9780142002407
    LC 2003286412
National Book Award Finalist: Nonfiction (2002)
"On a summer day in 1941 in Nazi-occupied Poland, half of the town of Jedwabne brutally murdered the other half: 1,600 men, women, and children-all but seven of the town's Jews. In this . . . study, historian Jan Gross pieces together eyewitness accounts as well as physical evidence into a comprehensive reconstruction of the horrific July day remembered well by locals but hidden to history." (Publisher's note)
Includes bibliographical references (p. 155-200) and index

Guttenplan, D. D.

The **Holocaust** on trial. Norton 2001 328p il hardcover o.p. pa $15.95   **940.53**
1. Trials 2. Historians 3. College teachers 4. Holocaust, 1933-1945 -- Historiography
ISBN 0-393-32292-0 pa
    LC 2001-30370
The author chronicles the "libel trial in Britain brought by historian David Irving. Irving, widely viewed as an apologist for Hitler, sued American scholar Deborah Lipstadt, whose Denying the Holocaust (1993) had labeled Irving as a right-wing extremist. . . . Interspersing essayistic diversions, the author presents a thoughtful work as well as a courtroom thriller." Booklist
Includes bibliographical references

Hackett, David A.

The **Buchenwald** report; translated, edited, and with an introduction by David A. Hackett; foreword by Frederick A. Praeger. Westview Press 1995 397p map hardcover o.p. pa $29   **940.53**
1. Buchenwald (Germany: Concentration camp) 2. Holocaust, 1933-1945 -- Personal narratives
ISBN 0-8133-1777-0; 0-8133-3363-6 pa
    LC 94-39714
"This seminal document, published here in its entirety for the first time, is a report compiled for the Allied Army from interviews with the inmates of the Buchenwald concentration camp, located near Weimar, Germany in April 1945, shortly after the camp's liberation. . . . It is immediate, direct, and, as the product of the testimony of many people, more inclusive and wide-ranging than any single individual's personal testament. A classic of Holocaust literature that should be in any library that covers European history." Libr J
Includes bibliographical references

Hamilton, Nigel, 1944-

Commander in chief; FDR's battle with Churchill, 1943. Nigel Hamilton. Houghton Mifflin Harcourt 2016 496 p. illustrations, maps (hardcover) $30   **940.53**
1. World War, 1939-1945 2. Command of troops -- Case studies 3. World War, 1939-1945 -- Campaigns 4. World War, 1939-1945

-- United States 5. World War, 1939-1945 -- Diplomatic history 6. Great Britain -- Foreign relations -- United States 7. United States -- Foreign relations -- Great Britain
ISBN 0544279115; 9780544279117
    LC 2015037253
This book, by Nigel Hamilton, presents a "look at Franklin Roosevelt's role in the Allied strategy midway through World War II, with an emphasis on his relations with Winston Churchill. Hamilton shows Roosevelt's clear vision of how to win the war and how to create a postwar society that would prevent such wars from recurring." (Kirkus Reviews)
"This is an outstanding contribution to understanding the wartime alliance and Roosevelt's role in it." Booklist
Includes bibliographical references and index

Hayes, Peter

Why? Explaining the Holocaust. Peter Hayes. W W Norton & Co Inc 2017 432 p. illustrations, maps (ebook) $50; (hardcover) $27.95   **940.53**
1. Antisemitism 2. Holocaust, 1939-1945 3. Germany -- History -- 1933-1945 4. Germany -- Ethnic relations 5. Holocaust, Jewish (1939-1945) 6. Holocaust, Jewish (1939-1945) -- Causes 7. Jews -- Germany -- History -- 20th century 8. Antisemitism -- Germany -- History -- 20th century 9. Jews -- Persecutions -- Europe -- History -- 20th century
ISBN 9780393254372; 9780393254365
    LC 2016031588
This book, by Peter Hayes, is a "new exploration that answers the most commonly asked questions about the Holocaust. Despite the outpouring of books, movies, museums, memorials, and courses devoted to the Holocaust, a coherent explanation of why such ghastly carnage erupted from the heart of civilized Europe in the twentieth century still seems elusive even seventy years later." (Publisher's note)
"In a narrative brimming with historical sources, Hayes's work is required reading for history scholars, amateur history buffs, and anyone interested in answering necessary questions surrounding this tragedy." LJ
Includes bibliographical references and index

Helm, Sarah

★ **Ravensbruck**; life and death in Hitler's concentration camp for women. Sarah Helm. Nan A. Talese/Doubleday 2014 656 p. 16 plates; illustrations; maps (hardback) $37.50 **940.53**
1. Concentration camps 2. Holocaust, 1939-1945 3. World War, 1939-1945 -- Women 4. Ravensbrück (Concentration camp) 5. Women prisoners -- Germany -- Ravensbrück 6. World War, 1939-1945 -- Prisoners and prisons, German 7. Women concentration camp inmates -- Germany -- Ravensbrück
ISBN 038552059X; 9780385520591
    LC 2014014974
This book by Sarah Helm focuses on "Ravensbrück, a concentration camp designed specifically for women by Heinrich Himmler, prime architect of the Holocaust. Using testimony unearthed since the end of the Cold War and interviews with survivors who have never talked before, . . . Helm has ventured into the heart of the camp, demonstrating for the reader in riveting detail how easily and quickly the unthinkable horror evolved." (Publisher's note)
"This book deserves significant attention, both for Helm's notable interviews of aging witnesses and as a beautifully written history of events that offers additional insight into Nazism and those caught in its path." Pub Wkly

Henderson, Bruce B., 1946-

Rescue at Los Banos; the most daring prison camp raid of

World War II. Bruce Henderson. William Morrow 2015 366 p.
illustrations (hardcover) $27.99   **940.53**
  1. World War, 1939-1945 -- Philippines 2. World War, 1939-1945
-- Aerial operations 3. World War, 1939-1945 -- Prisoners and
prisons 4. Los Baños Internment Camp 5. World War, 1939-1945
-- Campaigns -- Philippines 6. World War, 1939-1945 -- Prisoners
and prisons, Japanese 7. World War, 1939-1945 -- Aerial operations,
American -- Philippines 8. World War, 1939-1945 -- Amphibious
operations, American -- Philippines
  ISBN 006232506X; 9780062325068; 9780062325075;
9780062370020
                                              LC 2015007141
  This book by Bruce Henderson tells the "true story of one of the
greatest military rescues of all time, the 1945 World War II prison camp
raid at Los Baños in the Philippines. Combining personal interviews,
diaries, correspondence, memoirs, and archival research, [Henderson]
tells the story of a remarkable group of prisoners . . . and of the young
American soldiers and Filipino guerrillas who risked their lives to save
them." (Publisher's note)
  "This narrative of one event depicting the horrors of war and its resolution should broaden the perspective of general readers of 20th-century
military history. Although a monument, a ceremony, and a joint U.S.
congressional resolution honored this liberation on its 60th anniversary,
the event was underpublicized at the time since Joe Rosenthal's iconic
photograph of the raising of the American flag on Iwo Jima taken the
same day received more media coverage." LJ
  Includes bibliographical references and index

Herman, Arthur
  Freedom's forge; how American business produced victory
in World War II. Arthur Herman. Random House 2012 xiv,
413 p.p   **940.53**
  1. Economic policy -- United States 2. Industrial mobilization
-- United States 3. Manufacturing industries -- United States 4.
United States -- Economic conditions -- 1933-1945 5. World War,
1939-1945 -- Economic aspects -- United States 6. United States --
Economic policy -- 1933-1945 7. Industrial management -- United
States -- History -- 20th century 8. Industrial mobilization -- United
States -- History -- 20th century 9. Manufacturing industries --
Military aspects -- United States -- History -- 20th century
  ISBN 1400069645; 9780679604631; 9781400069644
                                              LC 2011040661
  In this book, "the author argues . . . against the conventional wisdom
that America's rearmament [during World War II] took place under the
guidance of a competent federal government. . . . The production of the
flood of war materiel that drowned the Axis was achieved by the voluntary cooperation of businesses driven as much by the profit motive as
by patriotism, solving problems through their own ingenuity rather than
waiting for government directives." (Kirkus Reviews)
  Includes bibliographical references (p. [387-399) and index

Hoffman, Eva
  After such knowledge; memory, history and the legacy of
the Holocaust. Public Affairs 2004 301p $25; pa $14 **940.53**
  1. Holocaust, 1933-1945
  ISBN 1-586-48046-4; 0-586-48304-8 pa
                                              LC 2003-66443
  The author "focuses on the consciousness and experience of the Holocaust's second generation—the children of survivors. . . . The book
considers such diverse concepts as how the 'trauma' of the Holocaust is
constructed, the role of emigration and national identity in shaping the
second generation's narratives of their lives. . . . Hoffman writes with a
subdued but vibrant passion." Publ Wkly

Includes bibliographical references

Horwitz, Gordon J.
  Ghettostadt; Lodz and the making of a Nazi city. The
Belknap Press of Harvard University Press 2008 395p il
map   **940.53**
  1. Holocaust, 1933-1945 2. Jews -- Persecutions 3. Lodz (Poland)
-- Ethnic relations
  ISBN 0-674-02799-X; 978-0-674-02799-2
                                              LC 2007-50934
  The author discusses how the Nazis transformed Lodz, whose popu-
lation was more than one-third Jewish, into a new German city called
Litzmannstadt. Index.
  "The Nazis' use of bureaucracy to achieve their genocidal aims
comes through clearly in this historical tour de force. The Nazis attempt-
ed to 're-engineer' the Polish city of Lodz, home to more than 230,000
Jews (one-third of the city's population) before the war, into a model—
and Judenfrei—German city embodying health and beauty they called
Litzmannstadt. This required forcing the Jews into a ghetto with the help
of Jewish leaders, especially the . . . reportedly lascivious industrialist
Chaim Rumkowski. . . . With a graceful style rare in academic history,
Horwitz . . . marshals a host of primary sources to highlight the gradual
destruction of the ghetto." Publ Wkly
  Includes bibliographical references

Jones, Michael
  After Hitler; the last ten days of World War II in Europe.
Michael Jones. NAL Caliber 2015 400 p. 16 plates; illustra-
tions; maps (hardback) $27.95   **940.53**
  1. World War, 1939-1945 -- Peace 2. World War, 1939-1945 --
Europe -- End 3. World War, 1939-1945 -- Diplomatic history
  ISBN 0451477014; 9780451477019
                                              LC 2015018149
  "After Hitler shines a light on ten fascinating days after that infamous suicide that changed the course of the twentieth century. Combining exhaustive research with masterfully paced storytelling, Michael
Jones recounts the Führer's frantic last stand; the devious maneuverings
of his handpicked successor, Karl Dönitz; the grudging respect Joseph
Stalin had for Churchill and FDR, as well as his distrust of Harry Truman; the bold negotiating by General Dwight D. Eisenhower that hastened Germany's surrender but drew the ire of the Kremlin; the journalist who almost scuttled the cease-fire; and the thousands of ordinary
British, American, and Russian soldiers caught in the swells of history,
from the Red Army's march on Berlin to the liberation of the Nazis'
remaining concentration camps. Through it all, Jones traces the shifting
loyalties between East and West that sowed the seeds of the Cold War
and nearly unraveled the Grand Alliance." From the Publisher
  "Unlike connoisseurs of military history, casual readers may not be
concerned with martial unit designations and some of the gritty details
of battle formation, but the exploits of the men and women they represented are engrossing, sometimes even heartbreaking. A skillful historian demonstrates how courage and hope characterized the last act of the
great campaign to bring peace to Europe 70 years ago." Kirkus

Joukowsky, Artemis
  Defying the Nazis; The Sharps' War. Artemis Joukowsky,
foreword by Ken Burns. Beacon Press 2016 255 p. illustrations (hardcover: alk. paper) $25.95; (ebook) $15.99 **940.53**
  1. Holocaust, 1939-1945 2. Righteous Gentiles in the Holocaust
3. World War, 1939-1945 -- Jews -- Rescue 4. Holocaust,
Jewish (1939-1945) 5. Righteous Gentiles in the Holocaust --
Massachusetts -- Wellesley Hills
  ISBN 080707182X; 9780807071823; 9780807071830

LC 2016007704

This book by Artemis Joukowsky, with foreword by Ken Burns, tells the story of the Reverend Waitstill Sharp, a young Unitarian minister, and his wife, Martha, "whose faith and commitment to social justice inspired them to undertake dangerous rescue and relief missions across war-torn Europe, saving the lives of countless refugees, political dissidents, and Jews on the eve of World War II." (Publisher's note)

"A harrowing and ultimately inspirational tribute to a brave couple." Booklist

Includes bibliographical references (pages 235-244) and index.

Karski, Jan, 1914-2000

★ **Story** of a secret state; my report to the world. Jan Karski; foreword by Madeleine Albright. Georgetown University Press 2013 464 p. (hbk.: alk. paper) $26.95   **940.53**
1. World War, 1939-1945 -- Poland 2. World War, 1939-1945 -- Personal narratives 3. Poland -- History -- Occupation, 1939-1945 4. World War, 1939-1945 -- Personal narratives, Polish
ISBN 1589019830; 9781589019836

LC 2012037549

This book, by Jan Karski, is a memoir of a diplomat who served during "World War II and the Holocaust. With elements of a spy thriller, documenting his experiences in the Polish Underground, and as one of the first accounts of the systematic slaughter of the Jews by the German Nazis, this volume is a remarkable testimony of one man's courage and a nation's struggle for resistance against overwhelming oppression." (Publisher's note)

Includes bibliographical references and index

Kershaw, Alex

Avenue of spies; a true story of terror, espionage, and one American family's heroic resistance in Nazi-occupied Paris. by Alex Kershaw. Crown 2015 304 p. 8 plates; ills; maps; ports. (hardback) $28   **940.53**
1. Spies 2. Americans -- France 3. Physicians -- Biography 4. Paris (France) -- History 5. World War, 1914-1918 -- France 6. Spies -- France -- Paris -- Biography 7. World War, 1939-1945 -- France -- Paris 8. Americans -- France -- Paris -- Biography 9. Physicians -- France -- Paris -- Biography 10. France -- History -- German occupation, 1940-1945 11. Paris (France) -- History, Military -- 20th century 12. World War, 1939-1945 -- Underground movements -- France -- Paris
ISBN 0804140030; 9780804140034

LC 2015016861

This book, by Alex Kershaw, is the "true story of an American doctor in Paris. . . . Avenue Foch, one of the most exclusive residential streets in Nazi-occupied France, was Paris's hotbed of daring spies, murderous secret police, amoral informers, and Vichy collaborators. So when American physician Sumner Jackson, who lived with his wife and young son Phillip at Number 11, found himself drawn into the Liberation network of the French resistance, he knew the stakes were impossibly high." (Publisher's note)

"Kershaw tells their story in an intense, moving account that also serves to vividly describe the life of ordinary Parisians under the occupation." Booklist

Kinney, David

The **devil's** diary; Alfred Rosenberg and the stolen secrets of the Third Reich. Robert K. Wittman and David Kinney. Harper 2016 528 p. illustrations (hardcover: alkaline paper) $35   **940.53**
1. National socialism 2. National socialists 3. Holocaust, 1939-

1945 4. Nazis -- Diaries 5. National socialism -- Philosophy 6. Holocaust, Jewish (1939-1945) -- Philosophy 7. Germany -- Foreign relations -- Soviet Union 8. Soviet Union -- Foreign relations -- Germany 9. United States. Federal Bureau of Investigation -- Officials and employees -- Biography
ISBN 9780062319012; 9780062319029

LC 2015036609

This book, by Robert K. Wittman and David Kinney, "investigates the disappearance of a private diary penned by one of Adolf Hitler's top aides—Alfred Rosenberg, his 'chief philosopher'—and mines its long-hidden pages to deliver a fresh, eye-opening account of the Nazi rise to power and the genesis of the Holocaust." (Publisher's note)

"Wittman and Kinney's chronicle of the efforts historians took to gain access to the diary feels like it's pulled from a movie, especially when they add in Rosenberg's story. This is an outstanding piece of journalism." Pub Wkly

Includes bibliographical references (pages [447]-494) and index.

Klein, Maury

A **call** to arms; mobilizing America for World War II. by Maury Klein. 1st U.S. ed. Bloomsbury 2013 912 p. (hardcover) $40.00   **940.53**
1. Military weapons 2. World War, 1939-1945 3. United States -- Armed forces 4. United States -- Economic policy -- 1933-1945 5. World War, 1939-1945 -- Economic aspects -- United States 6. Industrial mobilization -- United States -- History -- 20th century 7. United States -- Armed Forces -- Mobilization -- History -- 20th century
ISBN 1596916079; 9781596916074

LC 2012039497

This book, written by Maury Klein, examines U.S. efforts to "create, outfit, transport, and supply huge armies, navies, and air forces" for World War II. It looks at how American productivity, "American industry, and American workers, won World War II [and how it] [n]ot only . . . determine[d] the outcome of the war, but it transformed the American economy and society." (Publisher's note)

Includes bibliographical references and index.

Koker, David

At the edge of the abyss; a concentration camp diary, 1943-1944. David Koker; edited by Robert Jan van Pelt; translated from the Dutch by Michiel Horn and John Irons. Northwestern University Press 2012 xii, 396 p.p   **940.53**
1. Diaries 2. Jews -- Biography 3. World War, 1939-1945 -- Prisoners and prisons 4. Vught (Concentration camp) 5. Prisoners of war -- Netherlands -- Biography 6. World War, 1939-1945 -- Personal narratives, Dutch
ISBN 0810126362; 9780810126367

LC 2011026584

The book presents the diary of David Koker from 1943-1944. "During his time in the Vught concentration camp, the 21-year-old David recorded on an almost daily basis his observations, thoughts, and feelings. He mercilessly probed the abyss that opened around him and, at times, within himself. David's diary covers almost a year, both charting his daily life in Vught as it developed over time and tracing his spiritual evolution as a writer. Until early February 1944, David was able to smuggle some 73,000 words from the camp to his best friend Karel van het Reve, a non-Jew." (Publisher's note)

Includes bibliographical references

Kruk, Herman

The **last** days of the Jerusalem of Lithuania; chronicles from the Vilna ghetto and the camps, 1939-1944. edited and in-

troduced by Benjamin Harshav; translated by Barbara Harshav.
Yivo Inst. for Jewish Res. 2002 732p il maps $45   **940.53**
1. Jews -- Lithuania 2. Holocaust, 1933-1945 3. World War, 1939-
1945 -- Underground movements
ISBN 0-300-04494-1

LC 2002-16736

This a collection of Kruk's journals and other writings from the Jewish ghetto of Vilna and a labor camp in Estonia
This "is a major addition to Holocaust literature and Jewish history.
In 1961 a Yiddish edition of the Vilna diaries was published. This larger
new edition has been painstakingly assembled from those diaries and
other documents and writings by Kruk that were widely scattered and
only found since the 1961 edition; Harshav has also added a wealth of
new footnotes." Publ Wkly
Includes bibliographical references

Langer, Lawrence L.
Admitting the Holocaust; collected essays. Oxford Univ.
Press 1995 202p hardcover o.p. pa $14.95   **940.53**
1. Poets 2. Authors 3. Novelists 4. Dramatists 5. Holocaust,
1939-1945, in literature 6. Essayists 7. Short story writers 8.
Holocaust, 1933-1945 9. Nobel laureates for literature 10.
Holocaust, 1933-1945, in literature
ISBN 0-19-510648-2 pa

LC 94-13368

"A horribly bleak, undeniably important book." Booklist
Includes bibliographical references

Art from the ashes; a Holocaust anthology. edited by Lawrence L. Langer. Oxford Univ. Press 1995 689p il hardcover
o.p. pa $47.95; $76.95   **940.53**
1. Holocaust, 1939-1945, in literature 2. Holocaust, 1933-1945, in
literature 3. Holocaust, 1933-1945 -- Personal narratives
ISBN 0-19-507732-6 pa; 9780195077322

LC 94-11446

A "remarkable volume, perfectly suited for anyone studying the
Holocaust. . . . Compared with [the] firsthand accounts, fiction could
be, one would think, only a pallid version of reality. Yet the fiction Mr.
Langer collects . . . highlights the reality of the Holocaust with stunning
intensity." N Y Times Book Rev

Levi, Primo
★ **Survival** in Auschwitz; the Nazi assault on humanity.
translated from the Italian by Stuart Woolf; including "A conversation with Primo Levi" by Philip Roth. Touchstone 1997 187p
hardcover o.p. pa $16.00   **940.53**
1. Auschwitz (Poland: Concentration camp) 2. Holocaust, 1933-
1945 -- Personal narratives 3. World War, 1939-1945 -- Personal
narratives
ISBN 0-02-029192-2; 9780684826806 pa

LC 86-13656

Originally published 1958 in Italy; first United States editon published 1959 by Orion Press with title: If this is a man
This volume tells of the Italian Jewish chemist's ten months as a
concentration camp inmate

Lewy, Guenter
★ The **Nazi** persecution of the gypsies. Oxford Univ. Press
2000 306p il hardcover o.p. pa $24.95   **940.53**
1. National socialism 2. Romanies 3. World War, 1939-1945
-- Atrocities
ISBN 0-19-512556-8; 0-19-514240-3 pa

LC 98-52545

The author "begins with a brief history of the maltreatment of Gypsies all over Europe, from the fifteenth century onward; then, by dint of
exhaustive research, Lewy documents the horrors of their expulsions,
detentions, deportations, and deaths during the systematic madness of
the Holocaust." Booklist
Includes bibliographical references

Lipstadt, Deborah E.
Denying the Holocaust; the growing assault on truth and
memory. with a new preface by the author. Plume 1994 278p
pa $16   **940.53**
1. Antisemitism 2. Holocaust, 1933-1945 -- Historiography
ISBN 0-452-27274-2; 978-0-452-27274-3

LC 93-45586

First published 1993 by Free Press
"Lipstadt has written a disturbing book that deserves a wide reader-
ship." Libr J
Includes bibliographical references

★ **History** on trial; my day in court with David Irving.
Ecco 2005 xxi, 346p il $25.95; pa $14.95   **940.53**
1. Trials 2. Historians 3. Holocaust, 1933-1945 -- Historiography
ISBN 0-06-059376-8; 0-06-059377-6 pa

LC 2004-57533

"No one who cares about historical truth, freedom of speech or the
Holocaust will avoid a sense of triumph from Gray's decision—or a
sense of dismay that British libel laws allowed such intimidation by Irving of a historian and a publisher in the first place." Publ Wkly
Includes bibliographical references

Lower, Wendy
Hitler's Furies; German Women in the Nazi Killing Fields.
by Wendy Lower. Houghton Mifflin Harcourt 2013 288 p. illustrations, map $26   **940.53**
1. National socialists 2. World War, 1939-1945 -- Women 3. World
War, 1939-1945 -- Germany 4. HISTORY -- Holocaust 5. National
socialism and women 6. Holocaust, Jewish (1939-1945) 7. Women
war criminals -- Germany 8. SOCIAL SCIENCE -- Women's
Studies 9. World War, 1939-1945 -- Women -- Germany 10. World
War, 1939-1945 -- Participation, Female
ISBN 0547863381; 9780547863382

LC 2013026081

National Book Award Finalist: Nonfiction (2013)
National Book Award Finalist (2013)
Author Wendy Lower presents an "account of the role of German
women on the World War II Nazi eastern front powerfully revises history, proving that we have ignored the reality of women's participation
in the Holocaust. [He] builds a . . . picture of a morally 'lost generation'
of young women, born into a defeated, tumultuous post--World War I
Germany, and then swept up in the nationalistic fervor of the Nazi movement." (Publisher's note)
"Lower, a consultant for the Holocaust Memorial Museum in Washington, D.C., sheds some much-needed light on an aspect of WWII history that has remained in the shadows for decades. "The consensus in
Holocaust and genocide studies," the author writes, "is that the systems
that make mass murder possible would not function without the broad
participation of society, and yet nearly all histories of the Holocaust
leave out half of those who populated that society, as if women's history happens somewhere else." Based on two decades of research and
interviews, the book looks at the role of women in Nazi Germany, in particular women who participated in the Nazi extermination of the Jews...
Lower writes about horribly violent female concentration-camp guards;

of young girls trained in the use of firearms; of brutality that would rival anything perpetrated by their male counterparts. Surprising and deeply unsettling, the book is a welcome addition to the literature on the Holocaust." (Booklist)

Lukacs, John, 1924-

Five days in London, May 1940. Yale Univ. Press 1999 236p $19.95; pa $11.95   **940.53**
1. Diplomats 2. Statesmen 3. Historians 4. Prime ministers 5. Memoirists 6. Cabinet members 7. Government officials 8. Members of Parliament 9. Colonial administrators 10. Nobel laureates for literature 11. World War, 1939-1945 -- Great Britain 12. World war, 1939-1945 -- Great Britain 13. Great Britain -- Politics and government 14. World War, 1939-1945 -- Diplomatic history 15. Great Britain -- Politics and government -- 1936-1945 16. Great Britain -- Politics and government -- 20th century
ISBN 0-300-08030-1; 0-300-08466-8 pa
LC 99-27583
Lukacs discusses Prime Minister Winston Churchill's war policy during the five days between May 24 and May 28, 1940. "In that period, Belgium surrendered; and it became clear that France must shortly do the same. . . . Churchill also had to face a political threat within his own inner War Cabinet, from Lord Halifax. . . . Defiance of Hitler in those final days of May 1940 looked rash to Halifax. He wanted to discover what terms Hitler was prepared to offer, . . . and hinted that he might resign if Churchill refused to consider all options." (Natl Rev) Index.

This work focuses on the "chaotic few days during which, according to the author, Hitler came closest to winning the war. . . . Lukacs concentrates on the struggle within the British War Cabinet, which pitted the Prime Minister, Winston Churchill, against the Foreign Secretary, Lord Halifax, a Tory idol and a friend of the King. The point of contention was Halifax's belief that England should attempt to negotiate a general European settlement with Hitler. Churchill's stubborn refusal won out. The author's equally stubborn digging uncovered a stunning amount of defeatism and intrigue against Churchill by contemporary statesmen." New Yorker
Includes bibliographical references

Maitland, Leslie

Crossing the borders of time; a true story of war, exile, and love reclaimed. Leslie Maitland. Other Press 2012 494 p.   **940.53**
1. Jews -- France 2. Romance fiction 3. Jewish refugees -- Biography 4. World War, 1939-1945 -- Jews 5. Immigrants -- United States -- Biography 6. First loves -- France -- Biography 7. Jewish refugees -- United States -- Biography 8. World War, 1939-1945 -- Jews -- France -- Biography 9. World War, 1939-1945 -- Refugees -- France -- Biography
ISBN 1590514963; 9781590514962
LC 2011047110
This book focuses on "love lost in Alsace during World War II, rediscovered 50 years later in New Jersey. . . . [Author Leslie] Maitland's mother Janine, along with her German-speaking parents, sister and brother, originally fled in 1938 from Freiburg,. . . . The family then landed in Lyon, where Janine . . . reignited a friendship with a dashing Catholic law student, Roland Arcieri. After falling in love during their brief time together, Janine was yanked away again with her family." (Kirkus Reviews)
Includes bibliographical references (p. 489-492)

Mazower, Mark

Hitler's empire; how the Nazis ruled Europe. Penguin Press 2008 xl, 725p il map   **940.53**

1. National socialism 2. Europe -- History -- 1918-1945 3. Germany -- History -- 1918-1945 4. Germany -- History -- 1933-1945 5. World War, 1939-1945 -- Germany
ISBN 1-594-20188-9; 978-1-594-20188-2
LC 2008-26997
This is an account of how the Nazis designed, maintained, and ultimately lost their European empire. (Publisher's note) Index.

The author's compelling analysis of the contradictions underpinning the Nazis' dream of Lebensraum impressively demonstrates that the Nazis were destined to lose World War II. But he soberly reminds us that, inefficient as the Nazis may have been at running an empire, they were brutally effective at suppressing resistance to it. New Leader
Includes bibliographical references

Mazzeo, Tilar J.

★ **Irena's** children; the extraordinary story of the woman who saved 2,500 children from the Warsaw ghetto. Tilar J. Mazzeo. Gallery Books 2016 336 p. (hardcover: alk. paper) $26   **940.53**
1. World War, 1939-1945 -- Jews -- Rescue 2. Holocaust, Jewish (1939-1945) -- Poland 3. World War, 1939-1945 -- Jews -- Rescue -- Poland 4. Righteous Gentiles in the Holocaust -- Poland -- Biography
ISBN 1476778507; 9781476778501; 9781476778518
LC 2015051244
This book, by Tilar J. Mazzeo, gives the "account of . . . the 'female Oskar Schindler' who took staggering risks to save 2,500 children from death and deportation in Nazi-occupied Poland during World War II. In 1942, one young social worker, Irena Sendler, was granted access to the Warsaw ghetto as a public health specialist. While there, she reached out to the trapped Jewish families, going from door to door and asking the parents to trust her with their young children." (Publisher's note)

"Mazzeo chronicles a ray of hope in desperate times in this compelling biography of a brave woman who refused to give up." Kirkus
Includes bibliographical references and index.

McCarten, Anthony

Darkest hour; how Churchill brought England back from the brink. Anthony McCarten. HarperCollins 2017 xii, 316 p.p illustrations (hardcover) $26.99   **940.53**
1. World War, 1939-1945 2. Prime ministers -- Great Britain 3. World War, 1939-1945 -- England 4. Prime ministers -- Great Britain -- Biography 5. Great Britain -- History -- George VI, 1936-1952 6. Great Britain -- Politics and government -- 1936-1945
ISBN 9780062749543; 9780062749512; 006274951X
In this book, Anthony "McCarten exposes sides of . . . [Winston Churchill] never seen before. He reveals how he practiced and re-wrote his key speeches, from 'Blood, toil, tears and sweat' to 'We shall fight on the beaches'; his consideration of a peace treaty with Nazi Germany, and his underappreciated role in the Dunkirk evacuation; and, above all, how 25 days helped make one man an icon." (Publisher's note)

"A fresh, readable look at events and players that, though well-known to history, deserve to be studied for some time to come." Kirkus
Includes bibliographical references (pages 269-305) and index.

McConahay, Mary Jo

The **tango** war; the struggle for the hearts, minds and riches of Latin America during World War II. Mary Jo McConahay. St. Martin's Press 2018 336 p. (hardcover) $29.99   **940.53**
1. World War, 1939-1945 2. Latin America -- History 3. Latin America -- History -- 1898-1948 4. World War, 1939-1945 -- Latin America

ISBN 9781250091239

LC 2018011523

In this book, "Mary Jo McConahay fills an important gap in WWII history. Beginning in the thirties, both sides were well aware of the need to control not just the hearts and minds but also the resources of Latin America. The fight was often dirty: residents were captured to exchange for U.S. prisoners of war and rival spy networks shadowed each other across the continent. At all times it was a Tango War, in which each side closely shadowed the other's steps." (Publisher's note)

Includes bibliographic references and index

McDougall, Christopher

Natural Born Heroes; How a Daring Band of Misfits Mastered the Lost Secrets of Strength and Endurance. Christopher McDougall. Knopf 2015 368 p. map $26.95   **940.53**
1. Crete (Greece) 2. Heroes and heroines 3. World War, 1939-1945 -- Greece
ISBN 0307594963; 9780307594969

LC 2014047459

In this book Christopher McDougall explains how he "finds his next great adventure on the razor-sharp mountains of Crete, where a band of Resistance fighters in World War II plotted the daring abduction of a German general from the heart of the Nazi occupation. McDougall makes his way to the island to find the answer and retrace their steps, experiencing firsthand the extreme physical challenges the Resistance fighters and their local allies faced." (Publisher's note)

"As long as McDougall sticks to their exploits, this narrative is riveting. Unfortunately, his ruminations upon the nature of heroism and his efforts to link these men to ancient and modern heroes ring false. Still, at its best, this is a well-done recounting of a truly heroic episode of WWII." Booklist

Moorhouse, Roger

The **Devils'** Alliance; Hitler's Pact With Stalin, 1939-1941. by Roger Moorhouse. Basic Books 2014 432 p. 16 plates; illustrations; maps $29.99   **940.53**
1. World War, 1939-1945 -- Treaties 2. Soviet Union -- Foreign relations -- Germany
ISBN 0465030750; 9780465030750

LC 2012278241

This book, by Roger Moorhouse, "explores the causes and implications of the Nazi-Soviet Pact, a . . . covenant whose creation and dissolution were crucial turning points in World War II. Forged by the German foreign minister, Joachim von Ribbentrop, and his Soviet counterpart, Vyacheslav Molotov, the nonaggression treaty briefly united the two powers in a brutally efficient collaboration. Together, the Germans and Soviets quickly conquered and divided central and eastern Europe." (Publisher's note)

"Moorhouse's accessible prose and clear explication make this a great story for history readers, and his extensive research and documentation help create a critical text for academics focusing on World War II, German history, and Soviet history." LJ

Mortimer, Gavin

The **longest** night; the bombing of London on May 10, 1941. Berkley Caliber 2005 356p il $24.95   **940.53**
1. World War, 1939-1945 -- Great Britain 2. World War, 1939-1945 -- Aerial operations
ISBN 0-425-20557-6

LC 2005-45281

"This account is given special power and poignancy by using the recollections of surviving men and women who endured that terrible night. An outstanding addition to World War II collections." Booklist

Nagorski, Andrew

The **Nazi** hunters; Andrew Nagorski. Simon & Schuster 2016 416 p. illustrations (hardcover) $30   **940.53**
1. War criminals 2. Holocaust, 1939-1945 3. Fugitives from justice 4. World War, 1939-1945 -- Atrocities 5. Nuremberg Trial of Major German War Criminals, 1945-1946 6. Nazi hunters -- History 7. Holocaust, Jewish (1939-1945) 8. War criminals -- Germany -- History 9. Fugitives from justice -- Germany -- History
ISBN 9781476771861; 9781476771878

LC 2015027334

This book, by Andrew Nagorski, "reveals the experiences of the young American prosecutors in the Nuremberg and Dachau trials, Benjamin Ferencz and William Denson; the Polish investigating judge Jan Sehn, who handled the case of Auschwitz commandant Rudolf Höss; Germany's judge and prosecutor Fritz Bauer; . . . the Mossad agent Rafi Eitan, who was in charge of the Israeli team that nabbed Eichmann; and Eli Rosenbaum, who rose to head the US Justice Department's Office of Special Investigations." (Publisher's note)

"A detailed look at the grim work of tracking Nazis over the decades since World War II." Kirkus

Includes bibliographical references and index

Neiberg, Michael

Potsdam; the end of World War II and the remaking of Europe. Michael Neiber. Basic Books 2015 336 p. illustrations (hardcover: alk. paper) $29.99   **940.53**
1. World War, 1939-1945 -- Treaties 2. World War, 1939-1945 -- Armistices 3. World War, 1939-1945 -- Peace
ISBN 0465075258; 9780465075256

LC 2015007545

In this book author "Michael Neiberg brings the turbulent Potsdam conference to life, vividly capturing the delegates' personalities: Truman, trying to escape from the shadow of Franklin Roosevelt; Churchill, bombastic and seemingly out of touch; Stalin, cunning and meticulous. The delegates arrived at Potsdam determined to learn from the mistakes their predecessors made. But, riven by tensions and dramatic debates over how to end the most recent war, they only dimly understood that their discussions of peace were giving birth to a new global conflict." (Publisher's note)

"A must-have account for everyone from students of world history at the undergraduate and graduate levels to knowledgeable recreational readers." LJ

Includes bibliographical references and index

The **New** York Times complete World War II, 1939-1945; the coverage from the battlefields to the home front. edited by Richard Overy. Black Dog & Leventhal Pub 2013 611 p. $40   **940.53**
1. World War, 1939-1945 2. Newspapers -- United States
ISBN 1579129447; 9781579129446

This book, edited by Richard Overy, features "hundreds of . . . articles from the archives of the 'Times'—including firsthand accounts of major events and little-known anecdotes. . . . The book covers the biggest battles of the war, from the Battle of the Bulge to the Battle of Iwo Jima, as well as moving stories from the home front and profiles of noted leaders and heroes such as Winston Churchill and George Patton." (Publisher's note)

"This is a book to lose yourself in, to witness the war transmuted into print for the masses of readers living through it and anxious to follow its twists and turns." LJ

Olson, Lynne

Those angry days; Roosevelt, Lindbergh, and America's

fight over World War II, 1939-1941. by Lynne Olson. Random House Inc. 2013 576 p. (hardcover) $30.00; (ebook) $85.00 **940.53**

> 1. World War, 1939-1945 -- United States 2. United States -- Military policy 3. World War, 1939-1945 -- Diplomatic history 4. United States -- Foreign relations -- 1933-1945 5. United States -- Politics and government -- 1933-1945 6. Isolationism -- United States -- History -- 20th century 7. Intervention (International law) -- History -- 20th century 8. Political culture -- United States -- History -- 20th century
> ISBN 9781400069743; 1400069742; 9780679604716
> LC 2012025381

This book, by Lynne Olson, offers an "account of the debate over American intervention in World War II. . . . At the center of this controversy stood the two most famous men in America: President Franklin D. Roosevelt, who championed the interventionist cause, and aviator Charles Lindbergh, who as unofficial leader and spokesman for America's isolationists emerged as the president's most formidable adversary." (Publisher's note)

Includes bibliographical references (p. [509]-518) and index.

Orbach, Danny

The **plots** against Hitler; Danny Orbach. Houghton Mifflin Harcourt 2016 432 p. (hardcover) $28 **940.53**

> 1. Heads of state 2. World War, 1939-1945 -- Underground movements 3. Germany -- Politics and government -- 1933-1945 4. Heads of state -- Germany -- Biography 5. Assassins -- Germany -- History -- 20th century 6. Anti-Nazi movement -- Germany -- History -- 20th century 7. Opposition (Political science) -- Germany -- History -- 20th century
> ISBN 9780544714434
> LC 2015043037

This book, by Danny Orbach, is an "account of the anti-Nazi underground in Germany and its numerous efforts to assassinate Adolf Hitler. In 1933, Adolf Hitler became Chancellor of Germany. A year later, all parties but the Nazis had been outlawed. . . . Yet over the next few years, an unlikely clutch of conspirators emerged — soldiers, schoolteachers, politicians, diplomats, theologians, even a carpenter — who would try repeatedly to end the Fuhrer's genocidal reign." (Publisher's note)

"Likely to become the definitive general history of the subject and the starting place for all future research, Orbach's work is a fascinating story of courage and an excellent study of the struggle of individuals to act morally and honorably." Pub Wkly

Includes bibliographical references and index

Overy, Richard

Why the Allies won; {by} Richard Overy. W W Norton & Co Inc 1996 416 p. il maps hardcover o.p. (pbk.) $19.95 **940.53**

> 1. Strategy 2. World War, 1939-1945
> ISBN 039331619X; 978-0393316193
> LC 95-52444

This is an analysis of the reasons for the Allied victory over the Axis powers in 1945. "Professor Overy has chosen to divide his book into two . . . distinct parts. In the first part he gives summary accounts of the four military arenas which he considered decisive: the war at sea; the Eastern Front in 1942-3; the strategic air offensive; and the invasion of France in 1944. In the second part, he turns to the underlying political, social and industrial factors." (Times Lit Suppl) Bibliography. Index.

"Eschewing the belief that the Allies won solely because of their prodigious production of weapons and equipment, Mr. Overy points out that in the early stages of the war, before the Allies were fully mobilized, the Axis countries held the production advantage, yet failed to achieve

victory because Germany's management of supply logistics was far inferior to that of the Allies—frequently as a result of Hitler's wrongheaded interference. . . . Assiduously researched and concisely written, this is a highly perceptive study." N Y Times Book Rev

Includes bibliographical references

Pivnik, Sam

Survivor; Auschwitz, the Death March and My Fight for Freedom. Sam Pivnik. St. Martin's Press 2013 320 p. (hardcover) $26.99 **940.53**

> 1. Holocaust, 1939-1945
> ISBN 125002952X; 9781250029522

This book, by Sam Pivnik, presents a memoir of a Jewish Holocaust survivor. "On fourteen occasions he should have been killed, but luck, his physical strength, and his determination not to die all played a part in Sam Pivnik living to tell his . . . story. In 1939, . . . Pivnik's life changed forever when the Nazis invaded Poland. He survived the two ghettoes . . . , six months [in] Auschwitz . . . , [and] the brutal Fürstengrube mining camp." (Publisher's note)

Plokhy, S. M.

Yalta; the price of peace. [by] S.M. Plokhy. Viking 2010 xxviii, 451p il map **940.53**

> 1. Yalta Conference (1945) 2. World politics -- 1945-1991 3. World War, 1939-1945 -- Peace 4. World War, 1939-1945 -- Diplomatic history
> ISBN 978-0-670-02141-3
> LC 2009-26833

Plokhy "has produced a colorful and gripping portrait of the three aging leaders at their historic encounter." Wall Street J

Includes bibliographical references

Raghavan, Srinath

India's war; World War II and the making of modern South Asia. Srinath Raghavan. Basic Books 2016 592 p. illustrations (hardcover) $35 **940.53**

> 1. India -- History -- 20th century 2. World War, 1939-1945 -- Campaigns -- South Asia
> ISBN 9780465030224
> LC 2016933273

This book, by Srinath Raghavan, discusses the experience of World War II in India. The author "paints a compelling picture of battles abroad and of life on the home front, arguing that the war is crucial to explaining how and why colonial rule ended in South Asia. World War II forever altered the country's social landscape, overturning many Indians' settled assumptions and opening up new opportunities for the nation's most disadvantaged people." (Publisher's note)

"This book will be appreciated by scholars and general readers alike who wish to discover more answers to India's role in World War II." LJ

Includes bibliographical references and index.

Rees, Laurence

Auschwitz: a new history; Laurence Rees. Public Affairs 2005 xxii, 327p il $30; pa $16 **940.53**

> 1. Holocaust, 1933-1945 2. Auschwitz (Poland: Concentration camp)
> ISBN 1-586-48303-X; 1-586-48357-9 pa
> LC 2004-43196

For this history of the concentration camp, the author "interviewed 100 former Nazi perpetrators and survivors from the camp and drew on hundreds of interviews conducted for his previous research on the Third Reich, many with former members of the Nazi Party. . . . This is a significant contribution to our understanding of the intricacies of Nazi racial and ethnic policy that resulted in this ultimate abomination." Booklist

Includes bibliographical references

★ The **Holocaust**; a new history. Laurence Rees. Public Affairs 2017 xv, 509 p.p illustrations (some col.), map (hardcover) $32   **940.53**

1. Holocaust survivors 2. Holocaust, 1939-1945 3. Holocaust, Jewish (1939-1945) 4. World War, 1939-1945 -- Atrocities 5. Jews -- Europe -- History -- 20th century

ISBN 1610398440; 9781610398442; 9781568588100

LC 2017933355

Author "Laurence Rees has spent twenty-five years meeting the survivors and perpetrators of the 'Third Reich and the Holocaust.' In this sweeping history, he combines this testimony with the latest academic research to investigate how history's greatest crime was possible. Rees argues that while hatred of the Jews was at the epicenter of Nazi thinking, we cannot fully understand the Holocaust without considering Nazi plans to kill millions of non-Jews as well." (Publisher's note)

"Historian Rees . . . combines thorough scholarship of the Nazi era with his own vast archive of interviews with survivors, perpetrators, and bystanders to create a comprehensive, chilling, and readable history of the Holocaust." LJ

Includes bibliographical references and index.

Reeves, Richard

Infamy; the shocking story of the Japanese American internment in World War II. Richard Reeves. Henry Holt & Co. 2015 368 p. 16 plates; illustrations; maps (hardcover) $32   **940.53**

1. World War, 1939-1945 2. Japanese -- United States 3. Concentration camps -- United States 4. World War, 1939-1945 -- Japanese Americans 5. Japanese Americans -- Evacuation and relocation, 1942-1945

ISBN 0805094083; 9780805094084

LC 2014033329

In this book author "Richard Reeves provides an authoritative account of the internment of more than 120,000 Japanese-Americans and Japanese aliens during World War II. Reeves has interviewed survivors, read numerous private letters and memoirs, and combed through archives to deliver a sweeping narrative of this atrocity." (Publisher's note)

"Reeves mixes intimate narratives with historical documents to give an authoritative account of one of the darkest periods in American history." LJ

Includes bibliographical references and index

Reporting World War II. Library of Am. 1995 2v ea $35   **940.53**

1. World War, 1939-1945 2. Reporters and reporting

ISBN 1-883011-04-3 v1; 1-883011-05-1 v2

LC 94-45463

This "collection of some 200 entries by nearly 90 writers, drawn from newspapers, magazine articles, broadcast transcripts and book excerpts, recalls WW II campaigns and battles in all theaters but pays attention to the home front as well. It begins with an excerpt from William L. Shirer's Berlin Diary and ends with one from John Hersey's Hiroshima. . . . This is a treasure trove of war reporting, featuring writing of the highest order." Publ Wkly

Reynolds, David

In command of history; Churchill fighting and writing the Second World War. by David Reynolds. Random House 2005 xxiv, 631p il $35   **940.53**

1. Statesmen 2. Historians 3. Prime ministers 4. Memoirists 5. Cabinet members 6. Members of Parliament 7. Nobel laureates for literature 8. World War, 1939-1945 -- Historiography

ISBN 0-679-45743-7

LC 2004-51087

"Packed with detail and vivid characterizations . . . [this book is] a different take on one of the few men capable of both making history and writing it." Publ Wkly

Includes bibliographical references

Richmond Mouillot, Miranda

A **fifty**-year silence; love, war, and a ruined house in France. Miranda Richmond Mouillot. Crown Publishers 2015 288 p. illustrations, maps $26   **940.53**

1. Divorce 2. Grandparents 3. World War, 1939-1945 -- Refugees 4. Grandparents -- Biography 5. Jews -- France -- Biography 6. Divorced people -- Biography 7. World War, 1939-1945 -- France 8. Holocaust survivors -- Biography 9. Jews -- United States -- Biography 10. Holocaust, Jewish (1939-1945) -- France

ISBN 0804140642; 9780804140645

LC 2014015315

This book is an "account of [author] Miranda Richmond Mouillot's journey to find out what happened between her grandmother, a physician, and her grandfather, an interpreter at the Nuremberg Trials, who refused to utter his wife's name aloud after she left him. To discover the roots of their embittered and entrenched silence, Miranda abandons her plans for the future and moves to their stone house, now a crumbling ruin; immerses herself in letters, archival materials, and secondary sources." (Publisher's note)

"The corrosive effects of the Holocaust--upon those directly involved and generations thereafter--are illustrated vividly in this candid saga of familial love and misunderstanding." LJ

Rosenfeld, Oskar

In the beginning was the ghetto; 890 days in Lodz. edited and with an introduction by Hanno Loewy; translated from the German by Brigitte M. Goldstein. Northwestern Univ. Press 2002 xxxviii, 313p $40   **940.53**

1. Łódz (Poland) 2. Jews -- Poland 3. Holocaust, 1933-1945 -- Personal narratives

ISBN 0-8101-1488-7

LC 2001-6691

Original German edition, 1994

These entries from Rosenfeld's diary "contain vivid descriptions of daily life in the ghetto, including details about deportations, forced labor, hunger, diseases, cold, terror, and the struggle to maintain human dignity. . . . This book is one of the most important and lasting works documenting the horrors of the Holocaust." Booklist

Includes bibliographical references

Russell, Jan Jarboe, 1951-

The **Train** to Crystal City; FDR's Secret Prisoner Exchange Program and America's Only Family Internment Camp During World War II. Jan Jarboe Russell. Simon & Schuster 2015 416 p. 8 plates; illustrations; map $30   **940.53**

1. Crystal City (Tex.) -- History 2. Concentration camps -- United States 3. World War, 1939-1945 -- United States

ISBN 1451693664; 9781451693669

LC 2014030862

This book, by Jan Jarboe Russell, tells the history of "a secret FDR-approved American internment camp in Texas during World War II, where thousands of families . . . were incarcerated. . . . Focusing her story on two American-born teenage girls who were interned, [the] author . . . uncovers the details of their years spent in the camp." (Publisher's note)

"Based in part on interviews with camp survivors, Russell documents in chilling detail a shocking story of national betrayal." Kirkus

Sakamoto, Pamela Rotner, 1962-

Midnight in broad daylight; a Japanese American family caught between two worlds. Pamela Rotner Sakamoto. Harper 2016 464 p. 8 plates; portraits (hardback) $29.99 **940.53**
1. World War, 1939-1945 -- Japan 2. Japanese Americans -- Evacuation and relocation, 1942-1945 3. Soldiers -- Japan -- Biography 4. Japan -- Relations -- United States 5. United States -- Relations -- Japan 6. Translators -- United States -- Biography 7. World War, 1939-1945 -- Japanese Americans 8. World War, 1939-1945 -- Japan -- Hiroshima-shi 9. Japanese American families -- Washington -- Seattle
ISBN 9780062351937

LC 2015017943

This book, by Pamela Rotner Sakamoto, "alternating between the American and Japanese perspectives, . . . captures the uncertainty and intensity of those charged with the fighting [of World War II] as well as the deteriorating home front of Hiroshima . . . and provides a fresh look at the dropping of the first atomic bomb. . . . It is . . . a scathing examination of racism and xenophobia [and] an homage to the tremendous Japanese American contribution to the American war effort." (Publisher's note)

"A beautifully rendered work wrought with enormous care and sense of compassionate dignity." Kirkus

Includes bibliographical references and index

Scheyer, Moriz

Asylum; A Survivor's Flight from Nazi-Occupied Vienna Through Wartime France. Moriz Scheyer; P. N. Singer (translator, Epilogue) Little, Brown and Co. 2016 320 p. ill., maps, portraits $28 **940.53**
1. Asylum 2. Journalists 3. Holocaust survivors 4. World War, 1939-1945
ISBN 9780316272889

LC 2016932793

This memoir by Austrian Jewish writer Moriz Scheyer, translated and with an epilogue by P. N. Singer, provides an account of Scheyer's "flight, persecution, and clandestine life in wartime France. As arts editor for one of Vienna's principal newspapers, Scheyer knew many of the city's foremost artists, and was an important literary journalist. With the advent of the Nazis he was forced from both job and home. In 1943, . . . Scheyer began drafting what was to become this book." (Publisher's note)

"A well-written book full of desperate hope, intense fear, and a demand for vigilance against the mentality of hate." Kirkus

Includes bibliographical references (pages 304-305).

Shephard, Ben

The **long** road home; the aftermath of the Second World War. Alfred A. Knopf 2011 489p map $35; ebook $35 **940.53**
1. World War, 1939-1945 -- Refugees 2. World War, 1939-1945 -- Forced repatriation 3. United Nations Relief and Rehabilitation Administration
ISBN 978-1-4000-4068-1; 978-1-4000-4068-1 ebook

LC 2010-23894

First published 2010 in the United Kingdom

The book examines the experience of "roughly eleven million foreigners stranded in Germany [after World War II], often in ghastly conditions, after surviving years of hard labor and imprisonment in labor camps, concentration camps, death camps, and POW camps. . . . The Allied armies, chiefly the Americans, Soviets, and British, were faced with the kind of catastrophe left in the wake of most wars, but the scale in 1945 was unprecedented. . . . Shephard describes . . . the . . . confrontation of well-fed people from a relatively secure world with human beings who had indeed been reduced to a state that seemed lower than animals." (New York Review of Books)

"Ben Shephard's account of this demanding and important subject is a triumph. He has unearthed new and moving testimony by former DPs and has burrowed into official and personal papers without ever letting his deep scholarship get in the way of the riveting story he has to tell." Hist Today

Includes bibliographical references

Smith, Lyn

Remembering, voices of the holocaust; a new history in the words of the men and women who survived. [foreword by Laurence Rees] Carroll & Graf 2006 351p il map $27 **940.53**
1. Holocaust, 1933-1945 -- Personal narratives
ISBN 0-7867-1640-1

LC 2006-284769

First published 2005 in the United Kingdom

The author, "who has recorded the experiences of survivors for London's Imperial War Museum, weaves together more than 100 accounts to construct a narrative of Nazi persecutions from the first anti-Semitic measures in 1933 through the liberation of the concentration camps. . . . This is an extraordinary work of scholarship and a reminder of the power of individual stories, which can bring home the horrors of WWII more forcefully than abstract numbers." Publ Wkly

Includes bibliographical references

Snyder, Timothy D., 1969-

Black Earth; The Holocaust As History and Warning. Timothy Snyder. Random House Inc. 2015 480 p. maps $30 **940.53**
1. Atrocities 2. Holocaust, 1939-1945 3. World War, 1939-1945
ISBN 1101903457; 9781101903452

LC 2015016818

This book, by Timothy Snyder, exploring the legacy of the Jewish Holocaust, "presents a new explanation of the great atrocity of the twentieth century, and reveals the risks that we face in the twenty-first. Based on new sources from eastern Europe and forgotten testimonies from Jewish survivors, . . . [it] recounts the mass murder of the Jews as an event that is still close to us, more comprehensible than we would like to think, and thus all the more terrifying." (Publisher's note)

"Snyder brings two fresh elements to his dizzying, harrowing tale. The first is his extraordinarily wide and deep research into the remarkable stories, many unknown, of individual Holocaust survivors, the subject of the last half of his book. The second element, likely to be controversial, is his argument, asserted and reasserted, that, at its roots, the Holocaust was made possible by the failure of national states." Pub Wkly

Includes bibliographical references and index

Spiegelman, Art

★ **Maus**; a survivor's tale. Art Spiegelman. 25th anniversary ed. Pantheon Bks. 1996 295 p. 2v in 1 ill., maps (some col.) $35 **940.53**
1. Graphic novels 2. Biographical graphic novels 3. Holocaust, 1933-1945 -- Graphic novels
ISBN 0-679-40641-7

LC 96-32796

A combined edition of Maus I: My father bleeds history (1986) and Maus II: And here my troubles began (1991)

Pulitzer Prize Special Award (1992)

Harvey Award: Best Graphic Album of Previously Published Material (1992) for Maus II

Eisner Award: Best Graphic Album--Reprint for Maus II

Los Angeles Times Book Prize: Fiction (1992) for Maus II

"An undisputed classic and award-winning title (including a Pulitzer Prize in 1992) in which renowned cartoonist Spiegelman depicts his father's experiences as a World War II Nazi concentration camp survivor. The memoir is also a chronicle of Spiegelman's relationship with his father as we witness their visits and disagreements. The black-and-white drawings are straightforward, but with an interesting twist: all of the Jews are depicted as mice and the Nazis as cats." LJ

In this work "Spiegelman takes the comic book to a new level of seriousness, portraying Jews as mice and Nazis as cats. Depicting himself being told about the Holocaust by his Polish survivor father, Spiegelman not only explores the concentration-camp experience, but also the guilt, love, and anger between father and son." Rochman. Against borders

★ **MetaMaus**. Pantheon Books 2011 299p il $35 **940.53**
1. Authors 2. Cartoonists 3. Graphic novels 4. Autobiographical graphic novels 5. Nonfiction writers 6. Cartoonists -- Graphic novels 7. Holocaust survivors -- Graphic novels 8. Holocaust, 1933-1945 -- Graphic novels
ISBN 978-0-375-42394-9

LC 2010052045

The New York cartoonist traces the creative process that went into drawing his Pulitzer Prizewinning classic, revealing the sources of his inspiration and describing his parents' emotional struggles as Holocaust survivors after the end of World War II.

"Informative about everything you may or may not have thought to ask about Maus and the Spiegelmans, this exhaustive purgative has been well organized and packaged and succeeds in being grimly entertaining, indeed almost addictive." Libr J

Stargardt, Nicholas

Witnesses of war; children's lives under the Nazis. Distributed by Random House 2006 493p il map $30; pa $16.95 **940.53**
1. World War, 1939-1945 -- Children
ISBN 1-4000-4088-4; 978-1-4000-4088-9; 1-4000-3379-9 pa; 978-1-4000-3379-9 pa

LC 2005-50409

First published 2005 in the United Kingdom

This is "a sharp and taut account of misery." Publ Wkly

Includes bibliographical references

Takaki, Ronald T.

Double victory; a multicultural history of America in World War II. [by] Ronald Takaki. Little, Brown 2000 282p il hardcover o.p. pa $19.99 **940.53**
1. United States -- Race relations 2. World War, 1939-1945 -- United States
ISBN 0-316-83155-7; 0-316-83156-5 pa

LC 99-40374

"Takaki discusses the experiences of African Americans, Indians, Chicanos, Asian Americans from several nations, German and Italian Americans, and Jewish Americans. . . . Despite Jim Crow, internment camps, neglected slums, barrios, reservations, and rejection of Jewish refugees, the nation's not-quite-Americans fought bravely in World War II." Booklist

Includes bibliographical references

Tate, Tim

Hitler's forgotten children; a true story of the Lebensborn program and one woman's search for her real identity. Ingrid von Oelhafen and Tim Tate; with Dr. Dorothee Schmitz-Koster. Berkley Caliber 2016 288 p. illustrations, plates (hardback) $28 **940.53**
1. World War, 1939-1945 -- Children 2. Lebensborn e. V. (Germany) 3. World War, 1939-1945 -- Children -- Biography 4. Eugenics -- Germany -- History -- 20th century 5. World War, 1939-1945 -- Personal narratives, Yugoslav
ISBN 9780425283325

LC 2015034223

This book, by Ingrid von Oelhafen and Tim Tate, with Dorothee Schmitz-Koster, describes how "in the summer of 1942, parents across Nazi-occupied Yugoslavia were required to submit their children to medical checks designed to assess racial purity. One such child, Erika Matko, was . . . taken to Germany and placed with politically vetted foster parents, Erika was renamed Ingrid von Oelhafen. Many years later, Ingrid began to uncover the truth of her identity." (Publisher's note)

"This riveting, raw, and heart-wrenching story of misplaced identity and one woman's quest to find peace and hope in the darkest of times will intrigue a variety of readers interested in a mix of history nestled among personal memoir." LJ

Includes bibliographical references (page 275).

United States Holocaust Memorial Museum

The **Holocaust** and history; the known, the unknown, the disputed, and the reexamined. edited by Michael Berenbaum and Abraham J. Peck. Indiana Univ. Press 1998 836p $58.71; pa $35 **940.53**
1. Holocaust, 1933-1945
ISBN 0-253-33374-1; 0-253-21529-3 pa

LC 97-40030

"Papers collected here originated at a 1993 conference organized by the US Holocaust Memorial Museum's Research Institute. . . . The 50 contributors treat the subject from every conceivable angle: the role of antisemitism and racism; the politics of 'racial hygiene'; Nazi leadership and bureaucracy; the complicity of 'ordinary' people; the experiences of Gypsies, homosexuals, and blacks; the concentration camps; the Holocaust as reflected in international relations; the response of Jews, rescuers, and survivors. Recognizing the passionately controversial nature of the field, the editors have opted for variety over unanimity." Choice

Van Es, Bart

The **cut** out girl; a story of war and family, lost and found. Bart van Es. Penguin Press 2018 304 p. (hardback) $28 **940.53**
1. Jews -- Netherlands 2. Jewish children in the Holocaust 3. Jews -- Netherlands -- Biography 4. Holocaust, Jewish (1939-1945) -- Netherlands -- Biography 5. Jewish children in the Holocaust -- Netherlands -- Biography
ISBN 9780735222243

LC 2018006209

This book, by Bart van Es, presents the "true story of a young Jewish girl [named Lientje] in Holland under Nazi occupation who finds refuge in the homes of an underground network of foster families, one of them . . . [was van Es'] grandparents. . . . [The book] braids together a powerful recreation of that intensely harrowing childhood story of Lientje's with the present-day account of Bart's efforts to piece that story together." (Publisher's note)

Wachsmann, Nikolaus

Kl; A History of the Nazi Concentration Camps. Nikolaus

Wachsmann. Farrar, Straus & Giroux 2015 880 p. 32 plates; illustrations; maps $40 **940.53**
1. Holocaust, Jewish (1939-1945) 2. World War, 1939-1945 -- Concentration camps 3. World War, 1939-1945 -- Atrocities -- Germany 4. Concentration camps -- History -- 20th century 5. World War, 1939-1945 -- Prisoners and prisons, German
ISBN 0374118256; 9780374118259

LC 2014031269

Author Nicholas Wachusmann "presents startling revelations, based on many years of archival research, about the functioning and scope of the [Nazi concentration] camp system. Examining, close up, life and death inside the camps, and adopting a wider lens to show how the camp system was shaped by changing political, legal, social, economic, and military forces, Wachsmann produces a unified picture of the Nazi regime." (Publisher's note)

"A comprehensive, encyclopedic work that should be included in the collections of libraries, schools and other institutions." Kirkus

Includes bibliographical references (pages 779-826) and index

Weinberg, Gerhard L.
★ A **world** at arms; a global history of World War II. 2nd ed; Cambridge University Press 2005 xxix, 1178p map $65; pa $25.99 **940.53**
1. World War, 1939-1945
ISBN 0-521-85316-8; 978-0-521-85316-3; 0-521-61826-6 pa; 978-0-521-61826-7 pa

LC 2005-41954

First published 1994

"Weinberg's unrivaled command of archival sources combine with a smooth writing style to produce a definitive one-volume history of World War II." Libr J [review of 1994 edition]

Includes bibliographical references

Weissova, Helga, 1929-
Helga's diary; a young girl's account of life in a concentration camp. Helga Weiss; translated by Neil Bermel; Introduction by Francine Prose. 1st American ed. W.W. Norton & Co Inc. 2013 256 p. (hardcover) $24.95 **940.53**
1. Concentration camps 2. Terezin (Czechoslovakia: Concentration camp) 3. Holocaust, Jewish (1939-1945) 4. Jewish children in the Holocaust 5. Jews -- Czech Republic -- Prague 6. Theresienstadt (Concentration camp) 7. Prague (Czech Republic) -- Biography
ISBN 0393077977; 9780393077971

LC 2013003775

Helga Weiss "begins her diary as a frightened eight-year-old in a bomb shelter . . . . The scene sets the tone of fear and confusion that will dominate her life for the next several years, the bulk of which she spends in the Jewish ghetto, Terezín. Her writings describe both the torturous physical circumstances of daily life, as well as the psychological toll wrought by ceaseless anxiety, degradation, and survivor's guilt." (Publishers Weekly)

Includes bibliographical references.

Weller, George
Weller's war; a legendary foreign correspondent's saga of World War II on five continents. edited by Anthony Weller. Crown Publishers 2009 644p il map $30 **940.53**
1. World War, 1939-1945 -- Campaigns 2. World War, 1939-1945 -- Personal narratives
ISBN 978-0-307-40655-2; 0-307-40655-5

The author "wrote for the Chicago Daily News for 35 years, achieving fame for his widely ranging dispatches from the many fronts of World War II. He was captured by the Gestapo in Greece, escaped from Java on a boat strafed by Japanese fighters, marched with Belgian colonial troops fighting Italian colonial troops in Ethiopia, and slogged through swamps with Americans and Australians locked in grim struggles in New Guinea. Weller's war reporting won him the Pulitzer Prize in 1943. Here, his son assembles many of his dispatches, which add tremendously to our understanding of the war at ground level, the people's war." Libr J

West Point History of World War II; The United States Military Academy; Editors: Clifford J. Rogers, Ty Seidule, and Steve R. Waddell. Simon & Schuster 2015 432, 370 p.p 2 vol illustrations; color maps (hardcover) $55 **940.53**
1. World War, 1939-1945 2. United States Military Academy
ISBN 9781476782782 (v. 2); 9781476782737 (v. 1); 9781476782744 (v. 1); 9781476782775 (v. 2); 1476782733

LC 2015031711

This book, published by the United States Military Academy, edited by Clifford J. Rogers, Ty Seidule, and Steve R. Waddell, offers "an outstanding new military history of the first half of World War II, featuring a rich array of images, . . . graphics, . . . maps, and expert analysis commissioned by the United States Military Academy to teach the art of war to West Point cadets." (Publisher's note)

"An astonishing, important book that will inform and entertain all readers, this is an essential purchase. Fans of military history, strategy, warfare, and human conflict will reap the benefits of this work." LJ

Winik, Jay
1944; FDR and the year that changed history. Jay Winik. Simon & Schuster 2015 512 p. illustrations (hardcover) $35 **940.53**
1. World War, 1939-1945 2. Holocaust, Jewish (1939-1945) 3. World War, 1939-1945 -- United States 4. Political leadership -- United States -- History -- 20th century
ISBN 1439114080; 9781439114087; 9781501125362

LC 2015013912

This book by "author Jay Winik brings to life in gripping detail the year 1944, which determined the outcome of World War II and put more pressure than any other on an ailing yet determined President Roosevelt. [It] is the first book to tell these events with such moral clarity and unprecedented sweep, and a moving appreciation of the extraordinary struggles of the era's outsized figures." (Publisher's note)

"An accomplished popular historian unpacks the last full year of World War II and the excruciatingly difficult decisions facing Franklin Roosevelt. . . . A complex history rendered with great color and sympathy." Kirkus

Includes bibliographical references and index

★ A **woman** in Berlin; eight weeks in the conquered city: a diary. by Anonymous; translated by Philip Boehm. Metropolitan Books/Henry Holt 2005 261p $23 **940.53**
1. Berlin, Battle of, 1945 2. World War, 1939-1945 -- Women 3. World War, 1939-1945 -- Personal narratives
ISBN 0-8050-7540-2

LC 2005-41984

Original German edition, 2003; Expurgated edition translated by James Stern published 1954 by Harcourt, Brace

This "is one of the most important documents to emerge from World War II." N Y Times Book Rev

World War II; the definitive encyclopedia and document collection. Spencer C. Tucker, editor; Paul G. Pierpaoli Jr.,

associate editor; Timothy C. Dowling, assistant editor; William H. Van Husen, assistant editor; David T. Zabecki, assistant editor; Priscilla Roberts, documents editor; Gerhard L. Weinberg, foreword. ABC-CLIO, an imprint of ABC-CLIO, LLC 2016 5 volumes (lxxix, 2471 p.)p illustrations, maps (set: alk. paper) $520   **940.53**
1. World history -- 20th century 2. World War, 1939-1945 -- Sources 3. World War, 1939-1945 -- Encyclopedias 4. History, Modern -- 20th century -- Encyclopedias
ISBN 9781440845932; 9781440845949; 9781440845956; 9781440845963; 9781440845970; 9781851099689; 9781851099696

LC 2015046300

This five-volume collection, edited by Spencer C. Tucker, contains "more than 1,700 cross-referenced entries covering every aspect of World War II, the events and developments of the era, and myriad related subjects as well as a documents volume. . . . [It] provides a clear understanding of the causes of World War II, . . . examines home front developments in major countries . . . , [and] details the changing attitudes toward the war as expressed in film and literature." (Publisher's note)

"This exhaustive encyclopedia is highly recommended for public and academic libraries where budget allows, especially where there is interest in military history." Booklist

Includes bibliographical references and index

Yellin, Emily

Our mothers' war; American women at home and at the Front during World War II. Free Press 2004 447p il hardcover o.p. pa $14   **940.53**
1. World War, 1939-1945 -- Women
ISBN 0-7432-4514-8; 0-7432-4516-4 pa

LC 2004-40496

"Yellin reveals all of the responsibilities held by women, including helping to manufacture aircraft, ships, and other munitions; and, in the process, outproducing all of America's allies and enemies, by far. Readers see war brides who worked hard to maintain the morale of their husbands while surviving long separation, fear, and shortages of virtually everything necessary to support a family. . . . [This book] is an important book because the role played by women in World War II has been regularly ignored." SLJ

Includes bibliographical references

Zuccotti, Susan

Père Marie-Benoît and Jewish rescue; how a French priest together with Jewish friends saved thousands during the Holocaust. Susan Zuccotti. Indiana University Press 2013 280 p. (cloth: alkaline paper) $35   **940.53**
1. World War, 1939-1945 -- Jews -- Rescue 2. Marseille (France) -- Biography 3. Priests -- France -- Marseille -- Biography 4. Capuchins -- France -- Marseille -- Biography 5. Marseille (France) -- History -- 20th century 6. Holocaust, Jewish (1939-1945) -- France -- Marseille 7. Jews -- France -- Marseille -- History -- 20th century 8. World War, 1939-1945 -- Jews -- Rescue -- France -- Marseille 9. Righteous Gentiles in the Holocaust -- France -- Marseille -- Biography
ISBN 0253008530; 9780253008534

LC 2012047187

In this book, Susan Zuccotti offers an account "of the life of Capuchin priest Père Marie-Benoît and his successful efforts to save thousands of Jews." Her "approach begins before Marie-Benoît's birth in 1895, with a review of the geography and history of the region in France where he was born. She then moves on to profile the courageous priest

in the trenches of the First World War, . . . and afterward during his high-level religious studies in Rome after the war." (Publishers Weekly)

Includes bibliographical references and index

Under his very windows; the Vatican and the Holocaust in Italy. Yale Univ. Press 2000 408p il $29.95; pa $16.95 **940.53**
1. Popes 2. Jews -- Italy 3. Holocaust, 1933-1945 4. Catholic Church -- Relations -- Judaism
ISBN 0-300-08487-0; 0-300-09310-1 pa

LC 00-43307

Zuccotti's "aim is to show that whatever help was given to the Jews by the Catholic Church during the war resulted almost entirely from spontaneous acts by courageous individuals—priests, monks and nuns, and occasionally prelates—and not from any interventions by the Vatican. . . . Zuccotti makes her case strongly. . . . This is a serious and well-researched book." N Y Times Book Rev

Includes bibliographical references (p. 329-396) and index

940.531   Social, political, economic history; Holocaust

Goldberg, Rita

Motherland; growing up with the holocaust. Rita Goldberg. Halban 2014 xvi, 340 p.p illustrations $27.95 **940.531**
1. Holocaust survivors 2. Jews -- Netherlands 3. Holocaust, 1939-1945 4. World War, 1939-1945 -- Jewish resistance 5. Holocaust, Jewish (1939-1945) 6. World War, 1939-1945 -- Participation, Jewish 7. World War, 1939-1945 -- Underground movements 8. Holocaust survivors -- Netherlands -- Biography 9. Jews -- Netherlands -- 20th century -- Biography 10. Jews -- Netherlands -- Social conditions -- 20th century
ISBN 1620970732; 1905559623; 9781620970737; 9781905559626

LC 2013496141

This book, by Rita Goldberg, is a "deeply moving second-generation Holocaust memoir. . . . Proud of her mother and yet struggling to forge an identity in the shadow of such heroic accomplishments (in a family setting that included close relationships with the iconic Frank family), Goldberg reveals a little-explored aspect of Holocaust survival: the often-wrenching family and interpersonal struggles of the children and grandchildren whose own lives are haunted by historic tragedy." (Publisher's note)

"Of course, the family story, and especially the Frank connection, will draw readers (she knew Otto very well, right up to his postwar visits to the U.S.), who will be open to discussion of the big issues of perpetrators, victims, and, especially, bystanders, then and now." Booklist

Includes bibliographical references

Henderson, Bruce

Sons and soldiers; the untold story of the Jews who escaped the Nazis and returned with the U.S. Army to fight Hitler. Bruce Henderson. William Morrow, an imprint of HarperCollins Publishers 2017 xii, 429 p.p illustrations, portraits (hardcover) $28.99   **940.531**
1. Jews -- Germany 2. World War, 1939-1945 -- Jewish resistance 3. Jews, German -- United States 4. Jewish soldiers -- United States 5. World War, 1939-1945 -- Participation, Jewish 6. World War, 1939-1945 -- Military intelligence -- United States
ISBN 9780062419118; 9780062419095; 0062419099

LC 2017446169

This book, by Bruce Henderson, is about the "young German Jews, dubbed The Ritchie Boys, who fled Nazi Germany in the 1930s, came of age in America, and returned to Europe at enormous personal risk as members of the U.S. Army to play a key role in the Allied victory. . . . [It] draws on personal interviews with many surviving veterans and extensive archival research to bring this never-before-told chapter of the Second World War to light." (Publisher's note)

"A gripping addition to the literature of the period and an overdue tribute to these unique Americans." Kirkus

Includes bibliographical references (pages 411-418) and index.

Holden, Wendy

Born Survivors; Three Young Mothers and Their Extraordinary Story of Courage, Defiance, and Hope. Wendy Holden. HarperCollins 2015 400 p. map, illustrations $26.99 **940.531**
1. Mothers 2. Survival skills 3. Concentration camps
ISBN 0062370251; 9780062370259

This book by Wendy Holden "celebrates three mothers who defied death to give their children life. The Nazis murdered their husbands but concentration camp prisoners Priska, Rachel, and Anka would not let evil take their unborn children too." (Publisher's note) Holden draws on "interviews, letters, historical records, and personal visits to the sites where this story unfolded." (Kirkus Reviews)

"An engrossing, intense, and highly descriptive narrative chronicling the ghastly conditions three pregnant women suffered through at the hands of the Nazis." Kirkus

Simon, Marie Jalowicz

Underground in Berlin; A Young Woman's Extraordinary Tale of Survival in the Heart of Nazi Germany. Marie Jalowicz Simon; translated by Anthea Bell. Little, Brown & Co. 2015 384 p. illustrations, map $28 **940.531**
1. Jews -- Germany 2. Berlin (Germany) 3. Holocaust, 1939-1945
ISBN 0316382094; 9780316382090
LC 2015935821

This memoir tells how "in 1941, [author] Marie Jalowicz Simon, a nineteen-year-old Berliner, made an extraordinary decision. All around her, Jews were being rounded up for deportation, forced labor, and extermination. Marie took off her yellow star, turned her back on the Jewish community, and vanished into the city. In the years that followed, Marie lived under an assumed identity, forced to accept shelter wherever she found it." (Publisher's note)

Wallace, Max

In the name of humanity; the secret deal to end the Holocaust. Max Wallace. Two Rivers Distribution 2018 496 p. $26.99 **940.531**
1. Holocaust, 1939-1945 2. World War, 1939-1945 -- Poland 3. Auschwitz (Poland: Concentration camp)
ISBN 151073497X; 9781510734975

In this book, author Max Wallace "uncovers an astounding story involving the secret negotiations of an unlikely trio--a former fascist President of Switzerland, a courageous Orthodox Jewish woman, and [Heinrich] Himmler's Finnish osteopath--to end the Holocaust, aided by clandestine Swedish and American intelligence efforts. He documents their efforts to deceive Himmler, who, as Germany's defeat loomed, sought to enter an alliance with the West against the Soviet Union." (Publisher's note)

940.534

Fritzsche, Peter

An **iron** wind; Europe under Hitler. Peter Fritzsche. Basic Books 2016 376 p. (hardcover) $29.99; (ebook) $20.99 **940.534**
1. World War, 1939-1945 -- Europe 2. World War, 1939-1945 -- Occupied territories 3. Civilians in war -- Europe -- History -- 20th century 4. World War, 1939-1945 -- Personal narratives, European 5. Europe -- Social conditions -- 20th century 6. World War, 1939-1945 -- Social aspects -- Europe 7. War and society -- Europe -- History -- 20th century 8. Violence -- Social aspects -- Europe -- History -- 20th century
ISBN 9780465057740; 9780465096558
LC 2016018828

In this book about Europe during World War II, "historian Peter Fritzsche draws on diaries, letters, and other first-person accounts to show how civilians . . . struggled to understand this terrifying chaos. As the Third Reich targeted Europe's Jews for deportation and death, confusion and mistrust reigned. What were Hitler's aims? . . . Was collaboration or resistance the wisest response to occupation? . . . And where was God?" (Publisher's note)

"Fritzsche is adept at utilizing contemporary literature, memoirs, and correspondence to reconstruct the intellectual impact of Nazi occupation." LJ

Includes bibliographical references and index

Olson, Lynne

Last Hope Island; Britain, Occupied Europe, and the Brotherhood That Helped Turn the Tide of War. Lynne Olson. Random House Inc 2016 576 p. (hardback) $30 **940.534**
1. World War, 1939-1945 -- Europe 2. World War, 1939-1945 -- Diplomatic history 3. World War, 1939-1945 -- Governments in exile 4. World War, 1939-1945 -- Great Britain 5. Europe -- Politics and government -- 1918-1945 6. Exiles -- England -- London -- History -- 20th century 7. Europeans -- England -- London -- History -- 20th century 8. Government, Resistance to -- Europe -- History -- 20th century 9. Heads of state -- England -- London -- History -- 20th century 10. Political refugees -- England -- London -- History -- 20th century
ISBN 9780812997354
LC 2016019187

In this book, historian Lynne Olson "takes us back to those perilous days when the British and their European guests joined forces to combat the mightiest military force in history. Here we meet the courageous King Haakon of Norway, . . . his fiery Dutch counterpart, Queen Wilhelmina, . . . [and] the Earl of Suffolk, a swashbuckling British aristocrat. . . . [This book] recounts some of the Europeans' heretofore unsung exploits that helped tilt the balance against the Axis." (Publisher's note)

"The many individuals are finely drawn, major developments... are well covered, and the book provides an unusual and very insightful angle on the war." Booklist

Includes bibliographical references and index

940.54 Military history of World War II

Alperovitz, Gar

The **decision** to use the atomic bomb and the architecture of an American myth; {by} Gar Alperovitz with the assistance of Sanho Tree {et al.} Knopf 1995 843p hardcover o.p. pa $18 **940.54**
1. United States -- Foreign relations 2. World War, 1939-1945 -- United States 3. Hiroshima (Japan) -- Bombardment, 1945
ISBN 0-679-76285-X pa
LC 95-8778

"Alperovitz is the dean of revisionist scholars who argue that the nuclear bombing of Japan was unnecessary and that America bears a hefty responsibility for the cold war. . . . His main and probably most controversial contention is that certain documents pertaining to the decision were doctored, some by none other than Truman himself. Further, Alperovitz sees James Byrnes, Truman's Mephistophelian secretary of state, as a furtive player who nixed such alternative plans as modifying the unconditional-surrender demand and encouraging a Russian declaration of war." Booklist

Includes bibliographical references

Ambrose, Stephen E.

★ **Band** of brothers; E Company, 506th Regiment, 101st Airborne from Normandy to Hitler's Eagle's Nest. [by] Stephen Ambrose. Simon & Schuster 2001 333p il maps $25; pa $16 **940.54**

1. World War, 1939-1945 -- Europe 2. United States -- Army -- Parachute Infantry Regiment, 506th -- Company E

ISBN 0-7432-1638-5; 0-7432-2454-X pa

LC 2001-20134

A reissue of the title first published 1992

"Moving, poignant, and uplifting, this book is highly recommended for medium and large World War II collections." Booklist

Includes bibliographical references

Citizen soldiers; the U.S. Army from the Normandy beaches to the Bulge to the surrender of Germany, June 7, 1944-May 7, 1945. Simon & Schuster 1997 512p il maps hardcover o.p. pa $17 **940.54**

1. World War, 1939-1945 -- Campaigns -- France

ISBN 0-684-84801-5 pa

LC 97-23876

This continuation of D-Day focuses on the front-line experiences of American soldiers who fought in northwestern Europe in the war's last years

"These events have all been well documented, but in Ambrose's capable hands, the bloody and dramatic battles fought in northwest Europe in 1944-45 come alive as never before." N Y Times Book Rev

Includes bibliographical references

D-Day, June 6, 1944; the climactic battle of World War II. Simon & Schuster 1994 655p il maps $30; pa $17 **940.54**

1. Normandy (France), Attack on, 1944 2. World War, 1939-1945 -- Campaigns -- France

ISBN 0-671-88403-4; 0-684-80137-X pa

LC 93-40353

This is an account of the Allied invasion of Normandy in 1944. The author argues "that the invasion represented a triumph of the old United States Army, whose officers had transformed millions of civilians into a cohesive, highly trained and motivated mass army that, backed by a united nation, won with relative ease." (Christ Sci Monit) Index.

"Mr. Ambrose wonderfully illuminates the mind of the very young soldier of any nation anywhere who has never been in fighting before." N Y Times Book Rev

Includes bibliographical references

The **victors**; Eisenhower and his boys, the men of World War II. Simon & Schuster 1998 396p hardcover o.p. pa $16 **940.54**

1. Generals 2. Presidents 3. College presidents 4. United States -- Army 5. World War, 1939-1945 -- Campaigns

ISBN 0-684-85629-8 pa

LC 98-37808

"The author is a master of letting his subjects tell the story, of standing back and allowing the large lessons to unfold. The result is history with lasting impact." SLJ

Includes bibliographical references

The **wild** blue; the men and boys who flew the B-24s over Germany 1944-45. Simon & Schuster 2001 299p il $26; pa $16 **940.54**

1. Air pilots 2. B-24 bomber 3. Senators 4. Members of Congress 5. Government officials 6. Presidential candidates 7. World War, 1939-1945 -- Aerial operations

ISBN 0-7432-0339-9; 0-7432-2309-8 pa

LC 2001-20563

Ambrose presents profiles of American pilots who flew B-24 bombers focusing on the Dakota Queen piloted by future senator and presidential candidate George McGovern

"Ambrose's narrative flows smoothly, even as he manages to cover each man's story." Libr J

Includes bibliographical references

Atkinson, Rick, 1952-

★ An **army** at dawn; the war in North Africa, 1942-1943. Holt & Co. 2002 681p il maps (The liberation trilogy) $30; pa $16 **940.54**

1. Africa, North -- History, Military 2. World War, 1939-1945 -- North Africa 3. World War, 1939-1945 -- Campaigns -- North Africa 4. World War, 1939-1945 -- Campaigns -- Africa, North

ISBN 0-8050-6288-2; 0-8050-7448-1 pa

LC 2002-24130

This is the first volume of a projected World War II trilogy.

This "volume covers the conception of Operation Torch through the German surrender in Tunisia in May 1943. . . . An exemplary work that feeds anticipation of the succeeding volumes." Booklist

Includes bibliographical references

Followed by The day of battle (2007)

★ The **day** of battle; the war in Sicily and Italy, 1943-1944. H. Holt 2007 791p il map (The liberation trilogy) $35; pa $17 **940.54**

1. World War, 1939-1945 -- Campaigns -- Italy

ISBN 978-0-8050-6289-2; 0-805-06289-0; 978-0-8050-8861-8 pa; 0-8050-8861-X pa

LC 2007-7653

"The second volume of . . . [the author's] 'Liberation' trilogy, which began with the Pulitzer Prizewinning An Army at Dawn: The War in North Africa, 1942–1943, this is probably the most eagerly awaited World War II book of the year. Atkinson's clear prose, perceptive analysis, and grasp of the personalities and nuances of the campaigns make his book an essential purchase." Libr J

Includes bibliographical references

The **guns** at last light; the war in Western Europe, 1944-1945. Rick Atkinson. Henry Holt and Co. 2013 877 p. ill. (The liberation trilogy) $40 **940.54**

1. Generals 2. Soldiers 3. World War, 1939-1945 4. World War, 1939-1945 -- Campaigns -- Western Front

ISBN 0805062904; 9780805062908

LC 2012034312

This book concludes Rick Atkinson's series about World War II. "Peopling the pages [of the book] are German, British, French, Canadian, and (primarily) American generals and common soldiers. Excerpts from the letters of dead soldiers on both sides, as well as from the diaries of captain generals, fill out the story." (Publishers Weekly)

"[L]ively, occasionally lyric prose brings the vast theater of battle, from the beaches of Normandy deep into Germany, brilliantly alive." Pub Wkly

Includes bibliographical references (pages 813-841) and index

Bascomb, Neal

The **winter** fortress; the epic mission to sabotage Hitler's superbomb. Neal Bascomb. Houghton Mifflin Harcourt 2016 400 p. ill., portraits, maps (hardcover) $28　　**940.54**
　1. Atomic bomb　2. World War, 1939-1945　3. Atomic bomb -- Germany -- History　4. Sabotage -- Norway -- History -- 20th century　5. World War, 1939-1945 -- Germany -- Technology　6. World War, 1939-1945 -- Commando operations -- Norway　7. World War, 1939-1945 -- Underground movements -- Norway
ISBN 0544368053; 9780544368057

LC 2015042716

In this book, by Neal Bascomb, "It's 1942 and the Nazis are racing to be the first to build a weapon unlike any known before. They have the physicists, they have the uranium, and now all their plans depend on amassing a single ingredient: heavy water, which is produced in Norway's Vemork. . . . For the Allies, the plant must be destroyed. But how would they reach the castle fortress set on a precipitous gorge in one of the coldest, most inhospitable places on Earth?" (Publisher's note)

"Parts of the book read like an adventure novel, others like straightforward history, but the combination will appeal to readers of both WWII fiction and nonfiction." Booklist

Includes bibliographical references and index

Beevor, Antony, 1946-

Ardennes 1944; The Battle of the Bulge. by Antony Beevor. Penguin Group USA 2015 480 p. illustrations, maps $35　　**940.54**
　1. Ardennes (France), Battle of the, 1944-1945　2. World War, 1914-1918 -- Campaigns -- France
ISBN 0670025313; 9780670025312

LC 2015490442

In this book, historian Antony Beevor "reconstructs the Battle of the Bulge. . . . On December 16, 1944, Hitler launched his 'last gamble' in the snow-covered forests and gorges of the Ardennes in Belgium. . . . The allies, taken by surprise, found themselves fighting two panzer armies. Belgian civilians abandoned their homes. . . . Panic spread even to Paris. While some American soldiers, overwhelmed by the German onslaught, fled or surrendered, others held on heroically." (Publisher's note)

"Beevor skewers the pretensions and weaknesses of generals and details atrocities and mistreatment of both civilians and surrendering enemies by both sides. The author takes for granted more knowledge of the battle, the terrain, and the German language than general readers may possess, and he occasionally repeats information attentive readers will recall from previous mentions. But these are small quibbles. On the whole, this is a treasure of memorable portraits, striking details, fascinating revelations, and broad insights—likely to be the definitive account of the battle for years to come. Essential reading for anyone interested in World War II." Kirkus

The **Battle** of Arnhem; the deadliest airborne operation of WWII, 1944. Antony Beevor. Viking 2018 496 p. (hbk.) $31.50　　**940.54**
　1. Strategy　2. World War, 1939-1945　3. Arnhem, Battle of, Netherlands, 1944　4. Arnhem, Battle of, Arnhem, Netherlands, 1944
ISBN 9780525429821; 0525429824

In this book author Antony Beevor "reconstructs the devastating airborne battle of Arnhem. . . . Using often overlooked sources from Dutch, American, British, Polish, and German archives, [he] has reconstructed the terrible reality of the fighting, which General Student called 'The Last German Victory.' Yet The Battle of Arnhem, written with Beevor's inimitable style and gripping narrative, is about much more than a single dramatic battle--it looks into the very heart of war." (Publisher's note)

Includes bibliographical references and index

D-day; the Battle for Normandy. Viking 2009 591p il map $32.95　　**940.54**
　1. Normandy (France), Attack on, 1944
ISBN 978-0-670-02119-2

LC 2009-23574

This "is a vibrant work of history that honors the sacrifice of tens of thousands of men and women." Time

Includes bibliographical references

The **fall** of Berlin 1945. Viking 2002 xxxvii, 489p il maps $29.95; pa $16　　**940.54**
　1. Berlin, Battle of, 1945　2. World War, 1939-1945 -- Germany
ISBN 0-670-03041-4; 0-14-200280-1 pa

LC 2002-510674

The author "relies on material from American, German, British, French, and Swedish archives and documents from former Soviet files, making the book an invaluable and meticulous account." Booklist

Includes bibliographical references (p. 466-475) and index

The **Second** World War; Antony Beevor. Little, Brown & Co 2012 xii, 863 p.p　　**940.54**
　1. Military history　2. World War, 1939-1945　3. Europe -- History -- 1918-1945
ISBN 0316023744; 9780316023740

LC 2012007028

In this book on World War II Anthony Beevor describes how "the war was set in motion by a single person--Adolf Hitler--and its extension reflected specific decisions by specific people, and its course changed lives across the globe in ways impossible to predict. . . . And from heads of state to front-line riflemen, from field marshals to teenaged girls, Beevor's protagonists exercise choice in the context of 'the greatest man-made disaster in history.'" (Publishers Weekly)

Includes bibliographical references and index.

Blum, Howard

The **Last** Goodnight; A World War II Story of Espionage, Adventure, and Betrayal. Howard Blum. Harper Collins Publishers 2016 528 p. illustrations (hardcover) $28.99　**940.54**
　1. Women spies　2. World War, 1939-1945 -- Secret service　3. Women spies -- United States -- Biography　4. World War, 1939-1945 -- Secret service -- United States　5. Espionage, American -- Europe -- History -- 20th century
ISBN 9780062307675; 9780062307798; 9780062307804

LC 2015019329

This book, by Howard Blum, offers a "biography of Betty Pack, the dazzling American debutante who became an Allied spy during WWII and was hailed by OSS chief General 'Wild Bill' Donovan as 'the greatest unsung heroine of the war.' . . . Beneath Betty's cool, professional determination, Blum reveals a troubled woman conflicted by the very traits that made her successful." (Publisher's note)

"Occasionally breathless and torrid in description, this is a well-documented work that certainly never bores." Kirkus

Includes bibliographical references

Bradley, James

Flags of our fathers; [by] James Bradley with Ron Powers.
Bantam Bks. 2000 376p $24.95; pa $14   **940.54**

1. Iwo Jima, Battle of, 1945 2. Photojournalists 3. United States
-- Marine Corps

ISBN 0-553-11133-7; 0-553-38415-5 pa

LC 00-25803

This is the "story of the most famous photograph to come out of
World War II, the flag-raising on Mount Suribachi during the Battle of
Iwo Jima in February 1945. Bradley is the son of one of the six men
immortalized in that remarkable photo, and his gripping narrative, vivid
descriptions, and heartfelt style make this a powerful story of courage,
humility, and tragedy." Libr J

Includes bibliographical references

Breitman, Richard

Official secrets; what the Nazis planned, what the British
and Americans knew. Hill & Wang 1998 325p hardcover o.p.
pa $22   **940.54**

1. Holocaust, 1933-1945 2. World War, 1939-1945 -- Atrocities 3.
Germany -- Politics and government -- 1933-1945

ISBN 0-8090-3819-6; 0-8090-0184-5 pa

LC 98-7997

This "is a remarkable study, concise yet carefully nuanced." N Y
Times Book Rev

Includes bibliographical references

Brokaw, Tom

An **album** of memories; personal histories from the greatest generation. Random House 2001 314p il maps $29.95; pa
$14.95   **940.54**

1. United States -- History -- 1933-1945 2. World War, 1939-1945
-- Personal narratives

ISBN 0-375-50581-4; 0-375-76041-5 pa

LC 2001-273436

This volume "gathers letters written to Brokaw by Americans who
lived through the Depression and World War II and, in some cases,
letters written by their children. Brokaw provides a brief introduction
and a time line for each chapter; these cover the Depression, the war in
Europe and in the Pacific, and the wartime 'home front,' closing with
'Reflections.' The book is lavishly illustrated with reproductions of
photographs, drawings, documents, and other memorabilia of the era."
Booklist

Burgin, R. V.

Islands of the damned; a Marine at war in the Pacific. [by]
R.V. Burgin with William Marvel. New American Library 2010
296p il $24.95   **940.54**

1. World War, 1939-1945 -- Pacific Ocean 2. World War, 1939-
1945 -- Personal narratives

ISBN 978-0-451-22990-8

LC 2009-40454

"As this well-written, excellently detailed personal narrative makes
clear, some Marines who fought alongside him did not make it home
alive. They and thousands more died amid war's confusing and unspeakable horrors. Sometimes they were killed by the enemy, sometimes by
friendly fire, sometimes by accidents, and sometimes by shocking, split-
second decisions where one life was sacrificed to save others. . . . Time
is thinning the ranks of America's Pacific War veterans. But Islands of
the Damned is a taut, engrossing, haunting book that will help keep their
accomplishments and enormous sacrifices alive." Dallas Morning News

Burleigh, Michael

Moral combat; good and evil in World War II. Harper 2011
xxi, 650p il map $29.95   **940.54**

1. World War, 1939-1945 -- Ethical aspects

ISBN 978-0-06-058097-1; 0-06-058097-6

First published 2010 in the United Kingdom

"No-one with an interest in the Second World War should be without
this book; and indeed nor should anyone who cares about how our world
has come about." Daily Telegraph

Includes bibliographical references

Clark, Lloyd

Blitzkrieg; Myth, Reality, and Hitler's Lightning War:
France 1940. Lloyd Clark. Atlantic Monthly Press 2016 480
p. illustrations, maps $27   **940.54**

1. Military history 2. Strategy -- History 3. World War, 1939-
1945 4. Dunkerque (France), Battle of, 1940 5. Ardennes (France),
Battle of the, 1944-1945

ISBN 0802125131; 9780802125132

This book by Lloyd Clark delivers a new history of Germany's 1940
invasion of France. "Germans launched a military offensive in France .
. . that married superb intelligence, the latest military thinking, and new
technology to achieve . . . what their fathers had failed to achieve in . . .
the First World War. It was a . . . victory, altering the balance of power in
Europe in one stroke, and convinced the entire world that the Nazi war
machine was unstoppable." (Publisher's note)

"A solid, well-documented military history, Clark's newest work
will appeal to anyone interested in World War II and early operations on
the western front." LJ

Includes bibliographical references (pages 420-439) and index.

Conant, Jennet

A **covert** affair; Julia Child and Paul Child in the OSS.
Simon & Schuster 2011 395p il $28   **940.54**

1. Cooks 2. Artists 3. Diplomats 4. Intelligence service 5.
Anticommunist movements 6. Television personalities 7. Senators
8. Cookbook writers 9. Spouses of prominent persons 10. World
War, 1939-1945 -- Secret service 11. United States -- Office of
Strategic Services 12. United States -- Politics and government
-- 1945-1953 13. World War, 1939-1945 -- Secret service -- United
States 14. Anti-communist movements -- United States -- History
-- 20th century

ISBN 978-1-4391-6352-8; 978-1-4391-6850-9 ebook

LC 2011-02875

This is an "account of Julia and Paul Child's experiences as members of the Office of Strategic Services (OSS) in the Far East during
World War II." (Publisher's note) Index.

"Paul and Julia Child are merely supporting players in this book
about the Office of Strategic Services in World War II and the McCarthy
witch hunts that followed. Despite this blatant marketing ploy, the book
is a well-researched and well-written account of this period in American
history." Seattle Times

Includes bibliographical references

The **irregulars**; Roald Dahl and the British spy ring in
wartime Washington. Simon & Schuster 2008 xx, 393p il
$27.95   **940.54**

1. Authors 2. Children's authors 3. Short story writers 4.
Intelligence service -- Great Britain 5. World War, 1939-1945 --
Secret service

ISBN 978-0-7432-9458-4; 0-7432-9458-0

LC 2008-12483

Conant tells the story of young writer Roald Dahl who is assigned by His Majesty's Government to Washington, D.C. as a diplomat to gather intelligence about America's isolationist circles. In the course of his "spying," he meets or works closely with David Ogilvy, Ian Fleming, and the great spymaster William Stephenson (aka Intrepid).

"Entertaining social history that also reveals a little-known aspect of an important literary figure's life." Kirkus

Includes bibliographical references

Corera, Gordon

Operation Columba; the Secret Pigeon Service: the untold story of World War II resistance in Europe. Gordon Corera. William Morrow 2018 352 p. (hardcover) $28.99 **940.54**
1. Espionage 2. Homing pigeons -- War use 3. World War, 1939-1945 -- Military intelligence -- Great Britain 4. World War, 1939-1945 -- Communications 5. Homing pigeons -- War use -- Great Britain 6. Great Britain. MI6 -- History -- 20th century 7. World War, 1939-1945 -- Underground movements -- Belgium
ISBN 0062667076; 9780062667076
LC 2018017421

This book, by Gordon Corera, tells the "untold story of how British intelligence secretly used homing pigeons as part of a clandestine espionage operation to gather information, communicate, and coordinate with members of the Resistance to defeat the Nazis in occupied Europe during World War II. . . . Corera uses declassified documents and extensive original research to tell the story of the Operation Columba and the Secret Pigeon Service for the first time." (Publisher's note)

Includes bibliographical references and index

Costello, John

The **Pacific** War. Quill 1982 742p il $21.95 **940.54**
1. World War, 1939-1945 -- Pacific Ocean
ISBN 0-688-01620-0; 978-0-688-01620-3
LC 82-15054

First published 1981 by Rawson, Wade

A "history of World War II as it was played out in the Pacific theater. . . . Emphasizing the role played by Allied intelligence sources during the early period of the war, Costello analyzes the actual battles from Pearl Harbor to the atomic bombing of Japan." Booklist

Includes bibliographical references

Curtis, Brian

Fields of Battle; Pearl Harbor, the Rose Bowl, and the Boys Who Went to War. by Brian Curtis. St. Martin's Press 2016 320 p. $29.99 **940.54**
1. Football players 2. College football -- History 3. World War, 1939-1945 -- United States
ISBN 1250059585; 9781250059581
LC 2016020829

This book by Brian Curtis recalls how, "in the wake of the bombing of Pearl Harbor, the 1942 Rose Bowl was moved from Pasadena to Duke University out of fear of further Japanese attacks on the West Coast. Shortly after this unforgettable game, many of the players and coaches left their respective colleges, entered the military, and went on to serve around the world in famous battlegrounds, . . . where fate and destiny would bring them back together." (Publisher's note)

"A fine sports book with a stirring extra dimension." Kirkus

Includes bibliographical references and index.

Dando-Collins, Stephen

The **big** break; Stephen Dando-Collins. St. Martin's Press 2017 272 p. illustrations, maps (ebook) $60; (hardback)

$27.99 **940.54**
1. World War, 1939-1945 2. Soldiers -- United States -- Biography 3. World War, 1939-1945 -- Prisoners and prisons 4. Oflag 64 (Concentration camp) 5. Americans -- Poland -- Szubin -- Biography 6. United States. Army -- Officers -- Biography 7. Prisoners of war -- Poland -- Szubin -- Biography 8. World War, 1939-1945 -- Prisoners and prisons, German 9. World War, 1939-1945 -- Concentration camps -- Poland -- Szubin 10. Prisoner-of-war escapes -- Poland -- Szubin -- History -- 20th century
ISBN 9781250087577; 9781250087560
LC 2016037566

This book, by Stephen Dando-Collins, follows prisoners of war "including General Eisenhower's personal aide, General Patton's son-in-law, and Ernest Hemingway's eldest son as they struggled to be free. Military historian and Paul Brickhill biographer Stephen Dando-Collins expertly chronicles this gripping story of Americans determined to be free, brave Poles risking their lives to help them, and dogmatic Nazis determined to stop them." (Publisher's note)

"An exciting account from a passionate author who has done the necessary research." Kirkus

Includes bibliographical references and index

Daws, Gavan

Prisoners of the Japanese; POWs of World War II in the Pacific. Morrow 1994 462p il map hardcover o.p. pa $19.95 **940.54**
1. Prisoners of war 2. World War, 1939-1945 -- Pacific Ocean 3. World War, 1939-1945 -- Prisoners and prisons
ISBN 0-688-11812-7; 0-688-14370-9 pa
LC 93-49363

"Daws offers a well-written thoroughly researched account of these POWs. . . . An exceptionally worthwhile addition to the literature on the war in the Pacific." Booklist

Includes bibliographical references

Dimbleby, Jonathan

The **Battle** of the Atlantic; how the allies won the war. Jonathan Dimbleby. Oxford University Press 2016 560 p. illustrations, maps $34.95 **940.54**
1. World War, 1939-1945 -- Campaigns 2. World War, 1939-1945 -- Naval operations 3. World War, 1939-1945 -- Campaigns -- Atlantic Ocean 4. World War, 1939-1945 -- Naval operations -- Submarine
ISBN 9780190495855
LC 2015032726

This book, by Jonathan Dimbleby, focuses on the "Battle of the Atlantic and the men who fought it. . . . Had Germany succeeded in cutting off the supply of American ships, England might not have held out. Yet had Churchill siphoned reinforcements to the naval effort earlier, thousands of lives might have been preserved. The battle consisted of not one but hundreds of battles, ranging from hours to days in duration, and forcing both sides into constant innovation." (Publisher's note)

"The history of the battle for the Atlantic is well documented, but Dimbleby's work, with its emphasis on the strategic importance of the battle, is an excellent addition to the story, and expert historians as well as general readers can enjoy this effort." Pub Wkly

Includes bibliographical references and index

Doyle, William

PT 109; an American epic of war, survival, and the destiny of John F. Kennedy. William Doyle. William Morrow 2015 352 p. 8 plates; illustrations; maps (hardcover) $27.99 **940.54**
1. World War, 1939-1945 -- Naval operations 2. PT-109 (Torpedo

boat) 3. World War, 1939-1945 -- Naval operations, American 4. World War, 1939-1945 -- Campaigns -- Solomon Islands
ISBN 9780062346582; 9780062346599

LC 2015021575

This book, by William Doyle, tells "the extraordinary World War II story of shipwreck and survival that paved John F. Kennedy's path to power. . . . Author William Doyle has crafted a thrilling and definitive account of the sinking of PT 109 and its shipwrecked crew's heroics. . . . The story's second act . . . explores in new detail how this extraordinary episode shaped Kennedy's character and fate, proving instrumental to achieving his presidential ambitions." (Publisher's note)

"Dramatic and revealing. Readers unfamiliar with the Joe Kennedy back story will be startled to learn of his puppet master-like role in orchestrating JFK's rise to the presidency." Kirkus

Includes bibliographical references and index

Drury, Bob

Lucky 666; The Impossible Mission. by Bob Drury and Tom Clavin. Simon & Schuster 2016 368 p. illustrations, map (hardcover) $30 **940.54**

1. Bomber pilots -- United States -- Biography 2. World War, 1939-1945 -- Aerial operations -- United States 3. B-17 bomber 4. World War, 1939-1945 -- Campaigns -- Pacific Area 5. World War, 1939-1945 -- Aerial operations, American 6. World War, 1939-1945 -- Regimental histories -- United States 7. United States. Army Air Forces. Bombardment Group, 22nd -- Biography
ISBN 9781476774855; 9781476774862

LC 2016017924

This book, by Bob Drury and Tom Clavin, tells the "untold story of a daredevil bomber pilot and his misfit crew who fly their lone B-17 into the teeth of the Japanese Empire in 1943, engage in the longest dogfight in history, and change the momentum of the War in the Pacific--but not without making the ultimate sacrifice." (Publisher's note)

"Drury and Clavin offer a vivid slice of war history that WWII buffs and anyone who admires true acts of heroism will find riveting." Booklist

Includes bibliographical references and index

Duffy, James P., 1941-

War at the end of the world; Douglas MacArthur and the forgotten fight for New Guinea, 1942-1945. James P. Duffy. NAL Caliber 2016 448 p. illustrations, maps $28 **940.54**

1. World War, 1939-1945 -- Campaigns -- New Guinea
ISBN 9780451418302

LC 2015019828

This book, by James P. Duffy, is an "account of an epic, yet nearly forgotten, battle of World War II—General Douglas MacArthur's four-year assault on the Pacific War's most hostile battleground: the mountainous, jungle-cloaked island of New Guinea." (Publisher's note)

"Duffy's portrait of the South Pacific is an entertaining and well-researched war history that will satisfy intrigued novices and devoted students alike." Kirkus

Includes bibliographical references and index

Dunnigan, James F.

The **Pacific** War encyclopedia; {by} James F. Dunnigan and Albert A. Nofi. Facts on File 1998 2v il maps set $137.50 **940.54**

1. Reference books 2. World War, 1939-1945 -- Encyclopedias
ISBN 0-8160-3439-7

LC 97-15634

This work "is lively as well as informative, and . . . will be attractive to military buffs while still useful to more serious researchers." Libr J

Felton, Mark

Zero Night; the untold story of World War Two's greatest escape. Mark Felton. Thomas Dunne Books/St. Martin's Press 2015 320 p. illustrations, maps (hardcover) $25.99 **940.54**

1. Escapes 2. World War, 1939-1945 -- Prisoners and prisons 3. Oflag VI B (Concentration camp) 4. World War, 1939-1945 -- Germany -- Warburg 5. World War, 1939-1945 -- Prisoners and prisons, German 6. Prisoners of war -- Germany -- Warburg -- History -- 20th century 7. Prisoner-of-war escapes -- Germany -- Warburg -- History -- 20th century
ISBN 9781250073747

LC 2015017591

This book, by Mark Felton, describes how "on August 30, 1942 - 'Zero Night' - 40 Allied officers staged . . . [a] mass escape. . . . Months of meticulous planning and secret training hung in the balance during three minutes of mayhem as the officers boldly stormed the huge double fences at Oflag Prison. . . . The highly coordinated effort succeeded and set 36 men free into the German countryside." (Publisher's note)

"The author grippingly tracks the evaders' trek to freedom, an event that would warrant a book in itself. Even the epilogue will bring a smile. In this exciting book, Felton has captivatingly captured the bravery of the prisoners." Kirkus

Includes bibliographical references and index

Frank, Richard B.

★ **Downfall**; the end of the Imperial Japanese Empire. Penguin 2001 484p il map pa $18 **940.54**

1. Japan -- History -- 1868-1945 2. World War, 1939-1945 -- Japan 3. World War, 1939-1945 -- Aerial operations
ISBN 0-14-100146-1

First published 1999 by Random House

"Weaving together the strands of military and diplomatic events, Frank contends that absent the bombings of Hiroshima and Nagasaki the war would have continued for at least several more months, at a cost in Japanese and Allied civilian and combatant lives far in excess of the admittedly awful toll that the atomic bombs exacted. A powerful work of history." Libr J

Includes bibliographical references

Freeman, Sally Mott

The **Jersey** brothers; a missing naval officer in the Pacific and his family's quest to bring him home. Sally Mott Freeman. Simon & Schuster 2017 xiv, 588 p.p illustrations (hardcover) $28 **940.54**

1. Prisoners of war 2. World War, 1939-1945 -- Prisoners and prisons 3. Prisoners of war -- Philippines -- Biography 4. United States. Navy -- Officers -- Biography 5. World War, 1939-1945 -- Campaigns -- Philippines 6. World War, 1939-1945 -- Prisoners and prisons, Japanese 7. World War, 1939-1945 -- Concentration camps -- Philippines
ISBN 1501104144; 9781501104145; 9781501104176

LC 2016021592

This book, by Sally Mott Freeman, tells "the extraordinary, real-life adventure of three brothers [during] . . . World War II and their mad race to change history--and save one of their own. . . . [It] is a . . . story of agony and triumph--from the home front to Roosevelt's White House, and Pearl Harbor to Midway and Bataan. . . . And it is, above all, a story of brotherly love: of three men finding their loyalty to each other tested under the tortures of war." (Publisher's note)

"A grieving family ultimately finds closure in this meticulously researched and compelling history." Kirkus

Includes bibliographical references (pages 565-574).

Geroux, William

The **Mathews** Men; Seven Brothers and the War Against Hitler's U-boats. by William Geroux. Penguin Group USA 2016 400 p. ill., maps, portraits $28 **940.54**
1. Virginia -- History 2. Merchant marine -- United States 3. World War, 1939-1945 -- United States
ISBN 0525428151; 9780525428152

This book, by William Geroux, focuses on "One of the last unheralded heroic stories of World War II: the U-boat assault off the American coast against the men of the U.S. Merchant Marine who were supplying the European war, and one community's monumental contribution to that effort. Mathews County, Virginia, is a remote outpost on the Chesapeake Bay with little to offer except unspoiled scenery—but it sent an unusually large concentration of sea captains to fight in World War II." (Publisher's note)

"Geroux presents an unflinching, inspiring, and long-delayed tribute to the sacrifice of these men." Booklist

Includes bibliographical references (pages 371-375) and index.

Giangreco, D. M.

Hell to pay; Operation Downfall and the invasion of Japan, 1945-47. Naval Institute Press 2009 xxiii, 362p il map $36.95 **940.54**
1. World War, 1939-1945 -- Campaigns -- Japan
ISBN 978-1-59114-316-1

LC 2009-27766

"Illustrative of just how much the war with Japan was a close-run thing, this is essential reading." Libr J

Includes bibliographical references

Glass, Charles

The **deserters**; a hidden history of World War II. Charles Glass. The Penguin Press 2013 400 p. (hardcover) $27.95 **940.54**
1. Military desertion 2. World War, 1939-1945 3. Military policy -- United States 4. Combat -- Psychological aspects 5. World War, 1939-1945 -- Desertions 6. Military deserters -- History -- 20th century 7. World War, 1939-1945 -- Psychological aspects 8. Desertion, Military -- History -- 20th century
ISBN 1594204284; 9781101617816; 9781594204289

LC 2012046881

This book follows three World War II soldiers court-martialed for desertion. "Tracking in detail the wartime biographies of three privates in the infantry—Tennessee farm boy Alfred Whitehead, Brooklyner Steve Weiss and Britisher John Bain—the author constructs a frame for his much broader . . . discussion of military personnel policy." (Kirkus Reviews)

Includes bibliographical references and index

The **good** war; an oral history of World War Two. [edited by] Studs Terkel. New Press 1997 589p pa $16.95 **940.54**
1. World War, 1939-1945 -- Personal narratives
ISBN 1-56584-343-6

LC 2003-389322

First published 1984 by Pantheon Bks.

In a series of interviews Terkel depicts how WWII affected the lives of average Americans.

Grayling, A. C.

Among the dead cities; the history and moral legacy of the WWII bombing of civilians in Germany and Japan. Walker & Co. 2006 361p il maps $25.95 **940.54**
1. World War, 1939-1945 -- Ethical aspects 2. World War, 1939-1945 -- Aerial operations
ISBN 0-8027-1471-4

LC 2005-58597

"Was it wrong for the Allies to bomb German and Japanese civilians in World War II? In this book, . . . [the author] attends to one of the twentieth-century's largest unexploded moral conundrums. . . . Grayling's book builds careful, generous cases for and against the bombing, admitting as evidence both the experience of the bombed as well as the bombers." Booklist

Includes bibliographical references

Groom, Winston

The **generals**; Patton, MacArthur, Marshall, and the winning of World War II. by Winston Groom. National Geographic 2015 496 p. maps; 16 plates (hardcover: alk. paper) $30 **940.54**
1. Generals 2. World War, 1939-1945 -- United States 3. Generals -- United States -- Biography 4. World War, 1939-1945 -- United States -- Biography
ISBN 9781426215490

LC 2015021562

This book, by Winston Groom, "tells the intertwined and uniquely American tales of George Patton, Douglas MacArthur, and George Marshall - from the World War I battle that shaped them to their greatest victory: leading the allies to victory in World War II. These three remarkable men-of-arms who rose from the gruesome hell of the First World War to become the finest generals of their generation during World War II redefined America's ideas of military leadership." (Publisher's note)

"There is much material on the battle tactics of both World Wars, which should appeal to military buffs, while general readers will welcome a review of the facts about these men conveyed through felicitous prose." LJ

Includes bibliographical references and index

Ham, Paul

Hiroshima Nagasaki; the real story of the atomic bombings and their aftermath. Paul Ham. Doubleday 2012 ix, 629 p.p ill. (some color), maps (hbk.) $35 **940.54**
1. Atomic bomb -- History 2. Nagasaki (Japan) -- Bombardment, 1945 3. Hiroshima (Japan) -- Bombardment, 1945 4. Atomic bomb victims -- Japan 5. World War, 1939-1945 -- Japan -- Nagasaki-shi 6. World War, 1939-1945 -- Japan -- Hiroshima-shi 7. Atomic bomb -- Government policy -- United States -- History -- 20th century 8. Nagasaki-shi (Japan) -- History -- Bombardment, 1945 -- Moral and ethical aspects 9. Hiroshima-shi (Japan) -- History -- Bombardment, 1945 -- Moral and ethical aspects
ISBN 1250047110; 9781448126279; 1448126274; 9781250047113

LC 2012515240

"In this harrowing history of the Hiroshima and Nagasaki bombings, Paul Ham argues against the use of nuclear weapons, drawing on extensive research and hundreds of interviews to prove that the bombings had little impact on the eventual outcome of the Pacific War. More than 100,000 people were killed instantly by the atomic bombs. . . . Many hundreds of thousands more succumbed to their horrific injuries later, or slowly perished of radiation-related sickness." (Publisher's note)

"A valuable contribution to the literature of World War II that asks its readers to rethink much of what they've been taught about America's just cause." Kirkus

Includes bibliographical references and index

Hamilton, Nigel, 1944-

The **mantle** of command; FDR at war, 1941-1942. Nigel

Hamilton. Houghton Mifflin Harcourt 2014 528 p. illustrations, maps (hardcover) $30   **940.54**

1. Strategy 2. World War, 1939-1945 -- United States 3. World War, 1939-1945 -- Campaigns 4. Command of troops -- United States -- Case studies 5. World War, 1939-1945 -- United States -- Biography 6. United States -- Foreign relations -- Great Britain
ISBN 0547775245; 9780544227842; 9780547775241

LC 2013045586

National Books Award: Nonfiction Longlist (2014)

"Based on years of archival research and interviews with the last surviving aides and Roosevelt family members, Nigel Hamilton offers a definitive account of FDR's masterful--and underappreciated--command of the Allied war effort. Hamilton takes readers inside FDR's White House Oval Study--his personal command center--and into the meetings where he battled with Churchill about strategy and tactics and overrode the near mutinies of his own generals and secretary of war." (Publisher's note)

"Though it's a weighty tome, and is based extensively on Roosevelt's own notes, Hamilton keeps a brisk pace throughout to produce what will likely be seen as a definitive volume on this aspect of Roosevelt's career." Pub Wkly

Includes bibliographical references and index

Hammel, Eric

Two flags over Iwo Jima; solving the mystery of the U.S. Marine Corps' proudest moment. Eric Hammel. Casemate Publishers 2018 222 p. illustrations, plates, maps $29.95   **940.54**

1. Historical literature 2. Iwo Jima, Battle of, 1945
ISBN 1612006299; 9781612006291

In this book, author Eric Hammel "reveals the all-but-forgotten first-flag raising, and the aftermath of the popularization campaign undertaken by the post-WWII Marine Corps and national press. Hammel attempts to untangle the various battles which led up to the first and second flag raisings, as well as following the men of the 28th Marine Regiment in the events which took place after." (Publisher's note)

Includes bibliographical references and index

Hanson, Victor Davis, 1953-

The **second** world wars; how the first global conflict was fought and won. Victor Davis Hanson. Basic Books 2017 xxi, 652 p.p illustrations (hardcover) $40   **940.54**

1. World War, 1939-1945 2. World War, 1939-1945 -- Campaigns
ISBN 9781541698567; 0465066984; 9780465066988

LC 2017024227

This book on World War II, by Victor Davis Hanson, "examines how combat unfolded in the air, at sea, and on land to show how distinct conflicts among disparate combatants coalesced into one interconnected global war. . . . Hanson argues that despite its novel industrial barbarity, neither the war's origins nor its geography were unusual. Nor was its ultimate outcome surprising." (Publisher's note)

"An ingenious, always provocative analysis of history's most lethal war." Kirkus

Includes bibliographical references (pages 531-632) and index.

Harding, Stephen

Last to die; a defeated empire, a forgotten mission, and the last American killed in World War II. Stephen Harding. Da Capo Press 2015 vii, 253 p.p 16 plates; maps (hardcover: alk. paper) $26.99   **940.54**

1. World War, 1939-1945 -- Aerial operations -- Japan 2. Pottstown (Pa.) -- Biography 3. World War, 1939-1945 -- Aerial operations, American 4. World War, 1939-1945 -- Campaigns -- Japan -- Tokyo

5. World War, 1939-1945 -- Reconnaissance operations, American 6. United States. Army Air Forces -- Aerial gunners -- Biography 7. United States. Army Air Forces. Photo Reconnaissance Squadron, 20th -- Biography
ISBN 0306823381; 9780306823381

LC 2015003486

This book, by Stephen Harding, describes the events surrounding the final U.S. combat death of World War II. "Based on official American and Japanese histories, personal memoirs, and the author's exclusive interviews with many of the story's key participants, . . . [this book] is a . . . tale of air combat, bravery, cowardice, hubris, and determination, all set during the turbulent and confusing final days of World War II." (Publisher's note)

"Harding treats the youth with admiration and affection that elicit compassion without becoming cloying or melodramatic. This is a superb look at the life and death of one young man among millions of others who loved, were loved by others, and died too soon." Booklist

Includes bibliographical references (pages 213-221) and index

Hastings, Max

Armageddon: the battle for Germany, 1944-45. A.A. Knopf 2004 584p il maps $30   **940.54**

1. World War, 1939-1945
ISBN 0-375-41433-9

LC 2004-46468

The author "tells the grim tale of the final collapse of the Third Reich. It does so from the viewpoints of the upper millstone (the Western Allies), the lower millstone (the Russians) and the grain being ground in between (the Germans). The research includes previously untapped Russian archives (particularly in the accounts of Soviet veterans) and leads to a gripping and horrifying story that serious students of military history will find almost impossible to put down." Publ Wkly

Includes bibliographical references

Inferno; by Max Hastings. Alfred A. Knopf 2011 xx, 729 p.p [48] p. of plates ill maps   **940.54**

1. Military history 2. World War, 1939-1945 3. Military art and science -- History
ISBN 9780307273598

LC 2011013890

'This book "offers an account of the [Second World] war that concentrates on the lived experience of the men and women who took part in it. On almost every page there is . . . material from interviews, diaries, letters, memoirs and personal documents of many kinds. . . . This is at its core very much a military history, despite the space devoted to the experiences of civilians. . . . [Author Max] Hastings argues that the navies of the United Kingdom and the United States were their best fighting forces; he thinks the armies of the two Allied powers were mostly no match for the ruthless fighting prowess of the Germans and Japanese, whose willingness to sacrifice themselves contrasted with the care taken by Allied generals to minimize casualties among their own men. Red Army troops behaved in a manner not unlike that of the Germans, their reckless disregard for their own safety driven on by the knowledge that the Soviet secret police would shoot them if they hesitated." (N Y Times)

Includes bibliographical references and index.

Retribution; the battle for Japan, 1944-45. Alfred A. Knopf 2008 615p il map $35   **940.54**

1. World War, 1939-1945 -- Japan
ISBN 978-0-307-26351-3; 0-307-26351-7

LC 2007-34202

First published 2007 in the United Kingdom with title: Nemesis

This chronicle of the final year of the Pacific war discusses such topics as the events leading to Allied victory, Japan's war against China, and the decision to bomb Hiroshima and Nagasaki.

"Encompassing the British, Chinese, and Soviet roles in vanquishing Japan, Hastings is both comprehensive and finely acute in this masterful interpretive narrative." Booklist

Includes bibliographical references

The **secret** war; Spies, Ciphers, and Guerrillas, 1939-1945. by Max Hastings. HarperCollins 2016 640 p. illustrations $35 **940.54**
1. Spies 2. Espionage 3. Intelligence service 4. World War, 1939-1945 -- Military intelligence
ISBN 006225927X; 9780062259271

This book, by Max Hastings, "is a sweeping examination of one of the most important yet underexplored aspects of World War II—intelligence—showing how espionage successes and failures by the United States, Britain, Russia, Germany, and Japan influenced the course of the war and its final outcome." (Publisher's note)

"This wide-ranging account is filled with compelling characters, some admirable, others morally dubious. Hastings also illustrates that even great intelligence coups can be wasted by politicians who fail to properly utilize the information." Booklist

Includes bibliographical references (pages 579-585) and index.

Haynes, Fred
The **lions** of Iwo Jima; [by] Fred Haynes and James A. Warren. Henry Holt 2008 272p il map $26; pa $17 **940.54**
1. Iwo Jima, Battle of, 1945 2. World War, 1939-1945 -- Personal narratives 3. United States -- Marine Corps -- Marines, 28th
ISBN 978-0-8050-8325-5; 0-8050-8325-1; 978-0-8050-9017-8 pa; 0-8050-9017-7 pa

LC 2007-42245

"The account focuses on the experience of Combat Team 28, a unit of 4,500 marines; their best-known accomplishment was the raising of the flag atop Mount Suribachi. However, that event, immortalized by the classic photograph, occurred only four days into the monthlong battle. Ahead lay a cauldron of merciless slaughter, with marines inching forward against Japanese troops entrenched in a series of interlocking caves and tunnels. The authors capture the horror of their advance as close-range combat in confined areas became the norm. This is a disturbing, sometimes sickening chronicle, but the harsh face of war in the Pacific theater has rarely been portrayed so effectively." Booklist

Includes bibliographical references

Hellbeck, Jochen
Stalingrad; the city that defeated the Third Reich. Jochen Hellbeck. PublicAffairs 2015 500 p. illustrations (hardcover) $29.99 **940.54**
1. Stalingrad, Battle of, 1942-1943 2. World War, 1939-1945 -- Soviet Union 3. Stalingrad, Battle of, Volgograd, Russia, 1942-1943 4. Stalingrad, Battle of, Volgograd, Russia, 1942-1943 -- Personal narratives, German 5. Stalingrad, Battle of, Volgograd, Russia, 1942-1943 -- Personal narratives, Russian
ISBN 1610394968; 9781610394963

LC 2015002880

Author Jochen Hellbeck presents "a definitive new portrait of the most fateful battle of World War II. The turning point of World War II came at Stalingrad. During the battle and shortly after its conclusion, scores of Red Army commanders and soldiers, party officials and workers spoke with a team of historians who visited from Moscow to record their conversations. The tapestry of their voices provides groundbreaking insights into the thoughts and feelings of Soviet citizens during wartime." (Publisher's note)

Includes bibliographical references and index

Hersey, John
Hiroshima; a new edition with a final chapter written forty years after the explosion. Knopf 1985 196p il $26; pa $6.50 **940.54**
1. Atomic bomb 2. World War, 1939-1945 -- Japan 3. Hiroshima (Japan) -- Bombardment, 1945
ISBN 0-394-54844-2; 0-679-72103-7 pa

LC 85-40346

First published 1946

An account of the aftermath of the first atomic bomb as reflected in the lives of six survivors

Hervieux, Linda
Forgotten; the untold story of D-Day's Black heroes, at home and at war. Linda Hervieux. HarperCollins 2015 368 p. 16 plates; ills; portraits $27.99 **940.54**
1. African American soldiers 2. Normandy (France), Attack on, 1944 3. World War, 1939-1945 -- Campaigns -- France 4. African American soldiers -- Biography 5. World War, 1939-1945 -- Balloons -- United States 6. World War, 1939-1945 -- Campaigns -- France -- Normandy 7. World War, 1939-1945 -- Participation, African American 8. World War, 1939-1945 -- Regimental histories -- United States 9. United States. Army. Anti-Aricraft Barrage Balloon Battalion, 320th -- History
ISBN 9780062313799

LC 2015017941

This book, by Linda Hervieux, "pays tribute to the valor of an all-black battalion whose crucial contributions at D-Day have gone unrecognized. . . . [T]he 320th Barrage Balloon Battalion . . . landed on the beaches of France. Their orders were to man a curtain of armed balloons meant to deter enemy aircraft. One member . . . would be nominated for the Medal of Honor, an award he would never receive. The nation's highest decoration was not given to black soldiers in World War II. (Publisher's note)

"Recommended for aviation buffs, chroniclers of World War II, and anyone who wants a nondense military read." LJ

Includes bibliographical references and index

Hillenbrand, Laura, 1967-
Unbroken. Random House 2010 473p il map $27; ebook $27 **940.54**
1. Veterans 2. Prisoners of war 3. Evangelists 4. Olympic athletes 5. Air force officers 6. Runners (Athletes) 7. Biography, Individual 8. World War, 1939-1945 -- Aerial operations 9. World War, 1939-1945 -- Prisoners and prisons
ISBN 978-1-4000-6416-8; 1-4000-6416-3; 978-0-679-60375-7 ebook; 0-679-60375-1 ebook

LC 2010017517

This is an account of Army Air Force bomber Louis Zamperini's plane crash in 1943 and his abuse as a Japanese prisoner of war.

"Hillenbrand's triumph is that in telling Louie's story . . . she tells the stories of thousands whose suffering has been mostly forgotten. She restores to our collective memory this tale of heroism, cruelty, life, death, joy, suffering, remorselessness, and redemption." Publ Wkly

Includes bibliographical references

Hindley, Meredith
★ **Destination** Casablanca; exile, espionage, and the battle for North Africa in World War II. Meredith Hindley. PublicAffairs 2017 xviii, 491 p.p (hardcover) $30 **940.54**

1. Morocco 2. World War, 1939-1945 -- Campaigns 3. France -- Foreign relations -- United States 4. United States -- Foreign relations -- France 5. World War, 1939-1945 -- Campaigns -- Morocco 6. World War, 1939-1945 -- Intelligence service 7. World War, 1939-1945 -- Morocco -- Casablanca
ISBN 1610394054; 9781610394055

LC 2017018911

In this book, by Meredith Hindley, "in November 1942, as a part of Operation Torch, 33,000 American soldiers sailed undetected across the Atlantic and stormed the beaches of French Morocco. Seventy-four hours later, the Americans controlled the country and one of the most valuable wartime ports: Casablanca." (Publisher's note)

Includes bibliographical references (pages 430-480) and index.

Holland, James

Battle of Britain; five months that changed history, May-October 1940. St. Martin's Press 2011 677p il map $40; ebook $19.99   **940.54**
1. Britain, Battle of, 1940
ISBN 978-0-312-67500-4; 978-1-4299-1941-8 ebook

LC 2010-40646

First published 2010 in the United Kingdom

"This massive volume is informative, enthralling, and moving—often all three at once. It effectively combines narrative and analysis to tell the story of the confrontation between the Luftwaffe and RAF Fighter Command from May through October 1940." Booklist

Includes bibliographical references

The **rise** of Germany 1939-1941; The Rise of Germany, 1939-1941. James Holland. Atlantic Monthly Press 2015 512 p. illustrations (some color) $30   **940.54**
1. World War, 1939-1945 -- Germany
ISBN 080212397X; 9780802123978

This book, by James Holland, presents a reappraisal of traditional World War II historiography. "It is commonly held that at the outset of war, Germany had the best army in the world and Britain barely managed to hold out against it until the Americans declared war. . . . But the picture looked much different in 1939. . . . Hitler was bluffing when he called for the wholesale destruction of Poland, but his bet that Western Europe wouldn't get involved turned out to be fatally wrong." (Publisher's note)

"Holland skillfully integrates the broad political, diplomatic, economic, and military narrative with stories of individuals, civilians, and soldiers from all the belligerents." LJ

Hornfischer, James D.

Ship of ghosts; the story of the USS Houston, FDR's legendary lost cruiser, and the epic saga of her survivors. Bantam Books 2006 530p il map $26   **940.54**
1. Houston (Cruiser) 2. World War, 1939-1945 -- Naval operations
ISBN 0-553-80390-5; 978-0-553-80390-7

LC 2006-47530

This book "recounts the exploits of the Houston, mainstay of the skimpy Allied fleet opposing the Japanese onslaught in the war's early days, until her sinking in a desperate battle with overwhelming Japanese forces in the Java Sea in 1942. . . . The narrative then shifts gears to follow the Houston's several hundred survivors through Japanese POW camps in Southeast Asia, focusing on the labor camps on the Burma-Thailand railway (glamorized in the movie Bridge on the River Kwai). . . . [This is] a gripping, well-told memorial to Greatest Generation martyrdom." Publ Wkly

Includes bibliographical references

Hotta, Eri

Japan 1941; countdown to infamy. by Eri Hotta. Alfred A. Knopf 2013 352 p. (hardcover) $27.95   **940.54**
1. World War, 1939-1945 -- Japan 2. Japan -- Politics and government 3. Pearl Harbor (Oahu, Hawaii), Attack on, 1941 4. War -- Decision making 5. Pearl Harbor (Hawaii), Attack on, 1941 6. Japan -- Politics and government -- 1926-1945 7. Japan -- Military policy -- History -- 20th century 8. Military planning -- Japan -- History -- 20th century
ISBN 0307594017; 9780307594013

LC 2013014781

In this book, author Eri Hotta presents his attempt "to examine the lead up to the attack on Pearl Harbor from a Japanese perspective [and] portrays the dilemma faced by the Japanese government and military in 1941. She indicts American policy makers for their failure to understand Japan's views [and] condemns U.S. demands that Japan withdraw from China." (Booklist)

Includes bibliographical references and index

★ **Iwo** Jima; World War II veterans remember the greatest battle of the Pacific. [edited by] Larry Smith. W.W. Norton 2008 xxiv, 345p il map $26.95; pa $17.95   **940.54**
1. Iwo Jima, Battle of, 1945 2. World War, 1939-1945 -- Personal narratives
ISBN 978-0-393-06234-2; 0-393-06234-1; 978-0-393-33491-3 pa; 0-393-33491-0 pa

LC 2008-1301

This is "a superb collection of 22 oral histories from Iwo Jima veterans, including two Medal of Honor winners, a Navajo 'Code-Talker,' the last surviving flag raiser from the first flag raising on Mount Suribachi, a war correspondent, and an African American marine who served in an ammo company." Libr J

Jacobsen, Annie

Operation Paperclip; the secret intelligence program to bring Nazi scientists to America. Annie Jacobsen. Little Brown & Co 2014 544 p. illustrations (hardcover) $30   **940.54**
1. Cold war 2. German scientists 3. National socialists 4. Scientists -- Germany -- History 5. Scientists -- United States -- History
ISBN 031622104X; 9780316221047

LC 2013028255

This book by Annie Jacobsen describes how "in the chaos following World War II, the U.S. government faced many difficult decisions, including what to do with the Third Reich's scientific minds. These were the brains behind the Nazis' once-indomitable war machine. So began Operation Paperclip, a decades-long, covert project to bring Hitler's scientists and their families to the United States." (Publisher's note)

"Built upon archival records, court transcripts, declassified documents, and interviews, Jacobsen's impressive book plumbs the dark depths of this postwar recruiting and shows the historical truths behind the space race and postwar U.S. dominance." LJ

Includes bibliographical references and index

Jones, Michael K.

The **retreat**; Hitler's first defeat. [by] Michael Jones. Thomas Dunne Books/St. Martin's Press 2010 xxi, 328p il map $27.99   **940.54**
1. World War, 1939-1945 -- Campaigns -- Soviet Union
ISBN 978-0-312-62819-2

LC 2010-34784

First published 2009 in the United Kingdom

"Fluently written with good sourcing, this book covers both sides of a vast conflict that dwarfed any other in Western Europe." Libr J

Includes bibliographical references

Kaplan, Alice Yaeger

The **interpreter**; [by] Alice Kaplan. University of Chicago Press 2007 240p il map pa $15   **940.54**

1. Authors 2. Veterans 3. Novelists 4. Trials (Homicide) 5. African American soldiers 6. Army officers 7. World War, 1939-1945 -- African Americans

ISBN 978-0-226-42425-5; 0-226-42425-1

LC 2006-35822

First published 2005 by Free Press

This is an "account of the trials of two American soldiers accused of murdering French citizens in the waning days of World War II. One of the accused soldiers, a black man named James Hendricks, was sentenced to death, while the other, George Whittington, a white who had been proclaimed a war hero, was acquitted. French political novelist Louis Guilloux served as an interpreter at these trials, and Kaplan draws from Guilloux's diaries as well as from a novel he based upon the trials. . . . Inventive, moving, and beautifully written, this is a major contribution to investigative history." Libr J

Includes bibliographical references

Karnad, Raghu

Farthest field; an Indian story of the Second World War. Raghu Karnad. W W Norton & Co Inc. 2015 320 p. maps (hardcover) $25.95   **940.54**

1. War and civilization 2. World War, 1939-1945 3. Social change -- India 4. India -- History -- 1765-1947, British occupation 5. World War, 1939-1945 -- India 6. Soldiers -- India -- Biography 7. World War, 1939-1945 -- India -- Madras 8. World War, 1939-1945 -- India -- Calicut 9. Social change -- India -- History -- 20th century 10. War and society -- India -- History -- 20th century 11. Great Britain. Army. British Indian Army -- Biography 12. Great Britain. Army. British Indian Army -- History -- World War, 1939-1945

ISBN 0393248097; 9780393248098

LC 2015018733

This book, by journalist Raghu Karnad, "narrates the lost epic of India's [role in World War II], in which the largest volunteer army in history fought for the British Empire, even as its countrymen fought to be free of it. It carries us from Madras to Peshawar, Egypt to Burma—unfolding the saga of a young family amazed by their swiftly changing world and swept up in its violence." (Publisher's note)

"An appealing, if necessarily fictionalized in places, portrait of three officers who did their best fighting a war widely opposed by many countrymen and that provided little benefit to the nation and was quickly forgotten after Indian independence in 1947." Kirkus

Includes bibliographical references and index

Katz, Robert

The **battle** for Rome; the Germans, the allies, the partisans and the Pope, September 1943-June 1944. Simon & Schuster 2003 418p il map $28; pa $16   **940.54**

1. World War, 1939-1945 -- Italy

ISBN 0-7432-1642-3; 0-7432-5808-8 pa

LC 2003-45677

"This narrative history describes the Eternal City at a key time of struggle—the dark year of German occupation between the overthrow of Mussolini in 1943 and liberation by the Allies in 1944. Four parties wrestle for Rome: the ruthless yet wary German occupiers, the Holy See in self-preservation mode, a gutsy band of patriotic students with homemade explosives, and the U.S. Fifth Army under Mark Clark. . . . This is

challenging research presented fluidly, and Katz's fascination with a key moment for a fascinating city shines through." Booklist

Includes bibliographical references

Kennedy, Paul M., 1945-

Engineers of victory; the problem solvers who turned the tide in the Second World War. Paul Kennedy. Random House 2013 464 p. (alk. paper) $30   **940.54**

1. World War, 1939-1945 2. World War, 1939-1945 -- Campaigns 3. Germany -- Armed Forces -- Organization 4. World War, 1939-1945 -- Naval operations 5. World War, 1939-1945 -- Aerial operations 6. Bombing, Aerial -- History -- 20th century 7. Amphibious warfare -- History -- 20th century 8. World War, 1939-1945 -- Amphibious operations 9. World War, 1939-1945 -- Campaigns -- Pacific Area 10. Germany -- Armed Forces -- History -- World War, 1939-1945 11. Naval convoys -- Atlantic Ocean -- History -- 20th century

ISBN 1400067618; 9781400067619; 9781588368980

LC 2012024284

This book by Paul Kennedy "provides a new and unique look at how World War II was won." The book is a "nuts-and-bolts account of the strategic factors that led to Allied victory. Kennedy reveals how the leaders' grand strategy was carried out by the ordinary soldiers, scientists, engineers, and businessmen responsible for realizing their commanders' visions of success." (Publisher's note)

Includes bibliographical references and index

Kershaw, Alex

Escape from the deep; the epic story of a legendary submarine and her courageous crew. Da Capo Press 2008 270p il map $26; pa $15.95   **940.54**

1. Tang (Ship) 2. World War, 1939-1945 -- Pacific Ocean 3. World War, 1939-1945 -- Naval operations 4. World War, 1939-1945 -- Prisoners and prisons

ISBN 978-0-306-81519-5; 0-306-81519-2; 978-0-306-81790-8 pa; 0-306-81790-X pa

LC 2008-298762

Details the history of the U.S. Navy submarine Tang in the Pacific theater of World War II, the explosion that led to its sinking, the ordeal of its surviving crew members and their capture by the Japanese, followed by months of brutal captivity.

The author "has researched exhaustively, including interviewing the last two living survivors, and written compactly the portrait of nine Americans who rose to heroism and of a ship that well deserved its status . . . as a legend in the naval history of World War II." Booklist

Includes bibliographical references

Keuning-Tichelaar, An

Passing on the comfort; the war, the quilts, and the women who made a difference. [by] An Keuning-Tichelaar and Lynn Kaplanian-Buller. Good Books 2005 186p il pa $14.95 **940.54**

1. Quilts 2. World War, 1939-1945 -- Personal narratives

ISBN 1-561484-82-2

LC 2005-01932

This is the "narrative of a Dutch resistance operation during WWII conducted by Keuning-Tichelaar and her husband, Herman, a Mennonite minister. With the support of their townspeople, the two young newlyweds sheltered and saved the lives of Jewish adults and children, and others in danger from the Nazis. As part of a relief effort, quilts were created by women in North American Mennonite circles and sent to the Netherlands. Beautifully illustrated with 19 color photographs of the quilts, this book describes in an understated voice the harrowing events and the daily acts of courage that Keuning-Tichelaar undertook.

When, decades later, coauthor Kaplanian-Buller, a U.S. citizen living in Amsterdam, found the old quilts, she persuaded An to share her story." Publ Wkly

Includes bibliographical references

Korda, Michael, 1933-

★ **Alone**; Britain, Churchill, and Dunkirk: defeat into victory. Michael Korda. Liveright Publishing Company, a division of W W Norton & Co. 2017 xiv, 525 p.p illustrations, maps (hardcover) $29.95   **940.54**

1. World War, 1939-1945 -- Campaigns -- France 2. World War, 1939-1945 -- Personal narratives 3. World War, 1939-1945 -- Great Britain 4. Dunkirk, Battle of, Dunkerque, France, 1940 5. World War, 1939-1945 -- Personal narratives, English 6. World War, 1939-1945 -- Campaigns -- France -- Dunkerque
ISBN 9781631491337; 9781631491320

LC 2017017244

This book, by Michael Korda, "chronicles the outbreak of World War Two and the great events that led to Dunkirk. 'Alone' captures the heroism of World War II as movingly as any book in recent memory. . . . Korda, . . . chronicles the outbreak of hostilities, recalling as a prescient young boy the enveloping tension that defined pre-Blitz London, and then as a military historian the great events that would alter the course of the twentieth century." (Publisher's note)

"Korda succeeds in infusing straight history with the accessible tone of narrative nonfiction." Booklist

Includes bibliographical references (pages 465-489) and index

With wings like eagles; a history of the Battle of Britain. Harper 2009 322p il map $25.95   **940.54**

1. Britain, Battle of, 1940 2. Great Britain -- Royal Air Force 3. World War, 1939-1945 -- Aerial operations
ISBN 978-0-06-112535-5; 0-06-112535-0

LC 2008-09293

This "is a skillful, absorbing, often moving contribution to the popular understanding of one of the few episodes in history to live on untarnished and undiminished in the collective memory and to deserve the description 'heroic.'" Washington Post

Includes bibliographical references (p. 303-305)

Leckie, Robert, 1920-

Okinawa; the last battle of World War II. Viking 1995 220p il hardcover o.p. pa $13.95   **940.54**

1. World War, 1939-1945 -- Campaigns -- Okinawa Island
ISBN 0-670-84716-X; 0-14-017389-7 pa

LC 94-39145

In this history of the Battle of Okinawa "Leckie supplies an accessible historical overview of a perplexing war tactic, the kamikaze attack." Booklist

Lee, Bruce

Marching orders; the untold story of World War II. Da Capo Press 2001 608p map pa $24   **940.54**

1. Cryptography 2. World War, 1939-1945 -- Japan 3. World War, 1939-1945 -- Secret service
ISBN 978-0-306-81036-7; 0-306-81036-0

First published 1995 by Crown

"Many of the mysteries that have eluded historians since the end of the war are much clarified. . . . This is the most significant publication about World War II since the recent series of books on the Ultra revelations and should be purchased by all libraries." Libr J

Includes bibliographical references

Letts, Elizabeth

The **perfect** horse; The Daring U.S. Mission to Rescue the Priceless Stallions Kidnapped by the Nazis. Elizabeth Letts. Ballantine Books 2016 400 p. illustrations, map (hardcover: alk. paper) $28   **940.54**

1. Horses 2. World War, 1939-1945 -- Austria 3. Arabian horse -- Poland -- History -- 20th century 4. Lipizzaner horse -- Austria -- History -- 20th century 5. Spanische Reitschule (Vienna, Austria) -- History -- 20th century 6. United States. Army. Cavalry Regiment, Mechanized, 2nd -- History 7. World War, 1939-1945 -- Confiscations and contributions -- Germany 8. World War, 1939-1945 -- Confiscations and contributions -- United States 9. World War, 1939-1945 -- Commando operations -- Czech Republic -- Hostouň
ISBN 0345544803; 9780345544803

LC 2016010501

This book, by Elizabeth Letts, tells the "story of the heroic rescue of priceless horses in the closing days of World War II. . . . A small troop of . . . American soldiers captures a German spy and makes an astonishing find—his briefcase is empty but for photos of beautiful white horses that have been stolen and kept on a secret farm behind enemy lines. Hitler has stockpiled the world's finest purebreds in order to breed the perfect military machine—an equine master race." (Publisher's note)

"The author's elegant narrative conveys how the love for these amazing creatures transcends national animosities." Kirkus

Includes bibliographical references and index

Lewis, Damien

The **Dog** Who Could Fly; The Incredible True Story of a WWII Airman and the Four-legged Hero Who Flew at His Side. Damien Lewis. Pocket Books 2014 304 p. illustrations $26   **940.54**

1. Dogs 2. World War, 1939-1945 -- Aerial operations
ISBN 1476739145; 9781476739144

LC 2014015567

This book by Damien Lewis "is the true account of a German shepherd who was adopted by the Royal Air Force during World War II, joined in flight missions, and survived everything from crash-landings to parachute bailouts--ultimately saving the life of his owner and dearest friend. . . . Airman Robert Bozdech stumbled across the tiny German shepherd--whom he named Ant--after being shot down on a daring mission over enemy lines." (Publisher's note)

A "heartwarming and well-paced man-and-his-dog story. . . . Lewis has captured the spirit of the era and told the story using Bozdech's manuscript as source material without making it maudlin or sentimental." Pub Wkly

Includes bibliographical references

Liebling, A. J.

World War II writings. Library of America 2008 1089p map (The library of America) $40   **940.54**

1. World War, 1939-1945 -- Campaigns 2. World War, 1939-1945 -- Personal narratives
ISBN 978-1-59853-018-6

LC 2007-938791

"The war brought out the best in [Liebling]. Here he . . . relied on straightforward observation, delivered in a style less mannered than Hemingway's, less sentimental than Ernie Pyle's, less excitable than Michael Herr's. It's the kind of writing that looks easy, except that very few war correspondents have ever done it so well." N Y Times Book Rev

Includes bibliographical references

Lifton, Robert Jay

Hiroshima in America; a half century of denial. [by] Robert Jay Lifton & Greg Mitchell; with a new afterword by the authors. Avon Books 1996 427p il pa $18.95 **940.54**

1. Atomic bomb 2. Hiroshima (Japan) -- Bombardment, 1945
ISBN 978-0-380-72764-3; 0-380-72764-1

First published 1995 by Putnam with title: Hiroshima in America: fifty years of denial

Lifton and Mitchell examine "the reaction of the American people to the bombing of Hiroshima in 1945 and its domestic aftermath. The authors examine what they perceive to be a conspiracy by the government to mislead and suppress information about the actual bombing, Truman's decision to drop the bomb, and the birth and mismanagement of the beginning of the nuclear age." Libr J

Includes bibliographical references

Lineberry, Cate

The **secret** rescue; Cate Lineberry. Little, Brown and Co. 2013 320 p. $27 **940.54**

1. Nurses 2. World War, 1939-1945 3. Special forces (Military science) -- United States
ISBN 0316220221; 9780316220224

LC 2013934814

This book looks at the Medical Air Evacuation Transport Squadron during World War II. Cate Lineberry "looks in particular at the 807th MAETS, consisting of 25 female nurses, 24 medics and other enlisted men from all over the country. They were assembled at Bowman Field in Louisville, Ky., for training before being shipped off in mid-August 1943." When they were forced down over enemy territory, there "ensued many weeks of near-comical confusion" before a rescue took place. (Kirkus Reviews)

Lukacs, John D.

Escape from Davao; the forgotten story of the most daring prison break of the Pacific war. Simon & Schuster 2010 xiii, 433p il $27.99 **940.54**

1. Davao City (Philippines) 2. Soldiers -- United States 3. World War, 1939-1945 -- Philippines 4. World War, 1939-1945 -- Prisoners and prisons 5. World War, 1939-1945 -- Underground movements
ISBN 978-0-7432-6278-1; 0-7432-6278-6

LC 2010-03238

The author "is a gifted stylist and storyteller. He doesn't flinch at the grim or the gruesome. . . . At bottom, 'Escape From Davao' is a morality tale, not unlike the war movies of the 1940s and '50s, about pluck, luck, courage, comradeship, Yankee humor, ingenuity, and religious faith." Pittsburgh Post-Gazette

Includes bibliographical references

Lulushi, Albert

Donovan's Devils; OSS commandos behind enemy lines: Europe, World War II. Albert Lulushi. Arcade Pubishing 2016 398 p. illustrations, maps (hardcover: alk. paper) $25.99 **940.54**

1. World War, 1939-1945 -- Commando operations 2. World War, 1939-1945 -- Secret service -- United States 3. World War, 1939-1945 -- Commando operations -- Europe 4. United States. Office of Strategic Services -- History
ISBN 9781628725674

LC 2015037691

This book, by Albert Lulushi, presents a history of "the OSS—Office of Strategic Services—created under the command of William Donovan . . . [and] its cloak-and-dagger operations during World War II . . . as the precursor of the CIA. . . . [This book] provides the most comprehensive

account to date of the Operational Group activities, including a detailed narrative of the ill-fated Ginny mission, which resulted in the one of the OSS's gravest losses of the war." (Publisher's note)

"A proficient, well-wrought work that emphasizes the actual fighting men, their deeds, and their fates." Kirkus

Includes bibliographical references and index

Macintyre, Ben, 1963-

Double cross; the true story of the D-day spies. Ben Macintyre. Crown 2012 399 p. ill., maps **940.54**

1. Spies 2. World War, 1939-1945 3. Normandy (France), Attack on, 1944 4. Spies -- Europe -- Biography 5. World War, 1939-1945 -- Deception 6. World War, 1939-1945 -- Secret service 7. World War, 1939-1945 -- Military intelligence 8. Espionage -- Europe -- History -- 20th century 9. Deception (Military science) -- History -- 20th century 10. World War, 1939-1945 -- Campaigns -- France -- Normandy
ISBN 9780307888754; 9780307888761

LC 2012003089

This book looks at the "deceit operation [that] was aimed at convincing the Nazis that Calais and Norway, not Normandy, were the targets of the 150,000-strong [D-Day] invasion force. The deception involved every branch of Allied wartime intelligence - the Bletchley Park codebreakers, MI5, MI6, SOE, Scientific Intelligence, the FBI and the French Resistance. But at its heart was the 'Double Cross System', a team of double agents controlled by the secret Twenty Committee." The squad comprised "a bisexual Peruvian playgirl, a tiny Polish fighter pilot, a Serbian seducer, a wildly imaginative Spaniard with a diploma in chicken farming, and a hysterical Frenchwoman whose obsessive love for her pet dog very nearly wrecked the entire deception," as well as a "sixth spy." (Publisher's note)

Includes bibliographical references (p. [383]-386) and index.

Operation Mincemeat; how a dead man and a bizarre plan fooled the Nazis and assured an allied victory. Harmony Books 2010 400p il $25.99 **940.54**

1. Lawyers 2. Intelligence service agents 3. World War, 1939-1945 -- Secret service
ISBN 978-0-307-45327-3; 0-307-45327-8

LC 2009-47562

A "true WWII tale that reads like something by Ian Fleming. In fact, two of Fleming's fellow British intelligence officers hatched the title operation. They dressed a corpse in uniform and arranged for it to wash up on a Nazi-friendly stretch of the Spanish coast bearing a suitcase with false war plans. Against all odds, Operation Mincemeat succeeded — and helped convince the Germans that the Allies planned to invade Sardinia and Greece in 1943 instead of their real target, Sicily. Relying on a cache of once-classified documents, Macintyre provides the fullest account yet of this curious episode and enlivens his yarn with quirky details." Entertainment Wkly

Includes bibliographical references

★ **Rogue** Heroes; The History of the SAS, Britain's Secret Special Forces Unit That Sabotaged the Nazis and Changed the Nature of War. by Ben Macintyre. Random House Inc 2016 352 p. illustrations, maps (ebook) $65; $28 **940.54**

1. Special forces (Military science) 2. World War, 1939-1945 -- Great Britain
ISBN 9781101904176; 110190416X; 9781101904169

This book, by Ben Macintyre, shares the "untold story of WWII's greatest secret fighting force. . . . Britain's Special Air Service—or SAS—was the brainchild of David Stirling. . . . Where most of his colleagues looked at a battlefield map of World War II's African theater and saw a protracted struggle with Rommel's desert forces, Stirling saw an opportunity: given a small number of elite, well-trained men, he could parachute behind enemy lines and sabotage their airplanes and war material." (Publisher's note)

"He demonstrates that even in a global war, a few uniquely talented, imaginative, and bold individuals of relatively junior rank can have a major impact. Macintyre delivers a solid history and an enjoyable read that will appeal to those interested in military history as well as readers who enjoy real-life tales of adventure." Pub Wkly

Includes bibliographical references (pages 363-364) and index.

Maslov, Sasha

Veterans; faces of World War II. Sasha Maslov. Princeton Architectural Press 2017 142 p. (hardcover) $29.95 **940.54**

1. World War, 1939-1945 -- Veterans 2. World War, 1939-1945 -- Biography 3. World War, 1939-1945 -- Veterans -- Interviews 4. World War, 1939-1945 -- Veterans -- Pictorial works

ISBN 9781616895785; 9781616896133

LC 2016038694

This book, by Sasha Maslov, is "the outcome of a worldwide project by . . . [the author] to interview and photograph the last surviving combatants from World War II. Soldiers, support staff, and resistance fighters candidly discuss wartime experiences and their lifelong effects in this unforgettable, intimate record of the end of a cataclysmic chapter in world history and tribute to the members of an indomitable generation." (Publisher's note)

"The result is an outstanding photographic essay accompanied by moving stories. Without Maslov's intervention, this is a valuable piece of history that would have been lost." LJ

McKay, Sinclair

The **secret** lives of codebreakers; the men and women who cracked the Enigma code at Bletchley Park. Sinclair McKay. Penguin Group 2012 vi, 338 p.p (paperback) $16.00 **940.54**

1. Cryptography 2. World War, 1939-1945 -- Great Britain 3. World War, 1939-1945 -- Military intelligence 4. World War, 1939-1945 -- Cryptography 5. Bletchley Park (Milton Keynes, England) -- History 6. Great Britain. Government Communications Headquarters -- History 7. World War, 1939-1945 -- Electronic intelligence -- Great Britain

ISBN 0452298717; 9780452298712

LC 2012018408

This book by Sinclair McKay looks at the staff of "the Government Code & Cypher School, where [during World War II] British experts deciphered German communications, including those encrypted by the Enigma coding machine. . . . McKay presents a sociological history of the scientists, engineers, and other academics . . . thrown together at Bletchley Park with debutantes and ordinary workers, all with a common goal." (Library Journal)

Includes bibliographical references and index.

Merridale, Catherine

★ **Ivan's** war; life and death in the Red Army, 1939-1945. Metropolitan Books 2006 426p il map $30 **940.54**

1. Soviet Union -- Red Army 2. World War, 1939-1945 -- Soviet Union

ISBN 0-8050-7455-4

LC 2005-50457

The author discusses the life of the ordinary Russian soldier during World War II.

Merridale "succeeds admirably in fashioning a compelling portrait, helped immensely by her talent as a writer." Foreign Affairs

Includes bibliographical references

Miller, Nathan

War at sea; a naval history of World War II. Oxford University Press 1996 592p il map pa $29.95 **940.54**

1. World War, 1939-1945 -- Naval operations

ISBN 0-19-511038-2

LC 96-31787

First published 1995 by Scribner

"Miller's research—primarily on the Royal Navy—and a reading of hundreds of pertinent monographs has enabled him to fashion a briskly paced narrative that will both inform and entertain." Choice

Includes bibliographical references

Miller, Scott

Agent 110; An American Spymaster and the German Resistance in WWII. Scott Miller. Simon & Schuster 2017 384 p. (hardcover: alkaline paper) $28.00 **940.54**

1. Intelligence officers -- United States -- Biography 2. World War, 1939-1945 -- Secret service -- Switzerland 3. World War, 1939-1945 -- Secret service -- United States 4. Anti-Nazi movement -- Germany 5. Spies -- United States -- Biography 6. Germany -- Politics and government -- 1933-1945 7. United States. Office of Strategic Services -- Biography 8. Espionage, American -- Germany -- History -- 20th century

ISBN 9781451693386; 9781451693393

LC 2016025790

This book, by Scott Miller, presents "the secret and suspenseful account of how OSS spymaster Allen Dulles led a network of Germans conspiring to assassinate Hitler and negotiate surrender to bring about the end of World War II before the Soviet's advance. Agent 110 is Allen Dulles, a newly minted spy from an eminent family. . . . Miller shows how Dulles's negotiations fell short." (Publisher's note)

"Entertaining for bot h its historical insights into WWII and its dramatic narrative." Kirkus

Includes bibliographical references and index

Agent One Ten

Milton, Giles

Churchill's Ministry of Ungentlemanly Warfare; the mavericks who plotted Hitler's defeat. Giles Milton. St. Martin's Press 2017 368 p. illustrations (ebook) $60; $28 **940.54**

1. World War, 1939-1945 -- Secret service -- Great Britain

ISBN 9781250119049; 1250119022; 9781250119025

LC 2016039180

This book, by Giles Milton, narrates how, "in the spring of 1939, a top-secret organization was founded in London . . . to plot the destruction of Hitler's war machine through spectacular acts of sabotage. The guerrilla campaign that followed was every bit as extraordinary as the six men who directed it. . . . These men . . . formed a secret inner circle that, aided by a group of formidable ladies, single-handedly changed the course [of the] Second World War." (Publisher's note)

"An exciting, suspenseful tale of international intrigue." Kirkus

Includes bibliographical references (pages 313-339) and index.

Morris, Jan, 1926-

Battleship Yamato; of war, beauty and irony. Jan Morris. Liveright Publishing Corporation 2017 96 p. (hardcover) $15.95 **940.54**

1. Warships 2. World War, 1939-1945 3. Yamato (Battleship) 4. World War, 1939-1945--Naval operations, Japanese

ISBN 9781631493423; 1631493426

LC 2017035438

In this book, author Jan Morris, "tells the dramatic story of the . .

. . [battleship Yamato]--from secret wartime launch to futile sacrifice at Okinawa . . . [and] interprets the ship as an allegorical figure of . . . [World War II], in its splendor and its squalor, its heroism and its waste. Drawing on rich naval history and rhapsodic metaphors from international music and art, 'Battleship Yamato' is a work of grand ironic elegy." (Publisher's note)

Moses, Sam

At all costs; how a crippled ship and two American merchant mariners turned the tide of World War II. Random House 2006 335p il $25.95 **940.54**
    1. World War, 1939-1945 -- Naval operations 2. World War, 1939-1945 -- Mediterranean Sea
    ISBN 1-4000-6318-3
                              LC 2006-40425
"The remarkable heroism that won the day, as well as Moses' thorough retelling, makes this an exciting, imperative read for anyone interested in WWII." Publ Wkly
    Includes bibliographical references

Moynahan, Brian

Leningrad; Siege and Symphony: The Story of the Great City Terrorized by Stalin, Starved by Hitler, Immortalized by Shostakovich. Brian Moynahan. Atlantic Monthly Press 2014 496 p. 16 plates; illustrations; maps $30 **940.54**
    1. Symphony 2. World War, 1939-1945 -- Soviet Union
    ISBN 0802123163; 9780802123169
In this book author Brian Moynahan "sets the composition of Shostakovich's most famous work against the tragic canvas of the siege itself and the years of repression and terror that preceded it. In vivid . . . detail he tells the story of the cruelties heaped by the twin monsters of the twentieth century on a city of exquisite beauty and fine minds, and of its no less remarkable survival." (Publisher's note)
"Moynahan's rapturous commentary on the music at times amounts to puffery. Nonetheless an admirable tribute to the human spirit and artistic integrity. Highly recommended for all readers interested in the era and the wellsprings of artistic creation." LJ

Mulley, Clare

The Spy Who Loved; The Secrets and Lives of Christine Granville. Clare Mulley. St. Martin's Press 2013 xix, 426 p.p $26.99 **940.54**
    1. Spies -- Great Britain -- Biography 2. Women spies -- Great Britain -- Biography 3. World War, 1939-1945 -- Secret service -- Great Britain
    ISBN 1250030323; 9781250030320
                              LC 2013010210
Includes bibliographical references (pages [363]-411) and index

The women who flew for Hitler; a true story of soaring ambition and searing rivalry. Clare Mulley. St. Martin's Press 2017 xxiii, 470 p.p illustrations, maps (hardback) $27.99 **940.54**
    1. Women air pilots 2. World War, 1939-1945 -- Aerial operations -- Germany 3. Iron Cross -- Biography 4. Women air pilots -- Germany -- Biography 5. World War, 1939-1945 -- Women -- Germany 6. Air pilots, Military -- Germany -- Biography 7. Aeronautical engineers -- Germany -- Biography 8. World War, 1939-1945 -- Aerial operations, German
    ISBN 9781250133168; 9781250063670
                              LC 2017011483
This book, by Clare Mulley, looks at the lives of Hanna Reitsch and Melitta von Stauffenberg, "Nazi Germany's most highly decorated women pilots. . . . Hanna was middle-class, vivacious, and distinctly Aryan, while . . . Melitta came from an aristocratic Prussian family. . . . [Mulley provides an] account of their contrasting yet strangely parallel lives, against a changing backdrop of the 1936 Olympics, the Eastern Front, the Berlin Air Club, and Hitler's bunker." (Publisher's note)
"Absolutely gripping, Mulley's double portrait is a reminder that there are many more stories to tell from this oft-examined time." Booklist
    Includes bibliographical references (pages [435]-453) and index.

Mundy, Liza

Code girls; the untold story of the American women code breakers of World War II. Liza Mundy. Hachette Books 2017 xiv, 416 p.p illustrations (hardcover) $28 **940.54**
    1. Historical literature 2. World War, 1939-1945 -- Cryptography 3. World War, 1939-1945 -- Participation, Female 4. Cryptography -- United States -- History -- 20th century 5. Cryptographers -- United States -- History -- 20th century
    ISBN 9780316352499; 9780316352536; 9780316439893
                              LC 2017020069
This book, by Liza Mundy, is about female cryptographers during World War II. "Recruited by the U.S. Army and Navy from small towns and elite colleges, more than ten thousand women served as codebreakers during World War II. . . . Their efforts shortened the war, saved countless lives, and gave them access to careers previously denied to them." (Publisher's note)
"A well-researched, compellingly written, crucial addition to the literature of American involvement in World War II." Kirkus
    Includes bibliographical references (pages [363]-402) and index.

Murphy, Brian, 1959-

81 days below zero; the incredible survival story of a World War II pilot in Alaska's frozen wilderness. Brian Murphy. Da Capo Press 2015 264 p. 8 plates; illustrations (hardback) $24.99 **940.54**
    1. Survival skills 2. Wilderness survival 3. Survival after airplane accidents, shipwrecks, etc. 4. Wilderness survival -- Alaska 5. World War, 1939-1945 -- Alaska 6. Airplane crash survival -- Alaska 7. B-24 (Bomber) -- Accidents -- Alaska 8. Aeronautics, Military -- Accidents -- Alaska 9. Air pilots, Military -- United States -- Biography 10. World War, 1939-1945 -- Aerial operations, American
    ISBN 0306823284; 9780306823282; 9780306823299
                              LC 2015003484
This book by Brian Murphy tells how "shortly before Christmas in 1943, five Army aviators left Alaska's Ladd Field on a test flight. Only one ever returned: Leon Crane, a city kid from Philadelphia with little more than a parachute on his back when he bailed from his B-24 Liberator before it crashed into the Arctic. Alone in subzero temperatures, Crane managed to stay alive in the dead of the Yukon winter for nearly twelve weeks and, amazingly, walked out of the ordeal intact." (Publisher's note)
    Includes bibliographical references and index

Neiberg, Michael

The blood of free men; the liberation of Paris, 1944. Michael Neiberg. Basic Books, A Member of the Perseus Books Group 2012 309 p. (hardcover: alk. paper) $28.99 **940.54**
    1. World War, 1939-1945 -- France -- Paris 2. World War, 1939-1945 -- Campaigns -- France -- Paris
    ISBN 0465023991; 9780465023998
                              LC 2012016282

This book by Michael Neiber focuses on Paris, France during World War II. "As the Allies struggled inland from Normandy in August of 1944, the fate of Paris hung in the balance. Other jewels of Europe . . . were, or would soon be, reduced to rubble during attempts to liberate them. But Paris endured, thanks to a fractious cast of characters, from Resistance cells to Free French operatives to an unlikely assortment of diplomats, Allied generals, and governmental officials." (Publisher's note)

Includes bibliographical references and index.

Neitzel, Sönke, 1968-

Soldaten; On Fighting, Killing, and Dying: The Secret WWII Transcripts of German POWs. Sönke Neitzel and Harald Welzer; translated from the German by Jefferson Chase. Alfred A. Knopf 2012 x, 437 p.p $30.50   **940.54**

1. World War, 1939-1945 -- Prisoners and prisons, German 2. Eavesdropping -- Great Britain 3. World War, 1939-1945 -- Anecdotes 4. Soldiers -- Germany -- Attitudes -- Sources 5. Prisoners of war -- Germany -- Attitudes -- Sources 6. World War, 1939-1945 -- Prisoners and prisons, British 7. Prisoners of war -- Great Britain -- Attitudes -- Sources 8. Germany -- Armed Forces -- History -- 20th century -- Sources 9. World War, 1939-1945 -- Military intelligence -- Great Britain

ISBN 0307958124; 9780307958129

LC 2012005744

This book, by Sönke Neitzel and Herald Welzer, "closely examines. . . recorded interrogations of German POWs. . . and the casual, pitiless brutality omnipresent in them, from a historical and psychological perspective. What factors led to the degradation of the soldiers' sense of awareness and morality? How much did their social environments affect their interpretation of the war and their actions during combat? . . . [An] unflinching narrative of wartime experience emerges." (Publisher's note)

Includes bibliographical references (p. [397]-412)

Nelson, Craig

The **first** heroes; the extraordinary story of the Doolittle Raid--America's first World War II victory. Viking 2002 430p il $27.95; pa $15   **940.54**

1. Generals 2. Air force officers 3. World War, 1939-1945 -- Japan 4. United States -- Army Air Forces 5. World War, 1939-1945 -- Aerial operations

ISBN 0-670-03087-2; 0-14-200341-7 pa

LC 2002-28092

"The most interesting part of the book is the harrowing story of survival as crew members are forced to ditch their planes on the Asian mainland. This is a thrilling real-life saga that both informs and inspires." Booklist

Includes bibliographical references (p. {403}-415) and index

★ **Pearl** Harbor; from infamy to greatness. Craig Nelson. Scribner, an imprint of Simon & Schuster 2016 800 p. (hardcover) $32   **940.54**

1. United States -- Military history 2. Pearl Harbor (Oahu, Hawaii), Attack on, 1941 3. Pearl Harbor (Hawaii), Attack on, 1941

ISBN 9781451660494

LC 2016018490

This book, by Craig Nelson, is a "definitive account of the event that changed twentieth-century America—Pearl Harbor. . . . Beginning in 1914, . . . Craig Nelson maps the road to war, beginning with Franklin D. Roosevelt, then the Assistant Secretary of the Navy . . . , [and] traces Japan's leaders as they lurch into ultranationalist fascism, which culminates in their insanely daring yet militarily brilliant scheme to terrify

America with one of the boldest attacks ever waged." (Publisher's note)

"Nelson's well written history of Pearl Harbor will be enjoyed by the general reader and appropriately highlights the battle's historical significance." Pub Wkly

Includes bibliographical references

Norman, Elizabeth M.

★ **Tears** in the darkness; the story of the Bataan Death March and its aftermath. [by] Michael Norman and Elizabeth M. Norman. Farrar, Straus, and Giroux 2009 463p il $30   **940.54**

1. Prisoners of war 2. World War, 1939-1945 -- Atrocities 3. World War, 1939-1945 -- Prisoners and prisons 4. World War, 1939-1945 -- Campaigns -- Philippines 5. Prisoners of war -- Philippines -- Bataan (Province) 6. World War, 1939-1945 -- Prisoners and prisons, Japanese

ISBN 0-374-27260-3; 978-0-374-27260-9

LC 2008-47163

"For the first four months of 1942, U.S., Filipino, and Japanese soldiers fought what was America's first major land battle of World War II, the battle for the tiny Philippine peninsula of Bataan. It ended with the surrender of 76,000 Filipinos and Americans, the single largest defeat in American military history. The defeat, though, was only the beginning, as Michael and Elizabeth M. Norman [argue in this] . . . book. From then until the Japanese surrendered in August 1945, the prisoners of war suffered an ordeal of unparalleled cruelty and savagery: forty-one months of captivity, starvation rations, dehydration, hard labor, deadly disease, and torture." (Publisher's note) Index.

This book "is authoritative history. Ten years in the making, it is based on hundreds of interviews with American, Filipino and Japanese combatants. But it is also a narrative achievement. The book seamlessly blends a wide-angle view with the stories of many individual participants." N Y Times (Late N Y Ed)

Includes bibliographical references

Olson, Lynne

Citizens of London; the Americans who stood with Britain in its darkest, finest hour. Random House 2010 471p il $28   **940.54**

1. Diplomats 2. Governors 3. Radio reporters 4. Government officials 5. Television reporters 6. Television news anchors 7. World War, 1939-1945 -- Diplomatic history 8. Great Britain -- Foreign relations -- United States 9. United States -- Foreign relations -- Great Britain

ISBN 978-1-4000-6758-9

The story of how the United States forged its wartime alliance with Britain, told from the perspective of three key American players in London: Edward R. Murrow, Averell Harriman, and John Gilbert Winant.

A nuanced history that captures the intensity of life in a period when victory was not a foregone conclusion. Kirkus

Includes bibliographical references

Orr, Timothy

Never call me a hero; a legendary American dive-bomber pilot remembers the battle of Midway. N. Jack "Dusty" Kleiss; with Timothy Orr and Laura Orr. William Morrow, an imprint of HarperCollins Publishers 2017 xvii, 312 p.p illustrations, maps (hardcover) $26.99   **940.54**

1. Midway, Battle of, 1942 2. World War, 1939-1945 -- Aerial operations 3. Enterprise (Aircraft carrier: CV-6) 4. Dive bomber pilots -- United States -- Biography 5. World War, 1939-1945 -- Naval operations, American 6. World War, 1939-1945 -- Aerial

operations, American 7. United States. Navy. Scouting Squadron Six -- Biography 8. Midway, Battle of, 1942 -- Personal narratives, American

ISBN 9780062692351; 9780062692054; 9780062692368; 0062692054

Lt. Dusty Kleiss "worked on this book for years with naval historians Timothy and Laura Orr, aiming to publish 'Never Call Me a Hero' for Midway's seventy-fifth anniversary. . . . These pages are Dusty's remarkable legacy, providing a riveting eyewitness account of the Battle of Midway, and an inspiring testimony to the brave men who fought, died, and shaped history during those four extraordinary days in June, seventy-five years ago." (Publisher's note)

The **Pacific** War; from Pearl Harbor to Hiroshima. editor, Daniel Marston. Pbk. ed.; Osprey Pub. 2010 272p il map pa $19.95   **940.54**
  1. World War, 1939-1945 -- Campaigns -- Pacific Ocean
  ISBN 978-1-84908-382-9

                   LC 2010-292672

First published 2005 with title: The Pacific war companion

"These essays on the Pacific theater of WW II, written by a group of international scholars representing Australia, Great Britain, Japan, and the US, cover the wellknown events at Pearl Harbor, the Coral Sea, and Midway; MacArthur's push to the Philippines; Nimitz's island campaign in the central Pacific; Okinawa; and the dropping of the atomic bomb on Hiroshima and Nagasaki. . . . A chronology, detailed maps, and photographs greatly enhance this excellent volume on the Pacific phase of WW II." Choice

  Includes bibliographical references

Patton, George S.

  War as I knew it; by George S. Patton, Jr.; annotated by Paul D. Harkins. Houghton Mifflin 1947 425p il maps hardcover o.p. pa $18   **940.54**
  1. World War, 1939-1945 -- Campaigns
  ISBN 0-395-73529-7 pa

  An account of the General's WWII European campaigns from the fight for Sicily to the conquest of Germany based on a series of "open letters" written to his wife

Peffer, Randall

  Where divers dare; the hunt for the last U-boat. Randall Peffer. Berkley Calibre 2016 320 p. illustrations (hardback) $28   **940.54**
  1. Shipwrecks 2. Submarines 3. Marine salvage 4. World War, 1939-1945 -- Campaigns 5. U-550 (Submarine) 6. Shipwrecks -- North Atlantic Ocean 7. Salvage -- United States -- History 8. Divers -- United States -- Biography 9. Deep diving -- United States -- History 10. Underwater archaeology -- North Atlantic Ocean 11. Shipwrecks -- Massachusetts -- Nantucket Island 12. World War, 1939-1945 -- Naval operations, German 13. World War, 1939-1945 -- Naval operations -- Submarine 14. World War, 1939-1945 -- Campaigns -- North Atlantic Ocean
  ISBN 9780425276365

                   LC 2015028313

This book, by Randall Peffer, is the "true account of the search for German U-boat U-550. . . . In 2012, a team found it—the last undiscovered U-boat in dive-able waters off the Eastern Seaboard of the United States, more than three hundred feet below the surface. This is the story of their twenty-year quest to find this 'Holy Grail' of deep-sea diving and their tenacious efforts to dive on this treacherous wreck." (Publisher's note)

"Peffer conveys the tension, fear, and exhilaration of deep wreck diving in this uncomfortable true story of bravery, compassion, and death that characterized the violent last hours of U-550." Pub Wkly

Pellegrino, Charles

  To hell and back; the last train from Hiroshima. Charles Pellegrino. Rowman & Littlefield 2015 432 p. illustrations, map (Asia/Pacific/perspectives) (cloth: alk. paper) $29.95   **940.54**
  1. Atomic bomb 2. Atomic bomb victims 3. Hiroshima (Japan) -- Bombardment, 1945 4. Hiroshima-shi (Japan) -- Biography 5. Forensic archaeology -- Japan -- Hiroshima-shi 6. World War, 1939-1945 -- Japan -- Hiroshima-shi 7. Hiroshima-shi (Japan) -- History -- Bombardment, 1945 8. Atomic bomb victims -- Japan -- Hiroshima-shi -- Biography 9. Atomic bomb -- Social aspects -- Japan -- Hiroshima-shi -- History -- 20th century 10. Hiroshima-shi (Japan) -- History -- Bombardment, 1945 -- Personal narratives, Japanese
  ISBN 1442250585; 9781442250581

                   LC 2015014341

This book, by Charles Pellegrino, part of the "Asia/Pacific/Perspectives" series, "drawing on the voices of atomic bomb survivors and the new science of forensic archaeology, . . . describes the events and the aftermath of two days in August when nuclear devices, detonated over Japan, changed life on Earth forever. . . . At the narrative's core are eyewitness accounts of those who experienced the atomic explosions firsthand--the Japanese civilians on the ground." (Publisher's note)

"This is horrifying, painful, and necessary reading." Kirkus

Includes bibliographical references and index

Pleshakov, Konstantin

  ★ **Stalin's** folly; the tragic first ten days of World War II on the Eastern Front. [by] Constantine Pleshakov. Houghton Mifflin 2005 326p il map $26   **940.54**
  1. Heads of state 2. Communist leaders 3. Political leaders 4. World War, 1939-1945 -- Europe
  ISBN 0-618-36701-2

                   LC 2004-65133

This is an account of the German invasion of the Soviet Union in 1941.

This book "belongs in every World War II collection." Libr J

Includes bibliographical references

Prados, John

  Storm over Leyte; The Philippine Invasion and the Destruction of the Japanese Navy. John Prados. New American Library 2016 400 p. illustrations, map $28   **940.54**
  1. World War, 1939-1945 -- Campaigns -- Philippines 2. Leyte Gulf, Battle of, Philippines, 1944 3. Leyte Island (Philippines) -- History, Military 4. World War, 1939-1945 -- Campaigns -- Philippines -- Leyte Island
  ISBN 9780451473615

                   LC 2015047067

This book, by John Prados, presents the "story of the Battle of Leyte Gulf in World War II. . . . As Allied ships prepared for the invasion of the Philippine island of Leyte, every available warship, submarine and airplane was placed on alert while Japanese admiral Kurita Takeo stalked Admiral William F. Halsey's unwitting American armada." (Publisher's note)

"The work is exceedingly balanced and provides detailed portraits of the personalities of the Japanese commanders, their understanding of events, and their decision-making processes." Pub Wkly

Includes bibliographical references and index.

Read, Anthony

The **fall** of Berlin; [by] Anthony Read and David Fisher. Da Capo Press 1995 513p il map pa $18.50   **940.54**

1. Berlin, Battle of, 1945 2. Germany -- History -- 1933-1945 3. World War, 1939-1945 -- Germany

ISBN 0-306-80619-3; 978-0-306-80619-3

LC 94-47998

First published 1992 in the United Kingdom

A description of "the bombing of Berlin by the British and Americans and how the Russian Army fought its way toward and through Berlin in 1945. The authors intend no startling new interpretations or profound analysis. Instead, they offer vignettes, often based on diaries, to describe life in Berlin late in the war. They also retell the story of fanatical Nazi leaders and of the Wehrmacht's desperate efforts to defend the city. The result is a highly readable and, at the same time, sophisticated and reliable narrative history." Libr J

Includes bibliographical references

Roberts, Andrew, 1963-

Masters and commanders; how four titans won the war in the West, 1941-1945. HarperCollins 2009 xl, 673p il map $35   **940.54**

1. Generals 2. Governors 3. Statesmen 4. Historians 5. Presidents 6. Prime ministers 7. People with disabilities 8. Marshals 9. Memoirists 10. Philatelists 11. Cabinet members 12. Secretaries of state 13. Members of Parliament 14. Secretaries of defense 15. Nobel laureates for peace 16. Great Britain -- War Cabinet 17. Nobel laureates for literature 18. World War, 1939-1945 -- Campaigns 19. Strategy -- History -- 20th century 20. World War, 1939-1945 -- Military intelligence 21. World War, 1939-1945 -- Personal narratives, British 22. World War, 1939-1945 -- Personal narratives, American

ISBN 0-06-122857-5; 978-0-06-122857-5

First published 2008 in the United Kingdom with subtitle: how Roosevelt, Churchill, Marshall and Alanbrooke won the war in the West

Roberts examines the "history of the four men responsible for final decisions: FDR, Churchill, and their top military advisors, George Marshall and Alan Brooke, respectively. Both to humanize the pressure on figures now memorialized in bronze and to serve as Clio's arbiter of impassioned disagreements over the optimal strategy to defeat Nazi Germany, Roberts examines how arguments played out amongst the quartet and those in their orbit. . . . Roberts reinforces his reputation for high-quality military history with this comprehensive synthesis of primary sources about the fundamental strategic decisions of WWII." Booklist

The **storm** of war; a new history of the Second World War. HarperCollins 2011 lvi, 712p il map $29.99   **940.54**

1. World War, 1939-1945

ISBN 978-0-06-122859-9; 0-06-122859-1

First published 2009 in the United Kingdom

"In general, histories of the Second World War in the English language can be divided sharply into those written by Americans, which downplay the British role in the war, and those written by British historians, which downplay the role of the Americans (and also give less space and attention to the Pacific theater than the European theater). Roberts has managed to write a book that both strives and succeeds in giving more or less equal time to both, and also manages to include enough about events in China and the war on the Eastern Front to give the reader a well-balanced and excitingly written account of the whole war. . . . His scholarship is superb, and the 'packaging' of the book, with very good illustrations and ample first-class maps, makes it a real pleasure to read." Daily Beast

Includes bibliographical references

Roberts, Geoffrey

Stalin's general; the life of Georgy Zhukov. Geoffrey Roberts. Random House 2012 375 p. (alk. paper) $30   **940.54**

1. Biography 2. National socialism 3. Soviet Union -- History -- 1939-1945 4. World War, 1939-1945 -- Soviet Union 5. Marshals -- Soviet Union -- Biography

ISBN 1400066921; 9780679645177; 9781400066926

LC 2011040663

Author Geoffrey Roberts presents a "biography of the ruthless Red Army general who defeated the Nazis and then spent decades alternately disgraced and rehabilitated in Soviet Russia. . . . As [Georgy] Zhukov, a rising cavalry commander in the rapidly modernizing Red Army, managed to escape being a victim of the army purges of 1937-38 and was then appointed on his first important mission for Stalin: to 'conduct a purge' of the Japanese from the Mongolian-Manchurian border in 1939." (Kirkus Reviews)

Includes bibliographical references and index.

Rooney, Andrew A.

My war; [by] Andy Rooney. PublicAffairs 2000 333p il $20; pa $14   **940.54**

1. Authors 2. Humorists 3. Journalists 4. World War, 1939-1945 -- Personal narratives

ISBN 1-58648-010-3; 1-58648-159-2 pa

LC 00-59228

First published 1995 by Random House

The author "relates how he became a notable combat journalist in WW II, a war he calls 'the ultimate experience for anyone in it.' For the Army newspaper Stars and Stripes, he covered the air war over Germany, the D-Day invasion of Normandy and the Allied drive into Germany. Rooney's simple, ruminative style . . . grips the reader as he describes famous events of the war." Publ Wkly

Scott, James M.

Rampage; Macarthur, Yamashita, and the Battle of Manila. James M. Scott. W W Norton & Co Inc 2018 640 p. $32.95   **940.54**

1. World War, 1939-1945 -- Campaigns -- Philippines

ISBN 0393246949; 9780393246940

"The twenty-nine-day battle to liberate Manila resulted in the catastrophic destruction of the city and a rampage by Japanese forces that brutalized the civilian population. . . . Based on extensive research in the United States and the Philippines, including war-crimes testimony, after-action reports, and survivor interviews . . . [author James M. Scott] recounts one of the most heartbreaking chapters of Pacific war history." (Publisher's note)

Target Tokyo; Jimmy Doolittle and the raid that avenged Pearl Harbor. James M. Scott. W W Norton & Co Inc 2015 xv, 648 p.p ill. (hbk.) $35   **940.54**

1. World War, 1939-1945 -- Aerial operations -- Japan 2. Tokyo (Japan) -- History -- Bombardment, 1942 3. World War, 1939-1945 -- Aerial operations, American

ISBN 9780393089622; 0393089622

LC 2014043257

Pulitzer Prize Finalist: History (2016)

This book, by James M. Scott, describes the events of the U.S. Doolittle Raid on Japan in the aftermath of the Pearl Harbor bombing. "On April 18, 1942, sixteen U.S. Army bombers under the command of daredevil pilot Jimmy Doolittle lifted off from the deck of the USS Hornet on a one-way mission to pummel the enemy's factories, refineries, and dockyards and then escape to Free China." (Publisher's note)

"This popular history will appeal to fans of Laura Hillebrand's Unbroken and is comparable to other histories of the Tokyo Raid including Craig Nelson's The First Heroes and Carroll V. Glines's The Doolittle Raid." LJ

Includes bibliographical references (pages 613-622) and index.

Scott-Clark, Cathy

The **Amber** Room; the fate of the world's greatest lost treasure. [by] Catherine Scott-Clark & Adrian Levy. Walker & Co. 2004 386p il $26   **940.54**

1. Art thefts 2. World War, 1939-1945 -- Destruction and pillage

ISBN 0-8027-1424-2

LC 2004-49625

The authors "tell an exciting, intense, and surprising story. It is filled with episodes of cold-war intrigue, cynicism, amoral betrayal, and bureaucratic stalling that degenerates into absurdity." Booklist

Includes bibliographical references

Sebag-Montefiore, Hugh

Enigma: the battle for the code. Wiley 2000 422p il hardcover o.p. pa $16.95   **940.54**

1. Cryptography 2. World War, 1939-1945 -- Secret service

ISBN 0-471-40738-0; 0-471-49035-0 pa

LC 00-43920

This is the story of the German Enigma code.

"Describing the breaking of the German naval code during World War II, is both engrossing and exciting. Much of the information presented here is based on recently declassified documents." Booklist

Includes bibliographical references

Sheftall, Mordecai G.

Blossoms in the wind; the human legacy of the Kamikaze. [by] M.G. Sheftall. NAL Caliber 2005 480p il $24.95 **940.54**

1. Kamikaze airplanes 2. World War, 1939-1945 -- Aerial operations

ISBN 0-451-21487-0

LC 2004-27356

This account of the "design, training, and execution [of Japanese suicide missions] includes interviews with the families of dead pilots and, harder to reach, pilots who survived the missions." Booklist

Includes bibliographical references

Sides, Hampton

Ghost soldiers; the forgotten epic story of World War II's most dramatic mission. Doubleday 2001 342p il maps $24.95   **940.54**

1. World War, 1939-1945 -- Prisoners and prisons 2. United States -- Army -- Ranger Battalion, 6th 3. World War, 1939-1945 -- Campaigns -- Philippines

ISBN 0-385-49564-1

LC 2001-17337

"The author's excellent grasp of human emotions and bravery makes this a compelling book hard to put down." Publ Wkly

Smyth, Denis

Deathly deception; the real story of Operation Mincemeat. Oxford University Press 2010 xx, 367p il   **940.54**

1. Lawyers 2. Intelligence service agents 3. World War, 1939-1945 -- Secret service

ISBN 978-0-19-923398-4

LC 2010-923437

"When the Allies decided to invade Sicily in summer 1943, they floated the body of a British military officer ashore in German-friendly Spain with the hope that the documents he carried would influence the Germans to believe that the Greek islands or Sardinia would be the Allies' actual target—and the ruse appeared to work. . . . [This is an] administrative history of both sides."

"This superlative and almost unexpurgated account of Operation Mincemeat will enthrall serious students of WWII." Booklist

Includes bibliographical references

Snyder, Timothy D., 1969-

Bloodlands; Europe between Hitler and Stalin. Basic Books 2010 524p map $29.95   **940.54**

1. Genocide 2. Massacres 3. Heads of state 4. Nazi leaders 5. Eastern Europe 6. Communist leaders 7. Political leaders 8. Genocide -- Europe 9. Holocaust, 1933-1945 10. Soviet Union -- History 11. Holocaust, Jewish (1939-1945) 12. Germany -- History -- 1933-1945 13. World War, 1939-1945 -- Atrocities 14. Soviet Union -- History -- 1917-1936 15. Eastern Europe -- History -- 1918-1945

ISBN 9780465002399; 0465002390

LC 2010-16816

The book "tr[ies] to explain mass violence in parts of Eastern Europe in the twentieth century. . . . Snyder deals with territories that were ruled for some time by both Nazi Germany and the USSR from 1930 to 1953. He covers most of today's Poland and Ukraine (the focus of his interest), Belarus, the three Baltic countries, and the most western strip of Russia. . . . Snyder gives a[n] . . . account of political history. . . . [He] places . . . emphasis on the exploitation of the countryside and enforced hunger, which claimed half of the fourteen million victims in the 'bloodlands.' Economically speaking, he emphasizes the extraction of resources by imperialists as the cause of mass starvation." (American Historical Review)

"Mr. Snyder's book is revisionist history of the best kind: in spare, closely argued prose, with meticulous use of statistics, he makes the reader rethink some of the best-known episodes in Europe's modern history." Economist

Includes bibliographical references

Takaki, Ronald T.

Hiroshima; why America dropped the atomic bomb. [by] Ronald Takaki. Little, Brown 1995 193p il $28; pa $14.95   **940.54**

1. Atomic bomb 2. World War, 1939-1945 -- United States 3. Hiroshima (Japan) -- Bombardment, 1945

ISBN 0-316-83122-0; 0-316-83124-7 pa

LC 95-13546

This study of the bombings of Hiroshima and Nagasaki focuses on the psychological motivations of the American decision-makers, especially Harry Truman.

"Right or wrong, the study is a provocative addition to the unresolved debate over the dropping of the atomic bombs." Publ Wkly

Includes bibliographical references

Thomas, Evan

★ **Sea** of thunder; four commanders and the last great naval campaign, 1941-1945. Simon & Schuster 2006 415p il map $27   **940.54**

1. World War, 1939-1945 -- Naval operations 2. World War, 1939-1945 -- Campaigns -- Pacific Ocean

ISBN 978-0-7432-5221-8; 0-7432-5221-7

LC 2006-47511

This is an "account of the Battle of Leyte Gulf, October 1944, one of history's largest naval battles, where Admiral William 'Bull' Halsey, the commander of the U.S. Third Fleet, and his commander, Ernest Evans, met the forces of Japanese admirals Takeo Kurita and Matome Ugaki. . . . Thomas paints compelling portraits of these men, offering insight into their characters and actions throughout the war in the Pacific." Libr J

Includes bibliographical references

Toll, Ian W.

The **conquering** tide; war in the Pacific Islands, 1942-1944. Ian W. Toll. W. W. Norton & Company 2015 672 p. 32 plates; illustrations; maps (hardcover) $35   **940.54**
   1. World War, 1939-1945 -- Naval operations 2. World War, 1939-1945 -- Campaigns -- Pacific Ocean
ISBN 0393080641; 9780393080643

LC 2015009591

This book, by Ian W. Toll, "encompasses the heart of the Pacific War--the period between mid-1942 and mid-1944--when parallel Allied counteroffensives north and south of the equator washed over Japan's far-flung island empire like a 'conquering tide,' concluding with Japan's irreversible strategic defeat in the Marianas." (Publisher's note)

Pacific crucible; war at sea in the Pacific, 1941-1942. Ian W. Toll. W.W. Norton 2011 xxxvi, 597p il map $35   **940.54**
   1. United States -- Naval history 2. World War, 1939-1945 -- Naval operations 3. Pearl Harbor (Oahu, Hawaii), Attack on, 1941 4. World War, 1939-1945 -- Campaigns -- Pacific Ocean
ISBN 978-0-393-06813-9; 0-393-06813-7

LC 2011028907

In this book, "[p]rize-winning freelance naval historian [Ian W.] Toll . . . chronicles one of the U.S. Navy's finest performances of WWII in this . . . narrative of the months following the . . . attacks on Pearl Harbor. Eyewitness accounts and . . . research in American and Japanese print and archival sources" form the book's basis. (Publishers Weekly)

"The author makes vast quantities of technological and tactical concepts intelligible to all but the rankest beginner—for whom this book is not remotely suitable. A particular gift of the author is intelligent character portraits: Yamamoto, MacArthur, Halsey, and Nimitz (clearly one of the author's favorites). Add to all these other attributes a thorough scholarly apparatus, and it is difficult to think of a recent book on this subject that is of such consistently outstanding value." Booklist

Includes bibliographical references and index.

Twomey, Steve

Countdown to Pearl Harbor; The Twelve Days to the Attack. Steve Twomey. Simon & Schuster 2016 384 p. maps, illustrations (ebook) $20.99; (hardcover) $30   **940.54**
   1. United States. Navy 2. World War, 1939-1945 -- Causes 3. Pearl Harbor (Oahu, Hawaii), Attack on, 1941 4. Military intelligence -- United States -- History -- 20th century
ISBN 1476776466; 9781476776507; 9781476776460

LC 2016019080

This book, by Steve Twomey, offers "a fascinating look at the twelve days leading up to the Japanese attack on Pearl Harbor--the warnings, clues and missteps. . . . In Washington, DC, in late November 1941, admirals compose the most ominous message in Navy history to warn Hawaii of possible danger, but they write it too vaguely. They think precautions are being taken, but never check to see if they are." (Publisher's note)

"A well-researched study of an infamous moment that is still fascinating and controversial." Kirkus

Includes bibliographical references (pages 344-353) and index.

Weale, Adrian

Army of evil; a history of the SS. Adrian Weale. NAL

Caliber 2012 xiii, 459 p.p $28.95   **940.54**
   1. Waffen-SS 2. World War, 1939-1945 -- Germany 3. World War, 1939-1945 -- Regimental histories 4. National Socialism 5. Waffen-SS -- History 6. Germany -- Politics and government -- 1933-1945 7. World War, 1939-1945 -- Regimental histories -- Germany 8. Nationalsozialistische Deutsche Arbeiter-Partei. Schutzstaffel
ISBN 0451237919; 9780451237910

LC 2012014170

This book by Adrian Weale presents a "look at the formation of the Schutzstaffeln (aka the SS), from [Adolf] Hitler's early private bodyguards to Heinrich Himmler's elite extermination squads. Weale . . . plots the evolution of the SS as the embodiment and implementation of the Nazi racist ideology. . . . Weale delineates the consolidation of Himmler's power, including the implementation of the concentration camp system . . . as the SS soldiers evolved into instruments of genocide." (Kirkus Reviews)

Includes bibliographical references (p. 433-440) and index

Wilson, Kevin

Blood and Fears; How America's Bomber Boys of the 8th Air Force Saved World War II. Kevin Wilson. W W Norton & Co Inc 2017 560 p. illustrations (ebook) $50; $29.95 **940.54**
   1. World War, 1939-1945 -- Campaigns 2. World War, 1939-1945 -- Aerial operations
ISBN 9781681773797; 1681773198; 9781681773193

LC 2017005016

This book, by Kevin Wilson, presents the story of the US 8th Air Force. "From Operation Argument in February [1944]—targeting German aircraft production plants—to bringing the Luftwaffe to battle over Berlin, the combined US Air Force-Royal Air Force forces' round-the-clock campaign bottled up the German army in Normandy." (Publisher's note)

"A well-researched and well-written history of a significant aspect of World War II." LJ

Includes bibliographical references (pages 516-521) and index.

World War II; the definitive visual history: from Blitzkrieg to the atom bomb. senior editor, Alison Sturgeon. DK Publishing 2015 372 p. illustrations, color maps (hardcover) $40   **940.54**
   1. World War, 1939-1945
ISBN 9781465436023; 1465436022

LC 2015288118

This book, edited Alison Sturgeon and the Dorling Kindersley company, part of the Smithsonian Visual History series, "is a comprehensive, authoritative, yet accessible guide to the people, politics, events, and lasting effects of World War II. . . . [It] presents a complete overview of the war, including the rise of [Adolf] Hitler and the Nazi party, fascism, Pearl Harbor, Hiroshima, and the D-Day landings." (Publisher's note)

"This is a good quick-reference source for information on not just what happened in this great conflict but also on the causes and consequences of it as well. Additionally, it is attractively packaged and provides solid competition to similar Internet resources. The organization and layout are simple, clear, and intuitive." Booklist

Wukovits, John F., 1944-

Hell from the heavens; the epic story of the USS Laffey and World War II's greatest kamikaze attack. John F. Wukovits. Da Capo Press, a member of the Perseus Books Group 2015 336 p. 16 plates; illustrations (hardcover) $25.99   **940.54**
   1. World War, 1939-1945 -- Naval operations 2. World War, 1939-

1945 -- Aerial operations -- Japan 3. Laffey (Ship) 4. Kamikaze pilots -- Japan 5. Japan. Kaigun. Kamikaze Tokubetsu Kōgekitai 6. World War, 1939-1945 -- Campaigns -- Pacific Area 7. World War, 1939-1945 -- Naval operations, American 8. World War, 1939-1945 -- Aerial operations, Japanese
ISBN 0306823241; 9780306823244

LC 2014042127

This book, by John F. Wukovits, presents the story of "the largest single-ship kamikaze attack of World War II. On April 16, 1945, the crewmen of the USS Laffey were battle hardened and prepared. They had engaged in combat off the Normandy coast in June 1944. . . . But nothing could have prepared the crew for this moment--an eighty-minute ordeal in which the single small ship was targeted by no fewer than twenty-two Japanese suicide aircraft." (Publisher's note)

"For WWII buffs, surely, but also for general readers looking to understand the damage inflicted and the terror in s pired by the Japanese suicide squadrons." Kirkus

Includes bibliographical references and index

Zuckoff, Mitchell

Frozen in Time; An Epic Story of Survival and a Modern Quest for Lost Heroes of World War II. Mitchell Zuckoff. HarperCollins 2013 384 p. (hardcover) $28.99   **940.54**
1. Rescue work 2. Arctic regions
ISBN 0062133438; 9780062133434

This book, by Mitchell Zuckoff, tells of how "on November 5, 1942, a US cargo plane slammed into the Greenland Ice Cap." Several subsequent rescue attempts themselves crashed. This book "tells the story of these crashes and the fate of the survivors, bringing vividly to life their battle to endure 148 days of the brutal Arctic winter, until an expedition headed by famed Arctic explorer Bernt Balchen brought them to safety." (Publisher's note)

"Zuckoff's...complex narrative involves the fates of three downed missions to Greenland in late 1942, juxtaposed with the events of the modern-day search effort, led by an exploration company in August 2012 and joined by the author. As a result of the many competing strands and characters, some confusion in the details ensues--though maps and a cast of characters are included to help orient readers... An exhaustively layered but exciting account involving characters of enormous courage and stamina." Kirkus

Lost in Shangri-la. HarperCollins 2011 xii, 384p.p ill. $26.99   **940.54**
1. Primitive societies 2. Survival after airplane accidents, shipwrecks, etc. 3. New Guinea 4. Aircraft accidents -- New Guinea 5. Primitive societies -- New Guinea 6. World War, 1939-1945 -- Missing in action 7. World War, 1939-1945 -- Aerial operations, American 8. World War, 1939-1945 -- Search and rescue operations
ISBN 978-0-06-198834-9; 0-06-198834-0

LC 201034508

L.L. Winship/PEN New England Award: Nonfiction (2012)

This book describes "how three World War II sightseers survived a crash in remote New Guinea." (N Y Times Book Rev) Bibliography. Index.

"On May 13, 1945, an American transport plane carrying 24 servicemen and women crashed into a mountain in the tropical jungles of Dutch New Guinea (now Papua), leaving three survivors. Learning about the event while researching another subject, the author recognized the ingredients of a terrific tale: a beautiful young WAC, a hidden valley reminiscent of the Shangri-La in James Hilton's Lost Horizon, primitive tribal people and a daring air rescue. In this well-crafted book, Zuckoff turns the long-forgotten episode into an unusually exciting narrative. Drawing on the young WAC survivor Margaret Hastings' diary as well

as journals and interviews, the author hones in on life at the U.S. military base in Hollandia, on the northern coast of uncharted New Guinea; a soldier's chance discovery a year earlier of Baliem Valley, a verdant area about 150 miles into the interior, with its hundreds of native villages surrounded by gardens; and the doomed flight of officers and enlisted personnel out on a joy ride to view this much-talked-about land of Stone Age people from the air." Kirkus

Includes bibliographical references and index.

940.542   Campaigns and battles by theater

Summers, Anthony

A **Matter** of Honor; Pearl Harbor: Betrayal, Blame, and a Family's Quest for Justice. Anthony Summers, Robbyn Swan. HarperCollins 2016 464 p. illustrations, map $35; (ebook) $32.99   **940.542**
1. Pearl Harbor (Oahu, Hawaii), Attack on, 1941 2. World War, 1939-1945 -- Campaigns -- Hawaii -- History
ISBN 0062405519; 9780062405517; 9780062405531

This book by Anthony Summers and Robbyn Swan focuses on the efforts of "Admiral Husband Kimmel, Commander-in-Chief of the Pacific Fleet, [who] was relieved of command, accused of negligence and dereliction of duty, [and] publicly disgraced [following the attack on Pearl Harbor]. . . . Summers' and Swan's search for the truth has taken them far beyond the Kimmel story—to explore claims of duplicity and betrayal in high places in Washington." (Publisher's note)

"This sad story reads like a thriller, thanks to the authors' evocative prose and careful use of detail." Pub Wkly

Includes bibliographical references (pages [375]-492) and index.

940.545   Naval operations

Symonds, Craig L.

★ **World** War II at sea; a global history. Craig L. Symonds. Oxford University Press 2018 xxii, 770 p.p illustrations, map (hardback: alk. paper) $34.95   **940.545**
1. Strategy 2. Naval history 3. World War, 1939-1945 -- Naval operations
ISBN 9780190243678

LC 2017032532

In this book, author Craig L. Symonds, presents "a complete narrative of the naval war and all of its belligerents, on all of the world's oceans and seas, between 1939 and 1945 . . . [He] shows how any limitations on naval warfare would become irrelevant before the decade was up, as Europe erupted into conflict once more and its navies were brought to bear against each other." (Publisher's note)

"A veteran maritime historian delivers a satisfying one-volume history of 'the impact of sea services from all nations on the overall trajectory and even the outcome' of World War II." Kirkus

Includes bibliographical references (pages 653-741) and index.

940.55   Europe--1945-1999

Judt, Tony

Postwar; a history of Europe since 1945. Penguin Press 2005 878p il maps $39.95   **940.55**
1. Europe -- History -- 1945-
ISBN 1-59420-065-3

LC 2005-52126

"This is the best history we have of Europe in the postwar period and not likely to be surpassed for many years." Publ Wkly

Includes bibliographical references

Lowe, Keith

  Savage continent; Europe in the aftermath of World War II. St. Martin's Press 2012 460 p. $30.00   **940.55**

  1. Europe -- History -- 1945- 2. Reconstruction (1939-1951) 3. World War, 1939-1945 -- Occupied territories

  ISBN 1250000203; 9781250000200

                    LC 2011279703

Includes bibliographical references and index.

This book offers an "account of the violent and vengeful aftermath of the Second World War in Europe. . . . The aftermath was in part a product of inherited political tensions and ideological conflicts from before 1939 but chiefly a consequence of the massive destruction, displacement and criminality unleashed by Hitler's invasion of Poland and, perhaps more important, the Anglo-French decision to resist it." (New Statesman)

Mazower, Mark

  Dark continent: Europe's twentieth century. Knopf 1999 487p il maps hardcover o.p. pa $16   **940.55**

  1. Europe -- History -- 20th century

  ISBN 0-679-75704-X pa

                    LC 98-15886

The author's "relative unconcern with international and great-power politics probably accounts for a rather intra-European perspective . . . just as it contributes to some exaggeration of the points of comparison and convergence in East and West European economic history. . . . But these are minor defects, the price to be paid for a confident and unconventional work of historical interpretation." N Y Times Book Rev

Includes bibliographical references

940.554   History of Europe – 1945-1999

Feigel, Lara

  The **bitter** taste of victory; life, love and art in the ruins of the reich. Lara Feigel. St. Martin's Press 2016 464 p. illustrations, maps $32; (ebook) $66   **940.554**

  1. World War, 1939-1945 2. Reconstruction (1939-1951) 3. Germany -- History -- 1933-1945

  ISBN 9781632865519; 9781632865533; 1632865513

                    LC 2016020710

This book, by Lara Feigel, tells the never before told experiences of "Ernest Hemingway, Martha Gellhorn, Marlene Dietrich, George Orwell, Lee Miller, W. H. Auden, Stephen Spender, Billy Wilder, and others [who] undertook the challenge of reconfiguring German society. . . . The experiences of these celebrated figures, . . . offers an entirely fresh view of post-war Europe. [This book] is a brilliant and important addition to the literature of World War II." (Publisher's note)

"Many individuals had to come to terms with the evil they saw and with themselves, and Feigel does a masterful job in sorting it out. This is uniquely nuanced history." Booklist

Includes bibliographical references (pages [371]-420) and index.

941   British Isles

Burns, William E.

  A **brief** history of Great Britain. Facts On File 2010 xxiv, 296p il map (Brief history) $49.50; pa $19.95   **941**

  1. Great Britain -- History

  ISBN 978-0-8160-7728-1; 978-0-8160-8124-0 pa

                    LC 2009-8217

This book "narrates the history of Great Britain from the earliest times to the 21st century, covering the entire island—England, Wales, and Scotland—as well as associated archipelagos such as the Channel Islands, the Orkneys, and Ireland as they have influenced British history. The central story of this volume is the development of the British kingdom, including its rise and decline on the world stage." Publisher's note

Includes bibliographical references

Farquhar, Michael

  Behind the palace doors; five centuries of sex, adventure, vice, treachery, and folly from royal Britain. Random House Trade Paperbacks 2011 307p pa $15; ebook $11.99   **941**

  1. Great Britain -- Kings and rulers

  ISBN 978-0-8129-7904-6 pa; 978-0-679-60453-2 ebook

                    LC 2010-21116

The author "probes 500 years of monarchical mishaps and misdeeds, screaming headlines and gleeful attacks by cartoonists. He uncloaks secrets, schemes, scandals, blood-soaked sheets, public humiliations, intrigues, and adultery. Illustrated with lineage charts and chronologically organized, chapters cover the houses of Tudor, Stuart, Hanover, Saxe-Coburg-Gotha, and Windsor. . . . [His] style is a breezy pleasure throughout." Publ Wkly

Includes bibliographical references.

Fraser, Rebecca

  ★ The **story** of Britain; from the Romans to the present: a narrative history. Norton 2005 829p il map $35   **941**

  1. Great Britain -- History

  ISBN 0-393-06010-1

                    LC 2004-26049

First published 2003 in the United Kingdom with title: A people's history of Britain

The author's "narrative advances with the emphasis on the roles of a litany of historical icons, from Queen Boudica to Margaret Thatcher. For those readers who are primarily interested in the 'who, what, when, where, why' of British history, this is a valuable general study." Booklist

Includes bibliographical references

Guy, John

  The **Children** of Henry VIII. Oxford University Press 2013 272 p. (hardcover) $27.95   **941**

  1. Great Britain -- History -- 1485-1603, Tudors

  ISBN 0192840908; 9780192840905

This book by John Guy looks at "the heirs of Henry VIII. . . . Rather than attempt the massive undertaking of covering in depth the histories of Edward, Mary, and Elizabeth, Guy has chosen to give the most salient details regarding the monarchs . . . present[ing] an overall picture of their lives and upbringings under Henry's rule and during their later reigns. His particular focus is on how their relationships with each other -and . . . their father--affected them." (Library Journal)

Hunt, Tristram, 1974-

  Cities of empire; the British colonies and the creation of the urban world. Tristram Hunt. Metropolitan Books 2014 544 p. illustrations, maps (hardback) $35   **941**

  1. Colonies 2. City and town life 3. Great Britain -- Colonies 4. Cities and towns -- Case studies 5. Metropolitan areas -- Case studies 6. Imperialism -- History -- Case studies 7. Great Britain -- Colonies -- History -- Case studies

ISBN 0805093087; 9780805093087

LC 2014030024

Author Tristram Hunt presents a "history of the most enduring colonial creation, the city, explored through ten portraits of powerful urban centers the British Empire left in its wake. He traces the collaboration of cultures and traditions that produced these influential urban centers, the work of an army of administrators, officers, entrepreneurs, slaves, and renegades." (Publisher's note)

"A book to be enjoyed by an array of readers, including historians of various stripes, particularly those who have traveled to any of the book's cities." LJ

Includes bibliographical references and index

Lacey, Robert

★ **Great** tales from English history; the truth about King Arthur, Lady Godiva, Richard the Lionheart, and more. Little, Brown and Co. 2004 254p maps $22.95   **941**

1. Great Britain -- History
ISBN 0-316-10910-X

LC 2003-115660

First published 2003 in the United Kingdom

"This volume begins in 7150 BC with the life and death of Cheddar Man and ends in 1381 with Wat Tyler and the Peasants' Revolt." Publisher's note

Includes bibliographical references

★ **Great** tales from English history [2] Joan of Arc, the princes in the Tower, Bloody Mary, Oliver Cromwell, Sir Isaac Newton, and more. Little, Brown and Co. 2005 271p il map $23.95   **941**

1. Great Britain -- History
ISBN 0-316-10924-X

LC 2004-63351

First published 2004 in the United Kingdom

The author's "second volume on English history opens in 1348, the year of the Black Plague, which wiped out half of England's five million people, and proceeds through the astonishing scientific discoveries of Sir Isaac Newton in 1687. . . . Lacey's animated prose, energetic storytelling and spirited approach to British history bring the past to life." Publ Wkly

Includes bibliographical references

★ **Great** tales from English history [3] Captain Cook, Samuel Johnson, Queen Victoria, Charles Darwin, Edward the Abdicator, and more. Little, Brown and Co. 2006 305p $23.99   **941**

1. Great Britain -- History
ISBN 978-0-316-11459-2; 0-316-11459-6

LC 2006-931723

"The third volume in Lacey's series of edifying and entertaining stories from English history abounds in fascinating profiles. Industrial and agricultural pioneers such as Jethro Tull, James Hargreaves and Isambard Kingdom Brunel abide alongside human rights protestors such as Thomas Clarkson, who founded the British antislavery movement; feminist philosopher Mary Wollstonecraft; and journalist Annie Besant, who initiated a successful 1888 match girls' strike." Publ Wkly

Includes bibliographical references

The **Oxford** history of Britain; edited by Kenneth O. Morgan. Rev ed, New ed; Oxford University Press 2010 821p map pa $18.95   **941**

1. Great Britain -- History

ISBN 978-0-19-957925-9; 0-19-957925-3

LC 2010279308

Text based on The Oxford illustrated history of Britain, published 1984. This version first published 2001

This "volume tells the story of Britain and its people over two thousand years, from the coming of the Roman legions to the present day." Publisher's note

Includes bibliographical references

Schama, Simon

A **history** of Britain. Hyperion 2000 3v ea $40   **941**

1. Great Britain -- History
ISBN 0-7868-6675-6 v1; 0-7868-6752-3 v2; 0-7868-6899-6 v3

LC 00-61442

Schama "writes wonderfully, in an easygoing yet elegant manner, with an eye for the telling aesthetic detail, and throughout brimming with intelligence and passion." N Y Times Book Rev

Includes bibliographical references

941.009   British Isles -- Areas, regions places in general

Tinniswood, Adrian, 1954-

Behind the throne; a domestic history of the British royal household. Adrian Tinniswood. Basic Books 2018 416 p. (hardcover) $32   **941.009**

1. Monarchy 2. Historical literature 3. Great Britain -- Kings and rulers 4. Royal households -- Great Britain -- History
ISBN 9780465094028

LC 2018008384

In this book, "historian Adrian Tinniswood uncovers the reality of five centuries of life at the English court, taking the reader on a remarkable journey from one Queen Elizabeth to another and exploring life as it was lived by clerks and courtiers and clowns and crowned heads: the power struggles and petty rivalries, the tension between duty and desire, the practicalities of cooking dinner for thousands and of ensuring the king always won when he played a game of tennis." (Publisher's note)

Includes bibliographical references and index

941.06   House of Stuart and Commonwealth periods, 1603-1714

Ackroyd, Peter, 1949-

Rebellion; the history of England from James I to the Glorious Revolution. Peter Ackroyd. Thomas Dunne Books, an imprint of St. Martin's Press 2014 512 p. illustrations (some color) (hardcover) $29.99   **941.06**

1. Great Britain -- History -- 1603-1714, Stuarts 2. Great Britain -- History -- Stuarts, 1603-1714
ISBN 1250003636; 9781250003638

LC 2014026045

This book, by Peter Ackroyd, presents the "history of England, beginning the progress south of the Scottish king, James VI, who on the death of Elizabeth I became the first Stuart king of England, and ending with the deposition and flight into exile of his grandson, James II. . . . In addition to its account of England's royalty, [it] also gives us a very real sense of the lives of ordinary English men and women" (Publisher's note)

"Although general readers in the U.S. may find some of the names and places unfamiliar, this masterful work of popular history will remind them that the ideas that launched our own revolution were forged during this seminal period of English history." Booklist

Revolution; the history of England from the Battle of the Boyne to the Battle of Waterloo. by Peter Ackroyd. Thomas Dunne Books 2017 ix, 403 p.p illustrations (History of England) (hardcover) $29.99   **941.06**

1. Great Britain -- History 2. Great Britain -- History -- 1660-1714 3. Great Britain -- History -- 1714-1837 4. Great Britain -- History -- Revolution of 1688 5. Great Britain -- History -- Revolution of 1688 -- Influence

ISBN 9781466880160; 9781250003645; 1250003644

LC 2017027329

In this book in The History of England series, author Peter Ackroyd "takes readers from William of Orange's accession following the Glorious Revolution to the Regency, when the flamboyant Prince of Wales ruled in the stead of his mad father, George III, and England was--again--at war with France, a war that would end with the defeat of Napoleon at Waterloo." (Publisher's note)

"Ackroyd provides a readable and entertaining overview of the political, social, cultural, and economic changes in England from 1689 to 1815." Choice

Includes bibliographical references (pages 373-384) and index.

Long, James

The **plot** against Pepys; [by] James Long & Ben Long. Overlook Press 2008 322p il $27.95   **941.06**

1. Trials 2. Diarists 3. Military officials 4. Government officials 5. Members of Parliament 6. Great Britain -- History -- 1603-1714, Stuarts

ISBN 978-1-59020-069-8; 1-59020-069-1

First published 2007 in the United Kingdom

"The book is packed with marvellous asides that add colour to an already kaleidoscopic cavalcade of crass credulousness, court drama and crookery. . . . I couldn't put it down, and there aren't many books on the seventeenth century you can say that about." Hist Today

Includes bibliographical references

Pepys, Samuel

★ The **diary** of Samuel Pepys; edited and with a preface by Richard Le Gallienne; introduction by Robert Louis Stevenson. Modern Lib. 2001 xxxv, 310p $22; pa $15.95   **941.06**

1. Diarists 2. Military officials 3. Government officials 4. Members of Parliament

ISBN 0-679-64221-8; 0-8129-7071-3 pa

LC 00-54817

An abridged edition of Pepys' eleven-volume diary, originally written between 1660 and 1669.

Tomalin, Claire

Samuel Pepys; the unequalled self. Knopf 2002 xxiii, 470p il $30; pa $16.95   **941.06**

1. Diarists 2. Military officials 3. Government officials 4. Members of Parliament 5. Great Britain -- Social life and customs 6. Great Britain -- History -- 1603-1714, Stuarts

ISBN 0-375-41143-7; 0-375-72553-9 pa

LC 2002-75701

"Tomalin mines the diary, and she also expands upon the characters and events, great and small, that affected Pepys' life and livelihood to bring the man and his milieu to life—pungently as well as vibrantly." Booklist

Includes bibliographical references

941.066   Reign of Charles II, 1660-1685 (Restoration)

Jordan, Don

The **king's** revenge; Charles II and the Greatest Manhunt in British History. Don Jordan and Michael Walsh. Little, Brown & Co. 2012 383 p. illustrations $27.95   **941.066**

1. Great Britain -- History 2. Regicides -- England -- History -- 17th century 3. Great Britain -- History -- Charles II, 1660-1685 4. Great Britain -- History -- Puritan Revolution, 1642-1660

ISBN 1408703270; 1681771683; 9781408703274; 9781681771687

LC 2012545486

In this book, by Don Jordan and Michael Walsh, "when Charles I was executed, his son Charles II made it his role to seek out retribution, producing the biggest manhunt Britain had ever seen, one that would span Europe and America and would last for thirty years. . . . Many of the most senior figures in England were hanged, drawn and quartered; imprisoned for life; or consigned to a self-imposed exile, in constant fear of the assassin's bullet." (Publisher's note)

"Crafted like a spy novel as Charles II set about to find the living regicides, this work will intrigue readers with the breadth and ruthlessness of the king's search." LJ

Includes bibliographical references (p. [357]-360) and index

Mortimer, Ian

The **time** traveler's guide to Restoration Britain; a handbook for visitors to the seventeenth century: 1660-1700. Ian Mortimer. Pegasus Books 2017 454 p. illustrations (chiefly color) (hardcover) $28.95   **941.066**

1. Great Britain -- Social conditions -- History 2. Great Britain -- History -- 1660-1688, Restoration 3. Great Britain -- History -- 1660-1714 4. London (England) -- History -- 17th century 5. Great Britain -- History -- Restoration, 1660-1688 6. Great Britain -- Social conditions -- 17th century

ISBN 1681773546; 9781681773544; 9781681774008

This book, by Ian Mortimer, offers "an up-close-and-personal look at Britain between the Restoration of King Charles II in 1660 and the end of the century . . . Over these four dynamic decades, the last vestiges of medievalism are swept away and replaced by a tremendous cultural flowering. . . . [The author] delves into the nuances of daily life to paint a vibrant and detailed picture of society at the dawn of the modern world as only he can." (Publisher's note)

"This is a sure bet for history lovers and readers with a penchant for unusual travelogues." Booklist

Includes bibliographical references (pages 413-440) and index.

941.07   Period of House of Hanover, 1714-1837

Brewer, John

The **pleasures** of the imagination; English culture in the eighteenth century. University of Chicago Press 2000 721p il pa $20   **941.07**

1. Great Britain -- Civilization 2. Great Britain -- Intellectual life 3. Great Britain -- Social life and customs

ISBN 0-226-07419-6; 978-0-226-07419-1

LC 99-57059

First published 1997 by Farrar, Straus and Giroux

"A remarkable feat of scholarship, this volume will quickly establish itself as an indispensable reference." Booklist

Includes bibliographical references

Foreman, Amanda

Georgiana, Duchess of Devonshire. Random House 2000 454p hardcover o.p. pa $15.95　　**941.07**

1. Socialites 2. Spouses of prominent persons 3. Nobility -- Great Britain -- Biography 4. Women politicians -- Great Britain -- Biography 5. Great Britain -- Politics and government -- 1789-1820 6. Great Britain -- Social life and customs -- 18th century 7. Great Britain -- History -- George III, 1760-1820 -- Biography

ISBN 0-375-75383-4 pa

LC 99-23580

Georgiana "was the society leader of her day. Daughter of the fabulously wealthy Earl Spencer (and ancestor of the late princess of Wales) and married to the even more wealthy duke of Devonshire, Georgiana was watched, adored, and imitated. But she evolved herself into more than just a fashionable hostess; she got involved in Whig politics, to an extent unprecedented for women. . . . The tenor of the subject's time and place—in this instance, aristocratic Britain in the late 1700s and early 1800s—is both colorfully and meaningfully realized." Booklist

Includes bibliographical references

Fraser, Antonia, 1932-

The **King** and the Catholics; England, Ireland, and the fight for religious freedom, 1780-1829. Antonia Fraser. Nan A. Talese, Doubleday 2018 336 p. $29.95　　**941.07**

1. Catholics -- Great Britain 2. Church and state -- Great Britain 3. Great Britain -- History -- 1714-1837 4. Catholic emancipation 5. Catholic Church -- Great Britain -- History 6. Great Britain -- Politics and government -- 1714-1837

ISBN 9780385544528

LC 2018015523

This book, by Antonia Fraser, presents "the dramatic story of how Catholics in the United Kingdom won back their rights after two centuries of official discrimination. In the summer of 1780, mob violence swept through London. Nearly one thousand people were killed. . . . These were the Gordon Riots: the worst civil disturbance in British history, triggered by an act of Parliament designed to loosen two centuries of systemic oppression of Catholics in the British Isles." (Publisher's note)

McLynn, Frank

1759: the year Britain became master of the world. Atlantic Monthly Press 2004 422p il map $26　　**941.07**

1. Seven Years' War, 1756-1763 2. Great Britain -- Colonies 3. Great Britain -- Foreign relations

ISBN 0-87113-881-6

LC 2004-57397

First published 2004 in the United Kingdom

1759 "was the fourth [year] in the Seven Years War, a struggle between France and England for global dominance that was fought worldwide. McLynn focuses on the deadly conflict, contrasting the two nations' differing wartime policies and showing how the combination of Britain's maritime prowess and sheer good luck helped it emerge triumphant, albeit by a narrow margin. . . . Splendidly narrated, with balanced insights into the Native American aspect of the French and Indian Wars, McLynn's book will enthrall all lovers of history told well." Publ Wkly

Includes bibliographical references

941.08　Period of Victoria and House of Windsor, 1837-

McKillop, A. B.

The **spinster** & the prophet; H.G. Wells, Florence Deeks,

and the case of the plagiarized text. Four Walls Eight Windows 2002 477p il $26.95　　**941.08**

1. Authors 2. Novelists 3. Historians 4. Plagiarism 5. Historiography 6. Feminists 7. Writers on science 8. Writers on politics 9. Science fiction writers

ISBN 1-56858-236-6

LC 2002-71292

"When, in 1920, Florence Deeks finally received her rejected manuscript—a feminist history of the world—from Macmillan after eight months, she couldn't understand why it appeared in such bad condition. . . . Later that year, when she read H.G. Wells's new book, The Outline of History, published by Macmillan, she felt a chill. There were so many similarities to her own work: shared themes, organization, word choice, even the same mistakes. Florence made a dramatic decision—she would sue Wells and his publisher for plagiarism. . . . The author handles the dual story line brilliantly, weaving together two opposing characters into one altogether gripping tale of literary theft." Publ Wkly

Includes bibliographical references

Vallone, Lynne

Becoming Victoria. Yale Univ. Press 2001 256p il $26.95　　**941.08**

1. Queens 2. Great Britain -- History -- 19th century

ISBN 0-300-08950-3

LC 00-68561

"Analyzing Victoria's girlhood diaries, drawings and fiction, as well as records of her education and scores of accounts of her childhood, Valone . . . constructs a revisionist account of the princess's youthful persona but also traces the process by which Victoria was molded into the 'right' kind of adult: capable of assuming the throne and also a clear embodiment of all that was womanly and pure. . . . Well-researched, and with sophisticated cultural criticism, this sound scholarship will engage the interest of academics and nonacademics alike." Publ Wkly

Includes bibliographical references

941.081　British Isles--Reign of Victoria, 1837-1901

Cadbury, Deborah

Queen Victoria's matchmaking; the royal marriages that shaped Europe. Deborah Cadbury. First US edition Public Affairs 2017 382 p. illustrations (hardcover) $27　　**941.081**

1. Marriage 2. Kings and rulers 3. Marriages of royalty and nobility -- Europe -- History -- 19th century 4. Marriages of royalty and nobility -- Europe -- History -- 20th century

ISBN 9781610398473; 9781610398466

LC 2017952726

This book, by Deborah Cadbury, "travels through the glittering, decadent palaces of Europe from London to Saint Petersburg, weaving in scandals, political machinations and family tensions to enthralling effect. It is at once an intimate portrait of a royal family and an examination of the conflict caused by the marriages the Queen arranged. At the heart of it all is Victoria herself: doting grandmother one moment, determined Queen Empress the next." (Publisher's note)

"British historian and documentarian Cadbury (Princes at War) energetically reveals the extent of Queen Victoria's meddling in the marriage arrangements of her grandchildren in order to create the family's ideal British-German alliance." Pub Wkly

Includes bibliographical references (pages 331-369) and index.

Encyclopedia of the Victorian era; James Eli Adams, editor in chief; Tom Pendergast, Sara Pendergast, editors. Grolier Academic Reference 2004 4v il map set $499   **941.081**
1. Great Britain -- Civilization 2. Great Britain -- History -- 19th century
ISBN 0-7172-5860-2

LC 2003-57101

"Entries ranging in length from a few paragraphs to several pages are written by experts, treat topics from William Acton to zoological gardens, and seek to encompass the important issues, people, and events of the Victorian era.... While predictable figures such as Queen Victoria and Benjamin Disraeli appear, so too do social history topics such as the sporting life, penny dreadfuls, and cholera." Choice
Includes bibliographical references

Murphy, Paul Thomas
Shooting Victoria; madness, mayhem, and the rebirth of the British monarchy. Paul Thomas Murphy. Pegasus Books 2012 669 p. $35.00   **941.081**
1. Victoria, Queen of Great Britain, 1819-1901 -- Assassination attempts
ISBN 9781605983547; 1605983543

This book on various attempts to assassinate Queen Victoria of England "recounts ... how these deluded subjects managed to channel their mental instability or optimistic naïveté into assassination attempts with barely functioning pistols or stout canes.... [Paul Thomas] Murphy ... weaves their life stories in with the reactions of Victoria and Albert and other notables as the government struggled to define a policy for punishing assassins." (Publishers Weekly)

Summerscale, Kate
Mrs. Robinson's disgrace; the private diary of a Victorian lady. Kate Summerscale. Bloomsbury 2012 xvi, 303 p.p geneal. tables $26.00   **941.081**
1. Diaries 2. Divorce 3. Great Britain -- History -- Victoria, 1837-1901
ISBN 1608199134; 9781608199136

LC 2012451243

This book considers the experience of Victorian woman "Isabella Robinson [who] defended herself in the newly created English divorce court over a mislaid diary filled with passionate erotic entries, philosophical musings, and complaints against her husband.... In two sections, the book first describes Isabella's flowery, coy memories of [her lover] ...; the second part focuses on her trial on an adultery charge and the scrambling of her male friends to preserve their reputations." (Publishers Weekly)
Includes bibliographical references and index

Wilson, A. N.
The **Victorians**. Norton 2003 724p il $35; pa $17.95   **941.081**
1. Great Britain -- Civilization 2. Great Britain -- History -- 19th century
ISBN 0-393-04974-4; 0-393-32543-1 pa

LC 2002-33809

First published 2002 in the United Kingdom
"Even to fastidious readers, Wilson's failings are minor, and the colorful tapestry he presents of a smoky world peopled with the likes of Carlyle, Mill, Marx, Ruskin, and Darwin can hardly fail to enthrall. Both professional scholars and laypeople will love to relax with this book, although some knowledge of the age is a must." Choice
Includes bibliographical references

941.084   British Isles, 1936-1945

Cadbury, Deborah
Princes at war; the bitter battle inside Britain's royal family in the darkest days of wwii. Deborah Cadbury. PublicAffairs 2014 384 p. 16 plates; illustrations (hardcover) $28.99 **941.084**
1. Great Britain -- Kings and rulers 2. Great Britain -- History -- 20th century
ISBN 1610394038; 9781610394031; 9781610394048

LC 2014957933

This book, by Deborah Cadbury, explores how "In 1936, the British monarchy faced the greatest threats to its survival in the modern era--the crisis of abdication and the menace of Nazism. The fate of the country rested in the hands of George V's sorely unequipped sons.... [The book portrays] these four very different men ..., one of whom had to save the monarchy ... as the old order was overturned." (Publisher's note)
"Bias aside, this is an engaging, well-told history of England and its royals during its most fragile period; conveying wartime tensions, worldwide scandals, and familial devotions and rivalries with equal vividness." LJ

Clarke, Peter
Mr. Churchill's profession; the statesman as author and the book that defined the 'special relationship' Peter Clarke. 1st US ed. Bloomsbury Press 2012 xix, 347 p.p ill. (alk. paper) $30.00   **941.084**
1. Politicians' writings 2. Prime ministers -- Great Britain 3. Great Britain -- History -- 20th century 4. Prime ministers -- Great Britain -- Biography
ISBN 1608193721; 9781608193721

LC 2011044274

This book "traces the making of the ... work that occupied [Winston] Churchill for a quarter century, his four-volume 'History of the English-Speaking Peoples.' Churchill signed the contract for 'History' in 1932, at a time when his political career seemed over. His ... return to power when the Nazis swept across Europe meant the book went uncompleted until the 1950s. But long before he took office, the ... project was shaping his worldview, his speeches, and his leadership." (Publisher's note)
Includes bibliographical references (p.318 -331) and index

Maier, Thomas
When lions roar; the Churchills and the Kennedys. Thomas Maier. Crown Publishers 2014 784 p. 16 plates; illustrations $30   **941.084**
1. Kennedy family 2. Great Britain -- Relations -- United States 3. United States -- Relations -- Great Britain 4. Great Britain -- Politics and government -- 20th century 5. United States -- Politics and government -- 20th century
ISBN 0307956792; 9780307956798; 9780307956811

LC 2014007201

This book, by Thomas Maier, provides "the first comprehensive history of the deeply entwined personal and public lives of the Churchills and the Kennedys and what their 'special relationship' meant for Great Britain and the United States.... Thomas Maier tells this dynastic saga ... providing ... insight into the Churchill and Kennedy families and the profound forces of duty, loyalty, courage and ambition that shaped them." (Publisher's note)
"An excellent work for all history collections, especially those devoted to 20th-century political history." LJ
Includes bibliographical references and index
Churchills and the Kennedys

Morton, Andrew

17 carnations; the royals, the nazis and the biggest cover-up in history. Andrew Morton. Grand Central Publishing 2015 384 p. illustrations (hardcover) $28   **941.084**

1. Conspiracies -- Great Britain -- History -- 20th century
ISBN 9781455527090; 9781455527113; 9781478959151; 9781619695887

LC 2014957815

This book, by Andrew Morton, "tells the story of the feckless Edward VIII, later Duke of Windsor, his American wife, Wallis Simpson, the bizarre wartime Nazi plot to make him a puppet king after the invasion of Britain, and the attempted cover-up by Churchill, General Eisenhower, and King George VI of the duke's relations with Hitler." (Publisher's note)

Includes bibliographical references (pages [329]-362) and index.

Weir, Alison

The **children** of Henry VIII. Ballantine Bks. 1996 385p il hardcover o.p.   **941.084**

1. Queens 2. Kings 3. Great Britain -- History -- 1485-1603, Tudors

LC 96-14849

Published in the United Kingdom with title: Children of England

This "book covers the lives of Henry's children Mary Tudor and Edward VI, but it only takes Elizabeth up to her accession, and it also includes the entire short life of Jane Grey, the granddaughter of Henry's sister Mary. When Henry died in 1547, he left a country embroiled in several social problems brought about by the enclosure of common lands, the high cost of his European wars, and the closure of monasteries. How his heirs dealt with these problems, along with their relationships, makes interesting reading." Libr J

Includes bibliographical references

941.085   British Isles, 1945-1999

Andersen, Christopher

Game of crowns; Elizabeth, Camilla, Kate, and the throne. Christopher Andersen. Gallery Books 2016 352 p. color illustrations $28   **941.085**

1. Queens 2. Princesses 3. Great Britain -- Kings and rulers
ISBN 9781476743950; 9781476743974

LC 2015050619

This book, by Christopher Anderson, takes a "look into the relationships and rivalries of Queen Elizabeth, Camilla Parker Bowles, and Kate Middleton. Andersen reveals what transpires within the royal family away from the public's prying eyes; how the women actually feel about each other; how they differ as lovers, wives, and mothers; and how they are reshaping the landscape of the monarchy." (Publisher's note)

"With gaspworthy and laugh-out-loud moments revealing scandalous and sympathetic details of the royal family, Andersen humanizes this privileged yet embattled group." Kirkus

Includes bibliographical references (pages 315-319) and index.

Junor, Penny

The **Firm**: the troubled life of the House of Windsor. Thomas Dunne Books 2005 xxi, 442p il $25.95   **941.085**

1. Queens 2. Kings 3. Great Britain -- Kings and rulers
ISBN 0-312-35274-3

LC 2005-45528

"Readers of this interesting and occasionally jaw-dropping look at the world's most famous dysfunctional family will find plenty to engage them." Libr J

Includes bibliographical references

Kynaston, David

Austerity Britain; 1945-51. Walker & Co. 2008 692p il (Tales of a new Jerusalem) $45   **941.085**

1. Great Britain -- Social conditions 2. Great Britain -- History -- 1945-1952 3. Great Britain -- Politics and government -- 20th century
ISBN 978-0-8027-1693-4; 0-8027-1693-8

First published 2007 in the United Kingdom

"Drawing on a remarkable array of diaries, letters, memoirs, and surveys, Kynaston assembles a polyphonic history of a pivotal time." New Yorker

Includes bibliographic references

Family Britain, 1951-1957. Walker & Co 2010 776p il $47.50   **941.085**

1. Great Britain -- History -- 1952- 2. Great Britain -- Social conditions 3. Great Britain -- Politics and government -- 20th century
ISBN 978-0-8027-1797-9

"Picking up where the much-lauded Austerity Britain, 1945-1951 (2008) left off, Kynaston's latest presents a panoramic view of a transformative period. . . . Leading us on an immersive tour of headlines and correspondence, diaries and sociological studies, Kynaston narrates moments and motifs both great and small, among them the Festival of Britain, Council housing, the queen's coronation, pub culture, Kingsley Amis, smog, labor strikes, skiffle, the 'colour bar,' grammar schools, football, the Suez Crisis, young Mick Jagger, and the BBC." Booklist

Includes bibliographical references

941.1   Scotland

Herman, Arthur

How the Scots invented the modern world; the true story of how western Europe's poorest nation created our world & everything in it. Crown 2001 392p $25.95; pa $14.95 **941.1**

1. Scottish national characteristics 2. Scotland -- Civilization
ISBN 0-609-60635-2; 0-609-80999-7 pa

LC 2001-28951

"This is a worthwhile book for the general reader." Publ Wkly

Includes bibliographical references (p. 362-376) and index

Nicolson, Adam

Sea room: an island life in the Hebrides. North Point Press 2002 391p il maps $27; pa $14   **941.1**

1. Hebrides (Scotland) -- Social life and customs
ISBN 0-86547-636-5; 0-86547-667-5 pa

LC 2002-19816

First published 2001 in the United Kingdom

"Magnificent and poetic, this is a literary and ecological masterpiece." Booklist

Includes bibliographical references

Royle, Trevor

★ **Culloden**; Scotland's Last Battle and the Forging of the British Empire. Trevor Royle. W W Norton & Co Inc 2016 432 p. illustrations (hardcover) $28.95; (ebook) $50 **941.1**

1. Jacobite Rebellion, 1745-1746 2. Culloden, Battle of, Scotland, 1746 3. Scotland -- History -- 18th century 4. Great Britain --

History -- 1714-1837

ISBN 9781681772363; 9781681772813; 1681772361

"The Battle of Culloden in 1746 has gone down in history as the last major battle fought on British soil: a vicious confrontation between the English Royal Army and the Scottish forces supporting the Stuart claim to the throne.... In Trevor Royle's vivid and evocative narrative, we are drawn into the ranks, on both sides, alongside doomed Jacobites fighting fellow Scots dressed in the red coats of the Duke of Cumberland's Royal Army." (Publisher's note)

"Culloden's importance to Scotland's fortunes has never been doubted; Royle now demonstrates that its relevance to decades of British global supremacy cannot be questioned." Pub Wkly

Includes bibliographical references and index.

941.3   Southeastern Scotland

Robb, Graham

The **debatable** land; the lost world between Scotland and England. Graham Robb. W W Norton & Co Inc 2018 336 p. $27.95   **941.3**

1. Scotland -- History 2. Boundaries -- History 3. Great Britain -- History

ISBN 0393285324; 9780393285321

This book, by Graham Robb, "takes us from a time when neither England nor Scotland existed to the present day, when contemporary nationalism and political turmoil threaten to unsettle the cross-border community once more. With his customary charm, wit, and literary grace, . . . Robb proves the Debatable Land to be a crucial, missing piece in the puzzle of British history." (Publisher's note)

Stewart, Rory

The **Marches**; A Borderland Journey Between England and Scotland. by Rory Stewart. Houghton Mifflin Harcourt 2016 304 p. $26   **941.3**

1. England 2. Scotland 3. Boundaries

ISBN 0544108884; 9780544108882

This book, by Rory Stewart, is "an exploration of the Marches—the borderland between England and Scotland—and the people, history, and conflicts that have shaped it. . . . Following the lines of Neolithic standing stones, wading through floods and ruined fields, he walks Hadrian's Wall with soldiers who have fought in Afghanistan and visits the Buddhist monks who outnumber Christian monks in the Scottish countryside today." (Publisher's note)

941.5   Ireland

★ **Encyclopedia** of Irish history and culture; James S. Donnelly Jr., editor in chief; Karl S. Bottigheimer . . . [et al.], associate editors. Macmillan Reference USA 2004 2v il map set $270   **941.5**

1. Reference books 2. Ireland -- Encyclopedias

ISBN 0-02-865902-3

LC 2004-5353

"The A-Z entries are preceded by a chronology and followed by a selection of almost 150 primary documents ranging from the Confession of St. Patrick (c. 450) to the Belfast/Good Friday Agreement (1998). . . . Providing the latest in scholarship, entries are well written and cover the gamut of historical, social, and cultural topics." Booklist

Includes bibliographical references

Ferriter, Diarmaid

The **transformation** of Ireland. Overlook Press 2005 884p $37.50   **941.5**

1. Ireland -- History

ISBN 1-58567-681-0

LC 2005-49849

First published 2004 in the United Kingdom

"This book isn't a political history of 20th-century Ireland; it's more a chronicle of the social reaction to the events that shaped that century. . . . [The author] has written an informative, funny, at times derisive book that takes a fresh approach to 20th-century Ireland." Publ Wkly

Includes bibliographical references

Gibney, John

A **short** history of Ireland, 1500-2000; John Gibney. Yale University Press 2017 296 p. (alk. paper) $25   **941.5**

1. Ireland -- History 2. Historical literature 3. Great Britain -- History

ISBN 9780300208511

LC 2017941374

This book, by John Gibney, presents "a brisk, concise, and readable overview of Irish history from the Protestant Reformation to the dawn of the twenty-first century. . . . [It] covers important historical events, including the Cromwellian conquest and settlement, the Great Famine, and the struggle for Irish independence. Gibney's book explores major themes such as Ireland's often contentious relationship with Britain . . . and the global reach of the Irish diaspora." (Publisher's note)

Kelly, John

The **graves** are walking; the great famine and the saga of the Irish people. John Kelly. Henry Holt and Co. 2012 397 p.   **941.5**

1. Famines -- Ireland 2. Ireland -- History 3. Ireland -- Immigration and emigration 4. Ireland -- History -- Famine, 1845-1852 5. Famines -- Ireland -- History -- 19th century 6. Irish -- Migrations -- History -- 19th century 7. Ireland -- Emigration and immigration -- History -- 19th century

ISBN 080509184X; 9780805091847

LC 2012011493

This book, by John Kelly, offers an "account of . . . the Great Irish Potato Famine. . . . It started in 1845, . . . [a] perfect storm of bacterial infection, political greed, and religious intolerance. . . . But even more extraordinary . . . were its political underpinnings, and [the author] . . . provides . . . analysis on the role that Britain's nation-building policies played in exacerbating the devastation by attempting to use the famine to reshape Irish society and character." (Publisher's note)

Includes bibliographical references and index

Nic Dhiarmada, Bríona, 1957-

The **1916** Irish Rebellion; Bríona Nic Dhiarmada; foreword by Mary McAleese. University of Notre Dame Press 2016 ix, 205 p.p illustrations, map (hardcover: alk. paper) $45   **941.5**

1. Irish Americans 2. Ireland -- History -- 20th century 3. Irish question 4. Ireland -- History -- Easter Rising, 1916

ISBN 0268036144; 9780268036140

LC 2015042508

In this book, "scholar Bríona Nic Dhiarmada has seized the occasion of the centenary of the Irish Rising to reassess this event and its historical significance. Her book explores the crucial role of Irish Americans in both the lead-up to and the aftermath of the events in Dublin and places the Irish Rising in its European and global context, as an expression of the anti-colonialism that found its full voice in the wake of the First

World War." (Publisher's note)

"Rich in fascinating historical photographs and informative and poignant documents that capture each phase of the struggle and its inevitable and tragic outcome, this striking volume tells the complex tale of a singular chapter in the long war against colonialism in plain and ringing language." Booklist

Includes bibliographical references and index

State, Paul F.

A **brief** history of Ireland. Facts On File 2009 xxiv, 408p il map (Brief history) $49.50; pa $19.95   **941.5**
1. Ireland -- History
ISBN 978-0-8160-7516-4; 0-8160-7516-6; 978-0-8160-7517-1 pa; 0-8160-7517-4 pa

LC 2008-29243

The author "opens this vibrant reference with an introduction to Ireland's landscape, people, economics, natural resources, and current government. Following this essay-style overview are 11 chronologically organized chapters. Each is devoted to a significant historical watershed, tracing events from Ireland's prehistory to its contemporary prosperity. Appendixes provide at-a-glance portraits of Northern Ireland and the Irish Republic, including a list of presidents, prime ministers, and a time line of notable dates." Libr J

Includes bibliographical references

Walsh, Maurice

Bitter freedom; Ireland in a revolutionary world. Maurice Walsh. Liveright Publishing Corp., a division of W.W. Norton & Company 2016 544 p. (hardcover) $35   **941.5**
1. Revolutions 2. World politics 3. World War, 1914-1918 -- Influence 4. Ireland -- History -- 20th century 5. World politics -- 1919-1932 6. Ireland -- History -- 1910-1921 7. World War, 1914-1918 -- Ireland 8. Revolutions -- History -- 20th century 9. World War, 1914-1918 -- Political aspects 10. Ireland -- Politics and government -- 1910-1921 11. Ireland -- History -- War of Independence, 1919-1921 12. Ireland -- History -- War of Independence, 1919-1921 -- Social aspects
ISBN 1631491954; 9781631491955

LC 2016002970

This book, by Maurice Walsh, "places revolutionary Ireland within the panorama of nationalist movements born out of World War I. Beginning with the Easter Rising of 1916, [it] follows through from the War of Independence to the end of the post-partition civil war in 1924." (Publisher's note)

"An excellent history, but more importantly, a sharply written portrait of a people and their long struggle to survive." Kirkus

Includes bibliographical references and index

941.501   Early history to 1086

Cahill, Thomas

How the Irish saved civilization; the untold story of Ireland's heroic role from the fall of Rome to the rise of medieval Europe. {by} Thomas Cahill. Talese 1995 246p il maps $27.50; pa $12.95   **941.501**
1. Medieval civilization 2. Learning and scholarship 3. Ireland -- Civilization
ISBN 0-385-41848-5; 0-385-41849-3 pa

LC 94-28130

"Highly literate and affectionate, if somewhat rambling and indulgent. . . . As a freewheeling, witty popular history of Irish Christianity in the Dark Ages, this will amuse and enlighten." Libr J

Includes bibliographical references

941.505   Period under House of Tudor, 1485-1603

Ekin, Des

The **Last** Armada; Queen Elizabeth, Juan Del Águila, and the 100-day Invasion of England. by Des Ekin. W W Norton & Co Inc 2016 420 p. 8 plates; illustrations; maps $27.95 **941.505**
1. Naval battles 2. Spain -- History 3. Great Britain -- History
ISBN 1605989444; 9781605989440

This book, by Des Ekin, is the "story of the last great naval battle between England and Spain. . . . General Juan del Águila has been sprung from a prison cell to command the last great Spanish armada. His mission: to seize a bridgehead in Queen Elizabeth's England and hold it. Facing him is Charles Blount, a brilliant English strategist. . . . Meanwhile, Irish insurgent Hugh O'Neill knows that this is his final chance to drive the English out of Ireland." (Publisher's note)

"The author explains the terrain, battles, siege construction, and weaponry well enough to please any military historian, but the real prizes here are the author's discussions of the effect of the battle on Spain as its empire died and England's colonies grew, the end of Spain's religious wars, the shift of power in England, and the cataclysm as Gaelic Ireland declined and died. A fantastic book that finally assigns Kinsale its rightful place in history." Kirkus

941.6   Northern Ireland; Donegal, Monaghan, Cavan counties of Republic of Ireland

Campbell, Julieann

Setting the truth free; the inside story of the Bloody Sunday Justice Campaign. Julieann Campbell. Liberties Press 2012 219 p. ill. (some col.) (pbk.) $24.95   **941.6**
1. Civil rights demonstrations 2. Northern Ireland -- History 3. Bloody Sunday, Derry, Northern Ireland, 1972 4. Bloody Sunday Justice Campaign 5. Londonderry (Northern Ireland) -- History -- 20th century 6. Massacres -- Northern Ireland -- Londonderry -- History -- 20th century
ISBN 1907593373; 9781907593376

LC 2012379691

In this book about the "1972 Bloody Sunday massacre during a peaceful civil rights march in Derry, Northern Ireland .. . . [Julieann] Campbell, an Irish journalist . . . niece of the first person slain on that tragic day . . . [and] the press officer for the campaign to find justice for those killed and wounded, not only tells the tale of her murdered 17-year-old uncle, Jackie Duddy, but also details the planning of the march, the . . . slaughter by the British troops, and the traumatic remembrances of the survivors. . . . A need to seek justice, as Campbell writes, motivated the Irish community to protest and pressure the British government to launch a real inquiry into the shootings." (Publishers Weekly)

Coogan, Tim Pat

The **troubles**; Ireland's ordeal, 1966-1996, and the search for peace. Palgrave 2002 589p il map pa $22.95   **941.6**
1. Northern Ireland
ISBN 978-0-312-29418-2; 0-312-29418-2
First published 1995 in the United Kingdom
In this political history the author "examines all parties to the struggle. . . . He reconstructs the past 30 years, from the 1969 marching and riots to the H-Block protests, the MacBride Principles, the Anglo-Irish

agreement, and the recent paramilitary cease-fire. Coogan traces the current peace process, stalled by Great Britain's insistence that the IRA hand in its weapons, to the 1979 visit of Pope John Paul II." Libr J

Includes bibliographical references

942   England and Wales

Ackroyd, Peter

London: the biography. Talese 2001 xxvi, 801p il $45; pa $18.95   **942**

1. London (England) -- History
ISBN 0-385-49770-9; 0-385-49771-7 pa

LC 2001-27153

First published 2000 in the United Kingdom

"A sweeping, highly readable account of London's colorful and complicated history." Libr J

Includes bibliographical references

Thames; the biography. Nan A. Talese/Doubleday 2008 481p il map $40   **942**

1. Thames River (England) 2. London (England) -- History
ISBN 978-0-385-52623-4; 0-385-52623-7

LC 2008-02864

First published 2007 in the United Kingdom

"Eschewing standard organization, Ackroyd jumps from today's posh London banks to Roger Bacon's observatory at Grandpont to Dickens's 'deathlike and mysterious' waterway. We learn about the riverbank's many species of willow (white, weeping, crack, cane osier), and about the Retribution and the Belliqueux, eighteenth-century prison boats that each held hundreds of men. . . . A survey of the many ways in which the river can kill notes that most Thames suicides remain 'anonymous and unlamented.' Not every tidbit will appeal to every reader, but the book demands to be read as it was written, according to one's fancy." New Yorker

Includes bibliographical references

Cartwright, Justin

Oxford revisited. Bloomsbury 2009 223p pa $18   **942**

1. Oxford (England) 2. University of Oxford
ISBN 978-1-59691-093-5; 1-59691-093-3

First published 2008 in the United Kingdom with title: This secret garden

"A South African-born novelist who graduated from Oxford University in the 1960s, Cartwright returns to the medieval campus nearly four decades later on a combination nostalgic tour and journalistic inquiry. Seeking to define the university's greatness, Cartwright offers erudite meditations on everything from the solidity of its buildings . . . to the fiercely individualistic lives of its students. . . . He offers sharply observed homages to the thinkers and writers—Isaiah Berlin, J. R. R. Tolkien, Charles Dodgson—who shaped Oxford's discourse, and maps out the university's peculiar mix of silly rituals and sublime intellectual life. In addition, the book retraces Cartwright's own journey from callow teenager to confident young scholar-athlete." N Y Times Book Rev

Gott, Richard

Britain's empire; resistance, repression and revolt. Richard Gott. Verso Books 2011 vii, 568 p.p $34.95   **942**

1. Imperialism 2. Resistance to government 3. Great Britain -- Colonies 4. Imperialism -- History 5. Great Britain -- Civilization 6. Commonwealth countries -- History 7. Great Britain -- Colonies -- History 8. Government, Resistance to -- Commonwealth countries -- History 9. Government, Resistance to -- Great Britain

-- Colonies -- History
ISBN 1844677389; 9781844677382

LC 2011456112

This book, by Richard Gott, offers a "history of the foundation of the British empire, . . . punctur[ing] the still widely held belief that the British Empire was a . . . civilizing enterprise of great benefit to its subject peoples. Instead, [it] reveals a history of systemic repression . . . and . . . military dictatorship. . . . [But w]herever Britain tried to plant its flag, there was resistance. From Ireland to India, from the American colonies to Australia." (Publisher's note)

Includes bibliographical references and index.

Hollis, Leo

London rising; the men who made modern London. Walker & Co. 2008 390p il map $27.99   **942**

1. Authors 2. Architects 3. Economists 4. Physicians 5. Physicists 6. Philosophers 7. Diarists 8. Essayists 9. Biographers 10. College teachers 11. Members of Parliament 12. London (England) -- History 13. Political and social philosophers 14. St. Paul's Cathedral (London, England)
ISBN 978-0-8027-1632-3; 0-8027-1632-6

LC 2008-000179

"London in the mid-17th century remained a medieval city. The civil war, a plague that claimed 100,000 lives and the Great Fire of 1666 would have been sufficient to send it back to the Dark Ages. Instead, London was transformed into a modern metropolis. . . . Hollis controls the narrative by focusing on the five figures who best represent the spirit of the age. John Locke, the philosopher, outlined a daring theory of universal natural rights; social observer John Evelyn grappled with the specific meaning of Englishness; real estate developer and speculator Nicholas Barbon rebuilt the center of London (with designs by the scientific polymath Robert Hooke); and lastly, Christopher Wren, who created St. Paul's Cathedral, eternal symbol of the glittering city." Publ Wkly

Includes bibliographical references

Livingstone, Natalie

The **mistresses** of Cliveden; three centuries of scandal, power, and intrigue in an English stately home. Natalie Livingstone. Ballantine Books 2016 512 p. illustrations (hardback) $32   **942**

1. Nobility 2. Women -- England 3. Country homes -- England 4. Cliveden (England) -- History 5. Women -- England -- Biography 6. Cliveden (England) -- Biography 7. Nobility -- England -- Biography 8. Rich people -- England -- Biography
ISBN 9780553392074

LC 2015049927

In this book, by Natalie Livingstone, "five miles from Windsor Castle, home of the royal family, sits the Cliveden estate. . . . Throughout its storied history, Cliveden has been a setting for misbehavior, intrigue, and passion—from its salacious, deadly beginnings in the seventeenth century to the 1960s Profumo Affair, the sex scandal that toppled the British government." (Publisher's note)

"In her debut book, Livingstone ably avoids tabloidlike gossip to profile five remarkable women, and she provides a helpful cast of characters at the beginning of the story. Readers who enjoy English history will be happy to have this in their libraries." Kirkus

Includes bibliographical references and index

Nicolson, Juliet

The **perfect** summer; England 1911, just before the storm. Grove Press 2007 290p il $25; pa $15   **942**

1. Great Britain -- Social conditions 2. Great Britain -- History -- 20th century 3. Great Britain -- Social life and customs

ISBN 0-8021-1846-1; 978-0-8021-1846-2; 0-8021-4367-9 pa; 978-0-8021-4367-9 pa

LC 2006-48854

First published 2006 in the United Kingdom

"With her sparkling social history about Edwardian society on the brink of World War I, Nicolson has created the perfect beach reading for Anglophiles." Christ Sci Monit

Includes bibliographical references

Tombs, Robert

The **English** and their history; Robert Tombs. Knopf 2014 x, 1012 p.p 32 plates; illustrations; maps $45   **942**
1. Great Britain -- History 2. Great Britain -- Civilization 3. English
ISBN 1101874767; 1846140188; 9781101874769; 9781846140181

LC 2014486349

This book by Robert Tombs is an "account of the people who have a claim to be the oldest nation in the world. The English first came into existence as an idea, before they had a common ruler and before the country they lived in even had a name. They have lasted as a recognizable entity ever since, and their defining national institutions can be traced back to the earliest years of their history." (Publisher's note)

"All readers will benefit from a history that reveals the "connections and disconnections," the "continuities and discontinuities" that make the English who they think they are. Summing Up: Essential. All levels/libraries." Choice

Includes bibliographical references and index

942.01   England -- Early history to 1066

Adams, Max

In the Land of Giants; A Journey Through the Dark Ages. Max Adams. W W Norton & Co Inc 2016 416 p. color illustrations, maps $29.95   **942.01**
1. Great Britain -- History -- 0-1066 2. Great Britain -- Description and travel
ISBN 1681772183; 9781681772189

In this book, author Max Adams "explores Britain's lost early medieval past by walking its paths and exploring its lasting imprint on valley, hill, and field. From York to Whitby, from London to Sutton Hoo, from Edinburgh to Anglesey, and from Hadrian's Wall to Loch Tay, each of his ten walking narratives form free-standing chapters as well as parts of a wider portrait of a Britain of fort and fyrd, crypt and crannog, church and causeway, holy well and memorial stone." (Publisher's note)

"Myth and ancient magic meet with solid historical ground in Adams' voyage through a largely forgotten age." Kirkus

Includes bibliographical references (pages 443-444).

942.02   England--Norman period, 1066-1154

Morris, Marc

★ The **Norman** Conquest; The Battle of Hastings and the Fall of Anglo-saxon England. by Marc Morris. W W Norton & Co Inc 2013 464 p. $32   **942.02**
1. Hastings (East Sussex, England), Battle of, 1066 2. Great Britain -- History -- 1066-1154, Norman period
ISBN 1605984515; 9781605984513

This book by Marc Morris "explains why the Norman Conquest was the most significant cultural and military episode in English history. It

explain[s] why England was at once so powerful and yet so vulnerable to William the Conqueror's attack; why the Normans, in some respects less sophisticated, possessed the military cutting edge; how William's hopes of a united Anglo-Norman realm unraveled, dashed by English rebellions, Viking invasions, and the insatiable demands of his fellow conquerors." (Publisher's note)

Weir, Alison

★ **Queens** of the conquest; Book one England's medieval queens. Alison Weir. First U.S. Edition Ballantine Books 2017 xxxiv, 556 p., 16 unnumbered pages of platesp color illustrations, maps Hardcover $30   **942.02**
1. Queens -- Great Britain -- Biography 2. Great Britain -- Kings and rulers -- Biography 3. Monarchy -- Great Britain -- History -- To 1500 4. Great Britain -- History -- Norman period, 1066-1154
ISBN 9781101966662; 1101966661

LC 2017030167

This book in the England's Medieval Queens series, by Alison Weir, spans "the years from the Norman conquest in 1066 to the dawn of a new era in 1154, when Henry II succeeded to the throne and Eleanor of Aquitaine, the first Plantagenet queen, was crowned. . . . [It] brings to vivid life five women, including: Matilda of Flanders, wife of William the Conqueror, the first Norman king; Matilda of Scotland . . .; and Empress Maud, England's first female ruler." (Publisher's note)

Includes bibliographical references (pages 441-532) and index.

942.03   England--Period of House of Plantagenet, 1154-1399

Jones, Dan

★ The **Plantagenets**; the warrior kings and queens who made England. Dan Jones. Viking 2013 xxv, 534 p.p (hardcover) $36   **942.03**
1. Great Britain -- Kings and rulers 2. Great Britain -- History -- 1154-1399, Plantagenets 3. Great Britain -- Kings and rulers -- Biography 4. Great Britain -- History -- Plantagenets, 1154-1399 5. Great Britain -- Politics and government -- 1154-1399
ISBN 0670026654; 9780670026654

LC 2012039998

First published in Great Britain in 2012.

This book, by Dan Jones, examines how "the first Plantagenet king inherited a blood-soaked kingdom from the Normans and transformed it into an empire stretched at its peak from Scotland to Jerusalem. . . . We meet . . . Eleanor of Aquitaine, . . . her son, Richard the Lionheart, . . . and King John, a tyrant who was forced to sign Magna Carta. . . . This is the era of chivalry, . . . the Black Death, the founding of Parliament, . . . and the Hundred Year's War." (Publisher's note)

"The great battles against the Scots and French and the subjugation of the Welsh make for thrilling reading but so do the equally enthralling struggles over succession, the Magna Carta, and the Provisions of Oxford...Written with prose that keeps the reader captivated throughout accounts of the span of centuries and the not-always-glorious trials of kingship, this book is at all times approachable, academic, and entertaining." Booklist

Includes bibliographical references and index

Seward, Desmond

The **Demon's** Brood; A History of the Plantagenet Dynasty. by Desmond Seward. W W Norton & Co Inc 2014 400 p. 16 plates; ills; portraits (hardback) $28.95   **942.03**
1. Great Britain -- History -- 1154-1399, Plantagenets

ISBN 1605986186; 9781605986180; 9781605988696

This book, by Desmond Seward, offers a "history of the most dominant royal dynasty in English history, from Richard the Lionheart and Edward the Black Prince to Henry IV and Richard III. The Plantagenets reigned over England longer than any other family--from Henry II to Richard III. . . . Based on major contemporary sources and recent research, acclaimed historian Desmond Seward provides the first readable overview of the whole extraordinary dynasty, in one volume." (Publisher's note)

"Seward is a good author to turn to for ease in reading history; his writing style is quick, vibrant and delightfully pithy in its simplicity of phrase." Kirkus

942.04   England--Period of Houses of Lancaster and York, 1399-1485

Bicheno, Hugh

Blood Royal; The Wars of the Roses, 1462-1485. Hugh Bicheno. Pegasus Books 2017 xli, 390 p.p illustrations, maps (hardcover) $28.95   **942.04**
1. Monarchy 2. Great Britain -- History -- 1455-1485, War of the Roses 3. Great Britain -- History -- Wars of the Roses, 1455-1485
ISBN 9781681774282; 1681774283
Companion to: Battle Royal: The Wars of the Roses: 1440-1462 (2016)

This book "is the second part of a two-volume history of the dynastic wars fought between the houses of Lancaster and York for the English throne from 1450 until 1485. Hugh Bicheno tells the story of the Wars of the Roses as an enthralling, character-driven saga of interwoven families, narrating each chapter from the point of view of a key player in the wider drama.[It] describes three Lancastrian attempts to overthrow the Yorkists, ending with the death of Edward's successor, Richard III." (Publisher's note)

"A well-written conclusion to a history perfectly suited to scholars and students." Kirkus

Includes bibliographical references (pages 375-381) and index.

Gristwood, Sarah

Blood sisters; the women behind the Wars of the Roses. Sarah Gristwood. Basic Books, A Member of the Perseus Books Group 2013 432 p. (hard cover: alk. paper) $29.99   **942.04**
1. Courts and courtiers 2. Queens -- Great Britain 3. Great Britain -- History -- 1455-1485, Wars of the Roses 4. Great Britain -- History -- Henry VII, 1485-1509 5. Great Britain -- History -- Wars of the Roses, 1455-1485
ISBN 0465018319; 9780465018314

LC 2012044813

This book, by historian Sarah Gristwood, examines the female dynamics behind the War of the Roses. "While the events of this turbulent time are usually described in terms of the male leads who fought and died seeking the throne, a handful of powerful women would prove just as decisive as their kinfolks' clashing armies. . . . Gristwood traces the rise and rule of the seven most critical women in the wars." (Publisher's note)

Includes bibliographical references and index

Jones, Dan

The **Wars** of the Roses; the fall of the Plantagenets and the rise of the Tudors. Dan Jones. Viking 2014 416 p. ills., maps, genealogical tab. $36   **942.04**
1. Great Britain -- History -- 1455-1485, Wars of the Roses 2. Great

Britain -- History -- Wars of the Roses, 1455-1485 3. Great Britain -- History -- Lancaster and York, 1399-1485
ISBN 0670026670; 9780670026678

LC 2014010099

This book, by Dan Jones, describes how "the crown of England changed hands five times over the course of the fifteenth century, as two branches of the Plantagenet dynasty fought to the death for the right to rule. . . . [The volume chronicles] how the longest-reigning British royal family tore itself apart until it was finally replaced by the Tudors." (Publisher's note)

"This excellent and fairly accessible contribution to the history of the Wars of the Roses serves as a helpful corrective to previous mythologized versions. It is highly recommended for studies of British royal history and for readers of popular narrative nonfiction." LJ

Includes bibliographical references and index

Jones, Michael K.

Bosworth 1485; The Battle That Transformed England: the Rise of the Tudor Dynasty. Michael K. Jones. W W Norton & Co Inc. 2015 256 p. 16 plates; illustrations $27.95   **942.04**
1. Great Britain -- History -- 1455-1485, Wars of the Roses
ISBN 1605988596; 9781605988597

This book, by Michael K. Jones, offers an "authoritative reinterpretation of the Battle of Bosworth Field, where the Wars of the Roses ended and the Tudor dynasty began. . . . With startling detail of Henry Tudor's reliance on French mercenaries, plus a new account of the battle itself, the author turns Shakespeare on its head, painting an entirely fresh picture of the dramatic life and death of Richard III, England's most infamous monarch." (Publisher's note)

"Jones recounts the actual battle in easily understood terms for laymen and offers unusual insights into the role of foreign fighters. This is a well-done reexamination of the conflict that truly altered the course of history." Booklist

Weir, Alison

The **Wars** of the Roses. Ballantine Bks. 1995 462p il hardcover o.p. pa $15.95   **942.04**
1. Great Britain -- History -- 1455-1485, War of the Roses
ISBN 0-345-39117-9; 0-345-40433-5 pa

"No history collection should be do without this perfectly focused and beautifully unfolded account." Booklist

942.05   England--Period of House of Tudor, 1485-1603

Ackroyd, Peter, 1949-

Tudors; The History of England from Henry VIII to Elizabeth I. by Peter Ackroyd. Thomas Dunne Books 2013 512 p. (History of England) $29.99   **942.05**
1. England 2. Great Britain -- History -- 1485-1603, Tudors 3. Great Britain -- History -- Tudors, 1485-1603
ISBN 1250003628; 9781250003621

LC 2013024573

This book, the "second title in [Peter Ackroyd's] projected six-volume history of England," focuses on "the 16th-century religious reformation that began, as a dynastic matter, with Henry VIII's divorce from Katherine of Aragon in 1533. . . . The Reformation in England was marked by upheaval and bloodshed, as the Tudors imposed religious changes upon an initially reluctant populace." (Publishers Weekly)

Includes bibliographical references (pages 473-481) and index

Borman, Tracy

The **private** lives of the Tudors; uncovering the secrets of Britain's greatest dynasty. Tracy Borman. Grove Press 2016 464 p. illustrations, portraits (hardcover) $27.00; (ebook) $27   **942.05**

1. Kings and rulers 2. Great Britain -- History -- 1485-1603, Tudors
ISBN 9780802125996; 9780802189806; 0802125999

LC 2016047439

This book, by Tracy Borman, "delves deep behind the public face of the [Tudor] monarchs. . . . Drawing on the accounts of those closest to them, Borman examines Tudor life in fine detail. What did the monarchs eat? What clothes did they wear, and how were they designed, bought, and cared for? How did they practice their faith? And in earthlier moments, who did they love, and how did they give birth to the all-important heirs?" (Publisher's note)

"This Downton Abbey-like peek into the everyday lives of these privileged yet cloistered rulers and their households will appeal to both serious scholars and Tudor enthusiasts." Booklist

Includes bibliographical references (pages 381-426) and index.

Fletcher, Catherine

The **divorce** of Henry VIII; the untold story from inside the Vatican. Catherine Fletcher. Palgrave Macmillan 2012 xviv, 266 p.p ill., map (hardcover) $28   **942.05**

1. Great Britain -- Foreign relations 2. Catholic Church -- Foreign relations 3. Reformation -- England 4. Catholic Church -- Foreign relations -- Great Britain 5. Great Britain -- Foreign relations -- Catholic Church 6. Great Britain -- Politics and government -- 1509-1547 7. Church and state -- Great Britain -- History -- 16th century
ISBN 0230341519; 9780230341517

LC 2011050335

This book, by historian Catherine Fletcher, explores the history and politics of the formation of the Church of England from Vatican archive sources. "In 1533 . . . Henry VIII decided to divorce his wife of twenty years. . . . But getting his freedom involved a terrific web of intrigue. . . . Henry's man in Rome was a wily Italian diplomat named Gregorio Casali who drew no limits on skullduggery including kidnapping, bribery and theft to make his king a free man." (Publisher's note)

Includes bibliographical references and index

Goodman, Ruth

How to be a Tudor; a dawn-to-dusk guide to Tudor life. Ruth Goodman. Liveright Publishing Corporation 2016 336 p. illustrations (some color) (hardcover) $29.95   **942.05**

1. Great Britain -- Social life and customs 2. Great Britain -- History -- 1485-1603, Tudors 3. Great Britain -- History -- Tudors, 1485-1603 4. Great Britain -- Social conditions -- 16th century 5. Great Britain -- Social life and customs -- 16th century
ISBN 9781631491399

LC 2015038420

This book, by Ruth Goodman, is "an erudite romp through the intimate details of life in Tudor England. . . . Drawing on her own adventures living in re-created Tudor conditions, Goodman serves as our intrepid guide to sixteenth-century living. Proceeding from daybreak to bedtime, this . . . work celebrates the ordinary lives of those who labored through the era." (Publisher's note)

"Throughout, Goodman's palpable enthusiasm and clear appreciation for the resourcefulness of the era's people make these men and women entirely relatable and yet full of surprises." Pub Wkly

Includes bibliographical references and index

Lipscomb, Suzannah

★ A **Journey** Through Tudor England; Hampton Court Palace and the Tower of London to Stratford-upon-Avon and Thornbury Castle. by Suzannah Libscomb. 1st ed. W W Norton & Co Inc 2013 336 p. (hardcover) $26.95   **942.05**

1. Great Britain -- Description and travel 2. Great Britain -- History -- 1485-1603, Tudors
ISBN 1605984604; 9781605984605

This is "a guidebook that introduces readers to the history of the [Tudor] period through 50 of 'the best and most interesting' buildings associated with Tudor royalty. Each chapter tells the story of how a specific building served as the physical backdrop to the lives of those who inhabited it or to a particularly important visit from a famous personage." (Publishers Weekly)

Meyer, G. J.

The **Tudors**; the complete story of England's most notorious dynasty. Delacorte Press 2010 xxvi, 612p il map $30 **942.05**

1. Queens 2. Kings 3. Great Britain -- Kings and rulers 4. Great Britain -- History -- 1485-1603, Tudors
ISBN 978-0-385-34076-2

LC 2009-40032

"History buffs will savor Meyer's cheeky, nuanced, and authoritative perspective on an entire dynasty, and his study brims with enriching background discussions, ranging from class structure and the medieval Catholic Church to the Tudor connection to Spanish royalty." Publ Wkly

Includes bibliographical references

Mortimer, Ian

The **time** traveler's guide to Elizabethan England; Ian Mortimer. Viking 2013 416 p. (hardcover) $27.95   **942.05**

1. Great Britain -- Social conditions -- History 2. Great Britain -- History -- 1558-1603, Elizabeth 3. England -- Social conditions -- 16th century 4. Great Britain -- History -- Elizabeth, 1558-1603 5. England -- Social life and customs -- 16th century
ISBN 0670026077; 9780670026074

LC 2013001566

In this book, British historian Ian Mortimer offers an "account of life during Queen Elizabeth's 1558-1603 reign. The average Elizabethan paid little attention to politics but a great deal to domestic technology. Thus, bricks and clear glass became cheaper." Topic include the advent of chimneys, Elizabethan professionals, bathing habits, and personal hygiene. (Kirkus Reviews)

Includes bibliographical references and index

Ronald, Susan

Heretic queen; Queen Elizabeth I and the wars of religion. Susan Ronald. St. Martin's Press 2012 350 p. (hardcover) $27.99   **942.05**

1. Religious tolerance 2. War -- Religious aspects 3. Great Britain -- History -- 1485-1603, Tudors 4. Reformation -- England 5. England -- Church history -- 16th century 6. Great Britain -- History -- Elizabeth, 1558-1603
ISBN 0312645384; 9780312645380; 9781250015211

LC 2012010248

In this "companion volume to 'Pirate Queen,' [Susan] Ronald's 2007 study of . . . England's Elizabeth I , the author sets the Elizabethan age within the context of the Catholic-Protestant wars of religion" of "the latter half of the 16th century. Elizabeth had witnessed the religious divisions that marked the reigns of" Henry VIII, Edward VI, and Mary I, "so upon her ascension to the throne in 1558 she was eager to grant a measure of religious tolerance to her subjects." (Publishers Weekly)

Includes bibliographical references and index

Starkey, David

Six wives: the queens of Henry VIII. HarperCollins Pubs. 2003 xxvii, 852p il hardcover o.p. pa $16.95 **942.05**

1. Queens 2. Great Britain -- History -- 1485-1603, Tudors
ISBN 0-694-01043-X; 0-06-000550-5 pa

"Solidly researched and delightfully told, this is highly recommended." Libr J

Includes bibliographical references

Weir, Alison

Henry VIII; the king and his court. Ballantine Bks. 2001 632p il $28; pa $16.95 **942.05**

1. Kings 2. Great Britain -- History -- 1485-1603, Tudors
ISBN 0-345-43659-8; 0-345-43708-X pa

LC 2001-116042

In this biography of the Tudor king, the author "examines the minutiae of his daily life and gives prominence to the background players of his court.... At times, the weighty detail and numerous characters will make the work inaccessible; however, as a scholarly study it is a significant achievement." Libr J

Includes bibliographical references

The **life** of Elizabeth I. Ballantine Bks. 1998 532p il hardcover o.p. pa $15.95 **942.05**

1. Queens 2. Great Britain -- History -- 1485-1603, Tudors
ISBN 0-345-42550-2 pa

LC 98-34917

"Weir brings a fine sense of selection and considerable zest to her portrait of the self-styled Virgin Queen." Publ Wkly

Includes bibliographical references

The **six** wives of Henry VIII. Grove Weidenfeld 1992 643p il hardcover o.p. pa $15 **942.05**

1. Kings 2. Great Britain -- History -- 1485-1603, Tudors
ISBN 0-8021-3683-4 pa

LC 91-29522

First published 1991 in the United Kingdom

This is a collective biography of the wives of the Tudor king of England

"Wonderfully detailed, extensively researched.... The narrative is free flowing, humorous, informative, and readable." SLJ

Includes bibliographical references

942.055 Reign of Elizabeth I, 1558-1603

MacGregor, Neil, 1946-

Shakespeare's restless world; A Portrait of an Era in Twenty Objects. Neil MacGregor. Allen Lane 2012 xvi, 320 p.p ill. (some color), color maps $36 **942.055**

1. Great Britain -- Social conditions -- History 2. England -- Social conditions -- 16th century 3. England -- Social conditions -- 17th century
ISBN 0670026344; 9780670026340

LC 2013376339

This book, by Neil MacGregor, "brings the world of Shakespeare and the Tudor era of Elizabeth I into focus.... MacGregor and his team at the British Museum, working together in a landmark collaboration with the Royal Shakespeare Company and the BBC, bring us twenty objects that capture the essence of Shakespeare's universe.... This was

... [a] time when discoveries in science and technology altered the parameters of the known world." (Publisher's note)

"Beautifully illustrated, MacGregor's history offers a vibrant portrait of Shakespeare's dramatic, perilous and exhilarating world." Kirkus

Includes bibliographical references and index

942.06 England--House of Stuart and Commonwealth periods to present, 1603-

Fraser, Antonia

Faith and treason; the story of the Gunpowder Plot. Doubleday 1996 xxxv, 347p il hardcover o.p. pa $16 **942.06**

1. Gunpowder plot, 1605 2. Conspirators 3. Revolutionaries 4. Great Britain -- History -- 1603-1714, Stuarts
ISBN 0-385-47190-4 pa

LC 96-21709

"A small group of Roman Catholics planned to blow up Parliament on its opening day in 1605, when the Protestant King James and his older son would be present, and to proclaim the nine-year-old princess Elizabeth queen, raise her as a Catholic, and so restore Catholicism as the state religion.... The Gunpowder Plot was both cruel and crackpot, but Fraser does a wonderful job of conveying to the modern reader just why a few Catholics felt that it was justified and also was likely to succeed." New Yorker

Includes bibliographical references

942.081 England--1837-1901

Ackroyd, Peter, 1949-

Dominion; the history of England from the Battle of Waterloo to Victoria's Diamond Jubilee. Peter Ackroyd. Thomas Dunne Books/St. Martin's Press 2018 400 p. (hardcover) $29.99 **942.081**

1. Historical literature 2. Great Britain -- History -- 19th century
ISBN 9781250003652

LC 2018019772

This book, "the fifth volume of Peter Ackroyd's masterful History of England, begins in 1815 as national glory following the Battle of Waterloo gives way to a post-war depression and ends with the death of Queen Victoria in January 1901.... Ackroyd takes readers from the accession of the profligate George IV ... to the 'Sailor King' William IV whose reign saw the modernization of the political system and the abolition of slavery." (Publisher's note)

"With a large cast of historic figures, a chronicling of the coalescence of the middle class and changing labor concerns, the rise of secularism, and the expanse of the British empire, Ackroyd's deep and broad canvas is rich in informative details and will appeal to all readers interested in British history while especially pleasing those fascinated by this era." Booklist

Includes bibliographical references and index

942.1 London (England)

Flanders, Judith

The **Victorian** city; everyday life in Dickens' London. Judith Flanders. Thomas Dunne Books 2014 xxiii, 520 p.p 16 plates; illustrations; maps (hardback) $27.99 **942.1**

1. London (England) -- History 2. London (England) -- In literature 3. London (England) -- Intellectual life -- 19th century 4. London

(England) -- Social life and customs -- 19th century
ISBN 1250040213; 9781250040213

LC 2014007566

Los Angeles Times Book Prize Finalist: History (2014)

This book, by Judith Flanders, offers a "portrait of everyday life on the streets of [Victorian] London. . . . From the moment Charles Dickens . . . arrived in the city in 1822, he obsessively walked its streets. . . . Now, with him, Judith Flanders leads us through the markets, transport systems, sewers, . . . chop-houses and entertainment emporia of Dickens' London, to reveal the Victorian capital in all its variety, vibrancy, and squalor." (Publisher's note)

"This is a superb portrait of an exciting, thriving, and dangerous city." Booklist

Includes bibliographical references (pages 479-499)and index

Jones, Nigel

Tower; an epic history of the Tower of London. Nigel Jones. St. Martin's Press 2012 464 p. (hardcover) $35.00 **942.1**
1. Great Britain -- History 2. London (England) -- History 3. Prisons -- England -- London -- History 4. Tower of London (London, England) -- History 5. Fortification -- England -- London -- History 6. London (England) -- Buildings, structures, etc
ISBN 0312622961; 9780312622961; 9781250018144

LC 2012028273

The book presents a history of the Tower of London in which the author "seeks to conjure the many characters that have lived, been imprisoned and perished within its walls. His concern is not so much with the building itself: he pays only fleeting attention to its architectural development. Instead, he is interested in the 'great actors in the dramas of English history' who trod its passages." These include "Henry VII . . . Simon de Montfort . . . Elizabeth I . . . [and] Sir Walter Raleigh". (TLS)

Includes bibliographical references and index

Sinclair, Iain

The **last** London; true fictions from an unreal city. Iain Sinclair. Oneworld Publications 2018 324 p. illustrations (hardcover) $24.99 **942.1**
1. Travel writing 2. London (England) -- Description and travel 3. London (England) -- Intellectual life
ISBN 9781786071750; 9781786071743; 1786071746

In this book, author Iain Sinclair "strikes out on a series of solitary walks and collaborative expeditions to make a final reckoning with a capital stretched beyond recognition. . . . Travelling from the pinnacle of the Shard to the outer limits of the London Overground system at Croydon and Barking, from the Thames Estuary to the future ruins of Olympicopolis, Sinclair reflects on where London begins and where it ends." (Publisher's note)

"An unconventional, atmospheric exploration of London from one its most unique chroniclers." Kirkus

Includes bibliographical references (pages 317-318) and index.

942.106   London (England) -- 17ᵗʰ century

Jordan, Don

The **king's** city; a history of London during the Restoration: the city that transformed a nation. Don Jordan. Pegasus Books 2018 xvii, 526 p.p illustrations (hardcover) $29.95 **942.106**
1. London (England) -- History 2. Great Britain -- History -- 1603-1714, Stuarts 3. London (England) -- History -- 17th century 4. Great Britain -- History -- Charles II, 1660-1685
ISBN 1681776383; 9781681776385; 9781681777023

This book, by Don Jordan, reveals that "during the reign of Charles II, London was a city in flux. After years of civil war and political turmoil, England's capital became the center for major advances . . . that paved the way for the creation of the British Empire. . . . This book tells the gripping story of a city that defined a nation and birthed modern Britain--and how the vision of great individuals helped to build the richly diverse place we know today." (Publisher's note)

"A wonderful picture of 17th-century England, replete with the excitement of ideas and discoveries and the beginnings of the empire." Kirkus

Includes bibliographical references (pages 473-502) and index.

942.9   Wales

Morris, Jan

A **writer's** house in Wales. National Geographic Soc. 2002 143p (National Geographic directions) $25 **942.9**
1. Wales
ISBN 0-7922-6523-8

LC 2001-44731

The author "reflects on her home in Wales, its beautiful setting and the nature of being Welsh. . . . This slim and charming volume offers a crisp account of the turbulent history of the Welsh and their battle to maintain their language and culture in the shadow of their more powerful neighbor." Publ Wkly

942.901   Historical periods

Charles-Edwards, T. M.

Wales and the Britons, 350-1064; by T.M. Charles-Edwards. Oxford University Press 2013 xx, 795 p.p (The history of Wales) $185 **942.901**
1. Wales -- History 2. Great Britain -- History -- 0-1066 3. Wales -- History -- To 1063
ISBN 0198217315; 9780198217312

LC 2012376060

This book, by T.M. Charles-Edwards, "provides a detailed history of Wales in the period in which it was created out of the remnants of Roman Britain. It thus begins in the fourth century, with accelerating attacks from external forces, and ends shortly before the Norman Conquest of England. The narrative history is interwoven with chapters on the principal sources, the social history of Wales, the Church, the early history of the Welsh language, and its early literature, both in Welsh and in Latin." (Publisher's note)

Includes bibliographical references (p. [680]-739) and index

943   Germany and neighboring central European countries

Coy, Jason Philip

A **brief** history of Germany; [by] Jason P. Coy. Facts on File 2011 288p il map (Brief history) $49.50; pa $19.95 **943**
1. Germany -- History
ISBN 978-0-8160-8142-4; 978-0-8160-8329-9 pa

LC 2010-23139

This book provides an "account of the events, people, and special customs and traditions that have shaped Germany from ancient times to the present." Publisher's note

Includes bibliographical references

Fulbrook, Mary

★ A **concise** history of Germany; 2nd ed; Cambridge University Press 2004 277p il, maps (Cambridge concise histories) hardcover o.p. pa $22   **943**

1. Princes 2. Statesmen 3. Heads of state 4. Prime ministers 5. National socialism 6. Nazi leaders 7. Germany -- History

ISBN 0-521-83320-5; 0-521-54071-2 pa

LC 2004-271599

First published 1990 in the United Kingdom

This history of Germany "spans the early Middle Ages to the present day. . . . Mary Fulbrook explores the interrelationships between social, political and cultural factors in the light of the latest scholarly controversies." Publ Wkly

Includes bibliographical references

Gay, Ruth

The **Jews** of Germany; a historical portrait. with an introduction by Peter Gay. Yale Univ. Press 1992 297p il maps hardcover o.p. pa $35   **943**

1. Jews -- Germany

ISBN 0-300-05155-7; 0-300-06052-1 pa

LC 91-30235

This is a history of Germany's Jews from the first century to the Holocaust.

"Illustrated sumptuously with paintings, photographs and excerpts from letters and historical documents, . . . this affirming history survives the sad end of the centuries-old German Jewish way of life." N Y Times Book Rev

Gorra, Michael Edward

The **bells** in their silence; travels through Germany. {by} Michael Gorra. Princeton University Press 2004 211p $24.95   **943**

1. Germany -- Description and travel

ISBN 0-691-11765-9

Gorra's "account of his travels through Germany is shaped—perhaps even haunted—by figures from the past: historical, literary, personal. A captivating, unique work of synthesis." Booklist

Includes bibliographical references

Harding, Thomas

The **House** by the Lake; One House, Five Families, and a Hundred Years of German History. Thomas Harding. St. Martin's Press 2016 464 p. ill., maps, genealogical table (hardcover) $28   **943**

1. Houses 2. Germany

ISBN 1250065062; 9781250065063

LC 2015044339

"In the summer of 1993, [author] Thomas Harding traveled to Germany with his grandmother to visit a small house by a lake on the outskirts of Berlin. . . . Slowly he began to piece together the lives of the five families who had lived there: a wealthy landowner, a prosperous Jewish family, a renowned composer, a widow and her children, a Stasi informant. All had made the house their home, and all but one had been forced out." (Publisher's note)

"This personal saga centered on a family home will appeal to enthusiasts of German history, especially post-World War II division and reunification." LJ

Includes bibliographical references (pages 361-414) and index.

MacDonogh, Giles

Frederick the Great; a life in deed and letters. St. Martin's Press 2000 436p il hardcover o.p. pa $16.95   **943**

1. Kings

ISBN 0-312-27266-9 pa

LC 00-24799

First published 1999 in the United Kingdom

"Both general readers and those with a strong background in European history will find great value in this outstanding biography." Booklist

Includes bibliographical references

MacGregor, Neil, 1946-

Germany; memories of a nation. Neil MacGregor. Alfred A. Knopf 2015 656 p. color illustrations; maps (hardback) $40   **943**

1. Germany -- History 2. Germany -- Civilization

ISBN 1101875666; 9781101875667

LC 2014048396

In this book, Neil MacGregor presents a history of Germany in objects. The author "argues that, uniquely for any European country, no coherent, overarching narrative of Germany's history can be constructed, for in Germany both geography and history have always been unstable. . . . German history may be inherently fragmented, but it contains a large number of widely shared memories, awarenesses, and experiences; examining some of these is the purpose of this book." (Publisher's note)

"Most importantly, the author finds post-World War II Germany hyperattuned to the need for memorials to victims of terror and oppression—e.g., via the work of painter and printmaker Käthe Kollwitz. A comprehensive record jam-packed with visuals." Kirkus

Includes bibliographical references and index

Moorhouse, Roger

Berlin at war. Basic Books 2010 432p il $29.95   **943**

1. Berlin (Germany) -- History 2. World War, 1939-1945 -- Germany

ISBN 978-0-465-00533-8

LC 2010-907169

"Election results in the fading days of the Weimar Republic indicate that Berliners were not particularly sympathetic to Hitler or his movement. Yet Berlin endured horrible physical destruction, deprivation, and death. This included intense Allied bombings by day and night, and a siege and eventual ravaging by the Russian army. . . . [Moorhouse] begins with an almost idyllic scene as huge crowds in Berlin witness the celebration of Hitler's birthday in April 1939; at the time, of course, Germany seemed to have achieved its foreign-policy goals without firing a shot. As the fortunes of Germany and Berlin deteriorate, Moorhouse uses the testimonies of a variety of Berliners to describe some memorable scenes and struggles.This is a hard, unrelenting saga of the effects of total warfare on citizens just hoping to survive." Booklist

Includes bibliographical references

Watson, Peter, 1943-

The **German** genius; Europe's third renaissance, the second scientific revolution, and the twentieth century. Harper 2010 964p il $35   **943**

1. Germany -- Civilization 2. Germany -- Intellectual life

ISBN 0060760222; 9780060760229

LC 2010-06738

This is a "cultural history of German ideas and influence, from 1750 to the present day." (Publisher's note) Index.

This is "a panoramic review of German cultural and intellectual development from 1750 to the present. Examining the contributions of literally hundreds of German thinkers and doers and mapping the conceptual connections between them, the author demonstrates the breadth, volume, and influence of German output in philosophy, science, industry, art, literature, and all forms of scholarly activity. But Watson's true focus is the cultural crucible, forged in the eighteenth and nineteenth centuries and informed by notions of Bildung and inwardness, that gave rise to such accomplishments but also set the stage for the evil actions of the Third Reich. To some extent an effort to untether our understanding of German history from the conflicts of the twentieth century, this study is also a reminder that our modern Western worldview has deep German roots." Booklist

Includes bibliographical references

943.08   Germany since 1866

Evans, Richard J.

★ The **coming** of the Third Reich; a history. Penguin Press 2004 622p il map hardcover o.p. pa $18   **943.08**
1. National socialism 2. Germany -- History -- 1866-1918 3. Germany -- History -- 1918-1933
ISBN 1-594-20004-1; 0-14-303469-3 pa

LC 2003-63205
First published 2003 in the United Kingdom
"This is a first-rate narrative history that informs and educates and may inspire readers to delve even deeper into the subject." Booklist

Includes bibliographical references

Stern, Fritz Richard

Five Germanys I have known; [by] Fritz Stern. Farrar, Straus & Giroux 2006 546p il map $30   **943.08**
1. Germany -- History
ISBN 978-0-374-15540-7; 0-374-15540-2

LC 2006-60
In this "memoir, Stern looks back over the 'five Germanys' his generation has seen—the Weimar Republic, Nazi tyranny, the post-1945 Federal Republic, the Soviet-controlled German Democratic Republic and, lastly, the reunited Germany of the present—and explains how he came to reconcile himself with his birth country (which his Jewish family fled in 1938) as it has come to terms with its new place in today's more cohesive and peaceful Europe. . . . The book's intriguing structure makes it a wonderful combination of history, memoir, analysis and even poetry." Publ Wkly

943.085   Period of Weimar Republic, 1918-1933

Haffner, Sebastian

Defying Hitler; a memoir. translated from the German by Oliver Pretzel. Farrar, Straus & Giroux 2002 309p il $24; pa $14   **943.085**
1. Germany -- History -- 1918-1933
ISBN 0-374-16157-7; 0-312-42113-3 pa

LC 2002-17058
"In August 1938 a young German lawyer and journalist with the . . . name of Raimund Pretzel arrived in England. . . . Pretzel, a non-Jew, was fleeing to join and marry a Jewish woman pregnant with their first child. . . . Choosing a new name—Sebastian Haffner—to keep the Nazis from retaliating against his relatives, he went on to a . . . career as a journalist and historian in England, where he died in 1999. Afterward, while perusing his father's papers, Oliver Pretzel . . . found a . . . typescript in German. It was Haffner's unfinished memoir about his early years, begun in 1939, that sought through autobiography to understand how Hitler came to power." New Leader

King, David

The **trial** of Adolf Hitler; the Beer Hall Putsch and the rise of Nazi Germany. David King. W W Norton & Co Inc 2017 xxi, 455 p.p illustrations (hardcover) $27.95   **943.085**
1. Trials 2. Treason 3. True crime stories 4. Trials (Treason) -- Germany -- Munich 5. Germany -- History -- Beer Hall Putsch, 1923
ISBN 9780393242645; 9780393241693

LC 2017008985
This book, by David King, "tells the true story of the monumental criminal proceeding that followed when [Adolf] Hitler and nine other suspects were charged with high treason. . . . By its end, Hitler would transform the fiasco of the beer hall putsch into a stunning victory for the fledgling Nazi Party. It was this trial that thrust Hitler into the limelight, provided him with an unprecedented stage for his demagoguery, and set him on his improbable path to power." (Publisher's note)
"King . . . affirms his reputation as a first-rate narrative historian in this well-researched analysis of Adolf Hitler's trial for treason in the aftermath of the 1923 Beer Hall Putsch." Pub Wkly

Includes bibliographical references and index

943.086   Germany--Period of Third Reich, 1933-1945

Album of the damned; snapshots from the Third Reich. Academy Chicago Publishers 2008 408p il $50   **943.086**
1. Germany -- History -- 1933-1945 2. World War, 1939-1945 -- Pictorial works
ISBN 978-0-89733-576-8; 0-89733-576-7
"Photographed almost exclusively by amateurs — both soldiers and civilians — the pictures in Album of the Damned center on the daily life within the Third Reich, both at home and on the battlefield. . . . Garson assembled the exclusively black-and-white photos from private collections around the world, including many captured by the Soviets that only became available after the fall of the Soviet Union. . . . Critics might maintain that by focusing on showing how Nazis were 'human,' attention is diverted from their crimes against humanity. But it's impossible to thumb through the book on any page and not see the ghosts of the six million floating around every photo. A narrative that snakes through the book provides an overview of the time period and background on what's taking place in the photos." Jerusalem Post

Aycoberry, Pierre

The **social** history of the Third Reich; 1933-1945. translated from the French by Janet Lloyd. New Press 2000 380p $30; pa $15.95   **943.086**
1. National socialism 2. Germany -- Social conditions 3. Germany -- Politics and government -- 1933-1945
ISBN 1-56584-549-8; 1-56584-635-4 pa

LC 99-14059
"In examining the actions of individuals and social groups, {the author} illustrates that German citizens' response to the Nazi regime varied wildly. Some resisted bravely; others saw an opportunity for advancement. Most people sought merely to survive. In fact, what is extremely unsettling is how so many could maintain a semblance of normalcy in their lives. Aycoberry does not attempt to answer the unanswerable questions posed by the Nazi era, but his disturbing, brutally honest, and scrupulously fair work may be a landmark in the field." Booklist

Includes bibliographical references and index

Bascomb, Neal

Hunting Eichmann; how a band of survivors and a young

spy agency chased down the world's most notorious Nazi. Houghton Mifflin Harcourt 2009 390p il map $26 **943.086**

1. War criminals 2. Nazi leaders 3. Secret service -- Israel

ISBN 978-0-618-85867-5; 0-618-85867-9

LC 2008-35757

The author recounts the pursuit, capture, and abduction of Nazi war criminal Adolf Eichmann. "Bascomb spread a wide net in researching the 15-year hunt, and he fills his book with previously unknown or neglected details, utilizing the remembrances of former Mossad agents, German and American intelligence operatives, and Argentine Nazi sympathizers who tried to find Eichmann after his seizure. . . . This is an outstanding account of a sustained and worthy manhunt." Booklist

Includes bibliographical references

Burleigh, Michael

The **Third** Reich; a new history. Hill & Wang 2000 xxv, 965p il maps hardcover o.p. pa $18 **943.086**

1. Germany -- History -- 1933-1945

ISBN 0-8090-9326-X pa

LC 00-31838

"This brilliant and unique view of a great tyranny is an important addition to our understanding of the first half of the twentieth century." Booklist

Includes bibliographical references

Evans, Richard J.

★ The **Third** Reich in power, 1933-1939. Penguin Press 2005 941p il map hardcover o.p. pa $20 **943.086**

1. National socialism 2. Germany -- History -- 1933-1945

ISBN 1-594-20074-2; 0-14-303790-0 pa

LC 2005-52128

This "is a major achievement. No other recent synthetic history has quite the range and narrative power of Evans's work." Publ Wkly

Includes bibliographical references

Fritzsche, Peter

Life and death in the Third Reich. Belknap Press of Harvard University Press 2008 368p **943.086**

1. National socialism 2. Holocaust, 1933-1945 3. Germany -- Ethnic relations 4. Collective memory -- Germany 5. Holocaust, Jewish (1939-1945) 6. Germany -- History -- 1933-1945 7. Holocaust, Jewish (1939-1945) -- Germany

ISBN 0-674-02793-0; 0-674-03465-1 pa; 978-0-674-02793-0; 978-0-674-03465-5 pa

LC 2007-40552

This is a sequel to the author's Germans into Nazis (1998). In this study, Fritzsche seeks to explain the success of the ideology of Nazism. He argues that "its basic appeal lay in the Volksgemeinschaft—a 'people's community' that appealed to Germans to be part of a great project to redress the wrongs of the Versailles treaty, make the country strong and vital, and rid the body politic of unhealthy elements. The goal was to create a new national and racial self-consciousness among Germans. For Germany to live, others—especially Jews—had to die. . . . Fritzsche examines the efforts of Germans to adjust to new racial identities, to believe in the necessity of war, to accept the dynamic of unconditional destruction—in short, to become Nazis." (Publisher's note) Index.

"This book combines a compelling historical narrative with a thought-provoking analysis and will be of much interest to scholars in the field as well as a more general readership." Times Higher Ed

Includes bibliographical references

Johnson, Eric A.

What we knew; terror, mass murder and everyday life in Nazi Germany: an oral history. [by] Eric A. Johnson and Karl-Heinz Reuband. Basic Books 2005 xxiii, 434p $27.50 **943.086**

1. Holocaust, 1933-1945 2. Germany -- History -- 1933-1945

ISBN 0-465-08571-7

"The authors posit that 'far from living in a state of constant fear and discontent, most Germans led happy and even normal lives in Nazi Germany.' They believe that the Holocaust could not have been possible without the complicity of the majority of the German population. . . . This scholarly work is a major contribution to the understanding of life in Nazi Germany and a compelling narrative that is certain to be the standard work on the subject." Booklist

Includes bibliographical references

Kershaw, Ian

Hitler, 1936-1945: nemesis. Norton 2000 832p hardcover o.p. pa $25 **943.086**

1. Dictators 2. Heads of state 3. National socialism 4. Nazi leaders 5. Germany -- Politics and government -- 1933-1945

ISBN 0-393-04994-9; 0-393-32252-1 pa

"The second volume of Kershaw's biography of Hitler covers the period from the Anschluss with Austria to 1945. . . . By 1938, Hitler's word was the equivalent of written law. After 1936, Hitler also came to believe his own propaganda. . . . Without any reasonable restraint, he led Germany inexorably to destruction. . . . Kershaw's two volumes will probably be the standard source for many years." Libr J

Nelson, Anne

Red Orchestra; the story of the Berlin underground and the circle of friends who resisted Hitler. Random House 2009 388p il $27 **943.086**

1. National socialism 2. Rote Kapelle (Resistance group) 3. World War, 1939-1945 -- Underground movements

ISBN 978-1-4000-6000-9; 1-4000-6000-1

LC 2008-23465

The author "documents the wartime journey of Greta Kuckhoff, a young German, and her valiant colleagues who formed a potent resistance to the Hitler regime in its glory days. . . . Nelson's riveting book speaks proudly of Greta . . . and all of the nearly three million Germans who resisted Hitler's iron will, and gives the reader a somber view of hell from the inside." Publ Wkly

Includes bibliographical references

Ortner, Helmut

The lone assassin; the epic true story of the man who almost killed Hitler. Helmut Ortner; translated by Ross Benjamin. Skyhorse Pub. 2012 183 p. (hardcover: alk. paper) $24.95 **943.086**

1. World War, 1939-1945 -- Underground movements 2. Germany -- History -- 1933-1945 3. Anti-Nazi movement -- Germany -- Biography

ISBN 1616083832; 9781616083830

LC 2011049214

"In this book . . . author [Helmut] Ortner . . . lays out the story of Georg Elser, the carpenter who attempted to assassinate [Adolf] Hitler in 1939, courtesy of a bomb in the Munich Beer Hall. . . . Ortner examines Elser's life as well as covering the conditions that led to Hitler's rise to power, including the 1923 failed coup that made the Munich Beer Hall so symbolic to the Nazi regime." (Publishers Weekly)

The **Oxford** illustrated history of the Third Reich; [edited by] Robert Gellately. Oxford University Press 2018 384 p. (hardback: alk. paper) $39.95   **943.086**
1. Military history 2. Germany -- History -- 1933-1945
ISBN 9780198728283

LC 2017939066

This book in the Oxford Illustrated History series, edited by Robert Gellately, "provides a readable and fresh approach to the complex history of the Third Reich, from the coming to power of the Nazis in 1933 to the final collapse in 1945. Using photographs, paintings, propaganda images, and a host of other such materials from a wide range of sources, . . . it distills our ideas about the period and provides a balanced and accessible account of the whole era." (Publisher's note)

Parssinen, Terry M.

The **Oster** conspiracy of 1938; the unknown story of the military plot to kill Hitler and avert World War II. {by} Terry Parssinen. HarperCollins Pubs. 2003 xxii, 232p il map $27.95; pa $13.95   **943.086**
1. Generals 2. Heads of state 3. Nazi leaders 4. Underground leaders 5. Germany -- Politics and government -- 1933-1945
ISBN 0-06-019587-8; 0-06-095525-2 pa

LC 2002-68896

"A fascinating, blow-by-blow account of a seemingly feasible but failed attempt to prevent World War II. . . . Even knowing the outcome, readers feel suspense and hope as events unfold; alternate history buffs and history students alike will gain new insight into the past and into human character from this tragic story." SLJ
Includes bibliographical references

Rosenbaum, Ron

Explaining Hitler; the search for the origins of his evil. HarperPerennial 1999 444p pa $16   **943.086**
1. Heads of state 2. National socialism 3. Nazi leaders 4. Germany -- Politics and government -- 1933-1945
ISBN 0-06-095339-X; 978-0-06-095339-3

LC 99-25965

First published 1998 by Random House
This book examines interpretations of Hitler made by his contemporaries and by historians.
"In this brilliantly skeptical inventory of the world's Hitler-thinking, Rosenbaum analyzes not only the multiple Hitler theories but also the agendas and fantasies that the theorizers bring to their subject." Time
Includes bibliographical references

Shirer, William L.

The **rise** and fall of the Third Reich; a history of Nazi Germany. with a new afterword by the author. Simon & Schuster 1990 1249p hardcover o.p. pa $25   **943.086**
1. Heads of state 2. Nazi leaders 3. Germany -- History -- 1933-1945 4. World War, 1939-1945 -- Germany
ISBN 0-671-72868-7 pa

LC 90-221762

First published 1960
This is a comprehensive, documented history of Germany from the beginning of the Nazi party in 1918 to the World War II defeat of Germany in 1945. Here is a detailed account of the events, and the leading figures of the Nazi era, especially Adolf Hitler
Includes bibliographical references

Speer, Albert

Inside the Third Reich; memoirs. translated from the German by Richard and Clara Winston; introduction by Eugene Davidson. Simon & Schuster 1997 596p il pa $18   **943.086**
1. Heads of state 2. Nazi leaders 3. Germany -- History -- 1933-1945 4. World War, 1939-1945 -- Germany
ISBN 0-684-82949-5; 978-0-684-82949-4
Original German edition, 1969
The author, Hitler's "architect and later his armaments minister, was in the dictator's inner circle for almost 12 years. . . . After the war Speer used the enforced leisure of his 20 prison years as a war criminal to plan and write these memoirs." Libr J
Includes bibliographical references

Stargardt, Nicholas

The **German** War; A Nation Under Arms. Nicholas Stargardt. Basic Books, a member of the Perseus Books Group 2015 720 p. 24 plates; illustrations; maps $35   **943.086**
1. World War, 1939-1945 2. Germany -- History -- 1933-1945
ISBN 0465018998; 9780465018994

LC 2015945013

This book, by Nicholas Stargardt, "draws on an extraordinary range of primary source materials--personal diaries, court records, and military correspondence--to answer [why Germany continued World War II for 3 years after its strategic defeat.] . . . He offers an unprecedented portrait of wartime Germany, bringing the hopes and expectations of the German people--from infantrymen and tank commanders on the Eastern front to civilians on the home front--to vivid life." (Publisher's note)
"A well-researched, unsettling social history of war that will prove deeply thought-provoking—even worrying—for readers who wonder what they might have done under the same circumstances." Kirkus

★ The **Third** Reich; A History of Nazi Germany. Thomas Childers. Simon & Schuster 2017 651 p. illustrations, maps (hardback) $35   **943.086**
1. National socialism -- History 2. Germany -- History -- 1933-1945 3. National socialism 4. World War, 1939-1945 -- Causes 5. Germany -- Social conditions -- 1933-1945 6. Germany -- Politics and government -- 1933-1945
ISBN 9781451651157; 1451651139; 9781451651133

LC 2016019506

In this book, "Thomas Childers shows how the young Hitler became passionately political and anti-Semitic as he lived on the margins of society. Fueled by outrage at the punitive terms of the Versailles Treaty that ended the Great War, he found his voice and drew a following. As his views developed, Hitler attracted like-minded colleagues who formed the nucleus of the nascent Nazi party." (Publisher's note)
"A riveting study delves deeply into the conditions of the perfect storm that allowed Hitler and his Nazi party to seize and wield unprecedented power." Kirkus
Includes bibliographical references (pages 571-625) and index.

Tubach, Frederic C.

German voices; memories of life during Hitler's Third Reich. [by] Frederic C. Tubach with Sally Patterson Tubach. University of California Press 2011 273p il $26.95   **943.086**
1. National socialism 2. Germany -- History -- 1933-1945 3. World War, 1939-1945 -- Germany 4. Germany -- Social life and customs
ISBN 978-0-520-26964-4; 0-520-26964-0

LC 2010-51218

"Tubach approaches his mission with a nice, unobtrusive blend of sympathetic warmth and scholarly detachment. . . . The best recommendation I can make—and it is a warm one—is that readers go into German Voices prepared to treat it as one facet of a larger investigation into the phenomenon that was the Third Reich—as a uniquely accessible, honest and frequently thought-provoking window enabling some valuable ground-level insight into the much larger evil behavior that prevailed—until it imploded." PopMatters

Includes bibliographical references

943.087   Germany--1945-1990

Bessel, Richard

Germany 1945; from war to peace. HarperCollins 2009 522p il map $28.99   **943.087**
1. Reconstruction (1939-1951) 2. World War, 1939-1945 -- Peace 3. Germany -- History -- 1945-1990 4. World War, 1939-1945 -- Germany

ISBN 978-0-06-054036-4; 0-06-054036-2

This is an account of the German home front during the last months of the war. Bessel also writes about the country's path to economic recovery in the second half of 1945.

The author "does an excellent job of evoking the blasted landscape of a conquered Germany—the homelessness and the hunger, the rubble and the mass rape." New Yorker

Includes bibliographical references

Reeves, Richard

Daring young men; the heroism and triumph of the Berlin Airlift, June 1948-May 1949. Simon & Schuster 2010 316p il map $28   **943.087**
1. Air pilots 2. Air pilots -- Biography 3. Air pilots, Military -- History 4. Berlin (Germany) -- History -- Blockade, 1948-1949

ISBN 978-1-4165-4119-6; 1-4165-4119-5

LC 2009-15333

"'The American people will not allow the German people to starve,' Colonel Frank Howley, one of the top American commanders in Berlin, said in June, 1948, after the Soviets cut off all supply routes except an air corridor to the Western sectors of the city. But when the blockade began, as Reeves notes in his appealing account, almost no one believed that food and fuel for an urban population of more than two million could be delivered by air, and many American officials thought the question was how Berlin could be abandoned with the least embarrassment. Ten and a half months and a quarter-million American and British flights later—an unmatched act of politico-logistical bravado—the Soviets abandoned their blockade." New Yorker

Includes bibliographical references

Sarotte, Mary Elise

The **collapse**; the accidental opening of the Berlin Wall. Mary Elise Sarotte. Basic Books 2014 320 p. illustrations, maps (hardback) $27.99   **943.087**
1. Berlin Wall (1961-1989) 2. Berlin (Germany) -- History 3. Germany (East) -- Politics and government 4. Berlin Wall, Berlin, Germany,1961-1989 5. Berlin (Germany) -- History -- 1945-1990 6. Germany (East) -- Politics and government -- 1989-1990

ISBN 0465064949; 9780465064946

LC 2014026435

In this book on the factors contributing to the fall of the Berlin Wall, "historian Mary Elise Sarotte reveals how a perfect storm of decisions made by daring underground revolutionaries, disgruntled Stasi officers, and dictatorial party bosses sparked an unexpected series of events culminating in the chaotic fall of the Wall." (Publisher's note)

"Amply researched and emotive, this work shares the full narrative of events leading to the fall of the Berlin Wall in a way that both academ-

ics and lay readers will appreciate. Those already familiar with the subjects and time frames involved will definitely benefit from the author's extensive research and emphasis on personal narratives." LJ

Includes bibliographical references and index

Accidental opening of the Berlin Wall

Taylor, Frederick

Exorcising Hitler; the occupation and denazification of Germany. [by] Frederick Taylor. Bloomsbury Press 2011 xxxvii, 438p il $30   **943.087**
1. Nazi leaders 2. Denazification 3. Heads of state 4. Germany -- History -- 1945-1955 5. Germany -- History -- 1945-1990 6. Reconstruction (1939-1951) -- Germany 7. Germany -- Politics and government -- 1945-1990

ISBN 1-59691-536-6; 978-1-59691-536-7

LC 2010-46282

This is a "history of the birth of democracy in the ruins of Hitler's Germany." (Publisher's note) It "chronicles the bitter endgame of war, the murderous Nazi resistance, the vast displacement of people in Central and Eastern Europe, and the nascent cold war struggle between Soviet and Western occupiers". (New York Times Book Review)

This is a "history of the birth of democracy in the ruins of Hitler's Germany." Publisher's note

Includes bibliographical references

943.155   Berlin (Germany)

Mitchell, Greg

The **tunnels**; escapes under the Berlin Wall and the historic films the JFK White House tried to kill. Greg Mitchell. Crown Publishing 2016 400 p. illustrations, maps (ebook) $65; (hardback) $28   **943.155**
1. Escapes 2. Cold war 3. Refugees 4. Political activists 5. Berlin Wall (1961-1989) 6. Escapes -- Germany (East) -- History 7. Berlin Wall, Berlin, Germany, 1961-1989 8. Refugees -- Germany (East) -- Biography 9. National Broadcasting Company -- History 10. Columbia Broadcasting System, inc. -- History 11. Political activists -- Germany (West) -- Biography 12. Escapes -- Germany -- Berlin -- History -- 20th century 13. Tunnels -- Germany -- Berlin -- History -- 20th century 14. Documentary films -- Censorship -- United States -- History -- 20th century

ISBN 9781101903865; 9781101903858; 9781101903872

LC 2016013452

This book, by Greg Mitchell, is a "Cold War narrative of superpower showdowns, media suppression, and two escape tunnels beneath the Berlin Wall. In the summer of 1962, . . . a group of young West Germans risked prison, Stasi torture, and even death to liberate friends, lovers, and strangers in East Berlin by digging tunnels under the Wall. Then two U.S. television networks heard about the secret projects and raced to be first to document them from the inside." (Publisher's note)

"Mitchell's tense, fascinating account reveals how the U.S. undermined a freedom struggle for the sake of diplomacy." Pub Wkly

Includes bibliographical references and index.

943.7   Czech Republic and Slovakia

Goldstone, Nancy

Daughters of the winter queen; four remarkable sisters, the crown of Bohemia, and the enduring legacy of Mary, Queen of Scots. Nancy Goldstone. Little, Brown & Co. 2018 496 p.

$30 **943.7**

1. Queens -- Biography 2. Princesses -- Great Britain -- Biography
ISBN 9780316387910

LC 2017942373

This book, by Nancy Goldstone, tells "the . . . story of four . . . sisters and their glamorous mother, Elizabeth Stuart. . . . Forced into exile, the Winter Queen and her growing family found refuge in Holland, where the . . . art and culture of the Dutch Golden Age formed the backdrop to her daughters' education.. . . . Goldstone shows how these . . . women faced danger, tragic loss, and betrayal, and by refusing to surrender to adversity, changed the course of history." (Publisher's note)

943.703   1918-1992

McNamara, Kevin J.

Dreams of a great small nation; the mutinous army that threatened a revolution, destroyed an empire, founded a republic, and remade the map of Europe. Kevin J. McNamara. PublicAffairs 2016 416 p. maps (hardcover) $28.99   **943.703**

1. Slovenia 2. Revolutions 3. Czechoslovakia
ISBN 9781610394840; 9781610394857

LC 2016930908

This book, by Kevin J. McNamara, tells how "in 1917, two empires that had dominated much of Europe and Asia teetered on the edge of the abyss, exhausted by the ruinous cost in blood and treasure of the First World War. As Imperial Russia and Habsburg-ruled Austria-Hungary began to succumb, a small group of Czech and Slovak combat veterans stranded in Siberia saw an opportunity to realize their long-held dream of independence." (Publisher's note)

"McNamara's work presents a vital first entry that opens the doors on this integral part of World War I history and the shaping of the Soviet-influenced Eastern European political and social fabric." LJ

Includes bibliographical references (pages 331-379) and index.

943.71   Czech Republic

Eisen, Norman

The **last** palace; Europe's turbulent century in five lives and one legendary house. Norman L. Eisen. Crown 2018 416 p. $28   **943.71**

1. Historic buildings 2. Europe -- History -- 20th century 3. Prague (Czech Republic) -- History -- 20th century 4. Prague (Czech Republic) -- Buildings, structures, etc 5. Pražský hrad (Prague, Czech Republic) -- History 6. Schönbornský palác (Prague, Czech Republic) -- History
ISBN 9780451495785

LC 2018014382

This book, by Norman Eisen, presents "a sweeping yet intimate narrative about the last hundred years of turbulent European history, as seen through one of Mitteleuropa's greatest houses--and the lives of its occupants. . . . There was the optimistic Jewish financial baron, Otto Petschek, who built the palace . . .; Rudolf Toussaint, the cultured, compromised German general . . .; [and] Laurence Steinhardt, the first postwar US ambassador." (Publisher's note)

Includes bibliographical references and index

943.8   Poland

Swan, Oscar E.

Kaleidoscope of Poland; a cultural encyclopedia. Oscar E. Swan with Ewa Kołaczek-Fila, with a foreword by Adam Zamoyski. University of Pittsburgh Press 2015 xxvii, 366 p.p illustrations (some color) (Series in Russian and East European studies) (hardback: acid-free paper) $39.95   **943.8**

1. Europe -- History 2. Poland -- Encyclopedias 3. Encyclopedias and dictionaries 4. Poland -- History -- Encyclopedias 5. Poland -- Social life and customs -- Encyclopedias
ISBN 9780822944386

LC 2015013694

This book, in the Russian and East European Studies series, by Oscar E. Swan, "is a highly readable volume containing short articles on major personalities, places, events, and accomplishments from the thousand-year record of Polish history and culture. Featuring approximately 900 compact text entries and 600 illustrations. . . . [This] book is essentially a 'cultural dictionary'--offering a knowledge base that can be referred to time and time again." (Publisher's note)

"A balanced, splendidly illustrated survey of Polish history and culture." Booklist

943.9   Hungary

Michener, James A.

The **bridge** at Andau. Fawcett Crest 1983 277p pa $6.99   **943.9**

1. Hungarian refugees 2. Hungary -- History -- 1956, Revolution
ISBN 978-0-449-21050-5; 0-449-21050-2

First published 1957 by Random House

"The heroism, horror and tragedy of the 1956 Hungarian revolt is revealed through interviews with many refugees who crossed the bridge at Andau to freedom." Cleveland Public Libr

944   France and Monaco

Baldwin, Rosecrans, 1977-

Paris, I love you but you're bringing me down; Rosecrans Baldwin. Farrar, Straus and Giroux 2012 286 p.   **944**

1. Autobiographies 2. Americans -- France 3. Paris (France) -- Description and travel 4. Paris (France) -- Biography 5. Couples -- France -- Paris -- Biography 6. Americans -- France -- Paris -- Biography 7. Paris (France) -- Social life and customs
ISBN 0374146683; 9780374146689

LC 2011045886

This expatriate memoir by Rosecrans Baldwin presents an account of his time living in Paris, France. "Baldwin discovered some very French things about office life in Paris: You have to eat lunch, because the company docks a portion of your pay and returns it to you as meal coupons. . . . It's virtually impossible to get fired. . . . The author also discovered that French banks seem never to have heard of credit cards, and although he and wife qualified as legal residents for health-insurance coverage, the cards permitting them to actually use the insurance didn't arrive until a month before they left. Nonetheless, despite tight finances and loud construction work around their apartment, Baldwin fell in love just like everyone else." (Kirkus)

Buckley, Veronica

The **secret** wife of Louis XIV; Francoise d'Aubigne, Madame de Maintenon. Farrar, Straus and Giroux 2009 498p il map $35   **944**

    1. Kings 2. Royal favorites 3. France -- History -- 1589-1789, Bourbons

    ISBN 978-0-374-15830-9; 0-374-15830-4

                       LC 2008-16210

This is "a lively, sympathetic portrayal of the woman who, against all odds, succeeded in taming the royal tomcat." N Y Times Book Rev

    Includes bibliographical references

Downie, David

    A **passion** for Paris; romanticism and romance in the City of Light. David Downie. St. Martin's Press 2015 320 p. illustrations (hardback) $26.99   **944**

    1. Romanticism 2. Paris (France)

    ISBN 1250043158; 9781250043153

                       LC 2015007261

This memoir, by David Downie, is the author's "irreverent quest to uncover why Paris is the world's most romantic city--and has been for over 150 years. . . . Weaving together his own with the lives and loves of Victor Hugo, Georges Sand, Charles Baudelaire, Balzac, Nadar and other great Romantics, Downie delights in the city's secular romantic pilgrimage sites." (Publisher's note)

    "The author's encyclopedic knowledge of the city and its artists grants him a mystical gift of access: Doors left ajar and carriage gates left open foster his search for the city's magical story. Anyone who loves Paris will adore this joyful book. Readers visiting the city are advised to take it with them to discover countless new experiences." Kirkus

Fiennes, Ranulph, 1944-

    Agincourt; The Fight for France. Ranulph Fiennes. Pegasus 2015 336 p. plts; ills; mps; chrt; g tabls $26.95   **944**

    1. War 2. France -- History -- 1589-1789, Bourbons

    ISBN 1605989150; 9781605989150

Author Ranulph Fiennes "account of the Battle of Agincourt gives a unique perspective on one of the most significant battles in English history. With fascinating detail on the battle plans, weaponry, and human drama of Agincourt, this is a gripping evocation of a historical event integral to English identity. Six hundred years after the Battle of Agincourt, Sir Ranulph Fiennes casts new light on this epic event that has resonated throughout British and French history." (Publisher's note)

    "Despite its shortcomings, Fiennes's strong narrative style pulls readers along quickly, leaving plenty of time to tackle another more authoritative book on Agincourt such as Juliet Barker's Agincourt: Henry V and the Battle That Made England." Library Journal

Fraser, Antonia

    Marie Antoinette; the journey. Talese 2001 xxii, 512p il $35; pa $16.95   **944**

    1. Queens 2. France -- History -- 1589-1789, Bourbons

    ISBN 0-385-48948-X; 0-385-48949-8 pa

                       LC 2001-23493

"A well-researched biography that may cause one to rethink the role in which history has cast Marie Antoinette." Libr J

    Includes bibliographical references

Frieda, Leonie

    Francis I; the maker of modern France. Leonie Frieda. HarperCollins 2018 384 p. $29.99   **944**

    1. France -- History 2. France -- Kings and rulers

    ISBN 0061563099; 9780061563096

In this book, author Leonie Frieda "returns to sixteenth-century Europe in this evocative and entertaining biography that recreates a remarkable era of French history and brings to life a great monarch--Francis I--who turned France into a great nation. . . . With access to private archives that have never been used in a study of Francis I, Frieda explores the life of a man who was the most human of the monarchs of the period--and yet, remains the most elusive." (Publisher's note)

Goldstone, Nancy

    The **rival** queens; Catherine De' Medici, her daughter Marguerite De Valois, and the betrayal that ignited a kingdom. Nancy Goldstone. Little, Brown & Co. 2015 448 p. 8 plates; color ills., maps $30   **944**

    1. France -- History -- 1328-1589, House of Valois

    ISBN 0316409650; 9780316409650

                       LC 2014955135

This book by Nancy Goldstone is the "true story of mother-and-daughter queens Catherine de' Medici and Marguerite de Valois, whose wildly divergent personalities and turbulent relationship changed the shape of their tempestuous and dangerous century. Treacherous court politics, poisonings, inter-national espionage, and adultery form the background to a story that includes such celebrated figures as Elizabeth I, Mary, Queen of Scots, and Nostradamus." (Publisher's note)

    "This highly accessible account is recommended for general but serious readers interested in European history and royal biography." LJ

Gordon, Mary

    ★ **Joan** of Arc. Viking 2000 xxv, 180p (Penguin lives series) $19.95   **944**

    1. Saints 2. Christian saints 3. France -- History -- 1328-1589, House of Valois

    ISBN 0-670-88537-1

                       LC 99-55678

"This biography rehearses the well-known highlights in Joan's short life: the voices she heard who charged her with the mission to save France, her participation in the Battle of Orléans and the coronation of King Charles VII; her trial by an ecclesiastical court, where she was charged with witchcraft, heresy and idolatry. . . . The strength of this 'biographical meditation' lies in the penultimate chapter, in which Gordon investigates the numerous re-creations of Joan on stage and screen." Publ Wkly

    Includes bibliographical references

Green, David

    The **Hundred** Years War; a people's history. David Green. Yale University Press 2014 360 p. 16 plates; illustrations; maps (cl: alk. paper) $40   **944**

    1. Hundred Years' War, 1339-1453 2. France -- History -- 1328-1589, House of Valois 3. Great Britain -- History -- 1066-1485, Medieval period 4. France -- History, Military -- 1328-1589 5. France -- Foreign relations -- Great Britain 6. Great Britain -- Foreign relations -- France 7. Great Britain -- History, Military -- 1066-1485

    ISBN 0300134517; 9780300134513

                       LC 2014014233

This book, by David Green, profiles "the Hundred Years War (1337-1453) [which] dominated life in England and France for well over a century. . . . [The author] focuses on the ways the war affected different groups, among them knights, clerics, women, peasants, soldiers, peacemakers, and kings. He also explores how the long war altered governance in England and France and reshaped peoples' perceptions of themselves and of their national character." (Publisher's note)

    "This impressive survey ought to be included in any collection on the Middle Ages or the history of England and France. Summing Up:

Highly recommended. All levels/libraries." Choice

100 Years War

Horne, Alistair

★ La belle France; a short history. Knopf 2005 485p il map $30 **944**

1. France -- History

ISBN 1-4000-4140-6

LC 2004-42329

First published 2004 in the United Kingdom with title: Friend or foe: an Anglo-Saxon history of France

"This compelling narrative belongs in any public library needing an excellent, current one-volume history of France." Booklist

Includes bibliographical references

Seven ages of Paris. Knopf 2002 448p $35; pa $16 **944**

1. Paris (France)

ISBN 0-679-45481-0; 1-4000-3446-9 pa

LC 2002-29653

The author traces "the history of Paris through seven periods, beginning in the 12th century and ending with the death of Charles de Gaulle in 1969. . . . Each section includes fascinating insights into the social and cultural life of the age, fashions in clothing, architectural developments, leading personalities, and lifestyles of rich and poor alike. With the verve of a master storyteller, Horne captures Parisians' 'zest for living.'" Libr J

Includes bibliographical references

Jones, Colin

Paris; biography of a city. Colin Jones. Viking 2005 xxv, 566p il map $29.95 **944**

1. Paris (France)

ISBN 0-670-03393-6

LC 2004-53608

First published 2004 in the United Kingdom

"Moving from prehistoric tribal habitation through Roman times, medieval uncertainty and splendor, early modern religious wars, Enlightenment, revolution, and two world wars, Jones examines how rulers, economy, religion and violence have shaped the city. . . . Anyone who loves Paris will find connections and revelations here, a Paris of the mind that resonates through the centuries." Publ Wkly

Includes bibliographical references

Jonnes, Jill

Eiffel's tower; and the World's Fair where Buffalo Bill beguiled Paris, the artists quarreled, and Thomas Edison became a count. Viking 2009 354p il map $27.95 **944**

1. Structural engineers 2. Eiffel Tower (Paris, France) 3. Exposition Universelle de 1889 (Paris, France)

ISBN 978-0-670-02060-7; 0-670-02060-5

LC 2008-49839

"Not long after Gustave Eiffel, an engineer and builder of railway bridges, won the contract to build a centerpiece attraction for the 1889 World's Fair, he faced a barrage of criticism of its design as well as financial, architectural, mechanical, and political obstacles to its construction. Jonnes . . . captures the verve and personality of the Belle Epoque as Paris struggled to show the world its glory. . . . [She also] details the iconic figures who added to the allure of the fair—James McNeill Whistler, Paul Gauguin, Thomas Edison, Annie Oakley, and Buffalo Bill—and the excitement and ambitions of the era." Booklist

Includes bibliographical references

Kaplan, Alice

Dreaming in French; the Paris years of Jacqueline Bouvier Kennedy, Susan Sontag, and Angela Davis. Alice Kaplan. University of Chicago Press 2012 x, 289 p.p **944**

1. Paris (France) -- History 2. Foreign students -- France 3. Women -- United States -- Biography 4. Women -- United States -- Intellectual life 5. Students, Foreign -- France -- Paris -- Biography 6. United States -- Civilization -- French influences

ISBN 0226424383; 9780226424385

LC 2011026598

This book by Alice Kaplan offers a biographical account of the "transformative Parisian experiences of three strikingly different young women: Jacqueline Bouvier Kennedy, Susan Sontag, and Angela Davis. . . . In her comparisons of the three women's experiences, . . . she argues . . . about the impact of Paris on the rest of their lives: Bouvier's, aesthetic; Sontag's, intellectual; and Davis's, political." (Choice: Current Reviews for Academic Libraries)

Includes bibliographical references and index

Lever, Evelyne

Madame de Pompadour; translated from the French by Catherine Temerson. Farrar, Straus & Giroux 2002 310p il $26; pa $16.95 **944**

1. Royal favorites 2. France -- History -- 1589-1789, Bourbons

ISBN 0-374-11308-4; 0-312-31050-1 pa

LC 2002-22811

Original French edition, 2000

"Lever has crafted a detailed and fascinating portrait of the woman who pretty well ran France from 1745 to 1764." Publ Wkly

Includes bibliographical references

Moorehead, Caroline

Village of Secrets; Defying the Nazis in Vichy France. by Caroline Moorehead. HarperCollins 2014 384 p. illustrations, maps $27.99 **944**

1. World War, 1939-1945 -- France 2. World War, 1939-1945 -- Underground movements

ISBN 0062202472; 9780062202475

LC 2014497785

This book, by Caroline Moorehead, tells the "story of a French village that helped save thousands hunted by the Gestapo during World War II. . . . Le Chambon-sur-Lignon is a small village . . . high in the mountains of the Ardèche. . . . During the Second World War, the inhabitants of this tiny mountain village and its parishes saved thousands wanted by the Gestapo: resisters, freemasons, communists, OSS and SOE agents, and Jews." (Publisher's note)

"Moorehead not only recounts the heroics but also the everyday ordinariness of those involved, busting the embellished mythology while emphasizing the essential humanity of the entire operation." Booklist

Norwich, John Julius, 1929-2018

A history of France; John Julius Norwich. Atlantic Monthly Press 2018 400 p. (hardcover) $30 **944**

1. France -- History 2. Hundred Years' War, 1339-1453

ISBN 0802128904; 9780802128904

LC 2018026531

"This study of French history [by John Julius Norwich] comprises a cast of legendary characters--Charlemagne, Louis XIV, Napoleon, Joan of Arc and Marie Antionette, to name a few--as Norwich chronicles France's often violent, always fascinating history. From the French Revolution . . . to the storming of the Bastille, from the Vichy regime and the Resistance to the end of the Second World War, [this book] is packed with heroes and villains, battles and rebellion." (Publisher's note)

Paris was ours; thirty-two writers reflect on the City of Light. edited by Penelope Rowlands. Algonquin Books of Chapel Hill 2011 279p pa $15.95   **944**
  1. Paris (France) -- Description and travel
  ISBN 978-1-56512-953-5; 1-56512-953-9

           LC 2010-30560

In this anthology "Penelope Rowlands culled 32 essays, stories and poems, some original, some previously published, from writers who include professors, single mothers, gay men, a homeless woman, a wealthy Iranian and a poor young Cuban. The collection takes some of the shine off Paris but not the allure — not unlike the pull of a troubled but passionate lover who could never be more than a fling. . . . Ultimately, the writers fall in love with Paris, a city that embraces sorrow, depression, snarkiness, human frailty and living in the moment no matter the menial task that entails. In dismantling the dream of Paris, they reveal an infinitely more complex city and people." Minneapolis Star Tribune

Riding, Alan
  And the show went on; cultural life in Nazi-occcupied Paris. Alfred A. Knopf 2010 399p il map $28.95   **944**
  1. Popular culture -- France 2. World War, 1939-1945 -- France 3. France -- Social life and customs 4. Paris (France) -- Intellectual life 5. France -- History -- 1940-1945, German occupation
  ISBN 978-0-307-26897-6; 0-307-26897-7

           LC 2010-16841

"This engrossing work, rich in detail, should appeal to French historians and serious readers interested in 20th-century cultural history." Libr J
  Includes bibliographical references

Robb, Graham
  Parisians; an adventure history of Paris. W.W. Norton & Co. 2010 475p il map $28.95   **944**
  1. Paris (France) -- History
  ISBN 978-0-393-06724-8; 0-393-06724-6

           LC 2009-54279

Part history, part travelog, part Ripley's Believe It or Not!, this creative historical geography takes us on a tour of Paris via a series of chronologically arranged vignettes stretching from the eve of the Revolution of 1789 to the present. . . . The book records a series of moments and meetings when characters both obscure and famous interacted with key landmarks like the Palais Royal, Notre Dame, or Place de la Concorde. Robb . . . recreates the drama and turmoil of key events like the bloody horrors of the Commune, De Gaulle's triumphant 1944 entry into Paris, or the tumultuous student demonstrations of May 1968. Libr J
  Includes bibliographical references

Sante, Luc
  The **other** Paris; Luc Sante. Farrar, Straus & Giroux 2015 320 p. illustrations, map (hardback) $27   **944**
  1. Poverty 2. Paris (France) 3. France -- Social conditions 4. Poor -- France -- Paris 5. Paris (France) -- Social conditions 6. Criminals -- France -- Paris -- History 7. Paris (France) -- Description and travel 8. Working class -- France -- Paris -- History 9. City and town life -- France -- Paris -- History 10. Paris (France) -- Social life and customs -- 19th century 11. Paris (France) -- Social life and customs -- 20th century 12. Eccentrics and eccentricities -- France -- Paris -- History
  ISBN 0374299323; 9780374299323; 9781429944588

           LC 2015004988

In this book on Paris, France, author "Luc Sante gives us a panoramic view of that second metropolis, which has nearly vanished but whose traces are in the bricks and stones of the contemporary city, in the culture of France itself, and, by extension, throughout the world. Drawing on testimony from a great range of witnesses-from Balzac and Hugo to assorted boulevardiers, rabble-rousers, and tramps-Sante . . . takes the reader on a whirlwind tour." (Publisher's note)
  "A fascinating stroll through a vanished, wild past. Recommended for general readers." LJ
  Includes bibliographical references and index

Tuchman, Barbara Wertheim
  A **distant** mirror; the calamitous 14th century. {by} Barbara W. Tuchman. Knopf 1978 xx, 677p il maps hardcover o.p. pa $17.95   **944**
  1. Plague 2. Crusades 3. Medieval civilization 4. Women -- Europe 5. World history -- 14th century 6. Church history -- 600-1500, Middle Ages 7. France -- History -- 1328-1589, House of Valois 8. Great Britain -- History -- 1154-1399, Plantagenets
  ISBN 0-345-34957-1 pa

           LC 78-5985

The author traces the history of the fourteenth century by following the career of a "feudal lord, Enguerrand de Coucy VII, the seigneur of some 150 towns and villages in Picardy. He was born in 1340, and he died in captivity in 1397, having been made a prisoner by the Turks." Time
  Includes bibliographical references

Yalom, Marilyn
  How the French invented love; nine hundred years of passion and romance. HarperCollins 2012 416 p. $15.99   **944**
  1. Cultural critique 2. French literature 3. Love in literature
  ISBN 0062048317; 9780062048318
  This book offers author Marilyn Yalom's literary investigation into "how the French manage their romances, marriages, affairs, and obsession with love and sex." She "argues that it's not only gender-specific traits and roles that are socially constructed, but love, too. For example, 'Les liaisons dangereuses' . . . is still on the list of required reading in French high schools." (Publishers Weekly)

944.04   France since 1789

Burke, Edmund
  ★ **Reflections** on the Revolution in France; edited by J.C.D. Clark. Stanford Univ. Press 2001 446p $65; pa $29.95 **944.04**
  1. France -- History -- 1789-1799, Revolution
  ISBN 0-8047-3923-4; 978-0-8047-3923-8; 0-8047-4205-7 pa; 0-8047-4205-4 pa

           LC 00-63732

First published 1790
  "A treatise by Edmund Burke, written in the form of a letter to a Frenchman. It attacks the leaders and principles of the French Revolution for their violence and excesses, and urges reform, rather than rebellion, as a means of correcting social and political abuses." Benet's Reader's Ency. 4th edition
  Includes bibliographical references

McPhee, Peter
  ★ **Liberty** or death; the French Revolution, 1789-1799. Peter McPhee. Yale University Press 2016 488 p. (cloth: alk. paper) $35   **944.04**

1. France -- History -- 1789-1799, Revolution 2. France -- History -- Revolution, 1789-1799
ISBN 9780300189933

LC 2015040677

This book, by Peter McPhee, discusses "the French Revolution [which] has fascinated, perplexed, and inspired for more than two centuries. It was a seismic event that radically transformed France and launched shock waves across the world. In this . . . new history, Peter McPhee draws on a lifetime's study of eighteenth-century France and Europe to create an entirely fresh account of the world's first great modern revolution—its origins, drama, complexity, and significance." (Publisher's note)

"McPhee (emeritus, history, Univ. of Melbourne; Robespierre: A Life) has written on many aspects of the French Revolution but never more beneficially than in this articulate and perceptive volume. McPhee's revolution is truly national in scope; Paris interacting with the hinterlands rather than a case of Paris playing the dog and the rest of France the tail. The author also makes solid use of primary source materials from outside France. . . . Numerous histories of the French Revolution exist; while many are good, none is so current on the literature and lucidly presented as this. Scholars and history lovers will rejoice." LJ

Reiss, Tom, 1964-

★ The **Black** Count; glory, revolution, betrayal, and the real Count of Monte Cristo. Tom Reiss; [maps by David Lindroth Inc.] Crown Trade 2012 ix, 414 p.p maps (hardcover) $27 **944.04**
1. Generals -- France -- Biography 2. France. Armée -- Biography 3. France -- History, Military -- 1789-1815
ISBN 030738246X; 9780307382467; 9780307952950

LC 2012017633

Pulitzer Prize: Biography (2013)

This book by Tom Reiss, which won the Pulitzer Prize for biography presents the story of "General Alex Dumas, . . . the son of a black slave--who rose higher in the white world than any man of his race. . . . Born in Saint-Domingue (now Haiti), Alex Dumas was briefly sold into bondage but made his way to Paris where he was schooled as a sword-fighting member of the French aristocracy. Enlisting as a private, he rose to command armies at the height of the Revolution." (Publisher's note)

Includes bibliographical references (p. [341]-403) and index

944.05   Period of First Empire, 1804-1815

Johnson, Paul

★ **Napoleon**. Viking 2002 190p (Penguin lives series) hardcover o.p. pa $13 **944.05**
1. Emperors 2. France -- Kings and rulers
ISBN 0-670-03078-3; 0-14-303745-5 pa

LC 2001-45605

Johnson "presents a concise appraisal of Napoleon's career and a precise understanding of his enigmatic character. The author views Napoleon, not as an 'idea man' whose ideology was the ladder by which he propelled himself to heights of power, but as an opportunist who took advantage of a series of events and situations he could manipulate into achieving supreme control." Booklist

Includes bibliographical references

Schom, Alan

One hundred days; Napoleon's road to Waterloo. Oxford University Press 1993 398p pa $45 **944.05**
1. Emperors 2. Waterloo, Battle of, 1815

ISBN 978-0-19-508177-0; 0-19-508177-3

LC 93-11787

First published 1992 by Atheneum

This is an account of "Napoleon's escape from Elba in February 1815 and his return . . . to France. Rallying the nation behind him, he mustered his army and marched off to meet Wellington at Waterloo. . . . This is a first-class reconstruction of Napoleon's final campaign." Publ Wkly

Includes bibliographical references

944.081   Period of Third Republic, 1870-1945

Brown, Frederick

For the soul of France; culture wars in the age of Dreyfus. Alfred A. Knopf 2010 304p il $28.95 **944.081**
1. French national characteristics 2. Nationalism -- France 3. France -- History -- 1815-1914
ISBN 978-0-307-26631-6; 0-307-26631-1

LC 2009-30912

"Brown recounts the history of France, following its 1789 revolution, as an ongoing contest between the champions and foes of the Enlightenment. . . . The humiliating defeat of the Franco-Prussian War of 1870-71 was followed by the economic crash of 1882 and the Panama Company bribery scandal of 1893, both of which were reputedly executed by Jewish masters. . . . In 1894, an opportunity for revenge presented itself in the person of Alfred Dreyfus, a 34-year-old Jewish army officer. Accused of espionage on the flimsiest of evidence—fabrications, and forgeries—Dreyfus was twice tried and convicted. Dreyfus was eventually freed in 1906, one year after a law requiring the separation of church and state had passed. Secularism seemed to hold sway. But, as Brown demonstrates in his brilliant study, religious fervor and bellicose patriotism combined in World War I to shift the balance yet again." Boston Globe

Includes bibliographical references

Derfler, Leslie

★ The **Dreyfus** affair. Greenwood Press 2002 xxii, 167p il (Greenwood guides to historic events, 1500-1900) $44.95 **944.081**
1. Antisemitism 2. Army officers 3. France -- Politics and government -- 1815-1914
ISBN 0-313-31791-7

LC 2001-38365

"Following a chronology is a 'Historical Overview' containing several chapters of background and analysis. These chapters provide context for what is commonly known as the Dreyfus affair, discuss how anti-Semitism and socialism played into and were affected by the affair, and summarize how the affair has been viewed through history. The next section is an A-Z collection of biographies of almost 20 key individuals. . . . Primary documents comprise the next chapter and most documents are accompanied by short explanations. . . . This guide is useful for researchers who need more information than they can find in an encyclopedia." Booklist

Includes bibliographical references

Read, Piers Paul

The **Dreyfus** affair; the scandal that tore France in two. Piers Paul Read. Bloomsbury Press 2012 408 p. **944.081**
1. Treason 2. Scandals 3. Antisemitism 4. France -- History -- 1815-1914 5. France -- Intellectual life -- 19th century 6. Scandals -- France -- History -- 19th century 7. France -- History

-- Third Republic, 1870-1940 8. France -- Politics and government -- 1870-1940 9. Trials (Treason) -- Political aspects -- France 10. Antisemitism -- France -- History -- 19th century 11. Religion and politics -- France -- History -- 19th century
ISBN 1608194329; 9781608194322

LC 2011034456

This historical work by Piers Paul Read reviews the Dreyfus Affair. —Captain Alfred Dreyfus was a rising star in the French artillery command. . . . However, Dreyfus had enemies as a result of his ambition. . . . On the basis of flimsy evidence, Dreyfus was placed under arrest for the crime of high treason. Not long afterward, he was sentenced to spend the rest of his life on the legendary, lethal Devil's Island. The saga of Dreyfus's many trials . . . the fight to free him, and the intrigues on both sides, is a . . . story rife with heroes and villains. . . . The anti-Semitism and deceit on display in the Dreyfus case was an ominous prelude to the Holocaust and the long, bloody twentieth century to come." (Publisher's note)

Includes bibliographical references and index.

944.083   Period of Fifth Republic, 1958-

Mayle, Peter, 1939-2018

A **year** in Provence; illustrations by Judith Clancy. Knopf 1990 207p il $19.95   **944.083**
1. Provence (France) -- Social life and customs
ISBN 0394572300

LC 89-38475

First published 1989 in the United Kingdom

"Peter Mayle recently emigrated to the South of France, where he has bought and modernized a house close to the village of Ménerbes in the Lubéron. A Year in Provence is his account of a settler's experiences, beginning with his arrival in January and ending with a party for the builders to celebrate the house's completion the following Christmas." (Times Lit Suppl)

White, Edmund

The **flaneur**; a stroll through the paradoxes of Paris. Bloomsbury Pub. 2001 211p maps $16.95   **944.083**
1. Paris (France) -- Description and travel
ISBN 1-58234-135-4

LC 00-46812

"White is richly informed, and his evocative writing should appeal to both armchair travelers and visitors to Paris." Libr J

944.084 France-2000

Chirac, Jacques, 1932-

My life in politics; Jacques Chirac; edited by Catherine Spencer. Palgrave Macmillan 2012 352 p.   **944.084**
1. France -- Politics and government 2. Presidents -- France -- Biography 3. France -- Politics and government -- 1958-
ISBN 0230340881; 9780230340886

LC 2012018097

This book by "[t]wo-time president of France, mayor of Paris, and international politician—Jacques Chirac—covers the full scope of Chirac's political career of more than 50 years. . . . As mayor of Paris, Chirac was famed for his success in beautifying the City of Lights and keeping it whole during the heady days of the 1968 riots. As president in the 1990s and early 2000s, Chirac took controversial steps to privatize the economy and plan the European Union." (Publisher's note)

944.361   Paris

Baxter, John, 1939-

Saint-Germain-des-Pres; Paris's rebel quarter. HarperCollins 2016 256 p. illustrations (ebook) $14.99; $15.99 **944.361**
1. Neighborhood 2. Paris (France) -- History
ISBN 9780062431912; 0062431900; 9780062431905

In this book, author John "Baxter, an expat who has called Saint-Germain home for more than two decades, guides readers on an off-the-beaten-path journey through the quarter's history, landmarks, and delights.Today, the neighborhood, with its cobblestone streets, iconic cafes, and unique shopping destinations, is one of Paris's premier tourist attractions. And yet it retains its rebel soul—if you know where to look." (Publsiher's note)

"Although this book's most fortunate readers will undoubtedly be those who will soon be toting it in the City of Lights, those with no travel plans at all will still count themselves lucky to be in the company of such an engaging Paris pro." Booklist

Brassaï, 1899-1984

Brassai; Paris by Night. by Brassai. Random House Inc. 2012 96 p. illustrations $45   **944.361**
1. Night 2. Photography 3. Paris (France)
ISBN 2080200992; 9782080200990

In this book, by Brassai, "he sensed that photography was the tool that would allow him to document his vision of a dying society. Fascinated by the night, which he found disconcerting, enigmatic, and suggestive, Brassaï photographed its every aspect, from police to prostitutes to the homeless to socialites, all in a dreamlike and mysterious manner." (Publisher's note)

Verant, Samantha

How to make a French family; a memoir of love, food, and faux pas. Samantha Vérant. Sourcebooks Inc 2017 xxi, 308 p.p $15.99   **944.361**
1. Married people 2. Travel writing 3. Americans -- France 4. Cugnaux (France) -- Biography 5. Americans -- France -- Cugnaux -- Biography 6. France, Southwest -- Social life and customs
ISBN 1492638498; 9781492638490

LC 2016032663

In this memoir, Samantha Vérant, recalls her life when she moved to France to be with her French husband Jean-Luc and his kids. "But almost from the moment the plane touches down, Samantha realizes that there are a lot of things about her new home-- . . . that she hadn't counted on. . . . Samantha isn't sure if she really has what it takes to make it in la belle France. But when a second chance at life and love is on the line, giving up isn't an option." (Publisher's note)

"Verant combines one part second chance at romance, on part travelogue, and nearly three dozen recipes in this heartfelt account of how she...started life over in France with an instant family. " Pub Wkly.

944.9   Provence-Côte d'Azur, Monaco, Corsica

Lovell, Mary S.

The **Riviera** set; glitz, glamour, and the hidden world of high society. by Mary S. Lovell. Pegasus Books 2017 viii, 434 p.p illustrations (hardcover) $27.95   **944.9**
1. Social classes 2. Riviera (France) 3. France -- Social life and customs 4. Chateau de l'Horizon -- History 5. Rich people -- France -- History 6. France, Southern -- 20th century -- History 7. Riviera (France) -- 20th century -- History

ISBN 9781681775159; 9781681775791; 1681775158

This book, by Mary S. Lovell, "reveals the story of the group of people who lived, partied, bed-hopped and politicked at the Château de l'Horizon near Cannes, over the course of forty years from the time when Coco Chanel made southern French tans fashionable in the twenties to the death of the playboy Prince Aly Khan in 1960." (Publisher's note)

"Lovell bridges the Edwardian age and postwar Europe, as cultural and political shifts brought more Americans and money usurped style as the most valuable currency in the region." Pub Wkly

Includes bibliographical references (pages 395-408) and index.

Mayle, Peter, 1939-2018

My twenty-five years in Provence; reflections on then and now. Peter Mayle. Alfred A. Knopf 2018 192 p. (hardback) $25   **944.9**
1. France 2. Provence (France) -- Description and travel 3. Provence (France) -- Social life and customs
ISBN 9780451494528

LC 2018001245

In this book, author Peter Mayle "offers vivid recollections from his twenty-five years in the South of France--lessons learned, culinary delights enjoyed, and changes observed. Twenty-five years ago, Peter Mayle and his wife, Jennie, were rained out of a planned two weeks on the Côte d'Azur. In search of sunlight, they set off for Aix-en-Provence; enchanted by the world and life they found there, they soon decided to uproot their lives in England and settle in Provence." (Publisher's note)

945   Italy, San Marino, Vatican City, Malta

Berendt, John

The **city** of falling angels; a Venice story. Penguin Press 2005 414p $25.95; pa $15   **945**
1. Venice (Italy) -- Social life and customs
ISBN 1-59420-058-0; 1-59420-061-0 pa

LC 2005-47661

The author describes some of his encounters with contemporary Venetians. The starting point for his travels was the investigation of the fire which destroyed La Fenice opera house in 1996.

Berendt "delivers an urbane, beautifully fashioned book with much exotic charm. . . . [The author] makes erudite, inquisitive, nicely skeptical company as he leads the reader through the shadows of what was heretofore better known as a tourist attraction." N Y Times (Late N Y Ed)

Bosworth, R. J. B.

Mussolini's Italy; life under the dictatorship, 1915-1945. Penguin 2006 xxvi, 692p il map $35   **945**
1. Heads of state 2. Fascism -- Italy 3. Italy -- History -- 1914-1945
ISBN 1-59420-078-5

LC 2005-52127

First published 2005 in the United Kingdom

Bosworth "combines prodigious research with a clear writing style that will appeal to all readers interested in the Italy of Il Duce." Libr J

Includes bibliographical references

Capponi, Niccolo

The **Day** the Renaissance Was Saved; The Battle of Anghiari and Da Vinci's Lost Masterpiece. Niccolo Capponi; translated by Andre Naffis-Sahely. Random House Inc 2015 240 p. 16 plates; illustrations $26.95   **945**
1. Renaissance 2. Painting -- 15th and 16th centuries

ISBN 1612194605; 9781612194608

LC 2015955589

In this book author "Niccolò Capponi--a direct descendent of Niccolò Machiavelli, as well as of a Florentine general who was a key strategist of the campaign at Anghiari--weaves the story of da Vinci's lost masterpiece through the narrative of the history-changing battle, and offers context on the development of humanist thought and the political intrigues of fifteenth-century Italy." (Publisher's note)

"A significant survey of an important battle and its outcomes as retold by an expert of Italian Renaissance military and political history, this book will be of interest mostly to scholars, graduate students, and some general readers of the subject. For both large public and academic libraries." LJ

Clark, Robert

Dark water; flood and redemption in the city of masterpieces. Doubleday 2008 354p il $26   **945**
1. Floods 2. Florence (Italy)
ISBN 978-0-7679-2648-5; 0-7679-2648-X

LC 2008-1695

This is an account of the Florence flood of 1966.

The author "tells an enthralling true story in a way that makes it read like a novel." Economist

Includes bibliographical references

Crowley, Roger

★ **City** of fortune; how Venice ruled the seas. Roger Crowley. Random House 2011 xxix, 432 p.p (alk. paper) $32.00   **945**
1. Venice (Italy) 2. Italy -- History 3. Medieval civilization 4. Venice (Italy) -- Commerce -- History 5. Venice (Italy) -- History -- 697-1508 6. Merchants -- Italy -- Venice -- History 7. Mediterranean Region -- Commerce -- History 8. Venice (Italy) -- Economic conditions -- To 1797
ISBN 1400068207; 9780679644262; 9781400068203

LC 2011005529

Author Roger Crowley "narrate[s] the rise and apogee of the empire acquired by Venice [Italy] between 1000 and 1500 . . . [It discusses] . . . the collective nature of the medieval Venetian state, its organisation and its awe-inspiring effectiveness [and] . . . draws the substantive difference between Venice and Genoa in their centuries-long struggle for commercial and economic dominance." (History Today)

Includes bibliographical references (p. [407]-415) and index

Frieda, Leonie

The **Deadly** Sisterhood; A Story of Women, Power, and Intrigue in the Italian Renaissance, 1427-1527. Leonie Frieda. HarperCollins 2013 xi, 403 p.p (hardcover) $32.50   **945**
1. Renaissance 2. Women -- Biography 3. Italy -- History -- 0-1559
ISBN 0061563080; 9780061563089

This book, by Leonie Frieda, provides a biography of "eight women whose lives . . . encompass the spectacle, opportunity, and depravity of Italy's Renaissance. Lucrezia Turnabuoni, Clarice Orsini, Beatrice d'Este, Isabella d'Este, Caterina Sforza, Giulia Farnese, Isabella d'Aragona, and Lucrezia Borgia shared the riches of their birthright: wealth, political influence, and friendship, but none were not exempt from personal tragedies, exile, and poverty." (Publisher's note)

Hazzard, Shirley, 1931-2016

The **ancient** shore; dispatches from Naples. [by] Shirley Hazzard and Francis Steegmuller. University of Chicago Press

2008 129p il pa $13; $18   **945**

1. Authors 2. Novelists 3. Short story writers 4. Naples (Italy) -- Civilization 5. Italy -- Description and travel 6. Naples (Italy) -- Description and travel

ISBN 0-226-32202-5 pa; 0-2263-2201-7; 978-0-226-32202-5 pa; 978-0-2263-2201-8

LC 2008-15420

This book is a collection of " best of [Shirley] Hazzard's writings on Naples, along with a classic New Yorker essay by her late husband, Francis Steegmuller.... With Hazzard as our guide, we encounter Henry James, Oscar Wilde, and of course Goethe, but Hazzard's concern is primarily with the Naples of our own time--often violently unforgiving to innocent tourists, but able to transport the visitor who attends patiently to its rhythms and history." (Publisher's note)

"Much larger than all its parts, this book does full justice to a place, and a time, where 'nothing was pristine, except the light.'" Bookforum

Hibbert, Christopher

The **Borgias** and their enemies; 1431-1519. Harcourt, Inc. 2008 328p $26   **945**

1. Kings 2. Italy -- History

ISBN 978-0-15-101033-2; 0-15-101033-1

LC 2008-03076

"Lucrezia Borgia, on hearing that her father, Pope Alexander VI, was choosing her third husband, noted that her first two had been 'very unlucky.' Luck had little to do with it, as Hibbert shows in this vivid chronicle of the notoriously corrupt Renaissance family. One husband was killed on the orders of her brother Cesare, whose ruthlessness made him the model for Machiavelli's 'The Prince'; the other was discarded after ceasing to be politically useful to the Pope. Hibbert ably traces the web of alliances through which the Spanish-born Alexander hoped to secure his hold on Italy and his family's place in power." New Yorker

Includes bibliographical references

Hollingsworth, Mary

★ The **family** Medici; the hidden history of the Medici dynasty. Mary Hollingsworth. W W Norton & Co Inc 2018 528 p. $29.95   **945**

1. Italy -- Kings and rulers 2. Florence (Italy) -- History

ISBN 1681776480; 9781681776484

This book, by Mary Hollingsworth, presents a "revisionist narrative of the rise and fall of the House of Medici. Having founded the bank that became the most powerful in Europe in the fifteenth century, the Medici gained massive political power in Florence. . . . However, . . . Hollingsworth argues that the idea that the Medici were enlightened rulers of the Renaissance is a fiction that has now acquired the status of historical fact." (Publisher's note)

"A vital acquisition for anyone who studies the Renaissance and seeks the true role of the Medici in the history of Florence." Kirkus

Hughes, Robert

Rome; a cultural, visual, and personal history. Alfred A. Knopf 2011 498p il $35   **945**

1. Rome -- History

ISBN 978-0-307-26844-0; 0-307-26844-6

LC 2011-14600

The author "gives us a guided tour through the city in its many incarnations, excavating the geologic layers of its cultural past and creating an indelible portrait of a city in love with spectacle and power . . . . The reader need not agree with Mr. Hughes's acerbic assessments or even be interested in Rome as a destination on the map to relish this volume, so captivating is his narrative. Although his book is a biography of Rome, it is also an acutely written historical essay informed by his

wide-ranging knowledge of art, architecture and classical literature, and a thought-provoking meditation on how gifted artists (like Bernini and Michelangelo) and powerful politicians and church leaders (like Augustus, Mussolini and Pope Sixtus V) can reshape the map and mood of a city." n Y times Book Rev

Includes bibliographical references

Keahey, John

Seeking Sicily; a cultural journey through myth and reality in the heart of the Mediterranean. Thomas Dunne Books/St. Martin's Press 2011 312p il $27.99; ebook $14.99   **945**

1. Sicily (Italy) -- Description and travel 2. Sicily (Italy) -- Social life and customs

ISBN 978-0-312-59705-4; 978-1-4299-9067-7 ebook

LC 2011026786

The author "takes a meandering and inspiring tour through the history, culture, and landscape of Sicily, an island that has been a crossroads for the various peoples of the Mediterranean for millennia. . . . Keahey's thoroughly researched book will inspire any traveler to look past the Sicily of the traditional tourist's guide and appreciate its diverse, layered, and sometimes dark history." Libr J

Includes bibliographical references

Lee, Alexander

The **ugly** Renaissance; Alexander Lee. Doubleday 2013 448 p. 16 plts; ills; gen. tabl; map $30   **945**

1. Renaissance 2. Italy -- History -- 0-1559 3. Art -- 15th and 16th centuries 4. Renaissance -- Italy 5. Italy -- Civilization -- 1268-1559 6. Italy -- Social life and customs -- To 1500 7. Degeneration -- Social aspects -- Italy -- History -- To 1500

ISBN 0385536593; 9780385536592

LC 2013015480

This book, by Alexander Lee, offers "a . . . counterintuitive portrait of the sordid, hidden world behind the dazzling artwork of Michelangelo, Leonardo da Vinci, Botticelli, and more. . . . Renaissance scholar Alexander Lee illuminates the dark and titillating contradictions that were hidden beneath the surface of the period's best-known artworks." (Publisher's note)

"This highly inviting history should appeal widely to both scholars and casual readers." LJ

Includes bibliographical references and index

Leon, Donna

My Venice and Other Essays; by Donna Leon. Pgw 2013 240 p. $26   **945**

1. Venice (Italy)

ISBN 0802120369; 9780802120366

This book, by Donna Leon, presents "over fifty . . . essays that range from battles over garbage in the canals to the troubles with rehabbing Venetian real estate. She shares episodes from her life in Venice, explores her love of opera, and recounts tales from in and around her country house in the mountains. With pointed observations and humor, she also explores her family history and former life in New Jersey, and the idea of the Italian man." (Publisher's note)

Madden, Thomas F.

Venice; a new history. Thomas F. Madden. Viking 2012 xi, 446 p.p (hbk.: alk. paper) $35   **945**

1. Venice (Italy) -- History

ISBN 0670025429; 9780670025428

LC 2012005304

This book on the history of Venice by Thomas Madden "trac[es] an arc from the city's humble origins as a lagoon refuge to its apex as a vast maritime empire and Renaissance epicenter to its rebirth as a modern tourist hub. Madden explores all aspects of Venice's . . . achievements . . . its role as an economic powerhouse and birthplace of capitalism, its popularization of opera, the stunning architecture of its watery environs, and more." (Publisher's note)

Includes bibliographical references and index.

Strathern, Paul, 1940-

Death in Florence; the Medici, Savonarola and the battle for the soul of the Renaissance city. Paul Strathern. W W Norton & Co Inc 2015 464 p. 8 plates; color ills., maps $29.95 **945**

1. Martyrs 2. Renaissance 3. Florence (Italy) 4. Monks 5. Political leaders 6. Patrons of the arts 7. Writers on religion 8. Florence (Italy) -- History -- 1421-1737

ISBN 160598826X; 9781605988269

In this book on Florence, Italy author "Paul Strathern reveals the paradoxes, self-doubts, and political compromises that made the battle for the soul of the Renaissance city one of the . . . important moments in Western history. By the end of the fifteenth century . . . the ruling Medici embodied the progressive humanist spirit. In the form of Savonarola, an unprepossessing provincial monk, Lorenzo [de Medici] found his nemesis. The battle between these two men would be a fight to the death, a series of sensational events." (Publisher's note)

"Strathern brings his two opponents to life by including a great deal about their physicality (Lorenzo was plagued by gout and arthritis; Savonarola had a plain face but eyes that burned with intensity). The juxtaposition of Lorenzo's and Savonarola's lives and approaches to life adds to the sense of a 'cat and mouse game' throughout this riveting narrative history." Booklist

Taylor, Benjamin

Naples declared; a walk around the bay. Benjamin Taylor. G.P. Putnam's Sons 2012 240 p. **945**

1. Local history 2. Naples (Italy) 3. City and town life 4. Naples (Italy) -- History 5. Naples, Bay of (Italy) -- History 6. City and town life -- Italy -- Naples 7. Naples (Italy) -- Description and travel 8. Naples (Italy) -- Social life and customs 9. Naples, Bay of (Italy) -- Description and travel

ISBN 0399159177; 9780399159176

LC 2011049450

This book by Benjamin Taylor provides a description of Naples, Italy with "discussions of history, philosophy, religion, art, culture, literature, [and] customs. The book meanders between past and present, wanders in stream-of-thought fashion through the Naples streets, delves . . . into the city's stories, lives, and lore, and drops in for conversations with locals . . ." (Library Journal) "[including] present-day encounters with a fervently communist doctor, with a chain-smoking student of Faulkner, and with novelist Shirley Hazzard." (Kirkus)

Includes bibliographical references and index

945.091   Reign of Victor Emmanuel III, 1900-1946

Bosworth, R. J. B.

Mussolini. Oxford Univ. Press 2002 584p il hardcover o.p. pa $14.95 **945.091**

1. Heads of state 2. Fascism -- Italy 3. Italy -- Politics and government

ISBN 0-340-73144-3; 0-340-80988-4 pa

LC 2002-283267

This is "the definitive study of the Italian dictator and belongs in every public and academic library with a strong European history collection." Libr J

Includes bibliographical references

Corner, Paul

The **Fascist** Party and popular opinion in Mussolini's Italy; by Paul Corner. Oxford University Press 2012 302 p. (hbk.) $125 **945.091**

1. Public opinion 2. Fascism -- Italy 3. Fascism -- Italy -- History 4. Fascism -- Italy -- Public opinion 5. Partito nazionale fascista (Italy) 6. Public opinion -- Italy -- History -- 20th century

ISBN 0198730691; 9780198730699

LC 2012462711

Focusing on fascism in Italy, author Paul Corner "argues that 'real existing Fascism', as lived by a large part of the population, was in fact an increasingly negative experience and reflected few of those colourful and attractive features of fascist propaganda which have induced more favourable interpretations of the regime. Distinguishing clearly between the fascist project and its realisation, Corner examines the ways in which the fascist party asserted itself at the local level." (Publisher's note)

Moorehead, Caroline

A **bold** and dangerous family; the remarkable story of an Italian mother, her two sons, and their fight against fascism. Caroline Moorehead. Harper 2017 xv, 432 p.p illustrations (hardcover) $27.99 **945.091**

1. Fascism -- Italy 2. Italy -- History -- 1914-1945 3. Intellectuals -- Italy -- Biography 4. Fascism -- Italy -- History -- 20th century 5. Italy -- Politics and government -- 1914-1945 6. Anti-fascist movements -- Italy -- History -- 20th century

ISBN 0062308300; 9780062308306; 9780062308320

This book, by Caroline Moorehead, presents the "story of the aristocratic Italian family who stood up to Mussolini's fascism, and whose efforts helped define the path of Italy in the years between the World Wars--a profile in courage that remains relevant today. . . . [T]he Rosselli family, led by their fierce matriarch, Amelia, were vocal anti-fascists. . . . Amelia's sons Carlo and Nello led the opposition, taking a public stand against Il Duce." (Publisher's note)

"Based in part on letters preserved by the family and secret police files, Moorehead's account tells an extremely personal and engaging story about the price one family paid for its political resistance." LJ

Includes bibliographical references (pages 379-403) and index.

945.093   Italy 2000-

Hooper, John

The **Italians**; John Hooper. Penguin Group USA 2015 336 p. illustrations $28.95 **945.093**

1. Italians 2. Italy -- Civilization

ISBN 0525428070; 9780525428077

LC 2014038474

This book, by John Hooper, "a vivid and surprising portrait of the Italian people. . . . Digging deep into their history, culture, and religion, Hooper offers keys to understanding everything from their bewildering politics to their love of life and beauty. Looking at the facts that lie behind the stereotypes, he sheds new light on many aspects of Italian life." (Publisher's note)

"'Few countries,' writes the author, 'are as comprehensively associated with happiness as Italy. Just the mention of its name brings to mind sunny days, blue skies, glittering seas; delicious, comforting food; good-looking, well-dressed people; undulating hills topped with cypress trees; museums crammed with much of the best of Western art.' What's not to love? A thoroughly researched, well-written, ageless narrative of a fascinating people." Kirkus

945.51 Florence

Strathern, Paul, 1940-

The **Medici**; Power, Money, and Ambition in the Italian Renaissance. by Paul Strathern. W W Norton & Co Inc 2016 464 p. $28.95 **945.51**

1. Renaissance 2. Florence (Italy) -- History

ISBN 1605989665; 9781605989662

In this book, author Paul Strathern "explores the . . . rise and fall of the Medici family in Florence, as well as the Italian Renaissance which they did so much to sponsor and encourage. Strathern also follows the lives of many of the great Renaissance artists with whom the Medici had dealings, including Leonardo, Michelangelo and Donatello; as well as scientists like Galileo and Pico della Mirandola." (Publisher's note)

"A fantastically comprehensive history covering the breadth of the great learning, art, politics, and religion of the period." Kirkus

Includes bibliographical references (pages 413-417) and index.

945.6 Central Italy and Vatican City

Kneale, Matthew, 1960-

Rome; a history in seven sackings. Matthew Kneale. Simon & Schuster 2018 432 p. $30 **945.6**

1. Rome -- History 2. Rome (Italy) -- History, Military 3. Rome (Italy) -- History 4. Rome -- History, Military

ISBN 1501191098; 9781501191091

LC 2017045287

In this book, author Matthew Kneale "tells the story of the Eternal City--from the early Roman Republic through the Renaissance and the Reformation to Mussolini and the German occupation in World War Two--through pivotal moments that defined its history. . . . [He] uses seven of these crisis moments to create a powerful and captivating account of Rome's extraordinary history." (Publisher's note)

Includes bibliographical references and index

945.7 Southern Italy

Wilson, Katherine

Only in Naples; lessons in food and famiglia from my Italian mother-in-law. Katherine Wilson. Random House Inc 2016 304 p. (hardback: acid-free paper) $27 **945.731**

1. Naples (Italy) 2. Cooking -- Italy -- Naples 3. Families -- Italy -- Naples 4. Naples (Italy) -- Biography 5. Americans -- Italy -- Naples -- Biography 6. Naples (Italy) -- Social life and customs 7. Mothers-in-law -- Italy -- Naples -- Biography 8. Daughters-in-law -- Family relationships -- Italy -- Naples

ISBN 9780812998160

LC 2015016098

This memoir, by Katherine Wilson, "follows American-born Katherine Wilson on her adventures abroad. Thanks to a surprising romance—and a spirited woman who teaches her to laugh, to seize joy, and to love—a three-month rite of passage in Naples turns into a permanent embrace of this boisterous city on the Mediterranean." (Publisher's note)

"Each experience, each delicious meal is insightfully described as the reader follows Wilson's path toward carnale, becoming confident and comfortable in one's own skin." Booklist

945.8 Sicily and adjacent islands

Norwich, John Julius, 1929-2018

Sicily; John Julius Norwich. Random House 2015 400 p. 16 plates; color ills; map (hardback: acid-free paper) $32 **945.8**

1. Sicily (Italy) 2. Italy -- History 3. Sicily (Italy) -- History 4. Sicily (Italy) -- Civilization 5. Sicily (Italy) -- History, Military 6. Sicily (Italy) -- Kings and rulers -- History

ISBN 0812995171; 9780812995176

LC 2015007371

Author "John Julius Norwich's engrossing narrative is the first to knit together all of the colorful strands of Sicilian history into a single comprehensive study. Here is a vivid, erudite, page-turning chronicle of an island and the remarkable kings, queens, and tyrants who fought to rule it." (Publisher's note)

"This excellent, informative source on natural features, art and architecture, and regional lifestyles is not to be missed by armchair travelers, history lovers, and fans of Norwich's previous works." LJ

Includes bibliographical references and index

946 Spain, Andorra, Gibraltar, Portugal

Goodwin, Robert

Spain; The Center of the World 1519-1682. by Robert Goodwin. St. Martin's Press 2015 608 p. 16 plates; ills.; maps; ports. $40 **946**

1. Spain -- History

ISBN 1620403609; 9781620403600

LC 2014415759

This book, by Robert Goodwin, focuses on the "Golden Age of the Spanish Empire. . . . From scholars and playwrights, to poets and soldiers, Goodwin is in complete command of the history of this tumultuous and exciting period. But the superstars alone will not tell the whole tale--Goodwin delves deep to find previously unrecorded sources and accounts of how Spain's Golden Age would unfold, and ultimately, unravel." (Publisher's note)

"Anyone wanting a better idea of the feel of this phase of Spanish history will be well served by this title. Accompanying maps and a genealogical chart are helpful." LJ

Kurlansky, Mark

The **Basque** history of the world. Penguin 2001 387p il map pa $15 **946**

1. Basque Provinces (France and Spain)

ISBN 978-0-14-029851-2; 0-14-029851-7

First published 1999 by Walker & Co.

"This book traces the history of the Basques from their mysterious origins to their politically fraught existence in this century. . . . Kurlansky shows how Basques, famed for their geographic and linguistic isolation, have played significant roles in world history-as mercenaries in ancient Greece, whalers in the Middle Ages, explorers in the Americas, and even cautious supporters of modern European integration." New Yorker

Lowney, Chris

A **vanished** world; medieval Spain's golden age of enlightenment. Free Press 2005 320p il map $26 **946**

1. Spain -- Civilization

ISBN 0-7432-4359-5

LC 2004-56362

This is a history of Spain between the Muslim conquest in 711 and the driving of Muslims from Iberia in 1492, during which the author argues there was a tentative peace between Christians, Muslims, and Jews.

The author "successfully brings the story of medieval Spain to a wider audience and draws out of this rich history important lessons for the post-9/11 world." Christ Sci Monit

Includes bibliographical references

Tremlett, Giles

Ghosts of Spain; travels through Spain and its secret past. Walker 2007 386p $26.95   **946**

1. Spain -- Description and travel 2. Spain -- Social life and customs

ISBN 0-8027-1574-5; 978-0-8027-1574-6

First published 2006 in the United Kingdom

An "examination of the Franco years and their legacy make a somber backdrop for an otherwise cheery tale. Having summoned the ghosts, [the author] moves along to offer a guided tour of modern Spain, making stops at the usual journalistic destinations. The educational system, politics, health care, child rearing and the national character are dealt with in well-organized chapters that move the reader briskly along.... A highly informative, well-written introduction to post-Franco Spain." N Y Times (Late N Y Ed)

946.081   Period of Second Republic, 1931-1939

Hochschild, Adam

Spain in our hearts; Americans in the Spanish Civil War, 1936/1939. Adam Hochschild. Houghton Mifflin Harcourt 2016 464 p. illustrations, maps (hardcover) $30   **946.081**

1. Americans -- Spain 2. Spain -- History -- 1936-1939, Civil War

ISBN 9780547973180; 9780547974538

LC 2015037244

This book, by Adam Hochschild, offers "a sweeping history of the Spanish Civil War, told through a dozen [American expatriate] characters, including Ernest Hemingway and George Orwell: a tale of idealism, heartbreaking suffering, and a noble cause that failed.... It was in many ways the opening battle of World War II, and we still have much to learn from it." (Publisher's note)

"Hochschild ably explores subtle shades of the conflict that contemporary authors and participants did not want to consider." Kirkus

Includes bibliographical references and index

Lewis, Norman

The **tomb** in Seville; crossing Spain on the brink of civil war. introduction by Julian Evans. Carroll & Graf 2005 150p $20; pa $14.95   **946.081**

1. Spain -- Description and travel

ISBN 0-7867-1439-5; 0-7867-1687-8 pa

First published 2003 in the United Kingdom

"Reading the author's account of his travels in a country on the brink of war is almost as satisfying as being there." Booklist

Rhodes, Richard

Hell and Good Company; The Spanish Civil War and the World It Made. Richard Rhodes. Simon & Schuster 2015 384 p. 16 plates; illustrations; maps $30   **946.081**

1. War stories 2. Spain -- History -- 1936-1939, Civil War

ISBN 1451696213; 9781451696219

This book by Richard Rhodes looks at the "story of the Spanish Civil War through the eyes of the reporters, writers, artists, doctors, and nurses who witnessed it. He takes us into battlefields and bomb shelters, into the studios of artists, into the crowded wards of war hospitals, and into the hearts and minds of a rich cast of characters to show how the ideo-

logical, aesthetic, and technological developments that emerged in Spain changed the world forever." (Publisher's note)

"Despite the inclusion of a superb bibliography, the author's interpretation seems stuck in 1936. Other recent histories offer a more complicated and, in many instances, a more nuanced understanding of events and the actions of key personalities and groups. Summing Up: Recommended. General and undergraduate libraries." Choice

946.083   Reign of Juan Carlos I, 1975-

Stewart, Chris

Driving over lemons; an optimist in Andalucia. Pantheon Bks. 2000 248p il maps hardcover o.p. pa $13.95   **946.083**

1. Spain -- Description

ISBN 978-0-375-41028-4; 978-0-375-70915-9 pa; 0-375-70915-0 pa

LC 99-56675

"The ability to write hilarious travelogues featuring excruciating scenes of discomfort may well be a {British} national characteristic. It's certainly possessed by Chris Stewart." N Y Times Book Rev

946.89   Gibraltar

Adkins, Lesley

★ **Gibraltar**; the greatest siege in British history. Roy and Lesley Adkins. Penguin Group USA 2018 480 p. $30 **946.89**

1. Spain -- History 2. France -- Foreign relations -- History 3. Great Britain -- Foreign relations -- France -- History

ISBN 0735221626; 9780735221628

This book, by Roy and Lesley Adkins, describes how, "from 1779 to 1783, ... Gibraltar was besieged and blockaded, on land and at sea, by the overwhelming forces of Spain and France. It became the longest siege in British history, and the obsession with saving Gibraltar was blamed for the loss of the American colonies in the War of Independence. ... The everyday experiences of all those involved are brought vividly to life with eyewitness accounts and expert research." (Publisher's note)

" This intense account portrays the heroism and sufferings of the defenders while offering interesting vignettes that cover intriguing personalities on both sides. The Adkinses have created an absorbing examination of an important episode in British and European history." Booklist

947   Russia and neighboring east European countries

Applebaum, Anne

★ **Iron** curtain; the crushing of Eastern Europe, 1945-1956. Anne Applebaum. Doubleday 2012 xxxvi, 566 p.p (hardcover) $35.00   **947**

1. Communism -- Russia 2. Soviet Union -- Social conditions 3. Communist countries -- Social conditions 4. Europe, Eastern -- Relations -- Soviet Union 5. Soviet Union -- Relations -- Europe, Eastern 6. Communist countries -- Politics and government 7. Europe, Eastern -- Social conditions -- 20th century 8. Communism -- Europe, Eastern -- History -- 20th century 9. Europe, Eastern -- Politics and government -- 1945-1989 10. Political culture -- Europe, Eastern -- History -- 20th century 11. Political persecution -- Europe, Eastern -- History -- 20th century 12. Communism -- Social aspects -- Europe, Eastern -- History -- 20th century

ISBN 9780385515696; 0385515693

LC 2012022086

National Book Award Finalist: Nonfiction (2012)

In this book, "journalist Anne Applebaum delivers a . . . history of how Communism took over Eastern Europe after World War II." She "describes how the Communist regimes of Eastern Europe were created and what daily life was like once they were complete. She draws on newly opened East European archives, interviews, and personal accounts translated for the first time to portray . . . the dilemmas faced by millions of individuals." (Publisher's note)

Includes bibliographical references and index.

Drakulic, Slavenka

Cafe Europa; life after communism. Penguin Books 1999 213p pa $14   **947**

1. Eastern Europe -- Social conditions 2. Eastern Europe -- Politics and government

ISBN 978-0-14-027772-2; 0-14-027772-2

First published 1996 in the United Kingdom; first United States edition published 1997 by Norton

The author of these pieces is "at once critical of a culture that remains bleakly conformist in the aftermath of Communist rule and empathetic for its having known nothing else. With consistent equanimity, she examines the frustrating plight of the novice Balkan democracies. On a more quotidian level, too, she finds that much is wanting, measured against Western standards of richesse, congeniality, and even taxi service. Owing largely to Drakulic's knack for drawing humor from an abundance of anecdotes—whether about a toothpaste monopoly or the bureaucratic cartwheels required to purchase a vacuum cleaner—these essays read like stories." New Yorker

Erickson, Carolly

Great Catherine. St. Martin's Griffin 1995 392p pa $18.95   **947**

1. Empresses 2. Russia -- History 3. Russia -- Kings and rulers

ISBN 0-312-13503-3

LC 95-22619

First published 1994 by Crown

"Erickson's fluid, captivating portrait of Catherine the Great reads like a first-rate historical novel." Booklist

Figes, Orlando, 1959-

The **Crimean** War; a history. Metropolitan Books 2010 576p il map $35; e-book $16.99   **947**

1. Crimean War, 1853-1856

ISBN 978-0-8050-7460-4; 0-8050-7460-0; 978-1-4299-9724-9 e-book; 1-4299-9724-9 e-book

LC 2010-23152

Published in the United Kingdom with title: Crimea

This "is a complex tale, told vividly by Mr Figes. Perhaps it should serve as a healthy cold shower for any modern civilisational warrior who sets out to present the course of history as a simple tug-of-war between Christianity and Islam." Economist

Includes bibliographical references

Hosking, Geoffrey A.

★ **Russia** and the Russians; a history. {by} Geoffrey Hosking. Belknap Press 2001 718p il map $35; pa $18.95   **947**

1. Russia -- History 2. Soviet Union -- History

ISBN 0-674-00473-6; 0-674-01114-7 pa

LC 00-65085

"This is a high-quality overview, suitable for all libraries." Booklist

"From the Carpathians in the west to the Greater Khingan range in the east, a huge, flat expanse dominates the Eurasian continent. Here, over more than a thousand years, the history and destiny of Russia have

unfolded. In a sweeping narrative, one of the English-speaking world's leading historians of Russia follows this story from the first emergence of the Slavs in the historical record in the sixth century C.E. to the Russians' persistent appearances in today's headlines." (Publisher's note)

King, David

Red star over Russia; a visual history of the Soviet Union from the revolution to the death of Stalin: posters, photographs and graphics from the David King collection. Abrams 2009 345p il $50   **947**

1. Russian art 2. Soviet Union -- History -- Pictorial works

ISBN 978-0-8109-8279-6; 0-8109-8279-X

In this survey "the graphics used to promote the workers' paradise deserve admiration. But the rest of this extraordinarily illustrated book provides witness to the corrosive effects of ham-handed propaganda, and to the role of state-sanctioned imagery in demeaning and subjugating the arts. Red Star Over Russia is a mammoth collection of rare Soviet applied art and photographs . . . organized not into individual chapters, but into pages and spreads devoted to a range of themes addressed in graphic and photographic materials, including 'Political Abstraction,' 'Urban Proletariat' and 'Workers of the World, Unite.' Prominent artists like El Lissitzky and Gustav Klutsis are featured." N Y Times Book Rev

Kotkin, Stephen

Uncivil society; 1989 and the implosion of the communist establishment. with a contribution by Jan T. Gross. Modern Library 2009 197p il map (Modern Library chronicles) $24 **947**

1. Soviet Union -- Social conditions 2. Eastern Europe -- Social conditions 3. Soviet Union -- Politics and government 4. Eastern Europe -- Politics and government

ISBN 978-0-679-64276-3; 0-679-64276-5

LC 2009-12903

"Combining scholarship with sparkling prose, the authors recount a thoroughly satisfying historical struggle in which the good guys won." Publ Wkly

Includes bibliographical references

Massie, Robert K., 1929-

Catherine the Great; portrait of a woman. Robert K. Massie. Random House 2011 xiii, 625p ill. (some col.), maps **947**

1. Biography 2. Empresses 3. Russia -- Kings and rulers

ISBN 9780679456728; 9781588360441

LC 2011015279

Presents a reconstruction of the eighteenth-century empress's life that covers her efforts to engage Russia in the cultural life of Europe, her creation of the Hermitage, and her numerous scandal-free romantic affairs.

"Massie delivers a fascinating account of dog-eat-dog politics in 18th-century Europe and the larger-than-life Russian empress who gave as good as she got." Kirkus

Includes bibliographical references

Massie, Suzanne

Land of the firebird; the beauty of old Russia. Hearttree 1980 493p il pa $32   **947**

1. Russian art 2. Russia -- Civilization

ISBN 978-0-9644184-1-7; 0-9644184-1-X

First published 1980 by Simon & Schuster

The author's intent "is to give 'a sense of the whole, now-vanished culture of old Russia . . . to describe that beauty which the Russians once knew how to create, what they loved, and admired and how they once lived and rejoiced.'" N Y Times Book Rev

Includes bibliographical references

Pleshakov, Konstantin

There is no freedom without bread! 1989 and the civil war that brought down communism. [by] Constantine Pleshakov. Farrar, Straus, and Giroux 2009 289p $26 **947**

1. Communism 2. Berlin Wall (1961-1989) 3. Poland -- Politics and government 4. Soviet Union -- Politics and government 5. Eastern Europe -- Politics and government
ISBN 978-0-374-28902-7; 0-374-28902-6

LC 2009-10185

The author's "explanation of the 1989 collapse respects the complexity of Eastern Europe, yet his account is both clear and beautifully lyrical. His greatest strength lies in not being burdened by doctrine; he finds worth in communists and in Reagan. . . . Pleshakov writes history with a human face." Washington Post Book World

Includes bibliographical references

Polonsky, Rachel

Molotov's magic lantern; travels in Russian history. Farrar, Straus and Giroux 2011 390p map $27; ebook $14.99 **947**

1. Diplomats 2. Authors, Russian 3. Communism and literature 4. Cabinet members 5. Communist leaders 6. Soviet Union -- Intellectual life 7. Moscow (Russia) -- Description and travel 8. Russia (Federation) -- Description and travel
ISBN 978-0-374-21197-4; 978-1-4299-7490-5 ebook

LC 2010-23037

Polonsky "has produced a spectacular and enjoyable display of intellectual fireworks for the general reader. . . . Her finely drawn literary travelogues on Taganrog, Murmansk, Vologda, Irkutsk and other places depict squalor, pomp, misery, exhilaration, heroism and brutishness, each cameo framed in its historical, cultural and physical context. . . . She has a knack for putting herself into other people's shoes with empathy and skill. . . . The author has grit, charm and style—and a gift for traveller's tales." Economist

Riasanovsky, Nicholas V.

A **history** of Russia; 8th ed; Oxford University Press 2011 various paging il map pa $64.95 **947**

1. Russia -- History 2. Soviet Union -- History
ISBN 978-0-19-534197-3

LC 2010-23174

First published 1963

This narrative history includes discussions of economics, social organization, religion, and culture.

Includes bibliographical references

Sebestyen, Victor

Revolution 1989; the fall of the Soviet empire. Pantheon Books 2009 xxi, 451p il $30 **947**

1. Soviet Union -- Politics and government 2. Eastern Europe -- Politics and government
ISBN 978-0-375-42532-5; 0-375-42532-2

LC 2009-23045

"Numerous books have come out that attempt to synthesize the compelling story of the fall of communism, but Revolution 1989 comes closest to being the essential volume. Sebestyen's elegant narrative lays out in crisp episodes what was happening in Russia, Bulgaria, East Germany, Hungary, Czechoslovakia, and Afghanistan throughout the tumultuous 1980s. His portrait of Gorbachev is particularly sharp—and asks us to reconsider the Soviet leader's surprising role 20 years ago. As a refugee from Hungary in 1956, Sebestyen brings a personal touch to these historic moments." Daily Beast

Includes bibliographical references

947.08 Russia since 1855

Kurth, Peter

Tsar: the lost world of Nicholas and Alexandra; photographs by Peter Christopher. Little, Brown 1995 229p il hardcover o.p. pa $29.95 **947.08**

1. Emperors 2. Empresses 3. Russia -- History
ISBN 0-316-50787-3; 0-316-55788-9 pa

LC 95-12820

In text and photographs, this volume examines the lives of Tsar Nicholas II, the Empress Alexandra, and the Russian Imperial family.

"A large format and a profusion of illustrations ostensibly mark it a picture book; instead it is a remarkably comprehensive overview of the reign of the last czar and his consort. . . . Kurth sensitively documents the imperial family's suffering as prisoners of the Bolsheviks and their eventual execution." Booklist

Includes bibliographical references

Massie, Robert K., 1929-

The **Romanovs**; the final chapter. Random House 1995 308p il hardcover o.p. pa $14.95 **947.08**

1. Emperors 2. Empresses 3. Forensic anthropology 4. Impostors 5. Royal pretenders 6. Russia -- Kings and rulers
ISBN 0-394-58048-6; 0-345-40640-0 pa

LC 95-4718

This book "is divided into three major parts. The first segment—by far the most fascinating and original—focuses on the complex scientific process used in identifying the Romanovs' remains. . . . The second part concerns the various impostors who have claimed to be members of the Russian imperial family. . . . [The] third segment [is] a report on those Romanov émigrés—close relatives of the Czar's—who survived the Bolsheviks' persecution." N Y Times Book Rev

Includes bibliographical references

947.083 Reign of Nicholas II, 1894-1917

Rappaport, Helen

The **race** to save the Romanovs; the truth behind the secret plans to rescue the Russian imperial family. Helen Rappaport. St. Martin's Press 2018 400 p. $28.99 **947.083**

1. Russia -- History -- 1917-1925
ISBN 125015121X; 9781250151216

In this book investigating the murder of the Russian Imperial Family, author "Helen Rappaport embarks on a quest to uncover the various plots and plans to save them, why they failed, and who was responsible. The murder of the Romanov family in July 1918 horrified the world, and its aftershocks still reverberate today. . . . [The book] is sure to replace outdated classics as the final word on the fate of the Romanovs." (Publisher's note)

"Relying on fresh archival material, Rappaport dispels some mystery about secret Western rescue plans—that is to say, she clarifies that they were nonexistent. Regarding myriad Russian monarchist rescue plots, she admits that rumors and misinformation make unraveling the truth "an impossible task." This is a well-researched account of a colorful, suspenseful, and tragic series of events." Publishers' Weekly

Service, Robert, 1947-

The **Last** of the Tsars; Nicholas II and the Russia Revolu-

tion. Robert Service. Pegasus Books 2017 xviii, 382 p.p illustrations (some color) (hardcover) $29.95   **947.083**
1. Emperors 2. Russia -- History -- 1917-1921, Revolution 3.
Russia -- Kings and rulers -- Biography 4. Russia -- History --
Nicholas II, 1894-1917 5. Soviet Union -- History -- Revolution,
1917-1921
ISBN 9781681775722; 9781681775012; 1681775018
This book, by Robert Service, presents an "account of the last eighteen months of Tsar Nicholas II's life and reign. . . . The story has been
told many times, but Service's deep understanding of the period and
his forensic examination of previously untapped sources, including the
Tsar's diaries and recorded conversations, . . . shed remarkable new light
on his troubled reign, also revealing the kind of Russia that Nicholas
wanted to emerge from the Great War." (Publisher's note)
"A compelling work; organized, concise, and chilling." Kirkus
Includes bibliographical references (pages 301-362) and index.

Zygar, Mikhail
The **empire** must die; Russia's revolutionary collapse,
1900-1917. Mikhail Zygar. PublicAffairs 2017 xi, 558 p.p
illustrations, maps (hardcover) $30   **947.083**
1. Russia -- Kings and rulers 2. Russia -- History -- 0-1917 3.
Russia -- Politics and government 4. Russia -- History -- 1801-1917
ISBN 9781610398312; 9781610399227; 1610398319
LC 2017448549
In this book, by Mikhail Zygar, "in 1912, Russia experienced a flowering of liberalism and tolerance that placed it at the forefront of the
modern world: women were fighting for the right to vote in the elections
. . . [and] there was a vibrant free press and intellectual life. But a fatal
flaw was left uncorrected. . . . Its princes, archdukes, and generals bled
the country dry during the First World War and by 1917 the only consensus was that the Empire must die." (Publisher's note)
"A vivid, character-driven reconstruction of the period leading up to
the overthrow of the Romanovs and the birth of modern Russia." Kirkus
Includes bibliographical references (pages 521-530) and index

947.084   Russia (Soviet Union)--1917-1991

Amis, Martin
Koba the dread; laughter and the twenty million. Hyperion
2002 306p il $24.95   **947.084**
1. Heads of state 2. Communist leaders 3. Political leaders 4.
Soviet Union -- Politics and government
ISBN 0-7868-6876-7
"Amis create{s} a compelling narrative, summarizing vast amounts
of information and presenting it in a lucid, accessible form." New
York Times

Brent, Jonathan
Stalin's last crime; the plot against the Jewish doctors,
1948-1953. {by} Jonathan Brent and Vladimir P. Naumov.
HarperCollins 2003 399p $26.95; pa $14.95   **947.084**
1. Heads of state 2. Communist leaders 3. Political leaders 4.
Jews -- Persecutions
ISBN 0-06-019524-X; 0-06-093310-0 pa
LC 2002-191930
"This book points out suspicious inconsistencies in official accounts
of Stalin's death and fingers chief of secret police Beria as a likely assassin. . . . Brent and Naumov link Stalin's famously anti-Semitic 'Doctors' Plot,' in which Jewish doctors were unjustly accused of conspiring
to murder important politicians, to the ridiculous 'plan of the internal

blow,' another alleged conspiracy of officials supposedly aiding an
American plan to nuke the Kremlin itself. The authors argue that these
Stalin-engineered plots were to be used by the paranoid dictator as justification for nuclear war. Tales of Stalin's paranoia are nothing new,
but rarely are his subtle, yet relentless, machinations laid out in such
intricate detail." Booklist
Includes bibliographical references

Competing voices from the Russian Revolution; edited by Michael C. Hickey. Greenwood 2011 xiii, 599p ill. (alk.
paper) $65.00   **947.084**
1. History -- Sources 2. World War, 1914-1918 3. Russia --
History -- 1917-1921, Revolution 4. Social conflict -- Soviet Union
-- History -- Sources 5. Soviet Union -- History -- Revolution,
1917-1921 -- Sources 6. Soviet Union -- Politics and government
-- 1917-1936 -- Sources 7. Soviet Union -- History -- Revolution,
1917-1921 -- Personal narratives 8. Soviet Union -- History --
Revolution, 1917-1921 -- Social aspects -- Sources
ISBN 9780313385230; 0313385238; 9780313385247;
0313385246
LC 2010039676
This book "presents documents that underscore the . . . public discussion about key events and issues during the 1917 Russian Revolution, one of the pivotal events in modern history. . . . [T]he documents
. . . clarify the issues while revealing the broad range of ways in which
Russians understood the events unfolding around them. Focusing on
public rhetoric and debate in Russia from the outbreak of World War I
in 1914 through the dissolution of the Constituent Assembly in January
1918, the documents present the views not only of key political figures,
but also of ordinary men and women—mothers, soldiers, factory workers, peasants, students, businesspeople, and educated professionals."
(Publisher's note)
Includes bibliographical references (p. 583-588) and index.

Figes, Orlando
★ The **whisperers**; private life in Stalin's Russia. Metro-
politan Books 2007 xxxviii, 739p il map $35   **947.084**
1. Communism -- Soviet Union 2. Soviet Union -- Social conditions
ISBN 978-0-8050-7461-1; 0-8050-7461-9
LC 2007-24223
"This is a humbling monument to the evil and endurance of Russia's
Soviet past and, implicitly, a guide to its present." Economist
Includes bibliographical references

Gellately, Robert
Stalin's curse; battling for communism in war and Cold
War. by Robert Gellately. Knopf 2013 496 p. $32.50 **947.084**
1. Communism -- Russia 2. Communism -- Europe -- History
-- 20th century 3. Soviet Union -- Politics and government -- 1936-
1953
ISBN 0307269159; 9780307269157
LC 2012028768
Author Robert Gellately presents an "account based on newly re-
leased Russian documentation that reveals Joseph Stalin's true motives-
-and the extent of his enduring commitment to expanding the Soviet
empire--during the years in which he seemingly collaborated with
Franklin D. Roosevelt, Winston Churchill, and the capitalist West."
(Publisher's note)
Includes bibliographical references and index

Hochschild, Adam
The **unquiet** ghost; Russians remember Stalin. Houghton
Mifflin 2003 304p il map pa $14.95   **947.084**

1. Heads of state 2. Communist leaders 3. Political leaders 4. Soviet Union -- History
ISBN 978-0-618-25747-8; 0-618-25747-0
First published 1994 by Viking

In this look at Stalin's legacy the author "visits the ruins of the old prison camps of Kazakhstan and Kolyma, digs through the K.G.B. archives and spends a night at Stalin's seaside retreat. Most important, he interviews camp survivors, camp guards and the children of both. The questions he asks are of universal significance. . . . By asking these questions while traveling through today's Russia, Mr. Hochschild effectively places Stalinism in a modern context." N Y Times Book Rev

Includes bibliographical references

McMeekin, Sean

The **Russian** revolution; a new history. Sean McMeekin. Basic Books 2017 xxxi, 445 p.p illustrations, maps (hardback) $30   **947.084**
1. Historical literature 2. Soviet Union -- Military history 3. Russia -- History -- 1917-1921, Revolution 4. Soviet Union -- History -- Revolution, 1917-1921
ISBN 9781541698550; 9780465039906

LC 2016058361

This book, by Sean McMeekin, "traces the events which ended Romanov rule, ushered the Bolsheviks into power, and introduced Communism to the world. Between 1917 and 1922, Russia underwent a complete and irreversible transformation. . . . The Bolsheviks staged a hostile takeover of the Russian Imperial Army, promoting mutinies and mass desertions of men in order to fulfill [Vladimir] Lenin's program of turning the 'imperialist war' into civil war." (Publisher's note)

"McMeekin effectively shows how easily one man could undermine the foundations of a nation, and he makes the revolution comprehensible as he exposes the deviousness of its leader." Kirkus

Includes bibliographical references (pages 359-420) and index.

Medvedev, Roy Aleksandrovich, 1925-

★ **Let** history judge; the origins and consequences of Stalinism. {by} Roy Medvedev. rev and expanded ed; Columbia Univ. Press 1989 xxi, 903p $104; pa $35   **947.084**
1. Heads of state 2. Communist leaders 3. Political leaders 4. Political crimes and offenses 5. Soviet Union -- Politics and government 6. Soviet Union -- Politics and government -- 1925-1953
ISBN 0-231-06350-4; 0-231-06351-2 pa

LC 89-758

Original Russian edition copyrighted 1967; first United States edition published 1972 by Knopf

The first two parts of this book examine Stalin's rise in the Communist Party, and his assumption of power and reliance on repression. The last two sections consider the nature and causes of Stalinism as well as the effects of Stalin's dictatorship. Glossary. Index. For the first edition see BRD 1972.

"Never have Stalin's crimes against humanity been more forcefully or more thoroughly documented than in . . . {this book, which} distills firsthand testimonies of the mass arrests, torture, imprisonment and executions that befell millions of innocent Soviet citizens." Publ Wkly

Includes bibliographical references

Miéville, China, 1972-

October; the story of the Russian Revolution. China Miéville. Verso 2017 369 p. illustrations, maps (hardback) $26.95   **947.084**
1. Russia -- History -- 1917-1921, Revolution 2. Soviet Union -- History -- Revolution, 1917-1921

ISBN 9781784782771; 9781784782795

LC 2016051217

"In a panoramic sweep, stretching from St Petersburg and Moscow to the remotest villages of a sprawling empire, [author China] Miéville uncovers the catastrophes, intrigues and inspirations of 1917, in all their passion, drama and strangeness. Intervening in long-standing historical debates, but told with the reader new to the topic especially in mind, here is a breathtaking story of humanity at its greatest and most desperate." (Publisher's note)

"Miéville is an ideal guide through this complex historical moment, giving agency to obscure and better-known participants alike, and depicting the revolution as both a tragically lost opportunity and an ongoing source of inspiration." Pub Wkly

Includes bibliographical references (pages 330-341) and index

Pipes, Richard

A **concise** history of the Russian Revolution. Knopf 1995 431p il maps hardcover o.p. pa $16   **947.084**
1. Russia -- History
ISBN 0-679-74544-0 pa

LC 95-3127

A one volume condensation of the author's The Russian Revolution and Russia under the Bolshevik regime

"Forcefully showing why the 70-year-old Communist experiment failed {Pipes} provides the nonacademic reader with accurate historical events in a highly readable format." Libr J

Includes bibliographical references

Russia under the Bolshevik regime. Vintage Books 1995 587p il map pa $21   **947.084**
1. Heads of state 2. Revolutionaries 3. Communist leaders 4. Political leaders 5. Soviet Union -- History
ISBN 978-0-679-76184-6; 0-679-76184-5
First published 1994 by Knopf

"In this sequel to The Russian Revolution Pipes persuasively argues that Lenin's one-party dictatorship, through its terrorizing, suppression of the press, censorship and monopolistic control of cultural organizations, set the stage for Stalin's genocidal totalitarianism. . . . Pipes shows how both Hitler and Mussolini drew on Lenin's tyrannical methods, and he perceptively analyzes the mindset of Western fellow-travelers who wove fantasies of the U.S.S.R. as an egalitarian Eden while rationalizing its evils." Publ Wkly

Includes bibliographical references

Reed, John

Ten days that shook the world. Penguin Books 2007 368p (Penguin classics) pa $12   **947.084**
1. Soviet Union -- History -- 1917-1921, Revolution
ISBN 978-0-14-144212-9; 0-14-144212-3
First published 1919 by International Pubs.

"A reportorial, firsthand, and sympathetic account of the November Revolution in Russia (1917). . . . After prefatory explanation of political groups and other organizations, and of the background of the uprising, the work tells with graphic detail of the fall of the provisional government, the revolution and counterrevolution, the solidifying of power, and the resultant congress." Oxford Companion to Am Lit. 5th edition

Service, Robert

Lenin--a biography. Harvard Univ. Press 2000 xxv, 561p il maps $38.95; pa $19.95   **947.084**
1. Heads of state 2. Revolutionaries 3. Communist leaders 4. Political leaders
ISBN 0-674-00330-6; 0-674-00828-6 pa

LC 00-21394

This biography focuses "on Lenin the man. It draws on a wealth of new material to provide a subtle and complex portrait. . . . In particular, Service's account adds much to our knowledge of Lenin's early years and his final years as a man cut down by a series of strokes. . . . It is lucidly written, sharply observed, full of good sense, packed with vivid anecdote and, above all, succeeds—where so many have failed—in creating a Lenin who is believably human." Hist Today

Includes bibliographical references

947.085   Russia (Soviet Union)--1953-1991

Carlson, Peter

K blows top; a Cold War comic interlude starring Nikita Khrushchev, America's most unlikely tourist. PublicAffairs 2009 327p il $26.95   **947.085**
1. Cold war 2. Heads of state 3. Communist leaders 4. Political leaders 5. Soviet Union -- Foreign relations -- United States 6. United States -- Foreign relations -- Soviet Union
ISBN 9781586484972; 1-58648-497-4

LC 2008-39090

Recounts Khrushchev's 1959 trip across America against the backdrop of the Cold War and a capitalist America living under the shadow of the hydrogen bomb.

"Drawing on contemporary news reports, modern interviews, and memoirs written by some of the participants, [this is] . . . a story about a poorly educated but extraordinarily powerful man who became, for a brief time, a pop-culture icon. . . . A fine example of popular history at its most engaging—anecdotal but informative and written with great feeling for the comedic side of current events." Booklist

Includes bibliographical references

Gorbachev, Mikhail

On my country and the world; {by} Gorbachev. Columbia Univ. Press 1999 300p $50; pa $17.95   **947.085**
1. World politics -- 1965- 2. Soviet Union -- Politics and government 3. Russia (Federation) -- Politics and government
ISBN 0-231-11514-8; 0-231-11515-6 pa

LC 99-31273

The former Soviet leader presents an analysis of his country's Communist past and an account of his role in government in the 1980s. Gorbachev also includes ideas for political change

Gorbachev is "fresh and candid in its initial section on the pluses and minuses of the Revolution of 1917." Nation

Remnick, David

★ **Lenin's** tomb; Russia and the fall of Communism. Random House 1993 576p hardcover o.p. pa $15.95   **947.085**
1. Soviet Union -- Politics and government
ISBN 0-679-75125-4 pa

LC 92-56841

"This book is a record of almost four years beginning in 1988 when David Remnick, a Washington Post reporter, was assigned to Moscow. . . . He argues convincingly that what did in the old Soviet leadership, right down through Mikhail Gorbachev, was its unending assault not only on people but on memory. By making a secret of history, it made its people increasingly distracted, and desperate, until they overthrew it." N Y Times Book Rev

Satter, David

Age of delirium; the decline and fall of the Soviet Union.

Yale University Press 2001 424p pa $30   **947.085**
1. Soviet Union -- History
ISBN 0-300-08705-5; 978-0-300-08705-5
First published 1996 by Knopf

The author "appraises the Russians by writing about the travails of average people in the last decade of Soviet rule. Objects of the Communist ideology's enforced unanimity, his subjects include dissidents sent to psychiatric wards, persecuted religious people, a TASS journalist learning how to write the party line, and miners exploited by the workers' state. . . . An insightful from-the-ground-up view of typical Russians whom the top-down politicians are now courting." Booklist

Stokes, Gale

The **walls** came tumbling down; the collapse of communism in Eastern Europe. Oxford Univ. Press 1993 319p hardcover o.p. pa $31.95   **947.085**
1. Communism 2. Eastern Europe -- Politics and government
ISBN 0-19-506644-8; 0-19-506645-6 pa

LC 92-44862

This book "can be recommended as a coherent, well-written history that defines its time frame well, provides sound coverage, makes prudent judgments, and wears its analysis lightly. . . . Stokes's overview traces the ebb and flow of personalities and events in a manner that is both accessible to lay readers and informative to scholars." Libr J

947.086 Russia - 1991

Aleksievich, Svetlana, 1948-

★ **Secondhand** time; the last of the Soviets. Svetlana Alexievich; translated by Bela Shayevich. Random House 2016 496 p. (hardback: acid-free paper) $30   **947.086**
1. Russia 2. Oral history 3. Soviet Union -- Social conditions 4. Soviet Union -- Biography 5. Oral history -- Soviet Union 6. Russia (Federation) -- Biography 7. Oral history -- Russia (Federation) 8. Post-communism -- Russia (Federation) 9. Russia (Federation) -- Social conditions -- 1991-
ISBN 9780399588808

LC 2016005925

Author Svetlana Alexievich won the Nobel Prize in Literature in 2015.

This book, by Svetlana Alexievich, translated by Bela Shayevich, "chronicles the demise of communism. Everyday Russian citizens recount the past thirty years, showing us what life was like during the fall of the Soviet Union and what it's like to live in the new Russia left in its wake. Through interviews spanning 1991 to 2012, Alexievich takes us behind the propaganda and contrived media accounts, giving us a panoramic portrait of contemporary Russia and Russians." (Publisher's note)

"Journalist Alexievich (Voices from Chernobyl), who won the 2015 Nobel Prize in Literature, captures the heartache, excitement, and harsh realities of life at the end of the Soviet era and the birth of modern Russia. A collection of oral histories linked by topic, theme, and the author's own musings, this impassioned and critical study, originally published in Russian in 2013, documents the immense changes the Russian people underwent in the 1990s and 2000s. . . . A must for historians, lay readers, and anyone who enjoys well-curated personal narratives. All readers will appreciate the revelations about Russia's turbulent transition and present cultural and political status." LJ

Baker, Peter

Kremlin rising; Vladimir Putin's Russia and the end of

revolution. [by] Peter Baker and Susan Glasser. Scribner 2005
453p il $27.50   **947.086**
   1. Russia (Federation) -- Politics and government
   ISBN 0-743-26431-2

                          LC 2005-44157

The authors chronicle the transformation of contemporary Russia
under President Vladimir Putin.

"Well written, well reported and well organized, the book consists
of freestanding chapters that touch on the most important events and
trends in contemporary Russia, from the war in Chechnya to the spread
of AIDS and the dire state of the Russian judicial system." N Y Times
(Late N Y Ed)

Includes bibliographical references

Brent, Jonathan

   Inside the Stalin archives; discovering the new Russia. Atlas & Company 2008 335p il $26   **947.086**
   1. Heads of state 2. Communist leaders 3. Political leaders 4.
Russia (Federation) 5. Archives -- Soviet Union
   ISBN 978-0-9777-4333-9; 0-9777-4333-0

This work, which draws upon the author's fifteen years of unprecedented access to high-level Soviet Archives, "reveals as much about
the grim realities of post-Soviet life and bureaucracy as it does about
the archives themselves. Equipped with little Russian and few contacts,
but with an almost palpable sense of decency and honest intentions that
illuminate his book, Brent explains for the general reader as well as for
specialists how he went about his work in the new Russia." N Y Times
Book Rev

Conradi, Peter

   Who lost Russia? how the world entered a new cold war.
Peter Conradi. Oneworld Publications 2017 xiv, 370 p.p map
(hardcover) $27.99   **947.086**
   1. World politics 2. Russia -- History -- 1991- 3. Political culture
-- Russia (Federation) 4. Russia (Federation) -- Politics and
government -- 1991- 5. Russia (Federation) -- Foreign relations
-- Western countries 6. Western countries -- Foreign relations --
Russia (Federation)
   ISBN 1786070413; 9781786070418; 9781786070425

In this book, author Peter Conradi "charts the complex and turbulent
course of U.S.-Russia relations since the collapse of the U.S.S.R., and
investigates how the end of the Cold War failed to result in either con-
ciliation or superpower cooperation. . . . Conradi details how occasional
moments of tentative cooperation . . . have masked a relationship fraught
with tension, fundamentally different perspectives, and mutual misunderstandings." (Publishers Weekly)

"In this balanced and timely work, Sunday Times foreign editor Conradi (The Great Survivors) charts the complex and turbulent course of
U.S.-Russia relations since the collapse of the U.S.S.R. . . ." Pub Wkly

Includes bibliographical references (pages 345-361) and index.

Dawisha, Karen

   Putin's kleptocracy; who owns Russia? Karen Dawisha.
Simon & Schuster 2014 vii, 445 p.p illustrations $30 **947.086**
   1. Russia -- History -- 1991- 2. Racketeering -- Russia (Federation)
3. Political corruption -- Russia (Federation) 4. Russia (Federation)
-- Politics and government -- 1991-
   ISBN 1476795193; 9781476795195

                          LC 2014948969

Author Rachel Dawisha's book is "the result of years of research
into the KGB and the various Russian crime syndicates. [It] describes
and exposes the origins of [Vladimir] Putin's kleptocratic regime. She
presents extensive new evidence about the Putin circle's use of public

positions for personal gain even before Putin became president in 2000."
(Publisher's note)

"A rich and exhaustive account of Putin and his regime that supports
a forecast of its 'hard authoritarian' drift and dependence on 'European
public goods' for survival." LJ

Includes bibliographical references and index

Gessen, Masha

   ★ The **future** is history; how totalitarianism reclaimed
Russia. Masha Gessen. Riverhead Books 2017 400 p. hardcover $28   **947.086**
   1. Totalitarianism 2. Russia -- Politics and government
   ISBN 9781594634536; 9780698406209; 159463453X

                          LC 2017014363

National Book Award: Nonfiction (2017)

National Book Critics Circle Award Finalist: Nonfiction (2017)

In this book, author Masha Gessen "reveals how, in the space of a
generation, Russia surrendered to a more virulent and invincible new
strain of autocracy. . . . [She] follows the lives of four people born at
what promised to be the dawn of democracy. Each of them came of
age with unprecedented expectations, some as the children and grandchildren of the very architects of the new Russia, each with newfound
aspirations of their own." (Publisher's note)

"A superb, alarming portrait of a government that exercises outsize
influence in the modern world, at great human cost." Kirkus

Includes bibliographical references (pages 488-506) and index

Meier, Andrew

   Black earth; a journey through Russia after the fall. Norton
2003 511p il map $28.95; pa $15.95   **947.086**
   1. Russia (Federation)
   ISBN 0-393-05178-1; 0-393-32641-1 pa

                          LC 2003-6562

"After talking to scores of people—from survivors of the Aldy
massacre to a harrowed Russian lieutenant colonel who runs the body-
collection point closest to the Chechen battleground—Meier paints in
this heartbreaking book a devastating picture of contemporary life in a
country where, as one man put it, people have 'lived like the lowest dogs
for more than eighty years.'" Publ Wkly

Includes bibliographical references

Ostrovsky, Arkady

   The **invention** of Russia; from Gorbachev's freedom to Putin's war. Arkady Ostrovsky. Viking 2016 384 p. (hardcover)
$30   **947.086**
   1. Cold war 2. World politics -- 1945-1991 3. Russia -- Politics
and government 4. Russia -- History -- 1917-1991, Soviet Union
5. Russia (Federation) -- History -- 1991- 6. Nationalism -- Russia
(Federation) -- History 7. Social change -- Russia (Federation) --
History 8. Post-communism -- Russia (Federation) -- History 9.
Political culture -- Russia (Federation) -- History 10. Capitalism
-- Social aspects -- Russia (Federation) -- History
   ISBN 0399564160; 9780399564161

                          LC 2016008393

This book, by Arkady Ostrovsky, "reaches back to the darkest days
of the cold war to tell the story of the fight for the soul of a nation. With
the deep insight only possible of a native son, Ostrovsky introduces us
to the propagandists, oligarchs, and fixers who have set Russia's course
since the collapse of the Soviet Union, inventing a new and more ominous identity for a country where ideas are all too often wielded like a
cudgel." (Publisher's note)

"A troubling and superbly documented book that will make readers wonder what comes next for Russia and its propagandists." Booklist

Includes bibliographical references (pages [351]-355) and index.

Politkovskaya, Anna

A **Russian** diary; a journalist's final account of life, corruption, and death in Putin's Russia. translated by Arch Tait; foreword by Scott Simon. Random House 2007 369p map $25.95   **947.086**

1. Presidents 2. Prime ministers 3. Russia (Federation) -- Politics and government

ISBN 1-4000-6682-4; 978-1-4000-6682-7

LC 2007-296943

These are the journals kept by the Russian journalist who was killed in Moscow in 2006.

This is a "brilliant . . . portrayal of Russian life during the middle years of Putin's rule." New York Rev Books

Remnick, David

Resurrection; the struggle for a new Russia. Random House 1997 398p hardcover o.p. pa $15   **947.086**

1. Russia (Federation) -- Politics and government

ISBN 0-375-75023-1 pa

LC 96-47360

In this companion volume to Lenin's tomb, "Remnick concentrates on the post-Soviet scene and its prospects. . . . Chaotic uncertainty, massive corruption, and crime are notoriously present, yet the possibility of a different, better life also beckons. . . . This is an interesting, highly informative portrait of a country struggling toward a fateful future." Libr J

Includes bibliographical references

Richards, Susan

Lost and found in Russia; lives in a post-Soviet landscape. Other Press 2010 544p pa $15.95; ebook $15.95   **947.086**

1. Russia (Federation) -- Description and travel 2. Russia (Federation) -- Social life and customs

ISBN 978-1-59051-348-4 pa; 978-1-59051-369-9 ebook

First published 2010 in the United Kingdom

"During many trips from 1992 to 1998, Richards . . . traveled to visit friends in Russia, particularly in the southwestern towns of Saratov and Marx. . . . She fashions the narrative around the friends she met and lived with closely. Vera, follower of the Vissarion cult, was an inhabitant of Saratov, once called the Athens of the Volga, now a forsaken place closed to foreigners because of its military industry (presently defunct). In Marx, once the nexus of the Russian Germans, Richards stayed with Anna, a tensely coiled journalist—a pravednik, or 'truth bearer'—who had been punished for her honest writing; the volatile couple Natasha and Igor, lured to the dead-end town by Gorbachev's promise of a German homeland, now mostly unemployed and alcoholic; and the couple Misha and Tatiana, marooned in Marx after their engineering training, who became thriving entrepreneurs and part of the rising Russian middle class. . . . Other trips took her through Siberia and the Crimea to view the residues of Russian Orthodoxy, the Old Believers and folksy spiritualism. A patiently crafted glimpse 'through a crack in the wardrobe' of the devastation wrought on Russian society during the turbulent post-Communist '90s." Kirkus

Szablowski, Witold

Dancing bears; true stories of people nostalgic for life under tyranny. by Witold Szablowski; translated by Antonia Lloyd-Jones. Penguin Books 2018 xvii, 233 p.p illustrations (paperback) $16   **947.086**

1. Communist countries -- Social conditions 2. Bears -- Bulgaria 3. Cuba -- Civilization -- 21st century 4. Post-communism --

Psychological aspects 5. Bulgaria -- Civilization -- 21st century 6. Europe, Eastern -- Civilization -- 21st century

ISBN 9781101993385; 9780143129745; 0143129740

LC 2017043107

This book, by Witold Szablowski, translated by Antonia Lloyd-Jones, "uncovers remarkable stories of people throughout Eastern Europe and in Cuba who, like Bulgaria's dancing bears, are now free but who seem nostalgic for the time when they were not. His on-the-ground reporting . . . provides a fascinating portrait of social and economic upheaval and a lesson in the challenges of freedom and the seductions of authoritarian rule." (Publisher's note)

"A surprising look at societies grappling with profound change." Kirkus

Includes bibliographical references.

Treisman, Daniel

The **return**; Russia's journey from Gorbachev to Medvedev. Free Press 2011 523p il $30; ebook $14.99   **947.086**

1. Russia (Federation) -- Politics and government

ISBN 978-1-4165-6071-5; 1-4165-6071-8; 978-1-4516-0574-7 ebook; 1-4516-0574-9 ebook; 1416560718; 1451605749 ebook; 978141656071-5; 9781451605747 ebook

LC 2010011520

"The politics and economics of post-Communist Russia occupy this survey of the past two decades. Treisman . . . works commentary about Russia's successive leaders—Gorbachev, Yeltsin, Putin, and Medvedev—into the problems they confronted. . . . Encompassing foreign policy and Russian public opinion, Treisman's knowledgeable presentation is a reliable current-affairs source for Russia's economic revival and reassertion in international affairs." Booklist

Walker, Shaun

★ The **long** hangover; Putin's new Russia and the ghosts of the past. Shaun Walker. Oxford University Press 2018 278 p. maps (hardcover) $29.95   **947.086**

1. Russia -- History 2. Russia -- Politics and government 3. Russia (Federation) -- History 4. Russia (Federation) -- Politics and government -- 1991-

ISBN 9780190659240; 0190659246

LC 2017015739

In this book, author "Shaun Walker provides a deeply reported, bottom-up explanation of Russia's resurgence under [Vladimir] Putin. By cleverly exploiting the memory of the Soviet victory over fascism in World War II, Putin's regime has made ordinary Russians feel that their country is great again. . . . Walker provides new insight into contemporary Russia and its search for a new identity, telling the story through the country's troubled relationship with its Soviet past." (Publisher's note)

"Intelligent and ambitious, Walker's book succeeds in providing insight into the recent history of a nation at the center of world attention." Pub Wkly

Includes bibliographical references (pages 267-271) and index.

Zygar, Mikhail

All the Kremlin's men; inside the court of Vladimir Putin. Mikhail Zygar. PublicAffairs 2016 400 p. (ebook) $17.99; (hardback) $27.99   **947.086**

1. Russia -- History 2. Russia (Federation) -- History -- 1991- 3. Russia (Federation) -- Biography -- Interviews 4. Russia (Federation) -- Politics and government -- 1991-

ISBN 9781610397407; 9781610397391

LC 2016018443

This book, by Mikhail Zygar, "presents a radically different view of power and politics in Russia. The image of Putin as a strongman is dissolved. In its place is a weary figurehead buffeted--if not controlled--by the men who at once advise and deceive him. . . . [It] is a shocking revisionist portrait of the Putin era and a dazzling reconstruction of the machinations of courtiers running riot." (Publisher's note)

"This excellent book contains a continuous account of Putin's years in power seasoned with details that are poorly known to most readers, if known at all." LJ

Includes bibliographical references and index

947.43   Ural Mountains (Russia)

Garrels, Anne

Putin country; a journey into the real Russia. Anne Garrels. Farrar, Straus & Giroux 2015 240 p. (hardback) $26   **947.43**

1. Russia -- Description and travel 2. Cheliabinsk (Russia) -- Biography 3. Cheliabinsk (Russia) -- Social conditions 4. Cheliabinsk (Russia) -- Description and travel 5. Cheliabinsk (Russia) -- Social life and customs 6. Interviews -- Russia (Federation) -- Cheliabinsk 7. Subculture -- Russia (Federation) -- Cheliabinsk 8. Political culture -- Russia (Federation) -- Cheliabinsk
ISBN 9780374247720

LC 2015034644

In this book, the NPR correspondent Anne Garrels "began visiting a crumbling military-industrial center called Chelyabinsk that lies 1,000 miles east of Moscow. Here she profiles economic chaos, political corruption, and surging xenophobia, bursting cosmopolitanism and sudden wealth for rising professionals and Mafiosi. . . . All to clarify what the fall of communism has meant for the population at large. And she explains why so many Russians love Vladimir Putin." (Library Journal)

"This book will be of interest to general readers seeking to learn more about the country that exists beyond Moscow and St. Petersburg, as well as those wanting to gain better insight into its interior political and social conditions." LJ

947.5   Caucasus

Baiev, Khassan

The **Oath**; a surgeon under fire. [by] Khassan Baiev; with Ruth and Nicholas Daniloff. Walker & Co. 2003 376p il $26   **947.5**

1. Chechnya (Russia)
ISBN 0-8027-1404-8

LC 2003-52502

The author "is modest, which only adds to his heroism. But more than that, he has humanized the Chechens, whom others have portrayed as terrorists. Russian president Vladimir Putin has tried to equate Russia's fight against the Chechens with the U.S. battle against al-Qaida. Those who read this stirring memoir will be hard-pressed to see the situation so simply." Publ Wkly

Seierstad, Asne

The **angel** of Grozny; orphans of a forgotten war. translated by Nadia Christensen. Basic Books 2008 340p $25.95   **947.5**

1. Chechnya (Russia) -- History -- 1994- (Civil War)
ISBN 978-0-465-01122-3; 0-465-01122-5

LC 2008-925222

In the early hours of New Year's 1994, Russian troops invaded the Republic of Chechnya, plunging the country into a prolonged and bloody conflict that continues to this day. A foreign correspondent in Moscow at the time, Åsne Seierstad traveled regularly to Chechnya to report on the war, describing its affects on those trying to live their daily lives amidst violence.

"Seierstad's searing, evocative recounting brings Chechnya to life, especially the unimaginable suffering and strength of the Chechen people. Powerful, painful, and raw, . . . [this] is essential reading." Booklist

947.6   Moldova

Zipperstein, Steven J.

Pogrom; Kishinev and the tilt of history. Steven J. Zipperstein. Liveright Publishing Corporation 2018 288 p. (hardcover) $27.95   **947.6**

1. Jews 2. Judaism 3. Persecution 4. Chişinău (Moldova) -- Ethnic relations 5. Kishinev Massacre, Chişinău, Moldova, 1903 6. Jews -- Moldova -- Chişinău -- History -- 20th century 7. Pogroms -- Moldova -- Chişinău -- History -- 20th century 8. Massacres -- Moldova -- Chişinău -- History -- 20th century 9. Jews -- Persecutions -- Moldova -- Chişinău -- History -- 20th century
ISBN 9781631492693

LC 2017055798

This book, by Steven J. Zipperstein, explores "the aftereffects of Kishinev, the rampage that broke out in late-Tsarist Russia in April 1903, . . . In three days of violence, 49 Jews were killed and 600 raped or wounded, while more than 1,000 Jewish-owned houses and stores were ransacked and destroyed. . . . [the book] brings historical insight and clarity to a much-misunderstood event that would do so much to transform twentieth-century Jewish life and beyond." (Publisher's note)

Includes bibliographical references and index

947.7   Ukraine

Applebaum, Anne

Red famine; Stalin's war on Ukraine. by Anne Applebaum. Doubleday 2017 xxx, 461 p.p illustrations, maps (hardcover) $35   **947.7**

1. Ukraine -- History 2. Ukraine -- History -- Famine, 1932-1933 3. Famines -- Ukraine -- History -- 20th century 4. Genocide -- Ukraine -- History -- 20th century 5. Collectivization of agriculture -- Ukraine -- History
ISBN 9780385538862; 9780385538855; 0385538855

LC 2017029952

This book, by Anne Applebaum, is a "history of one of Stalin's greatest crimes--the consequences of which still resonate today. . . . In 1929 Stalin launched his policy of agricultural collectivization--in effect a second Russian revolution--which forced millions of peasants off their land and onto collective farms. The result was a catastrophic famine, the most lethal in European history." (Publisher's note)

"An authoritative history of national strife from a highly knowledgeable guide." Kirkus

Includes bibliographical references (pages [363]-434) and index.

Judah, Tim

In wartime; Stories from Ukraine. Tim Judah. Tim Duggan Books 2016 240 p. illustrations, maps (hbk.) $27   **947.7**

1. Ukraine -- History 2. War and civilization 3. Ukraine Conflict, 2014- 4. Ukraine Conflict, 2014- -- Social aspects 5. Ukraine Conflict, 2014- -- Personal narratives 6. Russia (Federation) -- Foreign relations -- Ukraine 7. Ukraine -- Foreign relations -- Russia (Federation) 8. War and society -- Ukraine -- History -- 21st century

ISBN 0241198828; 0451495470; 9780241198827; 9780451495471

LC 2016000368

This book, by Tim Judah, explores the geopolitical and social aspects of Ukraine in the 21st century. "Ever since Ukraine's violent 2014 revolution, followed by Russia's annexation of Crimea, the country has been at war. . . . lays bare the events that have turned neighbors against one another and mired Europe's second-largest country in a conflict seemingly without end." (Publisher's Note)

"Judah's special and timely book will provide lay readers with an apt introduction to Ukraine, and specialists will appreciate its atypical yet enlightening approach and its insights into the social aspects of ongoing conflicts." Pub Wkly

Includes bibliographical references (pages [247]-254).

King, Charles

Odessa; genius and death in a city of dreams. W.W. Norton & Co. 2011 336p il map $27.95 **947.7**

1. Jews -- Ukraine 2. Odessa (Ukraine) 3. Odessa (Ukraine) -- History 4. Jews -- Ukraine -- Odessa -- History 5. Odessa (Ukraine) -- Politics and government

ISBN 9780393070842; 0-393-07084-0

LC 2010-38000

This is a "finely written and evocative portrait of the city. . . . [Its] detail, coupled with a fine feel for the sweep of history . . . makes this book a worthy tribute to one of Europe's greatest and least-known cities." Economist

Includes bibliographical references

Kurtz, Glenn

Three minutes in Poland; discovering a lost world in a 1938 family film. Glenn Kurtz. Farrar, Straus & Giroux 2014 432 p. illustrations, maps (hardback) $30 **947.7**

1. Community life 2. Jews -- Poland 3. Holocaust, 1939-1945 4. Poland -- History -- 1918-1945 5. Nasielsk (Poland) -- Biography 6. Holocaust survivors -- Biography 7. Jews -- PolandHistory -- 20th century 8. Holocaust, Jewish (1939-1945) -- Poland 9. Nasielsk (Poland) -- History -- 20th century 10. Community life -- Poland -- Nasielsk -- History -- 20th century

ISBN 0374276773; 9780374276775

LC 2014008516

In this book, author "Glenn Kurtz stumbles upon an old family film in his parents' closet in Florida. . . . The film, shot long ago by his grandfather on a sightseeing trip to Europe, includes shaky footage of Paris and the Swiss Alps. . . . Astonishingly, David Kurtz also captured on color 16mm film the only known moving images of the thriving, predominantly Jewish town of Nasielsk, Poland, shortly before the community's destruction." (Publisher's note)

"Engrossing detective work and chance encounters--one casual online viewer recognized a 13-year-old boy in the film as her still-living grandfather--allowed Kurtz to assemble a vibrant portrait of Jewish Nasielsk, its homely shops, proud synagogue, quarreling Hasidim and Zionists, impish kids, and, not least, of its harrowing war-time dissolution. He also explores the resurrection of the community's history, as survivors find images of loved ones lost for generations and forge new bonds." Pub Wkly

947.98 Estonia

Theroux, Alexander

Estonia: a ramble through the periphery. Fantagraphics Books 2011 351p il $29.99 **947.98**

1. Estonia -- Description and travel

ISBN 978-1-60699-465-8; 1-60699-465-4

Theroux "follows his wife, Sarah, to [Estonia] in 2008, where she paints on her Fulbright grant scenes of its stolid towns. Brother of the equally waspish travel writer Paul, Alexander Theroux, meanwhile, skulks, fulminates, studies, and walks wherever he can, soaking up the frigid atmosphere of its people. . . . He deploys bombast, overkill, and ridicule to pepper his perennial pop-up targets of greed, lassitude, and stupidity. He includes here his caustic if characteristic habit of lists, ruminations, and rants. For all his predilection for careful observation of how people look, sound, and move, he inflates, if maybe in sly self-deprecation, the impact others have on him—rather than vice versa. . . . Full of endnotes, translating many phrases he quotes in their original languages, and graced by a few of the couple's photos and Sarahs plein air oil paintings, this provides a suitably quirky introduction to Theroux as an essayist and critic." PopMatters

948 Scandinavia

Booth, Michael

The **Almost** Nearly Perfect People. Jonathan Cape 2014 416 p. map $26 **948**

1. Scandinavia -- Civilization 2. Scandinavia -- Social conditions 3. Scandinavia -- Social life and customs

ISBN 0224089625; 9780224089623; 9781250061966; 1250061962

In this book, Michael Booth "covers the countries that invariably dominate the top ten lists of best/healthiest/most egalitarian places to live: Denmark, Finland, Iceland, Norway, and Sweden. Beginning with his adopted home of Denmark, Booth sets out to address whether the quality of life in Nordic countries is really so high. . . . He . . . discovers . . . some chinks in the utopian armor: isolationism, persistent racism . . . and growing fissures in a classless society." (Publishers Weekly)

"Thanks to Booth's good-natured description of his adventures—and his honest admiration—we may head for Scandinavia after all (bringing some elf-off spray, just in case)." Booklist

Ferguson, Robert

Scandinavians; in search of the soul of the North. Robert Ferguson. Overlook Press 2017 xxiii, 455 p.p illustrations (hardcover) $35 **948**

1. Scandinavia -- History 2. Scandinavia -- Social conditions 3. Scandinavia -- Politics and government

ISBN 9781468314830; 9781468314823; 1468314823

This book, by Robert Ferguson, follows "two millennia of Scandinavia's history, culture and society. . . . [T]he Vendel era of Swedish prehistory; the age of the Vikings; the Christian conversions of Denmark, Norway, Sweden and Iceland; the unified Scandinavian state of the late Middle Ages; the sea-change of the Reformation; the kingdom of Denmark-Norway; King Gustav Adolphus and the age of Sweden's greatness; . . . and the terror attacks of Anders Behring Breivik." (Publisher's note)

"In a free-wheeling love letter to the essence of Scandinavia, Ferguson (Life Lessons from Kierkegaard) takes readers on a leisurely jaunt through the collective, interconnected histories of Norway, Denmark, and Sweden." Pub Wkly

Includes bibliographical references (pages 431-443) and index.

The **Vikings**; a history. Viking 2009 450p il map **948**

1. Vikings 2. Europe -- History -- 476-1492

ISBN 978-0-670-02079-9

LC 2009-26818

"Ferguson's scholarly study requires close attention, but the intellectual rewards are plentiful. Provides a significant deepening of our knowledge of the Vikings." Kirkus
Includes bibliographical references

The **Oxford** illustrated history of the Vikings; edited by Peter Sawyer. Oxford Univ. Press 1997 298p il maps hardcover o.p. pa $27.50   **948**
1. Vikings
ISBN 0-19-820526-0; 0-19-285434-8 pa
LC 97-16649

This illustrated collection of articles includes discussion of the Vikings' impact on England, Iceland, Greenland, Russia, and the Frankish and Danish Empires; Viking ships and ship-building; Viking religion; and the ways in which Vikings have been portrayed throughout history. Significant archaeological finds are featured.
Includes bibliographical references

Roesdahl, Else
The **Vikings**; translated by Susan M. Margeson and Kirsten Williams. 2nd ed; Penguin Books 1998 324p il map pa $17   **948**
1. Vikings
ISBN 0-14-025282-7; 978-0-14-025282-8
Original Danish edition, 1987
A survey of Viking civilization from c.750-c.1050.
"About one-third of the book deals with Viking expansion into Russia, Normandy, the British Isles, Iceland, Greenland, etc. . . . Most of the book surveys the geography, people, society, religion, art, etc., of the Vikings' Scandinavian homelands." Libr J
Includes bibliographical references

948.97   Finland

Beach, Hugh
A **year** in Lapland; guest of the reindeer herders. with a new afterword by the author. University of Washington Press 2001 242p il map pa $25   **948.97**
1. Sami (European people) 2. Lapland
ISBN 0-295-98037-0; 978-0-295-98037-9
LC 00-47936

First published 1993 by Smithsonian Institution Press
The author "tells of his first year among the Saami reindeer herders of Swedish Lapland. His narrative interweaves adventure, descriptions of the harsh beauty of the landscape, supernatural tales and ancient myths. Beach also explores topics of change in the lives of the herders brought on by laws requiring village groups to move and by adaptations to new items such as rubber boots, seaplanes, and appliances." Libr J

Edwards, Robert
The **Winter** War; Russia's invasion of Finland, 1939-1940. Pegasus Books 2008 319p il map $27.95   **948.97**
1. Russo-Finnish War, 1939-1940 2. World War, 1939-1945 -- Finland
ISBN 978-1-933648-50-7
First published 2006 in the United Kingdom
"A brisk, efficient account of one of the most overlooked episodes of World War II. . . . Highly readable and informative." Kirkus
Includes bibliographical references

949.12   Iceland

Johanneson, Gudni Thorlacius
The **history** of Iceland; Guðni Thorlacius Jóhannesson. Greenwood 2013 xv, 172 p.p (The Greenwood Histories of the Modern Nations) (hardcopy: acid-free paper) $58   **949.12**
1. Iceland -- History
ISBN 0313376204; 9780313376207
LC 2012031759

This book divides the "history of Iceland into seven sections chronicling events and conditions in the country from 874 through mid-2012. . . . The author enlivens his coverage with . . . stories, such as one of an early chronicler who marveled that the midnight sun was so bright that lice could easily be picked out of clothing." (Booklist)
Includes bibliographical references (pages 157-160) and index

949.2   Netherlands

Shorto, Russell
Amsterdam; a history of the world's most liberal city. Russell Shorto. Doubleday 2013 368 p. $28.95   **949.2**
1. Liberalism 2. Netherlands -- History 3. Amsterdam (Netherlands) -- History 4. Liberalism -- Netherlands -- Amsterdam -- History
ISBN 0385534574; 9780385534574
LC 2013003544

Author Russell Shorto's book presents a history of the city of Amsterdam. "Weaving in his own experiences of his adopted home, Shorto provides" a "story of Amsterdam from the building of its first canals in the 1300s, through its brutal struggle for independence, its golden age as a vast empire, to its complex present in which its cherished ideals of liberalism are under siege." (Publisher's note)
Includes bibliographical references

949.5   Greece

Brownworth, Lars
Lost to the West; the forgotten Byzantine Empire that rescued Western civilization. Crown Publishers 2009 329p map $26; pa $15   **949.5**
1. Byzantine Empire
ISBN 978-0-307-40795-5; 978-0-307-40796-2 pa
"Brownworth delivers just enough of the big picture for interested readers to pursue specific events in greater detail. An energetic look at a still-misunderstood period in late antiquity." Kirkus
Includes bibliographical references

Mazower, Mark
Salonica, city of ghosts; Christians, Muslims, and Jews, 1430-1950. Knopf 2005 490p il maps $35   **949.5**
1. Thessalonike (Greece)
ISBN 0-375-41298-0
LC 2004-57690

First published 2004 in the United Kingdom
This is a history of the Greek city.
The author's "graceful, evocative prose, his deft attention to details and his empathetic presentation of all sides of the story add up to a magnificent tale of this unique city." Publ Wkly
Includes bibliographical references

949.6 Balkan Peninsula

Pamuk, Orhan, 1952-
Istanbul; memories and the city. translated from the Turkish by Maureen Freely. Knopf 2005 384p il $26.95 **949.6**
1. Authors 2. Novelists 3. Istanbul (Turkey) 4. Nobel laureates for literature 5. Istanbul (Turkey) -- Description and travel
ISBN 1-400-04095-7
LC 2004-61537
Original Turkish edition, 2003
The novelist writes about his life as a resident of Istanbul.
"The author mingles 'personal memoir with cultural history', and a fascinating read it is too for anyone who has even the slightest acquaintance with this fabled bridge between east and west." Economist

949.7 Serbia, Croatia, Slovenia, Bosnia and Hercegovina, Montenegro, Macedonia

Di Giovanni, Janine
Madness visible; a memoir of war. Knopf 2003 285p map hardcover o.p. pa $14 **949.7**
1. Kosovo (Serbia)
ISBN 0-375-41073-2; 978-0-375-72455-8 pa; 0-375-72455-9 pa
LC 2002-44820
This "narrative of the 1999 war in Kosovo, NATO's campaign against Serbia, and the ouster of Milosevic offers an unbiased view of the enormous suffering of Yugoslav Albanians and Serbs following the genocidal rage of the Belgrade regime against the Kosovo Liberation Army's (KLA) drive for an independent Kosovo.... This exciting work is highly recommended for all libraries." Libr J
Includes bibliographical references

Rieff, David
Slaughterhouse; Bosnia and the failure of the West. Simon & Schuster 1995 240p hardcover o.p. pa $18.95 **949.7**
1. Yugoslav War, 1991-1995 2. Bosnia and Hercegovina
ISBN 0-684-81903-1 pa
LC 94-40148
This account of the war in the former Yugoslavia grew out of Rieff's travels in the region from 1992 through 1994
"Slaughterhouse is perhaps the most powerful, passionate, and penetrating dissection of a Westerner of the ongoing Bosnian tragedy." Booklist

Rohde, David
Endgame; the betrayal and fall of Srebrenica, Europe's worst massacre since World War II. Westview Press 1998 450p il pa $20 **949.7**
1. Yugoslav War, 1991-1995 2. Srebrenica (Bosnia and Hercegovina)
ISBN 0-8133-3533-7; 978-0-8133-3533-9
LC 98-26127
First published 1997 by Farrar, Straus & Giroux
"Rohde argues that the fall of Srebrenica could have been prevented, but he is ultimately unable to explain the 'collective failure' of the United States, the United Nations, and NATO in stopping the massacre. His investigation is carefully documented by over 300 footnotes. This is an important and revealing book." Libr J
Includes bibliographical references

949.702 Yugoslavia, 1918-1991

Maass, Peter
Love thy neighbor; a story of war. Knopf 1996 305p hardcover o.p. pa $14 **949.702**
1. Yugoslav War, 1991-1995 2. Bosnia and Hercegovina
ISBN 0-679-76389-9 pa
LC 95-39250
This book on the Yugoslav conflict is based on Maass's experiences as the Washington Post's reporter in Bosnia
"Maass was only in Bosnia for about a year, from 1992 to 1993, but he saw a great deal. And he displays extraordinary sensitivity to the ambiguities of his position." Nation
Includes bibliographical references

949.703 Period as sovereign nations, 1991-

Clark, Wesley K.
★ **Waging** modern war; Bosnia, Kosovo, and the future of combat. PublicAffairs 2001 xxxi, 479p il map hardcover o.p. pa $18 **949.703**
1. Yugoslav War, 1991-1995 2. Kosovo (Serbia) -- History
ISBN 1-58648-139-8 pa
LC 01-19717
This is an account of the former Supreme Allied Commander's experiences during the Kosovo crises. "Clark tells a story of frustration with NATO allies, who had to approve each operation and target selection, and with U.S. policymakers as he tried to formulate a strategy that would achieve his military goals." Libr J

949.71 Serbia

McAllester, Matthew
Beyond the Mountains of the Damned; the war inside Kosovo. New York Univ. Press 2002 227p il $30; pa $17.95 **949.71**
1. Kosovo (Serbia) -- History
ISBN 0-8147-5660-3; 0-8147-5661-1 pa
LC 2001-4370
"McAllester's spare, understated prose ... is potent, as is his exploration of the human side of geopolitics and war." Publ Wkly
Includes bibliographical references

949.8 Romania

Kaplan, Robert D., 1952-
In Europe's shadow; two cold wars and a thirty-year journey through Romania and beyond. Robert D. Kaplan. Random House Inc 2015 336 p. 16 plates; illustrations; maps (hardcover) $28 **949.8**
1. Geopolitics 2. Romania -- Civilization 3. Europe -- History -- 20th century 4. Romania -- History -- 1989- 5. Romania -- History -- 1944-1989 6. Romania -- Description and travel
ISBN 9780812996814
LC 2015012726
This book, by Robert D. Kaplan, "illuminates the fusion of the Latin West and the Greek East that created Romania, the country that gave rise to ... [Adolf] Hitler's chief foreign accomplice during World War II, and

the country that was home to the most brutal strain of Communism. . . . Kaplan finds himself in dialogue with the great thinkers of the past, and with the Romanians of today, the philosophers, priests, and politicians— those who struggle to keep the flame of humanism alive in the era of a resurgent Russia." (Publisher's note)

"Despite the lack of a clear focus and the somewhat incoherent organization, this is a well-written, intriguing, and informative book." Pub Wkly

Includes bibliographical references and index

949.9 Bulgaria

Kassabova, Kapka, 1973-

Border; a journey to the edge of Europe. Kapka Kassabova. Graywolf Press 2017 xviii, 379 p.p map (paperback) $16   **949.9**

1. Bulgaria 2. Borderlands -- Greece 3. Borderlands -- Turkey 4. Borderlands -- Bulgaria 5. Borderlands -- Bulgaria -- History 6. Bulgaria -- Description and travel

ISBN 9781555977863; 9781555979782

LC 2017930112

National Book Critics Circle Award Finalist: Nonfiction (2017)

In this book, "Kapka Kassabova returns to Bulgaria, from where she emigrated as a girl twenty-five years previously, to explore the border it shares with Turkey and Greece. . . . Kassabova discovers a place that has been shaped by successive forces of history: the Soviet and Ottoman empires, and, older still, myth and legend. Her exquisite portraits of fire walkers, smugglers, treasure hunters, botanists, and border guards populate the book." (Publisher's note)

"Wild animals abound, myths mingle with reality, and Kassabova proves to be a penetrating and contemplative guide through rough terrain." Pub Wkly

950 History of Asia

Mishra, Pankaj

From the ruins of empire; the intellectuals who remade Asia. Pankaj Mishra. Farrar, Straus and Giroux 2012 368 p. ill. (alk. paper) $27.00; (pbk.) $18.00   **950**

1. Intellectuals

ISBN 9780374249595; 0374249598; 1250037719; 9781250037718

LC 2012940483

"Originally published in 2012 by Allen Lane, an imprint of Penguin Books, Great Britain as From the ruins of empire: the revolt against the West and the remaking of Asia"--Title page verso.

This book "looks at how, between about 1870 and 1940, 'some of the most intelligent and sensitive people in the East responded to the encroachments of the West (both physical and intellectual) on their societies.' In particular, he focuses on Jamal al-Din al-Afghani and Liang Qichao, intellectuals and political activists." (Publishers Weekly)

Includes bibliographical references (pages 311-340) and index.

Said, Edward W., 1935-2003

Orientalism; Edward W. Said. 1st Vintage books ed. Vintage Books 1979 xi, 368 p.p (paperback) $17   **950**

1. Imperialism 2. Orientalism 3. East and West 4. Asia -- Study and teaching 5. Middle East -- Study and teaching 6. Asia -- Foreign public opinion, Occidental 7. Middle East -- Foreign public opinion, Occidental

ISBN 9780394740676; 9780804153867; 039474067X

LC 79010497

This book, by Edward W. Said, is a "groundbreaking critique of the West's historical, cultural, and political perceptions of the East. . . . In this wide-ranging, intellectually vigorous study, Said traces the origins of 'orientalism' to the centuries-long period during which Europe dominated the Middle and Near East and, from its position of power, defined "the orient" simply as 'other than' the occident." (Publisher's note)

Includes bibliographical references and index

Weatherford, Jack

Genghis Khan and the Quest for God; How the World's Greatest Conqueror Gave Us Religious Freedom. by Jack Weatherford. Penguin Group USA 2016 304 p. $28   **950**

ISBN 0735221154; 9780735221154

This biography, by Jack Weatherford, "reveals how Genghis [Khan] harnessed the power of religion to rule the largest empire the world has ever known. . . . He created the world's greatest trading network, . . . but he knew that if his empire was going to last, he would need something stronger and more binding than trade. He needed religion. And so, unlike the Christian, Taoist and Muslim conquerors who came before him, he gave his subjects freedom of religion." (Publisher's note)

"This sound examination of Khan, his methods of rule, and his views on religious tolerance presents a valid and welcome addition to scholarship on the subject." LJ

951 China and adjacent areas

Bstan-'dzin-rgya-mtsho, Dalai Lama XIV, 1935-

My Tibet; text by His Holiness the fourteenth Dalai Lama of Tibet; photographs and introduction by Galen Rowell. University of Calif. Press 1990 162p il hardcover o.p. pa $34.95 **951**

1. Buddhism 2. Tibet (China) -- Pictorial works

ISBN 0-520-08948-0 pa

LC 90-10868

This is "a volume of photographs taken in recent years by Galen Rowell, with a text drawn from interviews with the Dalai Lama or essays written previously by him." N Y Times Book Rev

Fairbank, John King

★ **China**; a new history. [by] John King Fairbank and Merle Goldman. 2nd enl. ed.; Belknap Press of Harvard University Press 2006 560p il map pa $24   **951**

1. China -- History

ISBN 0-674-01828-1; 978-0-674-01828-0

LC 2005-53695

First published 1992

Fairbank covers the history of China from paleolithic cultures of 400,000 B.C. up to 1989. Goldman adds a chapter on events in the post-Mao period and an epilogue on China at the beginning of the 21st century.

Includes bibliographical references

Hessler, Peter

★ **Oracle** bones; a journey between China's past and present. HarperCollins 2006 491p il $26.95; pa $15.99   **951**

1. China -- Civilization 2. China -- Description and travel

ISBN 0-06-082658-4; 0-06-082659-2 pa

LC 2005-52607

National Book Award Finalist: Nonfiction (2006)

The author "has a marvelous sense of the intonations and gestures that give life to the moment; he knows when to join in the action and when simply to wait for things to happen. Today's China could have been made for him." N Y Times Book Rev

Includes bibliographical references

Meyer, Michael J.

The **last** days of old Beijing; life in the vanishing backstreets of a city transformed. [by] Michael Meyer. Walker & Company 2008 355p il map $25.99; pa $16   **951**

1. Beijing (China)

ISBN 978-0-8027-1652-1; 0-8027-1652-0; 978-0-8027-1750-4 pa; 0-8027-1750-4 pa

LC 2008-15546

This is a "revealing portrait of urban change, and the consequences of China's unquenchable thirst for modernization." Kirkus

Includes bibliographical references

Ming; 50 Years That Changed China. by Craig Clunas, Jessica Harrison-Hall. University of Washington Press 2014 304 p. color illustrations, color map (hardcover) $60   **951**

1. China -- History

ISBN 0295994509; 9780714124841; 9780295994505

This book, by Craig Clunas and Jessica Harrison-Hall, "by focusing on the significant years of the early Ming dynasty and through the themes of court people and their lives, extraordinary developments in culture, the military, religion, diplomacy and trade, . . . brings the wider history of this fascinating period to colorful life." (Publisher's note)

"For anyone interested in Chinese art and history." LJ

Palmer, James

Heaven cracks, earth shakes; James Palmer. Basic Books, a member of the Perseus Books Group 2012 ix, 273p.p ill. **951**

1. Earthquakes 2. China -- History -- 1949-1976

ISBN 9780465014781; 9780465023493

LC 2011934180

In this book, "Beijing-based author [James] Palmer . . . lays out the devastation wrought by 10 years of the Cultural Revolution, and how over the space of a few months the Chinese people managed to rebound and move forward. The year was scarred irrevocably by three events: the death in January of the people's beloved prime minister Zhou Enlai; the earthquake in Tangshan, which had been predicted several days before yet warnings ignored, flattening the coal-mining town in the space of 23 seconds and killing more than 650,000 people; and Mao's death in September, which set off a power struggle between the Gang of Four, led by Mao's widow, Jiang Qing, and the supporters of Deng Xiaoping." (Kirkus)

Includes bibliographical references (p. 261-264) and index.

Platt, Stephen R.

Autumn in the Heavenly Kingdom; China, the West, and the epic story of the Taiping Civil War. by Stephen R. Platt. Alfred A. Knopf 2012 468 p.   **951**

1. Manchus 2. China -- Foreign relations 3. Europeans -- China -- History 4. Christian missionaries -- History 5. China -- History -- 1850-1864, Taiping Rebellion 6. Ethnic conflict -- China 7. Americans -- China -- History -- 19th century

ISBN 9780307271730

LC 2011035137

The book is author Stephen R. Platt's account of "[t]he cataclysmic Taiping rebellion. . . . In 1837 a peasant named Hong Xiuquan announced that he was Jesus' younger brother, sent to rid China of 'devils' including its weak, corrupt, ethnically foreign Manchu rulers. His

charisma attracted a vast following that by the 1850s had conquered a large area, the Taiping Heavenly Kingdom, with a capital at Nanjing." (Publishers Weekly)

Includes bibliographical references

Preston, Diana

The **Boxer** Rebellion; the dramatic story of China's war on foreigners that shook the world in the summer of 1900. Walker & Co. 2000 xxvii, 436p il maps $28   **951**

1. China -- History

ISBN 0-8027-1361-0

LC 00-39243

"Preston's account, compiled from the many letters, diaries, and memoirs by European survivors of the siege, captures an odd strain of mordant humor." N Y Times Book Rev

Includes bibliographical references and index

Schell, Orville

Wealth and power; Orville Schell & John Delury. Random House Inc 2013 496 p. $30   **951**

1. China -- Social conditions 2. China -- Politics and government 3. China -- History -- 20th century -- Biography 4. China -- History -- 21st century -- Biography 5. China -- Politics and government -- 20th century 6. China -- Politics and government -- 21st century

ISBN 0679643478; 9780679643470

LC 2013002596

In this book, the authors "track the intellectual and political pursuit of fuqiang, or wealth and power, by Chinese thinkers and leaders in response to the humiliations heaped upon their country by Western powers, beginning with the Opium Wars of the mid-19th century. The work comprises chronologically ordered minibiographies, . . . with long sections devoted to Mao Zedong and Deng Xiaoping." (Publishers Weekly)

Includes bibliographical references and index

Spence, Jonathan D.

Treason by the book; {by} Jonathan Spence. Viking 2001 300p map $24.95; pa $14   **951**

1. China -- History 2. China -- Politics and government

ISBN 0-670-89292-0; 0-14-200041-8 pa

LC 00-43805

"Spence's story of emperor, officials, and conspirators is both rousingly unlikely and highly informative." Libr J

Tenzin Gyatso, Dalai Lama XIV, 1935-

My appeal to the world; in quest of truth and justice on behalf of the Tibetan people, 1961-2010.... Presented by Sofia Stril-Rever. Tibet House U.S. 2015 400 p. (hardback: alk. paper) $29.95   **951**

1. Peace 2. Tibet (China) 3. Tibetans -- Social conditions 4. Tibet Autonomous Region (China) -- History 5. Peace-building -- China -- Tibet Autonomous Region 6. Tibet Autonomous Region (China) -- Politics and goverment

ISBN 0967011566; 9780967011561

LC 2014034290

In this book, "[a]ll of the Dalai Lama's March 10th speeches, at their most poignant and eloquent, are collected, . . . introduced and historically contextualized by Sofia Stril-Rever, an author and scholar of Tibetan history and culture and Buddhist spirituality who has long served as his French translator." (Publisher's note)

"Those who wish to learn more about the late 20th-century history of Sino-Tibetan relations will find this a respectable resource, but it should be noted that this set of writings does not offer Chinese perspectives on

the thorny issue." Pub Wkly
Includes bibliographical references and index

951.033   China, 1796-1850

Platt, Stephen R.
Imperial twilight; the Opium War and the end of China's
last golden age. Stephen R. Platt. Alfred A. Knopf 2018 592 p.
(hardcover) $35   **951.033**
   1. China -- History -- 19th century 2. China -- History -- Opium
War, 1840-1842 3. China -- Foreign relations -- 19th century
   ISBN 9780307961730; 9780345803023

                                            LC 2017028172
This book, by Stephen R. Platt, "[tells] the story of [China's] last
age of ascendance and how it came to an end in the nineteenth-century
Opium War. . . . Platt sheds new light on the early attempts by Western
traders and missionaries to 'open' China . . . even as China's imperial
rulers were struggling to manage their country's decline and Confucian
scholars grappled with how to use foreign trade to China's advantage."
(Publisher's note)
   "Clear writing and an excellent sense of story and scene-setting
mark Platt's (Autumn in the Heavenly Kingdom, 2012) compelling reexamination of the causes of the First Opium War (1839–42)." Booklist
Includes bibliographical references

951.04   China--Period of Republic, 1912-1949

Chang, Iris
  ★ The **rape** of Nanking; the forgotten holocaust of World
War II. Penguin 1998 290p il pa $16   **951.04**
   1. Sino-Japanese Conflict, 1937-1945 2. Nanjing (Jiangsu Province,
China) massacre, 1937
   ISBN 0-14-027744-7; 978-0-14-027744-9

                                       LC 97-24137
First published 1997 by Basic Books
   "Chang's book is a memorial to the victims of Nanking, a damning
indictment of Japanese political historiography, a valuable addition to
Pacific war literature, and a literary model of how to speak about the
unspeakable." Booklist
Includes bibliographical references

Sun Shuyun
The **Long** March; the true history of Communist China's
founding myth. Doubleday 2007 270p il map $26   **951.04**
   1. Heads of state 2. Communist leaders 3. Political leaders 4.
China -- History -- 1912-1949
   ISBN 978-0-385-52024-9; 0-385-52024-7
First published 2006 in the United Kingdom
   "In 1934, surrounded by Chiang Kai-shek's forces in the south,
Mao's Red Army marched more than eight thousand miles to a new
base, in the northwest. The march, completed by only a fifth of the
original army, was a defeat in all ways but one: it returned Mao from
the political wilderness to power. Mao transformed the march into the
founding myth of modern China and, in doing so, created a new narrative around victories that never happened. Shuyun, a Chinese-born
BBC documentary producer, retraces the route and interviews the few
remaining survivors, in an account that shows the human cost of Mao's
revisionism." New Yorker

951.042   Period of nationalist government, 1927-1949

Kurtz-Phelan, Daniel
The **China** mission; George C. Marshall's unfinished war,
1945/1947. Daniel Kurtz-Phelan. W. W. Norton & Company
2018 496 p. (hardcover) $28.95   **951.042**
   1. Cold war 2. Generals -- United States
   ISBN 9780393240955

                                       LC 2017053909
This book, by Daniel Kurtz-Phelan, focuses on how the "conflict
between Chinese Nationalists and Communists threatened to suck in the
United States and escalate into revolution. [General George Marshall's]
assignment was to broker a peace, build a Chinese democracy, and prevent a Communist takeover, all while staving off World War III. . . .
[The book] traces this neglected turning point and forgotten interlude in
a heroic career." (Publisher's note)
Includes bibliographical references and index

951.05   China--Period of People's Republic, 1949-

Dikötter, Frank
Mao's great famine; the history of China's most devastating catastrophe, 1958-1962. Walker & Co. 2010 420p il map
$30   **951.05**
   1. Food supply 2. Heads of state 3. Famines -- China 4. Communist
leaders 5. Political leaders 6. Food supply -- China 7. Economic
policy -- China 8. China -- Economic policy -- 1949-1976
   ISBN 978-0-8027-7768-3; 0-8027-7768-6

                                      LC 2010-13141
This book on the 1958-1962 famine in China "focuses on describing
and conveying to the reader the stark effects of the famine at the local
level. . . . [T]he first two . . . parts retrace major events of the Great Leap
Forward disaster and famine. . . stressing the crucial role of the Lushan
Conference." Other chapters depict "survival strategies, repressive violence . . . the various ways in which people died, and the places where
most deaths occurred." (China Perspectives)
   The author parses this study of the Great Leap Forward into three
"components: Mao Zedong's bloody-minded resolve to implement the
accelerated collectivization of the countryside, and the stifling of all opposition; the effects of these devastating policies on agriculture, industry, trade, housing and nature; and the catastrophic human toll ('at least
45 million people died unnecessarily between 1958 and 1962')." Kirkus
Includes bibliographical references and index

Fallows, James M.
Postcards from Tomorrow Square; reports from China. [by]
James Fallows. Vintage Books 2009 262p pa $14.95 **951.05**
   1. China -- History -- 1976-
   ISBN 978-0-307-45624-3; 0-307-45624-2

                                       LC 2008-28083
   "In this series of articles, Fallows reports on interesting trends and
personalities in China—ambitious entrepreneurs and the rise in popularity of reality shows on state-run television. Despite the Western view of
a powerful, single-minded China, Fallows presents a portrait of a huge
and complex nation with such a vast range of ages and regional, geographic, and cultural differences that it defies simple definition." Booklist

Leibovitz, Liel
Fortunate sons; the 120 Chinese boys who came to America, went to school, and revolutionized an ancient civilization.

[by] Liel Leibovitz & Matthew Miller. W.W. Norton 2011
319p il $26.95   **951.05**
1. Educators 2. China -- History 3. Education -- China 4. China --
History -- 1861-1912 5. China -- Politics and government 6. China
-- History -- Reform movement, 1898 7. Chinese students -- United
States -- History 8. China -- Politics and government -- 19th century
ISBN 0-393-07004-2; 978-0-393-07004-0

LC 2010-37724

The book "begins with Yung Wing, who came to America in the
late 1840s. The first Chinese student admitted to Yale, he returned to his
homeland in 1854. . . . Under his tutelage, 120 Chinese boys crossed the
Pacific in the 1870s, intent on learning Western skills that might help
their country modernize." (N Y Times Book Rev) Index.

"A curious, little-known episode of Sino-American history vividly
told." Kirkus

Includes bibliographical references

Levine, Steven I.

★ **Mao**; the real story. Alexander V. Pantsov with Steven
I. Levine. 1st Simon & Schuster hardcover Simon & Schuster
2012 xix, 755 p.p $35   **951.05**
1. Communism -- China 2. China -- Politics and government
3. Heads of state -- China -- Biography 4. China -- Politics and
government -- 1949-1976
ISBN 1451654472; 9781451654479; 9781451654493

LC 2011053113

This book offers a biography of Communist leader Mao Zedong.
It relates "how Mao, who joined the Communist Party in 1920, fought
his way . . . to its leadership in the 1930s. . . . Taking power in 1949,
Mao established a Stalinist autocracy featuring purges, massive social
upheaval, and disastrous economic policies. . . . [Alexander V.] Pantsov
reveals that Mao took pains to remain a faithful follower until Stalin's
1952 death." (Publishers Weekly)

Includes bibliographical references and index

Ma Jian

Red dust; a path through China. translated from the Chinese by Flora Drew. Pantheon Bks. 2001 324p maps hardcover o.p. pa $14   **951.05**
1. China -- Description and travel
ISBN 0-385-72023-8 pa

LC 2001-21575

"Faced with imprisonment, Jian fled to the Chinese countryside,
eventually making his way to Tibet. His journey is presented as a combination travelogue and a narrative of sheer poetry and spirituality."
Booklist

Pomfret, John

Chinese lessons; five classmates and the story of the new
China. H. Holt 2006 315p il map $26   **951.05**
1. China
ISBN 978-0-8050-7615-8; 0-8050-7615-8

LC 2006-41211

This "is a highly personal, honest, funny and well-informed account
of China's hyperactive effort to forget its past and reinvent its future."
N Y Times Book Rev

Salzman, Mark

Iron & silk. Random House 1987 211p hardcover o.p. pa
$12.95   **951.05**
1. Martial arts 2. China -- Description and travel
ISBN 0-394-55156-7; 0-394-75511-1 pa

LC 86-11846

The author tells of his two years teaching English to medical students in China's Hunan Province following his graduation from Yale
University in 1982.

This book is "not so much a treatise on modern Chinese mores as
a series of telling vignettes. . . . [The author] describes his encounter
with Pan Qingfu, the country's foremost master of wushu, the traditional
Chinese martial art." Time

Schoppa, R. Keith

The **Columbia** guide to modern Chinese history. Columbia
Univ. Press 2000 356p il map (Columbia guides to Asian history) $49   **951.05**
1. China -- History
ISBN 0-231-11276-9

LC 99-53420

This narrative overview of Chinese history focuses on five areas:
domestic politics, society, the economy, culture, and relations with the
outside world. Contains approximately 500 annotated entries for further
research in English as well as electronic resources and films. A chronology, excerpts from primary documents, and numerous graphs and tables
are appended

Includes bibliographical references

Short, Philip

Mao; a life. Holt & Co. 2000 782p il maps hardcover o.p.
pa $20   **951.05**
1. Heads of state 2. Communist leaders 3. Political leaders 4.
China -- Politics and government
ISBN 0-8050-6638-1 pa

LC 99-41839

This biography "takes Mao from his 1893 birth in the village of
Shaoshan to school in Changsha, where he trained to be a teacher, and
then into revolutionary activity, the long fight with Chiang Kai-shek, and
leadership of the most populous nation on Earth." Booklist

Includes bibliographical references

Spence, Jonathan D.

Mao Zedong; {by} Jonathan Spence. Viking 1999 188p
map (Penguin lives series) $19.95   **951.05**
1. Heads of state 2. Communist leaders 3. Political leaders 4.
China -- Politics and government
ISBN 0-670-88669-6

LC 99-27739

"This specialist's book for nonspecialists concisely recounts the life
of the Communist leader who revolutionized China. Ideas travel fast:
Mao, a peasant son born in 1893, was able to read Darwin and Marx in
translation and add Western ideas to his heritage of classical Chinese
thought, and Spence helps us understand why he eventually embraced
Communism. What is less clear is why a gifted, high-minded youth became a ruthless, crackpot tyrant." New Yorker

Includes bibliographical references

Vogel, Ezra F.

Deng Xiaoping and the transformation of China; Ezra F.
Vogel. Belknap Press of Harvard University Press 2011 xxiv,
876p ill.   **951.05**
1. Communism -- China 2. China -- Economic conditions 3. China
-- Politics and government 4. Biography, Individual
ISBN 978-0-674-05544-5; 0-674-05544-6; 9780674062832

LC 2011006925

Lionel Gelber Prize (Canada) (2012)

This book, a 2012 Lionel Gelber Prize winner, offers a biography of Chinese politician Deng Xiaoping. "Deng was the pragmatic yet disciplined driving force behind China's radical transformation in the late twentieth century. He confronted the damage wrought by the Cultural Revolution, dissolved Mao's cult of personality, and loosened the economic and social policies that had stunted China's growth. Obsessed with modernization and technology, Deng opened trade relations with the West, which lifted hundreds of millions of his countrymen out of poverty. Yet at the same time he answered to his authoritarian roots, most notably when he ordered the crackdown in June 1989 at Tiananmen Square. . . . In the fifty years of his tumultuous rise to power, he endured accusations, purges, and even exile before becoming China's preeminent leader from 1978 to 1989 and again in 1992. When he reached the top, Deng saw an opportunity to creatively destroy much of the economic system he had helped build for five decades as a loyal follower of Mao—and he did not hesitate." (Publisher's note)

Includes bibliographical references and index

951.056   China, 1960-1969

Dikötter, Frank

The **Cultural** Revolution; A People's History, 1962-1976. by Frank Dikötter. St. Martin's Press 2016 432 p. map $32   **951.056**
1. China -- History -- 1949-1976
ISBN 1632864215; 9781632864215

This book on the Chinese Cultural Revolution, by Frank Dikötter, "draws for the first time on hundreds of previously classified party documents, from secret police reports to unexpurgated versions of leadership speeches. . . . Dikötter uses this wealth of material to undermine the picture of complete conformity that is often supposed to have characterized the last years of the Mao era." (Publisher's note)

"Dikotter tells a harrowing tale of unbelievable suffering. A potent combination of precise history and moving examples, plus a useful chronology of events." Kirkus

Includes bibliographical references and index.

951.06 -2000

Osnos, Evan

★ **Age** of ambition; chasing fortune, truth, and faith in the new China. Evan Osnos. 1st edition Farrar Straus & Giroux 2014 416 p. map (hardback) $27   **951.06**
1. China -- Social conditions 2. China -- Politics and government 3. China -- Civilization 4. Individualism -- China 5. Social change -- China 6. Authoritarianism -- China 7. Economic development -- China
ISBN 0374280746; 9780374280741

LC 2013041338

Pulitzer Prize Finalist: General Nonfiction (2015); National Book Award: Nonfiction (2014)

Author "Evan Osnos was on the ground in China for years, witness to profound political, economic, and cultural upheaval. In 'Age of Ambition,' he describes the greatest collision taking place in that country: the clash between the rise of the individual and the Communist Party's struggle to retain control." (Publisher's note)

"Osnos combines scintillating reportage with an eye for telling ironies that illuminate broader trends; without downplaying the uniqueness of Chinese society, he makes its tensions feel achingly familiar for Western readers." Pub Wkly

Includes bibliographical references index

951.132   Shanghai

Schmitz, Rob

Street of Eternal Happiness; big city dreams along a Shanghai road. Rob Schmitz. Crown Publishers 2016 336 p. maps (hardback) $28   **951.132**
1. Shanghai (China) 2. City and town life -- China -- Shanghai 3. Streets -- China -- Shanghai 4. Shanghai (China) -- Biography 5. Neighborhoods -- China -- Shanghai 6. Shanghai (China) -- Economic conditions 7. Americans -- China -- Shanghai -- Biography 8. Shanghai (China) -- Social life and customs
ISBN 9780553418088

LC 2015041162

This book, by Rob Schmitz, offers a "portrait of individuals who hope, struggle, and grow along a single street cutting through the heart of China's most exhilarating metropolis: . . . Modern Shanghai: a global city in the midst of a renaissance, where dreamers arrive each day to partake in a mad torrent of capital, ideas, and opportunity." (Publisher's note)

"Probing human-interest stories that mine the heart of today's China." Kirkus

Includes bibliographical references (pages 316-322) and index.

951.9   Korea

Brady, James

The **coldest** war; a memoir of Korea. St. Martin's Griffin 2000 248p il map pa $15.95   **951.9**
1. Korean War, 1950-1953 -- Personal narratives
ISBN 978-0-312-26511-3; 0-312-26511-5

First published 1990 by Orion Bks.

"From November 1951 to July 1952, the author was a marine lieutenant who frequently found himself called upon to fight and kill Chinese and North Korean soldiers on the battlefields of Korea. His memoir of that experience is a well-crafted piece told in a voice that skillfully mixes the sardonic insight of an older man looking back on a highly extraordinary episode of his past with the naivete of the young warrior he once was." Booklist

Cumings, Bruce

★ **Korea's** place in the sun; a modern history. Updated ed; W. W. Norton 2005 542p il map pa $16.95   **951.9**
1. Korea -- History
ISBN 0-393-32702-7; 0-393-31681-5

LC 2006-276040

First published 1997

This history of Korea from 1860 focuses primarily on the post-1945 period

"Mr. Cumings has pored over the historical documents and he argues intelligently. His book is important precisely because he marshals considerable evidence to challenge conventional understanding." N Y Times Book Rev

Includes bibliographical references

Cumings, Bruce, 1943-

The **Korean** War; a history. Modern Library 2010 288p il map (Modern Library chronicles)   **951.9**
1. Korean War, 1950-1953 2. Korean War, 1950-1953 -- United

States
ISBN 0-679-64357-5; 978-0-679-64357-9

LC 2010005629

This is a "revisionist history of America's intervention in Korea." (N Y Times (Late N Y Ed)) Index.

A "revisionist history of America's intervention in Korea. Beneath its bland title, Mr. Cumings's book is a squirm-inducing assault on America's moral behavior during the Korean War, a conflict that he says is misremembered when it is remembered at all. It's a book that puts the reflexive anti-Americanism of North Korea's leaders into sympathetic historical context. . . . [Cumings] mows down a host of myths about the war in his short new book, which is a distillation of his own scholarship and that of many other historians." N Y Times (Late N Y Ed)

Includes bibliographical references

Halberstam, David

★ The **coldest** winter; America and the Korean War. Hyperion 2007 719p map $35   **951.9**
1. Korean War, 1950-1953
ISBN 1-401-30052-9; 978-1-401-30052-4

LC 2007-1635

"Alive with the voices of the men who fought, Halberstam's telling is a virtuoso work of history." Publ Wkly

Includes bibliographical references

O'Donnell, Patrick K.

Give me tomorrow; the Korean War's greatest untold story--the epic stand of the marines of George Company. Da Capo 2010 261p il map $26   **951.9**
1. Korean War, 1950-1953 -- Campaigns
ISBN 978-0-306-81801-1
Includes bibliographical references

Oberdorfer, Don

The **two** Koreas; a contemporary history. New ed; Basic Bks. 2001 521p il map pa $21   **951.9**
1. Korea -- History
ISBN 0-465-05162-6

LC 2001-43486

First published 1997 by Addison-Wesley

This is a study of North and South Korean politics and an analysis of U.S. policy from the 1970s to the present

Includes bibliographical references and index

Peterson, Mark

A **brief** history of Korea; [by] Mark Peterson with Phillip Margulies. Facts On File 2010 328p il map (Brief history) $49.50   **951.9**
1. Korea -- History
ISBN 978-0-8160-5085-7

LC 2009-18889

This book "covers the history of Korea from the origins of the Korean people in prehistoric times to the economic and political situation in North and South Korea today." Publisher's note

Includes bibliographical references

951.904   1945-1999

Harden, Blaine

The **Great** Leader and the Fighter Pilot; The True Story of the Tyrant Who Created North Korea and the Young Lieuten-

ant Who Stole His Way to Freedom. by Blaine Harden. Penguin Group USA 2015 288 p. 16 plates; illustrations; maps $27.95   **951.904**
1. United States -- Foreign relations -- Korea (North)
ISBN 0670016578; 9780670016570

LC 2014038542

In this book, author Blaine Harden "tells the . . . story of how Kim Il Sung grabbed power and plunged his country into war against the United States while the youngest fighter pilot in his air force was playing a high-risk game of deception--and escape. As Kim ascended from Soviet puppet to godlike ruler, No Kum Sok noisily pretended to love his Great Leader. That is, until he swiped a Soviet MiG-15 and delivered it to the Americans." (Publisher's note)

"An enjoyable read that is highly recommended for those interested in Cold War or North Korean history, or for anyone who likes a strong narrative. Readers who enjoy this book might also appreciate No Kum-Sok's A MiG-15 to Freedom." LJ

Hickey, Michael

The **Korean** War; the West confronts communism. Overlook Press 2000 397p il maps $35   **951.904**
1. Korean War, 1950-1953 2. United Nations -- Armed Forces -- Korea
ISBN 1-58567-035-9

LC 00-27692

First published 1999 in the United Kingdom

An "analysis of both the military and political factors that caused the war and the conduct on all sides. . . . The author does not mince words when criticizing General MacArthur and other UN commanders. Using declassified documents as well as regimental and personal diaries, he wades through political intrigue and military disasters and triumphs to give us a memorable account." Libr J

Includes bibliographical references

Hutton, Robin

Sgt. Reckless; America's war horse. Robin Hutton. Regnery Publishing 2014 346 p. illustrations (alk. paper) $27.99   **951.904**
1. Horses 2. Animals -- War use 3. Korean War, 1950-1953 -- Biography 4. Korean War, 1950-1953 -- Campaigns 5. Korean War, 1950-1953 -- Artillery operations 6. United States. Marine Corps -- History 7. War horses -- Korea (South) -- History -- 20th century 8. War horses -- United States -- History -- 20th century 9. United States. Marine Corps. Marine Regiment, 5th -- Biography
ISBN 1621572633; 9781621572633

LC 2014019750

This book, by Robin Hutton, tells the story of "a Mongolian mare who was bred to be a racehorse . . . , purchased . . . and renamed . . . Reckless, for the Recoilless Rifles Platoon, Anti-Tank Division, of the 5th Marines she'd be joining. . . . This . . . equine became an American hero. Reckless was awarded two Purple Hearts for her valor and was officially promoted to staff sergeant twice, a distinction never bestowed upon an animal before or since." (Publisher's note)

"Hutton's passion and admiration for her subject (she also heads an effort to create a monument to Reckless) shines through in this sparkling and engaging portrait of a most remarkable and courageous animal." Pub Wkly

Includes bibliographical references and index
Sergeant Reckless, America's war horse

Makos, Adam

Devotion; An Epic Story of Heroism, Friendship, and Sacrifice. by Adam Makos. Random House Inc. 2015 464 p. 16 plates; illustrations; maps $28 **951.904**

ISBN 0804176582; 9780804176583

LC 2015023955

This book, by Adam Makos, "tells the inspirational story of the U.S. Navy's most famous aviator duo, Lieutenant Tom Hudner and Ensign Jesse Brown, and the Marines they fought to defend. A white New Englander from the country-club scene, Tom passed up Harvard to fly fighters for his country. An African American sharecropper's son from Mississippi, Jesse became the navy's first black carrier pilot, defending a nation that wouldn't even serve him in a bar." (Publisher's note)

Weintraub, Stanley, 1929-

A **Christmas** far from home; an epic tale of courage and survival during the Korean War. Stanley Weintraub. Da Capo Press, a member of the Perseus Books Group Press 2014 304 p. illustrations, maps (hardcover) $26.99 **951.904**

1. Christmas 2. United States. Army 3. Korean War, 1950-1953 4. Soldiers -- United States 5. Courage -- Korea (North) -- History -- 20th century 6. Escapes -- Korea (North) -- History -- 20th century 7. Marines -- United States -- History -- 20th century 8. Soldiers -- United States -- History -- 20th century 9. Survival -- Korea (North) -- History -- 20th century 10. Christmas -- Korea (North) -- History -- 20th century 11. United States. Army. Corps, 10th -- History -- 20th century 12. Korean War, 1950-1953 -- Regimental histories -- United States 13. Korean War, 1950-1953 -- Campaigns -- Korea (North) -- Changjin Reservoir

ISBN 0306822326; 9780306822322

LC 2014011944

In this book, by Stanley Weintraub, "five months into the Korean War, General Douglas MacArthur flew to American positions in the north and grandly announced an end-the-war-by-Christmas offensive. . . . Marching north in plunging temperatures, General Edward Almond's X Corps, which included a Marine division under the able leadership of General Oliver Smith, encountered little resistance. But thousands of Chinese . . . were lying in wait and would soon trap tens of thousands of US troops." (Publisher's note)

"The tragic tale of how the arrogance of a general led to disastrous consequences for the American troops in North Korea in 1950... Weintraub expertly delineates the unraveling disaster for the entrapped, frozen, dispirited troops on the ground." Kirkus

Includes bibliographical references and index

951.93 North Korea (People's Democratic Republic of Korea)

Cha, Victor

The **impossible** state; North Korea, past and future. Victor Cha. Ecco 2012 xii, 530 p.p illustrations (chiefly color) (hardcover) $29.99 **951.93**

1. Korea (North) 2. Political culture 3. Korea (North) -- Social conditions 4. Korea (North) -- Politics and government 5. Political culture -- Korea (North) -- History 6. Korea (North) -- Foreign relations -- United States 7. United States -- Foreign relations -- Korea (North)

ISBN 9780062200150; 9780061998508; 9780061998515; 0061998508

LC 2012009517

This book, by Victor Cha, offers a "look . . . at North Korea's history, the rise of the Kim family dynasty, and the obsessive personality cult that empowers them. He illuminates the repressive regime's complex economy and culture, its appalling record of human-rights abuses, and its belligerent relationship with the United States, and analyzes the regime's major security issues." (Publisher's note)

"A useful, pertinent work for understanding the human story behind the headlines." Kirkus

Includes bibliographical references and index

Demick, Barbara

★ **Nothing** to envy; ordinary lives in North Korea. Barbara Demick. Spiegel & Grau 2009 xii, 314 p.p illustrations, maps (hardcover) $27 **951.93**

1. Korea (North) 2. Korea (North) -- Social conditions -- 21st century 3. Korea (North) -- Economic conditions -- 21st century 4. Koreans -- Korea (North) -- Social conditions -- 21st century -- Case studies 5. Koreans -- Korea (North) -- Economic conditions -- 21st century -- Case studies

ISBN 9780385529617; 9780385523905; 0385523904

LC 2009022420

National Book Award Finalist: Nonfiction (2010)

This book, by Barbara Demick, "follows the lives of six North Korean citizens over fifteen years—a chaotic period that saw the death of Kim Il-sung, the rise to power of his son Kim Jong-il (the father of Kim Jong-un), and a devastating famine that killed one-fifth of the population." (Publisher's note)

"Strongly written and gracefully structured, Demick's potent blend of personal narratives and piercing journalism vividly and evocatively portrays courageous individuals and a tyrannized state within a saga of unfathomable suffering punctuated by faint glimmers of hope." Booklist

Includes bibliographical references (p. [299]-314)

Hassig, Ralph C.

The **hidden** people of North Korea; everyday life in the hermit kingdom. [by] Ralph Hassig and Kongdan Oh. Rowman & Littlefield Publishers 2009 300p il $39.95 **951.93**

1. Heads of state 2. Korea (North) 3. Communist leaders 4. Korea (North) -- Social conditions 5. Political culture -- Korea (North) 6. Korea (North) -- Economic conditions 7. Korea (North) -- Politics and government

ISBN 978-0-7425-6718-4; 0-7425-6718-4

LC 2009-29786

The authors "gather behind-the-curtain research to expose day-to-day life, and the powers that control it, in North Korea, a developed nation where meat is a luxury and the Internet doesn't exist for anyone but the dictator. . . . The uninformed will find much that's fascinating and shocking: a nation of castes and concentration camps, replete with a politics of fear that rivals the worst Orwell could imagine." Publ Wkly

Includes bibliographical references

Jeppesen, Travis

See you again in Pyongyang; a journey into Kim Jong Un's North Korea. Travis Jeppesen. Hachette Books 2018 304 p. (hardcover) $28 **951.93**

1. Korea (North) -- Social conditions 2. Korea (North) -- Description and travel

ISBN 9780316509138; 9780316509152; 9781549169137

LC 2018934067

In this book, author Travis Jeppesen, "the first American to complete a university program in North Korea, culls from his experiences living, traveling, and studying in the country to create a multifaceted portrait of the country and its idiosyncratic capital city in the Kim Jong Un Era. . . . Jeppesen takes readers behind the propaganda, showing how the North Korean system actually works in daily life." (Publisher's note)

Lankov, Andrei

The **real** North Korea; life and politics in the failed Stalinist utopia. Andrei Lankov. Oxford University Press 2013 304 p. (hardcover) $27.95   **951.93**

1. Korea (North) -- Social conditions 2. Korea (North) -- Politics and government 3. Korea (North) -- Foreign relations 4. Korea (North) -- Politics and government -- 1994-

ISBN 0199964297; 9780199964291

LC 2012046992

This first half of this book by Andrei Lankov "provides an overview of North Korea's past history, and discusses how it has changed in the years since the famine of the 1990s. The second half predicts that the North Korean regime will ultimately collapse, then discusses likely outcomes of this event." (Library Journal)

Includes bibliographical references and index

Pearson, James

North Korea confidential; private markets, fashion trends, prison camps, dissenters and defectors. Daniel Tudor and James Pearson. Tuttle Pub 2015 224 p. color illustrations (hardcover) $21.95   **951.93**

1. Crime -- Korea (North) 2. Korea (North) -- Social conditions 3. Korea (North) -- Politics and government 4. Fashion -- Korea (North) 5. Human rights -- Korea (North) 6. Korea (North) -- History -- 21st century 7. Korea (North) -- Social conditions -- 21st century 8. Korea (North) -- Economic conditions -- 21st century

ISBN 0804844585; 9781462915125; 9780804844581

LC 2016469265

This book, by Daniel Tudor and James Pearson, describes "how North Korea functions by opportunistic entrepreneurism abetted by bribery. After the North Korean economy and government failed in the 1990s, most of the population, from ordinary citizens to upper-level bureaucrats, survived by hustling--buying, selling, and stealing from the government--beneath the illusion of dictatorial control." (Kirkus Reviews)

"Rather than describing a gray, economically stagnant, and totalitarian society dominated by dictator Kim Jong Un, veteran journalists and coauthors Tudor and Pearson paint a vivid portrait of how North Korea functions by opportunistic entrepreneurism abetted by bribery." LJ

Includes bibliographical references and index.

952   Japan

Jansen, Marius B.

The **making** of modern Japan. Belknap Press 2000 871p il maps $35; pa $18.95   **952**

1. Japan -- History

ISBN 0-674-00334-9; 0-674-00991-6 pa

LC 00-41352

"Jansen has produced what is sure to become the standard narrative history of modern Japan. . . . In every way this is a remarkable book . . . and no reference collection on Japan can pretend to be complete without it." Choice

Includes bibliographical references

McClain, James L.

Japan, a modern history. Norton 2001 632p il maps $35; pa $31.25   **952**

1. Japan -- History

ISBN 0-393-04156-5; 0-393-97720-X pa

LC 2001-34545

"This is a well-written, well-researched, and easily readable survey of the modern history of a fascinating and important nation." Booklist

Includes bibliographical references

Mockett, Marie Mutsuki

Where the Dead Pause, and the Japanese Say Goodbye; A Journey. by Marie Mutsuki Mockett. W W Norton & Co Inc 2015 336 p. $26.95   **952**

1. Grief 2. Sendai Earthquake, Japan, 2011 3. Fukushima Nuclear Accident, Fukushima, Japan, 2011

ISBN 0393063011; 9780393063011

LC 2014032438

In this memoir, "Marie Mutsuki Mockett's family owns a Buddhist temple 25 miles from the Fukushima Daiichi nuclear power plant. In March 2011, after the earthquake and tsunami, radiation levels prohibited the burial of her Japanese grandfather's bones. As Japan mourned thousands of people lost in the disaster, Mockett also grieved for her American father, who had died unexpectedly. Seeking consolation, Mockett is guided by a colorful cast of Zen priests and ordinary Japanese." (Publisher's note)

"Mockett's involving and revelatory chronicle of Japanese spirituality in a time of crisis greatly enriches our perceptions of both a unique culture and the human longing for connection with the dead." Booklist

952.03   Japan--1868-1945

Buruma, Ian

Inventing Japan, 1853-1964. Modern Lib. 2003 194p hardcover o.p. pa $12.95   **952.03**

1. Japan -- History

ISBN 0-679-64085-1; 0-8129-7286-4 pa

LC 2002-26346

"Buruma traces the remarkable metamorphosis that transformed an isolated island shogunate into an expansive military empire and then into a pacified and prosperous democracy. . . . An excellent introductory study." Booklist

Includes bibliographical references

Gordon, Andrew

The **modern** history of Japan. Oxford University Press 2003 384p il $35; pa $29.95   **952.03**

1. Japan -- History

ISBN 0-19-511060-9; 0-19-511061-7 pa

LC 2002-70916

The author examines "Japan's political, economic, social, and cultural inventions of its modernity in evolving international contexts, incorporating inside viewpoints and debates. Beyond identifying the national stages (feudalism, militarism, democracy), the author innovatively emphasizes how labor unions, cultural figures, and groups in society (especially women) have been affected over time and have responded." Libr J

Includes bibliographical references and index

Keene, Donald

Emperor of Japan: Meiji and His world, 1852-1912. Columbia Univ. Press 2002 922p il $82.50; pa $27.95 **952.03**

1. Emperors 2. Japan -- History -- 1868-1945

ISBN 0-231-12340-X; 0-231-12341-8 pa

LC 2001-28826

This is a "biography-cum-history of Emperor Meiji and his times. . . . Meiji's reign saw Japan become fully industrialized under a brand new constitution, and with new economic and educational systems adopted. Despite the book's massive scale, Keene's graceful writing holds the reader's interest throughout." Booklist

Includes bibliographical references

Seagrave, Sterling

The **Yamato** dynasty; the secret history of Japan's Imperial family. Broadway Bks. 2000 394p il hardcover o.p. pa $23   **952.03**

1. Emperors 2. Japan -- Kings and rulers 3. Japan -- Politics and government

ISBN 0-7679-0497-4 pa

LC 99-49888

This "history of Japan from the mid-19th century to the present weaves together an iconoclastic historical narrative with a mostly caustic view of Japan's imperial family. The Seagraves depict modern Japan as a country consistently dominated by a closed financial oligarchy in league with politicians, bureaucrats, the imperial family, and underworld bosses." Libr J

Includes bibliographical references

952.05 Japan - 2000

Parry, Richard Lloyd

Ghosts of the Tsunami; Death and Life in Japan's Disaster Zone. Richard Lloyd Parry. MCD / Farrar, Straus and Giroux 2017 x, 295 p.p illustrations, maps (hardcover) $27 **952.05**

1. Tsunamis 2. Earthquakes -- Japan 3. Sendai Earthquake, Japan, 2011 4. Japan -- History -- Heisei period, 1989- 5. Tohoku Earthquake and Tsunami, Japan, 2011 6. Tsunamis -- Japan -- History -- 21st century

ISBN 0374253978; 9780374710934; 9780374253974

LC 2017021678

This book, by Richard Lloyd Parry, is "the definitive account of what happened, why, and above all how it felt, when catastrophe hit Japan. . . . On March 11, 2011, a powerful earthquake sent a 120-foot-high tsunami smashing into the coast of northeast Japan. By the time the sea retreated, more than eighteen thousand people had been crushed, burned to death, or drowned." (Publisher's note)

"A sobering and compelling narrative of calamity." Kirkus

Includes bibliographical references and index.

953 Arabian Peninsula and adjacent areas

Filiu, Jean-Pierre

Gaza; A History. Jean-Pierre Filiu; translated by John King. Oxford University Press 2014 384 p. maps $29.95 **953**

1. Gaza Strip 2. Gaza -- History 3. Arab-Israeli conflict 4. Gaza Strip -- History 5. Land settlement -- Gaza 6. Gaza Strip -- Social conditions 7. Gaza Strip -- Economic conditions 8. Gaza Strip -- Politics and government 9. Social conflict -- Gaza Strip -- History

ISBN 0190201894; 9780190201890

LC 2013497342

This book, by Jean-Pierre Filiu, presents the history of Gaza. "Wedged between the Negev and Sinai deserts on one side and the Mediterranean Sea on the other, Gaza was contested by the Pharaohs, Persians, Greeks, Romans, Byzantines, Arabs, Fatimids, Mamluks, Crusaders, and Ottomans. Then in 1948, 200,000 people sought refuge in Gaza. . . . It is here that Palestinian nationalism grew and sprouted into a dream of statehood, a journey much filled with strife." (Publisher's note)

"While the chronological account leaves out some significant discussions, such as everyday politics in Gaza, as in Asef Bayat's Life as Politics: How Ordinary People Change the Middle East (CH, Aug'10, 47-7167), Filiu is at his best when he engages with various sources in uncovering histories mostly ignored or even unknown to many. A must read for students and scholars of the modern Middle East, and anyone who wants to understand Palestinian history. Summing Up: Essential. All public and academic libraries." Choice

Includes bibliographical references (pages 375-379) and indexes

Krane, Jim

City of gold; Dubai and the dream of capitalism. St. Martin's Press 2009 356p il map $27.99 **953**

1. Dubai (United Arab Emirates)

ISBN 9780312535742

LC 2009-13188

The author "traces the historical roots and economic and political changes of 'a small Arab village that grew into a big city' and profiles the members of the ruling royal family—Sheikh Rashid, Sheikh Zayed, and Sheikh Mohammed—whose vision brought Dubai to where it is today. . . . This landmark work is recommended to those interested in the history, politics, and economics of the Middle East; an excellent choice for anyone who wishes to learn more about Dubai." Libr J

Includes bibliographical references

953.305 Yemen, 1918-

Kasinof, Laura

Don't be afraid of the bullets; an accidental war correspondent in Yemen. Laura Kasinof. Arcade Publishing 2014 304 p. map (hardcover) $24.95 **953.305**

1. Yemen 2. Protest movements 3. Arab Spring, 2010- 4. War correspondents 5. Americans -- Yemen (Republic) -- Biography 6. Ṣanʿāʾ (Yemen) -- Biography 7. Yemen (Republic) -- History -- 1990- -- Biography 8. War correspondents -- Yemen (Republic) -- Biography 9. Foreign correspondents -- Yemen (Republic) -- Biography 10. Yemen (Republic) -- Politics and government -- 21st century 11. Ṣanʿāʾ (Yemen) -- Description and travel 12. Protest movements -- Yemen (Republic) -- History -- 21st century 13. Ṣanʿāʾ (Yemen) -- Social conditions -- 21st century

ISBN 1628724455; 9781628724455

LC 2014019103

This memoir tells the story of freelance journalist Laura Kasinof. "When she first moved to [Yemen] in 2009, she was the only American reporter based in the country. . . . When antigovernment protests broke out in [2011], . . . she contacted the 'New York Times' to see if she could cover the rapidly unfolding events for the newspaper. Laura never planned to be a war correspondent, but found herself in the middle of brutal government attacks on peaceful protesters." (Publisher's note)

"By the book's end, she is sharper, savvier and a confirmed Yemenophile. Even if the reader doesn't fully grasp the appeal Yemen holds for Kasinof, her passion for the country still makes for a compelling tale."

953.8 Saudi Arabia

House, Karen Elliott

On Saudi Arabia; its people, past, religion, fault lines--and future. Karen Elliott House. 1st ed. Alfred A. Knopf 2012 x, 308 p.p ill., map (hardcover) $28.95 **953.8**

1. Saudi Arabia -- History 2. Saudi Arabia -- Politics and government

3. Saudi Arabia -- Religion 4. Saudi Arabia -- Civilization 5. Saudi Arabia -- Social life and customs
ISBN 0307272168; 9780307272164

LC 2012018977

This book, by Pulitzer Prize-winning reporter Karen Elliott House, "explores all facets of life in . . . [Saudi Arabia]: its tribal past, its complicated present, its precarious future. Through observation, anecdote, extensive interviews, and analysis Karen Elliot House navigates the maze in which Saudi citizens find themselves trapped and reveals the mysterious nation that is the world's largest exporter of oil, critical to global stability, and a source of Islamic terrorists." (Publisher's note)

Includes bibliographical references (p. 281-289)

Lacey, Robert

Inside the Kingdom; kings, clerics, modernists, terrorists, and the struggle for Saudi Arabia. Viking 2009 404p il map $27.95   **953.8**
1. Saudi Arabia -- Social conditions
ISBN 978-0-670-02118-5; 0-670-02118-0

LC 2009-08367

Sequel to The kingdom (1982)

The author's "eye for sweeping trends and the telling detail combined with the depth, breadth and evenhandedness of his research makes for an indispensable guide." Publ Wkly

Includes bibliographical references

Wynbrandt, James

A **brief** history of Saudi Arabia; foreword by Fawaz A. Gerges. 2nd ed; Facts On File 2010 364p il map (Brief history) $49.50; pa $19.95   **953.8**
1. Saudi Arabia -- History
ISBN 978-0-8160-7876-9; 978-0-8160-8250-6 pa

LC 2010-5466

First published 2004

This history of Saudi Arabia covers "pre-Islamic Arabia; Bedouin society and culture; the birth and spread of Islam; the development of and philosophy behind Wahhabism; the origins of House Saud; Saudi Arabia's role in the Middle East; Saudi Arabia's relationship to the United States; the battle between conservative and progressive elements in the monarchy today; [and] the reign of King Abdullah." Publisher's note

Includes glossary and bibliographical references

954 India and neighboring south Asian countries

Dalrymple, William

White Mughals; love and betrayal in the eighteenth-century India. Viking 2003 xlvii, 459p il map $34.95; pa $16   **954**
1. British -- India
ISBN 0-670-03184-4; 0-14-200412-X pa

LC 2002-191082

James Kirkpatrick was the Resident of the East India Company in Hyderabad. This book documents his marriage to Khair-un-Nissa, a Mughal aristocrat

This "book, ambitious in scope and rich in detail, demonstrates that a century before Kipling's 'never the twain'—and two centuries before neocons and radical Islamists trumpeted the clash of civilizations—the story of the Westerner in Muslim India was one not of conquest but of appreciation, adaptation, and seduction." New Yorker

Includes bibliographical references

Hajari, Nisid

Midnight's furies; the deadly legacy of India's partition. Nisid Hajari. Houghton Mifflin Harcourt 2015 304 p. 8 pages; illustrations (hardcover) $28   **954**
1. Pakistan -- History 2. India -- History -- 1947- 3. India-Pakistan Conflict, 1947-1949 4. India -- History -- Partition, 1947 5. Pakistan -- History -- 20th century
ISBN 0547669216; 9780547669212

LC 2014034426

This book, by Nisid Hajari, discusses the history of the partition of India and Pakistan. "Nobody expected the liberation of India and birth of Pakistan to be so bloody. . . . As the summer of 1947 approached, all three groups were heavily armed and on edge, and the British rushed to leave. . . . Some of the most brutal and widespread ethnic cleansing in modern history erupted on both sides of the new border, searing a divide between India and Pakistan that remains a root cause of many evils." (Publisher's note)

Includes bibliographical references and index

Khilnani, Sunil

Incarnations; a history of India in fifty lives. Sunil Khilnani. First American edition Farrar, Straus & Giroux 2016 ix, 449 p.p illustrations (chiefly color) (hardback) $30   **954**
1. India -- History 2. India -- Biography
ISBN 9780374715427; 9780374175498

LC 2016007101

This book, by Sunil Khilnani, "bring[s] to life fifty extraordinary men and women who changed both India and the world. Journeying across India in pursuit of their stories—visiting slum temples, ayurvedic call centers, Bollywood studios, textile mills, and Mughal fortresses—Khilnani offers trenchant portraits of emperors, warriors, philosophers, artists, iconoclasts, and entrepreneurs" (Publisher's note)

"Khilnani's essays are provocative and serious, a worthy rebuttal to the image of Indian history as 'curiously unpeopled.'" Pub Wkly

Includes bibliographical references (pages [401]-426) and index

Lapierre, Dominique

The **City** of Joy. Warner Books 1991 528p il pa $7.99 **954**
1. Calcutta (India) -- Social conditions
ISBN 0-446-35556-9

Original French edition, 1985

An account of life in the most squalid of Calcutta's slums, Anand Nagar (The City of Joy). The author focuses on the lives of a rickshaw driver, a Polish Catholic priest, an American doctor and an Assamese nurse.

Mehta, Suketu

★ **Maximum** city; Bombay lost and found. Alfred A. Knopf 2004 542p $27.95   **954**
1. Bombay (India)
ISBN 0-375-40372-8

LC 2004-48969

The author "explores various aspects of Bombay life, from setting up residence to exploring the hugely successful domestic film industry; from detailing Bombay's sex industry to profiling the reasons behind India's own 'September 11,' the 1993 riots and bombings that exposed a vast enmity between extremist Hindus and Muslims. . . . Mehta delivers a fresh and unblinking look at contemporary Bombay." Booklist

Rashid, Ahmed

Descent into chaos; the US and the failure of nation building in Pakistan, Afghanistan, and Central Asia. Viking 2008

lviii, 484p il map $27.95; pa $18   **954**
1. Pakistan -- Politics and government 2. Afghanistan -- Politics and government 3. Central Asia -- Foreign relations -- United States 4. United States -- Foreign relations -- Central Asia
ISBN 978-0-670-01970-0; 0-670-01970-4; 978-0-14-311557-1 pa; 0-14-311557-X pa

LC 2008-02949

This is a "lucid, insightful, and highly readable tome on the existent and emergent threats in Central Asia." Choice
Includes bibliographical references

Roy, Arundhati
Walking with the comrades. Penguin Books 2011 220p il map pa $15   **954**
1. Terrorism 2. Atrocities 3. Guerrillas 4. Social conflict 5. India -- Politics and government
ISBN 978-0-14-312059-9

LC 2011039307

The author "exposes the violent contradictions of India's economic miracle in this blistering critique of the Indian government's campaign against the Maoist insurgents in the country's central tribal lands encompassing several states. Roy, who recounts time spent on the move with a cadre of rebels, argues forcefully that Operation Green Hunt—launched by the state under the rubric of the threat of terrorism—is an all-out war to remove indigenous communities from lands already promised to corporations eager to exploit their extremely valuable resources. . . . Informed, impassioned, at times strident, and fleet and fascinating when describing life on the ground among the rebels, Roy's prose will both rouse and ruffle." Publ Wkly
Includes bibliographical references

Sen, Amartya Kumar
The **argumentative** Indian; writings on Indian history, culture, and identity. [by] Amartya Sen. Farrar, Straus and Giroux 2006 xx, 409p il   **954**
1. India -- Civilization
ISBN 0-374-10583-9

LC 2005-49460

"Sen's lucid reasoning and thoroughgoing humanism . . . ensure a lively and commanding defense of diversity and dialogue." Publ Wkly
Includes bibliographical references

Walsh, Judith E.
A **brief** history of India; 2nd ed.; Facts On File, Inc. 2010 414p il map (Brief history) $49.50; pa $19.95   **954**
1. India -- History
ISBN 978-0-8160-8143-1; 978-0-8160-8362-6 pa

LC 2010-26316

First published 2006

"The Brief History series introduces readers to the dramatic events, notable people, and special customs and traditions that have shaped many of the world's countries. Each engaging volume covers a specific country and offers a concise history of the struggles and triumphs of the peoples and cultures that have called that country home." (Publisher's note)

"The book surveys India's history in about 300 pages, with a number of pictures and short in-depth sidebars on items such as "Rajput Clans" and "Dowry Deaths." Walsh (SUNY, Old Westbury) begins with India's geography and concludes with a section on contemporary India. . . . The book is most suitable for those wanting a very quick, basic introduction to India's history and culture." Choice
Includes bibliographical references

Wolpert, Stanley A.
A **new** history of India; 7th ed; Oxford University Press 2004 530p il map $63.95; pa $43   **954**
1. Mogul Empire
ISBN 0-19-516677-9; 0-19-516678-7 pa

LC 2003-53589

First published 1977. Periodically revised

A comprehensive survey of Indian history from its early beginnings to the present. Includes discussion of the assassination of Rajiv Gandhi; violence in Kashmir, Punjab, and Assam; and the effects of rural development
Includes bibliographical references

954.03   India--Period of British rule, 1785-1947

Chadha, Yogesh
Gandhi; a life. Wiley 1998 546p il hardcover o.p. pa $19.95   **954.03**
1. Authors 2. Journalists 3. Essayists 4. Pacifists 5. Memoirists 6. Political leaders 7. Writers on politics 8. India -- Politics and government
ISBN 0-471-35062-1 pa

LC 97-37406

First published 1997 in the United Kingdom with title: Rediscovering Gandhi

"Chadha reexamines Gandhi's life with an eye to restoring its complications and contradictions, noting that 'to suppress his weaknesses would be to undermine his strengths.' And he succeeds in his mission, presenting the great leader not as a holy man but as a humanist and politician." Booklist
Includes bibliographical references

Wolpert, Stanley A.
★ **Gandhi's** passion; the life and legacy of Mahatma Gandhi. [by] Stanley Wolpert. Oxford Univ. Press 2001 308p il hardcover o.p. pa $17.95   **954.03**
1. Authors 2. Journalists 3. Essayists 4. Pacifists 5. Memoirists 6. Political leaders 7. Writers on politics 8. India -- Politics and government
ISBN 0-19-513060-X; 0-19-515634-X pa

LC 00-45298

"From his pampered childhood to his ascetic final years, the text follows the Mahatma ('Great Soul') on a paradoxical pilgrimage in which the deliberate acceptance of suffering endowed him with the power he needed to challenge the leading politicians of Europe, Africa, and Asia." Booklist
Includes bibliographical references

954.04   India 1947-1971

French, Patrick
India; a portrait. Alfred A. Knopf 2011 398p il $30 **954.04**
1. India -- History -- 1947-
ISBN 978-0-307-27243-0; 0-307-27243-5

LC 2011-03921

This work "combines deep research about the country's history with a series of vignettes culled from French's street-level reporting. Taken together, his reading of seminal texts and his interviews with politicians, pimps, businessmen, laborers, farmers, scholars and people from all levels of India's caste system result in a fittingly vigorous and colorful book about what it means to live in India six decades after the nation freed itself from British rule." San Francisco Chron

Includes bibliographical references

Guha, Ramachandra

India after Gandhi; the history of the world's largest democracy. Ecco 2007 893p il map $34.95   **954.04**

1. India -- History -- 1947-

ISBN 978-0-06-019881-7; 0-06-019881-8

            LC 2006-52180

This book documents India's transformation from a colonial state to independence.

The author "builds his story by making us witnesses of events as they occur, drawing on contemporary accounts. His voluminous account may seem daunting, but it is crucial for the understanding of modern India. . . . Guha is patient in his approach, gentle in his criticism, exasperated by what he does not like, and eclectic in drawing on evidence that supports his argument." New Statesman

Includes bibliographical references

Tharoor, Shashi

Nehru: the invention of India. Arcade Pub 2003 282p $24.95; pa $13.95   **954.04**

1. Prime ministers 2. Nonfiction writers 3. Prime ministers -- India

ISBN 1-559-70697-X; 1-559-70737-2 pa

            LC 2003-58274

The author touches "on key points in Nehru's life: his English education, the importance of guidance he received from his father and Gandhi, his prison years during the drive for independence, and his administration of the new Indian republic. He neatly pulls together the essence of Nehru's beliefs in democratic institution building, pan-Indian secularism, Socialist democratic economy, and the foreign policy of nonalignment. . . . If readers could choose only one narrative about Nehru, this would suffice." Libr J

Includes bibliographical references

954.05   India -- 1971

Deb, Siddhartha

The **beautiful** and the damned; Siddhartha Deb. Faber and Faber, Inc. 2011 253p.   **954.05**

1. Journalism 2. Globalization 3. Cultural critique 4. India -- Social conditions 5. India -- Civilization -- 21st century 6. India -- Social conditions -- 21st century 7. India -- Economic conditions -- 21st century 8. India -- Politics and government -- 21st century

ISBN 9780865478732; 0865478627; 9780865478626

            LC 2011024408

This book "examines India's many contradictions through various individual . . . perspectives. . . . [Author Siddhartha] Deb introduces the reader to an unforgettable group of Indians, including a Gatsby-like mogul in Delhi whose hobby is producing big-budget gangster films that no one sees; a wiry, dusty farmer named Gopeti whose village is plagued by suicides and was the epicenter of a riot; and a sad-eyed waitress named Esther who has set aside her dual degrees in biochemistry and botany to serve Coca-Cola to arms dealers at an upscale hotel called Shangri La." (Publisher's note)

Giridharadas, Anand

India calling; an intimate portrait of a nation's remaking. Times Books/Henry Holt and Co. 2011 273p $25; ebook $11.99   **954.05**

1. Journalists 2. India -- Civilization 3. Social change -- India 4. India -- Social conditions 5. India -- Civilization -- 1947- 6. India -- Description and travel 7. India -- Social life and customs 8. India -- Social conditions -- 1947- 9. National characteristics, East Indian

ISBN 0-8050-9177-7; 1-4299-5062-5 ebook; 978-0-8050-9177-9; 978-1-4299-5062-6 pa

            LC 2010-18447

The author, who is "an American, traces his parents' journey from India." (N Y Times Book Rev) Index.

This "is a fine book, elegant, self-aware and unafraid of contradictions and complexity. Giridharadas captures fundamental changes in the nature of family and class relationships and the very idea of what it means to be an Indian." N Y Times Book Rev

Mishra, Pankaj

★ **Temptations** of the West; how to be modern in India, Pakistan, Tibet, and beyond. Farrar, Straus & Giroux 2006 323p $25   **954.05**

1. South Asia -- Description and travel

ISBN 0-374-17321-4; 978-0-374-17321-0

            LC 2006-11987

"It is impossible in a short form to do justice to the density and complexity of . . . [the author's] arguments, to his comprehensive illustrations, to his scathing demolition of the comfort zones of both East and West, and to the intrepid and endlessly questioning spirit which lies behind his book." N Y Rev Books

954.1   Northeastern India

Black, George

On the Ganges; encounters with saints and sinners on India's mythic river. George Black. St. Martin's Press 2018 336 p. (hardcover) $29.99   **954.1**

1. Rivers -- India 2. Rivers -- Bangladesh 3. Ganges River (India and Bangladesh) -- Description and travel 4. Ganges River (India and Bangladesh) -- Social life and customs

ISBN 9781250057358

            LC 2018003985

This book, by George Black, "introduces us to a vivid and often eccentric cast of characters who worship the [Ganges] river, pollute it, and flock to it from all over the world in search of enlightenment and adventure. Black encounters those who run the corrupt cremation business, workers who eke out a living in squalid factories, religious fanatics, and Brits who continue to live as if the Raj had never ended." (Publisher's note)

"Black is a great storyteller, putting scenarios—some familiar, others verging on the surreal—into context. Never condescending or sensationalized, but always interesting, his vignettes capture India's continuing dependence on Ma Ganga, the great Ganges River." Booklist

954.9   Other jurisdictions

Napoli, Lisa

Radio Shangri-La; what I learned in the happiest kingdom on earth. Crown Publishers 2010 xx, 277p $25   **954.9**

1. Bhutan -- Description and travel

ISBN 978-0-307-45302-0; 978-0-307-45304-4 ebook

            LC 2009-49176

"The author provides a readable account of her life-changing decision to leave the comforts of her cosmopolitan Los Angeles life and serve as a volunteer at Kuzoo FM 90, a radio station for young people in the remote Himalayan kingdom of Bhutan. Disillusioned with her love life and fed up with her job as a public-radio commentator, Napoli took a chance on a mysterious stranger's offer of unpaid work in a country where '[b]eing, not having' and '[h]appiness above wealth' were the prevailing national philosophies. . . . The author's authentic voice and light, pleasant cultural insights make for a refreshingly uplifting book." Kirkus

Includes bibliographical references

954.91   Pakistan

Gull, Imtiaz
The **most** dangerous place; Pakistan's lawless frontier. Viking 2010 xxx, 282p map   **954.91**
1. Terrorism 2. Taliban 3. Al Qaeda (Organization)
ISBN 0-670-02225-X; 978-0-670-02225-0
LC 2010-01898
First published 2009 in India with title: The al Qaeda connection
Gul "tracks the Taliban and al-Qaeda insurgents into the mountainous tribal regions to investigate the tangle of perilous allegiances. The destabilized Afghanistan-Pakistan border region is constantly in the news as the Obama administration attempts to flush out the militants using the area as a base to train soldiers and launch terrorist attacks. In a dense, timely study, the author investigates the complicated makeup of these groups. . . . Informational rather than didactic, Gul's insider take will serve as an excellent resource." Kirkus
Includes bibliographical references

Inskeep, Steve
Instant city; life and death in Karachi. Penguin Press 2011 284p il map $27.95   **954.91**
1. Karachi (Pakistan) -- Social conditions 2. Karachi (Pakistan) -- Description and travel
ISBN 978-1-59420-315-2; 1-59420-315-6
LC 2011020673
Analyzes the growing metropolis of Karachi, Pakistan, including the importance of regional stability to American security interests, the terrorist bombing of a Shia religious procession, and the challenging religious, ethnic, and political divides.
"This is an intimate book about a megacity, and Inskeep succeeds by keeping his ambitions modest. By trying to understand the horrific event of one particular day, he keeps his narrative well paced and full of small surprises. The book sparkles when Inskeep takes an unexpected turn and follows a stranger, or when he tracks down a new trend to illuminate a new facet of the city." Publ Wkly
Includes bibliographical references

Lieven, Anatol
Pakistan; a hard country. PublicAffairs 2011   558p il $35   **954.91**
1. Pakistan -- History 2. Pakistan -- Social conditions 3. Pakistan -- Politics and government 4. Pakistan -- Politics and government -- 1988-
ISBN 978-1-61039-021-7; 1-61039-021-0
LC 2011-921821
"Lieven breaks down his study by specific region; considers the structures of justice, religion, the military and politics in turn; and, finally, in a skillful, insightful synthesis, addresses the history of and issues concerning the Taliban, both Pakistani and Afghani. A well-reasoned, welcome resource for Western 'experts' and lay readers alike." Kirkus

Schmidle, Nicholas
To live or to perish forever; two tumultuous years in Pakistan. Henry Holt and Co. 2009 254p il map $25   **954.91**
1. Pakistan -- Description and travel 2. Pakistan -- Politics and government
ISBN 978-0-8050-8938-7; 0-8050-8938-1
LC 2008-48373
"Schmidle offers a gripping, grim account of his two years as a journalism fellow in Pakistan, where his travels took him into the most isolated and unfriendly provinces, and into the thick of interests and beliefs that impede that nation's peace and progress. . . . Schmidle has, with this effort, established himself as a fresh, eloquent and informed contributor to the ongoing dialogue regarding Pakistan, terrorism and the strategic importance of engaging Central Asia in efforts toward peace and stability." Publ Wkly

954.93   Sri Lanka

Deraniyagala, Sonali
Wave; Sonali Deraniyagala. Alfred A. Knopf 2013 240 p. (hardcover) $24   **954.93**
1. Grief 2. Indian Ocean earthquake and tsunami, 2004 3. Bereavement 4. Parents -- Death 5. Children -- Death 6. Widows -- Biography 7. Indian Ocean Tsunami, 2004 8. Disaster victims -- Sri Lanka -- Biography
ISBN 0307962695; 9780307962690
LC 2012040980
National Book Critics Circle Award Finalist: Autobiography (2013)
This book offers author Sonali Deraniyagala's experience coping with the loss of her parents, husband, and two young sons, who perished in the "Indian Ocean tsunami that broke loose on December 26, 2004" and "killed something like 230,000 people." This is "an account of her coping with her grief while also celebrating the memories of those she loved. . . . She ranges over her childhood in Colombo, meeting her English husband at Cambridge, and the birth of her children." (Library Journal)

954.96   Nepal

Twigger, Robert
White mountain; a cultural adventure through the Himalayas. by Robert Twigger. First hardcover edition Pegasus Books 2017 458 p. illustrations, maps Hardcover $28.95   **954.96**
1. Himalaya Mountains 2. Explorers 3. Mountains 4. Mountaineers 5. Himalaya Mountains Region
ISBN 1681775352; 9781681775357
LC 2017039317
In this book, by Robert Twigger, "the Himalayas have always loomed tall in our imagination. . . . They are a central hub of the world's religion, as well as a climber's challenge and a traveler's dream. . . . Following a winding path across the Himalayas to its physical end in Nagaland on the Indian-Burmese border, Twigger encounters incredible stories from a unique cast of mountaineers and mystics, pundits and prophets." (Publisher's note)
Includes bibliographical references (pages 441-445) and index.

955   Iran

Follett, Ken

On wings of eagles. New American Library 1984 415p il
pa $7.99   **955**
1. Iran hostage crisis, 1979-1981
ISBN 0-451-16353-2; 978-0-451-16353-0
First published 1983 by Morrow
The author "recounts the efforts of successful Texas industrialist
Ross Perot to rescue from a Teheran jail two senior corporate executives
arrested during the anti-American and revolutionary period in Iran in
1979." Libr J

Housden, Roger

Saved by beauty; an American romantic in Iran. Broadway
Books 2011 290p map $24; ebook $11.99   **955**
1. Iran -- Description and travel 2. Iran -- Social life and customs
ISBN 978-0-307-58773-2; 978-0-307-58775-6 ebook
LC 2011003323
The author "documents his travels to Iran in late 2008 and early
2009. The narrative flows seamlessly as the author visits Tehran, paradise gardens in Shiraz, the Pasargadae archaeological site where Cyrus
the Great is buried, Persepolis, the Jewish quarter in Yazd, Esfaha-n,
Sanandaj, Mashhad, Neysha-bur, Tu-s, Kermanshah, Ahvaz, and Turkey's Bursa and Konya, as well as surrounding settlements, plains, deserts, and mountainous areas. . . . Poetry lovers and adventurers alike will
appreciate this work." Libr J

Peterson, Scott

Let the swords encircle me; Iran--a journey behind the headlines. Simon & Schuster 2010 732p il $32; ebook $16.99 **955**
1. Iran -- History -- 1979- 2. Iran -- Social conditions 3. Iran --
Politics and government 4. Iran -- Foreign relations -- United States
5. United States -- Foreign relations -- Iran
ISBN 978-1-4165-9728-5; 978-1-4165-9739-1 ebook
LC 2010-17761
"Reading 'Let the Swords Encircle Me' is like taking a seminar on
modern Iran with a patient guide who knows and loves both Iran and
the US, and wants only for them to reconcile. The book's deep under-
standing of the nuances and many shades of Iran are valuable." Christ
Sci Monit
Includes bibliographical references

Polk, William R.

Understanding Iran; everything you need to know, from
Persia to the Islamic Republic, from Cyrus to Ahmadinejad.
William R. Polk. Palgrave Macmillan 2011 xvii, 247 p.p illustrations, map (paperback) $18.99   **955**
1. Iran 2. Middle East 3. Iran -- History
ISBN 023010343X; 9780230103436; 9780230103238
LC 2009035743
This book on Iran, by William R. Polk, "provides an informative,
readable history of a country which is moving quickly toward becoming
the dominant power and culture of the Middle East. A former member of
the State Department's Policy Planning Council, Polk describes a country and a history misunderstood by many in the West." (Publisher's note)
Includes bibliographical references (p. [215]-237) and index.

Satrapi, Marjane

Embroideries. Pantheon Books 2005 134p il $16.95 **955**
1. Graphic novels 2. Iran -- Graphic novels 3. Women -- Iran
-- Graphic novels

ISBN 0-375-42305-2
LC 2004-58660
"Discussions of sex are frank and explicit and laced with high humor. . . . Satrapi's simple black-and-white cartooning style is tremendously effective, expertly portraying emotional nuances with just a few
lines." Libr J

Wright, Robert A.

Our man in Tehran; the true story behind the secret mission to save six Americans during the Iran Hostage Crisis and
the foreign ambassador who worked with the CIA to bring them
home. [by] Robert Wright. Other Press ed.; Other Press 2011
xxvi, 406p il $25.95; ebook $25.95   **955**
1. Escapes 2. Diplomats 3. Iran hostage crisis, 1979-1981 4. Iran
-- Foreign relations -- United States 5. United States -- Foreign
relations -- Iran
ISBN 978-1-59051-413-9; 978-1-59051-414-6 ebook
LC 2010-20376

First published 2010 in Canada
"Much of Iran's relationship with the West—and their mutual antipathy—stems from the muddled events of a single day: November
4, 1979, when Iranian militants overran the U.S. embassy in Tehran,
launching a 444-daylong hostage drama. What's often forgotten is that
six Americans evaded their would-be captors and were protected and
eventually extracted from Iran by Canadian diplomats. In this fascinating account of spycraft and compassion, Wright . . . puts newly unclassi-
fied documents to excellent use in recounting how Canadian ambassador
Ken Taylor hid the Americans who had slipped out a side door and gathered intelligence for the U.S. government." Publ Wkly
Includes bibliographical references

955.05   Iran--1906-2005

Abrahamian, Ervand

The coup; 1953, the CIA, and the roots of modern U.S.-
Iranian relations. Ervand Abrahamian. The New Press 2013
277 p. (hardcover) $26.95   **955.05**
1. Iran -- History -- 1941-1979 2. United States. Central Intelligence
Agency 3. Great Britain -- Foreign relations -- Iran 4. Iran --
Foreign relations -- Great Britain 5. Iran -- Foreign relations --
United States 6. Iran -- History -- Coup d'état, 1953 7. United
States -- Foreign relations -- Iran 8. Iran -- Politics and government
-- 1941-1979 9. United States. Central Intelligence Agency --
History -- 20th century 10. Petroleum industry and trade -- Political
aspects -- Iran -- History -- 20th century 11. Petroleum industry and
trade -- Political aspects -- United States -- History -- 20th century
ISBN 1595588264; 9781595588265
LC 2012031402
This book, by Ervand Abrahamian, profiles how "in August 1953,
the U.S. Central Intelligence Agency orchestrated the swift overthrow
of Iran's democratically elected leader and installed Muhammad Reza
Shah Pahlavi in his place. Over the next twenty-six years, the United
States backed the unpopular, authoritarian shah. . . . The blowback was
almost inevitable, as this new and revealing history of the coup and its
consequences shows." (Publisher's note)
Includes bibliographical references and index

Baglio, Matt

Argo; how the CIA and Hollywood pulled off the most audacious rescue in history. Antonio J. Mendez and Matt Baglio.
Viking 2012 viii, 310 p.p $26.95   **955.05**

1. Iran -- History 2. United States -- History 3. United States -- Foreign relations -- Iran 4. Iran Hostage Crisis, 1979-1981 5. Canada -- Foreign relations -- Iran 6. Iran -- Foreign relations -- Canada 7. United States. Central Intelligence Agency 8. Diplomats -- United States -- History -- 20th century
ISBN 0670026220; 9780670026227

LC 2012014991

In this book, Antonio J. Mendez tells the story of "November 4, 1979, [when] Iranian militants stormed the American embassy in Tehran and captured dozens of American hostages. . . . Disguising himself as a Hollywood producer, and supported by [under]cover CIA operatives . . . Mendez traveled to Tehran under the guise of scouting locations for a fake science fiction film called 'Argo.' While pretending to find the perfect film backdrops, Mendez and a colleague succeeded in contacting the escapees, and smuggling them out of Iran." (Publisher's note)
Includes bibliographical references and index.

Buchan, James

Days of God; the revolution in Iran and its consequences. James Buchan. Simon & Schuster 2013 432 p. illustrations, maps (hardcover) $27.99   **955.05**
1. Islam and politics 2. Iran -- History -- 1979- 3. Iran -- Politics and government -- 20th century 4. Iran -- History -- 1979-1997 5. Iran -- History -- Revolution, 1979 6. Iran -- History -- Revolution, 1979 -- Causes 7. Iran -- History -- Revolution, 1979 -- Influence 8. Political violence -- Iran -- History -- 20th century
ISBN 1416597778; 9781416597773

LC 2013008890

This book by James Buchan examines how "the Iranian Revolution of 1979 was a turning-point in modern history. The destruction of the Iranian monarchy not only upset the political order in the Middle East and brought on a quarter-century of warfare, but introduced a new way to look at history. In 'Days of God' James Buchan lives each moment of the revolution through the eyes of ordinary people." (Publisher's note)
Includes bibliographical references and index

Cooper, Andrew Scott

The **fall** of heaven; the Pahlavis and the final days of imperial Iran. Andrew Scott Cooper. Henry Holt & Co. 2016 624 p. (hardback) $35   **955.05**
1. Iran -- History 2. Iran -- History -- Mohammad Reza Pahlavi, 1941-1979
ISBN 9780805098976; 9780805098983

LC 2015046095

This book, by Andrew Scott Cooper, is an "account of the rise and fall of Iran's glamorous Pahlavi dynasty, written with the cooperation of the late Shah's widow, Empress Farah, Iranian revolutionaries and US officials from the Carter administration." (Publisher's note)
"A thorough new appraisal of an enigmatic ruler who died believing his people still loved him." Kirkus
Includes bibliographical references and index

Secor, Laura

Children of Paradise; The Struggle for the Soul of Iran. Laura Secor. Penguin Group USA 2016 528 p. map (hardcover) $30   **955.05**
1. Iran -- History -- 1979- 2. Iran -- Politics and government
ISBN 9781594487101; 1594487103
This book, by Laura Secor, presents a history of Iran from 1979 to the present. "Inside Iran, a breathtaking drama has unfolded since then, as religious thinkers, political operatives, poets, journalists, and activists have imagined and reimagined what Iran should be. They have drawn as deeply on the traditions of the West as of the East and have acted upon

their beliefs with urgency and passion, frequently staking their lives for them." (Publisher's note)
"Secor's clear writing offers a firm grounding in the last 40 years of Iranian political thought and the many actions it has inspired in a complicated and fascinating country." Pub Wkly
Includes bibliographical references (pages [470]-494) and index.

955.062   Administration of Hassan Rouhani, 2013-

Orth, Stephan

Couchsurfing in Iran; revealing a hidden world. Stephan Orth, translated by Jamie McIntosh. Greystone Books 2018 304 p. $16.95   **955.062**
1. Travel writing 2. Iran -- Description and travel 3. Iran -- Social life and customs
ISBN 1771642807; 9781771642804
In this book, "author Stephan Orth spends sixty-two days on the road in . . . [Iran] to provide a revealing, behind-the-scenes look at life in one of the world's most closed societies. Through the unsurpassed hospitality of twenty-two hosts, he skips the guidebooks and tourist attractions and travels from Persian carpet to bed to cot, covering more than 8,400 kilometers to recount 'this world's hidden doings.'" (Publisher's note.

956   Middle East (Near East)

Armenian Golgotha; translated by Peter Balakian with Aris Sevag. Alfred A. Knopf 2009 509p il map $35   **956**
1. Genocide 2. Armenian massacres, 1915-1923 3. Priests 4. Genocide -- Turkey 5. Biography, Individual 6. Armenian massacres, 1915-1923 -- Personal narratives
ISBN 0-307-26288-X; 978-0-307-26288-2

LC 2008-39957

This is a first-person account of the Armenian massacre. Chronology. Glossary. Bibliography. Index.
"On the night of April 24, 1915, Grigoris Balakian, an Armenian priest, and more than two hundred other Armenian politicians and intellectuals were arrested in Constantinople. Soon, Armenians across Turkey were massacred or forced to join a death march to the desert of Der Zor. Balakian walked among the displaced for months before he fled, disguising himself variously as a German engineer, a soldier, and a worker in the vineyards; he began this book while in hiding. (It was published in Armenian in 1922 and in 1959; the translator is Balakian's great-nephew.) Both a memoir and an attempt at a history of the genocide, it assumes considerable familiarity with Ottoman politics, but remains fascinating firsthand testimony to a monumental crime." New Yorker
Includes bibliographical references

Barr, James

A **line** in the sand. W. W. Norton & Co. 2012 xii, 450 p ill. 12 p. of plates   **956**
1. Diplomats 2. Middle East 3. World War, 1914-1918 4. Sykes-Picot Agreement 5. France -- Foreign relations -- Great Britain 6. Great Britain -- Foreign relations -- France 7. Middle East -- Foreign relations -- 20th century 8. Middle East -- Politics and government -- 1914-1945
ISBN 1-84737-453-0 Simon & Schuster; 978-1-84737-453-0 Simon & Schuster; 9780393070651 W.W. Norton & Co. 2012; 0393070654 W.W. Norton & Co., 2012

LC 2011038037

"In 1916, in the middle of the First World War, two men secretly agreed to divide the Middle East between them. Sir Mark Sykes was a visionary politician; François Georges-Picot a diplomat with a grudge. The deal they struck, which was designed to relieve tensions that threatened to engulf the Entente Cordiale, drew a line in the sand from the Mediterranean to the Persian frontier. Territory north of that stark line would go to France; land south of it, to Britain. . . . Their pact survived the war to form the basis for the postwar division of the region into five new countries Britain and France would rule. The creation of Britain's mandates of Palestine, Transjordan and Iraq, and France's in Lebanon and Syria, made the two powers uneasy neighbours for the following thirty years. . . . [This book] tells the story of the . . . era when Britain and France ruled the Middle East. It [aims to] explain . . . how the old antagonism between these two powers inflamed the . . . modern rivalry between the Arabs and the Jews, and ultimately led to war between the British and the French in 1941 and between the Arabs and the Jews in 1948." (Publisher's note)

Includes bibliographical references and index.

Finkel, Caroline

★ **Osman's** dream; the story of the Ottoman Empire, 1300-1923. Basic Books 2006 660p il map   **956**
1. Turkey -- History 2. Turkey -- History -- Ottoman Empire, 1288-1918

ISBN 0465023967; 9780465023967

First published 2005 in the United Kingdom

This is a history "of the Ottoman Empire from its origins in the thirteenth century through its destruction on the battlefields of World War I." (Publisher's note)

This is a history "of the Ottoman Empire from its origins in the thirteenth century through its destruction on the battlefields of World War I." Publisher's note

Includes bibliographical references

Friedman, Thomas L.

From Beirut to Jerusalem. Farrar, Straus & Giroux 1989 541p il maps $32   **956**
1. Jewish-Arab relations 2. Lebanon -- History 3. Israel -- Politics and government 4. Middle East -- Politics and government

ISBN 0-374-15895-9

LC 92-148666

First published 1989

The author presents an account of the political situation in the Middle East as he witnessed it in his years as a reporter in Lebanon and Jerusalem

"When recounting his frequently harrowing experiences in that troubled region, Friedman can be absolutely riveting; similarly, his historical insights, his explanation of the root causes of the Arab-Israeli conflict, and his impressions of people and places in the Holy Land never fail to fascinate." Booklist

Herzog, Chaim

The **Arab-**Israeli wars; war and peace in the Middle East from the 1948 War of Independence to the present. updated by Shlomo Gazit; introduction by Isaac Herzog and Michael Herzog. 2nd ed, rev and updated; Vintage Books 2005 476p il pa $16.95   **956**
1. Jewish-Arab relations

ISBN 1-4000-7963-2

LC 2005-280207

First published 1982 by Random House

This book traces "the Arab-Israeli wars and military conflicts from the 1948 War of Independence through the 1973 Yom Kippur War."

Libr J

Includes bibliographic references

Lewis, Bernard

The **Middle** East; a brief history of the last 2,000 years. Scribner 1995 433p il hardcover o.p. pa $16   **956**
1. Middle East -- History

ISBN 0-684-80712-2; 0-684-83280-1 pa

LC 96-4384

"Lewis has chosen to accentuate the social, economic, and cultural changes that have occurred over 20 centuries. He ranges from seemingly trivial concerns (changes in dress and manners in an Arab coffeehouse) to earth-shaking events (the Mongol conquest of Mesopotamia) in painting a rich, varied, and fascinating portrait of a region that is steeped in traditionalism while often forced by geography and politics to accept change." Booklist

Includes bibliographical references

Notes on a century; reflections of a Middle East historian. Bernard Lewis; with Buntzie Ellis Churchill. Viking 2012 388 p.   **956**
1. Autobiographies 2. International relations 3. Middle East -- Politics and government 4. Middle East -- Historiography 5. Middle East -- History -- 20th century 6. Middle East -- History -- 21st century 7. Middle East specialists -- Great Britain -- Biography

ISBN 0670023531; 9780670023530

LC 2011049267

This memoir by political consultant and historian Bernard Lewis provides the author's personal reflections on his international career and his views on the major themes of world politics spanning "World War II, up through the Arab Spring. . . . Lewis . . . was the first to warn of a coming 'clash of civilizations,' a term he coined in 1957, and has led [a] life, as much a political actor as a scholar of the Middle East." (Publisher's note)

Includes bibliographical references and index.

Meyer, Karl E.

Kingmakers; the invention of the modern Middle East. [by] Karl E. Meyer and Shareen Blair Brysac. Norton 2008 507p il map $27.95   **956**
1. Middle East -- History

ISBN 978-0-393-06199-4; 0-393-06199-X

LC 2008-07378

The authors "have written a timely and engrossing study of the men and women who were instrumental in giving birth to some of the nations, institutions, and chronic problems of the area." Booklist

Includes bibliographical references

★ The **Middle** East; Ellen Lust, editor. 14th edition CQ Press 2016 1020 p paperback $100   **956**
1. Middle East

ISBN 9781506329284

LC 2015045140

Covers topics such as oil, Islam, the Arab-Israeli conflict, the Persian Gulf, and the arms trade in the Middle East. Also presents profiles of Middle Eastern nations and twentieth-century leaders and includes documents such as UN resolutions and peace treaties.

956.01   Middle East – Early history to 1900

Lambert, Malcolm

God's Armies; Crusade and Jihad: Origins, History, Aftermath. Malcolm Lambert. W W Norton & Co Inc 2016 352 p. ill., map, genealogical tables $27.95; (ebook) $50   **956.01**
1. Jihad 2. Crusades 3. Military history
ISBN 1681772248; 9781681772240; 9781681772752

This book by Malcolm Lambert "traces the origins and development of crusade and jihad, showing . . . that jihad reflected internal tensions in Islam from its beginnings. . . . [It] reveals the ways in which crusade and jihad were used to disguise ambitions for power and to justify atrocity and yet also inspired acts of great chivalry and heroic achievement. The story brims with larger than life characters, among them Richard the Lionheart, Nur al-Din, . . . and Ghenghiz Khan." (Publisher's note)

"An all-encompassing introduction to the Christian-Islamic struggle for the armchair history buff." Kirkus

Includes bibliographical references (pages 276-282) and index.

956.04   Middle East--1945-1980

Fisk, Robert

The **great** war for civilisation; the conquest of the Middle East. Robert Fisk. Knopf 2005 1107 p.   **956.04**
ISBN 9781400041510; 1400041511

LC 2005049813
Includes bibliographical references (p. [1061]-1067) and index.

Gandt, Robert

Angels in the sky; how a band of volunteer airmen saved the new state of Israel. Robert Gandt. W W Norton & Co Inc 2017 xix, 442 p.p illustrations, map (hardcover) $26.95   **956.04**
1. Air pilots -- Biography 2. Israel-Arab War, 1948-1949 3. Fighter pilots -- Biography 4. Airplanes, Military -- Israel -- History 5. Israel. Ḥel ha-avir -- History 6. Israel-Arab War, 1948-1949 -- Aerial operations
ISBN 9780393254785; 9780393254778

LC 2017028807
This book, by Robert Gandt, tells the "story of how an all-volunteer air force helped defeat five Arab nations and protect the fledgling . . . state of Israel [in 1948]. . . . In the crucible of war they became brothers in a righteous cause. They flew, fought, died, and, against all odds, helped save a new nation. The saga of the volunteer airmen in Israel's war of independence stands as one of the most stirring--and untold--war stories of the . . . 20th] century." (Publisher's note)

"An exciting military chronicle packed with well-documented, intimate portraits of a group of brave pilots." Kirkus

Includes bibliographical references and index

MacFarquhar, Neil

The **media** relations department of Hizbollah wishes you a happy birthday; unexpected encounters in the changing Middle East. PublicAffairs 2009 387p il map $26.95; pa $15.95   **956.04**
1. Middle East -- Description and travel 2. Middle East -- Politics and government
ISBN 978-1-58648-635-8; 978-1-58648-811-6 pa

LC 2009-2004
The author "offers something fresh and unexpected for readers steeped in a decade of news reports about suicide bombers, absolutist imams and tyrannical despots. . . . [This book] is MacFarquhar's effort to write a funny (yet penetrating) account about real Arabs—and a few Persians—struggling against long odds to bring their societies into the modern age. . . . For those who care about the Middle East and want to start listening to weak but growing voices calling for reform and modernization on local rather than Western terms, MacFarquhar's account is a fine place to begin." N Y Times Book Rev

Includes bibliographical references

Oren, Michael

Six days of war; June 1967 and the making of the modern Middle East. {by} Michael B. Oren. Oxford Univ. Press 2002 446p il $30   **956.04**
1. Israel-Arab War, 1967
ISBN 0-19-515174-7

LC 2001-58823
This is a history of the June 1967 Arab-Israeli War

"What makes this book important is the breadth and depth of the research. Oren draws on archives, newly declassified documents, memoirs and interviews from Israel, America, Britain and what was then the Soviet Union." N Y Times Book Rev

Includes bibliographical references and index

Sacco, Joe

Footnotes in Gaza. Metropolitan Books 2009 418p il $29.95   **956.04**
1. Graphic novels 2. Massacres -- Graphic novels 3. Israel-Arab conflicts -- Graphic novels
ISBN 978-0-8050-7347-8; 0-8050-7347-7

LC 2009-28433
"Cartoonist and journalist Joe Sacco is the world's foremost creator of 'comics journalism'—a contemporary field he basically invented. . . . [This] book, whose 'footnotes' refer both to facts and metaphorically to history's forgotten people, is about two massacres of Palestinians in the Gaza Strip in November 1956. . . . Very little has been written about either event. Sacco conducted extensive research of U.N. documents and other materials, and additionally set out to interview as many eyewitnesses as he could track down. This is really the heart of this moving, precisely drawn work." Time Out N Y

Includes bibliographical references

Shlaim, Avi

The **iron** wall; Israel and the Arab world since 1948. Norton 1999 704p il hardcover o.p. pa $17.95   **956.04**
1. Israel-Arab conflicts 2. Jewish-Arab relations 3. Israel -- Foreign relations
ISBN 0-393-32112-6 pa

LC 99-23121
"A thorough analysis of Israel's relationships with the West as well as its neighbors from a controversial but thoughtful point of view." Booklist

Includes bibliographical references

Wright, Lawrence, 1947-

★ **Thirteen** Days in September; Carter, Begin, and Sadat at Camp David. Lawrence Wright. First edition Alfred A. Knopf 2014 368 p. illustrations, maps $27.95   **956.04**
1. Egypt -- History 2. Arab countries -- Foreign relations -- Israel 3. Camp David Agreements (1978) 4. Israel-Arab War, 1973 -- Peace 5. United States -- Foreign relations -- 1977-1981
ISBN 0385352034; 9780385352031

LC 2013497329
Los Angeles Times Book Prize Finalist: History (2014)

Carnegie Medal Shortlist: Nonfiction (2015)

This book by Lawrence Wright is a "day-by-day account of the 1978 Camp David conference, when President Jimmy Carter persuaded Israeli prime minister Menachem Begin and Egyptian president Anwar Sadat to sign the first peace treaty in the modern Middle East, one which endures to this day. . . . Wright draws vivid portraits of other fiery personalities who were present at Camp David--including Moshe Dayan, Osama el-Baz, and Zbigniew Brzezinski." (Publisher's note)

"The author alternates among each day's events, biographical sketches of the central and supporting players, and insightful sociopolitical essays on the three leaders and their countries as he explains the process that led to a Nobel Peace Prize for Sadat and Begin and laid the foundation for the subsequent Oslo Accords." LJ

Includes bibliographical references and index

956.05 Middle East (Near East) ---1980

Engel, Richard, 1973-

And then all hell broke loose; two decades in the Middle East. by Richard Engel. Simon & Schuster 2016 400 p. 8 plates; illustrations, maps (hardback) $27   **956.05**
1. Journalists 2. Middle East -- History 3. Middle East -- History -- 21st century 4. Foreign correspondents -- United States -- Biography 5. Middle East -- Politics and government -- 21st century
ISBN 9781451635119; 9781451635126; 9781451635133

LC 2015030898

This book, by journalist Richard Engel, is the "story of the Middle East revolutions, the Arab Spring, war, and terrorism. . . . Engel has been under fire, blown out of hotel beds, taken hostage. He has watched Mubarak and Morsi in Egypt arrested and condemned, reported from Jerusalem, been through the Lebanese war, covered the whole shooting match in Iraq, interviewed Libyan rebels who toppled Gaddafi, [and] reported from Syria as Al-Qaeda stepped in." (Publisher's note)

"Clear, candid, and concise, Engel's overview of the ongoing battleground should be required reading for anyone desiring a thorough and informed portrait of what the past has created and what the future holds for the Middle East and the world at large." Booklist

Hider, James

The **spiders** of Allah; travels of an unbeliever on the frontline of holy war. St. Martin's Griffin 2009 323p pa $14.95   **956.05**
1. Religion and politics 2. Religious fundamentalism 3. Terrorism -- Religious aspects 4. Middle East -- Description and travel 5. Middle East -- Politics and government
ISBN 978-0-312-56585-5; 0-312-56585-2

LC 2009-7378

"A British journalist's firsthand account of fanaticism and bloodshed in the Middle East. . . . [The author] loosely examines the ways in which radical Islam and fundamentalist Christianity have continually warped and damaged an already difficult situation. . . . The author's dense, vivid descriptions, frequently steeped in irony and humor, make for a slow but powerful read." Kirkus

Pope, Hugh

Dining with al-Qaeda; three decades exploring the many worlds of the Middle East. Thomas Dunne Books/St. Martin's Press 2010 332p il map $26.99   **956.05**
1. Middle East -- Description and travel 2. Middle East -- Politics and government
ISBN 978-0-312-38313-8

Pope's "criticisms of the invasion and of Israel may grate some readers, but those interested in the interpersonal rather than the international will enjoy Pope's bold curiosity in meeting people all over the Middle East." Booklist

Said, Edward W.

The **end** of the peace process; Oslo and after. Pantheon Bks. 2000 345p $27.50; pa $14   **956.05**
1. Israel-Arab conflicts 2. Jewish-Arab relations
ISBN 0-375-40930-0; 0-375-72574-1 pa

LC 99-44765

The author provides "analysis of the pitfalls of the Oslo agreement. Most of the essays in this collection have appeared in Cairo's al-Ahram Weekly and al-Hayat, London's Arabic-language daily. Each essay is Said's reflection on a dimension of the Palestinian predicament. . . . He is as critical of the corruption, incompetence, and authoritarianism of the Palestinian Authority as he is of American and Israeli postures." Libr J

Shavit, Ari, 1957-

My promised land; Ari Shavit. Spiegel & Grau 2013 464 p.   **956.05**
1. Zionism 2. Israel -- History 3. Israel-Arab conflicts 4. Israel -- Politics and government 5. Arab-Israeli conflict
ISBN 9780385521703; 9780812984644

LC 2012046122

In this book, "Israeli journalist [Ari] Shavit . . . presents a history of and meditation on Zionism's successes and failures. . . .He traces the rise and demise of the kibbutzim, the 1948 displacement of Palestinians, the shock of 1967's Six-Day War victory, and the near defeat in the 1973 Yom Kippur War." He asks, "Can Israel fully integrate its Arab citizens, do justice to the Palestinians, and assure security in the face of looming military and demographic threats? " (Library Journal)

Stack, Megan

Every man in this village is a liar; an education in war. [by] Megan K. Stack. Doubleday 2010 257p $26.95   **956.05**
1. War and civilization 2. War on terrorism 3. Middle East -- Description and travel
ISBN 978-0-385-52716-3; 0-385-52716-0

LC 2009-34473

National Book Award Finalist: Nonfiction (2010)

"As a 25-year-old correspondent for the Los Angeles Times, Stack covered Afghanistan in the days immediately following 9/11, then traveled to other outposts in the war on terror, from Iraq to Iran, Libya, and Lebanon. In a disquieting series of essays, Stack now takes readers deep into the carnage where she was exposed to the insanity, innocence, and inhumanity of wars with no beginning, middle, or end. Her soaring imagery sears itself into the brain, in acute and accurate tales that should never be forgotten by the wider world, and yet always are." Booklist

Weiss, Michael

Isis; inside the army of terror. Michael Weiss, Hassan Hassan. Regan Arts 2015 270 p. map $14; (hbk) $28.95 **956.05**
1. Iraq 2. Syria 3. Terrorism
ISBN 1682450201; 1941393578; 9781941393574; 9781682450291; 9781682450208

LC 2015930621

This book, by Michael Weiss and Hassan Hassan, presents a "look inside the world's most dangerous terrorist group . . . the Islamic State of Iraq and Syria (ISIS). . . . [The authors] explain how these violent extremists evolved from a nearly defeated Iraqi insurgent group into a jihadi army of international volunteers who behead Western hostages in slickly produced videos and have conquered territory equal to the size of

Great Britain." (Publisher's note)

Includes bibliographical references (pages 367-402) and index.

956.054   Middle East, 2000-

Bacevich, Andrew J., 1947-

★ **America's** war for the greater Middle East; a military history. Andrew J. Bacevich. Random House Inc 2016 480 p. maps (hardcover) $30   **956.054**

1. Middle East -- History 2. United States -- Military history 3. Middle East -- Foreign relations -- United States 4. United States -- Foreign relations -- Middle East 5. United States -- History, Military -- 20th century 6. United States -- History, Military -- 21st century

ISBN 9780553393941; 9780553393934

LC 2015038868

National Book Award Longlist: Nonfiction (2016)

This book, by Andrew J. Bacevich, "provides a searing reassessment of U.S. military policy in the Middle East over the past four decades. During the 1980s, Bacevich argues, a great transition occurred. As the Cold War wound down, the United States initiated a new conflict—a War for the Greater Middle East. Bacevich weaves a compelling narrative out of episodes as varied as the Beirut bombing of 1983, the Mogadishu firefight of 1993, the invasion of Iraq in 2003, and the rise of ISIS." (Publisher's note)

Includes bibliographical references and index

Wood, Graeme

The **way** of the strangers; encounters with the Islamic State. Graeme Wood. Random House Inc 2017 384 p. (ebook) $65; $28   **956.054**

1. Terrorists 2. IS (Organization) 3. Terrorism -- Middle East

ISBN 9780812988765; 0812988752; 9780812988758

LC 2016055880

This book, by Graeme Wood, "is an intimate journey into the minds of the Islamic State's true believers. . . . Graeme Wood interviews supporters, recruiters, and sympathizers of the group. . . . [We] learn about a prodigy of Islamic rhetoric, now stripped of the citizenship of the nation of his birth and determined to see it drenched in blood. Wood speaks with non-Islamic State Muslim scholars and jihadists, and explores the group's idiosyncratic, coherent approach to Islam." (Publisher's note)

Includes bibliographical references (pages 285-305) and index.

956.1   Turkey

Hughes, Bettany

Istanbul; a tale of three cities. Bettany Hughes. Da Capo Press 2017 xxix, 800 p.p illustrations (some color) (hardcover) $40   **956.1**

1. Istanbul (Turkey) 2. Turkey -- Civilization 3. Cities and towns -- Turkey 4. Istanbul (Turkey) -- History 5. Istanbul (Turkey) -- Civilization

ISBN 9780306825842; 9780306902635; 0306825848

In this book, author Bettany "Hughes takes us on a dazzling historical journey from the Neolithic to the present, through the many incarnations of one of the world's greatest cities--exploring the ways that Istanbul's influence has spun out to shape the wider world. [He] deftly guides readers through Istanbul's rich layers of history." (Publisher's note)

"Hughes balances especially well a study of one city with the commentary of greater time periods and historic events taking place simultaneously around the world; the rich, cultural, religious, and social pres-

ence of Istanbul's complex tale lends itself as an excellent focus." LJ

Includes bibliographical references and index.

Kinzer, Stephen

Crescent and star; Turkey between two worlds. Farrar, Straus & Giroux 2001 252p hardcover o.p. pa $14   **956.1**

1. Turkey -- Politics and government

ISBN 0-374-52866-7 pa

LC 2001-23298

The author "gives a concise introduction to Turkey: Kemal Atatürk's post-WWI establishment of the modern secular Turkish state; the odd makeup of contemporary society, in which the military enforces Atatürk's reforms. In stylized but substantive prose, he devotes chapters to the problems he sees plaguing Turkish society: Islamic fundamentalism, frictions regarding the large Kurdish minority and the lack of democratic freedoms." Publ Wkly

Mango, Andrew

The **Turks** today; Andrew Mango. 1st ed; Overlook Press 2004 292p map $29.95; pa $17.95   **956.1**

1. Turkey -- History

ISBN 1-585-67615-2; 1-585-67756-6 pa

LC 2004-58339

"This fascinating and timely survey is both a political history and a cultural examination of a diverse, dynamic society." Booklist

Includes bibliographical references

Ureneck, Lou

The **Great** Fire; One American's Mission to Rescue Victims of the 20th Century's First Genocide. HarperCollins 2015 496 p. 16 plates; ills.; maps; ports. $28.99   **956.1**

1. Genocide 2. Armenian massacres, 1915-1923

ISBN 0062259881; 9780062259882

This book by Lou Ureneck tells the story of Asa Jennings "a Methodist Minister and [Halsey Powell] a principled American naval officer who helped rescue more than 250,000 refugees during the genocide of Armenian and Greek Christians." (Publisher's note)

"This account is written with fans of popular narrative history in mind. Despite the muddled material, many will find this a worthwhile read. Students of this dark part of history, however, will most appreciate Ureneck's research." LJ

956.6   Eastern Turkey

Akcam, Taner

A **shameful** act; the Armenian genocide and the question of Turkish responsibility. translated by Paul Bessemer. Metropolitan Books 2006 483p map $30   **956.6**

1. Genocide 2. Armenian massacres, 1915-1923

ISBN 0-8050-7932-7; 978-0-8050-7932-6

LC 2005-58401

Original Turkish edition, 1999

"This groundbreaking and lucid account by a prominent Turkish scholar speaks forcefully to all." Publ Wkly

Includes bibliographical references

Balakian, Peter

★ The **burning** Tigris; the Armenian genocide and America's response. HarperCollins 2003 xx, 475p il $26.95; pa $14.95   **956.6**

1. Genocide 2. Armenian massacres, 1915-1923

ISBN 0-06-019840-0; 0-06-055870-9 pa

LC 2003-44986

"The book's real power derives from the eyewitness accounts of the genocide itself. The sheer volume of outsiders' testimony that Balakian compiles, and the horrifying similarity of their observations of men, women and children beaten, tortured, burned to death in churches or sent out into the desert to starve, is an overwhelmingly convincing retort to genocide deniers." N Y Times Book Rev

Includes bibliographical references

Suny, Ronald Grigor

They Can Live in the Desert but Nowhere Else; A History of the Armenian Genocide. by Ronald Grigor Suny. Princeton University Press 2015 520 p. illustrations, maps $35   **956.6**

1. Armenian massacres, 1915-1923

ISBN 0691147302; 9780691147307

LC 2014041347

In this book on the Armenian genocide, historian Ronald Grigor Suny "cuts through nationalist myths, propaganda, and denial to provide an unmatched account of when, how, and why the atrocities of 1915-16 were committed. . . . Drawing on archival documents and eyewitness accounts, this is an unforgettable chronicle of a cataclysm that set a tragic pattern for a century of genocide and crimes against humanity." (Publisher's note)

"Suny weaves this complex story into a nuanced, meticulously researched, and compellingly argued book. Summing Up: Highly recommended. Advanced undergraduate and graduate collections." Choice

956.7   Iraq

Allawi, Ali A.

The **occupation** of Iraq; winning the war, losing the peace. Yale University Press 2007 xxiv, 518p il map $28   **956.7**

1. Iraq War, 2003-2011 2. Iraq -- Politics and government

ISBN 978-0-300-11015-9; 0-300-11015-4

LC 2006-39445

This "scholarly yet immensely readable exposition of Iraqi society and politics will likely become the standard reference on post-9/11 Iraq." Publ Wkly

Includes bibliographical references

Atkinson, Rick

In the company of soldiers; a chronicle of combat. H. Holt 2004 319p il maps $25; pa $14   **956.7**

1. Iraq War, 2003-2011 2. United States -- Army -- Airborne Division, 101st

ISBN 0-8050-7561-5; 0-8050-7773-1 pa

LC 2003-67607

This is an eyewitness account of the war in Iraq. "In the spring of 2003, the author accompanied combat units to Iraq. He spent two months embedded with the 101st Airborne Division's headquarters staff, sharing their daily experiences from initial deployment out of Fort Campbell, KY, to overseas staging areas in Kuwait, and ultimately bearing witness to the unit's march on Baghdad. His view of the war was from a vantage point that permitted scrutiny of strategy, planning, and decision making at the senior command level." SLJ

Filkins, Dexter

★ The **forever** war. Alfred A. Knopf 2008 368p il $25   **956.7**

1. Iraq War, 2003-2011 2. Journalists 3. War on Terrorism, 2001-

4. Iraq War, 2003-2011 -- Personal narratives 5. Afghanistan -- Politics and government -- 2001-

ISBN 0-307-26639-7; 978-0-307-26639-2

LC 2008-11761

Filkins, a "New York Times correspondent, furnishes a firsthand account of the battle against Islamic fundamentalism, from the rise of the Taliban in the 1990s, to the terrorist attacks of 9/11, to the modern-day wars in Afghanistan and Iraq." (Publisher's note)

This is "wonderfully written and carefully researched [book]. . . . Filkins's gripping account gives readers a clear, though disturbing, view of what's happening on the ground in Iraq. And he has put himself in the middle of this madness to deliver a stunning and illuminating story." Christ Sci Monit

Includes bibliographical references

Finkel, David

The **good** soldiers. Sarah Crichton Books 2009 287p il $26   **956.7**

1. Iraq War, 2003-2011 2. United States -- Army 3. Counterinsurgency -- Iraq 4. Soldiers -- United States 5. Iraq War, 2003-2011 -- Campaigns 6. Soldiers -- United States -- Biography

ISBN 0-374-16573-4; 978-0-374-16573-4

LC 2009-19391

This is an account of the Iraq "war as experienced on the ground . . . by members of an Army battalion sent to Baghdad during the surge in 2007." (N Y Times (Late N Y Ed))

"Finkel's keen firsthand reportage, its grit and impact only heightened by the literary polish of his prose, gives us one of the best accounts yet of the American experience in Iraq." Publ Wkly

Frederick, Jim

Black hearts; one platoon's descent into madness in Iraq's triangle of death. Harmony Books 2010 439p il map $26 **956.7**

1. War crimes 2. Iraq War, 2003-2011 -- Atrocities 3. United States -- Army -- Airborne Division, 101st

ISBN 978-0-307-45075-3; 0-307-45075-9

LC 2009-35537

"Frederick recounts the events leading up to and following the rape and murder of 14-year-old Iraqi Abeer al-Janabi and the subsequent murder of her family—parents Qassim and Fakhriah and six-year-old sister Hadeel—committed by members of one U.S. Army deployment in Iraq's 'Triangle of Death.'" Publ Wkly

Includes bibliographical references

Gordon, Michael R., 1951-

The **endgame**; the inside story of the struggle for Iraq, from George W. Bush to Barack Obama. Michael R. Gordon and Bernard E. Trainor. Pantheon Books 2012 xix, 779 p.p $35 **956.7**

1. Iraq War, 2003-2011 2. Iraq -- Politics and government 3. Iraq -- Foreign relations -- United States 4. United States -- Foreign relations -- Iraq 5. Insurgency -- Iraq 6. Iraq -- Ethnic relations 7. Iraq -- Relations -- United States 8. United States -- Relations -- Iraq 9. Iraq -- Politics and government -- 21st century 10. United States -- Armed Forces -- Iraq -- History 11. Iraq War, 2003-2011 -- Political aspects -- United States

ISBN 0307377229; 9780307377227

LC 2012024746

This book by Michael R. Gordon and Bernard E. Trainor presents a "chronicle of the Iraq War, emphasizing military maneuvers and Iraqi participation at all levels." It offers a "record of the nine years of conflict between the 'inside-out' versus 'outside-in' strategies of the U.S. government in dealing with Iraqi intransigence and conversion to democracy. . . . The authors take great pains to delineate the makeup of the Iraqi government in the prickly transition to sovereignty." (Kirkus Reviews)

Includes bibliographical references and index.

Gourevitch, Philip

Standard operating procedure; [by] Philip Gourevitch and Errol Morris. Penguin Press 2008 286p il $25.95 **956.7**

1. Prisoners of war 2. Iraq War, 2003-2011 3. Abu Ghraib (Baghdad, Iraq: Prison)

ISBN 978-1-59420-132-5

LC 2008-10215

"This deft piece of reportage will stir readers' anger, at both the actions and the consequences. . . . A thorough, terrifying account of an American-made 'bedlam.'" Publ Wkly

Haass, Richard

War of necessity: war of choice; a memoir of two Iraq wars. by Richard N. Haass. Simon & Schuster 2009 336 p. $27 **956.7**

1. Iraq War, 2003-2011 2. Iraq War, 2003-2011 -- Causes 3. Persian Gulf War, 1991 -- Causes 4. United States -- Military policy 5. Iraq War, 2003-2011 -- Political aspects 6. Persian Gulf War, 1991 -- Political aspects 7. Middle East -- Foreign relations -- United States 8. United States -- Foreign relations -- Middle East

ISBN 978-1-4165-4902-4; 1-4165-4902-1; 1416549021; 9781416549024

LC 2009004495

"A unique perspective on how war policy was formed by two very different presidents." Kirkus

Includes bibliographical references and index

Hoffmann, Andrea C.

The **girl** who escaped ISIS; this is my story. Farida Khalaf, Andrea C. Hoffmann. Atria Books 2016 240 p. map (hardback) $24 **956.7**

1. Refugees 2. Terrorism 3. IS (Organization) 4. Iraq -- Refugees -- Biography 5. Yezidi women -- Iraq -- Biography

ISBN 1501131710; 9781501131714; 9781501152337

LC 2016022449

In this memoir, by Farida Khalaf with Andrea C. Hoffmann, translated from the German by Jamie Bulloch, the author "describes her world as it was [under the Islamic State.] . . . Held in a slave market in Syria and sold into the homes of several ISIS soldiers, she stubbornly attempts resistance at every turn. Farida is ultimately brought to an ISIS training camp in the middle of the desert, where she plots an against-all-odds escape for herself and five other girls." (Publisher's note)

Kennedy, Hugh

When Baghdad ruled the Muslim world; the rise and fall of Islam's greatest dynasty. Da Capo Press 2005 xxv, 326p il map hardcover o.p. pa $18.95 **956.7**

1. Islamic civilization 2. Baghdad (Iraq)

ISBN 0-306-81435-8; 978-0-306-81435-8; 0-306-81480-3 pa; 978-0-306-81480-8 pa

LC 2006-295518

First published 2004 in the United Kingdom with title: The Court of the Caliphs

The author "has written an informative and sobering lesson for those who idolize the past." Choice

Includes bibliographical references

Maurer, Kevin

Hunter Killer; Inside America's Unmanned Air War. T.

Mark McCurley and Kevein Maurer. Penguin Group USA 2014 352 p. illustrations $27.95 **956.7**

1. Drone aircraft 2. Military art and science

ISBN 0525954430; 9780525954439

LC 2015016824

Authors T. Mark McCurley and Kevin Maurer offer a "look at the US military's secretive Remotely Piloted Aircraft program. McCurley provides an unprecedented look at the aviators and aircraft that forever changed modern warfare. This is the first account by an RPA pilot, told from his unique-in-history vantage point supporting and executing Tier One counterterrorism missions." (Publisher's note)

"The author ably chronicles the tedious, routine work involving 'days drenched in blood,' and he gives a good sense of the evolution of the RPA since the 1990s and the intensive human element necessary to command it. An illuminating tale of a pilot on the cutting edge." Kirkus

Mills, Dan

Sniper one; on scope and under siege with a sniper team in Iraq. St. Martin's Press 2008 xxvi, 349p il map $26.95 **956.7**

1. Iraq War, 2003-2011 -- Personal narratives

ISBN 978-0-312-53126-3; 0-312-53126-5

LC 2008-20438

First published 2007 in the United Kingdom

"When a battalion of the Prince of Wales' Royal Regiment landed in Iraq in 2004, Mills commanded the 18 men of the sniper platoon. His gripping combat narrative covers how the platoon did more than its share of the fighting during the months when the Iraqis virtually besieged the battalion." Booklist

Packer, George

The **assassins'** gate; America in Iraq. Farrar, Straus & Giroux 2005 467p hardcover o.p. pa $15 **956.7**

1. Iraq War, 2003-2011 2. Iraq -- Politics and government 3. United States -- Politics and government -- 2001-

ISBN 0-374-29963-3; 0-374-53055-6 pa

LC 2005-11521

This "book rests on three main pillars: analysis of the intellectual origins of the Iraq war, summary of the political argument that preceded and then led to it, and firsthand description of the consequences on the ground. . . . The Iraq debate has long needed someone who is both tough-minded enough, and sufficiently sensitive, to register all its complexities. In George Packer's work, this need is answered." Publ Wkly

Includes bibliographical references

Raddatz, Martha

The **long** road home; a story of war and family. Putnam 2007 310p il map hardcover o.p. pa $15 **956.7**

1. Soldiers -- United States 2. United States -- Army -- Cavalry, 1st 3. Iraq War, 2003-2011 -- Personal narratives

ISBN 0-399-15382-9; 978-0-399-15382-2; 0-425-21934-8 pa; 978-0-425-21934-8 pa

LC 2006-37332

This "account has grit and high drama. . . . Sometimes the level of detail is astonishing." N Y Times (Late N Y Ed)

Ricks, Thomas E.

Fiasco: the American military adventure in Iraq. Penguin Press 2006 482p il map hardcover o.p. pa $16 **956.7**

1. Iraq War, 2003-2011

ISBN 0-14-303891-5 pa; 1-59420-103-X; 978-0-14-303891-7 pa; 978-1-59420-103-5

LC 2006-45357

This book is "not a political rant nor is it shrill. But in its low-key, extraordinarily well-sourced, highly-detailed portrait of the run-up to and conduct of the war it is devastating." Christ Sci Monit

Includes bibliographical references

Roe, William R.

★ **Understanding** Iraq; the whole sweep of Iraqi history, from Genghis Khan's Mongols to the Ottoman Turks to the British mandate to the American occupation. [by] William R. Polk. HarperCollins 2005 221p map $22.95; pa $13.95   **956.7**
1. Iraq -- History
ISBN 0-06-076468-6; 0-06-076469-4 pa
                                    LC 2005-281319

The author presents an account of the history of Iraq, from the Dark Ages to the American occupation that began in 2003.

This is "a sober and informed account of Iraq's history, culminating in a compelling critique of the U.S. intervention there." Foreign Affairs

Includes bibliographical references

Seierstad, Asne

A **hundred** and one days; a Baghdad journal. translated by Ingrid Christophersen. Basic Books 2005 321p il maps hardcover o.p. pa $14   **956.7**
1. Iraq War, 2003-2011 -- Personal narratives
ISBN 0-465-07600-9; 0-465-07601-7 pa
First published 2005 in the United Kingdom

The author "writes about her stay as a reporter for Scandinavian, Dutch, and German media in Baghdad in the days before the war in Iraq through the fall of Baghdad. . . . Seierstad puts a human face to and provides insight into the mosaic of the people of Iraq, the Bath party supporters, the dissidents, and the average person caught in the nightmare of the Saddam regime and the horrors of war." SLJ

Shadid, Anthony

Night draws near; Iraq's people in the shadow of America's war. Picador 2006 507p map pa $15   **956.7**
1. Iraq War, 2003-2011
ISBN 978-0-312-42603-3; 0-312-42603-8
First published 2005 by Holt & Co.

"Evenhanded and keenly observed, containing just enough (and no more) of the author to suggest a decent man worthy of our trust, . . . [this book] is written for the inexpert but has fresh material for scholars." Economist

Includes bibliographical references

Sheeler, Jim

Final salute; a story of unfinished lives. Penguin Press 2008 280p il $25.95   **956.7**
1. Death 2. Bereavement 3. Iraq War, 2003-2011 4. Military personnel -- United States
ISBN 978-1-59420-165-3; 1-59420-165-X
                                    LC 2007-44130
National Book Award Finalist: Nonfiction (2008)

This is a "tribute to the soldiers who have died in Iraq and their devastated families. The author spent two years shadowing Maj. Steve Beck, a marine in charge of casualty notification, as he delivered the news of battlefield death to families. Sheeler puts readers in Beck's shoes as he walks up to houses, delivers the knock on the door so dreaded by military families and tries to comfort distraught spouses and parents. . . . Sheeler's book is a devastating account of the sacrifices military families make and should be required reading for all Americans." Publ Wkly

Sky, Emma

The **Unraveling**; High Hopes and Missed Opportunities in Iraq. Emma Sky. PublicAffairs 2015 400 p. illustrations, maps, portraits (hardcover) $28.99   **956.7**
1. Iraq War, 2003-2011 2. Postwar reconstruction
ISBN 161039593X; 9781610395939
                                    LC 2015932207

This book, by Emma Sky, "provides unique insights into the US military as well as the complexities, diversity, and evolution of Iraqi society. [The memoir] . . . is an intimate insider's portrait of how and why the Iraq adventure failed and contains a unique analysis of the course of the war." (Publisher's note)

"At once informative and emotional, this book will find a wide audience of adult readers, especially those interested in global politics and current events." LJ

Stewart, Rory

The **prince** of the marshes; and other occupational hazards of a year in Iraq. Harcourt, Inc. 2006 396p il $25   **956.7**
1. Diplomats 2. Nonfiction writers 3. Iraq -- Social conditions 4. Iraq -- Description and travel 5. Iraq -- Politics and government
ISBN 0-15-101235-0; 978-0-15-101235-0
                                    LC 2006-06905

"In August 2003, at the age of thirty, Rory Stewart took a taxi from Jordan to Baghdad. A Farsi-speaking British diplomat who had recently completed an epic walk from Turkey to Bangladesh, he was soon appointed deputy governor of Amarah and then Nasiriyah, provinces in the remote, impoverished marsh regions of southern Iraq. He spent the next eleven months negotiating hostage releases, holding elections, and splicing together some semblance of an infrastructure for a population of millions. . . . The Prince of the Marshes tells the story of Stewart's year." (Publisher's note) Chronology.

"In 2003, Stewart, a former British diplomat, joined the Coalition Provisional Authority in Iraq and was posted to the southern province of Maysan, where he found himself the de-facto governor of a restive populace whose allegiances were split among fifty-four political parties, twenty major tribes, and numerous militias. Stewart's account of his attempts to placate the various local figures who continually threaten to kill each other, or him, is both shrewd and self-deprecating." New Yorker

Tripp, Charles

A **history** of Iraq; 3rd ed.; Cambridge University Press 2007 xxiii, 357p il map $70; pa $24.99   **956.7**
1. Iraq -- History
ISBN 978-0-521-87823-4; 978-0-521-70247-8 pa
                                    LC 2007-282451
First published 2000

This book traces the political history of Iraq from the Ottoman Empire to the fall of Saddam Hussein and the American occupation.

Includes bibliographical references

Woodward, Bob

★ **Plan** of attack. Simon & Schuster 2004 467p il map hardcover o.p. pa $14   **956.7**
1. Iraq War, 2003-2011 2. United States -- Politics and government -- 2001-
ISBN 0-7432-5547-X; 0-7432-5548-8 pa
                                    LC 2004-351204

The author "delivers an engrossing blow-by-blow of the run-up to war in Iraq. . . . With this book, Woodward . . . has delivered his most important and impressive work in years. Ultimately, this first-class work of contemporary history will be remembered for shedding needed light on the Iraq War." Publ Wkly

Wright, Evan

Generation kill; Devil Dogs, Iceman, Captain America, and the new face of American war. G.P. Putnam's Sons 2004 354p il maps hardcover o.p. pa $15   **956.7**

  1. Iraq War, 2003-2011 -- Personal narratives

  ISBN 0-399-15193-1; 0-425-20040-X pa

                  LC 2004-44682

The author discusses his experiences when embedded with the First Marine Division in Iraq. This book is based on a series of articles that originally appeared in Rolling Stone.

"This "account is a personality-driven, readable and insightful look at the Iraq War's first month from the Marine grunt's point of view." Publ Wkly

956.704 Iraq ---1920

Bolger, Daniel P.

Why We Lost; A General's Inside Account of the Iraq and Afghanistan Wars. Daniel Bolger. Houghton Mifflin Harcourt 2014 400 p. 16 plates; illustrations; maps $28   **956.704**

  1. Afghan War, 2001- 2. Iraq War, 2003-2011 3. United States -- Military history 4. Military personnel -- United States 5. Leadership -- United States 6. Afghan War, 2001- -- Campaigns 7. Iraq War, 2003-2011 -- Campaigns 8. Strategic culture -- United States 9. Afghan War, 2001- -- Personal narratives, American 10. Iraq War, 2003-2011 -- Personal narratives, American 11. War on Terrorism, 2001-2009 -- Personal narratives, American 12. Civil-military relations -- United States -- History -- 21st century

  ISBN 0544370481; 9780544370487

                  LC 2014026908

This book, by Daniel Bolger, is an "insider account of the U.S. wars in Iraq and Afghanistan, and how it all went wrong. Over a thirty-five-year career, . . . Bolger rose through the army infantry to become a three-star general, commanding in both theaters of the U.S. campaigns in Iraq and Afghanistan. . . . Now, as a witness to all levels of military command, Bolger offers a unique assessment of these wars, from 9/11 to the final withdrawal from the region." (Publisher's note)

"Bolger does a fine job of delineating the technical aspects of military workings (while making good fun of the euphemistic names of the various operations labeled by the 'guys in the Pentagon basement') and candidly describes America's efforts after a decade of attrition as 'global containment of Islamic threats.' With vigorous, no-nonsense prose and an impressive clarity of vision, this general does not mince blame in this chronicle o f failure." Kirkus

  Includes bibliographical references (pages 438-485) and index

Campbell, Deborah

Disappearance in Damascus; friendship and survival in the shadow of war. Deborah Campbell. Picador 2017 341 p.   **956.704**

  1. Refugees -- Syria 2. Iraq War, 2003-2011 3. Women journalists -- Biography 4. Refugees -- Iraq -- Biography 5. Refugees -- Syria -- Biography 6. Journalists -- Canada -- Biography 7. Political prisoners -- Syria -- Biography 8. Iraq War, 2003-2011 -- Refugees -- Syria -- Biography

  ISBN 9781250147899; 9781250147875

                  LC 2017027145

This book "begins in 2007, when Deborah Campbell travels undercover to Damascus to report on the exodus of Iraqis into Syria, following

the overthrow of Saddam Hussein. There she meets and hires Ahlam, a refugee working as a 'fixer'—providing Western media with trustworthy information and contacts to help get the news out. Ahlam has fled her home in Iraq after being kidnapped while running a humanitarian center." (Publisher's note)

"Campbell's captivating writing allows readers to see inside the life of a foreign correspondent and the bonds forged and broken through investigative reporting." Booklist

  Includes bibliographical references (pages 327-341)

Castner, Brian

The long walk; a story of war and the life that follows. Brian Castner. Doubleday 2012 222 p.   **956.704**

  1. Autobiographies 2. Ordnance disposal units 3. Post-traumatic stress disorder 4. Iraq War, 2003-2011 -- Personal narratives 5. Ordnance disposal units -- Iraq 6. Ordnance disposal units -- United States 7. United States. Air Force -- Officers -- Biography 8. Iraq War, 2003-2011 -- Personal narratives, American 9. Iraq War, 2003-2011 -- Veterans -- United States -- Biography

  ISBN 0385536208; 9780385536202

                  LC 2011052419

This memoir by Brian Castner describes his life during and after the Iraq War. "[A]s the commander of an Explosive Ordnance Disposal unit in Iraq . . . [d]ays and nights he and his team . . . would . . . engage in . . . disarming the deadly improvised explosive devices that had been discovered. . . . When Castner returned home to his wife and family, he began a struggle with . . . an unshakable feeling of fear and confusion and survivor's guilt that he terms The Crazy." (Publisher's note)

  Includes bibliographical references and index.

Chandrasekaran, Rajiv

Imperial life in the emerald city; inside Iraq's green zone. Rajiv Chandrasekaran. Alfred A. Knopf 2006 x, 320p maps (alk. paper) $25.95   **956.704**

  1. Iraq 2. Iraq War, 2003-2011 3. Political corruption 4. United States -- Politics and government 5. Iraq War, 2003- 6. Iraq -- Coalition Provisional Authority 7. United States -- Politics and government -- 2001- 8. United States -- Politics and government -- 2001-2009

  ISBN 1400044871; 9781400044870

                  LC 2006041014

  National Book Award Finalist: Nonfiction (2006)

  BBC Samuel Johnson Prize for Non-Fiction (2007)

  This book discusses "the Green Zone in Baghdad, headquarters for the American occupation in Iraq, . . . [and provides a] portrait of the Green Zone and the Coalition Provisional Authority (which ran Iraq's government from April 2003 to June 2004) that becomes a metaphor for the [U.S.] administration's larger failings in Iraq. An insular, often blinkered approach to decision making; a reluctance to listen to experts; Pollyannaish expectations leading to inadequate allocations of resources and staff; a willful ignorance of Iraqi culture and history; and an obliviousness to realities on the ground: all are on unfortunate display in the Emerald City." (New York Times)

"This is a clearly written, blessedly undidactic book. It should be read by anyone who wants to understand how things went so badly wrong in Iraq." N Y Times Book Rev

  Includes bibliographical references (p. [303]-306) and index.

Edmonds, Bill Russell

God Is Not Here; A Soldier's Struggle With Torture, Trauma, and the Moral Injuries of War. Bill Russell Edmonds. W.W. Norton & Co. Inc. 2015 312 p. illustrations $27.95 **956.704**

  1. War -- Ethical aspects 2. Iraq War, 2003-2011 -- Personal

narratives
ISBN 1605987743; 9781605987743

In this book, by Lieutenant Colonel Bill Russell Edmonds, "the focus is on a young man struggling to learn what is right when fighting wrong. [The author] . . . provides a disturbing and thought-provoking account of the morally ambiguous choices faced when living with and fighting within a foreign religion and culture, as well as the resulting psychological and spiritual impacts on a soldier." (Publisher's note)

"Edmonds doesn't reach the depth attained in recent books by Ben Fountain, Phil Klay, or Michael Pitre, but he does provide a useful adjunct to the work on PTSD done by Jonathan Shay and other writers and analysts. War is hell, and hell is other people. In this serviceable account, Edmonds assures us that both adage s are true." Kirkus

Fair, Eric

Consequence; A Memoir. Eric Fair. Henry Holt & Co. 2016 256 p. (hardcover) $26   **956.704**

1. Ethics 2. Iraq War, 2003-2011 3. Torture -- Iraq 4. Linguists -- Iraq -- Biography 5. Military interrogation -- Iraq 6. Iraq War, 2003-2011 -- Atrocities 7. Military interrogation -- United States 8. Government contractors -- United States -- Biography 9. Iraq War, 2003-2011 -- Personal narratives, American 10. Iraq War, 2003-2011 -- Prisoners and prisons, American 11. Heart -- Transplantation -- Patients -- United States -- Biography
ISBN 9781627795135; 9781627795142

LC 2015031396

In this memoir, author Eric Fair "questions everything--his faith, his morality, his country--as he recounts his experience as an interrogator in Iraq. It is a story of a man who chases his own demons from Egypt, where he served as an Army translator, to a detention center in Iraq, to seminary at Princeton, and eventually, to a heart transplant ward at the University of Pennsylvania." (Publisher's note)

"A startling debut from a haunted individual who wishes he had left Iraq earlier 'with my soul intact.' " Kirkus

Hornfischer, James D.

Service; a Navy SEAL at war. Marcus Luttrell; with James D. Hornfischer. Little, Brown and Co. 2012 xv, 364 p.p (hardcover) $27.99   **956.704**

1. War 2. Soldiers -- United States 3. Voluntary military service 4. Afghan War, 2001- -- Campaigns 5. Iraq War, 2003-2011 -- Campaigns 6. Afghan War, 2001- -- Personal narratives, American 7. United States. Navy. SEALs -- Officers -- Biography 8. Iraq War, 2003-2011 -- Personal narratives, American
ISBN 0316185361; 9780316185363

LC 2012904468

Author Marcus "Luttrell chronicles his missions preserving democracy for America . . . During their time in Iraq, his SEAL combat brothers killed perceived enemies, suffered countless wounds, and died at a rapid pace, making the narrative occasionally difficult to follow. In some chapters, battle tactics predominate, and the sentences are quick and graphic . . . Luttrell explains why some men answer the call of war no matter the risk to themselves or their loved ones. The author seeks to explain the honor of military service to . . . readers who have never experienced it." (Kirkus)

Includes bibliographical references.

Swofford, Anthony

Jarhead: a Marine's chronicle of the Gulf War and other battles. Scribner 2003 260p hardcover o.p. pa $15   **956.704**

1. United States -- Marine Corps 2. Persian Gulf War, 1991 -- Personal narratives
ISBN 0-7432-3535-5; 0-7432-8721-5 pa

LC 2002-30866

This book offers "an unflinching portrayal of the loneliness and brutality of modern warfare and sophisticated analyses of—and visceral reactions to—its politics." Publ Wkly

Thorpe, Helen

Soldier girls; the battles of three women at home and at war. Helen Thorpe. Scribner 2014 416 p. (hardcover: alk. paper) $28   **956.704**

1. Afghan War, 2001- 2. Iraq War, 2003-2011 3. United States. Army 4. Women in the military 5. United States -- National Guard 6. Women -- Indiana -- Biography 7. Afghan War, 2001- -- Campaigns 8. Iraq War, 2003-2011 -- Campaigns 9. Indiana. National Guard -- Biography 10. United States. Army -- Women -- Biography 11. Single mothers -- United States -- Biography 12. Women soldiers -- United States -- Biography 13. Women veterans -- United States -- Biography 14. Afghan War, 2001- -- Women -- United States -- Biography 15. Iraq War, 2003-2011 -- Women -- United States -- Biography
ISBN 1451668104; 9781451668100; 9781451668117

LC 2014000658

This book, by Helen Thorpe, is an "account of three women deployed to Afghanistan and Iraq, and how their military service affected their friendship, their personal lives, and their families. . . . These women, who are quite different in every way, become friends, and we watch their interaction and also what happens when they are separated. . . . We see them work extremely hard, deal with the attentions of men on base and in war zones, and struggle to stay connected to their families back home." (Publisher's note)

"Thorpe fills this gripping tale with the women's own words, texts, and letters (from friends and their children, as well), and the story is engrossing and heartbreaking at once. Thorpe notes in the acknowledgments that the women's full-bore contributions to the book were not just to enlighten readers but also to let other war veterans know that they are not alone in their struggle to put their lives back together after a deployment." Booklist

Battles of three women at home and at war

956.91   Syria

Abouzeid, Rania

No turning back; life, loss, and hope in wartime Syria. Rania Abouzeid. W W Norton & Co Inc 2018 384 p. $26.95 **956.910**

1. Civil war 2. Syria -- History -- Civil War, 2011-
ISBN 0393609499; 9780393609493

This book, by Rania Abouzeid, "dissects the tangle of ideologies and allegiances that make up the Syrian conflict. . . . When violence broke out in Homs, a poet named Abu Azzam became an unlikely commander in a Free Syrian Army militia. . . . Abouzeid [also] brings readers deep inside Assad's prisons, to covert meetings where foreign states and organizations manipulated the rebels, and to the highest levels of Islamic militancy and the formation of ISIS." (Publisher's note)

"A brilliant, detailed work on a devastating topic. For readers interested in narrative nonfiction, the Syrian war, the Middle East, and personal accounts." LJ

Alpeyrie, Jonathan

The shattered lens; a war photographer's true story of captivity and survival in Syria. Jonathan Alpeyrie with Stash Luczkiw and Bonnie Timmermann. Atria Books 2017 260 p.   **956.91**

1. French Americans -- Biography 2. Photojournalists -- Biography 3. War correspondents -- Biography 4. Torture -- Syria -- History -- 21st century 5. Survival -- Syria -- History -- 21st century 6. Kidnapping -- Syria -- History -- 21st century 7. Syria -- History -- Civil War, 2011- -- Biography
ISBN 9781501146503; 9781501146534

LC 2017016403

Bontinck, Dimitri

Rescued from Isis; the gripping true story of how a father saved his son. Dimitri Bontinck. St. Martin's Press 2017 278 p. color illustrations (hardcover) $26.99 **956.91**
1. Islam 2. Radicalism 3. Islamic literature 4. Islamic fundamentalism 5. Syria -- History -- Civil War, 2011- 6. IS (Organization) 7. Islamic fundamentalism -- Syria 8. Terrorists -- Recruiting -- Belgium 9. Radicalism -- Religious aspects -- Islam 10. Syria -- History -- Civil War, 2011- -- Personal narratives, Belgian
ISBN 1250147581; 9781250147585; 9781250147592

In this book, author Dimitri Bontinck, recounts how he traveled to the "Middle East to save his child from radical Islam. . . . His teenage son, introduced to Islam by his girlfriend, fell into the clutches of a radical mosque. . . . [He] set off on his own to save his son. Using only his military training, a lot of courage, and a little luck, he . . . embedded himself . . . into the Middle East. After months of searching . . . he was able to find his son." (Publisher's note)

"A moving personal account that offers profound insights into Islamic terrorism and the struggle against it." Kirkus

Crabapple, Molly

Brothers of the gun; a memoir of the Syrian War. by Marwan Hisham; illustrated by Molly Crabapple. Random House Inc 2018 320 p. $28 **956.91**
1. Biography 2. Syria -- Politics and government 3. Syria -- History -- Civil War, 2011-
ISBN 0399590625; 9780399590627

In this memoir, illustrated by Molly Crabapple, Marwan Hisham describes his experiences as "a young man coming of age during the Syrian war. [This book] is an intimate lens on the century's bloodiest conflict and a profound meditation on kinship, home, and freedom. . . . [It] offers a ground-level reflection on the Syrian revolution--and how it bled into international catastrophe and global war. ." (Publisher's note)

Di Giovanni, Janine

The **Morning** They Came For Us; Dispatches from Syria. Janine di Giovanni. W W Norton & Co Inc 2016 320 p. maps $25.95 **956.91**
1. Jihad 2. Syria 3. War correspondents
ISBN 0871407132; 9780871407139

LC 2016007537

In this book, journalist Janine di Giovanni "gives us a tour de force of war reportage [in Syria], all told through the perspective of ordinary people—among them a doctor, a nun, a musician, and a student. What emerges is an extraordinary picture of the devastating human consequences of armed conflict, one that charts an apocalyptic but at times the tender story of life in a jihadist war zone." (Publisher's note)

"Di Giovanni presents a devastating picture of the horrors of civil war and the disintegration of Syrian society. Her vivid depictions of suffering may be overwhelming for some readers." LJ

Includes bibliographical references (pages [173]-176) and index.

Erlich, Reese

Inside Syria; the backstory of their civil war and what the world can expect. Reese Erlich; foreword by Noam Chomsky. Prometheus Books 2014 287 p. 8 plates; illustrations; maps (hardback) $25 **956.91**
1. War 2. Syria -- Politics and government 3. Syria -- History -- Civil War, 2011- 4. Syria -- Politics and government -- 2000- 5. Protest movements -- Syria -- History -- 21st century 6. Political violence -- Syria -- History -- 21st century
ISBN 1616149485; 9781616149482

LC 2014015840

In this book author "Reese Erlich unravels the complex dynamics underlying the Syrian civil war. Through vivid, on-the-ground accounts and interviews with both rebel leaders and Syrian President Bashar al-Assad, Erlich gives the reader a better understanding of this momentous power struggle and why it matters." (Publisher's note)

"A timely, immediate description and explanation of social and political disintegration at huge human cost in war-torn Syria." LJ

Includes bibliographical references and index

Fleming, Melissa

A **hope** more powerful than the sea; one refugee's incredible story of love, loss, and survival. Melissa Fleming. Flatiron Books 2017 288 p. (ebook) $60; (hardcover) $25.99 **956.91**
1. Refugees -- Syria 2. Syria -- History -- Civil War, 2011- 3. Europe -- Emigration and immigration -- Government policy 4. Syria -- Emigration and immigration
ISBN 9781250106018; 9781250105998

LC 2016044107

Alex Award (2018)

This book, by Melissa Fleming, tells the story of Syrian refugee Doaa Al Zamel who, together with her young fiance, "hand their life savings to smugglers and board a dilapidated fishing vessel with five hundred other refugees, including a hundred children. After four horrifying days at sea, another ship, filled with angry men shouting insults, rams into Doaa's boat, sinking it and leaving the passengers to drown. That is where Doaa's struggle for survival really begins." (Publisher's note)

"This book amply demonstrates why she has since become a symbol of hope for other refugees. Fleming should be congratulated for bringing Al Zamel's inspiring and illuminating story to the page." Pub Wkly

Pearlman, Wendy

We crossed a bridge and it trembled; voices from Syria. Wendy Pearlman. Custom House 2017 liii, 290 p.p (hardcover) $24.99 **956.91**
1. Protest movements 2. Syria -- History -- Civil War, 2011- 3. Refugees -- Syria -- Interviews 4. Syria -- History -- 20th century 5. Syria -- History -- 21st century 6. Protest movements -- Syria -- History -- 21st century
ISBN 9780062654458; 9780062654618

LC 2016049210

This book, by Wendy Pearlman, discusses how "in 2011 hundreds of thousands of Syrians took to the streets demanding freedom, democracy and human rights. The government's ferocious response, and the refusal of the demonstrators to back down, sparked a brutal civil war . . . Based on interviews with hundreds of displaced Syrians . . . [the book] is a . . . mosaic of first-hand testimonials from the frontlines." (Publisher's note)

"This powerfully edifying work of witness is essential reading." Booklist

Samer (Author)

The **Raqqa** Diaries; Escape from "Islamic State" Samer;

edited by Mike Thomson; illustrations by Scott Coello; translation by Nader Ibrahim; co-edited by John Neal. Interlink Pub Group Inc 2017 106 p. illustrations (hardcover) $16.95 **956.91**

1. Islamic fundamentalism 2. Syria -- Social conditions -- 21st century 3. Refugees 4. IS (Organization) 5. Syria -- History -- Civil War, 2011-

ISBN 9781566560054; 1566560055

This book, by Samer, edited by Mike Thomson, illustrated by Scott Coelho, presents accounts of a man living inside the territory of the terrorist group ISIS. "No-one is allowed to speak to western journalists or leave Raqqa. . . . Those caught breaking the rules face death by beheading. Despite this, the BBC's Mike Thomson, with the help of the BBC Arabic Service, found a young man who is willing to risk his life to tell the world what is happening in his city." (Publisher's note)

"The details of Samer's experience are often times shocking yet provide an important document of this region's history." LJ

Seierstad, Åsne

Two sisters; a father, his daughters, and their journey into the Syrian jihad. Åsne Seierstad; translated from the Norwegian by Seán Kinsella. Farrar, Straus & Giroux 2018 vi, 418 p.p (hardcover) $27 **956.91**

1. Norway 2. Terrorists 3. Radicalism 4. IS (Organization) 5. Muslims -- Ethnic identity 6. Women terrorists -- Norway 7. Terrorists -- Norway -- Recruiting

ISBN 9780374716288; 0374279675; 9780374279677

LC 2017047949

This book, by Åsne Seierstad, "tells the unforgettable story of a family divided by faith. Sadiq and Sara, Somali immigrants raising a family in Norway, one day discover that their teenage daughters Leila and Ayan have vanished--and are en route to Syria to aid the Islamic State. Seierstad's riveting account traces the sisters' journey from secular, social democratic Norway to the front lines of the war in Syria, and follows Sadiq's harrowing attempt to find them." (Publisher's note)

"Seierstad's scrupulous reporting shines a revealing new light on the phenomenon of young Westerners becoming fervent supporters of terror." Pub Wkly

Includes bibliographical references

Warrick, Joby, 1960-

Black flags; the rise of ISIS. Joby Warrick. Doubleday 2015 368 p. 8 plates (hardback) $28.95 **956.91**

1. Islamic fundamentalism 2. Terrorism -- Middle East 3. IS (Organization) 4. Terrorism -- Iraq 5. Terrorism -- Religious aspects -- Islam 6. Middle East -- Politics and government -- 21st century

ISBN 0385538219; 9780385538213

LC 2015020949

Pulitzer Prize: General Nonfiction (2016)

This book, by Joby Warrick, "traces how the strain of militant Islam behind ISIS first arose in a remote Jordanian prison and spread with the unwitting aid of two American presidents. . . . Drawing on unique high-level access to CIA and Jordanian sources, Warrick weaves gripping, moment-by-moment operational details with the perspectives of diplomats and spies, generals and heads of state, many of whom foresaw a menace worse than al Qaeda and tried desperately to stop it." (Publisher's note)

"The author focuses on dramatic flashpoints and the roles of key players, creating an exciting tale with a rueful tone, emphasizing how the Iraq invasion's folly bir t hed ISIS and created many missed opportunities to stop al-Zarqawi quickly. Warrick stops short of offering policy solutions, but he provides a valuable, readable introduction to a pressing international security threat." Kirkus

Yassin-Kassab, Robin

Burning Country; Syrians in Revolution and War. Robin Yassin-Kassab and Leila Al-Shami. Pluto Press 2016 xii, 262 p.p maps (hardcover) $80 **956.91**

1. Syria -- Politics and government 2. Syria -- History -- Civil War, 2011- 3. Syria -- Politics and government -- 2000-

ISBN 0745336272; 9780745336275

LC 2017286184

This book by Robin Yassin-Kassab and Leila Al-Shami "explores the complicated reality of life in present-day Syria with unprecedented detail and sophistication, drawing on new first-hand testimonies from opposition fighters, exiles lost in an archipelago of refugee camps, and courageous human rights activists. Yassin-Kassab and Al-Shami expertly interweave these stories with an incisive analysis of the militarization of the uprising, the rise of the Islamists and sectarian warfare, and the role of Syria's government in exacerbating the brutalization of the conflict." (Publisher's note)

"This is the best book yet interpreting the tragedies that have befallen Syria since the outbreak of civil war in 2011. It proffers the best coverage of the war by two Syrian scholars and journalists who have participated in it." Choice

Includes bibliographical references (pages 226-257) and index.

956.92 Lebanon

Friedman, Matti

★ **Pumpkinflowers**; a soldier's story of a forgotten war. Matti Friedman. Algonquin Books of Chapel Hill 2016 256 p. map (hardcover) $25.95 **956.92**

1. Lebanon -- History -- 1975-1976, Civil War 2. Lebanon -- History -- Civil War, 1975-1990 -- Personal narratives, Israeli

ISBN 1616204583; 9781616204587

LC 2015031466

This book, by Matti Friedman, describes the author's experiences serving in the Israeli military during the Lebanese civil war. "Part memoir, part reportage, part history, . . . [it] captures the birth of today's chaotic Middle East and the rise of a twenty-first-century type of war in which there is never a clear victor and media images can be as important as the battle itself." (Publisher's note)

"A haunting yet wry tale of young people at war, cursed by political forces beyond their control, that can stand alongside the best narrative nonfiction coming out of Afghanistan and Iraq." Kirkus

Includes bibliographical references.

956.94 Palestine; Israel

Armstrong, Karen

Jerusalem; one city, three faiths. Knopf 1996 xxi, 471p il maps hardcover o.p. pa $17.95 **956.94**

1. Jerusalem -- History

ISBN 0-679-43596-4; 0-345-39168-3 pa

LC 96-75888

Armstrong's "overarching theme, that Jerusalem has been central to the experience and 'sacred geography' of Jews, Muslims and Christians and thus has led to deadly struggles for dominance, is a familiar one, yet she brings to her sweeping, profusely illustrated narrative a grasp of sociopolitical conditions seldom found in other books." Publ Wkly

Blincoe, Nicholas

Bethlehem; biography of a town. Nicholas Blincoe. Per-

seus Books Group 2017 288 p. $28 **956.94**
1. Israel -- History 2. Bible. New Testament 3. Palestine -- History
ISBN 1568585837; 9781568585833

In this book, author "Nicholas Blincoe tells . . . [Bethlehem's] history through the visceral experience of living there, taking readers through its stone streets and desert wadis, its monasteries, aqueducts, and orchards to show the city from every angle and era. His portrait of Bethlehem sheds light on one of the world's most intractable political problems." (Publisher's note)

"Deftly written, this narrative has something to offer a wide variety of readers, whether interested in history, archaeology, religious connection, or the Israeli-Palestinian conflict." (LJ)

Bregman, Ahron

A **history** of Israel. Palgrave Macmillan 2002 xx, 320p map (Palgrave essential histories) $70; pa $21.95 **956.94**
1. Israel -- History
ISBN 0-333-67631-9; 0-333-67632-7 pa
LC 2002-72304

"Bregman takes into account all the major issues involving Israel's history." Booklist
Includes bibliographical references

Carroll, James, 1943-

Jerusalem, Jerusalem; how the ancient city ignited our modern world. Houghton Mifflin Harcourt 2011 418p $20 **956.94**
1. Jerusalem
ISBN 978-0-547-19561-2; 0-547-19561-3
LC 2010-43034

"Carroll examines the enigma that is Jerusalem—the holiest and most blood-soaked spot on earth. . . . While various religions flourished all over the ancient world, it was in Jerusalem that God emerged. Not just a god, but God, one who recognizes how both the need for violence and the hatred of violence reside within the human spirit. These conflicting impulses are the subthemes that propel Carroll's story across the ages, through Jerusalem's wreckages and rebirths, as the three Abrahamic religions claim the city as its own. Carroll's writing is so compelling, so beautifully constructed, that, ironically, the book can be a very slow read. There is something on almost every page that makes the reader want to stop and contemplate." Booklist
Includes bibliographical references

Cohen, Rich

Israel is real. Farrar, Straus, and Giroux 2009 383p map $27; pa $16 **956.94**
1. Jews -- History 2. Israel -- Description and travel
ISBN 978-0-374-17778-2; 0-374-17778-3; 978-0-312-42976-8 pa; 0-312-42976-2 pa
LC 2008-49223

The author explains "the history of a people and its religion from the time Zealots revolted against their Roman occupiers to the rise of the Zionists, who helped build the current republic. . . . A must-read for those who want to understand the context of the modern Jewish state." Kirkus
Includes bibliographical references

Collins, Larry

O Jerusalem! {by} Larry Collins and Dominique Lapierre. Simon & Schuster 1972 637p il maps hardcover o.p. pa $17 **956.94**
1. Israel-Arab War, 1948-1949 2. Jerusalem -- History -- 1948, Siege
ISBN 0-671-66241-4 pa

This is an account of the struggle for the city of Jerusalem during the Israel-Arab War of 1948
Includes bibliographical references

Di Cintio, Marcello

Pay no heed to the rockets; life in contemporary Palestine. Marcello Di Cintio. Counterpoint 2018 272 p. map $26 **956.94**
1. Intifada, 1987-1992 2. Arabic literature -- Palestine -- History and criticism
ISBN 1640090819; 9781640090811

In this book, author Marcello Di Cintio "reveals . . . the Palestinian experience as seen through the lens of authors, books, and literature. Using the form of a political-literary travelogue, he explores what literature means to modern Palestinians and how Palestinians make sense of the conflict between a rich imaginative life and the daily tedium and violence of survival." (Publisher's note)

"Interweaving history and politics, the book introduces Western readers to the modern Palestinian literary scene while celebrating the rich diversity of voices that comprise it." Kirkus
Includes bibliographical references (pages 233-237)

Ephron, Dan

Killing a king; the assassination of Yitzhak Rabin and the remaking of Israel. Dan Ephron. W W Norton & Co Inc 2015 304 p. 8 plates; color illustrations (hardcover) $27.95 **956.94**
1. Assassination 2. Israel -- History 3. Israel -- Politics and government -- 1993-
ISBN 0393242099; 9780393242096
LC 2015025695

Los Angeles Times Book Prize: History (2015)

In this book author Dan Ephron "relates the parallel stories of [Israeli Prime Minister Yitzhak] Rabin and his stalker, Yigal Amir, over the two years leading up to the assassination, as one of them planned political deals he hoped would lead to peace, and the other plotted murder. Through the prism of the assassination, much about Israel today comes into focus, from the paralysis in peacemaking to the fraught relationship between current Prime Minister Benjamin Netanyahu and President Barack Obama." (Publisher's note)

"Fascinating characterizations of real people and intrigue make this book appealing to readers of both fiction and nonfiction thrillers and anyone interested in the history of Israel." LJ
Includes bibliographical references and index

Gordis, Daniel

Israel; A Concise History of a Nation Reborn. Daniel Gordis. HarperCollins 2016 560 p. ill. (some color), color maps $29.99; (ebook) $27.99 **956.94**
1. Israel -- History
ISBN 0062368745; 9780062368744; 9780062368768

This book about Israel, by Daniel Gordis, offers "a brief but thorough account of the cultural, economic, and political history of this complex nation, from its beginnings to the present. Accessible, levelheaded, and rigorous, . . . [it] sheds light on Israel's past so we can understand its future." (Publisher's note)

"A readable, concise history that effectively captures the sense of grand ideas in Israel's identity." Kirkus
Includes bibliographical references (pages 501-504) and index.

Hoffman, Adina

Till we have built Jerusalem; architects of a new city. Adina Hoffman. Farrar, Straus & Giroux 2016 368 p. illustrations (hardback) $28   **956.94**

1. Jerusalem 2. Architects 3. Architecture 4. Jerusalem -- Buildings 5. Architects -- Jerusalem -- Biography 6. Jerusalem -- History -- 20th century

ISBN 9780374289102; 9780374709785

LC 2015034650

This book, by Adina Hoffman, is a "journey into the very different lives of three architects who helped shape modern Jerusalem. The book unfolds as an excavation and opens with the arrival in 1930s Jerusalem of the celebrated Berlin architect Erich Mendelsohn. . . . Next we meet Austen St. Barbe Harrison, Palestine's chief government architect from 1922-1937. . . . And in the riveting . . . section, Hoffman herself sets out through the battered streets of today's Jerusalem." (Publisher's note)

"This is a well-done survey of the period and of a city that continues to attract and sadden both visitors and residents." Booklist

Hoffman, Bruce

Anonymous soldiers; the struggle for Israel, 1918-1947. Bruce Hoffman. Alfred A. Knopf, a division of Random House LLC 2015 640 p. 24 plates; illustrations $35   **956.94**

1. Zionism 2. Counterinsurgency 3. Israel -- History 4. Palestine -- History 5. World War, 1939-1945 6. Israel-Arab conflicts 7. Palestine -- History -- 1917-1948 8. World War, 1939-1945 -- Palestine 9. Zionism -- Palestine -- History -- 20th century 10. Palestine -- Politics and government -- 1917-1948 11. Counterinsurgency -- Palestine -- History -- 20th century

ISBN 0307594718; 9780307594716

LC 2014018177

This book, by Bruce Hoffman, is "based on newly available documents, of the battles between Jews, Arabs, and the British that led to the creation of Israel. . . . Hoffman . . . shines new light on the bombing of the King David Hotel, the assassination of Lord Moyne in Cairo, the leadership of Menachem Begin, the life and death of Abraham Stern, and much else. Above all, Hoffman shows exactly how the underdog 'anonymous soldiers' of Irgun and Lehi defeated the British." (Publisher's note)

"A must-read for anyone interested in the origins of the State of Israel." LJ

Kashua, Sayed

Native; dispatches from an Israeli-Palestinian life. Sayed Kashua. Grove Press 2016 304 p. (ebook) $23.99; (hardcover) $24   **956.94**

1. Essays 2. Palestinian Arabs

ISBN 9780802190185; 9780802124555; 9780802126290; 0802124550

LC 2016000992

In this essay collection, author Sayed Kashua, "an Arab-Israeli who lived in Jerusalem for most of his life, . . . started writing with the hope of creating one story that both Palestinians and Israelis could relate to. . . . He writes about his children's upbringing and encounters with racism, about fatherhood and married life, the Jewish-Arab conflict, . . . travels around the world as an author, and—more than anything—his love of books and literature." (Publisher's note)

"A wickedly ironic but humane collection." Kirkus

Mitchell, George J. (George John), 1933-

A **Path** to Peace; A Brief History of Israeli-Palestinian Negotiations and a Way Forward in the Middle East. George J. Mitchell; Alon Sachar. Simon & Schuster 2016 192 p. $26   **956.94**

1. Diplomacy 2. Palestine 3. Israel-Arab conflicts 4. Israel --

Foreign relations -- Arab countries

ISBN 1501153919; 9781501153914

LC 2016027278

This book by former US Special Envoy for Middle East Peace George J. Mitchell and Alon Sachar offers an "insider account of how the Israelis and the Palestinians have progressed (and regressed) in their negotiations through the years and outlines the specific concessions each side must make to finally achieve lasting peace." (Publisher's note)

"Mitchell's careful statements may simply seem inconclusive to the more casual reader, but this is only a testament to the level of nuance in this scrupulous book." Pub Wkly

Includes bibliographical references and index.

Montefiore, Sebag

Jerusalem; the biography. [by] Simon Sebag Montefiore. Knopf 2011 638p il map $35   **956.94**

1. Jerusalem -- History

ISBN 978-0-307-26651-4; 0-307-26651-6

"An epic history of the holy city at the heart of Judaism, Christianity and Islam is presented through the lives of its creators and conquerors from King David and Jesus to the Maccabees and Sir Moses Montefiore, in a chronicle that draws on new archival materials, current scholarship and family records. By the award-winning author of Stalin." (Publisher's note)

"If, as some have maintained, the word Jerusalem means "city of peace," it is a grand historical irony. For, as this beautifully written, absorbing, but often grim account shows, there are few stones of the city that have not been stained with the blood of its inhabitants during the past 3,000 years. Acclaimed historian and biographer Montefiore views Jerusalem as a living, breathing organism bearing the genetic imprint of many conquerors, including Jews, Greeks, Arabs, crusading Franks, Turks, and the British. . . . While sometimes painful to read, this is an essential book for those who wish to understand a city that remains a nexus of world affairs." Booklist

O'Malley, Padraig

The **two**-state delusion; Israel and Palestine: a tale of two narratives. Padraig O'Malley. Viking 2015 432 p. maps $30   **956.94**

1. Israel-Arab conflicts 2. Israel -- Politics and government 3. Jews -- Identity 4. Arab-Israeli conflict -- Causes 5. Israel -- History -- 21st century 6. Palestinian Arabs -- Ethnic identity 7. Arab-Israeli conflict -- 1993- -- Peace 8. Arab-Israeli conflict -- Political aspects 9. Palestinian Arabs -- History -- 21st century 10. Israel -- Politics and government -- 21st century 11. Palestinian Arabs -- Politics and government -- 21st century

ISBN 0670025054; 9780670025053

LC 2014038545

In this book author Padraig O'Malley "argues that a two-state solution is no longer a viable path to create lasting peace in Israel and Palestine. O'Malley concludes that even if such an agreement could be reached, it would be nearly impossible to implement given the staggering costs, Palestine's political disunity and the viability of its economy, rapidly changing demographics, Israel's continuing political shift to the right, global warming's effect on the water supply, and more." (Publisher's note)

"If O'Malley's out-of-the-box advice lacks a comprehensive one-state solution, it could galvanize readers to engage in the discussion in new and more creative ways." Booklist

Includes bibliographical references and index

Palestine Speaks; Voices from the West Bank and Gaza. edited by Cate Malek and Mateo Hoke. McSweeney's 2014 320 p. illustrations, map $16   **956.94**
1. Palestine 2. Military occupation
ISBN 1940450241; 9781940450247

LC 2015452323

In this "oral history collection" edited by Cate Malek and Mateo Hoke, "men and women from Palestine--including a fisherman, a settlement administrator, and a marathon runner--describe in their own words how their lives have been shaped by the historic crisis. The occupation of the West Bank and Gaza has been one of the world's most widely reported yet least understood human rights crises for over four decades." (Publisher's note)

"An absolute must for anyone interested in the Arab-Israeli conflict or with an interest in human rights. This book, similar to the other titles in the series, is an excellent way of developing a deeper understanding of people living the encounters about which we read in the papers and watch on the news." LJ

Tolan, Sandy

The **lemon** tree; an Arab, a Jew, and the heart of the Middle East. Bloomsbury Pub. 2006 362p $24.95   **956.94**
1. Israel-Arab conflicts
ISBN 1-58234-343-8; 978-1-58234-343-3

LC 2005-30360

The author "captures the Arab-Israeli struggle in this story of a house and the two families, first Palestinian and then Jewish, who successively lived in it. . . . This wonderful human story vividly depicts the depths of attachment to contested ground." Libr J

956.940 Palestine; Israel ---1948

Bar-On, Mordechai

Moshe Dayan; Israel's controversial hero. Mordechai Bar-On. 1st ed. Yale University Press 2012 xii, 247 p.p photograph (alk. paper) $25   **956.940**
1. Soldiers -- Israel 2. Israel -- Politics and government 3. Generals -- Israel -- Biography 4. Statesmen -- Israel -- Biography 5. Arab-Israeli conflict -- Biography
ISBN 0300149417; 9780300149418

LC 2012000595

"In this . . . biography [of Israeli leader Moshe Dayan], Mordechai Bar-On . . . offers a . . . view of Dayan's private life, public career, and political controversies, set against an . . . analysis of Israel's political environment from pre-Mandate Palestine through the early 1980s. . . . Drawing on . . . Israeli archives, accounts by Dayan and members of his circle, and firsthand experiences, Bar-On reveals Dayan as a man unwavering in his devotion to Zionism and . . . Israel." (Publisher's note)
Includes bibliographical references (p. 219-236) and index

Brenner, Michael

In search for Israel; the history of an idea. Michael Brenner. Princeton University Press 2018 392 p. $29.95   **956.940**
1. Judaism 2. Israel -- History 3. Israel 4. Judaism -- Israel
ISBN 9780691179285

LC 2017037393

This book, by Michael Brenner, offers a "major new history of the century-long debate over what a Jewish state should be. . . . Born from the ashes of genocide and a long history of suffering, Israel was conceived to be unique. . . . It is this paradox, says . . . Brenner--the Jewish people's wish for a homeland both normal and exceptional--that shapes

Israel's ongoing struggle to define itself and secure a place among nations." (Publisher's note)
"A lucid, valuable text about a homeland that may not yet be a light unto the nations but is surely unique." Kirkus
Includes bibliographical references and index

Cohen, Richard

Israel; Is It Good for the Jews? Richard Cohen. Simon & Schuster 2014 288 p. (hardback) $26   **956.940**
1. Israel 2. Jews -- History 3. Israel -- History
ISBN 1416575685; 9781416575689; 9781416575696

LC 2014021062

National Jewish Book Awards Finalist: Modern Jewish Thought and Experience (2014)

This book, by Richard M. Cohen, "is part reportage, part memoir--an intimate journey through the history of Europe's Jews, culminating in the establishment of Israel. A veteran, syndicated columnist for 'The Washington Post,' . . . [the author] began this journey as a skeptic, wondering in a national column whether the creation of a Jewish State was 'a mistake.'" (Publisher's note)

"A thoughtful study recommended for both general and academic readers of history." LJ

La Guardia, Anton

War without end; Israelis, Palestinians, and the struggle for a promised land. St. Martin's Griffin 2003 xxii, 436p il map pa $16.95   **956.940**
1. Zionism 2. Palestinian Arabs 3. Israel-Arab conflicts 4. Israeli national characteristics
ISBN 0-312-31633-X

LC 2003-41288

First published 2001 in the United Kingdom with title: Holy Land, unholy war: Israelis and Palestinians

"This is fundamentally an examination of two wounded peoples, neither of whom seems capable of surmounting national myths and past hatreds to forge a new future. La Guardia is evenhanded in his criticism of both Israeli and Palestinian leaders, but he does not spare ordinary people. . . . This is an absorbing but heartbreaking examination of a seemingly endless tragedy that continues to unfold before our eyes." Booklist [review of 2002 edition]
Includes bibliographical references

Rubin, Barry

Israel; an introduction. Barry Rubin. Yale University Press 2012 ix, 340 p.p (paperback: alk. paper) $30.00   **956.940**
1. Israel
ISBN 0300162308; 9780300162301

LC 2011028927

This book presents a "survey of the many . . . facets of Israeli history, society, government, economics and culture . . . Such issues include existential insecurity, ongoing Palestinian conflict, fluid borders, diverse immigrant population, living with daily terrorist violence and the sense of being "misunderstood by outside observers." . . . [Barry Rubin] reminds readers that Jews even in exile acted as a "national people, arguably the first such in history," and thus the establishment of Israel was "the continuation of a long historical process," not merely the result of the Holocaust." (Kirkus)
Includes bibliographical references and index

Shilon, Avi

Menachem Begin; a life. Avi Shilon; translated from the Hebrew by Danielle Zilberberg and Yoram Sharett. Yale Uni-

versity Press 2012 545 p. (clothbound: alk. paper) $40 **956.940**
1. Prime ministers -- Israel 2. Israel -- Politics and government
3. Prime ministers -- Israel -- Biography 4. Revisionist Zionists
-- Israel -- Biography 5. Israel -- Politics and government -- 20th
century
ISBN 0300162359; 9780300162356

LC 2012012189

Author Avi Shilon discusses Menachem Begin. "The book presents a
detailed new portrait of Israel's founding leader. Among the many topics
Avi Shilon holds up to new light are Begin's antagonistic relationship
with David Ben-Gurion, his controversial role in the 1982 Lebanon War,
his unique leadership style, the changes in his ideology over the years,
and the mystery behind the total silence he maintained at the end of his
career." (Publisher's note)
Includes bibliographical references and index

956.95   Jordan and West Bank

Ehrenreich, Ben
The **Way** to the Spring; Life and Death in Palestine. by
Ben Ehrenreich. Penguin Group USA 2016 448 p. illustra-
tions, maps $28   **956.95**
1. Palestine 2. West Bank 3. Journalists 4. Palestinian Arabs
ISBN 1594205906; 9781594205903

LC 2016016951

This book, by journalist Ben Ehrenreich, is an "immersion into the
everyday struggles of Palestinian life. . . . Ruled by the Israeli military,
set upon and harassed constantly by Israeli settlers who admit unapologetically to wanting to drive them from the land, forced to negotiate an
ever more elaborate and more suffocating series of fences, checkpoints,
and barriers that have sundered home from field, home from home, this
is a population whose living conditions are unique." (Publisher's note)

"Ehrenreich's journal conveys how the Israeli-Palestinian conflict
truly plays out at ground level, where "normal" might include the sounds
of screaming, being arrested and questioned for hours, or simply being
shot at." Booklist
Includes bibliographical references (pages 371-411) and index.

Grossman, David
The **yellow** wind; translated from the Hebrew by Haim
Watzman; {with a new afterword by the author} Picador 2002
222p map pa $13   **956.95**
1. Palestinian Arabs 2. Jewish-Arab relations 3. West Bank
ISBN 0-312-42098-6

LC 2002-67325

Original Hebrew edition, 1987; this translation first published 1988
"Grossman was assigned to report for a weekly newspaper on life for
both occupied and occupier on the West Bank during the 20th anniversary of its conquest. With an eye and ear for revealing detail, he argues
that the Jews are now doing to Palestinians what has been done to them
through the ages." Libr J

957   Siberia (Asiatic Russia)

Frazier, Ian
Travels in Siberia. Farrar, Straus and Giroux 2010 529p il
map $30   **957**
1. Siberia (Russia) -- Description and travel
ISBN 978-0-374-27872-4; 0-374-27872-4

LC 2010-05784

"Frazier records several visits [to Siberia]: a summer's trip via
cantankerous automobile across the entire region, in the company of a
couple of local companions; a winter's journey by train and car, during
which the car sometimes used frozen waterways for roads; and a return
visit to see the effects of the emerging Russian energy industry. . . . The
contrasts are stark—one day, he walked through the ruins of a remote,
frozen Soviet-era prison camp and later saw a ballet in St. Petersburg—
and the writing is consistently rich. A dense, challenging, dazzling work
that will leave readers exhausted but yearning for more." Kirkus
Includes bibliographical references

Gessen, Masha
Where the Jews aren't; The Sad and Absurd Story of Biro-
bidzhan, Russia's Jewish Autonomous Region. Masha Gessen.
Nextbook/Schocken 2016 192 p. map (hardback) $25 **957.7**
1. Jews -- Russia 2. Russia -- History 3. Birobidzhan (Russia) --
History 4. Jews -- Russia (Federation) -- Birobidzhan 5. Evreĭskaia
avtonomnaia oblast' (Russia) -- History
ISBN 9780805242461

LC 2015049370

This book, by Masha Gessen, tells the "story of the Jews in twentieth-century Russia . . . . In 1929, the Soviet Union declared the area
of Birobidzhan a homeland for Jews. It was championed by a group of
intellectuals who envisioned a place of post-oppression Jewish culture.
. . . After the Second World War, the newly named 'Jewish Autonomous
Region' received an influx of Jews dispossessed from what had once
been the Pale, most of whom had lost families in the Holocaust." (Publisher's note)

"Gessen ably tells one of the 20th century's most chilling stories of
struggle, perseverance, and despair." Pub Wkly
Includes bibliographical references (pages [151]-163) and index.

Thubron, Colin
In Siberia. HarperCollins Pubs. 2000 287p hardcover o.p.
pa $14   **957**
1. Siberia (Russia) -- Description and travel
ISBN 0-06-095373-X pa

LC 99-41346

"Thubron elegantly encompasses both awe-inspiring landscapes and
their dark histories as well as immersing himself in local eccentricities."
Times Lit Suppl

958.1   Afghanistan

Badkhen, Anna, 1976-
★ The **world** is a carpet; four seasons in an Afghan village.
Anna Badkhen. Riverhead Hardcover 2013 288 p. (hardback)
$26.95   **958.1**
1. Nomads 2. Afghanistan 3. Carpets -- Afghanistan 4. Weaving
-- Afghanistan 5. Women weavers -- Afghanistan 6. Rugs, Oriental
-- Afghanistan 7. Afghanistan -- Social life and customs 8. Women
-- Afghanistan -- Social conditions -- 21st century
ISBN 1594488320; 9781594488320

LC 2013003827

This book relates the year author Anna Badkhen spent in a "Balkh village in northern Afghanistan that could not be found on the map, where
the illiterate Turkoman women fashioned the most exquisite rugs in the
world." She chronicles "the hard lives of the inhabitant survivors," who
deal with opium addiction, poverty, and colonizers. (Kirkus Reviews)

Coll, Steve

Ghost wars; the secret history of the CIA, Afghanistan, and bin Laden, from the Soviet invasion to September 10, 2001. Penguin Press 2004 695p maps $29.95; pa $16   **958.1**
1. Terrorists 2. Afghanistan 3. United States -- Central Intelligence Agency
ISBN 1-594-20007-6; 0-14-303466-9 pa
LC 2003-58593
The author "has given us what is certainly the finest historical narrative so far on the origins of Al Qaeda in the post-Soviet rubble of Afghanistan." N Y Times Book Rev
Includes bibliographical references

Dalrymple, William

Return of a king; the battle for Afghanistan, 1839-42. William Dalrymple. 1st ed. Alfred A. Knopf 2013 xxix, 515 p.p ill. (some col.), maps (hardcover) $30   **958.1**
1. Afghan War, 2001- 2. Afghanistan -- History -- British Intervention, 1838-1842 3. Afghanistan -- History, Military -- 19th century 4. British -- Afghanistan -- History -- 19th century
ISBN 0307958280; 9780307958280
LC 2012040998
This book, by William Dalrymple, "gives us the . . . account yet of the spectacular first battle for Afghanistan: the British invasion of the remote kingdom in 1839. . . . Dalrymple takes us beyond the bare outline of this infamous battle, and . . . illuminates the uncanny similarities between the West's first disastrous entanglement with Afghanistan and the situation today." (Publisher's note)
Includes bibliographical references (pages 493-497) and index.

Elliot, Jason

An unexpected light; travels in Afghanistan. St. Martin's Press 2001 473p map hardcover o.p. pa $18   **958.1**
1. Afghanistan -- Description and travel
ISBN 0-312-28846-8 pa
LC 2001-50036
This "is an account of Elliot's two visits to Afghanistan. The first occurred when he joined the mujaheddin circa 1979 and was smuggled into Soviet-occupied Afghanistan; the second happened nearly ten years later, when he returned to the still war-torn land. The skirmishes that Elliot painstakingly describes here took place between the Taliban and the government of Gen. Ahmad Shah Massoud in Kabul. . . . Elliot traveled widely in the hinterland, visiting Faizabad in the north and Herat in the west. The result is some of the finest travel writing in recent years." Libr J

Ewans, Martin

Afghanistan; a short history of its people and politics. HarperCollins Pubs. 2002 244p il maps hardcover o.p. pa $13.95   **958.1**
1. Afghanistan -- History
ISBN 0-06-050508-7 pa
LC 2002-17342
"This is a fascinating story and the best book-length examination of Afghanistan's history we're likely to have for some time." Booklist
Includes bibliographical references

Feifer, Gregory

The **great** gamble; the Soviet war in Afghanistan. Harper 2009 326p il map $27.99   **958.1**
1. Afghanistan -- History -- Soviet occupation, 1979-1989
ISBN 978-0-06-114318-2; 0-06-114318-9
LC 2008-22594
This is a history of the Soviet Union's 1979-1989 war in Afghanistan. "Taking advantage of his skills, experience, and contacts . . . as a foreign correspondent, Feifer's narrative relies greatly on the experiences of those involved on all sides of the conflict—from Soviet political and military insiders to various participants in the mujahideen resistance and even former CIA operatives—but he leans most heavily on the poignant stories of Soviet veterans. Fortunately for the reader, Feifer's research also includes a prudent mix of combat analyses, contemporary reports, and historical studies that inform a balanced treatment of his complex subject." Open Letters
Includes bibliographical references

Guibert, Emmanuel

★ The **photographer**; [by] Emmanuel Guibert, Didier Lefèvre and Frédéric Lemercier; translated by Alexis Siegel. First Second 2009 267p il map pa $29.95   **958.1**
1. Graphic novels 2. Photojournalism -- Graphic novels 3. Médecins Sans Frontières (Organization) -- Graphic novels 4. Afghanistan -- History -- Soviet occupation, 1979-1989 -- Graphic novels
ISBN 978-1-59643-375-5; 1-59643-375-2
"In 1986, photographer Didier Lefèvre documented a seasoned Médecins sans Frontières (Doctors without Borders) team en route to a region in the way of the insurgents' war with the Soviet army supporting Afghanistan's then-Marxist government. This wedding of his photos and Guibert's European-realist comics records his arduous, frightening round trip from Normandy, where his mother lived." (Booklist)
"Originally published as three volumes in France from 2003 to 2006, this graphic novel follows photojournalist Didier Lefèvre during his three months in Pakistan and Afghanistan in 1986 as he documented the medical missions of Doctors without Borders. . . . The graphic novel combines traditional comic art with some of the four thousand photographs Lefevre shot while in Afghanistan. . . . Many images will stay with readers as both horrifying and glorious. The Afghan children being treated for burns, bullet wounds, and shrapnel are page by page next to the beauty of the Afghan mountainous landscapes. . . . [This book] has a powerful message and images of a part of the world that should be discussed more often." Voice Youth Advocates

Junger, Sebastian

War. Twelve 2010 287p map $26.99   **958.1**
1. Afghan War, 2001- -- Personal narratives 2. United States -- Army -- Airborne Brigade, 173rd
ISBN 978-0-446-55624-8
LC 2009-49493
"The war in Afghanistan contains brutal trauma but also transcendent purpose in this riveting combat narrative. Junger spent 14 months in 2007-2008 intermittently embedded with a platoon of the 173rd Airborne brigade in Afghanistan's Korengal Valley, one of the bloodiest corners of the conflict. . . . Junger experiences everything they do—nerve-racking patrols, terrifying roadside bombings and ambushes, stultifying weeks in camp when they long for a firefight to relieve the tedium. . . . The result is an unforgettable portrait of men under fire." Publ Wkly
Includes bibliographical references

Lemmon, Gayle Tzemach

Ashley's war; the untold story of a team of women soldiers on the Special Ops battlefield. Gayle Tzemach Lemmon. HarperCollins 2015 320 p. illustrations (hbk.) $26.99   **958.1**
1. Afghan War, 2001- 2. Women in the military 3. Special forces (Military science) -- United States
ISBN 006233381X; 9780062333810

LC 2015460337

This book, by Gayle Tzemach Lemmon, tells the "story of a groundbreaking team of female American warriors who served alongside Special Operations soldiers on the battlefield in Afghanistan—including Ashley White, a beloved soldier who died serving her country's cause. . . . The idea was that women could access places and people that had remained out of reach, and could build relationships—woman to woman—in ways that male soldiers in a conservative, traditional country could not." (Publisher's note)

"This compassionate and intimate exposé addressing the female battlefield experience will resonate with readers interested in the woman warriors of today's military." LJ

Rashid, Ahmed

Taliban; militant Islam, oil and fundamentalism in Central Asia. 2nd ed; Yale University Press 2010 319p map pa $17.95   **958.1**
1. Islam and politics 2. Islamic fundamentalism 3. Taliban 4. Afghanistan -- Politics and government
ISBN 978-0-300-16368-1; 0-300-16368-1

LC 2009-938249

First published 2000

The author explains "the Taliban's rise to power, its impact on Afghanistan and the region, its role in oil and gas company decisions, and the effects of changing American attitudes toward the Taliban. He also describes the new face of Islamic fundamentalism and explains why Afghanistan has become the world center for international terrorism." Publisher's note

Includes bibliographical references

Romesha, Clinton L., 1981-

★ **Red** platoon; a true story of American valor. Clinton Romesha. Penguin Group USA 2016 400 p. illustrations (hardcover) $28   **958.1**
1. Battles 2. Afghan War, 2001- -- Personal narratives 3. Taliban 4. Kamdesh, Battle of, Afghanistan, 2009
ISBN 9780525955054; 0525955054

This book is "the only comprehensive, firsthand account of the fourteen hour firefight at the Battle of Keating [in the Afghan War] by Medal of Honor recipient Clinton Romesha. . . . On October 3, 2009, after years of constant smaller attacks, the Taliban finally decided to throw everything they had at Keating. The ensuing 14-hour battle—and eventual victory—cost 8 men their lives." (Publisher's note)

"This firsthand account by former U.S. Army staff sergeant Romesha, who earned the Medal of Honor for his actions during this battle, expertly disentangles the complicated threads of the effort, accounting for the actions (and deaths) of every participant, including the massive air support, medical care, and command decisions related to the action. . . . A clear and expertly crafted account of an iconic fight during the Afghan War, this work is sure to be popular with readers of military history." LJ

Schroen, Gary C.

First in; an insider's account of how the CIA spearheaded the war on terror in Afghanistan. Presidio Press/Ballantine Books 2005 $25.95; pa $14.95   **958.1**
1. Afghanistan 2. United States -- Central Intelligence Agency
ISBN 0-89141-872-5; 0-89141-875-X pa

LC 2005-43171

The author describes his experiences after he "was tapped to lead the effort to establish contact with the Northern Alliance in the days following 9/11; the 35-year CIA veteran commanded the first American team on the ground in Afghanistan. . . . Schroen delivers what he advertises:

a powerful account that takes the reader inside war councils and 19th-century- style cavalry charges in the months just after 9/11." Publ Wkly

Seierstad, Asne

The **bookseller** of Kabul; translated by Ingrid Christophersen. Little, Brown 2003 287p $19.95; pa $12.95 **958.1**
1. Afghanistan 2. Women -- Afghanistan
ISBN 0-316-73450-0; 0-316-15941-7 pa

LC 2003-54643

The author "entered Kabul with Northern Alliance soldiers after they ousted the Taliban. She took the rare opportunity to live with and write a book about the extended family of Sultan Khan, bookseller and entrepreneur. The result, organized around events in the lives of individual members of Khan's large clan . . . provides appropriate information about recent Afghani history, a glimpse from the inside at an Islamic family, and an understanding of the harshness and difficulty of the daily grind in Afghanistan—both under the Taliban and after the U.S. antiterrorist campaign." Booklist

Shah, Saira

The **storyteller's** daughter. Knopf 2003 253p $24; pa $13.95   **958.1**
1. Afghanistan
ISBN 0-375-41531-9; 1-4000-3147-8 pa

LC 2004-295126

The author "weaves oral traditions with history to describe life as an Afghani raised in the West but with solid roots in the East. . . . We learn about Shah's documentary work in Afghanistan, the power of myth through which Afghanistan's tradition is born, the brave work of peoples and organizations such as the Revolutionary Association of the Women of Afghanistan (RAWA), and the West's (and even East's) misconceptions regarding Muslim teachings. . . . This rare personal and historic account of the region is a great addition to public and academic libraries." Libr J

Wahab, Shaista

★ A **brief** history of Afghanistan; [by] Shaista Wahab and Barry Youngerman. 2nd ed; Facts on File 2010 354p il map (Brief history) $49.50; pa $19.95   **958.1**
1. Afghanistan -- History
ISBN 978-0-8160-8218-6; 978-0-8160-8219-3 pa; 978-1-4381-0819-3 ebook

LC 2010-19656

First published 2006

This history of Afghanistan "examines this country's isolation and how it found itself involved in 30 years of war and anarchy. . . . [It] explores the culture and politics of the Pashtun tribes whose homeland extends across much of Afghanistan and northern Pakistan, as well as the Taliban insurgency and the relationship between local leaders and the central government in Kabul." Publisher's note

Includes bibliographical references

West, Bing

The **wrong** war; grit, strategy, and the way out of Afghanistan. [by] Bing West. Random House 2011 307p il map $28   **958.1**
1. Afghan War, 2001-
ISBN 978-1-4000-6873-9; 1-4000-6873-8

LC 2010043107

West argues that "the central premise of counterinsurgency doctrine holds that if the Americans sacrifice on behalf of the Afghan government, then the Afghan people will risk their lives for that same government in return. They will fight the Taliban. . . . This isn't happening. . . . [The author contends that] the Afghans are waiting to see who prevails, but prevailing is impossible without their help." (N Y Times Book Rev) Bibliography. Index.

This is "a crushing and seemingly irrefutable critique of the American plan in Afghanistan. It should be read by anyone who wants to understand why the war there is so hard." N Y Times Book Rev

Includes bibliographical references

958.104   Afghanistan--1919-

Bruning, John R.

Level zero heroes; the story of U.S. Marine Special Operations in Bala Murghab, Afghanistan. Michael Golembesky with John R. Bruning. St. Martin's Press 2014 320 p. 16 plates; illustrations; maps (hardcover) $26.99   **958.104**
1. Afghan War, 2001- 2. Special forces (Military science) -- United States 3. Taliban 4. Close air support -- History -- 21st century 5. Afghan War, 2001- -- Personal narratives, American 6. Bādghīs (Afghanistan) -- History, Military 7. Afghan War, 2001- -- Campaigns -- Afghanistan -- Bādghīs 8. United States. Marine Corps -- Non-commissioned officers -- Biography 9. Murgab River Region (Afghanistan and Turkmenistan) -- History, Military 10. United States. Marine Special Operations Command. Marine Special Operations Team 8222 -- Biography
ISBN 1250030404; 9781250030405

LC 2014016597

Author "Michael Golembesky follows the members of U.S. Marine Special Operations Team 8222 on their assignment to . . . Taliban stronghold known as Bala Murghab as they conduct special operations. [It] brings to life the mission of these selected few that fought side-by-side in Afghanistan, in a narrative as action-packed and emotional as anything to emerge from the Special Operations community contribution to the Afghan War." (Publisher's note)

"Readers who enjoy first-person accounts of battles laced with non-stop action will have a tough time putting this one down." LJ

Includes bibliographical references

Story of U.S. Marine Special Operations in Bala Murghab, Afghanistan

Castner, Brian

All the ways we kill and die; an elegy for a fallen comrade and the hunt for his killer. Brian Castner. Arcade Pub. 2016 356 p. (hardcover: alk. paper) $25.99   **958.104**
1. Explosives 2. Afghan War, 2001- 3. Military personnel -- United States 4. Afghan War, 2001- -- Campaigns 5. Ordnance disposal units -- Afghanistan 6. United States. Air Force -- Officers -- Biography 7. Afghan War, 2001- -- Personal narratives, American 8. Improvised explosive devices -- Detection -- Afghanistan
ISBN 1628726547; 9781628726541

LC 2015040029

In this memoir, author "Brian Castner, an Iraq War vet, learns that his friend and [explosive ordnance disposal] brother Matt has been killed by an IED in Afghanistan, he . . . begins a personal investigation. Is the bomb maker who killed Matt the same man American forces have been hunting since Iraq, known as the Engineer? Castner takes us inside the manhunt for this elusive figure, meeting maimed survivors, interviewing the forensics teams who gather post-blast evidence, [and] the wonks who collect intelligence." (Publisher's note)

"Castner's writing is evocative and engaging, completely absorbing from beginning to end. A must-read for military buffs and a should-read for anyone who has given even a cursory thought to the U.S. efforts in Afghanistan and Iraq." Kirkus

Includes bibliographical references

Coll, Steve, 1958-

Directorate S; the C.I.A. and America's secret wars in Afghanistan and Pakistan. Steve Coll. Penguin Press 2018 xxiii, 757 p.p illustrations (hardcover) $35.00   **958.104**
1. Afghan War, 2001- 2. United States. Central Intelligence Agency 3. Pakistan -- Foreign relations -- United States 4. Afghanistan -- Foreign relations -- United States 5. Taliban 6. Qaida (Organization) 7. Military intelligence -- Pakistan 8. Pakistan. Inter Services Intelligence 9. Military intelligence -- United States 10. Pakistan -- Military relations -- United States 11. United States -- Military relations -- Pakistan
ISBN 9781594204586; 9780525557302; 1594204586

LC 2017470649

This book, by Steve Coll, tells the "story of America's intelligence, military, and diplomatic efforts to defeat Al Qaeda and the Taliban in Afghanistan and Pakistan since 9/11. . . . Today we know that the war in Afghanistan would falter badly. . . . But more than anything, as Coll makes painfully clear, the war in Afghanistan was doomed because of the failure of the United States to apprehend the motivations and intentions of I.S.I.'s 'Directorate S.'" (Publisher's note)

"With his evenhanded approach, gift for limning character, and dazzling reporting skills, he has created an essential work of contemporary history." Booklist

Includes bibliographical references (pages 729-736) and index

Darack, Ed

The **final** mission of Extortion 17; special ops, helicopter support, SEAL Team Six, and the deadliest day of the U.S. war in Afghanistan. Ed Darack. Smithsonian Books 2017 x, 227 p.p illustrations, maps (hardcover) $24.95   **958.104**
1. Helicopters 2. Afghan War, 2001- 3. United States. Army 4. Military art and science 5. United States. Navy. SEALs 6. Afghan War, 2001- -- Campaigns 7. Chinook (Military transport helicopter) 8. Afghan War, 2001- -- Aerial operations, American 9. United States. Navy. SEALs -- History -- 21st century 10. United States. Naval Special Warfare Development Group -- History 11. United States. Army. Ranger Regiment, 75th -- History -- 21st century 12. Special operations (Military science) -- United States -- History -- 21st century
ISBN 9781588345905; 9781588345899; 1588345890

LC 2017001110

In this book, by Ed Darack, "on August 6, 2011, a U.S. Army CH-47D Chinook helicopter approached a landing zone in Afghanistan 40 miles southwest of Kabul. The helicopter, call sign Extortion 17, was on a mission to reinforce American and coalition special operations troops. It would never return. . . . Darack . . . uncovers the truth behind this mysterious tragedy. His account of the brave pilots, crew, and passengers of Extortion 17 . . . is interwoven into a rich, complex narrative." (Publisher's note)

"Darack delivers a respectful salute to the dead amid detailed exemplification of the bravery of those fighting America's protracted war in Afghanistan." Booklist

Includes bibliographical references and index

Gall, Carlotta

The **wrong** enemy; America in Afghanistan, 2001/2014. Carlotta Gall. Houghton Mifflin Harcourt 2014 352 p. illustrations $28   **958.104**
1. Taliban 2. Afghan War, 2001- 3. Qaida (Organization) 4.

Pakistan -- Politics and government 5. Pakistan. Inter Services Intelligence 6. Afghanistan -- Politics and government 7. Pakistan -- Foreign relations -- United States 8. United States -- Foreign relations -- Pakistan 9. Afghanistan -- Foreign relations -- United States 10. United States -- Foreign relations -- Afghanistan
ISBN 0544046692; 9780544046696

LC 2013044257

"Carlotta Gall has reported from Afghanistan and Pakistan for almost the entire duration of the American invasion and occupation, beginning shortly after 9/11. She knows just how much this war has cost the Afghan people, and how much damage can be traced to Pakistan and its duplicitous government and intelligence forces. Now that American troops are withdrawing, it is time to tell the full history of how we have been fighting the wrong enemy, in the wrong country." Publisher's Note

"The author offers a compelling account of the attack on bin Laden's compound, the repercussions of which are still being felt. Gall admirably never loses sight of the human element in this tragedy." Kirkus

Includes bibliographical references and index

Gopal, Anand, 1980-

No good men among the living; America, the Taliban, and the war through Afghan eyes. Anand Gopal. Metropolitan Books 2014 320 p. map (hardback) $27   **958.104**
1. Taliban 2. Afghan War, 2001- 3. Peace-building -- Afghanistan 4. Counterinsurgency -- Afghanistan 5. Internal security -- Afghanistan 6. United States -- Military policy 7. Afghan War, 2001 -- Personal narratives, Afghani
ISBN 0805091793; 9780805091793

LC 2014001384

Pulitzer Prize Finalist: General Nonfiction (2015); National Book Award Finalist: Nonfiction (2014)

In this book, "Anand Gopal traces in vivid detail the lives of three Afghans caught in America's war on terror. He follows a Taliban commander, who rises from scrawny teenager to leading insurgent; a US-backed warlord, who uses the American military to gain personal wealth and power; and a village housewife trapped between the two sides, who discovers the devastating cost of neutrality." (Publisher's note)

"Policymakers and informed readers will benefit immensely from this illuminating book." LJ

Grenier, Robert L.

88 days to Kandahar; a CIA diary. Robert L. Grenier. Simon & Schuster 2014 448 p. 16 plates; illustrations; maps (hardcover) $28   **958.104**
1. Taliban 2. Afghan War, 2001- 3. Intelligence service -- United States 4. United States. Central Intelligence Agency 5. Afghan War, 2001- -- Campaigns 6. Afghan War, 2001- -- Secret service 7. Pakistan -- Relations -- United States 8. United States -- Relations -- Pakistan 9. Afghan War, 2001- -- Personal narratives, American 10. Intelligence officers -- United States -- Biography 11. Afghanistan -- Politics and government -- 21st century 12. United States. Central Intelligence Agency -- Biography
ISBN 1476712077; 9781476712079; 9781476712086

LC 2014036555

This book focuses on the "First American-Afghan War, a CIA war, [that] was approved by President George W. Bush and directed by the author, Robert Grenier, the CIA station chief in Islamabad. Forging separate alliances with warlords, Taliban dissidents, and Pakistani Intelligence, Grenier launched the 'southern campaign,' orchestrating the final defeat of the Taliban and Hamid Karzai's rise to power in eighty-eight chaotic days." (Publisher's note)

"This eye-opening account of how things really "work" in the Middle East and in modern war will appeal to general readers and those interested in political science, war memoirs, contemporary battle accounts, American history, Middle Eastern politics, and books about spies/covert operations. Highly Recommended." LJ

Eighty eight days to Kandahar, a CIA diary

Lamb, Christina

Farewell Kabul; from Afghanistan to a more dangerous world. by Christina Lamb. William Collins 2016 640 p. color ill., maps, portraits $17.99   **958.104**
1. Afghan War, 2001-
ISBN 0007256949; 0008171521; 9780007256945; 9780008171520

LC 2016019208

This book, by Christina Lamb, "tells how the West turned success into defeat in the longest war fought by the United States in its history and by Britain since the Hundred Years War. It is the story of well-intentioned men and women going into a place they did not understand at all. . . . It has been a fiasco which has left Afghanistan still one of the poorest and most dangerous nations on earth." (Publisher's note)

"Lamb's focus on the facts... provides an intense primer to the various sides of a complicated war that readers intrigued by foreign policy and curious about the region will certainly find well worth their time." Booklist

Includes bibliographical references and index.

Levy, Adrian

The **exile**; the stunning inside story of Osama bin Laden and Al Qaeda in flight. Cathy Scott-Clark and Adrian Levy. Bloomsbury USA 2017 xx, 619 p.p color illustrations (hardback) $30   **958.104**
1. Terrorists 2. Qaida (Organization) 3. Terrorism 4. Terrorists -- Biography
ISBN 9781620409855; 9781620409848

LC 2017008379

This book, by Cathy Scott-Clark and Adrian Levy, presents "an intimate insider's story of Osama bin Laden's retinue in the ten years after 9/11, a family in flight and at war. . . . 'The Exile' tells the extraordinary inside story of that decade through the eyes of those who witnessed it: bin Laden's four wives and many children, his deputies and military strategists, his spiritual advisor, the CIA, Pakistan's ISI, and many others who have never before told their stories." (Publisher's note)

"This extensively researched, eminently readable work greatly enhances public knowledge of these dramatic years and will be welcomed by specialists and general readers alike." Pub Wkly

Includes bibliographical references (pages 525-597) and index.

Luttrell, Marcus, 1975-

Lone survivor; the eyewitness account of Operation Redwing and the lost heroes of SEAL Team 10. Marcus Luttrell; with Patrick Robinson. 1st ed.; Little, Brown & Co. 2007 390 p. ill., maps $28   **958.104**
1. Afghan War, 2001- 2. United States. Navy. SEALs 3. Afghan War, 2001- -- Campaigns 4. United States. Navy. SEALs -- Officers 5. Afghan War, 2001- -- Personal narratives, American
ISBN 0316067598; 9780316067591

LC 2007921207

This memoir by Marcus Luttrell, with Patrick Robinson, recalls how "in late June 2005, four U.S. Navy SEALs left their base in northern Afghanistan for the mountainous Pakistani border. Their mission was to capture or kill a notorious al Qaeda leader known to be ensconced in a Taliban stronghold surrounded by a small but heavily armed force. Less then twenty-four hours later, only one of those Navy SEALs remained alive." (Publisher's note)

Maurer, Kevin

No easy day; the autobiography of a Navy SEAL: the firsthand account of the mission that killed Osama Bin Laden. Mark Owen; with Kevin Maurer. Dutton 2012 xiii, 316 p.p $26.95 **958.104**

1. Afghan War, 2001- -- Personal narratives 2. Special forces (Military science) -- United States 3. Qaida (Organization) 4. United States. Navy. SEALs -- Biography 5. United States. Navy -- Commando troops -- Biography
ISBN 0525953728; 9780525953722

LC 2012371921

This book, by Mark Owen with Kevin Mauer, offers a "first-person account of the planning and execution of the Bin Laden raid from a Navy Seal" who was present on the mission. The book follows "Owen and the other handpicked members of the twenty-four-man team as they train[ed] for the biggest mission of their lives." It provides a "narrative of the assault, beginning with the helicopter crash . . . straight through to the radio call confirming Bin Laden's death." (Publisher's note)

Includes bibliographical references.

Nordland, Rod

The **Lovers**; Afghanistan's Romeo and Juliet, the True Story of How They Defied Their Families and Escaped an Honor Killing. HarperCollins 2016 384 p. chiefly col. ill., map $26.99 **958.104**

1. Love 2. Honor 3. Islamic law 4. Women -- Afghanistan
ISBN 0062378821; 9780062378828

This book, by Rod Nordland, tells the "story of a young couple. . . . Zakia and Ali were from different tribes, but they grew up on neighboring farms in the hinterlands of Afghanistan. By the time they were young teenagers, [they] had fallen in love. Defying their families, sectarian differences, cultural conventions, and Afghan civil and Islamic law, they ran away together only to live under constant threat from Zakia's large and vengeful family, who have vowed to kill her." (Publisher's note)

"Nordland offers a stark, eye-opening look at the deplorable state of women's rights in Afghanistan through the travails of a brave, determined young couple." Booklist

Includes bibliographical references and index.

Omar, Qais Akbar

A **fort** of nine towers; an Afghan family story. by Qais Akbar Omar. 1st ed. Farrar, Straus and Giroux 2013 396 p. maps (hardcover) $27.00 **958.104**

1. Family 2. Afghanistan -- Social conditions 3. Afghanistan -- Biography 4. Afghanistan -- Social conditions -- 20th century
ISBN 0374157642; 9780374157647

LC 2012034566

In this book, author Qais Akbar Omar presents a coming-of-age memoir about his experiences in Afghanistan during the Afghan Civil War. "With rockets falling around them, Omar's family fled, leaving behind everything they owned to take shelter in an old fort. As the violence escalated, Omar's father decided he must take his children out of the country to safety. Omar recounts terrifyingly narrow escapes and absurdist adventures, as well as moments of intense joy and beauty." (Publisher's note)

Partlow, Joshua

★ A **kingdom** of their own; The Family Karzai and the Afghan Disaster. Joshua Partlow. Alfred A. Knopf 2016 432 p. illustrations (hardback) $30 **958.104**

1. Afghan War, 2001- 2. Afghanistan -- Politics and government 3. United States -- Foreign relations -- Afghanistan 4. Afghanistan -- Foreign relations -- United States
ISBN 9780307962645

LC 2016007281

This book by Joshua Partlow focuses on the failed relationship between the powerful Karzai family and the United States. "The United States went to Afghanistan on a simple mission: avenge the September 11 attacks and drive the Taliban from power. . . . [In] the ensuing fight for power and money, . . . President Hamid Karzai and his brothers began the war as symbols of a new Afghanistan: . . . the antithesis of the brutish and backward Taliban regime." (Publisher's note)

"American military and political arrogance butts up against deep-rooted cultural customs and family networks throughout this excellent account of a vastly difficult topic." Pub Wkly

Includes bibliographical references (pages [391]-402) and index.

Slahi, Mohamedou Ould, 1970-

Guantanamo diary; Mohamedou Ould Slahi; edited by Larry Siems. Little, Brown & Co. 2015 400 p. $29 **958.104**

1. Torture 2. Prisoners 3. Guantanamo Bay Detention Camp 4. War on Terrorism, 2001-2009 -- Biography 5. Prisoners of war -- United States -- Diaries 6. Political prisoners -- United States -- Diaries 7. Guantánamo Bay Detention Camp -- Biography 8. Mauritanians -- Cuba -- Guantánamo Bay Naval Base -- Diaries 9. Political prisoners -- Cuba -- Guantánamo Bay Naval Base -- Diaries
ISBN 0316328685; 9780316328685

LC 2014023763

This memoir, edited by Larry Siems, tells how "since 2002, [author] Mohamedou Slahi has been imprisoned at the detention camp at Guantánamo Bay, Cuba. In all these years, the United States has never charged him with a crime. . . . Three years into his captivity Slahi began a diary. . . . His diary is not merely a vivid record of a miscarriage of justice, but a deeply personal memoir--terrifying, darkly humorous, and surprisingly gracious." (Publisher's note)

"Slahi may or may not be a reliable narrator; readers are called on to suspend disbelief. By his account, of course, he is not guilty. His memoir is essential reading for anyone concerned with human rights and the rule of law."

Smith, Graeme

The **Dogs** Are Eating Them Now; Our War in Afghanistan. by Graeme Smith. Knopf Canada 2013 320 p. illustrations, maps $26 **958.104**

1. Journalists 2. Afghan War, 2001-
ISBN 0307397807; 1619024799; 9780307397805; 9781619024793

LC 2014034083

This book, by foreign correspondent Graeme Smith, "is a highly personal narrative of our war in Afghanistan. . . . Smith was not simply embedded with the military: he operated independently and at great personal risk to report from inside the war, and the heroes of his story are the translators, guides, and ordinary citizens who helped him find the truth. They revealed sad, absurd, touching stories that provide the key to understanding why the mission failed to deliver peace and democracy." (Publisher's note)

"Recommended for readers of battlefield accounts and those seeking a better understanding of the Afghani people. For another excellent journalistic account, see Edward Giradet's Killing the Cranes." LJ

959.1   Myanmar

Thant Myint-U

The **river** of lost footsteps; histories of Burma. Farrar, Straus & Giroux 2006 361p il map $25; pa $15   **959.1**

1. Myanmar

ISBN 978-0-374-16342-6; 0-374-16342-1; 978-0-374-53116-4 pa; 0-374-53116-1 pa

LC 2006-09199

"This readable, reflective history will support revived interest in Burma." Booklist

Includes bibliographical references

959.3   Thailand

Krauss, Erich

Wave of destruction; the stories of four families and history's deadliest tsunami. Rodale 2006 244p il map $24.95 **959.3**

1. Tsunamis 2. Survival after airplane accidents, shipwrecks, etc. 3. Thailand

ISBN 1-59486-378-4

LC 2005-24531

The author provides an "account of four families in a Thai village devastated by the tsunami of December 26, 2004. . . . Passionately told, this tragic story portrays the full human cost of natural devastation." Publ Wkly

959.6   Cambodia

Brinkley, Joel, 1952-2014

Cambodia's curse; the modern history of a troubled land. PublicAffairs 2011 386p il $27.99   **959.6**

1. Heads of state 2. Communist leaders 3. Political leaders 4. Democracy -- Cambodia 5. Cambodia -- History -- 1979- 6. Cambodia -- Social conditions 7. Cambodia -- Politics and government 8. Cambodia -- Politics and government -- 1979-

ISBN 978-1-58648-787-4; 1-58648-787-6

LC 2010-44806

"Brinkley cuts a clear narrative path through the bewildering, cynical politics and violent social life of one of the worlds most brutalized and hard-up countries." Foreign Affairs

Includes bibliographical references

Ung, Loung

★ **First** they killed my father; a daughter of Cambodia remembers. HarperCollins Pubs. 2000 240p il hardcover o.p. pa $13.95   **959.6**

1. Cambodia -- History -- 1975-

ISBN 0-06-019332-8; 0-06-085626-2 pa

LC 99-34707

The author's father was a "high-ranking government official in Phnom Penh. She was only five when the Khmer Rouge stormed the city and her family was forced to flee. They sought refuge in various camps, hiding their wealth and education, always on the move and ever fearful of being betrayed. After 20 months, Ung's father was taken away, never to be seen again. Her story of starvation, forced labor, beatings, attempted rape, separations, and the deaths of her family members is one of horror and brutality." SLJ

959.604 -1949

Bizot, Francois

The **gate**; translated from the French by Euan Cameron; with a preface by John Le Carré. Knopf 2003 275p $24; pa $14   **959.604**

1. Atrocities 2. Communism -- Cambodia 3. Cambodia -- History -- 1970-1975, Civil War

ISBN 0-375-41293-X; 0-375-72723-X pa

LC 2002-69428

Original French edition, 2000

Bizot's "tale of his experiences, both in the camp and as translator at the gate of the French embassy, leaves readers with haunting images of the doomed." Booklist

Him, Chanrithy, 1965-

When broken glass floats; growing up under the Khmer Rouge. Norton 2000 330p il map hardcover o.p. pa $13.95   **959.604**

1. Refugees 2. Memoirists 3. Interpreters 4. Cambodia -- History 5. Political refugees -- Cambodia 6. Political atrocities -- Cambodia 7. Political refugees -- United States 8. Cambodia -- Politics and government -- 1975-1979

ISBN 0-393-32210-6 pa

LC 99-58417

This is an account of the author's experiences as a child in Cambodia under the Khmer Rouge. Him "watched {her} father hauled away to be killed, saw {her} mother and several siblings die by execution, starvation and disease. After the Khmer Rouge's downfall, {she} eventually escaped to Thailand and then to the United States." (N Y Times Book Rev)

Him "was 10 in 1975 when the Khmer Rouge overtook her country in what she calls the time of broken glass. Feeling a survivor's responsibility to do so, Him vividly recalls the brutality of the camps, the strict social control, and alienation from family that the Khmer Rouge enforced." Booklist

959.7   Vietnam

Blehm, Eric

Legend; A Harrowing Story from the Vietnam War of One Green Beret's Heroic Mission to Rescue a Special Forces Team Caught Behind Enemy Lines. Eric Blehm. Random House Inc. 2015 288 p. 16 plates; ills.; maps; ports. $27   **959.7**

1. Rescue work 2. Vietnam War, 1961-1975 3. Special forces (Military science) -- United States

ISBN 0804139512; 9780804139519

LC 2015451022

In this book, Eric Blehm looks at the Vietnam War through "a single mission that occurred on May 2, 1968. A twelve-man Special Forces team had been covertly inserted into a small clearing in the jungles of neutral Cambodia. Soon they found themselves surrounded by hundreds of NVA, under attack. When Special Forces Staff Sergeant Roy Benavidez heard the distress call, he jumped aboard the next helicopter bound for the combat zone." (Publisher's note)

"Overall, the narrative seems a good magazine article pulled into book length, with some slipshod moments (e.g., one doesn't get a master's degree in Shakespeare) and too many draggy stretches. In the hands of a Junger or Krakauer, this story might have taken more memorable form . Still, Vietnam War completists will be interested." Kirkus

Goscha, Christopher

Vietnam; Christopher Goscha. Basic Books 2016 592 p. illustrations, maps $35 **959.7**

1. Vietnam -- History 2. Vietnam -- Colonization
ISBN 9780465094363

LC 2016017630

In this book, author Christopher Goscha "tells the full history of Vietnam, from antiquity to the present day. Generations of emperors, rebels, priests, and colonizers left complicated legacies in this remarkable country. Periods of Chinese, French, and Japanese rule reshaped and modernized Vietnam, but so too did the colonial enterprises of the Vietnamese themselves as they extended their influence southward from the Red River Delta." (Publisher's note)

"A vigorous, eye-opening account of a country of great importance to the world, past and future." Kirkus

Includes bibliographical references and index

959.704   Vietnam--1945-

Appy, Christian G.

American Reckoning; The Vietnam War and Our National Identity. Christian G. Appy. Penguin Group USA 2015 416 p. $28.95 **959.704**

1. Vietnam War, 1961-1975 2. National characteristics 3. United States -- Politics and government
ISBN 0670025399; 9780670025398

LC 2014038477

In this book on the Vietnam War, Christian G. Appy argues "that the way the war was fought and its outcome put an indelible dent in the idea of American exceptionalism. The war, he argues, 'shattered the central tenet of American national identity--the broad faith that the United States is a unique force for good in the world.'" (Publishers Weekly)

"Appy paints with a broad brush and may interpret our national security needs too narrowly. Still, his assertion that our current policies could guarantee constant warfare deserves to be seriously considered." Booklist

Boot, Max

★ The **road** not taken; Edward Lansdale and the American tragedy in Vietnam. Max Boot. Liveright Publishing Corporation 2018 xxxix, 717 p.p illustrations, maps (hardcover) $35 **959.704**

1. United States. Central Intelligence Agency -- Officials and employees -- Biography 2. United States. Army -- Biography 3. Generals -- United States -- Biography 4. Vietnam War, 1961-1975 -- United States 5. United States. Air Force -- Officers -- Biography 6. Intelligence officers -- United States -- Biography
ISBN 9780871409430; 9780871409416; 0871409410

LC 2017047418

In this biography, author Max Boot describes "the adventurous life of legendary [U.S. Central Intelligence Agency] operative Edward Lansdale . . . [which] definitively reframes our understanding of the Vietnam War. . . . [Boot] demonstrates how Lansdale pioneered a 'hearts and mind' diplomacy, first in the Philippines, then in Vietnam. It was a visionary policy that, as Boot reveals, was ultimately crushed by America's giant military bureaucracy." (Publisher's note)

"A probing, timely study of wrong turns in the American conduct of the Vietnam War." Kirkus

Includes bibliographical references and index.

Bowden, Mark, 1951-

★ **Hue** 1968; a turning point of the American war in Vietnam. Mark Bowden. Atlantic Monthly Press 2017 610 p. (hardcover) $30 **959.704**

1. Tet Offensive, 1968 2. Vietnam War, 1961-1975 3. Hue, Battle of, Huế, Vietnam, 1968 4. Vietnam War, 1961-1975 -- Urban warfare -- United States
ISBN 9780802127006; 9780802189240

LC 2017022809

This book, by Mark Bowden, presents "the story of the centerpiece of the Tet Offensive and a turning point in the American War in Vietnam. . . . The lynchpin of Tet was the capture of Hue, Vietnam's intellectual and cultural capital, by 10,000 National Liberation Front troops who descended from hidden camps and surged across the city of 140,000. . . . Bowden narrates each stage of this crucial battle through multiple viewpoints." (Publisher's note)

"One of the best books on a single action in Vietnam, written by a tough, seasoned journalist who brings the events of a half-century past into sharp relief." Kirkus

Burns, Ken, 1953-

★ The **Vietnam** War; an intimate history. Geoffrey C. Ward; based on a documentary film by Ken Burns & Lynn Novick; with a preface by Ken Burns & Lynn Novick. Alfred A. Knopf 2017 xiii, 612 p.p illustrations, maps (hardcover) $60 **959.704**

1. War 2. Historical literature 3. Vietnam War, 1961-1975 4. World politics -- 1945-1989
ISBN 9781524733100; 9780307700254; 9780375712203

LC 2017015686

In this book, by Geoffrey C. Ward, based on a documentary by Ken Burns and Lynn Novick, "more than forty years after it ended, the Vietnam War continues to haunt our country. . . . The authors draw on dozens and dozens of interviews . . . to give us the perspectives of people involved at all levels of the war. . . . Rather than taking sides, the book seeks to understand why the war happened the way it did, and to clarify its complicated legacy." (Publisher's note)

"Accompanying the PBS series to be aired in September 2017, this is an outstanding, indispensable survey of the Vietnam War." Kirkus

Includes bibliographical references and index

Caputo, Philip

★ A **rumor** of war; with a twentieth anniversary postscript by the author. Henry Holt and Co. 1996 xxi, 356p pa $15 **959.704**

1. Vietnam War, 1961-1975 -- Personal narratives
ISBN 0-8050-4695-X

LC 96-19314

First published 1977 by Holt, Rinehart & Winston

These are "the combat recollections of a very young Marine officer in Vietnam in 1965-1966. Caputo later became a newspaperman. . . . He remembers himself as a patriotic youngster, eager to prove his manhood, and then . . . he takes us through his step-by-step discovery that war and manhood and their interrelation are more complicated than he had dreamed." New Yorker

Duiker, William J.

Ho Chi Minh; by William Duiker. Hyperion 2000 695p il maps $35; pa $16.95 **959.704**

1. Heads of state 2. Communist leaders 3. Political leaders
ISBN 0-7868-6387-0; 0-7868-8701-X pa

LC 00-26757

In this biography the author "examines Ho's life primarily in the context of his political activity in Paris, Moscow, southern China, and Vietnam, occasionally spiced with anecdotes of Ho's highly secretive personal life. . . . Duiker handles the complicated political and diplomatic issues with ease, and his narrative, though it sometimes strays from Ho's life to fill in the bigger picture, never bogs down." Booklist

Includes bibliographical references

Ellsberg, Daniel

Secrets: a memoir of Vietnam and the Pentagon papers. Viking 2002 498p il $29.95; pa $16   **959.704**
1. Vietnam War, 1961-1975 2. Pentagon Papers
ISBN 0-670-03030-9; 0-14-200342-5 pa

LC 2002-16874

Ellsberg recalls how he leaked "the Pentagon Papers, which documented U.S. foreign-policy failures and deceit in Vietnam from 1945 to 1968. . . . Ellsberg's autobiographical account provides insight into the disturbing abuses of presidential power that plagued the Vietnam/Watergate era." Libr J

Includes bibliographical references

FitzGerald, Frances

Fire in the lake; the Vietnamese and the Americans in Vietnam. Little, Brown 1972 491p maps hardcover o.p. pa $16.95   **959.704**
1. Vietnam War, 1961-1975 2. Vietnam -- Politics and government
ISBN 0-316-15919-0 pa

This book looks at the effects American intervention had on the Vietnamese social and intellectual landscape.

Includes bibliographical references

Hampton, Dan

The **hunter** killers; the extraordinary story of the first Wild Weasels, the band of maverick aviators who flew the most dangerous missions of the Vietnam War. Dan Hampton. William Morrow 2015 416 p. 16 plates; illustrations; maps (hardcover) $27.99   **959.704**
1. Air pilots 2. Electronic warfare 3. Vietnam War, 1961-1975 -- Aerial operations 4. Vietnam War, 1961-1975 -- Campaigns 5. Vietnam War, 1961-1975 -- Political aspects 6. Vietnam War, 1961-1975 -- Aerial operations, American 7. Electronic warfare aircraft -- United States -- History -- 20th century
ISBN 006237513X; 9780062375124; 9780062375131; 9780062392947

LC 2015007013

This book, by Dan Hampton, tells the story of how, "at the height of the Cold War, America's most elite aviators bravely volunteered for a covert program aimed at eliminating an impossible new threat. . . . Vietnam, 1965: . . . a USAF F-4 Phantom jet was suddenly blown from the sky by a mysterious and lethal weapon--a Soviet SA-2 surface-to-air missile (SAM). . . . the Pentagon ordered a top secret program called Wild Weasel I to counter the SAM problem." (Publisher's note)

"Hampton uses a lot of military terminology, some of which might be difficult for the lay reader to understand, but his overall writing style is excellent; in particular, his vivid, fast-paced combat narratives. His latest work will appeal to military history fans or anyone looking for an absorbing read." LJ

Includes bibliographical references and index

Extraordinary story of the first Wild Weasels, the band of maverick aviators who flew the most dangerous missions of the Vietnam War

Karnow, Stanley

Vietnam; a history. 2nd rev & updated ed; Penguin Bks. 1997 768p il maps pa $17.95   **959.704**
1. Vietnam War, 1961-1975 2. Vietnam -- History
ISBN 0-14-026547-3

First published 1983

A summation "of over two centuries of conflict in Indochina. Chronicling a tragic history, Karnow presents a balanced and sympathetic view of Vietnamese aspirations and the mishaps that led to American involvement in a 'war nobody won.'" Voice Youth Advocates [review of 1983 edition]

Includes bibliographical references

Kissinger, Henry

Ending the Vietnam War; a history of America's involvement in and extrication from the Vietnam War. Touchstone 2002 640p map pa $18   **959.704**
1. Vietnam War, 1961-1975
ISBN 0-7432-1532-X

LC 2002-17996

"Readers interested in the Vietnam period but unfamiliar with Kissinger's previous books will find this new volume worthwhile. . . . Kissinger's account of America's venture in Vietnam and his role in that shipwreck is factually accurate, eminently informed and masterfully crafted." Publ Wkly

Includes bibliographical references

Logevall, Fredrik, 1963-

★ **Embers** of War; The Fall of an Empire and the Making of America's Vietnam. Fredrik Logevall. Random House 2012 xxii, 839 p.p ill.   **959.704**
1. France -- Colonies 2. Vietnam War, 1961-1975 3. Indochinese War, 1946-1954 4. United States -- Foreign relations -- Vietnam 5. United States -- Politics and government -- 1961-1974
ISBN 0375504427; 9780375504426

LC 2011034971

Pulitzer Prize: History (2013)

This book examines "the [Vietnam] war's roots in the U.S. reaction to the French colonial experience." Discussing "the global changes wrought by WWII, the beginning of the cold war, and America's new role as the pre-eminent power in Asian and world affairs . . . [Fredrik] Logevall makes" the "case that America's Vietnam involvement replicated the French experience: the U.S. was fighting against an anticolonialist revolution and giving the Democratic Republic of Vietnam legitimacy." (Publishers Weekly)

Includes bibliographical references and index.

Maraniss, David

They marched into sunlight; war and peace in Vietnam and America, October 1967. Simon & Schuster 2003 592p il map hardcover o.p. pa $16   **959.704**
1. Vietnam War, 1961-1975
ISBN 0-7432-1780-2; 0-7432-6104-6 pa

LC 2003-52885

This is a "narrative by a reporter who juxtaposes a ghastly little battle in Vietnam with an antiwar and anti-Dow demonstration at the University of Wisconsin, Madison, on the same day; it captures moral ambiguity everywhere, without stereotyping or condescension." N Y Times Book Rev

Includes bibliographical references

McNamara, Robert S.

In retrospect; the tragedy and lessons of Vietnam. Vintage Bks. 1996 518p il map pa $16.95 **959.704**
1. Vietnam War, 1961-1975
ISBN 0-679-76749-5; 978-0-679-76749-7
First published 1995 by Times Books
"Former defense secretary McNamara seeks 'to put Vietnam in context' and counter 'the cynicism and even contempt with which so many people view our political institutions and leaders.' . . . He identifies 'eleven major causes for our disaster in Vietnam' and six points when the U.S. could legitimately have withdrawn. Certainly not the last word on this still-controversial subject but an essential acquisition for most libraries." Booklist
Includes bibliographical references

Moore, Harold G.

We are soldiers still; a journey back to the battlefields of Vietnam. [by] Harold G. Moore and Joseph L. Galloway. Harper 2008 248p il $24.95; pa $14.99 **959.704**
1. Vietnam -- Description and travel 2. Vietnam War, 1961-1975 -- Personal narratives
ISBN 978-0-06-114776-0; 0-06-114776-1; 978-0-06-114777-7 pa; 0-06-114777-X pa
LC 2008-11034
Sequel to We were soldiers once¿and young (1992)
"A worthy and wise successor to one of the best books ever about combat in Vietnam." Kirkus

Morgan, Ted

Valley of death; the tragedy at Dien Bien Phu that led America into the Vietnam War. Random House 2010 722p il map $35 **959.704**
1. Indochinese War, 1946-1954 2. Dien Bien Phu, Battle of, 1954 3. United States -- Foreign relations -- Vietnam 4. Vietnam -- Foreign relations -- United States
ISBN 978-1-4000-6664-3
LC 2009-19714
"This absorbing account of the prelude, battle, and aftermath that ended the 'first Viet Nam War' is a sad tale of misconception, missed opportunities, and massive blunders by French and even American military and civilian officials. . . . This is a superb chronicle of a sad and avoidable conflict that led to an even more destructive one." Booklist
Includes bibliographical references

Nguyen, Viet Thanh, 1971-

Nothing ever dies; Vietnam and the memory of war. Viet Thanh Nguyen. Harvard University Press 2016 356 p. illustrations $27.95 **959.704**
1. Vietnam War, 1961-1975 2. Art and war 3. War and society 4. Identity (Psychology) in art 5. Memory -- Sociological aspects 6. Vietnam War, 1961-1975 -- Social aspects 7. Vietnam War, 1961-1975 -- Art and the war
ISBN 9780674660342
LC 2015037444
National Book Award Finalist: Nonfiction (2016)
This book, by Viet Thanh Nguyen, "brings a comprehensive vision of the [Vietnam] war into sharp focus. At stake are ethical questions about how the war should be remembered by participants that include not only Americans and Vietnamese but also Laotians, Cambodians, South Koreans, and Southeast Asian Americans." (Publisher's note)
"Essentially a critical study, Nguyen's work is a powerful reflection on how we choose to remember and forget." Kirkus

Includes bibliographical references and index

Reston, James, 1941-

A **rift** in the Earth; art, memory, and the fight for a Vietnam War memorial. James Reston, Jr. Arcade Publishing 2017 xi, 267 p.p illustrations (some color) (hardcover: alk. paper) $24.99 **959.704**
1. National monuments 2. Vietnam Veterans Memorial (Washington, D.C.) 3. Washington (D.C.) -- Buildings, structures, etc 4. Vietnam Veterans Memorial (Washington, D.C.) -- History 5. Vietnam War, 1961-1975 -- Monuments -- Washington (D.C.)
ISBN 9781628728569; 9781628728583
LC 2017012314
This book, by James Reston, Jr., "tells the remarkable story of the ferocious 'art war' that raged between 1979 and 1984 over what kind of memorial should be built to honor the men and women who died in the Vietnam War. The story intertwines art, politics, historical memory, patriotism, racism, and a fascinating set of characters, from those who fought in the conflict and those who resisted it to politicians at the highest level." (Publisher's note)
"A gripping history of the fights over how to memorialize the Vietnam War." Kirkus
Includes bibliographical references and index

Sallah, Michael

Tiger Force; a true story of men and war. [by] Michael Sallah and Mitch Weiss. Little, Brown 2006 403p il map $25.95 **959.704**
1. Vietnam War, 1961-1975 2. United States -- Army -- Infantry Regiment, 327th -- Battalion, 1st
ISBN 0-316-15997-2; 978-0-316-15997-5
LC 2005-20921
"In 1967, the Tiger Force platoon of the 101st Airborne went on a seven-month-long rampage through South Vietnam's central highlands that left dead more than 325 civilians, mostly children, women, and old men. . . . [This] is a searing narrative, difficult to read yet difficult to put down, about Tiger Force's descent into a leaderless and ruthless unit, in which, as one of the ex-soldiers puts it to the authors, the objective was to 'kill anything that moves.'" Libr J
Includes bibliographical references

Stanton, Doug

The **odyssey** of Echo Company; the 1968 Tet Offensive and the epic battle to survive the Vietnam War. Doug Stanton. Scribner 2017 xix, 312 p.p illustrations, maps (hardcover) $30 **959.704**
1. Tet Offensive, 1968 2. Vietnam War, 1961-1975 -- Regimental histories 3. Tet Offensive, 1968 -- Personal narratives, American 4. Vietnam War, 1961-1975 -- Personal narratives, American 5. Vietnam War, 1961-1975 -- Regimental histories -- United States 6. United States. Army. Airborne Division, 101st -- History -- 20th century
ISBN 1476761914; 9781476761930; 9781476761916
This book, by Doug Stanton, presents "the harrowing, redemptive, and utterly unforgettable account of an American army reconnaissance platoon's fight for survival during the Vietnam War. . . . On a single night, January 31, 1968, as many as 100,000 soldiers in the North Vietnamese Army attacked thirty-six cities throughout South Vietnam. . . . Forty young American soldiers . . . are suddenly thrust into savage combat, having been in-country only a few weeks." (Publisher's note)
Includes bibliographical references (pages 301-312).

Talty, Stephan

Saving Bravo; the greatest rescue mission in Navy SEAL history. Stephan Talty. Houghton Mifflin Harcourt 2018 320 p. (hardback) $28   **959.704**

1. Rescue work 2. Vietnam War, 1961-1975 3. United States. Navy. SEALs 4. Search and rescue operations -- Vietnam 5. Vietnam War, 1961-1975 -- Search and rescue operations 6. United States. Navy. SEALs -- Search and rescue operations -- Vietnam

ISBN 9781328866721

LC 2018006365

This book, by Stephan Talty, tells "the untold story of the most important rescue mission not just of the Vietnam War, but the entire Cold War: one American aviator, who knew our most important secrets, crashed behind enemy lines and risked capture by both the North Vietnamese and the Soviets. One Navy SEAL and his Vietnamese partner had to sneak past them all to save him." (Publisher's note)

Includes bibliographical references and index

Thi, Kim Phuc Phan

★ **Fire** road; the Napalm girl's journey through the horrors of war to faith, forgiveness, and peace. Kim Phuc Phan Thi. Tyndale Momentum 2017 xv, 317 p.p (hc) $25.99   **959.704**

1. Christian biography 2. Vietnam War, 1961-1975 -- Women -- Biography 3. Vietnam War, 1961-1975 -- Children -- Biography 4. Napalm -- History 5. Women -- Vietnam -- Biography 6. Vietnamese -- Canada -- Biography 7. Women refugees -- Canada -- Biography 8. Chemical burns -- Patients -- Biography 9. Political refugees -- Canada -- Biography 10. Vietnam War, 1961-1975 -- Aerial operations, American

ISBN 9781496424297; 9781496424303

LC 2017021371

This book, by Kim Phuc Phan Thi, is about the horrors of the Vietnam War. "Get out! Run! We must leave this place! They are going to destroy this whole place! . . . These were the final shouts nine year-old Kim Phuc heard before her world dissolved into flames--before napalm bombs fell from the sky. . . . It's a moment forever captured, an iconic image that has come to define the horror and violence of the Vietnam War." (Publisher's note)

Includes bibliographical references.

Tucker, Spencer C.

The **encyclopedia** of the Vietnam War; a political, social, and military history. Spencer C. Tucker, editor. 2nd ed.; ABC-CLIO 2011 4v il map set $395   **959.704**

1. Reference books 2. Vietnam War, 1961-1975 -- Encyclopedias

ISBN 978-1-85109-960-3; 978-1-85109-961-0 ebook

LC 2011007604

First published 1998

"Written to provide multidimensional perspectives into the conflict, . . . [this encyclopedia] covers not only the American experience in Vietnam, but also the entire scope of Vietnamese history, including the French experience and the Indochina War, as well as the origins of the conflict, how the United States became involved, and the extensive aftermath of this prolonged war." Publisher's note

Includes bibliographical references

Ulander, Perry A.

Walking point; from the ashes of the Vietnam War. Perry A. Ulander. North Atlantic Books 2016 252 p. (trade pbk.) $18.95   **959.704**

1. United States. Army 2. Vietnam War, 1961-1975 3. Soldiers -- United States 4. Soldiers -- Drug use -- Vietnam 5. Soldiers --

United States -- Biography 6. Vietnam War, 1961-1975 -- Vietnam -- Central Highlands 7. Vietnam War, 1961-1975 -- Personal narratives, American 8. United States. Army. Airborne Brigade, 173rd. Bravo Company 9. United States. Army -- Military life -- History -- 20th century

ISBN 9781623170127

LC 2015022372

In this memoir, author "Perry A. Ulander chronicles . . . the bewildering predicament he confronted and the fellowship and guidance that transformed him during the year he served as an American GI in the jungles of Vietnam. Conveying . . . the harrowing experiences that shatter his core beliefs, Ulander also captures the camaraderie and humor of his platoon." (Publisher's note)

"Ulander's fine memoir should take a place among the best works in the Vietnam War autobiographical canon." Pub Wkly

The **Vietnam** War; editor, Mark Lawrence; introduction by David K. Shipler. Fitzroy Dearborn Pubs. 2001 2v il maps (New York Times 20th century in review) set $150 **959.704**

1. Vietnam War, 1961-1975

ISBN 1-57958-368-7

LC 2002-726953

"A must-have for all libraries." Recomm Ref Books for Small & Medium-sized Libr & Media Cent, 2003

Wolf, Marvin J.

Abandoned in hell; the fight for Vietnam's Fire Base Kate. Captain William Albracht (Ret.) and Captain Marvin J. Wolf (Ret.) NAL Caliber 2015 384 p. 16 plates; illustrations (hardback) $27.95   **959.704**

1. Vietnam War, 1961-1975 -- Personal narratives 2. Courage -- Case studies 3. Fire Base Kate (Vietnam) 4. Command of troops -- Case studies 5. Heroes -- United States -- Biography 6. Soldiers -- United States -- Biography 7. Vietnam War, 1961-1975 -- Personal narratives, American 8. United States. Army. Special Forces -- Officers -- Biography 9. Escapes -- Vietnam -- Central Highlands -- History -- 20th century

ISBN 0451468082; 9780451468086

LC 2014028501

This memoir, by William Albracht and Marvin J. Wolf, describes how "in October 1969, . . . the youngest Green Beret captain in Vietnam took command of a remote hilltop outpost called Fire Base Kate, held by only 27 American soldiers and 150 Montagnard militiamen. He found their defenses woefully unprepared. At dawn the next morning, three North Vietnamese Army regiments . . . crossed the Cambodian border and attacked." (Publisher's note)

"This fast-paced narrative encapsulates Vietnam War themes, significantly the bravery of grunts and company grade officers and their loyalty to one another, and also bureaucratic mistakes with tragic consequences made by inexperienced officers and government officials too far removed from front-line action. Ultimately, Firebase Kate, as Albracht says, was built in a vulnerable location and its men were "written off" when they could no longer defend it. Readers of such excellent battlefield works as Harold Moore and Joseph Galloway's We Were Soldiers Once And Young will delve into this one." LJ

Wright, James

★ **Enduring** Vietnam; an American generation and its war. James Wright. Thomas Dunne Books, an imprint of St. Martin's Press 2017 xvi, 445 p.p maps (hardcover) $29.99   **959.704**

1. Vietnam War, 1961-1975 2. Vietnam War, 1961-1975 -- Influence 3. Vietnam War, 1961-1975 -- United States

ISBN 9781250092489; 9781250092496

LC 2016038762

This book, by James Wrigh, "recounts the experiences of the young Americans who fought in Vietnam and of families who grieved those who did not return. By 1969 nearly half of the junior enlisted men who died in Vietnam were draftees. And their median age was 21—among the non-draftees it was only 20." (Publisher's note)

"Wright's worthy effort is a tribute to Americans who saw the worst that the Vietnam War offered, combined with a broad look at the domestic and geopolitical factors that led to the U.S. getting involved in the long, controversial conflict." Pub Wkly

Includes bibliographical references and index

959.8 Indonesia and East Timor

Hoffman, Carl

The **last** wild men of Borneo; a true story of death and treasure. Carl Hoffman. William Morrow 2018 347 p. (hardcover) $27.99 **959.8**

1. Caves 2. Travelers 3. Missing persons 4. Dayak (Bornean people) 5. Penan (Bornean people) 6. Borneo -- Description and travel

ISBN 9780062439048; 9780062439024; 0062439022

LC 2017033692

In this book, by Carl Hoffman, "two modern adventurers sought a treasure possessed by the legendary 'Wild Men of Borneo.' One found riches. The other vanished forever into an endless jungle. Had he shed civilization--or lost his mind? Global headlines suspected murder. Lured by these mysteries, . . . Hoffman journeyed to find the truth, discovering that nothing is as it seems in the world's last Eden, where the lines between sinner and saint blur into one." (Publisher's note)

"An expertly wrought tale of exploration, adventure, and mischief by Hoffman . . . who returns to the South Pacific island of Borneo to tell it." Kirkus

Includes bibliographical references and index.

959.9 Philippines

Jones, Gregg

Honor in the dust; Theodore Roosevelt, war in the Philippines, and the rise and fall of America's imperial dream. Gregg Jones. New American Library 2012 xvi, 430 p.p (hbk.) $26.95 **959.9**

1. Philippines -- History -- Philippine American War, 1899-1902 2. Philippines -- Annexation to the United States 3. Philippines -- History -- Philippine American War, 1899-1902 -- Atrocities 4. Philippines -- History -- Philippine American War, 1899-1902 -- Campaigns -- Philippines -- Samar 5. Philippines -- History -- Philippine American War, 1899-1902 -- Political aspects -- United States

ISBN 0451229045; 9780451229045

LC 2011033386

This book by Gregg Jones is the story of how "an up-and-coming Theodore Roosevelt set out to transform the U.S. into a major world power. The Spanish-American War would forever change America's standing in global affairs, and drive the young nation into its own imperial showdown in the Philippines. . . . [Jones] captures an era brimming with American optimism and confidence as the nation expanded its influence abroad." (Publisher's note)

Includes bibliographical references (p. 382-420) and index

960 History of Africa

Meredith, Martin

Born in Africa; by Martin Meredith. 1st ed.; PublicAffairs 2011 xxiv, 230p ill. **960**

1. Africa 2. Anthropology 3. Human origins

ISBN 9781586486631 pa; 9781610391054

LC 2010043985

This book presents an "account of human evolution and the fiercely competitive anthropologists who are unearthing our ancestors' remains and arguing over what they mean. . . . [It] describ[es] the nuts-and-bolts of field research, the meaning of the often headline-producing findings and the ever-changing variety of species who split off from the common ancestors of chimpanzees and hominids." (Kirkus) "Scientists . . . have firmly established Africa as the birthplace not only of humankind but of modern humans. They have revealed how early technology, language ability, and artistic endeavour all originated in Africa; and they have shown how small groups of Africans spread out from Africa in an exodus sixty thousand years ago to populate the rest of the world." (Publisher's note)

Includes bibliographical references (p. 199-218) and index.

The **fortunes** of Africa; a history of the continent over fifty centuries. Martin Meredith. PublicAffairs 2014 784 p. 16 plates; illustrations; maps (hardcover) $35 **960**

1. Africa -- History

ISBN 1610394593; 9781610394598; 9781610394604

LC 2014939816

This book, by Martin Meredith, "follows the fortunes of Africa over a period of 5,000 years. With compelling narrative, he traces the rise and fall of ancient kingdoms and empires; the spread of Christianity and Islam; the enduring quest for gold and other riches; the exploits of explorers and missionaries; and the impact of European colonization. He examines, too, the fate of modern African states and concludes with a glimpse of their future." (Publisher's note)

"A gripping tale of insatiable greed—personal and collective." Booklist

Pakenham, Thomas

The **scramble** for Africa; the White man's conquest of the dark continent from 1876 to 1912. Avon 1992 xxv, 738p il map pa $22.95 **960**

1. Africa -- History

ISBN 0-380-71999-1

First published 1991 by Random House

This book is an account of the colonization and conquest of Africa by five European nations—Great Britain, France, Belgium, Germany, and Italy.

This is a "sweeping narrative, refreshingly old fashioned in its appreciation of the fact that imperialism did have some virtues, which offers as good an introduction to the 'scramble' as has ever been written." Libr J

Includes bibliographical references

961.205 -2011

Wehrey, Frederic

★ The **burning** shores; inside the battle for the new Libya. Frederic Wehrey. Farrar, Straus & Giroux 2018 xiv, 326 p.p (hardcover) $28 **961.205**

1. Libya -- Politics and government 2. Libya -- History -- Civil

War, 2011- 3. Libya -- Economic conditions -- 21st century 4. Libya -- Politics and government -- 21st century 5. Libya -- History -- Civil War, 2011- -- Participation, American
ISBN 9780374715281; 9780374278243

LC 2017049275

"The death of Colonel Muammar Qadhafi freed Libya from forty-two years of despotic rule, raising hopes for a new era. But in the aftermath, the country descended into bitter rivalries and civil war, paving the way for the Islamic State and a catastrophic migrant crisis. In a fast-paced narrative that blends frontline reporting, analysis, and history, Frederic Wehrey tells the story of what went wrong." (Publisher's note)

"A searing tale of violence, chaos, and unintended consequences in post-Gadhafi Libya. . . . Essential reading for anyone interested in the facts of the Benghazi attacks and in the future of a definitively troubled region." Kirkus

Includes bibliographical references and index

962   Egypt, Sudan, South Sudan

Jeal, Tim

Explorers of the Nile; the triumph and tragedy of a great Victorian adventure. Yale 2011 510p il map $32.50   **962**
1. Explorers 2. East Africa -- History 3. Central Africa -- History 4. Nile River -- Exploration
ISBN 978-0-300-14935-7

LC 2011933872

In this book on Victorian "efforts to find the source of the [Nile River]," the author focuses on a "quintet of great Victorian explorers," namely David Livingstone, Henry Morton Stanley, John Hanning Speke, Richard Burton, and Samuel Baker. "He recreates the mosquito-infested journeys and reveals the complex personal relationships, as Livingstone's early ventures to Lake Nyasa give way to the rivalry between Burton and Speke, who ventured north to Lakes Tanganyika, Victoria and Albert." Details on "the geopolitical consequences of finding the source of the Nile" are also presented. (History Today)

"Jeal's judicious account is a must-read for anyone hoping to understand the internal dynamics of modern state-building in central Africa." Booklist

Includes bibliographical references

Morrison, Dan

The **black** Nile; one man's amazing journey through peace and war on the world's longest river. Viking 2010 307p il map $26.95   **962**
1. Canoes and canoeing 2. War and civilization 3. Nile River -- Social conditions 4. Nile River -- Description and travel
ISBN 978-0-670-02198-7

LC 2010-4709

A foreign correspondent traces the four-thousand-mile plank-board boat journey he took with an inexperienced childhood friend along the Nile River from Lake Victoria to the Mediterranean Sea.

"Morrison's account transcends the travel genre to provide authentic and timely information on a complicated part of the world." Libr J

Stothard, Peter

Alexandria; The Last Nights of Cleopatra. Penguin Group USA 2013 400 p. $26.95   **962**
1. Alexandria (Egypt) 2. Egypt -- Description and travel
ISBN 1468303708; 9781468303704

In this book, "when Peter Stothard, editor of the 'Times Literary Supplement,' finds himself stranded in Alexandria in the winter of 2010 after his flight to South Africa has been cancelled, he sets out to explore a nation on the brink of revolution. Guided by two native Egyptians, Stothard traces his own life-long interest in the history of Cleopatra, and his repeated failure to write the book about her that he had always wanted to." (Publisher's note)

Strathern, Paul

Napoleon in Egypt; Bantam hardcover ed; Bantam Books 2008 480p il map $30   **962**
1. Emperors 2. Egypt -- History -- 1798-1801, French occupation
ISBN 978-0-553-80678-6; 0-553-80678-5

LC 2008-28135

First published 2007 in the United Kingdom
"Strathern's skillful use of memoir and other primary sources brings to life one of the most fascinating campaigns in military history." Libr J
Includes bibliographical references (p. 429-460)

962.05   Egypt since 1922

Cambanis, Thanassis

Once upon a revolution; an Egyptian story. Thanassis Cambanis. Free Press 2015 274 p. (hardcover) $26   **962.05**
1. Revolutionaries 2. Egypt -- History 3. Arab Spring, 2010- 4. Political activists 5. Social change -- Arab countries 6. Civic leaders -- Egypt -- Biography 7. Egypt -- History -- Protests, 2011- 8. Revolutionaries -- Egypt -- Biography 9. Egypt -- History -- 1981- -- Biography 10. Political activists -- Egypt -- Biography 11. Social change -- Egypt -- History -- 21st century
ISBN 1451658990; 9781451658996; 9781451659009

LC 2014022751

This book, on the 2011 Egyptian revolution by Thanassis Cambanis, "follows two leaders of the uprising from the beginnings of their political involvement to the military coup that overthrew Mohamed Morsi. Basem, an unassuming architect, becomes one of the few liberal members of parliament, while Moaz, a Muslim Brother, grows increasingly disenchanted with political Islam." (Publishers Weekly)

"Cambanis is master of the compelling detail: for example, in relating that Kamel was born in 1937, he notes that this was the year King Farouk I was crowned, a king who ate oysters by the hundred in his palace while his people endured WWII bombings. Wonderfully readable and insightful." Booklist

Includes bibliographical references and index

Khalil, Ashraf

Liberation Square; Ashraf Khalil. St. Martin's Press 2012 x, 324p.p   **962.05**
1. Revolutions 2. Political corruption 3. Egypt -- History -- 1970- 4. Egypt -- History -- Protests, 2011 5. Egypt -- Politics and government -- 21st century
ISBN 9781250006691; 9781429962445

LC 2011038194

This book covers "the rise and fall of Hosni Mubarak's dictatorship. . . . The . . . combination of judicial corruption and police brutality began to awake significant opposition, and the tipping point was the brutal beating death of Khalid Saieed in Alexandria on June 6, 2010. . . . [Author Ashraf] Khalil's discussion of the role of the Internet and social media . . . [shows] how large numbers of people were organized to achieve specific objectives--for example, converging on Cairo's squares and other public areas. The author . . . examines how the opposition to Egypt's paramilitary police gained strength, and how American diplomacy contributed to the cause. Khalil closes with the battle for Tahrir Square and the overthrow of the dictatorship." (Kirkus)

962.4 Sudan and South Sudan

Deng, Benson

They poured fire on us from the sky; the true story of three lost boys from Sudan. [by] Benson Deng, Alephonsion Deng, Benjamin Ajak; with Judy Bernstein. Public Affairs 2005 xxiii, 311p map hardcover o.p. pa $13.95 **962.4**
 1. Refugees 2. Sudan
 ISBN 1-58648-269-6; 1-58648-388-9 pa

             LC 2005-42566

"This collection is moving in its depictions of unbelievable courage." Publ Wkly

962.404 -1956

Mahjoub, Jamal, 1960-

A **line** in the river; Khartoum, city of memory. Jamal Mahjoub. St. Martin's Press 2018 416 p. $30 **962.404**
 1. Autobiographies 2. Cities and towns -- HIstory 3. Khartoum (Sudan) -- History
 ISBN 1408885468; 9781408885468

"Hoping to pull together the fragments of his British and Sudanese identity into a cohesive whole, . . . [Jamal Mahjoub] explores his own memories of Khartoum, which leads him into an examination of Sudan's rich past and present. Writing with the lyricism and observation of a novelist, Mahjoub brings colonialism, religion, politics, and memoir together to create a layered and revelatory portrait of a complex country, with his own story at the heart of 'A Line in the River.'" (Publisher's note)

963 Ethiopia and Eritrea

Shah, Tahir

In search of King Solomon's mines. Little, Brown 2003 240p il map $24.95; pa $13.95 **963**
 1. Ethiopia -- Description and travel
 ISBN 1-55970-641-4; 1-55970-724-0 pa
 First published in 2002 in the United Kingdom

This is an account of the author's search for "the mysterious mines of Ophir, where King Solomon, the Bible's wisest king, was supposed to have buried a fortune in gold. . . . According to his reckoning, the mines should be in modern-day Ethiopia, so he set out on an adventure of a lifetime with a shifty bookseller named (no kidding) Ali Baba. Along the way, readers are treated to his accounts of everything from the California gold rush to a sadistic Sultan." Libr J
 Includes bibliographical references

964 Morocco, Ceuta, Melilla, Western Sahara, Canary Islands

Shah, Tahir

The **Caliph's** house; Tahir Shah. Bantam Books 2006 349p il $22 **964**
 1. Morocco -- Description and travel
 ISBN 0-553-80399-9

             LC 2005-53656

"Shah's picture of Moroccan society, its deeply held Islamic faith, its primitive superstition, and its raucous economy makes for endlessly fascinating reading." Booklist

965 Algeria

Camus, Albert, 1913-1960

Algerian chronicles; Albert Camus; translated by Arthur Goldhammer; with an introduction by Alice Kaplan. Harvard University Press 2013 240 p. (hardcover) $21.95 **965**
 1. Algeria -- History 2. French-Algerian War, 1954-1962 3. Algeria -- History -- Revolution, 1954-1962 4. Algeria -- Social conditions -- 20th century 5. Algeria -- Politics and government -- 20th century
 ISBN 0674072588; 9780674072589

             LC 2012036100

This book is "the first English translation of [Albert Camus'] 'Chroniques Algériennes' (1958)." It includes his "reportage of the 1939 famine in Kabylia" as well as other observations "fixed historically in the French-Algerian war." Camus' struggles "with the concept and conflicts of colonialism" are shared. (Publishers Weekly)
 Includes bibliographical references and index.

Evans, Martin

Algeria; France's undeclared war. Martin Evans. Oxford University Press 2012 xxi, 457 p.p (hardcover) $35.00 **965**
 1. Torture 2. Nationalism 3. War and civilization 4. Algeria -- Foreign relations 5. France -- Colonies -- Africa 6. France -- Foreign relations -- 1945- 7. Algeria -- Foreign relations -- France 8. France -- Foreign relations -- Algeria 9. Algeria -- History -- Revolution, 1954-1962 10. Algeria -- History -- Revolution, 1954-1962 -- Causes
 ISBN 0192803506; 9780192803504

             LC 2012371069

Author "Martin Evans argues that it was the Socialist led Republican Front, in power from January 1956 until May 1957, which was the defining moment in the [Algerian revolutionary] war [of 1954-1962 . . . [and] underlines the conflict of values between the Republican Front and Algerian nationalism, explaining how this clash produced patterns of thought and action, such as the institutionalization of torture and the raising of pro-French Muslim militias, which tragically polarized choices and framed all subsequent stages of the conflict." (Publisher's note)
 Includes bibliographical references (p. [415]-429) and index

966.23 Mali

English, Charlie

The **storied** city; the quest for Timbuktu and the fantastic mission to save its past. Charlie English. Riverhead Books 2017 400 p. illustrations, maps (hardcover) $28 **966.23**
 1. Antiquities 2. Tombouctou (Mali) 3. Tombouctou (Mali) -- Antiquities 4. Manuscripts, Arabic -- Mali -- Tombouctou 5. Tombouctou (Mali) -- Discovery and exploration 6. Cultural property -- Protection -- Mali -- Tombouctou 7. Islamic learning and scholarship -- Mali -- Tombouctou 8. Libraries -- Destruction and pillage -- Mali -- Tombouctou 9. Mali -- History -- Tuareg Rebellion, 2012- -- Destruction and pillage
 ISBN 9780698197145; 9781594634284

             LC 2016039192

This book, by Charlie English, tells how a team of librarians and archivists joined forces to hide ancient manuscripts of Timbuktu when al-Qaeda-linked jihadists entered Mali in 2012. "Timbuktu [is considered] a medieval center of learning, it was home to tens of thousands--according to some, hundreds of thousands--of ancient manuscripts, on subjects ranging from religion to poetry, law to history, pharmacology, and astronomy." (Publisher's note)

"With a clear-eyed and straightforward approach, English thoroughly dispels the myths about Timbuktu to reveal a truth that is, in many ways, even more remarkable." Booklist

Includes bibliographical references and index

966.62 Liberia

Dwyer, Johnny

American warlord; the true story of a father and son. Johnny Dwyer. Alfred A. Knopf 2015 368 p. 8 plates; illustrations, maps $27.95 **966.62**

1. Americans -- Africa 2. Soldiers -- Liberia 3. Political violence -- Liberia 4. Liberia -- Politics and government -- 1980- 5. Liberia -- History -- Civil War, 1989-1996 -- Atrocities 6. Liberia -- History -- Civil War, 1999-2003 -- Atrocities

ISBN 0307273482; 9780307273482

LC 2014025451

This book by Johnny Dwyer is the story of "Chucky Taylor . . . the American son of the infamous African dictator Charles Taylor. Raised by his mother in the Florida suburbs, at the age of 17 he followed his father to Liberia, where he ended up leading a murderous militia. Chucky is now in a federal penitentiary, the only American ever convicted of torture." (Publisher's note)

"Dwyer deftly captures both the larger implications of Taylor's reign and the human-scaled horror of his son's descent: "Chucky's story had been improbable and at times surreal, but its brutality was real." A dark triumph—a meticulous geopolitica l narrative and gripping tale of an American son lost to evil." Kirkus

966.68 Cote d'Ivoire (Ivory Coast)

Erdman, Sarah

Nine hills to Nambonkaha; two years in the heart of an African village. Holt & Co. 2003 322p $23; pa $14 **966.68**

1. Ivory Coast 2. Peace Corps (U.S.)

ISBN 0-8050-7381-7; 0-312-42312-8 pa

LC 2003-44955

"This is an engrossing, well-told tale certain to appeal to armchair travelers and to anyone—especially women—considering international volunteer work." Publ Wkly

966.905 -1960

Maier, Karl

This house has fallen; midnight in Nigeria. PublicAffairs 2000 xxxvii, 327p hardcover o.p. pa $18 **966.905**

1. Nigeria -- Politics and government

ISBN 0-8133-4045-4 pa

LC 00-28199

The author "explores the promise and paradox of Nigeria. {He} . . . recounts the history of this nation cobbled together from British colonial interests in its formative years and dominated by international oil interests in more recent years." Booklist

Includes bibliographical references

967.5 Democratic Republic of the Congo, Rwanda, Burundi

Hochschild, Adam

★ **King** Leopold's ghost; a story of greed, terror, and heroism in Colonial Africa. Houghton Mifflin 1998 366p il map hardcover o.p. pa $15 **967.5**

1. Atrocities 2. Belgium -- Colonies 3. Congo (Republic) -- History

ISBN 0-395-75924-2; 0-618-00190-5 pa

LC 98-16813

"Hochschild's impressively researched history records the roles of the famous and obscure, missionaries, journalists, opportunists, politicians, and royalty in this long-forgotten drama." Booklist

Includes bibliographical references

967.51 Democratic Republic of the Congo

Stearns, Jason K.

Dancing in the glory of monsters; the collapse of the Congo and the great war of Africa. PublicAffairs 2011 380p $28.99 **967.51**

1. Genocide 2. Massacres 3. Congo (Republic) 4. Massacres -- Congo (Democratic Republic) 5. Congo (Democratic Republic) -- History -- 1997- 6. Political violence -- Congo (Democratic Republic)

ISBN 978-1-58648-929-8; 1-58648-929-1

LC 2010-43075

This book does not tell "the story of the Rwanda genocide in 1994, in which 800,000 people—almost all civilians—were massacred by their ethnic rivals in the space of a hundred days. That great atrocity is now relatively well known. Instead, this book tells of the war that broke out in the same region two years later, and that was in many ways its consequence. . . . As the Rwandan invaders penetrated into the eastern Congo, atrocities broke out. The Rwandans murdered the Hutus who had not fled. . . . Robert Mugabe of Zimbabwe and Eduardo Dos Santos of Angola pulled their troops out of the war, warning Kabila to negotiate for peace. . . . As well as 'big men' actors, [Jason K.] Stearns questioned many survivors of battle and massacre." (New York Review of Books)

A "look at the war that began in Congo in 1996 and that eventually involved nine countries and 20 different rebel movements, resulting in the deaths of more than five million people. In sheer brutality, this mostly unremarked upon cataclysm ranks with the two world wars, the Great Leap Forward and the Cambodia genocide. . . . Mr. Stearns has spoken to everyone—villagers, child soldiers, Mobutu's commanders, Kabila's ministers, Rwandan intelligence officers. In these conversations he found gold, bringing clarity—and humanity—to a place that usually seems inexplicable and barbaric. "Dancing in the Glory of Monsters" is riveting and certain to become essential reading for anyone looking to understand Central Africa." Wall Street J

Sundaram, Anjan

Stringer; a reporter's journey in the Congo. Anjan Sundaram. Doubleday 2014 265 p. $25.95 **967.51**

1. Journalism 2. Congo (Democratic Republic) 3. Congo (Democratic Republic) -- Description and travel 4. Congo (Democratic Republic) -- Social conditions -- 21st century

ISBN 0385537751; 9780345806321; 9780385537759; 9780385537766

LC 2013000980

Author Anjan "Sundaram exchanged mathematics for journalism, starting out as a stringer in dangerous Congo with little in the way of experience or contacts. This memoir sees him struggling to learn his craft while battling malaria, isolation, financial woes, and the tendency of editors to send in name reporters when a big story breaks. In addition, Sundaram offers an intensely rendered account of the immeasurable sadness of Congo through the tumultuous 2006 elections. " (Library Journal)

"The author skillfully captures the smallest details of life in a destitute land, blending the sordid history of Congo with his battle to forge a career in a troubled and forsaken country." Pub Wkly

967.571   Rwanda

Gourevitch, Philip

We wish to inform you that tomorrow we will be killed with our families; stories from Rwanda. Farrar, Straus & Giroux 1998 355p hardcover o.p. pa $15   **967.571**
    1. Genocide 2. Rwanda -- Politics and government
ISBN 0-374-28697-3; 0-312-24335-9 pa

                 LC 98-22132

This work is "readable and moving, Gourevitch is an impassioned and thoughtful observer. But this is not a work that gives much pleasure or comfort. Nor are its arguments fool-proof, its evidence complete, or its documentation thorough. . . . Still Gourevitch does struggle to come close to a great mystery of evil, and he makes us attend to great crimes." Commonweal

Hatzfeld, Jean

The **antelope's** strategy; living in Rwanda after the genocide. a report by Jean Hatzfeld; translated from the French by Linda Coverdale. Farrar, Straus and Giroux 2009 242p map $25   **967.571**
    1. Genocide 2. Hutu (African people) 3. Tutsi (African people) 4. Rwanda
ISBN 978-0-374-27103-9; 0-374-27103-8

               LC 2008-52489

Original French edition, 2007
This "is a book that illustrates vividly the thorny realities that accompany survival and appeasement." Washington Post

Blood Papa; Rwanda's new generation. Jean Hatzfeld; translated from the French by Joshua David Jordan. Farrar, Straus & Giroux 2018 240 p. (hardcover) $26   **967.571**
    1. Genocide -- Rwanda 2. Hutu (African people) 3. Tutsi (African people) 4. Genocide -- Rwanda -- History -- 20th century 5. Rwanda -- History -- Civil War, 1994 -- Personal narratives 6. Tutsi (African people) -- Crimes against -- Rwanda -- History -- 20th century
ISBN 9780374279783

            LC 2018007632

This book, by Jean Hatzfeld, translated by Joshua David Jordan, is "the continuation of a . . . study of the Rwandan genocide, and the story of the survivor generation. . . . Hatzfeld . . . ask[s] what has become of the children. . . . Here their moving first-person accounts combined with Hatzfeld's arresting chronicles of everyday life form a testament to survival in a country devastated by the terrible crimes and trauma of the past." (Publisher's note)

"This book, more of an ethnography than a history, exposes the effects of the genocide's stubborn legacy on the next generation, but is not an introduction to the events of 1994. Readers approaching it without prior knowledge of the genocide or Hutu-Tutsi relations will have a hard time fully understanding it, but those who have context will find this an illuminating update." Pub Wkly

Machete season; the killers in Rwanda speak: a report. translated from the French by Linda Coverdale; preface by Susan Sontag. Farrar, Straus and Giroux 2005 253p il maps hardcover o.p. pa $14   **967.571**
    1. Genocide 2. Hutu (African people) 3. Tutsi (African people) 4. Rwanda
ISBN 0-374-28082-7; 0-312-42503-1 pa

            LC 2004-61600

Original French edition, 2003
"Steering clear of politics, this important book succeeds in offering the reader some grasp of how such unspeakable acts unfolded." Publ Wkly

967.6   Uganda and Kenya

Chretien, Jean-Pierre

★ The **great** lakes of Africa; two thousand years of history. translated by Scott Straus. Zone Books 2003 504p map $36   **967.6**
    1. Rwanda 2. Uganda 3. Burundi 4. East Africa
ISBN 1-89095-134-X

            LC 2002-191001

"This is an impressive and important book surveying 2,000 years of history. . . . The preeminence accorded Rwanda and Burundi . . . leads to the book's most significant contribution: to demonstrate that the region's recent interrelated conflicts claiming over four million lives are not based on ancient, unchanging 'ethnic' cleavages, most notably between Tutsi and Hutu." Choice
Includes bibliographical references

Rice, Andrew

The **teeth** may smile but the heart does not forget; murder and memory in Uganda. Metropolitan Books/Henry Holt and Co. 2009 363p il map $26   **967.6**
    1. Generals 2. Atrocities 3. Presidents 4. Uganda 5. Murderers 6. Murder victims 7. Government officials 8. Children of prominent persons
ISBN 978-0-8050-7965-4; 0-8050-7965-3

            LC 2008-41984

"At the core of the book is an unsolved disappearance: Eliphaz Laki, a local leader with ties to the anti-Amin opposition, vanished in the early days of the Amin regime. When his son, Duncan, uncovered a clue to his father's disappearance 30 years later, the investigation eventually implicated Amin's second-in-command, Maj. Gen. Yusuf Gowon. With Amin living out his years safely in Saudi Arabia, the trial of Gowon forced Uganda to confront its brutal past. Treating the Lakis' story as a microcosm of Uganda's own, the author weaves together the family's search for truth and justice with Uganda's history." Publ Wkly

967.61   Uganda

David, Saul

Operation Thunderbolt; Flight 139 and the Raid on Entebbe Airport, the Most Audacious Hostage Rescue Mission in History. Saul David. Little Brown & Co. 2015 464 p. 16 unnumbered pages of plates (hardcover) $30   **967.61**
    1. Hostages 2. Special forces (Military science) -- Israel

ISBN 9780316245418; 0316245410

LC 2015946917

This book, by Saul David, offers a "definitive account of one of the greatest Special Forces missions ever. . . . On June 27, 1976, an Air France flight from Tel Aviv to Paris was hijacked by a group of . . . terrorists. . . . The plane was forced to divert to Entebbe, in Uganda. . . . Days later, Israeli commandos disguised as Ugandan soldiers assaulted the airport terminal, killed all the terrorists, and rescued all the hostages but three who were killed in the crossfire." (Publisher's note)

"A definitive history of the Entebbe operation, likely to be popular among readers of military and terrorism works." LJ

967.62   Kenya

Dinesen, Isak

  ★ **Out** of Africa and Shadows on the grass. Vintage Bks. 1989 462p pa $13.95   **967.62**

1. Kenya

ISBN 0-679-72475-3

LC 89-40144

Out of Africa is a recording of the author's life on a Kenya coffee plantation. Shadows on the grass consists of four short essays which present the author's recollections of her servants in Africa

967.73   Somalia

Fergusson, James

  The **world's** most dangerous place; inside the outlaw state of Somalia. James Fergusson. Da Capo Press 2013 432 p. (hardcover) $27.50   **967.73**

1. Violence 2. Somalia -- Social conditions

ISBN 0306821176; 9780306821172

LC 2013933566

This book "investigates the civil war, foreign interventions and mass starvation of Somalia. . . . The vast majority of Somalians is illiterate, desperately poor and so committed to genetic ties within their particular geographic clan that pulling together as a nation seems hopeless. Many of the peacekeeping soldiers are from Uganda, ironic given that nation's recent bouts of sectarian violence." (Kirkus)

Rawlence, Ben

  ★ **City** of thorns; nine lives in the world's largest refugee camp. by Ben Rawlence. Picador 2016 352 p. (hardcover) $26   **967.73**

1. Refugees 2. Somali-Ethiopian Conflict, 1979- 3. Refugees -- Kenya 4. Refugees -- Somalia 5. Refugee camps -- Kenya

ISBN 1250067634; 9781250067630

LC 2015029505

Carnegie Medal Longlist: Nonfiction (2017)

In this book, by Ben Rawlence, "deep within the inhospitable desert of northern Kenya where only thorn bushes grow, Dadaab [refugee camp] is a city like no other. Its buildings are made from mud, sticks or plastic, its entire economy is grey, and its citizens survive on rations and luck. . . . Rawlence interweaves the stories of nine individuals to show what life is like in the camp and to sketch the wider political forces that keep the refugees trapped there." (Publisher's note)

968.04   1814-1910

Meredith, Martin

  Diamonds, gold, and war; the British, the Boers, and the making of South Africa. PublicAffairs 2007 570p il map $35   **968.04**

1. South African War, 1899-1902 2. South Africa -- History 3. Great Britain -- Colonies -- Africa

ISBN 978-1-58648-473-6; 1-58648-473-7

LC 2007-34540

A history of the tumultuous period leading up to the 1910 founding of the modern state of South Africa explores how the discovery of vast diamond and gold deposits led to a fierce struggle between the British and the Boers for control of the region.

"Meredith thoroughly involves us in this gripping history. Highly recommended for all libraries." Libr J

Includes bibliographical references (p. 540-550)

Millard, Candice

  ★ **Hero** of the empire; the Boer war, a daring escape, and the making of Winston Churchill. Candice Millard. Doubleday 2016 416 p. (hardcover) $30   **968.04**

1. South African War, 1899-1902 2. South African War, 1899-1902 -- Participation, British 3. South African War, 1899-1902 -- Prisoners and prisons, British

ISBN 0385535732; 9780385535731

LC 2015049806

In this book, Candice Millard presents a "narrative of Winston Churchill's . . . exploits during the Boer War. . . . Just two weeks after his arrival, the soldiers he was accompanying on an armored train were ambushed, and Churchill was taken prisoner. Remarkably, he pulled off a daring escape--but then had to traverse hundreds of miles of enemy territory, alone, with nothing but a crumpled wad of cash, four slabs of chocolate, and his wits to guide him." (Publisher's note)

"Here the author documents the equally risky adventures of Winston Churchill (1874–1965) during the Second Boer War, in which Churchill and his fellow soldiers were captured upon arriving in South Africa. Churchill managed an escape, eventually returning to South Africa to free the men with whom he was imprisoned. . . . Enjoyable for all readers, especially fans of Churchill, military and world history, narrative nonfiction, and survival stories." LJ

968.06   South Africa--Period as Republic, 1961-

Carlin, John

  Playing the enemy; Nelson Mandela and the game that made a nation. Penguin 2008 274p il $24.95   **968.06**

1. Presidents 2. Rugby football 3. Political prisoners 4. Rugby 5. Political leaders 6. Human rights activists 7. Nobel laureates for peace

ISBN 978-1-59420-174-5; 1-59420-174-9

LC 2008-298721

"Deftly sketched characters make up both an audience for the big game and a gallery of South Africa, through which Carlin will recount the absorbing story of a country emerging from its cruelly absurd racist experiment." N Y Times Book Rev

Includes bibliographical references

Duke, Lynne

  Mandela, Mobutu, and me; a newswoman's African journey. Doubleday 2003 294p $24   **968.06**

1. Generals 2. Presidents 3. Political prisoners 4. Political leaders 5. Human rights activists 6. Nobel laureates for peace 7. South Africa -- Politics and government

ISBN 0-385-50398-9

LC 2002-73365

The author covers "some of the bloodier postcolonial wars of southern Africa as well as one of the most constructive struggles: the shaping of a postapartheid government. Her interviews with Mandela and Mobutu 'bookend' . . . conversations with common folk: township women struggling for clean water, AIDS nurses battling superstitious villagers and even a quiet old Zulu man impressed to meet his 'first foreign black folk.' A consummate journalist, Duke gives readers concise but thorough background briefings on a country's relevant history before cutting to the chase: who's taken control now, why, and what that means for the balance of power. . . . She deftly combines solid information and personal perspective to produce a powerful, readable chronicle." Publ Wkly

Mandela, Nelson

Mandela; an illustrated autobiography. Little, Brown 1996 208p il map $29.95   **968.06**

1. Presidents 2. Political prisoners 3. Political leaders 4. Human rights activists 5. Nobel laureates for peace 6. South Africa -- Race relations 7. South Africa -- Politics and government

ISBN 0-316-55038-8

LC 96-77497

"The photos, from a variety of archives and journalistic sources, ably illustrate Mandela and, even more so, the South Africa around him." Libr J

The **prison** letters of Nelson Mandela; Nelson Mandela, Sahm Venter [editor] W W Norton & Co Inc 2018 640 p. $35   **968.06**

1. Political prisoners 2. Presidents -- South Africa

ISBN 1631491172; 9781631491177

Edited by Sahm Venter, "this collection of 255 prison letters written by the late revolutionary and former president of South Africa provides a unique glimpse of [Nelson] Mandela during his 27-year incarceration, which he served at four different prisons. Both intimate and diplomatic, these writings showcase Mandela's various roles as a husband, father, friend, and lawyer." (Library Journal)

Waldmeir, Patti

Anatomy of a miracle; the end of apartheid and the birth of the new South Africa. Rutgers University Press 1998 289p pa $22.95   **968.06**

1. South Africa -- Race relations 2. South Africa -- Politics and government

ISBN 0-8135-2582-9; 978-0-8135-2582-2

LC 98-15628

First published 1997 by W.W. Norton

Waldmeir traces the political and personal struggles that ultimately contributed to the dismantling of apartheid in South Africa

"Although Mandela attributes greatness to de Klerk for his courage, it is Mandela's own character that dominates this history. . . . Engrossing in its sweep, this account also describes the obstacles facing the regime." Publ Wkly

Includes bibliographical references

968.91   Zimbabwe

Lamb, Christina

House of stone; the true story of a family divided in war-torn Zimbabwe. Lawrence Hill Books 2007 290p il map   **968.91**

1. Farmers 2. Nannies 3. Zimbabwe -- Race relations

ISBN 978-1-55652-735-7; 1-55652-735-7

LC 2007-19814

"Through the parallel accounts of two people in Zimbabwe, one a poor black maid, one a rich white farmer, . . . Lamb tells the compelling story of a country ravaged first by colonial settlers and now by brutal civil war. . . . The anguished personal detail, true to the changing viewpoints, makes for a gripping read." Booklist

970   History of North America

Hogeland, William

Autumn of the Black Snake; The Creation of the U.S. Army and the Invasion That Opened the West. William Hogeland. Farrar, Straus & Giroux 2017 447 p. illustrations (hardcover) $28   **970**

1. United States. Army 2. Native Americans -- Wars 3. United States -- Military history 4. Wayne's Campaign, 1794

ISBN 0374107343; 9780374107345

LC 2016052193

Author William Hogeland "tells the overlooked story of how [George] Washington achieved his aim [of creating an army]. Hogeland conjures up the woodland battles and the hardball politics that formed the Legion of the United States, our first true standing army. His memorable portraits of leaders on both sides—from the daring war chiefs Blue Jacket and Little Turtle to the doomed commander Richard Butler and a steely, even ruthless Washington—drive a tale of horrific violence, brilliant strategizing, stupendous blunders, and valorous deeds." (Publisher's note)

"This is a scrupulously balanced account of a formative period in westward expansion." Booklist

Includes bibliographical references (pages 419-425) and index.

970.004   North American native peoples

Brown, Dee Alexander

★ **Bury** my heart at Wounded Knee; an Indian history of the American West. [by] Dee Brown. Thirtieth anniversary ed; Holt & Co. 2001 487p il hardcover o.p. pa $16   **970.004**

1. Generals 2. Civil engineers 3. Government officials 4. West (U.S.) -- History 5. Native Americans -- Wars 6. Native Americans -- West (U.S.)

ISBN 0-8050-6634-9; 0-8050-6669-1 pa

LC 00-40958

First published 1970

This is an account of the experience of the American Indian during the white man's expansion westward.

Includes bibliographical references

Bruchac, Joseph

Our stories remember; American Indian history, culture, & values through storytelling. Fulcrum 2003 192p map pa $16.95   **970.004**

1. Storytelling 2. Native Americans -- History

ISBN 1-555-91129-3

LC 2002-151236

"This important volume includes a wealth of traditional stories and solid information." SLJ

Includes bibliographical references

Deloria, Vine

Custer died for your sins; an Indian manifesto. by Vine Deloria, Jr. University of Oklahoma Press 1988 278p pa $19.95 **970.004**

1. Native Americans

ISBN 0-8061-2129-7

LC 87-40561

First published 1969 by Macmillan

The author examines how anthropologists, missionaries, and government agencies have mistreated American Indians.

Dunbar-Ortiz, Roxanne

An **indigenous** peoples' history of the United States; Roxanne Dunbar-Ortiz. Beacon Press 2014 296 p. (ReVisioning American history) (hardcover: alk. paper) $27.95 **970.004**

1. United States -- Race relations 2. Native Americans -- United States 3. United States -- History -- 1600-1775, Colonial period 4. United States -- Colonization 5. United States -- Politics and government

ISBN 080700040X; 9780807000403

LC 2013050262

This book, by Roxanne Dunbar-Ortiz, "offers a history of the United States told from the perspective of Indigenous peoples and reveals how Native Americans, for centuries, actively resisted expansion of the US empire. . . . [It] challenges the founding myth of the United States and shows how policy against the Indigenous peoples was colonialist and designed to seize the territories of the original inhabitants, displacing or eliminating them." (Publisher's note)

Includes bibliographical references and index

Encyclopedia of Native American wars and warfare; general editors, William B. Kessel, Robert Wooster. Facts on File 2005 398p il map $75; pa $21.95 **970.004**

1. Reference books 2. Native Americans -- Wars -- Encyclopedias

ISBN 0-8160-3337-4; 0-8160-6430-X pa

LC 00-56200

"This encyclopedia offers readers a wide range of information about Native American history in North America after 1492." Choice

Includes bibliographical references

Hirschfelder, Arlene B.

Native American almanac; More Than 50,000 Years of the Cultures and Histories of Indigenous Peoples. Yvonne Wakim Dennis, Arlene Hirschfelder and Shannon Rothenberger Flynn. Visible Ink Press 2016 xi, 643 p.p illustrations, map (ebook) $19.99; (pbk.: alk. paper) $24.95 **970.004**

1. Native Americans -- History 2. Native Americans -- North America 3. Native Americans -- Social life and customs 4. Indians of North America -- History 5. Indians of North America -- Social life and customs

ISBN 9781578596072; 9781578595075

LC 2015050881

This book, by Yvonne Wakim Dennis, Arlene Hirschfelder and Shannon Rothenberger Flynn, "traces the rich heritage of indigenous people. It is a fascinating mix of biography, pre-contact and post-contact history, current events, Tribal Nations' histories, enlightening insights

on environmental and land issues, arts, treaties, languages, education, movements, and more." (Publisher's note)

"This volume provides a solid beginning for students as well as general readers with no background in Native American studies." LJ

Includes bibliographical references (page 607-624) and index

Iverson, Peter

We are still here; American Indians in the twentieth century. Davidson, H. 1998 255p il (American history series) pa $14.95 **970.004**

1. Native Americans

ISBN 0-88295-940-9

LC 97-38321

The author "begins at Wounded Knee and tells the stories of Indian communities throughout the United States, including not only political leaders and activists, but also professionals, artists, soldiers and athletes." Publisher's note

Includes bibliographical references

Johnson, Michael G.

Encyclopedia of native tribes of North America; Michael Johnson; illustrator, Richard Hook. Compendium 2007 320 p. color illustrations; maps $49.95 **970.004**

1. Native Americans -- North America 2. Native Americans -- Encyclopedias

ISBN 1770854614; 190557374X; 9781770854611; 9781905573745

LC 2008360036

This book, by Michael Johnson, illustrated by Richard Hook, "offers the most up-to-date and essential facts on the identity, kinships, locations, populations and cultural characteristics of some 400 separately identifiable peoples native to the North American continent, both living and extinct, from the Canadian Arctic to the Rio Grande." (Publisher's note)

"The maps, photographs, and beautiful illustrations by Hook, combined with concise, accurate entries, make this volume a good purchase, especially for libraries that lack the 2007 edition. Summing Up: Recommended. Lower-division undergraduates and above; general readers." Choice

Ojibwa; people of forests and prairies. Michael G. Johnson. Firefly Books 2016 160 p. ill. (some color), color maps $35 **970.004**

1. Ojibwa Indians 2. Ojibwa Indians -- History 3. Ojibwa Indians -- Social life and customs

ISBN 9781770858008

LC 2016436367

This book, by Michael G. Johnson, "describes the history and culture of the [Ojibwa] people, and introduces their most important figures. It offers the most up-to-date and essential facts on identity, kinships, locations, populations and cultural characteristics. It presents extensive visual coverage of tribal dress and cultural artifacts, . . . regional maps that show prehistoric cultural and historic sites, and maps showing tribe distribution and major historical events." (Publisher's note)

"This study will appeal to anyone interested in First Nations people and would make a great addition to reference libraries." Pub Wkly

Includes bibliographical references and index

Josephy, Alvin M., 1915-2005

The **longest** trail; writings on American Indian history, culture, and politics. by Alvin M. Josephy, Jr.; edited by Marc Jaffe and Rich Wandschneider. Vintage Books, A Division of Penguin

Random House LLC 2015 544 p. (paperback) $16.95 **970.004**

1. Native Americans -- History 2. Native Americans -- Politics and government 3. Native Americans -- Social life and customs

ISBN 9780345806918

LC 2015010197

This book, by Alvin M. Josephy, Jr., edited by Marc Jaffe and Rich Wandschneider, reviews "five hundred years of Indian history in North America from first settlements in the East to the long trek of the Nez Perce Indians in the Northwest. The essays deal with the origins of still unresolved troubles with treaties and territories to fishing and land rights, and who should own archeological finds, as well as the ideologies that underpin our Indian policy." (Publisher's note)

"Essential for anyone interested in contemporary Native American history and culture and should be read alongside Josephy's autobiography A Walk Toward Oregon: A Memoir." LJ

McLoughlin, William Gerald

After the Trail of Tears; the Cherokees' struggle for sovereignty, 1839-1880. {by} William G. McLoughlin. University of N.C. Press 1993 439p maps hardcover o.p. pa $21.95 **970.004**

1. Cherokee Indians 2. Indian chiefs

ISBN 0-8078-4433-0 pa

LC 93-18532

The author "recounts the tragedy that continued to afflict the Cherokee Nation after their forced removal from their traditional home to Oklahoma during the 1820s and 1830s. In Oklahoma the Cherokee Nation set out to reconstruct their society, reestablishing their newspaper, which published in the Cherokee language, and governing themselves according to a constitution modeled on that of the United States. . . . McLoughlin vividly depicts the conflicts between 'full-bloods,' who sought to live by more traditional ways, and Cherokees of mixed ancestry who favored assimilation into the dominant culture." Publ Wkly

Includes bibliographical references

Milton, Giles

Big Chief Elizabeth; the adventures and fate of the First English Colonists in America. Farrar, Straus & Giroux 2000 358p il maps hardcover o.p. pa $14 **970.004**

1. Queens 2. Native Americans 3. Virginia -- History 4. America -- Exploration 5. Great Britain -- Colonies -- America

ISBN 0-312-42018-8 pa

LC 00-31522

"Nearly 500 years ago, a small group of white men landed on the shores of North America and named it Virginia (for the Virgin Queen [Elizabeth]). Their purpose was to capture some natives and bring them to England to learn their language and everything else they could about the country they wished to colonize. . . . [Milton] chronicles the century-long battle to establish a permanent settlement in Virginia." Christ Sci Monit

Includes bibliographical references

Philip, Neil

The **great** circle; a history of the First Nations. foreword by Dennis Hastings. Clarion Books 2006 153p il map $25 **970.004**

1. Native Americans

ISBN 978-0-618-15941-3; 0-618-15941-X

LC 2005032743

"Philip takes on a huge challenge here: to present a unified narrative that explains the complex and confrontational relationships between Native Americans and white settlers. . . . He pulls it off, however, thanks

to solid research, an engaging writing style, and a talent for making individual stories serve the whole. . . . Top marks, too, for the volume's photographs and historical renderings, which so intensely illustrate the pages." Booklist

Includes bibliographical references

Richter, Daniel K.

Facing east from Indian country; a Native history of early America. Harvard Univ. Press 2001 317p il maps $27.50; pa $15.95 **970.004**

1. Native Americans

ISBN 0-674-00638-0; 0-674-01117-1 pa

LC 2001-24997

The author "recasts early American history from the Native American point of view and in doing so illuminates as much about the Europeans as about the original Americans. . . . Exploring the varying complexities of different native people's relationships with England, France and Spain, he argues that the Native Americans were safer during the colonial era than after the Revolution. . . . Gracefully written and argued, Richter's compelling research and provocative claims make this an important addition to the literature for general readers of both Native American and U.S. studies." Publ Wkly

Includes bibliographical references

Treuer, Anton

Atlas of Indian nations; by Anton Treuer. National Geographic Books 2013 319 p. ills.; maps; photos (color) (hardcover: alk. paper) $40 **970.004**

1. Native Americans -- North America 2. Native Americans -- History

ISBN 1426211600; 9781426211607; 9781426212567

LC 2013036634

This book, by Anton Treuer, "is a comprehensive resource for those interested in Native American history and culture. Told through maps, photos, art, and archival cartography, this is the story of American Indians. . . . Organized by region, this encyclopedic reference details Indian tribes in these areas: beliefs, sustenance, shelter, alliances and animosities, key historical events, and more." (Publisher's note)

"'The land made the first people of North America,' insists Ojibwe scholar Treuer (Everything You Wanted to Know About Indians but Were Afraid to Ask), and in this gorgeously illustrated volume employs the atlas format to demonstrate this reality. Chock full of historical and contemporary maps, photographs, and paintings, this smart hybrid of art book and textbook is irresistible to leaf through because of the eye-catching images on every page. But Treuer's clear, accessible text is the complementary gem." Pub Wkly

Includes bibliographical references and index

Waldman, Carl

Atlas of the North American Indian; 3rd ed; Facts on File 2009 450p il map (Facts on file library of American history) $85; pa $24.95 **970.004**

1. Atlases 2. Reference books 3. Native Americans

ISBN 978-0-8160-6858-6; 0-8160-6858-5; 978-0-8160-6859-3 pa; 0-8160-6859-3 pa

LC 2008-40736

First published 1985

"This is a very well-designed book, a bargain for any library." Voice Youth Advocates [review of 2000 edition]

Includes glossary and bibliographical references

Encyclopedia of Native American tribes; 3rd rev ed; Facts

on File 2006 xxiv, 360p il map (Facts on File library of American history) $75; pa $21.95 **970.004**
1. Reference books 2. Native Americans -- Encyclopedias
ISBN 978-0-8160-6273-7; 0-8160-6273-0; 978-0-8160-6274-4 pa; 0-8160-6274-9 pa

LC 2006-12529

First published 1988
"This well-written and easily accessible encyclopedia of a good starting point for research on Native American tribes." Libr Media Connect
Includes bibliographical references

Weatherford, J. McIver
Native roots; how the Indians enriched America. [by] Jack Weatherford. Fawcett 1992 310p il map pa $13.95 **970.004**
1. Native Americans
ISBN 978-0-449-90713-9; 0-449-90713-9
First published 1991 by Crown
"A valuable corrective to the sentimentality with which we regard the first U.S. settlers and developers." Booklist
Includes bibliographical references

Woodard, Colin
American nations; a history of the eleven rival regional cultures of North America. Viking 2011 371p map $30 **970.004**
1. Multiculturalism 2. Regionalism -- North America 3. North America -- Race relations
ISBN 978-0-670-02296-0

LC 2011015196

The author's "take on American history identifies the original cultural settlements that became the United States, and proceeds with the thesis that these regional and cultural divisions are responsible for clashes stretching back to Revolutionary times. The 11 nations don't follow state or even country territory lines, but rather the paths taken by the earliest settlers of these areas; while later immigrants added to the mix, they didn't change the fundamental culture. . . . The book's compelling explanations and apt descriptions will fascinate anyone with an interest in politics, regional culture, or history." Publ Wkly
Includes bibliographical references

970.01 North America--Early history to 1599

Adovasio, J. M.
The **first** Americans; in pursuit of archaeology's greatest mystery. {by} J.M. Adovasio with Jake Page. Random House 2002 328p il maps hardcover o.p. pa $14.95 **970.01**
1. America -- Antiquities 2. Native Americans -- Origin
ISBN 0-375-75704-X pa

LC 2002-69766

"Readers get a lively, close-up view of how archaeologists study America's original discoverers." Booklist
Includes bibliographical references

Dillehay, Tom D.
★ The **settlement** of the Americas; a new prehistory. {by} Thomas D. Dillehay. Basic Bks. 2000 xxi, 371p il hardcover o.p. pa $22 **970.01**
1. America -- Antiquities 2. America -- Exploration
ISBN 0-465-07669-6 pa

LC 00-27572

This "is a seminal work in the field that is accessible to lay readers." Libr J

Includes bibliographical references

Horwitz, Tony
★ A **voyage** long and strange; rediscovering the new world. Henry Holt and Co. 2008 445p il map $27.50 **970.01**
1. Explorers 2. America -- Exploration
ISBN 978-0-8050-7603-5; 0-8050-7603-4

LC 2007-45883

"Realizing that his knowledge of American history between Columbus's discovery and Plymouth Rock over 100 years later was sketchy at best, . . . [the author] sets out to educate himself with his own explorations. He intertwines his experiences retracing the early conquistadors, adventurers, and entrepreneurs through such regions as Newfoundland, the Dominican Republic, and the American South, Southwest, and New England with thoroughly researched accounts of the territories themselves, the natives who were historically affected, and the motives of the explorers. . . . This readable and vastly entertaining history travelog is highly recommended for public libraries." Libr J
Includes bibliographical references

Mann, Charles C.
1491; new revelations of the Americas before Columbus. Knopf 2005 465p il maps **970.01**
1. America -- Antiquities 2. Native Americans -- History
ISBN 1-4000-3205-9 pa; 1-4000-4006-X

LC 2005-42178

This is a portrait "of the Americas before the arrival of the Europeans in 1492." (Publisher's note) Index.
"Mann navigates adroitly through the controversies. He approaches each in the best scientific tradition, carefully sifting the evidence, never jumping to hasty conclusions, giving everyone a fair hearing—the experts and the amateurs; the accounts of the Indians and their conquerors. And rarely is he less than enthralling." N Y Times Book Rev
Includes bibliographical references

National Museum of Natural History (U.S.)
Vikings: the North Atlantic saga; edited by William W. Fitzhugh and Elisabeth I. Ward. Smithsonian Institution Press 2000 432p il maps hardcover o.p. pa $34.95 **970.01**
1. Vikings 2. America -- Exploration
ISBN 1-56098-970-X; 1-56098-995-5 pa

LC 99-57983

This book is "well designed, heavily illustrated and almost encyclopedic in scope and detail." Publ Wkly
Includes bibliographical references

970.017 North America – English explorations

Butman, John
New world, inc. the making of America by England's merchant adventurers. John Butman & Simon Targett. Little, Brown & Co. 2018 xxv, 405 p.p illustrations (chiefly color) (hardcover) $29 **970.017**
1. United States -- History 2. Great Britain -- Colonies -- America 3. Colonial companies -- America -- History 4. America -- Discovery and exploration -- British 5. Great Britain -- Commerce -- History -- 16th century 6. Great Britain -- Colonies -- America -- History -- 16th century
ISBN 9780316307888; 9780316510127; 0316307882

LC 2017963936

This book, by John Butman and Simon Targett, "draws a portrait of life in London, on the Atlantic, and across the New World that offers a fresh analysis of the founding of American history. . . . Butman and Targett examine the enterprising spirit that inspired European settlement of America and established a national culture of entrepreneurship and innovation that continues to this day." (Publisher's note)

"An eye-opening and thoroughly enjoyable look at the roots of American ambition." Booklist

Includes bibliographical references (pages 337-353) and index.

970.3　Specific native peoples

Nabokov, Peter

How the World Moves; The Odyssey of an American Indian Family. Peter Nabokov. Penguin Group USA 2015 560 p. illustrations $32.95　　**970.3**

1. Immigrants 2. Pueblo Indians

ISBN 0670024880; 9780670024889

In this book author Peter Nabokov "narrates the . . . story of [Edward Proctor] Hunt's life within a multicultural and historical context. Chronicling Pueblo Indian life and Anglo/Indian relations over the last century and a half, he explores how this entrepreneurial family capitalized on the nation¿s passion for Indian culture. Nabokov dramatizes how the Hunts, like immigrants throughout history, faced anguishing decisions over staying put or striking out for economic independence." (Publisher's note)

"The pull of the Pueblo was always powerful, and the familial ties and love of ceremony and song were sufficient to bring them back often. The lure of the Land of Enchantment is irresistible, as Nabokov draws us into the simple, cooperative life of the Pueblo Indians and their magnificent territory. A great choice for lovers of the Southwest." Kirkus

971　Canada

Black, Conrad, 1944-

Rise to greatness; the history of Canada from Vikings to the present. Conrad Black. McClelland & Stewart 2014 1106 p. 24 plates; ills.; portraits (hardcover: alk. paper) $50　　**971**

1. Canada -- History

ISBN 1468309943; 9780771013546; 9780771013553

LC 2014944153

This book, by Conrad Black, "Spanning 874 to 2014, . . . challenges our perception of our history and Canada's role in the world. From Champlain to Carleton, Baldwin and Lafontaine, to MacDonald, Laurier, and King, Canada's role in peace and war, to Quebec's quest for autonomy, [author Conrad] Black takes on sweeping themes and vividly recounts the story of Canada's development from colony to dominion to country." (Publisher's note)

Gray, Charlotte

Gold diggers; striking it rich in the Klondike. Counterpoint 2010 413p il map $29.95　　**971**

1. Gold mines and mining 2. Klondike River valley (Yukon) -- Gold discoveries 3. Frontier and pioneer life -- Klondike River valley (Yukon)

ISBN 978-1-58243-611-1

LC 2010-17805

This is "an enchanting recitation of lives—and deaths—in the Klondike during the gold rush over 100 years ago. Combining a keen eye for detail and firsthand histories of contemporary witnesses, Gray sets forth the lives of six 'stampeders,' including Jack London (who almost died

in the wild before writing so wonderfully of those who did), Mountie Sam Steele, business wiz Belinda Mulrooney, highborn journalist Flora Shaw, devoted Jesuit priest William Judge, and, most of all, Bill Haskell, a simple soul who left America with a dream of exploration and riches." Libr J

Includes bibliographical references

MacDonald, Laura M.

Curse of the Narrows. Walker & Co. 2005 355p il maps $26　　**971**

1. Explosions 2. Halifax (N.S.)

ISBN 0-8027-1458-7

LC 2005-44255

This "book captures in vivid detail the history of this catastrophe." Booklist

Includes bibliographical references

Mowat, Farley

High latitudes; an Arctic journey. foreword by Margaret Atwood. Steerforth Press 2003 300p map pa $15.95　　**971**

1. Arctic regions 2. Natural history -- Canada

ISBN 1-58642-061-5

LC 2002-151151

First published 2002 in Canada

"In 1966, Mowat's publisher, Jack McClelland, sent Mowat into northern Canada to research an illustrated volume on the region. This book is the tale of that journey. Hopscotching by creaky plane from one isolated settlement to another, Mowat witnesses the devastation being wrought on the native peoples by encroaching white men, lured by a mirage of the north's supposedly limitless minerals and the raw beauty of the land and its people. A cavalcade of vivid, fiction-worthy characters fills these pages. . . . Voiced with a passionate sense of justice, this work is stirring reading from the bard of the Canadian north." Publ Wkly

Riendeau, Roger E.

A brief history of Canada; [by] Roger Riendeau. 2nd ed; Facts on File 2007 444p il map (Brief history) $45　　**971**

1. Canada -- History

ISBN 978-0-8160-6335-2

LC 2006-47130

First published 2000

This is a history of Canada "beginning with the exploration of the Northern American frontier and continuing through the rise and fall of the French and British empires to the foundations of Canadian nationhood and the present day." Publisher's note

Includes bibliographical references

971.01　Early history to 1763

Macleod, D. Peter

Northern Armageddon; the Battle of the Plains of Abraham and the making of the American Revolution. Peter MacLeod. Alfred A. Knopf 2016 448 p. (hardcover: alk. paper) $35　　**971.01**

1. Seven Years' War, 1756-1763 2. Canada -- History -- 1755-1763 3. Canada -- History -- To 1763 (New France) 4. Québec Campaign, Québec, 1759 5. Plains of Abraham, Battle of the, Québec, 1759

ISBN 0307269892; 9780307269898

LC 2015015893

In this book author Peter MacLeod "using original research--diaries, journals, letters, and firsthand accounts--and bringing to bear all of his extensive knowledge and grasp of warfare and colonial North American history, tells the epic story on a human scale. He writes of the British at Quebec through the eyes of a master's mate on one of the ships embroiled in the battle. And from the French perspective, as the British bombarded Quebec, of four residents of the city—a priest, a clerk, a nun, and a notary—caught in the crossfire." (Publisher's note)

"This is a superbly researched and written account of a seminal episode in world history." Booklist

Includes bibliographical references

971.6   Nova Scotia

Bacon, John U.

The **great** Halifax explosion; a World War I story of treachery, tragedy, and extraordinary heroism. John U. Bacon. William Morrow, an imprint of HarperCollins Publishers 2017 ix, 418 p.p illustrations (hardcover) $29.99   **971.6**

   1. Disasters 2. Halifax (N.S.) -- History 3. Halifax Explosion, Halifax, N.S., 1917 4. Halifax (N.S.) -- History -- 20th century
ISBN 9780062686992; 9780062666536; 9780062666550; 0062666533

This book, by John U. Bacon, offers "a gripping narrative history of the largest manmade detonation prior to Hiroshima: in 1917 a ship laden with the most explosives ever packed on a vessel sailed out of Brooklyn's harbor for the battlegrounds of World War I; when it stopped in Halifax, Nova Scotia, . . . [an] impact ignited the explosives below, resulting in a horrific blast that, in one fifteenth of a second, leveled 325 acres of Halifax." (Publisher's note)

"An absorbing history of disaster and survival." Kirkus

Includes bibliographical references (pages 393-397) and index.

971.9   Northern territories

Castner, Brian

★ **Disappointment** River; finding and losing the Northwest Passage. Brian Castner. Doubleday 2018 xii, 334 p.p (hardcover) $28.95   **971.9**

   1. Northwest Passage -- Exploration 2. Northwest Passage -- Description and travel 3. Northwest Passage -- Discovery and exploration 4. Mackenzie River (N.W.T.) -- Description and travel
ISBN 0385541627; 9780385541626

                        LC 2017033495

This book, by Brian Castner, "is a dual historical narrative and travel memoir. . . . Fourteen years before Lewis and Clark, [Alexander] Mackenzie set off to cross the continent of North America with a team of voyageurs and Chipewyan guides, to find a trade route to the riches of the East. What he found was a river that he named 'Disappointment.' Mackenzie died thinking he had failed. He was wrong." (Publisher's note)

A vital addition to the library of the far north and of exploration. --Kirkus (February 1, 2018)

Includes bibliographical references (pages 314-318) and index.

972   Mexico, Central America, West Indies, Bermuda

Coe, Michael D.

The **Maya**; Michael D. Coe. 7th ed fully rev and expanded; Thames and Hudson 2005 272p il map (Ancient peoples and places) pa $22.50   **972**

   1. Mayas
ISBN 978-0-500-28505-3; 0-500-28505-5
First published 1966 by Praeger

An illustrated survey of the Maya civilization, focusing on the achievements of the Classic Period, A.D. 300-900

Includes bibliographical references

Crutchfield, James A.

Revolt at Taos; The New Mexican and Indian Insurrection of 1847. James A. Crutchfield. Westholme Pub Llc 2015 400 p. illustrations, maps (hardcover) $29.95   **972**

   1. Insurgency 2. Taos (N.M.) -- History
ISBN 1594162239; 9781594162237

                        LC 2015451017

This book, by James A. Crutchfield, describes the events surrounding the New Mexican/Indian revolt of Taos in 1847 and its aftermath. "On the morning of January 19, 1847, Charles Bent, the newly appointed governor of the American-claimed territory of New Mexico, was savagely killed at his home in Don Fernando de Taos, a small, remote town located north of Santa Fe." (Publisher's note)

"This broad treatment of the Taos Revolt is a sincere attempt to view events and consequences from the perspectives of all peoples involved. Recommended for the examination of civil rights during the forced Americanization of established residents of New Mexico territory." LJ

Diaz del Castillo, Bernal

The **discovery** and conquest of Mexico, 1517-1521; translated by A.P. Maudslay. Da Capo Press 2003 478p il map pa $24   **972**

   1. Mexico -- History
ISBN 0-306-81319-X; 978-0-306-81319-1
First published 1956 by Farrar, Straus & Giroux

"The memoirs of an old man, who began to write of his experiences half a century after they occurred and completed his account at the age of 84, they are not free from minor inaccuracies, but they are the most reliable narrative that exists." Chicago Sunday Trib

Foster, Lynn V.

★ A **brief** history of Mexico; 4th ed; Facts On File 2009 324p il map (Brief history) $49.50; pa $19.95   **972**

   1. Mexico -- History
ISBN 978-0-8160-7405-1; 978-0-8160-7406-8 pa

                        LC 2009-18298

First published 1997

An overview of Mexican history covering pre-Columbian civilizations and contemporary indigenous cultures. Language, art, religion, politics and economics are discussed. A chronology and bibliography are included.

Includes bibliographical references

Kirkwood, Burton

The **history** of Mexico; 2nd ed.; Greenwood Press/ABC-CLIO 2010 258p il map (Greenwood histories of the modern nations) $49.95   **972**

   1. Mexico -- History
ISBN 978-0-313-36601-7; 0-313-36601-2

                        LC 2009036964

First published 2000

A historical survey of Mexico and its people from the arrival of the first humans in the Western Hemisphere to the first decade of the 21st century. Topics range from Mexico's cultural past to more current issues such as the war on drugs and the North American Free Trade Agreement.

Includes bibliographical references

Meyer, Michael C.

★ The **course** of Mexican history; [by] Michael C. Meyer, William L. Sherman, Susan M. Deeds. 8th ed.; Oxford University Press 2007 688p il map hardcover o.p. pa $64.95 **972**

1. Mexico -- History
ISBN 0-19-517835-1; 978-0-19-517835-7; 0-19-517836-X pa; 978-0-19-517836-4 pa

LC 2006-51741

A chronologically arranged survey of the political, economic, social, and cultural history of Mexico, ranging from the pre-Columbian period to the present.

Includes bibliographical references

The **Oxford** history of Mexico; edited by Michael C. Meyer and William H. Beezley. Oxford Univ. Press 2000 709p il maps $45 **972**

1. Mexico -- History
ISBN 0-19-511228-8

LC 99-56044

The editors "have compiled 20 previously unpublished essays by experts who explore Mexico from precolonial times to the present. . . . Examining the country with new and different approaches, the contributors challenge traditional historical concepts on a variety of issues." Libr J

Includes bibliographical references

Smith, Michael Ernest

The **Aztecs**; [by] Michael E. Smith. 2nd ed; Blackwell 2003 367p il maps (Peoples of America) hardcover o.p. pa $29.95 **972**

1. Aztecs 2. Mexico -- Antiquities
ISBN 0-631-23015-7; 0-631-23016-5 pa

LC 2001-6950

First published 1996

The author "summarizes the results of archaeological research conducted largely in the past 30 years into the everyday lives of ordinary people in the villages, hamlets, and farmsteads from many regions of central Mexico. His method permits a fresh view of such topics as agricultural methods, population size, market system, relations between city-states and the empire, and even human sacrifice. Smith carries his social account of these people through transformation under Spanish rule and their legacy in modern Mexico." Libr J [review of 1996 edition]

Includes bibliographical references

Townsend, Richard F.

The **Aztecs**; 3rd ed; Thames & Hudson 2009 256p il map (Ancient peoples and places) pa $24.95 **972**

1. Aztecs
ISBN 978-0-500-28791-0

LC 2008-908216

First published 1992

"Examines the history of these accomplished people through a review of the monuments and artifacts they left behind; exploring how their water-control projects worked, the purposes of their ceremonial centers, and the way they built their incredible ancient structures that still stand today." Publisher's note

Includes bibliographical references

972.02   Mexico – Conquest and colonial period, 1519-1810

Restall, Matthew

When Montezuma met Cortés; the true story of the meeting that changed history. Matthew Restall. Ecco, an imprint of HarperCollinsPublishers 2018 xxxiii, 526 p.p illustrations (chiefly color) (hardcover) $35 **972.02**

1. Mexico -- History 2. Mexico -- History -- Conquest, 1519-1540
ISBN 9780062427267; 0062427261

This book, by Matthew Restall, is "a comprehensive reevaluation of both [Hernando] Cortés and Montezuma. Drawing on rare primary sources and overlooked accounts by conquistadors and Aztecs alike, Restall explores Cortés's and Montezuma's posthumous reputations, their achievements and failures, and the worlds in which they lived--leading, step by step, to a dramatic inversion of the old story." (Publisher's note)

"Blending erudition with enthusiasm, Restall has achieved a rare kind of work—serious scholarship that is impossible to put down." Pub Wkly

Includes bibliographical references (pages 469-508) and index.

972.08   Mexico since 1867

Womack, John

Zapata and the Mexican Revolution. Knopf 1969 435p il hardcover o.p. pa $17 **972.08**

1. Revolutionaries 2. Mexico -- History
ISBN 0-394-70853-9 pa

The author reconstructs the "history of the agrarian revolution in southern Mexico from the late Diaz period to about 1920. The work is well written {and} carefully conceived." Choice

972.81   Guatemala

Carlsen, William

Jungle of Stone; The True Story of Two Men, Their Extraordinary Journey, and the Discovery of the Lost Civilization of the Maya. by William Carlsen (Author) HarperCollins 2016 496 p. ill. (some color), maps $28.99 **972.81**

1. Explorers 2. Ancient civilization 3. Mayas -- Antiquities 4. Central America -- Civilization
ISBN 0062407392; 9780062407399

In this book, by William Carlsen, "In 1839 rumors of . . . stone ruins buried within the unmapped jungles of Central America reached two of the world's most intrepid travelers. . . . [John Lloyd] Stephens and [Frederick] Catherwood . . . documented the remains of an astonishing civilization that had flourished in the Americas. . . . [They] were the first to grasp the significance of the Maya remains." (Publisher's note)

"A captivating history of two men who dramatically changed their contemporaries' view of the past." Kirkus

Includes bibliographical references (pages [467]-515) and index.

Coe, Michael D.

Royal cities of the ancient Maya; Michael D. Coe; photographs by Barry Brukoff. Vendome Press 2012 224 p. $50 **972.81**

1. Mayas -- History 2. Cities and towns -- HIstory 3. Maya architecture 4. Mayas -- Antiquities 5. Central America -- Antiquities
ISBN 0865652848; 9780865652842

LC 2011051139

This book presents the "history of Mayan civilization as seen through the development and decline of its many impressive city-states." It offers "glimpses, through dated stone monuments, into the hereditary lines of dynastic kings who ruled Mayan city-states and frequently did battle with each other." (Library Journal)

Includes bibliographical references

Encyclopedia of the ancient Maya; edited by Walter R. T. Witschey. Rowman & Littlefield 2015 574 p. (cloth: alk. paper) $95   **972.81**

1. Mayas 2. Mayas -- Encyclopedias
ISBN 9780759122840

LC 2015032712

This book, edited by Walter R. T. Witschey, "offers an A-to-Z overview of the ancient Maya culture from its inception around 3000 BC to the Spanish Conquest after AD 1600. Over two hundred entries written by more than sixty researchers explore subjects ranging from food, clothing, and shelter to the sophisticated calendar and now-deciphered Maya writing system." (Publisher's note)

"The work would be a valuable resource for undergraduate students of archaeology, anthropology, history, Latino studies, and art history." Booklist

Includes bibliographical references and index

Goldman, Francisco

The **art** of political murder; who killed the Bishop? Grove Press 2007 396p il map $25   **972.81**

1. Bishops 2. Trials (Homicide) 3. Murder victims 4. Human rights activists 5. Guatemala -- Politics and government
ISBN 978-0-8021-1828-8; 0-8021-1828-3

This book "is a tour de force, not just for . . . [the author's] reportorial tenacity . . . but because his novelist's eye and his deep understanding of Guatemalan society take you places no other reporter could." Nation

Includes bibliographical references

972.85   Nicaragua

Preston, Douglas

The **Lost** City of the Monkey God; a true story. Douglas Preston. Grand Central Publishing 2017 336 p. ill. (some color), maps (hardback) $28   **972.85**

1. Extinct cities 2. Mosquitia (Nicaragua and Honduras) 3. Native Americans -- Central America -- Antiquities 4. Mosquitia (Nicaragua and Honduras) -- Antiquities 5. Extinct cities -- Mosquitia (Nicaragua and Honduras) 6. Mosquitia (Nicaragua and Honduras) -- Description and travel 7. Cities and towns, Ancient -- Mosquitia (Nicaragua and Honduras) 8. Mosquitia (Nicaragua and Honduras) -- Discovery and exploration 9. Indians of Central America -- Mosquitia (Nicaragua and Honduras) -- Antiquities
ISBN 9781455540006; 9781455569410

LC 2016037247

This book, by Douglas Preston, focuses on the quest for "a lost city of immense wealth hidden somewhere in the Honduran interior, called the White City or the Lost City of the Monkey God. . . . Venturing into this raw, treacherous, but breathtakingly beautiful wilderness to confirm the discovery, Preston and [his] team battled torrential rains, quickmud, disease-carrying insects, jaguars, and deadly snakes. But it wasn't until they returned that tragedy struck." (Publisher's note)

Includes bibliographical references and index

972.87   Panama

McCullough, David G.

★ The **path** between the seas; the creation of the Panama Canal, 1870-1914. [by] David McCullough. Simon & Schuster 1977 698p il maps hardcover o.p. pa $18   **972.87**

1. Diplomats 2. Governors 3. Physicians 4. Presidents 5. Panama Canal 6. Vice-presidents 7. Army officers 8. Public health officials 9. Nobel laureates for peace
ISBN 0-671-24409-4

LC 76-57967

"Not only is this a well-told story of the building of the Panama Canal but it also supplies welcome background for the . . . debate on the canal's role in inter-American relations." Booklist

Includes bibliographical references

972.9   West Indies (Antilles) and Bermuda

Gibson, Carrie

Empire's Crossroads; A History of the Caribbean from Columbus to the Present Day. Carrie Gibson. Atlantic Monthly Press 2014 448 p. color illustrations; maps $28   **972.9**

1. World history 2. Caribbean Region
ISBN 0802126146; 9780802126146

LC 2015430678

In this book author "Carrie Gibson traces the story of [the Caribbean] from the northern rim of South America up to Cuba, and from discovery through colonialism to today, offering a . . . panoramic view of this complex region and its rich, important history. Gibson wields . . . . detail to combat the myths that have romanticized this region as one of uniform white sand beaches where the palm trees always sway." (Publisher's note)

"Alongside her stark descriptions of the slave economies, Gibson recounts geopolitical events that have periodically wracked the Caribbean Sea, from wars galore in the 1700s to the Cold War, as well as the supplanting of European suzerainty by American influence, expressed today more by cruise ship than by gunboat. Sympathetically attuned to the hard actualities of life in ostensibly paradisaical tropics, Gibson delivers a fine, faceted history for general-interest readers." Booklist

Jelly-Schapiro, Joshua

Island people; by Joshua Jelly-Schapiro. Alfred A. Knopf 2016 464 p. map (hardback) $28.95   **972.9**

1. Caribbean region -- History 2. Caribbean Region -- Civilization 3. Caribbean Region -- Intellectual life 4. Caribbean Area -- History 5. Caribbean Area -- Civilization 6. Caribbean Area -- Intellectual life
ISBN 9780385349772; 9780385349765

LC 2016010673

"A masterwork of travel literature and of history: voyaging from Cuba to Jamaica, Puerto Rico to Trinidad, Haiti to Barbados, and islands in between, [author] Joshua Jelly-Schapiro offers a kaleidoscopic portrait of each society, its culture and politics, connecting this region's common heritage to its fierce grip on the world's imagination." (Publisher's note)

"Though his arguments about the relationship between modernity, tourism, and branding are not always clear, Jelly-Schapiro writes joyfully about music and literature and how these arts reflect the Caribbean's hybrid and evolving culture." Pub Wkly

Includes bibliographical references (pages [437]-451).

Von Tunzelmann, Alex

Red heat; conspiracy, murder, and the Cold War in the Caribbean. Henry Holt 2011 449p il $30; ebook $14.99 **972.9**

1. Generals 2. Physicians 3. Presidents 4. Revolutionaries 5. Haiti -- History 6. Communist leaders 7. Political leaders 8. Cuba -- History -- 1959- 9. Caribbean region -- History 10. Dominican Republic -- History 11. Haiti -- History -- 1934-1986 12. Caribbean region -- History -- 1945- 13. Dominican Republic -- History -- 1930-1961 14. Caribbean region -- Foreign relations -- United States 15. United States -- Foreign relations -- Caribbean region

ISBN 978-0-8050-9067-3; 978-1-4299-6673-3 ebook

LC 2010-37585

"Three dictators, circa 1960—Castro in Cuba, François Duvalier in Haiti, and Rafael Trujillo in the Dominican Republic—are the principals in von Tunzelmann's political history. Recounting alarms that trio set off in Washington, she ponders how well the Eisenhower and Kennedy administrations understood situations on the islands of Cuba and Hispaniola. Not very realistically, runs the tenor of von Tunzelmann's narrative. . . . Punctuated by accounts of such major incidents as the Bay of Pigs, the assassination of Trujillo, the Cuban missile crisis, and LBJ's 1965 intervention in the Dominican Republic, von Tunzelmann's diligent work will widen the eyes of cold war buffs." Booklist

Includes bibliographical references

972.91 Cuba

Cooke, Julia

The **other** side of paradise; life in the new Cuba. Julia Cooke. Seal Press 2014 248 p. (paperback) $17 **972.91**

1. Havana (Cuba) 2. Cuba -- Social life and customs 3. Havana (Cuba) -- Biography 4. Cuba -- History -- 1990- -- Biography 5. Cuba -- Politics and government -- 1990- 6. Young adults -- Cuba -- Havana -- Biography 7. Havana (Cuba) -- Social conditions -- 21st century 8. Havana (Cuba) -- Social life and customs -- 21st century 9. Social change -- Cuba -- Havana -- History -- 21st century

ISBN 1580055311; 9781580055314

LC 2013044413

This book by Julia Cook describes how "[t]his last generation of Cubans raised under Fidel Castro animate life in a waning era of political stagnation as the rest of the world beckons: waiting out storms at rummy hurricane parties and attending raucous drag cabarets, planning ascendant music careers and black-market business ventures, trying to reconcile the undefined future with the urgent today." (Publisher's note)

"An absorbing and educational read about contemporary Cuba, the love of its people for their country, and their hope for opportunity." LJ

Includes bibliographical references

Guerriero, Leila

Cuba on the Verge; 12 writers on continuity and change in Havana and across the country. edited by Leila Guerriero. Ecco, an imprint of HarperCollins Publishers 2017 xi, 286 p.p (hardcover) $26.99 **972.91**

1. Essays 2. Cuba -- History 3. Cuba -- Foreign relations -- United States 4. Cuba -- Economic conditions -- 1990- 5. Cuba -- Politics and government -- 21st century

ISBN 9780062661081; 9780525563235; 9780062661067; 006266106X

This essay collection, by Leila Guerriero, offers "a timely look at a society's profound transformation--from inside and out. . . . These essays span the spectrum, from Carlos Manuel Álvarez's story of being among the last generation of Cubans to be raised under Fidel Castro

to Patricia Engel's look at how Cuba's capital has changed through her years of riding across it with her taxi driver friend." (Publisher's note)

"Guerriero's meticulously curated dozen essays offers an irresistibly beckoning window onto a nation just 90 miles from American shores, though far away in practice and culture." Booklist

Guevara March, Aleida, 1960-

Remembering Che; my life with Che Guevara. Aleida March; [translated by Pilar Aguilera] Ocean Press 2012 viii, 168 p.p ill. **972.91**

1. Cuba -- History -- 1958-1959, Revolution 2. Cuba -- History -- 1990- 3. Cuba -- History -- 1959-1990 4. Revolutionaries -- Latin America -- Biography 5. Revolutionaries' spouses -- Latin America -- Biography

ISBN 0987077937; 9780987077936; 9780987077998

LC 2011943980

Author Aleida March "evokes the memories of her partner, Ernesto Che Guevara. She describes their great romance and life together from the days when they first met as fellow guerrillas in Cuba's revolutionary war up to the tragic moment when she learned of Che's assassination in Bolivia less than a decade later. . . . She also describes her efforts to raise her four children as ordinary children despite their father's legendary status in Cuba and abroad." (Publisher's note)

Includes bibliographical references

Guillermoprieto, Alma

Dancing with Cuba; a memoir of the revolution. translated from the Spanish by Esther Allen. Pantheon 2004 290p $25; pa $13 **972.91**

1. Cuba -- Description and travel

ISBN 0-375-42093-2; 0-375-72581-4 pa

LC 2003-44200

"Guillermoprieto vividly and purposefully recounts her acute discomfort with the strained and ludicrous rhetoric of the revolution, her sorrow over Castro's catastrophic failures, her astonishment at the great valor of Cuba's people, and her gradual recognition of her true calling as a journalist." Booklist

Kurlansky, Mark, 1948-

Havana; a subtropical delirium. by Mark Kurlansky. St. Martin's Press 2017 xii, 259 p.p $26 **972.91**

1. Havana (Cuba) 2. Havana (Cuba) -- Description and travel

ISBN 163286391X; 9781632863911

LC 2016041072

This book, by Mark Kurlansky, "presents an insider's view of Havana: the elegant, tattered city he has come to know over more than thirty years. Part cultural history, part travelogue, with recipes, historic engravings, photographs, and Kurlansky's own pen-and-ink drawings throughout, Havana celebrates the city's singular music, literature, baseball, and food; its five centuries of outstanding, neglected architecture; and its extraordinary blend of cultures." (Publisher's note)

"An affectionate, richly detailed, brief biography of a unique city." Kirkus.

Includes bibliographical references and index.

Perez, Louis A.

Cuba; between reform and revolution. Oxford University Press 2006 442p il map (Latin American histories) $77.95; pa $34.95 **972.91**

1. Cuba -- History

ISBN 0-19-517911-0; 978-0-19-517911-8; 0-19-517912-9 pa; 978-0-19-517912-5 pa

LC 2004-65477

First published 1988

"A narrative history that emphasizes the antecedents of the Cuban revolution and concludes with an analysis of Fidel Castro's successes and failures." N Y Public Libr Book of How & Where to Look It Up [entry for 1988 edition]

Includes bibliographical references

Rasenberger, Jim

The **brilliant** disaster; JFK, Castro, and America's doomed invasion of Cuba's Bay of Pigs. Scribner 2011 460p il **972.91**

1. Presidents 2. Senators 3. Communist leaders 4. Members of Congress 5. Cuba -- History -- 1961, Invasion 6. Cuba -- Foreign relations -- United States 7. United States -- Foreign relations -- Cuba

ISBN 978-1-4165-9650-9

LC 2011-4178

"On Apr., 17, 1961, a CIA-trained brigade of 1,400 Cuban exiles, mostly students and former soldiers, made an unsuccessful amphibious assault on the Bay of Pigs, in southern Cuba, hoping to spur a popular revolt and overthrow the Castro regime. Fifty years later, Rasenberger . . . succeeds admirably in offering a nuanced view of the entire botched operation, from its planning in two U.S. administrations to the Cuban armed forces' quick defeat of the exiles, whose attack lacked air cover and the element of surprise." Kirkus

Includes bibliographical references

Suchlicki, Jaime

Cuba; from Columbus to Castro and beyond. {by} Jaime Suchlicki. 5th ed; Brassey's 2002 285p pa $24.95 **972.91**

1. Cuba -- History

ISBN 1-57488-436-0

LC 2002-3953

First published 1997

A summary of Cuba's development, with emphasis on the twentieth century and the factors that led to the Cuban revolution

Includes bibliographical references

Symmes, Patrick

The **boys** from Dolores; Fidel Castro's schoolmates from revolution to exile. Pantheon Books 2007 352p $26.95 **972.91**

1. Presidents 2. Communist leaders 3. Colegio de Dolores (Cuba) 4. Cuba -- Description and travel

ISBN 978-0-375-42283-6; 0-375-42283-8

LC 2006-30323

"The author writes of Castro's schoolmates from Dolores, the private Jesuit academy in Santiago de Cuba on the island's eastern end, and he visits several of them. . . . Among the Dolores students were Castro's brothers Raul and Ramon and a future star in North American television, Desi Arnaz. But it is Cuban intellectuals like Lundy Aguilar to whom Symmes turns for insights into Cuba before and after Castro's revolution. The result is a remarkable account of the country and its people." Libr J

972.94   Haiti

Dubois, Laurent

Haiti; the aftershocks of history. Laurent Dubois. 1st ed.; Henry Holt and Co. 2012 p. cm. $32 **972.94**

1. Haiti -- History

ISBN 978-0-8050-9335-3

LC 2011020162

"Building on his landmark synthesis of revolutionary Haiti. . . , Dubois summarizes colonial slave society and the liberation era, then thoroughly covers poorly understood 19th-century developments. Ongoing tensions between ruling elites and rural citizens characterized this period. Elites hoped to restore the plantation regime's coercive labor relations; peasants sought title to land for subsistence farming and local market production. Dubois persuasively argues that the resulting stalemate defines much of Haiti's history, shaping political as well as agricultural life." (Choice Reviews)

Includes bibliographical references

Laferriee, Dany

The **World** Is Moving Around Me; A Memoir of the Haiti Earthquake. Dany Laferrière; translated by David Homel. Arsenal Pulp Press 2013 192 p. $15.95 **972.94**

1. Natural disasters 2. Haiti Earthquake, Haiti, 2010

ISBN 1551524988; 9781551524986

LC 2012517880

This book by Dany Laferriere "is an eyewitness account of the [January 12, 2010 earth]quake and its aftermath. In a series of vignettes, Laferrière reveals the shock, rage, and grief experienced by those around him, the acts of heroism he witnessed, and his own sense of survivor guilt. This book is not only the chronicle of a natural disaster; it is also a personal meditation about the responsibility and power of the written word." (Publisher's note)

972.97   Leeward Islands

Kincaid, Jamaica, 1946-

A **small** place. Farrar, Straus & Giroux 1988 81p hardcover o.p. pa $11 **972.97**

1. Antigua and Barbuda 2. Antigua (Antigua and Barbuda)

ISBN 0-374-52707-5 pa

LC 88-376

The author of Annie John (BRD 1986) addresses foreign visitors to her country, the island of Antigua. In this essay, she discusses the poverty and political corruption of the island, which she views as a legacy of British colonialism and also as a result of an economy controlled by tourism.

973   United States

The **50s**; the story of a decade. The New Yorker; edited by Henry Finder; introduction by David Remnick. Random House 2015 784 p. illustrations (hardcover) $35 **973**

1. Nineteen fifties 2. United States -- Civilization -- 1945-

ISBN 9780679644811; 0679644814

LC 2015030067

In this book, edited by Henry Finder, articles from "The New Yorker" magazine from the 1950s are presented to chronicle the era. "In this . . . volume, classic works of reportage, criticism, and fiction are complemented by new contributions from the magazine's present all-star lineup of writers, including Jonathan Franzen, Malcolm Gladwell, and Jill Lepore." (Publisher's note)

Includes bibliographical references

Andersen, Kurt

★ **Fantasyland**; how America went haywire: a 500-year history. Kurt Andersen. Random House 2017 xiii, 462 p.p

Hardcover $30   **973**

1. Historical literature 2. United States -- Civilization 3. American national characteristics 4. National characteristics, American 5. Popular culture -- United States -- History

ISBN 1400067219; 9781400067213

LC 2017016052

This book, by Kurt Andersen, "shows that what's happening in our country today--this post-factual, 'fake news' moment we're all living through--is not something new, but rather the ultimate expression of our national character. America was founded by wishful dreamers, magical thinkers, and true believers, by hucksters and their suckers. Fantasy is deeply embedded in our DNA." (Publisher's note)

Ashby, Ruth

The **great** American documents; Volume 1, 1620-1830. Ruth Ashby; illustrated by Ernie Colón; editorial consultant Russell Motter. Hill and Wang 2014 160 p. col. ill. (hardcover) $40   **973**

1. United States -- History -- Sources 2. United States -- Politics and government -- Sources

ISBN 0809094606; 9780809094608

LC 2013956401

Written by Ruth Ashby and illustrated by Ernie Colón, "'The Great American Documents: Volume 1' introduces as series narrator none other than Uncle Sam, who walks us through twenty essential documents. Each document gets a chapter, in which Uncle Sam explains its key passages, its origins, how it came to be written, and its impact. This graphic primer is an indispensable resource for students and anyone else who wants the facts of American history close at hand." (Publisher's note)

"Colon uses well-designed, full-color panel layouts to eloquently blend charts and other informative graphics with straightforward images of events, clothing, and customs as well as clear, concise metaphors, all with an eye toward promoting a solid understanding of the basic facts and their impact." Booklist

Includes bibliographical references

Berger, Joseph

The **pious** ones; the world of Hasidim and their battles with America. Joseph Berger. Harper Perennial 2014 384 p. (paperback) $15.99   **973**

1. Ethnic relations 2. Jews -- New York (N.Y.) 3. Hasidim -- Social conditions 4. New York (N.Y.) -- Ethnic relations 5. Hasidim -- New York (State) -- New York -- Social conditions 6. Jews -- New York (State) -- New York -- Social life and customs

ISBN 0062123343; 9780062123343; 9780062123350

LC 2014011724

In this book, "journalist Joseph Berger takes us inside the notoriously insular world of the Hasidim to explore their origins, beliefs, and struggles--and the social and political implications of their expanding presence in America. . . . Berger traces their origins in eighteenth-century Eastern Europe, illuminating their dynamics and core beliefs that remain so enigmatic to outsiders." (Publisher's note)

"Through Berger's solid research and approachable writing, readers will gain a clear, well-rounded understanding of who the Hasidim are, where they came from and where they are going as a people." Kirkus

Boorstin, Daniel J.

The **Americans**: The colonial experience. Random House 1958 434p hardcover o.p. pa $15   **973**

1. Puritans 2. Americanisms 3. Society of Friends 4. American national characteristics 5. Georgia -- History 6. Law -- United States 7. United States -- Civilization 8. United States -- Intellectual life 9. Colleges and universities -- United States 10. United States -- History -- 1600-1775, Colonial period

ISBN 0-394-70513-0 pa

The first volume of the author's trilogy entitled: The Americans

"This study of colonial America attempts to show that it was not merely an offshoot of the mother country, but a new civilization. . . . The author centers his highly informative work on colonial education, the special qualities of American speech, and the growth of a distinct culture." Booklist

Includes bibliographical references

The **Americans**: The democratic experience. Random House 1973 717p hardcover o.p. pa $19   **973**

1. Advertising 2. American art 3. Americanisms 4. Higher education 5. Automobile industry 6. United States -- Civilization 7. Cities and towns -- United States 8. United States -- Social conditions 9. United States -- Economic conditions

ISBN 0-394-71011-8 pa

Concluding volume of the author's trilogy which began with The Americans: The colonial experience and continued with The Americans: The national experience

This volume is concerned with the democratization of the national character over the past hundred years and the growth of technology

Includes bibliographical references

The **Americans**: The national experience. Random House 1965 517p hardcover o.p. pa $16   **973**

1. Americanisms 2. Federal government 3. Heroes and heroines 4. American national characteristics 5. America -- Exploration 6. African Americans -- Religion 7. United States -- Civilization 8. United States -- Intellectual life 9. Constitutional history -- United States 10. Colleges and universities -- United States

ISBN 0-394-70358-8 pa

This is the second volume of the author's trilogy

A cultural interpretation of American history, this book traces "the roots of contemporary American life to the years between the Revolution and the Civil War." Booklist

Includes bibliographical references

Bracks, Lean'tin

African American almanac; 400 years of triumph, courage and excellence. Lean'tin Bracks. Visible Ink Press 2012 xiii, 543 p.p ill. (pbk.) $22.95   **973**

1. Almanacs 2. African Americans -- History 3. African Americans -- Encyclopedias 4. African Americans -- Biography -- Encyclopedias 5. African Americans -- Biography 6. African Americans -- Intellectual life 7. African Americans -- Social life and customs

ISBN 1578593239; 9781578593231

LC 2011038636

This reference book by Lean'tin Bracks "chronicles the African American experience from the arrival of the first Africans to North America in the early 1600s to the present day," including an almanac of topics such as Civil Rights, politics, and music, as well as biographies of various notable African Americans. "Bracks also gives context to less documented areas of African American history." (Booklist)

"This mostly excellent overview of African American contributions to the United States will be a welcome addition to school, public, and community college libraries." LJ

Includes bibliographical references (p. 469-477) and index

Cannon, Carl M.

On this date; from the Pilgrims to today, discovering America one day at a time. Carl M. Cannon. Twelve 2017 xi, 430 p.p illustrations (hardcover) $28 **973**

1. United States -- History

ISBN 9781455542307; 9781538760321; 145554230X

LC 2017935431

This book, by Carl Cannon, "is focused on fascinating -- and sometimes unknown -- stories behind specific dates in U.S. history: What inspired Abraham Lincoln to grow his famous beard, what Dwight Eisenhower really thought about playing football against the great Jim Thorpe, the legal grounds for the first American divorce, who wrote 'Rudolph, the Red-Nosed Reindeer' -- and who profited from it." (Publisher's note)

Churchill, Winston

The **great** republic; a history of America. edited by Winston S. Churchill. Random House 1999 454p hardcover o.p. pa $15.95 **973**

1. United States -- History

ISBN 0-375-50320-X; 978-0-375-75440-1 pa; 0-375-75440-7 pa

LC 99-28511

"The first half of the volume offers an old-fashioned narrative history of America's political development, from the age of exploration to the 1880s. The second half reprints articles that Churchill penned for English publications on such themes as Prohibition, the muckraking of Upton Sinclair, and the death of Franklin Delano Roosevelt." Libr J

Includes bibliographical references

Daily life through American history in primary documents; Randall M. Miller, general editor. Greenwood 2012 1099 p. **973**

1. Archives -- United States 2. United States -- History -- Chronology 3. United States -- Social life and customs

ISBN 161069032X; 1610690338; 9781610690324; 9781610690331

LC 2011040023

In this history book, "four volumes are organized chronologically and then thematically and present the 'many small things that made up Americans' daily life.' Volumes are 'The Colonial Period through the American Revolution,' 'The American Revolution to the Civil War,' 'The Civil War to World War I,' and 'World War I to the Present.' Each volume begins with a time line of selected events and a lengthy historical-overview essay describing significant themes, events, and concerns of the period. This is followed by about 100 primary documents that illustrate daily life." (Booklist)

Includes bibliographical references and index

Davis, Thomas J.

History of African Americans; exploring diverse roots. Thomas J. Davis. Greenwood, an imprint of ABC-CLIO, LLC 2016 xxxiii, 271 p.p (alk. paper) $58 **973**

1. African Americans -- History 2. African Americans -- Social life and customs 3. African Americans -- Race identity 4. Racism -- United States -- History 5. African Americans -- Social conditions

ISBN 0313385408; 9780313385407; 9780313385414

LC 2016025200

Author Thomas J. Davis presents this "cultural history of African Americans [that] outlines their travails, triumphs, and achievements in negotiating individual and collective identities to overcome racism, slavery, and the legacies of these injustices from colonial times to the present." (Publisher's note)

"Davis's book is mandatory reading for undergraduates and the general public, who tend to have only the most superficial understanding of

African American history." Choice

Includes bibliographical references and index

Dream a world anew; The African American Experience and the Shaping of America. edited by Kinshasha Holmes Conwill; introduction by Lonnie G. Bunch III. Smithsonian Books 2016 288 p. color illustrations $40 **973**

1. African Americans -- History 2. United States -- Civilization -- African American influences

ISBN 9781588345684

LC 2016015596

This book edited by Kinshasha Holmes Conwill with introduction by Lonnie G. Bunch III, "is the stunning gift book accompanying the opening of the Smithsonian National Museum of African American History and Culture. It combines informative narratives from leading scholars, curators, and authors with objects from the museum's collection to present a thorough exploration of African American history and culture." (Publisher's note)

"With the feel of an exhibition catalog rich with illustrations, this handsome work provides both a sweeping historical overview of African American history and a tantalizing glimpse of the artifacts, images, and stories NMAAHC promises to display from among its treasures." LJ

Includes bibliographical references and index.

Eyewitness to America; 500 years of America in the words of those who saw it happen. edited by David Colbert. Pantheon Bks. 1997 xxx, 599p hardcover o.p. pa $16.95 **973**

1. United States -- History -- Sources

ISBN 0-679-44224-3; 0-679-76724-X pa

LC 96-24150

This volume contains a "panorama of first-person accounts of moments in the country's story that stretch from an October 10, 1492, diary entry by one of Columbus's crewmen to a 1994 e-mail message from Bill Gates. The nearly 300 entries tend to be short, preceded by informative introductions. The result is a feeling for history that is both immediate and dramatic." Publ Wkly

Includes bibliographical references

Gates, Henry Louis, 1950-

100 amazing facts about the Negro; Henry Louis Gates, Jr. Pantheon Books 2017 xii, 476 p.p illustrations (some color) (hard cover: alk. paper) $40 **973**

1. Blacks -- History 2. African Americans -- History 3. Blacks -- History -- Miscellanea 4. African Americans -- History -- Miscellanea

ISBN 9780307908711; 9780307908728

LC 2016024453

This book, by Henry Louis Gates, Jr., "gives us a corrective yet loving homage to [Joel Augustus Roger's] work. Relying on the latest scholarship, Gates leads us on a romp through African, diasporic, and African-American history in question-and-answer format. Among the one hundred questions: Who were Africa's first ambassadors to Europe? Who was the first black president in North America? Did Lincoln really free the slaves?" (Publisher's note)

"Gates presents topics and facts that are fascinating and unique." LJ

Includes bibliographical references and index.

And Still I Rise; Black America Since MLK. Henry L. Gates, Kevin M. Burke. HarperCollins 2015 336 p. illustrations (chiefly color) (ebook) $32.99; (hardcover) $35 **973**

1. United States -- Race relations 2. African Americans -- Social conditions 3. African Americans -- History -- Chronology

ISBN 9780062427014; 0062427008; 9780062427007

This book by Henry L. Gates and Kevin M. Burke explores "the last half-century of the African American experience. More than fifty years after the passage of the Civil Rights Act and the birth of Black Power, the United States has both a black president and black CEOs running Fortune 500 companies—and a large black underclass beset by persistent poverty, inadequate education, and an epidemic of incarceration. . . . [Gates] raises . . . vital questions about this dichotomy." (Publisher's note)

"This is an amazing collection of images of achievement on the long road to equality in the U.S." Booklist

Includes bibliographical references (pages 287-307) and index.

Glass, Brent D.

50 great American places; essential historic sites across the U.S. Brent D. Glass. Simon & Schuster 2016 320 p. illustrations $16 **973**

1. Historic sites 2. United States -- Description and travel 3. Historic sites -- United States -- Guidebooks

ISBN 1451682034; 9781451682038

LC 2015031714

This book, by Brent D. Glass, is a "guide to fifty of the most important cultural and historic sites in the United States. From Massachusetts to Florida to Washington to California, [it] takes you on a journey through our nation's history. Sharing the inside stories of sites as old as Mesa Verde (Colorado) and Cahokia (Illinois) and as recent as Silicon Valley (California) and the Mall of America (Minnesota), each essay provides the historical context." (Publisher's note)

"This book will whet the appetite of history buffs interested in possible destinations, or anybody who would like to learn American history through the places where it happened." Library Journal

Includes bibliographical references and index

Gregory, Dick, 1932-2017

Defining moments in Black history; reading between the lies. Dick Gregory. Amistad 2017 236 p. (hardcover) $24.99 **973**

1. Civil rights 2. African Americans -- History 3. Civil rights -- United States 4. African Americans -- Civil rights -- History 5. Black nationalism -- United States -- History

ISBN 0062448692; 9780062448729; 9780062448699

"In this collection of . . . essays, [Dick] Gregory charts the complex and often obscured history of the African American experience. . . . [H]e moves from African ancestry and surviving the Middle Passage to the creation of the Jheri Curl, the enjoyment of bacon and everything pig, the headline-making shootings of black men, and the Black Lives Matter movement. . . . [The book] explores historical movements such as The Great Migration and the Harlem Renaissance." (Publisher's note)

"Gregory's devotion to civil rights and his global recognition add to his appealing writing style and clever sense of humor to make this a book for a wide audience." Kirkus

Hilgers, Lauren

★ **Patriot** number one; American dreams in Chinatown. Lauren Hilgers. Random House Inc 2018 336 p. $27 **973**

1. Chinese Americans -- New York (State) 2. Immigrants -- New York (State) -- New York

ISBN 0451496132; 9780451496133

In this book, author Lauren Hilgers follows Zhuang Liehong's "family through a world hidden in plain sight: a byzantine network of employment agencies and language schools, of underground asylum brokers and illegal dormitories that Flushing's Chinese community relies on for survival. As the irrepressibly opinionated Zhuang and the more pragmatic Little Yan pursue legal status and struggle to reunite with their son." (Publisher's note)

"This book is hard to put down. It would be easy to say that it is recommended for readers interested in Chinese-American communities, but at its heart is a highly readable story about starting over in a new land; a must-read for all." LJ

Hofstadter, Richard

The **American** political tradition, and the men who made it; with a foreword by Christopher Lasch. 25th anniversary ed; Knopf 1973 xxxiii, 378p hardcover o.p. pa $14 **973**

1. Authors 2. Lawyers 3. Generals 4. Governors 5. Statesmen 6. Architects 7. Presidents 8. Abolitionists 9. Philanthropists 10. Vice-presidents 11. People with disabilities 12. Orators 13. Essayists 14. Handicapped 15. Philatelists 16. Political leaders 17. State legislators 18. College presidents 19. Secretaries of war 20. Members of Congress 21. Secretaries of state 22. Presidential candidates 23. Secretaries of commerce 24. Nobel laureates for peace 25. United States -- Politics and government

ISBN 0-679-72315-3 pa

First published 1948

This volume contains twelve essays, ten of which analyze the political careers of Lincoln, Jefferson, Jackson, Calhoun, Wendell Phillips, Bryan, Theodore Roosevelt, Wilson, Hoover and Franklin D. Roosevelt.

Includes bibliographical references

Kendall, Joshua C.

First dads; parenting and politics from George Washington to Barack Obama. Joshua Kendall. Grand Central Publishing 2016 400 p. illustrations (hardcover) $27 **973**

1. Presidents -- United States -- Children 2. Presidents -- United States -- Biography 3. Presidents -- United States -- History 4. Children of presidents -- United States -- History 5. Children of presidents -- United States -- Biography 6. Presidents -- Family relationships -- United States -- History

ISBN 9781455551958

LC 2015050559

This book, by Joshua Kendall, explores how "every [U.S.] president has had some experience as a parent. . . . Each president's parenting style reveals much about his beliefs as well as his psychological make-up. . . . Based on research in archives around the country, Kendall shows presidential character in action." (Publisher's note)

"Kendall's research puts all the presidents and their parenting practices in perspective, giving readers great insight into these men and their children. Rich in detail, this informative book gives new understanding to our nation's leaders and their offspring." Kirkus

Includes bibliographical references and index

Lee, Erika

The **making** of Asian America; a history. by Erika Lee. Simon & Schuster 2015 416 p. illustrations, map (hardback) $29.95 **973**

1. Asian Americans -- History 2. Asians -- United States -- History 3. Racism -- United States -- History 4. United States -- Race relations -- History 5. United States -- Ethnic relations -- History 6. South Asia -- Emigration and immigration -- History 7. United States -- Emigration and immigration -- History

ISBN 9781476739403; 9781476739410

LC 2015010372

This book, by Erika Lee, "shows how generations of Asian immigrants and their American-born descendants have made and remade Asian American life in the United States: sailors who came on the first trans-Pacific ships in the 1500s; indentured 'coolies' who worked alongside African slaves in the Caribbean; and Chinese, Japanese, Filipino, Korean, and South Asian immigrants who were recruited to work in the United States only to face massive racial discrimination." (Publisher's note)

"An impressive work that details how this diverse population has both swayed and been affected by the United States." LJ

Lepore, Jill

★ The **mansion** of happiness; a history of life and death. Jill Lepore. 1st ed. Alfred A. Knopf 2012 xxxiii, 282 p.p $27.95 **973**
1. Life 2. Death 3. Popular culture 4. United States -- Intellectual life 5. United States -- Social conditions 6. United States -- Social life and customs 7. Popular culture -- United States -- History 8. Politics and culture -- United States -- History 9. Life -- Social aspects -- United States -- History 10. Death -- Social aspects -- United States -- History 11. Happiness -- Social aspects -- United States -- History 12. Life (Biology) -- Social aspects -- United States -- History 13. Life cycle, Human -- Social aspects -- United States -- History
ISBN 0307592995; 9780307592996
LC 2011050566

In this book Jill Lepore examines "the history of American ideas about life and death. . . . Lepore starts . . . with the story of a seventeenth-century Englishman who had the idea that all life begins with an egg and ends it with an American who, in the 1970s, began freezing the dead. . . . Investigating the surprising origins of the stuff of everyday life . . . Lepore argues that the age of discovery, Darwin, and the Space Age turned ideas about life on earth topsy-turvy." (Publisher's note)

Includes bibliographical references and index.

The **story** of America; essays on origins. Jill Lepore. Princeton University Press 2012 viii, 416 p.p (acid-free paper) $27.95 **973**
1. United States -- History 2. Democracy -- United States -- History 3. United States -- Politics and government 4. United States -- History -- Sources 5. United States -- Politics and government -- Sources
ISBN 069115399X; 9780691153995
LC 2012016854

In this book, "Jill Lepore investigates American origin stories . . . to show how American democracy is bound up with the history of print. . . . Part civics primer, part cultural history, 'The Story of America' excavates the origins of everything from the paper ballot and the Constitution to the I.O.U. and the dictionary. . . . From past to present, Lepore argues, Americans have wrestled with the idea of democracy by telling stories." (Publisher's note)

Includes bibliographical references and index.

★ **These** truths; a history of the United States. Jill Lepore. W W Norton & Co Inc 2018 960 p. $39.95 **973**
1. United States -- History 2. Equality -- United States 3. United States -- Politics and government
ISBN 0393635244; 9780393635249

In this book, author Jill Lepore "offers a magisterial account of the origins and rise of a divided nation. . . . Lepore's groundbreaking investigation places truth itself--a devotion to facts, proof, and evidence--at the center of the nation's history. The American experiment rests on three ideas-- . . . political equality, natural rights, and the sovereignty of the people. And it rests, too, on a fearless dedication to inquiry, Lepore argues." (Publisher's note)

"Lepore is a historian with wide appeal, and this comprehensive work will answer readers' questions about who we are as a nation."

Booklist

Loewen, James W.

Lies across America; what our historic sites get wrong. Simon & Schuster 2007 464p pa $16 **973**
1. Monuments 2. Historic sites
ISBN 978-0-7432-9629-8; 0-7432-9629-X
First published 1999 by New Press

"The book consists of 95 brief commentaries on specific sites from Alaska to Florida to Maine, sandwiched between essays that offer advice on how to interpret what you read or are told at historic sites." N Y Times Book Rev [review of 1999 edition]

McCullough, David G., 1933-

The **American** spirit; who we are and what we stand for. speeches by David McCullough. Simon & Schuster 2017 xv, 176 p.p illustrations (some color) (hardcover) $25 **973**
1. American speeches 2. United States -- Civilization 3. American national characteristics 4. National characteristics, American 5. Speeches, addresses, etc., American
ISBN 9781501174209; 9781501174216; 1501174215
LC 2017002640

This collection of speeches, by Pulitzer Prize, National Book Awards and Presidential Medal of Freedom awardee David McCullough, "reminds us of fundamental American principles. . . . Now, at a time of self-reflection in America following a bitter election campaign that has left the country divided, McCullough has collected some of his most important speeches in a brief volume designed to identify important principles and characteristics that are particularly American." (Publisher's note)

"Historian McCullough . . . presents this collection of 15 inspiring speeches in which he celebrates America's talent for curiosity, intelligence, goodwill, and humanity." LJ

Meacham, Jon

★ The **soul** of America; the battle for our better angels. Jon Meacham. Random House Inc 2018 416 p. (hardback) $30 **973**
1. United States -- Civilization 2. American national characteristics 3. National characteristics, American
ISBN 9780399589812
LC 2018010451

In this book, author Jon Meacham "shows us how what Abraham Lincoln called the 'better angels of our nature' have repeatedly won the day. Painting surprising portraits of Lincoln and other presidents . . . and illuminating the courage of such influential citizen activists as Martin Luther King, Jr., early suffragettes Alice Paul and Carrie Chapman Catt . . . and Army-McCarthy hearings lawyer Joseph N. Welch, Meacham brings vividly to life turning points in American history." (Publisher's note)

"An excellent work by a skilled historian and worthy of all library collections." Library Journal

Includes bibliographical references and index

Olson, James Stuart

Encyclopedia of the industrial revolution in America; {by} James S. Olson; technical editor: Robert L. Shadle. Greenwood Press 2002 xxv, 313p il $69.95 **973**
1. Reference books 2. Industrial revolution -- Encyclopedias
ISBN 0-313-30830-6
LC 00-52129

"A well-organized and comprehensive ready reference." Voice Youth Advocates

Includes bibliographical references

Prothero, Stephen

The **American** Bible; how our words unite, divide, and define a nation. Stephen Prothero. 1st ed. HarperOne 2012 vii, 533 p.p (hardback) $29.99 **973**

1. American national characteristics 2. United States -- Politics and government 3. American literature -- History and criticism 4. Group identity in literature 5. United States -- Civilization 6. National characteristics, American 7. Language and culture -- United States 8. Nationalism and literature -- United States 9. National characteristics, American, in literature 10. Literature and society -- United States -- History 11. Rhetoric -- Political aspects -- United States -- History 12. Speeches, addresses, etc., American -- History and criticism

ISBN 0062123432; 9780062123435

LC 2012005054

In this book, Stephen Prothero has "assembl[ed] a version of the American canon: 'Not the books I revere but those that Americans themselves have made sacred.' His scripture comprises a set of essays, speeches and fiction that, in his judgment, have largely influenced the United States' self-image. By recovering their teachings, he believes, we can heal the divisiveness and self-interest that ail our politics." (Washington Post)

Includes bibliographical references (p. 491-510) and index.

Puleo, Stephen

American treasures; The Secret Efforts to Save the Declaration of Independence, the Constitution and the Gettysburg Address. Stephen Puleo. St. Martin's Press 2016 432 p. illustrations (hardback) $28.99 **973**

1. Historic preservation 2. United States. Constitution 3. Democracy -- United States -- History 4. United States. Declaration of independence 5. United States -- History -- Sources 6. Hiding places -- United States -- History 7. United States. Declaration of Independence 8. United States -- Politics and government -- Sources 9. Historic preservation -- Political aspects -- United States -- History 10. Manuscripts -- Collection and preservation -- United States -- History 11. United States -- Antiquities -- Collection and preservation -- History

ISBN 9781250065742

LC 2016003702

This book, by Stephen Puleo, focuses on how "FDR set about hiding the country's valuables: . . . the Declaration of Independence, the Constitution, the Gettysburg Address, and more, guarded by a battery of agents and bound for safekeeping in the nation's most impenetrable hiding place." (Publisher's note)

"This unique, easily digestible, well-researched saga is ideal for general readers." Booklist

Includes bibliographical references and index

State by state; a panoramic portrait of America. edited by Matt Weiland & Sean Wilsey. Ecco 2008 xxxi, 572p il map $29.95 **973**

1. United States

ISBN 978-0-06-147090-5; 0-06-147090-2

LC 2008-300642

"Taking as their inspiration the state guides published by the Federal Writers' Project during and shortly after the Great Depression, Weiland and Wilsey assembled 50 of America's finest writers and asked them to contribute essays on the same general theme: why my state is special—or not. The result is a funny, moving, rousing collection, greater than the sum of its excellent parts, a convention of literary super-delegates, each one boisterously nominating his or her piece of the Republic." N Y Times Book Rev

Steinbeck, John

Travels with Charley; in search of America. Viking 1962 246p hardcover o.p. pa $14 **973**

1. United States -- Civilization 2. United States -- Description and travel

ISBN 0-670-72508-0; 0-14-200070-1 pa

The Nobel laureate recounts his impressions and observations of America gathered during a trip through forty states in the company of his French poodle Charley

Taylor, Elizabeth Dowling

The **original** black elite; Daniel Murray and the story of a forgotten era. Elizabeth Dowling Taylor. Amistad 2017 498 p. illustrations (hardcover) $27.99 **973**

1. African Americans -- History 2. National Afro-American Council 3. African Americans -- Washington (D.C.) 4. African American librarians -- Biography 5. Upper class African Americans -- History 6. African Americans -- History -- 1877-1964 7. United States -- Race relations -- History 8. African American intellectuals -- History -- 19th century 9. African American intellectuals -- History -- 20th century

ISBN 0062346091; 9780062346094; 9780062346117

This cultural biography, by Elizabeth Dowling Taylor, "chronicles a critical yet overlooked chapter in American history: the inspiring rise and calculated fall of the black elite, from Emancipation through Reconstruction to the Jim Crow Era--embodied in the experiences of an influential figure of the time, academic, entrepreneur, and political activist and black history pioneer Daniel Murray." (Publisher's note)

"The level of detail and research sheds light on a period that is mostly forgotten, revealing much-needed insight into African Americans' role and response in the shaping of American culture and politics." LJ

Includes bibliographical references (pages 421-464) and index.

Vowell, Sarah

Assassination vacation. Simon & Schuster 2005 258p il hardcover o.p. pa $14 **973**

1. United States -- Local history 2. United States -- Description and travel 3. Presidents -- United States -- Assassination

ISBN 0-7432-6003-1; 0-7432-6004-X pa

LC 2004-59134

"[Vowell] has done her homework, providing lucid descriptions of the murders and agile summations of the scholarly assessments of each era." America

Wilkins, Robert Leon

Long road to hard truth; the 100 year mission to create the National Museum of African American History and Culture. Robert L, Wilkins. Proud Legacy Pub. 2016 160 p. (ebook) $9.99; (alk. paper) $26.99 **973**

1. Museums -- Social aspects -- United States -- History 2. African Americans -- Museums -- Washington (D.C.) -- Planning 3. National Museum of African American History and Culture (U.S.)

ISBN 9780997910421; 9780997910407; 9780997910414

LC 2016950268

This book, by Robert L. Wilkins, "tells the story of how his curiosity about why there wasn't a national museum dedicated to African American history and culture became an obsession . . . [and a] mission to help the museum become a reality. . . . Wilkins follows the endless obstacles through the decades, culminating in his honor of becoming a member of the Presidential Commission that wrote the plan for creating the museum and how . . . Congress finally authorized [it]." (Publisher's note)

"Given all the historical minutiae that Wilkins provides, it's a surprisingly gripping historical drama. A delightful, edifying tale written with intelligence and emotional sensitivity." Kirkus

Zimmermann, Warren

First great triumph; how five Americans made their country a world power. Farrar, Straus & Giroux 2002 562p il $30; pa $15   **973**

1. Poets 2. Lawyers 3. Admirals 4. Diplomats 5. Governors 6. Statesmen 7. Historians 8. Presidents 9. Vice-presidents 10. Spanish-American War, 1898 11. Senators 12. Biographers 13. Secretaries of war 14. Secretaries of state 15. Nobel laureates for peace 16. United States -- History -- 1898-1919
ISBN 0-374-17939-5; 0-374-52893-4 pa

                       LC 2002-25015

The author credits five men "for the vision, determination and political skill that first gave the United States its global ambition. His book is a history of the American rise to power and a collective biography of [his] five heroes: Theodore Roosevelt, the assistant secretary of the Navy and later president; Alfred T. Mahan, the naval strategist; Senator Henry Cabot Lodge of Massachusetts; Secretary of State John Hay; and the first American colonial administrator, Elihu Root." N Y Times (Late N Y Ed)

Includes bibliographical references

Zinn, Howard, 1922-2010

★ A people's history of the United States; 1492-present. Howard Zinn. HarperCollins 2003 729 p.   **973**

1. United States -- History
ISBN 0060528427

                       LC 2002032895

"According to this classic of revisionist American history, narratives of national unity and progress are a smoke screen disguising the ceaseless conflict between elites and the masses whom they oppress and exploit. Historian [Howard] Zinn sides with the latter group in chronicling Indians' struggle against Europeans, blacks' struggle against racism, women's struggle against patriarchy, and workers' struggle against capitalists." (Publishers Weekly)

Includes bibliographical references (p. [689]-708) and index

973.049

Wills, Shomari

Black Fortunes; The Story of the First Six African Americans Who Escaped Slavery and Became Millionaires. by Shomari Wills. Amistad 2018 xv, 300 p.p illustrations (hardcover) $26.99   **973.049**

1. Millionaires 2. Rich -- United States 3. African Americans -- History 4. African American businesspeople -- Biography 5. Success in business -- United States -- Case studies 6. African American businesspeople -- United States -- History -- 19th century
ISBN 9780062437594; 9780062437549; 0062437593

This book, by Shomari Wills, tells the "untold history of America's first black millionaires—former slaves who endured incredible challenges to amass and maintain their wealth for a century, from the Jacksonian period to the Roaring Twenties—self-made entrepreneurs whose unknown success mirrored that of American business heroes such as Henry Ford, John D. Rockefeller, and Thomas Edison." (Publisher's note)

"Wills' storytelling is infectious, his subjects are irresistible, and his

broad coverage invites readers to venture further into the events and historical context he so vividly introduces." Booklist

Includes bibliographical references and index.

973.09   Presidents--United States

Carlson, Brady

Dead presidents; an American adventure into the strange deaths and surprising afterlives of our nation's leaders. Brady Carlson. W W Norton & Co Inc 2016 336 p. illustrations (hardcover) $26.95   **973.09**

1. Monuments -- United States 2. Presidents -- United States -- Death and burial 3. Presidents -- United States -- Death 4. Presidents -- United States -- Biography
ISBN 9780393243932

                       LC 2015032329

This book, by Brady Carlson, offers an "exploration into the death stories of our nation's greatest leaders—and the wild ways we choose to remember and memorialize them. . . . With an engaging mix of history and contemporary reporting, Carlson recounts the surprising origin stories of the Washington Monument, Mount Rushmore, Grant's Tomb, and JFK's Eternal Flame." (Publisher's note)

"A brisk, lighthearted travelogue with an exuberant guide." Kirkus
Includes bibliographical references and index

Freedman, Eric

Presidents and Black America; a documentary history. Stephen A. Jones, Eric Freedman. CQ Press 2011 xxxiv, 546 p.p (cloth: alk. paper) $145   **973.09**

1. African Americans 2. Presidents -- Attitudes 3. Presidents -- United States 4. African Americans -- Political activity 5. United States -- Race relations -- History 6. African Americans -- Attitudes -- History -- Sources 7. Presidents -- United States -- Racial attitudes -- Sources 8. Presidents -- Relations with African Americans -- History -- Sources
ISBN 1608710084; 9781608710089

                       LC 2011032618

This reference book "features a mixture of primary source material with introductory essays outlining each president's views on blacks in America. . . . The work is arranged in chronological order, with each chapter covering a president. . . . Chapters open with an introductory essay. . . . One can clearly see how the successive Republican presidencies of Harding, Coolidge, and Hoover turned American blacks . . . to the Democratic party of Franklin Roosevelt." (Booklist)

Includes bibliographical references and index.

973.099   United States Presidents

Goodwin, Doris Kearns, 1943-

★ Leadership; in turbulent times. Doris Kearns Goodwin. Simon & Schuster 2018 352 p. (hardcover) $18   **973.099**

1. Presidents -- United States 2. Political leadership -- United States 3. United States -- Politics and government 4. Political leadership -- United States -- Case studies 5. United States -- Politics and government -- Case studies
ISBN 9781476795928; 9781476795942; 1476795924

                       LC 2018020283

In this book, Doris Kearns Goodwin "draws upon the four presidents she has studied most closely--Abraham Lincoln, Theodore Roosevelt, Franklin D. Roosevelt, and Lyndon B. Johnson (in civil rights)--to show

how they recognized leadership qualities within themselves and were recognized as leaders by others. By looking back to their first entries into public life, we encounter them at a time when their paths were filled with confusion, fear, and hope." (Publisher's note)

"Goodwin draws on 50 years of scholarship in this strong and resonant addition to the literature of the presidency." Booklist

Greenberg, David

Republic of spin; an inside history of the American presidency. David Greenberg. W.W. Norton & Co. 2016 560 p. 16 plates; illustrations (hardcover) $35   **973.099**
  1. Presidents -- United States   2. United States -- Politics and government   3. Critics -- United States -- Biography   4. Presidents -- United States -- History   5. Presidents -- United States -- Biography   6. Spin doctors -- United States -- Biography   7. Political consultants -- United States -- Biography   8. Communication in politics -- United States -- History   9. Presidents -- United States -- Public opinion -- History   10. Public relations and politics -- United States -- History   11. Public opinion -- Political aspects -- United States -- History
  ISBN 0393067068; 9780393067064

                   LC 2015031998

In this book author David Greenberg "recounts the rise of the White House spin machine, from Teddy Roosevelt to Barack Obama. His sweeping, startling narrative takes us behind the scenes to see how the tools and techniques of image making and message craft work. Greenberg also examines the profound debates Americans have waged over the effect of spin on our politics. Does spin help our leaders manipulate the citizenry? Or does it allow them to engage us more fully in the democratic project?" (Publisher's note)

"This revealing account of politics as image in U.S. presidential culture should be read by any student of the American presidency and American politics." LJ

Includes bibliographical references and index

973.2   United States--Colonial period, 1607-1775

Anderson, Fred

The **crucible** of war; the Seven Years' War and the fate of empire in British North America, 1754-1766. with illustrations from the William L. Clements Library. Knopf 2000 862p il hardcover o.p. pa $21   **973.2**
  1. Seven Years' War, 1756-1763   2. United States -- History -- 1600-1775, Colonial period
  ISBN 0-375-70636-4 pa

                   LC 99-18512

The author "demonstrates that the conflict was more than just a peripheral squabble that anticipated the American Revolution. Not only did the war decisively alter relations among the French, the English and the Native American allies of the two powers, who for decades had played the English and French off one another to their own advantage, but just as critical, argues Anderson, the war also changed the character of British imperialism, with the mother country trying to reshape the terms of empire and the colonists' place in it." Publ Wkly

The **dominion** of war; empire and liberty in North America, 1500-2000. [by] Fred Anderson and Andrew Cayton. Viking 2005 520p il maps $27.95; pa $16   **973.2**
  1. United States -- Military history   2. United States -- Territorial expansion
  ISBN 0-670-03370-7; 0-14-303651-3 pa

The authors provide an "account of the U.S. rise to global preeminence over five centuries. Central to their thesis is the assertion that military conflict has been essential in determining the cultural and political evolution of North America. . . . Anderson and Cayton have provided a well-written and important reinterpretation of our past." Booklist

Includes bibliographical references

Bailyn, Bernard

★ The **barbarous** years; the peopling of British North America: the conflict of civilizations, 1600-1675. Bernard Bailyn. Alfred A. Knopf 2012 614 p. $35   **973.2**
  1. Colonization   2. Immigration and emigration   3. Great Britain -- Colonies -- America   4. United States -- History -- 1600-1775, Colonial period   5. Canada -- History -- To 1763 (New France)   6. North America -- Civilization -- 17th century   7. Immigrants -- North America -- History -- 17th century   8. United States -- History -- Colonial period, ca. 1600-1775   9. Great Britain -- Colonies -- America -- History -- 17th century
  ISBN 0394515706; 9780394515700

                   LC 2012034223

This book, by Bernard Bailyn, presents an account of the 17th century colonial migrations to North America. "They moved . . . from different social backgrounds and cultures . . . and circumstances. . . . They came hoping to re-create if not to improve these diverse lifeways in a remote . . . environment. But their stories are mostly of confusion, failure, violence, and the loss of civility as they sought to normalize abnormal situations and recapture lost worlds." (Publisher's note)

Includes bibliographical references and index.

Dolin, Eric Jay

Black flags, blue waters; the epic history of America's most notorious pirates. Eric Jay Dolin. W W Norton & Co Inc 2018 400 p. $29.95   **973.2**
  1. Maritime history   2. Piracy -- History   3. United States -- History
  ISBN 1631492101; 9781631492105

This book, by Eric Jay Dolin, "reveals the dramatic and surprising history of American piracy's "Golden Age"--spanning the late 1600s through the early 1700s--when lawless pirates plied the coastal waters of North America and beyond. Best-selling author . . . Dolin illustrates how American colonists at first supported these outrageous pirates in an early display of solidarity against the Crown, and then violently opposed them." (Publisher's note)

Hawke, David Freeman

Everyday life in early America. Harper & Row 1988 195p il (Everyday life in America) hardcover o.p. pa $13   **973.2**
  1. United States -- Social life and customs   2. United States -- History -- 1600-1775, Colonial period
  ISBN 0-06-091251-0 pa

                   LC 87-17667

The author "provides enlightening and colorful descriptions of early Colonial Americans and debunks many widely held assumptions about 17th century settlers." Publ Wkly

Includes bibliographical references

Philbrick, Nathaniel

★ **Mayflower**; a story of courage, community, and war. Viking 2006 461p il $29.95; pa $16   **973.2**
  1. Pilgrims (New England colonists)   2. Massachusetts -- History -- 1600-1775, Colonial period
  ISBN 0-670-03760-5; 978-0-670-03760-5; 978-0-14-311197-9 pa; 0-14-311197-3 pa

                   LC 2005-58470

The author "has written a judicious, fascinating work of revisionist history. 'Mayflower' is a surprise-filled account of what are supposed to be some of the best-known events in this country's past but are instead an occasion for collective amnesia." N Y Times (Late N Y Ed)

Includes bibliographical references

973.3 United States--Periods of Revolution and Confederation, 1775-1789

Allen, Danielle

Our Declaration; A Reading of the Declaration of Independence in Defense of Equality. Danielle Allen. W W Norton & Co Inc 2014 288 p. illustrations $27.95 **973.3**
1. Freedom 2. United States. Declaration of independence 3. Equality -- United States 4. United States. Declaration of Independence -- Criticism, Textual
ISBN 087140690X; 9780871406903

LC 2014009825

"Troubled by the fact that so few Americans actually know what it says, Danielle Allen . . . set out to explore the arguments of the Declaration, reading it with both adult night students and University of Chicago undergraduates. Keenly aware that the Declaration is riddled with contradictions--liberating some while subjugating slaves and Native Americans--Allen and her students nonetheless came to see that the Declaration makes a coherent and riveting argument about equality." (Publisher's note)

"As if conducting a friendly conversation, sentence by sentence, [Allen] takes readers through all the text's words, and she proves a patient, informed and friendly guide." Kirkus

Includes bibliographical references and index

The **American** Revolution: writings from the War of Independence. Library of Am. 2001 878p $40 **973.3**
1. United States -- History -- 1775-1783, Revolution
ISBN 1-88301-191-4

LC 00-45373

"This work will serve as a marvelous research tool for specialists, but general readers with an interest in American history will also find fascinating gems." Booklist

Includes bibliographical references

Bobrick, Benson

Angel in the whirlwind; the triumph of the American Revolution. Penguin Bks. 1998 553p map pa $18 **973.3**
1. United States -- History -- 1775-1783, Revolution
ISBN 0-14-027500-2; 978-0-14-027500-1

LC 97-11320

First published 1997 by Simon & Schuster

"Many of the stories are familiar—Paul Revere's ride, Arnold's descent into infamy—but the book's strength lies in its many lesser-known details on the battlefield and beyond. . . . Though the format demands only brief treatment of complicated issues, what emerges is a highly impressive show of exhaustive research and engaging storytelling." Publ Wkly

Includes bibliographical references

Breen, T. H.

American insurgents, American patriots; the revolution of the people. Hill and Wang 2010 337p $27 **973.3**
1. United States -- History -- 1775-1783, Revolution 2. United States -- Militia -- History -- Revolution, 1775-1783 3. United States -- History -- Revolution, 1775-1783 -- Social aspects 4. United States -- History -- Revolution, 1775-1783 -- Committees of safety
ISBN 978-0-8090-7588-1; 0-8090-7588-1

LC 2009-42496

Breen "uses correspondence, diaries, outtakes from clergy sermons and newspaper reports to build a mosaic representation of the popular mood, and the escalating willingness to take up arms. . . . [The] book shows an energetic and necessarily untidy process of invention on the part of a people, and captures well its improvisatory nature." Chicago Trib

Includes bibliographical references and index

Bunker, Nick

★ An **empire** on the edge; how Britain came to fight America. Nick Bunker. 1st edition Alfred A. Knopf 2014 448 p. illustrations, map hbk $30 **973.3**
1. Boston Tea Party, 1773 2. Great Britain -- Foreign relations -- United States 3. United States -- Foreign relations -- Great Britain 4. United States -- History -- 1600-1775, Colonial period 5. United States -- History -- 1775-1783, Revolution -- Causes
ISBN 030759484X; 9780307594846

LC 2014001032

Pulitzer Prize Finalist: History (2015)

This book, by Nick Bunker, "tells the story of the last three years of mutual embitterment that preceded the outbreak of America's war for independence in 1775. . . . At the heart of the book lies the Boston Tea Party, an event that arose from fundamental flaws in the way the British managed their affairs. . . . By the late summer of 1774, when the rebels in New England began to arm themselves, the descent into war had become irreversible." (Publisher's note)

"Bunker's book argues that, for the British, America was 'a continent she did not comprehend and could not hope to rule.' The author is particularly attuned to economic context and concerned with how events unfolded in practice, rather than what was said in theory." LJ

Includes bibliographical references and index

Cox, Caroline

★ **Boy** soldiers of the American Revolution; Caroline Cox; with a foreword by Robert Middlekauff. University of North Carolina Press 2016 xvi, 211 p.p (cloth: alk. paper) $29.95 **973.3**
1. Child soldiers 2. Historical literature 3. United States -- History -- 1775-1783, Revolution 4. Child soldiers -- United States -- History -- 18th century 5. Children -- United States -- Social life and customs -- 18th century 6. United States -- History -- Revolution, 1775-1783 -- Participation, Juvenile
ISBN 9781469627533

LC 2015039985

In this book, author "Caroline Cox reconstructs the lives and stories of this young subset of early American soldiers, focusing on how these boys came to join the army and what they actually did in service. Giving us a rich and unique glimpse into colonial childhood, Cox traces the evolution of youth in American culture in the late eighteenth century, as the accepted age for children to participate meaningfully in society--not only in the military--was rising dramatically." (Publisher's note)

Includes bibliographical references (pages 159-202) and index.

Daughan, George C.

Lexington and Concord; the battle heard round the world. George C. Daughan. W W Norton & Co Inc 2018 368 p. (hardcover) $27.95 **973.3**

1. Concord (Mass.), Battle of, 1775 2. Lexington (Mass.), Battle of, 1775 3. United States -- History -- 1775-1783, Revolution 4. Concord, Battle of, Concord, Mass., 1775 5. Lexington, Battle of, Lexington, Mass., 1775 6. United States -- History -- Revolution, 1775-1783 -- Causes 7. United States -- History -- Revolution, 1775-1783 -- Economic aspects
ISBN 9780393245745

LC 2017060269

In this book, author George C. Daughan presents a "detailed account of the Battle of Lexington and Concord [that] challenges the prevailing narrative of the American War of Independence. It was, Daughan argues, based as much in economic concerns as political ones. When Massachusetts militiamen turned out in overwhelming numbers to fight the British, they believed they were fighting for their farms and livelihoods, as well as for liberty." (Publisher's note)

Includes bibliographical references and index

DuVal, Kathleen

★ **Independence** Lost; Lives on the Edge of the American Revolution. Kathleen DuVal. Random House Inc. 2015 464 p. illustrations, maps $28   **973.3**
1. United States -- History -- 1775-1783, Revolution 2. West Florida -- History, Military -- 18th century 3. Gulf Coast (U.S.) -- History, Military -- 18th century 4. United States -- History -- Revolution, 1775-1783 -- Biography 5. United States -- History -- Revolution, 1775-1783 -- Social aspects 6. Autonomy -- Social aspects -- Gulf Coast (U.S.) -- History -- 18th century
ISBN 1400068959; 9781400068951

LC 2014042511

"Focusing on the frontier struggle in the Gulf of Mexico region, DuVal . . . illustrates how multipronged the American Revolution was. It involved three empires (Britain, France, and Spain), several major Native American peoples, and both free and enslaved Africans. DuVal personalizes the conflict by tracing the fates of eight individuals: two tribal leaders, a loyalist couple, a merchant couple backing the colonists, a transplanted pro-colonist Acadian, and a slave who served as a cattle driver and later as a courier for the Spanish." (Publishers Weekly)

"By describing these lives and how the revolution affected them, DuVal accurately theorizes that independence was lost by many, and that the idea of 'empire' was often a place of security and affluence." LJ

Includes bibliographical references and index

Egerton, Douglas R.

Death or liberty; African Americans and revolutionary America. Oxford University Press 2009 342p il map $29.95   **973.3**
1. Slavery -- United States 2. African Americans -- History 3. United States -- History -- 1775-1783, Revolution
ISBN 978-0-19-530669-9; 0-19-530669-4

LC 2008-27862

The author "traverses the rise and the debatable inevitability of slavery in the United States between the end of the Seven Years' War (1763) and Jefferson's election (1800), arguing that the 'division of the Republic into free wage labor sections and proslavery regions did not have to happen that way.'" Publ Wkly

Includes bibliographical references and index

Ellis, Joseph J.

American creation; triumphs and tragedies at the founding of the republic. A. A. Knopf 2007 283p   **973.3**
1. United States -- History -- 1783-1809 2. United States -- History -- 1775-1783, Revolution 3. United States -- Politics and government -- 1783-1809 4. United States -- Politics and government -- 1775-

1783, Revolution
ISBN 978-0-307-26369-8; 0-307-26369-X

LC 2007-5273

The author "selects 'certain propitious moments' from the American Revolution and early republic, dramatizes them, and analyzes their crucial ramifications for America's future. . . . A history bound for phenomenal popularity." Booklist

Includes bibliographical references

★ **American** dialogue; the founding fathers and us. Joseph J. Ellis. Knopf 2018 304 p. (hardback) $27.95   **973.3**
1. Political culture -- United States 2. Founding Fathers of the United States 3. United States -- Politics and government 4. Political culture -- United States -- History 5. United States -- Politics and government -- 2017- -- Philosophy 6. United States -- Politics and government -- 1775-1783 -- Philosophy
ISBN 9780385353427

LC 2017050340

In this book, author Joseph J. Ellis "gives us a deeply insightful examination of the relevance of the views of George Washington, Thomas Jefferson, James Madison, and John Adams to some of the most divisive issues in America today. . . . He discusses Jefferson and the issue of racism, Adams and the specter of economic inequality, Washington and American imperialism, Madison and the doctrine of original intent." (Publisher's note)

"Drawing from his intimate knowledge of the Founding Fathers, Ellis addresses four 21st-century obstacles to reveal truths from their writings that should infuse wisdom into present-day debate: Thomas Jefferson's inconsistency on slavery and race; John Adams's warnings about financial aristocracy and economic inequality; James Madison's politically expedient concessions and the idea of original intent; and George Washington's approach to national and foreign policy, and the incompatibility of American imperialism with revolutionary ideals." LJ

The **Quartet**; Orchestrating the Second American Revolution, 1783-1789. Joseph J. Ellis. Knopf 2015 320 p. $27.95   **973.3**
1. Founding Fathers of the United States 2. United States -- Politics and government -- 1783-1809 3. Constitutional history -- United States 4. Statesmen -- United States -- Biography 5. Politicians -- United States -- Biography 6. United States -- Politics and government -- 1783-1789 7. Federal government -- United States -- History -- 18th century 8. Confederation of states -- United States -- History -- 18th century
ISBN 0385353405; 9780385353403

LC 2014034503

In this book, author Joseph J. Ellis presents "the story of this second American founding and of the men most responsible--George Washington, Alexander Hamilton, John Jay, and James Madison. These men, with the help of Robert Morris and Gouverneur Morris, shaped the contours of American history by diagnosing the systemic dysfunctions created by the Articles of Confederation." (Publisher's note)

"Ellis's approach employs deft characterizations and insights into these politicians and philosophers. . . . With his usual skill, Ellis brings alive what otherwise might seem dry constitutional debates, with apt quotations and bright style." Pub Wkly

Includes bibliographical references and index

★ **Revolutionary** summer; the birth of American independence. by Joseph J. Ellis. 1st ed. Alfred A. Knopf 2013 xiii, 219 p., 8 unnumbered pages of platesp col. ill., map (hardcover) $26.95   **973.3**
1. Founding Fathers of the United States 2. United States -- History

-- 1775-1783, Revolution 3. United States -- History -- Revolution, 1775-1783

ISBN 0307701220; 9780307701220

LC 2012026140

This book, by Pulitzer-winning historian Joseph Ellis, discusses "the summer months of 1776 . . . in the story of our country's founding. . . . The Continental Congress and the Continental Army were forced to make decisions on the run, improvising as history congealed around them. . . . Ellis . . . examines the most influential figures in this propitious moment . . . [and] weaves together the political and military experiences as two sides of a single story." (Publisher's note)

Includes bibliographical references (pages 189-208) and index.

Ferling, John

Apostles of revolution; Jefferson, Paine, Monroe and the struggle against the old order in America and Europe. John Ferling. St. Martin's Press 2018 496 p. $35   **973.3**

1. France -- History -- 1789-1799, Revolution 2. United States -- History -- 1775-1783, Revolution

ISBN 1632862093; 9781632862099

This book, by John Ferling, "spans a crucial period in Western Civilization ranging from the American insurgency against Great Britain to the Declaration of Independence, from desperate engagements on American battlefields to the threat posed to the ideals of the Revolution by the Federalist Party. With the French Revolution devolving into anarchy in the background, the era culminates with the 'Revolution of 1800,' Jefferson's election as president." (Publisher's note)

Whirlwind; the American Revolution and the war that won it. John Ferling. Bloomsbury 2015 432 p. 16 plates; illustrations; maps (alk. paper) $30   **973.3**

1. United States -- History -- 1775-1783, Revolution 2. United States -- History -- Revolution, 1775-1783 3. United States -- History -- Revolution, 1775-1783 -- Campaigns

ISBN 162040172X; 9781620401729

LC 2014033315

This book, by John Ferling, "is a fast-paced and scrupulously told one-volume history of [the American Revolution]. Balancing social and political concerns of the period and perspectives of the average American revolutionary with a careful examination of the war itself, Ferling has crafted . . . a book about the causes of the American Revolution, the war that won it, and the meaning of the Revolution overall." (Publisher's note)

"Ferling has created another accessible yet scholarly work on the American Revolution. While its primary appeal is to history buffs, academics looking for an introductory survey history should also find this work useful." LJ

Includes bibliographical references and index

Fischer, David Hackett

Paul Revere's ride. Oxford Univ. Press 1994 445p il maps $37.50; pa $19.95   **973.3**

1. Concord (Mass.), Battle of, 1775 2. Lexington (Mass.), Battle of, 1775 3. Artisans 4. Metalworkers 5. Revolutionaries

ISBN 0-19-508847-6; 0-19-509831-5 pa

LC 93-25739

"Fischer's solid study of Paul Revere and his infamous ride debunks the myths surrounding the event, reconstructing the circumstances leading to the Battle of Lexington and Concord. Fischer's extensive use of primary sources affords an intimate glimpse of the participants' thoughts and feelings." Booklist

Includes bibliographical references

Washington's crossing. Oxford University Press 2004 564p il maps (Pivotal moments in American history) $35; pa $16.95   **973.3**

1. Generals 2. Presidents 3. United States -- History -- 1775-1783, Revolution -- Campaigns

ISBN 0-19-517034-2; 0-19-518159-X pa

LC 2003-19858

National Book Award Finalist: Nonfiction (2004)

The author describes how "Washington, his officers, and their men turn the early military defeats of Long Island and New York City into victory at Trenton and Princeton. The opening chapter is devoted to the painting Washington Crossing the Delaware. Then the author discusses the British, Hessian, and American military units that were involved in these campaigns and gives background on their officers. This is Fischer's strong suit: he tells stories and gives details that bring history alive. . . . In the hands of such a thorough researcher and talented writer, this is powerful stuff." SLJ

Includes bibliographical references

Fried, Stephen

Rush; madness, medicine, and the visionary doctor who became a founding father. Stephen Fried. Crown Publishers 2018 608 p. (hardcover) $30   **973.309**

1. Statesmen -- United States 2. Founding Fathers of the United States 3. United States. Declaration of independence 4. United States -- History -- 1775-1783, Revolution

ISBN 9780804140065; 9780804140089

LC 2018016147

This book, by, Stephen Fried, looks at the "monumental life of Benjamin Rush, medical pioneer and one of our most provocative and unsung Founding Fathers. . . . From improbable beginnings as the son of a Philadelphia blacksmith, Rush grew into an internationally renowned writer, reformer, and medical pioneer who touched virtually every page in the story of the nation's founding." (Publisher's note)

Includes bibliographical references and index

Hoock, Holger

Scars of independence; America's violent birth. Holger Hoock. Crown Publishing 2017 xiv, 559 p.p illustrations, maps (hardcover) $30   **973.3**

1. Violence -- History 2. United States -- History -- 1775-1783, Revolution 3. National characteristics, American 4. United States -- Civilization -- 1783-1865 5. Violence -- United States -- History -- 18th century 6. United States -- History -- Revolution, 1775-1783 -- Influence 7. United States -- History -- Revolution, 1775-1783 -- Social aspects

ISBN 9780804137294; 9780804137287; 9780804137300

LC 2016031348

In this book, author Holger Hoock "writes the violence back into the story of the [American] Revolution. American Patriots persecuted and tortured Loyalists. British troops massacred enemy soldiers and raped colonial women. Prisoners were starved on disease-ridden ships and in subterranean cells. African-Americans fighting for or against independence suffered disproportionately, and Washington's army waged a genocidal campaign against the Iroquois." (Publisher's note)

"An accomplished, powerful presentation of the American Revolution as it was, rather than as we might wish to remember it." Kirkus

Includes bibliographical references and index

Jasanoff, Maya

Liberty's exiles; Maya Jasanoff. Alfred A. Knopf 2011 xvi, 460p.p col. ill., maps $30   **973.3**

1. Refugees 2. American Loyalists 3. American loyalists 4. Great Britain -- Colonies 5. United States -- History -- 1775-1783, Revolution 6. United States -- History -- Revolution, 1775-1783
ISBN 978-1-4000-4168-8; 1-4000-4168-6; 978-0-307-59530-0 e-book

LC 201023514

National Book Critics Circle Award: General Nonfiction (2011)
This book offers a "global history of the [American] loyalist exodus to Canada, the Caribbean, Sierra Leone, India, and beyond. . . . [Loyalists discussed include] Elizabeth Johnston, a young mother from Georgia, who led her growing family to Britain, Jamaica, and Canada, questing for a home; black loyalists . . . and Mohawk Indian leader Joseph Brant, who tried to find autonomy for his people in Ontario." (Publisher's note)

The author "examines the effects of the American Revolution on those whose loyalty to the Crown compelled them to flee the new United States." Kirkus

Includes bibliographical references and index.

Maier, Pauline

American scripture; making the Declaration of Independence. Knopf 1997 xxi, 304p hardcover o.p. pa $14 **973.3**
1. United States -- Declaration of Independence 2. United States -- Politics and government -- 1775-1783, Revolution
ISBN 0-679-77908-6 pa

LC 97-2769

"In the spring of 1776, with a British invasion fleet on its way, the Second Continental Congress appointed a committee to compose a statement explaining America's decision to seek independence. Thomas Jefferson was the principal drafter of the statement, but Maier makes it clear that his task was to express the sentiments of the Congress, not his personal views, and she shows that when the congressmen edited his draft they improved it greatly (rather than 'mangling' it, as Jefferson ever after maintained). The Declaration of Independence is, she argues, a profoundly collective document, both in its origins and in our still-evolving interpretation of its self-evident truths." New Yorker

McCullough, David G., 1933-

★ **1776**; [by] David McCullough. Simon & Schuster 2005 386p il map $32 **973.3**
1. United States -- History -- 1775-1783, Revolution
ISBN 0-7432-2671-2

LC 2005-42505

"This is a narrative tour de force, exhibiting all the hallmarks the author is known for: fascinating subject matter, expert research and detailed, graceful prose." Publ Wkly
Includes bibliographical references

Middlekauff, Robert

★ The **glorious** cause; the American Revolution, 1763-1789. Rev. and expanded ed.; Oxford University Press 2004 736p il map (Oxford history of the United States) $37.50 **973.3**
1. United States -- History -- 1775-1783, Revolution
ISBN 0-19-516247-1

LC 2004-16295

First published 1982
"This is narrative history at its best, written in a conversational and engaging style." Libr J
Includes bibliographical references

O'Donnell, Patrick K.

Washington's Immortals; The Untold Story of an Elite Regiment Who Changed the Course of the Revolution. by Pat-

rick K. O'Donnell. Atlantic Monthly Press 2016 336 p. ill. (some color), maps $28 **973.3**
1. United States -- History -- 1775-1783, Revolution
ISBN 0802124593; 9780802124593

This book, by Patrick K. O'Donnell, focuses on the U.S. revolutionary war "regiment, famously known as the 'Immortal 400.' . . . O'Donnell pieces together the stories of these brave men--their friendships, loves, defeats, and triumphs. He explores their arms and tactics, their struggles with hostile loyalists and shortages of clothing and food, their development into an elite unit, and their dogged opponents, including British General Lord Cornwallis." (Publisher's note)

"Using primary sources from both sides of the Atlantic, O'Donnell effectively traces the story of Maryland's immortals, describing the battles authentically along with the precariousness of the American cause." LJ

Includes bibliographical references (pages 387-442) and index.

Parkinson, Robert G.

The **common** cause; Creating Race and Nation in the American Revolution. by Robert G. Parkinson. Univ. of North Carolina Pr. for the Omohundro Inst. of Early Am. History & Culture 2016 768 p. illustrations, map (cloth: alk. paper) $45 **973.3**
1. Racism -- History 2. United States -- Race relations -- History 3. United States -- History -- 1775-1783, Revolution 4. Racism -- United States -- History -- 18th century 5. United States -- History -- Revolution, 1775-1783 -- Propaganda 6. United States -- History -- Revolution, 1775-1783 -- Social aspects
ISBN 9781469626635

LC 2016000574

In this book, author Robert G. Parkinson "argues that to unify the patriot side, political and communications leaders linked British tyranny to colonial prejudices, stereotypes, and fears about insurrectionary slaves and violent Indians. Manipulating newspaper networks, Washington, Jefferson, Adams, Franklin, and their fellow agitators broadcast stories of British agents inciting African Americans and Indians to take up arms against the American rebellion." (Publisher's note)
Includes bibliographical references and index

Paul, Joel R.

Unlikely allies; how a merchant, a playwright, and a spy saved the American Revolution. [by] Joel Richard Paul. Riverhead Books 2009 405p il $25.95 **973.3**
1. Spies 2. Authors 3. Diplomats 4. Dramatists 5. Cross-dressers 6. Saratoga Campaign, 1777 7. Transvestites 8. Secret service -- United States 9. United States -- History -- 1775-1783, Revolution
ISBN 978-1-59448-883-2; 1-59448-883-5

LC 2009-34986

"A rip-roaring account of the American Revolution, told from a fresh, and undeniably offbeat, perspective." Booklist
Includes bibliographical references (p. 384-396)

Philbrick, Nathaniel

Bunker Hill; A City, a Siege, a Revolution. Nathaniel Philbrick. Viking Adult 2013 400 p. (hardcover) $32.95 **973.3**
1. Boston (Mass.) -- History 2. Bunker Hill (Boston, Mass.), Battle of, 1775 3. United States -- History -- 1775-1783, Revolution 4. Bunker Hill, Battle of, Boston, Mass., 1775 5. Boston (Mass.) -- History -- Revolution, 1775-1783
ISBN 0670025445; 9780670025442

LC 2013001534

This book, by Nathaniel Philbrick, profiles the history of the Battle of Bunker Hill. "After the Boston Tea Party, British and American soldiers and Massachusetts residents have warily maneuvered around each other until April 19, [1775] when violence finally erupts. . . . In June, . . . skirmishes give way to outright war in the Battle of Bunker Hill. It would be the bloodiest battle of the Revolution to come, and the point of no return for the rebellious colonists." (Publisher's note)

Includes bibliographical references and index

★ **Valiant** Ambition; George Washington, Benedict Arnold, and the Fate of the American Revolution. by Nathaniel Philbrick. Penguin Group USA 2016 448 p. ill., maps, portraits $30   **973.3**

1. United States -- History -- 1775-1783, Revolution

ISBN 0525426787; 9780525426783

This book, by Nathaniel Philbrick, is an "account of the middle years of the American Revolution, and the tragic relationship between George Washington and Benedict Arnold. . . . As a country wary of tyrants suddenly must figure out how it should be led, Washington's unmatched ability to rise above the petty politics of his time enables him to win the war that really matters." (Publisher's note)

"Philbrick weaves exciting accounts of Arnold's impulsive battlefield exploits with the activities of self-interested military and civil associates into the demythified story of the circumstances of a tragic betrayal." LJ

Includes bibliographical references (pages 329-403) and index.

Phillips, Kevin, 1940-

1775; a good year for revolution. Kevin Phillips. Viking 2012 656 p. $36   **973.3**

1. Great Britain -- History 2. United States -- History -- 1775-1783, Revolution 3. United States -- Foreign relations -- Great Britain 4. United States. Continental Congress 5. Concord, Battle of, Concord, Mass., 1775 6. Fort Ticonderoga (N.Y.) -- Capture, 1775 7. Lexington, Battle of, Lexington, Mass., 1775 8. Boston (Mass.) -- History -- Siege, 1775-1776 9. United States -- History -- Revolution, 1775-1783 10. United States -- Politics and government -- 1775-1783

ISBN 0670025127; 9780670025121

LC 2012001786

Author Kevin Phillips looks at "the myth that 1776 was the watershed year of the American Revolution. He suggests that the great events and confrontations of 1775--Congress's belligerent economic ultimatums to Britain . . . and the new provincial congresses and hundreds of local committees that quickly reconstituted local authority in Patriot hands--achieved a sweeping Patriot control of territory and local government that Britain was never able to overcome." (Publisher's note)

Includes bibliographical references and index.

Raphael, Ray

★ A **people's** history of the American Revolution; how common people shaped the fight for independence. 1st Perennial ed; Perennial 2002 506p pa $13.95   **973.3**

1. United States -- History -- 1775-1783, Revolution

ISBN 0-06-000440-1

LC 2002-16992

First published 2001 by New Press

"Moving from broad overviews to stories of small groups or individuals, Raphael's study is impressive in both its sweep and its attention to the particular." Publ Wkly

Includes bibliographical references

The **spirit** of 74; how the American Revolution began.

Ray Raphael and Marie Raphael. The New Press 2015 288 p. (hardcover: alk. paper) $26.95   **973.3**

1. United States -- Politics and government 2. United States -- History -- 1775-1783, Revolution 3. Massachusetts -- History -- Revolution, 1775-1783 4. United States -- History -- Revolution, 1775-1783 -- Causes

ISBN 9781620971260; 1620971267

LC 2015008420

This book by Ray Raphael and Marie Raphael "fills in this gap in our nation's founding narrative, showing how in these mislaid months, step by step, real people made a revolution. A 'Spirit of '74' initiated the American Revolution, much as the better-known 'Spirit of '76' sparked independence." (Publisher's note)

The Raphaels expertly contextualize how the outbreak of a shooting war at Lexington and Concord marked a crucial 'turning point' in, rather than the beginning of, the American Revolution." Pub Wkly

Includes bibliographical references and index

Shorto, Russell

Revolution Song; a story of American freedom. by Russell Shorto. W W Norton & Co Inc 2017 xii, 621 p.p illustrations, map (hardcover) $28.95   **973.3**

1. United States -- History -- 1775-1783, Revolution 2. United States -- History -- Revolution, 1775-1783

ISBN 9780393245547; 9780393245554; 0393245543

In this book, "Russell Shorto takes us back to the founding of the American nation, drawing on diaries, letters and autobiographies to flesh out six lives that cast the era in a fresh new light. They include an African man who freed himself and his family from slavery, a . . . young woman who abandoned her abusive husband to chart her own course and a certain Mr. Washington, who was admired for his social graces but . . . criticized for his often-disastrous military strategy." (Publisher's note)

"This important addition to popular literature on the revolution enables readers to engage these issues on many levels." Booklist

Includes bibliographical references (pages 557-578) and index.

Spero, Patrick

Frontier rebels; the fight for independence in the American West, 1765-1776. Patrick Spero. W W Norton & Co Inc 2018 288 p. (hardcover) $27.95   **973.3**

1. Frontier and pioneer life -- United States 2. United States -- History -- 1775-1783, Revolution 3. United States -- History -- 1600-1775, Colonial period 4. Black Boys Rebellion, 1765 5. Insurgency -- Pennsylvania -- 18th century 6. Pennsylvania -- History -- Colonial period, ca. 1600-1775

ISBN 0393634701; 9780393634709

LC 2018024793

"Drawing on largely forgotten manuscript sources from archives across North America, Patrick Spero recasts the familiar narrative of the American Revolution, moving the action from the Eastern Seaboard to the treacherous western frontier. In spellbinding detail, 'Frontier Rebels' reveals an often-overlooked truth: the West played a crucial role in igniting the flame of American independence."

"For professional and casual historians of early American government, military, and citizen protest movements, this well-researched and concisely written monograph takes a timely look back at the history and spirit of dissent." LJ

Includes bibliographical references and index

Taylor, Alan

American revolutions; a continental history, 1750-1804. Alan Taylor. W W Norton & Co Inc 2016 736 p. (hardcover)

$37.5   **973.3**

1. United States -- History -- 1775-1783, Revolution 2. United States -- History -- 1600-1775, Colonial period

ISBN 0393082814; 9780393082814

LC 2016011418

This book, by Alan Taylor, "gives us a different creation story in this magisterial history of the nation's founding. Taylor's Revolution builds like a ground fire overspreading Britain's mainland colonies, fueled by local conditions, destructive, hard to quell. Taylor skillfully draws France, Spain, and native powers into a comprehensive narrative of the war that delivers the major battles, generals, and common soldiers with insight and power." (Publisher's note)

"A clear, authoritative, well-organized look at the messy Colonial march toward revolution and self-rule." Kirkus

Tuchman, Barbara Wertheim

The **first** salute; [by] Barbara W. Tuchman. Knopf 1988 347p il maps hardcover o.p. pa $16.95 **973.3**

1. United States -- History -- 1775-1783, Revolution

ISBN 0-394-55333-0; 0-345-33667-4 pa

LC 88-45216

"The book is a tightly woven narrative, ingeniously structured. It is not a blow-by-blow account of the conflict; familiarity with issues and events is assumed. Instead, Tuchman takes a specific incident and through it elucidates the course and outcome of the war." Christ Sci Monit

Includes bibliographical references

Unger, Harlow Giles

American tempest; how the Boston Tea Party sparked a revolution. [by] Harlow Giles Unger. Da Capo Press 2011 288p il map $26 **973.3**

1. Boston Tea Party, 1773 2. United States -- History -- 1775-1783, Revolution -- Causes

ISBN 978-0-306-81962-9; 0-306-819627

LC 2010-47734

"As Unger makes clear, the true impact of the Boston Tea Party came from Britain's ill-advised overreaction to the symbolic act of vandalism. It was exactly the response [Sam] Adams had dreamed of, with an enraged British government closing the port of Boston, sending more troops, imposing martial law, and requiring permits for any large Boston meetings. These 'Coercive Acts,' along with Adams's constant drumbeat of anti-British propaganda, helped unify the colonies around the idea of independence. Unger ends the book with British soldiers marching out to Lexington and Concord hoping to arrest Adams and Hancock (who, tipped off by Paul Revere, had fled). The rest, as they say, is history, and Unger has brought it brilliantly to life." Boston Globe

Includes bibliographical references

Vowell, Sarah, 1969-

Lafayette in the Somewhat United States; by Sarah Vowell. Penguin Group USA 2015 288 p. illustrations $27.95 **973.3**

1. United States -- History -- 1775-1783, Revolution

ISBN 1594631743; 9781594631740

LC 2015024639

This book, by Sarah Vowell, is an "account of George Washington's trusted officer and friend, that swashbuckling teenage French aristocrat the Marquis de Lafayette. Chronicling General Lafayette's years in Washington's army, Vowell reflects on the ideals of the American Revolution versus the reality of the Revolutionary War." (Publisher's note)

"In this crash course on the fledgling nation's teenaged French general, undoubtedly the only American Revolution narrative to offhandedly drop a Ferris Bueller reference, Vowell . . . retains her familiar casual

tone and displays her crow-like ability to find the shiny, nearly forgotten historical details." Pub Wkly

Wood, Gordon S., 1933-

Friends divided; John Adams and Thomas Jefferson. by Gordon S. Wood. Penguin Press 2017 502 p. illustrations (hardcover) $35 **973.3**

1. Founding Fathers of the United States 2. Presidents -- United States -- Biography 3. Founding Fathers of the United States -- Biography 4. United States -- Politics and government -- 1775-1783 5. United States -- Politics and government -- 1783-1809

ISBN 0735224714; 9780735224728; 9780735224711

LC 2017025116

This book, by Gordon S. Wood, is a "dual biography of two of America's most enduringly fascinating figures, whose partnership helped birth a nation, and whose subsequent falling out did much to fix its course. Thomas Jefferson and John Adams could scarcely have come from more different worlds. . . . Jefferson . . . was an aristocratic Southern slaveowner, while Adams, the overachiever from New England's rising middling classes, . . . was a skeptic about popular rule." (Publisher's note)

"Wood glides through the political intricacies and intrigues of the times, offering incisive analyses, especially of the ongoing debate over slavery, finely illuminating the minds of Adams and Jefferson." Pub Wkly

Includes bibliographical references (pages 437-484) and index.

Wren, Christopher S. (Christopher Sale), 1936-

Those turbulent sons of freedom; Ethan Allen's Green Mountain boys and the American Revolution. Christopher S. Wren. Simon & Schuster 2018 320 p. (hardback) $26 **973.3**

1. Vermont 2. United States -- Militia 3. United States -- History -- 1775-1783, Revolution 4. Vermont -- Militia 5. Vermont -- History -- To 1791 6. Ticonderoga (N.Y.) -- History -- Revolution, 1775-1783 7. United States -- History -- Revolution, 1775-1783 -- Regimental histories

ISBN 9781416599555; 9781416599562

LC 2017053023

In this book, author "[Christopher S.] Wren overturns the myth of Ethan Allen as a legendary hero of the American Revolution and a patriotic son of Vermont and offers a different portrait of Allen and his Green Mountain Boys. They were ruffians who joined the rush for cheap land on the northern frontier of the colonies in the years before the American Revolution." (Publisher's note)

Includes bibliographical references and index

973.385   American secret service and spies

Nagy, John A.

George Washington's secret spy war; The Making of America's First Spymaster. John A. Nagy. St. Martin's Press 2016 384 p. illustrations (ebook) $60; (hardcover) $27.99 **973.385**

1. Spies -- United States 2. American espionage -- History 3. United States -- History -- 1775-1783, Revolution 4. Spies -- United States -- Biography 5. Espionage -- United States -- History -- 18th century 6. United States -- History -- Revolution, 1775-1783 -- Secret service

ISBN 9781250096821; 9781250096814

LC 2016021588

This book by John A. Nagy tells "how George Washington took a disorderly, ill-equipped rabble and defeated the best trained and best equipped army of its day in the Revolutionary War. . . . Using George

Washington's diary as the primary source, Nagy tells the story of Washington's experiences during the French and Indian War and his first steps in the field of espionage." (Publisher's note)

"Nagy's fast-paced chronicle reveals a little-known side of America's Revolutionary War hero." Pub Wkly

Includes bibliographical references and index

973.4   United States--Constitutional period, 1789-1809

Burstein, Andrew

Madison and Jefferson; [by] Andrew Burstein and Nancy Isenberg. Random House 2010 809p il map $35; e-book $35   **973.4**

1. Architects 2. Presidents 3. Vice-presidents 4. Essayists 5. Members of Congress 6. Secretaries of state 7. Presidents -- United States 8. United States -- Politics and government -- 1783-1865 9. United States -- Politics and government -- 1775-1783, Revolution
ISBN 978-1-4000-6728-2; 978-0-679-60410-5 e-book

LC 2010-5884

This "dual biography promotes Madison from junior partner to full-fledged colleague of the 'more magnetic' Jefferson. According to the authors, Madison's popular image peaked in 1789 as 'father of the Constitution.' But Burstein . . . and Isenberg . . . see him as a canny, effective politician for four decades, from the Continental Congress through his two terms as America's fourth president. . . . An important, thoughtful, and gracefully written political history from the viewpoint of the young nation's two most intellectual founding fathers." Publ Wkly

Includes bibliographical references and index

Ellis, Joseph J.

Founding brothers; the revolutionary generation. Knopf 2000 288p $26.95; pa $14   **973.4**

1. United States -- Biography 2. Presidents -- United States 3. United States -- History -- 1783-1809 4. United States -- Politics and government -- 1783-1809
ISBN 0-375-40544-5; 0-375-70524-4 pa

LC 99-59304

"Ellis' essays are angled, fascinating, and perfect for general-interest readers." Booklist

Includes bibliographical references

Gordon-Reed, Annette

Thomas Jefferson and Sally Hemings; an American controversy. University Press of Va. 1997 xx, 288p hardcover o.p. pa $14.95   **973.4**

1. Slaves 2. Architects 3. Presidents 4. Vice-presidents 5. Essayists 6. Mistresses
ISBN 0-8139-1833-2 pa

LC 96-34550

The author presents "evidence for and against the proposition that Jefferson was the father of several children born to his household slave Sally Hemings." (Libr J) Bibliography. Index.

"Hemings, a slave who was one-quarter African, was also a half sister of Jefferson's deceased wife, and she lived at Monticello for many years. In this understated, brilliant study an African-American law professor examines the allegation that Jefferson was the father of Hemings' children." New Yorker

Includes bibliographical references

Hamilton, Alexander

Writings. Library of Am. 2001 1108p $40   **973.4**

1. United States -- Politics and government -- 1783-1809 2. United States -- Politics and government -- 1775-1783, Revolution
ISBN 1-931082-04-9

LC 2001-23043

"The text consists of more than 170 letters, speeches, essays, reports, and memoranda written between 1769 and 1804, including all of Hamilton's material presented in The Federalist. This additionally sports several conflicting eyewitness accounts of Hamilton's lethal duel with Aaron Burr." Libr J

Includes bibliographical references

Hogeland, William

★ The **Whiskey** Rebellion; George Washington, Alexander Hamilton, and the frontier rebels who challenged America's newfound sovereignty. Scribner 2006 302p map $26.95; pa $16   **973.4**

1. Whiskey Rebellion, Pa., 1794
ISBN 978-0-7432-5490-8; 0-7432-5490-2; 978-0-7432-5491-5 pa; 0-7432-5491-0 pa

LC 2005-56340

"Soon after Americans ousted inequitable British taxation, Secretary of Finance Alexander Hamilton, hatched a plan to put the new nation on steady financial footing by imposing the first American excise tax, on whiskey makers. The tax favored large distillers over small farmers with stills in the mountains of Pennsylvania, Maryland and Virginia, and the farmers fomented their own new revolution—a challenge to the sovereignty of the new government and the power of the wealthy eastern seaboard. In a fast-paced, blow-by-blow account of this 'primal national drama,' journalist Hogeland energetically chronicles the skirmishes that made the Whiskey Rebellion from 1791 to 1795 a symbol of the conflict between republican ideals and capitalist values." Publ Wkly

Includes bibliographical references

Kukla, Jon

A **wilderness** so immense; the Louisiana Purchase and the destiny of America. Knopf 2003 430p il map $30; pa $16   **973.4**

1. Louisiana Purchase
ISBN 0-375-40812-6; 0-375-70761-1 pa

LC 2002-27395

"This judicious, aptly illustrated work will gratify all its readers. Rarely does a work of history combine grace of writing with such broad authority." Publ Wkly

Includes bibliographical references

Purcell, Sarah J.

The **early** national period; [by] Sarah Purcell. Facts on File 2004 420p il map (Eyewitness history) $75   **973.4**

1. United States -- History -- 1783-1865
ISBN 0-8160-4769-3

LC 2003-14969

"A serious history student will find this book invaluable." Libr Media Connect

Includes bibliographical references

Sedgwick, John

War of two; Alexander Hamilton, Aaron Burr, and the duel that stunned the nation. John Sedgwick. Berkley Books 2015 480 p. color illustrations (hardcover: alk. paper) $27.95 **973.4**

1. United States -- Politics and government -- 1783-1809 2. Burr-Hamilton Duel, Weehawken, N.J., 1804 3. United States -- Politics and government -- 1801-1809

ISBN 9781592408528

LC 2015014275

This book, by John Sedgwick, is an "investigation into the rivalry between Alexander Hamilton and Aaron Burr, whose infamous duel left the Founding Father dead and turned a sitting Vice President into a fugitive. . . . A series of letters between Burr and Hamilton suggest the duel was fought over an unflattering comment made at a dinner party. But another letter . . . provides critical insight into his true motivation. It was addressed to former Speaker of the House Theodore Sedgwick." (Publisher's note)

"A fine rendition of a storied episode in American history." Booklist

Includes bibliographical references and index

Vidal, Gore

Inventing a nation: Washington, Adams, Jefferson. Yale University Press 2003 224p $22; pa $14   **973.4**

1. Generals 2. Architects 3. Presidents 4. Vice-presidents 5. Essayists

ISBN 0-300-10171-6; 0-300-10592-4 pa

LC 2003-015612

Vidal offers "characteristically brilliant and acerbic reflections on power and personality. . . . This entertaining and enlightening reappraisal of the Founders is a must for buffs of American civilization and its discontents." Booklist

Wiencek, Henry

★ An **imperfect** god; George Washington, his slaves, and the creation of America. Farrar, Straus and Giroux 2003 404p il map $26; pa $15   **973.4**

1. Generals 2. Presidents 3. Presidents -- United States

ISBN 0-374-17526-8; 0-374-52951-5 pa

LC 2003-6984

"This work of stylish scholarship and genealogical investigation makes Washington an even greater and more human figure than he has seemed before." Publ Wkly

Includes bibliographical references

★ **Master** of the mountain; Thomas Jefferson and his slaves. Henry Wiencek. Farrar, Straus and Giroux 2012 352 p. ill. maps, geneal. tables (alk. paper) $28.00   **973.4**

1. Slavery -- United States 2. United States -- History -- 1775-1865 3. Monticello (Va.) -- History 4. Slaves -- Virginia -- Albemarle County -- History 5. Plantation life -- Virginia -- Albemarle County -- History

ISBN 0374299560; 9780374299569

LC 2011052231

In this book, Henry Wiencek "explores the economic calculus behind [Thomas] Jefferson's gradual cooling toward emancipation and eventual acceptance of human capital as a great 'investment opportunity.' Wiencek argues . . . that Jefferson not only failed to follow the advice and example of his peers . . . and embrace emancipation but was in fact a 'pioneer in the monetizing of slaves' and went to great lengths to impose 'his own reality' on his 'little familial empire.'" (Library Journal)

"Wiencek's insightful and engaging account is recommended to both the illustrious Virginian's detractors and to his devotees." LJ

Includes bibliographical references (p.305-315) and index.

Wood, Gordon S., 1933-

★ **Empire** of liberty; a history of the early Republic, 1789-1815. Oxford University Press 2009 778p il map (Oxford history of the United States) $35   **973.4**

1. United States -- Civilization 2. National characteristics, American 3. United States -- Civilization -- 1783-1865 4. United States -- Politics and government -- 1783-1809 5. United States -- Politics and government -- 1783-1865

ISBN 978-0-19-503914-6

LC 2009-10762

"Skillfully traversing seminal topics such as slavery, westward expansion, social leveling, diplomacy, evangelicalism, the arts and sciences, and the transformation of the American legal system, Wood's authoritative and compelling narrative presents a picture of early Americans engaged in pursuit of cultural, social, and economic self-discovery. . . . [This is] a brilliant, definitive, and thought-provoking historical synthesis; sure to become indispensable to any study of the era." Libr J

Includes bibliographical references

Yaeger, Don

★ **George** Washington's secret six; the spy ring that saved the American Revolution. Brian Kilmeade and Don Yaeger. Sentinel 2013 256 p. illustrations, map $27.95   **973.4**

1. American espionage 2. United States -- History -- 1775-1783, Revolution 3. Spies -- United States -- History -- 18th century 4. Spies -- New York (State) -- History -- 18th century 5. United States -- History -- Revolution, 1775-1783 -- Secret service 6. New York (State) -- History -- Revolution, 1775-1783 -- Secret service

ISBN 159523103X; 9781595231031

LC 2013032285

This book by Brian Kilmeade and Don Yaeger examines the American Revolution and General George Washington's "little-known, top-secret group called the Culper Spy Ring. Kilmeade and . . . Yaeger have painted compelling portraits of George Washington's secret six [including]: Robert Townsend, the reserved Quaker merchant . . . Austin Roe, the tavern keeper . . . [and] Agent 355, a woman whose identity remains unknown." (Publisher's note)

"While Kilmeade and Yaeger don't provide deep analysis, the narrative should please enthusiastic fans of the upheaval surrounding the founding of the United States. In a slim, quick-moving book, the authors bring attention to a group that exerted an enormous influence over events during the Revolutionary War." Kirkus

Includes bibliographical references and index

Zacks, Richard

The **pirate** coast; Thomas Jefferson, the first marines, and the secret mission of 1805. Hyperion 2005 432p il map $25.95; pa $15.95   **973.4**

1. Diplomats 2. Architects 3. Presidents 4. Vice-presidents 5. Essayists 6. Army officers 7. United States -- History -- 1801-1805, Tripolitan War

ISBN 1-401-30003-0; 1-401-30849-X pa

LC 2004-60635

"This is the book that Captain Eaton has long deserved." Publ Wkly

Includes bibliographical references

973.41   Administration of George Washington, 1789-1797

Avlon, John

Washington's farewell; the founding father's warning to future generations. by John Avlon. Simon & Schuster 2017 368 p. illustrations (ebook) $18.99; (hardback) $27   **973.41**

1. American national characteristics 2. Presidents -- United States -- Messages 3. National characteristics, American

ISBN 9781476746487; 9781476746463; 9781476746470

LC 2016045258

This book, by John Avlon, offers a "portrait of our first president and his battle to save America from self-destruction. At the end of his second term, Washington surprised Americans by publishing his Farewell message in a newspaper. The President called for unity among 'citizens by birth or choice,' advocated moderation, defended religious pluralism, proposed a foreign policy of independence (not isolation), and proposed that education is essential to democracy." (Publisher's note)

"A solid analysis of our first president and his farewell to the American people." LJ

Includes bibliographical references and index

973.44   Administration of John Adams, 1797-1801

Ekirch, A. Roger, 1950-

American Sanctuary; Mutiny, Martyrdom, and National Identity in the Age of Revolution. A. Roger Ekirch. Pantheon Books 2017 320 p. illustrations (hardcover) $30; (ebook) $65   **973.44**

1. Hermione Mutiny, 1797   2. Fugitives from justice -- Great Britain -- Biography   3. United States -- Politics and government -- 1797-1801   4. Political refugees -- United States -- Biography   5. Nationalism -- United States -- History -- 18th century   6. Asylum, Right of -- United States -- History -- 18th century   7. Mutiny -- Political aspects -- United States -- History -- 18th century   8. Martyrdom -- Political aspects -- United States -- History -- 18th century

ISBN 9780307379900; 9781101871737

LC 2016015119

This book, by A. Roger Ekirch, lays out in full detail the story of how the execution of British Royal Navy mutineer and American citizen Jonathan Robbins "and the presidential campaign of 1800 inflamed the new nation and set in motion a constitutional crisis, resulting in [John] Adams's defeat and [Thomas] Jefferson's election as the third president of the United States." (Publisher's note)

"The Robbins controversy featured arguments about alien rights, asylum, national identity, and the meaning and scope of American citizenship, all of which persist and all of which Ekirch handles with remarkable dexterity." Kirkus

Includes bibliographical references and index

973.5   United States--1809-1845

Brands, H. W.

★ **Heirs** of the founders; the epic rivalry of Henry Clay, John Calhoun and Daniel Webster, the second generation of American giants. H. W. Brands. Doubleday, a division of Penguin Random House LLC 2018 432 p. (hardback) $30 **973.5**

1. Constitutional history -- United States   2. Statesmen -- United States -- Biography   3. United States -- Politics and government -- 1801-1815   4. United States -- Politics and government -- 1815-1861

ISBN 9780385542531

LC 2018010542

This book, by H. W. Brands, tells the "story of how America's second generation of political giants--Henry Clay, Daniel Webster, and John Calhoun--battled to complete the unfinished work of the Founding Fathers and decide the shape of our democracy.... Together this second generation of American founders took the country to war, battled one another for the presidency, and tasked themselves with finishing the work the Founders had left undone." (Publisher's note)

"Requiring of readers no prior knowledge of the period or the players, this fascinating history illuminates rifts that still plague the country today." Pub Wkly

Includes bibliographical references and index

Cook, Jane Hampton

American phoenix; John Quincy and Louisa Adams, the War of 1812, and the exile that saved American independence. Jane Hampton Cook. Thomas Nelson 2013 x, 502 p.p ill. (some col.) (hardcover) $26.99   **973.5**

1. Diplomats -- United States -- Biography   2. Presidents -- United States -- Biography   3. Russia -- Foreign relations -- United States   4. United States -- Foreign relations -- Russia   5. United States -- History -- War of 1812 -- Peace   6. Presidents' spouses -- United States -- Biography   7. United States -- History -- War of 1812 -- Biography   8. United States -- History -- War of 1812 -- Diplomatic history

ISBN 1595555412; 9781595555410

LC 2012039898

This is a "dual biography of John Quincy and Louisa Adams during the former's service as United States envoy to Russia (1809-1814) and throughout his negotiations with Britain that produced the Treaty of Ghent and ended the War of 1812." Jane Hampton Cook "draws heavily from diaries and voluminous correspondences to render the couple's daily and inner struggles." (Publishers Weekly)

Includes bibliographical references and index

Daughan, George C.

1812: the Navy's war; George C. Daughan. Basic Books 2011 xxix, 491p il map $32.50   **973.5**

1. War of 1812   2. United States -- Navy -- History

ISBN 978-0-465-02046-1; 978-0-465-02808-5 ebook

LC 2011020923

This book provides an account of "the U.S. Navy's surprising performance in the war that finally reconciled the British to America's independence.... If the U.S. Navy ... didn't win the War of 1812, it probably kept the nation from losing. The ... exploits of outstanding officers like Isaac Hull, David Porter, Stephen Decatur and Oliver Hazard Perry earned new respect for America's fleet; victories by the Essex, the Hornet and the Constitution ... set off national celebrations. Daughan supplies ... the big picture-the dismal struggles of both armies, Napoleon's off-stage machinations that determined so much of the war's progress, the outcome of domestic political squabbles upon which the navy's survival depended ... but he focuses on the personalities, ships and battles that prevented the British from suffocating the infant nation's maritime ambitions." (Kirkus)

"Daughan narrates the story of the War of 1812, focusing on the tiny, 20-ship U.S. Navy. In doing so, from the poorly conducted chase of HMS Belvidera by Commodore John Rogers in June 1812 to the capture of HMS Penguin by USS Hornet in March 1815, Daughan also traces the development of the U.S. Navy." Libr J

Includes bibliographical references

Groom, Winston

★ **Patriotic** fire; Andrew Jackson and Jean Laffite at the Battle of New Orleans. Alfred A. Knopf 2006 xxiv, 292p il map $26   **973.5**

1. Pirates   2. Generals   3. Presidents   4. New Orleans (La.), Battle of, 1815

ISBN 1-4000-4436-7; 978-1-4000-4436-8

LC 2005-51001

"This is a beautifully written and exciting work of popular history." Booklist

Includes bibliographical references

Hahn, Steven

A **nation** without borders; the United States and its world in an age of civil wars, 1830-1910. Steven Hahn; edited by Eric Foner. Penguin Group USA 2016 608 p. (hardcover) $35 **973.5**

    1. Capitalism 2. Mexican War, 1846-1848 3. United States -- History -- 19th century 4. United States -- History -- 1861-1865, Civil War

    ISBN 0670024686; 9780670024681

LC 2016018053

This book by Pulitzer Prize-winning historian Steven Hahn "takes on the conventional histories of the nineteenth century and offers a perspective that promises to be as enduring as it is controversial. It begins and ends in Mexico and, throughout, is internationalist in orientation. . . . It places the Civil War in the context of many domestic rebellions against state authority. . . . It reconfigures the history of capitalism." (Publisher's note)

"Given Hahn's unimpeachable body of knowledge, readers can be confident that they're getting the most current understanding of the history of the U.S." Pub Wkly

Howe, Daniel Walker, 1937-

    ★ **What** hath God wrought; the transformation of America, 1815-1848. Oxford University Press 2007 904p il map (Oxford history of the United States) $35 **973.5**

    1. Social change -- United States 2. United States -- History -- 1815-1861 3. United States -- Foreign relations -- 1815-1861 4. United States -- Politics and government -- 1815-1861

    ISBN 978-0-19-507894-7; 0-19-507894-2

LC 2007-12370

The author "narrates a crucial period in U.S. history—a time of territorial growth, religious revival, booming industrialization, a recalibrating of American democracy and the rise of nationalist sentiment. . . . Supported by engaging prose, Howe's achievement will surely be seen as one of the most outstanding syntheses of U.S. history published this decade." Publ Wkly

Includes bibliographical references

Inskeep, Steve

    Jacksonland; President Andrew Jackson, Cherokee Chief John Ross, and a Great American Land Grab. by Steve Inskeep. Penguin Group USA 2015 448 p. 8 plates; ills.; maps; ports. $29.95 **973.5**

    1. Cherokee Indians 2. Land settlement -- United States

    ISBN 1594205566; 9781594205569

LC 2015300789

This book, by Steve Inskeep, "is the thrilling narrative history of two men-- President Andrew Jackson and Cherokee chief John Ross-- who led their respective nations at a crossroads of American history. Five decades after the Revolutionary War, the United States approached a constitutional crisis. At its center stood two former military comrades locked in a struggle that tested the boundaries of our fledgling democracy." (Publisher's note)

"This superb book is highly recommended for readers interested in Native American studies or Southern history. For more on Catherine Beecher and her movement, see Alisse Portnoy's Their Right To Speak: Women's Activism in the Indian and Slave Debates." LJ

Langguth, A. J., 1933-2014

    Driven West; Andrew Jackson and the Trail of Tears to the Civil War. Simon & Schuster 2010 466p il map $30; ebook $14.99 **973.5**

    1. Generals 2. Presidents 3. Trail of Tears, 1838-1839 4. Native Americans -- Relocation 5. United States -- History -- 1815-1861

    ISBN 978-1-4165-4859-1; 1-4165-4859-9; 978-1-4391-9327-3 ebook; 1-4391-9327-4 ebook

LC 2010-20455

Langguth argues "that the passage of the Indian Removal Act of 1830, Jackson's breaking of Indian treaties and his support of the Southern states, especially Georgia, in resisting a Supreme Court ruling in favor of the Cherokees were 'salvos . . . fired in the nation's first civil war'." (N Y Times Book Rev) Bibliography. Index.

"A disturbing reconsideration of a key period of history and a powerful indictment of its main actors." Kirkus

Includes bibliographical references

Lincoln, Abraham

    ★ **Speeches** and writings, 1832-1858; speeches, letters, and miscellaneous writings: the Lincoln Douglas debates. Library of Am. 1989 898p $35 **973.5**

    1. Lincoln-Douglas debates, 1858 2. United States -- Politics and government -- 1815-1861

    ISBN 0-940450-43-7

LC 88-82723

Based on the "eight volumes of 'The Collected Works of Abraham Lincoln,' edited by Roy P. Basler, Marion Dolores Pratt and Lloyd A. Dunlap, the present . . . [volume contains] all seven of the Lincoln-Douglas debates, as well as the . . . speeches, before and after the debates, that attacked the repeal of the Missouri Compromise of 1820 and 'squatter sovereignty' in the territories." N Y Times Book Rev

Includes bibliographical references

Reynolds, David S.

    Waking giant; America in the age of Jackson. Harper 2008 466p il $29.95 **973.5**

    1. Generals 2. Presidents 3. United States -- History -- 1815-1861

    ISBN 978-0-06-082656-7

LC 2007-51751

This is "a terrific introduction of succinct length to . . . a time when the foundations of much of modern America were laid." N Y Times (Late N Y Ed)

Includes bibliographical references

Smith, Gene Allen

    The **slaves'** gamble; choosing sides in the War of 1812. Gene Allen Smith. Palgrave Macmillan 2013 272 p. $27 **973.5**

    1. War of 1812 2. Slavery -- United States

    ISBN 0230342086; 9780230342088

LC 2012045726

This book by Gene Allen Smith explains that "in the [19th] century's first two decades, the [United States] waged war against Britain, Spain, and various Indian tribes. Slaves played a role in the military operations, and the different sides viewed them as a potential source of manpower. While surprising numbers did assist the Americans, the wars created opportunities for slaves to find freedom among the Redcoats, the Spaniards, or the Indians." (Publisher's note)

Includes bibliographical references and index.

Stewart, David O.

    Madison's Gift; Five Partnerships That Built America. David O. Stewart. Simon & Schuster 2015 432 p. 24 plates; illustrations $28 **973.5**

1. Founding Fathers of the United States 2. Statesmen -- United States -- Biography 3. Presidents -- United States -- Biography 4. United States -- Politics and government -- 1775-1783 5. United States -- Politics and government -- 1783-1865 6. Friendship -- Political aspects -- United States -- History
ISBN 145168858X; 9781451688580

LC 2014021393

In this book, author David O. Stewart "examines [James Madison] from a fresh angle, looking at the ways in which Madison's associations with George Washington, Alexander Hamilton, Thomas Jefferson, James Monroe, and his wife, Dolley, helped create the United States. Stewart illuminates much about the history-making relationships among these celebrated figures." (Publisher's Weekly)

Includes bibliographical references and index

Taylor, Alan

★ The **civil** war of 1812; American citizens, British subjects, Irish rebels, & Indian allies. Alfred A. Knopf 2010 620p il map $35; e-book $35   **973.5**

1. War of 1812 2. Ontario -- History -- War of 1812 3. United States -- History -- War of 1812 4. Northern boundary of the United States -- History
ISBN 978-1-4000-4265-4; 1-4000-4265-8; 978-0-307-59459-4 e-book

LC 2010-12783

In this book, Alan "Taylor examines themes pertinent to the period and the war [of 1812], blending narrative with analysis. He sees this upheaval, and the earlier American Revolution, as part of an anglophone civil war that defined America, Canada, and the British Empire in the nineteenth century. It was a peculiar type of civil war, to be certain, as it involved more than one state and more than one culture. . . . Many Canadians were in fact displaced American loyalists who hoped to undo the revolution. . . . Taylor draws on the conceptual frameworks created in the burgeoning field of borderlands history to construct his study. He uses this approach to situate the character of the war along the American-Canadian border, which he sees as central to the entire conflict." (American Historical Review)

"Instead of a traditional narrative of the war from its beginnings in June 1812 to its end in early 1815, [this] book is structured topically. . . . Such a neat and methodical organization helps Taylor bring the confused and chaotic events of the war under control. It also allows him to present an enormous amount of material—on persons, events, and stories—without overwhelming the reader. And the amount of material is enormous." N Y Rev Books

Includes bibliographical references

Tocqueville, Alexis de

Democracy in America; with an introduction by Alan Ryan. Knopf 1994 lxxii, 434, xi, 394p (Everyman's library) $27   **973.5**

1. Democracy 2. American national characteristics 3. United States -- Social conditions 4. United States -- Politics and government
ISBN 978-0-679-43134-3; 0-679-43134-9

LC 94-1752

First part originally published in France, 1835; the second in 1840

Based partly on the French author's observations of American political and social conditions during a visit in 1831-1832. "It remains the best philosophical discussion of Democracy illustrated by the experience of the United States, up to the time when it was written, which can be found in any language." Pratt Alcove

Includes bibliographical references

Vogel, Steve

Through the perilous fight; six weeks that saved the nation. Steve Vogel. Random House Inc 2013 560 p. (acid-free paper) $30   **973.5**

1. War of 1812 2. Baltimore, Battle of, Baltimore, Md., 1814 3. Maryland -- History -- War of 1812 -- Campaigns 4. United States -- History -- War of 1812 -- Campaigns 5. Washington (D.C.) -- History -- Capture by the British, 1814
ISBN 1400069130; 9780679603474; 9781400069132

LC 2012039797

This book is a "chronicle of the critical closing months of the War of 1812—specifically, the British attacks on Washington and Baltimore." Steve Vogel "begins in the summer of 1814 with the British planning their attack. They were eager for payback after the American invasion of Canada two years earlier. Vogel focuses on Rear Adm. George Cockburn—a figure he revisits throughout—who was especially intent on capturing and torching Washington." (Kirkus Reviews)

Includes bibliographical references and index

Yaeger, Don

Andrew Jackson and the miracle of New Orleans; the battle that shaped America's destiny. Brian Kilmeade and Don Yaeger. Sentinel, an imprint of Penguin Random House 2017 256 p. (hard cover: alk. paper) $28   **973.5**

1. War of 1812 2. New Orleans (La.), Battle of, 1815 3. Generals -- United States -- Biography 4. New Orleans, Battle of, New Orleans, La., 1815 5. United States -- History -- War of 1812 -- Campaigns
ISBN 0735213232; 9780735213234

LC 2017027754

Includes bibliographical references and index

973.6   United States--1845-1861

Bordewich, Fergus M.

America's great debate; Henry Clay, Stephen A. Douglas, and the compromise that preserved the Union. Fergus M. Bordewich. Simon & Schuster 2012 x, 480 p.p   **973.6**

1. Debates and debating 2. Slavery -- United States -- History 3. United States -- History -- 1861-1865, Civil War 4. United States -- Politics and government -- 1861-1865 5. Compromise of 1850 6. Slavery -- United States -- History -- 19th century 7. United States -- Politics and government -- 1815-1861 8. United States -- History -- Civil War, 1861-1865 -- Causes
ISBN 1439124604; 9781439124604; 9781439141687

LC 2011029547

In this book, "Historian [Fergus M.] Bordewich . . . recounts the amazing story of the cliffhanging compromise hammered out in both houses of Congress in 1850 that pitted the rival pro- and antislavery factions against each other and saved the country, temporarily, from dissolution. . . . Bordewich portrays a colorful cast of characters--Democrats, Whigs, Free Soilers and abolitionists--whose passionate rhetoric attained lyrical heights and brought the debate about America's very identity to the forefront. Chief architect Henry Clay . . . warned his colleagues of the dire consequences of disunion. . . . Warring factions . . . threatened to defeat the omnibus bill, until the rhetorical arm-wringing by . . . Stephen A. Douglas squeezed a compromise and the necessary passage." (Kirkus)

Includes bibliographical references (p. [403]-463) and index

Guelzo, Allen C.

Lincoln and Douglas; the debates that defined America.

Simon & Schuster 2008 xxvii, 383p il map $26   **973.6**
1. Lawyers 2. Presidents 3. Lincoln-Douglas debates, 1858 4. Senators 5. Political leaders 6. State legislators 7. Members of Congress 8. Presidential candidates 9. United States -- Politics and government -- 1815-1861
ISBN 978-0-7432-7320-6; 0-7432-7320-6

LC 2007-44254

"This Lincoln-Douglas rendition will engage every interest in Civil War and black history." Booklist
Includes bibliographical references

Wineapple, Brenda

Ecstatic nation; confidence, crisis, and compromise, 1848-1877. Brenda Wineapple. Harper 2013 736 p. $35   **973.6**
1. United States -- History 2. Slavery -- United States -- History 3. United States -- History -- 1849-1877 4. Reconstruction (U.S. history, 1865-1877) 5. United States -- History -- Civil War, 1861-1865 6. Slavery -- United States -- History -- 19th century 7. United States -- History -- Civil War, 1861-1865 -- Causes 8. Antislavery movements -- United States -- History -- 19th century 9. United States -- Territorial expansion -- History -- 19th century
ISBN 0061234575; 9780061234576

LC 2012051538

Author Brenda Wineapple's book focuses on the history of the U.S. and discusses people "such as P. T. Barnum, Walt Whitman, George Armstrong Custer, Horace Greeley, and Jefferson Davis." The book discusses "slavery through the devastations of the Civil War and its aftermath. It explores the terrible complexities of Reconstruction and the fledgling hope that women would share equally in a new definition of American citizenship, and it traces the lust for land and the lure of its beauty from a frenzied rush to riches to the displacement of Indians." (Publisher's note)
Includes bibliographical references and index

973.7   Administration of Abraham Lincoln, 1861-1865

Abbott, Karen

Liar, Temptress, Soldier, Spy; Four Women Undercover in the Civil War. by Karen Abbott. HarperCollins Publishers 2014 368 p. illustrations, map $27.99   **973.7**
1. American espionage 2. Women -- United States -- History 3. United States -- History -- 1861-1865, Civil War
ISBN 0062092898; 9780062092892

LC 2014013602

In this book, author Karen Abbott "illuminates . . . little known aspects of the Civil War: the stories of four courageous women--a socialite, a farmgirl, an abolitionist, and a widow--who were spies. . . . Using a wealth of primary source material and interviews with the spies' descendants, Abbott seamlessly weaves the adventures of these four heroines throughout the tumultuous years of the war." (Publisher's note)
"Remarkable, brave lives rendered in a fluidly readable, even romantic history lesson." Kirkus
Includes bibliographical references and index

Ash, Stephen V.

Firebrand of liberty; the story of two Black regiments that changed the course of the Civil War. W.W. Norton & Co. 2008 282p il map $25.95   **973.7**
1. African American soldiers 2. United States -- Army -- South Carolina Volunteers, 1st 3. United States -- History -- 1861-1865, Civil War -- Campaigns 4. United States -- Army -- South Carolina

Volunteers, 2nd (1863-1864)
ISBN 978-0-393-06586-2; 0-393-06586-3

LC 2008-2503

"The titular firebrand in this revealing history is not an individual but a curious and ambitious project: the establishment, in March 1863, of a permanent Union outpost in Florida to serve as a haven for fugitive slaves and to 'help ignite the destruction of Southern slavery from within.' In readable prose and relying exclusively on primary sources, historian Ash . . . tells the little-known but crucial story of how 900 newly freed slaves, under the leadership of white abolitionist officers, captured Jacksonville." Publ Wkly
Includes bibliographical references (p. [256]-265) and index.

Ayers, Edward L., 1953-

★ The **thin** light of freedom; the Civil War and emancipation in the heart of America. Edward L. Ayers. W W Norton & Co Inc 2017 xxiii, 576 p.p illustrations, maps (hardcover) $35   **973.7**
1. Virginia -- History -- 1861-1865, Civil War 2. United States -- History -- 1861-1865, Civil War 3. Slaves -- Emancipation -- United States 4. Augusta County (Va.) -- History -- 19th century 5. Franklin (Venango County, Pa.) -- History -- 19th century 6. Shenandoah River Valley (Va. and W. Va.) -- History -- Civil War, 1861-1865
ISBN 9780393292640; 0393292630; 9780393292633

LC 2017021653

This book, by Edward L. Ayers, "restores the drama of the unexpected to the history of the Civil War. He does this by setting up at ground level in the Great Valley counties of Augusta, Virginia, and Franklin, Pennsylvania, communities that shared a prosperous landscape but were divided by the Mason-Dixon Line." (Publisher's note)
"Ayers focuses on the thoughts, fears, and hopes of normal people struggling to stay alive and make sense of the murderous events taking place around them. The result is a superb, readable work of history." Pub Wkly
Includes bibliographical references and index

Berg, Scott W.

★ **38** nooses; Lincoln, Little Crow, and the beginning of the frontier's end. Scott W. Berg. Pantheon Books 2012 384 p. $27.95   **973.7**
1. Native Americans -- Wars 2. United States -- History -- 1775-1865 3. Native Americans -- Government relations -- History 4. Dakota Indians -- Relocation 5. Dakota Indians -- Wars, 1862-1865 6. Dakota Indians -- Government relations -- History -- 19th century 7. Executions and executioners -- United States -- History -- 19th century
ISBN 0307377245; 9780307377241

LC 2012002807

Author Scott W. Berg discusses "events within the larger context of the Civil War, the history of the Dakota people, and the subsequent United States-Indian wars. . . . In August 1862, after decades of broken treaties, increasing hardship, and relentless encroachment on their lands, a group of Dakota warriors convened a council at the tepee of their leader, Little Crow. . . . So began six weeks of intense conflict along the Minnesota frontier as the Dakotas clashed with settlers and federal troops, all the while searching for allies in their struggle." (Publisher's note)
Includes bibliographical references and index.

Blanton, DeAnne

They fought like demons; women soldiers in the American Civil War. {by} DeAnne Blanton and Lauren M. Cook. Loui-

siana State Univ. Press 2002 277p il (Conflicting worlds) $29.95   **973.7**
     1. Women soldiers 2. United States -- History -- 1861-1865, Civil War
     ISBN 0-8071-2806-6

LC 2002-4441

"The authors reconstruct the reasons why women entered the armed forces: many were simply patriotic, while others followed their husbands or lovers and yet others yearned to break free from the constraints that Victorian society had laid on them as women. Blanton and Cook detail women soldiers in combat, on the march, in camp and in the hospital, where many were discovered after getting sick. Some even wound up in grim prisons kept by both sides, while a few hid pregnancies and were only discovered after giving birth. . . . Solid research by the authors, including a look at the careers of a few women soldiers after the war, makes this a compelling book that belongs in every Civil War library." Publ Wkly

Includes bibliographical references and index

Boatner, Mark Mayo

The **Civil** War dictionary; by Mark Mayo Boatner III; maps and diagrams by Allen C. Northrop and Lowell I. Miller. 1st Vintage Civil War Library ed.; Vintage Civil War Library 1991 974p il map pa $24   **973.7**
     1. Reference books 2. United States -- History -- 1861-1865, Civil War -- Encyclopedias
     ISBN 0-679-73392-2; 978-0-679-73392-8

LC 91-50013

First published 1959 by McKay

"With more than 4,000 entries . . . this dictionary remains the most comprehensive and consistently accurate reference tool on the American Civil War. In addition to the biographical sketches there are entries relating to campaigns and battles, naval engagements, weapons, issues and incidents, military terms and definitions, politics, literature, and statistics." Choice

Includes bibliographical references

Bordewich, Fergus M.

★ **Bound** for Canaan; the epic story of the underground railroad, America's first integrated civil rights movement. Fergus M. Bordewich. Amistad 2005 540p il map $27.95; pa $14.95   **973.7**
     1. Underground railroad 2. Slavery -- United States
     ISBN 0-06-052430-8; 0-06-052431-6 pa

LC 2004-52082

"The men and women of this remarkable account will remain with readers for a long time to come." Publ Wkly

Includes bibliographical references

Boritt, G. S.

The **Gettysburg** gospel; the Lincoln speech that nobody knows. Simon & Schuster 2006 415p il $28   **973.7**
     1. Lawyers 2. Presidents 3. State legislators 4. Members of Congress
     ISBN 978-0-7432-8820-0; 0-7432-8820-3

LC 2006-50578

"The author sets the speech in its contemporary context and, most interestingly, demonstrates that it was not only minimally noticed by Lincoln's peers and the press at the time but was virtually forgotten to history until the 20th century. He addresses many of the myths surrounding the address, such as that Lincoln wrote it in haste on the train to Gettysburg. In fact, it went through a number of careful revisions.

He includes images of the known copies of the handwritten address, broadsides and programs relating to the dedication ceremony at Gettysburg, selections of photos from the era, and a line-byline analysis of the various drafts of the address. Boritt's narrative style will appeal to lay readers . . . , while his extensive research and insightful conclusions will appeal to scholars." Libr J

Brewster, Todd

Lincoln's Gamble; The Tumultuous Six Months That Gave America the Emancipation Proclamation and Changed the Course of the Civil War. Todd Brewster. Simon & Schuster"||"Scribner 2014 368 p. illustrations $27   **973.7**
     1. Emancipation Proclamation 2. United States -- History -- 1861-1865, Civil War 3. Slaves -- Emancipation -- United States 4. United States -- Politics and government -- 1861-1865 5. United States. President (1861-1865: Lincoln). Emancipation Proclamation
     ISBN 1451693869; 9781451693867

LC 2013497336

Author Todd Brewster offers an "account of the most critical six months in Abraham Lincoln's presidency, when he penned the Emancipation Proclamation and changed the course of the Civil War. Brewster focuses on these critical six months to ask: was it through will or by accident, intention or coincidence, personal achievement or historical determinism that he freed the slaves?" (Publisher's note)

"Featuring vignettes of figures who met Lincoln during his formulation of the proclamation, Brewster's work illuminates Lincoln's lines of thought during this turning point in American history." Booklist

Includes bibliographical references (pages 321-335) and index

The **Causes** of the Civil War; edited by Kenneth M. Stampp. 3rd rev ed; Simon & Schuster 1991 255p pa $14   **973.7**
     1. Nationalism 2. State rights 3. Slavery -- United States 4. Southern States -- Economic conditions 5. United States -- History -- 1861-1865, Civil War -- Causes 6. United States -- History -- 1861-1865, Civil War -- Sources
     ISBN 0-671-75155-7

LC 91-36819

First published 1959 by Prentice-Hall

This book integrates the conclusions of various post-war historians with the thoughts of contemporary commentators like Jefferson Davis, Horace Greeley, and Lincoln. Political, cultural and economic aspects are emphasized

Includes bibliographical references

★ The **Civil** War; the first year told by those who lived it. edited by Brooks D. Simpson, Stephen W. Sears, Aaron Sheehan-Dean. Library of America 2011 xxv, 814p map $37.50   **973.7**
     1. United States -- History -- 1861-1865, Civil War -- Sources 2. United States -- History -- Civil War, 1861-1865 -- Sources 3. United States -- History -- 1861-1865, Civil War -- Personal narratives
     ISBN 978-1-59853-088-9; 1-59853-088-7

LC 2010-931718

"Drawing on diaries, letters, speeches, newspaper reports and editorials, memoirs, songs, poems, and other sources, the editors bring together a rich variety of voices relating or remembering the crisis of the Union from Lincoln's election in 1860 through the first year of war. . . . Readable and riveting, this 'you are there' collection makes real the sense of urgency that gripped Americans as the nation came apart and as the war began, 175 years ago. An excellent primer on why the Civil War mattered to those living it." Libr J

Includes bibliographical references

The **Civil** War: a visual history; [produced in association with the Smithsonian Institution] DK Publishing 2011 360p il map $40 **973.7**
1. United States -- History -- 1861-1865, Civil War -- Pictorial works
ISBN 978-0-7566-7185-3

"Drawing on Smithsonian Institution collections, this fact-filled and richly illustrated history brings the war fully to life, along with time lines, sidebars on particular issues, chapter introductions, lengthy captions, and detailed maps. The emphasis throughout is on the military. Multiple examples of weapons, supplies, uniforms, camp life necessities, transport, and battle scenes dominate and show the variety, complexity, and prolixity of making war. Espionage, the home front, and politics get a nod, but this book is for those wanting to smell the sulfur and hear the thunder of guns." Libr J

Davis, Burke
Sherman's march. Random House 1980 335p il maps hardcover o.p. pa $14 **973.7**
1. Generals 2. Bentonville (N.C.), Battle of, 1865 3. Memoirists 4. Secretaries of war 5. United States -- History -- 1861-1865, Civil War -- Campaigns
ISBN 0-394-75763-7 pa

LC 79-5550

The author "reconstructs Sherman's infamous, but vastly consequential march through Georgia and the Carolinas, which sent the Confederacy into its death throes. Basing his narrative on eyewitness accounts, Davis brings the event down to a personal level." Booklist

Includes bibliographical references

To Appomattox; nine April days, 1865. Burford Books 2002 433p map pa $18.95 **973.7**
1. Appomattox Campaign, 1865 2. United States -- History -- 1861-1865, Civil War
ISBN 1-580-80097-1; 978-1-580-80097-6

LC 2001-56744

First published 1959 by Rinehart

"The story of the last nine days of the Civil War from the march on Richmond to the surrender at Appomattox. Quotations from diaries, letters, newspapers and military reports create a sense of immediacy as the reader follows each day's events in the city, in the Confederate camp, and with the Union Army." Publ Wkly

Includes bibliographical references

Davis, William C.
Battle at Bull Run; a history of the first major campaign of the Civil War. Louisiana State University Press 1981 298p il map pa $19.95 **973.7**
1. Bull Run, 1st Battle of, 1861
ISBN 978-0-8071-0867-3; 0-8071-0867-7

First published 1977 by Doubleday

In this account of the war's first major engagement Davis' "sketches of the commanders, which will particularly delight Civil War enthusiasts, delve into the officer's backgrounds and unusual characteristics and include critical appraisals of their leadership capabilities. In addition, Davis includes fascinating human interest stories about the troops." Libr J

Includes bibliographical references

Doyle, Don H.
The **Cause** of All Nations; An International History of the American Civil War. by Don H. Doyle. Basic Books 2014 400 p. illustrations $29.99 **973.7**

1. War -- Public opinion 2. United States -- History -- 1861-1865, Civil War
ISBN 0465029671; 9780465029679

LC 2014024140

In this book, "historian Don H. Doyle explains that the Civil War was viewed abroad as part of a much larger struggle for democracy that spanned the Atlantic Ocean, and had begun with the American and French Revolutions. While battles raged, . . . a parallel contest took place abroad, both in the marbled courts of power and in the public square. Foreign observers held widely divergent views on the war--from radicals such as Karl Marx and Giuseppe Garibaldi, . . . to aristocratic monarchists." (Publisher's note)

Egerton, Douglas R.
Thunder at the gates; Douglas R. Egerton. Basic Books 2016 448 p. illustrations, maps, portraits (ebook) $20.99; (hardcover) $32.00 **973.7**
1. United States. Army 2. United States -- History -- 1861-1865, Civil War 3. United States -- History -- Civil War, 1861-1865 -- Campaigns 4. United States. Army. Massachusetts Cavalry Regiment, 5th (1864-1865) 5. African American soldiers -- Massachusetts -- History -- 19th century 6. United States. Army. Massachusetts Infantry Regiment, 54th (1863-1865) 7. United States. Army. Massachusetts Infantry Regiment, 55th (1863-1865) 8. United States. Army -- African American troops -- History -- 19th century 9. Massachusetts -- History -- Civil War, 1861-1865 -- Participation, African American 10. United States -- History -- Civil War, 1861-1865 -- Participation, African American
ISBN 9780465096657; 9780465096640

LC 2016032057

In this book author "Douglas Egerton chronicles the formation and battlefield triumphs of the 54th and 55th Massachusetts Infantry and the 5th Massachusetts Cavalry-regiments led by whites but composed of black men born free or into slavery. He argues that the most important battles of all were won on the field of public opinion, for in fighting with distinction the regiments realized the long-derided idea of full and equal citizenship for blacks." (Publisher's note)

"A thoroughly researched, comprehensive look at the Civil War regiments who took the first step in the struggle to make their countrymen see them as intelligent, capable men." Kirkus

Includes bibliographical references and index

★ **Encyclopedia** of the American Civil War; a political, social, and military history. David S. Heidler and Jeanne T. Heidler, editors; foreword by James W. McPherson; David J. Coles, associate editor; Gary W. Gallagher, James M. McPherson, Mark E. Neely, Jr., editorial board. ABC-CLIO 2000 5v il maps set $425 **973.7**
1. Reference books 2. United States -- History -- 1861-1865, Civil War -- Encyclopedias
ISBN 1-57607-066-2

LC 00-11195

ALA RUSA Dartmouth Medal honorable mention (2001)

"The editors have compiled a comprehensive source that provides a first-stop reference on broad areas or specific topics on the Civil War. The contemporary photographs and lithographs bring the human element into the encyclopedia, a type of reference known more for facts and figures than emotions. The primary-source-documents volume brings obscure resources together, which will further illumine the period for students."—"Outstanding Reference Sources." American Libraries, May 2001

Includes bibliographical references

Faust, Drew Gilpin

Mothers of invention; women of the slaveholding South in the American Civil War. University of N.C. Press 1996 326p il $37.50; pa $19.95 **973.7**

1. Women -- Southern States 2. United States -- History -- 1861-1865, Civil War -- Women

ISBN 0-8078-2255-8; 0-8078-5573-1 pa

LC 95-8896

Based on journals, letters and memoirs, this is an "analysis of the impact of secession, invasion and conquest on Southern white women. Antebellum images based on helplessness and dependence were challenged as women assumed an increasing range of social and economic responsibilities. . . . Faust's provocative analysis of a complex subject merits a place in all collections of U.S. history." Publ Wkly

Includes bibliographical references

Faust, Drew Gilpin, 1947-

This republic of suffering; death and the American Civil War. Alfred A. Knopf 2008 346p il $27.95 **973.7**

1. Death 2. Burial -- History 3. Death -- Social aspects -- United States 4. United States -- History -- 1861-1865, Civil War 5. United States -- History -- Civil War, 1861-1865 -- Influence 6. United States -- History -- Civil War, 1861-1865 -- Social aspects

ISBN 0-375-40404-X; 978-0-375-40404-7

LC 2007-14658

National Book Award Finalist: Nonfiction (2008)

The author "surveys the many ways the Civil War generation coped with the trauma: the concept of the Good Death—conscious, composed and at peace with God; the rise of the embalming industry; the sad attempts of the bereaved to get confirmation of a soldier's death, sometimes years after war's end; the swelling national movement to recover soldiers' remains and give them decent burials; the intellectual quest to find meaning—or its absence—in the war's carnage. . . . The result is an insightful, often moving portrait of a people torn by grief." Publ Wkly

Includes bibliographical references

Foner, Eric

The **fiery** trial; Abraham Lincoln and American slavery. W.W. Norton 2010 426p il map $29.95 **973.7**

1. Lawyers 2. Presidents 3. State legislators 4. Members of Congress 5. Biography, Individual 6. Slavery -- United States 7. Slaves -- Emancipation -- United States

ISBN 978-0-393-06618-0; 0-393-06618-5

LC 2010-23425

The author "explores the evolution—from frontier lawyer to Great Emancipator—of Lincoln's thought about and response to slavery. The book . . . showcases Foner's engaging style and insight, while keeping a tight focus on Lincoln in his own historical context. [This work] explains how a man who was more skilled politician than reformer came to issue one of the most sweeping, consequential edicts in American history." Am Scholar

Includes bibliographical references

★ **Gateway** to Freedom; The Hidden History of the Underground Railroad. Eric Foner. W W Norton & Co Inc 2015 320 p. ill, maps, port hbk $26.95 **973.7**

1. Fugitive slaves 2. Underground railroad 3. Slavery -- United States

ISBN 0393244075; 9780393244076

LC 2014036993

Author Eric Foner examines "the dramatic story of fugitive slaves and the antislavery activists who defied the law to help them reach free-

dom. [He] elevates the underground railroad from folklore to sweeping history. The story is inspiring--full of memorable characters making their first appearance on the historical stage--and significant--the controversy over fugitive slaves inflamed the sectional crisis of the 1850s." (Publisher's note)

"The author eschews the common approach of documenting the phenomenon from the South, instead centering his monograph on New York City. Through individuals such as abolitionist Sydney Howard Gay and minister Charles Ray, he demonstrates that ferrying escaped slaves from the city's waterfront to other locales throughout the North was fraught with extreme danger." LJ

Includes bibliographical references and index

Foote, Shelby

The **Civil** War; a narrative. Random House 1958 3v maps set $165; pa $75 **973.7**

1. United States -- History -- 1861-1865, Civil War

ISBN 0-394-49517-9; 0-394

"In objectivity, in range, in mastery of detail, in beauty of language and feeling for the people involved, this work surpasses anything else on the subject." New Repub

Includes bibliographical references

The **Civil** War, a narrative; by Shelby Foote. Vintage Books 1986 (pbk.: v. 1): $15.95; $50.00 **973.7**

1. United States -- History -- 1861-1865, Civil War 2. United States -- History -- Civil War, 1861-1865

ISBN 0394746236 (per vol.); 0394749138 (set); 9780394746210; 9780394746227; 9780394746234

LC 86040135

This book, by Shelby Foote, presents a reprint of a multi-volume narrative history of the U.S. Civil War written between 1958 and 1974. In it the author covers the political and social forces, the battles, and the major figures of the conflict from its beginning at the siege of Fort Sumpter to the final battle of Appomattox.

Includes bibliographies and indexes

Stars in their courses; the Gettysburg campaign, June-July 1863. Shelby Foote. Modern Library 1994 viii, 290 p.p maps $23 **973.7**

1. Gettysburg (Pa.), Battle of, 1863 2. Gettysburg Campaign, 1863

ISBN 0679601120; 9780679601128

LC 94196068

This book, by Shelby Foote, "brilliantly re-creates the three-day conflict [at Gettysburg]: it is a masterly treatment of a key great battle and the events that preceded it - not as legend has it but as it really was, before it became distorted by controversy and overblown by remembered glory." (Publisher's note)

Ford, Lacy K.

Deliver us from evil; the slavery question in the old South. Oxford University Press 2009 673p $34.95 **973.7**

1. Slavery -- United States 2. Southern States -- History 3. Southern States -- Race relations 4. Slavery -- United States -- History

ISBN 0-19-511809-X; 978-0-19-511809-4

LC 2008-47533

This book focuses "on the period from the drafting of the federal consitution in 1787 through the age of Jackson. . . . [Ford] examines the political, intellectual, economic , and social thought of leading white southerners." (N Y Times Book Rev) Index.

This book provides "an intricate, textured argument about the intellectual, social, and political interests shaping 'the slavery question,' as well as a reminder that Southern white commitment to a hardened proslavery position was not preordained or one-dimensional. Essential for all students of this subject." Libr J

Includes bibliographical references

Foreman, Amanda

A **world** on fire; Britain's crucial role in the American Civil War. Random House 2011 958p il map $35   **973.7**

1. United States -- History -- 1861-1865, Civil War 2. Great Britain -- Foreign relations -- United States 3. United States -- Foreign relations -- Great Britain 4. United States -- History -- Civil War, 1861-1865 -- Participation, British 5. United States -- History -- Civil War, 1861-1865 -- Foreign public opinion, British

ISBN 0-375-50494-X; 978-0-375-50494-5

First published 2010 in the United Kingdom

Amanda Foreman tells the "story of the American Civil War and the major role played by Britain and its citizens in that struggle. . . . Between 1861 and 1865, thousands of British citizens volunteered for service on both sides of the Civil War. From the first cannon blasts on Fort Sumter to Lee's surrender at Appomattox, they served as officers and infantrymen, sailors and nurses, blockade runners and spies." (Publisher's note)

"Ranging from the drawing rooms of Washington and London to the battlefields of Gettysburg and Antietam, to the high seas, and to Confederate and Union home fronts, Foreman has written a diplomatic, military, and social kaleidoscope of the Civil War. She superbly conveys the horror, pathos, and chaos of battle, the political and moral ambiguities, and the devotion of those who fought. She has also restored an international dimension missing from many histories. The fall of Fort Sumter in April 1861 set off a furious diplomatic contest between North and South for the favors of Great Britain, then the world's superpower. Britain had a tangle of economic interests in the United States; it was bound to the South by cotton, which kept the British textile industry spinning, and British investors held millions in stocks and securities." Boston Globe

Fredriksen, John C.

Civil War almanac. Facts on File, Inc. 2007 858p il map (Almanacs of American wars) $85   **973.7**

1. United States -- History -- 1861-1865, Civil War

ISBN 0-8160-6459-8; 978-0-8160-6459-5

LC 2006-29985

First published 1983 under the editorship of John Stewart Bowman

This book contains a "day-by-day chronology of the events and people of this monumental war, along with an A-to-Z dictionary offering biographical information on leading military and political figures involved in the conflict." Publisher's note

Includes bibliographical references

Freeman, Joanne B.

The **field** of blood; violence in congress and the road to civil war. Joanne B. Freeman. Farrar, Straus & Giroux 2018 480 p. $27   **973.7**

1. United States -- History -- 1861-1865, Civil War 2. United States -- Politics and government -- 1783-1865

ISBN 0374154775; 9780374154776

In this book, author Joanne B. Freeman "recovers the long-lost story of physical violence on the floor of the U.S. Congress. Drawing on an extraordinary range of sources, she shows that the Capitol was rife with conflict in the decades before the Civil War. Legislative sessions were often punctuated by mortal threats, canings, flipped desks, and all-out slugfests. When debate broke down, congressmen drew pistols and waved Bowie knives." (Publisher's note)

Gallagher, Gary W.

The **union** war. Harvard University Press 2011 215p il $27.95   **973.7**

1. United States -- History -- 1861-1865, Civil War 2. United States -- History -- Civil War, 1861-1865 3. United States -- Politics and government -- 1861-1865 4. Popular culture -- United States -- History -- 19th century

ISBN 978-0-674-04562-0; 0-674-04562-9

LC 2010-51977

In this book, "Gary Gallagher argues . . . that Northerners, ranging from President Lincoln all the way down to the conscripts in the Army of the Potomac, didn't fight the Civil War to free the slaves or to topple white supremacy in the South. Instead, they fought for the Union, an admittedly diffuse concept, Gallagher admits, but nevertheless their central animating principle." (Times Literary Supplement)

"Gallagher offers not so much a history of wartime patriotism as a series of meditations on the meaning of the Union to Northerners, the role of slavery in the conflict and how historians have interpreted (and in his view misinterpreted) these matters." N Y Times Book Rev

Includes bibliographical references

Gienapp, William E.

Abraham Lincoln and Civil War America; a biography. Oxford Univ. Press 2001 239p il maps hardcover o.p. pa $24.95   **973.7**

1. Lawyers 2. Presidents 3. State legislators 4. Members of Congress 5. Presidents -- United States 6. United States -- History -- 1861-1865, Civil War

ISBN 0-19-515099-6; 0-19-515100-3 pa

LC 2001-50056

This biography focuses on the American president's leadership during the Civil War.

"In spite of the book's size, its discriminating history of Lincoln's life is surprisingly rich, and the narrative of his presidency and the unfolding of the war is crisp and coherent." Bookmarks

Includes bibliographical references

Goldfield, David R.

★ **America** aflame; how the Civil War created a nation. [by] David Goldfield. Bloomsbury Press 2011 632p il $35   **973.7**

1. United States -- History -- 1861-1865, Civil War -- Causes 2. United States -- History -- Civil War, 1861-1865 -- Causes 3. United States -- History -- Civil War, 1861-1865 -- Campaigns 4. United States -- History -- Civil War, 1861-1865 -- Influence 5. United States -- History -- Civil War, 1861-1865 -- Social aspects 6. United States -- History -- 1861-1865, Civil War -- Religious aspects

ISBN 978-1-59691-702-6; 1-59691-702-4

LC 2010-25241

"A provocatively written, scrupulously researched, and well-framed consideration of evangelical religion's questionable role in the antebellum, Civil War, and Reconstruction periods of our history." Libr J

Includes bibliographical references

Goodheart, Adam

★ **1861**; the Civil War awakening. 1st ed.; Alfred A. Knopf 2011 481p il $28.95   **973.7**

1. United States -- Intellectual life 2. United States -- Politics and government -- 1861-1865 3. United States -- History -- 1861-1865, Civil War -- Causes

ISBN 978-1-4000-4015-5; 1-4000-4015-9

LC 2010-51326

"Goodheart leads us on a journey through the frenzied, frightening months between Abraham Lincoln's election to the presidency in 1860 — followed with breakneck speed by the secession of the Confederate States and the outbreak of war — and July 4, 1861, when President Lincoln delivered his first message to Congress, laying out the case not only for the necessity of war, but for a more democratic vision of the United States. The election of Lincoln and the secession crisis is, of course, familiar terrain. But Goodheart's version is at once more panoramic and more intimate than most standard accounts, and more inspiring. This is fundamentally a history of hearts and minds, rather than of legislative bills and battles." N Y Times Book Rev

Gopnik, Adam

Angels and ages; a short book about Darwin, Lincoln, and modern life. Alfred A. Knopf 2009 211p $24.95   **973.7**
1. Lawyers 2. Presidents 3. Naturalists 4. Modern civilization 5. Travel writers 6. State legislators 7. Writers on science 8. Members of Congress
ISBN 978-0-307-27078-8; 0-307-27078-5
LC 2008-36224

"The book is worth reading . . . for the author's unquestioned skill as a craftsman and the light he sheds on what has become, for many, settled history." Bookmarks

Groom, Winston

Shiloh, 1862; the first great and terrible battle of the civil war. Winston Groom. National Geographic Books 2012 446 p.   **973.7**
1. Shiloh (Tenn.), Battle of, 1862 2. Tennessee -- History -- 1861-1865, Civil War 3. United States -- History -- 1861-1865, Civil War -- Campaigns 4. Shiloh, Battle of, Tenn., 1862 5. Tennessee -- History -- Civil War, 1861-1865 -- Campaigns 6. United States -- History -- Civil War, 1861-1865 -- Campaigns
ISBN 9781426208744
LC 2012372339

This book "presents Shiloh, fought on April 6-7 in western Tennessee, as a turning point in the [U.S. Civil War]." (Kirkus) "[Winston] Groom . . . compels the reader to appreciate the enormous toll to both sides owing to advanced arms, outmoded battle tactics, and poor generalship. Although Groom lays responsibility on both sides, he especially blames General [Ulysses] Grant and General [William] Sherman . . . for failure to fortify positions, properly reconnoiter, read the signs of enemy advances, and have a battle plan in case of attack. . . . Groom sees Shiloh as a learning experience for Grant, who finally understood that no single battle, no matter how costly or geographically significant, could end the rebellion: the Union could be restored only through the total conquest of the South." (Libr J)

Includes bibliographical references (p. 409-419) and index

Vicksburg, 1863. Alfred A. Knopf 2009 482p il $30 **973.7**
1. Vicksburg (Miss.) -- Siege, 1863 2. United States -- History -- 1861-1865, Civil War -- Campaigns
ISBN 978-0-307-26425-1
LC 2008-45984

"Rarely has the story of such a lengthy and complicated campaign been told with such clarity and grace." Washington Post

Includes bibliographical references

Guelzo, Allen C.

Gettysburg; the last invasion. by Allen C. Guelzo. 1st ed. Alfred A. Knopf 2013 xix, 632 p., 16 unnumbered pages of platesp ill., maps (hardcover) $35   **973.7**
1. Gettysburg (Pa.), Battle of, 1863 2. United States -- History

-- 1861-1865, Civil War 3. Gettysburg, Battle of, Gettysburg, Pa., 1863
ISBN 0307594084; 9780307594082
LC 2012047013

The book offers an account of the battle of Gettysburg. Though "the battle site was not inevitable, the actual battle was . . . . The Union had reason to be concerned, but, as [Allen C.] Guelzo documents, their foe was scattered and divided, with rivalries and miscommunication . . . keeping James Longstreet from attacking, J.E.B. Stuart from arriving on the battlefield in time, and the much-disliked George Pickett from enjoying a better fate than being cannon fodder." (Kirkus Reviews)

Includes bibliographical references (pages 483-599) and index.

Harper, Judith E.

Women during the Civil War; an encyclopedia. Routledge 2003 472p il map $170; pa $59.95   **973.7**
1. Reference books 2. United States -- History -- 1861-1865, Civil War -- Women -- Encyclopedias
ISBN 0-415-93723-X; 0-415-95574-2 pa
LC 2003-7181

"The 128 entries range in length from 400 to 4000 words, and include biographies of women from all regions of the U.S. Well-known figures such as Harriet Tubman, Clara Barton, Louisa May Alcott, and Mary Todd Lincoln are represented but so too are African-American sculptor Edmonia Lewis, poet Lucy Larcom, and Emma LeConte. . . . As well as biographies, there are superb thematic entries on women living in the West, prostitutes, industrial workers, family life, and invasion and occupation. . . . This encyclopedia is a welcomed addition to reference collections." SLJ

Includes bibliographical references

Holzer, Harold

The **Civil** War in 50 objects; Harold Holzer and the New-York Historical Society; with an introduction by Eric Foner. Viking 2013 416 p. (hardcover) $36   **973.7**
1. United States -- Antiquities 2. United States -- History -- 1861-1865, Civil War 3. New-York Historical Society 4. United States -- History -- Civil War, 1861-1865 -- Museums 5. United States -- History -- Civil War, 1861-1865 -- Anecdotes 6. United States -- History -- Civil War, 1861-1865 -- Antiquities 7. United States -- History -- Civil War, 1861-1865 -- Collectibles
ISBN 067001463X; 9780670014637
LC 2013001532

This book, by Harold Holzer, explores the U.S. Civil War through a set of preserved objects "from a soldier's diary with the pencil still attached to John Brown's pike, the Emancipation Proclamation, a Confederate Palmetto flag, and the leaves from Abraham Lincoln's bier. . . . Lincoln scholar Harold Holzer sheds new light on the war by examining fifty objects from the New-York Historical Society's acclaimed collection." (Publisher's note)

Includes bibliographical references and index

Lincoln and the power of the press; the war for public opinion. Harold Holzer. Simon & Schuster 2014 768 p. illustrations (hardcover) $37.50   **973.7**
1. Press 2. Presidents -- United States -- Press relations 3. United States -- Politics and government -- 1861-1865 4. Press and politics -- United States -- History -- 19th century 5. United States -- History -- Civil War, 1861-1865 -- Journalists 6. United States -- History -- Civil War, 1861-1865 -- Press coverage
ISBN 1439192715; 9781439192719; 9781439192726
LC 2014021392

This book by Harold Holzer describes how, "From his earliest days,

[U.S. President Abraham] Lincoln devoured newspapers. As he started out in politics he wrote editorials and letters to argue his case. He spoke to the public directly through the press. He even bought a German-language newspaper to appeal to that growing electorate in his state. Lincoln alternately pampered, battled, and manipulated the three most powerful publishers of the day." (Publisher's note)

Includes bibliographical references (pages 665-697) and index

Horwitz, Tony

Confederates in the attic; dispatches from the unfinished Civil War. Pantheon Bks. 1998 406p map hardcover o.p. pa $14.95 **973.7**

1. United States -- History -- 1861-1865, Civil War
ISBN 0-679-75833-X pa

LC 97-26759

This "is the work of a skilled journalist looking at how—and why—the War Between the States continues to live in so many issues still with us." Libr J

Howard, David

Lost rights; the misadventures of a stolen American relic. Houghton Mifflin Harcourt 2009 344p $26 **973.7**

1. Theft 2. Manuscripts 3. United States -- Constitution -- 1st-10th amendments
ISBN 978-0-618-82607-0; 0-618-82607-6

LC 2009-18046

"The tale pulsates with dynamic personalities greatly affected by their connection to one of the rarest, most influential and valuable documents in American history. Howard has produced a marvelously compelling read." Publ Wkly

Includes bibliographical references

Hyslop, Stephen G.

Atlas of the Civil War; a comprehensive guide to the tactics and terrain of battle. edited by Neil Kagan; narrative by Stephen G. Hyslop; introduction by Harris J. Andrews. National Geographic Society 2009 255p il map $40 **973.7**

1. Reference books 2. Historical atlases 3. United States -- History -- 1861-1865, Civil War -- Maps
ISBN 978-1-4262-0347-3

LC 2008-35066

"Arranged chronologically, this atlas combines period photographs and illustrations, rare period maps and modern cartography, with just enough narrative to explain the two-page spread devoted to each subject (the majority being about particular battles or campaigns). . . . The text also features numerous sidebars throughout, offering micro-timelines, biographies, and images showing the human side of the war. All of these special features make this large-format atlas a superior choice for Civil War buffs as well as those new to the subject." Libr J

Jordan, Brian Matthew, 1986-

Marching Home; Union Veterans and Their Unending Civil War. Brian Matthew Jordan. W W Norton & Co Inc 2015 384 p. illustrations $28.95 **973.7**

1. Veterans 2. United States -- History -- 1861-1865, Civil War
ISBN 0871407817; 9780871407818

LC 2014032544

Pulitzer Prize Finalist: History (2016)

In this book, U.S. "Civil War historian Brian Matthew Jordan" looks at Union veterans, who, "tending rotting wounds, battling alcoholism, campaigning for paltry pensions . . . tragically realized that they stood as unwelcome reminders to a new America. Mining previously untapped

archives, Jordan uncovers anguished letters and diaries, essays by amputees, and gruesome medical reports, all deeply revealing of the American psyche." (Publisher's note)

Kaplan, Fred, 1937-

Lincoln and the Abolitionists; John Quincy Adams, Slavery, and the Civil War. Fred Kaplan. HarperCollins 2017 xvi, 395 p.p illustrations, portraits (hardcover) $28.99 **973.7**

1. Slavery -- United States 2. Abolitionists -- United States 3. Racism -- United States -- History -- 19th century 4. Slavery -- United States -- History -- 19th century 5. United States -- History -- Civil War, 1861-1865 -- Causes 6. Antislavery movements -- United States -- History -- 19th century
ISBN 9780062440006; 9780062440013; 0062440004

This biography, by Fred Kaplan, presents "a thought-provoking exploration of how Abraham Lincoln's and John Quincy Adams' experiences with slavery and race shaped their differing viewpoints, provides both perceptive insights into these two great presidents and a revealing perspective on race relations in modern America." (Publisher's note)

"A fresh look at John Quincy Adams, Abraham Lincoln, the Civil War, abolitionism, and other related American history." Kirkus

Includes bibliographical references (pages [341]-366) and index.

Keegan, John

The **American** Civil War; a military history. Alfred A. Knopf 2009 396p il map $35 **973.7**

1. Military geography -- United States 2. United States -- History -- 1861-1865, Civil War -- Campaigns
ISBN 978-0-307-26343-8; 0-307-26343-6

LC 2009-19469

The author "provides the single best one-volume assessment of the military character and conduct of America's ordeal by fire." Libr J

Includes bibliographical references

Krauthamer, Barbara

Envisioning emancipation; Black Americans and the end of slavery. Deborah Willis and Barbara Krauthamer. Temple University Press 2013 223 p. ill. (cloth: alk. paper) $35 **973.7**

1. Slaves -- Emancipation 2. Slavery -- United States 3. African Americans -- Portraits 4. Documentary photography -- United States 5. Historiography and photography -- United States 6. African Americans -- History -- 1863-1877 -- Pictorial works 7. United States -- History -- Civil War, 1861-1865 -- African Americans -- Pictorial works
ISBN 1439909857; 9781439909850

LC 2012032600

This book is a collection "of nearly 150 photographs reaching from the mid-19th to the early 20th century" that are meant to help readers "contemplate not only the history of slavery and emancipation but also our continued ties to that history and its legacies." Subjects include the "escaped slave Dolly pictured on a reward notice, a group gathered for a 1916 slave reunion, Emancipation Day celebrations, fugitives fording a river, chimney sweeps, family groups, and penal slavery crews." (Publishers Weekly)

Includes bibliographical references and index

Levine, Bruce

The **fall** of the house of Dixie; how the Civil War remade the American South. Bruce Levine. Random House 2013 xix, 439 p., [16] p. of platesp ill., map $30 **973.7**

1. Confederate States of America -- History 2. United States -- History -- 1861-1865, Civil War 3. Confederate States of

America 4. Confederate States of America -- Social conditions 5. Confederate States of America -- Economic conditions 6. United States -- History -- Civil War, 1861-1865 -- Social aspects 7. United States -- History -- Civil War, 1861-1865 -- Economic aspects 8. Elite (Social sciences) -- Southern States -- History -- 19th century 9. Slavery -- Social aspects -- Southern States -- History -- 19th century 10. Slavery -- Economic aspects -- Southern States -- History -- 19th century
ISBN 1400067030; 9780679645351; 9781400067039

LC 2011048310

In this book Bruce Levine tells the "story of how [the American Civil War] upended the economic, political, and social life of the old South, utterly destroying the Confederacy and the society it represented and defended. Told through the words of the people who lived it, 'The Fall of the House of Dixie' illuminates the way a war undertaken to preserve the status quo became a second American Revolution whose impact on the country was as strong and lasting as that of our first." (Publishing note)

Includes bibliographical references (p. [377]-415) and index.

Lincoln, Abraham

★ **Speeches** and writings, 1859-1865; speeches, letters, and miscellaneous writings, presidential messages and proclamations. Library of Am. 1989 xxxiii, 787p $35   **973.7**
1. United States -- Politics and government -- 1861-1865
ISBN 0-940450-63-1

LC 89-45349

This volume is based upon The Collected Works of Abraham Lincoln. It includes public statements, business letters, "poems, personal letters, telegrams to generals in the field, and other [writings]." Libr J

Includes bibliographical references

Masur, Louis P.

The **Civil** War: a concise history. Oxford University Press 2011 118p il $18.95   **973.7**
1. United States -- History -- 1861-1865, Civil War
ISBN 978-0-19-974048-2

LC 2010-19460

The author provides "a concise but compelling narrative of the Civil War era, packing in the critical information to track the trajectory of secession, war, emancipation, and Reconstruction. He focuses on the political and the military, with Lincoln, Jefferson Davis, and the generals especially getting their due." Libr J

Includes bibliographical references

McPherson, James M.

Abraham Lincoln and the second American Revolution. Oxford Univ. Press 1991 173p hardcover o.p. pa $16.95 **973.7**
1. Lawyers 2. Presidents 3. State legislators 4. Members of Congress 5. United States -- History -- 1861-1865, Civil War
ISBN 0-19-507606-0 pa

LC 90-6885

The author "examines Lincoln's role in the transformation wrought by the Civil War—the liberation of four million slaves, the overthrow of the social and political order of the South." Publ Wkly

Includes bibliographical references

Hallowed ground; a walk at Gettysburg. Crown Publishers 2003 144p map (Crown Journeys series) $16   **973.7**
1. Gettysburg (Pa.), Battle of, 1863
ISBN 0-609-61023-6

LC 2002-35154

"If it were only a pointer to the physical ground and commemorative markers, this guide would be ordinary, but McPherson so articulately

injects reminders—as of a free black farmer who fled the approaching battle lest Confederates enslave him—of what the Civil War was about as to display the crystalline style that has made him one of our finest Civil War historians." Booklist

★ **This** mighty scourge; perspectives on the Civil War. Oxford University Press 2007 260p $28   **973.7**
1. Lawyers 2. Presidents 3. State legislators 4. Members of Congress 5. United States -- History -- 1861-1865, Civil War
ISBN 0-19-531366-6

LC 2006-35523

These essays "stand as a remarkably elegant and clarifying narrative exploration of the most basic questions concerning the Civil War, issues over which scholars and activists still contend. . . 'This Mighty Scourge,' in fact, is an exemplary exercise in the contribution a great historian and eloquent writer can make to a people's understanding of themselves." Los Angeles Times

McPherson, James M., 1936-

Battle cry of freedom; the Civil War era. Oxford Univ. Press 1988 904p il maps (Oxford history of the United States) $47.50; pa $18.95   **973.7**
1. United States -- History -- 1861-1865, Civil War
ISBN 0-19-503863-0; 0-19-516895-X pa

LC 87-11045

This narrative covers events "from the Mexican War through Appomattox. . . . {There are} political and economic discussions . . . {as well as} descriptions of military campaigns and personalities." (Libr J) Bibliography. Index.

This volume "is comprehensive yet succinct, scholarly without being pedantic, eloquent but unrhetorical. It is compellingly readable." N Y Times Book Rev

Includes bibliographical references

The **war** that forged a nation; why the Civil War still matters. James M. McPherson. Oxford University Press 2015 232 p. (hardback) $27.95   **973.7**
1. United States -- History -- 1861-1865, Civil War 2. Social change -- United States -- History 3. War and society -- United States -- History 4. National characteristics, American -- History 5. United States -- History -- Civil War, 1861-1865 -- Influence 6. United States -- History -- Civil War, 1861-1865 -- Social aspects 7. United States -- History -- Civil War, 1861-1865 -- Psychological aspects
ISBN 0199375771; 9780199375776

LC 2014018008

In this book "historian James M. McPherson considers why the Civil War remains so deeply embedded in our national psyche and identity. The drama and tragedy of the war, from its scope and size--an estimated death toll of 750,000, far more than the rest of the country's wars combined--to the nearly mythical individuals involved--Abraham Lincoln, Robert E. Lee, Stonewall Jackson--help explain why the Civil War remains a topic of interest." (Publisher's note)

"In a discussion of Lincoln and slavery, the author agrees with Eric Foner that the president was anti-slavery (deeming it a violation of natural rights) but not an abolitionist (he expected slavery would eventually die out). These authoritative essays, most of which appeared previously in various formats, will appeal mainly to serious students and specialists." Kirkus

Includes bibliographical references and index

Meyer, Eugene L.

Five for freedom; the African American soldiers in John

Brown's army. Eugene L. Meyer. Lawrence Hill Books, an imprint of Chicago Review Press Inc. 2018 304 p. (cloth: alk. paper) $26.99 **973.7**

    1. African Americans 2. Abolitionists -- Biography 3. African Americans -- Biography 4. Slavery -- United States -- History 5. African American abolitionists -- History -- 19th century 6. Harpers Ferry (W. Va.) -- History -- John Brown's Raid, 1859

    ISBN 9781613735718

                      LC 2017045333

    This book, by Eugene L. Meyer, tells the story of five African Americans who participated "on [the] October 16, 1859 . . . ill-fated attempt to incite a slave insurrection . . . [led by John Brown. The book recounts] the circumstances in which they were born and raised, how they came together at this fateful time and place, and the legacies they left behind. It is an American story that continues to resonate." (Publisher's note)

    Includes bibliographical references and index

The **New** York Times disunion; A History of the Civil War. edited by Edward L. Widmer, with Clay Risen and George Kalogerakis. Oxford University Press 2016 392 p. illustrations $34.95 **973.7**

    1. United States -- History -- 1861-1865, Civil War 2. United States -- History -- Civil War, 1861-1865

    ISBN 9780190621834

                      LC 2016015114

    This book, edited by Edward L. Widmer, presents "a series [of New York Times articles] marking the long string of anniversaries around the Civil War. . . . Moving chronologically and thematically across all four years of hostilities, this comprehensive and engrossing work examines secession, slavery, battles, and domestic and global politics." (Publisher's note)

    (Noted academics, scholars, editors, and historians contribute to a collection of fresh, provocative essays on the Civil War." (Kirkus)

    Includes bibliographical references and index

Nofi, Albert A.

    The **blue** & gray almanac; the Civil War in facts and figures, recipes and slang. Albert Nofi. Casemate Pub & Book Dist Llc 2017 304 p. $32.95 **973.7**

    1. United States -- History -- 1861-1865, Civil War

    ISBN 1612005527; 9781612005522

    "Written by notable military historian [Albert] Nofi, this browsable book is not a traditional reference work, yet it is not a typical history book either. Twelve chapters are devoted to subjects like the naval war, generals, troops, medicine, and the attention-grabbing money, graft, and corruption. Through anecdotes, brief essays, and the unearthing of unusual and little-known details, Nofi relays an entertaining and illuminating story of the [American Civil] War." (Choice)

Oakes, James

    Freedom national; the destruction of slavery in the United States, 1861-1865. James Oakes. W. W. Norton & Co. 2013 608 p. (hardcover) $29.95 **973.7**

    1. Slavery -- United States 2. Slaves -- Emancipation -- United States 3. United States -- History -- 1861-1865, Civil War 4. Slavery -- United States -- History 5. United States -- History -- Civil War, 1861-1865 6. Antislavery movements -- United States -- History 7. United States. President (1861-1865: Lincoln). Emancipation Proclamation

    ISBN 0393065316; 9780393065312

                      LC 2012035601

    This book by James Oakes "shows how deftly [Abraham] Lincoln and congressional Republicans pursued antislavery throughout the [American Civil] war, pragmatic in policy but steadfast on principle. . . . As the devastating war continued with slavery still entrenched, Republicans embraced a more aggressive military emancipation, triggered by the Emancipation Proclamation. Finally it took a constitutional amendment on abolition to achieve the Union's primary goal in the war." (Publisher's note)

    Includes bibliographical references and index

Paludan, Phillip S.

    The **presidency** of Abraham Lincoln; {by} Phillip Shaw Paludan. University Press of Kan. 1994 xx, 384p (American presidency series) $29.95; pa $15.95 **973.7**

    1. Lawyers 2. Presidents 3. State legislators 4. Members of Congress 5. United States -- Politics and government -- 1861-1865

    ISBN 0-7006-0671-8; 0-7006-0745-5 pa

                      LC 93-46830

    The author "traces the year-by-year chronology of a Presidency engaged with recruiting, placating, appeasing and coercing the various and competing factions of the war years, and sees in Lincoln 'a commitment to the political-constitutional system that would itself move the nation toward its highest ambitions.' . . . Equally interesting is Mr. Paludan's depiction of how the war transformed the national Government, not only establishing the foundations for the Gilded Age but more subtly strengthening and enriching the role of government." NY Times Book Rev

    Includes bibliographical references

Perry, James M.

    Touched with fire; five presidents and the Civil War battles that made them. PublicAffairs 2003 335p il map $26; pa $16 **973.7**

    1. Generals 2. Governors 3. Presidents 4. Senators 5. Members of Congress 6. Presidents -- United States 7. United States -- History -- 1861-1865, Civil War

    ISBN 1-586-48114-2; 1-586-48290-4 pa

                      LC 2003-46625

    "All chief executives during the Gilded Age volunteered for the Union in the Civil War (excluding Grover Cleveland, who paid for a substitute). Perry here recounts their war records with an eye to the subsequent electoral advertising of their bravery and patriotism. . . . Perry, a wry storyteller, delivers the regimental-level detail that buffs crave while dusting events with the skepticism that presidential electoral campaigning invites." Booklist

    Includes bibliographical references

Pryor, Elizabeth Brown, 1951-2015

    Six Encounters with Lincoln; A President Confronts Democracy and Its Demons. by Elizabeth Brown Pryor. Penguin Group USA 2017 496 p. illustrations, portraits (ebook) $65; $35 **973.7**

    1. United States -- Politics and government -- 1861-1865

    ISBN 9780735222793; 0670025909; 9780670025909

                      LC 2016042837

    This book, by Elizabeth Brown Pryor, "examines six intriguing, mostly unknown encounters that Abraham Lincoln had with his constituents. Taken together, they reveal his character and opinions in unexpected ways, illustrating his difficulties in managing a republic and creating a presidency. Pryor probes both the political demons that Lincoln battled in his ambitious exercise of power and the demons that arose from the very nature of democracy itself." (Publisher's note)

"Deeply researched, telling moments in the life of arguably the most written-about man in American history." Kirkus

Includes bibliographical references and index.

Rable, George C.

God's almost chosen peoples; a religious history of the American Civil War. University of North Carolina Press 2010 586p il (Littlefield history of the Civil War era) $35   **973.7**

1. United States -- History -- 1861-1865, Civil War -- Religious aspects

ISBN 978-0-8078-3426-8; 0-8078-3426-2

LC 2010-23646

"Rable draws upon newspapers, sermons, diaries, letters, and journals to show that many people on both sides of the conflict turned to faith to help explain the war's causes, course, and consequences. Rable demonstrates that both Northerners and Southerners tried to make sense of the brutal war by thumbing through their Bibles, listening to their preachers, and interpreting battles as a fulfillment of a divine plan. . . . Because of its thorough research and its chronicle of the lives of ordinary people, Rable's engrossing study of the role of religion in the Civil War will stand as the definitive religious history of America's most divisive conflict." Publ Wkly

Includes bibliographical references and index

Sarna, Jonathan D.

Lincoln and the Jews; a history. by Jonathan Sarna and Benjamin Shapell. Thomas Dunne Books 2015 288 p. color illustrations; map (hardcover) $40   **973.7**

1. Jews -- United States 2. Jews -- United States -- History -- 19th century 3. United States -- History -- Civil War, 1861-1865 -- Jews

ISBN 1250059534; 9781250059536

LC 2014033453

In this book, authors "Jonathan D. Sarna and collector Benjamin Shapell reveal how Lincoln's remarkable relationship with American Jews impacted both his path to the presidency and his policy decisions as president. The volume uncovers a new and previously unknown feature of Abraham Lincoln's life, one that broadened him, and, as a result, broadened America." (Publishers' note)

"The authors provide extensive discussion of Lincoln's efforts to restrain anti-Semitic attitudes in the army, most notably General Ulysses Grant's infamous expulsion order, and extensive prejudice by General Benjamin Butler. This attractive volume featuring a plethora of primary documents highlights the political contributions of numerous Jews to Lincoln's decisions both small and momentous." Choice

Includes bibliographical references and index

Sears, Stephen W.

★ **Chancellorsville**. Houghton Mifflin 1996 593p hardcover o.p. pa $17   **973.7**

1. Generals 2. Chancellorsville (Va.), Battle of, 1863

ISBN 0-395-87744-X pa

LC 96-31220

In this history of the campaign that ended in Chancellorsville, the author argues that "a chain of errors, assumptions, and communications failures combined with the genuine brilliance and good luck of the Confederates to lead to a stinging if indecisive Union defeat." Booklist

Includes bibliographical references

★ **Gettysburg**. Houghton Mifflin 2003 623p il map $30; pa $17   **973.7**

1. Gettysburg (Pa.), Battle of, 1863

ISBN 0-395-86761-4; 0-618-48538-4 pa

LC 2002-191259

This is an "assessment of the battle of Gettysburg and the events leading up to it. . . . Sears examines several turning points during the battle's buildup and three-day duration. The resulting insights add to the excellent and dramatic narrative flow. . . . For all Civil War collections and academic libraries." Libr J

Includes bibliographical references

★ **Landscape** turned red; the Battle of Antietam. Houghton Mifflin 2003 431p il pa $17   **973.7**

1. Antietam (Md.), Battle of, 1862

ISBN 978-0-618-34419-2; 0-618-34419-5

First published 1983 by Ticknor & Fields

This "account of the Battle of Antietam, the bloodiest day of the Civil War, is wide-ranging, detailed, and copiously documented. Stephen Sears . . . describes the tension-filled days preceding September 17, 1862, especially the political climate of Union pessimism and Confederate optimism. . . . The battle itself is then exhaustively recounted." Booklist

Lincoln's lieutenants; the high command of the Army of the Potomac. Stephen W. Sears. Houghton Mifflin Harcourt 2017 ix, 884 p.p illustrations, maps (hardcover) $38   **973.7**

1. United States -- History -- 1861-1865, Civil War 2. Generals -- United States -- Biography 3. United States. Army of the Potomac -- Officers -- Biography 4. United States -- History -- Civil War, 1861-1865 -- Biography 5. United States -- History -- Civil War, 1861-1865 -- Campaigns

ISBN 0618428259; 9780544826250; 9780618428250

LC 2017288442

This book, by Stephen W. Sears, is "a multilayered group biography of the commanders who led the Army of the Potomac. The high command of the Army of the Potomac was a changeable, often dysfunctional band of brothers, going through the fires of war under seven commanding generals in three years, until Grant came east in 1864." (Publisher's note)

"A staggering work of research by a masterly historian." Kirkus

Includes bibliographical references (pages 846-858) and index.

To the gates of Richmond; the peninsula campaign. Mariner 2001 468p il map pa $17   **973.7**

1. Peninsular Campaign, 1862

ISBN 978-0-618-12713-9; 0-618-12713-5

First published 1992 by Ticknor & Fields

"The campaign on the peninsula between the James and York rivers in Virginia in the spring of 1862 was McClellan's major strategic effort and the first major Union offensive in the East. . . . Sears does an outstanding job in making intelligible an extremely complex campaign." Booklist

Includes bibliographical references

Slotkin, Richard, 1942-

Long Road to Antietam; how the Civil War became a revolution. Richard Slotkin. Liveright Publishing Corporation 2012 512 p. (hardcover) $32.95   **973.7**

1. Emancipation Proclamation 2. United States -- History -- 1861-1865, Civil War 3. Antietam, Battle of, Md., 1862 4. United States. President (1861-1865: Lincoln). Emancipation Proclamation

ISBN 0871404117; 9780871404114

LC 2012007795

This book looks at the germination of the U.S. Civil War which "became a revolution in summer 1862, when Lincoln acknowledged that peaceful compromise was at that point impossible and thoroughly committed himself to war. First up in this new strategy: the Emancipation Proclamation. As Lincoln clashed with ambitious general George McClellan, the country started on the bloody road to Antietam." (Library Journal)

Includes bibliographical references and index

Snodgrass, Mary Ellen

★ The **Underground** Railroad; an encyclopedia of people, places, and operations. Sharpe Reference 2007 2v il map set $199   **973.7**

   1. Reference books 2. Underground railroad -- Encyclopedias 3. Slavery -- United States -- Encyclopedias

   ISBN 978-0-7656-8093-8

LC 2007-9199

The author "has compiled an important and extensively researched encyclopedia of the Underground Railroad. Beginning with a concise, informative general introduction, this ambitious two-volume set neatly identifies the key people, places, documents, organizations, and publications of the Underground Railroad movement, along with significant actions, events, and ideas underlying it in the US and Canada. Offering photographs, bookplates, sketches, and handbills, the set is visually attractive." Choice

Includes bibliographical references

Snow, Richard

Iron dawn; The Monitor, the Merrimack, and the Civil War Sea Battle that Changed History. Richard Snow. Scribner 2016 384 p. illustrations $30; (ebook) $20.99   **973.7**

   1. Hampton Roads, Battle of, Va., 1862 2. Warships -- United States -- History 3. United States -- History -- 1861-1865, Civil War -- Naval operations 4. Monitor (Ironclad) 5. Virginia (Ironclad)

   ISBN 9781476794181; 9781476794204

LC 2016006965

This book, by Richard Snow, focuses on the sea battle "at Hampton Roads, Virginia, in March 1862. The Confederacy . . . built an iron fort containing ten heavy guns on the hull of a captured Union frigate named the Merrimack. The North got word of the project . . . [and] commissioned an eccentric inventor named John Ericsson to build the Monitor, an entirely revolutionary iron warship. . . . She fought the Merrimack to a standstill, and saved the Union cause." (Publisher's note)

"A thorough and enthusiastic treatment, Snow's account will capture the naval-history and Civil War readership." Booklist

Includes bibliographical references and index.

Stout, Harry S.

Upon the altar of the nation: a moral history of the American Civil War. Viking 2006 552p il $29.95   **973.7**

   1. United States -- History -- 1861-1865, Civil War

   ISBN 0-670-03470-3

LC 2005-42420

"Impeccably sourced and highly engaging, the book will surely be controversial—the best histories often are." Booklist

Includes bibliographical references

Swanson, Mark

Atlas of the Civil War, month by month; major battles and troop movements. maps by Mark Swanson, with Jacqueline D. Langley. University of Georgia Press 2004 141p il map $39.95   **973.7**

   1. Reference books 2. Historical atlases 3. United States -- History -- 1861-1865, Civil War -- Maps

   ISBN 0-8203-2658-5

LC 2004-12264

This Civil War atlas depicts "multiple aspects of the war's action in a month-by-month sequence from April 1861 to June 1865. . . . An absolute must for Civil War studies." Univ Press Books for Public and Second Sch Libr, 2006

Includes bibliographical references

Walters, Kerry

The **Underground** Railroad; a reference guide. Kerry Walters. ABC-CLIO 2012 x, 223 p.p ill. (hardcover: acid-free paper) $58.00; (ebook) $58.00   **973.7**

   1. Abolitionists 2. Slavery -- United States -- History 3. Underground railroad -- Encyclopedias 4. Underground railroad 5. Fugitive slaves -- United States -- History 6. Abolitionists -- United States -- History -- 19th century 7. Antislavery movements -- United States -- History -- 19th century

   ISBN 1598846477; 9781598846478; 9781598846485

LC 2011041517

"This book, part of the Guides to Historic Events in America series, brings into perspective what the Underground Railroad did and how it operated. This guide begins with a chronology from 1690 to 1870, followed by an introduction that attempts to separate the legends from the reality of the times. Subsequent chapters cover the major aspects of slavery and the Underground Railroad." (Booklist)

Includes bibliographical references and index.

Ward, Andrew

The **slaves'** war; the Civil War in the words of former slaves. Houghton Mifflin Co. 2008 386p il $28   **973.7**

   1. Slavery -- United States 2. Freedmen -- United States 3. Slaves -- Southern States -- Biography 4. United States -- History -- Civil War, 1861-1865 -- Social aspects 5. United States -- History -- Civil War, 1861-1865 -- African Americans 6. United States -- History -- 1861-1865, Civil War -- Personal narratives 7. United States -- History -- Civil War, 1861-1865 -- Personal narratives

   ISBN 0-618-63400-2; 978-0-618-63400-2

LC 2008-1532

Collected from "interviews, diaries, letters, and memoirs, here is the Civil War as seen from not only battlefields, capitals, and camps, but also slave quarters, kitchens, roadsides, farms, towns, and swamps." (Publisher's note) Index.

The author "has provided a . . . narrative that gives voice to the experiences and attitudes of slaves who endured the conflict. Ward utilizes testimonials, diaries, and letters, and organizes them in chronological order from the months before the commencement of hostilities to the aftermath of the surrender at Appomattox. . . . This is a work that will interest both scholars and general readers." Booklist

Includes bibliographical references

Ward, Geoffrey C.

The **Civil** War; an illustrated history. {by} Geoffrey C. Ward with Ken Burns and Ric Burns. Knopf 1990 425p il maps $75; pa $29.95   **973.7**

   1. United States -- History -- 1861-1865, Civil War

   ISBN 0-394-56285-2; 0-679-74277-8 pa

LC 89-43475

"A companion to a nine-part Public Broadcasting System documentary, this superbly designed book easily stands on its own." N Y Times Book Rev

Includes bibliographical references

The **West** Point History of the Civil War; by The United States Military Academy with Colonel Ty Seidule and Clifford

Rogers. Simon & Schuster 2014 352 p. color illustrations, maps (hardcover) $55   **973.7**
1. Military art and science 2. United States Military Academy 3. United States -- History -- 1861-1865, Civil War
ISBN 9781476782621; 1476782628

This book, published by United States Military Academy, with Colonel Ty Seidule and Clifford Rogers, offers a "definitive military history of the Civil War, featuring the same exclusive images, tactical maps, and expert analysis commissioned by The United States Military Academy to teach the history of the art of war to West Point cadets." (Publisher's note)

Williams, David

★ **Bitterly** divided; the South's inner Civil War. David Williams. New Press 2008 310p ill., ports. (hbk.) o.p.; (pbk.) $14; (hbk.) o.p.   **973.7**
1. Social conflict 2. Southern States -- History 3. Secession -- Southern States 4. Confederate States of America 5. United States -- History -- 1861-1865, Civil War 6. Social conflict -- Southern States -- History -- 19th century
ISBN 1-59558-108-1; 978-1595584755; 9781595581082
LC 2007045285

In this book, author and "historian David Williams lays bare the myth of a united confederacy, revealing that the South was in fact fighting two civil wars--an external one that we know so much about and an internal one about which there is scant literature and virtually no public awareness. . . . [The book] shows that from the Confederacy's very beginnings white Southerners were as likely to have opposed secession as supported it, and they undermined the Confederate war effort at nearly every turn. In just one of many telling examples in . . . narrative history, Williams shows that when planters grew too much cotton and tobacco and exempted themselves from the draft, plain folk called the conflict a 'rich man's war' and rioted. Many formed armed anti-Confederate bands. Southern blacks, in what W.E.B. DuBois called 'a general strike against the Confederacy,' resisted in increasingly overt ways, escaped by the thousands, and forced a change in the war's direction that led to emancipation." (Publisher's note)

"Williams marshals abundant evidence to demonstrate that the Confederacy also lost an internal civil war during 1861-65. . . . This firm repudiation of the myth of the solid Confederate South is absolutely essential Civil War reading." Booklist
Includes bibliographical references (p. [275]-291) and index

Wills, Garry

Lincoln at Gettysburg; the words that remade America. Simon & Schuster 1992 317p hardcover o.p. pa $14   **973.7**
1. Lawyers 2. Presidents 3. State legislators 4. Members of Congress
ISBN 0-671-86742-3 pa
LC 92-3546

This is a "tour de force that will cause much discussion and argument." Libr J
Includes bibliographical references

Woodworth, Steven E.

Atlas of the Civil War; by Steven Woodworth and Kenneth J. Winkle; foreword by James M. McPherson. Oxford University Press 2004 400p il map $75   **973.7**
1. Reference books 2. Historical atlases 3. United States -- History -- 1861-1865, Civil War -- Maps
ISBN 0-19-522131-1
LC 2004-53112

"Richly illustrated, this publication will be wanted by all types of libraries. . . . The text entries are useful, while the maps and illustrations are both informative and eye-catching." Choice

973.711   Civil War – Causes

Manning, Chandra

Troubled refuge; Struggling for Freedom in the Civil War. Chandra Manning. Alfred A. Knopf 2016 416 p. illustrations, maps $30   **973.711**
1. Slaves -- Emancipation -- United States 2. United States -- History -- 1861-1865, Civil War 3. United States -- History -- Civil War, 1861-1865 -- Social aspects 4. United States -- History -- Civil War, 1861-1865 -- African Americans
ISBN 9780307271204
LC 2015039724

This book, by Chandra Manning, is "a vivid portrait of the Union army's escaped-slave refugee camps and how they shaped the course of emancipation and citizenship in the United States. . . . Drawing on records of the Union and Confederate armies, the letters and diaries of soldiers, transcribed testimonies of former slaves, and more, . . . Manning allows us to accompany the black men, women, and children who sought out the Union army in hopes of achieving autonomy." (Publisher's note)

"An essential contribution to the history of the Civil War and its aftermath." Booklist
Includes bibliographical references

Sinha, Manisha

The **Slave's** cause; a history of abolition. Manisha Sinha. Yale University Press 2016 784 p. illustrations $37.50 **973.711**
1. Abolitionists 2. Slaves -- Emancipation 3. Slavery -- United States
ISBN 9780300181371
LC 2015948091

National Book Awards Longlist: Nonfiction (2016)

"Drawing on extensive archival research, including newly discovered letters and pamphlets, [author Manisha] Sinha documents the influence of the Haitian Revolution and the centrality of slave resistance in shaping the ideology and tactics of abolition. This book is a comprehensive new history of the abolition movement in a transnational context." (Publisher's note)

"Sinha's book is a tour de force that surpasses all previous works in scope, scale, and scholarship." LJ
Includes bibliographic references and index.

973.73   Civil War -- Operations

Murray, Williamson

★ A **savage** war; A Military History of the Civil War. Williamson Murray and Wayne Hsieh. Princeton University Press 2016 616 p. maps (hardback: alk. paper) $35   **973.73**
1. United States -- Military history 2. United States -- History -- 1861-1865, Civil War -- Campaigns 3. United States -- History -- Civil War, 1861-1865 -- Campaigns
ISBN 9780691169408
LC 2016008730

This book on the American Civil War by Williamson Murray and Wayne Hsieh shows how "waging war was made possible by the powerful historical forces unleashed by the Industrial Revolution and the

French Revolution. . . . [Despite] material superiority, a Union victory remained in doubt for most of the war. Murray and Hsieh paint indelible portraits of Abraham Lincoln, Ulysses S. Grant, . . . and other major figures . . . [who played] decisive roles in the fate of a nation." (Publisher's note)

"This expertly written narrative will draw in anyone with an interest in the Civil War at any knowledge level. A great resource for public and academic libraries." LJ

Includes bibliographical references and index

973.775 Civil War – Medical services

Toler, Pamela D.
Heroines of Mercy Street; the real nurses of the Civil War. Pamela D. Toler. Little, Brown & Co. 2016 287 p. illustrations $27   973.775
   1. Nurses 2. United States -- History -- 1861-1865, Civil War
   ISBN 0316392073; 9780316392075
                                                LC 2015953905
This book, by Pamela D. Toler, " tells the true stories of the nurses at Mansion House, the Alexandria, Virginia, mansion turned war-time hospital and setting for the new PBS drama 'Mercy Street.' Among the Union soldiers, doctors, wounded men from both sides, freed slaves, politicians, speculators, and spies who passed through the hospital in the crossroads of the Civil War, were nurses who gave their time freely and willingly to save lives and aid the wounded." (Publisher's note)

"Accessible and well researched, Toler's book coincides with the recent PBS series Mercy Street and successfully illustrates the beginnings of nursing as a designated field of medical practice." LJ

Includes bibliographical references (pages 263-274) and index.

973.8 United States--Reconstruction period, 1865-1901

Algeo, Matthew
   The **president** is a sick man; wherein the supposedly virtuous Grover Cleveland survives a secret surgery at sea and vilifies the courageous newspaperman who dared expose the truth. Chicago Review Press 2011 255p il $24.95   973.8
   1. Mayors 2. Governors 3. Journalism 4. Presidents 5. Journalists 6. District attorneys 7. United States -- Politics and government -- 1865-1898
   ISBN 978-1-56976-350-6; 1-56976-350-X
                                                LC 2010-44639
"Incredibly, shortly after his second term began in 1893, Cleveland boarded a friend's yacht and sailed into the Long Island Sound where surgeons, in a makeshift operating theater, cut away cancerous tissue in his mouth and part of his jawbone. . . . Cancer was virtually taboo in Cleveland's day. He didn't want to lose public confidence or become a spectacle like former President Grant, who had died from cancer. Also, Cleveland was in a contentious political struggle over whether the U.S. should return to the gold standard to back its money (his position), or continue with a policy that also accepted silver, the view of his vice president, Adlai Stevenson. Cleveland feared that should he become incapacitated, Stevenson would assume power and sway the country's financial direction. The yacht's crew and surgeons kept mum, except for a dentist serving as anesthetist, who told a fellow doctor. Word found its way to Philadelphia Press reporter E.J. Edwards, who confirmed enough of the tale to print it. Cleveland's circle squatted on the scoop and undermined the reporter's reputation. . . . Only decades later would one of the surgeons tell all in an article, and make amends to Edwards for the harm done to him." Milwaukee J Sentinel

Includes bibliographical references

Donovan, James
   A **terrible** glory; Custer and the Little Bighorn-- the last great battle of the American West. [by] James Donovan. Little, Brown and Co. 2008 528p il map pa $16.99; $26.99 973.8
   1. Generals 2. Little Bighorn, Battle of the, 1876 3. Army officers 4. Western States -- History, Military 5. Native Americans -- Government relations 6. Little Bighorn, Battle of the, Mont., 1876
   ISBN 0-316-06747-4 pa; 0-316-15578-0; 978-0-316-06747-8 pa; 978-0-316-15578-6
                                                LC 2007-26156
The author "collects the multiple threads that led to the 1876 massacre at Little Big Horn. . . . Exhaustive research, lively prose and fresh interpretation make for a valuable addition to literature on this otherwise well-trodden historical event." Publ Wkly

Includes bibliographical references (p. [487]-511) and index

Douglass, Frederick, 1817-1895
   The **portable** Frederick Douglass; Frederick Douglass; edited with an introduction and notes by John Stauffer and Henry Louis Gates. Penguin Books 2016 xxxvi, 579 p.p (Penguin classics) (paperback) $22   973.8
   1. Abolitionists -- Biography 2. Slaves -- United States -- Biography 3. African American abolitionists -- Biography 4. Speeches, addresses, etc., American -- African American authors 5. Antislavery movements -- United States -- History -- 19th century
   ISBN 0143106813; 9780143106814; 9781101992265
                                                LC 2016006199
This book in the Penguin Classic series, by Frederick Douglass, edited by John Stauffer and Henry Louis Gates, "offers a full course on the remarkable, diverse career of Frederick Douglass. . . . [It] includes the full range of Douglass's works: [such as] . . . 'Narrative of the Life of Frederick Douglass,' . . . the brilliant speeches that launched his political career and that constitute the greatest oratory of the Civil War era; and his journalism." (Publisher's note)

Includes bibliographical references.

Foner, Eric, 1943-
   Forever free; the story of emancipation and Reconstruction. illustrations edited and with commentary by Joshua Brown. Knopf 2005 xxx, 268p il $27.50; pa $15   973.8
   1. Reconstruction (1865-1876) 2. Slavery -- United States 3. United States -- Politics and government -- 1865-1898
   ISBN 0-375-40259-4; 978-0-375-40259-3; 0-375-70274-1 pa; 978-0-375-70274-7 pa
                                                LC 2005-40706
This "is an invaluable and timely book about a subject central to U.S. history and still of obvious significance today—slavery, the Civil War, emancipation, Reconstruction, and both the immediate aftermath and longer-term consequences of those things." Rev Am Hist

Includes bibliographical references

Franklin, John Hope, 1915-2009
   Reconstruction after the Civil War; John Hope Franklin; with a new foreword by Eric Foner. 3rd edition University of Chicago Press 2013 279 p. $20   973.8
   1. Reconstruction (1865-1876) 2. United States -- History -- 1865-1898

ISBN 9780226923376; 0226923371

LC 2012010482

This is an "account of American life in a time of great challenge, unfamiliar problems, and uncertain leadership. Discusses the Radicals' effort to secure racial justice in the South, the fact that corruption existed not only in the South, and that some worthwhile measures emerged from 'carpetbag' legislatures." Guide to Read in Am Hist {review of 1961 edition}

Grua, David W.

★ **Surviving** Wounded Knee; the Lakotas and the politics of memory. David W. Grua. Oxford University Press 2016 ix, 276 p.p (hardcover: alk. paper) $36.95   **973.8**
1. Memorialization 2. Collective memory 3. Dakota Indians -- Wars 4. Dakota Indians -- Claims 5. South Dakota -- Race relations 6. Memorialization -- South Dakota 7. Collective memory -- South Dakota 8. Dakota Indians -- Wars, 1890-1891 9. Wounded Knee Massacre, S.D., 1890 10. Dakota Indians -- Government relations 11. Wounded Knee Massacre, S.D., 1890 -- Claims 12. Memory -- Political aspects -- United States 13. Memorialization -- Political aspects -- United States
ISBN 9780190249038

LC 2015035931

This book, by David W. Grua, "argues that Wounded Knee serves as a window into larger debates over how the United States' conquest of the indigenous peoples should be remembered. During the five decades after Wounded Knee, the survivors pursued historical justice in the form of compensation, in accordance with traditional Lakota conflict resolution practices and treaty provisions that required compensation for past wrongs." (Publisher's note)

Includes bibliographical references (pages [183]-260) and index.

Grumet, Bridget Hall

Reconstruction era: primary sources; Lawrence W. Baker, project editor. UXL 2004 xxv, 228p il (Reconstruction Era reference library) $60   **973.8**
1. Reconstruction (1865-1876)
ISBN 0-7876-9219-0

LC 2004-17309

This book "contains 19 complete or partial documents, such as the Fourteenth Amendment of the U.S. Constitution and Rutherford B. Hayes' inaugural address. Each document is accompanied by an introduction, keys to reading the document, a discussion of subsequent events related to the document, and other material." Booklist

Includes bibliographical references

Howes, Kelly King

Reconstruction era: almanac; Lawrence W. Baker, project editor. UXL 2004 xxxvii, 228p il map (Reconstruction Era reference library) $60   **973.8**
1. Reconstruction (1865-1876)
ISBN 0-7876-9217-4

LC 2004-17301

This book "covers the political and social aspects of Reconstruction, including carpetbaggers and scalawags, amnesty for white Southerners, 'Black Codes,' the impeachment of President Johnson, the rise of the Ku Klux Klan, attempts to restore the old order in the South and much more." Publisher's note

Includes bibliographical references

Langguth, A. J., 1933-2014

After Lincoln; how the north won the Civil War and lost the peace. A. J. Langguth. Simon & Schuster 2014 464 p. illustrations (hardcover) $28   **973.8**
1. Reconstruction (1865-1876) 2. United States -- Politics and government -- 1865-1898 3. Reconstruction (U.S. history, 1865-1877) 4. United States -- Politics and government -- 1865-1877
ISBN 1451617321; 9781451617320; 9781451617337

LC 2013051340

This book, by A. J. Langguth, "tells the story of the Reconstruction, which set back black Americans and isolated the South for a century. . . . President Andrew Johnson, a former slave owner from Tennessee, was challenged by Northern Congressmen, Radical Republicans led by Thaddeus Stephens and Charles Sumner, who wanted to punish the defeated South. . . . By the 1868 election, united Republicans nominated Ulysses Grant, Lincoln's winning Union general." (Publisher's note)

"The power of the Ku Klux Klan to strike fear was very real, no matter how foreign it seems today. This is a cogent, well-researched, well-told history of that important period. Langguth shows rather than explains, and the result is a rich history of an understudied period of American history." Kirkus

Includes bibliographical references and index

Millard, Candice

The **destiny** of the republic; Candice Millard. Doubleday 2011 x, 319 p., [16] p. of platesp ill.   **973.8**
1. United States -- History -- 1865-1898 2. Presidents -- United States -- Assassination 3. Presidents -- United States -- Biography 4. Medicine -- United States -- History -- 19th century 5. United States -- Politics and government -- 1881-1885 6. Political culture -- United States -- History -- 19th century 7. Power (Social sciences) -- United States -- History -- 19th century 8. Presidents -- Medical care -- United States -- History -- 19th century 9. Medical instruments and apparatus -- United States -- History -- 19th century
ISBN 9780307939654; 0385535007; 9780385526265; 9780385535007

LC 2011001549

This book explores U.S. history during the presidency and assassination of U.S. president James Garfield. "As [the author] . . . builds to the president's fatal encounter with his assassin, she details the intra-party struggle among Republicans that led to Garfield's surprise 1880 nomination. . . . During the nearly three excruciating months Garfield lay dying, Alexander Graham Bell . . . scrambled to perfect his induction balance (a metal detector) in time to locate the lead bullet lodged in the stricken president's back. Meanwhile, Garfield's medical team persistently failed to observe British surgeon Joseph Lister's methods of antisepsis--the American medical establishment rejected the idea of invisible germs as ridiculous--a neglect that almost surely killed the president." (Kirkus)

Includes bibliographical references (p. 313-323) and index

Miller, Scott

The **President** and the assassin; McKinley, terror, and empire at the dawn of the American century. Random House 2011 422p il   **973.8**
1. Governors 2. Presidents 3. Anarchism and anarchists 4. Murderers 5. Anarchists 6. Members of Congress 7. Anarchism -- United States -- History 8. United States -- Social conditions -- 1865-1918 9. United States -- Politics and government -- 1865-1898 10. United States -- Politics and government -- 1897-1901 11. United States -- Politics and government -- 1898-1919 12. United States -- Territorial expansion -- History -- 19th century
ISBN 1-4000-6752-9; 978-1-4000-6752-7

LC 2010-38857

"Miller examines the social, economic and political forces that underlay the transformation of the U.S. after the Civil War from a feeble newcomer in world affairs to the global power we know today in a way that keeps you learning and turning pages at the same time. Rewarding as it is to be able to grasp at last such late 19th-century mysteries as the monetary debates that have befuddled college students ever since, what makes the book compelling is neither the narrative nor the explanations but the sense of familiarity that pervades it all. Indeed, so many of the circumstances and events of the earlier time have parallels in our own that the experience of reading it is practically eerie." Oregonian

Includes bibliographical references (p. [385]-403) and index

Philbrick, Nathaniel

★ The **last** stand; Custer, Sitting Bull, and the Battle of the Little Bighorn. Viking 2010 466p il map $30   **973.8**
   1. Generals 2. Dakota Indians 3. Little Bighorn, Battle of the, 1876 4. Army officers 5. Indian chiefs 6. Dakota Indians -- Wars, 1876 7. Little Bighorn, Battle of the, Mont., 1876
   ISBN 978-0-670-02172-7

LC 2009-47209

The author "writes a lively narrative that brushes away the cobwebs of mythology to reveal the context and realities of Custer's unexpected 1876 defeat at the hands of his Indian enemies under Sitting Bull, and the character of each leader. Judicious in his assessments of events and intentions, Philbrick offers a rounded history of one of the worst defeats in American military history, a story enhanced by his minute examination of the battle's terrain and interviews with descendants in both camps." Publ Wkly

Includes bibliographical references

Rauchway, Eric

Murdering McKinley; the making of Theodore Roosevelt's America. Hill & Wang 2003 250p il $25; pa $14   **973.8**
   1. Governors 2. Presidents 3. Vice-presidents 4. Murderers 5. Anarchists 6. Members of Congress 7. Nobel laureates for peace 8. United States -- Politics and government -- 1898-1919
   ISBN 0-8090-7170-3; 0-8090-1638-9 pa

LC 2003-40666

The author "uses a search for the motive of President William McKinley's assassin as a means to comment on the Progressive Era and show how Theodore Roosevelt manipulated the emotions of rage and despair after the tragic event to give it meaning, thereby advancing his own political vision. . . . Novel in its conception and well written, the book is appropriate for public as well as academic libraries." Choice

Includes bibliographical references

Tuccille, Jerome

The **roughest** riders; the untold story of the Black soldiers in the Spanish-American War. Jerome Tuccille. Chicago Review Press 2015 304 p. illustrations, maps (cloth) $26.95   **973.8**
   1. African American soldiers 2. Spanish-American War, 1898 3. United States -- Military history 4. Spanish-American War, 1898 -- Campaigns 5. African American soldiers -- History -- 19th century 6. Spanish-American War, 1898 -- Participation, African American
   ISBN 1613730462; 9781613730461

LC 2015001414

This book, by Jerome Tuccille, "is the inspiring story of the first African American soldiers to serve during the post-slavery era, first in the West and later in Cuba, when full equality, legally at least, was still a distant dream. They fought heroically and courageously, making [Teddy] Roosevelt's campaign [in the Spanish-American War] a great success that added to the future president's legend as a great man of words and action." (Publisher's note)

"Tuccille's excellent descriptions give readers a graphic feel for the vicissitudes of jungle warfare and the grim racial and social realities that these men endured." Pub Wkly

Includes bibliographical references and index

Welch, James

Killing Custer; the Battle of the Little Bighorn and the fate of the Plains Indians. by James Welch with Paul Stekler. Norton 1994 320p il hardcover o.p. pa $14.95   **973.8**
   1. Little Bighorn, Battle of the, 1876 2. Native Americans -- Wars
   ISBN 0-393-32939-9 pa

LC 94-5617

"Welch produced this history of the Indian wars of the northern plains as a by-product of his work scripting a television documentary on the Battle of the Little Bighorn. In addition to military history, it contains long sections describing the life of the Plains Indians, accounts of contemporary Indian radical groups, and Welch's reactions while visiting the various historic sites in the area." Libr J

Includes bibliographical references

West, Elliott

The **last** Indian war; the Nez Perce story. Oxford University Press 2009 397p il map (Pivotal moments in American history)   **973.8**
   1. Indian chiefs 2. Nez Percé War, 1877 3. Big Hole, Battle of the, 1877 4. Nez Percé Indians -- Wars, 1877 5. Nez Percé Indians -- History -- 19th century
   ISBN 9780195136753

LC 2008051382

This is an account of the 1877 war between the Nez Perce Indians and the United States government. Chronology. Index.

The author "uses the story of the Nez Percé War of 1877 and its origins and aftermath to illuminate the era of expansion and consolidation between 1845 and 1877 that forged the American identity, a period he calls the 'Greater Reconstruction.' . . . This well-written book is an excellent place to start in understanding the Nez Percé War and is highly recommended for all libraries." Libr J

Includes bibliographical references (p. 325-328) and index.

White, Richard, 1947-

The **republic** for which it stands; the United States during Reconstruction and the Gilded Age, 1865-1896. Richard White. Oxford University Press 2017 xx, 941 p.p illustrations (some color) (Oxford history of the United States) (hardcover: alk. paper) $35   **973.8**
   1. Reconstruction (1865-1876) 2. United States -- Politics and government -- 19th century 3. United States -- History -- 1865-1921 4. Reconstruction (U.S. history, 1865-1877) 5. United States -- Politics and government -- 1865-1933
   ISBN 9780190619060; 9780199735815

LC 2017002719

This book in The Oxford History of the United States series, by Richard White, "offers a fresh and integrated interpretation of Reconstruction and the Gilded Age as the seedbed of modern America. . . . White narrates the conflicts and paradoxes of these decades of disorienting change and mounting unrest, out of which emerged a modern nation whose characteristics resonate with the present day." (Publisher's note)

"White . . . seamlessly incorporates political, economic, social, and legal history to show the birth of the modern US. Throughout, he includes fascinating anecdotes that captivate readers." Choice

Includes bibliographical essay (pages 873-901) and index.

973.9   United States--1901-

Boorstin, Daniel J. (Daniel Joseph), 1914-2004

The **image**; a guide to pseudo-events in America. Daniel J. Boorstin. Vintage Books, a division of Random House, Inc. 2012 x, 321 p.p (pbk.) $16   **973.9**

1. Fame 2. Popular culture -- United States 3. National characteristics, American 4. United States -- Civilization -- 1945- 5. Popular culture -- United States -- History -- 20th century

ISBN 0679741801; 9780679741800

LC 2012464128

This book, by Daniel J. Boorstin, "first published in 1962, . . . introduced the notion of 'pseudo-events'--events such as press conferences and presidential debates, which are manufactured solely in order to be reported--and the contemporary definition of celebrity. . . . Since then Daniel J. Boorstin's prophetic vision of an America inundated by its own illusions has become an essential resource for any reader who wants to distinguish the manifold deceptions of our culture." (Publisher's note)

Menand, Louis

The **Metaphysical** Club. Farrar, Straus & Giroux 2001 546p il $30; pa $15   **973.9**

1. Educators 2. Metaphysics 3. Philosophers 4. Psychologists 5. Logicians 6. Writers on science 7. Metaphysics -- History 8. Supreme Court justices 9. National characteristics, American 10. United States -- Intellectual life 11. United States -- Intellectual life -- 20th century

ISBN 0-374-19963-9; 0-374-52849-7 pa

LC 00-66279

"In January of 1872, a group of young intellectuals in Cambridge, Mass., formed a conversation society. One of them, a prodigy in math, science and philosophy named Charles Sanders Peirce, said later that they called themselves the Metaphysical Club 'half-ironically, half-defiantly.' . . . Among the other members were William James . . . and Oliver Wendell Holmes." (N Y Times Book Rev) Index.

"Menand brings rare common sense and graceful, witty prose to his richly nuanced reading of American intellectual history." N Y Times Book Rev

Includes bibliographical references

Tintori, Karen

Trapped: the 1909 Cherry Mine disaster. Simon & Schuster 2002 273p il $25; pa $14   **973.9**

1. Coal mines and mining -- Accidents

ISBN 0-7434-2194-9; 0-7434-2195-7 pa

LC 2002-104596

"On November 13, 1909, a fire trapped 480 coal miners . . . 400 feet below ground in a mine at Cherry, Illinois. Only 221 escaped. . . . Tintori describes the life-and-death struggle of the miners below ground and the terror of the women and children gathered at the mine's entrance. . . . Tintori's graphic account of this tragedy is a sad but gripping story." Booklist

973.91   United States--1901-1953

Allen, Frederick Lewis

Only yesterday; an informal history of the 1920's. Wiley 1997 285p (Wiley investment classics) $21.95   **973.91**

1. United States -- Social conditions 2. United States -- History -- 1919-1933 3. United States -- Economic conditions -- 1919-1933

ISBN 0-471-18952-9

LC 97-19930

A reissue of the title first published 1931 by Harper and Brothers

"An account of the years from the spring of 1919 to . . . {1931}. It is a kaleidoscopic picture of American politics, society, manners, morals, and economic conditions." Booklist

Includes bibliographical references

Beam, Alex

A **great** idea at the time; the rise, fall, and curious afterlife of the Great Books. PublicAffairs 2008 245p il $24.95 **973.91**

1. Books and reading 2. United States -- Intellectual life 3. Great books of the Western world (Franklin Center, Pa.)

ISBN 978-1-58648-487-3; 1-58648-487-7

LC 2008-33115

This is a "look at the marketing phenomenon and cultural-icon status of the Great Books of Western Civilization, a 54-volume collection compiled by university-affiliated academics. . . . Beam's book will have readers looking at volumes in the series from a whole new perspective owing to its witty handling of popular culture." Libr J

Includes bibliographical references (p. 223-228) and index

Fraser, Steve, 1945-

The **age** of acquiescence; the life and death of American resistance to organized wealth and power. Steve Fraser. Little, Brown & Co. 2015 480 p. (hardback) $28   **973.91**

1. Income 2. Power (Social sciences) 3. United States -- Social conditions 4. Acquiescence (Psychology) -- History 5. Social conflict -- United States -- History 6. Protest movements -- United States -- History 7. Social psychology -- United States -- History 8. Income distribution -- United States -- History 9. United States -- Politics and government -- 1945- 10. Elite (Social sciences) -- United States -- History 11. Power (Social sciences) -- United States -- History

ISBN 0316185434; 9780316185431

LC 2014020466

This book by Steve Fraser "examines the rise of American capitalism, the visionary attempts to protect the democratic commonwealth, and the great surrender to today's delusional fables of freedom and the politics of fear. Mass movements envisioned a new world supplanting dog-eat-dog capitalism. But over the last half-century that political will and cultural imagination have vanished. Why? [Fraser] seeks to solve that mystery." (Publisher's note)

"Though the implications for both present and future are bleak, few books feature such an ambitious premise or cover as much historical ground over such a complex era as skillfully as does Fraser's. Summing Up: Highly recommended. All levels/libraries."

Gardner, Mark Lee

Rough Riders; Theodore Roosevelt, his cowboy regiment, and the immortal charge up San Juan Hill. Mark Lee Gardner. William Morrow 2016 352 p. illustrations (hardcover) $26.99   **973.91**

1. Spanish-American War, 1898 -- Regimental histories 2. San Juan Hill, Battle of, Cuba, 1898 3. United States. Army. Volunteer Cavalry, 1st 4. Spanish-American War, 1898 -- Campaigns -- Cuba

ISBN 9780062312082; 9780062312099; 9780062466433

LC 2015046230

This narrative history book, by Mark Lee Gardner, profiles Theodore Roosevelt and his Rough Riders cavalry regiment. "In February 1898, Congress authorized President McKinley to recruit a volunteer army to drive the Spaniards from Cuba. From this army emerged the legendary 'Rough Riders,' a mounted regiment drawn from America's western territories and led by the indomitable Theodore Roosevelt."

(Publisher's note)

"Gardner provides some terrifying, exhilarating stories of the battle, including the valiant charge up San Juan Hill through enemy gunfire. Throughout, Gardner celebrates Roosevelt, who as a postwar commander-in-chief never forgot the lesson of war and the heroic sacrifices of the fighters." Pub Wkly

Giorgione, Michael

Inside Camp David; the private world of the presidential retreat. Michael Giorgione. Little, Brown & Co. 2017 320 p. (hc) $28   **973.91**
   1. Historic sites 2. Presidents -- United States -- Homes
   ISBN 9780316509619
                                              LC 2017936280
In this book "former Camp David commander Rear Admiral Michael Giorgione, CEC, USN (Ret.), takes us deep into this enigmatic and revered sanctuary. Combining fascinating first-person anecdotes of the presidents and their families with storied history and interviews with commanders both past and present, he reveals the intimate connection felt by the First Families with this historic retreat." (Publisher's note)

Goodwin, Doris Kearns, 1943-

★ The **Bully** Pulpit; Theodore Roosevelt, William Howard Taft, and the Golden Age of Journalism. Doris Kearns Goodwin. Simon & Schuster 2013 848 p. illustrations $40 **973.91**
   1. Journalism -- United States -- History 2. United States -- Politics and government -- 1901-1909 3. United States -- Politics and government -- 1909-1913 4. Republican Party (U.S.: 1854-) -- History -- 20th century 5. Press and politics -- United States -- History -- 20th century 6. Progressivism (United States politics) -- History -- 20th century
   ISBN 141654786X; 9781416547860
                                              LC 2013032709
LA Times Book Prize Finalist: History (2013)
Andrew Carnegie Medal for Excellence in Nonfiction (2014)
This book, by Doris Kearns Goodwin, examines "the friendship of two very different Presidents, [Theodore] Roosevelt and William Howard Taft. . . . Though the book is primarily concerned with the intervening private lives of two politicians, a prominent second narrative emerges as Goodwin links both presidents' fortunes to the rise of 'muckraking' journalism, specifically the magazine 'McClure's' and its influence over political and social discussion." (Publishers Weekly)

"By shining a light on a little-discussed President and a much-discussed one, Goodwin manages to make history very much alive and relevant." Pub Wkly

Includes bibliographical references (pages 753-867) and index

Lunde, Darrin

The **naturalist**; Theodore Roosevelt, a lifetime of exploration, and the triumph of American natural history. Darrin Lunde. Crown 2016 352 p. illustrations, map (hardback) $28 **973.91**
   1. Presidents -- United States -- Biography 2. Nature conservation -- United States -- History 3. Nature conservation -- United States 4. Natural history museums -- United States 5. Naturalists -- United States -- Biography 6. Conservationists -- United States -- Biography
   ISBN 9780307464309
                                              LC 2015036683
This book, by Darrin Lunde, is a "captivating new account of how Theodore Roosevelt's lifelong passion for the natural world set the stage for America's wildlife conservation movement and determined his legacy as a founding father of today's museum naturalism." (Publisher's note)

"Colloquially and anecdotally written, sometimes graphically detailing the pursuit and skinning of game, this book is accessible to the lay reader and authenticated for the historian." LJ

Includes bibliographical references and index.

Millard, Candice

The **river** of doubt; Theodore Roosevelt's darkest journey. Doubleday 2005 416p il map $26   **973.91**
   1. Governors 2. Presidents 3. Vice-presidents 4. Amazon River valley 5. Nobel laureates for peace 6. Roosevelt-Rondon Scientific Expedition (1913-1914)
   ISBN 0-385-50796-8
                                              LC 2005-46541
This is an account of the Amazon expedition Theodore Roosevelt undertook in 1912, with his son Kermit and the Brazilian explorer Col. Candido Rondon.

The author "turns this incredible story into one that easily matches an Indiana Jones screen adventure." Libr J

Includes bibliographical references

Pietrusza, David

1920: the year of the six presidents. Carroll & Graf 2007 533p il $28.95   **973.91**
   1. Presidents -- United States -- Election -- 1920
   ISBN 978-0-78671-622-7; 0-7867-1622-3
"Six men—a sitting president, former president, and four eventual presidents—competed in the 1920 presidential election. . . . [The author] contends that this election marked the birth of modern American politics. . . . The many issues and forces that swirled during that time, from the fear of Communists and Socialists and the terrorism they allegedly perpetrated to technological advances and Prohibition, make for a fascinating and compelling tale of an often-overlooked election in our history." Libr J

Includes bibliographical references

Smith, Hedrick

Who stole the American dream? Hedrick Smith. Random House 2012 xxxi, 557 p.p   **973.91**
   1. American dream 2. Middle class -- United States 3. United States -- Politics and government 4. Public interest -- United States 5. Divided government -- United States 6. Income distribution -- United States 7. Polarization (Social sciences) -- United States 8. United States -- Politics and government -- 1989- 9. Middle class -- Political activity -- United States 10. Middle class -- United States -- Economic conditions 11. United States -- Politics and government -- 1945-1989 12. Political culture -- United States -- History -- 20th century 13. Political culture -- United States -- History -- 21st century
   ISBN 1400069661; 9780679604648; 9781400069668
                                              LC 2012005865
This book, by Pulitzer Prize winner Hedrick Smith, offers an "account of how, over the past four decades, the American Dream has been dismantled. . . . Smith reveals how pivotal laws and policies were altered while the public wasn't looking, how Congress often ignores public opinion, why moderate politicians got shoved to the sidelines, and how Wall Street often wins politically by hiring over 1,400 former government officials as lobbyists." (Publisher's note)

Includes bibliographical references (p. [527]-538) and index

Terkel, Studs, 1912-2008

★ **Hard** times; an oral history of the great depression. Norton 2000 462p pa $14.95   **973.91**
   1. Great Depression, 1929-1939 2. United States -- Social

conditions 3. United States -- Economic conditions -- 1919-1933
4. United States -- Economic conditions -- 1933-1945
ISBN 1-56584-656-7

LC 2003-389318

A reissue of the title first published 1970 by Pantheon Bks.

"Persons of all ages, occupations, and classes scattered across the U.S. remember what they experienced or were told about the economic crisis of the 1930's. The result is a social document of immense interest." Booklist

973.917   Administration of Franklin Delano Roosevelt, 1933-1945

The **40s**; the story of a decade. The New Yorker; edited by Henry Finder with Giles Harvey; introduction by David Remnick. Random House Inc 2014 720 p. illustrations (acid-free paper) $30   **973.917**
1. Nineteen forties 2. New York (N.Y.) -- Intellectual life 3. United States -- In literature 4. New Yorker (New York, N.Y.: 1925) 5. United States -- History -- 1933-1945 6. United States -- History -- 1945-1953 7. United States -- Social customs -- 1945- 8. United States -- Social customs -- 1933-1945 9. United States -- Social life and customs -- 20th century
ISBN 0679644792; 9780679644798; 9780679644804

LC 2013047082

"The 1940s were when 'The New Yorker' came of age. A magazine that was best known for its humor and wry social observation would extend itself, offering the first in-depth reporting from Hiroshima and introducing American readers to the fiction of Vladimir Nabokov and the poetry of Elizabeth Bishop. In this . . . book, . . . contributions from the . . . writers who graced [the magazine's] pages throughout the decade are placed in history by the magazine's current writers." (Publisher's note)

"Readers are certain to enjoy the beautiful writing, clever thinking and insightful thoughts across a vast range of topics." Kirkus

Cook, Blanche Wiesen

Eleanor Roosevelt. v1 Penguin Bks. 1993 587p v1 il pa $18   **973.917**
1. Diplomats 2. Columnists 3. Humanitarians 4. Social activists 5. Spouses of presidents 6. United Nations officials 7. Presidents' spouses -- United States
ISBN 0-14-009460-1

LC 87040632

First published 1992

This first volume of a two-volume biography of Eleanor Roosevelt "spans the years from Eleanor's birth to her husband Franklin Delano's inauguration." Publisher's note

Includes bibliographical references

Fullilove, Michael

Rendezvous with destiny; how Franklin D. Roosevelt and five extraordinary men took America into the war and into the world. Michael Fullilove. The Penguin Press 2013 480 p. (hardcover) $29.95   **973.917**
1. World War, 1939-1945 -- United States 2. World War, 1939-1945 -- Diplomatic history 3. United States -- Foreign relations -- 1933-1945
ISBN 1594204357; 9781594204357

LC 2012047003

This book by Michael Fullilove looks at the lead-up to the U.S. entry in to World War II. President Franklin D. Roosevelt "had to jump some big hurdles: he had to convince his fellow Americans of the necessity of getting involved, and he had to support Britain's efforts to keep Hitler from overwhelming the U.K.'s skies and shores. In 1940, Roosevelt enlisted five capable men to cross the Atlantic to visit, negotiate, observe the war-weary British, and assess how the U.S. could help." (Publishers Weekly)

Includes bibliographical references and index

Golay, Michael

★ **America** 1933; the Great Depression, Lorena Hickok, Eleanor Roosevelt, and the shaping of the New Deal. by Michael Golay. Free Press 2013 336 p. $26.99   **973.917**
1. Great Depression, 1929-1939 2. United States -- History -- 1919-1933 3. Depressions -- 1929 -- United States 4. United States -- History -- 1933-1945 5. United States -- Social conditions -- 1918-1945 6. United States -- Economic conditions -- 1918-1945 7. Investigative reporting -- United States -- History -- 20th century
ISBN 143919601X; 9781439196014

LC 2012041139

In this book, author Michael Golay "writes of the 1933-34 cross-country trip undertaken by Lorena Hickok to evaluate and report to the new Federal Emergency Relief Administration (FERA) on how the Great Depression was impacting ordinary families. . . . She had been an Associated Press reporter; her friendship with Eleanor Roosevelt (ER) helped her to create FERA reports that captured President Roosevelt's attention. Golay focuses here on the grinding poverty that Hickok witnessed." (Library Journal)

Includes bibliographical references and index

Jordan, Jonathan W.

American warlords; how Roosevelt's high command led America to victory in World War II. Jonathan W. Jordan. NAL Caliber 2015 624 p. illustrations $28.95   **973.917**
1. Generals 2. World War, 1939-1945 -- Campaigns 3. World War, 1939-1942 -- United States 4. Generals -- United States -- Biography 5. Presidents -- United States -- Biography 6. Command of troops -- History -- 20th century 7. United States -- Politics and government -- 1933-1945
ISBN 0451414578; 9780451414571

LC 2014036427

This book by Jonathan W. Jordan "explores the relationship between Franklin D. Roosevelt and his top military advisers, extending the analysis to the Asian and South Pacific dimension of World War II. Focusing on the leadership tension of the era, the author proves how Roosevelt was often pitted against his Secretary of War Henry Stimson, Army Chief of Staff George C. Marshall, and Chief of Naval Operations Ernest J. King." (Library Journal)

"Jordan's wonderful new insight into the leaders shows how lucky we were regarding Stimson's prescient warnings about nuclear war, Marshall's long-suffering, self-effacing loyalty, and King's rough-and-ready fighting abilities. In addition to World War II buffs, other readers will enjoy the intrigue, back-stabbing, action, and diplomacy in this well-written book." Kirkus

Includes bibliographical references and index

Simon, James F.

FDR and Chief Justice Hughes; the president, the Supreme Court, and the epic battle over the New Deal. James F. Simon. Simon & Schuster 2012 461 p. ill. $28   **973.917**
1. New Deal, 1933-1939 2. Presidents -- United States 3. United States -- Foreign relations 4. United States. Supreme Court -- Biography 5. United States -- Politics and government -- 1933-1945 6. Executive power -- United States -- History -- 20th century

7. Political questions and judicial power -- United States -- History -- 20th century

ISBN 9781416573289; 9781416573296; 9781416578895

LC 2011028825

Author James F. Simon focuses on "the struggle between FDR and Chief Justice Charles Evans Hughes that decided the fate of the New Deal. . . . In 1936, FDR was reelected by a landslide and the exasperated president proposed legislation to relieve, he said, the overburdened and elderly justices of their heavy workload. He proposed the appointment of an additional justice for each sitting member over seventy years old. . . . The proposal would have permitted the president to stack the Court with justices favorable to the New." (Publisher's note)

Includes bibliographical references and index.

973.918 Administration of Harry S Truman, 1945-1953

Baime, A. J.

The **accidental** president; Harry S. Truman and the four months that changed the world. by A. J. Baime. Houghton Mifflin Harcourt 2017 xvi, 431 p.p illustrations (hardcover) $30 **973.918**

1. Presidents -- United States 2. United States -- Politics and government -- 1945- 3. World War, 1939-1945 4. Presidents -- United States -- Biography 5. United States -- Politics and government -- 1945-1953

ISBN 9780544617346; 9780544618480; 0544617347

LC 2017044086

This book, by A. J. Baime, presents the "story of Harry Truman's first four months in office, when this unlikely president had to take on Germany, Japan, Stalin, and the atomic bomb, with the fate of the world hanging in the balance. . . . Chosen as FDR's fourth term Vice President, . . .Harry S. Truman--a Midwesterner who had no college degree . . . --was the prototypical ordinary man. That is, until he was shockingly thrust in over his head." (Publisher's note)

Includes bibliographical references and index.

Brands, H. W.

★ The **General** Vs. the President; MacArthur and Truman at the Brink of Nuclear War. by H.W. Brands. Random House Inc 2016 448 p. illustrations, maps (ebook) $65; $30 **973.918**

1. Nuclear weapons -- United States -- History 2. United States -- Politics and government -- 1945-

ISBN 9780385540582; 0385540574; 9780385540575

LC 2016021412

This book, by H.W. Brands, presents the "story of how President Harry Truman and General Douglas MacArthur squared off to decide America's future in the aftermath of World War II. . . . In the nuclear era, when the Soviets, too, had the bomb, the specter of a catastrophic third World War lurked menacingly close on the horizon." (Publisher's note)

"An exciting, well-written comparison study of two American leaders at loggerheads during the Korean War crisis." Kirkus

Includes bibliographical references and index.

Weisbrode, Kenneth

The **Year** of Indecision, 1946; A Tour Through the Crucible of Harry Truman's America. by Kenneth Weisbrode. Penguin Group USA 2016 320 p. $28 **973.918**

1. Nineteen forties 2. United States -- History -- 20th century

ISBN 0670016845; 9780670016846

This book, by Kenneth Weisbrode, is an "account of America at the pivot point of the postwar era, Harry Truman's first full year in office. .

. . Relations broke down with the Soviet Union, and nearly did with the British. The United States suffered shortages and strikes of a magnitude it had not seen in years. In November 1946, the Democrats lost both houses of Congress. The tension between fear and optimism expressed itself too in popular culture." (Publisher's note)

"A solid, fact-filled study, especially relevant for those who thought life was better then." Kirkus

Includes bibliographical references (pages [267]-285) and index.

973.92 United States--1953-2001

Duffy, Michael

★ The **presidents** club; inside the world's most exclusive fraternity. Nancy Gibbs and Michael Duffy. Simon & Schuster 2012 vii, 641 p.p **973.92**

1. Interpersonal relations 2. Presidents -- United States 3. United States -- Politics and government -- 1945- 4. Presidents -- United States -- History 5. Ex-presidents -- United States -- History

ISBN 1439127700; 9781439127704

LC 2011042047

This book "chart[s] the zigzag arc of relationships among the men who have occupied the White House since the mid 20th century. . . . [T]he authors present numerous instances of presidents warming to their predecessors. . . . Sometimes mutual admiration was already in place (Truman and Eisenhower--though it later disintegrated); sometimes, antipathy (Clinton and Bush II). But almost always the sitting presidents found in their predecessors some solace, willing ears and sound advice." (Kirkus)

Includes bibliographical references.

Freeman, Joshua B., 1949-

American empire, 1945-2000; the rise of a global power, the democratic revolution at home. Joshua Freeman. Viking 2012 512 p. **973.92**

1. United States -- History -- 1945- 2. United States -- Foreign relations 3. United States -- Politics and government -- 1945- 4. United States -- Economic conditions -- 20th century 5. United States -- Foreign relations -- 1989- 6. United States -- Economic conditions -- 1945- 7. United States -- Foreign relations -- 1945-1989 8. United States -- Politics and government -- 1989- 9. United States -- Politics and government -- 1945-1989

ISBN 0670023787; 9780670023783

LC 2011049263

In this book, author Joshua B. Freeman examines a postwar dominant America . . . . Covering the glory years of 1945-2000, Freeman . . . turns his critical eye on America's turbulent internal affairs, delving into Truman's contested Fair Deal reforms, the McCarthy communist witch-hunts, Eisenhower's cautious civil rights record, LBJ's ambitious Great Society programs, Nixon's Watergate disgrace, the return of 'corporate capitalism' and Reagan conservatism. Freeman deals with the Clinton administration's economic policies . . . followed by the Republican victory in 2000. Though at its peak, America's power exceeded that of the Roman and British empires in cultural, economic, military, and political terms, the nation's postwar dreams were never completely fulfilled, says Freeman." (Publishers Weekly)

Includes bibliographical references and index

Frum, David

How we got here; the 70's: the decade that brought you modern life (for better or worse) Basic Bks. 2000 xxiv, 418p il hardcover o.p. pa $18.95 **973.92**

1. United States -- Civilization -- 1970-
ISBN 0-465-01496-5 pa

The author "aims 'to describe—and to judge' the transformation of American values during the '70s. Surveying politics, legal cases and opinion polls as well as popular culture, he links what he sees as America's loss of faith in government, the rise of 'sourness and cynicism' and the culture of licentiousness and divorce, among other social changes, to events in that decade." Publ Wkly

Includes bibliographical references

Halberstam, David

The **fifties**. Villard Bks. 1993 800p il hardcover o.p. pa
$17.95 **973.92**

1. Popular culture -- United States 2. United States -- Social life and customs 3. United States -- Politics and government -- 20th century
ISBN 0-449-90933-6 pa

LC 92-56815

This is a social history of the United States during the 1950s

The author's "sources are secondary and derivative, but his instinct for the revealing anecdote, his ear for the memorable quote, and his awesome powers of organization add up to a variegated overview that moves seamlessly between the serious shenanigans of Chief Justice Earl Warren and the frivolous ones of . . . Grace Metalious." Natl Rev

Includes bibliographical references

Hayden, Tom

The **long** sixties; from 1960 to Barack Obama. Paradigm Publishers 2009 272p $26.95 **973.92**

1. Lawyers 2. Presidents 3. Social change 4. Social movements 5. Senators 6. State legislators 7. Nobel laureates for peace 8. United States -- Social conditions 9. United States -- History -- 1961-1974
ISBN 978-1-59451-739-6; 1-59451-739-8

"With elements of a new Rules for Radicals and knowing takes on such old New Left moments as The Port Huron Statement, Hayden's book could be a worthy foundational document." Kirkus

Includes bibliographical references

King, Martin Luther, Jr., 1929-1968

The **trumpet** of conscience; [by] Martin Luther King, Jr. Beacon Press 2010 80p (King legacy series) $22; pa $12 **973.92**

1. United States -- Social conditions
ISBN 978-0-8070-0071-7; 0-8070-0071-X; 978-0-8070-0170-7 pa; 0-8070-0170-8 pa

LC 2010007881

First published 1968 by Harper & Row

"In November and December 1967, Dr. Martin Luther King, Jr., delivered five lectures for the renowned Massey Lecture Series of the Canadian Broadcasting Corporation. The collection was immediately released as a book under the title Conscience for Change, but after King's assassination in 1968, it was republished as The Trumpet of Conscience. The collection . . . is his final testament on racism, poverty, and war. Each oration in this volume encompasses a distinct theme, . . . addressing issues of equality, conscience and war, the mobilization of young people, and nonviolence." Publisher's note

Kuralt, Charles

Charles Kuralt's America. Anchor Books 1996 279p il pa $14.95 **973.92**

1. United States -- Description and travel 2. United States -- Social life and customs

ISBN 0-385-48510-7; 978-0-385-48510-4

LC 96-18992

First published 1995 by Putnam

"Kuralt is not in search of crises or epiphanies; he values nature and good food, neighborliness and craftsmanship, quaintness and quirkiness. Though no literary match for American chroniclers like Calvin Trillin, the effable Kuralt does, in un-fancy style, convey his enthusiasm and his engagement." Publ Wkly

On the road with Charles Kuralt. Fawcett 1986 363p il pa $19 **973.92**

1. United States -- Description and travel 2. United States -- Social life and customs
ISBN 0-449-00740-5; 978-0-449-00740-2

First published 1985 by Putnam

"As a CBS reporter specializing in 'soft' news, Kuralt has been roaming around the U.S. since 1967 in search of 'just plain folks.' Some 100 of the television interviews that resulted from that search have been transcribed for this collection. Loosely organized by themes emphasizing the individuality, altruism, and humor that characterize small town and rural Americans, the interviews and anecdotes are consistently entertaining." Booklist

Patterson, James T.

Grand expectations; the United States, 1945-1974. James T. Patterson. Oxford Univ. Press 1996 xviii, 829p ill., maps (pbk.) $27.95; o.p. **973.92**

1. United States -- History -- 1945- 2. United States -- Economic conditions 3. United States -- Politics and government -- 1945-
ISBN 9780195117974; 019507680X

LC 9513878

Bancroft Prize (1996)

In this book, author "James T. Patterson['s] . . . work . . . weaves [together] the major political, cultural, and economic events of . . . America from 1945 through Watergate. . . . [The book explores events from] the bloody campaigns in Korea and . . . McCarthyism to the assassinations of the Kennedys and Martin Luther King, to the Vietnam War, Watergate, and Nixon's resignation. Patterson . . . portray[s] the . . . [economic] growth after World War II . . . as well as the resultant buoyancy of spirit reflected in everything from streamlined toasters, to big, flashy cars, to the soaring, butterfly roof of TWA's airline terminal in New York. . . . [A]n important thread running through the book is a . . . depiction of the civil rights movement--from the electrifying Brown v. Board of Education decision, to the violent confrontations in Little Rock, Birmingham, and Selma, to the landmark civil rights acts of 1964 and 1965." (Publisher's note)

Includes bibliographical references (p. 791-802) and index.

Pietrusza, David

1960: LBJ vs. JFK vs. Nixon; the epic campaign that forged three presidencies. Union Square Press 2008 xx, 523p il $24.95 **973.92**

1. Presidents 2. Vice-presidents 3. Senators 4. Nonfiction writers 5. Members of Congress 6. Presidents -- United States -- Election -- 1960
ISBN 978-1-402-76114-0

LC 2009-291219

"The 1960 presidential campaign season was dominated by the personalities of three men, each of whom became president. . . . Pietrusza chronicles their roles and character in a stirring, hard-edged political saga." Booklist

Includes bibliographical references

Postwar America; an encyclopedia of social, political, cultural, and economic history. James Ciment, editor. M.E. Sharpe 2006 4v il set $399 **973.92**
1. Reference books 2. United States -- Civilization -- Encyclopedias
ISBN 0-7656-8067-X; 978-0-7656-8067-9

LC 2004-13120

"A-Z entries address specific persons, groups, concepts, events, geographical locations, organizations, and cultural and technological phenomena. Sidebars highlight primary source materials, items of special interest, statistical data, and other information; and Cultural Landmark entries chronologically detail the music, literature, arts, and cultural history of the era. Bibliographies covering literature from the postwar era and about the era are also included, as well as illustrations and specialized indexes." Publisher's note

Includes bibliographical references

Shelley, Fred M.
Atlas of American politics, 1960-2000; [by] Fred M. Shelley [et al.] CQ Press 2002 242p maps $156.25 **973.92**
1. United States -- Politics and government -- Maps
ISBN 1-56802-665-X

LC 2001-18267

This work "examines U.S. government and politics at the congressional district, state, and national levels from a combined historical, geographical, and political perspective. More than 200 maps from a variety of government and private sources show the relationship between the nation's geography and its political life.... This book provides a unique look at U.S. politics during the last 40 years and will be useful to students and researchers from the high-school level up." Booklist

Includes bibliographical references

Thomas, Evan
★ **Ike's** bluff; president Eisenhower's secret battle to save the world. Evan Thomas. Little, Brown and Co. 2012 496 p. $29.99 **973.92**
1. Generals 2. Presidents -- United States 3. Cold war -- Diplomatic history 4. United States -- Foreign relations -- 1953-1961 5. National security -- United States -- History -- 20th century 6. Nuclear warfare -- Government policy -- United States -- History -- 20th century 7. Nuclear weapons -- Government policy -- United States -- History -- 20th century
ISBN 0316091049; 9780316091046; 9780316224161

LC 2012019640

In this book about U.S. President Dwight Eisenhower, Evan Thomas makes a "case for the way that Eisenhower, the World War II Allied forces' supreme commander and one of the greatest shoo-ins in American electoral history, brought his military instincts from the battlefield to the White House . . . Eisenhower's combination of courage, petulance and cunning are hard qualities to reconcile." (New York Times)

Includes bibliographical references and index.

Von Tunzelmann, Alex
Blood and Sand; Suez, Hungary, and Eisenhower's Campaign for Peace. by Alex von Tunzelmann. HarperCollins 2016 560 p. illustrations, maps $32.50 **973.92**
1. Cold war 2. World politics 3. Hungary -- History -- 1956, Revolution
ISBN 006224924X; 9780062249241

This book by Alex von Tunzelmann "tells the story of both the Suez Crisis and the Hungarian Revolution of 1956—a tale of conspiracy and revolutions, spies and terrorists, kidnappings and assassination plots, the fall of the British Empire and the rise of American hegemony under the

heroic leadership of President Dwight D. Eisenhower—which shaped the Middle East and Europe we know today." (Publisher's note)

"This is an outstanding reexamination of these sad, history-altering events." Booklist

Includes bibliographical references (pages 503-509) and index.

Whipple, Chris
The **gatekeepers**; how the White House chiefs of staff define every presidency. Chris Whipple. Crown 2017 365 p. illustrations (some color) (hardback) $28 **973.92**
1. Presidents -- United States -- Staff 2. United States -- Officials and employees 3. United States -- Politics and government 4. United States. White House Office -- Officials and employees
ISBN 9780804138246; 9780804138260; 9780804138253

LC 2016046233

This book, by Chris Whipple, presents "the first in-depth, behind-the-scenes look at the White House Chiefs of Staff, whose actions--and inactions--have defined the course of our country. . . . [Whipple shows] us how James Baker's expert managing of the White House, the press, and Capitol Hill paved the way for the Reagan Revolution--and, conversely, how Watergate, the Iraq War, and even the bungled Obamacare rollout might have been prevented by a more effective chief." (Publisher's note)

"In this page-turner of a history, readers will discover new facets of historical events that they felt they already knew." Pub Wkly

Includes bibliographical references (pages 301-342) and index.

Woodward, Bob
Shadow; five presidents and the legacy of Watergate. Simon & Schuster 1999 592p il hardcover o.p. pa $16 **973.92**
1. Actors 2. Diplomats 3. Governors 4. Presidents 5. Vice-presidents 6. Watergate Affair, 1972-1974 7. Senators 8. Nonfiction writers 9. Members of Congress 10. Parents of presidents 11. United Nations officials 12. Nobel laureates for peace 13. Presidents -- United States 14. United States -- Politics and government -- 1989- 15. United States -- Politics and government -- 1974-1989
ISBN 0-684-85263-2 pa

LC 99-37045

Woodward examines the long-term effect of the Watergate Affair on the presidencies of Gerald Ford, Jimmy Carter, Ronald Reagan, George Bush, and Bill Clinton

The author is an "effective investigative journalist. These skills are on full display in Shadow.... {The book} is most interesting as a reconstruction of the many scandals that have troubled the Clinton Administration." Nation

Includes bibliographical references

973.921 Administration of Dwight David Eisenhower, 1953-1961

Branch, Taylor
★ **Parting** the waters: America in the King years, 1954-63. Simon & Schuster 1988 1064p il hardcover o.p. pa $22 **973.921**
1. Clergy 2. Nonfiction writers 3. Civil rights activists 4. Nobel laureates for peace 5. African Americans -- Civil rights 6. United States -- History -- 1953-1961
ISBN 0-671-46097-8; 0-671-68742-5 pa

LC 88-24033

This history of the American civil rights movement from 1954 to

1963 focuses on the life of Dr. Martin Luther King.

The author "has searched out the hidden reality and often tragic human drama of the King years. On his best pages, the past, miraculously, seems to spring back to life. King himself appears human, all too human. Yet when the reader is done, his remarkable virtues and ordinary vices seem of a piece, the component parts of a coherent, towering personality." Newsweek

Includes bibliographical references

Gellman, Irwin F.

The **President** and the Apprentice; Eisenhower and Nixon, 1952-1961. Yale University Press 2015 816 p. 16 plates; illustrations $40   **973.921**

1. Nixon, Richard M. (Richard Milhous), 1913-1994
ISBN 0300181051; 9780300181050

LC 2015935011

This book by Irwin F. Gellman "reveals a different [Dwight] Eisenhower, and a different [Richard] Nixon. Ike trusted and relied on Nixon, sending him on many sensitive overseas missions. Based on twenty years of research in numerous archives, many previously untouched, this book offers a fresh and surprising account of the Eisenhower presidency." (Publisher's note)

"Although he doesn't discount Nixon's character flaws, Gellman asserts that Eisenhower respected Nixon and valued his views on a variety of issues. This is hardly the final word on their relationship, but Gellman has certainly made a worthy effort at reappraisal." Booklist

Hitchcock, William I.

The **age** of Eisenhower; America and the world in the 1950s. William I. Hitchcock. Simon & Schuster 2018 xx, 650 p.p illustrations (hardcover) $35   **973.921**

1. United States -- Politics and government -- 1953-1961 2. United States -- Foreign relations -- 1953-1961
ISBN 9781439175668; 9781451698435; 1439175667

LC 2017026867

This book, by William I. Hitchcock, "is the definitive account of . . . [Dwight D. Eisenhower's] presidency, drawing extensively on declassified material from the Eisenhower Library, the CIA and Defense Department, and troves of unpublished documents. . . . Hitchcock shows how Ike shaped modern America, and he astutely assesses Eisenhower's close confidants, from Attorney General Brownell to Secretary of State Dulles." (Publisher's note)

Includes bibliographical references and index

Nichols, David A.

Ike and McCarthy; Dwight Eisenhower's secret campaign against Joseph McCarthy. David A. Nichols. Simon & Schuster 2017 400 p. $27.95   **973.921**

1. United States -- Politics and government -- 1953-1961 2. Anti-communist movements -- United States -- History -- 20th century 3. Presidents -- United States -- Biography 4. Cold War -- Social aspects -- United States
ISBN 1451686609; 9781451686609

LC 2016037570

This book, by David A. Nichols, reveals "how President Dwight Eisenhower masterminded the downfall of the anti-Communist demagogue Senator Joseph McCarthy. . . . [in] 1954, McCarthy was arguably the most powerful member of the Senate. By the end of that year, he had been censured by his colleagues for unbecoming conduct. Eisenhower's covert operation had discredited the senator . . . , exploiting the controversy that resulted from the televised Army-McCarthy hearings." (Publisher's note)

"A thorough, well-written, and surprising picture of a man who was

much more than a 'do-nothing' president." Kirkus

Includes bibliographical references and index

Simon, James F.

Eisenhower vs. Warren; the battle for civil rights and liberties. James F. Simon. Liveright Publishing Corporation 2018 xvii, 427 p.p illustrations (hardcover) $35   **973.921**

1. Civil rights 2. United States -- Politics and government -- 1953-1961 3. African Americans -- Civil rights -- History -- 20th century 4. School integration -- United States -- History -- 20th century 5. Civil rights movements -- United States -- History -- 20th century
ISBN 9780871407559; 9780871407665; 0871407558

In this book, "author James F. Simon examines the years of strife between . . . [President Dwight D. Eisenhower and Chief Justice Earl Warren] that led Eisenhower to say that his biggest mistake as president was appointing that 'dumb son of a bitch Earl Warren.' This momentous, poisonous relationship is presented here at last in one volume. . . . [The book] brings to vivid life the clash that continues to reverberate in political and constitutional debates today." (Publisher's note)

"This is a cogently written book, especially given the complexity of many of the issues. Simon does great justice to an important segment of a critical period in American history." Booklist

Includes bibliographical references and index.

Smith, Jean Edward

Eisenhower; in war and peace. by Jean Edward Smith. Random House 2012 950 p. (hbk: alk. paper) $40.00 **973.921**

1. Biography 2. Presidents -- United States -- Biography 3. Generals 4. Presidents 5. College presidents 6. Presidents -- United States 7. United States. Army -- Biography 8. United States -- Politics and government -- 1953-1961
ISBN 9781400066933; 140006693X; 9780679644293

LC 2011008605

This book presents a biography of former U.S. President Dwight D. Eisenhower. Jean Edward Smith "provides . . . insight into Ike's . . . apprenticeship under Douglas MacArthur in Washington and the Philippines. Then the whole panorama of World War II unfolds, with Eisenhower's . . . generalship forging the Allied path to victory. . . . Domestically, Eisenhower reduced defense spending, balanced the budget, constructed the interstate highway system, and provided social security coverage for millions who were self-employed." (Publisher's note)

Includes bibliographical references

973.922   Administration of John Fitzgerald Kennedy, 1961-1963

Branch, Taylor, 1947-

★ **Pillar** of fire; America in the King years, 1963-65. Simon & Schuster 1998 746p il hardcover o.p.   **973.922**

1. Clergy 2. Nonfiction writers 3. Civil rights activists 4. Nobel laureates for peace 5. African Americans -- Civil rights 6. United States -- History -- 1961-1969 7. United States -- History -- 1961-1974 8. Afro-Americans -- Civil rights -- History -- 20th century
ISBN 0-684-84809-0 pa

LC 97-46076

"Branch began telling the story of the civil rights movement in his . . . Parting the Waters: America in the King Years, 1954-63. Here he picks up where he left off, narrating the history of the years 1963-65, when the movement won . . . the Civil Rights Act of 1964 and the Voting Rights Act of 1965." (Commonweal) Bibliography. Index.

"Branch's research is impeccable and his knowledge of his material solid. . . . The book is significant for marshaling so much information, particularly the profiles of all the many individuals involved in the race issues of that time." Booklist

Includes bibliographical references

Brinkley, Douglas

JFK; A Vision for America. edited by Stephen Kennedy Smith and Douglas Brinkley. HarperCollins 2017 493 p. illustrations (some color) (hardcover) $45   **973.922**

    1. Presidents of the United States 2. United States -- History -- 1961-1969 3. United States -- Politics & government -- 1953-1961 4. United States -- Politics & government -- 1961-1963

    ISBN 9780062668844; 0062668846

This book "is the definitive compendium of JFK's most important and brilliant speeches, accompanied by commentary and reflections by leading American and international figures—including Senator Elizabeth Warren, David McCullough, Kofi Annan, and the Dalai Lama—and edited by JFK's nephew Stephen Kennedy Smith and renowned historian Douglas Brinkley." (Publisher's note)

"Amid the stream of JFK books to be released for the centennial, this work should emerge as one of the most complete and useful." Kirkus

Bugliosi, Vincent

Reclaiming history; the assassination of President John F. Kennedy. W.W. Norton & Co. 2007 xlv, 1612p il $49.95   **973.922**

    1. Presidents 2. Conspiracies 3. Senators 4. Murderers 5. Members of Congress

    ISBN 978-0-393-04525-3; 0-393-04525-0

                                           LC 2007-01545

The author argues that Lee Harvey Oswald was the lone assassin of John F. Kennedy.

"Destined to be the most significant challenge (save the Warren Report) to conspiracy theories, Bugliosi's study will provoke controversy and debate." Booklist

Includes bibliographical references

Cohen, Andrew

Two days in June; John F. Kennedy and the 48 hours that changed history. Andrew Cohen. McClelland & Stewart 2014 416 p. (hardcover: alk. paper) $29.95   **973.922**

    ISBN 0771023871; 9780771023873; 9780771023880

                                           LC 2014944155

This book, by Andrew Cohen, focuses on how "on two consecutive days in June 1963, in two lyrical speeches, John F. Kennedy . . . [addressed] the two greatest issues of his time: nuclear arms and civil rights. . . . His speech on June 10 leads to the Limited Nuclear Test Ban Treaty of 1963; his speech on June 11 to the Civil Rights Act of 1964." (Publisher's note)

"This book is a page-turner. Undoubtedly, Kennedy supporters will love it. More important, it serves as a first-rate introduction to why the president made such a significant impression on the nation and the world despite his brief tenure." LJ

Coleman, David G.

The **fourteenth** day; JFK and the aftermath of the Cuban Missile Crisis. David G. Coleman. 1st ed. W.W. Norton & Co. 2012 192 p. (hardcover) $25.95   **973.922**

    1. Cuban Missile Crisis, 1962 2. United States -- History -- 1961-1974 3. United States -- Foreign relations -- Soviet Union 4. Cuban Missile Crisis, 1962 -- Influence 5. United States -- Foreign relations -- 1961-1963 6. Soviet Union -- Foreign relations -- United States

7. United States -- Politics and government -- 1961-1963

    ISBN 0393084418; 9780393084412

                                           LC 2012025397

In this book on the aftermath of the 1962 Cuban Missile Crisis, "[David G.] Coleman . . . reveals that the possibility of a U.S.-USSR war did not end . . . when . . . [John F.] Kennedy lifted the naval blockade. The author draws on Kennedy's 260 hours of secret White House tapes and presidential and foreign relations records to offer a narrative covering from October 29, 1962, through February 1963, when tensions subsided and relations between the two superpowers began to improve." (Library Journal)

Includes bibliographical references and index.

Dobbs, Michael

★ **One** minute to midnight; Kennedy, Khrushchev, and Castro on the brink of nuclear war. Alfred A. Knopf 2008 426p $28.95   **973.922**

    1. Cuban Missile Crisis, 1962

    ISBN 978-1-4000-4358-3; 1-4000-4358-1

                                           LC 2007-52250

The author discusses the Cuban Missile Crisis of 1962.

This book "is filled with . . . insights that will change the views of experts and help inform a new generation of readers." N Y Times Book Rev

Includes bibliographical references

Halberstam, David

The **best** and the brightest; foreword by John McCain. Modern Library ed; Modern Lib. 2001 xxviii, 780p $24.95; pa $16,95   **973.922**

    1. Authors 2. Generals 3. Diplomats 4. Educators 5. Statesmen 6. Presidents 7. Vice-presidents 8. Bankers 9. Senators 10. Army officers 11. College teachers 12. Nonfiction writers 13. Members of Congress 14. Foundation officials 15. Government officials 16. Political scientists 17. Secretaries of state 18. Presidential advisers 19. Secretaries of defense 20. Nobel laureates for peace 21. International organization officials 22. United States -- Foreign relations -- Vietnam 23. Vietnam -- Foreign relations -- United States 24. United States -- Politics and government -- 1961-1974

    ISBN 0-679-64099-1; 0-449-90870-4 pa

                                           LC 2001-31261

A reissue of the title first published 1972

"The author describes analytically rather than narratively, how the Kennedy-Johnson intellectual (McNamara, Bundy, Rusk, Ball, Taylor, et al.) men praised as 'the best and the brightest' men of this century, became the architects of the disastrous American policy of Indochina." Libr J

Includes bibliographical references

Hill, Clint

Five days in November; Clint Hill and Lisa McCubbin. Gallery Books 2013 256 p. (hardback) $30   **973.922**

    1. Kennedy, John F. (John Fitzgerald), 1917-1963 -- Assassination 2. United States. Secret Service -- Officials and employees -- Biography

    ISBN 1476731497; 9781476731490; 9781476731506

                                           LC 2013019272

Author Clint Hill presents a book of photographs pertaining to the day that President John F. Kennedy was assassinated. Through the pictures, "we witness three-year-old John Kennedy Jr.'s pleas to come to Texas with his parents and the rapturous crowds of mixed ages and races that greeted the Kennedys at every stop in Texas. We stand beside a shaken Lyndon Johnson as he is hurriedly sworn in as the new president.

We experience the first lady's steely courage when she insists on walking through the streets of Washington, D.C., in her husband's funeral procession." (Publisher's note)

Mrs. Kennedy and me; Clint Hill; with Lisa McCubbin. Gallery Books 2012 viii, 343 p.p **973.922**
1. Bodyguards -- Biography 2. Secret service -- United States 3. Presidents' spouses -- United States 4. Presidents -- United States -- Assassination 5. Presidents' spouses -- Protection -- United States 6. United States. Secret Service -- Officials and employees -- Biography
ISBN 1451648448; 9781451648447; 9781451648461
LC 2011051017
This book is a "memoir of guarding First Lady Jacqueline Kennedy through the young and sparkling years of the Kennedy presidency and the dark days following the assassination. Secret Service Special Agent [Clint] Hill . . . first met a young and pregnant soon-to-be First Lady in November 1960. For the next four years Hill would seldom leave her side. Theirs would be an odd relationship of always-proper formality combined with deep intimacy crafted through close proximity and mutual trust and respect. . . . When the bullet ripped into the president's brain with Hill not five feet away, he remained with her, through the public and private mourning. . . . Soon after, both would go on with their lives, but Hill would . . . never stop feeling he could have done more to save the president." (Kirkus)

Kennedy, Caroline, 1957-
Jacqueline Kennedy; foreword by Caroline Kennedy; introduction and annotations by Michael Beschloss. Hyperion 2011 xxxii, 368 p.p 8 sound discs **973.922**
1. Interviews 2. Presidents' spouses -- United States 3. United States -- History -- 1953-1961 4. Presidents -- United States -- Biography 5. Presidents' spouses -- Interviews 6. United States -- Politics and government -- 1961-1963
ISBN 9781401324254; 1401324258
LC 2012372265
This book, accompanied by a set of 8 compact discs (CDs), presents "seven historic interviews" by U.S. First Lady Jacqueline Kennedy "about her life with John F. Kennedy" (JFK). Recorded in 1964, "shortly after President . . . Kennedy's assassination," the interviews discuss JFK's political career and his views on various subjects, "including his thoughts and feelings about his brothers Robert and Ted, and his take on world leaders past and present." (Publisher's note) Other topics include JFK's reading habits, U.S. relations with Cuba, and Kennedy's relationship with her husband.
Includes bibliographical references and index.

Kennedy, Robert F., 1925-1968
Make gentle the life of this world; the vision of Robert F. Kennedy. edited and with an introduction by Maxwell Taylor Kennedy. Broadway Books 1999 188p il pa $15 **973.922**
1. Quotations
ISBN 0-7679-0371-4
LC 98-55988
First published 1998 by Harcourt Brace & Co.
This is a collection of quotations by Robert F. Kennedy and the authors who inspired him
"Chapters are arranged by issues that were most important to Kennedy and remain timely today—the responsibilities of citizens to their government, the tragedy of poverty in the midst of plenty, the importance of dissent in a democratic society, and work as the solution for the welfare crises. The book's haunting photos convey Kennedy's spirit as successfully as the words." Libr J

Includes bibliographical references

Leaming, Barbara
Mrs. Kennedy; the missing history of the Kennedy years. Free Press 2001 406p il $25; pa $14 **973.922**
1. Editors 2. Socialites 3. Spouses of presidents
ISBN 0-684-86209-3; 0-7432-2749-2 pa
LC 2001-40442
"Asserting that Jacqueline Kennedy's role in shaping her husband's presidency has been under-examined, Leaming . . . offers a corrective in this intimate look at a very private woman. Initially inclined to keep herself as much in the background as possible, says Leaming, Jacqueline Kennedy became an increasingly visible and vocal first lady as she realized how effective she could be as an image maker. It's in this capacity that Leaming convincingly depicts her as being instrumental in shaping the course of her husband's administration." Publ Wkly
Includes bibliographical references

Matthews, Chris
Kennedy & Nixon; the rivalry that shaped postwar America. {by} Christopher Matthews. Simon & Schuster 1996 377p il hardcover o.p. pa $14 **973.922**
1. Presidents 2. Vice-presidents 3. Senators 4. Nonfiction writers 5. Members of Congress 6. United States -- Politics and government -- 20th century
ISBN 0-684-83246-1 pa
LC 96-15677
This exploration of the rift between Kennedy and Nixon "shows how these two anti-New Dealers, anti-Communists, and freshmen members of Congress in 1946 became enemies as their political careers advanced." Libr J
Includes bibliographical references

Minutaglio, Bill
Dallas 1963; Bill Minutaglio, Steven L. Davis. Twelve 2013 336 p. (hardcover) $28 **973.922**
1. Conspiracies 2. Kennedy, John F. (John Fitzgerald), 1917-1963 -- Assassination
ISBN 9781455522095; 9781455522118; 9781619692794
LC 2013939303
Author Bill Minutaglio's book focuses on the assassination of President John F. Kennedy. "Beginning with the campaign for Kennedy's election and set against a nation in transition, Bill Minutaglio and Steven L. Davis ingeniously explore the swirling forces that led numerous friends and aides to warn the president against stopping in Dallas on his fateful trip to Texas." (Publisher's note)
Includes bibliographical references (pages 341-362) and index

Neff, James
Vendetta; Bobby Kennedy Versus Jimmy Hoffa. by James Neff. Little, Brown & Co. 2015 384 p. illustrations $28 **973.922**
1. United States -- Politics and government -- 20th century
ISBN 0316738344; 9780316738347
LC 2015939408
In this book, author James Neff "brings to life the . . . clash of two American titans: Robert Kennedy and his nemesis Jimmy Hoffa. . . . Kennedy's battle with Hoffa burst into the public consciousness with the 1957 Senate Rackets Committee hearings and intensified when his brother named him attorney general in 1961. RFK put together a . . . squad within the Justice Department, devoted to destroying [him]. But Hoffa, with nearly unlimited Teamster funds, was not about to roll over."

(Publisher's note)

"This enthralling account, based mostly on archival research, will appeal to Kennedy followers, true crime fans, and students and scholars of modern American history." LJ

Posner, Gerald L.

Case closed; Lee Harvey Oswald and the assassination of JFK. [by] Gerald Posner. Anchor Books 2003 608p il pa $17.95 **973.922**

    1. Presidents 2. Senators 3. Murderers 4. Members of Congress

ISBN 1-400-03462-0; 978-1-400-03462-8

                        LC 2003-283539

First published 1993

In this book Posner argues that Lee Harvey Oswald was solely responsible for the assassination of President Kennedy and that none of the theories alleging conspiracy is valid.

"One of the strongest and most important features of the book, indeed, is Posner's painstaking dissection of each and every one of the competing conspiracy theories. None of them stands up under scrutiny." Natl Rev

    Includes bibliographical references

Sherman, Casey

Above and beyond; John F. Kennedy and America's most dangerous Cold War spy mission. Casey Sherman and Michael J. Tougias. PublicAffairs 2018 360 p. $28 **973.922**

    1. Cold war 2. United States -- History

ISBN 1610398041; 9781610398046

This book, by Casey Sherman and Michael J. Tougias, is the "story of President John F. Kennedy and two U-2 pilots . . . who risked their lives to save America during the Cuban Missile Crisis. . . . On October 27, 1962, . . . Chuck Maultsby . . . steered his plane into Soviet airspace. . . . [And then] another U-2 [in Cuba] had gone missing, this one belonging to Rudy Anderson. . . . For the president, any wrong move could turn the Cold War nuclear." (Publisher's note)

Swanson, James L.

End of Days; The Assassination of John F. Kennedy. James L. Swanson. HarperCollins 2013 416 p. illustrations, map $29.99 **973.922**

    1. Kennedy, John F. (John Fitzgerald), 1917-1963 -- Assassination

ISBN 0062083481; 9780062083487

                        LC 2013498445

This book, by James L. Swanson, on the assassination of U.S. President John F. Kennedy "follows the event hour-by-hour, from the moment Lee Harvey Oswald conceived of the crime three days before its execution, to his own murder two days later at a Dallas Police precinct at the hands of Jack Ruby, a two-bit nightclub owner." (Publisher's note)

"Drawing on the decades of technological advances that have deepened the knowledge of the assassination, the author presents the stunning unfolding of the event in punchy, poignant vignettes, following one character after another to the inexorable conclusion." Kirkus

    Includes bibliography and index

Wilkie, Curtis

  ★ The **road** to Camelot; inside JFK's five-year campaign. Thomas Oliphant and Curtis Wilkie. Simon & Schuster 2017 x, 433 p.p illustrations (hardback) $28 **973.922**

    1. Presidents -- United States -- Election -- 1960 2. Presidential candidates -- United States -- Biography 3. United States -- Politics and government -- 1953-1961 4. Political campaigns -- United States -- History -- 20th century

ISBN 9781501105586; 9781501105562; 9781501105579

                        LC 2016050682

This book, by Thomas Oliphant and Curtis Wilkie, presents "a behind-the-scenes, revelatory account of John F. Kennedy's wily campaign to the White House, beginning with his bold, failed attempt to win the vice presidential nomination in 1956. A young and undistinguished junior plots his way to the presidency and changes the way we nominate and elect presidents." (Publisher's note)

"The authors add a new perspective to literature on Kennedy by focusing on his electioneering efforts rather than his persona and policy outcomes." LJ

    Includes bibliographical references and index.

Zapruder, Alexandra, 1969-

Twenty-six seconds; A Personal History of the Zapruder Film. Alexandra Zapruder. Twelve 2016 480 p. illustrations (some color) (ebook) $81; (hardcover) $27.00 **973.922**

    1. Amateur films 2. Kennedy, John F. (John Fitzgerald), 1917-1963 -- Assassination 3. Motion pictures and history 4. Memory -- Political aspects -- United States 5. Amateur films -- Texas -- Dallas -- History -- 20th century

ISBN 9781455540600; 9781455574810

                        LC 2016025786

This book, by Alexandra Zapruder, is the "untold family story behind Abraham Zapruder's film footage of the Kennedy assassination. . . . Abraham Zapruder didn't know when he began filming President Kennedy's motorcade on November 22, 1963 that his home movie would change not only his family's life but American culture and history, as well. Now his granddaughter tells the whole story of the Zapruder film for the first time." (Publisher's note)

"This well-written exploration of conspiracy, propriety, copyright, and public good versus private gain is seen through the prism of the world's most famous home movie." Pub Wkly

    Includes bibliographical references and index

    Personal history of the Zapruder film

973.923   Administration of Lyndon Baines Johnson, 1963-1969

Branch, Taylor, 1947-

  ★ At Canaan's edge; America in the King years, 1965-68. Simon & Schuster 2006 1039p il hardcover o.p. **973.923**

    1. Clergy 2. Nonfiction writers 3. Civil rights activists 4. Civil rights movements 5. Nobel laureates for peace 6. African Americans -- Civil rights 7. United States -- History -- 1961-1969 8. United States -- History -- 1961-1974 9. African Americans -- Civil rights -- History -- 20th century 10. Civil rights movements -- United States -- History -- 20th century

ISBN 0-684-85712-X; 0-684-85713-8 pa

                        LC 2005-40177

National Book Award Finalist: Nonfiction (2006)

This is "the third and final volume of Taylor Branch's . . . history of the life and times of King." (N Y Times (Late N Y Ed)) Index.

In this history that follows the life of Martin Luther King "from the protest at Selma and the 1966 Meredith March through King's expanding political concern for the poor to his 1968 assassination in Memphis, Tenn., Branch gives us not only the civil rights leader's life but also the rapidly changing pulse of American culture and politics. . . . This magisterial book is a fitting tribute to a magisterial man." Publ Wkly

    Includes bibliographical references

The **Columbia** guide to America in the 1960s; David Farber and Beth Bailey, editors. Columbia Univ. Press 2001 508p il map (Columbia guides to American history and cultures) $60; pa $25   **973.923**
1. United States -- Social conditions 2. United States -- History -- 1961-1974
ISBN 0-231-11372-2; 0-231-11373-0 pa

                                        LC 00-65577
This reference work includes "a dictionary, an extensive annotated bibliography, a chronology of the era, and statistical information [and] two extraordinary bonuses: a section 'Debating the Sixties,' which includes ten essays by prominent historians . . . and an excellent 77-page history of the 1960s. This book is a fine addition to any library's collection." Choice
Includes bibliographical references

Ishizuka, Karen L.
  ★ **Serve** the people; making Asian America in the long Sixties. Karen L. Ishizuka. Verso 2016 xiii, 270 p.p $29.95   **973.923**
1. Asian Americans -- History 2. Civil rights -- United States
ISBN 1781688621; 9781781688625
This book, by Karen Ishizuka, "tells the story of the social and cultural movement that knit . . . [the Asian American] communities into a political identity, the history of how--and why--the double consciousness of Asian America came to be. . . . [T]he book evokes the feeling of growing up alien in a society rendered in black and white, and recalls the intricate memories and meanings of the Asian American movement." (Publisher's note)
Includes bibliographical references and index.

Patterson, James T.
  The **eve** of destruction; how 1965 transformed America. James T. Patterson. Basic Books 2012 344 p. (hardcover: alk. paper) $28.99   **973.923**
1. Vietnam War, 1961-1975 2. United States -- History -- 1961-1974 3. Civil rights -- United States -- History 4. United States -- Politics and government -- 1961-1974 5. United States -- History -- 1961-1969 6. Vietnam War, 1961-1975 -- United States 7. United States -- Social conditions -- 1960-1980 8. United States -- Politics and government -- 1963-1969
ISBN 0465013589; 9780465013586; 9780465033485

                               LC 2012033786
In this book, James T. Patterson "asserts that 1965 was 'a pivotal year in American life.' He sets the stage with a picture of 'buoyant and confident' white America in late 1964, before addressing the 'shifts of mood . . . politics, culture, and foreign policies' that many found unsettling and divisive. . . . The bulk of his attention is turned toward the civil rights movement . . . the Great Society programs of President Johnson and the escalation of the Vietnam War." (Publishers Weekly)

Taking charge; the Johnson White House tapes, 1963-1964. edited and with commentary by Michael R. Beschloss. Simon & Schuster 1997 591p il hardcover o.p. pa $16 **973.923**
1. Presidents 2. Vice-presidents 3. Senators 4. Members of Congress 5. United States -- Politics and government -- 1961-1974
ISBN 0-684-84792-2 pa

                               LC 97-26749
This book is a "selection of conversations taped by Lyndon B. Johnson during the first nine months of his Presidency—beginning on the day of the Kennedy assassination and continuing through the close of the Democratic National Convention in 1964. . . . There are no stun-

ning revelations and no recorded moments of epochal importance. But 'Taking Charge' is a riveting book nevertheless. This is partly because it has been superbly edited and annotated by the historian Michael R. Beschloss, who has made everything—even the most arcane references—accessible to ordinary readers." N Y Times Book Rev

Woods, Randall B.
  Prisoners of hope; Lyndon B. Johnson, the Great Society, and the limits of liberalism. Randall B. Woods. Basic Books 2016 480 p. illustrations (hardback) $32   **973.923**
1. Social policy -- United States 2. United States -- Economic policy -- 1961-1971 3. United States -- Social policy -- 20th century 4. United States -- Politics and government -- 1963-1969 5. Liberalism -- United States -- History -- 20th century 6. Social legislation -- United States -- History -- 20th century 7. Economic assistance, Domestic -- United States -- History -- 20th century
ISBN 9780465050963

                               LC 2015040042
This book, by Randall B. Woods, "presents the first comprehensive history of the Great Society [policies of U.S. President Lyndon B. Johnson], exploring both the breathtaking possibilities of visionary politics, as well as its limits. . . . A cautionary tale about the unintended consequences of even well-intentioned policy, . . . [the book] offers a nuanced portrait of America's most ambitious--and controversial--domestic policy agenda since the New Deal." (Publisher's note)
"A sympathetic but also gimlet-eyed scholar's look at a towering physical and political presence who learned, to his sorrow, that good intentions were insufficient." Kirkus
Includes bibliographical references and index

Zeitz, Joshua
  Building the great society; inside Lyndon Johnson's White House. Joshua Zeitz. Viking 2018 xviii, 378 p.p (hardcover) $30   **973.923**
1. Economic policy -- United States 2. United States -- Politics and government -- 1961-1974 3. United States -- Economic policy -- 1961-1971 4. United States -- Social policy -- 20th century 5. United States -- Politics and government -- 1963-1969
ISBN 9780698191594; 9780525428787; 052542878X
This book, by Joshua Zeitz, "is the story of how one of the most competent White House staffs in American history - serving one of the most complicated presidents ever to occupy the Oval Office - fundamentally changed everyday life for millions of citizens and forged a legacy of compassionate and interventionist government." (Publisher's note)
"Zeitz's lucid account yields engrossing insights into one of America's most hopeful, productive, and tragic political eras." Pub Wkly Annex
Includes bibliographical references (pages 353-361) and index.

973.924   Administration of Richard Milhous Nixon, 1969-1974

Bernstein, Carl
  All the president's men; {by} Carl Bernstein, Bob Woodward. Simon & Schuster 1999 349p il hardcover o.p. pa $14   **973.924**
1. Watergate Affair, 1972-1974 2. Washington post
ISBN 0-684-86355-3; 0-671-89441-2 pa

                               LC 98-54773
A reissue of the title first published 1974
The two Washington Post reporters whose investigative journal-

ism first revealed the Watergate scandal tell the way it happened from the first suspicions, through the trail of false leads, lies, secrecy, and high-level pressure, to the final moments when they were able to put the pieces of the puzzle together and write the series that won the Post a Pulitzer Prize

Dean, John W. (John Wesley), 1938-

The **Nixon** Defense; What He Knew and When He Knew It. John W. Dean. Viking 2014 416 p. $35   **973.924**
  1. Watergate Affair, 1972-1974   2. Nixon, Richard M. (Richard Milhous), 1913-1994
ISBN 0670025364; 9780670025367

LC 2014020821

In this book, author and former White House Counsel John W. Dean "connects the dots between what we've come to believe about Watergate and what actually happened. . . . [He] draws on his own transcripts of almost a thousand conversations, a wealth of Nixon's secretly recorded information, and more than 150,000 pages of documents in the National Archives and the Nixon Library to provide the definitive answer to the question: What did President Nixon know and when did he know it?" (Publisher's note)

"[O]ne of the best and fullest accounts of the Watergate cover-up, one that conveys in Nixon's own voice the casual criminality of his troubled presidency." Pub Wkly

Includes bibliographical references (pages 661-719) and index

Hughes, Ken

Chasing shadows; the Nixon tapes, the Chennault affair, and the origins of Watergate. Ken Hughes. University of Virginia Press 2014 x, 228 p.p (cloth: acid-free paper) $24.95 **973.924**
  1. Watergate Affair, 1972-1974   2. Nixon, Richard M. (Richard Milhous), 1913-1994   3. Audiotapes   4. United States -- Politics and government -- 1961-1963   5. United States -- Politics and government -- 1963-1969   6. United States -- Politics and government -- 1969-1974
ISBN 0813936632; 9780813936635

LC 2014013429

This book, by by Ken Hughes, explores the larger picture surrounding the Watergate Scandal of the Richard Nixon administration. The author "unearth[s] a pattern of actions by Nixon . . . that begins during the 1968 campaign, when Nixon, concerned about the impact on his presidential bid of the Paris peace talks with the Vietnamese, secretly undermined the negotiations through a Republican fundraiser named Anna Chennault." (Publisher's note)

"Through its foremost practitioners in Johnson and Nixon, Hughes reveals the realities of see American politics as a blood sport." Pub Wkly

Includes bibliographical references and index

The **Nixon** tapes; 1973. edited and annotated by Douglas Brinkley and Luke A. Nichter. Houghton Mifflin Harcourt 2015 848 p. 8 plates; color illustrations (hardcover) $35 **973.924**
  1. Sound recordings   2. Presidents -- United States -- Archives   3. Nixon, Richard M. (Richard Milhous), 1913-1994   4. Audiotapes   5. United States -- Foreign relations -- 1969-1974 -- Sources   6. United States -- Politics and government -- 1969-1974 -- Sources
ISBN 0544610539; 9780544610538

LC 2015028189

In this book, authors Douglas Brinkley and Luke A. Nichter "conclude their project of publishing highlights from Richard Nixon's infamous tapes. . . . This volume finds Nixon often exulting publicly thanks to the emerging success of his rapprochement and trip to China, the winding down of the Vietnam War, and growing détente with the Soviet Union. Some of the most affecting conversations on these tapes take place between Nixon and Soviet Premier Leonid Brezhnev." (Kirkus Reviews)

"General readers might prefer earlier transcription efforts, such as Watergate principal John Dean's 2014 The Nixon Defense, since the excerpts in that book are shorter and more context is given. Even so, these longer excerpts resemble an oddly fascinating reality show, and historians will like that Brinkley and Nichter worked with the most complete body of recordings and used audio equipment of the highest quality to ensure transcription accuracy." LJ

Olson, Keith W.

Watergate; the presidential scandal that shook America. University Press of Kansas 2003 220p il $35; pa $15.95   **973.924**
  1. Watergate Affair, 1972-1974
ISBN 0-7006-1250-5; 0-7006-1251-3 pa

LC 2002-38058

The author describes "the White House-approved break-in at Democratic National Committee headquarters in Washington's Watergate complex and its aftermath—most importantly, the dramatic proceedings of the Senate Watergate Committee. . . . {This} book provides an excellent, compact narrative of a crucial moment in the history of the American presidency." Publ Wkly

Includes bibliographical references

Packer, George

★ The **unwinding**; an inner history of the new America. George Packer. Farrar Straus & Giroux 2013 448 p. (hardcover) $27   **973.924**
  1. Economics -- History   2. United States -- Economic conditions   3. Crises -- United States   4. United States -- Biography   5. Social problems -- United States   6. United States -- History -- 1969-   7. Celebrities -- United States -- Biography   8. Politicians -- United States -- Biography   9. United States -- Social conditions -- 1980-   10. United States -- Politics and government -- 1989-
ISBN 0374102414; 9780374102418

LC 2013004431

National Book Critics Circle Award Finalist: Nonfiction (2013)
National Book Award: Nonfiction (2013)

In this book, George Packer "charts the erosion of the social compact that kept the country stable and middle class. Readers experience three decades of change via the personal histories of an Ohio factory worker, a Washington political operative, a North Carolinian small businessman, and an Internet billionaire. Their lives follow the ups and downs of a changing country, where manufacturing jobs vanish, businesses thrive and fail, and political fortunes crest and recede." (Publishers Weekly)

Includes bibliographical references (pages 431-434)

Perlstein, Rick, 1969-

The **Invisible** Bridge; The Fall of Nixon and the Rise of Reagan. by Rick Perlstein. Simon & Schuster 2014 800 p. illustrations (some color) $37.50   **973.924**
  1. Conservatism -- United States   2. United States -- History -- 20th century   3. Nixon, Richard M. (Richard Milhous), 1913-1994
ISBN 1476782415; 9781476782416

LC 2014381509

This book, by Rick Perlstein, is a "portrait of America on the verge of a nervous breakdown in the tumultuous political and economic times of the 1970s. In January of 1973 Richard Nixon announced the end of the Vietnam War and prepared for a triumphant second term--until televised Watergate hearings revealed his White House as little better than a mafia den." Ronald Reagan was "inventing the new conservative political culture we know now." (Publisher's note)

"Although the book only goes up to Reagan's loss of the 1976 Republican nomination to President Gerald Ford, the scope of the work never feels limited. . . . A compelling, astute chronicle of the politics and culture of late-20th-century America." Kirkus

★ **Nixonland**; the rise of a president and the fracturing of America. Scribner 2008 881p il   **973.924**

1. Presidents 2. Vice-presidents 3. Senators 4. Nonfiction writers 5. Members of Congress 6. Presidents -- United States 7. United States -- Politics and government -- 1961-1974 8. United States -- Politics and government -- 1969-1974 9. United States -- Politics and government -- 1974-1977

ISBN 0743243021; 074324303X; 9780743243025; 9780743243032 pa

LC 20080273706

This book focuses on U.S. President Richard Nixon, from the "tumultuous years of 1965, on the eve of the Watts Riot, through Nixon's landslide victory in 1972. [Rick] Perlstein has twin objectives. First, he develops a . . . narrative about how Richard Nixon . . . came to epitomize and personify the values of the 'silent majority.' Second, Nixon's ability to exploit voters' anxieties about race, poverty, law and order, and patriotism has produced bitter partisan divisions." (Choice: Current Reviews for Academic Libraries)

This "is an exceptionally broad and thorough social, cultural and political history of eight tumultuous years. . . . It sings with outstanding storytelling and insight." Washington Monthly

Includes bibliographical references

Weiner, Tim

One man against the world; the tragedy of Richard Nixon. Tim Weiner. Henry Holt & Co. 2015 384 p. illustration (hardcover) $30   **973.924**

1. Presidents -- United States 2. Nixon, Richard M. (Richard Milhous), 1913-1994 3. Presidents -- United States -- Biography 4. United States -- Politics and government -- 1969-1974

ISBN 1627790837; 9781627790833

LC 2015012381

In this book, author Tim Weiner argues that "President Richard Nixon's (1913-94) most tragic flaw was his idea that the presidency was above the law; a delusion that drove him to the "gutter politics" that led to the Watergate scandal in 1972 and his inevitable resignation in 1974." The book draws on "archival documents that were not declassified until the 21st century . . . notably about bombings in Southeast Asia and a near-nuclear confrontation with the former Soviet Union." (Library Journal)

"Those seeking to understand America in the second half of the twentieth century and, distressingly, beyond would do well to begin here. The tragedy was not Nixon's alone, but his role in it has never been portrayed more vividly." Booklist

Includes bibliographical references (pages [325]-356) and index.

Woodward, Bob

The **final** days; {by} Bob Woodward, Carl Bernstein. Simon & Schuster 1976 476p il hardcover o.p. pa $16 **973.924**

1. Presidents 2. Vice-presidents 3. Watergate Affair, 1972-1974 4. Senators 5. Nonfiction writers 6. Members of Congress 7. United States -- Politics and government -- 1961-1974

ISBN 0-7432-7406-7 pa

The title refers to the final days of the Nixon Presidency. The authors have "constructed a two-part narrative, the first half covering the period from April 30, 1973—the day John Dean was fired as White House counsel—until late July 1974, and the second half covering the last two weeks in detail." N Y Times Book Rev

973.925   Administration of Gerald Rudolph Ford, 1974-1977

Schulman, Bruce J.

The **seventies**; the great shift in American culture, society, and politics. Da Capo 2002 334p pa $17.95   **973.925**

1. United States -- Civilization -- 1970-

ISBN 0-306-81126-X; 978-0-306-81126-5

First published 2001 by Free Press

"This is an important contribution to modern American social history and the literature of popular culture." Publ Wkly

Includes bibliographical references

973.926   Administration of Jimmy (James Earl) Carter, 1977-1981

Eizenstat, Stuart, 1943-

★ **President** Carter; the White House years. Stuart E. Eizenstat; foreword by Madeleine Albright. Thomas Dunne Books, St. Martin's Press 2018 xxi, 999 p.p (hardback) $35   **973.926**

1. Presidents -- United States -- Biography 2. United States -- Politics and government 3. United States -- Politics and government -- 1977-1981

ISBN 9781250104571; 1250104556; 9781250104557

LC 2017043521

In this book, author Stuart E. Eizenstat, "reveals the grueling negotiations behind [United States President Jimmy] Carter's peace between Israel and Egypt, what led to the return of the Panama Canal, and how Carter made human rights a presidential imperative. He follows Carter's passing of America's first comprehensive energy policy, and his deregulation of the oil, gas, transportation, and communications industries. And he details the creation of the modern vice-presidency." (Publisher's note)

"A compelling reassessment of an oft-maligned chief executive." Booklist

Includes bibliographical references and index.

973.927   Administration of Ronald Reagan, 1981-1989

Brokaw, Tom

The **time** of our lives; past, present, promise. Random House 2011 xxii, 291p il $26; ebook $12.99   **973.927**

1. Social problems 2. American national characteristics 3. United States -- Social conditions 4. United States -- Politics and government -- 1989-

ISBN 978-1-4000-6458-8; 978-0-679-64392-0 ebook

LC 2011022825

"At this troubled point in the nation's history, . . . Brokaw offers a perspective from his own life and career. Drawing on interviews and observations, he ponders how the U.S. has come to a point where the country is suffering from eroding confidence, a financial crisis, declining education, and fears about China's progress. . . . Through the prism of his family and career, Brokaw looks back on the Great Depression, the civil rights era, the Cold War, and more recent history and looks forward to the future for his grandchildren and the nation. With commonsense values, he appeals to Americans to recommit to family and community, increase civic engagement, and make sacrifices in an effort to ensure some security for generations to come. An engaging recollection of the achievements of the past, the realities of the present, and the promise of the future." Booklist

Mann, James

The **rebellion** of Ronald Reagan; a history of the end of the Cold War. [by] James Mann. Viking 2009 396p il **973.927**
1. Actors 2. Cold war 3. Governors 4. Presidents 5. Cold War 6. Cabinet members 7. Communist leaders 8. Nobel laureates for peace 9. Soviet Union -- Foreign relations -- United States 10. United States -- Foreign relations -- Soviet Union 11. Political leadership -- United States -- History -- 20th century
ISBN 0670020540; 9780670020546

LC 2008029029

Ronald Reagan did not win the Cold War, nor was he just historically lucky, as two contrasting viewpoints would sometimes have it. Instead, . . . [the author writes,] after a career of hard line anticommunism Reagan proved more flexible and visionary than many other leaders of American foreign policy and more opportunistic and insightful into the motives of Mikhail Gorbachev when the Soviet leader signaled change in the USSR's own conventional hard-line position. . . . Mann bases his argument upon impressive original research, including interviews with principals who range from George Shultz, to Colin Powell, to Helmut Kohl, to Nancy Reagan. Libr J

Includes bibliographical references

973.928 Administration of George Bush, 1989-1993

Woodward, Bob

The **commanders**. Simon & Schuster 1991 398p il hardcover o.p. pa $16 **973.928**
1. Diplomats 2. Presidents 3. Vice-presidents 4. Persian Gulf War, 1991 5. Members of Congress 6. Parents of presidents 7. United Nations officials 8. United States -- Dept. of Defense 9. United States -- Foreign relations
ISBN 0-671-41367-8; 0-7432-3475-8 pa

LC 91-13037

This book discusses "top-level White House [and] Pentagon decisionmaking, first in the attack on Panama, and then in the 5½ months of diplomatic and especially military maneuvering that preceded the [1991] war with Iraq." Christ Sci Monit

973.929 Administration of Bill Clinton, 1993-2001

Gormley, Ken

The **death** of American virtue; Clinton vs. Starr. Crown Publishers 2010 789p il $35 **973.929**
1. Judges 2. Lawyers 3. Governors 4. Presidents 5. Political ethics 6. Misconduct in office 7. Interns 8. Senators 9. Law teachers 10. Presidential aides 11. Government officials 12. Secretaries of state 13. Spouses of presidents 14. Presidential candidates 15. Clothing industry executives 16. Whitewater Inquiry, 1993-2000 17. Special prosecutors -- United States 18. Misconduct in office -- United States 19. Governmental investigations -- United States
ISBN 0-307-40944-9; 978-0-307-4094-4

The author presents an analysis of the events leading up to the impeachment trial of President William Jefferson Clinton, from Ken Starr's initial Whitewater investigation through the Paula Jones sexual harassment suit to the Monica Lewinsky affair. . . . [The book includes material from interviews with] Bill Clinton, Ken Starr, Monica Lewinsky, Paula Jones, [and] Susan McDougal. (Publisher's note) Index.

For those wishing to understand exactly what happened during this confusing, dismal time, Gormley's informed reporting and evenhanded analysis is the place to start. The entire nightmare vividly recalled. Kirkus

Includes bibliographical references

Toobin, Jeffrey R.

A **vast** conspiracy; the real story of the sex scandal that nearly brought down a president. 1st Touchstone ed.; Simon & Schuster 2000 422p pa $20 **973.929**
1. Governors 2. Presidents 3. United States -- Politics and government -- 1989-
ISBN 0-7432-0413-1; 978-0-7432-0413-2

LC 00-59524

First published 1999 by Random House

"Even for those who disagree with [Toobin's] assessment, the book is still hugely entertaining. There are plenty of scandal pellets to be found scattered throughout the analysis." Christ Sci Monit

Includes bibliographical references

973.93 United States--2001-

Baker, Peter

Days of fire; Bush and Cheney in the White House. by Peter Baker. Doubleday 2013 816 p. (hardback) **973.93**
1. United States -- Politics and government -- 2001- -- United States -- 21st Century
ISBN 0385525184; 9780385525183

LC 2013018745

Author Peter Baker presents a "study of the inner workings, conflicts, and critical policy decisions made during the eight years of [George W.] Bush and [Dick] Cheney['s] governance. Baker sees [Bush] as a man trapped by events, whose hopes for a more 'modest' foreign policy and a 'compassionate conservatism' domestic affairs were frustrated by the vast shadows cast by 9/11." (Booklist)

Includes bibliographical references (pages 659-774) and index

Caputo, Philip

The **longest** road; overland in search of America from Key West to the Arctic Ocean. by Philip Caputo. Henry Holt and Company 2013 352 p. $28 **973.93**
1. Travel writing 2. United States -- Social conditions 3. United States -- Biography 4. National characteristics, American 5. United States -- Description and travel 6. United States -- Social conditions -- 21st century 7. United States -- Social life and customs -- 21st century
ISBN 0805094466; 9780805094466

LC 2012050451

In this book author Philip Caputo takes a "journey across America, Airstream in tow, and asks everyday Americans what unites and divides a country as endlessly diverse as it is large. What he found is a story [designed to] entertain and inspire readers as much as it informs them about the state of today's United States, the glue that holds us all together, and the conflicts that could cause us to pull apart." (Publisher's note)

973.931 Administration of George W. Bush, 2001-2009

Bernstein, Richard

Out of the blue; the story of September 11, 2001, from Jihad to Ground Zero. {by} Richard Bernstein and the staff of the New York Times. Times Bks. 2002 287p il hardcover o.p. pa

$15   **973.931**

1. Terrorism 2. September 11 terrorist attacks, 2001
ISBN 0-8050-7240-3; 0-8050-7410-4 pa

LC 2002-20396

This account of the September 11, 2001 terrorist attacks focuses "on the personal—the victims, the perpetrators and heroes whose lives became tangled in catastrophe. . . . It uses these stories as a jumping-off point for a comprehensive look at the terror attacks—the reactions of New Yorkers, the nation and the world; the criticism of U.S. government agencies; the lingering effects of the tragedy. While some of this information has been published elsewhere, it has not been gathered so comprehensively—nor has it been written so well." Publ Wkly

Bruni, Frank

Ambling into history: the unlikely odyssey of George W. Bush. HarperCollins Pubs. 2002 278p hardcover o.p. pa $12.95   **973.931**

1. Governors 2. Presidents 3. Baseball executives 4. Children of presidents 5. Energy industry executives 6. Presidents -- United States
ISBN 0-06-093782-3 pa

The author, who covered Bush's 2000 presidential campaign for the New York Times, focuses on Bush's personality and mannerisms as well as his basic interactions with family, friends, and the public.

"Given [Bruni's] familiarity with Bush, one would expect his book to contain revealing insights, and this superb, incisive, and surprising account does not disappoint." Booklist
Includes bibliographical references

Eichenwald, Kurt

500 days; secrets and lies in the terror wars. by Kurt Eichenwald. 1st Touchstone hardcover ed. Touchstone 2012 xxiii, 611 p.p (hardcover) $30.00; (paperback) $18.00   **973.931**

1. International relations 2. Terrorism -- Prevention 3. September 11 terrorist attacks, 2001 4. War on Terrorism, 2001-2009 5. World politics -- 21st century 6. September 11 Terrorist Attacks, 2001
ISBN 1451669380; 9781451669381; 9781451674132; 9781451669398

LC 2012001214

This book offers an "episodic reconstruction of the fallout from 9/11 in the highest spheres of terrorist strategy. Former 'New York Times' reporter [Kurt] Eichenwald . . . chronicles the entire post-9/11 year-and-a-half spectacular, demonstrating literally how the anti-terrorist hysteria in the United States, and the hatred of America and general global paranoia, forged the 'trauma that haunts the world to this day.'" (Kirkus Reviews)
Includes bibliographical references (p. [525]-576) and index.

Farmer, John J.

The **ground** truth; the untold story of America under attack on 9/11. [by] John Farmer. Riverhead Books 2009 388p $26.95   **973.931**

1. Terrorism 2. September 11 terrorist attacks, 2001
ISBN 978-1-59448-894-8; 1-59448-894-0

LC 2009-23297

The author "presents a dismaying catalogue of incompetence and dissembling before and after the attack on the World Trade Center and the Pentagon. The author makes excellent use of declassified primary-source documents from 9/11—including transcriptions of frantic last-minute phone calls of air-traffic controllers—to demonstrate how a massively funded national-security system, a relic of the Cold War, failed to counter a small band of terrorists. . . . An important systematic brief on how an elaborately constructed national-defense system was penetrated,

and why lessons of that day for disaster response remain dimly understood." Kirkus
Includes bibliographical references

Franks, Tommy

American soldier; [by] Tommy Franks, with Malcolm McConnell. Regan Bks. 2004 590p il map $27.95; pa $16.95   **973.931**

1. Generals
ISBN 0-06-073158-3; 0-06-077954-3 pa

LC 2004-558617

"The real value of 'American Soldier' . . . is not what it says about the war on terror, but what it reveals about Tommy Franks. . . . The chapter on Vietnam, where Franks spent a year in brutal combat as a field artillery officer, is a cleareyed, mordant memoir." N Y Times Book Rev

Greenberg, Karen J.

The **torture** papers; the road to Abu Ghraib. edited by Karen J. Greenberg, Joshua L. Dratel; introduction by Anthony Lewis. Cambridge University Press 2005 xxxiv, 1249p il $30   **973.931**

1. Iraq War, 2003-2011 2. Iraq War, 2003-2011 -- Atrocities 3. Abu Ghraib (Baghdad, Iraq: Prison)
ISBN 0-521-85324-9

"A gripping and alarming read about the use of government power." Choice
Includes bibliographical references

Hersh, Seymour M.

★ **Chain** of command; the road from 9/11 to Abu Ghraib. HarperCollins 2004 394p map $25.95; pa $14.95   **973.931**

1. Iraq War, 2003-2011 2. September 11 terrorist attacks, 2001 3. War on terrorism 4. Abu Ghraib (Baghdad, Iraq: Prison)
ISBN 0-06-019591-6; 0-06-095537-6 pa

"This sobering book is the closest anyone without a security clearance will get to operatives in the inner sanctums of America's intelligence, military, political and diplomatic worlds." Publ Wkly

Kaplan, Robert D.

Imperial grunts; the American military on the ground. Random House 2005 421p maps $27.95   **973.931**

1. Soldiers -- United States 2. Military policy -- United States
ISBN 1-4000-6132-6

LC 2004-61466

Kaplan's "on-the-ground reportage makes for riveting reading." N Y Times (Late N Y Ed)
Includes bibliographical references

Mayer, Jane

The **dark** side; the inside story of how the war on terror turned into a war on American ideals. Doubleday 2008 392p il $27.50   **973.931**

1. September 11 terrorist attacks, 2001 2. War on terrorism 3. United States -- Politics and government -- 2001-
ISBN 978-0-385-52639-5; 0-385-52639-3

LC 2008-299452

National Book Award Finalist: Nonfiction (2008)

This is an account of how the Bush administration has fought the war on terror.

This is a "brilliantly researched and deeply unsettling book." N Y Times Book Rev
Includes bibliographical references (p. 361-369)

Miller, John

The **cell**: inside the 9/11 plot and why the FBI and CIA failed to stop it; {by} John Miller and Michael Stone, with Chris Mitchell. Hyperion 2002 336p $24.95; pa $13.95 **973.931**
1. Terrorism 2. September 11 terrorist attacks, 2001 3. Intelligence service -- United States 4. United States -- Central Intelligence Agency 5. United States -- Federal Bureau of Investigation
ISBN 0-7868-6900-3; 0-7868-8782-6 pa

LC 2002-27322

The authors analyze the circumstances inside and outside the United States that culminated in the September 11 terrorist attack. Included is an account of Miller's face-to-face meeting with Osama bin Laden in Afghanistan in 1998.

This is a "frightening and important book." Publ Wkly

National Commission on Terrorist Attacks Upon the United States

★ The **9** /11 Commission report; final report of the National Commission on Terrorist Attacks Upon the United States. Norton 2004 567p il $19.95; pa $10 **973.931**
1. Terrorism 2. September 11 terrorist attacks, 2001 3. War on terrorism 4. Qaida (Organization) 5. National security -- United States
ISBN 0-393-06041-1; 0-393-32671-3 pa

LC 2004-57564

National Book Award Finalist: Nonfiction (2004)

This work aims to describe how the terrorist attacks of September 11, 2001 occurred and to provide recommendations for the prevention of future attacks.

This book "reads like a Shakespearean drama. . . . This multi-author document produces an absolutely compelling narrative intelligence, one with clarity, a sense of shared mission and an overriding desire to do something about the situation." Publ Wkly

Includes bibliographical references

No day shall erase you; The Story of 9/11 as Told at the September 11 Museum. Alice M. Greenwald, foreword by Michael R. Bloomberg. Skira Rizzoli, an imprint of Rizzoli International Publications, Inc. 2016 226 p. illustrations (chiefly color) (pbk.: alk. paper) $24.95 **973.931**
1. Historical museums 2. September 11 terrorist attacks, 2001 3. National September 11 Memorial & Museum (Organization)
ISBN 9780847849475; 9780847849482

LC 2016939352

This book, by Alice M. Greenwald, with foreword by Michael R. Bloomberg, "is the definitive, official companion volume to the National September 11 Memorial & Museum. It provides visitors with a lasting record of their experience at the museum, and tells the story of September 11 through essays on and photographs of the installations and thoughtfully curated artifacts that serve as touchstones to the day and its aftermath." (Publisher's note)

"Vivid photos and several insightful essays by museum staff complement text written respectfully and with understated authority by Greenwald, the memorial and museum's director and executive vice president for exhibitions, collections, and education." Pub Wkly

Includes bibliographical references (page 216).

Ramo, Joshua Cooper

The **age** of the unthinkable; why the new world disorder constantly surprises us and what we can do about it. Little, Brown and Company 2009 279p $25.99 **973.931**
1. World politics -- 1991- 2. Military policy -- United States 3.

United States -- Foreign relations
ISBN 978-0-316-11808-8; 0-316-11808-7

LC 2009-00854

This is "a fascinating look at various aspects of today's complicated world and how interconnecting systems often come to bear in unexpected ways." Libr J

Includes bibliographical references

Smith, Jean Edward

Bush; Jean Edward Smith. Simon & Schuster 2016 768 p. $35 **973.931**
1. Presidents -- United States 2. United States -- Politics and government -- 2001-2009
ISBN 1476741190; 9781476741192

LC 2015034690

This book, by Jean Edward Smith "demonstrates that it was not Dick Cheney, Donald Rumsfeld, or Condoleezza Rice, but President [George W.] Bush himself who took personal control of foreign policy. Bush drew on his deep religious conviction that important foreign-policy decisions were simply a matter of good versus evil. Domestically, he overreacted to 9/11 and endangered Americans' civil liberties." (Publisher's note)

"This is a superb recap and critical analysis of Bush's controversial administration." Pub Wkly

Includes bibliographical references and index

Soufan, Ali H.

★ The **black** banners; the inside story of 9/11 and the war against Al-Qaeda. [by] Ali H. Soufan; with Daniel Freedman. W.W. Norton & Co. 2011 xxvi, 572p il map $26.95 **973.931**
1. Terrorism 2. September 11 terrorist attacks, 2001 3. War on terrorism 4. Al Qaeda (Organization) 5. War on Terrorism, 2001-6. Terrorism -- United States -- Prevention
ISBN 978-0-393-07942-5; 0-393-07942-2

LC 2011026938

A former FBI special agent offers an insider's account of how the September 11th attacks could have been prevented, as well as his role in the war on terror.

"The best and most original book published in the West on al-Qaeda, this is highly recommended." Libr J

Includes bibliographical references

Spiegelman, Art

In the shadow of no towers. Pantheon Books 2004 il $19.95 **973.931**
1. Graphic novels 2. September 11 terrorist attacks, 2001 -- Graphic novels
ISBN 0-375-42307-9

LC 2004-43870

The author "provides a hair-raising and wry account of his family's frantic efforts to locate one another on September 11 as well as a morbidly funny survey of his trademark sense of existential doom. . . . This is a powerful and quirky work of visual storytelling by a master comics artist." Publ Wkly

Suskind, Ron

The **one** percent doctrine; deep inside America's pursuit of its enemies since 9/11. Simon & Schuster 2006 367p $27 **973.931**
1. Terrorism 2. War on terrorism 3. United States -- Politics and government -- 2001-
ISBN 0-7432-7109-2; 978-0-7432-7109-7

LC 2006-279373

"Relying on . . . access to former and current government officials, this book [seeks to] . . . reveal for the first time how the U.S. government—from President Bush on down—is frantically improvising to fight a new kind of war." Publisher's note

Woodward, Bob

State of denial. Simon & Schuster 2006 560p il hardcover o.p. pa $16   **973.931**

1. Governors 2. Presidents 3. Iraq War, 2003-2011 4. Baseball executives 5. Children of presidents 6. Energy industry executives
ISBN 0-7432-7223-4; 978-0-7432-7223-0; 0-7432-7224-2 pa; 978-0-7432-7224-7 pa

LC 2006-285190

This is a critique of the Bush administration's handling of the war in Iraq.

"If journalism is the first page of history, then Woodward's opus will be required reading for any would-be historians of the time." Publ Wkly
Includes bibliographical references

Wright, Lawrence, 1947-

★ The **looming** tower; Al Qaeda and the road to 9/11. Knopf 2006 469p map $27.95   **973.931**

1. Terrorism 2. September 11 terrorist attacks, 2001 3. Al Qaeda (Organization) 4. Intelligence service -- United States 5. Terrorism -- Government policy -- United States
ISBN 0-375-41486-X; 9780375414862

LC 2006-41032

National Book Award Finalist: Nonfiction (2006)

This is a "narrative history of the events leading to 9/11." (Publisher's note)

The author "goes back—way back—to 1948 to dissect the personal influences and political radicalization that would lead to al Qaeda's attack on America." Libr J
Includes bibliographical references

973.932   Administration of Barack Obama, 2009-

Berry, Mary Frances

Power in words; the stories behind Barack Obama's speeches, from the state house to the White House. [by] Mary Frances Berry, Josh Gottheimer; foreword by Ted Sorensen. Beacon Press 2010 xxxiii, 267p $24.95   **973.932**

1. American speeches 2. Presidents -- United States -- Election -- 2008 3. United States -- Politics and government -- 2001-
ISBN 978-0-8070-0104-2

LC 2010004085

Collection of 18 of Obama's most memorable speeches between 2002 and 2008, each introduced by Berry and Gottheimer with political analysis, historical context, and commentary from the speechwriters.

"A book to savor and return to for subsequent readings." Kirkus
Includes bibliographical references

Chait, Jonathan

Audacity; how Barack Obama defied his critics and created a legacy that will prevail. Jonathan Chait. Custom House 2017 272 p. (ebook) $26.99; (hardback) $27.99   **973.932**

1. Presidents -- United States 2. United States -- Politics and government -- 2009- 3. United States -- Foreign relations -- 2009-
ISBN 9780062426994; 9780062426970

LC 2016038527

In this book, author Jonathan Chait "digs deep into [President

Barack] Obama's record on major policy fronts--the economy, the environment, domestic reform, health care, race, and foreign policy--to demonstrate why history will judge our forty-fourth president as among our greatest. Chait explains why so many observers . . . missed the enormous evidence of progress amidst the smoke screen of extremist propaganda and the confinement of short-term perspective." (Publisher's note)

"Chait offers a well-organized, clearly written case that will be valuable to future historians in their assessments." Kirkus

Chozick, Amy

Chasing Hillary; ten years, two presidential campaigns, and one intact glass ceiling. Amy Chozick. HarperCollins 2018 400 p. $27.99   **973.932**

1. Women presidential candidates -- United States 2. Presidential candidates -- United States -- Biography
ISBN 0062413597; 9780062413598

This book presents "the dishy, rollicking, and deeply personal story of what really happened in the 2016 election, as seen through the eyes of the New York Times reporter [Amy Chozick] who gave eight years of her life to covering the First Woman President who wasn't. . . . Chozick's candor and clear-eyed perspective . . . provide fresh intrigue and insights into the story we thought we all knew." (Publisher's note)

Coates, Ta-Nehisi, 1975-

★ **We** were eight years in power; an American tragedy. Ta-Nehisi Coates. One World 2017 xvii, 367 p.p (hardcover) $28   **973.932**

1. American essays 2. United States -- Politics and government -- 2009-2017 3. African Americans -- Social conditions -- 21st century 4. United States -- Race relations -- History -- 21st century 5. African Americans -- Politics and government -- 21st century
ISBN 9780399590566; 9780399590580; 0399590560

LC 2017039343

"In this sweeping collection of new and selected essays, [author] Ta-Nehisi Coates explores the tragic echoes of that history in our own time: the unprecedented election of a black president followed by a vicious backlash that fueled the election of the man Coates argues is America's 'first white president.' . . . Coates powerfully examines the events of the Obama era from his intimate and revealing perspective." (Publisher's note)

"Biting cultural and political analysis from the award-winning journalist. . . . Emotionally charged, deftly crafted, and urgently relevant essays." Kirkus

D'Antonio, Michael

A **consequential** president; The Legacy of Barack Obama. Michael D'Antonio. Thomas Dunne Books 2017 320 p. illustrations (hardcover) $27.99; (ebook) $60   **973.932**

1. United States -- Politics and government -- 2009-
ISBN 9781250081391; 9781466893276

LC 2016045029

This book, by Michael D'Antonio, "tallies President [Barack] Obama's long record of achievement, recalling both his major successes and less-noticed ones that nevertheless contribute to his legacy. The record includes Obama's role as an inspirational leader who was required to navigate race relations as the first black president and had to function in an atmosphere that included both racial acrimony from his critics and unfair expectations among supporters." (Publisher's note)

"Obama's historic presidency during a time of great divisiveness in Washington and the country is an important time in American history, and D'Antonio offers a terrific summary." Booklist
Includes bibliographical references and index

Isikoff, Michael

Russian roulette; the inside story of Putin's war on America and the election of Donald Trump. Michael Isikoff and David Corn. Grand Central Pub 2018 352 p. $30   **973.932**

1. Elections -- Corrupt practices
ISBN 1538728753; 9781538728758

LC 2018001213

This book, by Michael Isikoff and David Corn, "is a story of political skullduggery unprecedented in American history. It weaves together tales of international intrigue, cyber espionage, and superpower rivalry. After U.S.-Russia relations soured, as Vladimir Putin moved to reassert Russian strength on the global stage, Moscow trained its best hackers and trolls on U.S. political targets and exploited WikiLeaks to disseminate information that could affect the 2016 election." (Publisher's note)

"The way the text builds from the 2016 election to the present—covering how those in the Obama administration and the intelligence services dealt with the interference issue (or, in some cases, didn't)—makes for thought-provoking reading. A smart, solid, even-handed book that future historians will use as a starting point." Booklist

Johnston, David Cay

The **making** of Donald Trump; David Cay Johnston. Melville House 2016 xvi, 263 p.p (hardcover) $24.99   **973.932**

1. Businessmen -- Biograpy 2. Businessmen -- United States -- Biography 3. Celebrities -- United States -- Biography 4. Real estate developers -- United States -- Biography 5. Presidential candidates -- United States -- Biography 6. Television personalities -- United States -- Biography 7. Political campaigns -- United States -- History -- 21st century
ISBN 1612196322; 9781612196329

LC 2016947664

This book, by David Cay Johnston, is the "culmination of nearly 30 years of reporting on Donald Trump. . . . Covering the long arc of Trump's career, Johnston tells the full story of how a boy from a quiet section of Queens, NY would become an entirely new, and complex, breed of public figure. Trump is a man of great media savvy, entrepreneurial spirit, and political clout. Yet his career has been plagued by legal troubles and mounting controversy." (Publisher's note)

"By exposing what he argues is Trump's strategic flouting of the law, as well as his belief in revenge as a 'guiding principle' and his strategy of 'sowing doubt and threatening litigation,' Johnston hopes that his book will prompt readers to carefully 'evaluate the prospect of a Trump presidency.' " Booklist

Includes bibliographic references (pages 215-258) and index

Kantor, Jodi, 1975-

The **Obamas**; Jodi Kantor. Little, Brown and Co. 2012 viii, 359 p.p $16   **973.932**

1. Presidents -- United States -- Family 2. White House (Washington, D.C.) 3. Presidents -- United States -- Biography
ISBN 0316098760; 9780316098755; 9780316098762

LC 2011940240

This book profiles the marriage of U.S. President Barack Obama and his wife Michelle. Author Jodi Kantor, "a 'New York Times' Washington correspondent, offers a prolonged peek behind the curtain at the evolving role of the Obama marriage as a driver of White House East and West Wing sensibility." (AudioFile)

Includes bibliographical references (p. 343-347) and index

Litt, David

★ **Thanks,** Obama; my hopey changey White House years. David Litt. Ecco 2017 310 p. (hardback) $27.99   **973.932**

1. Speechwriters -- United States -- Biography 2. Political satire, American 3. Obama, Barack -- Friends and associates 4. Humorists, American -- 21st century -- Biography 5. Presidents -- United States -- Staff -- Biography 6. United States -- Politics and government -- 2009- -- Humor
ISBN 0062568450; 9780062568458

LC 2017019330

In this memoir, David Litt narrates, how, "after graduating from college in 2008, he went straight to the Obama campaign. In 2011, he became one of the youngest White House speechwriters in history. Until leaving the White House in 2016, he wrote on topics from healthcare to climate change to criminal justice reform. As President [Barack] Obama's go-to comedy writer, he also took the lead on the White House Correspondents' Dinner, the so-called 'State of the Union of jokes.'" (Publisher's note)

Rhodes, Benjamin J., 1977-

The **world** as it is; a memoir of the Obama White House. Ben Rhodes. Random House 2018 480 p. (hbk.) $30 **973.932**

1. Presidents -- United States 2. United States -- Politics and government -- 2009-
ISBN 9780525509356; 0525509356

In this book, author Ben Rhodes "shows what it was like to be . . . [at the White House]--from the early days of the Obama campaign to the final hours of the presidency. It is a story populated by such characters as Susan Rice, Samantha Power, Hillary Clinton, Bob Gates, and--above all--Barack Obama, who comes to life on the page in moments of great urgency and disarming intimacy." (Publisher's note)

Souza, Pete

Obama; an intimate portrait. Pete Souza; foreword by Barack Obama. Little, Brown & Co. 2017 349 p. color illustrations (hardcover) $50   **973.932**

1. Presidents -- United States -- Pictorial works 2. Presidents -- United States -- Biography
ISBN 9780316512602; 9780316512589; 0316512583

LC 2017941348

This book is a "visual biography of Barack Obama's historic Presidency, captured in unprecedented detail by his White House photographer. . . . Pete Souza served as Chief Official White House Photographer for President Obama's full two terms. He was with the President during more crucial moments than anyone else--and he photographed them all. Souza took nearly two million photographs of President Obama, capturing moments both highly classified and disarmingly candid." (Publisher's note)

"In addition to being a collection of masterfully crafted images, the volume is a time capsule, capturing an era in pictures—one still fresh in collective memory." Pub Wkly Annex

Taibbi, Matt

Griftopia; bubble machines, vampire squids, and the long con that is breaking America. Spiegel & Grau 2010 252p $26   **973.932**

1. Despotism 2. Political corruption 3. Global Financial Crisis, 2008-2009 4. United States -- Politics and government -- 2001-
ISBN 978-0-385-52995-2; 978-0-385-52997-6 ebook

LC 2010-15067

This is a study of the causes and consequences of the 2008 financial crisis.

"Taibbi's glib prose is punctuated with just enough irreverence and wit to allow him to appeal to more casual readers while providing sufficient detail to satisfy those looking for a serious discussion of the high-level manipulation of the economy. Recommended for anyone interested in understanding the economy and how it got that way." Libr J

973.933   Administration of Donald Trump, 2017-

Dionne, E. J., 1952-

★ **One** nation after Trump; a guide for the perplexed, the disillusioned, the desperate, and the not-yet deported. E.J. Dionne Jr., Norman J. Ornstein, and Thomas E. Mann. St. Martin's Press 2017 344 p. $25.99   **973.933**

1. Political participation -- United States 2. United States -- Politics and government -- 21st century
ISBN 1250164052; 9781250164056

In this book, authors E.J. Dionne Jr., Norman J. Ornstein and Thomas E. Mann explain "the danger [Donald Trump's] administration poses to our free institutions. They also offer encouragement to . . . Americans now experiencing a new sense of citizenship and engagement and argue that our nation needs a unifying alternative to Trump's dark and divisive brand of politics--an alternative rooted in a New Economy, a New Patriotism, a New Civil Society, and a New Democracy." (Publisher's note)

Ultimately, the authors seek to develop a new concept of patriotism, a new sense of civic-mindedness, a new civil society, and a new democracy. Of course, this is all exceedingly difficult in the current climate, but the authors are seasoned guides and provide good jumping-off points for moving beyond the noxious atmosphere of Trumpism.

Includes bibliographical references (pages 294-327) and index.

Frances, Allen

★ **Twilight** of American sanity; a psychiatrist analyzes the age of Trump. Allen Frances, MD. HarperCollins 2017 336 p. $27.99   **973.933**

1. Psychiatry 2. United States -- Social conditions 3. Psychology 4. United States 5. Political ethics 6. Presidents -- Psychology 7. Political leadership -- Psychological aspects
ISBN 0062394509; 9780062394507

In this book, psychiatrist Allen Frances "analyzes the [U.S.] nation, viewing the rise of Donald J. Trump as darkly symptomatic of a deeper societal distress that must be understood if we are to move forward. . . . Frances argues that Trump is 'bad, not mad'--and that the real question to wrestle with is how we as a country could have chosen him as our leader." (Publisher's note)

Includes bibliographical references and index.

Frum, David

Trumpocracy; the corruption of the American republic. David Frum. HarperCollins 2018 320 p. $25.99   **973.933**

1. Democracy 2. United States -- Politics and government
ISBN 0062796739; 9780062796738

For this book, author "David Frum has . . . collect[ed] the lies, obfuscations, and flagrant disregard for the traditional limits placed on the office of the presidency. . . . [H]e documents how [Donald] Trump and his administration are steadily damaging the tenets and accepted practices of American democracy. . . . [He] outlines how Trump could push America toward illiberalism, what the consequences could be for our nation . . . and what we can do to prevent it." (Publisher's note)

"Highly recommended for anyone who cares about the republic and its future." LJ

Johnston, David Cay

It's even worse than you think; what the Trump administration is doing to America. David Cay Johnston. Simon & Schuster 2018 320 p. $28   **973.933**

1. Social policy -- United States 2. United States -- Politics and government -- 2009-
ISBN 1501174169; 9781501174162

LC 2017045101

In this book, author "David Cay Johnston shines a light on the political termites who have infested . . . [the U.S.] government under the Trump Administration, destroying it from within and compromising . . . jobs, safety, finances, and more. . . . [It] goes inside the administration to show how the federal agencies that touch the lives of all Americans are being undermined." (Publisher's note)

"Thoroughly depressing - but urgent, necessary reading, at least for those who aren't true believers in the Trumpite cause." Kirkus

Includes bibliographical references and index

Kurtz, Howard

Media madness; Donald Trump, the press, and the war over the truth. Howard Kurtz. Regnery Pub 2018 288 p. $28.99   **973.933**

1. Journalism -- United States 2. Mass media -- Political aspects
ISBN 1621577260; 9781621577263

In this book, author "Howard Kurtz offers a stunning exposé of how supposedly objective journalists, alarmed by [U.S. President Donald] Trump's success, have moved into the opposing camp. Kurtz's exclusive, in-depth, behind-the-scenes interviews with reporters, anchors, and insiders within the Trump White House reveal the unprecedented hostility between the media and the president they cover." (Publisher's note)

"Alongside Kurtz's lively, entertaining narrative of vitriolic news cycles is a penetrating critique of a liberal news establishment that, he contends, has abandoned objectivity for a hysterical partisanship that galvanizes Trump's support among the conservative voters it disdains." Pub Wkly

Wolff, Michael, 1953-

★ **Fire** and fury; inside the Trump White House. Michael Wolff. Henry Holt & Co. 2018 336 p. (hardcover) $30 **973.933**

1. Presidents -- United States -- Staff 2. United States -- Politics and government 3. Presidents -- United States 4. United States -- Politics and government -- 2017- 5. United States -- Politics and government -- 2009-2017
ISBN 9781250158062

LC 2017050324

This book, by Michael Wolff, is a "riveting and explosive account of [Donald] Trump's administration [that] provides a wealth of new details about the chaos in the Oval Office, including: what President Trump's staff really thinks of him, what inspired Trump to claim he was wiretapped by President Obama [and] why FBI director James Comey was really fired." (Publisher's note)

"While Wolff's use of anonymous 'deep background' sources may give readers reservations about the accuracy of every detail, this explosive account will undoubtedly remain a topic of conversation for the near future." Pub Wkly

974   Specific states of United States

Vowell, Sarah

The **wordy** shipmates. Riverhead Books 2008 254p map $25.95   **974**

1. Puritans 2. Pilgrims (New England colonists) 3. New England -- History -- 1600-1775, Colonial period
ISBN 978-1-59448-999-0; 1-59448-999-8

LC 2008-30491

"Focusing on the Puritans who settled in 1692 in the Massachusetts

Bay Colony, Vowell laments their image as 'boring killjoys' when in fact they were 'fascinating killjoys.' A book dense with detail, insight, and humor." Booklist

974.1 Maine

Finkel, Michael

The **stranger** in the woods; the extraordinary story of the North Pond hermit. by Michael Finkel. Alfred A. Knopf 2017 224 p. $25.95 **974.1**

1. Hermits 2. Solitude 3. Solitude -- Case studies 4. Survival -- Case studies 5. Smithfield Region (Me.) -- Biography 6. Hermits -- Maine -- Smithfield Region -- Biography 7. Thieves -- Maine -- Smithfield Region -- Biography 8. Recluses -- Maine -- Smithfield Region -- Biography

ISBN 9781101875681; 9781471152115

LC 2016029910

This book, by Michael Finkel, tells "the remarkable true story of a man who lived alone in the woods of Maine for 27 years, making this dream a reality—not out of anger at the world, but simply because he preferred to live on his own. . . . It is a gripping story of survival that asks fundamental questions about solitude, community, and what makes a good life, and a deeply moving portrait of a man who was determined to live his own way, and succeeded." (Publisher's note)

"With inevitable comparisons to Jon Krakauer's Into the Wild, this book will appeal to recreational readers interested in outdoor adventure, survival stories, or escaping the mainstream." LJ

974.4 Massachusetts

Bradford, William

Of Plymouth Plantation, 1620-1647; the complete text, with notes and an introduction by Samuel Eliot Morison. Knopf 1952 xliii, 448p maps $25 **974.4**

1. Pilgrims (New England colonists) 2. Massachusetts -- History -- 1600-1775, Colonial period

ISBN 0-394-43895-7

Written between 1630 and 1650; first published 1856 with title: History of Plymouth Plantation

"The opening book sketches the origin of the Separatist movement, the flight from England to Holland, the settlement at Leiden, the plans for the settlement in New England, and the Mayflower voyage. The second book, which includes the major part of the history, is in the form of annals from 1620 to 1646, and describes every aspect of the life of the Pilgrims. Besides being a primary historical source, the work has artistic value because of its dignified, sonorous style, deriving from the Geneva Bible." Oxford Companion to Am Lit. 5th edition

Bremer, Francis J.

John Winthrop; America's forgotten founding father. Oxford University Press 2003 478p il hardcover o.p. pa $21.95 **974.4**

1. Clergy 2. Government officials 3. Colonial administrators

ISBN 0-19-514913-0; 978-0-19-517981-1 pa; 0-19-517981-1 pa

LC 2002-38143

"Bremer's definitive biography gracefully portrays Winthrop as a man of his time, whose influence in the new colony grew out of his own struggles to establish his identity before he left England." Publ Wkly

Includes bibliographical references

Bunker, Nick

★ **Making** haste from Babylon; the Mayflower Pilgrims and their world: a new history. Alfred A. Knopf 2010 489p il map $30 **974.4**

1. Pilgrims (New England colonists) 2. Mayflower (Ship) 3. Pilgrims (New Plymouth Colony) 4. Massachusetts -- History -- New Plymouth, 1620-1691 5. Massachusetts -- History -- 1600-1775, Colonial period

ISBN 978-0-307-26682-8; 0-307-26682-6

LC 2009038520

This is an "account of the Mayflower project and the first decade of the Plymouth Colony." (Publisher's note)

"Never before has such a comprehensive and thoroughly researched study of the subject appeared. . . . [This book] scoops up every relevant character and links all to the basic tale of indomitable courage, religious faith, commercial ambition, international rivalry, and domestic politics. The results are stunning. Certain to be the dominating work on the Pilgrims for decades." Publ Wkly

Includes bibliographical references

Cliff, Nigel

The **Shakespeare** riots; revenge, drama, and death in nineteenth-century America. Random House 2007 312p il $26.95 **974.4**

1. Poets 2. Actors 3. Authors 4. Dramatists 5. Riots -- New York (N.Y.) 6. Astor Place (New York, N.Y.) 7. New York (N.Y.) -- Social life and customs

ISBN 9780345486943; 0-345-48694-3

LC 2006-49139

"Cliff argues persuasively that 'the Astor Place riot,' as it came to be known, marked a turning point in America's search for a national identity. . . . [This] is an intriguing, thought-provoking book." Washington Post Book World

Includes bibliographical references

Fraser, Rebecca

★ The **Mayflower**; the families, the voyage, and the founding of America. Rebecca Fraser. St. Martin's Press 2017 xiii, 358 p.p (hardcover) $29.99 **974.4**

1. Mayflower (Ship) -- Juvenile literature 2. Mayflower (Ship) 3. Pilgrims (New Plymouth Colony) 4. Massachusetts -- History -- New Plymouth, 1620-1691

ISBN 9781250108562

LC 2017026873

This book, by Rebecca Fraser, is a "narrative history of the Mayflower and of the Winslow family, who traveled to America in search of a new world. . . . Edward Winslow, an apprentice printer, fled England and then Holland for a life of religious freedom and opportunity. Despite the intense physical trials of settlement, he found America exotic, enticing, and endlessly interesting." (Publisher's note)

Includes bibliographical references and index

Kidder, Tracy

Home town. Washington Square Press 2000 432p pa $14.95 **974.4**

1. City and town life 2. Northampton (Mass.)

ISBN 978-0-671-78521-5; 0-671-78521-4

First published 1999 by Random House

This "acutely observed, crisply written, and utterly absorbing documentary proves that there is nothing on this spinning earth more amazing and full of grace than everyday life." Booklist

Includes bibliographical references

Manegold, Catherine

Ten Hills Farm; the forgotten history of slavery in the North. [by] C.S. Manegold. Princeton University Press 2010 317p il map $29.95   **974.4**

1. Slaves -- Massachusetts 2. Massachusetts -- History 3. Slavery -- Massachusetts 4. Slavery -- United States 5. Slave trade -- Massachusetts

ISBN 978-0-691-13152-8; 0-691-13152-X

LC 2009030875

This book tells the story "of five generations of slave owners in colonial New England. Settled in 1630, . . . Ten Hills Farm, a six-hundred-acre estate just north of Boston, passed from the Winthrops to the Ushers, to the Royalls—all . . . dynasties tied to the Native American and Atlantic slave trades." (Publisher's note) Index.

"Full of rich historical detail, this is a story that needed to be told." Kirkus

Includes bibliographical references

974.5   Rhode Island

Barry, John M.

Roger Williams and the creation of the American soul; church, state, and the birth of liberty. John M. Barry. Viking 2012 464 p.   **974.5**

1. Puritans 2. Religion and politics -- United States 3. United States -- History -- 1600-1775, Colonial period 4. United States -- History -- 17th century 5. United States -- Civilization -- 17th century

ISBN 0670023051; 9780670023059

LC 2011032995

This book by John M. Barry offers a "look at how Roger Williams shaped the nature of religion, political power, and individual rights in America. . . . Americans have [always] wrestled with . . . two concepts that define the nature of the nation: the proper relation between church and state and between a free individual and the state. These debates began with the extraordinary thought and struggles of Roger Williams. . . . This is a story . . . set against Puritan America and the English Civil War. Williams's interactions with King James, Francis Bacon, Oliver Cromwell, and his mentor Edward Coke set his course, but his fundamental ideas came to fruition in America, as Williams, though a Puritan, collided with John Winthrop's vision of his 'City upon a Hill.'" (Publisher's note)

Includes bibliographical references (p. 427-438) and index

974.502   Rhode Island--1620-1776

Warren, James A.

God, war, and providence; the epic struggle of Roger Williams and the Narragansett Indians against the Puritans of New England. James A. Warren. Simon & Schuster 2018 304 p. $30   **974.502**

1. Puritans -- History 2. Narragansett Indians 3. Rhode Island -- History

ISBN 150118041X; 9781501180415

In this book, author "James A. Warren tells the remarkable and little-known story of the alliance between Roger Williams's Rhode Island and the Narragansett Indians, and how they joined forces to retain their autonomy and their distinctive ways of life against Puritan encroachment. Deeply researched, vividly written, this account of the Narragansetts' courageous resistance campaign, aided by Williams, serves as a telling

precedent for white-Native American encounters." (Publisher's note)

974.7   New York

★ **After** the fall; edited by Mary Marshall Clark ... [et al.] New Press 2011 xxiii, 263 p.p $26.95   **974.7**

1. September 11 terrorist attacks, 2001 -- Personal narratives

ISBN 978-1-59558-647-6; 9781595586476

LC 2011012833

This book was produced by "Columbia University's Oral History Research Office, headed by [the book's editor,] Mary Marshall Clark, [who] went to work immediately after September 11, 2001, and has now issued a selection from its hundreds of interviews with those most directly involved—first responders, victims' families, residents of lower Manhattan. . . . The interviews make clear the distance between those who will go on distressfully reliving their experience forever and those of us who were merely bystanders." (Columbia Journalism Review)

"The Columbia Center for Oral History (CCOH) is committed to building 'repositories of living memory,' and after 9/11 began to gather narratives from a variety of New York survivors and witnesses, eventually collecting over 600 histories. The skilled interviewers . . . are trained in oral history methods and richly summon forth from interviewees the repercussions of the attack on individuals, families, and communities. Those interviewed reflect a variety of perspectives, including both professional and unskilled workers in the Twin Towers, neighbors, first responders, and many of New York's immigrant groups, including Muslims." Libr J

Alexiou, Alice Sparberg

Devil's mile; the rich, gritty history of the Bowery. Alice Sparberg Alexiou. St. Martin's Press 2018 304 p. $28.99 **974.7**

1. Historical literature 2. New York (N.Y.) -- History 3. Architecture -- 19th century

ISBN 1250021383; 9781250021380

In this book, author "Alice Sparberg Alexiou tells the story of The Bowery, starting with its origins, when forests covered the surrounding area, and through the pre-Civil War years, when country estates of wealthy New Yorkers lined this thoroughfare. She then describes The Bowery's deterioration in stunning detail, starting in the post-bellum years." (Publisher's note)

" New York buffs, especially those nostalgic for a grittier time, will find this a learned pleasure." Kirkus

Burns, Cherie

The great hurricane-1938. Atlantic Monthly Press 2005 240p il $24   **974.7**

1. Hurricanes 2. Northeastern States

ISBN 0-8711-3893-X

LC 2005-41211

The author discusses the hurricane of September 1938, which affected the northeastern United States from Long Island to Providence, Rhode Island.

The author "has dug up old newspaper accounts and local histories to reconstruct the terror and destruction that accompanied the 1938 hurricane. Those who suffered the most, of course, did not survive to tell their tales. Nearly 700 people died, and about 63,000 were left homeless. . . . Survivor's stories, however, give ample feeling for the power of the rain, tide, and wind." Nat Hist

Calhoun, Ada

St. Marks Is Dead; The Many Lives of America's Hippest

Street. by Ada Calhoun. W.W. Norton & Co. Inc. 2015 400 p. illustrations, map (ebook) $50; $27.95   **974.7**
    1. Counterculture 2. Manhattan (New York, N.Y.)
    ISBN 9780393249798; 039324038X; 9780393240382
                    LC 2015028040
This book, by Ada Calhoun, is a "narrative history of three hallowed Manhattan blocks . . . St. Marks Place. . . . Calhoun profiles iconic characters from W. H. Auden to Abbie Hoffman, from Keith Haring to the Beastie Boys, among many others. She argues that St. Marks has variously been an elite address, an immigrants' haven, a mafia warzone, a hippie paradise, and a backdrop to the film Kids—but it has always been a place that outsiders call home." (Publisher's note)
"As Calhoun traces the neighborhood's evolution from wealthy and respectable to gritty and poverty-stricken and back again, she shows how one street can become a microcosm of America's political and cultural history." Pub Wkly
    Includes bibliographical references (pages 341-397) and index.

Daughan, George C.
    Revolution on the Hudson; New York City and the Hudson River Valley in the American War of Independence. George C. Daughan. W W Norton & Co Inc 2016 432 p. ill., maps, portraits (hardcover) $28.95   **974.7**
    1. Hudson River (N.Y. and N.J.) -- History 2. United States -- History -- 1775-1783, Revolution
    ISBN 9780393245721; 0393245721
                    LC 2016007017
This book, by George C. Daughan, tells "the untold story of the fight for the Hudson River Valley, control of which, both the Americans and the British firmly believed, would determine the outcome of the Revolutionary War. . . . It unpacks intricate military maneuvers on land and sea, introduces the personalities presiding over each side's strategy, and reinterprets the vagaries of colonial politics." (Publisher's note)
"A stimulating look at the American Revolution by a diligent historian and talented writer." Kirkus
    Includes bibliographical references (pages [355]-395) and index.

Dwyer, Jim
    102 minutes; the untold story of the fight to survive inside the Twin Towers. [by] Jim Dwyer and Kevin Flynn. Times Books 2005 322p il $26; pa $15   **974.7**
    1. September 11 terrorist attacks, 2001 2. World Trade Center terrorist attack, 2001
    ISBN 0-8050-7682-4; 0-8050-8032-5 pa
                    LC 2004-55321
Dwyer and Flynn have "given us a fitting tribute to the people caught up in one of the great dramas of our time. And for people still haunted by the events of that day, reading '102 Minutes' provides a cathartic release." N Y Times Book Rev

Friend, David
    Watching the world change; the stories behind the images of 9/11. Farrar, Straus and Giroux 2006 435p il $30   **974.7**
    1. Documentary photography 2. World Trade Center (New York, N.Y.) 3. September 11 terrorist attacks, 2001 -- Pictorial works
    ISBN 978-0-374-29933-0; 0-374-29933-1
                    LC 2005-36158
In this "analysis of how images of 9/11 and the 'war on terror' have altered our understanding of power, world politics, religion and identity, . . . [the author] successfully merges reportage and analysis as he interprets the images of falling towers, panic in Manhattan streets and prisoners at Abu Ghraib that have been burned into our brains." Publ Wkly

    Includes bibliographical references

Gage, Beverly
    The **day** Wall Street exploded; a story of America in its first age of terror. Oxford University Press 2009 400p il   **974.7**
    1. Bombings 2. Terrorism 3. Wall Street (New York, N.Y.) 4. Terrorism -- New York (N.Y.) 5. Terrorism -- United States -- History
    ISBN 0-19-514824-X; 978-0-19-514824-4
                    LC 2008022074
This is an account of the "1920 terrorist attack on Wall Street—why it happened [and] how it shaped American politics." (Publisher's note) Index.
"Gage has performed a real service, both in presenting such a complicated case in such a fair and balanced way and in reminding readers how large a space terrorism once occupied on the political landscape." San Francisco Chron
    Includes bibliographical references

Gill, Jonathan
    Harlem; the four hundred year history from Dutch village to capital of black America. Grove Press 2011 520p il map $29.95   **974.7**
    1. New York (N.Y.) -- Harlem
    ISBN 978-0-8021-1910-0
"Comprehensive and compassionate—an essential text of American history and culture." Kirkus
    Includes bibliographical references

Gopnik, Adam
    At the strangers' gate; arrivals in New York. Adam Gopnik. Alfred A. Knopf 2017 272 p. (hardback) $26.95   **974.7**
    1. Travel 2. Friendship 3. Family life 4. New York (N.Y.) -- Biography 5. New York (N.Y.) -- Description and travel 6. New York (N.Y.) -- Social life and customs -- 20th century
    ISBN 9781400041800; 9781400075744
                    LC 2017016651
In this memoir, "when Adam Gopnik and his soon-to-be-wife, Martha, left the comforts of home in Montreal for New York, the city then, much like today, was a pilgrimage site for the young, the arty, and the ambitious. But it was also becoming a city of greed, where both life's consolations and its necessities were increasingly going to the highest bidder." (Publisher's note)

Griswold, Mac
    The **Manor**; Three Centuries at a Slave Plantation on Long Island. Mac Griswold. Farrar Straus & Giroux 2013 304 p. $28   **974.7**
    1. Plantations 2. Slavery -- United States 3. Long Island (N.Y.) -- History 4. Long Island (N.Y.) -- Biography 5. Shelter Island (N.Y.) -- History 6. Sylvester Manor Plantation Site (N.Y.) 7. Slavery -- New York (State) -- Long Island -- History 8. Plantations -- New York (State) -- Long Island -- History 9. Excavations (Archaeology) -- New York (State) -- Long Island 10. Plantation life -- New York (State) -- Long Island -- History 11. Plantation owners -- New York (State) -- Long Island -- Biography
    ISBN 0374266298; 9780374266295
                    LC 2013005463
This book is Mac Griswold's exploration of a 1652 plantation house on Long Island. She uncovers the histories of "those who lived in it or passed through its grounds: Native Americans, generation after generation of Sylvesters (the original owners), and—most surprisingly,

considering that the Sylvesters were Quakers—the family's slaves." (Publishers Weekly)

Includes bibliographical references and index

In the Catskills; a century of Jewish experience in the mountains. Phil Brown, editor. Columbia University Press 2002 xvi, 415 p.p illustrations $60   **974.7**

1. Jews -- United States 2. Catskill Mountains (N.Y.) 3. Catskill Mountains Region (N.Y.)/Social life and customs 4. Jews/Recreation/New York (State)/Catskill Mountains region 5. Catskill Mountains Region (N.Y.) -- Social life and customs 6. Jews/New York (State)/Catskill Mountains Region/Social life and customs

ISBN 0231123604; 9780231123600

LC 2001042319

"Through fiction, memoir, music, and art, this book offers a glimpse of the Catskills experience over a century and assesses its continuing impact on American culture. The book features contributions from such writers as Isaac Bashevis Singer and Vivian Gornick; and original contributions from historians, sociologists, and scholars of American and Judaic studies." Publisher's Note

"This is a great look at the history of Catskill culture for readers new to the material, but those looking for more depth will be disappointed." Pub Wkly

Includes bibliographical references (p. 393-412)

Khan, Yasmin Sabina

Enlightening the world; the creation of the Statue of Liberty. Cornell University Press 2010 231p il $24.95   **974.7**

1. Artists 2. Sculptors 3. National monuments 4. Statue of Liberty (New York, N.Y.) 5. France -- Foreign relations -- United States 6. United States -- Foreign relations -- France

ISBN 978-0-8014-4851-5; 0-8014-4851-4

LC 2009035711

This is "a lucid account connecting France's widespread grief over Abraham Lincoln's 1865 assassination with that country's own struggles to establish a lasting democracy. Khan shows how Édouard-René Lefebvre de Laboulaye, a legal scholar and celebrant of French-American friendship, led others to design and construct what was officially called Liberty Enlightening the World. . . . An important book for general audiences." Publ Wkly

Includes bibliographical references

Langewiesche, William

American ground, unbuilding the World Trade Center. North Point Press 2002 205p $22; pa $13   **974.7**

1. September 11 terrorist attacks, 2001 2. World Trade Center (New York, N.Y.)

ISBN 0-86547-582-2; 0-86547-675-6 pa

LC 2002-75153

First published as a three part series of articles in Atlantic Monthly

"This is a genuinely monumental story, told without melodrama, an intimate depiction of ordinary Americans reacting to grand-scale tragedy at their best—and sometimes their worst." Publ Wkly

Lepore, Jill

New York burning; liberty, slavery, and conspiracy in an eighteenth-century Manhattan. Alfred A. Knopf 2005 323p il maps $26.95   **974.7**

1. Slavery -- United States 2. New York (N.Y.) -- History

ISBN 1-4000-4029-9

LC 2004-57625

"In this first-rate social history, Lepore not only adroitly examines the case's travesty, questioning whether such a conspiracy ever existed,

but also draws a splendid portrait of the struggles, prejudices and triumphs of a very young New York City in which fully 'one in five inhabitants was enslaved.'" Publ Wkly

Includes bibliographical references

MacColl, Gail

To marry an English Lord; by Gail MacColl and Carol McD. Wallace. Workman Pub. 1989 x, 403 p.p ill. (pbk.) $15.95; o.p.   **974.7**

1. Marriage 2. Nobility 3. Great Britain -- History 4. Women -- Social conditions 5. Women -- United States -- History 6. England -- Social life and customs

ISBN 9780761171959; 0894809393

LC 85040529

This book traces how "[f]rom the Gilded Age until 1914, more than 100 American heiresses invaded Britannia and swapped dollars for titles--just like Cora Crawley, Countess of Grantham, the first of the Downton Abbey characters Julian Fellowes was inspired to create [for the television program] after reading 'To Marry An English Lord.' Filled with . . . personalities, . . . anecdotes, grand houses, and . . . period details--plus photographs, illustrations, quotes, and the finer points of Victorian and Edwardian etiquette--'To Marry An English Lord' is [a] social history." (Publisher's note)

Martin, Wednesday

Primates of Park Avenue; a memoir. Wednesday Martin, Ph.D. Simon & Schuster 2015 256 p. (hardcover) $26 **974.7**

1. Mothers 2. Upper class 3. New York (N.Y.) 4. Primates -- Behavior 5. New York (N.Y.) -- Biography 6. Primates -- Behavior -- Miscellanea 7. New York (N.Y.) -- Social life and customs 8. Upper East Side (New York, N.Y.) -- Biography 9. Mothers -- New York (State) -- New York -- Biography 10. Interpersonal relations -- New York (State) -- New York 11. Upper East Side (New York, N.Y.) -- Social life and customs 12. Mothers -- New York (State) -- New York -- Social life and customs

ISBN 1476762627; 9781476762623; 9781476762715

LC 2014041481

In this memoir, "Wednesday Martin decodes the primate social behaviors of Upper East Side mothers. . . . After marrying a man from the Upper East Side and moving to the neighborhood, . . . Martin struggled to fit in. Drawing on her background in anthropology and primatology, she tried looking at her new world through that lens, and suddenly things fell into place. . . . [S]he analyzed tribal migration patterns; display rituals; physical adornment, mutilation, and mating practices." (Publisher's note)

"This anthropological journey into the wilds of New York City's most exclusive zip code could have easily devolved into condescension, but instead it proves that mothers everywhere want the same thing: health and happiness for their progeny." LJ

Includes bibliographical references

McCourt, Malachy

Singing my him song. HarperCollins Pubs. 2000 242p hardcover o.p. pa $14   **974.7**

1. Actors

ISBN 0-06-095548-1 pa

LC 00-59774

In this sequel to A monk swimming, "McCourt tells us the rest of his story; how he got from there to here, how he went from living the headlong and heedless life of a world-class drunk to becoming a sober, loving father and grandfather, still happily married after thirty-five years." Publisher's note

Miller, Donald L.

Supreme city; How Jazz Age Manhattan gave birth to modern America. Donald L. Miller. Simon & Schuster 2014 784 p. illustrations, map $37.50 **974.7**

1. Manhattan (New York, N.Y.) 2. New York (N.Y.) -- History 3. New York (N.Y.) -- History -- 20th century 4. New York (N.Y.) -- Politics and government -- 1898-1951 5. New York (N.Y.) -- Social life and customs -- 20th century
ISBN 1416550194; 9781416550198

LC 2013020154

This book, by Donald L. Miller, "is the story of Manhattan's growth and transformation in the 1920s and the brilliant people behind it. . . . As mass communication emerged, the city moved from downtown to midtown through a series of engineering triumphs--Grand Central Terminal . . . the Holland Tunnel, and the modern skyscraper. In less than ten years Manhattan became the social, cultural, and commercial hub of the country. The 1920s was the Age of Jazz and the Age of Ambition." (Publisher's note)

"Conveying the panoramic sweep of the era with wit, illuminating details, humor, and style, Miller illustrates how Midtown Manhattan became the nation's communications, entertainment, and commercial epicenter." Pub Wkly

Includes bibliographical references and index

Stanton, Brandon

Humans of New York; Brandon Stanton. St. Martin's Press 2013 304 p. color illustrations (hardback) $29.99 **974.7**

1. Photography 2. Street life 3. New York (N.Y.) 4. Photography, Artistic 5. New York (N.Y.)-- Pictorial works 6. Street photography -- New York (State) -- New York 7. City and town life -- New York (State) -- New York -- Hisotry -- 21st century -- Pictorial works
ISBN 9781250038814; 9781250038821; 1250038820

LC 2013027586

This book, by photographer Brandon Stanton, is "inspired by the blog [of the same name]. With four hundred color photos, including exclusive portraits and all-new stories, 'Humans of New York' is a stunning collection of images that showcases the outsized personalities of New York." (Publisher's note)

"There's the Yugoslavian janitor who studied for 12 years to earn his classics degree; Banana George, the world's oldest barefoot water-skier who's now in a wheelchair; Muslims in prayer; and shots of adorable kids, crazy fashionistas, and young lovers, all paired with a comment from Stanton or from the subjects themselves. There's no judgment, just observation and in many cases reverence, making for an inspiring reading and visual experience." Pub Wkly

Humans of New York: stories; Brandon Stanton. St. Martin's Press 2015 432 p. chiefly color illustrations (hardcover) $29.99 **974.7**

1. New York (N.Y.) 2. Portrait photography 3. New York (N.Y.)-- Biography 4. Interviews-- New York (State) -- New York 5. New York (N.Y.) -- Biography -- Pictorial works 6. Street photography -- New York (State)-- New York 7. New York (N.Y.) -- Social life and customs -- Pictorial works 8. City and town life -- New York (State) -- New York -- Pictorial works
ISBN 9781250058904; 9781466886964; 1250058902

LC 2015025568

Alex Award (2016)

"In the summer of 2010, photographer Brandon Stanton began an ambitious project--to single-handedly create a photographic census of New York City. The photos he took and the accompanying interviews became the blog Humans of New York. Ever since Brandon began interviewing people on the streets of New York, the dialogue he's had with them has increasingly become as in-depth, intriguing and moving as the photos themselves." (Publisher's note)

"Photographer and author Stanton returns with a companion volume to Humans of New York (2013), this one with similarly affecting photographs of New Yorkers but also with some tales from his subjects' mouths. . . . A wondrous mix of races, ages, genders, and social classes, and on virtually every page is a surprise." Kirkus

Strausbaugh, John

The **Village**; 400 Years of Beats and Bohemians, Radicals and Rogues, a History of Greenwich Village. HarperCollins 2013 640 p. (hardcover) $29.99 **974.7**

1. Bohemianism -- New York (N.Y.) 2. Greenwich Village (New York, N.Y.) -- History 3. Greenwich Village (New York, N.Y.) -- Social life and customs
ISBN 0062078194; 9780062078193

In this book, author John Strausbaugh "traces the history of [Greenwich Village, New York City] . . . from its early settlement in the 1600s to the present day. He examines its role in the arts within the context of broader issues and periods such as Prohibition, World War II, McCarthyism, organized crime, and gay liberation. Among the writers, artists, and musicians discussed are Amy Lowell, Maxwell Bodenheim, Norman Mailer, Allen Ginsberg . . . and Edward Albee." (Library Journal)

Taylor, Alan

The **divided** ground; Indians, settlers and the northern borderland of the American Revolution. Alfred A. Knopf 2006 542p il maps $35; pa $16.95 **974.7**

1. Iroquois Indians -- History 2. New York (State) -- History 3. United States -- History -- 1775-1783, Revolution
ISBN 0-679-45471-3; 1-4000-7707-9 pa

LC 2005-43582

"Taylor's exquisite writing and thorough research in both Canadian and US archives and manuscript collections make this a major work." Choice

Includes bibliographical references

Von Drehle, Dave

★ **Triangle**: the fire that changed America. Atlantic Monthly Press 2003 340p il hardcover o.p. pa $14 **974.7**

1. Fires 2. Factories 3. Clothing industry 4. New York (N.Y.) 5. Triangle Shirtwaist Company, Inc.
ISBN 0-87113-874-3; 0-8021-4151-X pa

LC 2003-41835

"Von Drehle's engrossing account, which emphasizes the humanity of the victims and the theme of social justice, brings on of the pivotal and most shocking episodes of American labor history to life." Publ Wkly

Includes bibliographical references

974.71   New York (N.Y.)

Anbinder, Tyler

★ **City** of Dreams; Tyler Anbinder. Houghton Mifflin Harcourt 2016 768 p. illustrations, maps (ebook) $35; (hardcover) $35 **974.71**

1. Immigrants -- New York (State) -- New York -- History 2. New York (N.Y.) -- Emigration and immigration -- History
ISBN 9780544103856; 9780544104655; 054410465X

This book about immigrants features "memorable characters both beloved and unfamiliar, whose lives unfold in rich detail. . . . [Author] Tyler Anbinder's story is one of innovators and artists, revolutionaries and rioters, staggering deprivation and soaring triumphs, all playing out against the powerful backdrop of New York City, at once ever-changing and profoundly, permanently itself." (Publisher's note)

"An endlessly fascinating kaleidoscope of American history. A fantastic historical resource" Kirkus

Includes bibliographical references (pages 579-700) and index.

Gopnik, Adam

Through the children's gate; a home in New York. Alfred A. Knopf 2006 318p $25   **974.71**

1. New York (N.Y.) -- Description and travel 2. New York (N.Y.) -- Social life and customs. 3. Home -- Social aspects -- New York (State) -- New York.

ISBN 1-4000-4181-3; 978-1-4000-4181-7

LC 2006-45260

"Gopnik writes about returning to New York after five years in Paris." (N Y Times Book Rev)

"You don't have to be a New Yorker or even necessarily an enthusiast of the city to be alternately amused, touched, and charmed by Gopnik's well-crafted pieces." Christ Sci Monit

Wallace, Mike

Greater Gotham; a history of New York City from 1898 to 1919. Mike Wallace. Oxford University Press 2017 xi, 1182 p.p (hardback: acid-free paper) $45   **974.71**

1. New York (N.Y.) -- History 2. United States -- History -- 1898-1919 3. New York (N.Y.) -- History -- 1898-1951

ISBN 9780195116359

LC 2017005224

Follow-up to: Gotham (1998)

In this book, in The History of NYC Series, author Mike Wallace "captures the swings of prosperity and downturn, from the 1898 skyscraper-driven boom to the Bankers' Panic of 1907, the labor upheaval, and violent repression during and after the First World War. Here is New York on a whole new scale, moving from national to global prominence -- an urban dynamo driven by restless ambition, boundless energy, immigrant dreams, and Wall Street greed." (Publisher's note)

"Wallace shapes this sprawl into a coherent, engrossing narrative that's nicely balanced between historical sweep and colorful detail. The result sets a standard for urban history, capturing both New York's particularities and its protean dynamism." Pub Wkly

Includes bibliographical references and indexes.

974.8   Pennsylvania

Pennsylvania: a history of the Commonwealth; edited by Randall M. Miller and William Pencak. Pennsylvania State Univ. Press 2002 xxxi, 654p il maps $49.95; pa $29.95 **974.8**

1. Pennsylvania -- History

ISBN 0-271-02213-2; 0-271-02214-0 pa

LC 2002-5457

"More than half of this book is an unusual and inspired hybrid of history and nine other disciplines from geography to literature. . . . The editors profess to discover the sources of Pennsylvania's greatness and significance but also expose its faults and declining significance in the 20th century. They succeed at both." Choice

Roker, Al, 1954-

Ruthless tide; the heroes and villains of the Johnstown flood, America's astonishing gilded age disaster. Al Roker. HarperCollins 2017 320 p. illustrations $28.99   **974.8**

1. Dams -- United States 2. Floods -- United States

ISBN 0062445510; 9780062445513

This book, by Al Roker, presents a "narrative . . . of the 1889 Johnstown Flood--the deadliest flood in US history. . . . [It] follows a . . . cast of characters whose fates converged because of that tragic day, including John Parke, the engineer whose heroic efforts failed to save the dam; Henry Clay Frick, the robber baron whose . . . sport fishing resort was responsible for modifications that weakened the structure; and Clara Barton, the founder of the American Red Cross." (Publisher's note)

"Roker is especially adept at focusing on key individuals--residents, politicians, movers and shakers, rescue workers--and letting their stories represent the myriads of others. . . . An exciting, tragic story seasoned with sensitive social analysis and criticism." Kirkus

Includes bibliographical references (pages 285-292) and index

975   Southeastern United States (South Atlantic states)

Blount, Roy

Long time leaving; dispatches from up South. [by] Roy Blount, Jr. Knopf 2007 383p $25   **975**

1. Southern States -- Humor 2. Southern States -- Civilization

ISBN 978-0-307-26618-7; 0-307-26618-4

LC 2007-6799

"This delightful collection is not only fun and funny but insightful as well." Libr J

Bragg, Rick

Ava's man. Knopf 2001 259p $25; pa $13   **975**

1. Carpenters 2. Factory workers

ISBN 0-375-41062-7; 0-375-72444-3 pa

LC 2001-32677

In this account of his maternal grandfather's life as a roofer and bootlegger in Appalachia, the author "creates a soulful, poignant portrait of working-class Southern life." Publ Wkly

Lemann, Nicholas

Redemption: the last battle of the Civil War. Farrar, Straus and Giroux 2006 257p $24   **975**

1. African Americans -- Segregation 2. Southern States -- Race relations

ISBN 978-0-374-24855-0; 0-374-24855-9

LC 2006-91

This book "offers a vigorous, necessary reminder of how racist reaction bred an American terrorism that suppressed black political activity and crushed Reconstruction in the South." N Y Times Book Rev

Includes bibliographical references

Southern living 50 years; a celebration of people, places, and culture. Sid Evans and the editors of Southern Living Magazine. Oxmoor House 2015 320 p. color illustrations (hardcover) $40   **975**

1. Southern cooking 2. Southern States -- Description and travel

ISBN 9780848744144; 0848744144

LC 2015942383

This book, by Sid Evans and the editors of the "Southern Living" magazine, celebrates the magazine's 50-year anniversary by profiling the Southern States. "Filled with evocative images, fascinating stories, revealing explorations, and time-honored recipes, [This book] . . . is about how Southerners live, what they value, how they cook, how they welcome people into their homes." (Publisher's note)

Theroux, Paul, 1941-

Deep South; four seasons on back roads. Paul Theroux. Houghton Mifflin Harcourt 2015 464 p. 16 unnumbered pages of plates (hardcover: alkaline paper) $29.95   **975**

1. Southern States 2. United States -- Description and travel 3. Seasons -- Southern States 4. Southern States -- Biography 5. Scenic byways -- Southern States 6. Southern States -- Social conditions 7. Southern States -- Description and travel 8. Southern States -- Social life and customs

ISBN 0544323521; 9780544323520

LC 2015006631

In this book author Paul Theroux "explores a piece of America -- the Deep South. He finds there a paradoxical place, full of incomparable music, unparalleled cuisine, and yet also some of the nation's worst schools, housing, and unemployment rates. It's these parts of the South, so often ignored, that have caught Theroux's keen traveler's eye." (Publisher's note)

"Theroux's books always appear on the best-seller list, and his latest may prove to be his most popular book yet." Booklist

Includes bibliographical references and index

975.004   Southeastern United States – Ethnic and national groups

Sedgwick, John

Blood moon; an American epic of war and splendor in the Cherokee Nation. by John Sedgwick. Simon & Schuster 2018 512 p. (hardcover) $30   **975.004**

1. Cherokee Indians 2. United States -- History -- 1861-1865, Civil War 3. Trail of Tears, 1838-1839 4. Cherokee Indians -- History -- 19th century

ISBN 9781501128691; 9781501128714

LC 2017041911

This book, by John Sedgwick, "is the story of the century-long blood feud between two rival Cherokee chiefs from the early years of the United States through the infamous Trail of Tears and into the Civil War. The two men's mutual hatred, while little remembered today, shaped the tragic history of the tribe far more than anyone, even the reviled President Andrew Jackson, ever did." (Publisher's note)

Includes bibliographical references and index

975.044   Southeastern States – 2000-

Catte, Elizabeth

★ **What** you are getting wrong about Appalachia; Elizabeth Catte. Belt Publishing 2018 146 p. $16.95   **975.044**

1. Human geography 2. Appalachian Region

ISBN 0998904147; 9780998904146

This book, by Elizabeth Catte, "is a frank assessment of America's recent fascination with the people and problems of the [Appalachian] region. The book analyzes trends in contemporary writing on Appalachia, presents a brief history of Appalachia with an eye toward unpacking Appalachian stereotypes, and provides examples of writing, art, and policy created by Appalachians as opposed to for Appalachians." (Publisher's note)

Includes bibliographical references (pages 135-142)

975.3   District of Columbia (Washington)

Brower, Kate Andersen

The **residence**; inside the private world of the White House. Kate Andersen Brower. Harper 2015 320 p. 16 plates; color illustrations $27.99   **975.3**

1. Presidents -- United States 2. White House (Washington, D.C.) 3. Presidents -- United States -- Biography -- Anecdotes 4. Washington (D.C.) -- Social life and customs -- Anecdotes 5. Presidents' spouses -- United States -- Biography -- Anecdotes 6. Presidents -- Family relationships -- United States -- Anecdotes 7. Children of presidents -- United States -- Biography -- Anecdotes 8. White House (Washington, D.C.) -- History -- 20th century -- Anecdotes 9. Household employees -- Washington (D.C.) -- Social life and customs -- Anecdotes

ISBN 0062305190; 9780062305190

LC 2014040404

This book by Kate Brower Anderson "reveals daily life in the White House as it is really lived through the voices of the maids, butlers, cooks, florists, doormen, engineers, and others who tend to the needs of the President and First Family. She reveals the intimacy between the First Family and the people who serve them, as well as tension that has shaken the staff over the decades." (Publisher's note)

"Fans of Downton Abbey will find this look into the secret world of the White House fascinating. History buffs who would like to learn more about the personal lives of the presidents and their families will definitely enjoy all the intriguing vignettes." LJ

Gordon, John S., 1944-

Washington's monument; and the fascinating history of the obelisk. John Steele Gordon. Bloomsbury USA 2016 224 p. illustrations (hardback) $27   **975.3**

1. Monuments 2. Washington Monument (Washington, D.C.) 3. Washington (D.C.) -- Buildings, structures, etc 4. Washington Monument (Washington, D.C.) -- History

ISBN 1620406500; 9781620406502

LC 2015036462

This book, by John Steele Gordon, examines the history of the Washington Monument. "The story behind its construction is a largely untold and intriguing piece of American history, which acclaimed historian John Steele Gordon relates with verve, connecting it to the colorful saga of the ancient obelisks of Egypt. Nobody knows how many obelisks were crafted in ancient Egypt, or even exactly how they were created. Their stories illuminate that of the Washington Monument." (Publisher's note)

"Filled with fascinating facts and interesting anecdotes, this is a book that will delight history and architecture buffs and enrich both past and planned visits to Washington, D.C., and its sights." Booklist

Includes bibliographical references (pages 215-216) and index.

Gugliotta, Guy

Freedom's cap; Guy Gugliotta. Hill and Wang 2012 viii, 486 p.p   **975.3**

1. Capitols 2. Historic buildings -- United States 3. United States -- History -- 1815-1861 4. United States -- History -- 1849-1877 5. Washington (D.C.) -- Buildings, structures, etc. 6. United States Capitol (Washington, D.C.) -- History

ISBN 9780809046812

LC 2011025750

This book takes place in "Washington [in the] 1850s. . . . [Author Guy Gugliotta provides an] account of the transformation of the U. S. Capitol from a[n] . . . inadequate . . . structure into today's massive marble symbol of democracy. . . . The author begins in the mid-1850s with the issue of Thomas Crawford's statue, 'Freedom,' now perched atop the Capitol dome. The . . . contest that Gugliotta outlines was between Army engineer Montgomery C. Meigs and architect Thomas Ustick Walter, both of whom would, at times, have control of the project. Both had ferocious work ethics, as well as enormous egos. . . . Gugliotta . . . includ[es] stories about marble quarries and ironworks; John Brown (whom he labels a terrorist); Presidents Fillmore, Pierce, Buchanan and Lincoln; and the many artisans and artists, principally Constantino Brumidi." (Kirkus)

Includes bibliographical references and index

Lusane, Clarence

The **Black** history of the White House. City Lights Books 2011 575p il (Open Media series)   **975.3**
1. Slavery -- United States 2. White House (Washington, D.C.) 3. United States -- Race relations 4. Presidents -- United States -- Staff 5. African Americans -- Washington (D.C.)
ISBN 978-0-8728-6532-7
            LC 2010-36925

The author "offers a comprehensive and well-documented account of African Americans who have graced the White House as builders, slaves, servants, entertainers, policy professionals, and finally as the nation's First Family. . . . This is an important work of historical scholarship, bringing together chronicles of the African Americans who have played major roles in the annals of the presidential mansion." Libr J

Includes bibliographical references

Monkman, Betty C.

★ The **White** House; its historic furnishings and first families. principal photography by Bruce White. Abbeville Press 2000 320p il $65   **975.3**
1. White House (Washington, D.C.)
ISBN 0-7892-0624-2
            LC 00-27085

"Monkman, the White House curator, documents the furnishings and decorative objects as well as the metamorphoses of White House interiors. The impact of the presidents and first ladies is particularly intriguing." Libr J

Includes bibliographical references

Official guide to the Smithsonian National Museum of African American History & Culture; National Museum of African American History and Culture; Kathleen M. Kendrick. Smithsonian Books 2017 175 p. color illustrations (paperback) $14.95   **975.3**
1. Museums -- Guidebooks 2. National Museum of African American History and Culture (U.S.) 3. National Museum of African American History and Culture (U.S.) -- Guidebooks
ISBN 9781588345936
            LC 2016038059

This book, by the National Museum of African American History and Culture with Kathleen M. Kendrick, "takes visitors on a journey through the richness and diversity of African American culture and the history of a people whose struggles, aspirations, and achievements have shaped the nation. Opened in September 2016, the National Museum of African American History and Culture welcomes all visitors who seek to understand, remember, and celebrate this history." (Publisher's note)

Includes bibliographical references.

Snow, Peter

When Britain burned the White House; the 1814 invasion of Washington. Peter Snow. Thomas Dunne Books/St. Martin's

Press 2014 320 p. 8 plates; illustrations; maps (hardcover: alk. paper) $25.99   **975.3**
1. War of 1812 2. United States -- Foreign relations -- Great Britain 3. Maryland -- History -- War of 1812 -- Campaigns 4. United States -- History -- War of 1812 -- Campaigns 5. Washington (D.C.) -- History -- Capture by the British, 1814
ISBN 1250048281; 9781250048288
            LC 2014010743

In this book on the War of 1812, author "Peter Snow recounts the fast-changing fortunes of that summer's extraordinary confrontations. Drawing from a wealth of material, including eyewitness accounts, Snow describes the colorful personalities on both sides of those spectacular events: including the beleaguered President James Madison and First Lady Dolley, American heroes such as Joshua Barney and Sam Smith, and flawed military leaders like Army Chief William Winder." (Publisher's note)

"Although the author ultimately tells a riveting true story, he offers little new about the campaign, which is disappointing. Summing Up: Recommended. Public libraries/general collections." Choice

Includes bibliographical references and index

975.5   Virginia

Horn, James P. P.

A **land** as God made it; Jamestown and the birth of America. [by] James Horn. Basic Books 2005 337p il maps $26 **975.5**
1. Jamestown (Va.) -- History
ISBN 0-465-03094-7
            LC 2005-13054

"Possessing Jamestown's inherent drama, this is a solid rendition of the saga." Booklist

Includes bibliographical references

Kelly, Joseph

Marooned; Jamestown, shipwreck, and the epic story of the first Americans. Joseph Kelly. Bloomsbury Publishing 2018 512 p. $32   **975.5**
1. Jamestown (Va.) -- History 2. Virginia -- History -- 1600-1775, Colonial period 3. Frontier and pioneer life -- Virginia -- Jamestown 4. Jamestown (Va.) -- History -- 17th century 5. Virginia -- History -- Colonial period, ca. 1600-1775
ISBN 9781632867773
            LC 2018003587

"Joseph Kelly reexamines the history of Jamestown and comes to a radically different and decidedly American interpretation of these first Virginians. . . . Kelly argues that the colonists at Jamestown were literally and figuratively marooned, cut loose from civilization, and cast into the wilderness. The British caste system meant little on this frontier: those who wanted to survive had to learn to . . . intermingle with the nearby native populations." (Publisher's note)

"Discovering seeds of democracy in Massachusetts' zealots or Virginia's autocratic patricians has never been easy, but Kelly's lively, heavily researched, frequently gruesome account gives a slight nod to Jamestown as the 'better place to look for the genesis of American ideals.'" Kirkus

Includes bibliographical references

Lingan, John

Homeplace; a Southern town, a country legend, and the last days of a mountaintop honky-tonk. John Lingan. Houghton Mifflin Harcourt 2018 272 p. (hardcover) $27   **975.5**

1. Social classes 2. Mountain people 3. Manners and customs 4. Winchester (Va.) -- Social conditions 5. Social classes -- Virginia -- Winchester 6. Winchester (Va.) -- Social life and customs 7. Mountain people -- Virginia -- Winchester -- Social conditions
ISBN 9780544932531

LC 2017050068

This book, by John Lingan, presents "an intimate account of country music, social change, and a vanishing way of life as . . . [the] Shenandoah town [of Winchester, Virginia] collides with the twenty-first century. . . . 'Homeplace'. . . illuminates questions that now dominate our national conversation--about how we move into the future without pretending our past doesn't exist, about what we salvage and what we leave behind." (Publisher's note)

"Readers interested in Patsy Cline and the Shenandoah Valley will appreciate the history and in-depth details of various localities." LJ

Includes bibliographical references

McElya, Micki
The **politics** of mourning; death and honor in Arlington National Cemetery. Micki McElya. Harvard University Press 2016 395 p. illustrations (hardcover) $29.95 **975.5**
1. Nationalism -- United States 2. Arlington National Cemetery (Va.) 3. Nationalism -- United States -- History 4. Arlington National Cemetery (Arlington, Va.) -- History 5. National cemeteries -- Virginia -- Arlington -- History
ISBN 9780674974067; 9780674737242

LC 2016008043

Pulitzer Prize Finalist: General Nonfiction (2017)
This book, by Micki McElya, shows the political role played by the Arlington National Cemetery in shaping the country's national identity. "The cemetery was seen primarily as a memorial to the white Civil War dead until its most famous monument was erected in 1921: the Tomb of the Unknown Soldier. . . . [It] encompasses the most inspiring and the most shameful aspects of American history." (Publisher's note)

"McElya diligently unravels the American desire to honor the dead, preserve history and custom, and devise symbols of what the cemetery should represent in the minds of its citizens." LJ

Includes bibliographical references (pages 315-371) and index

Poole, Robert M.
Section 60; Arlington National Cemetery: where war comes home. Robert M. Poole. Bloomsbury 2014 256 p. illustrations, map (alk. paper) $27 **975.5**
1. Afghan War, 2001- 2. Iraq War, 2003-2011 3. Arlington National Cemetery (Va.) 4. Memorial Day 5. Families of military personnel -- United States 6. Afghan War, 2001- -- Casualties -- United States 7. Iraq War, 2003-2011 -- Casualties -- United States 8. Arlington National Cemetery (Arlington, Va.) -- History -- 21st century
ISBN 1620402939; 9781620402931

LC 2014017528

Author Robert M. Poole's book on Arlington National Cemetary presents a "biography of a five-acre plot where many of those killed in Iraq and Afghanistan have been laid to rest alongside service members from earlier wars. Poole recounts stories of courage and sacrifice by fallen heroes, and explores the ways in which soldiers' comrades, friends, and families honor and remember those lost to war-carrying on with life in the aftermath of wartime tragedy." (Publisher's note)

"Nonfiction enthusiasts will appreciate this work; it will especially satisfy those with an interest in the human condition. It is a book that will linger in the reader's mind." LJ

Includes bibliographical references and index
Section 60, Arlington National Cemetery
Arlington National Cemetery, where war comes home

Price, David
★ **Love** and hate in Jamestown; John Smith, Pocahontas, and the heart of a new nation. {by} David A. Price. Knopf 2003 305p maps $25.95; pa $14.95 **975.5**
1. Princesses 2. Colonists 3. Indian leaders 4. Travel writers 5. Jamestown (Va.) -- History
ISBN 0-375-41541-6; 1-4000-3172-9 pa

LC 2002-43437

"For those general readers who wish to move beyond the myths and obtain a better understanding of them and the early years of the colony, this book will be an enjoyable and valuable tool." Booklist

Includes bibliographical references

Taylor, Alan
★ The **internal** enemy; slavery and war in Virginia, 1772-1832. Alan Taylor. W.W. Norton & Co. Inc. 2013 624 p. (hardcover) $35 **975.5**
1. Virginia -- History 2. Slavery -- United States -- History 3. United States -- History -- 1783-1815 4. Virginia -- History -- War of 1812 5. Slaves -- Virginia -- Tidewater (Region) -- History 6. Slavery -- Virginia -- Tidewater (Region) -- History 7. Plantation life -- Virginia -- Tidewater (Region) -- History 8. United States -- History -- War of 1812 -- Naval operations, British 9. United States -- History -- War of 1812 -- Participation, African American
ISBN 0393073718; 9780393073713

LC 2013009643

Pulitzer Prize: History (2014); National Book Award Finalist: Nonfiction (2013); LA Times Book Prize Finalist: History (2013)
Author Alan Taylor "illustrates that a great factor in the liberation of thousands of slaves was the policy and intervention of the British government and military. Taylor concentrates on the six decades between the American Revolution and the slave revolt of Nat Turner, and he focuses on the Chesapeake region of Virginia. The area is dotted with numerous rivers flowing to the bay, and here hundreds of slaves paddled out to British warships, especially during the War of 1812." (Booklist)

Includes bibliographical references and index

975.6 North Carolina

Horn, James
A **kingdom** strange; the brief and tragic history of the lost colony of Roanoke. [by] James Horn. Basic Books 2010 296p il map $26 **975.6**
1. Roanoke Island (N.C.) -- History
ISBN 978-0-465-00485-0

LC 2010-563

"The author creates an engaging, you-are-there feel to the narrative, with rich descriptions of European politics, colonists' daily struggles and the vagaries of relations between Native American tribes. . . . A satisfying recounting of some of the earliest American history." Kirkus

Includes bibliographical references

Kiernan, Denise
★ The **last** castle; the epic story of love, loss, and American royalty in the nation's largest home. Denise Kiernan. Touchstone 2017 vii, 388 p.p illustrations (hardcover) $28 **975.6**
1. Mansions -- United States 2. Biltmore Estate (Asheville, N.C.) -- History
ISBN 9781476794068; 9781476794044; 9781476794051

LC 2017015229

This book, by Denise Kiernan, tells the "true story behind the magnificent Gilded Age mansion Biltmore--the largest, grandest residence ever built in the United States. . . . Edith Stuyvesant Dresser . . . grew up in Newport and Paris, and her engagement and marriage to George Vanderbilt was one of the most watched events of Gilded Age society. But none of this prepared her to be mistress of Biltmore House." (Publisher's note)

"Kiernan (The Girls of Atomic City) presents an intriguing history of the largest private U.S. residence: the Biltmore House." LJ

Includes bibliographical references (pages 309-363) and index.

Lawler, Andrew

The **secret** token; myth, obsession, and the search for the lost colony of Roanoke. Andrew Lawler. Doubleday 2018 448 p. (hardcover) $29.95   **975.6**
1. Roanoke Island (N.C.) -- History 2. Great Britain -- Colonies -- America 3. United States -- History -- 1600-1775, Colonial period 4. Roanoke Colony 5. Roanoke Island (N.C.) -- History -- 16th century
ISBN 9780385542012

LC 2017045395

This book, by Andrew Lawler, provides "a sweeping account of America's oldest unsolved mystery, the people racing to unearth its answer, and the sobering truths--about race, gender, and immigration--exposed by the Lost Colony of Roanoke. In 1587, 115 men, women, and children arrived at Roanoke Island on the coast of North Carolina. . . . But when the colony's leader, John White, returned to Roanoke from a resupply mission, his settlers were nowhere to be found." (Publisher's note)

"This detailed historical inquiry will powerfully intrigue early American history buffs." Booklist

Includes bibliographical references

975.7   South Carolina

Ball, Edward

Slaves in the family. Ballantine Books 1999 505p il map pa $17.95   **975.7**
1. Plantation life 2. Slaveholders 3. South Carolina 4. Plantation owners 5. Slavery -- United States 6. United States -- Race relations
ISBN 978-0-345-43105-9; 0-345-43105-7
First published 1998 by Farrar, Straus & Giroux

"For nearly a hundred and seventy years before the Civil War, members of the Ball family owned a string of plantations worked by slaves along South Carolina's Cooper River. After the war, the author's ancestors lost or sold their land and scattered to make new lives, but he wondered what happened to the slaves. This book, a brilliant blend of archival research and oral history, tells what he found." New Yorker

Includes bibliographical references

Kytle, Ethan J.

Denmark Vesey's garden; slavery and memory in the cradle of Confederacy. Ethan J. Kytle and Blain Roberts. The New Press 2018 464 p. (alk. paper) $28.99   **975.7**
1. Slavery -- History 2. Charleston (S.C.) -- History 3. Emanuel AME Church (Charleston, S.C.) 4. Slavery -- South Carolina -- Charleston -- History 5. Charleston (S.C.) -- History -- Slave Insurrection, 1822 6. Memory -- Social aspects -- South Carolina -- Charleston
ISBN 1620973650; 9781620973653

LC 2017041546

This book, by Ethan J. Kytle and Blain Roberts, "reveals the deep roots of . . . [the] controversies [over Confederate symbols] and traces them to the heart of slavery in the United States: Charleston, South Carolina, where almost half of the U.S. slave population stepped onto our shores, where the first shot at Fort Sumter began the Civil War, and where Dylann Roof shot nine people at Emanuel A.M.E. Church." (Publisher's note)

Includes bibliographical references and index

975.8   Georgia

Berendt, John

Midnight in the garden of good and evil; a story of Savannah. Random House 1994 388p $25; pa $14   **975.8**
1. Savannah (Ga.)
ISBN 0-679-42922-0; 0-679-75152-1 pa

LC 93-3955

"Berendt has fashioned a Baedeker to Savannah that, while it flirts with condescension, is always contagiously affectionate. Few cities have been introduced more seductively." Newsweek

★ **Foxfire** 40th anniversary book; faith, family, and the land. edited by Angie Cheek, Lacy Hunter Nix, and Foxfire students. Anchor Books 2006 xxxix, 512p il pa $17.95 **975.8**
1. Handicraft 2. Country life -- Georgia 3. Appalachian region -- Social life and customs
ISBN 0-307-27551-5; 978-0-307-27551-6

LC 2006-45311

"Drawing on the magazine's published talks by local high school students with elderly rural inhabitants, the books have explored the crafts, cooking, music, gardening and stories that have been passed down through the generations. The focus in this anniversary volume is on devotion to religion, family and the land. Collecting pieces from 40 years' worth of the magazine, the book inevitably covers topics covered in previous Foxfire collections, including snake handling, childhood toys and recipes. But the spoken words remain captivating, eloquent if plainspoken." Publ Wkly

Jones, Jacqueline

Saving Savannah; the city and the Civil War. Alfred A. Knopf 2008 510p il map $30   **975.8**
1. Savannah (Ga.) 2. United States -- History -- 1861-1865, Civil War
ISBN 978-1-4000-4293-7; 1-4000-4293-3

LC 2008-11508

"Synthesizing the perspectives of the mercantile elite, the aristocratic upper crust and the downtrodden, . . . [the author has] fashioned a compelling social and political history." Washington Post Book World

Includes bibliographical references

Phillips, Jessica

Travels with Foxfire; stories of people, passions, and practices from Southern Appalachia. Phil Hudgins and Foxfire student Jessica Phillips. Anchor Books, a division of Random House LLC 2018 336 p. (pbk.: alk. paper) $19.95   **975.8**
1. Country life -- Appalachian Region 2. Southern States -- Social life and customs 3. Appalachian Region -- Social life and customs 4. Handicraft -- Southern States 5. Interviews -- Southern States 6. Country life -- Southern States 7. Southern States -- Civilization 8. Handicraft -- Appalachian Region 9. Interviews -- Appalachian Region 10. Appalachian Region -- Civilization
ISBN 9780525436294

LC 2017056227

In this book in the Foxfire Series, author "Phil Hudgins and Foxfire student Jessica Phillips travel from Georgia to the Carolinas, Tennessee to Kentucky, collecting the stories of the men and women who call the region home. Across more than thirty essays, we discover the secret origins of stock car racing, the story behind the formation of the Great Smoky Mountains National Park, . . . and the recipes of an award-winning cookbook writer." (Publisher's note)

"Some readers may be surprised by the breadth of material encompassed here; there are some chapters on African-American artistry and some on award-winning regional cooking (often including recipes). The collection ends abruptly, with no closing chapter, but anyone with an interest in Americana, history, or nature will appreciate these poignant and enjoyable stories of shared knowledge and traditions." Publishers' Weekly

Pressly, Paul M.

★ **On** the rim of the Caribbean; colonial Georgia and the British Atlantic world. Paul M. Pressly. University of Georgia Press 2013 xii, 354 p.p (hardcover: alk. paper) $69.95 **975.8**
1. Georgia -- History 2. International trade 3. United States -- History -- 1600-1775, Colonial period 4. Georgia -- Economic conditions -- 18th century 5. Plantations -- Georgia -- History -- 18th century 6. Georgia -- History -- Colonial period, ca. 1600-1775 7. Georgia -- Commerce -- West Indies, British -- History -- 18th century 8. West Indies, British -- Commerce -- Georgia -- History -- 18th century
ISBN 0820335673; 0820345032; 9780820335674; 9780820345031

LC 2012033964

In this book, "Paul M. Pressly interprets Georgia's place in the Atlantic world in light of recent work in transnational and economic history." He "examines the ways in which Georgia came to share many of the characteristics of the sugar islands, how Savannah developed as a 'Caribbean' town, the dynamics of an emerging slave market, and the role of merchant-planters as leaders in forging a highly adaptive economic culture open to innovation." (Publisher's note)

"This richly documented, analytically complex, and well-written book is a major contribution to the study of Colonial Georgia and the 18th-century Atlantic world." Choice

Includes bibliographical references (p. [301]-335) and index

Sherrod, Shirley

The **courage** to hope; how I stood up to the right wing media, the Obama administration, and the forces of fear. Shirley Sherrod; with Catherine Whitney. 1st Atria Books hardcover ed. Atria Books 2012 240 p., [8] p. of plates p col. ill. (hardcover: alk. paper) $24.99; (trade paper: alk. paper) $15.00 **975.8**
1. Rural development 2. Sherrod, Shirley, 1948- 3. United States -- Race relations 4. Rural poor -- Georgia 5. Georgia -- Rural conditions 6. Rural development -- Georgia 7. Farmers -- Georgia -- Economic conditions 8. Mass media -- Objectivity -- United States 9. African American farmers -- Georgia -- Economic conditions 10. United States. Dept. of Agriculture -- Officials and employees -- Biography
ISBN 1451650949; 9781451650945; 9781451651010; 9781451651027

LC 2011050718

In this memoir, "[Shirley] Sherrod sets the record straight on her forced resignation from the Department of Agriculture in 2010. The author . . . was director for the USDA's Rural Development in Georgia when conservative political blogger Andrew Breitbart attacked her for allegedly reverse racist comments she made at an NAACP event. The threat of exposure on national TV was enough to send the USDA running for cover, and she was dismissed. Sherrod decided she had to fight back." (Kirkus Reviews)

Includes bibliographical references and index.

975.9 Florida

Barry, Dave, 1947-

Best. State. Ever. A Florida Man Defends His Homeland. by Dave Barry. G. P. Putnam's Sons 2016 229 p. illustrations $27 **975.9**
1. Florida 2. Wit and humor 3. Florida -- Humor
ISBN 1101982608; 9781101982600

LC 2016027545

This book, by Dave Barry, is a "funny exploration of the Sunshine State from the man who knows it best. . . . Somehow, the state's acquired an image as a subtropical festival of stupid, and as a loyal Floridian, Dave begs to differ. Sure, there was the 2000 election. And people seem to take their pants off for no good reason. And it has flying insects the size of LeBron James. But it is a great state, and Dave is going to tell you why." (Publisher's note)

"Readers may not embrace Florida the way the author has, but they will understand why a humorist loves it." Kirkus.

Gaines, Steven S.

Fool's paradise; players, poseurs, and the culture of excess in South Beach. Crown Publishers 2009 274p il $25.95 **975.9**
1. South Beach (Miami Beach, Fla.) -- Social life and customs
ISBN 978-0-307-34627-8; 0-307-34627-7

LC 2008-36067

This is a "terrific social history buffet. . . . [Gaines is] a gifted storyteller. He fills the book with telling anecdotes and bons mots, but the narrative never gets off track. It would be easy to focus on the drug-and-sleaze aspect of South Beach. But Gaines lets a little bit go a long way. He could fill the book with stupid celebrity tricks. But again, less is more. This book succeeds not because of star power but because of story power. The centerpiece of the book is a war of dueling architects and builders fighting to build the iconic Fontainebleau hotel and then to destroy it out of spite." St. Petersburg Times

Includes bibliographical references

Grunwald, Michael

The **swamp**; the Everglades, Florida, and the politics of paradise. Simon & Schuster 2005 450p il map hardcover o.p. pa $15 **975.9**
1. Everglades (Fla.)
ISBN 0-7432-5105-9; 978-0-7432-5105-1; 978-0-7432-5107-5 pa; 0-7432-5107-5 pa

LC 2005-56329

This is a "chronicle of the history of the Everglades. . . . [This] is a riveting tale of ambition versus ecological reality, politics versus science, and, on the upside, our gradual awakening to the true nature of nature." Booklist

Includes bibliographical references

976.1 Alabama

Agee, James, 1909-1955

★ **Cotton** Tenants; Three Families. Random House Inc 2013 224 p. $24.95 **976.1**

1. Farm family -- Alabama -- History -- 20th century 2. Farm tenancy -- Alabama -- History -- 20th century
ISBN 1612192122; 9781612192123

This book, written during the Great Depression, was "commissioned by Fortune magazine' as a 'report on working conditions of poor white farmers in the deep south.' The report itself was never published. . . . It follows the lives of three impoverished tenant farmers--Floyd Burroughs, Bud Fields, and Frank Tingle--and their families". Topics include "diet, shelter, and labor". (Publishers Weekly)

Let us now praise famous men; [by] James Agee, Walker Evans; with an introduction to the new edition by John Hersey. Houghton Mifflin 2000 il $30; pa $18   **976.1**
1. Farm tenancy 2. Alabama -- Social conditions
ISBN 978-0-395-95771-4; 0-395-95771-0; 978-0-618-12749-8 pa; 0-618-12749-6 pa
First published 1941

This work documents "the ways of life of three Alabama tenant-farming families. . . . It is a unique and complex book, deeply honest and compassionate, and remarkable for its extraordinary descriptive, lyric, and meditative prose." Benet's Reader's Ency of Am Lit

McWhorter, Diane
Carry me home; Birmingham, Alabama: the climactic battle of the civil rights revolution. Simon & Schuster 2001 701p il hardcover o.p. pa $17   **976.1**
1. African Americans -- Civil rights 2. Birmingham (Ala.) -- Race relations
ISBN 0-684-80747-5; 0-7432-1772-1 pa
LC 00-53827

McWhorter presents an account of the struggle for civil rights in Birmingham, Ala., both from a personal and societal perspective

"A daughter of Birmingham's privileged elite, McWhorter weaves a personal narrative through this startling account of the history, events, and major players on both sides of the civil rights battle in that city." Booklist
Includes bibliographical references

976.3   Louisiana

Baum, Dan
Nine lives; death and life in New Orleans. Spiegel & Grau 2009 335p $26   **976.3**
1. New Orleans (La.) -- Social life and customs
ISBN 978-0-385-52319-6; 0-385-52319-X
LC 2008-31483

"Baum's in-depth reporting (he was on scene during Katrina, even turning himself in at the Convention Center to chronicle the out-of-sight outrages) is evident on every page." Booklist
Includes bibliographical references

Brinkley, Douglas
The **great** deluge; Hurricane Katrina, New Orleans, and the Mississippi Gulf Coast. Morrow 2006 716p il hardcover o.p. pa $17.95   **976.3**
1. Disaster relief 2. Hurricane Katrina, 2005
ISBN 0-06-112423-0; 0-06-114849-0 pa
LC 2006-43338

This is an account of Hurricane Katrina, which ravaged the Gulf Coast in late summer 2005.

The author "captures the human toll of Katrina as graphically as the

most vivid newspaper and television accounts did, and by pulling together a huge, choral portrait of what happened during that first week of havoc and distress (from Saturday, Aug. 27, through Saturday, Sept. 3), he gives the reader a richly detailed timeline of disaster—a timeline in which the sheer cumulative power of details impresses upon us, again, just how abysmally inept relief efforts were on every level, from FEMA to the Red Cross to the New Orleans police department, from the federal government to state and local authorities." N Y Times (Late N Y Ed)

Dyson, Michael Eric
Come hell or high water; Hurricane Katrina and the color of disaster. Basic Civitas 2006 258p $23; pa $14.95   **976.3**
1. Disaster relief 2. Hurricane Katrina, 2005 3. African Americans -- Social conditions
ISBN 978-0-465-01761-4; 0-465-01761-4; 978-0-465-01772-0 pa; 0-465-01772-X pa
LC 2007-310210

This book on Hurrican Katrina "not only chronicles what happened when, it also argues that the nation's failure to offer timely aid to Katrina's victims indicates deeper problems in race and class relations. . . . [The author's] contention that Katrina exposed a dominant culture pervaded not only by 'active malice' toward poor blacks but also by a long history of 'passive indifference' to their problems is both powerful and unsettling." Publ Wkly
Includes bibliographical references

Horne, Jed
★ **Breach** of faith; Hurricane Katrina and the near death of a great American city. Random House 2006 412p map hardcover o.p. pa $16   **976.3**
1. Disaster relief 2. Hurricane Katrina, 2005 3. New Orleans (La.) -- Description and travel
ISBN 978-1-4000-6552-3; 1-4000-6552-6; 978-0-8129-7650-2 pa; 0-8129-7650-9 pa
LC 2006-46468

This book does "an admirable job of detailing the design flaws that left New Orleans underwater." New Repub
Includes bibliographical references

Krist, Gary
Empire of sin; a story of sex, jazz, murder, and the battle for modern New Orleans. Gary Krist. Crown 2014 432 p. illustrations (hardback) $26   **976.3**
1. Prostitution 2. Crime -- United States 3. New Orleans (La.) -- History 4. New Orleans (La.) -- History -- 20th century 5. New Orleans (La.) -- Social conditions -- 20th century 6. Storyville (New Orleans, La.) -- History -- 20th century 7. Crime -- Louisiana -- New Orleans -- History -- 20th century 8. Murder -- Louisiana -- New Orleans -- History -- 20th century 9. Corruption -- Louisiana -- New Orleans -- History -- 20th century 10. Sex customs -- Louisiana -- New Orleans -- History -- 20th century 11. Storyville (New Orleans, La.) -- Social conditions -- 20th century 12. Jazz -- Social aspects -- Louisiana -- New Orleans -- History -- 20th century
ISBN 0770437060; 9780770437060; 9780770437084
LC 2014003191

This book, by Gary Krist, "re-creates the remarkable story of New Orleans' thirty-years war against itself, pitting the city's elite 'better half' against its powerful and long-entrenched underworld of vice, perversity, and crime. This early-20th-century battle centers on one man: Tom Anderson, the undisputed czar of the city's Storyville vice district, who fights desperately to keep his empire intact as it faces onslaughts from all sides." (Publisher's note)

"Krist's lively book is only marred by an overlong section devoted to a series of axe murders that plagued the city. A wild, well-told tale." Kirkus

Includes bibliographical references (pages 333-344) and index

Lane, Charles

The **day** freedom died; the Colfax massacre, the Supreme Court, and the betrayal of Reconstruction. Henry Holt and Co. 2008 326p il map $27   **976.3**
   1. Massacres 2. Trials (Homicide) 3. Reconstruction (1865-1876) 4. Louisiana -- Race relations 5. African Americans -- History 6. United States -- Supreme Court
   ISBN 978-0-8050-8342-2; 0-8050-8342-1

LC 2007-37514

"The Colfax Massacre . . . took place on an Easter Sunday afternoon in 1873. Within four hours, at least eighty black American men had been brutally murdered by white vigilantes in Colfax, La. Journalist Lane's groundbreaking and persuasive work illustrates this 'pivotal event in the political and constitutional history of post-Civil War America' and its social, political and judicial aftermath. . . . Students of American and African-American history will find it particularly valuable; fans of American history will find it a moving and instructive drama." Publ Wkly

Includes bibliographical references

Neufeld, Josh

A.D. New Orleans after the deluge. Pantheon Books 2009 193p il $24.95   **976.3**
   1. Graphic novels 2. New Orleans (La.) -- Graphic novels 3. Hurricane Katrina, 2005 -- Graphic novels
   ISBN 978-0-307-37814-9; 0-307-37814-4

LC 2008-55687

"Graphic artist Neufeld paints an emotive portrait of New Orleans during and after Hurricane Katrina, as seen through the eyes of seven of the city's citizens. The opening panels coalesce into a long cinematic pan, a thrumming setup for the disaster. The half-page and quarter-page panels—satellite views of weather patterns and close inspections of neighborhoods—are crisp, and the two-page spreads are softly focused. . . . Neufeld's words and images are commensurable and rhythmic, and the vernacular is sharp. Bristling with attitude and pungent with social awareness." Kirkus

Rasmussen, Daniel

American uprising; the untold story of America's largest slave revolt. Harper 2011 276p map   **976.3**
   1. Slavery -- United States 2. New Orleans (La.) -- History 3. African Americans -- Louisiana 4. New Orleans (La.) -- Race relations 5. Slavery -- Louisiana -- New Orleans 6. African Americans -- Louisiana -- New Orleans 7. Slave insurrections -- Louisiana -- New Orleans
   ISBN 0061995215; 0062084356; 9780061995217; 9780062084354

LC 2010017855

This is a history of the 1811 slave rebellion in New Orleans. Bibliography. Index.

This is an "account of a large-scale, three-day slave revolt on the sugar plantations near New Orleans during the 1811 Carnival (Mardi Gras) season. The author argues that the slave-rebels, who had learned warfare tactics in their native Africa, were inspired by the successful Haitian revolution. . . . This is a welcome addition to popular history and an engaging read for anyone interested in this important chapter in the tragic story of American slavery." Libr J

Includes bibliographical references

Rivlin, Gary

Katrina; After the Flood. Gary Rivlin. Simon & Schuster 2015 480 p. maps $27   **976.3**
   1. New Orleans (La.) 2. Hurricane Katrina, 2005
   ISBN 1451692226; 9781451692228

LC 2015431412

In this book, "ten years after Hurricane Katrina made landfall in southeast Louisiana--on August 29, 2005--journalist Gary Rivlin traces the storm's immediate damage, the city of New Orleans's efforts to rebuild itself, and the storm's lasting affects not just on the city's geography and infrastructure--but on the psychic, racial, and social fabric of one of this nation's great cities." (Publisher's note)

"Rivlin captures the snark, the bellyaching, and the outright denial of those in charge—and many aimed to be in charge (while many dodged responsibility as well). A fascinating lesson in urban planning in the face of calamity and financial shenanigans about what has been deemed 'the most expensive disaster in history.'" Booklist

Van Heerden, Ivor Ll.

The **storm**; what went wrong and why during Hurricane Katrina. [by] Ivor van Heerden and Mike Bryan. Viking 2006 308p il map hardcover o.p. pa $15   **976.3**
   1. Disaster relief 2. Hurricane Katrina, 2005
   ISBN 0-670-03781-8; 0-14-311213-9 pa

LC 2006-44727

This book focuses on public mismanagement relating to Hurricane Katrina.

"This serious, scientific explanation of what exactly happened in the hours—and years—leading up to Hurricane Katrina's devestation of New Orleans brings a fresh perspective to a tragedy that has generated remarkably similar news accounts over the past eight months." Publ Wkly

Includes bibliographical references

976.4 Texas

Donovan, James

The **blood** of heroes; the 13-day struggle for the Alamo--and the sacrifice that forged a nation. James Donovan. 1st ed. Little, Brown and Co. 2012 x, 500 p.p ill., maps $29.99 **976.4**
   1. Texas -- History 2. Alamo (San Antonio, Tex.) -- History 3. Alamo (San Antonio, Tex.) -- Siege, 1836
   ISBN 0316053740; 9780316053747

LC 2011050067

This book chronicles "the Battle of the Alamo" which the author characterizes as "the signal event of the Texas struggle for independence. . . . [James] Donovan's . . . story focuses on the 13-day standoff, but he also supplies . . . context, helping us to understand the history of the breakaway province and notable characters in the revolution like [Sam] Houston, Stephen Austin, Ben Milam and James C. Neill." (Kirkus Reviews)

Includes bibliographical references (p. [467]-488) and index.

Hodge, Roger D.

★ **Texas** blood; seven generations among the outlaws, ranchers, Indians, missionaries, soldiers, and smugglers of the borderlands. by Roger D. Hodge. Alfred A. Knopf 2017 353 p. (hardcover) $28.95   **976.4**
   1. Texas -- History 2. Texas -- Description and travel 3. Texas -- History, Local 4. Mexican-American Border Region -- History, Local 5. Mexican-American Border Region -- Description and

travel
ISBN 9780307961402

LC 2016053188

This book, by Roger D. Hodge, is an "attempt to grapple with all that makes Texas so magical, punishing, and polarizing. Here is a spellbindingly evocative portrait of the borderlands . . .; where stories of death and drugs and desperation play out daily. And here is a contemplation of what it means that the ranching industry that has sustained families like Hodge's for almost two centuries is quickly fading away." (Publisher's note)

Includes bibliographical references and index

McCollom, James P.

The **last** sheriff in Texas; a true tale of violence and the vote. James McCollom. Counterpoint Press 2017 272 p. $26　　　**976.4**

1. Texas -- History　2. Police corruption　3. Beeville (Tex.) -- History -- 20th century　4. Sheriffs -- Texas -- Beeville -- Case studies　5. Elections -- Texas -- Beeville -- Case studies　6. Beeville (Tex.) -- Social conditions -- 20th century　7. Police misconduct -- Texas -- Beeville -- Case studies　8. Beeville (Tex.) -- Politics and government -- 20th century

ISBN 1619029960; 9781619029965

LC 2017024770

In this book, by James McCollom, "Beeville, Texas, was the most American of small towns. . . . Old West justice ruled, as evidenced by a 1947 shootout when outlaws surprised popular sheriff Vail Ennis at a gas station and shot him five times, point-blank, in the belly. Ennis managed to draw his gun and put three bullets in each assailant; he reloaded and shot them three times more." (Publisher's note)

"Of interest to students of Texas history as well as aspiring law enforcement officers, who should read it as an example of how not to conduct themselves." Kirkus Reviews

Roker, Al, 1954-

The **storm** of the century; tragedy, heroism, survival, and the epic true story of America's deadliest natural disaster: the great Gulf hurricane of 1900. Al Roker. William Morrow 2015 320 p. 8 plates; ills., maps (hardcover) $27.99　　　**976.4**

1. Storms　2. Natural disasters -- United States　3. Galveston (Tex.) -- History -- 20th century　4. Hurricanes -- Texas -- Galveston -- History -- 20th century

ISBN 0062364650; 9780062364654; 9780062364661

LC 2015007009

In this book, author Al Roker "brings to life the Great Gulf Hurricane of 1900, the deadliest natural disaster in American history. Exploring the impact of the disaster on a rising nation's confidence--the pain and trauma of the loss and the determination of the response--Al Roker illuminates both the energy and the limitations of the American Century, and of nature itself." (Publisher's note)

"Roker's account will interest readers who previously knew nothing about the Galveston hurricane. However, Isaac's Storm is not out of date and deserves its place as the recommended version." Kirkus

Includes bibliographical references

Valby, Karen

Welcome to Utopia; notes from a small town. Spiegel & Grau 2010 238p il $25　　　**976.4**

1. City and town life　2. Utopia (Tex.)

ISBN 978-0-385-52286-1; 0-385-52286-X

LC 2009-37970

"Entertainment Weekly magazine sent intrepid reporter Karen Valby into the great flyover zone in 2006 in search of a 'small town somewhere in America without popular culture.' She found Utopia, a town of a few hundred souls 90 miles west of the nation's seventh-largest city, San Antonio. Utopia is not exactly off the grid, and one suspects that its name appealed to Valby more than its isolation. Her book . . . is a pleasant moment-in-time postcard of a typical U.S. town." Minneapolis Star Tribune

Includes bibliographical references

976.6　Oklahoma

Anderson, Sam

Boom town; the fantastical saga of Oklahoma city, its chaotic founding... its purloined basketball team, and the dream of becoming a world-class metropolis. Sam Anderson. Crown 2018 432 p. (hardback) $28　　　**976.6**

1. Urbanization　2. Cities and towns　3. Oklahoma City (Okla.) -- History　4. Oklahoma City (Okla.) -- Social life and customs

ISBN 9780804137317; 9780804137331

LC 2017054583

In this book, author Sam Anderson "unfolds an idiosyncratic mix of American history, sports reporting, urban studies, gonzo memoir, and much more to tell the strange but compelling story of . . . [Oklahoma City] whose unique mix of geography and history make it a fascinating microcosm of the democratic experiment. Filled with [popular] characters . . . , 'Boom Town' offers a remarkable look at the urban tapestry woven from control and chaos, sports and civics." (Publisher's note)

"Anderson's lively and empathetic saga captures the outsize ambitions, provincial realities, and vibrant history of a quintessentially American city." Pub Wkly

Field, Kendra Taira

★ **Growing** up with the country; family, race, and nation after the civil war. Kendra Taira Field. Yale University Press 2017 256 p. (hardback: alk. paper) $38　　　**976.6**

1. African Americans　2. Internal migration　3. Immigrants -- United States -- History

ISBN 9780300180527

LC 2017932063

Part of The Lamar Series in Western History, "Kendra Field's epic family history chronicles the westward migration of freedom's first generation in the fifty years after emancipation. Drawing on decades of archival research and family lore within and beyond the United States, Field traces their journey out of the South to Indian Territory, where they participated in the development of black and black Indian towns and settlements." (Publisher's note)

"A masterpiece in the areas of personal narration, family genealogy, and African American historiography. Highly recommended for U.S. Civil War/Reconstruction and African American scholars and enthusiasts, genealogical specialists, and all readers." LJ

Grann, David

★ **Killers** of the flower moon; the Osage murders and the birth of the FBI. David Grann. Doubleday 2016 352 p. (hardcover) $28.95　　　**976.6**

1. Osage Indians -- Crimes against -- Case studies　2. Murder -- Oklahoma -- Osage County -- Case studies　3. United States. Federal Bureau of Investigation -- Case studies　4. Osage County (Okla.) -- History -- 20th century　5. Homicide investigation -- Oklahoma -- Osage County -- Case studies

ISBN 9780385534246; 0385534248

LC 2016021407

National Book Award Finalist: Nonfiction (2017)

Carnegie Medal Finalist: Nonfiction (2018)

In this book on the Osage Indian nation murders of the 1920s, author David Grann "revisits a shocking series of crimes in which dozens of people were murdered in cold blood. Based on years of research and startling new evidence, the book is a masterpiece of narrative nonfiction, as each step in the investigation reveals a series of sinister secrets and reversals." (Publisher's note)

"Grann employs you-are-there narrative effects to set readers right in the action, and he relays the humanity, evil, and heroism of the people involved. His riveting reckoning of a devastating episode in American history deservedly captivates." Booklist

Hirsch, James S.

Riot and remembrance; the Tulsa race war and its legacy. Houghton Mifflin 2002 358p il $25; pa $14   **976.6**

   1. Riots 2. Tulsa (Okla.) -- Race relations 3. African Americans -- Tulsa (Okla.)

   ISBN 0-618-10813-0; 0-618-34076-9 pa

LC 2001-51615

"Hirsch unearths an important episode in U.S. history with verve, intelligence and compassion." Publ Wkly

Includes bibliographical references

976.8   Tennessee

Kiernan, Denise

The **girls** of atomic city; the secret history of the women who built WWII's most powerful weapon. by Denise Kiernan. Simon & Schuster 2013 400 p. $26   **976.8**

   1. Atomic bomb 2. Women -- Tennessee -- Oak Ridge -- History 3. World War, 1939-1945 -- Tennessee -- Oak Ridge 4. Oak Ridge (Tenn.) -- History -- 20th century

   ISBN 1451617526; 9781451617528

LC 2012045467

This book by Denise Kiernan tells the "story of the young women of Oak ridge, Tennessee, who unwittingly played a crucial role in . . . enriching uranium for the atomic bomb. . . . Few could piece together the true nature of their work until the bomb 'Little Boy' was dropped over Hiroshima, Japan, and the secret was out. Kiernan traces the astonishing story of these unsung WWII workers through interviews with dozens of surviving women and other Oak Ridge residents." (Publisher's note)

Includes bibliographical references

Lauterbach, Preston

Beale Street Dynasty; Sex, Song, and the Struggle for the Soul of Memphis. Preston Lauterbach. W W Norton & Co Inc 2015 368 p. 8 plates; ills.; maps $26.95   **976.8**

   1. Race relations 2. Political corruption 3. Memphis (Tenn.) -- History

   ISBN 0393082571; 9780393082579

LC 2014039928

Author Preston Lauterbach presents this "history of Beale Street . . . and the battle for the soul of Memphis. Following the Civil War, Beale Street in Memphis, Tennessee, thrived as a cauldron of sex and song, violence and passion. But out of this turmoil emerged a center of black progress, optimism, and cultural ferment. Lauterbach tells this . . . story through the multigenerational saga of a family whose ambition, race pride, and moral complexity indelibly shaped the city." (Publisher's note)

"While sex and song (as promised in the book's subtitle) are present at times, this account is really about politics and power in a major Southern city. Recommended for all readers interested in Memphis or in African American history." LJ

976.9   Kentucky

Snyder, Christina

Great Crossings; Indians, Settlers, and Slaves in the Age of Jackson. Christina Snyder. Oxford University Press 2017 416 p. illustrations, maps (hardcover: alk. paper) $29.95   **976.9**

   1. Kentucky 2. Choctaw Indians 3. Slaves -- United States -- 19th century 4. Choctaw Indian Academy -- History 5. Great Crossing (Ky.) -- History -- 19th century 6. Slaves -- Kentucky -- Great Crossing -- History -- 19th century 7. Great Crossing (Ky.) -- Race relations -- History -- 19th century 8. United States -- Territorial expansion -- History -- 19th century 9. Community life -- Kentucky -- Great Crossing -- History -- 19th century 10. Choctaw Indians -- Kentucky -- Great Crossing -- History -- 19th century 11. Imperialism -- Social aspects -- United States -- History -- 19th century 12. African Americans -- Kentucky -- Great Crossing -- History -- 19th century

   ISBN 9780199399062

LC 2016024418

This book, by Christina Snyder, "reinterprets the history of Jacksonian America. Most often, this drama focuses on whites who turned west to conquer a continent, extending 'liberty' as they went. Great Crossings also includes Native Americans from across the continent seeking new ways to assert anciently-held rights and people of African descent who challenged the United States to live up to its ideals." (Publisher's note)

"This is a well-researched, engagingly written, and remarkable work of scholarship." Pub Wkly

Includes bibliographical references and index

977   North central United States

Boissoneault, Lorraine

The **Last** Voyageurs; Retracing La Salle's Journey Across America: Sixteen Teenagers on an Adventure of a Lifetime. by Lorraine Boissoneault. W W Norton & Co Inc 2016 368 p. color illustrations, map $27.95   **977**

   1. Teachers 2. Mississippi River 3. Voyages and travels

   ISBN 1605989762; 9781605989761

In this book, by Lorraine Boissoneault, "Reid Lewis never wanted to be an ordinary French teacher. With the approach of the American Bicentennial, he decided to . . . [recreate] the voyage of René Robert Cavelier, Sieur de La Salle, the first European to travel from Montreal to the end of the Mississippi River. Lewis' crew of modern voyageurs was comprised of 16 high school students and 6 teachers." (Publisher's note)

"All the elements of an exciting adventure story are here. Boissoneault describes interesting, complicated people facing life-threatening perils, and in alternating Lewis's story with that of La Salle's journey, she makes fascinating historical comparisons." Pub Wkly

Cox, Anna-Lisa

The **bone** and sinew of the land; America's forgotten black pioneers and the struggle for equality. Anna-Lisa Cox. PublicAffairs 2018 304 p. (hardcover) $28   **977**

   1. Slaves -- Emancipation 2. African Americans -- History 3. Farmers -- United States -- HIstory 4. Northwest, Old -- Race relations 5. Frontier and pioneer life -- Ohio 6. Frontier and pioneer life -- Indiana 7. Northwest, Old -- History -- 1775-1865 8.

Frontier and pioneer life -- Northwest, Old 9. African Americans -- Northwest, Old -- History 10. African Americans -- Ohio -- History -- 19th century 11. African Americans -- Indiana -- History -- 19th century 12. African Americans -- Social conditions -- Northwest, Old
ISBN 9781610398107

LC 2017056938

This book, by Anna-Lisa Cox, reveals the "truth about America's black pioneers, the frontier they settled, and their fight for a better nation. . . . Starting in our nation's earliest years, thousands of free African Americans were building hundreds of settlements in the Northwest Territory, a territory that banned slavery and gave equal voting rights to all men. This groundbreaking work of research reveals the lost history of the nation's first Great Migration." (Publisher's note)

Includes bibliographical references and index

Dennis, Jerry

The **living** Great Lakes; searching for the heart of the inland seas. Thomas Dunne Bks. 2003 296p il maps hardcover o.p. pa $14.95   977

1. Great Lakes
ISBN 0-312-25193-9; 0-312-33103-7 pa

LC 2002-32500

The author offers a "description of being a crew member on the schooner Malabar on a six-week trip through the waters of Lakes Huron, Ontario, Michigan, Erie and Superior. . . . Dennis weaves anecdotes from his childhood, such as a family-fishing trip on Lake Michigan, together with informed commentary on the natural history of the lakes and the people who live there." Publ Wkly

Includes bibliographical references

Laskin, David

The **children's** blizzard; . HarperCollins 2004 307p map $24.95; pa $13.95   977

1. Blizzards
ISBN 0-06-052075-2; 0-06-052076-0 pa

LC 2005-295018

"An adroit, sensitive drama and a skillful addition to a popular genre." Booklist

Includes bibliographical references

977.1   Ohio

Gup, Ted

A **secret** gift; how one man's kindness--and a trove of letters--revealed the hidden history of the Great Depression. Penguin Press 2010 365p il $25.95   977.1

1. Charity 2. Businesspeople 3. Philanthropists 4. Great Depression, 1929-1939 5. Canton (Ohio)
ISBN 978-1-59420-270-4; 1-59420-270-2

LC 2010-17302

"As Gup interweaves the sagas of recipient families with the life of their anonymous benefactor, 'A Secret Gift' never fails to entertain, inform and sometimes astound." Cleveland Plain Dealer

Ryan, Terry

The **prize** winner of Defiance, Ohio; how my mother raised 10 kids on 25 words or less. foreword by Suze Orman. Simon & Schuster 2001 351p il $24; pa $13   977.1

1. Homemakers 2. Prizewinners 3. Defiance (Ohio) -- Biography 4. Prize contests in advertising

ISBN 0-7432-1122-7; 0-7432-1123-5 pa

LC 2001-18379

"Although Terry Ryan's father, Kelly Ryan, drank away most of his weekly machinist's paycheck, her mother responded by finding a use for her skill with words {by entering and winning contests}." (Women's Rev Books)

The author recounts the life of her mother, "a small-town Ohio housewife in the nineteen-fifties who lived on the brink of dire poverty, thanks to a brood of ten kids and an ineffectual drunk of a husband. Since Evelyn couldn't work outside her home, she worked inside it, penning hundreds of product jingles and entering them in the national contests that drove the advertising industry of the day." New Yorker

977.3   Illinois

Abbott, Karen

Sin in the Second City; madams, ministers, playboys, and the battle for America's soul. Random House 2007 xxiv, 356p il $25.95   977.3

1. Prostitution 2. Madams 3. Everleigh Club (Chicago, Ill.) 4. Prostitution -- Illinois -- Chicago 5. Chicago (Ill.) -- Social life and customs
ISBN 1-4000-6530-5; 978-1-4000-6530-1

LC 2006-51878

This book by Karen Abbott examines "the history of the Everleigh Club that operated on Chicago's Near South Side from 1900 to 1911. At this renowned high-class brothel, enterprising sisters Ada and Minna Everleigh challenged the stereotype of the victimized immature woman by hiring only willing adults whose comportment, education, meals, and health they closely monitored." (Library Journal)

"Lavish in her details, nicely detached in her point of view, [and with] scrupulous concern for historical accuracy, Ms. Abbott has written an immensely readable book. Sin in the Second City offers much in the way of reflection for those interested in the unending puzzle that goes by the name of human nature." Wall Street Journal

Includes bibliographical references

Cohen, Adam

American pharaoh: Mayor Richard J. Daley: his battle for Chicago and the nation; {by} Adam Cohen and Elizabeth Taylor. Little, Brown 2000 614p map hardcover o.p. pa $16.95   977.3

1. Mayors 2. Political party leaders 3. Chicago (Ill.) -- Politics and government
ISBN 0-316-83489-0 pa

LC 99-42157

"Penetrating, nonsensationalistic and exhaustive, this is an impressive and important biography." Publ Wkly

Includes bibliographical references

Dyja, Thomas

The **third** coast; when Chicago built the American dream. Thomas Dyja. The Penguin Press 2013 xxxiv, 544 p.p ill. (hardcover) $29.95   977.3

1. Chicago (Ill.) -- History -- 20th century 2. Chicago (Ill.) -- Social conditions -- 20th century 3. Chicago (Ill.) -- Relations -- United States 4. Chicago (Ill.) -- Intellectual life -- 20th century
ISBN 1594204322; 9781594204326

LC 2012039710

This book, by Thomas Dyja, explores the industrial and cultural history of Chicago, Illinois in the mid-20th century. "Much of what defined the nation as it grew into a superpower was produced in Chicago.... Yet even as Chicago led the way in creating mass-market culture, its artists pushed back in their own distinct voices.... Thomas Dyja re-creates the story of the city in its postwar prime and explains its profound impact on modern America." (Publisher's note)

"A readable, richly detailed history of America's second city." Kirkus

Includes bibliographical references and index

977.4 Michigan

LeDuff, Charlie

Detroit; an American autopsy. Charlie LeDuff. Penguin Press 2013 xvi, 286 p.p ill. (hardcover) $27.95   **977.4**
1. Detroit (Mich.) -- History 2. Detroit (Mich.) -- Economic conditions 3. Detroit (Mich.) -- Social conditions 4. Detroit (Mich.) -- Politics and government 5. Journalists -- Michigan -- Detroit -- Biography
ISBN 1594205345; 9781594205347
LC 2012030924
LA Times Book Prize Finalist: Current Interest (2013)

In this book, Charlie LeDuff profiles Detroit, Michigan. "Having led us on the way up, Detroit now seems to be leading us on the way down. Once the richest city in America, Detroit is now the nation's poorest. Once the vanguard of America's machine age . . . , Detroit is now America's capital for unemployment, illiteracy, dropouts, and foreclosures. . . . LeDuff sets out to uncover what destroyed his city." (Publisher's note)

Maraniss, David

Once in a great city; a Detroit story. David Maraniss. Simon & Schuster 2015 512 p. 16 plates; illustrations; maps (hardcover) $32.50   **977.4**
1. Detroit (Mich.) -- Economic conditions
ISBN 9781476748382; 1476748381
LC 2015017134

This book, by David Maraniss, "highlights the class and race frictions that demarcated and defined the city [of Detroit in the mid-20th century] and gives readers a glimpse of the colorful life of mobsters and moguls, entertainers and entrepreneurs. Among the famous Detroiters he highlights are Henry Ford II, Lee Iacocca, Berry Gordy Jr., George Romney, and the Reverend C. L. Franklin. Maraniss captures Detroit just as it is both thriving and dying." (Booklist)

"Although overstuffed with facts (for example, that Cavanagh 'kept four extra suits, thirteen striped ties,' and abundant shirts in his office for a quick change), and sometimes breaching the city's boundaries to become a history of the whole country, Maraniss' brawny narrative evokes a city still 'vibrantly alive' and striving for a renaissance. An illuminating history of a golden era in a city desperately seeking to reclaim the glory." Kirkus

Martelle, Scott

Detroit; a biography. Scott Martelle. Chicago Review Press 2012 xvi, 288 p.p   **977.4**
1. Detroit (Mich.) -- History 2. Detroit (Mich.) -- Population 3. Detroit (Mich.) -- Economic conditions 4. African Americans -- Detroit (Mich.) -- History 5. African Americans -- Michigan -- Detroit -- History
ISBN 156976526X; 9781569765265
LC 2011041173

This book on Detroit, Michigan "recounts the rise and downfall of a once-great city, from its origins as a French military outpost to protect fur traders and tame local Indian tribes, to the industrial giant, known

colloquially as Motown, and now when its "economy seized up like an engine run dry." Founded by a French naval officer named Cadillac, the city became a vibrant river town with the Erie Canal's opening, exporting both to the east and westward to Chicago. The 1855 opening of Lake Superior later expanded its postbellum shipping capacity and brought heavy industry.... But a series of downturns ravaged the city: the 1973 OPEC oil embargo helped destroy the city's auto-industry dominance, and drug-dealing gangs caused a murder rate that far out-stripped New York's." (Publishers Wkly)

Includes bibliographical references (p. 261-280) and index

McDonnell, Michael A.

Masters of Empire; Great Lakes Indians and the Making of America. Michael McDonnell. Farrar, Straus & Giroux 2015 402 p. illustrations, maps $35   **977.4**
1. Great Lakes region 2. Native Americans -- United States
ISBN 0809029537; 9780809029532
LC 2015022331

This book, by Michael A. McDonnell, "reveals the pivotal role played by the native peoples of the Great Lakes in the history of North America. Though less well known than the Iroquois or Sioux, the Anishinaabeg, who lived across Lakes Michigan and Huron, were equally influential. Masters of Empire charts the story of one group, the Odawa, who settled at the straits between those two lakes." (Publisher's note)

"McDonnell's scholarly yet compelling history will be a valuable addition to American history and Native American collections." Booklist

Includes bibliographical references and index.

Miles, Tiya

The **dawn** of Detroit; a chronicle of slavery and freedom in the city of the straits. Tiya Miles. The New Press 2017 336 p. illustrations, maps (hardcover) $27.95   **977.4**
1. Slavery 2. Race relations 3. Detroit (Mich.) -- History 4. Slavery -- Michigan 5. Detroit (Mich.) -- Race relations 6. Detroit (Mich.) -- History -- 18th century 7. Detroit (Mich.) -- History -- 19th century
ISBN 9781620972328; 9781620972311
LC 2017018381

In this book, author Tiya Miles "reveals that slavery was at the heart of the Midwest's iconic city: Detroit.... [She] has pieced together the experience of the unfree--both native and African American--in the frontier outpost of Detroit, a place wildly remote yet at the center of national and international conflict.... [Miles also] introduces new historical figures and unearths struggles that remained hidden from view until now." (Publisher's note)

"Diligently researched and well written, this provocative exploration of slavery in frontier-era Detroit proves illuminating." Choice

Includes bibliographical references and index

977.434 Detroit

Boyd, Herb

Black Detroit; a people's history of self-determination. Herb Boyd. Amistad 2017 xii, 416 p.p illustrations (hardcover) $27.99   **977.434**
1. Detroit (Mich.) -- History 2. African Americans -- History 3. Detroit (Mich.) -- Biography 4. Detroit (Mich.) -- History -- 20th century 5. African Americans -- Michigan -- Detroit -- History -- 20th century
ISBN 9780062346629; 9780062346636; 9780062346643;

0062346628

LC 2017302465

This book, by Herb Boyd, "looks at the evolving culture, politics, economics, and spiritual life of Detroit--a blend of memoir, love letter, history, and clear-eyed reportage that explores the city's past, present, and future and its significance to the African American legacy and the nation's fabric. . . . [The author] reflects on his life and this landmark place, in search of understanding why Detroit is a special place for black people." (Publisher's note)

"An inspiring, illuminating book that will interest students of urban history and the black experience." Kirkus

Includes bibliographical references (pages 353-397) and index.

978   Western United States

Brown, Dee Alexander

The **American** West; photos edited by Martin F. Schmitt. Scribner 1994 461p il maps hardcover o.p. pa $17   **978**

1. Rodeos 2. Cowhands 3. Kiowa Indians 4. Apache Indians 5. Dakota Indians 6. Cheyenne Indians 7. Little Bighorn, Battle of the, 1876 8. Outlaws 9. Indian chiefs 10. Nez Percé Indians 11. West (U.S.) -- History 12. Frontier and pioneer life -- West (U.S.)

ISBN 0-684-80441-7 pa

LC 94-37444

"This narrative history of westward expansion paints a vivid portrait of the settlers, pioneers, entrepreneurs, and Native Americans of the old West. Useful as collateral research material and for recreational reading." Booklist

Includes bibliographical references

Buck, Rinker

The **Oregon** Trail; an American journey. Rinker Buck. Simon & Schuster 2015 464 p. illustrations, maps (hardcover) $28   **978**

1. Oregon Trail 2. Frontier and pioneer life -- West (U.S.) 3. Oregon National Historic Trail

ISBN 1451659164; 9781451659160; 9781451659177

LC 2015001159

This book, by Rinker Buck, presents an "account of traveling the length of the Oregon Trail the old-fashioned way. . . . Spanning two thousand miles and traversing six states from Missouri to the Pacific coast, the Oregon Trail is the route that made America. In the fifteen years before the Civil War, . . . it united the coasts, doubled the size of the country, and laid the groundwork for the railroads. Today, amazingly, the trail is all but forgotten." (Publisher's note)

"Recommended for folk interested in the Oregon Trail, pioneer history, or mules." LJ

Calloway, Colin G.

One vast winter count; the Native American West before Lewis and Clark. University of Nebraska Press 2003 631p il (History of the American West) $39.95   **978**

1. West (U.S.) -- History 2. Native Americans -- West (U.S.)

ISBN 0-8032-1530-4

LC 2003-44757

"Calloway concentrates on the Indian experience from the Appalachians to the Pacific, in a time frame from prehistory to the 18th century. The scope is staggering, but Calloway masters it, demonstrating a remarkable command of a broad spectrum of historical, ethnographic and archeological sources including printed material and oral traditions." Publ Wkly

Includes bibliographical references

Egan, Timothy

The **worst** hard time; the untold story of those who survived the great American dust bowl. Timothy Egan. Houghton Mifflin Co. 2006 340p ill., map $28; $28   **978**

1. Dust storms 2. Great Depression, 1929-1939 3. United States -- History -- 20th century 4. Great Plains -- History 5. Great Plains -- Social conditions -- 20th century

ISBN 061834697X; 9780618346974

LC 2005-08057

National Book Awards: Nonfiction (2006), Oklahoma Book Awards: Nonfiction Category (2006), Western Heritage Award: Outstanding Nonfiction (2007)

This book presents an "account of how America's . . . plains turned to dust, and how the ferocious plains winds stirred up an endless series of 'black blizzards' . . . in what became known as the Dust Bowl. But the plague was man-made, as Egan shows: the plains weren't suited to farming, and plowing up the grass to plant wheat, along with a confluence of economic disaster—the Depression—and natural disaster—eight years of drought—resulted in an ecological and human catastrophe. . . . [The author] grounds his tale in portraits of the people who settled the plains: hardy Americans and immigrants desperate for a piece of land to call their own and lured by the lies of promoters who said the ground was arable." (Publishers Weekly)

"With characters who seem to have sprung from a novel by Sinclair Lewis or Steinbeck, and Egan's powerful writing, this account will long remain in readers' minds." Publ Wkly

Includes bibliographical references (p. 315-327) and index

Faulkner, Steven

Bitterroot; Echoes of Beauty & Loss. by Steven Faulkner. Midpoint Trade Books Inc 2016 384 p. illustrations, map $24.95   **978**

1. Pacific Northwest 2. Lewis and Clark Expedition (1804-1806)

ISBN 0825307929; 9780825307928

In this book, "using the letters of the 19th-century explorer Pierre Jean De Smet, Steven Faulkner and his eighteen-year-old son, Alex, follow De Smet across the High Plains to the fur trappers' rendezvous on the Green River, then on to the Lewis and Clark Trail. . . . By road, foot, mountain bike, and canoe, Steven and Alex experience the vast landscape and try to capture an understanding of the Wild Northwest." (Publisher's note)

"Faulkner's verbs vivify, his quotes enlarge his experience, and his poetic descriptions exploit all five senses colorfully; still, keener editing would have pared the backwoods baroque." Pub Wkly

Schmidt, Thomas

The **Lewis** & Clark Trail; foreword by Stephen E. Ambrose. Bicentennial ed completely rev; National Geographic Soc. 2002 192p il maps pa $16   **978**

1. Lewis and Clark Expedition (1804-1806) 2. West (U.S.) -- Description and travel

ISBN 0-7922-6471-1

LC 2001-7003

First published 1998

Color photographs and maps provide a guide to the Lewis and Clark National Historic Trail

Sides, Hampton

Blood and thunder; an epic of the American West. Doubleday 2006 460p il $26.95   **978**

1. Navajo Indians 2. Scouts 3. Pioneers 4. West (U.S.) -- History 5. United States -- Territorial expansion 6. Frontier and pioneer life -- West (U.S.)

ISBN 978-0-385-50777-6; 0-385-50777-1

LC 2006-16579

This book "will surely capture readers, and it ought to. It's a riveting account of a vast swath of history with which few Americans are familiar." New Yorker

Includes bibliographical references

Slatta, Richard W.

The **cowboy** encyclopedia. Norton 1996 474p il pa $17 **978**

1. Reference books 2. Cowhands -- Encyclopedias

ISBN 0-393-31473-1

LC 94-19824

First published 1994 by ABC-CLIO

"Focusing on the cowboy experience in North and South America, The Cowboy Encyclopedia provides history, definitions, and commentary in an A-to-Z arrangement with major topics such as saddles and cowboy films receiving longer topical entries. Excellent cross-references and an extensive index provide easy access to all aspects of a topic. Appendixes cover cowboy films and videotape sources, museums, periodicals, and western cultural happenings." Am Libr

Slaughter, Thomas P.

Exploring Lewis and Clark; reflections on men and wilderness. Knopf 2003 231p il maps $24; pa $14 **978**

1. Slaves 2. Explorers 3. Lewis and Clark Expedition (1804-1806) 4. Interpreters 5. Guides (Persons) 6. Territorial governors 7. West (U.S.) -- Exploration

ISBN 0-375-40078-8; 0-375-70071-4 pa

LC 2002-69376

"It may be easy to dismiss as a nitpicking revisionist potshot at our beloved heroes, but as the expedition's bicentennial approaches, this book's perspective will help keep our understanding well nuanced and grounded in fact." Booklist

Includes bibliographical references

Stark, Peter

Astoria; John Jacob Astor and Thomas Jefferson's lost Pacific empire: a story of wealth, ambition, and survival. by Peter Stark. HarperCollins Publishers 2014 366 p. ill. (some col.), maps, port $27.99 **978**

1. Scientific expeditions 2. United States -- Exploring expeditions

ISBN 0062218298; 9780062218292

The launch -- The journey -- Pacific Empire and war -- Fate of the Astorians

This book, by Peter Stark, relates how "in 1810, entrepreneur John Jacob Astor proposed to Thomas Jefferson that Astor start a trading colony in what is now Oregon.... [Peter] Stark ... chronicles Astor's mad dash to establish a fur-trading company, Astoria, which would capture the territory's wealth and allow Jefferson to inaugurate his vision of a democracy from sea to shining sea." (Publishers Weekly)

"A fast-paced, riveting account of exploration and settlement, suffering and survival, treachery and death." Kirkus

Includes bibliographical references and index

Stillman, Deanne

Blood brothers; the story of the strange friendship between Sitting Bull and Buffalo Bill. Deanne Stillman. Simon & Schuster 2017 286 p. (hardback) $27 **978**

1. Buffalo Bill's Wild West Show 2. Entertainers -- United States -- Biography 3. Wild west shows -- History -- 19th century 4. Buffalo Bill's Wild West Company -- Biography 5. Dakota Indians -- Kings and rulers -- Biography

ISBN 9781476773520; 9781476773537

LC 2017006041

This book, by Deanne Stillman, tells the "unlikely friendship of two famous figures of the American West--Buffalo Bill Cody and Sitting Bull--told through their time in Cody's Wild West show in the 1880s.... Stillman unearths little told details about the two men and their tumultuous times. Their alliance was eased by none other than Annie Oakley. ... When Cody died in 1917, a large contingent of Native Americans attended his public funeral." (Publisher's note)

"Thoughtful and thoroughly well-told—just the right treatment for a subject about which many books have been written before, few so successfully." Kirkus.

Includes bibliographical references and index

Wallis, Michael, 1945-

The **best** land under heaven; the Donner party in the age of Manifest Destiny. Michael Wallis. Liveright Publishing Corp., a division of W.W. Norton & Co. 2017 xx, 455 p.p illustrations (hardcover) $27.95 **978**

1. Donner party 2. Overland journeys to the Pacific 3. Frontier and pioneer life -- West (U.S.) 4. Donner Party 5. Pioneers -- California -- History -- 19th century 6. Pioneers -- West (U.S.) -- History -- 19th century 7. Sierra Nevada (Calif. and Nev.) -- History -- 19th century

ISBN 9780871407696

LC 2017012937

In this book, biographer Michael Wallis "reclaims the horrific story of the infamously ill-fated wagon train from the annals of sensationalism.... The Donner Party's struggles and determination continue to fascinate, and Wallis's comprehensive account of bravery, luck, and failure illuminates the realities of westward expansion." (Publishers Weekly)

"Solid Western history that enhances the understanding of a tragic tale by highlighting the strong human dimension through the accounts of participants before, during, and after the expedition." Kirkus

Includes bibliographical references and index

978.004 Western United States--American native peoples

Jackson, Joe

Black Elk; The Life of an American Visionary. Joe Jackson. Farrar, Straus & Giroux 2016 624 p. illustrations, maps, portraits (hardback) $30 **978.004**

1. Oglala Indians -- Religion 2. Oglala Indians -- Biography 3. Lakota Indians

ISBN 9780374253301; 9780374709617

LC 2016016695

This book by Joe Jackson presents a biography of Black Elk, the Native American holy man. "Born in an era of rising violence between the Sioux, white settlers, and U.S. government troops, Black Elk killed his first man at the Little Bighorn, witnessed the death of his second cousin Crazy Horse, and traveled to Europe with Buffalo Bill's Wild West show. ... But Black Elk was not a warrior, instead accepting the path of a healer and holy man." (Publisher's note)

"Of much literary and historical merit and a fine addition to the shelves of anyone interested in this part of America's unhappy past." Kirkus

Includes bibliographical references and index

978.02   Western United States – 1800-1899

Cozzens, Peter

The **earth** is weeping; The Epic Story of the Indian Wars for the American West. by Peter Cozzens. Alfred A. Knopf 2016 576 p. illustrations, maps (ebook) $65; $35   **978.02**

1. West (U.S.) -- History 2. Native Americans -- Wars 3. Native Americans -- West (U.S.) -- History 4. West (U.S.) -- History -- 1860-1890 5. Indians of North America -- Wars -- 1866-1895

ISBN 9780307958051; 9780307958044

LC 2015044077

This book, by Peter Cozzens, is an "account . . . of how the West was won and lost. . . . With the end of the Civil War, the nation recommenced its expansion onto traditional Indian tribal lands, setting off a wide-ranging conflict that would last more than three decades. Cozzens gives us both sides in comprehensive and singularly intimate detail. He illuminates the encroachment experienced by the tribes and the tribal conflicts over whether to fight or make peace." (Publisher's note)

"This is a beautifully written work of understanding and compassion that will be a treasure for both general readers and specialists." Booklist

Includes bibliographical references

978.1   Kansas

Frank, Thomas

What's the matter with Kansas? how conservatives won the heart of America. Metropolitan Books 2004 306p map $24; pa $14   **978.1**

1. Conservatism 2. Kansas

ISBN 0-8050-7339-6; 0-8050-7774-X pa

LC 2004-44824

This is "a brilliant book, one of the best so far this decade on American politics." Nation

Includes bibliographical references

978.176   Dodge City (Kansas)

Clavin, Tom

Dodge City; Wyatt Earp, Bat Masterson, and the wickedest town in the American West. Tom Clavin. St. Martin's Press 2017 xiii, 384 p.p illustrations (hardback) $29.99   **978.176**

1. Thieves 2. Criminals 3. Frontier and pioneer life 4. Dodge City (Kan.) -- Biography 5. Dodge City (Kan.) -- History -- 19th century 6. Frontier and pioneer life -- Kansas -- Dodge City 7. Peace officers -- Kansas -- Dodge City -- Biography 8. Outlaws -- Kansas -- Dodge City -- History -- 19th century

ISBN 9781250071484

LC 2016038741

This book, by Tom Clavin, "brims with a colorful collection of real outlaws, sex workers, gamblers, and chorus dancers whose personalities, deeds, and even nicknames help readers understand why the Western legend entranced the nation in the first place. To know the history of Dodge City is to understand how the West was won, and this history is often just as captivating and strange as the legends that have supplanted it." (Publishers Weekly)

"This is an enjoyable saga, appealing to both Old West aficionados and general readers." Booklist.

Includes bibliographical references (pages [365]-369) and index.

978.3   South Dakota

Mort, Terry

Thieves' Road; The Black Hills Betrayal and Custer's Path to Little Bighorn. Terry Mort. Random House Inc 2015 340 p. 8 plates; illustrations; maps $25   **978.3**

1. Native Americans -- Wars

ISBN 1616149604; 9781616149604

LC 2014035457

This book, by Terry Mort, describes how "in the summer of 1874, Brevet Major General George Armstrong Custer led an expedition of some 1,000 troops and more than one hundred wagons into the Black Hills of South Dakota. This . . . work of narrative history tells the little-known story of this exploratory mission and reveals how it set the stage for the climactic Battle of the Little Bighorn two years later." (Publisher's note)

"This highly readable and insightful work is recommended as an essential backstory to Custer's subsequent downfall at the aforementioned battle." LJ

978.7   Wyoming

Black, George

Empire of shadows; the epic story of Yellowstone. George Black. St. Martin's Press 2012 548 p   **978.7**

1. West (U.S.) -- Exploration 2. Yellowstone National Park -- History 3. United States -- History -- 19th century 4. Native Americans -- West (U.S.) -- History 5. Yellowstone National Park -- Discovery and exploration

ISBN 9780312383190; 9781429989749

LC 2011041351

This book is an "account of the discovery and imaginative creation of Yellowstone National Park is told through the lives of the park's colorful and often tragically egotistic explorers and promoters. . . . Waging an irreverent battle against now traditional fakelore, [George] Black particularly emphasizes Native American presence in the region of geysers, hot springs, and the headwaters of the Yellowstone River and the role of Lt. Gustavus Doane's military exploration, which opened the wonderland to international attention." (Libr J) "Divided into five sections and beginning with the familiar expedition of Lewis and Clark, the book spans nearly the entire 19th century. . . . As the book continues, the government enters with paleontologists, entomologists, botanists, and mineralogists, among others." (Kirkus)

Includes bibliographical references

Meyer, Judith L.

The **spirit** of Yellowstone; the cultural evolution of a national park. photographs by Vance Howard. Roberts Rinehart 2003 145p il pa $19.95   **978.7**

1. Human influence on nature 2. Yellowstone National Park

ISBN 1-570-98395-X

LC 2002-156320

First published 1996 by Rowman & Littlefield

The author "pays tribute to the park and all its glories, covering the park's history, its prime landmarks, and its prominence in art. The photographs are truly striking and not the typical landscape fare. Howard plays with light and texture to capture images that will amaze even those already familiar with the park's unprecedented beauty." Libr J

Includes bibliographical references

978.8   Colorado

Enss, Chris

Mochi's war; the tragedy of Sand Creek. Chris Enss and Howard Kazanjian. TwoDot, an imprint of Rowman & Littlefield Publishers 2015 184 p. illustrations (pbk.) $16.95 **978.8**

1. Cheyenne Indians 2. Prisoners of war 3. Sand Creek, Battle of, 1864 4. Cheyenne Indians -- Biography 5. Cheyenne Indians -- Wars, 1864 6. Native Americans -- Relocation 7. Sand Creek Massacre, Colo., 1864 8. Sand Creek Massacre National Historic Site (Colo.) 9. Prisoners of war -- Florida -- Castillo de San Marcos National Monument (Saint Augustine) -- Biography

ISBN 9780762760770; 076276077X

LC 2015005372

This book, by Chris Enss and Howard Kazanjian, focuses on "the brutal and unprovoked massacre of a sleeping village of Cheyenne and Arapaho peoples at Sand Creek (present-day Colorado) by troops of the Colorado Volunteers in November 1864. This still controversial military engagement sets the background in which Mochi, a Cheyenne woman, lost her entire family and barely survived herself, by killing a soldier and then fleeing her camp." (Library Journal)

"Highly recommended for adult readers of Western and Native American history, this biographical account provides a counterpoint to the many works that have mythologized such women as Pocahontas and Sacajawea." LJ

Includes bibliographical references and index

978.9   New Mexico

Childs, Craig Leland

House of rain; tracking a vanished civilization across the American Southwest. [by] Craig Childs. Little, Brown and Co. 2006 496p il map $24.99 **978.9**

1. Pueblo Indians 2. Southwestern States -- Antiquities 3. Chaco Culture National Historical Park (N.M.)

ISBN 978-0-316-60817-6; 0-316-60817-3

LC 2006-19112

"Beginning at the monumental cultural center of Chaco Canyon, where the Anasazi flourished, Childs's quest to understand their apparent disappearance leads him to the numerous great houses of New Mexico, such as Pueblo Bonito, to the Four Corners area of northeastern Arizona, southern Colorado and Utah, and beyond to northern Mexico. In these places, he identifies features that had not appeared prior to the apparent abandonment of Chaco (thus implying that the Anasazi migrated to these areas). Childs vividly weaves his personal narrative, imbued with a deep respect for the geography and cultural landscape, with scientific research and numerous interactions with foremost scholars." Libr J

979   Great Basin and Pacific Slope region of United States

Hutton, Paul Andrew

The **Apache** wars; the hunt for Geronimo, the Apache Kid, and the captive boy who started the longest war in American history. by Paul Andrew Hutton. Crown Publishing 2016 528 p. illustrations, map (hardcover) $30 **979**

1. Apache Indians -- Wars

ISBN 9780770435813; 9780770435837

LC 2015050712

This book, by Paul Andrew Hutton, is a "historical account of the manhunt for Geronimo and the 25-year Apache struggle for their home-

land. They called him Mickey Free. His kidnapping started the longest war in American history, and both sides--the Apaches and the white invaders—blamed him for it. A mixed-blood warrior who moved uneasily between the worlds of the Apaches and the American soldiers, he was never trusted by either but desperately needed by both." (Publisher's note)

"What happened to Felix Ward is less important to the larger historical picture than how the situation with the Apaches was resolved, but Hutton provides an unexpected twist that keeps the story fresh until the end." Pub Wkly

Includes bibliographical references and index

Neely, Nick

Coast range; a collection from the Pacific edge. Nick Neely. Soft Skull Press, an imprint of Counterpoint Press 2016 200 p. illustrations (ebook) $25; (hardback) $25 **979**

1. Nature -- Essays 2. Natural history -- Northwest, Pacific 3. Northwest, Pacific -- Description and travel

ISBN 9781619028593; 9781619028364

LC 2016020226

This book by Nick Neely presents a collection of essays set in the California and Oregon coastal ranges. "Each essay explores an iconic organism (a few geologic), so that, on the whole, the collection becomes a curiosity cabinet that freshly embodies this Pacific Northwest landscape. But the book also employs a playful range of forms. Just as forest gives way to bluff and ocean, here narrative journalism adjoins memoir and lyric essay." (Publisher's note)

"Neely capably explores the complexity of his subjects with polish and finesse, looking carefully and thinking deeply." Kirkus

979.1   Arizona

Brooks, James F.

Mesa of sorrows; a history of the Awat'ovi massacre. James F. Brooks. W W Norton & Co Inc 2016 224 p. illustrations, maps (ebook) $50; (hardcover) $26.95 **979.1**

1. Massacres -- Southwest, New 2. Hopi Indians -- Arizona -- Awatovi -- History 3. Excavations (Archeology) -- Social aspects -- Arizona -- Awatovi 4. Hopi Indians -- Religion 5. Awatovi (Ariz.) -- History 6. Violence -- Southwest, New 7. Awatovi (Ariz.) -- Antiquities 8. Social archaeology -- Southwest, New 9. Indians of North America -- Missions -- Arizona 10. Excavations (Archaeology) -- Social aspects -- Arizona -- Awatovi

ISBN 9780393292534; 9780393061253

LC 2015037504

In this book, author James F. Brooks offers an "investigation of the mysterious massacre of Hopi Indians at Awat'ovi, and the event's echo through American history. . . . Piecing together three centuries of investigation, he offers insight into why some were spared—women, mostly, and taken captive—and others sacrificed. He weighs theories that the attack was in retribution for Awat'ovi having welcomed Franciscan missionaries or for the residents' practice of sorcery." (Publisher's note)

"An occasionally repetitive but fully illuminating account for any who relish the rich history and traditions of the Hopi." Kirkus

Includes bibliographical references and index

History of the Awat'ovi massacre

Dolnick, Edward

Down the great unknown; John Wesley Powell's 1869 journey of discovery and tragedy through the Grand Canyon. HarperCollins Pubs. 2001 367p il maps $27.50; pa $13.95 **979.1**

1. Explorers 2. Geologists 3. Large print books 4. Grand Canyon (Ariz.) 5. Colorado River (Colo.-Mexico) 6. Explorers -- United States -- Biography 7. Grand Canyon (Ariz.) -- Description and travel 8. Grand Canyon (Ariz.) -- Discovery and exploration 9. Colorado River (Colo.-Mexico) -- Discovery and exploration
ISBN 006019619X; 0060955864

LC 2001-24819

This is an account of Major John Wesley Powell's survey of the Grand Canyon. "Powell (one-armed since Shiloh) and nine men, six of them Civil War veterans, set out on May 24, 1869, at Green River Station on the Union Pacific Railroad in what was then Wyoming Territory. . . . One day before they reached the end of the canyon, three deserted, thinking that a rapids they could see ahead was certain death. These three climbed the walls of the canyon and were never seen again. The survivors came out into the flat country at the mouth of the Virgin River, ninety-nine days after they had set out." (Harpers)

"Dolnick, a science journalist who has rafted down the Grand, turns in a most estimable rendition of that storied expedition. It skillfully integrates the notes and journals of expedition members with technical insight about the perils of roiling whitewater." Booklist

Includes bibliographical references

Pasternak, Judy

Yellow dirt; an American story of a poisoned land and a people betrayed. Free Press 2010 317p il map $26; ebook $12.99   **979.1**
1. Navajo Indians 2. Uranium mines and mining
ISBN 1416594825; 1439100462; 9781416594826; 9781439100462

LC 2010-5546

"In the 1940s, when the U.S. government was embarking on developing atomic weapons, it discovered huge uranium deposits in Navajo territory covering parts of Utah, New Mexico, and Arizona. . . . The Navajo themselves saw little of the huge profits from uranium but as workers and land dwellers would suffer radiation exposure four times that of the Japanese targeted by the A-bomb. . . . Pasternak follows four generations of Navajo families, from the patriarch who warned against violating the land to those tempted by the prospects of jobs and money. . . . A stunning look at a shameful chapter in American history with long-lasting implications for all Americans concerned with environmental justice." Booklist

Includes bibliographical references

979.2   Utah

Leonard, Glen M.

★ **Massacre** at Mountain Meadows; an American tragedy. by Ronald W. Walker, Richard E. Turley, Jr., [and] Glen M. Leonard. Oxford University Press 2008 430p il map $29.95   **979.2**
1. Mountain Meadows Massacre, 1857 2. Mormons -- History
ISBN 978-0-19-516034-5

LC 2008-14451

"On September 11, 1857, a band of Mormon militia, under a flag of truce, lured unarmed members of a party of emigrants from their fortified encampment and, with their Paiute allies, killed them. More than 120 men, women, and children perished. . . . The book [aims to] shed light on factors contributing to the [killings], . . . including the war hysteria that overcame the Mormons after President James Buchanan dispatched federal troops to Utah Territory to put down a supposed rebellion, the suspicion and conflicts that polarized the perpetrators and victims, and the reminders of attacks on Mormons in earlier settlements in Missouri

and Illinois. It also analyzes the influence of Brigham Young's rhetoric and military strategy during the . . . 'Utah War' and the role of local Mormon militia leaders in enticing Paiute Indians to join in the attack." (Publisher's note) Index.

The authors tell the story of "the titular 1857 tragedy in which 157 emigrants traveling to California were killed by local Mormons. With its understated prose, an essential purchase." Libr J

Includes bibliographical references

979.3   Nevada

Crouch, Gregory

The **bonanza** king; John Mackay and the battle over the greatest riches in the American West. Gregory Crouch. Simon & Schuster 2018 384 p. illustrations $30   **979.3**
1. Gold mines and mining 2. Silver mines and mining 3. Capitalists and financiers
ISBN 1501108190; 9781501108198

This book, by Gregory Crouch, is "the rags-to-riches American frontier tale of an Irish immigrant who outwits, outworks, and outmaneuvers thousands of rivals to take control of Nevada's Comstock Lode--the rich body of gold and silver so immensely valuable that it changed the destiny of the United States. . . . [It] is a dazzling tour de force, a riveting history of Virginia City, Nevada, the Comstock Lode, and America itself." (Publisher's note)

D'Agata, John

About a mountain. W. W. Norton 2010 236p $23.95 **979.3**
1. Yucca Mountain Repository (Nev.) 2. Las Vegas metropolitan area (Nev.) -- Social life and customs
ISBN 978-0-393-06818-4; 0-393-06818-8

LC 2009-39295

D'Agata "uses the federal government's highly controversial (and recently rejected) proposal to entomb the U.S.'s nuclear waste located in Yucca Mountain, near Las Vegas, as his way into a spiraling and subtle examination of the modern city, suicide, linguistics, Edvard Munch's The Scream, ecological and psychic degradation, and the gulf between information and knowledge. Acting as a counterpoint to Yucca is the story of a teenager named Levi who leapt to his death off Las Vegas' Stratosphere Motel. . . . A sublime reading experience, aesthetically rewarding and marked by moral courage and humility." Publ Wkly

Denton, Sally

The **money** and the power; the making of Las Vegas and its hold on America, 1947-2000. by Sally Denton and Roger Morris. Knopf 2001 479p hardcover o.p. pa $15   **979.3**
1. Gambling 2. Organized crime 3. Political corruption 4. Las Vegas (Nev.)
ISBN 0-375-70126-5 pa

LC 00-62011

"The idea of Las Vegas as the epitome of crass American pop culture has become at least a surface truism in most circles. But Denton and Morris . . . go much deeper than the surface in this sobering account of the famous Nevada resort town." Booklist

Includes bibliographical references

979.4   California

Brands, H. W.

The **Age** of Gold; The California Gold Rush & the New

American Dream. by H.W. Brands. Anchor Books 2003 549 p. 16 plates; illustrations; maps $19.95 **979.4**
> 1. California -- History 2. California -- Gold discoveries 3. United States -- Civilization -- 1783-1865 4. United States -- Social conditions -- To 1865 5. California -- Gold discoveries -- Social aspects
> ISBN 0385720882; 9780385720885

LC 200223776

This book, by H.W. Brands, focuses on the "gold rush of 1848. . . . For most of the hundreds of thousands who flocked to California, though, life in the mines of the Sierras was hard and rarely paid off. Yet the hopeful kept coming not only from the East but from around the world, with profound implications for California and the rest of the country." (Publishers Weekly)

"Combining this wealth of ideas with vivid biographies of actors great and small in the expansionist drama, Brands has produced a work that stands far above the tide of mostly forgettable titles that accompanied the 150th anniversary of the Gold Rush three years ago. A lucid, literate survey of events that transformed the nation, for better and worse." Kirkus

Didion, Joan
Where I was from. Knopf 2003 226p $23; pa $13.95 **979.4**
> 1. American national characteristics 2. California -- History 3. California -- Social conditions
> ISBN 0-679-43332-5; 0-679-75286-2 pa

LC 2002-43325

This "is a complex and challenging memoir, difficult to enter into but just as difficult to put down. . . . Those who have long admired the clarity and precision of her prose will not be disappointed with this partly autobiographical, partly historical, but fully engrossing account." Libr J

Krist, Gary
The **mirage** factory; illusion, imagination, and the invention of Los Angeles. Gary Krist. Crown Publishers 2018 416 p. (hardback) $27 **979.4**
> 1. Cities and towns 2. Los Angeles (Calif.) -- History
> ISBN 9780451496386

LC 2017049682

This book, by Gary Krist, is about the visionaries behind the rise of the city of Los Angeles. "William Mulholland . . . designed the massive aqueduct that would make urban life here possible. D.W. Griffith, who transformed the motion picture from a vaudeville-house novelty into a cornerstone of American culture, gave L.A. its signature industry. And Aimee Semple McPherson, a charismatic evangelist . . . , cemented the city's identity as a center for spiritual exploration. (Publisher's note)

Lee, Helie
In the absence of sun; a Korean American woman's promise to reunite three lost generations of her family. Harmony Bks. 2002 342p il maps hardcover o.p. pa $18.95 **979.4**
> 1. Korean Americans 2. Korea (North)
> ISBN 0-449-91171-3 pa

LC 2002-1680

"Lee's Still Life with Rice (1996) was a novelized account of her grandmother's life and escape from what would become North Korea. As she now recounts her and her father's struggles to get other people out of the North, she continues to wrestle with her own Korean heritage—in particular, the paternalistic and patronizing attitudes toward women." Booklist

Menuez, Doug
Fearless genius; the digital revolution in Silicon Valley, 1985-2000. by Doug Menuez; foreword by Elliott Erwitt; introduction by Kurt Andersen. Atria Books 2014 192 p. illustrations (hardcover: alk. paper) $39.99 **979.4**
> 1. Microelectronics 2. High technology industry 3. Computer industry -- United States 4. Santa Clara Valley (Santa Clara County, Calif.) 5. Santa Clara Valley (Santa Clara County, Calif.) -- Pictorial works 6. Documentary photography -- California -- Santa Clara Valley (Santa Clara County) 7. High technology -- California -- Santa Clara Valley (Santa Clara County) -- History 8. Microelectronics industry -- California -- Santa Clara Valley (Santa Clara County) -- History
> ISBN 1476752699; 9781476752693

LC 2013045228

This book, by Doug Menuez, is a "chronicle of the Silicon Valley technology boom, capturing key moments in the careers of Steve Jobs and more than seventy other leading innovators . . . [including] John Warnock at Adobe, John Sculley at Apple, Bill Gates at Microsoft, John Doerr at Kleiner Perkins, Bill Joy at Sun Microsystems, Gordon Moore and Andy Grove at Intel, Marc Andreessen at Netscape." (Publisher's note)

"Menuez even makes the innovators' solitude--sequestered behind drawn blinds for days or cordoned off from the rest of the pack in lonely cubicles--surprisingly compelling. The accompanying text is both complementary and instructive." Kirkus

Includes bibliographical references and index

Pawel, Miriam
The **Browns** of California; the family dynasty that transformed a state and shaped a nation. Miriam Pawel. Bloomsbury Publishing 2018 496 p. illustrations, maps hardcover $35 **979.4**
> 1. Governors -- California 2. Governors -- California -- Biography
> ISBN 9781632867339

LC 2018011464

In this book, "journalist and scholar Miriam Pawel weaves a narrative history that spans four generations, from August Schuckman, the Prussian immigrant who crossed the Plains in 1852 and settled on a northern California ranch, to his great-grandson Jerry Brown, who reclaimed the family homestead one hundred forty years later. Through the prism of their lives, we gain an essential understanding of California and an appreciation of its importance." (Publisher's note)

Includes bibliographical references (pages 425-429) and index

Randall, David K.
The **King** and Queen of Malibu; The True Story of the Battle for Paradise. by David K. Randall. W W Norton & Co Inc 2016 256 p. illustrations $26.95 **979.4**
> 1. California -- History 2. United States -- History
> ISBN 0393240991; 9780393240993

LC 2015038696

This book, by David K. Randall, "traces the path of one family as the country around them swept off the last vestiges of the Civil War and moved into what we would recognize as the modern age. The story of Malibu ranges from the halls of Harvard to the Old West in New Mexico to the beginnings of San Francisco's counter culture amid the Gilded Age, and culminates in the glamour of early Hollywood." (Publisher's note)

"An engaging story about wealth, entitlement, property rights, change, loss, and pain." Kirkus

Includes bibliographical references.

Winchester, Simon

A **crack** in the edge of the world; America and the great California earthquake of 1906. HarperCollins 2005 462p il maps $27.95   **979.4**

1. Earthquakes -- California 2. San Francisco (Calif.) -- History 3. San Francisco (Calif.) -- Earthquake, 1906 4. Earthquakes -- California -- San Francisco -- History -- 20th century

ISBN 0-06-057199-3

LC 2005-46009

"Winchester writes about the earthquake and fire that destroyed San Francisco almost 100 years ago." (N Y Times Book Rev)

"In this brawny page-turner, . . . [the author] has crafted a magnificent testament to the power of planet Earth and the efforts of humankind to understand her." Publ Wkly

Includes bibliographical references

979.494   Los Angeles (Calif.)

Ross, Steven J.

★ **Hitler** in Los Angeles; how Jews foiled Nazi plots against Hollywood and America. Steven J. Ross. Bloomsbury USA 2017 414 p. illustrations, maps (hardcover) $30 **979.494**

1. National socialism -- History 2. Los Angeles (Calif.) -- History 3. Jews -- United States -- History 4. National socialism and motion pictures 5. Los Angeles (Calif.) -- Ethnic relations 6. Jews -- California -- Los Angeles -- History -- 20th century 7. Jewish Federation Council of Greater Los Angeles -- Political activity 8. Motion pictures -- Political aspects -- United States -- History -- 20th century

ISBN 9781620405642; 1620405628; 9781620405628

LC 2017012324

Pulitzer Prize Finalist: History (2018)

This book, by Steven J. Ross, is the "story of the rise of Nazism in Los Angeles, and the Jewish leaders . . . who stopped it. . . . The Nazis plotted to kill the city's Jews and to sabotage the nation's military installations: plans existed for hanging twenty prominent Hollywood figures; . . . for driving through Boyle Heights and machine-gunning as many Jews as possible; and for blowing up defense installations and seizing munitions from National Guard armories along the Pacific Coast." (Publisher's note)

"Ross puts his experience in film history to good use, and he creates lively portraits of the men and women whom Lewis recruited as spies and who succeeded in putting some dangerous Nazis behind bars." Kirkus

Includes bibliographical references

979.5   Oregon

Sharfstein, Daniel J.

★ **Thunder** in the mountains; Chief Joseph, Oliver Otis Howard, and the Nez Perce War. Daniel J. Sharfstein. W.W. Norton & Company, Inc. 2017 xvii, 613 p.p ills., maps, portraits (hardcover) $29.95   **979.5**

1. Nez Perce War, 1877 2. Reconstruction (1865-1876) 3. Civil rights -- United States 4. Nez Percé Indians -- Wars, 1877 5. Political culture -- United States -- History -- 19th century 6. United States -- Race relations -- Political aspects -- History 7. Indians of North America -- Civil rights -- History -- 19th century

ISBN 9780393634181; 9780393239416

LC 2016055352

This book, by Daniel J. Sharfstein, narrates the "epic clash of two American legends--their brutal war and a battle of ideas that defined America after Reconstruction. Oliver Otis Howard. . . . was entrusted with the era's most crucial task: helping millions of former slaves claim the rights of citizens. . . . [His] plans . . . ran headlong into the resistance of Chief Joseph, a young Nez Perce leader in northeastern Oregon who refused to leave his ancestral land." (Publisher's note)

"Sharfstein has provided a scrupulously researched and detailed revisiting of one of the most moving and saddest sagas in American history." Booklist

Includes bibliographical references (pages [509]-592) and index.

979.7   Washington

Krist, Gary

The **white** cascade; the Great Northern Railway disaster and America's deadliest avalanche. Henry Holt and Company 2007 315p il map $26   **979.7**

1. Avalanches 2. Railroad accidents

ISBN 978-0-8050-7705-6; 0-8050-7705-7

LC 2006-49047

"This is a tale in which snow falls, a mountain looms, and most of the protagonists simply sit. The outcome is predetermined. Mr. Krist does wonders with this unpromising material, however. Adopting a restrained, documentary tone, he slowly builds a picture of massing natural forces and helpless humanity, brought closer and closer to catastrophe with each tick of the clock. The pacing is expertly judged, and the potentially confusing narrative threads, involving multiple actors in scattered locations, are tied together neatly." N Y Times (Late N Y Ed)

Includes bibliographical references

Sone, Monica

Nisei daughter; Monica Sone; introduction to the 2014 edition by Marie Rose Wong; introduction to the 1979 edition by S. Frank Miyamoto; preface to the 1979 edition by the author. University of Washington Press 2014 238 p. (paperback: alkaline paper) $18.95   **979.7**

1. World War, 1939-1945 -- United States 2. Japanese Americans -- Evacuation and relocation, 1942-1945 3. Seattle (Wash.) -- Biography 4. Puyallup Assembly Center (Puyallup, Wash.) 5. Japanese Americans -- Washington (State) -- Seattle -- Biography

ISBN 9780295993553

LC 2013036826

In this memoir, author Monica Sone "tells what it was like to grow up Japanese American on Seattle's waterfront in the 1930s and to be subjected to 'relocation' during World War II. Along with over one hundred thousand other persons of Japanese ancestry — most of whom were U.S. citizens — Sone and her family were uprooted from their home and imprisoned in a camp." (Publisher's note)

979.8   Alaska

Borneman, Walter R.

★ **Alaska**: saga of a bold land. HarperCollins Pubs. 2003 608p il maps $34.95; pa $16.95   **979.8**

1. Alaska -- History

ISBN 0-06-050306-8; 0-06-050307-6 pa

LC 2002-27271

"Separated into nine chronologically based chapters, the text explores a recurring theme in Alaska's development: conflict among disparate groups over how the land would be used for personal enrichment. . . . Engaging chapters detail the important events and those who helped shape Alaska's history. . . . This expansive, comprehensive history is recommended for all libraries." Libr J

Includes bibliographical references

Heacox, Kim

Rhythm of the wild; a life inspired by Alaska's Denali National Park. Kim Heacox. Lyons Press 2015 304 p. (hardcover: alkaline paper) $25.95   **979.8**

1. National parks and reserves -- Alaska 2. Denali National Park and Preserve (Alaska) -- History 3. Natural history -- Alaska -- Denali National Park and Preserve 4. Denali National Park and Preserve (Alaska) -- Description and travel 5. Denali National Park and Preserve (Alaska) -- Environmental conditions 6. Nature conservation -- Alaska -- Denali National Park and Preserve (Alaska) 7. Landscape protection -- Alaska -- Denali National Park and Preserve (Alaska)

ISBN 1493003895; 9781493003891

LC 2014048442

This book, by Kim Heacox, is "an Alaska memoir focused on Denali National Park. . . . an Alaska memoir focused on Denali National Park. . . . We hitchhike with Kim through Idaho, camp on the Colorado Plateau, and fly off the sand cliffs of Hangman Creek with a little terrier named Super Max, the Wonder Dog." (Publisher's note)

"The park's wildlife—moose, eagles, red fox, sandhill cranes, grizzly bears, porcupines and wolves—share the stage with human actors in Heacox's chronicle. Top-notch environmental writing to shelve alongside George Perkins Marsh, Aldo Leopold, Robert Marshall and Barry Lopez." Kirkus

Includes bibliographical references and index

Jenkins, Peter

Looking for Alaska. St. Martin's Press 2002 434p il $25.95; pa $14.95   **979.8**

1. Alaska -- Description and travel 2. Alaska -- Social life and customs

ISBN 0-312-26178-0; 0-312-30289-4 pa

LC 2001-48871

This book "sparkles with adventure, quirky characters, unbelievable hardships, and indescribable beauty." Libr J

980   History of South America

Casey, Michael

Che's afterlife; the legacy of an image. Vintage Books 2009 388p il pa $15.95   **980**

1. Physicians 2. Photographers 3. Revolutionaries

ISBN 978-0-307-27930-9; 0-307-27930-8

LC 2008-32186

Casey "has written a book that is not only a cultural history of an image, but also a sociopolitical study of the mechanisms of fame. It is a book about how ideas travel and mutate in this age of globalization, how concepts of political ideology have increasingly come to be trumped by notions of commerce and cool and chic, and how the historical Che Guevara gave way, postmortem, to a host of other Ches." N Y Times (Late N Y Ed)

Includes bibliographical references.

Chasteen, John Charles

Born in blood and fire; a concise history of Latin America.

2nd ed; W.W. Norton 2006 372p il map pa $43.25   **980**

1. Latin America -- History

ISBN 978-0-393-92769-6; 0-393-92769-5

LC 2005-48248

First published 2000

"Chasteen focuses on major political, social and economic topics and trends that helped shape Latin America, including liberalism, the caste system, the mixing of races, nationalism and the Western notion of 'Progress'; he also examines the role that Europe and the United States played in the development of these phenomena. Also refreshing is Chasteen's examination of the periods he covers from the perspective of women." Publ Wkly [review of 2000 edition]

Includes bibliographical references

980.03   1830-1999

Vargas Llosa, Mario, 1936-

Sabers and utopias; visions of Latin America. Mario Vargas Llosa; translated from the Spanish by Anna Kushner. Farrar, Straus & Giroux 2018 xxiii, 275 p.p (hardcover) $28   **980.03**

1. Essays 2. Latin America 3. Arts, Latin American 4. Latin America -- Politics and government -- 1980- 5. Latin American literature -- History and criticism 6. Latin America -- Politics and government -- 1948-1980

ISBN 9780374708917; 9780374253738; 0374253730

LC 2017038306

This book, by Mario Vargas Llosa, translated by Anna Kushner, is a "collection of essays on the Nobel laureate's conception of Latin America, past, present, and future. . . . Reflecting the intellectual development of the writer himself, these essays distill the great events of Latin America's recent history, analyze political groups like FARC and Sendero Luminoso, and evaluate the legacies of infamous leaders such as Papa Doc Duvalier and Fidel Castro." (Publisher's note)

"After nearly a half century of literary output, Vargas Llosa still has few equals when it comes to power of expression and clearheaded conviction." Booklist

981   Brazil

Reel, Monte

The **last** of the tribe; the epic quest to save a lone man in the Amazon. Scribner 2010 273p il map $26   **981**

1. Native Americans -- Brazil 2. Guapore River valley (Brazil and Bolivia)

ISBN 978-1-4165-9474-1; 1-4165-9474-4

LC 2009-37974

"In the opening scene of Monte Reel's 'The Last of the Tribe,' Brazilian government workers approach the deep jungle hideout of an Amazonian Indian they suspect to be the last living member of his tribe. The Indian sits in his hut, cornered, an arrow drawn on his bow, and waits. After two hours, the standoff ends. The government workers leave; the Indian disappears into the jungle. Again. 'The Last of the Tribe' is the story of the 20-year pursuit of that solitary Indian by aid workers who want to contact and protect him, and by loggers and miners who want him dead or moved before he gives the government a reason to protect more land from resource extraction. . . . Reel's tale is expertly told: perfectly timed, thoroughly researched and descriptively written." San Francisco Chron

Includes bibliographical references

Whitaker, Robert

The **mapmaker's** wife; a true tale of love, murder, and survival in the Amazon. Basic Books 2004 352p il maps $25 **981**
  1. Travelers 2. Scientific expeditions 3. Amazon River valley
ISBN 0-7382-0808-6; 978-0-7382-0808-4

                           LC 2003-26902

"The harrowing journey of Isabel Godin across the Andes and down the Amazon to rejoin her husband after a 20-year separation is only a small part of the extended history of the Charles-Marie de la Condamine expedition, which in turn is set within its context of the history of Enlightenment science, 18th-century mapping methods, the debate over the shape of the earth, and the sorry history of the Spanish and Portuguese conquest of South America." Sci Books Films

Includes bibliographical references

981.53

Barbassa, Juliana

Dancing With the Devil in the City of God; Rio de Janeiro and the Olympic Dream. Juliana Barbassa. Simon & Schuster 2015 336 p. color illustrations, map (ebook) $16.99; (hardback: alkaline paper) $27   **981.53**
  1. Social problems -- Brazil -- Rio de Janeiro 2. City and town life -- Brazil -- Rio de Janeiro 3. Rio de Janeiro (Brazil) -- Economic conditions 4. Economic development -- Brazil -- Rio de Janeiro
ISBN 9781476756271; 1476756252; 9781476756257

                           LC 2014042530

In this book by Juliana Barbassa, "Rio has always aspired to the pantheon of global capitals, and under the spotlight of the 2014 World Cup and the 2016 Olympic Games it seems that its moment has come. But in order to prepare itself for the world stage, Rio must vanquish the entrenched problems that Barbassa recalls from her childhood. Turning this beautiful but deeply flawed place into a pristine showcase of the best that Brazil has to offer." (Publisher's note)

"Her interviews with police, prostitutes, drug dealers, ecologists, businesspeople, academics, movers and shakers, and the moved and shaken offer a fascinating look at the people who live in and aspire to change one of the world's most impressive cities." Booklist

Includes bibliographical references and index.

982   Argentina

Brown, Jonathan C.

A **brief** history of Argentina; 2nd ed; Facts On File 2010 354p il map (Brief history) $49.50; pa $19.95   **982**
  1. Argentina -- History
ISBN 978-0-8160-7796-0; 978-0-8160-8361-9 pa; 978-1-4381-3111-5 ebook

                           LC 2010004887

First published 2002

This book covers "Argentina's diverse geography and its varied natural resources; the origins of the deep-seated practices of discrimination, which continue today; the effects of neoliberalism on Argentina's large working class and urban poor, culminating in the caserola movement, the piqueteros movement, and the birth of the cartoneros; the impact a changing global economy has had within Argentina's borders; [and] the rich culture of Argentina, which has created five Nobel laureates, vibrant cities that draw millions of tourists annually, and sports teams that have won multiple world championships." Publisher's note

Includes bibliographical references

Parrado, Nando

 ★ **Miracle** in the Andes; 72 days on the mountain and my long trek home. [by] Nando Parrado with Vince Rause. Crown Publishers 2006 291p il map hardcover o.p. pa $13.95 **982**
  1. Survival after airplane accidents, shipwrecks, etc. 2. Andes
ISBN 1-4000-9767-3; 978-1-4000-9767-8; 1-4000-9769-X pa; 978-1-4000-9769-2 pa

                           LC 2005-21629

"In October 1972, a plane carrying an Uruguayan rugby team crashed in the Andes. Not immediately rescued, the survivors turned to cannibalism to survive and after 72 days were saved. Rugby team member Parrado has written a beautiful story of friendship, tragedy and perseverance." Publ Wkly

985   Peru

Adams, Mark

Turn right at Machu Picchu. Dutton 2011 333p il map $26.95   **985**
  1. Explorers 2. Governors 3. Historians 4. Senators 5. Machu Picchu (Peru) 6. Peru -- Antiquities
ISBN 978-0-525-95224-4; 0-525-95224-1

                           LC 2011-10211

Traces the author's recreation of Hiram Bingham III's discovery of the ancient citadel, Machu Picchu, in the Andes Mountains of Peru, describing his struggles with rudimentary survival tools and his experiences at the sides of local guides.

"While some readers may prefer a more straightforward version of Bingham's exploits . . . , those favoring a quirkier retelling will relish Mr. Adams's wry, revealing romp through the Andes." Wall Street J

Bingham, Hiram

 ★ **Lost** city of the Incas; the story of Machu Picchu and its builders. with an introduction by Hugh Thomson; photographs by Hugh Thomson. Sterling 2002 274p il hardcover o.p. pa $12.95   **985**
  1. Incas 2. Machu Picchu (Peru) 3. Peru -- Antiquities
ISBN 0-2976-0759-6; 1-84212-585-0 pa

                           LC 2002-483039

A reissue of the title first published 1948 by Duell

"In 1911 Bingham, an American explorer, found the Inca city of Machu Picchu, which had been lost for 300 years. In this volume he tells of its origin, how it came to be lost and how it was finally discovered." Libr J

Includes bibliographical references

Hunefeldt, Christine

A **brief** history of Peru; 2nd ed; Facts On File 2010 xx, 332p il map (Brief history) $49.50   **985**
  1. Peru -- History
ISBN 978-0-8160-8144-8; 978-1-4381-0828-5 ebook

                           LC 2010-20748

First published 2004

This is a history of Peru ranging "from its ancient peoples and the Inca Empire through . . . recent political, social, and economic developments." Publisher's note

Includes bibliographical references

Moseley, Michael Edward

 ★ The **Incas** and their ancestors; the archaeology of Peru. rev ed; Thames & Hudson 2001 288p il maps $27.50 **985**

1. Incas 2. Peru -- Antiquities
ISBN 0-500-28277-3

LC 00-108866

First published 1992

This account of Andean prehistory and archaeology takes us from the first settlement of 10,000 years ago to the Spanish conquest

"Clearly presented, with a generous ration of maps and illustrations, {the volume} is thoughtful and welcome." Times Lit Suppl {review of 1992 edition}

Includes bibliographical references

Thomson, Hugh

The **white** rock; an exploration of the Inca heartland. Overlook Press 2003 316p il map $27.95; pa $16.95   **985**

1. Incas
ISBN 1-585-67355-2; 1-585-67503-2 pa

LC 2002-34606

First published 2001 in the United Kingdom

"So entertaining and appealing is Thomson's story of his exploration of the Inca empire that readers will wish they could take off and follow in his footsteps. . . . Thomson's wit, eye for detail and reverence for humanity set him apart from the average travel-adventure writer—he is as good a companion as a traveler could hope for." Publ Wkly

Includes bibliographical references

990   History of Australasia, Pacific Ocean islands, Atlantic Ocean islands, Arctic islands, Antarctica, extraterrestrial worlds

Michener, James A.

Return to paradise. Random House 1951 437p hardcover o.p. pa $7.99   **990**

1. Islands of the Pacific
ISBN 0-449-20650-5 pa

"Alternate chapters describe each island followed by a short story set against the region described." Ont Libr Rev

Treister, Kenneth

Easter Island's silent sentinels; the sculpture and architecture of Rapa Nui. Kenneth Treister, Patricia Vargas Casanova, and Claudio Cristino; foreword by Daniel Libeskind; maps and illustrations by Roberto Izaurieta and Kenneth Treister. University of New Mexico Press 2013 xv, 144 p.p color illustrations (cloth: alk. paper) $45   **990**

1. Sculpture 2. Architecture 3. Easter Island
ISBN 0826352642; 9780826352644

LC 2013013728

Written by Kenneth Treister, Patricia Vargas Casanova, and Claudio Cristino, "this richly illustrated book of the history, culture, and art of Easter Island is the first to examine in detail the island's vernacular architecture, often overshadowed by its giant stone statues. It shows the conjecturally reconstructed prehistoric pole houses . . . and the Easter Island Statue Project's inventory of the colossal moai sculptures." (Publisher's note)

Includes bibliographical references (pages 123-132) and index

994   Australia

Clendinnen, Inga

Dancing with strangers; Europeans and Australians at first contact. Inga Clendinnen. Cambridge University Press 2005 324p il map $60; pa $21.99   **994**

1. Aboriginal Australians 2. Australian national characteristics 3. Australia -- Race relations 4. Great Britain -- Colonies -- Australia
ISBN 0-5218-5137-8; 0-5216-1681-6 pa

LC 2005-11523

First published 2003 in Australia

"In January 1788, the First Fleet arrived in New South Wales, Australia and a thousand British men and women encountered the people who would be their new neighbors. . . . [This book] tells the story of what happened between the first British settlers of Australia and these Aborigines." Publisher's note

Includes bibliographical references

Hughes, Robert

The **fatal** shore. Knopf 1987 688p il maps hardcover o.p. pa $18   **994**

1. Penal colonies 2. Australia -- History
ISBN 0-394-75366-6 pa

LC 86-45272

"This epic account chronicles the history of Australia during the 80 years (1788-1868) of England's convict transportation system, when some 160,000 convicts reached 'the fatal shore.' Interweaving his own lucid narrative with untapped original sources—including the diaries and letters of the prisoners themselves—Hughes shows the evolution of the system and of the fledgling nation that emerged from the brutal penal colony." Libr J

Includes bibliographical references

Keneally, Thomas

A **commonwealth** of thieves; the improbable birth of Australia. Nan A. Talese/Doubleday 2006 385p map hardcover o.p. pa $15.95   **994**

1. Admirals 2. Penal colonies 3. Australia -- History 4. Colonial administrators 5. Frontier and pioneer life -- Australia
ISBN 0-385-51459-X; 978-0-385-51459-0; 1-4000-7956-X pa; 978-1-4000-7956-8 pa

LC 2006-44470

First published 2005 in Australia

This "book offers an engaging treatment of a subject which over the years has provoked a long and sometimes heated debate." Times Lit Suppl

Includes bibliographical references

995   New Guinea and neighboring countries of Melanesia

Hoffman, Carl

★ A **Savage** Harvest; A Tale of Cannibals, Colonialism, and Michael Rockefeller's Tragic Quest for Primitive Art. by Carl Hoffman. HarperCollins 2014 304 p. illustrations $26.99   **995**

1. New Guinea 2. Cannibalism 3. Missing persons
ISBN 0062116150; 9780062116154

This book, by Carl Hoffman, focuses on "the mysterious disappearance of Michael Rockefeller in New Guinea in 1961. . . . Soon after his disappearance, rumors surfaced that he'd been killed and ceremonially eaten by the local Asmat--a native tribe of warriors whose complex culture was built around sacred, reciprocal violence, head hunting, and ritual cannibalism. The Dutch government and the Rockefeller family denied the story, and Michael's death was officially ruled a drowning." (Publisher's note)

"[An] unforgettable story of a soothing and politically expedient cover-up and a brutal and tragic collision of cultures." Booklist

Includes bibliographical references (pages 310-312) and index.

996   Polynesia and other Pacific Ocean islands

Alexander, Caroline

   ★ The **Bounty**: the true story of the mutiny on the Bounty. Viking 2003 491p il hardcover o.p. pa $17   **996**
1. Admirals 2. Explorers 3. Oceania 4. Mutineers 5. Bounty (Ship) 6. Naval officers 7. Government officials 8. Colonial administrators
ISBN 978-0-670-03133-7; 0-670-03133-X; 978-0-14-200469-2 pa; 0-14-200469-3 pa
                LC 2003-50158
"A rollicking sea adventure told with enormous confidence and style." Booklist

Includes bibliographical references

996.18

Preston, Diana

Paradise in chains; the Bounty Mutiny and the founding of Australia. Diana Preston. Bloomsbury 2017 xii, 333 p.p illustrations (hardcover) $30   **996.18**
1. Bounty Mutiny, 1789 2. Australia -- History -- 1788-1851 3. Escapes -- History -- 18th century 4. Ocean travel -- History -- 18th century 5. Survival at sea -- History -- 18th century 6. Prisoners -- Travel -- History -- 18th century 7. Islands of the Pacific -- Description and travel 8. Islands of the Pacific -- History -- 18th century 9. Prisoners -- Australia -- Botany Bay (N.S.W.) -- History -- 18th century
ISBN 9781632866127; 9781632866103
                LC 2017002518
This book, by Diana Preston, is an "account of the mutiny of the Bounty and the flight of convicts from the Australian penal colony. . . . Preston provides the background and context to explain the thrilling open-boat voyages each party survived and the Pacific Island nations each encountered on their journey to safety." (Publisher's note)

"A wonderful look into the beginnings of Australia and the remarkable strength of the survivors of these dangerous voyages." Kirkus

Includes bibliographical references (pages 293-300) and index

996.9   Hawaii and neighboring north central Pacific Ocean islands

Haley, James L.

Captive paradise; the United States and Hawai'i. James L. Haley. St. Martin's Press 2014 448 p. illustrations (hardcover: alk. paper) $29.99   **996.9**
1. Hawaii -- History 2. United States -- History 3. Hawaii -- Annexation to the United States
ISBN 0312600658; 9780312600655
                LC 2014026108

This book "focuses on Hawaii's annexation by the United States. Weaving a vast web of culture clashes amid the military and ideological conquests that turned native Hawaiians into 'strangers in their own land,' [James L.] Haley delivers his narrative through big personalities: royalty, missionaries, and conquerors of various backgrounds." (Publishers Weekly)

"Haley underscores how remarkable it was that the islands were able to withstand coercion by French, British and American forces for as long as they did. A pertinent work of keen understanding of the complex Hawaiian story." Kirkus

Includes bibliographical references and index

Moore, Susanna, 1948-

Paradise of the Pacific; approaching Hawaii. Susanna Moore. Farrar, Straus & Giroux 2015 320 p. illustrations, map (hardback) $26   **996.9**
1. Hawaii -- History 2. Folklore -- Hawaii 3. Hawaii -- Description and travel 4. Legends -- Hawaii 5. Hawaii -- History -- 18th century 6. Hawaii -- Social conditions -- 18th century 7. Hawaii -- Social life and customs -- 18th century 8. Acculturation -- Hawaii -- History -- 18th century 9. Social change -- Hawaii -- History -- 18th century 10. Culture conflict -- Hawaii -- History -- 18th century 11. Hawaii -- Emigration and immigration -- History -- 18th century
ISBN 0374298777; 9780374298777
                LC 2015002967

NBA Longlist

Author Susanna Moore "pieces together the elusive, dramatic story of late-eighteenth-century Hawaii—its kings and queens, gods and goddesses, missionaries, migrants, and explorers—a not-so-distant time of abrupt transition, in which an isolated pagan world of human sacrifice and strict taboo, without a currency or a written language, was confronted with the equally ritualized world of capitalism, Western education, and Christian values." (Publisher's note)

"Moore's background in storytelling radiates throughout this work, creating a quick- paced and well-crafted narrative. Highly recommended for the armchair historian and those intrigued by Hawaiian history, maritime exploration, and the history of Christian missionaries. For readers with a continued fascination in the development of the Hawaiian Islands, perusing Julia Flynn Siler's Lost Kingdom might also prove a rewarding endeavor." LJ

Includes bibliographical references and index

Vowell, Sarah, 1969-

Unfamiliar fishes. Riverhead Books 2011 238p il map $25.95   **996.9**
1. Hawaii -- History 2. United States -- Territorial expansion 3. Hawaii -- Annexation to the United States
ISBN 978-1-59448-787-3
                LC 2010-47943
"While Vowell's take on Hawaii's Americanization is abbreviated, it's never bereft of substance—her repartee manages to be filling, her insights astute and comprehensive." N Y Times Book Rev

Includes bibliographical references

998   Arctic islands and Antarctica

Alexander, Caroline

   ★ The **Endurance**; Shackleton's legendary Antarctic expedition. Knopf 1998 211p il $29.95   **998**
1. Explorers 2. Endurance (Ship) 3. Antarctica -- Exploration 4. Imperial Trans-Antarctic Expedition (1914-1917)

ISBN 0-375-40403-1

In 1914, Sir Ernest Shackleton "sailed to Antarctica with 27 men in hopes of being the first human to transverse the continent. But his ship, the Endurance, was trapped, then crushed, by ice in the Weddell Sea, propelling the party into a nightmare of cold and near starvation. Alexander, relying extensively on journals by crew members, some never published, as well as on myriad other sources, delivers a spellbinding story of human courage. . . . What makes this book especially exciting, however, are the 170 previously unpublished photos by the expedition's photographer, Frank Hurley." Publ Wkly

Ehrlich, Gretel

This cold heaven; seven seasons in Greenland. Pantheon Bks. 2001 377p il maps hardcover o.p. pa $14   **998**
    1. Inuit 2. Greenland
    ISBN 0-679-44200-6; 0-679-75852-6 pa

LC 00-69277

"Ehrlich began traveling to Greenland during her recovery from a nearly fatal lightning strike, and her keen, often poetic responses to the beauty of the frigid landscape and the warmth of Inuit families, combined with a profound immersion in Greenland history, infuse her captivating account with both drama and reflection." Booklist

Includes bibliographical references

Emmerson, Charles

The **future** history of the Arctic. PublicAffairs 2010 405p il map   **998**
    1. Geopolitics 2. Arctic regions
    ISBN 978-1-58648-636-5

LC 2009-35094

"It's easy to romanticise the Arctic, and over the years plenty of authors have. Oddly though, given the region's increasing geopolitical significance, it's rare to find books that treat it as something other than a chilly adventure playground or an excuse for reams of purple prose. Thank goodness, then, for Charles Emmerson. In this book he looks at how the frozen north has played a key role in world affairs in the past and how it could prove more important in the years to come." Scotsman

Includes bibliographical references

The **ends** of the earth; an anthology of the finest writing on the Arctic and the Antarctic. Bloomsbury 2007 2v in 1 map $29.95   **998**
    1. Antarctica 2. Polar regions 3. Arctic regions
    ISBN 1-59691-443-2; 978-1-59691-443-8

The editors "present an anthology of writings about the Arctic and Antarctic, which is actually two books in one. Halfway through, readers can turn the book upside down for writings about the opposite end of the earth. . . . Included are primary-source accounts by early explorers such as Ernest Shackleton, John Franklin, and Kund Rasmussen, nature writings by Barry Lopez and Gretel Ehrlich, excerpts from novels by Jules Verne, Jack London, and H.P. Lovecraft, and essays by journalists and scientists. Each excerpt is just long enough to whet the reader's appetite. Great reading for the armchair adventurer." Libr J

Kavenna, Joanna

The **ice** museum; in search of the lost land of Thule. Viking 2006 294p il map $24.95; pa $15   **998**
    1. Arctic regions -- Exploration
    ISBN 0-670-03473-8; 0-14-303846-X pa
    First published 2005 in the United Kingdom
The author "chronicles her personal journey into the myth and real-ity of the legendary Arctic land of Thule. . . . [This book] transcends all genre description, and holds its own as a journey into a world that somehow vibrantly exists on paper and nowhere else." Booklist

McGonigal, David

Antarctica; secrets of the southern continent. chief consultant, David McGonigal. Firefly Books 2008 400p il map $59.95   **998**
    1. Antarctica
    ISBN 978-1-55407-398-6; 1-55407-398-7

This "book covers all aspects of the continent, including ecology, geography, wildlife, and exploration. . . . Sumptuously illustrated with photos, maps, and paintings, this will be the go-to reference on Antarctica for years to come. A truly superb production." Booklist

Riffenburgh, Beau

Shackleton's forgotten expedition; the voyage of the Nimrod. by Beau Riffenburgh. Bloomsbury, Distributed to the trade by Holtzbrinck Publishers 2004 xxiv, 358p il map $25.95; pa $15.95   **998**
    1. Explorers 2. Antarctica -- Exploration
    ISBN 1-58234-488-4; 1-58234-611-9 pa

LC 2004-11999

The author recounts Shackleton's "voyage to the Antarctic from 1907 to 1909, during which he led a small group of men to within 97 miles of the South Pole. . . . For those who thrilled to the Endurance saga, Riffenburgh offers an equally gripping adventure, which laid the foundations of Shackleton's capacity for brilliant leadership under pressure." Publ Wkly

Includes bibliographical references

Smith, Roff

Life on the ice; no one goes to Antarctica alone. National Geographic 2005 208p pa $16   **998**
    1. Antarctica -- Description and travel
    ISBN 0-7922-9345-2

LC 2005-298454

First published 2002 in Australia

"Smith is the most exceptional of travel writers: his portraits of people are deeply sympathetic, while his language is at once lyrical and knowledgeable. Not to be missed." Booklist

Streever, Bill

Cold; adventures in the world's frozen places. Little, Brown and Co. 2009 292p $24.99; pa $14.99   **998**
    1. Cold 2. Arctic regions -- Description and travel
    ISBN 978-0-316-04291-8; 0-316-04291-9; 978-0-316-04292-5 pa; 0-316-04292-7 pa

LC 2008-45350

Strever "delivers a poetic, anecdotal narrative complete with polar expeditions, Ice Age mysteries, igloos, permafrost and hailstorms. . . . This is a wonderful collection of one man's first-rate observations and commentary about the history and importance of cold to the earth and its occupants." Publ Wkly

Includes bibliographical references

Turney, Chris

1912; the year the world discovered Antarctica. Pgw 2012 358 p. $27   **998**
    1. Explorers 2. Antarctica -- Exploration
    ISBN 1582437890; 9781582437897

This book by Chris Turney presents "an in-depth look at a year in which five different expeditions set out to explore Antarctica. . . . The continent would see no fewer than five different national exploration teams during that year, and geologist Turney . . . examines each expedition in turn, after outlining some of the earliest attempts at exploring Antarctica, including Ernest Shackleton's 1907-1909 expedition." (Kirkus Reviews)

Includes bibliographical references and index.

AUTHOR, TITLE, AND SUBJECT INDEX

This index to the books in the Classified Collection includes author, title, and subject entries; added entries for publishers' series, illustrators, joint authors, and editors of works entered under title; and name and subject cross-references; all arranged in one alphabet.

The number or symbol in bold face type at the end of each entry refers to the Dewey Decimal Classification or to the Fiction (Fic) or Story Collection (S C), or Easy Books (E) section where the main entry for the book will be found. Works classed in 92 will be found under the headings for the biographies' subject.

AUTHOR, TITLE, AND SUBJECT INDEX
SEVENTEENTH EDITION

The **addiction** solution. Sederer, L. I.   362.29

ADDICTS -- REHABILITATION
Fletcher, A. M. Inside rehab   362.29
Jamison, L. The recovering   616.86

ADDICTS -- REHABILITATION -- UNITED STATES
Dresner, A. My fair junkie   92

ADDICTS -- UNITED STATES -- BIOGRAPHY
Dresner, A. My fair junkie   92

Adding value to libraries, archives, and museums. Matthews, J. R. | 025.1

ADDITIVES, FOOD *See* Food additives

Addonizio, Kim
Mortal trash   811

ADDRESSES *See* Lectures and lecturing; Speeches

Adeliza, of Louvain, Queen, consort of Henry I, King of England, approximately 1109-1151
About
Weir, A. Queens of the conquest   942.02

Adelman, Carol A.
(jt. auth) Michener, D. C. Peony   635.9

Adelson-Goldstein, Jayme
The Oxford picture dictionary   423

Aderkas, P. von
Turner, N. J. The North American guide to common poisonous plants and mushrooms   581.6

ADHD does not exist. Saul, R.   618.92

ADHD nation. Schwarz, A.   618.92

ADHESIVES
See also Materials

Adichie, Chimamanda Ngozi, 1977-
Dear Ijeawele, or a feminist manifesto in fifteen suggestions   305.42
We should all be feminists   305.42

Adimando, Stacy
Nopalito   641.59

Adjonyoh, Zoe
Zoe's Ghana kitchen   641.5

ADJUSTMENT (PSYCHOLOGY)
Brizendine, J. Stunned by grief   248
Cacciatore, J. Bearing the unbearable   155.937
Gonzales, L. Surviving survival   155.9
Kingma, D. R. The ten things to do when your life falls apart   155.9
Lieberman, D. J. Never get angry again   152.47
Rehm, D. On my own   92
Seligman, M. E. P. Learned optimism   155.2
Sonenshein, S. Stretch   153.35
Thomas, A. What Comes Next and How to Like It   92
Tuck, S. Getting from me to we   155.4
Winch, G. How to fix a broken heart   155.9

ADJUSTMENT (PSYCHOLOGY)
See also Psychology

ADJUSTMENT (PSYCHOLOGY) IN CHILDREN
Janis-Norton, N. Calmer, easier, happier screen time   649.1
Tuck, S. Getting from me to we   155.4

ADJUSTMENT, SOCIAL *See* Social adjustment

Adkin, Mark
The Trafalgar companion   940.2

Adkins, Lesley
Gibraltar   946.89

Adkins, Roy (Roy A.), 1951-
(jt. auth) Adkins, L. Gibraltar   946.89

Adler, Carlye
(jt. auth) Warren, J. Meditation for fidgety skeptics   158.12
(jt. auth) Webb, M. G. Dear founder   658

Adler, Julian
(jt. auth) Berman, G. Start here   364.609

Adler, Margot
Drawing down the moon   133.4

Adler, Mortimer J.
How to think about the great ideas   080

Adler, Moshe
Economics for the rest of us   330

Adler, Robert E.
Medical firsts   610

Adler, Stella
Stella Adler on America's master playwrights   812
Stella Adler: the art of acting   792

Adler, Stephen J.
Grunwald, L. Women's letters   305.4

Adler, William M.
The man who never died   92

ADMINISTRATION *See* Civil service; Management; Public administration

ADMINISTRATION OF CRIMINAL JUSTICE
Benforado, A. Unfair   364.3
Bogira, S. Courtroom 302   345
Burns, S. The Central Park Five   364.1
Dreisinger, B. Incarceration nations   365
Encyclopedia of crime and punishment   346
Feige, D. Indefensible   345
Morris, E. A wilderness of error   364.152
Stevenson, B. Just Mercy   353.4

ADMINISTRATION OF CRIMINAL JUSTICE
See also Administration of justice; Criminal law

ADMINISTRATION OF CRIMINAL JUSTICE -- UNITED STATES
Anatomy of innocence   364.973
Berman, G. Start here   364.609
The divide   303.3
Edelman, P. Not a crime to be poor   362.5
Forman, J. Locking up our own   364.973
Garrett, B. L. Too big to jail   345.73
Hylton, D. A little piece of light   92
Smith, C. S. The injustice system   345.73
Trainum, J. L. How the police generate false confessions   345.73

ADMINISTRATION OF JUSTICE
Legal systems of the world   340

ADMINISTRATION OF JUSTICE
See also Law

ADMINISTRATION OF JUSTICE -- UNITED STATES

1930

Linn, S. The case for make believe   **155.4**

ADVICE COLUMNISTS

Dickinson, A. The mighty queens of Freeville   **92**

Life stories   **920**

ADVICE COLUMNISTS -- UNITED STATES -- BIOGRA-PHY

Dickinson, A. Strangers tend to tell me things   **92**

ADVICE COLUMNS

   See also Counseling; Newspapers -- Sections, columns, etc.

ADVICE LITERATURE

Anders, G. You can do anything   **331.702**

Bradley, M. J. Crazy-stressed   **306.874**

DeClaire, J. Enlightened aging   **612.67**

Moore, D. W. The story cure   **808.3**

Ockwell-Smith, S. Gentle discipline   **649.64**

Rossen, J. Rossen to the rescue   **640.73**

Waters, L. The strength switch   **306.874**

Weathington, M. Gardening in the South   **635.9**

Advice not given. Epstein, M.   **294.3**

ADVOCACY (POLITICAL SCIENCE)

Dufton, E. Grass roots   **362.295**

Nasty women   **305.42**

Tolokonnikova, N. Rules for rulebreakers   **782.421**

Turshen, J. Feed the resistance   **641.5**

ADVOCACY (POLITICAL SCIENCE)

   See also Political science

The **Aeneid.** Virgil   **873**

Aerial geology. Morton, M. C.   **557**

AERIAL PHOTOGRAPHY

Malin, G. Beaches   **779.3**

AERIAL PHOTOGRAPHY

   See also Photography

AERIAL PROPELLERS

   See also Airplanes

AERIAL RECONNAISSANCE

   See also Military aeronautics; Remote sensing

AERIAL ROCKETS *See* Rockets (Aeronautics)

AERIALISTS -- UNITED STATES -- BIOGRAPHY

Jensen, D. Queen of the air   **791.3**

AERODYNAMICS, SUPERSONIC -- RESEARCH -- UNITED STATES

Hampton, D. Chasing the demon   **629.132**

AERONAUTICAL ENGINEERS

Clary, D. A. Rocket man   **92**

Hargittai, I. The Martians of science   **920**

AERONAUTICAL ENGINEERS -- GERMANY -- BIOG-RAPHY

Mulley, C. The women who flew for Hitler   **940.54**

AERONAUTICAL INSTRUMENTS

   See also Scientific apparatus and instruments

AERONAUTICAL SPORTS

Higgins, M. Bird dream   **797.5**

AERONAUTICAL SPORTS

   See also Aeronautics; Sports

AERONAUTICS

Alexander, D. E. Why don't jumbo jets flap their

wings?   **629.13**

Cassutt, M. The astronaut maker   **629.4**

Hampton, D. Chasing the demon   **629.132**

McCullough, D. The Wright brothers   **92**

Ryan, C. Sonic wind   **92**

AERONAUTICS

   See also Engineering; Locomotion

AERONAUTICS -- ACCIDENTS *See* Aircraft accidents

AERONAUTICS -- CHINA

Fallows, J. China airborne   **387.7**

AERONAUTICS -- COMPETITIONS

Jackson, J. Atlantic fever   **629.130**

AERONAUTICS -- FLIGHTS

Botting, D. Dr. Eckener's dream machine   **629.133**

Lindbergh, C. The spirit of St. Louis   **629.13**

AERONAUTICS -- FLIGHTS

   See also Voyages and travels

AERONAUTICS -- FLIGHTS -- HISTORY

Hampton, D. The flight   **629.13**

AERONAUTICS -- HAWAII -- HISTORY -- 20TH CEN-TURY

Ryan, J. Race to Hawaii   **629.13**

AERONAUTICS -- HISTORY

Goldstone, L. Birdmen   **629.13**

Jackson, J. Atlantic fever   **629.130**

AERONAUTICS -- PILOTING *See* Airplanes -- Piloting

AERONAUTICS -- POPULAR WORKS

Vanhoenacker, M. Skyfaring   **629.132**

AERONAUTICS -- SAFETY MEASURES

McGee, W. J. Attention all passengers   **387.7**

AERONAUTICS -- SAFETY MEASURES -- RESEARCH -- UNITED STATES -- HISTORY -- 20TH CENTURY

Ryan, C. Sonic wind   **92**

AERONAUTICS -- UNITED STATES -- BIOGRAPHY

McCullough, D. The Wright brothers   **92**

AERONAUTICS -- UNITED STATES -- HISTORY

Kessner, T. The flight of the century   **92**

AERONAUTICS -- UNITED STATES -- HISTORY -- 20TH CENTURY

Groom, W. The aviators   **920**

McCullough, D. The Wright brothers   **92**

AERONAUTICS AND CIVILIZATION

   See also Aeronautics; Civilization

AERONAUTICS IN AGRICULTURE

   See also Aeronautics; Agriculture; Spraying and dust-ing

AERONAUTICS, COMMERCIAL -- CHINA

Fallows, J. China airborne   **387.7**

AERONAUTICS, MILITARY -- ACCIDENTS -- ALASKA

Murphy, B. 81 days below zero   **940.54**

AERONAUTICS, MILITARY -- TECHNOLOGICAL IN-NOVATIONS -- HISTORY -- 20TH CENTURY

Bruning, J. R. Indestructible   **92**

AERONAUTICS, MILITARY -- UNITED STATES -- HIS-TORY -- 20TH CENTURY

Groom, W. The aviators   **920**

AEROPLANES *See* Airplanes

Abdul-Jabbar, K. Coach Wooden and me   **92**

AFRICAN AMERICAN BOXERS -- BIOGRAPHY

Assael, S. The murder of Sonny Liston   **796.83**

Gildea, W. The longest fight   **796.83**

Runstedtler, T. Jack Johnson, rebel sojourner   **796.83**

Stratton, W. K. Floyd Patterson   **92**

Tyson, M. Iron ambition   **92**

AFRICAN AMERICAN BOXERS -- UNITED STATES -- BIOGRAPHY

Montville, L. Sting like a bee   **92**

AFRICAN AMERICAN BOYS

Our black sons matter   **305.242**

AFRICAN AMERICAN BUSINESS PEOPLE *See* African American businesspeople

AFRICAN AMERICAN BUSINESSPEOPLE

White, S. Prince of darkness   **92**

AFRICAN AMERICAN BUSINESSPEOPLE

See also Black businesspeople; Businesspeople

AFRICAN AMERICAN BUSINESSPEOPLE -- BIOGRAPHY

Wills, S. Black Fortunes   **973.049**

AFRICAN AMERICAN CARTOONISTS -- BIOGRAPHY

Tisserand, M. Krazy   **92**

AFRICAN AMERICAN CHILDREN

See also Black children; Children

AFRICAN AMERICAN CHILDREN -- EDUCATION

Tough, P. Whatever it takes   **362.7**

AFRICAN AMERICAN CIVIL RIGHTS WORKERS

Lewis, J. March   **92**

Sugrue, T. J. Sweet land of liberty   **323**

AFRICAN AMERICAN CIVIL RIGHTS WORKERS -- BIOGRAPHY

Rosenbloom, J. Redemption   **92**

AFRICAN AMERICAN CIVIL RIGHTS WORKERS -- HISTORY -- 20TH CENTURY

Dyson, M. E. What truth sounds like   **305.8**

AFRICAN AMERICAN COLLEGE GRADUATES

Hobbs, J. The short and tragic life of Robert Peace   **92**

AFRICAN AMERICAN COLLEGE TEACHERS -- BIOGRAPHY

Harris, J. B. My soul looks back   **92**

Stewart, J. C. The new Negro   **92**

AFRICAN AMERICAN COMEDIANS -- BIOGRAPHY

Hart, K. I can't make this up   **92**

AFRICAN AMERICAN COOKING

Afro-vegan   **641.59**

Chambers, V. Between Harlem and Heaven   **641.59**

Harris, J. B. My soul looks back   **92**

Miller, A. Soul food   **641.59**

Soul food love   **641.59**

Terry, B. Vegan Soul kitchen   **641.5**

Twitty, M. The cooking gene   **641.59**

AFRICAN AMERICAN COOKING -- HISTORY

Deetz, K. F. Bound to the fire   **641.59**

AFRICAN AMERICAN COOKS

Edna Lewis   **641.597**

AFRICAN AMERICAN COOKS -- BIOGRAPHY

Harris, J. B. My soul looks back   **92**

AFRICAN AMERICAN COOKS -- UNITED STATES -- BIOGRAPHY

Chambers, V. Yes, chef   **92**

AFRICAN AMERICAN COOKS -- VIRGINIA -- BIOGRAPHY

Deetz, K. F. Bound to the fire   **641.59**

AFRICAN AMERICAN COOKS -- VIRGINIA -- HISTORY

Deetz, K. F. Bound to the fire   **641.59**

African American cultural theory and heritage [series]

Inaba, M. Willie Dixon   **92**

AFRICAN AMERICAN DANCERS

See also African Americans; Dancers

AFRICAN AMERICAN DANCERS -- BIOGRAPHY

Copeland, M. Life in motion   **92**

AFRICAN AMERICAN EDUCATORS

Harlan, L. R. Booker T. Washington: the making of a black leader, 1856-1901   **92**

Harlan, L. R. Booker T. Washington: the wizard of Tuskegee, 1901-1915   **92**

McCluskey, A. T. A forgotten sisterhood   **370.9**

Norrell, R. J. Up from history   **92**

Smock, R. W. Booker T. Washington   **92**

Uncle Tom or new Negro   **370**

Walker, V. S. The lost education of Horace Tate   **370.92**

Washington, B. T. Up from slavery   **92**

AFRICAN AMERICAN EDUCATORS

See also African Americans; Educators

AFRICAN AMERICAN EDUCATORS -- SOUTHERN STATES -- BIOGRAPHY

McCluskey, A. T. A forgotten sisterhood   **370.9**

AFRICAN AMERICAN ENGINEERS -- BIOGRAPHY

Paul, R. We could not fail   **920**

AFRICAN AMERICAN ENTERTAINERS -- BIOGRAPHY

Common One day it'll all make sense   **92**

AFRICAN AMERICAN FAMILIES -- HISTORY

Williams, H. A. Help me to find my people   **306.3**

AFRICAN AMERICAN FAMILIES.

Haley, A. Roots   **920**

AFRICAN AMERICAN FARMERS -- GEORGIA -- ECONOMIC CONDITIONS

Sherrod, S. The courage to hope   **975.8**

AFRICAN AMERICAN FEMINISTS -- BIOGRAPHY

Bell-Scott, P. The firebrand and the First Lady   **92**

Cooper, B. Eloquent rage   **305.48**

African American folklore.   **398.2**

AFRICAN AMERICAN FOOTBALL PLAYERS

Ross, C. K. Mavericks, money, and men   **796.332**

AFRICAN AMERICAN GAY MEN

Arceneaux, M. I can't date Jesus   **306.76**

AFRICAN AMERICAN GAY MEN -- BIOGRAPHY

Moore, D. L. No ashes in the fire   **92**

AFRICAN AMERICAN GENERALS -- BIOGRAPHY

Powell, C. L. It worked for me   **92**

AFRICAN AMERICAN GIRLS -- ILLINOIS -- CHICAGO

AFRICAN AMERICANS -- ATTITUDES -- HISTORY -- SOURCES

Freedman, E. Presidents and Black America   **973.09**

AFRICAN AMERICANS -- BIOGRAPHY

Baylor, E. Hang time   **92**

Buckley, G. L. The Black Calhouns   **92**

Honey, M. K. To the promised land   **323**

Jacoby, K. The strange career of William Ellis   **92**

Laymon, K. Heavy   **92**

Macy, B. Truevine   **791.3**

Meyer, E. L. Five for freedom   **973.7**

Moore, W. The work   **92**

Motley, E. L. Madison Park   **92**

Perry, T. Higher is waiting   **92**

Reed, A. The life and the adventures of a haunted convict   **365.34**

Smith, J. Blood brothers   **92**

White, S. Prince of darkness   **92**

AFRICAN AMERICANS -- BIOGRAPHY -- DICTIONARIES

African American national biography   **920.003**

Notable black American men, book II   **920.003**

Who's who among African Americans   **920.003**

AFRICAN AMERICANS -- BIOGRAPHY -- ENCYCLOPEDIAS

Bracks, L. African American almanac   **973**

AFRICAN AMERICANS -- BIOGRAPHY.

Haley, A. Roots   **920**

AFRICAN AMERICANS -- CHICAGO (ILL.)

Common One day it'll all make sense   **92**

Michaeli, E. The defender   **071**

AFRICAN AMERICANS -- CIVIL RIGHTS

Kantrowitz, S. More than freedom   **323.1**

Lowery, W. They can't kill us all   **305.896**

Martin, T. Rest in power   **92**

Morris, J. M. Eye on the Struggle   **92**

Mosnier, J. Julius Chambers   **92**

Peck, R. I am not your negro   **323.1**

Rieder, J. Gospel of freedom   **323.1**

Sokol, J. All eyes are upon us   **323.1**

Stratton, W. K. Floyd Patterson   **92**

AFRICAN AMERICANS -- CIVIL RIGHTS

See also Blacks -- Civil rights; Civil rights

AFRICAN AMERICANS -- CIVIL RIGHTS -- ALABAMA -- BIRMINGHAM

Rieder, J. Gospel of freedom   **323.1**

AFRICAN AMERICANS -- CIVIL RIGHTS -- ALABAMA -- MONTGOMERY -- HISTORY -- 20TH CENTURY

Brinkley, D. Rosa Parks   **92**

Theoharis, J. The rebellious life of Mrs. Rosa Parks   **92**

AFRICAN AMERICANS -- CIVIL RIGHTS -- GRAPHIC NOVELS

Lewis, J. R. March   **92**

Lewis, J. March   **92**

AFRICAN AMERICANS -- CIVIL RIGHTS -- HISTORIOGRAPHY

Theoharis, J. A more beautiful and terrible history   **323.1**

AFRICAN AMERICANS -- CIVIL RIGHTS -- HISTORY

Theoharis, J. A more beautiful and terrible history   **323.1**

AFRICAN AMERICANS -- CIVIL RIGHTS -- HISTORY -- 19TH CENTURY

Blackmon, D. A. Slavery by another name   **305.8**

Douglass, F. Frederick Douglass: selected speeches and writings   **326**

AFRICAN AMERICANS -- CIVIL RIGHTS -- HISTORY -- 20TH CENTURY

Blackmon, D. A. Slavery by another name   **305.8**

Boyle, K. Arc of justice   **345**

Branch, T. At Canaan's edge   **973.923**

Dyson, M. E. I may not get there with you: the true Martin Luther King, Jr   **323**

Honey, M. K. To the promised land   **323**

Joseph, P. E. Waiting 'til the midnight hour   **323.1**

Katznelson, I. When affirmative action was white   **323.1**

King, M. L. The autobiography of Martin Luther King, Jr   **323**

Levingston, S. Kennedy and King   **920**

Lewis, A. B. The shadows of youth   **323.1**

Peck, R. I am not your negro   **323.1**

Rosenbloom, J. Redemption   **92**

Simon, J. F. Eisenhower vs. Warren   **973.921**

Sugrue, T. J. Sweet land of liberty   **323**

Sullivan, P. Lift every voice   **323.1**

Theoharis, J. A more beautiful and terrible history   **323.1**

AFRICAN AMERICANS -- CIVIL RIGHTS -- HISTORY -- 20TH CENTURY -- PICTORIAL WORKS

Kelley, K. Let Freedom Ring   **323.1**

AFRICAN AMERICANS -- CIVIL RIGHTS -- MASSACHUSETTS -- BOSTON REGION -- HISTORY -- 19TH CENTURY

Kantrowitz, S. More than freedom   **323.1**

AFRICAN AMERICANS -- CIVIL RIGHTS -- NORTH CAROLINA -- HISTORY -- 20TH CENTURY

Mosnier, J. Julius Chambers   **92**

AFRICAN AMERICANS -- CIVIL RIGHTS -- NORTHEASTERN STATES -- HISTORY -- 20TH CENTURY

Sokol, J. All eyes are upon us   **323.1**

AFRICAN AMERICANS -- CIVIL RIGHTS -- POETRY

Wright, C. D. One with others   **811**

AFRICAN AMERICANS -- CIVIL RIGHTS -- SOUTHERN STATES -- HISTORY

McCluskey, A. T. A forgotten sisterhood   **370.9**

Remembering Jim Crow   **305.896**

AFRICAN AMERICANS -- CIVIL RIGHTS -- SOUTHERN STATES -- HISTORY -- 20TH CENTURY

Arsenault, R. Freedom riders   **323**

Sokol, J. There goes my everything   **305.8**

AFRICAN AMERICANS -- CRIMES AGAINST

Morrison, M. S. Murder on Shades Mountain   **345.761**

Tyson, T. B. The blood of Emmett Till   **364.134**

AFRICAN AMERICANS -- CRIMES AGAINST -- MISSISSIPPI

Anderson, D. S. Emmett Till   **364.1**

Tyson, T. B. The blood of Emmett Till   **364.134**

AFRICAN AMERICANS -- DETROIT (MICH.) -- HIS-

AFRICAN AMERICANS -- INTELLECTUAL LIFE -- BIBLIOGRAPHY
African American literature   **810.9**

AFRICAN AMERICANS -- KENTUCKY -- GREAT CROSSING -- HISTORY -- 19TH CENTURY
Snyder, C. Great Crossings   **976.9**

AFRICAN AMERICANS -- LOUISIANA
Rasmussen, D. American uprising   **976.3**

AFRICAN AMERICANS -- MICHIGAN -- DETROIT
Boyle, K. Arc of justice   **345**

AFRICAN AMERICANS -- MICHIGAN -- DETROIT -- HISTORY
Martelle, S. Detroit   **977.4**

AFRICAN AMERICANS -- MICHIGAN -- DETROIT -- HISTORY -- 20TH CENTURY
Boyd, H. Black Detroit   **977.434**

AFRICAN AMERICANS -- MICHIGAN -- DETROIT -- SOCIAL CONDITIONS -- 21ST CENTURY
Philp, D. A $500 house in Detroit   **307.3**

AFRICAN AMERICANS -- MIGRATIONS -- HISTORY
Berlin, I. The making of African America   **305.8**

AFRICAN AMERICANS -- MIGRATIONS -- HISTORY -- 20TH CENTURY
Wilkerson, I. The warmth of other suns   **307**

AFRICAN AMERICANS -- MISSISSIPPI
Evers, M. W. The autobiography of Medgar Evers: a hero's life and legacy revealed through his writings, letters, and speeches   **92**

Ferris, W. Give my poor heart ease   **781.643**

Lomax, A. The land where the blues began   **781.643**

Trethewey, N. D. Beyond Katrina   **818**

AFRICAN AMERICANS -- MISSISSIPPI -- GREENWOOD -- BIOGRAPHY
Johnson, Y. The song and the silence   **305.896**

AFRICAN AMERICANS -- MUSEUMS -- WASHINGTON (D.C.) -- PLANNING
Wilkins, R. L. Long road to hard truth   **973**

AFRICAN AMERICANS -- OHIO -- HISTORY -- 19TH CENTURY
Cox The bone and sinew of the land   **977**

AFRICAN AMERICANS -- PENNSYLVANIA -- PITTSBURGH -- HISTORY
Whitaker, M. Smoketown   **305.896**

AFRICAN AMERICANS -- PICTORIAL WORKS
The Scurlock Studio and Black Washington   **779**

AFRICAN AMERICANS -- POETRY
Clifton, L. The collected poems of Lucille Clifton 1965-2010   **811**

Smith, P. Incendiary art   **811.54**

Wicker, M. Silencer   **811**

Young, K. Brown   **811**

AFRICAN AMERICANS -- POLITICAL ACTIVITY
The Black Panthers   **322.42**

Freedman, E. Presidents and Black America   **973.09**

AFRICAN AMERICANS -- POLITICAL ACTIVITY
See also Blacks -- Political activity; Political participation

AFRICAN AMERICANS -- POLITICS AND GOVERNMENT
Dyson, M. E. The Black presidency   **305.8**

AFRICAN AMERICANS -- POLITICS AND GOVERNMENT -- 20TH CENTURY -- SOURCES
The Black Panthers   **322.42**

AFRICAN AMERICANS -- POLITICS AND GOVERNMENT -- 21ST CENTURY
Coates We were eight years in power   **973.932**

Dyson, M. E. The Black presidency   **305.8**

Lebron, C. J. The making of Black lives matter   **305.896**

AFRICAN AMERICANS -- PORTRAITS
Krauthamer, B. Envisioning emancipation   **973.7**

AFRICAN AMERICANS -- RACE IDENTITY
Davis, T. J. History of African Americans   **973**

Ellison, R. The collected essays of Ralph Ellison   **814**

Jefferson, M. Negroland   **92**

Robinson, E. Disintegration   **305.8**

Sandweiss, M. A. Passing strange   **92**

Smith, T. K. Ordinary light   **92**

AFRICAN AMERICANS -- RACE IDENTITY
See also Blacks -- Race identity; Race awareness

AFRICAN AMERICANS -- RACE RELATIONS
Young, R. J. Let it bang   **305.896**

AFRICAN AMERICANS -- RELIGION
Blum, E. J. The color of Christ   **232**

AFRICAN AMERICANS -- RELIGION
See also Blacks -- Religion; Religion

AFRICAN AMERICANS -- RELIGION -- ENCYCLOPEDIAS
The Encyclopedia of African and African-American religions   **299.6**

AFRICAN AMERICANS -- REPARATIONS
Berry, M. F. My face is black is true   **92**

AFRICAN AMERICANS -- SEGREGATION
Rothstein, R. The color of law   **305.8**

AFRICAN AMERICANS -- SEGREGATION
See also Blacks -- Segregation; Segregation

AFRICAN AMERICANS -- SEGREGATION -- NORTHEASTERN STATES -- HISTORY
Sokol, J. All eyes are upon us   **323.1**

AFRICAN AMERICANS -- SEGREGATION -- SOUTHERN STATES
Arsenault, R. Freedom riders   **323**

AFRICAN AMERICANS -- SEGREGATION -- SOUTHERN STATES -- HISTORY
McCluskey, A. T. A forgotten sisterhood   **370.9**

Remembering Jim Crow   **305.896**

AFRICAN AMERICANS -- SOCIAL CONDITIONS
Coates Between the World and Me   **305.8**

Forman, J. Locking up our own   **364.973**

Gates, H. L. And Still I Rise   **973**

Hobbs, J. The short and tragic life of Robert Peace   **92**

Sokol, J. The heavens might crack   **323.092**

Trillin, C. Jackson, 1964   **305.8**

Whitaker, M. Smoketown   **305.896**

AFRICAN AMERICANS -- SOCIAL CONDITIONS

1600-1775, Colonial period

AMERICAN COLONIZATION SOCIETY

Davis, D. B.   The problem of slavery in the age of emancipation   **306.3**

AMERICAN COMPOSERS *See* Composers -- United States

American cookie. Byrn, A.   **641.86**

AMERICAN COOKING

101 classic cookbooks   **641**

Acheson, H.   The broad fork   **641.597**

Acheson, H.   A New Turn in the South   **641.59**

Ahern, S. J.   Gluten-Free Girl American classics reinvented   **641.597**

America--farm to table   **641.597**

The America's test kitchen do-it-yourself cookbook   **641.597**

The America's Test Kitchen healthy family cookbook   **641.5**

The America's Test Kitchen new family cookbook   **641.5**

The Beetlebung Farm cookbook   **641**

Brennan, K.   Keepers   **641.5**

Bring it!   **641.597**

Brioza, S.   State Bird Provisions   **641.597**

Brock, S.   Heritage   **641.59**

Brownson, J.   Dinner at home   **641.5**

Cooking my way back home   **641.5**

Cook's Country eats local   **641.597**

Currence, J.   Pickles, pigs & whiskey   **641.59**

Diaz, V.   Coconuts and collards   **641.597**

Disbrowe, P.   Down south   **641.59**

Dixon, K.   The Tutka Bay Lodge cookbook   **641.59**

Dupree, N.   Mastering the art of Southern cooking   **641.59**

Erickson, R.   A boat, a whale, and a walrus   **641.597**

Foose, M. H.   A southerly course   **641.59**

Friedman, A.   Chefs, drugs and rock & roll   **647.957**

Gartland, A.   Heartlandia   **641.597**

Hamilton, G.   Prune   **641.3**

Harris, J. B.   My soul looks back   **92**

Hesser, A.   Food52 a new way to dinner   **641.5**

Home   **641.5**

Humm, D.   I love New York   **641.59**

The immigrant cookbook   **641.59**

Jamison, B.   The border cookbook   **641.59**

Jennings, M.   Homegrown   **641.5**

Kostow, C.   A new Napa cuisine   **641.59**

Langholtz, G.   America   **641.597**

Lee, M.   The Lee Bros. Charleston kitchen   **641.59**

Mario Batali Big American cookbook   **641.597**

McMillan, T.   The American way of eating   **338.4**

Miller, A.   Soul food   **641.59**

Moore, C.   Little Flower baking   **641.815**

Moore, R.   This is Camino   **641.5**

Moulton, S.   Sara Moulton's Home Cooking 101   **641.5**

My perfect pantry   **641.5**

Parks, R.   Guerrilla Tacos   **641.84**

Parks, S.   BraveTart   **641.86**

Phillips, M.   The Chelsea Market cookbook   **641.59**

Prueitt, E.   Tartine all day   **641.5**

Red Rooster Cookbook   **641.5**

Ridge, B.   The Beekman 1802 heirloom dessert cookbook   **641.5**

Rodgers, R.   The essential James Beard cookbook   **641.597**

Rollins, K.   A taste of cowboy   **641.597**

Selengut, B.   Good fish   **641.6**

Selengut, B.   How to taste   **641.597**

Sewall, J.   The New England kitchen   **641.597**

The Silver Palate cookbook   **641.5**

Thompson-Anderson, T.   Texas on the Table   **641.597**

Victuals   **641.5**

Wilson, M.   The Alaska from scratch cookbook   **641.597**

Yeh, M.   Molly on the range   **641.5**

AMERICAN COOKING

See also Cooking

AMERICAN COOKING -- HISTORY

Coe, A.   A square meal   **641.5**

Edge, J. T.   The potlikker papers   **641.5**

Lee, E.   Buttermilk graffiti   **641.59**

Lohman, S.   Eight Flavors   **641.5**

AMERICAN COOKING -- SOUTHERN STYLE *See* Southern cooking

American creation. Ellis, J. J.   **973.3**

American crucifixion. Beam, A.   **289.3**

American dance. Fuhrer, M.   **792.8**

American Diabetes Association

(comp) Ask the experts   **616.4**

American Diabetes Association complete guide to diabetes   **616.4**

American Diabetes Association complete guide to diabetes. American Diabetes Association   **616.4**

American dialogue. Ellis, J. J.   **973.3**

AMERICAN DIARIES

See also American literature; Diaries

American Dietetic Association complete food and nutrition guide. Duyff, R. L.   **613.2**

AMERICAN DIPLOMATIC AND CONSULAR SERVICE

Neu, C. E.   Colonel House   **92**

AMERICAN DRAMA -- 20TH CENTURY

Gurney, A. R.   Love letters and two other plays: The golden age and What I did last summer   **812**

AMERICAN DRAMA -- 20TH CENTURY -- HISTORY AND CRITICISM

Adler, S.   Stella Adler on America's master playwrights   **812**

Playwrights at work   **812**

AMERICAN DRAMA -- AFRICAN AMERICAN AUTHORS -- HISTORY AND CRITICISM

Lane, S. F.   Black Broadway   **792**

AMERICAN DRAMATISTS

Adler, S.   Stella Adler on America's master playwrights   **812**

Dowling, R. M.   Eugene O'Neill   **92**

Gelb, B.   By women possessed   **92**

Lahr, J.   Tennessee Williams   **92**

AMERICAN DRAMATISTS

See also American authors; Dramatists

AMERICAN DRAWING

Eggers, D.   Ungrateful mammals   **700.411**

BANKS AND BANKING -- WASHINGTON (STATE) -- SEATTLE -- HISTORY

Grind, K. The lost bank   332.3

BANKS AND BANKING, INTERNATIONAL

Rhodes, W. R. Banker to the world   92

Bankston, Carl L.

(ed) Great lives from history: Notorious lives   920.003

BANNED BOOKS *See* Books -- Censorship

Banned in the U.S.A. Foerstel, H. N.   025.2

Bannerman, Stacy

Homefront 911   362.86

BANNERS *See* Flags

Bannon, Stephen K

About

Wolff, M. Fire and fury   973.933

Green, J. Devil's bargain   324.973

Bannos, Pamela

Vivian Maier   92

BANQUETS *See* Dining; Dinners

Banville, John

About

Banville, J. Time pieces   92

Banyas, Stephanie

Brunch @ Bobby's   641.5

(jt. auth) Flay, B. Bobby Flay fit   641.5

Bao Pu

(tr) Prisoner of the state   92

Baptist, Edward E.

The half has never been told   306.3

BAPTISTS -- UNITED STATES -- CLERGY -- BIOGRAPHY

Dyson, M. E. I may not get there with you: the true Martin Luther King, Jr   323

King, M. L. The autobiography of Martin Luther King, Jr   323

Rosenbloom, J. Redemption   92

BAR *See* Lawyers

Bar Book.   641.87

BAR MITZVAH

See also Judaism -- Customs and practices

Bar Tartine. Balla, N.   641.59

BAR TARTINE (SAN FRANCISCO, CALIF.)

Balla, N. Bar Tartine   641.59

Bar-Itzhak, Haya

(ed) Encyclopedia of Jewish folklore and traditions   398.2

Bar-On, Mordechai

Moshe Dayan   956.940

Bara, Brett

(ed) Crochet at home   746.43

Barack Obama. Maraniss, D.   92

Baraka, Imamu Amiri

Dutchman, and The slave   812

The LeRoi Jones/Amiri Baraka reader   818

Baranczak, Stanislaw

Monologue of a dog   891.8

Szymborska, W. Poems, new and collected, 1957-1997   891.8

Barash, David P.

The myth of monogamy   306.7

BARBADOS -- HISTORY

Stuart, A. Sugar in the Blood   338.1

Barbarian Days. Finnegan, W.   92

Barbarian lost. Trudeau, A.

Barbarisi, Daniel

Dueling with kings   793.93

The **barbarous** years. Bailyn, B.   973.2

Barbash, Tom

Lutnick, H. On top of the world   332.6

Barbassa, Juliana

Dancing With the Devil in the City of God   981.53

Barbe, Karen

Colour confident stitching   746.4

BARBECUE COOKING

Batali, M. Italian grill   641.5

Bittman, M. How to grill everything   641.76

Blonder, G. Meathead   641.7

Byres, T. Smoke   641.6

Carroll, J. Feeding the fire   641.7

Carruthers, J. Eat street   641.76

Cool smoke   641.7

Cramby, J. Tex-Mex from Scratch   641.59

The essential New York times grilling cookbook   641.5

The grilling book   641.5

Kaminsky, P. Charred & scruffed   641.7

Korean BBQ   641.595

Lang, A. P. Serious barbecue   641.5

Mackay, J. Franklin barbecue   641.7

Mallmann, F. Seven fires   641.5

Master of the grill   641.578

Meyer, L. Great vegan bbq without a grill   641.563

Neely, P. Down home with the Neelys   641.5

The one true barbecue   641.5

Praise the lard   641.7

Purviance, J. Weber's greatest hits   641.5

Raichlen, S. The barbecue! bible   641.5

Raichlen, S. Project fire   641.7

Raichlen, S. Project smoke   641.6

Symon, M. Michael Symon's playing with fire   641.7

BARBECUE COOKING

See also Outdoor cooking

The **barbecue!** bible. Raichlen, S.   641.5

BARBECUING

Bittman, M. How to grill everything   641.76

Blonder, G. Meathead   641.7

Carroll, J. Feeding the fire   641.7

Carruthers, J. Eat street   641.76

Cool smoke   641.7

The essential New York times grilling cookbook   641.5

Kaminsky, P. Charred & scruffed   641.7

Kaminsky, P. Mallmann on fire   641.598

Korean BBQ   641.595

Mackay, J. Franklin barbecue   641.7

Master of the grill   641.578

Praise the lard   641.7

Purviance, J. Weber's greatest hits   641.5

Raichlen, S. Project fire   641.7

Basketball. MacMullan, J. | 796.323
BASKETBALL
Baylor, E. Hang time | 92
Blais, M. In these girls, hope is a muscle | 796.323
Bradburd, R. All the dreams we've dreamed | 92
Colton, L. Counting coup | 796.323
Davis, S. When March went mad | 796.323
Dohrmann, G. Play their hearts out | 796.323
Feinstein, J. Last dance | 796.323
FreeDarko presents the macrophenomenal pro basketball almanac | 796.323
McCallum, J. Golden days | 796.323
Merlino, D. The hustle | 796.323
Reynolds, B. Hope | 796.323
Simmons, B. The book of basketball | 796.323
Smith, S. Hard Labor | 796.323
Swidey, N. The assist | 796.323
Wideman, J. E. Hoop roots | 813
BASKETBALL
See also Ball games; Sports
BASKETBALL -- BIOGRAPHY
Lazenby, R. Jerry West | 92
BASKETBALL -- CALIFORNIA -- HISTORY
McCallum, J. Golden days | 796.323
BASKETBALL -- ECONOMIC ASPECTS -- UNITED STATES
Glockner, A. Chasing perfection | 796.323
Smith, S. Hard Labor | 796.323
BASKETBALL -- HISTORY
Fury, S. Rise & fire | 796.323
McCallum, J. Dream team | 796.323
Windhorst, B. Return of the king | 796.323
BASKETBALL -- OHIO -- COLUMBUS -- HISTORY
Haygood, W. Tigerland | 796.323
BASKETBALL -- UNITED STATES -- FINANCE
Smith, S. Hard Labor | 796.323
BASKETBALL -- UNITED STATES -- HISTORY
MacMullan, J. Basketball | 796.323
BASKETBALL COACHES
Abdul-Jabbar, K. Coach Wooden and me | 92
Bradburd, R. All the dreams we've dreamed | 92
Cornelius, M. M. The final season | 92
Davis, S. Getting to us | 796.07
Feinstein, J. The legends club | 796.323
BASKETBALL COACHES -- OKLAHOMA -- BIOGRAPHY
Reeder, L. Dust bowl girls | 796.323
BASKETBALL COACHES -- UNITED STATES -- BIOGRAPHY
Abdul-Jabbar, K. Coach Wooden and me | 92
Cornelius, M. M. The final season | 92
Davis, S. Wooden | 92
Feinstein, J. The legends club | 796.323
BASKETBALL DRAFT
Abrams, J. Boys among men | 796.323
BASKETBALL EXECUTIVES
Lazenby, R. Jerry West | 92

BASKETBALL FOR WOMEN
Reeder, L. Dust bowl girls | 796.323
BASKETBALL FOR WOMEN
See also Sports for women
BASKETBALL FOR WOMEN -- OKLAHOMA -- HISTORY
Reeder, L. Dust bowl girls | 796.323
BASKETBALL PLAYERS
Abdul-Jabbar, K. On the shoulders of giants | 92
Dohrmann, G. Play their hearts out | 796.323
Kriegel, M. Pistol | 92
Lazenby, R. Jerry West | 92
Smith, T. Called for traveling | 796.323
BASKETBALL PLAYERS -- RECRUITING -- UNITED STATES
Abrams, J. Boys among men | 796.323
BASKETBALL PLAYERS -- SALARIES, ETC. -- UNITED STATES -- HISTORY
Smith, S. Hard Labor | 796.323
BASKETBALL PLAYERS -- UNITED STATES -- BIOGRAPHY
Arkush, M. From the outside | 92
Baylor, E. Hang time | 92
Lazenby, R. Michael Jordan | 92
Lazenby, R. Showboat | 92
McCallum, J. Dream team | 796.323
Smith, T. Called for traveling | 796.323
Walton, B. Back from the dead | 92
Williams, J. Life is not an accident | 92
BASKETBALL TEAMS
Feinstein, J. The legends club | 796.323
Glockner, A. Chasing perfection | 796.323
Malinowski, E. Betaball | 796.323
BASKETBALL TEAMS
See also Basketball; Sports teams
BASKETBALL TEAMS -- NORTH CAROLINA -- HISTORY
Feinstein, J. The legends club | 796.323
BASKETS
See also Containers
The **Basque** book. | 641.5
BASQUE COOKING
The Basque book | 641.5
Hirigoyen, G. Pintxos | 641.8
The **Basque** history of the world. Kurlansky, M. | 946
BASQUE PROVINCES (FRANCE AND SPAIN)
The Basque book | 641.5
BASS (FISH)
Greenberg, P. Four fish | 333.95
Bass, Amy
One goal | 796.334
Bass, Diana Butler
Grateful | 241
Grounded | 231
Bass, Ellen
The courage to heal | 616.85
Bass, Gary Jonathan, 1969-

BIOGRAPHY & AUTOBIOGRAPHY -- CULTURAL HERITAGE

BIOGRAPHY & AUTOBIOGRAPHY -- PRESIDENTS & HEADS OF STATE

BIOGRAPHY (AS A LITERARY FORM) *See* Biography as a literary form

BIOGRAPHY -- 20TH CENTURY

BIOGRAPHY -- BIBLIOGRAPHY

BIOGRAPHY -- DICTIONARIES

BIOGRAPHY -- DICTIONARIES

See also Encyclopedias and dictionaries

BIOGRAPHY -- HISTORY AND CRITICISM *See* Biography as a literary form

The **Black** history of the White House. Lusane, C.   **975.3**

Black hole. Bartusiak, M.   **523.8**

Black hole blues and other songs from outer space. Levin, J.   **539.7**

The **black** hole war. Susskind, L.   **530.1**

BLACK HOLES (ASTRONOMY)

Bartusiak, M. Black hole   **523.8**

Fletcher, S. Einstein's shadow   **523.8**

Hawking, S. My brief history   **92**

Impey, C. Einstein's monsters   **523.8**

Levin, J. Black hole blues and other songs from outer space   **539.7**

Miller, A. I. Empire of the stars   **520**

Pretorius, F. The little book of black holes   **523.8**

Rovelli, C. Seven Brief Lessons on Physics   **530**

Scharf, C. Gravity's engines   **523.8**

Susskind, L. The black hole war   **530.1**

Thorne, K. S. Black holes and time warps   **530.1**

Tyson, N. d. Death by black hole   **523.8**

BLACK HOLES (ASTRONOMY)

See also Astronomy; Astrophysics; Stars

BLACK HOLES (ASTRONOMY) -- POPULAR WORKS

Impey, C. Einstein's monsters   **523.8**

Black holes and baby universes and other essays. Hawking, S.   **523.1**

Black holes and time warps. Thorne, K. S.   **530.1**

BLACK HUMOR (LITERATURE)

See also Fiction; Literature; Wit and humor

Black is the new white. Mooney, P.   **92**

Black Kettle, Cheyenne Chief, 1803?-1868
About

Brown, D. A. The American West   **978**

Black klansman. Stallworth, R.   **92**

BLACK LEAD *See* Graphite

BLACK LEGION

Stanton, T. Terror in the city of champions   **364.152**

BLACK LIBRARIANS

See also Librarians

Black like me. Griffin, J. H.   **305.8**

BLACK LITERATURE (AMERICAN) *See* American literature -- African American authors

Black literature criticism.   **809**

BLACK LIVES MATTER MOVEMENT

Bandele, A. When they call you a terrorist   **92**

Lebron, C. J. The making of Black lives matter   **305.896**

Our black sons matter   **305.242**

BLACK LIVES MATTER MOVEMENT -- UNITED STATES

Carruthers, C. A. Unapologetic   **305.488**

Black maestro. Drape, J.   **92**

BLACK MAGIC (WITCHCRAFT) *See* Magic; Witchcraft

Black Man in a White Coat. Tweedy, D.   **92**

The **black** Maria. Girmay, A.   **811.6**

BLACK MARKET

Voigt, E. The dragon behind the glass   **597.176**

BLACK MARKET -- UNITED STATES -- CASE STUDIES

Bilton, N. American kingpin   **364.16**

BLACK MUSIC

See also Music

BLACK MUSICIANS

Smith, J. E. Becoming Belafonte   **92**

BLACK MUSICIANS

See also Musicians

BLACK MUSLIM LEADERS

Evanzz, K. The messenger: the rise and fall of Elijah Muhammad   **297.8**

Gardell, M. In the name of Elijah Muhammad   **297**

Gates, H. L. Thirteen ways of looking at a black man   **920.71**

Levinsohn, F. H. Looking for Farrakhan   **297.8**

Marable, M. Malcolm X   **92**

BLACK MUSLIMS -- BIOGRAPHY

Evanzz, K. The messenger: the rise and fall of Elijah Muhammad   **297.8**

Smith, J. Blood brothers   **92**

BLACK NATIONALISM

See also African Americans -- Political activity; African Americans -- Race identity; Blacks -- Political activity; Blacks -- Race identity

BLACK NATIONALISM -- UNITED STATES -- HISTORY

Gregory, D. Defining moments in Black history   **973**

Marable, M. Malcolm X   **92**

Black nature.   **808**

The **black** Nile. Morrison, D.   **962**

BLACK PANTHER PARTY

The Black Panthers   **322.42**

BLACK PANTHER PARTY -- HISTORY

The Black Panthers   **322.42**

BLACK POETRY (AMERICAN) *See* American poetry -- African American authors

Black postcards. Wareham, D.   **92**

BLACK POWER

Black Power 50   **323.1**

Carruthers, C. A. Unapologetic   **305.488**

Joseph, P. E. Waiting 'til the midnight hour   **323.1**

Black Power 50.   **323.1**

The **Black** presidency. Dyson, M. E.   **305.8**

The **Black** Prince. Jones, M.   **92**

Black profiles in courage. Abdul-Jabbar, K.   **920**

BLACK SABBATH (MUSICAL GROUP)

Osbourne, O. I am Ozzy   **92**

BLACK SEA REGION -- HISTORY

Mayor, A. The Poison King   **92**

Black stars [series]

Haskins, J. African American religious leaders   **920**

The **black** swan. Taleb, N. N.   **003**

Black trials. Weiner, M. S.   **342**

Black wings. Hardesty, V.   **920**

BLACK WOMEN

Black girls rock!   **305.488**

Lewis, R. C. Voyage of the Sable Venus and other poems   **811**

BLACK WOMEN

See also Women

Black women in America.   **920.003**

Black women writers (1950-1980)   **810**

CHRISTMAS
See also Christian holidays; Holidays

CHRISTMAS
Brown, S. Glitterville's handmade Christmas   **745.594**
Flanders, J. Christmas   **394.266**
Forbes, B. D. Christmas   **394.26**
Weintraub, S. A Christmas far from home   **951.904**

CHRISTMAS -- HISTORY
Standiford, L. The man who invented Christmas   **823**

CHRISTMAS -- KOREA (NORTH) -- HISTORY -- 20TH CENTURY
Weintraub, S. A Christmas far from home   **951.904**

CHRISTMAS -- WALES
Thomas, D. A child's Christmas in Wales   **828**

CHRISTMAS CARDS
See also Greeting cards

CHRISTMAS COOKING
Oliver, J. Jamie Oliver's cookbook Christmas   **641.5**

CHRISTMAS DECORATIONS
Christmas with Southern Living 2017   **745.594**

CHRISTMAS DECORATIONS
See also Decoration and ornament; Holiday decorations

CHRISTMAS ENTERTAINMENTS
See also Amusements; Christmas
A **Christmas** far from home. Weintraub, S.   **951.904**

CHRISTMAS TREES
Brown, C. The new Christmas tree   **745.594**
Flanders, J. Christmas   **394.266**

CHRISTMAS TREES
See also Christmas decorations; Trees
Christmas with Southern Living 2017.   **745.594**
Christopher Marlowe. Honan, P.   **92**

Christopher, Thomas
Essential perennials   **635.9**
Garden revolution   **577**

CHROMOSOME ABNORMALITIES
See also Chromosomes; Variation (Biology)

CHROMOSOMES
Sykes, B. DNA USA   **559.9**
Wapner, J. The Philadelphia chromosome   **616.99**

CHROMOSOMES
See also Genetics; Heredity

CHRONIC DISEASE
Snyder, R. d. 1. What you must know about dialysis   **617.4**

CHRONIC DISEASES
Bland, J. S. The disease delusion   **615.5**
Horowitz, R. I. Why can't I get better?   **616.9**
Monte, T. Unexpected recoveries   **616.029**
Steinhart, A. H. Crohn's & colitis diet guide   **616.3**

CHRONIC DISEASES
See also Diseases

CHRONIC DISEASES -- PATIENTS -- CARE
Mangalik, A. Dealing with doctors, denial, and death   **616.044**

CHRONIC FATIGUE SYNDROME
Murphree, R. H. Treating and beating fibromyalgia and chronic fatigue syndrome   **616**
Nicholls, H. Sleepyhead   **616.849**

CHRONIC FATIGUE SYNDROME
See also Diseases

CHRONIC PAIN
Kaplan, G. Total recovery   **616**
Parks, T. Teach us to sit still   **616**

CHRONIC PAIN
See also Chronic diseases; Pain

CHRONICALLY ILL
Khakpour, P. Sick   **92**

CHRONICALLY ILL -- CARE
Mangalik, A. Dealing with doctors, denial, and death   **616.044**

CHRONICLE HISTORY (DRAMA) *See* Historical drama
The **chronicle** of jazz. Cooke, M.   **781.65**
CHRONICLE PLAYS *See* Historical drama
Chronicles. Dylan, B.   **92**

CHRONOLOGY
See also Astronomy; History; Time
The **Chronology** of American literature.   **810**
CHRONOLOGY, HISTORICAL *See* Historical chronology
CHRONOMETERS *See* Clocks and watches

CHRYSLER CORP.
Vlasic, B. Once upon a car   **338.4**

Chu, Jeff
About
Chu, J. Does Jesus Really Love Me?   **261.8**

Chu, Lenora
Little soldiers   **307.951**

Chua, Amy, 1962-
About
Chua, A. Battle hymn of the tiger mother   **306.874**

Chua-Eoan, Howard
(jt. auth) Hargrove, J. Beneath the surface   **599.53**

Chuck D presents This day in rap and hip-hop history. Chuck D   **782.421**

Chuck D, 1960-
Chuck D presents This day in rap and hip-hop history   **782.421**
Chuck Klosterman X. Klosterman, C.   **909.83**

Chudnovsky, D. (David), 1947-
About
Life stories   **920**

Chudnovsky, G. (Gregory), 1952-
About
Life stories   **920**

Chura, David
I don't wish nobody to have a life like mine   **371.9**

CHURCH
McKnight, S. Kingdom conspiracy   **231.7**
Pattison, J. Slow church   **253**

CHURCH AND SOCIAL PROBLEMS
Volf, M. Public faith in action   **261.7**

CHURCH AND SOCIAL PROBLEMS
See also Church; Social problems

CHURCH AND STATE
Greenawalt, K. Does God belong in public schools?   **379**
Wexler, J. Holy hullabaloos   **342**

CHURCH AND STATE
See also Church; State, The

Closing the courthouse door. Chemerinsky, E.   **347.732**

Closing the ring. Churchill, W.   **940.53**

CLOTH *See* Fabrics

CLOTHES *See* Clothing and dress

Clothes, Clothes, Clothes. Music, Music, Music. Boys, Boys, Boys. Albertine, V.   **92**

CLOTHIERS *See* Clothing industry

CLOTHING AND DRESS

Halbreich, B. I'll drink to that   **92**

Herzog, A. Knit wear love   **746.432**

Murphy, M. Woven to wear   **746.1**

One-yard wonders   **646.2**

Stevenson, N. J. Fashion   **391.009**

CLOTHING AND DRESS

   See also Manners and customs

CLOTHING AND DRESS -- AFRICA -- HISTORY

Clarke, D. African textiles   **746**

CLOTHING AND DRESS -- ALTERATION -- PICTORIAL WORKS

Veblen, S. The complete photo guide to perfect fitting   **646.4**

CLOTHING AND DRESS -- HISTORY

Cox, C. The world atlas of street fashion   **391.009**

CLOTHING AND DRESS -- HISTORY -- 18TH CENTURY

Stowell, L. The american duchess guide to 18th century dressmaking   **646**

CLOTHING AND DRESS MEASUREMENTS

Herzog, A. Knit to flatter   **746.43**

CLOTHING AND DRESS MEASUREMENTS -- PICTORIAL WORKS

Veblen, S. The complete photo guide to perfect fitting   **646.4**

CLOTHING DESIGNERS *See* Fashion designers

CLOTHING INDUSTRY

Gross, M. Focus   **770.92**

Snyder, R. L. Fugitive denim   **382**

Von Drehle, D. Triangle: the fire that changed America   **974.7**

Ziegler, M. Wild company   **381**

CLOTHING INDUSTRY

   See also Industries

CLOTHING INDUSTRY EXECUTIVES

Crowe, L. G. The towering world of Jimmy Choo   **391**

Gormley, K. The death of American virtue   **973.929**

CLOTHING TRADE *See* Clothing industry

CLOTHING TRADE -- UNITED STATES

Jacobs, B. Life is good   **650.1**

Ziegler, M. Wild company   **381**

CLOUD COMPUTING

Arora, P. To the cloud   **004.67**

CLOUD SEEDING *See* Weather control

Cloud, Abigail

Sylph   **811**

CLOUDS

Hamblin, R. The invention of clouds   **551.57**

CLOUDS

   See also Atmosphere; Meteorology

Clouds of Glory. Korda, M.   **92**

Clough, Arthur Hugh

(ed) Plutarch: the lives of the noble Grecians and Romans   **920**

Cloutier, Mark

(ed) National electrical code handbook 2017   **621.3**

Clover, Charles

The end of the line   **333**

CLOWNS

   See also Circus; Entertainers

CLUBS

   See also Associations

Clunas, Craig

(ed) Ming   **951**

Clyde, 1909-1934

About

Guinn, J. Go down together   **364.1**

Co-Mix. Spiegelman, A.   **741.5**

COACH DRIVERS

Smardz Frost, K. I've got a home in glory land   **92**

Coach Wooden and me. Abdul-Jabbar, K.   **92**

COACH-ATHLETE RELATIONSHIPS -- UNITED STATES

Abdul-Jabbar, K. Coach Wooden and me   **92**

Coache, Christopher D.

(ed) National electrical code handbook 2017   **621.3**

COACHING *See* Coaching (Athletics); Horsemanship

COACHING (ATHLETICS)

Davis, S. Getting to us   **796.07**

Langton, J. Full circle   **364.133**

Walker, S. The captain class   **796.077**

COACHING (ATHLETICS)

   See also Athletics; Physical education; Sports

COAL

Rhodes, R. Energy   **333.79**

COAL

   See also Fuel

COAL GASIFICATION

   See also Coal

COAL LIQUEFACTION

   See also Coal

COAL MINERS

   See also Miners

COAL MINES AND MINING

Biggers, J. Reckoning at Eagle Creek   **333.73**

Galuszka, P. A. Thunder on the Mountain   **363.11**

House, S. Something's rising   **338.2**

Laskas, J. M. Hidden America   **305.5**

COAL MINES AND MINING

   See also Coal; Mines and mineral resources

COAL MINES AND MINING -- ACCIDENTS

Tintori, K. Trapped: the 1909 Cherry Mine disaster   **973.9**

COAL MINES AND MINING -- APPALACHIAN REGION

Galuszka, P. A. Thunder on the Mountain   **363.11**

COAL OIL *See* Petroleum

COAL TAR PRODUCTS

   See also Petroleum

COAL TRADE -- APPALACHIAN REGION

Galuszka, P. A. Thunder on the Mountain   **363.11**

COAL TRADE -- CORRUPT PRACTICES -- WEST VIRGINIA

COMPASSION

Armstrong, K. Twelve steps to a compassionate life **177**

Beam, C. I feel you **152.4**

Cousineau, T. The kindness cure **177.7**

Doty, J. R. Into the Magic Shop **92**

How to be compassionate **294.3**

Rakel, D. The compassionate connection **610.1**

Wicks, R. J. Night call **155.24**

COMPASSION

See also Emotions

The **compassionate** connection. Rakel, D. **610.1**

COMPENSATION *See* Pensions; Salaries, wages, etc.; Workers' compensation

COMPENSATION FOR JUDICIAL ERROR -- UNITED STATES

Hinton, A. R. The sun does shine **92**

COMPETENCE *See* Performance

Competing voices from the Russian Revolution. **947.084**

COMPETITION

See also Business; Business ethics; Commerce

COMPETITION (PSYCHOLOGY)

Rosenbaum, D. A. It's a jungle in there **153**

COMPETITION (PSYCHOLOGY)

See also Interpersonal relations; Motivation (Psychology); Psychology

COMPETITION, INTERNATIONAL

Newman, K. S. The accordion family **306.874**

The **Complacent** Class. Cowen, T. **305.513**

COMPLEMENTARY THERAPIES -- ENCYCLOPEDIAS -- ENGLISH

The Gale encyclopedia of alternative medicine **615.5**

The **complete** book of food counts. Netzer, C. T. **613.2**

Complete book of home preserving. **641.4**

The **complete** book of jewelry making. Codina, C. **739.27**

The **Complete** book of pasta and noodles. **641.8**

The **complete** book of pickling. Mackenzie, J. **641.4**

The **complete** book of polymer clay. Pavelka, L. **738.1**

The **complete** Calvin and Hobbes. Watterson, B. **741.5**

The **complete** cartoons of the New Yorker. **741.5**

The **complete** cat breed book. **636.8**

The **complete** classical music guide. **780**

The **complete** collected poems of Maya Angelou. Angelou, M. **811**

The **complete** compost gardening guide. Pleasant, B. **631.8**

Complete crochet course. Mullett-Bowlsby, S. **746.43**

Complete do-it-yourself manual. Reader's Digest Association, I. **643**

Complete do-it-yourself manual. **643**

The **complete** game. Darling, R. **92**

The **complete** gods and goddesses of ancient Egypt. Wilkinson, R. H. **299**

Complete gods and goddesses of ancient Egypt. Wilkinson, R. H. **299.31**

Complete Greek tragedies [series]

Aeschylus Aeschylus **882**

Euripides Euripides **882**

Euripides Euripides [2] **882**

Sophocles Sophocles **882**

The **complete** guide to acquisitions management. Lewis, L. K. **025.2**

The **complete** guide to finishing basements. **643**

Complete guide to fitness & health. **613.7**

The **complete** guide to hunting, butchering, and cooking big game. **799.2**

The **Complete** Guide to Hunting, Butchering, and Cooking Wild Game. **799.2**

The **complete** guide to national symbols and emblems. Minahan, J. **929.9**

The **complete** guide to patios & walkways. Black & Decker Corp. **690**

The **complete** guide to plumbing. Black & Decker Corp. **696**

The **complete** guide to plumbing. **696**

Complete Guide to Prescription & Nonprescription Drugs. Griffith, H. W. **615**

The **complete** guide to roofing & siding. **695**

The **complete** guide to roofing, siding & trim. Black & Decker Corp. **695**

Complete Guide to Stargazing. Scagell, R. **520**

The **complete** guide to upholstery. Dobson, C. **684.1**

The **complete** guide to wiring. **621.319**

The **complete** houseplant survival manual. Pleasant, B. **635.9**

The **complete** IEP guide. Siegel, L. M. **371.9**

The **complete** jewelry making course. McGrath, J. **739.27**

The **complete** lesbian & gay parenting guide. Lev, A. I. **649**

The **complete** library technology planner. Cohn, J. M. **025**

The **complete** major prose plays. Ibsen, H. **839.8**

The **complete** odes of Pindar. Pindar **884**

The **complete** operas of Mozart. Osborne, C. **792.5**

The **complete** operas of Puccini. Osborne, C. **792.5**

The **complete** operas of Richard Wagner. Osborne, C. **792.5**

The **complete** outdoor builder. **690**

The **complete** Persepolis. Satrapi, M. **741.5**

The **Complete** Photo Guide to Cardmaking. Watanabe, J. **745.594**

The **complete** photo guide to crochet. Hubert, M. **746.43**

The **complete** photo guide to framing & displaying artwork. Kistler, V. C. **749**

The **complete** photo guide to home improvement. Black & Decker Corp. **643**

The **complete** photo guide to home repair. Black & Decker Corp. **643**

The **complete** photo guide to perfect fitting. Veblen, S. **646.4**

The **complete** photo guide to sewing. Creative Publishing International, I. **646.2**

The **complete** photo guide to window treatments. **646.2**

Complete plays. O'Neil, E. **812**

The **complete** plays. Aristophanes **882**

The **complete** plays. Synge, J. M. **822**

The **complete** plays. Chekhov, A. P. **891.7**

The **complete** plays. Plays **822**

The **complete** poems. **811**

The **complete** poems. Coleridge, S. T. **821**

The **complete** poems. Lawrence, D. H. **821**

The **complete** poems. Jonson, B. **821**

The America's test kitchen do-it-yourself cookbook **641.597**
The America's Test Kitchen healthy family cookbook **641.5**
The America's Test Kitchen new family cookbook **641.5**
Ancient grains for modern meals **641.59**
Ansel, D. Dominique Ansel **641.86**
Austin, M. Maggie Austin cake **641.86**
The autoimmune solution cookbook **641.5**
Balla, N. Bar Tartine **641.59**
Bastianich, J. Healthy pasta **641.82**
Bastianich, L. M. Lidia's celebrate like an Italian **641.5**
Bastianich, L. M. Lidia's commonsense Italian cooking **641.59**
Bastianich, L. M. Lidia's family table **641.5**
Bastianich, L. M. Lidia's favorite recipes **641.594**
Battista, M. Food gift love **642**
Beddia, J. Pizza camp **641.82**
Ben-Ishay, M. Cakes by Melissa **641.86**
Beranbaum, R. L. The baking Bible **641.81**
Beranbaum, R. L. Rose's baking basics **641.81**
Berry, M. Baking with Mary Berry **641.865**
Berry, M. Cooking with Mary Berry **641.5**
Besh, J. Cooking from the heart **641.5**
Besh, J. My New Orleans **641.59**
The Best Casserole cookbook ever **641.8**
The best recipe **641.5**
Better Homes and Gardens New Cook Book **641.5**
Betty Crocker cookbook **641.5**
Bevill, A. World spice at home **641.6**
Bilderback, L. No-churn ice cream **641.86**
Birdsall, J. Hawker Fare **641.595**
Bishara, R. Levant **641.59**
Bishara, R. Olives, lemons & za'atar **641.59**
Bittman, M. How to Bake Everything **641.86**
Bittman, M. How to Cook Everything Fast **641.5**
Bittman, M. How to cook everything vegetarian **641.5**
Bittman, M. How to grill everything **641.76**
Bittman, M. Mark Bittman's kitchen matrix **641.5**
Bjork, K. From the north **641.594**
Blais, R. So good **641.5**
Blonder, G. Meathead **641.7**
The book of greens **641.654**
Bouchon Bakery **641.59**
Bourdain, A. Appetites **641**
Boyle, T. The cake book **641.8**
Boyle, T. Flavorful **641.86**
Bragg, R. The best cook in the world **92**
Breakfast at Huckleberry **641.5**
Brennan, K. Keepers **641.5**
Brock, S. Heritage **641.59**
Brown, A. Everydaycook **641.5**
Brule, J. Learn to cook 25 Southern classics 3 ways **641.5**
Bruni, F. A meatloaf in every oven **641.824**
Bryant, G. The paleo kitchen **641.5**
Burgers **641.66**
But I could never go **641.5**
Byres, T. Smoke **641.6**
Byrn, A. American cake **641.86**

Carrillo Arronte, M. Mexico **641.59**
Carroll, J. Feeding the fire **641.7**
Castanho, T. Brazilian Food **641.598**
Cavallari, K. True roots **641.563**
Chambers, V. Between Harlem and Heaven **641.59**
Chang, J. Myers + Chang at home **641.595**
Chaplin, A. At home in the whole food kitchen **641.3**
Chitnis, C. Little bites **641.5**
Clark, M. Dinner **641.5**
Clark, M. Franny's **641.594**
Classic home desserts **641.8**
Coffey, B. Chocolate every day **641**
Colwin, L. Home cooking **641.5**
Colwin, L. More home cooking **642**
Cook, S. Zahav **641.59**
Cooking my way back home **641.5**
The cook's illustrated meat book **641.6**
The country cooking of France **641.59**
Couscous and other good food from Morocco **641.59**
Crapanzano, A. The London cookbook **641.5**
Currence, J. Pickles, pigs & whiskey **641.59**
Davies, K. Q. What Katie Ate **641.5**
Day, C. Back in the Day Bakery, made with love **641.81**
De Laurentiis, G. Giada's Italy **641.594**
Del Mar Sacasa, M. Summer cocktails **641.87**
Digregorio, S. Adventures in slow cooking **641.5**
Dining in **641.52**
Duguid, N. Burma **641.59**
Dunlop, F. Every grain of rice **641.59**
Dunlop, F. Land of fish and rice **641.5**
Dupree, N. Mastering the art of Southern cooking **641.59**
Dusoulier, C. Tasting Paris **641.594**
Eating from the ground up **641.6**
Eckhardt, R. Istanbul & beyond **641.5**
Edna Lewis **641.597**
Erway, C. The food of Taiwan **641.595**
Esposito, J. Jennifer's way kitchen **641.563**
The essential New York times grilling cookbook **641.5**
Falk, D. The hungry fan's game day cookbook **641.5**
The Farm Cooking School **641.564**
Fearnley-Whittingstall, H. River Cottage Veg **641.5**
Ferroni, L. Doughnuts **641.86**
Fertig, J. The back in the swing cookbook **641.5**
Fine cooking appetizers **641.8**
Firth, H. Bosh! **641.5**
Flay, B. Bobby Flay fit **641.5**
Flores, E. K. Adventures in chicken **641.665**
The food of Morocco **641.59**
Food processor perfection **641.589**
Foose, M. H. A southerly course **641.59**
Forkish, K. Flour water salt yeast **641.81**
Fraioli, J. O. Culinary birds **641.6**
Fuentes, L. The best homemade kids' lunches on the planet **641.5**
Gaines, J. Magnolia table **641**
Galarza, D. Beyond the plate **641.5**
Garten, I. Cook like a pro **641.5**

The complete guide to hunting, butchering, and cooking big game **799.2**

COOKING (GAME) -- TECHNIQUE

Canterbury, D. The Bushcraft field guide to trapping, gathering, and cooking in the wild **641.691**

COOKING (GREENS)

The book of greens **641.654**

COOKING (HERBS)

Hemphill, I. The spice & herb bible **641.3**

Spices of life **641.5**

COOKING (HONEY)

Jones, R. A. The beekeeper's bible **638**

COOKING (MEAT)

Burgers **641.66**

Carreño, C. Meat **641.6**

Charcuteria **641.594**

The cook's illustrated meat book **641.6**

Guggiana, M. Primal cuts **641.6**

Recipes from an Italian butcher **641.66**

Symon, M. Michael Symon's playing with fire **641.7**

COOKING (NATURAL FOODS)

The Blue Apron cookbook **641.5**

Britton, S. My new roots **641.3**

Britton, S. Naturally nourished **641.5**

DiSpirito, R. Rocco's healthy & delicious **641.3**

Esposito, J. Jennifer's way kitchen **641.563**

The family cooks **641.3**

Fong, H. Nom nom paleo **641.5**

Fong, H. Ready or not! **641.563**

Hamshaw, G. Choosing raw **641.3**

Katzen, M. The heart of the plate **641.5**

Lederman, M. Forks over knives family **641.5**

Lillien, L. Hungry girl clean & hungry **641.302**

Mills, E. Natural Feasts **641.563**

Moosewood Restaurant cooks at home **641.5**

The Moosewood Restaurant table **641.5**

The naked cookbook **641.302**

Nutritious delicious **641.3**

Patalsky, K. Healthy happy vegan kitchen **641.5**

Rathbone, O. The Occidental Arts and Ecology Center cookbook **641.3**

Seo, D. Naturally, delicious **641.302**

The sprouted kitchen **641.3**

The sprouted kitchen bowl and spoon **641.3**

Two Moms in the Raw **641.5**

The very best of recipes for health **641.5**

COOKING (NATURAL FOODS) -- POPULAR WORKS

Smith, M. The Whole Smiths good food cookbook **641.5**

COOKING (PASTA)

Bastianich, J. Healthy pasta **641.82**

Green, A. Making artisan pasta **641.82**

Henry, C. Back pocket pasta **641.822**

Pasta by hand **641.82**

COOKING (PEPPERS)

Presilla, M. E. Peppers of the Americas **641.6**

COOKING (POTATOES)

Iyer, R. Smashed, mashed, boiled, and baked-and fried, too! **641.6**

COOKING (POULTRY)

Fraioli, J. O. Culinary birds **641.6**

COOKING (QUINOA)

Del Mar Sacasa, M. The quinoa [keen-wah] cookbook **641.3**

COOKING (SEAFOOD)

Pollinger, B. School of fish **641.6**

Rick Stein's complete seafood **641.6**

Selengut, B. Good fish **641.6**

COOKING (SMOKED FOODS)

Raichlen, S. Project smoke **641.6**

COOKING (SPICES)

Bevill, A. World spice at home **641.6**

Duguid, N. Burma **641.59**

Hemphill, I. The spice & herb bible **641.3**

Selengut, B. How to taste **641.597**

Sugar and spice **641.86**

COOKING (TEA)

Tea **641.3**

COOKING (VEGETABLES)

Complete book of home preserving **641.4**

Dinki, N. Meat on the side **641.35**

Eating from the ground up **641.6**

Jacoby, K. Vedge **641.6**

Madison, D. Vegetable literacy **641.6**

Ottolenghi, Y. Plenty more **641.6**

Thug Kitchen **641.5**

COOKING (WILD FOODS)

Viljoen, M. Forage, harvest, feast **641.6**

COOKING (WILD FOODS) -- TECHNIQUE

Canterbury, D. The Bushcraft field guide to trapping, gathering, and cooking in the wild **641.691**

COOKING (YOGURT)

Rule, C. S. Yogurt culture **641.6**

COOKING -- ALASKA

Dixon, K. The Tutka Bay Lodge cookbook **641.59**

COOKING -- APPALACHIAN REGION, SOUTHERN

Victuals **641.5**

COOKING -- BLOGS

Galarza, D. Beyond the plate **641.5**

COOKING -- CALIFORNIA -- SAN FRANCISCO

Moore, R. This is Camino **641.5**

COOKING -- CHEESE

World cheese book **641.3**

COOKING -- CHOCOLATE

Coffey, B. Chocolate every day **641**

Giller, M. Bean-to-bar chocolate **641.6**

Higgins, K. Chocolate-covered Katie **641.6**

Masonis, T. Making chocolate **641.6**

Mast Brothers Chocolate **641.6**

COOKING -- COMPETITIONS

Friedman, A. Knives at dawn **641.5**

COOKING -- CURRY

Iyer, R. 660 curries **641.5**

COOKING -- EGGS

All about eggs **641.6**

Ruhlman, M. Egg **641.675**

Grigson, J. Charcuterie and French pork cookery   **641.6**

COOKING -- PORTUGAL -- LISBON

Mendes, N. My Lisbon   **641.594**

COOKING -- POTATOES

Iyer, R. Smashed, mashed, boiled, and baked-and fried, too!   **641.6**

COOKING -- POULTRY

Fraioli, J. O. Culinary birds   **641.6**

COOKING -- POULTRY

See also Poultry

COOKING -- RESEARCH

López-Alt, J. K. The food lab   **664**

COOKING -- SEAFOOD

Pollinger, B. School of fish   **641.6**

Rick Stein's complete seafood   **641.6**

Seaver, B. Two if by sea   **641.692**

Selengut, B. Good fish   **641.6**

Thompson, J. T. Fresh Fish   **641.692**

COOKING -- SEAFOOD

See also Seafood

COOKING -- SOUTH CAROLINA -- CHARLESTON

Lee, M. The Lee Bros. Charleston kitchen   **641.59**

COOKING -- SOUTHERN STATES

Add a Pinch cookbook   **641.59**

COOKING -- SOUTHWESTERN STYLE

Jamison, B. The border cookbook   **641.59**

COOKING -- SYRIA -- ALEPPO

Matar, M. The Aleppo cookbook   **641.595**

COOKING -- TECHNIQUE

Clair, J. Six basic cooking techniques   **641.5**

COOKING -- TEXAS

Thompson-Anderson, T. Texas on the Table   **641.597**

COOKING -- UNITED STATES

Ganeshram, R. Future Chefs   **641.3**

COOKING -- VEGETABLES

Anthony, M. V Is for Vegetables   **641.6**

A beautiful mess   **641.563**

The book of greens   **641.654**

Clair, J. Six basic cooking techniques   **641.5**

Coscarelli, C. Chloe flavor   **641.5**

Dinki, N. Meat on the side   **641.35**

Donofrio, J. The Love and Lemons Cookbook   **641.5**

Eating from the ground up   **641.6**

The Farm Cooking School   **641.564**

Jacoby, K. Vedge   **641.6**

La Place, V. Verdura   **641.6**

Lang, R. The Southern vegetable book   **641.65**

Madison, D. In my kitchen   **641.5**

Malone, H. The Power of Pulses   **635.65**

Mangini, C. The Vegetable Butcher   **641.65**

McFadden, J. Six seasons   **641.5**

Moosewood restaurant favorites   **641.5**

Rosen, I. Saladish   **641.83**

Simply vibrant   **641.5**

Thug Kitchen   **641.5**

Viljoen, M. Forage, harvest, feast   **641.6**

Wilkinson, M. Mr. Wilkinson's vegetables   **641.65**

COOKING -- VEGETABLES

See also Vegetables

COOKING -- YUCATAN PENINSULA

Sterling, D. Yucatán   **641.59**

Cooking at home with Bridget & Julia. Davison, J. C.   **641.5**

Cooking dirty. Sheehan, J.   **92**

Cooking for Jeffrey. Garten, I.   **641.5**

COOKING FOR LARGE NUMBERS *See* Quantity cooking

COOKING FOR ONE

Hunt, L. M. Healthyish   **641.5**

COOKING FOR ONE

See also Cooking

COOKING FOR THE SICK

Katz, R. The cancer-fighting kitchen   **641.5**

COOKING FOR THE SICK

See also Cooking; Diet in disease; Nursing; Sick

COOKING FOR TWO

Lane, C. Dessert for Two   **641.86**

COOKING FOR TWO

See also Cooking

Cooking from the heart. Besh, J.   **641.5**

The **cooking** gene. Twitty, M.   **641.59**

Cooking light cooking that counts.   **641.5**

Cooking light global kitchen. Joachim, D.   **641.59**

Cooking my way back home.   **641.5**

COOKING TEACHERS

Hazan, M. Amarcord, Marcella remembers   **92**

COOKING UTENSILS *See* Kitchen utensils

Cooking with Italian grandmothers. Theroux, J.   **641.5**

Cooking with Mary Berry. Berry, M.   **641.5**

COOKING, AFRICAN

Afro-vegan   **641.59**

COOKING, AMERICAN

Ahern, S. J. Gluten-Free Girl American classics reinvented   **641.597**

America--farm to table   **641.597**

The America's test kitchen do-it-yourself cookbook   **641.597**

The America's Test Kitchen healthy family cookbook   **641.5**

The America's Test Kitchen new family cookbook   **641.5**

Brennan, K. Keepers   **641.5**

Bring it!   **641.597**

Cook's Country eats local   **641.597**

Gartland, A. Heartlandia   **641.597**

Gluten-Free Girl American classics reinvented   **641.597**

Guarnaschelli, A. The home cook   **641.597**

Harris, J. B. My soul looks back   **92**

Hesser, A. Food52 a new way to dinner   **641.5**

Humm, D. I love New York   **641.59**

The immigrant cookbook   **641.59**

Kahan, P. Cheers to the Publican, repast and present   **641.594**

Mario Batali Big American cookbook   **641.597**

McMillan, T. The American way of eating   **338.4**

Moore, C. Little Flower baking   **641.815**

Phillips, M. The Chelsea Market cookbook   **641.59**

Ridge, B. The Beekman 1802 heirloom dessert cookbook   **641.5**

Rodgers, R. The essential James Beard cookbook   **641.597**

My pantry	641.594
Olney, R. Simple French food	641.59
Payard, F. Payard cookies	641.86
Peltre, B. My French family table	641.5
Shulman, M. R. The art of French pastry	641.86
Spitz, B. Dearie	92
Thorisson, M. French country cooking	641.5
Thorisson, M. A kitchen in France	641.594

COOKING, FRENCH -- PROVENCAL STYLE

Olney, R. Simple French food	641.59

COOKING, GEORGIAN (SOUTH CAUCASIAN)

Duguid, N. Taste of Persia	641.5

COOKING, GERMAN

Classic German baking	641.5
Nolen, J. German cooking now	641.594

COOKING, GHANAIAN

Adjonyoh, Z. Zoe's Ghana kitchen	641.5

COOKING, GREEK

Hoffman, S. The olive and the caper	641.594
Kochilas, D. Ikaria	641.594

COOKING, ICELANDIC

Eddy, J. North	641.59

COOKING, INDIC

Bajaj, A. Rasika	641.5
Fresh India	641.595
Helou, A. Feast	641.595
Iyer, R. Indian cooking unfolded	641.59
Jaffrey, M. An invitation to Indian cooking	641.59
Jaffrey, M. Vegetarian India	641.595
Thomas, D. Deepa's secrets	641.5

COOKING, IRANIAN

Duguid, N. Taste of Persia	641.5

COOKING, IRISH

McDonnell, I. The Farmette cookbook	641.5

COOKING, ISRAELI

Cook, S. Zahav	641.59
The Palomar cookbook	641.5
Shaya, A. Shaya	641.595

COOKING, ITALIAN

Bastianich, J. Healthy pasta	641.82
Bastianich, L. M. Lidia's celebrate like an Italian	641.5
Bastianich, L. M. Lidia's favorite recipes	641.594
Bastianich, L. M. Lidia's mastering the art of Italian cuisine	641.594
Bastianich, L. M. My American dream	92
Clark, M. Franny's	641.594
De Laurentiis, G. Giada's Italy	641.594
Friedman, A. Classico e moderno	641.59
Lahey, J. The Sullivan Street Bakery cookbook	641.815
Marchetti, D. The glorious pasta of Italy	641.82
Minchilli, E. Eating Rome	641.594
Mohammadi, K. Bella figura	641.01
Mozza at home	641.5
Ray, R. Everyone is Italian on Sunday	641.59
Recipes from an Italian butcher	641.66
Rustic Italian food	641.59
Solfrini, V. Naturally vegetarian	641.563

COOKING, ITALIAN -- NORTHERN STYLE

Necchio, V. Veneto	641.594

COOKING, ITALIAN -- TUSCAN STYLE

River Cafe London	641.594

COOKING, ITALIAN -- VENETIAN STYLE

Necchio, V. Veneto	641.594

COOKING, JAPANESE

Hiroko Shimbo Hiroko's American kitchen	641.59

COOKING, KOREAN

Chattman, L. Maangchi's real Korean cooking	641.595
Deuki Hong Koreatown	641.59
Korean BBQ	641.595
Korean food made simple	641.595

COOKING, KOREAN -- COMIC BOOKS, STRIPS, ETC

Ha, R. Cook Korean!	641.595

COOKING, KURDISH

Duguid, N. Taste of Persia	641.5

COOKING, LAO

Birdsall, J. Hawker Fare	641.595

COOKING, LATIN AMERICAN

Gran cocina latina	641.597
New World kitchen	641.59

COOKING, LEBANESE

Man'oushé	641.5

COOKING, MEDITERRANEAN

Ancient grains for modern meals	641.59
Goldstein, J. The new Mediterranean Jewish table	641.5
Lawson, N. At my table	641.59
Ottolenghi, Y. Nopi	641.5
Psilakis, M. Live to eat	641.59
Ronnen, T. Crossroads	641.59
Wolfert, P. Mediterranean clay pot cooking	641.59

COOKING, MEXICAN

Adimando, S. Nopalito	641.59
Bayless, R. Authentic Mexican	641.597
Bayless, R. Mexican everyday	641.597
Bayless, R. More Mexican everyday	641.597
Gerson, F. Mexican ice cream	641.86
Gran cocina latina	641.597
Jinich, P. Mexican today	641.5
Mena, J. C. Tacopedia	641.84
Santibañez, R. Truly Mexican	641.59
Stupak, A. Tacos	641.84
Turnip greens & tortillas	641.597
Valladolid, M. Casa Marcela	641.5
Werner, E. Hartwood	641.597

COOKING, MIDDLE EASTERN

Bishara, R. Levant	641.59
Ghayour, S. Persiana	641.595
Helou, A. Feast	641.595
Maffei, Y. My halal kitchen	641.595
Ottolenghi, Y. Jerusalem	641.5
Ottolenghi, Y. Nopi	641.5
Ottolenghi, Y. Sweet	641.86

COOKING, MOROCCAN

Couscous and other good food from Morocco	641.59
The food of Morocco	641.59

Deb, Siddhartha

The beautiful and the damned   **954.05**

Debaise, Colleen

Start a successful business   **658.1**

The **debatable** land. Robb, G.   **941.3**

The **Debate** on the Constitution.   **342**

DEBATES AND DEBATING

Bordewich, F. M. America's great debate   **973.6**

Fish, S. E. Winning arguments   **808**

DEBATES AND DEBATING

See also Public speaking; Rhetoric

DeBenedetti, Christian

Beer bites   **641.5**

DEBIT CARDS

See also Banks and banking

Debord, Matthew

Return to Glory   **796.72**

DEBRIS IN SPACE *See* Space debris

DEBT

Atwood, M. Payback   **332.7**

Tamanaha, B. Z. Failing law schools   **340**

DEBT

See also Finance

DEBT -- MORAL AND ETHICAL ASPECTS

Atwood, M. Payback   **332.7**

DEBTOR *See* Debtor and creditor

DEBTOR AND CREDITOR

Leonard, R. Solve your money troubles   **346**

DEBTOR AND CREDITOR

See also Commercial law

DEBTS, PUBLIC -- UNITED STATES

Johnson, S. White House burning   **336.3**

DEBUTANTE BALLS

See also Dance

DeBuys, William

The last unicorn   **591.68**

A great aridness   **551.6**

Decade of the wolf. Smith, D. W.   **599.77**

DECATHLETES

Anderson, L. Carlisle vs. Army   **796.332**

Crawford, B. All American   **92**

DECEASED *See* Dead

DECEIT *See* Deception; Fraud

December 8, 1980. Greenberg, K. E.   **92**

The **December** Project. Davidson, S.   **296.7**

DECEPTION

Ariely, D. The honest truth about dishonesty   **177**

Konnikova, M. The Confidence Game   **364.163**

Rabin-Havt, A. Lies, Incorporated   **320.6**

Triandis, H. C. Fooling ourselves   **155.2**

DECEPTION

See also Truthfulness and falsehood

DECEPTION (MILITARY SCIENCE) -- HISTORY -- 20TH CENTURY

Macintyre, B. Double cross   **940.54**

DECEPTION -- PSYCHOLOGICAL ASPECTS

Trivers, R. The folly of fools   **153.4**

DECEPTION -- SOCIAL ASPECTS

Trivers, R. The folly of fools   **153.4**

DECEPTIVE ADVERTISING

See also Advertising; Business ethics

Dech, Stefan

(jt. auth) Messner, R. Mountains   **551.432**

Décharné, Max

Vulgar tongues   **427**

Decherney, Peter

Hollywood's copyright wars   **346.73**

DECIMAL SYSTEM

See also Numbers

DECISION MAKING

Berger, J. Invisible Influence   **302.13**

Dennett, D. C. Freedom evolves   **153.8**

Dobelli, R. The art of thinking clearly   **153.4**

Duhigg, C. Smarter faster better   **158**

Duke, A. Thinking in bets   **658.4**

Gladwell, M. Blink: the power of thinking without thinking   **153.4**

Groopman, J. E. Your medical mind   **610**

Hall, S. S. Wisdom   **179**

Huston, T. How women decide   **155.333**

Iyengar, S. The art of choosing   **153.8**

Johnson, S. Farsighted   **153.8**

Kahneman, D. Thinking, fast and slow   **153.4**

Kowitz, B. Sprint   **658.4**

Lehrer, J. How we decide   **153.8**

MacMillan, M. Dangerous games   **901**

Martin, R. L. Creating great choices   **658.4**

McKeown, G. Essentialism   **153.8**

Meyer, J. Decision quality   **658.4**

Michelson, L. D. The patient's playbook   **610.69**

Miller, P. The smart swarm   **156**

Mlodinow, L. Elastic   **612.807**

Mlodinow, L. Subliminal   **154.2**

Mudd, P. The Head Game   **153.4**

Partnoy, F. Wait   **153.8**

Rhodes, W. R. Banker to the world   **92**

Rice, C. Political risk   **658.15**

Schulz, K. Being wrong   **153**

DECISION MAKING -- PERSONAL NARRATIVES

Ilse, S. The prenatal bombshell   **618.3**

DECISION MAKING -- PSYCHOLOGICAL ASPECTS

Huston, T. How women decide   **155.333**

DECISION MAKING -- SEX DIFFERENCES

Huston, T. How women decide   **155.333**

Decision points. Bush, G. W. (. W.   **92**

Decision quality. Meyer, J.   **658.4**

The **decision** to use the atomic bomb and the architecture of an American myth. Alperovitz, G.   **940.54**

The **Decisive** Moment. Cartier-Bresson, H.   **770**

DECKS (ARCHITECTURE, DOMESTIC) -- DESIGN AND CONSTRUCTION -- AMATEURS' MANUALS

Toht, D. Stanley decks   **690**

DECKS (DOMESTIC ARCHITECTURE) *See* Patios

DeClaire, Joan

DeFelice, Jim
West like lightning   **383.143**
Defend the realm. Andrew, C. M.   **327.12**
The **defender.** Michaeli, E.   **071**
Defenders of the faith. Reston, J.   **940.2**
Defending professionalism.   **020**
DEFENSE INDUSTRY
    See also Industries
DEFENSE MECHANISMS (PSYCHOLOGY)
    Walker, B. F. Anxiety Relief for Kids   **649.1**
DEFENSIVE (MILITARY SCIENCE)
    Emlen, D. J. Animal weapons   **591.47**
Defiance. Taylor, S.   **92**
DEFIANCE (OHIO) -- BIOGRAPHY
    Ryan, T. The prize winner of Defiance, Ohio   **977.1**
DEFICIENCIES *See* Scarcity
DEFICIT FINANCING
    See also Public finance
DEFICIT FINANCING -- UNITED STATES
    Johnson, S. White House burning   **336.3**
Defining moments in Black history. Gregory, D.   **973**
The **definitive** book of body language. Pease, A.   **153.6**
The **definitive** guide to thriving after cancer. Gazella, K. A.   **616.99**
DEFLATION (FINANCE)
    See also Finance
Defoe, Daniel, 1661?-1731
      About
    Frank, K. Crusoe   **823**
Defoe, Daniel, 1661?-1731. Robinson Crusoe
      About
    Frank, K. Crusoe   **823**
Deford, Frank, 1938-2017
      About
    Deford, F. Over time   **92**
DEFORESTATION
    See also Forests and forestry
Defying Hitler. Haffner, S.   **943.085**
Defying the Nazis. Joukowsky, A.   **940.53**
DeGarmo, John
    The foster parenting manual   **306.874**
Degas. Hauptman, J.   **709**
Degas, Edgar, 1834-1917
      About
    Hauptman, J. Degas   **709**
DeGategno, Paul J.
    Critical companion to Jonathan Swift   **828**
DEGENERATION -- SOCIAL ASPECTS -- ITALY -- HISTORY -- TO 1500
    Lee, A. The ugly Renaissance   **945**
DeGeneres, Ellen, 1958-
    Home   **747**
Degraaf, Leonard
    Edison and the rise of innovation   **92**
Degrees of inequality. Mettler, S.   **378.73**
DEGREES OF LATITUDE AND LONGITUDE *See* Geodesy; Latitude; Longitude

Deheane, Stanislas
    Reading in the brain   **418**
DEISM
    See also Religion; Theology
DEITIES *See* Gods and goddesses
DeJean, Joan E.
    The essence of style   **391**
DEJECTION *See* Depression (Psychology)
Del Bosque, Melissa
    Bloodlines   **364.1**
Del Giocondo, Lisa, 1479-
      About
    Hales, D. Mona Lisa   **759.5**
Del Mar Sacasa, María
    The quinoa [keen-wah] cookbook   **641.3**
    Summer cocktails   **641.87**
Del Negro, Janice M.
    Folktales aloud   **027.62**
The **Del** Posto cookbook. Ladner, M.   **641.5**
Delahunty, Andrew
    (ed) Adonis to Zorro   **422**
    Oxford dictionary of nicknames   **929.4**
    (ed) From bonbon to cha-cha   **422**
Delambre, J. B. J., 1749-1822
      About
    Alder, K. The measure of all things   **526**
Delancey. Wizenberg, M.   **647.95**
DELANCEY (PIZZERIA : SEATTLE, WASH.)
    Wizenberg, M. Delancey   **647.95**
Delano, Amasa, 1763-1823
      About
    Grandin, G. The empire of necessity   **306.3**
Delany, Mary Granville Pendarves, 1700-1788
      About
    Peacock, M. The paper garden   **92**
Delbanco, Andrew
    College   **378.73**
    Melville   **92**
Delbruck, Max
      About
    Segrè, G. Ordinary geniuses   **572.8**
Delehanty, Hugh
    Caring for your parents   **362.6**
Deliberate prose. Ginsberg, A.   **814**
Delicious dump cakes. Moore, K.   **641.86**
Delights & shadows. Kooser, T.   **811**
DeLillo, Don
      About
    Remnick, D. Reporting   **814**
DELINQUENCY, JUVENILE *See* Juvenile delinquency
DELINQUENTS *See* Criminals
Delish. Saltz, J.   **641.5**
Delisle, Guy
    Pyongyang: a journey in North Korea   **741.5**
    Hostage   **364.15**
Deliver us from evil. Ford, L. K.   **973.7**
DELIVERY OF HEALTH CARE *See* Medical care

McCarter, J. Young radicals   **322.4**

Easto, Jessica

Craft coffee   **641.877**

EASY AND QUICK COOKING *See* Quick and easy cooking

An **easy** burden. Young, A.   **92**

Easy fair isle knitting. Storey, M.   **746.432**

Easy Gourmet. Le, S.   **641.5**

Easy information sources for ESL, adult learners, & new readers. Riechel, R.   **016**

EASY READING MATERIALS

> *See also* Children's literature; Reading materials

Easy soups from scratch with breads to match.   **641.813**

Easy to love, difficult to discipline. Bailey, R. A.   **155**

Eat a little better. Kass, S.   **641.3**

Eat it up! Vinton, S. B.   **641.5**

The **Eat** Like a Man Guide to Feeding a Crowd.   **641.5**

Eat Mexico. Tellez, L.   **641.597**

Eat street. Carruthers, J.   **641.76**

Eat that frog! Tracy, B.   **640**

Eat the apple. Young, M.   **92**

Eat to live quick and easy cookbook. Fuhrman, J.   **641.5**

Eat what you watch. Rea, A.   **641.5**

Eat, pray, love. Gilbert, E.   **92**

Eat, sleep, poop. Cohen, S. W.   **618.92**

Eataly Srl

(comp) How to eataly   **641.594**

Eathorne, Alison Malone

(jt. auth) Malone, H. The Power of Pulses   **635.65**

EATING *See* Dining; Gastronomy

Eating animals. Foer, J. S.   **641.3**

EATING CUSTOMS

Altmann, T. R. What to feed your baby   **649.3**

Animal, vegetable, miracle   **641**

Barber, D. The third plate   **641.3**

Behr, E. The Food and Wine of France   **641.5**

Campbell, T. C. The China study   **613.2**

Carroll, A. The bad food bible   **613.2**

Collingham, E. M. (. M. Curry   **394.1**

Consider the fork   **643**

First bite   **641.01**

The food of a younger land   **394.1**

Fuhrman, J. Eat to live quick and easy cookbook   **641.5**

Goulding, M. Grape, olive, pig   **394.1**

Hyman, M. Food   **613.2**

Kauffman, J. Hippie food   **394.12**

Lappé, A. Diet for a hot planet   **641**

Mayle, P. French lessons   **394.1**

McWilliams, J. E. Just food   **394.1**

Nesheim, M. Why calories count   **613.2**

Pollan, M. The omnivore's dilemma   **394.1**

Rosenstrach, J. Dinner   **642**

Rude, E. Tastes Like Chicken   **636.5**

Smith, M. The Whole Smiths good food cookbook   **641.5**

Standage, T. An edible history of humanity   **394.1**

Stone, D. The food explorer   **92**

The story of food   **641**

Tye, D. Baking as biography   **92**

Wrangham, R. W. Catching fire   **641.3**

EATING CUSTOMS

> *See also* Diet; Human behavior; Nutrition

EATING CUSTOMS -- UNITED STATES -- HISTORY

Lohman, S. Eight Flavors   **641.5**

Eating disorders. Lask, B.   **616.85**

EATING DISORDERS

> *See also* Abnormal psychology

EATING DISORDERS

Brzezinski, M. Obsessed   **362.196**

Bulik, C. M. Midlife eating disorders   **616.85**

Can I tell you about eating disorders?   **616.85**

Gay, R. Hunger   **92**

The Hungry Brain   **616.85**

Laymon, K. Heavy   **92**

Lock, J. Help your teenager beat an eating disorder   **616.85**

EATING DISORDERS -- PATIENTS -- UNITED STATES -- BIOGRAPHY

Collins, J. Cravings   **616.85**

Laymon, K. Heavy   **92**

EATING DISORDERS IN ADOLESCENCE

Lask, B. Eating disorders   **616.85**

Lock, J. Help your teenager beat an eating disorder   **616.85**

Eating from the ground up.   **641.6**

EATING HABITS

Brzezinski, M. Obsessed   **362.196**

Caldesi, G. Around the world in 120 salads   **641.83**

Consider the fork   **643**

Copeland, M. Ballerina body   **613.71**

Fisher, M. F. K. (. F. K. The art of eating   **641**

Fuentes, L. The best homemade kids' snacks on the planet   **641.5**

Mann, T. Secrets from the eating lab   **613.2**

Milk Bar Life   **641.86**

Mitchell, A. Eating in the middle   **641.3**

Wansink, B. Mindless eating   **616.85**

EATING HABITS -- ECONOMIC ASPECTS

Cowen, T. An economist gets lunch   **394.1**

Eating in the middle. Mitchell, A.   **641.3**

Eating on the wild side. Robinson, J.   **306.4**

Eating Rome. Minchilli, E.   **641.594**

Eating the sun. Morton, O.   **572**

Eatingwell (Company)

(comp) Eatingwell Vegetables   **641.65**

Eatingwell Vegetables.   **641.65**

Eatman, Nick

Friday, Saturday, Sunday in Texas   **796.332**

Eaton, Jan

350+ crochet tips, techniques, and trade secrets   **746.43**

(jt. auth) Thomas, M. Mary Thomas's dictionary of embroidery stitches   **746.44**

Eaton, Jonathan

(ed) Chapman piloting & seamanship   **623.88**

Eaton, William, 1764-1811

About

Zacks, R. The pirate coast   **973.4**

Eats, shoots & leaves. Truss, L.   **421**

Faster, Higher, Farther. Ewing, J.   **338.7**

Faster, higher, stronger. McClusky, M.   **613.7**

FASTING

See also Asceticism; Diet

FASTS AND FEASTS *See* Religious holidays

FASTS AND FEASTS -- JUDAISM

Axelrod, M. Your guide to the Jewish holidays   **296.4**

Goldman, A. L. Being Jewish   **296.4**

Pogrebin, A. My Jewish year   **296.43**

FASTS AND FEASTS -- JUDAISM *See* Jewish holidays

Fasulo, Linda M.

An insider's guide to the UN   **341.23**

The **fat** man and infinity. Antunes, A. L.   **869**

Fat witch bake sale. Baker, L.   **641.81**

FAT WITCH BAKERY

Baker, L. Fat witch bake sale   **641.81**

Fatal discord. Massing, M.   **270.609**

Fatal invention. Roberts, D.   **305.8**

Fatal risk. Boyd, R.   **368**

The **fatal** shore. Hughes, R.   **994**

Fatal vision. McGinniss, J.   **364.1**

FATALLY ILL CHILDREN *See* Terminally ill children

FATALLY ILL PATIENTS *See* Terminally ill

FATE AND FATALISM

Jakes, T. D. Destiny   **248.4**

May, R. Freedom and destiny   **158**

FATE AND FATALISM

See also Philosophy

FATE AND FATALISM -- RELIGIOUS ASPECTS -- CHRISTIANITY

Jakes, T. D. Destiny   **248.4**

The **Fate** of Gender. Browning, F.   **305.3**

The **fate** of nature. Wohlforth, C.   **304.2**

The **fate** of Rome. Harper, K.   **937**

FATHER AND CHILD -- UNITED STATES

Levs, J. All in   **306.3**

FATHER AND CHILD

Austin, P. Beautiful eyes   **92**

FATHER AND CHILD *See* Father-child relationship

FATHER AND CHILD -- ANECDOTES

McGlynn, D. One day you'll thank me   **306.874**

FATHER AND CHILD -- CALIFORNIA -- LOS ANGELES

Leap, J. Project Fatherhood   **306.874**

FATHER AND CHILD -- HUMOR

McGlynn, D. One day you'll thank me   **306.874**

The **father** of us all. Hanson, V. D.   **355**

FATHER'S DAY

See also Holidays

FATHER-CHILD RELATIONSHIP

Davis, T. Handy dad   **745.592**

Levs, J. All in   **306.3**

McGlynn, D. One day you'll thank me   **306.874**

FATHER-CHILD RELATIONSHIP

See also Children; Fathers; Parent-child relationship

FATHER-DAUGHTER RELATIONSHIP

Anderson, S. The Hostage's Daughter   **92**

Babul, D. D. The fatherless daughter project   **306.874**

Brennan-Jobs, L. Small fry   **92**

Brodak, M. Bandit   **92**

Cooper, E. Falling   **92**

Donlan, C. The inward empire   **92**

Faludi, S. In the Darkroom   **818**

Foreman, T. My year of running dangerously   **92**

Shaw, B. Major Barbara   **822**

Spring   **839.823**

Tyler, C. Soldier's heart   **741.5**

Venegas, M. Bulletproof vest   **364.109**

Wetherall, T. No way home   **92**

Wickersham, J. The suicide index   **155.9**

FATHER-DAUGHTER RELATIONSHIP

See also Daughters; Father-child relationship; Fathers

FATHER-SON RELATIONSHIP

Abad, H. Oblivion   **868**

Bartholomew, R. Two and two   **92**

Biden, J. Promise me, Dad   **92**

Bragg, R. The prince of Frogtown   **92**

Burns, E. The Golden Lad   **92**

Chabon, M. Pops   **306.874**

Cockburn, H. Henry's demons   **92**

Edmundson, M. Why football matters   **92**

The fall   **616.8**

Giffels, D. Furnishing eternity   **306.874**

Giraldi, W. The Hero's Body   **92**

Harding, T. Kadian Journal   **155.9**

Kozol, J. The theft of memory   **616.8**

Matar, H. The return   **92**

Mendelsohn, D. An odyssey   **92**

Molina, B. Molina   **92**

Ollestad, N. Crazy for the storm   **92**

Pardlo, G. Air traffic   **811**

Phillips, P. Elegy for a broken machine   **811**

Thomson, D. Try to tell the story   **92**

Tóibín, C. Mad, bad, dangerous to know   **820.9**

FATHER-SON RELATIONSHIP

See also Father-child relationship; Fathers; Sons

FATHERHOOD

Chabon, M. Pops   **306.874**

Donlan, C. The inward empire   **92**

Falcone, B. Being a dad is weird   **92**

McGlynn, D. One day you'll thank me   **306.874**

Spring   **839.823**

When I first held you   **306.874**

Yousafzai, Z. Let her fly   **92**

FATHERHOOD

See also Parenthood

FATHERHOOD -- ANECDOTES

Falcone, B. Being a dad is weird   **92**

McGlynn, D. One day you'll thank me   **306.874**

FATHERHOOD -- CALIFORNIA -- LOS ANGELES

Leap, J. Project Fatherhood   **306.874**

FATHERHOOD -- HUMOR

McGlynn, D. One day you'll thank me   **306.874**

The **fatherless** daughter project. Babul, D. D.   **306.874**

FATHERS

Nabokov, V. V. Lectures on literature 808.3
Flavor. Holmes, B. 612.8
FLAVOR
Holmes, B. Flavor 612.8
Selengut, B. How to taste 641.597
The **flavor** bible. Page, K. 641.5
Flavor flours. 641.3
Flavorful. Boyle, T. 641.86
FLAVORING ESSENCES
See also Cooking; Essences and essential oils; Food
Flawless. Campbell, G. 364.1
Flaxman, Larry
(jt. auth) Jones, M. D. Demons, the devil, and fallen angels 133.4
Flay, Bobby, 1964-
Brunch @ Bobby's 641.5
Bobby Flay fit 641.5
Flea market fabulous. Spencer, L. 747
FLEA MARKETS
Lee, V. Kitchenalia 747
Spencer, L. Flea market fabulous 747
Stanton, M. Killer stuff and tons of money 381
FLEA MARKETS
See also Markets; Secondhand trade
Fleck, Ludwik, 1896-1961
About
Allen, A. The fantastic laboratory of Dr. Weigl 614.5
Fledge. Yoder, B. L. 248.8
Fleming, Fergus
Ninety degrees North 919
Fleming, James Rodger
Fixing the sky 551.6
Fleming, Melissa
A hope more powerful than the sea 956.91
Fleming, Victor, 1883-1949
About
Sragow, M. Victor Fleming 92
Fletcher, Anne M.
Inside rehab 362.29
Fletcher, Catherine
The divorce of Henry VIII 942.05
Fletcher, Colin, 1922-2007
About
Fletcher, C. The man who walked through time 917
Fletcher, Joann
The Story of Egypt 932
Cleopatra the great 92
Fletcher, Seth
Bottled lightning 621.31
Einstein's shadow 523.8
FLEXIBLE WORK ARRANGEMENTS
Mulcahy, D. The gig economy 650.1
Flexner, James Thomas
George Washington and the new nation, 1783-1793 92
George Washington: anguish and farewell 1793-1799 92
George Washington: the forge of experience, 1732-1775 92
FLIES

McAlister, E. The secret life of flies 595.77
FLIES
See also Household pests; Insects; Pests
FLIES -- POPULAR WORKS
McAlister, E. The secret life of flies 595.77
FLIES, ARTIFICIAL
Gathercole, P. Fly tying for beginners 688.7
Gathercole, P. The fly-tying bible 688.7
FLIES, ARTIFICIAL *See* Artificial flies
FLIES, ARTIFICIAL -- HISTORY
The history of fly fishing in fifty flies 799.124
Higgins, M. Bird dream 797.5
Holmes, R. Falling upwards 387.7
The **flight.** Hampton, D. 629.13
Flight 232. Gonzales, L. 363.12
FLIGHT ATTENDANTS
See also Airlines
The **flight** of the century. Kessner, T. 92
Flight path. Palmer, H. 92
FLIGHT TO THE MOON *See* Space flight to the moon
FLIGHT TRAINING *See* Aeronautics -- Study and teaching; Airplanes -- Piloting
Flight: 100 years of aviation. Grant, R. G. 629.13
Flink, David
Thinking Differently 371.9
FLINT (MICH.)
Clark, A. The poisoned city 363.61
FLINT (MICH.) -- ENVIRONMENTAL CONDITIONS
Hanna-Attisha, M. What the eyes don't see 92
Flippin, Royce
The diabetes reset 616.4
Floating collections. Bartlett, W. K. 025.2
Flock, Elizabeth
The heart is a shifting sea 306.81
FLOOD FORECASTING
Goodell, J. The water will come 551.45
FLOODPLAIN MANAGEMENT -- UNITED STATES -- HISTORY
Doyle, M. The source 333.91
FLOODS
Clark, R. Dark water 945
Goodell, J. The water will come 551.45
FLOODS
See also Meteorology; Natural disasters; Rain; Water
FLOODS -- MISSISSIPPI RIVER
Welky, D. The thousand-year flood 363.34
FLOODS -- OHIO RIVER VALLEY
Welky, D. The thousand-year flood 363.34
FLOODS -- UNITED STATES
Roker, A. Ruthless tide 974.8
FLORA *See* Botany; Plants
Flora illustrata. 016
Flora, Joseph M.
(ed) The Companion to southern literature 810
FLORAL DECORATION *See* Flower arrangement
Florence. 759.5
FLORENCE (ITALY)

G

Croom, E. A. The genealogist's companion and source-book **929**

Gates, H. L. In search of our roots **305.8**

Greenwood, V. D. The researcher's guide to American genealogy **929**

Jacobs, A. J. It's all relative **929.1**

Kemp, T. J. Virtual roots 2.0 **929**

Laskin, D. The Family **92**

Mann, S. Hold Still **92**

Marshall, S. Reunited **362.82**

McCarthy, A. Journeys home **929.1**

Neighbors, J. The family tree cemetery field guide **929.5**

Pennavaria, K. Genealogy **929.1**

Simpson, J. Basics of genealogy reference **929**

Sykes, B. DNA USA **559.9**

Wagner, A. Futureface **92**

Well, F. Family trees **929.2**

GENEALOGY -- ANECDOTES
McCarthy, A. Journeys home **929.1**

GENEALOGY -- HUMOR
Jacobs, A. J. It's all relative **929.1**

GENEALOGY -- UNITED STATES -- HISTORY
Well, F. Family trees **929.2**

General Mills Inc.
(comp) Betty Crocker cookbook **641.5**

GENERAL MOTORS CORP.
Vlasic, B. Once upon a car **338.4**

GENERAL MOTORS CORP. -- BANKRUPTCY
Lutz, B. Car guys vs. bean counters **338.7**

GENERAL RELATIVITY (PHYSICS)
Greene, B. (. The hidden reality **530.1**

Susskind, L. The black hole war **530.1**

GENERAL STORES
See also Retail trade; Stores

GENERAL SURGERY -- HISTORY -- PENNSYLVANIA
Aptowicz, C. O. Dr. Mütter's Marvels **92**

GENERAL SURGERY -- PENNSYLVANIA -- BIOGRAPHY
Aptowicz, C. O. Dr. Mütter's Marvels **92**

The **general** theory of employment, interest and money. Keynes, J. M. **330.1**

A **general** theory of love. Lewis, T. **152.4**

The **General** Vs. the President. Brands, H. W. **973.918**

The **generalissimo**. Taylor, J. **92**

The **generals**. Groom, W. **940.54**

GENERALS
Ambrose, S. E. Eisenhower **92**

Ambrose, S. E. The victors **940.54**

Anderson, L. Carlisle vs. Army **796.332**

Atkinson, R. The guns at last light **940.54**

Bell, M. S. Toussaint Louverture **92**

Blount, R. Robert E. Lee **92**

Brands, H. W. Andrew Jackson **92**

Brighton, T. Patton, Montgomery, Rommel **920**

Brown, D. A. Bury my heart at Wounded Knee **970.004**

Bunting, J. Ulysses S. Grant **92**

Davis, B. Sherman's march **973.7**

De Young, K. Soldier: the life of Colin Powell **92**

Donovan, J. A terrible glory **973.8**

Duke, L. Mandela, Mobutu, and me **968.06**

Ellis, J. J. His Excellency **92**

Fellman, M. Citizen Sherman **92**

Fellman, M. The making of Robert E. Lee **92**

Fischer, D. H. Washington's crossing **973.3**

Flexner, J. T. George Washington and the new nation, 1783-1793 **92**

Flexner, J. T. George Washington: anguish and farewell 1793-1799 **92**

Flexner, J. T. George Washington: the forge of experience, 1732-1775 **92**

Frank, R. B. MacArthur **92**

Franks, T. American soldier **973.931**

Freeman, D. S. Lee **92**

Gaines, J. R. For liberty and glory **92**

Gates, H. L. Thirteen ways of looking at a black man **920.71**

Geary, R. The Lindbergh child **364.1**

Goldsworthy, A. K. Antony and Cleopatra **92**

Groom, W. The generals **940.54**

Groom, W. Patriotic fire **973.5**

Groom, W. Vicksburg, 1863 **973.7**

Halberstam, D. The best and the brightest **973.922**

Hanson, V. D. The soul of battle **355**

Hibbert, C. Wellington **92**

Hofstadter, R. The American political tradition, and the men who made it **973**

Jackson, J. De Gaulle **92**

Johnson, P. George Washington: the Founding Father **92**

Jordan, J. W. American warlords **973.917**

Keneally, T. American scoundrel: the life of the notorious Civil War General Dan Sickles **92**

Kennett, L. B. Sherman **92**

Kessner, T. The flight of the century **92**

Kissinger, H. Diplomacy **327.2**

Korda, M. Ulysses S. Grant: the unlikely hero **92**

Langguth, A. J. Driven West **973.5**

Lemann, N. Redemption: the last battle of the Civil War **975**

Lindbergh, C. The spirit of St. Louis **629.13**

Lindbergh, R. Under a wing **92**

Linklater, A. An artist in treason **92**

Meacham, J. American lion **92**

Moore, H. G. We are soldiers still **959.704**

Morris, R. Fraud of the century **324.9**

Nelson, C. The first heroes **940.54**

O'Connell, R. L. The ghosts of Cannae **937**

Pakula, H. The last empress **92**

Palmer, J. The bloody white baron **92**

Parssinen, T. M. The Oster conspiracy of 1938 **943.086**

Perry, J. M. Touched with fire **973.7**

Philbrick, N. The last stand **973.8**

Remini, R. V. Andrew Jackson **92**

Reynolds, D. S. Waking giant **973.5**

Rice, A. The teeth may smile but the heart does not forget **967.6**

Ricks, T. E. The generals **355.009**

Gender medicine   362.108

Glickman, Elaine Rose

Your kid's a brat and it's all your fault   649.1

GLIDERS (AERONAUTICS)

See also Aeronautics; Airplanes

GLIDING AND SOARING

See also Aeronautics

Glier, Ray

(jt. auth) Savage, P. 4th and goal every day   796.332

Glinert, Lewis

The story of Hebrew   429.4

Glitter and Glue. Corrigan, K.   92

Glitterville's handmade Christmas. Brown, S.   745.594

Glitterville's handmade Halloween. Brown, S.   745.594

Global crisis. Parker, G.   909

Global Discontents. Chomsky, N.   410.92

GLOBAL ENVIRONMENTAL CHANGE

Barnosky, A. D. Tipping point for planet earth   304.2

Biello, D. The unnatural world   304.2

Cullen, H. The weather of the future   551.63

Global weirdness   577.2

Gore, A. The future   303.4

Hertsgaard, M. Hot   304.2

Kolbert, E. Field notes from a catastrophe   363.7

Macdougall, J. D. Frozen earth   551.7

Montaigne, F. Fraser's penguins   577.2

Vince, G. Adventures in the anthropocene   577.27

GLOBAL ENVIRONMENTAL CHANGE -- ECONOMIC ASPECTS

Klein, N. This changes everything   363.738

GLOBAL ENVIRONMENTAL CHANGE -- SOCIAL ASPECTS

Vince, G. Adventures in the anthropocene   577.27

GLOBAL FINANCIAL CRISIS, 2008-2009

Bartiromo, M. The weekend that changed Wall Street   330.9

Bernanke, B. The Courage to Act   92

Blinder, A. S. After the music stopped   330.973

Dayen, D. Chain of title   330.973

Garson, B. Down the up escalator   339.2

Gasparino, C. The sellout   332

Hudson, M. The monster   332.6

Kolhatkar, S. Black edge   364.16

Lanchester, J. I.O.U.   330.9

Lewis, M. The big short   330.9

Lowenstein, R. The end of Wall Street   332.6

McGee, S. Chasing Goldman Sachs   332.6

McLean, B. All the devils are here   330.9

Morgenson, G. Reckless endangerment   332.7

Paulson, H. M. On the brink   330.9

Sharma, R. The rise and fall of nations   330.9

Sorkin, A. R. Too big to fail   330.9

Stiglitz, J. E. The price of inequality   305.5

Taibbi, M. Griftopia   973.932

Wessel, D. In Fed we trust   332.1

A **global** history of architecture.   720.9

GLOBAL POSITIONING SYSTEM

Bray, H. You are here   910.285

GLOBAL POSITIONING SYSTEM

See also Navigation

GLOBAL SATELLITE COMMUNICATIONS SYSTEMS

See Artificial satellites in telecommunication

GLOBAL WARMING

Climate change   363.738

Coll, S. Private empire   338.7

Flannery, T. F. The weather makers   363.7

Fleming, J. R. Fixing the sky   551.6

The global warming reader   363.738

Global weirdness   577.2

Gore, A. An inconvenient sequel   363.738

Gore, A. An inconvenient truth   363.7

Hertsgaard, M. Hot   304.2

Kolbert, E. Field notes from a catastrophe   363.7

McKibben, B. Eaarth   253

Nuccitelli, D. Climatology versus pseudoscience   577.276

Smith, Z. Feel free   824.92

Stager, C. Deep future   363.7

Vince, G. Adventures in the anthropocene   577.27

Vollmann, W. T. No immediate danger   333.79

Weart, S. R. The discovery of global warming   551.6

GLOBAL WARMING

See also Climate; Solar radiation

GLOBAL WARMING -- ENCYCLOPEDIAS

Encyclopedia of global warming & climate change   363.738

GLOBAL WARMING -- POLITICAL ASPECTS

Bloomberg, M. R. Climate of hope   363.7

Mooney, C. Storm world   363.7

The **global** warming reader.   363.738

Global weirdness.   577.2

GLOBALIZATION

Bacon, D. Illegal people   331.6

Borzutzky, D. The performance of becoming human   811.6

Deb, S. The beautiful and the damned   954.05

Epping, R. C. The 21st century economy   330.9

Foer, F. How soccer explains the world   303.482

Friedman, T. L. Thank you for being late   303.483

Hoekstra, J. M. The atlas of global conservation   333.95

Jacques, M. When China rules the world   327

Novogratz, J. The blue sweater   339.4

Stiglitz, J. E. Globalization and its discontents   337

Yergin, D. The quest   333.79

GLOBALIZATION

See also International relations

GLOBALIZATION -- ECONOMIC ASPECTS

Newman, K. S. The accordion family   306.874

GLOBALIZATION -- ECONOMIC ASPECTS -- CASE STUDIES

Goldstein, N. Globalization and free trade   382

GLOBALIZATION -- SOCIAL ASPECTS

Bacon, D. Illegal people   331.6

Glenny, M. McMafia   364.1

Goldhagen, D. J. The Devil That Never Dies   305.892

Globalization and free trade. Goldstein, N.   382

Globalization and its discontents. Stiglitz, J. E.   337

Globe Newspaper Co.

-- HISTORY
Adkins, L. Gibraltar ... 946.89
GREAT BRITAIN -- FOREIGN RELATIONS -- IRAN
Abrahamian, E. The coup ... 955.05
GREAT BRITAIN -- FOREIGN RELATIONS -- SPAIN
Ferreiro, L. D. Brothers at arms ... 327.73
GREAT BRITAIN -- FOREIGN RELATIONS -- TURKEY
Brotton, J. The sultan and the queen ... 327.42
GREAT BRITAIN -- FOREIGN RELATIONS -- UNITED STATES
Bunker, N. An empire on the edge ... 973.3
GREAT BRITAIN -- HISTORY
Ackroyd, P. Revolution ... 941.06
De Lisle, L. The White King ... 92
Ekin, D. The Last Armada ... 941.505
Gibney, J. A short history of Ireland, 1500-2000 ... 941.5
Jones, M. The Black Prince ... 92
Jones, N. Tower ... 942.1
Jordan, D. The king's revenge ... 941.066
MacColl, G. To marry an English Lord ... 974.7
Manchester, W. The last lion, Winston Spencer Churchill ... 92
Phillips, K. 1775 ... 973.3
Robb, G. The debatable land ... 941.3
Tombs, R. The English and their history ... 942
Woolley, B. The king's assassin ... 92
GREAT BRITAIN -- HISTORY -- 0-1066
Adams, M. In the Land of Giants ... 942.01
Charles-Edwards, T. M. Wales and the Britons, 350-1064 ... 942.901
Higgins, C. Under another sky ... 936
Morris, M. A Great & Terrible King ... 92
GREAT BRITAIN -- HISTORY -- 1066-1154, NORMAN PERIOD
Guy, J. Thomas Becket ... 92
Morris, M. The Norman Conquest ... 942.02
GREAT BRITAIN -- HISTORY -- 1066-1485, MEDIEVAL PERIOD
Green, D. The Hundred Years War ... 944
GREAT BRITAIN -- HISTORY -- 1154-1399, PLANTAGENETS
Jones, D. The Plantagenets ... 942.03
Seward, D. The Demon's Brood ... 942.03
GREAT BRITAIN -- HISTORY -- 1455-1485, WARS OF THE ROSES
Bicheno, H. Blood Royal ... 942.04
Gristwood, S. Blood sisters ... 942.04
Jones, D. The Wars of the Roses ... 942.04
Jones, M. K. Bosworth 1485 ... 942.04
GREAT BRITAIN -- HISTORY -- 1485-1603, TUDORS
Ackroyd, P. Tudors ... 942.05
Borman, T. The private lives of the Tudors ... 942.05
Borman, T. Thomas Cromwell ... 92
Goodman, R. How to be a Tudor ... 942.05
Guy, J. The Children of Henry VIII ... 941
Lipscomb, S. A Journey Through Tudor England ... 942.05
MacCulloch, D. Thomas Cromwell ... 92
Norton, E. The Temptation of Elizabeth Tudor ... 92

Ronald, S. Heretic queen ... 942.05
Starmore, A. Tudor roses ... 746.432
Tallis, N. Crown of Blood ... 92
Weir, A. The lost Tudor princess ... 92
GREAT BRITAIN -- HISTORY -- 1558-1603, ELIZABETH
Brotton, J. The sultan and the queen ... 327.42
Guy, J. Elizabeth ... 92
Hilton, L. Elizabeth ... 92
Mortimer, I. The time traveler's guide to Elizabethan England ... 942.05
GREAT BRITAIN -- HISTORY -- 1603-1714, STUARTS
Ackroyd, P. Rebellion ... 941.06
Jordan, D. The king's city ... 942.106
GREAT BRITAIN -- HISTORY -- 1642-1660, CIVIL WAR AND COMMONWEALTH
Spencer, C. E. M. S. Prince Rupert ... 92
GREAT BRITAIN -- HISTORY -- 1660-1688, RESTORATION
Mortimer, I. The time traveler's guide to Restoration Britain ... 941.066
GREAT BRITAIN -- HISTORY -- 1660-1714
Ackroyd, P. Revolution ... 941.06
Mortimer, I. The time traveler's guide to Restoration Britain ... 941.066
GREAT BRITAIN -- HISTORY -- 1714-1837
Fraser, A. The King and the Catholics ... 941.07
Royle, T. Culloden ... 941.1
GREAT BRITAIN -- HISTORY -- 1853-1856, CRIMEAN WAR See Crimean War, 1853-1856
GREAT BRITAIN -- HISTORY -- 18TH CENTURY
Byrne, P. Belle ... 92
GREAT BRITAIN -- HISTORY -- 1945-1952
Kynaston, D. Austerity Britain ... 941.085
GREAT BRITAIN -- HISTORY -- 1952-
Queen Elizabeth II and the Royal Family ... 92
GREAT BRITAIN -- HISTORY -- 19TH CENTURY
Ackroyd, P. Dominion ... 942.081
GREAT BRITAIN -- HISTORY -- 20TH CENTURY
Cadbury, D. Princes at war ... 941.084
GREAT BRITAIN -- HISTORY -- ANNE, 1702-1714
Somerset, A. Queen Anne ... 92
GREAT BRITAIN -- HISTORY -- CHARLES I, 1625-1649
De Lisle, L. The White King ... 92
GREAT BRITAIN -- HISTORY -- CHARLES II, 1660-1685
Jordan, D. The king's city ... 942.106
Jordan, D. The king's revenge ... 941.066
Pepys, S. The diary of Samuel Pepys ... 941.06
Spencer, C. E. M. S. Prince Rupert ... 92
GREAT BRITAIN -- HISTORY -- CIVIL WAR, 1642-1649
De Lisle, L. The White King ... 92
Spencer, C. E. M. S. Prince Rupert ... 92
GREAT BRITAIN -- HISTORY -- EDWARD I, 1272-1307
Morris, M. A Great & Terrible King ... 92
GREAT BRITAIN -- HISTORY -- EDWARD III, 1327-1377
Ormrod, W. M. Edward III ... 92
GREAT BRITAIN -- HISTORY -- EDWARD VI, 1547-1553
Rounding, V. The burning time ... 272.6

National Geographic the national parks 363.6

About

Heacox, K. Rhythm of the wild 979.8

HEAD

See also Anatomy

HEAD -- WOUNDS AND INJURIES

Laskas, J. M. Concussion 617.5

Head ball coach. Finebaum, P. 92

The **Head** Game. Mudd, P. 153.4

Head off & split. Finney, N. 811

Head, Anthony

Gentry, A. The Real Food Daily cookbook 641.5

Head, Dominic

(ed) The Cambridge guide to literature in English 820

The Cambridge introduction to modern British fiction, 1950-2000 823

HEADACHE

See also Pain

Heade, Martin Johnson, 1819-1904

About

Benfey, C. E. G. A summer of hummingbirds 920

Headlee, Celeste

We need to talk 153.6

Headley, Brooks

Superiority Burger cookbook 641.5

HEADS OF STATE

Amis, M. Koba the dread 947.084

Berthon, S. Warlords 940.53

Bosworth, R. J. B. Mussolini 945.091

Bosworth, R. J. B. Mussolini's Italy 945

Breitman, R. The architect of genocide 92

Brent, J. Inside the Stalin archives 947.086

Brent, J. Stalin's last crime 947.084

Brinkley, J. Cambodia's curse 959.6

Carlson, P. K blows top 947.085

Chang, J. Mao: the unknown story 92

Cornwell, J. Hitler's pope: the secret history of Pius XII 92

Dikötter, F. Mao's great famine 951.05

Dobbs, M. One minute to midnight 973.922

Duiker, W. J. Ho Chi Minh 959.704

Fulbrook, M. A concise history of Germany 943

Gordin, M. D. Red cloud at dawn 355

Hassig, R. C. The hidden people of North Korea 951.93

Hochschild, A. The unquiet ghost 947.084

Kershaw, I. Hitler 92

Kershaw, I. Hitler, 1936-1945: nemesis 943.086

Kissinger, H. Diplomacy 327.2

Medvedev, R. A. Let history judge 947.084

Montefiore, S. Stalin: the court of the red tsar 92

Montefiore, S. Young Stalin 92

Nikita Khrushchev 92

Parssinen, T. M. The Oster conspiracy of 1938 943.086

Pipes, R. Russia under the Bolshevik regime 947.084

Pleshakov, K. Stalin's folly 940.54

Pomper, P. Lenin's brother 92

Pringle, P. The murder of Nikolai Vavilov 92

Rosenbaum, R. Explaining Hitler 943.086

Ryback, T. W. Hitler's private library 027

Service, R. Lenin--a biography 947.084

Service, R. Stalin 92

Shirer, W. L. The rise and fall of the Third Reich 943.086

Snyder, T. D. Bloodlands 940.54

Speer, A. Inside the Third Reich 943.086

Spence, J. D. Mao Zedong 951.05

Strathern, P. The artist, the philosopher, and the warrior 920

Sun Shuyun The Long March 951.04

Taylor, F. Exorcising Hitler 943.087

Weber, T. Hitler's first war 940.4

HEADS OF STATE

See also Executive power; Statesmen

HEADS OF STATE -- CHINA -- BIOGRAPHY

Levine, S. I. Mao 951.05

Short, P. Mao 951.05

Spence, J. D. Mao Zedong 951.05

HEADS OF STATE -- ENGLAND -- LONDON -- HISTORY -- 20TH CENTURY

Olson, L. Last Hope Island 940.534

HEADS OF STATE -- FRANCE -- BIOGRAPHY

Gueniffey, P. Bonaparte 92

HEADS OF STATE -- GERMANY -- BIOGRAPHY

Hitler 92

Orbach, D. The plots against Hitler 940.53

Weber, T. Becoming Hitler 92

HEADS OF STATE -- SOUTH AMERICA -- BIOGRAPHY

Arana, M. Bolivar 92

HEADS OF STATE -- SOVIET UNION -- BIOGRAPHY

Taubman, W. Gorbachev 92

HEALING

Kaur, R. Milk and honey 811.6

Monte, T. Unexpected recoveries 616.029

HEALING

See also Therapeutics

HEALING -- PSYCHOLOGICAL ASPECTS

Rakel, D. The compassionate connection 610.1

Healing children. Newman, K. 92

The **healing** of America. Reid, T. R. 362.1

The **healing** self. Tanzi, R. E. 615.8

HEALING, MENTAL *See* Mental healing

HEALING, SPIRITUAL *See* Spiritual healing

HEALTH

Bittman, M. The food matters cookbook 641.3

Budig, K. Aim true 613.7

Buettner, D. The Blue Zones solution 613.2

Carroll, A. The bad food bible 613.2

Collen, A. 10% human 612.3

Complete guide to fitness & health 613.7

Dietert, R. The human superorganism 613

Enayati, A. Seeking serenity 155.9

Flay, B. Bobby Flay fit 641.5

Gazella, K. A. The definitive guide to thriving after cancer 616.99

Grigore, A. Skin cleanse 613

Hanoch, D. The yoga lifestyle 613.7

Helwig, J. Smoothie-licious 641.87

Pawel, M. The Crusades of Cesar Chavez   92

HISPANIC AMERICANS AND LIBRARIES
Moller, S. C. Library service to Spanish speaking patrons   027.6

HISPANIC AMERICANS IN LITERATURE
Latino and Latina writers   810

Hissing cousins. Peyser, M.   92

HISTORIANS
See also Authors

HISTORIANS -- BIOGRAPHY
Aldous, R. Schlesinger   92

HISTORIANS -- UNITED STATES
Schlesinger, A. M. (. M. Journals: 1952-2000   92
Schlesinger, A. M. (. M. A life in the twentieth century   92

HISTORIANS -- UNITED STATES -- BIOGRAPHY
Aldous, R. Schlesinger   92
Crais, C. History lessons   92
Duberman, M. Howard Zinn   92

HISTORIC BUILDINGS
Eisen, N. The last palace   943.71

HISTORIC BUILDINGS
See also Buildings; Historic sites; Monuments

HISTORIC BUILDINGS -- NEW YORK (N.Y.)
Freeland, D. Automats, taxi dances, and vaudeville

HISTORIC BUILDINGS -- UNITED STATES
Gugliotta, G. Freedom's cap   975.3

HISTORIC HOUSES *See* Historic buildings

Historic lives [series]
Brown, M. T.E. Lawrence   92

HISTORIC PRESERVATION
Puleo, S. American treasures   973

HISTORIC SITES
Caro, I. Paris to the past   914
Giorgione, M. Inside Camp David   973.91
Glass, B. D. 50 great American places   973
Hunt, P. Ten discoveries that rewrote history   930.1
Loewen, J. W. Lies across America   973

HISTORIC SITES
See also Archeology; History

HISTORIC SITES -- NEW YORK (STATE) -- NEW YORK
Bartholomew, R. Two and two   92

HISTORIC SITES -- UNITED STATES -- GUIDEBOOKS
Glass, B. D. 50 great American places   973
Historical atlas of Central Europe. Magocsi, P. R.   911
Historical atlas of the American West. Hayes, D.   911
A Historical atlas of the Jewish people.   909
Historical atlas of the North American railroad. Hayes, D.   385
Historical atlas of the United States. Hayes, D.   911

HISTORICAL ATLASES
Atlas of the Civil War   973.7
Davidson, P. Atlas of empires   909
Hayes, D. Historical atlas of the American West   911
Hayes, D. Historical atlas of the North American railroad   385
Smithsonian atlas of world aviation   629.13
Swanson, M. Atlas of the Civil War, month by month   973.7
Woodworth, S. E. Atlas of the Civil War   973.7

HISTORICAL ATLASES

See also Atlases

HISTORICAL CHRONOLOGY
Grun, B. The timetables of history   902
National Geographic concise history of the world   909
Timelines of history   902.02
The timetables of American history   902

HISTORICAL CHRONOLOGY
See also Chronology; History

Historical dictionaries of religions, philosophies, and movements [series]
Olson, C. Historical dictionary of Buddhism   294.3
Historical dictionary of Buddhism. Olson, C.   294.3
Historical dictionary of U.S. Constitution. Conley, R. S.   342.73

HISTORICAL DRAMA
McCarter, J. Hamilton   782.1

HISTORICAL DRAMA
See also Drama

Historical encyclopedia of American labor.   331.8

HISTORICAL FICTION
Baker, J. S. The readers' advisory guide to historical fiction   026
Johnson, S. L. Historical fiction II   016

HISTORICAL FICTION
See also Fiction

HISTORICAL FICTION -- BIBLIOGRAPHY
Hooper, B. Read on....historical fiction   016
Historical fiction II. Johnson, S. L.   016
Historical gazetteer of the United States. Hellmann, P. T.   911

HISTORICAL GEOGRAPHY
See also Geography; History

HISTORICAL GEOGRAPHY -- MAPS *See* Historical atlases

HISTORICAL GEOLOGY
Stager, C. Deep future   363.7

HISTORICAL GEOLOGY
See also Geology

HISTORICAL LITERATURE
Ackroyd, P. Dominion   942.081
Alexiou, A. S. Devil's mile   974.7
Andersen, K. Fantasyland   973
Bollywood   791.430
Burns, K. The Vietnam War   959.704
Conn, D. The fall of the house of FIFA   796.334
Cox, C. Boy soldiers of the American Revolution   973.3
Dean, J. The taking of K-129   359.93
Everett, D. L. How language began   401
Fager, J. Fifty years of 60 minutes   791.457
Gibney, J. A short history of Ireland, 1500-2000   941.5
Hammel, E. Two flags over Iwo Jima   940.54
Koehn, N. Forged in crisis   303.34
Lashinsky, A. Wild ride   338.76
Marques, L. The United States and the slave trade to the Americas, 1776-1867   306.362
McMeekin, S. The Russian revolution   947.084
Mundy, L. Code girls   940.54
Satia, P. Empire of guns   330.941
Schoenberger, N. Wayne and Ford   791.43

HUMAN BEINGS -- SEXUAL BEHAVIOR See Sex

HUMAN BIOLOGY

Provine, R. R. Curious behavior	152.3
The **Human** body.	612

HUMAN BODY

See also Human beings; Self

HUMAN BODY

Francis, G. Adventures in human being	612
Herzog, A. Knit to flatter	746.43
Lieberman, D. The story of the human body	612
Provine, R. R. Curious behavior	152.3
Shubin, N. H. The universe within	550

HUMAN BODY -- POETRY

Powell, D. A. Useless landscape	811
Sinclair, S. Cannibal	811.6
The **human** brain book. Carter, R.	612.8

HUMAN CAPITAL

See also Capital

Human chain. Heaney, S.	821

HUMAN CLONING

Kurpinski, K. How to defeat your own clone	660.6
Wilmut, I. After Dolly	176

HUMAN CLONING

See also Cloning

HUMAN CLONING -- ETHICAL ASPECTS

See also Ethics

HUMAN COMFORT -- DENMARK

Brits, L. T. The book of hygge	747

HUMAN COMMUNICATION WITH ANIMALS See Human-animal communication

Human dark with sugar. Shaughnessy, B.	811

HUMAN ECOLOGY

Ackerman, D. The Human Age	304.2
Barnosky, A. D. Dodging extinction	576.8
Biello, D. The unnatural world	304.2
Brown, C. S. A big history	909
Dunn, R. The wild life of our bodies	579
Fagan, B. Elixir	553.7
Gore, A. An inconvenient truth	363.7
Gore, A. Our choice	363.7
Guzman, A. T. Overheated	363.738
Owen, D. Green metropolis	304.2
Roberts, C. The ocean of life	551.46
Safina, C. The view from Lazy Point	508
Williams, F. Breasts	612.6
Wilson, E. O. In search of nature	113
Worster, D. Shrinking the Earth	304.2
Zuk, M. Riddled with life	616.07

HUMAN ECOLOGY

See also Sociology

HUMAN ECOLOGY -- ALASKA

Wohlforth, C. The fate of nature	304.2

HUMAN ECOLOGY -- MEXICO, GULF OF

Davis, J. E. The Gulf	909

HUMAN ECOLOGY -- POPULAR WORKS

Frank, A. Light of the stars	523.1

HUMAN ECOLOGY -- UNITED STATES -- PHILOSO-PHY

Williams, T. T. The hour of land	333.78

HUMAN ECOLOGY -- WASHINGTON (STATE) -- OLYMPIC PENINSULA

Freeman, S. Saving Tarboo Creek	333.72

HUMAN ENCOUNTERS WITH ALIENS See Human-alien encounters

HUMAN ENGINEERING

Norman, D. The design of everyday things	745.2
Human evolution. Dunbar, R.	155.7

HUMAN EVOLUTION

Eldredge, N. Why we do it	155.3
Johanson, D. C. From Lucy to language	599.93
Martin, R. How we do it	612.6
Miller, K. R. The human instinct	155.7
Pagel, M. Wired for culture	303.4
Prum, R. O. The evolution of beauty	591.56
Pyne, L. Seven skeletons	569.9
Sang-Hee Lee Close encounters with humankind	569.9
Sarmiento, E. The last human	569.9
Shlain, L. Sex, time, and power	306.7
Switek, B. Written in stone	576.8
Wade, N. Before the dawn	599.93
Walter, C. Last ape standing	569.9
Wrangham, R. W. Catching fire	641.3
Zuk, M. Riddled with life	616.07

HUMAN EVOLUTION -- PHILOSOPHY

Wilson, E. O. The social conquest of earth	599.93

HUMAN EXPERIMENTATION -- HISTORY -- UNITED STATES

Masterson, K. M. The malaria project	616.9

HUMAN EXPERIMENTATION IN MEDICINE

Masterson, K. M. The malaria project	616.9
Roach, M. Stiff	611
Skloot, R. The immortal life of Henrietta Lacks	92
Tucker, T. The great starvation experiment	174.2
Wadman, M. The vaccine race	614.523
Washington, H. A. Medical apartheid	174.2

HUMAN EXPERIMENTATION IN MEDICINE

See also Medical ethics; Medicine -- Research

HUMAN FERTILITY

Martin, R. How we do it	612.6
Weschler, T. Taking charge of your fertility	613.9

HUMAN FERTILITY

See also Birth rate; Fertility; Population

The **human** figure. Vanderpoel, J. H.	743.4

HUMAN FIGURE IN ART

Bradley, B. Drawing people	743.4
Hart, C. Human anatomy made amazingly easy	743.4

HUMAN FIGURE IN ART See Artistic anatomy; Figure drawing; Figure painting; Nude in art

HUMAN FOSSILS See Fossil hominids

HUMAN GENETICS

Epstein, D. The sports gene	613.7

HUMAN GENETICS -- MISCELLANEA

Kean, S. The violinist's thumb	572.8

HUMAN GENETICS -- POPULAR WORKS

I

Brick, M. Saving the school   **373.22**

John Huston. Meyers, J.   **92**

John James Audubon. Rhodes, R.   **92**

John Lennon. Norman, P.   **92**

John Marshall. Unger, H. G.   **92**

John Muir and the ice that started a fire. Heacox, K.   **92**

John Osborne. Heilpern, J.   **92**

John Paul II. Flynn, R.   **B**

John Paul II, Pope, 1920-2005
About
Flynn, R. John Paul II   **B**

O'Connor, G. Universal Father: a life of John Paul II   **92**

Weigel, G. Lessons in hope   **282.092**

John Paul Jones. Thomas, E.   **92**

John Quincy Adams. Traub, J.   **92**

John Quincy Adams. Remini, R. V.   **92**

John Quincy Adams. Unger, H. G.   **92**

John Quincy Adams. Kaplan, F.   **92**

John Shaw's nature photography field guide. Shaw, J.   **778.9**

John Steinbeck.   **813**

John Tyler. Crapol, E. P.   **92**

John Tyler. May, G.   **92**

John Wayne: the life and legend. Eyman, S.   **92**

John Wesley. Tomkins, S.   **287**

John Winthrop. Bremer, F. J.   **974.4**

John, King of England, 1167-1216
About
Morris, M. King John   **92**

John, Lauren Z.

Running book discussion groups   **374**

Johnny Appleseed. Means, H. B.   **92**

Johnny Cash. Kleist, R.   **92**

Johnny Cash. Light, A.   **92**

Johnny Cash. Hilburn, R.   **92**

Johnny Cash. Streissguth, M.   **92**

The **Johns** Hopkins guide to diabetes. Rubin, R. R.   **616.4**

Johns Hopkins patients' guide to colon and rectal cancer. Ahuja, N.   **616.99**

Johns Hopkins Press health book [series]

Mace, N. L. The 36-hour day   **618.97**

Thomas, D. E. The lupus encyclopedia   **616.7**

Yosipovitch, G. Living with itch   **616.5**

Johnsen, Gregory D.

The last refuge   **363.325**

Johnsen, Ole

Minerals of the world   **549**

Johnson, Alex

Improbable libraries   **027**

Johnson, Andrew, 1808-1875
About
Gordon-Reed, A. Andrew Johnson   **92**

Johnson, Catherine

Grandin, T. Animals in translation   **591.5**

Grandin, T. Animals make us human   **636**

Johnson, Charles

The way of the writer   **808.3**

Johnson, Clarence L., 1910-1990

About
Reel, M. A brotherhood of spies   **327.127**

Johnson, Daniel

(jt. auth) Johnson, S. How to build chicken coops   **636.5**

Johnson, Doug

The indispensable librarian   **025.1**

Johnson, Elaine

(ed) Sunset the great outdoors cookbook   **641.5**

Johnson, Eric A.

What we knew   **943.086**

Johnson, George

Miss Leavitt's stars   **92**

A shortcut through time   **004.1**

The ten most beautiful experiments   **507.8**

Johnson, Gus, 1913-2000
About
Dance, S. The world of Count Basie   **920**

Johnson, Harriet McBryde
About
Johnson, H. M. Too late to die young   **92**

Johnson, Hugh

The world of trees   **582.16**

Hugh Johnson on wine   **641.22**

Johnson, Ian

A mosque in Munich   **297**

The souls of China   **200.951**

Johnson, J. J.

(jt. auth) Chambers, V. Between Harlem and Heaven   **641.59**

Johnson, Jack, 1878-1946
About
Runstedtler, T. Jack Johnson, rebel sojourner   **796.83**

Ward, G. C. Unforgivable blackness   **92**

Johnson, Jaclyn

WorkParty   **650.1**

Johnson, James Weldon

Complete poems   **811**

The essential writings of James Weldon Johnson   **818**

Johnson, Jean

Where did the jobs go-- and how do we get them back?   **331.1**

Johnson, Jenny

In full velvet   **811**

Johnson, Joyce, 1935-

The voice is all   **818**

Johnson, Kendall

Haralson, E. L. Critical companion to Henry James   **813**

Johnson, Kirk Wallace

The feather thief   **364.162**

Johnson, L. S. (Lonni Sue)
About
Lemonick, M. D. The perpetual now   **616.8**

Johnson, Lacy M.

The other side   **92**

Johnson, Lacy M., 1978-
About
Johnson, L. M. The other side   **92**

Johnson, Lady Bird, 1912-2007
About

Porter, R. Madness   **616.89**

Shroder, T. Acid test   **615.7**

Slater, L. Prozac diary   **616.89**

Smoller, J. The other side of normal   **591.5**

Washington, H. A. Infectious madness   **616.89**

Whitaker, R. Anatomy of an epidemic   **616.89**

MENTAL ILLNESS

    See also Abnormal psychology; Diseases

MENTAL ILLNESS -- DRUG THERAPY

Pollan, M. How to change your mind   **615.788**

MENTAL ILLNESS -- DRUG THERAPY

    See also Drug therapy

MENTAL ILLNESS -- HISTORY

Scull, A. Madness in civilization   **616.89**

MENTAL ILLNESS -- HUMOR

Lawson, J. Furiously happy   **92**

MENTAL ILLNESS -- PHYSIOLOGICAL ASPECTS

    See also Physiology

MENTAL ILLNESS -- TREATMENT

Frank, L. The pleasure shock   **92**

Horn, S. Damnation island   **362.2**

MENTAL ILLNESS -- TREATMENT -- NEW YORK (STATE) -- NEW YORK -- 19TH CENTURY -- HISTORY

Horn, S. Damnation island   **362.2**

MENTAL ILLNESS -- UNITED STATES

Sederer, L. I. The family guide to mental health care   **616.89**

Whitaker, R. Anatomy of an epidemic   **616.89**

MENTAL INSTITUTIONS *See* Mentally ill -- Institutional care

MENTAL PATIENTS *See* Mentally ill

MENTAL PROCESSES -- PHYSIOLOGY

Kandel, E. R. The disordered mind   **616.89**

MENTAL RETARDATION

    See also Abnormal psychology

MENTAL STEREOTYPE *See* Stereotype (Social psychology)

MENTAL STRESS *See* Stress (Psychology)

MENTAL SUGGESTION

    See also Mind and body; Parapsychology; Subconsciousness

MENTAL TESTS *See* Intelligence tests; Psychological tests

MENTAL TYPES *See* Typology (Psychology)

MENTAL WORK

Newport, C. Deep work   **650.1**

MENTALLY DEPRESSED *See* Depression (Psychology)

MENTALLY DERANGED *See* Mentally ill

MENTALLY HANDICAPPED *See* People with mental disabilities

MENTALLY ILL

Montross, C. Falling into the fire   **616.89**

Murphy, T. W. Life in rewind   **92**

Nathan, D. Sybil exposed   **616.85**

Powers, R. No One Cares About Crazy People   **362.26**

Smith, T. A balanced life   **362.1**

Torrey, E. F. (. F. Surviving schizophrenia   **616.89**

Von Ziegesar, P. The looking glass brother   **92**

Winchester, S. The professor and the madman   **423**

MENTALLY ILL

    See also Sick

MENTALLY ILL -- BIOGRAPHY

Allen, S. A kind of mirraculas paradise   **92**

MENTALLY ILL -- FAMILY RELATIONSHIPS

Earley, P. Resilience   **616.89**

MENTALLY ILL -- INSTITUTIONAL CARE

Ronson, J. The psychopath test   **616.85**

MENTALLY ILL -- PSYCHOLOGY

Stryker, K. Ask   **302**

MENTALLY ILL -- UNITED STATES

Roth, A. Insane   **364.38**

MENTALLY ILL -- UNITED STATES -- BIOGRAPHY

Shroder, T. Acid test   **615.7**

Smith, D. Monkey mind   **616.85**

MENTALLY ILL -- WASHINGTON (STATE) -- SEATTLE -- BIOGRAPHY

Guppy, J. My fluorescent God   **92**

MENTALLY ILL CHILDREN *See* Emotionally disturbed children

MENTALLY ILL OFFENDERS -- WASHINGTON (STATE) -- SEATTLE -- CASE STUDIES

Sanders, E. While the city slept   **364.152**

MENTALLY ILL PERSONS -- PSYCHOLOGY -- PERSONAL NARRATIVES

Montross, C. Falling into the fire   **616.89**

MENTALLY RETARDED *See* People with mental disabilities

MENTALLY RETARDED CHILDREN *See* Children with mental disabilities

MENTORING

Chertavian, G. A Year Up   **331.25**

Edelman, M. W. Lanterns   **92**

MENTORING

    See also Counseling

Menuez, Doug

Fearless genius   **979.4**

MENUS

Bayless, R. Fiesta at Rick's   **641.5**

Brennan, K. Keepers   **641.5**

Garten, I. Barefoot Contessa at home   **641**

Henry, D. How to eat a peach   **641.5**

Tanis, D. Heart of the artichoke and other kitchen journeys   **641.5**

Tanis, D. A platter of figs and other recipes   **641.5**

MENUS

    See also Cooking; Diet

Merali, Zeeya

A big bang in a little room   **523.1**

MERCANTILE LAW *See* Commercial law

MERCEDES AUTOMOBILES

Klara, R. The Devil's Mercedes   **629.222**

MERCEDES AUTOMOBILES -- HISTORY -- 20TH CENTURY

Klara, R. The Devil's Mercedes   **629.222**

MERCENARY SOLDIERS

(comp) The Mood guide to fabric and fashion   **746.9**

The **Mood** guide to fabric and fashion.   **746.9**

Moody, Anne, 1940-2015

The children money can buy   **362.73**

Moody, Raymond A.

Life after life   **133.9**

MOON

> *See also* Astronomy; Solar system

MOON -- EXPLORATION

Kluger, J. Apollo 8   **629.45**

MOON -- EXPLORATION

> *See also* Space flight to the moon

MOON -- MAPS

> *See also* Maps

MOON -- PICTORIAL WORKS

> *See also* Space photography

MOON WORSHIP

> *See also* Religion

Moon, Rachel Y.

(ed) Sleep   **618.92**

MOON, VOYAGES TO *See* Space flight to the moon

Moondust. Smith, A.   **920**

Moonen, Rick

Fish without a doubt   **641.6**

Mooney, Chris

Storm world   **363.7**

Mooney, Jonathan

> **About**

Mooney, J. The short bus   **92**

Mooney, Paul

> **About**

Mooney, P. Black is the new white   **92**

A **moonless,** starless sky. Okeowo, A.   **363.321**

Moonlight. Walsh, J. E.   **345**

MOONS *See* Satellites

Moonwalking with Einstein. Foer, J.   **153.1**

Moore, Alexis

Cyber self-defense   **613.6**

Moore, Christine

Little Flower baking   **641.815**

Moore, Colten

(jt. auth) O'Brien, K. Catching the Sky   **796.94**

Moore, Darnell L.

No ashes in the fire   **92**

Moore, Dinty W.

The story cure   **808.3**

Moore, Dorothy Rudd, 1940-

> **About**

Walker-Hill, H. From spirituals to symphonies   **780**

Moore, Gerald

(ed) The Penguin book of modern African poetry   **896**

Moore, Harold G.

We are soldiers still   **959.704**

Moore, Honor

(ed) Lowell, A. Selected poems   **811**

(ed) Poems from the women's movement   **811**

Moore, John Allphin

Encyclopedia of the United Nations   **341.23**

Moore, Kate

The radium girls   **363.17**

Moore, Kathy

Delicious dump cakes   **641.86**

Moore, Kenneth

(ed) The revolt of the masses   **901**

Moore, Lorrie, 1957-

See what can be done   **801**

Moore, Marianne, 1887-1972

Marshall, M. Elizabeth Bishop   **811.54**

New collected poems   **811**

The poems of Marianne Moore   **811**

> **About**

Jarrell, R. No other book   **809**

Leavell, L. Holding on upside down   **92**

Moore, Mary Tyler

> **About**

Moore, M. T. Growing up again   **92**

Moore, Michael Scott

The desert and the sea   **364.154**

Moore, Minyon

(jt. auth) Brazile, D. For colored girls who have considered politics   **92**

Moore, R. Laurence

(jt. auth) Kramnick, I. Godless citizens in a godly republic   **211**

Moore, Rachel S.

The artist's compass   **791**

Moore, Richard

The Bolt supremacy   **796.422**

Moore, Robin

In search of lost frogs   **597.8**

Moore, Russell

Onward   **230**

This is Camino   **641.5**

Moore, Stephen W.

(jt. auth) Griffith, H. W. Complete Guide to Prescription & Nonprescription Drugs   **615**

Moore, Steven, 1978-

The novel   **809**

Moore, Susanna, 1948-

Paradise of the Pacific   **996.9**

Moore, Thomas, 1940-

Ageless soul   **155.67**

Moore, Thurston

No wave   **781.66**

Moore, Tim

The Cyclist Who Went Out in the Cold   **796.6**

Gironimo!   **796.6**

Moore, Undine Smith, 1904-1989

> **About**

Walker-Hill, H. From spirituals to symphonies   **780**

Moore, Wendy

How to create the perfect wife   **823**

Moore, Wes, 1975-

> **About**

My dead parents. Yurchyshyn, A.   **92**

My dearest friend. Adams, J.   **92**

My dyslexia. Schultz, P.   **92**

My face is black is true. Berry, M. F.   **92**

My fair junkie. Dresner, A.   **92**

My father before me. Forhan, C.   **92**

My father's paradise. Sabar, A.   **305.8**

My father's people. Rubin, L. D.   **920**

My fellow citizens.   **352.23**

My Fellow Soldiers. Carroll, A.   **940.4**

My fight / your fight. Rousey, R.   **92**

My fluorescent God. Guppy, J.   **92**

My French family table. Peltre, B.   **641.5**

My friend Dahmer. Backderf, D.   **741.5**

My generation. Styron, W.   **814**

My girls. Fisher, T.   **92**

My grandfather would have shot me.   **929.2**

My halal kitchen. Maffei, Y.   **641.595**

My happiness bears no relation to happiness. Hoffman, A.   **92**

My invented country. Allende, I.   **863**

My Isl@m. Nasr, A. A.   **297.09**

My Jewish year. Pogrebin, A.   **296.43**

My kitchen year. Reichl, R.   **641.5**

My Korean deli. Howe, B. R.   **92**

My life. Duncan, I.   **92**

My life. Clinton, B.   **92**

My life in France. Child, J.   **92**

My life in Middlemarch. Mead, R.   **823**

My life in politics. Chirac, J.   **944.084**

My life on the road. Steinem, G.   **92**

My life with Bob. Paul, P.   **92**

My life with Pablo Neruda. Urrutia, M.   **92**

My life with the saints. Martin, J.   **920**

My Life, My Love, My Legacy. Reynolds, B.   **92**

My Lisbon. Mendes, N.   **641.594**

My lives. White, E.   **813**

My losing season. Conroy, P.   **796.323**

My Lost Brothers. McDonough, B.   **363.379**

My Lunches With Orson. Biskind, P.   **791.43**

My marathon. Shorter, F.   **92**

My master recipes. Wells, P.   **641.5**

My mother/my self. Friday, N.   **155.6**

My name on his tongue. Halaby, L.   **811**

My New Orleans. Besh, J.   **641.59**

My new roots. Britton, S.   **641.3**

My own words. Ginsburg, R. B.   **92**

My pantry.   **641.594**

My Paris kitchen.   **641.59**

My patients and other animals. Fincham-Gray, S.   **636.089**

My perfect pantry.   **641.5**

My plastic brain. Williams, C.   **612.8**

My poets. McLane, M. N.   **811**

My prison, my home. Esfandiari, H.   **92**

My promised land. Shavit, A.   **956.05**

My Salinger year. Smith Rakoff, J.   **92**

My sister, guard your veil; my brother guard, your eyes. Azam Zanganeh, L.   **305**

My song. Belafonte, H.   **92**

My soul looks back. Harris, J. B.   **92**

My squirrel days. Kemper, E.   **792.7**

My stroke of insight. Taylor, J. B.   **362.19**

My sweet Mexico. Gerson, F.   **641.5**

My Tibet. Bstan-'dzin-rgya-mtsho, D. L. X.   **951**

My Tiny Veg Plot.   **635**

My twenty-five years in Provence. Mayle, P.   **944.9**

My two Souths. Foose, M. H.   **641.5**

My Venice and Other Essays. Leon, D.   **945**

My vocabulary did this to me. Spicer, J.   **811**

My war. Rooney, A. A.   **940.54**

My year of flops. Rabin, N.   **791.43**

My year of running dangerously. Foreman, T.   **92**

MYANMAR

Duguid, N. Burma   **641.59**

MYANMAR -- POLITICS AND GOVERNMENT

Wintle, J. Perfect hostage   **92**

Myers + Chang at home. Chang, J.   **641.595**

MYERS+CHANG

Chang, J. Myers + Chang at home   **641.595**

Myers, Allen C.

(ed) Eerdmans dictionary of the Bible   **220.3**

Myers, Amy

The autoimmune solution cookbook   **641.5**

The autoimmune solution   **616.97**

Myers, Elsie Palmer, 1872-1955

About

Lucey, D. M. Sargent's women   **920**

Myers, Gary

Brady vs Manning   **92**

Myers, Isabel Briggs

Gifts differing   **155.2**

Myers, Marc

Why jazz happened   **781.65**

Myers, Peter B.

Myers, I. B. Gifts differing   **155.2**

Myers, Steven Lee

The new tsar   **92**

MYERS-BRIGGS TYPE INDICATOR

Emre, M. The personality brokers   **155.2**

Myerson, Joel

(ed) Transcendentalism   **810**

Myles, Eileen

I Must Be Living Twice   **811.54**

Myles, Eileen

About

Myles, E. Afterglow   **636.7**

Myne. Presley, F.   **821**

Myrdal, Gunnar, 1898-1987

About

Ellison, R. The collected essays of Ralph Ellison   **814**

Myrna Loy. Leider, E. W.   **92**

Myron, Vicki

Dewey   **636.8**

Myself with others. Fuentes, C.   **864**

MYSPACE (WEBSITE)

Iacoboni, M. Mirroring people   **573.8**
Kandel, E. R. In search of memory   **153**
Kosik, K. S. Outsmarting alzheimer's   **616.8**
Ropper, A. H. Reaching down the rabbit hole   **616.8**
Sacks, O. The mind's eye   **616.85**
Wolf, N. Vagina   **305.42**

NERVOUS SYSTEM
    See also Anatomy; Physiology

NERVOUS SYSTEM -- DISEASES
Eichenwald, K. A mind unraveled   **92**
McAuliffe, K. This is your brain on parasites   **612.8**

NERVOUS SYSTEM -- DISEASES
    See also Diseases

Nesbit, Evelyn, 1884-1967
        About
Baatz, S. The girl on the velvet swing   **364.152**

Nesheim, Malden
Why calories count   **613.2**

Nesmith, Michael
        About
Nesmith, M. Infinite Tuesday   **92**

Ness, Eliot
        About
Collins, M. A. Scarface and the untouchable   **920**

NEST BUILDING
Zickefoose, J. Baby Birds   **598**

NEST BUILDING
    See also Animal behavior; Animals -- Habitations

Nesteroff, Kliph
The Comedians   **792.7**

NESTING (ANIMAL BEHAVIOR) *See* Nest building

NESTING BEHAVIOR *See* Nest building

The **nesting** place. Smith, M.   **248.4**

Nestle, Marion
(jt. auth) Nesheim, M. Why calories count   **613.2**

Nestor, James
Deep   **797.2**

The **Netanyahu** years. Caspit, B.   **92**

Netanyahu, Benjamin
        About
Remnick, D. Reporting   **814**
Caspit, B. The Netanyahu years   **92**

NETHERLANDS
Buruma, I. Murder in Amsterdam   **364.152**

NETHERLANDS -- HISTORY
Shorto, R. Amsterdam   **949.2**

NETHERLANDS -- HISTORY -- 1940-1945, GERMAN OCCUPATION
Barnouw, D. The diary of Anne Frank: the critical edition   **92**
Frank, A. The diary of a young girl: the definitive edition   **92**
Gies, M. Anne Frank remembered   **92**

NETHERLANDS -- HISTORY -- 1940-1945, GERMAN OCCUPATION -- DRAMA
Goodrich, F. The diary of Anne Frank   **812**

Netherlands State Institute for War Documentation
Barnouw, D. The diary of Anne Frank: the critical edition   **92**

NETHERLANDS. STATEN-GENERAAL -- BIOGRAPHY
Hirsi Ali, A. Nomad   **92**

Nettle, Daniel
Happiness   **152.4**

Nettles, Brenda S.
(jt. auth) Ahuja, N. Johns Hopkins patients' guide to colon and rectal cancer   **616.99**

NETWORK THEORY *See* System analysis

Networked. Wellman, B.   **006.7**

NETWORKS (ASSOCIATIONS, INSTITUTIONS, ETC.)
    See Associations

NETWORKS, COMPUTER *See* Computer networks

NETWORKS, INFORMATION *See* Information networks

Netzer, Corinne T.
The complete book of food counts   **613.2**

Neu, Charles E.
Colonel House   **92**

Neubauer, Alexander
(ed) Poetry in person   **809.1**

Neubauer, Linda
(ed) The complete photo guide to window treatments   **646.2**

Neuburger, Emily K.
Show me a story   **741.6**

Neufeld, Josh
Gladstone, B. The influencing machine   **302.23**
A.D.   **976.3**

Neufeld, Michael J.
(ed) Milestones of space   **629.4**

Neufeld, Michael J.
Von Braun   **92**

NEURASTHENIA
    See also Mental illness

NEUROANATOMY
Taylor, J. B. My stroke of insight   **362.19**

NEUROBIOLOGY
Sapolsky, R. M. Behave   **612.8**

Neurocomic. Ros, H.   **612.82**

NEUROLOGIC MANIFESTATIONS -- POPULAR WORKS
Kean, S. The tale of the dueling neurosurgeons   **617.4**

NEUROLOGICAL SCIENCES *See* Neurosciences

NEUROLOGISTS
Quiñones-Hinojosa, A. Becoming Dr. Q   **92**
Sacks, O. W. Uncle Tungsten   **616.8**

NEUROLOGISTS -- BIOGRAPHY
Sacks, O. Gratitude   **306.9**

NEUROLOGISTS -- ENGLAND -- BIOGRAPHY
Sacks, O. W. Uncle Tungsten   **616.8**
Sacks, O. On the move   **92**

NEUROLOGISTS -- GREAT BRITAIN -- BIOGRAPHY
Lewis, C. The enlightened Mr. Parkinson   **92**

NEUROLOGISTS -- MASSACHUSETTS -- BOSTON -- BIOGRAPHY
Ropper, A. H. Reaching down the rabbit hole   **616.8**

NEUROLOGISTS -- UNITED STATES -- BIOGRAPHY
Sacks, O. On the move   **92**

The **new** Jerusalem Bible. 220.5

The **new** joys of Yiddish. Rosten, L. 422

The **new** librarianship field guide. Lankes, R. D. 020.1

New life, no instructions. Caldwell, G. 92

A **new** literary history of America. 810

A **new** map of wonders. Henderson, C. 031.02

The **new** mediterranean cookbook. Wadi, S. 641.59

The **new** Mediterranean diet cookbook. Jenkins, N. H. 641.5

The **new** Mediterranean Jewish table. Goldstein, J. 641.5

NEW MEXICO

Connors, P. Fire season 634.9

NEW MEXICO -- ECONOMIC CONDITIONS -- 21ST CENTURY

Martínez, R. Desert America 330.9

NEW MEXICO -- RACE RELATIONS

Martínez, R. Desert America 330.9

NEW MEXICO -- SOCIAL CONDITIONS -- 21ST CENTURY

Martínez, R. Desert America 330.9

The **New** Midwestern table. Thielen, A. 641.59

The **new** mind of the South. Thompson, T. 305.8

A **new** model. Graham, A. 92

A **new** Napa cuisine. Kostow, C. 641.59

New narratives in American history [series]

Franklin, J. H. In search of the promised land 929

The **new** Negro. Stewart, J. C. 92

NEW NEGRO MOVEMENT *See* Harlem Renaissance

The **New** new journalism. Boynton, R. S. 071

The **new** normal. Wann, D. 306

NEW ORLEANS (LA.)

Rivlin, G. Katrina 976.3

NEW ORLEANS (LA.) -- BIOGRAPHY

Baum, D. Nine lives 976.3

Crais, C. History lessons 92

Gisleson, A. The futilitarians 92

Perry, T. Higher is waiting 92

NEW ORLEANS (LA.) -- DESCRIPTION AND TRAVEL

Horne, J. Breach of faith 976.3

NEW ORLEANS (LA.) -- GRAPHIC NOVELS

Neufeld, J. A.D. 976.3

NEW ORLEANS (LA.) -- HISTORY -- 20TH CENTURY

Krist, G. Empire of sin 976.3

NEW ORLEANS (LA.) -- POLITICS AND GOVERNMENT

Landrieu, M. In the shadow of statues 305.8

NEW ORLEANS (LA.) -- RACE RELATIONS

Rasmussen, D. American uprising 976.3

NEW ORLEANS (LA.) -- SOCIAL CONDITIONS -- 20TH CENTURY

Krist, G. Empire of sin 976.3

NEW ORLEANS (LA.) -- SOCIAL LIFE AND CUSTOMS

Besh, J. My New Orleans 641.59

NEW ORLEANS (LA.), BATTLE OF, 1815

Yaeger, D. Andrew Jackson and the miracle of New Orleans 973.5

New Oxford American dictionary. 423

The **New** Oxford book of Irish verse. 821

The **New** Oxford book of literary anecdotes. 828

The **new** Oxford book of war poetry. 808.81

The **new** Partridge dictionary of slang and unconventional English. 427

New poems. Rilke, R. M. 831

The **new** Portuguese table. Leite, D. 641.5

NEW PRODUCT DEVELOPMENT *See* New products

NEW PRODUCTS

Duffy, S. Launch! 658.1

Kolko, J. Well-designed 658.5

NEW PRODUCTS

See also Commercial products; Industrial research; Marketing

NEW PRODUCTS -- MORAL AND ETHICAL ASPECTS

Wachter-Boettcher, S. Technically wrong 303.483

The **new** religious intolerance. Nussbaum, M. C. 201

The **new** retirement. Cullinane, J. 646.7

The **new** rules of the roost. Litt, R. 636.5

The **new** rum. Bauer, B. T. 641.2

New selected poems. Levine, P. 811

A **new** selected poems. Kinnell, G. 811

The **new** sewing essentials. 646.2

The **new** solar system. Daniels, P. 523.2

The **New** Southern Living Garden Book. 635.9

The **new** Stokes field guide to birds. Stokes, D. 598

The **new** Stokes field guide to birds. Stokes, D. 598

The **new** terrarium. Martin, T. 635.9

NEW THOUGHT

James, W. The varieties of religious experience 210

The **new** time travelers. Toomey, D. M. 530.1

The **new** tsar. Myers, S. L. 92

A **New** Turn in the South. Acheson, H. 641.59

New vegetarian [series]

Hart, A. Good veg 641.5

The **new** vegetarian cooking for everyone. Madison, D. 641.5

A **new** way to bake. 641.815

NEW WORDS

Metcalf, A. A. Predicting new words 420

NEW WORDS

See also Vocabulary

New World kitchen. 641.59

New world, inc. Butman, J. 970.017

NEW YEAR

See also Holidays

NEW YORK (N.Y.)

Christgau, R. Going Into the City 92

Clegg, B. Ninety days 362.29

Gooch, B. Smash Cut 92

Harmon, K. You are here NYC 912.747

Highbrow, Lowbrow, Brilliant, Despicable 051

Invisible City 779

Martin, W. Primates of Park Avenue 974.7

Stanton, B. Humans of New York 974.7

Stanton, B. Humans of New York: stories 974.7

Winder, E. Pain, Parties, Work 811

NEW YORK (N.Y.) -- BIOGRAPHY

Stanton, B. Humans of New York: stories 974.7

NONFICTION, CREATIVE *See* Creative nonfiction

Nong's Thai kitchen. Greeley, A. **641.595**

NONGRADED SCHOOLS

See also Ability grouping in education; Education -- Experimental methods; Schools

NONINDIGENOUS PESTS

Hamilton, G. Super species **578.6**

NONINDIGENOUS PESTS

See also Biological invasions; Pests

NONLINGUISTIC COMMUNICATION *See* Nonverbal communication

NONPRESCRIPTION DRUGS

PDR for nonprescription drugs **615**

NONPRESCRIPTION DRUGS

See also Drugs

NONPROFIT ORGANIZATIONS

Smith, G. S. Cost control for nonprofits in crisis **025.1**

NONPROFIT ORGANIZATIONS

See also Associations

NONPROFIT ORGANIZATIONS -- COST CONTROL

Smith, G. S. Cost control for nonprofits in crisis **025.1**

NONPROFIT ORGANIZATIONS -- COST EFFECTIVE- NESS

Smith, G. S. Cost control for nonprofits in crisis **025.1**

NONPROFIT ORGANIZATIONS -- MANAGEMENT -- DECISION MAKING

Smith, G. S. Cost control for nonprofits in crisis **025.1**

NONPROFIT ORGANIZATIONS -- UNITED STATES -- FINANCE

Smith, G. S. Cost control for nonprofits in crisis **025.1**

Campbell, T. C. The China study   613.2

Davis, B. Becoming vegan   613.2

Duyff, R. L. American Dietetic Association complete food and nutrition guide   613.2

The family cooks   641.3

Flanagan, S. Run fast, eat slow   641.5

Gibney, M. Something to chew on   616.02

Hartwig, M. Food Freedom Forever   613.2

Hyman, M. Food   613.2

Kass, S. Eat a little better   641.3

Le, S. One hundred million years of food   641.3

Mercola, J. M. Effortless healing   613.2

Morris, J. Superfood Kitchen   641.5

Mullen, S. Real food heals   641.563

Nesheim, M. Why calories count   613.2

Olmsted, L. Real food/fake food   641.3

Parker, L. The Louise Parker Method   613.25

Price, C. Vitamania   612.3

Robinson, J. Eating on the wild side   306.4

Sacks, S. What the fork are you eating?   641.3

Schatzker, M. The Dorito effect   641.3

Taubes, G. The case against sugar   613.2

Wolf, R. Wired to eat   613.28

NUTRITION
See also Health; Physiology; Therapeutics

NUTRITION -- ECONOMIC ASPECTS -- UNITED STATES
Moss, M. Salt, sugar, fat   613.2

NUTRITION -- POPULAR WORKS
Carroll, A. The bad food bible   613.2

Masley, S. The better brain solution   612.82

Olmsted, L. Real food/fake food   641.3

Smith, M. The Whole Smiths good food cookbook   641.5

The whole30   613.2

The whole30 fast & easy   641.563

NUTRITION -- TABLES
Netzer, C. T. The complete book of food counts   613.2

NUTRITION -- UNITED STATES -- PSYCHOLOGICAL ASPECTS
Price, C. Vitamania   612.3

NUTRITION POLICY -- HISTORY -- 20TH CENTURY
Collingham, L. The taste of war   940.53

NUTRITION POLICY -- UNTIED STATES
Bittman, M. A bone to pick   338.1

Nutrition Stripped. Hill, M.   641.302

NUTRITIONAL SUPPLEMENTS See Dietary supplements

NUTRITIONALLY INDUCED DISEASES
Campbell, T. C. The China study   613.2

NUTRITIONALLY INDUCED DISEASES -- POPULAR WORKS
Taubes, G. The case against sugar   613.2

Nutritious delicious.   641.3

NUTS
See also Food; Seeds

Nutt, Amy Ellis

(jt. auth) Jensen, F. E. The teenage brain   612.6

Becoming Nicole   306.76

Nuttall, A. D.

Shakespeare the thinker   822.3

Nutter, Tommy, 1943-1992

About

Richardson, L. House of Nutter   92

Nyad, Diana

About

Nyad, D. Find a way   92

Nyberg, Amanda Jean

(jt. auth) Arkison, C. Sunday morning quilts   746.46

No scrap left behind   746.46

Nye, Bill, 1955-

Everything all at once   153.4

Undeniable   576.8

Nye, Naomi Shihab

You & yours: poems   811

O

O Jerusalem! Collins, L.   956.94

O'Brady, Tara

Seven spoons   641.597

O'Brian, Patrick

About

King, D. Patrick O'Brian   823

O'Brien, David M.

Storm center   347

O'Brien, Edna

James Joyce   823

About

O'Brien, E. Country Girl   92

Country Girl   92

O'Brien, Geoffrey

Bartlett's familiar quotations   808.88

O'Brien, Jack

About

Swidey, N. The assist   796.323

O'Brien, J. Jack be nimble   92

O'Brien, Keith

Catching the Sky   796.94

Fly girls   920

O'Brien, Michael

Mrs. Adams in winter   940.2

O'Brien, Patricia

Goodman, E. I know just what you mean   158.2

O'Brien, Timothy L.

TrumpNation   92

O'Clair, Robert

Ramazani, J. The Norton anthology of modern and contemporary poetry   821

O'Connell, Mark

To be a machine   306.461

O'Connell, Robert L.

The ghosts of Cannae   937

O'Conner, Patricia T.

Woe is I   428

O'Connor, Anne-Marie

Brown, D. J. The Boys in the Boat   797.12
Schaap, J. Triumph   92
OLYMPIC GAMES, 1968 (MEXICO CITY, MEX.)
Hoffer, R. Something in the air   796.4
OLYMPIC GAMES, 2000 (SYDNEY, AUSTRALIA)
Mullen, P. H. Gold in the water   797.2
OLYMPIC GAMES, 2012 (LONDON, ENGLAND)
   See also Olympic games
OLYMPICS *See* Olympic games
OLYMPICS -- HISTORY -- 20TH CENTURY
Legler, C. Godspeed   92
OLYMPICS, SPECIAL *See* Special Olympics
Omar, Qais Akbar
About
Omar, Q. A. A fort of nine towers   958.104
Omdahl, Kristin
The finer edge   746.43
Omeros. Walcott, D.   811
The **omnivore's** dilemma. Pollan, M.   394.1
Omrani, Bijan
Caesar's footprints   936.4
On a farther shore. Souder, W.   92
On architecture. Huxtable, A. L.   724
On Augustine. Williams, R.   92
On Becoming a Mother. McConville, B.   306.874
On becoming a novelist. Gardner, J.   808.3
On becoming baby wise. Ezzo, G.   649
On being human. Fromm, E.   150.19
On children and death. Kubler-Ross, E.   155.9
On Conan Doyle; or, The whole art of storytelling. Dirda, M.   823
On death and dying. Kubler-Ross, E.   155.9
On desire. Irvine, W. B.   128
On edge. Petersen, A.   616.85
On grand strategy. Gaddis, J. L.   355.4
On Hinduism. Doniger, W.   294.5
On His Own Terms. Smith, R. N.   92
On immunity. Biss, E.   616.07
On living. Egan, K.   170.44
On monsters. Asma, S. T.   398.2
On my country and the world. Gorbachev, M.   947.085
On my own. Rehm, D.   92
On paper. Basbanes, N. A.   676
On politics. Ryan, A.   320.01
On Saudi Arabia. House, K. E.   953.8
On second thought. Herbert, W.   153.4
On the backroad to heaven. Kraybill, D. B.   289.7
On the brink. Paulson, H. M.   330.9
On the burning edge. Dickman, K.   363.37
On the bus with Rosa Parks. Dove, R.   811
On the courthouse lawn. Ifill, S. A.   364.1
On the edge. Koch, K.   811
On the eve. Wasserstein, B.   305.892
On the Ganges. Black, G.   954.1
On the good life. Cicero, M. T.   878
On the Irish waterfront. Fisher, J. T.   331.7
On the law of nations. Moynihan, D. P.   327

On the line. Ripert, E.   647
On the Map. Garfield, S.   912
On the move. Sacks, O.   92
On the natural history of destruction. Sebald, W. G.   838
On the nature of things: De rerum natura. Lucretius Carus, T.   187
On the origin of species. Darwin, C.   576.8
On the origin of stories. Boyd, B.   809
On the rim of the Caribbean. Pressly, P. M.   975.8
On the road & off the record with Leonard Bernstein. Harmon, C.   92
On the road with Charles Kuralt. Kuralt, C.   973.92
On the road with Janis Joplin. Cooke, J. B.   92
On the shoulders of giants. Abdul-Jabbar, K.   92
On the side. Smith, E.   641.81
On the spectrum of possible deaths. Perillo, L.   811
On the surface of things. Frankel, F.   530.4
On the trail. Chamberlin, S.   796.51
ON THE WATERFRONT (MOTION PICTURE)
Fisher, J. T. On the Irish waterfront   331.7
On this date. Cannon, C. M.   973
On top of the world. Lutnick, H.   332.6
On truth. Blackburn, S.   121
On tyranny. Snyder, T. D.   321.9
On ugliness.   111
On war. Clausewitz, C. v.   355
On wings of eagles. Follett, K.   955
On writing. King, S.   813
On Your Case. Green, L.   344
Onassis, Jacqueline Kennedy, 1929-1994
About
Bowles, H. Jacqueline Kennedy   92
Hill, C. Five days in November   973.922
Hill, C. Mrs. Kennedy and me   973.922
Jacqueline Kennedy   973.922
Kaplan, A. Dreaming in French   944
Leaming, B. Jacqueline Bouvier Kennedy Onassis   92
Leaming, B. Mrs. Kennedy   973.922
McKeon, K. Jackie's girl   92
Taraborrelli, J. R. Jackie, Janet & Lee   920
Once in a great city. Maraniss, D.   977.4
Once upon a car. Vlasic, B.   338.4
Once upon a country. David, A.   92
Once upon a revolution. Cambanis, T.   962.05
Once upon a time. Bell, I.   92
Once Upon a Time in Russia. Mezrich, B.   330
Once we were sisters. Kohler, S.   92
ONCOLOGISTS -- JERUSALEM -- BIOGRAPHY
Waldman, E. This narrow space   616.99
ONCOLOGISTS -- UNITED STATES -- BIOGRAPHY
DeVita-Raeburn, E. The death of cancer   92
Ross, T. A cancer in the family   616.99
Ondra, Nancy J.
Grasses   635.9
The **one.** Smith, R. J.   92
ONE ACT PLAYS
The Best American short plays   812

PHYSICAL FITNESS FOR WOMEN
Dawn, K. Tone it up   **613.7**
Pagano, J. Strength training exercises for women   **613.7**
PHYSICAL GEOGRAPHY
Oxford Atlas of the world   **912**
PHYSICAL GEOGRAPHY
See also Geography; Geology
PHYSICAL GEOGRAPHY -- YELLOWSTONE NATIONAL PARK -- MAPS
Atlas of Yellowstone   **912.09**
PHYSICAL SCIENCES
Ball, P. Patterns in nature   **500.2**
Miodownik, M. Stuff matters   **620.1**
PHYSICAL SCIENCES
See also Science
PHYSICAL STAMINA *See* Physical fitness
PHYSICAL THERAPY
See also Therapeutics
PHYSICAL TRAINING *See* Physical education
PHYSICIAN AND PATIENT
Berger, Z. Talking to your doctor   **610.69**
Brokaw, T. A Lucky Life Interrupted   **92**
Mangalik, A. Dealing with doctors, denial, and death **616.044**
Roth, A. J. Managing prostate cancer   **616.99**
PHYSICIAN'S ROLE -- PERSONAL NARRATIVES
Reilly, B. One doctor   **610.69**
PHYSICIAN-ASSISTED SUICIDE *See* Assisted suicide
PHYSICIAN-NURSE RELATIONS -- UNITED STATES -- PERSONAL NARRATIVES
The nurses   **362.17**
Robbins, A. The nurses   **362.17**
PHYSICIAN-NURSE RELATIONS -- UNITED STATES -- POPULAR WORKS
The nurses   **362.17**
Robbins, A. The nurses   **362.17**
PHYSICIAN-PATIENT RELATIONS
Epstein, R. Attending   **610.695**
Kore   **610**
Volandes, A. E. The conversation   **616.02**
Wachter, R. The digital doctor   **610.28**
PHYSICIAN-PATIENT RELATIONS -- PERSONAL NARRATIVES
Montross, C. Falling into the fire   **616.89**
Ofri, D. What doctors feel   **610.69**
Reilly, B. One doctor   **610.69**
PHYSICIAN-PATIENT RELATIONSHIP
Berger, Z. Talking to your doctor   **610.69**
Fischer-Wright, H. Back to balance   **610.69**
Groopman, J. E. The anatomy of hope   **616**
Groopman, J. E. Your medical mind   **610**
Mangalik, A. Dealing with doctors, denial, and death **616.044**
Montross, C. Falling into the fire   **616.89**
Ofri, D. What doctors feel   **610.69**
Reilly, B. One doctor   **610.69**
Wachter, R. The digital doctor   **610.28**
PHYSICIANS
Boyle, K. Arc of justice   **345**

Brock, P. Charlatan   **92**
Callow, P. Chekhov, the hidden ground   **891.7**
Casey, M. Che's afterlife   **980**
Chekhov, A. P. Anton Chekhov's life and thought   **92**
Groopman, J. E. How doctors think   **610**
Halberstam, D. The children   **323.1**
Hanna-Attisha, M. What the eyes don't see   **92**
Hollis, L. London rising   **942**
Jarrell, R. No other book   **809**
Jauhar, S. Doctored   **92**
Johnson, S. The ghost map   **614.5**
Kean, S. The tale of the dueling neurosurgeons   **617.4**
Kluger, J. Splendid solution: Jonas Salk and the conquest of polio   **92**
Lattin, D. The Harvard Psychedelic Club   **920**
Leibowitz, H. A. Something urgent I have to say to you: the life and works of William Carlos Williams   **92**
Malcolm, J. Reading Chekhov   **891.7**
Marion, R. Genetic rounds   **92**
McCullough, D. G. The path between the seas   **972.87**
McGoogan, K. Race to the Polar Sea   **92**
Nuland, S. B. The doctors' plague   **92**
Ofri, D. What doctors feel   **610.69**
Orbinski, J. An imperfect offering   **610**
Sacks, O. W. Uncle Tungsten   **616.8**
Sagan, C. Broca's brain   **500**
Starr, D. The killer of little shepherds   **364.152**
Sweet, V. God's hotel   **610.92**
Tweedy, D. Black Man in a White Coat   **92**
Von Tunzelmann, A. Red heat   **972.9**
Webster, C. Paracelsus   **92**
PHYSICIANS
See also Medical personnel
PHYSICIANS -- ATTITUDES
Teresi, D. The undead   **610**
PHYSICIANS -- BIOGRAPHY
Aptowicz, C. O. Dr. Mutter's Marvels   **92**
Bartolo, P. Tears of salt   **92**
Franscell, R. Morgue   **616.07**
Kershaw, A. Avenue of spies   **940.53**
Manheimer, E. Twelve patients   **362.11**
Newman, K. Healing children   **92**
Waldman, E. This narrow space   **616.99**
PHYSICIANS -- COLOMBIA -- BIOGRAPHY
Abad, H. Oblivion   **868**
PHYSICIANS -- DIRECTORIES
See also Directories
PHYSICIANS -- FRANCE -- PARIS -- BIOGRAPHY
Kershaw, A. Avenue of spies   **940.53**
PHYSICIANS -- GREAT BRITAIN -- BIOGRAPHY
Sims, M. Arthur and Sherlock   **823.8**
PHYSICIANS -- HISTORY
Frank, L. The pleasure shock   **92**
PHYSICIANS -- HISTORY -- POPULAR WORKS
Kean, S. The tale of the dueling neurosurgeons   **617.4**
PHYSICIANS -- ITALY -- LAMPEDUSA -- BIOGRAPHY
Bartolo, P. Tears of salt   **92**

See also Antiquities; Archeology; Human beings

PREHISTORIC PEOPLES -- FOOD

Le, S. One hundred million years of food   **641.3**

Wrangham, R. W. Catching fire   **641.3**

PREHISTORIC PEOPLES -- NORTH AMERICA

Childs, C. Atlas of a lost world   **551.7**

PREHISTORIC PEOPLES -- NUTRITION

Fong, H. Nom nom paleo   **641.5**

Fong, H. Ready or not!   **641.563**

Mullen, S. Real food heals   **641.563**

Well fed   **641.5**

PREHISTORY *See* Archeology; Fossil hominids; Prehistoric peoples

Prejean, Helen

The death of innocents   **364.66**

PREJUDICE *See* Prejudices

PREJUDICE-MOTIVATED CRIMES *See* Hate crimes

PREJUDICES

Goldhagen, D. J. Worse than war   **364.1**

Griffin, J. H. Black like me   **305.8**

Rosling, H. Factfulness   **155.9**

PREJUDICES

See also Attitude (Psychology); Emotions; Interpersonal relations

Prelude to bruise. Jones, S.   **811**

PREMATURE BURIAL

See also Burial

PREMATURE INFANTS

French, T. Juniper   **618.92**

Linden, D. W. Preemies   **618.92**

PREMATURE INFANTS -- CARE

Linden, D. W. Preemies   **618.92**

PREMATURE INFANTS -- HOSPITAL CARE

Understanding the NICU   **618.92**

PREMENSTRUAL SYNDROME

See also Menstruation; Syndromes

The **prenatal** bombshell. Ilse, S.   **618.3**

PRENATAL CARE

Ilse, S. The prenatal bombshell   **618.3**

Mayo Clinic guide to a healthy pregnancy   **618.2**

PRENATAL CARE

See also Pregnancy

PRENATAL DIAGNOSIS

See also Diagnosis

PRENATAL DIAGNOSIS -- PSYCHOLOGY -- PERSONAL NARRATIVES

Ilse, S. The prenatal bombshell   **618.3**

Prentice, Rachel

(jt. auth) Keene, N. Your Child in the Hospital   **362.1**

PREPARATION GUIDES FOR EXAMINATIONS *See* Examinations -- Study guides

PREPARATORY SCHOOL STUDENTS -- NEW YORK (STATE) -- NEW YORK -- BIOGRAPHY

Weiss, P. You all grow up and leave me   **92**

PREPAREDNESS -- UNITED STATES

Koppel, T. Lights out   **363.11**

Preparing for baby. Choudhri, N. K.   **332.024**

PREPPIES -- NEW YORK (STATE) -- NEW YORK -- BIOGRAPHY

Weiss, P. You all grow up and leave me   **92**

PRESBYTERIAN CHURCH -- SERMONS

See also Sermons

PRESCHOOL CHILDREN *See* Children

Preschool clues. Santomero, A. C.   **305.233**

PRESCHOOL EDUCATION

Christakis, E. The Importance of Being Little   **372.21**

Vanover, S. T. Finding Quality Early Childcare   **362.71**

PRESCHOOL EDUCATION

See also Education

Prescott, Matthew

Food is the solution   **613.2**

PRESCRIPTION DRUG ABUSE *See* Medication abuse

Prescription for the people. Quigley, F.   **338.4**

PRESCRIPTION PRICING -- UNITED STATES

Quigley, F. Prescription for the people   **338.4**

Presence. Cuddy, A.   **158.1**

Present at the creation. Aczel, A. D.   **539.7**

Present Shock. Rushkoff, D.   **303.48**

Presentation zen. Reynolds, G.

PRESENTISM (PHILOSOPHY)

The order of time   **530.11**

PRESENTS *See* Gifts

PRESERVATION OF BIODIVERSITY *See* Biodiversity conservation

PRESERVATION OF BOTANICAL SPECIMENS *See* Plants -- Collection and preservation

PRESERVATION OF FOOD *See* Food -- Preservation

PRESERVATION OF FORESTS *See* Forest conservation

PRESERVATION OF HISTORICAL RECORDS *See* Archives

PRESERVATION OF LIBRARY RESOURCES *See* Library resources -- Conservation and restoration

PRESERVATION OF NATURAL RESOURCES *See* Conservation of natural resources

PRESERVATION OF NATURAL SCENERY *See* Landscape protection; Natural monuments; Nature conservation

PRESERVATION OF SPECIMENS *See* Taxidermy

PRESERVATION OF WILDLIFE *See* Wildlife conservation

PRESERVATION OF ZOOLOGICAL SPECIMENS *See* Zoological specimens -- Collection and preservation

PRESERVATIONISM (HISTORIC PRESERVATION) *See* Historic preservation

PRESERVING *See* Canning and preserving

The **presidency** of Abraham Lincoln. Paludan, P. S.   **973.7**

The **President** and the Apprentice. Gellman, I. F.   **973.921**

The **President** and the assassin. Miller, S.   **973.8**

President Carter. Eizenstat, S.   **973.926**

The **president** is a sick man. Algeo, M.   **973.8**

President McKinley. Merry, R. W.   **92**

The **president's** book of secrets. Priess, D.   **327.127**

PRESIDENTIAL ADVISERS

Dallek, R. Nixon and Kissinger   **92**

Feldman, N. Scorpions   **920**

Greenspan, A. The age of turbulence   **92**

PRESIDENTS -- ARAB COUNTRIES -- HISTORY

PRESIDENTS -- ATTITUDES
PRESIDENTS -- CHINA
**PRESIDENTS -- DWELLINGS -- UNITED STATES -- PIC-
TORIAL WORKS**
**PRESIDENTS -- FAMILY -- UNITED STATES -- BIOGRA-
PHY**
**PRESIDENTS -- FAMILY RELATIONSHIPS -- UNITED
STATES -- ANECDOTES**
**PRESIDENTS -- FAMILY RELATIONSHIPS -- UNITED
STATES -- HISTORY**
PRESIDENTS -- FRANCE -- BIOGRAPHY
**PRESIDENTS -- LEGAL STATUS, LAWS, ETC. -- UNIT-
ED STATES**
PRESIDENTS -- LIBERIA -- BIOGRAPHY
**PRESIDENTS -- MEDICAL CARE -- UNITED STATES --
HISTORY -- 19TH CENTURY**
PRESIDENTS -- MIDDLE EAST -- HISTORY
PRESIDENTS -- POWERS *See* Executive power
PRESIDENTS -- PRESS COVERAGE -- UNITED STATES
PRESIDENTS -- PROTECTION -- UNITED STATES
PRESIDENTS -- PSYCHOLOGY
**PRESIDENTS -- RELATIONS WITH AFRICAN AMERI-
CANS -- HISTORY -- SOURCES**
**PRESIDENTS -- RUSSIA (FEDERATION) -- BIOGRA-
PHY**
PRESIDENTS -- SOUTH AFRICA
PRESIDENTS -- SOUTH AFRICA -- BIOGRAPHY
PRESIDENTS -- TAIWAN
**PRESIDENTS -- TRAVEL -- UNITED STATES -- HISTO-
RY -- 18TH CENTURY**
PRESIDENTS -- UNITED STATES

and representation

PROPOSAL WRITING FOR GRANTS -- UNITED STATES

MacKellar, P. H. Writing successful technology grant proposals **025.1**

PROPOSAL WRITING FOR GRANTS -- UNITED STATES -- HANDBOOKS, MANUALS, ETC

Gerding, S. K. Winning grants **025.1**

PROPOSAL WRITING IN LIBRARY SCIENCE -- UNITED STATES

MacKellar, P. H. Writing successful technology grant proposals **025.1**

PROPOSAL WRITING IN LIBRARY SCIENCE -- UNITED STATES -- CASE STUDIES

Gerding, S. K. Winning grants **025.1**

PROPOSAL WRITING IN LIBRARY SCIENCE -- UNITED STATES -- HANDBOOKS, MANUALS, ETC

Gerding, S. K. Winning grants **025.1**

PROPRIETARY RIGHTS See Intellectual property

ProQuest LLC

(comp) ProQuest Statistical Abstract of the United States **300**

ProQuest Statistical Abstract of the United States. **300**

PROSE LITERATURE -- AUTHORSHIP

Kidder, T. Good prose **808.02**

PROSE LITERATURE, AMERICAN See American prose literature

PROSE POETRY

Grass, G. Of All That Ends **838**

Reed, J. P. Indecency **811**

PROSE POETRY

See also Poetry

Prose, Francine

Reading like a writer **808**

What to read and why **028.9**

Anne Frank **839.3**

Caravaggio **92**

PROSECUTION -- CORRUPT PRACTICES

Cohan, W. D. The price of silence **364.15**

PROSECUTION -- DECISION MAKING

Eisinger, J. The chickenshit club **364.168**

PROSECUTION -- UNITED STATES

Eisinger, J. The chickenshit club **364.168**

Garrett, B. L. Too big to jail **345.73**

Prosek, Jen

Raising Can-Do Kids **649.7**

PROSPECTING

See also Gold mines and mining; Mines and mineral resources; Silver mines and mining

Prosper, David

(jt. auth) White, V. The Total Skywatcher's Manual **523.8**

PROSPERITY (PA.) -- SOCIAL CONDITIONS

Griswold, E. Amity and prosperity **363.73**

PROSTATE -- CANCER

Walsh, P. C. Dr. Patrick Walsh's guide to surviving prostate cancer **616.99**

PROSTATE -- CANCER -- PSYCHOLOGICAL ASPECTS

Roth, A. J. Managing prostate cancer **616.99**

PROSTATE -- CANCER -- UNITED STATES

Roth, A. J. Managing prostate cancer **616.99**

PROSTHESIS -- SOCIAL ASPECTS

O'Connell, M. To be a machine **306.461**

PROSTITUTES -- IRELAND -- DUBLIN -- BIOGRAPHY

Moran, R. Paid for **306.74**

PROSTITUTION

Abbott, K. Sin in the Second City **977.3**

Kolker, R. Lost Girls **364.152**

Krist, G. Empire of sin **976.3**

PROSTITUTION

See also Sexual ethics; Social problems; Women -- Social conditions

PROSTITUTION -- CALIFORNIA

Phelps, C. Runaway girl **362.74**

PROSTITUTION -- ILLINOIS -- CHICAGO

Abbott, K. Sin in the Second City **977.3**

PROSTITUTION -- IRELAND

Moran, R. Paid for **306.74**

Protecting America's health. Hilts, P. J. **353.9**

Protecting intellectual freedom in your public library. Pinnell-Stephens, J. **025.2**

PROTECTION AGAINST BURGLARY See Burglary protection

PROTECTION OF ANIMALS See Animal welfare

PROTECTION OF BIRDS See Birds -- Protection

PROTECTION OF CHILDREN See Child welfare

PROTECTION OF ENVIRONMENT See Environmental protection

PROTECTION OF NATURAL SCENERY See Landscape protection; Natural monuments; Nature conservation

PROTECTION OF PLANTS See Plant conservation

PROTECTION OF WILDLIFE See Wildlife conservation

PROTECTIVE CUSTODY

Rushdie, S. Joseph Anton **92**

Proteinaholic. Jacobson, H. **613.2**

PROTEINS

See also Biochemistry; Nutrition

PROTEINS IN HUMAN NUTRITION

Jacobson, H. Proteinaholic **613.2**

PROTEST MOVEMENTS

Hedges, C. Wages of rebellion **303.48**

Razsa, M. Bastards of Utopia **303.48**

Together we rise **305.42**

Vinen, R. 1968 **909.82**

PROTEST MOVEMENTS

See also Social movements

PROTEST MOVEMENTS -- SYRIA -- HISTORY -- 21ST CENTURY

Erlich, R. Inside Syria **956.91**

Pearlman, W. We crossed a bridge and it trembled **956.91**

PROTEST MOVEMENTS -- UNITED STATES -- HISTORY

Fraser, S. The age of acquiescence **973.91**

Young, R. Dissent **303.48**

PROTEST MOVEMENTS -- YEMEN (REPUBLIC) -- HIS-

Strunk, W. The elements of style **808**

RHETORIC

See also Language and languages

RHETORIC -- POLITICAL ASPECTS -- UNITED STATES -- HISTORY

Prothero, S. The American Bible **973**

Rhett & Link's book of mythicality. McLaughlin, R. **302.231**

RHEUMATISM

See also Diseases

RHINOCEROS

Orenstein, R. Ivory, horn and blood **333.95**

RHINOCEROS HORN INDUSTRY -- CORRUPT PRACTICES

Orenstein, R. Ivory, horn and blood **333.95**

Rhinoceros, and other plays. Ionesco, E. **842**

RHINOCEROSES -- EFFECT OF POACHING ON

Orenstein, R. Ivory, horn and blood **333.95**

RHODE ISLAND -- HISTORY

Warren, J. A. God, war, and providence **974.502**

Rhoden, William C.

$40 million slaves **796**

Rhodes, Benjamin J., 1977-

The world as it is **973.932**

Rhodes, Mike

(jt. auth) Todd, B. Ultimate guide to Google AdWords **659.144**

Rhodes, Richard

Energy **333.79**

Hedy's folly **92**

Hell and Good Company **946.081**

John James Audubon **92**

Arsenals of folly **355**

Rhodes, William Reginald

About

Rhodes, W. R. Banker to the world **92**

RHYME

See also Poetics; Versification

RHYMES *See* Limericks; Nonsense verses; Nursery rhymes; Poetry -- Collections

RHYTHM

See also Aesthetics; Poetics

RHYTHM AND BLUES MUSIC

See also Popular music

Rhythm of the wild. Heacox, K. **979.8**

Rhythms of life. Foster, R. G. **571.7**

Riasanovsky, Nicholas V.

A history of Russia **947**

RIBBON WORK

A-z of Ribbon Embroidery **746.44**

RIBBON WORK

See also Handicraft

Ribowsky, Mark

Dreams to remember **92**

Hank **92**

The last cowboy **92**

Ricardo, David, 1772-1823

About

Heilbroner, R. L. The worldly philosophers **330.1**

Ricca, Brad

Mrs. Sherlock Holmes **92**

Super boys **741.5**

Ricciardi, Holly

(jt. auth) Harris, M. Magpie **641.86**

Rice, Andrew

The teeth may smile but the heart does not forget **967.6**

Rice, Anne, 1941-

About

Rice, A. Called out of darkness **92**

Rice, Condoleezza, 1954-

Democracy **321.8**

No higher honor

Political risk **658.15**

Rice, noodle, fish. Goulding, M. **394.12**

Rice, Stanley A.

Encyclopedia of biodiversity **578.7**

RICH

Freeland, C. Plutocrats **305.5**

Oppenheimer, J. The Kardashians **920**

Tough, P. How children succeed **372.21**

RICH

See also Social classes

RICH -- UNITED STATES

Callahan, D. The givers **361.7**

Mayer, J. Dark money **320.52**

Wills, S. Black Fortunes **973.049**

RICH PEOPLE *See* Rich

RICH PEOPLE -- BIOGRAPHY

Buck, J. J. The price of illusion **92**

RICH PEOPLE -- CONDUCT OF LIFE

Freeland, C. Plutocrats **305.5**

RICH PEOPLE -- ENGLAND -- BIOGRAPHY

Livingstone, N. The mistresses of Cliveden **942**

RICH PEOPLE -- FRANCE -- HISTORY

Lovell, M. S. The Riviera set **944.9**

RICH PEOPLE -- UNITED STATES

Callahan, D. The givers **361.7**

The divide **303.3**

RICH PERSONS *See* Rich

Rich, Adrienne

(ed) Rukeyser, M. Selected poems **811**

Rich, Adrienne, 1929-2012

Essential essays **811**

Collected poems **811.54**

The school among the ruins: poems, 2000-2004 **811**

Rich, Mari

World authors, 2000-2005 **920.003**

The Richard Ellmann lectures in modern literature [series]

Eco, U. Confessions of a young novelist **808.3**

Richard III. Skidmore, C. **92**

Richard III. Horspool, D. **92**

Richard III, King of England, 1452-1485

About

Horspool, D. Richard III **92**

Shah, Saira
The storyteller's daughter   958.1

Shah, Sonia
The fever   614.5
Pandemic   362.1
The body hunters   362.1
The fever   614.5

Shah, Tahir
The Caliph's house   964
In search of King Solomon's mines   963

Shahidi, Afshin
Prince   92

Shahnameh. Firdawsi   891

SHAHNAMEH (EPIC POEM)
Jubber, N. Drinking arak off an ayatollah's beard   915

Shake Shack. Garutti, R.   641.5

SHAKE SHACK (RESTAURANT CHAIN)
Garutti, R. Shake Shack   641.5

Shake the devil off. Brown, E.   364.152
Shakespeare. Bryson, B.   822.3
Shakespeare after all. Garber, M.   822.3

SHAKESPEARE AND COMPANY
The letters of Sylvia Beach   92

Shakespeare and modern culture. Garber, M.   822.3
The **Shakespeare** riots. Cliff, N.   974.4
Shakespeare the thinker. Nuttall, A. D.   822.3
The **Shakespeare** thefts. Rasmussen, E.   822.3
The **Shakespeare** wars. Rosenbaum, R.   822.3
Shakespeare's first folio. Smith, E.   822.33
Shakespeare's kings. Norwich, J. J.   822.3
Shakespeare's language. Kermode, F.   822.3
Shakespeare's personalities [series]
Bloom, H. Lear   822.33
Shakespeare's restless world. MacGregor, N.   942.055

Shakespeare, Nicholas
Bruce Chatwin   823
Under the sun   92

Shakespeare, Nicholas, 1957-
(ed) Under the sun   92

Shakespeare, William, 1564-1616
The complete works   822.3

About
Baker, W. The facts on file companion to Shakespeare   822.3
Bate, J. Soul of the age   822.3
Bloom, H. Lear   822.33
Bloom, H. Hamlet: poem unlimited   822.3
Bloom, H. Shakespeare: the invention of the human   822.3
Bloom, H. The Western canon   809
Boyce, C. Critical companion to William Shakespeare   822.3
Bryson, B. Shakespeare   822.3
Butler, C. The practical Shakespeare   822.3
Cliff, N. The Shakespeare riots   974.4
Collins, P. The book of William   822.3
Dromgoole, D. Hamlet Globe to globe   792.9
Falk, D. The Science of Shakespeare   822.3
Garber, M. Shakespeare after all   822.3
Garber, M. Shakespeare and modern culture   822.3

Greenblatt, S. J. Will in the world   822.3
Greenblatt, S. Tyrant   822.33
The Greenwood companion to Shakespeare   822.3
Heylin, C. So long as men can breathe   822.3
Keenan, J. Sex With Shakespeare   306.7
Kenji Yoshino A thousand times more fair   822.3
Kermode, F. Shakespeare's language   822.3
Lamb, C. Tales from Shakespeare   822.3
Living with Shakespeare   822.3
MacGregor, N. Shakespeare's restless world   942.055
Mays, A. E. The millionaire and the bard   822.3
Norwich, J. J. Shakespeare's kings   822.3
Nuttall, A. D. Shakespeare the thinker   822.3
The Oxford companion to Shakespeare   822.3
Rasmussen, E. The Shakespeare thefts   822.3
Rosenbaum, R. The Shakespeare wars   822.3
Scarry, E. Naming thy name   821.3
Shapiro, J. Contested Will   822.3
Shapiro, J. A year in the life of William Shakespeare, 1599   822.3
Shapiro, J. The year of Lear   822.33
Smith, E. Shakespeare's first folio   822.33
Wells, S. W. Shakespeare: for all time   822.3
Wills, G. Verdi's Shakespeare   822.3

Shakespeare: for all time. Wells, S. W.   822.3
Shakespeare: the invention of the human. Bloom, H.   822.3

Shakur, Tupac

About
Dyson, M. E. Holler if you hear me: searching for Tupac Shakur   92

Shalaby, Carla
Troublemakers   371.93

SHALE GAS INDUSTRY
Raimi, D. The fracking debate   363.11
Wilber, T. Under the surface   333.8
Zuckerman, G. The frackers   338.2

SHALE GAS RESERVOIRS -- POPULAR WORKS
Prud'homme, A. Hydrofracking   622

Shaler's fish. Macdonald, H.   811

Shales, Tom
(jt. auth) Miller, J. A. Those guys have all the fun   791.45
Live from New York   791.45

Shall we play that one together? De Barros, P.   92
Shallcross. Wright, C. D.   811.54

SHAMANISM
See also Religions

SHAMANS
Black Elk Black Elk speaks   92

SHAME
Ronson, J. So you've been publicly shamed   152.4
Tanenbaum, L. I Am Not a Slut   305.23

SHAME
See also Emotions

SHAME -- SOCIAL ASPECTS
Scheff, S. Shame nation   302.34
Shame and wonder. Searcy, D.   814.54
Shame nation. Scheff, S.   302.34

SHERPA (NEPALESE PEOPLE)
Zuckerman, P. Buried in the sky   796.522

Sherr, Lynn
Sally Ride   92

Sherratt, Yvonne
Hitler's philosophers   193

Sherrod, Shirley, 1948-
About
Sherrod, S. The courage to hope   975.8

Sherwin, Martin J.
Bird, K. American Prometheus   92

Shesol, Jeff
Supreme power   347

Shestov, Lev, 1866-1938
About
Milosz, C. To begin where I am   891.8

Shetlar, David
(jt. auth) Cranshaw, W. Garden insects of North America **635**

Shetreat-Klein, Maya
The Dirt Cure   618.92

Shetterly, Caitlin
Modified   664

Shetterly, Margot Lee, 1969-
Hidden Figures   510.92

Shetterly, Susan Hand
Settled in the wild   508

Shevelow, Kathryn
For the love of animals   179

SHI'AH
Hazleton, L. After the prophet   297
Nasr, V. The Shia revival   297
The **Shia** revival. Nasr, V.   297

Shida, Hitomi
Japanese knitting stitch bible   746.432

Shields, Carol
Jane Austen   92

Shields, Charles J.
And so it goes: Kurt Vonnegut: a life   92

Shields, David
(ed) The Inevitable   814

Shields, David S.
(ed) American poetry: the seventeenth and eighteenth centuries   811

Shifflett C. M.
(jt. auth) Esty, M. L. Conquering Concussion   617.4

Shiffman, John
Wittman, R. Priceless   364.1
The **shift.** Brown, T.   616.02

Shih, Bryan
(ed) The Black Panthers   322.42

SHIITES
See also Islamic sects

Shiller, Robert J., 1946-
Irrational exuberance   332.63
Shiloh, 1862. Groom, W.   973.7

SHILOH, BATTLE OF, TENN., 1862
Groom, W. Shiloh, 1862   973.7

Shilon, Avi
Menachem Begin   956.940

Shilts, Randy
And the band played on   362.1

Shim, Jae K.
Accounting handbook   657

Shimoda, Naoko
Artfully embroidered   746.44
Shine. Hallowell, E. M.   658.3

Shing-Tung Yau
(jt. auth) Nadis, S. The shape of inner space   530.1
Shinto. Hardacre, H.   299.561

SHINTO
Eastern religions   200.9

SHINTO
See also Religions

SHINTO -- HISTORY
Hardacre, H. Shinto   299.561
Shiny objects. Roberts, J. A.   339.4

SHIP CAPTAINS
Blainey, G. Sea of dangers   92
Harris, J. W. The hanging of Thomas Jeremiah   92

SHIP CAPTAINS -- UNITED STATES -- BIOGRAPHY
Lineberry, C. Be free or die   92
Ship of ghosts. Hornfischer, J. D.   940.54

SHIP SALVAGE *See* Marine salvage

Shipler, David K.
Freedom of speech   323.44
The rights of the people   323

Shipp, Steve
Latin American and Caribbean artists of the modern era   920.003

SHIPPING
See also Transportation

SHIPPING -- UNITED STATES -- HISTORY -- 19TH CENTURY
Ujifusa, S. Barons of the sea   387.5

SHIPPING EXECUTIVES
Millard, C. The river of doubt   973.91
Renehan, E. J. Commodore   92

SHIPS -- HISTORY
Graham, I. Fifty ships that changed the course of history **387.2**

SHIPS -- SAFETY REGULATIONS
See also Maritime law; Safety regulations
The **shipwreck** hunter. Mearns, D. L.   910.452

SHIPWRECK VICTIMS
Wilson, P. Lusitania   910.4

SHIPWRECK VICTIMS -- NORTH ATLANTIC OCEAN -- ANECDOTES
Wilson, P. Lusitania   910.4

SHIPWRECKS
Beneath the seven seas   930.1
Chowdhury, B. The last dive   363.14
Junger, S. The perfect storm   910.4
Lord, W. A night to remember   910.4
Mearns, D. L. The shipwreck hunter   910.452
Peffer, R. Where divers dare   940.54

Stourton, James
  Kenneth Clark   **92**
Stout, Glenn
  Fenway 1912   **796.357**
Stout, Harry S.
  Upon the altar of the nation : a moral history of the American Civil War   **973.7**
Stout, Janis
  (ed) Cather, W. The selected letters of Willa Cather   **813**
Stover, Kaite Mediatore
  (jt. auth) Moyer, J. E. The readers' advisory handbook **025.5**
Stow, Dorrik A. V.
  Oceans: an illustrated reference   **551.46**
The **stowaway**. Shapiro, L. G.   **919.89**
STOWAWAYS -- ANTARCTICA -- BIOGRAPHY
  Shapiro, L. G. The stowaway   **919.89**
Stowe, Calvin Ellis, 1802-1886
  About
  Wilson, E. Patriotic gore   **810**
Stowe, Harriet Beecher, 1811-1896
  About
  Benfey, C. E. G. A summer of hummingbirds   **920**
  Reynolds, D. S. Mightier than the sword   **813**
  Wilson, E. Patriotic gore   **810**
Stowell, Lauren
  The american duchess guide to 18th century dressmaking **646**
Strachan, Hew
  The First World War   **940.3**
Strachey, James
  (tr) Freud, S. Civilization and its discontents   **150.19**
Straight. Blank, H.   **306.76**
Straight to Hell. Lefevre, J.   **332.1**
STRAIN (PSYCHOLOGY) *See* Stress (Psychology)
Stranahan, Susan Q.
  (jt. auth) Lyman, E. Fukushima   **363.17**
Strand, Jessica
  (ed) Upstairs at the Strand   **808.02**
Strand, Mark
  (ed) 100 great poems of the twentieth century   **821**
  (ed) The Making of a poem   **821**
  Collected poems   **811**
Strang, Dean A.
  Worse than the devil   **345**
Strange angel. Pendle, G.   **92**
The **strange** career of William Ellis. Jacoby, K.   **92**
Strange glory. Marsh, C.   **92**
Strange glow. Jorgensen, T. J.   **539.2**
The **strange** order of things. Damasio, A.   **612.022**
Strange stars. Heller, J.   **781.66**
A **strange** stirring. Coontz, S.   **305.42**
Stranger. Ramos, J.   **325.73**
The **stranger** beside me. Rule, A.   **92**
The **stranger** from paradise: a biography of William Blake. Bentley, G. E.   **821**
The **stranger** in the woods. Finkel, M.   **974.1**
Stranger to history. Taseer, A.   **915.6**
A **stranger's** mirror. Hacker, M.

Stranger, Tom
  About
  Elva, T. South of forgiveness   **362.883**
Strangers in their own land. Hochschild, A. R.   **320.52**
Strangers tend to tell me things. Dickinson, A.   **92**
Strangers: homosexual love in the nineteenth century. Robb, G.   **306.76**
Strassler, Robert B.
  (ed) Herodotus, c. 4. B. B. C. The landmark Herodotus **938**
  (ed) The Landmark Xenophon's Hellenika   **938**
STRATEGIC ALLIANCES
  Ryckman, P. Stiletto network   **331.4**
STRATEGIC CULTURE -- CHINA
  French, H. W. Everything under the heavens   **327.51**
STRATEGIC CULTURE -- UNITED STATES
  Bolger, D. P. Why We Lost   **956.704**
  Brooks, R. How everything became war and the military became everything   **355**
STRATEGIC DEFENSE INITIATIVE
  See also Military policy -- United States; Space warfare; United States -- Defenses
STRATEGIC MANAGEMENT *See* Strategic planning
STRATEGIC MATERIALS *See* Materials
STRATEGIC PLANNING
  Collins, J. C. Good to great   **658**
  Debaise, C. Start a successful business   **658.1**
  Duke, A. Thinking in bets   **658.4**
  Galloway, S. The four   **338.7**
  Goldfayn, A. The revenue growth habit   **658.15**
  Johnson, W. Disrupt yourself   **658.4**
  Matthews, J. R. Scorecards for results   **027.4**
  Peters, T. The excellence dividend   **658.4**
  Webb, A. The signals are talking   **658.4**
STRATEGIC PLANNING
  See also Planning
Strategic vision. Brzezinski, Z.   **327.1**
Strategize to win. Harris, C. A.   **650.1**
STRATEGY
  Beevor, A. The Battle of Arnhem   **940.54**
  Collingham, L. The taste of war   **940.53**
  D'Este, C. Warlord   **92**
  Hamilton, N. The mantle of command   **940.54**
  Overy, R. Why the Allies won   **940.53**
  Preston, D. A higher form of killing   **940.4**
  Symonds, C. L. World War II at sea   **940.545**
STRATEGY
  See also Military art and science; Naval art and science
STRATEGY -- HISTORY
  Clark, L. Blitzkrieg   **940.54**
  Gaddis, J. L. On grand strategy   **355.4**
STRATEGY -- HISTORY -- 20TH CENTURY
  Roberts, A. Masters and commanders   **940.54**
Stratemeyer, Edward, 1862-1930
  About
  Rehak, M. Girl sleuth   **813**
Strathern, Paul
  The artist, the philosopher, and the warrior   **920**

STREET TRAFFIC *See* City traffic; Traffic engineering

Street vegan. **641.5**

Street-fighting mathematics. Mahajan, S. **510**

A **streetcar** named desire. Williams, T. **812**

STREETS

> *See also* Cities and towns; Civil engineering; Transportation

STREETS -- CHINA -- SHANGHAI

Schmitz, R. Street of Eternal Happiness **951.132**

STREETS -- LIGHTING

> *See also* Lighting

Streever, Bill

Heat **551.41**

Cold **998**

Streicher, Lauren F., 1956-

The essential guide to hysterectomy **618.1**

Streiff, Fritz

The art of simple food **641.5**

Streisand, Barbra

About

Mann, W. J. Hello, gorgeous **92**

Streissguth, Michael

Johnny Cash **92**

Strength in stillness. Roth, B. **158.1**

Strength in what remains. Kidder, T. **92**

The **strength** switch. Waters, L. **306.874**

Strength to love. King, M. L. **252**

STRENGTH TRAINING *See* Weight lifting

Strength training exercises for women. Pagano, J. **613.7**

Strengths based marriage. Evans, J. **248.844**

STRESS (PHYSIOLOGY)

Benson, H. The relaxation response **155.9**

Gambaro, J. The truth about carpal tunnel syndrome **616.85**

Goldman, B. Brain fitness **153.1**

STRESS (PHYSIOLOGY)

> *See also* Adaptation (Biology); Physiology

STRESS (PSYCHOLOGY)

Benson, H. The relaxation response **155.9**

Taylor, S. E. The tending instinct **304.5**

Van der Kolk, B. A. The body keeps the score **616.85**

STRESS (PSYCHOLOGY)

> *See also* Mental health; Psychology

STRESS DISORDERS, POST-TRAUMATIC -- THERAPY

Van der Kolk, B. A. The body keeps the score **616.85**

STRESS MANAGEMENT

Dell'Antonia, K. J. How to be a happier parent **306.874**

Goldman, B. Brain fitness **153.1**

Hanoch, D. The yoga lifestyle **613.7**

Harris, D. 10% happier **158.1**

Langshur, E. Start here **158**

Roth, B. Strength in stillness **158.1**

Tanzi, R. E. The healing self **615.8**

STRESS MANAGEMENT

> *See also* Health

STRESS MANAGEMENT FOR CHILDREN

Johnson, N. The self-driven child **155.4**

Stretch. Sonenshein, S. **153.35**

STRETCHING EXERCISES

Liebman, H. 1,500 stretches **613.7**

STRETCHING EXERCISES

> *See also* Exercise

Strickland, Carol

The annotated Mona Lisa **709**

Strictly science fiction. Herald, D. T. **016**

STRIKES

Loomis, E. A history of America in ten strikes **331.892**

STRIKES

> *See also* Industrial relations; Labor disputes

STRIKES AND LOCKOUTS *See* Strikes

STRIKES AND LOCKOUTS -- UNITED STATES -- HISTORY

Loomis, E. A history of America in ten strikes **331.892**

Strindberg. Prideaux, S. **839.7**

Strindberg, August, 1849-1912

About

Prideaux, S. Strindberg **839.7**

STRING FIGURES

> *See also* Amusements

STRING MODELS

Nadis, S. The shape of inner space **530.1**

Randall, L. Warped passages **530**

Smolin, L. The trouble with physics **530.1**

STRING MODELS *See* String theory

String theory. Wallace, D. F. **796.342**

STRING THEORY

Greene, B. R. The elegant universe **539.7**

Hawking, S. The grand design **530.1**

Kaku, M. Parallel worlds **523.1**

Nadis, S. The shape of inner space **530.1**

Smolin, L. The trouble with physics **530.1**

STRING THEORY

> *See also* Particles (Nuclear physics)

STRINGED INSTRUMENTS

> *See also* Musical instruments

Stringer. Sundaram, A. **967.51**

STRIPTEASE

Abbott, K. American rose **92**

STRIPTEASERS

Abbott, K. American rose **92**

Strobel, Lee

The Case for Grace **234**

Strogatz, Steven, 1959-

The joy of X **510**

STROKE

Pataki, A. Beauty in the broken places **92**

STROKE

> *See also* Brain -- Diseases

STROKE PATIENTS

Taylor, J. B. My stroke of insight **362.19**

Strøksnes, Morten

Shark drunk **799.173**

Strom, Yale

The book of Klezmer **781.62**

Stromberg, Lisen

TRENT AFFAIR, 1861
See also United States -- History -- 1861-1865, Civil War
Trethewey, Natasha D., 1966-
Beyond Katrina — 818
Tretick, Stanley
About
Kelley, K. Let Freedom Ring — 323.1
Treuer, Anton
Atlas of Indian nations — 970.004
Everything you wanted to know about Indians but were afraid to ask — 909
Treviño Morales, José, 1966-
About
Tone, J. Bones — 364.1
Treviño Morales, Miguel, 1970-
About
Tone, J. Bones — 364.1
Del Bosque, M. Bloodlines — 364.1
The **trial**. Kadri, S. — 345
TRIAL MARRIAGE *See* Unmarried couples
The **trial** of Adolf Hitler. King, D. — 943.085
The **trial** of Socrates. Stone, I. F. (. F. — 183
TRIALS
Barrett, P. M. Law of the jungle — 344
Great American trials — 347
Guttenplan, D. D. The Holocaust on trial — 940.53
Heard, A. The eyes of Willie McGee — 364.66
Hoffer, P. C. The Salem witchcraft trials — 345
Kadri, S. The trial — 345
King, D. The trial of Adolf Hitler — 943.085
Lipstadt, D. E. History on trial — 940.53
Long, J. The plot against Pepys — 941.06
McGinty, B. Lincoln's Greatest Case — 346
Newton, M. A. Enemy of the state — 345
Rabinowitz, D. No crueler tyrannies — 345
Strang, D. A. Worse than the devil — 345
Strebeigh, F. Equal — 342
Toobin, J. The run of his life — 345.73
Walsh, J. E. Moonlight — 345
Waterfield, R. Why Socrates died — 183
Weiner, M. S. Black trials — 342
Wise, S. M. Though the heavens may fall — 342
TRIALS (ANARCHY) -- NEW YORK (STATE) -- NEW YORK -- HISTORY -- 20TH CENTURY
Healy, T. The great dissent — 342.73
TRIALS (CONSPIRACY) -- ENGLAND -- LONDON
Preston, J. A very English scandal — 364.152
TRIALS (HOMICIDE)
Anderson, D. S. Emmett Till — 364.1
Baatz, S. The girl on the velvet swing — 364.152
Balko, R. The cadaver king and the country dentist — 614
Boyle, K. Arc of justice — 345
Bryan, P. L. Midnight assassin — 364.152
Collins, P. Duel With the Devil — 364.152
Colquhoun, K. Did she kill him? — 364.152
Davis, K. The brain defense — 345.747
Goldman, F. The art of political murder — 972.81

Kaplan, A. Y. The interpreter — 940.54
Lane, C. The day freedom died — 976.3
Lebsock, S. A murder in Virginia — 364.1
Liebman, J. S. The wrong Carlos — 364.152
Malcolm, J. Iphigenia in Forest Hills — 345
Martin, T. Rest in power — 92
Nelson, M. The red parts — 362.88
Parry, R. L. People who eat darkness — 364.152
Rule, A. --and never let her go — 364.1
Smith, C. S. The injustice system — 345.73
Starr, D. The killer of little shepherds — 364.152
Temkin, M. The Sacco-Vanzetti Affair — 345
Toobin, J. The run of his life — 345.73
Watson, B. Sacco and Vanzetti — 345
TRIALS (HOMICIDE)
See also Homicide; Trials
TRIALS (MURDER) *See* Trials (Homicide)
TRIALS (MURDER) -- ALABAMA -- BESSEMER
Hinton, A. R. The sun does shine — 92
TRIALS (MURDER) -- ARIZONA -- MARICOPA COUNTY
Siegel, B. Manifest injustice — 364.152
TRIALS (MURDER) -- FLORIDA
Smith, C. S. The injustice system — 345.73
TRIALS (MURDER) -- MASSACHUSETTS -- DEDHAM
Temkin, M. The Sacco-Vanzetti Affair — 345
TRIALS (MURDER) -- MISSISSIPPI
Balko, R. The cadaver king and the country dentist — 614
TRIALS (MURDER) -- MISSISSIPPI -- SUMNER
Anderson, D. S. Emmett Till — 364.1
Tyson, T. B. The blood of Emmett Till — 364.134
TRIALS (MURDER) -- NEW YORK (STATE) -- NEW YORK
Baatz, S. The girl on the velvet swing — 364.152
Davis, K. The brain defense — 345.747
TRIALS (MURDER) -- QUEENS (NEW YORK, N.Y.)
Malcolm, J. Iphigenia in Forest Hills — 345
TRIALS (MURDER) -- TEXAS
Graves, A. Infinite hope — 345.764
Liebman, J. S. The wrong Carlos — 364.152
TRIALS (RAPE)
Balko, R. The cadaver king and the country dentist — 614
Krakauer, J. Missoula — 362.883
TRIALS (RAPE) -- ALABAMA -- BIRMINGHAM
Morrison, M. S. Murder on Shades Mountain — 345.761
TRIALS (RAPE) -- MISSISSIPPI
Balko, R. The cadaver king and the country dentist — 614
TRIALS (RAPE) -- UNITED STATES
Winslow, E. Jane Doe January — 362.883
TRIALS (RIOTS) -- WISCONSIN -- MILWAUKEE -- HISTORY -- 20TH CENTURY
Strang, D. A. Worse than the devil — 345
TRIALS (SEDITIOUS LIBEL) -- NEW YORK (STATE)
Kluger, R. Indelible ink — 686.2
TRIALS (SODOMY) -- TEXAS
Carpenter, D. Flagrant conduct — 342.73
TRIALS (TREASON) -- GERMANY -- MUNICH

Hawkins, L. Raw **92**

U.S. BORDER PATROL -- OFFICIALS AND EMPLOY-EES -- BIOGRAPHY

Cantú, F. The line becomes a river **92**

U.S. Chess Federation's official rules of chess. **794.1**

The U.S. Constitution A to Z. Maddex, R. L. **342**

U.S. FISH AND WILDLIFE SERVICE -- FORENSICS LABORATORY

Neme, L. A. Animal investigators **363.2**

The U.S. House of Representatives. Spieler, M. **328.73**

U.S. Immigration Made Easy. Bray, I. M. **342**

UAVS (UNMANNED AERIAL VEHICLES) *See* Drone aircraft

UBER (FIRM)

Lashinsky, A. Wild ride **338.76**

Stone, B. The upstarts **338.04**

Uberti, Oliver

(jt. auth) Cheshire, J. Where the animals go **591.479**

UCHI (AUSTIN, TEX.: RESTAURANT)

Cole, T. Uchi: the cookbook **641.6**

Uchi: the cookbook. Cole, T. **641.6**

Uebbing, James J.

(ed) Love had a compass **811**

UFOS *See* Unidentified flying objects

UFOs, chemtrails, and aliens. Prothero, D. R. **001.94**

UGANDA

Chretien The great lakes of Africa **967.6**

Rice, A. The teeth may smile but the heart does not forget **967.6**

Uglow, Jennifer S.

A gambling man **92**

Nature's engraver **92**

The ugly Renaissance. Lee, A. **945**

Uhlberg, Myron

About

Uhlberg, M. Hands of my father **92**

Uhls, Yalda T.

Media moms & digital dads **306.874**

Ujifusa, Steven

Barons of the sea **387.5**

A man and his ship **623.8**

UKRAINE

Hercules, O. Mamushka **641.594**

UKRAINE -- FOREIGN RELATIONS -- RUSSIA (FEDERATION)

Judah, T. In wartime **947.086**

UKRAINE -- HISTORY

Applebaum, A. Red famine **947.7**

Judah, T. In wartime **947.086**

UKRAINE -- HISTORY -- FAMINE, 1932-1933

Applebaum, A. Red famine **947.7**

UKRAINE -- POLITICS AND GOVERNMENT -- 1945-1991

Plokhy, S. The man with the poison gun **327.12**

UKRAINE CONFLICT, 2014-

Judah, T. In wartime **947.086**

UKRAINE CONFLICT, 2014- -- PERSONAL NARRA-

TIVES

Judah, T. In wartime **947.086**

UKRAINE CONFLICT, 2014- -- SOCIAL ASPECTS

Judah, T. In wartime **947.086**

UKRAINIANS -- GERMANY -- BIOGRAPHY

Plokhy, S. The man with the poison gun **327.12**

Ulander, Perry A., 1948-

About

Ulander, P. A. Walking point **959.704**

Ulanski, Stan L.

The Gulf Stream **551.46**

Ulbricht, Ross William, 1985-

About

Bilton, N. American kingpin **364.16**

Ulianov, Aleksandr, 1886-1887

About

Pomper, P. Lenin's brother **92**

Ullman, Ellen

About

Ullman, E. Life in code **92**

Ullrich, Volker

Hitler **92**

Ulrich, Laurel

Well-behaved women seldom make history **305.4**

ULTIMATE (GAME)

Gessner, D. Ultimate glory **92**

Ultimate bar book. Hellmich, M. **641.8**

The ultimate bicycle owner's manual. Weiss, E. **796.6**

The Ultimate Book of Family Card Games. Ho, O. **795.4**

The ultimate book of modern juicing. Kirk, M. **663**

Ultimate crochet bible. Crowfoot, J. **746.43**

The Ultimate Encyclopedia of Aquarium Fish & Fish Care. Bailey, M. **639.34**

ULTIMATE FIGHTING CHAMPIONSHIP (ORGANIZA-TION)

Wertheim, L. J. Blood in the cage **92**

Ultimate glory. Gessner, D. **92**

Ultimate guide : home repair and improvement. **643**

The ultimate guide to dog training. Anderson, T. **636.7**

Ultimate guide to Google AdWords. Todd, B. **659.144**

Ultimate guide to plumbing.

The ultimate guide to raising teens and tweens. Haddad, D. **373.236**

Ultimate guide: porches. Cory, S. **690**

The Ultimate Jack the Ripper companion. **364.15**

The ultimate Picasso. Leal, B. **759**

Ultimate punishment. Turow, S. **345**

The ultimate quotable Einstein. Einstein, A. **530**

Ultimate Star wars. Wallace, D.

The ultimate student cookbook. Goodall, T. **641.5**

Ultimate travel. **910.2**

ULTRA-ORTHODOX JEWS -- NEW YORK (STATE) -- NEW YORK -- BIOGRAPHY

Vincent, L. Cut me loose **305.892**

ULTRASONICS

See also Sound

ULTRAVIOLET RAYS

UNITED STATES -- FOREIGN RELATIONS -- ISRAEL

Ross, D. B. Doomed to succeed 327.73

UNITED STATES -- FOREIGN RELATIONS -- JAPAN

Nimura, J. P. Daughters of the Samurai 920.72

UNITED STATES -- FOREIGN RELATIONS -- KOREA (NORTH)

Harden, B. The Great Leader and the Fighter Pilot 951.904

UNITED STATES -- FOREIGN RELATIONS -- MIDDLE EAST

Bacevich, A. J. America's war for the greater Middle East 956.054

Haass, R. War of necessity: war of choice 956.7

Nasr, V. The dispensable nation 327.73

UNITED STATES -- FOREIGN RELATIONS -- MORAL AND ETHICAL ASPECTS

O'Toole, P. The moralist B

UNITED STATES -- FOREIGN RELATIONS -- PAKISTAN

Gall, C. The wrong enemy 958.104

UNITED STATES -- FOREIGN RELATIONS -- RELIGIOUS ASPECTS

Preston, A. Sword of the spirit, shield of faith 322

UNITED STATES -- FOREIGN RELATIONS -- RUSSIA

McFaul, M. A. From Cold War to hot peace 327.73

UNITED STATES -- FOREIGN RELATIONS -- RUSSIA (FEDERATION)

McFaul, M. A. From Cold War to hot peace 327.73

UNITED STATES -- FOREIGN RELATIONS -- SOUTH ASIA

Bass, G. J. The Blood telegram 327.73

UNITED STATES -- FOREIGN RELATIONS -- SOVIET UNION

Blum, H. In the enemy's house 327.124

Budiansky, S. Code warriors 327.73

Coleman, D. G. The fourteenth day 973.922

Service, R. The End of the Cold War, 1985-1991 909.82

UNITED STATES -- FOREIGN RELATIONS -- TREATIES

See also Treaties

UNITED STATES -- FOREIGN RELATIONS -- VIETNAM

Logevall, F. Embers of War 959.704

UNITED STATES -- GAZETTEERS

Hellmann, P. T. Historical gazetteer of the United States 911

UNITED STATES -- GAZETTEERS

See also Gazetteers

UNITED STATES -- GENEALOGY

Greenwood, V. D. The researcher's guide to American genealogy 929

Simpson, J. Basics of genealogy reference 929

UNITED STATES -- GENEALOGY -- ANECDOTES

McCarthy, A. Journeys home 929.1

UNITED STATES -- GENEALOGY -- HANDBOOKS, MANUALS, ETC

Croom, E. A. The genealogist's companion and sourcebook 929

McCarthy, A. Journeys home 929.1

Neighbors, J. The family tree cemetery field guide 929.5

UNITED STATES -- GEOGRAPHY

See also Geography

UNITED STATES -- GOVERNMENT See United States -- Politics and government

UNITED STATES -- GOVERNMENT EMPLOYEES See United States -- Officials and employees

UNITED STATES -- GUIDEBOOKS

McAlester, V. S. A field guide to American houses 728

National Geographic Guide to the State Parks of the United States 917.3

UNITED STATES -- HISTORIC BUILDINGS See Historic buildings -- United States

UNITED STATES -- HISTORICAL GEOGRAPHY -- DICTIONARIES

Hellmann, P. T. Historical gazetteer of the United States 911

UNITED STATES -- HISTORICAL GEOGRAPHY -- MAPS

Hayes, D. Historical atlas of the United States 911

UNITED STATES -- HISTORIOGRAPHY

See also Historiography

UNITED STATES -- HISTORY

Baglio, M. Argo 955.05

Butman, J. New world, inc. 970.017

Cannon, C. M. On this date 973

Dolin, E. J. Black flags, blue waters 973.2

Dolin, E. J. When America first met China 382

Gillette, M. L. Lady Bird Johnson 92

Haley, J. L. Captive paradise 996.9

Han, L. C. Handbook to American democracy 320.4

Koppel, L. The Astronaut Wives Club 629.45

Lepore, J. The story of America 973

Lepore, J. These truths 973

Lind, M. Land of promise 330.973

Mires, C. Capital of the world 341.23

Nielsen, K. E. A disability history of the United States 362.4

Randall, D. K. The King and Queen of Malibu 979.4

Sherman, C. Above and beyond 973.922

Warren, W. New England Bound 306.362

Wineapple, B. Ecstatic nation 973.6

Young, R. Dissent 303.48

UNITED STATES -- HISTORY -- 1600-1775, COLONIAL PERIOD

Bailyn, B. The barbarous years 973.2

Barry, J. M. Roger Williams and the creation of the American soul 974.5

Bunker, N. An empire on the edge 973.3

Dunbar-Ortiz, R. An indigenous peoples' history of the United States 970.004

Lawler, A. The secret token 975.6

Pressly, P. M. On the rim of the Caribbean 975.8

Spero, P. Frontier rebels 973.3

Taylor, A. American revolutions 973.3

UNITED STATES -- HISTORY -- 1755-1763, FRENCH AND INDIAN WAR

Cohen, E. A. Conquered into liberty 355

UNITED STATES -- HISTORY -- 1755-1763, FRENCH AND INDIAN WAR

Ellis, J. J. American dialogue **973.3**

UNITED STATES -- POLITICS AND GOVERNMENT -- 20TH CENTURY

Brazile, D. For colored girls who have considered politics **92**

Frank, B. Frank **92**

Judt, T. Thinking the twentieth century **320**

Neff, J. Vendetta **973.922**

Tirella, J. Tomorrow-land **607**

UNITED STATES -- POLITICS AND GOVERNMENT -- 21ST CENTURY

Dionne, E. J. One nation after Trump **973.933**

Frank, B. Frank **92**

Hayes, C. Twilight of the elites **305.5**

Kasich, J. Two paths **324.973**

Nasty women **305.42**

Nussbaum, M. C. The monarchy of fear **306.209**

Sexton, J. Y. The people are going to rise like the waters upon your shore **324.973**

Weisman, J. (((Semitism))) **305.892**

UNITED STATES -- POLITICS AND GOVERNMENT -- 21ST CENTURY -- HUMOR

Leary, D. Why we don't suck **818.602**

UNITED STATES -- POLITICS AND GOVERNMENT -- ANECDOTES

Dickerson, J. Whistlestop **324.973**

UNITED STATES -- POLITICS AND GOVERNMENT -- CASE STUDIES

Moss, D. A. Democracy **320.473**

UNITED STATES -- POLITICS AND GOVERNMENT -- DICTIONARIES

Conley, R. S. Historical dictionary of U.S. Constitution **342.73**

UNITED STATES -- POLITICS AND GOVERNMENT -- ENCYCLOPEDIAS, JUVENILE

Encyclopedia of the U.S. presidency **352.23**

UNITED STATES -- POLITICS AND GOVERNMENT -- HANDBOOKS, MANUALS, ETC

Han, L. C. Handbook to American democracy **320.4**

UNITED STATES -- POLITICS AND GOVERNMENT -- HISTORY

Lawrence, J. A. The class of '74 **328.73**

UNITED STATES -- POLITICS AND GOVERNMENT -- HUMOR

Leary, D. Why we don't suck **818.602**

UNITED STATES -- POLITICS AND GOVERNMENT -- MAPS

Shelley, F. M. Atlas of American politics, 1960-2000 **973.92**

UNITED STATES -- POLITICS AND GOVERNMENT -- PUBLIC OPINION

Fallows, J. Our towns **306.097**

Salvanto, A. Where did you get this number? **303.38**

UNITED STATES -- POLITICS AND GOVERNMENT -- SOURCES

Ashby, R. The great american documents **973**

UNITED STATES -- POPULAR CULTURE *See* Popular culture -- United States

UNITED STATES -- POPULATION

Peake, R. Mapping Census 2010 **304.6**

Sykes, B. DNA USA **559.9**

UNITED STATES -- POPULATION

See also Population

UNITED STATES -- RACE RELATIONS

Asch, C. M. Chocolate City **305.8**

Brown, A. C. I'm still here **305.896**

Coates Between the World and Me **305.8**

DeWolf, T. N. Gather at the table **306.3**

Dunbar-Ortiz, R. An indigenous peoples' history of the United States **970.004**

Dyson, M. E. The Black presidency **305.8**

Dyson, M. E. Tears We Cannot Stop **305.8**

Dyson, M. E. What truth sounds like **305.8**

The Fire This Time **305.896**

Gates, H. L. And Still I Rise **973**

Gillon, S. M. Separate and unequal **363.32**

Hill, M. L. Nobody **306.09**

Kendi, I. X. Stamped from the beginning **305.8**

Leamer, L. The lynching **364.134**

Lebron, C. J. The making of Black lives matter **305.896**

Lehr, D. The Birth of a Nation **305.8**

Lythcott-Haims, J. Real American **92**

Oluo, I. So you want to talk about race **305.8**

Rankine, C. Citizen **811**

Savoy, L. Trace **917.3**

Sherrod, S. The courage to hope **975.8**

Thomas, E. We matter **796.089**

Trillin, C. Jackson, 1964 **305.8**

UNITED STATES -- RACE RELATIONS

See also Race relations

UNITED STATES -- RACE RELATIONS -- 21ST CENTURY

Hill, M. L. Nobody **306.09**

Saslow, E. Rising out of hatred **92**

UNITED STATES -- RACE RELATIONS -- HISTORIOGRAPHY

Theoharis, J. A more beautiful and terrible history **323.1**

UNITED STATES -- RACE RELATIONS -- HISTORY

Anderson, C. (. E. White Rage **305.8**

Davis, T. J. Plessy v. Ferguson **342**

Freedman, E. Presidents and Black America **973.09**

Haney Lopez, I. Dog whistle politics **323.119**

Parkinson, R. G. The common cause **973.3**

Phillips, P. Blood at the root **305.8**

Sokol, J. The heavens might crack **323.092**

Theoharis, J. A more beautiful and terrible history **323.1**

White, S. Prince of darkness **92**

UNITED STATES -- RACE RELATIONS -- HISTORY -- 19TH CENTURY

Reed, A. The life and the adventures of a haunted convict **365.34**

White, S. Prince of darkness **92**

UNITED STATES -- RACE RELATIONS -- HISTORY -- 20TH CENTURY

Anderson, D. S. Emmett Till **364.1**

Gordon, L. The second coming of the KKK **322.42**

Kramer, A. S. Breaking through bias   **650.1**
Licht, A. Leave Your Mark   **650.1**
McKenna, A. Nontraditional careers for women and men   **331.702**
Morgan, G. Undecided   **371.4**
Mulcahy, D. The gig economy   **650.1**
Parini, J. The art of teaching   **371.1**
Raskin, D. The dirty little secrets of getting your dream job   **650.14**
Shell, G. R. Springboard   **650.1**
Smith, L. R. No fears, no excuses   **650.1**
Steib, M. The career manifesto   **650.1**

VOCATIONAL GUIDANCE
    See also Counseling; Vocational education

VOCATIONAL GUIDANCE -- ENCYCLOPEDIAS
J.G. Ferguson Publishing Company Encyclopedia of careers and vocational guidance   **331.7**

VOCATIONAL GUIDANCE -- INFORMATION SERVICES
Jerrard, J. Crisis in employment   **025.5**

VOCATIONAL GUIDANCE -- UNITED STATES
Anders, G. You can do anything   **331.702**

VOCATIONAL GUIDANCE -- UNITED STATES -- HISTORY -- 21ST CENTURY
Chideya, F. The episodic career   **650.1**

VOCATIONAL GUIDANCE -- UNITED STATES -- JUVENILE LITERATURE
McKenna, A. Nontraditional careers for women and men   **331.702**

VOCATIONAL GUIDANCE FOR PEOPLE WITH DISABILITIES
    See also People with disabilities; Vocational guidance

VOCATIONAL GUIDANCE FOR WOMEN
Downey, A. Here's the plan   **306.36**
Kramer, A. S. Breaking through bias   **650.1**

VOCATIONAL TRAINING *See* Occupational training

VOCATIONS *See* Occupations; Professions

VODUN *See* Voodooism

Vogel, Ezra F.
Deng Xiaoping and the transformation of China   **951.05**

Vogel, Kenneth P.
Big money   **324.7**

Vogel, Steve
Through the perilous fight   **973.5**
The Pentagon   **355.6**

Vogel, Steven, 1940-2015
The life of a leaf   **575.5**

Vogler, Amy
Lang, A. P. Serious barbecue   **641.5**

Vogt, William, 1902-1968
        About
Mann, C. C. The wizard and the prophet   **363.7**

VOGUE
Buck, J. J. The price of illusion   **92**
Vogue and the Metropolitan Museum of Art Costume Institute. Bowles, H.   **391**
Vogue knitting.   **746.432**

Vogue Knitting (Company)
(comp) Vogue knitting   **746.432**

VOICE
    See also Language and languages; Throat
The voice at 3:00 a.m. Simic, C.   **811**

VOICE CULTURE
    See also Public speaking; Singing; Speech
The voice is all. Johnson, J.   **818**
Voice lessons for parents. Mogel, W.   **649.1**
Voice of America. Heil, A. L.   **384.54**

VOICE OF AMERICA
Heil, A. L. Voice of America   **384.54**
The voice of reason; essays in objectivist thought. Rand, A.   **191**
Voices in our blood.   **323.1**
Voices in the Ocean. Casey, S.   **599.53**

Voices of an era [series]
Voices of early Christianity   **270.1**
Voices of early Christianity.   **270.1**
Voices of war.   **355**

Voices that matter [series]
Reynolds, G. Presentation zen

Voigt, Emily
The dragon behind the glass   **597.176**

Volandes, Angelo E., 1971-
The conversation   **616.02**

VOLATILE OILS *See* Essences and essential oils

VOLCANIC ERUPTIONS
McGuire, B. Waking the giant   **551.5**

VOLCANIC ERUPTIONS -- WASHINGTON (STATE)
Olson, S. Eruption   **363.34**
Volcano cowboys. Thompson, D.   **551.21**

VOLCANOES
Gates, A. E. Encyclopedia of earthquakes and volcanoes **551.2**
Olson, S. Eruption   **363.34**
Oppenheimer, C. Eruptions that shook the world   **551.2**
Scarth, A. Vesuvius: a biography   **551.2**
Thompson, D. Volcano cowboys   **551.21**
Winchester, S. Krakatoa: the day the world exploded, August 27, 1883   **551.2**

VOLCANOES
    See also Geology; Mountains; Physical geography

VOLCANOES -- ENCYCLOPEDIAS
Gates, A. E. Encyclopedia of earthquakes and volcanoes **551.2**

VOLCANOES -- WASHINGTON (STATE)
Olson, S. Eruption   **363.34**

Volf, Miroslav
Public faith in action   **261.7**

Volger, Lukas
Bowl   **641.81**

Volk, Audrey Morgen
        About
Volk, P. Shocked   **92**

Volk, Patricia
        About
Volk, P. Shocked   **92**

Volkov, Solomon

Who thought this was a good idea? Mastromonaco, A.   **92**

Who's afraid of Virginia Woolf? Albee, E.   **812**

Who's who 2008.   **920.003**

Who's who among African Americans.   **920.003**

Who's who in America.   **920.003**

Who's who in American art, 2008.   **920.003**

Who's who in American politics 2007-2008. Jaques Cattell Press   **920.003**

Who's who in finance and business 2008-2009.   **920.003**

Who's who in the Jewish Bible. Mandel, D.   **920.003**

Who's who of American women 2007.   **920.003**

The **who,** what, and where of America.   **317.3**

Whoa, baby! Rowland, K.   **618.2**

WHODUNITS *See* Mystery and detective plays; Mystery fiction; Mystery films; Mystery radio programs; Mystery television programs

The **whole** death catalog. Schechter, H.   **306.9**

The **whole** equation. Thomson, D.   **791.43**

The **whole** foods allergy cookbook. Pascal, C.   **641.5**

The **whole** heart solution. Khan, J.   **616.1**

WHOLE LANGUAGE

     See also Education -- Experimental methods; Language arts

The **Whole** Smiths good food cookbook. Smith, M.   **641.5**

The **whole-brain** child. Siegel, D. J.   **649**

The **whole30.**   **613.2**

The **whole30** fast & easy.   **641.563**

WHOLISTIC MEDICINE *See* Holistic medicine

Why "A" Students Work for "C" Students and Why "B" Students Work for the Government. Kiyosaki, R. T.   **332.024**

Why be happy when you could be normal? Winterson, J.   **823**

Why be Jewish? Bronfman, E. M.   **296**

Why beauty is truth. Stewart, I.   **539.7**

Why Bob Dylan Matters. Thomas, R. F.   **782.4**

Why Buddhism is true. Wright, R.   **294.3**

Why calories count. Nesheim, M.   **613.2**

Why can't I get better? Horowitz, R. I.   **616.9**

Why can't I meditate? Wellings, N.   **158.12**

Why cant U teach me 2 read? Fertig, B.   **372.4**

Why cats land on their feet. Levi, M.   **530**

Why courage matters. McCain, J. S.   **179**

Why did the chicken cross the world? Lawler, A.   **636.5**

Why Dinosaurs Matter. Lacovara, K.   **567.9**

Why does the world exist? Holt, J.   **113**

Why don't jumbo jets flap their wings? Alexander, D. E.   **629.13**

Why don't you want my stuff? Levine, J.   **155**

Why evolution is true. Coyne, J. A.   **576.8**

Why football matters. Edmundson, M.   **92**

Why Homer matters. Nicolson, A.   **883**

Why I came West. Bass, R.   **92**

Why jazz happened. Myers, M.   **781.65**

Why Mahler? Lebrecht, N.   **92**

Why nations fail. Acemoglu, D.   **330**

Why not me? Kaling, M.   **92**

Why organizations struggle so hard to improve so little. Klubeck, M.   **658.4**

Why people believe weird things. Shermer, M.   **001.9**

Why read Moby-Dick? Philbrick, N.   **813**

Why read the classics? Calvino, I.   **809**

Why Socrates died. Waterfield, R.   **183**

Why the Allies won. Overy, R.   **940.53**

Why the Dalai Lama matters. Thurman, R. A. F.   **294.3**

Why the right went wrong. Dionne, E. J.   **320.52**

Why the West rules--for now. Morris, I.   **909**

Why this world. Moser, B.   **92**

Why time flies. Burdick, A.   **529.2**

Why translation matters. Grossman, E.   **418**

Why we buy. Underhill, P.   **658.8**

Why we can't wait. King, M. L.   **323.1**

Why we do it. Eldredge, N.   **155.3**

Why we don't suck. Leary, D.   **818.602**

Why we get fat and what to do about it. Taubes, G.   **613.7**

Why We Lost. Bolger, D. P.   **956.704**

Why we make mistakes. Hallinan, J. T.   **153**

Why we sleep. Walker, M.   **612.8**

Why X matters [series]

     Grossman, E. Why translation matters   **418**

Why? Livio, M.   **153.3**

Why? Hayes, P.   **940.53**

Whybrow, P. J.

     (ed) Travels with the fossil hunters   **560**

Whyte, Kenneth

     Hoover   **92**

     The uncrowned king   **92**

WICA *See* Wicca

WICCA

     Callow, J. Embracing the darkness   **299**

     Pearson, J. Belief beyond boundaries   **209**

WICCA

     See also Paganism

WICCA -- UNITED STATES

     Mar, A. Witches of America   **299**

WICCANS -- MASSACHUSETTS -- SALEM

     Ocker, J. W. A season with the witch   **133.4**

'wichcraft. Colicchio, T.   **641.8**

Wichman, Emily T.

     Librarian's guide to passive programming   **025.5**

Wick, Myra

     (ed) Mayo Clinic guide to a healthy pregnancy   **618.2**

The **Wicked** Boy. Summerscale, K.   **364.152**

Wicked bugs. Stewart, A.   **632**

The **wicked** healthy cookbook. Joachim, D.   **641.563**

WICKEDNESS *See* Good and evil

Wicker, Marcus

     Silencer   **811**

Wickersham, Joan

     The suicide index   **155.9**

Wickham, Chris

     The inheritance of Rome   **940.1**

Wicks, Robert J.

     Night call   **155.24**

Wideman, John Edgar

         About

     Wideman, J. E. Writing to save a life   **364.152**

WOMEN -- PSYCHOLOGY -- POPULAR WORKS
Kinsman, K. Hi, anxiety   **616.85**

WOMEN -- RELATIONS WITH MEN *See* Man-woman relationship

WOMEN -- RELIGIOUS ASPECTS -- CHRISTIANITY
Jaynes, S. When you feel you're not enough   **248.8**

WOMEN -- RELIGIOUS LIFE
Earhardt, A. The light within me   **92**
Hatmaker, J. Of mess and moxie   **248.8**

WOMEN -- RELIGIOUS LIFE
    See also Religious life

WOMEN -- RELIGIOUS LIFE -- CHRISTIANITY
Hatmaker, J. Of mess and moxie   **248.8**

WOMEN -- RELIGIOUS LIFE -- SOUTHERN STATES
Circling faith   **200.8**

WOMEN -- ROME
Freisenbruch, A. Caesars' wives   **937**

WOMEN -- SELF-DEFENSE *See* Self-defense for women

WOMEN -- SEXUAL BEHAVIOR
Angel, K. Unmastered   **828**
Bergner, D. What Do Women Want?   **305**
Koenig, E. Moan   **306.7**
McLaughlin, A. Girl boner   **306.708**
Nagoski, E. Come as you are   **613.9**
Wolf, N. Vagina   **305.42**

WOMEN -- SOCIAL CONDITIONS
Adichie, C. N. Dear Ijeawele, or a feminist manifesto in fifteen suggestions   **305.42**
Armstrong, J. K. Sexy feminism   **305.42**
Chocano, C. You play the girl   **305.42**
Hernández, D. A cup of water under my bed   **920.009**
Jerkins, M. This will be my undoing   **305.896**
MacColl, G. To marry an English Lord   **974.7**
Orenstein, P. Don't call me princess   **305.42**
Ryckman, P. Stiletto network   **331.4**
Spar, D. L. Wonder Women   **305.42**

WOMEN -- SOCIAL CONDITIONS
    See also Social conditions

WOMEN -- SOCIAL CONDITIONS -- 21ST CENTURY
Rosin, H. The end of men   **305.42**

WOMEN -- SOUTH AFRICA
Burge, K. The born frees   **305.242**

WOMEN -- SOUTH AFRICA -- BIOGRAPHY
Kohler, S. Once we were sisters   **92**

WOMEN -- SOUTHERN STATES
Faust, D. G. Mothers of invention   **973.7**

WOMEN -- SPORTS *See* Sports for women

WOMEN -- SUFFRAGE
Dudden, F. E. Fighting chance   **324.6**
Ginzberg, L. D. Elizabeth Cady Stanton   **92**
Goldsmith, B. Other powers   **92**

WOMEN -- SUFFRAGE
    See also Suffrage; Women's rights

WOMEN -- SUFFRAGE -- HISTORY
Ginzberg, L. D. Elizabeth Cady Stanton   **92**

WOMEN -- SUFFRAGE -- UNITED STATES
Weiss, E. The woman's hour   **324.623**

WOMEN -- TENNESSEE -- OAK RIDGE -- HISTORY
Kiernan, D. The girls of atomic city   **976.8**

WOMEN -- TEXAS -- HOUSTON -- SOCIAL LIFE AND CUSTOMS -- 20TH CENTURY
Koppel, L. The Astronaut Wives Club   **629.45**

WOMEN -- TRAVEL
Baggett, J. The lost girls   **910.4**
Howell, G. Gertrude Bell   **92**

WOMEN -- UNITED STATES
Kaplan, C. Miss Anne in Harlem   **700.92**

WOMEN -- UNITED STATES -- BIOGRAPHY
American   women
Brower, K. A. First women   **920**
Gubar, S. Memoir of a debulked woman   **616.99**
Livingston, S. Ladies night at the Dreamland   **920.72**
Lucey, D. M. Sargent's women   **920**
Mackrell, J. Flappers   **920**
Smith, C. B. The rules of inheritance   **616.99**

WOMEN -- UNITED STATES -- HISTORY
Abbott, K. Liar, Temptress, Soldier, Spy   **973.7**
Kerrison, C. Jefferson's daughters   **920**
Livingston, S. Ladies night at the Dreamland   **920.72**
MacColl, G. To marry an English Lord   **974.7**

WOMEN -- UNITED STATES -- HISTORY -- 18TH CENTURY
Kerrison, C. Jefferson's daughters   **920**

WOMEN -- UNITED STATES -- HISTORY -- 19TH CENTURY
Kerrison, C. Jefferson's daughters   **920**
Roberts, C. Capital dames   **793.7**

WOMEN -- UNITED STATES -- HISTORY -- SOURCES
Grunwald, L. Women's letters   **305.4**

WOMEN -- UNITED STATES -- INTELLECTUAL LIFE
Kaplan, A. Dreaming in French   **944**

WOMEN -- UNITED STATES -- INTERVIEWS
Schnall, M. What will it take to make a woman president?   **305.4**

WOMEN -- UNITED STATES -- SOCIAL CONDITIONS
Livingston, S. Ladies night at the Dreamland   **920.72**
Traister, R. All the single ladies   **306.81**

WOMEN -- UNITED STATES -- SOCIAL CONDITIONS -- 18TH CENTURY
Lepore, J. Book of ages   **92**

WOMEN -- UNITED STATES -- SOCIAL CONDITIONS -- 19TH CENTURY
Berkin, C. Civil War wives   **920**

WOMEN -- UNITED STATES -- SOCIAL CONDITIONS -- 20TH CENTURY
Coontz, S. A strange stirring   **305.42**
May, E. T. America and the pill   **363.9**

WOMEN -- UNITED STATES -- SOCIAL CONDITIONS -- 21ST CENTURY
Nasty women   **305.42**

WOMEN -- VIETNAM -- BIOGRAPHY
Thi, K. P. P. Fire road   **959.704**

WOMEN -- VIOLENCE AGAINST
The mother of all questions   **305.42**

WRITERS ON THE SEA
Writers on writers [series]
WRITING
WRITING
See also Communication; Language and languages; Language arts
WRITING (AUTHORSHIP) See Authorship; Creative writing
WRITING -- HISTORY
WRITING -- MATERIALS AND INSTRUMENTS
WRITING -- STUDY AND TEACHING See Handwriting
WRITING MATERIALS AND INSTRUMENTS
WRITING OF NUMERALS
See also Handwriting; Numerals; Writing
WRITINGS OF GAY MEN See Gay men's writings
WRITINGS OF LESBIANS See Lesbians' writings
Wroe, Ann